Best Books
for Children

Best Books for Children

PRESCHOOL THROUGH GRADE 6
10th Edition

Catherine Barr
and
Jamie Campbell Naidoo

Children's and Young Adult Literature Reference

 LIBRARIES UNLIMITED

AN IMPRINT OF ABC-CLIO, LLC
Santa Barbara, California • Denver, Colorado • Oxford, England

Library of Congress Cataloging-in-Publication Data
Barr, Catherine, 1951–
  Best books for children, preschool through grade 6 / Catherine Barr. — Tenth edition.
    pages cm. — (Children's and young adult literature reference)
  Includes bibliographical references and index.
  ISBN 978-1-59884-781-9 (hardback) — ISBN 978-1-4408-3744-9 (ebook)
  1. Children—Books and reading—United States. 2. Children's literature—Bibliogra-
phy. 3. Best books—United States. I. Naidoo, Jamie Campbell. II. Title.
  Z1037.G48 2015
  011.62—dc23   2014015174

ISBN: 978-1-59884-781-9
EISBN: 978-1-4408-3744-9

19 18 17 16 15   1 2 3 4 5

This book is also available on the World Wide Web as an eBook.
Visit www.abc-clio.com for details.

Libraries Unlimited
An Imprint of ABC-CLIO, LLC

ABC-CLIO, LLC
130 Cremona Drive, P.O. Box 1911
Santa Barbara, California 93116-1911

This book is printed on acid-free paper ∞⃝
Manufactured in the United States of America

Contents

Biography

The Arts and Language

Personal Development

Physical and Applied Sciences

CONTENTS

ix

Recreation

Major Subjects Arranged Alphabetically

Preface

Librarians and other specialists in children's literature have available, through print and online sources, a large number of bibliographies that recommend books suitable for young people. Unfortunately, these sources vary widely in quality and usefulness. The Best Books series was created to furnish authoritative, reliable, and comprehensive bibliographies for use in libraries that collect materials for readers from preschool through grade 12. The series currently consists of three volumes: *Best Books for Children, Best Books for Middle School and Junior High Readers,* and *Best Books for High School Readers.*

Best Books for Children contains books recommended for preschool through grade 6, *Best Books for Middle School and Junior High Readers* supplies information on books recommended for readers in grades 6 through 9 or roughly ages 11 through 15, and *Best Books for High School Readers* covers grades 9 through 12.

As every librarian knows, reading levels are elastic. There is no such thing, for example, as a fifth-grade book. Instead there are only fifth-grade readers who, in their diversity, can represent a wide range of reading abilities and interests. This bibliography contains a liberal selection of entries that, we hope, will accommodate readers in these early grades and allow for their great range of tastes and reading competencies. Gifted fifth- and sixth-grade readers may find suitable recommendations in *Best Books for Middle School and Junior High Readers.*

In selecting books for inclusion, deciding on their arrangement, and collecting the information supplied on each, our intention is to reflect the current needs and interests of young readers while keeping in mind the latest trends and curricular emphases in today's schools.

General Scope and Criteria for Inclusion

Of the 26,405 titles in this tenth edition of *Best Books for Children,* 25,138 are individually numbered entries. The remaining 1,267 titles — those cited within the annotations — are additional recommended titles by the main entry author.

Excluded from this bibliography are general reference works, such as dictionaries and encyclopedias, except for a few single-volume works that are so heavily illustrated and attractive that they can also be used in the general circulation collection. Also excluded are professional books for librarians and teachers and mass market series such as the Nancy Drew and Hardy Boys books.

For most fiction and nonfiction, a minimum of two recommendations were required from the current reviewing sources consulted for a title to be considered for listing. However, there were a number of necessary exceptions. For example, in some reviewing journals only a few representative titles from extensive nonfiction series are reviewed even though others in the series will also be recommended. In such cases a single favorable review was enough for inclusion. As well as favorable reviews, additional criteria such as availability, currency, accuracy, usefulness, and relevance were considered. An asterisk following a review citation denotes an outstanding recommendation from that source. Many awards are also cited.

Sources Used

Several sources were used to compile this annotated bibliography. At the outset, there was a thorough perusal and evaluation of the entries in the ninth (2010) edition of *Best Books for Children* and its supplement. The other sources consulted were numerous and varied. The major tools were current reviewing periodicals, principally *Booklist, Bulletin of the Center for Children's Books, Horn Book, Library Media Connection,* and *School Library Journal.*

Uses of This Book

It is hoped that this bibliography will be used in four different ways: (1) as a tool to evaluate the adequacy of existing collections; (2) as a book selection instrument for beginning and expanding collections; (3) as an aid for giving reading guidance to children; and (4) as a base for the preparation of bibliographies and reading lists. To increase the book's usefulness, particularly in the two latter areas, the chosen titles are arranged under broad interest areas or, as in the case of nonfiction works, by curriculum-oriented subjects rather than by the Dewey Decimal Classification System.

For example, a book on religious practices in colonial America might be cataloged under religion, but in this book it would be included with other books on "Colonial Period (U.S.)." In this way, analogous titles that otherwise would be in separate sections are brought together and can be seen in relation to other books on the same broad topic.

Arrangement

In general, the titles that appear in the section Books for Younger Readers are those usually read to children or used in assisted-reading situations. The one exception in this section is the listing of "Books for Beginning Readers." This area contains books of fiction easy enough to be read by beginning readers; non-fiction beginning readers are integrated into the appropriate subject areas with mention in the annotation that the work is suitable for beginning readers. Interactive books, such as books containing tabs, pop-ups, or flaps, are integrated into appropriate sections but their annotations mention the nature of their format.

The "Imaginative Stories" section in the Picture Books area is divided into two categories: Fantasies and Imaginary Animals. The first contains both books that depict humans, usually children, in fanciful, unrealistic situations (many bordering on the supernatural) and books that include (as characters) such mythical creatures as dragons and unicorns. The Imaginary Animals category includes stories about anthropomorphized animals that engage in human activities (such as pigs going to school) and display human motivations and behavior.

Simple chapter books and similar nonfiction titles that bridge the reading abilities and interests of children in the upper primary grades and early middle grades are integrated into the appropriate sections for older readers and their annotations indicate that they are easily read.

In the Fiction for Older Readers areas, only general anthologies of short stories are included under "Short Stories and Anthologies." Collections of short stories on a single topic, such as sports stories, are found under that specific topic. In the nonfiction Biography section under "African Americans," "Hispanic Americans," and "Native Americans," only those individuals who have been associated primarily with race-related activities are included. For example, a biography of Martin Luther King, Jr., would be found under "African Americans" but a life story of athlete Wilma Rudolph would be under sports biographies. Also in the nonfiction area, general books of science projects and experiments are found under "General Science — Experiments and Projects," but books of activities relating to a specific area of science are included in that area.

We have introduced some changes in categories with this edition. A new section called Traditional Literature embraces Fairy Tales and Folklore; Mythology; Nursery Rhymes; and Poetry. Another change is that fantasy and science fiction titles are listed together under Fantasy, Science Fiction, and the Supernatural.

A listing of "Major Subjects Arranged Alphabetically" provides both the range of entry numbers and page numbers for the largest subject areas covered in the volume.

Entry Information

Titles in the main section of the book are assigned an entry number. Entries contain the following information where applicable: (1) author or editor; (2) title; (3) suitable grade levels; (4) adapter or translator; (5) indication of illustrations or illustrator's name (usually only for picture books); (6) series title; (7) date of publication; (8) publisher and price of hardbound edition (LB=library binding); (9) ISBN of hardbound edition; (10) paperback (paper) publisher (if no publisher is listed, it is the same as the hardbound edition) and price; (11) ISBN of paperback edition; (12) number of pages; (13) annotation; (14) awards;

(15) audio version; (16) ebook version; (17) Lexile; (18) review citations; (19) Dewey Decimal number.

Review citations are given where available. The following abbreviations are used:

Booklist (BL)
Bulletin of the Center for Children's Books (BCCB)
Horn Book (HB)
Horn Book Guide (HBG)
Library Media Connection (LMC)
School Library Journal (SLJ)

The citing of only one review does not necessarily mean that the book received only a single recommendation; it might also have been listed in one or more of the other sources consulted. Books without review citations or Dewey numbers are pre-1985 imprints and reprints of older recommended books recently brought back into print (the original publication date is indicated within the annotation if it was readily available).

An asterisk following a review citation denotes an outstanding recommendation from that source.

Lexile measures may be preceded by a code, as in AD310. The codes are defined below; more information is available at lexile.com.

AD   Adult Directed
NC   Non-Conforming
HL   High-Low
IG   Illustrated Guide
GN   Graphic Novel
BR   Beginning Reading
NP   Non-Prose

Indexes

Best Books for Children includes three indexes: author/illustrator, book title, and subject/grade level. Authors and illustrators are listed alphabetically by last name, followed by book titles and entry numbers; fiction titles are indicated by (F). The Title Index includes both main entry titles and internal titles cited within the annotation, all with entry numbers and (F) notations.

The Subject/Grade Level Index includes thousands of subject headings. Within each subject, entries are listed according to grade-level suitabilities. For example, under the subject Humorous Stories there may be numerous entry numbers given first for Primary (P) readers; then for the Primary-Intermediate (PI) group; for the Intermediate (I) group; for the Intermediate-Junior High (IJ) readers; and finally for all readers, covering grades from preschool through grade 8 (All). This will enable the professional to select the most appropriate titles for use. Biographical entries are listed in this index by the last name of the subject of the biography. The following codes are used to give approximate grade level:

P   (Primary) preschool through grade 3
PI   (Primary-Intermediate) grades 2 through 4
I   (Intermediate) grades 4 through 6
IJ   (Intermediate-Junior High) grades 5 through 8 (or in a few cases some higher grades)
All   (All readers) preschool through grade 8 (or higher)

Specific, more exact grade-level suitabilities are given (parenthetically) for each book in its main text entry. To facilitate quick reference, all listings in all indexes refer the user to entry number, not page number.

With this edition, I am delighted to announce my new coauthor/editor, Jamie Campbell Naidoo. Jamie is a professor of library studies and a children's literature scholar. He has written several well-received books relating to children's literature and librarianship, three of them part of this Children's and Young Adult Literature Reference series. He brings years of experience connecting children and teens with the "best books" in both school and public library settings. We welcome his expertise and his contributions to all the titles in the Best Books series.

Many people were involved in the preparation of this bibliography. We are especially grateful to Barbara Ittner and Emma Bailey of Libraries Unlimited for their encouragement and support, and to Christine McNaull, who makes production of this large book possible. Kristina Strain, Chelsea Smith, and Jane Higgins also made significant contributions.

Catherine Barr

Literature

Books for Younger Readers

Alphabet, Concept, and Counting Books

Alphabet Books

1 *ABC USA* (K–2). Illus. by Martin Jarrie. 2005, Sterling $14.95 (978-1-4027-1619-5). 32pp. A strikingly illustrated celebration of American culture and history, from alligator to Zydeco. (Rev: BL 2/15/05; SLJ 5/05) [421.1]

2 Agee, Jon. *Z Goes Home* (1–3). Illus. by author. 2003, Hyperion $16.95 (978-0-7868-1987-4). Offering much for both the visually and verbally inclined, this offbeat alphabet book follows the letter Z home after a day's work on the zoo sign. (Rev: HB 11/03; HBG 4/04; SLJ 9/03)

3 Allen, Susan, and Jane Lindaman. *Read Anything Good Lately?* (K–2). Illus. by Vicky Enright. 2003, Millbrook LB $22.90 (978-0-7613-2322-8). 32pp. From "an atlas at the airport" to "the zodiac at the zoo," this alphabet book suggests places and ways to read. (Rev: BL 5/15/03; HBG 10/03; SLJ 7/03) [028]

4 Allen, Susan, and Jane Lindaman. *Written Anything Good Lately?* (1–4). Illus. by Vicky Enright. 2006, Millbrook LB $15.95 (978-0-7613-2426-3). 32pp. This attractive alphabet book introduces different types of writing — an autobiography, a brilliant book report, detailed directions, Valentine's verses, and so forth. (Rev: HBG 10/06; LMC 11/06; SLJ 4/06) [808]

5 Ashman, Linda. *M Is for Mischief: An A to Z of Naughty Children* (K–2). Illus. by Nancy Carpenter. 2008, Dutton $16.99 (978-0-525-47564-4). From Angry Abby to Zany Zelda this is an entertaining catalog of bad behavior. (Rev: BCCB 7–8/08; BL 8/08; LMC 11/08)

6 Aylesworth, Jim. *Little Bitty Mousie* (PS–2). Illus. by Michael Hague. 2007, Walker $16.95 (978-0-8027-9637-0). 32pp. A little mouse explores the house she lives in, finding everything from an Apple to a cat Z'ing. (Rev: BL 10/15/07; SLJ 10/07)

7 Aylesworth, Jim. *Naughty Little Monkeys* (PS–1). Illus. by Henry Cole. 2003, Dutton $16.99 (978-0-525-46940-7). When the (human) parents go out for the evening, their 26 little monkeys run riot — Andy making paper planes, Brooke bouncing, Carla eating cake, and so forth. (Rev: BL 9/1/03; HBG 4/04; SLJ 8/03)

8 Aylesworth, Jim. *Old Black Fly* (PS–2). Illus. by Stephen Gammell. 1992, Holt $16.95 (978-0-8050-1401-3). 32pp. A fun alphabet book that describes the 26 awful things Old Black Fly did one day. (Rev: BCCB 7–8/92; BL 2/15/92*; HB 5/92; SLJ 4/92*)

9 Azarian, Mary. *A Gardener's Alphabet* (K–2). Illus. by author. 2000, Houghton $17.00 (978-0-618-03380-5). Stunning black woodcuts hand-tinted with watercolors are featured in this handsome alphabet book that uses words associated with gardens and gardening. (Rev: BCCB 9/00; BL 4/15/00; HBG 10/00; SLJ 6/00)

10 Babypants, Caspar. *Augie to Zebra* (PS–K). Illus. by Kate Endle. 2012, Sasquatch $16.99 (978-1-570-61750-8). 32pp. An attractive alliterative alphabet book full of action and creative animal and human diversity. (Rev: BL 8/12; SLJ 10/12)

11 Baker, Keith. *LMNO Peas* (PS–1). Illus. by author. 2010, Simon & Schuster $16.99 (978-1-4169-9141-0). 40pp. An entertaining pea-oriented alphabetical introduction to occupations. (Rev: BL 2/1/10; SLJ 3/1/10*)

12 Bar-El, Dan. *Alphabetter* (PS–1). Illus. by Graham Ross. 2006, Orca $17.95 (978-1-55143-439-1). The alphabet and the 26 children taking part in an activity are out of synch; the child holding A needs an item held by B and so forth; a humorous and interesting approach. (Rev: SLJ 12/06)

13 Basher, Simon. *ABC Kids* (PS–2). Illus. by author. 2011, Kingfisher $17.99 (978-0-7534-6495-3). 64pp. Beautifully designed illustrations accompany alliterative introductions to the letters of the alphabet. (Rev: BL 5/1/11; SLJ 3/1/11)

14 Bataille, Marion. *ABC3D* (1–4). Illus. by author. 2008, Roaring Brook $19.95 (978-1-59643-425-7). 32pp. A three-dimensional alphabet book full of surprises and delights. (Rev: BLO 12/16/08)

15 Beccia, Carlyn. *Who Put the B in Ballyhoo?* (2–4). Illus. 2007, Houghton $16.00 (978-0-618-71718-7). 32pp. From A for awesome to Z for zippy, this is an alphabetical tour of circus acts of the past. (Rev: BL 4/1/07)

16 Blackstone, Stella. *Alligator Alphabet* (PS). Illus. by Stephanie Bauer. 2005, Barefoot Books $16.99 (978-1-84148-494-5). A bright A to Z of animal parent-and-baby pairs. (Rev: SLJ 1/06)

17 Bonder, Dianna. *Accidental Alphabet* (K–2). Illus. by author. 2003, Whitecap $16.95 (978-1-55285-394-8). A bouncy rhyming text accompanies detailed illustrations. (Rev: SLJ 5/03)

18 Bottner, Barbara. *An Annoying ABC* (PS–1). Illus. by Michael Emberley. 2011, Knopf $17.99 (978-0-375-86708-8); LB $20.99 (978-037596708-5). 32pp. Adelaide annoys Bailey first, then Bailey blames Clyde, and so forth to Zelda, when a chain of apologies starts. (Rev: BL 11/15/11; HB 11–12/11; SLJ 10/1/11*)

19 Brown, Margaret Wise. *Goodnight Moon ABC: An Alphabet Book* (PS–K). Illus. by Clement Hurd. 2010, HarperCollins $16.99 (978-0-06-189484-8). Unpaged. Well-known images and items from the beloved bedtime book are featured in this attractive alphabet book. (Rev: SLJ 7/1/10) [421]

20 Bruel, Nick. *Bad Kitty* (K–2). 2005, Roaring Brook $15.95 (978-1-59643-069-3). 40pp. In this cleverly conceived alphabet book, a cat misbehaves wildly when she discovers that the only foods in the house are unappealing vegetables ranging from asparagus to zucchini. (Rev: BL 12/15/05; SLJ 10/05)

21 Bruel, Nick. *A Bad Kitty Christmas* (K–3). Illus. by author. 2011, Roaring Brook $15.99 (978-159643668-8). 40pp. A rowdy alphabetical take on "The Night Before Christmas" in which Bad Kitty goes on a rampage after but eventually learns the true meaning of Christmas. (Rev: BLO 11/15/11; HB 11–12/11; SLJ 10/1/11)

22 Bruel, Nick. *Poor Puppy* (PS–2). Illus. by author. 2007, Roaring Brook $16.95 (978-1-59643-270-3). 40pp. Counting and alphabet are combined when Kitty won't play with Puppy and Puppy must amuse himself. (Rev: BL 9/1/07; SLJ 1/08)

23 Bunting, Eve. *Girls A to Z* (K–3). Illus. by Suzanne Bloom. 2002, Boyds Mills $15.95 (978-1-56397-147-1). An alphabet book filled with girls pretending to be grown-ups with interesting jobs (such as astronauts and gondoliers). (Rev: BL 9/15/02; HBG 3/03; SLJ 10/02)

24 Butler, Dori. *F Is for Firefighting* (PS–1). Illus. by Joan C. Waites. 2007, Pelican $15.95 (978-1-58980-420-3). This alphabet book introduces firefighting tools and vehicles in an entertaining format. (Rev: SLJ 6/07)

25 Buzzeo, Toni. *"R" Is for Research* (2–4). Illus. by Nicole Wong. 2008, Upstart $17.95 (978-1-60213-030-2). Students researching cats learn how to use the resources of the library as the humorous tabby called Cal D. Cat comments on their progress. (Rev: LMC 11/08*; SLJ 9/08) [027.62]

26 *C Is for Caboose: Riding the Rails from A to Z* (PS–1). Illus. 2007, Chronicle $14.95 (978-0-8118-5643-0). 32pp. A simple alphabet book that offers lots of railroad lore and an attractive vintage look. (Rev: BL 4/15/07) [385]

27 Cabatingan, Erin. *A Is for Musk Ox* (1–3). Illus. by Matthew Myers. 2012, Roaring Brook $16.99 (978-1-59643-676-3). 40pp. An indignant zebra listens as a vainglorious musk ox claims all the letters of the alphabet can be used to describe his wonderful characteristics. **e** Lexile AD470L (Rev: BL 12/1/12; LMC 3–4/13; SLJ 10/12)

28 Capucilli, Alyssa Satin. *Mrs. McTats and Her Houseful of Cats* (PS–1). Illus. by Joan Rankin. 2001, Simon & Schuster $16.00 (978-0-689-83185-0). 32pp. Mrs. McTats adds alphabetically named stray cats (and one dog) to her household in this nicely illustrated and humorous book that teaches numbers as well. (Rev: BL 9/1/01; HBG 10/01; SLJ 8/01)

29 Castella, Krystina, and Brian Boyl. *Discovering Nature's Alphabet* (2–6). Photos by authors. 2006, Heyday $15.95 (978-1-59714-021-8). Photographs of letters of the alphabet formed by nature will fascinate children and adults. (Rev: SLJ 5/06)

30 Catalanotto, Peter. *Matthew A.B.C.* (PS–2). Illus. 2002, Simon & Schuster $14.95 (978-0-689-84582-6). 32pp. There is a Matthew for every letter of the alphabet in Mrs. Tuttle's class, and each boy has a special characteristic to match his letter. (Rev: BL 7/02; HB 7/02; HBG 10/02; SLJ 6/02)

31 Cheney, Lynne. *America: A Patriotic Primer* (2–4). 2002, Simon & Schuster $16.95 (978-0-689-85192-6). 40pp. The wife of the former vice president presents an alphabet book for older children that outlines the virtues of America's democracy. (Rev: BCCB 3/02; BL 6/1–15/02; HBG 3/03; SLJ 7/02) [973]

32 Chesworth, Michael. *Alphaboat* (2–4). Illus. 2002, Farrar $16.00 (978-0-374-30244-3). 32pp. Spirited rhyming wordplay and cartoon illustrations take the crew of the Alphaboat on a lively journey in search of lost treasure. (Rev: BL 10/15/02; HBG 10/03; SLJ 9/02)

33 Chung, Hyechong. *K Is for Korea* (K–3). Illus. by Prodeepta Das. 2008, Frances Lincoln $16.95 (978-1-84507-789-1). An alphabetical introduction to Korea and its culture. (Rev: BL 12/1/08; SLJ 12/08) [951.905]

34 Cleary, Brian P. *Peanut Butter and Jellyfishes: A Very Silly Alphabet Book* (PS–2). Illus. by Betsy E. Snyder. 2007, Millbrook LB $15.95 (978-0-8225-6188-0). Children will enjoy searching for letters of the alphabet hidden in this book of alphabetical nonsense verse. (Rev: SLJ 5/07)

35 Cline-Ransome, Lesa. *Quilt Alphabet* (PS–1). Illus. by James Ransome. 2001, Holiday House $17.95 (978-0-8234-1453-6). 32pp. In this alphabet picture book, the letters are incorporated into quilt squares and accompanied by riddles. (Rev: BL 9/1/01; HBG 3/02; SLJ 11/01) [811]

36 Compestine, Ying Chang. *D Is for Dragon Dance* (K–1). Illus. by YongSheng Xuan. 2006, Holiday $17.95 (978-0-8234-1887-9). 32pp. Bright illustrations are the highlight of this alphabet book about the Chinese New Year. (Rev: BL 2/1/06; SLJ 3/06) [394.261]

37 Cronin, Doreen. *Click, Clack, Quackity-Quack: An Alphabetical Adventure* (PS). Illus. by Betsy Lewin. 2005, Simon & Schuster $12.95 (978-0-689-87715-5). 24pp. Set in a barnyard and featuring the cows that type (from *Click, Clack, Moo*), this appealing alphabet book follows preparations for a picnic. (Rev: BL 9/15/05; SLJ 11/05*)

38 Czekaj, Jef. *A Call for a New Alphabet* (K–2). Illus. by author. 2011, Charlesbridge $12.95 (978-1-58089-228-5); paper $5.95 (978-1-58089-229-2). 44pp. A disgruntled letter X complains about his place in the world — always stuck in the middle, hardly ever fronting words — until he realizes how much more responsibility the other letters have, and decides to stay just where he is. Lexile GN520L (Rev: BL 2/1/11; HB 5–6/11; SLJ 3/1/11)

39 Delessert, Etienne. *A Was an Apple Pie: An English Nursery Rhyme* (PS–2). Illus. 2005, Creative Editions $18.95 (978-1-56846-196-0). 32pp. Colorful modern art graces this alphabet book based on a 17th-century nursery rhyme. (Rev: BL 1/1–15/06; SLJ 1/06) [428.1]

40 Demarest, Chris L. *Alpha Bravo Charlie: The Military Alphabet* (K–3). Illus. 2005, Simon & Schuster $16.95 (978-0-689-86928-0). 40pp. From Alpha to Zulu, this large-format book introduces the military alphabet and corresponding U.S. Navy signal flags with many full-color illustrations of military scenes. (Rev: BL 5/15/05) [355]

41 Demarest, Chris L. *Firefighters A to Z* (PS–K). Illus. 2000, Simon & Schuster $16.95 (978-0-689-83798-2). 40pp. Beginning with "A is for Alarm," this is a large-format alphabet book showing fire fighters, their equipment, and their activities. (Rev: BL 7/00; HB 7/00; HBG 3/01; SLJ 12/00)

42 deRubertis, Barbara. *Alexander Anteater's Amazing Act* (PS–1). Illus. by R. W. Alley. Series: Animal Antics A to Z. 2010, Kane LB $22.60 (978-1-57565-304-4); paper $7.95 (978-1-57565-300-6). 32pp. With a little help and encouragement from his friends, Alexander the Anteater practices and perfects a balancing routine for the school talent show in this vocabulary-building alphabet book, the first in a series of 26. (Rev: BL 3/15/10; LMC 5–6/10; SLJ 5/1/10)

43 DiTerlizzi, Tony. *G Is for One Gzonk! An Alpha-Number-Bet Book* (K–3). Illus. by author. 2006, Simon & Schuster $16.95 (978-0-689-85290-9). This clever tribute to Dr. Seuss and Edward Lear takes readers on a chaotic romp through a poetic alphabet full of fantastic beings and unruly numbers. (Rev: SLJ 10/06)

44 Doran, Ella, et al. *A Is for Artist: An Alphabet* (PS–2). Illus. 2005, Abrams $19.95 (978-1-85437-556-8). 56pp. This striking alphabet book introduces young readers to art in a wide array of forms, ranging from a simple black-and-white photograph to the multicolored paint spatters of an abstract painting. (Rev: BL 11/1/05)

45 Downie, Mary Alice. *A Pioneer ABC* (K–2). Illus. by Mary Jane Gerber. 2005, Tundra $15.95 (978-0-88776-688-6). This attractive alphabet book shows young readers what life was like for Loyalists who migrated to Canada after the American Revolution. (Rev: SLJ 11/05)

46 Dugan, Joanne. *ABC NYC: A Book About Seeing New York City* (K–3). Photos by author. 2005, Abrams $14.95 (978-0-8109-5854-8). An urban ABC that introduces New York's sites, shapes, and sounds. (Rev: SLJ 6/05)

47 Edwards, Richard. *Amazing Animal Alphabet* (PS–1). Illus. 1999, Orchard $14.95 (978-0-531-30123-4). Arranged in alphabetical order, different animals are found hiding under flaps in this interactive book. (Rev: BL 12/15/99; SLJ 6/99)

48 Edwards, Wallace. *Alphabeasts* (PS–K). Illus. 2002, Kids Can $15.95 (978-1-55337-386-5). 32pp. Rhyming couplets caption lavish, full-page illustrations of animals from alligator to zebra. (Rev: BL 11/1/02; HBG 3/03; SLJ 12/02)

49 Ehlert, Lois. *Eating the Alphabet: Fruits and Vegetables from A to Z* (PS–1). Illus. by author. 1989, Harcourt $16.00 (978-0-15-224435-4); paper $5.95 (978-0-15-201036-2). 32pp. An eye-catching alphabet book. (Rev: BL 3/15/89; HB 5/89; SLJ 6/89)

50 Elya, Susan Middleton. *F Is for Fiesta* (K–2). Illus. by G. Brian Karas. 2006, Putnam $12.99 (978-0-399-24225-0). 32pp. This small, bright alphabet book presents Spanish words relating to celebrations within a mainly English text. (Rev: BL 2/1/06; SLJ 2/06)

51 Elya, Susan Middleton, and Merry Banks. *N Is for Navidad* (PS–2). Illus. by Joe Cepeda. 2007, Chronicle $14.95 (978-0-8118-5205-0). 32pp. Readers follow a Mexican family through their Christmas celebration in this rhyming alphabet book that introduces many Spanish words. (Rev: BCCB 1/08; BL 11/1/07; HB 11/07; LMC 5/08)

52 Ernst, Lisa Campbell. *The Turn-Around, Upside-Down Alphabet Book* (PS–2). Illus. by author. 2004, Simon & Schuster $15.95 (978-0-689-86585-5). Each letter becomes three different objects as the book is turned; for example, the A is also a beak, an ice cream cone, and the point of a star. (Rev: HB 7/04; LMC 1/05; SLJ 8/04) [428.1]

53 Evans, Nate, and Stephanie Gwyn Brown. *Bang! Boom! Roar! A Busy Crew of Dinosaurs* (PS–2). Illus. by Christopher Santoro. 2012, HarperCollins $15.99 (978-0-06-087960-0). 40pp. Combining dinosaurs, heavy equipment, and ABCs, this attractive book about creating a playground uses rhyming, alliterative text. Lexile 390L (Rev: BLO 10/1/12; SLJ 8/12)

54 Farrell, John. *Stargazer's Alphabet: Night-Sky Wonders from A to Z* (3–5). 2007, Boyds Mills $16.95 (978-1-59078-466-2). 32pp. Photographs of heavenly bodies accompany rhyming text describing astronomical wonders from A to Z. Based on a song from the author's CD *Oh, Yeah!* (Rev: SLJ 5/07)

55 Faulkenberry, Lauren. *What Do Animals Do on the Weekend? Adventures from A to Z* (K–3). Illus. by author. 2002, Novello Festival $17.95 (978-0-9708972-4-4). An alliterative approach to animal activities, where kangaroos kayak and penguins picnic, that also conveys factual information. (Rev: SLJ 10/02)

56 Fisher, Valorie. *Ellsworth's Extraordinary Electric Ears and Other Amazing Alphabet Anecdotes* (PS–2). 2003, Simon & Schuster $16.95 (978-0-689-85030-1). This fun-packed alphabet book introduces readers to 26 wildly diverse scenes and stories. (Rev: HBG 10/03; SLJ 7/03)

57 Fleming, Denise. *Alphabet Under Construction* (PS–2). Illus. 2002, Holt $16.95 (978-0-8050-6848-1). An industrious mouse assembles an alphabet using actions that start with each letter. (Rev: BCCB 10/02; BL 8/02; HB 9/02; HBG 3/03; SLJ 9/02)

58 Floca, Brian. *The Racecar Alphabet* (PS–2). Illus. by author. 2003, Simon & Schuster $15.95 (978-0-689-85091-2). Sports cars, stock cars, Formula 1 — they're all included in this attractive, alliterative alphabet book. (Rev: HB 11/03; HBG 4/04; SLJ 11/03)

59 Frampton, David. *My Beastie Book of ABC: Rhymes and Woodcuts* (PS–3). Illus. by author. 2002, HarperCollins LB $15.89 (978-0-06-028824-2). Animals from A to Z are introduced with a letter, rhyme, and illustration. (Rev: BCCB 9/02; HBG 10/02; SLJ 5/02)

60 Fuge, Charles. *Astonishing Animal ABC* (K–2). Illus. by author. 2011, Sterling $14.95 (978-1-4027-8645-7). 32pp. Full of alliteration, this entertaining alphabet book introduces animals from aardvark to an imaginary zak. (Rev: BLO 6/21/11; SLJ 7/11) [590]

61 Geisert, Arthur. *Country Road ABC: An Illustrated Journey Through America's Farmland* (PS–3). Illus. by author. 2010, Houghton Mifflin $17 (978-0-547-19469-1). 64pp. This alphabet book for older readers reveals much about rural life in the United States. (Rev: BL 4/15/10; SLJ 4/1/10) [630.973]

62 Gelber, Lisa, and Jody Roberts. *P Is for Peanut: A Photographic ABC* (4–6). 2007, Getty $9.95 (978-0-89236-878-5). A selection of black-and-white photographs from the J. Paul Getty Museum is presented in an imaginative alphabetical format. For lovers of photography as well as for children. (Rev: SLJ 5/07)

63 Girnis, Meg. *A B C for You and Me* (PS–2). Illus. by Shirley Leamon Green. 2000, Whitman $16.99 (978-0-8075-0101-6). 32pp. Using photographs of children with Down syndrome, this alphabet book celebrates the beauty of all kinds of children. (Rev: BL 7/00; HB 5/00; HBG 10/00; SLJ 4/00)

64 Grassby, Donna. *A Seaside Alphabet* (1–3). Illus. by Susan Tooke. 2000, Tundra $19.95 (978-0-88776-516-2). Picture puzzles and nautical scenes featuring the seaside introduce the alphabet. (Rev: HBG 10/00; SLJ 6/00)

65 Gritz, Ona. *Tangerines and Tea: My Grandparents and Me* (PS–K). Illus. by Yumi Heo. 2005, Abrams $15.95 (978-0-8109-5871-5). 32pp. An alliterative alphabet book featuring two preschoolers visiting their grandparents' farm. (Rev: BL 5/15/05)

66 Grobler, Piet. *Little Bird's ABC* (PS). Illus. 2005, Front St. $8.95 (978-1-932425-52-9). 32pp. A small, square beautifully illustrated alphabet of birds making often humorous sounds. (Rev: BL 11/15/05; SLJ 12/05) [411]

67 Grossman, Bill. *My Little Sister Hugged an Ape* (K–3). Illus. by Kevin Hawkes. 2004, Knopf LB $18.99 (978-0-517-80018-8). A little girl hugs a variety of unlikely animals from apes to zebras. (Rev: HB 11/04; SLJ 11/04)

68 Gutierrez, Elisa. *Letter Lunch* (K–2). Illus. by author. 2014, OwlKids $16.95 (978-177147000-1). 32pp. A visual treat involving two hungry children hunting for letters for lunch. (Rev: BL 3/1/14; SLJ 2/14)

69 Haas, Jessie. *Appaloosa Zebra: A Horse Lover's Alphabet* (PS–3). Illus. by Margot Apple. 2002, HarperCollins LB $15.89 (978-0-688-17881-9). 40pp. This informative alphabet book for girls who love horses features a different breed for almost every letter. (Rev: BL 1/1–15/02; HBG 10/02; SLJ 2/02)

70 Hanson, Anders. *Nan and Nick* (PS–1). Series: First Sounds. 2005, ABDO LB $19.93 (978-1-59679-176-3). 23pp. An alphabet book, part of a series, featuring photographs of items that begin with the letter N, followed by simple rebus sentences using the words. (Rev: SLJ 7/05) [428.1]

71 Heder, Thyra. *Fraidyzoo* (K–2). Illus. by author. 2013, Abrams $16.95 (978-1-41970776-6). 48pp. In this imaginative and humorous alphabet book, Little T's family acts out animals from A to Z in an effort to find out why she's frightened of the zoo. ALA Notable Children's Book. (Rev: BL 12/1/13; LMC 3–4/14; SLJ 10/13)

72 Herzog, Brad. *A Is for Amazing Moments: A Sports Alphabet* (2–4). Illus. by Melanie Rose. 2009, Sleeping Bear $17.95 (978-1-58536-360-5). 40pp. Four-line rhymed verses, each accompanied by a lively oil painting and brief information, range from Amazin' Mets to a clock approaching Zero. (Rev: BLO 1/13/09) [796]

73 Herzog, Brad. *G Is for Gold Medal: An Olympics Alphabet* (2–4). Illus. by Doug Bowles. 2011, Sleeping Bear $15.95 (978-158536462-6). 32pp. This alphabet book with alliterative verses includes lots of information on the games, the athletes, and related traditions. (Rev: BL 12/1/11) [796.48]

74 Herzog, Brad. *H Is for Home Run: A Baseball Alphabet* (1–4). Illus. by Melanie Rose. 2004, Sleeping Bear $16.95 (978-1-58536-219-6). An alphabet book full of alliteration and baseball lore. (Rev: SLJ 8/04) [796.357]

75 Hobbie, Holly. *Toot and Puddle: Puddle's ABC* (PS–1). Illus. 2000, Little, Brown $14.95 (978-0-316-36593-2). 48pp. To teach Otto the turtle the alphabet, little pig Puddle paints 26 clever pictures that illustrate the letters. (Rev: BCCB 12/00; BL 9/15/00; HBG 3/01; SLJ 11/00)

76 Hopkins, Lee Bennett. *Alphathoughts: Alphabet Poems* (2–6). Illus. by Marla Baggetta. 2003, Boyds Mills $15.95 (978-1-56397-979-8). An alphabet book that can be used on several levels with brief verses that describe the chosen words. (Rev: BL 4/1/03; HBG 10/03; SLJ 3/03)

77 Howell, Theresa. *A Is for Airplane / A es para Avión* (PS–2). Illus. by David Brooks. 2003, Rising Moon $6.95 (978-0-87358-831-7). A bilingual alphabet book with bright illustrations. (Rev: SLJ 3/03)

78 Howell, Will C. *Zoo Flakes ABC* (PS–2). Illus. 2002, Walker LB $16.85 (978-0-8027-8827-6). 32pp. Clever cut-paper snowflakes depict the alphabet in animal forms — O is for Octopus, for example — and children will enjoy finding the elusive animals hidden in each flake. Also includes directions on making snowflake cut-outs. (Rev: BL 12/1/02; HBG 3/03; SLJ 3/03) [736]

79 Hudes, Quiara Alegría. *Welcome to My Neighborhood! A Barrio ABC* (PS–K). Illus. by Shino Arihara. 2010, Scholastic $16.99 (978-0-545-09424-5). 32pp. From "abuela" to "Z street," this alphabet book gives a gritty but warm image of an urban neighborhood. (Rev: BL 7/10; LMC 1–2/11; SLJ 10/1/10)

80 Inkpen, Mick. *Kipper's A to Z: An Alphabet Adventure* (PS–2). Illus. 2001, Harcourt $16.95 (978-0-15-202594-6). 56pp. Arnold the pig and Kipper the dog find animals, sounds, and actions that run from A to Z. (Rev: BL 5/15/01; HBG 10/01; SLJ 6/01*)

81 Jackson, Woody. *A Cow's Alfalfa-Bet* (PS–1). Illus. by author. 2003, Houghton $15.00 (978-0-618-16599-5). Striking watercolors of New England countryside illustrate an interesting choice of alphabet words. (Rev: HBG 4/04; SLJ 9/03) [428.1]

82 Jirankova-Limbrick, Martina. *The Artful Alphabet* (PS–2). Illus. 2003, Candlewick $16.99 (978-0-7636-2187-2). 72pp. This highly visual alphabet book offers lots of interest for young eyes. (Rev: BL 2/1/04; HBG 4/04; SLJ 1/04) [428.1]

83 Jocelyn, Marthe. *ABC x 3: English, Español, Français* (PS–K). Illus. by Tom Slaughter. 2005, Tundra $12.95 (978-0-88776-707-4). This multilingual alphabet book gives words in English, French, and Spanish, often underlining their similarity. (Rev: BL 12/15/05; SLJ 10/05) [411]

84 Johnson, Stephen T. *Alphabet City* (4–7). 1995, Viking $16.99 (978-0-670-85631-2). A sophisticated alphabet book that consists of a series of paintings, each of which represents a letter. (Rev: BCCB 11/95; BL 1/1–15/96; HB 11–12/95; SLJ 1/96*) [421]

85 Johnston, Tony. *P Is for Piñata: A Mexico Alphabet* (K–4). Illus. by John Parra. 2008, Sleeping Bear $17.95 (978-1-58536-144-1). A colorful alphabet-book introduction to Mexico with rhymed lines for younger readers and detailed sidebars for older readers. (Rev: BL 12/15/08; SLJ 1/09)

86 Kalman, Maira. *What Pete Ate from A to Z* (1–3). Illus. 2001, Penguin $16.99 (978-0-399-23362-3). 40pp. Pete the dog eats everything in sight — all the way through the alphabet. (Rev: BL 9/1/01; HB 1/02; HBG 3/02; SLJ 9/01*)

87 Kirk, David. *Miss Spider's ABC* (PS–3). Illus. 1998, Scholastic $16.95 (978-0-590-28279-6). 32pp. An ABC book in which a number of creatures, mainly bugs, prepare a surprise party for Miss Spider. (Rev: BL 12/1/98; HBG 3/99; SLJ 12/98)

88 Kontis, Alethea. *Alpha Oops! The Day Z Went First* (K–2). Illus. by Bob Kolar. 2006, Candlewick $15.99 (978-0-7636-2728-7). 56pp. Z is tired of being last in the alphabet, and other letters also decide they want better places. (Rev: BL 9/1/06; SLJ 9/06)

89 Korman, Susan. *P Is for Philadelphia* (1–5). Illus. 2005, Temple Univ. $16.95 (978-1-59213-107-5). An alphabetical tour of a city full of diversity, with text on the left and illustrations by local schoolchildren on the right. (Rev: SLJ 6/05)

90 Krull, Kathleen. *M Is for Music* (PS–3). Illus. by Stacy Innerst. 2003, Harcourt $16.00 (978-0-15-201438-4). From anthem/accordion to zydeco/zither/zippy, Krull and Innerst provide a lively introduction to musical concepts. (Rev: HBG 4/04; SLJ 9/03)

91 Layne, Steven L., and Deborah Dover Layne. *T Is for Teachers: A School Alphabet* (K–4). Illus. by Doris Ettlinger. 2005, Sleeping Bear $16.95 (978-1-58536-159-5). An informative, rhyming alphabet book celebrating the joys of school. (Rev: SLJ 8/05)

92 Lear, Edward. *An Edward Lear Alphabet* (1–2). Illus. by Vladimir Radunsky. 1999, HarperCollins LB $14.89 (978-0-06-028114-4). Introduces the nonsense alphabet of Edward Lear accompanied by droll illustrations. (Rev: BL 4/1/99; HBG 10/99; SLJ 6/99) [821]

93 Lear, Edward, and Suse MacDonald. *A Was Once an Apple Pie* (PS–K). Illus. 2005, Scholastic $12.99 (978-0-439-66056-3). 32pp. Lear's nonsense alphabet is only slightly altered in this version with bright, folksy artwork. (Rev: BL 8/05; SLJ 8/05*) [821]

94 Leopold, Niki Clark. *K Is for Kitten* (PS–2). Illus. by Susan Jeffers. 2002, Penguin $15.99 (978-0-399-23563-4). An alphabet book about a girl and her kitten, with lovely artwork. (Rev: BL 9/15/02; HBG 3/03; SLJ 9/02) [811.6]

95 Leuck, Laura. *Jeepers Creepers: A Monstrous ABC* (PS–K). Illus. by David Parkins. 2003, Chronicle $15.95 (978-0-8118-3509-1). Twenty-six goofy monsters go through the typical daily routine of preschoolers. (Rev: BCCB 9/03; HBG 4/04; SLJ 12/03)

96 Lichtenheld, Tom, and Ezra Fields Meyer. *E-mergency!* (1–3). Illus. by Tom Lichtenheld. 2011, Chronicle $16.99 (978-0-8118-7898-2). 40pp. Rushing downstairs for breakfast, the letter E falls and injures herself, leaving O to take her place and causing worldwide chaos. (Rev: BL 12/1/11*; SLJ 12/1/11)

97 Lobel, Anita. *Animal Antics: A to Z* (PS). Illus. 2005, Greenwillow LB $16.89 (978-0-06-051815-8). 32pp. Striking circus-themed illustrations spotlight animals from "adoring alligators" to "zany zebras." (Rev: BL 11/1/05; SLJ 9/05) [791.3]

98 Lobel, Arnold. *On Market Street* (PS–1). Illus. by Anita Lobel. 1981, Greenwillow $17.89 (978-0-688-84309-0); Morrow paper $6.99 (978-0-688-08745-6). 40pp. A merry alphabet book with objects from apples to zippers.

99 Maass, Robert. *A Is for Autumn* (PS–2). Illus. 2011, Henry Holt $16.99 (978-0-8050-9093-2). 32pp. An alphabetical introduction to fall and its features — fallen leaves, back-to-school, Halloween, and so forth. (Rev: BL 9/1/11; SLJ 10/1/11)

100 Maccarone, Grace. *The Three Bears ABC* (PS–1). Illus. by Hollie Hibbert. 2013, Whitman $16.99 (978-0-8075-7823-0). 32pp. The story of Goldilocks is told in A to Z format. Lexile AD360 (Rev: BL 3/15/13; LMC 3–4/14; SLJ 2/13)

101 MacDonald, Suse. *Alphabet Animals: A Slide-and-Peek Adventure* (PS–K). Illus. by author. 2008, Simon & Schuster $12.99 (978-1-4169-5045-5). Animals in the shape of letters give clues and pull-out panels reveal the animal itself and its name. (Rev: SLJ 12/08)

102 McGuirk, Leslie. *If Rocks Could Sing: A Discovered Alphabet* (PS–3). Illus. by author. 2011, Tricycle $17.99 (978-1-58246-370-4); LB $20.99 (978-1-58246-395-7). 32pp. This unique alphabet book uses rocks that the author found on the beach to illustrate the letters. (Rev: BL 5/1/11; SLJ 5/1/11)

103 McLeod, Bob. *Superhero ABC* (K–3). Illus. 2006, HarperCollins $17.99 (978-0-06-074514-1). From Astro-Man ("Astro-Man Is Always Alert for an Alien Attack") to the Zinger, this alphabet book leaps off the pages. (Rev: BCCB 2/06; BL 1/1–15/06*; HB 3/06; HBG 10/06; SLJ 2/06*)

104 McLimans, David. *Gone Wild: An Endangered Animal Alphabet* (3–6). Illus. by author. 2006, Walker $16.95 (978-0-8027-9563-2). This strikingly illustrated alphabet book introduces a different endangered animal for each letter from A to Z. Caldecott Honor Book, 2007. (Rev: SLJ 11/06)

105 Madden, Caolan. *Let's Have Fun with Alphabet Riddles* (K–2). Series: Let's Find Out. 2007, Children's Pr. LB $18.00 (978-0-531-14868-6). These clever riddles, one for each letter of the alphabet, will build the skills of young children, who will find that the letters are formed from the answers. (Rev: SLJ 7/07)

106 Marino, Gianna. *Zoopa: An Animal Alphabet* (PS–2). Illus. by author. 2005, Chronicle $14.95 (978-0-8118-4789-6). This clever, colorful title introduces a menagerie of animals, from ant to zebra. (Rev: SLJ 10/05)

107 Martin, Bill, Jr., and John Archambault. *Chicka Chicka Boom Boom* (PS–2). Illus. by Lois Ehlert. 1989, Simon & Schuster $15.00 (978-0-671-67949-1). The letters of the alphabet enjoy a series of adventures. (Rev: BL 10/15/89*; HB 1/90*; SLJ 11/89)

108 Melmed, Laura K. *New York, New York! The Big Apple from A to Z* (PS–2). Illus. by Frane Lessac. 2005, HarperCollins LB $17.89 (978-0-06-054876-6). From American Museum of Natural History to Bronx Zoo, this is a lively alphabetical guide to New York, full of factoids and interesting features, plus a useful map. (Rev: SLJ 6/05)

109 Milich, Zoran. *The City ABC Book* (PS–2). Illus. 2001, Kids Can $15.95 (978-1-55074-942-7). 32pp. A Canadian photojournalist cleverly uses pictures of city structures to introduce the letters of the alphabet. (Rev: BCCB 3/01; BL 4/15/01; HB 7/01; HBG 10/01; SLJ 6/01)

110 Moncure, Jane Belk. *My "a" Sound Box* (K–1). Illus. by Colin King. Series: New Sound Box Library. 2000, Child's World LB $22.79 (978-1-56766-767-7). 30pp. Many words beginning with the letter "a" are found and put in the "a" sound box. Others in this series are *My "c" Sound Box,"* and *My "d" Sound Box* (both 2000). (Rev: SLJ 3/01)

111 Mora, Pat. *¡Marimba! Animales from A to Z* (PS–1). Illus. by Doug Cushman. 2006, Clarion $16.00 (978-0-618-19453-7). 32pp. A happy A to Z of animals frolic down the street in English and Spanish. (Rev: SLJ 11/06)

112 Morales, Yuri. *Just in Case* (K–3). Illus. by author. 2008, Roaring Brook $16.95 (978-1-59643-329-8). 32pp. Part trickster story, part ghost story, and part Mexican American alphabet book, this follows a well-dressed skeleton who collects presents from A to Z for Grandma Beetle's birthday party. (Rev: BCCB 12/08; BL 9/15/08; HB 1/09; LMC 5/09; SLJ 9/08)

113 Most, Bernard. *A B C T-Rex* (PS–K). Illus. 2000, Harcourt $13.00 (978-0-15-202007-1). A comical ABC book in which a suburban dinosaur eats his way through the alphabet. (Rev: BL 4/1/00; HBG 10/00; SLJ 4/00)

114 Murphy, Liz. *ABC Doctor* (PS–K). Illus. 2007, Blue Apple $15.95 (978-1-59354-593-2). 36pp. Introduces the ABCs of a visit to the doctor's office, with reassuring explanations. (Rev: BL 4/1/07)

115 Murray, Alison. *Apple Pie ABC* (PS–1). Illus. by author. 2011, Hyperion/Disney $16.99 (978-1-4231-3694-1). 32pp. A simple story about a dog and an apple pie is told in one-line phrases beginning with sequential letters of the alphabet. (Rev: BLO 6/21/11; HB 7–8/11; SLJ 7/11)

116 *Museum ABC: The Metropolitan Museum of Art* (K–3). Illus. 2002, Little, Brown $16.95 (978-0-316-07170-3). 60pp. The artwork is stunning in this simple alphabet book from the Metropolitan Museum of Art. (Rev: BL 11/15/02; HBG 3/03; SLJ 9/02) [708.147]

117 Napier, Matt. *Z Is for Zamboni: A Hockey Alphabet* (K–4). Illus. by Melanie Rose. 2002, Sleeping Bear $19.95 (978-1-58536-065-9). Historical highlights and facts about the game are presented in a simple A to Z using Canadian spellings. (Rev: SLJ 4/03)

118 Nickle, John. *Alphabet Explosion! Search and Count from Alien to Zebra* (PS–2). Illus. by author. 2006, Random $16.95 (978-0-375-83598-8). 40pp. A hunt-and-seek game in which young readers search for animals and objects whose names begin with each letter of the alphabet. (Rev: BL 10/1/06; SLJ 9/06) [428.1]

119 O'Connell, Rebecca. *Danny Is Done with Diapers: A Potty ABC* (PS). Illus. by Amanda Gulliver. 2010, Whitman $16.99 (978-0-8075-1466-5). 32pp. From Adam to Zach, children learn the ABCs of using a toilet, washing hands, getting dressed, and so forth. (Rev: BL 3/15/10; SLJ 3/1/10)

120 O'Keefe, Susan Heyboer. *Hungry Monster ABC* (K–2). Illus. by Lynn Munsinger. 2007, Little, Brown $12.99 (978-0-316-15574-8). Ten monsters (from *One Hungry Monster*) create chaos at school in this rhyming alphabet book that includes alphabet flash cards. (Rev: SLJ 6/07)

121 Osornio, Catherine L. *The Declaration of Independence from A to Z* (1–4). Illus. by Layne Johnson. 2010, Pelican $16.99 (978-1-58980-676-4). Unpaged. This simple, alphabetical introduction will be a useful supplement for those studying the document. (Rev: LMC 8–9/10; SLJ 4/1/10)

122 Pallotta, Jerry. *The Construction Alphabet Book* (PS–2). Illus. by Rob Bolster. 2006, Charlesbridge $16.95 (978-1-57091-437-9); paper $7.95 (978-1-57091-438-6). 32pp. From aerial lift to zipper, this volume offers arresting illustrations plus pertinent facts. (Rev: BL 7/06; SLJ 8/06) [624]

123 Pearson, Debora. *Alphabeep: A Zipping, Zooming ABC* (PS–K). Illus. by Edward Miller. 2003, Holiday House $17.95 (978-0-8234-1722-3). From "ambulance" to "zamboni," this is a celebration of moving vehicles and road signs. (Rev: HBG 4/04; SLJ 9/03)

124 Pinto, Sara. *The Alphabet Room* (PS). Illus. 2003, Bloomsbury $16.95 (978-1-58234-841-4). Flaps lift to reveal a room that gradually fills up with all the items mentioned — apples, bowl, cat, and so forth. (Rev: BL 2/1/04*) [428.1]

125 Plant, Andrew. *Could a Tyrannosaurus Play Table Tennis?* (K–4). Illus. by author. 2006, Kane paper $8.95 (978-1-929132-97-3). Combines the merits of an alphabet book and a guide to dinosaurs, introducing a prehistoric reptile for every letter from A to Z and profiling each featured dinosaur by era, size, diet, and habitat, along with a lighthearted illustration. (Rev: SLJ 8/06)

126 Raczka, Bob. *3-D ABC: A Sculptural Alphabet* (PS–2). Illus. Series: Bob Raczka's Art Adventures. 2006, Lerner LB $23.93 (978-0-7613-9456-3). 32pp. This cleverly crafted alphabet book introduces a wide array of 20th-century sculptures. (Rev: BL 11/1/06; SLJ 11/06*) [730]

127 Rash, Andy. *Agent A to Agent Z* (PS–2). Illus. 2004, Scholastic $16.95 (978-0-439-36882-7). 40pp. From A to Z, spies undertake often-ridiculous missions and end up in bizarre situations; an imaginatively illustrated, hard-boiled offering. (Rev: BL 1/1–15/04; HB 3/04; SLJ 2/04)

128 Rey, H. A. *Curious George Learns the Alphabet* (K–2). Illus. by author. 1963, Houghton $16.00 (978-0-395-16031-2); paper $6.95 (978-0-395-13718-5). 72pp. George makes learning the alphabet a wonderful and amusing game.

129 Rosenthal, Amy Krouse. *Al Pha's Bet* (PS–1). Illus. by Delphine Durand. 2011, Putnam $16.99 (978-0-399-24601-2). 32pp. Faced with a disorganized mess of recently invented letters, Al Pha takes responsibility for arranging them just so in this fun, quirky story. (Rev: BL 8/11; LMC 11–12/11; SLJ 6/11)

130 Rumford, James. *There's a Monster in the Alphabet* (1–4). Illus. 2002, Houghton $16.00 (978-0-618-22140-0). 40pp. An imaginative and complex alphabet book that looks at the origins of the letters, incorporating mythology and the Phoenician alphabet, with attractive Grecian-style illustrations. (Rev: BL 12/1/02; SLJ 10/02) [398.2]

131 Salzmann, Mary Elizabeth. *Ann and Alan* (PS–1). Series: First Sounds. 2005, ABDO LB $19.93 (978-1-59679-126-8). 23pp. An alphabet book, part of a series, featuring photographs of items that begin with the letter A, followed by simple rebus sentences using the words. Also use *Deb and Dan* (2005). (Rev: SLJ 7/05)

132 Schaefer, Carole Lexa. *ABCers* (PS–1). Illus. by Pierr Morgan. 2012, Viking $16.99 (978-0-670-01231-2). 40pp. A bright alphabet book showing diverse children in activities from A to Z. ℮ (Rev: BL 9/1/12*; SLJ 8/12)

133 Schafer, Kevin. *Penguins ABC* (PS–K). Photos by author. 2002, NorthWord $14.95 (978-1-55971-831-8). An alphabet book that will please penguin lovers. (Rev: SLJ 1/03)

134 Scillian, Devin. *P Is for Passport: A World Alphabet* (2–5). Illus. 2003, Sleeping Bear $19.95 (978-1-58536-157-1). Two dozen artists illustrated this alphabetical look at travel and at things that are part of the lives of people everywhere — B is for Bread, for example, and M is for music. (Rev: HBG 4/04; SLJ 3/04) [910]

135 Seeger, Laura Vaccaro. *Walter Was Worried* (PS–2). 2005, Roaring Brook $15.95 (978-1-59643-066-2). The weather provokes different reactions in children whose names start with each letter of the alphabet. (Rev: SLJ 8/05)

136 Seuss, Dr. *Dr. Seuss' ABC* (K–2). Illus. by author. 1963, Random $11.99 (978-0-394-90030-8). 72pp. A master author creates a strikingly popular alphabet book.

137 Shapiro, Zachary. *We're All in the Same Boat* (K–3). Illus. by Jack E. Davis. 2009, Putnam $16.99 (978-0-399-24393-6). 32pp. When Noah is fed up with the alphabetical miseries of the animals on the ark — complaining camels, grumpy giraffes — he reminds them that they're all in the same situation and the alphabet turns to enthusiastic elephants, foxes telling fables . . . . (Rev: BL 1/1–15/09; SLJ 1/09)

138 Shindler, Ramon, and Wojciech Graniczewski. *Found Alphabet* (1–3). Illus. 2005, Houghton $16.00 (978-0-618-44232-4). Brief verses and appealing photographs show found objects from airplane to zebra. (Rev: BL 6/1–15/05; SLJ 7/05)

139 Shoulders, Michael. *The ABC Book of American Homes* (1–3). Illus. by Sarah S. Brannen. 2008, Charlesbridge $17.95 (978-1-57091-565-9); paper $7.95 (978-1-57091-566-6). 32pp. An alphabetical look at American dwellings — from apartment to pueblo to White House to yurt. (Rev: BL 8/08; LMC 11/08) [728.0973]

140 Shulman, Mark. *A Is for Zebra* (1–3). Illus. by Tamara Petrosino. 2006, Sterling $14.95 (978-1-4027-3494-6). 32pp. With colorful cartoons, this funny variation on the traditional alphabet book turns the spotlight on the final letter of each word, as in the title example. (Rev: BL 3/15/06) [428.1]

141 Shulman, Mark. *AA Is for Aardvark: Double the Letters, Double the Fun* (PS–3). Illus. by Tamara Petrosino. 2005, Sterling LB $14.95 (978-1-4027-2871-6). Letters appearing twice in a row are the focus of this inventive and effective alphabet book. (Rev: SLJ 2/06)

142 Siddals, Mary McKenna. *Compost Stew: An A to Z Recipe for the Earth* (PS–2). Illus. by Ashley Wolff. 2010, Tricycle $15.99 (978-1-58246-316-2). 32pp. A rhyming, alphabetical recipe — with an engaging chorus — for making compost. (Rev: BL 2/15/10; SLJ 4/1/10)

143 Sierra, Judy. *The Sleepy Little Alphabet: A Bedtime Story from Alphabet Town* (PS–1). Illus. by Melissa Sweet. 2009, Knopf $16.99 (978-0-375-84002-9). 40pp. Uppercase parents and lowercase children humorously struggle through familiar bedtime routines in a book filled with amusing, detailed illustrations and rhyming text. (Rev: BL 7/09; SLJ 6/09)

144 Smith, Marie, and Roland Smith. *Z Is for Zookeeper: A Zoo Alphabet* (K–4). Illus. by Henry Cole. 2005, Sleeping Bear $16.95 (978-1-58536-158-8). "Animals," "brooms," and "quarantine" are only three of the letters in this text that also includes additional information for the curious reader. (Rev: SLJ 9/05)

145 Sobel, Jane. *Shiver Me Letters: A Pirate ABC* (PS–2). Illus. by Henry Cole. 2006, Harcourt $16.00 (978-0-15-216732-5). 32pp. Animal buccaneers may have to walk the plank if they don't manage to track down every letter from A to Z. (Rev: BL 6/1–15/06; SLJ 6/06)

146 Sobel, June. *B Is for Bulldozer: A Construction ABC* (PS–K). Illus. by Melissa Iwai. 2003, Harcourt $16.00 (978-0-15-202250-1). This appealing alphabet book focuses on the construction of a roller coaster, introducing a new tool, material, or piece of construction equipment for each letter of the alphabet. (Rev: HBG 10/03; SLJ 7/03)

147 Spirin, Gennady. *A Apple Pie* (PS–2). Illus. 2005, Philomel $16.99 (978-0-399-23981-6). 32pp. This whimsical alphabet book full of lovely, detailed watercolor paintings revives a 17th-century nursery rhyme and introduces verbs for the letters from A to Z. (Rev: BL 11/1/05; SLJ 9/05)

148 Stewig, John W. *The Animals Watched: An Alphabet Book* (K–2). Illus. by Rosanne Litzinger. 2007, Holiday $16.95 (978-0-8234-1906-7). 32pp. Animal pairs from aardvarks to zebras (and including urodeles and other unfamiliar animals) give their viewpoints on the voyage aboard Noah's ark. (Rev: BL 11/1/07; SLJ 9/07)

149 *T Is for Tugboat: Navigating the Seas from A to Z* (PS–2). Illus. 2008, Chronicle $15.99 (978-0-8118-6094-9). 32pp. With an attractive mix of vintage and contemporary images, this alphabet book covers all things nautical, starting with "Anchor," "Ahoy!," and "Aground." (Rev: BL 5/1/08; SLJ 7/08) [623.8]

150 Ulmer, Wendy. *A Isn't for Fox: An Isn't Alphabet* (PS–K). Illus. by Laura Knorr. 2008, Sleeping Bear $16.95 (978-1-58536-319-3). 32pp. Rhyming couplets

tell what a letter does not stand for before offering a word that does start with it. (Rev: BL 4/15/08; LMC 10/08; SLJ 7/08)

151 Vidrine, Beverly Barras. *Thanksgiving Day Alphabet* (1–3). Illus. by Alison Davis Lyne. 2006, Pelican paper $7.95 (978-1-58980-338-1). This colorful Thanksgiving alphabet book introduces people, places, and things related to the holiday's history. (Rev: SLJ 11/06) [394.2649]

152 Wallace, Nancy Elizabeth. *Alphabet House* (PS–2). Illus. 2005, Marshall Cavendish $16.95 (978-0-7614-5192-1). Inside Alphabet House, which is home to a rabbit family, young readers will find multiple examples of words that begin with each letter of the alphabet. (Rev: BL 11/1/05; SLJ 10/05)

153 Watterson, Carol. *An Edible Alphabet: 26 Reasons to Love the Farm* (PS–2). Illus. by Michela Sorrentino. 2011, Tricycle $16.99 (978-1-58246-421-3); LB $19.99 (978-1-58246-422-0). 48pp. From "Ants on Asparagus" to "Zoom Zoom Zucchini," rich collage illustrations and clever wordplay add appeal to this informative, farm-centric alphabet book. (Rev: BL 6/1/11; SLJ 7/11) [530]

154 Wells, Rosemary. *Max's ABC* (PS–K). 2006, Viking $15.99 (978-0-670-06074-0). 32pp. Brief episodes featuring rabbit siblings Max and Ruby introduce every letter from A to Z. (Rev: BL 6/1–15/06; SLJ 5/06)

155 Werner, Sharon. *Alphabeasties and Other Amazing Types* (K–4). Illus. by Sarah Forss. 2009, Blue Apple $19.99 (978-1-934706-78-7). Unpaged. Multiple typefaces grace this joyful alphabetical exploration of animals and vocabulary. (Rev: LMC 11–12/09; SLJ 10/1/09)

156 Wilbur, Helen L. *M Is for Meow* (3–6). Illus. by Robert Papp. (2007, Sleeping Bear $17.95. Realistic illustrations accompany facts about all sorts of cats in this installment in this alphabet series. (Rev: SLJ 5/07)

157 Winter, Jeanette. *Calavera Abecedario: A Day of the Dead Alphabet Book* (K–3). Illus. 2004, Harcourt $16.00 (978-0-15-205110-5). 48pp. With a story about preparing for Mexico's Dia de los Muertos as a backdrop, Winter presents an alphabet celebrating the skeletons that mark the holiday. (Rev: BL 11/1/04; SLJ 5/05) [394.266]

158 Wisnewski, Andrea. *A Cottage Garden Alphabet* (2–4). Illus. 2003, Godine $18.95 (978-1-56792-229-5). 64pp. Beautiful cut-paper illustrations of a garden's bounty accompany each letter of the alphabet. (Rev: BL 2/15/03; HBG 10/03; SLJ 5/03) [635]

159 Wojtowycz, David. *Animal ABC* (K–1). Illus. by author. 2000, David & Charles $14.95 (978-1-86233-107-5). A host of animals from an athletic aardvark to a zigzag zebra introduce the alphabet. (Rev: SLJ 9/00)

160 Wood, Audrey. *Alphabet Adventure* (PS–2). Illus. by Bruce Wood. 2001, Scholastic $16.95 (978-0-439-08069-9). 40pp. The 26 letters are on their way to teach a child the alphabet when they encounter some difficulties in this inventive book illustrated with glowing, computer-generated graphics. (Rev: BL 9/1/01; HBG 3/02; SLJ 9/01)

161 Wood, Audrey. *Alphabet Mystery* (PS–2). Illus. by Bruce Wood. 2003, Scholastic $16.99 (978-0-439-44337-1). When Little x disappears, the other 25 letters of the alphabet launch a search. (Rev: BL 12/1/03; HBG 4/04; SLJ 11/03)

162 Wood, Audrey. *Alphabet Rescue* (PS–2). Illus. by Bruce Wood. 2006, Scholastic $15.99 (978-0-439-85316-3). 40pp. Readers join the lowercase letters of the alphabet as they repair an old fire truck and come to the rescue of other letters that need help. (Rev: BL 11/15/06; SLJ 10/06)

163 Ziefert, Harriet. *ABC Dentist* (K–3). Illus. by Liz Murphy. 2008, Blue Apple $15.95 (978-1-934706-31-2). 36pp. An alphabetical reassurance that a visit to the dentist is not going to be a horrible experience. (Rev: BL 11/15/08; SLJ 11/08) [617.6]

Concept Books

GENERAL

164 Aber, Linda Williams. *Grandma's Button Box* (K–1). Illus. by Page Eastburn O'Rourke. 2002, Kane paper $4.95 (978-1-57565-110-1). When a young girl drops her grandmother's button box, she and her cousins try different ways of sorting them out in this simple concept book. (Rev: BL 4/15/02)

165 Abramson, Beverley. *Off We Go!* (PS). Photos by author. 2006, Tundra $15.95 (978-0-88776-728-9). Multicultural children enjoy a multitude of energetic activities in this book of few words. (Rev: HBG 10/06; SLJ 6/06)

166 Alda, Arlene. *Hello, Good-bye* (PS–K). Illus. by author. 2009, Tundra $16.95 (978-0-88776-900-9). 32pp. A great conversation starter, this concept book features eye-catching color photographs that demonstrate opposites such as "straight" and "slanted" and "old" and "new." (Rev: BL 1/1–15/09; SLJ 5/09)

167 Alda, Arlene. *Here a Face, There a Face* (PS–3). Illus. 2008, Tundra $14.95 (978-0-88776-845-3). 24pp. Here Alda looks at the "faces" we see in all sorts of objects. (Rev: BL 2/15/08; SLJ 6/08)

168 Aliki. *Push Button* (PS). Illus. by author. 2010, Greenwillow $16.99 (978-0-06-167308-5). 40pp. Only when his finger hurts too much does this toddler stop pushing any available buttons and consider other forms of entertainment. (Rev: BL 2/15/10*; HB 7–8/10; SLJ 4/1/10)

169 Aliki. *Feelings* (K–2). Illus. 1984, Greenwillow $16.89 (978-0-688-03832-8); Morrow paper $6.99 (978-0-688-06518-8). 32pp. An introduction to various emotions.

170 *American Babies* (PS). Illus. 2010, Charlesbridge $6.95 (978-158089280-3). 16pp. A companion volume to *Global Babies,* this board book offers close-up photographs of diverse babies accompanied by brief text. (Rev: BL 5/1/10*)

171 Asim, Jabari. *Whose Knees Are These?* (PS). Illus. by LeUyen Pham. 2006, Little, Brown $6.99 (978-0-316-73576-6). A happy brown-skinned baby rejoices in bending knees in this board book with simple rhymes and lively illustrations. Also use *Whose Toes Are Those?* (2006). (Rev: SLJ 6/06)

172 Baeten, Lieve. *Little Witch's Magic Word Book* (PS–2). Illus. by author. 2012, NorthSouth $9.95 (978-073584102-4). 14pp. This large-format board book based on the Little Witch series features large illustrations and a find-the-object game. (Rev: BLO 9/1/12)

173 Baker, Alan. *Little Rabbit's First Time Book* (PS–K). Illus. 1999, Kingfisher $10.95 (978-0-7534-5220-2). 16pp. The activities of three bunnies throughout a day illustrate the passage of hours, which can be traced by using the movable hands on a clock. (Rev: BL 12/1/99; SLJ 2/00)

174 Baker, Keith. *Just How Long Can a Long String Be?* (PS–2). Illus. by author. 2009, Scholastic $16.99 (978-0-545-08661-5). 32pp. Ant and Bird consider the various uses of string (for a banjo, a balloon, a yoyo, a fishing line, and so forth) and the lengths needed. (Rev: BL 4/15/09; HB 7/09; SLJ 5/09)

175 Barraclough, Sue. *Fast and Slow* (PS–K). Illus. Series: How Do Things Move? 2006, Raintree LB $14.95 (978-1-4109-2261-8). 24pp. The concept of speed is illustrated in spreads depicting two objects moving at different paces. (Rev: BL 4/1/06) [531]

176 Bauer, Marion Dane. *One Brown Bunny* (PS–K). Illus. by Ivan Bates. 2009, Scholastic $14.99 (978-0-439-68010-3). 32pp. This double-duty concept book does colors and numbers from 1 through 10. (Rev: BL 12/1/08; SLJ 4/09)

177 Bauer, Marion Dane. *Thank You for Me!* (PS–1). Illus. by Kristina Stephenson. 2010, Simon & Schuster $14.99 (978-0-689-85788-1). 32pp. Vibrantly illustrated, this book features rhymed text celebrating all the wondrous things a body is capable of. (Rev: BL 1/1/10; SLJ 2/1/10)

178 Bauer, Marion Dane. *Toes, Ears, and Nose!* (PS). Illus. by Karen Katz. 2003, Simon & Schuster $5.99 (978-0-689-84712-7). In this colorful lift-the-flap title, preschoolers are introduced to various parts of the human body. (Rev: SLJ 6/03)

179 Beaton, Clare. *Daisy Gets Dressed* (PS–K). Illus. 2005, Barefoot Books $15.99 (978-1841487939). A seek-and-find book that requires the reader to identify among many patterns the right pieces of clothing to complete Daisy's outfit. (Rev: BL 5/1/05)

180 Beaton, Clare. *How Big Is a Pig?* (PS–K). Illus. 2000, Barefoot Books $14.99 (978-1-84148-077-0). 32pp. Double-page spreads are used in this amusing book that illustrates opposites in animals — fast and slow dogs and quiet and jumpy frogs. (Rev: BL 10/1/00; HBG 3/01; SLJ 12/00)

181 Beeke, Tiphanie. *Roar Like a Lion! A First Book About Sounds* (PS). Illus. 2001, Sterling $7.95 (978-1-86233-143-3). 16pp. This fun-filled book about a mouse trying to find friends will have preschoolers making all kinds of jungle noises. (Rev: BL 3/1/02)

182 Behrens, Janice. *Let's Find Rain Forest Animals: Up, Down, Around* (PS–1). Illus. Series: Let's Find Out. 2007, Scholastic LB $18.00 (978-0-531-14874-7). 32pp. Readers guess which rain forest animals are shown in cropped photographs and in the process learn "position" words; factual information is appended. (Rev: BL 4/1/07) [591.734]

183 Bender, and Bender. *Ribbit! Flip and See Who Froggy Can Be* (K–3). Illus. by authors. 2007, HarperCollins $16.99 (978-0-06-113820-1). Flip pages divided into three horizontal sections allow children to "dress" Froggy in different zany outfits. (Rev: SLJ 8/07)

184 Berkes, Marianne. *Over in a River: Flowing Out to the Sea* (PS–2). Illus. by Jill Dubin. 2013, Dawn paper $8.95 (978-15846933-0-7). 32pp. This counting book introduces 10 North American rivers and the animals that live there; with collage illustrations and a surprise on each spread. (Rev: BLO 9/15/13; LMC 3–4/14; SLJ 10/13)

185 Bernhard, Durga. *To and Fro, Fast and Slow* (PS–2). Illus. 2001, Walker LB $16.85 (978-0-8027-8783-5). 32pp. This clever, well-illustrated concept book uses a girl's visits to her mother's country home and her father's city apartment to show opposites. (Rev: BL 11/1/01; HBG 3/02; SLJ 9/01)

186 Bond, Felicia. *Big Hugs, Little Hugs* (PS). Illus. by author. 2012, Philomel $16.99 (978-0-399-25614-1). 32pp. Illustrations of all kinds of loving animals, both wild and domestic, show that there are many different ways to hug. (Rev: BL 1/12; SLJ 12/1/11)

187 Boutignon, Beatrice. *Not All Animals Are Blue* (PS–K). Illus. by author. 2009, Kane $15.95 (978-1-933605-96-8). 48pp. Which sentences describe which animals? Each spread offers five animals and five questions. (Rev: BL 3/15/09; HB 5/09; SLJ 5/09)

188 Brocket, Jane. *Spiky, Slimy, Smooth: What Is Texture?* (PS–2). Illus. by author. Series: Clever Concepts. 2011, Millbrook LB $25.26 (978-0-7613-4614-2). 32pp. Brocket introduces the concept of texture using evocative words and bright, eye-catching photographs of various objects and foods. (Rev: BL 4/15/11; SLJ 5/1/11) [612.8]

189 Bullard, Lisa. *Long and Short: An Animal Opposites Book* (K–2). Series: A+ Books: Animal Opposites. 2005, Capstone LB $23.93 (978-0-7368-4275-4). Animal pairings — a python and a bat, for example — introduce the concept of opposites. Also use *Loud and Quiet* (2005). (Rev: SLJ 1/06) [590]

190 Butler, John. *Can You Growl Like a Bear?* (PS–K). Illus. by author. 2007, Peachtree $15.95 (978-1-56145-396-2). 32pp. From the click of a dolphin to the howl of a wolf, this "sound-along" picture book highlights 10 animals, ending with a suggestion of the sound of sleep. (Rev: BL 9/1/07; SLJ 9/07)

191 Butler, John. *If You See a Kitten* (PS). Illus. by author. 2003, Peachtree $13.95 (978-1-56145-108-1). Cuddly kittens, pudgy pigs, and slithery snakes are among the animals introduced with suggested one-word responses — "Ahhh!" or "Yikes," for example. (Rev: BL 3/03; HBG 10/03; SLJ 5/03)

192 Carle, Eric. *From Head to Toe* (PS). Illus. 1997, HarperCollins LB $17.89 (978-0-06-023516-1). Children make the same movements as animals in this concept book illustrated with lively collages. (Rev: BCCB 6/97; BL 4/15/97; SLJ 4/97) [613.7]

193 Carle, Eric. *My Very First Book of Words* (PS–1). Illus. by author. 1985, HarperCollins $2.95 (978-0-690-57368-8). 10pp. A nicely illustrated beginning word book, printed on heavy stock cards.

194 Cendrars, Blaise. *Shadow* (K–3). Trans. and illus. by Marcia Brown. 1982, Macmillan $17.00 (978-0-684-17226-2). 40pp. This Caldecott winner (1983) explores the mysterious world of shadows.

195 Clark, Emma Chichester. *Mimi's Book of Opposites* (PS). Illus. by author. Series: A Mimi Book. 2003, Charlesbridge $9.95 (978-1-57091-574-1). In this appealing concept book, Mimi the monkey and her little brother explore the world of opposites. (Rev: HBG 4/04; SLJ 11/03)

196 Cocca-Leffler, Maryann. *Rain Brings Frogs: A Little Book of Hope* (PS–2). Illus. by author. 2011, HarperCollins $9.99 (978-0-06-196106-9). 32pp. Nate, a little boy who sees everything on the bright side, helps show readers see the good things in life. (Rev: BL 2/15/11; SLJ 2/1/11)

197 Costello, David Hyde. *I Can Help* (PS–K). Illus. by author. 2010, Farrar $12.99 (978-0-374-33526-7). 32pp. In this simple, charming story, the pattern of being the rescuer and rescued is repeated as one animal after another calls on his friends for help. (Rev: BL 1/1/10; LMC 1–2/10; SLJ 1/1/10)

198 Cousins, Lucy. *Maisy's Amazing Big Book of Learning* (PS–K). Illus. by author. 2011, Candlewick $14.99 (978-076365481-8). 48pp. Maisy the mouse's life is full of concepts as she counts, makes noises, jumps, watches the weather, and so forth; this oversize book has lots of lift-the-flap features. (Rev: BL 9/1/11)

199 Crowther, Robert. *Opposites* (PS–1). Illus. 2005, Candlewick $12.99 (978-0-7636-2783-6). 16pp. Bright collage artwork and clever, sturdy pull-tab and lift-the-flap features illustrate opposites — happy and sad, full and empty, and so forth. (Rev: BL 9/1/05; SLJ 9/05) [428.1]

200 Cumpiano, Ina. *Quinito, Day and Night / Quinito, día y noche* (PS–K). Illus. by José Ramírez. 2008, Children's Book Pr. $16.95 (978-0-89239-226-1). A bright, bilingual look at opposites, presented by the little boy last seen in *Quinito's Neighborhood* (2005). (Rev: BL 7/08; SLJ 9/08)

201 Davis, Nancy. *A Garden of Opposites* (PS–K). Illus. by author. 2009, Random $10.99 (978-0-375-85666-2). 26pp. This concept book uses a farm garden to show eight sets of opposites. (Rev: BLO 5/15/09; SLJ 4/09)

202 Emberley, Ed. *Where's My Sweetie Pie?* (PS–1). Illus. by author. 2010, Little, Brown $7.99 (978-031601891-3). 14pp. Readers raise die-cut flaps as they hunt through the pages for the missing sweetie pie. (Rev: BL 2/1/10)

203 Emberley, Rebecca. *My Opposites / Mis Opuestos* (PS). 2000, Little, Brown $5.95 (978-0-316-23345-3). 20pp. A concept board book that introduces opposites in English and Spanish. (Rev: BCCB 12/00*; HBG 3/01; SLJ 9/00)

204 Falconer, Ian. *Olivia's Opposites* (PS). Illus. 2002, Simon & Schuster $6.99 (978-0-689-85088-2). 12pp. A simple board book featuring Olivia the pig that demonstrates the concept of opposites. (Rev: BL 7/02; HBG 10/02; SLJ 6/02)

205 Fisher, Valorie. *Everything I Need to Know Before I'm Five* (PS–K). Illus. by author. 2011, Random House $17.99 (978-0-375-86865-8). 40pp. An appealing concept book covering numbers, opposites, shapes, colors, seasons, weather, and the alphabet. (Rev: BL 7/11; HB 7–8/11; SLJ 7/11)

206 Fleming, Denise. *The Everything Book* (PS). Illus. 2000, Holt $18.95 (978-0-8050-6292-2). 64pp. This book offers all sorts of information on topics ranging from the seasons and days of the week to parts of the body plus poems, songs, and games. (Rev: BCCB 10/00; BL 7/00; HBG 3/01; SLJ 10/00)

207 Fleming, Denise. *Shout! Shout It Out!* (PS–1). 2011, Henry Holt $16.99 (978-0-8050-9237-0). 40pp. Readers are encouraged to vocalize with enthusiasm their knowledge of numbers, the alphabet, colors, animal names, and so forth. ℮ (Rev: BL 3/1/11; HB 3–4/11; SLJ 2/1/11)

208 Freymann, Saxton, and Joost Elffers. *Food for Thought: The Complete Book of Concepts for Growing Minds* (PS). Illus. 2005, Scholastic $14.95 (978-0-439-11018-1). Colors, letters, numbers, opposites, and shapes are all introduced using the authors' signature fruits and vegetables. (Rev: BL 1/1–15/05; SLJ 3/05)

209 Friday, Mary Ellen. *It's a Bad Day* (PS–K). Illus. by Glin Dibley. 2006, Rising Moon $15.95 (978-0-87358-904-8). Discouraging events that can turn a good day into a bad day are put into perspective in this simple and charming book. (Rev: SLJ 5/07)

210 Gabriel, Nat. *Sam's Sneaker Squares* (1–2). Illus. by Ron Fritz. 2002, Kane paper $4.95 (978-1-57565-114-9). 32pp. In this concept book, Sam learns about measurements to determine the cost of mowing lawns. (Rev: BL 4/15/02)

211 George, Patrick. *I See . . .* (PS–K). Illus. by author. 2013, IPG $12.99 (978-1-908473-04-2). 36pp. A simple introduction to the sense of sight, cheerfully depicting the different ways people can see: up, down, upside down, near, and far. (Rev: BLO 10/1/13; SLJ 7/13)

212 Gordon, Sharon. *Dirty Clean* (PS–2). Series: Bookworms: Just the Opposite. 2003, Benchmark LB $21.36 (978-0-7614-1569-5). 23pp. A primer in the contrast between things that are dirty and things that are clean and how they might get that way. (Rev: HBG 4/04; SLJ 3/04)

213 Gordon, Sharon. *Fast Slow* (PS–2). Series: Bookworms: Just the Opposite. 2003, Benchmark LB $21.36 (978-0-7614-1570-1). The contrast between fast and slow is explored through various means of transportation, from rollerskates to cars. (Rev: HBG 4/04; SLJ 3/04)

214 Got, Yves. *Sweet Dreams, Sam* (PS). Illus. 2000, Chronicle $8.95 (978-0-8118-2985-4). This interactive book uses different textures to explore the sense of touch, such as simulating the crinkly skin of an elephant. (Rev: BL 12/1/00)

215 Gravett, Emily. *Orange Pear Apple Bear* (PS–1). Illus. by author. 2007, Simon & Schuster $12.99 (978-1-4169-3999-3). A brown bear stars in this book about shapes, colors, and sequence. (Rev: SLJ 4/07*)

216 Greve, Meg. *Integrity* (PS–K). Illus. Series: Little World Social Skills. 2012, Rourke LB $22.79 (978-161810137-2); paper $7.95 (9781618102706). 24pp. With simple text and photographs, plus a quiz, this volume introduces the concept of integrity. (Rev: BLO 9/1/12)

217 Gurth, Per-Henrik. *Hockey Opposites* (PS). Illus. by author. 2010, Kids Can $15.95 (978-155453241-4). 24pp. A simple introduction to opposites using ice hockey examples — out/in, win/lose, big/small, and so forth. (Rev: BL 9/1/10)

218 Hall, Michael. *My Heart Is Like a Zoo* (PS). Illus. by author. 2010, Greenwillow $16.99 (978-0-06-191510-9); LB $17.89 (978-0-06-191511-6). 32pp. Readers consider various emotions as they explore bright collages of zoo animals showing expressions such as "eager as a beaver," "angry as a bear," "brave as a lion." (Rev: BL 11/15/09; SLJ 2/1/10)

219 Harper, Charise Mericle. *Amy and Ivan* (PS). Illus. by author. 2006, Tricycle $12.95 (978-1-58246-134-2). 24pp. Amy is planning a surprise party for her friend Ivan in this bright, square, lift-the-flap book with numbers and colors for children to name. (Rev: BL 5/15/06; SLJ 9/06)

220 Harper, Jamie. *Splish Splash, Baby Bundt* (PS). Illus. by author. 2007, Candlewick $6.99 (978-0-7636-3240-3). A board book recipe for a successful bathtime — 1 sticky Baby Bundt, 1 family of rubber ducks . . . (Rev: SLJ 1/08)

221 Hartman, Gail. *As the Crow Flies: A First Book of Maps* (PS–1). Illus. by Harvey Stevenson. 1993, Aladdin paper $5.99 (978-0-689-71762-8). 32pp. The concept of maps is introduced by using the environments of different animals. (Rev: BL 3/1/91; HB 5/91; SLJ 3/91)

222 Henry, Jed. *I Speak Dinosaur* (PS–K). Illus. by author. 2012, Abrams $14.95 (978-141970233-4). 32pp. A young boy who has adopted the manners and roars of a dinosaur learns there might be better ways to behave in public. (Rev: BLO 3/1/12; LMC 8–9/12; SLJ 4/12)

223 Herman, Gail. *Bad Luck Brad* (1–2). Illus. by Stephanie Roth. Series: Math Matters. 2002, Kane paper $4.95 (978-1-57565-112-5). 32pp. The concept of probability is explored when a series of misfortunes occur to Brad on a single day. (Rev: BL 5/1/02)

224 Hicks, Barbara Jean. *I Like Black and White* (PS). Illus. by Lila Prap. 2006, ME Media $9.95 (978-1-58925-057-4). Simple black-and-white art (with color accents) and brief, rhyming text depict animals, patterns, and shapes. (Rev: BL 5/15/06)

225 Hills, Tad. *What's Up, Duck?* (PS). Illus. by author. Series: Duck and Goose. 2008, Random $6.99 (978-0-375-84738-7). 22pp. Duck, Goose, and Thistle illustrate nine opposites — loud and quiet, front and back, and so forth — in this board book. (Rev: BL 4/1/08) [428.1]

226 Hoban, Tana. *Black on White* (PS). Illus. 1993, Greenwillow $6.99 (978-0-688-11918-8). The photographs show black objects on a white background. A companion book is *White on Black* (1993). (Rev: HB 7/93; SLJ 8/93)

227 Hoban, Tana. *What Is That?* (PS). Illus. 1994, Greenwillow paper $6.99 (978-0-688-12920-0). 12pp. Using silhouettes, a number of common animals are pictured in this board book. Also use *Who Are They?* (1994). (Rev: BL 12/1/94; HB 11/94; SLJ 11/94)

228 Holland, Gini. *Light and Heavy* (K–1). Series: I Know Opposites. 2007, Gareth Stevens LB $17.27 (978-0-8368-8295-7); paper $4.50 (978-0-8368-8300-8). 16pp. Bright photographs and simple text illustrate such opposites as a light toy truck and a heavy fire truck. Also use *Soft and Hard* and *Alive and Not Alive* (both 2007). (Rev: SLJ 12/07) [530.8]

229 Horowitz, Dave. *Twenty-six Princesses* (PS–2). Illus. by author. 2008, Putnam $15.99 (978-0-399-24607-4). From Alice to Zaire, 26 royal young ladies — presented in portraits and rhyming couplets that capture their nature — set off to meet the prince (er, frog). (Rev: BCCB 6/08; LMC 11/08; SLJ 4/08)

230 Hudson, Cheryl W. *Hands Can* (PS). Photos by John-Francis Bourke. 2003, Candlewick $14.99 (978-0-7636-1667-0). Bright colors and eye-catching photos draw readers into this display of movements and expressions made with hands. (Rev: BL 10/1/03; HBG 4/04; SLJ 12/03)

231 Hutchins, Hazel. *A Second Is a Hiccup: A Child's Book of Time* (PS–2). Illus. by Kady M. Denton. 2007, Scholastic $16.99 (978-0-439-83106-2). Children will recognize the many examples given here for seconds, minutes, and hours and what can be accomplished within their parameters. (Rev: BL 1/1–15/07; SLJ 3/07*)

232 Isadora, Rachel. *Say Hello!* (PS–1). Illus. by author. 2010, Putnam $16.99 (978-0-399-25230-3). 32pp. Carmelita and her mother greet their multicultural neighbors in a variety of languages, while their dog Manny sticks to "woof." (Rev: BL 2/15/10; LMC 5–6/10; SLJ 3/1/10)

233 Jocelyn, Marthe. *A Day with Nellie* (PS). Illus. by author. 2002, Tundra $15.95 (978-0-88776-600-8). 24pp. Numbers, colors, the alphabet, and other concepts are introduced as readers follow preschooler Nellie through the activities of her ordinary day. (Rev: BL 12/1/02; HBG 3/03; SLJ 1/03)

234 Jocelyn, Marthe. *Same Same* (PS–K). Illus. by Tom Slaughter. 2009, Tundra $15.95 (978-0-88776-885-9). 24pp. Bright illustrations depict sets of three objects that are alike — "round things," for example, and "things that make music." (Rev: BCCB 2/09; BL 3/1/09; SLJ 3/09)

235 Jocelyn, Marthe, and Nell Jocelyn. *Ones and Twos* (PS–1). Illus. by Marthe Jocelyn. 2011, Tundra $15.95 (978-1-77049-220-2). 24pp. Rhyming couplets follow a bird and a girl as they go about their everyday activities, highlighting instances of ones and twos. (Rev: BL 4/15/11; HB 9–10/11; SLJ 5/1/11*) [513.2]

236 Jolivet, Joëlle. *Almost Everything* (PS–2). Illus. 2005, Roaring Brook $19.95 (978-1-59643-090-7). 40pp. This large-format collection of images, a follow-up to *Zoo-ology* (2003), is organized into 13 categories, including tools, the human body, historical costumes, and trees and flowers. (Rev: BL 11/1/05; SLJ 11/05) [423]

237 Katz, Karen. *Ten Tiny Tickles* (PS). Illus. 2005, Simon & Schuster $14.95 (978-0-689-85976-2). 32pp. A simple book that celebrates the various parts of a baby and offers counting opportunities as well. (Rev: BL 7/05; SLJ 7/05)

238 Krensky, Stephen. *I Know a Lot!* (PS). Illus. by Sara Gillingham. 2013, Abrams/Appleseed $6.95 (978-1-4197-0938-8). 12pp. A little girl's understanding of opposites gives her confidence in herself in this charming board book. (Rev: BL 11/15/13; SLJ 10/13)

239 Kroll, Steven. *That Makes Me Mad!* (PS–1). Illus. by Christine Davenier. 2002, North-South LB $16.50 (978-1-58717-184-0). A newly illustrated edition of the 1976 story about Nina and everything that makes her mad. (Rev: HBG 3/03; SLJ 8/02)

240 Laden, Nina. *Grow Up!* (PS). Illus. 2003, Chronicle $6.95 (978-0-8118-3761-3). 26pp. A well-illustrated, rhyming board book about growing up in which a kitten becomes a cat, a puppy becomes a dog, a seedling become a tree, and so forth. (Rev: BL 5/15/03)

241 Lewis, J. Patrick. *Big Is Big (and Little, Little): A Book of Contrasts* (PS–1). Illus. by Bob Barner. 2007, Holiday House $16.95 (978-0-8234-1909-8). Big, sad, fat, dark, and hot animals meet their opposites in this delightfully illustrated book. (Rev: SLJ 5/07)

242 Lewison, Wendy Cheyette. *Two Is for Twins* (PS). Illus. by Hiroe Nakata. 2006, Viking $16.99 (978-0-670-06128-0). 40pp. This bright picture book celebrates things that come in pairs, especially twins. (Rev: BL 5/15/06; SLJ 4/06)

243 Lobel, Anita. *Ten Hungry Rabbits: Counting and Color Concepts* (PS). Illus. by author. 2012, Knopf $9.99 (978-037586864-1); LB $12.99 (978-037596864-8). 24pp. A herd of 10 young bunnies are sent into the garden to gather a variety of different-colored fruits and vegetables for dinner in this numbers and colors concept story. (Rev: BL 1/1/12; HB 1–2/12; SLJ 1/12)

244 Mamada, Mineko. *Which Is Round? Which Is Bigger?* (PS–2). Illus. by author. 2013, Kids Can $16.95 (978-1-55453-973-4). 24pp. An inventive and eye-catching look at some basic concepts. (Rev: BL 5/1/13*; SLJ 4/13) [516]

245 Manceau, Edouard. *Windblown* (PS–K). Trans. by Sarah Quinn. Illus. by author. 2013, OwlKids $16.95 (978-1-926973-77-7). 32pp. Scraps of paper — of different colors and shapes — morph into animals that claim ownership of the paper before the wind comes along again; an unusual and eye-catching book that will engage young children. Lexile AD590 (Rev: BL 3/15/13; HB 5–6/13; SLJ 7/13)

246 Marks, Jennifer L. *Sorting by Size* (K–3). Series: Sorting. 2006, Capstone LB $23.93 (978-0-7368-6740-5). 32pp. Simple text and everyday examples show how to sort by size; also use *Sorting Money* and *Sorting Toys* (both 2006). (Rev: SLJ 4/07)

247 Marzollo, Jean. *I Spy School Days: A Book of Picture Riddles* (PS–2). Illus. by Walter Wick. Series: I Spy. 1995, Scholastic $13.99 (978-0-590-48135-9). 38pp. Riddles and puzzles using photographs are featured, each related to school activities. (Rev: BL 12/1/95; SLJ 10/95)

248 Miura, Taro. *Tools* (PS–K). Illus. 2006, Chronicle $15.95 (978-0-8118-5519-8). 40pp. This attractive introduction to a wide array of tools offers children the chance to guess which occupations they are used in. (Rev: BL 11/1/06; SLJ 10/06) [621.9]

249 Mora, Pat. *Gracias / Thanks* (PS–2). Trans. by Adriana Dominguez. Illus. by John Parra. 2009, Lee & Low $17.95 (978-160060258-0). 32pp. In this bilingual picture book, a young boy gives thanks for all the simple and often taken-for-granted things in his life, like his pajamas and the crickets that sing at night. (Rev: BL 11/1/09*; HB 1–2/10; LMC 3–4/10)

250 Murphy, Stuart J. *It's About Time!* (PS–2). Illus. Series: MathStart. 2005, HarperCollins $16.99 (978-0-06-055768-3); paper $5.99 (978-0-06-055769-0). 40pp. Introduces time-telling by linking everyday activities to the time of day; both analog and digital clocks are featured. (Rev: BL 3/1/05) [529]

251 Newman, Jeff. *Hand Book* (PS–K). Illus. by author. 2011, Simon & Schuster $15.99 (978-1-4169-5013-4). 40pp. A tale of the role of hands in our lives, from very basic toddler functions to adult uses. (Rev: BL 7/11; SLJ 7/11)

252 Nilsen, Anna. *My Best Friends* (PS–K). Illus. by Emma Dodd. 2003, Gingham Dog $15.95 (978-0-7696-3159-2). Brightly colored cartoon characters illustrate the importance — and challenges — of friendship. (Rev: HBG 4/04; SLJ 1/04)

253 O'Connell, Rebecca. *Baby Parade* (PS). Illus. by Susie Poole. 2013, Whitman $15.99 (978-0-8075-0509-0). 24pp. Diverse brightly dressed babies are shown in various happy situations in this appealing book full of motion. (Rev: BL 3/1/13; SLJ 3/13)

254 Olson-Brown, Ellen. *Ooh La La Polka-Dot Boots* (PS–K). Illus. by Christiane Engel. 2010, Ten Speed/Tricycle $14.99 (978-1-58246-287-5). 36pp. A game of dress-up in book form, this book features a multicultural

array of characters showing off their favorite outfits in bright illustrations including polka-dot boots. (Rev: BL 1/1/10; SLJ 4/1/10)

255 Olson, Nathan. *Animal Patterns* (1–2). Series: Finding Patterns. 2006, Capstone LB $23.93 (978-0-7368-6728-3). 32pp. Patterns that appear on animals (or that are made by them) are featured in large color photographs on well-designed pages. Also use *City Patterns, Food Patterns,* and *People Patterns.* (Rev: SLJ 5/07)

256 Patricelli, Leslie. *Baby Happy Baby Sad* (PS). Illus. by author. Series: Leslie Patricelli board books . 2008, Candlewick $6.99 (978-0-7636-3245-8). 24pp. Happiness (holding a balloon) and sadness (seeing ice cream hit the ground) are concepts easily understood from these pages. (Rev: BCCB 4/08; SLJ 4/08)

257 Patricelli, Leslie. *Faster! Faster!* (PS–2). Illus. by author. 2012, Candlewick $15.99 (978-0-7636-5473-3). 32pp. The little girl we met in *Higher! Higher!* (2009) now urges her father to carry her faster and faster as she imagines he is a dog, a cheetah, an ostrich, and so forth. (Rev: BLO 10/15/11; SLJ 3/1/12)

258 Patricelli, Leslie. *No No Yes Yes* (PS). Illus. by author. Series: Leslie Patricelli board books . 2008, Candlewick $6.99 (978-0-7636-3244-1). Patricelli illustrates opposites while showing a toddler behaving appropriately and inappropriately in a variety of everyday situations. (Rev: BCCB 4/08; SLJ 4/08) [428.1]

259 Payne, Nina. *Four in All* (PS–3). Illus. by Adam Payne. 2001, Front St $15.95 (978-1-886910-16-4). A girl takes an imaginary journey in this richly illustrated, captivating verse for younger readers that uses four-word lines to present items that come in fours (such as north, east, south, and west) and is wonderfully illustrated by the author's son. (Rev: BCCB 12/01; BL 1/1–15/02; HBG 3/02; SLJ 12/01*)

260 Pearson, Susan. *Hooray for Feet!* (PS–1). Illus. by Roxanna Baer-Block. 2005, Blue Apple $12.95 (978-1-59354-093-7). In this rhyming text, this appealing picture book celebrates feet and the many wonders they can perform. (Rev: SLJ 11/05)

261 Penner, Lucille R. *Where's That Bone?* (PS–2). Illus. by Lynn Adams. Series: Math Matters. 2000, Kane paper $4.95 (978-1-57565-097-5). 32pp. A dog forgets where he has buried his bones so Jill draws him a map in this concept book about distance and maps. (Rev: SLJ 2/01)

262 Penner, Lucille R. *X Marks the Spot!* (1–2). Illus. by Jerry Smath. 2002, Kane paper $4.95 (978-1-57565-111-8). 32pp. Brothers Leo and Jake learn to read charts to find treasures in their new hometown in this clever concept book. (Rev: BL 4/15/02)

263 Petelinsek, Kathleen, and E. Russell Primm. *Opposites / Los contrarios* (K–2). Illus. by Nichole Day Diggins. Series: Talking Hands. 2006, The Child's World LB $21.36 (978-1-59296-454-3). 24pp. Students demonstrate simple words using American Sign Language; the text is in both English and Spanish. (Rev: SLJ 6/06) [419]

264 Pinto, Sara. *Apples and Oranges: Going Bananas with Pairs* (PS–2). Illus. by author. 2008, Bloomsbury Children's $16.95 (978-1-59990-103-9). 32pp. A humorous introduction to "compare and contrast" thinking that could lead to interesting out-of-the-box discussions. (Rev: BL 1/1–15/08; LMC 1/08; SLJ 1/08)

265 Raschka, Chris. *Five for a Little One* (PS–K). Illus. by author. 2006, Simon & Schuster $16.95 (978-0-689-84599-4). A thoughtful young bunny shares the glories of the five senses in this picture book with unusual, eye-catching illustrations. (Rev: BL 6/1–15/06; SLJ 7/06)

266 Redding, Sue. *Up Above and Down Below* (PS). Illus. by author. 2006, Chronicle $14.95 (978-0-8118-4876-3). 32pp. Worlds above and below — hikers and cavers, golfers and gophers, cruise passengers and crew, for example — are contrasted in this imaginative book for preschoolers. (Rev: BL 5/15/06; SLJ 7/06)

267 Reidy, Hannah. *All Sorts of Clothes* (PS). Illus. by Emma Dodd. Series: All Sorts of Things. 2005, Picture Window LB $25.26 (978-1-4048-1063-1). This toddler-friendly book helps little ones identify different articles of clothing. (Rev: BL 4/1/05)

268 Reidy, Hannah. *All Sorts of Noises* (PS). Illus. by Emma Dodd. Series: All Sorts of Things. 2005, Picture Window LB $25.26 (978-1-4048-1064-8). 24pp. Introduces noises of all kinds, from birds chirping to alarm clocks and street sounds. (Rev: SLJ 6/05)

269 Rosenthal, Amy Krouse. *Duck! Rabbit!* (PS–1). Illus. by Tom Lichtenheld. 2009, Chronicle $16.99 (978-0-8118-6865-5). 40pp. Is it a duck or a rabbit? A visual debate full of fun and color. (Rev: BL 4/1/09; HB 5/09; LMC 8/09; SLJ 5/09)

270 Rosenthal, Amy Krouse. *Wumbers: It's a Word Cr8ed with a Number!* (K–2). Illus. by Tom Lichtenheld. 2012, Chronicle $16.99 (978-1-4521-1022-6). 40pp. Uses double-page vignettes to present various situations that allow for inventive wordplay and will please young children once they have mastered the "ba6." ℮ (Rev: BL 9/1/12; HB 11–12/12; SLJ 8/12) [793.73]

271 Rotner, Shelley. *Lots of Feelings* (PS–1). Photos by author. 2003, Millbrook LB $21.90 (978-0-7613-2896-4). Close-up photographs show children displaying a variety of emotions. (Rev: HBG 4/04; SLJ 4/04)

272 Rotner, Shelley. *Shades of People* (PS–3). Illus. by Sheila M. Kelly. 2009, Holiday House $16.95 (978-0-8234-2191-6). 32pp. Celebrates the many different skin tones found around the world. ALSC Notable Children's Book, 2010. (Rev: BL 8/09; SLJ 9/1/09)

273 Rubin, Susan G. *Matisse: Dance for Joy* (PS–K). Illus. by author. 2008, Chronicle $6.99 (978-0-8118-6288-2). 24pp. A board-book introduction to the work of Matisse, using the artist's cutout collages and rhythmic text. (Rev: BLO 6/17/08) [709.2]

274 Rueda, Claudia. *Is It Big or Is It Little?* (PS–1). Illus. by author. 2013, Eerdmans $14 (978-0-8028-5423-0). 26pp. A cat and a mouse explore concepts such as depth and weight in this stylish book that uses opposites effectively. (Rev: BL 7/13; SLJ 10/13)

275 Savadier, Elivia. *Will Sheila Share?* (PS–K). Illus. by author. 2008, Roaring Brook $12.95 (978-1-59643-289-5). 24pp. Sheila finds sharing very difficult until her grandmother shows her sharing will make her happy. (Rev: SLJ 4/08)

276 Schaefer, Lola M. *What's Up, What's Down?* (PS–2). Illus. by Barbara Bash. 2002, HarperCollins $17.99 (978-0-06-029757-2). 32pp. A fascinating and innovative approach that involves turning the book sideways and following arrows up and down to see the world from the point of view of various plants and animals. (Rev: BL 12/1/02; HBG 3/03; SLJ 1/03) [500]

277 Schwartz, David M. *If You Hopped Like a Frog* (K–4). Illus. by James Warhola. 1999, Scholastic $16.95 (978-0-590-09857-1). This picture book discusses the concepts of ratio and proportion, using animal facts to explore topics such as relative strength. (Rev: BCCB 12/99; BL 11/15/99; HBG 3/00; SLJ 11/99) [513.2]

278 Seeger, Laura Vaccaro. *Black? White! Day? Night!* (PS–2). Illus. 2006, Roaring Brook $16.95 (978-1-59643-185-0). 24pp. A creative introduction to opposites using full-page flaps, cutouts, and bright colors. (Rev: BCCB 11/06; BL 11/1/06; HBG 4/07; SLJ 11/06*) [428.1]

279 Seeger, Laura Vaccaro. *First the Egg* (PS–K). Illus. by author. 2007, Roaring Brook $14.95 (978-1-59643-272-7). 32pp. Die-cut pages and cleverly layered images integrated with spare text present examples of development in nature (from egg to chicken, tadpole to frog) and in the making of a story (word, story, paint, picture). Caldecott Honor Book. ∩ [571.8]

280 Seeger, Laura Vaccaro. *What If?* (PS–K). Illus. by author. 2010, Roaring Brook $15.99 (978-1-59643-398-4). 32pp. In this simple yet thought-provoking, almost wordless story about friendship and sharing, Seeger explores the different outcomes possible when three seals play with a beach ball. (Rev: BL 2/1/10; LMC 5–6/10; SLJ 4/1/10*)

281 Selig, Josh. *Red and Yellow's Noisy Night* (PS–2). Illus. by Little Airplane Productions. 2012, Sterling $14.95 (978-140279070-6). 28pp. Characters Red and Yellow learn about simple conflict resolution when Red decides to play a quiet song instead of loud music to help his friend to sleep. (Rev: BL 4/1/12; SLJ 5/1/12)

282 Sheehan, Monica. *Love Is You and Me* (PS–1). Illus. by author. 2013, Simon & Schuster $14.99 (978-144243607-7). 48pp. A visually pleasing appreciation of the value of love. (Rev: BL 11/15/13; SLJ 2/14)

283 Silvano, Wendi. *What Does the Wind Say?* (PS–K). Illus. by Joan M. Delehanty. 2006, NorthWord $15.95 (978-1-55971-954-4). A gentle book with watercolor illustrations and rhyming text that poses questions about various parts of nature — "What do the stars do?" "What does the moon play?" (Rev: SLJ 11/06)

284 Siminovich, Lorena. *I Like Vegetables* (PS). Illus. by author. 2011, Candlewick $6.99 (978-0-7636-5283-8). 10pp. With tactile fabric sections in collages, this square board book introduces a variety of vegetables. (Rev: BL 7/11; SLJ 9/1/11)

285 Slate, Joseph. *Miss Bindergarten Celebrates the 100th Day of Kindergarten* (PS–1). Illus. by Ashley Wolff. 1998, Dutton $16.99 (978-0-525-46000-8). 32pp. Superteacher Miss Bindergarten asks her students to bring 100 things to class to celebrate the 100th day of kindergarten in this combination alphabet and counting book. (Rev: BL 10/15/98; HBG 3/99; SLJ 9/98)

286 Snicket, Lemony. *Thirteen Words* (K–2). Illus. by Maira Kalman. 2010, HarperCollins $16.99 (978-0-06-166465-6). 40pp. A quirky, playful book involving 13 words, a despondent bird, a dog, and a mezzo-soprano. (Rev: BL 9/1/10; SLJ 12/1/10)

287 Soltis, Sue. *Nothing Like a Puffin* (PS–2). Illus. by Bob Kolar. 2011, Candlewick $15.99 (978-0-7636-3617-3). 40pp. This exercise in similarities and differences compares a puffin to everything from a newspaper to a pair of blue jeans. (Rev: BL 12/1/11; SLJ 9/1/11)

288 Sper, Emily. *The Kids' Fun Book of Jewish Time* (1–4). Illus. by author. 2006, Jewish Lights $16.99 (978-1-58023-311-8). Lift-the-flap and pull-the-tab features add interest to this introduction to the Jewish calendar. (Rev: SLJ 11/06) [296.4]

289 Spicer, Maggee, and Richard Thompson. *We'll All Go Flying* (PS–K). Illus. by Kim LaFave. 2002, Fitzhenry & Whiteside $16.95 (978-1-55041-698-5). Colors, shapes, sounds, and animals are all presented from the platform of a hot-air balloon in this counting book with movable flaps. (Rev: SLJ 12/02)

290 Spurr, Elizabeth. *Farm Life* (PS–1). Illus. by Steve Björkman. 2003, Holiday House $16.95 (978-0-8234-1777-3). 32pp. Basic colors and numbers 1 to 10 are taught by exploring the buildings on a farm. (Rev: BL 3/15/03; HBG 10/03; SLJ 6/03)

291 Steggall, Susan. *Red Car, Red Bus* (PS–K). Illus. by author. 2012, Frances Lincoln $17.99 (978-1-84780-184-5). 32pp. Torn-paper illustrations and minimal text introduce concepts of color and pattern. (Rev: BLO 10/1/12; SLJ 12/12) [388]

292 Stinson, Kathy. *A Pocket Can Have a Treasure in It* (PS–K). Illus. by Deirdre Betteridge. 2008, Annick LB $18.95 (978-1-55451-126-6); paper $6.95 (978-1-55451-125-9). 32pp. A friendly concept book — with a new sibling twist — about things found inside other things. (Rev: BCCB 9/08; SLJ 9/08)

293 Tafuri, Nancy. *All Kinds of Kisses* (PS–K). Illus. by author. 2012, Little, Brown $16.99 (978-0-316-12235-1). 32pp. This large-format picture book celebrates different kinds of kisses that animals — and people — share around the world. (Rev: BL 1/1/12; HB 1–2/12; SLJ 12/1/11)

294 Tillman, Nancy. *The Crown on Your Head* (PS). Illus. by author. 2011, Feiwel & Friends $16.99 (978-0-312-64521-2). 32pp. Celebrates the unique qualities endowed on every child, using a crown as an illustration. (Rev: BL 9/15/11; SLJ 9/1/11)

295 Timmers, Leo. *Who Is Driving?* (PS–K). Illus. 2007, Bloomsbury $12.95 (978-1-59990-021-6). 32pp. Readers must guess which animal is driving each of seven vehicles in this interesting picture puzzle with clue-laden illustrations. (Rev: BL 12/15/06)

296 Tullet, Hervé. *The Book with a Hole* (PS–2). 2011, Abrams paper $14.50 (978-1-85437-946-7). Unpaged. This board book features a large hole in the middle of each illustration, which gives readers opportunities for interaction; simple text provides encouragement. Other books in this attractive, inventive series include *The Game of Finger Worms, The Game of Let's Go!, The Game of Light, The Game of Mix and Match, The Game of Mix-Up Art,* and *The Game of Patterns* (all 2011). (Rev: SLJ 9/1/11)

297 Tullet, Hervé. *Press Here* (PS–2). Illus. by author. 2011, Chronicle $14.99 (978-0-8118-7954-5). 56pp. This sturdy book encourages readers to tilt, twist, press, and blow on the pages to see colored dots move. (Rev: BL 4/1/11; HB 7–8/11; SLJ 4/11*)

298 Underwood, Deborah. *The Loud Book!* (PS). Illus. by Renata Liwska. 2011, Houghton Mifflin $12.99 (978-0-547-39008-6). 32pp. Noises from burping to whistling are celebrated in this book featuring the lively stuffed animals first seen in *The Quiet Book* (2010). (Rev: BL 1/1–15/11; SLJ 5/1/11*)

299 Underwood, Deborah. *The Quiet Book* (PS–K). Illus. by Renata Liwska. 2010, Houghton Mifflin $12.95 (978-0-547-21567-9). 32pp. Using young animals as characters, this picture book explores different kinds of quiet. (Rev: BL 2/15/10; SLJ 3/1/10*)

300 Van Fleet, Matthew. *Moo* (PS). Illus. by Brian Stanton. 2011, Simon & Schuster $16.99 (978-1-4424-3503-2). 18pp. This interactive board book looks at barnyard animals using simple text, tabs, flaps, and touch-and-feel elements. (Rev: BLO 11/15/11; SLJ 10/1/11) [636]

301 Verdick, Elizabeth. *Calm-Down Time* (PS). Illus. by Marieka Heinlen. Series: Toddler Tools. 2010, Free Spirit paper $7.95 (978-1-57542-316-6). Unpaged. This board book introduces the importance of calming down when overexcited and various strategies to use. (Rev: SLJ 6/1/10) [152.4]

302 Walsh, Joanna. *The Biggest Kiss* (PS–1). Illus. by Judi Abbot. 2011, Simon & Schuster $12.99 (978-1-4424-2769-3). 32pp. This tribute to kisses celebrates all different kinds, from fish kisses to penguin kisses to the sweetest kisses of all. (Rev: BL 12/15/11; SLJ 11/1/11)

303 Wan, Joyce. *Hug You, Kiss You, Love You* (PS). Illus. 2013, Scholastic $6.99 (978-054554045-2). 14pp. A board book celebration of the various ways in which parents express their love for their children. (Rev: BL 11/15/13)

304 Weakland, Mark. *How Heavy? Wacky Ways to Compare Weight* (PS–2). Illus. by Bill Bolton. Series: Wacky Comparisons. 2013, Picture Window LB $27.32 (978-140488322-2); paper $7.95 (9781479519125). 24pp. Imaginative cartoon-style illustrations compare such things as a bulldog to hamburgers, a school bus to hippos. (Rev: BL 10/1/13; LMC 5–6/14; SLJ 11/4/13) [530.8]

305 Whitman, Candace. *Lines That Wiggle* (PS–1). Illus. by Steve Wilson. 2009, Blue Apple $14.99 (978-1-934706-54-1). A concept book that explores in rhyme a deceptively simple line. (Rev: BL 6/1–15/09)

306 Wild, Margaret. *Itsy-Bitsy Babies* (PS). Illus. by Jan Ormerod. 2010, IPG/Little Hare $15.99 (978-1-921541-36-0). 24pp. A simple and charming rhyming celebration of the things that babies and toddlers do. (Rev: BL 11/1/10; SLJ 12/1/10)

307 Wormell, Christopher. *Teeth, Tales and Tentacles: An Animal Counting Book* (PS–3). 2004, Running Pr. $18.95 (978-0-7624-2100-8). 64pp. This clever animal-themed counting book operates on several levels, serving as an introduction to numbers for preschoolers, an overview of 20 different animal species from around the world, and a collection of fascinating facts and figures about those animals and their behavior. (Rev: BL 10/1/04*)

308 Yoon, Salina. *Do Cows Meow?* (PS). Illus. by author. 2012, Sterling $9.95 (978-1-4027-8956-4). 18pp. This attractive lift-the-flap book introduces preschoolers to a variety of animal sounds. (Rev: BLO 11/15/12; SLJ 12/12)

309 Yoon, Salina. *Opposnakes: A Lift-the-Flap Book About Opposites* (PS–K). Illus. by author. 2009, Simon & Schuster $9.99 (978-1-4169-7875-6). 16pp. Simple text, funny illustrations, and a deft structure work together to teach about opposites. (Rev: SLJ 6/09)

COLORS

310 Austin, Mike. *Monsters Love Colors* (K–1). Illus. by author. 2013, HarperCollins $15.99 (978-0-06-212594-1). 40pp. Four happy little monsters have great fun mixing colors. (Rev: BL 11/15/12; SLJ 1/13)

311 Barry, Frances. *Duckie's Rainbow* (PS). Illus. by author. 2004, Candlewick $7.99 (978-0-7636-2066-0). Duckie passes many vivid colors as she hurries home in this fan-shaped board book with collage art. (Rev: SLJ 7/04) [813.6]

312 Basher, Simon. *Colors* (PS). Illus. by author. Series: Go! Go! BoBo. 2011, Kingfisher $6.99 (978-0-7534-6493-9). Unpaged. BoBo, a childlike character, plunges into six basic colors in this appealing board book. (Rev: BL 7/11; SLJ 8/1/11) [535.6]

313 *Big Yellow Trucks and Diggers: Colors* (PS). 2003, Chronicle $6.95 (978-0-8118-4030-9). Colors are introduced through eye-catching photographs of appealing machines. (Rev: SLJ 1/04) [624]

314 Brocket, Jane. *Ruby, Violet, Lime: Looking for Color* (PS–2). Photos by author. Series: Jane Brocket's Clever Concepts. 2011, Millbrook LB $25.26 (978-0-7613-4612-8). 32pp. Bright photographs and vivid text illustrate the primary colors plus a few extras. **e** (Rev: SLJ 9/1/11)

315 Carle, Eric. *Hello, Red Fox* (K–3). Illus. 1998, Simon & Schuster $16.00 (978-0-689-81775-5). 32pp. The author invites readers to experience a simple story by employing the phenomenon whereby staring at a color and then at a blank white page reveals a complementary color as if by magic. (Rev: BCCB 7–8/98; BL 4/1/98; HBG 10/98; SLJ 7/98)

316 Catalanotto, Peter. *Kitten Red, Yellow, Blue* (PS–K). Illus. 2005, Simon & Schuster $15.95 (978-0-689-86562-6). 32pp. Both colors and professions are introduced in this clever story that involves color-coding a batch of kittens according to their owners. (Rev: BL 2/15/05; SLJ 3/05)

317 *Color* (K–3). Photos and illus. by Ella Doran, et al. 2006, Abrams $19.95 (978-1-85437-697-8). Primary colors, complementary colors, hue, tint, and many other concepts about color are all covered here, in a fittingly colorful package with some movable features. (Rev: SLJ 6/07)

318 Ehlert, Lois. *Color Zoo* (PS–2). Illus. by author. 1989, HarperCollins LB $17.89 (978-0-397-32260-2). 32pp. How basic shapes can be combined to make familiar objects. (Rev: BL 5/15/89; SLJ 4/89)

319 Emberley, Rebecca. *My Colors / Mis Colores* (PS). 2000, Little, Brown $5.95 (978-0-316-23347-7). 20pp. A board book in English and Spanish introduces the basic colors. (Rev: BCCB 12/00*; HBG 3/01; SLJ 9/00)

320 Fontes, Justine. *Black Meets White* (PS–2). Illus. by Geoff Waring. 2005, Candlewick $12.99 (978-0-7636-1933-6). Cutouts and lift-the-flap features highlight this tale of two colors, which cleverly introduces various patterns. (Rev: SLJ 11/05)

321 Fox, Christyan, and Diane Fox. *What Color Is That, PiggyWiggy?* (PS–K). Illus. 2001, Handprint $5.95 (978-1-929766-17-8). 20pp. In this book about colors, PiggyWiggy dons articles of clothing of different hues until he becomes a perfect circus clown. (Rev: BL 4/1/01; SLJ 8/01)

322 Gibbs, Edward. *I Spy with My Little Eye* (PS–1). Illus. by author. 2011, Candlewick $14.99 (978-0-7636-5284-5). Unpaged. Part seek-and-find, part practice with colors, this engaging book features brightly colored illustrations and die-cut holes. (Rev: SLJ 6/11*)

323 Gunzi, Christiane. *My Very First Look at Colors* (PS–K). Illus. by Steve Gorton. Series: My Very First Look. 2001, Two-Can $8.95 (978-1-58728-236-2); paper $5.95 (978-1-58728-276-8). 24pp. A concept book that uses photographs of everyday objects to teach preschoolers about colors. (Rev: BL 2/15/02; HBG 10/02; SLJ 2/02) [535.6]

324 Harrison, Carlos. *Ruben's Rainbow / El Arco Iris de Ruben* (K–2). Illus. by Grizelle Paz. 2001, Globo Libros $15.95 (978-0-9706953-0-7). Ruben tumbles from a world of black and white into a world full of color in this bilingual text accompanied by a CD. (Rev: SLJ 1/02)

325 Hoban, Tana. *Colors Everywhere* (PS–K). Illus. 1995, Greenwillow $17.89 (978-0-688-12763-3). 32pp. A wordless picture book that identifies the colors found in each of the photographs used. (Rev: BCCB 3/95; BL 5/1/95; HB 7/95; SLJ 7/95)

326 Hoban, Tana. *Red, Blue, Yellow Shoe* (PS). Illus. by author. 1986, Greenwillow paper $6.99 (978-0-688-06563-8). 12pp. A very simple introduction to color in a board book. (Rev: BCCB 1/87; BL 10/15/86; HB 11/86)

327 Holm, Sharon L. *Zoe's Hats: A Book of Colors and Patterns* (PS–1). Illus. 2003, Boyds Mills $13.95 (978-1-59078-042-8). 32pp. Zoe has fun trying on all manner of hats in this simple book for the very young. (Rev: BL 2/1/03; HBG 10/03; SLJ 2/03)

328 Horacek, Petr. *Strawberries Are Red* (PS). Illus. by author. 2001, Candlewick $4.99 (978-0-7636-1461-4). Fruit and colors are introduced on brightly illustrated double-page spreads. Also use *What Is Black and White?* (2001). (Rev: SLJ 8/01)

329 Houblon, Marie. *A World of Colors: Seeing Colors in a New Way* (PS–2). Illus. 2009, National Geographic $16.95 (978-1-4263-0556-6); LB $25.90 (978-1-4263-0559-7). 48pp. In this sophisticated color book, each color is presented in a variety of different shades and tints while questions encourage readers to expand their perceptions. (Rev: BL 11/15/09; SLJ 10/1/09) [535.6]

330 Jay, Alison. *Red, Green, Blue: A First Book of Colors* (PS–3). Illus. by author. 2010, Dutton $16.99 (978-0-525-42303-4). 40pp. Children are introduced to colors through familiar nursery rhyme characters, from the three little (pink) pigs to Little Bo Peep's white sheep and Miss Muffet's scary black spider. (Rev: BL 5/15/10; SLJ 6/1/10)

331 Jonas, Ann. *Color Dance* (PS–K). Illus. 1989, Greenwillow $17.89 (978-0-688-05991-0). 32pp. Dancers wave colored scarves and introduce various colors. (Rev: BL 8/89; SLJ 12/89)

332 Lionni, Leo. *Little Blue and Little Yellow* (PS–1). Illus. by author. 1959, Astor-Honor $14.95 (978-0-8392-3018-2). All the characters are blobs of color; an ingenious story intended to give the young child an awareness of color.

333 MacDonald, Suse. *Shape by Shape* (PS–2). Illus. by author. 2009, Simon & Schuster $14.99 (978-1-4169-7147-4). Progressive, bright die-cut shapes finally reveal a whole dinosaur on a fold-out spread. (Rev: BL 5/1/09; SLJ 6/09)

334 MacKinnon, Debbie. *Eye Spy Colors* (PS–K). Illus. by Anthea Sieveking. 1998, Charlesbridge $8.95 (978-0-88106-334-9). 24pp. Colors are introduced through a series of double-page spreads and peepholes. (Rev: BL 1/1–15/99; HBG 3/99)

335 Martin, Bill, Jr. *Brown Bear, Brown Bear, What Do You See?* (PS–1). Illus. by Eric Carle. 1992, Holt $15.95 (978-0-8050-1744-1). This brightly illustrated easy-reader book first appeared in 1967 and is a fine introduction to colors. (Rev: BL 3/1/92; SLJ 5/92)

336 Micklethwait, Lucy. *I Spy Colors in Art* (K–3). Illus. 2007, Greenwillow $19.99 (978-0-06-134837-2). 40pp. Images by artists including Magritte and Picasso invite

children to look closely at colors. (Rev: BL 9/15/07; SLJ 9/07) [752]

337 Milich, Zoran. *City Colors* (PS–1). Photos by author. 2004, Kids Can $14.95 (978-1-55337-542-5). Starting with basic colors (a red bus, a blue wall), the author works through a city's spectrum (from a green swing to a pink conduit) in this attractive concept book. (Rev: SLJ 5/04) [535.6]

338 Mockford, Caroline. *Cleo's Color Book* (PS). Illus. by author. 2006, Barefoot Books $15.99 (978-1-905236-30-5). 32pp. The orange cat featured in *Cleo's Alphabet Book* and *Cleo's Counting Book* (both 2003) observes the colors around her in this beginning concept book. (Rev: BL 5/15/06; SLJ 4/06)

339 Nunn, Daniel. *Yellow* (PS–K). Illus. Series: Colors All Around Us. 2012, Raintree LB $25.32 (978-143295748-3); paper $8.95 (978-143295757-5). 24pp. Yellow objects of all kinds — yolks, trucks, sunflowers, ducklings — are on display here. (Rev: BLO 3/1/12) [535.6]

340 Otoshi, Kathryn. *One* (PS–K). Illus. by author. 2008, KO Kids $16.95 (978-0-9723946-4-2). The color Red is a successful bully until One turns up and challenges Red's ascendance; in turn the other colors become numbers too — Yellow is two, Green is three — and support the bullied, quiet Blue. (Rev: BL 11/15/08*; LMC 3/08*; SLJ 12/08)

341 Park, Linda Sue. *What Does Bunny See? A Book of Colors and Flowers* (PS). Illus. by Maggie Smith. 2005, Clarion $15.00 (978-0-618-23485-1). Poppies, violets, primroses, and lilies are among the flowers Bunny sees in a colorful garden in this rhyming presentation of blossoms and their colors. (Rev: BL 3/1/05; SLJ 6/05)

342 Robertson, Patrisha. *Cirque du Soleil: Parade of Colors* (K–4). Photos by Cirque du Soleil. 2003, Abrams $15.95 (978-0-8109-4515-9). 32pp. In this lushly illustrated concept book, young readers are introduced to colors in a parade of performers from the famed Cirque du Soleil. (Rev: HBG 4/04; SLJ 1/04)

343 Rodrigue, George. *Why Is Blue Dog Blue?* (PS–3). Illus. 2002, Stewart, Tabori & Chang $16.95 (978-1-58479-162-1). The artist explains why he paints his dog different colors depending on the situation. (Rev: BL 6/1–15/02; HBG 10/02)

344 Rowe, Jeannette. *YoYo's Colors* (PS). Illus. by author. Series: YoYo. 2002, Tiger Tales $3.95 (978-1-58925-682-8). YoYo the yellow dog introduces preschoolers to other vividly colored creatures in this board book. Also use *YoYo's Numbers* and *YoYo's Toys* (both 2002). (Rev: SLJ 6/03)

345 Salzano, Tammi. *One Rainy Day* (PS). Illus. by Hannah Wood. 2011, ME Media/Tiger Tales $8.95 (978-158925860-0). 24pp. A duckling goes out for a walk in the rain in this padded board book designed to reinforce the names of colors. (Rev: BL 7/11)

346 Seeger, Laura Vaccaro. *Lemons Are Not Red* (PS–2). Illus. 2004, Roaring Brook $14.95 (978-1-59643-008-2). 32pp. Various objects introduce colors in this attractive small book that ends with a bedtime message. (Rev: BL 1/1–15/05)

347 Shahan, Sherry. *Spicy Hot Colors / Colores Picantes* (PS–1). Illus. by Paula Barragán. 2004, August House $16.95 (978-0-87483-741-4). Spicy-hot art and rhythmic descriptions introduce colors in both English and Spanish. (Rev: BL 9/15/04; SLJ 11/04) [535.6]

348 Shannon, George. *White Is for Blueberry* (PS–K). Illus. by Laura Dronzek. 2005, Greenwillow LB $17.89 (978-0-06-029276-8). 40pp. Plants and animals are linked to unexpected colors (for instance, crows are pink . . . when newly hatched from their eggs) in this lushly illustrated book. (Rev: BL 3/15/05; SLJ 5/05)

349 Sterling, Kristin. *Blue Everywhere* (K–2). Series: Lightning Bolt Books — Colors Everywhere. 2010, Lerner LB $25.26 (978-0-7613-4588-6). 32pp. Highlights the presence of blue in the everyday world and its connection to emotional expression. Also use *Red Everywhere* and *Silver and Gold Everywhere* (both 2010). (Rev: LMC 3–4/10; SLJ 2/1/10) [535.6]

350 Stockland, Patricia M. *Pink* (PS–K). Illus. by Julia Woolf. 2011, ABDO LB $18.95 (978-161641138-1). 24pp. A simple approach to the color pink and the places it is often found. Also use *Orange, Gray,* and *Brown* (all 2011). (Rev: BL 5/1/11) [535.6]

351 Swinburne, Stephen. *What Color Is Nature?* (PS–K). Illus. 2002, Boyds Mills $15.95 (978-1-56397-967-5); paper $9.95 (978-1-59078-008-4). Using bright photographs of children, animals, and plants, different colors are introduced. (Rev: BL 6/1–15/02; HBG 10/02)

352 Tafuri, Nancy. *Blue Goose* (PS–K). Illus. by author. 2008, Simon & Schuster $15.99 (978-1-4169-2834-8). 32pp. Blue Goose, Red Hen, Yellow Chick, and White Duck decide to add color to their stark surroundings, first working alone and then blending their colors to create purple doors, orange shutters, and even green grass. (Rev: BCCB 2/08; BL 11/15/07; SLJ 1/08)

353 Thong, Roseanne. *Red Is a Dragon: A Book of Colors* (PS–2). Illus. by Grace Lin. 2001, Chronicle $18.95 (978-0-8118-3177-2). 180pp. This concept book, a companion to *A Book of Shapes* (2000), is illustrated with Chinese American images. (Rev: BL 11/15/01; HBG 3/02; SLJ 1/02)

354 Weakland, Mark. *Football Colors* (PS–1). Illus. Series: SI Kids Rookie Books. 2013, Capstone LB $22.65 (978-142969959-4). 32pp. This book about colors uses effective photographs from *Sports Illustrated*. (Rev: BL 4/1/13)

355 Wolff, Ashley. *Baby Bear Sees Blue* (PS–K). Illus. by author. 2012, Simon & Schuster $16.99 (978-144241306-1). 40pp. Baby Bear sees colors all around him — yellow light, blue birds, red strawberries, orange butterflies, and more. **e** (Rev: BL 2/1/12; HB 3–4/12; SLJ 1/12)

356 Wood, Audrey. *The Deep Blue Sea: A Book of Colors* (PS). Illus. by Bruce Wood. 2005, Scholastic $15.99 (978-0-439-75382-1). Bright tropical artwork introduces basic colors. (Rev: BL 7/05; SLJ 8/05)

PERCEPTION

357 Averbeck, Jim. *Except If* (PS–1). Illus. by author. 2011, Atheneum $12.99 (978-1-4169-9544-9). 40pp. An egg will become a baby bird, except if . . . . This intriguing book presents many alternative scenarios. (Rev: BL 12/1/10; HB 1–2/11; SLJ 2/1/11)

358 Carter, David A. *One Red Dot* (K–2). Illus. by author. 2005, Simon & Schuster $19.95 (978-0-689-87769-8). This attractive pop-up book challenges readers to find the single red dot that is hidden somewhere in each of its 10 paper sculptures. (Rev: SLJ 11/05)

359 Ciboul, Adele. *The Five Senses* (PS–K). Trans. by Anthea Bell. Illus. by Clementine Colliner. Series: Explore Your World. 2006, Firefly $15.95 (978-1-55407-007-7). 28pp. An appealing, interactive introduction to the senses, with lots of pullouts, flaps, pictures, and photos. (Rev: BL 10/15/06) [612.8]

360 Hoban, Tana. *Is It Rough? Is It Smooth? Is It Shiny?* (PS). Illus. by author. 1984, Greenwillow $17.99 (978-0-688-03823-6). 32pp. Textures are explored in a series of photographs.

361 Kuskin, Karla. *Green as a Bean* (PS–2). Illus. by Melissa Iwai. 2007, HarperCollins $17.99 (978-0-06-075332-0). Thought-provoking "what if" questions challenge young readers to consider what they might be if they were different colors, textures, shapes, sounds, or sizes; previously published as *Square as a House*. (Rev: BL 11/1/06; SLJ 2/07)

362 Maccaulay, David. *Black and White* (2–6). Illus. 1990, Houghton $17.00 (978-0-395-52151-9). 32pp. With thought-provoking illustrations, four short stories are presented. Caldecott Medal winner, 1991. (Rev: BCCB 5/90; BL 4/1/90*; HB 9/90)

363 *Peek-a-Boo What?* (PS). Illus. by Elliot Kreloff. Series: Begin Smart. 2009, Sterling $10.95 (978-193461850-9). 18pp. Simple collage illustrations and die-cut holes enhance this repetitive rhymed board-book game of peek-a-boo. (Rev: BLO 11/15/09)

364 Robert, Francois, and Jean Robert. *Find a Face* (PS–2). 2004, Chronicle $15.95 (978-0-8118-4338-6). Faces are everywhere in this inventive collection of photographs of objects ranging from light switches to shoe heels. (Rev: SLJ 8/04) [779]

365 Shaw, Charles. *It Looked Like Spilt Milk* (K–2). Illus. by author. 1947, HarperCollins LB $17.89 (978-0-06-025565-7); paper $6.99 (978-0-06-443159-0). 30pp. White material appears on each page, but its identity is not revealed until the end. Originally published in 1947.

SIZE AND SHAPE

366 Aber, Linda Williams. *Carrie Measures Up* (K–2). Illus. by Joy Allen. Series: Math Matters. 2001, Kane paper $4.95 (978-1-57565-100-2). 32pp. Carrie gets totally carried away measuring things around the house. (Rev: SLJ 6/01)

367 Basher, Simon. *Shapes* (PS). Illus. by author. Series: Go! Go! BoBo. 2011, Kingfisher $6.99 (978-0-7534-

6494-6). 16pp. BoBo, the bouncy baby with a Band-Aid on his head, explores various shapes. (Rev: BLO 11/15/11; SLJ 8/1/11) [516]

368 Blackstone, Stella. *Ship Shapes* (PS). Illus. by Siobhan Bell. 2006, Barefoot Books $15.99 (978-1-905236-34-3). Two children and a dog set sail on a raft and encounter a variety of different shapes. (Rev: SLJ 8/06)

369 Carter, David. *Whoo? Whoo?* (PS–1). Illus. by author. 2007, Simon & Schuster $12.99 (978-1-4169-3816-3). Stylized animals made from shapes are hiding here, and young readers will build visualization skills trying to see them. (Rev: SLJ 8/07)

370 Dodd, Emma. *I Am Small* (PS). Illus. by author. 2011, Scholastic $8.99 (978-0-545-35370-0). 24pp. A baby penguin finds the size of the world quite scary, but recognizes that he feels quite safe in his mother's arms. (Rev: BL 12/15/11; SLJ 10/1/11)

371 Emberley, Rebecca. *My Shapes / Mis Formas* (PS). 2000, Little, Brown $5.95 (978-0-316-23355-2). 20pp. Different shapes are introduced in English and Spanish in this board book. (Rev: BCCB 12/00*; HBG 3/01; SLJ 9/00)

372 Ernst, Lisa Campbell. *Round Like a Ball* (PS–2). Illus. by author. 2008, Blue Apple $15.95 (978-1-934706-01-5). 36pp. What is this round thing shaped like a ball? A family follows bold visual cues. (Rev: BL 4/1/08; LMC 10/08)

373 Florian, Douglas. *A Pig Is Big* (PS–K). Illus. 2000, Greenwillow $17.99 (978-0-688-17125-4). Using animals as subjects, this book explores the concept of comparative size. (Rev: BCCB 12/00*; BL 9/15/00; HB 11/00; HBG 3/01; SLJ 10/00)

374 Fox, Christyan, and Diane Fox. *What Shape Is That, PiggyWiggy?* (PS). Illus. by authors. 2002, Handprint $5.95 (978-1-929766-44-4). Shapes including squares, circles, arches, triangles, and diamonds are demonstrated as a pig and his teddy bear build a house in this board book. (Rev: SLJ 6/02)

375 Frazier, Craig. *Lots of Dots* (PS–K). Illus. by author. 2010, Chronicle $15.99 (978-0-8118-7715-2). Unpaged. Colorful, punchy illustrations show how dots and circles — scoops of ice cream, traffic signals, spotted animals, and more — can be seen everywhere. (Rev: SLJ 12/1/10)

376 Gordon, Sharon. *Big Small* (PS–2). Series: Bookworms: Just the Opposite. 2003, Benchmark LB $21.36 (978-0-7614-1568-8). 23pp. A young girl's various possessions are bigger than her little brother's in this exploration of the concept of size. (Rev: HBG 4/04; SLJ 3/04) [155.7]

377 Hall, Michael. *Perfect Square* (PS–3). Illus. by author. 2011, Greenwillow $16.99 (978-0-06-191513-0). 40pp. A perfect red square is transmogrified into a variety of new shapes in this satisfyingly simple square picture book. (Rev: BL 4/15/11; HB 3–4/11; SLJ 4/11*)

378 Hoban, Tana. *Cubes, Cones, Cylinders, and Spheres* (PS–K). Illus. 2000, Greenwillow LB $18.89 (978-0-688-15326-7). 24pp. Delightful pictures introduce different shapes in everyday objects. (Rev: BCCB 12/00; BL 10/15/00; HBG 3/01; SLJ 10/00) [513]

379 Hoban, Tana. *Shapes, Shapes, Shapes* (PS–1). Illus. by author. 1986, Greenwillow $17.89 (978-0-688-05833-3). 32pp. Eleven shapes are sought in the color photos. (Rev: BCCB 4/86; BL 3/1/86; HB 5/86)

380 Hutchins, Pat. *Shrinking Mouse* (PS–K). Illus. 1997, Greenwillow $15.89 (978-0-688-13962-9). 32pp. A clever exploration of space and perspective using woodland animals and birds. (Rev: BL 2/15/97; SLJ 4/97*)

381 Intriago, Patricia. *Dot* (PS–K). Illus. by author. 2011, Farrar $14.99 (978-0-374-31835-2). 40pp. This inventive book explores the versatile possibilities of a simple dot; fresh, direct language and comic illustrations add humor. (Rev: BLO 8/11; HB 9–10/11; SLJ 8/1/11*)

382 Jenkins, Steve. *Big and Little* (PS–2). Illus. 1996, Houghton $16.00 (978-0-395-72664-8). 32pp. The concept of size is explored in this book that contrasts various animals. (Rev: BL 10/1/96; SLJ 10/96*)

383 Long, Ethan. *Up! Tall! and High!* (PS–1). Illus. by author. 2012, Putnam $15.99 (978-0-399-25611-0). 40pp. A group of different birds try to outdo each other by being the tallest and flying the highest in this nicely illustrated story with lift-the-flap surprises. (Rev: BL 3/15/12; SLJ 2/1/12)

384 MacDonald, Suse. *Sea Shapes* (PS–K). Illus. 1994, Harcourt $13.95 (978-0-15-200027-1); paper $6.00 (978-0-15-201700-2). 32pp. Sea creatures and attractive collages are used to introduce a number of shapes. (Rev: BL 9/1/94; HB 11/94; SLJ 11/94)

385 MacKinnon, Debbie. *Eye Spy Shapes: A Peephole Book* (PS). Photos by Anthea Sieveking. 2000, Charlesbridge $6.95 (978-0-88106-135-2). In this interactive book, various shapes are introduced through a peephole guessing game. (Rev: HBG 10/01; SLJ 9/00)

386 Micklethwait, Lucy. *I Spy: Shapes in Art* (PS–2). 2004, Greenwillow $19.99 (978-0-06-073193-9). 40pp. A variety of shapes can be identified in beautiful reproductions of well-known works of art. (Rev: BL 8/04; SLJ 9/04) [701]

387 Montague-Smith, Ann. *First Shape Book* (PS–1). Illus. by Mandy Stanley. 2002, Kingfisher $12.95 (978-0-7534-5433-6). 47pp. Cartoon illustrations and a series of questions and games introduce shapes, mirror images, pairs, and size in a way that encourages identification, matching, and counting. (Rev: SLJ 7/02)

388 Murphy, Chuck. *Slide 'n Seek: Shapes* (PS–K). Illus. Series: Slide 'n Seek. 2001, Simon & Schuster $5.99 (978-0-689-84477-5). 12pp. This small board book introduces shapes using pull-tabs and clear, bright illustrations. (Rev: BL 12/15/01) [513]

389 Murphy, Stuart J. *Let's Fly a Kite* (PS–3). Illus. by Brian Floca. 2000, HarperCollins LB $15.89 (978-0-06-028035-2); paper $5.99 (978-0-06-446737-7). 40pp. Geometry and symmetry in everyday life are the concepts explored in this picture book about two quarreling siblings. (Rev: BL 9/15/00; HBG 3/01; SLJ 11/00)

390 *Museum Shapes* (PS–2). Illus. 2005, Little, Brown $16.99 (978-0-316-05698-4). Using artifacts from the collections of New York's Metropolitan Museum of Art, this concept book introduces readers to 10 geometric forms, including the square, circle, rectangle, triangle, crescent, heart, star, and diamond. (Rev: BL 10/1/05; SLJ 12/05) [516]

391 Nagel, Karen. *Shapes That Roll* (PS–2). Illus. by Steve Wilson. 2009, Blue Apple $14.99 (978-1-934706-81-7). Unpaged. A triangle, circle, and square have fun exploring and talking about other different kinds of shapes, from diamonds and stars to bananas and catchers' mitts in this bright, introduction to shapes. Lexile AD310 (Rev: SLJ 1/1/10)

392 Neuschwander, Cindy. *Pastry School in Paris: An Adventure in Capacity* (PS–3). Illus. by Bryan Langdo. 2009, Holt $16.95 (978-0-8050-8314-9). 32pp. Twins Bibi and Matt attend classes at a small Parisian cooking school and learn about measurements. (Rev: BL 6/1–15/09)

393 Olson, Nathan. *Spheres* (K–2). Illus. Series: 3-D Shapes. 2007, Capstone LB $23.93 (978-1-4296-0052-1). Using child-friendly examples (bubbles, oranges, snowballs), this book introduces the nature of a sphere and includes well-known examples of spheres plus a craft project. Also use *Pyramids* and *Cylinders* (both 2007). (Rev: SLJ 2/08) [516]

394 Pollack, Pam, and Meg Belviso. *Chickens on the Move* (1–2). Illus. by Lynn Adams. 2002, Kane paper $4.95 (978-1-57565-113-2). 32pp. In this witty concept book, three children use 24 feet of fencing to create coops of different shapes to house their grandfather's three chickens. (Rev: BL 4/15/02)

395 Rau, Dana Meachen. *Rectangles* (PS–2). Illus. Series: Bookworms: The Shape of the World. 2006, Marshall Cavendish $22.79 (978-0-7614-2282-2). 23pp. A bright, small-format introduction to rectangles with minimal text. (Rev: BL 10/15/06; SLJ 1/07) [516]

396 Rau, Dana Meachen. *A Star in My Orange: Looking for Nature's Shapes* (PS–2). Illus. 2002, Millbrook LB $22.90 (978-0-7613-2414-0). 32pp. Through colorful photographs and simple text, this book explores shapes such as stars and spirals as they occur in nature. (Rev: BL 2/1/02; HBG 10/02; SLJ 5/02) [516]

397 Ray, Mary Lyn. *Stars* (PS–2). Illus. by Marla Frazee. 2011, Simon & Schuster $16.99 (978-1-4424-2249-1). 40pp. A celebration of the wonder of stars and the many places we find their shapes in our lives. (Rev: BL 10/15/11*; SLJ 10/1/11*)

398 Rayner, Catherine. *Ernest, the Moose Who Doesn't Fit* (PS–1). Illus. by author. 2010, Farrar $15.99 (978-0-374-32217-5). 32pp. An enormous moose struggles to solve his problem of being too big — too big, even, for a picture book spread — by enlisting the help of a chipmunk friend in this funny book with a gatefold. (Rev: BL 12/1/10; SLJ 10/1/10*)

399 Rissman, Rebecca. *Shapes in Sports* (PS–1). Illus. Series: Spot the Shape. 2009, Heinemann LB $14.50 (978-143292170-5). 24pp. Using crisp photographs, Rissman identifies a lot of interesting shapes found in sporting equipment and venues. (Rev: BL 9/1/09*) [516]

400 Schoonmaker, Elizabeth. *Square Cat* (PS–1). Illus. by author. 2011, Simon & Schuster $14.99 (978-1-4424-0619-3). 32pp. A square cat named Eula has a difficult life and longs to be like the other cats, and they — after first trying to minimize her squareness — work to convince her that her shape has its advantages. (Rev: BL 2/1/11; SLJ 1/1/11)

401 Scott, Janine. *The Shape of Things* (K–2). Illus. Series: Spyglass Books. 2003, Compass Point LB $19.93 (978-0-7565-0453-3). 24pp. This photo-filled concept book introduces young readers to a wide array of different shapes, including circles, boxes, and stars. (Rev: SLJ 10/03) [516]

402 Scott, Janine. *Take a Guess: A Look at Estimation* (K–2). Illus. Series: Spyglass Books. 2003, Compass Point LB $19.93 (978-0-7565-0446-5). 24pp. This photo-filled volume introduces the concept of estimation and making approximations. (Rev: SLJ 12/03) [519.5]

403 Shea, Susan A. *Do You Know Which Ones Will Grow?* (PS–2). Illus. by Tom Slaughter. 2011, Blue Apple $16.99 (978-1-60905-062-7). 38pp. This flap book posits a variety of playful questions about size, shape, and growth. (Rev: BL 5/1/11; SLJ 6/11*)

404 Thong, Roseanne. *Round Is a Mooncake* (PS–1). Illus. by Grace Lin. 2000, Chronicle $13.95 (978-0-8118-2676-1). An Asian American girl looks at shapes she sees in her neighborhood in this book that explores circles, squares, and rectangles. (Rev: BL 12/1/00; HBG 3/01; SLJ 8/00)

405 Thong, Roseanne Greenfield. *Round Is a Tortilla* (PS–1). Illus. by John Parra. 2013, Chronicle $16.99 (978-145210616-8). 40pp. Full of Spanish words, this rhyming picture book introduces a variety of shapes — and some interesting foods. (Rev: BL 4/15/13; LMC 11–12/13; SLJ 4/13*)

406 Walsh, Ellen S. *Mouse Shapes* (PS–K). Illus. by author. 2007, Harcourt $16.00 (978-0-15-206091-6). 40pp. Three mice use colorful, assorted shapes to frighten away a pesky cat. (Rev: BL 7/07; HB 7/07; SLJ 7/07)

407 Wilson, Zachary. *A Circle in the Sky* (K–2). Illus. by JoAnn Aldinolfi. 2006, Children's Pr. LB $19.50 (978-0-531-12570-0). 32pp. A small girl's imaginative ideas serve as a framework for introducing four basic shapes. (Rev: BL 11/15/06)

Counting and Number Books

408 Andreasen, Dan. *The Baker's Dozen: A Counting Book* (PS). Illus. by author. 2007, Holt $16.95 (978-0-8050-7809-1). Numbers of tasty treats are created by a lively baker in this well-illustrated counting book. (Rev: BL 7/07; SLJ 9/07)

409 Anno, Mitsumasa. *Anno's Counting Book: An Adventure in Imagination* (PS–K). Illus. by author. 1977, HarperCollins LB $17.89 (978-0-690-01288-0); paper

$6.99 (978-0-06-443123-1). An appealing book on numbers in which the same landscapes are used throughout; houses, birds, trees, and people are added as the seasons progress.

410 Appelt, Kathi. *Bats on Parade* (K–3). Illus. by Melissa Sweet. 1999, Morrow LB $15.89 (978-0-688-15666-4). Basic multiplication is introduced in this story about a bat parade told with rhymes and peppy illustrations. (Rev: BL 4/1/99; HBG 10/99; SLJ 6/99)

411 Armstrong-Ellis, Carey F. *Ten Creepy Monsters* (PS–1). Illus. by Carey Armstrong-Ellis. 2012, Abrams $14.95 (978-1-4197-0433-8). 32pp. Counting and Halloween, humor and spookiness are combined in this appealing volume featuring rhyming text and a series of monsters that meet a succession of fates until the last one climbs into bed dropping his bag of candy. e (Rev: BLO 9/1/12; SLJ 9/12)

412 Bailey, Linda. *Goodnight, Sweet Pig* (PS–2). Illus. by Josee Masse. 2007, Kids Can LB $16.95 (978-1-55337-844-0). Poor pig is trying to sleep, but her bed is crowded by noisy pigs arriving one after the other. (Rev: SLJ 6/07)

413 Baker, Keith. *1-2-3 Peas* (PS–2). Illus. by author. 2012, Simon & Schuster $16.99 (978-144244551-2). 40pp. The peas introduced in *LMNO Peas* (2010) are back, teaching numbers from 1 to 10, and then by tens up to 100. (Rev: BLO 8/12; SLJ 7/12)

414 Baker, Keith. *Quack and Count* (PS–1). Illus. 1999, Harcourt $14.00 (978-0-15-292858-2). 24pp. This book shows how to have fun with the number seven while counting ducks in various combinations to reach that number. (Rev: BL 10/15/99; HBG 3/00; SLJ 11/99)

415 Bang, Molly. *Ten, Nine, Eight* (PS–1). Illus. by author. 1983, Greenwillow $17.89 (978-0-688-00907-6); Morrow paper $6.99 (978-0-688-10480-1). A counting-down book (from 10 to 1) involving an African American child going to bed. (Rev: BL 11/15/98)

416 Barnett, Mac. *Count the Monkeys* (PS–2). Illus. by Kevin Cornell. 2013, Disney/Hyperion $16.99 (978-1-4231-6065-6). 32pp. A funny counting book featuring a variety of animals that have frightened the monkeys off the pages. ALA Notable Children's Book. (Rev: BL 6/13; SLJ 5/13)

417 Barry, Frances. *Duckie's Ducklings: A One-to-Ten Counting Book* (PS). Illus. 2005, Candlewick $7.99 (978-0-7636-2514-6). 32pp. As Mother Duckie searches desperately for her 10 ducklings, one by one, members of her brood line up directly behind her. (Rev: BL 2/15/05)

418 Bates, Ivan. *Five Little Ducks* (PS). Illus. 2006, Scholastic $12.99 (978-0-439-74693-9). 24pp. Based on the classic children's song, this counting book follows a mother duck as she tries to round up her wandering ducklings. (Rev: BL 1/1–15/06; SLJ 2/06)

419 Beaton, Clare. *One Moose, Twenty Mice* (PS–1). Illus. 1999, Barefoot Books $14.95 (978-1-902283-37-1). A counting book containing different animals from 1

to 20, but posing the question "Where's the cat?" (Rev: BCCB 7–8/99; BL 5/15/99; SLJ 6/99)

420 Beaty, Andrea. *Hide and Sheep* (PS–2). Illus. by Bill Mayer. 2011, Simon & Schuster $15.99 (978-1-4169-2544-6). 32pp. A sleepy farmer's sheep escape to various locations in order to avoid shearing in this rhymed book that counts down from 10. (Rev: BL 4/1/11; SLJ 4/11)

421 Berkes, Marianne. *Over in Australia: Amazing Animals Down Under* (PS–2). Illus. by Jill Dubin. 2011, Dawn $16.95 (978-1-58469-135-8); paper $8.95 (978-1-58469-136-5). 32pp. A wombat and a crocodile are among the animals presented in this rhyming counting book based on "Over in the Meadow"; includes facts and activities. (Rev: BL 3/15/11; LMC 10/11; SLJ 6/11)

422 Berkes, Marianne. *Over in the Arctic: Where the Cold Winds Blow* (PS–1). Illus. by Jill Dubin. 2008, Dawn $16.95 (978-1-58469-109-9); paper $8.95 (978-1-58469-110-5). 32pp. This rhyming counting book based on "Over in the Meadow" showcases Arctic animals and their babies. (Rev: SLJ 9/08)

423 Berkes, Marianne. *Over in the Forest: Come and Take a Peek* (PS–2). Illus. by Jill Dubin. 2012, Dawn $16.95 (978-158469162-4); paper $8.95 (978-15846916-3-1). 32pp. Introduces woodland animals using a refrain based on "Over in the Meadow" and offering many opportunities for counting. (Rev: BLO 4/15/12; SLJ 7/12)

424 Berkes, Marianne. *Over in the Jungle: A Rainforest Rhyme* (PS–3). Illus. by Jeanette Canyon. 2007, Dawn $16.95 (978-1-58469-091-7); paper $8.95 (978-1-58469-092-4). Animals and plants of the rain forest fashioned from clay are featured in this fact-filled counting book. (Rev: SLJ 5/07)

425 Berry, Lynne. *Duck Dunks* (PS–K). Illus. by Hiroe Nakata. 2008, Holt $16.95 (978-0-8050-8128-2). 32pp. Five little ducks have fun at the seaside in this appealing companion to the counting book *Duck Skates* (2005). (Rev: BLO 7/29/08; SLJ 6/08)

426 Berry, Lynne. *Duck Skates* (PS–K). Illus. by Hiroe Nakata. 2005, Holt $15.95 (978-0-8050-7219-8). 32pp. Simple math concepts and numbers from 1 to 10 are integrated into this appealing picture-book story of five ducks enjoying a snowy day. (Rev: BL 10/1/05; SLJ 11/05)

427 Blackstone, Stella. *Cleo's Counting Book* (PS). Illus. by Caroline Mockford. 2003, Barefoot Books $15.99 (978-1-84148-207-1). Cleo the cat counts what she sees in the great outdoors. (Rev: HBG 10/03; SLJ 9/03)

428 Blackstone, Stella. *Counting Cockatoos* (PS–K). Illus. by Stephanie Bauer. 2006, Barefoot Books $16.99 (978-1-905236-31-2). Beautifully painted birds and other animals frolic on the pages of this book that counts from 1 to 12. (Rev: SLJ 5/06)

429 Blechman, Nicholas. *Night Light* (PS–K). Illus. by author. 2013, Scholastic $16.99 (978-0-545-46263-1). 48pp. A counting book with die-cut pages that allows readers to guess which vehicles are represented by a series of lights. (Rev: BL 7/13*; HB 7–8/13; SLJ 4/13)

430 Boueri, Marijean. *Lebanon 1-2-3* (PS–2). Illus. by Mona Trad Dabaji. 2005, Publishing Works $16.95 (978-1-933002-03-3). 32pp. Set in Lebanon, this brightly illustrated, trilingual (Arabic, English, and French) counting book introduces the numbers from 1 to 10. (Rev: BL 11/1/05; SLJ 11/05) [513.2]

431 Bowen, Betsy. *Gathering: A Northwoods Counting Book* (K–4). Illus. by author. 1999, Houghton $16.00 (978-0-395-98133-7); paper $6.95 (978-0-395-98134-4). This counting book shows preparations taken in the North for a long, hard winter, starting in the spring with planting a garden. (Rev: HBG 3/00; SLJ 9/99)

432 Brooks, Alan. *Frogs Jump: A Counting Book* (PS–1). Illus. by Steven Kellogg. 1996, Scholastic $15.95 (978-0-590-45528-2). 48pp. Madcap animals introduce basic numbers through unusual activities. (Rev: BL 10/15/96; SLJ 10/96)

433 Burns, Marilyn. *How Many Feet? How Many Tails? A Book of Math Riddles* (1–2). Illus. by Lynn Adams. 1996, Scholastic paper $3.99 (978-0-590-67360-0). 32pp. During a walk with Grandpa, a child learns about numbers in this easy-to-read book. (Rev: BL 2/1/97)

434 Burton, Katherine. *One Gray Mouse* (PS). Illus. by Kim Fernandes. 1997, Kids Can $12.95 (978-1-55074-225-1). Different numbers of animals are presented in this pleasant picture book that teaches the concepts of counting and colors. (Rev: BL 11/15/97; SLJ 12/97) [513.2]

435 Butler, John. *Ten in the Den* (PS–1). Illus. by author. 2005, Peachtree $15.95 (978-1-56145-344-3). Taking a cue from the rhyme "Ten in the Bed," 10 cuddly animals roll one by one down a hill and settle in for a nap. (Rev: SLJ 9/05)

436 Byrd, Lee Merrill. *Lover Boy / Juanito el cariñoso: A Bilingual Counting Book* (PS–2). Trans. by David Dorado Romo. Illus. by Francisco Delgado. 2006, Cinco Puntos $15.95 (978-0-938317-38-8). A little boy enjoys giving kisses to everyone he sees (whether they enjoy it or not) in this book that counts kisses in English and Spanish. (Rev: SLJ 6/06)

437 Cabrera, Jane. *Over in the Meadow* (PS). Illus. 2000, Holiday House $16.95 (978-0-8234-1490-1). Readers learn numbers while naming animals and copying their actions in this fresh new treatment of the traditional counting song. (Rev: BCCB 5/00; BL 2/1/00; HBG 10/00; SLJ 4/00) [513.2]

438 Carle, Eric. *Roosters Off to See the World* (PS–K). Illus. by author. 1991, Picture Book $16.95 (978-0-88708-042-5). 28pp. In this counting book originally published in 1972, a rooster gathers together a group of animals to explore the world. Addition and subtraction are also introduced.

439 Catalanotto, Peter. *Daisy 1, 2, 3* (PS–1). Illus. by author. 2003, Simon & Schuster $15.95 (978-0-689-85457-6). Mrs. Tuttle, who has 20 Dalmatians — all called Daisy — in her obedience class, comes up with an ingenious way to tell them apart. (Rev: BL 11/1/03; HBG 4/04; SLJ 12/03)

440 Cato, Sheila. *Addition* (1–4). Illus. by Sami Sweeten. Series: A Question of Math Book. 1999, Carolrhoda LB $25.26 (978-1-57505-320-2). 32pp. Using cartoon characters and one addition problem per double-page spread, this book demonstrates the basic processes of addition. Also use *Subtraction* and *Counting and Numbers* (both 1999). (Rev: HBG 3/00; SLJ 11/99)

441 Cato, Sheila. *Division* (1–4). Illus. by Sami Sweeten. Series: A Question of Math Book. 1999, Carolrhoda LB $25.26 (978-1-57505-319-6). 32pp. Using a series of problems followed by clear answers and explanations, the principles of division are covered. Also use *Multiplication* (1999). (Rev: HBG 3/00; SLJ 11/99)

442 Cave, Kathryn. *One Child, One Seed: A South African Counting Book* (K–2). Photos by Gisele Wulfson. 2003, Holt $16.95 (978-0-8050-7204-4). Cave interweaves basic counting skills with information about life in rural Natal in this innovative book that features beautiful photographs. (Rev: BL 5/1/03; HBG 10/03; SLJ 8/03) [513.2]

443 Chaconas, Dori. *One Little Mouse* (PS–K). Illus. by LeUyen Pham. 2002, Viking $15.99 (978-0-670-88947-1). A little mouse searching for a new house visits other animals' homes before deciding that his own is best of all, in a rhyming text that teaches children to count up to 10 and back down again. (Rev: BL 9/1/02; HBG 10/02; SLJ 8/02)

444 Chae, In Seon. *How Do You Count a Dozen Ducklings?* (PS–1). Illus. by Seung Ha Rew. 2006, Albert Whitman $16.95 (978-0-8075-1718-5). 32pp. A mother duck uses various math strategies to keep track of her newly hatched ducklings. (Rev: BL 9/15/06; SLJ 9/06)

445 Chall, Marsha Wilson. *One Pup's Up* (PS–K). Illus. by Henry Cole. 2010, Simon & Schuster $16.99 (978-1-4169-7960-9). 32pp. Readers can count up to 10 and back again as a litter of puppies tumble and play. (Rev: BL 4/15/10; SLJ 6/1/10)

446 Chandra, Deborah. *Miss Mabel's Table* (PS–2). Illus. by Max Grover. 1994, Harcourt $14.95 (978-0-15-276712-9). 32pp. A counting book about Miss Mabel, her restaurant, and the food she serves. (Rev: BCCB 4/94; BL 3/15/94; SLJ 6/94)

447 Cheng, Andrea. *Grandfather Counts* (PS–3). Illus. by Ange Zhang. 2000, Lee & Low $15.95 (978-1-58430-010-6). 32pp. In this unusual counting book, Helen, a little Chinese-American girl, and her grandfather count the cars on a passing train in both English and Chinese. (Rev: BL 12/15/00; HBG 3/01; SLJ 11/00)

448 Chorao, Kay. *Number One Number Fun* (PS–1). Illus. 1995, Holiday House LB $15.95 (978-0-8234-1142-9). 32pp. Simple arithmetic is highlighted through a series of clever rhymes involving addition and subtraction. (Rev: BCCB 2/95; BL 2/15/95; SLJ 3/95)

449 Christelow, Eileen. *Five Little Monkeys Go Shopping* (PS–2). Illus. by author. 2007, Clarion $16.00 (978-0-618-82161-7). 32pp. Will Mom bring the right number of monkeys home from the back-to-school sale? (Rev: SLJ 10/07)

450 Christelow, Eileen. *Five Little Monkeys Sitting in a Tree* (PS–K). Illus. 1991, Houghton $16.00 (978-0-395-54434-1). The numbers 1 through 5 are taught through the antics of five little monkeys. A sequel is: *Don't Wake Up Mama!* (1992). (Rev: BL 5/15/91; SLJ 8/91)

451 Christelow, Eileen, retel. *Five Little Monkeys Jumping on the Bed* (PS–K). Illus. by Eileen Christelow. 1989, Ticknor $15.00 (978-0-89919-769-2); paper $5.95 (978-0-395-55701-3). An exuberant rendition of the favorite nursery rhyme. (Rev: BL 6/1/89)

452 Clark, Emma Chichester. *Mimi's Book of Counting* (PS). Illus. by author. Series: A Mimi Book. 2003, Charlesbridge $9.95 (978-1-57091-573-4). In this appealing counting book, Mimi the monkey and her visiting grandmother find everyday household items that they count from 1 to 10. (Rev: HBG 4/04; SLJ 11/03)

453 Clements, Andrew. *A Million Dots* (K–3). Illus. by Mike Reed. 2006, Simon & Schuster $16.95 (978-0-689-85824-6). 48pp. The million dots on these pages will give young readers a feeling for the magnitude of the number, enhanced by the numerical facts/trivia scattered through the book. (Rev: BL 6/1–15/06; SLJ 7/06) [513.2]

454 Coats, Lucy. *Down in the Daisies: A Baby Animal Counting Book* (PS–1). Illus. by Emily Bolam. 2003, Orion $16.95 (978-1-85881-513-8). This beautifully illustrated counting book spotlights baby animals and their mothers in all kinds of weather. (Rev: SLJ 10/03)

455 Cohn, Scotti. *One Wolf Howls* (PS–2). Illus. by Susan Detwiler. 2009, Sylvan Dell $16.95 (978-1-934359-92-1); paper $8.95 (978-1-60718-037-1). This rhyming picture book combines counting — by month and number of wolves — up to 12 with basic information about wolves' lives, behavior, and endangered status. (Rev: BL 4/1/09; SLJ 6/09) [599.773]

456 Coleman, Michael. *One, Two, Three, Oops!* (PS–K). Illus. by Gwyneth Williamson. 1999, Little Tiger $14.95 (978-1-888444-45-2). 32pp. When Mr. Rabbit begins to count his children, he has to work out which ones have been counted and which haven't. (Rev: BL 1/1–15/99; HBG 10/99; SLJ 3/99)

457 Cotten, Cynthia. *At the Edge of the Woods: A Counting Book* (PS–2). Illus. by Reg Cartwright. 2002, Holt $16.95 (978-0-8050-6354-7). 32pp. Gentle verse and bright, primitive paintings are used in this incremental tale of a forest day, in which 1 chipmunk, 2 young deer, and then more and more animals appear. (Rev: BL 12/1/02; HBG 3/03; SLJ 6/03)

458 Crews, Donald. *Ten Black Dots* (PS–K). Illus. by author. 1986, Greenwillow $17.89 (978-0-688-06068-8). 32pp. Dots form an integral part of this counting book, originally published in 1968, such as "five dots make buttons on a coat." (Rev: BL 3/1/86; SLJ 5/86)

459 Cronin, Doreen. *Click, Clack, Splish, Splash: A Counting Adventure* (PS). Illus. by Betsy Lewin. 2006, Simon & Schuster $12.95 (978-0-689-87716-2). 24pp. A cumulative counting book about farm animals sneaking off for a secret fishing trip. (Rev: BL 1/1–15/06; SLJ 1/06)

460 *Curious George Learns to Count from 1 to 100* (PS–2). Illus. by Anna Grossnickle Hines. 2005, Houghton $16.00 (978-0-618-47602-2). 64pp. As part of his town's centennial celebration, the inquisitive little monkey learns how to count to 100. (Rev: BL 9/15/05; SLJ 10/05)

461 Cuyler, Margery. *Guinea Pigs Add Up* (PS–2). Illus. by Tracey Campbell Pearson. 2010, Walker $16.99 (978-0-8027-9795-7). 32pp. Class pet guinea pigs offer a lesson in counting as they multiply. (Rev: BL 5/1/10; LMC 8–9/10; SLJ 7/1/10)

462 Cuyler, Margery. *100th Day Worries* (K–2). Illus. by Arthur Howard. 2000, Simon & Schuster $16.00 (978-0-689-82979-6). 32pp. In this counting book, 1st-grader Jessica is asked to bring 100 objects to celebrate the 100th day of school. (Rev: BCCB 2/00; BL 11/1/99; HBG 10/00; SLJ 1/00)

463 Dahl, Michael. *Eggs and Legs: Counting by Twos* (PS–2). Illus. by Todd Ouren. Series: Know Your Numbers. 2005, Picture Window LB $25.26 (978-1-4048-0945-1). Counting by twos to 20 is the focus of a lively story with bright cartoons and numerals hidden within the text and illustrations. Also use *Pie for Piglets: Counting by Twos* (2005). (Rev: SLJ 6/05)

464 Dahl, Michael. *One Big Building: A Counting Book About Construction* (PS–K). Illus. by Todd Ouren. Series: Know Your Numbers. 2004, Picture Window LB $25.26 (978-1-4048-0580-4). "Fun Facts" about construction are included along with numbers from 1 to 12 — "one big plan" and "twelve stories tall." Also use *From the Garden: A Counting Book About Growing Food* (2004). (Rev: BL 4/1/04; SLJ 6/04) [513.2]

465 Dahl, Michael. *Pie for Piglets: Counting by Twos* (PS–K). Illus. Series: Know Your Numbers. 2005, Picture Window LB $25.26 (978-1-4048-0943-7). 24pp. An entertaining introduction to counting by 2, with numbers hidden within the text and illustrations. Other titles in this series include *Hands Down: Counting by Fives* and *Lots of Ladybugs! Counting by Fives* (2005). (Rev: SLJ 6/05)

466 Degman, Lori. *One Zany Zoo* (K–1). Illus. by Colin Jack. 2010, Simon & Schuster $15.99 (978-1-4169-8990-5). Unpaged. A rollicking counting book in which the zoo animals are freed from their cages. (Rev: LMC 8–9/10; SLJ 7/1/10)

467 Delessert, Etienne. *Hungry for Numbers* (PS–2). Illus. by author. 2006, Creative Editions $18.95 (978-1-56846-198-4). Ten hungry creatures eat delicious fruit — from 1 banana to 10 blueberries. (Rev: SLJ 11/06)

468 Demarest, Chris L. *Smokejumpers One to Ten* (PS–1). Illus. 2002, Simon & Schuster $17.00 (978-0-689-84120-0). 32pp. A counting book featuring courageous and hardworking parachuting fire fighters. (Rev: BCCB 7–8/02; BL 7/02; HBG 10/02; SLJ 7/02) [634.9]

469 Denise, Anika. *Pigs Love Potatoes* (PS–K). Illus. by Christopher Denise. 2007, Philomel $15.99 (978-0-399-

24036-2). 40pp. Mama enlists the help of her family of pigs to wash, peel, and cook potatoes in this charming counting book. (Rev: BCCB 9/07; BL 6/1–15/07; SLJ 7/07)

470 Dickinson, Rebecca. *Over in the Hollow* (PS–K). Illus. by Stephan Britt. 2009, Chronicle $15.99 (978-0-8118-5035-3). Unpaged. Count from 1 spider to 13 ghosts in this spooky and comic Halloween tale. (Rev: LMC 1–2/10; SLJ 10/1/09)

471 Donaldson, Julia. *One Ted Falls Out of Bed* (PS–2). Illus. by Anna Currey. 2006, Holt $15.95 (978-0-8050-7787-2). 32pp. An impressive assortment of toys and three mice come to the aid of a teddy bear that's fallen out of his owner's bed, giving the reader the opportunity to count up to 10 and down again. (Rev: BL 6/1–15/06; SLJ 6/06)

472 Durango, Julia. *Cha-Cha-Chimps* (PS–K). Illus. by Eleanor Taylor. 2006, Simon & Schuster $15.95 (978-0-689-86456-8). 32pp. Ten little chimps go to Mambo Jamba's for a lively dance session in this rhythmic counting book. (Rev: BL 1/1–15/06; SLJ 2/06)

473 Durango, Julia. *Go-Go Gorillas* (PS–K). Illus. by Eleanor Taylor. 2010, Simon & Schuster $15.99 (978-1-4169-3779-1). 32pp. King Big Daddy's relatives are summoned to the Great Gorilla Villa in this lively, bouncy counting book that shows gorillas arriving in buses, hot-air balloons, and planes. Lexile AD530L (Rev: BL 5/1/10; SLJ 3/1/10)

474 Ehlert, Lois. *Fish Eyes: A Book You Can Count On* (PS–K). Illus. 1990, Harcourt $14.95 (978-0-15-228050-5). 32pp. Compelling color and design introduce this counting book. (Rev: BL 3/1/90*; SLJ 5/90)

475 Ehrhardt, Karen. *This Jazz Man* (PS–2). Illus. by R. G. Roth. 2006, Harcourt $16.00 (978-0-15-205307-9). 32pp. The well-known song "This Old Man" is presented here with a lively jazz theme, featuring different jazz musicians as children rhyme and count to nine. (Rev: BL 11/15/06; SLJ 12/06)

476 Elliott, David. *One Little Chicken: A Counting Book* (PS–K). Illus. by Ethan Long. 2007, Holiday $16.95 (978-0-8234-1983-8). 24pp. Bouncy rhyming text and expressive illustrations show chickens flapping their wings to different dance styles: "Three chickens practice their ballet. Four chickens swing the night away." (Rev: BL 11/15/07; SLJ 12/07)

477 Emberley, Rebecca. *My Numbers / Mis Numeros* (PS). 2000, Little, Brown $5.95 (978-0-316-23350-7). 20pp. This counting board book introduces the numbers in both English and Spanish. (Rev: BCCB 12/00*; HBG 3/01; SLJ 9/00)

478 Emberley, Rebecca, and Ed Emberley. *Ten Little Beasties* (PS–1). Illus. by authors. 2011, Roaring Brook $12.99 (978-1-59643-627-5). Unpaged. Count little beasties up to 10 and back again to the tune of "Ten Little Indians" or to the original melody offered on a related Web site. (Rev: SLJ 10/1/11)

479 Ewing, Susan. *Ten Rowdy Ravens* (PS–6). Illus. by Evon Zerbetz. 2005, Alaska Northwest $15.95 (978-0-88240-606-0); paper $8.95 (978-0-88240-610-7). The mischievous nature of ravens is highlighted in this entertaining counting book. (Rev: SLJ 1/06)

480 Falconer, Ian. *Olivia Counts* (PS). Illus. 2002, Simon & Schuster $6.99 (978-0-689-85087-5). 12pp. A simple board book featuring Olivia the pig with 1 beach ball, 2 bows, and so forth up to 10. (Rev: BCCB 6/02; BL 7/02; HBG 10/02; SLJ 6/02)

481 Falwell, Cathryn. *Turtle Splash! Countdown at the Pond* (PS–K). Illus. 2001, Greenwillow LB $17.89 (978-0-06-029463-2). 32pp. A rhythmic countdown to bedtime as one turtle after another — for a total of 10 — splashes into a lake as evening comes closer and animals arrive at the water's edge. (Rev: BL 8/01; HBG 3/02; SLJ 9/01*)

482 Fox, Mem. *Let's Count Goats!* (PS–K). Illus. by Jan Thomas. 2010, Simon & Schuster $16.99 (978-1-4424-0598-1). 40pp. Goats in different shapes, sizes, colors, and numbers populate brightly colored, comic spreads, while simple text encourages readers to search, find, and count. (Rev: BL 10/1/10; SLJ 11/1/10)

483 Franco, Betsy. *Birdsongs* (PS–2). Illus. by Steve Jenkins. 2007, Simon & Schuster $16.99 (978-0-689-87777-3). 32pp. Nature lesson and counting book are combined in this beautifully illustrated collection of avian collages. (Rev: BL 1/1–15/07; SLJ 1/07)

484 Franco, Betsy. *Double Play* (PS–1). Illus. by Doug Cushman. 2011, Tricycle $15.99 (978-158246384-1); LB $18.99 (978-158246396-4). 32pp. At recess, Jill and Jake's activities offer the chance to count, add, and double numbers from 1 to 10. (Rev: BL 7/11; SLJ 6/11)

485 Franco, Betsy. *Zero Is the Leaves on the Tree* (PS–2). Illus. by Shino Arihara. 2009, Tricycle $15.99 (978-1-58246-249-3). 32pp. The concept of zero is introduced in a variety of creative ways. (Rev: BL 9/15/09; LMC 3–4/10; SLJ 9/1/09) [513]

486 Fromental, Jean-Luc, and Joëlle Jolivet. *365 Penguins* (PS–2). Illus. 2006, Abrams $17.95 (978-0-8109-4460-2). 32pp. A family's problems — and mathematical calculations — multiply when an additional penguin arrives every day for a year; a lively, oversize picture book. (Rev: BL 1/1–15/07; SLJ 12/06)

487 Fuller, Jill. *Springtime Addition* (PS–K). Series: Rookie Read-about Math. 2004, Children's Pr. LB $20.50 (978-0-516-24422-8). 31pp. A simple, colorful, and interesting introduction to addition featuring outdoor attractions. Also use *Toy Box Subtraction* and *A Garden Full of Sizes* (both 2004). (Rev: SLJ 3/05) [513.2]

488 Garland, Michael. *How Many Mice?* (PS–2). Illus. by author. 2007, Dutton $15.99 (978-0-525-47833-1). Prompted by questions in the text, children will count and seek hidden clues in this appealing story about mice dodging a fox, an owl, and other dangers as they carry food back to their home. (Rev: BL 6/1–15/07; SLJ 6/07)

489 Gayzagian, Doris K. *One White Wishing Stone: A Beach Day Counting Book* (PS). Illus. by Kristina Swarner. 2006, National Geographic $16.95 (978-0-

7922-5110-1). In this gentle counting book, a little girl spending a day at the beach with her mother counts off the wondrous treasures she discovers for her sandcastle. (Rev: SLJ 11/06)

490 Gershator, Phillis. *Zoo Day ¡Olé! A Counting Book* (PS–1). Illus. by Santiago Cohen. 2009, Marshall Cavendish $17.99 (978-0-7614-5462-5). 32pp. Combining counting, Spanish words, and animals, this is an enjoyable trip to the zoo. (Rev: BL 5/1/09; SLJ 4/09) [513.2]

491 Geser, Gretchen. *One Bright Ring* (PS–2). Illus. by author. 2013, Henry Holt $16.99 (978-0-8050-9279-0). 32pp. A little girl catches a ring that falls out of a man's pocket, and she and her mother pursue him, conquering various obstacles in their path, which count up to 20. (Rev: BLO 7/13; SLJ 5/13)

492 Giganti, Paul. *Each Orange Had Eight Slices* (PS–3). Illus. by Donald Crews. 1992, Greenwillow $17.89 (978-0-688-10429-0). This well-designed book challenges young readers to think analytically about what it portrays. (Rev: BCCB 4/92; BL 3/15/92; SLJ 3/92) [513.5]

493 Giganti, Paul. *How Many Blue Birds Flew Away? A Counting Book with a Difference* (PS–K). Illus. by Donald Crews. 2005, Greenwillow LB $16.89 (978-0-06-000763-8). 32pp. Attractive colorful illustrations pose addition and subtraction puzzles. (Rev: BL 10/15/05; SLJ 9/05)

494 Gillham, Bill. *How Many Sharks in the Bath?* (PS). Illus. by Christyan Fox. 2005, Frances Lincoln $14.95 (978-1-84507-288-9). The zany animal antics in this colorful counting book give readers an opportunity to practice numbers from 0 to 10. (Rev: SLJ 1/06)

495 Ginkel, Anne. *I've Got an Elephant* (PS–2). Illus. by Janie Bynum. 2006, Peachtree $16.95 (978-1-56145-373-3). 32pp. A little girl's elephant gets lonely when she goes to school and invites an elephant friend over, and then another, and then another — until this rhyming counting book reaches 10. (Rev: BL 9/15/06; SLJ 9/06)

496 Giogas, Valarie. *In My Backyard* (PS–3). Illus. by Katherine Zecca. 2007, Sylvan Dell $15.95 (978-0-9777423-1-8); paper $8.95 (978-1-9343591-7-4). As well as counting to 10, readers become familiar with the names of 10 animals and learn facts about them and about how to deal with injured animals. (Rev: LMC 11/07; SLJ 11/07) [591.5]

497 Girnis, Meg. *1, 2, 3 for You and Me* (PS–1). Photos by Shirley Leamon Green. 2001, Whitman LB $16.99 (978-0-8075-6107-2). Smiling children with Down's syndrome are shown holding toys and everyday objects in this simple counting book. (Rev: HBG 10/01; SLJ 7/01)

498 Goldstone, Bruce. *100 Ways to Celebrate 100 Days* (PS–2). Illus. by author. 2010, Henry Holt $16.99 (978-0-8050-8997-4). 48pp. Bolstering reading and counting skills, this volume presents a wide variety of simple ways to celebrate the first 100 days of school. (Rev: BL 9/1/10; LMC 10/10; SLJ 7/1/10) [513]

499 Gravett, Emily. *The Rabbit Problem* (1–4). Illus. by author. 2010, Simon & Schuster $17.99 (978-1-4424-

1255-2). Unpaged. If a pair of baby rabbits are put into a field, how many pairs will there be: a) At the end of each month? b) After one year? This book takes a clever and humorous approach to the Fibonacci problem. (Rev: HB 1–2/11; SLJ 12/1/10)

500 Guy, Ginger F. *¡Fiesta!* (PS–2). Illus. by Rene King Moreno. 1996, Greenwillow $16.99 (978-0-688-14331-2). Numbers are introduced in English and Spanish in this book about collecting articles to celebrate a Mexican fiesta. (Rev: SLJ 9/96)

501 Halfmann, Janet. *Eggs 1, 2, 3: Who Will the Babies Be?* (PS–2). Illus. by Betsy Thompson. 2012, Blue Apple $17.99 (978-1-60905191-4). 32pp. Eggs of various animals — and the resulting hatchlings — are featured in gatefolds that teach numbers from 1 penguin to 10 ostriches. (Rev: BL 8/12; SLJ 7/12) [591.4]

502 Harris, Trudy. *Jenny Found a Penny* (K–3). Illus. by John Hovell. Series: Math Is Fun! 2007, Millbrook LB $23.93 (978-0-8225-6725-7). 32pp. Jenny's story of earning, saving, and spending is interwoven with a lesson on counting money. (Rev: SLJ 10/07)

503 Harris, Trudy. *100 Days of School* (PS–K). Illus. by Beth Griffis Johnson. 1999, Millbrook LB $22.90 (978-0-7613-1271-0). 32pp. Various combinations of familiar objects are used to reach the number 100 in this innovative counting book. (Rev: BL 11/15/99; HBG 3/00; SLJ 11/99)

504 Harris, Trudy. *20 Hungry Piggies: A Number Book* (PS–2). Illus. by Andrew N. Harris. 2007, Millbrook LB $15.95 (978-0-8225-6370-9). Twenty little piggies unwittingly foil the plans of a hungry wolf in this funny take on the original toe-counting nursery game. (Rev: SLJ 5/07)

505 Helman, Andrea. *1, 2, 3 Moose: A Pacific Northwest Counting Book* (PS–2). Illus. by Art Wolfe. 1996, Sasquatch $15.95 (978-1-57061-078-3). 32pp. A 1-to-20 counting book that employs the flora and fauna of the Pacific Northwest. (Rev: BL 11/1/96; SLJ 1/97) [428.1]

506 Himmelman, John. *Ten Little Hot Dogs* (PS–1). Illus. by author. 2010, Marshall Cavendish $12.99 (978-0-7614-5797-8). 32pp. Lively little dachshunds leap, play, pile, and snooze in this counting book. (Rev: BL 12/1/10; SLJ 9/1/10)

507 Hoban, Tana. *Let's Count* (PS–1). Illus. 1999, Greenwillow $16.99 (978-0-688-16008-1). Amazing photos are used in this counting book to highlight objects from 1 to 15, then by tens to 50, and finally to 100. (Rev: BL 9/15/99; HBG 3/00; SLJ 9/99) [513.2]

508 Hughes, Shirley. *Alfie's 1-2-3* (PS). Illus. 2000, Lothrop $15.95 (978-0-688-17705-8). 32pp. Playful activities of a preschooler's day form the framework of this simple counting book. (Rev: BL 4/15/00; HBG 10/00; SLJ 5/00)

509 Hutchins, Pat. *Ten Red Apples* (PS–2). Illus. 2000, Greenwillow $17.99 (978-0-688-16797-4). A charming counting book about a farmer and his apple crop. (Rev: BL 5/1/00; HBG 10/00; SLJ 5/00)

510 Jay, Alison. *1 2 3: A Child's First Counting Book* (K–2). Illus. by author. 2007, Dutton $15.99 (978-0-525-47836-2). 40pp. A little girl falls asleep with a book of fairy tales open in her hands and dreams she appears in 10 fairy-tale scenes in this picture book with beautiful illustrations. (Rev: BL 9/15/07; SLJ 9/07)

511 Jocelyn, Marthe. *One Some Many* (PS–K). Illus. by Tom Slaughter. 2004, Tundra $11.95 (978-0-88776-675-6). A counting book in rhyme that creatively introduces the differences between "many," "few," "some," "none," and "more." (Rev: SLJ 6/04)

512 Katz, Karen. *Mommy Hugs* (PS). Illus. 2006, Simon & Schuster $12.95 (978-0-689-87772-8). 32pp. This appealing counting book deals in the hugs that a baby gets throughout the day. (Rev: BL 2/15/06; SLJ 4/06)

513 Katz, Karen. *Ten Tiny Babies* (PS). Illus. by author. 2008, Simon & Schuster $14.99 (978-1-4169-3546-9). 32pp. This rhythmic and colorful counting book follows 10 babies through simple activities, ending with a bath and bedtime. (Rev: BL 7/08; SLJ 9/08)

514 Keller, Laurie. *Grandpa Gazillion's Number Yard* (PS–K). Illus. 2005, Holt $16.95 (978-0-8050-6282-3). 32pp. Junkyard owner Grandpa Gazillion sees numbers in very different ways, introducing his concepts for using 1 through 20. (Rev: BL 11/15/05; SLJ 11/05)

515 Kellogg, Steven. *Give the Dog a Bone* (K–3). Illus. 2000, North-South LB $15.88 (978-1-58717-002-7). 40pp. A riotous counting book that involves a grand total of 250 dogs (and 1 chicken). (Rev: BL 12/1/00; HBG 3/01; SLJ 11/00)

516 Kelly, Mij. *One More Sheep* (PS–2). Illus. by Russell Ayto. 2006, Peachtree $16.95 (978-1-56145-378-8). 30pp. Sam always falls asleep when he tries to count his herd of 10 sheep, and one night when a wolf (dressed in sheep's clothing) tries to sneak in, the sheep must work hard to keep Sam awake so he can count to 11. (Rev: BL 11/15/06; SLJ 10/06)

517 Kimmelman, Leslie. *How Do I Love You?* (PS–1). Illus. by Lisa McCue. 2005, HarperCollins $14.99 (978-0-06-001200-7). In this counting-book celebration of parental love, an adult crocodile lists 20 reasons why it loves its child. (Rev: SLJ 2/06)

518 Law, Diane. *Come Out and Play* (PS). 2006, North-South $9.95 (978-0-7358-2060-9). 24pp. A counting book that incorporates multiculturalism through language (each number is shown in English, Spanish, German, French, and Chinese) and through the characters (the children are of different ethnicities and live in different settings). (Rev: BL 5/1/06; SLJ 7/06)

519 Lee, Huy Voun. *1, 2, 3, Go!* (PS–1). Illus. 2001, Holt $16.00 (978-0-8050-6205-2). 32pp. This introduction to Chinese numbers gives the Chinese characters for 1 to 10 and for the words used to illustrate each number. (Rev: BL 2/1/01; HBG 10/01) [495.1]

520 Leedy, Loreen. *Fraction Action* (K–2). Illus. 1994, Holiday House LB $17.95 (978-0-8234-1109-2). 32pp. How to divide various objects and the meaning of fractions are explored in this simple, colorful arithmetic book. (Rev: BCCB 3/94; BL 3/15/94) [513.2]

521 Leedy, Loreen. *Missing Math: A Number Mystery* (K–2). Illus. by author. 2008, Marshall Cavendish $16.99 (978-0-7614-5385-7). 32pp. Ack! How does a town cope when it's deprived of all its numbers? (Rev: BL 4/1/08; LMC 8/08; SLJ 6/08)

522 Leedy, Loreen. *Subtraction Action* (1–3). Illus. 2000, Holiday House $17.95 (978-0-8234-1454-3). 32pp. In seven short chapters, Miss Prime and her class learn how to do subtraction. (Rev: BL 9/15/00; HBG 3/01; SLJ 9/00)

523 Lessac, Frane. *Island Counting 123* (PS–K). Illus. 2005, Candlewick $12.99 (978-0-7636-1960-2). 24pp. Set in the Caribbean, this counting book features warm island scenes. (Rev: BL 5/15/05)

524 Ljungkvist, Laura. *Follow the Line* (K–2). Illus. by author. 2006, Viking $16.99 (978-0-670-06049-8). The line leads through all sorts of settings, encouraging children to count objects ranging from fire hydrants to babies sleeping in a village. (Rev: SLJ 5/06)

525 Lodge, Bernard. *How Scary!* (PS–K). Illus. 2001, Houghton $15.00 (978-0-618-11547-1). One growling giant, 2 dreadful dragons, and so on up to 10 rattling robots all add up to a satisfying Halloween counting book. (Rev: BL 9/1/01; HBG 3/02; SLJ 9/01)

526 Long, Ethan. *One Drowsy Dragon* (PS–2). Illus. by author. 2010, Scholastic $16.99 (978-0-545-16557-0). Unpaged. An adult dragon is kept awake by 10 rambunctious youngsters in this bright counting book full of onomatopoeia. (Rev: LMC 10/10; SLJ 7/1/10)

527 MacDonald, Margaret Read, and Nadia Jameel Taibah. *How Many Donkeys? An Arabic Counting Tale* (K–2). Illus. by Carol Liddiment. 2009, Whitman $16.99 (978-0-8075-3424-3). 32pp. Jouha is having trouble counting his 10 donkeys in this eye-catching tale set in the Middle East and featuring both English and Arabic. (Rev: BL 9/15/09; LMC 11–12/09; SLJ 10/1/09) [398.2]

528 MacDonald, Suse. *Fish, Swish! Splash, Dash! Counting Round and Round* (PS–2). Illus. by author. 2007, Simon & Schuster $8.99 (978-1-4169-3605-3). Young children will enjoy counting 10 colorful fish, then turning the book and counting back down to 1. Die-cut pages contribute to the entertaining design. (Rev: SLJ 6/07)

529 McFarland, Lyn Rossiter. *Mouse Went Out to Get a Snack* (PS–1). Illus. by Jim McFarland. 2005, Farrar $16.00 (978-0-374-37672-7). One piece of cheese, 2 plump plums — these are just the first of the luxury items the mouse hopes to get back to his hole. (Rev: LMC 8/05*; SLJ 3/05)

530 McGrath, Barbara Barbieri. *Teddy Bear Counting* (PS). Illus. by Tim Nihoff. 2010, Charlesbridge $16.95 (978-1-58089-215-5); paper $7.95 (978-1-58089-216-2). Unpaged. This colorful book uses appealing bear illustrations to present basic counting (1 to 12) as well as colors, shapes, addition and subtraction, and grouping numbers in sets. (Rev: SLJ 2/1/10)

531 Maloney, Peter, and Felicia Zekauskas. *One Foot Two Feet: An EXCEPTIONal Counting Book* (PS–K). 2011, Putnam $12.99 (978-0-399-25446-8). 48pp. Counting and vocabulary are combined in this interactive book that emphasizes how plural nouns differ from singular ones. (Rev: BL 6/1/11; SLJ 7/11*) [372.72]

532 Mannis, Celeste Davidson. *One Leaf Rides the Wind: Counting in a Japanese Garden* (PS–2). Illus. by Susan Kathleen Hartung. 2002, Viking $15.99 (978-0-670-03525-0). A Japanese girl counts the plants and objects in a traditional garden in this elegant book that also introduces haiku and the tea ceremony. (Rev: HBG 3/03; SLJ 10/02)

533 Mariconda, Barbara. *Sort It Out!* (PS–2). Illus. by Sherry Rogers. 2008, Sylvan Dell $16.95 (978-1-934359-11-2); paper $8.95 (978-1-934359-32-7). 32pp. Packrat enjoys sorting his belongings in a variety of ways in this rhyming introduction to basic set theory. (Rev: SLJ 9/08)

534 Marino, Gianna. *One Too Many: A Seek and Find Counting Book* (PS–2). Illus. by author. 2010, Chronicle $16.99 (978-0-8118-6908-9). 40pp. A wordless, cumulative — and beautifully illustrated — counting book in which groups of animals from 1 to 12 congregate on the pages until a final addition (a skunk) is just one too many. (Rev: BL 4/15/10; LMC 10/10; SLJ 5/1/10)

535 Markle, Sandra. *How Many Baby Pandas?* (K–3). Illus. 2009, Walker $15.99 (978-0-8027-9783-4). Readers can count pandas as they learn about young pandas' diet, physical characteristics, and behavior. (Rev: BCCB 5/09; BL 4/1/09; SLJ 4/09) [599.789]

536 Marzollo, Jean. *Help Me Learn Numbers 0–20* (PS–1). Illus. 2011, Holiday House $15.95 (978-0-8234-2334-7). 32pp. Photographs and interactive rhymes that become more difficult as they progress teach children to count to 20. (Rev: BL 11/1/11; SLJ 9/1/11) [513.2]

537 Marzollo, Jean. *Ten Little Christmas Presents* (PS–K). Illus. by author. 2008, Scholastic paper $9.99 (978-0-545-02791-5). 32pp. Ten small animals gather to see what's inside the 10 Christmas presents labeled with their names and their pictures in this counting book that has a matching game at the end. (Rev: BL 9/1/08)

538 Matzke, Ann H. *Make It 100!* (PS–K). Illus. Series: Little World Math Concepts. 2011, Rourke $22.79 (978-161741765-8); paper $7.96 (978-16174196-7-6). 24pp. Bright illustrations show a variety of ways to count to hundred. Also use *Plus 0, Minus 0* and *Plus 2, Minus 2* (both 2011). (Rev: BL 11/1/11)

539 May, Eleanor. *The Mousier the Merrier* (PS–1). Illus. by Deborah Melmon. Series: Mouse Math. 2012, Kane $22.60 (978-157565447-8); paper $7.95 (9781575654409). 32pp. Mouse siblings Wanda and Albert invite friends over to play in this appealing counting book. (Rev: BL 9/1/12; SLJ 11/12)

540 Melville, Kirsty. *Splash! A Penguin Counting Book* (PS–1). Illus. by Jonathan Chester. 2001, Tricycle paper $6.95 (978-1-58246-042-0). 32pp. A slight story teaches counting from 1 to 10 using charming penguins. (Rev: BL 1/1–15/01)

541 Modesitt, Jeanne. *Oh, What a Beautiful Day! A Counting Book* (PS). Illus. by Robin Spowart. 2009, Boyds Mills $16.95 (978-1-56397-409-0). 24pp. A young girl enjoys a beautiful day as she counts the animals around her and plays with them. (Rev: BL 3/1/09; SLJ 6/09)

542 Modesitt, Jeanne. *One, Two, Three Valentine's Day* (PS–1). Illus. by Robin Spowart. 2002, Boyds Mills $15.95 (978-1-56397-868-5). 32pp. A counting book in which Mr. Mouse takes valentine gifts to his friends, to 1 frog, 2 pigs, and so forth up to his 10 little sons. (Rev: BL 1/1–15/03; HBG 3/03; SLJ 1/03)

543 Mora, Pat. *Uno, Dos, Tres: One, Two, Three* (PS–2). Illus. by Barbara Lavallee. 1996, Clarion $15.00 (978-0-395-67294-5). 43pp. The numbers 1 to 10 are introduced in English and Spanish. (Rev: BL 6/1–15/96; HB 5/96; SLJ 4/96)

544 Morales, Yuri. *Just a Minute: A Trickster Tale and Counting Book* (PS–2). Illus. by author. 2003, Chronicle $15.95 (978-0-8118-3758-3). This satisfying book combines counting — in both English and Spanish — and Spanish culture with Grandma's success in sending death away for another year. (Rev: BL 12/1/03*; HBG 4/04; SLJ 12/03) [398.2]

545 *Mother Goose: Numbers on the Loose* (PS–2). Illus. by Leo Dillon. 2007, Harcourt $17.00 (978-0-15-205676-6). 56pp. Twenty-four rhythmic counting rhymes caper across pages illustrated with lively characters. (Rev: BCCB 11/07; BL 9/1/07; HB 11/07; LMC 1/08; SLJ 10/07) [398.8]

546 Murphy, Stuart J. *Jack the Builder* (PS). Illus. by Michael Rex. Series: MathStart. 2006, HarperCollins paper $5.99 (978-0-06-055775-1). As Jack keeps adding more blocks, he can make more and more sophisticated constructions. Also use *A Fair Bear Share* (1998), which introduces groups of 10; *The Penny Pot* (1998), about counting coins; *Henry the Fourth* (1999), which introduces ordinal numbers; *Double the Ducks* (2003), *Leaping Lizards* (2005), which teaches counting by multiples of 5 and 10. (Rev: BL 1/1–15/06) [513.2]

547 Napoli, Donna Jo, and Richard Tchen. *Corkscrew Counts: A Story About Multiplication* (K–3). Illus. by Anna Currey. 2008, Holt $16.95 (978-0-8050-7664-6). 32pp. This story follows 12 children and a parrot who go to Corkscrew the pig's birthday party and play a variety of games that require teams of different numbers. (Rev: BLO 8/28/08)

548 Norman, Kim. *Ten on the Sled* (PS–2). Illus. by Liza Woodruff. 2010, Sterling $14.95 (978-1-4027-7076-0). 24pp. A sled careening down a frozen hill with 10 animals aboard gradually becomes a vehicle for 1 lonely caribou as the other passengers tumble out. (Rev: BLO 10/15/10; SLJ 12/1/10)

549 O'Keefe, Susan Heyboer. *One Hungry Monster: A Counting Book in Rhyme* (PS–K). Illus. by Lynn Munsinger. 2001, Little, Brown $5.95 (978-0-316-60804-6).

16pp. A little boy tries to keep 10 hungry monsters out of trouble. (Rev: BL 3/1/01)

550 Oldland, Nicholas. *Dinosaur Countdown* (PS–K). Illus. by author. 2012, Kids Can $15.95 (978-1-55453-834-8). 24pp. Counting down from 10 to 1, this book features velociraptors, tyrannosaurus, and other extinct animals enjoying life. (Rev: BL 10/1/12; SLJ 11/12)

551 Olson, K. C. *Construction Countdown* (PS–1). Illus. by David Gordon. 2004, Holt $14.95 (978-0-8050-6920-4). Rhyming text and colorful illustrations of big construction trucks appear on double-page spreads, counting down from 10. (Rev: BL 5/15/04; SLJ 7/04) [629.22]

552 Otoshi, Kathryn. *Zero* (PS–3). Illus. by author. 2010, KO Kids $17.95 (978-0-9723946-3-5). 32pp. Zero has difficulty accepting her role, envying numbers that have value, but eventually realizes her real importance in this story with a message about being true to oneself. (Rev: BL 9/15/10*; LMC 3–4/11; SLJ 11/1/10)

553 Oxley, Jennifer. *The Chicken Problem* (PS–1). Illus. by Billy Aronson. 2012, Random House $16.99 (978-0-375-86989-1). 32pp. This funny tale combined with math lesson features 100 loose chickens. (Rev: BL 10/15/12; SLJ 10/12)

554 Pallotta, Jerry. *Ocean Counting: Odd Numbers* (PS–2). Illus. by Shennen Bersani. 2005, Charlesbridge $16.95 (978-0-88106-151-2); paper $6.95 (978-0-88106-150-5). 32pp. Facts about marine animals are interwoven into this lively counting book that concentrates on odd numbers. (Rev: BL 2/1/05; SLJ 3/05) [513.2]

555 Pallotta, Jerry. *Underwater Counting: Even Numbers* (1–3). Illus. by David Biedrzycki. 2001, Charlesbridge $16.95 (978-0-88106-952-5); paper $6.95 (978-0-88106-800-9). 32pp. A variety of underwater creatures are introduced in this counting book that gives even numbers from zero to 50. (Rev: BL 3/1/01; HBG 10/01)

556 Parenteau, Shirley. *One Frog Sang* (K–2). Illus. by Cynthia Jabar. 2006, Candlewick $15.99 (978-0-7636-2394-4). From 1 to 10, and down again, groups of frogs enjoy a spring evening. (Rev: SLJ 4/07)

557 Parker, Kim. *Counting in the Garden* (PS). Illus. 2005, Scholastic $16.95 (978-0-439-69452-0). 32pp. Colorful garden scenes shelter animals in groups from 1 to 10. (Rev: BL 6/1–15/05; SLJ 4/05)

558 Perl, Erica S. *Ninety-Three in My Family* (K–3). Illus. by Mike Lester. 2006, Abrams $15.95 (978-0-8109-5760-2). In a funny story full of counting opportunities, a young boy identifies the members of his extended family that includes his parents, two sisters, and a mind-boggling assortment of pets and other creatures, including a pygmy hippo. (Rev: SLJ 10/06)

559 Pinczes, Elinor J. *Inchworm and a Half* (PS–3). Illus. by Randall Enos. 2001, Houghton $15.00 (978-0-395-82849-6). 32pp. The concept of fractions is explored in this amusing book about different-sized inchworms and the objects they measure. (Rev: BCCB 3/01; BL 3/15/01; HBG 10/01)

560 Pinczes, Elinor J. *One Hundred Hungry Ants* (K–3). Illus. by Bonnie Mackain. 1993, Houghton $16.00 (978-0-395-63116-4). Ants group and regroup on their march to a picnic site. (Rev: BL 3/1/93; SLJ 8/93)

561 Raffi. *Five Little Ducks* (PS–1). Illus. by Jose Aruego and Ariane Dewey. 1988, Crown paper $5.99 (978-0-517-58360-9). 32pp. Mother Duck and her ducklings waddle "over the hills and far away" in this addition to the Songs to Read series. (Rev: BL 6/1/89; HB 5/89)

562 Rathmann, Peggy. *10 Minutes till Bedtime* (K–2). Illus. 1998, Penguin $17.99 (978-0-399-23103-2). 46pp. A very active counting book involving a 10-minute countdown to bed for a little boy and 10 mischievous hamsters numbered 1 through 10. (Rev: BCCB 12/98; BL 10/15/98; HB 9/98; HBG 3/99; SLJ 9/98)

563 Reidy, Hannah. *All Sorts of Numbers* (PS). Illus. by Emma Dodd. Series: All Sorts of Things. 2005, Picture Window LB $25.26 (978-1-4048-1062-4). A bright introduction to numbers from 1 to 5. (Rev: SLJ 6/05)

564 Reiser, Lynn. *Hardworking Puppies* (PS–2). 2006, Harcourt $16.00 (978-0-15-205404-5). 40pp. In this attractive countdown tale, 10 bored puppies — one by one — are assigned professional tasks such as guide dog, sled dog, therapy dog. (Rev: BL 6/1–15/06; SLJ 4/06)

565 Root, Phyllis. *One Duck Stuck* (PS–1). Illus. by Jane Chapman. 1998, Candlewick $15.99 (978-0-7636-0334-2). 40pp. In this counting book that uses alliterative rhymes, different animals try to free a duck that gets stuck in the muck. (Rev: BL 4/1/98; HBG 10/98; SLJ 6/98)

566 Rose, Deborah L. *One Nighttime Sea* (PS–2). Illus. by Steve Jenkins. 2003, Scholastic $16.95 (978-0-439-33906-3). 40pp. This counting book uses rhyming text to introduce young readers to numbers from 1 to 10 as well as common marine animals. (Rev: HBG 4/04; SLJ 9/03) [513.2]

567 Rose, Deborah L. *The Twelve Days of Kindergarten: A Counting Book* (PS–1). Illus. by Carey Armstrong-Ellis. 2003, Abrams $14.95 (978-0-8109-4512-8). The wonders of kindergarten are introduced along with numbers from 1 alphabet to 12 eggs. (Rev: HBG 4/04; SLJ 8/03) [372.21]

568 Rose, Deborah L. *The Twelve Days of Springtime: A School Counting Book* (PS–1). Illus. by Carey Armstrong-Ellis. 2009, Abrams $15.95 (978-0-8109-8330-4). Spring is the focus of this entertaining counting book featuring a rambunctious kindergarten class. (Rev: SLJ 4/09)

569 Rose, Deborah L. *The Twelve Days of Winter: A School Counting Book* (K–3). Illus. by Carey Armstrong-Ellis. 2006, Abrams $14.95 (978-0-8109-5472-4). The melody of "The Twelve Days of Christmas" provides the framework for this cumulative counting verse that celebrates the joys of winter. (Rev: SLJ 10/06)

570 Savage, Steven. *Ten Orange Pumpkins* (PS–1). Illus. by author. 2013, Dial $16.99 (978-0-80373938-3). 48pp. A Halloween counting book in which ten pumpkins are removed one by one by suitably spooky characters. ALA Notable Children's Book. (Rev: BL 10/15/13; SLJ 11/13)

571 Sayre, April P., and Jeff Sayre. *One Is a Snail, Ten Is a Crab: A Counting by Feet Book* (PS–2). Illus. by Randy Cecil. 2003, Candlewick $15.99 (978-0-7636-1406-5). Readers count up to 10 and then in multiples of 10 to 100, using animal feet as units. (Rev: HBG 10/03; SLJ 7/03) [513.2]

572 Schafer, Kevin. *Penguins 123* (PS–K). Photos by author. 2002, NorthWord $14.95 (978-1-55971-830-1). A counting book that will grab the attention of penguin lovers. (Rev: SLJ 1/03)

573 Schulman, Janet. *Ten Easter Egg Hunters: A Holiday Counting Book* (PS). Illus. by Linda Davick. 2011, Knopf $8.99 (978-0-375-86787-3); LB $11.99 (978-0-375-96787-0). 32pp. An Easter bunny hides a basket full of eggs, and watches from a distance as a group of children hunts and finds them in this colorful counting book. e (Rev: BL 2/1/11; SLJ 2/1/11)

574 Schulman, Janet. *10 Trick-or-Treaters: A Halloween Counting Book* (PS–K). Illus. by Linda Davick. 2005, Knopf $9.95 (978-0-375-83225-3). Ten little trick-or-treaters head out into the night, but one by one are scared off by various Halloween creatures. (Rev: SLJ 8/05)

575 Sebe, Masayuki. *Let's Count to 100!* (PS–2). Illus. by author. 2011, Kids Can $16.95 (978-1-55453-661-0). 24pp. Attractive spreads show 100 animals, people, or objects organized in groups of 10, making the task of counting to 100 less daunting. (Rev: BLO 9/1/11; SLJ 9/1/11) [513.2]

576 Sebe, Masayuki. *100 Animals on Parade!* (PS–2). Illus. by author. 2013, Kids Can $16.95 (978-155453871-3). 24pp. A lively counting book with challenges on each page. (Rev: BL 6/13) [513.2]

577 Seeger, Laura Vaccaro. *One Boy* (PS–3). Illus. by author. 2008, Roaring Brook $14.95 (978-1-59643-274-1). Part counting book, part eye-catching picture book, and part clever die-cut exploration of words within words. (Rev: BL 10/15/08*; HB 11/08; LMC 1/09; SLJ 10/08)

578 Shahan, Sherry. *Cool Cats Counting* (K–3). Illus. by Paula Barragán. 2005, August House $16.95 (978-0-87483-757-5). Lively illustrations and rhythmic text introduce numbers from 1 to 10, with a translation of the key words into Spanish. (Rev: SLJ 10/05)

579 Shea, Pegi Deitz, and Cynthia Weill. *Ten Mice for Tet* (PS–2). Illus. by To Ngoc Trang and Pham Vi t Dinh. 2003, Chronicle $15.95 (978-0-8118-3496-4). This handsome counting book introduces numbers 1 through 10 plus the traditions of the Vietnamese New Year. (Rev: HBG 4/04; SLJ 12/03) [394.2]

580 Singer, Marilyn. *City Lullaby* (PS–2). Illus. by Carll Cneut. 2007, Clarion $16.00 (978-0-618-60703-7). 32pp. In this counting book set in the city, a baby sleeps happily through the blare of 10 horns and the roar of 2 motorbikes but is woken by the sound of 1 bird. (Rev: BL 10/15/07; HB 1/08; SLJ 10/07)

581 Singer, Marilyn. *Quiet Night* (PS–K). Illus. by John Manders. 2002, Clarion $15.00 (978-0-618-12044-4). A riotous romp of a counting book in which the quiet of night turns into a symphony of animal noises. (Rev: BCCB 6/02; BL 3/15/02; HBG 10/02; SLJ 3/02)

582 Siy, Alexandra. *One Tractor: A Counting Book* (PS). Illus. by Jacqueline Rogers. 2008, Holiday $16.95 (978-0-8234-1923-4). A little boy's dreams are populated with 1 tractor, 2 airplanes, 3 floating boats, and so on, and he helps with the action at every point. (Rev: BL 3/1/08; SLJ 2/08)

583 Skinner, Daphne. *All Aboard!* (1–3). Illus. by Jerry Smath. Series: Math Matters. 2007, Kane paper $4.95 (978-1-57565-239-9). 32pp. Two children and their grandmother must stick to a schedule as they travel to a wedding. Readers will be challenged by the math problems about time that are integrated into the story. (Rev: SLJ 6/07)

584 Slaughter, Tom. *1 2 3* (PS–K). Illus. by author. 2003, Tundra $11.95 (978-0-88776-664-0). A cleverly designed counting book that introduces the numbers 1 through 10. (Rev: SLJ 11/03) [513.2]

585 Smith, Danna. *Two at the Zoo: A Counting Book* (PS–K). Illus. by Valeria Petrone. 2009, Harcourt $16.00 (978-0-547-04982-3). 32pp. Clear rhyming text and colorful illustrations lead the reader through the zoo counting from 1 to 10 with a little boy and his grandfather. (Rev: SLJ 2/09)

586 Stiegemeyer, Julie. *Gobble Gobble! Crash!* (PS–2). Illus. by Valeri Gorbachev. 2008, Dutton $16.99 (978-0-525-47959-8). 32pp. A flock of wild turkeys wake up a drowsy barnyard in this rhyming counting book with watercolor illustrations. (Rev: BLO 8/28/08; SLJ 8/08)

587 Stutson, Caroline. *Cats' Night Out* (PS–K). Illus. by Jon Klassen. 2010, Simon & Schuster $15.99 (978-1-4169-4005-0). 32pp. Captivating, retro illustrations enhance this hip counting book in which cats dance the night away, doing the tango, rumba, boogie . . . (Rev: BL 2/15/10; SLJ 2/1/10)

588 Tafuri, Nancy. *The Big Storm: A Very Soggy Counting Book* (PS–K). Illus. by author. 2009, Simon & Schuster $15.99 (978-1-4169-6795-8). 32pp. Readers count from 1 to 10 as they watch animals seeking shelter from a storm. (Rev: BLO 5/27/09)

589 Tang, Greg. *Math Fables* (PS–1). Illus. by Heather Cahoon. 2004, Scholastic $16.95 (978-0-439-45399-8). 40pp. Groupings of numbers are shown through rhyming stories with colorful art. (Rev: BL 2/1/04; SLJ 3/04) [513.2]

590 Thompson, Lauren. *How Many Cats?* (K–2). Illus. by Robin Eley. 2009, Hyperion $15.99 (978-1-4231-0801-6). 32pp. Count to 20 with this houseful of energetic and mischievous cats. (Rev: BL 4/1/09; LMC 5/09; SLJ 5/09)

591 Thornhill, Jan, adapt. *Over in the Meadow* (PS–2). Illus. by Jan Thornhill. 2004, Maple Tree $16.95 (978-1-897066-08-9). Unusual illustrations add to the charm of this inventive rendition of a traditional counting song. (Rev: SLJ 1/05)

592 *Toddler Two* (PS). Illus. by Winnie Cheon. 2000, Lee & Low $6.95 (978-1-58430-015-1). The concept of two

31

is explored in this interactive board book with flaps and pop-ups. (Rev: SLJ 1/01)

593 *Trucks and Diggers One to Ten: Counting* (PS). 2003, Chronicle $6.95 (978-0-8118-4029-3). Numbers are introduced through eye-catching photographs of appealing machines. (Rev: SLJ 1/04)

594 van Lieshout, Maria. *Flight 1-2-3* (PS–1). Illus. by Maria van Lieshout. 2013, Chronicle $14.99 (978-1-45211-6624.). 40pp. A counting book focusing on airports and planes, and ranging from 1 to 10 and then up to 33,000 feet. (Rev: BLO 6/13; SLJ 5/13)

595 Verdick, Elizabeth. *Peep Leap* (PS–1). Illus. by John Bendall-Brunello. 2013, Amazon/Two Lions $16.99 (978-1-4778-1640-0). 30pp. Ten fledgling wood ducks bravely make it down into the pond in this nicely illustrated, rhyming counting book. (Rev: BL 4/1/13; SLJ 6/13)

596 Waber, Bernard. *Lyle Walks the Dogs: A Counting Book* (PS–K). Illus. by Paulis Waber. 2010, Houghton Mifflin $12.99 (978-0-547-22323-0). 24pp. Well-intentioned crocodile Lyle struggles to keep his 10 canine charges in line in his new job as dog-walker. (Rev: BLO 4/15/10; SLJ 5/1/10)

597 Wadsworth, Olive A. *Over in the Meadow: A Counting Rhyme* (PS–1). Illus. by Anna Vojtech. 2002, North-South $15.95 (978-0-7358-1596-4). This classic nursery counting rhyme is given a fresh look with double-page spreads and stunning watercolors. (Rev: BL 4/15/02; HBG 10/02; SLJ 4/02)

598 Wallace, Nancy Elizabeth. *Planting Seeds* (PS). Illus. 2010, Marshall Cavendish $7.99 (978-0-7614-5643-8). 24pp. A rabbit family plants, grows, and harvests carrots — and generously shares the feast — in this warm, clearly illustrated book that counts from 1 to 10. (Rev: BLO 4/1/10; SLJ 4/1/10)

599 Walsh, Ellen S. *Mouse Count* (PS–K). Illus. 1991, Harcourt $13.00 (978-0-15-256023-2). 32pp. In this counting book, 10 little mice fall asleep unaware that a hungry snake is nearby. (Rev: BL 2/15/91; HB 5/91; SLJ 5/91*)

600 Williams, Rozanne Lanczak. *Adding* (PS–1). Illus. Series: I Can Do Math. 2004, Gareth Stevens LB $22.00 (978-0-8368-4108-4). A question-and-answer format and abundant photographs introduce addition. Also use *Subtracting*, *Crayola Counting*, and *Learning About Coins* (all 2004).

601 Wilson, Karma. *A Frog in the Bog* (PS–2). Illus. by Joan Rankin. 2003, Simon & Schuster $16.95 (978-0-689-84081-4). A humorous counting book in which a hungry frog consumes progressively larger swamp snacks, including "one tick," "two fleas," "three flies," and "four slugs." (Rev: BL 11/1/03; HBG 4/04; SLJ 12/03)

602 Winter, Jeanette. *Josefina* (PS–3). Illus. 1996, Harcourt $15.00 (978-0-15-201091-1). An original counting book that features the Mexican woman Josefina and her amazing collection of clay figures. (Rev: BCCB 10/96; BL 10/15/96*; SLJ 10/96)

603 Wolff, Ashley. *Baby Bear Counts One* (PS–K). Illus. by author. 2013, Simon & Schuster $16.99 (978-1-4424-4158-3). 40pp. In this engaging story Baby Bear counts different animals as they go about their preparations for winter. (Rev: BL 10/1/13; SLJ 8/13)

604 Young, Cybele. *Ten Birds* (1–3). Illus. by author. 2011, Kids Can $16.95 (978-1-55453-568-2). 32pp. Counts down from 10 as small black birds use different contraptions to cross a river, collecting the hardware from a heap that subsides with the countdown. (Rev: BL 5/1/11; SLJ 4/11)

605 Young, Cybele. *Ten Birds Meet a Monster* (PS–1). Illus. by author. 2013, Kids Can $16.95 (978-1-55453-955-0). 32pp. Ten birds who think they see a monster find various ways to frighten it in this unusual counting book. Lexile 420 (Rev: BLO 10/1/13; SLJ 9/13)

606 Ziefert, Harriet. *A Dozen Ducklings Lost and Found* (K–2). Illus. by Donald Dreifuss. 2003, Houghton $15.00 (978-0-618-14175-3). 32pp. While proudly parading her dozen ducklings through the barnyard, Mother Duck loses some in newly dug postholes. (Rev: BL 3/15/03; HBG 10/03; SLJ 3/03)

607 Ziefert, Harriet. *Knick-Knack Paddywhack* (PS–K). Illus. by Emily Bolam. 2005, Sterling $5.95 (978-1-4027-2292-9). A boy, a dog, some bones, and an old man figure in this appealing counting-oriented version of the familiar song. (Rev: SLJ 10/05)

Bedtime Books

608 Adler, David A. *It's Time to Sleep, It's Time to Dream* (PS–K). Illus. by Kay Chorao. 2009, Holiday $16.95 (978-0-8234-1924-1). Poetic text and illustrations evoke the four seasons in this gentle bedtime book. (Rev: BL 3/1/09; SLJ 4/09)

609 Alborough, Jez. *Yes* (PS). Illus. 2006, Candlewick $15.99 (978-0-7636-3183-3). 40pp. Bobo, the chimp seen in *Hug* (2000), is back and this time he's excited about having a bath but definitely not ready to go to bed. (Rev: BL 11/15/06; SLJ 10/06)

610 Apperley, Dawn. *Good Night, Sleep Tight, Little Bunnies* (PS). Illus. by author. 2002, Scholastic $9.95 (978-0-439-22525-0). A rhyming refrain and cartoon images depict young animals settling down for the night. (Rev: HBG 10/02; SLJ 5/02)

611 Arro, Lena. *Good Night, Animals* (PS–1). Trans. by Joan Sandin. Illus. by Catarina Kruusval. 2002, Farrar $15.00 (91-29-65654-0). 28pp. A cumulative bedtime story in which two children who decide to camp out soon find their tent packed with animals. (Rev: BCCB 12/02; BL 12/15/02; HBG 3/03; SLJ 2/03)

612 Ashman, Linda. *Starry Safari* (PS–K). Illus. by Jeff Mack. 2005, Harcourt $16.00 (978-0-15-204766-5). 40pp. A little girl with a vivid imagination turns bedtime into an exciting safari. (Rev: BL 8/05; SLJ 7/05)

613 Averbeck, Jim. *In a Blue Room* (PS–1). Illus. by Tricia Tusa. 2008, Harcourt $16.00 (978-0-15-205992-7). 32pp. Alice wants to sleep in a blue room and despite her mother's efforts to lull her to sleep it is only when the moon bathes the room in a blue light that Alice is ready to dream. (Rev: BCCB 5/08; BL 4/1/08; SLJ 6/08) ⌒

614 Banks, Kate. *The Bear in the Book* (PS–K). Illus. by Georg Hallensleben. 2012, Farrar $16.99 (978-0-374-30591-8). 40pp. At bedtime a little boy and his mother share a book about a black bear and its hibernation. **e** (Rev: BL 10/15/12*; SLJ 10/12*)

615 Banks, Kate. *Close Your Eyes* (PS). Illus. by Georg Hallensleben. 2002, Farrar $16.00 (978-0-374-31382-1). A thoroughly enjoyable, dreamily illustrated story about a little tiger who doesn't want to fall asleep, and his mother's patient reassurances. (Rev: BL 10/15/02; HB 9/02; HBG 3/03; SLJ 7/02)

616 Bardhan-Quallen, Sudipta. *Chicks Run Wild* (PS–1). Illus. by Ward Jenkins. 2011, Simon & Schuster $15.99 (978-1-4424-0673-5). 32pp. A mama hen finally manages to exhaust her energetic brood of chicks in this funny bedtime story. (Rev: BL 1/1–15/11; SLJ 1/1/11)

617 Beaton, Clare. *Mrs. Moon: Lullabies for Bedtime* (PS–1). Illus. by author. 2003, Barefoot Books $19.99 (978-1-84148-176-0). 48pp. This collection of lullabies and bedtime poetry includes many old favorites and is accompanied by a musical CD. (Rev: HBG 4/04; SLJ 1/04) [782.4]

618 Beaumont, Karen. *Baby Danced the Polka* (PS). Illus. by Jennifer Plecas. 2004, Dial $12.99 (978-0-8037-2587-4). Baby prefers dancing to sleeping in this lively bedtime book with flaps hiding stuffed animal dancing partners. (Rev: BL 2/15/04; HB 5/04; SLJ 6/04)

619 Beaumont, Karen. *No Sleep for the Sheep!* (PS–2). Illus. by Jackie Urbanovic. 2011, Harcourt $16.99 (978-0-15-204969-0). 32pp. A sleepy sheep must deal with one interruption after another as his barnyard friends decide to join him, one at a time; excellent for read-alouds, with humorous and expressive artwork. Lexile AD650L (Rev: BL 4/15/11; HB 3–4/11; SLJ 4/11*)

620 Beck, Andrea. *Elliot's Noisy Night* (PS–1). Illus. 2002, Kids Can $12.95 (978-1-55337-011-6). 32pp. Elliot the toy moose infects his friends with his fears about the noises at night and they all end up sleeping in Elliot's room. (Rev: BL 1/1–15/03; HBG 3/03)

621 Becker, Bonny. *A Bedtime for Bear* (PS–3). Illus. by Kady MacDonald Denton. 2010, Candlewick $16.99 (978-0-7636-4101-6). 48pp. A sleepover with Mouse proves challenging to Bear's usual bedtime routine, but in the end he's glad to have his friend. (Rev: BL 10/15/10; SLJ 8/1/10*)

622 Blomgren, Jennifer. *Where Do I Sleep? A Pacific Northwest Lullaby* (PS–2). Illus. by Andrea Gabriel. 2001, Sasquatch $15.95 (978-1-57061-258-9). 32pp. A peaceful bedtime book featuring animals native to the Pacific Northwest bedding down for the night. (Rev: BL 11/1/01; HBG 3/02; SLJ 11/01)

623 Boelts, Maribeth. *Looking for Sleepy* (PS). Illus. by Bernadette Pons. 2004, Whitman LB $14.95 (978-0-8075-0447-5). A bedtime picture book starring Little Bear and his patient father. (Rev: SLJ 4/04)

624 Boelts, Maribeth. *Sweet Dreams, Little Bunny!* (PS). Illus. by Kathy Parkinson. 2010, Whitman $7.99 (978-080754589-8). 14pp. A mama bunny gently guides her little one off to bed in this board book. (Rev: BL 1/1–15/11)

625 Bogan, Paulette. *Goodnight Lulu* (PS–2). Illus. by author. 2003, Bloomsbury $15.95 (978-1-58234-803-2). A mother hen reassures her chick that she will protect her from any potential dangers in this delightful bedtime book. (Rev: HBG 10/03; SLJ 7/03)

626 Bradman, Tony. *Daddy's Lullaby* (PS). Illus. by Jason Cockcroft. 2002, Simon & Schuster $16.95 (978-0-689-84295-5). 32pp. Late at night, a father tries to soothe his baby to sleep by quietly making his way around the house with the child in his arms. (Rev: BL 4/15/02; HBG 10/02; SLJ 5/02)

627 Braun, Sebastien. *Back to Bed, Ed!* (PS–1). Illus. by author. 2010, Peachtree $15.95 (978-1-56145-518-8). Unpaged. A little mouse learns the secret to staying safe and comfortable in his own bed: a bevy of stuffed animal friends alongside. (Rev: SLJ 3/1/10*)

628 Brian, Janeen. *Where Does Thursday Go?* (PS–K). Illus. by Stephen M. King. 2002, Clarion $14.00 (978-0-618-21264-4). A little bear and his friend search for Thursday, wondering where the day goes when nighttime comes, in this attractive book that makes a great bedtime story. (Rev: BL 3/1/02; HBG 10/02; SLJ 4/02)

629 Bright, Paul. *Under the Bed* (PS). Illus. by Ben Cort. 2004, Good Bks. $16.00 (978-1-56148-436-2). A boy is afraid of creatures under his bed, and it turns out they are also afraid of him, in this book with amusing illustrations. (Rev: SLJ 8/04)

630 Brisson, Pat. *Star Blanket* (PS–1). Illus. by Erica Magnus. 2003, Boyds Mills $15.95 (978-1-56397-889-0). Laura's father tells her the familiar story of the time-worn, star-studded blanket on her bed. (Rev: HBG 4/04; SLJ 12/03)

631 Brown, Margaret Wise. *Goodnight Moon* (PS). Illus. by Clement Hurd. 1947, HarperCollins LB $16.89 (978-0-06-020706-9); paper $6.99 (978-0-06-443017-3). 32pp. A soothing go-to-sleep story.

632 Brown, Margaret Wise. *Sheep Don't Count Sheep* (PS). Illus. by Benrei Huang. 2003, Simon & Schuster $14.95 (978-0-689-83346-5). 32pp. A little lamb can't get to sleep because there's too much going on in the field, so his mother tells him to count butterflies. (Rev: BL 1/1–15/03; HBG 10/03; SLJ 3/03)

633 Butler, John. *Bedtime in the Jungle* (PS). Illus. by author. 2009, Peachtree $16.95 (978-1-56145-486-0). 32pp. As dusk arrives, the animals of the jungle settle down for the night; with verses inspired by "Over in the Meadow" and stunning illustrations. (Rev: BL 9/15/09; SLJ 9/1/09)

634 Butler, John. *Hush, Little Ones* (PS). Illus. 2002, Peachtree $15.95 (978-1-56145-269-9). 32pp. A very visual bedtime book full of sleeping animals — birds in nests, monkeys up trees, a penguin between his father's feet. (Rev: BL 11/15/02; HBG 3/03; SLJ 10/02)

635 Cabrera, Jane. *Ten in the Bed* (PS). Illus. 2006, Holiday $16.95 (978-0-8234-2027-8). 32pp. In a good-night countdown, 10 stuffed animals with different occupations strut their stuff. (Rev: BL 10/1/06; SLJ 9/06)

636 Capucilli, Alyssa Satin. *Little Spotted Cat* (PS–K). Illus. by Dan Andreasen. 2005, Dial $14.99 (978-0-8037-2692-5). 32pp. A traditional story book about a kitten who gets into all sorts of trouble when his mother tells him that it's nap time. (Rev: BL 3/15/05; SLJ 6/05)

637 Child, Lauren. *I Am Not Sleepy and I Will Not Go to Bed* (PS–3). Illus. Series: Charlie and Lola. 2001, Candlewick $16.99 (978-0-7636-1570-3). 32pp. Charlie tries to get his imaginative little sister to go to bed. (Rev: BL 8/01; HBG 3/02; SLJ 9/01)

638 Christelow, Eileen. *Five Little Monkeys Reading in Bed* (PS–2). Illus. by author. 2011, Clarion $16.99 (978-0-547-38610-2). 40pp. Reading is so much fun that the five little monkeys just don't feel sleepy. (Rev: BL 10/15/11; SLJ 9/1/11)

639 Cohen, Caron Lee. *Martin and the Giant Lion* (PS–K). Illus. by Elizabeth Sayles. 2002, Clarion $15.00 (978-0-618-04908-0). 32pp. After he is tucked into bed, Martin travels via his purple truck to a land where he plays with a family of lions. (Rev: BL 4/15/02; HBG 10/02; SLJ 7/02)

640 Cooper, Elisha. *Bear Dreams* (PS). 2006, Greenwillow $16.99 (978-0-06-087428-5). 40pp. It's almost time to hibernate, but Bear, a cub, has places to go and things to do, until finally he tires himself out. (Rev: BL 10/1/06; SLJ 9/06)

641 Cowell, Cressida. *What Shall We Do with the Boo-Hoo Baby?* (PS–1). Illus. by Ingrid Godon. 2000, Scholastic $15.95 (978-0-439-15311-9). 32pp. Animals try different tactics to hush a crying baby and become so tired that they nap, which causes the baby to smile. (Rev: BCCB 2/01; BL 1/1–15/01; HBG 3/01; SLJ 3/01)

642 Crum, Shutta. *All on a Sleepy Night* (K–2). Illus. by Sylvie Daigneault. 2002, Stoddart $15.95 (978-0-7737-3315-2). 24pp. The sounds of his grandparents' house lull a young boy to sleep in this rhyming picture book. (Rev: BL 9/15/02; HBG 3/03; SLJ 5/02)

643 DaCosta, Barbara. *Nighttime Ninja* (PS–2). Illus. by Ed Young. 2012, Little, Brown $16.99 (978-0-316-20384-5). 32pp. A little boy sneaks ninja-style through the house at midnight, intent on getting some ice cream. ALA Notable Children's Book. Lexile AD150L (Rev: BL 10/1/12*; HB 11–12/12; LMC 3–4/13; SLJ 9/12)

644 Daddo, Andrew. *Goodnight, Me* (PS). Illus. by Emma Quay. 2007, Bloomsbury $11.95 (978-1-59990-153-4). At the end of a busy day, a baby orangutan says good night to every part of his body from his toes to his nose. (Rev: SLJ 12/07)

645 Dahl, Michael. *Goodnight Baseball* (PS–2). Illus. by Christina Forshay. 2013, Capstone $14.95 (978-1-62370-000-3). 32pp. A boy reviews all the highlights of a day at the ballpark with his father in this rhythmic, rhyming bedtime story. Lexile AD410L (Rev: BL 3/1/13; SLJ 5/13)

646 Dahl, Michael. *Nap Time for Kitty* (PS). Illus. by Oriol Vidal. 2011, Capstone $7.99 (978-140485216-7). 20pp. A young kitten with no interest in nap time is finally persuaded to go to sleep. (Rev: BL 7/11)

647 Davies, Jacqueline. *The Night Is Singing* (PS–K). Illus. by Kyrsten Brooker. 2006, Dial $16.99 (978-0-8037-3004-5). 40pp. The sounds of the night lull a little girl to sleep in this rhyming, soothing picture book. (Rev: BL 5/15/06; SLJ 6/06)

648 de Vries, Maggie. *How Sleep Found Tabitha* (PS–K). Illus. by Sheena Lott. 2002, Orca $16.95 (978-1-55143-193-2). 32pp. Pastel watercolor illustrations provide an excellent backdrop for this story of a sleepless child. (Rev: BL 8/02; HBG 10/02; SLJ 8/02)

649 Deniers, Dominique. *Every Single Night* (PS–K). Trans. by Sarah Quinn. Illus. by Nicolas Debon. 2006, Groundwood $17.95 (978-0-88899-699-2). 32pp. Little Simon simply can't fall asleep until his father completes their nighttime ritual full of images of a wonderful world full of nature. (Rev: BL 3/15/06; SLJ 5/06)

650 Docherty, Helen. *The Snatchabook* (PS–1). Illus. by Thomas Docherty. 2013, Sourcebooks/Jabberwocky $16.99 (978-1-4022-9082-4). 32pp. A lonely little creature is persuaded to return all the books he has stolen from the woodland creatures and finds himself invited to lovely bedtime storytimes. (Rev: BL 10/1/13; SLJ 10/13)

651 Dodd, Emma. *Forever* (PS–1). Illus. by author. 2013, Candlewick $12.99 (978-0-7636-7132-7). 24pp. In this bedtime tale a mother polar bear reassures her cub that her love will last forever. (Rev: BL 11/15/13; SLJ 10/13)

652 Dodds, Dayle Ann. *The Prince Won't Go to Bed!* (PS–K). Illus. by Kyrsten Brooker. 2007, Farrar $16.00 (978-0-374-36108-2). 32pp. The whole royal household struggles to get the teeny-tiny Prince to go to bed until his sister gives him a good night kiss. (Rev: BL 10/1/07; HB 1/08; SLJ 12/07)

653 Dragonwagon, Crescent. *All the Awake Animals Are Almost Asleep* (PS–1). Illus. by David McPhail. 2012, Little, Brown $16.99 (978-0-316-07045-4). 40pp. This alliterative alphabet/bedtime book portrays a mother lulling her child to sleep as she describes sleepy animals from antelope to zebra. (Rev: BL 11/1/12; HB 1–2/13; SLJ 10/12)

654 Dragonwagon, Crescent. *Is This a Sack of Potatoes?* (PS–1). Illus. by Catherine Stock. 2002, Marshall Cavendish $15.95 (978-0-7614-5089-4). Charlie hides under the covers at bedtime in this lift-the-flap book with charming watercolor illustrations. (Rev: BL 12/15/02; HBG 3/03; SLJ 11/02)

655 Dunbar, Joyce. *Tell Me Something Happy Before I Go to Sleep* (PS). Illus. by Debi Gliori. 1998, Harcourt

$16.00 (978-0-15-201795-8). A young bunny has trouble getting to sleep until she begins thinking of all the nice things that will happen to her the next day. (Rev: HBG 3/99; SLJ 11/98)

656 Durand, Hallie. *Mitchell's License* (PS). Illus. by Tony Fucile. 2011, Candlewick $15.99 (978-0-7636-4496-3). 40pp. Three-year-old Mitchell gets to drive his father to bed, riding on his shoulders; a funny, active but satisfying bedtime book. (Rev: BL 3/1/11; SLJ 4/11)

657 Durango, Julia, and Katie Belle Trupiano. *Dream Away* (PS–2). Illus. by Robert Goldstrom. 2011, Simon & Schuster $16.99 (978-1-4169-8702-4). 32pp. A young boy is lulled to sleep as he and his father read a bedtime story about sailing through the stars. (Rev: BLO 7/11; SLJ 7/11)

658 Dyer, Jane. *Animal Crackers: A Delectable Collection of Pictures, Poems, and Lullabies for the Very Young* (PS). Illus. 1996, Little, Brown $17.95 (978-0-316-19766-3). 64pp. An immensely appealing collection of lullabies, poems, and nursery rhymes accompanied by muted illustrations. (Rev: BCCB 3/96; BL 4/15/96; SLJ 5/96)

659 Egielski, Richard. *The Sleepless Little Vampire* (PS–2). Illus. 2011, Scholastic $16.99 (978-0-545-14597-8). 32pp. A little vampire who can't sleep wonders which creature is keeping him up. Is it the werewolf? The spider? The skeletons? (Rev: BL 9/1/11; SLJ 7/11)

660 Ehrlich, Fred. *Does a Baboon Sleep in a Bed?* (PS). Illus. by Emily Bolam. Series: Early Experiences. 2006, Blue Apple $13.50 (978-1-59354-142-2); paper $5.95 (978-1-59354-143-9). 32pp. Where do animals sleep? Not in beds, as people do, informs this bedtime book, which offers factual information about the sleeping habits of six different kinds of animals. (Rev: BL 5/15/06) [649]

661 Emberley, Ed. *Go Away, Big Green Monster!* (PS–1). Illus. 1993, Little, Brown $15.95 (978-0-316-23653-9). 32pp. This toy book deals with a child's nighttime fears in a lighthearted way that will be both a joy and a comfort to young people. (Rev: BCCB 3/93; BL 4/15/93*; HB 7/93)

662 Emberley, Ed. *Nighty Night, Little Green Monster* (PS). Illus. by author. 2013, Little, Brown $8.99 (978-031621041-6). 32pp. A series of shapes detail Little Green Monster as the stars come out, signifying that it's Little Green Monster's bedtime. (Rev: BLO 9/15/13; SLJ 7/13)

663 Feiffer, Kate. *No Go Sleep!* (K–3). Illus. by Jules Feiffer. 2012, Simon & Schuster $16.99 (978-144241683-3). 32pp. A stubborn baby is finally charmed into sleep by a pastel cast of forest animals, celestial bodies, and more in this sweet bedtime story. e (Rev: BL 2/15/12; HB 3–4/12; SLJ 5/1/12*)

664 Ferreri, Della Ross. *How Will I Ever Sleep in This Bed?* (PS). Illus. by Capucine Mazille. 2005, Sterling LB $12.95 (978-1-4027-1492-4). Unable to adjust to his new, larger bed, a young boy fills it up with his stuffed toys, leaving no room for himself. (Rev: SLJ 1/06)

665 Fleming, Denise. *Sleepy, Oh So Sleepy* (PS). Illus. by author. 2010, Henry Holt $16.99 (978-0-8050-8126-8). 32pp. Baby animals go to sleep in this effective bedtime book. (Rev: BL 6/10*; HB 7–8/10; SLJ 7/1/10)

666 Fore, S. J. *Tiger Can't Sleep* (PS–1). Illus. by R. W. Alley. 2006, Viking $15.99 (978-0-670-06078-8). 32pp. An imaginative little boy tries to get the noisy tiger in his closet to quiet down so he can get some sleep. (Rev: BL 12/15/05; SLJ 2/06)

667 Fox, Mem. *Sleepy Bears* (PS–2). Illus. by Kerry Argent. 1999, Harcourt $16.00 (978-0-15-202016-3). 32pp. Mama Bear sings a different lullaby to each of her six cubs as they settle in for a winter's sleep. (Rev: BL 11/15/99; HBG 3/00; SLJ 10/99)

668 Fox, Mem. *Tell Me about Your Day Today* (PS–1). Illus. by Lauren Stringer. 2012, Simon & Schuster $17.99 (978-1-4169-9006-2). 40pp. At bedtime a little boy's stuffed animals tell him what they have done during the day before the boy himself reviews events. e Lexile AD250L (Rev: BL 11/1/12; SLJ 9/12)

669 Fox, Mem. *Time for Bed* (PS). Illus. by Jane Dyer. 1993, Harcourt $16.00 (978-0-15-288183-2). 32pp. Various animals put their babies to sleep in this quiet bedtime book. (Rev: BCCB 10/93; BL 10/1/93; SLJ 10/93)

670 Fox, Mem. *Where the Giant Sleeps* (PS–2). Illus. by Vladimir Radunsky. 2007, Harcourt $16.00 (978-0-15-205785-5). 32pp. The slumbering places of giants, wizards, and other fairy tale characters are revealed in two-page spreads mimicking the view through a spyglass. (Rev: BL 11/15/07; LMC 1/08; SLJ 11/07)

671 Frampton, David. *The Whole Night Through: A Lullaby* (PS–1). Illus. 2001, HarperCollins LB $15.89 (978-0-06-028826-6). 32pp. A boisterous little leopard is determined to stay awake. (Rev: BL 5/15/01; HBG 10/01; SLJ 6/01*)

672 Fraser, Mary Ann. *Pet Shop Lullaby* (PS–2). Illus. by author. 2009, Boyds Mills $16.95 (978-1-59078-618-5). 32pp. A hamster spinning his exercise wheel disturbs his fellow pet shop inhabitants in this please-go-to-bed story. (Rev: BL 11/1/09; HB 1–2/10; SLJ 11/1/09)

673 Frederick, Heather Vogel. *Hide and Squeak* (PS). Illus. by C. F. Payne. 2011, Simon & Schuster $16.99 (978-0-689-85570-2). Unpaged. A father mouse patiently follows his young one's pre-bedtime capers before finally persuading him to sleep. (Rev: BL 1/1–15/11; SLJ 2/1/11)

674 Freedman, Claire. *Good Night, Sleep Tight* (PS–K). Illus. by Rory Tyger. 2003, Abrams $14.95 (978-0-8109-4513-5). In this heartwarming bedtime story, Grandma Bear gets little Archie to sleep when she tells him stories about putting his mother to bed. (Rev: BL 12/15/03; HBG 4/04; SLJ 12/03)

675 Gabriel, Andrea. *My Favorite Bear* (PS–1). Illus. 2003, Charlesbridge $15.95 (978-1-58089-038-0). 32pp. To get her little bear to sleep, a mother bear sings a song about different kinds of bears. (Rev: BL 2/15/03; HBG 10/03; SLJ 2/03)

676 Gal, Susan. *Night Lights* (PS–1). Illus. by author. 2009, Knopf LB $14.99 (978-0-375-95862-5). 32pp. A little girl, her mother, and dog share a variety of quiet evening activities on a summer night in this book that is wordless apart from the names of the various lights they see (street, fire, candle, star). (Rev: BL 12/1/09; SLJ 11/1/09*)

677 Gay, Michel. *Zee Is Not Scared* (PS–2). Trans. from French by Marie Mianowski. Illus. by author. 2004, Clarion $15.00 (978-0-618-43931-7). 29pp. A little zebra can't settle down to sleep in this translation of a French story, and decides to dress up as a ghost and scare his parents. (Rev: SLJ 4/04)

678 George, Lindsay Barrett. *My Bunny and Me* (PS–2). Illus. 2001, Greenwillow LB $15.89 (978-0-688-16075-3). 32pp. A boy draws a bunny that comes to life and the two play together until the boy goes to bed and the bunny hops off into a field. (Rev: BL 1/1–15/01; HBG 10/01)

679 Gerber, Carole. *Firefly Night* (PS–3). Illus. by Marty Husted. 2000, Charlesbridge $16.95 (978-1-58089-051-9); paper $6.95 (978-1-58089-066-3). 32pp. Based on some lines from Longfellow's *Hiawatha*, this is the gentle story of a young Chippewa girl who is guided home at night by a firefly. (Rev: BL 11/1/00; HBG 3/01; SLJ 1/01)

680 Gershator, Phillis. *Moo, Moo, Brown Cow! Have You Any Milk?* (PS–2). Illus. by Giselle Potter. 2011, Random House $16.99 (978-0-375-86744-6); LB $19.99 (978-0-375-96744-3). 40pp. A sheep contributes wool for a blanket, a cow milk for a bedtime snack, and so forth in this soothing barnyard bedtime story. (Rev: BL 6/1/11; HB 9–10/11; SLJ 6/11)

681 Gershator, Phillis, and Mim Green. *Who's Awake in Springtime?* (PS–2). Illus. by Emilie Chollat. 2010, Henry Holt $16.99 (978-0-8050-6390-5). 32pp. In this cumulative bedtime story with a find-and-seek twist, a host of animals playfully evades bedtime until it proves irresistible. (Rev: BL 12/15/09; LMC 1–2/10; SLJ 2/1/10)

682 Glass, Beth Raisner, and Susan Lubner. *Noises at Night* (PS–1). Illus. by Bruce Whatley. 2005, Abrams $15.95 (978-0-8109-5750-3). In this unusual bedtime story told in rhyming couplets, the mysterious sounds of nighttime inspire a young boy to dream of grand adventures with his teddy bear. (Rev: SLJ 10/05)

683 Gorbachev, Valeri. *Shhh!* (PS–1). Illus. by author. 2011, Philomel $16.99 (978-0-399-25429-1). 32pp. A little boy tiptoes around the house while his brother naps, asking all his toys (clown, knights, tiger) to keep quiet. (Rev: BLO 10/15/11; SLJ 9/1/11)

684 Gravett, Emily. *Again!* (PS–1). Illus. by author. 2013, Simon & Schuster $17.99 (978-1-4424-5231-2). 32pp. At bedtime little Cedric the dragon asks his mother to read his favorite story again and again; his mother alters the story with each rereading and eventually falls asleep herself, leaving one very annoyed Cedric. (Rev: BL 5/1/13; HB 7–8/13; SLJ 6/13)

685 Greenberg, David T. *Enchanted Lions* (PS–2). Illus. by Kristina Swarner. 2009, Dutton $16.99 (978-0-525-47938-3). 32pp. A young girl sets off for a nighttime adventure on the back of an enchanted lion. (Rev: BL 5/15/09; SLJ 6/09)

686 Guthrie, James. *Last Song* (PS–K). Illus. by Eric Rohmann. 2010, Roaring Brook $10.99 (978-1-59643-508-7). 28pp. A squirrel family settles in for the night after a busy day in this nicely illustrated story based on a Scottish verse. (Rev: BL 10/15/10; SLJ 10/1/10)

687 Guy, Ginger F. *Go Back to Bed!* (K–2). Illus. by James Bernardin. 2006, Carolrhoda LB $15.95 (978-1-57505-750-7). Edwin comes up with lots of excuses not to go to sleep and imagines exciting things happening downstairs. (Rev: SLJ 6/06)

688 Hague, Kathleen. *Good Night, Fairies* (PS–3). Illus. by Michael Hague. 2002, North-South $15.95 (978-1-58717-134-5). 40pp. This magical bedtime book has a mother explaining to her child all the jobs performed by fairies. (Rev: BL 3/15/02; HBG 10/02)

689 Harris, Peter. *The Night Pirates* (PS–K). Illus. by Deborah Allwright. 2006, Scholastic $17.99 (978-0-439-79959-1). A boy named Tom joins a band of tough girl pirates in this rhyming bedtime story full of humor. (Rev: BL 2/1/06; SLJ 3/06)

690 Harris, Robie H. *Maybe a Bear Ate It!* (PS–2). Illus. by Michael Emberley. 2008, Scholastic $15.99 (978-0-439-92961-5). 40pp. As a small animal gets ready for bed, he realizes that his favorite book is missing and imagines many improbable reasons for its disappearance. (Rev: BL 12/15/07; LMC 1/08; SLJ 1/08)

691 Harshman, Marc. *All the Way to Morning* (PS–3). Illus. by Felipe Davalos. 1999, Marshall Cavendish $15.95 (978-0-7614-5042-9). 32pp. On a camping trip, a father tells his son what children in other countries such as Israel, Japan, and Kenya hear as they go to sleep at night. (Rev: BL 9/15/99; HBG 3/00; SLJ 11/99)

692 Hayes, Geoffrey. *The Bunny's Night-Light: A Glow-in-the-Dark Search* (PS–K). Illus. by author. 2012, Random House $11.99 (978-0-375-86926-6); LB $14.99 (978-0-375-96926-3). 32pp. Bunny and his dad search the woods for the perfect night-light, dismissing the moon and fireflies before his mom figures out the perfect solution to the problem. (Rev: BL 1/1/12; SLJ 12/1/11)

693 Henry, Jed. *Good Night, Mouse!* (PS–1). Illus. by author. 2013, Houghton Mifflin $16.99 (978-0-547-98156-7). 32pp. In this sequel to *Cheer Up, Mouse!* (2013), Mouse has trouble falling asleep and his forest friends try to help. (Rev: BLO 10/1/13; HB 9–10/13; SLJ 8/13)

694 Henry, Rohan. *Good Night, Baby Ruby* (PS). Illus. by author. 2009, Abrams $14.95 (978-0-8109-8323-6). 32pp. Toddler Ruby is much too active to go to bed, and evades her mother at every turn. (Rev: SLJ 3/09)

695 Hest, Amy. *Kiss Good Night* (PS–1). Illus. by Anita Jeram. 2001, Candlewick $15.99 (978-0-7636-0780-7). 32pp. Sam, a little bear, cannot fall asleep without his mother's goodnight kiss. (Rev: BL 10/1/01; HBG 3/02; SLJ 11/01*)

36

696 Hill, Susanna Leonard. *Can't Sleep Without Sheep* (PS–1). Illus. by Mike Wohnoutka. 2010, Walker $16.99 (978-0-8027-2066-5). Unpaged. Ava just can't sleep, but the disgruntled sheep are exhausted and try to find suitable replacements, without success. (Rev: SLJ 9/1/10)

697 Ho, Minfong. *Hush! A Thai Lullaby* (PS–3). Illus. by Holly Meade. 1996, Orchard LB $16.99 (978-0-531-08850-0). 32pp. In this lullaby, a mother quiets the animals, one by one, so that her baby can sleep. (Rev: BCCB 4/96; BL 4/15/96; HB 11/96; SLJ 3/96)

698 Holub, Joan. *Bed, Bats, and Beyond* (2–3). Illus. by Mernie Gallagher-Cole. 2008, Darby Creek $14.95 (978-1-58196-077-8). 64pp. Its morning and time for bed but young bat Fink can't get to sleep, so the whole bat family pitches in with stories. (Rev: SLJ 12/08)

699 Howland, Naomi. *Princess Says Goodnight* (PS–K). Illus. by David Small. 2010, HarperCollins $16.99 (978-0-06-145525-4). 32pp. A little girl imagines herself a princess as she gets ready for bed, eating chocolate éclairs and practicing her curtsies. (Rev: BL 4/1/10; SLJ 4/1/10)

700 Hurd, Thacher. *The Weaver* (PS–2). Illus. by Elisa Kleven. 2010, Farrar $16.99 (978-0-374-38254-4). 32pp. High above the Earth, a young girl in a red dress sits on a cloud and weaves her observations of life below during the day and evening before going home to her own family. (Rev: BL 4/15/10; LMC 8–9/10; SLJ 6/1/10)

701 Imai, Ayano. *The 108th Sheep* (PS–K). Illus. by author. 2007, ME Media $15.95 (978-1-58925-063-5). 32pp. An oversize bedtime/counting book in which sleepless young Emma decides to count sheep. (Rev: BL 6/1–15/07; SLJ 5/07)

702 Inches, Alison. *The Stuffed Animals Get Ready for Bed* (PS–K). Illus. by Bryan Langdo. 2006, Harcourt $16.00 (978-0-15-216466-9). 32pp. It's bedtime, but the stuffed animals aren't sleepy yet and it's up to their young owner to get them settled down. (Rev: BL 8/06; SLJ 9/06)

703 Ives, Penny. *Rabbit Pie* (PS). Illus. 2006, Viking $15.99 (978-0-670-05951-5). 32pp. A mother rabbit follows nightly rituals as she readies her six little bunnies for sleep. (Rev: BL 1/1–15/06; SLJ 5/06)

704 Iwamura, Kazuo. *Bedtime in the Forest* (PS–1). Illus. by author. 2010, NorthSouth $16.95 (978-0-7358-2310-5). 32pp. A trio of young squirrels want to stay up past their bedtimes to play with their owl friends, but eventually figure out an even better way to interact. (Rev: BL 8/10; SLJ 1/1/11)

705 Jadoul, Emile. *Good Night, Chickie* (PS). Illus. by author. 2011, Eerdmans $13.99 (978-0-8028-5378-3). 26pp. Finally reassured by Mother Hen that all is well, little Chickie tells his toy bunny that it's time to go to sleep. (Rev: BL 5/1/11; SLJ 2/1/11)

706 Jennings, Sharon. *No Monsters Here* (PS–K). Illus. by Ruth Ohi. 2004, Fitzhenry & Whiteside $14.95 (978-1-55041-787-6). 24pp. A young boy reassures his fearful father, checking there are no monsters under his father's bed before he settles down for the night. (Rev: BL 9/1/04; SLJ 10/04)

707 Jewel. *Sweet Dreams* (PS). Illus. by Amy June Bates. 2013, Simon & Schuster $17.99 (978-144248931-8). 32pp. In this charming lullaby by singer Jewel, a mother and her child go for a boat ride through the evening sky and while the mother sings an enchanting lullaby, they make constellations by stringing stars together with silver thread. (Rev: BL 11/15/13; SLJ 11/13)

708 Joosse, Barbara. *Lovabye Dragon* (PS–1). Illus. by Randy Cecil. 2012, Candlewick $15.99 (978-0-7636-5408-5). 32pp. A dragon and a little girl, both lonely, find each other and become devoted companions in this poetic bedtime book. (Rev: BL 9/1/12*; HB 9–10/12; SLJ 10/12)

709 Joosse, Barbara M. *In the Night Garden* (PS–K). Illus. by Elizabeth Sayles. 2008, Holt $16.95 (978-0-8050-6671-5). Bedtime slips into surreal dream time for three little girls who imagine themselves impressive animals. (Rev: SLJ 12/08)

710 Joosse, Barbara M. *Roawr!* (PS–K). Illus. by Jan Jutte. 2009, Philomel $16.99 (978-0-399-24777-4). An exciting bedtime story featuring a boy who must first trap a bear. (Rev: BL 12/1/08; SLJ 3/09)

711 Kanevsky, Polly. *Sleepy Boy* (K–2). Illus. by Stephanie Anderson. 2006, Simon & Schuster $15.95 (978-0-689-86735-4). A small boy remembers the lion cub he saw at the zoo as he cuddles with his daddy in this charming bedtime book. (Rev: BL 4/15/06; SLJ 5/06)

712 Katz, Karen. *Counting Kisses* (PS). Illus. 2001, Simon & Schuster $14.00 (978-0-689-83470-7). 32pp. Every family member showers a baby with kisses until the young child peacefully drops off to sleep. (Rev: BCCB 2/01; BL 2/1/01; HBG 10/01; SLJ 2/01)

713 Katz, Karen. *Princess Baby, Night-Night* (PS–K). Illus. by author. 2009, Random $14.99 (978-0-375-84462-1). Princess Baby is not tired and to prove it she falls asleep on the floor. (Rev: BL 12/1/08; SLJ 1/09)

714 Kavanagh, Peter. *I Love My Mama* (PS–1). Illus. by Jane Chapman. 2003, Simon & Schuster $12.95 (978-0-689-85691-4). A mother elephant and her baby spend their day traversing the beautiful African landscape before settling down to sleep in the grass. (Rev: HBG 10/03; SLJ 4/03)

715 Kempter, Christa. *When Mama Can't Sleep* (PS). Illus. by Natascha Rosenberg. Series: Tuff Books. 2011, NorthSouth $6.95 (978-0-7358-4015-7). Unpaged. Mama can't sleep; nor can Papa, or Max, or teddy, or the dog. The only thing to do is all crawl into bed together. (Rev: SLJ 8/1/11)

716 Kono, Erin Eitter. *Hula Lullaby* (PS–2). Illus. 2005, Little, Brown $15.99 (978-0-316-73591-9). 32pp. In her mother's lap, a Hawaiian girl listens to descriptions of the warm world around her until she falls asleep. (Rev: BL 5/1/05)

717 Lamb, Albert. *Tell Me the Day Backwards* (PS–1). Illus. by David McPhail. 2011, Candlewick $15.99 (978-0-7636-5055-1). 40pp. Before bed, a little bear and his mother lovingly rehash their eventful day. (Rev: BL 3/1/11; SLJ 3/1/11)

718 LaRochelle, David. *The Haunted Hamburger and Other Ghostly Stories* (PS–2). Illus. by Paul Meisel. 2011, Dutton $16.99 (978-0-525-42272-3). 40pp. A daddy ghost tells his offspring three short scary bedtime stories; fortunately, what's scary to ghosts is funny to readers. (Rev: BLO 8/11; HB 9–10/11; LMC 11–12/11; SLJ 8/1/11)

719 Levine, Joan. *Topsy-Turvy Bedtime* (K–3). Illus. by Tony Auth. 2008, Candlewick $14.99 (978-0-7636-3008-9). 32pp. Arathusela must put her parents to bed and they prove very difficult, wanting to watch TV, asking for another drink . . . (Rev: BCCB 5/08; BL 6/1–15/08)

720 Lewis, Kim. *Good Night, Harry* (PS–K). Illus. by author. 2004, Candlewick $15.99 (978-0-7636-2206-0). Harry the elephant can't sleep, so Lulu and Ted — also soft toy animals — sit up with him until he drifts off. (Rev: SLJ 4/04)

721 Lewis, Paeony. *No More Yawning!* (PS–1). Illus. by Brita Granström. 2008, Scholastic $16.99 (978-0-545-02957-5). 32pp. Seems like Florence and her toy monkey Arnold need a hundred things before they can go to sleep; includes endnotes with tips on falling asleep. (Rev: BL 1/1–15/08; SLJ 4/08)

722 Lindbergh, Reeve. *Our Nest* (PS–1). Illus. by Jill McElmurry. 2004, Candlewick $15.99 (978-0-7636-1286-3). 32pp. The comforts of all sorts of nests — from birds in trees to fish in water and boats in harbors — are celebrated in this gentle book. (Rev: BL 4/15/04*; SLJ 5/04)

723 Logue, Mary. *Sleep Like a Tiger* (PS–1). Illus. by Pamela Zagarenski. 2012, Houghton Mifflin $16.99 (978-0-547-64102-7). 40pp. A little girl who is not sleepy is nonetheless interested in how animals sleep. Caldecott Honor; ALA Notable Children's Book; Booklist Editors' Choice: Books for Youth. ❤ (Rev: BL 10/1/12*; HB 11–12/12; SLJ 12/12*)

724 London, Jonathan. *Froggy Goes to Bed* (PS–K). Illus. by Frank Remkiewicz. 2000, Viking $15.99 (978-0-670-88860-3). 32pp. The nighttime rituals become so prolonged that Froggy's mother falls asleep before he does. (Rev: BL 3/1/00; HBG 10/00; SLJ 6/00)

725 Long, Sylvia. *Hush Little Baby* (PS–1). Illus. 1997, Chronicle $12.95 (978-0-8118-1416-4). This song, a tender lullaby, focuses on the relationship between a mother and her baby bunny. (Rev: BL 6/1–15/97)

726 Lyon, George E. *Sleepsong* (PS–K). Illus. by Peter Catalanotto. 2009, Atheneum $16.99 (978-0-689-86973-0). 40pp. A little girl's parents get her ready for bed. (Rev: BL 12/1/08; SLJ 1/09)

727 McCain, Becky Ray. *Grandmother's Dreamcatcher* (K–2). Illus. by Stacey Schuett. 1998, Whitman $15.95 (978-0-8075-3031-3). 32pp. A young Chippewa boy goes to live with his grandmother, who cures him of having bad dreams by placing a dreamcatcher above his bed. (Rev: BL 10/1/98; HBG 3/99; SLJ 12/98)

728 MacDonald, Margaret Read. *The Squeaky Door* (PS–2). Illus. by Mary Newell Depalma. 2006, HarperCollins $15.99 (978-0-06-028373-5). 40pp. A funny retelling of the story of a boy who can't sleep because he's scared of his squeaking door, with eye-catching typography and bright cartoon illustrations. (Rev: BL 12/1/05; SLJ 1/06)

729 MacDonald, Margaret Read. *Tuck-Me-In Tales: Bedtime Stories from Around the World* (PS–1). Illus. by Yvonne Davis. 1996, August House $19.95 (978-0-87483-461-1). Five traditional bedtime stories from around the world are lavishly illustrated. (Rev: BL 10/1/96; SLJ 11/96) [398.2]

730 MacLachlan, Patricia. *Lala Salama: A Tanzanian Lullaby* (PS–K). Illus. by Elizabeth Zunon. 2011, Candlewick $16.99 (978-0-7636-4747-6). 32pp. As evening falls, a mother recalls the events of the day for her baby as they sit on the banks of Lake Tanganyika. (Rev: BL 12/1/11; SLJ 11/1/11)

731 MacLachlan, Patricia. *Who Loves Me?* (PS). Illus. by Amanda Sheperd. 2005, HarperCollins LB $15.89 (978-0-06-027977-6). 40pp. A little girl and her cat check off all the people who love her. (Rev: BL 6/1–15/05; SLJ 5/05)

732 Marlow, Layn. *Hurry Up and Slow Down* (PS–2). Illus. by author. 2009, Holiday $16.95 (978-0-8234-2178-7). 32pp. Hare and Tortoise are good friends who find their differences are easily conquered. (Rev: BL 2/1/09; SLJ 2/09)

733 Martin, Bill, and Michael Sampson. *Kitty Cat, Kitty Cat, Are You Going to Sleep?* (PS–K). Illus. by Laura J. Bryant. 2011, Marshall Cavendish $15.99 (978-0-7614-5946-0). 24pp. A young kitten reluctantly follows her mother's patient prompts about the process of getting ready for bed. (Rev: BL 3/15/11; SLJ 5/1/11)

734 Martin, Ruth. *Moon Dreams* (PS–K). Illus. by Olivier Latyk. 2010, Candlewick $15.99 (978-0-7636-5012-4). 32pp. Luna wonders where the moon goes during the day and dreams up fanciful, beautifully illustrated, scenarios. (Rev: BL 7/10; SLJ 4/11)

735 Matheis, Mickie. *Bedtime for Boo* (PS–1). Illus. by Bonnie Leick. 2012, Random House $10.99 (978-0-375-86991-4). 32pp. The various sounds of his ghost family's house comfort Boo as he settles down to sleep after a game of hide-and-seek among the clouds. ❤ (Rev: BL 9/1/12; SLJ 8/12)

736 Meadows, Michelle. *Piggies in Pajamas* (PS–1). Illus. by Ard Hoyt. 2013, Simon & Schuster $15.99 (978-1-4169-4982-4). 32pp. Alert for their mother coming upstairs, five little piglets enjoy boisterous play before bed. Lexile AD360 (Rev: BL 3/15/13; SLJ 3/13)

737 Melling, David. *Good Knight Sleep Tight* (PS–2). Illus. 2006, Barron's $14.99 (978-0-7641-5878-0). 32pp. The baby princess cannot sleep because the cat has destroyed her pillow, so an intrepid young knight is sent in search of suitably fluffy material. (Rev: BL 2/1/06; SLJ 3/06)

738 Meng, Cece. *Bedtime Is Canceled* (K–2). Illus. by Aurelie Neyret. 2012, Clarion $16.99 (978-0-547-

63668-9). 32pp. Maggie and her brother write a note declaring that "Bedtime is canceled" — with unexpectedly wide-ranging consequences. (Rev: BL 9/1/12; SLJ 11/12)

739 Millen, C. M. *Blue Bowl Down: An Appalachian Rhyme* (PS–1). Illus. by Holly Meade. 2004, Candlewick $16.99 (978-0-7636-1817-9). 32pp. Appealing cut-paper art and a lullaby rhyme depict an Appalachian mother and her toddler son step by step as they prepare bread dough for baking early the next morning. (Rev: BL 5/1/04; SLJ 9/04)

740 Morales, Yuyi. *Little Night* (PS–2). Illus. 2007, Roaring Brook $16.95 (978-1-59643-088-4). Although she doesn't want to go to bed, Little Night has a bath in falling stars and a nightdress crocheted from clouds. (Rev: BL 2/1/07)

741 Morgan, Mary. *Sleep Tight, Little Mouse* (PS). Illus. by author. 2003, Knopf LB $14.99 (978-0-375-92308-1). As he gets ready for bed, Little Mouse considers other options — such as a bird's nest or kangaroo's pouch — but decides that the best sleeping place is his own. (Rev: BL 5/15/03; HBG 10/03; SLJ 8/03)

742 Mortensen, Denise Dowling. *Good Night Engines* (PS). Illus. by Melissa Iwai. 2003, Clarion $15.00 (978-0-618-13537-0). 32pp. At bedtime, a variety of forms of transport come to a halt and settle down for the night. (Rev: BL 12/15/03; HBG 4/04; SLJ 12/03)

743 Murray, Alison. *Little Mouse* (PS–K). Illus. by author. 2013, Disney/Hyperion $16.99 (978-142314330-7). 32pp. A feisty little girl describes all the nicknames that would apply to her better than "little mouse." (Rev: BL 5/15/13*; SLJ 6/13)

744 Myers, Tim. *Dark Sparkle Tea: And Other Bedtime Poems* (2–4). Illus. by Kelley Cunningham. 2006, Boyds Mills $16.95 (978-1-59078-288-0). 32pp. Rhythmic poems featuring funny, lively wordplay describe bouncy bedtimes. (Rev: BL 3/15/06; SLJ 6/06) [811]

745 Nakamura, Katherine Riley. *Song of Night: It's Time to Go to Bed* (PS). Illus. by Linnea Riley. 2002, Scholastic $15.95 (978-0-439-26678-9). 40pp. Animal parents help their beloved children get ready for bed in this charming bedtime book. (Rev: BL 2/1/02; HBG 10/02; SLJ 5/02)

746 Neubecker, Robert. *Beasty Bath* (PS–1). Illus. by author. 2005, Scholastic $14.99 (978-0-439-64000-8). As she has a bath and gets ready for bed, a little girl imagines herself as many beasts and monsters. (Rev: SLJ 1/06)

747 Newman, Lesléa. *Daddy's Song* (PS–1). Illus. by Karen Ritz. 2007, Holt $16.95 (978-0-8050-6975-4). A father sings an imaginative, loving song to his daughter as he puts her to bed. Bright, beautiful illustrations bring the song to life. (Rev: SLJ 6/07)

748 Noll, Amanda. *I Need My Monster* (K–2). Illus. by Howard McWilliam. 2009, Flashlight $16.95 (978-0-9799746-2-5). 32pp. Ethan can't sleep when his under-the-bed monster Gabe goes fishing, so he interviews a

series of replacement monsters. (Rev: BL 3/15/09; LMC 8/09; SLJ 4/09)

749 Numeroff, Laura. *When Sheep Sleep* (PS–K). Illus. by David McPhail. 2006, Abrams $15.95 (978-0-8109-5469-4). A little girl, struggling to fall asleep, decides to try counting sheep but is disheartened to find that all the sheep are already asleep. (Rev: BL 9/1/06; SLJ 10/06)

750 Oppenheim, Joanne. *The Prince's Bedtime* (PS–1). Illus. by Miriam Latimer. 2006, Barefoot Books $16.99 (978-1-84148-597-3). The prince refuses to go to sleep despite many inducements until a wise woman arrives with bedtime stories. (Rev: SLJ 12/06)

751 Owens, Mary Beth. *Panda Whispers* (PS–2). Illus. by author. 2007, Dutton $16.99 (978-0-525-47171-4). After a succession of animals wish their babies happy dreams, a father does the same to his human child. (Rev: SLJ 4/07)

752 Paul, Ann Whitford. *If Animals Kissed Goodnight* (PS–2). Illus. by David Walker. 2008, Farrar $16.95 (978-0-374-38051-9). 40pp. A mother and her child preparing for bed discuss how various animals behave at nighttime. (Rev: BL 6/1–15/08; SLJ 6/08)

753 Peck, Jan. *Way Up High in a Tall Green Tree* (PS–1). Illus. by Valeria Petrone. 2005, Simon & Schuster $15.95 (978-1-4169-0071-9). A girl says good-night to all sorts of jungle animals, then settles down to sleep in her bed full of similar rainforest toys. (Rev: SLJ 9/05)

754 Pendziwol, Jean K. *Once Upon a Northern Night* (K–2). Illus. by Isabelle Arsenault. 2013, Groundwood $17.95 (978-155498138-0). 36pp. A quiet celebration of a chilly northern night and the animals that populate it as a child sleeps in a cozy bed. USBBY Outstanding International Book. **e** Lexile AD1250 (Rev: BL 12/15/13*; SLJ 10/13*)

755 Perl, Erica S. *Chicken Bedtime Is Really Early* (PS). Illus. by George Bates. 2005, Abrams $14.95 (978-0-8109-4926-3). 32pp. Baby farm animals — chicks, calves, bunnies, hamsters — turn in early to get some rest before the rooster crows in this bedtime picture book. (Rev: BL 3/15/05; SLJ 4/05)

756 Perlman, Willa. *Good Night, World* (PS). Illus. by Carolyn Fisher. 2011, Simon & Schuster $16.99 (978-1-4424-0197-4). 40pp. A small child wishes good night to everything from the sun and the stars to his neighborhood and family. (Rev: BL 7/11; HB 9–10/11; SLJ 6/11)

757 Peters, Lisa Westberg. *Sleepyhead Bear* (PS). Illus. by Ian Schoenherr. 2006, Greenwillow $16.99 (978-0-06-059675-0). 32pp. Little Bear, glad to find some friendly butterflies after being bothered by pesky bugs, settles down for a good night's sleep in this simple bedtime book. (Rev: BL 5/15/06; SLJ 5/06)

758 Pfister, Marcus. *Bertie at Bedtime* (PS–1). Illus. by author. 2008, North-South $16.95 (978-0-7358-2194-1). A young hippo called Bertie resists bedtime until his father is totally worn out. (Rev: BL 4/15/08; SLJ 5/08)

759 Pfister, Marcus. *Good Night, Little Rainbow Fish* (PS–1). Illus. by author. 2012, NorthSouth $18.95 (978-0-7358-4082-9). 32pp. Mommy reassures Little Rainbow Fish that she will be there to rescue him from a number of scary scenarios, and gradually the little one relaxes. (Rev: BLO 12/15/12; SLJ 11/12)

760 Pitcher, Caroline. *The Winter Dragon* (K–2). Illus. by Sophy Williams. 2004, Lincoln $15.95 (978-1-84507-322-0). 36pp. Young Rory's dragon warms the winter nights, leaving the boy with memories of comfort and companionship when spring arrives. (Rev: BL 10/15/04; SLJ 1/05)

761 Puttock, Simon. *Earth to Stella!* (PS–2). Illus. by Philip Hopman. 2006, Clarion $16.00 (978-0-618-58535-9). 32pp. As she brushes her teeth and gets ready for bed, young Stella alternates between her fantasy of outer space and the reality of her attentive father. (Rev: SLJ 3/06)

762 Radzinski, Kandy. *Where to Sleep* (PS–K). Illus. by author. 2009, Sleeping Bear $15.95 (978-1-58536-436-7). 32pp. A kitten finds a comfy spot at the feet of its "best friend" in this nap/bedtime book set on a farm. (Rev: BL 4/1/09; SLJ 5/09)

763 Reidy, Jean. *Light Up the Night* (K–2). Illus. by Margaret Chodos-Irvine. 2011, Hyperion/Disney $16.99 (978-1-4231-2024-7). 40pp. A little boy takes a magic blanket tour of the universe before returning to his comfortable bed. (Rev: BL 11/15/11; HB 9–10/11; SLJ 9/1/11)

764 Rex, Michael. *You Can Do Anything, Daddy!* (PS–K). Illus. 2007, Putnam $14.99 (978-0-399-24298-4). When a little boy at bedtime asks his tie-wearing dad if he'd save him if pirates took him, the action morphs into an adventurous rescue full of pirates, snakes, robots, and more, with the son proffering apple juice and bandages at its end; detail-filled illustrations emulate comics. (Rev: BL 1/1–15/07)

765 Rinker, Sherri Duskey. *Goodnight, Goodnight, Construction Site* (PS–K). Illus. by Tom Lichtenheld. 2011, Chronicle $16.99 (978-0-8118-7782-4). 32pp. As the sun sets, five construction site vehicles end their working day and bed down for the night. (Rev: BL 9/1/11*; SLJ 7/11*)

766 Rinker, Sherri Duskey. *Steam Train, Dream Train* (PS–K). Illus. by Tom Lichtenheld. 2013, Chronicle $16.99 (978-145210920-6). 40pp. A train is slowly loaded up and chugs away toward dreamland in this rhyming bedtime book. Lexile AD720 (Rev: BL 5/15/13*; SLJ 6/13*)

767 Robbins, Maria Polushkin. *Mother, Mother, I Want Another* (PS–2). Illus. by Jon Goodell. 2005, Knopf LB $16.99 (978-0-375-92588-7). 32pp. A newly illustrated edition of the bedtime story in which Mrs. Mouse misinterprets her son's request. (Rev: BL 2/15/05; SLJ 3/05)

768 Rock, Lois. *I Wish Tonight* (PS–2). Illus. by Anne Wilson. 2000, Good Bks. $16.00 (978-1-56148-315-0). In bed at night, a young boy wishes on a star and travels into a world of make-believe. (Rev: SLJ 12/00)

769 Rockwell, Anne. *Here Comes the Night* (PS–K). Illus. by author. 2006, Holt $16.95 (978-0-8050-7663-9).

A little boy's mommy helps him get ready for bed and drift off to dreamland. (Rev: SLJ 6/06)

770 Roep, Nanda. *Kisses* (PS). Illus. by Marijke Ten Cate. 2002, Front St. $15.95 (978-1-886910-85-0). Goodnight kisses are the focus of this richly illustrated, gentle story. (Rev: HBG 3/03; SLJ 1/03)

771 Rose, Deborah Lee. *Someone's Sleepy* (PS–K). Illus. by Dan Andreasen. 2013, Abrams $16.95 (978-1-4197-0539-7). 32pp. A soothing bedtime book that reviews pre-bedtime rituals. (Rev: BL 6/13; SLJ 6/13)

772 Rosenthal, Amy Krouse. *Bedtime for Mommy* (PS–K). Illus. by LeUyen Pham. 2010, Bloomsbury $16.99 (978-1-59990-341-5). 32pp. A determined child oversees her mother's progress to bed in this humorous role-reversal story. (Rev: BL 2/15/10; LMC 1–2/10; SLJ 3/1/10)

773 Rosenthal, Amy Krouse. *Little Hoot* (PS–2). Illus. by Jen Corace. 2008, Chronicle $12.99 (978-0-8118-6023-9). 36pp. Little Hoot's mean parents make him stay up late playing, when he'd rather be asleep like all his friends. (Rev: BCCB 3/08; SLJ 4/08)

774 Ross, Tony. *I Want My Light On! A Little Princess Story* (PS–1). Illus. by author. 2010, Andersen $16.95 (978-0-7613-6443-6). 32pp. Little Princess is petrified of ghosts until she meets one and discovers that it's as afraid of her as she is of it. (Rev: BL 7/10; SLJ 8/1/10)

775 Ruddell, Deborah. *Who Said Coo?* (PS). Illus. by Robin Luebs. 2010, Simon & Schuster $16.99 (978-1-4169-8510-5). 40pp. Various animal sounds interrupt Lulu the Pig as she's trying to sleep in this comic lullaby with a sweet ending. (Rev: BL 6/10; LMC 8–9/10; SLJ 8/1/10) [811.6]

776 Russo, Marisabina. *The Bunnies Are Not in Their Beds* (K–2). Illus. by author. 2006, Random $15.99 (978-0-375-83961-0). Three bunny siblings are too full of energy to go to sleep despite their parents' frequent admonitions. (Rev: BL 2/1/07; SLJ 12/06)

777 Saltzberg, Barney. *Cornelius P. Mud, Are You Ready for Bed?* (PS). Illus. 2005, Candlewick $15.99 (978-0-7636-2399-9). 32pp. Asked many pre-bed questions ("Have you used the bathroom?"), Cornelius the pig blithely lies "yes" but the illustrations tell the truth. (Rev: BL 5/1/05; SLJ 3/05)

778 Sanroman, Susana. *Señora Reganona* (PS–3). Illus. by Domi. 1998, Douglas & McIntyre $14.95 (978-0-88899-320-5). 32pp. A child conquers her fear of the dark, which she calls "Señora Reganona," when she flies into the sky one night and makes a friend of the Señora. (Rev: BL 8/98; HBG 10/98; SLJ 9/98)

779 Sartell, Debra. *Time for Bed, Baby Ted* (PS–K). Illus. by Kay Chorao. 2010, Holiday House $16.95 (978-0-8234-1968-2). 32pp. Toddler Ted is an expert at prolonging his bedtime routine, impersonating different animals and enticing his patient, good-natured dad to guess the correct animal before tucking him in. (Rev: BL 1/1/10; SLJ 3/1/10)

780 Saunders, Karen. *Baby Badger's Wonderful Night* (PS–2). Illus. by Dubravka Kolanovic. 2011, Egmont

$16.99 (978-1-60684-172-3). Unpaged. Baby badger's dad takes him on a beautiful nighttime walk through the forest and shows him that the dark is not frightening after all. (Rev: SLJ 4/11)

781 Sayles, Elizabeth. *The Goldfish Yawned* (PS–1). Illus. by author. 2005, Holt $16.95 (978-0-8050-7624-0). A sleepy young child sets sail on a magical boat trip. (Rev: SLJ 1/06)

782 Schaefer, Carole Lexa. *Who's There?* (PS–1). Illus. by Pierr Morgan. 2011, Viking $15.99 (978-0-670-01241-1). 32pp. Alone in the dark with his teddy bear, a little rabbit imagines all kinds of sources for the noises he hears; the illustrations are of completely unscary monsters. (Rev: BL 5/1/11; SLJ 7/11)

783 Schroeder, Lisa. *Baby Can't Sleep* (PS). Illus. by Viviana Garofoli. 2005, Sterling LB $12.95 (978-1-4027-2171-7). Counting sheep doesn't always put babies to sleep! (Rev: SLJ 1/06)

784 Schwartz, Amy. *Lucy Can't Sleep* (PS–K). Illus. by author. 2012, Roaring Brook $16.99 (978-1-59643-543-8). 32pp. Lucy finds lots of ways to have fun when she can't sleep — looking for lost toys, raiding the fridge, playing with clothes — until she tires herself out. **℮** (Rev: BL 9/1/12; HB 9–10/12; SLJ 8/12)

785 Scotton, Rob. *Russell the Sheep* (PS–1). Illus. by author. 2005, HarperCollins LB $18.89 (978-0-06-059849-5). Russell the sheep just can't sleep; he tries counting feet — and then stars — and then sheep . . . (Rev: SLJ 4/05)

786 Shea, Bob. *Dinosaur vs. Bedtime* (PS–K). Illus. by author. 2008, Hyperion $15.99 (978-1-4231-1335-5). 40pp. A plucky little dinosaur conquers most challenges of the day but finds bedtime the hardest of all. (Rev: BCCB 10/08; HB 9/08; SLJ 11/08)

787 Shea, Bob. *Race You to Bed* (PS–1). Illus. by author. 2010, HarperCollins $16.99 (978-0-06-170417-8). 32pp. A hyperactive rabbit leads readers on a frenetic race — over hills, through a swamp, on a train — to bed in this rather energetic bedtime story. (Rev: BL 4/1/10; SLJ 2/1/10)

788 Shulevitz, Uri. *So Sleepy Story* (PS). Illus. by author. 2006, Farrar $16.00 (978-0-374-37031-2). 32pp. A magical dance in the middle of the night enlivens a small boy's room. (Rev: BCCB 10/06; BL 7/06; HB 1/07; HBG 4/07; SLJ 8/06*)

789 Smee, Nicola. *No Bed Without Ted* (PS–1). Illus. by author. 2005, Bloomsbury $14.95 (978-1-58234-963-3). A girl heading for bed can't find her favorite teddy bear without her mother's help in this lift-the-flap book. (Rev: SLJ 7/05)

790 Smith, Danna. *Pirate Nap: A Book of Colors* (PS–K). Illus. by Valeria Petrone. 2011, Clarion $14.99 (978-0-574-57531-5). 40pp. Two brothers intent on seeing pirate possibilities all around the house strongly resist the idea that they should take a nap. (Rev: SLJ 8/1/11)

791 Sobel, June. *The Goodnight Train* (PS–K). Illus. by Laura Huliska-Beith. 2006, Harcourt $16.00 (978-0-15-205436-6). The Goodnight Train picks up a cast of colorful characters as it counts down the time until lights-out. (Rev: SLJ 10/06)

792 Spinelli, Eileen. *When Papa Comes Home Tonight* (PS). Illus. by David McPhail. 2009, Simon & Schuster $16.99 (978-1-4169-1028-2). 32pp. A young boy describes the things that he and Papa do at the close of day. (Rev: BL 4/1/09; SLJ 4/09)

793 Srinivasan, Divya. *Little Owl's Night* (PS–K). Illus. by author. 2011, Viking $16.99 (978-0-670-01295-4). 32pp. Little Owl is having such a good time foraging through the night that he's sad to see the sun come up and realize that it's time for bed. (Rev: BL 10/15/11*; SLJ 11/1/11)

794 Steigemeyer, Julie. *Seven Little Bunnies* (PS). Illus. by Laura J. Bryant. 2010, Marshall Cavendish $15.99 (978-0-7614-5600-1). 24pp. Seven little bunnies resist bedtime with frenzied activities that eventually tire them out. (Rev: BL 2/15/10; SLJ 4/1/10)

795 Steinbrenner, Jessica. *My Sleepy Room* (PS). Illus. by Elizabeth Wolf. 2004, Handprint $15.95 (978-1-59354-007-4). Bess's "sleepy room" is a comforting place where she reads, plays with toys, and sometimes sleeps. (Rev: SLJ 7/04)

796 Stevenson, James. *What's Under My Bed?* (1–3). Illus. by author. 1983, Greenwillow LB $15.89 (978-0-688-02327-0); Morrow paper $4.95 (978-0-688-09350-1). A grandfather helps reduce his grandchildren's fears. A sequel is: *Worse Than Willy!* (1984).

797 Stills, Caroline, and Sarcia Stills Blott. *The House of 12 Bunnies* (PS–1). Illus. by Judith Rossell. 2012, Holiday House $16.95 (978-0-8234-2422-1). 24pp. Sophia the bunny searches the whole house for her book before finding it under her pillow in this book that offers counting and seek-and-find opportunities. (Rev: BL 3/1/12; SLJ 4/1/12)

798 Symes, Sally. *Yawn* (PS). Illus. by Nick Sharratt. 2011, Candlewick $7.99 (978-076365725-3). 24pp. Sean gives a yawn that passes to a cat, leading to a domino effect and general sleepiness. (Rev: BLO 11/15/11; HB 1–2/12; SLJ 1/12)

799 Tafuri, Nancy. *I Love You, Little One* (PS–1). Illus. 1998, Scholastic $15.95 (978-0-590-92159-6). 32pp. In this bedtime story, different animal mothers try to tell their children how much they love them. (Rev: BL 2/1/98; HBG 10/98; SLJ 3/98)

800 Thomas, Jan. *Let's Sing a Lullaby with the Brave Cowboy* (PS–2). Illus. by author. 2012, Simon & Schuster $12.99 (978-144244276-4). 40pp. A bouncy, funny "lullaby" that still ends up with a bedtime tone. **℮** (Rev: BL 11/1/12)

801 Thompson, Lauren. *Little Quack's Bedtime* (PS–K). Illus. by Derek Anderson. 2005, Simon & Schuster $14.95 (978-0-689-86894-8). Mama Duck succeeds in getting four of her ducklings off to sleep, but Little Quack needs special attention. (Rev: SLJ 2/05)

802 Trapani, Iza. *Shoo Fly!* (PS–1). Illus. by author. 2000, Charlesbridge LB $15.95 (978-1-58089-052-6). This adaptation of a perky song concerns a little mouse and pesky fly and how they are both tucked in at night. (Rev: SLJ 1/01)

803 van Genechten, Guido. *No Ghost Under My Bed* (PS). Illus. by author. 2010, Clavis $16.95 (978-1-60537-069-9). 30pp. A little penguin named Jake asks his father to check around his room repeatedly before finally feeling safe enough to sleep. (Rev: BL 11/1/10; SLJ 10/1/10)

804 Verdick, Elizabeth. *Bedtime* (PS). Illus. by Marieka Heinlen. Series: Toddler Tools. 2010, Free Spirit paper $7.95 (978-1-57542-315-9). Unpaged. This board book introduces the importance of bedtime and various actions that can make children sleepy. (Rev: SLJ 6/1/10)

805 Watson, Wendy. *Bedtime Bunnies* (PS). Illus. by author. 2010, Clarion $15.99 (978-0-547-22312-4). 32pp. Five little bunnies get ready for bed in this lively book with minimal, onomatopoeic text. ℮ (Rev: BL 12/1/10; HB 11–12/10; SLJ 12/1/10*)

806 Watts, Frances. *Kisses for Daddy* (PS). Illus. by David Legge. 2008, Trafalgar $15.95 (978-1-921272-43-1). Father Bear succeeds in persuading a cranky young bear to go to bed as he shows all the ways baby animals kiss their dads. Children's Book Council of Australia Honour Book, 2006. (Rev: BL 6/1–15/08)

807 Weeks, Sarah. *Counting Ovejas* (2–4). Illus. by David Diaz. 2006, Simon & Schuster $16.95 (978-0-689-86750-7). 40pp. A young insomniac learns to count sheep in English and Spanish. (Rev: BL 6/1–15/06; SLJ 6/06)

808 Wells, Rosemary. *Goodnight Max* (PS). Illus. by author. 2000, Viking $11.99 (978-0-670-88707-1). In this board book that contains touch-and-feel surprises Max the rabbit has to change his pajamas three times before he can get to sleep. (Rev: BL 6/1–15/03; HBG 10/03; SLJ 4/00)

809 Wells, Rosemary. *Max and Ruby's Bedtime Book* (PS–1). Illus. by author. 2010, Viking $17.99 (978-0-670-01141-4). 48pp. At their bedtime, Grandma tells three stories about young rabbits Max and Ruby. (Rev: BL 7/10; HB 9–10/10; SLJ 6/11)

810 Whybrow, Ian. *The Noisy Way to Bed* (PS–1). Illus. by Tiphanie Beeke. 2004, Scholastic $16.95 (978-0-439-55689-7). A little boy collects a parade of noisy farm animals on his way to bed. (Rev: SLJ 3/04)

811 Wild, Margaret. *Nighty Night!* (PS–1). Illus. by Kerry Argent. 2001, Peachtree $15.95 (978-1-56145-246-0). 32pp. Simple, rhythmic text and rich, humorous illustrations describe animal babies resisting their parents' efforts to put them to bed. (Rev: BCCB 9/01; BL 9/1/01; HBG 3/02; SLJ 9/01)

812 Wiles, Deborah. *One Wide Sky: A Bedtime Lullaby* (PS–K). Illus. by Tim Bowers. 2003, Harcourt $16.00 (978-0-15-202334-8). In this appealing bedtime and counting story, three children and two young squirrels enjoy the delights of the leafy backyard. (Rev: HBG 10/03; SLJ 6/03)

813 Willems, Mo. *Time to Sleep, Sheep the Sheep!* (PS–K). Illus. by author. 2010, HarperCollins $10.99 (978-0-06-172847-1). 32pp. Cat the Cat has a slumber party

at which most of her friends (Sheep, Pig, Giraffe, and others) are all happy to get to bed — except Owl. (Rev: BL 5/1/10; HB 7–8/10; SLJ 7/1/10)

814 Wilson, Karma. *Sleepyhead* (PS). Illus. by John Segal. 2006, Simon & Schuster $15.95 (978-1-4169-1241-5). 32pp. A kitten tries to get her teddy bear ready to go to bed but he keeps putting it off with pleas for more hugs, kisses, books, drinks, and so forth. (Rev: BL 11/15/06; SLJ 10/06)

815 Wing, Natasha. *Go to Bed, Monster!* (PS). Illus. by Sylvie Kantorovitz. 2007, Harcourt $16.00 (978-0-15-205775-6). 40pp. A little girl who is not ready for bed draws herself a playmate monster, but after they play she is tired and must stay awake drawing pictures of things that will satisfy the monster and eventually get him to sleep. (Rev: BL 11/1/07; SLJ 10/07)

816 Wright, Michael. *Jake Stays Awake* (PS–2). Illus. by author. 2007, Feiwel & Friends $16.95 (978-0-312-36797-8). 32pp. When Jake insists on sleeping with Mom and Dad, they counteroffer with alternative sleeping places for all three that Jake considers unsuitable. (Rev: BL 9/1/07; SLJ 9/07)

817 Yolen, Jane. *Creepy Monsters, Sleepy Monsters: A Lullaby* (PS–1). Illus. by Kelly Murphy. 2011, Candlewick $14.99 (978-0-7636-4201-3). 32pp. Diverse young monsters complete their daily dinner-bath-bedtime routine in this story with detailed illustrations. (Rev: BL 5/1/11; SLJ 6/11)

818 Yolen, Jane. *How Do Dinosaurs Say Goodnight?* (PS–1). Illus. by Mark Teague. 2000, Scholastic $16.99 (978-0-590-31681-1). A bedtime book that features all sorts of baby dinosaurs behaving like human children at bedtime. (Rev: BCCB 6/00; BL 4/1/00*; HBG 10/00; SLJ 6/00)

819 Yolen, Jane. *Sleep, Black Bear, Sleep* (K–2). Illus. by Brooke Dyer. 2007, HarperCollins $15.99 (978-0-06-081560-8). 32pp. A lulling rhyme and snuggly illustrations of animals in various beds grace this bedtime book. (Rev: BL 11/15/06; SLJ 2/07)

820 Ziefert, Harriet. *Mommy, I Want to Sleep in Your Bed!* (PS). Illus. by Elliot Kreloff. 2005, Blue Apple $15.95 (978-1-59354-103-3). 40pp. Charlie the puppy begs to sleep with his parents but finally is happily tucked in after a story. (Rev: BL 12/15/05; SLJ 11/05)

Stories Without Words

821 Andreasen, Dan. *The Treasure Bath* (PS). Illus. by author. 2009, Holt $16.99 (978-0-8050-8686-7). 40pp. An imaginative boy bakes with his mother and then takes a bath in this wordless picture book. (Rev: BL 6/1–15/09)

822 Armstrong, Jennifer. *Once Upon a Banana* (PS–2). Illus. by David Small. 2006, Simon & Schuster $16.95 (978-0-689-84251-1). A hilarious chain of accidents results when a monkey carelessly discards a banana peel on a busy sidewalk; rhyming street signs serve as captions for this wordless story. (Rev: BCCB 12/06; BL 11/1/06; HB 1/07; HBG 4/07; LMC 1/07; SLJ 12/06*)

823 Baker, Jeannie. *Mirror* (PS–3). Illus. by author. 2010, Candlewick $18.99 (978-0-7636-4848-0). 40pp. Boys on opposite sides of the world — in Sydney, Australia, and in rural Morocco — are shown spending the day with their families in parallel wordless stories. (Rev: BL 2/15/11; SLJ 1/1/11*)

824 Bang, Molly. *The Grey Lady and the Strawberry Snatcher* (PS–1). Illus. by author. 1984, Macmillan $16.00 (978-0-02-708140-4). The snatcher tries to get the strawberries from the Grey Lady.

825 Banyai, Istvan. *Zoom* (1–3). Illus. 1995, Viking $16.99 (978-0-670-85804-0). 64pp. A clever picture book that begins with small objects and zooms to larger perspectives. (Rev: BCCB 2/95; BL 2/1/95; SLJ 3/95)

826 Becker, Aaron. *Journey* (1–4). Illus. by author. 2013, Candlewick $15.99 (978-076366053-6). 40pp. A young girl embarks on a journey through a magical realm in this wordless story of escape from boredom. ALA Notable Children's Book. (Rev: BL 8/13*; LMC 1–2/14*; SLJ 7/13*)

827 Bossio, Paula. *The Line* (PS–K). Illus. by author. 2013, Kids Can $16.95 (978-189478684-3). 32pp. This imaginative wordless story highlights a young girl's journey with a line that turns into many things. (Rev: BLO 9/15/13; SLJ 10/13)

828 Boyd, Lizi. *Inside Outside* (PS–2). Illus. by author. 2013, Chronicle $15.99 (978-1-4521-0644-1). 40pp. A wordless picture book about a boy and his pets playing both inside and outside. (Rev: BL 7/13*; HB 7–8/13; SLJ 6/13*)

829 Briggs, Raymond. *The Snowman* (K–3). Illus. by author. 1978, Random $17.00 (978-0-394-83973-8); paper $7.99 (978-0-394-88466-0). 32pp. A small boy has adventures with the snowman he has made.

830 Carle, Eric. *Do You Want to Be My Friend?* (PS–K). Illus. by author. 1971, HarperCollins LB $18.89 (978-0-690-01137-1); paper $6.99 (978-0-06-443127-9). 32pp. The end of an animal's tail appears on each page, and the child must guess the animal before turning the page to see the rest of it.

831 Carmi, Giora. *A Circle of Friends* (K–2). Illus. by author. 2003, Star Bright $15.95 (978-1-932065-00-8). In this heartwarming, wordless picture book, a young boy unknowingly sets in motion a circle of kindness when he shares his muffin with a homeless man he finds sleeping on a park bench. (Rev: HBG 4/04; SLJ 1/04)

832 Cole, Henry. *Unspoken: A Story from the Underground Railroad* (2–4). Illus. by author. 2012, Scholastic $16.99 (978-0-545-39997-5). 32pp. In this wordless picture book set in the Civil War, a young Virginia farm girl discovers a runaway slave hiding in the barn and decides to help him. ALA Notable Children's Book. (Rev: BL 12/1/12; HB 11–12/12; LMC 5–6/13*; SLJ 11/12*)

833 Cooper, Elisha. *Beaver Is Lost* (PS–2). Illus. by author. 2010, Random House $17.99 (978-0-375-85765-2). 40pp. A beaver hitches a ride on a logging truck and

ends up having a big and sometimes frightening adventure in the big city, eventually finding his way home across a big lake. (Rev: BL 6/10; LMC 11–12/10; SLJ 6/1/10)

834 Crews, Donald. *Truck* (1–3). Illus. by author. 1980, Greenwillow $17.89 (978-0-688-84244-4); Morrow paper $6.99 (978-0-688-10481-8). 32pp. This picture book traces a truck trip from loading dock to its San Francisco destination.

835 Day, Alexandra. *Carl's Snowy Afternoon* (PS). Illus. by author. 2009, Farrar $12.99 (978-0-374-31086-8). 32pp. With the babysitter preoccupied, Carl the Rottweiler and his young charge sneak off to attend a pond party on a snowy afternoon. (Rev: BL 11/15/09; SLJ 12/1/09)

836 Desrosiers, Sylvie. *Hocus Pocus Takes the Train* (PS–2). Illus. by Remy Simard. 2013, Kids Can $16.95 (978-155453956-7). 32pp. Hocus Pocus is a busy magician's bunny: not only does he have to return a stuffed bunny to a young child, but his magician has left him behind, and Hocus Pocus has to track him down with the help of the magician's cantankerous canine assistant, Dog; a nearly wordless book with cartoon images. **e** (Rev: BLO 9/15/13; SLJ 8/13)

837 Doremus, Gaetan. *Bear Despair* (PS–2). Illus. by author. 2012, Enchanted Lion $14.95 (978-1-59270-125-4). 32pp. Bear's teddy bear is stolen, and a series of animals suffer the consequences until a friendly octopus gets it back — and the animals Bear has eaten are dramatically restored to life. (Rev: BL 12/15/12; LMC 5–6/13; SLJ 10/12*)

838 Dudley, Rebecca. *Hank Finds an Egg* (PS–1). 2013, Peter Pauper $16.99 (978-1-4413-1158-0). 40pp. In this wordless story, Hank — a little stuffed animal — finds an egg in the woods and cares for it through the night; the next day he finally has success in findings its real home. (Rev: BL 5/1/13*; LMC 11–12/13; SLJ 6/13)

839 Faller, Regis. *Polo and Lily* (PS–2). Illus. by author. 2009, Roaring Brook $9.95 (978-1-59643-496-7). 32pp. A wordless picture book in which Polo, a floppy-eared puppy who lives happily in a large tree, makes friends with a rabbit named Lily. (Rev: LMC 8/09; SLJ 7/09)

840 Faller, Regis. *Polo and the Dragon* (PS–K). Illus. by author. 2009, Roaring Brook $9.99 (978-1-59643-498-1). 32pp. A young dog named Polo becomes trapped in ice when out sailing but a friendly dragon helps him get home safely; a wordless picture book. (Rev: BLO 11/1/09; SLJ 11/1/09)

841 Faller, Regis. *Polo: The Runaway Book* (PS–2). Illus. by author. 2006, Roaring Brook $16.95 (978-1-59643-189-8). 80pp. In this almost-wordless picture-book adventure, Polo the dog chases an alien that has run off with his new book. (Rev: BL 12/1/06; SLJ 1/07*)

842 Frazier, Craig. *Bee and Bird* (PS–1). Illus. by author. 2011, Roaring Brook $16.99 (978-1-59643-660-2). 40pp. A wordless tale about a bird and a bee sharing a journey using various forms of transportation. (Rev: BL 5/1/11; SLJ 7/11)

843 Geisert, Arthur. *Hogwash* (K–3). Illus. by author. 2008, Houghton $16.00 (978-0-618-77332-9). 32pp. Mama pigs put their piglets through an intricate cleaning process in this wordless book with detailed illustrations. (Rev: BL 1/1–15/08)

844 Geisert, Arthur. *Ice* (PS–2). Illus. by author. 2011, Enchanted Lion $14.95 (978-1-59270-098-1). 32pp. A group of adventurous pigs running short of water leave their sunny island in search of an iceberg in this wordless adventure. (Rev: BL 4/15/11; SLJ 5/1/11)

845 Geisert, Arthur. *Oops* (K–3). 2006, Houghton $16.00 (978-0-618-60904-8). 32pp. Just a little spilled milk sets off a chain of events that destroys a pig family's house in this wordless story. (Rev: BL 9/1/06; SLJ 10/06)

846 Gordon, Domenica More. *Archie* (PS–1). Illus. by author. 2012, Bloomsbury $17.99 (978-1-59990-936-3). 32pp. Archie, a dog who has his own dog, starts a successful business creating clothes for dogs, attracting even the attention of the queen; a wordless offering with appealing watercolor illustrations. (Rev: BL 11/15/12; SLJ 11/12*)

847 Guilloppe, Antoine. *One Scary Night* (2–4). Illus. 2005, Milk & Cookies $15.95 (978-0-689-04636-0). 32pp. In this scary, wordless picture book, a young boy wandering through the snowy woods alone at night is being followed by a creature that in the last spread turns out to be a friendly dog. (Rev: BL 11/1/05; SLJ 11/05)

848 Gutiérrez, Elisa. *Picturescape* (PS–2). Illus. by author. 2005, Simply Read $16.95 (978-1-894965-24-8). A boy's trip to an art museum turns into a magical excursion as each colorful painting transports him to a thrilling new location; a beautifully illustrated wordless book. (Rev: SLJ 2/06)

849 Hogrogian, Nonny. *Cool Cat* (PS–1). Illus. by author. 2009, Roaring Brook $17.99 (978-1-59643-429-5). Unpaged. Cool Cat is tired of his dreary neighborhood and transforms it with some paint and a lot of help from friends who appreciate the new, beautiful world. (Rev: HB 1–2/10; LMC 11–12/09; SLJ 10/1/09)

850 Idle, Molly. *Flora and the Flamingo* (PS–2). Illus. by author. 2013, Chronicle $16.99 (978-1-4521-1006-6). Flora and a flamingo become friends and dance together in this wordless book. ALA Notable Children's Book. (Rev: SLJ 4/13*)

851 Khing, T. T. *Where Is the Cake Now?* (PS–K). Illus. by author. 2009, Abrams $12.95 (978-0-8109-8926-9). 32pp. Picnicking animals are dismayed when they discover their dessert is missing yet again and begin pointing fingers at each other in this entertaining, wordless adventure. (Rev: BLO 6/16/09; HB 7/09; SLJ 6/09)

852 Kim, Patti. *Here I Am* (K–3). Illus. by Sonia Sanchez. 2013, Capstone $14.95 (978-162370036-2). 40pp. A young boy journeys to America and while at first he feels overwhelmed and confused by all of the new sights and sounds, he eventually finds friendship and comfort in this wordless picture book. (Rev: BLO 9/15/13; LMC 3–4/2014*; SLJ 11/13)

853 King, Stephen Michael. *Leaf* (PS–1). Illus. by author. 2009, Roaring Brook $14.95 (978-1-59643-503-2). 64pp. An appealing, wordless book in which a bird drops a seed on a little boy's long-haired, messy head and the boy and his dog carefully nurture the seed's growth. (Rev: BCCB 6/09; LMC 10/09; SLJ 4/09)

854 Lee, Suzy. *Shadow* (PS–1). Illus. by author. 2010, Chronicle $15.99 (978-0-8118-7280-5). Unpaged. This nearly wordless story that is read horizontally features a girl playing with shadows in a dark attic. (Rev: SLJ 11/1/10*)

855 Lee, Suzy. *Wave* (K–3). Illus. by author. 2008, Chronicle $15.99 (978-0-8118-5924-0). 40pp. A little girl learns to dance with the sea during a day at the beach in this wordless picture book. (Rev: SLJ 5/08)

856 Lehman, Barbara. *Museum Trip* (PS–2). Illus. 2006, Houghton $15.00 (978-0-618-58125-2). 40pp. A boy on a visit to an art museum suddenly finds himself inside a series of artistic mazes; a wordless book with clever illustrations. (Rev: BL 4/15/06*; HB 5/06; HBG 10/06; LMC 1/07; SLJ 5/06)

857 Lehman, Barbara. *The Red Book* (PS–2). Illus. by author. 2004, Houghton $12.95 (978-0-618-42858-8). 32pp. A story without words in which a red book connects children across the world. Caldecott Honor Book. (Rev: BL 10/1/04*; HB 9/04; SLJ 11/04*)

858 Lehman, Barbara. *The Secret Box* (PS–2). Illus. by author. 2011, Houghton Mifflin $15.99 (978-0-547-23868-5). 48pp. In a school dormitory in the early 20th century, a young boy hides a mysterious box under the floorboards; as the generations roll by, the scenery around the dormitory changes, until the box is rediscovered by a modern-day boy; this wordless story is told in detailed watercolors. (Rev: BL 2/1/11; HB 7–8/11; SLJ 5/1/11)

859 Lehman, Barbara. *Trainstop* (PS–2). Illus. by author. 2008, Houghton $16.00 (978-0-618-75640-7). 32pp. A girl on a train ride daydreams of rescuing an aviator in a world of little people in this story told entirely in pictures. (Rev: BL 1/1–15/08; SLJ 7/08)

860 McCully, Emily Arnold. *Picnic* (PS–2). Illus. by author. 1984, HarperCollins LB $16.89 (978-0-06-024100-1). An eventful picnic for the mouse family.

861 McCully, Emily Arnold. *School* (PS–1). Illus. by author. 1987, HarperCollins LB $15.89 (978-0-06-024133-9); paper $5.95 (978-0-06-443233-7). 32pp. The littlest mouse decides to follow her siblings to school to see what it's like. (Rev: BL 9/1/87; SLJ 10/87)

862 Martin, Rafe. *Will's Mammoth* (K–2). Illus. by Stephen Gammell. 1989, Penguin $17.99 (978-0-399-21627-5). 32pp. A boy named Will travels back in time to when mammoths and saber-toothed tigers roamed the earth. (Rev: BCCB 11/89; BL 9/15/89; HB 3/90*; SLJ 10/89*)

863 Mayer, Mercer. *Octopus Soup* (K–2). Illus. by author. 2011, Marshall Cavendish $16.99 (978-0-7614-5812-8). Unpaged. An octopus has a series of misadventures in this wordless picture book. (Rev: SLJ 4/11)

864 Newgarden, Mark. *Bow-Wow Bugs a Bug* (1–3). Illus. by Megan Montague Cash. 2007, Harcourt $12.95 (978-0-15-205813-5). This wordless picture book is designed like a giant comic strip that follows the adventures of a dog and a bug. (Rev: HB 7/07; SLJ 7/07)

865 Nolan, Dennis. *Sea of Dreams* (PS–4). Illus. by author. 2011, Roaring Brook $16.99 (978-1-59643-470-7). Unpaged. In this magical realism story, the inhabitants of a young girl's sandcastle escape at night, as the tide comes in and their home is washed away. (Rev: LMC 1–2/12; SLJ 11/1/11)

866 Nyeu, Tao. *Wonder Bear* (PS–1). Illus. by author. 2008, Dial $17.99 (978-0-8037-3328-2). 48pp. Two children grow a giant white bear with a magic hat that produces all kinds of wonders. (Rev: BL 9/15/08; SLJ 9/08)

867 Pinkney, Jerry. *The Lion and the Mouse* (PS–1). Illus. by author. 2009, Little, Brown $16.99 (978-0-316-01356-7). 40pp. Jerry Pinkney's lively, wordless retelling of Aesop's famous fable unfolds through beautiful watercolor illustrations. (Rev: BCCB 11/09; BL 7/09*; HB 11/09; SLJ 9/09)

868 Raschka, Chris. *A Ball for Daisy* (PS–K). Illus. by author. 2011, Random House $16.99 (978-0-375-85861-1); LB $19.99 (978-0-375-95861-8). 32pp. A playful little dog gets depressed when another dog punctures her favorite ball in this effective wordless story. Caldecott Medal. (Rev: BL 6/1/11; HB 9–10/11; SLJ 8/1/11*)

869 Raschka, Chris. *Daisy Gets Lost* (PS–K). Illus. by author. 2013, Random House $17.99 (978-044981741-4). 32pp. Daisy, the lovable dog of the Caldecott-winning *A Ball for Daisy* (2011), gets lost in the woods after chasing a squirrel and is ecstatic when she is reunited with her young owner. (Rev: BL 9/1/13; SLJ 9/13*)

870 Rodriguez, Beatrice. *The Chicken Thief* (PS–2). Illus. by author. 2010, Enchanted Lion $14.95 (978-1-59270-092-9). 32pp. A chicken's friends — a bear, a rabbit, and a rooster — set off in hot pursuit when she is captured by a fox in this wordless story. (Rev: BL 6/10; SLJ 8/1/10*)

871 Rodriguez, Béatrice. *Fox and Hen Together* (PS–1). Illus. by author. 2011, Enchanted Lion $14.95 (978-1-59270-109-4). Unpaged. Hen leaves Fox in charge of their egg and heads off on an ill-fated fishing trip with Crab; the entertaining, wordless sequel to *The Chicken Thief* (2010). The final volume in the trilogy is *Rooster's Revenge* (2011). (Rev: SLJ 7/11*)

872 Rogers, Gregory. *Midsummer Knight* (K–2). 2007, Roaring Brook $16.95 (978-1-59643-183-6). 32pp. A wordless story in which an Elizabethan bear enters a world reminiscent of Shakespeare's *A Midsummer Night's Dream* and finds himself embroiled in royal intrigue. (Rev: BL 4/1/07)

873 Schories, Pat. *Breakfast for Jack* (PS–2). Illus. by author. 2004, Front St. $13.95 (978-1-932425-16-1). Jack the dog is very worried when his family leaves in the morning without giving him breakfast in this wordless book. Also use *Jack and the Missing Piece* (2004). (Rev: HB 1/05; SLJ 11/04)

874 Schories, Pat. *Jack and the Night Visitors* (PS–K). Illus. 2006, Front St. $13.95 (978-1-932425-33-8). 32pp. Jack the dog and his young master entertain aliens in this wordless but very expressive picture book, the third in a series. (Rev: BL 4/15/06; SLJ 6/06)

875 Schories, Pat. *Jack Wants a Snack* (PS–2). Illus. by author. 2008, Front St. $13.95 (978-1-59078-546-1). A bright dog named Jack disrupts a little girl's tea party in this lively, wordless picture book. (Rev: HB 9/08; SLJ 9/08)

876 Schories, Pat. *When Jack Goes Out* (PS–K). Illus. by author. 2010, Boyds Mills $13.95 (978-1-59078-652-9). 32pp. Jack the dog enjoys a night cavorting with fun-loving aliens, but does he want to go home with them? A wordless book. (Rev: BL 2/15/10; LMC 5–6/10; SLJ 2/1/10*)

877 Schubert, Ingrid, and Dieter Schubert. *The Umbrella* (PS–2). Illus. by authors. 2011, Lemniscaat $16.95 (978-1-9359-5400-2). Unpaged. A small black dog with a red umbrella takes readers on a trip through all Earth's climate zones, from arctic tundra to tropical rain forest in this wordless picture book. (Rev: SLJ 11/1/11)

878 Sís, Peter. *Dinosaur!* (PS–K). Illus. 2000, Greenwillow $16.99 (978-0-688-17049-3). 24pp. In this wordless book, the bath a boy takes with his toy dinosaur is suddenly transformed into a prehistoric scene where many dinosaurs are roaming in their native habitat. (Rev: BCCB 6/00; BL 3/15/00; HB 7/00; HBG 10/00; SLJ 6/00)

879 Staake, Bob. *Bluebird* (PS–1). Illus. by author. 2013, Random House $17.99 (978-037587037-8). 40pp. A beautiful, wordless picture book about a friendship between a bird and a young boy, in which tragedy turns to hope. (Rev: BL 4/15/13*; LMC 10/13; SLJ 3/13)

880 Thomson, Bill. *Chalk* (K–3). Illus. by author. 2010, Marshall Cavendish $15.99 (978-0-7614-5526-4). 40pp. A wordless picture book in which three children find some chalk and draw pictures on a playground that come to life. ℮ (Rev: BLO 3/1/10; SLJ 4/1/10*)

881 Tolman, Marije, and Ronald Tolman. *The Tree House* (PS–1). Illus. by authors. 2010, Boyds Mills $17.95 (978-1-59078-806-6). Unpaged. A variety of different animals have carefree and kindhearted adventures in a magnificent treehouse in this wordless story. (Rev: SLJ 4/1/10)

882 Van Allsburg, Chris. *The Mysteries of Harris Burdick* (2–5). Illus. by author. 1984, Houghton $18.95 (978-0-395-35393-6). 32pp. A group of pictures are presented and youngsters are asked to supply the stories.

883 van Ommen, Sylvia. *The Surprise* (PS–1). Illus. by author. 2007, Front St. $15.95 (978-1-932425-85-7). 32pp. This wordless book presents many mysteries in its story about a sheep who dyes her wool red and then shears it off. What is she doing? (Rev: BL 5/15/07; SLJ 5/07)

884 Varon, Sara. *Chicken and Cat* (PS–2). Illus. 2006, Scholastic $16.99 (978-0-439-63406-9). 20pp. Cat comes to visit Chicken in New York City but is not impressed with urban life, and the two decide to plant a garden; a wordless story that manages to cover a number of themes. (Rev: BL 2/1/06; SLJ 5/06*)

885 Villa, Alvaro F. *Flood* (K–3). Illus. by Alvaro F. Villa. 2013, Capstone $15.95 (978-1-62370-001-0). 32pp. Gripping illustrations take the place of words in this story of a family that has to abandon its home in a fierce storm. (Rev: BLO 3/15/13; SLJ 4/13)

886 Weitzman, Jacqueline Preiss. *You Can't Take a Balloon into the Metropolitan Museum* (K–3). Illus. by Robin P. Glasser. 1998, Dial $18.99 (978-0-8037-2301-6). 35pp. In this wordless picture book, a guard tends a balloon for a girl who is visiting the Metropolitan Museum of Art. When it gets loose, he chases it around Central Park and into the Plaza Hotel. (Rev: BL 11/15/98*; HB 11/98; HBG 3/99; SLJ 12/98)

887 Weitzman, Jacqueline Preiss. *You Can't Take a Balloon into the Museum of Fine Arts* (K–3). 2002, Dial $18.99 (978-0-8037-2570-6). 40pp. In this wordless book, a runaway balloon causes mishaps as it floats around the city of Boston. (Rev: BL 6/1–15/02*; HBG 10/02; SLJ 8/02)

888 Wiesner, David. *Flotsam* (PS–2). Illus. 2006, Clarion $17.00 (978-0-618-19457-5). 40pp. On a visit to the seaside a young boy finds an old-fashioned camera containing a film full of amazing images among the flotsam tossed on the beach in this inventive wordless book. Caldecott Medal, 2007. (Rev: BCCB 9/06; BL 8/06; HB 9/06; HBG 4/07; LMC 1/07; SLJ 9/06*)

889 Wiesner, David. *Free Fall* (PS–K). Illus. by author. 1988, Lothrop LB $17.89 (978-0-688-05584-4); paper $6.99 (978-0-688-10990-5). 32pp. An atlas falls from a boy's lap as he sleeps and opens his imagination to exotic places. (Rev: BCCB 5/88; BL 6/1/88; SLJ 6–7/88)

890 Wiesner, David. *Mr. Wuffles!* (K–3). Illus. by author. 2013, Clarion $17.99 (978-061875661-2). 32pp. Magically surreal, marvelously illustrated, and playfully wordless, this visual story book pits Mr. Wuffles, the standoffish cat, against a tiny spaceship full of alien explorers as they try to plot an escape from being his next prey. ALA Notable Children's Book; Caldecott Honor Book. e (Rev: BL 9/1/13*; LMC 1–2/14*; SLJ 9/13*)

Picture Books

Imaginative Stories

FANTASIES

891 Ada, Alma Flor. *With Love, Little Red Hen* (K–3). Illus. by Leslie Tryon. 2001, Simon & Schuster $16.00 (978-0-689-82581-1). Little Red Hen writes to Hetty Henny about moving to the Hidden Forest, where her neighbors are other characters from children's stories. Third in a series including *Dear Peter Rabbit* (1994) and *Yours Truly, Goldilocks* (1998). (Rev: BL 9/15/01; HB 1/02; HBG 3/02; SLJ 10/01)

892 Ahlberg, Allan. *The Pencil* (K–2). Illus. by Bruce Ingman. 2008, Candlewick $16.99 (978-0-7636-3894-8). 48pp. It's amazing how much trouble a lonely pencil can get into when it starts to draw things — and then to try to erase them. (Rev: BCCB 9/08; HB 1/09; 11/08; SLJ 9/08)

893 Ahlberg, Allan. *Shopping Expedition* (PS–1). Illus. by André Amstutz. 2005, Candlewick $16.99 (978-0-7636-2586-3). 32pp. A fanciful little girl describes how a shopping expedition goes dramatically awry in this story involving blizzards, floods, and jungles. (Rev: BL 5/1/05)

894 Almond, David. *Kate, the Cat and the Moon* (PS–2). Illus. by Steve Lambert. 2005, Doubleday $15.95 (978-0-385-74691-5). 32pp. On a night with a full moon, Kate is transformed into a cat and joins her own pet on a journey through magical scenes under the stars; includes a fold-out. (Rev: BCCB 10/05; BL 7/05; HBG 4/06; LMC 1/06; SLJ 9/05)

895 Anderson, Derek. *Story County: Here We Come!* (PS–1). Illus. by author. 2011, Scholastic $16.99 (978-0-545-16844-1). 40pp. A farmer, a dog, a cow, a pig, and a chicken team up to create a colorful farm with crops such as jelly beans and pizza, all in a bouncy day. Lexile AD190L (Rev: BLO 1/1–15/11; SLJ 2/1/11)

896 Andreae, Giles. *Captain Flinn and the Pirate Dinosaurs* (1–3). Illus. by Russell Ayto. 2005, Simon & Schuster $15.95 (978-1-4169-0713-8). 32pp. A schoolboy finds a pirate crying in his classroom's supply closet and volunteers to help the hapless buccaneer regain control of his ship, which has been stolen by dinosaurs. (Rev: BCCB 12/05; BL 12/1/05; HBG 4/06; SLJ 12/05)

897 Andres, Kristina. *Good Little Wolf* (PS–K). Illus. by author. 2008, North-South $12.95 (978-0-7358-2210-8). 32pp. A toy wolf emphasizes all the characteristics that make him a good wolf in this picture book with tiny, fine illustrations. (Rev: BL 12/1/08; SLJ 12/08)

898 Argueta, Manlio. *Magic Dogs of the Volcanoes: Los Perros Mágicos de los Volcanes* (K–3). Illus. by Elly Simmons. 1990, Children's Book Pr. $14.95 (978-0-89239-064-9). 30pp. From El Salvador, this dual-language book tells the story of the magical dogs that live at the foot of volcanoes. (Rev: SLJ 2/91)

899 Arnold, Caroline. *The Terrible Hodag and the Animal Catchers* (1–3). Illus. by John Sandford. 2006, Front St. $15.95 (978-1-59078-166-1). Olee Swenson and his lumberjack friends help to protect the Hodag, a blueberry-eating monster, from capture. (Rev: BL 4/1/06; HBG 10/06; LMC 1/07; SLJ 3/06)

900 Arrou-Vignod, Jean-Philippe. *Rita and Whatsit* (PS–2). Illus. by Olivier Tallec. 2009, Chronicle $14.99 (978-0-8118-6550-0). 32pp. A talking dog soothes a very grumpy girl. (Rev: BL 6/1–15/09)

901 Ashburn, Boni. *Over at the Castle* (PS–1). Illus. by Kelly Murphy. 2010, Abrams $15.95 (978-0-8109-8414-1). 32pp. The song "Over in the Meadow" is recast in a medieval setting in which the occupants of a castle go about their daily activities until dragons offer a fire display; a counting component adds an extra dimension. (Rev: BL 3/1/10; SLJ 5/1/10)

902 Ashman, Linda. *Rub-a-Dub Sub* (K–2). Illus. by Jeff Mack. 2003, Harcourt $16.00 (978-0-15-202658-5). Rhyming text complemented by vivid artwork follows a little boy on an underwater fantasy in a bright orange submarine. (Rev: HBG 10/03; SLJ 7/03)

903 Auch, Mary Jane. *Monster Brother* (PS–2). Illus. 1994, Holiday House LB $15.95 (978-0-8234-1095-8). 32pp. Rodney is visited by a monster every night, but his brother, Sidney, has a unique solution. (Rev: BCCB 11/94; BL 11/15/94; SLJ 11/94)

904 Averbeck, Jim. *Oh No, Little Dragon* (PS–1). Illus. by author. 2012, Atheneum $14.99 (978-1-41699545-6). 14.99pp. Little Dragon accidentally puts out his flame in the bathtub, and only his mother can bring it back. e (Rev: BL 9/1/12; SLJ 5/1/12)

905 Avi. *Things That Sometimes Happen: Very Short Stories for Little Listeners* (PS). Illus. by Marjorie Priceman. 2002, Simon & Schuster $16.95 (978-0-689-83914-6). 40pp. Lively new illustrations enhance this collection of nine varied stories originally published in 1970. (Rev: BL 10/1/02; HBG 10/03; SLJ 11/02)

906 Aylesworth, Jim. *The Full Belly Bowl* (K–3). Illus. by Wendy A. Halperin. 1999, Simon & Schuster $16.00 (978-0-689-81033-6). 40pp. In this handsomely illustrated tale, an old man who is always hungry is given a magical food bowl by a tiny creature he has saved from being eaten by a fox. (Rev: BCCB 12/99; BL 11/1/99*; HBG 3/00; SLJ 10/99)

907 Aylesworth, Jim. *The Tale of Tricky Fox* (PS–2). Illus. by Barbara McClintock. 2001, Scholastic $16.95 (978-0-439-09543-3). 32pp. Tricky Fox, who thinks he has caught a pig for dinner, is outwitted by an old woman who puts a ferocious bulldog in the fox's sack instead. (Rev: BCCB 3/01; BL 2/1/01; HB 3/01*; HBG 10/01; SLJ 3/01)

908 Babin, Claire. *Gus Is a Tree* (K–3). Illus. by Olivier Tallec. 2008, Enchanted Lion $14.95 (978-1-59270-078-3). Gus drowses in the schoolyard and dreams he is a big tree feeling wind, night, and rain. (Rev: SLJ 12/08)

909 Baca, Ana. *Benito's Sopaipillas / La sopaipillas de Benito* (2–4). Trans. from Spanish by Carolina Villarroel. Illus. by Anthony Accardo. 2007, Arte Publico $15.95 (978-1-55885-370-6). Cristina's aunt tells her the story of her great-grandfather Benito and how he made it rain by making sopaipillas, a kind of fried pastry. In English and Spanish. (Rev: SLJ 7/07)

910 Baeten, Lieve. *The Clever Little Witch* (PS–2). Illus. by Wietse Fossey. 2012, NorthSouth $16.95 (978-0-7358-4079-9). 32pp. Lizzy's efforts to open a mysterious suitcase by using spells do not work, so she consults older witches and, with their advice, succeeds — to find a letter inviting her to attend Witch School. (Rev: BLO 4/15/12; SLJ 4/1/12)

911 Baeten, Lieve. *The Curious Little Witch* (PS–2). Illus. by author. 2010, NorthSouth $16.95 (978-0-7358-2305-1). 32pp. An over-curious young witch named Lizzy finds herself in the home of benevolent older witches, who enhance her broken broomstick and send her on her way. Also use *Happy Birthday, Little Witch* (2011) in which Lizzy searches for her missing black cat. (Rev: BL 9/15/10; LMC 1–2/11; SLJ 11/1/10)

912 Baicker, Karen. *Pea Pod Babies* (PS). Illus. by Sam Williams. 2003, Handprint $15.95 (978-1-59354-003-6). In this appealing rhyming story, three babies growing up in a pea pod resent their similarity and go their own ways. (Rev: BL 11/15/03; HBG 4/04; SLJ 12/03)

913 Baker, Ken. *Old MacDonald Had a Dragon* (PS–K). Illus. by Christopher Santoro. 2012, Amazon $16.99 (978-0-7614-6175-3). 32pp. Old MacDonald has expanded his farm, and when he starts singing about his new dragon, the other animals begin to complain until the dragon eats them and the farmer; luckily, they know just what to do to convince the dragon to let them go. e (Rev: SLJ 1/13)

914 Baker, Lisa. *Harold and the Purple Crayon: Dinosaur Days* (PS–1). Illus. Series: Harold and the Purple Crayon. 2002, HarperCollins $14.99 (978-0-06-000541-2). 40pp. Harold uses his crayon to journey to a jungle and play with dinosaurs. (Rev: BL 2/15/03; HBG 3/03; SLJ 1/03)

915 Balouch, Kristen. *Mystery Bottle* (K–3). Illus. 2006, Hyperion $15.99 (978-0-7868-0999-8). 32pp. A mysterious bottle whisks a 7-year-old boy on a fantastical journey to Iran and a meeting with his grandfather. (Rev: BL 2/1/06)

916 Bang, Molly. *The Paper Crane* (PS–1). 1985, Greenwillow paper $6.99 (978-0-688-07333-6). 32pp. A paper crane left by a thankful stranger leads to good fortune for a restaurant owner down on his luck. (Rev: BCCB 3/86; BL 1/15/86; HB 1/86)

917 Banks, Kate. *The Eraserheads* (PS–2). Illus. by Boris Kulikov. 2010, Farrar $16.99 (978-0-374-39920-7). 40pp. Three animal-shaped erasers find themselves on a fantastic and dangerous trip as they try to help a young boy with his homework. (Rev: BL 1/1/10; SLJ 5/1/10)

918 Banks, Kate. *Max's Dragon* (PS–2). Illus. by Boris Kulikov. 2008, Farrar $16.95 (978-0-374-39921-4). Max's interest in wordplay draws his croquet-playing brothers in when his supposed dragon in the clouds is closely followed by a thunderstorm. (Rev: BL 3/1/08; HB 3/08; SLJ 2/08)

919 Barnett, Mac. *Extra Yarn* (K–2). Illus. by Jon Klassen. 2012, HarperCollins $16.99 (978-0-06-195338-5). 40pp. Annabelle has a seemingly unending supply of yarn and knits sweaters for all the people, animals, and buildings of the town . . . and then an evil archduke arrives. Boston Globe–Horn Book Award. (Rev: BL 12/15/11*; HB 1–2/12; SLJ 12/1/11)

920 Barrett, Judith. *Cloudy with a Chance of Meatballs* (K–3). Illus. by Ron Barrett. 1978, Macmillan $16.00 (978-0-689-30647-1); paper $5.99 (978-0-689-70749-0). 32pp. In the land of ChewandSwallow, food falls from the skies.

921 Barrett, Judith. *Pickles to Pittsburgh: The Sequel to Cloudy with a Chance of Meatballs* (K–2). Illus. by Ron Barrett. 1997, Simon & Schuster $16.00 (978-0-689-80104-4). The people of the town of Chewandswallow take all their excess food and distribute it around the world — for example, eggplants to Ecuador and pickles to Pittsburgh. (Rev: HBG 3/98; SLJ 11/97)

922 Bartoletti, Susan Campbell. *Naamah and the Ark at Night* (PS–1). Illus. by Holly Meade. 2011, Candlewick $16.99 (978-0-7636-4242-6). 32pp. In this reimagined story with rhyming text, Bartoletti pictures Noah's wife as a soothing singer who helps calm the animals and people aboard the Ark. (Rev: BL 11/1/11*; SLJ 7/11)

923 Bateman, Teresa. *Fiona's Luck* (K–5). Illus. by Kelly Murphy. 2007, Charlesbridge $15.95 (978-1-57091-651-9). A leprechaun king gets upset with humans' profligate use of luck and steals the luck away, leaving an unhappy population and a girl called Fiona who is determined to get it back; set against the backdrop of the potato famine. (Rev: SLJ 4/07) ◯

924 Bateman, Teresa. *Harp O' Gold* (PS–2). Illus. by Jill Weber. 2001, Holiday House $16.95 (978-0-8234-1523-6). 32pp. When Irish minstrel Tom trades his old harp for a new bright gold one owned by a leprechaun, he knows he has made a good exchange but still longs for his old harp. (Rev: BL 3/1/01; HBG 10/01)

925 Bateman, Teresa. *Keeper of Soles* (K–2). Illus. by Yayo. 2006, Holiday $16.95 (978-0-8234-1734-6). 32pp. Colin the cobbler outsmarts the Grim Reaper, persuading him he needs "soles" not "souls" and offering him progressively more impressive footwear. (Rev: BL 3/1/06; SLJ 4/06)

926 Bateman, Teresa. *The Merbaby* (1–3). Illus. by Patience Brewster. 2001, Holiday House $16.95 (978-0-8234-1531-1). A fisherman catches a merbaby and is rewarded when he returns it to the sea. (Rev: BCCB 9/01; BL 9/15/01; HBG 3/02; SLJ 1/02)

927 Bauer, Marion Dane. *If Frogs Made Weather* (PS–2). Illus. by Dorothy Donohue. 2005, Holiday House $16.95 (978-0-8234-1622-6). A boy speculates about how the weather would be if the animals had their way. (Rev: SLJ 5/05)

928 Bauer, Marion Dane. *If You Had a Nose Like an Elephant's Trunk* (PS–3). Illus. by Susan Winter. 2001, Holiday House $16.95 (978-0-8234-1589-2). 32pp. A girl playfully imagines what she could do if she had the features or attributes of different animals. (Rev: BL 9/15/01; HBG 3/02; SLJ 9/01)

929 Baum, L. Frank. *The Wizard of Oz* (K–3). Illus. by Lisbeth Zwerger. 1996, North-South $19.95 (978-1-55858-638-3). 103pp. A Viennese artist reworks this classic tale with unusual, refreshing illustrations and an abridged text. (Rev: BL 10/15/96; SLJ 11/96*)

930 Baumgart, Klaus. *Laura's Secret* (PS–2). Trans. from German by Judy Waite. Illus. by author. 2003, Tiger Tales $16.95 (978-1-58925-031-4). Laura makes a wish on her secret star and soon the kite she and her younger brother Tommy made is flying high. (Rev: SLJ 1/04)

931 Baynton, Martin. *Jane and the Dragon* (K–3). Illus. by author. 2007, Candlewick paper $4.99 (978-0-7636-3570-1). In her zeal to become a knight despite those who say all knights are men, Jane sets out to rescue the prince from a dragon, becomes a great friend of the dragon, and goes on to become a real knight; a tie-in to an animated TV series. (Rev: SLJ 4/07)

932 Beaty, Andrea. *When Giants Come To Play* (PS–2). Illus. by Kevin Hawkes. 2006, Abrams $16.95 (978-0-8109-5759-6). 32pp. Young Anna whiles away an idyllic summer afternoon in the company of two very large playmates. (Rev: BL 9/15/06; SLJ 10/06)

933 Beck, Andrea. *Elliot Digs for Treasure* (PS–2). Illus. 2001, Kids Can $12.95 (978-1-55074-806-2). 32pp. When stuffed toy Elliot Moose and his friends decide to dig for buried treasure they get stuck in the hole, and only persistence and cooperation can get them out. (Rev: BL 11/1/01; HBG 3/02; SLJ 11/01)

934 Beck, Andrea. *Elliot's Emergency* (PS–2). Illus. 1998, Kids Can $12.95 (978-1-55074-441-5). 32pp. Elliot Moose, a stuffed toy, panics when he snags his fur on a nail. His friend Beaverton sews him up good as new. (Rev: BL 11/15/98; HBG 3/99; SLJ 12/98)

935 Beck, Ian. *Teddy's Snowy Day* (PS–K). Illus. 2002, Scholastic $15.95 (978-0-439-17520-3). 32pp. The simple story of a teddy bear who gets left out in the snow, has a wonderful time at first, and happily finds a ride home when he tires. (Rev: BL 10/1/02; HBG 3/03; SLJ 10/02)

936 Bee, William. *Beware of the Frog* (1–4). Illus. by author. 2008, Candlewick $15.99 (978-0-7636-3920-4). A frog protects old Mrs. Collywobbles, gobbling up those who threaten her — Greedy Goblin, Smelly Troll, and Giant Hungry Ogre. (Rev: LMC 1/09; SLJ 7/08)

937 Bell, Cece. *Sock Monkey Boogie-Woogie: A Friend Is Made* (PS–2). Illus. 2004, Candlewick $14.99 (978-0-7636-2392-0). 32pp. Sock Monkey creates the dance partner of his dreams — out of argyle socks — in this energetic romp about a Big Celebrity Dance. (Rev: BL 1/1–15/05; SLJ 1/05)

938 Bell, Cece. *Sock Monkey Goes to Hollywood: A Star Is Bathed* (PS–K). Illus. by author. 2003, Candlewick $13.99 (978-0-7636-1962-6). When Sock Monkey is nominated for an Oswald Award as Best Supporting Toy in a motion picture, he faces the challenge of getting clean enough to attend. (Rev: HBG 4/04; SLJ 12/03)

939 Bell, Cece. *Sock Monkey Rides Again* (PS–2). Illus. by author. 2007, Candlewick $13.99 (978-0-7636-3089-8). Cast in a starring role as a singing cowboy, Sock Monkey seems poised to make it big, but his future begins to look a little shaky when he can't bring himself to kiss the leading lady. (Rev: SLJ 1/07)

940 Bently, Peter. *King Jack and the Dragon* (PS–K). Illus. by Helen Oxenbury. 2011, Dial $17.99 (978-0-8037-3698-6). 32pp. Three diapered boys build a cardboard castle and fight dragons in this imaginative adventure with spare, rhyming text. (Rev: BL 9/1/11; SLJ 9/1/11*)

941 Berger, Lou. *The Elephant Wish* (PS–3). Illus. by Ana Juan. 2008, Random $16.99 (978-0-375-83962-7). 48pp. Eliza gets her birthday wish and sets off on an elephant-borne adventure only to find an elderly neighbor has followed her. (Rev: BL 12/1/08; SLJ 9/08)

942 Bergman, Mara. *Snip Snap! What's That?* (PS–2). Illus. by Nick Maland. 2005, Greenwillow $16.99 (978-0-06-077754-8). 32pp. When an alligator creeps into their apartment, three children frighten him back into a manhole in this picture book with a refrain made for shouting. (Rev: BL 3/1/05; SLJ 6/05)

943 Berkeley, Jon. *Chopsticks* (2–4). Illus. 2005, Random $16.95 (978-0-375-83309-0). 32pp. When the moon is full over Hong Kong, Chopsticks the mouse and a wooden dragon he helped to free take off on wonderful adventures. (Rev: BL 12/1/05; SLJ 12/05)

944 Bernheimer, Kate. *The Girl in the Castle Inside the Museum* (PS–1). Illus. by Nicoletta Ceccoli. 2008, Random $16.99 (978-0-375-83606-0). 32pp. A lonely little girl who lives in a tiny castle inside a snow globe, inside a museum, tries to think of a way to find some friends. (Rev: BCCB 2/08; BL 6/1–15/08; LMC 3/08; SLJ 2/08)

945 Bertrand, Lynne. *Granite Baby* (K–2). Illus. by Kevin Hawkes. 2005, Farrar $16.00 (978-0-374-32761-3). 40pp. A tall tale set in New Hampshire about five giant sisters who learn to care for a tiny baby one of them carves from granite. (Rev: BL 4/1/05; SLJ 4/05)

946 Biedrzycki, David. *Me and My Dragon* (K–2). Illus. by author. 2011, Charlesbridge $16.95 (978-1-58089-278-0); paper $7.95 (978-1-58089-279-7). Unpaged. A young boy imagines all the fun he could have with a pet dragon. ℮ (Rev: SLJ 7/11)

947 Bird, Betsy. *Giant Dance Party* (K–3). Illus. by Brandon Dorman. 2013, Greenwillow $17.99 (978-0-06-196083-3). 32pp. Lexy loves to dance but has stage fright, so she opts to teach instead, but her only customers are a herd of furry blue giants. (Rev: BL 6/13; SLJ 4/13)

948 Blackstone, Stella. *An Island in the Sun* (K–3). Illus. by Nicoletta Ceccoli. 2002, Barefoot Books $15.99 (978-1-84148-193-7). 24pp. A boy in a small sailboat visits an island where he plays with a polka-dot dog before taking him home at night. (Rev: BL 5/1/02; HBG 10/02; SLJ 7/02)

949 Blaikie, Lynn. *Beyond the Northern Lights* (PS–2). Illus. 2006, Fitzhenry & Whiteside $16.95 (978-1-55005-123-0). 32pp. A young girl imagines wonderful flights with a raven to the seas and skies of the north of the world. (Rev: BL 1/1–15/07; SLJ 3/07)

950 Bond, Rebecca. *The Great Doughnut Parade* (PS–K). Illus. by author. 2007, Houghton $17.00 (978-0-618-77705-1). A small boy with a doughnut tied to his belt attracts a parade of human and animal followers. (Rev: BL 10/1/07; SLJ 9/07)

951 Bowen, Anne. *I Know an Old Teacher* (K–3). Illus. by Stephen Gammell. 2008, Carolrhoda $16.95 (978-0-8225-7984-7). 32pp. As her students watch in horror, their teacher eats the class pets she has taken home for the weekend; told in a traditional cumulative pattern. (Rev: BCCB 9/08; BL 8/08; LMC 3/09; SLJ 9/08)

952 Bowen, Anne. *Tooth Fairy's First Night* (K–2). Illus. by Jon Berkeley. 2005, Carolrhoda $15.95 (978-1-57505-753-8). A young tooth fairy finds her first assignment more taxing than she expected. (Rev: SLJ 6/05)

953 Bradman, Tony. *Red Riding Hood Takes Charge* (2–5). Illus. by Sarah Warburton. Series: After Happily Ever After. 2009, Stone Arch $17.99 (978-1-4342-1308-2). 56pp. After her bad experience with the wolf, Little Red's grandmother is lonely and her granddaughter searches for ways to cheer her up. (Rev: BLO 3/19/09; SLJ 6/09)

954 Breathed, Berkeley. *Mars Needs Moms!* (PS–2). Illus. 2007, Philomel $16.99 (978-0-399-24736-1). After Milo's mom is abducted by Martians, he learns to appreciate all the things mothers do in this hilarious and brightly illustrated book. (Rev: BCCB 4/07; BL 5/1/07; SLJ 5/07)

955 Brennan-Nelson, Denise. *He's Been a Monster All Day!* (PS–K). Illus. by Cyd Moore. 2013, Sleeping Bear $14.99 (978-1-58536-827-3). 32pp. A mother's complaint spawns many fantasies in a little boy's mind. (Rev: BL 3/15/13; SLJ 8/13)

956 Briant, Ed. *Don't Look Now* (K–2). Illus. by author. 2009, Roaring Brook $16.95 (978-1-59643-345-8). 32pp. This graphic novel fantasy of few words features two brothers who learn to work together. (Rev: HB 5/09; SLJ 6/09)

957 Bright, Rachel. *Love Monster* (PS–K). Illus. by author. 2013, Farrar $16.99 (978-037434646-1). 32pp. Monster decides that he must find someone to love him, but this is hard in the town of Cutesville, where children prefer bunnies and kittens to googly-eyed monsters. (Rev: BL 11/1/13; SLJ 11/13)

958 Brisson, Pat. *Tap-Dance Fever* (PS–2). Illus. by Nancy Cote. 2005, Boyds Mills $15.95 (978-1-59078-290-3). 32pp. Annabelle Applegate's nonstop tap dancing annoys her neighbors — until the day her tapping charms the rattlesnakes. (Rev: BL 3/1/05; SLJ 3/05)

959 Bromley, Nick. *Open Very Carefully: A Book with Bite* (PS–1). Illus. by Nicola O'Byrne. 2013, Candlewick $15.99 (978-0-7636-6163-2). 32pp. A hungry crocodile wreaks havoc when he falls into a picture book. (Rev: BLO 6/13; SLJ 4/13)

960 Brown, Calef. *Tippintown: A Guided Tour* (PS–2). Illus. by author. 2003, Houghton $16.00 (978-0-618-14972-8). This rollicking, brightly illustrated story, told in rhyme, transports young readers to the magical world of Tippintown, where the guide has an elephant's trunk and the gargoyles play games. (Rev: HBG 10/03; SLJ 5/03)

961 Brown, Jeff. *Flat Stanley* (K–3). Illus. by Scott Nash. 2006, HarperCollins $16.99 (978-0-06-112904-9). Flattened to a thickness of half an inch, Stanley Lambchop discovers that his new shape has some decided advantages in this new version of the book published in 1964. (Rev: SLJ 12/06)

962 Brown, Jeff. *Invisible Stanley* (2–3). Illus. by Steve Björkman. 1996, HarperCollins paper $4.25 (978-0-06-442029-7). 81pp. When Stanley suddenly becomes invisible, he performs many humanitarian acts, including foiling a bank robbery. (Rev: SLJ 12/96)

963 Browne, Anthony. *My Dad* (PS–3). Illus. 2001, Farrar $16.00 (978-0-374-35101-4). A little boy imagines all the things his dad could do if he wanted — walk on a tightrope or sing in the opera, for example. (Rev: BL 3/1/01; HBG 10/01)

964 Brownlow, Mike. *Mickey Moonbeam* (PS–2). Illus. by author. 2006, Bloomsbury $16.95 (978-1-58234-704-2). Mickey Moonbeam receives a distress call from his pen pal Quiggle and rushes in his spaceship to the rescue, only to discover that Quiggle is gigantic! (Rev: SLJ 11/06)

965 Brumbeau, Jeff. *The Quiltmaker's Journey* (K–3). Illus. by Gail de Marken. 2005, Scholastic $17.95 (978-0-439-51219-0). 56pp. Readers find out what prompted a young girl to become the Quiltmaker in this prequel to *The Quiltmaker's Gift* (1999); with bright quilt-themed illustrations. (Rev: BL 3/1/05; SLJ 4/05)

966 Bryan, Sean. *A Boy and His Bunny* (PS–1). Illus. by Tom Murphy. 2005, Arcade $14.95 (978-1-55970-725-1). A boy wakes up with a bunny on his head but allays his mother's concerns with the reassurance that this will in no way limit his activities. (Rev: SLJ 6/05)

967 Buehner, Caralyn. *Snowmen at Night* (PS). Illus. by Mark Buehner. 2002, Penguin $15.99 (978-0-8037-2550-8). 32pp. Captivating illustrations and breezy text put snowmen into action (sledding, playing baseball, and drinking iced cocoa), revealing why snowmen look so tuckered out in the mornings. (Rev: BL 10/15/02; HBG 3/03; SLJ 10/02)

968 Bunting, Eve. *My Robot* (K–2). Illus. by Dagmar Fehlau. Series: Green Light Reader. 2006, Harcourt $12.95 (978-0-15-205593-6). 24pp. In this beginning reader with brief sentences and a repetitive refrain, a young African American boy describes the attributes of Cecil, the robot who is his best friend. (Rev: BL 3/15/06; SLJ 6/06)

969 Bunting, Eve. *Night of the Gargoyles* (PS–3). Illus. by David Wiesner. 1994, Clarion $16.00 (978-0-395-66553-4). A horror story in which gargoyles come alive at night. (Rev: BCCB 11/94; BL 10/1/94; SLJ 10/94*)

970 Bunting, Eve. *Pirate Boy* (PS–1). Illus. by Julie Fortenberry. 2011, Holiday House $16.95 (978-0-8234-2321-7). 32pp. Danny wonders about becoming a pirate but has his doubts about the wisdom of this plan; his mother reassures him that she will always come and get him. (Rev: BL 10/15/11; SLJ 9/1/11)

971 Bunting, Eve. *That's What Leprechauns Do* (PS–2). Illus. by Emily Arnold McCully. 2006, Clarion $16.00 (978-0-618-35410-8). 32pp. The job of three leprechauns is to place the pot of gold at the end of rainbows, but mischief often diverts them, and nobody ever finds the gold anyway. (Rev: BL 1/1–15/06; SLJ 2/06)

972 Burell, Sarah. *Diamond Jim Dandy and the Sheriff* (K–1). Illus. by Bryan Langdo. 2010, Sterling $14.95 (978-1-4027-5737-2). 32pp. Dustpan, Texas, finds itself in a tizzy when a friendly and talented rattlesnake comes to town. (Rev: BL 2/15/10; LMC 5–6/10; SLJ 3/1/10)

973 Burningham, John. *The Magic Bed* (PS). Illus. by author. 2003, Knopf LB $18.99 (978-0-375-92423-1). Georgie chooses an antique bed to replace his crib and soon finds his nights are full of magical adventures. (Rev: HBG 4/04; SLJ 10/03)

974 Burningham, John. *Mr. Grumpy's Outing* (PS–K). Illus. 2001, Holt $6.95 (978-0-8050-6629-6). 20pp. A board-book version of the tale of Mr. Grumpy and the animals he takes for a trip down the river. (Rev: BL 4/1/01; HBG 3/02)

975 Burns, Marilyn. *The Greedy Triangle* (K–3). Illus. by Gordon Silveria. 1995, Scholastic $16.95 (978-0-590-48991-1). A little triangle is tired of his shape and becomes a quadrilateral. (Rev: BCCB 3/95; BL 2/1/95; SLJ 3/95)

976 Calvert, Pam. *Princess Peepers Picks a Pet* (K–2). Illus. by Tuesday Mourning. 2011, Marshall Cavendish $16.99 (978-0-7614-5815-9). Unpaged. Princess Peepers loses her glasses on a trip to the forest to select a nice animal for the pet show at the Royal Academy for Perfect Princesses and mistakes a dragon for a unicorn. (Rev: SLJ 4/11)

977 Carle, Eric. *Draw Me a Star* (PS–2). Illus. 1992, Penguin $16.99 (978-0-399-21877-4). The story of creation is told through the artist's drawings of various objects. (Rev: BCCB 12/92; BL 9/15/92; SLJ 10/92)

978 Carle, Eric. *Little Cloud* (PS–K). Illus. 1996, Penguin $16.99 (978-0-399-23034-9). 32pp. A little cloud transforms itself into a variety of shapes and finally produces rain. (Rev: BL 4/1/96; HB 5/96; SLJ 5/96)

979 Carle, Eric. *Papa, Please Get the Moon for Me* (PS–K). Illus. by author. 1986, Picture Book $19.00 (978-0-88708-026-5). 32pp. A little girl's father gets a high ladder to climb to the moon, but has to admit it's too large to bring home. (Rev: BL 6/1/86; SLJ 8/86)

980 Carle, Eric. *10 Little Rubber Ducks* (PS–1). Illus. 2005, HarperCollins LB $20.89 (978-0-06-074076-4). Ten rubber ducks fall off a ship and float off in different directions; the tenth is adopted by a mother duck despite the fact that it can only squeak, not quack. (Rev: BL 5/1/05; SLJ 1/05)

981 Carr, Jan. *Greedy Apostrophe: A Cautionary Tale* (1–3). Illus. by Ethan Long. 2007, Holiday House $16.95 (978-0-8234-2006-3). Greedy Apostrophe keeps showing up where he shouldn't in this amusing story about a commonly misused punctuation mark. (Rev: SLJ 7/07)

982 Carroll, Lewis. *Alice's Adventures in Wonderland* (K–6). Illus. by Robert Sabuda. 2003, Simon & Schuster $24.95 (978-0-689-84743-1). Dazzling — but perhaps delicate — pop-ups adorn this faithful adaptation of Lewis Carroll's classic story. (Rev: BL 3/15/04; HB 11/03; HBG 4/04; SLJ 11/03)

983 Casanova, Mary. *One-Dog Sleigh* (PS–1). Illus. by Ard Hoyt. 2013, Farrar $16.99 (978-037435639-2). 32pp. A young girl and her dog set off for a ride in their little red sleigh, but the sleigh becomes increasingly crowded as a multitude of animals ask to come along in this rhyming cumulative tale. **e** (Rev: BLO 9/15/13; LMC 3–4/14; SLJ 9/13)

984 Chabon, Michael. *The Astonishing Secret of Awesome Man* (PS–2). Illus. by Jake Parker. 2011, HarperCollins $17.99 (978-0-06-191462-1). 40pp. A young superhero describes and then demonstrates his amazing powers, admitting at the same time that Mom is always waiting at the Fortress of Awesome with cheese and crackers and chocolate milk. (Rev: BL 9/15/11; SLJ 8/1/11*)

985 Chang, Grace. *Jin Jin the Dragon* (1–3). Illus. by Chong Chang. 2008, Enchanted Lion $16.95 (978-1-59270-102-5). 45pp. Jin Jin, a golden dragon, meets many animals on his quest to find his true identity in this well-written book that features Chinese watercolors and information on dragons' importance in China. (Rev: LMC 11/08; SLJ 7/08)

986 Charlip, Remy, and Burton Supree. *Mother Mother I Feel Sick Send for the Doctor Quick Quick Quick* (PS–K). Illus. 2001, Tricycle $16.95 (978-1-58246-043-7). 48pp. A boy who complains of being sick is operated on and objects including a teapot and a bicycle are removed from his stomach. (Rev: BL 3/1/01; HBG 10/01)

987 Child, Lauren. *Who's Afraid of the Big Bad Book?* (K–3). Illus. by author. 2003, Hyperion $16.99 (978-0-7868-0926-4). While reading his favorite book of fairy tales, young Herb falls asleep and awakes to find himself in the middle of a fairy tale world in which the characters scold him for treating their book badly. (Rev: BCCB 1/04; BL 1/1–15/04; HBG 4/04; SLJ 12/03)

988 Christelow, Eileen. *The Desperate Dog Writes Again* (PS–2). Illus. by author. 2010, Clarion $16.99 (978-0-547-24205-7). 40pp. Worried about her human's relationship with another human, Emma the dog consults Queenie, the canine advice columnist. (Rev: BL 10/15/10; SLJ 1/1/11)

989 Cleminson, Katie. *Cuddle Up, Goodnight* (PS–K). Illus. by author. 2011, Hyperion/Disney $15.99 (978-1-4231-3844-0). 32pp. A young boy and his animal friends — an elephant, a raccoon, a hippo, a polar bear — have a variety of daytime adventures, including mealtime, naptime, play time, and bath time, ending up with bedtime. (Rev: BL 1/1–15/11; HB 1–2/11; LMC 3/1/11; SLJ 2/1/11)

990 Clibbon, Meg. *Imagine You're a Mermaid!* (K–4). Illus. by Lucy Clibbon. Series: Imagine This! 2003, Annick $19.95 (978-1-55037-791-0); paper $7.95 (978-1-55037-790-3). A pun-filled book all about mermaids and what they're really like. (Rev: SLJ 3/04)

991 Cohen, Caron Lee. *Broom, Zoom!* (PS–K). Illus. by Sergio Ruzzier. 2010, Simon & Schuster $12.99 (978-1-4169-9113-7). 32pp. After an initial disagreement about who needs the broom most, Little Witch and Little Monster agree to share and cooperate. (Rev: BL 9/1/10; HB 9–10/10; SLJ 9/1/10)

992 Cole, Babette. *Princess Smartypants Rules* (1–3). Illus. Series: Princess Smartypants. 2005, Penguin $15.99 (978-0-399-24349-3). 32pp. A superbaby turns Princess Smartypants' world upside-down in this zany tale that includes dragons, an evil count, and a prince. (Rev: BL 3/1/05; SLJ 3/05)

993 Cole, Brock. *Good Enough to Eat* (PS–3). Illus. by author. 2007, Farrar $16.00 (978-0-374-32737-8). 32pp. Frightened villagers offer a helpless girl with no name to a giant ogre, but the girl gets the best of them all with a little magic. (Rev: BCCB 11/07; BL 10/1/07; HB 9/07; SLJ 1/08)

994 Collins, Ross. *Doodleday* (PS–K). Illus. by author. 2011, Whitman $16.99 (978-0-8075-1683-6). 32pp. Henry is warned not to draw on Doodleday but he goes ahead and draws a fly, then a spider, and more; each successive animal comes to life and risks creating havoc until his mother rushes home to save the day. (Rev: BL 3/1/11; SLJ 5/1/11)

995 Coplestone, Lis. *Noah's Bed* (PS–2). Illus. by Jim Coplestone. 2004, Frances Lincoln $14.95 (978-1-84507-002-1). Frightened by the torrential rainstorm, various animals sneak one by one into bed with Noah, Mrs. Noah, and grandson Eber. (Rev: SLJ 6/04)

996 Coristine, Philip. *Serena and the Wild Doll* (K–3). Illus. by Julia Gukova. 2000, Annick LB $19.95 (978-1-55037-649-4); paper $6.95 (978-1-55037-648-7). 32pp. Serena, a proper doll who lives in an attic, is joined by a wild doll in a tattered dress and a fox, and the three venture out to see the city. (Rev: BL 2/15/01; HBG 3/01; SLJ 11/00)

997 Cottringer, Anne. *Eliot Jones, Midnight Superhero* (PS–2). Illus. by Alex T. Smith. 2009, Tiger Tales $15.95 (978-1-58925-083-3); paper $7.95 (978-1-58925-416-9). Unpaged. Eliot becomes a superhero each night at midnight and embarks on a mission to save Earth from a giant meteor. (Rev: LMC 11–12/09; SLJ 9/1/09)

998 Cowen-Fletcher, Jane. *Nell's Elf* (K–2). Illus. by author. 2006, Candlewick $14.99 (978-0-7636-2391-3). A little girl bored on a rainy day cheers up when the elf she draws comes alive and shows her how to enjoy life. (Rev: SLJ 4/06)

999 Cowley, Joy. *Chicken Feathers* (3–5). Illus. by David Elliot. 2008, Philomel $15.99 (978-0-399-24791-0). 160pp. While Josh's mother is in hospital awaiting the arrival of a new baby, Josh is also preoccupied with his talking pet hen, Semolina, who alerts him to a fox plot. (Rev: BL 5/15/08; HB 5/08; LMC 8/08; SLJ 4/08)

1000 Cowley, Joy. *Mrs. Wishy-Washy's Farm* (PS–1). Illus. by Elizabeth Fuller. 2003, Philomel $15.99 (978-0-399-23872-7). Obsessed with cleanliness, Mrs. Wishy-Washy decides it's time to scrub all the animals on the farm; to escape their date with the tub, her cow, duck, and pig run off, only to find themselves in loads of trouble and longing to be reunited with their master. (Rev: HBG 10/03; SLJ 7/03)

1001 Crew, Gary. *Pig on the Titanic: A True Story* (K–2). Illus. by Bruce Whatley. 2005, HarperCollins LB $18.89 (978-0-06-052306-0). 32pp. A music-box pig named Maxixe describes the sinking of the *Titanic* and how his music keeps up the spirits of the children in his lifeboat in this compelling story based on reality. (Rev: BL 6/1–15/05; SLJ 5/05)

1002 Crummel, Susan Stevens. *All in One Hour* (PS–1). Illus. by Dorothy Donohue. 2003, Marshall Cavendish $16.95 (978-0-7614-5129-7). 32pp. Paper-cut collage illustrations tell a "This Is the House That Jack Built" type story featuring a mouse, a cat, a dog, a dogcatcher, a robber, and a police officer. (Rev: BL 3/15/03; HBG 10/03; SLJ 5/03)

1003 Cullen, Lynn. *Little Scraggly Hair: A Dog on Noah's Ark* (PS–3). Illus. by Jacqueline Rogers. 2003, Holiday House $16.95 (978-0-8234-1772-8). With an Appalachian flair, this tells the story of Noah's ark and as a bonus explains why dogs have wet noses. (Rev: BCCB 2/04; BL 11/1/03; HBG 4/04; SLJ 12/03)

1004 Cumming, Hannah. *The Red Boat* (PS–1). Illus. by author. 2012, Child's Play $16.99 (978-1-84643-493-8). 32pp. A red rowboat takes Posy and her dog George on magical journeys in this nicely illustrated book about a girl who has just moved and is lonely. (Rev: BL 11/1/12; SLJ 1/13)

1005 Cuyler, Margery. *Monster Mess!* (PS). Illus. by S. D. Schindler. 2008, Simon & Schuster $14.99 (978-0-689-86405-6). 40pp. A tired monster feels he has to clean up a little boy's bedroom before he can go to sleep. (Rev: BL 6/1–15/08; SLJ 7/08)

1006 Czernecki, Stefan. *Lilliput 5357* (PS–2). Illus. by author. 2006, Simply Read $16.95 (978-1-894965-32-3). Driven from his playground by a bunch of bullies, Lilliput 5357, a diminutive robot, searches desperately for somewhere new to play. (Rev: SLJ 4/06)

1007 Davies, Jacqueline. *The House Takes a Vacation* (1–3). Illus. by Lee White. 2007, Marshall Cavendish $16.99 (978-0-7614-5331-4). Readers who enjoy puns will appreciate this story about a house that decides it deserves a vacation as much as its residents do. (Rev: SLJ 5/07)

1008 Davol, Marguerite W. *The Paper Dragon* (PS–3). Illus. by Robert Sabuda. 1997, Simon & Schuster $18.00 (978-0-689-31992-1). This story set in China tells how Mi Fei accomplishes his task of putting a destructive dragon to sleep. (Rev: BL 10/15/97*; HBG 3/98; SLJ 11/97)

1009 de Monfreid, Dorothée. *Dark Night* (PS–K). Illus. by author. 2009, Random $14.99 (978-0-375-85687-7). 40pp. Scared by the animals in the forest, little Felix ends up in a rabbit's home and there finds a devil's mask with which he manages to escape — but then there are a lot of frightened beasts to reassure. (Rev: BL 7/09)

1010 Deeble, Jason. *Sir Ryan's Quest* (K–3). Illus. by author. 2009, Roaring Brook $16.95 (978-1-59643-330-4). With saucepan-helmet on head, little Sir Ryan sets out on a knightly household adventure. (Rev: BL 4/1/09; SLJ 4/09)

1011 Deedy, Carmen A. *The Library Dragon* (K–2). Illus. by Michael P. White. 1994, Peachtree $16.95 (978-1-56145-091-6). The new librarian is a real fire-breathing dragon who in time learns to trust children with her books. (Rev: BCCB 2/95; SLJ 12/94)

1012 DeFelice, Cynthia. *One Potato, Two Potato* (1–3). 2006, Farrar $16.00 (978-0-374-35640-8). 32pp. A poor elderly Irish couple used to sharing their one chair, their one coat, are down to their last potato when they discover a magic pot in this appealing adaptation of a Chinese folk tale. (Rev: BL 9/1/06; SLJ 8/06)

1013 Demi. *The Boy Who Painted Dragons* (K–2). Illus. by author. 2007, Simon & Schuster $21.99 (978-1-4169-2469-2). 52pp. A boy named Ping paints dragons everywhere, but is secretly afraid of them and is forced to face his fears. (Rev: BL 9/15/07; LMC 11/07; SLJ 9/07)

1014 Demi. *Liang and the Magic Paintbrush* (2–4). Illus. by author. 1980, Holt paper $5.95 (978-0-8050-0801-2). 32pp. A boy in old China finds that everything he dreams comes to life.

1015 dePaola, Tomie. *Angels, Angels Everywhere* (PS). Illus. by author. 2005, Putnam $14.99 (978-0-399-24370-7). DePaola presents angels who provide guidance for children in almost every aspect of daily life — including "the wake up angel," "the popcorn angel," and "the babysitting angel." (Rev: SLJ 10/05)

1016 dePaola, Tomie. *Big Anthony: His Story* (PS–3). Illus. 1998, Penguin $16.99 (978-0-399-23189-6). 32pp. Klutzy Big Anthony goes out on his own to earn his fortune and finds himself at the door of the Italian witch Strega Nona. (Rev: BL 11/15/98; HBG 3/99; SLJ 11/98)

1017 dePaola, Tomie. *Bill and Pete* (K–2). Illus. by author. 1996, Penguin paper $6.99 (978-0-698-11400-5). 32pp. Pete is a toothbrush (alias a bird) who helps young Bill in a series of world misadventures.

1018 dePaola, Tomie. *Jamie O'Rourke and the Pooka* (PS–3). Illus. 2000, Penguin $16.99 (978-0-399-23467-5). 32pp. A humorous original folktale about the laziest man in Ireland and the strange donkey-like beast, the pooka, that helps clean his house. (Rev: BL 1/1–15/00; HBG 10/00; SLJ 3/00)

1019 dePaola, Tomie. *Strega Nona Meets Her Match* (K–2). Illus. 1993, Penguin $17.99 (978-0-399-22421-8). 34pp. Strega Amelia comes to town and takes away business from the town's other witch, Strega Nona. (Rev: BCCB 12/93; BL 11/1/93; HB 11/93)

1020 dePaola, Tomie. *Strega Nona Takes a Vacation* (K–3). Illus. 2000, Penguin $16.99 (978-0-399-23562-7). 32pp. While Strega Nona is away on vacation, Big Anthony uses too many bath crystals and creates enough soapsuds to flow into town. (Rev: BL 10/15/00; HBG 3/01; SLJ 10/00)

1021 dePaola, Tomie. *Strega Nona's Harvest* (PS–3). Illus. by author. 2009, Putnam $16.99 (978-0-399-25291-4). 32pp. When Big Anthony grows more vegetables than he can handle, he leaves them for Strega Nona, who turns them into a grand feast. Lexile AD690L (Rev: BL 11/1/09; SLJ 10/1/09)

1022 Ditchfield, Christin. *Cowlick!* (PS–K). Illus. by Rosalind Beardshaw. 2007, Random $14.99 (978-0-375-83540-7). 40pp. Interpreting its title literally, this rhyming romp depicts a cow depositing drooly kisses upon slumbering children's heads, with predictable results next morning. (Rev: BL 1/1–15/07; SLJ 1/07)

1023 Docherty, Thomas. *Little Boat* (PS–K). Illus. by author. 2009, Candlewick $15.99 (978-0-7636-4428-4). A courageous little tugboat sets out into the vast and dangerous sea to find its companions. (Rev: BL 5/15/09; SLJ 8/09)

1024 Doherty, Berlie. *Jinnie Ghost* (2–4). Illus. by Jane Ray. 2005, Frances Lincoln $16.95 (978-1-84507-292-6). 44pp. Jinnie Ghost visits sleeping children throughout the night, leaving each one with a different dream. (Rev: BL 10/15/05; SLJ 2/06)

1025 Donaldson, Julia. *Charlie Cook's Favorite Book* (PS–2). Illus. by Axel Scheffler. 2006, Dial $16.99 (978-0-8037-3142-4). Charlie is led through 10 different fairy tales by the books' characters themselves in this amusing circular take on some familiar stories. (Rev: BL 5/1/06; SLJ 7/06)

1026 Donohue, Moira Rose. *Alfie the Apostrophe* (1–3). Illus. by JoAnn Adinolfi. 2006, Albert Whitman $16.95 (978-0-8075-0255-6). 32pp. A lively tale about a little apostrophe who makes his mark trying out for a school talent show directed by Mr. Asterisk. (Rev: BL 8/06; SLJ 8/06)

1027 Donohue, Moira Rose. *Penny and the Punctuation Bee* (1–3). Illus. by Jenny Law. 2008, Albert Whitman $16.95 (978-0-8075-6477-6). 32pp. A humorous look at punctuation, in which Penny, a period, and Quentin, a question mark, prepare for a contest against an irritating exclamation mark. (Rev: BL 7/08; LMC 8/08; SLJ 5/08)

1028 Dorros, Arthur. *Abuela* (K–2). Illus. by Elisa Kleven. 1991, Dutton $16.99 (978-0-525-44750-4). Rosalba and her grandmother fly over New York City in her imagination. (Rev: BCCB 9/92; BL 10/15/91*; HB 11/91*; SLJ 10/91)

1029 Doyle, Malachy. *The Dancing Tiger* (K–2). Illus. by Steve Johnson and Lou Fancher. 2005, Viking $15.99 (978-0-670-06020-7). A girl and a tiger dance together by the full moon in this nicely illustrated story with poetic text. (Rev: SLJ 7/05)

1030 Duddle, Jonny. *The King of Space* (1–3). Illus. by author. 2013, Candlewick $15.99 (978-0-7636-6435-0). 32pp. In this action-packed story, 6-year-old Rex — with the help of his alien sidekick Blip — builds a dung ray and overcomes the Western Spiral resistance; despite the fact that he has crowned himself the king of space, he needs his mother's help to sort everything out. Lexile AD680 (Rev: BLO 4/1/13; SLJ 4/13)

1031 Duddle, Jonny. *The Pirate Cruncher* (PS–2). Illus. by author. 2010, Candlewick $15.99 (978-0-7636-4876-3). 38pp. Greedy pirates follow a mysterious fiddler who

promises rich treasures, but a monster awaits instead. (Rev: BL 4/15/10; SLJ 5/1/10)

1032 Dunbar, Polly. *Hello Tilly* (PS). Illus. by author. Series: Tilly and Friends. 2008, Candlewick $12.99 (978-0-7636-4109-2). 32pp. For toddlers, this is a pleasing book about Tilly, who lives with five animal friends in a little yellow house and enjoy simple pleasures. (Rev: SLJ 6/09)

1033 Dunbar, Polly. *Penguin* (PS). Illus. by author. 2007, Candlewick $15.99 (978-0-7636-3404-9). 40pp. Ben goes to great lengths trying to get his new pet penguin to talk, but the mute penguin finds a way to communicate after saving Ben from the jaws of a lion. (Rev: BL 6/1–15/07; SLJ 7/07)

1034 Dyer, Sarah. *Five Little Fiends* (K–3). Illus. 2002, Bloomsbury $15.95 (978-1-58234-751-6). 32pp. In this unusual picture book, the little fiends of the title emerge from statues to steal parts of the environment, until they realize the error of their ways. (Rev: BL 9/1/02; SLJ 9/02)

1035 Dyer, Sarah. *Monster Day at Work* (PS–1). Illus. by author. 2010, Frances Lincoln $16.95 (978-1-84780-069-5). 28pp. It's Bring Your Child to Work Day and Monster Dad takes Monster Son (and the dog) along with him in this humorous story seen from the child's perspective. (Rev: BL 10/15/10; SLJ 1/1/11)

1036 Edwards, Pamela Duncan. *The Leprechaun's Gold* (PS–2). Illus. by Henry Cole. 2004, HarperCollins LB $16.89 (978-0-06-623975-0). 32pp. Young Tom's determination to become the finest harpist in Ireland is foiled by leprechauns. (Rev: BL 1/1–15/04; SLJ 2/04)

1037 Edwards, Pamela Duncan. *The Old House* (PS–1). Illus. by Henry Cole. 2007, Dutton $16.99 (978-0-525-47796-9). 32pp. A lonely old house becomes a happy home when a family fixes it up and moves in. (Rev: BL 10/1/07; LMC 1/08; SLJ 11/07)

1038 Eeckhout, Emmanuelle. *There's No Such Thing as Ghosts!* (PS–1). Illus. by author. 2008, Kane $13.95 (978-1-933605-91-3). 32pp. Readers get lots of laughs as a little boy hunting ghosts explores a haunted house, butterfly net in hand, but fails to see any of the many phantoms hovering there. (Rev: HB 1/09; SLJ 11/08)

1039 Egielski, Richard. *Captain Sky Blue* (PS–1). Illus. by author. 2010, Scholastic $17.95 (978-054521342-4). 32pp. In this action-packed, imaginative story, a young boy's favorite toy pilot becomes lost at sea but eventually makes it back home thanks to his bravery and some help from Santa. Lexile AD580L (Rev: BL 9/15/10; HB 11–12/10)

1040 Egielski, Richard. *Itsy Bitsy Spider* (PS–K). Illus. by author. 2012, Atheneum $19.99 (978-1-4169-9895-2). 12pp. This pop-up version of the classic rhyme features a little boy in a baseball cap as the spider. (Rev: BLO 11/15/12; SLJ 12/12)

1041 Einhorn, Edward. *A Very Improbable Story* (1–3). Illus. by Adam Gustavson. 2008, Charlesbridge $16.95 (978-1-57091-871-1); paper $7.95 (978-1-57091-872-8). 32pp. What are the chances you'll wake up with a talking cat named Odds on your head? This feline will not go away until Ethan wins a game of probability. (Rev: BL 2/1/08; LMC 10/08; SLJ 2/08)

1042 Eitzen, Ruth. *Tara's Flight* (K–2). Illus. by Allan Eitzen. 2008, Boyds Mills $16.95 (978-1-59078-563-8). 32pp. The story of Noah's ark is retold through the eyes of Noah's grandson, Aram, whose pet dove serves as a useful messenger. (Rev: BL 2/15/08; SLJ 3/08)

1043 Ellery, Amanda. *If I Had a Dragon* (PS–2). Illus. by Tom Ellery. 2006, Simon & Schuster $14.95 (978-1-4169-0924-8). 40pp. A boy imagines what would happen if his baby brother were a dragon, and decides he likes having a human sibling better. (Rev: BL 7/06; SLJ 7/06)

1044 Ellery, Amanda. *If I Were a Jungle Animal* (PS–1). Illus. by Tom Ellery. 2009, Simon & Schuster $15.99 (978-1-4169-3778-4). Bored in the outfield, Morton imagines himself as a variety of animals until his teammates interrupt him. (Rev: LMC 8/09; SLJ 4/09)

1045 Elliott, George. *The Boy Who Loved Bananas* (PS–2). Illus. by Andrej Krystoforski. 2005, Kids Can $15.95 (978-1-55337-744-3). After watching the monkeys at the zoo, Matthew vows only to eat bananas, which is fine until he morphs into a monkey himself. (Rev: SLJ 6/05)

1046 Ellis, Andy. *When Lulu Went to the Zoo* (PS–1). Illus. by author. 2010, Andersen $16.95 (978-0-7613-5499-4). 32pp. Empathetic 4-year-old Lulu invites the zoo's animals home with her in this zany, whimsical tale with eye-catching illustrations. (Rev: BL 1/1/10; SLJ 3/1/10)

1047 Elya, Susan Middleton. *Fairy Trails: A Story Told in English and Spanish* (PS). Illus. by Mercedes McDonald. 2005, Bloomsbury $16.95 (978-1-58234-927-5). 32pp. On their way to their aunt's house, Miguel and Maria meet a variety of fairy-tale characters — Aladdin, Cinderella, and so forth — in a rhyming text sprinkled with Spanish words and names. (Rev: BL 5/15/05)

1048 Enderle, Dotti. *The Library Gingerbread Man* (PS–2). Illus. by Colleen M. Madden. 2010, Upstart $17.95 (978-1-60213-048-7). 32pp. A gingerbread man escapes from his story on the shelf at the library, and manages to elude a host of other literary characters in his pursuit for a grand adventure. (Rev: BLO 4/15/10; LMC 10/10; SLJ 6/1/10)

1049 Engle, Margarita. *Tiny Rabbit's Big Wish* (PS–2). Illus. by David Walker. 2014, Houghton Mifflin $16.99 (978-054785286-7). 32pp. A tiny rabbit longs to be bigger, more like other animals, until he comes to recognize that his size and his large ears do offer benefits. e (Rev: BL 3/1/14; LMC 8–9/14; SLJ 1/1/14)

1050 Fancher, Lou, adapt. *The Velveteen Rabbit* (PS–2). Illus. by Steve Johnson and Lou Fancher. 2002, Simon & Schuster $16.95 (978-0-689-84134-7). With appealing illustrations and very readable text, Fancher retells the story of a stuffed rabbit that becomes real. (Rev: HBG 3/03; SLJ 12/02)

1051 Farley, Brianne. *Ike's Incredible Ink* (PS–3). Illus. by author. 2013, Candlewick $16.99 (978-076366296-7). 32pp. Ike the inkblot wants to write a book, but he has some trouble finding the right ink to use, not realizing that along with the perfect ink, he has had the creativity inside himself all along; a quirky look at procrastination and imagination. e Lexile AD340 (Rev: BLO 9/15/13; LMC 1–2/14; SLJ 7/13)

1052 Federspiel, Jürg. *Alligator Mike* (1–3). Illus. by Petra Rappo. 2007, North-South $15.95 (978-0-7358-2124-8). Mike discovers that New York City is full of unhappy alligators that want to go home to Florida and decides to do what he can to help. (Rev: SLJ 4/07)

1053 Fenton, Joe. *Boo!* (PS–1). Illus. by author. 2010, Simon & Schuster $12.99 (978-1-4169-7936-4). Unpaged. A little ghost does his best to scare his family but fails until he wanders into a white sheet. (Rev: SLJ 7/1/10)

1054 Fenton, Joe. *What's Under the Bed?* (K–2). Illus. by author. 2008, Simon & Schuster $15.99 (978-1-4169-4943-5). 32pp. Fred finally realizes that the monster under the bed is his teddy bear, but uncomfortable questions remain. (Rev: SLJ 9/08)

1055 Fernandes, Eugenie. *Sleepy Little Mouse* (PS–K). Illus. by Kim Fernandes. 2000, Kids Can $12.95 (978-1-55074-701-0). 24pp. When Little Mouse cries at nap time, she produces so many tears that her bed floats down a river and into the sea where she is found by sea creatures. (Rev: BL 10/1/00; HBG 3/01)

1056 Flaherty, A. W. *The Luck of the Loch Ness Monster: A Tale of Picky Eating* (K–3). Illus. by Scott Magoon. 2007, Houghton $16.00 (978-0-618-55644-1). A young girl's refusal to eat oatmeal on an ocean trip to Scotland, and a sea worm's hunger, apparently gave birth to a legend. (Rev: BL 10/1/07; SLJ 9/07)

1057 Fleischman, Paul. *Sidewalk Circus* (K–3). Illus. by Kevin Hawkes. 2004, Candlewick $15.99 (978-0-7636-1107-1). Triggered by posters advertising an upcoming circus, a young girl's imagination transforms the events of everyday life into a dizzying series of colorful circus performances. (Rev: BL 4/15/04*; HB 5/04; SLJ 7/04)

1058 Fleischman, Paul. *Weslandia* (K–3). Illus. by Kevin Hawkes. 1999, Candlewick $15.99 (978-0-7636-0006-8). 40pp. In this offbeat fantasy, unconventional Wesley cultivates magical seeds that serve as the basis of a new civilization. (Rev: BCCB 7–8/99; BL 7/99*; HB 3/99; HBG 10/99; SLJ 6/99)

1059 Fletcher, Ralph. *The Sandman* (PS–K). Illus. by Richard Cowdry. 2008, Holt $16.95 (978-0-8050-7726-1). A miniature man named Tor discovers the secret of sleep and in his mouse-drawn carriage travels far and wide helping insomniac children. (Rev: BL 7/08; SLJ 5/08)

1060 Florczak, Robert. *Yikes!!!* (PS). Illus. by author. 2003, Scholastic $15.95 (978-0-590-05043-2). A young child encounters some fearsome creatures on an imaginary journey and utters suitable cries of dismay. (Rev: BL 11/15/03; HBG 4/04; SLJ 12/03)

1061 Floyd, Madeleine. *Cold Paws, Warm Heart* (PS). Illus. 2005, Candlewick $15.99 (978-0-7636-2761-4). A little girl named Hannah seeks to warm up a lonely polar bear named Cold Paws. (Rev: BL 12/1/05; SLJ 7/06)

1062 Foley, Greg. *Willoughby and the Lion* (PS–2). Illus. by author. 2009, HarperCollins $17.99 (978-0-06-154750-8). 40pp. A beautiful golden lion grants young Willoughby 10 wishes but warns that unless the boy chooses the most wonderful thing of all, the lion will remain trapped on his rock in the backyard forever; counting opportunities arise as Willoughby struggles to find the perfect wish. (Rev: BL 1/1–15/09; SLJ 2/09)

1063 Foley, Greg. *Willoughby and the Moon* (K–2). Illus. by author. 2010, HarperCollins $18.99 (978-0-06-154753-9). 40pp. Willoughby can't sleep when the moon disappears and discovers the moon in his closet with a giant snail that is looking for his lost silver ball; shining illustrations enhance this quirky tale about fears and imagination. (Rev: BL 2/15/10; SLJ 5/1/10)

1064 Fore, S. J. *Read to Tiger* (PS–1). Illus. by R. W. Alley. 2010, Viking $15.99 (978-0-670-01140-7). Unpaged. A little boy absorbed in his book is constantly disturbed by an annoying tiger, but finally convinces him that the story is worth listening to. (Rev: LMC 11–12/10; SLJ 8/1/10)

1065 Foreman, Michael. *Fortunately, Unfortunately* (PS–2). Illus. by author. 2011, Andersen $16.95 (978-0-7613-7460-2). 32pp. On the way to return his grandmother's umbrella, young Milo has a number of lucky and unlucky encounters (with a whale, a pirate, dinosaurs, friendly aliens, and so forth). e Lexile AD530L (Rev: BL 3/1/11; SLJ 2/1/11)

1066 Foreman, Michael. *Superfrog and the Big Stink!* (PS–K). Illus. by author. 2013, IPG/Andersen $16.99 (978-184939516-8). 32pp. Superfrog — who is propelled by his own gas — flies into action to save the world from pollution, accompanied by a group of children. (Rev: BLO 7/13; SLJ 12/13)

1067 Fowles, Shelley. *Climbing Rosa* (PS–2). Illus. 2006, Frances Lincoln $15.95 (978-1-84507-079-3). 32pp. Brightly colored artwork enlivens this tale of Rosa, a poor young woman who climbs a towering tree to win the hand of a prince. (Rev: BL 4/1/06; SLJ 5/06)

1068 Fox, Mem. *The Magic Hat* (PS–1). Illus. by Tricia Tusa. 2002, Harcourt $16.00 (978-0-15-201025-6). 32pp. A magic hat transforms the people on whose heads it lands into a variety of different animals in this charming fantasy. (Rev: BCCB 7–8/02; BL 4/15/02; HBG 10/02; SLJ 4/02)

1069 Franson, Scott E. *Un-Brella* (PS–3). Illus. by author. 2007, Roaring Brook $15.95 (978-1-59643-179-9). A little girl enjoys a day at the beach although it's snowing out and conversely a day in the snow during a hot summer, all with the help of her "un-brella." (Rev: SLJ 4/07)

1070 Frazier, Craig. *Stanley Goes Fishing* (PS–1). Illus. by author. Series: Stanley. 2006, Chronicle $15.95 (978-0-8118-5244-9). Stanley, having no luck fishing in a stream, tries to fish in the sky instead and there they are! (Rev: SLJ 6/06)

1071 Frazier, Craig. *Stanley Goes for a Drive* (PS–3). Illus. by author. 2004, Chronicle $15.95 (978-0-8118-4429-1). Out for a drive in his pickup on a hot summer day, Stanley milks a spotted cow, tosses the milk to the sky, and enjoys the resulting clouds and rain; the simple text is enhanced by wonderful illustrations. (Rev: SLJ 9/04)

1072 Freedman, Deborah. *Scribble* (K–2). Illus. by author. 2007, Knopf $15.99 (978-0-375-83966-5). Lucie's scribbles on her big sister's drawing create a story about a scribbled cat and a princess that live happily every after. (Rev: SLJ 6/07)

1073 Freymann, Saxton, and Joost Elffers. *Gus and Button* (PS–3). 2001, Scholastic $15.95 (978-0-439-11015-0). 32pp. This tale about a bland-colored mushroom boy and his mushroom dog on a quest to find a colorful place that contrasts with his life is artfully illustrated with computer-enhanced photographs of vegetables. (Rev: BL 11/15/01; HBG 3/02; SLJ 12/01)

1074 Gackenbach, Dick. *Harry and the Terrible Whatzit* (PS–2). Illus. by author. 1979, Houghton $16.00 (978-0-395-28795-8); paper $7.95 (978-0-89919-223-9). 32pp. Harry follows his mother into the dark cellar to confront the terrible two-headed Whatzit.

1075 Gaiman, Neil. *Crazy Hair* (PS–3). Illus. by Dave McKean. 2009, HarperCollins $18.99 (978-0-06-057908-1). This is a surreal story about a man who claims his madcap tresses are home to a wide variety of residents. (Rev: BL 3/15/09; SLJ 6/09)

1076 Gaiman, Neil. *The Dangerous Alphabet* (1–4). Illus. by Gris Grimly. 2008, HarperCollins $17.99 (978-0-06-078333-4). This unusual alphabet story follows two Victorian children and their gazelle on a treasure hunt through darkly funny sewers. (Rev: BL 3/1/08; HB 7/08; SLJ 5/08)

1077 Gaiman, Neil. *The Wolves in the Walls* (3–6). Illus. by Dave McKean. 2003, HarperCollins $16.99 (978-0-380-97827-4). Lucy says there are wolves in the walls of her house, but her family doesn't believe her — until the wolves come out — in this imaginatively illustrated story. (Rev: BL 2/1/04; HBG 4/04; SLJ 9/03)

1078 Gall, Chris. *Dear Fish* (1–4). Illus. by author. 2006, Little, Brown $16.99 (978-0-316-05847-6). All sorts of fish venture onto land to visit Peter after he sends them an invitation in the form of a message in a bottle. (Rev: SLJ 5/06)

1079 Gammell, Stephen. *Mudkin* (PS–1). Illus. by author. 2011, Carolrhoda $16.95 (978-0-7613-5790-2). 32pp. A strange, muddy little creature invites a young girl to join him in a glorious day of mud-filled activities in this almost wordless story. (Rev: BL 1/1–15/11*; SLJ 3/1/11)

1080 Garland, Michael. *Miss Smith and the Haunted Library* (1–3). Illus. by author. 2009, Dutton $16.99 (978-0-525-42139-9). 32pp. The magical storybook first seen in *Miss. Smith's Incredible Storybook* (2003) comes to life again in a spooky library, generating characters such as Count Dracula and Captain Hook who cause chaos, delight, and suspense. (Rev: BLO 6/16/09; SLJ 7/09)

1081 Garland, Michael. *Miss Smith Reads Again!* (K–3). Illus. by author. Series: Miss Smith. 2006, Dutton $15.99 (978-0-525-47722-8). This follow-up to *Miss Smith's Incredible Storybook* finds Miss Smith's class transported to the age of the dinosaurs when she reads from Arthur Conan Doyle's *The Lost World*. (Rev: SLJ 7/06)

1082 Garland, Michael. *Miss Smith's Incredible Storybook* (1–4). Illus. by author. 2003, Dutton $16.99 (978-0-525-47133-2). A magic story book that brings the characters to life proves too much for the substitute teacher. (Rev: HBG 4/04; SLJ 10/03)

1083 Gay, Marie-Louise. *On My Island* (PS–1). Illus. 2001, Groundwood $16.95 (978-0-88899-396-0). 32pp. In this fantasy set on an island, a young boy who shares his home with a variety of animals claims nothing ever happens, but the opposite is true. (Rev: BL 3/15/01)

1084 Gebhard, Wilfried. *What Eddie Can Do* (PS–1). Illus. 2004, Kane $15.95 (978-1-929132-60-7). 32pp. Eddie doesn't have time to learn to tie his shoelaces as he's too busy enjoying his elaborate imaginary adventures; shoelace tying instructions included. (Rev: BL 3/1/04; SLJ 7/04)

1085 Gerstein, Mordicai. *A Book* (K–3). Illus. by author. 2009, Roaring Brook $16.95 (978-1-59643-251-2). 48pp. A little girl whose family lives in a book wanders through a variety of stories — fairy tales, mysteries, adventures, and so forth — searching for a story of her own. (Rev: BCCB 7–8/09; BL 3/15/09; HB 5/09; LMC 8/09; SLJ 5/09)

1086 Gerstein, Mordicai. *Carolinda Clatter!* (PS–2). Illus. 2005, Roaring Brook $16.95 (978-1-59643-063-1). When Carolinda Clatter is born, her penchant for noise threatens the whole town of Pupickton, which is perched atop a sleeping giant's stomach. (Rev: BL 6/1–15/05)

1087 Gerstein, Mordicai. *Minifred Goes to School* (PS–3). Illus. by author. 2009, HarperCollins $17.99 (978-0-06-075889-9). 32pp. Minifred the kitten grows into a cat who goes to school with the human children and learns well but shows a total disregard for rules. (Rev: BCCB 9/09; BL 4/1/09; SLJ 6/09)

1088 Gillmor, Don. *Yuck, a Love Story* (K–4). Illus. by Marie-Louise Gay. 2000, Stoddart $14.95 (978-0-7737-3218-6). Austin Grouper develops a crush on the girl next door and, to prove his love, lassos the moon as a gift. (Rev: SLJ 11/00)

1089 Gleeson, Libby. *The Great Bear* (2–4). Illus. by Armin Greder. 2011, Candlewick $16.99 (978-0-7636-5136-7). Unpaged. A captive dancing bear in a medieval circus endures neglect and abuse until it finally rebels and escapes up into the sky. (Rev: SLJ 9/1/11)

1090 Gliori, Debi. *The Trouble with Dragons* (K–4). Illus. by author. 2008, Walker $16.99 (978-0-8027-9789-6). 32pp. Dragons threaten the environment by overpopulation, cutting down trees, building expansively, generating garbage, and blowing hot air until the other animals convince them of the errors of their ways and they start to conserve, reduce, reuse, and recycle. (Rev: LMC 3/09; SLJ 11/08)

1091 Goldberg, Myla. *Catching the Moon* (PS–2). Illus. by Chris Sheban. 2007, Scholastic $16.99 (978-0-439-57686-4). The moon assists an old fisherwoman by helping her keep the tides away from her house and dock. The moon's light is beautifully depicted in the illustrations. (Rev: SLJ 6/07)

1092 Gordon, David. *Smitten* (PS–2). Illus. by author. 2007, Simon & Schuster $15.99 (978-1-4169-2440-1). A single pink mitten and a lonely blue sock team up to look for their other halves but discover that all they need is each other. (Rev: BCCB 12/07; SLJ 2/08)

1093 Gore, Leonid. *The Wonderful Book* (PS–1). Illus. by author. 2010, Scholastic $16.99 (978-0-545-08598-4). 32pp. A red object is used for various purposes by the animals in the forest (a hat, a picnic table) before a little boy turns up and reads a story from it. (Rev: BL 10/15/10; LMC 1–2/11; SLJ 11/1/10)

1094 Graham, Bob. *April and Esme, Tooth Fairies* (PS–2). Illus. by author. 2010, Candlewick $16.99 (978-0-7636-4683-7). Unpaged. Two young fairies are asked to make their first expedition, to collect Daniel Dangerfield's tooth. (Rev: BL 10/1/10*; HB 9–10/10*; LMC 1–2/11; SLJ 9/1/10)

1095 Gralley, Jean. *The Moon Came Down on Milk St* (PS–1). Illus. by author. 2004, Holt $16.95 (978-0-8050-7266-2). A variety of community workers rush to help when the moon falls out of the sky and breaks into pieces. (Rev: SLJ 11/04)

1096 Grambling, Lois G. *Can I Bring My Pterodactyl to School, Ms. Johnson?* (PS–K). Illus. by Judy Love. 2006, Charlesbridge $16.95 (978-1-58089-044-1); paper $6.95 (978-1-58089-141-7). 32pp. A boy tries to convince his teacher to let him bring a pterodactyl to school. (Rev: BL 12/15/05; SLJ 3/06)

1097 Grandits, John. *The Travel Game* (K–2). Illus. by R. W. Alley. 2009, Clarion $16.00 (978-0-618-56420-0). 32pp. Rather than take a nap, Tad plays the travel game with his grandmother, and this time they choose Hong Kong and take an imaginary trip there. (Rev: BLO 6/23/09; SLJ 7/09)

1098 Gravel, Elise. *Adopt a Glurb!* (1–3). Illus. by author. Series: Balloon Toons. 2010, Blue Apple $10.99 (978-160905037-5). 40pp. Gravel describes the benefits and drawbacks of adopting a glurb — a smelly little monster — in this funny book with cartoon illustrations. (Rev: BL 11/15/10)

1099 Graves, Keith. *Three Nasty Gnarlies* (K–3). Illus. by author. 2003, Scholastic $16.95 (978-0-439-24090-1). Although inspired by a beautiful butterfly to improve their appearance, three nasty gnarlies — Grubby Gurgle, Stanky Stoo, and Ooga-Mooga — have little success. (Rev: BCCB 1/04; BL 11/15/03; HBG 4/04; SLJ 12/03)

1100 Gravett, Emily. *Monkey and Me* (PS–K). Illus. by author. 2008, Simon & Schuster $15.99 (978-1-4169-5457-6). 32pp. A little girl plays with her stuffed monkey and imagines them meeting a series of wild animals. (Rev: BL 2/1/08; HB 5/08; LMC 3/08; SLJ 4/08)

1101 Grey, Mini. *Ginger Bear* (PS–K). Illus. by author. 2007, Knopf $15.99 (978-0-375-84253-5). 32pp. A gingerbread bear comes to life and bakes some other animals so he can have friends. (Rev: BCCB 9/07; BL 7/07; HB 7/07; SLJ 6/07)

1102 Grey, Mini. *Toys in Space* (PS–2). Illus. by author. 2013, Knopf $16.99 (978-0-307-97812-7). 32pp. Left outside overnight a group of scared toys ask WonderDoll to tell them a story, which involves lost toys, aliens, and space travel. ℮ (Rev: BL 5/1/13; HB 5–6/13; SLJ 6/13*)

1103 Grey, Mini. *Traction Man and the Beach Odyssey* (PS–2). Illus. by author. 2012, Knopf $16.99 (978-0-224-08364-5); LB $19.99 (978-037596952-2). 32pp. Action toy Traction Man and his sidekick Scrubbing Brush have an exciting adventure at the beach and meet Beach Time Brenda. (Rev: BL 4/15/12*; HB 7–8/12; SLJ 4/1/12*)

1104 Grey, Mini. *Traction Man Is Here!* (PS–2). Illus. 2005, Knopf LB $17.99 (978-0-375-93191-8). 32pp. A little boy's action figure sets off on adventures all around the house as the boy uses household objects for imaginative play. (Rev: BL 3/1/05; SLJ 6/05)

1105 Grey, Mini. *Traction Man Meets Turbodog* (PS–2). Illus. by author. 2008, Knopf $16.99 (978-0-375-85583-2). 32pp. The robotic Turbodog turns out to be no replacement for Traction Man's sidekick Scrubbing Brush in this humorous and satisfying sequel to *Traction Man Is Here!* (2005). (Rev: BL 9/1/08; HB 1/09; SLJ 8/08)

1106 Grindley, Sally. *Mucky Duck* (PS). Illus. by Neal Layton. 2003, Bloomsbury $13.95 (978-1-58234-821-6). Oliver Dunkley enjoys spending time with Mucky Duck, who lives in a pond behind Oliver's house and seems to create mess wherever she goes. (Rev: HBG 10/03; SLJ 7/03)

1107 Grobler, Piet. *Hey, Frog!* (PS–K). Illus. 2002, Front St. $15.95 (978-1-886910-84-3). 32pp. Humorous illustrations and fast-reading text tell the story of a greedy frog who drinks all the water on the African savannah, leaving the other thirsty animals to plot their revenge, including the tickly eels. (Rev: BL 1/1–15/03; HB 1/03; HBG 3/03; SLJ 1/03)

1108 Gruelle, Johnny. *Raggedy Ann Stories* (PS–3). Illus. 1993, Macmillan LB $16.00 (978-0-02-737585-5). 96pp. This story features the lovable rag doll. A reissue. Also use: *Raggedy Andy Stories* (1993).

1109 Gutierrez, Akemi. *The Pirate and Other Adventures of Sam and Alice* (K–2). Illus. by author. Series: Sam and Alice. 2007, Houghton $17.00 (978-0-618-73737-6). Three Sam and Alice stories appear in this book: "Space Patrol," "The Genius Crocodile," and "The Pirate," all full of adventure and unlikely events. (Rev: SLJ 6/07)

1110 Haas, Irene. *Bess and Bella* (PS–K). Illus. 2006, Simon & Schuster $14.95 (978-1-4169-0013-9). 32pp. A bird called Bella drops in with a suitcase of goodies and cheers Bess's lonely winter. (Rev: BL 12/15/05*; HBG 10/06; SLJ 2/06)

1111 Hächler, Bruno. *What Does My Teddy Bear Do All Night?* (PS–K). Trans. from German by Charise Myngher. Illus. by Birte Müller. 2005, Minedition $14.99 (978-0-698-40029-0). A young girl and her teddy bear play together long after the child's bedtime, and even after the child finally falls asleep her faithful stuffed animal keeps watch over her. (Rev: SLJ 12/05)

1112 Hakala, Marjorie Rose. *Mermaid Dance* (PS–2). Illus. by Mark Jones. 2009, Blue Apple $16.99 (978-1-934706-47-3). 40pp. Mermaids have a party on the first night of summer. (Rev: SLJ 6/09)

1113 Hale, Nathan. *Yellowbelly and Plum Go to School* (PS–1). Illus. by author. 2007, Putnam $16.99 (978-0-399-24624-1). Yellowbelly takes his teddy bear, Plum, to the first day of school and together they learn some new games to play. (Rev: SLJ 8/07)

1114 Harper, Charise Mericle. *Cupcake: A Journey to Special* (PS–1). Illus. by author. 2010, Hyperion/Disney $14.99 (978-1-4231-1897-8). 32pp. A plain vanilla cupcake receives advice from a friendly candle on how to decorate himself. (Rev: BL 3/1/10; HB 3–4/10; SLJ 6/1/10)

1115 Harrison, Carlos. *Ruben's Jungle / La selva de Ruben* (PS–2). Illus. by Grizelle Paz. 2003, Globo Libros $16.95 (978-0-9706953-1-4). Ruben visits the jungle in this appealing bilingual story, packaged with an audio CD. (Rev: SLJ 7/03)

1116 Harvey, Matthea. *Cecil the Pet Glacier* (K–2). Illus. by Giselle Potter. 2012, Random House $17.99 (978-0-375-86773-6). 40pp. On a trip to Norway with her eccentric parents and her three dolls named Jennifer, young Ruby inadvertently acquires a devoted pet — a small glacier named Cecil. ℮ Lexile AD820L (Rev: BL 9/15/12; HB 9–10/12; SLJ 8/12)

1117 Hazen, Barbara S. *Who Is Your Favorite Monster, Mama?* (PS–2). Illus. by Maryann Kovalski. 2006, Hyperion $15.99 (978-0-7868-1810-5). 32pp. Mama Monster reassures little Harry when he feels slighted by the attention she gives to his siblings. (Rev: BL 7/06; SLJ 4/06)

1118 Heap, Sue. *Danny's Drawing Book* (PS–1). Illus. by author. 2008, Candlewick $9.99 (978-0-7636-3654-8). 32pp. Danny and his friend Ettie use his sketchbook to create an illustrated story about the animals at the zoo. (Rev: BL 5/15/08; SLJ 3/08)

1119 Heidbreder, Robert. *I Wished for a Unicorn* (PS–3). Illus. by Kady M. Denton. 2000, Kids Can $14.95 (978-1-55074-543-6). 32pp. A young girl's dog is transformed into a unicorn and together they travel into a magic land. (Rev: BCCB 5/00; BL 4/15/00; HBG 10/00; SLJ 8/00)

1120 Heidbreder, Robert. *Lickety-Split* (PS–2). Illus. by Dusan Petricic. 2007, Kids Can $15.95 (978-1-55337-710-8). 32pp. A boy's imaginary adventures are described in inventive wordplay. (Rev: SLJ 10/07)

1121 Heidbreder, Robert. *A Sea-Wishing Day* (PS–2). Illus. by Kady M. Denton. 2007, Kids Can $15.95 (978-1-55337-707-8). 32pp. A little boy's imagination carries him and his dog, Skipper, on an exciting high-seas adventure. (Rev: BL 3/15/07)

1122 Heine, Theresa. *Star Seeker: A Journey to Outer Space* (2–4). Illus. by Victor Tavares. 2006, Barefoot Books $16.99 (978-1-905236-36-7). 32pp. Strong illustrations of the planets and other bodies enhance the rhyming text in this fantasy of travel into space aboard a series of unlikely conveyances — including armchairs, hobby horses, and paper airplanes. (Rev: BL 4/15/06; SLJ 3/07)

1123 Heller, Linda. *Today Is the Birthday of the World* (PS–K). Illus. by Alison Jay. 2009, Dutton $16.99 (978-0-525-47905-5). 32pp. On the world's birthday, God celebrates animals' attributes. (Rev: BL 5/1/09; SLJ 6/09)

1124 Henkes, Kevin. *My Garden* (PS–1). Illus. by author. 2010, Greenwillow $17.99 (978-0-06-171517-4); LB $18.89 (978-0-06-171518-1). 40pp. A young girl imagines her ideal garden, complete with never-dying flowers and chocolate rabbits. (Rev: BL 1/1/10; HB 3–4/10; SLJ 3/1/10*)

1125 Hennessy, B. G. *Claire and the Unicorn Happy Ever After* (K–3). Illus. by Susan Mitchell. 2006, Simon & Schuster $12.95 (978-1-4169-0815-9). Claire and her toy unicorn journey to a land full of literary characters and ask what it takes to make someone happy ever after. (Rev: SLJ 2/06)

1126 Herrera, Juan Felipe. *Super Cilantro Girl / La Supernina del Cilantro* (K–3). Illus. by Honorio Robledo Tapia. 2003, Children's Book Pr. $16.95 (978-0-89239-187-5). 30pp. Transformed into a giant green superheroine, 8-year-old Esmeralda Sinfronteras uses her newfound powers to rescue her mother, who can't return to the United States without a green card. (Rev: HBG 4/04; SLJ 12/03)

1127 Hicks, Barbara Jean. *Jitterbug Jam: A Monster Tale* (1–3). Illus. by Alexis Deacon. 2005, Farrar $16.00 (978-0-374-33685-1). A monster is frightened by the little boy under his bed in this picture book with amusing artwork. (Rev: BL 3/1/05)

1128 High, Linda Oatman. *Cool Bopper's Choppers* (K–3). Illus. by John O'Brien. 2007, Boyds Mills $16.95 (978-1-59078-379-5). When Cool Bopper's dentures fly out of his mouth and end up down the drain, the sax player heads to the beach, where he spies them blowing a tune on a seashell. (Rev: SLJ 5/07)

1129 Highet, Alistair. *The Yellow Train* (K–3). Illus. by François Roca. 2000, Creative $17.95 (978-1-56846-128-1). Theo and Grandpa travel back in time and embark on a magical journey through unspoiled landscapes as they ride the Yellow Train with Grandpa at the controls. (Rev: BL 12/15/00; HBG 3/01; SLJ 12/00)

1130 Hines, Anna Grossnickle. *I Am a Tyrannosaurus* (PS). Illus. by author. 2011, Tricycle $14.99 (978-1-58246-413-8); LB $15.99 (978-1-58246-414-5). 40pp. A little boy has a day of imaginative play, acting out the behaviors of various dinosaurs. (Rev: BLO 3/14/11; SLJ 8/1/11)

1131 Hissey, Jane. *Old Bear* (PS–K). Illus. by author. 2013, Tundra $19.99 (978-177049481-7). 36pp. Old Bear simply must be rescued from the attic, and Bramwell Brown, Duck, Rabbit, and Little Bear hatch an plan to do just that, so that they can be reunited with their friend in the nursery. Lexile AD700 (Rev: BLO 9/15/13)

1132 Hoban, Russell. *Rosie's Magic Horse* (PS–2). Illus. by Quentin Blake. 2013, Candlewick $15.99 (978-0-7636-6400-8). 40pp. Rosie adds a new ice-pop stick to her collection and is rewarded when the horse she built out of the sticks appears in a dream and whisks her off in search of a treasure that will help solve her family's problems. (Rev: BL 12/15/12; SLJ 2/13)

1133 Hoberman, Mary Ann. *Miss Mary Mack* (PS). Illus. by Nadine Bernard Westcott. 2001, Little, Brown $5.95 (978-0-316-36642-7). 24pp. This bouncy board book presents a clapping rhyme that features Miss Mary Mack and her pet elephant. (Rev: BL 2/15/01; HBG 3/02)

1134 Hogg, Gary. *Beautiful Buehla and the Zany Zoo Makeover* (PS–1). Illus. by Victoria Chess. 2006, HarperCollins $15.99 (978-0-06-009420-1). It's picture day at the zoo, and Beautiful Buehla gives the reluctant animals quite extreme makeovers. (Rev: BL 5/1/06; SLJ 5/06)

1135 Holwitz, Peter. *Stick Kid* (PS–2). Illus. by author. 2003, Philomel $13.99 (978-0-399-24163-5). A stick figure child comes to life and grows up in this imaginative story with rhyming text. (Rev: SLJ 4/04)

1136 Horn, Emily. *Excuse Me . . . Are You a Witch?* (PS–3). Illus. by Pawel Pawlak. 2003, Charlesbridge LB $15.95 (978-1-58089-093-9). Having read that witches favor black cats as companions, Herbert the black kitten searches long and hard for a witch but is about to give up when a class of aspiring witches adopts him. (Rev: HBG 4/04; SLJ 8/03)

1137 Howe, James. *Brontorina* (PS–2). Illus. by Randy Cecil. 2010, Candlewick $15.99 (978-0-7636-4437-6). 32pp. An enormous dinosaur named Brontorina is determined to become a ballerina despite her many drawbacks. (Rev: BL 5/15/10*; LMC 10/10; SLJ 7/1/10)

1138 Hughes, Shirley. *Jonadab and Rita* (PS–2). Illus. by author. 2011, IPG/Red Fox paper $11.99 (978-1-86-230-313-3). 32pp. Minnie neglects her toy donkey Jonadab and he flies off for an exciting adventure. (Rev: BLO 8/11; SLJ 6/11)

1139 Hughes, Vi. *Aziz the Storyteller* (K–3). Illus. by Stefan Czernecki. 2002, Crocodile $15.95 (978-1-56656-456-4). Aziz, a lover of storytelling, trades the family's donkey for a special carpet, which proves worthwhile despite his father's ire. (Rev: HBG 10/02; SLJ 11/02)

1140 Ichikawa, Satomi. *Come Fly with Me* (PS–1). Illus. by author. 2008, Philomel $15.99 (978-0-399-24679-1). Cosmos, a wooden toy plane, and Woggy, a black-and-white stuffed dog, escape their limited environment and fly out of the toy box to explore the rooftops of Paris. (Rev: BL 2/1/08; SLJ 4/08)

1141 Ichikawa, Satomi. *La La Rose* (PS). Illus. 2004, Penguin $15.99 (978-0-399-24029-4). Atmospheric illustrations draw readers into the adventures of a pink stuffed rabbit who is separated from her young owner in Paris's Luxembourg Gardens. (Rev: BL 1/1–15/04; SLJ 2/04)

1142 Ichikawa, Satomi. *My Little Train* (PS–1). Illus. by author. 2010, Philomel $15.99 (978-0-399-25453-6). 40pp. A toy train travels across the broad expanse of living room carpet, depositing its animal passengers at different locales: a potted plant, the fishbowl, the couch. (Rev: BL 10/1/10; SLJ 11/1/10)

1143 Issacs, Anne. *Pancakes for Supper!* (PS–2). Illus. by Mark Teague. 2006, Scholastic $15.99 (978-0-439-64483-9). 40pp. Alone in the wilderness after falling from her parents' wagon, young Toby uses her wits — and most of her clothes — to bargain her way back to civilization in this entertaining tall tale with arresting illustrations. (Rev: BCCB 11/06; BL 10/15/06; HB 11/06; HBG 4/07; LMC 3/07; SLJ 10/06*)

1144 Jackson, Ellen. *The Seven Seas* (PS–2). Illus. by Bill Slavin and Esperança Melo. 2011, Eerdmans $15.99 (978-0-8028-5341-7). 36pp. As his teacher talks about geography, a young rabbit daydreams about exploring fantasy seas — a Pink Sea with flamingos and cotton candy clouds, and so forth. (Rev: BL 2/15/11; SLJ 2/1/11)

1145 Janisch, Heinz. *Why Is the Snow White?* (K–3). Trans. by Rebecca K. Morrison. Illus. by Silke Leffler. 2012, NorthSouth $17.95 (978-0-7358-4092-8). 32pp. Father Snow, who has been seeking a color for his transparent substance, is rejected by a variety of flowers before he comes across a generous snowdrop. (Rev: BL 12/1/12; SLJ 12/12)

1146 Janisch, Heinz, and Silke Leffler. *"I Have a Little Problem," Said the Bear* (PS–2). Illus. by Silke Leffler. 2009, North-South $16.95 (978-0-7358-2235-1). Bear has a problem but everybody's got more advice to offer than time to listen. (Rev: BL 12/15/08; LMC 10/09; SLJ 3/09)

1147 Jarman, Julia. *Class Three at Sea* (PS). Illus. by Lynne Chapman. 2008, Carolrhoda $16.95 (978-0-8225-7617-4). A class field trip turns into adventure in this pirate fantasy. (Rev: SLJ 9/08)

1148 Jeffers, Oliver. *The Hueys in the New Sweater* (PS–1). Illus. by author. 2012, Philomel $10.99 (978-039925767-4). 32pp. A population of identical, humdrum creatures called Hueys finds a new perspective on life when a Huey named Rupert knits himself an orange sweater in this paean to individuality. (Rev: BL 5/15/12*)

1149 Jeffers, Oliver. *The Incredible Book Eating Boy* (PS–3). Illus. by author. 2007, Philomel $16.99 (978-0-399-24749-1). Facts and stories get all jumbled up in Henry when he eats too many books, so he decides it would be smarter to read them instead. Varied typefaces and collages make the illustrations appealing. (Rev: SLJ 6/07)

1150 Jeffers, Oliver. *Up and Down* (K–2). Illus. by author. 2010, Philomel $16.99 (978-0-399-25545-8). 40pp. A

boy and his penguin friend share board games and make music together until the penguin decides he must learn to fly, and must do so alone. (Rev: SLJ 12/1/10*)

1151 Jeffers, Oliver. *The Way Back Home* (PS–1). Illus. by author. 2008, Philomel $16.99 (978-0-399-25074-3). 32pp. A little boy flies an airplane to the moon, where he runs out of gas; luckily a young Martian also arrives there by spacecraft and after initial uncertainty the two become friends and help each other out of their predicaments. (Rev: BL 4/15/08; LMC 5/08; SLJ 4/08)

1152 Jenkins, Emily. *Toys Come Home: Being the Early Experiences of an Intelligent Stingray, a Brave Buffalo, and a Brand-New Someone Called Plastic* (K–2). Illus. by Paul O. Zelinsky. 2011, Random House $16.99 (978-0-375-86200-7); LB $19.99 (978-0-375-96200-4). 144pp. A prequel to *Toys Go Out* (2006) and *Toy Dance Party* (2008), this book explores the history of the toys that came to be cherished by the Girl. (Rev: BL 9/15/11*; SLJ 10/1/11)

1153 Jennings, Sharon. *The Happily Ever Afternoon* (PS–K). Illus. by Ron Lightburn. 2006, Annick LB $19.95 (978-1-55037-945-7); paper $7.95 (978-1-55037-944-0). 24pp. As his parents prepare for his birthday party, an imaginative little boy battles dragons — the family cat and dog — to get to the treasure, a kitchen full of birthday treats. (Rev: BL 8/06)

1154 Johnson, Angela. *The Day Ray Got Away* (PS–2). Illus. by Luke LaMarca. 2010, Simon & Schuster $16.99 (978-0-689-87375-1). 40pp. A strong-willed parade balloon shaped like the sun makes a break for freedom — inspiring the other parade balloons to attempt an "uprising." Lexile AD610L (Rev: BL 8/10; HB 9–10/10; SLJ 9/1/10)

1155 Johnson, D. B. *Palazzo Inverso* (K–3). Illus. by author. 2010, Houghton Mifflin $16 (978-0-15-23999-6.). 32pp. Channeling Escher, this picture book full of shifting perspectives features young Mauk, whose contributions to the design of a grand Palazzo are dizzy-making. (Rev: BL 2/15/10; SLJ 5/1/10)

1156 Joosse, Barbara. *Old Robert and the Sea-Silly Cats* (PS–2). Illus. by Jan Jutte. 2012, Philomel $16.99 (978-0-399-25430-7). 40pp. A lonely old sailor's life is changed when a group of cats — three performing, and one an endearing little soul with no apparent talents — moves in. (Rev: BL 4/1/12; LMC 10/12; SLJ 4/1/12)

1157 Joyce, William. *The Man in the Moon* (PS–3). Illus. by author. Series: Guardians of Childhood. 2011, Atheneum $17.99 (978-1-4424-3041-9). 56pp. When he was a child in the Golden Age, the Man in the Moon (MiM) was attacked by Pitch, the King of Nightmares, and escaped to a faraway galaxy where he made friends with guardians including the Tooth Fairy and the Sandman to look after the children of Earth. (Rev: BL 10/1/11; SLJ 10/1/11)

1158 Joyce, William. *Sleepy Time Olie* (PS–K). Illus. 2001, HarperCollins LB $15.89 (978-0-06-029614-8). 48pp. This brightly colored, rollicking picture book about space-kid Olie (first seen in *Rolie Polie Olie*

[1999] and *Snowie Rolie* [2000]) finds him building a laugh-ray to fix his grandfather's broken smile. (Rev: BL 11/15/01; HBG 3/02; SLJ 10/01)

1159 Judge, Lita. *Red Sled* (PS–2). Illus. by author. 2011, Simon & Schuster $16.99 (978-1-4424-2007-6). Unpaged. A diverse group of animals enjoy a little girl's red sled during the night in this almost-wordless book. (Rev: LMC 1–2/12*; SLJ 10/1/11*)

1160 Jukes, Mavis. *You're a Bear* (PS–2). Illus. by Steve Johnson and Lou Fancher. 2003, Knopf LB $18.99 (978-0-375-90267-3). A young girl dons a furry hooded jacket and pretends to be a bear. (Rev: BL 12/1/03; HBG 4/04; SLJ 12/03)

1161 Juster, Norton. *The Odious Ogre* (PS–1). Illus. by Jules Feiffer. 2010, Scholastic $17.95 (978-0-545-16202-9). 32pp. An ogre used to terrorizing villages is undone by a beautiful young girl who refuses to fear him; the illustrations add to the humor. **e** Lexile AD880L (Rev: BL 9/15/10; HB 11–12/10; LMC 1–2/11; SLJ 10/1/10*)

1162 Kain, Karen. *The Nutcracker* (1–3). Illus. by Rajka Kupesic. 2005, Tundra $18.95 (978-0-88776-696-1). In this handsome adaptation of "The Nutcracker" based on a National Ballet of Canada production, Marie and her brother Misha watch the toys battle and visit the Sugar Plum Fairy's palace. (Rev: BL 11/1/05; SLJ 10/05) [792.8]

1163 Kann, Victoria. *Emeraldalicious* (K–2). Illus. by author. 2013, HarperCollins $17.99 (978-0-06-178126-1). 40pp. Pinkalicious and her brother Peter transform a garbage-filled park into a glorious and palatial garden. Lexile 400 (Rev: BLO 4/1/13; SLJ 4/13)

1164 Kann, Victoria, and Elizabeth Kann. *Pinkalicious* (K–2). 2006, HarperCollins $17.99 (978-0-06-077639-8). 40pp. Despite warnings from her parents, a little girl gobbles up so many pink cupcakes that she turns pink herself. (Rev: BL 6/1–15/06; SLJ 8/06)

1165 Karlins, Mark. *Starring Lorenzo, and Einstein Too* (K–2). Illus. by Sandy Nichols. 2009, Dial $16.99 (978-0-8037-3220-9). 32pp. Little Lorenzo, budding scientist and reluctant member of his family's vaudeville act, takes off with Albert Einstein to explore the universe but finds himself homesick. (Rev: BL 4/1/09; LMC 8/09; SLJ 4/09)

1166 Kasbarian, Lucine, reteller. *The Greedy Sparrow: An Armenian Tale* (PS–2). Illus. by Maria Zaikina. 2011, Marshall Cavendish $17.99 (978-0-7614-5821-2). 32pp. A greedy sparrow keeps trading up the goods he's able to con his neighbors out of, eventually receiving well-deserved comeuppance in the end. **e** Lexile AD640L (Rev: BLO 2/14/11; SLJ 3/1/11)

1167 Kastner, Jill. *Princess Dinosaur* (PS–K). Illus. 2001, Greenwillow LB $15.89 (978-0-688-17046-2). 32pp. An action-filled picture book about the adventures of Princess Dinosaur and her friends Cowboy Tex, a toy, and Bettina, a doll. (Rev: BCCB 5/01; BL 4/15/01; HBG 10/01; SLJ 5/01)

1168 Keller, Laurie. *The Scrambled States of America* (K–3). Illus. 1998, Holt $16.95 (978-0-8050-5802-4).

In this lighthearted introduction to the 50 states, Kansas and Nebraska decide to have a party where the states exchange places, but complications occur when, for example, Minnesota gets a sunburn while Florida is freezing. (Rev: BCCB 10/98; BL 1/1–15/99; HBG 3/99; SLJ 11/98)

1169 Keller, Laurie. *The Scrambled States of America Talent Show* (K–3). Illus. by author. 2008, Holt $16.95 (978-0-8050-7997-5). 40pp. The states have a wild time at their talent show, providing additional facts in this companion to *The Scrambled States of America* (1998). (Rev: BL 8/08; SLJ 8/08)

1170 Kellogg, Steven. *The Missing Mitten Mystery* (PS–1). Illus. 2000, Dial $16.99 (978-0-8037-2566-9). 32pp. In this reworking of the 1974 title, a little girl sets off with her dog Oscar to find a lost mitten and discovers it is acting as the heart of a snowman. (Rev: BL 10/15/00*; HBG 3/01)

1171 Kelly, L. J. R. *Blanket and Bear, a Remarkable Pair* (PS–1). Illus. by Yoko Tanaka. 2013, Putnam $16.99 (978-039925681-3). 32pp. A moving story about lost toys involving a boy and his beloved blanket and bear, with both boy and blanket and bear finding ways to cope. **e** (Rev: BL 9/1/13; SLJ 12/13)

1172 Kennedy, Kim. *Pirate Pete* (K–3). Illus. by Doug Kennedy. 2002, Abrams $15.95 (978-0-8109-4356-8). 32pp. Pete and his parrot share a series of swashbuckling adventures after he steals a treasure map from a queen. (Rev: BL 6/1–15/02; HBG 10/02)

1173 Kennedy, Kim. *Pirate Pete's Talk Like a Pirate* (K–2). Illus. by Doug Kennedy. 2007, Abrams $15.95 (978-0-8109-9348-8). 40pp. This third book in the series features Pirate Pete and his parrot searching for a crew on Rascal Island. (Rev: BL 12/1/07; SLJ 4/08)

1174 Kennedy, Kim. *Pirate Peter's Giant Adventure* (PS–2). Illus. by Doug Kennedy. 2006, Abrams $15.95 (978-0-8109-5965-1). Pirate Pete and his trusty parrot sidekick brave the perils of Thunder Island to rescue the Sea-Fairy Sapphire and return it to the sea; a sequel to *Pirate Pete* (2002). (Rev: BL 6/1–15/06)

1175 Kent, Allegra. *Ballerina Swan* (PS–3). Illus. by Emily Arnold McCully. 2012, Holiday House $16.95 (978-0-8234-2373-6). 32pp. A young swan named Sophie who is eager to be a ballerina works hard and is eventually awarded a part in *Swan Lake*. (Rev: BL 3/15/12; SLJ 4/1/12*)

1176 Ketteman, Helen. *Bubba, The Cowboy Prince: A Fractured Texas Tale* (K–3). Illus. by James Warhola. 1997, Scholastic $16.95 (978-0-590-25506-6). 32pp. A Western version of the Cinderella story in which a cow is the fairy godmother. (Rev: BL 12/1/97; HBG 3/98)

1177 Ketteman, Helen. *Heat Wave* (K–3). Illus. by Scott Goto. 1998, Walker LB $16.85 (978-0-8027-8645-6). 32pp. In this hilarious fantasy, a heat wave gets stuck on a rural weather vane causing a great upheaval for plants and animals. (Rev: BL 2/1/98; HBG 10/98; SLJ 3/98)

1178 Kimmel, Eric A. *The Erie Canal Pirates* (K–3). Illus. by Andrew Glass. 2002, Holiday House $16.95

(978-0-8234-1657-8). 32pp. A humorous tale about a captain battling pirates on the Erie Canal, using the traditional folk song as a base. (Rev: BCCB 11/02; BL 10/15/02; HBG 3/03; SLJ 11/02)

1179 Kimmel, Eric A. *The Tale of Ali Baba and the Forty Thieves: A Story from the Arabian Nights* (1–3). Illus. by Will Hillenbrand. 1996, Holiday House LB $15.95 (978-0-8234-1258-7). 30pp. Ali Baba and the story of his amazing treasure trove are covered in colorful prose. (Rev: BCCB 2/97; BL 12/1/96; SLJ 12/96)

1180 Kipling, Rudyard. *Rikki-Tikki-Tavi* (1–3). Illus. by Lambert Davis. 1992, Harcourt $18.00 (978-0-15-267015-3). 44pp. A mongoose overcomes snakes that live in the garden of an English family in India. (Rev: BL 9/15/92)

1181 Kirk, Daniel. *Honk Honk! Beep Beep!* (PS–K). Illus. by author. 2010, Hyperion $15.99 (978-1-4231-2486-3). 32pp. A young boy's toys — father and son — enjoy a secret adventure before he awakens. (Rev: BL 6/10; SLJ 11/1/10)

1182 Kirk, Daniel. *Library Mouse: A Friend's Tale* (K–3). Illus. by author. 2009, Abrams $15.95 (978-0-8109-8927-6). 32pp. Sam, library mouse and author/illustrator, gains a young friend and collaborator. (Rev: BL 5/15/09; SLJ 4/09)

1183 Kleven, Elisa. *The Paper Princess* (K–2). Illus. 1994, Dutton $16.99 (978-0-525-45231-7). 32pp. A paper princess created by a little girl flies over the city and learns about life. (Rev: BL 7/94; SLJ 6/94*)

1184 Kleven, Elisa. *The Paper Princess Finds Her Way* (PS–1). Illus. by author. 2003, Dutton $16.99 (978-0-525-46911-7). Ignored by the now-grown girl who made her, a paper princess flies off in search of new adventures. (Rev: HBG 4/04; SLJ 10/03)

1185 Kleven, Elisa. *The Paper Princess Flies Again: (With Her Dog!)* (K–2). Illus. 2005, Tricycle $15.95 (978-1-58246-146-5). 32pp. The Paper Princess (a paper doll) and her faithful canine companion embark on an adventure-filled search for a gift to give to Lucy, their owner. (Rev: BL 12/1/05; SLJ 12/05)

1186 Knapman, Timothy. *Mungo and the Spiders from Space* (K–3). Illus. by Adam Stower. 2009, Dial $16.99 (978-0-8037-3277-3). 32pp. When Mungo finds that the last page of his superhero book is missing, his mother suggests that he make up the rest. (Rev: BL 2/1/09; SLJ 4/09)

1187 Knudsen, Michelle. *Argus* (PS–3). Illus. by Andrea Wesson. 2011, Candlewick $15.99 (978-0-7636-3790-3). 32pp. Sally is presented with an odd egg in her class's egg-hatching project; it turns out to be a dragon, presenting a wealth of funny situations and challenging problems. Lexile AD420L (Rev: BL 1/1–15/11; LMC 5–6/11; SLJ 2/1/11)

1188 Kohara, Kazuno. *Ghosts in the House!* (PS–1). Illus. by author. 2008, Roaring Brook $12.95 (978-1-59643-427-1). Undeterred by the fact that she and her cat have moved into a haunted house, the young witch

catches the ghosts, tosses them in the washer, and makes some lovely linens. (Rev: BL 9/1/08; HB 1/09)

1189 Kraegel, Kenneth. *King Arthur's Very Great Grandson* (K–2). Illus. by author. 2012, Candlewick $15.99 (978-076365311-8). 40pp. A young knight who is a descendant of King Arthur sets out on his 6th birthday to find adventure and combat against dragons and other monsters, but finds himself making friends instead. Lexile 720AD (Rev: BL 8/12; SLJ 7/12)

1190 Krause, Ute. *Oscar and the Very Hungry Dragon* (1–3). Illus. by author. 2010, NorthSouth $16.95 (978-0-7358-2306-8). Unpaged. Unlucky Oscar is sent from his village as a peace offering to a hungry dragon; fortunately his cunning and his cooking abilities trick the beast into eating haute cuisine rather than human flesh. (Rev: LMC 11–12/10; SLJ 10/1/10)

1191 Krauss, Ruth. *The Carrot Seed* (K–1). Illus. by Crockett Johnson. 1945, HarperCollins LB $17.89 (978-0-06-023351-8); paper $6.99 (978-0-06-443210-8). 24pp. A young boy is convinced that the seeds he plants will grow, in spite of his family's doubts.

1192 Krensky, Stephen. *Noah's Bark* (K–2). Illus. by Roge. 2010, Carolrhoda $16.95 (978-082257645-7). 32pp. Noah's animals make too many confusing sounds and Noah induces order by making them each choose their own sound. Lexile AD470L (Rev: BL 3/1/10; LMC 8–9/10)

1193 Kroll, Steven. *Super-Dragon* (PS–2). Illus. by Douglas Holgate. 2011, Marshall Cavendish $16.99 (978-0-7614-5819-7). 32pp. Little Drago gets a bird to teach him to fly so he can enter a contest, at which he surprises and impresses his whole family. (Rev: BLO 3/25/11; LMC 8–9/11; SLJ 5/1/11)

1194 Kroll, Steven. *The Tyrannosaurus Game* (K–2). Illus. by S. D. Schindler. 2010, Marshall Cavendish $17.99 (978-0-7614-5603-2). 32pp. Stuck inside on a rainy day, 12 students craft a progressive story about an imaginary dinosaur to pass the time. (Rev: BLO 3/1/10; LMC 8–9/10; SLJ 4/1/10)

1195 Krosoczka, Jarrett J. *Ollie the Purple Elephant* (1–2). Illus. by author. 2011, Knopf $16.99 (978-0-375-86654-8); LB $19.99 (978-0-375-96654-5). Unpaged. A cat and an unhappy neighbor scheme to get rid of the purple elephant living in the McLaughlins' New York City apartment. ❻ (Rev: SLJ 12/1/11)

1196 Kvasnosky, Laura McGee. *Really Truly Bingo* (PS–1). Illus. by author. 2008, Candlewick $15.99 (978-0-7636-3210-6). 32pp. Bea's imaginary dog named Bingo gets her into lots of trouble as they play together in the garden. (Rev: BCCB 6/08; BL 4/15/08; HB 5/08; SLJ 7/08)

1197 Landry, Leo. *Space Boy* (PS–1). Illus. by author. 2007, Houghton $16.00 (978-0-618-60568-2). 32pp. It's too noisy to go to sleep, so young Nicholas takes off for the moon instead, where he enjoys a picnic before returning home to a peaceful house. (Rev: BL 10/15/07; HB 9/07; SLJ 10/07)

1198 Langdo, Bryan. *Tornado Slim and the Magic Cowboy Hat* (K–2). Illus. by author. 2011, Marshall Cavendish $17.99 (978-0-7614-5962-0). 32pp. A hat presented to Tornado Slim by a coyote brings nothing but trouble on a journey to Fire Gulch City. e (Rev: BLO 11/15/11; LMC 1–2/12; SLJ 9/1/11)

1199 LaReau, Kara. *Otto: The Boy Who Loved Cars* (K–3). Illus. by Scott Magoon. 2011, Roaring Brook $15.99 (978-1-59643-484-4). 32pp. A little boy obsessed with race cars turns into one in this quirky fantasy that encourages readers to try new things. (Rev: BL 7/11; SLJ 8/1/11)

1200 LaRochelle, David. *It's a Tiger* (PS–1). Illus. by Jeremy Tankard. 2012, Chronicle $16.99 (978-0-8118-6925-6). 36pp. An imaginative little boy sees a tiger everywhere he looks in this colorful picture book. (Rev: BL 8/12; LMC 3–4/13; SLJ 9/12*)

1201 Lawler, Janet. *If Kisses Were Colors* (PS–1). Illus. by Alison Jay. 2003, Dial $15.99 (978-0-8037-2617-8). 32pp. A fanciful series of characterizations of kisses — as colors, pebbles, comets, flowers, and more — are accompanied by appealing illustrations. (Rev: BL 3/1/03; HBG 10/03; SLJ 3/03)

1202 Lawson, Janet. *Audrey and Barbara* (K–2). Illus. 2002, Simon & Schuster $13.95 (978-0-689-83896-5). 32pp. A little girl and her reluctant cat take a pretend voyage to India in a bathtub. (Rev: BL 9/15/02; HB 5/02; HBG 10/02; SLJ 7/02)

1203 Lazo, Caroline. *Someday When My Cat Can Talk* (K–2). Illus. by Kyrsten Brooker. 2008, Random $16.99 (978-0-375-83754-8). 32pp. A little girl imagines all the fun her cat could have on a trip to Europe. (Rev: BL 3/15/08; SLJ 3/08)

1204 Lechner, John. *Sticky Burr: Adventures in Burrwood Forest* (K–3). Illus. by author. 2007, Candlewick $15.99 (978-0-7636-3054-6). 48pp. This fast-paced, graphic-novel-style book chronicles the adventures of a tiny forest burr who is bullied by the other burrs but eventually gets to show his real mettle. (Rev: BL 7/07; SLJ 7/07)

1205 Lee, Suzy. *The Zoo* (2–5). Illus. by author. 2007, Kane $15.95 (978-1-933605-28-9). The animals sneak out of their cages for a special play time with a little girl during her family's visit to the zoo. (Rev: SLJ 6/07)

1206 Lee, YJ. *The Little Moon Princess* (PS–3). Illus. by author. 2010, HarperCollins $16.99 (978-0-06-154736-2). 32pp. A sparrow and a princess work together to spread bright stars throughout the night sky in this beautifully illustrated story. (Rev: BL 5/1/10; SLJ 4/1/10)

1207 Leedahl, Shelley A. *The Bone Talker* (PS–2). Illus. by Bill Slavin. 2000, Red Deer $15.95 (978-0-88995-214-0). 32pp. To help cheer up elderly Grandmother Bones, a little girl gets her to begin making a quilt that later becomes a patchwork of fields across the Great Plains. (Rev: BL 4/15/00)

1208 Leedy, Loreen. *Follow the Money!* (1–3). Illus. 2002, Holiday House $17.95 (978-0-8234-1587-8). 32pp. George, a newly minted quarter, has a busy day and experiences many exciting adventures, from delivery at the bank to his eventual return there. (Rev: BCCB 4/02; BL 4/15/02*; HBG 10/02; SLJ 5/02)

1209 Lehman, Barbara. *Rainstorm* (PS–2). Illus. 2007, Houghton $16.00 (978-0-618-75639-1). On a rainy, shut-in day, a boy finds a chest and a key that lead him down a ladder, up some stairs, and onto a sunny island with playmates at the ready; sophisticated, boldly lined art captures the recurrent adventures in this wordless fantasy. (Rev: BL 1/1–15/07)

1210 Leonard, Marie. *Tibili: The Little Boy Who Didn't Want to Go to School* (K–3). Illus. by Andree Prigent. 2002, Kane $15.95 (978-1-929132-20-1). An African child is reluctant to start school but, when the animals show him how important reading is, he changes his mind. (Rev: BL 6/1–15/02; HBG 10/02; SLJ 4/02)

1211 Lerner, Harriet, and Susan Goldhor. *Franny B. Kranny, There's a Bird in Your Hair!* (PS–3). Illus. by Helen Oxenbury. 2001, HarperCollins LB $15.89 (978-0-06-029503-5). 40pp. A bird settles in Franny's hair when her overabundant locks are put up for a special occasion, and she refuses to dislodge it. (Rev: BCCB 9/01; BL 6/1–15/01; HB 7/01; HBG 10/01; SLJ 6/01)

1212 Leslie, Amanda. *Who's That Scratching at My Door? A Peekaboo Riddle Book* (PS–K). Illus. by author. 2001, Handprint $12.95 (978-1-929766-19-2). A young boy is looking for a friend, but the animals that keep showing up at the door (actually, under the flap) are never quite right until a puppy turns up. (Rev: HBG 10/01; SLJ 7/01)

1213 Lester, Julius. *The Hungry Ghosts* (K–1). Illus. by Geraldo Valério. 2009, Dial $16.99 (978-0-8037-2513-3). 40pp. Young Malcolm, who lives beside a graveyard, realizes that three ghosts are only making eerie noises because they're hungry. But what do ghosts eat? (Rev: BL 5/15/09; SLJ 8/09)

1214 Lester, Julius. *Shining* (K–3). Illus. by John Clapp. 2003, Harcourt $17.00 (978-0-15-200773-7). Shunned by her fellow villagers because she refuses to speak, Shining eventually finds her voice and becomes the leader of her people. (Rev: BCCB 12/03; HBG 4/04; SLJ 11/03)

1215 Leuck, Laura. *My Monster Mama Loves Me So* (PS). Illus. by Mark Buehner. 1999, Lothrop LB $15.93 (978-0-688-16867-4). A slight, humorous tale in which a little monster tells the ways his mother loves him — like attending his beastball games. (Rev: HBG 3/00; SLJ 1/00)

1216 Levert, Mireille. *An Island in the Soup* (PS). Illus. 2001, Groundwood $15.95 (978-0-88899-403-5). 32pp. Victor of the Noodle experiences great danger while traveling through his soup. (Rev: BL 7/01; HBG 10/01; SLJ 6/01)

1217 Levine, Gail C. *Betsy Who Cried Wolf!* (PS–2). Illus. by Scott Nash. 2002, HarperCollins LB $16.89 (978-0-06-028764-1). A wolf tries to outwit the new shepherd, 8-year-old Betsy, but she manages to make him an ally. (Rev: BCCB 10/02; BL 7/02; HBG 10/02; SLJ 6/02)

1218 Levine, Gail Carson. *Betsy Red Hoodie* (K–3). Illus. by Scott Nash. 2010, HarperCollins $16.99 (978-0-06-146870-4). 40pp. Shepherd Betsy (of 2002's *Betsy Who Cried Wolf!*) is off to Grandma's house along with the sheep and her colleague Zimmo the wolf in this funny fractured tale. Lexile AD210L (Rev: BL 9/15/10; HB 9–10/10; SLJ 9/1/10)

1219 Lewis, Kim. *Hooray for Harry* (PS–2). 2006, Candlewick $15.99 (978-0-7636-2962-5). 32pp. Accompanied by his friends Lulu the lamb and Ted the teddy bear, Harry the stuffed elephant goes in search of his missing blanket. (Rev: BL 6/1–15/06; SLJ 4/06)

1220 Lewis, Paul Owen. *The Jupiter Stone* (PS–3). Illus. by author. 2003, Tricycle $15.95 (978-1-58246-107-6). When a boy discovers a strange rock of extraterrestrial origin that has laid undiscovered on the Earth's surface for millions of years, he enlists the help of NASA to see that the stone is returned to the vastness of outer space. (Rev: SLJ 9/03)

1221 Lichtenheld, Tom. *Cloudette* (PS–2). Illus. by author. 2011, Henry Holt $16.99 (978-0-8050-8776-5). 40pp. A kindhearted cloud too little to quench a whole field of crops finds a perfect application for her altruistic spirit: a tiny pond with a lone parched frog. **e** Lexile AD660L (Rev: BL 2/1/11; SLJ 2/1/11)

1222 Light, Steve. *The Shoemaker Extraordinaire* (PS–1). Illus. 2003, Abrams $14.95 (978-0-8109-4236-3). 32pp. The tale of Hans Crispin, who makes magical shoes for a giant named Barefootus. (Rev: BL 3/15/03; HBG 4/04; SLJ 7/03)

1223 Light, Steve. *Zephyr Takes Flight* (PS–2). Illus. by author. 2012, Candlewick $16.99 (978-0-7636-5695-9). 40pp. Airplane-mad Zephyr is sent to her room after making a mess and finds herself in a strange land full of flying machines. (Rev: BLO 10/15/12; LMC 3–4/13; SLJ 9/12)

1224 Lillegard, Dee. *Tiger, Tiger* (PS–2). Illus. by Susan Guevara. 2002, Penguin $16.99 (978-0-399-22633-5). 32pp. Dramatic illustrations add to this exciting story, in which lonely Pocu finds a magic feather in the hot jungle and uses it and his imagination to create a tiger — a very hungry tiger. (Rev: BL 1/1–15/03; HBG 3/03; SLJ 12/02)

1225 Lindenbaum, Pija. *Bridget and the Gray Wolves* (PS–2). Illus. 2001, Farrar $14.00 (91-29-65395-9). 24pp. Timid little Bridget always expects the worst, but when she becomes surrounded by wolves she surprisingly becomes leader of the pack in this humorous reversal full of funny lupines. (Rev: BCCB 9/01; BL 12/15/01; HBG 3/02; SLJ 11/01)

1226 Lindenbaum, Pija. *Bridget and the Moose Brothers* (PS–1). Trans. from Swedish by Kjersti Board. Illus. by author. 2004, R&S $16.00 (91-29-66046-7). Bridget wants a baby brother or sister, but what she gets instead is a trio of uncouth moose. (Rev: SLJ 5/04)

1227 Lindenbaum, Pija. *Bridget and the Muttonheads* (PS–2). Trans. by Kjersti Board. Illus. 2002, Farrar $16.00 (91-29-65650-8). 28pp. Little Bridget, on vaca-

tion with her parents and bored by the pool, wanders off to find an adventure of her own in this imaginative tale. (Rev: BL 8/02; HB 11/02; HBG 3/03; SLJ 1/03)

1228 Lindgren, Astrid. *Mirabelle* (PS–2). Trans. from Swedish by Elisabeth Kallick Dyssegaard. Illus. by Pija Lindenbaum. 2003, R&S $15.00 (91-29-65821-7). Translated into English, this charming Swedish tale tells how 8-year-old Britta plants a seed given to her by a stranger and is pleasantly surprised when the seed sprouts into a doll like the one she has long been wanting. (Rev: BL 5/15/03; HBG 10/03; SLJ 8/03) [839.7]

1229 Lindgren, Astrid. *Most Beloved Sister* (2–4). Trans. by Elisabeth Kallick Dyssegaard. Illus. by Hans Arnold. 2002, Farrar $15.00 (91-29-65502-1). When her baby brother is born, Barbara's imaginary twin sister, Lalla-Lee, comes to her rescue and the two have a day of magical adventures together in this vividly illustrated story that was originally published a half-century ago. (Rev: BL 7/02; HBG 10/02; SLJ 8/02)

1230 Lloyd-Jones, Sally. *Old MacNoah Had an Ark* (K–2). Illus. by Jill Newton. 2008, HarperBlessings $16.99 (978-0-06-055717-1). Lloyd-Jones uses "Old MacDonald Had a Farm" as a base for a rollicking view of the animals aboard Noah's ark. (Rev: BL 6/1–15/08; SLJ 4/08)

1231 Loki. *Jake Greenthumb* (PS–2). Illus. by Jason Gaillard. 2002, Mondo $15.95 (978-1-59034-186-5). 32pp. Jake's thumb is so green that the plants he is looking after threaten to take over his room. (Rev: HBG 10/02; SLJ 9/02)

1232 Long, Loren. *Otis and the Puppy* (PS–1). Illus. by author. 2013, Philomel $17.99 (978-0-399-25469-7). 40pp. A tractor called Otis and a little puppy become friends even before Otis rescues the puppy when he is lost in the woods. ♫ **e** Lexile AD820 (Rev: BL 3/1/13; SLJ 3/13)

1233 Long, Loren. *Otis and the Tornado* (PS–2). Illus. by author. 2011, Philomel $17.99 (978-0-399-25477-2). 40pp. When a tornado looms over the farm, Otis the tractor comes to the aid of the recalcitrant and ornery bull. (Rev: BL 9/1/11; SLJ 10/1/11)

1234 Long, Melinda. *How I Became a Pirate* (PS–3). Illus. by David Shannon. 2003, Harcourt $16.00 (978-0-15-201848-1). The charms of a life aboard a pirate ship wane as Jeremy Jacob realizes he misses bedtime stories and goodnight kisses. (Rev: HBG 4/04; SLJ 9/03)

1235 López, Brigitta Garcia. *Dreamflight* (K–2). Trans. by Marianne Martens. Illus. 2005, North-South $16.95 (978-0-7358-2024-1). Young Max awakens one night to discover his rather plump guardian angel driving around his bedroom in a racing car. (Rev: BL 12/15/05)

1236 Lowell, Susan. *The Bootmaker and the Elves* (K–4). Illus. by Tom Curry. 1997, Orchard LB $16.99 (978-0-531-33044-9). 32pp. The old folktale is given a new setting, the Old West, and a new subject, cowboy boots. (Rev: BL 9/15/97; HB 11/97; HBG 3/98; SLJ 11/97)

1237 Lucas, David. *Nutmeg* (1–3). 2006, Knopf $16.95 (978-0-375-83519-3). 32pp. Pigtailed Nutmeg is tired of the same old fare for breakfast, lunch, and dinner, but things get a little crazy after she receives a magic spoon. (Rev: BL 8/06; SLJ 8/06)

1238 Lucas, David. *Whale* (PS–1). Illus. by author. 2007, Knopf $16.99 (978-0-375-84338-9). 32pp. When a tsunami leaves a beached whale in its wake, Joe and his grandma consult the mystical powers of nature to solve the problem. (Rev: BCCB 9/07; BL 6/1–15/07; LMC 8/07; SLJ 6/07)

1239 Luján, Jorge. *Sky Blue Accident / Accidente celeste* (K–1). Trans. from Spanish by Elisa Amado. Illus. by Piet Grobler. 2007, Groundwood $16.95 (978-0-88899-805-7). This story in English and Spanish has a boy accidentally breaking off a bit of the sky when he falls off his bike. (Rev: SLJ 7/07)

1240 Lund, Deb. *Monsters on Machines* (PS–1). Illus. by Robert Neubecker. 2008, Harcourt $16.00 (978-0-15-205365-9). 40pp. Bright, lively illustrations add to the appeal of this story about young monsters using construction machines to build a haunted house. (Rev: SLJ 9/08)

1241 Lyon, George E. *My Friend, the Starfinder* (K–2). Illus. by Stephen Gammell. 2008, Atheneum $16.99 (978-1-4169-2738-9). 40pp. A little girl listens to her neighbor tell the fairytale like story of how, as a boy, he met a star and found himself at the end of a rainbow. (Rev: BCCB 3/08; BL 1/1–15/08; HB 3/08; LMC 3/08*; SLJ 3/08) ⌒

1242 McAllister, Angela. *Mama and Little Joe* (PS). Illus. by Terry Milne. 2007, Simon & Schuster $15.99 (978-1-4169-1631-4). Timeworn and tattered, stuffed kangaroos Mama and Little Joe get the cold shoulder from the newer, brighter stuffed toys at their new home; but when Little Joe is accidentally discarded the newer toys rise to the occasion and offer to help find him. (Rev: BL 4/1/07)

1243 McAllister, Angela. *Yuck! That's Not a Monster* (PS–2). Illus. by Alison Edgson. 2010, Good Books $16.99 (978-156148683-0). 32pp. Two warty and frightful monsters are miffed when their third egg hatches into something adorable. (Rev: BLO 5/15/10; SLJ 8/10)

1244 McCarty, Peter. *The Monster Returns* (PS–K). Illus. by author. 2012, Henry Holt $16.99 (978-080509030-7). 40pp. In this sequel to *Jeremy Draws a Monster* (2009), the monster created in a drawing threatens to return and Jeremy asks his friends to help create new monsters — and a hospitable atmosphere. (Rev: BLO 12/15/11; SLJ 1/12)

1245 McCaughrean, Geraldine. *Blue Moon Mountain* (1–3). Illus. by Nicki Palin. 2007, Simply Read $16.95 (978-1-894965-56-9). 32pp. Joy follows a moonlit path to Blue Mountain, the magical home of the fantastical creatures of myth, legend, and literature. (Rev: BL 3/15/07; SLJ 4/1/07)

1246 McClintock, Barbara. *Dahlia* (PS–2). Illus. 2002, Farrar $16.00 (978-0-374-31678-5). 32pp. When Charlotte is given a frilly doll named Dahlia, she includes her in her tomboy adventures in this picture book set in the Victorian age. (Rev: BCCB 10/02; BL 9/1/02; HB 9/02*; HBG 3/03; SLJ 11/02*)

1247 McDaniels, Preston. *A Perfect Snowman* (PS–1). Illus. by author. 2007, Simon & Schuster $15.99 (978-1-4169-1026-8). 40pp. Built by a wealthy boy, every element of the snowman seems perfect, but the real value comes when the snowman shares what he has with those around him. (Rev: BL 12/1/07; SLJ 10/07)

1248 McDonald, Megan. *Ant and Honey Bee: What a Pair!* (PS–2). Illus. by G. Brian Karas. 2005, Candlewick $13.99 (978-0-7636-1265-8). 32pp. Ant and Honey Bee set off happily for the costume party, but rain ruins their efforts and they must improvise hastily. (Rev: BL 2/15/05; SLJ 4/05)

1249 McDonald, Megan. *It's Picture Day Today!* (PS–K). Illus. by Katherine Tillotson. 2009, Atheneum $16.99 (978-1-4169-2434-0). 32pp. A class made up of art materials — squiggles, sequins, pom-poms, buttons, glue, and so forth — is very excited on Picture Day. (Rev: BL 5/1/09; HB 7/09; SLJ 6/09)

1250 McDonald, Megan. *When the Library Lights Go Out* (PS–2). Illus. by Katherine Tillotson. 2005, Simon & Schuster $16.95 (978-0-689-86170-3). 40pp. After the library has closed for the night, storytime puppets Rabbit and Lion launch a search for their friend Hermit Crab. (Rev: BL 11/1/05; SLJ 11/05)

1251 MacDonald, Ross. *Bad Baby* (K–2). Illus. 2005, Roaring Brook $16.95 (978-1-59643-064-8). 32pp. Superhero Jack, first seen in *Another Perfect Day* (2002), begins to rethink his wish for a little sister when the reality turns out to be far different than he had imagined. (Rev: BCCB 11/05; BL 10/1/05*; HB 9/05; HBG 4/06; SLJ 9/05)

1252 McDonnell, Patrick. *The Monsters' Monster* (K–2). Illus. by author. 2012, Little, Brown $16.99 (978-0-316-04547-6). 40pp. Three little monsters — Grouch, Grump, and Gloom 'n' Doom, who cannot agree on which is the biggest and baddest — create a huge monster who surprisingly just wants to have fun. (Rev: BL 10/1/12; LMC 3–4/13; SLJ 10/12*)

1253 McElligott, Matthew. *Even Monsters Need Haircuts* (PS–2). Illus. by author. 2010, Walker $14.99 (978-0-8027-8819-1). 40pp. Monsters do need haircuts, and once a month a normally obedient boy provides this service in his father's barbershop. (Rev: BL 8/10; SLJ 9/1/10)

1254 McKinlay, Meg. *No Bears* (K–2). Illus. by Leila Rudge. 2012, Candlewick $15.99 (978-076365890-8). 32pp. Ella is determined to write a story without bears, but one keeps cropping up despite her best intentions and even plays a key role in this book with fairy-tale themes. (Rev: BL 4/1/12; HB 5–6/12; LMC 10/12; SLJ 5/1/12)

1255 McKissack, Patricia C. *Ol' Clip-Clop: A Ghost Story* (K–3). Illus. by Eric Velasquez. 2013, Holiday $16.95 (978-0-8234-2265-4). 32pp. Using dark and appropriately creepy illustrations, McKissack tells the story of John Leep, a selfish landlord who in 1741 happily sets out to evict a poor widow and is followed by the eerie clip-clop of a ghostly horse. Lexile AD630 (Rev: BL 10/1/13; SLJ 9/13)

1256 McKissack, Patricia C. *Where Crocodiles Have Wings* (K–2). Illus. by Bob Barner. 2005, Holiday $16.95 (978-0-8234-1748-3). 32pp. A rhyming fantasy set in a land where "surprises grow on trees" full of happy animals engaging in unusual activities. (Rev: BL 9/15/05; SLJ 10/05)

1257 McKissack, Patricia C., and Onawumi Jean Moss. *Precious and the Boo Hag* (K–2). Illus. by Kyrsten Brooker. 2005, Simon & Schuster $16.95 (978-0-689-85194-0). 40pp. Precious, stuck home alone with a stomachache when her mother and brother must leave, resists multiple attempts by the Boo Hag to gain entry to the house. (Rev: BL 2/1/05; SLJ 3/05)

1258 Maclear, Kyo. *Spork* (PS–2). Illus. by Isabelle Arsenault. 2010, Kids Can $7.95 (978-1-55337-736-8). 32pp. Frustrated with never fitting in, young Spork (who is part spoon and part fork) vies for acceptance until a new development makes the misfit utensil just what everyone needs. Lexile 740L (Rev: BL 9/15/10; SLJ 2/1/11)

1259 McMullan, Kate. *I Stink!* (PS–3). Illus. by James McMullan. 2002, HarperCollins LB $17.89 (978-0-06-029849-4). In this boldly illustrated picture book, a garbage truck describes its activities during its nightly rounds. (Rev: BCCB 6/02; BL 6/1–15/02; HB 5/02*; HBG 10/02; SLJ 5/02)

1260 McNamara, Margaret. *The Three Little Aliens and the Big Bad Robot* (PS–2). Illus. by Mark Fearing. 2011, Random House $16.99 (978-0-375-86689-0); LB $19.99 (978-0-375-96689-7). 40pp. In this story reminiscent of the Three Little Pigs, three lovable aliens — Bork, Gork, and Nklxwcyz — set off into space to build their own homes, taking care to watch out for the big, bad robot. (Rev: BL 10/15/11; SLJ 9/1/11)

1261 McNaughton, Janet. *Brave Jack and the Unicorn* (K–3). Illus. by Susan Tooke. 2005, Tundra $15.95 (978-0-88776-677-0). 32pp. Drawing on traditional Newfoundland tales, this is the story of Jack, who is sent off in search of his older brothers and succeeds in finding them — as well as a wife — with the help of plants and animals that reward him with magical gifts. (Rev: BL 6/1–15/05)

1262 McPhail, David. *Boy on the Brink* (PS–2). Illus. by author. 2006, Holt $15.95 (978-0-8050-7618-9). 32pp. In his dreams, a boy reviews and expands dramatically on the day's events. (Rev: BL 5/15/06; SLJ 5/06)

1263 McPhail, David. *Edward and the Pirates* (PS–3). Illus. 1997, Little, Brown $15.95 (978-0-316-56344-4). The pirates that Edward is reading about come alive and kidnap him. (Rev: BCCB 7–8/97; BL 4/15/97; SLJ 5/97)

1264 McPhail, David. *Edward in the Jungle* (PS–3). Illus. 2002, Little, Brown $15.95 (978-0-316-56391-8). 32pp. While reading about Tarzan, Edward is transported to Africa where he is saved from a menacing crocodile by the Lord of the Jungle. (Rev: BCCB 4/02; BL 4/1/02; HBG 10/02; SLJ 3/02)

1265 MacRae, Tom. *The Opposite* (1–3). Illus. by Elena Odriozola. 2006, Peachtree $15.95 (978-1-56145-371-9). After the Opposite, a strange-looking creature, appears in his bedroom one morning, Nate finds that everything he does turns out the opposite of what he intended. (Rev: SLJ 10/06)

1266 Mahy, Margaret. *Bubble Trouble* (PS–1). Illus. by Polly Dunbar. 2009, Clarion $16.00 (978-0-547-07421-4). It takes a human ladder, a slingshot, and a good catch to save a baby who is floating away in a bubble. (Rev: BL 4/15/09; HB 5/09; SLJ 5/09)

1267 Mahy, Margaret. *The Green Bath* (PS–2). Illus. by Steven Kellogg. 2013, Scholastic $16.99 (978-0-545-20667-9). 40pp. A new green bathtub whisks Sammy off on a whirlwind adventure while he is supposed to be getting clean for his grandmother's visit. Lexile AD640 (Rev: BL 7/13; LMC 1–2/14; SLJ 7/13)

1268 Mahy, Margaret. *The Man from the Land of Fandango* (PS–1). Illus. by Polly Dunbar. 2012, Clarion $16.99 (978-0-547-81988-4). 32pp. A whimsical rhyming tale about a roly-poly man who springs to life from a painting to lead two children on a lively, imaginative romp. (Rev: BL 11/1/12; SLJ 9/12)

1269 Marciano, John Bemelmans. *Madeline at the White House* (PS–1). Illus. by author. 2011, Viking $17.99 (978-0-670-01228-2). 48pp. Madeline and her orphan friends arrive from Paris to cheer up neglected First Daughter Candle in this magical Capitol Hill romp. Lexile AD540L (Rev: BL 1/1–15/11; SLJ 3/1/11)

1270 Marciano, John Bemelmans. *There's a Dolphin in the Grand Canal* (K–2). Illus. 2005, Viking $15.99 (978-0-670-05987-4). Bored despite the fact that he lives in Venice, Luca gets a thrilling ride over the city on the back of a dolphin. (Rev: BL 6/1–15/05)

1271 Mayer, Mercer. *The Bravest Knight* (PS–2). Illus. 2007, Dial $16.99 (978-0-8037-3206-3). 32pp. A young boy dreams of living in the olden days, in a world of knights, castles, dragons, and — um — scary trolls — in this newly illustrated update of Mayer's *Terrible Troll* (1968). (Rev: BL 5/1/07; SLJ 6/07)

1272 Mayer, Mercer. *Too Many Dinosaurs* (K–2). Illus. by author. 2011, Holiday House $16.95 (978-0-8234-2316-3). 32pp. A little boy who desperately wants a puppy ends up with a dinosaur egg instead, with interesting consequences. (Rev: BL 9/15/11; SLJ 9/1/11)

1273 Mayhew, James. *Ella Bella Ballerina and Swan Lake* (PS–3). Illus. by author. 2011, Barron's $14.99 (978-0-7641-6407-1). 32pp. A music box transports young Ella Bella into Tchaikovsky's ballet, where she sees the story unfold. Lexile AD670L (Rev: BLO 7/11; SLJ 8/1/11)

1274 Mayhew, James. *Ella Bella Ballerina and the Nutcracker* (PS–2). Illus. by author. 2012, Barron's $14.99 (978-0-7641-6581-8). 32pp. Madame Rosa's magic music box transports Ella Bella and her ballet class to the world of the *Nutcracker*; the 4th in the series. (Rev: BLO 10/15/12; SLJ 1/13)

1275 Mayhew, James. *Katie and the Mona Lisa* (K–3). Illus. 1999, Orchard $15.95 (978-0-531-30177-7). 32pp. In the company of Mona Lisa, Katie enters several famous Renaissance paintings to regain Mona Lisa's famous smile. (Rev: BCCB 9/99; BL 9/1/99; HBG 3/00; SLJ 12/99)

1276 Mayhew, James. *Katie and the Sunflowers* (K–3). Illus. 2001, Scholastic $16.95 (978-0-531-30325-2). 32pp. Katie's museum escapades continue with a romp through Van Gogh, Gauguin, and Cezanne canvases that involves sunflowers, still lifes, and a chase through a cafe. (Rev: BL 6/1–15/01; HBG 10/01; SLJ 7/01)

1277 Mayhew, James. *The Knight Who Took All Day* (K–2). Illus. by author. 2005, Scholastic $15.99 (978-0-439-74829-2). Determined to impress a princess by vanquishing a dragon, a self-centered knight has so much trouble finding one that the princess tames the beast herself. (Rev: SLJ 10/05)

1278 Meadows, Michelle. *Pilot Pups* (PS–K). Illus. by Dan Andreasen. 2008, Simon & Schuster $15.99 (978-1-4169-2484-5). 32pp. Toy dogs take to the air to rescue a toy train that has been abandoned outside. (Rev: BL 7/08; SLJ 4/08)

1279 Meadows, Michelle. *Traffic Pups* (PS–K). Illus. by Dan Andreasen. 2011, Simon & Schuster $15.99 (978-1-4169-2485-2). 32pp. Canine motorcyclists police their toy community's roads, helping where needed, and disciplining the occasional offender in this sequel to *Pilot Pups* (2008). (Rev: BLO 8/11; SLJ 6/11)

1280 Meddaugh, Susan. *The Witch's Walking Stick* (PS–2). Illus. 2005, Houghton $16.00 (978-0-618-52948-3). 32pp. Bullied by her older brother and sister, Margaret runs away and happens upon a magic stick (acquiring a new canine friend in the process); she then uses the stick to cast suitably awful spells on her evil siblings. (Rev: BL 7/05; SLJ 9/05)

1281 Melling, David. *The Kiss That Missed* (PS–2). Illus. by author. 2002, Barron's $14.95 (978-0-7641-5451-5). A royal kiss goes astray and must be retrieved from a spooky forest full of dangers. (Rev: HBG 3/03; SLJ 12/02)

1282 Meshon, Aaron. *Tools Rule!* (PS–1). Illus. by author. 2014, Atheneum $16.99 (978-144249601-9). 40pp. A team of tools decide they need their own shed and set to the task cooperatively. ℮ (Rev: BL 3/1/14; HB 3–4/14; LMC 5–6/14*; SLJ 2/14)

1283 Metzger, Steve. *Detective Blue* (PS–2). Illus. by Tedd Arnold. 2011, Scholastic $16.99 (978-0-545-17286-8). 32pp. Detective (Little Boy) Blue searches for the missing Miss Muffet and encounters a variety of familiar nursery rhyme characters along the way. (Rev: BL 8/11; HB 9–10/11; LMC 11–12/11; SLJ 7/11*)

1284 Milgrim, David. *Another Day in the Milky Way* (PS–1). Illus. by author. 2007, Putnam $15.99 (978-0-399-24548-0). Upset when he wakes up on the wrong planet, young Monty looks desperately for someone who can help him get back to Earth and then remembers he's been in this situation before. (Rev: BL 2/15/07; SLJ 2/07)

1285 Milord, Susan. *The Ghost on the Hearth* (PS–2). Illus. by Lydia Dabcovich. 2003, Vermont Folklife Center $15.95 (978-0-916718-18-3). 32pp. A well-illustrated ghost story set in early 19th-century Quebec, in which a young girl returns from the dead to the house in which she worked. (Rev: BL 2/1/04; HBG 4/04; SLJ 12/03)

1286 Milord, Susan. *Pebble: A Story About Belonging* (PS–2). Illus. by author. 2007, HarperCollins $15.99 (978-0-06-085807-0). 32pp. On a rocky coastline a small round pebble longs to become something special and its dream comes true when a young boy visits the beach with his family and selects the pebble as a keepsake. (Rev: BL 11/15/07; SLJ 2/08)

1287 Mitchell, Adrian. *Nobody Rides the Unicorn* (1–4). Illus. by Stephen Lambert. 2000, Scholastic $16.95 (978-0-439-11204-8). 32pp. An evil king tricks a young girl into capturing the unicorn, but when she realizes what has happened she is able to free him. (Rev: BCCB 2/00; BL 4/15/00; HBG 10/00; SLJ 1/01)

1288 Moore, Jodi. *When a Dragon Moves In* (PS–2). Illus. by Howard McWilliam. 2011, Flashlight $16.95 (978-0-979974-67-0). Unpaged. A dragon moves into a boy's sandcastle and the two have great fun together but nobody will believe that he's there. (Rev: LMC 10/11*; SLJ 9/1/11)

1289 Morgan, Mary. *Dragon Pizzeria* (PS–3). Illus. by author. 2008, Knopf $16.99 (978-0-375-82309-1). A pizzeria run by dragons in Fairy Tale Land allows readers many chances for guessing. Who would have ordered a topping of magic beans? Porridge? (Rev: SLJ 4/08)

1290 Morris, Jackie. *Little Evie in the Wild Wood* (1–3). Illus. by Catherine Hyde. 2013, Frances Lincoln $18.99 (978-184780371-9). 36pp. When Little Evie begins her walk home through the woods, it seems mysterious and a little scary, but she soon meets a wolf with whom she has jam tarts to share, and in return he carries Little Evie home to her waiting mother in this fractured fairy tale. (Rev: BL 11/1/13; SLJ 2/14)

1291 Morrissey, Dean. *The Wizard Mouse* (K–2). Illus. by author. 2011, HarperCollins $16.99 (978-0-06-008066-2). Unpaged. A young field mouse named Rollie agrees to assist an aging wizard in keeping his kingdom of Muddmoor safe from attack. (Rev: SLJ 12/1/11)

1292 Morrissey, Dean, and Stephen Krensky. *The Crimson Comet* (PS–2). Illus. by Dean Morrissey. 2006, HarperCollins LB $17.89 (978-0-06-008070-9). Nora becomes alarmed when the light of the moon suddenly blinks out, so she and her brother Jack board a rocket and head off to see if they can offer assistance to the Man-in-the-Moon. (Rev: SLJ 12/06)

1293 Morrow, Tara Jaye. *Just Mommy and Me* (PS). Illus. by Katy Bratun. 2004, HarperCollins LB $13.89 (978-0-06-000725-6). Told in rhyme, with an imaginative graphic layout, this is the story of a little boy who thinks about what fun it would be if he and his mother were monkeys. (Rev: SLJ 4/04)

1294 Mortimer, Rachael. *Song for a Princess* (PS–1). Illus. by Maddy McClellan. 2010, Scholastic $17.99 (978-0-545-24835-8). Unpaged. A little brown bird manages to cheer up a sad princess by using the happy words he has collected from her stories. Lexile AD650L (Rev: LMC 1–2/11; SLJ 11/1/10)

1295 Moser, Lisa. *The Monster in the Backpack* (1–2). Illus. by Noah Z. Jones. 2006, Candlewick $14.99 (978-0-7636-2390-6). 40pp. Initially startled to discover a monster in her backpack, Annie soon develops a warm spot in her heart for the strange and mischievous yet endearing creature. (Rev: SLJ 8/06)

1296 Mull, Brandon. *Pingo* (K–2). Illus. by Brandon Dorman. 2009, Shadow Mountain $17.95 (978-1-60641-109-4). Unpaged. A young boy's imaginary friend becomes resentful when he's put aside for more mature interests, mischievously sabotaging Chad's life until, many years later, Chad returns to his old friend for company. (Rev: SLJ 1/1/10)

1297 Murphy, Stuart J. *A Pair of Socks* (PS–1). Illus. by Lois Ehlert. 1996, HarperCollins LB $15.89 (978-0-06-025880-1). A sock sets out to find its lost mate. (Rev: BL 10/1/96; SLJ 12/96)

1298 Murray, Laura. *The Gingerbread Man Loose in the School* (K–2). Illus. by Mike Lowery. 2011, Putnam $16.99 (978-0-399-25052-1). 32pp. The Gingerbread Man is upset when the class that created him takes off for recess, leaving him on his own. (Rev: BL 8/11*; SLJ 8/1/11)

1299 Murray, Martine. *Henrietta Gets a Letter* (1–3). Illus. by author. 2010, IPG/Allen & Unwin paper $8.99 (978-17417545-1-3). 92pp. Henrietta recovers from a tantrum when she discovers a small fairy under her bed in this third installment in the series. (Rev: BL 1/1–15/11)

1300 Muth, Jon J. *Zen Ghosts* (K–3). Illus. by author. 2010, Scholastic $17.99 (978-0-439-63430-4). 40pp. On Halloween, Stillwater the Zen Buddhist panda tells his three sibling friends a thought-provoking and spooky story. ♫ Lexile AD530L (Rev: BL 9/15/10; SLJ 11/1/10)

1301 Muth, Jon J. *Zen Ties* (K–3). Illus. by author. 2008, Scholastic $17.99 (978-0-439-63425-0). 40pp. Stillwater the giant panda, in the company of his nephew Koo, persuades his three young friends to befriend a cranky elderly neighbor. (Rev: BL 2/15/08; SLJ 4/08)

1302 Namioka, Lensey. *The Hungriest Boy in the World* (K–3). Illus. by Aki Sogabe. 2001, Holiday House $16.95 (978-0-8234-1542-7). 32pp. A little Japanese boy swallows a hunger monster that causes the boy to eat everything in sight. (Rev: BL 4/1/01; HB 5/01; HBG 10/01; SLJ 4/01)

1303 Nara, Yoshitomo. *The Lonesome Puppy* (PS). Illus. by author. 2008, Chronicle $17.99 (978-0-8118-5640-9). 40pp. A puppy so large he spans the Pacific Ocean is lonely until a little girl climbs high enough to recognize him for what he is. (Rev: BL 6/1–15/08; SLJ 7/08)

1304 Neubecker, Robert. *Courage of the Blue Boy* (PS–K). Illus. 2006, Tricycle $15.95 (978-1-58246-182-3).

32pp. A blue boy and his blue cow search for lands with other colors and eventually find a multicolor city that has no blue; it's up to the boy to add this. (Rev: BL 11/1/06; SLJ 11/06)

1305 Nez, John. *One Smart Cookie* (PS–2). 2006, Albert Whitman $16.99 (978-0-8075-6099-0). 32pp. Cookie the dog comes to school and outshines Duffy and Nash in reading and writing ability. (Rev: BL 9/15/06; SLJ 10/06)

1306 Nielsen-Fernlund, Susin. *Hank and Fergus* (PS–2). 2003, Orca $16.95 (978-1-55143-245-8). Hank, always conscious of his birthmark, conjures up an imaginary dog called Fergus, who keeps him company until he finds a real friend. (Rev: HBG 4/04; SLJ 2/04)

1307 Niemann, Christoph. *The Police Cloud* (PS–2). Illus. 2007, Random $15.99 (978-0-375-83963-1). A little white cloud dreams of being a police officer but discovers fire fighting may be better suited to his skills. (Rev: BL 5/1/07; HB 3/07; SLJ 6/07)

1308 Nolen, Jerdine. *Big Jabe* (1–4). Illus. by Kadir Nelson. 2000, Lothrop LB $16.89 (978-0-688-13663-5). 32pp. An original tall tale about a man of unusual strength who could lead slaves to freedom. (Rev: BCCB 9/00; BL 4/1/00; HB 7/00; HBG 10/00; SLJ 6/00)

1309 Nolen, Jerdine. *Hewitt Anderson's Great Big Life* (K–3). Illus. by Kadir Nelson. 2005, Simon & Schuster $16.95 (978-0-689-86866-5). Born into a family of giants, little Hewitt fails to develop properly, but despite his diminutive size he constantly proves his worth. (Rev: BL 3/1/04; SLJ 5/05)

1310 Nolen, Jerdine. *Raising Dragons* (PS–2). Illus. by Elise Primavera. 1998, Harcourt $16.00 (978-0-15-201288-5). 32pp. An African American child raises a dragon named Hank on her parents' farm and teaches him to perform useful chores. Eventually, though, she must take him to a land where he will be with his own kind. (Rev: BCCB 6/98; BL 4/1/98; HB 3/98; HBG 10/98; SLJ 4/98)

1311 Nolen, Jerdine. *Thunder Rose* (K–3). Illus. by Kadir Nelson. 2003, Harcourt $16.00 (978-0-15-216472-0). Born during a fierce thunderstorm, Thunder Rose is an African American child of extraordinary talent and magical ability in this vividly illustrated story set in the West. (Rev: HBG 4/04; SLJ 9/03)

1312 Norac, Carl. *Monster, Don't Eat Me!* (1–3). Trans. from Dutch by Elisa Amado. Illus. by Carll Cneut. 2007, Groundwood $18.95 (978-0-88899-800-2). Poor Alex, a little well-dressed piglet, is nearly eaten by a monster but saved when the monster's mother stops her son from snacking. (Rev: SLJ 8/07)

1313 Norling, Beth. *The Stone Baby* (K–2). Illus. by author. 2003, Lothian $18.95 (978-0-7344-0353-7). A little girl protects a stone baby through a series of adventures, including encounters with wild animals and pirates. (Rev: SLJ 5/04)

1314 Novak, Matt. *No Zombies Allowed* (K–2). Illus. by author. 2002, Simon & Schuster $16.95 (978-0-689-84130-9). Witch Wizzle and Witch Woddle are busy crossing names off their monster party guest list because of bad behavior the year before. (Rev: BCCB 9/02; HB 9/02; HBG 3/03; SLJ 8/02)

1315 O'Connor, George. *Sally and the Something* (PS–2). 2006, Roaring Brook $16.95 (978-1-59643-141-6). 32pp. Bored young Sally sets off for the pond where she befriends a strange-looking creature and they try to find activities they both enjoy. (Rev: BL 6/1–15/06; SLJ 3/06)

1316 Oldland, Nicholas. *Big Bear Hug* (K–2). Illus. by author. 2009, Kids Can $16.95 (978-1-55453-464-7); paper $4.99 (978-1-55453-482-1). Unpaged. An environmentally minded tree-hugging bear must make a decision when he comes across a man with an axe — and decides on the usual hug. (Rev: LMC 11–12/09; SLJ 10/1/09)

1317 O'Malley, Kevin, and Patrick O'Brien. *Captain Raptor and the Space Pirates* (1–3). Illus. by Patrick O'Brien. 2007, Walker $16.95 (978-0-8027-9571-7). 32pp. Captain Raptor's mission is to save his home planet from raiding space pirates in this new graphic novel adventure that will appeal to reluctant readers. (Rev: BL 9/1/07; SLJ 9/07)

1318 Oram, Hiawyn. *Rubbaduck and Ruby Roo* (PS–1). Illus. by David Lucas. 2005, Boyds Mills $15.95 (978-1-59078-356-6). 32pp. Rubbaduck is angry when rag doll Ruby Roo eats up everything in his kitchen and trades away his coat, but all ends well when Ruby's magic turns to gold. (Rev: BL 3/1/05; SLJ 3/05)

1319 Ormerod, Jan. *Maudie and Bear* (PS–1). Illus. by Freya Blackwood. 2012, Putnam $16.99 (978-039925709-4). 48pp. A charmingly self-centered little girl leans on her accommodating, loyal friend Bear in this series of five short stories. (Rev: BL 1/1/12*; SLJ 1/12)

1320 Ormondroyd, Edward. *Theodore: The Adventures of a Smudgy Bear* (PS–1). Illus. by Juli Kangas. 2009, Dial $16.99 (978-0-8037-3163-9). 32pp. A well-loved teddy bear has to find a way back home when he is unexpectedly laundered and becomes unrecognizable to Lucy; a new edition of a story first published in 1966, with bright illustrations. (Rev: BLO 6/23/09; SLJ 7/09)

1321 Owen, Karen. *I Could Be, You Could Be* (PS–1). Illus. by Barroux. 2011, Barefoot $16.99 (978-1-84686-405-6). 32pp. A young boy and girl have an adventure in imagination, mulling over the various things they could be — astronauts, dragons, chimps, and so forth. (Rev: BL 4/15/11; SLJ 5/1/11)

1322 Palatini, Margie. *Goldie and the Three Hares* (PS–2). Illus. by Jack E. Davis. 2011, HarperCollins $16.99 (978-0-06-125314-0). 32pp. A family of hares finds itself with a bossy housemate — Goldilocks — and calls the Bears' house in desperation for advice on how to get her to leave. e Lexile AD610L (Rev: BL 1/1–15/11; SLJ 3/1/11)

1323 Palatini, Margie. *Piggie Pie!* (K–3). Illus. by Howard Fine. 1995, Clarion $16.00 (978-0-395-71691-5). 32pp. Gritch the Witch is off to Old MacDonald's farm in search of eight plump pigs for her favorite pie. (Rev: BL 9/1/95*; SLJ 11/95*)

1324 Paquette, Ammi-Joan. *The Tiptoe Guide to Tracking Fairies* (PS–2). Illus. by Christa Unzner. 2009, Tanglewood $15.95 (978-1-933718-20-0). 32pp. All you need to know about the places where fairies like to hide. (Rev: BL 5/1/09; SLJ 9/09)

1325 Park, Barbara. *Ma! There's Nothing to Do Here!* (PS–K). Illus. by Viviana Garofoli. 2007, Random $15.99 (978-0-375-83852-1). A baby waiting to be born humorously complains about being bored. (Rev: BL 12/15/07; SLJ 3/08)

1326 Pawagi, Manjusha. *The Girl Who Hated Books* (K–3). Illus. by Leanne Franson. 1999, Beyond Words $14.95 (978-1-896764-11-5). 24pp. When nonreader Meena accidentally frees a lot of book characters, such as Humpty Dumpty and Ali Baba, from the pages of their books, she has to read the whole family library to find where they belong. (Rev: BL 11/1/99; SLJ 6/99)

1327 Pearce, Clemency. *Frangoline and the Midnight Dream* (K–2). Illus. by Rebecca Elliott. 2011, Scholastic $16.99 (978-0-545-31426-8). Unpaged. Frangoline is good by day but gets wild by night until she scares herself to the point where she wants to go home. (Rev: LMC 11–12/11; SLJ 7/11)

1328 Pearson, Susan. *We're Going on a Ghost Hunt* (PS–3). Illus. by S. D. Schindler. 2012, Amazon Children's $16.99 (978-0-7614-6307-8). 32pp. Four children head out into the mildly scary night to a refashioned *We're Going on a Bear Hunt*. (Rev: BLO 10/15/12; SLJ 12/12)

1329 Peck, Jan. *Way Far Away on a Wild Safari* (PS–K). Illus. by Valeria Petrone. 2006, Simon & Schuster $15.95 (978-1-4169-0072-6). A little boy's safari through the African savannah turns out to be a date with Grandma's animal cookies. (Rev: SLJ 6/06)

1330 Peet, Bill. *Big Bad Bruce* (K–3). Illus. by author. 1982, Houghton $17.00 (978-0-395-25150-8); paper $8.95 (978-0-395-32922-1). Bruce encounters a witch and is shrunk to the size of a chipmunk.

1331 Peet, Bill. *The Caboose Who Got Loose* (K–3). Illus. by author. 1980, Houghton $17.00 (978-0-395-14805-1); paper $8.95 (978-0-395-28715-6). 48pp. When Katy Caboose is jarred loose from the rest of the train, she gets her wish to be a "cabin in the trees," free from noise and smoke.

1332 Pendziwol, Jean, and Martine Gourbault. *No Dragons for Tea: Fire Safety for Kids (and Dragons)* (PS–1). Illus. 1999, Kids Can $14.95 (978-1-55074-569-6). 32pp. A young girl's pet dragon sneezes, and her experiences with the ensuing blaze teach fire safety to readers. (Rev: BCCB 4/99; BL 2/1/99; HBG 10/99; SLJ 4/99)

1333 Perl, Erica S. *Dotty* (K–2). Illus. by Julia Denos. 2010, Abrams $16.95 (978-0-8109-8962-7). 32pp. Ida is a little embarrassed by her imaginary friend Dotty until she learns that her teacher also has a special friend. (Rev: BL 7/10; LMC 11–12/10; SLJ 8/1/10)

1334 Perret, Delphine. *The Big Bad Wolf and Me* (1–3). Illus. 2006, Sterling $9.95 (978-1-4027-3725-1). With his confidence almost gone, Big Bad Wolf is not very scary at all, so Boy takes pity and tries to help poor animal to recoup. (Rev: BL 11/1/06)

1335 Pickering, Jimmy. *Skelly the Skeleton Girl* (PS–3). Illus. by author. 2007, Simon & Schuster $12.99 (978-1-4169-1192-0). A slightly spooky little girl goes looking for the owner of a lost bone in this Halloween-y story. (Rev: SLJ 8/07)

1336 Pilkey, Dav. *Ricky Ricotta's Giant Robot* (2–4). Illus. by Martin Ontiveros. 2000, Scholastic $16.95 (978-0-590-30719-2). 111pp. Ricky Ricotta, a tiny mouse, is a victim of bullying until he becomes friends with a large robot who protects him. (Rev: BCCB 5/00; HBG 10/00; SLJ 4/00)

1337 Pilkey, Dav. *Ricky Ricotta's Giant Robot vs. the Mutant Mosquitoes from Mercury* (1–3). Illus. by Martin Ontiveros. 2000, Scholastic paper $4.99 (978-0-590-30722-2). 127pp. Ricky the mouse and his robot friend fight extraterrestrial insects and an evil robot. (Rev: SLJ 10/00)

1338 Pilkey, Dav. *Ricky Ricotta's Mighty Robot vs. the Stupid Stinkbugs from Saturn* (2–4). Illus. by Martin Ontiveros. 2003, Scholastic $16.99 (978-0-439-37644-0); paper $4.99 (978-0-439-37645-7). 125pp. After the evil Sergeant Stinkbug kidnaps his cousin Lucy, Ricky Ricotta, stalwart mouse, and his trusty robot friend come to the rescue. (Rev: HBG 4/04; SLJ 1/04)

1339 Pinder, Eric. *If All the Animals Came Inside* (PS–K). Illus. by Marc Brown. 2012, Little, Brown $16.99 (978-0-316-09883-0). 40pp. A little boy imagines inviting a noisy and boisterous group of zoo animals into his house, and eventually decides the mess and chaos is too much for him and that a dog and cat are quite enough. (Rev: BL 4/15/12; SLJ 4/1/12*)

1340 Pinkney, Andrea D. *Peggony-Po: A Whale of a Tale* (K–2). Illus. by Brian Pinkney. 2006, Hyperion $16.99 (978-0-7868-1958-4). Peggony-Po, a young boy carved from a piece of driftwood by a peg-legged African American sailor, tries to retrieve the leg of his creator from the whale that ate it in this action-packed tall tale. (Rev: BL 4/1/06; SLJ 6/06*)

1341 Pinkwater, Daniel. *Bear's Picture* (K–3). Illus. by D. B. Johnson. 2008, Houghton $16.00 (978-0-618-75923-1). A standoff between an artistic bear and a couple of opinionated gentlemen demonstrates the importance of creativity and belief in oneself; a newly illustrated edition of a 1972 title. (Rev: BCCB 5/08; BL 2/1/08; SLJ 4/08)

1342 Pinkwater, Daniel. *I Am the Dog* (PS–1). Illus. by Jack E. Davis. 2010, HarperCollins $16.99 (978-0-06-055505-4). 32pp. Young Jacob trades places with his dog in this zany romp. Lexile AD220L (Rev: BL 10/15/10; SLJ 10/1/10)

1343 Plecas, Jennifer. *Pretend* (PS–1). Illus. by author. 2011, Philomel $15.99 (978-0-399-23430-9). 32pp. A boy and his father enjoy a fantasy that begins with the living room sofa being a boat at sea. (Rev: BL 5/1/11; SLJ 7/11)

1344 Plourde, Lynn. *Dino Pets* (PS–1). Illus. by Gideon Kendall. 2007, Dutton $15.99 (978-0-525-47778-5). A little boy's efforts to find the perfect dinosaur pet result in a houseful of dinos. Facts about dinosaurs accompany the humorous story. (Rev: SLJ 6/07)

1345 Plourde, Lynn. *Spring's Sprung* (PS–1). Illus. by Greg Couch. 2002, Simon & Schuster $16.00 (978-0-689-84229-0). March, April, and May are querulous siblings who test Mother Earth's patience in this ode to spring. (Rev: HBG 10/02; SLJ 3/02)

1346 Polacco, Patricia. *Emma Kate* (PS–2). Illus. 2005, Philomel $16.99 (978-0-399-24452-0). 32pp. A little girl and her elephant best friend do everything together — even having their tonsils out at the same time — and it may take readers some time to work out that it is the girl who is imaginary, not the elephant. (Rev: BL 9/15/05; SLJ 11/05)

1347 Polacco, Patricia. *Rechenka's Eggs* (K–2). Illus. by author. 1988, Penguin $16.99 (978-0-399-21501-8). 32pp. Old Babushka saves a wild goose, and when her decorated eggs are broken, the goose repays her kindness by laying her own decorated eggs. (Rev: BCCB 6/88; BL 4/1/88; SLJ 5/88)

1348 Portis, Antoinette. *Not a Stick* (PS–K). Illus. by author. 2008, HarperCollins $12.99 (978-0-06-112325-2). 32pp. An imaginative little pig demonstrates the many things a stick can be other than a stick (a sword, a fishing rod, and so forth). (Rev: BL 2/15/08; HB 3/08; SLJ 1/08)

1349 Prelutsky, Jack. *The Wizard* (K–2). Illus. by Brandon Dorman. 2007, Greenwillow $16.99 (978-0-06-124076-8). 32pp. A wicked suburban wizard ponders evil deeds and casts spells in this richly illustrated book. (Rev: BL 9/1/07; SLJ 7/07)

1350 Pulver, Robin. *Happy Endings: A Story About Suffixes* (K–3). Illus. by Lynn Rowe Reed. 2011, Holiday House $16.95 (978-0-8234-2296-8). 32pp. Hearing that Mr. Wright's class is to "tackle" suffixes, the suffixes take fright and disappear, leading the students on an interesting chase. Lexile AD430L (Rev: BL 4/15/11; LMC 11–12/11; SLJ 3/1/11)

1351 Pulver, Robin. *Silent Letters Loud and Clear* (K–3). Illus. by Lynn Rowe Reed. 2008, Holiday $16.95 (978-0-8234-2127-5). 32pp. The silent letters (in knee, wrong, and so forth) take offense when the students in Mr. Wright's class deride them, and they decide to fight back. (Rev: BLO 8/28/08; HB 5/08; SLJ 6/08)

1352 Puttock, Simon. *Yours Truly, Louisa* (PS–2). Illus. by Jo Kiddie. 2009, HarperCollins $17.99 (978-0-06-136634-5). 32pp. This barn yarn follows a fastidious pig in her quest for cleanliness from farm to city and back to farm again. (Rev: BLO 2/9/09; SLJ 2/09)

1353 Pym, Tasha. *Have You Ever Seen a Sneep?* (PS–K). Illus. by Joel Stewart. 2009, Farrar $16.95 (978-0-374-32868-9). 32pp. Have you ever seen a Sneep? A Snook? A Grullock or a Floon? Apparently if you have you will remember the encounter. (Rev: BL 9/15/09; LMC 11–12/09; SLJ 11/1/09)

1354 Quattlebaum, Mary. *The Hungry Ghost of Rue Orleans* (K–2). Illus. by Patricia Castelao. 2011, Random House $15.99 (978-0-375-86207-6); LB $18.99 (978-0-375-96207-3). 32pp. Fred is a very happy ghost in his New Orleans home until it is turned into a restaurant, and his efforts to scare the customers away seem counterproductive. (Rev: BL 9/15/11; SLJ 9/1/11)

1355 Ramos, Mario. *I Am So Handsome* (PS–2). Illus. by author. 2012, Gecko $17.95 (978-187757919-6). 28pp. A wolf with a high opinion of himself struts through the forest boosting his own ego through the other residents (Little Red Riding Hood, the three little pigs, Snow White) until he meets a less sycophantic little dragon. Lexile AD420L (Rev: BLO 9/15/12; SLJ 11/12)

1356 Rasmussen, Halfdan. *The Ladder* (K–3). Trans. by Marilyn Nelson. Illus. by Pierre Pratt. 2006, Candlewick $17.99 (978-0-7636-2282-4). A ladder sets off to view more of the world and encounters many people who wish to climb it. (Rev: BL 6/1–15/06)

1357 Rawson, Katherine. *If You Were a Parrot* (K–2). Illus. by Sherry Rogers. 2006, Sylvan Dell $15.95 (978-0-9764943-9-3). Illustrations of children with parrot features — beaks, feet, voice, and feathers — show the power of imagination and inform about parrots' physical and behavioral characteristics. (Rev: SLJ 12/06)

1358 Ray, Jane. *The Apple-Pip Princess* (PS–2). Illus. by author. 2008, Candlewick $16.99 (978-0-7636-3747-7). 32pp. Planting a tiny apple seed from a box of her dead mother's treasures, Serenity transforms her dustbowl kingdom into a lush paradise. (Rev: BL 3/15/08; SLJ 4/08)

1359 Ray, Jane. *Can You Catch a Mermaid?* (PS–2). Illus. by author. 2008, Orchard $12.95 (978-1-84616-269-5). 32pp. Lonely Eliza is happy to become friends with mermaid Freya, but does she have the strength to help her friend return to her own home? (Rev: BL 1/1–15/09)

1360 Ray, Jane. *The Dollhouse Fairy* (PS–3). Illus. by author. 2010, Candlewick $16.99 (978-0-7636-4411-6). 32pp. When Rosy's beloved father goes to the hospital, she misses the time they used to spend on her dollhouse and, playing there by herself, she discovers that a fairy with a broken wing has moved in. (Rev: BL 6/10*; SLJ 8/1/10)

1361 Ray, Mary L. *All Aboard!* (PS–2). Illus. by Amiko Hirao. 2002, Little, Brown $14.95 (978-0-316-73507-0). 32pp. The rabbit named Mr. Barnes, who appears to be traveling alone, belongs in fact to the little girl on the same train. (Rev: BL 11/1/02; HBG 3/03; SLJ 10/02)

1362 Rayner, Catherine. *Sylvia and Bird* (PS–2). Illus. by author. 2009, Good Bks. $16.95 (978-1-56148-661-8). 32pp. A lonely dragon called Sylvia befriends a little yellow bird. (Rev: BL 5/1/09)

1363 Reed, Neil. *The Midnight Unicorn* (K–2). Illus. by author. 2006, Sterling LB $14.95 (978-1-4027-3218-8). Millie and her dog Casper go on a wonderful journey when the statue of a unicorn springs to life. (Rev: SLJ 1/07)

1364 Rennert, Laura. *Dragon Dreams* (1–3). Illus. by Melanie Florian. Series: Royal Princess Academy. 2012, Dial $16.99 (978-0-8037-3750-1). 112pp. This early chapter book features Emma, an atypical princess, who prefers soccer to dance and is happy to investigate the malaise afflicting the kingdom's dragons. **ℯ** (Rev: BLO 9/15/12; SLJ 1/13)

1365 Rex, Adam. *Moonday* (PS–1). Illus. by author. 2013, Disney/Hyperion $16.99 (978-142311920-3). 40pp. The moon follows a young girl and her family home, refusing to leave and let day dawn until the family comes up with a plan to get the moon back into the sky and allow the sun to rise for the next day. (Rev: BL 11/1/13; SLJ 10/13)

1366 Rex, Michael. *My Freight Train* (PS–K). Illus. 2002, Holt $15.95 (978-0-8050-6682-1). A little boy segues from playing with his toy train to a day as engineer of a real freight train, and explains every detail of the train and his duties. (Rev: BL 11/15/02; HBG 3/03; SLJ 11/02)

1367 Reynolds, Aaron. *Snowbots* (PS–1). Illus. by David Barneda. 2010, Knopf $16.99 (978-0-375-85873-4); LB $19.99 (978-0-375-95873-1). Unpaged. A gaggle of robot children enjoy a frosty day of outdoor play in this lively, rhyming story. (Rev: SLJ 11/1/10)

1368 Reynolds, Aaron. *Superhero School* (K–3). Illus. by Andy Rash. 2009, Bloomsbury $16.99 (978-1-59990-166-4). 32pp. When the teachers at Leonard's superhero school are kidnapped by ice zombies, the young students rise to the occasion and defeat the foe using their math skills. (Rev: SLJ 9/1/09)

1369 Reynolds, Adrian. *Pete and Polo's Farmyard Adventure* (PS–K). Illus. 2002, Scholastic $16.95 (978-0-439-30913-4). A boy named Pete and his toy polar bear search for missing ducks after they discover the pond has dried up. (Rev: BL 8/02; HBG 10/02; SLJ 7/02)

1370 Reynolds, Peter H. *The North Star* (K–3). Illus. by author. 2009, Candlewick $16.99 (978-0-7636-3677-7). 64pp. A bright star guides a little boy as he travels through the world. (Rev: BL 6/1–15/09; SLJ 5/09)

1371 Reynolds, Peter H. *So Few of Me* (K–3). Illus. by author. 2006, Candlewick $14.00 (978-0-7636-2623-5). Young Leo feels so overburdened that he wishes there were more of him to handle all his tasks, but when his wish is granted — many times over — he soon finds himself longing for the good old days. (Rev: SLJ 12/06)

1372 Ringgold, Faith. *Tar Beach* (PS–2). Illus. 1991, Crown LB $18.99 (978-0-517-58031-8). 32pp. A little girl on the rooftop of her apartment building dreams of soaring over New York City. (Rev: BCCB 3/91; BL 1/1/91; HB 5/91*; SLJ 2/91*)

1373 Robertson, M. P. *The Dragon Snatcher* (PS–2). Illus. 2005, Dial $16.99 (978-0-8037-3103-5). 32pp. George and his dragon sidekick work to foil an evil wizard who's determined to rid the world of dragons; the third installment in a series that began with *The Egg* (2001) and *The Great Dragon Rescue* (2004). (Rev: BL 12/1/05; SLJ 10/05)

1374 Robles, Anthony D. *Lakas and the Manilatown Fish / Si Lakas at ang Isdang Manilatown* (K–3). Trans. by Eloisa D. de Jesus and Magdalena de Guzman. Illus. by Carl Angel. 2003, Children's Book Pr. $16.95 (978-0-89239-182-0). 32pp. In this whimsical bilingual (English and Tagalog) story, a young Filipino boy and his father race through the streets of San Francisco in pursuit of a fish that can talk, jump, and play. (Rev: HB 5/03; HBG 10/03; SLJ 10/03)

1375 Rocco, John. *Moonpowder* (PS–1). Illus. by author. 2008, Hyperion $15.99 (978-1-4231-0011-9). 48pp. Eli prides himself on his ability to fix things but suffers from continuing bad dreams until Mr. Moon asks his help repairing the Moonpowder Factory; rich, inventive illustrations add to the story's appeal. (Rev: BL 6/1–15/08; LMC 3/08; SLJ 4/08)

1376 Rohmann, Eric. *Clara and Asha* (PS–2). Illus. 2005, Roaring Brook $16.95 (978-1-59643-031-0). 40pp. This story of a little girl's friendship with an imaginary giant fish named Asha features arresting illustrations. (Rev: BL 7/05; SLJ 8/05)

1377 Root, Phyllis. *Big Momma Makes the World* (PS–2). Illus. by Helen Oxenbury. 2003, Candlewick $16.99 (978-0-7636-1132-3). 48pp. Glowing illustrations depict the take-charge Big Momma, baby on hip, as she creates the world and admires her work, though she does have to keep an eye on the humans to make sure they "straighten up." (Rev: BCCB 2/03; BL 1/1–15/03*; HB 3/03*; HBG 10/03; SLJ 3/03)

1378 Root, Phyllis. *Grandmother Winter* (PS–2). Illus. by Beth Krommes. 1999, Houghton $16.00 (978-0-395-88399-0). 32pp. When Grandmother Winter shakes out her quilt and causes a snowfall, all nature responds to the coming of winter. (Rev: BCCB 10/99; BL 11/15/99; HB 9/99; HBG 3/00; SLJ 9/99)

1379 Root, Phyllis. *Lucia and the Light* (K–3). Illus. by Mary GrandPré. 2006, Candlewick $16.99 (978-0-7636-2296-1). Brave Lucia battles frightening trolls in order to rescue the sun and bring back the daylight that has disappeared from her northern winter. (Rev: BL 12/1/06*; SLJ 12/06)

1380 Rosen, Michael. *Bear Flies High* (PS–K). Illus. by Adrian Reynolds. 2009, Bloomsbury $16.99 (978-1-59990-386-6). 32pp. A bear who has always longed to fly meets four children who take him to an amusement park and have a great time. (Rev: BL 12/15/09; SLJ 2/1/10*)

1381 Rosen, Michael. *Red Ted and the Lost Things* (PS–K). Illus. by Joel Stewart. 2009, Candlewick $16.99 (978-0-7636-4537-3); paper $8.99 (978-0-7636-4624-0). 40pp. A teddy bear and a stuffed crocodile at the Lost and Found bond over being abandoned and set out to find the bear's owner. (Rev: SLJ 11/1/09)

1382 Rosenberg, Liz. *Tyrannosaurus Dad* (K–2). Illus. by Matthew Myers. 2011, Roaring Brook $16.99 (978-1-59643-531-5). 32pp. A young boy's Tyrannosaurus rex father turns out to be just the thing to save the day

when there's bully trouble at school. (Rev: BL 4/15/11; LMC 10/11; SLJ 5/1/11)

1383 Rosenthal, Amy Krouse. *Spoon* (PS–1). Illus. by Scott Magoon. 2009, Hyperion $15.99 (978-1-4231-0685-2). 40pp. A spoon called Spoon has self-esteem problems in this humorous insider's look at cutlery. (Rev: BL 12/1/08; SLJ 6/09)

1384 Ross, Fiona. *Chilly Milly Moo* (PS–K). Illus. by author. 2011, Candlewick $15.99 (978-0-7636-5693-5). 32pp. Milly Moo, unlike the other cows, dislikes warm weather and has a special ability in cold weather — producing ice cream rather than milk. (Rev: BL 10/1/11; SLJ 11/1/11)

1385 Rumford, James. *The Nine Animals and the Well* (1–3). Illus. 2003, Houghton $16.00 (978-0-618-30915-3). 32pp. Nine animals bear birthday gifts for the raja (three almond cakes, four sugar cones), each worried that his gift is not good enough, in this combination of charming text and counting book. (Rev: BL 7/03; HB 5/03; HBG 10/03; SLJ 6/03)

1386 Rusch, Elizabeth. *A Day with No Crayons* (PS–2). Illus. by Chad Cameron. 2007, Rising Moon $15.95 (978-0-87358-910-9). 32pp. When Liza runs out of paper and expands onto the wall, her crayons are confiscated and the world loses its bright colors. (Rev: SLJ 4/08)

1387 Ryan, Pam Muñoz. *Mice and Beans* (PS–2). Illus. by Joe Cepeda. 2001, Scholastic $16.95 (978-0-439-18303-1). Readers get a mouse's perspective in this story of mice helping Rosa Maria prepare for her grandchild's birthday celebration that interweaves Spanish expressions. (Rev: BCCB 10/01; BL 9/15/01; HBG 3/02; SLJ 10/01)

1388 Rylant, Cynthia. *Dog Heaven* (PS–1). Illus. 1995, Scholastic $16.95 (978-0-590-41701-3). 32pp. In dog heaven, dogs run and play and wait for their absent friends. (Rev: BCCB 10/95; BL 8/95; HBG 4/04; SLJ 10/95)

1389 Sabuda, Robert. *Peter Pan: A Classic Collectible Pop-Up* (1–4). Illus. by author. 2008, Simon & Schuster $29.99 (978-0-689-85364-7). 14pp. Striking pop-ups are combined with inset envelopes that retell the original story. (Rev: BLO 12/16/08)

1390 Sauer, Tammi. *Mostly Monsterly* (PS–2). Illus. by Scott Magoon. 2010, Simon & Schuster $14.99 (978-1-4169-6110-9). 40pp. A monster with a tender heart, Bernadette has trouble fitting in with her peers. e Lexile AD270L (Rev: BL 7/10; LMC 11–12/10; SLJ 8/1/10)

1391 Say, Allen. *Stranger in the Mirror* (3–6). Illus. 1995, Houghton $16.95 (978-0-395-61590-4). In this fantasy, Sam one morning discovers that he has the face of an old, wrinkled man. (Rev: BCCB 11/95; BL 10/1/95; SLJ 10/95*)

1392 Schaefer, Lola M. *Frankie Stein* (PS–1). Illus. by Kevan Atteberry. 2007, Marshall Cavendish $14.99 (978-0-7614-5358-1). Frankie is born cute and there's little mom and dad can do to make him scary until he figures it out for himself. (Rev: BL 9/15/07; SLJ 9/07)

1393 Schaefer, Lola M. *Frankie Stein Starts School* (PS–1). Illus. by Kevan Atteberry. 2010, Marshall Cavendish $15.99 (978-0-7614-5656-8). 32pp. Frankie Stein angles for acceptance at the Ghoul Academy by making grotesque faces and howling like a coyote. ℮ (Rev: BLO 7/10; SLJ 10/1/10)

1394 Schanzer, Rosalyn. *Davy Crockett Saves the World* (K–3). Illus. 2001, HarperCollins LB $17.89 (978-0-688-16992-3). 32pp. Davy Crockett is called upon to battle Halley's Comet in this tall tale rich with colorful illustrations. (Rev: BCCB 2/02; BL 11/15/01; HBG 10/02; SLJ 8/01)

1395 Schertle, Alice. *Little Blue Truck* (1–3). Illus. by Jill McElmurry. 2008, Harcourt $16.00 (978-0-15-205661-2). 32pp. Animals rush to the rescue when a friendly little blue pickup truck gets into trouble, whereas an uppity big dump truck finds itself without support but does learn a valuable lesson. (Rev: BL 4/1/08; HB 5/08; SLJ 7/08)

1396 Schneider, Howie. *Chewy Louie* (PS–1). Illus. 2000, Rising Moon $15.95 (978-0-87358-765-5). 32pp. Louie can't stop chewing things, but when he starts on the family car and the house, his family must act to stop him. (Rev: BL 8/00; HBG 10/00; SLJ 11/00)

1397 Schubert, Ingrid, and Dieter Schubert. *There's a Crocodile Under My Bed!* (PS–1). Illus. by authors. 2005, Front St. $15.95 (978-1-932425-48-2). Little Peggy overcomes her fears and befriends the crocodile beneath her bed. (Rev: SLJ 12/05)

1398 Schwartz, Amy, and Leonard Marcus. *Oscar: The Big Adventure of a Little Sock Monkey* (K–3). Illus. by Amy Schwartz. 2006, HarperCollins $16.99 (978-0-06-072622-5). 32pp. Oscar the sock monkey braves the wilds of New York City to get to his owner, Susie, when she forgets to take an important item to school. (Rev: BL 5/15/06; SLJ 6/06)

1399 Schwarz, Viviane. *Timothy and the Strong Pajamas* (PS–2). Illus. by author. 2008, Scholastic $16.99 (978-0-545-03329-9). 40pp. A little lemur named Timothy Smallbeast dons reconditioned pajamas and gains super abilities — until the pajamas rip, his amazing powers evaporate, and he needs help to rescue his toy monkey. (Rev: BCCB 3/08; BL 2/1/08; HB 5/08; LMC 3/08; SLJ 3/08)

1400 Scieszka, Jon. *Smash! Crash!* (PS–K). Illus. by David Gordon. 2008, Simon & Schuster $16.99 (978-1-4169-4133-0). 42pp. Jack Truck and Dump Truck Dan are having fun smashing and crashing when who should turn up but Wrecking Crane Rosie, who actually needs their help to demolish a building. (Rev: BCCB 3/08; BL 11/15/07; SLJ 1/08)

1401 Selick, Henry. *Moongirl* (K–2). Illus. by Peter Chan. 2006, Candlewick $22.99 (978-0-7636-3068-3). 48pp. Out for a night of fishing with his squirrel friend, Leon finds himself pulled into a magical adventure on the moon; based on the animated short by the same name, this edition includes a DVD. (Rev: BL 11/1/06; SLJ 12/06)

1402 Sendak, Maurice. *Outside Over There* (PS–3). Illus. by author. 1981, HarperCollins paper $9.95 (978-0-06-443185-9). 40pp. Goblins steal Ira's baby sister and leave another made of ice.

1403 Sendak, Maurice. *Where the Wild Things Are* (K–3). Illus. by author. 1988, HarperCollins LB $18.89 (978-0-06-025493-3); paper $8.95 (978-0-06-443178-1). The few moments' wild reverie of a small unruly boy who has been sent supperless to his room. Caldecott Medal winner, 1964.

1404 Seuss, Dr. *And to Think That I Saw It on Mulberry Street* (K–3). Illus. by author. 1989, Random LB $15.99 (978-0-394-94494-4). A rhyme about what Marco saw on Mulberry Street.

1405 Seuss, Dr. *Bartholomew and the Oobleck* (K–2). Illus. by author. 1949, Random LB $12.99 (978-0-394-90075-9). What happens when sticky green stuff begins falling instead of snow? Also use: *McElligot's Pool* (1947).

1406 Seuss, Dr. *The Butter Battle Book* (K–2). Illus. by author. 1984, Random LB $14.99 (978-0-394-96580-2). 48pp. A warning about the nuclear arms race in words and pictures.

1407 Seuss, Dr. *The 500 Hats of Bartholomew Cubbins* (K–2). Illus. by author. 1989, Random $15.99 (978-0-394-94484-5). 48pp. What happened when Bartholomew couldn't take his hat off before the king.

1408 Shannon, David. *Jangles: A Big Fish Story* (K–3). Illus. by author. 2012, Scholastic $17.99 (978-0-545-14312-7). 32pp. A father tells his son about a gigantic trout covered with lures and hooks; when the father caught Jangles as a boy he enjoyed a mystical journey to the bottom of the lake. Lexile AD900L (Rev: BL 9/1/12; HB 9–10/12; LMC 1–2/13; SLJ 10/12)

1409 Shannon, George. *A Very Witchy Spelling Bee* (K–3). Illus. by Mark Fearing. 2013, Harcourt $16.99 (978-015206696-3). 32pp. Determined young witch Cordelia takes on the 203-year-old champion Beulah Divine at the Witches' Double Spelling Bee in this delightful picture book with humorous illustrations and a playfully effective use of language perfect for reinforcing concepts of spelling. Lexile AD590 (Rev: BLO 9/1/13; HB 9–10/13; LMC 10/13; SLJ 7/13)

1410 Shea, Bob. *Big Plans* (K–3). Illus. by Lane Smith. 2008, Hyperion $17.99 (978-1-4231-1100-9). 48pp. A little boy in an empty classroom dreams about impressing the world with his big plans. (Rev: BL 2/15/08; LMC 1/08; SLJ 6/08)

1411 Shea, Pegi Deitz. *The Boy and the Spell* (K–3). Illus. by Serena Riglietti. Series: Musical Stories. 2007, Pumpkin House $16.95 (978-0-964601-04-8). 32pp. When Thomas has a tantrum in his bedroom, his various possessions rebel and set out to teach him a lesson; based on the story line of the opera *L'Enfant et les Sortilèges* with music by Maurice Ravel and libretto by Colette. (Rev: BL 4/1/07)

1412 Shields, Carol Diggory. *Food Fight!* (PS–2). Illus. by Doreen Gay-Kassel. 2002, Handprint $15.95 (978-

1-929766-29-1). Pun-filled fun for the contents of the kitchen while the humans are asleep. (Rev: HBG 3/03; SLJ 10/02)

1413 Shields, Gillian. *The Perfect Bear* (PS–1). Illus. by Gary Blythe. 2008, Simon & Schuster $16.99 (978-1-4169-5363-0). 26pp. A white teddy bear who is proud of his looks is upset when his young owner gets him dirty, but when he becomes lost, he realizes how much he misses her. (Rev: SLJ 4/08)

1414 Shulevitz, Uri. *When I Wore My Sailor Suit* (K–3). Illus. by author. 2009, Farrar $16.95 (978-0-374-34749-9). 32pp. A boy's imagination sets sail on a neighbor's model ship. (Rev: BL 6/1–15/09; SLJ 8/09)

1415 Sís, Peter. *Madlenka* (PS–3). Illus. 2000, Farrar $17.00 (978-0-374-39969-6). 48pp. When Madlenka finds she has a loose tooth, she wanders through her culturally diverse neighborhood telling everyone about her condition in this, at times surreal, picture book. (Rev: BCCB 10/00; BL 9/1/00; HB 9/00; HBG 3/01; SLJ 10/00)

1416 Sís, Peter. *Madlenka's Dog* (PS–2). Illus. 2002, Farrar $17.00 (978-0-374-34699-7). 40pp. A flap book in which many of Madlenka's friends imagine what her invisible dog looks like. (Rev: BCCB 6/02; BL 4/1/02*; HB 3/02*; HBG 10/02; SLJ 4/02*)

1417 Slack, Michael. *Elecopter* (PS–1). Illus. by author. 2013, Henry Holt $15.99 (978-080509304-9). 32pp. Elecopter is part-elephant and part-helicopter in this delightfully illustrated, charming picture book that follows her roving rescue missions across the African savanna in a quest to help any creature in need. ℮ (Rev: BL 9/1/13; SLJ 9/13)

1418 Slate, Jenny, and Dean Fleischer Camp. *Marcel the Shell with Shoes On: Things About Me* (K–2). Illus. by Amy Lind. 2011, Penguin $18.99 (978-1-59514-455-3). 40pp. Marcel, the tiny shell with shoes, takes readers on a tour of his home. ⌒ (Rev: BL 11/15/11; SLJ 12/1/11)

1419 Smith, Lane. *Abe Lincoln's Dream* (K–3). Illus. by author. 2012, Roaring Brook $16.99 (978-1-59643-608-4). 32pp. While taking a tour of the White House, an African American schoolgirl named Quincy meets a tall ghost with a stovepipe hat and together they share jokes, dreams, and a history update. ℮ Lexile AD390L (Rev: BL 9/15/12; HB 11–12/12*; SLJ 12/12*)

1420 Smith, Lane. *Pinocchio the Boy; or, Incognito in Collodi* (K–3). Illus. 2002, Viking $16.99 (978-0-670-03585-4). What happens after Pinocchio is turned into a real boy is the subject of this inventive picture book. (Rev: BL 8/02; HB 9/02; HBG 3/03; SLJ 9/02*)

1421 Smith, Linda. *Mrs. Biddlebox* (PS–2). Illus. by Marla Frazee. 2002, HarperCollins LB $17.89 (978-0-06-029782-4). Mrs. Biddlebox is having a bad day and decides to cook it away, making a cake of the various components — gloom, fog, sky, and so on — and eating the result before happily greeting the night. (Rev: BCCB 1/03; BL 11/15/02; HB 11/02; HBG 3/03; SLJ 10/02)

1422 Smith, Stu. *Goldilocks and the Three Martians* (PS–2). Illus. by Michael Garland. 2004, Dutton $15.99 (978-0-525-46972-8). In search of a planet that's just right, Goldilocks investigates a house on Mars. (Rev: SLJ 8/04)

1423 Soman, David, and Jacky Davis. *The Amazing Adventures of Bumblebee Boy* (PS–2). Illus. by David Soman. 2011, Dial $16.99 (978-0-8037-3418-0). 40pp. Sam, who imagines himself the superhero Bumblebee Boy, discovers the advantages of collaboration when he's confronted by some creepy aliens and his younger brother offers to help. (Rev: BL 12/1/11; SLJ 11/1/11)

1424 Sorel, Edward. *Johnny on the Spot* (K–4). Illus. 1998, Simon & Schuster $16.00 (978-0-689-81293-4). When Johnny's ancient radio starts receiving tomorrow's news, he becomes an overnight sensation. (Rev: BL 8/98; HBG 3/99; SLJ 11/98)

1425 Spangler, Brie. *The Grumpy Dump Truck* (PS–2). Illus. by author. 2009, Knopf $15.99 (978-0-375-85839-0). 40pp. Bertand the dump trunk is cranky and clanky until he meets a porcupine construction worker. (Rev: BL 6/1–15/09; SLJ 6/09)

1426 Speck, Katie. *Maybelle in the Soup* (1–3). Illus. by Paul Ratz de Tagyos. 2007, Holt $15.95 (978-0-8050-8092-6). 58pp. Maybelle the cockroach decides to sample some soup from the Peabodys' table and her appearance sets off a chaotic melee that ends with surprisingly happy results for herself and her friend Henry the flea. (Rev: BL 11/15/07; HB 11/07; SLJ 12/07)

1427 Sperring, Mark. *Find-a-Saurus* (PS–1). Illus. by Alexandra Steele-Morgan. 2003, Scholastic $15.95 (978-0-439-53162-7). Despite his mother's insistence that all dinosaurs are extinct, Marty is convinced that the creatures are just good at hiding, so he sets off to find one. (Rev: HBG 4/04; SLJ 1/04)

1428 Sperring, Mark. *Mermaid Dreams* (PS–K). Illus. by Pope Twins. 2006, Scholastic $16.99 (978-0-439-79610-1). As her mother gets her ready for bed, young Meriam recounts the undersea adventures of her day. (Rev: SLJ 8/06)

1429 Sperring, Mark. *The Sunflower Sword* (PS–3). Illus. by Miriam Latimer. 2011, Andersen $16.95 (978-0-7613-7486-2). 32pp. A little knight armed with a flower charms instead of slays a giant dragon, and the two become friends in a land where dragon-human conflict was common. (Rev: BL 5/1/11; SLJ 2/1/11)

1430 Sperring, Mark. *Wanda's First Day* (K–2). Illus. by Kate Pope. 2004, Scholastic $15.95 (978-0-439-62773-3). 32pp. On her first day in a new school, Wanda, a youthful witch, finds herself the only pupil of her kind in a classroom full of fairies. (Rev: BL 8/04; SLJ 7/04)

1431 Spinelli, Eileen. *Sophie's Masterpiece: A Spider's Tale* (PS–2). Illus. by Jane Dyer. 2001, Simon & Schuster $16.00 (978-0-689-80112-9). 32pp. As her last project, an unappreciated spider named Sophie weaves a beautiful baby blanket for a pregnant woman. (Rev: BL 4/15/01*; HB 7/01; HBG 10/01; SLJ 5/01)

1432 Spires, Ashley. *Small Saul* (PS–3). Illus. by author. 2011, Kids Can $16.95 (978-1-55453-503-3). Unpaged. Small Saul — too short to join the Navy — trains as a pirate instead, but his gentle, caring nature means he has an uncertain future. (Rev: SLJ 4/11)

1433 Stein, David Ezra. *Monster Hug!* (PS–K). Illus. by author. 2007, Putnam $15.99 (978-0-399-24637-1). A boisterous romp in which two large monsters have great fun playing together before morphing into human children. (Rev: BL 10/15/07; SLJ 9/07)

1434 Stein, Mathilde. *Mine!* (PS–2). Illus. by Mies van Hout. 2007, Boyds Mills $16.95 (978-1-59078-506-5). A greedy ghost finally learns to share when he is befriended by Charlotte, the little girl whose house he is "haunting." (Rev: SLJ 8/07)

1435 Stewart, Joel. *Dexter Bexley and the Big Blue Beastie* (PS–2). Illus. 2007, Holiday $16.95 (978-0-8234-2068-1). Dexter Bexley runs into a voracious Big Blue Beastie who threatens to eat the boy, but Dexter resourcefully comes up with one idea after another to keep the creature otherwise occupied. (Rev: BL 4/1/07)

1436 Stoop, Naoko. *Red Knit Cap Girl to the Rescue* (PS–1). Illus. by author. 2013, Little, Brown $17 (978-031622885-5). 40pp. Red Knit Cap Girl and her friends must rescue a polar bear and reunite him with his mother with the help of the wise moon. (Rev: BL 11/1/13; SLJ 9/13)

1437 Strom, Maria Diaz. *Rainbow Joe and Me* (1–3). Illus. 1999, Lee & Low $15.95 (978-1-880000-93-9). 32pp. In this picture book using African American characters, a blind musician shows painter Eloise how he creates colors through his music. (Rev: BL 11/15/99; HBG 3/00; SLJ 11/99)

1438 Sturgis, Brenda Reeves. *Ten Turkeys in the Road* (PS–K). Illus. by David Slonim. 2011, Marshall Cavendish $16.99 (978-0-7614-5847-0). 32pp. Ten turkeys rehearsing circus acts block the road, holding up an impatient farmer in this colorful story that offers plenty of opportunities for counting practice. (Rev: BLO 11/15/11; LMC 1–2/12; SLJ 10/1/11)

1439 Suen, Anastasia. *Raise the Roof!* (PS–1). Illus. by Elwood H. Smith. 2003, Viking $15.99 (978-0-670-89282-2). 32pp. A house is constructed despite a dog's "help" in this picture book with cartoon-like, stylized illustrations. (Rev: BCCB 2/03; BL 2/15/03; HB 3/03; HBG 10/03; SLJ 2/03)

1440 Sussman, Michael. *Otto Grows Down* (PS–1). Illus. by Scott Magoon. 2009, Sterling $14.95 (978-1-4027-4703-8). 36pp. On his 6th birthday, Otto wishes his baby sister had never been born and the clock starts moving backward, taking Otto along with it. (Rev: BL 4/15/09; LMC 10/09; SLJ 4/09)

1441 Tauss, Marc. *Superhero* (PS–2). Illus. 2005, Scholastic $16.99 (978-0-439-62734-4). Maleek, an African American boy with a secret identity, springs into action when his city's parks and playgrounds start mysteriously disappearing. (Rev: BL 8/05; SLJ 12/05)

1442 Teague, David. *Franklin's Big Dreams* (PS–1). Illus. by Boris Kulikov. 2010, Hyperion $16.99 (978-1-4231-1919-7). 40pp. A beautifully illustrated story about a young boy's dreams full of dramatic construction activity in his bedroom. (Rev: BL 6/10*; SLJ 7/1/10)

1443 Teague, Mark. *The Secret Shortcut* (PS–3). Illus. 1996, Scholastic $14.95 (978-0-590-67714-1). Pirates, space aliens, and a plague of frogs are only three of the obstacles that prevent Wendell and Floyd from getting to school on time. (Rev: BL 9/15/96; SLJ 11/96)

1444 Tegen, Katherine. *The Story of the Leprechaun* (PS–2). Illus. by Sally Anne Lambert. 2011, HarperCollins $12.99 (978-0-06-143086-2). 40pp. An industrious leprechaun shoemaker outwits a plot to steal his gold. **e** Lexile 780L (Rev: BL 1/1–15/11; SLJ 2/1/11)

1445 Thomas, Shelley Moore. *A Cold Winter's Good Knight* (PS–2). Illus. by Jennifer Plecas. 2008, Dutton $15.99 (978-0-525-47964-2). 32pp. The three little dragons who have previously appeared in an easy-reader series attend a fancy ball and learn about manners in this picture book. (Rev: BL 2/1/09; HB 1/09; SLJ 12/08)

1446 Thomas, Shelley Moore. *A Good Knight's Rest* (K–2). Illus. by Jennifer Plecas. 2011, Dutton $16.99 (978-0-525-42195-5). Unpaged. The Good Knight has worked hard and deserves a rest but makes the mistake of taking his three little dragon friends with him. (Rev: HB 7–8/11; SLJ 6/11)

1447 Thomson, Bill. *Fossil* (1–3). Illus. by author. 2013, Amazon/Two Lions $17.99 (978-147784700-8). 48pp. A young boy and his dog find themselves facing a big problem when fossils emerge alive from the rocks on a beach — and one of these rocks contains a dinosaur foot. **e** (Rev: BL 11/1/13; LMC 5–6/14; SLJ 11/13)

1448 Thomson, Sarah L. *Imagine a Day* (3–6). Illus. by Rob Gonsalves. 2005, Simon & Schuster $16.95 (978-0-689-85219-0). 40pp. Surrealist images are accompanied by brief text in this large-format volume that is a companion to *Imagine a Night* (2003). (Rev: BL 1/1–15/05; SLJ 4/05)

1449 Tillman, Nancy. *On the Night You Were Born* (PS). Illus. by author. 2006, Feiwel & Friends $16.95 (978-0-312-34606-5). 32pp. The wind, rain, moon, and a variety of creatures big and small welcome the wondrous arrival of a baby, and celebrate its uniqueness. (Rev: BL 12/1/06)

1450 Timmers, Leo. *Happy with Me* (K–2). Illus. 2002, Tallfellow/Smallfellow $16.95 (978-1-931290-08-1). After considering the ups and downs of being different animals, a little boy decides he's happy being himself in this colorful picture book. (Rev: BL 7/02)

1451 Tompert, Ann. *Grandfather Tang's Story* (K–3). Illus. by Robert Andrew Parker. 1990, Crown LB $17.99 (978-0-517-57272-6). 32pp. As a Chinese grandfather tells his granddaughter a tale about two foxes, he arranges Chinese puzzles to form the animals' shapes. (Rev: BCCB 4/90; BL 4/15/90; SLJ 5/90)

1452 Tonatiuh, Duncan. *Pancho Rabbit and the Coyote: A Migrant's Tale* (PS–1). Illus. by author. 2013, Abrams $16.95 (978-1-4197-0583-0). 32pp. A young rabbit named Pancho heads to *El Norte* to find his father when he fails to return home from his work in the fields; along the way Pancho meets a coyote who offers to guide him, and the following events closely parallel the experiences of many migrants headed north — but with a happy ending. Belpré Honor; ALA Notable Children's Book. ∩ (Rev: BL 6/13; LMC 10/13; SLJ 4/13)

1453 Tusa, Tricia. *Follow Me* (PS–2). Illus. by author. 2011, Harcourt $16.99 (978-0-547-27201-6). 40pp. A young girl soars from a swing into the sky and travels over the Earth through a palette of colors. (Rev: BL 3/1/11; SLJ 4/11)

1454 Vamos, Samantha R. *The Cazuela That the Farm Maiden Stirred* (PS–1). Illus. by Rafael Lopez. 2011, Charlesbridge $17.95 (978-1-58089-242-1). 32pp. This happy, cumulative tale involving farm animals includes many Spanish vocabulary words as it shows the process for making *arroz con leche,* or rice pudding. ALSC Notable Children's Book, 2012; Pura Belpre Illustrator Honor Book, 2012. (Rev: BL 4/15/11; SLJ 3/1/11*)

1455 Van Allsburg, Chris. *Ben's Dream* (2–4). Illus. by author. 1982, Houghton $16.95 (978-0-395-32084-6). 32pp. Ben dreams that he is in a flood and passing the great landmarks of the world.

1456 Van Allsburg, Chris. *Jumanji* (1–4). Illus. by author. 1981, Houghton $18.95 (978-0-395-30448-8). A board game that two children play brings out a jungle world. Caldecott Medal winner, 1982.

1457 Van Allsburg, Chris. *Just a Dream* (K–3). Illus. 1990, Houghton $18.95 (978-0-395-53308-6). 48pp. Walter, who doesn't recycle his trash, takes a trip into the future and finds the situation bleak. (Rev: BCCB 11/90; BL 10/15/90; HB 1/91; SLJ 12/90)

1458 Van Allsburg, Chris. *The Sweetest Fig* (3–6). Illus. 1993, Houghton $18.95 (978-0-395-67346-1). All of his wildest dreams come true when a cruel dentist eats the figs given him in payment by a poor woman. (Rev: BCCB 11/93; BL 10/1/93*; SLJ 11/93*)

1459 Van Allsburg, Chris. *The Widow's Broom* (K–2). Illus. 1992, Houghton $18.95 (978-0-395-64051-7). 32pp. In this tale of good and evil, a witch's broom falls from the sky with the witch still on it. (Rev: BCCB 10/92*; BL 9/15/92*; HB 1/93; SLJ 11/92*)

1460 Vaughan, Richard Lee. *Eagle Boy: A Pacific Northwest Native Tale* (PS–3). Illus. by Lee Christiansen. 2000, Sasquatch $16.95 (978-1-57061-171-1). When Eagle Boy is left behind by his people, the eagles with whom he has shared his fishing catch bring him food. (Rev: BL 1/1–15/01; HBG 10/01; SLJ 12/00)

1461 Viorst, Judith. *Lulu and the Brontosaurus* (1–4). Illus. by Lane Smith. 2010, Atheneum $15.99 (978-1-4169-9961-4). 128pp. Lulu demands a pet brontosaurus for her birthday and, when her parents deny her this, leaves home in search of one; when she finally happens upon one in the woods, the beast insists the girl become *his* pet instead. ☉ Lexile 910L (Rev: BL 9/1/10; LMC 1–2/11; SLJ 9/1/10)

1462 Viva, Frank. *A Long Way Away* (PS–1). Illus. by author. 2013, Little, Brown $16.99 (978-0-316-22196-2). 40pp. With continuous vertical art, this innovative book can be read either front-to-back — which follows an alien as he travels from space to the sea — or back-to-front — which follows a journey in the reverse direction. (Rev: BLO 7/13; HB 5–6/13; SLJ 4/13*)

1463 Voake, Steve. *Daisy Dawson and the Secret Pond* (1–3). Illus. by Jessica Meserve. 2009, Candlewick $14.99 (978-0-7636-4009-5). 88pp. Daisy, who can communicate with animals, and her friends Boom the dog and Cyril the squirrel set out on a mission to photograph wild otters. Also in this series is *Daisy Dawson and the Big Freeze* (2010), in which Daisy rescues a lamb. (Rev: SLJ 12/1/09)

1464 Voake, Steve. *Daisy Dawson Is on Her Way!* (2–4). Illus. by Jessica Meserve. 2008, Candlewick $14.99 (978-0-7636-3740-8). 112pp. On her way to school, trying not to be late as usual, Daisy Dawson meets a butterfly that bestows on her the ability to communicate with animals — and many adventures ensue. (Rev: BCCB 6/08; BL 5/1/08; LMC 10/08; SLJ 4/08)

1465 von Olfers, Sibylle. *Mother Earth and Her Children* (PS–1). Trans. by Jack Zipes. Illus. by Sieglinde Schoen Smith. 2007, Breckling $17.95 (978-1-933308-18-0). 32pp. A translation of a German story about Mother Earth's children who sleep underground during the winter and emerge in the spring; illustrated with sections of a quilt that appears in full at the end. (Rev: BLO 1/15/08; SLJ 2/08)

1466 Wallace, Ian. *The Sleeping Porch* (K–2). Illus. by author. 2008, Groundwood $18.95 (978-0-88899-826-2). 32pp. A boy and a cat have wonderful adventures in this sleep fantasy with stunning artwork. (Rev: LMC 3/09; SLJ 9/08)

1467 Walter, Mildred P. *Brother to the Wind* (K–2). Illus. by Leo Dillon and Diane Dillon. 1985, Lothrop LB $15.89 (978-0-688-03812-0). 32pp. A folklike tale set in Africa about a boy who wants to fly. (Rev: BCCB 3/85; HB 7/85; SLJ 5/85)

1468 Ward, Lindsay. *Please Bring Balloons* (PS–1). Illus. by author. 2013, Dial $16.99 (978-080373878-2). 32pp. Emma finds a note under the saddle of the polar bear on the carousel saing "Please bring a balloon" — and thereby starts a magnificent adventure. (Rev: BL 11/1/13; SLJ 9/13)

1469 Watt, Mélanie. *You're Finally Here!* (PS–1). Illus. by author. 2011, Hyperion/Disney $15.99 (978-1-4231-3486-2). 40pp. An enthusiastic but finicky rabbit narrates this short, amusing story, beginning by first chastising the reader for not showing up sooner. (Rev: BL 4/15/11; SLJ 3/1/11)

1470 Wells, Philip. *Daddy Island* (PS–K). Illus. by Niki Daly. 2001, Barefoot Books $15.99 (978-1-84148-197-5). 24pp. A boy imagines himself as all kinds of things — a crab, a wild storm, a rock — as he completes the mundane task of getting ready for bed. (Rev: BL 11/15/01; HBG 3/02; SLJ 12/01)

1471 Whybrow, Ian. *Sammy and the Robots* (PS–1). Illus. by Adrian Reynolds. 2001, Scholastic $15.95 (978-0-531-30327-6). Sammy's robot is off being mended and when Sammy's grandmother must go into the hospital, Sammy realizes she needs a robot to look after her. (Rev: HBG 10/01; SLJ 7/01)

1472 Wiesner, David. *June 29, 1999* (PS–3). Illus. 1992, Houghton $16.00 (978-0-395-59762-0). 32pp. Holly sends small growing vegetables into space in balloons and reaps a fantastic harvest. (Rev: BCCB 11/92; BL 10/15/92; HB 1/93*; SLJ 11/92*)

1473 Wiesner, David. *Sector 7* (K–4). Illus. 1999, Clarion $16.00 (978-0-395-74656-1). In an almost wordless fantasy, a young boy who enjoys drawing is taken to a cloud terminal where clouds are hoping they will be made into new exciting shapes. Caldecott Honor Book, 2000. (Rev: BCCB 1/00*; BL 9/15/99; HB 9/99; HBG 3/00; SLJ 9/99)

1474 Wiesner, David, and Kim Kahng. *The Loathsome Dragon* (PS–2). Illus. by David Wiesner. 2005, Clarion $16.00 (978-0-618-54359-5). 32pp. A revised edition of the fairy tale about a beautiful princess who is turned into a dragon by her jealous stepmother, the queen, and must await the return of her wandering brother to free her from the evil spell. (Rev: BL 2/15/05; SLJ 4/05) [398.2]

1475 Willard, Nancy. *The Sorcerer's Apprentice* (1–4). Illus. by Leo Dillon and Diane Dillon. 1993, Scholastic $16.95 (978-0-590-47329-3). 32pp. Sylvia, the sorcerer's apprentice, is overcome when she is directed to make clothes for the many creatures found in the magician's house. (Rev: BCCB 1/94; BL 11/1/93; SLJ 1/94)

1476 Williams, C. K. *How the Nobble Was Finally Found* (K–2). Illus. by Stephen Gammell. 2009, Harcourt $17.00 (978-0-15-205460-1). In which a winged, long-eared creature who spends a lot of time in the space between Wednesday and Thursday, and with no experience with humans, ventures into the real world and finds friends. (Rev: BL 6/1–15/09; SLJ 9/09)

1477 Williams, Linda. *The Little Old Lady Who Was Not Afraid of Anything* (PS–1). Illus. by Megan Lloyd. 1986, HarperCollins LB $17.89 (978-0-690-04586-4); paper $6.99 (978-0-06-443183-5). 32pp. The scary tale of a little old woman who comes upon two big shoes in the forest going clomp clomp all by themselves. (Rev: BCCB 10/86; BL 10/1/86; SLJ 1/87)

1478 Williams, Margery. *The Velveteen Rabbit* (1–3). Illus. by Gennady Spirin. 2011, Marshall Cavendish $17.99 (978-0-7614-5848-7). 48pp. A handsome version of the classic children's story, with a tribute to the author at the end of the book. (Rev: BL 5/1/11; SLJ 5/1/11)

1479 Wojtowicz, Jen. *The Boy Who Grew Flowers* (1–3). Illus. by Steve Adams. 2005, Barefoot Books $16.99 (978-1-84148-686-4). In this story of differences and self-acceptance, Rink Bowagon, a boy who sprouts flowers from his body during the full moon, courts Angelina Quiz, a new girl at school who has a short right leg. (Rev: BL 10/15/05; SLJ 2/06)

1480 Wood, Audrey. *The Bunyans* (K–3). Illus. by David Shannon. 1996, Scholastic $15.95 (978-0-590-48089-5). 32pp. Meet the rest of the Bunyan family, including two

gigantic children. (Rev: BCCB 1/97; BL 9/15/96; SLJ 12/96*)

1481 Wood, Audrey. *Elbert's Bad Word* (PS–1). Illus. by author. 1988, Harcourt $15.00 (978-0-15-225320-2). 32pp. A bad word flies into Elbert's mouth, which gets him in trouble, so he goes to the local wizard for help. (Rev: BL 10/1/88; HB 1/89; SLJ 10/88)

1482 Wood, Audrey. *The Rude Giants* (PS–3). Illus. 1993, Harcourt $13.95 (978-0-15-269412-8). 32pp. Clever Gerda convinces two dirty, ugly, rude giants to clean up the castle before they eat everybody. (Rev: BCCB 6/93; BL 3/1/93*; SLJ 5/93)

1483 Wood, Audrey, and Don Wood. *Piggies* (PS–K). Illus. by Don Wood. 1991, Harcourt $16.00 (978-0-15-256341-7). 32pp. Fingers can become piggies in this imaginative book with elaborate artwork. (Rev: BCCB 4/91*; BL 3/1/91*; SLJ 5/91*)

1484 Yee, Paul. *Ghost Train* (3–5). Illus. by Harvey Chan. 1996, Douglas & McIntyre $15.95 (978-0-88899-257-4). In this historical fantasy, a Chinese girl comes to the United States and discovers that her father has been killed while working as a railroad construction laborer. (Rev: BCCB 2/97; BL 11/1/96)

1485 Yolen, Jane. *Waking Dragons* (PS–3). Illus. by Derek Anderson. 2012, Simon & Schuster $16.99 (978-1-4169-9032-1). 32pp. Before leaving for school a small knight must help his dragons get up, brush their teeth, get dressed, and have breakfast. Lexile AD430L (Rev: BLO 9/15/12; SLJ 9/12)

1486 Yoo, Taeeun. *The Little Red Fish* (PS–2). 2007, Dial $15.99 (978-0-8037-3145-5). 40pp. On a trip to a library with his grandfather, a young boy falls into a fantasy world when he awakes to find his pet fish is missing; a beautiful and unusual book, much of it wordless. (Rev: BL 4/15/07)

1487 Yorinks, Arthur. *Homework* (K–2). Illus. by Richard Egielski. 2009, Walker $16.99 (978-0-8027-9585-4). Tony's homework has not been done yet again, so his pencils, pens, ruler, and so on decide to do it for him. (Rev: BL 5/1/09; HB 7/09; SLJ 7/09)

1488 Young, Cybèle. *A Few Blocks* (PS–1). Illus. by author. 2011, Groundwood $18.95 (978-0-88899-995-5). Unpaged. Ferdie doesn't want to go to school but his older sister Viola makes it easier by making the journey an exciting fantasy involving sailing ships, knights, and dragons. (Rev: SLJ 11/1/11)

1489 Ziefert, Harriet. *Bunny's Lessons* (PS–2). Illus. by Barroux. 2011, Blue Apple $16.99 (978-1-60905-028-3). 40pp. A toy rabbit describes what he has learned from his boy about emotions, responsibility, apologies, and consequences. (Rev: BL 5/1/11; SLJ 5/1/11)

1490 Ziefert, Harriet. *By the Light of the Harvest Moon* (PS–2). Illus. by Mark Jones. 2009, Blue Apple $16.99 (978-193470669-5). 40pp. Under the harvest moon, the leaf people gather to celebrate fall and then fly on the wind. (Rev: BLO 11/15/09; LMC 3–4/10)

1491 Ziefert, Harriet. *Mighty Max* (PS). Illus. by Elliot Kreloff. 2008, Blue Apple $15.95 (978-1-934706-36-

7). 40pp. In his role as Mighty Max, the little superhero saves the day over and over again — rebuilding a sand castle, rescuing lunch from gulls. (Rev: BL 12/1/08; SLJ 2/09)

IMAGINARY ANIMALS

1492 Abrahams, Peter. *Quacky Baseball* (PS–2). Illus. by Frank Morrison. 2011, HarperCollins $16.99 (978-0-06-122978-7). 32pp. The littlest duckling on the baseball team copes with anxiety and pressure as he tries to do his very best for his team. (Rev: BL 3/1/11; SLJ 2/1/11)

1493 Adams, Jean Ekman. *Clarence Goes Out West and Meets a Purple Horse* (K–2). Illus. 2000, Rising Moon $15.95 (978-0-87358-753-2). 32pp. Smoky, a purple horse, introduces a tenderfoot piglet named Clarence to all the fun of line dancing, card playing, and other cowboy pleasures. (Rev: BL 4/1/00; HBG 10/00; SLJ 6/00)

1494 Agee, Jon. *Milo's Hat Trick* (PS–2). Illus. 2001, Hyperion $15.95 (978-0-7868-0902-8). 32pp. Milo isn't much of a magician until he meets a bear who knows hat tricks. (Rev: BL 7/01; HB 5/01*; HBG 10/01; SLJ 5/01*)

1495 Alborough, Jez. *Some Dogs Do* (PS–2). Illus. by author. 2003, Candlewick $15.99 (978-0-7636-2201-5). In this whimsical tale told in rhyming verse, a puppy named Sid takes flight on his way to school one day. (Rev: HBG 4/04; SLJ 12/03)

1496 Alborough, Jez. *Super Duck* (PS–1). Illus. by author. 2009, Kane $15.95 (978-1-933605-89-0). 32pp. A book called *Super Duck* inspires Duck to adopt the guise of superhero in this sixth adventure. Earlier installments in the series include *Duck in the Truck* (2000), *Fix-It Duck* (2002), *Duck's Key, Where Can It Be?* (2005), and *Hit the Ball Duck* (2006). (Rev: BL 5/1/09; SLJ 3/09)

1497 Alexander, Claire. *Back to Front and Upside Down* (PS–2). Illus. by author. 2012, Eerdmans $16 (978-0-8028-5414-8). 26pp. Stan the puppy struggles with writing a birthday card and finally admits he needs help from his teacher. Lexile 800 (Rev: BL 8/12; SLJ 9/12)

1498 Alexander, Claire. *Small Florence: Piggy Pop Star!* (PS–1). Illus. by author. 2010, Whitman $16.99 (978-0-8075-7455-3). 32pp. Florence, a young pig in awe of her older sisters, manages to finally display her own talents when they lose their nerve during an American Idol-like audition. Lexile AD660L (Rev: BL 4/15/10; SLJ 2/1/10)

1499 Alexander, Kwame. *Acoustic Rooster and His Barnyard Band* (1–3). Illus. by Tim Bowers. 2011, Sleeping Bear $15.95 (978-1-58536-688-0). 32pp. Acoustic Rooster forms a jazz band with Duck Ellington, Bee Holliday, and Pepe Ernesto Cruz to compete in the Barnyard Talent Show against the likes of Thelonius Monkey and Mules Davis in this swingin' story. (Rev: BLO 11/15/11; SLJ 11/1/11)

1500 Allard, Harry. *Starlight Goes to Town* (K–2). Illus. by George Booth. 2008, Farrar $16.95 (978-0-374-37187-6). 32pp. When Ethel AKA Starlight, a little Tennessee chicken, dreams of a glamorous life, a fairy godmother appears right on cue and Starlight begins laying eggs filled with dreams come true; ink-and-watercolor artwork. (Rev: BL 9/15/08; SLJ 9/08)

1501 Allen, Jonathan. *I'm Not Cute!* (PS–K). Illus. 2006, Hyperion $14.99 (978-0-7868-3720-5). 32pp. Baby Owl rejects all compliments, asserting that he is really "a huge, sleek hunting machine," until his mother agrees that he's not cute and realizes that it's definitely time for bed. (Rev: BCCB 6/06; BL 4/15/06; HBG 10/06; SLJ 3/06)

1502 Allen, Jonathan. *"I'm Not Scared!"* (PS). Illus. 2007, Hyperion $14.99 (978-0-7868-3722-9). 32pp. Baby Owl knows that owls stay up all night and is indignant at the idea that he might be scared of the dark. (Rev: BL 5/1/07; SLJ 7/07)

1503 Alter, Anna. *Abigail Spells* (K–2). Illus. by author. 2009, Knopf $16.99 (978-0-375-85617-4). George the bear helps Abigail practice for a spelling bee and cheers her up when she flubs the world "elephant." (Rev: BL 3/15/09; SLJ 6/09)

1504 Alter, Anna. *Disappearing Desmond* (PS–2). Illus. by author. 2010, Knopf $17.99 (978-0-375-86684-5); LB $20.99 (978-0-375-96684-2). 40pp. A shy cat who prefers to disappear behind camouflage gains self-confidence when he makes friends with a gregarious rabbit. (Rev: BL 11/15/10; SLJ 9/1/10)

1505 Alter, Anna. *A Photo for Greta* (PS–1). Illus. by author. 2011, Knopf $16.99 (978-0-375-85618-1); LB $19.99 (978-0-375-95618-8). 40pp. A bunny named Greta misses her photographer father when he's away on assignment but enjoys all the more the times they do spend together. (Rev: BLO 9/1/11; SLJ 8/1/11)

1506 Altes, Marta. *My Grandpa* (PS–K). Illus. by author. 2013, Abrams $15.95 (978-1-4197-0588-5). 32pp. A lovely story about the mutual love of a young bear and his aging grandfather, who is showing signs of dementia. (Rev: BLO 4/1/13; SLJ 4/13)

1507 Anaya, Rudolfo. *Roadrunner's Dance* (K–3). 2000, Hyperion $15.99 (978-0-7868-0254-8). 32pp. The bully Snake is defeated when Desert Woman creates Roadrunner, who is able to get the best of Snake through his unique dance. (Rev: BCCB 12/00; BL 12/15/00; HBG 3/01; SLJ 9/00)

1508 Andreae, Giles. *Cock-a-doodle-doo! Barnyard Hullabaloo* (PS). Illus. by David Wotjowycz. 2000, Little Tiger $14.95 (978-1-888444-75-9). 32pp. Singsong verses describe the activities of some farmyard animals and the sounds they make. (Rev: BL 3/15/00; HBG 10/00; SLJ 5/00)

1509 Andres, Kristina. *Elephant in the Bathtub* (K–1). Illus. by author. 2010, NorthSouth $12.95 (978-0-7358-2291-7). Unpaged. Elephant and his animal friends have an adventure in the bathtub. (Rev: SLJ 6/1/10)

1510 Anholt, Catherine, and Laurence Anholt. *Happy Birthday Chimp and Zee* (PS). Illus. by authors. 2006, Frances Lincoln $15.95 (978-1-84507-507-1). For Chimp and Zee, monkey twins, the highlight of their birthday is a party thrown by their friends, a party they almost miss when they become lost in a swamp. (Rev: SLJ 4/06)

1511 Appelt, Kathi. *Oh, My Baby, Little One* (PS–K). Illus. by Jane Dyer. 2000, Harcourt $16.00 (978-0-15-200041-7). 32pp. When baby bird goes off to school, Mama misses her and begins to worry about her well-being. (Rev: BL 3/1/00; HBG 10/00; SLJ 4/00)

1512 Arnold, Marsha Diane. *Prancing, Dancing Lily* (PS–2). Illus. by John Manders. 2004, Dial $16.99 (978-0-8037-2823-3). Lily the cow may soon be the leader of her herd, but first she sets off on a long journey to gain experience; cartoon illustrations add to the fun. (Rev: SLJ 3/04)

1513 Arnold, Marsha Diane, and Vernise Elaine Pelzel. *Hugs on the Wind* (PS–K). Illus. by Elsa Warnick. 2006, Abrams $15.95 (978-0-8109-5968-2). A gentle story of Little Cottontail, who misses his grandfather and decides to send him hugs and kisses via the wind. (Rev: HBG 10/06; SLJ 3/06)

1514 Arnold, Tedd. *Green Wilma, Frog in Space* (PS–2). Illus. by author. 2009, Dial $16.99 (978-0-8037-2698-7). 32pp. Wilma the frog is mistaken for an alien child and takes an unscheduled trip into space. (Rev: BL 5/1/09; SLJ 6/09)

1515 Aroner, Miriam. *Clink, Clank, Clunk!* (PS). Illus. by Dominic Catalano. 2006, Boyds Mills $15.95 (978-1-59078-270-5). Rabbit's car is on its last legs, but he manages to drive his animal friends to town one last time before junking the vehicle and buying a shiny red auto to replace it. (Rev: HBG 10/06; SLJ 4/06)

1516 Asch, Frank. *Moondance* (PS–K). Illus. 1993, Scholastic $12.95 (978-0-590-45487-2). 32pp. Bear wants to dance with the moon, but doesn't feel worthy of the honor. (Rev: BL 2/15/93; SLJ 6/93)

1517 Asch, Frank. *Mrs. Marlowe's Mice* (2–4). Illus. by David Asch. 2007, Kids Can $17.95 (978-1-55453-022-9). 32pp. Mrs. Marlowe, a cat who works as a librarian, hides a large and happy family of mice in her apartment in this beautifully illustrated book. (Rev: BL 10/1/07; SLJ 10/07)

1518 Asch, Frank. *Sand Cake* (K–2). Illus. by author. 1979, Parents LB $5.95 (978-0-8193-0986-0). 48pp. On the beach, Papa Bear makes a sand cake.

1519 Asher, Sandy. *Here Comes Gosling!* (PS–2). Illus. by Keith Graves. 2009, Philomel $16.99 (978-0-399-25085-9). 32pp. Eye-catching illustrations and believable toddler behavior entertain in this tale of friends Froggie and Rabbit who wait expectantly for the arrival of the baby gosling. (Rev: BLO 6/16/09; SLJ 6/09)

1520 Asher, Sandy. *What a Party!* (PS–1). Illus. by Keith Graves. 2007, Philomel $15.99 (978-0-399-24496-4). Excited about the birthday party for his grandfather, Froggie doesn't want all the fun to end. (Rev: BL 2/1/07; SLJ 2/07)

1521 Auch, Mary Jane. *Bantam of the Opera* (K–3). Illus. 1997, Holiday House LB $16.95 (978-0-8234-1312-6). 32pp. Luigi, a bantam rooster with a huge voice, gets his

chance at the Cosmopolitan Opera Company. (Rev: BL 10/1/97; HBG 3/98; SLJ 10/97*)

1522 Auch, Mary Jane. *Eggs Mark the Spot* (PS–3). Illus. 1996, Holiday House $16.95 (978-0-8234-1242-6). 32pp. A hen copies onto her eggs some portraits painted by famous artists. (Rev: BL 3/15/96; SLJ 5/96)

1523 Auch, Mary Jane. *Peeping Beauty* (PS–3). Illus. 1993, Holiday House LB $16.95 (978-0-8234-1001-9). 32pp. Poulette the hen decides she wants to be a ballerina. (Rev: BL 3/1/93; SLJ 4/93*)

1524 Auch, Mary Jane. *Poultrygeist* (PS–1). Illus. by Mary Jane Auch and Herm Auch. 2003, Holiday House $17.95 (978-0-8234-1756-8). Upset by the noise made by rowdy roosters Rudy and Ralph, Clarissa the cow and Sophie the pig dress up as a spooky "poultrygeist." (Rev: HBG 4/04; SLJ 9/03)

1525 Auch, Mary Jane. *Souperchicken* (K–2). Illus. by Herm Auch. 2003, Holiday House $16.95 (978-0-8234-1704-9). 32pp. Talented hen Henrietta saves her aunts from the "Souper Soup Co." truck on their way to what they think is a free vacation, but is in fact the soup pot. (Rev: BL 3/15/03; HBG 10/03; SLJ 5/03)

1526 Avi. *A Beginning, a Muddle, and an End: The Right Way to Write Writing* (1–3). Illus. by Tricia Tusa. 2008, Harcourt $14.95 (978-0-15-205555-4). Full of fun and wordplay, this sequel to *The End of the Beginning: Being the Adventures of a Small Snail (and an Even Smaller Ant)* (2004), follows Avon the Snail and Edward the Ant in their writing efforts. (Rev: BCCB 5/08; BL 7/08; LMC 11/08)

1527 Axelrod, Amy. *Pigs at Odds: Fun with Math and Games* (2–4). Illus. by Sharon McGinley-Nally. 2000, Simon & Schuster $14.00 (978-0-689-81566-9). In this entertaining concept book starring the Pig family at a carnival, the concept of probability is explored. (Rev: HBG 3/01; SLJ 1/01)

1528 Axelrod, Amy. *Pigs in the Pantry: Fun with Math and Cooking* (PS–2). Illus. by Sharon McGinley-Nally. 1997, Simon & Schuster $14.00 (978-0-689-80665-0). 40pp. The story of Mr. Pig's disastrous cooking spree, with some added math facts about measuring ingredients. (Rev: BCCB 5/97; BL 3/1/97; SLJ 4/97)

1529 Axelrod, Amy. *Pigs on a Blanket* (K–3). Illus. by Sharon McGinley-Nally. 1996, Simon & Schuster paper $14.00 (978-0-689-80505-9). 32pp. Unforeseen problems cause delays for a pig family that wants to spend a day at the beach. (Rev: BL 5/15/96; SLJ 6/96)

1530 Axelrod, Amy. *Pigs Will Be Pigs* (K–3). Illus. by Sharon McGinley-Nally. 1994, Four Winds paper $14.00 (978-0-02-765415-8). 40pp. To finance a dinner out, the pig family engages in a money hunt around the house. (Rev: BCCB 2/94; BL 2/15/94; SLJ 5/94*)

1531 Aylesworth, Jim. *Aunt Pitty Patty's Piggy* (PS–K). Illus. by Barbara McClintock. 1999, Scholastic $15.95 (978-0-590-89987-1). A delightful cumulative tale involving Aunt Pitty Patty's efforts to get her pig home and the many animals she asks for help. (Rev: BCCB 12/99; BL 9/15/99*; HB 9/99; HBG 3/00; SLJ 10/99)

1532 Badescu, Ramona. *Big Rabbit's Bad Mood* (PS–1). Illus. by Delphine Durand. 2009, Chronicle $16.99 (978-0-8118-6666-8). 32pp. Big Rabbit's mood is so horrible that it becomes an actual ugly thing that won't go away until his friends and his mother show up, surprising Big Rabbit with cake and presents for his birthday. (Rev: BL 7/09; SLJ 6/09)

1533 Badescu, Ramona. *Pomelo Begins to Grow* (1–3). Trans. from French by Claudia Bedrick. Illus. by Benjamin Chaud. 2011, Enchanted Lion $16.95 (978-1-59270-111-7). Unpaged. A little elephant contends with the many concerns he has about growing up — will all his parts grow equally? Will he have to stop clowning around? (Rev: SLJ 8/1/11)

1534 Baicker-McKee, Carol. *Mimi* (PS–K). Illus. by author. 2008, Bloomsbury $15.95 (978-1-59990-065-0). 32pp. Readers follow Mimi, a little pig, as she navigates through the events of a busy day without her pet roly-poly bug, Frank. (Rev: BLO 12/30/08; SLJ 8/08)

1535 Bailey, Linda. *The Farm Team* (PS–2). Illus. by Bill Slavin. 2006, Kids Can $16.95 (978-1-55337-850-1). The animals from Farmer Stolski's farm compete valiantly in a championship hockey game against their archrivals, the Bush League Bandits, a team made up of creatures from the wild. (Rev: BL 10/1/06; SLJ 11/06)

1536 Baker, Barbara. *One Saturday Evening* (1–3). Illus. by Kate Duke. 2007, Dutton $13.99 (978-0-525-47103-5). 48pp. In this easy-to-read chapter book, Mama and Papa Bear at last have some peace and quiet after enduring the happy chaos of putting their four bear cubs to bed; a sequel to 1994's *One Saturday Morning*. (Rev: BCCB 10/07; BL 7/07; SLJ 8/07)

1537 Baker, Keith. *My Octopus Arms* (PS–1). Illus. by author. 2013, Simon & Schuster $16.99 (978-1-4424-5843-7). 40pp. An octopus demonstrates what he can do with his eight arms, from playing the banjo and doing chores to giving hugs and building things, in this vivid and cheerfully illustrated picture book with rhyming text. e (Rev: BLO 10/1/13; LMC 1–2/14; SLJ 8/13)

1538 Baker, Keith. *No Two Alike* (PS–2). Illus. by author. 2011, Simon & Schuster $16.99 (978-1-4424-1742-7). 40pp. In rhyming text and appealing illustrations, two little red birds enjoy a snowy day and remark on how everything they see around them is unique. (Rev: BL 11/1/11*; SLJ 9/1/11)

1539 Bardhan-Quallen, Sudipta. *Duck, Duck, Moose!* (PS–1). Illus. by Noah Z. Jones. 2014, Hyperion $16.99 (978-142317110-2). 32pp. Two tidy ducks try to prepare for a party only to have all their efforts ruined by their clumsy housemate Moose. (Rev: BL 12/15/13; LMC 8–9/14*; SLJ 12/13)

1540 Bardhan-Quallen, Sudipta. *Hampire!* (K–2). Illus. by Howard Fine. 2011, HarperCollins $16.99 (978-0-06-114239-0). 32pp. The much-feared Hampire — a caped pig — turns out to be fairly harmless in this suspensefully comic barnyard tale. (Rev: BL 8/11; SLJ 8/1/11)

1541 Base, Graeme. *Jungle Drums* (PS–2). Illus. 2004, Abrams $18.95 (978-0-8109-5044-3). 40pp. A diminutive warthog named Ngiri Mdogo makes his mark when he acquires magical drums in this brightly illustrated, oversize book. (Rev: BL 9/1/04; SLJ 10/04)

1542 Battersby, Katherine. *Squish Rabbit* (PS–1). Illus. by author. 2011, Viking $12.99 (978-0-670-01267-1). 40pp. A lonely and fearful little bunny has trouble finding a friend until he comes across a squirrel. (Rev: BL 10/15/11; SLJ 8/1/11)

1543 Battut, Eric. *The Fox and the Hen* (PS–1). Illus. by author. 2010, Boxer $16.95 (978-1-907152-02-3). 32pp. When an innocent red hen trades her first egg to a sly fox for a worm, her barnyard friends rally round, offering their own precious objects to the fox in an attempt to win back the egg. (Rev: BLO 2/1/10; SLJ 3/1/10*)

1544 Battut, Eric. *Little Mouse's Big Secret* (PS–K). Illus. by author. 2011, Sterling $12.95 (978-1-4027-7462-1). 24pp. A little mouse buries an apple, keeping it a secret for himself, but over the years it grows into a tree and produces enough fruit for all the friends who wondered what he was hiding. (Rev: BL 3/15/11; SLJ 8/1/11)

1545 Baum, Louis. *The Mouse Who Braved Bedtime* (PS). Illus. by Sue Hellard. 2006, Bloomsbury $16.95 (978-1-58234-691-5). Troubled by a persistent nightmare, Milo the mouse seeks advice from family members but in the end must find the courage to confront his fears. (Rev: SLJ 10/06)

1546 Baumgart, Klaus. *Where Are You, Little Green Dragon?* (PS–2). Illus. by author. 1993, Hyperion $12.95 (978-1-56282-344-3); paper $4.95 (978-0-7868-1073-4). The Little Green Dragon with his friendly fly share many adventures. (Rev: SLJ 8/93)

1547 Bearn, Emily. *Tumtum and Nutmeg: Adventures Beyond Nutmouse Hall* (2–4). Illus. by Nick Price. 2009, Little, Brown $16.99 (978-0-316-02703-8). 512pp. Three adventures involve Tumtum and Nutmeg, a married pair of mice who try to look after the human children who share their house. (Rev: BL 4/15/09; SLJ 5/09)

1548 Beaty, Andrea. *Doctor Ted* (K–2). Illus. by Pascal LeMaitre. 2008, Simon & Schuster $14.99 (978-1-4169-2820-1). After bumping his knee, a little bear called Ted decides to become a doctor, but his professional skills do not meet with immediate appreciation. (Rev: BCCB 4/08; BL 6/1–15/08; HB 5/08; SLJ 4/08)

1549 Beaty, Andrea. *Firefighter Ted* (K–2). Illus. by Pascal Lemaitre. 2009, Simon & Schuster $15.99 (978-1-4169-2821-8). Unpaged. The good-hearted but bumbling bear last seen in *Doctor Ted* (2008) decides to become a firefighter in this funny story. (Rev: HB 9–10/09; SLJ 9/1/09)

1550 Beaumont, Karen. *Duck, Duck, Goose! (A Coyote's on the Loose!)* (PS–1). Illus. by Jose Aruego and Ariane Dewey. 2004, HarperCollins $17.99 (978-0-06-050802-9). 32pp. Fear of a coyote in their midst (in fact, a dirty bunny) spreads through the farmyard animals like wildfire. (Rev: BL 3/1/04; SLJ 2/04)

1551 Beaumont, Karen. *Move Over, Rover!* (PS–K). Illus. by Jane Dyer. 2006, Harcourt $16.00 (978-0-15-201979-2). 40pp. Rover the dog offers shelter in his doghouse during a rainstorm and it gets very crowded until Skunk arrives. (Rev: BL 9/1/06; SLJ 9/06)

1552 Beaumont, Karen. *Who Ate All the Cookie Dough?* (PS–1). Illus. by Eugene Yelchin. 2008, Holt (978-0-8050-8267-8). Who did eat that dough? A variety of animals tell Kanga they did not do it and in the end a lift-up flap reveals the culprit — Kanga's own little joey. (Rev: SLJ 7/08)

1553 Bechtold, Lisze. *Sally and the Purple Socks* (PS–2). Illus. by author. 2008, Philomel $15.99 (978-0-399-24734-7). 40pp. Sally the duck gets some new purple socks that grow and grow — becoming first a scarf and cap, then curtains, then a blanket, then a tent — until a rain shower returns them to foot-size. (Rev: BL 6/1–15/08; SLJ 6/08)

1554 Becker, Bonny. *The Sniffles for Bear* (PS–2). Illus. by Kady MacDonald Denton. 2011, Candlewick $16.99 (978-0-7636-4756-8). 32pp. Bear has a dreadful cold and will not be cheered up, even by Mouse. (Rev: BLO 9/15/11; HB 9–10/11; SLJ 8/1/11)

1555 Becker, Bonny. *A Visitor for Bear* (PS–2). Illus. by Kady M. Denton. 2008, Candlewick $16.99 (978-0-7636-2807-9). 56pp. Bear doesn't want any visitors but after a persistent mouse wears down his resistance, Bear discovers the pleasures of having company. (Rev: BL 2/15/08; HB 3/08; SLJ 2/08)

1556 Beiser, Tim. *Bradley McGogg: The Very Fine Frog* (PS–K). Illus. by Rachel Berman. 2009, Tundra $17.95 (978-0-88776-864-4). A hungry frog sets out to visit his neighbors only to find that they eat the most disgusting things! (Rev: SLJ 3/09)

1557 Bell, Cece. *Bee-Wigged* (K–2). Illus. by author. 2008, Candlewick $16.99 (978-0-7636-3614-2). 40pp. Jerry the bee's very large size has prejudiced others against him, but when he dons a wig (actually a guinea pig) he is suddenly accepted. (Rev: SLJ 3/09)

1558 Bell, Cece. *Itty Bitty* (PS–1). Illus. by author. 2009, Candlewick $9.99 (978-0-7636-3616-6). 32pp. Itty Bitty, a very small dog, works hard to make his home in a huge bone, and despite his size, confidently travels into the city to find just the right items to decorate and cozily furnish his space. (Rev: BL 7/09)

1559 Bently, Peter. *The Great Sheep Shenanigans* (K–2). Illus. by Mei Matsuoka. 2012, Andersen $16.95 (978-076138990-3). 32pp. A wolf called Lou Pine is determined to make really tasty food out of a flock of lambs and tries various whacky disguises. (Rev: BL 4/15/12; SLJ 5/1/12)

1560 Berenstain, Stan, and Jan Berenstain. *The Berenstain Bears in the Dark* (PS–2). Illus. by authors. 1982, Random paper $3.25 (978-0-394-85443-4). Brother and Sister Bear in one of a very large series of books.

1561 Berger, Carin. *Forever Friends* (PS). Illus. by author. 2010, Greenwillow $16.99 (978-0-06-191528-4); LB $17.89 (978-0-06-191529-1). 40pp. A young rabbit and its bluebird friend are separated for a long, lonely winter but are reunited when spring arrives and the bird flies back north. (Rev: BL 3/1/10; HB 3–4/10; SLJ 3/1/10)

1562 Berger, Joe. *Bridget Fidget and the Most Perfect Pet* (PS–2). Illus. by author. 2009, Dial $16.99 (978-0-8037-3405-0). 32pp. Bridget Fidget is sure that the box they just delivered must contain her unicorn. (Rev: BL 6/1–15/09; SLJ 6/09)

1563 Berger, Samantha. *Martha Doesn't Share!* (PS). Illus. by Bruce Whatley. 2010, Little, Brown $16.99 (978-0-316-07367-7). Unpaged. Martha the difficult young otter learns about the value of sharing in this simple story. (Rev: HB 9–10/10; LMC 1–2/11; SLJ 10/1/10)

1564 Berner, Rotraut Susanne. *Hound and Hare* (PS–2). Trans. by Shelley Tanaka. Illus. by author. 2011, Groundwood $18.95 (978-0-88899-987-0). 80pp. A new generation of hounds and hares begins to question their families' long-standing feud. (Rev: BL 6/1/11; LMC 10/11; SLJ 6/11)

1565 Berry, Lynne. *Duck Tents* (PS–K). Illus. by Nakata Hiroe. 2009, Holt $16.95 (978-0-8050-8696-6). 32pp. Five little ducks set off on a backyard camping adventure, have fun toasting marshmallows, and worry about the sounds of the night in this charming story that includes counting guidance. (Rev: BCCB 9/09; BL 4/1/09; SLJ 4/09)

1566 Berry, Lynne. *Ducking for Apples* (PS–K). Illus. by Hiroe Nakata. Series: Duck. 2010, Henry Holt $16.99 (978-0-8050-8935-6). 32pp. In this cheerful story, the five little ducklings ride their bikes to an apple tree, where they gather fruit to make a pie. ℮ (Rev: BLO 7/10; SLJ 8/1/10)

1567 Billingsley, Franny. *Big Bad Bunny* (PS–2). Illus. by G. Brian Karas. 2008, Atheneum $16.99 (978-1-4169-0601-8). 40pp. Mama Mouse tucks in her brood while a fearsome bunny is on the loose; the nature of this scary personage (actually a baby mouse in a bunny suit) is revealed at the end. (Rev: BL 3/15/08; HB 3/08; SLJ 4/08)

1568 Birney, Betty. *Surprises According to Humphrey* (2–4). 2008, Putnam $14.99 (978-0-399-24730-9). 192pp. Humphrey, the classroom hamster, faces new pleasures and challenges — a hamster ball, a janitor replaced by an alien (?), and a teacher considering retirement. (Rev: BL 2/1/08; SLJ 2/08)

1569 Björkman, Steve. *Supersnouts!* (PS–1). Illus. 2004, Holiday House $16.95 (978-0-8234-1810-7). 32pp. A young pig named Hamlet gets a chance to join the Superhero Pig Patrol in this pun- and action-packed story. (Rev: BL 4/1/04; SLJ 5/04)

1570 Blackaby, Susan. *Rembrandt's Hat* (PS–3). 2002, Houghton $15.00 (978-0-618-11452-8). Rembrandt the bear has lost his hat and tries many inventive substitutes before finding one that suits him. (Rev: BCCB 5/02; BL 4/15/02; HBG 10/02; SLJ 7/02)

1571 Blackstone, Stella. *Bear's Birthday* (PS–K). Illus. by Debbie Harter. 2011, Barefoot $6.99 (978-1-84686-515-2); paper $6.99 (978-1-84686-516-9). 24pp. A bear and his friends have a busy birthday party in this lively board book. (Rev: BL 6/1/11; SLJ 6/11)

1572 Blathwayt, Benedict. *Dinosaur Chase!* (PS–1). Illus. by author. 2006, Hutchinson $16.99 (978-0-09-189293-7). Fin the dinosaur is having a good time with his friends when a group of bullies tries to break up their fun; detailed illustrations enhance the story. (Rev: SLJ 9/06)

1573 Blight, Peter. *The Lonely Giraffe* (PS). Illus. by Michael Terry. 2005, Bloomsbury $16.99 (978-0-7475-6894-0). The story of a previously ignored giraffe who uses his long neck to help others and make new friends. (Rev: SLJ 7/05)

1574 Bloom, Suzanne. *A Mighty Fine Time Machine* (PS–1). Illus. by author. 2009, Boyds Mills $16.95 (978-1-59078-527-0). 24pp. Samantha, an anteater, helps her aardvark friend Grant and armadillo friend Antoine but they cannot make their newly acquired time machine work, so Samantha turns it into a bookmobile. (Rev: BL 5/1/09; SLJ 3/09)

1575 Bloom, Suzanne. *Oh! What a Surprise!* (PS–1). Illus. by author. 2012, Boyds Mills $16.95 (978-1-59078-892-9). 32pp. Goose and Bear are making presents, but will any of them be suitable for Fox? (Rev: BLO 10/1/12; SLJ 9/12)

1576 Bloom, Suzanne. *A Splendid Friend, Indeed* (PS–2). Illus. 2005, Boyds Mills $15.95 (978-1-59078-286-6). 32pp. Goose is talkative and outgoing, while Bear is quiet and introverted, but somehow the two manage to strike up a lasting friendship. (Rev: BL 2/15/05; SLJ 5/05)

1577 Bloom, Suzanne. *Treasure* (PS–2). Illus. by author. 2007, Boyds Mills $15.95 (978-1-59078-457-0). Goose mistakes Bear's tic-tac-toe game for a treasure map and insists that they immediately start digging; the treasure they find is an enjoyable day together. (Rev: LMC 1/08; SLJ 2/08)

1578 Bloom, Suzanne. *What About Bear?* (PS–1). Illus. by author. 2010, Boyds Mills $16.95 (978-1-59078-528-7). 32pp. Goose acts as a mediator between Bear and Little Fox, who eventually discover that they have more in common than they thought. (Rev: BL 3/15/10; SLJ 6/1/10*)

1579 Bogan, Paulette. *Lulu the Big Little Chick* (PS–K). Illus. by author. 2009, Bloomsbury $16.99 (978-1-59990-343-9). 24pp. Lulu resents being small and tries to assert her independence. (Rev: BL 5/1/09)

1580 Bond, Felicia. *Tumble Bumble* (PS–K). Illus. 1996, Front St. $13.95 (978-1-886910-15-7). 32pp. A simple rhyme about the adventures of a bug that goes for a walk. (Rev: BL 11/15/96; SLJ 10/96)

1581 Bond, Michael. *Paddington Bear* (PS–2). Illus. by R. W. Alley. 1998, HarperCollins $15.99 (978-0-06-027854-0). 32pp. A simple version of the first Paddington story in which the bear meets the Brown family in Paddington Station. (Rev: BL 1/1–15/99; HBG 3/99)

1582 Bonwill, Ann. *Bug and Bear: A Story of True Friendship* (PS–K). Illus. by Layn Marlow. 2011, Marshall Cavendish $17.99 (978-0-7614-5902-6). 32pp. Bear is testy when his friend Bug annoys him on his way to naptime, and later regrets his sharp words. (Rev: BL 5/1/11; SLJ 5/1/11)

1583 Bornstein, Ruth. *Little Gorilla* (PS). Illus. by author. 1986, Houghton $15.00 (978-0-395-28773-6); paper $5.95 (978-0-89919-421-9). 32pp. Even though Little Gorilla grows into a big gorilla, everyone still loves him.

1584 Boyle, Bob. *Hugo and the Really, Really, Really Long String* (PS–1). Illus. by author. 2010, Random House $15.99 (978-0-375-83423-3); LB $18.99 (978-0-375-93423-0). Unpaged. A friendly hippo decides to follow a long red thread he spies one day; his friends join him one by one, expecting a great surprise and treasure at the end. (Rev: LMC 5–6/10; SLJ 2/1/10)

1585 Bradley, Kimberly Brubaker. *Ballerino Nate* (PS–K). Illus. by R. W. Alley. 2006, Dial $16.99 (978-0-8037-2954-4). Nate the puppy's desire to become a ballet dancer is diminished when his older brother insists that only girls can be ballerinas. (Rev: BL 2/1/06; SLJ 3/06)

1586 Braun, Sebastien. *I Love My Daddy* (PS). Illus. by author. 2004, HarperCollins $12.99 (978-0-06-054311-2). The story of Baby Bear's day and all the things he does with his father. (Rev: SLJ 4/04)

1587 Breen, Steve. *Pug and Doug* (PS–1). Illus. by author. 2013, Dial $16.99 (978-080373521-7). 32pp. Dogs Pug and Doug manage to maintain a close friendship despite their differences and the occasional misunderstanding. (Rev: BL 1/13; LMC 8–9/13*; SLJ 2/13)

1588 Brett, Jan. *Comet's Nine Lives* (PS–3). Illus. 1996, Penguin $16.99 (978-0-399-22931-2). 30pp. Comet, a white cat, has many adventures on Nantucket Island until finding a permanent home in a lighthouse. (Rev: BL 10/15/96; SLJ 12/96)

1589 Brett, Jan. *The Hat* (PS–3). Illus. 1997, Penguin $16.99 (978-0-399-23101-8). 32pp. When a red wool stocking is blown onto the head of Hedgie the hedgehog, he maintains that it is his new hat. (Rev: BL 9/1/97*; HBG 3/98; SLJ 9/97)

1590 Brett, Jan. *Hedgie Blasts Off!* (PS–2). 2006, Putnam $16.99 (978-0-399-24621-0). 32pp. Hedgie's dream of becoming an astronaut comes true when the diminutive hedgehog is dispatched to the planet Mikkop on a mission to repair a malfunctioning volcano. (Rev: BL 8/06; SLJ 9/06)

1591 Brett, Jan. *Hedgie's Surprise* (PS–1). Illus. 2000, Penguin $16.99 (978-0-399-23477-4). Henny wants to have family but a hungry troll named Tomten keeps stealing her eggs until she gets help from Hedgie the hedgehog. (Rev: BCCB 10/00; BL 9/1/00; HBG 3/01; SLJ 9/00)

1592 Brett, Jan. *The Three Little Dassies* (PS–2). Illus. by author. 2010, Putnam $17.99 (978-0-399-25499-4). 32pp. In this Three Little Pigs adaptation, three fancifully dressed African rock hyraxes or dassies — Timbi, Mimibi, and Pimbi — defend their Namibian homes from a hungry eagle. (Rev: BL 9/1/10; LMC 1–2/11; SLJ 10/1/10)

1593 Brett, Jan. *Town Mouse, Country Mouse* (PS–3). Illus. 1994, Penguin LB $16.99 (978-0-399-22622-9). 32pp. A town cat and a country owl, both of whom enjoy mice for dinner, decide to change places. (Rev: BL 9/1/94; SLJ 9/94)

1594 Bridwell, Norman. *Clifford's Good Deeds* (PS–1). Illus. by author. 1985, Scholastic paper $3.99 (978-0-590-44292-3). 32pp. Clifford is a large shaggy dog whose efforts to be helpful result in comic mishaps. Also use: *Clifford Takes a Trip* (1985); *Clifford's Tricks* (1986); *Clifford the Big Red Dog* (1988); *Clifford the Small Red Puppy* (1990); *Clifford at the Circus* (1985); *Clifford Goes to Hollywood* (1986).

1595 Brooks, Erik. *Polar Opposites* (PS–2). Illus. by author. 2010, Marshall Cavendish $16.99 (978-0-7614-5685-8). 32pp. Two pen pals — an Arctic polar bear and a demure penguin from Antarctica — meet up at the Galapagos islands to share a happy vacation together despite their differences. Lexile AD170L (Rev: BL 10/1/10; LMC 1–2/11; SLJ 10/1/10)

1596 Brown, Marc. *Arthur Lost and Found* (PS–K). Illus. 1998, Little, Brown $15.95 (978-0-316-10912-3). 32pp. In a balanced tale of fun and caution, Arthur and his pal Buster get lost on the wrong side of town. Also included in this series are *Arthur and the Crunch Cereal Contest* and *Arthur's Mystery Envelope* (both 1998). (Rev: BL 12/1/98; HBG 3/99; SLJ 1/99)

1597 Brown, Marc. *Arthur Turns Green* (K–3). Illus. by author. 2011, Little, Brown $16.99 (978-0-316-12924-4). 32pp. Arthur the aardvark is focusing on the environment but D.W. worries that she will turn green too. Lexile 580L (Rev: BL 3/1/11; SLJ 3/1/11)

1598 Brown, Marc. *Arthur Writes a Story* (PS–3). Illus. 1996, Little, Brown $15.95 (978-0-316-10916-1). 32pp. Arthur's classmates embellish the simple story of how he got his puppy. Also use *Arthur's New Puppy* (1993), *Arthur's Chicken Pox* (1994), and *Arthur's Computer Disaster* (1997). (Rev: BL 9/15/96; SLJ 9/96)

1599 Brown, Marc. *Arthur's Underwear* (PS–1). Illus. 1999, Little, Brown $15.95 (978-0-316-11012-9). 32pp. Arthur experiences the ultimate embarrassment when his pants rip and reveal his underwear. (Rev: BL 1/1–15/00; HBG 3/00)

1600 Brown, Marc. *D.W.'s Guide to Perfect Manners* (PS–2). Illus. by author. 2006, Little, Brown $15.99 (978-0-316-12106-4). Arthur the aardvark challenges little sister D.W. to be the model of good behavior for a full 24 hours. (Rev: SLJ 8/06)

1601 Brown, Marc. *D.W.'s Library Card* (PS–2). Illus. by author. 2001, Little, Brown $14.95 (978-0-316-11013-6). Arthur the aardvark teaches little sister D.W. how to look after — and enjoy — library books. (Rev: HBG 3/02; SLJ 12/01)

1602 Brown, Marc. *D.W.'s Lost Blankie* (PS). Illus. 1998, Little, Brown $13.95 (978-0-316-10914-7). 24pp. Arthur's little sister, D.W., is inconsolable when she loses her beloved blankie. Luckily, Mom knows where to find it. (Rev: BL 5/15/98; HBG 10/98; SLJ 5/98)

1603 Brown, Marc, and Laurie Krasny Brown. *The Bionic Bunny Show* (2–3). Illus. by Marc Brown. 1984, Little, Brown $14.95 (978-0-316-11120-1). An ordinary rabbit becomes a super TV star thanks to makeup magic.

1604 Brown, Margaret Wise. *The Runaway Bunny* (PS–K). Illus. by Clement Hurd. 1972, HarperCollins LB $16.89 (978-0-06-020766-3); paper $6.99 (978-0-06-443018-0). 40pp. With nine colorful illustrations, this new edition of an old favorite is a charming story of mother bunny's love for her restless youngster, who keeps trying to escape but is always found.

1605 Brown, Peter. *Mr. Tiger Goes Wild* (PS–2). Illus. by author. 2013, Little, Brown $17.99 (978-031620063-9). 48pp. With delightfully detailed illustrations, this funny story follows Mr. Tiger's rebellion against proper Victorian city life. ALA Notable Children's Book. Lexile AD170 (Rev: BL 9/1/13*; HB 11–12/13; SLJ 7/13*)

1606 Browne, Anthony. *Me and You* (PS–3). Illus. by author. 2010, Farrar $16.99 (978-0-374-34908-0). 32pp. The story of Goldilocks is retold here in parallel narratives — one from the baby bear's point of view — and given an urban setting and moody, evocative illustrations. (Rev: BL 9/15/10; HB 11–12/10; SLJ 11/1/10*)

1607 Bruchac, Joseph. *Turtle's Race with Beaver: A Traditional Seneca Story* (1–3). Illus. by Jose Aruego and Ariane Dewey. 2003, Penguin $15.99 (978-0-8037-2852-3). 32pp. Turtle and Beaver compete for ownership of a pond in this variant on a Seneca Indian tale that resembles Aesop's story of the tortoise and the hare. (Rev: BL 9/15/03; HBG 4/04; SLJ 10/03)

1608 Bruss, Deborah. *Book! Book! Book!* (PS–K). Illus. by Tiphanie Beeke. 2001, Scholastic $16.95 (978-0-439-13525-2). 40pp. A crew of bored animals head to the library and try to make the librarian understand what they need. (Rev: BCCB 2/01; BL 5/15/01; HBG 10/01; SLJ 5/01)

1609 Bunting, Eve. *Have You Seen My New Blue Socks?* (PS–1). Illus. by Sergio Ruzzier. 2013, Clarion $16.99 (978-0-547-75267-9). 32pp. In repetitive, rhyming text, the reader follows a little green duck as he searches for his missing socks. Lexile AD290L (Rev: BL 3/1/13; HB 3–4/13; SLJ 3/13*)

1610 Bunting, Eve. *Hey Diddle Diddle* (PS–2). Illus. by Mary Ann Fraser. 2011, Boyds Mills $16.95 (978-1-59078-768-7). 32pp. This catchy version of the familiar rhyme features a troupe of lively instrument-playing animals. (Rev: BL 6/1/11; SLJ 4/11)

1611 Bunting, Eve. *Hurry! Hurry!* (PS–K). Illus. by Jeff Mack. 2007, Harcourt $16.00 (978-0-15-205410-6). 40pp. All the animals of the farmyard gather to greet a new chick into the world. (Rev: BL 2/1/07)

1612 Bunting, Eve. *Mouse Island* (K–2). Illus. by Dominic Catalano. 2008, Boyds Mills $15.95 (978-1-59078-447-1). Lonely Mouse lives by himself on an island until he rescues a creature — a cat! — from a sinking ship. (Rev: BL 3/15/08; SLJ 4/08)

1613 Bunting, Eve. *Tweak Tweak* (PS–K). Illus. by Sergio Ruzzier. 2011, Clarion $14.99 (978-0-618-99851-7).

40pp. A little elephant on a walk with her mother learns about what makes her unique as they talk about other animals — a frog, a bird, a butterfly, a crocodile. (Rev: BL 3/1/11; SLJ 5/1/11)

1614 Burkert, Rand. *Mouse and Lion* (PS–2). Illus. by Nancy Ekholm Burkert. 2011, Scholastic $17.95 (978-0-545-10147-9). 32pp. In this retelling of the classic Aesop fable the mouse plays the leading role. ALSC Notable Children's Book, 2012. (Rev: BL 12/1/11*; HB 11–12/11; LMC 1–2/12; SLJ 8/1/11*)

1615 Burleigh, Robert. *Hit the Road, Jack* (K–2). Illus. by Ross MacDonald. 2012, Abrams $17.95 (978-1-4197-0399-7). 48pp. A rabbit named Jack travels across an earlier United States visiting various sites and hearing many stories in this book loosely based on the experiences of Jack Kerouac. e (Rev: BL 10/1/12; LMC 3–4/13; SLJ 8/12)

1616 Burningham, John. *It's a Secret!* (PS–1). Illus. by author. 2009, Candlewick $16.99 (978-0-7636-4275-4). Where do cats go at night? Out cat dancing. (Rev: BCCB 9/09; BL 6/1–15/09; SLJ 6/09)

1617 Bynum, Janie. *Kiki's Blankie* (PS–K). Illus. by author. 2009, Sterling $14.95 (978-1-4027-5910-9). 32pp. Kiki, a little monkey, finds her missing blankie but it's in a tree above a crocodile. Will Kiki find a way to get it back? (Rev: BL 5/15/09; SLJ 6/09)

1618 Calhoun, Mary. *Cross-Country Cat* (K–2). Illus. by Erick Ingraham. 1979, Morrow paper $6.99 (978-0-688-06519-5). 40pp. A Siamese cat named Henry sets out on a cross-country skiing adventure.

1619 Calhoun, Mary. *Hot-Air Henry* (PS–4). Illus. by Erick Ingraham. 1981, Morrow paper $6.99 (978-0-688-04068-0). 40pp. Siamese cat Henry sneaks into the basket of a hot-air balloon.

1620 Cannon, Janell. *Crickwing* (1–4). Illus. 2000, Harcourt $16.00 (978-0-15-201790-3). 48pp. Crickwing, a starving cockroach-artist, joins forces with some plucky leafcutter ants to rout a group of voracious army ants in this gripping story set in a rain forest. (Rev: BL 10/15/00*; HBG 3/01; SLJ 11/00)

1621 Cannon, Janell. *Stellaluna* (PS–3). Illus. 1993, Harcourt $16.00 (978-0-15-280217-2). 48pp. Stellaluna, a fruit bat, is separated from her mother and raised by birds. (Rev: BL 4/1/93; SLJ 6/93)

1622 Cannon, Janell. *Verdi* (K–3). Illus. 1997, Harcourt $16.00 (978-0-15-201028-7). 48pp. A baby python named Verdi has fun and adventures when he travels alone in the rain forest. (Rev: BCCB 6/97; BL 4/15/97; SLJ 5/97)

1623 Capucilli, Alyssa Satin. *Katy Duck* (PS). Illus. by Henry Cole. 2007, Simon & Schuster $7.99 (978-1-4169-1901-8). Katy Duck loves to dance at home but is a little unsure of ballet class until she sees what fun it can be. (Rev: SLJ 7/07)

1624 Capucilli, Alyssa Satin. *Katy Duck Is a Caterpillar* (PS–2). Illus. by Henry Cole. 2009, Simon & Schuster $14.99 (978-1-4169-6061-4). Katy Duck is devastated

when she is given the role of a caterpillar in the spring dance recital. (Rev: BL 12/1/08; SLJ 2/09)

1625 Carle, Eric. *The Grouchy Ladybug* (PS–K). Illus. by author. 1977, HarperCollins $15.00 (978-0-690-01391-7). 48pp. A grouchy ladybug, who is looking for a fight, challenges every insect and animal she meets regardless of size. Brilliantly illustrated in collage, the pages vary in size with the size of the animal.

1626 Carle, Eric. *The Mixed-Up Chameleon* (PS–2). Illus. by author. 1984, HarperCollins LB $18.89 (978-0-690-04397-6); paper $6.99 (978-0-06-443162-0). 32pp. A new edition of the story of a chameleon who finally decides to be himself.

1627 Carle, Eric. *"Slowly, Slowly, Slowly," Said the Sloth* (K–3). Illus. by author. 2002, Philomel $16.99 (978-0-399-23954-0). A sloth explains to a variety of jungle animals the reasons why he likes to take things easy in this beautifully illustrated book. (Rev: HBG 3/03; SLJ 9/02)

1628 Carle, Eric. *The Very Busy Spider* (PS–K). Illus. by author. 1989, Penguin $21.99 (978-0-399-21166-9). 32pp. A spider spins its web in this striking picture book. Also use the story of a crab that outgrows his shell in: *A House for Hermit Crab* (1991, Picture Book). (Rev: BCCB 5/85; BL 6/1/85; SLJ 5/85)

1629 Carle, Eric. *The Very Clumsy Click Beetle* (PS–1). Illus. 1999, Penguin $21.99 (978-0-399-23201-5). 32pp. A click beetle learns to use its lifesaving device of clicking to turn over when it is on its back, but only in the nick of time. (Rev: BL 10/1/99; HBG 3/00; SLJ 11/99)

1630 Carle, Eric. *The Very Hungry Caterpillar* (PS–2). Illus. by author. 1981, Penguin $21.99 (978-0-399-20853-9). 32pp. A caterpillar eats a great deal and then spins its cocoon.

1631 Carle, Eric. *The Very Lonely Firefly* (PS–1). Illus. 1995, Penguin $22.99 (978-0-399-22774-5). 32pp. A little firefly searches for some of his own kind but is confused by such lights as candles and fireworks. (Rev: BCCB 7–8/95; BL 5/15/95; HB 9/95; SLJ 8/95)

1632 Carle, Eric. *The Very Quiet Cricket* (PS–1). Illus. 1990, Penguin $22.99 (978-0-399-21885-9). 48pp. A newly hatched cricket has a problem getting his wings to chirp. (Rev: BCCB 11/90; BL 10/1/90; HB 1/91; SLJ 12/90)

1633 Carlson, Nancy. *First Grade, Here I Come!* (PS–1). 2006, Viking $15.99 (978-0-670-06127-3). 32pp. Henry the mouse reviews his experiences on the first day in 1st grade and realizes he quite enjoyed it after all. (Rev: BL 8/06; SLJ 7/06)

1634 Carlson, Nancy. *Henry and the Bully* (K–2). Illus. by author. 2010, Viking $15.99 (978-0-670-01148-3). Unpaged. Young 1st-grade mouse Henry finds a way to stand up to the 2nd-grade Sam (a poodle) who is bullying him. (Rev: LMC 11–12/10; SLJ 7/1/10)

1635 Carlson, Nancy. *I Like Me!* (PS–K). Illus. by author. 1988, Puffin paper $6.99 (978-0-14-050819-2). 32pp. An exuberant book that teaches how to appreciate oneself. (Rev: BL 6/15/88; SLJ 9/88)

1636 Carlson, Nancy. *Look Out, Kindergarten, Here I Come! / ¡Preparate Kindergarten! Alla voy!* (PS–3). Trans. by Teresa Mlawer. Illus. 2004, Viking $15.99 (978-0-670-03673-8). 32pp. A bilingual story about Henry the mouse's ambivalence toward his first day of kindergarten. (Rev: BL 3/1/04; SLJ 9/04)

1637 Carlson, Nancy. *Loudmouth George Earns His Allowance* (PS–2). Illus. 2007, Carolrhoda $15.95 (978-0-8225-6560-4). George the rabbit ends up doing more work after his brothers "help" him with his chores in this brightly illustrated book. (Rev: BL 5/1/07)

1638 Carlson, Nancy. *Start Saving, Henry!* (K–2). Illus. by author. 2009, Viking $15.99 (978-0-670-01147-6). 32pp. A 7-year-old mouse named Henry really wants a Super Robot Dude, but his mother won't pay for it. Can he save enough to buy it himself? (Rev: BL 9/15/09; SLJ 10/1/09)

1639 Carman, Patrick. *Saving Mister Nibbles!* (1–3). Illus. by Jim Madsen. 2008, Scholastic $12.99 (978-0-545-01930-9). 74pp. Eliot the squirrel and his friends are horrified to see a stuffed squirrel being presented as a birthday gift and determine to rescue it from a life in captivity. (Rev: BL 6/1–15/08; LMC 3/08) 🎧

1640 Carrer, Chiara. *Otto Carrotto* (K–3). Illus. by author. 2011, Eerdmans $16 (978-0-8028-5393-6). 26pp. A carrot-obsessed rabbit finds his singular diet has physical repercussions and decides to switch to spinach. (Rev: BL 11/1/11; SLJ 10/1/11)

1641 Carrick, Carol. *What Happened to Patrick's Dinosaurs?* (K–2). Illus. by Donald Carrick. 1988, Houghton $16.00 (978-0-89919-406-6); paper $5.95 (978-0-89919-797-5). Patrick explains to his young brother his theory of how dinosaurs disappeared: they left by spaceship. (Rev: HB 8–9/86; SLJ 5/86)

1642 Cash, John Carter. *The Cat in the Rhinestone Suit* (K–2). Illus. by Scott Nash. 2012, Simon & Schuster $17.99 (978-1-4169-7483-3). 32pp. A cat with a taste for sparkles has a long-standing feud with a snake called Del Moore until the cat is in danger and Del comes to the rescue; with a twangy rhythm, this colorful tale is written by the son of June Carter and Johnny Cash. (Rev: BL 4/1/12; SLJ 4/1/12)

1643 Cazet, Denys. *Will You Read to Me?* (PS–2). Illus. 2007, Atheneum $16.99 (978-1-4169-0935-4). Hamlet's fellow pigs refuse to listen to his stories or read to him, so he goes to the pond and there finds an appreciative audience. (Rev: BL 5/1/07; SLJ 7/07)

1644 Cecil, Randy. *Duck* (PS–1). Illus. by author. 2008, Candlewick $15.99 (978-0-7636-3072-0). 40pp. A wooden carousel duck nurses a real duckling until he grows old enough to fly, which is a challenge for them both; but Duck's rewards come when a fully grown Duckling returns and takes Duck up into the air. (Rev: BL 2/1/08; LMC 3/08; SLJ 3/08)

1645 Chaconas, Dori. *Cork and Fuzz: The Swimming Lesson* (PS–2). Illus. by Lisa McCue. Series: Viking Easy-to-Read. 2011, Viking $13.99 (978-0-670-01281-7). 32pp. Fuzz the possum overcomes his fear of water in

order to visit his pal Cork, the muskrat, and then offers to teach Cork to climb. (Rev: HB 7–8/11; SLJ 7/11)

1646 Chaconas, Dori. *Mousie Love* (K–2). Illus. by Josee Masse. 2009, Bloomsbury $16.99 (978-1-59990-111-4). A charming tale of old-fashioned romance between mice Tully and Frill. (Rev: BL 5/1/09)

1647 Charles, Faustin, and Michael Terry. *The Selfish Crocodile* (PS–2). Illus. 1999, Little Tiger $14.95 (978-1-888444-56-8). 32pp. A selfish crocodile won't allow any animals in his river until a little mouse helps him and he realizes the value of friendship. (Rev: BL 6/1–15/99)

1648 Chaud, Benjamin. *The Bear's Song* (PS–K). Illus. by author. 2013, Chronicle $17.99 (978-145211424-8). 32pp. Papa Bear is settling down for a long winter when he realizes that Little Bear has disappeared, and must track him down at the Opera House. USBBY Outstanding International Book. (Rev: BL 12/15/13*; LMC 5–6/14; SLJ 9/13)

1649 Chen, Chih-Yuan. *The Featherless Chicken* (K–3). Illus. by author. 2006, Heryin $16.95 (978-0-9762056-9-2). A featherless young chicken agonizes about his looks and his rejection by his peers. (Rev: SLJ 10/06)

1650 Chen, Chih-Yuan. *Guji Guji* (PS–3). Illus. by author. 2004, Kane $15.95 (978-1-929132-67-6). Guji Guji, a crocodile raised by a duck, faces difficult decisions when he grows to maturity. (Rev: SLJ 11/04)

1651 Cherry, Lynne. *How Groundhog's Garden Grew* (PS–3). Illus. 2003, Scholastic $16.99 (978-0-439-32371-0). 40pp. Squirrel shows Groundhog how to plant a garden, with delicious results come harvest time. (Rev: BL 2/1/03; HBG 10/03; SLJ 2/03)

1652 Chivers, Natalie. *Rhino's Great Big Itch!* (PS–1). Illus. by author. 2010, Good Books $16.99 (978-1-56148-684-7). 32pp. After several animals fail to help him, a friendly bird proves just the right size to help a rhinoceros with a pesky itch in the ear. (Rev: BL 5/1/10; SLJ 5/1/10)

1653 Christelow, Eileen. *Five Little Monkeys Wash the Car* (PS–1). Illus. 2000, Clarion $15.00 (978-0-395-92566-9). 33pp. Mama, a monkey, gets help from her five little monkeys when she decides to sell the rickety old family car. (Rev: BL 5/1/00; HBG 10/00; SLJ 5/00)

1654 Christelow, Eileen. *Five Little Monkeys with Nothing to Do* (PS–1). Illus. 1996, Clarion $16.00 (978-0-395-75830-4). Five little monkeys prepare for their Grandma Bessie's visit. (Rev: BCCB 12/96; BL 9/1/96; SLJ 11/96)

1655 Church, Caroline Jayne. *One Smart Goose* (PS–2). Illus. 2005, Scholastic $16.95 (978-0-439-68765-2). 32pp. A clever goose uses camouflage to hide from a fox, earning the respect of his fellow geese. (Rev: BL 3/1/05; SLJ 5/05)

1656 Church, Caroline Jayne. *Ruff! And the Wonderfully Amazing Busy Day* (PS–1). Illus. by author. 2013, HarperCollins $17.99 (978-0-06-201498-6). 32pp. Ruff the dog makes new friends when he digs a pond in his backyard. (Rev: BL 6/13; SLJ 6/13)

1657 Clark, Leslie Ann. *Peepsqueak!* (PS–K). Illus. by author. 2012, HarperCollins $12.99 (978-006207801-8). 32pp. Peepsqueak the newborn chick hatches with a determination to fly despite advice from Big Brown Cow, Big, Sheep, and others; after failing several times he receives some help from a kindly goose. (Rev: BL 1/1/12; SLJ 1/12)

1658 Cooper, Helen. *Delicious!* (PS–1). Illus. by author. 2007, Farrar $16.00 (978-0-374-31756-0). 32pp. What can you do with a picky eater when Duck's favorite pumpkin soup is out of season? Cat and Squirrel must use their imaginations in this third book in the series that began with *Pumpkin Soup* (1999). (Rev: BL 9/1/07; SLJ 9/07)

1659 Cooper, Helen. *A Pipkin of Pepper* (PS–2). Illus. 2005, Farrar $16.00 (978-0-374-35953-9). 32pp. Duck gets lost when he accompanies friends Cat and Squirrel to the city to buy salt for the soup in this companion to *Pumpkin Soup* (1997). (Rev: BL 8/05; SLJ 9/05)

1660 Costello, David Hyde. *Little Pig Joins the Band* (PS–K). Illus. by author. 2011, Charlesbridge $14.95 (978-1-58089-264-3). 32pp. Jacob the pig is too little for any of the available instruments in the marching band, so he takes on the role of leader of his older siblings. (Rev: BL 5/1/11; SLJ 7/11)

1661 Côté, Geneviève. *Starring Me and You* (PS–1). Illus. by author. 2014, Kids Can $16.95 (978-189478639-3). 32pp. Piggy and Bunny are going to put on a play, but first they have to agree on the subject in this sequel to *Me and You* (2009) and *Without You* (2011). Lexile AD300 (Rev: BL 3/1/14; SLJ 3/14)

1662 Cousins, Lucy. *I'm the Best* (PS–K). Illus. by author. 2010, Candlewick $14.99 (978-0-7636-4684-4). 32pp. With exuberant bravado, a showoff dog claims to be better than all his animal friends, not realizing he's hurting their feelings until the end, when he apologizes, they forgive him, and all is well. (Rev: BL 5/1/10*; SLJ 5/1/10*)

1663 Cousins, Lucy. *Maisy Goes on Vacation* (PS–K). Illus. by author. 2010, Candlewick $12.99 (978-0-7636-4752-0). Unpaged. Maisy packs her suitcase and travels to the beach with her friend Cyril, where they have fun by the ocean and then return to their hotel. (Rev: SLJ 9/1/10)

1664 Cousins, Lucy. *Maisy Goes Swimming* (PS). Illus. 1990, Little, Brown $13.95 (978-0-316-15834-3). Maisy, a mouse, goes to a swimming pool in this book that contains many flaps and tabs. Also use: *Maisy Goes to Bed* (1990). (Rev: BCCB 10/90*; SLJ 9/90)

1665 Cousins, Lucy. *Maisy Goes to the Library* (PS–K). Illus. 2005, Candlewick $12.99 (978-0-7636-2669-3). 32pp. In this colorfully illustrated picture book, Maisy the mouse goes to the library in search of a book about fish and a peaceful setting in which to read it. (Rev: BL 8/05; SLJ 8/05)

1666 Cousins, Lucy. *Maisy, Charley, and the Wobbly Tooth*. Series: Maisy. 2006, Candlewick $12.99 (978-0-7636-2904-5). 32pp. Supportive mouse Maisy accompanies her crocodile friend Charlie to the dentist, where he learns about brushing his teeth. (Rev: BL 5/1/06)

1667 Cowley, Joy. *Snake and Lizard* (K–4). Illus. by Gavin Bishop. 2008, Kane $14.95 (978-1-933605-83-8). 85pp. In 15 short, funny episodes Snake and Lizard enjoy their unlikely friendship and resolve each and every conflict. (Rev: HB 11/08; LMC 3/08; SLJ 12/08*)

1668 Cox, Judy. *Snow Day for Mouse* (PS–2). Illus. by Jeffrey Ebbeler. 2012, Holiday $16.95 (978-0-8234-2408-5). 32pp. Mouse and Cat find themselves swept out into the snow, where Mouse has a series of adventures while avoiding Cat. Lexile AD510L (Rev: BLO 10/1/12; SLJ 11/12)

1669 Craig, Lindsey. *Dancing Feet!* (PS–K). Illus. by Marc Brown. 2010, Knopf $16.99 (978-0-375-86181-9). 40pp. Vibrant collage illustrations of dancing animals enhance this book of rhythm and movement. (Rev: BL 4/1/10; SLJ 4/1/10)

1670 Crimi, Carolyn. *Dear Tabby* (K–3). Illus. by David Roberts. 2011, HarperCollins $16.99 (978-0-06-114245-1). 32pp. Tabby D. Cat provides wholesome advice to a variety of different animals suffering from common emotional situations in this comic story. Lexile AD820L (Rev: BL 1/1–15/11; SLJ 2/1/11)

1671 Crimi, Carolyn. *Henry and the Buccaneer Bunnies* (PS–2). Illus. by John Manders. 2005, Candlewick $15.99 (978-0-7636-2449-1). More interested in books than buccaneering, Henry the bunny endures the taunts of his shipmates but saves the day with his book smarts when their pirate ship is wrecked on a desert island. (Rev: BL 12/1/05; SLJ 11/05)

1672 Crimi, Carolyn. *Rock 'n' Roll Mole* (K–2). Illus. by Lynn Munsinger. 2011, Dial $16.99 (978-0-8037-3166-0). 32pp. Mole is a cool rock-and-roll musician — until he has to perform in front of an audience. (Rev: BLO 10/1/11; SLJ 8/1/11)

1673 Cronin, Doreen. *Click, Clack, Moo: Cows That Type* (PS–3). Illus. by Betsy Lewin. 2000, Simon & Schuster $15.00 (978-0-689-83213-0). 32pp. In this humorous tale, barnyard animals go on strike for better working conditions including electric blankets for cold nights. Caldecott Honor Book, 2001. (Rev: BCCB 9/00; BL 4/1/00; HB 3/00; HBG 10/00)

1674 Cronin, Doreen. *Duck for President* (K–3). Illus. by Betsy Lewin. 2004, Simon & Schuster $15.95 (978-0-689-86377-6). Bored with his life, Duck arranges and wins an election to replace Farmer Brown as head of the farm and then winds up running the country; voting problems and Duck's campaign techniques add to the fun for adults. (Rev: SLJ 3/04)

1675 Cronin, Doreen. *Giggle, Giggle, Quack* (PS–1). Illus. by Betsy Lewin. 2002, Simon & Schuster $15.00 (978-0-689-84506-2). 32pp. A hilarious cartoon story about novice Bob and his attempts to care for some farm animals in spite of the intervention of bossy Duck. (Rev: BCCB 6/02; BL 4/15/02; HB 5/02; HBG 10/02; SLJ 6/02)

1676 Cronin, Doreen. *Rescue Bunnies* (PS–1). Illus. by Scott Menchin. 2010, HarperCollins $16.99 (978-0-06-112871-4). 32pp. A rescue bunny-in-training named Newbie learns about courage and teamwork when she helps rescue a giraffe who's stuck in the mud in this quirky, funny picture book. (Rev: BL 7/10; HB 9–10/10; SLJ 9/1/10)

1677 Cronin, Doreen. *Stretch* (PS–1). Illus. by Scott Menchin. 2009, Atheneum $15.99 (978-1-4169-5341-8). 40pp. Stretch is a lively dog who leads a yoga class and clearly demonstrates many ways of stretching. (Rev: BL 5/15/09; SLJ 8/09)

1678 Cronin, Doreen. *Thump, Quack, Moo: A Whacky Adventure* (PS–2). Illus. by Betsy Lewin. 2008, Atheneum $16.99 (978-1-4169-1630-7). 42pp. The ever-inventive Duck has his own ideas about the design of Farmer Brown's contribution to the annual Corn Maze Festival. (Rev: BL 7/08; SLJ 8/08)

1679 Crummel, Susan Stevens. *Ten-Gallon Bart* (K–2). Illus. by Dorothy Donohue. 2006, Marshall Cavendish $16.95 (978-0-7614-5246-1). Ten-Gallon Bart, the canine sheriff of Dog City, is convinced to put his retirement plans on hold when he hears that Billy the Kid, an outlaw goat, is headed for town; colorful language and humorous collage illustrations capture the feel of the Old West. (Rev: BL 4/1/06; SLJ 4/06)

1680 Crummel, Susan Stevens. *Ten-Gallon Bart and the Wild West Show* (K–2). Illus. by Dorothy Donohue. 2008, Marshall Cavendish $16.99 (978-0-7614-5391-8). 40pp. Bart, the former sheriff of Dog City first seen in *Ten-Gallon Bart* (2006) enters a bull-riding competition that poses interesting challenges. (Rev: BL 4/1/08; SLJ 5/08)

1681 Crummel, Susan Stevens. *Ten-Gallon Bart Beats the Heat* (K–2). Illus. by Dorothy Donohue. 2010, Marshall Cavendish $17.99 (978-0-7614-5634-6). 40pp. Dog City sheriff Bart, tired of the heat in the South, heads north to Alaska and finds new adventures — from pulling a sled to ice-fishing to panning for gold — along the way. **e** Lexile AD510L (Rev: BL 4/15/10; SLJ 3/1/10)

1682 Cuyler, Margery. *Groundhog Stays Up Late* (PS–2). Illus. by Jean Cassels. 2005, Walker $16.95 (978-0-8027-8939-6). 32pp. Awake during a cold and lonely winter, Groundhog tricks his sensible, hibernating friends into waking up early only to have them plot an effective revenge. (Rev: BL 12/1/05; SLJ 12/05)

1683 Czekaj, Jef. *Cat Secrets* (PS–1). Illus. by author. 2011, HarperCollins $16.99 (978-0-06-192088-2). 32pp. Secretive cats are determined not to share their precious lore with non-cats and readers must prove they are real cats. **e** (Rev: BL 12/15/10; SLJ 1/1/11)

1684 Czekaj, Jef. *Hip and Hop, Don't Stop!* (PS–2). Illus. by author. 2010, Hyperion $16.99 (978-1-4231-1664-6). 40pp. Two very different wannabe rappers — a turtle and a rabbit — team up with terrific results in this lively book about sharing and working together. (Rev: BL 6/10; HB 5–6/10; LMC 8–9/10; SLJ 4/1/10)

1685 D'Amico, Carmela. *Ella Sets the Stage* (PS–1). Illus. by Steve D'Amico. 2006, Scholastic $16.99 (978-0-439-83152-9). 48pp. Ella the elephant is initially afraid of the forthcoming talent show, but discovers that she has a distinct gift for organization and planning. (Rev: BL 10/15/06; SLJ 10/06)

1686 D'Amico, Carmela. *Ella Takes the Cake* (PS–K). Illus. by Steven D'Amico. 2005, Scholastic $16.99 (978-0-439-62794-8). 48pp. Ella the elephant wants to help out in her mother's bakery and finally proves she can be useful when she successfully delivers a cake to a customer. (Rev: BL 8/05; SLJ 9/05)

1687 D'Amico, Carmela, and Steve D'Amico. *Ella Sets Sail* (PS–1). Illus. by Carmela D'Amico. 2008, Scholastic $16.99 (978-0-439-83155-0). 48pp. When Ella the elephant goes off to sea to retrieve her lucky red hat, she finds herself very lucky to find her way safely home again. (Rev: BL 8/08; SLJ 7/08)

1688 D'Amico, Carmela, and Steven D'Amico. *Suki the Very Loud Bunny* (PS–1). 2011, Dutton $16.99 (978-0-525-42230-3). 32pp. A noisy young bunny's loud voice ends up saving the day when she's lost in the woods at night. (Rev: BL 2/1/11; SLJ 2/1/11)

1689 Dahl, Roald. *The Enormous Crocodile* (K–3). Illus. by Quentin Blake. 1978, Puffin paper $5.99 (978-0-14-036556-6). 48pp. Animals band together to save a group of children from becoming a crocodile's lunch.

1690 Dale, Penny. *Dinosaur Rescue!* (PS–K). Illus. by author. 2013, Candlewick $15.99 (978-0-7636-6829-7). 32pp. The Dinosaur Rescue team is called to help in a desperate effort to save a pickup truck stuck on the railroad tracks, even as a train is approaching; a brightly illustrated tale full of tension and with a satisfying resolution. (Rev: BL 11/15/13; SLJ 10/13)

1691 Daly, Niki. *Welcome to Zanzibar Road* (PS–3). 2006, Clarion $16.00 (978-0-618-64926-6). 32pp. A gentle story about the animals living in the busy community of Zanzibar Road, including Mama Jumbo, who adopts chicken Little Chiko. (Rev: BL 5/1/06; SLJ 7/06) ∩

1692 Darbyshire, Kristen. *Put It On the List!* (PS–K). Illus. by author. 2009, Dutton $16.99 (978-0-525-47906-2). 32pp. A family of chickens learns to keep a shopping list after getting tired of running out of essential items like syrup and toilet paper. (Rev: BL 2/1/09; SLJ 2/09)

1693 Davis, Jerry, and Katie Davis. *Little Chicken's Big Day* (PS–K). Illus. by Katie Davis. 2011, Simon & Schuster $14.99 (978-1-4424-1401-3). 40pp. Little Chicken knows his mother is watching him throughout the day. (Rev: BL 3/15/11*; HB 5–6/11; SLJ 4/11)

1694 Day, Alexandra. *Carl's Christmas* (PS–K). Illus. 1990, Farrar $12.95 (978-0-374-31114-8). 32pp. On Christmas Eve, Carl, a big black dog, takes the baby he is caring for out to greet the world. (Rev: BCCB 10/90; BL 11/1/90)

1695 De Beer, Hans. *Little Polar Bear and the Big Balloon* (K–2). Trans. from German by Rosemary Lanning. Illus. by author. 2002, North-South LB $16.50 (978-0-

7358-1533-9). Little polar bear Lars and a puffin friend take a trip in a brightly colored hot-air balloon. (Rev: HBG 3/03; SLJ 11/02)

1696 De Brunhoff, Jean. *The Story of Babar, the Little Elephant* (PS). Illus. by author. 1937, Random LB $5.99 (978-0-394-90575-4). A time-tested reading favorite about the little French elephant. (Rev: HBG 3/03)

1697 De Brunhoff, Laurent. *Babar's Museum of Art* (K–3). Illus. by author. 2003, Abrams $16.95 (978-0-8109-4597-5). 44pp. Babar and Celeste set up an art museum in Celesteville's abandoned train station and fill it with works of art from their personal collection — which boasts pachyderm versions of many classics. (Rev: HBG 4/04; SLJ 11/03)

1698 De Brunhoff, Laurent. *Babar's World Tour* (PS–2). Illus. Series: Babar. 2005, Abrams $16.95 (978-0-8109-5780-0). 48pp. Babar and Celeste take their children on a round-the-world tour in this large-format picture book. (Rev: BL 10/1/05; SLJ 1/06)

1699 DeGroat, Diane. *Ants in Your Pants, Worms in Your Plants! (Gilbert Goes Green)* (K–2). Illus. by author. 2011, HarperCollins $16.99 (978-0-06-176511-7). 32pp. Gilbert the opossum can come up with no ideas for Earth Day until his teacher mentions ants. **e** (Rev: BL 3/15/11; SLJ 2/1/11)

1700 deGroat, Diane. *Brand-New Pencils, Brand-New Books* (PS–2). Illus. Series: Gilbert. 2005, HarperCollins $15.99 (978-0-06-072613-3). 32pp. Gilbert's excitement about starting 1st grade is mixed with fears; but at the end of the day he recognizes that it wasn't all bad. (Rev: BL 8/05; SLJ 9/05)

1701 deGroat, Diane. *Good Night, Sleep Tight, Don't Let the Bedbugs Bite!* (PS–K). Illus. Series: Gilbert. 2002, North-South LB $15.88 (978-1-58717-129-1). Gilbert's spooky first night at camp reveals that other campers are just as fearful as he. (Rev: BL 7/02; HB 7/02; HBG 10/02; SLJ 8/02)

1702 deGroat, Diane. *No More Pencils, No More Books, No More Teacher's Dirty Looks!* (K–2). Series: Gilbert. 2006, HarperCollins $15.99 (978-0-06-079114-8). 32pp. As the end-of-school awards ceremony nears, Gilbert the possum worries there will be no prize for him. (Rev: BL 6/1–15/06; SLJ 6/06)

1703 Dempsey, Kristy. *Mini Racer* (PS–1). Illus. by Bridget Strevens-Marzo. 2010, Bloomsbury $16.99 (978-1-59990-170-1). 32pp. A group of snazzy race cars piloted by a variety of different animals fall away one by one, until only a pokey snail is left to cross the finish line. (Rev: BL 12/15/10; SLJ 1/1/11*)

1704 Denim, Sue. *The Dumb Bunnies* (K–2). Illus. by Dav Pilkey. 1994, Scholastic $13.95 (978-0-590-47708-6). 32pp. The story of the three dumb bunnies and their hectic misadventures. (Rev: BL 1/15/94; SLJ 3/94)

1705 Denim, Sue. *The Dumb Bunnies Go to the Zoo* (1–3). Illus. by Dav Pilkey. 1997, Scholastic $13.95 (978-0-590-84735-3). 32pp. The three Dumb Bunnies go to the zoo, where they create havoc. (Rev: BL 4/1/97; SLJ 3/97)

1706 Denim, Sue. *Make Way for Dumb Bunnies* (1–3). Illus. by Dav Pilkey. 1996, Scholastic $12.95 (978-0-590-58286-5). 32pp. A slapstick tale about the misadventures of an unthinking rabbit family. (Rev: BL 2/1/96; SLJ 3/96)

1707 dePaola, Tomie. *Bill and Pete Go Down the Nile* (K–3). Illus. by author. 1987, Penguin $16.99 (978-0-399-21395-3); paper $6.99 (978-0-698-11401-2). 32pp. A crocodile and a bird in a delightful romp down the Nile. (Rev: BL 5/1/87; SLJ 9/87)

1708 dePaola, Tomie. *Four Friends in Autumn* (PS–2). Illus. by author. 2004, Simon & Schuster $14.95 (978-0-689-85980-9). In this tale adapted from *Four Stories for Four Seasons* (1980), four friends — Missy Cat, Mistress Pig, Master Dog, and Mister Frog — gather for dinner at Mistress Pig's house. (Rev: SLJ 11/04)

1709 dePaola, Tomie. *The Knight and the Dragon* (1–3). Illus. by author. 1998, Penguin $17.99 (978-0-399-20707-5); paper $5.99 (978-0-698-11623-8). An inexperienced knight and an inexperienced dragon prepare themselves to do battle.

1710 dePaola, Tomie. *Little Grunt and the Big Egg: A Prehistoric Fairy Tale* (PS–2). Illus. by author. 2006, Putnam $16.99 (978-0-399-24529-9). 32pp. A new edition of the story about the prehistoric boy who adopts a dinosaur called George. (Rev: BL 5/15/06)

1711 dePaola, Tomie. *Meet the Barkers: Morgan and Moffat Go to School* (PS–1). Illus. 2001, Penguin $13.99 (978-0-399-23708-9). 32pp. Terrier siblings Morgie and Moffie have always been different — Moffie is smart, Morgie gregarious — and these characteristics hold true when they start school. (Rev: BL 6/1–15/01; HBG 3/02; SLJ 8/01)

1712 dePaola, Tomie. *A New Barker in the House* (PS–2). Illus. Series: The Barkers. 2002, Penguin $13.99 (978-0-399-23865-9). 32pp. When the Barker family adopts Spanish-speaking Marcos, twins Morgie and Moffie try hard to make him feel comfortable in this book full of Spanish words and charming art. (Rev: BL 7/02; HBG 10/02; SLJ 6/02)

1713 dePaola, Tomie. *T-Rex Is Missing!* (1–2). Illus. by author. 2002, Grosset paper $3.99 (978-0-448-42870-3). 32pp. The disappearance of a toy dinosaur causes a major falling out between two animal friends. (Rev: HBG 10/03; SLJ 2/03)

1714 dePaola, Tomie. *Trouble in the Barkers' Class* (K–2). Illus. by author. 2003, Penguin $14.99 (978-0-399-24164-2). Moffie and Morgie Barker, twin terriers, are disappointed when the newcomer to their class, Carole Anne, turns out to be an ill-tempered bully. (Rev: HBG 4/04; SLJ 10/03)

1715 Derom, Dirk. *Pigeon and Pigeonette* (K–2). Illus. by Sarah Verroken. 2009, Enchanted Lion $16.95 (978-1-59270-087-5). Unpaged. A small pigeon with undersize wings finds a friend to help her fly south — a big pigeon who can't see — and together they set off for warmer climes. (Rev: LMC 1–2/10; SLJ 11/1/09)

1716 deRubertis, Barbara. *Kylie Kangaroo's Karate Kickers* (K–1). Illus. by R. W. Alley. Series: Animal Antics A to Z. 2011, Kane $22.60 (978-157565332-7); paper $7.95 (978-15756532-3-5). 32pp. A young kangaroo works hard to learn karate, eventually learning to put her faith in training and practice rather than luck. (Rev: BLO 8/11)

1717 Dewdney, Anna. *Llama Llama Home with Mama* (PS). Illus. by author. 2011, Viking $17.99 (978-0-670-01232-9). Unpaged. Llama Llama's mother takes care of him when he gets sick; and when mom herself gets sick, the little llama knows exactly how to take care of her. (Rev: SLJ 9/1/11)

1718 Dewdney, Anna. *Llama Llama Misses Mama* (PS–K). Illus. by author. Series: Llama Llama. 2009, Viking $16.99 (978-0-670-06198-3). 40pp. Little Llama Llama approaches the start of school with some trepidation but finds it's not as bad as he feared. (Rev: SLJ 6/09)

1719 Dewdney, Anna. *Llama Llama Time to Share* (PS–K). Illus. by author. 2012, Viking $17.99 (978-0-670-01233-6). 40pp. Llama is able to share his blocks with his new young neighbor, but when Nelly Gnu plays with his beloved doll, his possessiveness flares up. e Lexile AD250L (Rev: BLO 11/1/12; SLJ 8/12)

1720 Dewdney, Anna. *Nobunny's Perfect* (PS–1). Illus. by author. 2008, Viking $12.99 (978-0-670-06288-1). Young rabbits exhibit amazingly childlike bad behaviors. (Rev: BL 1/1–15/08; SLJ 8/08)

1721 Dewdney, Anna. *Roly Poly Pangolin* (PS). Illus. by author. 2010, Viking $16.99 (978-0-670-01160-5). Unpaged. A young pangolin full of fears rolls into a tight ball at the slightest provocation, but eventually discovers how much fun it can be to make new friends; a note at the end provides information on these endangered animals. (Rev: BL 2/1/10; SLJ 2/1/10)

1722 DiCamillo, Kate. *Mercy Watson Goes for a Ride* (PS–2). Illus. by Chris Van Dusen. Series: Mercy Watson. 2006, Candlewick $12.99 (978-0-7636-2332-6). 80pp. Plump pig Mercy gives Mr. Watson an unexpectedly exciting ride in his pink Cadillac. (Rev: BL 5/1/06; SLJ 6/06)

1723 DiCamillo, Kate. *Mercy Watson Thinks Like a Pig* (PS–2). Illus. by Chris Van Dusen. 2008, Candlewick $12.99 (978-0-7636-3265-6). 80pp. The animal control officer is called when Mercy the pig eats the Lincoln sisters' petunias. Can Mercy elude capture? (Rev: BL 6/1–15/08; SLJ 8/08)

1724 Diesen, Deborah. *The Pout-Pout Fish in the Big-Big Dark* (PS–K). Illus. by Dan Hanna. 2010, Farrar $16.99 (978-0-374-30798-1). 32pp. Mr. Fish conquers his fear of the dark and rescues Ms. Clam's lost pearl from the sea floor with the help of Miss Shimmer and Mr. Lantern. Lexile AD670L (Rev: BLO 7/10; SLJ 9/1/10)

1725 Dillard, Sarah. *Perfectly Arugula* (PS–K). Illus. by author. 2009, Sterling $14.95 (978-1-4027-5954-3). 36pp. Arugula is a hedgehog with a passion for tidiness and order, which doesn't exactly fit with her party plans. (Rev: BLO 3/24/09)

1726 DiPucchio, Kelly. *Gilbert Goldfish Wants a Pet* (PS–2). Illus. by Bob Shea. 2011, Dial $16.99 (978-0-8037-3394-7). 32pp. A lonely goldfish yearns for a pet, but after trying a dog, a mouse, and a fly, he's unsure about trying a fourth option; fortunately, a cat turns out to be just right. (Rev: BL 7/11; SLJ 7/11)

1727 Dodd, Emma. *Dog's Noisy Day: A Story to Read Aloud* (PS–K). Illus. 2003, Dutton $14.99 (978-0-525-47015-1). Dog tries to imitate the sounds he hears around the farm, from a rooster's crow to a bee's buzz. (Rev: BL 2/15/03; HBG 10/03; SLJ 3/03)

1728 Dodd, Emma. *Just Like You* (PS). Illus. by author. Series: Templar Bks. 2008, Dutton $10.99 (978-0-525-47933-8). 24pp. A baby bear enumerates why he loves big bear. (Rev: SLJ 4/08)

1729 Dodd, Emma. *Meow Said the Cow* (PS–K). Illus. by author. 2011, Scholastic $16.99 (978-0-545-31861-7). 40pp. A cat disgruntled by a noisy rooster puts a spell on all the farm animals, swapping their voices. (Rev: BLO 8/11; LMC 11–12/11; SLJ 7/11)

1730 Dodd, Emma. *No Matter What* (PS). Illus. by author. 2008, Dutton $10.99 (978-0-525-47932-1). A simple story about a mother elephant and her love for her child. (Rev: BL 4/1/08; SLJ 2/08)

1731 Dominguez, Angela. *Let's Go, Hugo!* (PS–K). Illus. by author. 2013, Dial $16.99 (978-0-8037-3864-5). 40pp. Hugo, a bird who enjoys his life in Paris apart from his fear of flying, finally seeks help and is happy to tackle the Eiffel Tower with the lovely Lulu. (Rev: BL 3/1/13; LMC 8–9/13; SLJ 3/13)

1732 Donaldson, Julia. *The Fish Who Cried Wolf* (PS–K). Illus. by Axel Scheffler. 2008, Scholastic $15.99 (978-0-439-92825-0). 40pp. Tiddler, a little fish given to elaborate excuses, finds his tall tales useful when he winds up far from home. (Rev: BCCB 6/08; BL 8/08; LMC 10/08; SLJ 6/08)

1733 Donaldson, Julia. *The Highway Rat* (K–2). Illus. by Axel Scheffler. 2013, Scholastic $16.99 (978-0-545-47758-1). 32pp. A rat highwayman successfully steals food from travelers until a brave duck intercedes and he learns the evil of his ways. Lexile AD850 (Rev: BL 4/1/13; HB 5–6/13; LMC 10/13; SLJ 3/13*)

1734 Donaldson, Julia. *What the Ladybug Heard* (PS–1). Illus. by Lydia Monks. 2010, Henry Holt $16.99 (978-0-8050-9028-4). 32pp. A shy, silent ladybug becomes empowered to speak up and protect her farm friends when she hears bad men plotting to steal the prize cow. (Rev: BL 2/15/10; SLJ 4/1/10)

1735 Donaldson, Julia. *Where's My Mom?* (PS–1). Illus. by Axel Scheffler. 2008, Dial $16.99 (978-0-8037-3228-5). 32pp. A butterfly tries to help a lost monkey find his mother but misunderstandings about the mother's anatomy abound. (Rev: SLJ 5/08)

1736 Donnio, Sylviane. *I'd Really Like to Eat a Child* (PS–K). Trans. from French by Leslie Martin. Illus. by Dorothée de Monfreid. 2007, Random $14.99 (978-0-375-83761-6). A small crocodile tired of the food his mother offers says he would prefer to eat a child and sets off to do so. (Rev: SLJ 4/07)

1737 Dotlich, Rebecca Kai. *Grandpa Loves* (PS–K). Illus. by Kathryn Brown. 2005, HarperCollins LB $16.89 (978-0-06-029406-9). 32pp. A young pig describes all the things her grandfather loves — billiards, backpacking, flipping pancakes, and so forth. (Rev: BL 6/1–15/05; SLJ 5/05)

1738 Dotlich, Rebecca Kai. *Mama Loves* (PS–1). Illus. by Kathryn Brown. 2004, HarperCollins $14.99 (978-0-06-029407-6). 32pp. A tally of all the things that Mama Pig loves to do with her baby daughter. (Rev: BL 3/1/04)

1739 Downey, Lynn. *Matilda's Humdinger* (1–3). Illus. by Tim Bowers. 2006, Knopf $15.95 (978-0-375-82403-6). Matilda the cat is a terrible waitress but a great storyteller. (Rev: SLJ 10/06)

1740 Downey, Lynn. *The Tattletale* (PS–K). Illus. by Pam Paparone. 2006, Holt $16.95 (978-0-8050-7152-8). 32pp. Humorous art adds to the fun in this story about two pig brothers that carries a message about telling tales and bullying. (Rev: BL 11/1/06; SLJ 11/06)

1741 Downing, Julie. *No Hugs Till Saturday* (PS–1). Illus. by author. 2008, Clarion $16.00 (978-0-618-91078-6). 32pp. A little dragon named Felix clearly demonstrates his displeasure when his mother punishes him for misbehavior but comes to realize he is also depriving himself. (Rev: BL 7/08; SLJ 7/08)

1742 Doyle, Malachy. *Big Pig* (PS–2). Illus. by John Bendall-Brunello. 2006, Simon & Schuster $19.95 (978-0-689-87484-0); paper $9.99 (978-0-689-87485-7). Pig has grown too big to keep in the house, so John Henry must take the ample porker to the local pig farm, but when John Henry has a mishap on the way home, Pig comes to the rescue. (Rev: SLJ 11/06)

1743 Drachman, Eric. *Bad Rats* (PS–2). Illus. by James Muscarello. 2008, Kidwick $18.95 (978-0-9703809-4-4). Five little rats who love art and music are told that this is bad behavior and sent to Professor Perimeter for reeducation; luckily the professor recognizes their creativity and in fact learns instead from them. Comes with a CD of the story. (Rev: BL 6/1–15/08; SLJ 5/08)

1744 Dubosarsky, Ursula. *The Terrible Plop* (PS–K). Illus. by Andrew Joyner. 2009, Farrar $15.95 (978-0-374-37428-0). 40pp. Falling apples cause concern to lounging animals in this entertaining picture book full of rhyme and repetition. (Rev: BL 7/09)

1745 Duke, Kate. *Ready for Pumpkins* (K–2). Illus. by author. 2012, Knopf $16.99 (978-037587068-2). 40pp. Guinea pig Hercules, a first-grade class pet, and his rabbit friend Daisy grow a garden together. e (Rev: BL 8/12; HB 9–10/12; SLJ 6/1/12)

1746 Duke, Kate. *The Tale of Pip and Squeak* (PS–2). Illus. by author. 2007, Dutton $16.99 (978-0-525-47777-8). Two little mice — Pip, who likes to paint, and Squeak, who likes to sing — realize that their talents are best used together to throw a party for their friends. (Rev: SLJ 5/07)

1747 Dunbar, Joyce. *A Chick Called Saturday* (PS–1). Illus. by Brita Granström. 2003, Eerdmans $16.00 (978-0-8028-5260-1). Saturday, an inquisitive chick, is disappointed in life until he discovers that he's got a real talent for crowing. (Rev: HBG 4/04; SLJ 8/03)

1748 Dunbar, Joyce. *Oddly* (K–2). Illus. by Patrick Benson. 2009, Candlewick $16.99 (978-0-7636-4274-7). 40pp. Strange creatures form a bond with a little boy on the beach. (Rev: BL 6/1–15/09; SLJ 7/09)

1749 Dunbar, Joyce. *Tell Me What It's Like to Be Big* (K–3). Illus. by Debi Gliori. 2001, Harcourt $16.00 (978-0-15-202564-9). 32pp. Detailed, vivid images illustrate the story of Willa the rabbit, who is frustrated because she is too little to reach the food on the table. (Rev: BL 12/15/01; HBG 3/02; SLJ 9/01)

1750 Dunbar, Joyce. *Where's My Sock?* (PS–2). Illus. by Sanja Rescek. 2006, Scholastic $15.99 (978-0-439-74831-5). 32pp. Pippin the mouse can't find his yellow sock and enlists the help of Tog the cat; they find socks all over the house and match them all up (in a very colorful fold-out) only to discover the missing sock where they least expected. (Rev: BL 1/1–15/06; SLJ 2/06)

1751 Dunrea, Olivier. *Gossie and Gertie* (PS). Illus. 2002, Houghton $9.95 (978-0-618-17676-2). 32pp. A little gosling named Gossie learns a lesson in individuality when her best friend Gertie no longer wants to do everything she does. Also use *Gossie* (2002). (Rev: BL 8/02; HB 1/03*; HBG 3/03; SLJ 9/02*)

1752 Dunrea, Olivier. *Little Cub* (PS–2). Illus. by author. 2012, Philomel $16.99 (978-0-399-24235-9). 32pp. Lonely Little Cub and equally unhappy Old Bear find mutual comfort and friendship. (Rev: BL 11/1/12; HB 11–12/12; LMC 5–6/13; SLJ 10/12*)

1753 Dunrea, Olivier. *Old Bear and His Cub* (PS–1). Illus. by author. 2010, Philomel $16.99 (978-0-399-24507-7). 32pp. Old Bear and Little Bear reverse roles — bossy and submissive — according to who needs help most. (Rev: BL 11/1/10*; HB 1–2/11; SLJ 11/1/10*)

1754 Dunrea, Olivier. *Ollie* (PS–1). Illus. by author. 2003, Houghton $9.95 (978-0-618-33928-0). Goslings Gossie and Gertie grow impatient waiting for their sibling Ollie to hatch from his egg. (Rev: HBG 4/04; SLJ 7/03)

1755 Dunrea, Olivier. *Ollie's Easter Eggs* (PS–K). Illus. by author. Series: Gossie and Friends. 2010, Houghton Mifflin $9.99 (978-0-618-53243-8). 32pp. When Ollie the gosling sees the brightly colored Easter eggs his friends have dyed, he is overcome with desire to have them all. (Rev: BL 1/1/10; SLJ 3/1/10)

1756 Durango, Julia. *Pest Fest* (PS–2). Illus. by Kurt Cyrus. 2007, Simon & Schuster $16.99 (978-0-689-85569-6). Who will win the title Best Pest of the Year at the Pest Fest talent show? Readers will enjoy the rhyming text that extols the virtues of many insects and the beautiful illustrations that accompany it. (Rev: LMC 10/07; SLJ 7/07)

1757 Edwards, Pamela Duncan. *McGillycuddy Could!* (PS). Illus. by Sue Porter. 2005, HarperCollins LB $15.89 (978-0-06-029002-3). Kangaroo McGillycuddy's ability to hop, jump, bounce, and kick fails to impress the other animals at the farm. (Rev: BCCB 2/05; HB 3/05; SLJ 3/05)

1758 Edwards, Pamela Duncan. *The Mixed-Up Rooster* (PS). Illus. by Megan Lloyd. 2006, HarperCollins $15.99 (978-0-06-028999-7). 32pp. A rooster who prefers to stay up at night finds a new position on the farm in this entertaining story. (Rev: BL 7/06; SLJ 8/06)

1759 Edwards, Pamela Duncan. *Ms. Bitsy Bat's Kindergarten* (PS–K). Illus. by Henry Cole. 2005, Hyperion $15.99 (978-0-7868-0669-0). 32pp. The second day of kindergarten proves stressful when the students learn that Mr. Fox won't be back. (Rev: BL 8/05; SLJ 8/05)

1760 Egan, Tim. *Dodsworth in Paris* (K–3). Illus. by author. 2008, Houghton $15.00 (978-0-618-98062-8). 48pp. A mouse named Dodsworth and a wacky duck are off to Paris where the duck tries hard, really, not to get into trouble. (Rev: BL 9/1/08; HB 1/09)

1761 Egan, Tim. *Roasted Peanuts* (1–3). Illus. 2006, Houghton $16.00 (978-0-618-33718-7). 32pp. Sam the horse and Jackson the cat are best friends who love baseball but although Jackson is a great pitcher only Sam is talented enough to make the team; Jackson gets a job selling peanuts, however, and his throwing skills have results. (Rev: BL 4/15/06; SLJ 5/06)

1762 Ehlert, Lois. *Mole's Hill* (PS–2). Illus. 1994, Harcourt $15.00 (978-0-15-255116-2). 32pp. Fox demands that Mole move from her hill, but she is able to outwit him and remain. (Rev: BCCB 4/94; BL 3/15/94; HB 7/94; SLJ 5/94)

1763 Ehlert, Lois. *Nuts to You!* (PS–2). Illus. 1993, Harcourt $16.00 (978-0-15-257647-9). A rural squirrel shows how he gathers food in the big city. (Rev: BL 3/1/93; HB 3/93; SLJ 4/93)

1764 Elwell, Peter. *Adios Oscar! A Butterfly Fable* (K–2). Illus. by author. 2009, Scholastic $16.99 (978-0-545-07159-8). 32pp. When a caterpillar becomes a gray moth rather than a monarch butterfly, he is disappointed, but with support, he still follows his dream of being with the monarchs in Mexico. (Rev: LMC 10/09; SLJ 5/09)

1765 Elya, Susan Middleton. *Eight Animals Bake a Cake* (2–4). Illus. by Lee Chapman. 2002, Penguin $15.99 (978-0-399-23468-2). 32pp. Too many animals almost spoil the cake in this appealing picture book that introduces Spanish words and includes a recipe for pineapple upside-down cake. (Rev: BL 7/02; HBG 3/03; SLJ 8/02)

1766 Elya, Susan Middleton. *Eight Animals on the Town* (1–3). Illus. by Lee Chapman. 2000, Penguin $15.99 (978-0-399-23437-8). 32pp. English and Spanish words are mixed in this delightful story about eight animals who head into town for dinner. (Rev: BCCB 1/01; BL 12/1/00; HBG 3/01; SLJ 9/00)

1767 Emberley, Ed. *The Red Hen* (PS–K). Illus. by Rebecca Emberley. 2010, Roaring Brook $17.99 (978-1-59643-492-9). 32pp. Red Hen can't find anyone to help her make a "simply splendid cake" although her friends are quite happy to help eat it in this twist on the classic tale. (Rev: BL 10/15/10; SLJ 10/1/10)

1768 Emberley, Rebecca. *The Ant and the Grasshopper* (PS–2). Illus. by Ed Emberley. 2012, Roaring Brook $16.99 (978-1-59643-493-6). 32pp. A jazzy band of bugs led by a grasshopper cheers an ant who enjoys the music but feels a sense of duty toward her colony; a lighthearted New Orleans-flavored version of the classic tale. **e** Lexile AD790L (Rev: BL 12/1/12; LMC 3–4/13; SLJ 10/12)

1769 Emmett, Jonathan. *I Love You Always and Forever* (PS–K). Illus. by Daniel Howarth. 2007, Scholastic $14.99 (978-0-439-91654-7). Father mouse Longtail and daughter Littletail spend an enjoyable day together that ends with reassurances of love; wonderful illustrations blend with the gentle text. (Rev: SLJ 4/07)

1770 Emmett, Jonathan. *No Place Like Home* (PS–1). Illus. by Vanessa Cabban. 2005, Candlewick $15.99 (978-0-7636-2554-2). Mole's friends all recommend new homes for him, but each has disadvantages, so Mole decides to return underground. (Rev: SLJ 3/05)

1771 Emmett, Jonathan. *This Way, Ruby!* (PS). Illus. by Rebecca Harry. 2007, Scholastic $16.99 (978-0-439-87992-7). Ruby the duckling moves more slowly than her siblings but her powers of observation are keen, which proves a godsend when there is an unexpected storm. (Rev: BL 12/15/06; SLJ 2/07)

1772 Empson, Jo. *Rabbityness* (PS–2). Illus. by author. 2012, Child's Play $16.99 (978-1-84643-492-1). 32pp. In many ways Rabbit is a typical rabbit, but he has some unusual creative instincts and his art and music cheer his companions when he suddenly disappears. (Rev: BL 11/15/12; SLJ 2/13)

1773 Erlbruch, Wolf. *Duck, Death and the Tulip* (K–3). Trans. by Catherine Chigey. Illus. by author. 2011, Gecko $17.95 (978-1-877579-02-8). 36pp. A duck becomes spooked when she realizes she's being followed by Death personified; reassuringly, the character turns out to be sensitive to her concerns, and together the two discuss the afterlife. (Rev: BLO 11/15/11; SLJ 10/1/11)

1774 Ernst, Lisa Campbell. *Sylvia Jean, Drama Queen* (PS–2). Illus. 2005, Dutton $16.99 (978-0-525-46962-9). 40pp. When a town-wide costume party is announced, everyone assumes that Sylvia Jean, a fashion-conscious piglet, will take home the grand prize for best costume. (Rev: BL 9/15/05; SLJ 9/05)

1775 Ernst, Lisa Campbell. *Sylvia Jean, Scout Supreme* (PS–2). Illus. by author. 2010, Dutton $16.99 (978-0-525-47873-7). 32pp. Sylvia Jean gets a little over-enthusiastic when her Pig Scout leader challenges the troop to perform good deeds to earn a badge. (Rev: BL 12/1/09; LMC 1–2/10; SLJ 2/1/10)

1776 Esbaum, Jill. *Stanza* (PS–2). Illus. by Jack E. Davis. 2009, Harcourt $16.00 (978-0-15-205998-9). 32pp. Stanza, a fearsome dog with the heart of a poet, persuades his two brothers to tap their creative juices and stop terrorizing the neighborhood. (Rev: BL 5/1/09; SLJ 5/09)

1777 Escoffier, Michael. *Rabbit and the Not-So-Big-Bad Wolf* (K–3). Illus. by Kris Di Giacomo. 2013, Holiday

$16.95 (978-0-8234-2813-7). 32pp. Rabbit has problems drawing the Not-So-Big-Bad-Wolf, but when his subject actually turns up, Rabbit finds he's not so scary. (Rev: BL 4/1/13; SLJ 4/13)

1778 Evans, Cambria. *Martha Moth Makes Socks* (PS–2). Illus. by author. 2006, Houghton $16.00 (978-0-618-55745-5). In preparation for her birthday celebration with friends Flit and Flora, Martha Moth samples some of the delectable clothing items she plans to serve at the party, but she overdoes it, leaving little to share with her guests. (Rev: BL 5/1/06; SLJ 4/06)

1779 Evans, Lezlie. *The Bunnies' Trip* (PS–K). Illus. by Kay Chorao. 2008, Hyperion $16.99 (978-0-7868-1898-3). 32pp. Eight little bunnies struggle to pack for a journey. (Rev: BL 4/1/08)

1780 Evans, Lezlie. *Who Loves the Little Lamb?* (PS–K). Illus. by David McPhail. 2010, Hyperion $15.99 (978-1-4231-1659-2). 32pp. Animal mothers love their children even when they are not at their best. (Rev: BL 4/15/10; SLJ 6/1/10)

1781 Falconer, Ian. *Olivia* (PS–K). Illus. 2000, Simon & Schuster $16.00 (978-0-689-82953-6). 40pp. An outstanding picture book about Olivia, a delightful little pig, who is a bundle of energy and talent. Caldecott Honor Book 2001. (Rev: BCCB 11/00*; BL 8/00*; HBG 3/01; SLJ 9/00)

1782 Falconer, Ian. *Olivia . . . and the Missing Toy* (PS–1). Illus. by author. 2003, Simon & Schuster $16.95 (978-0-689-85291-6). When her favorite stuffed animal mysteriously disappears, Olivia the pig turns sleuth in this story with witty illustrations. (Rev: BL 9/1/03*; HBG 4/04; SLJ 10/03)

1783 Falconer, Ian. *Olivia and the Fairy Princesses* (PS–1). Illus. by author. 2012, Atheneum $17.99 (978-1-4424-5027-1). 40pp. Olivia is in crisis — she doesn't want to be a princess like all the other girls — and tries out a variety of identities before deciding on Queen. Lexile 630 (Rev: BL 8/12; SLJ 8/12)

1784 Falconer, Ian. *Olivia Forms a Band* (PS–1). Illus. by author. 2006, Simon & Schuster $17.95 (978-1-4169-2454-8). 50pp. Disconsolate when she learns that there will be no band performing at the fireworks exhibition, Olivia the energetic pig comes up with a plan to supply the music all by herself. (Rev: BL 6/1–15/06; SLJ 6/06*)

1785 Falconer, Ian. *Olivia Goes to Venice* (PS–1). Illus. by author. 2010, Atheneum $17.99 (978-1-4169-9674-3). 48pp. Olivia the porcine adventurer explores Venice: gondola rides, gelato, walking tours, and beautiful palazzos. (Rev: BL 9/1/10; SLJ 9/1/10)

1786 Falconer, Ian. *Olivia Saves the Circus* (PS–1). Illus. 2001, Simon & Schuster $16.00 (978-0-689-82954-3). 32pp. Olivia, the little pig full of talented energy, describes how she took over each and every role when the circus was hit by a rash of earaches. (Rev: BCCB 11/01; BL 8/01; HB 11/01; HBG 3/02; SLJ 10/01)

1787 Falkenstern, Lisa. *A Dragon Moves In* (K–2). Illus. by author. 2011, Marshall Cavendish $16.99 (978-0-7614-5947-7). 32pp. Initially thrilled with their discovery of a dragon hatchling, Hedgehog and Rabbit find themselves facing serious problems as their friend grows larger and larger. (Rev: BL 11/1/11; SLJ 9/1/11)

1788 Faulkner, Keith. *The Wide-Mouthed Frog* (PS–1). Illus. by Jonathan Lambert. 1996, Dial $13.99 (978-0-8037-1875-3). 14pp. An interactive book that pictures a variety of animals and their eating habits. (Rev: BL 2/1/96; SLJ 4/96)

1789 Fearnley, Jan. *Martha in the Middle* (PS). Illus. by author. 2008, Candlewick $15.99 (978-0-7636-3800-9). 40pp. Tired of feeling neglected as the middle child, Martha the mouse decides to run away but at the end of the garden meets a clever frog who explains that being in the middle can be special. (Rev: BL 6/1–15/08; SLJ 7/08)

1790 Feeney, Tatyana. *Little Owl's Orange Scarf* (PS–2). Illus. by author. 2013, Knopf $16.99 (978-0-449-81411-6). 32pp. Little Owl lives a generally happy life — except for the detested, exceedingly long, very orange scarf that his mother has wished on him; he finally finds a solution when he spots a giraffe at the zoo. ✪ (Rev: BL 6/13; SLJ 6/13)

1791 Feiffer, Jules. *Bark, George* (PS–3). Illus. 1999, HarperCollins LB $18.89 (978-0-06-205186-8). 32pp. When puppy George is asked to bark by his mother, he manages to produce a range of animal sounds including a "meow" and a "moo," but never an "arf." (Rev: BCCB 11/99; BL 8/99*; HBG 3/00; SLJ 9/99)

1792 Finlay, Lizzie. *Little Croc's Purse* (K–3). Illus. by author. 2011, Eerdmans $14.99 (978-0-8028-5392-9). Unpaged. Little Croc is rewarded for doing the right thing when he finds a purse full of money in this subtle character education story. ✪ Lexile AD570L (Rev: LMC 10/11; SLJ 5/1/11)

1793 Fleming, Candace. *Gator Gumbo* (K–3). Illus. by Sally Anne Lambert. 2004, Farrar $16.00 (978-0-374-38050-2). 32pp. Aging Monsieur Gator, taunted by his animal neighbors in the swamp, turns the table on them when he decides to cook up a pot of gumbo "just like Maman used to make." (Rev: BL 4/1/04; HB 3/04; SLJ 2/04)

1794 Fleming, Denise. *The Cow Who Clucked* (PS–2). 2006, Holt $16.95 (978-0-8050-7265-5). 40pp. Cow awakens to find that she is clucking like a chicken and sets out to track down her missing "moo." (Rev: BL 9/1/06; SLJ 8/06*)

1795 Fleming, Denise. *Lunch* (PS–K). Illus. 1992, Holt $16.95 (978-0-8050-1636-9). 30pp. A mouse samples all the goodies on a banquet table and gets fatter and fatter. (Rev: BCCB 12/92; BL 11/1/92; HB 1/93; SLJ 12/92*)

1796 Fleming, Denise. *Mama Cat Has Three Kittens* (PS–K). Illus. 1998, Holt $15.95 (978-0-8050-5745-4). Two of Mama Cat's kittens are well behaved, but the third, Boris, just loves to nap. (Rev: BCCB 12/98; BL 11/15/98; HBG 3/99; SLJ 11/98)

1797 Foley, Greg. *Good Luck Bear* (PS). Illus. by author. 2009, Viking $15.99 (978-0-670-06258-4). Bear searches for a four-leaf clover and the promised luck it will bring despite the discouraging attitude of many of his animal friends. (Rev: BL 11/15/08; SLJ 3/09)

1798 Foley, Greg. *I Miss You Mouse* (PS–1). Illus. by author. 2010, Viking $12.99 (978-0-670-01238-1). Unpaged. Mouse is looking for her friend Bear and can't find him anywhere until she returns to her own house in this charming flap book. (Rev: SLJ 2/1/11)

1799 Foley, Greg. *Purple Little Bird* (PS–1). Illus. by author. 2011, HarperCollins $14.99 (978-0-06-200828-2). 32pp. A purple bird limited by his own perfectionism is aided by a variety of animal friends and eventually learns to loosen up. (Rev: BL 5/1/11; SLJ 7/11)

1800 Foley, Greg. *Thank You Bear* (PS–K). Illus. 2007, Viking $15.99 (978-0-670-06165-5). 32pp. Bear is quite pleased with his latest find — a tiny, empty box — and is disappointed by his friends' reactions until he shows it to Mouse, who promptly curls up in it. (Rev: BL 4/15/07; SLJ 3/07*)

1801 Folgueira, Rodrigo. *Ribbit!* (PS–1). Illus. by Poly Bernatene. 2013, Knopf $15.99 (978-0-307-98146-2). 32pp. A pig sitting in their pond and saying "Ribbit!" sparks a flurry of speculation among the resident animals about his intentions, until a wise old beetle solves the puzzle — he just wants to make friends. Lexile AD500 (Rev: BL 3/15/13; SLJ 3/13)

1802 Ford, Bernette. *Christmas Recital* (PS–K). Illus. by Sam Williams. Series: Ballet Kitty. 2012, Sterling $16.95 (978-190715212-2). 32pp. Rivalry over who will dance the role of the Sugar Plum Fairy causes friction between Kitty and Princess Pussycat. (Rev: BLO 12/15/12)

1803 Ford, Bernette. *No More Pacifier for Piggy!* (PS). Illus. by Sam Williams. 2008, Sterling $12.95 (978-1-905417-89-6). 26pp. An appealing young pig learns to get along without his pacifier through a game of peekaboo. (Rev: BLO 7/29/08; SLJ 8/08)

1804 Foreman, Michael. *Friends* (PS–2). Illus. by author. 2012, Andersen $16.95 (978-1-4677-0317-8). 32pp. Cat worries that life is too restricted for Bubble the goldfish, but Bubble rejects various alternatives on the grounds that at least in his small world he has a friend. (Rev: BL 9/1/12; SLJ 9/12)

1805 Foreman, Michael. *The Littlest Dinosaur* (PS–K). Illus. by author. 2008, Walker $16.95 (978-0-8027-9759-9). 32pp. The littlest dinosaur may be small but he's sensitive and brave, and his actions — and friendship with a lonely tall dinosaur — rescue the rest of his larger family. (Rev: BL 5/15/08; LMC 8/08; SLJ 5/08)

1806 Foreman, Michael. *The Littlest Dinosaur's Big Adventure* (PS–K). Illus. by author. 2009, Walker $16.99 (978-0-8027-9545-8). 32pp. The Littlest Dinosaur, a triceratops, is in the scary woods when he meets a young pterodactyl who is also nervous and discovers that he has some courage after all. (Rev: BL 5/1/09; SLJ 5/09)

1807 Fox, Christyan, and Diane Fox. *Astronaut PiggyWiggy* (PS). Illus. by authors. 2002, Handprint $9.95 (978-1-929766-41-3). The ever-imaginative Piggy-

Wiggy looks through his telescope and pictures himself blasting off and visiting distant places in this book with fold-out flaps. For other career options, consider *Goodnight PiggyWiggy* (2000), *Bathtime PiggyWiggy* and *Fire Fighter PiggyWiggy* (2001), and *Pirate PiggyWiggy* (2003). (Rev: HBG 10/02; SLJ 7/02)

1808 Fox, Diane, and Christyan Fox. *Tyson the Terrible* (PS–2). Illus. by authors. 2007, Bloomsbury $12.95 (978-1-58234-734-9). Far less formidable than the reputation that precedes him, Tyson the little Tyrannosaurus rex turns out to be just a lonely dinosaur looking for some friends. (Rev: SLJ 2/07)

1809 Fox, Mem. *Hattie and the Fox* (PS–K). Illus. by Patricia Mullins. 1987, Macmillan $16.00 (978-0-02-735470-6); paper $5.99 (978-0-689-71611-9). 32pp. A cumulative tale about a big black hen who spies a fox in the farmyard. (Rev: BL 3/15/87; HB 5/87; SLJ 5/87)

1810 Fox, Mem. *Hunwick's Egg* (PS–2). Illus. by Pamela Lofts. 2005, Harcourt $16.00 (978-0-15-216318-1). A kindly bandicoot adopts and cares for an egg that is actually a stone in this strikingly illustrated book that shows the plants and animals of Australia's desert habitat. (Rev: BL 2/15/05; SLJ 3/05)

1811 Fox, Mem. *Koala Lou* (PS–2). Illus. by Pamela Lofts. 1989, Harcourt $15.00 (978-0-15-200502-3). 32pp. A young koala named Koala Lou finds that her mother is too busy with her younger children to shower the same affection on her as before. (Rev: BL 11/15/89; HB 11/89; SLJ 1/90)

1812 Fox, Mem. *Possum Magic* (K–2). Illus. by Julie Vivas. 1990, Harcourt $15.00 (978-0-15-200572-6); paper $6.00 (978-0-15-263224-3). 32pp. Grandmother Opossum makes Hush invisible, and then forgets how she did it in this tale from Down Under. (Rev: BL 12/1/87; SLJ 12/87)

1813 Fox, Mem. *Where Is the Green Sheep?* (PS–1). Illus. by Judy Horacek. 2004, Harcourt $15.00 (978-0-15-204907-2). A beginning reader in rhyme featuring sheep in all kinds of activities, with the added fillip of a search for the green sheep. (Rev: HB 5/04; SLJ 4/04)

1814 Freedman, Claire. *Follow That Bear If You Dare!* (PS–2). Illus. by Alison Edgson. 2008, Good Bks. $16.00 (978-1-56148-588-8). 28pp. Hare is very interested in bears and asks his rabbit friend Rumbly to accompany him on a bear hunt, following the advice in *The Best Book of Bear Hunting*; it's only after an encounter with a bear cub — and when they turn to the last page of the book — that the two adventurers realize that bears eat rabbits. (Rev: BL 6/1–15/08; SLJ 8/08)

1815 Freedman, Deborah. *Blue Chicken* (PS–2). Illus. by author. 2011, Viking $15.99 (978-0-670-01293-0). 40pp. A white chicken intent on helping the artist who created her hops off the page and tips over a pot of blue paint, transforming barnyard and animals. **e** Lexile AD270L (Rev: BL 11/1/11*; HB 1–2/12; SLJ 9/1/11*)

1816 Freeman, Don. *Corduroy* (PS–1). Illus. by author. 1968, Puffin paper $6.99 (978-0-14-050173-5). 32pp. The amusing story of a toy bear whose one missing button from his green corduroy overalls almost costs him the opportunity of belonging to someone. A sequel is: *A Pocket for Corduroy* (1978).

1817 Freeman, Don. *Earl the Squirrel* (PS–K). Illus. 2005, Viking $15.99 (978-0-670-06019-1). Earl the squirrel must learn to find acorns on his own in this funny, action-packed posthumous story by the author of *Corduroy*. (Rev: BL 9/15/05; SLJ 10/05)

1818 Freeman, Don. *Gregory's Shadow* (PS–1). Illus. 2000, Viking $15.99 (978-0-670-89328-7). 32pp. Gregory Groundhog doesn't want to be separated from his shadow nor does he want six more weeks of winter — what a dilemma! (Rev: BL 1/1–15/01; HBG 3/01; SLJ 2/01)

1819 Freeman, Don. *Manuelo the Playing Mantis* (K–2). Illus. 2004, Viking $15.99 (978-0-670-03684-4). Manuelo the praying mantis longs to make music but is frustrated in his efforts until a clever spider helps him construct a cello. (Rev: BL 4/15/04; SLJ 4/04)

1820 Freeman, Tor. *Olive and the Bad Mood* (PS). Illus. by author. 2013, Candlewick $15.99 (978-076366657-6). 32pp. An unhappy cat inflicts her gloom on all her friends and then cannot understand why they too are feeling down. (Rev: BL 9/1/13; SLJ 11/13)

1821 French, Jackie. *Diary of a Baby Wombat* (K–3). Illus. by Bruce Whatley. 2010, Clarion $16.99 (978-0-547-43005-8). 32pp. Baby Wombat writes about his life and the fact that he and his mother need a new burrow in this sequel to *Diary of a Wombat* (2003). (Rev: BL 12/1/10; HB 9–10/10; SLJ 10/1/10)

1822 French, Jackie. *Diary of a Wombat* (K–2). Illus. by Bruce Whatley. 2003, Clarion $14.00 (978-0-618-38136-4). A wombat relates her daily life in her diary; most entries deal with eating and sleeping until some friendly humans arrive. (Rev: HBG 4/04; SLJ 8/03)

1823 French, Jackie. *Josephine Wants to Dance* (K–2). Illus. by Bruce Whatley. 2007, Abrams $15.95 (978-0-8109-9431-7). 32pp. Josephine the kangaroo, who loves to dance, gets the chance she's dreamed of when the prima ballerina twists her ankle. (Rev: BL 11/1/07; SLJ 11/07)

1824 French, Jackie. *Too Many Pears!* (PS–1). Illus. by Bruce Whatley. 2003, Star Bright $16.95 (978-1-932065-47-3). Pamela the cow develops a real love for pears in this humorously illustrated picture book. (Rev: HBG 4/04; SLJ 11/03)

1825 Friend, Catherine. *The Perfect Nest* (K–2). Illus. by John Manders. 2007, Candlewick $16.99 (978-0-7636-2430-9). Jack the cat has a longing for a lovely omelet and builds a perfect nest, which succeeds in drawing a chicken, a duck, and a goose, but sadly Jack's plan just won't work. (Rev: SLJ 3/07*)

1826 Futterer, Kurt. *Emile* (PS–2). Trans. by Bronwen Gray Sepcht and Ingrid MacGillis. Illus. by Ralf Futterer. 2004, MacAdam $17.95 (978-1-931561-95-2). 32pp. Emile, a white cat who lives in a pristine home, finds himself covered in color after a visit to van Gogh's stu-

dio and his new appearance inspires his owners to adopt a brighter life. (Rev: BL 1/1–15/05)

1827 Gaiman, Neil. *Chu's Day* (PS–K). Illus. by Adam Rex. 2013, HarperCollins $17.99 (978-0-06-201781-9). 32pp. Bad things tend to happen when little panda sneezes, and unfortunately a lot of factors can cause this. Lexile AD210L (Rev: BL 11/1/12; SLJ 1/13)

1828 Gantos, Jack. *The Nine Lives of Rotten Ralph* (K–3). Illus. by Nicole Rubel. 2009, Houghton $16.00 (978-0-618-80046-9). 32pp. According to the vet, Ralph has used eight of his nine lives; can Sarah get the disobedient cat to change his ways? (Rev: BL 4/1/09; HB 5/09; SLJ 4/09)

1829 Gantos, Jack. *Rotten Ralph* (K–3). Illus. by Nicole Rubel. 1976, Houghton $16.00 (978-0-395-24276-6); paper $7.95 (978-0-395-29202-0). 48pp. Ralph is truly a nasty cat — mean and disruptive — until he is reformed under unusual circumstances. Sequels include *Worse Than Rotten, Ralph* (1982), *Back to School for Rotten Ralph* (1998), and *Wedding Bells for Rotten Ralph* (1999).

1830 Garza, Xavier. *Juan and the Chupacabras / Juan y el Chupacabras* (2–4). Trans. by Carolina Villarroel. Illus. by April Ward. 2006, Piñata $15.95 (978-1-55885-454-3). Cousins Luz and Juan don't know whether to believe their grandfather's tales of confrontations with the dreaded Chupacabras, so they decide to search out one of the bloodsucking demons themselves. (Rev: SLJ 10/06)

1831 Gavril, David. *Penelope Nuthatch and the Big Surprise* (PS–2). Illus. 2006, Abrams $14.95 (978-0-8109-5762-6). 32pp. Penelope Nuthatch thinks her friend Luther is taking her to the ballet and spends time and money preening and primping; so she is very disappointed to find that her "unforgettable surprise" is a trip to a water park, and it takes a while for her to recover and join in. (Rev: BL 1/1–15/06; SLJ 2/06)

1832 Gay, Marie-Louise. *Caramba* (K–3). Illus. 2005, Groundwood $16.95 (978-0-88899-667-1). Caramba the cat is sad that he cannot to fly like the other cats, but then he finds out that unlike them he is able to swim! (Rev: BL 10/1/05; SLJ 11/05)

1833 Gay, Marie-Louise. *Caramba and Henry* (K–3). Illus. by author. 2011, Groundwood $17.95 (978-1-55498-097-0). 40pp. Caramba, the cat who cannot fly, is assigned to guard his younger brother, and ends up having to rescue him; a sequel to *Caramba* (2005). (Rev: BL 10/15/11; SLJ 11/1/11)

1834 Gay, Marie-Louise. *Roslyn Rutabaga and the Biggest Hole on Earth!* (PS–1). Illus. by author. 2010, Groundwood $16.95 (978-0-88899-994-8). Unpaged. A young rabbit meets obstacles when she sets out to dig the world's biggest hole. (Rev: SLJ 9/1/10)

1835 Geisert, Arthur. *Lights Out* (K–3). Illus. 2005, Houghton $16.00 (978-0-618-47892-7). 32pp. In this compelling, nearly wordless picture book, an ingenious little pig who's afraid of the dark figures out an elaborate contraption that will turn off his bedroom light after he's already fallen asleep. (Rev: BCCB 10/05; BL 11/1/05*; HB 11/05; HBG 4/06; SLJ 12/05)

1836 Geisert, Arthur. *Mystery* (2–4). Illus. by author. 2003, Houghton $16.00 (978-0-618-27293-8). 32pp. The illustrations are the focus of this story about a little pig who investigates the theft of paintings from the art museum. (Rev: HBG 4/04; SLJ 10/03)

1837 George, Lindsay Barrett. *Alfred Digs* (PS–2). Illus. by author. 2008, Greenwillow $16.99 (978-0-06-078760-8). 40pp. Alfred the aardvark has a pet ant called Itty Bitty who heads off to the zoo one day; Alfred sets off in pursuit and encounters many letters of the alphabet on the way (the action takes place within a dictionary). (Rev: BL 4/1/08; SLJ 6/08)

1838 George, Lindsay Barrett. *The Secret* (PS–2). Illus. by author. 2005, HarperCollins LB $16.89 (978-0-06-029600-1). Mr. Snail whispers his secret to a mouse, who whispers it to a beetle, who passes it on to a turtle, and so forth until the secret ("I love you") finally makes it to Miss Snail. (Rev: BL 3/1/04; SLJ 5/05)

1839 George, Lucy M. *Back to School Tortoise* (PS–2). Illus. by Merel Eyckerman. 2011, Whitman $15.99 (978-0-8075-0510-6). 24pp. An anxious tortoise dreads the first day of school in this story with a twist — the tortoise is the teacher. (Rev: BL 8/11; SLJ 7/11)

1840 Giovanni, Nikki. *The Grasshopper's Song: An Aesop's Fable Revisited* (3–6). Illus. by Chris Raschka. 2008, Candlewick $16.99 (978-0-7636-3021-8). 56pp. In this retelling set in a courtroom, a grasshopper sues the ants when he is denied his share of the harvest, claiming that it was his music that enabled them to work efficiently. (Rev: BL 5/15/08; LMC 10/08*; SLJ 6/08)

1841 Glass, Beth Raisner. *Blue-Ribbon Dad* (PS–2). Illus. by Margie Moore. 2011, Abrams $14.95 (978-0-8109-9727-1). Unpaged. A young squirrel prepares a special surprise present for the dad who does so much for him. (Rev: BL 4/15/11; SLJ 5/1/11)

1842 Glenn, Sharlee. *Just What Mama Needs* (PS–2). Illus. by Amiko Hirao. 2008, Harcourt $16.00 (978-0-15-205759-6). 32pp. Abby is an inventive young dog who takes on a different role — a pirate on Monday, a detective on Tuesday — every day except Sunday, when she is just herself but continues to help her mother with chores. (Rev: BL 4/15/08; SLJ 5/08)

1843 Gliori, Debi. *Flora's Blanket* (PS). Illus. 2001, Scholastic $15.95 (978-0-531-30305-4). Flora, a young bunny, cannot sleep because her favorite blanket has disappeared. (Rev: BL 5/15/01; HBG 10/01; SLJ 7/01*)

1844 Gliori, Debi. *Mr. Bear to the Rescue* (PS–1). Illus. 2000, Orchard $15.95 (978-0-531-30276-7). 32pp. When bunny Flora is missing, Mr. Bear loads his tools into his carriage and sets off to help. (Rev: BL 11/15/00; HBG 10/01; SLJ 11/00)

1845 Gliori, Debi. *Where Did That Baby Come From?* (PS–2). Illus. 2005, Harcourt $16.00 (978-0-15-205373-4). A tiger cub wonders where his new sibling came from — a store? outer space? the zoo? — but happily accepts his presence in the end. (Rev: BL 3/1/05; SLJ 4/05)

1846 Goodman, Joan Elizabeth. *Bernard Wants a Baby* (PS–K). Illus. by Dominic Catalano. 2004, Boyds Mills $15.95 (978-1-59078-088-6). Although he has expressed a wish for siblings, young elephant Bernard is uncertain when triplets arrive. (Rev: SLJ 7/04)

1847 Gorbachev, Valeri. *Dragon Is Coming!* (PS–2). Illus. by author. 2009, Harcourt $16.00 (978-0-15-205196-9). 44pp. Misunderstanding and panic ensue when the animals think a storm cloud is a dragon, but all is well once the storm is over and they realize what has happened. (Rev: BL 7/09; SLJ 5/09)

1848 Gorbachev, Valeri. *Heron and Turtle* (PS–2). Illus. by author. 2006, Philomel $15.99 (978-0-399-24321-9). Heron and Turtle are close friends despite their difference in size. (Rev: SLJ 11/06)

1849 Gorbachev, Valeri. *Molly Who Flew Away* (PS–1). Illus. by author. 2009, Philomel $16.99 (978-0-399-25211-2). 32pp. Molly the mouse enjoys a day at the country fair with her friends — until she buys too many balloons and is wafted aloft. (Rev: BL 5/15/09; SLJ 6/09)

1850 Gorbachev, Valeri. *That's What Friends Are For* (PS–1). Illus. 2005, Philomel $15.99 (978-0-399-23966-3). 32pp. When Goat sees Pig crying, he imagines all kinds of disasters that might explain the situation. (Rev: BL 5/15/05)

1851 Gorbachev, Valeri. *What's the Big Idea, Molly?* (PS–2). Illus. by author. 2010, Philomel $16.99 (978-0-399-25428-4). 32pp. Molly Mouse has writer's block and she and her friends struggle to come up with a suitable birthday present for Turtle. (Rev: BL 6/10; LMC 11–12/10; SLJ 7/1/10)

1852 Gorbachev, Valeri. *Whose Hat Is It?* (PS–K). Illus. by author. 2004, HarperCollins LB $15.89 (978-0-06-053435-6). A turtle patiently seeks the owner of a pink hat found swept away by the wind. (Rev: SLJ 7/04)

1853 Gordon, Gus. *Herman and Rosie* (PS–2). Illus. by author. 2013, Roaring Brook $17.99 (978-1-59643-856-9). 32pp. Set in New York City, this book tells the romantic tale of neighbors Herman Schubert, a crocodile who plays the oboe, and Rosie Bloom, a deer who sings jazz, who meet when they lose their respective jobs and bond over their love of music. Booklist Editors' Choice: Books for Youth, 2013. ❡ Lexile AD720 (Rev: BL 10/1/13*; LMC 3–4/14; SLJ 10/13)

1854 Gore, Leonid. *Mommy, Where Are You?* (PS–K). Illus. by author. 2009, Atheneum $16.99 (978-1-4169-5505-4). A little mouse named Ozzy looks everywhere for his mother. (Rev: BCCB 4/09; BL 5/1/09; SLJ 5/09)

1855 Gormley, Greg. *Dog in Boots* (PS–1). Illus. by Roberta Angaramo. 2011, Holiday House $17.95 (978-0-8234-2347-7). 32pp. Inspired by "Puss in Boots," Dog decides to go shoe shopping but finds it more challenging than he expected. Lexile AD680L (Rev: BL 3/15/11; SLJ 3/1/11*)

1856 Gravett, Emily. *Blue Chameleon* (PS–K). Illus. by author. 2011, Simon & Schuster $16.99 (978-1-4424-1958-2). 32pp. A chameleon lonely for a friend transforms himself without success until he finally finds what he's been seeking — another chameleon. (Rev: BL 3/15/11; HB 3–4/11; SLJ 3/1/11)

1857 Gravett, Emily. *The Odd Egg* (PS–2). Illus. by author. 2009, Simon & Schuster $15.99 (978-1-4169-6872-6). 32pp. Duck is happy to find an egg to sit on, even though it's a suspicious-looking green-spotted giant of an egg that draws general derision. What will pop out? (Rev: BCCB 1/09; BL 1/1–15/09; HB 1/09; LMC 5/09; SLJ 1/09)

1858 Gravett, Emily. *Wolves* (PS–2). Illus. by author. 2006, Simon & Schuster $15.95 (978-1-4169-1491-4). A rabbit is so engrossed in reading the book about wolves that he borrowed from the library that he doesn't realize he's face to face with a real live wolf. (Rev: BL 12/1/06; SLJ 8/06*)

1859 Green, Alison. *The Fox in the Dark* (K–2). Illus. by Deborah Allwright. 2010, Tiger Tales $15.95 (978-1-58925-091-8). Unpaged. Rabbit offers his den as shelter for a group of animals running from a fox; when the fox knocks, it turns out he is just as in need of shelter as they are. (Rev: SLJ 11/1/10)

1860 Greene, Stephanie. *Pig Pickin'* (1–3). Illus. by Joe Mathieu. Series: Moose and Hildy. 2006, Marshall Cavendish $14.99 (978-0-7614-5324-6). 56pp. Hildy the pig asks Moose to join her on a trip down south to a pig pickin', an event she mistakenly believes is a porcine beauty contest. (Rev: SLJ 10/06)

1861 Gretz, Susanna. *Riley and Rose in the Picture* (K–3). Illus. 2005, Candlewick $16.99 (978-0-7636-2681-5). 32pp. Riley the dog and Rose the cat, natural antagonists, try to get along by drawing pictures inside on a rainy day. (Rev: BL 8/05; SLJ 9/05)

1862 Grey, Mini. *Three by the Sea* (PS–2). Illus. by author. 2011, Knopf $17.99 (978-0-375-86784-2); LB $20.99 (978-0-375-96784-9). 32pp. A dog, a cat, and a mouse used to sharing household duties are tested when a fox from the Winds of Change Trading Company stirs up discord. (Rev: BL 2/1/11; SLJ 4/11*)

1863 Guarino, Deborah. *Is Your Mama a Llama?* (PS–K). Illus. by Steven Kellogg. 1989, Scholastic $14.95 (978-0-590-41387-9). 32pp. A pleasing study of who belongs to whom, as a koala and her baby clutch each other or an opossum ambles off with babies aboard her back. (Rev: BCCB 11/89; BL 10/1/89; SLJ 10/89)

1864 Guest, Elissa Haden. *Harriet's Had Enough* (PS–2). Illus. by Paul Meisel. 2009, Candlewick $15.99 (978-0-7636-3454-4). Harriet, a little raccoon, has an argument with her mother about picking up her toys and decides to run away from home. (Rev: BL 4/1/09; SLJ 4/09)

1865 Guion, Melissa. *Baby Penguins Everywhere!* (PS–1). Illus. by author. 2012, Philomel $16.99 (978-0-399-25535-9). 32pp. A lonely penguin is surprised and a little alarmed to find herself joined by a horde of little penguins, making her happy but also a little wistful for her peaceful solitary life. **℮** (Rev: BL 12/15/12; SLJ 12/12)

1866 Hager, Sarah. *Dancing Matilda* (PS–2). Illus. by Kelly Murphy. 2005, HarperCollins $15.99 (978-0-06-051452-5). A little kangaroo named Matilda dances her way through the pages of this book with rhyming text and lovely illustrations. (Rev: SLJ 8/05)

1867 Hall, Algy Craig. *Fine as We Are* (PS). Illus. by author. 2008, Boxer Bks. $14.95 (978-1-905417-72-8). 32pp. Happy as an only child, Little Frog suddenly finds himself overrun with noisy little siblings who follow him everywhere. (Rev: LMC 8/08; SLJ 4/08)

1868 Hample, Stoo. *I Will Kiss You: Lots and Lots and Lots!* (PS). 2005, Candlewick $15.99 (978-0-7636-2787-4). A mother bunny enumerates the many opportunities each day offers for planting a kiss on her toddler. (Rev: BL 2/1/06; SLJ 5/06)

1869 Harper, Anita. *It's Not Fair!* (PS–K). Illus. by Mary McQuillan. 2007, Holiday $16.95 (978-0-8234-2094-0). 32pp. A young cat is jealous that her new baby brother gets all the attention, but the roles are later reversed when the baby grows older and is frustrated that he can't do all the fun things his big sister can do; originally published in 1986, this edition features new illustrations. (Rev: BL 7/07; SLJ 10/07)

1870 Harper, Charise Mericle. *Pink Me Up* (PS–2). Illus. by author. 2010, Knopf $16.99 (978-0-375-85607-5). 40pp. When bunny Violet's mother comes down with a fever, she recruits her dad to take her to a "Pink-nic," decorating his clothing with pink so he'll fit in. (Rev: BL 4/15/10; SLJ 4/1/10)

1871 Harper, Charise Mericle. *When Randolph Turned Rotten* (PS–2). Illus. by author. 2007, Knopf $16.99 (978-0-375-84071-5). 40pp. Jealous of Ivy the goose's invitation to an all-girls party, friend Randolph the beaver loads her down with "essential" items, which — it turns out — save the day. (Rev: BL 11/15/07; HB 1/08; LMC 1/08; SLJ 12/07*)

1872 Harper, Lee. *Snow! Snow! Snow!* (PS–K). Illus. by author. 2009, Simon & Schuster $14.99 (978-1-4169-8454-2). 40pp. Two puppies and their father enjoy a day frolicking in the snow in this cartoon-like, lighthearted offering. (Rev: BL 11/1/09; SLJ 10/1/09)

1873 Harrison, David L. *A Perfect Home for a Family* (PS–2). Illus. by Roberta Angaramo. 2013, Holiday $16.95 (978-0-8234-2338-5). 32pp. Raccoon parents-to-be awaiting the arrival of twins search for a suitable new home with the help of a squirrel realtor; their choice of an attic turns out — horrors! — to have humans and a dog below, and they return happily to their former tree. Well-paced for beginning readers. (Rev: BL 4/1/13; LMC 11–12/13; SLJ 5/13)

1874 Heide, Florence Parry. *The One and Only Marigold* (PS–3). Illus. by Jill McElmurry. 2009, Random $16.99 (978-0-375-84031-9). 40pp. Four linked stories follow the deepening friendship of Marigold, a contrary 2nd-grade monkey, and her hippo friend, Maxine, whose only desire is to fit in. (Rev: BCCB 1/09; BL 2/1/09; LMC 5/09; SLJ 2/09)

1875 Heide, Florence Parry, and Sylvia Van Clief. *That's What Friends Are For* (PS–2). Illus. by Holly Meade. 2003, Candlewick $15.99 (978-0-7636-1397-6). 40pp. Poor Theodore the elephant has hurt his leg and gets totally useless advice from most of the animals in the forest. (Rev: BL 3/15/03; HBG 10/03; SLJ 5/03)

1876 Heinz, Brian. *Red Fox at McCloskey's Farm* (K–4). Illus. by Chris Sheban. 2006, Creative Editions $17.95 (978-1-56846-195-3). 30pp. In this action-packed rhyming tale, Farmer McCloskey and his hound dog foil Fox's plan to raid the hen house. (Rev: SLJ 11/06)

1877 Helakoski, Leslie. *Big Chickens Fly the Coop* (PS–2). Illus. by Henry Cole. 2008, Dutton $15.99 (978-0-525-47915-4). Four adventurous chickens set off into the wide world to find the farmhouse, but they mistake many other buildings for this structure, which turns out to be right next to the coop. (Rev: BL 1/1–15/08; SLJ 6/08)

1878 Helakoski, Leslie. *Fair Cow* (PS–2). Illus. by author. 2010, Marshall Cavendish $16.99 (978-0-7614-5684-1). 32pp. Petunia the pig helps Effie the cow primp for the state fair beauty competition in this pun-filled romp. Lexile AD430L (Rev: BL 9/1/10; LMC 1–2/11; SLJ 9/1/10)

1879 Helakoski, Leslie. *Woolbur* (PS–1). Illus. by Lee Harper. 2008, HarperCollins $16.99 (978-0-06-084726-5). 32pp. Woolbur the sheep is a nonconformist who would rather run with the dogs than hang with the flock. (Rev: BL 1/1–15/08; SLJ 1/08) ∩

1880 Helquist, Brett. *Bedtime for Bear* (PS–1). Illus. by author. 2010, HarperCollins $16.99 (978-0-06-050205-8). Unpaged. Bear is persuaded by his raccoon friends to spend one last day playing in the snow before settling in for the winter. (Rev: BL 10/15/10; SLJ 2/1/11*)

1881 Hendra, Sue. *Barry, the Fish with Fingers* (K–2). Illus. by author. 2010, Knopf $15.99 (978-0-375-85894-9); LB $18.99 (978-0-375-95894-6). Unpaged. Barry's fingers allow him to do amazing things. (Rev: LMC 11–12/10; SLJ 7/1/10)

1882 Henkes, Kevin. *Chrysanthemum* (PS–1). Illus. 1991, Greenwillow $17.89 (978-0-688-09700-4). Other mouse children make fun of Chrysanthemum's name until her music teacher helps out. (Rev: BCCB 10/92; BL 8/91; HB 9/91*; SLJ 9/91*)

1883 Henkes, Kevin. *Julius, the Baby of the World* (PS–3). Illus. 1990, Greenwillow $17.89 (978-0-688-08944-3). 32pp. Lilly, a girl mouse, has a fit of jealousy when her baby brother gets all the attention in the family. (Rev: BCCB 11/90; BL 11/1/90; HB 1/91*; SLJ 10/90*)

1884 Henkes, Kevin. *Kitten's First Full Moon* (PS). Illus. by author. 2004, Greenwillow LB $16.89 (978-0-06-058829-8). A kitten mistakes the moon for a bowl of milk and is determined to lap it up. Caldecott Medal winner, 2005. (Rev: BL 2/15/04*; HB 5/04; SLJ 4/04)

1885 Henkes, Kevin. *Owen* (PS). Illus. 1993, Greenwillow $17.89 (978-0-688-11450-3). 24pp. Owen, a mouse, loves his fuzzy yellow blanket more than anything. (Rev: BL 8/93*)

1886 Henkes, Kevin. *Sheila Rae, the Brave* (PS–1). Illus. by author. 1987, Greenwillow $17.89 (978-0-688-07156-1). Sheila Rae, a mouse, fears nothing until she takes the wrong way home. (Rev: BL 9/1/87; SLJ 9/87)

1887 Henkes, Kevin. *Wemberly Worried* (PS–1). Illus. 2000, Greenwillow $17.99 (978-0-688-17027-1). Wemberly, a little mouse girl, is a real worrywart until she makes a new friend at school who makes the world look less scary. (Rev: BCCB 9/00; BL 8/00; HB 9/00; HBG 3/01; SLJ 8/00)

1888 Hest, Amy. *Guess Who, Baby Duck!* (PS–K). Illus. by Jill Barton. 2004, Candlewick $14.99 (978-0-7636-1981-7). When Baby Duck has a cold, her grandfather brings an album of pictures to cheer her up. (Rev: SLJ 5/04)

1889 Hest, Amy. *Little Chick* (PS–K). Illus. by Anita Jeram. 2009, Candlewick $17.99 (978-0-7636-2890-1). Three short stories present Little Chick tackling different situations: waiting impatiently for a carrot to grow, learning to fly a kite, and trying to catch a star. (Rev: BL 4/15/09; SLJ 5/09)

1890 Hill, Susanna Leonard. *April Fool, Phyllis!* (K–3). Illus. by Jeffrey Ebbeler. 2011, Holiday House $16.95 (978-0-8234-2270-8). 32pp. It's the first day of April and nobody believes Phyllis the groundhog when she says a blizzard is on its way; a sequel to *Punxsutawney Phyllis* (2006). (Rev: BL 3/15/11; SLJ 5/1/11)

1891 Hill, Susanna Leonard. *Punxsutawney Phyllis* (K–3). Illus. by Jeffrey Ebbeler. 2005, Holiday $17.95 (978-0-8234-1872-5). 32pp. Punxsutawney Phyllis, a groundhog, hopes to take over the weather forecasting duties long performed by her Uncle Phil. (Rev: BL 12/1/05; SLJ 10/05)

1892 Hillenbrand, Will. *Louie!* (K–3). Illus. by author. 2009, Philomel $16.99 (978-0-399-24707-1). Louie the pig's artistic talents are generally ignored until he is sent to work in a hotel, and there his illustrations — of a girl with appendicitis who lives in a convent school where the students walk in lines of two — are appreciated; based loosely on the life of Ludwig Bemelmans. (Rev: BCCB 6/09; BL 3/15/09; LMC 8/09; SLJ 3/09)

1893 Hillenbrand, Will. *Spring Is Here* (PS–2). Illus. by author. 2011, Holiday House $16.95 (978-0-8234-1602-8). 32pp. At the end of winter Mole wakes his friend Bear up from hibernation by baking a sumptuous breakfast. (Rev: BL 2/15/11; HB 3–4/11; SLJ 3/1/11)

1894 Hills, Tad. *Duck and Goose Find a Pumpkin* (PS). Illus. by author. 2009, Random House $6.99 (978-037585813-0). 20pp. Duck and Goose like their friend Thistle's pumpkin and decide to find one of their own. (Rev: BL 9/15/09; SLJ 8/1/09)

1895 Hills, Tad. *Duck and Goose: How Are You Feeling?* (PS). Illus. by author. 2009, Schwartz & Wade $6.99 (978-0-375-84629-8). 22pp. Duck and Goose display a variety of emotions as they face a storm and try to build structures in this appealing board book. (Rev: BLO 1/13/09; SLJ 3/09)

1896 Hills, Tad. *Duck, Duck, Goose* (PS–1). Illus. by author. 2006, Random $14.95 (978-0-375-83611-4). A foolish duck and a goose squabble over a spotted ball they think is an egg, but finally realize their mistake and become friends. (Rev: BL 3/1/07; SLJ 1/06)

1897 Hills, Tad. *How Rocket Learned to Read* (K–2). Illus. by author. 2010, Random House $17.99 (978-0-375-85899-4). 40pp. A smart yellow bird enthusiastically teaches a willing dog how to read, starting with learning the alphabet. (Rev: BL 5/15/10; LMC 11–12/10; SLJ 7/1/10)

1898 Hobbie, Holly. *Toot and Puddle: I'll Be Home for Christmas* (PS–2). Illus. by author. 2001, Little, Brown $15.95 (978-0-316-36623-6). While Puddle the pig has been eagerly preparing for Toot's return from a trip to Scotland, Toot is spared from a disappointing delay when a sleigh mysteriously picks him up and wafts him home to a happy reunion. (Rev: HBG 3/02; SLJ 10/01)

1899 Hobbie, Holly. *Toot and Puddle: Top of the World* (PS–2). Illus. 2002, Little, Brown $15.95 (978-0-316-36513-0). 32pp. Toot and Puddle, the friendly pigs, visit France and Nepal before deciding that home beckons. Also use *Toot and Puddle: Charming Opal* (2003). (Rev: BL 10/1/02; HBG 3/03)

1900 Hobbie, Holly. *Toot and Puddle: Wish You Were Here* (PS–3). Illus. by author. 2005, Little, Brown $16.99 (978-0-316-36602-1). Stung by a bee while off on an exotic trip, Toot the pig turns violet and must be nursed back to health by his friends Puddle and Opal. (Rev: SLJ 10/05)

1901 Hobbie, Holly. *Toot and Puddle: You Are My Sunshine* (PS–2). Illus. by author. 1999, Little, Brown $14.95 (978-0-316-36562-8). In this story about friendship, two little piglets, Tulip and Puddle, try to cheer up their friend Toot, who is feeling blue. (Rev: BCCB 9/99; HBG 3/00; SLJ 8/99)

1902 Hodgkinson, Jo. *The Talent Show* (K–3). Illus. by author. 2011, Andersen $16.95 (978-0-7613-7487-9). 32pp. A band composed of a bear, a crocodile, a lion, and a snake finds the perfect vocalist: a tiny red bird who is not too small after all. ℯ (Rev: BL 2/15/11; SLJ 2/1/11)

1903 Hodgkinson, Leigh. *Boris and the Wrong Shadow* (K–2). Illus. by author. 2009, Tiger Tales $15.95 (978-1-58925-082-6). Unpaged. Boris the cat wakes up to find that his shadow is all wrong — and that his mouse friend Vernon seems to be in possession of a cat shadow. (Rev: SLJ 9/1/09)

1904 Hodgkinson, Leigh. *Introducing Limelight Larry* (PS–2). Illus. by author. 2011, Tiger Tales $15.95 (978-1-58925-102-1). Unpaged. An attention-hogging peacock tries everything to exclude his friends from this book, resulting in a comic message about the importance of sharing the spotlight. (Rev: SLJ 11/1/11)

1905 Holabird, Katharine. *Angelina at the Palace* (K–2). Illus. by Helen Craig. Series: Angelina Ballerina. 2005, Viking $13.99 (978-0-670-06048-1). When her dance teacher falls ill, Angelina the mouse must teach a spe-

cial dance to three of Mouseland's princesses. (Rev: SLJ 10/05)

1906 Holt, Kimberly Willis. *Skinny Brown Dog* (PS–2). Illus. by Donald Saaf. 2007, Holt $16.95 (978-0-8050-7587-8). 40pp. A stray dog finally succeeds in persuading Benny, a polar bear who owns a bakery, to give him a home. (Rev: BL 7/07; LMC 11/07; SLJ 6/07)

1907 Hood, Susan. *Spike, the Mixed-up Monster* (PS–2). Illus. by Melissa Sweet. 2012, Simon & Schuster $16.99 (978-1-4424-0601-8). 40pp. Spike, a Mexican salamander, fancies himself as a monster but nobody seems to be afraid of him; Spanish words are sprinkled throughout the text. ℯ Lexile AD470L (Rev: BL 11/1/12; LMC 1–2/13; SLJ 8/12)

1908 Hood, Susan. *The Tooth Mouse* (PS–K). Illus. by Janice Nadeau. 2012, Kids Can $16.95 (978-1-55453-565-1). 32pp. Sophie, a little French mouse, is determined to prove that she can take on the important role of Tooth Mouse in this nicely illustrated picture book. ℯ Lexile AD580L (Rev: BL 9/1/12*; LMC 5–6/13; SLJ 10/12)

1909 Horacek, Petr. *Look Out, Suzy Goose* (PS–1). Illus. by author. 2008, Candlewick $14.99 (978-0-7636-3803-0). 32pp. Tired of the noise made by her fellow geese, Suzy (of *Silly Suzy Goose* [2006]) wanders into the woods by herself; it is her own loud honking that brings rescue from the predators on her track. (Rev: BL 8/08; SLJ 7/08)

1910 Horacek, Petr. *Puffin Peter* (PS–K). Illus. by author. 2013, Candlewick $16.99 (978-0-7636-6572-2). 40pp. When a young puffin named Peter is lost in a storm, his friend Paul teams up with a friendly whale to search for him. (Rev: BL 3/15/13; SLJ 6/13)

1911 Horacek, Petr. *Silly Suzy Goose* (PS–1). Illus. 2006, Candlewick $14.99 (978-0-7636-3040-9). 32pp. Suzy Goose longs to be different and imagines herself as all kinds of other animals, but a frightening encounter with a lion convinces her that there is safety in numbers; exuberant art enhances the fun. (Rev: BL 2/15/06*; HBG 10/06; SLJ 4/06)

1912 Horowitz, Dave. *Duck Duck Moose* (PS–2). Illus. by author. 2009, Putnam $16.99 (978-0-399-24782-8). Unpaged. A reluctant moose follows his feathered friends south for the winter and is surprised to discover how much he likes the sunshine. (Rev: BL 9/1/09; SLJ 10/1/09)

1913 Howe, James. *Horace and Morris But Mostly Dolores* (PS–2). Illus. by Amy Walrod. 1999, Simon & Schuster $16.00 (978-0-689-31874-0). 32pp. Three mice — two boys and a girl — decide to join unisex clubs, but in time they leave them for a day of exploring together. (Rev: BCCB 3/99; BL 2/15/99*; HBG 10/99; SLJ 3/99)

1914 Howe, James. *Rabbit-cadabra!* (2–4). Illus. by Jeff Mack. Series: Bunnicula and Friends. 2006, Simon & Schuster $14.95 (978-0-689-85727-0). 42pp. An easy chapter book about Chester, Howie, and Harold's plan to outsmart a magician who's bringing his vampire-bunny act to Toby's school. (Rev: SLJ 6/06)

1915 Hume, Lachie. *Clancy the Courageous Cow* (PS–2). Illus. 2007, Greenwillow $16.99 (978-0-06-117249-6). 32pp. An outcast among his fellow Belted Galloway cattle because he has no belt, Clancy is in despair until he uses his unique appearance to infiltrate the neighboring Hereford herd, with which the Belted Galloways have long been feuding. (Rev: BL 3/15/07; SLJ 3/07)

1916 Huneck, Stephen. *Sally Goes to the Farm* (PS–2). Illus. 2002, Abrams $17.95 (978-0-8109-4498-5). 40pp. Sally the dog visits a farm and has a wonderful time with Molly and other animal friends in this picture book with simple text and large, bold pictures that add to the story. (Rev: BL 7/02; HBG 10/02; SLJ 7/02)

1917 Hunter, Jana Novotny. *I Can Do It!* (PS). Illus. by Lucy Richards. 2006, Frances Lincoln $15.95 (978-1-84507-127-1). Little Guinea Pig has a satisfying day at preschool, finding perfect activities to match his moods. (Rev: SLJ 8/06)

1918 Hurd, Thacher. *Mama Don't Allow: Starring Miles and the Swamp Band* (PS–1). Illus. by author. 1984, HarperCollins LB $16.89 (978-0-06-022690-9); paper $6.99 (978-0-06-443078-4). The Swamp Band finds that the only audience that likes them is the alligator.

1919 Hutchins, Pat. *Little Pink Pig* (PS–1). Illus. 1994, Greenwillow $15.95 (978-0-688-12014-6). 32pp. Little Pig fails to heed his mother's call for bedtime because he is busy chasing a butterfly. (Rev: BL 4/1/94; HB 5/94; SLJ 5/94)

1920 Hutchins, Pat. *Rosie's Walk* (K–2). Illus. by author. 1968, Macmillan LB $16.00 (978-0-02-745850-3); paper $5.99 (978-0-02-043750-5). 32pp. Rosie the hen miraculously escapes capture by a fox.

1921 Irbinskas, Heather. *How Jackrabbit Got His Very Long Ears* (K–3). Illus. by Kenneth J. Spengler. 1994, Northland LB $15.95 (978-0-87358-566-8). 32pp. When Jackrabbit fails to follow the instructions of the Great Spirit, he is given big ears so that he can hear better. (Rev: BL 6/1–15/94)

1922 Ives, Penny. *Celestine, Drama Queen* (PS–K). Illus. by author. 2009, Scholastic $16.99 (978-0-545-08149-8). 32pp. Convinced of her future as a star, young duck Celestine is distressed when she suffers from stage fright. (Rev: BL 2/1/09; SLJ 2/09)

1923 Iwamura, Kazuo. *Hooray for Spring!* (PS–K). Illus. by author. 2009, North-South $15.95 (978-0-7358-2228-3). 32pp. Three young squirrels — Mick, Mack, and Molly — try to feed a hungry baby bird and are surprised that it chooses to eat a worm. (Rev: BL 4/15/09; SLJ 6/09)

1924 Iwamura, Kazuo. *Hooray for Summer!* (PS–1). Illus. by author. 2010, NorthSouth $16.95 (978-0-7358-2285-6). 32pp. Three squirrel siblings take refuge in a cave during a thunderstorm and make friends with a rabbit and two mice. Lexile AD420L (Rev: BLO 4/15/10; HB 7–8/10; SLJ 5/1/10)

1925 Jahn-Clough, Lisa. *Felicity and Cordelia: A Tale of Two Bunnies* (PS–K). Illus. by author. 2011, Farrar $16.99 (978-0-374-32300-4). 40pp. Adventuresome rabbit Felicity returns safely home after a ride in a hot air balloon, where her more cautious bunny friend Cordelia is waiting, with pie. (Rev: BL 2/15/11; SLJ 3/1/11)

1926 Jarman, Julia. *Two Shy Pandas* (PS–2). Illus. by Susan Varley. 2013, Andersen $16.95 (978-1-4677-1141-8). 32pp. Pandas Panda and Pandora live next door to each other but are too shy to make friends. **e** (Rev: BLO 3/15/13; SLJ 3/13)

1927 Jeffers, Oliver. *The Great Paper Caper* (PS–K). Illus. by author. 2009, Philomel $17.99 (978-0-399-25097-2). 40pp. Forest animals investigate why branches and trees are disappearing and find a bear who has been using them to make paper airplanes for a contest. (Rev: BL 12/15/08; LMC 5/09; SLJ 1/09)

1928 Jenkins, Emily. *Love You When You Whine* (PS). Illus. by Sergio Ruzzier. 2006, Farrar $15.00 (978-0-374-34652-2). A mother cat loves her little daughter no matter what mischief she does — from whining and painting the walls to having a terrible tantrum. (Rev: SLJ 10/06)

1929 Jennewein, Lenore. *Chick-o-saurus Rex* (PS–2). Illus. by Daniel Jennewein. 2013, Simon & Schuster $16.99 (978-1-4424-5186-5). 32pp. The idea that he is a descendent of a T. rex gives Little Chick new confidence in dealing with farmyard bullies. **e** Lexile AD640 (Rev: BL 7/13; SLJ 6/13)

1930 Johansen, Hanna. *Henrietta and the Golden Eggs* (1–3). Trans. by John S. Barrett. Illus. by Kathi Bhend. 2002, Godine $16.95 (978-1-56792-210-3). 64pp. The story of Henrietta, a chicken with dreams of freedom, is told with intricate pen-and-ink drawings. (Rev: BL 3/15/03; HBG 10/03)

1931 Johnson, D. B. *Henry Builds a Cabin* (PS–3). Illus. 2002, Houghton $15.00 (978-0-618-13201-0). 32pp. A sensible bear called Henry convinces his friends that a Thoreau-style cabin, and the great outdoors, is all that he needs to be happy. (Rev: BCCB 5/02; BL 3/15/02*; HB 7/02; HBG 10/02; SLJ 3/02)

1932 Johnson, D. B. *Henry Climbs a Mountain* (K–3). Illus. by author. 2003, Houghton $15.00 (978-0-618-26902-0). In this third picture book based on the life of Thoreau, Henry the bear is jailed for nonpayment of taxes and escapes into the scenery he has drawn on the wall, joining a stranger who is traveling north to freedom. (Rev: BL 10/1/03*; HBG 4/04; SLJ 9/03)

1933 Johnson, D. B. *Henry Hikes to Fitchburg* (PS–3). Illus. 2000, Houghton $16.00 (978-0-395-96867-3). 32pp. Henry the bear decides to take a nature walk to Fitchburg while his friend will ride the train in this amusing take-off on Thoreau's attitudes and his New England circle. (Rev: BCCB 7–8/00; BL 4/15/00*; HB 5/00; HBG 10/00; SLJ 6/00)

1934 Joyce, William. *Bently and Egg* (PS–3). Illus. 1992, HarperCollins $17.95 (978-0-06-020385-6); paper $7.99 (978-0-06-443352-5). Bently, a frog, is asked to egg-sit for his friend the duck. (Rev: BCCB 3/92; BL 1/1/92; HB 3/92; SLJ 4/92*)

1935 Joyner, Andrew. *Boris for the Win* (K–2). Illus. by author. 2013, Scholastic $15.99 (978-054548448-0); paper $4.99 (978-05454844-9-7). 80pp. Boris the warthog has trained hard for the coming field day, determined to win; but when the time comes he has to consider sportsmanship as well as competitive ambitions. Notable Australian Children's Book. Lexile 230 (Rev: BLO 9/15/13)

1936 Kaczman, James. *A Bird and His Worm* (PS–2). Illus. 2002, Houghton $15.00 (978-0-618-09460-8). 32pp. A bird and his friend, a worm, learn a lesson about strangers in their travels south. (Rev: BCCB 12/02; BL 9/15/02; HBG 3/03; SLJ 9/02)

1937 Kaplan, Michael B. *Betty Bunny Didn't Do It* (K–3). Illus. by Stephane Jorisch. 2013, Dial $16.99 (978-0-8037-3858-4). 32pp. When she breaks a lamp, Betty Bunny initially blames the accident on the tooth fairy, prompting a lesson about honesty. **e** Lexile AD660L (Rev: BLO 12/15/12; LMC 8–9/13; SLJ 2/13)

1938 Kaplan, Michael B. *Betty Bunny Loves Chocolate Cake* (K–3). Illus. by Stephane Jorisch. 2011, Dial $16.99 (978-0-8037-3407-4). 32pp. A chocolate-crazed young bunny has a variety of comic misadventures when she stuffs a piece of cake in her pocket. (Rev: BL 6/1/11; SLJ 6/11*)

1939 Kaplan, Michael B. *Betty Bunny Wants Everything* (K–3). Illus. by Stephane Jorisch. 2012, Dial $16.99 (978-080373408-1). 32pp. Stubborn Betty throws a fit when she's told she can only have one toy at the store. (Rev: BL 2/1/12; SLJ 1/12)

1940 Kasza, Keiko. *Badger's Fancy Meal* (PS–2). Illus. 2007, Putnam $16.99 (978-0-399-24603-6). 32pp. This creatively designed volume features Badger's unsuccessful attempts to capture a mole, a rat, and a rabbit — who ironically end up in his den and eat up his stores of food. (Rev: BL 5/1/07; HB 5/07; SLJ 7/07)

1941 Kasza, Keiko. *Don't Laugh, Joe!* (PS–1). Illus. 1997, Penguin $17.99 (978-0-399-23036-3). 32pp. A young opossum has an unusual problem: He can't stop giggling while playing dead. (Rev: BL 8/97; SLJ 6/97)

1942 Kasza, Keiko. *The Mightiest* (1–3). Illus. 2001, Penguin $16.99 (978-0-399-23586-3). 32pp. Lion, Bear, and Elephant argue about who among them is the mightiest, but they are all outdone by an old woman. (Rev: BL 9/1/01; HBG 3/02; SLJ 11/01)

1943 Kasza, Keiko. *A Mother for Choco* (PS–1). Illus. 1992, Penguin LB $15.99 (978-0-399-21841-5). 32pp. A little bird sets out to find his mother and is adopted by a kindly bear. (Rev: BCCB 4/92; BL 3/15/92; HB 5/92; SLJ 4/92*)

1944 Kasza, Keiko. *My Lucky Day* (K–2). Illus. by author. 2003, Penguin $15.99 (978-0-399-23874-1). A hungry fox can't believe his luck when a piglet comes knocking, but the little pig has many sensible suggestions and in the end the fox is too tired to eat. (Rev: HB 9/03; HBG 4/04; SLJ 9/03)

1945 Kasza, Keiko. *Ready for Anything!* (PS–2). Illus. by author. 2009, Putnam $16.99 (978-0-399-25235-8). 32pp. A group of animal friends consider both the best-case and worst-case scenarios before heading out on a picnic. (Rev: BL 9/15/09; SLJ 9/1/09)

1946 Keller, Holly. *Geraldine's Blanket* (PS–2). Illus. by author. 1988, Morrow paper $6.99 (978-0-688-07810-2). 32pp. A little pig named Geraldine becomes extremely attached to a blanket her aunt gave her.

1947 Keller, Holly. *Nosy Rosie* (PS). 2006, Greenwillow $16.99 (978-0-06-078758-5). 32pp. Nosy Rosie's super-sensitive fox nose comes in handy one day when a baby is lost in the woods. (Rev: BL 7/06; SLJ 9/06*)

1948 Keller, Holly. *Pearl's New Skates* (PS–2). Illus. 2005, Greenwillow LB $17.89 (978-0-06-056281-6). 24pp. Pearl the rabbit is delighted with her new ice skates but finds them surprisingly difficult to use. (Rev: BL 1/1–15/05; SLJ 2/05)

1949 Keller, Holly. *Sophie's Window* (PS–2). Illus. 2005, Greenwillow $15.99 (978-0-06-056282-3). 32pp. When Caruso, a little pigeon who is afraid to fly, is blown out of his family home, he is rescued by a nice dog called Sophie. (Rev: BL 9/15/05; SLJ 8/05)

1950 Kelley, Ellen A. *My Life as a Chicken* (PS–2). Illus. by Michael Slack. 2007, Harcourt $16.00 (978-0-15-205306-2). 40pp. In this action-packed picture-book story told in rhyming text, chicken Pauline Poulet is constantly on the move, bouncing from one near-tragedy to the next in an adventure that includes pirates, a typhoon, and a balloon ride. (Rev: BL 4/1/07)

1951 Kelley, True. *Blabber Mouse* (1–3). Illus. 2001, Dutton $15.99 (978-0-525-46742-7). 32pp. Blabber Mouse's classmates finally are forced to devise a solution to stop his chatter when he reminds teacher that she forgot to assign homework. (Rev: BL 12/1/01; HBG 3/02; SLJ 10/01)

1952 Kelley, True. *The Blabber Report* (1–3). Illus. by author. 2007, Dutton $15.99 (978-0-525-47809-6). 32pp. Young Blabber Mouse, first seen in the eponymous 2001 title, here learns — with the help of his friends — about preparing classroom presentations. (Rev: BL 9/1/07; SLJ 7/07)

1953 Kellogg, Steven. *The Mysterious Tadpole: 25th Anniversary Edition* (PS–2). Illus. 2002, Dial $16.99 (978-0-8037-2788-5). 36pp. This anniversary edition brings a slightly longer text and new illustrations to the story of the tadpole that won't stop growing. (Rev: BL 11/1/02; HBG 3/03)

1954 Kellogg, Steven, retel. *Chicken Little* (1–3). Illus. by Steven Kellogg. 1985, Morrow paper $6.99 (978-0-688-07045-8). 32pp. A wacky version of the old favorite. (Rev: BCCB 11/85; BL 9/1/85; SLJ 10/85)

1955 Kelly, Mark. *Mousetronaut Goes to Mars* (PS–K). Illus. by C. F. Payne. 2013, Simon & Schuster $16.99 (978-144248426-9). 40pp. Disappointed not to be chosen for the Mars mission, Meteor decides to sneak on board anyway, and eventually saves the entire mission. (Rev: BL 11/1/13; SLJ 10/13)

1956 Kempter, Christa. *Dear Little Lamb* (PS–2). Trans. from German by Michelle Maczka. Illus. by Frauke Weldin. 2006, North-South $16.95 (978-0-7358-2086-9). A clever wolf strikes up a pen-pal relationship with a young lamb, hoping eventually for a tasty meal, but the lamb's smart mother sees the danger and scuppers the wolf's plot. (Rev: SLJ 10/06)

1957 Kempter, Christa. *Wally and Mae* (PS–2). Illus. by Frauke Weldin. 2008, North-South $16.95 (978-0-7358-2208-5). 32pp. Two unlikely friends — a bunny and a bear — figure out how to work with, through, and around each other's quirky habits. (Rev: SLJ 9/08)

1958 Kennedy, Kim. *Hee-Haw-Dini and the Great Zambini* (K–3). Illus. by Doug Kennedy. 2009, Abrams $15.95 (978-0-8109-7025-0). 32pp. A donkey named Hee-Haw and a mouse named Chester persist in their dream of becoming magicians — and a lucky find helps them along the way. (Rev: BL 4/1/09; SLJ 4/09)

1959 Ketteman, Helen. *Armadillo Tattletale* (K–3). Illus. by Keith Graves. 2000, Scholastic $16.99 (978-0-590-99723-2). 32pp. In this original folktale, Armadillo's ears are cut down to a proper size to stop him from hearing — and passing on — gossip. (Rev: BCCB 11/00; BL 12/15/00; HBG 3/01; SLJ 9/00)

1960 Ketteman, Helen. *If Beaver Had a Fever* (PS–1). Illus. by Kevin O'Malley. 2011, Marshall Cavendish $16.99 (978-0-7614-5951-4). 32pp. A little bear wonders how his mom would treat a variety of sick animals. (Rev: BLO 11/15/11; LMC 1–2/12; SLJ 9/1/11)

1961 Kherdian, David. *Come Back, Moon* (PS). Illus. by Nonny Hogrogian. 2013, Simon & Schuster $16.99 (978-144245887-1). 32pp. Bear has stolen the moon, believing it is the reason for his insomnia, but the other animals want it back and their search for a solution finally leads them to wise Owl. (Rev: BL 11/1/13; LMC 5–6/14*; SLJ 11/13*)

1962 Kilaka, John. *Fresh Fish: A Tale from Tanzania* (K–3). Illus. by author. 2005, Groundwood $16.95 (978-0-88899-656-5). 28pp. Despite Sokwe Chimpanzee's generosity, Dog steals fish from him and is put on trial by the other animals; he is sentenced, makes his penance, and all is forgiven. (Rev: BCCB 6/05; SLJ 6/05)

1963 Kim, Byung-Gyu, and K. T. Hao. *The 100th Customer* (PS–2). Illus. by Giuliano Ferri. 2005, Purple Bear $15.95 (978-1-933327-03-7). 32pp. In this heartwarming tale about the power of generosity, Ben Bear and Chris Croc, co-owners of a pizza restaurant arrange to help a hungry boy and his grandmother. (Rev: BL 11/1/05; SLJ 1/06)

1964 Kimura, Ken. *999 Frogs Wake Up* (PS–2). Illus. by Yasunari Murakami. 2013, NorthSouth $17.95 (978-0-7358-4108-6). 48pp. A mother frog and 998 of her froglets wake up on a spring morning; once the 999th has finally joined them, they set about waking the other animals, including unfortunately a snake. (Rev: BL 3/1/13; HB 5–6/13; SLJ 2/13)

1965 Kimura, Ken. *Nine Hundred Ninety-nine Tadpoles* (PS–3). Illus. by Yasunari Murakami. 2011, NorthSouth $16.95 (978-0-7358-4013-3). 48pp. Things get too crowded in the pond when Mother and Father Frog produce 999 youngsters, and they all set off on a dangerous (and funny) journey to a bigger home. (Rev: BL 7/11; HB 7–8/11; SLJ 6/11)

1966 Kinerk, Robert. *Clorinda* (PS–2). Illus. by Steven Kellogg. 2003, Simon & Schuster $15.95 (978-0-689-86449-0). After a very brief stint as a performer, Clorinda the cow heads back to the farm and there shares her knowledge of ballet. (Rev: BL 11/1/03; HBG 4/04; SLJ 11/03)

1967 Kirk, Daniel. *Library Mouse* (K–3). Illus. by author. 2007, Abrams $32.00 (978-0-8109-9346-4). Sam the mouse lives in the library and one night places his own book on the shelves for the children to read. (Rev: BL 9/1/07; SLJ 10/07)

1968 Kirk, Daniel. *Library Mouse: Home Sweet Home* (K–2). Illus. by author. 2013, Abrams $16.95 (978-141970544-1). 40pp. Sam and Sarah, library mice, must find temporary lodging while the library is being renovated, so together they gather books about architecture and supplies from the library to make houses ranging from yurts and geodesic domes to more classical structures. Lexile AD670 (Rev: BL 9/15/13; SLJ 8/13)

1969 Kirk, Daniel. *A Museum Adventure* (K–2). Illus. by author. Series: Library Mouse. 2012, Abrams $16.95 (978-141970173-3). 32pp. Mouse friends Sam and Sarah leave the library to visit a museum where they have adventures and see different kinds of art. (Rev: BLO 4/15/12)

1970 Kirk, David. *Little Miss Spider* (PS–1). Illus. 1999, Scholastic $12.95 (978-0-439-08389-8). 32pp. After hatching, Little Miss Spider sets out to find her mother and is helped by a kindly green beetle named Betty; introduces a new smaller format. Also use *Little Miss Spider at Sunny Patch School* (2000). (Rev: BL 12/1/99; HBG 3/00; SLJ 11/99)

1971 Kirk, David. *Miss Spider's Wedding* (K–4). Illus. 1995, Scholastic $16.95 (978-0-590-56866-1). Miss Spider finds she is very wrong when she thinks handsome Spiderus Reeves is "Mr. Right." A sequel to *Miss Spider's Tea Party* (1993) and followed by *Miss Spider's New Car* (1997). (Rev: BL 10/1/95; SLJ 10/95)

1972 Kirsch, Vincent X. *Freddie and Gingersnap* (PS–1). Illus. by Vincent X. Kirsch. 2014, Disney/Hyperion $16.99 (978-142315958-2). 40pp. After initial hostilities a dragon and a dinosaur find that friendship and cooperation actually benefit them both. (Rev: BL 11/15/13; LMC 8–9/14; SLJ 11/13)

1973 Klassen, Jon. *I Want My Hat Back* (K–2). Illus. by author. 2011, Candlewick $15.99 (978-0-7636-5598-3). 40pp. A frustrated bear looking for his missing red hat asks various other animals but totally ignores the fact that his friend Rabbit has been wearing it all along. (Rev: BL 11/1/11; SLJ 8/1/11)

1974 Klassen, Jon. *This Is Not My Hat* (K–2). Illus. by author. 2012, Candlewick $15.99 (978-0-7636-5599-0). 40pp. A diminutive minnow only thinks he's gotten away with hat theft, while readers will see the hat's rightful owner — an ominously big fish — following right behind him. Caldecott Medal; ALA Notable Children's Book; Kate Greenaway Medal. Lexile 340AD (Rev: BL 8/12*; HB 9–10/12; LMC 1–2/13*; SLJ 9/12*)

1975 Klausmeier, Jesse. *Open This Little Book* (PS–K). Illus. by Suzy Lee. 2013, Chronicle $16.99 (978-0-8118-6783-2). 40pp. Designed as a series of books within books, this unusual title features animals reading stories that lead into each other. (Rev: BLO 3/15/13; HB 7–8/13; SLJ 4/13*)

1976 Kleven, Elisa. *Sun Bread* (PS–1). Illus. 2001, Dutton $16.99 (978-0-525-46674-1). Longing for sun, the baker makes a sun-shaped loaf so enticing that the animals cheer up and sun breaks through the clouds. (Rev: BL 5/1/01; HBG 10/01; SLJ 6/01)

1977 Kleven, Elisa. *Welcome Home, Mouse* (PS–K). Illus. by author. 2010, Tricycle $15.99 (978-1-58246-277-6). 32pp. A clumsy elephant apologizes for knocking down a mouse's house and builds a new one out of found materials. Lexile AD530L (Rev: BL 1/1–15/11; SLJ 9/1/10)

1978 Klise, Kate. *Grammy Lamby and the Secret Handshake* (PS–1). Illus. by M. Sarah Klise. 2012, Henry Holt $16.99 (978-0-8050-9313-1). 32pp. A little lamb named Larry learns to love his grandmother when he sees how good she is at fixing roofs. Lexile 560AD (Rev: BL 8/12; HB 9–10/12; LMC 11–12/12; SLJ 8/12)

1979 Klise, Kate. *Little Rabbit and the Meanest Mother on Earth* (1–3). Illus. by M. Sarah Klise. 2010, Harcourt $17 (978-0-15-206201-9). 32pp. Convinced he has the meanest mother on Earth, Little Rabbit suggests to a circus ringmaster that he might want to put her on display. (Rev: BLO 5/15/10; SLJ 3/1/10)

1980 Klise, Kate. *Little Rabbit and the Night Mare* (K–2). Illus. by M. Sarah Klise. 2008, Harcourt $16.00 (978-0-15-205717-6). 32pp. Plucky Little Rabbit conquers his Night Mare and even uses it as the subject of his dreaded class report. (Rev: BLO 6/17/08; SLJ 8/08)

1981 Klise, Kate. *Why Do You Cry? Not a Sob Story* (PS–2). Illus. by M. Sarah Klise. 2006, Holt $16.95 (978-0-8050-7319-5). 32pp. Little Rabbit finds out that crying's OK when others reveal what makes them cry. (Rev: BL 5/1/06; SLJ 7/06)

1982 Knudsen, Michelle. *Big Mean Mike* (K–2). Illus. by Scott Magoon. 2012, Candlewick $15.99 (978-0-7636-4990-6). 40pp. Big Mean Mike, one tough dog with a cool car, is initially threatened by the sweet fluffy bunnies that appear in his hot rod. Lexile AD520L (Rev: BL 9/1/12; LMC 1–2/13; SLJ 10/12)

1983 Knudsen, Michelle. *Library Lion* (PS–2). Illus. by Kevin Hawkes. 2006, Candlewick $15.99 (978-0-7636-2262-6). 48pp. Miss Merriweather, the head librarian, is very particular about the library's rules, but she's not sure what to do when a lion pays a visit. (Rev: BL 8/06; SLJ 8/06*)

1984 Koehler, Fred. *How to Cheer Up Dad* (PS–K). Illus. by author. 2014, Dial $16.99 (978-080373922-2). 32pp. Little Jumbo, a young elephant with a talent for creating chaos, is unhappy when his Dad seems to be downcast. (Rev: BL 3/1/14*; SLJ 4/14)

1985 Kohuth, Jane. *Duck Sock Hop* (PS–K). Illus. by Jane Porter. 2012, Dial $16.99 (978-080373712-9). 32pp. Once a week the ducks get together, choose colorful socks from the box, and dance to the music! (Rev: BL 5/15/12; SLJ 6/1/12)

1986 Kohuth, Jane. *Ducks Go Vroom* (PS–K). Illus. by Viviana Garofoli. 2011, Random House paper $3.99 (978-0-375-86-560-2). 32pp. For beginning readers, this onomatopoeic story about a family of lively ducks visiting a goose relative uses repetition, large type, and bright cartoon illustrations. **℮** (Rev: BL 12/15/10; SLJ 2/1/11)

1987 Kolanovic, Dubravka. *Everyone Needs a Friend* (PS–2). Illus. by author. 2010, Price Stern Sloan $9.99 (978-0-8431-9918-5). 32pp. Jack, a lonely wolf, would like a friend, but is Walter the mouse exactly right? (Rev: BL 10/1/10; SLJ 9/1/10)

1988 Kolar, Bob. *Big Kicks* (PS–3). Illus. by author. 2008, Candlewick $16.99 (978-0-7636-3390-5). 40pp. Biggie Bear is a quiet stamp collector who succeeds in the most unexpected way when he reluctantly agrees to help the local soccer team. (Rev: BL 9/1/08; SLJ 9/08)

1989 Kolar, Bob. *Racer Dogs* (PS–2). Illus. by author. 2003, Dutton $16.99 (978-0-525-45939-2). 32pp. Dogs zoom racecars around a track and end up in a jumbled pileup in this funny picture book. (Rev: BL 2/1/03; HBG 10/03; SLJ 3/03)

1990 Koller, Jackie F. *Baby for Sale* (PS–2). Illus. by Janet Pedersen. 2002, Marshall Cavendish $16.95 (978-0-7614-5106-8). 32pp. Rabbit Peter, fed up with his baby sister, tries to sell her to the neighbors but finally decides to keep her when he realizes that he loves her. (Rev: BL 9/1/02; HBG 3/03; SLJ 9/02)

1991 Kono, Erin Eitter. *Caterina and the Perfect Party* (PS–K). Illus. by author. 2013, Dial $16.99 (978-0-8037-3902-4). 32pp. Despite her love of planning, Caterina, a small, brown bird, is surprised and disappointed when rain disrupts her carefully organized outdoor party. (Rev: BLO 7/13; SLJ 6/13)

1992 Koontz, Robin Michal. *The Case of the Missing Goldfish* (K–2). Illus. by author. Series: Short Tales: Furlock & Muttson Mysteries. 2010, ABDO LB $22.78 (978-1-60270-561-6). 32pp. Furry detectives Furlock and Muttson are hot on the trail of a goldfish-napper in this entertaining story. Also use *The Case of the Mystery Museum* and *The Case of the Shifting Stacks* (both 2010). (Rev: SLJ 4/1/10)

1993 Korda, Lerryn. *Into the Wild* (PS). Illus. by author. Series: Playtime with Little Nye. 2010, Candlewick $7.99 (978-0-7636-4812-1). 26pp. Little Nye's friend Gracie prepares for an expedition to the edge of the yard and her friends beg to come along. (Rev: BL 4/15/10; SLJ 4/1/10)

1994 Korda, Lerryn. *It's Vacation Time* (PS). Illus. by author. Series: Playtime with Little Nye. 2010, Candlewick $8.99 (978-0-7636-4813-8). Unpaged. Little Nye's friend Nella struggles to shut a bulging suitcase in this entertaining story about getting ready for vacation. (Rev: SLJ 4/1/10)

1995 Kraus, Robert. *Leo the Late Bloomer* (PS–K). Illus. by Jose Aruego. 1971, HarperCollins LB $17.89 (978-0-87807-043-5). 32pp. Leo, a lion, is just a late bloomer, as Mother tells Father, but Father is worried. Finally Leo blooms — he can read, write, and eat neatly. A beguiling, humorous story.

1996 Kraus, Robert. *Mouse in Love* (PS–2). Illus. by Jose Aruego and Ariane Dewey. 2000, Orchard LB $16.99 (978-0-531-33297-9). 32pp. Mouse searches high and low for the mouse of his dreams and finds that she lives next door. (Rev: BCCB 11/00; BL 9/15/00; HBG 3/01; SLJ 8/00)

1997 Krauss, Ruth. *And I Love You* (PS–1). Illus. by Steven Kellogg. 2010, Scholastic $16.99 (978-0-439-02459-4). 40pp. Originally published as *Big and Little* in 1987, this story featuring a kitten and his mother conveys the comforting message that big people love and appreciate youngsters everywhere. (Rev: BL 9/15/10; SLJ 9/1/10)

1998 Krishnaswami, Uma. *Remembering Grandpa* (K–3). Illus. by Layne Johnson. 2007, Boyds Mills $16.95 (978-1-59078-424-2). A little rabbit tries to ease her grandmother's grief over her husband's death. (Rev: SLJ 4/07)

1999 Kroll, Steven. *Jungle Bullies* (PS–1). Illus. by Vincent Nguyen. 2006, Marshall Cavendish $16.99 (978-0-7614-5297-3). Mama Monkey teaches the bullying bigger animals a lesson about sharing. (Rev: SLJ 11/06)

2000 Kroll, Virginia. *On the Way to Kindergarten* (PS–2). Illus. by Elisabeth Schlossberg. 2006, Putnam $15.99 (978-0-399-24168-0). 32pp. As Bear gets ready to go to kindergarten, rhyming couplets celebrate the many milestones in his first five years of development. (Rev: BL 2/15/06; SLJ 3/06)

2001 Kroll, Virginia. *Really Rabbits* (PS–2). Illus. by Philomena O'Neill. 2006, Charlesbridge $16.95 (978-1-57091-897-1); paper $6.95 (978-1-57091-898-8). 32pp. Pet rabbits Tulip and Snuggle mystify their human owners when they help out around the house during the night in hopes of getting more attention during the day. (Rev: BL 7/06; SLJ 8/06)

2002 Kromhout, Rindert. *Little Donkey and the Baby-Sitter* (PS–K). Trans. by Marianne Martens. Illus. by Annemarie van Haeringen. 2006, North-South $15.95 (978-0-7358-2057-9). A little donkey causes all sorts of trouble for his hen baby-sitter in this gentle and amusing book. (Rev: SLJ 7/06)

2003 Krupinski, Loretta. *Pirate Treasure* (PS–2). Illus. 2006, Dutton $15.99 (978-0-525-47579-8). 40pp. When a storm drives their pirate ship upriver, Captain Oliver and First Mate Rosie, both mice, decide to trade their buccaneering ways for life as farmers. (Rev: BL 2/15/06; SLJ 3/06)

2004 Kurtz, Rob. *Seamus McNamus: The Goat Who Would Be King* (PS–2). Illus. by Mike Lester. 2009, IDW $16.99 (978-1-60010-337-7). 40pp. When things

on the farm get tough, a plucky young goat sets out to find work. (Rev: BL 6/1–15/09)

2005 Laden, Nina. *When Pigasso Met Mootisse* (K–2). Illus. 1998, Chronicle $15.95 (978-0-8118-1121-7). 40pp. Two painters, Pigasso, a pig, and Mootisse, a bull, become rivals in the art world in this takeoff on the Picasso-Matisse feud. (Rev: BL 11/1/98; HBG 3/99; SLJ 11/98)

2006 Lakin, Patricia. *Camping Day!* (PS–2). Illus. by Scott Nash. 2009, Dial $16.99 (978-0-8037-3309-1). The crocodile friends seen in *Snow Day* (2002) go on an exciting camping trip that turns sour when spooky nighttime sounds and shadows send them scrambling home to finish the trip in the safe familiarity of their own backyards. (Rev: BLO 6/16/09; SLJ 6/09)

2007 Lakin, Patricia. *Clarence the Copy Cat* (PS–2). Illus. by John Manders. 2002, Doubleday LB $17.99 (978-0-385-90854-2). 32pp. Clarence the cat is a pacifist and won't catch mice, which makes it difficult for him to find a home until he discovers the library, but even there a mouse finally turns up and causes much hilarity. (Rev: BL 11/1/02; HBG 3/03; SLJ 10/02)

2008 Lakin, Patricia. *Snow Day!* (PS–1). Illus. by Scott Nash. 2002, Dial $15.99 (978-0-8037-2642-0). 32pp. There's a twist to this story of four crocodiles playing in the snow — they're all school principals. (Rev: BL 11/15/02; HBG 3/03; SLJ 11/02)

2009 Lamb, Albert. *Sam's Winter Hat* (PS). Illus. by David McPhail. 2006, Scholastic $6.99 (978-0-439-79304-9). 32pp. Sam Bear is very forgetful and needs the help of his family and friends to find all of his misplaced items, including the blue winter hat his Grandma made. (Rev: BL 12/1/06; SLJ 10/06)

2010 Lamb, Rosy. *Paul Meets Bernadette* (PS–2). Illus. by author. 2013, Candlewick $14 (978-076366130-4). 40pp. Bored goldfish Paul's world expands when he is joined by an imaginative new companion called Bernadette; humor and lush illustrations add to the appeal of this picture book. Lexile AD350 (Rev: BL 11/15/13; LMC 8–9/14*; SLJ 1/1/14*)

2011 Landolf, Diane Wright. *Hog and Dog* (PS–K). Illus. by Jennifer Beck Harris. Series: Step into Reading. 2005, Random LB $11.99 (978-0-375-93165-9); paper $3.99 (978-0-375-83165-2). 32pp. Hog and Dog are good friends despite the occasional disagreement in this fast-paced book for beginning readers. (Rev: BL 10/15/05)

2012 Landry, Leo. *Grin and Bear It* (K–3). Illus. by author. 2011, Charlesbridge $12.95 (978-1-57091-745-5). 48pp. A shy bear who knows how to write jokes and an outgoing hummingbird who knows how to deliver them make an unlikely comic duo in this story about facing your fears. (Rev: BL 7/11; HB 9–10/11; SLJ 7/11)

2013 Landstrom, Lena. *Boo and Baa Have Company* (PS–2). Trans. by Joan Sandin. Illus. by Olof Landstrom. 2006, Farrar $15.00 (91-29-66546-9). 40pp. Comical mishaps ensue when sheep Boo and Baa attempt to rescue a cat stuck in a tree and to do some vacuuming. (Rev: BL 8/06; HB 9/06; HBG 4/07; SLJ 9/06)

2014 Landstrom, Lena. *A Hippo's Tale* (PS–2). Illus. 2007, Farrar $15.00 (91-29-66603-1). In this gentle story, Mrs. Hippopotamus discovers a clever solution to deal with the intruders on her private beach. (Rev: BL 5/1/07; SLJ 7/07)

2015 LaRochelle, David. *Moo!* (PS–2). Illus. by Mike Wohnoutka. 2013, Walker $16.99 (978-080273409-9). 40pp. Full of repetition and rhyme, this is a bouncy tale about a cow who takes the farmer's car for a joyride. ALA Notable Children's Book. e (Rev: BL 9/1/13; SLJ 8/13*)

2016 Lasky, Kathryn. *Poodle and Hound* (1–3). Illus. by Mitch Vane. 2009, Charlesbridge $12.95 (978-1-58089-322-0). 48pp. In the three stories in this book, Poodle and Hound discover that even though they often are annoyed by each other, their differences can be interesting and helpful. (Rev: BL 7/09; SLJ 7/09)

2017 Lasky, Kathryn. *Tumble Bunnies* (K–2). Illus. by Marylin Hafner. 2005, Candlewick $15.99 (978-0-7636-2265-7). Clyde, a bunny who never seems to get picked for the team, is pleased to discover the pleasure of individual events such as trampoline. (Rev: SLJ 4/05)

2018 Lass, Bonnie, and Philemon Sturges. *Who Took the Cookies from the Cookie Jar?* (PS–K). Illus. by Ashley Wolff. 2000, Little, Brown $14.95 (978-0-316-82016-5). 32pp. A little skunk, dressed as a cowboy, becomes a detective and inquires of various animals who stole the cookies from the cookie jar. (Rev: BCCB 12/00; BL 10/15/00; HBG 3/01; SLJ 10/00)

2019 Latimer, Alex. *Lion vs. Rabbit* (PS–2). Illus. by author. 2013, Peachtree $15.95 (978-156145709-0). 32pp. Lion won't stop bullying the animals of the jungle, and they simply don't know what to do, but luckily, Rabbit has just the cure, besting Lion at multiple contests that reward wit and guile. (Rev: BLO 9/15/13; LMC 3–4/14; SLJ 9/13)

2020 Latimer, Alex. *Penguin's Hidden Talent* (PS–1). Illus. by author. 2012, Peachtree $15.95 (978-1-56145-629-1). 32pp. Unsure of his own talents, Penguin decides to take charge of organizing the community talent show — and thereby discovers his own skills. Lexile AD500L (Rev: BL 12/15/12; SLJ 2/13)

2021 Lawrence, John. *This Little Chick* (PS–K). Illus. 2002, Candlewick $15.99 (978-0-7636-1716-5). 32pp. A little chick learns the many languages of the barnyard as he visits his animal friends. (Rev: BCCB 4/02; BL 2/1/02; HBG 10/02; SLJ 3/02*)

2022 Layton, Neal. *Hot Hot Hot* (K–3). Illus. by author. 2004, Candlewick $15.99 (978-0-7636-2148-3). A light-hearted story about a pair of woolly mammoths, Oscar and Arabella, and how they try to keep cool when summer suddenly comes in the middle of the Ice Age. (Rev: HB 7/04; SLJ 6/04)

2023 Layton, Neal. *The Mammoth Academy* (2–4). 2008, Holt $16.95 (978-0-8050-8708-6). 160pp. Woolly mammoth Oscar isn't happy about starting school but soon

finds a friend in Fox in this funny, fast-paced book set in the Ice Age. (Rev: BLO 9/2/08)

2024 Leaf, Munro. *The Story of Ferdinand* (K–4). Illus. by Robert Lawson. 1936, Puffin paper $7.99 (978-0-14-050234-3). 72pp. The classic story of the bull who wants only to sit and smell flowers.

2025 Lee, Ho Baek. *While We Were Out* (PS–1). Illus. by author. 2003, Kane $15.95 (978-1-929132-44-7). An adventurous white rabbit finds herself home alone and decides to try some of the luxuries of human life. (Rev: BL 4/15/03*; HB 7/03; HBG 10/03; SLJ 6/03)

2026 Leedy, Loreen. *The Furry News: How to Make a Newspaper* (1–4). Illus. 1990, Holiday House LB $17.95 (978-0-8234-0793-4). Big Bear becomes disgusted with his local newspaper and decides to publish his own. (Rev: BCCB 5/90; BL 5/1/90)

2027 Leedy, Loreen. *The Great Trash Bash* (K–2). Illus. 1991, Holiday House LB $17.95 (978-0-8234-0869-6). Mayor Hippo discovers that his town has too much trash. (Rev: SLJ 5/91)

2028 Leedy, Loreen. *The Monster Money Book* (2–4). Illus. 1992, Holiday House LB $17.95 (978-0-8234-0922-8). 32pp. Sarah joins a monster club and learns about various denominations of money. (Rev: BCCB 3/92; BL 3/15/92; SLJ 6/92)

2029 Leeuwen, Jean Van. *Five Funny Bunnies: Three Bouncing Tales* (PS–1). Illus. by Anne Wilsdorf. 2012, Marshall Cavendish $17.99 (978-0-7614-6114-2). 32pp. In three stories five young rabbit siblings visit their grandmother, practice jumping, and enjoy storytime; with charming watercolor-and-ink illustrations. e (Rev: BLO 4/1/12; SLJ 4/1/12)

2030 Lester, Helen. *All for Me and None for All* (PS–1). Illus. by Lynn Munsinger. 2012, Houghton Mifflin $16.99 (978-054768834-3). 32pp. A greedy pig named Gruntly learns to share when he realizes his pushy, grab-by ways make him do things without thinking. (Rev: BL 3/15/12*; SLJ 5/1/12)

2031 Lester, Helen. *Batter Up Wombat* (PS–K). Illus. by Lynn Munsinger. 2006, Houghton $16.00 (978-0-618-73784-0). 32pp. Wordplay abounds in this story of an Australian wombat whose efforts to play ball are unusual, but whose skill at digging tunnels is much appreciated when the National Wildlife League game is interrupted by a tornado. (Rev: BL 9/15/06; SLJ 10/06)

2032 Lester, Helen. *Hooway for Wodney Wat* (PS–2). Illus. by Lynn Munsinger. 1999, Houghton $16.00 (978-0-395-92392-4). A humorous story about Wodney Wat and his problems pronouncing the letter *r*. (Rev: BL 5/1/99; HB 7/99; HBG 10/99; SLJ 5/99)

2033 Lester, Helen. *A Porcupine Named Fluffy* (PS–K). Illus. by Lynn Munsinger. 1986, Houghton $16.00 (978-0-395-36895-4); paper $6.95 (978-0-395-52018-5). Fluffy's ridiculous name leads to a friendship with a rhino, with another ridiculous name — Hippo. (Rev: BL 4/15/86; SLJ 8/86)

2034 Lester, Helen. *The Sheep in Wolf's Clothing* (PS–2). Illus. by Lynn Munsinger. 2007, Houghton $16.00 (978-

103

0-618-86844-5). 32pp. The sheepish tale of young and insecure Ewetopia whose skill at dressing up saves the day as well as the flock. (Rev: BCCB 10/07; BL 10/1/07; SLJ 9/07)

2035 Lester, Helen. *Wodney Wat's Wobot* (PS–2). Illus. by Lynn Munsinger. 2011, Houghton Mifflin $16.99 (978-0-547-36756-9). 32pp. Young rat Wodney gets a talking robot (wobot) for his birthday that turns out to be a useful foil for the class bully Camilla. (Rev: BL 9/1/11; SLJ 8/1/11)

2036 Levy, Janice. *Gonzalo Grabs the Good Life* (K–2). Illus. by Bill Slavin. 2009, Eerdmans $17.50 (978-0-8028-5328-8). 32pp. Gonzalo the rooster wins the lottery and promptly leaves his farm job and heads for the high life in this humorous book full of wordplay. (Rev: BL 3/1/09; SLJ 3/09)

2037 Lewis, Kevin. *Dinosaur Dinosaur* (PS–2). Illus. by Daniel Kirk. 2006, Scholastic $15.99 (978-0-439-60371-3). 32pp. A dinosaur kid has a typical dinosaur (human) day in rhyming text and humorous art full of details like "The Dinosaur Times" newspaper, Dino Puffs cereal, and a "trilobite farm." (Rev: BL 2/1/06; SLJ 3/06)

2038 Lewis, Kevin. *My Truck Is Stuck!* (PS–K). Illus. by Daniel Kirk. 2002, Hyperion $14.99 (978-0-7868-0534-1). When their dump truck gets stuck, the two dogs hauling a load of bones seek help, in this amusing, brightly illustrated book with a teasing subplot and some basic counting reminders. (Rev: BL 11/1/02; HBG 3/03; SLJ 10/02)

2039 Lewis, Kim. *Seymour and Henry* (PS). Illus. by author. 2009, Candlewick $15.99 (978-0-7636-4243-3). 32pp. Soft pastel illustrations enhance this gentle tale of two ducklings who disobediently run off and hide, become cold, wet, and scared, and return to their mother who lovingly tucks them into bed. (Rev: BLO 6/19/09; SLJ 5/09)

2040 Leznoff, Glenda. *Pigmalion* (K–2). Illus. by Rachel Berman. 2002, Tradewind $15.95 (978-1-896580-20-3). Little pig Juliet is a skilled singer, actor, and dancer but so shy that she must rehearse in private when she's chosen for the part of Eliza Piglittle. (Rev: SLJ 8/02)

2041 Lies, Brian. *Bats at the Ballgame* (K–2). Illus. by author. 2010, Houghton Mifflin $16.99 (978-0-547-24970-4). 32pp. In this fanciful trip to the baseball diamond, furry bats flit around the bases while their fans eat "mothdogs" and hang upside down in the stands. (Rev: BLO 7/10; SLJ 8/1/10)

2042 Lies, Brian. *Bats at the Beach* (K–2). 2006, Houghton $16.00 (978-0-618-55744-8). 32pp. A family of bats spends a pleasant night at the beach, using "moon-tan lotion" and eating "bug-mallows." (Rev: BL 8/06; SLJ 6/06)

2043 Lin, Grace. *Olvina Flies* (PS–1). Illus. 2003, Holt $15.95 (978-0-8050-6711-8). 32pp. Olvina, a hen, is reluctant to take her first airplane ride but finds a friend in a fellow traveler, a penguin. (Rev: BL 2/1/03; HB 5/03; HBG 10/03; SLJ 4/03)

2044 Lincoln, Hazel. *Little Elephant's Trunk* (PS–K). Illus. by author. 2006, Albert Whitman $15.95 (978-0-8075-4591-1). A baby elephant unsure what to do with his trunk watches his elders and experiments. (Rev: SLJ 10/06)

2045 Lindgren, Barbro. *Oink, Oink Benny* (PS). Trans. by Elisabeth Kallick Dyssegaard. Illus. by Olof Landstrom. 2008, Farrar $16.00 (91-29-66855-7). 28pp. Benny and Binky, young pig brothers, head for the mudhole despite their mother's admonitions. (Rev: BCCB 5/08; BL 4/1/08; HB 5/08; SLJ 5/08)

2046 Lionni, Leo. *Alexander and the Wind-Up Mouse* (K–2). Illus. by author. 1969, Pantheon paper $5.99 (978-0-394-82911-1). Alexander, a real mouse, envies Willy, a toy, windup mouse, who is loved and cuddled.

2047 Lionni, Leo. *The Biggest House in the World* (PS–2). Illus. by author. 1968, Knopf paper $5.99 (978-0-394-82740-7). 32pp. A young snail, desiring a larger shell, receives fatherly advice and decides that small accommodations are an asset in regaining his mobility.

2048 Lionni, Leo. *Frederick* (PS–2). Illus. by author. 1967, Knopf LB $18.99 (978-0-394-91040-6); paper $5.99 (978-0-394-82614-1). A field mouse appears to be ignoring the coming of winter, but actually he is not.

2049 Lionni, Leo. *Inch by Inch* (PS–2). Illus. by author. 1962, Astor-Honor $15.95 (978-0-8392-3010-6). When the birds demand that he measure the length of a nightingale's song, this clever, captive inchworm inches his way to freedom.

2050 Lionni, Leo. *Swimmy* (PS–1). Illus. by author. 1963, Knopf paper $5.99 (978-0-394-82620-2). 40pp. A remarkable little fish instructs the rest of his school in the art of protection — swim in the formation of a gigantic fish! Beautiful, full-color illustrations.

2051 Lithgow, John. *Mahalia Mouse Goes to College* (PS–2). Illus. by Igor Oleynikov. 2007, Simon & Schuster $17.99 (978-1-4169-2715-0). 40pp. Mahalia Mouse crashes a Harvard science class, befriends a professor, and earns her degree in this charming story that was part of Lithgow's commencement address at Harvard in 2005; with CD. (Rev: BL 6/1–15/07; SLJ 5/07)

2052 Liwska, Renata. *Red Wagon* (PS–1). Illus. by author. 2011, Philomel $16.99 (978-0-399-25237-2). 32pp. Lucy the fox and her animal friends have a fanciful adventure on their way into town with a shopping list and her little red wagon. (Rev: BL 2/15/11*; HB 1–2/11; SLJ 2/1/11)

2053 Lloyd, Sam. *Mr. Pusskins and Little Whiskers* (PS–1). Illus. by author. 2008, Atheneum $15.99 (978-1-4169-5796-6). 32pp. Mr. Pusskins's contented new life is threatened when Emily brings a rambunctious kitten home. (Rev: BLO 7/29/08; SLJ 5/08)

2054 Lloyd, Sam. *Mr. Pusskins: A Love Story* (PS–2). Illus. by author. 2006, Simon & Schuster $14.95 (978-1-4169-2517-0). 32pp. Tired of the smothering love of his young owner, Mr. Pusskins the cat sets off to see what life is like outside his narrowly defined world, but he soon longs for the comforts of home. (Rev: BL 11/1/06; HBG 4/07; SLJ 1/07)

2055 Lobel, Arnold. *Fables* (2–4). Illus. by author. 1980, HarperCollins LB $17.89 (978-0-06-023974-9); paper $6.99 (978-0-06-443046-3). 48pp. An Americanized Aesop with excellent illustrations. Caldecott Medal winner, 1981.

2056 Lobel, Gill. *Too Small for Honey Cake* (PS–2). Illus. by Sebastien Braun. 2006, Harcourt $16.00 (978-0-15-206097-8). 32pp. Little Fox is sad when he thinks the new baby has taken his place in Daddy Fox's heart. (Rev: BL 9/1/06; SLJ 10/06)

2057 Lobel, Gillian. *Little Honey Bear and the Smiley Moon* (PS–2). Illus. by Tim Warnes. 2006, Good Bks. $16.00 (978-1-56148-533-8). Little Honey Bear, Lily Long Ears, and Teeny Tiny Mouse hope to visit the moon but become lost in the dark woods and are eventually rescued by Mommy Bear. (Rev: SLJ 11/06)

2058 London, Jonathan. *Froggy Goes to Hawaii* (PS–1). Illus. by Frank Remkiewicz. 2011, Viking $15.99 (978-067001221-3). 32pp. Froggy has a very exciting time when he and his family visit Hawaii. (Rev: BLO 5/1/11)

2059 London, Jonathan. *Froggy Plays Soccer* (PS–1). Illus. by Frank Remkiewicz. 1999, Viking $15.99 (978-0-670-88257-1). Froggy is a failure during the soccer game to win the City Cup until he gets a reminder from Dad and kicks the winning goal. Also use *Let's Go, Froggy!* (1994), *Froggy Goes to School* (1996), *Froggy's First Kiss* (1998), *Froggy Eats Out* (2001), *Froggy Plays in the Band* and *Froggy Goes to the Doctor* (2002), *Froggy's Day with Dad* (2004), and *Froggy Plays T-Ball* (2007). (Rev: BL 3/1/99; HBG 10/99; SLJ 3/99)

2060 Long, Ethan. *Chamelia* (PS–2). Illus. by author. 2011, Little, Brown $16.99 (978-031608612-7). 40pp. Bored with blending in, Chamelia the Chameleon starts dressing to stand out; eventually she realizes she can be herself and still find acceptance amongst the other lizards. (Rev: BL 4/1/11; LMC 10/11)

2061 Long, Ethan. *Pig Has a Plan* (PS–2). Illus. by author. Series: I Like to Read. 2012, Holiday $14.95 (978-0-8234-2428-3). 32pp. Pig wants to take a nap, but the other animals in the farmyard are just too noisy. (Rev: BLO 10/1/12; SLJ 9/12)

2062 Loomis, Christine. *Hattie Hippo* (PS). Illus. by Robert Neubecker. 2006, Scholastic $16.99 (978-0-439-54340-8). 32pp. Four episodes follow Hattie the young hippo through a series of minor mishaps. (Rev: BL 8/06; SLJ 8/06)

2063 Lord, Cynthia. *Happy Birthday, Hamster* (PS–K). Illus. by Derek Anderson. 2011, Scholastic $16.99 (978-0-545-25522-6). 40pp. Convinced his friends have forgotten his birthday, a hamster doesn't notice the birthday-party-supplies shopping going on in the background; a companion to *Hot Rod Hamster* (2010). (Rev: BLO 9/1/11; SLJ 10/1/11)

2064 Lord, Cynthia. *Hot Rod Hamster* (PS–K). Illus. by Derek Anderson. 2010, Scholastic $16.99 (978-0-545-03530-9). 40pp. In this lively rhymed book, a speed-

demon hamster prepares for and competes in a big race. (Rev: BL 12/1/09; LMC 5–6/10; SLJ 1/1/10)

2065 Loth, Sebastian. *Clementine* (PS–2). Illus. by author. 2011, NorthSouth $14.95 (978-0-7358-4009-6). 32pp. Clementine, a snail with a devotion to round things, and her friend, a snake, make two failed attempts to reach the moon using a trampoline and a slingshot before they decide on a rocket. (Rev: BL 4/1/11; SLJ 5/1/11)

2066 Loth, Sebastian. *Remembering Crystal* (PS–K). Illus. by author. 2010, NorthSouth $14.95 (978-0-7358-2300-6). 64pp. A goose named Zelda mourns her turtle friend and remembers the good times they had together. (Rev: BL 8/10; LMC 10/10; SLJ 6/1/10)

2067 Lowell, Susan. *The Three Little Javelinas* (PS–3). Illus. by Jim Harris. 1992, Northland LB $15.95 (978-0-87358-542-2). 32pp. This Americanized version of the "Three Little Pigs" features a coyote instead of the wolf. (Rev: BL 1/1/93)

2068 Lucas, David. *Peanut* (PS–2). Illus. by author. 2008, Candlewick $15.99 (978-0-7636-3925-9). 32pp. A tiny monkey is filled with fear — he is afraid of wild animals, rain, the setting sun — until a beetle causes him to fall and he recognizes his own abilities. (Rev: SLJ 3/09)

2069 Lund, Deb. *All Aboard the Dinotrain* (K–2). Illus. by Howard Fine. 2006, Harcourt $16.00 (978-0-15-205237-9). 40pp. In this spirited sequel to *Dinosailors* (2003), a band of adventurous dinosaurs goes for a memorable ride on a runaway train. (Rev: BL 4/1/06; SLJ 5/06)

2070 Lund, Deb. *Dinosailors* (K–2). Illus. by Howard Fine. 2003, Harcourt $16.00 (978-0-15-204609-5). 40pp. Six dinosaurs set out to sea with humorous results told in rhyming verse. (Rev: BL 9/1/03; HBG 4/04; SLJ 9/03)

2071 McAllister, Angela. *Barkus, Sly and the Golden Egg* (K–2). Illus. by Sally Anne Lambert. 2002, Bloomsbury $15.95 (978-1-58234-764-6). Three crafty chickens plan a clever escape from two dastardly foxes and alert the townspeople to the foxes' thieving ways. (Rev: SLJ 9/02)

2072 McAllister, Angela. *Brave Bitsy and the Bear* (PS–3). Illus. by Tiphanie Beeke. 2006, Clarion $16.00 (978-0-618-63994-6). 29pp. Grateful for the help of a big bear who helped her to get back home when she was lost in the woods, Bitsy the toy bunny finds a way to repay his kindness. (Rev: SLJ 10/06)

2073 McAllister, Angela. *Take a Kiss to School* (PS). Illus. by Sue Hellard. 2006, Bloomsbury $15.95 (978-1-58234-702-8). 32pp. Digby the mole's mother gives him a reassuring collection of kisses to build up his courage for his second day at school. (Rev: BL 8/06; SLJ 7/06)

2074 McBratney, Sam. *There, There* (PS). Illus. by Ivan Bates. 2013, Candlewick $15.99 (978-076366702-3). 40pp. Hansie Bear loves to play, and each time he gets hurt, his father is there to offer advice and sympathy, telling him, "There there . . ." and giving him a hug —

but when Dad gets hurt, it's Hansie who is there to comfort his father. (Rev: BL 9/15/13; SLJ 9/13)

2075 McBratney, Sam. *Yes We Can!* (PS–K). Illus. by Charles Fuge. 2007, HarperCollins $16.99 (978-0-06-121515-5). Little Roo, Quacker Duck, and Country Mouse find out that it's no fun when friends tease one another and learn to encourage one another instead. (Rev: SLJ 7/07)

2076 McCarty, Peter. *Chloe* (PS–1). Illus. by author. 2012, HarperCollins $16.99 (978-006114291-8). 40pp. Rabbit Chloe and her brothers and sisters decide they'd rather rely on their creativity for fun than watch their family's new television. (Rev: BL 4/15/12*; SLJ 5/1/12*)

2077 McCarty, Peter. *Henry in Love* (K–2). Illus. by author. 2010, HarperCollins $16.99 (978-0-06-114288-8); LB $17.89 (978-0-06-114289-5). 48pp. Lovestruck cat Henry shamelessly courts a pretty young bunny, resorting to all sorts of over-the-top antics in this humorous story. (Rev: BL 12/1/09; SLJ 1/1/10*)

2078 McClements, George. *Dinosaur Woods* (PS–1). Illus. by author. 2009, Simon & Schuster $16.99 (978-1-4169-8626-3). 40pp. Threatened by destruction of their habitat, a group of canny (and endangered) animals create a fierce dinosaur to scare off the demolition team. (Rev: BL 5/1/09; LMC 10/09; SLJ 6/09)

2079 McClements, George. *Ridin' Dinos with Buck Bronco* (1–3). Illus. by author. 2007, Harcourt $16.00 (978-0-15-205989-7). 32pp. All you need to know about riding and caring for dinosaurs of various kinds. (Rev: BL 10/15/07; SLJ 9/07)

2080 McCullough, Sharon Pierce. *Bunbun at the Fair* (PS). Illus. by author. 2002, Barefoot Books $14.99 (978-1-84148-900-1). Bunbun, a mischievous little rabbit, goes missing at the fair and his siblings search for him. (Rev: HBG 3/03; SLJ 12/02)

2081 McCully, Emily Arnold. *School* (PS–K). Illus. 2005, HarperCollins $15.99 (978-0-06-623856-2). 32pp. Bitty the mouse follows her older siblings to school and has a happy time in this new version of the 1987 wordless classic that features brief text and a larger format. (Rev: BL 8/05; SLJ 9/05)

2082 MacDonald, Margaret Read. *Pickin' Peas* (PS–3). Illus. by Pat Cummings. 1998, HarperCollins LB $15.89 (978-0-06-027970-7). 32pp. Little Girl uses various tactics to prevent Mr. Rabbit from picking the peas in her garden. (Rev: BL 7/98; HBG 10/98; SLJ 10/98)

2083 McDonald, Megan. *Hen Hears Gossip* (PS–2). Illus. by Joung Un Kim. 2008, Greenwillow $16.99 (978-0-06-113876-8). 32pp. Hen's gossip is passed around the farm until the facts are totally unrecognizable. (Rev: BL 7/08; SLJ 4/08)

2084 McElligott, Matthew. *Bean Thirteen* (K–3). Illus. by author. 2007, Putnam $15.99 (978-0-399-24535-0). How to evenly share thirteen beans? This is the challenge that bugs Flora and Ralph face, and what gets them thinking about division. A wonderful introduction to division for young learners. (Rev: SLJ 6/07)

2085 McElligott, Matthew. *The Lion's Share* (1–3). Illus. by author. 2009, Walker $16.99 (978-0-8027-9768-1). A sensitive ant turns the tables on impolite and greedy animals who have been invited to the king of the jungle's annual party; the story offers opportunities to practice division and multiplication. (Rev: BL 1/1–15/09; SLJ 2/09)

2086 McEvoy, Anne. *Betsy B. Little* (PS–1). Illus. by Jacqueline Rogers. 2009, HarperCollins $17.99 (978-0-06-059337-7). 32pp. Betsy, a cheerful giraffe, is exceedingly tall and unsuited to her dream of being a ballerina but she eventually learns to deal with her height in a highly satisfying way. (Rev: BL 1/1–15/09; SLJ 1/09)

2087 McKee, David. *Elmer and Rose* (PS–1). Illus. by author. 2010, Andersen $16.95 (978-0-7613-5493-2). Unpaged. Patchwork elephant Elmer meets a pink elephant called Rose who is lost, in this story about being different. (Rev: LMC 8–9/10; SLJ 3/1/10)

2088 McKee, David. *Elmer and the Big Bird* (PS–2). Illus. by author. 2012, Andersen $16.95 (978-146770319-2). 32pp. Patchwork elephant Elmer uses his imagination to deal with a bully. (Rev: BLO 12/15/12)

2089 McKee, David. *Elmer and the Kangaroo* (PS–K). Illus. 2000, HarperCollins $15.99 (978-0-688-17951-9). 32pp. Elmer, a patchwork elephant, helps a kangaroo newly arrived in the forest to gain confidence about his jumping ability. (Rev: BL 5/15/00; HBG 10/00; SLJ 5/00)

2090 McKee, David. *Elmer and the Lost Teddy Bear* (PS–K). Illus. 1999, Lothrop $15.99 (978-0-688-16912-1). Elmer, the patchwork elephant, helps Baby Elephant who is sad because he has lost his teddy bear. (Rev: BL 6/1–15/99; HBG 10/99; SLJ 7/99)

2091 McKee, David. *Elmer in the Snow* (PS–1). Illus. by author. 1995, Lothrop $15.99 (978-0-688-14596-5). In this picture book, a patchwork elephant takes some other elephants to snow-covered mountains so they will appreciate the meaning of cold. (Rev: SLJ 12/95)

2092 McKee, David. *Elmer's Special Day* (PS–2). Illus. by author. 2009, Andersen $16.95 (978-0-7613-5154-2). Unpaged. The other animals are jealous of the annual parade of decorated elephants, and Elmer invites them to join in. (Rev: SLJ 10/1/09)

2093 McMillan, Bruce. *The Problem with Chickens* (PS–2). Illus. by Gunnella. 2005, Houghton $16.00 (978-0-618-58581-6). 32pp. The chickens bought by the women of an Icelandic village begin to act more like their owners than like birds. (Rev: BL 9/15/05; SLJ 9/05*)

2094 McMullan, Kate. *Bulldog's Big Day* (K–2). Illus. by Pascal Lemaitre. 2011, Scholastic $16.99 (978-0-545-17155-7). 32pp. A bulldog eager to find his place in the world tries a variety of occupations before discovering that his talent for baking cookies offers an opportunity. Lexile AD540L (Rev: BL 2/15/11*; SLJ 2/1/11)

2095 McMullan, Kate. *I'm Big!* (PS–1). Illus. by Jim McMullan. 2010, HarperCollins $16.99 (978-0-06-122974-9). 40pp. A giant purple sauropod wakes up late and discovers his herd has disappeared, leaving him to face scary predators alone. (Rev: BL 10/15/10; SLJ 8/1/10)

2096 McPhail, David. *The Bear's Toothache* (PS–K). Illus. by author. 1972, Little, Brown paper $5.95 (978-0-316-56325-3). 32pp. A very funny story of a little boy's attempt to help extract a bear's tooth and rid him of his toothache.

2097 McPhail, David. *Big Brown Bear Goes to Town* (PS–1). Illus. by author. 2006, Harcourt $16.00 (978-0-15-205317-8). 40pp. Big Brown Bear has an idea to protect his friend Rat's car from the elements, so together the two go into town to get the necessary materials. (Rev: BL 6/1–15/06; SLJ 5/06)

2098 McPhail, David. *Big Brown Bear's Up and Down Day* (PS). Illus. by author. 2003, Harcourt $16.00 (978-0-15-216407-2). Big Brown Bear is not at all happy when Rat tries to trick him out of his slipper, but in time the two become friends who share. (Rev: BCCB 10/03; BL 11/03; HBG 4/04; SLJ 11/03)

2099 McPhail, David. *Drawing Lessons from a Bear* (PS–2). Illus. 2000, Little, Brown $14.95 (978-0-316-56345-1). An old bear reminisces about his life as a cub and how he decided to devote his life to drawing and teaching others the love of drawing. (Rev: BCCB 3/00; BL 2/15/00; HBG 10/00; SLJ 5/00)

2100 McPhail, David. *Lost!* (PS–K). Illus. 1990, Little, Brown $14.95 (978-0-316-56329-1). A young boy tries to help a bear get home from the big city. (Rev: BL 4/1/90; HB 5/90; SLJ 6/90)

2101 McPhail, David. *Pig Pig Meets the Lion* (PS–1). Illus. by author. 2012, Charlesbridge $15.95 (978-158089358-9). 32pp. A lion that has escaped from the zoo follows Pig Pig around the house as his mother obliviously goes about her morning tasks. Lexile AD420L (Rev: BL 2/1/12; SLJ 1/12)

2102 McPhail, David. *Pig Pig Returns* (PS–K). Illus. by author. 2011, Charlesbridge $16.95 (978-1-58089-356-5). 32pp. Despite his initial worries, Pig Pig enjoys cross-country travel with his aunt and uncle and has mixed feelings about coming home. (Rev: BL 5/1/11; SLJ 7/11)

2103 McPhail, David. *Waddles* (PS–2). Illus. by author. 2011, Abrams $15.95 (978-0-8109-8415-8). 32pp. Waddles, a fat raccoon, pines for his friend Emily the duck during her long winter away, but celebrates their reunion each spring. (Rev: BL 2/15/11; LMC 8–9/11; SLJ 4/11)

2104 Marino, Gianna. *Too Tall Houses* (PS–3). Illus. by author. 2012, Viking $16.99 (978-0-670-01314-2). 40pp. Friends and neighbors Rabbit and Owl indulge in a building contest as they fret about getting enough sunlight and views. Lexile 420L (Rev: BLO 9/1/12; LMC 3–4/13; SLJ 8/12*)

2105 Markel, Michelle. *Tyrannosaurus Math* (1–3). Illus. by Doug Cushman. 2009, Tricycle $15.99 (978-1-58246-282-0). 32pp. A young math-loving T. Rex drives his family crazy with his constant calculating until one day he uses his math abilities to save his sister. (Rev: BL 7/09)

2106 Marshall, James. *George and Martha* (PS–1). Illus. by author. 1972, Houghton $16.00 (978-0-395-16619-2); paper $6.95 (978-0-395-19972-5). 48pp. The friendship of two hippos leads to some very humorous situations. Also use the sequels: *George and Martha Encore* (1973); *George and Martha Rise and Shine* (1977); *George and Martha One Fine Day* (1982); *George and Martha Back in Town* (1984); *George and Martha Tons of Fun* (1986).

2107 Martin, Bill, Jr. *A Beasty Story* (PS–3). Illus. by Steven Kellogg. 1999, Harcourt $17.00 (978-0-15-201683-8). 40pp. Four mice explore a dark, dark house to find the beast they know lives inside. (Rev: BL 9/15/99; HBG 3/00; SLJ 9/99)

2108 Martin, Bill, Jr., and John Archambault. *Barn Dance!* (PS–2). Illus. by Ted Rand. 1986, Holt $16.95 (978-0-8050-0089-4); paper $6.95 (978-0-8050-0799-2). 32pp. The animals are holding a lively barn dance on a full-moon night. (Rev: BL 1/15/87; SLJ 2/87)

2109 Martin, Bill, Jr., and Michael Sampson. *Kitty Cat, Kitty Cat, Are You Waking Up?* (PS–1). Illus. by Laura J. Bryant. 2008, Marshall Cavendish $14.99 (978-0-7614-5438-0). 24pp. A mother cat struggles to get her young kitten up and off to school in this humorous rhyming narrative enhanced by lively watercolors. (Rev: BL 7/08; SLJ 9/08)

2110 Martin, David. *All for Pie, Pie for All* (PS–2). Illus. by Valeri Gorbachev. 2006, Candlewick $15.99 (978-0-7636-2393-7). 32pp. After the cat family enjoys an apple pie cooked by Grandma Cat, the remaining piece is carted away by Grandma Mouse, who sees that her whole family is fed, leaving a tiny piece that provides a satisfying meal for a family of ants. (Rev: BL 9/15/06)

2111 Martin, David. *Piggy and Dad Go Fishing* (PS–2). Illus. by Frank Remkiewicz. 2005, Candlewick $14.99 (978-0-7636-2506-1). Piggy is a sensitive soul and can't bring himself to put a worm on a hook or keep a fish once he has caught it. (Rev: SLJ 5/05)

2112 Masurel, Claire. *Domino* (PS–1). Illus. by David Walker. 2007, Candlewick $8.99 (978-0-7636-2862-8). Little Domino can go where the big dogs can't, a skill that comes in handy when a ball rolls under a fence. A cheerful tale for very young children. (Rev: SLJ 5/07)

2113 Matsuoka, Mei. *Footprints in the Snow* (PS–3). Illus. by author. 2008, Holt $16.95 (978-0-8050-8792-5). 32pp. Tired of the bad rap, Wolf begins to write a story about a nice wolf, which in turn frames a secondary story whose twists surprise even Wolf. (Rev: BL 9/15/08; LMC 1/09)

2114 Meadows, Michelle. *Hibernation Station* (PS–2). Illus. by Kurt Cyrus. 2010, Simon & Schuster $16.99 (978-1-4169-3788-3). 40pp. In this imaginative story, a train made of hollow logs rolls through the forest, collecting pajama-clad animals for their winter sleep. **e** Lexile 310L (Rev: BL 8/10; LMC 10/10; SLJ 7/1/10)

2115 Meadows, Michelle. *Piggies in the Kitchen* (PS–2). Illus. by Ard Hoyt. 2011, Simon & Schuster $14.99 (978-1-4169-3787-6). 32pp. Piggie children take over the kitchen when their mother leaves the house, creating cookies, cake, and pie — and a disastrous mess — before cleaning up in the nick of time. (Rev: BL 2/15/11; SLJ 2/1/11)

2116 Melling, David. *Don't Worry, Douglas!* (PS–1). Illus. by author. 2011, Tiger Tales $12.95 (978-1-58925-106-9). Unpaged. Douglas the bear accidentally destroys the wool hat his father gave him; in the end, he comes clean, is forgiven, and receives a new hat. (Rev: SLJ 11/1/11)

2117 Melling, David. *Hugless Douglas* (PS–1). Illus. by author. 2010, Tiger Tales $15.95 (978-1-58925-098-7). Unpaged. A funny story in which a bear cub in need of a hug tries various sources that prove uncomfortable. (Rev: SLJ 10/1/10)

2118 Meschenmoser, Sebastian. *Waiting for Winter* (PS–2). Illus. by author. 2009, Kane/Miller $15.99 (978-1-935279-04-4). 56pp. Young Squirrel is impatient for the arrival of snow but afraid that he will sleep through this new experience. (Rev: BL 11/1/09; LMC 1–2/10; SLJ 9/1/09)

2119 Middleton, Charlotte. *Nibbles: A Green Tale* (K–2). Illus. by author. 2010, Marshall Cavendish $17.99 (978-0-7614-5791-6). 32pp. A guinea pig village nearly eats its favorite food — dandelions — into extinction in this subtle parable about overconsumption and scarcity. **e** (Rev: BL 5/1/10; LMC 8–9/10; SLJ 5/1/10)

2120 Miller, Pat. *Substitute Groundhog* (K–3). Illus. by Kathi Ember. 2006, Albert Whitman $16.99 (978-0-8075-7643-4). Sidelined by the flu just before his big weather-predicting day, Groundhog auditions other animals to replace him. (Rev: SLJ 12/06)

2121 Mitton, Tony. *Dinosaurumpus!* (PS). Illus. by Guy Parker-Rees. 2003, Scholastic $15.95 (978-0-439-39514-4). Party with the dinosaurs in this joyous, energetic picture book with vivid, comical illustrations showing the dancing dinos in all their scaly glory. (Rev: BL 1/1–15/03; HBG 10/03; SLJ 3/03)

2122 Mitton, Tony. *Down by the Cool of the Pool* (PS–2). Illus. by Guy Parker-Rees. 2002, Scholastic $16.99 (978-0-439-30915-8). A group of animals dance and leap around the pool until they all fall in — and continue to party in the water. (Rev: HBG 10/02; SLJ 7/02)

2123 Mitton, Tony. *A Very Curious Bear* (PS–1). Illus. by Paul Howard. 2009, Random $16.99 (978-0-375-85083-7). 32pp. A little bear is full of questions — "Why does the sun come and light up the day?" — that are asked and answered in rhyme. (Rev: BL 4/1/09; SLJ 5/09)

2124 Modarressi, Mitra. *Taking Care of Mama* (PS–2). Illus. by author. 2010, Putnam $16.99 (978-0-399-25216-7). 32pp. When Mama is in bed with a cold, Papa and the three young raccoons are initially eager to shoulder her responsibilities; a sequel to *Stay Awake, Sally* (2007). (Rev: BL 2/1/10; SLJ 4/1/10)

2125 Monroe, Chris. *Monkey with a Tool Belt* (K–3). Illus. by author. 2008, Carolrhoda LB $16.95 (978-0-8225-7631-0). A mechanically minded monkey named Chico Bon Bon puts his tool belt to good effect when

he is captured by an organ grinder. (Rev: BCCB 6/08; SLJ 2/08)

2126 Monroe, Chris. *Monkey with a Tool Belt and the Noisy Problem* (PS–2). Illus. by author. 2009, Carolrhoda $16.95 (978-0-8225-9247-1). Using the tools in his trusty belt, Chico the monkey rescues an elephant named Clark from the laundry chute; detailed illustrations add to the appeal. (Rev: BCCB 7–8/09; BL 4/1/09; SLJ 3/09)

2127 Monroe, Chris. *Sneaky Sheep* (PS–1). Illus. by author. 2010, Carolrhoda LB $16.95 (978-0-7613-5615-8). 32pp. Two mischievous sheep, Rocky and Blossom, escape from the sheepdog, but their greener pasture proves to harbor a wolf and suddenly they need that kindly and brave dog. (Rev: BL 10/15/10; SLJ 9/1/10)

2128 Moore, Inga. *A House in the Woods* (PS–2). Illus. by author. 2011, Candlewick $16.99 (978-0-7636-5277-7). 48pp. After their home is accidentally destroyed by Bear and Moose, two little pigs recruit the help of some beavers to build a new abode. (Rev: BL 12/1/11; SLJ 10/1/11)

2129 Morgan, Michaela. *Brave, Brave Mouse* (PS–K). Illus. by Michelle Cartlidge. 2004, Whitman $15.95 (978-0-8075-0869-5). 32pp. Little Mouse fights his many fears by silently repeating rhymes that reinforce his inner strength. (Rev: BL 1/1–15/05; SLJ 11/04)

2130 Morgan, Michaela. *Bunny Wishes* (K–2). Illus. by Caroline Jayne Church. 2007, Scholastic $16.99 (978-0-439-91812-1). The wind carries Teeny and Tino's wish lists into the hands of the baby mice who play with the words until a new message is revealed in this sequel to *Dear Bunny* (2006). (Rev: BL 11/1/07)

2131 Morgan, Michaela. *Dear Bunny* (K–2). Illus. by Caroline Jayne Church. 2006, Scholastic $15.99 (978-0-439-74833-9). 32pp. Tino and Teeny, two shy but lovestruck bunnies, leave each other love notes that are shredded by a family of mice building a nest; all ends well when the mice realize what they have done and make amends. (Rev: BL 2/1/06; SLJ 1/06)

2132 Morrow, Barbara Olenyik. *Mr. Mosquito Put on His Tuxedo* (K–2). Illus. by Ponder Goembel. 2009, Holiday $16.95 (978-0-8234-2072-8). 32pp. The exquisitely dressed Mr. Mosquito saves the day at the insect-only royal ball and is dubbed the "Royal Pest" in this nicely illustrated tale. (Rev: BL 1/1–15/09; HB 5/09; SLJ 2/09)

2133 Mortimer, Anne. *Pumpkin Cat* (PS–2). Illus. by author. 2011, HarperCollins $14.99 (978-0-06-187485-7). 24pp. A mouse teaches his cat friend how to plant and tend a pumpkin vine all through spring and summer; the story culminates with carving jack o'lanterns. (Rev: BLO 8/11; SLJ 7/11)

2134 Moss, Miriam. *A Babysitter for Billy Bear* (PS–1). Illus. by Anna Currey. 2008, Dial $16.99 (978-0-8037-3269-8). 32pp. Billy Bear and his toy rabbit experience their first evening with a babysitter. (Rev: BL 7/08; SLJ 6/08)

2135 Moss, Miriam. *Bare Bear* (PS–2). Illus. by Mary McQuillan. 2005, Holiday House $16.95 (978-0-8234-1934-0). 32pp. Busby the bear finds himself bare after the wind blows his clothes off a clothesline; during his search to find the garments he meets some oddly dressed animals and an ogre. (Rev: BL 3/15/05; SLJ 3/05)

2136 Moss, Miriam. *Don't Forget I Love You* (PS–2). Illus. by Anna Currey. 2004, Dial $15.99 (978-0-8037-2920-9). 32pp. A mother bear and her son have a difficult morning when they get off to a late start. (Rev: BL 1/1–15/04; SLJ 2/04)

2137 Moss, Miriam. *Matty in a Mess!* (PS–2). Illus. by Jane Simmons. 2010, IPG/Andersen $16.99 (978-1-84270-812-5). 32pp. Bossy, tidy Matty is always after his messy sister to clean up, but when a scary storm threatens their house, it's kind, gentle Milly who saves the day. Another book in the series is *Matty Takes Off!* (2010). (Rev: BL 1/1/10; SLJ 2/1/10)

2138 Moss, Miriam. *The Snow Bear* (PS–1). Illus. by Maggie Kneen. 2001, Dutton $15.99 (978-0-525-46658-1). Winter scenes and spare, poetic text depict a polar bear cub who gets help from other animals in his search for his mother. (Rev: HBG 3/02; SLJ 10/01)

2139 Müller, Birte. *I Can Dress Myself!* (PS–K). Trans. by Marianne Martens. Illus. by author. 2007, North-South $16.95 (978-0-7358-2128-6). 32pp. Mother tries to be patient as Daisy, a young rabbit, insists on getting herself dressed. (Rev: BL 5/15/07; SLJ 6/07)

2140 Muntean, Michaela. *Do Not Open This Book!* (K–3). Illus. by Pascal LeMaitre. 2006, Scholastic $15.99 (978-0-439-66037-2). 32pp. The action here centers on a cranky pink pig/would-be author who objects to those who are trying to read his work in progress; the simple process of turning the pages draws the reader into the story. ALA Notable Children's Book. (Rev: BL 3/15/06)

2141 Murguia, Bethanie Deeney. *Snippet: The Early Riser* (K–1). Illus. by author. 2013, Knopf $15.99 (978-1-58246-460-2). 40pp. Readers will learn about snails and their beautiful shells as they enjoy this entertaining story about a young snail who has difficulty waking his sleepy family. e (Rev: BLO 3/15/13; SLJ 3/13)

2142 Murray, Marjorie Dennis. *Hippo Goes Bananas!* (PS–1). Illus. by Kevin O'Malley. 2006, Marshall Cavendish $14.95 (978-0-7614-5224-9). Hippo has a toothache, and his strange behavior unnerves the other animals in this cumulative tale. (Rev: SLJ 5/06)

2143 Muth, Jon J. *Zen Shorts* (K–3). Illus. 2005, Scholastic $17.99 (978-0-439-33911-7). 40pp. A beautifully illustrated introduction to Zen thinking through Stillwater the panda, who tells three children meaningful stories that make them see the world and each other in new ways. Caldecott Honor Book, 2006. (Rev: BL 3/1/05; SLJ 2/05)

2144 Myers, Walter Dean. *The Blues of Flats Brown* (K–3). Illus. by Nina Laden. 2000, Holiday House $16.95 (978-0-8234-1480-2). 32pp. Two junkyard dogs, the musical Flats Brown and his friend Caleb, escape their mean owner — who wants to make them fighting dogs — by means of Flats' great blues playing. (Rev: BCCB 2/00; BL 3/1/00*; HBG 10/00; SLJ 3/00)

2145 Myers, Walter Dean. *Looking for the Easy Life* (K–2). Illus. by Lee Harper. 2011, HarperCollins $16.99 (978-0-06-054375-4). 40pp. Led by Uh-Huh Freddie and Oswego Pete, five monkeys on Monkey Island set out to find "the easy life" but discover that maybe a little hard work isn't so bad after all; features African American dialect and cartoon illustrations. Lexile 750L (Rev: BL 3/15/11; SLJ 2/1/11)

2146 Na, Il Sung. *The Thingamabob* (PS–K). Illus. by author. 2010, Knopf $15.99 (978-0-375-86106-2). 24pp. Hilarity and confusion ensue when an innocent elephant happens upon a red umbrella in this humorous tale with compelling illustrations. (Rev: BL 2/1/10; LMC 5–6/10; SLJ 3/1/10)

2147 Nishimura, Kae. *Bunny Lune* (K–2). Illus. by author. 2007, Clarion $15.00 (978-0-618-71606-7). 32pp. After learning about a Japanese lunar celebration, Bunny Lune becomes preoccupied with the moon and comes up with harebrained schemes to raise money for his own lunar voyage. (Rev: BL 5/15/07; SLJ 8/07)

2148 Nitto, Tomio. *The Red Rock: A Graphic Fable* (K–2). 2006, Groundwood $15.95 (978-0-88899-669-5). 32pp. To save his beloved valley from destruction by developers, Old Beaver and his animal friends mount a campaign to block the project. (Rev: BL 4/15/06; LMC 11/06)

2149 Noguès, Jean-Come. *House for a Mouse* (PS–2). Trans. by J. Alison James. Illus. by Anne Velghe. 2005, North-South $15.95 (978-0-7358-2017-3). While searching for a home of her own, Little Mouse encounters an artist and agrees to pose as his model. (Rev: SLJ 11/05)

2150 Nolan, Janet. *A Father's Day Thank You* (PS–K). Illus. by Kathi Ember. 2007, Albert Whitman $16.99 (978-0-8075-2291-2). 32pp. For Father's Day, Harvey the bear cub decides to do a drawing of all the things his dad has done for him. (Rev: BL 4/1/07)

2151 Nolan, Lucy. *A Fairy in a Dairy* (PS–2). Illus. by Laura J. Bryant. 2003, Marshall Cavendish $16.95 (978-0-7614-5130-3). Decked out in a pink tutu, Pixie the cow brings dairy magic to the town of Buttermilk Hollow, which finds itself in dire financial straits. (Rev: HBG 4/04; SLJ 11/03)

2152 Numeroff, Laura. *If You Give a Dog a Donut* (PS–2). Illus. by Felicia Bond. 2011, HarperCollins $16.99 (978-0-06-026683-7). 32pp. This circular story features a donut-toting dog seeking one thing after another until he ends up where he left off. (Rev: BLO 11/15/11; SLJ 10/1/11)

2153 Numeroff, Laura. *If You Give a Moose a Muffin* (PS–2). Illus. by Felicia Bond. Series: If You Give a . . . 1991, HarperCollins LB $17.89 (978-0-06-024406-4). This circular tale begins with a moose being lured to a boy's house to receive a muffin. (Rev: BCCB 9/91; BL 7/91; SLJ 12/91*)

2154 Numeroff, Laura. *If You Give a Mouse a Cookie* (PS–K). Illus. by Felicia Bond. Series: If You Give a . . . 1985, HarperCollins LB $17.89 (978-0-06-024587-0).

32pp. A little mouse asks for a variety of things until the floor is a clutter of goods. This is followed by *If You Take a Mouse to the Movies* (2000) and *If You Take a Mouse to School* (2002). (Rev: BCCB 7–8/85; BL 6/1/85; HBG 10/01; SLJ 5/85)

2155 Numeroff, Laura. *If You Give a Pig a Pancake* (PS–1). Illus. by Felicia Bond. Series: If You Give a . . . 1998, HarperCollins LB $16.89 (978-0-06-026687-5). 32pp. Giving a pig a pancake leads from one consequence to another until we get back to a new plate of pancakes. A sequel is *If You Give a Pig a Party* (2000), in which the enthusiastic protagonist wants a better and better party. (Rev: BCCB 6/98; BL 5/15/98; HBG 10/98; SLJ 7/98)

2156 Numeroff, Laura. *Otis and Sydney and the Best Birthday Ever* (PS–1). Illus. by Dan Andreasen. 2010, Abrams $16.95 (978-0-8109-8959-7). 32pp. Best bear friends Sydney and Otis are happy to share Sydney's birthday party themselves when the party invitations go awry. (Rev: BL 9/1/10; SLJ 12/1/10)

2157 Numeroff, Laura. *What Mommies Do Best / What Daddies Do Best* (PS–1). Illus. by Lynn Munsinger. 1998, Simon & Schuster $13.00 (978-0-689-80577-6). 40pp. In these two stories the reader discovers that both parents do all of the activities pictured — making snowmen, reading stories, watching the sunset — equally well. (Rev: BL 4/1/98; HBG 3/99; SLJ 4/98)

2158 Numeroff, Laura, and Nate Evans. *The Jellybeans and the Big Art Adventure* (K–2). Illus. by Lynn Munsinger. Series: The Jellybeans. 2012, Abrams $16.95 (978-1-4197-0171-9). 32pp. When Bitsy the paint-loving pig is asked to create a mural, she invites her differently talented friends along to help and provide support; the fourth installment in the series. (Rev: BLO 1/25/12; SLJ 4/1/12)

2159 Numeroff, Laura, and Nate Evans. *The Jellybeans and the Big Camp Kickoff* (K–2). Illus. by Lynn Munsinger. Series: The Jellybeans. 2011, Abrams $16.95 (978-0-8109-9765-3). Unpaged. At Camp Pook-A-Woo the four animal friends with different talents and abilities all try to use them to best effect, although Nicole (a cat) is initially disappointed that there is no soccer. (Rev: SLJ 5/1/11)

2160 Nyeu, Tao. *Bunny Days* (PS). Illus. by author. 2010, Dial $16.99 (978-0-8037-3330-5). 48pp. Three gentle tales of easily reparable mishaps feature a group of bunnies, a helpful bear, and familiar household appliances; quilt-like art adds atmosphere. (Rev: BL 1/1/10; SLJ 12/1/09)

2161 Odanaka, Barbara. *A Crazy Day at the Critter Café* (K–2). Illus. by Lee White. 2009, Simon & Schuster $16.99 (978-1-4169-3914-6). 32pp. A quiet day at the Critter Café is interrupted when a busload of rude and hungry animals arrives. (Rev: BL 5/1/09; SLJ 6/09)

2162 Odanaka, Barbara. *Smash! Mash! Crash! There Goes the Trash!* (PS–2). Illus. by Will Hillenbrand. 2006, Simon & Schuster $15.95 (978-0-689-85160-5). 32pp. From their bedroom, two little pigs watch a pair of garbage trucks making their early morning rounds, pick-

ing up everything from old furniture to stinky diapers; rhyming text and expressive illustrations add to the fun. (Rev: BL 12/1/06; SLJ 11/06)

2163 Oh, Jiwon. *Mr. Monkey's Classroom* (K–2). Illus. 2005, HarperCollins LB $15.89 (978-0-06-055722-5). 32pp. On his first day at school, Mouse becomes jealous when his friend Cat — one year older — rushes off to join old friends; a sequel to *Cat and Mouse: A Delicious Tale* (2003). (Rev: BL 8/05)

2164 Ohi, Ruth. *A Trip with Grandma* (PS–1). Illus. by author. 2007, Annick LB $19.95 (978-1-55451-072-6); paper $5.95 (978-1-55451-071-9). 32pp. Frightened at first by the prospect of being separated from his parents, young gerbil Sprout comes to enjoy a road trip with his sister and Grandma. (Rev: BL 5/15/07)

2165 O'Keefe, Susan Heyboer. *Baby Day* (PS). Illus. by Robin Spowart. 2006, Boyds Mills $15.95 (978-1563979811). A day in the life of a baby bear looked after by loving parents. (Rev: BL 3/1/06)

2166 Oldland, Nicholas. *The Busy Beaver* (PS–K). Illus. by author. 2011, Kids Can $16.95 (978-1-55453-749-5). Unpaged. An eager and previously thoughtless beaver realizes apologies are due to his animal friends who have been injured or annoyed by his chewing trees down willy-nilly. (Rev: SLJ 9/1/11)

2167 Oldland, Nicholas. *Making the Moose Out of Life* (PS–2). Illus. by author. 2010, Kids Can $16.95 (978-1-55453-580-4). 32pp. A reserved and timid moose is inspired to participate more fully in life after a scary experience at sea. (Rev: SLJ 10/1/10)

2168 O'Malley, Kevin. *Leo Cockroach . . . Toy Tester* (PS–2). Illus. 1999, Walker LB $16.85 (978-0-8027-8690-6). 32pp. Leo Cockroach feels he is unappreciated as a prize toy tester, so he decides to move on. (Rev: BCCB 6/99; BL 4/15/99; HBG 10/99; SLJ 4/99)

2169 Ormerod, Jan. *If You're Happy and You Know It!* (PS). Illus. by Lindsey Gardiner. 2003, Star Bright $15.95 (978-1-932065-07-7); paper $5.95 (978-1-932065-10-7). 32pp. Animals demonstrate ways to show happiness in this update of the classic song. (Rev: BL 3/15/03; HBG 10/03; SLJ 5/03)

2170 Ormerod, Jan. *When an Elephant Comes to School* (PS–2). Illus. 2005, Scholastic $16.95 (978-0-439-73967-2). 32pp. An elephant's first day at school is made easier by thoughtful actions on the part of other students. (Rev: BL 6/1–15/05)

2171 Palatini, Margie. *Bad Boys* (K–2). Illus. by Henry Cole. 2003, HarperCollins LB $16.89 (978-0-06-000103-2). Willy and Wally Wolf, on the run from the Three Little Pigs and Little Red Riding Hood, dress up in sheep's clothing in the hope of fooling Trudie Ewe and Meryl Sheep. (Rev: BCCB 11/03; BL 11/15/03; HBG 4/04; LMC 3/04; SLJ 11/03)

2172 Palatini, Margie. *Boo-Hoo Moo* (K–2). Illus. by Keith Graves. 2009, HarperCollins $17.99 (978-0-06-114375-5). 32pp. Whimsical, colorful illustrations and clever text tell a funny tale of farm animal friends who hold singing auditions for a chorus to accompany sad Hilda Mae Heifer's despondent mooing. (Rev: SLJ 2/09)

2173 Palatini, Margie. *Earthquack!* (PS–1). Illus. by Barry Moser. 2002, Simon & Schuster $15.95 (978-0-689-84280-1). The barnyard becomes alarmed, Henny-Penny-style, when the animals feel what they think is an earthquake in this rhyming tale. (Rev: BCCB 7–8/02; BL 7/02; HBG 10/02; SLJ 6/02)

2174 Palatini, Margie. *Gorgonzola: A Very Stinkysaurus* (PS–2). Illus. by Tim Bowers. 2007, HarperCollins $16.99 (978-0-06-073897-6). 32pp. A stinky dinosaur with a sad history learns about soap, toothpaste, and mouthwash in this funny take on cleanliness. (Rev: SLJ 5/08)

2175 Palatini, Margie. *Hogg, Hogg, and Hog* (K–3). Illus. by author. 2011, Simon & Schuster $15.99 (978-1-4424-0322-2). 32pp. Three trendsetting pigs head to the big city to launch the "next big thing" — OINK — but must come up with a new idea after that initial fad fizzles. (Rev: BL 2/1/11; SLJ 4/11)

2176 Palatini, Margie. *Lousy Rotten Stinkin' Grapes* (PS–2). Illus. by Barry Moser. 2009, Simon & Schuster $15.99 (978-0-689-80246-1). Fox's rigid plans for reaching the grapes on a high vine are rejected by all the animals whose aid he enlists. (Rev: BL 6/1–15/09; LMC 10/09; SLJ 7/09)

2177 Palatini, Margie. *No Biting, Louise* (PS–K). Illus. by Matthew Reinhart. 2007, HarperCollins $16.99 (978-0-06-052627-6). 32pp. Young alligator Louise struggles to rid herself of her nasty habit of biting, and when she overcomes the problem, it changes to burping. (Rev: BL 11/1/07; SLJ 9/07)

2178 Palatini, Margie. *Stinky Smelly Feet: A Love Story* (PS–3). Illus. by Ethan Long. 2004, Dutton $15.99 (978-0-525-47201-8). Love between ducks Douglas and Dolores prevails despite Douglas's extremely smelly feet. (Rev: BCCB 6/04; SLJ 6/04)

2179 Palatini, Margie. *Stuff* (PS–1). Illus. by Noah Z. Jones. 2011, HarperCollins $16.99 (978-0-06-171921-9). 32pp. Edward, a rabbit with more possessions than friends, finally comes to the conclusion that he'd be happier with less stuff and more company. (Rev: BL 9/15/11; SLJ 9/1/11)

2180 Parenteau, Shirley. *Bears on Chairs* (PS–K). Illus. by David Walker. 2009, Candlewick $15.99 (978-0-7636-3588-6). 32pp. Four chairs and one-too-many bears create a simple, comic problem. (Rev: BL 11/1/09; SLJ 10/1/09)

2181 Park, Linda Sue. *Xander's Panda Party* (PS–3). Illus. by Matt Phelan. 2013, Houghton Mifflin $16.99 (978-0-54755865-3). 40pp. As he is the only panda at the zoo, Xander must find invitees to his birthday party among the other animals — but how to select them? Includes an author note on pandas' endangered status. ALA Notable Children's Book. e Lexile AD380 (Rev: BL 8/13; LMC 1–2/14; SLJ 8/13*)

2182 Parker, Marjorie Blain. *Mama's Little Duckling* (PS). Illus. by Mike Wohnoutka. 2008, Dutton $15.99 (978-0-525-47950-5). A little duck named Dandelion seeks independence but is only allowed to go off by himself after he has warned his mother of impending danger. (Rev: SLJ 2/08)

2183 Parr, Todd. *Otto Goes to Bed* (PS–K). Illus. by author. 2003, Little, Brown $9.95 (978-0-316-73873-6). The title character, a yellow dog with one red ear and one blue ear, does everything he can to put off going to bed, but his attitude changes when he discovers how much fun he can have in his dreams. (Rev: HBG 10/03; SLJ 7/03)

2184 Parr, Todd. *Otto Goes to School* (PS). Illus. 2005, Little, Brown $9.99 (978-0-316-83533-6). 24pp. Otto, the colorful dog with many human characteristics, heads off for his first day at school. (Rev: BL 8/05; SLJ 9/05)

2185 Parr, Todd. *Otto Goes to the Beach* (PS–K). Illus. by author. 2003, Little, Brown $9.95 (978-0-316-73870-5). Otto, a most unusually colored dog, goes to the beach in search of friends and after rejections by an ill-tempered crab and a surfing cat finally finds a kindred spirit in a purple poodle with a pink coiffure. (Rev: HBG 10/03; SLJ 7/03)

2186 Patricelli, Leslie. *The Patterson Puppies and the Midnight Monster Party* (PS–2). Illus. by author. 2010, Candlewick $14.99 (978-0-7636-3243-4). Unpaged. Her puppy siblings try to help Petra overcome her fear of the dark and conviction that a monster is lurking. (Rev: SLJ 5/1/10)

2187 Peet, Bill. *Cowardly Clyde* (K–2). Illus. by author. 1984, Houghton paper $8.95 (978-0-395-36171-9). 48pp. A horse named Clyde quivers in fear at the thought of fighting a dragon with his master, Sir Galavant. Other titles by this author and publisher are: *Ant and the Elephant* (1980); *The Luckiest One of All* (1985); *No Such Things* (1985); *Pamela Camel* (1986); *Farewell to Shady Glade* (1991).

2188 Peet, Bill. *Eli* (1–3). Illus. by author. 1984, Houghton paper $8.95 (978-0-395-36611-0). 48pp. An old lion is saved from hunters by playing dead. Others by Bill Peet and published by Houghton are: *Hubert's Hair-Raising Adventure* (1959); *Ella* (1964); *Chester the Worldly Pig* (1978); *Kermit the Hermit* (1980); *Cyrus the Unsinkable Sea Serpent* (1982).

2189 Pennypacker, Sara. *Pierre in Love* (PS–2). Illus. by Petra Mathers. 2007, Scholastic $16.99 (978-0-439-51740-9). 40pp. Pierre the mouse/fisherman is smitten with Catherine the rabbit/ballet teacher but has trouble plucking up courage to declare his love. (Rev: BL 12/15/06; SLJ 3/07)

2190 Perez, Monica. *Curious George Saves His Pennies* (PS–2). Illus. by Mary O'Keefe Young. 2013, Houghton Mifflin $12.99 (978-054763231-5). 32pp. George saves up for a $5 train only to lose his piggy bank; happily, a girl returns it and he shares the contents with her. e (Rev: BLO 12/1/12)

2191 Petz, Moritz. *Wish You Were Here* (PS–2). Illus. by Quentin Greban. 2005, North-South $15.95 (978-0-7358-2005-0). 32pp. Separated for five long days, friends Hedgehog and Mouse exchange letters and eagerly anticipate their reunion. (Rev: BL 10/1/05; SLJ 12/05)

2192 Pfanner, Louise. *Little Lucie's Diary* (PS). Illus. by author. 2008, Trafalgar $12.95 (978-1-877003-68-4). Little Lucie and Pip, mouse friends, have simple adventures together in this book that is made up partly of diary entries. (Rev: BL 6/1–15/08)

2193 Pfister, Marcus. *Bertie: Just Like Daddy* (PS–1). Illus. by author. 2009, North-South $16.95 (978-0-7358-2224-5). 32pp. A little hippo called Bertie wants to do everything just like Dad. (Rev: BLO 1/21/09; SLJ 3/09)

2194 Pfister, Marcus. *Happy Birthday, Bertie!* (PS–2). Illus. by author. 2010, NorthSouth $16.95 (978-0-7358-2280-1). 32pp. Bertie the hippo eagerly anticipates his birthday party, waiting as his family decorates, bakes a cake, and invites his animal buddies over to join in the fun. (Rev: BL 1/1/10; LMC 1–2/10; SLJ 1/1/10)

2195 Pfister, Marcus. *Rainbow Fish and the Big Blue Whale* (PS–K). Trans. by J. Alison James. Illus. 1998, North-South LB $18.88 (978-0-7358-1010-5). 32pp. Rainbow Fish and his friends are afraid that a whale who arrives in their area will eat all the krill and then eat them. Earlier books in the series include *The Rainbow Fish* (1992) and *Rainbow Fish to the Rescue!* (1995). (Rev: BL 9/15/98; HBG 3/99; SLJ 9/98)

2196 Pichon, Liz. *The Three Horrid Little Pigs* (PS–2). Illus. by author. 2008, Tiger Tales $15.95 (978-1-58925-077-2). 32pp. This happily fractured tale tells the story of three horrid little pigs and the sincerely kind wolf who teaches them how to build homes of their own. (Rev: BLO 9/17/08; LMC 1/09)

2197 Pilkey, Dav. *Dog Breath: The Horrible Trouble with Hally Tosis* (PS–2). Illus. 1994, Scholastic $16.99 (978-0-590-47466-5). 32pp. Hally Tosis, a dog with terrible breath, uses his affliction to capture two burglars. (Rev: BL 9/15/94; HB 11/94; SLJ 1/95)

2198 Pinkwater, Daniel. *Bad Bears and a Bunny: An Irving and Muktuk Story* (K–2). Illus. by Jill Pinkwater. 2005, Houghton $16.00 (978-0-618-33926-6). 32pp. Irving and Muktuk, the two naughty polar bears who live in a New Jersey zoo, come up against one tough rabbit. (Rev: BL 2/15/05; SLJ 3/05)

2199 Pinkwater, Daniel. *Bad Bears in the Big City: An Irving and Muktuk Story* (K–3). Illus. by Jill Pinkwater. 2004, Houghton $16.00 (978-0-618-25208-4). In a sequel to *Two Bad Bears* (2001), the unrepentant duo, now confined to their quarters at a New Jersey zoo, break out and embark on a muffin hunt. (Rev: BL 3/1/04; SLJ 4/04)

2200 Pinkwater, Daniel. *Bear in Love* (PS–1). Illus. by Will Hillenbrand. 2012, Candlewick $15.99 (978-07636-4569-4). 40pp. Lovely illustrations enhance this story of a gentle bear who nurtures a friendship with a rabbit as they exchange carrots and honeycombs. **e** (Rev: BL 10/1/12; HB 7–8/12; SLJ 9/12*)

2201 Pinkwater, Daniel. *Irving and Muktuk: Two Bad Bears* (PS–3). Illus. by Jill Pinkwater. 2001, Houghton

$15.00 (978-0-618-09334-2). 32pp. Two polar bears plot to steal the main attraction from a town's blueberry muffin festival. (Rev: BL 9/15/01; HBG 3/02; SLJ 9/01)

2202 Plecas, Jennifer. *Olive's Perfect World: A Friendship Story* (PS–K). Illus. by author. 2013, Philomel $16.99 (978-0-399-25287-7). 32pp. Young cat Olive's world is perfect when she and Emily are BFFs, but then new girl Eva enters the picture and Olive finds it hard to adjust. (Rev: BL 7/13; SLJ 8/13)

2203 Plourde, Lynne. *You're Wearing That to School?!* (PS–1). Illus. by Sue Cornelison. 2013, Disney/Hyperion $16.99 (978-1-4231-5510-2). 32pp. Tiny the mouse is older and less exuberant than his friend Penelope, a hippo, and feels confident enough to offer her advice on correct behavior and attire for her first day of school. (Rev: BLO 7/13; LMC 10/13; SLJ 5/13)

2204 Pochocki, Ethel. *The Blessing of the Beasts* (K–3). Illus. by Barry Moser. 2007, Paraclete $18.95 (978-1-55725-502-0). 32pp. Francesca, a cockroach, and Martin, a skunk, make their way to St. John the Divine in New York City for the annual blessing of the animals. (Rev: BL 10/1/07)

2205 Portis, Antoinette. *A Penguin Story* (PS–2). Illus. by author. 2009, HarperCollins $17.99 (978-0-06-145688-6). 40pp. Edna, a little penguin, sets off to find something more colorful than black and white and blue. (Rev: BL 11/15/08; HB 3/09; SLJ 1/09)

2206 Postgate, Daniel. *Smelly Bill: Love Stinks* (PS–1). Illus. by author. Series: Smelly Bill. 2010, Whitman $16.99 (978-0-8075-7464-5). 32pp. At the sight of poodle Peachy Snugglekins, scruffy Bill's knees go weak and he decides to clean up his act. (Rev: BL 12/1/10; LMC 1–2/11; SLJ 9/1/10)

2207 Posthuma, Sieb. *Benny* (PS–1). Illus. 2003, Kane $15.95 (978-1-929132-43-0). 32pp. A dog's sniffing ability is impaired when he comes down with a cold. (Rev: BCCB 3/03; BL 2/15/03; HB 7/03; HBG 10/03; SLJ 8/03)

2208 Potter, Beatrix. *The Complete Adventures of Peter Rabbit* (K–3). Illus. by author. 1982, Puffin paper $8.99 (978-0-14-050444-6). 96pp. An omnibus of the Peter Rabbit stories.

2209 Potter, Beatrix. *The Tales of Peter Rabbit and Benjamin Bunny* (1–2). Adapted by Sindy McKay. Illus. by author. Series: We Both Read. 1998, Treasure Bay $7.99 (978-1-891327-01-8). Two texts, one for parents and the other for children, face each other in this version that uses the original illustrations. (Rev: SLJ 3/99)

2210 Pritchett, Dylan. *The First Music* (K–3). Illus. by Erin Bennett Banks. 2006, August House $16.95 (978-0-87483-776-6). 32pp. All the animals of the jungle, each with their own sound, join together to create music in this rhythmic cumulative African tale. (Rev: BL 11/15/06; SLJ 1/07)

2211 Proimos, James. *Swim! Swim!* (PS). Illus. by author. 2010, Scholastic $16.99 (978-0-545-09419-1). 32pp. A lonely goldfish called Lerch thinks he's finally found a friend when a cat hops up to chat; "Lerch" is a pseudonym for James Proimos. (Rev: BL 5/15/10; LMC 10/10; SLJ 7/1/10)

2212 Protopopescu, Orel. *Thelonious Mouse* (PS–2). Illus. by Anne Wilsdorf. 2011, Farrar $16.99 (978-0-374-37447-1). 32pp. Thelonious can't help making music wherever he goes, which attracts the scary attentions of Fat Cat, but eventually the two find bebop companionship at the piano. (Rev: BL 5/1/11; SLJ 8/1/11)

2213 Puttock, Simon. *Miss Fox* (PS–1). Illus. by Holly Swain. 2007, Frances Lincoln $15.95 (978-1-84507-475-3). 32pp. Even though the other animal children like the substitute teacher, Lily Lamb is rightly suspicious of Miss Fox's motives. (Rev: BCCB 1/08; BL 11/1/07)

2214 Ramos, Mario. *I Am So Strong* (K–2). Trans. from French by Jean Anderson. Illus. by author. 2011, Gecko $16.95 (978-0-9582-7877-5). Unpaged. A big bad wolf used to asserting his strength meets his match when he picks on a small creature that turns out to be a baby dragon — and his mother is not pleased. (Rev: LMC 5–6/12; SLJ 10/1/11)

2215 Rathmann, Peggy. *Good Night, Gorilla* (PS–1). Illus. 1994, Penguin $14.99 (978-0-399-22445-4). After the zookeeper says good night to his animals, a playful gorilla lets them out of their cages. (Rev: BCCB 5/94; BL 7/94; HB 7/94; SLJ 7/94)

2216 Rawlinson, Julia. *Fletcher and the Falling Leaves* (PS–2). Illus. by Tiphanie Beeke. 2006, Greenwillow $16.99 (978-0-06-113401-2). 32pp. When his favorite tree begins to lose its leaves, Fletcher the fox becomes convinced that the tree is sick. (Rev: BL 8/06; SLJ 8/06*)

2217 Rawlinson, Julia. *Mule School* (PS–2). Illus. by Lynne Chapman. 2008, Good Bks. $16.95 (978-1-56148-597-0). 32pp. Stomper the mule doesn't toe the line at Mule School, but his contrariness proves an advantage when a dam bursts and floods the valley. (Rev: BLO 7/30/08; SLJ 8/08)

2218 Rayner, Catherine. *Augustus and His Smile* (PS–2). Illus. by author. 2006, Good Bks. $16.00 (978-1-56148-510-9). Augustus the tiger travels the world looking for his lost smile only to find it while looking into a puddle. (Rev: SLJ 8/06)

2219 Rayner, Catherine. *The Bear Who Shared* (PS–1). Illus. by author. 2011, Dial $16.99 (978-0-8037-3576-7). 32pp. A bear, a mouse, and a raccoon wait impatiently for a luscious fruit to ripen; when it finally falls, they share it evenly. Lexile AD400L (Rev: BL 4/1/11; SLJ 3/1/11)

2220 Rayner, Catherine. *Solomon Crocodile* (PS–2). Illus. by author. 2011, Farrar $15.99 (978-0-374-38064-9). 32pp. Roughhousing Solomon the Crocodile can't find anyone to play with in the river and rejoices when one of his own turns up. (Rev: BL 12/15/11; HB 11–12/11; SLJ 11/1/11)

2221 Regan, Dian Curtis. *The Snow Blew Inn* (PS–K). Illus. by Doug Cushman. 2011, Holiday House $16.95 (978-0-8234-2351-4). 32pp. An excited kitten eagerly anticipates the arrival of her cousin and aunt at the inn; but there is a blizzard and the inn is filling up with travelers — when will Abby and her mother get there and where will they sleep? Lexile AD560L (Rev: BL 10/15/11; SLJ 10/1/11)

2222 Reibstein, Mark. *Wabi Sabi* (K–3). Illus. by Ed Young. 2008, Little, Brown $16.99 (978-0-316-11825-5). 40pp. Wabi Sabi, a Japanese cat, sets out to discover what her name means and learns about the link between beauty and simplicity; this handsome book is illustrated with arresting collages. (Rev: BL 9/1/08; HB 1/09; SLJ 9/08) ∩

2223 Reid, Barbara. *The Subway Mouse* (PS–2). Illus. 2005, Scholastic $15.95 (978-0-439-72827-0). 40pp. Nib the mouse, who has lived his entire life in a busy subway station, sets out to find what lies beyond the confines of his subterranean world; clever 3-D photo-collages bring the story to life. (Rev: BL 9/1/05*; HBG 10/05; LMC 10/05; SLJ 8/05)

2224 Reidy, Jean. *All Through My Town* (PS–K). Illus. by Leo Timmers. 2013, Bloomsbury $14.99 (978-1-59990-785-7). 32pp. A bouncy, rhyming look around a town full of anthropomorphic characters. e (Rev: BL 3/15/13; SLJ 2/13)

2225 Rey, H. A. *Curious George* (K–4). Illus. by author. 1941, Houghton $16.00 (978-0-395-15993-4); paper $6.95 (978-0-395-15023-8). 56pp. A small monkey finds himself in difficulties due to his mischievous curiosity. Also use by the same author: *Curious George Takes a Job* (1947); *Curious George Rides a Bike* (1952); *Curious George Gets a Medal* (1957).

2226 Rey, Margaret. *Curious George Flies a Kite* (K–2). Illus. by H. A. Rey. 1973, Houghton $16.00 (978-0-395-16965-0); paper $6.95 (978-0-395-25937-5). 80pp. More predicaments are encountered by this fun-loving monkey. Also use by the same author: *Curious George Goes to the Hospital* (1973).

2227 Roberts, Bethany. *Double Trouble Groundhog Day* (PS–2). Illus. by Lorinda Bryan Cauley. 2008, Holt $16.95 (978-0-8050-8280-7). 40pp. Groundhog twins Gregory and Greta must decide which of them will assume their grandfather's duties as weather forecaster; when February 2 rolls around Gregory finds he needs his sister's support. (Rev: BLO 7/30/08)

2228 Rocco, John. *Wolf! Wolf!* (K–3). Illus. by author. 2007, Hyperion $15.99 (978-1-4231-0012-6). The Aesop fable about a boy who cries wolf is reconfigured in an Asian setting with humorous twists. (Rev: SLJ 2/07)

2229 Rockwell, Anne. *Brendan and Belinda and the Slam Dunk!* (PS–1). Illus. by Paul Meisel. 2007, HarperCollins $15.99 (978-0-06-028443-5). 40pp. Young pigs Brendan and Belinda's lives are so entwined with basketball that they can't even find time to play in the snow. (Rev: BL 7/07; SLJ 12/07)

2230 Rodman, Mary Ann. *Surprise Soup* (PS–1). Illus. by G. Brian Karas. 2009, Viking $15.99 (978-0-670-06274-4). Kevie the bear's culinary efforts come under some criticism as he, his older brother, and father make soup while they're waiting for the new baby to arrive. (Rev: BCCB 6/09; BL 3/15/09; SLJ 3/09)

2231 Rodriguez, Edel. *Sergio Makes a Splash!* (PS–1). Illus. by author. 2008, Little, Brown $15.99 (978-0-316-06616-7). 32pp. Even equipped with life preserver, floaties, and snorkel, a young penguin named Sergio is reluctant to get in the water. (Rev: BL 5/15/08; SLJ 4/08)

2232 Rodriguez, Edel. *Sergio Saves the Game* (PS–2). Illus. by author. 2009, Little, Brown $15.99 (978-0-316-06617-4). Sergio the penguin finally finds his place in the game of soccer after trying and failing several times. (Rev: BLO 6/16/09; HB 7/09; SLJ 7/09)

2233 Rohmann, Eric. *A Kitten Tale* (PS). Illus. by author. 2008, Knopf $15.99 (978-0-517-70915-3). 32pp. Four kittens contemplate the coming of winter with mixed expectations — three fear the cold, while the fourth "can't wait" for the snow — and when the snow arrives the brave one persuades his mates to play in it. (Rev: BCCB 1/08; BL 11/1/07; LMC 1/08; SLJ 2/08)

2234 Rohmann, Eric. *My Friend Rabbit* (PS–3). Illus. by author. 2007, Square Fish paper $6.99 (978-0-312-36752-7). 32pp. A paperback edition of the funny 2002 book about a mouse who plays with his friend Rabbit despite Rabbit's tendency to attract trouble. Caldecott Medal, 2003. (Rev: BL 3/02; SLJ 5/02)

2235 Root, Phyllis. *Toot Toot Zoom!* (PS–K). Illus. by Matthew Cordell. 2009, Candlewick $15.99 (978-0-7636-3452-0). 40pp. Pierre the fox hopes to make friends on the other side of the mountain, but instead he ends up finding several friends along the way. (Rev: BCCB 6/09; SLJ 5/09)

2236 Rosen, Michael. *Bear's Day Out* (PS–2). Illus. by Adrian Reynolds. 2007, Bloomsbury $16.95 (978-1-59990-007-0). 32pp. A large and chatty bear travels from the seaside to the city only to find it's too noisy there. (Rev: BL 9/1/07; SLJ 10/07)

2237 Rosenthal, Amy Krouse. *Little Oink* (PS–2). Illus. by Jen Corace. 2009, Chronicle $14.99 (978-0-8118-6655-2). 36pp. To his parents' despair, Little Oink likes to be clean and tidy. (Rev: BCCB 6/09; BLO 5/15/09)

2238 Rosoff, Meg. *Meet Wild Boars* (PS–2). Illus. by Sophie Blackall. 2005, Holt $15.95 (978-0-8050-7488-8). 32pp. Wild boars Morris, Boris, Horace, and Doris make for very impolite house guests in this outrageously funny picture book. (Rev: BL 3/15/05)

2239 Roth, Judith L. *Serendipity and Me* (4–7). 2013, Viking $16.99 (978-0-670-01440-8). 320pp. A white kitten brings comfort to 12-year-old Sara in the aftermath of her mother's death in this novel told in verse. Lexile 690 (Rev: BL 3/1/13; SLJ 3/13)

2240 Roth, Susan L. *Great Big Guinea Pigs* (K–2). Illus. 2006, Bloomsbury $17.95 (978-1-58234-724-0). 32pp. To help her son fall asleep, a mother guinea pig tells him a tale about their oversized prehistoric ancestors; this is fiction served full of facts. (Rev: BL 10/15/06; HBG 4/07; LMC 3/07; SLJ 11/06)

2241 Rubel, Nicole. *Ham and Pickles: First Day of School* (K–2). 2006, Harcourt $16.00 (978-0-15-205039-9). 32pp. Pickles the guinea pig is worried about her first day of school and her older brother Ham is definitely not helping. (Rev: BL 8/06; SLJ 7/06)

2242 Rubin, Vicky. *The Three Swingin' Pigs* (1–4). Illus. by Rhode Montijo. 2007, Holt $16.95 (978-0-8050-7335-5). The three little pigs are now a jazz trio whose music is appreciated by even the big bad wolf in this take on the fairy tale. (Rev: SLJ 6/07)

2243 Rueda, Claudia. *No* (PS). Trans. by Elisa Amado. Illus. by author. 2010, Groundwood $18.95 (978-0-88899-991-7). 44pp. Reluctant to hibernate, little bear is determined to brave out the winter cold — but realizes in the end that safe and snug is where he wants to be. (Rev: BL 11/1/10*; SLJ 9/1/10*)

2244 Ruelle, Karen Gray. *Dear Tooth Fairy* (K–2). Illus. by author. Series: A Harry and Emily Adventure. 2006, Holiday House $14.95 (978-0-8234-1929-6). 32pp. Emily, a kitten, is thrilled when her loose tooth finally comes out and she receives a visit from the Tooth Fairy. (Rev: BL 3/1/06; SLJ 5/06)

2245 Rumford, James. *Calabash Cat and His Amazing Journey* (K–3). Illus. by author. 2003, Houghton $16.00 (978-0-618-22423-4). Calabash Cat, searching for the point where the world ends, travels farther and farther afield with different animals serving as his guide for each leg of the journey. (Rev: HB 11/03; HBG 4/04; SLJ 9/03)

2246 Runton, Andy. *Owly and Wormy: Friends All Aflutter!* (PS–1). Illus. by author. 2011, Simon & Schuster $15.99 (978-1-4169-5774-4). 40pp. Owly and Wormy decide to plant flowers that will attract butterflies and then are disappointed when caterpillars turn up instead in this almost-wordless picture book about the comic book characters. ❸ (Rev: BL 2/15/11; LMC 8–9/11; SLJ 5/1/11)

2247 Russell, Natalie. *Brown Rabbit in the City* (PS–1). Illus. by author. 2010, Viking $16.99 (978-0-670-01234-3). 40pp. Brown Rabbit goes to visit Little Rabbit in the city but finds her schedule totally exhausting, and the two must negotiate more time together. (Rev: BL 4/15/10; SLJ 6/1/10)

2248 Russell, Natalie. *Moon Rabbit* (PS–1). Illus. by author. 2009, Viking $16.99 (978-0-670-01170-4). In a big city a lonely little rabbit finds a kindred spirit in the park. (Rev: BL 4/15/09; SLJ 6/09)

2249 Russo, Marisabina. *Peter Is Just a Baby* (1–3). Illus. by author. 2012, Eerdmans $16 (978-080285384-4). 32pp. A young bear lists her own accomplishments and expresses frustration with her messy baby brother but comes to recognize that he will soon grow to become more fun. (Rev: BL 1/1/12; SLJ 1/12)

2250 Russo, Marisabina. *A Very Big Bunny* (PS–1). Illus. by author. 2010, Random House $17.99 (978-0-375-84463-8); LB $20.99 (978-0-375-94463-5). 40pp. A oversize bunny and an undersize bunny become fast friends in this story about bullying and accepting differences. (Rev: BL 11/1/09; HB 1–2/10; LMC 1–2/10; SLJ 2/1/10)

2251 Ruzzier, Sergio. *Bear and Bee* (PS–1). Illus. by author. 2013, Disney/Hyperion $14.99 (978-1-4231-5957-5). 48pp. A bear who is frightened by his image of bees is pleasantly surprised in the end and enjoys sharing the honey. (Rev: BL 3/1/13; HB 5–6/13; SLJ 5/13)

2252 Ruzzier, Sergio. *Hey, Rabbit!* (K–2). Illus. by author. 2010, Roaring Brook $16.99 (978-1-59643-502-5). 32pp. A rabbit surprises his woodland friends when he pulls one magical gift after another out of his suitcase. (Rev: BL 12/1/09; LMC 1–2/10; SLJ 2/1/10)

2253 Ryan, Candace. *Ribbit Rabbit* (PS–1). Illus. by Mike Lowery. 2011, Walker $12.99 (978-0-8027-2180-8). 32pp. Frog and Bunny are best friends even though they sometimes have disputes over toys. (Rev: BLO 2/14/11; LMC 3–4/11; SLJ 3/1/11)

2254 Ryan, Pam Muñoz. *Nacho and Lolita* (1–3). Illus. by Claudia Rueda. 2005, Scholastic $16.99 (978-0-439-26968-1). This charming story, inspired by a Mexican folk tale, features a rare and beautiful pitacohi bird that falls in love with a swallow and uses his colorful feathers to guide her home to San Juan Capistrano after her annual migration. (Rev: BL 10/1/05; SLJ 10/05)

2255 Ryan, Pam Muñoz. *Tony Baloney* (PS–1). Illus. by Edwin Fotheringham. 2011, Scholastic $16.99 (978-0-545-23135-0). 40pp. Middle penguin child Tony contends with the many woes and frustrations of being overlooked. Lexile AD880L (Rev: BL 2/1/11; HB 3–4/11; SLJ 2/1/11)

2256 Ryder, Joanne. *Bear of My Heart* (PS). Illus. by Margie Moore. 2006, Simon & Schuster $12.95 (978-0-689-85947-2). A mother bear expresses her love for her cub in tender words and lovely illustrations. (Rev: SLJ 2/07)

2257 Ryder, Joanne. *Dance by the Light of the Moon* (PS–2). Illus. by Guy Francis. 2007, Hyperion $15.99 (978-0-7868-1820-4). Weaving in the chorus from the song "Buffalo Gals," this upbeat rhyming tale centers on a moonlit barn dance attended by gussied-up animals. (Rev: BL 1/1–15/07; SLJ 1/07)

2258 Rylant, Cynthia. *The Octopus* (2–4). Illus. by Preston McDaniels. 2005, Simon & Schuster $14.95 (978-0-689-86246-5). 64pp. The Lighthouse Family, consisting of Pandora the mother cat, Sebold the father dog, and two mice children, forges a friendship with Cleo, a shy octopus. (Rev: BL 10/1/05)

2259 Sacre, Antonio. *The Barking Mouse* (PS–1). Illus. by Alfredo Aguirre. 2003, Whitman LB $16.99 (978-0-8075-0571-7). A mouse mother impresses her family with her barking abilities when a cat threatens them in this attractively illustrated retelling of a Cuban tale. (Rev: HBG 10/03; SLJ 6/03)

2260 Sakai, Komako. *Mad at Mommy* (PS–1). Illus. by author. 2010, Scholastic $16.99 (978-0-545-21209-0). 40pp. A young bunny's frustration and anger with his mom — for sleeping late, for enforcing bedtimes, for not giving him what he wants — is the focus of this beautifully illustrated story. (Rev: BL 9/15/10; HB 11–12/10; SLJ 11/1/10)

2261 Sakai, Komako. *The Snow Day* (PS–K). Illus. by author. 2009, Scholastic $16.99 (978-0-545-01321-5). 40pp. A 5-year-old bunny who lives in a high-rise apartment wakes up one morning to discover a magically transformed world, one that offers both inconvenience and delights. (Rev: BCCB 2/09; BL 1/1–15/09; SLJ 12/08)

2262 Salley, Coleen. *Epossumondas* (PS–3). Illus. by Janet Stevens. 2002, Harcourt $16.00 (978-0-15-216748-6). 40pp. A bumbling little possum can't seem to get anything right in this uproarious adaptation of a classic Louisiana tale. (Rev: BCCB 10/02; BL 8/02; HB 11/02; HBG 3/03; SLJ 9/02*)

2263 Salley, Coleen. *Epossumondas Plays Possum* (PS–1). Illus. by Janet Stevens. 2009, Harcourt $16 (978-0-15-206420-4). 40pp. Epossumondas ignores his mother's warning and heads into the swamp alone, where he must play dead when he thinks he hears the scary loup-garou. ∩ Lexile AD620L (Rev: BL 9/15/09; HB 9–10/09; SLJ 10/1/09*)

2264 Salley, Coleen. *Epossumondas Saves the Day* (K–3). Illus. by Janet Stevens. 2006, Harcourt $16.00 (978-0-15-205701-5). It's his birthday and Mama is baking biscuits for Epossumondas the possum when she realizes she needs sody sallyratus; several guests head out to the store but fail to return, so the birthday boy goes to investigate. (Rev: SLJ 12/06*)

2265 Saltzberg, Barney. *Cornelius P. Mud, Are You Ready for Baby?* (PS–K). Illus. by author. 2009, Candlewick $15.99 (978-0-7636-3596-1). Cornelius the pig greets his new baby brother with a distinct lack of enthusiasm and asks if the baby can be returned. (Rev: BL 3/1/09; SLJ 2/09)

2266 Saltzberg, Barney. *Stanley and the Class Pet* (PS–2). Illus. by author. 2008, Candlewick $15.99 (978-0-7636-3595-4). Stanley the hamster is allowed to take the class bird home for the weekend but is persuaded by his friend Larry to let Figgy out of his cage. (Rev: BL 8/08; SLJ 7/08)

2267 Saltzberg, Barney. *Star of the Week* (K–2). Illus. 2006, Candlewick $15.99 (978-0-7636-2914-4). Stanley the hamster's turn as Star of the Week at school does not start off well. (Rev: BL 2/1/06; SLJ 2/06)

2268 Sandall, Ellie. *Birdsong* (PS–1). Illus. by author. 2011, Egmont $16.99 (978-1-60684-193-8). 32pp. One bird after another lands on a tree branch, too involved in twittering together to notice the bough bending . . . but it is a tiny butterfly that deals the final blow. (Rev: BLO 8/11; SLJ 6/11)

2269 Sattler, Jennifer. *Chick 'n' Pug* (PS–1). 2010, Bloomsbury $14.99 (978-1-59990-534-1); LB $15.89 (978-1-59990-535-8). Unpaged. A brassy little chick decides he's a lazy pug's new best friend and ably frightens off a cat threatening to usurp the limelight. (Rev: LMC 11–12/10; SLJ 11/1/10)

2270 Sattler, Jennifer. *Pig Kahuna* (PS–2). Illus. by author. 2011, Bloomsbury $14.99 (978-1-59990-635-5). 32pp. An anxious young piglet faces his fear of water to save his brother's special surfboard. Lexile AD490L (Rev: BL 4/15/11; SLJ 5/1/11*)

2271 Sattler, Jennifer. *Sylvie* (PS–2). Illus. by author. 2009, Random $15.99 (978-0-375-85708-9). 40pp. A young flamingo who wonders why she is always in the pink, tries out other colors. (Rev: BCCB 7–8/09; BL 6/1–15/09; SLJ 4/09)

2272 Sauer, Tammi. *Mr. Duck Means Business* (PS–2). Illus. by Jeff Mack. 2011, Simon & Schuster $15.99 (978-1-4169-8522-8). 32pp. A tranquility-obsessed duck learns to be more tolerant of his friends' boisterous activities in this lively barnyard story. ℮ Lexile AD320L (Rev: BLO 1/1–15/11; LMC 5–6/11; SLJ 1/1/11)

2273 Sauer, Tammi. *Nugget and Fang: Friends Forever – or Snack Time?* (K–2). Illus. by Michael Slack. 2013, Harcourt $16.99 (978-0-547-85285-0). 40pp. The friendship between a minnow and a shark begins to unravel when the minnow hears constant stories about sharks' bad behavior; but all turns out well in the end. Lexile 300 (Rev: BL 3/15/13; LMC 8–9/13; SLJ 3/13)

2274 Scanlon, Liz Garton. *Noodle and Lou* (PS–1). Illus. by Arthur Howard. 2011, Simon & Schuster $15.99 (978-1-4424-0288-1). 32pp. Noodle the worm's gloomy mood can only be cleared away by the efforts of his friend Lou the bird in this cheerful ode to friendship that features humorous details in the illustrations. (Rev: BL 3/1/11; SLJ 5/1/11)

2275 Schachner, Judith Byron. *The Grannyman* (PS–3). Illus. 1999, Dutton $15.99 (978-0-525-46122-7). 32pp. In this fantasy an old cat fondly remembers all his activities as a youngster including stalking wildebeest and playing Bach. (Rev: BCCB 1/00; BL 3/15/00; HBG 3/00; SLJ 11/99)

2276 Schachner, Judy. *Skippyjon Jones Class Action* (K–3). Illus. by author. 2011, Dutton $17.99 (978-0-525-42228-0). Unpaged. Skippyjon Jones, the Siamese who sees himself as a chihuahua, longs to go to dog obedience class in this zany story. (Rev: SLJ 7/11)

2277 Schachner, Judy. *Skippyjon Jones Lost in Spice* (K–3). Illus. by author. 2009, Dutton $16.99 (978-0-525-47965-9). Unpaged. Skippyjon has a zany adventure to Mars, which includes a sock-monkey tug-of-war and the discovery that the planet is covered with chili powder. (Rev: SLJ 11/1/09)

2278 Schindler, S. D. *Spike and Ike Take a Hike* (PS–1). Illus. by S. D. Schindler. 2013, Penguin $16.99 (978-0-399-24495-7). 32pp. A hedgehog and a coatimundi enjoy a walk through the countryside, with comments throughout on the animals and scenery around them. (Rev: BL 4/1/13; SLJ 3/13)

2279 Schmid, Paul. *Hugs from Pearl* (PS–K). Illus. by author. 2011, HarperCollins $14.99 (978-0-06-180434-2). Unpaged. Hug-loving Pearl the porcupine finds an inventive way to get all the affection she needs without hurting anyone. (Rev: SLJ 11/1/11)

2280 Schoenherr, Ian. *Pip and Squeak* (PS–1). Illus. by author. 2007, HarperCollins $16.99 (978-0-06-087253-3). Pip and Squeak, mice on the way to rabbit Gus's birthday party, realize they have forgotten the present (a lump of cheese) and must find a substitute; the illustrations offer interesting perspectives. (Rev: BL 1/1/07; SLJ 1/07)

2281 Schoenherr, Ian. *Read It, Don't Eat It!* (PS–1). Illus. by author. 2009, HarperCollins $17.99 (978-0-06-172455-8). 32pp. Featuring animals demonstrating various behaviors, this is book of easy rules for enjoying books and the library. (Rev: BL 4/1/09; SLJ 4/09)

2282 Schubert, Dieter, and Ingrid Schubert. *Ophelia* (PS–K). Illus. by Ingrid Schubert. 2009, Boyds Mills $16.95 (978-1-59078-659-8). 24pp. As Ophelia the hippo rushes to help her friend Kevin the alligator, who has butterflies in his stomach, she explains to other animals what's happening and each misinterprets what she says. (Rev: BL 3/15/09; LMC 8/09; SLJ 3/09)

2283 Schwartz, Amy. *Tiny and Hercules* (PS–2). Illus. by author. 2009, Roaring Brook $16.95 (978-1-59643-253-6). 32pp. Tiny, the elephant, and Hercules, the mouse, are just another odd couple headed for happiness. (Rev: BL 6/1–15/09; HB 5/09; SLJ 5/09)

2284 Schwartz, Corey Rosen, and Tali Klein. *Hop! Plop!* (PS–2). Illus. by Olivier Dunrea. 2006, Walker $15.95 (978-0-8027-8056-0). 32pp. Elephant and Mouse are friends, but they find it difficult to play together. (Rev: BL 4/15/06; SLJ 5/06)

2285 Schwartz, Roslyn. *The Vole Brothers* (PS–2). Illus. by author. 2011, OwlKids $16.95 (978-1-926818-83-2). Unpaged. Two vole brothers smell a delicious slice of pizza, but discover there's stiff competition for this prize; this well-illustrated book includes lots of onomatopoeia. (Rev: LMC 1–2/12; SLJ 8/1/11)

2286 Scotton, Rob. *Russell and the Lost Treasure* (PS–2). 2006, HarperCollins $15.99 (978-0-06-059851-8). 32pp. Armed with the Super-Duper Treasure Seeker, Russell the sheep sets off to track down the lost treasure of Frogsbottom and at first believes he has only found junk; a sequel to *Russell the Sheep* (2005). (Rev: BL 6/1–15/06; SLJ 5/06)

2287 Scotton, Rob. *Secret Agent Splat!* (PS–1). Illus. by author. Series: Splat the Cat. 2012, HarperCollins $16.99 (978-0061978-71-5). 40pp. Splat the Cat sets out to discover who's been stealing his toy ducks in this brightly illustrated, humorous story. ☊ (Rev: BLO 4/15/12; SLJ 6/1/12)

2288 Scotton, Rob. *Splat the Cat* (PS–1). Illus. by author. 2008, HarperCollins $16.99 (978-0-06-083154-7). 40pp. Splat the cat does not want to go to school and takes along his pet mouse Seymour, only to learn that cats are supposed to chase mice; detailed illustrations add to the humor of this simple story. (Rev: BL 7/08; SLJ 7/08)

2289 Scotton, Rob. *Splish, Splash, Splat!* (PS–1). Illus. by author. Series: Splat the Cat. 2011, HarperCollins $16.99 (978-0-06-197868-5); LB $17.89 (978-0-06-197869-2). Unpaged. At-odds cat friends Splat and Spike find common ground in their shared hatred of water in this comic story. (Rev: SLJ 8/1/11)

2290 Scotton, Rob, and Annie Auerbach. *On with the Show* (PS–1). Illus. by Rob Scotton. Series: Splat the Cat. 2013, HarperCollins paper $3.99 (978-00620901-0-2). 24pp. Splat the Cat gets a leading role in the school play, *Cinderpaws,* with unexpected results. (Rev: BLO 4/1/13)

2291 Segal, John. *Alistair and Kip's Great Adventure!* (PS–2). Illus. by author. 2008, Simon & Schuster $15.99 (978-1-4169-0280-5). 32pp. An orange cat named Alexander and a shy beagle called Kip set off on a hair-raising nautical adventure. (Rev: SLJ 5/08)

2292 Segal, John. *Carrot Soup* (PS–2). Illus. 2006, Simon & Schuster $12.95 (978-0-689-87702-5). 32pp. Rabbit loves carrots and looks after his garden carefully, so he is very upset when all his carrots disappear, but his unhappiness evaporates when he gets home and finds all his friends there with bowls of soup. (Rev: BL 2/15/06; SLJ 5/06)

2293 Segal, John. *Far Far Away!* (PS–1). Illus. by author. 2009, Philomel $16.99 (978-0-399-25007-1). When Piggie says he's leaving, Mother Pig does everything she can to help him. (Rev: BL 6/1–15/09)

2294 Segal, John. *Pirates Don't Take Baths* (PS–K). Illus. by author. 2011, Philomel $16.99 (978-0-399-25425-3). 32pp. A stubborn young pig devises one fantasy scenario after another in order to avoid getting a bath. (Rev: BL 7/11; SLJ 3/1/11)

2295 Sendak, Maurice. *Bumble-Ardy* (PS–2). Illus. by author. 2011, HarperCollins $17.95 (978-0-06-205198-1). 40pp. A little piggy hosts a raucous birthday party for himself after his aunt goes off to work. (Rev: BL 7/11; SLJ 8/1/11*)

2296 Serfozo, Mary. *Whooo's There?* (PS–2). Illus. by Jeffrey Scherer. 2007, Random $9.99 (978-0-375-84050-0). An owl notes fellow animals that are out at night in this rhyming book about nocturnal activity. (Rev: SLJ 8/07)

2297 Serwacki. *Doorknob the Rabbit and the Carnival of Bugs* (PS–2). Illus. by author. 2005, Tricycle $14.95 (978-1-58246-143-4). Doorknob foolishly opens the door without checking who's there and in come 6,000 bugs; Doorknob's efforts to get rid of them include mice, who move in too, followed by cats, who also show no signs of leaving. (Rev: SLJ 5/05)

2298 Seuss, Dr. *Horton Hears a Who!* (K–3). Illus. by author. 1954, Random LB $16.99 (978-0-394-90078-0). The children's favorite elephant discovers a whole town of creatures so small that they live on a speck of dust. Other titles by Dr. Seuss: *Horton Hatches the Egg* (1940); *If I Ran the Zoo* (1950); *If I Ran the Circus* (1956); *Yertle the Turtle and Other Stories* (1958).

2299 Shannon, David. *Duck on a Bike* (PS–1). Illus. 2002, Scholastic $16.99 (978-0-439-05023-4). A funny tale about a duck who dares to ride a bike, and the reactions of his farm-animal friends. (Rev: BCCB 3/02; BL 2/15/02; HB 3/02; HBG 10/02; SLJ 3/02*)

2300 Shannon, George. *Tippy-Toe Chick, Go!* (PS–K). Illus. by Laura Dronzek. 2003, HarperCollins LB $17.89 (978-0-06-029824-1). Little Chick is a dreamer, but she saves the day when a dog threatens Mother Hen and her brood. (Rev: BCCB 3/03; BL 1/1–15/03; HB 1/03*; HBG 10/03; SLJ 2/03)

2301 Sharkey, Niamh. *The Ravenous Beast* (PS–2). Illus. by author. 2003, Candlewick $16.99 (978-0-7636-2182-7). In this fantastical but reassuringly upbeat tale, the Ravenous Beast, a dinosaur-like creature, takes on all challengers to the title of "hungriest animal of all." (Rev: HBG 4/04; SLJ 12/03)

2302 Sharmat, Mitchell. *Gregory, the Terrible Eater* (PS–3). Illus. by Jose Aruego and Ariane Dewey. 1980, Macmillan $16.00 (978-0-02-782250-2); Scholastic paper $4.99 (978-0-590-43350-1). Gregory, a young goat, prefers a diet of fruit and vegetables to paper, shoes, and clothing.

2303 Shaw, Hannah. *School for Bandits* (PS–1). Illus. by author. 2011, Knopf $16.99 (978-0-375-86768-2); LB $19.99 (978-0-375-96768-9). 32pp. Ralph the Raccoon is just too nice and is sent off to bandit school by his well-meaning parents, who just want him to be more like the other raccoons. ℯ Lexile AD610L (Rev: BL 8/11*; SLJ 8/1/11)

2304 Shaw, Hannah. *Sneaky Weasel* (K–3). Illus. by author. 2009, Knopf $15.99 (978-0-375-85625-9). 32pp. When nobody comes to his party, Weasel, both sneaky and a bully, must reconsider the way he treats others; the funny text is extended by detailed illustrations of Weasel's misdeeds. (Rev: BL 4/15/09; SLJ 6/09)

2305 Shaw, Nancy. *Sheep Blast Off!* (PS–1). Illus. by Margot Apple. 2008, Houghton $15.00 (978-0-618-13168-6). 32pp. The sheep we know from books including *Sheep in a Jeep* (1986) find a spaceship and decide to explore. (Rev: BL 8/08; SLJ 4/08)

2306 Shaw, Nancy. *Sheep Take a Hike* (PS–1). Illus. by Margot Apple. 1994, Houghton $15.00 (978-0-395-68394-1). When they get lost in the woods, a flock of sheep find their way home because of bits of wool left on bushes. (Rev: BL 9/15/94; HB 11/94; SLJ 9/94*)

2307 Shea, Bob. *Cheetah Can't Lose* (PS–1). 2013, HarperCollins $17.99 (978-0-06-173083-2). 40pp. A competitive cheetah is overly confident that he will win a race against two kittens. (Rev: BL 3/15/13; SLJ 3/13)

2308 Shea, Bob. *New Socks* (PS–2). Illus. by author. 2007, Little, Brown $12.99 (978-0-316-01357-4). A self-confident little chicken flaunts his spiffy new orange socks, which will give him great prestige — even gaining recognition from the president. (Rev: SLJ 4/07)

2309 Shea, Bob. *Oh, Daddy!* (PS–K). Illus. by author. 2010, HarperCollins $16.99 (978-0-06-173080-1). 40pp. A young hippo shows his dad how to accomplish everyday tasks such as getting dressed, watering flowers, and opening a car door. (Rev: BL 2/15/10; SLJ 4/1/10*)

2310 Sherry, Kevin. *I'm the Biggest Thing in the Ocean* (PS). Illus. by author. 2007, Dial $16.99 (978-0-8037-3192-9). A giant squid insists that he is bigger than anything else in the ocean, even when he's swallowed by a whale. Bathtub stickers are included. (Rev: SLJ 5/07)

2311 Shields, Carol Diggory. *Wombat Walkabout* (PS–2). Illus. by Sophie Blackall. 2009, Dutton $16.99 (978-0-525-47865-2). 32pp. Set in the Australian outback, this rhyming story involves six little wombats who are being trailed by a hungry dingo but are smart enough to outwit him. (Rev: BL 1/1–15/09; HB 3/09; LMC 5/09; SLJ 2/09)

2312 Shields, Gillian. *When the World Was Waiting for You* (PS). Illus. by Anna Currey. 2011, Bloomsbury $14.99 (978-1-59990-531-0); LB $15.89 (978-1-59990-532-7). Unpaged. A rabbit family eagerly awaits the arrival of its newest member. (Rev: SLJ 7/11)

2313 Shireen, Nadia. *Hey, Presto!* (K–2). Illus. by author. 2012, Knopf $16.99 (978-0-375-86905-1). 32pp. The friendship between a cat named Presto and a dog named Monty is jeopardized when fame and money turn Monty's head. **e** (Rev: BLO 11/15/12; LMC 3–4/13; SLJ 10/12)

2314 Sierra, Judy. *Counting Crocodiles* (PS–1). Illus. by Will Hillenbrand. 1997, Harcourt $16.00 (978-0-15-200192-6). 40pp. A hungry monkey wants bananas from a neighboring island, but she is afraid that crocodiles will catch her if she tries to swim. (Rev: BL 9/1/97; HBG 3/98; SLJ 10/97)

2315 Sierra, Judy. *Good Night Dinosaurs* (PS–1). Illus. by Victoria Chess. 1996, Clarion $15.00 (978-0-395-65016-5). 32pp. Stylized drawings of dinosaurs portray them in humorous day-to-day activities, such as snoozing in the mud and sucking on baby bottles. (Rev: BCCB 3/96; BL 1/1–15/96; HB 7/96; SLJ 4/96)

2316 Sierra, Judy. *Preschool to the Rescue* (PS–K). Illus. by Will Hillenbrand. 2001, Harcourt $15.00 (978-0-15-202035-4). A group of animal preschoolers come to the rescue of a pizza van and other vehicles that are stuck in a huge mud puddle. (Rev: BCCB 4/01; BL 4/15/01; HB 5/01; HBG 10/01; SLJ 5/01)

2317 Sierra, Judy. *We Love Our School!* (PS–1). Illus. by Linda Davick. 2011, Knopf $7.99 (978-0-375-86728-6); LB $10.99 (978-0-375-96728-3). 24pp. Frog, Duck, Mouse, and Snail celebrate everything they love about their school on their first day of classes in this book with rhyming text and rebus pictures. (Rev: BL 6/1/11; SLJ 6/11)

2318 Sierra, Judy. *ZooZical* (PS–2). Illus. by Marc Brown. 2011, Knopf $17.99 (978-0-375-86847-4). 40pp. A city zoo's cast of animal characters decides to put on a musical to get themselves through the dark, lonely winter. (Rev: BL 7/11; SLJ 7/11)

2319 Siminovich, Lorena. *Alex and Lulu: Two of a Kind* (PS–1). Illus. by author. 2009, Candlewick $14.99 (978-0-7636-4423-9). 32pp. A young girl cat named Lulu and a boy dog called Alex consider their differences but decide that they don't matter. (Rev: BL 5/1/09; SLJ 5/09)

2320 Simmons, Jane. *Together* (PS–K). Illus. by author. 2007, Knopf $15.99 (978-0-375-84339-6). 32pp. Even though they are friends, dogs Mousse and Nut have a disagreement and must learn to accept each other's differences. (Rev: BL 7/07; SLJ 8/07)

2321 Slate, Joseph. *Miss Bindergarten Plans a Circus with Kindergarten* (PS–2). Illus. by Ashley Wolff. 2002, Dutton $16.99 (978-0-525-46884-4). Miss Bindergarten and her alphabetical charges each have a role to play in the circus. (Rev: HBG 3/03; SLJ 12/02)

2322 Smallman, Steve. *The Lamb Who Came for Dinner* (PS–K). Illus. by Joelle Dreidemy. 2007, Tiger Tales $15.95 (978-1-58925-506-3). 32pp. A little lamb knocks on an old wolf's door just in time for dinner, but the lamb's sweet nature saves it from the cooking pot. (Rev: SLJ 10/07)

2323 Smallman, Steve. *The Very Greedy Bee* (PS–K). Illus. by Jack Tickle. 2007, Tiger Tales $15.95 (978-1-58925-065-9). A greedy bee learns to share when he is too full of honey to move and kindhearted insects help him home. (Rev: SLJ 5/07)

2324 Smee, Nicola. *Clip-Clop* (PS–K). Illus. by author. 2006, Boxer Bks. $18.95 (978-1-905417-09-4). Mr. Horse takes his animal friends on a rollicking ride that ends with a fall into a haystack. (Rev: SLJ 6/06*)

2325 Smee, Nicola. *What's the Matter, Bunny Blue?* (PS). Illus. by author. 2010, Boxer $14.95 (978-1-906250-91-1). 32pp. With help from other animals, Bunny Blue searches for his missing grandmother. (Rev: BL 3/1/10; SLJ 4/1/10)

2326 Smith, Alex T. *Foxy and Egg* (K–2). Illus. by author. 2011, Holiday House $17.95 (978-0-8234-2330-9). 32pp. Foxy has evil plans when she offers Egg a place to stay the night, but gets her comeuppance when the egg hatches not a chicken but an alligator. (Rev: BL 3/15/11; SLJ 3/1/11)

2327 Smith, Alex T. *Home* (PS–2). Illus. by author. 2010, ME Media/Tiger Tales $15.95 (978-1-58925-088-8). 32pp. In this zany fantasy, four animal friends take parts of their collective home to disparate locations in order to pursue their dreams, only to realize how lonely they are without each other. (Rev: BLO 6/10; LMC 8–9/10; SLJ 5/1/10)

2328 Sneed, Brad. *Deputy Harvey and the Ant Cow Caper* (K–3). Illus. by author. 2005, Dial $16.99 (978-0-8037-3023-6). Deputy Harvey of Ant Hill vows to track down the culprits responsible for rustling half of the community's herd of ant cows. (Rev: SLJ 11/05)

2329 Soto, Gary. *Chato Goes Cruisin'* (PS–2). Illus. by Susan Guevara. 2005, Penguin $16.99 (978-0-399-23974-8). 32pp. Disappointed to find themselves on a dog-only cruise, Chato and Novio Boy, cool cats from LA, nonetheless set off in search for help when the dogs all fall ill. (Rev: BL 5/1/05; SLJ 6/05)

2330 Soto, Gary. *Chato's Kitchen* (PS–3). Illus. by Susan Guevara. 1995, Penguin $16.99 (978-0-399-22658-8). 32pp. In his Los Angeles barrio home, the cat Chato extends an invitation to some mice to come to dinner. (Rev: BL 3/1/95; HB 9/95; SLJ 7/95*)

2331 Spanyol, Jessica. *Little Neighbors on Sunnyside Street* (PS). Illus. by author. 2007, Candlewick $16.99 (978-0-7636-2986-1). Sunnyside Street is a busy place, with animal neighbors enjoying all kinds of activities, attending a party, and heading for bed. (Rev: BL 7/07)

2332 Spinelli, Eileen. *A Big Boy Now* (PS–2). Illus. by Megan Lloyd. 2012, HarperCollins $16.99 (978-006008673-2). 32pp. A young rabbit proud of his growing accomplishments gets carried away and pulls the training wheels off his bike, learning a lesson in the process. (Rev: BL 2/1/12; SLJ 1/12)

2333 Spinelli, Eileen. *Buzz* (PS–1). Illus. by Vincent Nguyen. 2010, Simon & Schuster $15.99 (978-1-4169-4925-1). 32pp. A newspaper headline leads Buzz the bumblebee to doubt her flying abilities, but an emergency proves that she has no problems. (Rev: BL 6/10; LMC 10/10; SLJ 6/1/10)

2334 Spinelli, Eileen. *Callie Cat, Ice Skater* (PS–2). Illus. by Anne Kennedy. 2007, Albert Whitman $16.95 (978-0-8075-1042-1). Callie is a little cat who loves ice skating and agrees to enter a competition even though she is happiest when skating purely for pleasure. (Rev: BCCB 12/08; BL 10/15/07; SLJ 12/07)

2335 Spinelli, Eileen. *Miss Fox's Class Earns a Field Trip* (K–3). Illus. by Anne Kennedy. 2010, Whitman $16.99 (978-0-8075-5169-1). 32pp. Miss Fox's class encounters setbacks — involving a certain visiting author — as it works toward its goal of raising $135 for a field trip to a roller coaster park in this funny book involving addition and subtraction. (Rev: BL 4/15/10; SLJ 4/1/10)

2336 Spinelli, Eileen. *Miss Fox's Class Shapes Up* (K–3). Illus. by Anne Kennedy. 2011, Whitman $16.99 (978-0-8075-5171-4). 32pp. Miss Fox helps her class to become more healthy — eating properly, sleeping well, and exercising more. Lexile AD500L (Rev: BL 8/11; SLJ 7/11)

2337 Spinelli, Eileen. *Peace Week in Miss Fox's Class* (PS–2). Illus. by Anne Kennedy. 2009, Albert Whitman $16.99 (978-0-8075-6379-3). 32pp. Peace Week — no quarrels, be nice to others — proves challenging but possible for Miss Fox's animal class. (Rev: BL 4/15/09; LMC 10/09; SLJ 5/09)

2338 Spinelli, Eileen. *Princess Pig* (PS–2). Illus. by Tim Bowers. 2009, Knopf $16.99 (978-0-375-84571-0). 40pp. When the wind bestows a princess's scarf on a young pig, she decides she is indeed royal. (Rev: BL 5/1/09; SLJ 6/09)

2339 Stadler, Alexander. *Beverly Billingsly Borrows a Book* (PS–2). Illus. 2002, Harcourt $16.00 (978-0-15-202510-6). 32pp. Beverly is thrilled to have her own library card, until she hears some scary rumors about what happens to children with overdue books. (Rev: BL 3/15/02; HBG 3/03; SLJ 4/02)

2340 Stadler, Alexander. *Beverly Billingsly Takes the Cake* (PS–2). Illus. 2005, Harcourt $16.00 (978-0-15-205357-4). When Beverly's attempts to make a perfect cake are foiled, her mother helps her come up with a solution. (Rev: BL 4/1/05; SLJ 4/05)

2341 Stamp, Jorgen. *Flying High* (K–2). Illus. by author. 2009, Enchanted Lion $16.95 (978-1-59270-089-9). Unpaged. An ambitious and ungenerous giraffe is more

appreciative of his turtle friend after his airplane crashes into the water. (Rev: LMC 11–12/09; SLJ 9/1/09)

2342 Stead, Philip C. *Bear Has a Story to Tell* (PS–1). Illus. by Erin E. Stead. 2012, Roaring Brook $16.99 (978-1-59643-745-6). 32pp. A bear with a story to tell patiently waits for just the perfect time to tell his animal friends, only to find he's forgotten what it was. ALA Notable Children's Book. Lexile AD540 (Rev: BL 8/12; LMC 1–2/13; SLJ 8/12*)

2343 Stead, Philip C. *Hello, My Name Is Ruby* (PS–2). Illus. by Philip C. Stead. 2013, Roaring Brook $16.99 (978-159643809-5). 40pp. A tiny bird named Ruby pluckily sets out to find a friend and perseveres despite many setbacks, eventually finding success. (Rev: BL 8/13*; LMC 3–4/14; SLJ 9/13)

2344 Stead, Philip Christian. *A Sick Day for Amos McGee* (PS–2). Illus. by Erin E. Stead. 2010, Roaring Brook $16.99 (978-1-59643-402-8). 32pp. When the animals' favorite zookeeper is out sick with a cold, they ride the city bus to his house to take care of him. Caldecott Medal. (Rev: BL 5/1/10; LMC 8–9/10; SLJ 5/1/10)

2345 Steffensmeier, Alexander. *Millie Waits for the Mail* (K–2). Illus. by author. 2007, Walker $16.95 (978-0-8027-9662-2). Millie the cow loves to get mail — so much so that in her enthusiasm she crushes the mailman's bike. Funny illustrations add to the story. (Rev: SLJ 8/07)

2346 Steig, William. *Doctor De Soto* (K–3). Illus. by author. 1982, Farrar $16.00 (978-0-374-31803-1). A mouse dentist outwits a fox.

2347 Steig, William. *Sylvester and the Magic Pebble* (K–3). Illus. by author. 1988, Simon & Schuster paper $5.99 (978-0-671-66269-1). A donkey who collects pebbles finds a red stone that will grant wishes — and off Sylvester goes on a series of adventures. Caldecott Medal winner, 1970.

2348 Stein, David Ezra. *Dinosaur Kisses* (PS–1). Illus. by author. 2013, Candlewick $15.99 (978-076366104-5). 32pp. Dinah is learning everything that a baby dinosaur needs to know, how to eat and walk, but when she tries to learn how to kiss, she ends up causing several minor disasters — until she meets her baby sibling. (Rev: BLO 9/15/13; SLJ 9/13)

2349 Stein, David Ezra. *Interrupting Chicken* (PS–3). Illus. by author. 2010, Candlewick $16.99 (978-0-7636-4168-9). 40pp. A rooster papa attempts to read fairy tales to his young daughter, who keeps interrupting the stories — which include Hansel and Gretel and Chicken Little — to intervene and save the characters from their fates. Caldecott Honor Book. Lexile AD300L (Rev: BL 9/15/10; LMC 11–12/10; SLJ 7/1/10)

2350 Stein, David Ezra. *Love, Mouserella* (PS–1). Illus. by author. 2011, Penguin $15.99 (978-0-399-25410-9). 32pp. Mouserella writes a heartfelt letter to her grandmouse in this book formatted like a letter on a pad and including drawings and photographs. (Rev: BL 11/1/11; SLJ 10/1/11)

119

2351 Steinberg, Laya. *Thesaurus Rex* (PS–3). Illus. by Debbie Harter. 2003, Barefoot Books $15.99 (978-1-84148-042-8). Readers follow Thesaurus Rex, a little turquoise-colored dinosaur, through a typical, vocabulary-expanding day of junior dino antics. (Rev: HBG 4/04; LMC 1/04; SLJ 12/03)

2352 Stevens, April. *Edwin Speaks Up* (PS–1). Illus. by Sophie Blackall. 2011, Random House $16.99 (978-0-375-85337-1). 40pp. A babbling baby ferret's jumbled rambles hold the key to remembering important items during the family's trip to the grocery store. (Rev: BL 5/1/11; SLJ 7/11*)

2353 Stevens, Janet, and Susan Stevens Crummel. *Cook-a-Doodle-Doo!* (PS–3). Illus. 1999, Harcourt $17.00 (978-0-15-201924-2). 48pp. A group of farm animals are happy to help Big Brown Rooster prepare strawberry shortcake in this delightful farce. (Rev: BCCB 7–8/99; BL 4/15/99*; HB 5/99; HBG 10/99; SLJ 4/99)

2354 Stevenson, James. *The Most Amazing Dinosaur* (PS–3). Illus. 2000, Greenwillow LB $15.89 (978-0-688-16433-1). When Wilfred, a rat, takes refuge from a snowstorm in a natural history museum, he is given a tour by other resident creatures. (Rev: BL 7/00; HBG 10/00; SLJ 6/00)

2355 Stewart, Amber. *I'm Big Enough* (PS–K). Illus. by Layn Marlow. 2007, Scholastic $12.99 (978-0-439-90666-1). Bean hides her beloved Blankie for safekeeping, then forgets where she left it and realizes she can do without it. (Rev: SLJ 5/07)

2356 Stewart, Amber. *No Babysitters Allowed* (PS–1). Illus. by Laura Rankin. 2008, Bloomsbury $16.99 (978-1-59990-154-1). Just the thought of an evening with a new babysitter gives Hopscotch the bunny a tummy ache. (Rev: SLJ 11/08)

2357 Stewart, Amber. *Rabbit Ears* (PS–2). Illus. by Laura Rankin. 2006, Bloomsbury $16.95 (978-1-58234-959-6). 32pp. Hopscotch will do almost anything to avoid having his ears washed and it comes as a revelation when he sees his older cousin Bobtail washing his own. (Rev: BL 2/1/06; SLJ 4/06)

2358 Stiegemeyer, Julie. *Cheep! Cheep!* (PS–K). Illus. by Carol Baicker-McKee. 2006, Bloomsbury $9.95 (978-1-58234-682-3). A simple story for very young children about three chicks who fall asleep while watching over an egg. (Rev: SLJ 3/06)

2359 Stileman, Kali. *Roly-Poly Egg* (PS–2). Illus. by author. 2011, ME Media/Tiger Tales $12.95 (978-1-58925-852-5). 32pp. Splotch the bird is careless in her excitement over her new, perfect egg, and it rolls off to have scary adventures before finally returning to her intact and hatching a polka-dot blue chick; dotted lines make the egg's travels easy to follow. (Rev: BLO 5/1/11; SLJ 5/1/11)

2360 Stock, Catherine. *A Porc in New York* (PS–2). Illus. 2007, Holiday $16.95 (978-0-8234-1994-4). Having already been introduced to the delights of Paris in *A Spree in Paree* (2004), French farmer Monmouton's farm animals decide it's time to see New York City and see such wonders as "Blooming Dells." (Rev: BL 3/15/07; HBG 10/07)

2361 Stock, Catherine. *A Spree in Paree* (PS–2). Illus. 2004, Holiday House $16.95 (978-0-8234-1720-9). 32pp. Monsieur Monmouton is persuaded to take his farm animals to Paris, where they act like crass tourists and generally have a great time throwing their weight around. (Rev: BL 3/15/04; SLJ 5/04)

2362 Stoeke, Janet Morgan. *Minerva Louise and the Red Truck* (PS–1). Illus. 2002, Dutton $14.99 (978-0-525-46909-4). The silly hen Minerva Louise gets taken for a ride in the farm truck and, as usual, misinterprets everything she sees. (Rev: BL 12/1/02; HB 11/02; HBG 3/03; SLJ 9/02)

2363 Stoeke, Janet Morgan. *Pip's Trip* (PS–K). Illus. by author. 2012, Dial $16.99 (978-080373708-2). 32pp. Pip the chicken hitches a solitary ride on the farm's truck when hen pals Midge and Dot are too scared, but Pip is secretly relieved when the truck goes nowhere. Lexile AD210L (Rev: BL 1/1/12; SLJ 1/12)

2364 Storms, Patricia. *The Pirate and the Penguin* (PS–2). Illus. by author. 2009, OwlKids $16.95 (978-1-897349-67-0). 32pp. A pirate and penguin, both seeking an escape from their dissatisfying lives, have a chance encounter amid the ice floes and swap identities — with hilarious, happily-ever-after results. (Rev: BL 1/1/10; LMC 1–2/10; SLJ 11/1/09)

2365 Sturges, Philemon. *This Little Pirate* (PS–K). Illus. by Amy Walrod. 2005, Dutton $16.99 (978-0-525-46440-2). 40pp. Colorful illustrations and humorous text follow two bands of pig pirates fighting over a box until they become so tired they declare a truce and settle down to enjoy its contents. (Rev: BL 6/1–15/05)

2366 Sutton, Jane. *Don't Call Me Sidney* (K–2). Illus. by Renata Gallio. 2010, Dial $16.99 (978-0-8037-2753-3). 32pp. Unhappy that his name only rhymes with "kidney," Sidney the pig experiments with being Joe until finally settling for Sid. (Rev: BL 6/10; LMC 11–12/10; SLJ 6/1/10)

2367 Swallow, Pamela C. *Groundhog Gets a Say* (K–2). Illus. by Denise Brunkus. 2005, Putnam $15.99 (978-0-399-23876-5). 40pp. A proud groundhog expounds on the attributes of his species in this humorous text with excellent illustrations. (Rev: BL 12/15/05; SLJ 1/06)

2368 Tafuri, Nancy. *The Busy Little Squirrel* (PS–K). Illus. by author. 2007, Simon & Schuster $15.99 (978-0-689-87341-6). 32pp. Attractive illustrations abound in this autumn-themed story about a busy squirrel preparing for the winter in spite of his friends' offers of fun. (Rev: BL 6/1–15/07; SLJ 11/07)

2369 Tafuri, Nancy. *Have You Seen My Duckling?* (PS–2). Illus. by author. 1984, Greenwillow $17.89 (978-0-688-02798-8); Morrow paper $6.99 (978-0-688-10994-3). 24pp. Mother Duck asks a number of animals if they have seen her missing duckling.

2370 Tafuri, Nancy. *Where Did Bunny Go?* (PS). 2001, Scholastic $15.95 (978-0-439-16959-2). 32pp. Bunny disappears during a game of hide-and-seek and his friends worry that he is angry until he returns to reassure them of his friendship in this gentle story. (Rev: BL 12/1/01; HBG 3/02; SLJ 12/01)

2371 Tankard, Jeremy. *Boo Hoo Bird* (K–3). Illus. by author. 2009, Scholastic $14.99 (978-0-545-06570-2). 32pp. When Boo Hoo Bird gets a boo-boo, all the other animals try to offer consolation. (Rev: BL 4/1/09; HB 5/09; SLJ 4/09)

2372 Tashiro, Chisato. *Five Nice Mice* (PS–2). Trans. by Sayako Uchida. Illus. by author. 2007, Penguin $16.99 (978-0-698-40058-0). 32pp. Gorgeous watercolor and pastel illustrations bring to life this story of five mice who, after being rejected by the frogs' orchestra, decide to form their own musical ensemble. (Rev: BL 5/15/07; SLJ 6/07)

2373 Taylor, Eleanor. *Beep, Beep, Let's Go!* (PS). Illus. 2005, Bloomsbury $15.95 (978-1-58234-973-2). 32pp. Various animals use various forms of transport to get to the beach, where they have a wonderful time. (Rev: BL 5/1/05)

2374 Taylor, Eleanor. *My Friend the Monster* (PS–K). Illus. by author. 2008, Bloomsbury $16.95 (978-1-59990-232-6). 32pp. When his family moves to a new house, a lonely little fox befriends the giant monster he finds hiding beneath his bed. (Rev: BL 9/1/08; SLJ 9/08)

2375 Taylor, Sean. *Huck Runs Amuck!* (PS–3). Illus. by Peter H. Reynolds. 2011, Dial $16.99 (978-0-8037-3261-2). 48pp. Huck the goat has a huge appetite for flowers and when he finds himself in the town of North Skettyfolk, he sees flowers in unexpected places. (Rev: BL 5/1/11; SLJ 5/1/11)

2376 Taylor, Sean. *The Ring Went Zing! A Story That Ends with a Kiss* (PS–2). Illus. by Jill Barton. 2010, Dial $16.99 (978-0-8037-3311-4). 40pp. A funny cumulative tale in which a frog presents his chicken love with a golden ring that falls to the ground and rolls away, followed by a growing procession of helpful animals. (Rev: LMC 11–12/10; SLJ 7/1/10)

2377 Taylor, Thomas. *Little Mouse and the Big Cupcake* (PS–K). Illus. by Jill Barton. 2010, Boxer $16.95 (978-1-907152-47-4). 32pp. Little Mouse asks his animal friends to help him get a monstrous cupcake home — and they do help, but not quite as he envisaged. (Rev: BL 12/1/10; LMC 3–4/11; SLJ 12/1/10)

2378 Teague, Mark. *Firehouse!* (PS–K). Illus. by author. 2010, Scholastic $16.99 (978-0-439-91500-7). 32pp. Lovable but scatterbrained bulldog Edward and his sensible cousin Judy visit a firehouse and learn about procedures there from the Dalmatian firefighters. (Rev: BL 5/15/10; SLJ 7/1/10)

2379 Teague, Mark. *Funny Farm* (PS–K). Illus. by author. 2009, Scholastic $16.99 (978-0-439-91499-4). Edward, a big city dog, gets a dose of country living when he visits the farm. (Rev: BL 11/15/08; SLJ 4/09)

2380 Teague, Mark. *Pigsty* (PS–3). Illus. 1994, Scholastic $15.95 (978-0-590-45915-0). 32pp. Even messy Wendell, a pig, resents his friends creating chaos in his room. (Rev: BL 9/15/94; SLJ 10/94*)

2381 Teckentrup, Britta. *Big Smelly Bear* (PS). Illus. by author. 2007, Boxer Bks. $12.95 (978-1-905417-37-3). Big Smelly Bear makes a friend after he finally takes a bath in this cheery book about the value of cleanliness. (Rev: SLJ 6/07)

2382 Teckentrup, Britta. *Little Wolf's Song* (PS–2). Illus. by author. 2010, Boxer $16.95 (978-1-907152-33-7). 32pp. A young wolf impatiently waits for his voice to develop so he can join his family in howling; when he gets lost in the woods, his wish is granted. (Rev: BL 10/1/10; SLJ 11/1/10)

2383 Tekavec, Heather. *Storm Is Coming!* (PS–1). Illus. by Margaret Spengler. 2002, Dial $16.99 (978-0-8037-2626-0). 32pp. A group of frightened animals bunch together in the barn, anticipating the arrival of Storm and comforted by the fact that the howling wind, flashing light, and rain will scare him away. (Rev: BL 3/1/02; HBG 10/02; SLJ 3/02)

2384 Tellegen, Toon. *Letters to Anyone and Everyone* (PS–3). Illus. by Jessica Ahlberg. 2010, Sterling $12.95 (978-1-906250-95-9). 156pp. First published in the Netherlands, this is a whimsical and compelling collection of stories in which animals communicate with each other by letter. (Rev: BL 5/15/10; LMC 5–6/10; SLJ 4/1/10)

2385 Thompson, Emma. *The Further Tale of Peter Rabbit* (PS–2). Illus. by Eleanor Taylor. 2012, Warne $20.00 (978-0-72326-710-2). 72pp. After complaining of boredom Peter Rabbit finds himself in Scotland, eating porridge and taking part in some strange games; lovers of the original Potter stories will enjoy the illustrations. (Rev: BL 12/1/12; SLJ 11/12)

2386 Thompson, Lauren. *Leap Back Home to Me* (PS–K). Illus. by Matthew Cordell. 2011, Simon & Schuster $15.99 (978-1-4169-0664-3). 32pp. A frog encourages her young one to leap higher and higher, farther and farther, and is always there for him when he comes home. **e** (Rev: BL 4/1/11; SLJ 3/1/11)

2387 Thompson, Lauren. *Mouse's First Day of School* (PS). Illus. by Buket Erdogan. 2003, Simon & Schuster $12.95 (978-0-689-84727-1). Mouse finds many items of interest when he finds his way into the classroom in this small book with large, bold type. (Rev: BL 7/03; HBG 4/04; SLJ 9/03)

2388 Thompson, Lauren. *Mouse's First Fall* (PS). Illus. by Buket Erdogan. 2006, Simon & Schuster $12.95 (978-0-689-85837-6). 32pp. In this picture-book celebration of fall, Mouse and his sister Minka frolic among the brightly colored leaves. Also use *Mouse's First Summer* (2004) and *Mouse's First Spring* and *Mouse's First Snow* (both 2005). (Rev: BL 9/15/06; SLJ 10/06)

2389 Thompson, Lauren. *Wee Little Chick* (PS–1). Illus. by John Butler. 2008, Simon & Schuster $14.99 (978-1-4169-3468-4). She may be small but the wee little chick has big ambitions. (Rev: BL 5/15/08; SLJ 1/08)

2390 Thoms, Susan Collins. *Cesar Takes a Break* (1–3). Illus. by Rogé. 2008, Sterling $14.95 (978-1-4027-3653-7). 32pp. It's spring break and the children are all gone, but Cesar the 2nd-grade class iguana finds there's lots of fun things to do around school. (Rev: BL 5/1/08; SLJ 6/08)

2391 Thomson, Pat. *Drat That Fat Cat* (PS–1). Illus. by Ailie Busby. 2003, Scholastic $15.95 (978-0-439-47195-4). In this bright and bouncy cumulative tale, a very fat cat grows even fatter as, one by one, he consumes virtually everything he encounters. (Rev: BCCB 1/04; BL 1/1–15/04; HB 1/04; HBG 4/04; SLJ 12/03)

2392 Timmers, Leo. *The Magical Life of Mr. Renny* (PS–3). Illus. by author. 2012, Gecko $17.95 (978-1-8775-7920-2). 36pp. A dog named Mr. Renny loves to paint but makes no money and one day idly wishes that he could consume what he painted; a cautionary tale. (Rev: BLO 10/15/12; LMC 3–4/13; SLJ 12/12)

2393 Tone, Satoe. *The Very Big Carrot* (PS–K). Illus. by author. 2013, Eerdmans $12 (978-080285426-1). 26pp. Six rabbits dig up an enormous carrot, and they explore multiple uses for it (a boat, an airplane, and a garden decoration) before finally deciding to eat it. (Rev: BL 9/15/13; SLJ 12/13)

2394 Trewin, Trudie. *I Lost My Kisses* (PS–K). Illus. by Nick Bland. 2008, Scholastic $14.99 (978-0-545-05557-4). An Australian cow in polka-dot tights searches high and low for her lost kisses. (Rev: BL 3/15/08; SLJ 4/08)

2395 Trivizas, Eugene. *The Three Little Wolves and the Big Bad Pig* (K–4). Illus. by Helen Oxenbury. 1993, Macmillan $17.00 (978-0-689-50569-0). 32pp. In this role-reversal story, three wolves are menaced by a big, bad pig who knocks their house down with a sledgehammer when huffing and puffing won't do the trick. (Rev: BCCB 9/93; BL 9/1/93; SLJ 12/93*)

2396 Tseng, Kevin. *Ned's New Home* (PS–1). Illus. by author. 2009, Tricycle $14.99 (978-1-58246-297-4). Unpaged. Ned the worm finds himself in need of a new home when the apple he's living in begins to decompose. (Rev: LMC 1–2/10; SLJ 9/1/09)

2397 Tucker, Lindy. *Porkelia: A Pig's Tale* (PS–2). Illus. by author. 2011, Charlesbridge $9.95 (978-1-934133-28-6). Unpaged. Porkelia is an ambitious pig and heads for New York City with dreams of becoming a Rockette — and it all comes true. (Rev: BL 5/1/11; SLJ 4/11)

2398 Turnbull, Ann. *Too Tired* (K–2). Illus. by Emma Chichester Clark. 1994, Harcourt $13.95 (978-0-15-200549-8). 32pp. There is a crisis on the ark when Noah discovers that the sloths are too tired to board. (Rev: BL 3/15/94; SLJ 4/94)

2399 Twohy, Mike. *Poindexter Makes a Friend* (PS–1). Illus. by author. 2011, Simon & Schuster $15.99 (978-1-4424-0965-1). 32pp. Shy Poindexter the pig makes friends with a bashful turtle called Shelby, and together the two read books to their stuffed animals. e Lexile AD740L (Rev: BL 4/1/11; SLJ 4/11*)

2400 Underwood, Deborah. *A Balloon for Isabel* (PS–1). Illus. by Laura Rankin. 2010, Greenwillow $16.99 (978-0-06-177987-9). 32pp. It's graduation day and every animal will receive a balloon — except the porcupines.

Can Isabel find a solution? Lexile AD510L (Rev: BL 4/15/10; SLJ 4/1/10)

2401 Urbanovic, Jackie. *Duck at the Door* (PS–2). 2007, HarperCollins $17.99 (978-0-06-121438-7). 32pp. Max the duck, left behind when his flock flies south, takes refuge in a house already full of pets and makes a bit of a nuisance of himself. (Rev: BL 4/1/07; SLJ 3/07)

2402 Urbanovic, Jackie. *Duck Soup* (PS–2). Illus. by author. 2008, HarperCollins $16.99 (978-0-06-121441-7). 32pp. There's a feather in the soup! Could Duck have fallen in? In a chaotic panic his friends attempt to save him. (Rev: BCCB 2/08; BL 1/1–15/08; SLJ 1/08)

2403 Urbanovic, Jackie. *Sitting Duck* (PS–2). Illus. by author. 2010, HarperCollins $17.99 (978-0-06-176583-4); LB $18.89 (978-0-06-176584-1). 40pp. Max the Duck gets in over his head when he offers to babysit a rambunctious puppy. (Rev: BL 5/1/10; SLJ 5/1/10)

2404 Valckx, Catharina. *Lizette's Green Sock* (PS–K). Illus. 2005, Clarion $15.00 (978-0-618-45298-9). 32pp. A little bird is thrilled to find a single green sock, and sports it on her foot before moving it to her head. (Rev: BL 5/1/05; SLJ 5/05)

2405 Van Allsburg, Chris. *Two Bad Ants* (1–4). Illus. by author. 1988, Houghton $18.95 (978-0-395-48668-9). 32pp. The story of two adventuresome ants. (Rev: BCCB 12/88; BL 10/1/88; SLJ 11/88)

2406 Van Lieshout, Maria. *Hopper and Wilson* (PS–2). Illus. by author. 2011, Philomel $16.99 (978-0-399-25184-9). 40pp. An elephant and a mouse set off in a boat to discover the end of the world, weather a storm, become separated, and are finally reunited. (Rev: BLO 7/11; SLJ 7/11)

2407 van Lieshout, Maria. *Peep! A Little Book About Taking a Leap* (PS–K). Illus. by author. Series: A Little Book. 2009, Feiwel & Friends $12.99 (978-0-312-36915-6). 48pp. On a walk with his family a little yellow chick called Peep is scared to jump off a high curb. (Rev: BL 5/1/09; SLJ 3/09)

2408 Van Patter, Bruce. *Tucker Took It!* (PS–1). 2010, Boyds Mills $16.95 (978-1-59078-698-7). Unpaged. Tucker the goat is automatically blamed when various articles of clothing go missing on the farm, but in fact he's not eating them but rather creating a scarecrow. (Rev: LMC 5–6/10; SLJ 4/1/10)

2409 Van Straaten, Harmen. *Duck's Tale* (K–2). Trans. from Dutch by Marianne Martens. Illus. by author. 2007, North-South $16.95 (978-0-7358-2133-0). Duck can't write and Toad can't read, but they can pretend, so Toad "reads" a story that Duck has "written" to a group of their animal friends. (Rev: SLJ 5/07)

2410 Van Straaten, Harmen. *For Me?* (PS–3). Trans. by MaryChris Bradley. Illus. by author. 2007, North-South $16.95 (978-0-7358-2163-7). 32pp. Seeking to make new friends, a newcomer sends Duck and each of his neighbors an anonymous red rose. (Rev: BL 2/15/08; SLJ 1/08)

2411 Verburg, Bonnie. *The Kiss Box* (PS–K). Illus. by Henry Cole. 2011, Scholastic $16.99 (978-0-545-11284-

0). 32pp. A mama bear and her little one prepare to be apart for the afternoon by talking about it and sharing kisses. (Rev: BL 12/15/11; SLJ 10/1/11)

2412 Vere, Ed. *Banana!* (PS–2). Illus. by author. 2010, Henry Holt $12.99 (978-0-8050-9214-1). Unpaged. This nearly wordless book (the only words are "banana" and "please") features two monkeys, one banana, and the idea of sharing. (Rev: LMC 3–4/11; SLJ 11/1/10)

2413 Vere, Ed. *The Getaway* (K–2). Illus. by author. 2007, Simon & Schuster $16.99 (978-1-4169-4789-9). 32pp. In this adventure, a mouse cheese thief named Fingers McGraw asks readers to be on the lookout for an elephant, Detective Jumbo Wayne, Jr., who chases him through street scenes illustrated with bright mixed-media. (Rev: BCCB 9/07; BL 11/15/07; SLJ 1/08)

2414 Villeneuve, Anne. *The Red Scarf* (K–2). Illus. by author. 2010, Tundra $17.95 (978-0-88776-989-4). 40pp. In this lively, nearly wordless, adventure, good-natured taxi driver Turpin (a white mole) finds himself taking part in a circus in his efforts to return a scarf left in his cab. (Rev: BL 1/1/10; SLJ 1/1/10)

2415 Vischer, Phil. *Sidney and Norman: A Tale of Two Pigs* (K–3). Illus. by Justin Gerard. 2006, Thomas Nelson $15.99 (978-1-4003-0834-7). 32pp. In this fable-like tale of two very different pigs who are invited to visit God, young readers learn some valuable lessons about the pitfalls of judging others. (Rev: BL 10/1/06)

2416 Von Buhler, Cynthia. *But Who Will Bell the Cats?* (K–2). Illus. by author. 2009, Houghton $16.00 (978-0-618-99718-3). 32pp. With detailed, creepy illustrations, this is an ingenious followup to Aesop's tale in which a clever mouse prevails against terrible odds to attain his goal in a battle against the cats. (Rev: BL 7/09; HB 8–10/09; SLJ 9/09)

2417 Waber, Bernard. *Bearsie Bear and the Surprise Sleepover Party* (PS–K). Illus. 1997, Houghton $16.00 (978-0-395-86450-0). 40pp. A number of animals are given shelter for the night; but when the porcupine tries to bed down, everybody leaves. (Rev: BL 10/1/97; HB 9/97; HBG 3/98; SLJ 10/97)

2418 Waber, Bernard. *The House on East 88th Street* (K–2). Illus. by author. 1973, Houghton $16.00 (978-0-395-18157-7); paper $6.95 (978-0-395-19970-1). The adventures of a pet crocodile (Lyle) who lives with a family in a New York City brownstone. Other books about Lyle include *Lyle, Lyle, Crocodile* (1965), *Lyle and the Birthday Party* (1966), *Lyle Finds His Mother* (1974), *Lovable Lyle* (1977), and *Funny, Funny Lyle* (1987).

2419 Waber, Bernard. *Ira Says Goodbye* (K–2). Illus. 1988, Houghton $16.00 (978-0-395-48315-2); paper $6.99 (978-0-395-58413-2). 40pp. Ira is sad because his best friend is moving away. (Rev: BCCB 10/88; BL 9/1/88; SLJ 9/88)

2420 Waber, Bernard. *Lyle at the Office* (PS–3). Illus. 1994, Houghton $16.00 (978-0-395-70563-6). 46pp. Lyle becomes very popular when he spends a day helping out in Mr. Primm's office. (Rev: BL 6/1–15/94; SLJ 9/94*)

2421 Waber, Bernard. *The Mouse That Snored* (PS–3). Illus. 2000, Houghton $15.00 (978-0-395-97518-3). 32pp. A mouse who has a terrible snore moves into a house where everyone hates noise so much they won't even eat celery. (Rev: BL 8/00; HB 11/00; HBG 3/01; SLJ 10/00)

2422 Waddell, Martin. *Captain Small Pig* (PS–K). Illus. by Susan Varley. 2010, Peachtree $15.95 (978-1-56145-519-5). 32pp. Old Goat and Turkey agree to go for a row on Blue Lake with Small Pig, whose whims they indulge despite their impracticality. (Rev: BL 2/15/10*; SLJ 3/1/10)

2423 Waddell, Martin. *Owl Babies* (PS–1). Illus. by Patrick Benson. 1992, Candlewick $15.99 (978-1-56402-101-4). Three small owls, left alone by their mother, wonder if she is coming back. (Rev: BL 12/1/92; HB 3/93; SLJ 12/92)

2424 Waddell, Martin. *Sleep Tight, Little Bear* (PS–K). Illus. by Barbara Firth. Series: Little Bear. 2005, Candlewick $15.99 (978-0-7636-2439-2). 32pp. Little Bear finds a small cave and makes it his own special place; when he gets permission to spend the night there alone, however, he finds himself thinking of home. (Rev: BL 1/1–15/06; SLJ 12/05)

2425 Wallace, Nancy Elizabeth. *The Kindness Quilt* (PS–2). 2006, Marshall Cavendish paper $16.99 (978-0-7614-5313-0). 48pp. After hearing the Aesop's fable about the lion and the mouse, Minna the bunny and her classmates are inspired to show kindness to others and to make a giant kindness quilt. (Rev: BL 10/1/06; SLJ 11/06)

2426 Wallace, Nancy Elizabeth. *Look! Look! Look! at Sculpture* (K–3). Illus. by author. 2012, Marshall Cavendish $17.99 (978-0-7614-6132-6). 40pp. Three mice sneak into an art museum and find themselves inspired by the range of sculpture styles they see, deciding to create their own. (Rev: BL 4/15/12; SLJ 4/1/12)

2427 Wallace, Nancy Elizabeth. *Pond Walk* (PS–3). Illus. by author. 2011, Marshall Cavendish $17.99 (978-0-7614-5816-6). 40pp. Buddy Bear and his mother spend a quiet day sketching and observing nature at a pond. ℮ (Rev: BL 3/15/11; SLJ 4/11)

2428 Wallace, Nancy Elizabeth. *Pumpkin Day!* (PS–2). Illus. 2002, Marshall Cavendish $16.95 (978-0-7614-5128-0). 32pp. A rabbit family visits a pumpkin farm to learn how they grow, before picking some for carving and eating. (Rev: BCCB 10/02; BL 8/02; HBG 3/03; SLJ 11/02)

2429 Wallace, Nancy Elizabeth. *Seeds! Seeds! Seeds!* (K–3). Illus. 2004, Marshall Cavendish $16.95 (978-0-7614-5159-4). A package from Grandpa gets Buddy Bear involved in a variety of activities involving seeds. (Rev: BL 4/15/04; SLJ 6/04)

2430 Wallace, Nancy Elizabeth. *Shells! Shells! Shells!* (PS–2). Illus. by author. 2007, Marshall Cavendish $16.99 (978-0-7614-5332-1). Buddy the bear learns all about shells during a walk along the beach with his mother; back matter includes facts and an activity. (Rev: BL 5/15/07; SLJ 5/07)

2431 Wallace, Nancy Elizabeth, and Linda K. Friedlaender. *Look! Look! Look!* (K–3). 2006, Marshall Cavendish $16.95 (978-0-7614-5282-9). 40pp. Three mice are so inspired by a beautiful postcard that they learn to make their own pictures; followed by instructions on making a self-portrait postcard. (Rev: BL 5/1/06; SLJ 3/06)

2432 Walsh, Ellen S. *Mouse Paint* (PS–K). Illus. 1989, Harcourt $14.00 (978-0-15-256025-6). 32pp. Three mice paint themselves as camouflage and find they like their new look. (Rev: BL 5/15/89; HB 7/89; SLJ 9/89)

2433 Walsh, Ellen Stoll. *Balancing Act* (PS–K). Illus. by author. 2010, Simon & Schuster $16.99 (978-1-4424-0757-2). 32pp. Two mice enjoying a seesaw made of a stick and a rock are joined by other animals who cause balancing problems until eventually the whole thing collapses. **e** Lexile AD110L (Rev: BL 8/10; HB 9–10/10; SLJ 8/1/10)

2434 Walton, Rick. *Bunny School: A Learning Fun-for-All* (PS–K). Illus. by Paige Miglio. 2005, HarperCollins $16.99 (978-0-06-057508-3). 32pp. At Cottontail School, the bunnies enjoy their first day; rhyming verses and detailed illustrations depict typical experiences. (Rev: BL 8/05; SLJ 9/05)

2435 Walton, Rick. *What Do We Do with the Baby?* (PS–K). Illus. by Paige Miglio. 2008, HarperCollins $16.99 (978-0-06-008419-6). 32pp. A rabbit family takes care of its new baby bunny; the illustrations add to the gentle fun. (Rev: BL 2/15/08; SLJ 3/08)

2436 Ward, Helen. *The Rooster and the Fox: A Tale from Chaucer* (K–3). Illus. 2003, Millbrook LB $24.90 (978-0-7613-2920-6). 40pp. "The Nun's Priest's Tale" about the proud rooster and the wily fox is adapted here in an effective tale using elegant, readable text and realistic watercolor art that makes the various animals come to life. (Rev: BCCB 2/03; BL 1/1–15/03; HBG 10/03; SLJ 10/04)

2437 Ward, Helen. *The Town Mouse and the Country Mouse* (K–2). Illus. by author. 2012, Candlewick $16.99 (978-0-7636-6098-7). 48pp. Set in 1930s New York at Christmas, this is a beautifully illustrated retelling of the story about two mice from very different backgrounds. (Rev: BL 10/1/12; LMC 3–4/13*; SLJ 8/12*)

2438 Warnes, Tim. *Chalk and Cheese* (K–2). Illus. by author. 2008, Simon & Schuster $16.99 (978-1-4169-1378-8). 32pp. Cheese, an English country mouse, visits his pen pal Chalk, a dog, and together they form an unusual friendship as they enjoy the energy and sights of New York City. (Rev: BCCB 12/08; BL 9/15/08; LMC 1/09)

2439 Watson, Richard Jesse. *The Magic Rabbit* (PS–1). Illus. 2005, Scholastic $16.99 (978-0-590-47964-6). 40pp. A white rabbit pops out of a hat and discovers that he's got some pretty amazing magical abilities, but somehow all this isn't much fun without a friend to share it. (Rev: BL 1/1–15/05; SLJ 4/05)

2440 Watt, Mélanie. *Chester's Back!* (K–2). Illus. by author. 2008, Kids Can $18.95 (978-1-55453-287-2). 32pp. The calico cat first seen in *Chester* (2007) tussles with the author for control of a fairy tale. (Rev: BCCB 12/08; SLJ 9/08)

2441 Watt, Mélanie. *Scaredy Squirrel* (1–3). 2006, Kids Can $14.95 (978-1-55337-959-1). Imagining all the dangers around him, Scaredy Squirrel doesn't dare venture from his tree — until the day he discovers he can fly. (Rev: BL 5/1/06; SLJ 6/06)

2442 Watt, Mélanie. *Scaredy Squirrel at the Beach* (1–3). Illus. by author. 2008, Kids Can $15.95 (978-1-55453-225-4). Scaredy Squirrel is so frightened by the idea of being at the beach that he decides to create his own seaside at the base of his favorite tree, but what he really needs is a seashell. What to do? (Rev: BL 6/1–15/08; SLJ 5/08)

2443 Watt, Mélanie. *Scaredy Squirrel Goes Camping* (1–3). Illus. by author. 2013, Kids Can $16.95 (978-1-894786-86-7). 32pp. Scaredy Squirrel has to do a lot of meticulous planning when he gets a new TV. Lexile AD560 (Rev: BL 5/1/13; SLJ 7/13)

2444 Watt, Mélanie. *Scaredy Squirrel Has a Birthday Party* (K–2). Illus. by author. 2011, Kids Can $16.95 (978-1-55453-468-5). Unpaged. Scaredy Squirrel plans to celebrate his birthday in solitary fashion as usual, but his friends have other ideas. (Rev: SLJ 5/1/11)

2445 Watt, Mélanie. *Scaredy Squirrel Makes a Friend* (PS–3). Illus. by author. 2007, Kids Can $14.95 (978-1-55453-181-3). A timid squirrel discovers that finding good friends may mean putting aside his fears. (Rev: SLJ 5/07)

2446 Watts, Leslie Elizabeth. *The Baabaasheep Quartet* (PS–2). Illus. 2005, Fitzhenry & Whiteside $16.95 (978-1-55041-890-3). 32pp. Four sheep have difficulty adjusting to life in the city but are optimistic when they see a singing contest they mistakenly believe is for sheep only. (Rev: BL 12/15/05; SLJ 2/06)

2447 Webster, Christine. *Otter Everywhere* (PS–1). Illus. by Tim Nihoff. 2007, Candlewick $15.99 (978-0-7636-2921-2); paper $5.99 (978-0-7636-2922-9). 40pp. Beginning readers will enjoy these simple stories about a friendly little otter. (Rev: SLJ 8/07)

2448 Weeks, Sarah. *Bunny Fun* (PS–K). Illus. by Sam Williams. 2008, Harcourt $14.00 (978-0-15-205838-8). 40pp. On a rainy day, young rabbit and his mouse friend enjoy a pillow fight and a game of dress-up. (Rev: BL 2/15/08; SLJ 12/07)

2449 Weeks, Sarah. *Catfish Kate and the Sweet Swamp Band* (PS–2). Illus. by Elwood H. Smith. 2009, Atheneum $16.99 (978-1-4169-4026-5). 32pp. The all-girl Sweet Swamp Band has a fine time playing jazzy music but the Skunktail Boys prefer to read and find the noise annoying; can a compromise be reached? (Rev: BL 5/15/09; LMC 10/09; SLJ 5/09)

2450 Weeks, Sarah. *I'm a Pig* (PS–2). Illus. by Holly Berry. 2005, HarperCollins LB $16.89 (978-0-06-074344-4). Appealing illustrations accompany a pig's expressions of happiness with her life and herself. (Rev: SLJ 5/05)

2451 Weeks, Sarah. *Overboard!* (PS). Illus. by Sam Williams. 2006, Harcourt $14.00 (978-0-15-205046-7). 40pp. Rhythmic text and colorful artwork celebrate a toddler's fascination with tossing objects of every kind "overboard." (Rev: BL 2/15/06; SLJ 4/06)

2452 Weigelt, Udo. *Super Guinea Pig to the Rescue* (K–3). Illus. by Nina Spranger. 2007, Walker $16.95 (978-0-8027-9705-6). 32pp. A little guinea pig hopes to impress his fellow pets by donning the role of his TV hero Super Guinea Pig. (Rev: BCCB 1/08; BL 10/1/07; SLJ 10/07)

2453 Wells, Rosemary. *Felix and the Worrier* (PS–2). Illus. by author. 2003, Candlewick $12.99 (978-0-7636-1405-8). Felix the guinea pig starts to fret about all sorts of things when a strange yellow creature called the Worrier begins bothering him. (Rev: HBG 4/04; SLJ 10/03)

2454 Wells, Rosemary. *Following Grandfather* (1–3). Illus. by Christopher Denise. 2012, Candlewick $14.99 (978-0-7636-5069-8). 64pp. When her grandfather dies, young mouse Jenny finds herself seeing him everywhere she turns and this reminds her of her immigrant origins. (Rev: BL 8/12; SLJ 3/13)

2455 Wells, Rosemary. *Max and Ruby's Treasure Hunt* (PS–1). Illus. by author. 2012, Viking $17.99 (978-0-670-06317-8). 32pp. A large lift-the-flap book in which seven clues guide readers through a treasure hunt Grandma creates for little rabbits Max and Ruby. (Rev: BL 9/1/12*; SLJ 10/12)

2456 Wells, Rosemary. *Max Cleans Up* (PS–3). Illus. 2000, Viking $15.99 (978-0-670-89218-1). Max's idea of cleaning up his room is to stuff everything into the front pocket of his overalls in this story about a delightful rabbit. (Rev: BL 2/1/01; HBG 10/01; SLJ 12/00)

2457 Wells, Rosemary. *Max's Bunny Business* (PS–1). Illus. by author. 2008, Viking $15.99 (978-0-670-01105-6). 32pp. Little rabbit Ruby and her friend Louise set up a lemonade stand to earn money to buy matching rings, but Ruby's brother Max foils their plan. (Rev: BL 3/1/08; HB 5/08; SLJ 6/08)

2458 Wells, Rosemary. *Otto Runs for President* (K–2). Illus. by author. 2008, Scholastic $15.99 (978-0-545-03722-8). 32pp. Will popular poodle Tiffany or athletic bulldog Charlie walk off with the election for president at Barkadelphia School? Or does Otto, a thoughtful mutt, stand a chance? (Rev: BL 7/08; SLJ 8/08)

2459 Wells, Rosemary. *Ruby's Beauty Shop* (PS–K). Illus. 2002, Viking $16.99 (978-0-670-03553-3). 32pp. Max the bunny gets a beauty makeover from his big sister Ruby and her friend Louise — and then Max does his own. (Rev: BCCB 11/02; BL 8/02; HBG 3/03; SLJ 10/02)

2460 Wells, Rosemary. *Yoko Finds Her Way* (K–3). Illus. by author. 2013, Disney/Hyperion $16.99 (978-1-4231-6512-5). 32pp. Young cat Yoko's ability to read signs helps her when she and her mother are separated at an airport. (Rev: BL 3/1/13; SLJ 9/13)

2461 Wells, Rosemary. *Yoko Learns to Read* (PS–1). Illus. by author. 2012, Hyperion $15.99 (978-1-4231-3823-5). 32pp. The Japanese American kitten only has three books at home and they are all in Japanese — how will she learn to read English? A teacher and librarian help out. (Rev: BL 12/15/11; SLJ 2/1/12)

2462 Wells, Rosemary. *Yoko's Show-and-Tell* (PS–1). Illus. by author. 2010, Hyperion $15.99 (978-1-4231-1955-5). 40pp. Against her mother's wishes, Yoko the cat brings her antique doll to school for show and tell, where the doll is tossed around and broken; fortunately, the doll is repaired and all is made well in the end. (Rev: BL 4/15/10; SLJ 7/1/10)

2463 Weninger, Brigitte. *Davy, Soccer Star!* (1–3). Illus. by Eve Tharlet. 2008, North-South $16.95 (978-0-7358-2196-5). 32pp. Davy and his Wild Rabbits hop to the task of getting into shape for the big match with the Bad Badgers. (Rev: BLO 8/28/08)

2464 Weninger, Brigitte. *Stay in Bed, Davy* (PS–1). Trans. by Marianne Martens. Illus. by Eve Tharlet. 2006, North-South $15.95 (978-0-7358-2048-7). Davy the rabbit is sick and his mother has told him to stay in bed, but his friend Eddie and cousin Kiki still find ways to have fun. (Rev: SLJ 3/06)

2465 Weston, Carrie. *The New Bear at School* (PS–2). Illus. by Tim Warnes. 2008, Scholastic $12.99 (978-0-545-05783-7). 32pp. A class full of cuddly little animals are surprised to find their new classmate is not a dear little teddy bear but a "hairy, scary grizzly bear." (Rev: BL 8/08; LMC 10/08; SLJ 7/08)

2466 Wheeler, Lisa. *Castaway Cats* (K–2). Illus. by Ponder Goembel. 2006, Simon & Schuster $16.95 (978-0-689-86232-8). 32pp. Stranded on a desert island, 15 independently minded cats decide to build a boat, and although they don't succeed in this they do set aside their differences and eventually decide to stay on the island. (Rev: BL 8/06; SLJ 6/06*)

2467 Wheeler, Lisa. *Dino-Baseball* (PS–2). Illus. by Barry Gott. 2010, Carolrhoda LB $16.95 (978-0-7613-4429-2). 32pp. The Rib-Eye Reds (carnivores) compete with the Green Sox (herbivores) in this action-packed rhyming romp. Also use *Dino-Basketball* (2011). (Rev: BL 3/1/10; SLJ 4/1/10)

2468 Wheeler, Lisa. *Dino-Hockey* (PS–2). Illus. by Barry Gott. 2007, Carolrhoda $16.95 (978-0-8225-6191-0). 32pp. It's Meat-Eaters versus Veggiesaurs in this fast and furious hockey game full of fun and facts. (Rev: BL 9/1/07; LMC 1/08; SLJ 12/07)

2469 Wheeler, Lisa. *Sailor Moo: Cow at Sea* (1–3). Illus. by Ponder Goembel. 2002, Simon & Schuster $16.95 (978-0-689-84219-1). A rhyming, humorous picture book about a young cow who longs to have a life at sea and ends up on a cattle barge turned pirate ship. (Rev: BL 5/1/02; HBG 3/03; SLJ 8/02)

2470 Wheeler, Lisa. *Ugly Pie* (PS–2). Illus. by Heather Solomon. 2010, Harcourt $16 (978-0-15-216754-7). 32pp. Ol' Bear collects unwanted ingredients from his friends and bakes a delicious Ugly Pie, which his friends happily help him eat; includes a recipe. Lexile AD670L (Rev: BL 7/10; HB 7–8/10; SLJ 7/1/10)

2471 Whybrow, Ian. *Bella Gets Her Skates On* (PS–K). Illus. by Rosie Reeve. 2007, Abrams $15.95 (978-0-8109-9416-4). Bella Rabbit worries when she faces a new task but with the loving support of Daddy Rabbit, she finds her confidence. (Rev: BL 12/1/07; SLJ 11/07)

2472 Wiesner, David. *Art and Max* (K–3). Illus. by author. 2010, Clarion $17.99 (978-0-618-75663-6). 40pp. Max's artistic aspirations have unexpected results in this compelling story about two lizard friends. (Rev: BL 10/15/10*; HB 11–12/10; LMC 1–2/11; SLJ 9/1/10*)

2473 Wiesner, David. *Tuesday* (PS–2). Illus. 1991, Houghton $17.00 (978-0-395-55113-4). Frogs have a wonderful time on Tuesday. Will the pigs have as great a time one week later? Caldecott Medal winner, 1992. (Rev: BCCB 5/91; BL 5/1/91; SLJ 5/91*)

2474 Wild, Margaret. *Piglet and Mama* (PS–K). Illus. by Stephen Michael King. 2005, Abrams $14.95 (978-0-8109-5869-2). 32pp. Poor piglet searches all over the farm for his mama, leading to a joyous reunion. (Rev: BL 3/1/05; SLJ 6/05)

2475 Wild, Margaret. *Piglet and Papa* (PS–K). Illus. by Stephen Michael King. 2007, Abrams $14.95 (978-0-8109-1476-6). 32pp. Piglet worries that her papa has stopped loving her, and she finds comfort and reassurance in this tender story. (Rev: BL 5/1/07; SLJ 7/07)

2476 Willems, Mo. *A Big Guy Took My Ball!* (PS–2). Illus. by author. Series: Elephant and Piggie. 2013, Disney/Hyperion $8.99 (978-1-4231-7491-2). 64pp. When a gigantic whale takes Piggie's ball, Gerald the elephant is not quite sure what to do. ALA Notable Children's Book. Lexile AD80 (Rev: BL 5/1/13; SLJ 7/13)

2477 Willems, Mo. *Can I Play Too?* (PS–2). Illus. by author. Series: Elephant and Piggie. 2010, Hyperion $8.99 (978-1-4231-1991-3). 64pp. Gerald the elephant and Piggie are playing catch — but can their armless new friend Snake join in? Lexile 70L (Rev: BLO 7/10; SLJ 8/1/10)

2478 Willems, Mo. *Cat the Cat, Who Is That?* (PS–1). Illus. by author. 2010, HarperCollins $12.99 (978-0-06-172840-2); LB $14.89 (978-0-06-172841-9). 32pp. Readers are introduced to a bright and outgoing cast of animal characters by the likable and effervescent Cat the Cat. (Rev: BL 3/15/10; HB 5–6/10; SLJ 2/1/10)

2479 Willems, Mo. *Don't Let the Pigeon Stay Up Late!* (PS). Illus. 2006, Hyperion $12.99 (978-0-7868-3746-5). 32pp. The irrepressible pigeon of *Don't Let the Pigeon Drive the Bus!* is not tired and has no intention of going to bed. (Rev: BL 2/15/06; SLJ 4/06*)

2480 Willems, Mo. *Happy Pig Day!* (PS–1). Illus. by author. Series: Elephant and Piggie. 2011, Hyperion $8.99 (978-1-4231-4342-0). 64pp. Gerald the elephant feels left out while his friend Piggie celebrates Pig Day with his porcine friends; in the end, however, Gerald realizes he can participate as well. (Rev: BL 10/15/11; SLJ 11/1/11)

2481 Willems, Mo. *I Am Going!* (PS–2). Illus. by author. Series: Elephant and Piggie. 2010, Hyperion $8.99 (978-1-4231-1990-6). 64pp. Gerald the elephant gets severe separation anxiety when best friend Piggie announces she is leaving. (Rev: BL 12/15/09; SLJ 6/1/10)

2482 Willems, Mo. *I Broke My Trunk!* (PS–2). Illus. by author. Series: Elephant and Piggie. 2011, Hyperion $8.99 (978-1-4231-3309-4). 64pp. Gerald the elephant tries to explain to Piggie the rather complicated story of how his trunk got broken. (Rev: BL 4/15/11; SLJ 5/1/11*)

2483 Willems, Mo. *I Love My New Toy!* (K–2). Illus. by author. Series: Elephant and Piggie. 2008, Hyperion $8.99 (978-1-4231-0961-7). 64pp. A "mishap" with a new toy threatens the friendship between Elephant and Piggie. Also use *I Will Surprise My Friend!* (2008). (Rev: BL 7/08)

2484 Willems, Mo. *I'm a Frog!* (PS–1). Illus. by author. 2013, Disney/Hyperion $8.99 (978-142318305-1). 64pp. Piggie has no success in getting Gerald to join him in a game of pretend. (Rev: BL 11/1/13; SLJ 12/13)

2485 Willems, Mo. *Let's Go for a Drive!* (PS–2). Illus. by author. Series: Elephant and Piggie. 2012, Hyperion $8.99 (978-1-42316482-1). 64pp. Gerald the elephant and Piggie spend a happy time planning what they need for a drive but eventually realize they have overlooked a very necessary item. ALSC Notable Book. (Rev: BL 10/1/12; SLJ 10/12*)

2486 Willems, Mo. *Listen to My Trumpet!* (PS–1). Illus. by author. Series: Elephant and Piggie. 2012, Hyperion $8.99 (978-1-4231-5404-4). 64pp. When Gerald the elephant summons the heart to tell Piggie her new trumpet makes an awful racket, she responds with grace and humor. (Rev: BL 2/1/12; SLJ 4/1/12*)

2487 Willems, Mo. *My Friend Is Sad* (PS–1). Illus. Series: Elephant and Piggie. 2007, Hyperion $8.99 (978-1-4231-0297-7). 64pp. Gerald the elephant is sad and Piggie, dressing in costumes, does his best to cheer him up but fails because Gerald does not recognize his best friend, and believes Piggie is missing all the fun. (Rev: BCCB 7–8/07; BL 4/1/07; HB 5/07)

2488 Willems, Mo. *Pigs Make Me Sneeze!* (PS–1). Illus. by author. Series: Elephant and Piggie. 2009, Hyperion $8.99 (978-1-4231-1411-6). 64pp. Convinced he must be allergic to his friend Piggie, Gerald the elephant is relieved when the doctor informs him the sniffles are only a cold. (Rev: BL 12/1/09; SLJ 12/1/09*)

2489 Willems, Mo. *That Is Not a Good Idea!* (PS–1). Illus. by author. 2013, HarperCollins $17.99 (978-006220309-0). 48pp. A fox slowly lures a naive duck back to his kitchen, only to have the tables turned on him in this silent-movie-style story book. Lexile AD230 (Rev: BL 5/15/13; SLJ 4/13*)

2490 Willems, Mo. *We Are in a Book!* (PS–2). Illus. by author. Series: Elephant and Piggie. 2010, Hyperion $8.99 (978-1-4231-3308-7). 64pp. In their latest clever adventure, Gerald the elephant and Piggie realize that they are in a book and someone is reading about them. (Rev: BL 9/15/10; LMC 3–4/11; SLJ 11/1/10*)

2491 Williams, Barbara. *Albert's Gift for Grandmother* (K–2). Illus. by Doug Cushman. 2006, Candlewick $15.99 (978-0-7636-2097-4). Downcast because he doesn't have a gift for his grandmother's birthday, Albert the turtle, first seen in *Albert's Impossible Toothache* (2003), finally comes up with an idea that he thinks will please her. (Rev: BL 11/1/06; SLJ 12/06)

2492 Willis, Jeanne. *Cottonball Colin* (PS–2). Illus. by Tony Ross. 2008, Eerdmans $16.00 (978-0-8028-5331-8). 26pp. The smallest mouse in the family, who has been overprotected by his mother, gets more adventure than he bargains for after he has been wrapped in cotton wool for safety. (Rev: BCCB 3/08; LMC 11/08; SLJ 4/08)

2493 Willis, Jeanne. *Gorilla! Gorilla!* (PS–2). Illus. by Tony Ross. 2006, Simon & Schuster $15.95 (978-1-4169-1490-7). A mouse who has lost her baby is chased around the world by a fierce gorilla — who is only trying to help. (Rev: SLJ 7/06)

2494 Willis, Jeanne. *Misery Moo* (PS–2). Illus. by Tony Ross. 2005, Holt $16.95 (978-0-8050-7672-1). Misery Moo won't be cheered despite a little lamb's best efforts, so he gives up and goes off in a state of depression of his own. (Rev: BL 5/15/04; SLJ 6/05)

2495 Willis, Jeanne. *Mommy Do You Love Me?* (PS). Illus. by Jan Fearnley. 2008, Candlewick $15.99 (978-0-7636-3470-4). Little Chick tests his mother's love with a series of challenges only to keep getting the same results. (Rev: BL 3/15/08; SLJ 4/08)

2496 Willis, Jeanne. *Tadpole's Promise* (K–4). Illus. by Tony Ross. 2005, Simon & Schuster $15.95 (978-0-689-86524-4). A caterpillar and a tadpole declare undying love and promise that neither of them will ever change. (Rev: BCCB 7–8/05; SLJ 5/05)

2497 Wilson, Karma. *Bear Feels Scared* (PS–1). Illus. by Jane Chapman. 2008, Simon & Schuster $16.99 (978-0-689-85986-1). Lost in a storm in the forest, a frightened Bear frets about the strange noises while back home his worried friends send out a rescue party. (Rev: BLO 9/2/08; SLJ 9/08) 🎧

2498 Wilson, Karma. *Bear Snores On* (PS–1). Illus. by Jane Chapman. 2002, Simon & Schuster $16.00 (978-0-689-83187-4). On a cold winter night, animals gather in a sleeping bear's cave to share food and warmth in this charming story told in rhyme. (Rev: BL 1/1–15/02; HBG 10/02; SLJ 1/02*)

2499 Wilson, Karma. *Bear Wants More* (PS–2). Illus. by Jane Chapman. 2003, Simon & Schuster $16.95 (978-0-689-84509-3). When spring comes, Bear wakes up and is extremely hungry. (Rev: BCCB 3/03; BL 4/15/03; HBG 10/03; SLJ 2/03)

2500 Wilson, Karma. *The Cow Loves Cookies* (PS–2). Illus. by Marcellus Hall. 2010, Simon & Schuster $16.99 (978-1-4169-4206-1). 40pp. The animals on the farm have very different tastes in food, but it's only the cow who likes cookies — why? (Rev: BL 4/15/10; LMC 8–9/10; SLJ 8/1/10)

2501 Wilson, Karma. *Hogwash!* (PS–1). Illus. by Jim McMullan. 2011, Little, Brown $16.99 (978-0-316-98840-7). 40pp. A mud bath is in the future for a farmer determined to give his reluctant pigs a wash; humorous illustrations add to the fun. (Rev: BL 6/1/11; SLJ 4/11)

2502 Wilson, Karma. *Mortimer's First Garden* (PS–2). Illus. by Dan Andreasen. 2009, Simon & Schuster $16.99 (978-1-4169-4203-0). 32pp. Mortimer the mouse plants a sunflower seed and, with some help from God, reaps a bountiful harvest. (Rev: BCCB 3/09; BL 2/1/09; SLJ 3/09)

2503 Wilson, Karma. *Who Goes There?* (PS–K). Illus. by Anna Currey. 2013, Simon & Schuster $16.99 (978-141698002-5). 40pp. Lewis Mouse is settling into his winter home when he hears strange noises and wonders who it can be; after imagining many possible creatures that might threaten him, he is relieved to find that it is just another mouse, Joy, who has been disturbed by his shouting. ℮ Lexile AD430 (Rev: BL 10/1/13; SLJ 12/13)

2504 Wise, William. *Christopher Mouse: The Tale of a Small Traveler* (3–5). Illus. by Patrick Benson. 2004, Bloomsbury $15.95 (978-1-58234-878-0). 152pp. Christopher Mouse, who learned his mother's lessons well, relates with humor and intelligence the ups and downs of his varied life. (Rev: BL 4/1/04*; SLJ 6/04)

2505 Wise, William. *Zany Zoo* (K–2). Illus. by Lynn Munsinger. 2006, Houghton $16.00 (978-0-618-18891-8). 32pp. Wacky animals and even wackier wordplay are presented in this appealing blend of rhyming verse and colorful artwork. (Rev: BL 4/15/06; SLJ 8/06)

2506 Wishinsky, Frieda. *Maggie Can't Wait* (PS–1). Illus. by Dean Griffiths. 2009, Fitzhenry & Whiteside $17.95 (978-1-55455-103-3). 32pp. A little cat girl is excited about the kitten her family is planning to adopt but this joy is deflated by her friends' lack of enthusiasm about the baby's picture. (Rev: BLO 11/15/09; SLJ 4/1/10)

2507 Wollman, Jessica. *Andrew's Bright Blue T-Shirt* (PS–2). Illus. by Ana L. Escriva. 2002, Doubleday $14.95 (978-0-385-74616-8). 32pp. A young fox named Andrew dreams of playing soccer and wears his brother's hand-me-down soccer T-shirt every day, until he tragically grows out of it — and his brother says he's now old enough to play. (Rev: BL 10/1/02; HBG 3/03; SLJ 10/02)

2508 Wood, A. J. *The Little Penguin* (PS–2). Illus. by Stephanie Boey. 2002, Dutton $15.99 (978-0-525-47023-6). 32pp. A visually appealing, tender book about a young, fuzzy penguin who longs for his father's refined look. (Rev: BL 10/15/02; HBG 3/03; SLJ 12/02)

2509 Wood, Audrey. *Jubal's Wish* (PS–3). Illus. by Don Wood. 2000, Scholastic $17.99 (978-0-439-16964-6). 32pp. Jubal wants his friends to join him on a picnic but they are too busy to attend in this story about friendship. (Rev: BL 12/1/00; HBG 3/01; SLJ 10/00)

2510 Wood, Audrey. *Little Penguin's Tale* (PS–2). Illus. 1989, Harcourt $13.95 (978-0-15-246475-2). 32pp. Little Penguin's escapades result in his being swallowed by a whale. (Rev: BL 11/15/89)

2511 Wood, Audrey. *Piggy Pie Po* (PS–K). Illus. by author. 2010, Harcourt $16.99 (978-0-15-202494-9). 32pp. Piggy Pie Po is a messy, rambunctious, happy-go-lucky piglet in these three rhyming and exuberant vignettes. ❢ (Rev: BL 6/10; SLJ 8/1/10)

2512 Wood, Audrey. *Silly Sally* (PS). Illus. 1992, Harcourt $16.00 (978-0-15-274428-1). This delightful nonsense book tells of Silly Sally and her trip into town walking backwards and upside down. (Rev: BCCB 6/92; BL 3/15/92*; SLJ 4/92)

2513 Wood, Douglas. *What Grandmas Can't Do* (PS–K). Illus. by Doug Cushman. 2005, Simon & Schuster $14.95 (978-0-689-84647-2). A follow-up to *What Moms Can't Do* (2001) and *What Dads Can't Do* (2000), this loving picture book features a dinosaur grandma who can't hug without a kiss, but is capable of plenty of other things. (Rev: SLJ 7/05)

2514 Wood, Douglas. *What Teachers Can't Do* (PS–2). Illus. by Doug Cushman. 2002, Simon & Schuster $14.95 (978-0-689-84644-1). A young dinosaur looks at all the silly and odd things teachers can't do — be late for school, add 2 + 2, for example. (Rev: BL 8/02; HBG 3/03; SLJ 10/02)

2515 Wormell, Christopher. *Henry and the Fox* (K–2). Illus. by author. 2008, Trafalgar $19.95 (978-0-224-07044-7). 32pp. Henry the cowardly cockerell's plan to show himself in a brave light takes an unexpected turn and, to his surprise, convinces the other animals of his courage. (Rev: BLO 5/30/08; SLJ 2/08)

2516 Wright, Johanna. *The Secret Circus* (PS–K). Illus. by author. 2009, Roaring Brook $16.95 (978-1-59643-403-5). 32pp. A mouse family travels to see a tiny circus in Paris that is known only to mice. (Rev: BL 4/15/09; SLJ 4/09)

2517 Wright, Maureen. *Sleep, Big Bear, Sleep!* (PS–1). Illus. by Will Hillenbrand. 2009, Marshall Cavendish $16.99 (978-0-7614-5560-8). Unpaged. Big Bear misunderstands Old Man Winter's instructions to hibernate in this nicely illustrated story. Also use *Sneeze, Big Bear, Sneeze* (2011). (Rev: HB 1–2/10; SLJ 9/1/09)

2518 Wu, Liz. *Rosa Farm* (2–4). Illus. by Matt Phelan. 2006, Knopf $15.95 (978-0-375-83681-7). 134pp. Gallileon, a young rooster, is nervous about filling in for his father, but welcoming the rising sun turns out to be only the beginning of a difficult day. (Rev: SLJ 1/07)

2519 Yaccarino, Dan. *Unlovable* (PS–1). Illus. by author. 2002, Holt $15.95 (978-0-8050-6321-9). 32pp. A puppy who is teased unmercifully about his funny looks befriends a dog he can't see — and who can't see him — on the other side of the fence. (Rev: BL 11/15/01; HBG 10/02; SLJ 1/02)

2520 Yamaguchi, Kristi. *Dream Big, Little Pig!* (PS–1). Illus. by Tim Bowers. 2011, Sourcebooks $16.99 (978-1-4022-5275-4). 32pp. Discouraged from planning a life in ballet, persistent Poppy the pig decides to become an ice-skating star. (Rev: BL 5/1/11; SLJ 5/1/11)

2521 Yamashita, Haruo. *Seven Little Mice Go to School* (PS–2). Illus. by Kazuo Iwamura. 2011, NorthSouth $16.95 (978-0-7358-4012-6). 44pp. Seven little mice nurture different fears about the first day of school, but they gain courage as they form a Mouse Train on their way through the forest. Lexile AD500L (Rev: BL 8/11; SLJ 6/11)

2522 Yates, Louise. *A Small Surprise* (PS–K). Illus. by author. 2009, Knopf $16.99 (978-0-375-85698-3). 40pp. Little rabbit would like to do more grown up things but all he can manage is a few disappearing tricks. (Rev: BL 6/1–15/09; SLJ 5/09)

2523 Yee, Wong H. *Abracadabra!* (K–3). Illus. by author. 2007, Houghton $15.00 (978-0-618-75926-2). 48pp. In this sequel to *Upstairs Mouse, Downstairs Mole,* Minkus the Magnificent's performance disappoints magic-fan Mole who then questions magic's existence, but Mouse soon convinces Mole that magic is all around them — in tadpoles turning into frogs, in the full moon, in fireflies, and so forth. (Rev: BL 11/1/07; HB 11/07; SLJ 12/07)

2524 Yee, Wong H. *Mouse and Mole, Fine Feathered Friends* (K–3). Illus. by author. Series: Mouse and Mole. 2009, Houghton Mifflin $15 (978-0-547-15222-6). 48pp. Mouse and Mole contrive a unique way to attract birds so they can observe and sketch them. Also use *Mouse and Mole: A Winter Wonderland* (2010). ❢ (Rev: BL 9/15/09; SLJ 2/1/10)

2525 Yee, Wong H. *A Winter Wonderland* (K–3). Illus. by author. Series: Mouse and Mole. 2010, Houghton Mifflin paper $15 (978-05473415-2-1). 48pp. After a contrary start, Mouse and Mole come together to enjoy a snowy day. Lexile 410L (Rev: BL 11/15/10; SLJ 11/10)

2526 Yolen, Jane. *Dimity Duck* (PS). Illus. by Sebastien Braun. 2006, Philomel $15.99 (978-0-399-24632-6). 32pp. Appealing art and rhyming verse follow Dimity Duck through a satisfying day, including playtime with her friend Frumity Frog then happily climbing into her nest for bedtime. (Rev: BL 6/1–15/06; SLJ 6/06)

2527 Yolen, Jane. *How Do Dinosaurs Get Well Soon?* (PS–1). Illus. by Mark Teague. 2003, Scholastic $16.99 (978-0-439-24100-7). 40pp. Humorous, full-color illustrations are coupled with rhyming text to show giant young dinosaurs who must learn how to behave while ill (taking medicine, resting, and so forth). Also use *How Do Dinosaurs Eat Their Food?* (2005) and *How Do Dinosaurs Go to School?* (2007). (Rev: BL 1/1–15/03*; HB 3/03; HBG 10/03; SLJ 2/03)

2528 Yolen, Jane. *How Do Dinosaurs Say I Love You?* (PS–K). Illus. by Mark Teague. 2009, Scholastic $16.99 (978-0-545-14314-1). 40pp. Parent dinosaurs forgive their children for misbehaving in various ways. Lexile AD520L (Rev: BL 11/1/09; SLJ 10/1/09)

2529 Yolen, Jane. *Off We Go!* (PS–K). Illus. by Laurel Molk. 2000, Little, Brown $12.95 (978-0-316-90228-1). A bouncy picture book about several animals, all of whom are on their way to visit their grandmothers. (Rev: BCCB 3/00; BL 3/15/00; HBG 10/00; SLJ 5/00)

2530 Yoon, Salina. *Penguin on Vacation* (PS–1). Illus. by author. 2013, Walker $14.99 (978-0-8027-3397-9). 40pp. Penguin needs a break from snow and ice and decides to head to the tropics, where he meets Crab and they have all sorts of fun together; so Penguin invites Crab to visit him. **e** Lexile 310 (Rev: BLO 4/1/13; HB 7–8/13; SLJ 4/13)

2531 Yorinks, Arthur. *Hey, Al* (2–4). Illus. 1986, Farrar $17.00 (978-0-374-33060-6); paper $5.95 (978-0-374-42985-0). 32pp. Eddie the dog wants to change his life, but when a bird takes him and Al the janitor to a bird-inhabited island, Eddie isn't quite so sure. Caldecott Medal winner, 1987. (Rev: BL 1/1/87; SLJ 3/87)

2532 Young, Ned. *Zoomer's Summer Snowstorm* (K–2). Illus. by author. 2011, HarperCollins $16.99 (978-0-06-170092-7). 32pp. A snow-cone machine overflow turns into a hot summer day delight for pooch Zoomer and his friends. (Rev: BL 4/15/11; SLJ 5/1/11)

2533 Zalben, Jane Breskin. *Mousterpiece* (PS–3). Illus. by author. 2012, Roaring Brook $16.99 (978-1-59643-549-0). 40pp. A little mouse named Janson is inspired to paint by the modern art in her museum, and does so well that the museum director gives Janson her own show. (Rev: BL 9/15/12*; LMC 3–4/13; SLJ 8/12)

2534 Zane, Alexander. *The Wheels on the Race Car* (PS–K). Illus. by James Warhola. 2005, Scholastic LB $14.95 (978-0-439-59080-8). In an exciting, action-packed combination of bright illustrations and compelling verse, rambunctious animals pilot racecars around a track, stopping for fill-ups and tune-ups. (Rev: BL 2/1/05; LMC 8/05; SLJ 3/05)

2535 Ziefert, Harriet. *Egad Alligator!* (PS–3). Illus. by Todd McKie. 2002, Houghton $16.00 (978-0-618-14171-5). 40pp. Little Gator doesn't understand why people are afraid of him until he experiences fear himself when he sits on a python. (Rev: BCCB 9/02; BL 4/15/02; HBG 10/02; SLJ 4/02)

2536 Zolotow, Charlotte. *Mr. Rabbit and the Lovely Present* (PS–3). Illus. by Maurice Sendak. 1977, HarperCollins paper $6.95 (978-0-06-443020-3). 32pp. A little girl meets Mr. Rabbit, and together they find the perfect birthday gift for her mother.

Realistic Stories

ADVENTURE STORIES

2537 Agee, Jon. *Terrific* (K–2). Illus. 2005, Hyperion $15.95 (978-0-7868-5184-3). 32pp. Stranded on a desert island when his cruise ship sinks, Eugene Mudge — who views life through the lens of his pessimism — begins to change his negative attitude when a talking parrot takes him under his wing. (Rev: BL 10/15/05; HB 11/05; LMC 1/06; SLJ 9/05)

2538 Ahlberg, Allan. *It Was a Dark and Stormy Night* (K–3). Illus. by Janet Ahlberg. 1994, Viking $13.99 (978-0-670-85159-1). A young captive of robbers escapes in the confusion caused by their acting out a story that he has told them. (Rev: BCCB 7–8/94; BL 5/1/94)

2539 Axtell, David. *We're Going on a Lion Hunt* (PS–1). Illus. 2000, Holt $15.95 (978-0-8050-6159-8). 32pp. In this variation on the familiar chant, two African girls go out on a lion hunt. (Rev: BCCB 5/00; BL 2/15/00; HBG 10/00; SLJ 5/00)

2540 Base, Graeme. *The Legend of the Golden Snail* (2–4). Illus. by author. 2010, Abrams $19.95 (978-0-8109-8965-8). 48pp. In this inventive, compassionate story, a kind-hearted little boy sets off in search of a fantastical ship, encountering many small creatures who need his help along the way. Lexile AD690L (Rev: BL 9/15/10; LMC 1–2/11; SLJ 10/1/10)

2541 Bauer, Hans, and Catherine Masciola. *Fishtale* (4–7). Illus. by Catherine Masciola. 2012, Amazon Children's $16.99 (978-076146223-1). 220pp. In the Mississippi bayou, 12-year-old Sawyer — with his sister and friends — sets out to find a legendary catfish that may have his widowed mother's missing wedding ring. ∩ **e** (Rev: BL 10/15/12; LMC 5–6/13; SLJ 1/13)

2542 Blake, Robert J. *Swift* (K–3). Illus. by author. 2007, Philomel $16.99 (978-0-399-23383-8). 48pp. After a grizzly attacks his father, Johnnie and his dog Swift set out across the Alaskan wilderness to get help. (Rev: BL 9/15/07; HB 9/07; SLJ 9/07)

2543 Buzzeo, Toni. *Adventure Annie Goes to Work* (PS). Illus. by Amy Wummer. 2009, Dial $16.99 (978-0-8037-3233-9). 32pp. Annie (aka Adventure Girl) turns a trip to Mommy's office into an opportunity to show her skills. (Rev: BL 2/1/09; SLJ 1/09)

2544 Caines, Jeannette. *Just Us Women* (PS–2). Illus. by Pat Cummings. 1984, HarperCollins paper $6.99 (978-0-06-443056-2). 32pp. A little African American girl is looking forward to a car ride she is going to take with her aunt.

2545 Carter, Anne Laurel. *Under a Prairie Sky* (PS–3). Illus. by Alan Daniel and Lea Daniel. 2002, Orca $16.95 (978-1-55143-226-7). 32pp. A Canadian boy gets a taste of being a Mountie when he rescues his younger brother from a coming storm. (Rev: BL 5/15/02; HBG 10/02; SLJ 6/02)

2546 Crowley, Ned. *Nanook and Pryce: Gone Fishing* (PS–2). Illus. by Larry Day. 2009, HarperCollins $17.99 (978-0-06-133641-6). 32pp. Two children and their dog drift all the way around the world on a chunk of glacial ice, having many exciting experiences. (Rev: BL 9/1/09; SLJ 1/1/10)

2547 Cummings, Pat. *Harvey Moon, Museum Boy* (K–2). Illus. by author. 2008, HarperCollins $16.99 (978-0-688-17889-5). 32pp. Harvey Moon's class trip to the museum becomes an adventure when his pet lizard, Zippy, escapes and Harvey spends an exciting night in the museum complete with encounters with mummies and dinosaurs. (Rev: BL 12/1/07; SLJ 3/08)

2548 Doyen, Denise. *Once Upon a Twice* (PS–1). Illus. by Barry Moser. 2009, Random $16.99 (978-0-375-85612-9). 32pp. Young Jam disregards the adults' warnings and ventures at night into the swamp where many perils await in this slightly scary book filled with rich nonsensical language. (Rev: BL 7/09)

2549 Duddle, Jonny. *The Pirates Next Door* (K–2). Illus. by author. 2012, Candlewick $15.99 (978-0-7636-5842-7). 44pp. Dull-on-Sea, a town full of staid old folks, receives a comic and surprising upset when pirates move in next door to Matilda, one of the few children. (Rev: BL 2/1/12; LMC 8–9/12*; SLJ 3/1/12)

2550 English, Karen. *Big Wind Coming!* (PS–2). Illus. by Cedric Lucas. 1996, Whitman LB $14.95 (978-0-8075-0726-1). A severe windstorm and its effects on an African American family as seen through the eyes of the young daughter. (Rev: BCCB 1/97; BL 10/15/96; SLJ 11/96)

2551 Fagan, Cary. *Thing-Thing* (K–2). Illus. by Nicolas Debon. 2008, Tundra $18.95 (978-0-88776-839-2). 32pp. A rejected little stuffed creature's long fall ends happily; illustrations full of scary perspectives add to this lighthearted tale. (Rev: HB 9/08; SLJ 9/08)

2552 Fleming, Candace. *Clever Jack Takes the Cake* (PS–2). Illus. by G. Brian Karas. 2010, Random House $17.99 (978-0-375-84979-4). 40pp. En route to the princess's birthday party, the cake Jack baked is slowly demolished in a series of mishaps, until all he has left to give the princess is the story of his day. Fortunately, it ends up being the best gift of all. e Lexile AD600L (Rev: BL 7/10*; LMC 11–12/10; SLJ 7/1/10*)

2553 Fleming, Candace. *Sunny Boy! The Life and Times of a Tortoise* (K–2). Illus. by Anne Wilsdorf. 2005, Farrar $16.00 (978-0-374-37297-2). 40pp. In this fact-based picture book, Sunny Boy, a 100-year-old tortoise, tells about the many adventures in his life, including a trip over Niagara Falls in a barrel with his daredevil owner. (Rev: BL 8/05; SLJ 8/05)

2554 Fox, Mem. *Tough Boris* (PS–3). Illus. by Kathryn Brown. 1994, Harcourt $16.00 (978-0-15-289612-6). 32pp. Boris is a rough and tough pirate, but when his parrot dies, he cries. (Rev: BL 3/1/94; HB 5/94; SLJ 5/94)

2555 Funke, Cornelia. *Pirate Girl* (K–2). Illus. by Kerstin Meyer. 2005, Scholastic $15.99 (978-0-439-71672-7). 32pp. A band of pirates meet their match when they kidnap young Molly. (Rev: BL 6/1–15/05)

2556 Garland, Michael. *Super Snow Day Seek and Find* (2–4). Illus. by author. Series: A Look Again Book. 2010, Dutton $16.99 (978-0-525-42245-7). 32pp. A young boy follows his aunt's rhymed clues to explore a winter wonderland in this story enhanced by seek-and-find illustrations. (Rev: BL 1/1–15/11; SLJ 12/1/10)

2557 Hallowell, George, and Joan Holub. *Wagons Ho!* (1–3). Illus. by Lynne Avril. 2011, Whitman $16.99 (978-0-8075-8612-9). 32pp. Two parallel stories chronicle trips from Missouri to Oregon; the one featuring Jenny in 1846 takes five months while Katie's journey in 2011 takes five days. (Rev: BL 10/1/11; SLJ 8/1/11)

2558 Jardine, Alan. *Sloop John B: A Pirate's Tale* (PS–1). Illus. by Jimmy Pickering. 2005, Milk & Cookies $17.95 (978-0-689-03596-8). A boy and his grandfather

fight off pirates aboard the *John B* in this beautifully illustrated book inspired by the traditional folk song; comes with a music CD. (Rev: SLJ 7/05)

2559 Lamb, Albert. *The Abandoned Lighthouse* (PS–2). Illus. by David McPhail. 2011, Roaring Brook $15.99 (978-1-59643-525-4). 32pp. A bear, a boy, and a dog end up at an abandoned lighthouse, where they catch some fish, eat dinner, and have a snooze, waking up just in time to get the light working again and avert a disaster. (Rev: BL 5/1/11; SLJ 6/11)

2560 Lane, Adam J. B. *Stop Thief!* (K–2). Illus. by author. 2012, Roaring Brook $16.99 (978-159643693-0). 32pp. After announcing that he's too grown up for his stuffed pig, young Randall nonetheless comes to its rescue when a burglar takes off with it and conducts a dramatic chase. (Rev: BL 5/1/12; SLJ 6/1/12)

2561 Look, Lenore. *Ruby Lu, Brave and True* (1–3). Illus. by Anne Wilsdorf. 2004, Simon & Schuster $15.95 (978-0-689-84907-7). 112pp. Ruby, a Chinese American 8-year-old, deals with family, school, and cultural problems in this appealing book with a glossary of terms. (Rev: BL 1/1–15/04; SLJ 2/04)

2562 Lumry, Amanda, and Laura Hurwitz. *Amazon River Rescue* (K–4). Illus. by Sarah McIntyre. Series: Adventures of Riley. 2004, Eaglemont Pr. $15.95 (978-0-9662257-9-2). Riley and Alice come across animals including a jaguar when they get lost in the Amazon; lots of sidebars supply factual information. (Rev: SLJ 11/04)

2563 Martin, Bill, Jr., and John Archambault. *White Dynamite and Curly Kidd* (1–3). Illus. by Ted Rand. 1986, Holt paper $6.95 (978-0-8050-1018-3). 48pp. A nervous fan carries on a conversation with a bull rider who is about to break out of the chute on White Dynamite. (Rev: BL 7/86; SLJ 4/86)

2564 Mauner, Claudia, and Elisa Smalley. *Zoe Sophia in New York: The Mystery of the Pink Phoenix Papers* (1–3). 2006, Chronicle $14.95 (978-0-8118-4877-0). 32pp. Zoe Sophia's Great-Aunt Dorothy comes to New York for a visit, during which they see many sites and search for a missing diary; a sequel to *Zoe Sophia's Scrapbook* (2003). (Rev: BL 6/1–15/06; SLJ 4/06)

2565 Mayhew, James. *Miranda the Explorer: A Magical Round-the-World Adventure* (1–3). Illus. by author. 2003, Orion $16.95 (978-1-84255-000-7). Another adventure for the plucky Miranda of *Miranda the Castaway,* this time involving a perilous round-the-world trip by hot-air balloon, sprinkled with foreign words and images. (Rev: BL 1/1–15/04; SLJ 6/04)

2566 Meyers, Susan. *Bear in the Air* (PS–K). Illus. by Amy June Bates. 2010, Abrams $15.95 (978-0-8109-8398-4). 32pp. A baby's teddy bear has exciting adventures after being dropped out of the pram. (Rev: BL 5/1/10; LMC 10/10; SLJ 5/1/10)

2567 Mitton, Tony. *Once Upon a Tide* (PS–K). Illus. by Selina Young. 2006, Random $16.95 (978-0-385-75100-1). Two small children have an adventurous and imaginative day at the beach searching for buried treasure. (Rev: SLJ 5/06)

2568 Quattlebaum, Mary. *Pirate vs. Pirate: The Terrific Tale of a Big, Blustery Maritime Match* (PS–2). Illus. by Alexandra Boiger. 2011, Hyperion/Disney $16.99 (978-1-4231-2201-2). 40pp. Two pirates — Bad Bart and his female counterpart Mean Mo — battle to show who is the strongest in this buccaneer romp with humor and romance. Lexile AD510L (Rev: BL 3/1/11; LMC 8–9/11; SLJ 3/1/11)

2569 Rosen, Michael J. *We're Going on a Bear Hunt* (PS–2). Illus. by Helen Oxenbury. 1989, Macmillan $17.00 (978-0-689-50476-1). The storytelling favorite is re-created with expansive pictures that capture the enthusiasm of the story. (Rev: BCCB 9/89; BL 8/89*; HB 11/89*; SLJ 8/89*)

2570 Rosenthal, Eileen. *Bobo the Sailor Man!* (PS–1). Illus. by Marc Rosenthal. 2013, Atheneum $15.99 (978-144244443-0). 40pp. Willy's cat, Earl, must come to the rescue when the young boy puts his sock monkey in a bucket in the river. **e** Lexile AD470 (Rev: BLO 9/15/13; SLJ 8/13)

2571 San Souci, Daniel. *The Amazing Ghost Detectives* (1–4). Illus. by author. Series: Clubhouse Books. 2006, Tricycle $15.95 (978-1-58246-165-6). Danny and the rest of the gang return to find someone has been in their clubhouse but the lock is untouched; could it be a ghost? (Rev: SLJ 4/07)

2572 Sauer, Tammi. *Cowboy Camp* (PS–2). Illus. by Mike Reed. 2005, Sterling $14.95 (978-1-4027-2224-0). 32pp. Avery seems an unlikely candidate for Cowboy Camp, but he eventually proves his worth when he foils an evil scheme by Black Bart. (Rev: BL 2/15/06; SLJ 3/06)

2573 Shannon, David. *How Georgie Radbourn Saved Baseball* (1–5). Illus. 1994, Scholastic $14.95 (978-0-590-47410-8). 32pp. A rich and powerful wheeler-dealer decides to ban baseball, and it's up to young Georgie Radbourn to save it. (Rev: BL 1/15/94; SLJ 4/94*)

2574 Stead, Philip Christian. *Jonathan and the Big Blue Boat* (PS–2). Illus. by author. 2011, Roaring Brook $16.99 (978-1-59643-562-9). 32pp. Jonathan has a series of adventures on his worldwide quest for the teddy bear his parents have taken away. (Rev: BL 6/1/11; LMC 11–12/11; SLJ 6/11)

2575 Stevenson, James. *"Could Be Worse!"* (K–3). Illus. by author. 1977, Morrow paper $6.99 (978-0-688-07035-9). 32pp. Grandpa's response to minor catastrophes is always the same.

2576 Swanson, Diane. *The Balloon Sailors* (2–4). Illus. by Krystyna Lipka-Sztarballo. 2003, Annick LB $15.95 (978-1-55037-809-2). A family in a kingdom divided by a guarded stone wall decides to fly over it in a hot-air balloon; a postscript likens the situation to Berlin after World War II. (Rev: SLJ 3/04)

2577 Trueman, Terry. *Hurricane* (5–7). 2008, HarperCollins $15.99 (978-0-06-000018-9). 144pp. José is 13 when Hurricane Mitch hits his village in Honduras and he must deal with the death and destruction left behind. (Rev: BL 12/1/07; SLJ 3/08)

2578 Van Camp, Katie. *CookieBot! A Harry and Horsie Adventure* (PS–1). Illus. by Lincoln Agnew. 2011, HarperCollins $16.99 (978-006197445-8). 32pp. Harry and his toy horse create a robot designed to help them get into the cookie jar, but the robot runs amok. (Rev: BL 6/1/11; SLJ 6/11)

2579 Van Dusen, Chris. *Randy Riley's Really Big Hit* (1–3). Illus. by author. 2012, Candlewick $15.99 (978-076364946-3). 32pp. Gifted in both science and baseball, Randy finds a way to save his town from an encroaching fireball from space. (Rev: BL 2/1/12; LMC 8–9/12; SLJ 1/12)

2580 Ward, Helen. *The Boat* (1–3). Illus. by Ian Andrew. 2005, Simply Read $16.95 (978-1-894965-18-7). 32pp. When flooding threatens an old man and his menagerie of animals, it is a young boy who tries to save them all. (Rev: BL 6/1–15/05)

2581 Wheeler, Lisa. *Seadogs: An Epic Ocean Operetta* (PS–2). Illus. by Mark Siegel. 2004, Simon & Schuster $16.95 (978-0-689-85689-1). In Victorian times, a little girl dog enjoys going to an operetta about and starring seagoing dogs in this comic-book-style story for the youngest readers. (Rev: BL 2/1/04; HB 3/04; SLJ 3/04)

2582 Williams, Vera B. *Three Days on a River in a Red Canoe* (K–3). Illus. by author. 1981, Greenwillow $16.89 (978-0-688-84307-6); Morrow paper $6.99 (978-0-688-04072-7). 32pp. A little girl describes a canoe trip with her cousins and their mother.

COMMUNITY AND EVERYDAY LIFE

2583 Addasi, Maha. *Time to Pray* (K–3). Trans. by Nuha Albitar. Illus. by Ned Gannon. 2010, Boyds Mills $17.95 (978-1-59078-611-6). 32pp. Visiting her mother in the Middle East, young Yasmin learns about various Muslim traditions that she can take home with her; with parallel text in Arabic. (Rev: BLO 10/15/10; SLJ 9/1/10)

2584 Ahlberg, Allan. *Hooray for Bread* (PS–1). Illus. by Bruce Ingman. 2013, Candlewick $15.99 (978-0-7636-6311-7). 32pp. A rhyming look at the life of a single loaf of bread and all the people and animals it feeds. (Rev: BL 3/15/13; LMC 8–9/13; SLJ 4/13)

2585 Ajmera, Maya. *Global Babies* (PS). Illus. 2007, Charlesbridge $6.95 (978-1-58089-174-5). 18pp. Many ethnic groups are represented in this book consisting of close-up photographs of babies' faces. (Rev: BL 7/07)

2586 Alda, Arlene. *Lulu's Piano Lesson* (K–3). Illus. by Lisa Desimini. 2010, Tundra $16.95 (978-0-88776-930-6). 32pp. Lulu's piano teacher manages to circumvent the fact the young girl has not practiced all week. (Rev: BL 8/10; SLJ 7/1/10)

2587 Aliki. *Hello! Good-bye!* (PS–2). Illus. 1996, Greenwillow $14.89 (978-0-688-14334-3). 32pp. The many ways of saying "hello" and "good-bye" around the world. (Rev: BCCB 12/96; BL 7/96; SLJ 9/96)

2588 Aliki. *Quiet in the Garden* (PS–K). Illus. by author. 2009, Greenwillow $17.99 (978-0-06-155207-6). 32pp. A little boy quietly watches the animals in his garden, imagining their conversations. (Rev: BCCB 3/09; BL 11/15/08; SLJ 2/09)

2589 Allen, Kit. *Slide, Already!* (PS–2). Illus. 2005, Houghton $12.00 (978-0-618-49643-3). 32pp. A simple story about the fears and joys involved in a boy's first experience on a slide. (Rev: BL 6/1–15/05)

2590 Alsdurf, Phyllis. *It's Milking Time* (K–2). Illus. by Steve Johnson. 2012, Random House $16.99 (978-0-375-86911-2); LB $19.99 (978-037596911-9). 40pp. A young girl helps her father with the regular, twice-daily cycle of milking in this gentle, detailed story. (Rev: BL 4/1/12; SLJ 4/1/12)

2591 Amado, Elisa. *Tricycle* (PS–2). Illus. by Alfonso Ruano. 2007, Groundwood $17.95 (978-0-88899-614-5). 32pp. When Margarita, a child of privilege in Guatemala, sees her friend Rosario steal her bicycle, she says nothing, keenly aware of the poverty in which her friend lives. (Rev: BL 4/1/07; SLJ 6/07)

2592 Anderson, Sara. *A Day at the Market* (PS–2). Illus. by author. 2006, Handprint $14.95 (978-1-59354-149-1). The sights and sounds of Seattle's Pike Place Market are depicted in rhyme and artistic collages in this large-format board book. (Rev: SLJ 5/06)

2593 Ashburn, Boni. *I Had a Favorite Dress* (1–3). Illus. by Julia Denos. 2011, Abrams $16.95 (978-1-4197-0016-3). 32pp. A young girl's favorite dress is constantly refashioned as she grows and grows. (Rev: BLO 8/11; SLJ 8/1/11)

2594 Aylesworth, Jim. *Cock-a-Doodle-doo, Creak, Pop-pop, Moo* (PS–1). Illus. by Brad Sneed. 2012, Holiday House $16.95 (978-082342356-9). 32pp. Rhyming text and bright illustrations show life on a farm in days gone by. (Rev: BL 4/15/12; SLJ 5/1/12)

2595 Ayres, Katherine. *Matthew's Truck* (PS). Illus. by Hideko Takahashi. 2005, Candlewick $8.99 (978-0-7636-2269-5). 24pp. A toddler-friendly board book about a little boy imagining himself the driver of his toy dump truck. (Rev: BL 3/1/05)

2596 Baguley, Elizabeth. *Meggie Moon* (PS–2). Illus. by Gregoire Mabire. 2005, Good Bks $16.00 (978-1-56148-474-4). Digger and Tiger spurn Meggie Moon's overtures because she's a girl, but they change their tune when she constructs a snappy-looking race car from scraps and refuse. (Rev: SLJ 10/05)

2597 Baicker, Karen. *You Can Do It Too!* (PS). Illus. by Ken Wilson-Max. 2005, Handprint $13.95 (978-1-59354-080-7). 24pp. A girl encourages her little brother to do as she is doing. (Rev: BL 6/1–15/05)

2598 Baker, Jeannie. *Home* (K–3). Illus. 2004, Greenwillow $16.99 (978-0-06-623935-4). Without a single word, Baker tells a compelling story of the value of conservation and environmental action. (Rev: BL 3/15/04*; HB 3/04; SLJ 3/04)

2599 Baker, Jeannie. *Window* (2–4). Illus. 1991, Greenwillow $17.89 (978-0-688-08918-4). The changes from a rural to an urban setting are traced in the changes seen through a window. (Rev: BCCB 3/91; BL 4/15/91; HB 5/91; SLJ 3/91*)

2600 Bang, Molly. *Yellow Ball* (PS–1). Illus. 1991, Morrow LB $15.89 (978-0-688-06315-3). 24pp. The yellow ball over the sea on the jacket becomes the focus of a game of catch. (Rev: BCCB 4/91; BL 3/1/91*; SLJ 5/91)

2601 Barber, Barbara E. *Saturday at The New You* (PS–3). Illus. by Anna Rich. 1994, Lee & Low $14.95 (978-1-880000-06-9). 32pp. Shauna, an African American girl, has fun on Saturdays helping at her mother's beauty shop. (Rev: BCCB 12/94; BL 12/1/94; SLJ 1/95)

2602 Barrett, Mary Brigid. *Shoebox Sam* (1–3). Illus. by Frank Morrison. 2011, Zondervan $15.99 (978-0-310-71549-8). 32pp. Two children learn the value of generosity by watching and assisting a kindly shoe-shop proprietor. (Rev: BL 7/11; SLJ 8/1/11)

2603 Barton, Chris. *Shark vs. Train* (PS–1). Illus. by Tom Lichtenheld. 2010, Little, Brown $16.99 (978-0-316-00762-7). 40pp. Two boys face-off in a spirited toy chest showdown in this wacky, imaginative story. (Rev: BL 4/15/10; SLJ 4/1/10*)

2604 Bateson-Hill, Margaret. *Shota and the Star Quilt* (PS–3). Illus. by Christine Fowler. 1998, Zero to Ten $14.95 (978-1-84089-021-1). Shota, a Lakota girl, and her friend Esther persuade their landlord not to tear down their apartment building, by showing him a star quilt that celebrates their apartment home. (Rev: BL 2/1/99; HBG 3/99)

2605 Bean, Jonathan. *At Night* (PS–K). Illus. by author. 2007, Farrar $15.00 (978-0-374-30446-1). Shadows and light expressed in this book's watercolor illustrations complement the gentle text about a young girl seeking the peace and open air of her rooftop at night. (Rev: BCCB 10/07; BL 7/07; HB 1/09; SLJ 9/07)

2606 Beaumont, Karen. *I Like Myself!* (PS–1). Illus. by David Catrow. 2004, Harcourt $16.00 (978-0-15-202013-2). Bright illustrations enliven the humorous verse about a girl who likes herself both inside and out. (Rev: BCCB 7–8/04; SLJ 7/04)

2607 Berger, Carin. *A Perfect Day* (PS–1). Illus. by author. 2012, Greenwillow $16.99 (978-0-06-201580-8). 40pp. With effective collage illustrations, this book celebrates the fun children have on a snow day. Lexile AD280L (Rev: BL 12/15/12; SLJ 10/12)

2608 Berger, Joe. *My Special One and Only* (PS–2). Illus. by author. 2012, Dial $16.99 (978-0-8037-3410-4). 32pp. Bridget Fidget is much distressed when she loses her favorite toy, Captain Cat — and greatly delighted when it is finally found. (Rev: BLO 9/1/12; SLJ 8/12)

2609 Berner, Rotraut Susanne. *In the Town All Year 'Round* (PS–2). Illus. by author. 2008, Chronicle $16.99 (978-0-8118-6474-9). 72pp. An intriguing look at how the activities of people in a town change with the seasons. (Rev: BL 11/15/08; SLJ 12/08)

2610 Bertram, Debbie, and Susan Bloom. *The Best Book to Read* (K–2). Illus. by Michael Garland. 2008, Random $14.99 (978-0-375-84702-8). 32pp. On a trip to the library, a young boy learns that there are lots of kinds of books, something for everyone. (Rev: BL 4/15/08; LMC 8/08; SLJ 6/08)

2611 Bertram, Debbie, and Susan Bloom. *The Best Time to Read* (K–2). Illus. by Michael Bloom. 2005, Random LB $16.99 (978-0-375-93025-6). 32pp. The whole family — even the dog — seems to have better things to do than listen to a little boy read. (Rev: BL 5/15/05)

2612 Best, Cari. *Red Light, Green Light, Mama and Me* (PS–2). Illus. by Niki Daly. 1995, Orchard LB $16.99 (978-0-531-08752-7). 32pp. Lizzie spends an exciting day with her mother, who is a children's librarian in a big downtown library. (Rev: BCCB 9/95; BL 9/1/95; SLJ 10/95)

2613 Best, Cari. *Sally Jean, the Bicycle Queen* (K–2). Illus. by Christine Davenier. 2006, Farrar $16.00 (978-0-374-36386-4). Sally Jean comes up with her own solution when her parents can't afford to buy her a new bike. (Rev: BL 5/1/06; SLJ 5/06*)

2614 Blackstone, Stella. *Making Minestrone* (K–3). Illus. by Nan Brooks. 2000, Barefoot Books $15.99 (978-1-84148-211-8). 32pp. A group of multiethnic kids get together under the supervision of a lonely boy to make a fine batch of minestrone soup. (Rev: BL 10/1/00; HBG 3/01; SLJ 10/00)

2615 Bloom, Suzanne. *Feeding Friendsies* (PS). Illus. by author. 2011, Boyds Mills $16.95 (978-1-59078-529-4). Unpaged. A trio of boisterous preschoolers whip up a feast featuring mud pie and raindrop soup. (Rev: SLJ 11/1/11)

2616 Boelts, Maribeth. *Those Shoes* (K–3). Illus. by Noah Z. Jones. 2007, Candlewick $15.99 (978-0-7636-2499-6). 40pp. African American Jeremy longs for the cool high-top sneakers that many of the kids are wearing, but with the help of his grandmother, learns the meaning of "wants," "needs," and compassion, and finally enjoys new boots to wear in the snow. (Rev: BCCB 12/07; BL 11/1/07; HB 11/07; LMC 1/08; SLJ 12/07)

2617 Bogart, Jo Ellen. *Jeremiah Learns to Read* (K–3). Illus. by Laura Fernandez. 1999, Orchard $15.95 (978-0-531-30190-6). 32pp. An elderly farmer named Jeremiah is taught to read by the local teacher and children in a one-room school, and in exchange he shares with them some of his animal lore. (Rev: BL 9/15/99; HBG 3/00; SLJ 10/99)

2618 Borden, Louise. *The Lost-and-Found Tooth* (K–2). Illus. by Adam Gustavson. 2008, Simon & Schuster $16.99 (978-1-4169-1814-1). Mr. Reilly uses the losing of teeth as the basis for learning a number of skills, and 2nd-grader Lucy longs to be able to add her name to the roster. (Rev: BL 7/08; SLJ 8/08)

2619 Boswell, Addie. *The Rain Stomper* (PS). Illus. by Eric Velasquez. 2008, Marshall Cavendish $16.99 (978-0-7614-5393-2). 32pp. When a heavy storm rains on Jazmin's parade, the little African American girl tries to chase the rain away. (Rev: BL 9/1/08; SLJ 9/08)

2620 Bottner, Barbara. *Miss Brooks Loves Books! (And I Don't)* (PS–2). Illus. by Michael Emberley. 2010, Knopf $17.99 (978-0-375-84682-3). 40pp. William Steig's *Shrek* is the book that finally interests a 1st-grade girl in

reading. ℮ (Rev: BL 3/1/10; HB 5–6/10; LMC 5–6/10; SLJ 2/1/10*)

2621 Boudreau, Hélène. *I Dare You Not to Yawn* (PS–2). Illus. by Serge Bloch. 2013, Candlewick $15.99 (978-0-7636-5070-4). 32pp. Using an instructional format, this book gives advice on how to avoid those infectious yawns and prevent being sent to bed. (Rev: BL 3/1/13; HB 5–6/13; SLJ 2/13)

2622 Boynton, Sandra. *Hey! Wake Up!* (PS). Illus. by author. 2000, Workman $6.95 (978-0-7611-1976-0). A board book about morning activities like yawning, stretching, breakfast, and getting dressed. Also use *Pajama Time!* (2000). (Rev: SLJ 2/01)

2623 Bradford, Wade. *Why Do I Have to Make My Bed? A History of Messy Rooms* (K–3). Illus. by Johanna van der Sterre. 2011, Tricycle $16.99 (978-1-58246-327-8); LB $19.99 (978-1-58246-388-9). Unpaged. A boy dubious about the merits of making a bed that's only going to get messed up again gets a history lesson from his mother on bed making — and other children's chores — through the ages. (Rev: BL 1/1–15/11; SLJ 3/1/11)

2624 Bregoli, Jane. *The Goat Lady* (2–4). Illus. by author. 2004, Tilbury House $16.95 (978-0-88448-260-4). Wonderful paintings enhance this story of an elderly French Canadian woman who was not accepted by the people of her Massachusetts town because she raised goats and failed to fit in. (Rev: SLJ 3/05) [759.13]

2625 Brennan-Nelson, Denise. *Willow and the Snow Day Dance* (K–2). Illus. by Cyd Moore. 2010, Sleeping Bear $16.95 (978-1-58536-522-7). 32pp. Willow's grumpy and elusive neighbor doesn't respond to her attempts to include him in her friendly community activities, but he does provide her (anonymously) with a recipe for a dance to make the snow fall. ℮ (Rev: BLO 1/1–15/11; SLJ 4/11)

2626 Brown, Margaret Wise. *Another Important Book* (PS–1). Illus. by Chris Raschka. 1999, HarperCollins LB $16.89 (978-0-06-026283-9). 32pp. In a series of rhymes, this book identifies important achievements and developments in the first six years of a child's life. (Rev: BCCB 1/00; BL 10/15/99; HB 9/99; HBG 3/00; SLJ 9/99)

2627 Brown, Margaret Wise. *A Child's Good Morning Book* (PS). Illus. by Karen Katz. 2009, HarperCollins $17.99 (978-0-06-128864-7). 32pp. A new edition of the classic picture-book story about a new day dawning for plants, animals, and children. (Rev: BL 11/15/08; SLJ 1/09)

2628 Brown, Margaret Wise. *Red Light, Green Light* (PS–K). Illus. by Leonard Weisgard. 1994, Scholastic paper $4.95 (978-0-590-44559-7). 40pp. This introduction to traffic signs was first published in 1944.

2629 Brown, Peter. *The Curious Garden* (PS–2). Illus. by author. 2009, Little, Brown $16.99 (978-0-316-01547-9). 40pp. A little boy named Liam decides to look after a few sad plants alongside a train track in a gray and gloomy city and his efforts result in a citywide renaissance. (Rev: BL 5/15/09; SLJ 4/09)

2630 Bunting, Eve. *Smoky Night* (K–3). Illus. by David Diaz. 1994, Harcourt $16.00 (978-0-15-269954-3). 32pp. Two families, one Korean American and the other African American, reach out to one another during the terrible Los Angeles riots. Caldecott Medal winner, 1995. (Rev: BCCB 3/94; BL 3/1/94; HB 5/94; SLJ 5/94*)

2631 Burleigh, Robert. *Clang! Clang! Beep! Beep! Listen to the City* (PS–1). Illus. by Beppe Giacobbe. 2009, Simon & Schuster $14.99 (978-1-4169-4052-4). A day in the sounds of the city — from garbage can bang to the last slamming door. (Rev: BL 6/1–15/09; SLJ 5/09)

2632 Burleigh, Robert. *I Love Going Through This Book* (PS–K). Illus. by Dan Yaccarino. 2001, HarperCollins $15.99 (978-0-06-028805-1). This boisterous excursion through a book, courtesy of a young boy and animal friends, introduces young readers to the parts of a book and the fun of reading. (Rev: BCCB 6/01; BL 6/1–15/01; HBG 10/01; SLJ 6/01)

2633 Burningham, John. *Edwardo: The Horriblest Boy in the Whole Wide World* (PS–3). Illus. by author. 2007, Knopf $16.99 (978-0-375-84053-1). The power of positive reinforcement is emphasized in this story of Edwardo, whose behavior becomes worse and worse the more he is criticized but improves dramatically when he is praised. (Rev: BL 1/1–15/07; SLJ 2/07*)

2634 Burton, Virginia Lee. *The Little House* (1–3). Illus. by author. 1978, Houghton $16.00 (978-0-395-18156-0); paper $7.99 (978-0-395-25938-2). Story of a little house in the country that over the years witnesses change and progress. Caldecott Medal winner, 1943. (Rev: HBG 10/03)

2635 Buzzeo, Toni. *Penelope Popper Book Doctor* (1–3). Illus. by Jana Christy. 2011, Upstart $17.95 (978-1-60213-054-8). Unpaged. A little girl determined to be a doctor is guided instead toward looking after damaged books in the library. (Rev: LMC 3–4/12; SLJ 11/1/11)

2636 Capucilli, Alyssa Satin. *The Potty Book for Boys* (PS). 2000, Barron's $5.95 (978-0-7641-5232-0). 32pp. The male narrator explains how he receives his own potty, how he sits on it, and how he is rewarded if successful. The same story from a girl's point of view is in *The Potty Book for Girls* (2000). (Rev: SLJ 9/00)

2637 Caraballo, Samuel. *Estrellita en la Ciudad Grande / Estrellita in the Big City* (K–3). Illus. by Pablo Torrecilla. 2008, Piñata $15.95 (978-1-55885-498-7). 32pp. Estrellita is an immigrant in New York City and her growing understanding of the English language and her new home is shown through her many conversations with her grandmother in Puerto Rico. (Rev: SLJ 2/09)

2638 Carle, Eric. *The Artist Who Painted a Blue Horse* (PS–2). Illus. by author. 2011, Philomel $17.99 (978-0-399-25713-1). 32pp. A young boy enjoys a playful day of painting using unexpected colors for various animals in this homage to painter Franz Marc that includes an author's note about his work. (Rev: BL 10/15/11*; HB 1–2/12; LMC 3–4/12; SLJ 10/1/11)

2639 Carlson, Nancy. *Get Up and Go!* (PS–K). Illus. 2006, Viking $15.99 (978-0-670-05981-2). 32pp. Carlson emphasizes the importance of exercise and examines its many benefits. (Rev: BL 12/1/05; SLJ 2/06)

2640 Carlson, Nancy. *I Don't Like to Read!* (K–2). Illus. by author. 2007, Viking $15.99 (978-0-670-06191-4). Frustrated by the difficulty of learning to read, Henry the mouse tries to mask his feelings by saying that reading is "boring" and "dumb." (Rev: BL 7/07; LMC 11/07; SLJ 7/07)

2641 Carlson, Nancy. *There's a Big, Beautiful World Out There!* (K–2). Illus. 2002, Viking $15.99 (978-0-670-03580-9). 32pp. Written just after September 11, 2001, this book uses cheery illustrations and a chatty approach to potential terrors to reassure children that anxieties are normal and the world is still a good place. (Rev: BL 10/1/02; HBG 3/03; SLJ 11/02)

2642 Carluccio, Maria. *I'm 3! Look What I Can Do* (PS). 2010, Henry Holt $10.99 (978-0-80508313-2). 24pp. A young brother and sister celebrate all the things they are able to do (eat with fork and spoon, hang up my coat . . .). (Rev: BL 7/10; SLJ 8/1/10)

2643 Carluccio, Maria. *The Sounds Around Town* (PS). Illus. by author. 2008, Barefoot Books $16.99 (978-1-905236-28-2). 24pp. A look at the sounds of a toddler's day — birds, cars, kittens, bathwater, and so forth. (Rev: BL 5/15/08; SLJ 7/08)

2644 Carter, Anne Laurel. *My Home Bay* (PS). Illus. by Alan Daniel and Lea Daniel. Series: Northern Lights Books for Children. 2004, Red Deer $17.95 (978-0-88995-284-3). When her family moves clear across Canada from Vancouver to Nova Scotia, young Gwyn is initially disdainful of her new surroundings. (Rev: BL 2/1/04; SLJ 8/04)

2645 Chessa, Francesca. *Holly's Red Boots* (PS–2). Illus. by author. 2008, Holiday $16.95 (978-0-8234-2158-9). 32pp. Holly's search for her red boots takes so long that by the time she finds them, the snow has melted, but now she can go out and puddle jump with Mom. (Rev: BL 9/1/08; SLJ 9/08)

2646 Child, Lauren. *But I've Used All of My Pocket Change* (PS–1). Illus. by author. 2012, Dial $16.99 (978-0-8037-3728-0). 32pp. Charlie and his sister Lola take different approaches to a trip to the zoo, Charlie saving for the book he wants and Lola splurging on immediate gratification. Lexile AD560L (Rev: BLO 11/15/12; SLJ 9/12)

2647 Chinn, Karen. *Sam and the Lucky Money* (PS–2). Illus. by Cornelius Van Wright and Ying-Hwa Hu. 1995, Lee & Low $15.95 (978-1-880000-13-7). Sam decides that the money he has received at Chinese New Year would be best used by giving it to a poor stranger. (Rev: SLJ 12/95)

2648 Choung, Euh-hee. *Minji's Salon* (PS). Illus. by author. 2008, Kane $15.95 (978-1-933605-67-8). 36pp. Minji goes to work on her dog's hair while her mother is at the beauty salon, trying out many styles and techniques (including an ice cream rinse); double-page spreads show the parallel primping. (Rev: BL 7/08; SLJ 8/08)

2649 Christensen, Bonnie. *Plant a Little Seed* (PS–1). Illus. by author. 2012, Roaring Brook $17.99 (978-1-59643-550-6). 32pp. Tells the yearlong story of a community garden, including its resident rabbits, and its harvest; facts about plants and harvest festivals are appended. (Rev: BL 4/1/12; HB 5–6/12; LMC 10/12; SLJ 8/12)

2650 Clanton, Ben. *Vote for Me!* (K–2). Illus. by author. 2012, Kids Can $16.95 (978-1-55453-822-5). 40pp. A donkey and an elephant compete for votes in this parody of the American political process. (Rev: BL 4/1/12; LMC 10/12; SLJ 4/1/12)

2651 Clary, Margie Willis. *A Sweet, Sweet Basket* (K–4). Illus. by Dennis L. Brown. 1995, Sandlapper $15.95 (978-0-87844-127-3). 40pp. An older woman explains to her granddaughter how baskets are woven from the sweetgrass that grows in South Carolina. (Rev: BL 9/1/95)

2652 Cohn, Diana. *¡Sí, Se Puede! / Yes, We Can! Janitor Strike in L.A.* (PS–3). Illus. by Francisco Delgado. 2002, Cinco Puntos $15.95 (978-0-938317-66-1). Mexican American boy Carlitos supports his janitor mother in seeking to start a union, in this bilingual picture book based on a Los Angeles strike in 2000. (Rev: BL 10/1/02; HBG 3/03; SLJ 11/02*)

2653 Cole, Joanna. *My Big Boy Potty Book* (PS). Illus. by Maxie Chambliss. 2000, HarperCollins $6.99 (978-0-688-17042-4). In this reassuring picture book, Michael is told that he will succeed in potty training because practice makes perfect. The female counterpart is *My Big Girl Potty Book* (2000). (Rev: BL 2/1/01; HBG 3/01; SLJ 11/00)

2654 Cole, Joanna. *My Friend the Doctor* (PS–K). Illus. by Maxie Chambliss. 2005, HarperCollins $6.99 (978-0-06-050500-4). Cartoon illustrations and brief text depict a little girl's visit to the doctor for a checkup that includes getting a shot. (Rev: BL 7/05; SLJ 9/05)

2655 Collier, Bryan. *Uptown* (PS–3). Illus. 2000, Holt $15.95 (978-0-8050-5721-8). 32pp. A young boy points out the sights and delights of Harlem — shopping on 125th Street and going to a jazz club. (Rev: BCCB 11/00; BL 6/1–15/00; HBG 10/00; SLJ 7/00)

2656 Conahan, Carolyn. *The Big Wish* (PS–2). Illus. by author. 2011, Chronicle $16.99 (978-0-8118-7040-5). 36pp. Young Molly is nurturing her dandelions in hopes of achieving a world-record-breaking wish. (Rev: BLO 8/11; SLJ 7/11)

2657 Cooper, Barbara. *Alan Apostrophe* (2–4). Illus. by Maggie Raynor. Series: Meet the Puncs: A Remarkable Punctuation Family. 2005, Gareth Stevens LB $24.00 (978-0-8368-4223-4). Alan Apostrophe, captain of a fishing boat, wears an eye patch in the shape of an apostrophe and his speech, with many dropped letters, involves much use of the punctuation for which he is named. Also in this series from Britain: *Christopher

Comma and *Emma Exclamation Point* (both 2005). (Rev: SLJ 4/05)

2658 Cooper, Elisha. *Beach* (K–2). 2006, Scholastic $16.99 (978-0-439-68785-0). 40pp. Double-page watercolor spreads and a simple text celebrate the joys of a day at the beach. (Rev: BL 6/1–15/06; SLJ 7/06)

2659 Cooper, Elisha. *Farm* (PS–3). Illus. by author. 2010, Scholastic $17.99 (978-0-545-07075-1). 48pp. Cooper portrays farm life from spring through fall, showing children and adults involved in a variety of activities. (Rev: BL 2/1/10; HB 5–6/10*; LMC 5–6/10; SLJ 3/1/10)

2660 Cooper, Elisha. *A Good Night Walk* (PS). 2005, Scholastic $16.99 (978-0-439-68783-6). 40pp. This gentle picture book captures the ebb and flow of neighborhood life as a parent and child take an evening stroll. (Rev: BCCB 10/05; BL 11/1/05*; HB 11/05; HBG 4/06; SLJ 9/05)

2661 Copeland, Cynthia L. *What Are You Waiting For?* (K–1). Illus. by Mike Gordon. Series: Silly Millies. 2003, Millbrook LB $17.90 (978-0-7613-2804-9). 31pp. As a young boy surveys the site for a new playground, he approaches construction workers as they arrive and urges them to get busy. (Rev: HBG 10/03; SLJ 6/03)

2662 Cotten, Cynthia. *Rain Play* (PS–2). Illus. by Javaka Steptoe. 2008, Holt $16.95 (978-0-8050-6795-8). 32pp. Cotton highlights the pleasures and dangers of a thunderstorm in this simple story of a rainy day. (Rev: BL 2/15/08; SLJ 6/08)

2663 Coulman, Valerie. *I Am a Ballerina* (PS–1). Illus. by Sandra Lamb. 2004, Lobster $15.95 (978-1-894222-91-4). The engaging tale of aspiring ballerina Molly. (Rev: BL 2/1/05; SLJ 3/05)

2664 Cousins, Lucy. *Maisy's Amazing Big Book of Words* (PS). Illus. by author. 2007, Candlewick $14.99 (978-0-7636-0794-4). This oversized volume with a colorful, lift-the-flap format introduces words relating to everyday categories such as transport, food, and clothes. (Rev: BL 6/1–15/07; SLJ 8/07)

2665 Cowell, Cress. *That Rabbit Belongs to Emily Brown* (PS–K). Illus. by Neal Layton. 2007, Hyperion $16.99 (978-1-4231-0645-6). 40pp. Young Emily loves her tattered old stuffed rabbit named Stanley, with whom she has many adventures, and refuses to give him up even when offered much newer toys. (Rev: BL 4/1/07)

2666 Crews, Donald. *Shortcut* (PS–3). Illus. 1992, Greenwillow $17.89 (978-0-688-06437-2). 32pp. Seven children follow a railroad track back home as the train gets closer and closer. (Rev: BCCB 10/92*; BL 10/15/92*; HB 1/93*; SLJ 11/92)

2667 Crews, Nina. *Below* (PS–K). Illus. 2006, Holt $16.95 (978-0-8050-7728-5). 32pp. Striking photographs tell the story of Jack's efforts to rescue Guy, his action figure, when Guy falls through a hole in the stairs. (Rev: BL 3/1/06; SLJ 3/06)

2668 Crews, Nina. *One Hot Summer Day* (PS–K). Illus. 1995, Greenwillow $14.89 (978-0-688-13394-8). 24pp. Using collages, the author illustrates the many activities associated with a hot summer's day. (Rev: BCCB 6/95; BL 6/1–15/95; HB 7/95; SLJ 6/95)

2669 Crews, Nina. *Snowball* (PS–1). Illus. 1997, Greenwillow $14.89 (978-0-688-14929-1). This is the story of an African American child in a city and how she gets her wish for snow. (Rev: BL 12/1/97; HBG 3/98; SLJ 9/97)

2670 Crum, Shutta. *Mine!* (PS). Illus. by Patrice Barton. 2011, Knopf $16.99 (978-0-375-86711-8). 32pp. Two very young children and a dog learn about sharing in this almost wordless funny story. (Rev: BL 7/11; SLJ 6/11*)

2671 Crum, Shutta. *Thunder-Boomer* (PS–2). Illus. by Carol Thompson. 2009, Clarion $16.00 (978-0-618-61865-1). Vibrant illustrations add atmosphere as a welcome summer thunderstorm hits a farm and brings a new kitten to live with the family. (Rev: BL 7/09; SLJ 6/09)

2672 Cummins, Julie. *Country Kid, City Kid* (K–2). Illus. by Ted Rand. 2002, Holt $16.95 (978-0-8050-6467-4). Ben's life on the farm and Jody's life in the city are contrasted on facing pages. (Rev: HBG 3/03; SLJ 11/02)

2673 Cupiano, Ina. *Quinito's Neighborhood / El vecindario de Quinito* (PS–2). Illus. by José Ramírez. 2005, Children's Book Pr. $16.95 (978-0-89239-209-4). Readers meet Quinito's neighbors and find out what they all do in warm illustrations and bilingual text. (Rev: BL 12/1/05; SLJ 10/05*)

2674 Curtis, Carolyn. *I Took the Moon for a Walk* (PS–2). Illus. by Alison Jay. 2004, Barefoot Books $16.99 (978-1-84148-611-6). 32pp. A young boy enjoys a nighttime stroll around his neighborhood with the moon as his companion; antique-looking panoramic illustrations add to the dreamlike text. (Rev: BL 4/1/04; SLJ 6/04)

2675 Curtis, Jamie Lee. *I'm Gonna Like Me: Letting Off a Little Self-Esteem* (1–3). Illus. by Laura Cornell. 2002, HarperCollins LB $17.89 (978-0-06-028762-7). 32pp. Humorous, detailed illustrations and rhyming text show a boy and girl taking turns liking themselves. (Rev: BL 10/1/02; HBG 3/03; SLJ 10/02)

2676 Curtis, Jamie Lee. *Is There Really a Human Race?* (K–2). Illus. by Laura Cornell. 2006, HarperCollins $16.99 (978-0-06-075346-7). 40pp. When did this race start? Where is it going? Is it important to win? A mother thoughtfully helps her son unravel these difficult questions. (Rev: BL 9/15/06; SLJ 8/06*)

2677 Cuyler, Margery. *Please Play Safe! Penguin's Guide to Playground Safety* (PS). 2006, Scholastic $15.99 (978-0-439-52832-0). 32pp. Penguin and his friend cleverly demonstrate the do's and don'ts of playground behavior. (Rev: BL 8/06; SLJ 8/06)

2678 Danneberg, Julie. *First Day Jitters* (K–4). Illus. by Judy Love. 2000, Charlesbridge $16.95 (978-1-58089-054-0). 32pp. A little girl imagines all the terrible things that could happen to her on her first day of school, but is pleasantly surprised with the real thing. (Rev: BL 3/15/00; HBG 10/00; SLJ 5/00)

2679 Davis, Aubrey. *A Hen for Izzy Pippik* (K–2). Illus. by Marie Lafrance. 2012, Kids Can $16.95 (978-155453243-8). 32pp. When Shaina finds a lost hen, she looks after it, its eggs, and all the subsequent offspring,

bringing prosperity to the community in the process; and when the owner of the hen returns, she offers to return the hen to everyone's dismay; based on a traditional tale. (Rev: BL 2/15/12; LMC 10/12; SLJ 5/1/12)

2680 de Anda, Diane. *The Patchwork Garden / Pedacitos de huerto* (K–3). Illus. by Oksana Kemarskaya. 2013, Arte Publico $16.95 (978-155885763-6). 32pp. A patchwork quilt is the seed from which sprouts a community effort to grow vegetables in this bilingual book. (Rev: BLO 5/1/13; LMC 11–12/13)

2681 Devine, Monica. *Carry Me, Mama* (PS–1). Illus. by Pauline Paquin. 2002, Stoddart $15.95 (978-0-7737-3317-6). A beautifully illustrated story of a mother gently persuading her child to walk further and further. (Rev: HB 5/02; HBG 10/02; SLJ 7/02)

2682 Diesen, Deborah. *The Barefooted, Bad Tempered Baby Brigade* (PS–K). Illus. by Tracy Dockray. 2010, Ten Speed/Tricycle $15.99 (978-1-58246-274-5). 32pp. Pictures of rebellious babies carrying picket signs propel this funny, rhythmic story. (Rev: BL 1/1/10; SLJ 2/1/10)

2683 Dole, Mayra L. *Drum, Chavi, Drum ! / Toca, Chavi, Toca!* (2–3). Illus. by Tonel. 2003, Children's Book Pr. $16.95 (978-0-89239-186-8). 32pp. In this charming and rhythmic bilingual book, Chavi sets out to prove that being a girl doesn't mean she can't be a great drummer. (Rev: BL 8/03; HBG 4/04; SLJ 12/03)

2684 Doughty, Rebecca. *Lost and Found* (K–2). Illus. 2005, Putnam $12.99 (978-0-399-24177-2). 32pp. Always in a rush, young Lucy is forever losing things; after looking under her bed, she resolves to take more time in the future. (Rev: BL 8/05)

2685 Doughty, Rebecca. *Oh No! Time To Go! A Book of Goodbyes* (PS–2). Illus. by author. 2009, Random $15.99 (978-0-375-84981-7). 40pp. How many ways are there to say goodbye? A young boy reviews many choices and describes the worst of his goodbye experiences. (Rev: BL 3/1/09; SLJ 4/09)

2686 Doyle, Malachy. *Get Happy* (PS–1). Illus. by Caroline Uff. 2011, Walker $14.99 (978-0-8027-2271-3). 32pp. Grumble less, giggle more. Doyle offers various simple tips on enjoying life and being happy. (Rev: BL 8/11; SLJ 6/11)

2687 Drescher, Henrik. *McFig and McFly: A Tale of Jealousy, Revenge, and Death (with a Happy Ending)* (K–3). Illus. by author. 2008, Candlewick $17.99 (978-0-7636-3386-8). 40pp. Neighbors McFig and McFly are so focused on their efforts to outbuild each other that they fail to notice that their children Anton and Rosie have fallen in love. (Rev: BL 6/1–15/08; LMC 10/08; SLJ 5/08)

2688 Drummond, Allan. *Tin Lizzie* (PS–3). Illus. by author. 2008, Farrar $16.95 (978-0-374-32000-3). 32pp. Eliza and her siblings go for a ride in Grandpa's restored Model T and look with dismay at all the changes cars have made to the landscape and atmosphere in the years since the old car was built. (Rev: BL 7/08; SLJ 7/08)

2689 Dunn, Todd. *We Go Together!* (PS–K). Illus. by Miki Sakamoto. 2007, Sterling $12.95 (978-1-4027-3260-7). 24pp. A rhyming text describes familiar items that go together like "leaves and fall" and "horse and wagon." (Rev: BL 12/1/07; SLJ 12/07)

2690 Earnhardt, Donna W. *Being Frank* (K–2). Illus. by Andrea Castellani. 2012, Flashlight $16.95 (978-1-9362611-9-2). 32pp. Frank takes honesty beyond the limits of kindness and eventually learns to temper the truth with sensitivity. (Rev: BLO 10/15/12; SLJ 12/12)

2691 Edwards, Pamela Duncan. *Jack and Jill's Treehouse* (K–3). Illus. by Henry Cole. 2008, HarperCollins $16.99 (978-0-06-009077-7). 24pp. In this cumulative tale with a familiar ring, Jack and Jill build a tree house and their work is duplicated by a pair of robins constructing their own nest. (Rev: BL 5/15/08; SLJ 5/08)

2692 Edwardson, Debby Dahl. *Whale Snow* (PS–2). Illus. by Annie Patterson. 2003, Charlesbridge $15.95 (978-1-57091-393-8). Amiqaqq, a young Inupiat boy, attends the first whaling feast of the winter season and learns about the important role the whale plays in Inupiat culture and the welfare of his small Alaskan village. (Rev: BL 8/03; HBG 4/04; LMC 1/04; SLJ 12/03)

2693 Ehlert, Lois. *Growing Vegetable Soup* (PS–K). Illus. by author. 1987, Harcourt $15.00 (978-0-15-232575-6); paper $6.00 (978-0-15-232580-0). 40pp. Father and child plant seeds and sprouts "to grow vegetable soup." Also use: *Planting a Rainbow* (1988). (Rev: BL 3/1/87; SLJ 3/87)

2694 Ehlert, Lois. *Market Day: A Story Told with Folk Art* (PS–2). Illus. 2000, Harcourt $16.00 (978-0-15-202158-0). 36pp. This picture book depicts a day when the farmers load their trucks with goods and go to the market to buy and sell, and work and play. (Rev: BCCB 7–8/00; BL 5/15/00; HBG 10/00; SLJ 7/00)

2695 Ellis, Sarah. *Next Stop!* (PS–K). Illus. by Ruth Ohi. 2000, Fitzhenry & Whiteside $13.95 (978-1-55041-539-1). Little Claire helps the bus driver by calling out the names of the streets and the special attractions found at each stop. (Rev: BL 12/1/00; SLJ 1/01)

2696 Elya, Susan Middleton. *Bebé Goes Shopping* (K–2). Illus. by Steven Salerno. 2006, Harcourt $16.00 (978-0-15-205426-7). 40pp. A child's visit to the supermarket with his mother introduces a number of Spanish vocabulary words in the rhyming text, which is enhanced by retro-style illustrations. (Rev: BCCB 6/06; BL 2/15/06*; HBG 10/06; SLJ 5/06)

2697 Elya, Susan Middleton. *Fire! Fuego! Brave Bomberos* (PS–1). Illus. by Dan Santat. 2012, Bloomsbury $16.99 (978-159990461-0). 40pp. This bilingual story captures a brave team of firefighters' response to an alarm call; action-packed illustrations add energy. (Rev: BL 4/15/12)

2698 Elya, Susan Middleton. *Tooth on the Loose* (PS–1). Illus. by Jenny Mattheson. 2008, Putnam $16.99 (978-0-399-24459-9). 32pp. Will a little girl's tooth fall out in time for her to buy a gift for her father's birthday? Told in English and Spanish, this is a charming rhyming story with glossary, pronunciation guide, and evocative illustrations. (Rev: BL 7/08; SLJ 8/08)

2699 Ericsson, Jennifer A. *A Piece of Chalk* (PS–1). Illus. by Michelle Shapiro. 2007, Roaring Brook $16.95 (978-1-59643-057-0). 32pp. A cheerful story about a little girl with a brand new box of chalk and a long driveway. (Rev: BL 9/1/07; SLJ 10/07)

2700 Erlbruch, Wolf. *The Big Question* (K–3). 2005, Europa paper $14.95 (978-1-933372-03-7). 52pp. A variety of answers to life's biggest question — why am I here? — can be found in the pages of this tall, creative book that won the 2004 Ragazzi Award at the Bologna Book Fair. (Rev: BL 1/1–15/06)

2701 Fair, Sylvia. *The Bedspread* (K–2). Illus. by author. 1982, Morrow $16.95 (978-0-688-00877-2). 32pp. Two old ladies decide to embroider their bedspreads.

2702 Falwell, Cathryn. *Mystery Vine: A Pumpkin Surprise* (PS–2). Illus. by author. 2009, HarperCollins $16.99 (978-0-06-177198-9). 32pp. Activities and recipes are included in this cheerful rhyming story about a brother and sister planting, tending, and harvesting a pumpkin vine. (Rev: BLO 6/19/09)

2703 Fitzgerald, Joanne. *This Is Me and Where I Am* (PS–2). Illus. 2004, Fitzhenry & Whiteside $14.95 (978-1-55041-819-4). A young child gradually focuses in on his small point in the universe and then expands his view again. (Rev: BL 10/1/04; SLJ 11/04)

2704 Fitzpatrick, Marie-Louise. *There* (PS–2). Illus. by author. 2009, Roaring Brook $17.95 (978-1-59643-087-7). 32pp. A little girl reflects on eternal questions including "When will I get There?" and "Will it take long to get There?" (Rev: BLO 5/27/09; SLJ 5/09)

2705 Formento, Alison. *This Tree Counts!* (PS–2). Illus. by Sarah Snow. 2010, Whitman $16.99 (978-0-8075-7890-2). 32pp. Formento provides a gentle science/counting lesson about the life cycle of trees along with a story about a tree-planting elementary school class. Lexile AD480L (Rev: BL 1/1/10; LMC 5–6/10; SLJ 2/1/10)

2706 Fox, Mem. *Hello Baby!* (PS). Illus. by Steve Jenkins. 2009, Simon & Schuster $16.99 (978-1-4169-8513-6). 32pp. Rhyming questions and eye-catching art ask young readers to consider just who they are, comparing themselves with a variety of animals. (Rev: BCCB 9/09; BL 5/15/09; SLJ 4/09)

2707 French, Lisa S. *The Terrible Trash Trail: Eco-Pig Stops Pollution* (PS–2). Illus. by Barry Gott. 2009, ABDO $18.95 (978-160270663-7). 32pp. Eco-Pig wakes up to find his beautiful mountaintop town has been covered in trash. (Rev: BL 2/15/10; LMC 3–4/10)

2708 Friedman, Laurie. *A Style All Her Own* (PS–1). Illus. by Sharon Watts. 2004, Carolrhoda $15.95 (978-1-57505-599-2). Isabelle Ashley Parker McBride likes to dress in her own style, even when she's asked to be a flower girl, but her aunt manages to negotiate a compromise. (Rev: SLJ 4/05)

2709 Fucile, Tony. *Let's Do Nothing!* (1–3). Illus. by author. 2009, Candlewick $16.99 (978-0-7636-3440-7). 40pp. Sal and Frankie try very hard to do nothing after exhausting themselves doing everything else in this lively, vividly illustrated book. (Rev: BL 7/09; SLJ 7/09)

2710 Garland, Sarah. *Eddie's Toolbox and How to Make and Mend Things* (K–3). Illus. by author. 2011, Frances Lincoln $17.95 (978-1-84780-053-4). 36pp. Eddie learns lots of new skills when a new family moves in next door and needs help with simple home repairs. (Rev: BL 9/1/11; SLJ 5/1/11)

2711 Gary, Meredith. *Sometimes You Get What You Want* (PS–2). Illus. by Lisa Brown. 2008, HarperCollins $16.99 (978-0-06-114015-0). 32pp. A brother and sister acknowledge the times during the day when they do and don't get what they want. (Rev: BL 5/15/08; HB 5/08; SLJ 4/08)

2712 Gauch, Patricia Lee. *Tanya and the Red Shoes* (PS–2). Illus. by Satomi Ichikawa. 2002, Penguin $16.99 (978-0-399-23314-2). 40pp. Young ballet dancer Tanya finds out that graduating to toe shoes isn't everything she thought it would be. (Rev: BL 3/1/02; HB 5/02; HBG 10/02; SLJ 3/02)

2713 Gay, Marie-Louise. *When Stella Was Very, Very Small* (PS–K). Illus. by author. Series: Stella. 2009, Groundwood $16.95 (978-0-88899-906-1). Stella's fans will enjoy getting to see her as a baby and growing through various stages, and appreciate her ever-plucky attitude toward the world around her. (Rev: BL 7/09)

2714 George, Kristine O'Connell. *Book!* (PS). Illus. by Maggie Smith. 2001, Clarion $9.95 (978-0-395-98287-7). 32pp. A toddler finds great joy in his first picture book in this engaging package of friendly text and lively illustrations. (Rev: BL 12/1/01; HBG 3/02; SLJ 10/01) [811]

2715 Geras, Adele. *Time for Ballet* (PS–2). Illus. by Shelagh McNicholas. 2004, Dial $16.99 (978-0-8037-2978-0). 32pp. Soft watercolors illustrate the tale of Tilly, an aspiring dancer, as she and the other members of her ballet class prepare for a recital. (Rev: BL 2/1/04*; SLJ 2/04)

2716 Gershator, Phillis. *Listen, Listen* (PS–2). Illus. by Alison Jay. 2007, Barefoot Books $16.99 (978-1-84686-084-3). 32pp. A tour of the sounds of the changing seasons in a country town. (Rev: BL 11/15/07; LMC 3/08; SLJ 11/07)

2717 Gershator, Phillis, and David Gershator. *Summer Is Summer* (PS–K). Illus. by Sophie Blackall. 2006, Holt $16.95 (978-0-8050-7444-4). In this gentle picture book, two girls — one African American, the other white — and their brothers make the most of summer, finding countless ways to have fun. (Rev: BL 4/15/06; SLJ 6/06*)

2718 Gerstein, Mordicai. *Leaving the Nest* (PS–2). Illus. by author. 2007, Farrar $16.00 (978-0-374-34369-9). In a single backyard youngsters — a kitten, a blue jay, a squirrel, and a girl — experiment with new skills under the watchful eyes of their mothers. (Rev: BL 3/1/07; SLJ 4/07)

2719 Godwin, Laura. *The Ring Bearer* (K–2). Illus. by John Wallace. 2006, Hyperion $12.99 (978-0-7868-5510-0). In this colorful picture book, rhymed couplets outline the responsibilities of the ring bearer during a wedding ceremony; a companion to *The Flower Girl* (2000). (Rev: SLJ 2/06)

2720 Godwin, Laura. *This Is the Firefighter* (PS–K). Illus. by Julian Hector. 2009, Hyperion $15.99 (978-1-4231-0800-9). 32pp. Rhyming couplets and bright illustrations show how fire fighters respond to a call for help. (Rev: BL 3/15/09; HB 3/09; SLJ 3/09)

2721 Gold, August. *Thank You, God, for Everything* (PS–2). Illus. by Wendy A. Halperin. 2009, Putnam $16.99 (978-0-399-24049-2). 32pp. Young Daisy appreciates and is grateful for all the things in her world. (Rev: BL 12/15/08; SLJ 1/09)

2722 Gomi, Taro. *Everyone Poops* (PS). Trans. by Amanda M. Stinchecum. Illus. Series: Can You Believe It! 1993, Kane $12.95 (978-0-916291-45-7). 28pp. This book shows that all animals poop and that this is a natural part of life. (Rev: BCCB 4/93; BL 5/15/93) [612]

2723 Goodhart, Pippa. *You Choose* (K–2). Illus. by Nick Sharratt. 2012, Kane/Miller paper $7.99 (978-16106707-6-0). 32pp. With spreads full of pictorial options, this book challenges young children to make choices in many areas of life — to select a pet, a dream home, a mode of transportation, and so forth. (Rev: BL 4/15/12; SLJ 6/1/12)

2724 Graham, Bob. *A Bus Called Heaven* (K–2). Illus. by author. 2012, Walker $16.99 (978-0-7636-5893-9). 40pp. A neighborhood comes together to help young Stella bring an abandoned bus to life with paint, yard chairs, and games; when a tow truck threatens to remove the bus, the neighbors pull together again to save it. Lexile AD570L (Rev: BL 2/15/12*; HB 5–6/12; SLJ 4/1/12)

2725 Graham, Bob. *The Silver Button* (PS–1). Illus. by author. 2013, Candlewick $16.99 (978-076366437-4). 32pp. A bird's-eye view of the world offers a chance for readers to see that the biggest things in one person's world — such as Jodie's brother taking his first steps — are all part of a bigger world made up of similar magic moments. USBBY Outstanding International Book. Lexile AD720 (Rev: BL 9/15/13; SLJ 9/13*)

2726 Grahn, Geoffrey. *What's Going on in There?* (K–3). Illus. by author. 2005, Scholastic $14.95 (978-0-439-57495-2). Readers must take time to examine each spread and identify what is really taking place in Grahnville (the pizza cook is really assembling a dinosaur, for example). (Rev: SLJ 3/05)

2727 Grambling, Lois G. *My Mom Is a Firefighter* (K–2). Illus. by Jane Manning. 2007, HarperCollins $16.99 (978-0-06-058640-9). 32pp. A young boy with a firefighter mom describes the duties of a firefighter and station-house life. (Rev: BL 10/1/07; SLJ 10/07)

2728 Gray, Libba M. *When Uncle Took the Fiddle* (PS–2). Illus. by Lloyd Bloom. 1999, Orchard $15.95 (978-0-531-30137-1). Although it's bedtime, an Appalachian family and their neighbors come to life when Uncle picks up his fiddle and starts to play. (Rev: BCCB 11/99; BL 9/15/99; HBG 3/00; SLJ 11/99)

2729 Gray, Nigel. *My Dog, My Cat, My Mama, and Me!* (PS). Illus. by Bob Graham. 2007, Candlewick LB $8.99

(978-0-7636-3639-5). 24pp. A lift-the-flap book that allows the reader to view the arrival of new puppies, new kittens, and finally new babies. (Rev: BL 12/15/07; SLJ 1/08)

2730 Gray, Rita. *Nonna's Porch* (PS–2). Illus. by Terry Widener. 2004, Hyperion $15.99 (978-0-7868-1613-2). On her porch, Nonna knits a blanket that depicts the summer scene. (Rev: SLJ 11/04)

2731 Greenberg, Melanie Hope. *Mermaids on Parade* (K–2). Illus. by author. 2008, Putnam $16.99 (978-0-399-24708-8). 32pp. This happy story about a young girl taking part in the Coney Island Mermaid Parade paints a bright picture of the beginning of summer. (Rev: BL 6/1–15/08; LMC 11/08; SLJ 7/08)

2732 Greenfield, Eloise. *Big Friend, Little Friend* (PS). Illus. by Jan S. Gilchrist. 1991, Writers & Readers $4.95 (978-0-86316-204-6). 12pp. This is one of a series of board books about the everyday activities of some African American children. Also use: *Daddy and I; I Make Music;* and *My Doll, Keshia* (all 1991). (Rev: BL 12/15/91; SLJ 12/91)

2733 Grimes, Nikki. *Come Sunday* (PS–3). Illus. by Michael Bryant. 1996, Eerdmans $16.00 (978-0-8028-5108-6); paper $8.00 (978-0-8028-5134-5). 32pp. Young Latasha finds that going to church on Sunday is an exciting adventure. (Rev: BCCB 3/97; BL 6/1–15/96*; SLJ 6/97)

2734 Guidone, Thea. *Drum City* (PS–3). Illus. by Vanessa Brantley-Newton. 2010, Tricycle $15.99 (978-1-58246-308-7). 32pp. One boy beating on a pot in his backyard snowballs into an exuberant parade of rhythm and music in this catchy story. (Rev: BL 5/15/10; LMC 1–2/11; SLJ 7/1/10)

2735 Gutierrez, Amy. *Smarty Marty's Got Game* (1–3). Illus. by Adam McCauley. 2013, Cameron + Co. $17.95 (978-193735951-5). 40pp. Marty takes her younger brother Mikey to a ball game and explains the rules and strategy to him. (Rev: BLO 11/15/13; SLJ 12/13)

2736 Guy, Ginger Foglesong. *¡Bravo!* (PS–K). Illus. by Rene King Moreno. 2010, Greenwillow $16.99 (978-006173180-8). 32pp. A young boy and girl gather seemingly unrelated objects around their yard and find enough for an impromptu musical celebration in this brightly illustrated bilingual story. (Rev: BL 11/1/10; SLJ 9/10)

2737 Hannigan, Katherine. *Emmaline and the Bunny* (1–3). Illus. by author. 2009, Greenwillow $17.99 (978-0-06-162654-8). 112pp. Tidiness is the rule in Neatasapin but when shunned young Emmaline seeks friendship with a wild bunny, things begin changing for the better; inventive wordplay adds to the fun. (Rev: BL 1/1–15/09; HB 3/09; SLJ 3/09)

2738 Harper, Charise Mericle. *Henry's Heart: A Boy, His Heart, and a New Best Friend* (K–2). Illus. by author. 2011, Henry Holt $16.99 (978-0-8050-8989-9). 40pp. Heartbroken when he is denied a puppy, sad young Henry is taken to the doctor — who prescribes a dog! With

factual information about the heart. Lexile AD420L (Rev: BLO 11/15/11; LMC 1–2/12; SLJ 11/1/11)

2739 Harper, Jamie. *Miles to Go* (PS–K). Illus. by author. 2010, Candlewick $12.99 (978-0-7636-3598-5). 32pp. Preschooler Miles drives his play car down the driveway, along the street, and down the sidewalk to school. (Rev: BL 12/15/10; SLJ 5/1/11)

2740 Harper, Jessica. *I Barfed on Mrs. Kenly* (K–3). Illus. by Jon Berkeley. Series: Uh-Oh, Cleo. 2010, Putnam $14.99 (978-039924673-9). 64pp. Cleo gets carsick on the way to a friend's birthday party, but Mrs. Kenley is kind about it despite the mess on her fur coat and encourages Cleo to show off her diving skills. (Rev: BLO 11/1/09; HB 3–4/10)

2741 Harris, Robie H. *Who's in My Family? All About Our Families* (PS–1). Illus. by Nadine Bernard Westcott. 2012, Candlewick $15.99 (978-0-7636-3631-9). 40pp. A wide variety of possible family compositions are discussed as young Gus and Nellie visit the zoo. (Rev: BL 11/1/12; SLJ 9/12)

2742 Hartland, Jessie. *Night Shift* (K–2). Illus. by author. 2007, Bloomsbury $16.95 (978-1-59990-025-4). Fourteen wee-hour occupations are highlighted, one per double-page spread, providing a new look at all the work that gets done while most people sleep. (Rev: BCCB 11/07; BL 11/15/07; HB 1/08; LMC 11/07; SLJ 12/07)

2743 Havill, Juanita. *Jamaica's Find* (PS–1). Illus. by Anne S. O'Brien. 1986, Houghton $16.00 (978-0-395-39376-5); paper $6.95 (978-0-395-45357-5). 32pp. Jamaica finds a stuffed dog, which she brings home, but her parents make her return it to the park where she found it, and where she also finds its true owner. Also use: *Jamaica Tag-Along* (1989). (Rev: BCCB 5/86; BL 4/1/86; SLJ 8/86)

2744 Helldorfer, M. C. *Got to Dance* (PS). Illus. by Hiroe Nakata. 2004, Doubleday LB $17.99 (978-0-385-90865-8). A young girl with a lot of energy loves to dance in this story set in a city in the heat of summer. (Rev: SLJ 8/04)

2745 Heller, Linda. *How Dalia Put a Big Yellow Comforter Inside a Tiny Blue Box: And Other Wonders of Tzedakah* (K–3). Illus. by Stacey Dressen McQueen. 2011, Tricycle $16.99 (978-1-58246-378-0); LB $19.99 (978-1-58246-402-2). 32pp. The Jewish tradition of *tzedakah* boxes is illustrated as Dalia shows her younger brother Yossi about helping those in need. (Rev: BLO 8/11; HB 9–10/11; SLJ 7/11)

2746 Hennessy, B. G. *Because of You* (PS–2). Illus. by Hiroe Nakata. 2005, Candlewick $15.99 (978-0-7636-1926-8). 24pp. A picture book focusing on what children can do to serve others and to make the world a better place. (Rev: BL 3/1/05)

2747 Herrera, Juan Felipe. *Grandma and Me at the Flea / Los Meros Meros Remateros* (2–4). Illus. by Anita De Lucio-Brock. 2002, Children's Book Pr. $15.95 (978-0-89239-171-4). A bilingual story about a boy named Juanito who helps his grandmother at a California flea market. (Rev: BL 4/1/02; HBG 10/02)

2748 Hershenhorn, Esther. *Chicken Soup by Heart* (K–3). Illus. by Rosanne Litzinger. 2002, Simon & Schuster $16.95 (978-0-689-82665-8). 32pp. Rudie and his mother make chicken soup with some special additives for Mrs. Gittel, Rudie's elderly neighbor and babysitter. (Rev: BCCB 1/03; BL 9/1/02; HBG 3/03; SLJ 11/02)

2749 Hesse, Karen. *Come On, Rain!* (K–2). Illus. by Jon J. Muth. 1999, Scholastic $17.99 (978-0-590-33125-8). 32pp. A delightful book about a group of children who enjoy a cloudburst during a sweltering day in the big city. (Rev: BCCB 4/99; BL 2/1/99; HB 7/99; HBG 10/99; SLJ 3/99)

2750 Hest, Amy. *The Reader* (PS–2). Illus. by Lauren Castillo. 2012, Amazon Children's $16.99 (978-0-7614-6184-5). 32pp. A small boy and his dog climb a hill, dragging a sled through the snow; at the top, they play in the snow, share a snack, read their favorite book, and then sled back down. e (Rev: BL 10/15/12; SLJ 12/12)

2751 Hest, Amy. *When You Meet a Bear on Broadway* (PS–1). Illus. by Elivia Savadier. 2009, Farrar $16.99 (978-0-374-40015-6). 40pp. A young girl encounters a sad and lost bear cub in the middle of the city, and orchestrates a happy reunion with its mama. (Rev: BL 11/1/09*; SLJ 10/1/09)

2752 Hilb, Nora, and Sharon Jennings. *Wiggle Giggle Tickle Train* (PS–K). Illus. by Nora Hilb. Photos by Marcela Cabezas Hilb. 2009, Annick $19.95 (978-1-55451-210-2); paper $8.95 (978-1-55451-209-6). Unpaged. Readers enjoy seeing a group of children playing at various games throughout the day, with appealing images paired with bouncy rhyming text. (Rev: BL 10/15/09; SLJ 12/1/09)

2753 Hindley, Judy. *Baby Talk* (PS). Illus. by Brita Granström. 2006, Candlewick $15.99 (978-0-7636-2971-7). 32pp. A day in the life of a toddler is chronicled in rhyming verse and appealing illustrations. (Rev: BL 2/15/06; SLJ 3/06)

2754 Hoberman, Mary Ann. *All Kinds of Families!* (K–3). Illus. by Marc Boutavant. 2009, Little, Brown $16.99 (978-0-316-14633-3). 40pp. In rhyming text, Hoberman looks at all the kinds of families there are — from human families to socks in the drawer. (Rev: BLO 5/15/09; SLJ 8/09)

2755 Hoffmann, E. T. A. *The Nutcracker* (PS). Illus. by Thea Kliros. 2003, HarperCollins $5.99 (978-0-06-052745-7). 22pp. A simplified, attractively illustrated version of the story behind Tchaikovsky's world-famous ballet. (Rev: SLJ 10/03)

2756 Hoppe, Paul. *Hat* (PS–1). Illus. by author. 2009, Bloomsbury $14.99 (978-1-59990-247-0). 32pp. Henry finds a hat and wonders at its amazing attributes but worries that its owner might want it back. (Rev: BL 3/1/09; SLJ 4/09)

2757 Hosford, Kate. *Infinity and Me* (K–3). Illus. by Gabi Swiatkowska. 2012, Carolrhoda $16.95 (978-0-7613-6726-0). 32pp. Young Uma struggles with the notion of infinity and is reassured that friends and family seem unconcerned by the concept and often have interest-

ing ways of seeing it. ALA Notable Children's Book. e Lexile AD670L (Rev: BL 10/15/12; HB 1–2/13; SLJ 10/12)

2758 Hubbell, Patricia. *Black All Around!* (PS–2). Illus. by Don Tate. 2003, Lee & Low $16.95 (978-1-58430-048-9). 32pp. An African American girl looks around to discover that the world is full of lovely things that are black, such as a lake at night and her Momma's cheek. (Rev: BL 2/15/03; HBG 10/03; SLJ 5/03)

2759 Hubbell, Patricia. *Check It Out! Reading, Finding, Helping* (PS–1). Illus. by Nancy Speir. 2011, Marshall Cavendish $16.99 (978-0-7614-5803-6). 32pp. With simple rhyming text, this book introduces the work of a children's librarian and shows how they inspire young people to read. (Rev: BLO 3/14/11; LMC 8–9/11; SLJ 3/1/11)

2760 Hubbell, Patricia. *Snow Happy!* (PS–1). Illus. by Hiroe Nakata. 2010, Tricycle $15.99 (978-1-58246-329-2). 32pp. A group of neighborhood children enjoy a snow day in this bouncy story with dynamic illustrations. (Rev: BL 10/15/10; SLJ 10/1/10)

2761 Hudson, Cheryl W., and Bernette G. Ford. *Bright Eyes, Brown Skin* (PS). Illus. by George Ford. 1990, Just Us Bks. $12.95 (978-0-940975-10-1). This book features four African American children on a typical day in preschool. (Rev: BL 12/1/90*; SLJ 1/91)

2762 Hughes, Shirley. *Alfie and the Big Boys* (PS–1). Illus. by author. 2008, Random $17.95 (978-0-370-32884-3). 32pp. Preschooler Alfie admires the popular Ian from afar until the day comes when he can help the older boy. (Rev: BL 9/15/08)

2763 Hughes, Shirley. *Bobbo Goes to School* (PS–K). Illus. by author. 2013, Candlewick $16.99 (978-0-7636-6524-1). 32pp. Young Lily tosses her stuffed dog into the air and he lands on a school bus, starting a very interesting day for Bobbo and a lot of angst for Lily. (Rev: BL 3/1/13; SLJ 3/13)

2764 Hughes, Shirley. *Don't Want to Go!* (PS). Illus. by author. 2010, Candlewick $16.99 (978-0-7636-5091-9). 32pp. Furious at having to spend the day at a friend's house, young Lily eventually comes around and enjoys herself; when the day is done, she doesn't want to leave. (Rev: BL 10/1/10; SLJ 11/1/10*)

2765 Hutchins, Pat. *Bumpety Bump* (PS–K). Illus. 2006, Greenwillow $15.99 (978-0-06-055999-1). A young boy and his grandfather harvest fruits and vegetables from the garden watched by a little red hen that later provides them with an egg; cross-sections show the plants above and below ground. (Rev: BL 2/1/06; SLJ 4/06)

2766 Hutchins, Pat. *The Doorbell Rang* (K–2). Illus. by author. 1986, Greenwillow $17.89 (978-0-688-05252-2); Morrow paper $6.99 (978-0-688-09234-4). Every time the doorbell rings, it means more of Ma's cookies are eaten, which leaves less for Victoria and Sam — until Grandma arrives with a package. (Rev: BCCB 3/86; BL 6/15/86; SLJ 4/86)

2767 Isadora, Rachel. *Peekaboo Bedtime* (PS). Illus. by author. 2008, Putnam $16.99 (978-0-399-24384-4). The

African American toddler seen in *Peekaboo Morning* (2002) is now playing peekaboo before going to bed. (Rev: BCCB 9/08; BL 6/1–15/08; SLJ 6/08)

2768 Isadora, Rachel. *Peekaboo Morning* (PS–K). Illus. 2002, Penguin $15.99 (978-0-399-23602-0). 32pp. An African American toddler plays peekaboo with friends, relatives, and family pets in this delightful book for preschoolers. (Rev: BCCB 7–8/02; BL 3/1/02; HBG 10/02; SLJ 7/02)

2769 Isadora, Rachel. *Uh-Oh!* (PS). Illus. by author. 2008, Harcourt $16.00 (978-0-15-205765-7). 32pp. "Uh oh!" is this African American toddler's response to the many small mishaps of a day. (Rev: BL 2/15/08; HB 5/08; SLJ 7/08)

2770 Isadora, Rachel. *Yo, Jo!* (PS–K). Illus. 2007, Harcourt $16.00 (978-0-15-205783-1). Young Jomar is a street-savvy kind with vocabulary to match in this evocative book. (Rev: BL 2/1/07)

2771 Jacobs, Paul Dubois, and Jennifer Swender. *My Subway Ride* (K–3). Illus. by Selina Alko. 2004, Gibbs Smith $15.95 (978-1-58685-357-0). New York City's subway comes alive in the rhythmic text and bright illustrations that depict landmark sites. (Rev: SLJ 9/04)

2772 Janovitz, Marilyn. *Play Baby Play!* (PS). Illus. by author. 2012, Sourcebooks $7.99 (978-140226224-1). 24pp. A baby attends play group and enjoys playing with the other babies in this simple, rhymed story. (Rev: BLO 4/15/12; SLJ 5/1/12)

2773 Javernick, Ellen. *What If Everybody Did That?* (K–2). Illus. by Collen M. Madden. 2010, Marshall Cavendish $12.99 (978-0-7614-5686-5). Unpaged. In this character education story, a boy is encouraged to think before acting impulsively through a series of scenarios. (Rev: LMC 8–9/10; SLJ 4/1/10)

2774 Jenkins, Emily. *Lemonade in Winter: A Book about Two Kids Counting Money* (PS–3). Illus. by G. Brian Karas. 2012, Random House $16.99 (978-0-375-85883-3). 40pp. A lemonade stand on a cold winter day proves unprofitable (as their parents predicted) but Pauline and John-John learn some valuable lessons and end up with enough to buy two Popsicles. e Lexile AD410L (Rev: BL 9/1/12; HB 9–10/12; SLJ 8/12*)

2775 Jenkins, Emily. *Water in the Park: A Book about Water and the Times of the Day* (PS–2). Illus. by Stephanie Graegin. 2013, Random House $16.99 (978-0-375-87002-6). 40pp. A look at a hot day at a city park and the various animals and people that enjoy the pond, a sprinkler, and a drinking fountain. e (Rev: BL 3/15/13*; HB 5–6/13; SLJ 5/13)

2776 Jenkins, Emily. *What Happens on Wednesdays* (PS–1). Illus. by Lauren Castillo. 2007, Farrar $16.00 (978-0-374-38303-9). 40pp. A young child catalogs the events of a typical Wednesday — getting up, her father taking her to school, her mother picking her up after lunch, and so forth. (Rev: BCCB 11/07; BL 10/15/07; SLJ 8/07)

2777 Jennings, Sharon. *Into My Mother's Arms* (PS–K). Illus. by Ruth Ohi. 2000, Fitzhenry & Whiteside $14.95 (978-1-55041-533-9). 32pp. A mother and her daughter

spend a busy day, starting with breakfast, continuing with activities like going shopping, and finally coming home to bed. (Rev: BL 5/15/00; SLJ 7/00)

2778 Jesset, Aurore. *Loopy* (PS–2). Illus. by Barbara Korthues. 2008, North-South $16.95 (978-0-7358-2175-0). 32pp. After leaving a favorite toy at the doctor's office, a child imagines all sorts of terrible fates that may befall it. (Rev: BL 6/1–15/08; SLJ 7/08)

2779 Johnson, Angela. *Lily Brown's Paintings* (K–2). Illus. by E. B. Lewis. 2007, Scholastic LB $16.99 (978-0-439-78225-8). Young Lily Brown's paintbrush takes her from everyday scenes into a world of imagination. (Rev: BL 2/1/07; SLJ 2/07)

2780 Johnson, Angela. *Rain Feet* (PS). Illus. by Rhonda Mitchell. 1994, Orchard $5.99 (978-0-531-06849-6). 12pp. A little African American boy enjoys splashing through puddles in this board book. Also use *Mama Birds, Baby Birds* (1994). (Rev: BL 12/1/94; HB 9/94; SLJ 1/95)

2781 Johnson, Angela. *Shoes Like Miss Alice's* (PS–K). Illus. by Ken Page. 1995, Orchard LB $16.99 (978-0-531-08664-3). 32pp. Sally resents her baby-sitter Miss Alice until she sees her wide assortment of shoes. (Rev: BL 3/15/95; SLJ 7/95)

2782 Johnson, Angela. *Violet's Music* (PS–2). Illus. 2004, Dial $16.99 (978-0-8037-2740-3). 32pp. Violet has always loved music and is thrilled when she finally meets some kindred spirits. (Rev: BL 3/15/04; SLJ 2/04)

2783 Johnson, D. B. *Eddie's Kingdom* (PS–2). Illus. 2005, Houghton $16.00 (978-0-618-56299-2). 32pp. Through his art, young Eddie resolves the complaints of his neighbors and brings peace to their apartment building. (Rev: BL 10/15/05; SLJ 11/05)

2784 Johnson, David. *Snow Sounds: An Onomatopoeic Story* (PS–2). Illus. 2006, Houghton $16.00 (978-0-618-47310-6). 32pp. Illustrations and onomatopoeias tell the story of a young boy's snowy morning. (Rev: BL 9/1/06; SLJ 10/06)

2785 Johnston, Tony. *The Quilt Story* (PS–2). Illus. by Tomie dePaola. 1996, Penguin paper $5.99 (978-0-698-11368-8). 32pp. The star of this book is the quilt, which gives fun, warmth, and comfort to two generations. (Rev: BCCB 7–8/85; BL 8/85; SLJ 9/85)

2786 Joosse, Barbara M. *Love Is a Good Thing to Feel* (PS–2). Illus. by Jennifer Plecas. 2008, Philomel $12.99 (978-0-399-25168-9). 32pp. A little girl with a stuffed bunny friend bounces through this book discussing the many ways to show and enjoy love. (Rev: BL 1/1–15/09; SLJ 12/08)

2787 Joosse, Barbara M. *Please Is a Good Word to Say* (PS–2). Illus. by Jennifer Plecas. 2007, Philomel $12.99 (978-0-399-24217-5). 32pp. Amusing illustrations and text enliven this manners handbook that presents illustrative anecdotes. (Rev: BL 6/1–15/07; SLJ 7/07)

2788 Juster, Norton. *Neville* (PS–3). Illus. by G. Brian Karas. 2011, Random House $17.99 (978-0-375-86765-1). 32pp. A young boy anxious about starting over in a new neighborhood finds a simple way to involve the whole community in a compelling hunt for the mysterious "Neville." **e** Lexile AD600L (Rev: BL 10/15/11*; HB 9–10/11; LMC 11–12/11; SLJ 9/1/11*)

2789 Karas, G. Brian. *The Village Garage* (PS–3). Illus. by author. 2010, Henry Holt $16.99 (978-0-8050-8716-1). 32pp. This look at a village garage crew through the seasons as they deal with various challenges and use different machines. (Rev: BL 4/15/10; SLJ 6/1/10)

2790 Katz, Karen. *Can You Say Peace?* (PS). Illus. by author. 2006, Holt $15.95 (978-0-8050-7893-0). 32pp. Drawings of children from around the world are featured along with collages representing their country of origin and the word for "peace" in their native language. (Rev: BL 5/15/06; SLJ 9/06)

2791 Katz, Karen. *Now I'm Big!* (PS). Illus. by author. 2013, Simon & Schuster $15.99 (978-1-4169-3547-6). 32pp. A toddler celebration of things learned (mastering zippers, using cutlery, etc.) (Rev: BL 3/1/13; SLJ 3/13)

2792 Katz, Karen. *A Potty for Me! A Lift-the-Flap Instruction Manual* (PS). Illus. by author. 2005, Simon & Schuster $7.99 (978-0-689-87423-9). A child learns to use the potty in this encouraging book with entertaining flaps to lift. (Rev: SLJ 8/05)

2793 Katz, Karen. *Twelve Hats for Lena: A Book of Months* (PS–3). Illus. by author. 2002, Simon & Schuster $16.95 (978-0-689-84873-5). Lena creates hats that are suitable for each month of the year, and hat-making directions are included. (Rev: HBG 3/03; SLJ 10/02)

2794 Kerley, Barbara. *One World, One Day* (PS–3). Illus. 2009, National Geographic $17.95 (978-1-4263-0460-6). 48pp. Clear color photographs show how children around the world live their lives — from what they eat for breakfast to where they go to school, the games they play, and so forth. (Rev: BL 5/15/09; SLJ 6/09) [305.23409]

2795 Kittinger, Jo S. *The House on Dirty-Third Street* (K–3). Illus. by Thomas Gonzalez. 2012, Peachtree $16.95 (978-1-56145-619-2). 32pp. A young girl's prayer for her mother to keep the faith in restoring their rundown house results in the church congregation pitching in to help. (Rev: BL 2/15/12; SLJ 4/1/12)

2796 Klinting, Lars. *What Do You Want?* (PS). Illus. 2006, Groundwood $15.95 (978-0-88899-636-7). 36pp. This import from Sweden with charming, simple illustrations explores the desires of various animate and inanimate objects, including a bird, bee, chair, chicken, and pillow. (Rev: BL 3/1/06; SLJ 4/06)

2797 Konnecke, Ole. *Anthony and the Girls* (PS–2). Trans. by Nancy Seitz. 2006, Farrar $15.00 (978-0-374-30376-1). Little Anthony's attempts to win the attention of two girls in a nearby sandbox all fail until he bursts into tears, bringing them running to his side. (Rev: BL 6/1–15/06; SLJ 2/06)

2798 Kooser, Ted. *Bag in the Wind* (1–3). Illus. by Barry Root. 2010, Candlewick $17.99 (978-076363001-0). 48pp. This thoughtful, and nicely illustrated, story about the life cycle of a simple plastic grocery bag offers messages about ecology, economy, and the importance of recycling. ⌒ (Rev: BL 1/1/10; LMC 5–6/10; SLJ 1/10)

2799 Kooser, Ted. *House Held Up by Trees* (K–3). Illus. by Jon Klassen. 2012, Candlewick $16.99 (978-076365107-7). 32pp. As a house abandoned by its former proud owners slowly falls apart, trees grow up around it, ultimately saving it and holding it aloft. (Rev: BL 2/15/12*; HB 3–4/12; LMC 8–9/12; SLJ 5/1/12)

2800 Krauss, Ruth. *The Growing Story* (PS–K). Illus. by Helen Osenbury. 2007, HarperCollins $16.99 (978-0-06-024716-4). In this new edition of Krauss's classic story published in 1947, a young boy observes growth everywhere around him and wonders if he is growing too. (Rev: BL 4/1/07; SLJ 7/1/07)

2801 Krebs, Laurie. *The Beeman* (PS–2). Illus. by Valeria Cis. 2008, Barefoot Books $16.99 (978-1-84686-146-8). 40pp. This new edition of the book in which a beekeeper shows his granddaughter around his hives and explains how honey is made features new illustrations and appended information. (Rev: BL 4/15/08; SLJ 6/08)

2802 Kroll, Virginia. *Cristina Keeps a Promise* (1–3). Illus. by Enrique O. Sánchez. Series: The Way I Act. 2006, Albert Whitman $15.99 (978-0-8075-1350-7). Cristina gives up a chance to meet her favorite author so she can keep a promise and attend her brother's Special Olympics track meet. (Rev: SLJ 1/07)

2803 Kroll, Virginia. *Everybody Has a Teddy* (PS–K). Illus. by Sophie Allsopp. 2007, Sterling $12.95 (978-1-4027-3580-6). 32pp. A little boy describes his classmates' teddy bears in detail and then his own — not a teddy bear but a toy monkey called Muh. (Rev: BL 3/15/07)

2804 Kroll, Virginia. *Good Neighbor Nicholas* (1–3). Illus. by Nancy Cote. Series: The Way I Act. 2006, Albert Whitman $15.99 (978-0-8075-2998-0). Nicholas clashes with his cranky, older neighbor on a number of occasions until he begins to understand some of the reasons the older man is so unhappy. (Rev: SLJ 1/07)

2805 Kroll, Virginia. *Jason Takes Responsibility* (1–3). Illus. by Nancy Cote. Series: The Way I Act. 2005, Albert Whitman $15.99 (978-0-8075-2537-1). Jason loses one of the invitations to his grandmother's birthday party on his way to the post office, but he does his best to make things right on the day. (Rev: SLJ 1/06)

2806 Kroll, Virginia. *Makayla Cares About Others* (PS–1). Illus. by Nancy Cote. 2007, Albert Whitman $15.99 (978-0-8075-4945-2). 32pp. Young Makayla overcomes her fear of bugs to help her neighbor Mrs. MacFee dig a memory garden for her cat. (Rev: BL 4/1/07)

2807 Kruusval, Catarina. *Franny's Friends* (PS–K). Trans. by Joan Sandin. Illus. by author. 2008, Farrar $16.00 (978-91-296-6836-0). 32pp. Franny and her friends — seven stuffed animals — set off on a picnic outing but Little Heddy Hedgehog and Itty Bitty Kitty go missing when they fall into a hole. (Rev: BL 6/1–15/08; SLJ 5/08)

2808 Lachtman, Ofelia Dumas. *Pepita Packs Up / Pepita empaca* (PS–2). Trans. by Gabriela Baeza Ventura. Illus.

by Alex Pardo DeLange. 2005, Piñata $15.95 (978-1-55885-431-4). In this appealing bilingual picture book, a little girl faces moving day with mixed emotions — sadness at leaving her old friends and neighbors behind but anticipation about what awaits at her new home. (Rev: SLJ 2/06)

2809 LaRochelle, David. *Arlo's ARTrageous Adventure!* (PS–2). Illus. by author. 2013, Sterling $14.95 (978-1-4027-9226-7). 28pp. Arlo's grandmother drags the young boy to the art museum in this engaging flap-book. (Rev: BL 11/15/13; LMC 3–4/14; SLJ 10/13)

2810 Lee, Spike, and Tonya Lewis Lee. *Giant Steps to Change the World* (2–5). Illus. by Sean Qualls. 2011, Simon & Schuster $16.99 (978-0-689-86815-3). 40pp. Motivational quotations from various luminaries, spreads with colorful illustrations, and poetic text profile people who have made significant contributions and encourage young people to follow in their footsteps. (Rev: BL 2/1/11; LMC 5–6/11; SLJ 2/1/11)

2811 Lewis, J. Patrick. *The Fantastic 5 and 10¢ Store: A Rebus Adventure* (1–2). Illus. by Valorie Fisher. 2010, Random House $17.99 (978-0-375-85878-9); LB $20.99 (978-0-375-95878-6). 40pp. This story about a store with many magical goods makes good use of rebuses and rhyming wordplay. (Rev: BL 10/1/10; LMC 1–2/11; SLJ 5/1/11)

2812 Lin, Grace. *Dim Sum for Everyone* (PS–K). Illus. 2001, Knopf $14.95 (978-0-375-81082-4). Text and appealing illustrations show an Asian family enjoying a meal at a dim sum restaurant in Chinatown. (Rev: BL 6/1–15/01; HBG 3/02; SLJ 7/01)

2813 Lin, Grace. *Fortune Cookie Fortunes* (K–2). Illus. 2004, Knopf $15.95 (978-0-375-81521-8). 32pp. The fortune cookies that follow a meal are the focus of this story featuring the family from *Dim Sum for Everyone* (2001). (Rev: BL 2/15/04; SLJ 6/04)

2814 Lomas Garza, Carmen. *In My Family / En Mi Familia* (1–4). Illus. 1996, Children's Book Pr. $15.95 (978-0-89239-138-7). 32pp. In 13 paintings labeled bilingually, the artist portrays his childhood in Kingsville, Texas. (Rev: BL 11/1/96; HB 11/96)

2815 London, Jonathan. *I'm a Truck Driver* (PS–1). Illus. by David Parkins. 2010, Henry Holt $12.99 (978-0-8050-7989-0). 32pp. Different kinds of trucks, from street sweepers to garbage trucks, are introduced in appealing illustrations and simple rhymes. (Rev: BL 5/1/10; SLJ 7/1/10)

2816 Lord, Janet. *Albert the Fix-It Man* (PS–2). Illus. by Julie Paschkis. 2008, Peachtree $15.95 (978-1-56145-433-4). When Albert the "Fix-It Man" gets ill, the neighbors join together to offer support. (Rev: BL 3/15/08; HB 5/08; SLJ 4/08)

2817 Lovell, Patty. *Have Fun, Molly Lou Melon* (PS–1). Illus. by David Catrow. 2012, Putnam $16.99 (978-0399-25406-2.). 32pp. Molly Lou's grandmother encourages the girl to use her imagination rather than depending on fancy toys, and Molly Lou passes this enthusiasm on to

her neighbor Gertie. Lexile AD820L (Rev: BL 11/1/12; SLJ 12/12)

2818 Lyon, George E. *Weaving the Rainbow* (K–2). Illus. by Stephanie Anderson. 2004, Simon & Schuster $15.95 (978-0-689-85169-8). 40pp. A well-illustrated, step-by-step picture-book story of an artist who raises sheep, shears the wool, processes it, and finally produces a woven work of art. (Rev: BL 2/15/04; SLJ 2/04)

2819 Lyons, Kelly Starling. *One Million Men and Me* (PS–2). Illus. by Peter Ambush. 2007, Just Us Bks. $16.95 (978-1-933491-07-3). 32pp. The 1995 Million Man March in Washington, D.C., is described from the perspective of a little girl attending with her father. (Rev: BL 10/15/07; SLJ 11/07)

2820 Macaulay, David. *Shortcut* (K–4). Illus. 1995, Houghton $15.95 (978-0-395-52436-7). 64pp. The lives of six people cross in a series of different stories. The author also uses this method of overlapping storytelling in *Black and White* (1990). (Rev: BCCB 9/95; BL 10/15/95; HB 3/95; SLJ 9/95*)

2821 Maccarone, Grace. *Miss Lina's Ballerinas and the Wicked Wish* (PS–3). Illus. by Christine Davenier. 2012, Feiwel & Friends $16.99 (978-1-250-00580-9). 40pp. Regina is disappointed to learn she will be a rat in the upcoming performance of *Sleeping Beauty* but everything turns out all right in the end. ℮ Lexile AD840L (Rev: BLO 9/1/12; SLJ 10/12)

2822 McCarty, Peter. *Baby Steps* (PS–K). Illus. 2000, Holt $16.00 (978-0-8050-5953-3). 32pp. Using clear pencil illustrations, this book traces the growth of baby Suki from one day old to her first steps at one year old. (Rev: BCCB 10/00; BL 10/1/00; HBG 3/01; SLJ 10/00)

2823 McCarty, Peter. *Fall Ball* (PS–1). Illus. by author. 2013, Henry Holt $16.99 (978-080509253-0). 32pp. A simple story about the joys of playing football after school on a beautiful fall day. Lexile AD290 (Rev: BL 11/15/13; SLJ 11/13)

2824 McClure, Nikki. *To Market, to Market* (PS–3). Illus. by author. 2011, Abrams $17.95 (978-0-8109-9738-7). 40pp. Tasked with gathering the items on a shopping list, a mother and son visit one farmer's market stall after another and learn about the farmers and techniques that produced these goods. (Rev: BL 4/1/11; LMC 8–9/11; SLJ 4/11)

2825 McGhee, Alison. *Bye-bye, Crib* (PS–K). Illus. by Ross MacDonald. 2008, Simon & Schuster $16.99 (978-1-4169-1621-5). 32pp. With the help of his blanket, pillow, and stuffed animal Baby Kitty, a little boy summons the courage to move into a big, real bed. (Rev: BCCB 6/08; BL 4/15/08; SLJ 2/08)

2826 McGhee, Alison. *So Many Days* (PS–3). Illus. by Taeeun Yoo. 2010, Atheneum $15.99 (978-1-4169-5857-4). 40pp. A child and a dog explore their world as a narrator emphasizes all the opportunities that await us in life. Lexile AD420L (Rev: BL 2/1/10; SLJ 3/1/10)

2827 McGowan, Michael. *Sunday Is for God* (1–3). Illus. by Steve Johnson. 2010, Random House $17.99 (978-0-375-84188-0); LB $20.99 (978-0-375-94591-5). 40pp.

A young African American boy describes how he spends his Sundays, some of them enjoyable and others a bit trying, but offering opportunity for imagination. (Rev: BL 11/15/09; SLJ 1/1/10)

2828 Mack, Jeff. *The Things I Can Do* (PS–2). Illus. by author. 2013, Roaring Brook $16.99 (978-1-59643-675-6). 32pp. In a flamboyantly illustrated autobiography, Jeff shows all the things he can do — fix his own lunch, brush his teeth, choose his clothes, and so forth; readers will enjoy the disparity between the images and the truth. (Rev: BL 7/13; SLJ 6/13)

2829 McKee, David. *The Conquerors* (K–3). Illus. by author. 2004, Handprint $16.95 (978-1-59354-078-4). The ruler of a large country conquers neighboring nations "so they can be like us" but fails to recognize that the culture sometimes flows in the other direction. (Rev: BCCB 1/05; HB 1/05; SLJ 2/05)

2830 Macken, JoAnn Early. *Waiting Out the Storm* (PS–2). Illus. by Susan Gaber. 2010, Candlewick $15.99 (978-0-7636-3378-3). 32pp. With striking, impressionistic illustrations and gentle text, this book follows a mother and daughter as they retreat inside when a storm arrives and discuss how the animals manage to keep safe. (Rev: BL 1/1/10*; LMC 5–6/10; SLJ 4/1/10)

2831 MacLachlan, Patricia. *Snowflakes Fall* (PS–2). Illus. by Steven Kellogg. 2013, Random House $17.99 (978-038537693-8). 32pp. Created as a tribute to the victims of the 2012 school shootings in Newtown, Connecticut, this poignant picture book uses poetry and illustrations beautifully to tell stories with motifs of snow, seasons, and nature's cycles to help children understand the power of healing, memory, hope, and rebirth. Lexile AD600 (Rev: BL 9/1/13*; HB 11–12/13; SLJ 9/13*)

2832 MacLean, Kole. *Even Firefighters Hug Their Moms* (PS–K). Illus. by Mike Reed. 2002, Dutton $16.99 (978-0-525-46996-4). A young boy is so immersed in his elaborate role-playing (as fire fighter, police officer, doctor) that he's too busy to give his mother the requested hug. (Rev: BL 11/15/02; HBG 3/03; SLJ 10/02)

2833 MacLennan, Cathy. *Chicky Chicky Chook Chook* (PS–1). Illus. by author. 2007, Boxer Bks. LB $12.95 (978-1-905417-40-7). An onomatopoeic story full of animal sounds and creative rhymes, featuring a group of animals as the weather changes from warm sun to rain. (Rev: SLJ 4/07*)

2834 McMenemy, Sarah. *Jack's New Boat* (PS–K). Illus. 2005, Candlewick $15.99 (978-0-7636-2477-4). With bright collage-and-gouache illustrations, this is the story of young Jack's new toy boat, which is lost almost as soon as he gets it but luckily is later found. (Rev: BL 5/1/05)

2835 McNamara, Margaret. *Earth Day* (PS–1). Illus. by Mike Gordon. Series: Robin Hill School Ready-to-Read. 2008, Aladdin LB $13.89 (978-1-4169-5536-8); paper $3.99 (978-1-4169-5535-1). Emma decides to start her environmental efforts slowly — brushing without the water running, recycling, and so forth. (Rev: BLO 4/14/09)

2836 McNaughton, Colin. *Potty Poo-Poo Wee-Wee!* (PS). Illus. 2005, Candlewick $9.99 (978-0-7636-2781-2). 40pp. Littlesaurus, a young dinosaur, is having problems with toilet training and further confounds matters with his potty mouth. (Rev: BL 8/05; SLJ 8/05)

2837 McPhail, David. *Bella Loves Bunny* (PS). Illus. by author. 2013, Abrams/Appleseed $8.95 (978-141970543-4). 22pp. Bella enjoys spending the day with her stuffed bunny in this gentle board-book companion to *Ben Loves Bear* (2013). (Rev: BL 3/15/13)

2838 McPhail, David. *NO!* (K–3). Illus. by author. 2009, Roaring Brook $16.95 (978-1-59643-288-8). 48pp. A little boy living in a war zone sets off to mail a letter to the president in this compelling, almost wordless story. (Rev: BL 3/15/09; SLJ 5/09)

2839 McPhail, David. *The Teddy Bear* (PS–2). Illus. 2002, Holt $15.95 (978-0-8050-6414-8). 32pp. A young boy generously gives his teddy bear to a homeless man who has become attached to it. (Rev: BL 5/1/02*; HBG 10/02; SLJ 6/02)

2840 McQuinn, Anna. *Lola at the Library* (PS). Illus. by Rosalind Beardshaw. 2006, Charlesbridge paper $6.95 (978-1-58089-142-4). A trip to the library with her mother is a treat for little Lola. (Rev: SLJ 7/06)

2841 Manushkin, Fran. *The Belly Book* (PS). Illus. by Dan Yaccarino. 2011, Feiwel & Friends $16.99 (978-0-312-64958-6). 32pp. This playful book celebrates the human midsection — belly buttons, stomachs, perfect for belly-flopping, and so on. (Rev: BLO 11/15/11; SLJ 12/1/11)

2842 Marsalis, Wynton. *Squeak, Rumble, Whomp! Whomp! Whomp! A Sonic Adventure* (PS–2). Illus. by Paul Rogers. 2012, Candlewick $15.99 (978-0-7636-3991-4). 32pp. A rhythmic introduction to a variety of sounds and musical instruments, with illustrations that extend the mood as a young boy explores his neighborhood. ℮ (Rev: BL 11/15/12*; LMC 5–6/13; SLJ 9/12*)

2843 Martin, Amy. *Symphony City* (1–3). Illus. by author. 2011, McSweeney's $17.95 (978-1-936365-39-5). 48pp. A young girl gets separated from her adult escort en route to a concert in the city and decides to follow the sound of music, discovering in the process that there is music everywhere. (Rev: BLO 8/11; LMC 5–6/12; SLJ 11/1/11)

2844 Martin, David. *We've All Got Bellybuttons!* (PS–K). Illus. by Randy Cecil. 2005, Candlewick $15.99 (978-0-7636-1775-2). Cartoon animals explore their bodies and ask the reader to mimic their movements (clapping, closing eyes, opening mouths, and so forth). (Rev: BCCB 2/05; SLJ 2/05)

2845 Martin, Jacqueline B. *On Sand Island* (PS–2). Illus. by David A. Johnson. 2003, Houghton $16.00 (978-0-618-23151-5). Carl, who lives on an island in Lake Superior, dreams of having a boat and, with the help of the community, he succeeds in building one. (Rev: BCCB 10/03; BL 8/03; HBG 4/04; LMC 3/04; SLJ 11/03)

2846 May, Eleanor. *Who Needs It?* (K–3). Illus. by Blanche Sims. Series: Social Studies Connects. 2009,

Kane paper $5.95 (978-1-57565-281-8). 32pp. Gus and Mickey have very different ideas about what to take on a camping trip in this funny story that includes sidebars about basic human needs. (Rev: BL 3/1/09)

2847 Mayer, Pamela. *Don't Sneeze at the Wedding* (PS–K). Illus. by Martha Aviles. 2013, Lerner/Kar-Ben $17.95 (978-1-4677-0428-1). 32pp. Flower girl Anna gets lots of advice on how to control her cold in this story that introduces Jewish wedding rituals. ℮ (Rev: BL 11/15/13; LMC 3–4/14; SLJ 9/13)

2848 Menchin, Scott. *Taking a Bath with the Dog and Other Things That Make Me Happy* (PS–K). Illus. by author. 2007, Candlewick $15.99 (978-0-7636-2919-9). Sweet Pea surveys her friends and neighbors (some human, some animal) to find out what makes them happy and also figures out what she most enjoys. (Rev: SLJ 7/07)

2849 Meng, Cece. *I Will Not Read This Book* (K–2). Illus. by Joy Ang. 2011, Clarion $16.99 (978-0-547-04971-7). 32pp. A charming reluctant reader outlines all the things he will do to avoid reading this book. (Rev: BL 9/1/11; SLJ 11/1/11)

2850 Merz, Jennifer. *Playground Day!* (PS–1). Illus. by author. 2007, Clarion $16.00 (978-0-618-81696-5). 32pp. A little girl enjoys an afternoon at the playground imagining herself a variety of different animals. (Rev: BL 10/1/07; SLJ 10/07)

2851 Meshon, Aaron. *Take Me Out to the Yakyu* (PS–2). Illus. by author. 2013, Atheneum $15.99 (978-144244177-4). 40pp. A young boy with grandfathers in both Japan and the United States celebrates baseball and the surrounding rituals in each country. ALA Notable Children's Book. ℮ Lexile AD610 (Rev: BL 2/15/13*; LMC 8–9/13; SLJ 2/13*)

2852 Meyerhoff, Jenny. *Third Grade Baby* (2–4). Illus. by Jill Weber. 2008, Farrar $15.00 (978-0-374-37482-2). 112pp. When Polly starts 3rd grade she is the only child who hasn't lost a tooth; is she too old for the tooth fairy? (Rev: BCCB 11/08; BL 12/1/08; SLJ 11/08)

2853 Meyers, Susan. *Everywhere Babies* (PS). Illus. by Marla Frazee. 2001, Harcourt $16.00 (978-0-15-202226-6). 32pp. A charming representation of the first year of a baby's life with a rhyming text and watercolors showing babies being fed and playing games like peek-a-boo. (Rev: BL 3/1/01; HB 5/01*; HBG 10/01)

2854 Meyers, Susan. *This Is the Way a Baby Rides* (PS–2). Illus. by Hiroe Nakata. 2005, Abrams $15.95 (978-0-8109-5763-3). 40pp. A lively toddler has fun at a picnic and his many movements are mimicked by animal babies on parallel spreads. (Rev: BL 10/1/05; SLJ 12/05)

2855 Mikkelsen, Jon. *Kids Against Hunger* (1–3). Illus. by Nathan Lueth. 2008, Stone Arch LB $15.95 (978-1-4342-0790-6). 40pp. This illustrated easy chapter book follows three boys who volunteer for a nonprofit organization feeding the needy. (Rev: BLO 12/4/08; SLJ 2/09)

2856 Milgrim, David. *Amelia Makes a Movie* (K–2). Illus. by author. 2008, Putnam $16.99 (978-0-399-24670-8). 32pp. Amelia and her little brother join forces to make a movie, which is shown in comic-strip panels; technical details will attract young readers. (Rev: BL 2/1/08; SLJ 4/08)

2857 Milgrim, David. *Time to Get Up, Time to Go* (PS–K). Illus. by author. 2006, Clarion $15.00 (978-0-618-51998-9). 32pp. A very busy young boy looks after himself and his stuffed doll during an activity-filled day; the minimal text and eye-focusing illustrations work well together. (Rev: SLJ 4/06)

2858 Millard, Glenda. *And Red Galoshes: A Story about a Rainy Day* (PS–1). Illus. by Jonathan Bentley. 2013, IPG/Little Hare $16.99 (978-1-921541-46-9). 24pp. Well, what do you do when your red galoshes are too big? Turns out they have lots of uses — collecting mud, as oars, as unlikely kites . . . (Rev: BL 3/15/13; SLJ 3/13)

2859 Miller, Pat. *We're Going on a Book Hunt* (PS–2). Illus. by Nadine Bernard Westcott. 2008, Upstart $17.95 (978-1-60213-007-4). A lively introduction to the library featuring a bear cub class, adapted from *We're Going on a Bear Hunt*. (Rev: BL 7/08; LMC 11/08)

2860 Minor, Wendell. *How Big Could Your Pumpkin Grow?* (PS–3). Illus. by author. 2013, Penguin $16.99 (978-039924684-5). 32pp. Gouache and watercolor art illustrates just how big pumpkins could grow (like to block the Brooklyn Bridge?), at the same time displaying key American landmarks and introducing comparisons of size; a concluding spread provides factual information. (Rev: BL 9/1/13; LMC 11–12/13; SLJ 7/13)

2861 Miranda, Anne. *To Market, to Market* (K–2). Illus. by Janet Stevens. 1997, Harcourt $16.00 (978-0-15-200035-6). 36pp. A wildly funny picture book about market day misunderstandings. (Rev: BL 11/1/97; HB 11/97; HBG 3/98; SLJ 1/98)

2862 Mitchell, Lori. *Different Just Like Me* (K–3). Illus. 1999, Charlesbridge LB $15.95 (978-0-88106-975-4). April's experiences during the week, when she meets new people, help her appreciate her much-anticipated weekend visit with her Grammie. (Rev: BL 3/1/99; HBG 10/99; SLJ 3/99)

2863 Mitchell, Margaree King. *Uncle Jed's Barber Shop* (2–5). Illus. by James Ransome. 1993, Simon & Schuster $16.00 (978-0-671-76969-7); paper $6.99 (978-0-689-81913-1). Uncle Jed, an African American barber in the 1920s, hopes to open his own shop, but his generosity always prevents him from saving enough money. (Rev: BCCB 9/93; BL 9/1/93; HB 11/93; SLJ 10/93)

2864 Mizzoni, Chris. *Clancy with the Puck* (PS–2). Illus. by author. 2007, Raincoast $16.95 (978-1-55192-804-3). 32pp. Told in rhyming couplets, this is the story of a gifted yet arrogant hockey star who helps move the Hogtown Maple Buds to the Stanley Cup finals only to fall short when he gets a chance at the winning goal. (Rev: BL 11/1/07; LMC 1/08; SLJ 1/08)

2865 Mora, Pat. *The Beautiful Lady: Our Lady of Guadalupe* (K–3). Illus. by Steve Johnson. 2012, Knopf $16.99 (978-0-375-86838-2). 40pp. The story of the miracles associated with Our Lady of Guadalupe is revealed as a contemporary family prepares to celebrate her feast day on December 12; an author's note provides additional background. **e** Lexile AD630L (Rev: BL 11/15/12; LMC 8–9/13; SLJ 2/13)

2866 Mora, Pat. *Maria Paints the Hills* (K–3). Illus. by Maria Hesch. 2002, Museum of New Mexico paper $9.95 (978-0-89013-410-8). 32pp. A simple story and stunning folk-art illustrations capture the life of a little girl in New Mexico. (Rev: BL 12/15/02; HBG 3/03)

2867 Morris, Ann. *Hats, Hats, Hats* (PS–1). Illus. by Ken Heyman. 1989, Morrow paper $6.99 (978-0-688-12274-4). A full-color display of varieties of hats. Also use: *Bread, Bread, Bread* (1989). (Rev: BL 4/15/89; SLJ 5/89)

2868 Morris, Ann. *Houses and Homes* (PS–1). Illus. 1992, Lothrop LB $16.89 (978-0-688-10169-5). 32pp. A fascinating look at how houses are built around the world. (Rev: BCCB 12/92; BL 10/1/92)

2869 Morris, Carla. *The Boy Who Was Raised by Librarians* (K–2). Illus. by Brad Sneed. 2007, Peachtree $16.95 (978-1-56145-391-7). 32pp. Melvin spends so much time at the library that the librarians become like family. (Rev: BL 5/1/07; LMC 10/07; SLJ 6/07)

2870 Mortensen, Denise Dowling. *Ohio Thunder* (PS–3). Illus. by Kate Kiesler. 2006, Clarion $16.00 (978-0-618-59542-6). 32pp. Rhyming verse and dramatic artwork describe a summer thunderstorm above the fields of an Ohio farm. (Rev: BL 4/15/06; SLJ 5/06)

2871 Muirhead, Margaret. *Mabel, One and Only* (PS–1). Illus. by Lynne Avril. 2009, Dial $16.99 (978-0-8037-3198-1). When their adult friends are all too busy to play, Mabel and her dog Jack turn a box into a spaceship; when the adults turn up she generously invites them into her game. (Rev: BLO 2/2/09; SLJ 4/09)

2872 Muldrow, Diane. *We Planted a Tree* (K–3). Illus. by Bob Staake. 2010, Good Books $17.99 (978-0-375-86432-2). 40pp. Nature, conservation, and family life are celebrated in this story of families around the world planting trees and the benefits these trees bring to them and to the environment. (Rev: BL 2/15/10; LMC 5–6/10; SLJ 3/1/10)

2873 Munsch, Robert. *Ribbon Rescue* (PS–1). Illus. by Eugenie Fernandes. 1999, Scholastic $11.95 (978-0-590-89012-0). 32pp. A Mohawk girl named Jillian is so helpful to all the members of a wedding party that they make her the flower girl. (Rev: BL 7/99; HBG 10/99; SLJ 6/99)

2874 Murphy, Stuart J. *Freda Is Found* (PS–K). Illus. by Tim Jones Illustration. Series: Stuart J. Murphy's I See I Learn. 2011, Charlesbridge $14.95 (978-1-58089-462-3); paper $6.95 (978-1-58089-463-0). Unpaged. This story of a young girl seeking help when she finds herself lost offers good advice on safety and decision-making. **e** (Rev: SLJ 7/11)

2875 Nevius, Carol. *Soccer Hour* (1–3). Illus. by Bill Thomson. 2011, Marshall Cavendish $16.99 (978-0-7614-5689-6). 32pp. A child narrator tells readers all about what takes place at a soccer practice session in this simple story. (Rev: BL 6/1/11; SLJ 4/11)

2876 Newman, Lesléa. *Miss Tutu's Star* (PS–2). Illus. by Carey Armstrong-Ellis. 2010, Abrams $16.95 (978-0-8109-8396-0). 32pp. A reassuring ballet teacher coaches anxious but passionate Selena through her first recital in this colorful story told in rhyming couplets. (Rev: BL 9/1/10; LMC 11–12/10; SLJ 8/1/10)

2877 Nikola-Lisa, W. *America: My Land, Your Land, Our Land* (K–3). Illus. 1997, Lee & Low $15.95 (978-1-880000-37-3). 32pp. A handsome picture book that shows many of the contrasts that are present in the United States. (Rev: BL 9/1/97; SLJ 7/97)

2878 Nikola-Lisa, W. *Summer Sun Risin'* (PS–1). Illus. by Don Tate. 2002, Lee & Low $16.95 (978-1-58430-034-2). A gentle story of a young African American boy's busy day on the farm — looking after the animals, plowing, picnicking, fishing, and bedtime stories. (Rev: HBG 10/02; SLJ 5/02)

2879 Nye, Naomi Shihab. *Baby Radar* (PS). Illus. by Nancy Carpenter. 2003, Greenwillow LB $16.89 (978-0-688-15949-8). The world is seen from the low-down viewpoint of a toddler in a stroller on a fine fall day. (Rev: HBG 4/04; SLJ 9/03)

2880 Ohi, Ruth. *Pants Off First!* (PS). Illus. Series: Early Bird Boardbook. 2001, Fitzhenry & Whiteside $6.95 (978-1-55041-667-1). As a little boy undresses, he puts his clothes on his pets in this humorous story that ends with a twist. (Rev: BL 7/01)

2881 Olsen, Sylvia. *Yetsa's Sweater* (PS–3). Illus. by Joan Larson. 2006, Sono Nis $17.95 (978-1-55039-155-8). Yetsa and her grandmother clean, card, and spin fleece into wool in this story featuring Cowichan traditions in British Columbia. (Rev: SLJ 5/07)

2882 Omololu, Cynthia Jaynes. *When It's Six O'Clock in San Francisco: A Trip Through Time Zones* (K–3). Illus. by Randy DuBurke. 2009, Clarion $16 (978-0-618-76827-1). 32pp. This story shows children around the world conducting activities appropriate to their time zones. (Rev: BL 9/15/09; SLJ 10/1/09)

2883 O'Neill, Alexis. *Estela's Swap* (K–3). Illus. by Enrique O. Sánchez. 2002, Lee & Low $16.95 (978-1-58430-044-1). Colorful illustrations accompany this story of Estela, a Hispanic girl who wants to sell a music box to earn money for dance lessons. (Rev: BL 12/15/02; HBG 3/03; SLJ 10/02)

2884 Oxenbury, Helen. *Pig Tale* (K–2). Illus. 2005, Simon & Schuster $16.95 (978-1-4169-0277-5). 32pp. Two pigs, Briggs and his wife Bertha, are thrilled when they become rich but soon find that money isn't everything after all. (Rev: BL 5/15/05)

2885 Parr, Todd. *The Feel Good Book* (PS–2). Illus. by author. 2002, Little, Brown $14.95 (978-0-316-07206-9). A list of things that make you feel good is illustrated with lively art. (Rev: HBG 3/03; SLJ 10/02)

2886 Parr, Todd. *It's Okay to Be Different* (PS–2). Illus. by author. 2001, Little, Brown $14.95 (978-0-316-66603-9). Readers learn that it's OK to be adopted, to wear glasses, to have an unusual nose, to lose a race — and to have a pet worm. (Rev: HBG 3/02; SLJ 10/01)

2887 Parr, Todd. *Reading Makes You Feel Good* (PS–K). Illus. 2005, Little, Brown $15.99 (978-0-316-16004-9). 32pp. This brightly colored picture book examines the many benefits of reading and the many places you can read, alone or with others. (Rev: BL 12/1/05; SLJ 9/05)

2888 Paschkis, Julie. *Apple Cake: A Recipe for Love* (PS–1). Illus. by author. 2012, Harcourt $16.99 (978-054780745-4). 32pp. Alfonso bakes a cake in an effort to finally attract the lovely Ida's attention in this beautifully drawn, simple story. (Rev: BL 9/1/12; SLJ 7/12)

2889 Patricelli, Leslie. *Binky* (PS). Illus. by author. 2005, Candlewick $6.99 (978-0-7636-2364-7). A board book about losing a beloved pacifier. Also use *Blankie* (2005). (Rev: SLJ 7/05)

2890 Patricelli, Leslie. *Blankie* (PS). 2005, Candlewick $6.99 (978-0-7636-2363-0). 24pp. A toddler-friendly board book about a child and a much-loved blanket. (Rev: BL 4/1/05)

2891 Patricelli, Leslie. *Tubby* (PS). Illus. by author. 2010, Candlewick $6.99 (978-0-7636-4567-0). Unpaged. A bald, smiling baby has a wonderful time in the bathtub (barring a small incident when soap gets in an eye) in this appealing board book. Also use *Potty* (2010). (Rev: HB 1–2/11; SLJ 1/1/11)

2892 Paul, Alison. *The Crow (A Not So Scary Story)* (PS–2). Illus. by author. 2007, Houghton $16.00 (978-0-618-66380-4). A young boy conjures up all kinds of scary scenarios after peaking at a crow outside the window. (Rev: BL 10/1/07; SLJ 11/07)

2893 Paul, Ann Whitford. *Word Builder* (K–3). Illus. by Kurt Cyrus. 2009, Simon & Schuster $16.99 (978-1-4169-3981-8). 32pp. This clever extended metaphor follows a boy in a hard hat as he works step-by-step from letter to word to sentence to paragraph to chapter until finally he has a full book. (Rev: BL 1/1–15/09; SLJ 1/09)

2894 Pearson, Debora. *Sophie's Wheels* (PS). Illus. by Nora Hilb. 2006, Annick LB $18.95 (978-1-55451-038-2); paper $6.95 (978-1-55451-037-5). Sophie, the sister of Leo in *Leo's Tree* (2004), appreciates the importance of wheels in her life — on strollers, on supermarket carts, on tricycles and bicycles. (Rev: BL 12/1/06; SLJ 3/07)

2895 Pearson, Susan. *How to Teach a Slug to Read* (K–2). Illus. by David Slonim. 2011, Marshall Cavendish $16.99 (978-0-7614-5805-0). 32pp. With appealing, cartoonish illustrations, this is a quirky guide to how to teach slugs, with advice to read out loud, choose favorite poems, explain vocabulary, and be patient. (Rev: BLO 2/15/11; SLJ 5/1/11)

2896 Perez, Amada Irma. *My Very Own Room / Mi propio cuartito* (1–3). Illus. by Maya Christina Gonzalez. 2000, Children's Book Pr. $15.95 (978-0-89239-164-6). 32pp. A bilingual story about a young Mexican American girl who is looking for a little privacy in her crowded home. (Rev: BCCB 11/00; BL 7/00; HB 11/00; HBG 3/01; SLJ 8/00)

2897 Peschke, Marci. *Blueberry Queen* (K–2). Illus. by Tuesday Mourning. Series: Kylie Jean. 2011, Picture Window LB $21.32 (978-1-4048-6756-7); paper $4.95 (978-1-4048-6615-7). 112pp. Kylie Jean aspires to be the Blueberry Festival Pageant queen in this story set in Texas. Also use *Drama Queen* (2011). (Rev: LMC 10/11; SLJ 7/11)

2898 Phillips, Christopher. *Ceci Ann's Day of Why* (PS–K). Illus. by Shino Arihara. 2006, Tricycle $14.95 (978-1-58246-171-7). 32pp. Vivid illustrations are paired with questions about everything in a little girl's life. (Rev: BL 1/1–15/07)

2899 Pilkey, Dav. *The Paperboy* (PS–1). Illus. 1996, Orchard LB $15.99 (978-0-531-08856-2). 32pp. This book reflects the thoughts of a young boy when he makes early-morning rounds on his paper route with his dog. (Rev: BCCB 3/96; BL 3/1/96*; HB 7/96; SLJ 3/96*)

2900 Pilutti, Deb. *The City Kid and the Suburb Kid* (PS–3). Illus. by Linda Bleck. 2008, Sterling LB $14.95 (978-1-4027-4002-2). 38pp. Which is better — city or suburb? This "flip the book over" volume allows readers to experience urban Jack's visit to the 'burbs and his cousin Adam's time in the city. (Rev: SLJ 5/08)

2901 Pinkney, Sandra L. *Read and Rise* (K–3). Photos by Myles C. Pinkney. Illus. 2006, Scholastic $15.99 (978-0-439-30929-5). 40pp. Part of the National Urban League's Read and Rise literacy campaign, this blend of verse and color photography emphasizes the importance of reading. (Rev: BL 2/1/06; SLJ 1/06)

2902 Pinkney, Sandra L. *Shades of Black: A Celebration of Our Children* (PS–2). Illus. by Myles C. Pinkney. 2000, Scholastic $17.99 (978-0-439-14892-4). This book of beautiful photographs shows children whose skin is of various shades of black and whose eyes and hair also show a diversity. (Rev: BCCB 1/01; BL 11/1/00; HBG 3/01; SLJ 12/00)

2903 Piven, Hanoch. *My Best Friend Is as Sharp as a Pencil* (K–3). Illus. by author. 2010, Random House $17.99 (978-0-375-85338-8); LB $20.99 (978-0-375-95629-4). 40pp. A girl uses collages and sculptures to answer her grandmother's questions about school in this inventive story. e (Rev: BL 3/1/10; LMC 8–9/10; SLJ 4/1/10)

2904 Plourde, Lynn. *Field Trip Day* (PS–2). Illus. by Thor Wickstrom. 2010, Dutton $16.99 (978-0-525-47994-9). 40pp. A rollicking (and quite mathematical) look at organic farming through Mrs. Shepherd's class and the vocal and wayward student named Juan. Lexile 1050 (Rev: BL 1/1/10; LMC 5–6/10; SLJ 3/1/10)

2905 Polacco, Patricia. *Bun Bun Button* (PS–2). Illus. by author. 2011, Putnam $17.99 (978-0-399-25472-7). 40pp. Young Paige Darling's favorite stuffed rabbit is carried away when she attaches it to a helium balloon but the family's luck holds out and brings Bun Bun Button home. (Rev: BL 11/15/11; LMC 3–4/12; SLJ 10/1/11)

2906 Pollak, Barbara. *Our Community Garden* (PS–3). Illus. by author. 2004, Beyond Words $15.95 (978-1-58270-109-7). A group of children tend the vegetables in their plots and enjoy a feast at harvest time. (Rev: SLJ 11/04)

2907 Portis, Antoinette. *Not a Box* (PS–K). Illus. by author. 2007, HarperCollins $12.99 (978-0-06-112322-1). With a little imagination, a box is not just a box. (Rev: BL 12/1/06; SLJ 1/07)

2908 Preller, James. *Mighty Casey* (PS–3). Illus. by Matthew Cordell. 2009, Feiwel & Friends $16.95 (978-0-312-36764-0). 32pp. The Delmar Dogs, never a great team, are having a bad day (bees, scraped knees, and needs to pee add to their woes) until Casey Jenkins — one of the poorest players — comes up to bat and saves the day. (Rev: BL 4/1/09; SLJ 3/09)

2909 Raschka, Chris. *Everyone Can Learn to Ride a Bicycle* (PS–2). Illus. by author. 2013, Random House $16.99 (978-037587007-1). 32pp. A father and daughter share the experience of choosing a bicycle and then learning to ride it despite the inevitable setbacks. ℮ (Rev: BL 4/15/13*; LMC 10/13; SLJ 3/13*)

2910 Ray, Mary L. *Christmas Farm* (K–2). Illus. by Barry Root. 2008, Harcourt $17.00 (978-0-15-216290-0). 32pp. Five-year-old Parker helps his neighbor plant 744 Christmas trees and in the years that follow, both the trees and the boy grow. (Rev: BCCB 12/08; BL 9/15/08; HB 11/08; LMC 11/08)

2911 Ray, Mary L. *Red Rubber Boot Day* (PS). Illus. by Lauren Stringer. 2000, Harcourt $16.00 (978-0-15-213756-4). Told from a child's point of view, this book gives details on the indoor and outdoor activities that are possible on a rainy day. (Rev: BL 3/15/00; HBG 10/00; SLJ 4/00)

2912 Reed, Lynn Rowe. *Big City Song* (PS). 2006, Holiday $16.95 (978-0-8234-1988-3). 32pp. Bright illustration and simple rhythms celebrate the sights and sounds of urban life. (Rev: BL 9/15/06)

2913 Reichert, Amy. *While Mama Had a Quick Little Chat* (K–3). Illus. by Alexandra Boiger. 2005, Simon & Schuster $15.95 (978-0-689-85170-4). Rose's mother is on the phone for ages, and Rose, who is supposed to be getting ready for bed, is unable to stop hordes of visitors from taking over their home. (Rev: BL 6/1–15/05)

2914 Reidy, Jean. *Too Purpley!* (PS–K). Illus. by Genevieve Leloup. 2010, Bloomsbury $11.99 (978-1-59990-307-1). 32pp. A little girl critiques all her outfit choices — "too matchy," "too stripey" — until she finds one that's "so comfy." (Rev: BL 1/1/10; SLJ 1/1/10)

2915 Reynolds, Aaron. *Metal Man* (K–3). Illus. by Paul Hoppe. 2008, Charlesbridge $15.95 (978-1-58089-150-9). 32pp. A man who makes sculptures from scrap metal helps young Devon, an African American boy, to create his own work. (Rev: BCCB 7–8/08; BLO 9/2/08; SLJ 7/08)

2916 Rim, Sujean. *Birdie's Big-Girl Shoes* (PS–1). Illus. by author. 2009, Little, Brown $15.99 (978-0-316-04470-7). 40pp. A young girl is excited to try on her mom's fancy shoes, until she discovers how awkward they are for playing and dancing. (Rev: BL 11/1/09*; SLJ 9/1/09)

2917 Robberecht, Thierry. *Sarah's Little Ghosts* (PS–2). Illus. by Philippe Goossens. 2007, Houghton $16.00 (978-0-618-89210-5). 32pp. When Sarah lies about breaking her mother's necklace, little ghosts start to plague her. (Rev: SLJ 11/07)

2918 Robles, Anthony D. *Lakas and the Makibaka Hotel* (2–4). Trans. by Eloisa D. de Jesus. Illus. by Carl Angel. 2006, Children's Book Pr. $16.95 (978-0-89239-213-1). Based on a real-life incident, this lively bilingual (English and Tagalog) picture book tells the story of a group of Filipino Americans fighting to prevent the sale of the hotel in which they live. (Rev: BL 2/15/06; SLJ 4/06)

2919 Roche, Suzzy. *Want to Be in a Band?* (1–3). Illus. by Giselle Potter. 2013, Random House $17.99 (978-0-375-86879-5). 40pp. An inventive account of what it takes to become a successful band member, featuring a young girl with older sisters. ℮ Lexile AD760L (Rev: BL 11/1/12; SLJ 3/13)

2920 Rockwell, Anne. *At the Supermarket* (PS–1). Illus. by author. 2010, Henry Holt $16.99 (978-0-8050-7662-2). 32pp. Rockwell updates her 1997 *The Supermarket,* about a young boy's shopping trip with his mother, offering new illustrations and revised text. (Rev: BLO 1/1/10; SLJ 3/1/10)

2921 Roosa, Karen. *Beach Day* (PS–K). Illus. by Maggie Smith. 2001, Clarion $16.00 (978-0-618-02923-5). 32pp. Lively art and detailed illustrations depict a day at the beach for a group of multicultural children. (Rev: BL 5/1/01; HBG 10/01; SLJ 4/01)

2922 Rosenberry, Vera. *Vera Goes to the Dentist* (PS–3). Illus. 2002, Holt $16.95 (978-0-8050-6668-5). 32pp. Vera is so frightened by her first trip to the dentist that she runs out of the office, but she is finally caught and becomes calm enough to finish the examination. (Rev: BL 4/1/02; HBG 10/02; SLJ 5/02)

2923 Rosenberry, Vera. *Vera Rides a Bike* (K–2). Illus. 2004, Holt $16.95 (978-0-8050-7125-2). 32pp. Vera makes the daunting transition from a tricycle to a two-wheeler. (Rev: BL 5/15/04; HB 5/04; SLJ 7/04)

2924 Rosenstiehl, Agnes. *Silly Lilly in What Will I Be Today?* (PS). Illus. by author. 2011, TOON $12.95 (978-193517908-5). 32pp. Lilly tries out a variety of occupations in this simple graphic novel for emerging readers. (Rev: BL 3/15/11; SLJ 5/1/11)

2925 Rosenthal, Amy Krouse. *Little Pea* (PS–2). Illus. by Jen Corace. 2005, Chronicle $12.95 (978-0-8118-4658-5). Little Pea is a happy child until it comes to meals, when he struggles through the candy courses waiting with anticipation for the dessert of spinach. (Rev: BL 3/1/04; SLJ 5/05)

2926 Rosenthal, Amy Krouse. *One of Those Days* (K–3). Illus. by Rebecca Doughty. 2006, Putnam $13.99 (978-0-399-24365-3). 32pp. This whimsical picture book imagines dozens of ways in which a child's day can take a turn for the worse but holds out hope that things will turn around tomorrow. (Rev: BL 6/1–15/06; SLJ 5/06)

2927 Rosenthal, Amy Krouse. *One Smart Cookie: Bite-Size Lessons for the School Years and Beyond* (PS–1). Illus. by Jane Dyer. 2010, HarperCollins $12.99 (978-0-06-142970-5). 40pp. A fourth volume in the series that uses cookies and baking to tie together words and life lessons. (Rev: BL 9/1/10; SLJ 9/1/10)

2928 Rosenthal, Amy Krouse. *This Plus That: Life's Little Equations* (PS–3). Illus. by Jen Corace. 2011, HarperCollins $14.99 (978-0-06-172655-2). 40pp. A variety of familiar conceptual equations, such as barefoot + screen door + popsicles = summer! are portrayed in this lighthearted book about math and life. (Rev: BL 3/15/11*; LMC 10/11; SLJ 5/1/11)

2929 Rosenthal, Amy Krouse. *Yes Day!* (PS–1). Illus. by Tom Lichtenheld. 2009, HarperCollins $14.99 (978-0-06-115259-7). 40pp. Once a year on Yes Day a young child gets to do everything he wants. (Rev: BL 4/1/09; SLJ 5/09)

2930 Rosenthal, Betsy R. *Which Shoes Would You Choose?* (PS–K). Illus. by Nancy Cote. 2010, Putnam $15.99 (978-0-399-25013-2). 32pp. A simple guessing game in which Sherman wears a variety of footwear — flip-flops, hiking boots, galoshes, slippers — depending on his activities. (Rev: BL 3/1/10; SLJ 4/1/10)

2931 Rosenthal, Eileen. *I Must Have Bobo!* (PS–K). Illus. by Marc Rosenthal. 2011, Simon & Schuster $14.99 (978-1-4424-0377-2). 40pp. Young Willy must cope with his cat Earl's endless fascination with his favorite sock monkey, Bobo. e (Rev: BL 3/15/11; SLJ 3/1/11)

2932 Ross, Michael Elsohn. *Play with Me* (PS–1). Illus. by Julie Downing. 2009, Tricycle $12.99 (978-1-58246-255-4). Animals and people at play with their babies. (Rev: SLJ 6/09)

2933 Roth, Julie Jersild. *Knitting Nell* (2–4). Illus. by author. 2006, Houghton $16.00 (978-0-618-54033-4). Nell, a quiet girl, finds added confidence when her knitting talent is recognized at the county fair. (Rev: SLJ 7/06)

2934 Ruiz-Flores, Lupe. *Let's Salsa/Bailemos salsa* (1–3). Illus. by Robert Casilla. 2013, Arte Publico $17.95 (978-155885762-9). 32pp. When Estela is told she's too young to join the adult class, she petitions the mayor to start salsa classes for children; in both English and Spanish. (Rev: BL 11/1/13; LMC 5–6/14*)

2935 Rule, Rebecca. *The Iciest, Diciest, Scariest Sled Ride Ever!* (K–3). Illus. by Jennifer Thermes. 2012, Islandport $17.95 (978-1-934031-88-9). 36pp. Seven children struggle to get an old-fashioned sled up an icy slope, and when they succeed they enjoy a very exciting trip back down. (Rev: BLO 11/15/12; SLJ 12/12)

2936 Ryder, Joanne. *Won't You Be My Hugaroo?* (PS–K). Illus. by Melissa Sweet. 2006, Harcourt $16.00 (978-0-15-205778-7). 40pp. Hugs of all kinds — from the job-well-done hug to a parent's loving bedtime hug — are shown with happy animal characters. (Rev: BL 3/1/06)

2937 Rylant, Cynthia. *All in a Day* (PS–1). Illus. by Nikki McClure. 2009, Abrams $17.95 (978-0-8109-8321-2). 32pp. What might happen in a day? This is an old-fashioned, poetic look at the various ways to enjoy a new day. (Rev: BL 4/1/09; SLJ 5/09)

2938 Sakai, Komako. *Emily's Balloon* (PS). Illus. by author. 2006, Chronicle $14.95 (978-0-8118-5219-7). A young girl is saddened when her helium-filled balloon is blown high into the branches of a tree in her backyard. (Rev: SLJ 4/06)

2939 Salat, Cristina. *Peanut's Emergency* (K–2). Illus. by Tammie Lyon. 2002, Charlesbridge $16.95 (978-1-57091-440-9); paper $6.95 (978-1-57091-441-6). 32pp. Peanut seeks help when her mother is late picking her up from school in this story about what to do in an "emergency." (Rev: BL 9/15/02; HBG 3/03)

2940 Scanlon, Liz Garton. *All the World* (PS–1). Illus. by Marla Frazee. 2009, Simon & Schuster $17.99 (978-1-4169-8580-8). 40pp. Rhyme, rhythm, and expressive illustrations relate the mundane aspects of life to the larger surrounding world in a book good for reading aloud. (Rev: BCCB 10/09; BL 7/09; HB 9/09; LMC 10/09; SLJ 8/09)

2941 Schaefer, Carole Lexa. *The Bora-Bora Dress* (PS–3). Illus. by Catherine Stock. 2005, Candlewick $16.99 (978-0-7636-1234-4). Lindsay is upset when she's told she must wear a dress for a party at her aunt's house, but a brightly colored island frock soon catches her eye. (Rev: BL 8/05*)

2942 Schertle, Alice. *All You Need for a Snowman* (PS–K). Illus. by Barbara Lavallee. 2002, Harcourt $16.00 (978-0-15-200789-8). 32pp. As the text describes the essentials for making a successful snowman, a group of children are shown building two gigantic examples. (Rev: BCCB 1/03; BL 11/15/02; HB 11/02; HBG 3/03; SLJ 12/02)

2943 Schrock, Jan West. *Give a Goat* (1–3). Illus. by Aileen Darragh. 2008, Tilbury House $16.95 (978-0-88448-301-4). Inspired by a story of giving, a 5th-grade class sets about earning enough money to make their own contribution; the work of Heifer International is the focus of this book. (Rev: BL 6/1–15/08; LMC 1/09)

2944 Schwartz, Ellen. *Abby's Birds* (PS–3). Illus. by Sima Elizabeth Shefrin. 2007, Tradewind $16.95 (978-1-896580-86-9). 32pp. Abby learns to fold paper cranes from her elderly Japanese neighbor, Mrs. Naka, and then fills a winter tree with numerous paper cranes to welcome Mrs. Naka home after a hospital stay. (Rev: BL 12/1/07; LMC 3/08)

2945 Schwartz, Howard. *Gathering Sparks* (PS–3). Illus. by Kristina Swarner. 2010, Roaring Brook $16.99 (978-1-59643-280-2). 32pp. In this story based on Jewish folklore, a man tells his grandson about the importance of good deeds, which restore light and hope to the night sky. (Rev: BL 8/10; LMC 11–12/10; SLJ 8/1/10)

2946 Sears, William, et al. *You Can Go to the Potty* (PS). Illus. by Renée Andriani. 2002, Little, Brown $12.95 (978-0-316-78888-5). 32pp. This introduction to toilet training is designed for adults to read with children, combining text for the young with sidebars for the adults. (Rev: BL 11/15/02; HBG 3/03; SLJ 11/02)

2947 Senning, Cindy Post, and Peggy Post. *Emily's Out and About Book* (PS–1). Illus. by Leo Landry. 2009, Collins $16.99 (978-006111700-8). 32pp. Emily and her mother spend the day in town — visiting the doctor and the library, having lunch, and so forth — in this simple story that emphasizes the importance of good manners. (Rev: BL 11/1/09)

2948 Seskin, Steve, and Allen Shamblin. *A Chance to Shine* (PS–2). Illus. by R. Gregory Christie. 2006, Tricycle $16.95 (978-1-58246-167-0). 32pp. This attractive picture-book version of a 1991 song tells how an African American father's act of kindness helps his son to look beyond color and social status in judging others. (Rev: BL 4/15/06)

2949 Seuss, Dr. *Oh, the Places You'll Go!* (PS–3). Illus. 1990, Random LB $17.99 (978-0-679-90527-1). This book of advice for youngsters tells them that in spite of problems, they can succeed. (Rev: BL 1/1/90*; SLJ 3/90)

2950 Shea, Bob. *Dinosaur vs. the Potty* (PS). Illus. by author. 2010, Hyperion/Disney $15.99 (978-1-4231-3339-1). 40pp. A stubborn young red dinosaur stages a spirited rebellion against the potty. (Rev: BL 10/15/10; SLJ 10/1/10)

2951 Shelby, Anne. *The Someday House* (PS–2). Illus. by Rosanne Litzinger. 1996, Orchard LB $16.99 (978-0-531-08860-9). 32pp. Three children imagine living in a variety of different houses and settings. (Rev: BL 3/1/96; SLJ 4/96)

2952 Shewchuk, Pat. *In Lucia's Neighborhood* (PS–2). Illus. by Marek Colek. 2013, Kids Can $16.95 (978-1-55453-420-3). 32pp. Seven-year-old Lucia takes readers through her neighborhood and the activities there in this book set in Toronto. Lexile AD360 (Rev: BL 4/1/13; SLJ 4/13)

2953 Shulevitz, Uri. *Snow* (PS). Illus. 1998, Farrar $16.00 (978-0-374-37092-3). 32pp. A young child is able to see the beauty in a single snowflake whereas the more sophisticated adults cannot. (Rev: BCCB 1/99; BL 10/15/98*; HB 1/99; HBG 3/99; SLJ 12/98)

2954 Shulman, Lisa. *The Moon Might Be Milk* (PS–2). Illus. by Will Hillenbrand. 2007, Dutton $16.99 (978-0-525-47647-4). Rosie asks a number of animals what the moon is made of and they all have different ideas — the cat says milk, the hen says an egg, the dog says butter — and then Rosie's grandmother combines all these ingredients to make moon-shaped sugar cookies; includes a recipe. (Rev: BL 2/15/07*)

2955 Sierra, Judy. *Ballyhoo Bay* (PS–2). Illus. by Derek Anderson. 2009, Simon & Schuster $16.99 (978-1-4169-5888-8). 40pp. When art teacher Mirra Bella learns that a new development threatens Ballyhoo Beach, she organizes a protest and an alternate plan. (Rev: BLO 6/17/09; LMC 8/09; SLJ 2/09)

2956 Sierra, Judy. *Born to Read* (PS–2). Illus. by Marc Brown. 2008, Knopf $16.99 (978-0-375-84687-8). 40pp. A little boy named Sam's inordinate love of reading makes this a good choice for literacy units. (Rev: BL 8/08; LMC 3/09)

2957 Singer, Marilyn. *Shoe Bop!* (PS–2). Illus. by Hiroe Nakata. 2008, Dutton $15.99 (978-0-525-47939-0). 32pp. What does a young girl do when her favorite

sneakers die? A series of rhyming couplets explores the possibilities. (Rev: BL 9/1/08; SLJ 7/08)

2958 Sís, Peter. *Madlenka, Soccer Star* (PS–2). Illus. by author. 2010, Farrar $16.99 (978-0-374-34702-4). 40pp. Young Madlenka dreams of being a soccer star and is willing to play with anyone and anything in this imaginative story with humorous illustrations. (Rev: BL 9/1/10; HB 11–12/10; LMC 3–4/11; SLJ 11/1/10)

2959 Skultety, Nancy. *From Here to Here* (PS–K). Illus. by Tammie Lyon. 2005, Boyds Mills $15.95 (978-1-59078-092-3). 32pp. Farmer Dibble asks for a new road and he gets just that, with its construction and all the equipment involved well documented. (Rev: BL 5/15/05; SLJ 5/05)

2960 Smith, Cynthia Leitich. *Jingle Dancer* (PS–2). Illus. by Cornelius Van Wright and Ying-Hwa Hu. 2000, Morrow LB $17.89 (978-0-688-16242-9). 32pp. Jenna, a Native American girl, gathers metal jingles to sew onto her dress so she can make pleasant sounds when she dances in the next powwow. (Rev: BCCB 7–8/00; BL 5/15/00; HBG 10/00; SLJ 7/00)

2961 Smith, Dana Kessimakis. *A Brave Spaceboy* (PS–2). Illus. by Laura Freeman. 2005, Hyperion $15.99 (978-0-7868-0933-2). On moving day, a boy and his younger sibling invest an empty box with spaceship powers and imagine themselves exploring the stars. (Rev: BL 3/1/04; HB 3/04; SLJ 5/05)

2962 Smith, Lois T. *Carrie and Carl Play* (PS). Illus. by author. 2007, Candlewick paper $5.99 (978-0-7636-1690-8). Young children will enjoy lifting flaps to discover what Carrie and Carl are up to next during a fun day of play. (Rev: SLJ 7/07)

2963 Spetter, Jung-Hee. *Lily and Trooper's Fall* (PS–K). Illus. 1999, Front St. $8.95 (978-1-886910-38-6). 32pp. Lily and her fun-loving dog Trooper enjoy such fall activities as jumping in a pile of leaves. Also use *Lily and Trooper's Winter* (1999). (Rev: BL 12/1/99; HBG 3/00; SLJ 10/99)

2964 Spinelli, Eileen. *The Best Time of Day* (PS–2). Illus. by Bryan Langdo. 2005, Harcourt $16.00 (978-0-15-205051-1). In rhyming text, farm residents — both human and animal — muse about their favorites time of day. (Rev: BL 10/15/05; SLJ 1/06)

2965 Spinelli, Eileen. *Cold Snap* (PS–2). Illus. by Marjorie Priceman. 2012, Knopf $17.99 (978-0-375-85700-3). 40pp. The icicle hanging from the nose of the statue in the town square of Toby Mills provides a gauge of just how cold it is in this wintry portrayal of a community coping with adversity. Booklist Editors' Choice: Books for Youth, 2012. ℮ (Rev: BL 9/1/12*; LMC 1–2/13; SLJ 10/12)

2966 Spinelli, Eileen. *Someday* (PS–2). Illus. by Rosie Winstead. 2007, Dial $16.99 (978-0-8037-2941-4). A young girl imagines herself accomplishing amazing feats in the future, even while she is enjoying her daily life. (Rev: BCCB 9/07; BL 6/1–15/07; SLJ 5/07)

2967 Spinelli, Jerry. *I Can Be Anything* (PS–K). Illus. by Jimmy Liao. 2010, Little, Brown $16.99 (978-

031616226-5). 32pp. A little boy considers what he might be when he grows up, in fact reviewing options available to him already (paper-plane folder, mixing-bowl licker, and so forth). (Rev: BL 1/1/10; SLJ 3/10)

2968 Stainton, Sue. *The Chocolate Cat* (PS–1). Illus. by Anne Mortimer. 2007, HarperCollins $16.99 (978-0-06-057245-7). 32pp. A cranky chocolate maker and his lazy cat live a dull existence until the confectioner decides to make a batch of scrumptious chocolate mice, inspiring a frenzy of chocolate creativity that cheers up the whole town. (Rev: BL 11/1/07; SLJ 1/08)

2969 Stein, David Ezra. *Because Amelia Smiled* (PS–1). Illus. by author. 2012, Candlewick $16.99 (978-0-7636-4169-6). 40pp. Young Amelia's appealing smile prompts Mrs. Higgins to send cookies to her grandson in Mexico, who shares them with his class . . . and a chain of happy events follow each other around the world. Lexile AD760L (Rev: BL 10/15/12; HB 9–10/12; SLJ 9/12)

2970 Stevens, Jan R. *Carlos Digs to China / Carlos Excava Hasta la China* (K–2). Trans. by Mario Lamo-Jimenez. Illus. by Jeanne Arnold. 2001, Rising Moon LB $15.95 (978-0-87358-764-8). A bilingual story in which Carlos decides to dig to China so that he can taste all that wonderful food. (Rev: HBG 10/01; SLJ 6/01)

2971 Stevens, Janet, and Susan Stevens Crummel. *Plaidypus Lost* (PS–1). Illus. by Janet Stevens. 2004, Holiday House $16.95 (978-0-8234-1561-8). 40pp. A little girl keeps finding and losing the platypus her Grandma made from an old plaid shirt. (Rev: BL 3/15/04; SLJ 5/04)

2972 Stevenson, James. *Popcorn* (2–5). Illus. 1998, Greenwillow $16.99 (978-0-688-15261-1). Daily life in a small seaside town is captured in a series of quiet, moving poems illustrated with exquisite watercolors. (Rev: BCCB 4/98; BL 5/1/98*; HB 5/98; HBG 10/98; SLJ 5/98)

2973 Stewart, Sarah. *The Library* (K–3). Illus. by David Small. 1995, Farrar $16.00 (978-0-374-34388-0). 32pp. The life story of a woman who loved reading books so much that eventually a library was named after her. (Rev: BCCB 5/95; BL 3/15/95; HB 7/95; SLJ 9/95)

2974 Stinson, Kathy. *The Man with the Violin* (K–1). Illus. by Dusan Petricic. 2013, Annick $19.95 (978-155451565-3). 32pp. Loosely based on the true story of violinist Joshua Bell, who accepted the challenge of playing in a train station dressed as a street musician, this book centers on a young boy named Dylan who wants to linger and enjoy the beautiful music but is dragged away by his harried mother. Lexile AD560 (Rev: BL 11/15/13; LMC 3–4/14; SLJ 10/13)

2975 Stock, Catherine. *Island Summer* (K–2). Illus. 1999, Lothrop $16.00 (978-0-688-12780-0). 32pp. After a cold winter, an island springs back to life when the summer residents arrive, only to become quiet again when they leave in the fall. (Rev: BL 10/15/99; HBG 3/00; SLJ 9/99)

2976 Strickland, Michael R. *Haircuts at Sleepy Sam's* (PS–2). Illus. by Keaf Holliday. 1998, Boyds Mills $15.95 (978-1-56397-562-2). Although two African

American brothers have a note from their mother for the barber telling him how to cut their hair, the barber, Sam, gives them the cut they want. (Rev: BL 10/15/98; HBG 3/99; SLJ 11/98)

2977 Sturges, Philemon. *I Love Tools!* (PS–1). Illus. by Shari Halpern. 2006, HarperCollins LB $14.89 (978-0-06-009288-7). Various tools are introduced as a family works to build a birdhouse. (Rev: SLJ 6/06)

2978 Swanson, Susan Marie. *The House in the Night* (PS–K). Illus. by Beth Krommes. 2008, Houghton $16.00 (978-0-618-86244-3). 40pp. A beautifully illustrated cumulative tale celebrating night and a reassuring sense of order. Caldecott Medal, 2009. (Rev: BL 4/15/08; SLJ 4/08)

2979 Taback, Simms. *Postcards from Camp* (1–3). Illus. by author. 2011, Penguin $17.99 (978-0-399-23973-3). 40pp. The story of a boy's summer at camp is told through the shared correspondence between the boy and his father in this appealing book with removable pieces. (Rev: BL 7/11; SLJ 9/1/11)

2980 Tafolla, Carmen. *Fiesta Babies* (PS–K). Illus. by Amy Cordova. 2010, Tricycle $12.99 (978-1-58246-319-3). 24pp. A crowd of multicultural babies participate exuberantly in the joys of a fiesta in this small, square book with bold art and a sprinkling of Spanish words. (Rev: BL 2/15/10; SLJ 3/1/10)

2981 Tafolla, Carmen. *What Can You Do with a Paleta?* (PS–3). Illus. by Magaly Morales. 2009, Tricycle $14.99 (978-1-58246-221-9). 32pp. On a warm night in the barrio, the bell of the paleta wagon signals the welcome popsicle treat; bright illustrations add to the appeal. (Rev: BL 5/15/09)

2982 Takabayashi, Mari. *I Live in Brooklyn* (1–2). Illus. 2004, Houghton $16.00 (978-0-618-30899-6). 32pp. Michelle, 6, lives in Brooklyn and describes the routines of her life there. (Rev: BL 2/15/04; HB 7/04; SLJ 4/04)

2983 Tarpley, Natasha A. *Bippity Bop Barbershop* (PS–1). Illus. by E. B. Lewis. 2002, Little, Brown $15.95 (978-0-316-52284-7). 32pp. Miles accompanies his father to the local barbershop for his first haircut. (Rev: BCCB 3/02; BL 2/15/02; HBG 10/02; SLJ 2/02)

2984 Tarpley, Natasha A. *I Love My Hair!* (PS–1). Illus. by E. B. Lewis. 1998, Little, Brown $15.95 (978-0-316-52275-5). 32pp. A young African American girl has fun creating different styles with her hair. (Rev: BCCB 4/98; BL 2/15/98; HBG 10/98; SLJ 2/98)

2985 Tarpley, Todd. *Ten Tiny Toes* (PS). Illus. by Marc Brown. 2012, Little, Brown $16.99 (978-0-316-12921-3). 32pp. Appealing illustrations and rhythmic text draw readers into this celebration of babies and their toes. (Rev: BLO 9/15/12; SLJ 8/12)

2986 Terasaki, Todd. *Ghosts for Breakfast* (2–4). Illus. by Shelly Shinjo. 2002, Lee & Low $16.95 (978-1-58430-046-5). 32pp. The Troublesome Trio informs Farmer Tanaka that there are ghosts in his field, so the farmer investigates, only to find that the ghosts are daikon radishes hanging to dry. (Rev: BL 1/1–15/03; HBG 3/03; SLJ 10/02)

2987 Terry, Sonya. *"L" Is for Library* (1–3). Illus. by Nicole Wong. 2006, Upstart $16.95 (978-1-932146-44-8). A cat conducts a tour of the library, introducing print and nonprint resources for every letter from A to Z. (Rev: SLJ 8/06)

2988 Thompson, Lauren. *Chew, Chew, Gulp!* (PS). Illus. by Jarrett J. Krosoczka. 2011, Simon & Schuster $14.99 (978-1-4169-9744-3). 32pp. This book follows four young children as they eat a variety of foods and make a variety of onomatopoeic accompanying sounds. **e** (Rev: BL 4/15/11; SLJ 5/1/11)

2989 Thong, Roseanne. *Gai See: What You Can See in Chinatown* (1–3). Illus. by Yangsook Choi. 2007, Abrams $16.95 (978-0-8109-9337-2). 40pp. Readers get a rhyming tour of a typical Chinatown *gai see* or street market. (Rev: BL 9/1/07; SLJ 11/07)

2990 Tildes, Phyllis L. *Billy's Big-Boy Bed* (PS). Illus. by author. 2002, Charlesbridge LB $15.95 (978-1-57091-475-1). Billy gets a new, big bed but prefers to remain in his crib for the time being. (Rev: HBG 10/02; SLJ 3/02)

2991 Torrey, Richard. *Almost* (PS–K). Illus. by author. 2009, HarperCollins $17.99 (978-0-06-156166-5). 40pp. Jack, nearly 6 years old, can almost do everything but it's the "almost" that frustrates him. (Rev: BL 4/1/09; SLJ 4/09)

2992 Torrey, Richard. *Why?* (PS–2). Illus. by author. 2010, HarperCollins $16.99 (978-0-06-156170-2). 40pp. A young boy asks questions all day in this book that touches on everything from science to haircuts. (Rev: BL 4/15/10; SLJ 5/1/10)

2993 Train, Mary. *Time for the Fair* (K–2). Illus. by Karel Hayes. 2005, Down East $15.95 (978-0-89272-694-3). Grace learns a little about the rhythms of the seasons as she anxiously awaits the arrival of the annual farmer's fair. (Rev: SLJ 12/05)

2994 Trent, Shanda. *Farmers' Market Day* (PS–2). Illus. by Jane Dippold. 2013, ME Media/Tiger Tales $12.95 (978-158925115-1). 32pp. Watercolor illustrations and rhythmic, rhyming text sweep the reader through a little girl's excited outing to the local farmers' market with her parents and her piggy bank. Lexile AD390 (Rev: BL 9/1/13; LMC 1–2/14; SLJ 6/13)

2995 Tutu, Archbishop Desmond, and Douglas Carlton Abrams. *God's Dream* (PS–K). Illus. by LeUyen Pham. 2008, Candlewick $16.99 (978-0-7636-3388-2). 40pp. This picture book shows a group of multicultural toddlers learning about empathy and sharing. (Rev: BL 8/08)

2996 Uhlberg, Myron. *A Storm Called Katrina* (1–4). Illus. by Colin Bootman. 2011, Peachtree $17.95 (978-1-56145-591-1). 40pp. Ten-year-old Louis Daniel's cornet comes in handy when his home is flooded and his family moves to the Superdome during Hurricane Katrina. (Rev: BL 9/1/11*; SLJ 9/1/11)

2997 Upjohn, Rebecca. *Lily and the Paper Man* (PS–2). Illus. by Renné Benoit. 2007, Second Story $14.95 (978-1-897187-19-7). 24pp. Although Lily has avoided the homeless man in her neighborhood, when the weather turns cold, she demonstrates true compassion by collecting warm clothing for him. (Rev: BL 12/1/07; LMC 3/08)

2998 Van Der Heide, Iris. *The Red Chalk* (PS–2). Illus. by Marije Tolman. 2006, Front St. $19.95 (978-1-932425-79-6). 32pp. Bored with her red chalk, Sara swaps it with Tim for his marbles, but the marbles soon lose their allure and she continues to trade until she finds something that suits her — red chalk. (Rev: BL 9/1/06; SLJ 1/07)

2999 Van Der Heide, Iris. *A Strange Day* (K–2). Illus. by Marijke ten Cate. 2007, Boyds Mills $16.95 (978-1-932425-94-9). Jack unwittingly helps his neighbors while wandering through town on a windy day in this story set in the Netherlands. (Rev: SLJ 5/07)

3000 Van Wert, Faye. *Empty Pockets* (PS–1). Illus. by author. 2000, Greene Bark $16.95 (978-1-880851-61-6). When Stevie's mother discovers a frog in his dresser drawer, she puts a stop to his hobby of bringing home everything he finds. (Rev: SLJ 3/01)

3001 Verde, Susan. *The Museum* (PS–2). Illus. by Peter H. Reynolds. 2013, Abrams $16.95 (978-1-4197-0594-6). 32pp. A young girl describes her emotions as she tours the exhibits in an art museum. (Rev: BL 3/15/13; LMC 10/13*; SLJ 4/13)

3002 Viorst, Judith. *Just in Case* (K–2). Illus. by Diana Cain Bluthenthal. 2006, Simon & Schuster $15.95 (978-0-689-87164-1). Charlie likes to be prepared for any eventuality, but when his friends throw him a birthday party he discovers that surprises can be fun. (Rev: BL 12/1/05; SLJ 1/06)

3003 Wahl, Jan. *The Art Collector* (PS–3). Illus. by Rosalinde Bonnet. 2011, Charlesbridge $15.95 (978-1-58089-270-4). 32pp. A little boy entranced by art but disappointed by his own efforts decides to become an art collector. Lexile AD450L (Rev: BL 7/11; SLJ 7/11)

3004 Walker, Nan. *The Midnight Kid* (1–3). Illus. by Barry Gott. Series: Science Solves It! 2007, Kane paper $4.99 (978-1-57565-238-2). 32pp. Peter performs a mini experiment — trying not to sleep for three nights — and discovers that sleep is important to his health. Facts about sleep are presented in sidebars. (Rev: SLJ 5/07)

3005 Walton, Rick. *A Very Hairy Scary Story* (K–3). Illus. by David Clark. 2004, Penguin $15.99 (978-0-399-23858-1). On her way home later than promised, a girl sees lots of scary things in the night. (Rev: SLJ 8/04)

3006 Warwick, Dionne, and David Freeman Wooley. *Little Man* (1–3). Illus. by Fred Willingham. 2011, Charlesbridge $19.95 (978-1-57091-731-8). Unpaged. A little African American boy in an urban neighborhood pursues his love of drums despite the lack of encouragement from others apart from his dad; comes with a CD of Dionne Warwick reading the story and drum playing by David Wooley. **e** (Rev: SLJ 11/1/11)

3007 Weatherford, Carole Boston. *Jazz Baby* (PS). Illus. by Laura Freeman. 2002, Lee & Low $11.95 (978-1-58430-039-7). A crew of ethnically diverse youngsters dances to the beat of a lively rhyme and jazz instruments. (Rev: HBG 10/02; SLJ 6/02)

3008 Weaver, Tess. *Frederick Finch, Loudmouth* (PS–2). Illus. by Debbie Tilley. 2008, Clarion $16.00 (978-0-618-45239-2). 32pp. After many failures, Frederick's loud voice finally helps him to win a competition at the state fair. (Rev: BL 6/1–15/08; SLJ 6/08)

3009 Weeks, Sarah. *If I Were a Lion* (PS–1). Illus. by Heather Solomon. 2004, Simon & Schuster $15.95 (978-0-689-84836-0). 40pp. A little girl who has been criticized for her "wild" behavior goes on the defensive and imagines what truly wild behavior would involve. (Rev: BL 3/15/04; SLJ 4/04)

3010 Wellington, Monica. *Ana cultiva manzanas / Apple Farmer Annie* (PS–2). Illus. by author. 2004, Dutton LB $10.99 (978-0-525-47252-0). The Spanish translation appears in large type above the smaller-type English original about a happy apple farmer. (Rev: BL 9/04; SLJ 9/04)

3011 Wellington, Monica. *Pizza at Sally's* (PS–K). 2006, Dutton $14.99 (978-0-525-47715-0). 32pp. This brightly illustrated picture book follows Sally the pizzeria owner as she goes through all the steps of making a pizza; a recipe is appended. (Rev: BL 8/06; SLJ 6/06)

3012 Wellington, Monica. *Truck Driver Tom* (PS–2). Illus. by author. 2007, Dutton $15.99 (978-0-525-47831-7). 32pp. Tom picks up produce on a farm and delivers it in the city before spending the night in his cab; the bright detailed illustrations invite close examination. (Rev: BL 11/1/07; SLJ 11/07)

3013 Whiting, Sue. *The Firefighters* (PS–2). Illus. by Donna Rawlins. 2008, Candlewick $15.99 (978-0-7636-4019-4). Miss Iverson's class has a great time playing fire fighters and afterward gets a surprise tour of a real fire engine with real firemen. (Rev: BL 9/1/08)

3014 Wickstrom, Sylvie. *I Love You, Mister Bear* (PS–1). Illus. by author. 2004, HarperCollins LB $15.89 (978-0-06-029332-1). Young Sosha rescues a dilapidated stuffed bear from a yard sale and takes it home for some special care and love. (Rev: BL 1/1–15/04; SLJ 1/04)

3015 Willems, Mo. *Time to Pee!* (PS). Illus. by author. 2003, Hyperion $12.99 (978-0-7868-1868-6). This useful guide to toilet training is enlivened by illustrations of tiny mice carrying signs with helpful advice and words of reassurance. (Rev: HBG 4/04; SLJ 12/03) [649]

3016 Williams, Carol Ann. *Booming Bella* (K–3). Illus. by Tatjana Mai-Wyss. 2008, Putnam $16.99 (978-0-399-24277-9). 32pp. Bella's loud comments on everything around her are criticized during a trip to the art museum, but her big voice proves useful when she realizes she's on the wrong bus. (Rev: BL 6/1–15/08; LMC 10/08; SLJ 7/08)

3017 Williams, Laura E. *The Can Man* (K–3). Illus. by Craig Orback. 2010, Lee & Low $18.95 (978-1-60060-266-5). 40pp. Tim collects and cashes in tin cans with the intention of buying himself a skateboard, but in the end gives his earnings to a homeless man. (Rev: BL 3/15/10; LMC 8–9/10; SLJ 5/1/10)

3018 Williams, Sue. *I Went Walking* (PS–K). Illus. by Julie Vivas. 1990, Harcourt $13.95 (978-0-15-200471-2). 32pp. This book involves guessing the identity of animals hidden in pictures during a boy's afternoon walk. (Rev: BCCB 12/92; BL 9/1/90*; HB 11/90; SLJ 10/90*)

3019 Williams, Vera B. *Cherries and Cherry Pits* (K–3). Illus. by author. 1986, Morrow paper $6.99 (978-0-688-10478-8). 40pp. Three tales and pictures from young Bidemmi, a black girl, about giving, loving, and making art. (Rev: BL 10/15/86; HB 9/86; SLJ 10/86)

3020 Willson, Sarah. *Hocus Focus* (2–3). Illus. by Amy Wummer. Series: Science Solves It! 2004, Kane paper $4.99 (978-1-57565-136-1). Jack and Gina, one nearsighted and the other far-sighted, decide to work together rather than wear glasses and suffer taunts; an eye chart and scientific information are appended. (Rev: BL 3/15/04; SLJ 6/04)

3021 Wilson, Karma. *How to Bake an American Pie* (PS–2). Illus. by Raúl Colón. 2007, Simon & Schuster $16.99 (978-0-689-86506-0). 40pp. A cat and a dog whip up a recipe consisting of such ingredients as purple mountain majesty, liberty, courage, and fruited plains. (Rev: BL 4/1/07)

3022 Wolf, Karina. *The Insomniacs* (PS–2). Illus. by The Brothers Hilts. 2012, Putnam $16.99 (978-0-399-25665-3). 32pp. When they move 12 time zones from home the Insomniacs — mother, father, and young Mika — have trouble adapting to their new hours and eventually decide to sleep during the day and conduct their lives in the dark. (Rev: BL 9/1/12; LMC 1–2/13; SLJ 8/12*)

3023 Wolfe, Frances. *One Wish* (PS–1). 2004, Tundra $15.95 (978-0-88776-662-6). 32pp. A young girl dreams of having a cottage by the sea in this gentle story with detailed oil paintings. (Rev: BL 6/1–15/04; SLJ 6/04)

3024 Wolff, Nancy. *Tallulah in the Kitchen* (K–2). Illus. 2005, Holt $16.95 (978-0-8050-7463-5). 32pp. Tallulah, a cat, and her sidekicks crocodile Freddie and pig Roxie whip up some pancakes and impart information about cooking in general. (Rev: BL 6/1–15/05)

3025 Wong, Janet S. *The Dumpster Diver* (1–3). Illus. by David Roberts. 2007, Candlewick $16.99 (978-0-7636-2380-7). 32pp. The children of an apartment complex enjoy helping Steve the electrician dive for buried treasure in the dumpster in the back alley; the group then creates new and inventive objects from the retrieved "junk." (Rev: BL 2/15/07*)

3026 Wood, Douglas. *Nothing to Do* (PS–2). Illus. by Wendy A. Halperin. 2006, Dutton $16.99 (978-0-525-47656-6). 32pp. Nothing to do? Try reading a book, sailing a toy boat, walking through the woods, or any of the other low-tech activities that children may find unexpectedly satisfying. (Rev: BL 5/1/06; SLJ 5/06)

3027 Wood, Douglas. *The Secret of Saying Thanks* (PS–2). Illus. by Greg Shed. 2005, Simon & Schuster $16.95 (978-0-689-85410-1). This beautifully illustrated picture book underlines the importance of showing gratitude for the wonders around us. (Rev: BL 10/15/05; SLJ 10/05)

3028 Wright, Michael. *Jake Goes Peanuts* (K–2). Illus. by author. 2010, Feiwel & Friends $16.99 (978-0-312-54967-1). 48pp. Jake won't eat anything but peanut butter until his parents come up with a brilliant strategy. (Rev: BL 11/15/10; LMC 11–12/10; SLJ 8/1/10)

3029 Yashima, Taro. *Umbrella* (PS–1). Illus. by author. 1958, Puffin paper $6.99 (978-0-14-050240-4). A 3-year-old Japanese American girl, born in New York City, longs for a rainy day so she can use her new blue umbrella and red rubber boots.

3030 Yee, Wong H. *Tracks in the Snow* (PS). Illus. by author. 2003, Holt $15.95 (978-0-8050-6771-2). A simple story, told in rhyming text, about a young girl who traces tracks in the snow to see who made them and finally realizes she made them herself the day before. (Rev: BL 12/1/03; HB 11/03; HBG 4/04; SLJ 12/03)

3031 Yee, Wong H. *Who Likes Rain?* (PS–1). Illus. by author. 2007, Holt $14.95 (978-0-8050-7734-6). 32pp. A little girl heads outdoors on a rainy day and discovers that many plants and animals really like rain — but not all. (Rev: BL 3/1/07*)

3032 Yolen, Jane. *Mama's Kiss* (PS–1). Illus. by Daniel Baxter. 2008, Chronicle $14.99 (978-0-8118-6683-5). 32pp. One of Mama's thrown kisses misses its mark and travels hither and thither before ending up where it was intended. (Rev: BL 12/15/08; SLJ 2/09)

3033 Yolen, Jane, and Heidi E. Y. Stemple. *Not All Princesses Dress in Pink* (PS–1). Illus. by Anne-Sophie Lanquetin. 2010, Simon & Schuster $15.99 (978-1-4169-8018-6). Unpaged. Some princesses wear baseball jerseys and spend their time building tree houses, doing carpentry, and getting muddy, according to this book that portrays a wide variety of princess activities. (Rev: LMC 8–9/10; SLJ 6/1/10)

3034 Young, Amy. *Belinda Begins Ballet* (PS–2). Illus. by author. 2008, Viking $15.99 (978-0-670-06244-7). 32pp. When an insensitive school talent show director casts Belinda as a clown because of her huge feet, Belinda stays true to her love of ballet and enchants her audience with a surprise performance. (Rev: BL 11/1/07; SLJ 4/08)

3035 Young, Amy. *Belinda in Paris* (PS–2). Illus. 2005, Viking $15.99 (978-0-670-03693-6). 32pp. Belinda, the big-footed ballerina, arrives in Paris for a big performance only to discover that her specially made pointe shoes are on their way to Pago Pago. (Rev: BL 1/1–15/05; SLJ 4/05)

3036 Young, Amy. *Belinda the Ballerina* (PS–2). Illus. 2003, Viking $15.95 (978-0-670-03549-6). 32pp. Belinda is rejected by ballet judges because of her huge feet, and she sadly abandons dance until a band arrives at Fred's Fine Food and her feet can't resist. (Rev: BL 3/1/03; HBG 10/03; SLJ 3/03)

3037 Zalben, Jane Breskin. *Baby Shower* (PS–2). Illus. by author. 2010, Roaring Brook $16.99 (978-1-59643-465-3). 32pp. Pet-obsessed Zoe dreams of young animals falling from the sky when she learns she will help with her aunt's baby shower. (Rev: BL 2/1/10*; SLJ 3/1/10)

3038 Ziefert, Harriet. *Circus Parade* (PS–2). Illus. by Tanya Roitman. 2005, Blue Apple $15.95 (978-1-

59354-088-3). A parade of circus characters, ranging from majorettes and clowns to elephants and horses, march through a colorful town to a lively rhyming chant. (Rev: SLJ 10/05)

3039 Ziefert, Harriet. *My Forever Dress* (K–2). Illus. by Liz Murphy. 2009, Blue Apple $16.99 (978-1-934706-45-9). 40pp. As a girl grows, her grandmother recycles her favorite dress into something that will fit. (Rev: BLO 5/27/09; SLJ 6/09)

3040 Zimmerman, Andrea. *Fire Engine Man* (PS–K). Illus. by David Clemesha. 2007, Holt $15.95 (978-0-8050-7905-0). 32pp. A boy affectionately includes his little brother in his dreams of someday becoming a firefighter. (Rev: BL 5/1/07; SLJ 7/07)

FAMILY STORIES

3041 Ackerman, Karen. *Song and Dance Man* (K–3). Illus. by Stephen Gammell. 1988, Knopf LB $16.99 (978-0-394-99330-0); paper $6.99 (978-0-679-81995-0). 32pp. Up in the attic, Grandpa shows three children what it's like to be a song-and-dance man. Caldecott Medal winner, 1989. (Rev: BCCB 11/88; BL 10/1/88; HB 11/88)

3042 Ada, Alma Flor. *I Love Saturdays y Domingos* (PS–3). Illus. by Elivia Savadier. 2002, Simon & Schuster $16.95 (978-0-689-31819-1). A little girl visits Grandma and Grandpa on Saturday and Abuelito and Abuelita on Sunday in this multicultural story that incorporates Spanish words and phrases. (Rev: BL 2/1/02; HBG 10/02; SLJ 1/02)

3043 Adams, Diane. *I Can Do It Myself!* (PS–K). Illus. by Nancy Hayashi. 2009, Peachtree $15.95 (978-1-56145-471-6). 32pp. Emily Pearl takes pride in her ability (sort of) to look after herself until bedtime comes and her independence evaporates. (Rev: BL 3/15/09; SLJ 4/09)

3044 Adler, David A. *It's a Baby, Andy Russell* (3–5). Illus. by Leanne Franson. 2005, Harcourt $14.00 (978-0-15-216742-4). Andy and his sister Rachel are glad that the new baby is arriving but worried about coexisting with Aunt Janet while their mother is in hospital. (Rev: BL 5/15/05; SLJ 3/05)

3045 Adler, Victoria. *All of Baby, Nose to Toes* (PS). Illus. by Hiroe Nakata. 2009, Dial $14.99 (978-0-8037-3217-9). 32pp. From head to toe this cheerful volume celebrates all things baby. (Rev: BL 5/15/09; SLJ 7/09)

3046 Adoff, Arnold. *Black Is Brown Is Tan* (K–3). Illus. by Emily Arnold McCully. 1973, HarperCollins $15.95 (978-0-06-020083-1). A story in rhyme, which needs to be read aloud for greater understanding, depicts the warmth and companionship of an interracial family.

3047 Akin, Sara Laux. *Three Scoops and a Fig* (PS–2). Illus. by Susan Kathleen Hartung. 2010, Peachtree $15.95 (978-1-56145-522-5). 32pp. Banished from her family's Italian kitchen, little Sofia comes up with something she can efficiently contribute to celebrate the arrival of Nonna and Nonno. Lexile AD550L (Rev: BL 11/1/10; SLJ 8/1/10)

3048 Allen, Janet. *Best Little Wingman* (K–3). Illus. by Jim Postier. 2005, Boyds Mills $15.95 (978-1-59078-197-5). Janny is happy to help her father plowing the roads in rural Maine. (Rev: SLJ 3/05)

3049 Altman, Alexandra Jessup. *Waiting for Benjamin: A Story About Autism* (1–4). Illus. by Susan Keeter. 2008, Albert Whitman $15.95 (978-0-8075-7364-8). 32pp. Alexander has trouble accepting the extra attention paid to his younger brother Benjamin, who is autistic. (Rev: BL 7/08; LMC 8/08; SLJ 7/08)

3050 Altman, Linda J. *Singing with Momma Lou* (2–5). Illus. by Larry Johnson. 2002, Lee & Low $16.95 (978-1-58430-040-3). 32pp. Tamika uses photograph albums to help her grandmother, who suffers from Alzheimer's disease, remember some of her past. (Rev: BL 5/15/02; HBG 10/02; SLJ 6/02)

3051 Amado, Elisa. *Cousins* (1–4). Illus. by Luis Garay. 2004, Groundwood $16.95 (978-0-88899-459-2). The narrator is a little girl who has difficulty living in two cultures — her extended family is of different ethnic backgrounds. (Rev: SLJ 5/04) [813]

3052 Anderson, Rachel. *Hello Peanut* (PS). Illus. by Debbie Harter. Series: Hodder Toddler. 2004, Hodder paper $8.95 (978-0-340-85248-4). A toddler follows the progress of her mother's pregnancy with great interest. (Rev: SLJ 2/04)

3053 Andreae, Giles. *I Love My Mommy* (PS). Illus. by Emma Dodd. 2011, Hyperion/Disney $12.99 (978-1-4231-4327-7). 32pp. A toddler explains all the reasons he loves his mother in this bright oversize book. (Rev: SLJ 3/1/11)

3054 Andrews, Julie, and Emma Walton Hamilton. *The Very Fairy Princess* (PS–K). Illus. by Christine Davenier. 2010, Little, Brown $16.99 (978-0-316-04050-1). 32pp. Geraldine encounters many people who doubt her true princess nature but she maintains her royalness throughout the day. **e** (Rev: BL 4/15/10; SLJ 5/1/10)

3055 Anholt, Laurence. *Seven for a Secret* (1–3). Illus. by Jim Coplestone. 2006, Frances Lincoln $15.95 (978-1-84507-300-8). 32pp. A dying man leaves a treasure for his granddaughter, whose family has been enduring a financial crisis. (Rev: BL 5/1/06; SLJ 6/06)

3056 Appelt, Kathi. *Brand-New Baby Blues* (PS–2). Illus. by Kelly Murphy. 2010, HarperCollins $16.99 (978-0-06-053233-8). 32pp. A young girl adjusts to the arrival of her baby brother, going from resentful to accepting. (Rev: BL 11/15/09; SLJ 2/1/10)

3057 *Are We There Yet?* (K–2). Illus. by Dale Gottlieb. Series: I'm Going to Read! 2005, Sterling $11.95 (978-1-4027-2714-6); paper $3.95 (978-1-4027-2713-9). 32pp. This beginning reader portrays a girl and her younger brother pestering their father as he drives them to the toy store. (Rev: BL 10/15/05)

3058 Argueta, Jorge. *Xochitl and the Flowers / Xochitl, la nina de las flores* (K–3). Illus. by Carl Angel. 2003, Children's Book Pr. $16.95 (978-0-89239-181-3). 31pp. Newly arrived in San Francisco from their native El Salvador, Xochitl Flores and her family have problems adapting to their new home but find joy in the flowers they grow and sell. (Rev: BL 12/1/03; HBG 4/04; SLJ 12/03)

3059 Armas, Teresa. *Remembering Grandma / Recordando a Abuela* (1–3). Trans. by Gabriela Baeza Ventura. Illus. by Pauline Rodriguez Howard. 2003, Piñata $14.95 (978-1-55885-344-7). Lorena brings comfort to her grandfather when they share her dead grandmother's prized belongings in this appealing bilingual story. (Rev: BL 5/15/03; SLJ 7/03)

3060 Ashman, Linda. *Mama's Day* (PS). Illus. by Jan Ormerod. 2006, Simon & Schuster $15.95 (978-0-689-83475-2). 32pp. The bond between mothers and their babies is celebrated in a charming blend of verse and ink-and-gouache illustrations. (Rev: BL 3/15/06; SLJ 5/06)

3061 Ashman, Linda. *When I Was King* (PS–1). Illus. by David McPhail. 2008, HarperCollins $16.99 (978-0-06-029051-1). A boy used to being the only child in the house — the king — expresses his discontent directly to his new baby brother. (Rev: BL 10/1/08; SLJ 10/08)

3062 Asim, Jabari. *Daddy Goes to Work* (PS–2). Illus. by Aaron Boyd. 2006, Little, Brown $15.99 (978-0-316-73575-9). 32pp. The story of a young African American girl's day at work with her father is told in rhyming couplets. (Rev: BL 2/1/06; SLJ 6/06)

3063 Aska, Warabe. *Tapicero Tap Tap* (PS–2). Illus. 2006, Tundra $16.95 (978-0-88776-760-9). 24pp. Spanish furniture maker Tapicero Tap Tap tells his grandson how he put aside his boyhood dreams of travel to care for his family after his father was killed. (Rev: BL 3/1/06)

3064 Aston, Dianna. *Mama Outside, Mama Inside* (PS–K). Illus. by Susan Gaber. 2006, Holt $15.95 (978-0-8050-7716-2). 32pp. This appealing picture book explores the parallels between two expectant mothers — one a bird and the other a human. (Rev: BL 2/15/06; SLJ 3/06)

3065 Baca, Ana. *Chiles for Benito / Chiles para Benito* (K–3). Trans. by Jose Juan Colin. Illus. by Anthony Accardo. 2003, Piñata $15.95 (978-1-55885-389-8). In New Mexico, Cristina hears stories about her ancestor's magic seeds as she and her grandmother string red chiles to dry. (Rev: BL 12/15/03; SLJ 12/03)

3066 Bang, Molly. *In My Heart* (PS–2). Illus. 2006, Little, Brown $15.99 (978-0-316-79617-0). 32pp. A mother emphasizes to her child that she is always in her heart, throughout the day. (Rev: BL 1/1–15/06; SLJ 1/06)

3067 Banks, Kate. *Max's Words* (K–3). Illus. by Boris Kulikov. 2006, Farrar $16.00 (978-0-374-39949-8). 32pp. When Max's older brothers refuse to share their stamp and coin collections with him, the young boy starts a very special collection of his own. (Rev: BL 9/1/06; SLJ 9/06*)

3068 Banks, Kate. *Max's Castle* (K–2). Illus. by Boris Kulikov. 2011, Farrar $16.99 (978-0-374-39919-1). Unpaged. Often-maligned younger brother Max proves his worth to his older brothers when his skills with wordplay saves them from certain disaster in the adventure-filled fantasy world they've created. ℮ (Rev: SLJ 9/1/11)

3069 Banks, Kate. *That's Papa's Way* (PS–1). Illus. by Lauren Castillo. 2009, Farrar $16.95 (978-0-374-37445-7). 40pp. A simple, gentle story about a little girl and her father who enjoy a quiet day fishing together even though they tackle the worms differently; soothing pastel illustrations add atmosphere. (Rev: BL 2/1/09; SLJ 5/09)

3070 Barbour, Karen. *Little Nino's Pizzeria* (PS–2). Illus. by author. 1990, Harcourt paper $6.00 (978-0-15-246321-2). 32pp. When his father's business turns big, Tony is only in the way. (Rev: BL 9/15/87; SLJ 11/87)

3071 Barnwell, Ysaye M. *No Mirrors in My Nana's House* (PS–3). Illus. by Synthia Saint James. 1998, Harcourt $18.00 (978-0-15-201825-2). 32pp. The idea that people can find beauty in humble surroundings and can rise above a demeaning environment is presented in this picture book about an African American family. (Rev: BL 9/15/98; HBG 3/99; SLJ 10/98)

3072 Baryshnikov, Mikhail. *Because . . .* (K–3). Illus. by Vladimir Radunsky. 2007, Simon & Schuster $16.99 (978-0-689-87582-3). A story by the famous ballet dancer about a grandmother who can't keep herself from dancing. (Rev: SLJ 5/07)

3073 Bastianich, Lidia. *Nonna's Birthday Surprise* (K–2). Illus. by Renee Graef. Series: Lidia's Family Kitchen. 2013, Running Press $16.95 (978-0-7624-4655-1). 60pp. The chef and her five grandchildren make a surprise birthday meal; includes 18 recipes that will appeal to children but will require adult participation. (Rev: BLO 6/13; SLJ 6/13)

3074 Battle-Lavert, Gwendolyn. *The Music in Derrick's Heart* (PS–3). Illus. by Colin Bootman. 2000, Holiday House $16.95 (978-0-8234-1353-9). 32pp. The power of music is explored in this gentle story about a young African American boy who is learning to play the harmonica by taking lessons from his uncle Booker T. (Rev: BCCB 3/00; BL 2/15/00*; HBG 10/00; SLJ 3/00)

3075 Bean, Jonathan. *Building Our House* (K–3). Illus. by author. 2013, Farrar $17.99 (978-037438023-6). 48pp. It takes a year and a half for a family, with the help of friends, to build a cozy new home in the country in this picture book based on personal experience. ALA Notable Children's Book; Boston Globe–Horn Book Award. ℮ Lexile AD820 (Rev: BL 1/13; LMC 11–12/13; SLJ 2/13*)

3076 Beaty, Andrea. *Rosie Revere, Engineer* (K–2). Illus. by David Roberts. 2013, Abrams $16.95 (978-141970845-9). 32pp. Second-grader Rosie is a shy inventor with big ideas she's too afraid to share, but with the help of her Great-Great Aunt Rose, she learns that failing is the first step to success. Amelia Bloomer. ℮ (Rev: BL 9/15/13; SLJ 9/13)

3077 Beaty, Daniel. *Knock Knock: My Dad's Dream for Me* (PS–2). Illus. by Bryan Collier. 2013, Little, Brown $18 (978-031620917-5). 40pp. One day, when a boy's father does not show up for their daily game, the son

slowly realizes that his father is not going to return. ALA Notable Children's Book. Lexile AD780 (Rev: BL 11/1/13; HB 11–12/13; SLJ 10/13)

3078 Beiton, Sandra. *Beauty, Her Basket* (1–4). Illus. by Cozbi A. Cabrera. 2004, Greenwillow $16.99 (978-0-688-17821-5). 32pp. As she learns from her grandmother how to weave baskets from the grasses of the Sea Islands off the coast of Georgia, a young girl also becomes more familiar with her African ancestry. (Rev: BL 3/1/04; SLJ 6/04)

3079 Benjamin, Floella. *My Two Grannies* (PS–1). Illus. by Margaret Chamberlain. 2008, Frances Lincoln $16.95 (978-1-84507-643-6). Granny Vero was born in Trinidad and Granny Rose in Yorkshire, and their differences really show when they both come to look after Alvina when her parents are away. (Rev: SLJ 12/08)

3080 Bennett, Kelly. *Dad and Pop: An Ode to Fathers and Stepfathers* (PS–2). Illus. by Paul Meisel. 2010, Candlewick $15.99 (978-0-7636-3379-0). 40pp. A young girl points out the differences and similarities between her two dads — one is a stepfather — in this positive, comforting book about blended families. (Rev: BL 2/15/10; LMC 5–6/10; SLJ 3/1/10)

3081 Bennett, Kelly. *Vampire Baby* (PS–2). Illus. by Paul Meisel. 2013, Candlewick $15.99 (978-076364691-2). 32pp. Tootie's teeth are coming in, and her big brother is sure that means she's turning into a vampire, but when a vampire family decides they want to take her home, he realizes that Tootie is his sister and he loves her, even if he still thinks she might be a vampire baby. (Rev: BLO 9/15/13; SLJ 6/13)

3082 Bennett, Kelly. *Your Daddy Was Just Like You* (PS–1). Illus. by David Walker. 2010, Putnam $16.99 (978-0-399-25258-7). 32pp. A grandmother reminisces with her grandson and his father as they look through a scrapbook. (Rev: BL 2/1/10; SLJ 3/1/10)

3083 Bergström, Gunilla. *Very Tricky, Alfie Atkins,* (PS–K). Trans. from Swedish by Elisabeth Kallick Dyssegaard. Illus. by author. 2005, Farrar $15.00 (91-29-66152-8). 27pp. Alfie is allowed to play with his father's tools but only gets his father's attention when he needs the forbidden saw; a charming story first published in Sweden in the 1970s. (Rev: SLJ 9/05)

3084 Bernardo, Anilú. *Un día con mis tías / A Day with My Aunts* (2–4). Illus. by Christina Rodriguez. 2006, Piñata $15.95 (978-1-55885-374-4). A young Latina girl spends a fun-filled day with her aunts in this appealing bilingual book that includes empanada recipes. (Rev: SLJ 10/06)

3085 Berry, Matt. *Up on Daddy's Shoulders* (PS). Illus. by Lucy Corvino. 2006, Scholastic paper $6.99 (978-0-439-67045-6). 32pp. This picture book beautifully captures a young boy's joy and feelings of invincibility as he rides tall on his father's shoulders. (Rev: BL 9/1/06; SLJ 6/06)

3086 Bertram, Debbie. *The Best Place to Read* (PS–1). Illus. by Michael Garland. 2003, Random $14.95 (978-0-375-82293-3). 32pp. The poor protagonist searches for a good spot to settle down and read his new book, and eventually finds the perfect place with his mother. (Rev: BL 1/1–15/03; HBG 10/03; SLJ 5/03)

3087 Bertrand, Diane Gonzales. *The Empanadas That Abuela Made / Las empanadas que hacia la abuela* (K–2). Trans. by Gabriela Baeza Ventura. Illus. by Alex Pardo DeLange. 2003, Piñata $15.95 (978-1-55885-388-1). Presented in the form of a cumulative rhyme, this bilingual tale suitable for beginning and ESL readers follows Abuela step-by-step as she prepares her popular pumpkin empanadas. (Rev: SLJ 12/03)

3088 Bertrand, Diane Gonzales. *Sip, Slurp, Soup, Soup / Caldo, Caldo, Caldo* (K–3). Illus. by Alex P. DeLange. 1997, Piñata $14.95 (978-1-55885-183-2). A simple bilingual book about a family making soup. (Rev: HBG 3/98; SLJ 8/97)

3089 Best, Cari. *Are You Going to Be Good?* (PS–2). Illus. by G. Brian Karas. 2005, Farrar $16.00 (978-0-374-30394-5). 32pp. With illustrations that show a child's perspective this is the story of Robert's first grown-up party and the number of "don'ts" he has to remember. (Rev: BL 9/1/05; SLJ 9/05)

3090 Best, Cari. *Easy as Pie* (PS–2). Illus. by Melissa Sweet. 2010, Farrar $16.99 (978-0-374-39929-0). 40pp. Young Jacob concentrates on making a peach pie for his parents' anniversary — and serves it before they all go out for dinner. (Rev: BL 2/1/10; LMC 5–6/10; SLJ 2/1/10)

3091 Best, Cari. *What's So Bad About Being an Only Child?* (PS–1). Illus. by Sophie Blackall. 2007, Farrar $16.00 (978-0-374-39943-6). 32pp. Rosemary, an only child, attempts to resolve the frustrations that come with being the sole focus of her parents' attention. (Rev: BL 9/1/07; SLJ 11/07)

3092 Best, Cari. *When We Go Walking* (PS–1). Illus. by Kyrsten Brooker. 2013, Amazon/Two Lions $17.99 (978-1-4778-1648-6). 32pp. Wendy finds all sorts of treasures on the walks she enjoys on Rambling Road with her family. (Rev: BL 5/1/13; SLJ 7/13)

3093 Birdsall, Jeanne. *Flora's Very Windy Day* (K–3). Illus. by Matt Phelan. 2010, Clarion $16 (978-0-618-98676-7). 32pp. When Flora's irritating little brother Crispin is swept away by the wind, she finds she can't let him go after all. ℮ Lexile AD590L (Rev: BL 7/10*; LMC 10/10; SLJ 7/1/10)

3094 Blackall, Sophie. *Are You Awake?* (PS). Illus. by author. 2011, Henry Holt $12.99 (978-0-8050-7858-9). 40pp. A little boy's mother resists his efforts to wake her up when he can't sleep. (Rev: BL 5/1/11; SLJ 6/11*)

3095 Bond, Rebecca. *Just Like a Baby* (PS–2). Illus. 1999, Little, Brown $14.95 (978-0-316-10416-6). 32pp. Everyone in the family contributes to preparing a cradle for the new baby, and the baby responds by sleeping happily in it. (Rev: BCCB 9/99; BL 9/15/99; HBG 3/00; SLJ 9/99)

3096 Bonwill, Ann. *Naughty Toes* (PS–1). Illus. by Teresa Murfin. 2011, Tiger Tales $15.95 (978-1-58925-103-8). 32pp. Belinda seems to be a ballet natural but her sister Chloe's feet don't seem to work until she discovers tap dancing. Lexile AD560L (Rev: BLO 10/15/11; SLJ 11/1/11)

3097 Bootman, Colin. *Fish for the Grand Lady* (PS–2). 2006, Holiday $16.95 (978-0-8234-1898-5). 32pp. The natural beauty and lilting speech of Trinidad are showcased in this gentle tale of two brothers who set out to catch some fish for their grandmother to cook. (Rev: BL 10/15/06; SLJ 10/06)

3098 Borden, Louise. *Big Brothers Don't Take Naps* (PS–1). Illus. by Emma Dodd. 2011, Simon & Schuster $16.99 (978-1-4169-5503-0). 32pp. Nicholas adores his older brother James, who goes to school and no longer takes naps; Nicholas is soon to learn that he himself will soon be an older brother. (Rev: BL 6/1/11; SLJ 5/1/11)

3099 Bouchard, David. *Nokum Is My Teacher* (K–3). Illus. by Allen Sapp. 2007, Fitzhenry & Whiteside $21.95 (978-0-88995-367-3). 32pp. A young Cree boy's grandmother helps him to understand why he has to go to school with white people; the text is in both Cree and English. (Rev: BL 4/15/07)

3100 Bourgeois, Paulette. *Oma's Quilt* (PS–3). Illus. by Stephane Jorisch. 2001, Kids Can $15.95 (978-1-55074-777-5). 32pp. Grumpy Oma hates her new life in a nursing home, so granddaughter Emily and her mother decide to make her a special quilt. (Rev: BCCB 12/01; BL 12/15/01; HBG 3/02; SLJ 11/01)

3101 Bowen, Anne. *How Did You Grow So Big, So Soon?* (PS–2). Illus. by Marni Backer. 2003, Carolrhoda LB $15.95 (978-0-87614-024-6). A little boy and his mother, on the eve of his starting school, talk about his life so far. (Rev: HBG 4/04; SLJ 3/04)

3102 Boyd, Lizi. *I Love Mommy* (PS). Illus. by author. 2004, Candlewick $8.99 (978-0-7636-2216-9). A frog mother and child spend a happy day together in this simple, attractive book. Also use *I Love Daddy* (2004), about a similarly happy day. (Rev: SLJ 6/04)

3103 Boyden, Linda. *The Blue Roses* (K–3). Illus. by Amy Córdova. 2002, Lee & Low $16.95 (978-1-58430-037-3). 32pp. When her beloved grandfather dies, Rosalie remembers the lessons he taught her in the garden. (Rev: BCCB 9/02; BL 5/15/02; HBG 10/02; SLJ 6/02)

3104 Brannen, Sarah S. *Uncle Bobby's Wedding* (PS–2). Illus. by author. 2008, Putnam $15.99 (978-0-399-24712-5). 32pp. Little guinea pig Chloe is worried that her favorite uncle won't have time for her when he marries his boyfriend, Jamie. (Rev: BL 1/1–15/08; SLJ 4/08)

3105 Braun, Sebastien. *I Love My Mommy* (PS). Illus. by author. 2004, HarperCollins $15.99 (978-0-06-054310-5). An oversized format, large print, and bright colors enhance this look at relationships between mothers and children, using animals as the storytellers. (Rev: SLJ 4/04)

3106 Briant, Ed. *A Day at the Beach* (PS–1). Illus. by author. 2005, HarperCollins LB $17.89 (978-0-06-079982-3). A panda family planning a day at the beach has to go home to pick up forgotten items so many times that before they know it, the entire day is gone. (Rev: SLJ 6/06)

3107 Bringsvaerd, Tor Age. *When Two Get Up* (PS–K). Illus. by Tina Soli. 2009, MacKenzie Smiles $14.95 (978-0-9815761-4-5). 36pp. A toddler and her father go through regular morning activities all the while pretending to be all manner of stuffed and real animals and objects. (Rev: BLO 1/14/09)

3108 Brisson, Pat. *Hobbledy-Clop* (PS–K). Illus. by Maxie Chambliss. 2003, Boyds Mills $15.95 (978-1-56397-888-3). In the repetitive style of an old Irish folktale, this is the story of Brendan O'Doyle's visit to his grandmother, accompanied by a growing troop of animals. (Rev: HBG 10/03; SLJ 2/03)

3109 Brown, Tameka Fryer. *My Cold Plum Lemon Pie Bluesy Mood* (PS–2). Illus. by Shane W. Evans. 2013, Viking $16.99 (978-0-670-01285-5). 32pp. The young narrator effectively uses colors and rhyming text to describe his changing moods. (Rev: BL 4/1/13; SLJ 3/13)

3110 Browne, Anthony. *My Mom* (PS–2). Illus. 2005, Farrar $16.00 (978-0-374-35098-7). 32pp. The mom in this book with clever illustrations is sometimes frazzled, sometimes dazzling, but always her child's hero. (Rev: BL 3/1/05; SLJ 6/05)

3111 Bruchac, Joseph. *My Father Is Taller Than a Tree* (PS–1). Illus. by Wendy Anderson Halperin. 2010, Dial $16.99 (978-0-8037-3173-8). 32pp. Two-page spreads featuring brief rhyming text and soft-palette illustrations celebrate close relationships between diverse fathers and sons. (Rev: BL 1/1/10; LMC 3–4/10; SLJ 3/1/10)

3112 Bryne, Gayle. *Sometimes It's Grandmas and Grandpas, Not Mommies and Daddies* (PS–1). Illus. by Mary Haverfield. 2009, Abbeville $15.95 (978-0-7892-1028-9). 32pp. A young narrator explains all about what it's like being raised by grandparents. (Rev: BL 11/15/09; SLJ 1/1/10)

3113 Bunting, Eve. *Flower Garden* (PS–1). Illus. by Kathryn Hewitt. 1994, Harcourt $16.00 (978-0-15-228776-4). A girl and her father create a window box of flowers as a birthday present for her mother. (Rev: BL 2/15/94*; HB 5/94; SLJ 4/94*)

3114 Bunting, Eve. *The Memory String* (K–3). Illus. by Ted Rand. 2000, Clarion $16.00 (978-0-395-86146-2). 32pp. Laura begins to accept her stepmother, Jane, after Jane helps Laura search for lost buttons from her collection, each of which is associated with a member of her family. (Rev: BL 8/00; HBG 3/01; SLJ 8/00)

3115 Bunting, Eve. *My Mom's Wedding* (K–3). Illus. by Lisa Papp. 2006, Sleeping Bear $16.95 (978-1-58536-288-2). Pinky's mom is getting remarried and Pinky has mixed feelings about the wedding and her new stepfather. (Rev: SLJ 3/07)

3116 Bunting, Eve. *Sunshine Home* (K–3). Illus. by Diane deGroat. 1994, Clarion $16.00 (978-0-395-63309-0). 32pp. Timmie is unhappy when he visits his grandmother in her nursing home for the first time. (Rev: BCCB 4/94; BL 3/15/94; SLJ 4/94)

3117 Bunting, Eve. *The Wall* (K–2). Illus. by Ronald Himler. 1990, Houghton $16.00 (978-0-395-51588-4). A picture book on the subject of the Vietnam Veterans War Memorial. (Rev: BCCB 7–8/92; BL 4/1/90*; HB 7/90; SLJ 5/90*)

3118 Bunting, Eve. *The Wednesday Surprise* (PS–2). Illus. by Donald Carrick. 1989, Houghton $16.00 (978-0-89919-721-0); paper $5.95 (978-0-395-54776-2). 32pp. Anna is proudest of Grandma's surprise — Grandma has learned to read, and Anna has taught her. (Rev: BCCB 3/89; BL 3/1/89; SLJ 6/89)

3119 Bunting, Eve. *Will It Be a Baby Brother?* (PS–K). Illus. by Beth Spiegel. 2010, Boyds Mills $16.95 (978-1-59078-439-6). 32pp. A young boy eager for a little brother must adjust his expectations when his new sibling turns out to be a girl. (Rev: BL 10/1/10; SLJ 11/1/10)

3120 Burningham, John. *There's Going to Be a Baby* (PS). Illus. by Helen Oxenbury. 2010, Candlewick $16.99 (978-0-7636-4907-4). 48pp. A young boy wonders how his life will change when the new baby arrives, and discusses this with his mother as the months pass. (Rev: BL 11/1/10*; SLJ 10/1/10*)

3121 Burrowes, Adjoa J. *Grandma's Purple Flowers* (PS–3). Illus. 2000, Lee & Low $15.95 (978-1-880000-73-1). A young African American girl grieves after her beloved grandmother's death but gains acceptance when, in the spring, her grandmother's flowers bloom. (Rev: BL 11/1/00; HBG 3/01; SLJ 12/00)

3122 Busse, Sarah Martin, and Jacqueline B. Martin. *Banjo Granny* (PS). Illus. by Barry Root. 2006, Houghton $16.00 (978-0-618-33603-6). 32pp. A rhythmic tall tale in which a banjo-toting bluegrass-loving grandmother travels far and wide to pay a visit to her newborn grandchild. (Rev: BL 11/1/06; SLJ 12/06*)

3123 Buzzeo, Toni. *The Sea Chest* (2–4). Illus. by Mary GrandPré. 2002, Dial $16.99 (978-0-8037-2703-8). 32pp. An elderly aunt tells her niece, who is eagerly awaiting an adopted sister, about the girl her family found in a sea chest and adopted many years ago. (Rev: BL 9/15/02; HBG 3/03; SLJ 8/02)

3124 Cabrera, Jane. *Mommy, Carry Me Please!* (PS–1). Illus. by author. 2006, Holiday House $16.95 (978-0-8234-1935-7). Shows the many different and special ways in which animal and human mothers carry their babies. (Rev: SLJ 2/06)

3125 Carlstrom, Nancy White. *Before You Were Born* (PS–2). Illus. by Linda Saport. 2002, Eerdmans $17.00 (978-0-8028-5185-7). 32pp. This exceptional story inspired by Psalm 139 celebrates the bond between parents and children. (Rev: BL 2/1/02; HBG 10/02; SLJ 6/02)

3126 Caseley, Judith. *In Style with Grandma Antoinette* (K–2). Illus. by author. 2005, Tanglewood $15.95 (978-0-9749303-4-3). Little Rosie is at first hesitant to spend the day at the hair salon where her grandmother works, but once there she pitches in to help and has a wonderful time. (Rev: SLJ 1/06)

3127 Castellucci, Cecil. *Grandma's Gloves* (K–3). Illus. by Julia Denos. 2010, Candlewick $15.99 (978-0-

7636-3168-0). 32pp. A girl and her grandmother enjoy gardening together until the elderly woman dies and the girl inherits her gardening gloves. (Rev: BL 8/10; SLJ 8/1/10)

3128 Cates, Karin. *The Secret Remedy Book: A Story of Comfort and Love* (PS–2). Illus. by Wendy A. Halperin. 2003, Scholastic $16.95 (978-0-439-35226-0). 32pp. Auntie Zep produces the perfect remedy for Lolly's homesickness. (Rev: HBG 4/04; SLJ 8/03)

3129 Catherine, Maria. *Time Together: Me and Dad* (PS–K). Illus. by Pascal Campion. 2014, Capstone $8.95 (978-147952253-8). 32pp. A gentle picture book showing a father and child enjoying various activities together. (Rev: BL 3/1/14; SLJ 4/14)

3130 Chaconas, Dori. *Dancing with Katya* (K–3). Illus. by Constance R. Bergum. 2006, Peachtree $16.95 (978-1-56145-376-4). When Katya, who has dreamed of being a ballerina, is stricken by polio and forced to wear heavy braces, her older sister Anna tries to keep her from surrendering to despair; set in the early 20th century. (Rev: BL 9/1/06; SLJ 9/06)

3131 Chall, Marsha Wilson. *Sugarbush Spring* (PS–1). Illus. by Jim Daly. 2000, Lothrop LB $16.89 (978-0-688-14908-6). A little girl in Minnesota tells about the annual collection of sap from the family sugar bush and how the sap is turned into syrup. (Rev: BL 1/1–15/04; HBG 10/00; SLJ 3/00)

3132 Charlip, Remy. *A Perfect Day* (PS–1). 2007, Greenwillow $16.99 (978-0-06-051972-8). 40pp. A gentle story about all the things a boy and his father can enjoy in a day. (Rev: BL 5/1/07; SLJ 5/07*)

3133 Cheng, Andrea. *Goldfish and Chrysanthemums* (PS–2). Illus. by Michelle Chang. 2003, Lee & Low $16.95 (978-1-58430-057-1). To cheer up her Chinese-born grandmother, Nancy builds a fishpond and borders it with chrysanthemums, just like Ni Ni had as a child. (Rev: HBG 10/03; SLJ 6/03)

3134 Cheng, Andrea. *The Lemon Sisters* (PS–2). Illus. by Tatjana Mai-Wyss. 2006, Putnam $16.99 (978-0-399-24023-2). 32pp. The sight of three young sisters playing together in the snow gladdens the heart of an elderly woman who recalls fun with her own sisters who have long since moved away. (Rev: BL 12/15/05; SLJ 1/06)

3135 Cheng, Andrea. *When the Bees Fly Home* (PS–2). Illus. by Joline McFadden. 2002, Tilbury House $16.95 (978-0-88448-238-3). 32pp. A boy who lacks self-confidence finds he has an unsuspected talent as he works to help his bee-keeping family in this novel that includes plenty of bee facts and lovely watercolors. (Rev: BL 7/02; HBG 3/03)

3136 Chessa, Francesca. *The Mysterious Package* (PS–1). Illus. by author. 2007, Bloomsbury $16.95 (978-1-59990-028-5). 32pp. The arrival of a large box sets twins Charlie and Frances fighting over what it is, who it's for, etc.; however, it turns out the package was delivered in error and sibling rivalry dissipates when the real, much smaller package arrives, allowing the twins to accomplish something together. (Rev: BL 7/07; SLJ 7/07)

3137 Child, Lauren. *I Really, Really Need Actual Ice Skates* (PS–1). Illus. by author. Series: Charlie and Lola. 2010, Dial $16.99 (978-0-8037-3451-7). Unpaged. Lola promises she will use her new ice skates if she gets them, but finds it hard to live up to this when she finds skating more difficult than expected — perhaps a scooter would have been better after all! (Rev: SLJ 1/1/11)

3138 Clark, Julie Aigner. *You Are the Best Medicine* (K–3). Illus. by Jana Christy. 2010, HarperCollins $16.99 (978-0-06-195644-7). 32pp. A mother who has cancer gently tells her child about the treatment she will undergo. (Rev: BL 10/15/10; SLJ 11/1/10)

3139 Clark, Karen Henry. *Sweet Moon Baby: An Adoption Tale* (PS–K). Illus. by Patrice Barton. 2010, Knopf $17.99 (978-0-375-85709-6); LB $20.99 (978-0-375-95709-3). Unpaged. The moon looks over a baby Chinese girl whose parents cannot look after her as her new family prepares for her arrival. (Rev: SLJ 1/1/11)

3140 Clements, Andrew. *Because Your Daddy Loves You* (PS–K). Illus. by R. W. Alley. 2005, Clarion $16.00 (978-0-618-00361-7). 32pp. A daddy is shown helping a child in many ways in this picture book that celebrates the everyday things fathers do. (Rev: BL 3/1/05)

3141 Clements, Andrew. *Because Your Mommy Loves You* (PS–2). Illus. by R. W. Alley. 2012, Clarion $16.99 (978-0-547-25522-4). 32pp. A boy and his mother share a camping adventure in this companion to *Because Your Daddy Loves You* (2005) that teaches preparation and self-reliance. ℮ (Rev: BLO 2/15/12; SLJ 4/1/12)

3142 Cobb, Rebecca. *Missing Mommy: A Book about Bereavement* (PS–2). Illus. by author. 2013, Henry Holt $16.99 (978-0-8050-9507-4). 32pp. A little boy's drawings and writings express his feelings after the death of his mother. (Rev: BLO 3/15/13; HB 3–4/13; SLJ 3/13)

3143 Coffelt, Nancy. *Catch That Baby!* (PS). Illus. by Scott Nash. 2011, Aladdin $16.99 (978-1-4169-9148-9). 40pp. Spirited baby Ruby takes off after his bath and leads his family on a merry chase as he resists getting dressed. (Rev: BL 5/1/11; SLJ 6/11)

3144 Coffelt, Nancy. *Fred Stays with Me!* (PS–K). Illus. by Tricia Tusa. 2007, Little, Brown $16.99 (978-0-316-88269-9). 32pp. A little girl copes with her parents' divorce by clinging tenaciously to her dog Fred, who, despite his sometimes unfortunate behavior, is a source of comfort. (Rev: BCCB 9/07; BL 5/1/07; HB 1/09; SLJ 6/07)

3145 Cohen, Caron Lee. *Everything Is Different at Nonna's House* (PS). Illus. by Hiroe Nakata. 2003, Clarion $16.00 (978-0-618-07335-1). A little city boy delights in his grandparents' farm far from the hustle-bustle of his urban home. (Rev: HBG 10/03; SLJ 7/03)

3146 Cohen, Deborah Bodin. *Papa Jethro: A Story of Moses' Interfaith Family* (PS–1). Illus. by Jane Dippold. 2007, Kar-Ben $17.95 (978-1-58013-250-3); paper $7.95 (978-1-58013-252-7). 32pp. Rachel, who is Jewish, wonders why her grandfather goes to church and he tells her the biblical story of Jethro and his grandson

Gershom and how they loved each other despite their different religions. (Rev: BL 10/1/07; SLJ 10/07)

3147 Cohen, Miriam. *My Big Brother* (PS–2). Illus. by Ronald Himler. 2004, Star Bright $15.95 (978-1-59572-007-8). 40pp. When the older brother he idolizes joins the army, a young African American boy assumes the "big brother" role for his younger sibling. (Rev: BL 1/1–15/05)

3148 Colato Laínez, René. *Playing Lotería / El juego de la lotería* (1–3). Illus. by Jill Arena. 2005, Luna Rising $15.95 (978-0-87358-881-2). In this engaging bilingual picture book, a young boy visits his grandmother in Mexico and agrees to teach her some English words if she will tutor him in Spanish. (Rev: SLJ 10/05)

3149 Conway, David. *The Most Important Gift of All* (PS–K). Illus. by Karen Littlewood. 2006, School Specialty $15.95 (978-0-7696-4618-3). 32pp. Excited about the birth of her brother, a young Kenyan girl wanders in search of love, a gift she wants to give to her new sibling; the story is told in a traditional folktale style with large, warm illustrations. (Rev: BL 4/1/06; SLJ 5/06)

3150 Cook, Stephen. *Day Out with Daddy* (PS–1). Illus. by author. 2006, Walker $16.95 (978-0-8027-8059-1). A mischievous boy tells his own version of his special day with his father; the illustrations show something closer to the truth. (Rev: SLJ 5/06)

3151 Cooke, Trish. *Full, Full, Full, of Love* (PS–1). Illus. by Paul Howard. 2003, Candlewick $15.99 (978-0-7636-1851-3). 32pp. A young boy enjoys a family dinner at his grandmother's house in this happy, cozy picture book. (Rev: BCCB 3/03; BL 2/15/03; HBG 10/03; SLJ 2/03)

3152 Cooper, Floyd. *Max and the Tag-Along Moon* (PS–2). Illus. by author. 2013, Philomel $16.99 (978-0-399-23342-5). 32pp. Max's grandfather promises that the moon will always shine for the boy, and indeed it follows him home until it is briefly obscured by clouds; an effective bedtime story. (Rev: BL 6/13; HB 7–8/13; LMC 1–2/14; SLJ 6/13)

3153 Cooper, Melrose. *Gettin' Through Thursday* (1–3). Illus. by Nneka Bennett. 1998, Lee & Low $15.95 (978-1-880000-67-0). In this sweet story of a single-parent African American family, Mama is proud that her 3rd-grade son makes the honor roll, but the family is too poor to have a celebration. (Rev: HBG 10/99; SLJ 1/99)

3154 Cora, Cat. *A Suitcase Surprise for Mommy* (PS–K). Illus. by Joy Allen. 2011, Dial $16.99 (978-0-8037-3332-9). 32pp. Little Zoran copes with separation anxiety by giving his mother a picture to take with her on a trip to New York City. (Rev: BL 2/15/11; SLJ 3/1/11)

3155 Coste, Marion. *Finding Joy* (PS–2). Illus. by Yong Chen. 2006, Boyds Mills $16.95 (978-1-59078-192-0). 32pp. This story opens with Chinese parents sadly leaving their baby girl and closes with the same girl, renamed Joy, at home with her new American parents. (Rev: BL 1/1–15/07; SLJ 11/06)

3156 Cowen-Fletcher, Jane. *Mama Zooms* (PS–1). Illus. 1994, Scholastic $19.95 (978-0-590-72848-5); paper

$4.99 (978-0-590-45775-0). 32pp. Mama's "zooming machine" turns out to be her wheelchair. (Rev: BL 4/15/93; SLJ 5/93)

3157 Cox, Judy. *My Family Plays Music* (PS–1). Illus. by Elbrite Brown. 2003, Holiday House $16.95 (978-0-8234-1591-5). A young girl from a multiracial musical family introduces each person and the instrument and kind of music played. (Rev: HBG 4/04; SLJ 10/03)

3158 Coyle, Carmela LaVigna. *Do Princesses Really Kiss Frogs?* (PS–3). Illus. by Mike Gordon and Carl Gordon. 2005, Rising Moon $15.95 (978-0-87358-880-5). While on a walk with her father and the family dog, a little girl peppers her dad with questions. (Rev: SLJ 11/05)

3159 Coyle, Carmela LaVigna. *Do Princesses Wear Hiking Boots?* (PS–1). Illus. by Mike Gordon. 2003, Rising Moon $15.95 (978-0-87358-828-7). In this charming tale, presented in rhyming text, a little girl asks her mother what princesses are like and discovers, to her surprise, that they're not all that different from her. (Rev: SLJ 8/03)

3160 Crews, Donald. *Bigmama's* (PS–2). Illus. 1991, Greenwillow $17.89 (978-0-688-09951-0). 32pp. A family's annual summer trip to grandparents' house in the country is a celebration of childhood memories. (Rev: BCCB 11/91*; BL 11/15/91*; HB 9/91; SLJ 10/91) [921]

3161 Crews, Nina. *Sky-High Guy* (PS–2). Illus. by author. 2010, Henry Holt $16.99 (978-0-8050-8764-2). Unpaged. Brothers Jack and Gus work together to rescue Guy, Jack's action figure, when he gets stuck in a tree while "skydiving"; drawings on photographs blend reality and imagination. (Rev: HB 5–6/10; SLJ 4/1/10)

3162 Crow, Kristyn. *The Middle-Child Blues* (K–2). Illus. by David Catrow. 2009, Putnam $16.99 (978-0-399-24735-4). Unpaged. A neglected middle child finds his niche when he whips out his guitar and starts to play the blues at the county fair. (Rev: HB 11–12/09; SLJ 11/1/09)

3163 Crowe, Carole. *Turtle Girl* (K–2). Illus. by Jim Postier. 2008, Boyds Mills $16.95 (978-1-59078-262-0). 32pp. Magdalena's efforts to help the sea turtles that arrive on their island make her feel connected to the beloved grandmother who recently died. (Rev: BL 2/15/08; LMC 3/08; SLJ 4/08)

3164 Cruise, Robin. *Little Mamá Forgets* (PS–2). Illus. by Stacey Dressen-McQueen. 2006, Farrar $16.00 (978-0-374-34613-3). 40pp. Lucy's Mexican American grandmother is losing her memory and Lucy must remind her how to do simple things, but the older woman still manages to remember some of the important things in life. (Rev: BL 1/1–15/06; HBG 10/06; LMC 1/07; SLJ 8/06)

3165 Crum, Shutta. *Dozens of Cousins* (PS–2). Illus. by David Catrow. 2013, Clarion $16.99 (978-061815874-4). 32pp. An extended family spends a fun-filled day together eating, swimming, and playing games, all described from a child's point of view. (Rev: BL 9/15/13; SLJ 7/13)

160

3166 Crum, Shutta. *My Mountain Song* (K–3). Illus. by Ted Rand. 2004, Clarion $16.00 (978-0-618-15970-3). 32pp. Brenda Gail collects favorite memories to make her very own song in this story set in her great-grandparents' home in the Kentucky highlands. (Rev: BL 5/1/04; SLJ 6/04)

3167 Cummings, Pat. *Angel Baby* (PS–2). Illus. 2000, Lothrop LB $15.89 (978-0-688-14822-5). 24pp. Amanda Lynn, who has to take care of her baby brother, knows he isn't the angel baby everyone thinks he is. (Rev: BCCB 7–8/00; BL 6/1–15/00; HBG 10/00; SLJ 6/00)

3168 Cunha, Francisco. *My Very Own Lighthouse* (PS–2). Illus. 2006, Winged Chariot $16.95 (978-1-905341-01-6). 32pp. Worried about her fisherman father out at sea, a young girl builds a lighthouse in her window to help guide her father home. (Rev: BL 11/15/06)

3169 Curtis, Jamie Lee. *My Mommy Hung the Moon: A Love Story* (PS–2). Illus. by Laura Cornell. 2010, HarperCollins $16.99 (978-0-06-029016-0). 40pp. A young boy celebrates his wonderful mother in this bouncy book. Lexile AD400L (Rev: BL 11/15/10; SLJ 1/1/11)

3170 Curtis, Marci. *Big Brother, Little Brother* (K–3). Illus. 2004, Dial $12.99 (978-0-8037-2870-7). 40pp. As this photoessay shows, brothers come in all shapes, sizes, colors, and temperaments. (Rev: BL 5/15/04; SLJ 7/04)

3171 de Anda, Diane. *A Day without Sugar / Un dia sin azucar* (K–3). Illus. by Janet Montecalvo. 2012, Arte Publico paper $17.95 (978-15588570-2-5). 32pp. Tía Sofía and the rest of Tito's Latino family help him make healthy food choices when he learns he's consuming too much sugar in this bilingual book. (Rev: BL 8/12; LMC 3–4/13; SLJ 10/12)

3172 De Smet, Marian. *I Have Two Homes* (PS–2). Illus. by Nynke Mare Talsma. 2012, Clavis $15.95 (978-160537102-3). 32pp. Young Nina narrates the story of her parents' divorce, from bitter separation to the new normal of her life: a positive place where she knows both love her even though they can't love each other. (Rev: BLO 5/15/12; SLJ 6/1/12)

3173 Dempsey, Sheena. *Bye-Bye Baby Brother!* (PS–K). Illus. by author. 2013, Candlewick $15.99 (978-0-7636-6241-7). 32pp. Tired of the attention her baby brother is getting, young Ruby dreams of many ways of having him disappear — some of which (such as sending him to the moon) actually seem quite appealing to Ruby herself. (Rev: BL 5/1/13; SLJ 5/13)

3174 dePaola, Tomie. *The Baby Sister* (PS–1). Illus. 1996, Penguin $17.99 (978-0-399-22908-4). When Tommy's mother has a baby, his grandmother comes to stay. (Rev: BL 3/15/96; HB 5/96; SLJ 5/96)

3175 dePaola, Tomie. *Tom* (K–2). Illus. 1993, Penguin LB $16.99 (978-0-399-22417-1). A picture book about the special relationship between the author/artist and his grandfather. (Rev: BCCB 5/93; BL 1/15/93*; HB 7/93*; SLJ 4/93)

3176 Derby, Sally. *No Mush Today* (PS). Illus. by Nicole Tadgell. 2008, Lee & Low $16.95 (978-1-60060-238-2).

32pp. Fed up with daily routine and her wailing baby brother, Nonie, a young African American girl, seeks refuge with her grandmother, but by the end of the day recognizes that maybe home is best. (Rev: BL 9/1/08; SLJ 9/08)

3177 Ditchfield, Christin. *"Shwatsit!"* (PS–K). Illus. by Rosalind Beardshaw. 2009, Random House $15.99 (978-0-375-84181-1); LB $18.99 (978-0-375-94351-5). Unpaged. A family tries desperately to make sense of the baby's favorite word. (Rev: SLJ 11/1/09)

3178 Dorros, Arthur. *Mama and Me* (PS–K). Illus. by Rudy Gutierrez. 2011, HarperCollins $16.99 (978-0-06-058160-2). 32pp. A young girl helps her mother with basic tasks during the day, but emphasizes that she wants to do things by herself; the reason eventually becomes clear — she has been planning a party for her Mama; integrates many Spanish words and phrases. (Rev: BL 5/1/11; SLJ 5/1/11)

3179 Dorros, Arthur. *Papa and Me* (PS–K). Illus. by Rudy Gutierrez. 2008, HarperCollins $16.99 (978-0-06-058156-5). 32pp. A warm story of a Latino boy and his father as they spend an enjoyable day together; with glowing illustrations and Spanish words. (Rev: BL 3/15/08; SLJ 5/08)

3180 Downes, Belinda. *Baby Days: A Quilt of Rhymes and Pictures* (PS–K). Illus. 2006, Candlewick $14.99 (978-0-7636-2786-7). 32pp. Embroidered into the pages of this picture book, each of which resembles a quilt square, are snippets of poetry and song; game pieces; images of objects children love; and pictures of children at play. (Rev: BL 2/1/06)

3181 Doyle, Malachy. *Too Noisy!* (PS–2). Illus. by Ed Vere. 2012, Candlewick $15.99 (978-0-7636-6226-4). 40pp. Sam is the sole quiet member of the Bungle family, but when he wanders into the woods to get away from the din he gets lost and realizes he must make some noise himself. (Rev: BLO 10/15/12; SLJ 10/12)

3182 Doyle, Roddy. *Her Mother's Face* (K–3). Illus. by Freya Blackwood. 2008, Scholastic $16.99 (978-0-439-81501-7). 32pp. Set in Dublin, this sensitive story tells of Siobhan's longing to fill the painful emptiness left by her mother's death. (Rev: BL 9/15/08; LMC 1/09)

3183 Driscoll, Laura. *Super Specs* (K–2). Illus. by Barry Gott. 2005, Kane paper $4.95 (978-1-57565-145-3). 32pp. Molly, fed up with her younger brother's teasing about her new glasses, uses her math skills to convince her sibling that the glasses give her special powers. (Rev: BL 8/05)

3184 Duble, Kathleen Benner. *Pilot Mom* (PS–3). Illus. by Alan Marks. 2003, Charlesbridge LB $15.95 (978-1-57091-555-0). Jenny's mother, an Air Force pilot, is due to leave on a mission to Europe and the two make preparations for her departure. (Rev: HBG 4/04; SLJ 1/04)

3185 Duke, Shirley Smith. *No Bows!* (PS). Illus. by Jenny Mattheson. 2006, Peachtree $15.95 (978-1-56145-356-6). 32pp. A strong-minded little girl makes her preferences quite clear throughout the day. (Rev: BL 7/06; SLJ 4/06)

161

3186 Duncan, Alice Faye. *Honey Baby Sugar Child* (PS). Illus. by Susan Keeter. 2005, Simon & Schuster $15.95 (978-0-689-84678-6). 32pp. An African American mother expresses love for her toddler in reassuring colloquial text accompanied by warm illustrations. (Rev: BL 2/1/05; SLJ 3/05)

3187 Edwards, Michelle. *Room for the Baby* (K–3). Illus. by Jana Christy. 2012, Random House $17.99 (978-0-375-87090-3). 32pp. A little Jewish boy worries that his mother's sewing room is too full for the new baby, but Mom makes many presents for holidays and gradually the room empties. **e** (Rev: BLO 10/1/12; SLJ 9/12)

3188 Egan, Kate. *Kate and Nate Are Running Late!* (PS–1). Illus. by Dan Yaccarino. 2012, Feiwel & Friends $16.99 (978-1-250-00080-4). 40pp. Nate's mother Kate oversleeps and there is bedlam in the household as pets get loose, breakfast is thrown together, and clothes are donned — but wait, isn't it Saturday? No school? **e** Lexile AD370L (Rev: BL 10/15/12; HB 11–12/12; LMC 5–6/13; SLJ 10/12)

3189 Elliott, Rebecca. *Just Because* (PS–2). Illus. by author. 2011, Lion $14.99 (978-0-7459-6267-2). Unpaged. A little boy explains all the things he loves about his older sister, even though she's mute and wheelchair-bound. (Rev: SLJ 8/1/11)

3190 Elya, Susan Middleton. *Adiós, Tricycle* (PS–K). Illus. by Elisabeth Schlossberg. 2009, Putnam $16.99 (978-0-399-24522-0). 32pp. A young pig catalogs the items in his family's yard sale; Spanish words with glossary. (Rev: BL 6/1–15/09)

3191 Elya, Susan Middleton. *Oh No, Gotta Go!* (PS–1). Illus. by G. Brian Karas. 2003, Penguin $15.99 (978-0-399-23493-4). A young girl's outing turns into a frantic search for a bathroom in this amusing book that introduces several Spanish words and phrases into the poetic text. (Rev: HBG 10/03; SLJ 7/03)

3192 Enderle, Judith, and Stephanie Jacob Gordon. *Smile, Principessa!* (PS–1). Illus. by Serena Curmi. 2007, Simon & Schuster $16.99 (978-1-4169-1004-6). 40pp. "Dethroned" siblings will relate to Principessa, who feels insecure as her new baby brother is lavished with attention. (Rev: BL 6/1–15/07; SLJ 7/07)

3193 England, Kathryn. *Grandfather's Wrinkles* (PS–2). Illus. by Richard McFarland. 2007, Flashlight $15.95 (978-0-9729225-9-3). Grandfather explains how he got his wrinkles, formed on happy occasions on which he smiled. (Rev: LMC 1/08; SLJ 2/08)

3194 Eschbacher, Roger. *Road Trip* (K–3). Illus. by Thor Wickstrom. 2006, Dial $16.99 (978-0-8037-2927-8). 40pp. A rhyming story about a family's road trip and all its boredom, anticipation, excitement, and surprises. (Rev: BL 5/15/06; SLJ 7/06)

3195 Evans, Kristina. *What's Special About Me, Mama?* (PS–K). Illus. by Javaka Steptoe. 2011, Disney $16.99 (978-0-7868-5274-1). 32pp. An African American mother lists her son's physical attributes and the wonderful ways in which he behaves. (Rev: BL 2/1/11; SLJ 1/1/11)

3196 Fearnley, Jan. *Milo Armadillo* (K–2). Illus. by author. 2009, Candlewick $15.99 (978-0-7636-4575-5). Unpaged. Tallulah's grandmother's well-intentioned knitting efforts result in a pink armadillo toy named Milo; initially resistant, Tallulah comes to cherish her new friend. (Rev: SLJ 2/1/10)

3197 Feiffer, Kate. *My Mom Is Trying to Ruin My Life* (1–3). Illus. by Diane Goode. 2009, Simon & Schuster $16.99 (978-1-4169-4100-2). 32pp. Young Emma is embarrassed by her parents and dreams of having them thrown in jail, but finally recognizes that they can actually be useful to have around. (Rev: BL 3/15/09; SLJ 5/09)

3198 Feiffer, Kate. *My Side of the Car* (K–2). Illus. by Jules Feiffer. 2011, Candlewick $16.99 (978-0-7636-4405-5). 32pp. Sadie is determined to finally get to the zoo and refuses to recognize that it is raining — definitely not on her side of the car. (Rev: BL 3/1/11; HB 3–4/11; LMC 5–6/11; SLJ 3/1/11)

3199 Finkelstein, Ruth. *Big Like Me! A New Baby Story* (PS–K). Illus. by Esther Touson. 2001, Hachai $10.95 (978-1-929628-04-9). 32pp. Benny has just learned some basic skills from his older brother when a new baby joins his Orthodox Jewish family. (Rev: BL 8/01; HBG 3/02; SLJ 1/02)

3200 Fisher, Valorie. *My Big Brother* (PS–K). Illus. 2002, Simon & Schuster $14.95 (978-0-689-84327-3). 40pp. The amazing feats of one big brother, from the point of view of his baby sibling. (Rev: BCCB 7–8/02; BL 9/15/02; HBG 3/03; SLJ 7/02)

3201 Fisher, Valorie. *My Big Sister* (PS–1). Photos by author. 2003, Simon & Schuster $14.95 (978-0-689-85479-8). A baby's comical view of his big sister is enhanced by the effective photographs. (Rev: HBG 4/04; SLJ 11/03)

3202 Fitzpatrick, Marie-Louise. *Silly Mommy, Silly Daddy* (PS–1). Illus. by author. 2006, Frances Lincoln $15.95 (978-1-84507-547-7). Young Beth is downcast and all attempts to cheer her up prove unsuccessful until her sister appears and starts making faces. (Rev: SLJ 9/06)

3203 Fleischman, Paul. *The Birthday Tree* (K–3). Illus. by Barry Root. 2008, Candlewick $16.99 (978-0-7636-2604-4). A tree that mirrors the well-being of their fourth child brings worry and comfort to parents whose three older sons died at sea; a reissue of a 1979 publication, with new illustrations. (Rev: BL 1/1–15/08; SLJ 2/08)

3204 Fleischman, Paul. *Lost! A Story in String* (1–4). Illus. by C. B. Mordan. 2000, Holt $15.95 (978-0-8050-5583-2). 30pp. When the electricity goes off during a storm, Grandmother entertains her little granddaughter with an adventure story. (Rev: BCCB 10/00; BL 7/00; HBG 10/00; SLJ 6/00)

3205 Fleischman, Paul. *The Matchbox Diary* (1–3). Illus. by Bagram Ibatoulline. 2013, Candlewick $16.99 (978-0-7636-46011.). 40pp. An Italian American great grandfather explains to his great granddaughter the importance of all his little matchboxes and their contents.

Lexile AD420 (Rev: BL 4/1/13*; LMC 8–9/13; SLJ 3/13*)

3206 Fletcher, Ralph. *Grandpa Never Lies* (PS–2). Illus. by Harvey Stevenson. 2000, Clarion $16.00 (978-0-395-79770-9). 32pp. A little girl has a special relationship with her grandparents and when her grandmother dies, the little girl and Grandpa mourn together. (Rev: BL 12/15/00; HBG 3/01; SLJ 11/00)

3207 Fournier Le Ray, Anne-Laure. *Grandparents!* (PS–K). Illus. by Roser Capdevila. 2003, Kane $10.95 (978-1-929132-46-1). A gentle look at grandparents and the ways in which they differ and are the same. (Rev: SLJ 6/03)

3208 Fox, Mem. *Ten Little Fingers and Ten Little Toes* (PS–K). Illus. by Helen Oxenbury. 2008, Harcourt $16.00 (978-0-15-206057-2). 32pp. This appealing picture book features groups of multicultural babies in their different environments. (Rev: BL 11/15/08; HB 1/09; SLJ 12/08)

3209 Fox, Mem. *Whoever You Are* (K–3). Illus. by Leslie Staub. 1997, Harcourt $16.00 (978-0-15-200787-4). A reassuring book for children that tells them that, regardless of their situations, there are others like them all over the world. (Rev: BL 10/1/97; HBG 3/98; SLJ 10/97)

3210 Friedman, Darlene. *Star of the Week: A Story of Love, Adoption, and Brownies with Sprinkles* (PS–3). Illus. by Roger Roth. 2009, HarperCollins $17.99 (978-0-06-114136-2). 32pp. Six-year-old Cassidy-Li uses photographs and her own drawings to tell the story of her adoption from China. (Rev: BL 4/1/09; SLJ 6/09)

3211 Friedman, Ina R. *How My Parents Learned to Eat* (2–4). Illus. by Allen Say. 1987, Houghton $16.00 (978-0-395-35379-0); paper $6.99 (978-0-395-44235-7). 32pp. John, an American, and Aiko, a Japanese girl, learn each other's eating habits.

3212 Funke, Cornelia. *The Wildest Brother* (PS–2). Trans. by Chantal Wright. Illus. by Kerstin Meyer. 2006, Scholastic $16.99 (978-0-439-82862-8). 32pp. Imaginative young Ben is a brave boy during the day, protecting his sister from dragons and other imaginary creatures, but he still needs her reassurance at night. (Rev: BL 7/06; SLJ 6/06)

3213 Gadot, A. S. *The First Gift* (K–2). Illus. by Marie Lafrance. 2006, Lerner $15.95 (978-1-58013-146-9); paper $6.95 (978-1-58013-149-0). 24pp. This appealing picture book provides an introduction to the origins of names and also takes a brief look at the diversity of first names found in different parts of the globe; includes information on Jewish naming customs. (Rev: BL 10/1/06)

3214 Galindo, Mary Sue. *Icy Watermelon / Sandia fria* (PS–3). Illus. by Pauline Rodriguez Howard. 2000, Arte Publico $14.95 (978-1-55885-306-5). 32pp. In this bilingual English and Spanish book, three Latino children share stories and jokes with their parents and grandparents on a porch where they are eating watermelon. (Rev: BL 12/15/00; SLJ 1/01)

3215 Garden, Nancy. *Molly's Family* (PS–2). Illus. by Sharon Wooding. 2004, Farrar $16.00 (978-0-374-35002-4). Although hurt by a classmate's remark about the makeup of her family — "no one has two mommies" — Molly comes to see that families come in all sorts of packages. (Rev: BL 4/15/04; HB 7/04; SLJ 5/04)

3216 Garland, Michael. *Grandpa's Tractor* (PS–2). Illus. by author. 2011, Boyds Mills $16.95 (978-1-59078-762-5). Unpaged. In this beautifully illustrated story, Grandpa Joe and Timmy visit the now-abandoned family farm. Lexile AD890L (Rev: SLJ 5/1/11)

3217 Gay, Marie-Louise. *What Are You Doing, Sam?* (PS). Series: Stella and Sam. 2006, Groundwood $14.95 (978-0-88899-734-0). 32pp. Red-headed big sister Stella keeps a close eye on her younger brother Sam as he tries to teach new tricks to Fred the dog. Earlier books in the series include *Stella, Star of the Sea* (1999), *Stella, Queen of the Snow* (2000), *Stella, Fairy of the Forest* (2002), *Good Morning, Sam* and *Good Night, Sam* (2003), and *Stella, Princess of the Sky* (2004). (Rev: BL 9/1/06; SLJ 9/06)

3218 George, Kristine O'Connell. *Up!* (PS). Illus. by Niroe Nakata. 2005, Clarion $15.00 (978-0-618-06489-2). 32pp. A little girl and her daddy enjoy a day at the park in this rhyming picture book. (Rev: BL 3/1/05; SLJ 3/05)

3219 Gerdner, Linda, and Sarah Langford. *Grandfather's Story Cloth: Yawg Daim Paj Ntaub Dab Neeg* (K–3). Illus. by Stuart Loughridge. 2008, Shen's $16.95 (978-1-885008-34-3). 32pp. Chersheng's grandfather has Alzheimer's but he can still remember the past as he "reads" the story cloth of how the family fled from soldiers; English and Hmong appear side by side. (Rev: BL 9/1/08; SLJ 9/08)

3220 Gibala-Broxholm, Scott. *Maddie's Monster Dad* (K–2). Illus. by author. 2011, Marshall Cavendish $16.99 (978-0-7614-5846-3). Unpaged. Fed up with her dad's busy schedule, Maddie decides to build a Monster Dad to play with her; her real Dad gets the message and makes space in his day for play. (Rev: LMC 1–2/12; SLJ 10/1/11)

3221 Gilchrist, Jan Spivey. *Indigo and Moonlight Gold* (K–3). Illus. 1993, Black Butterfly $13.95 (978-0-86316-210-7). 32pp. A tender moment between a mother and child is described in moving prose and beautiful oil paintings. (Rev: BCCB 2/94; BL 3/1/94; SLJ 5/94)

3222 Gillard, Denise. *Music from the Sky* (PS–1). Illus. by Stephen Taylor. 2001, Douglas & McIntyre $15.95 (978-0-88899-311-3). 32pp. A music-loving young African American girl spends time with her grandpa, who makes her a flute so she can make her own music. (Rev: BL 2/15/01; HBG 10/01)

3223 Gilles, Almira Astudillo. *Willie Wins* (PS–3). Illus. by Carl Angel. 2001, Lee & Low $16.00 (978-1-58430-023-6). 32pp. Willie isn't much interested in his father's stories of his youth in the Philippines, but when he needs a money bank for a school project, the coconut alkansiya his father gives him has a surprise in it. (Rev: BL 5/1/01; HBG 10/01; SLJ 6/01)

3224 Gilmore, Rachna. *A Gift for Gita* (2–3). Illus. by Alice Priestley. 2002, Tilbury House paper $7.95 (978-0-88448-239-0). 24pp. When Gita's father is offered a job back in their native India, the immigrant family must make a choice. (Rev: BL 9/15/02)

3225 Gilmore, Rachna. *Making Grizzle Grow* (K–3). Illus. by Leslie Elizabeth Watts. 2008, Fitzhenry & Whiteside $16.95 (978-1-55041-885-9). 32pp. After her father says he can't come out and play with her, a very angry Emily builds a very scary snow dinosaur that threatens to eat her father up. (Rev: BL 1/1–15/08; SLJ 3/08)

3226 Goode, Diane. *The Most Perfect Spot* (PS–2). 2006, HarperCollins $16.99 (978-0-06-072697-3). 32pp. Jack and his Mama try to enjoy a picnic at the park and end up wet, muddy — and the new owners of a stray puppy. (Rev: BL 5/1/06; SLJ 5/06*)

3227 Gore, Leonid. *When I Grow Up* (PS). Illus. by author. 2009, Scholastic $16.99 (978-0-545-08597-7). 32pp. A little boy wonders what he will be when he grows up and considers many options (a raindrop becoming a river, a caterpillar becoming a butterfly) before deciding that he'll be like his father. (Rev: BL 4/15/09; SLJ 6/09)

3228 Greenfield, Eloise. *First Pink Light* (PS–1). Illus. by Jan S. Gilchrist. 1991, Writers & Readers $13.95 (978-0-86316-207-7). A young African American boy waits in a rocking chair to greet his father, who has been away for a year. (Rev: BL 12/15/91; SLJ 1/92)

3229 Greenfield, Eloise. *Grandpa's Face* (K–3). Illus. by Floyd Cooper. 1988, Philomel $16.99 (978-0-399-21525-4); Penguin paper $6.99 (978-0-698-11381-7). 32pp. Tamika worries about her grandfather's reactions. (Rev: BL 11/15/88; HB 3/89; SLJ 11/88)

3230 Greenfield, Eloise. *She Come Bringing Me That Little Baby Girl* (K–2). Illus. by John Steptoe. 1990, HarperCollins paper $6.99 (978-0-06-443296-2). 32pp. Kevin resents all the attention the new baby is getting; most of all he resents the fact that she is a girl.

3231 Grimes, Nikki. *Welcome, Precious* (PS–2). Illus. by Bryan Collier. 2006, Scholastic $16.99 (978-0-439-55702-3). 32pp. A young African American family welcomes a new baby to the many wonders of the world. (Rev: BL 9/1/06; SLJ 11/06)

3232 Grossmann-Hensel, Katharina. *Papa Is a Pirate* (K–2). Illus. by author. 2009, North-South $16.95 (978-0-7358-2237-5). 32pp. Here is a fun twist on the pirate story that has a gentle father telling his doubtful son that he is in fact a dashing pirate, not an office worker. (Rev: SLJ 5/09)

3233 Gurley, Nan. *Twice Yours: A Parable of God's Gift* (K–3). Illus. by Bill Farnsworth. 2002, Zondervan $14.99 (978-0-310-70194-1). A grandfather tells his grandson a story relating to the words of the apostle Peter. (Rev: BL 2/1/02)

3234 Guy, Ginger F. *My Grandma / Mi abuelita* (PS–1). Illus. by Vivi Escriva. 2007, HarperCollins $15.99 (978-0-06-079098-1). A father, son, and daughter fly from

their city to Grandmother's tropical home in this engagingly illustrated bilingual story. (Rev: BL 1/1–15/07)

3235 Hanrahan, Brendan. *My Sisters Love My Clothes* (PS–2). Illus. by Lise Stork. 1992, Perry Heights Pr. $12.95 (978-0-9630181-0-6). 32pp. Young Louie has a smart wardrobe, but his sisters keep borrowing his clothes. (Rev: BCCB 4/92; BL 9/1/92)

3236 Hardin, Melinda. *Hero Dad* (PS–1). Illus. by Bryan Langdo. 2010, Marshall Cavendish $12.99 (978-0-7614-5713-8). 24pp. A young boy enthusiastically describes his dad's "super powers" — night vision, flying, and the endurance that comes from being a soldier. e (Rev: BL 12/15/10; LMC 1–2/11; SLJ 10/1/10)

3237 Harper, Jessica. *I Like Where I Am* (PS–2). Illus. by G. Brian Karas. 2004, Penguin $15.99 (978-0-399-23479-8). 32pp. A little boy faces the trauma of moving in this playfully illustrated book with a happy ending. (Rev: BL 2/15/04; SLJ 3/04)

3238 Harper, Jessica. *Lizzy's Do's and Don'ts* (1–3). Illus. by Lindsay Harper duPont. 2002, HarperCollins LB $15.89 (978-0-06-623861-6). 40pp. Cartoon art helps to convey the messages of this book, in which a mother and daughter realize they say "don't" to each other far too often. (Rev: BL 3/15/02; HBG 10/02; SLJ 7/02)

3239 Harper, Jessica. *Uh-oh, Cleo* (K–3). Illus. by Jon Berkeley. 2008, Putnam $14.99 (978-0-399-24671-5). 64pp. This appealing chapter book features 8-year-old Cleo, one of six children in a warm family, who has a stitches party after getting hit in the head. (Rev: BL 4/1/08; LMC 3/08; SLJ 8/08)

3240 Harper, Jessica. *Uh-oh, Cleo: Underpants on My Head* (K–3). Illus. by Jon Berkeley. 2009, Putnam $14.99 (978-0-399-24672-2). 64pp. Eight-year-old Cleo Small and her family get caught in a freak summer snowstorm at the top of Mount Baldy. (Rev: BL 2/1/09; SLJ 3/09)

3241 Harrington, Janice N. *Roberto Walks Home* (K–2). Illus. by Jody Wheeler. 2008, Viking $15.99 (978-0-670-06316-1). Forced to walk home alone after his brother forgets to pick him up from school, an angry Roberto falls asleep and dreams a sweet revenge. (Rev: BL 11/15/08; SLJ 12/08)

3242 Harris, Robie H. *The Day Leo Said I Hate You!* (K–3). Illus. by Molly Bang. 2008, Little, Brown $16.99 (978-0-316-06580-1). Leo and his mother allow their mutual frustration to escalate until Leo blurts out the dreaded words. (Rev: BL 9/1/08; SLJ 8/08)

3243 Harris, Robie H. *Don't Forget to Come Back!* (PS–2). Illus. by Harry Bliss. 2004, Candlewick $15.99 (978-0-7636-1782-0). 40pp. A little girl strongly protests her parents' departure for the evening but ends up having a delightful time with the baby-sitter; a newly illustrated version of a 1978 title. (Rev: BL 3/1/04; HB 3/04; SLJ 3/04)

3244 Harshman, Marc. *Roads* (PS–2). 2002, Marshall Cavendish $16.95 (978-0-7614-5112-9). 32pp. A thoughtful picture book about traveling from a child's perspective. (Rev: BL 10/15/02; HBG 3/03; SLJ 9/02)

3245 Hartt-Sussman, Heather. *Here Comes Hortense!* (K–2). Illus. by Georgia Graham. 2012, Tundra $17.95 (978-177049221-9). 32pp. A young boy is delighted to join his grandmother and her new husband on a trip to the theme park until he realizes that bratty young Hortense is coming too and monopolizes Nana. (Rev: BLO 4/15/12; SLJ 4/12)

3246 Haseley, Dennis. *The Skywriter* (PS–2). Illus. by Dennis Nolan. 2008, Roaring Brook $16.95 (978-1-59643-252-9). 32pp. A boy named Charles recognizes the joy he derived from his now-abandoned toys and decides to save them for a new younger brother. (Rev: BLO 7/29/08; LMC 1/09; SLJ 10/08)

3247 Hector, Julian. *The Little Matador* (PS–2). Illus. by author. 2008, Hyperion $15.99 (978-1-4231-0779-8). 40pp. A little boy just wants to draw but his parents want him to follow family tradition and fight bulls, and amazingly the Little Matador manages to combine the two. (Rev: BL 5/15/08; LMC 1/09)

3248 Henderson, Kathy. *And the Good Brown Earth* (PS). Illus. by author. 2004, Candlewick $15.99 (978-0-7636-2301-2). A well-illustrated story about Joe and his grandmother enjoying all four seasons in the garden. (Rev: SLJ 4/04)

3249 Henderson, Kathy. *Look at You!* (PS). 2007, Candlewick $15.99 (978-0-7636-2745-4). Diverse babies and toddlers explore the world, eat, play, crawl, and clap in soft, oversize watercolors. (Rev: BL 2/15/07*)

3250 Henson, Heather. *Grumpy Grandpa* (K–2). Illus. by Ross MacDonald. 2009, Atheneum $16.99 (978-1-4169-0811-1). Grandpa is a grouch until he and his grandson go fishing. (Rev: BL 5/15/09; HB 9/09; SLJ 7/09)

3251 Heo, Yumi. *Father's Rubber Shoes* (PS–3). Illus. 1995, Orchard LB $16.99 (978-0-531-08723-7). 32pp. Yungsu's father tells his lonely son why the family has moved to the United States. (Rev: BL 9/15/95; HB 11/95; SLJ 11/95)

3252 Heo, Yumi. *One Sunday Morning* (PS–1). Illus. 1999, Orchard LB $16.99 (978-0-531-33156-9). 32pp. Minho dreams that he and his father spend a day in the park experiencing its sights and sounds. (Rev: BCCB 5/99; BL 4/1/99; HB 3/99; HBG 10/99; SLJ 4/99)

3253 Heo, Yumi. *Ten Days and Nine Nights* (PS–2). Illus. by author. 2009, Random $16.99 (978-0-375-84718-9). 40pp. A little girl marks off the days on her calendar in anticipation of the upcoming arrival of her new adopted sister from Korea. (Rev: BL 4/1/09; HB 5/09; SLJ 5/09)

3254 Herman, Charlotte. *The Memory Cupboard: A Thanksgiving Story* (PS–2). Illus. by Ben F. Stahl. 2003, Whitman LB $16.95 (978-0-8075-5055-7). Katie is upset when she breaks her grandmother's gravy boat, but Grandma shows her that memories are more important than possessions. (Rev: BL 9/1/03; HBG 4/04; SLJ 11/03)

3255 Hesse, Karen. *Poppy's Chair* (K–3). Illus. by Kay Life. 1993, Macmillan LB $14.95 (978-0-02-743705-8). 32pp. Leah learns from her grandmother how to accept her grandfather's death. (Rev: BL 3/15/93; SLJ 7/93)

3256 Hesse, Karen. *Spuds* (PS–2). Illus. by Wendy Watson. 2008, Scholastic $16.99 (978-0-439-87993-4). A warm free-verse story about three hungry children who set out to gather potatoes left after the harvest but instead come home with stones. (Rev: BCCB 12/08; BL 9/15/08; LMC 1/09; SLJ 9/08)

3257 Hest, Amy. *When Charley Met Grampa* (PS–1). Illus. by Helen Oxenbury. 2013, Candlewick $15.99 (978-076365314-9). 40pp. Henry's worried about what Grampa will think of his new puppy Charley, but when Charley saves the day (or at least Grampa's hat), Henry realizes that Charley has made a new friend. ℮ Lexile AD550 (Rev: BL 9/15/13*; HB 11–12/13; SLJ 8/13*)

3258 Hines, Anna Grossnickle. *Daddy Makes the Best Spaghetti* (PS–K). Illus. by author. 1986, Houghton paper $5.95 (978-0-89919-794-4). The story of the warm relationship between a father and son as they spend time together doing things at home. (Rev: BL 3/1/86; HB 9/86; SLJ 5/86)

3259 Hines, Anna Grossnickle. *My Grandma Is Coming to Town* (PS–K). Illus. by Melissa Sweet. 2003, Candlewick $13.99 (978-0-7636-1237-5). 24pp. When grandma visits Albert for the first time since he was a baby, he is shy and hides while grandma waits patiently. (Rev: BL 3/15/03; HBG 10/03; SLJ 7/03)

3260 Hoberman, Mary Ann. *I'm Going to Grandma's* (PS–K). Illus. by Tiphanie Beeke. 2007, Harcourt $16.00 (978-0-15-216592-5). 32pp. A gentle story about a child's nervousness the first time she spends the night with Grandma and Grandpa. (Rev: BL 4/1/07)

3261 Hodgkinson, Leigh. *Smile!* (K–2). Illus. by author. 2010, HarperCollins $16.99 (978-0-06-185269-5). Unpaged. Sunny loses her smile when told not to eat more cookies before dinner and must look for it all over the house, discovering quite a bit in her search. (Rev: SLJ 2/1/10)

3262 Hoestlandt, Jo. *Gran, You've Got Mail!* (3–6). Illus. by Aurelie Abolivier. 2008, Delacorte $14.99 (978-0-385-73565-0). 128pp. Annabelle and her great-grandmother form a friendship through writing letters. (Rev: BL 11/15/08; LMC 11/09; SLJ 9/08)

3263 Holman, Sandy Lynne. *Grandpa, Is Everything Black Bad?* (PS–3). Illus. by Lela Kometiani. 1998, Culture C.O.-O.P. $18.95 (978-0-9644655-0-3). 32pp. A child named Montsho thinks that black is often associated with things that are bad, but his beloved grandfather assures him that black is beautiful. (Rev: BL 1/1–15/99; SLJ 12/98)

3264 Holmberg, Bo R. *A Day with Dad* (K–3). Illus. by Eva Eriksson. 2008, Candlewick $15.99 (978-0-7636-3221-2). 32pp. Young Tim spends a happy day with his visiting father. (Rev: BL 4/15/08; HB 5/08; SLJ 8/08)

3265 Holt, Kimberly Willis. *Waiting for Gregory* (PS–2). Illus. by Gabi Swiatkowska. 2006, Holt $16.95 (978-0-8050-7388-1). Young Iris eagerly awaits the birth of her new cousin, a boy to be named Gregory. (Rev: BL 2/1/06; SLJ 3/06)

3266 Hooks, Bell. *Homemade Love* (PS). Illus. by Shane W. Evans. 2002, Hyperion $16.99 (978-0-7868-0643-0). 32pp. An African American girl revels in the love of her supportive parents in this brightly illustrated book. (Rev: BCCB 2/03; BL 2/1/03; HBG 3/03; SLJ 12/02)

3267 Horrocks, Anita. *Silas' Seven Grandparents* (PS–3). Illus. by Helen Flook. 2010, Orca $19.95 (978-1-55143-561-9). 32pp. A lucky child with seven grandparents struggles to decide how to spend his time when he's invited to all of their houses at once. (Rev: BL 5/15/10; LMC 11–12/10; SLJ 9/1/10)

3268 Horse, Harry. *Little Rabbit's New Baby* (PS–1). Illus. by author. 2008, Peachtree $15.95 (978-1-56145-431-0). 32pp. Little Rabbit struggles with his new role as a big brother. (Rev: SLJ 4/08)

3269 Howard, Elizabeth F. *Flower Girl Butterflies* (PS–2). Illus. by Christiane Kromer. 2004, Greenwillow $15.99 (978-0-688-17809-3). 32pp. Sarah is scared of being a flower girl until she actually starts down the aisle. (Rev: BL 3/1/04; SLJ 4/04)

3270 Howard, Elizabeth F. *What's in Aunt Mary's Room?* (PS–2). Illus. by Cedric Lucas. 1996, Clarion $16.00 (978-0-395-69845-7). 32pp. Aunt Flossie explains the importance in the life of this African American family of the book stored in Aunt Mary's room, the family Bible. A sequel to *Aunt Flossie's Hats (and Crab Cakes Later)* (1991). (Rev: BL 2/15/96; SLJ 5/96)

3271 Howard, Elizabeth F. *When Will Sarah Come?* (PS–K). Illus. by Nina Crews. 1999, Greenwillow LB $15.89 (978-0-688-16181-1). On Sarah's first day at school, younger brother Jonathan waits impatiently for her return. (Rev: BCCB 10/99; BL 10/15/99; HBG 3/00; SLJ 9/99)

3272 Hughes, Shirley. *The Big Alfie and Annie Rose Storybook* (2–3). Illus. by author. 1989, Lothrop $18.00 (978-0-688-07672-6). 64pp. Stories, poems, and eye-catching artwork featuring Alfie and his little sister. (Rev: BCCB 4/89; BL 3/15/89; HB 5/89)

3273 Hughes, Shirley. *The Big Alfie Out of Doors Storybook* (PS–2). Illus. 1992, Lothrop $17.00 (978-0-688-11428-2). 64pp. Four-year-old Alfie has four happy experiences with different members of his family. (Rev: BCCB 10/92*; BL 10/15/92; HB 1/93; SLJ 10/92)

3274 Hundal, Nancy. *Camping* (PS–3). Illus. by Brian Deines. 2002, Fitzhenry & Whiteside $16.95 (978-1-55041-668-8). 32pp. Luminous illustrations form the backdrop for a young girl's discovery that camping in the wilderness has its delights after all. (Rev: BL 12/1/02; SLJ 11/02)

3275 Hunter, Jana Novotny. *When Daddy's Truck Picks Me Up* (PS–1). Illus. by Carol Thompson. 2006, Albert Whitman $15.95 (978-0-8075-8914-4). A little boy at preschool can't concentrate for anticipating the moment when his dad will pick him up in his big tanker truck. (Rev: SLJ 10/06)

3276 Hurwitz, Johanna. *The Two and Only Kelly Twins* (1–3). Illus. by Tuesday Mourning. 2013, Candlewick $14.99 (978-076365602-7). 96pp. Identical twins Arlene and Ilene feel special until a set of triplets arrives at their school; and will Arlene and Ilene remain the same when one of them has her appendix out? **e** Lexile 600 (Rev: BL 9/1/13; LMC 5–6/14; SLJ 11/13)

3277 Hutchins, Hazel. *I'd Know You Anywhere* (PS). Illus. by Ruth Ohi. 2002, Annick LB $19.95 (978-1-55037-747-7); paper $7.95 (978-1-55037-746-0). 24pp. A father reassures his son that he'd know him no matter how he was disguised in this book for very young readers. (Rev: BL 12/15/02; HBG 3/03; SLJ 4/03)

3278 Hutchins, Pat. *Titch* (K–3). Illus. by author. 1971, Macmillan paper $5.99 (978-0-689-71688-1). Titch, the youngest in the family, enjoys a moment of triumph. A sequel is: *You'll Soon Grow into Them, Titch* (1983, Greenwillow).

3279 Igus, Toyomi. *Two Mrs. Gibsons* (K–3). Illus. by Daryl Wells. 1996, Children's Book Pr. $14.95 (978-0-89239-135-6). 32pp. The two Mrs. Gibsons in a young girl's life are her mother and her grandmother. (Rev: BCCB 5/96; BL 5/15/96; SLJ 10/96)

3280 Igus, Toyomi. *When I Was Little* (K–3). Illus. by Higgins Bond. 1992, Just Us Bks. $14.95 (978-0-940975-32-3). 32pp. Noel finds it hard to believe there was no television and other things he takes for granted when his African American grandfather was growing up. (Rev: BL 3/1/93)

3281 Iwai, Melissa. *Soup Day* (PS–1). Illus. by author. 2010, Henry Holt $12.99 (978-0-8050-9004-8). 32pp. On a snowy day, a young girl helps her mother choose and prepare vegetables for soup; when Dad gets home, they all share the meal together. (Rev: BL 10/15/10; SLJ 9/1/10)

3282 Jabar, Cynthia. *Wow! It Sure Is Good to Be You!* (PS–2). Illus. by author. 2006, Houghton $9.95 (978-0-618-58132-0). Phone calls and letters help a little girl realize that even if the people you love are far away, they can still be with you. (Rev: SLJ 6/06)

3283 Jacobs, Julie. *My Heart Is a Magic House* (PS–K). Illus. by Bernadette Pons. 2007, Albert Whitman $16.99 (978-0-8075-5335-0). A young squirrel called Stephanie worries about being supplanted by the new sibling that's on the way, but her mother reassures her that she will simply add another room to her heart. (Rev: SLJ 4/07)

3284 Jagtenberg, Yvonne. *Jack's Kite* (K–2). Illus. by author. 2004, Roaring Brook LB $22.90 (978-0-7613-2904-6). Jack has a kite but he is waiting — and waiting — for his father to come and show him how to fly it. (Rev: HB 1/05; SLJ 2/05)

3285 James, Simon. *Nurse Clementine* (PS–1). Illus. by author. 2013, Candlewick $15.99 (978-0-7636-6382-7). 40pp. Everyone in the family (even the dog) cooperates with young Clementine's desire to practice bandaging and other first aid skills, except her little brother Tommy. Lexile AD390 (Rev: BL 3/15/13; HB 5–6/13; SLJ 5/13)

3286 Jenkins, Emily. *Daffodil* (PS–2). Illus. by Tomek Bogacki. 2004, Farrar $16.00 (978-0-374-31676-1). Rose, Violet, and Daffodil are triplets, and their mother likes to dress them in clothes that match their names until Daffodil rebels and the trio finally get to choose their own clothes. (Rev: BL 3/15/04; HB 5/04; SLJ 5/04)

3287 Jenkins, Emily. *Daffodil, Crocodile* (PS–2). Illus. by Tomek Bogacki. 2007, Farrar $16.00 (978-0-374-39944-3). 32pp. Tired of being lumped into a category with her sisters, Daffodil dons a handmade crocodile head and enjoys a day of wild individuality and self-expression; a sequel to *Daffodil* (2004). (Rev: BCCB 6/07; BL 5/15/07; HB 5/07; SLJ 7/07)

3288 Jenkins, Emily. *Five Creatures* (PS–K). Illus. by Tomek Bogacki. 2001, Farrar $16.00 (978-0-374-32341-7). 32pp. Child-like drawings are used in this book that describes the everyday activities of a family and their two cats in an entertaining format that is also an exercise in reasoning. (Rev: BCCB 2/01; BL 3/15/01*; HB 3/01*; HBG 10/01)

3289 Johnson, Angela. *The Aunt in Our House* (PS–3). Illus. by David Soman. 1996, Orchard LB $16.99 (978-0-531-08852-4). An aunt brings new life and interesting talents during a visit to her brother's biracial family. (Rev: BL 3/1/96; SLJ 4/96)

3290 Johnson, Angela. *Lottie Paris Lives Here* (PS–K). Illus. by Scott M. Fischer. 2011, Simon & Schuster $16.99 (978-0-689-87377-5). 32pp. Follows a day in the life of an imaginative young African American girl who lives with her Papa Pete. e (Rev: BL 8/11; SLJ 8/1/11)

3291 Johnson, Angela. *One of Three* (PS–K). Illus. by David Soman. 1991, Orchard paper $6.99 (978-0-531-07061-1). A young African American girl remembers the good times growing up with two older sisters. (Rev: BL 7/91; SLJ 10/91)

3292 Johnson, Angela. *The Wedding* (K–2). Illus. by David Soman. 1999, Orchard LB $17.99 (978-0-531-33139-2). Through the eyes of young Daisy, the reader experiences all the excitement of the preparations for her sister's wedding. (Rev: BCCB 3/99; HBG 10/99; SLJ 3/99)

3293 Johnson, Angela. *When I Am Old with You* (PS–2). Illus. by David Soman. 1990, Orchard LB $16.99 (978-0-531-08484-7); paper $6.95 (978-0-531-07035-2). 32pp. A young African American boy daydreams of all the things he and his grandfather can do when the youngster grows older. (Rev: BL 9/1/90; SLJ 9/90*)

3294 Johnson, Dolores. *Grandma's Hands* (1–3). Illus. by author. 1998, Marshall Cavendish $15.95 (978-0-7614-5025-2). Initially unhappy at having to live with his grandmother on her farm, a young African American boy grows to love her and her home. (Rev: HBG 10/98; SLJ 5/98)

3295 Johnson, Lindan Lee. *The Dream Jar* (PS–2). Illus. by Serena Curmi. 2005, Houghton $16.00 (978-0-618-17698-4). With the help of her older sister, a young girl learns the secret of transforming nightmares into pleasant dreams. (Rev: BL 12/1/05; SLJ 12/05)

3296 Johnston, Tony. *My Abuelita* (1–3). Illus. by Yuyi Morales. 2009, Harcourt $16 (978-015216330-3). 32pp. With many Spanish words sprinkled throughout, a boy

and his mother prepare for her day and job as a storyteller. (Rev: BL 8/09; LMC 5–6/10; SLJ 8/1/09)

3297 Johnston, Tony. *Uncle Rain Cloud* (PS–3). Illus. by Fabricio Vandenbroeck. 2001, Charlesbridge $15.95 (978-0-88106-371-4). A touching picture about Carlos' cranky Uncle Tomas who becomes animated and happy only when telling stories about his homeland, Mexico, and its culture. (Rev: BL 2/15/01*; HBG 10/01)

3298 Joosse, Barbara. *Sleepover at Gramma's House* (PS–1). Illus. by Jan Jutte. 2010, Philomel $17.99 (978-0-399-25261-7). 40pp. A little elephant packs her trunk and heads to her grandmother's cottage in the country, where the two have a delightful sleepover. (Rev: BL 5/1/10*; SLJ 6/1/10)

3299 Joosse, Barbara M. *Grandma Calls Me Beautiful* (PS–2). Illus. by Barbara Lavallee. 2008, Chronicle $16.99 (978-0-8118-5815-1). A Hawaiian grandmother tells her granddaughter how much she is loved; a glossary defines Hawaiian words and the illustrations evoke island life. (Rev: BL 6/1–15/08; SLJ 6/08)

3300 Joosse, Barbara M. *I Love You the Purplest* (PS–1). Illus. by Mary Whyte. 1996, Chronicle $15.95 (978-0-8118-0718-0). 32pp. Two young brothers compete for the attention of their mother, who demonstrates that she loves them equally. (Rev: BL 10/15/96; SLJ 5/97)

3301 Joosse, Barbara M. *Mama, Do You Love Me?* (PS–2). Illus. by Barbara Lavallee. 1991, Chronicle $14.95 (978-0-87701-759-2). An Eskimo girl asks her mother if she will still be loved even when she is naughty. (Rev: BCCB 12/91; HB 11/91; SLJ 11/91)

3302 Joosse, Barbara M. *Papa, Do You Love Me?* (PS–2). Illus. by Barbara Lavallee. 2005, Chronicle $15.95 (978-0-8118-4265-5). 32pp. A Maasai father happily repeats expressions of unconditional love for his son. (Rev: BL 7/05; SLJ 8/05)

3303 Jukes, Mavis. *Like Jake and Me* (2–3). Illus. by Lloyd Bloom. 1987, Knopf paper $7.99 (978-0-394-89263-4). Alex and his stepfather explore the meaning of fear.

3304 Juster, Norton. *The Hello, Goodbye Window* (PS–2). Illus. by Chris Raschka. 2005, Hyperion $15.95 (978-0-7868-0914-1). A little girl enjoys visiting Nanna and Poppy's house and looking out their special window. Caldecott Medal, 2006. (Rev: BL 3/15/05; SLJ 3/05)

3305 Katz, Karen. *Princess Baby* (PS–1). Illus. by author. 2008, Random $14.99 (978-0-375-84119-4). A little girl prefers to be addressed with her proper title, not silly names like "Buttercup" and "Cupcake." (Rev: BL 1/1–15/08; SLJ 3/08)

3306 Keane, Dave. *Daddy Adventure Day* (PS–1). Illus. by Sue Ramá. 2011, Philomel $15.99 (978-0-399-24627-2). 32pp. A patient father and his overeager son share a day at the baseball stadium. Lexile AD680L (Rev: BL 2/15/11; SLJ 3/1/11)

3307 Keller, Holly. *Miranda's Beach Day* (PS–K). Illus. by author. 2009, HarperCollins $17.99 (978-0-06-158298-1). Miranda and her Mom spend a happy day at the beach in this simple, reassuring story. (Rev: BL 4/1/09; SLJ 4/09)

3308 Kennedy, Frances. *The Just-Right, Perfect Present* (K–3). Illus. by Sheila Aldridge. 2007, Tricycle $14.95 (978-1-58246-199-1). After Donna's nasty cousin steals her choice of poem to read at their grandparents' anniversary celebration, Donna's family pitches in so she can learn another poem, which turns out to be even better. (Rev: BL 7/07; LMC 11/07; SLJ 11/07)

3309 Khan, Rukhsana. *Big Red Lollipop* (PS–2). Illus. by Sophie Blackall. 2010, Viking $16.99 (978-0-670-06287-4). 40pp. Pakistani American Rubina knows how to act in her new country but it's difficult to persuade her mother to adopt new customs. Charlotte Zolotow Award. (Rev: BL 2/1/10*; SLJ 3/1/10)

3310 Kleven, Elisa. *Cozy Light, Cozy Night* (PS–1). Illus. by author. 2013, Creston $16.99 (978-1-939547-02-6). 32pp. This gentle book full of vivid watercolor images takes readers through the four seasons and emphasizes the coziness of family life. (Rev: BLO 11/15/13; SLJ 9/13)

3311 Knister. *Sophie's Dance* (K–3). Illus. by Mandy Schlunt. 2007, Penguin $16.99 (978-0-698-40056-6). 32pp. Sophie and her grandma dance the night away in this enjoyable, carefree book. (Rev: BL 6/1–15/07)

3312 Knowlton, Laurie Lazzaro. *A Young Man's Dance* (K–3). Illus. by Layne Johnson. 2006, Boyds Mills $15.95 (978-1-59078-259-0). Now that his beloved grandmother has been institutionalized with Alzheimer's disease, her young grandson is reluctant to visit her, but he discovers that although the old woman no longer remembers much about her earlier life she still loves to dance. (Rev: SLJ 4/06)

3313 Krishnaswami, Uma. *Bringing Asha Home* (1–3). Illus. by Jamel Akib. 2006, Lee & Low $16.95 (978-1-58430-259-9). 32pp. Arun, a young Indian American boy, eagerly awaits the arrival of a new sister, who is being adopted from his father's native country of India. (Rev: BL 10/15/06; SLJ 11/06)

3314 Krosoczka, Jarrett J. *Giddy Up, Cowgirl* (PS–K). Illus. 2006, Viking $15.99 (978-0-670-06050-4). Lively illustrations add to the humor of this story about a little girl who is determined to help her mother and the often less-than-helpful results. (Rev: BL 1/1–15/06; SLJ 2/06)

3315 Kurtz, Jane. *Faraway Home* (PS–3). Illus. by E. B. Lewis. 2000, Harcourt $16.00 (978-0-15-200036-3). 32pp. In this moving family story, a young African American girl has to adjust to the fact that her father must return home to Ethiopia to care for his sick mother. (Rev: BCCB 5/00; BL 2/15/00*; HBG 10/00; SLJ 4/00)

3316 Kurtz, Jane. *In the Small, Small Night* (PS–2). Illus. by Rachel Isadora. 2005, Greenwillow LB $17.89 (978-0-06-623813-5). 32pp. Abena tells her little brother, Kofi, stories from Ghana, their homeland, to help him fall asleep and to calm his fears about adjusting to their new country. (Rev: BL 3/15/05; SLJ 2/05)

3317 LaChanze. *Little Diva* (PS–2). Illus. by Brian Pinkney. 2010, Feiwel & Friends $16.99 (978-0-312-37010-7). 32pp. Likable, determined Nena dreams of a Broadway career like her mother's and works hard to achieve it in this picture book with detailed illustrations and a CD of the author singing and reading. (Rev: BL 3/15/10; LMC 5–6/10; SLJ 3/1/10)

3318 LaMarche, Jim. *Up* (PS–3). 2006, Chronicle $16.95 (978-0-8118-4445-1). A magical tale about a boy who discovers he has a special power (levitation) and uses it to prove to his father and older brother that he's big and can be a fisherman too. (Rev: BL 11/15/06)

3319 Laminack, Lester L. *Saturdays and Teacakes* (PS–2). Illus. by Chris Soentpiet. 2004, Peachtree $16.95 (978-1-56145-303-0). 32pp. In this nostalgic tale set in 1960s Alabama, a boy rides his bicycle to his grandmother's house, where he mows the lawn and enjoys her teacakes. (Rev: BL 4/1/04; SLJ 4/04)

3320 Laminack, Lester L. *The Sunsets of Miss Olivia Wiggins* (K–4). Illus. by Constance R. Bergum. 1998, Peachtree $15.95 (978-1-56145-139-5). 32pp. Although it appears that Miss Olivia Wiggins, an Alzheimer's disease sufferer, does recognize her daughter and great-grandson when they visit her at a nursing home, inwardly she is recalling pleasant times from the past. (Rev: BL 5/1/98; HBG 10/98; SLJ 7/98)

3321 Landolf, Diane Wright. *What a Good Big Brother!* (PS–K). Illus. by Steve Johnson. 2009, Random $16.99 (978-0-375-84258-0). 40pp. There's a new little sister in the house and only helpful Cameron has the magic to soothe the crying baby. (Rev: BL 2/1/09; SLJ 2/09)

3322 Langley, Karen. *Shine* (K–2). Illus. by Jonathan Langley. 2002, Marshall Cavendish $15.95 (978-0-7614-5127-3). Jimmy worries that his busy father won't come to see him as the star of Bethlehem. (Rev: HBG 3/03; SLJ 1/03)

3323 Larsen, Andrew. *The Imaginary Garden* (PS–1). Illus. by Irene Luxbacher. 2009, Kids Can $16.95 (978-1-55453-279-7). 32pp. Theodora's grandfather has moved to an apartment and no longer has a garden, so he and Theo decide to create an imaginary one, starting with a stone wall painted on a large canvas. (Rev: BL 3/15/09; SLJ 3/09)

3324 Lasky, Kathryn. *Before I Was Your Mother* (PS–2). Illus. by LeUyen Pham. 2003, Harcourt $16.00 (978-0-15-201464-3). 40pp. Ruby's mother tells Ruby tales about her own childhood and her friends and activities. (Rev: BL 3/15/03; HBG 10/03; SLJ 5/03)

3325 Lawler, Janet. *A Father's Song* (PS). Illus. by Lucy Corvino. 2006, Sterling $12.95 (978-1-4027-2501-2). 24pp. In rhyming verse, a father expresses love for his son as the two spend a day together in the park. (Rev: BL 3/1/06; SLJ 3/06)

3326 Lawler, Janet. *A Mother's Song* (PS–K). Illus. by Kathleen Kemly. 2010, Sterling $14.95 (978-1-4027-6968-9). 24pp. A rhyming verse companion to 2006's *A Father's Song*, in which a mother encourages her daughter to enjoy nature's wonders throughout the seasons. (Rev: BL 5/1/10; SLJ 6/1/10)

3327 Lears, Laurie. *Megan's Birthday Tree: A Story About Open Adoption* (K–3). Illus. by Bill Farnsworth. 2005, Whitman $15.95 (978-0-8075-5036-6). 32pp. Megan worries that she will be forgotten when her birth mother, Kendra, moves to a new house, but she is reassured that they will still see one another. (Rev: BL 3/1/05; SLJ 6/05)

3328 Lee, Spike, and Tonya Lewis Lee. *Please, Baby, Please* (K–2). Illus. by Kadir Nelson. 2002, Simon & Schuster $16.95 (978-0-689-83233-8). 32pp. An appealing picture book by movie director Spike Lee and his producer wife that shows a mother continually pleading with her toddler to behave, until at bedtime it's the little one who begs for a goodnight kiss. (Rev: BCCB 2/03; BL 12/1/02; HBG 3/03; SLJ 12/02)

3329 Leijten, Aileen. *Hugging Hour!* (PS–2). Illus. by author. 2009, Philomel $15.99 (978-0-399-24680-7). 32pp. Drew (or "Drool") is nervous about spending the night at Grandma's house for the first time. (Rev: BCCB 1/09; BL 2/1/09)

3330 Lester, J. D. *Mommy Calls Me Monkeypants* (PS–K). Illus. by Hiroe Nakata. 2009, Robin Corey $7.99 (978-0-375-84502-4). A lighthearted board-book exploration of affectionate nicknames. (Rev: BLO 4/24/09; SLJ 3/09)

3331 Leuck, Laura. *I Love My Pirate Papa* (PS–2). Illus. by Kyle M. Stone. 2007, Harcourt $16.00 (978-0-15-205664-3). 32pp. A little boy tells of his life aboard ship with his pirate father. (Rev: BL 9/15/07; SLJ 9/07)

3332 Levine, Abby. *Daddies Give You Horsey Rides* (PS–1). Illus. by John Bendall-Brunello. 2004, Whitman $16.95 (978-0-8075-1429-0). 32pp. Animal fathers display the varied ways in which they add value to their children's lives in this simple book with a lively rhyme and humorous illustrations. (Rev: BL 3/15/04; SLJ 5/04)

3333 Levine, Arthur A. *Monday Is One Day* (PS–1). Illus. by Julian Hector. 2011, Scholastic $16.99 (978-0-439-78924-0). 32pp. This book celebrates all the ways in which working parents can enjoy time with their children during the week, while anticipating the joy of the weekend. (Rev: BL 2/1/11*; SLJ 4/11)

3334 Lin, Grace. *Kite Flying* (K–3). 2002, Knopf $14.95 (978-0-375-81520-1). A Chinese girl describes the family ritual of making and flying kites. (Rev: BL 6/1–15/02; HBG 10/02; SLJ 7/02)

3335 Lin, Grace. *The Ugly Vegetables* (K–2). Illus. 1999, Charlesbridge LB $16.95 (978-0-88106-336-3). 32pp. A Chinese American girl is disappointed in the dullness of her family garden compared with the lovely flowers she sees in other gardens — until harvest time when her mother makes a delicious soup from all the unusual Chinese vegetables. (Rev: BL 9/15/99; HB 9/99; HBG 3/00; SLJ 9/99)

3336 Lindahl, Inger. *Bertil and the Bathroom Elephants* (PS–K). Trans. from Swedish by Elisabeth Kallick Dyssegaard. Illus. by Eva Lindstrom. 2003, R&S $15.00 (91-29-65944-2). Three-year-old Bertil starts to believe that his invented elephants really do exist under the bathtub and refuses to use the bathroom at all. (Rev: HB 9/03; HBG 4/04; SLJ 12/03)

3337 Lloyd-Jones, Sally. *How to Be a Baby — By Me, the Big Sister* (K–3). Illus. by Sue Heap. 2007, Random $15.99 (978-0-375-83843-9). An older sister lists the many, many things that babies can't do before realizing that there are a few benefits to babies as well. (Rev: BCCB 4/07; BL 11/15/06*; HB 1/07; HBG 10/07; SLJ 2/07)

3338 Lloyd, Jennifer. *Looking for Loons* (PS–2). Illus. by Kirsti Anne Wakelin. 2007, Simply Read $16.95 (978-1-894965-54-5). 32pp. A family gathers one by one on the front porch to watch for the loons arriving on the lake. (Rev: BL 2/15/08; SLJ 1/08)

3339 Lo, Ginnie. *Mahjong All Day Long* (PS–2). Illus. by Beth Lo. 2005, Walker LB $17.85 (978-0-8027-8942-6). 32pp. The game of mahjong is important in a Chinese family's rituals and enjoyment of life. (Rev: BL 2/15/05; SLJ 5/05)

3340 Londner, Renee. *Stones for Grandpa* (K–3). Illus. by Martha Aviles. 2013, Lerner/Kar-Ben $17.95 (978-0-7613-7495-4); paper $7.95 (978-0-7613-7-496-1). 24pp. A year after Grandpa's death, a little boy's Jewish family gathers at the cemetery for a dedication ceremony. (Rev: BLO 4/1/13; LMC 10/13; SLJ 5/13)

3341 Long, Kathy. *Christopher Sat Straight Up in Bed* (PS–1). Illus. by Patricia Cantor. 2013, Eerdmans $16 (978-0-8028-5359-2). 33pp. A loud "Honk-shoo!" wakes young Christopher while staying at his grandparents' house, and he gets up to investigate — is it an elephant? a monster? a dinosaur? (Rev: BL 4/1/13; SLJ 4/13)

3342 Look, Lenore. *Uncle Peter's Amazing Chinese Wedding* (K–2). Illus. by Yumi Heo. 2006, Simon & Schuster $16.95 (978-0-689-84458-4). As her Chinese American family prepares for Peter's wedding, Jenny worries she will lose her special relationship with her uncle. (Rev: BCCB 1/06; BL 12/15/05*; HBG 10/06; LMC 8/06; SLJ 1/06)

3343 Lopez, Susana. *The Best Family in the World* (PS–3). Illus. by Ulises Wensell. 2010, Kane/Miller $15.99 (978-1-935279-47-1). 28pp. Young Carlota prepares to meet her adoptive parents, imagining the most exciting possibilities. (Rev: BL 4/1/10; LMC 8–9/10; SLJ 5/1/10)

3344 Lord, Janet. *Here Comes Grandma!* (PS–K). Illus. by Julie Paschkis. 2005, Holt $12.95 (978-0-8050-7666-0). 32pp. A grandmother goes to great lengths to visit her beloved grandchild. (Rev: BL 10/1/05; SLJ 9/05)

3345 Louie, Therese On. *Raymond's Perfect Present* (K–2). Illus. by Suling Wang. 2002, Lee & Low $16.95 (978-1-58430-055-7). 32pp. A tender story about a boy who can't afford flowers for his sick mother, but instead plants seeds. (Rev: BL 10/15/02; HBG 3/03; SLJ 11/02)

3346 Luthardt, Kevin. *Flying* (PS–1). Illus. by author. 2009, Peachtree $15.95 (978-1-56145-430-3). 32pp. "Why can't I fly?" asks a little African American boy, and he and his father set off on an imaginative trip. (Rev: BL 3/15/09; SLJ 4/09)

3347 Lyon, George E. *No Dessert Forever!* (PS–K). Illus. by Peter Catalanotto. 2006, Simon & Schuster $16.95 (978-1-4169-0385-7). 40pp. A young girl vents her frustrations with life through discussions with her doll; the brief text is amplified by the realistic, warm watercolors. (Rev: BL 11/1/06; SLJ 12/06)

3348 Lyons, Kelly Starling. *Tea Cakes for Tosh* (PS–3). Illus. by E. B. Lewis. 2012, Putnam $16.99 (978-039925213-6). 32pp. As he spends time with his grandmother baking tea cakes, young Tosh hears story of his family's history back to the days of slavery. Lexile 780 (Rev: BL 2/1/13; LMC 1–2/13*; SLJ 11/12)

3349 McAllister, Angela. *My Mom Has X-Ray Vision* (K–2). Illus. by Alex T. Smith. 2011, ME Media paper $7.95 (978-1-58925-428-2). 32pp. Matthew's mother always knows what he's doing — but how does she do it? Matthew decides to investigate. (Rev: BL 5/1/11; SLJ 4/11)

3350 McCloskey, Robert. *One Morning in Maine* (1–3). Illus. by author. 1952, Puffin paper $6.99 (978-0-14-050174-2). An exciting day, the loss of Sal's first tooth, is realistically recaptured by this fine storyteller and in the large, extraordinary blue-pencil drawings of Penobscot Bay. Also use: *Blueberries for Sal* (1948).

3351 McConnell, Sarah. *Don't Mention Pirates* (PS–2). Illus. by author. 2006, Barron's $14.99 (978-0-7641-5945-9). Although the Silver family has renounced its pirate past, it quickly reconsiders matters after young Scarlet discovers some buried gold. (Rev: SLJ 8/06)

3352 McCormack, Caren McNelly. *The Fiesta Dress: A Quinceañera Tale* (K–2). Illus. by Martha Aviles. 2009, Marshall Cavendish $17.99 (978-0-7614-5467-0). 40pp. Little Lolo, used to being the center of attention, is feeling neglected on her older sister's 15th birthday, but when her dog steals Eva's white sash it's Lolo who is suddenly in the forefront. (Rev: BCCB 5/09; BLO 3/5/09; SLJ 3/09)

3353 McCormick, Wendy. *The Night You Were Born* (PS–2). Illus. by Sophy Williams. 2000, Peachtree $15.95 (978-1-56145-225-5). 32pp. While waiting for news of the arrival of a sibling, Jamie listens to a story about the night he was born. (Rev: BL 1/1–15/01; HBG 3/01; SLJ 12/00)

3354 McDonald, Rae A. *A Fishing Surprise* (PS–2). Illus. by Kathleen Kemly. 2007, NorthWord $16.95 (978-1-55971-977-3). 32pp. A quiet summer day of fishing unexpectedly ends with an apple pie. (Rev: SLJ 10/07)

3355 McDonnell, Christine. *Goyangi Means Cat* (PS–2). Illus. by Steve Johnson. 2011, Viking $16.99 (978-0-670-01179-7). 32pp. An adopted Korean girl finds life in America bewildering but bonds with the family cat. (Rev: BL 5/1/11; SLJ 7/11*)

3356 McElroy, Lisa. *Love, Lizzie: Letters to a Military Mom* (1–3). Illus. by Diane Paterson. 2005, Albert Whitman $16.99 (978-0-8075-4777-9). 32pp. In letters to her mom, a soldier serving overseas, young Lizzie describes her life — the good things and the bad — and includes maps that show details of key events. (Rev: BL 9/1/05; SLJ 10/05)

3357 McGhee, Alison. *Little Boy* (PS–K). Illus. by Peter H. Reynolds. 2008, Atheneum $15.99 (978-1-4169-5872-7). 40pp. "Your yellow cup . . . your big cardboard box" and "a puddle to jump/sand to dump" — these are a few of the things a father appreciates in his son's life in this poetic reflection illustrated with images of a lively child. (Rev: BL 6/1–15/08; LMC 5/08; SLJ 6/08)

3358 MacK, Todd. *Princess Penelope Takes Charge!* (PS–2). Illus. by Julia Gran. 2006, Scholastic $16.99 (978-0-439-67380-8). Penelope wanted a baby sister and is not very excited when Dexter arrives instead, until she decides to welcome him into her personal kingdom. (Rev: SLJ 6/06)

3359 McKay, Hilary. *Lulu and the Cat in the Bag* (2–4). Illus. by Priscilla Lamont. 2013, Whitman $13.99 (978-080754804-2). 112pp. Lulu's grandmother isn't pleased when a large orange cat is found in a bag on their doorstep, but Lulu is determined to welcome the newcomer. Lexile 670 (Rev: BL 7/13; SLJ 2/14)

3360 Macken, JoAnn Early. *Baby Says "Moo!"* (PS). Illus. by David Walker. 2011, Hyperion/Disney $15.99 (978-1-4231-3400-8). Unpaged. Out in the car with her family, Baby constantly answers questions about various animals' sounds with "Moo!" (Rev: SLJ 3/1/11)

3361 McKenna, Sharon. *Good Morning, Sunshine: A Grandpa Story* (PS–1). 2007, Red Cygnet $17.95 (978-1-60108-003-5). 32pp. Grandpa's happy morning routine brightens his granddaughter's mood in this brightly illustrated picture book. (Rev: BL 5/1/07)

3362 Mackintosh, David. *The Frank Show* (K–2). Illus. by author. 2012, Abrams $16.95 (978-1-4197-0393-5). 32pp. A young boy's dread turns to surprise when his outwardly dull grandfather launches into an exciting story at show-and-tell; cartoon-style illustrations add to the humor. Lexile 780AD (Rev: BLO 8/12; LMC 5–6/13; SLJ 10/12)

3363 McKissack, Patricia C. *Stitchin' and Pullin': A Gee's Bend Quilt* (3–5). Illus. by Cozbi A. Cabrera. 2008, Random $17.99 (978-0-375-83163-8). 48pp. The free-verse story of a young African American girl choosing fabrics for her quilt draws in details of her personal history and heritage. (Rev: BL 12/15/08; HB 11/08; LMC 11/08; SLJ 11/08)

3364 MacLachlan, Patricia. *You Were the First* (PS). Illus. by Stephanie Graegin. 2013, Little, Brown $17 (978-031618533-2). 40pp. A young boy is told multiple times how he was the first child in the family to do many things, such as cry, smile, and crawl. (Rev: BL 9/15/13*; SLJ 9/13)

3365 MacLachlan, Patricia. *Your Moon, My Moon: A Grandmother's Words to a Faraway Child* (PS–2). Illus. by Bryan Collier. 2011, Simon & Schuster $16.99 (978-1-4169-7950-0). 32pp. A New England grandmother reflects on the bond she feels with her African grandchild in this evocative book about family bonds spanning great distances. (Rev: BL 8/11; SLJ 8/1/11)

3366 Maclear, Kyo. *Virginia Wolf* (K–2). Illus. by Isabelle Arsenault. 2012, Kids Can $16.95 (978-1-55453-649-8).

32pp. When young Virginia awakes "feeling wolfish," her sister Vanessa sets about creating a beautiful setting full of flowers and birds to cheer her up; inspired by the relationship between Virginia Woolf and her artist sibling. (Rev: BL 2/15/12; SLJ 4/1/12*)

3367 Macomber, Debbie, and Mary Lou Carney. *The Truly Terrible Horrible Sweater . . . That Grandma Knit* (PS–1). Illus. by Vincent Nguyen. 2009, HarperCollins $17.99 (978-006165093-2). 32pp. Cameron finally comes to appreciate the sweater his grandmother knitted for his birthday when she explains the importance of the pattern. ℮ (Rev: BLO 11/1/09; SLJ 11/09)

3368 McQuinn, Anna. *Lola Loves Stories* (PS–1). Illus. by Rosalind Beardshaw. 2010, Charlesbridge LB $15.95 (978-1-58089-258-2); paper $6.95 (978-1-58089-259-9). Unpaged. An African American girl gains inspiration from the stories her daddy reads her every night. ⌒ ℮ (Rev: SLJ 7/1/10*)

3369 Magenta, Emma. *Orlando on a Thursday* (PS–1). Illus. by author. 2010, Candlewick $15.99 (978-0-7636-4560-1). 32pp. Orlando's sad on Thursdays when his Mami goes to town, but his Papi keeps him happy and busy. (Rev: BL 9/1/10; SLJ 8/1/10)

3370 Mahoney, Daniel J. *A Really Good Snowman* (K–3). Illus. by author. 2005, Clarion $15.00 (978-0-618-47554-4). Happy to be free of his little sister Nancy for a while, Jack enters a snowman-building contest with two of his friends, but he quickly abandons this to come to her aid when older boys harass her. (Rev: SLJ 11/05)

3371 Mahy, Margaret. *A Busy Day for a Good Grandmother* (PS–3). Illus. by Margaret Chamberlain. 1993, Macmillan $14.95 (978-0-689-50595-9). 32pp. Mrs. Oberon is an unconventional grandmother who rides skateboards and fights vultures and alligators. (Rev: BL 10/15/93; SLJ 9/93)

3372 Makhijani, Pooja. *Mama's Saris* (PS–2). Illus. by Elena Gomez. 2007, Little, Brown $16.99 (978-0-316-01105-1). A young Indian American girl admires her mother's saris and wants to wear one herself. (Rev: BL 4/15/07)

3373 Manning, Mick, and Brita Granström. *Supermom* (PS–K). Illus. 2001, Whitman $16.99 (978-0-8075-7666-3). 32pp. Using both humans and animals as subjects, this book explores the many tasks that mothers perform. (Rev: BL 3/15/01; HBG 10/01)

3374 Manushkin, Fran. *How Mama Brought the Spring* (K–3). Illus. by Holly Berry. 2008, Dutton $16.99 (978-0-525-42027-9). 32pp. Mom gets a winter-weary Rosie out of her bed with the story of how the little girl's Russian Grandma brought spring to Mintz; includes a blintz recipe. (Rev: BCCB 2/08; BL 1/1–15/08; LMC 3/08; SLJ 1/08)

3375 Many, Paul. *Dad's Bald Head* (PS–2). Illus. by Kevin O'Malley. 2007, Walker $15.95 (978-0-8027-9579-3). Pete is a bit taken aback when his dad shaves his head (although Dad was already nearly bald) but slowly gets used to the new look. (Rev: SLJ 6/07)

3376 Manzano, Sonia. *A Box Full of Kittens* (PS–2). Illus. by Matt Phelan. 2007, Atheneum $16.99 (978-0-689-83089-1). Young Ruthie, aspiring superhero, feels confident of her ability to look after her pregnant aunt, but a box of kittens distract her attention. (Rev: BL 5/1/07; SLJ 8/07)

3377 Marshall, Linda Elovitz. *The Mitzvah Magician* (PS–1). Illus. by Christiane Engel. 2012, Lerner/KarBen $17.95 (978-0-7613-5656-1); paper $7.95 (978-0-7613-5-655-4). 32pp. Gabriel's efforts to practice magic are not very successful until his mother tells him he must do things that make people happy. (Rev: BLO 10/15/12; SLJ 3/13)

3378 Martin, Jacqueline B. *The Water Gift and the Pig of the Pig* (K–2). Illus. by Linda S. Wingerter. 2003, Houghton $15.00 (978-0-618-07436-5). When the pig that is an important part of their family history disappears, Isabel discovers that — like her grandfather — she has the ability to locate precious things. (Rev: HB 5/03; HBG 10/03; SLJ 6/03)

3379 Matthies, Janna. *The Goodbye Cancer Garden* (1–3). Illus. by Kristi Valiant. 2011, Whitman $16.99 (978-0-8075-2994-2). 32pp. Janie and her brother decide to plant a garden to represent their mom's slow triumph over breast cancer. Lexile AD660L (Rev: BL 2/15/11; SLJ 2/1/11*)

3380 Mauner, Claudia, and Elisa Smalley. *Zoe Sophia's Scrapbook: An Adventure in Venice* (1–4). Illus. by Claudia Mauner. 2003, Chronicle $14.95 (978-0-8118-3606-7). Nine-year-old Zoe Sophia, accompanied by her dachshund Mickey, explores the wonders of Venice during a visit to her Great-Aunt Dorothy in this picture book for older readers using a diary format. (Rev: BL 5/15/03; HBG 10/03; SLJ 8/03)

3381 May, Kathy L. *Molasses Man* (PS–3). Illus. by Felicia Marshall. 2000, Holiday House $16.95 (978-0-8234-1438-3). 32pp. Seen through the eyes of a young African American boy, this is the story of how his family makes molasses under the supervision of Grandpa, the Molasses Man. (Rev: BL 10/1/00; HBG 3/01; SLJ 10/00)

3382 Mazer, Norma Fox. *Has Anyone Seen My Emily Greene?* (PS–1). Illus. by Christine Davenier. 2007, Candlewick $15.99 (978-0-7636-1384-6). 32pp. Little Emily Greene makes her dad play a boisterous game of hide-and-seek before she'll eat lunch. (Rev: BL 5/1/07; SLJ 6/07)

3383 Medina, Meg. *Tía Isa Wants a Car* (PS–2). Illus. by Claudio Muñoz. 2011, Candlewick $15.99 (978-0-7636-4156-6). 32pp. A young Latina girl helps save money for the car her aunt so badly wants to get to the beach that reminds her of her island home; also available in Spanish. Ezra Jack Keats New Writer Award. (Rev: BL 6/1/11; HB 7–8/11; SLJ 6/11)

3384 Melmed, Laura K. *A Hug Goes Around* (PS–k). Illus. by Betsy Lewin. 2002, HarperCollins LB $15.89 (978-0-688-14681-8). 32pp. In spite of minor disasters, a family muddles through because they can comfort each other with hugs. (Rev: BL 6/1–15/02)

3385 Meltzer, Amy. *A Mezuzah on the Door* (K–2). Illus. by Janice Fried. 2007, Kar-Ben $17.95 (978-1-58013-249-7); paper $7.95 (978-1-58013-251-0). 32pp. Noah is having trouble adjusting to his new home in the suburbs, but he feels much better after they celebrate Hanukkat Habayit and he and his old friends touch the mezuzah. (Rev: BL 11/1/07; SLJ 10/07)

3386 Mennen, Ingrid. *One Round Moon and a Star for Me* (PS–1). Illus. by Niki Daly. 1994, Orchard LB $16.99 (978-0-531-08654-4). In this tale that takes place in Lesotho, a young boy needs reassurance when a new baby arrives in the family. (Rev: BCCB 4/94; BL 2/15/94; SLJ 9/94)

3387 Meserve, Jessica. *Can Anybody Hear Me?* (1–3). Illus. by author. 2008, Clarion $16.00 (978-0-547-02834-7). 32pp. Jack is too quiet to get much attention in his rambunctious family and nobody pays attention to him when he says he's going up the mountain; only when he becomes lost and calls for help does his family finally hear him. (Rev: SLJ 11/08)

3388 Meserve, Jessica. *Small Sister* (PS–2). Illus. by author. 2007, Clarion $16.00 (978-0-618-77658-0). A little sister seems a little bigger when she rescues her big sister's pet parrot. (Rev: SLJ 6/07)

3389 Michelson, Richard. *Oh No, Not Ghosts!* (1–3). Illus. by Adam McCauley. 2006, Harcourt $16.00 (978-0-15-205186-0). 44pp. As a boy and his little sister try to settle down to sleep, the brother teasingly escalates all the horrors they might face — ghosts, demons, goblins, giants, and skeletons. (Rev: SLJ 8/06)

3390 Michelson, Richard. *Too Young for Yiddish* (K–4). Illus. by Neil Waldman. 2002, Charlesbridge $15.95 (978-0-88106-118-5). 32pp. A young boy wants his grandfather to teach him the Yiddish language in this poignant tale that is part history, part family story. (Rev: BL 3/1/02; HBG 10/02; SLJ 3/02)

3391 Miller, William. *Zora Hurston and the Chinaberry Tree* (PS–3). Illus. by Cornelius Van Wright and Ying-Hwa Hu. 1994, Lee & Low $15.95 (978-1-880000-14-4); paper $6.99 (978-1-880000-33-5). 32pp. A picture book that explores the trauma experienced by the author Zora Hurston when her beloved mother died when the girl was only nine. (Rev: BL 10/15/94; SLJ 12/94) [813]

3392 Milord, Susan. *Love That Baby!* (PS). Illus. 2005, Houghton $7.95 (978-0-618-56323-4). This delightful lift-the-flap book celebrates the interaction between babies and their parents. (Rev: BL 10/1/05; SLJ 11/05)

3393 Mitchell, Rhonda. *The Talking Cloth* (PS–2). Illus. 1997, Orchard LB $16.99 (978-0-531-33004-3). 32pp. When Amber drapes her aunt's cloth from Ghana around herself, she pretends she is an Ashanti princess. (Rev: BCCB 6/97; BL 2/15/97; SLJ 7/97)

3394 Monk, Isabell. *Blackberry Stew* (PS–2). Illus. by Janice L. Porter. 2005, Carolrhoda $15.95 (978-1-57505-605-0). 32pp. Hope learns that she can keep her grandfather alive in her memory in this story of a warm African American family. (Rev: BL 2/1/05; SLJ 6/05)

3395 Monk, Isabell. *Family* (PS–2). Illus. by Janice L. Porter. 2001, Carolrhoda $15.95 (978-1-57505-485-8). 32pp. Celebrates the fun and food of an African American family reunion (complete with recipes). (Rev: BL 2/15/01; HBG 10/01)

3396 Monk, Isabell. *Hope* (K–3). Illus. by Janice L. Porter. 1999, Carolrhoda LB $15.95 (978-1-57505-230-4). Hope's great aunt Poogee tells the little girl that she should be proud of her biracial background and that her white father and African American mother represent two important cultures. (Rev: HBG 10/99; SLJ 6/99)

3397 Montanari, Eva. *Tiff, Taff, and Lulu* (K–2). Illus. by author. 2004, Houghton $16.00 (978-0-618-40238-0). Three monster sisters put aside their differences when their mother is injured in an accident. (Rev: SLJ 9/04)

3398 Moore-Mallinos, Jennifer. *Mom Has Cancer!* (K–2). Illus. by Marta Fàbrega. 2008, Barron's paper $6.99 (978-0-7641-4074-7). 32pp. Here is a straightforward and comforting look at a little boy's struggles to cope when his mother is sick. (Rev: SLJ 5/09)

3399 Mora, Pat. *Let's Eat! / ¡A Comer!* (PS–2). Illus. by Maribel Suárez. Series: My Family / Mi familia. 2008, HarperCollins $12.99 (978-0-06-085038-8). 24pp. In English and Spanish, a family gathers to enjoy a meal together. (Rev: BL 4/1/08; SLJ 4/08)

3400 Mora, Pat. *Pablo's Tree* (PS–3). Illus. by Cecily Lang. 1994, Macmillan paper $16.00 (978-0-02-767401-9). 32pp. Ever since his daughter adopted young Pablo, grandfather decorates a tree on the anniversary of the boy's arrival. (Rev: BCCB 9/94; BL 11/1/94; HB 11/94)

3401 Morris, Richard. *Bye-Bye, Baby!* (PS). Illus. by Larry Day. 2009, Walker $16.99 (978-0-8027-9772-8). 40pp. Felix does not adjust well to the arrival of his baby sister and fantasizes about grim ends for her. (Rev: BL 9/15/09; SLJ 11/1/09*)

3402 Morrison, Toni, and Slade Morrison. *Peeny Butter Fudge* (K–1). Illus. by Joe Cepeda. 2009, Simon & Schuster $16.99 (978-1-4169-8332-3). 32pp. Three happy children spend the day with their grandmother who disregards their mother's strict list and instead provides many fun activities culminating in the making of fudge, which softens the mother's attitude when the smell reminds her of long ago. (Rev: BL 7/09; SLJ 9/09)

3403 Moser, Lisa. *Watermelon Wishes* (K–2). Illus. by Stacey Schuett. 2006, Clarion $16.00 (978-0-618-56433-0). 32pp. In this appealing story, a young boy and his grandfather spend the summer tending a watermelon patch they planted together, and the boy hopes to harvest one very special melon that will grant him a wish: to spend another summer of fun with his granddad. (Rev: SLJ 12/06)

3404 Napoli, Donna Jo. *The Wishing Club: A Story About Fractions* (1–3). Illus. by Anna Currey. 2007, Holt $16.95 (978-0-8050-7665-3). 32pp. Wishing upon a star, four siblings use fractions to work out how to get the pet they want. (Rev: BL 6/1–15/07; LMC 1/08; SLJ 9/07)

3405 Nelson, Vaunda Micheaux. *Who Will I Be, Lord?* (PS–2). Illus. by Sean Qualls. 2009, Random House

$16.99 (978-0-375-84342-6); LB $19.99 (978-0-375-94342-3). Unpaged. A young African American girl looking to create her future looks to the lives of her older relatives and ancestors for inspiration. (Rev: BL 11/15/09; HB 11–12/09; SLJ 10/1/09)

3406 Neubecker, Robert. *Winter Is for Snow* (PS–1). Illus. by author. 2013, Disney/Hyperion $16.99 (978-142317831-6). 32pp. A young boy loves winter, but his sister can't stand the cold weather, and it is up to him to show her how wonderful the season can be with a little imagination. Lexile AD270 (Rev: BL 11/1/13; SLJ 9/13)

3407 Nevius, Carol. *Building with Dad* (PS–2). Illus. by Bill Thomson. 2006, Marshall Cavendish $16.99 (978-0-7614-5312-3). 32pp. Eye-catching vertical spreads illustrate this story about a young boy who accompanies his contractor dad to the construction site of a new school. (Rev: BL 9/1/06; SLJ 10/06)

3408 Newman, Lesléa. *Daddy, Papa, and Me* (PS). Illus. by Carol Thompson. 2009, Tricycle $7.99 (978-1-58246-262-2). Unpaged. Two fathers and their child enjoy a day full of fun in this board book. Also use *Mommy, Mama, and Me* (2009). (Rev: HB 5–6/09; SLJ 11/1/09)

3409 Newman, Lesléa. *Donovan's Big Day* (PS–2). Illus. by Mike Dutton. 2011, Tricycle $15.99 (978-1-58246-332-2). 32pp. A young boy feels proud and a little nervous about his upcoming role as ring bearer in his two moms' wedding. Lexile AD1540L (Rev: BL 4/1/11; SLJ 4/11)

3410 Newman, Lesléa. *Felicia's Favorite Story* (PS–1). Illus. by Adriana Romo. 2003, Two Lives paper $9.95 (978-0-9674468-5-1). Felicia, who was born in Guatemala, loves to hear her adoptive parents — two women — tell her how she came to be a member of their family. (Rev: SLJ 10/03)

3411 Newman, Marjorie. *Just Like Me* (PS). Illus. by Ken Wilson-Max. 2006, Walker $15.95 (978-0-8027-8080-5). Tom resents his new baby brother because the infant is suddenly the center of attention, but when his parents explain that the baby will grow up just as he has, the older boy accepts his role as big brother. (Rev: SLJ 4/06)

3412 Newman, Nanette. *What Will You Be, Grandma?* (PS–2). Illus. by Emma Chichester Clark. 2012, Candlewick $15.99 (978-076366099-4). 32pp. Lily speculates about the roles her grandmother can play when she grows up. (Rev: BLO 9/15/12)

3413 Nichols, Grace. *Whoa, Baby, Whoa!* (PS). Illus. by Eleanor Taylor. 2012, Bloomsbury $15.99 (978-159990742-0). 32pp. A baby used to being warned not to do something hears a new cry — "Go, Baby, go!" — when he ventures to take a couple of upright steps. (Rev: BL 3/1/12)

3414 Nielsen-Fernlund, Susin. *Mormor Moves In* (PS–1). 2004, Orca $16.95 (978-1-55143-291-5). Astrid has a hard time adapting to the arrival of her bereaved Swedish grandmother. (Rev: SLJ 11/04)

3415 Nolen, Jerdine. *Pitching In for Eubie* (PS–2). Illus. by E. B. Lewis. 2007, HarperCollins $16.99 (978-0-688-14917-8). 32pp. Lily's older sister Eubie gets a scholarship to college, and Lily tries to find a way to contribute to her room and board like everyone else in the family; set in rural America, this is a warm family story. (Rev: BCCB 1/08; BL 10/15/07; SLJ 12/07)

3416 Norac, Carl. *My Daddy Is a Giant* (PS). Illus. by Ingrid Godon. 2005, Clarion $16.00 (978-0-618-44399-4). Eye-catching illustrations draw readers into this simple story of a boy who idolizes his father. (Rev: BL 6/1–15/05; SLJ 5/05)

3417 Norman, Geoffrey. *Stars Above Us* (K–3). Illus. by E. B. Lewis. 2009, Putnam $16.99 (978-0-399-24724-8). 32pp. A young girl, who used to be afraid of the dark, looks at the glowing stars her dad helped affix to her bedroom ceiling and thinks of him when he's away fighting in the military. (Rev: BL 9/15/09; LMC 11–12/09; SLJ 10/1/09)

3418 North, Sherry. *Because I Am Your Daddy* (PS). Illus. by Marcellus Hall. 2010, Abrams $15.95 (978-0-8109-8392-2). 32pp. Daddy is shown doing fanciful things — flying his daughter to school, building a high-tech tree house — in this simple book celebrating the love between parent and child. (Rev: BL 3/1/10; SLJ 4/1/10)

3419 North, Sherry. *Because You Are My Baby* (PS). Illus. by Marcellus Hall. 2008, Abrams $15.95 (978-0-8109-9482-9). 32pp. In rhythmic rhyming text, a mother describes the ways she would love her baby if she were a skywriter, a chef, a mountaineer, and so forth. (Rev: BL 4/1/08)

3420 Novak, Matt. *A Wish for You* (PS–K). Illus. by author. 2010, Greenwillow $16.99 (978-0-06-155202-1); LB $17.89 (978-006155203-8). 32pp. Two parents get ready for and celebrate the arrival of their new baby in this lively book that celebrates birth and family. (Rev: BL 1/1/10; SLJ 3/1/10)

3421 Numeroff, Laura. *What Brothers Do Best / What Sisters Do Best* (PS–K). Illus. by Lynn Munsinger. 2009, Chronicle $15.99 (978-0-8118-6545-6). Unpaged. This flip book celebrates all the good things about having a brother or sister. (Rev: BL 9/15/09; SLJ 12/1/09)

3422 Numeroff, Laura. *What Grandmas Do Best / What Grandpas Do Best* (PS–K). Illus. by Lynn Munsinger. 2000, Simon & Schuster $14.00 (978-0-689-80552-3). 40pp. This is an upside-down book that if read one way shows children happy with their grandmothers and, when turned over, shows similar scenes with grandfathers. (Rev: BL 11/15/00; HBG 3/01; SLJ 10/00)

3423 O'Brien, Anne Sibley. *A Path of Stars* (2–4). Illus. by author. 2012, Charlesbridge $15.95 (978-157091735-6). 40pp. Cambodian American Dara enjoys hearing her refugee grandmother's stories about the homeland, and offers comfort when she receives sad news about her brother, who still lived there. ℮ Lexile 780L (Rev: BL 3/1/12)

3424 O'Connor, Jane. *Ready, Set, Skip!* (PS–1). Illus. by Ann James. 2007, Viking $15.99 (978-0-670-06216-4). With help from her mother, a young girl finally learns how to skip. (Rev: BL 7/07; HB 5/07; SLJ 7/07)

3425 O'Connor, Jane. *The Snow Globe Family* (PS–2). Illus. by S. D. Schindler. 2006, Putnam $16.99 (978-0-399-24242-7). 40pp. Two families — a large one living in a house and a tiny one living on the mantelpiece within a snow globe — enjoy a winter storm. (Rev: BL 10/1/06; SLJ 12/06)

3426 O'Connor, Joe. *Where Did Daddy's Hair Go?* (PS–2). Illus. by Henry Payne. 2006, Random $14.95 (978-0-375-83571-1). Daddy has "lost" his hair. Where did it go? Did it hurt? Does it matter? (Rev: SLJ 4/06)

3427 Oelschlager, Vanita. *A Tale of Two Mommies* (PS–K). Illus. by Mike Blanc. 2011, Vanita $15.95 (978-098263666-4). 40pp. A young boy answers his friends' questions about living with two mommies. (Rev: BL 12/15/11)

3428 O'Hair, Margaret. *Star Baby* (PS). Illus. by Erin Eitter Kono. 2005, Clarion $16.00 (978-0-618-30668-8). 32pp. This gentle picture book chronicles in rhythmic rhyming text and soft acrylic artwork a day in the life of a mother and child. (Rev: BL 10/15/05; SLJ 10/05)

3429 O'Hair, Margaret. *Twin to Twin* (PS). Illus. by Thierry Courtin. 2003, Simon & Schuster $15.95 (978-0-689-84494-2). Toddler twins — brother and sister — are shown going about their daily lives in a friendly text and lively illustrations. (Rev: BL 6/1–15/03; HBG 10/03; SLJ 5/03)

3430 Ohi, Ruth. *And You Can Come Too* (PS–2). Illus. 2005, Annick $19.95 (978-1-55037-905-1); paper $5.95 (978-1-55037-904-4). After her father scolds her for squabbling with her little sister, Sara decides to run away from home but allows her younger sibling to come along, and Dad even helps with building a tent in the backyard. (Rev: BL 10/1/05)

3431 Ohi, Ruth. *Me and My Brother* (PS–1). Illus. by author. 2007, Annick LB $19.95 (978-1-55451-092-4); paper $5.95 (978-1-55451-091-7). 24pp. Warm and realistic, this rhyming book captures the ups and downs of life with a little brother. (Rev: BL 11/1/07)

3432 Ohi, Ruth. *Me and My Sister* (PS–K). Illus. by author. 2005, Annick LB $19.95 (978-1-55037-893-1); paper $5.95 (978-1-55037-892-4). In simple rhyming text, a girl describes the events — good and bad — of a day with her toddler sister. (Rev: BL 7/05; SLJ 10/05)

3433 Okimoto, Jean D., and Elaine M. Aoki. *The White Swan Express: A Story About Adoption* (K–3). Illus. by Meilo So. 2002, Clarion $16.00 (978-0-618-16453-0). 32pp. This story alternates between adoptive parents in North America and the children awaiting adoption in China, with information on the legalities of adopting children and on China's policies on childbirth. (Rev: BL 11/1/02; HBG 3/03; SLJ 2/03)

3434 O'Leary, Sara. *When I Was Small* (PS–2). Illus. by Julie Morstad. 2012, Simply Read $16.95 (978-1-897476-38-3). 32pp. Henry's mother Dorothea tells her son all about when she was small and called Dot. (Rev: BLO 11/1/12; SLJ 12/12)

3435 O'Leary, Sara. *When You Were Small* (1–3). Illus. by Julie Morstad. 2006, Simply Read $16.95 (978-1-894965-36-1). When Henry was small, he was *really* small, according to his father, who tells tales of Henry once fitting in his shirt pocket in this imaginatively illustrated book. (Rev: BL 5/1/06; SLJ 10/06)

3436 Ormerod, Jan. *Ballet Sisters: The Duckling and the Swan* (PS–2). Illus. by author. 2007, Scholastic paper $5.99 (978-0-439-82281-7). 32pp. For beginning readers, this is the story of a graceful older sister who takes ballet lessons and an awkward younger sister who wants to dance. (Rev: BL 12/1/06; SLJ 1/07)

3437 Ormerod, Jan. *Molly and Her Dad* (PS–2). Illus. by Carol Thompson. 2008, Roaring Brook $17.95 (978-1-59643-285-7). 32pp. Molly doesn't know much about her dad and loves to imagine what he's like; then he finally arrives and although he's not quite what she expected they get along just fine. (Rev: BCCB 9/08; BL 1/1–15/09; LMC 1/09; SLJ 9/08)

3438 Orona-Ramirez, Kristy. *Kiki's Journey* (K–2). Illus. by Jonathan Warm Day. 2006, Children's Book Pr. $16.95 (978-0-89239-214-8). 32pp. A young Native American girl who was born on a reservation but has grown up in Los Angeles travels back to the Taos Pueblo where she learns some important lessons about her heritage. (Rev: BL 9/1/06; SLJ 10/06)

3439 Orr, Wendy. *The Princess and Her Panther* (PS–2). Illus. by Lauren Stringer. 2010, Simon & Schuster $16.99 (978-1-4169-9780-1). 40pp. A brave girl (the princess) and her younger sister (the panther) confront the "monsters" lurking outside while on a backyard camp-out. Lexile AD720L (Rev: BL 7/10; LMC 8–9/10; SLJ 7/1/10)

3440 Pak, Soyung. *Dear Juno* (PS–2). Illus. by Susan Kathleen Hartung. 1999, Viking $17.99 (978-0-670-88252-6). 32pp. Although he can't read Korean, Juno is able to piece together clues about the contents of the letter he has received from his grandmother in Seoul. (Rev: BCCB 1/00; BL 11/15/99; HBG 3/00; SLJ 12/99)

3441 Paradis, Susan. *Snow Princess* (PS–2). Illus. 2005, Front St. $16.95 (978-1-932425-31-4). Waiting for her father's return from work on a snowy day, a little girl lets her imagination run wild. (Rev: BL 11/1/05; SLJ 1/06)

3442 Park, Frances, and Ginger Park. *The Have a Good Day Cafe* (1–3). Illus. by Katherine Potter. 2005, Lee & Low $16.95 (978-1-58430-171-4). Concerned about his grandmother's homesickness for her native Korea, young Mike suggests her ethnic foods might revive business at their food cart. (Rev: BL 9/1/05; SLJ 8/05)

3443 Parkhurst, Carolyn. *Cooking with Henry and Elliebelly* (PS–2). Illus. by Dan Yaccarino. 2010, Feiwel & Friends $16.99 (978-0-312-54848-3). 32pp. Five-year-old Henry and his 2-year-old sister pretend they are making "raspberry-marshmallow-peanut butter waffles with barbecued banana bacon" on a television show. (Rev: BL 10/15/10; SLJ 10/1/10)

3444 Parr, Todd. *The Daddy Book* (PS–K). Illus. 2002, Little, Brown $14.95 (978-0-316-60799-5). 32pp. A bright, simple book that points out the differences, and the similarities, between fathers. Also use the companion volume *The Mommy Book* (2002). (Rev: BL 3/15/02; HBG 10/02; SLJ 5/02)

3445 Parr, Todd. *The Family Book* (PS–2). Illus. by author. 2003, Little, Brown $15.95 (978-0-316-73896-5). Families of all kinds are celebrated in bright, humorous illustrations. (Rev: HBG 4/04; SLJ 12/03)

3446 Parr, Todd. *The Grandma Book* (1–4). Illus. by author. 2006, Little, Brown $9.99 (978-0-316-05802-5). A simple celebration of all kinds of grandmothers and the different ways they show love to their grandchildren. Also use *The Grandpa Book* (2006). (Rev: SLJ 4/06)

3447 Parr, Todd. *We Belong Together: A Book About Adoption and Families* (PS–K). Illus. by author. 2007, Little, Brown $15.99 (978-0-316-01668-1). With humor and warmth, Parr looks at the many ways in which families come together. (Rev: BL 7/07; SLJ 10/07)

3448 Partridge, Elizabeth. *Whistling* (PS–2). Illus. by Anna Grossnickle Hines. 2003, Greenwillow LB $16.89 (978-0-06-050236-2). A beautifully illustrated portrait of the close relationship between a father and son as they enjoy a camping trip. (Rev: HBG 10/03; SLJ 4/03)

3449 Paschkis, Julie. *Mooshka: A Quilt Story* (PS–2). Illus. by author. 2012, Peachtree $16.95 (978-156145620-8). 32pp. New big sister Karla discovers the joy of sharing her family's special quilt with her baby sister Hannah in this nostalgic family story. (Rev: BL 3/1/12*; HB 5–6/12; SLJ 6/1/12)

3450 Patrick, Denise Lewis. *Ma Dear's Old Green House* (PS–2). Illus. by Sonia Lynn Sadler. 2004, Just Us Bks. $16.95 (978-0-940975-55-2). 32pp. A young African American girl recalls the joys of a summer spent at her grandmother's house in the South. (Rev: BL 2/1/05; SLJ 1/05)

3451 Patrick, Denise Lewis. *Red Dancing Shoes* (PS–2). Illus. by James Ransome. 1993, Morrow $15.89 (978-0-688-10393-4). Grandma gives her young granddaughter a new pair of dancing shoes. (Rev: BL 3/1/93; SLJ 3/93)

3452 Pearson, Debora. *Leo's Tree* (PS–K). Illus. by Nora Hilb. 2004, Annick LB $19.95 (978-1-55037-845-0); paper $5.95 (978-1-55037-844-3). Leo and the linden tree planted when he was a baby grow together; when sister Sophie arrives, another sapling is added. (Rev: SLJ 6/04)

3453 Peete, Holly Robinson, and Ryan Elizabeth Peete. *My Brother Charlie* (K–3). Illus. by Shane W. Evans. 2010, Scholastic $16.99 (978-0-545-09466-5). 40pp. Callie speaks lovingly — and frankly — about what it's like to have an autistic twin brother in this story of a family dealing with disability. e Lexile AD540L (Rev: BL 3/1/10; LMC 5–6/10; SLJ 3/1/10)

3454 Pellegrini, Nina. *Families Are Different* (PS–3). Illus. 1991, Holiday House LB $16.95 (978-0-8234-0887-0). 32pp. Two adopted Korean girls gradually adjust to their new American family. (Rev: BL 12/15/91; SLJ 10/91)

3455 Pelley, Kathleen T. *Inventor McGregor* (PS). Illus. by Michael Chesworth. 2006, Farrar $16.00 (978-0-374-33606-6). 32pp. Prolific inventor Hector McGregor is

moved to a new office in the city but finds that without his family and his country home, his muse has deserted him. (Rev: BL 2/15/06; SLJ 4/06)

3456 Pelton, Mindy L. *When Dad's at Sea* (PS–1). Illus. by Robert G. Steele. 2004, Whitman $16.99 (978-0-8075-6339-7). 32pp. Emily learns to deal with feelings of loss and fear during the six months her father is deployed at sea as a Navy pilot. (Rev: BL 3/15/04; SLJ 7/04)

3457 Perez, Amada Irma. *My Diary from Here to There / Mi Diario de Aqui Hasta Alla* (2–4). Trans. by Consuelo Hernandez. Illus. by Maya Christina Gonzalez. 2002, Children's Book Pr. $16.95 (978-0-89239-175-2). 32pp. Amada tells her diary her worries about moving from Mexico to California in this bilingual book with appealing illustrations. (Rev: BL 11/1/02; HB 9/02; HBG 3/03)

3458 Perez, Amada Irma. *Nana's Big Surprise / Nana, Que Sorpresa!* (1–3). Illus. by Maya Christina Gonzalez. 2007, Children's Book Pr. $16.95 (978-0-89239-190-5). 24pp. In this brightly illustrated bilingual picture book, Amada and her siblings hope a gift of some baby chicks will lift the spirits of their visiting grandmother who's still grieving the death of her husband. (Rev: BL 3/15/07)

3459 Perkins, Lynne Rae. *The Broken Cat* (PS–2). Illus. 2002, Greenwillow LB $16.89 (978-0-06-029264-5). 32pp. While Frank waits with his injured cat at the vet's office, his mother, aunt, and grandmother distract him with a story about the time his mother broke her arm. (Rev: BL 3/15/02; HB 5/02*; HBG 10/02; SLJ 6/02)

3460 Perkins, Lynne Rae. *Pictures from Our Vacation* (K–2). Illus. 2007, Greenwillow $16.99 (978-0-06-085097-5). 40pp. The daughter narrates this story, documented with photographs and maps, of a family's vacation and its mixture of boredom and welcome surprises. (Rev: BCCB 7–8/07; BL 5/1/07; HB 1/08; SLJ 6/07)

3461 Perl, Erica S. *Chicken Butt!* (PS–K). Illus. by Henry Cole. 2009, Abrams $12.95 (978-0-8109-8325-0). 32pp. A small boy tests his father's endurance with constant questions along the lines of "You know why?" "Chicken thigh!" (Rev: BL 4/15/09; SLJ 4/09)

3462 Perry, Elizabeth. *Think Cool Thoughts* (PS–2). Illus. by Linda Bronson. 2005, Clarion $16.00 (978-0-618-23493-6). 32pp. Angel, her mother, and her aunt flee the heat downstairs to spend a lovely summer night watching the stars from the roof of their apartment building. (Rev: BL 7/05; SLJ 8/05)

3463 Pettitt, Linda, and Sharon Darrow. *Yafi's Family: An Ethiopian Boy's Journey of Love, Loss, and Adoption* (PS–2). Illus. by Jan Spivey Gilchrist. 2010, Amharic $17.95 (978-0-9797481-4-1). 32pp. In this tender international adoption story, a young Ethiopian boy and his adoptive parents reminisce about their first meeting, and talk about the love he feels for both families. Lexile AD660L (Rev: BL 10/15/10; SLJ 1/1/11)

3464 Pham, LeUyen. *Big Sister, Little Sister* (PS–2). Illus. 2005, Hyperion $15.99 (978-0-7868-5182-9). 40pp. The tensions between younger and older sisters are captured in simple text and lively illustrations. (Rev: BL 6/1–15/05)

3465 Piven, Hanoch. *My Dog Is as Smelly as Dirty Socks: And Other Funny Family Portraits* (K–3). Illus. 2007, Random $15.99 (978-0-375-84052-4). A child describes family members in similes that are shown in portraits — Dad is "jumpy as a spring" and so forth. (Rev: BL 5/1/07; SLJ 6/07*)

3466 Piven, Hanoch. *The Scary Show of Mo and Jo* (PS–2). Illus. by author. 2005, Running Pr. $18.95 (978-0-7624-2097-1). Two siblings try to outdo one another with creative disguises that are artfully conceived in Piven's collages. (Rev: SLJ 11/05)

3467 Plourde, Lynn. *Dad, Aren't You Glad?* (PS–2). Illus. by Amy Wummer. 2005, Dutton $12.99 (978-0-525-47362-6). A little boy tries to give his father a treat by taking over his chores, with predictable consequences. (Rev: SLJ 3/05)

3468 Plourde, Lynn. *Thank You, Grandpa* (K–3). Illus. by Jason Cockcroft. 2003, Dutton $15.99 (978-0-525-46992-6). 32pp. When a girl's grandfather dies, she uses what she learned on their nature walks together to say good-bye. (Rev: BL 2/15/03; HBG 10/03; SLJ 4/03)

3469 Polacco, Patricia. *In Our Mothers' House* (1–4). Illus. by author. 2009, Philomel $17.99 (978-0-399-25076-7). 48pp. An African American narrator, one of three adopted multicultural siblings, recalls the happy childhood they had with their mothers Marmee and Meema. (Rev: BL 5/1/09; LMC 10/09; SLJ 5/09)

3470 Polacco, Patricia. *My Rotten Redheaded Older Brother* (K–3). Illus. 1994, Simon & Schuster $16.00 (978-0-671-72751-2). 30pp. A young girl engages in a fierce rivalry with her brother in spite of an underlying love. (Rev: BL 9/15/94; SLJ 10/94*)

3471 Polacco, Patricia. *Rotten Richie and the Ultimate Dare* (1–3). 2006, Philomel $16.99 (978-0-399-24531-2). 48pp. Tired of her brother Richie's teasing about her ballet classes, Trish challenges her obnoxious sibling to show what he can do on the dance floor; a companion to *My Rotten Redheaded Older Brother* (1999). (Rev: BL 4/15/06; SLJ 5/06)

3472 Polacco, Patricia. *Thunder Cake* (PS–3). Illus. 1990, Penguin $16.99 (978-0-399-22231-3). 32pp. A grandmother helps her young granddaughter conquer her fears of electrical storms by eating Thunder Cake. (Rev: BCCB 3/90; BL 2/15/90*; HB 3/90; SLJ 3/90*)

3473 Polacco, Patricia. *When Lightning Comes in a Jar* (2–4). Illus. 2002, Penguin $16.99 (978-0-399-23164-3). 40pp. An autobiographical remembrance of fun, games, and traditions at family reunions. (Rev: BL 8/02; HBG 10/02; SLJ 6/02)

3474 Pomerantz, Charlotte. *The Chalk Doll* (PS–1). Illus. by Frane Lessac. 1989, HarperCollins paper $6.99 (978-0-06-443333-4). Rose is sick, and Mother tells her stories of her Jamaican girlhood. (Rev: BL 5/15/89; HB 7/89)

3475 Pow, Tom. *Tell Me One Thing, Dad* (PS–1). Illus. by Ian Andrew. 2004, Candlewick $15.99 (978-0-7636-

2474-3). 32pp. To postpone the moment when her bedroom light will be turned off for the night, young Molly asks her father about a variety of real and imaginary creatures. (Rev: BL 4/1/04*; SLJ 6/04)

3476 Price, Mara. *Grandma's Chocolate / El Chocolate de Abuelita* (K–2). Illus. by Lisa Fields. 2010, Arte Publico $16.95 (978-155885587-8). 32pp. In this bilingual story, a granddaughter welcomes her grandmother's visit from Mexico, and the culturally significant gifts she brings along. (Rev: BLO 11/1/10; SLJ 1/11)

3477 Prigger, Mary Skillings. *Aunt Minnie and the Twister* (PS–2). Illus. by Betsy Lewin. 2002, Clarion $15.00 (978-0-618-11136-7). 32pp. Aunt Minnie and her nine nieces and nephews run to the root cellar to escape a twister that turns their house completely around. (Rev: BL 2/15/02; HB 5/02; HBG 10/02; SLJ 4/02)

3478 Prigger, Mary Skillings. *Aunt Minnie McGranahan* (PS–2). Illus. by Betsy Lewin. 1999, Clarion $15.00 (978-0-395-82270-8). 32pp. Minnie McGranahan accepts nine orphaned nieces and nephews into her household, and although she regulates their schedules, there is always time for fun. (Rev: BCCB 5/99; BL 5/1/99; HBG 10/99; SLJ 5/99)

3479 Proimos, James. *Todd's TV* (K–2). Illus. by author. 2010, HarperCollins $15.99 (978-0-06-170985-2). 40pp. Todd watches so much TV that the appliance has offered to adopt him; when Todd's parents realize what's happening, they finally cut back on TV in favor of family time. (Rev: BL 2/15/10; SLJ 5/1/10*)

3480 Pullen, Zachary. *Friday My Radio Flyer Flew* (PS–2). Illus. by author. 2008, Simon & Schuster $16.99 (978-1-4169-3983-2). 32pp. A little boy and his father enjoy restoring an old Radio Flyer and envisaging what it might be able to do. (Rev: SLJ 5/08)

3481 Purmwell, Ann. *Christmas Tree Farm* (PS–2). Illus. by Jill Weber. 2006, Holiday $16.95 (978-0-8234-1886-2). 32pp. A warm story about a Christmas tree farm, the excitement during the winter holidays, and the work that continues all year round. (Rev: BL 9/1/06; SLJ 10/06)

3482 Quigley, Mary. *Granddad's Fishing Buddy* (PS–2). Illus. by Stephane Jorisch. 2007, Dial $16.99 (978-0-8037-2942-1). Charmingly written and illustrated, this story about a young girl who goes fishing with her grandfather highlights the simple joy of spending quality time with older family members. (Rev: BL 5/15/07; SLJ 6/07)

3483 Raven, Margot Theis. *Circle Unbroken* (PS–3). Illus. by E. B. Lewis. 2004, Farrar $16.00 (978-0-374-31289-3). A grandmother teaches her granddaughter how to make Gullah baskets and tells her about her African heritage. (Rev: BL 5/15/04; SLJ 4/04)

3484 Reid, Margarette S. *The Button Box* (K–3). Illus. by Sarah Chamberlain. 1990, Dutton $16.99 (978-0-525-44590-6). 24pp. A boy imagines interesting stories behind the different buttons in his grandmother's button box. (Rev: BCCB 3/90; BL 4/15/90; SLJ 9/90)

3485 Reiser, Lynn. *My Baby and Me* (PS). Illus. by Penny Gentieu. 2008, Knopf $16.99 (978-0-375-85205-3).

32pp. Toddlers are shown interacting with their younger siblings in large-format pages with photographs and simple text. (Rev: BL 5/15/08; SLJ 8/08)

3486 Reiser, Lynn. *You and Me, Baby* (PS–1). Photos by Penny Gentieu. 2006, Knopf $15.95 (978-0-375-83401-1). Simple text accompanies a collection of appealing photographs of babies from diverse backgrounds and their parents. (Rev: SLJ 10/06)

3487 Reynolds, Peter. *Ish* (PS–2). Illus. 2004, Candlewick $14.00 (978-0-7636-2344-9). 32pp. Ramon is an aspiring young artist who nearly quits when his older brother belittles his work; fortunately, his little sister has better taste. (Rev: BL 11/1/04; SLJ 1/05*)

3488 Reynolds, Peter. *My Very Big Little World* (PS–K). Illus. 2006, Simon & Schuster $15.95 (978-0-689-87621-9). 40pp. SugarLoaf, a captivating middle child, introduces young readers to the important people and places in her life. (Rev: BL 4/15/06; SLJ 1/06)

3489 Reynolds, Peter H. *The Best Kid in the World* (PS–2). Illus. by author. 2006, Simon & Schuster $15.95 (978-0-689-87624-0). Jealous that her older brother once received a "Best Kid in the World" award, Sugar-Loaf sets out to do a number of good deeds, but things don't go exactly as she planned. (Rev: SLJ 8/06)

3490 Ries, Lori. *Fix It, Sam* (PS–K). Illus. by Sue Ramá. 2007, Charlesbridge $15.95 (978-1-57091-598-7); paper $6.95 (978-1-57091-722-6). 32pp. Little Petey relies on big brother Sam for lots of help, but discovers that he can fix things, too; bright mixed media art extends the text. (Rev: BL 1/1–15/07; SLJ 2/07)

3491 Ries, Lori. *Punk Wig* (K–3). Illus. by Erin Eitter Kono. 2008, Boyds Mills $16.95 (978-1-59078-486-0). 32pp. A little boy describes how his mother's cancer has affected his life. (Rev: BL 3/1/08; SLJ 4/08)

3492 Ries, Lori. *Super Sam!* (PS–1). 2004, Charlesbridge $14.95 (978-1-58089-041-0). When he dons a blankie cape, Sam becomes a superhero and his toddler brother Petey is full of awe. (Rev: SLJ 9/04)

3493 Robberecht, Thierry. *Back into Mommy's Tummy* (PS–K). Illus. by Philippe Goossens. 2005, Clarion $15.00 (978-0-618-58106-1). A 5-year-old girl whose mother is pregnant says she wants to go back into Mommy's tummy, where the center of attention is. (Rev: BL 12/1/05; SLJ 2/06)

3494 Rocco, John. *Blackout* (PS–1). Illus. by author. 2011, Hyperion/Disney $16.99 (978-1-4231-2190-9). 40pp. A bored young boy gets the quality family time he seeks when the power goes out. (Rev: BL 6/1/11; SLJ 7/11*)

3495 Rockwell, Anne. *Father's Day* (PS–2). Illus. by Lizzy Rockwell. 2005, HarperCollins LB $15.89 (978-0-06-051378-8). 40pp. A class of children write books about their fathers, showing the wide diversity of family situations. (Rev: BL 5/15/05; SLJ 5/05)

3496 Rodman, Mary Ann. *A Tree for Emmy* (PS–2). Illus. by Tatjana Mai-Wyss. 2009, Peachtree $15.95 (978-1-56145-475-4). Eager to have a tree like her grandmother's mimosa for her birthday, Emmy is initially

distressed to learn it will take years for a sapling to bear flowers. (Rev: BL 5/15/09; SLJ 3/09)

3497 Rodowsky, Colby. *The Next-Door Dogs* (2–4). Illus. by Amy June Bates. 2005, Farrar $15.00 (978-0-374-36410-6). 112pp. Sara overcomes her fear of dogs in order to help her new next-door neighbor. (Rev: BL 3/1/05; SLJ 6/05)

3498 Root, Phyllis. *Creak! Said the Bed* (PS–K). Illus. by Regan Dunnick. 2010, Candlewick $15.99 (978-0-7636-2004-2). 32pp. Onomatopoeia enhances this comic rhyming cumulative tale about a creaking, groaning, overcrowded bed. (Rev: BL 3/1/10; SLJ 3/1/10)

3499 Root, Phyllis. *The Name Quilt* (PS–1). Illus. by Margot Apple. 2003, Farrar $16.00 (978-0-374-35484-8). 32pp. When Sadie stays at Grandma's, she sleeps under a patchwork quilt embroidered with names and listens to Grandma's stories about these relatives. (Rev: BL 3/15/03; HBG 10/03; SLJ 5/03)

3500 Rose, Naomi C. *Tashi and the Tibetan Flower Cure* (K–3). Illus. by author. 2011, Lee & Low $18.95 (978-1-60060-425-6). 40pp. A Tibetan American girl administers a traditional flower-pollen cure when her grandfather becomes ill; the treatment process draws the community together and shows the family how much support they have in their new home. (Rev: BL 11/15/11; LMC 3–4/12; SLJ 11/1/11)

3501 Rosen, Michael J. *A Drive in the Country* (K–3). Illus. by Marc Burckhardt. 2007, Candlewick $16.99 (978-0-7636-2140-7). 32pp. A family of five, plus one dog, takes a gentle Sunday drive in the country and finds lots to enjoy. (Rev: BL 9/15/07; SLJ 11/07)

3502 Rosenbaum, Andria Warmflash. *A Grandma Like Yours / A Grandpa Like Yours* (PS–1). Illus. by Barb Björnson. 2006, Lerner LB $16.95 (978-1-58013-167-4); paper $6.95 (978-1-58013-168-1). One side of this flipbook extols the virtues of Jewish grandmas (in the guise of friendly animals), and the other, Jewish grandpas. (Rev: SLJ 5/06)

3503 Rosenberg, Liz. *The Silence in the Mountains* (1–3). Illus. by Chris K. Soentpiet. 1999, Orchard LB $16.99 (978-0-531-33084-5). 32pp. Iskander and his family must leave their war-torn country and find peace in America. (Rev: BL 2/1/99; HBG 10/99; SLJ 7/99)

3504 Rosenberg, Liz. *This Is the Wind* (PS–2). Illus. by Renee Reichert. 2008, Roaring Brook $16.95 (978-1-59643-268-0). 32pp. Imitating the structure of "This Is the House that Jack Built," this is the story of a child's birth on a windy night on a farm. (Rev: BLO 1/13/09; SLJ 10/08)

3505 Rosenberg, Madelyn. *The Schmutzy Family* (PS–2). Illus. by Paul Meisel. 2012, Holiday $16.95 (978-0-8234-2371-2). 32pp. The six Schmutzy children are gloriously messy until Friday rolls around each week and they clean themselves up for Shabbat. Lexile AD860L (Rev: BL 9/15/12; SLJ 11/12)

3506 Roth, Carol. *All Aboard to Work — Choo-Choo!* (PS–K). Illus. by Steve Lavis. 2009, Whitman $16.99 (978-0-8075-0271-6). Unpaged. A diverse array of parents dressed for work are shown commuting aboard a train and returning home each night to shower their families with affection. (Rev: SLJ 11/1/09)

3507 Rouss, Sylvia. *My Baby Brother* (K–2). Illus. by Liz Goulet Dubois. 2002, Jonathan David $14.95 (978-0-8246-0445-5). 24pp. Sarah, a young Jewish girl, initially resists the description of her new baby brother as a "miracle." (Rev: BL 10/1/02)

3508 Russo, Marisabina. *The Trouble with Baby* (PS–1). Illus. by author. 2003, Greenwillow LB $16.89 (978-0-06-008925-2). Siblings Hannah and Sam have always had a good time playing together, but when Hannah gets a new doll named Baby, Sam gets jealous and refuses to play; eventually Hannah comes up with a solution that brings sister and brother together again. (Rev: HBG 10/03; SLJ 6/03)

3509 Ryder, Jeanne. *My Mother's Voice* (K–2). Illus. by Peter Catalanotto. 2006, HarperCollins $15.99 (978-0-06-029509-7). 32pp. This gentle picture book celebrates the role of a mother's voice in a loving relationship with her daughter. (Rev: BL 4/15/06; SLJ 4/06)

3510 Sacre, Antonio. *A Mango in the Hand: A Story Told Through Proverbs* (K–3). Illus. by Sebastià Serra. 2011, Abrams $16.95 (978-0-8109-9734-9). Unpaged. Young Francisco wants mangoes for dessert on his saint day, and Papá's proverbs guide him through his efforts, teaching him about generosity; in Spanish and English. (Rev: SLJ 7/11)

3511 Saenz, Benjamin Alire. *A Gift from PapaDiego* (K–4). Illus. by Geronimo Garcia. 1998, Cinco Puntos paper $10.95 (978-0-938317-33-3). 40pp. Little Diego wants a Superman suit so he can fly to Mexico to visit with his beloved grandfather. When that fails, his disappointment is lessened by the news that his grandfather is coming to visit. (Rev: BL 5/1/98; HB 7/98)

3512 Saenz, Benjamin Alire. *A Perfect Season for Dreaming / Un tiempo perfecto para soñar* (K–3). Illus. by Esau Andrade Valencia. 2008, Cinco Puntos $17.95 (978-1-933693-01-9). 40pp. At the age of 78, Octavio Rivera is experiencing wonderful dreams, which he shares with his 6-year-old granddaughter; readers learn to count to 10 in both Spanish and English with this bilingual book. (Rev: HB 1/09; SLJ 4/09)

3513 Salonen, Roxane Beauclair. *First Salmon* (K–3). Illus. by Jim Fowler. 2005, Boyds Mills $15.95 (978-1-59078-171-5). 32pp. Charlie, a young Native American boy still grieving over the death of his beloved Uncle Joe, finds it hard to get excited about the annual First Salmon celebration. (Rev: BL 10/15/05; SLJ 11/05)

3514 Samuels, Barbara. *Happy Valentines Day, Dolores* (K–2). Illus. 2006, Farrar $16.00 (978-0-374-32844-3). 32pp. Despite her promise to quit snooping in her older sister's room, Dolores simply can't resist trying on a necklace she finds in a valentine box, with disastrous consequences; the detailed cartoon illustrations add to the fun. (Rev: BL 11/15/05*; HBG 10/06; SLJ 1/06*)

3515 Sandburg, Carl. *The Huckabuck Family and How They Raised Popcorn in Nebraska and Quit and Came Back* (K–3). Illus. by David Small. 1999, Farrar $16.00 (978-0-374-33511-3). 40pp. This story, part of the author's *Rootabaga Stories,* tells of the Huckabuck family, their trials and tribulations, travels, and eventual return to their farm. (Rev: BCCB 9/99; BL 9/15/99; HB 9/99; HBG 3/00; SLJ 8/99)

3516 Sanders-Wells, Linda. *Maggie's Monkeys* (K–2). Illus. by Abby Carter. 2009, Candlewick $16.99 (978-0-7636-3326-4). Maggie's big brother will not pretend that there are pink monkeys living in their refrigerator until the day his friends tease Maggie and, out of love, he defends Maggie and her monkeys. (Rev: BCCB 6/09; SLJ 5/09)

3517 Savadier, Elivia. *Time to Get Dressed!* (PS). Illus. 2006, Roaring Brook $14.95 (978-1-59643-161-4). Simple text and charming pictures depict Dad's patience as he struggles to get his toddler dressed for day care. (Rev: BL 4/1/06; SLJ 3/06)

3518 Say, Allen. *Grandfather's Journey* (PS–3). Illus. by author. 1993, Houghton $16.95 (978-0-395-57035-7). 32pp. An autobiographical story that chronicles the passages of generations of the author's family as they moved between Japan and the United States. Winner of the 1994 Caldecott Medal. (Rev: BL 7/93*; SLJ 9/98)

3519 Schertle, Alice. *Down the Road* (PS–3). Illus. by E. B. Lewis. 1995, Harcourt $16.00 (978-0-15-276622-1). Hetty accidentally breaks the eggs that she has been carefully carrying from the store for her family's breakfast. (Rev: BCCB 12/95; BL 9/15/95*; SLJ 4/96)

3520 Schlein, Miriam. *The Story About Me* (PS–1). Illus. by Kristina Stephenson. 2004, Whitman $16.99 (978-0-8075-7631-1). A grandmother tells her granddaughter about all the anticipation and happiness that preceded the little girl's birth. (Rev: BL 5/1/04; SLJ 5/04)

3521 Schmid, Paul. *Peanut and Fifi Have a Ball* (PS–K). Illus. by Randall de Seve. 2013, Dial $15.99 (978-0-8037-3578-1). 32pp. Two sisters enjoy imaginary play after they have an initial difference over sharing a new blue ball in this nicely illustrated book. (Rev: BL 4/1/13; SLJ 3/13*)

3522 Schotter, Roni. *The House of Joyful Living* (PS–2). Illus. by Terry Widener. 2008, Farrar $16.95 (978-0-374-33429-1). A young girl loves the diverse community in her New York tenement building and the parties they have on the roof; but the forthcoming new baby makes her worry that this world will change. (Rev: BCCB 1/09; BL 11/15/08; SLJ 11/08)

3523 Schotter, Roni. *Mama, I'll Give You the World* (1–3). Illus. by S. Saelig Gallagher. 2006, Random $16.95 (978-0-375-83612-1). To repay her mother for all her loving kindness, young Maria plans a very special birthday surprise. (Rev: BL 8/06; SLJ 9/1/06*)

3524 Schubert, Leda. *Feeding the Sheep* (PS–K). Illus. by Andrea U'Ren. 2010, Farrar $16.99 (978-0-374-32296-0). 32pp. A mother explains to her little daughter all the steps involved in making a sweater, starting with feeding the sheep. (Rev: BL 3/15/10; LMC 5–6/10; SLJ 3/1/10)

3525 Schubert, Leda. *The Princess of Borscht* (PS–2). Illus. by Bonnie Christensen. 2011, Roaring Brook $17.99 (978-1-59643-515-5). 32pp. When Ruthie's grandmother is in hospital and insists on having some homemade borscht, the young girl enlists some help in devising a recipe. (Rev: BL 9/15/11; SLJ 11/1/11)

3526 Schwartz, Amy. *Dee Dee and Me* (PS–1). Illus. by author. 2013, Holiday $16.95 (978-0-8234-2524-2). 32pp. Sisters Dee Dee and Hannah resolve their differences in this effective story about sibling rivalry. **e** (Rev: BL 11/15/13*; HB 9–10/13; SLJ 8/13)

3527 Schwartz, Joanne. *Our Corner Grocery Store* (PS–2). Illus. by Laura Beingessner. 2009, Tundra $19.95 (978-0-88776-868-2). 32pp. Anna Maria gets to play store for real on Saturday at her grandparents' grocery store. (Rev: BCCB 6/09; BL 5/15/09; SLJ 5/09)

3528 Scrimger, Richard. *Eugene's Story* (PS–1). Illus. by Gillian Johnson. 2003, Tundra $15.95 (978-0-88776-544-5). Eugene triumphs over his bossy big sister in this imaginative tale. (Rev: HBG 4/04; SLJ 3/04)

3529 Shahan, Sherry. *That's Not How You Play Soccer, Daddy!* (K–2). Illus. by Tatjana Mai-Wyss. 2007, Peachtree $15.95 (978-1-56145-416-7). 32pp. Young Mikey takes soccer very seriously while Dad is happy just to play for fun. (Rev: BL 9/1/07; SLJ 10/07)

3530 Shannon, David. *No, David!* (PS–K). Illus. 1998, Scholastic $16.99 (978-0-590-93002-4). It seems that everything young David does is met with a "No!" from his mother, but in spite of her criticism, he knows she loves him. (Rev: BCCB 9/98; BL 9/1/98; HBG 3/99; SLJ 8/98)

3531 Shannon, David. *Oh, David! A Diaper David Book* (PS). Illus. by author. 2005, Scholastic $6.99 (978-0-439-68881-9). In a board book prequel to the preschool David, we see the toddler unrolling toilet paper, refusing food, and filling his diaper, before a last cuddle with his long-suffering mother. Also use *Oops! A Diaper David Book* (2005). (Rev: BCCB 3/05; SLJ 3/05)

3532 Shapiro, Jody Fickes. *Up, Up, Up! It's Apple-Picking Time* (K–3). Illus. by Kitty Harvill. 2003, Holiday House $16.95 (978-0-8234-1610-3). Author Jody Fickes Shapiro beautifully evokes all the color and wonder of autumn and harvest in this story of a family's visit to the apple farm of Grandma and Grandpa. (Rev: HBG 4/04; SLJ 9/03)

3533 Sheridan, Sara. *I'm Me!* (PS–K). Illus. by Margaret Chamberlain. 2011, Scholastic $17.99 (978-0-545-28222-2). 32pp. Young Imogen doesn't want to play pretend this time she visits Auntie Sara — she just wants to be herself. (Rev: BL 3/15/11; SLJ 3/1/11)

3534 Sheth, Kashmira. *The No-Dogs-Allowed Rule* (1–3). Illus. by Carl Pearce. 2012, Whitman $14.99 (978-0-8075-5694-8). 128pp. Ishan, a 3rd grader, wants a dog very badly but his efforts to convince his mother to allow this generally misfire. **e** Lexile 470L (Rev: BL 10/1/12; LMC 3–4/13; SLJ 11/12)

3535 Shipton, Jonathan. *Baby Baby Blah Blah Blah!* (PS–2). Illus. by Francesca Chessa. 2009, Holiday $16.95 (978-0-8234-2213-5). 32pp. When Emily hears there's a new baby coming, she works her way through a list of pros and cons until she gets to the heart of the matter: what about me? (Rev: BCCB 4/09; BLO 2/9/09; SLJ 3/09)

3536 Siegel, Randy. *Grandma's Smile* (PS–2). Illus. by DyAnne DiSalvo. 2010, Roaring Brook $15.99 (978-1-59643-438-7). 32pp. A 6-year-old boy travels to visit his grandmother and help her locate her missing smile. (Rev: BL 7/10; SLJ 11/1/10)

3537 Singer, Marilyn. *Didi and Daddy on the Promenade* (PS–K). Illus. by Marie-Louise Gay. 2001, Clarion $14.00 (978-0-618-04640-9). 32pp. Didi and her father love to walk and play on Sunday mornings on the Brooklyn Heights Promenade that overlooks the Manhattan skyline. (Rev: BCCB 4/01; BL 4/1/01; HBG 10/01; SLJ 5/01)

3538 Singer, Marilyn. *The One and Only Me* (PS–K). Illus. by Nicole Rubel. 2000, HarperCollins $9.95 (978-0-694-01279-4). A little girl explains how she is like various members of her extended family in this charming family story illustrated with brightly colored cartoons. (Rev: HBG 10/00; SLJ 7/00)

3539 Singer, Marilyn. *Tallulah's Solo* (PS–3). Illus. by Alexandra Boiger. 2012, Clarion $16.99 (978-0-547-33004-4). 40pp. Though initially jealous when her brother lands a bigger ballet role than she does, Tallulah helps him rehearse and ends up celebrating his success. **e** (Rev: BLO 1/25/12; SLJ 4/1/12)

3540 Sinykin, Sheri. *Zayde Comes to Live* (PS–2). Illus. by Kristina Swarner. 2012, Peachtree $16.95 (978-1-56145-631-4). 32pp. Young Rachel struggles to understand what will happen to her grandfather when he dies, weighing conflicting information from her rabbi and her Christian and Muslim friends. Lexile AD490L (Rev: BL 11/15/12*; SLJ 10/12)

3541 Sitomer, Alan Lawrence. *Daddies Do It Different* (PS–2). Illus. by Abby Carter. 2012, Hyperion $16.99 (978-1-4231-3315-5). 40pp. A young girl revels in the more chaotic but ultimately more fun ways her dad takes care of her, from dressing to bathing. (Rev: BL 2/15/12; SLJ 4/1/12)

3542 Skeers, Linda. *The Impossible Patriotism Project* (1–3). Illus. by Ard Hoyt. 2007, Dial $16.99 (978-0-8037-3138-7). 32pp. In this touching yet humorous book, a boy discovers the true nature of patriotism as he honors his father, who is serving overseas in the military, as part of a school project. (Rev: BL 5/1/07; SLJ 8/07)

3543 Smalls, Irene. *Kevin and His Dad* (PS–1). Illus. by Michael Hays. 1999, Little, Brown $15.95 (978-0-316-79899-0). 32pp. An African American boy and his dad spend a day together — first helping around the house, then playing baseball, and going to a movie. (Rev: BCCB 5/99; BL 2/15/99; HBG 10/99; SLJ 5/99)

3544 Smalls, Irene. *My Nana and Me* (PS–K). Illus. by Cathy Ann Johnson. 2005, Little, Brown $15.99 (978-0-316-16821-2). 32pp. An African American preschooler tells about a very special day spent with her grandmother. (Rev: BL 11/1/05; SLJ 10/05)

3545 Smith, Lane. *Grandpa Green* (K–2). Illus. by author. 2011, Roaring Brook $16.99 (978-1-59643-607-7). 32pp. A great-grandson celebrates his Grandpa Green's spectacular topiaries and what they convey about his long life. Caldecott Honor Book. ℮ (Rev: BL 7/11; HB 9–10/11; LMC 11–12/11; SLJ 8/1/11*)

3546 Smith, Patricia. *Janna and the Kings* (PS–2). Illus. by Aaron Boyd. 2003, Lee & Low $16.95 (978-1-58430-088-5). Janna, a young African American girl, hesitantly returns to the barbershop her grandfather loved before he died. (Rev: BL 11/15/03; HBG 4/04; SLJ 11/03)

3547 Smith, Will. *Just the Two of Us* (PS–1). Illus. by Kadir Nelson. 2001, Scholastic $16.95 (978-0-439-08792-6). 32pp. Smith uses his song "Just the Two of Us" as the foundation for this celebration of a father's love for his son. (Rev: BL 7/01; HBG 10/01; SLJ 6/01)

3548 Smothers, Ethel Footman. *Auntee Edna* (K–3). Illus. by Wil Clay. 2001, Eerdmans $16.00 (978-0-8028-5154-3). Tokee doesn't look forward to staying the night with elderly Auntee Edna but has a wonderful time. (Rev: HBG 10/01; SLJ 8/01)

3549 Soman, David, and Jacky Davis. *Ladybug Girl* (PS–2). Illus. by David Soman. 2008, Dial $16.99 (978-0-8037-3195-0). 32pp. Lulu, wearing red-and-black polka-dot wings, is on her own for the morning and must make up her own diversions. (Rev: BL 4/1/08; SLJ 3/08)

3550 Soto, Gary. *If the Shoe Fits* (PS–3). Illus. by Terry Widener. 2002, Penguin $16.99 (978-0-399-23420-0). 32pp. Rigo, who is sick of wearing hand-me-downs, gets a new pair of loafers for his ninth birthday. (Rev: BCCB 3/02; BL 1/1–15/02; HB 7/02; HBG 10/02; SLJ 1/02)

3551 Spalding, Andrea. *Bottled Sunshine* (1–3). Illus. by Ruth Ohi. 2005, Fitzhenry & Whiteside $16.95 (978-1-55041-703-6). A young boy's memories of his last visit with his grandmother provide comfort after her death; the illustrations complement the gentle story. (Rev: SLJ 10/05)

3552 Spalding, Andrea. *The Most Beautiful Kite in the World* (PS–2). Illus. by Leslie Watts. 2003, Fitzhenry & Whiteside $15.95 (978-1-55041-716-6). Jenny is disappointed when her father gives her a homemade kite, but she forgets her pique as she learns to add enhancements. (Rev: SLJ 8/03)

3553 Spinelli, Eileen. *When You Are Happy* (PS–2). Illus. by Geraldo Valério. 2006, Simon & Schuster $16.95 (978-0-689-86251-9). 40pp. Members of a family reassure a little girl that they love her. (Rev: BL 3/1/06; SLJ 3/06)

3554 Spiro, Ruth. *Lester Fizz, Bubble-Gum Artist* (2–4). Illus. by Thor Wickstrom. 2008, Dutton $16.99 (978-0-525-47861-4). Lester, an untalented individual in a family full of artists, finally finds inspiration in a mouthful of gum; a funny story full of wordplay. (Rev: BLO 10/7/08; SLJ 10/08)

3555 Springstubb, Tricia. *Phoebe and Digger* (PS). Illus. by Jeff Newman. 2013, Candlewick $16.99 (978-0-7636-5281-4). 32pp. Phoebe is mollified about the annoying presence of a new baby brother when she is given a toy earthmover, only to have it taken temporarily by a bullying older girl. (Rev: BL 3/15/13; HB 3–4/13; SLJ 2/13)

3556 Stanton, Karen. *Papi's Gift* (PS–2). Illus. by Rene King Moreno. 2007, Boyds Mills $16.95 (978-1-59078-422-8). 32pp. Graciela desperately misses her father, who has left their village in Mexico to pick fruit in California; she treasures their weekly phone calls and prays for his return. (Rev: BL 4/15/07)

3557 Steptoe, John. *Baby Says* (PS). Illus. by author. 1988, Lothrop LB $17.89 (978-0-688-07424-1). An almost wordless picture book catching the exchange between a baby and a big brother. (Rev: BL 4/1/88; HB 7/88; SLJ 3/88)

3558 Steptoe, John. *Stevie* (PS–2). Illus. by author. 1969, HarperCollins paper $6.99 (978-0-06-443122-4). A small African American boy eloquently expresses his resentment at having to share his possessions and mother with a temporary younger boarder who becomes "kinda like a little brother"; illustrated in bold line and color.

3559 Stewart, Sarah. *The Friend* (1–3). Illus. by David Small. 2004, Farrar $16.00 (978-0-374-32463-6). Belle, daughter of wealthy and distant parents, and Bea, African American housekeeper, spend much of their time together at the family's house on the beach. (Rev: BL 8/04; SLJ 8/04)

3560 Stoeke, Janet Morgan. *Waiting for May* (K–3). Illus. by author. 2005, Dutton $16.99 (978-0-525-47098-4). A family adopting a girl from China waits impatiently for the journey there to begin. (Rev: SLJ 6/05)

3561 Stott, Ann. *I'll Be There* (PS–2). Illus. by Matt Phelan. 2010, Candlewick $14.99 (978-0-7636-4711-7). 32pp. A young son eagerly lists the things he no longer needs his mom to do for him, then asks for reassurance that she'll still be there, whether he needs her or not. (Rev: BL 2/1/11; SLJ 3/1/11)

3562 Struve-Bodeen, Stephanie. *The Best Worst Brother* (K–4). Illus. by Charlotte Fremaux. 2005, Woodbine $15.95 (978-1-890627-68-3). Emma discovers that it will take hard work to teach Isaac, her little brother who has Down's syndrome, to use sign language in this sequel to *We'll Paint the Octopus Red* (1998). (Rev: SLJ 9/05)

3563 Sturges, Philemon. *How Do You Make a Baby Smile?* (PS–1). Illus. by Bridget Strevens-Marzo. 2007, HarperCollins $16.99 (978-0-06-076072-4). This story uses animals and rhyming text to show young children different ways to make babies smile. (Rev: BL 7/07; SLJ 7/07)

3564 Stuve-Bodeen, Stephanie. *We'll Paint the Octopus Red* (PS–2). Illus. by Pam DeVito. 1998, Woodbine $15.95 (978-1-890627-06-5). 28pp. A young girl thinks of all the things that she and her new baby brother can do together. When she is told that he has Down syndrome, she maintains that they still will do those things, though now each activity might take a little longer. (Rev: BL 9/15/98; HBG 3/99; SLJ 12/98)

3565 Sugarman, Brynn Olenberg. *Rebecca's Journey Home* (PS–2). Illus. by Michelle Shapiro. 2006, Lerner $17.95 (978-1-58013-157-5). 32pp. This tender story of a Jewish American family adopting a Vietnamese baby girl also provides insight into both cultures. (Rev: BL 1/1–15/07; SLJ 11/06)

3566 Sullivan, Sarah. *Dear Baby: Letters from Your Big Brother* (PS–K). Illus. by Paul Meisel. 2005, Candlewick $14.99 (978-0-7636-2126-1). During the first year of his baby sister's life, her big brother records his thoughts about her development and his growing love for her. (Rev: BL 9/15/05; SLJ 9/05)

3567 Sullivan, Sarah. *Once Upon a Baby Brother* (K–3). Illus. by Tricia Tusa. 2010, Farrar $16.99 (978-0-374-34635-5). 32pp. Only when her baby brother goes away for the weekend does Lizzie realize the annoying child was actually inspiring the stories she loves to tell. (Rev: BL 5/1/10; LMC 11–12/10; SLJ 7/1/10)

3568 Taylor, Ann. *Baby Dance* (PS). Illus. by Marjorie van Heerden. Series: Harper Growing Tree. 1999, HarperCollins $6.99 (978-0-694-01206-0). In this board book, an African American dad and his baby daughter play to a series of catchy rhymes. (Rev: BCCB 5/99; SLJ 3/99)

3569 Tessler, Manya. *Yuki's Ride Home* (K–3). Illus. by author. 2008, Bloomsbury $16.95 (978-1-59990-023-0). 32pp. After spending the day with her grandmother, a Japanese girl faces a bicycle ride in the dark. (Rev: BL 4/1/08; LMC 3/08; SLJ 2/08)

3570 Thiel, Annie. *Chloe's New Baby Brother* (1–4). Illus. by William M. Edwards and Karen Marjoribanks. 2006, Playdate Kids $14.95 (978-1-933721-01-9). Only child Chloe learns that the arrival of a new sibling will not affect her parents' love for her. (Rev: SLJ 9/06)

3571 Thomas, Eliza. *The Red Blanket* (PS–2). Illus. by Joe Cepeda. 2004, Scholastic $15.95 (978-0-439-32253-9). 32pp. This endearing tale of a young woman's journey to China to adopt a child is based on events from the author's life. (Rev: BL 5/15/04; SLJ 7/04)

3572 Thomas, Naturi. *Uh-oh! It's Mama's Birthday!* (PS–3). Illus. by Keinyo White. 1997, Whitman LB $13.95 (978-0-8075-8268-8). 24pp. An African American boy gives his mother what she really wants on her birthday: a big hug. (Rev: BL 2/15/97; HB 3/97; SLJ 5/97)

3573 Thomas, Patricia. *Red Sled* (PS–2). Illus. by Chris L. Demarest. 2008, Boyds Mills $16.95 (978-1-59078-559-1). A father and son go sledding at night in this simple story told in rhyming pairs of words. (Rev: BL 9/1/08; HB 9/08; SLJ 8/08)

3574 Thong, Roseanne. *Tummy Girl* (PS–K). Illus. by Sam Williams. 2007, Holt $15.95 (978-0-8050-7609-7). 32pp. Rhyming text and a photo-album format celebrate a baby growing into a toddler and then into a schoolgirl. (Rev: BL 4/1/07)

3575 Tillman, Nancy. *Wherever You Are: My Love Will Find You* (PS–2). Illus. by author. 2010, Feiwel &

Friends $16.99 (978-031254966-4). 32pp. This sweetly reassuring rhyming picture book reinforces the message that all children are loved. (Rev: BL 9/15/10)

3576 Tonatiuh, Duncan. *Dear Primo: A Letter to My Cousin* (1–3). Illus. by author. 2010, Abrams $15.95 (978-0-8109-3872-4). 32pp. Urban American Charlie exchanges letters with his Cousin Carlitos, who lives in rural Mexico; Spanish words and details of Mexican culture are integrated, and the illustrations are based on Mixtec art. (Rev: BL 2/1/10; SLJ 3/1/10)

3577 Toten, Teresa. *Bright Red Kisses* (PS–K). Illus. by Deirdre Betteridge. 2005, Annick LB $19.95 (978-1-55037-909-9); paper $7.95 (978-1-55037-908-2). 32pp. A young girl helps her mother prepare for an evening out, from running the bath to choosing the best lipstick, which will kiss her when her mother returns. (Rev: BL 1/1–15/06)

3578 Trottier, Maxine. *Migrant* (PS–2). Illus. by Isabelle Arsenault. 2011, Groundwood $18.95 (978-0-88899-975-7). 40pp. Anna's Mennonite family travels from Mexico to Canada each year to work in the fields, and the young girl imagines herself as a variety of animals in an effort to cope with the constant moving. (Rev: BL 4/1/11; LMC 10/11; SLJ 5/1/11)

3579 Tuck, Justin. *Home-Field Advantage* (K–2). Illus. by Leonardo Rodriguez. 2011, Simon & Schuster $16.99 (978-1-4424-0369-7). 40pp. New York Giants defensive end Tuck offers a comic vignette from his childhood: the day he let his sisters cut his hair. Lexile AD540L (Rev: BLO 9/1/11; SLJ 9/1/11)

3580 Turner-Denstaedt, Melanie. *The Hat That Wore Clara B.* (K–3). Illus. by Frank Morrison. 2009, Farrar $16.95 (978-0-374-32794-1). Even though she has been told not to touch the impressive hat that her grandmother wears to a special Sunday service, Clara secretly attempts to try it on, accidentally crushes it, and is generously forgiven. (Rev: BCCB 7–8/09; SLJ 5/09)

3581 Underwood, Deborah. *Bad Bye, Good Bye* (PS–2). Illus. by Jonathan Bean. 2014, Houghton Mifflin $16.99 (978-054792852-4). 32pp. A simple book about a family moving to a new town and the emotions they experience. **e** (Rev: BL 3/1/14*; LMC 8–9/14; SLJ 3/14)

3582 Urdahl, Catherine. *Emma's Question* (PS–K). Illus. by Janine Dawson. 2009, Charlesbridge $16.95 (978-1-58089-145-5); paper $7.95 (978-1-58089-146-2). 32pp. Emma's grandmother is in the hospital, and Emma has lots of questions, including "Are you going to die?" (Rev: BCCB 2/09; BL 2/1/09; SLJ 5/09)

3583 Vamos, Samantha R. *Before You Were Here, Mi Amor* (PS–2). Illus. by Santiago Cohen. 2009, Viking $15.99 (978-0-670-06301-7). 32pp. In English interlaced with Spanish words, a mother tells her unborn child how the happy family is preparing for the little one's arrival. (Rev: BCCB 4/09; BL 2/15/09; SLJ 3/09)

3584 Van den Abeele, Veronique. *Still My Grandma* (K–2). Illus. by Claude K. Dubois. 2007, Eerdmans $16.00 (978-0-8028-5323-3). 28pp. Camille watches her grandma sink into Alzheimer's disease and tries to help and

181

show her love when she can. (Rev: BL 10/15/07; SLJ 10/07)

3585 Van Leeuwen, Jean. *Benny and Beautiful Baby Delilah* (PS–K). Illus. by LeUyen Pham. 2006, Dial $16.99 (978-0-8037-2891-2). 32pp. Bennie finds his "beautiful" baby sister very trying until he succeeds in making her smile; excellent artwork adds to the heartwarming story. (Rev: BL 2/1/06; SLJ 3/06*)

3586 Velasquez, Eric. *Grandma's Gift* (1–3). Illus. by author. 2010, Walker $16.99 (978-080272082-5). 32pp. This companion to the autobiographical *Grandma's Records* (2001) describes young Eric's activities — including a visit to the Metropolitan Museum of Art — with his Puerto Rican grandmother during a winter break in New York City; Spanish phrases are included in the text. (Rev: BL 11/15/10; LMC 11–12/10; SLJ 10/10)

3587 Velasquez, Eric. *Grandma's Records* (K–3). Illus. 2001, Walker LB $17.85 (978-0-8027-8761-3). 32pp. A young boy enjoys summers full of Latin music with his grandmother in Spanish Harlem in this novel based on the author's own memories. (Rev: BL 5/15/01; HBG 10/01; SLJ 9/01)

3588 Vestergaard, Hope. *Driving Daddy* (PS–1). Illus. by Thierry Courtin. 2003, Dutton $6.99 (978-0-525-47032-8). 24pp. A small-format book in which a little boy gets to ride on his father's shoulders. (Rev: BL 3/1/03; HBG 10/03; SLJ 3/03)

3589 Vigil-Pinon, Evangelina. *Marina's Muumuu / El Muumuu de Marina* (2–5). Illus. by Pablo Torrecilla. 2001, Arte Publico $14.95 (978-1-55885-350-8). 32pp. A bilingual story about a girl named Marina who dreams of wearing a colorful, tropical muumuu like those from her grandmother's home. (Rev: BL 1/1–15/02; SLJ 1/02)

3590 Viorst, Judith. *Alexander and the Terrible, Horrible, No Good, Very Bad Day* (K–3). Illus. by Ray Cruz. 1972, Macmillan LB $14.00 (978-0-689-30072-1); paper $4.99 (978-0-689-71173-2). Alexander wakes up to a bad day and things get progressively worse as the hours wear on, until he thinks he may escape it all and go to Australia.

3591 Viorst, Judith. *Alexander, Who's Not (Do You Hear Me? I Mean It!) Going to Move* (PS–3). Illus. by Robin P. Glasser. 1995, Simon & Schuster LB $15.00 (978-0-689-31958-7). 42pp. Alexander of bad-day fame, faces another crisis when he adamantly refuses to move to the family's new home. (Rev: BCCB 11/95; BL 8/95*; SLJ 10/95*)

3592 Viorst, Judith. *Nobody Here but Me* (PS–2). Illus. by Christine Davenier. 2008, Farrar $16.95 (978-0-374-35540-1). It's almost dinnertime and everybody in the house is busy as a little boy wanders around trying to get their attention in this cheerful look at how families operate. (Rev: BL 9/15/08; SLJ 8/08)

3593 Voake, Charlotte. *Hello Twins* (PS). Illus. by author. 2006, Candlewick $15.99 (978-0-7636-3003-4). Little Charlotte and Simon may be twins, but they are different and they like it that way. (Rev: BL 5/15/06; SLJ 7/06)

3594 Waboose, Jan B. *Firedancers* (1–4). Illus. by C. J. Taylor. 2000, Stoddart $14.95 (978-0-7737-3138-7). 32pp. A young Ojibwa girl visits Smooth Rock Island at night and joins her grandmother as a Firedancer. (Rev: BL 7/00)

3595 Wadham, Tim. *The Queen of France* (PS–3). Illus. by Kady MacDonald Denton. 2011, Candlewick $16.99 (978-0-7636-4102-3). 32pp. A young girl imagines herself the Queen of France, and considers all the ways her life might be easier before settling on being what she's most familiar with: herself. Lexile 400L (Rev: BL 4/15/11; HB 5–6/11; SLJ 2/1/11*)

3596 Waldherr, Kris. *Harvest* (PS–1). Illus. 2001, Walker LB $16.85 (978-0-8027-8793-4). A girl and her mother harvest and prepare fruits and vegetables from the garden in order to prepare for winter in this simple yet memorable autumn story. (Rev: BL 11/15/01; HBG 3/02; SLJ 11/01)

3597 Walton, Rick. *Baby's First Year!* (PS). Illus. by Caroline Jayne Church. 2011, Putnam $15.99 (978-0-399-25025-5). 32pp. In rhyming text and bright art, this book celebrates the key events of a baby's first year. (Rev: BL 2/15/11; SLJ 3/1/11)

3598 Walvoord, Linda. *Razzamadaddy* (PS–1). Illus. by Sachiko Yoshikawa. 2004, Marshall Cavendish $14.95 (978-0-7614-5158-7). A father and son enjoy a day at the beach, depicted in rhyming text and vivid illustrations. (Rev: SLJ 7/04)

3599 Wangerin, Walter. *I Am My Grandpa's Enkelin* (1–3). Illus. by Don Tate. 2007, Paraclete $18.95 (978-1-55725-468-9). 32pp. A young girl describes her German immigrant grandfather's farm and the lessons he has taught her in this fictional memoir that extends into the girl's adult years. (Rev: BL 2/15/08; SLJ 6/08)

3600 Wells, Rosemary. *Love Waves* (PS–1). Illus. by author. 2011, Candlewick $15.99 (978-0-7636-4989-0). 32pp. A young rabbit's parents send warm thoughts — love waves — home to him while they're out at work. (Rev: BL 9/1/11; SLJ 9/1/11)

3601 Weston, Tamson. *Hey, Pancakes!* (PS–1). Illus. by Stephen Gammell. 2003, Harcourt $17.00 (978-0-15-216502-4). Rhyming verse and mixed-media artwork portray three siblings energetically cooking up a sloppy batch of pancakes. (Rev: HBG 4/04; SLJ 9/03)

3602 Wewer, Iris. *My Wild Sister and Me* (PS–2). Illus. by author. 2011, NorthSouth $16.95 (978-0-7358-4003-4). 32pp. A young boy and his older sister enjoy imaginative games together until a friend interrupts them, spoiling his day — until later. Lexile AD570L (Rev: BL 3/1/11; SLJ 3/1/11)

3603 Wheeler, Lisa. *Jazz Baby* (PS–1). Illus. by R. Gregory Christie. 2007, Harcourt $16.00 (978-0-15-202522-9). 40pp. A bouncing African American baby enjoys music along with the rest of the family in this rhythmic volume with vibrant illustrations. (Rev: BCCB 12/07; BL 10/15/07; HB 1/08; SLJ 1/08)

3604 Whelan, Gloria. *Jam and Jelly by Holly and Nelly* (K–2). Illus. by Gijsbert van Frankenhuyzen. 2002,

Sleeping Bear $17.95 (978-1-58536-109-0). 48pp. A captivating story of a mother's determination to buy her daughter a coat so she can go to school in the cold. (Rev: BL 12/15/02; SLJ 1/03)

3605 Wigersma, Tanneke. *Baby Brother* (PS–1). Illus. by Nynke Mare Talsma. 2005, Front St. $16.95 (978-1-932425-55-0). In a letter to her grandmother, little Mia focuses on her cat's delivery of five kittens, only mentioning the birth of her baby brother at the end; illustrations fill in the gaps. (Rev: SLJ 11/05)

3606 Wild, Margaret. *Our Granny* (PS–1). Illus. by Julie Vivas. 1994, Ticknor $17.00 (978-0-395-67023-1). All kinds of grandmothers from the glamorous and kinky to cuddly and plain are celebrated in this lively picture book. (Rev: BCCB 5/94; BL 1/15/94*; HB 5/94; SLJ 4/94*)

3607 Willhoite, Michael. *Daddy's Roommate* (PS–2). Illus. 1990, Alyson paper $10.95 (978-1-55583-118-9). 32pp. After his parents' divorce, a young boy finds that his father has a male partner and on weekends the boy enjoys visiting the two of them. (Rev: BCCB 2/91; BL 3/1/91; SLJ 4/91)

3608 Williams, Karen Lynn. *Circles of Hope* (PS–K). Illus. by Linda Saport. 2005, Eerdmans $16.00 (978-0-8028-5276-2). 32pp. In Haiti, a boy called Facile struggles to grow a tree as a gift for his new baby sister, finally building a protective circle of stones. (Rev: BL 5/15/05; SLJ 4/05)

3609 Williams, Linda E. *The Best Winds* (K–3). Illus. by Eujin Kim Neilan. 2006, Boyds Mills $16.95 (978-1-59078-274-3). 32pp. Jinho ignores his grandfather's stories of ancient Korean traditions as the two work to create a kite, but when the young boy carelessly damages the kite he learns to appreciate his cultural heritage. (Rev: BL 4/1/06; SLJ 3/06)

3610 Williams, Vera B. *A Chair for Always* (PS–2). Illus. by author. 2009, HarperCollins $16.99 (978-0-06-172279-0). 40pp. The rose-covered chair first featured in *A Chair for My Mother* (1982) plays an important role in this fourth book, in which Rosa is anticipating a new cousin and there is tension about the dilapidated state of the beloved chair. (Rev: BL 5/15/09; SLJ 5/09) ∩

3611 Williams, Vera B. *A Chair for My Mother* (PS–2). Illus. by author. 1982, Greenwillow $17.89 (978-0-688-00915-1). After fire destroys their home, Rose and her mother and grandmother save to buy a nice new chair. Two sequels are: *Something Special for Me* (1983); *Music, Music for Everyone* (1984).

3612 Williams, Vera B. *Lucky Song* (PS–K). Illus. 1997, Greenwillow $14.89 (978-0-688-14460-9). 24pp. Evie is a lucky girl because all of her wants and needs are satisfied by her loving family. (Rev: BL 10/1/97*; HB 9/97; HBG 3/98; SLJ 8/97*)

3613 Wilson, Karma. *Mama Always Comes Home* (PS). Illus. by Brooke Dyer. 2005, HarperCollins LB $16.89 (978-0-06-057506-9). A mother tells her child that she will always come home, using animal stories as reassuring examples. (Rev: SLJ 5/05)

3614 Wilson, Sarah. *Friends and Pals and Brothers, Too* (PS–1). Illus. by Leo Landry. 2008, Holt $16.95 (978-0-8050-7643-1). Two young brothers play together throughout the year in this engaging picture book. (Rev: BL 5/15/08; SLJ 5/08)

3615 Winch, John. *Keeping Up with Grandma* (PS–3). Illus. 2000, Holiday House $16.95 (978-0-8234-1563-2). 32pp. Grandma wants to start mountain climbing, whitewater canoeing, and hot-air ballooning but she and Grandpa later decide that their usual quiet life is better. (Rev: BL 11/15/00; HBG 3/01; SLJ 11/00)

3616 Wing, Natasha L. *Jalapeno Bagels* (PS–2). Illus. by Robert Casilla. 1996, Simon & Schuster $15.00 (978-0-689-80530-1). Pablo, who comes from a racially mixed family, finds his life is enriched by both cultures. (Rev: BL 6/1–15/96; SLJ 7/96)

3617 Winstanley, Nicola. *Cinnamon Baby* (PS–2). Illus. by Janice Nadeau. 2011, Kids Can $16.95 (978-1-55337-821-1). 32pp. Miriam's cinnamon bread attracts a violinist named Sebastian, and the two get married; their beautiful baby cries and cries until the smell of baking bread finally solves the problem. Lexile AD930L (Rev: BL 2/15/11; SLJ 4/11)

3618 Winthrop, Elizabeth. *Squashed in the Middle* (K–3). Illus. by Pat Cummings. 2005, Holt $16.95 (978-0-8050-6497-1). Middle child Daisy gets her family's attention when she goes to a friend's house all on her own. (Rev: BL 4/1/05; SLJ 6/05)

3619 Wissinger, Tamera Will. *Gone Fishing* (1–4). Illus. by Matthew Cordell. 2013, Houghton Mifflin $15.99 (978-0-547-82011-8). 128pp. Sam is looking forward to a fishing trip with his father until his little sister Lucy announces she's coming too in this novel told in verse. ALA Notable Children's Book. (Rev: BL 3/15/13; SLJ 7/13*)

3620 Witte, Anna. *Lola's Fandango* (K–3). Illus. by Micha Archer. 2011, Barefoot $16.99 (978-1-84686-174-1); paper $9.99 (978-1-84686-681-4). 48pp. Lola, living in the shadow of her older sister, decides to learn flamenco dancing as a way of differentiating herself from Clementina. (Rev: BL 8/11*; SLJ 12/1/11)

3621 Wolff, Ashley. *Me Baby, You Baby* (PS). Illus. by author. 2004, Dutton $14.99 (978-0-525-46952-0). This book follows two toddlers (a white girl and a black boy) and their mothers through a busy day, including a visit to the zoo. (Rev: BL 3/1/04*; HB 3/04; SLJ 3/04)

3622 Wong, Janet S. *Homegrown House* (K–3). Illus. by E. B. Lewis. 2009, Simon & Schuster $16.99 (978-0-689-84718-9). 40pp. A little girl reluctantly prepares for yet another move to yet another house. (Rev: BL 6/1–15/09; SLJ 7/09)

3623 Woo, Alan. *Maggie's Chopsticks* (PS–1). Illus. by Isabelle Malenfant. 2012, Kids Can $16.95 (978-1-55453-619-1). 32pp. Young Maggie struggles with using chopsticks, and eventually comes up with her own technique in this Asian American family story. Lexile AD740 (Rev: BLO 8/12; LMC 5–6/13; SLJ 9/12)

3624 Wood, Douglas. *Grandad's Prayers of the Earth* (K–3). Illus. by P. J. Lynch. 1999, Candlewick $16.99 (978-0-7636-0660-2). 32pp. A boy and his grandfather talk about prayer, and after the old man's death, the boy remembers his gentle ways and his loving faith. (Rev: BL 12/1/99; HBG 3/00; SLJ 1/00)

3625 Wood, Douglas. *When a Dad Says "I Love You"* (PS–2). Illus. by Jennifer A. Bell. 2013, Simon & Schuster $16.99 (978-068987532-8). 32pp. A charming tribute to fathers' abilities to communicate with their children in a variety of ways. Lexile AD660 (Rev: BLO 3/15/13; SLJ 1/1/14)

3626 Woodson, Jacqueline. *Pecan Pie Baby* (PS–1). Illus. by Sophie Blackall. 2010, Putnam $16.99 (978-0-399-23987-8). 32pp. Gia's single-parent mother is pregnant, and Gia is jealous of the attention the pending arrival is getting. Boston Globe–Horn Book Award. Lexile AD710L (Rev: BL 8/10; HB 11–12/10; LMC 1–2/11; SLJ 10/1/10)

3627 Woodson, Jacqueline. *Visiting Day* (K–2). Illus. by James Ransome. 2002, Scholastic $15.95 (978-0-590-40005-3). 32pp. This is a gentle family story of a little African American girl's visit to her father in prison. (Rev: BCCB 12/02; BL 11/1/02; HB 11/02; HBG 3/03; SLJ 9/02)

3628 Yaccarino, Dan. *Every Friday* (PS–K). Illus. 2007, Holt $16.95 (978-0-8050-7724-7). 32pp. A father and son enjoy their weekly Friday breakfast together. (Rev: BL 2/1/07)

3629 Yeh, Kat. *The Magic Brush: A Story of Love, Family, and Chinese Characters* (K–3). Illus. by Huy Voun Lee. 2011, Walker $16.99 (978-080272178-5). 40pp. A young Chinese American girl, Jasmine, is sad after the death of the grandfather who taught her calligraphy and told her stories, but she soon realizes that her younger brother would also be interested and shares what she has learned with him. (Rev: BL 12/15/10; LMC 3–4/11; SLJ 4/11)

3630 Yolen, Jane. *My Father Knows the Names of Things* (PS–2). Illus. by Stephane Jorisch. 2010, Simon & Schuster $15.99 (978-1-4169-4895-7). 32pp. A young boy enumerates the amazing things that his father knows — the names of dogs, seven words that mean blue, the names of the planets — in this well-illustrated rhyming text. (Rev: BL 2/1/10; LMC 5–6/10; SLJ 3/1/10)

3631 Yolen, Jane. *Soft House* (PS–K). Illus. by Wendy A. Halperin. 2005, Candlewick $15.99 (978-0-7636-1697-7). 32pp. To fight boredom on a rainy day, a girl and her younger brother use household items to build a cozy fort. (Rev: BL 11/1/05)

3632 Young, Cybele. *A Few Bites* (PS–2). Illus. by author. 2012, Groundwood $18.95 (978-1-55498-295-0). 48pp. Ferdie's older sister Viola does her best to convince him that dinosaurs loved broccoli and that carrots give aliens their super vision. (Rev: BLO 10/1/12; SLJ 11/12)

3633 Young, Ed. *My Mei Mei* (PS–2). Illus. 2006, Philomel $16.99 (978-0-399-24339-4). A moving story about Antonia — who herself was adopted from China

— and her difficult adjustment to life with her newly adopted infant sister, also from China. (Rev: BL 1/1–15/06; SLJ 2/06*)

3634 Yum, Hyewon. *There Are No Scary Wolves* (PS–K). Illus. by author. 2010, Farrar $16.99 (978-0-374-38060-1). 40pp. Balancing a young boy's imagination with reassuring scenes of everyday life, this book about seeing people as wolves capitalizes on the safety and comfort of family and the familiar. (Rev: BL 11/15/10; SLJ 10/1/10)

3635 Yum, Hyewon. *The Twins' Blanket* (PS–2). Illus. by author. 2011, Farrar $16.99 (978-0-374-37972-8). 40pp. Five-year-old twin girls getting separate beds for the first time decide to divide their favorite blanket into two pieces. (Rev: BL 8/11; SLJ 8/1/11*)

3636 Zalben, Jane Breskin. *Baby Babka, the Gorgeous Genius* (K–4). Illus. by Victoria Chess. 2004, Clarion $15.00 (978-0-618-23489-9). 38pp. Beryl is disappointed when the new baby is another boy, but Uncle Morty has a solution. (Rev: SLJ 11/04)

3637 Zamorano, Ana. *Let's Eat!* (PS–2). Illus. by Julie Vivas. 1997, Scholastic $15.95 (978-0-590-13444-6). 32pp. A loving Spanish family enjoys Mama's food even more when she returns home from the hospital with baby Rosa. (Rev: BCCB 4/97; BL 5/15/97; SLJ 4/97*)

3638 Zemach, Margot. *Eating up Gladys* (PS–2). Illus. by Kaethe Zemach. 2005, Scholastic $16.99 (978-0-439-66490-5). 32pp. When Gladys, their bossy older sister, pushes them just a little too far, younger siblings Rose and Hilda plot a spectacular revenge. (Rev: BL 9/1/05; SLJ 9/05)

3639 Zia, F. *Hot, Hot Roti for Dada-ji* (1–3). Illus. by Ken Min. 2011, Lee & Low $17.95 (978-1-60060-443-0). 32pp. Grandfather Dada-ji's adventurous stories inspire young Aneel to make roti — flat, Indian bread — in this story full of Hindi culture. Lexile AD680L (Rev: BL 6/1/11; LMC 10/11; SLJ 6/11)

3640 Ziefert, Harriet. *Bigger than Daddy* (PS). Illus. by Elliot Kreloff. 2006, Blue Apple $15.95 (978-1-59354-147-7). 36pp. On a trip to the park, Edward wants to switch roles with his daddy and do grown-up things. (Rev: BL 5/1/06; SLJ 8/06)

3641 Ziefert, Harriet. *Grandma, It's for You!* (PS–1). Illus. by Lauren Browne. 2006, Blue Apple $15.95 (978-1-59354-109-5). Little Lulu fashions a very special hat to give to her grandmother. (Rev: SLJ 8/06)

3642 Ziefert, Harriet. *Grandma's Wedding Album* (K–3). Illus. by author. 2011, Blue Apple $17.99 (978-1-60905-058-0). 40pp. A grandmother shares her wedding album with her grandchildren; includes details of the engagement and wedding and covers wedding traditions around the world. (Rev: BLO 8/11; LMC 10/11; SLJ 6/11)

3643 Ziefert, Harriet. *My Friend Grandpa* (K–3). Illus. by Robert Wurzburg. 2004, Blue Apple $15.95 (978-1-59354-063-0). A celebration of the close relationship Emma shares with her grandfather and the happy times they spend in the country. (Rev: SLJ 11/04)

3644 Ziefert, Harriet. *A New Coat for Anna* (K–3). Illus. by Anita Lobel. 1986, Knopf paper $6.99 (978-0-394-

89861-2). 40pp. It's been a long time since Anna has had a new coat, and her mother vows to get one for her in this story of post-World War II Europe. (Rev: BCCB 3/87; BL 12/15/86; SLJ 12/86)

3645 Ziefert, Harriet. *31 Uses for a Mom* (PS–K). Illus. by Rebecca Doughty. 2003, Penguin $12.99 (978-0-399-23862-8). 32pp. Moms turn out to be fairly useful things in this list that covers a wide range of attributes. (Rev: BL 1/1–15/03; HBG 10/03; SLJ 3/03)

3646 Zisk, Mary. *The Best Single Mom in the World: How I Was Adopted* (PS–K). Illus. by author. 2001, Whitman LB $16.99 (978-0-8075-0666-0). A little girl and her mother tell the tale of her adoption across the sea. (Rev: HBG 3/02; SLJ 1/02)

3647 Zolotow, Charlotte. *A Father Like That* (K–3). Illus. by LeUyen Pham. 2007, HarperCollins $16.99 (978-0-06-027864-9). 40pp. First published in 1971 and now updated with new illustrations, this is the story of a young African American boy who imagines the father who left before he was born. (Rev: BL 5/15/07; SLJ 7/07)

3648 Zolotow, Charlotte. *If It Weren't for You* (PS–2). Illus. by G. Brian Karas. 2006, HarperCollins $15.99 (978-0-06-027875-5). As big sister fantasizes about what life would be like without her younger sibling, her younger sister behaves with such uncharacteristic kindness that the older girl decides she'd just as soon keep her around. (Rev: SLJ 10/06)

3649 Zolotow, Charlotte. *The Quarreling Book* (K–2). Illus. by Arnold Lobel. 1963, HarperCollins paper $6.99 (978-0-06-443034-0). 32pp. Father's failure to kiss mother one morning triggers a series of quarrels, but the pet dog sets things right. Also use: *The Hating Book* (1969).

3650 Zolotow, Charlotte. *William's Doll* (PS–3). Illus. by William Pene du Bois. 1972, HarperCollins paper $6.99 (978-0-06-443067-8). 32pp. William wanted a doll, much to his father's dismay; but when Grandma comes to visit she presents William with a doll, saying that now he will have an opportunity to practice being a good father.

3651 Zuckerman, Linda. *I Will Hold You 'til You Sleep* (PS). Illus. by Jon J. Muth. 2006, Scholastic $16.99 (978-0-439-43420-1). With poetic text and gentle illustrations, this book celebrates parents' love for a child throughout the years. (Rev: SLJ 10/06)

3652 Zuppardi, Sam. *The Nowhere Box* (PS–2). Illus. by author. 2013, Candlewick $15.99 (978-0-7636-6367-4). 40pp. An empty washing machine box provides a refuge for poor George, who is tired of his two little brothers — until he finds that he's lonely. (Rev: BLO 10/1/13; SLJ 10/13)

3653 Zweibel, Alan. *Our Tree Named Steve* (1–3). Illus. by David Catrow. 2005, Penguin $15.99 (978-0-399-23722-5). A sad story about a beloved tree knocked down by a storm. (Rev: BL 2/1/04; SLJ 4/05)

FRIENDSHIP STORIES

3654 Al Abdullah, Her Majesty Queen Rania, and Kelly DiPucchio. *The Sandwich Swap* (PS–2). Illus. by Tricia Tusa. 2010, Hyperion $16.99 (978-1-4231-2484-9). 32pp. Best friends Lily and Salma swap sandwiches — pita and hummus for peanut butter and jelly — and are pleasantly surprised by what they find. (Rev: BL 2/15/10; LMC 8–9/10; SLJ 4/1/10)

3655 Allen, Joy. *Princess Party* (PS–K). Illus. by author. 2009, Putnam $16.99 (978-0-399-25259-4). Unpaged. Two little girls — one dressed in frills and the other wearing cowboy boots and T-shirt — host a princess party attended by diverse ethnicities wearing many styles. (Rev: SLJ 11/1/09)

3656 Appelbaum, Diana. *Cocoa Ice* (2–5). Illus. by Holly Meade. 1997, Orchard LB $17.99 (978-0-531-33040-1). Two girls, one in Santo Domingo and the other in Maine, are linked by world trade, which brings chocolate to one and ice to the other. (Rev: BCCB 3/98; BL 11/1/97*; HBG 3/98; SLJ 1/98*)

3657 Appelt, Kathi. *Bubba and Beau, Best Friends* (PS–K). Illus. by Arthur Howard. 2002, Harcourt $16.00 (978-0-15-202060-6). 32pp. Bubba, a little boy, and Beau, his puppy, are unhappy when the smelly blanket they love is washed and now smells of soap. (Rev: BCCB 4/02; BL 4/1/02; HBG 10/02; SLJ 7/02)

3658 Atwood, Margaret. *Up in the Tree* (PS–2). Illus. 2006, Groundwood $14.95 (978-0-88899-729-6). 32pp. In this engaging two-color picture book first published in 1976, the Canadian author tells the story of two boys who make their home in a tree. (Rev: BL 4/1/06)

3659 Baker, Roberta. *Olive's First Sleepover* (1–3). Illus. by Debbie Tilley. 2007, Little, Brown $16.99 (978-0-316-73418-9). 32pp. Olive's first sleepover at her friend Lizard's house is full of fun and, when the lights go out, spooky sounds. (Rev: BL 7/07; SLJ 7/07)

3660 Barrows, Annie. *Bound to Be Bad* (1–3). Illus. by Sophie Blackall. 2008, Chronicle $14.99 (978-0-8118-6265-3). 124pp. Ivy learns about St. Francis and resolves to reform herself as well as Bean and the bully Matt. (Rev: BL 2/1/09; HB 3/09) ∩

3661 Bateman, Teresa. *Paul Bunyan vs. Hals Halson: The Giant Lumberjack Challenge!* (PS–2). Illus. by C. B. Canga. 2011, Whitman $16.99 (978-0-8075-6367-0). 32pp. Paul Bunyan eventually succeeds in making friends with the lumberjack who has been doing his best to prove that he is better and stronger. (Rev: BL 4/15/11; SLJ 2/1/11)

3662 Beaumont, Karen. *Being Friends* (PS–2). Illus. by Joy Allen. 2002, Dial $16.99 (978-0-8037-2529-4). Two girls, best friends despite their different personalities, have fun together in this rhyming picture book. (Rev: BL 9/15/02; HBG 10/02; SLJ 7/02)

3663 Blabey, Aaron. *Pearl Barley and Charlie Parsley* (K–1). Illus. by author. 2008, Front St. $16.95 (978-1-59078-596-6). 32pp. Pearl and Charlie are best friends even though they are different in every way. (Rev: BCCB 11/08; SLJ 9/08)

3664 Blake, Quentin. *Fantastic Daisy Artichoke* (PS–1). Illus. by author. 2001, Red Fox paper $11.00 (978-0-09-940006-6). Rhythmic text and bright, lively drawings tell the story of the fun two children had when they met their friend Daisy. (Rev: SLJ 10/01)

3665 Bley, Anette. *A Friend* (PS–1). Illus. by author. 2009, Kane $14.95 (978-1-935279-00-6). 36pp. Diverse scenarios demonstrate the value of friendship. (Rev: BL 3/1/09)

3666 Bottner, Barbara. *Rosa's Room* (PS–1). Illus. by Beth Spiegel. 2004, Peachtree $15.95 (978-1-56145-302-3). 32pp. Rosa's room in her new house seems strangely empty until she finds a friend to share it. (Rev: BL 4/1/04; SLJ 5/04)

3667 Brown, Laurie Krasny. *How to Be a Friend: A Guide to Making Friends and Keeping Them* (K–3). Illus. by Marc Brown. 1998, Little, Brown $14.95 (978-0-316-10913-0). 32pp. Using humanlike dinosaurs as subjects, this practical guide shows how to make friends and keep their friendship. (Rev: BL 10/15/98; HB 11/98; HBG 3/99; SLJ 9/98)

3668 Budnitz, Paul. *The Hole in the Middle* (PS–1). Illus. by Aya Kakeda. 2011, Hyperion/Disney $16.99 (978-1-4231-3761-0). 40pp. A self-centered young boy with a hole in his middle that leaves him feeling empty finds that the hole shrinks when he does something kind for a friend. (Rev: BL 6/1/11; SLJ 7/11)

3669 Bunge, Daniela. *Cherry Time* (K–2). Trans. from German by Kathryn Bishop. Illus. by author. 2007, Minedition $16.99 (978-0-698-40057-3). A boy overcomes his shyness with the help of his dog in this story translated from the German. (Rev: SLJ 7/07)

3670 Carle, Eric. *Friends* (PS–K). Illus. by author. 2013, Philomel $17.99 (978-039916533-7). 32pp. Carle's signature artwork is effective in this story about a boy's affection for his best friend, and his journey to find her when she moves away. (Rev: BL 9/1/13; SLJ 9/13)

3671 Catalanotto, Peter. *Monkey and Robot* (1–3). Illus. by author. 2013, Atheneum $12.99 (978-1-4424-2978-9). 64pp. Best friends Monkey and Robot have fun together watching a movie and playing games. e Lexile 460L (Rev: BL 3/1/13; HB 1–2/13; SLJ 9/13)

3672 Chodos-Irvine, Margaret. *Best Best Friends* (PS–K). Illus. by author. 2006, Harcourt $16.00 (978-0-15-205694-0). 40pp. In this charming story for the very young, preschool jealousy briefly interrupts Clare and Mary's best-friendship. (Rev: BCCB 9/06; BL 5/1/06; HB 5/06; HBG 10/06; SLJ 6/06)

3673 Cuyler, Margery. *I Repeat, Don't Cheat!* (K–2). Illus. by Arthur Howard. 2010, Simon & Schuster $15.99 (978-1-4169-7167-2). 32pp. Jessica learns the fine line between helping her friend and letting her cheat. (Rev: BL 5/15/10; SLJ 6/1/10)

3674 Demers, Dominique. *Today, Maybe* (K–3). Trans. by Sheila Fischman. Illus. by Gabrielle Grimard. 2011, Orca $19.95 (978-155469400-6). 32pp. Lovely paintings enhance this story about a young girl who is waiting for a special "someone" to turn up and dispatches vis-

iting characters from children's literature, who include thieves, a wolf, a prince, and a witch. (Rev: BL 4/15/11)

3675 DiPucchio, Kelly. *Crafty Chloe* (1–3). Illus. by Heather Ross. 2012, Atheneum $16.99 (978-1-4424-2123-3). 40pp. Unlike most of the other girls, Chloe's talent is making things, and this ability allows her to come to the rescue of an unkind classmate. e (Rev: BL 12/15/11; LMC 5–6/12; SLJ 3/1/12)

3676 DiPucchio, Kelly. *Crafty Chloe: Dress-Up Mess-Up* (PS–K). Illus. by Heather Ross. 2013, Simon & Schuster $16.99 (978-144242124-0). 40pp. Do-it-yourself heroine Chloe is back in this romp about friendship, creativity, and deciding which costume — and which friend — to choose for the Parade of Books dress-up day at school. Lexile AD510 (Rev: BLO 9/1/13; SLJ 7/13)

3677 Donofrio, Beverly. *Where's Mommy?* (PS–K). Illus. by Barbara McClintock. 2014, Random House $17.99 (978-037584423-2). 32pp. This nicely illustrated book depicts the parallel lives of friends Maria (upstairs) and Mouse Mouse (under the floor). Lexile AD550 (Rev: BL 3/1/14; HB 3–4/14; SLJ 3/14)

3678 English, Karen. *Nikki and Deja* (1–3). Illus. by Laura Freeman. 2008, Clarion $15.00 (978-0-618-75238-6). 80pp. Two African American 3rd-grade girls struggle to keep their friendship afloat when a new girl moves into the neighborhood. (Rev: BL 2/1/08; SLJ 6/08)

3679 Fagan, Carl. *Mr. Zinger's Hat* (K–2). Illus. by Dusan Petricic. 2012, Tundra $17.95 (978-1-77049-253-0). 32pp. A little boy named Leo and an elderly writer named Mr. Zinger create a relevant tale when Leo sends the man's hat flying. (Rev: BL 10/1/12; SLJ 12/12)

3680 Fagan, Cary. *Ella May and the Wishing Stone* (PS–1). Illus. by Geneviève Côté. 2011, Tundra $17.95 (978-1-77049-225-7). Unpaged. Ella May works to make amends after belittling her friends' efforts to imitate her "magical" wishing stone. (Rev: SLJ 8/1/11)

3681 Failing, Barbara Larmon. *Lasso Lou and Cowboy McCoy* (PS–2). Illus. by Tedd Arnold. 2003, Dial $16.99 (978-0-8037-2578-2). McCoy's 10-gallon hat is not enough to turn him into a cowboy, but Lasso Lou is patient and helps him to learn the ropes. (Rev: HBG 4/04; SLJ 10/03)

3682 Feldman, Eve B. *Billy and Milly, Short and Silly* (PS–2). Illus. by Tuesday Mourning. 2009, Putnam $16.99 (978-0-399-24651-7). 32pp. A collection of 13 tightly rhymed little stories (mostly four words long) about a little girl and boy, with satisfying visual interplays. (Rev: HB 9/09; SLJ 7/09*)

3683 Foley, Greg. *Don't Worry Bear* (PS). Illus. by author. 2008, Viking $19.99 (978-0-670-06245-4). A soothing story about Bear's emotional changes as his friend Caterpillar goes through a big change. (Rev: BL 1/1–15/08; SLJ 2/08)

3684 Foreman, Jack. *Say Hello* (PS–1). Illus. by Michael Foreman. 2008, Candlewick $15.99 (978-0-7636-3657-9). 32pp. A lonely dog gets to play with a group of children and then invites a lonely boy to join them too. (Rev: BL 8/08*; SLJ 7/08)

3685 Fox, Mem. *Wilfrid Gordon McDonald Partridge* (K–2). Illus. by Julie Vivas. 1989, Kane $14.95 (978-0-916291-04-4); paper $7.95 (978-0-916291-26-6). 32pp. The heartwarming story of the boy with four names who collects memorabilia in a box to take to his friend with four names in a nursing home because he has heard she is losing her memory. (Rev: BL 2/15/86; HB 1/86; SLJ 2/86)

3686 Galbraith, Kathryn O. *Two Bunny Buddies* (PS–1). Illus. by Joe Cepeda. 2014, Houghton Mifflin $16.99 (978-054417652-2). 32pp. Two bunnies can't agree on where to have lunch, but after they quarrel immediately miss each other. (Rev: BL 3/1/14; SLJ 2/14)

3687 Gleeson, Libby. *Half a World Away* (K–2). Illus. by Freya Blackwood. 2007, Scholastic $15.99 (978-0-439-88977-3). Best friends Louie and Amy are devastated when Amy moves from Australia to New York City, but they find a way to communicate nonetheless. (Rev: BL 3/1/07*; SLJ 2/07)

3688 Gonzalez, Rigoberto. *Soledad Sigh-Sighs / Soledad Suspiros* (1–3). Trans. by Jorge Argueta. Illus. by Rosa Ibarra. 2003, Children's Book Pr. $16.95 (978-0-89239-180-6). 32pp. Latchkey child Soledad lives a lonely life with an imaginary companion until two neighboring sisters befriend her and even envy her solitude, in this bilingual novel set in Brooklyn. (Rev: BL 5/15/03; HBG 10/03; SLJ 3/03)

3689 Greenfield, Eloise. *The Friendly Four* (PS–2). Illus. by Jan Spivey Gilchrist. 2006, HarperCollins $16.99 (978-0-06-000759-1). Drum has been dreading a dull summer and is happily surprised when three other African American children move into the neighborhood and they all become friends; an upbeat story told in a series of free-verse poems. (Rev: BL 4/15/06; SLJ 8/06)

3690 Grimes, Nikki. *Danitra Brown, Class Clown* (K–3). Illus. by E. B. Lewis. 2005, HarperCollins $16.99 (978-0-688-17290-9). 32pp. Zuri worries about her ailing mother and about the new school year in this latest story — presented in simple rhyming verses with expressive watercolors — about her close friendship with Danitra Brown. (Rev: BL 8/05; SLJ 9/05*)

3691 Harper, Charise Mericle. *Mimi and Lulu: Three Sweet Stories, One Forever Friendship* (PS–K). Illus. by author. 2009, HarperCollins $16.99 (978-0-06-17553-5). 40pp. Two friends share friction and rivalry in these three simple stories. (Rev: BL 11/15/09; SLJ 11/1/09)

3692 Havill, Juanita. *Brianna, Jamaica, and the Dance of Spring* (PS–3). Illus. by Anne S. O'Brien. 2002, Houghton $16.00 (978-0-618-07700-7). 32pp. Asian American Brianna longs to play the role of butterfly in the dance recital. (Rev: BL 3/15/02; HBG 10/02; SLJ 4/02)

3693 Havill, Juanita. *Jamaica and Brianna* (PS–1). Illus. by Anne S. O'Brien. 1993, Houghton $16.00 (978-0-395-64489-8). 32pp. Jamaica is upset when her friend, Brianna, makes fun of her hand-me-down boots. (Rev: BCCB 11/93; BL 10/15/93; HB 11/93; SLJ 10/93)

3694 Henkes, Kevin. *Chester's Way* (PS–2). Illus. by author. 1988, Greenwillow $17.89 (978-0-688-07608-5).

32pp. Chester and Wilson are best friends and will have nothing to do with new girl Lilly, until she bails them out of trouble. (Rev: BL 9/1/88; HB 9/88; SLJ 9/88)

3695 Horvath, David. *Bossy Bear* (PS–1). Illus. by author. 2007, Hyperion $12.99 (978-1-4231-0336-3). A bossy bear learns that being bossy is no way to make friends. Contemporary, anime-like illustrations add to the appeal. (Rev: SLJ 6/07)

3696 Hudson, Cheryl Willis. *My Friend Maya Loves to Dance* (PS–3). Illus. by Eric Velasquez. 2010, Abrams $16.95 (978-0-8109-8328-1). 32pp. Vivid oil painting illustrations depict an African American girl who absolutely loves to dance. (Rev: BL 4/1/10; SLJ 6/1/10)

3697 Hughes, Susan. *Earth to Audrey* (1–3). Illus. by Stéphanie Poulin. 2005, Kids Can $16.95 (978-1-55337-843-3). Audrey, a summer visitor to Ray's town, is so different that at first he thinks she's an alien, and as time goes by she teaches him a new way of looking at the world. (Rev: SLJ 1/06)

3698 Jahn-Clough, Lisa. *Alicia's Best Friends* (PS–1). Illus. 2003, Houghton $15.00 (978-0-618-23951-1). Alicia must find a solution when her four close friends insist she choose one as her best friend. (Rev: BL 3/15/03; HBG 10/03; SLJ 3/03)

3699 Jahn-Clough, Lisa. *Little Dog* (PS–2). Illus. 2006, Houghton $16.00 (978-0-618-57405-6). 32pp. An artist named Rosa and a hungry Little Dog used to living on the streets find happiness and friendship in the countryside. (Rev: BL 4/15/06; SLJ 5/06)

3700 Jeffers, Dawn. *Vegetable Dreams / Huerto soñado* (K–2). Trans. by Eida de la Vega. Illus. by Claude Schneider. 2006, Raven Tree $16.95 (978-0-9741992-9-0). 32pp. A little girl plants a vegetable garden with the help of a kind, elderly neighbor and together they watch it grow; in Spanish and English. (Rev: SLJ 6/06)

3701 Jeffers, Oliver. *Lost and Found* (PS–K). Illus. 2006, Philomel $15.99 (978-0-399-24503-9). 32pp. Finding a penguin on his doorstep, a little boy decides to take him home to the South Pole; it is only when he has put the penguin ashore that he realizes that all the bird wanted was a friend. (Rev: BL 12/15/05; SLJ 1/06)

3702 Joosse, Barbara. *Friends (Mostly)* (PS–1). Illus. by Tomaso Milian. 2010, Greenwillow $16.99 (978-0-06-088221-1). 32pp. Readers hear both sides of the story from Ruby and Henry, two friends whose relationship is sometimes rocky. (Rev: BL 10/1/10; SLJ 9/1/10)

3703 Jules, Jacqueline. *Picnic at Camp Shalom* (K–3). Illus. by Deborah Melmon. 2011, Lerner/Kar-Ben $17.95 (978-0-7613-6661-4); paper $7.95 (978-0-7613-6-662-1). 32pp. A misunderstanding threatens the new friendship between Carly and Sara in this Jewish camp story. Lexile AD560L (Rev: BL 6/1/11; SLJ 6/11)

3704 Keats, Ezra Jack. *Whistle for Willie* (PS–1). Illus. by author. 1964, Puffin paper $6.99 (978-0-14-050202-2). After many false starts, Peter at last learns to whistle.

3705 Kirsch, Vincent. *Forsythia and Me* (PS–2). Illus. by author. 2011, Farrar $16.99 (978-0-374-32438-4). 40pp. Chester has always admired his friend Forsythia from afar but feels closer to her when she is ill and he succeeds in entertaining her. **e** Lexile AD680L (Rev: BL 1/1–15/11; LMC 5–6/11; SLJ 3/1/11)

3706 Kostecki-Shaw, Jenny Sue. *Same, Same but Different* (PS–1). Illus. by author. 2011, Henry Holt $16.99 (978-0-8050-8946-2). 40pp. An American pen pal and his Indian counterpart exchange letters noting the similarities and differences in their cultures; they both, for example, enjoy climbing trees and going to school. (Rev: BLO 9/1/11; SLJ 8/1/11)

3707 Kroll, Virginia. *Forgiving a Friend* (PS–K). Illus. by Paige Billin-Frye. Series: The Way I Act. 2005, Albert Whitman $15.95 (978-1-80750-618-6). 32pp. Seth, furious with Jacob for damaging his toy truck, refuses to accept his friend's apology, but soon learns an important lesson about forgiveness when he accidentally breaks a lamp himself. (Rev: BL 10/1/05)

3708 Krosoczka, Jarrett J. *My Buddy, Slug* (PS–2). Illus. by author. 2006, Knopf $15.95 (978-0-375-83342-7). Alex upsets his friend the slug and must make an apology. (Rev: SLJ 9/06)

3709 Lester, Alison. *Tessa Snaps Snakes* (K–2). Illus. by author. 1991, Houghton paper $13.95 (978-0-685-52551-7). In double-page spreads, seven little children reveal their secrets and pet dislikes. (Rev: HB 11/91; SLJ 12/91)

3710 Lindenbaum, Pija. *Mini Mia and Her Darling Uncle* (K–2). Trans. from Swedish by Elisabeth Kallick Dyssegaard. Illus. by author. 2007, Farrar $16.00 (978-91-29-66734-9). 40pp. Little Mia struggles with having to share her beloved uncle with his friend Fergus until Fergus plays soccer with her. (Rev: SLJ 12/07)

3711 McCormick, Wendy. *Daniel and His Walking Stick* (PS–2). Illus. by Constance R. Bergum. 2005, Peachtree $15.95 (978-1-56145-330-6). On a trip to the country, Jesse meets a friend of her dead grandfather and the two become good friends, taking daily walks and talking about nature. (Rev: BL 3/1/04; HB 7/04; SLJ 5/05)

3712 McGhee, Alison. *Making a Friend* (PS–K). Illus. by Marc Rosenthal. 2011, Atheneum $16.99 (978-1-4169-8998-1). 40pp. A simple story about a boy who builds a snowman, and even when it melts continues to feel its presence in his world. (Rev: BL 10/1/11; SLJ 10/1/11)

3713 Mackintosh, David. *Marshall Armstrong Is New to Our School* (PS–2). Illus. by author. 2011, Abrams $16.95 (978-1-4197-0036-1). 32pp. Marshall, the new kid — and misfit — at school gains acceptance when he invites his classmates over to his house full of telescopes, instruments, and other fun gadgets. (Rev: BL 8/11; LMC 1–2/12; SLJ 8/1/11)

3714 Manushkin, Fran. *Best Season Ever* (K–2). Illus. by Tammie Lyon. Series: Katie Woo. 2010, Picture Window LB $19.99 (978-1-4048-5730-8). 32pp. Katie and her friends Pedro and JoJo share their opinions about the different seasons, agreeing to disagree where necessary. (Rev: SLJ 5/1/10)

3715 Marx, Patricia. *Dot in Larryland: The Big Little Book of an Odd-Sized Friendship* (PS–3). Illus. by Roz

Chast. 2009, Bloomsbury $16.99 (978-1-59990-181-7). 40pp. An unexpected friendship forms between minuscule Dot and extra-large Larry. (Rev: BCCB 1/09; BL 11/15/08; LMC 5/09; SLJ 2/09)

3716 Michelin, Linda. *Zuzu's Wishing Cake* (PS). Illus. by D. B. Johnson. 2006, Houghton $16.00 (978-0-618-64640-1). Zuzu loves to make things and uses all her creative energies in an effort to make the new boy next door smile. (Rev: BL 10/1/06; SLJ 10/06)

3717 Michelson, Richard. *Across the Alley* (1–3). 2006, Putnam $16.99 (978-0-399-23970-0). 32pp. Abe, a young Jewish boy, and Willie, his African American neighbor across the alley, nurture their friendship and their dreams, and discover unsuspected talents for baseball and the violin. (Rev: BL 9/1/06; SLJ 10/06)

3718 Miller, Pat Zietlow. *Sophie's Squash* (PS–2). Illus. by Anne Wilsdorf. 2013, Random House $16.99 (978-0307978-96-7). 40pp. Sophie is devoted to her squash, named Bernice; they do everything together until fall, when difficult decisions must be made. **e** Lexile AD550 (Rev: BL 8/13*; HB 11–12/13; SLJ 7/13*)

3719 Munson, Derek. *Enemy Pie* (K–3). Illus. by Tara Calahan King. 2000, Chronicle $14.95 (978-0-8118-2778-2). A young boy is nice to a boy he doesn't like and ends up having a good time. (Rev: BCCB 1/01; HBG 3/01; SLJ 12/00)

3720 Negron, Ray. *The Greatest Story Never Told: The Babe and Jackie* (K–3). Illus. by Laura Seeley. 2008, HarperCollins $17.99 (978-0-06-147161-2). 40pp. A batboy takes two hospitalized boys on a journey to meet baseball greats Babe Ruth and Jackie Robinson and helps them understand that people of different races can get along just fine. (Rev: BL 9/1/08)

3721 Noyes, Deborah. *Prudence and Moxie: A Tale of Mismatched Friends* (K–3). Illus. by AnnaLaura Cantone. 2009, Houghton $16.00 (978-0-618-41607-3). 32pp. Prudence and Moxie, both aptly named, maintain a close friendship despite their differences and help each other conquer their fears. (Rev: BL 4/15/09; SLJ 4/09)

3722 Okimoto, Jean D. *Dear Ichiro* (K–2). Illus. by Doug Keith. 2002, Kumagai $16.95 (978-1-57061-373-9). 32pp. Grampa's comments about the end of hostile feelings between Americans and Japanese make Henry reconsider his recent rupture with his friend Oliver. (Rev: BL 11/15/02; HBG 3/03; SLJ 3/03)

3723 Perkins, Lynne Rae. *The Cardboard Piano* (PS–K). Illus. by author. 2008, Greenwillow $17.99 (978-0-06-154265-7). 32pp. Despite their different ethnic backgrounds, Debbie and Tina enjoy their friendship until piano lessons get in the way. (Rev: BCCB 11/08; BL 1/1–15/09; HB 1/09; SLJ 11/08)

3724 Polacco, Patricia. *Mrs. Katz and Tush* (K–4). Illus. 1992, Bantam $15.00 (978-0-553-08122-0). 32pp. A lonely Jewish widow is befriended by an African American boy who brings her a kitten to love. (Rev: BCCB 7–8/92; BL 4/15/92; HB 11/92; SLJ 7/92)

3725 Primavera, Elise. *Louise the Big Cheese and the Ooh-la-la Charm School* (K–2). Illus. by Diane Goode.

2012, Simon & Schuster $16.99 (978-144240599-8). 40pp. Eager for attention, Louise finds herself comically duped by a trendy new girl who purports to be from Paris. ℮ (Rev: BL 2/1/12; SLJ 1/12)

3726 Rand, Gloria. *A Pen Pal for Max* (K–3). Illus. by Ted Rand. 2005, Holt $16.95 (978-0-8050-7586-1). Maximiliano, who lives on a Chilean fruit farm, slips a note into a box of grapes bound for the United States and is delighted when he gets a letter from 10-year-old Maggie; their friendship grows and Maggie's school helps when Max's is hit by an earthquake. (Rev: BL 10/15/05; SLJ 10/05)

3727 Raschka, Chris. *Yo! Yes?* (K–4). Illus. 1993, Orchard LB $16.99 (978-0-531-08619-3). 32pp. This picture book consists of a conversation between two boys, one white, one African American. (Rev: BCCB 4/93; BL 3/15/93; HB 5/93; SLJ 5/93*)

3728 Redbank, Tennant. *Which Way, Wendy?* (1–3). Illus. by Rebecca Thornburgh. Series: Social Studies Connects. 2005, Kane paper $4.99 (978-1-57565-147-7). 32pp. New girl Wendy makes some friends by reading and returning a map they lost; ends with a page on how to read maps. (Rev: BL 3/1/05)

3729 Reid, Barbara. *Perfect Snow* (K–3). Illus. by author. 2011, Whitman $16.99 (978-0-8075-6492-9). 32pp. Scott and Jim, friends despite their different personalities, discover they can achieve a better snowman creation when they work together. (Rev: BL 10/1/11*; SLJ 8/1/11)

3730 Reiser, Lynn. *My Way / A mi manera: A Margaret and Margarita Story / Un cuento de Margarita y Margaret* (PS–K). Illus. 2007, Greenwillow $15.99 (978-0-06-084101-0). 32pp. This bilingual picture book focuses on a friendship: although each friend has her own style, each learns from the other; refreshingly, Reiser emphasizes commonalities rather than differences. (Rev: BL 1/1–15/07)

3731 Reynolds, Peter H. *I'm Here* (PS–2). Illus. by author. 2011, Atheneum $15.99 (978-1-4169-9649-4). 32pp. A young boy who lives in his own world and feels alone even among a group of children makes an airplane out of a piece of paper and sends it off, surprised to find it returned to him by a girl. (Rev: BL 9/15/11; SLJ 10/1/11)

3732 Robbins, Jacqui. *The New Girl . . . and Me* (PS–2). Illus. by Matt Phelan. 2006, Simon & Schuster $16.95 (978-0-689-86468-1). Shy Mia hangs back at first but mention of a pet iguana gives her the courage to approach new girl Shakeeta and the two become friends. (Rev: BCCB 9/06; BL 7/06*; SLJ 7/06)

3733 Rodman, Mary Ann. *My Best Friend* (PS–2). Illus. by E. B. Lewis. 2005, Viking $15.99 (978-0-670-05989-8). 32pp. Lily, 6, is crushed when Tamika, one of the girls she sees each week at the pool, doesn't want to be best friends. (Rev: BL 3/15/05; SLJ 5/05)

3734 Rosenbluth, Roz. *Getting to Know Ruben Plotnick* (K–3). Illus. by Maurie J. Manning. 2005, Flashlight $15.95 (978-0-9729225-5-5). David worries what will

happen when his new friend Ruben — the most popular boy in class — meets David's grandmother, whose dementia has made her behavior erratic. (Rev: SLJ 11/05)

3735 Rumford, James. *Tiger and Turtle* (1–3). Illus. by author. 2010, Roaring Brook $17.99 (978-1-59643-416-5). 32pp. A tiger and a turtle initially quarrel over a fallen flower but in the end learning an important lesson about friendship and sharing. Lexile AD950L (Rev: HB 5–6/10; LMC 5–6/10; SLJ 4/1/10)

3736 Russo, Marisabina. *Sophie Sleeps Over* (PS–2). Illus. by author. 2014, Roaring Brook $16.99 (978-159643933-7). 32pp. Sophie, a little bunny, heads for a sleepover at her best friend Olive's house and is surprised to find that Olive has invited another friend too. ℮ (Rev: BL 3/1/14; SLJ 3/14)

3737 Ruzzier, Sergio. *Too Busy* (PS–1). Illus. by author. Series: Bear and Bee. 2014, Disney/Hyperion $14.99 (978-142315961-2). 48pp. Bee is always busy when Bear wants to play, and then Bear is sleeping when Bee wants to gaze at the moon; can they two find a compromise? ℮ (Rev: BL 3/1/14; SLJ 2/14)

3738 Ryan, Pam Muñoz. *A Box of Friends* (K–2). Illus. by Mary Whyte. 2003, Gingham Dog $14.95 (978-1-57768-420-6). Annie's grandmother helps her put together a box of memories, to cheer her after a move to a new house. (Rev: HBG 10/03; SLJ 9/03)

3739 San Souci, Daniel. *The Mighty Pigeon Club* (K–2). Illus. by author. Series: Clubhouse Books. 2007, Tricycle $15.95 (978-1-58246-213-4). Taking in a flock of pigeons proves much more problematic than the children in this clubhouse expected. (Rev: BL 9/1/07; LMC 3/08)

3740 Scieszka, Jon. *Cowboy and Octopus* (PS–2). Illus. by Lane Smith. 2007, Viking $16.99 (978-0-670-91058-8). 40pp. Cowboy and Octopus enjoy an unlikely friendship and some perfectly silly adventures. (Rev: BCCB 9/07; BL 7/07; HB 9/07; LMC 11/07; SLJ 9/07)

3741 Shields, Gillian. *Library Lily* (PS–1). Illus. by Francesca Chessa. 2011, Eerdmans $16 (978-0-8028-5401-8). 26pp. Young Lily loves to read and young Milly loves outdoor adventures, and together the two grow older and share their passions. (Rev: BL 11/1/11; SLJ 8/1/11)

3742 Shriver, Maria. *What's Wrong with Timmy?* (K–3). Illus. by Sandra Spieled. 2001, Little, Brown $14.95 (978-0-316-23337-8). 48pp. Eight-year-old Kate makes friends with Timmy, a boy who is mentally retarded, and wonders what it feels like to be Timmy. (Rev: BL 10/1/01; HBG 3/02; SLJ 1/02)

3743 Sif, Birgitta. *Oliver* (PS–2). Illus. by author. 2012, Candlewick $16.99 (978-0-7636-6247-9). 40pp. Oliver is a solitary child who shares his life and imagination with his toys until he meets a girl who is also a "bit different." (Rev: BL 10/1/12; LMC 3–4/13; SLJ 11/12)

3744 Smallcomb, Pam. *I'm Not* (PS–1). Illus. by Robert Weinstock. 2011, Random House $15.99 (978-0-375-86115-4); LB $18.99 (978-0-375-96115-1). 32pp. Two friends learn to appreciate their differences in this nicely illustrated story. (Rev: BL 1/1–15/11; HB 3–4/11; SLJ 3/1/11)

189

3745 Snihura, Ulana. *I Miss Franklin P. Shuckles* (K–3). Illus. by Leanne Franson. 1998, Annick LB $15.95 (978-1-55037-517-6); paper $5.95 (978-1-55037-516-9). When school starts, Molly decides to drop Franklin as a friend, but when she does she realizes how much she misses him. (Rev: SLJ 6/98)

3746 Steptoe, John. *Creativity* (PS–3). Illus. by E. B. Lewis. 1997, Clarion $17.00 (978-0-395-68706-2). 32pp. An African American boy wonders why a new class member who is as dark-skinned as himself can only speak Spanish. (Rev: BL 2/15/97; SLJ 4/97)

3747 Sydor, Colleen. *Timmerman Was Here* (K–3). Illus. by Nicolas Debon. 2009, Tundra $19.95 (978-0-88776-890-3). 32pp. A young girl is resentful of the boarder who moves into her grandfather's room, and is initially suspicious of the boarder's nocturnal activities; after her new friend departs, spring reveals that he was planting tulips around the neighborhood. (Rev: BL 11/15/09; SLJ 11/1/09)

3748 Teevin, Toni. *What to Do? What to Do?* (PS–2). Illus. by Janet Pedersen. 2006, Clarion $16.00 (978-0-618-44632-2). 32pp. When too many birds begin clamoring for lonely Sophie's home-baked bread, she consults a fortune teller and makes new friends. (Rev: BL 5/1/06; SLJ 7/06)

3749 Whitcomb, Mary E. *Odd Velvet* (K–3). Illus. by Tara Calahan King. 1998, Chronicle $13.95 (978-0-8118-2004-2). 32pp. Because she dresses and behaves differently than other children in her school, Velvet is ignored by them, but gradually they change their ways. (Rev: BCCB 1/99; BL 11/1/98; HBG 3/99; SLJ 1/99)

3750 Wiles, Deborah. *Freedom Summer* (K–3). Illus. by Jerome Lagarrigue. 2001, Simon & Schuster $16.00 (978-0-689-83016-7). 32pp. Set in the South during desegregation, this is the story of the friendship between John Henry Waddell, an African American boy, and the narrator, who is white. (Rev: BCCB 2/01; BL 2/15/01; HB 5/01; HBG 10/01; SLJ 2/01)

3751 Willems, Mo. *Hooray for Amanda and Her Alligator* (PS–2). Illus. by author. 2011, HarperCollins $17.99 (978-0-06-200400-0). 72pp. Amanda's stuffed alligator is used to having her for himself and must make adjustments when she brings home a stuffed panda. Lexile AD360L (Rev: BL 4/1/11; HB 7–8/11; LMC 10/11; SLJ 5/1/11*)

3752 Wishinsky, Frieda. *You're Mean, Lily Jean!* (PS–2). Illus. by Kady MacDonald Denton. 2011, Whitman $16.99 (978-0-8075-9476-6). 32pp. Sandy always played with her little sister Carly until Lily Jean moved in next door and demoted Carly to subsidiary roles. Lexile AD350L (Rev: BL 2/1/11; SLJ 2/1/11)

3753 Woloson, Eliza. *My Friend Isabelle* (PS–1). Illus. by Bryan Gough. 2003, Woodbine House $14.95 (978-1-890627-50-8). Charlie describes his friendship with Isabelle, a girl with Down syndrome, emphasizing that the differences between them (he's tall, she's short; he's fast, she's slow) help to make their relationship even more rewarding. (Rev: HBG 4/04; SLJ 12/03)

3754 Woodson, Jacqueline. *The Other Side* (K–3). Illus. by E. B. Lewis. 2001, Penguin $16.99 (978-0-399-23116-2). 32pp. The story of a white girl and a black girl who form a friendship despite the barrier between their houses. (Rev: BCCB 2/01; BL 2/15/01*; HBG 10/01; SLJ 1/01)

3755 Yoon, Salina. *Penguin and Pinecone: A Friendship Story* (PS–1). Illus. by author. 2012, Walker $12.99 (978-0-8027-2843-2). 40pp. A penguin comes across a pinecone and the two form a bond that endures even when Penguin returns Pinecone to the forest. ℮ (Rev: BLO 10/15/12; LMC 11–12/12; SLJ 9/12)

3756 Zolotow, Charlotte. *I Know a Lady* (PS–2). Illus. by James Stevenson. 1984, Morrow paper $6.99 (978-0-688-11519-7). 24pp. Sally loves a kind old lady who lives in the neighborhood.

HUMOROUS STORIES

3757 Ackerman, Karen. *Bean's Big Day* (K–4). Illus. by Paul Mombourquette. 2004, Kids Can $15.95 (978-1-55337-444-2). Someone in the small early-20th-century town of Bean, Pennsylvania, is going to be chosen to be in a movie in this story told by an 8-year-old narrator called Cricket. (Rev: SLJ 5/04)

3758 Agee, Jon. *Mr. Putney's Quacking Dog* (K–2). Illus. by author. 2010, Scholastic $16.95 (978-0-545-16203-6). 48pp. A pun-filled book of animal jokes revolving around names. (Rev: BL 7/10; HB 7–8/10; LMC 10/10; SLJ 7/1/10)

3759 Agee, Jon. *Nothing* (K–3). Illus. by author. 2007, Hyperion $16.99 (978-0-7868-3694-9). 32pp. The customer is always right, so when a rich woman wants to buy "nothing" Otis the shopkeeper complies. (Rev: BL 9/1/07; SLJ 8/07)

3760 Agee, Jon. *The Other Side of Town* (K–2). Illus. by author. 2012, Scholastic $17.95 (978-0-545-16204-3). 32pp. A New York cab driver has a weird experience when he picks up an odd little man who wants to go to the other side of town and finds himself in a strange pink-and-green world where nothing is quite right; the illustrations add to the fun. Lexile AD350L (Rev: BL 11/1/12; HB 1–2/13; LMC 5–6/13; SLJ 12/12)

3761 Agee, Jon. *The Retired Kid* (K–3). Illus. by author. 2008, Hyperion $16.99 (978-1-4231-0314-1). At the age of 8, Brian decides he's had enough of school, music lessons, babysitting, and so forth, and takes off to Florida and the Happy Sunset Retirement Community. (Rev: BCCB 7–8/08; BL 4/15/08; LMC 5/08; SLJ 6/08)

3762 Ahlberg, Allan. *The Runaway Dinner* (PS–3). Illus. by Bruce Ingman. 2006, Candlewick $15.99 (978-0-7636-3142-0). A sausage called Melvin decides he does not want to be eaten by young Banjo Cannon and takes flight, setting the stage for a frantic chase as the boy, his parents, the rest of the meal, kitchen furniture, and cutlery follow in pursuit. (Rev: BCCB 11/06; HBG 4/07; SLJ 12/06)

3763 Allard, Harry. *The Stupids Have a Ball* (K–3). Illus. by James Marshall. 1984, Houghton paper $6.95 (978-

0-395-36169-6). The whole Stupid family decides to celebrate when the children bring home terrible report cards from school. Two others in the series: *The Stupids Step Out* (1974); *The Stupids Die* (1981).

3764 Allard, Harry. *The Stupids Take Off* (K–3). Illus. by James Marshall. 1989, Houghton $17.00 (978-0-395-50068-2). 32pp. The irresistible noodleheads set off on a fourth adventure, this time to avoid a visit from Uncle Carbuncle. (Rev: BCCB 10/89; BL 10/1/89; SLJ 10/89)

3765 Allen, Elanna. *Itsy Mitsy Runs Away* (PS–K). Illus. by author. 2011, Atheneum $16.99 (978-1-4424-0671-1). 40pp. A little girl is so fed up with bedtime that she decides to run away from home, and her kindhearted father helps her pack, reminding her just how much she will need to take with her. (Rev: BL 6/1/11; SLJ 5/1/11)

3766 Amato, Mary. *The Chicken of the Family* (PS–1). Illus. by Delphine Durand. 2008, Putnam $16.99 (978-0-399-24196-3). 32pp. A zany story in which Henrietta's older sisters manage to convince her that she is not a child but a chicken. (Rev: BCCB 3/08; BL 2/1/08; SLJ 3/08)

3767 Anderson, Brian, and Liam Anderson. *Monster Chefs* (K–2). Illus. by Brian Anderson. 2014, Roaring Brook $16.99 (978-159643808-8). 32pp. Bored with eyeballs and ketchup, a monster king sends his four monster chefs out into the world to find new kinds of food. (Rev: BL 3/1/14)

3768 Anderson, Derek. *Gladys Goes Out to Lunch* (PS–2). Illus. by author. 2005, Simon & Schuster $15.95 (978-0-689-85688-4). Gladys the gorilla leaves the zoo in search of the source of a delicious smell, and tests various food (pizza, ice cream) before finding a cart selling banana bread. (Rev: SLJ 8/05)

3769 Anderson, Laurie Halse. *The Hair of Zoe Fleefenbacher Goes to School* (K–2). Illus. by Ard Hoyt. 2009, Simon & Schuster $16.99 (978-0-689-85809-3). 32pp. Zoe's hair is both talented and determined (it learned to open the cookie jar at the age of 2, after all) but the 1st-grade teacher's strict rules pose a real problem. (Rev: BL 4/15/09; LMC 10/09)

3770 Anderson, Peggy Perry. *Chuck's Band* (PS–1). Illus. by author. 2008, Houghton $16.00 (978-0-618-96506-9). 32pp. When farmer Chuck buys himself a banjo and a mandolin for his goat, all the other animals want in on the fun except for Fat Cat Pat, who has special demands. (Rev: BL 2/15/08; HB 5/08; SLJ 3/08)

3771 Anderson, Peggy Perry. *Chuck's Truck* (PS–2). Illus. by author. 2006, Houghton $16.00 (978-0-618-66836-6). 32pp. A rhyming story about a farmer whose truck is overfull of friendly animals, with lively illustrations. (Rev: HB 5/06; HBG 10/06; SLJ 5/06)

3772 Andreae, Giles. *Pants* (PS–2). Illus. by Nick Sharratt. 2003, Random $12.95 (978-0-385-75014-1). Cartoon-style illustrations highlight a rambunctious look at undergarments of all patterns and sizes. (Rev: HBG 4/04; SLJ 11/03)

3773 Angleberger, Tom. *Crankee Doodle* (K–3). Illus. by Cece Bell. 2013, Clarion $16.99 (978-0-547-81854-2).

32pp. A cranky colonial man and his goofy pony argue about the benefits of a trip into town in this funny take-off of the traditional song. (Rev: BL 6/13; LMC 8–9/13; SLJ 6/13)

3774 Angleberger, Tom. *Princess Labelmaker to the Rescue!* (4–6). Illus. by author. 2014, Abrams/Amulet $13.95 (978-141971052-0). 208pp. The students of McQuarrie Middle School battle against the imposition of FunTime — a maliciously named program that promises good standardized test results. Can Principal Rabbski help? (Rev: BLO 3/1/14; SLJ 5/14)

3775 Appelt, Kathi. *Bubba and Beau Meet the Relatives* (PS–2). Illus. by Arthur Howard. 2004, Harcourt $16.00 (978-0-15-216630-4). Newly clean, Baby Bubba and Beau the dog greet the arriving relatives before heading straight back to the mudhole, this time with baby Arlene in tow. (Rev: BL 3/15/04; HB 7/04; SLJ 5/04)

3776 Arnold, Marsha Diane. *Roar of a Snore* (PS). Illus. by Pierre Pratt. 2006, Dial $16.99 (978-0-8037-2936-0). Jack is being kept awake by a loud snoring sound, so he awakens the rest of his family, along with the dog and farm animals, and together they try to find out who's responsible. (Rev: HBG 4/0; SLJ 8/06*)

3777 Arnold, Tedd. *Dirty Gert* (PS–1). Illus. by author. 2013, Holiday $16.95 (978-0-8234-2404-7). 40pp. Little Gert loves dirt and spends so long playing in it that she puts out roots and sprouts leaves. (Rev: BLO 3/15/13; LMC 10/13; SLJ 5/13)

3778 Arnold, Tedd. *The Twin Princes* (K–3). Illus. by author. 2007, Dial $16.99 (978-0-8037-2696-3). 32pp. Twin chicken princes — one good, one bad — compete to inherit the kingdom in this pun-filled story. (Rev: BL 3/1/07*)

3779 Asch, Frank. *Monsieur Saguette and His Baguette* (PS–1). Illus. by author. 2004, Kids Can $14.95 (978-1-55337-461-9). A loaf of French bread assists in all sorts of adventures in this humorous Parisian romp. (Rev: SLJ 6/04)

3780 Asch, Frank, and Devin Asch. *The Daily Comet: Boy Saves Earth from Giant Octopus!* (2–4). Illus. by Frank Asch. 2010, Kids Can $16.95 (978-1-55453-281-0). 32pp. A science-minded boy refuses to believe the stories his tabloid editor father writes for the *Daily Comet* until he accompanies his dad on Go to Work With a Parent Day and beholds a giant octopus and other weird wonders; with effective retro illustrations. (Rev: BL 11/1/10; LMC 1–2/11; SLJ 6/11)

3781 Ashman, Linda. *No Dogs Allowed* (PS–2). Illus. by Kristin Sorra. 2011, Sterling $14.95 (978-1-4027-5837-9). 32pp. This nearly wordless picture book tells the story of a restaurant with a "no dogs" policy that is forced to expand this to cover a wide range of outlandish animals brought by pet owners. (Rev: BL 9/1/11; SLJ 9/1/11)

3782 Ashman, Linda. *Samantha on a Roll* (PS–1). Illus. by Christine Davenier. 2011, Farrar $16.99 (978-0-374-36399-4). 40pp. On her brand new skates for the first time, Samantha takes a fast, crazy trip through town. (Rev: BL 12/1/11; SLJ 9/1/11)

3783 Ashman, Linda. *To the Beach!* (PS). Illus. by Nadine Bernard Wescott. 2005, Harcourt $16.00 (978-0-15-216490-4). So many things are forgotten that the anticipated day at the beach ends up being a day in the backyard. (Rev: BL 5/1/05; SLJ 6/05)

3784 Atwood, Margaret. *Bashful Bob and Doleful Dorinda* (K–3). Illus. by Dusan Petricic. 2006, Bloomsbury Children's $17.95 (978-1-59990-004-9). 32pp. Alliteration and clever use of color enhance this Cinderella-like story of two hard-done-by children who wind up heroes. (Rev: BL 11/1/06)

3785 Baker, Keith. *Hide and Snake* (PS–K). Illus. 1991, Harcourt $15.00 (978-0-15-233986-9). 32pp. A snake hides in each of the double-page spreads depicting everyday life. (Rev: BL 11/15/91; SLJ 12/91*)

3786 Bardhan-Quallen, Sudipta. *Snoring Beauty* (PS–2). Illus. by Jane Manning. 2014, HarperCollins $17.99 (978-006087403-2). 32pp. When Prince Max arrives to wake the sleeping princess, he is put off by her snoring; so Mouse, who has been kept awake himself by the loud noise, decides to kiss her himself with unexpected results. (Rev: BL 3/1/14; SLJ 3/14)

3787 Barnett, Mac. *Chloe and the Lion* (K–3). Illus. by Adam Rex. 2012, Hyperion $16.99 (978-1-4231-1334-8). 48pp. Author and illustrator have creative differences about their book, and it is up to Chloe, the protagonist, to set them on the right track. (Rev: BL 4/1/12; LMC 5–6/12; SLJ 4/1/12*)

3788 Barnett, Mac. *Mustache!* (K–2). Illus. by Kevin Cornell. 2011, Hyperion/Disney $16.99 (978-1-4231-1671-4). 40pp. A vain king's subjects find a clever solution to their leader's unchecked narcissism. (Rev: BL 12/1/11; SLJ 9/1/11)

3789 Barrett, Judi. *Never Take a Shark to the Dentist and Other Things Not to Do* (PS–2). Illus. by John Nickle. 2008, Atheneum $16.99 (978-1-4169-0724-4). Advice such as "Never hold hands with a lobster" is paired with full-page illustrations showing the reasons underlying the tip. (Rev: BL 4/1/08; LMC 8/08; SLJ 5/08)

3790 Bartram, Simon. *Bob's Best-Ever Friend* (PS–3). Illus. by author. 2009, Candlewick $16.99 (978-0-7636-4425-3). 32pp. Astronaut Bob is back and focused on looking for a pet to be his best friend while all sorts of crazy things (shown in the illustrations) happen around him. (Rev: BL 7/09; SLJ 5/09)

3791 Beard, Alex. *The Jungle Grapevine* (K–2). Illus. by author. 2009, Abrams $16.95 (978-0-8109-8001-3). 48pp. An offhand remark by Turtle starts a rumor that morphs and escalates as it travels across the savanna in this amusing story paralleling a game of telephone. (Rev: BL 9/15/09; LMC 8–9/10; SLJ 9/1/09)

3792 Beaty, Andrea. *Artist Ted* (PS–2). Illus. by Pascal Lemaitre. 2012, Simon & Schuster $15.99 (978-141695374-6). 32pp. Young Ted's sudden passion for art and his choice of materials (ketchup, mustard) meet

less-than-appreciative reactions at home and at school. e Lexile AD430L (Rev: BL 2/15/12; LMC 8–9/12)

3793 Becker, Suzy. *Manny's Cows: The Niagara Falls Tale* (PS–2). 2006, HarperCollins $15.99 (978-0-06-054152-1). Disaster strikes when Manny, a farm boy who tends a herd of 500 cows, takes them with him on a vacation trip to Niagara Falls. (Rev: BL 6/1–15/06; SLJ 6/06)

3794 Bendall-Brunello, Tiziana. *I Wish I Could Read! A Story About Making Friends* (PS). Illus. by John Bendall-Brunello. 2011, Amicus LB $16.95 (978-1-60992-109-5). 24pp. A young pig finds a book and is frustrated at his friends' inability to teach him to read but finally finds a boy who can give him what he wants. (Rev: BLO 10/15/11; SLJ 3/1/12)

3795 Bernheimer, Kate. *The Girl Who Wouldn't Brush Her Hair* (PS–1). Illus. by Jake Parker. 2013, Random House $17.99 (978-037586878-8). 40pp. A young girl decides that she simply won't brush her hair, but when a menagerie of mice decide to take up residence atop her head she faces a dilemma. e (Rev: BL 9/15/13; LMC 3–4/14; SLJ 9/13)

3796 Berry, Lynne. *The Curious Demise of a Contrary Cat* (K–2). Illus. by Luke LaMarca. 2006, Simon & Schuster $12.95 (978-1-4169-0211-9). 40pp. Repetition and predictability are hallmarks of this wacky story about Cat's refusal to pitch in and help Witch with her party. (Rev: BL 11/1/06; SLJ 8/06)

3797 Berry, Lynne. *What Floats in a Moat?* (PS–2). Illus. by Matthew Cordell. 2013, Simon & Schuster $17.99 (978-1-4169-9763-4). 48pp. A funny story about a goat and a hen determined to get across a moat without using the drawbridge, teaching young readers some basic principles of physics. e Lexile AD400 (Rev: BLO 7/13; LMC 11–12/13; SLJ 6/13)

3798 Black, Michael Ian. *A Pig Parade Is a Terrible Idea* (PS–2). Illus. by Kevin Hawkes. 2010, Simon & Schuster $16.99 (978-1-4169-7922-7). 40pp. A pig parade may sound like an excellent idea, but this funny book makes clear it should be avoided. e Lexile AD970L (Rev: BL 8/10*; LMC 1–2/11; SLJ 12/1/10*)

3799 Black, Michael Ian. *The Purple Kangaroo* (PS–2). Illus. by Peter Brown. 2010, Simon & Schuster $16.99 (978-1-4169-5771-3). 32pp. A cheeky, captivating monkey claims to be a mind-reader in this energetic story, challenging readers to put his considerable, though zany, skills to the test. Lexile AD630L (Rev: BL 1/1/10; LMC 5–6/10; SLJ 2/1/10)

3800 Blackwood, Freya. *Ivy Loves to Give* (PS). Illus. by author. 2010, Scholastic $15.99 (978-0-545-23467-2). Unpaged. Ivy is immensely generous but her gifts are not always appropriate. (Rev: HB 11–12/10; SLJ 10/1/10)

3801 Blake, Quentin. *Mrs. Armitage: Queen of the Road* (PS–2). Illus. by author. 2003, Peachtree $15.95 (978-1-56145-287-3). The adventurous Mrs. Armitage and her dog set off in an old jalopy and take it in their stride when it starts losing parts and winds up a mere skeleton of a car. (Rev: HBG 4/04; SLJ 10/03)

3802 Blankenship, Lee Ann. *Mr. Tuggle's Troubles* (K–3). Illus. by Karen Dugan. 2005, Boyds Mills $15.95 (978-1-59078-196-8). Mr. Tuggle has trouble looking after his clothes and looks stranger and stranger as he devises various replacements. (Rev: SLJ 10/05)

3803 Bliss, Harry. *Bailey* (PS–2). Illus. by author. 2011, Scholastic $16.99 (978-0-545-23344-6). Unpaged. Bailey the dog is the favorite pupil at his elementary school in this funny book with appealing cartoon illustrations. (Rev: HB 11–12/11; SLJ 9/1/11*)

3804 Bloch, Serge. *Butterflies in My Stomach and Other School Hazards* (PS–2). Illus. by author. 2008, Sterling $12.95 (978-1-4027-4158-6). 32pp. A little boy's first day of school is made more confusing by the profusion of new, incomprehensible phrases in this funny look at the use of language. (Rev: BL 8/08; LMC 3/09; SLJ 9/08)

3805 Bluemle, Elizabeth. *My Father the Dog* (PS–2). Illus. by Randy Cecil. 2006, Candlewick $15.99 (978-0-7636-2222-0). 32pp. A girl (convincingly) equates her father's habits with those of her pet dog in this entertaining picture book. (Rev: BL 5/15/06; SLJ 7/06)

3806 Bock, Lee. *Oh, Crumps! / Ay, caramba!* (PS–2). Trans. by Eida de la Vega. Illus. by Morgan Midgett. 2003, Raven Tree LB $16.95 (978-0-9720192-4-8). 32pp. A humorous tale, in both English and Spanish, about an exhausted farmer trying to keep up with his never-ending tasks and "repair the cow, climb the fence, milk the hay, and mow the silo." (Rev: HBG 10/03; SLJ 7/03)

3807 Bowen, Anne. *What Do Teachers Do (After YOU Leave School?)* (K–3). Illus. by Barry Gott. 2006, Carolrhoda LB $15.95 (978-1-57505-922-8). Visions of teachers gone wild — dancing in the gym, roller-skating down the corridors, writing on the walls — may convince young children that teachers don't really live in the school. (Rev: SLJ 11/06)

3808 Brennan, Eileen. *Dirtball Pete* (1–3). Illus. by author. 2010, Random House $15.99 (978-0-375-83425-7). 32pp. A mother's attempts to scrub her dirty son go for naught when his script for the school assembly is blown away and he ends up as muddy as ever. **e** (Rev: BL 7/10; LMC 11–12/10; SLJ 7/1/10)

3809 Bright, Paul. *I'm Not Going Out There!* (K–2). Illus. by Ben Cort. 2006, Good Bks. $16.00 (978-1-56148-535-2). A little boy hides beneath his bed and refuses to come out, but he makes it clear that it's not the fearsome creatures in his bedroom that are keeping him there but rather his annoying sister. (Rev: SLJ 11/06)

3810 Broach, Elise. *Cousin John Is Coming!* (K–3). Illus. by Nate Lilly. 2006, Dial $16.99 (978-0-8037-3013-7). Ben and his cat recall the various horrors of Cousin John's last visit while Ben's mother rhapsodizes about John's forthcoming arrival; cartoon illustrations provide much of the humor. (Rev: SLJ 7/06)

3811 Broach, Elise. *When Dinosaurs Came with Everything* (PS–1). Illus. by David Small. 2007, Atheneum $16.99 (978-0-689-86922-8). 40pp. Want a dinosaur? They're available — free — at every store in this funny book. (Rev: BCCB 10/07; BL 9/15/07; HB 1/08; LMC 11/07; SLJ 9/07)

3812 Brockenbrough, Martha. *The Dinosaur Tooth Fairy* (PS–2). Illus. by Israel Sanchez. 2013, Scholastic $16.99 (978-0-545-24466-4). 32pp. A Dinosaur Tooth Fairy and a Human Tooth Fairy compete for a little girl's tooth. (Rev: BL 7/13; LMC 1–2/14; SLJ 7/13)

3813 Brown, Calef. *Boy Wonders* (PS–2). Illus. by author. 2011, Atheneum $16.99 (978-1-4169-7877-0). 40pp. "Is water scared of waterfalls?" "Are phones annoyed if no one calls?" Brown tackles these and other vexing questions and provides suitably appealing illustrations. (Rev: BL 6/1/11; SLJ 6/11)

3814 Brown, Peter. *Children Make Terrible Pets* (PS–2). Illus. by author. 2010, Little, Brown $16.99 (978-0-316-01548-6). 40pp. In this funny role-reversal story, a young bear called Lucy comes to the difficult realization that humans do not make good pets. (Rev: BL 10/1/10; LMC 1–2/11*; SLJ 9/1/10)

3815 Brown, Peter. *Chowder* (PS–2). 2006, Little, Brown $15.99 (978-0-316-01180-8). 32pp. Chowder is a bulldog with unusual talents and has little in common with the other dogs in his neighborhood, but he finally finds friends when a petting zoo opens nearby. (Rev: BL 9/1/06; HBG 4/07; LMC 3/07; SLJ 9/06)

3816 Brown, Peter. *Flight of the Dodo* (K–2). Illus. by author. 2005, Little, Brown $15.99 (978-0-316-11038-9). Penguin and a handful of other flightless birds join forces to invent a flying machine; both text and illustrations are full of fun. (Rev: SLJ 12/05)

3817 Brown, Peter. *You Will Be My Friend!* (PS–2). Illus. by author. 2011, Little, Brown $16.99 (978-0-316-07030-0). Unpaged. Lucy the bear last seen in *Children Make Terrible Pets* (2010) is determined to make a new friend but many potential pals find her approach off-putting. (Rev: SLJ 9/1/11)

3818 Brown, Ruth. *The Big Sneeze* (PS–K). Illus. by author. 1997, Morrow paper $4.95 (978-0-688-15282-6). 32pp. A fly lands on a farmer's nose; he sneezes, and havoc breaks out in the barnyard. (Rev: BCCB 2/86; BL 9/15/85; SLJ 10/85)

3819 Bruel, Nick. *Who Is Melvin Bubble?* (K–4). Illus. by author. 2006, Roaring Brook $16.95 (978-1-59643-116-4). This humorous profile of Melvin Bubble contains sometimes contradictory views of Melvin from his parents, dog, teddy bear, Santa Claus, and even a monster that lives in Melvin's closet. (Rev: SLJ 8/06)

3820 Bryan, Ashley. *Can't Scare Me!* (K–3). Illus. by author. 2013, Atheneum $16.99 (978-144247657-8). 40pp. A fearless little boy finally finds something really scary (dreadful off-key singing) in this cautionary/trickster tale from the Antilles. **e** Lexile AD570 (Rev: BL 9/1/13; HB 11–12/13; LMC 3–4/14; SLJ 10/13)

3821 Bryan, Sean. *A Girl and Her Gator* (K–2). Illus. by Tom Murphy. 2006, Arcade $14.99 (978-1-55970-798-5). A silly story about Claire, who is unsettled at first when she discovers an alligator on her head, but, assured that the gator should cause no change in her activities, the young girl blithely carries on with her everyday routine. (Rev: SLJ 8/06)

3822 Buckley, Michael. *Kel Gilligan's Daredevil Stunt Show* (PS–2). Illus. by Dan Santat. 2012, Abrams $16.95 (978-1-4197-0379-9). 40pp. Brave Kel Gilligan tackles such stunts as eating broccoli, getting dressed, and going to bed without checking for monsters. e (Rev: BLO 12/15/12; SLJ 10/12)

3823 Buehner, Caralyn. *The Queen of Style* (K–3). Illus. by Mark Buehner. 2008, Dial $16.99 (978-0-8037-2878-3). 40pp. A charming tale about a quirky queen who enrolls in beauty school and practices on her subjects and their sheep. (Rev: SLJ 9/08)

3824 Byars, Betsy. *The Golly Sisters Go West* (1–3). Illus. by Sue Truesdell. 1986, HarperCollins LB $16.89 (978-0-06-020884-4); paper $3.99 (978-0-06-444132-2). 64pp. In six stories, two adventurous women take on frontier life and the Wild West. (Rev: BCCB 11/86)

3825 Campbell, K. G. *Lester's Dreadful Sweaters* (K–3). Illus. by author. 2012, Kids Can $16.95 (978-1-55453-770-9). 32pp. Poor Lester, what is he to do when Cousin Clara moves in and starts knitting him a series of hideous sweaters that his parents encourage him to wear — desperate measures ensue. e Lexile AD670L (Rev: BL 9/1/12; LMC 5–6/13*; SLJ 10/12)

3826 Carrier, Lisa, and Lenore Hart. *T. Rex at Swan Lake* (PS–1). Illus. by Chris Demarest. 2004, Dutton $16.99 (978-0-525-47177-6). A dinosaur skeleton tired of being on display in a museum decides to try her hand at ballet. (Rev: BL 8/04; SLJ 8/04)

3827 Chaconas, Dori. *Don't Slam the Door!* (PS–2). Illus. by Will Hillenbrand. 2010, Candlewick $15.99 (978-0-7636-3709-5). 32pp. A funny cumulative, rhyming tale that starts with a slamming door that wakes a cat and leads to a series of chaotic events on a farm. (Rev: BL 8/10; LMC 11–12/10; SLJ 7/1/10)

3828 Chaconas, Dori. *Virginnie's Hat* (K–2). Illus. by Holly Meade. 2007, Candlewick $16.99 (978-0-7636-2397-5). 32pp. Intent on retrieving her hat from a tall tree in the bayou, Virginnie seems unaware that animals are showing a great deal of interest in her toes. (Rev: BL 6/1–15/07; SLJ 5/07)

3829 Charlip, Remy. *Little Old Big Beard and Big Young Little Beard* (PS). Illus. by Tamara Rettenmund and Tamara Rettenmund. 2003, Marshall Cavendish $16.95 (978-0-7614-5142-6). Two bearded cowboys embark on a search for their missing cow, but they are so inept that the cow has to find them. (Rev: HBG 4/04; SLJ 10/03)

3830 Charlip, Remy. *Why I Will Never Ever Ever Ever Have Enough Time to Read This Book* (K–3). Illus. by Jon J. Muth. 2000, Tricycle $14.95 (978-1-58246-018-5). 40pp. A humorous book about a little girl who has so many things to do, like homework and calling friends, that she will never to able to finish the big book that is always at her side. (Rev: BL 1/1–15/01; HBG 3/01; SLJ 9/00)

3831 Chartrand, Lili. *Taming Horrible Harry* (K–3). Trans. from French by Susan Ouriou. Illus. by Rogé. 2006, Tundra $16.95 (978-0-88776-772-2). What the monster called Harry enjoys most is scaring children — until he learns to read and discovers the joy of books; offbeat illustrations add to the appeal. (Rev: SLJ 7/06)

3832 Child, Lauren. *But Excuse Me That Is My Book* (PS–2). Illus. Series: Charlie and Lola. 2006, Dial $16.99 (978-0-8037-3096-0). 32pp. Colorful collage-style art portrays the story of little Lola, who is deeply disappointed when she discovers that the book she absolutely loves best has been checked out of the library by somebody else; eventually her big — and very patient — brother Charlie helps her find a substitute. (Rev: BL 4/1/06; SLJ 4/06*)

3833 Child, Lauren. *Clarice Bean, That's Me* (PS–2). Illus. by author. 1999, Candlewick $16.99 (978-0-7636-0961-0). 32pp. Clarice Bean's house is so crowded that she hopes she will be sent to her room as a punishment so she can be alone for a while. Also use *Clarice Bean, Guess Who's Babysitting?* (2001) and *What Planet Are You From, Clarice Bean?* (2002). (Rev: HBG 3/00; SLJ 12/99)

3834 Child, Lauren. *I Want a Pet* (PS–1). Illus. 1999, Tricycle $13.95 (978-1-883672-82-9). 24pp. A hilarious story about a family that cannot agree on the perfect pet. (Rev: BL 4/15/99; HB 5/99; HBG 10/99; SLJ 5/99)

3835 Child, Lauren. *I Will Never Not Ever Eat a Tomato* (PS–2). Illus. by author. Series: Charlie and Lola. 2000, Candlewick $15.99 (978-0-7636-1188-0). Charlie gets his fussy little sister to eat by calling the food by exotic names. (Rev: HBG 3/01; SLJ 11/00)

3836 Chodos-Irvine, Margaret. *Ella Sarah Gets Dressed* (PS). Illus. by author. 2003, Harcourt $16.00 (978-0-15-216413-3). Toddler Ella Sarah will not accept the fashion advice of her family, preferring to dress herself in vivid attire for her tea party. Caldecott Honor Book, 2004. (Rev: BL 6/1–15/03*; HBG 10/03; SLJ 7/03)

3837 Christelow, Eileen. *Letters from a Desperate Dog* (PS–2). 2006, Clarion $16.00 (978-0-618-51003-0). 32pp. Emma the dog feels badly treated by her owner George and seeks the advice of a canine columnist in the *Weekly Bone*. (Rev: BL 10/1/06; SLJ 11/06)

3838 Clanton, Benjamin. *The Table Sets Itself* (PS–2). Illus. by author. 2013, Walker $16.99 (978-0-8027-3447-1). 40pp. A funny story about setting the table with wayward utensils who have other ideas about their roles. Lexile AD710 (Rev: BL 10/1/13; SLJ 9/13)

3839 Clement, Rod. *Grandpa's Teeth* (PS–3). Illus. 1998, HarperCollins $16.99 (978-0-06-027671-3). 32pp. When Grandpa's false teeth are stolen, a nationwide search is begun. (Rev: BL 2/15/98; HBG 10/98; SLJ 3/98*)

3840 Clifford, Rowan. *Rodeo Ron and His Milkshake Cows* (K–2). Illus. 2005, Knopf LB $17.99 (978-0-375-

93195-6). 32pp. When Rodeo Ron rides into the town of Cavity with his four cows of different hues, the soda bar owners challenge him to a shake-off — milkshakes vs. soft drinks — with the children as judges. (Rev: BL 6/1–15/05; SLJ 6/05)

3841 Collins, Ross. *Dear Vampa* (K–2). Illus. by author. 2009, HarperCollins $16.99 (978-0-06-135534-9). 32pp. The Pires, a four-vampire family, are displeased when the sun-loving, boisterously cheerful Wolfsons move in next door in this funny story that ends with a twist (the Wolfsons are in fact werewolves). (Rev: BL 6/1–15/09)

3842 Copp, Jim. *Jim Copp, Will You Tell Me a Story? Three Uncommon Clever Tales* (K–2). Illus. by Lindsay duPont. 2008, Harcourt $17.95 (978-0-15-206331-3). 56pp. Three humorous short stories by Jim Copp are illustrated in the book and performed by the late Copp on the accompanying CD. (Rev: BL 12/1/08; SLJ 11/08)

3843 Cordsen, Carol Foskett. *Market Day* (PS–1). Illus. by Douglas B. Jones. 2008, Dutton $16.99 (978-0-525-47883-6). 32pp. It is definitely not a good idea for the Benson family to leave for the market without feeding the cow! (Rev: BCCB 9/08; BL 5/15/08; LMC 8/08; SLJ 6/08)

3844 Cote, Genevieve. *What Elephant?* (K–3). Illus. by author. 2006, Kids Can $16.95 (978-1-55337-875-4). When his neighbors express skepticism, George decides that perhaps he was mistaken when he saw an elephant in his house. (Rev: SLJ 12/06)

3845 Cox, Judy. *Pick a Pumpkin, Mrs. Millie!* (PS–2). Illus. by Joe Mathieu. 2009, Marshall Cavendish $15.99 (978-0-7614-5573-8). 32pp. Mrs. Millie, the teacher with funny language difficulties, takes her class on a field trip to a pumpkin farm. ♫ ℮ Lexile AD390L (Rev: BL 11/1/09; SLJ 9/1/09)

3846 Crandall, Court. *Hugville* (PS–1). Illus. by Joe Murray. 2005, Random $13.95 (978-0-375-82418-0). The mayor of Hugville proudly conducts a tour of his town, pointing out all the different types of hugs that are practiced there. (Rev: SLJ 1/06)

3847 Crimi, Carolyn. *The Louds Move In!* (K–2). Illus. by Regan Dunnick. 2006, Marshall Cavendish $14.95 (978-0-7614-5221-8). Although the neighbors have been annoyed by the noise created by the Loud family, they become worried when the din suddenly subsides. (Rev: SLJ 5/06)

3848 Cronin, Doreen. *Bounce* (PS). Illus. by Scott Menchin. 2007, Simon & Schuster $14.00 (978-1-4169-1627-7). 40pp. In this appealing sequel to *Wiggle* (2005), simple, rhyming text and colorful artwork combine to capture the essence of bouncing. (Rev: BL 3/15/07)

3849 Cronin, Doreen. *Diary of a Fly* (PS–2). Illus. by Harry Bliss. 2007, HarperCollins $15.99 (978-0-06-000156-8). 40pp. Fly shares her worries about her first day of school and interacts with characters from *Diary of a Worm* (2003) and *Diary of a Spider* (2005) in this humorous book with lots of gross aspects. (Rev: BL 11/1/07; HB 1/08; SLJ 10/07)

3850 Cronin, Doreen. *Diary of a Spider* (PS–3). Illus. by Harry Bliss. 2005, HarperCollins $15.99 (978-0-06-000153-7). A young spider's diary reveals typical concerns — molting, reassuring unhappy friends, worries about strange food, relations with flies, and vacuum drills. (Rev: SLJ 8/05)

3851 Cronin, Doreen. *Diary of a Worm* (PS–1). Illus. by Harry Bliss. 2003, HarperCollins LB $17.89 (978-0-06-000151-3). Presented in the form of a diary, this amusing title features a young earthworm who muses about the pros and cons of life as a worm. (Rev: BL 10/1/03; HB 11/03; HBG 4/04; SLJ 10/03)

3852 Cronin, Doreen. *M.O.M. (Mom Operating Manual)* (2–4). Illus. by Laura Cornell. 2011, Atheneum $16.99 (978-1-4169-6150-5). 56pp. A humorous guide to the care and feeding of mothers, with chapters on "Outdoor Use" and "Troubleshooting" and advice on danger signals. (Rev: BL 10/1/11; SLJ 10/1/11)

3853 Crunk, Tony. *Railroad John and the Red Rock Run* (1–3). Illus. by Michael Austin. 2006, Peachtree $16.95 (978-1-56145-363-4). Train engineer John overcomes some daunting challenges to deliver passenger Lonesome Bob to his wedding on time; illustrations reminiscent of daguerreotypes complement this tall tale. (Rev: BL 4/1/06; SLJ 5/06)

3854 Cummings, Troy. *The Eensy Weensy Spider Freaks Out (Big Time)* (K–3). Illus. by author. 2010, Random House $16.99 (978-0-375-86582-4). 40pp. Eensy the spider initially decides to retire from climbing after being washed out of the waterspout, but gradually regains her nerve with help from her ladybug friend. (Rev: BL 4/1/10; LMC 8–9/10; SLJ 4/1/10)

3855 Cutbill, Andy. *The Cow That Laid an Egg* (PS–2). Illus. by Russell Ayto. 2008, HarperCollins $16.99 (978-0-06-137295-7). 32pp. With the help of some friendly chickens, an ordinary cow named Marjorie lays an extraordinary egg that soon hatches into chicken who says "moo." (Rev: BL 2/15/08; SLJ 2/08)

3856 Cuyler, Margery. *Skeleton for Dinner* (PS–2). Illus. by Will Terry. 2013, Whitman $16.99 (978-080757398-3). 32pp. When Skeleton hears Big Witch say to Little Witch "we must have Skeleton for dinner" he thinks that he is the one on the menu, and it isn't until he's run away and convinced his friends that they too are in danger that he realizes his error. ℮ Lexile AD520 (Rev: BL 10/1/13; HB 9–10/13; SLJ 12/13)

3857 Cuyler, Margery. *Skeleton Hiccups* (2–4). Illus. by S. D. Schindler. 2002, Simon & Schuster $14.95 (978-0-689-84770-7). 32pp. A skeleton tries to rid himself of a bad case of hiccups and is finally scared out of them by looking in the mirror. (Rev: BCCB 9/02; BL 9/15/02; HB 9/02; HBG 3/03; SLJ 10/02)

3858 Cuyler, Margery. *That's Good! That's Bad!* (PS–K). Illus. by David Catrow. 1993, Holt paper $6.95 (978-0-8050-2954-3). 32pp. A boy's red balloon whisks him aloft for a series of adventures. (Rev: BCCB 12/91; BL 12/1/91; SLJ 11/91)

3859 Cuyler, Margery. *That's Good! That's Bad! In the Grand Canyon* (K–3). Illus. by David Catrow. 2002, Holt $16.95 (978-0-8050-5975-5). 32pp. A boy visiting the Grand Canyon has some "BAD" (but funny) close calls before he catches up with his grandmother. (Rev: BL 5/15/02; HBG 10/02; SLJ 6/02)

3860 Davidson, Ellen Dee. *Princess Justina Albertina: A Cautionary Tale* (PS–1). Illus. by Michael Chesworth. 2007, Charlesbridge $15.95 (978-1-57091-652-6). The willful Princess Justina Albertina wants a pet — a perfect pet — and is satisfied with none until her faithful nanny brings her a gryphon; and then the trouble begins. (Rev: SLJ 3/07)

3861 Daywalt, Drew. *The Day the Crayons Quit* (K–3). Illus. by Oliver Jeffers. 2013, Philomel $17.99 (978-0-399-25537-3). 40pp. Duncan's crayons have had it with him, and they convey their various grievances in nicely illustrated letters to their owner. ALA Notable Children's Book. Lexile AD730 (Rev: BL 7/13; LMC 1–2/14; SLJ 7/13*)

3862 De Sève, Randall. *The Duchess of Whimsy: An Absolutely Delicious Fairy Tale* (K–2). Illus. by Peter de Sève. 2009, Philomel $17.99 (978-0-399-25095-8). 40pp. The Duchess of Whimsy and the Earl of Norm find common ground despite their eccentric differences when he introduces her to grilled cheese sandwiches. (Rev: BL 10/1/09; SLJ 11/1/09)

3863 Deacon, Alexis. *A Place to Call Home* (PS–1). Illus. by Viviane Schwarz. 2011, Candlewick $16.99 (978-0-7636-5360-6). Unpaged. Seven overcrowded hamster siblings set out in search of a bigger home and have many adventures — crossing a sea (a puddle), climbing a mountain (a desk), and so forth. (Rev: LMC 11–12/11; SLJ 9/1/11)

3864 DeFelice, Cynthia. *Old Granny and the Bean Thief* (K–2). Illus. by Cat B. Smith. 2003, Farrar $16.00 (978-0-374-35614-9). When a thief steals some of Old Granny's beans and the sheriff is out of town, she enlists the help of a motley crew, including an alligator and a cactus. (Rev: HB 9/03; HBG 4/04; SLJ 9/03)

3865 deGroat, Diane, and Shelley Rotner. *Homer* (1–3). Illus. by Diane deGroat. 2012, Scholastic $15.99 (978-054533272-9). 32pp. Homer the golden retriever sneaks out at night to play baseball in a contest between the Doggers and the Hounds in this funny story. (Rev: BL 3/1/12; SLJ 5/1/12)

3866 Depalma, Mary Newell. *Uh-Oh!* (PS–1). Illus. by author. 2011, Eerdmans $14 (978-0-8028-5372-1). Unpaged. A young dinosaur gets himself into a series of funny "uh-oh!" situations in this nearly wordless book. (Rev: SLJ 8/1/11)

3867 Derby, Sally. *Whoosh Went the Wind!* (K–3). Illus. by Vincent Nguyen. 2006, Marshall Cavendish $16.99 (978-0-7614-5309-3). 32pp. In this lively picture book, an imaginative little boy explains to his skeptical teacher how the wind made him late for school. (Rev: BL 10/15/06; SLJ 10/06)

3868 DiCamillo, Kate, and Alison McGhee. *Bink and Gollie* (K–3). Illus. by Tony Fucile. 2010, Candlewick $15.99 (978-0-7636-3266-3). 96pp. Two oddball roller-skating friends — short Bink and tall Gollie — enjoy three humorous adventures in this picture book/graphic novel. Theodore Seuss Geisel Award. Lexile AD270L (Rev: BL 9/15/10; HB 1–2/11; LMC 11–12/10; SLJ 8/1/10)

3869 DiCamillo, Kate, and Alison McGhee. *Bink and Gollie: Best Friends Forever* (K–3). Illus. by Tony Fucile. 2013, Candlewick $15.99 (978-0-7636-3497-1). 96pp. A new trio of amusing stories about the mismatched friends in which Gollie boasts of royal blood, Bink tries a Stretch-o-Matic, and the two aim to become record holders. Lexile 420 (Rev: BL 3/15/13; HB 3–4/13; SLJ 4/13)

3870 DiCamillo, Kate, and Alison McGhee. *Two for One* (K–3). Illus. by Tony Fucile. 2012, Candlewick $15.99 (978-076363361-5). 96pp. Friends Bink and Gollie enjoy a day at the state fair, despite the mishaps they encounter. (Rev: BL 5/1/12; HB 5–6/12; SLJ 5/1/12*)

3871 DiPucchio, Kelly. *Zombie in Love* (K–2). Illus. by Scott Campbell. 2011, Atheneum $12.99 (978-1-4424-0270-6). 32pp. A lonely little zombie who longs for love has no luck until the night of the Cupid's Ball. (Rev: BLO 8/11; SLJ 8/1/11)

3872 Dodds, Dayle Ann. *Where's Pup?* (PS–K). Illus. by Pierre Pratt. 2003, Dial $12.99 (978-0-8037-2744-1). A clown makes the rounds of his fellow circus performers in a frantic search for his missing puppy; a final fold-out page reveals the pup's location atop a pyramid of acrobats. (Rev: HB 3/03*; HBG 10/03; SLJ 7/03)

3873 Dormer, Frank W. *Socksquatch* (PS–2). Illus. by author. 2010, Henry Holt $14.99 (978-0-8050-8952-3). Unpaged. A cold-footed monster storms a castle in search of the perfect sock in this comic story. (Rev: SLJ 12/1/10)

3874 Dunbar, Polly. *Where's Tumpty?* (PS–K). Illus. by author. Series: Tilly and Friends. 2009, Candlewick $12.99 (978-0-7636-4273-0). 32pp. A very funny story about a large blue elephant's efforts to disappear. (Rev: BL 3/1/09; SLJ 5/09)

3875 Durant, Alan. *Burger Boy* (PS–2). Illus. by Mei Matsuoka. 2006, Clarion $16.00 (978-0-618-71466-7). 32pp. Benny's mother warns him that if he eats nothing but burgers he'll turn into one and that's just what happens in this hilarious picture book. (Rev: BL 11/15/06; SLJ 10/06)

3876 Duval, Kathy. *Take Me to Your BBQ* (K–2). Illus. by Adam McCauley. 2013, Disney/Hyperion $16.99 (978-1-4231-2255-5). 40pp. Farmer Willy's delicious barbecue attracts a bunch of green three-eyed aliens eager to eat and make merry; the tables are turned when Willy takes off in their spaceship and they are left to look after the turnips. Lexile AD360 (Rev: BL 3/15/13; LMC 3–4/13; SLJ 3/13)

3877 Eaton, Jason Carter. *How to Train a Train* (PS–2). Illus. by John Rocco. 2013, Candlewick $16.99 (978-0-

7636-6307-0). 48pp. Got a longing to train a train? Here you will learn about trains' habitat, diet, and likes and dislikes. Lexile AD520 (Rev: BL 7/13*; SLJ 8/13*)

3878 Eaton, Maxwell, III. *The Mystery* (K–2). Illus. by Eaton. Series: The Adventures of Max and Pinky. 2008, Knopf $12.99 (978-0-375-83807-1). Max and Pinky together painted the barn red, so who has since been repainting it? A funny story with elaborate devices to catch the perp. (Rev: SLJ 12/08)

3879 Egan, Tim. *The Trial of Cardigan Jones* (K–3). Illus. by author. 2004, Houghton $16.00 (978-0-618-40237-3). Although he only sniffed the pie, Cardigan, a moose who is clumsy with his antlers, is put on trial for theft. (Rev: BCCB 10/04; SLJ 9/04)

3880 Elkin, Mark. *Samuel's Baby* (PS–2). Illus. by Amy Wummer. 2010, Tricycle $15.99 (978-1-58246-301-8). Unpaged. A young boy prepares for the arrival of his baby sister by sharing his anxiety with his kindergarten class in this funny and reassuring picture book. (Rev: SLJ 7/1/10)

3881 Ellis, Sarah. *The Queen's Feet* (K–2). Illus. by Dusan Petricic. 2006, Red Deer $17.95 (978-0-88995-320-8). 32pp. Queen Daisy's unruly feet finally get totally out of line and she has to rein them in this humorous story full of wordplay. (Rev: BL 5/1/06; SLJ 4/06)

3882 Elya, Susan Middleton. *Cowboy Jose* (K–1). Illus. by Tim Raglin. 2005, Penguin $15.99 (978-0-399-23570-2). 32pp. In bouncy rhyming English and Spanish, a poor Mexican cowboy seeks the money to impress Rosita but in the end decides to spend it on his faithful horse. (Rev: BL 2/1/05; SLJ 4/05)

3883 Emmett, Jonathan. *Someone Bigger* (PS–1). Illus. by Adrian Reynolds. 2004, Clarion $16.00 (978-0-618-44397-0). 32pp. Dad says Sam is too little to handle the kite, it needs someone bigger; and of course so it proves as a whole string of people and animals are pulled into the air until Sam acts to save the day. (Rev: BL 3/1/04; SLJ 5/04)

3884 Ernst, Lisa Campbell. *The Gingerbread Girl Goes Animal Crackers* (PS–1). Illus. by author. 2011, Dutton $16.99 (978-0-525-42259-4). 32pp. Initially thrilled with a gift box of animal crackers, Gingerbread Girl unleashes considerable chaos when the animated animals are let out of their box; a sequel to *The Gingerbread Girl* (2006). (Rev: BLO 10/1/11; SLJ 12/1/11)

3885 Ernst, Lisa Campbell. *Stella Louella's Runaway Book* (PS–2). Illus. 1998, Simon & Schuster $16.00 (978-0-689-81883-7). 40pp. Stella Louella traces the whereabouts of her lost library book by questioning various townspeople who have read it and passed it along. (Rev: BCCB 12/98; BL 8/98; HBG 3/99; SLJ 9/98)

3886 Esbaum, Jill. *Estelle Takes a Bath* (PS–2). Illus. by Mary Newell Depalma. 2006, Holt $16.95 (978-0-8050-7741-4). Estelle's comfortable bath is rudely interrupted by a little field mouse. (Rev: BL 1/1–15/07; SLJ 11/06)

3887 Esbaum, Jill. *Stink Soup* (1–4). Illus. by Roger Roth. 2004, Farrar $16.00 (978-0-374-37252-0). While on vacation at grandmother's farm, Willie keeps misbehaving

(and letting older sister Annabelle take the blame) — until he encounters a skunk. (Rev: SLJ 3/04)

3888 Espinosa, Laura. *Otis and Rae and the Grumbling Splunk* (PS–3). Illus. by Leo Espinosa. 2008, Houghton $12.95 (978-0-618-98206-6). 32pp. Adventurous Rae goes to sleep and careful Otis attempts to brave the dark night in this story featuring a Grumbling Splunk. (Rev: HB 5/08; SLJ 5/08)

3889 Fallon, Jimmy. *Snowball Fight!* (PS–1). Illus. by Adam Stower. 2005, Dutton $15.99 (978-0-525-47456-2). A boy and his younger sister enjoy a snow day off school in this book with action-packed cartoon illustrations. (Rev: SLJ 11/05)

3890 Fearnley, Jan. *The Search for the Perfect Child* (PS–K). Illus. by author. 2006, Candlewick $15.99 (978-0-7636-3231-1). The coolest dog in the world is searching for a perfect child and has a number of criteria laid out. (Rev: BL 12/1/06; SLJ 11/06)

3891 Feiffer, Jules. *By the Side of the Road* (2–4). 2002, Hyperion $15.95 (978-0-7868-0908-0). 64pp. A boy becomes so fed up with being bossed around by his dad that he decides to set out on his own. (Rev: BCCB 9/02; BL 6/1–15/02*; HBG 10/02; SLJ 5/02)

3892 Feiffer, Kate. *But I Wanted a Baby Brother!* (K–3). Illus. by Diane Goode. 2010, Simon & Schuster $16.99 (978-1-4169-3941-2). 32pp. Instead of the baby brother he expected, Oliver is disappointed when his mom has a girl, and attempts to change the child for a baby boy. (Rev: BL 4/15/10; SLJ 6/1/10)

3893 Feiffer, Kate. *Double Pink* (K–3). Illus. by Bruce Ingman. 2005, Simon & Schuster $15.95 (978-0-689-87190-0). Young Madison's single-minded love for the color pink gets out of control. (Rev: SLJ 11/05)

3894 Feiffer, Kate. *Henry, the Dog with No Tail* (K–2). Illus. by Jules Feiffer. 2007, Simon & Schuster $16.99 (978-1-4169-1614-7). 32pp. Sad, tailless Henry visits a tailor to have one made and goes to Battery Park for a device that will make it wag, but after the tail wags out of control he decides to do without, retaining only a "tale" to tell. (Rev: BL 11/1/07; SLJ 10/07)

3895 Feiffer, Kate. *President Pennybaker* (PS–1). Illus. by Diane Goode. 2008, Simon & Schuster $16.99 (978-1-4169-1354-2). 32pp. Life just isn't fair, so Luke runs for president — with his dog as running mate — and discovers that even being the boss doesn't mean he will get enough time for TV. (Rev: BL 8/08; LMC 10/08; SLJ 8/08)

3896 Fleming, Candace. *Muncha! Muncha! Muncha!* (PS–2). Illus. by G. Brian Karas. 2002, Simon & Schuster $16.00 (978-0-689-83152-2). 32pp. Mr. McGreely goes to great lengths to defend his vegetable garden from a group of clever rabbits in this hilarious story. (Rev: BCCB 3/02; BL 1/1–15/02; HBG 10/02; SLJ 2/02*)

3897 Fleming, Candace. *Tippy-Tippy-Tippy, Hide!* (PS–K). Illus. by G. Brian Karas. 2007, Simon & Schuster $16.99 (978-0-689-87479-6). 40pp. In this sequel to *Muncha! Muncha! Muncha!* (2002), Mr. McGreely is determined to keep the rabbits out of his cozy house and barricades it so thoroughly that he can't get out when spring finally arrives. (Rev: BL 12/15/06; SLJ 1/07)

3898 Foreman, Mark. *Granpa Jack's Tattoo Tales* (1–3). Illus. by author. 2007, Farrar $16.00 (978-0-374-32768-2). 40pp. Chloe can always count on Granpa Jack for a tall tale about one of hismany elaborate tattoos. (Rev: BL 1/1–15/08; SLJ 12/07)

3899 Foreman, Michael. *Oh! If Only . . .* (K–3). Illus. by author. 2013, Andersen $16.95 (978-1-4677-1213-2). 32pp. Totally embarrassed by the events of a day, a young lad wishes he hadn't decided to play ball with a bouncy dog, triggering a series of misfortunes that wind up ruining the queen's birthday. ℮ (Rev: BL 5/1/13; SLJ 3/13)

3900 Fox, Mem. *A Particular Cow* (PS–2). Illus. by Terry Denton. 2006, Harcourt $16.00 (978-0-15-200250-3). Out for her Saturday walk, a cow collides with a clothes-line, ends up with a pair of bloomers on her head, and slapstick mayhem follows. (Rev: SLJ 9/06)

3901 Frazee, Marla. *The Boss Baby* (K–2). Illus. by author. 2010, Simon & Schuster $16.99 (978-1-4424-0167-9). 40pp. A tyrannical baby in a suit-style onesie runs the household in corporate executive style, exhausting his weary parents. (Rev: BL 7/10; HB 7–8/10; SLJ 7/1/10*)

3902 Frazee, Marla. *A Couple of Boys Have the Best Week Ever* (K–3). Illus. by author. 2008, Harcourt $16.00 (978-0-15-206020-6). 40pp. Best friends James and Eamon attend nature camp each day but the enthusiastic reports they give to Eamon's grandparents differ quite a lot from reality; the illustrations add to the fun. Caldecott Honor Book, 2009. (Rev: BL 3/1/08; HB 3/08; SLJ 3/08*)

3903 Frazee, Marla. *Walk On! A Guide for Babies of All Ages* (PS–K). Illus. 2006, Harcourt $16.00 (978-0-15-205573-8). 40pp. A humorous how-to guide for babies who are just learning to walk. (Rev: BL 4/1/06; SLJ 4/06*)

3904 Freedman, Claire. *Pirates Love Underpants* (PS–2). Illus. by Ben Cort. 2013, Aladdin $15.99 (978-144248512-9). 32pp. The pirates must have the Pants of Gold, but in their haste to steal the treasure, they decide to cut through the elastic of the underwear, with predictably hilarious consequences. Lexile AD540 (Rev: BLO 9/15/13; SLJ 8/13)

3905 Freedman, Michelle. *The Ravioli Kid: An Original Spaghetti Western* (K–3). Illus. by Jason Abbott. 2005, Gibbs Smith $15.95 (978-1-58685-438-6). In this rollicking, pun-filled western tale, 7-year-old Stellina Pomodoro faces off against Angel Hair and the Anti-Pasta Gang. (Rev: SLJ 4/06)

3906 French, Jackie. *Pete the Sheep-Sheep* (PS–1). Illus. by Bruce Whatley. 2005, Clarion $14.00 (978-0-618-56862-8). 32pp. Shaun, a newly arrived sheep shearer at Shaggy Gully, shows the old timers that he can easily outperform them and their sheepdogs with the help of Pete, his "sheep-sheep." (Rev: BL 1/1–15/06; SLJ 11/05)

3907 Funke, Cornelia. *Princess Pigsty* (K–2). Trans. from German by Chantal Wright. Illus. by Kerstin Meyer. 2007, Scholastic $16.99 (978-0-439-88554-6). Princess Isabella is bored with her privileged life and longs to be normal; when she throws her crown away and refuses to cooperate, her father punishes her with work that she thoroughly enjoys. (Rev: SLJ 4/07)

3908 Gantos, Jack. *Three Strikes for Rotten Ralph* (1–3). Illus. by Nicole Rubel. Series: Rotten Ralph Rotten Reader. 2011, Farrar $16.99 (978-0-374-36354-3). 48pp. Rotten Ralph the cat has baseball aspirations that are subdued when he gets hit in the head, and he settles for being the team's "cat boy" instead. (Rev: BL 2/15/11; SLJ 1/1/11)

3909 Geist, Ken. *The Three Little Fish and the Big Bad Shark* (PS–1). Illus. by Julia Gorton. 2007, Scholastic $6.99 (978-0-439-71962-9). This spoof of the three little pigs story takes place in the ocean, with fish instead of pigs and the role of the big bad wolf played by a shark. (Rev: LMC 10/07; SLJ 6/07)

3910 Gemignani, Tony. *Tony and the Pizza Champions* (PS–3). Illus. by Matthew Trueman. 2009, Chronicle $16.99 (978-0-8118-6162-5). 44pp. Full of energy and puns, this is the story — based on fact — of an American pizza making team competing in the World Pizza Championship in Italy; includes recipes. (Rev: SLJ 6/09)

3911 Germein, Katrina. *My Dad Thinks He's Funny* (K–2). Illus. by Tom Jellett. 2013, Candlewick $14.99 (978-0-7636-6522-7). 32pp. A funny story about a father who just plain won't stop with his lame wisecracks. (Rev: BLO 6/13; SLJ 6/13)

3912 Gerstein, Mordicai. *How to Bicycle to the Moon to Plant Sunflowers: A Simple but Brilliant Plan in 24 Easy Steps* (PS–3). Illus. by author. 2013, Roaring Brook $16.99 (978-1-59643-512-4). 40pp. Determined to cheer up the moon, a young boy lays out the detailed 24-step plan he has made to plant sunflowers there; the colorful cartoon-style illustrations add to the fun. Lexile 690 (Rev: BL 3/15/13*; HB 5–6/13; LMC 10/13; SLJ 4/13)

3913 Gibbons, Faye. *Emma Jo's Song* (K–3). Illus. by Sherry Meidell. 2001, Boyds Mills $15.95 (978-1-56397-935-4). Emma Jo is the hit of the family reunion when she sings a duet with a howling dog. (Rev: BL 4/1/01; HBG 10/01; SLJ 5/01)

3914 Gibbons, Faye. *Mama and Me and the Model T* (PS–3). Illus. by Ted Rand. 1999, Morrow LB $15.89 (978-0-688-15299-4). In this delightful sequel to *Mountain Wedding,* Mama shows that it's not just the menfolk who can drive the new Model T around the farm. (Rev: BL 11/15/99; HBG 3/00; SLJ 11/99)

3915 Gibbons, Faye. *Mountain Wedding* (K–4). Illus. by Ted Rand. 1996, Morrow $16.89 (978-0-688-11349-0). 40pp. A series of humorous mishaps delay the wedding of widow Searcy and widower Long. (Rev: BCCB 9/96; BL 4/1/96; HB 5/96; SLJ 4/96)

3916 Gifford, Peggy. *Moxy Maxwell Does Not Love Stuart Little* (2–4). Illus. 2007, Random $12.99 (978-0-375-83915-3). 112pp. A fast-paced, funny tale about a girl who will do just about anything except finish reading her assigned summer book: *Stuart Little*. (Rev: BCCB 7–8/07; BL 7/07; HB 9/07; SLJ 7/07)

3917 Goodhart, Pippa. *Arthur's Tractor: A Fairy Tale with Mechanical Parts* (PS–2). Illus. by Colin Paine. 2003, Bloomsbury $15.95 (978-1-58234-847-6). 32pp. While Arthur is busy working on his tractor, he stumbles into a funny fairy tale. (Rev: BL 2/15/03; HBG 10/03; SLJ 3/03)

3918 Gordon, Domenica More. *Archie's Vacation* (PS–1). Illus. by author. 2014, Bloomsbury $17.99 (978-161963190-8). 32pp. Archie the dog designer decides to go on vacation. But what to take with him? He ends up with so many alternatives that his suitcase finally explodes. (Rev: BL 3/1/14; LMC 8–9/14; SLJ 3/14)

3919 Graham, Bob. *Dimity Dumpty* (PS–2). Illus. by author. 2007, Candlewick $15.99 (978-0-7636-3078-2). 40pp. Dimity is Humpty Dumpty's diffident little sister who conquers her timidity when her brother needs help. (Rev: BL 12/1/06)

3920 Graves, Keith. *Loretta: Ace Pinky Scout* (1–2). Illus. 2002, Scholastic $16.95 (978-0-439-36831-5). 40pp. Loretta discovers that not everyone can be perfect when she fails to earn her marshmallow toasting badge in this bright and silly spoof about scouting. (Rev: BL 10/15/02; HBG 3/03; SLJ 12/02)

3921 Graves, Keith. *The Unexpectedly Bad Hair of Barcelona Smith* (K–3). Illus. by author. 2006, Philomel $16.99 (978-0-399-24273-1). Barcelona sees dangers all around him and takes all precautions until the day his hair takes over. (Rev: SLJ 6/06)

3922 Gravett, Emily. *Spells* (K–3). Illus. by author. 2009, Simon & Schuster $16.99 (978-1-4169-8270-8). Unpaged. A small, ambitious frog researches a spell that will turn him into a prince, but doesn't pay sufficient attention. (Rev: LMC 11–12/09; SLJ 10/1/09*)

3923 Gray, Kes. *006 and a Half* (K–2). Illus. by Nick Sharratt. 2007, Abrams $10.95 (978-0-8109-1719-4). Daisy goes undercover as a secret agent but is frustrated when no one seems to be able to decipher her secret coded language. (Rev: BL 4/1/07)

3924 Greenberg, David. *Crocs!* (K–2). Illus. by Lynn Munsinger. 2008, Little, Brown $15.99 (978-0-316-07306-6). 32pp. A little boy leaves the city to get away from the roaches, pigeons, and other critters only to find himself on an island overrun with crocodiles. (Rev: BL 4/15/08; LMC 1/09; SLJ 4/08)

3925 Griffin, Kitty, and Kathy Combs. *The Foot-Stomping Adventures of Clementine Sweet* (K–2). Illus. by Mike Wohnoutka. 2004, Clarion $15.00 (978-0-618-24746-2). 32pp. The feisty Clementine Sweet makes her presence felt in her Texas town. (Rev: BL 3/1/04; SLJ 3/04)

3926 Grogan, John. *Marley Goes to School* (K–3). Illus. by Richard Cowdrey. 2009, HarperCollins $17.99 (978-0-06-156151-1); LB $18.89 (978-0-06-156152-8). Unpaged. Marley the dog follows his owner Cassie to school, where hilarity and mayhem ensue. (Rev: SLJ 11/1/09)

3927 Gutch, Michael. *Sticky, Sticky, Stuck!* (PS–2). Illus. by Steve Bjorkman. 2013, HarperCollins $17.99 (978-0-06-199818-8). 32pp. This whole family has a sticky problem — Annie's parents and siblings are always glued to their computers and they don't immediately notice when the little girl decides to make a peanut butter-and-honey sandwich, which gets stuck to the dog, which gets stuck to Annie, who gets stuck to Mom, and so on until they have to call the fire department. (Rev: BL 6/13; SLJ 6/13)

3928 Hale, Dean. *Scapegoat: The Story of a Goat Named Oat and a Chewed-Up Coat* (K–2). Illus. by Michael Slack. 2011, Bloomsbury $16.99 (978-1-59990-468-9). Unpaged. A kindhearted neighbor intervenes on behalf of Patsy Petunia Oat the goat, who's getting unjustly blamed for Jimmy Choat's frequent misdeeds. (Rev: BL 4/15/11; LMC 10/11; SLJ 6/11)

3929 Hall, Michael. *Cat Tale* (PS–K). Illus. by author. 2012, Greenwillow $16.99 (978-0-06-191516-1). 40pp. Three cats — Lillian, Tilly, and William J. — enjoy adventures full of nonsense wordplay in this quirky book with colorful, geometric illustrations. (Rev: BLO 10/1/12; SLJ 9/12)

3930 Hamburg, Jennifer. *A Moose That Says Moo* (PS–2). Illus. by Sue Truesdell. 2013, Farrar $16.99 (978-037435058-1). 32pp. As a little girl imagines the zoo that she would create, full of adorably unique animals with unexpected personalities, she realizes her imagination may have gotten out of hand. (Rev: BL 11/1/13; SLJ 9/13)

3931 Hamilton, Arlene. *Only a Cow* (PS–2). Illus. by Dean Griffiths. 2006, Fitzhenry & Whiteside $16.95 (978-1-55041-871-2). 32pp. A boisterous cow called Lucille longs to run, and gets her chance when she finds herself in a horse race at the county fair. (Rev: BL 1/1–15/07)

3932 Hanson, Warren. *It's Monday, Mrs. Jolly Bones!* (PS–2). Illus. by Tricia Tusa. 2013, Simon & Schuster $16.99 (978-1-4424-1229-3). 32pp. This quirky rhyming story follows Mrs. Jolly Bones through her week of unusual household activities. e Lexile AD480L (Rev: BL 3/1/13; HB 3–4/13; LMC 10/13; SLJ 2/13)

3933 Harley, Bill. *Dirty Joe, the Pirate: A True Story* (PS–2). Illus. by Jack E. Davis. 2008, HarperCollins $16.99 (978-0-06-623780-0). 32pp. Dirty Joe and his crew happily sail the seas searching for dirty socks until they come up against Stinky Annie and her impressive loot of underwear; in the ensuing melee it turns out that Joe and Annie are siblings! (Rev: SLJ 5/08)

3934 Harper, Charise Mericle. *Just Grace and the Flower Girl Power* (2–4). Illus. by author. 2012, Houghton Mifflin $15.99 (978-054757720-3). 208pp. Disappointed not to be picked as flower girl at her neighbor's wedding, Grace nonetheless decides that a trained cat can substitute. Lexile 660 (Rev: BL 8/12)

3935 Harrington, Janice N. *The Chicken-Chasing Queen of Lamar County* (PS–2). 2007, Farrar $16.00 (978-0-374-31251-0). 32pp. A young African American girl who enjoys chasing chickens decides to forgo the fun when she finds her main target tending to a flock of new chicks. (Rev: BL 2/1/07)

3936 Harris, Teresa E. *Summer Jackson: Grown Up* (K–3). Illus. by AG Ford. 2011, HarperCollins $16.99 (978-0-06-185757-7). Unpaged. Summer, a 7-year-old African American girl who is overeager for adult responsibilities, realizes maturity isn't all it's cracked up to be when her parents agree to let her take over their chores for a day. (Rev: SLJ 8/1/11)

3937 Harrison, Joanna. *Grizzly Dad* (PS–1). Illus. by author. 2009, Random $16.99 (978-0-385-75173-5). 32pp. It takes a day of play to retrieve the real Dad from the grizzly bear that woke up that morning. (Rev: BL 5/15/09; SLJ 8/09)

3938 Hartman, Bob. *The Wolf Who Cried Boy* (PS–2). Illus. by Tim Raglin. 2002, Penguin $16.99 (978-0-399-23578-8). 32pp. The cautionary tale is turned inside-out in this humorous story in which a wolf spots a pack of boy scouts. (Rev: BCCB 7–8/02; BL 7/02; HB 5/02; HBG 10/02; SLJ 6/02)

3939 Harvey, Matt. *Shopping with Dad* (PS–3). Illus. by Miriam Latimer. 2008, Barefoot Books $16.99 (978-1-84686-172-7). 32pp. A little girl's sneeze in the grocery store causes a series of unhappy events in this funny story. (Rev: SLJ 9/08)

3940 Haseley, Dennis. *The Invisible Moose* (PS–2). Illus. by Steven Kellogg. 2006, Dial $16.99 (978-0-8037-2892-9). 40pp. A shy Canadian moose in love with a lovely girl moose who is captured by a trapper uses an invisibility potion to follow her to New York City; a funny story of magic, romance, and adventure. (Rev: BL 2/1/06; SLJ 3/06)

3941 Hassett, Ann. *Mouse in the House* (PS–2). Illus. by John Hassett. 2004, Houghton $15.00 (978-0-618-35317-0). 32pp. Nana Quimby's discovery of a mouse in the house leads to even greater headaches as family members introduce one animal after another to rid the dwelling of an unwelcome guest. (Rev: BL 4/15/04*; HB 5/04; SLJ 3/04)

3942 Hassett, Ann. *Too Many Frogs!* (K–2). Illus. by John Hassett. 2011, Houghton Mifflin $16.99 (978-0-547-36299-1). 32pp. Overwhelmed by frogs emerging from her basement, Nana Quimby gets advice from neighborhood children but in the end has to solve the problem herself. (Rev: BLO 8/11; HB 7–8/11; SLJ 8/1/11)

3943 Havill, Juanita. *Just Like a Baby* (PS–2). Illus. by Christine Davenier. 2009, Chronicle $15.99 (978-0-8118-5026-1). It's hard to think about what you'll grow up when you're still in your crib. (Rev: SLJ 6/09)

3944 Hawkes, Kevin. *The Wicked Big Toddlah* (PS–1). Illus. 2007, Knopf $16.99 (978-0-375-82427-2). 40pp. A baby of gargantuan proportions is born in Maine, posing daunting challenges for the normal-sized people who must care for him. (Rev: BL 4/15/07)

3945 Hayes, Joe. *The Gum-Chewing Rattler* (K–3). Illus. by Antonio Castro L. 2006, Cinco Puntos $16.95 (978-

0-938317-99-9). In this amusing tall tale, inspired by the author's childhood in small-town Arizona, a young boy is saved from the bite of a rattlesnake by a wad of bubble gum. (Rev: SLJ 1/07)

3946 Heide, Florence Parry. *A Promise Is a Promise* (K–2). Illus. by Tony Auth. 2007, Candlewick $15.99 (978-0-7636-2285-5). George's parents promised he could have a pet — so why do they keep objecting to the creatures he brings home? (Rev: SLJ 6/07)

3947 Heide, Florence Parry, and Roxanne Heide Pierce. *Always Listen to Your Mother* (K–2). Illus. by Kyle M. Stone. 2010, Hyperion $15.99 (978-1-4231-1395-9). 32pp. Ernest, an obedient son of a demanding mother, finds a whole new outlook on life when spooky Vlapid and his mother move in next door. (Rev: BL 6/10; LMC 11–12/10; SLJ 7/1/10)

3948 Helakoski, Leslie. *Big Chickens* (PS–4). Illus. by Henry Cole. 2006, Dutton $15.99 (978-0-525-47575-0). 32pp. When a wolf is spotted in the barnyard, four hens run for their lives but find they gain courage when it's really needed. (Rev: BL 2/1/06; SLJ 2/06)

3949 Helakoski, Leslie. *Big Chickens Go to Town* (PS–2). Illus. by Henry Cole. 2010, Dutton $16.99 (978-0-525-42162-7). 32pp. The four funny chickens accidentally hitch a ride into town in the farmer's truck and are overwhelmed by the sights in this exuberant romp full of wordplay. (Rev: BL 1/1/10; SLJ 2/1/10)

3950 Henkes, Kevin. *Lilly's Big Day* (PS–K). Illus. 2006, Greenwillow $16.99 (978-0-06-074236-2). 40pp. Lilly is beside herself with excitement at the thought of being flower girl at her teacher's wedding, but there's a slight problem — he hasn't asked her. (Rev: BL 3/1/06*; SLJ 4/06*)

3951 Heos, Bridget. *Mustache Baby* (PS–1). Illus. by Joy Ang. 2013, Clarion $16.99 (978-0-547-77357-5). 40pp. Baby Billy is born with a mustache that evolves as he grows, going from a good-guy mustache to a bad-guy mustache, at which point he becomes a cat burglar and a cereal criminal; pun-filled and with cartoon illustrations that underline the slapstick humor. (Rev: BLO 5/1/13; SLJ 6/13)

3952 Hicks, Barbara Jean. *The Secret Life of Walter Kitty* (PS–2). Illus. by Dan Santat. 2007, Knopf $16.99 (978-0-375-83196-6). Poor Walter Kitty dreams of being a superhero cat; his owner does not see this potential and insists on cuddling Walter and calling him "Snookums." (Rev: BCCB 6/07; SLJ 7/07)

3953 Hill, Susanna Leonard. *No Sword Fighting in the House* (1–3). Illus. by True Kelley. 2007, Holiday $14.95 (978-0-8234-1916-6). 32pp. Readers will enjoy this funny story about two brothers who decide to "joust" atop two cows and end up ruining their mother's prized daffodils. (Rev: BL 5/1/07; HB 5/07; SLJ 8/07)

3954 Himmelman, John. *Chickens to the Rescue* (PS–2). Illus. 2006, Holt $16.95 (978-0-8050-7951-7). 32pp. Farmer Greenstalk's chickens come to the rescue of farm residents — both human and animal — in this entertaining romp. (Rev: BL 11/1/06; SLJ 10/06*)

3955 Himmelman, John. *Cows to the Rescue* (PS–2). Illus. by author. 2011, Henry Holt $16.99 (978-0-8050-9249-3). 32pp. When the family's car won't start, their farm animals willingly provide them with transportation to the county fair in this humorous romp. ℮ Lexile AD510L (Rev: BLO 10/15/11; SLJ 8/1/11)

3956 Himmelman, John. *Pigs to the Rescue* (PS–2). Illus. by author. 2010, Henry Holt $16.99 (978-0-8050-8683-6). 32pp. The pigs — and then the cows — overextend themselves in helping solve problems around the Greenstalk farm in this zany sequel to *Chickens to the Rescue* (2006). (Rev: BL 2/1/10; SLJ 4/1/10)

3957 Hoberman, Mary Ann. *The Seven Silly Eaters* (PS–3). Illus. by Marla Frazee. 1997, Harcourt $16.00 (978-0-15-200096-7). 40pp. A humorous picture book about Mrs. Peters and her brood of picky eaters. (Rev: BCCB 5/97; BL 3/1/97; HB 5/97; SLJ 3/97)

3958 Hodgkinson, Leigh. *Goldilocks and Just One Bear* (PS–3). Illus. by author. 2012, Candlewick $15.99 (978-0-7636-6172-4). 32pp. Baby Bear is all grown up and on a trip to the city when he seeks shelter and finds himself in the house of a familiar-looking woman with golden hair. (Rev: BLO 10/1/12; SLJ 11/12)

3959 Hodgkinson, Leigh. *Troll Swap* (PS–2). Illus. by author. 2014, Candlewick $15.99 (978-076367101-3). 32pp. A polite and tidy troll and a messy girl named Tabitha decide to swap places, which initially pleases their families — but eventually a level of dullness seeps in. (Rev: BL 3/1/14; LMC 8–9/14; SLJ 3/14)

3960 Hogg, Gary. *Look What the Cat Dragged In!* (K–3). Illus. by Mike Wohnoutka. 2005, Dutton $15.99 (978-0-525-46984-1). When the slothful Lazybones family begins to talk of replacing their faithful cat with a dog, the hardworking feline plots revenge. (Rev: BL 11/1/05; SLJ 2/06)

3961 Holt, Kimberly Willis. *The Adventures of Granny Clearwater and Little Critter* (K–3). Illus. by Laura Huliska-Beith. 2010, Henry Holt $16.99 (978-0-8050-7899-2). 32pp. In this hyperbolic Old West tall tale, Granny and Little Critter have some run-ins with outlaws on their way west to California. Lexile AD920L (Rev: BL 11/1/10; LMC 1–2/11; SLJ 9/1/10)

3962 Holub, Joan. *Little Red Writing* (K–3). Illus. by Melissa Sweet. 2013, Chronicle $16.99 (978-081187869-2). 36pp. Little Red is not a young girl in this tale, but a young pencil who must write a story, and with her basket of 15 words, sets off to do just that — but wait — the story she must write is fraught with grammar worries galore, and Little Red might just be the only one who can rescue Principal Granny from the Wolf 3000 pencil sharpener. Lexile AD740 (Rev: BL 9/15/13; HB 1–2/14; LMC 3–4/14; SLJ 9/13*)

3963 Hooper, Meredith. *Celebrity Cat* (K–3). Illus. by Bee Willey. 2006, Frances Lincoln $15.95 (978-1-84507-290-2). 36pp. Felissima, a cat with a passion for art, creates her own renditions of famous paintings to include cats in each one. (Rev: BL 11/15/06; SLJ 12/06)

3964 Hopkins, Jackie Mims. *The Gold Miner's Daughter: A Melodramatic Fairy Tale* (K–2). Illus. by Jon Goodell. 2006, Peachtree $15.95 (978-1-56145-362-7). 32pp. In this modern-day fable presented in the form of a stage production, Gracie Pearl encounters a series of classic fairy tale characters as she struggles to find a way to save her home and mine from an evil banker. (Rev: BL 2/15/06; SLJ 4/06)

3965 Horowitz, Dave. *Buy My Hats!* (K–2). Illus. by author. 2010, Putnam $16.99 (978-0-399-25275-4). 32pp. Washed-up hat salesmen Frank and Carl cheer a change in the weather that makes their wares fly off the shelves in this comic story about consumer whims. (Rev: BL 6/10; LMC 11–12/10; SLJ 6/1/10)

3966 Horowitz, Dave. *Five Little Gefiltes* (PS–2). Illus. by author. 2007, Putnam $12.99 (978-0-399-24608-1). In this Yiddish-flavored takeoff on "Five Little Ducklings," five young gefilte fish swim off on their own and explore the delights of New York City in the early 20th century. (Rev: SLJ 2/07)

3967 Horse, Harry. *The Last Polar Bears* (1–4). Illus. by author. 2007, Peachtree $12.95 (978-1-56145-379-5). 104pp. Through letters from Grandfather to his grandchild, readers learn about his expedition — with his faithful dog Roo, who seems unsuited to this task — to see the last polar bears before they become extinct. (Rev: LMC 1/08; SLJ 12/07)

3968 Horton, Joan. *Math Attack* (1–3). Illus. by Kyrsten Brooker. 2009, Farrar $16.95 (978-0-374-34861-8). 40pp. This entertaining picture book in rhyme tells what happens when a little girl is asked to answer one more math question than she can handle. (Rev: BL 1/1–15/09; SLJ 3/09)

3969 Horton, Joan. *Working Mummies* (K–2). Illus. by Drazen Kozjan. 2012, Farrar $12.99 (978-037438524-8). 32pp. What problems do mummy mothers face in their jobs? Graveyard shifts, sharpening claws, filling cavities in fangs, selling haunted houses, and much more in this pun-filled romp. (Rev: BLO 8/12; SLJ 7/12)

3970 Hosford, Kate. *Big Bouffant* (PS–2). Illus. by Holly Clifton-Brown. 2011, Carolrhoda $16.95 (978-0-7613-5409-3). 32pp. Bored with ordinary hairstyles, Annabelle decides to adopt a bouffant hairdo and ends up starting a school-wide trend. ℮ Lexile AD550L (Rev: SLJ 4/11)

3971 Howard, Arthur. *Serious Trouble* (PS–2). Illus. by author. 2003, Harcourt $16.00 (978-0-15-202664-6). Despite his serious parents, Prince Ernest is determined to become a jester, and he shows some talent at this when he coaxes a laugh from a three-headed dragon and thereby saves the kingdom. (Rev: HB 11/03; HBG 4/04; SLJ 11/03)

3972 Howe, James. *Horace and Morris Say Cheese (Which Makes Dolores Sneeze!)* (K–2). Illus. by Amy Walrod. 2009, Simon & Schuster $16.99 (978-0-689-83940-5). 32pp. Dolores suddenly becomes allergic to cheese but can she give it up? (Rev: BL 8/09; HB 7/09; SLJ 7/09)

3973 Huget, Jennifer LaRue. *The Best Birthday Party Ever* (K–1). Illus. by LeUyen Pham. 2011, Random House $16.99 (978-0-375-84763-9); LB $19.99 (978-0-375-95763-5). 32pp. A fanciful 6-year-old girl begins planning her birthday party five months in advance; comic illustrations add appeal. (Rev: BL 4/15/11; SLJ 4/11)

3974 Huget, Jennifer LaRue. *How to Clean Your Room in 10 Easy Steps* (K–3). Illus. by Edward Koren. 2010, Random House $16.99 (978-0-375-84410-2). 40pp. An entertaining guide to a tiresome chore. (Rev: BL 5/15/10; LMC 8–9/10; SLJ 4/1/10)

3975 Hughes, Ted. *My Brother Bert* (PS–1). Illus. by Tracey Campbell Pearson. 2009, Farrar $16.95 (978-0-374-39982-5). 40pp. Bert's little sister finds more than she expected when she invades her brother's room in this poem with riotous illustrations of a menagerie running wild. (Rev: BL 2/1/09; HB 5/09; SLJ 5/09)

3976 Hurd, Thacher. *Bad Frogs* (PS–2). Illus. by author. 2009, Candlewick $15.99 (978-0-7636-3253-3). 40pp. These misbehaving frogs — all 170 of them — get up to constant mischief in this brightly illustrated book. (Rev: BCCB 4/09; SLJ 6/09)

3977 Hutchins, Pat. *Don't Forget the Bacon!* (K–3). Illus. by author. 1976, Morrow paper $6.99 (978-0-688-08743-2). 32pp. A young boy mixes up the shopping list on a trip to the grocery store.

3978 Idle, Molly. *Tea Rex* (K–2). Illus. by author. 2013, Viking $16.99 (978-0-670-01430-9). 40pp. A lesson on proper tea party etiquette is combined with the difficulties of entertaining an enormous dinosaur in this amusing book. (Rev: BL 4/1/13; SLJ 3/13)

3979 Isaacs, Anne. *Dust Devil* (PS–2). Illus. by Paul O. Zelinsky. 2010, Random House $17.99 (978-0-375-86722-4). 48pp. In this tall tale sequel to 1994's *Swamp Angel,* the outsized Angelica tames a dust storm and rides off on a giant horse to defeat some desperadoes; set in 1835 Montana. **e** Lexile AD900L (Rev: BL 9/1/10*; LMC 1–2/11*; SLJ 9/1/10*)

3980 Isaacs, Anne. *Swamp Angel* (K–4). Illus. by Paul Zelinsky. 1994, Dutton $17.99 (978-0-525-45271-3). 40pp. Angelica Longrider is a true tall-tale heroine because, among her many accomplishments, she is able to lasso a tornado. (Rev: BCCB 11/94; BL 10/15/94*; SLJ 12/94*)

3981 Jackson, Alison. *Thea's Tree* (1–3). Illus. by Janet Pedersen. 2008, Dutton $16.99 (978-0-525-47443-2). 32pp. When the seed Thea planted for her science project sprouts a vine bearing a golden egg, a singing harp, gold coins, and other marvels, Thea consults experts from scientists to bankers; the illustrations add to the zany humor. (Rev: BL 7/08; LMC 10/08; SLJ 4/08)

3982 James, Simon. *Baby Brains and RoboMom* (PS–2). Illus. by author. 2008, Candlewick $15.99 (978-0-7636-3463-6). 32pp. The talented young Baby Brains invents a robot to help his mother with her chores, but RoboMom soon takes on too much. (Rev: BL 4/1/08; SLJ 5/08)

3983 James, Simon. *Baby Brains Superstar* (PS). Illus. 2005, Candlewick $15.99 (978-0-7636-2894-9). 32pp. In this appealing sequel to *Baby Brains* (2004), young Baby, a musical prodigy because Mom wore earphones on her belly, decides to pursue a career in rock 'n' roll, performing before a massive audience. (Rev: BL 9/15/05; SLJ 11/05)

3984 Jarka, Jeff. *Love That Kitty! The Story of a Boy Who Wanted to Be a Cat* (PS–2). Illus. by author. 2010, Henry Holt $12.99 (978-0-8050-9053-6). 32pp. Peter decides to become a cat in this sequel to *Love That Puppy! The Story of a Boy Who Wanted to Be a Dog* (2009), and his parents patiently deal with his phases. (Rev: BL 10/1/10; SLJ 9/1/10)

3985 Jarka, Jeff. *Love That Puppy! The Story of a Boy Who Wanted to Be a Dog* (PS–1). Illus. by author. 2009, Holt $12.95 (978-0-8050-8741-3). 32pp. A pleasantly silly story that will give readers something to chew on. (Rev: SLJ 6/09)

3986 Jeffers, Oliver. *Stuck* (PS–3). Illus. by author. 2011, Philomel $16.99 (978-0-399-25737-7). 32pp. A cumulative tale in which young Floyd throws increasingly large objects — all the way from a shoe up to a house, a fire truck, and a whale — into a tree trying to dislodge his kite. **e** (Rev: BL 12/1/11; LMC 5–6/12; SLJ 12/1/11)

3987 Jinkins, Jim. *Shrinky Pinky!* (1–3). Illus. Series: Pinky Dinky Doo. 2005, Random $12.95 (978-0-375-83234-5). 48pp. Pinky tells her younger brother a tall tale about how she dealt with a bully named Lane Puppytray. (Rev: BL 12/1/05)

3988 Johnson, Paul B. *Little Bunny Foo Foo* (PS–1). Illus. 2004, Scholastic $15.95 (978-0-439-37301-2). 32pp. In a lively adaptation full of eye-catching vehicles, the Good Fairy describes the transgressions of naughty bunny Foo Foo; music, lyrics, and suggested movements are included. (Rev: BL 1/1–15/04; SLJ 4/04)

3989 Johnson, Paul B. *On Top of Spaghetti* (PS–2). Illus. 2006, Scholastic $15.99 (978-0-439-74944-2). 32pp. The lyrics of Tom Glazer's song about spaghetti provide the framework for this tale of a runaway meatball. (Rev: BL 4/15/06; SLJ 5/06)

3990 Joyce, William. *A Day with Wilbur Robinson* (PS–2). 2006, HarperCollins $16.99 (978-0-06-089098-8). 40pp. A young friend visits Wilbur Robinson at home, meets his extraordinary family, and gets swept up in some unforgettable adventures in this wacky romp, an expanded version of the 1990 title. (Rev: BL 8/06)

3991 Kanninen, Barbara. *A Story with Pictures* (K–3). Illus. by Lynn Rowe Reed. 2007, Holiday House $16.95 (978-0-8234-2049-0). 32pp. A young author engages in a humorous battle with her illustrator for control of her story, teaching readers much about the structure of books in the process. (Rev: LMC 1/08; SLJ 10/07)

3992 Kaplan, Bruce. *Monsters Eat Whiny Children* (K–3). Illus. by author. 2010, Simon & Schuster $15.99 (978-1-4169-8689-8). 40pp. In this cautionary tale, two whiny children are kidnapped by a monster intending to eat them for dinner. Lexile AD660L (Rev: BL 8/10; SLJ 9/1/10*)

3993 Katz, Alan. *Don't Say That Word!* (PS–1). Illus. by David Catrow. 2007, Simon & Schuster $16.99 (978-0-689-86971-6). 40pp. Michael almost says seven bad words as he tells his mom about his school day in this hilariously picture book. (Rev: BCCB 9/07; BL 7/07; LMC 10/07; SLJ 7/07)

3994 Keane, Dave. *Bobby Bramble Loses His Brain* (1–3). Illus. by David Clark. 2009, Clarion $16.00 (978-0-547-05644-9). 32pp. When Bobby falls and knocks the top off his head, his brain takes off, prompting a frantic chase. (Rev: BCCB 6/09; BL 4/15/09; SLJ 6/09)

3995 Kelly, Mij. *Where's My Darling Daughter?* (PS). Illus. by Katharine McEwen. 2006, Good Bks. $16.00 (978-1-56148-537-6). Certain that he has misplaced his baby daughter (who is on her father's back the whole time), Poppa Bombola sets off on a frantic search. (Rev: SLJ 12/06)

3996 Kimmel, Eric A. *The Great Texas Hamster Drive* (PS–2). Illus. by Bruce Whatley. 2007, Marshall Cavendish $16.99 (978-0-7614-5357-4). Legendary cowboy Pecos Bill orders a pair of pet hamsters for his daughter without sufficient forethought and ends up herding their offspring clear up to Chicago. (Rev: BL 10/1/07; LMC 1/08; SLJ 10/07)

3997 Kimmel, Eric A. *I Took My Frog to the Library* (PS–K). Illus. by Blanche Sims. 1992, Puffin paper $5.99 (978-0-14-050916-8). 32pp. A number of different animals create havoc when they visit the library. (Rev: BL 2/15/90; SLJ 3/90)

3998 Kimmel, Eric A. *Little Britches and the Rattlers* (K–2). Illus. by Vincent Nguyen. 2008, Marshall Cavendish $16.99 (978-0-7614-5432-8). 32pp. Little Britches must negotiate with seven threatening rattlesnakes on her way to the rodeo in this humorous repetitive story. (Rev: BL 9/15/08; LMC 3/09; SLJ 9/08)

3999 Kirsch, Vincent X. *Natalie and Naughtily* (K–3). Illus. by author. 2008, Bloomsbury $16.99 (978-1-59990-269-2). 32pp. Twins Natalie and Naughtily, who live above a department store, disobey the rules and decide to go and "help" the customers. (Rev: LMC 3/09; SLJ 11/08)

4000 Kloske, Geoffrey. *Once Upon a Time, the End (Asleep in 60 Seconds)* (K–3). Illus. by Barry Blitt. 2005, Simon & Schuster $15.95 (978-0-689-86619-7). 40pp. An exhausted father tells his insatiable child hilariously abbreviated versions of fairy tales and nursery rhymes. (Rev: BCCB 12/05; BL 11/15/05*; HBG 4/06; SLJ 10/05)

4001 Koller, Jackie F. *Horace the Horrible: A Knight Meets His Match* (PS–3). Illus. by Jackie Urbanovic. 2003, Marshall Cavendish $16.95 (978-0-7614-5150-1). The humorous tale of Horace's knightly efforts to entertain his unhappy niece, the Princess Minuette. (Rev: BCCB 12/03; HBG 4/04; SLJ 11/03)

4002 Koller, Jackie F. *Peter Spit a Seed at Sue* (PS–3). Illus. by John Manders. 2008, Viking $15.99 (978-0-670-06309-3). 32pp. Four friends turn a dull summer day into a watermelon-seed-spitting adventure that infects the whole town. (Rev: LMC 11/08*; SLJ 9/08)

4003 Konnecke, Ole. *Anton and the Battle* (PS–1). Trans. by Catherine Chidgey. Illus. by author. 2013, Gecko $17.95 (978-1-8775-7926-4). 32pp. Young Anton and Luke compete to see who is stronger, louder, braver — until a little dog interrupts their rivalry. (Rev: BLO 7/13; SLJ 3/13)

4004 Könnecke, Ole. *Anton Can Do Magic* (PS–2). Illus. by author. 2011, Gecko $17.95 (978-1-8774-6737-0). Unpaged. Illustrations and text combine to tell the story of an aspiring magician with a wonky turban. (Rev: LMC 1–2/12; SLJ 10/1/11)

4005 Kopelke, Lisa. *The Younger Brother's Survival Guide: By Matt* (PS–3). Illus. by author. 2006, Simon & Schuster $15.95 (978-0-689-86249-6). Matt offers helpful and humorous advice on how to survive life with an older sibling. (Rev: SLJ 3/06)

4006 Kraft, Jim. *The No-Good Do-Good Pirates* (PS–2). Illus. by Lynne Avril. 2008, Albert Whitman $16.99 (978-0-8075-5695-5). 32pp. A thoroughly silly story in which four young pirates wreak havoc as they try to figure out how to do a good deed; cartoon illustrations add to the fun. (Rev: BCCB 11/08; SLJ 9/08)

4007 Krasnesky, Thad. *That Cat Can't Stay* (K–2). Illus. by David Parkins. 2010, Flashlight $16.95 (978-0-9799746-5-6). Unpaged. Mom loves cats and keeps taking in strays despite Dad's objections — until Dad finally comes home with a dog. (Rev: LMC 9–10/10; SLJ 5/1/10)

4008 Krensky, Stephen. *Big Bad Wolves at School* (PS–2). Illus. by Brad Sneed. 2007, Simon & Schuster $15.99 (978-0-689-83799-9). 32pp. Rufus, a happy-go-lucky young wolf, finds classes at the Big Bad Wolf Academy a little too challenging for his tastes; energetic illustrations add to the hilarity. (Rev: BL 4/1/07)

4009 Kulka, Joe. *My Crocodile Does Not Bite* (K–2). Illus. 2013, Carolrhoda $16.95 (978-0-7613-8937-8). 32pp. Ernest's crocodile entertains everyone at the annual pet show, except Cindy Lou — with surprising results. Lexile 420 (Rev: BL 3/15/13; LMC 11–12/13; SLJ 3/13)

4010 Kuskin, Karla. *A Boy Had a Mother Who Bought Him a Hat* (PS–1). Illus. by Kevin Hawkes. 2010, HarperCollins $16.99 (978-0-06-075330-6). 32pp. In this updated version of the 1976 classic, a young boy receives a series of bizarre gifts from his mother, and insists on wearing or using them all at once — a cello, a mouse, a hat, fancy shoes, skis, a Halloween mask, and an elephant. (Rev: BL 2/15/10; SLJ 3/1/10)

4011 Kyle, Tracey. *Gazpacho for Nacho* (K–3). Illus. by Carolina Farias. 2014, Amazon/Two Lions $16.99 (978-147781727-8). 32pp. Nacho will only eat gazpacho, so his mother takes him to the market hoping to inspire him to try something new; in English sprinkled with Spanish words, plus a glossary. ℮ (Rev: BLO 3/1/14; SLJ 4/14)

4012 Lasky, Kathryn. *Two Bad Pilgrims* (2–4). Illus. by John Manders. 2009, Viking $16.99 (978-0-670-06168-

6). 40pp. Fact and fiction are interwoven in this graphic-novel-style account of the Billington family (known for "generally poor behavior" aboard the *Mayflower*) in which sons Johnny and Francis get a chance to correct the record. (Rev: BL 7/09)

4013 Latimer, Alex. *The Boy Who Cried Ninja* (PS–2). Illus. by author. 2011, Peachtree $15.95 (978-0-56145-579-9). 32pp. A young boy tired of getting blamed for the mischief caused by his absurd and rambunctious friends invites them all over so his parents can see the truth. Lexile AD740L (Rev: BL 4/1/11; SLJ 3/1/11)

4014 Lehrhaupt, Adam. *Warning: Do Not Open This Book!* (PS–2). Illus. by Matthew Forsythe. 2013, Simon & Schuster $16.99 (978-144243582-7). 40pp. Each page of the book offers the reader a chance to see why they shouldn't have opened it, with ensuing hilarity as all the animals escape from a zoo. (Rev: BLO 9/15/13; SLJ 7/13)

4015 Lendler, Ian. *An Undone Fairy Tale* (K–3). Illus. by Whitney Martin. 2005, Simon & Schuster $15.95 (978-0-689-86677-7). 32pp. A fairy tale involving a princess locked in a tower spins out of control when the illustrator and narrator can't keep up. (Rev: BL 1/1–15/06; SLJ 12/05)

4016 Lerman, Josh. *How to Raise Mom and Dad: (Instructions from Someone Who Figured It Out)* (K–3). Illus. by Greg Clarke. 2009, Dutton $16.99 (978-0-525-47870-6). 32pp. An older sister instructs her younger brother in the art of dealing with parents. (Rev: BCCB 4/09; BL 3/1/09; SLJ 2/09)

4017 Lester, Helen. *It Wasn't My Fault* (PS–1). Illus. by Lynn Munsinger. 1985, Houghton $17.00 (978-0-395-35629-6). 32pp. Nerdy Murdley Gurdson tries to discover why an ostrich laid an egg on his head. (Rev: BCCB 6/85; BL 3/1/85; SLJ 5/85)

4018 Lester, Helen. *Tacky Goes to Camp* (PS–2). Illus. by Lynn Munsinger. 2009, Houghton $16.00 (978-0-618-98812-9). 32pp. Tacky the penguin saves the day when a bear threatens Camp Whoopihaha. Earlier books featuring Tacky include *Tacky the Penguin* (1988), *Three Cheers for Tacky* (1994), *Tacky in Trouble* (1998), *Tacky and the Emperor* (2000), *Tackylocks and the Three Bears* (2002), and *Tacky and the Winter Games* (2005). (Rev: BL 4/1/09; HB 5/09; SLJ 4/09)

4019 Levine, Martha Peaslee. *Stop That Nose!* (PS–1). Illus. by Lee White. 2006, Marshall Cavendish $14.95 (978-0-7614-5280-5). Dad's nose flies off in a sneezing fit and young David chases valiantly after it as it continues to sneeze, ejecting all sorts of things en route. (Rev: SLJ 4/06)

4020 Levinthal, David. *Who Pushed Humpty Dumpty? And Other Notorious Nursery Tale Mysteries* (K–3). Illus. by John Nickle. 2012, Random House $17.99 (978-0-375-84195-8). 40pp. A toad detective called Binky investigates various cases including the poisoning of Snow White, an intruder bothering the Bear family, and who pushed Humpty Dumpty. ⊖ (Rev: BL 9/15/12; HB 9–10/12; LMC 1–2/13*; SLJ 9/12)

4021 Lewis, Jill. *Don't Read This Book!* (2–4). Illus. by Deborah Allwright. 2010, ME Media/Tiger Tales $15.95 (978-1-58925-094-9). 32pp. A fat, belligerent king threatens his Royal Storyteller — who seems in the midst of writing some of best-loved fairy tales of all times — in this funny fractured fairy tale. Lexile AD530L (Rev: BL 11/15/10; LMC 1–2/11; SLJ 10/1/10)

4022 Lewis, Kevin. *Not Inside This House* (K–2). Illus. by David Ercolini. 2011, Scholastic $16.99 (978-043943981-7). 40pp. Livingstone Columbus Magellan Crouse's increasingly ambitious naturalist interests are not appreciated by his parents! (Rev: BLO 8/11)

4023 Lillegard, Dee. *Balloons Balloons Balloons* (PS–1). Illus. by Bernadette Pons. 2007, Dutton $16.99 (978-0-525-45940-8). Children and adult react in different ways when a town is inundated with colorful balloons. (Rev: SLJ 2/07)

4024 Lloyd-Jones, Sally. *How to Get a Job — by Me, the Boss* (PS–2). Illus. by Sue Heap. 2011, Random House $17.99 (978-0-375-86664-7); LB $20.99 (978-0-375-96664-4). Unpaged. The narrator from *How to Be a Baby — By Me, the Big Sister* (2007) explains to friends and baby brother the various kinds of jobs there are (president of the world, magician, cowboy, engineer) and how to go about getting one. ⊖ (Rev: SLJ 8/1/11)

4025 Lloyd-Jones, Sally. *How to Get Married . . . by Me, the Bride* (K–2). Illus. by Sue Heap. 2009, Random $16.99 (978-0-375-84118-7). 40pp. An entertaining primer for little bridal wannabes, with advice on such topics as picking a spouse and then good places to wed (a castle, a playroom . . .) . (Rev: BCCB 6/09; BLO 5/27/09; SLJ 4/09)

4026 Lloyd, Sam. *Chief Rhino to the Rescue* (PS–1). Illus. by author. 2009, Holt $14.99 (978-0-8050-8821-2). 32pp. Fire Chief Rhino rushes to put out a fire only to discover it's the 100 candles on Great-Granny Wrinkles' birthday cake; detailed illustrations add to the fun. (Rev: BL 7/09; SLJ 9/09)

4027 Long, Kathy. *The Runaway Shopping Cart* (PS–2). Illus. by Susan Estelle Kwas. 2007, Dutton $16.99 (978-0-525-47187-5). When the shopping cart Kaleb's sitting in gets loose and starts rolling through town it attracts a train of followers, Gingerbread Man-style. (Rev: SLJ 4/07)

4028 Lorbiecki, Marybeth. *Paul Bunyan's Sweetheart* (1–3). Illus. by Renee Graef. 2007, Sleeping Bear $16.95 (978-1-58536-289-9). 32pp. Paul Bunyan pursues his dream girl Lucette, who is as big a hero as Bunyan (literally), and must pass her love test in this story written in true tall-tale style. (Rev: BL 11/15/07; SLJ 9/07)

4029 Lord, John Vernon. *The Giant Jam Sandwich* (PS–2). Illus. by author. 1987, Houghton $17.00 (978-0-395-16033-6); paper $6.95 (978-0-395-44237-1). A rhymed verse about the citizens of Itching Down who make a giant jam sandwich to attract wasps.

4030 Low, Alice. *Aunt Lucy Went to Buy a Hat* (PS–1). Illus. by Laura Huliska-Beith. 2004, HarperCollins $15.99 (978-0-06-008971-9). 32pp. An imaginative and well-illustrated story told in rhyme about forgetful Aunt Lucy's search for a hat. (Rev: BL 2/1/04; SLJ 3/04)

4031 Lubner, Susan. *Ruthie Bon Bair, Do Not Go to Bed with Wringing Wet Hair!* (PS–3). Illus. by Bruce Whatley. 2006, Abrams $15.95 (978-0-8109-5470-0). Little Ruthie refuses to follow her mother's advice and ends up with all kinds of horrid hair problems. (Rev: SLJ 11/06)

4032 Lucas, David. *Halibut Jackson* (PS–1). Illus. 2004, Knopf $16.95 (978-0-375-82690-0). 32pp. Shy Halibut aims to be invisible and wears clothes intended to blend in to his surroundings, but he misinterprets a royal invitation and attracts a lot of attention. (Rev: BL 2/1/04; SLJ 3/04)

4033 Luckhurst, Matt. *Paul Bunyan and Babe the Blue Ox: The Great Pancake Adventure* (K–3). Illus. by author. 2012, Abrams $17.95 (978-1-4197-0420-8). 48pp. A surfeit of pancakes eventually curtails Paul Bunyan's progress across the continent with Babe the Blue Ox and they retreat to Mom's farm where they eat healthy vegetables. (Rev: BL 10/1/12; LMC 5–6/13; SLJ 10/12)

4034 Lum, Kate. *Princesses Are Not Perfect* (PS–3). Illus. by Sue Hellard. 2010, Bloomsbury $16.99 (978-1-59990-432-0); LB $17.89 (978-159990433-7). 32pp. Three princesses with specific talents switch roles for a day with chaotic results. (Rev: BL 12/1/09; LMC 3–4/10; SLJ 3/1/10)

4035 Maccarone, Grace. *Miss Lina's Ballerinas* (PS–3). Illus. by Christine Davenier. 2010, Feiwel & Friends $16.99 (978-0-312-38243-8). 40pp. In the European city of Messina, Miss Lina has eight students (whose names all end in "ina") and must find a way to settle them down when a ninth girl — Regina — joins the class and disrupts the system of dancing in pairs. e Lexile AD610L (Rev: BL 11/1/10*; SLJ 12/1/10*)

4036 Maccarone, Grace. *Miss Lina's Ballerinas and the Prince* (PS–3). Illus. by Christine Davenier. 2011, Feiwel & Friends $16.99 (978-0-312-64963-0). 40pp. Miss Lina's budding ballerinas are excited when they hear a boy will be joining the class, imagining him as a prince, but the reality is somewhat different. e Lexile AD790L (Rev: BL 10/15/11; SLJ 11/1/11*)

4037 McClements, George. *Baron von Baddie and the Ice Ray Incident* (K–2). Illus. by author. 2008, Harcourt $16.00 (978-0-15-206138-8). 40pp. Being bad is just no fun if you don't have good guys to go up against. (Rev: BCCB 9/09; BL 11/15/08; LMC 3/09; SLJ 9/08)

4038 McClements, George. *Night of the Veggie Monster* (PS–3). Illus. by author. 2008, Bloomsbury $14.95 (978-1-59990-061-2). Ack! A pea on the plate! This is a funny story about a critical moment. (Rev: BCCB 1/08; HB 3/08; LMC 3/08; SLJ 2/08)

4039 McCloskey, Robert. *Burt Dow, Deep-Water Man* (K–3). Illus. by author. 1963, Puffin paper $6.99 (978-0-14-050978-6). 64pp. The humorous tale of an old Maine fisherman who caught a whale by the tail and then used a multicolored Band-Aid to cover the hole.

4040 McCloskey, Robert. *Lentil* (K–3). Illus. by author. 1940, Puffin paper $6.99 (978-0-14-050287-9). 64pp. Tale of a boy who can't carry a tune, yet learns to play the harmonica.

4041 MacDonald, Alan. *Trolls, Go Home!* (2–4). Illus. by Mark Beech. Series: Troll Trouble. 2007, Bloomsbury $14.95 (978-1-59990-077-3); paper $5.95 (978-1-59990-078-0). 128pp. When the Trolls move in next door, the Priddles are initially very uncomfortable. (Rev: BCCB 9/07; BL 5/1/07; SLJ 10/07)

4042 McDonald, Megan. *Beetle McGrady Eats Bugs!* (PS–2). Illus. by Jane Manning. 2005, HarperCollins LB $17.89 (978-0-06-001355-4). Beetle is an adventurous soul and for Fun with Food Week declares that she will eat an ant. (Rev: BL 3/1/04; SLJ 5/05)

4043 MacDonald, Ross. *Henry's Hand* (PS–1). Illus. by author. 2013, Abrams $16.95 (978-1-4197-0527-4). 48pp. Henry is a zombie who keeps losing his body parts and relies on his right hand to retrieve them; but then one day Hand gets fed up with being taken for granted and runs away to the city; how will Henry cope? e Lexile AD570 (Rev: BL 10/1/13; LMC 5–6/14; SLJ 9/13)

4044 McElligott, Matthew. *Backbeard and the Birthday Suit: The Hairiest Pirate Who Ever Lived* (K–2). Illus. 2006, Walker $16.95 (978-0-8027-8065-2). 32pp. Blackbeard the pirate trades his dilapidated buccaneering duds for a stylish new outfit much to the surprise of his crew. (Rev: BL 4/15/06; SLJ 4/06)

4045 McElmurry, Jill. *I'm Not a Baby!* (PS–2). 2006, Random $16.95 (978-0-375-83614-5). 32pp. Leo Leotardi, the youngest member of his family, has difficulty convincing family members that he's no longer a baby; Victorian-era illustrations of Leo bursting out of his baby clothes add to the fun. (Rev: BL 6/1–15/06; HBG 4/07; SLJ 7/06*)

4046 McEvoy, Greg. *The Ice Cream King* (K–3). Illus. by author. 1998, Stoddart $13.95 (978-0-7737-3069-4). After graduating from King School, Lionel finds there are few openings, so he compromises and becomes an ice-cream seller known as "The Ice Cream King." (Rev: SLJ 12/98)

4047 McGee, Marni. *Winston the Book Wolf* (PS–2). Illus. by Ian Beck. 2006, Walker $16.95 (978-0-8027-9569-4). In this amusing send-up of the Little Red Riding Hood story, the wolf has an appetite for books, behavior that infuriates the librarian, but he's shown the error of his ways and taught to read — and not eat — the books by a little girl named Rosie who just happens to be wearing a red hood. (Rev: SLJ 12/06)

4048 McGhee, Alison. *The Case of the Missing Donut* (PS–1). Illus. by Isabel Roxas. 2013, Dial $16.99 (978-0-8037-3925-3). 32pp. A very young sheriff charged with collecting donuts from the bakery can't understand how everyone knows he helped himself to one on the way home. (Rev: BL 7/13; SLJ 6/13)

4049 McKy, Katie. *Pumpkin Town! (Or, Nothing Is Better and Worse Than Pumpkins)* (K–3). Illus. by Pablo Bernasconi. 2006, Houghton $16.00 (978-0-618-60569-9). José and his brothers don't know quite what to do when the pumpkin seeds they discarded at the end of the last growing season take root and threaten to overrun the town. (Rev: SLJ 11/06)

4050 McMullan, Kate. *I'm Bad!* (PS–1). Illus. by Jim McMullan. 2008, HarperCollins $16.99 (978-0-06-122971-8). 40pp. A hungry tyrannosaurus boasts about his size and badness but fails to find anything to eat in this funny book that ends with a foldout of his much huger mother. (Rev: BL 4/1/08; HB 5/08; SLJ 5/08)

4051 McNaughton, Colin. *Captain Abdul's Little Treasure* (K–3). Series: Captain Abdul. 2006, Candlewick $14.99 (978-0-7636-3045-4). The treasure on Captain Abdul's ship is a baby, and his pirate baby-sitters love playing with him despite their gruff appearances. (Rev: BL 5/1/06)

4052 McNaughton, Colin. *We're Off to Look for Aliens* (PS–3). Illus. by author. 2008, Candlewick $15.99 (978-0-7636-3636-4). A pleasing story within a story with a surprise ending, this title features humorous rhyming text and illustrations. (Rev: LMC 11/08; SLJ 9/08)

4053 Madison, Alan. *The Littlest Grape Stomper* (K–2). Illus. by Giselle Potter. 2007, Random $16.99 (978-0-375-83675-6). This whimsical tall tale describes the story behind the Grape Lakes, in which a boy called Sixto Poblano — disinclined to use the six toes he has on each foot to stomp grapes — squishes a huge vatful and then spills it out, creating a massive flood. (Rev: SLJ 4/07)

4054 Madison, Alan. *Pecorino Plays Ball* (K–2). Illus. by AnnaLaura Cantone. 2006, Simon & Schuster $15.95 (978-0-689-86522-0). 40pp. Although he's never caught or pitched a baseball before, young Pecorino Sasquatch looks forward to his first Little League game. (Rev: BL 2/1/06; SLJ 3/06)

4055 Madison, Alan. *Pecorino's First Concert* (K–2). Illus. by AnnaLaura Cantone. 2005, Simon & Schuster $15.95 (978-0-689-85952-6). Pecorino goes to the orchestra and gets trapped in a tuba in this amusing tale. (Rev: SLJ 8/05)

4056 Mahy, Margaret. *Down the Back of the Chair* (PS–2). Illus. by Polly Dunbar. 2006, Clarion $16.00 (978-0-618-69395-5). 32pp. A family in search of lost car keys discovers lots more under the chair cushions (including a diamond ring, a ski, and a lion) in this rhyming jaunt. (Rev: BL 5/1/06; SLJ 6/06)

4057 Manning, Maurie J. *The Aunts Go Marching* (PS–1). Illus. 2003, Boyds Mills $15.95 (978-1-59078-026-8). 32pp. Aunts (rather than the usual ants) march to town in this version of the familiar children's song. (Rev: BL 2/1/03; HB 5/03; HBG 10/03; SLJ 4/03)

4058 Manushkin, Fran. *The Shivers in the Fridge* (PS–1). Illus. by Paul Zelinsky. 2006, Dutton $16.99 (978-0-525-46943-8). 40pp. Readers may take some time to work out that the very cold characters In this fanciful picture book are actually members of a family of refrigerator magnets. (Rev: BCCB 10/06; BL 10/15/06; HB 11/06; HBG 4/07; SLJ 10/06)

4059 Marciano, John Bemelmans. *Madeline and the Old House in Paris* (PS–2). Illus. by author. 2013, Viking $17.99 (978-0-670-78485-1). 48pp. In this addition to the Madeline series set in Paris, Madeline and her friend Pepito meet a ghost in the attic, an astronomer who has been looking for the return of the comet that killed him, and they help him retrieve his stolen telescope. (Rev: BL 10/1/13; SLJ 9/13)

4060 Martin, Bill, Jr., and Michael Sampson. *Little Granny Quarterback* (K–3). Illus. by Michael Chesworth. 2001, Boyds Mills $15.95 (978-1-56397-930-9). A zany story in which Granny Whiteoak, a star football player in her day, saves her team from defeat. (Rev: HBG 3/02; SLJ 12/01)

4061 Martins, Isabel Minhos. *My Neighbor Is a Dog* (PS–1). Trans. by John Herring. Illus. by Madalena Matoso. 2013, OwlKids $16.95 (978-1-926973-68-5). 32pp. A little girl is happy when a dog moves into her apartment building, followed by a pair of elephants, and even an alligator; her parents, however, decide to move elsewhere — a fact made all the stranger because it turns out her parents are giraffes! Lexile AD640 (Rev: BL 3/15/13; LMC 10/13; SLJ 6/13)

4062 Meddaugh, Susan. *Martha Blah Blah* (PS–2). Illus. 1996, Houghton $16.00 (978-0-395-79755-6). 32pp. Martha the dog, who talks after eating alphabet soup, finds her vocabulary constricted when the soup company reduces the letters in each can. Other installments in this series are *Martha Calling* (1994), *Martha Walks the Dog* (1998), *Martha and Skits* (2000), and *Perfectly Martha* (2004). (Rev: BCCB 12/96; BL 9/15/96; HB 11/96; SLJ 11/96*)

4063 Meddaugh, Susan. *Martha Speaks* (PS–3). Illus. 1992, Houghton $16.99 (978-0-395-63313-7). 32pp. Helen feeds her dog alphabet soup, and suddenly Martha can talk! (Rev: BCCB 11/92*; BL 9/1/92*; HB 1/93*; SLJ 12/92)

4064 Melling, David. *The Scallywags* (PS–2). Illus. 2007, Barron's $14.99 (978-0-7641-5991-6). 32pp. The wolf family known as the Scallywags decide to reform their behavior after the other animals totally reject them, but they go much too far in the other direction. (Rev: BL 2/1/07)

4065 Menchin, Scott. *Harry Goes to Dog School* (PS–1). Illus. by author. 2012, HarperCollins $16.99 (978-006195801-4). 32pp. A little boy who wants to be a dog is happy when his parents drop him off at Pavlov Royal Academy for dogs — until lunchtime comes around. (Rev: BLO 8/12; SLJ 6/1/12)

4066 Mickelson, Scott. *Artichoke Boy* (PS–2). Illus. by author. 2009, Boyds Mills $16.95 (978-1-59078-605-5). 32pp. A boy with an unusual affection for artichokes sees them everywhere; mixed-media collages and cartoon illustrations extend the lighthearted rhymes. (Rev: BL 2/1/09; SLJ 3/09)

4067 Middleton, Julie. *Are the Dinosaurs Dead, Dad?* (PS–2). Illus. by Russell Ayto. 2013, Peachtree $16.95 (978-1-56145-690-1). 32pp. The dinosaurs in the natural history museum contradict Dave's dad in this funny story. (Rev: BL 3/1/13; SLJ 3/13)

4068 Milgrim, David. *Eddie Gets Ready for School* (PS–2). Illus. by author. 2011, Scholastic $8.99 (978-0-545-27329-9). 32pp. Eddie has a checklist for school days that all young readers will recognize: "Wake up." "Fall back asleep." "Wake up again." (Rev: BL 8/11; HB 7–8/11; SLJ 7/11)

4069 Miller, Bobbi. *Miss Sally Ann and the Panther* (K–3). Illus. by Megan Lloyd. 2012, Holiday $16.95 (978-0-8234-1833-6). 32pp. Fierce pioneer woman Sally Ann Thunder Ann Whirlwind and a panther have an all-out fight on the prairie, in this tall tale that ends with the two reaching a truce. ❂ Lexile AD780 (Rev: BL 8/12; SLJ 11/12)

4070 Monroe, Chris. *Cookie, the Walker* (PS–2). Illus. by author. 2013, Carolrhoda $16.95 (978-0-7613-5617-2). 32pp. Cookie the dog's ability to walk on her hind legs leads to her fame and fortune — and to a realization that staying on four legs may well be preferable. ❂ Lexile AD350 (Rev: BL 3/15/13; LMC 10/13; SLJ 3/13)

4071 Mora, Pat. *Doña Flor: A Tall Tale About a Giant Woman with a Great Big Heart* (PS–2). Illus. by Raúl Colón. 2005, Knopf $15.95 (978-0-375-82337-4). When the cries of a fearsome beast frighten her fellow villagers, Doña Flor, a woman of monumental stature, sets off to find out what's causing the animal's distress only to discover the perpetrator is much less threatening than expected. (Rev: BL 12/1/05; SLJ 10/05)

4072 Morales, Yuyi. *Nino Wrestles the World* (PS–1). Illus. by author. 2013, Roaring Brook $16.99 (978-1-59643-604-6). 40pp. His baby sisters prove to be tougher than his imaginary opponents when young Nino dons his *lucha libre* wrestling costume. ALA Notable Children's Book; Pura Belpre Award (illustration). Lexile 260 (Rev: BL 7/13; LMC 10/13*; SLJ 6/13)

4073 Morgan, Christopher. *Pirates Eat Porridge* (1–3). Illus. by Neil Curtis. 2007, Roaring Brook $12.95 (978-1-59643-304-5). 80pp. After a wayward treasure map blows into Billy and Heidi's treehouse, its demanding pirate owner comes to claim it and the treehouse is transformed into a ship, whisking them off to an island where the children learn pirate ways. (Rev: BL 11/15/07; SLJ 3/08)

4074 Mortensen, Lori. *Cowpoke Clyde and Dirty Dawg* (PS–2). Illus. by Michael Allen Austin. 2013, Clarion $16.99 (978-0-547-23993-4). 32pp. Cowpoke Clyde's dog is covered with mud but is totally resistant to the idea of a bath, prompting a chase that involves the whole barnyard. (Rev: BLO 5/1/13; LMC 8–9/13; SLJ 4/13)

4075 Moser, Lisa. *Cowboy Boyd and Mighty Calliope* (PS–2). Illus. by Sebastiaan Van Doninck. 2013, Random House $17.99 (978-037587056-9). 40pp. Cowboy Boyd and his loving, sensitive, yet clumsy rhinoceros Calliope team up for well-intentioned antics at the Double R Ranch in this Wild West picture book that has a good balance of illustrations, humor, and story. ❂ (Rev: BLO 9/1/13; SLJ 7/13)

4076 Moser, Lisa. *Perfect Soup* (PS–1). Illus. by Ben Mantle. 2010, Random House $16.99 (978-0-375-86014-0). 40pp. Murray the mouse needs a carrot for his Perfect Soup, and there begins a cumulative tale involving everyone from a farmer to a horse, a shopkeeper, and a snowman. (Rev: BLO 12/1/10; SLJ 11/1/10)

4077 Munsch, Robert. *Alligator Baby* (PS–2). Illus. by Michael Martchenko. 1997, Scholastic $10.95 (978-0-590-21101-7). 29pp. An amusing story about overwrought parents who bring different baby animals home from the zoo, thinking each is their child. (Rev: HBG 3/98; SLJ 11/97)

4078 Munsch, Robert. *Munschworks 2: The Second Munsch Treasury* (PS–2). Illus. by Michael Martchenko and Helene Desputeaux. 1999, Annick $19.95 (978-1-55037-553-4). This anthology contains five of Robert Munsch's picture books including *Purple, Green and Yellow*, *Pigs*, and *Something Good*. (Rev: BL 1/1–15/00; HBG 3/00)

4079 Munsch, Robert. *Munschworks: The First Munsch Collection* (PS–3). Illus. by Michael Martchenko. 1998, Annick $19.95 (978-1-55037-523-7). 128pp. This omnibus volume includes five of Robert Munsch's popular picture books, including *The Paper Bag Princess*, *David's Father*, and *Thomas' Snowsuit*. (Rev: BL 1/1–15/99)

4080 Munsch, Robert. *Stephanie's Ponytail* (1–3). Illus. by Michael Martchenko. 1996, Firefly $16.95 (978-1-55037-485-8); paper $5.95 (978-1-55037-484-1). Stephanie is annoyed when every one of her style changes is copied by class members and her teacher. (Rev: SLJ 11/96)

4081 Munsch, Robert, and Michael Kusugak. *Munschworks 3: The Third Munsch Treasury* (PS–2). Illus. by Vladyana Krykorka and Michael Martchenko. 2000, Annick $19.95 (978-1-55037-633-3). 144pp. A large book that is a compilation of five of Munsch's previously published picture books including *Stephanie's Ponytail* (1986), *Angela's Airplane* (1988), and *A Promise Is a Promise* (1988). (Rev: BL 2/1/01; HBG 10/01) [813]

4082 Murguia, Bethanie Deeney. *Zoe Gets Ready* (PS–K). Illus. by author. 2012, Scholastic $16.99 (978-054534215-5). 40pp. It's Saturday — the day when young fashionista Zoe is allowed to choose her own clothes — and the little girl has trouble making a decision because the day offers so many possibilities. (Rev: BL 5/1/12; SLJ 6/1/12)

4083 Myers, Tim. *Down at the Dino Wash Deluxe* (PS–2). Illus. by Macky Pamintuan. 2013, Sterling $14.95 (978-140277798-1). 48pp. A humorous romp in which a bunch of dirty dinosaurs get a jolly good wash. (Rev: BLO 6/13; SLJ 12/13)

4084 Nedwidek, John. *Ducks Don't Wear Socks* (K–3). Illus. by Lee White. 2008, Viking $15.99 (978-0-670-06136-5). 32pp. A serious-minded little girl learns to laugh through her relationship with a nattily dressed duck. (Rev: BL 6/1–15/08; SLJ 5/08)

4085 Nesbitt, Kenn. *More Bears!* (PS–2). Illus. by Troy Cummings. 2010, Sourcebooks $12.99 (978-1-4022-3835-2). Unpaged. An author tries to write a story without bears, but his young (unseen) audience disagrees with this choice and demands more bears until things get totally out of control. (Rev: LMC 1–2/11; SLJ 1/1/11)

4086 Newman, Jeff. *Hippo! No, Rhino* (K–2). Illus. by author. 2006, Little, Brown $15.99 (978-0-316-15573-1). A rhino at the zoo is mistakenly labeled a hippo in this almost-wordless tale. (Rev: SLJ 7/06)

4087 Noble, Trinka Hakes. *Jimmy's Boa and the Bungee Jump Slam Dunk* (K–3). Illus. by Steven Kellogg. 2003, Dial $16.99 (978-0-8037-2600-0). Jimmy and his pet boa constrictor create havoc when they visit the school gym, where dance lessons are taking place. (Rev: HBG 4/04; SLJ 9/03)

4088 Noble, Trinka Hakes. *Meanwhile, Back at the Ranch* (PS–1). Illus. by Tony Ross. 1987, Puffin paper $6.99 (978-0-14-054564-7). 32pp. A humorous Western adventure concerning Rancher Hicks and his drive into Sleepy Gulch for some excitement. (Rev: BL 4/1/87; SLJ 5/87)

4089 Novak, Matt. *Too Many Bunnies* (PS–K). Illus. by author. 2005, Roaring Brook $7.95 (978-1-59643-038-9). Enhanced by a die-cut format, this is the story of five overcrowded bunnies who spy an invitingly empty hole across the field and one by one hop over there only to find they are no better off. (Rev: BCCB 2/05; HB 3/05; SLJ 6/05)

4090 O'Connor, George. *Uncle Bigfoot* (K–2). Illus. by author. 2008, Roaring Brook $15.95 (978-1-59643-271-0). 32pp. When the gigantic and hairy Uncle Bernie comes to stay, a young boy learns that people are not all the same. (Rev: BL 5/1/08; LMC 11/08; SLJ 6/08)

4091 O'Connor, Jane. *Bonjour Butterfly* (PS). Illus. by Robin P. Glasser. Series: Fancy Nancy. 2008, Harper-Collins $16.99 (978-0-06-123588-7). 32pp. The little glamor queen is displeased when she has to miss her friend's butterfly party and go to her grandparents' anniversary party. (Rev: BL 3/15/08; SLJ 5/08)

4092 O'Connor, Jane. *Fancy Nancy* (PS–2). Illus. by Robin P. Glasser. 2006, HarperCollins $17.99 (978-0-06-054209-2). 32pp. Nancy, a fashion-obsessed young girl, is determined to give the rest of her family a badly needed makeover. (Rev: BL 1/1–15/06; SLJ 2/06)

4093 O'Connor, Jane. *Fancy Nancy: Aspiring Artist* (1–3). Illus. by Robin Preiss Glasser. Series: Fancy Nancy. 2011, HarperCollins $12.99 (978-006191526-0). 32pp. Inspired by the paintings hanging in her ballet classroom, Fancy Nancy stages an exhibition. (Rev: BL 6/1/11)

4094 O'Connor, Jane. *Fancy Nancy: Fanciest Doll in the Universe* (PS–2). Illus. by Robin Preiss Glasser. 2013, HarperCollins $17.99 (978-006170384-3). 32pp. Nancy is very annoyed when her younger sister draws a pirate skull tattoo on her favorite doll, and her mother has to find a way to mollify the girl. ∩ Lexile 420 (Rev: BLO 6/13)

4095 O'Connor, Jane. *Fancy Nancy: Ooh La La! It's Beauty Day* (PS–2). Illus. by Robin Preiss Glasser. Series: Fancy Nancy. 2010, HarperCollins $12.99 (978-

0-06-191525-3). Unpaged. For her mother's birthday, Nancy converts the backyard into a spa and gives her mother a beauty treatment. (Rev: SLJ 11/1/10)

4096 Offill, Jenny. *Eleven Experiments That Failed* (K–2). Illus. by Nancy Carpenter. 2011, Random House $16.99 (978-0-375-84762-2); LB $19.99 (978-0-375-95762-8). Unpaged. A young scientist undertakes a variety of ill-fated science experiments in this humorous tale rooted in scientific method. **e** (Rev: SLJ 11/1/11)

4097 Offill, Jenny. *17 Things I'm Not Allowed to Do Anymore* (PS–K). Illus. by Nancy Carpenter. 2006, Schwartz & Wade $15.99 (978-0-375-83596-4). The mischievous narrator of this appealing picture book recounts some of the things she's been forbidden to do — stapling her brother's hair to the pillow, freezing flies in ice cubes, and so forth. (Rev: BL 11/1/06; SLJ 11/06*)

4098 Oller, Erika. *The Cabbage Soup Solution* (PS–2). Illus. 2004, Dutton $15.99 (978-0-525-47005-2). 32pp. Old Elsie's cats solve the mystery of who has been tampering with the cabbage crop — rabbits. (Rev: BL 2/15/04; SLJ 2/04)

4099 Olson, David J. *The Thunderstruck Stork* (PS–2). Illus. by Lynn Munsinger. 2007, Albert Whitman $15.95 (978-0-8075-7910-7). 32pp. After Webster the stork collides with a hot-air balloon, families start receiving unlikely babies (sparrows get a piglet, for example) but everyone adapts happily. (Rev: BL 10/15/07; LMC 1/08; SLJ 9/07)

4100 O'Malley, Kevin. *Animal Crackers Fly the Coop* (K–3). Illus. by author. 2010, Walker $16.99 (978-0-8027-9837-4). 40pp. In this humorous take-off of "The Bremen Town Musicians," Hen, Dog, Cat, and Cow set off to become comedians and find themselves embroiled with a bunch of robbers. (Rev: BL 2/15/10; LMC 1–2/10; SLJ 2/1/10*)

4101 O'Malley, Kevin. *Gimme Cracked Corn and I Will Share* (K–2). Illus. by author. 2007, Walker $16.95 (978-0-8027-9684-4). Corny jokes and wordplays add to the humor of this story of a chicken searching for food. (Rev: BL 12/1/07; HB 1/08; LMC 1/08; SLJ 8/07)

4102 Opel-Gotz, Susann. *Now We Are Cool* (K–2). Illus. by author. 2012, Fitzhenry & Whiteside $18.95 (978-155455235-1). 28pp. Brothers Leo and Mug decide to become cool, but are not quite sure how to do it in this appealing import from Germany. (Rev: BL 11/1/12; LMC 5–6/13)

4103 Oppel, Kenneth. *The King's Taster* (K–3). Illus. by Lou Fancher. 2009, HarperCollins $17.99 (978-0-06-075372-6). 32pp. In this story about picky eating, a dog called Max is the king's food taster and is puzzled by the new monarch's fussiness. (Rev: BL 3/15/09; HB 7/09; SLJ 6/09)

4104 Orlean, Susan. *Lazy Little Loafers* (K–2). Illus. by G. Brian Karas. 2008, Abrams $16.95 (978-0-8109-7027-4). An older sister has a critical point of view regarding the value of babies. (Rev: BL 9/1/08)

4105 Orloff, Karen Kaufman. *I Wanna New Room* (PS–2). Illus. by David Catrow. 2010, Putnam $16.99 (978-0-

399-25405-5). 32pp. A little boy, tired of crowding and chaos, campaigns for his own room through illustrated letters to his parents. (Rev: BL 10/15/10; LMC 3–4/11*; SLJ 12/1/10)

4106 Palatini, Margie. *The Cheese* (K–3). Illus. by Steve Johnson. 2007, HarperCollins $16.99 (978-0-06-052630-6). 32pp. This wonderfully silly book turns "The Farmer in the Dell" on its head, telling the story of the song's characters as they puzzle over why "the cheese stands alone." (Rev: BCCB 9/07; BL 5/15/07; SLJ 6/07)

4107 Palatini, Margie. *The Perfect Pet* (PS–2). Illus. by Bruce Whatley. 2003, HarperCollins LB $16.89 (978-0-06-000109-4). When Elizabeth's parents reject every suggestion for a new pet, the young girl adopts a tiny bug that she names Doug. (Rev: BL 7/03; HBG 10/03; SLJ 5/03)

4108 Palatini, Margie. *Three French Hens* (PS–2). Illus. by Richard Egielski. 2005, Hyperion $15.99 (978-0-7868-5167-6). 40pp. Three French hens — Collette, Poulette, and Fifi — sent as a gift to M. Philippe Renard end up instead in the clutches of Phil Fox, who welcomes the trio as potential food but is soon transformed by their kind attentions. (Rev: BCCB 11/05; BL 11/1/05; HB 11/05; HBG 4/06; LMC 11/05; SLJ 10/05*)

4109 Palatini, Margie. *The Three Silly Billies* (PS–2). Illus. by Barry Moser. 2005, Simon & Schuster $15.95 (978-0-689-85862-8). 32pp. A troll stops characters from different fairy tales from crossing his bridge in this rollicking takeoff on the Billy Goats Gruff story. (Rev: BL 3/1/05)

4110 Parpan, Justin. *Gwango's Lonesome Trail* (1–5). Illus. by author. 2006, Red Cygnet $17.95 (978-1-60108-004-2). Gwango, a lonely dinosaur, wanders the contemporary Southwest in search of a friend; handsome paintings show the landscape and the humorous text has a retro feel. (Rev: SLJ 12/06)

4111 Patricelli, Leslie. *Be Quiet, Mike!* (PS–1). Illus. by author. 2011, Candlewick $14.99 (978-0-7636-4477-2). Unpaged. Young monkey Mike is constantly annoying people with his incessant drumming and banging until he creates a pots and pans drum set that changes minds. (Rev: HB 9–10/11; SLJ 8/1/11)

4112 Pearce, Emily Smith. *Slowpoke* (1–3). Illus. by Scot Ritchie. 2010, Boyds Mills $16.95 (978-1-59078-705-2). 40pp. Fed up with their daughter's slow poke pace of life, toddler Fiona's parents enroll her in speed school in this comically exaggerated story about the breakneck pace of modern life. Lexile 370L (Rev: BL 10/15/10; SLJ 11/1/10)

4113 Peck, Jan. *Giant Peach Yodel!* (K–3). Illus. by Barry Root. 2012, Pelican $16.99 (978-158980980-2). 32pp. Little Buddy Earl's yodeling skills save the family's reputation at the Peach Pickin' Festival in this retelling of a Russian folk tale set in the American South. (Rev: BL 4/1/12; SLJ 7/12)

4114 Peirce, Lincoln. *Big Nate Flips Out* (3–6). Illus. by author. Series: Big Nate (Chapter Books). 2013, HarperCollins $13.99 (978-006199663-4). 224pp. In an un-usual turn of events Nate becomes an obsessive neat freak and has other misadventures. Lexile 420 (Rev: BLO 6/13)

4115 Perry, Andrea. *The Bicklebys' Birdbath* (PS–2). Illus. by Roberta Angaramo. 2010, Atheneum $16.99 (978-1-4169-0624-7). 40pp. In this zany cumulative story, a series of animal-related mishaps concludes with a bewildered mailman in the Bicklebys' birdbath. (Rev: BL 2/1/10; LMC 3–4/10; SLJ 3/1/10)

4116 Perry, John. *The Book That Eats People* (PS–3). Illus. by Mark Fearing. 2009, Tricycle $15.99 (978-1-58246-268-4). Unpaged. A panicked narrator warns readers about a hungry book that is on a rampage, eating both children and grown-ups. (Rev: SLJ 11/1/09)

4117 Phillipps, J. C. *Monkey Ono* (PS–1). Illus. by J. C. Phillipps. 2013, Viking $16.99 (978-0-670-78505-6). 40pp. Disappointed to be left behind on Beach Day, a toy monkey comes up with many unsuccessful strategies to rejoin his boy. (Rev: BL 3/1/13; SLJ 3/13)

4118 Pinkwater, Daniel. *Bad Bear Detectives: An Irving and Muktuk Story* (PS–2). Illus. by Jill Pinkwater. Series: Irving and Muktuk. 2006, Houghton $16.00 (978-0-618-43125-0). 32pp. Who stole the muffins? Two falsely accused polar bears set out to find the real suspects. (Rev: BL 7/06; SLJ 8/06)

4119 Pinkwater, Daniel. *Bad Bears Go Visiting* (K–3). Illus. by Jill Pinkwater. 2007, Houghton $16.00 (978-0-618-43126-7). 32pp. Naughty polar bears Irving and Muktuk break out of the zoo and pay an unexpected and rowdy visit to the Beachball family. (Rev: BL 4/1/07)

4120 Pinkwater, Daniel. *Mrs. Noodlekugel and Four Blind Mice* (K–2). Illus. by Adam Stower. 2013, Candlewick $14.99 (978-076365054-4). 96pp. When Mrs. Noodlekugel discovers that her four mice need glasses, she takes them, neighboring children Maxine and Nick (and Mr. Fuzzface the cat) to the eye doctor, where the mice are given glasses — but the real surprise is when Mr. Fuzzface is reunited with his father. e Lexile AD630 (Rev: BLO 9/15/13; SLJ 11/13)

4121 Pinkwater, Daniel. *Sleepover Larry* (PS–2). Illus. by Jill Pinkwater. 2007, Marshall Cavendish $16.99 (978-0-7614-5314-7). 32pp. Larry the polar bear has a sleepover and his friends enjoy dancing, a movie, pizza, and other delicacies. Earlier books about Larry include *Bongo Larry* (1998), *Ice Cream Larry* (1999), and *Dancing Larry* (2006). (Rev: SLJ 11/07)

4122 Pizzoli, Greg. *The Watermelon Seed* (PS–1). Illus. by author. 2013, Disney/Hyperion $16.99 (978-1-4231-7101-0). 40pp. A funny story about a crocodile panicked because he has swallowed a watermelon seed. ALA Notable Children's Book; Theodor Seuss Geisel Award. (Rev: BLO 5/1/13; LMC 10/13; SLJ 5/13*)

4123 Plourde, Lynn. *Dino Pets Go to School* (PS–1). Illus. by Gideon Kendall. 2011, Dutton $16.99 (978-0-525-42232-7). 32pp. A young boy brings his dinosaurs to Pet Day at school with unpredictable and comical results; "Dino Facts" are appended. (Rev: BL 8/11; SLJ 7/11)

4124 Plourde, Lynn. *Grandpappy Snippy Snappies* (PS–K). Illus. by Christopher Santoro. 2009, HarperCollins $17.99 (978-0-06-028050-5). 32pp. Grandpappy's cure-all snappy suspenders fail to work when Grandmammy is hauled off by crows in this lively story full of wordplay. (Rev: BL 4/15/09; SLJ 5/09)

4125 Plourde, Lynn. *A Mountain of Mittens* (PS–1). Illus. by Mitch Vane. 2007, Charlesbridge $15.95 (978-1-57091-585-7). 32pp. A humorous tale about a mountainous lost-and-found box full of mittens and a townful of frustrated parents. (Rev: BL 6/1–15/07; SLJ 10/07)

4126 Polacco, Patricia. *Ginger and Petunia* (K–3). Illus. by author. 2007, Philomel $16.99 (978-0-399-24539-8). 40pp. Petunia's sitter is a no-show and the pampered pet pig is left to her own devices, with comical results. (Rev: BL 5/1/07; SLJ 6/07)

4127 Polhemus, Coleman. *The Crocodile Blues* (PS–2). Illus. by author. 2007, Candlewick $16.99 (978-0-7636-3543-5). 48pp. A nearly wordless tale in which a man and his pet cockatoo discover, much to their dismay, the true nature of the egg they bring home from the store. (Rev: SLJ 11/07)

4128 Portis, Antoinette. *Princess Super Kitty* (PS–1). Illus. by author. 2011, HarperCollins $14.99 (978-0-06-182725-9). 40pp. Young Maggie has a creative imagination that inflates her status and her needs until she is Water Lily Hula Porpoise Princess Super Kitty of the Sea. (Rev: BL 10/15/11; SLJ 10/1/11)

4129 Powell, Anna. *Don't Say That, Willy Nilly!* (K–2). Illus. by David Roberts. 2005, Good Bks. $16.00 (978-1-56148-488-1). Willy Nilly has an amazing knack for saying the wrong thing at the wrong time. (Rev: SLJ 10/05)

4130 Poydar, Nancy. *Mailbox Magic* (PS–2). Illus. 2000, Holiday House $15.95 (978-0-8234-1525-0). 32pp. Will, who longs to get mail, collects box tops to send away for a cereal bowl. (Rev: BL 6/1–15/00; HBG 10/01; SLJ 9/00)

4131 Primavera, Elise. *Thumb Love* (PS–2). Illus. by author. 2010, Random House $16.99 (978-0-375-84481-2); LB $19.99 (978-037595182-4). 48pp. A devoted thumb-sucker devises a 12-step recovery program for fellow addicts in this humorous story. (Rev: BL 10/15/10; SLJ 10/1/10)

4132 Pulver, Robin. *Axle Annie* (PS–3). Illus. by Tedd Arnold. 1999, Dial $15.99 (978-0-8037-2096-1). Shifty Rhodes and friends conspire to get extra ice and snow on a steep hill so that the school bus, driven by Axle Annie, will not be able to make it and there will be, at long last, a snow day in Burskyville. (Rev: BL 2/15/00; HBG 3/00; SLJ 10/99)

4133 Pulver, Robin. *Punctuation Takes a Vacation* (1–3). Illus. by Lynn Rowe Reed. 2003, Holiday House $17.95 (978-0-8234-1687-5). 32pp. Punctuation marks take offense at a teacher's comment and disappear, leaving children unable to write properly. (Rev: BL 3/1/03; HB 5/03; HBG 10/03; SLJ 4/03)

4134 Raczka, Bob. *Fall Mixed Up* (K–3). Illus. by Chad Cameron. 2011, Carolrhoda $17.95 (978-0-7613-4606-7). 40pp. An entertaining introduction to the joys and images of autumn, with mixed-up facts that will keep children guessing. (Rev: BLO 10/1/11; LMC 1–2/12; SLJ 11/1/11)

4135 Radunsky, Vladimir, and Eugenia Radunsky. *Yucka Drucka Droni* (1–3). Illus. 1998, Scholastic $15.95 (978-0-590-09837-3). 40pp. A European tale that is a tongue twister about three brothers who marry three sisters and have children with strange names. (Rev: BCCB 7–8/98; BL 2/1/98; HBG 10/98; SLJ 3/98*)

4136 Ransom, Jeanie Franz. *Grandma U* (K–2). Illus. by Lucy Corvino. 2002, Peachtree $15.95 (978-1-56145-214-9). Molly McCool goes to Grandma University to prepare for an impending arrival in this entertaining tale. (Rev: HBG 3/03; SLJ 12/02)

4137 Ransom, Jeanie Franz. *What Do Parents Do? (When You're Not Home)* (PS–2). Illus. by Cyd Moore. 2007, Peachtree $16.95 (978-1-56145-409-9). 32pp. Apparently parents get up to all sorts of things in their children's absence — jumping on the bed, dressing up the dog . . . (Rev: BL 4/1/07)

4138 Ransom, Jeanie Franz. *What Really Happened to Humpty?* (1–4). Illus. by Stephen Axelsen. 2009, Charlesbridge $15.95 (978-1-58089-109-7). 32pp. Humpty's brother Joe, a tough detective, investigates who pushed Humpty in this funny mystery set in Mother Gooseland. (Rev: BL 5/1/09; SLJ 5/09)

4139 Rash, Andy. *Are You a Horse?* (PS–2). Illus. by author. 2009, Scholastic $16.99 (978-0-439-72417-3). 32pp. Aspiring cowboy Roy has got himself a hat and he's got himself a saddle but he hasn't got a clue as to what he's supposed to put it on. (Rev: BL 1/1–15/09; SLJ 2/09)

4140 Rathmann, Peggy. *The Day the Babies Crawled Away* (K–2). Illus. by author. 2003, Penguin $17.99 (978-0-399-23196-4). A picture book with effective oversize illustrations and a simple story about a toddler who comes to the rescue after babies crawl away from their preoccupied parents. (Rev: BCCB 12/03; BL 9/15/03; HB 9/03; HBG 4/04; LMC 3/04; SLJ 11/03)

4141 Rausch, Molly. *My Cold Went on Vacation* (PS–2). Illus. by Nora Krug. 2011, Putnam $16.99 (978-0-399-25474-1). 32pp. When a young boy's cold goes away, he imagines the adventures it's having without him. (Rev: BL 1/1–15/11; SLJ 3/1/11)

4142 Reed, Lynn Rowe. *Please Don't Upset P.U. Zorilla* (PS–1). Illus. by author. 2006, Knopf $15.95 (978-0-375-83654-1). P.U. Zorilla, a skunk, finds it hard to hold down a job until his stinky spray succeeds in foiling a robbery and Mayor Tootlebee offers him a job as police chief. (Rev: SLJ 10/06)

4143 Rennert, Laura Joy. *Buying, Training and Caring for Your Dinosaur* (K–2). Illus. by Marc Brown. 2009, Knopf $16.99 (978-0-375-83679-4). Unpaged. Various species of dinosaur are profiled in this tongue-in-cheek guide to keeping dinosaurs as pets. (Rev: BL 10/1/09; SLJ 10/1/09)

4144 Rex, Adam. *Pssst!* (K–3). Illus. by author. 2007, Harcourt $16.00 (978-0-15-205817-3). 40pp. Animals at the zoo burden a young girl with a lot of seemingly wacky requests in this funny book with unusual artwork. (Rev: BCCB 10/07; HB 1/08; SLJ 10/07)

4145 Reynolds, Aaron. *Buffalo Wings* (K–3). Illus. by Paulette Bogan. 2007, Bloomsbury $16.95 (978-1-59990-062-9). 32pp. In preparation for the big game on TV, a misguided rooster sets off in search of something called Buffalo Wings. (Rev: LMC 11/07; SLJ 12/07)

4146 Reynolds, Aaron. *Pirates vs. Cowboys* (PS–2). Illus. by David Barneda. 2013, Knopf $16.99 (978-0-375-85874-1). 40pp. Pirates trying to hide their treasure make a mistake when they choose Cheyenne, a town full of outlaw cowboys in this romp peopled by anthropomorphic animals. ℮ (Rev: BL 3/1/13; LMC 10/13; SLJ 2/13)

4147 Robertson, M. P. *Hieronymus Betts and His Unusual Pets* (PS–1). Illus. by author. 2005, Frances Lincoln $15.95 (978-1-84507-289-6). Hieronymus Betts introduces his menagerie of unusually awful pets, but he asserts that there's one thing that's even worse — a little brother! (Rev: SLJ 2/06)

4148 Robinson, Fay. *Faucet Fish* (PS–2). Illus. by Wayne Anderson. 2005, Dutton $15.99 (978-0-525-47166-0). 32pp. Elizabeth can't seem to get her parents' attention, even when all types of fish begin to come out of the bathroom faucet. (Rev: BL 8/05; SLJ 8/05)

4149 Robinson, Fiona. *What Animals Really Like: A New Song Composed and Conducted by Mr. Herbert Timberteeth* (1–2). Illus. by author. 2011, Abrams $15.95 (978-0-8109-8976-4). 24pp. Mr. Herbert Timberteeth has trouble getting the National Animal Choir to perform his song as it was written in this supremely silly book. (Rev: BL 9/15/11; LMC 1–2/12; SLJ 9/1/11)

4150 Rocco, John. *Super Hair-o and the Barber of Doom* (K–2). Illus. by author. 2013, Disney/Hyperion $16.99 (978-1-4231-2189-3). 32pp. Young Rocco has a wonderful Afro that he believes gives him superpowers — until he is captured and taken (oh, no!) to the barbershop. (Rev: BL 5/1/13; LMC 10/13; SLJ 4/13)

4151 Root, Phyllis. *Paula Bunyan* (K–2). Illus. by Kevin O'Malley. 2009, Farrar $16.95 (978-0-374-35759-7). 32pp. Paul Bunyan's younger sister Paula, who is "as tall as a pine tree and as strong as a dozen moose," finds her size a great inconvenience and spends her time in the North Woods rescuing forests. (Rev: BCCB 6/09; BL 3/1/09; SLJ 3/09)

4152 Rosen, Michael. *Tiny Little Fly* (PS–K). Illus. by Kevin Waldron. 2010, Candlewick $15.99 (978-0-7636-4681-3). 32pp. An elephant, a tiger, and a hippo struggle mightily to catch a pesky little fly. (Rev: BL 12/15/10; HB 1–2/11; SLJ 2/1/11*)

4153 Rosenthal, Amy Krouse. *Exclamation Mark* (K–3). Illus. by Tom Lichtenheld. 2013, Scholastic $17.99 (978-054543679-3). 56pp. Poor young exclamation point just can't blend in until he meets a question mark and builds self-confidence. ALA Notable Children's Book. Lexile 90 (Rev: BL 2/15/13*; SLJ 2/13*)

4154 Rosenthal, Marc. *Phooey!* (PS–K). Illus. by author. 2007, HarperCollins $16.99 (978-0-06-075248-4). A boy unwittingly sets off a chain of wildly funny events after he declares in a fit of boredom that "nothing ever happens around here." (Rev: BCCB 9/07; BL 7/07; HB 9/07; SLJ 9/07)

4155 Rosoff, Meg. *Jumpy Jack and Googily* (PS–1). Illus. by Sophie Blackall. 2008, Holt $16.95 (978-0-8050-8066-7). 32pp. A snail called Jumpy Jack, who is afraid of monsters, relies on his friend Googily (who is actually a monster) to check behind trees and under tables. (Rev: BL 3/15/08; LMC 11/08*; SLJ 5/08)

4156 Ross, Tony. *I Don't Want to Go to the Hospital!* (PS–K). Illus. by author. Series: Little Princess. 2013, Andersen $16.95 (978-1-4677-1155-5). 32pp. The Little Princess does not — not! — want to go to the hospital, but after being forced through the experience she finds that she is treated like real royalty by the medical staff. ℮ (Rev: BLO 6/13; LMC 11–12/13; SLJ 4/13)

4157 Ross, Tony. *I Want a Party!* (PS–2). Illus. by author. 2011, Andersen $16.95 (978-0-7613-8089-4). 32pp. Little Princess makes great preparations for her party but forgets, alas, to send the invitations; fortunately, one friend does turn up by accident and she proves enough. (Rev: BLO 12/15/11; SLJ 10/1/11)

4158 Ross, Tony. *I Want My Tooth* (K–2). Illus. by author. 2005, Kane paper $4.95 (978-1-929132-85-0). When the Little Princess loses one of her teeth, she orders everyone in the castle to search for it. (Rev: SLJ 10/05)

4159 Ross, Tony. *I Want to Do It Myself! A Little Princess Story* (PS–2). Illus. by author. 2011, Andersen $16.95 (978-0-7613-7412-1). 32pp. Little Princess sets off from her castle on a solo camping trip completely ill-prepared — her friends save the day, and she returns no wiser, obstinate as ever. ℮ (Rev: BL 3/15/11; SLJ 2/1/11)

4160 Rubin, Adam. *Secret Pizza Party* (PS–1). Illus. by Daniel Salmieri. 2013, Dial $16.99 (978-080373947-5). 40pp. Using vibrant illustrations and humor to tell the story of Raccoon and his frenzied love of pizza, this picture book is full of zany scenarios and delightful absurdity. ◯ ℮ Lexile AD430 (Rev: BL 9/1/13; SLJ 8/13*)

4161 Rubin, Adam. *Those Darn Squirrels and the Cat Next Door* (K–4). Illus. by Daniel Salmieri. 2011, Clarion $16.99 (978-0-547-42922-9). Unpaged. Grumpy old Fookwire rejoices when his pesky squirrels hatch a plan to deal with the new cat in the neighborhood; a sequel to *Those Darn Squirrels* (2008). Lexile AD810L (Rev: SLJ 5/1/11)

4162 Rumford, James. *Don't Touch My Hat* (K–2). Illus. 2007, Knopf $16.99 (978-0-375-83782-1). Sheriff John relies on his lucky 10-gallon hat until the night he rushes off to catch some bad men wearing his wife's fancy plumed chapeau. (Rev: BL 12/15/06; SLJ 1/07)

4163 Ruurs, Margriet. *Wake Up, Henry Rooster!* (PS–2). Illus. by Sean Cassidy. 2006, Fitzhenry & Whiteside

$16.95 (978-1-55041-952-8). 32pp. Henry the rooster is no early bird and the farm life gets out of whack as he sleeps off his late nights. (Rev: BL 5/15/06; SLJ 7/06)

4164 Rylant, Cynthia. *Alligator Boy* (PS–2). Illus. by Diane Goode. 2007, Harcourt $16.00 (978-0-15-206092-3). 32pp. A boy decides to wear an alligator costume and delights in being different in this well-illustrated, rhyming tale. (Rev: BL 5/15/07; LMC 8/07; SLJ 6/07)

4165 Sadler, Marilyn. *Alice from Dallas* (K–2). Illus. by Ard Hoyt. 2014, Abrams $16.95 (978-141970790-2). 40pp. Dedicated cowgirl Alice, who lives in Dallas (Pennsylvania), is taken aback when a new cowgirl, Lexis, arrives from Texas, leading to showdowns at school. **e** (Rev: BL 3/1/14; SLJ 3/14)

4166 Salerno, Steven. *Harry Hungry!* (PS). Illus. by author. 2009, Houghton $16.00 (978-0-15-206257-6). 40pp. Harry the toddler eats his way through all the alphabet cookies, the mailbox, a mountain, and even a piece of the sky in this brightly illustrated tribute to the intensity of a child's hunger. (Rev: BCCB 3/09; BLO 1/14/09; HB 3/09; SLJ 2/09)

4167 Samuels, Barbara. *Dolores Meets Her Match* (1–3). Illus. by author. Series: Dolores and Duncan. 2007, Farrar $16.00 (978-0-374-31758-4). Dolores is confident of her cat Duncan's unique abilities until new girl Hillary arrives with the remarkable Harold. (Rev: BL 2/15/08; HB 11/07; SLJ 11/07)

4168 Sauer, Tammi. *Princess in Training* (PS–1). Illus. by Joe Berger. 2012, Harcourt $16.99 (978-0-15-206599-7). 40pp. Viola Louise Hassenfeffer is a princess out of control (she enjoys diving into the moat, skateboarding, and karate) so she goes to Camp Princess to learn to be "the darling of her kingdom." **e** Lexile 540L (Rev: BLO 10/15/12; LMC 10/12; SLJ 11/12)

4169 Savage, Stephen. *Where's Walrus?* (PS–K). Illus. by author. 2011, Scholastic $16.99 (978-0-439-70049-8). 32pp. An escaped zoo walrus cleverly evades capture by donning a series of funny disguises. (Rev: BL 5/1/11; SLJ 2/1/11)

4170 Scamell, Ragnhild. *Ouch!* (PS–1). Illus. by Michael Terry. 2006, Good Bks. $16.00 (978-1-56148-511-6). Poor Hedgehog has an apple stuck in her spines and all her friends' efforts to help her backfire until she comes across Goat. (Rev: SLJ 7/06)

4171 Schertle, Alice. *The Adventures of Old Bo Bear* (PS–2). Illus. by David Parkins. 2006, Chronicle $16.95 (978-0-8118-3476-6). 28pp. After his favorite teddy bear loses an ear in a much-needed washing, his owner takes him off for some energetic play that involves quite a lot of dirt plus some potential explanations for the missing appendage. (Rev: BL 2/1/06; SLJ 2/06)

4172 Schmid, Paul. *Petunia Goes Wild* (PS–2). Illus. by author. 2012, HarperCollins $12.99 (978-006196334-6). 40pp. Tired of all the rules imposed on human children, Petunia decides to start living the life of a wild animal. (Rev: BLO 2/1/12; SLJ 1/12)

4173 Schneider, Josh. *The Meanest Birthday Girl* (K–3). Illus. by author. 2013, Clarion $14.99 (978-0-547-

83814-4). 48pp. A birthday gift of a large elephant proves more troublesome than the self-involved Dana anticipated. Lexile AD580 (Rev: BL 5/1/13; HB 7–8/13; SLJ 3/13)

4174 Schotter, Roni. *The Boy Who Loved Words* (2–4). Illus. by Giselle Potter. 2006, Random $16.95 (978-0-375-83601-5). 40pp. A boy called Selig loves words, and after collecting many on scraps of paper — and suffering the scorn of his classmates — he decides to distribute them around. (Rev: BL 2/1/06; SLJ 4/06*)

4175 Schwartz, Corey Rosen. *The Three Ninja Pigs* (PS–3). Illus. by Dan Santat. 2012, Putnam $16.99 (978-0-399-25514-4). 40pp. The three little pigs — two boys and a girl — take up martial arts in an effort to combat the pesky wolf blowing houses down, but only the sister pig has taken the training seriously; this funny fractured tale is told in bouncy rhyming text and colorful images. Lexile AD630L (Rev: BL 12/1/12; LMC 1–2/13; SLJ 9/12)

4176 Schwarz, Viviane. *Shark and Lobster's Amazing Undersea Adventure* (PS–2). 2006, Candlewick $15.99 (978-0-7636-2910-6). 40pp. Shark and Lobster convince their undersea friends to build a fortress to protect themselves against tigers, then realize the folly of their phobia. (Rev: BL 7/06)

4177 Scieszka, Jon. *Baloney (Henry P.)* (1–4). Illus. by Lane Smith. 2001, Viking $16.99 (978-0-670-89248-8). 32pp. A small green alien comes up with a humdinger of an excuse for being late to school in this story full of humor. (Rev: BCCB 5/01; BL 5/15/01*; HB 5/01; HBG 10/01; SLJ 5/01)

4178 Scieszka, Jon. *The Stinky Cheese Man: And Other Fairly Stupid Tales* (2–6). Illus. by Lane Smith. 1992, Viking $17.99 (978-0-670-84487-6). 56pp. Lots of fun with fractured fairy tales. (Rev: BCCB 10/92*; BL 9/1/92; HB 11/92*; HBG 10/02; SLJ 9/92*)

4179 Scillian, Devin. *Brewster the Rooster* (K–3). Illus. by Lee White. 2007, Sleeping Bear $16.95 (978-1-58536-311-7). 32pp. A nearsighted rooster crows at inappropriate times of day until little Julie suggests that he needs glasses. (Rev: BL 7/07; SLJ 8/07)

4180 Sendak, Maurice. *Chicken Soup with Rice: A Book of Months* (K–3). Illus. by author. 1962, HarperCollins LB $16.89 (978-0-06-025535-0). 48pp. A rhyming story that takes one through each of the months with the always suitable chicken soup with rice.

4181 Seuss, Dr., and Jack Prelutsky. *Hooray for Diffendoofer Day!* (K–4). Illus. by Lane Smith. 1998, Knopf LB $18.99 (978-0-679-99008-6). 56pp. With this story about an unusual teacher named Miss Bonkers, Prelutsky and Smith complete the sketches Dr. Seuss left when he died in 1991. (Rev: BCCB 6/98; BL 5/1/98; HBG 10/98; SLJ 6/98)

4182 Shannon, David. *Bugs in My Hair!* (K–2). Illus. by author. 2013, Scholastic $17.99 (978-0-545-14313-4). 32pp. Help! How do I get rid of lice in my hair? A little boy goes through the whole process with horror and humor. Lexile 390 (Rev: BL 7/13; SLJ 7/13)

4183 Shannon, David. *David Gets in Trouble* (PS–1). Illus. 2002, Scholastic $16.99 (978-0-439-05022-7). 32pp. David of *No, David* (1998) and *David Goes to School* (1999) denies any responsibility for the trouble he causes — until bedtime, when he finally apologizes to Mom. (Rev: BL 9/15/02; HB 1/03; HBG 3/03; SLJ 9/02*)

4184 Shea, Bob. *I'm a Shark* (PS–1). Illus. by author. 2011, HarperCollins $16.99 (978-0-06-199846-1). 40pp. A shark boasts that he's not afraid of anything until someone brings up the subject of spiders. (Rev: BL 4/1/11; SLJ 4/11)

4185 Shea, Bob. *Unicorn Thinks He's Pretty Great* (PS–2). Illus. by author. 2013, Disney/Hyperion $15.99 (978-1-4231-5952-0). 40pp. Rivalry between Goat and Unicorn eventually turns to friendship in this funny, nicely illustrated picture book. Lexile AD400 (Rev: BL 5/1/13*; SLJ 4/13)

4186 Shulman, Mark. *Mom and Dad Are Palindromes* (1–4). Illus. by Adam McCauley. 2006, Chronicle $15.95 (978-0-8118-4328-7). Once Bob finds out what palindromes are, he sees them everywhere — more than 100 in all. (Rev: SLJ 6/06)

4187 Sierra, Judy. *Mind Your Manners, B. B. Wolf* (PS–2). Illus. by J. Otto Seibold. 2007, Knopf $16.99 (978-0-375-83532-2). 40pp. A seriously fractured fairy tale about the big bad wolf learning manners so that he can attend the library tea. (Rev: BL 9/1/07; HB 7/07; LMC 11/07; SLJ 8/07)

4188 Sierra, Judy. *The Secret Science Project That Almost Ate the School* (1–3). Illus. by Stephen Gammell. 2006, Simon & Schuster $16.95 (978-1-4169-1175-3). A young girl orders a science fair project by mail, but neglects to read the directions on its package carefully. (Rev: SLJ 11/06)

4189 Sierra, Judy. *Tell the Truth, B. B. Wolf* (PS–3). Illus. by J. Otto Seibold. 2010, Knopf $16.99 (978-0-375-85620-4); LB $19.99 (978-0-375-95620-1). 40pp. The retired Big Bad Wolf receives a phone call from a librarian asking for the "true" story of how he met the three little pigs in this sequel to *Mind Your Manners, B.B. Wolf* (2007). (Rev: BL 9/15/10; HB 9–10/10; LMC 11–12/10; SLJ 7/1/10)

4190 Sierra, Judy. *Thelonius Monster's Sky-High Fly Pie: A Revolting Rhyme* (PS–2). Illus. by Edward Koren. 2006, Knopf $16.95 (978-0-375-83218-5). 40pp. Thelonius invites friends to enjoy a pie of flies, but the fly takes off before he can enjoy it in this funny rhyming story illustrated in cartoonist Koren's signature style. (Rev: BL 5/1/06; SLJ 5/06*)

4191 Simms, Laura. *Rotten Teeth* (K–3). Illus. by David Catrow. 1998, Houghton $16.00 (978-0-395-82850-2). 32pp. Melissa has many things she could bring to school for show-and-tell, such as the alligator that lives in her family's doghouse. But her final choice is so disgusting that she will be remembered forever in the school's history. (Rev: BCCB 12/98; BL 9/1/98; HBG 3/99; SLJ 9/98)

4192 Skeers, Linda. *Tutus Aren't My Style* (PS–3). Illus. by Anne Wilsdorf. 2010, Dial $16.99 (978-0-8037-3212-4). 32pp. Outdoorsy, adventuresome Emma tries to learn how to be a ballerina when her uncle sends her a frilly pink tutu by mistake. (Rev: BLO 3/1/10; LMC 3–4/10; SLJ 2/1/10)

4193 Slater, Dashka. *Baby Shoes* (PS). Illus. by Hiroe Nakata. 2006, Bloomsbury $15.95 (978-1-58234-684-7). 32pp. Baby's new white shoes are soon covered in multicolor stains as he and his mother take a walk. (Rev: BL 5/1/06; HBG 10/06; SLJ 5/06)

4194 Slobodkina, Esphyr. *Caps for Sale* (K–3). Illus. by author. 1947, HarperCollins LB $17.89 (978-0-06-025778-1); paper $6.99 (978-0-06-443143-9). 48pp. When some monkeys engage in a bit of monkey business, the cap peddler must use his imagination to retrieve his wares.

4195 Smith, Cynthia Leitich. *Holler Loudly* (PS–2). Illus. by Barry Gott. 2010, Dutton $16.99 (978-0-525-42256-3). Unpaged. Holler's loud voice generally gets him in trouble until a tornado threatens and his hollering saves the day. (Rev: HB 1–2/11; LMC 1–2/11*; SLJ 1/1/11)

4196 Smith, Lane. *It's a Book* (1–3). Illus. by author. 2010, Roaring Brook $12.99 (978-1-59643-606-0). 32pp. In this droll, tech-savvy satire, a monkey and a donkey debate and compare the merits of books versus computers. (Rev: BL 7/10; HB 9–10/10; LMC 11–12/10; SLJ 8/1/10*)

4197 Smith, Lane. *Madam President* (K–2). Illus. by author. 2008, Hyperion $16.99 (978-1-4231-0846-7). 40pp. A little girl fantasizes about her duties as president — giving orders (for waffles), negotiating treaties (between a cat and dog), appointing a cabinet made up of toys, and generally behaving in exemplary fashion. (Rev: BCCB 7–8/08; BL 5/1/08; LMC 3/08; SLJ 7/08) 🎧

4198 Smith, Linda. *The Inside Tree* (PS–2). Illus. by David Parkins. 2010, HarperCollins $16.99 (978-0-06-028241-7); LB $17.89 (978-0-06-029818-0). 32pp. Mr. Potter's life becomes more complicated when he decides to move his dog — and the tree he sleeps under — inside his house. (Rev: BLO 6/10; HB 3–4/10; SLJ 1/1/10)

4199 Smith, Stu. *The Bubble Gum Kid* (K–2). Illus. by Julia Woolf. 2006, Running Pr. $15.95 (978-0-7624-2046-9). Billy Bob Glum asks his sister to teach him how to blow a bubble so he can impress an annoying bully named Double Chin Dan; a fast-paced story told in rhyming text. (Rev: SLJ 12/06)

4200 Snicket, Lemony. *The Lump of Coal* (1–3). Illus. by Brett Helquist. 2008, HarperCollins $12.99 (978-0-06-157428-3). 40pp. A tuxedo-wearing lump of coal with an artistic bent sets off in search of a purpose in life in this small volume. (Rev: BL 9/15/08; HB 11/08)

4201 Sonnenblick, Jordan. *Dodger for Sale* (4–6). 2010, Feiwel & Friends $16.99 (978-031237795-3). 176pp. Willie, his friend Lizzie, and their blue chimpanzee pal Dodger lobby to save a patch of nearby woods while contending with leprechauns that capture Willie's little sister. (Rev: BLO 3/1/10; SLJ 5/10)

4202 Spinelli, Eileen. *Silly Tilly* (PS–2). Illus. by David Slonim. 2009, Marshall Cavendish $16.99 (978-0-7614-5525-7). 32pp. Tilly is a very silly goose indeed, but when the other animals on the farm ask her to behave, they find they miss her antics. (Rev: BL 3/15/09; SLJ 3/09)

4203 Steffensmeier, Alexander. *Millie and the Big Rescue* (PS–K). Illus. by author. 2013, Walker $16.99 (978-0-8027-3402-0). 40pp. A barnyard game of hide-and-seek ends with cow Millie stuck in a tree and everyone else in similar predicaments, including the farmer. (Rev: BLO 7/13; SLJ 7/13)

4204 Steig, Jeanne. *Fleas!* (PS–2). Illus. by Britt Spencer. 2008, Philomel $16.99 (978-0-399-24756-9). 32pp. A cumulative/circular tale in which a dog gives a farmer fleas and the farmer swaps the fleas for a young lady's troublesomely talkative uncle and the trades continue until we're back with the fleas. (Rev: BL 5/15/08; SLJ 5/08)

4205 Steig, William. *The Amazing Bone* (K–2). Illus. by author. 1983, Farrar $17.00 (978-0-374-30248-1). A bone that talks saves a piglet from being eaten by a fox in this nonsensical and witty story.

4206 Steig, William. *Pete's a Pizza* (PS–K). Illus. 1998, HarperCollins $16.99 (978-0-06-205157-8). 32pp. Pete is in a terrible mood until his parents pretend he is a pizza and begin kneading him, tossing him in the air, and sprinkling him with flour. (Rev: BL 10/1/98*; HB 9/98; HBG 3/99; SLJ 11/98)

4207 Stein, David Ezra. *Ol' Mama Squirrel* (PS–2). Illus. by author. 2013, Penguin $16.99 (978-0-399-25672-1). 32pp. A mother squirrel must call in reinforcements when a grizzly bear threatens her offspring; a funny, energetic story. Lexile AD570 (Rev: BL 5/1/13; SLJ 4/13)

4208 Stevens, Janet, and Susan Stevens Crummel. *The Little Red Pen* (PS–2). Illus. by Janet Stevens. 2011, Houghton Harcourt $16.99 (978-0-15-206432-7). 56pp. In this schoolroom take on "The Little Red Hen," a red pen falls into the trash from exhaustion after marking papers all night and is eventually rescued by the highlighter, the stapler, and other previously unhelpful occupants. (Rev: BL 3/1/11; HB 3–4/11; LMC 10/11; SLJ 3/1/11)

4209 Stoeke, Janet Morgan. *The Loopy Coop Hens* (PS–1). Illus. by author. 2011, Dutton $16.99 (978-0-525-42190-0). Unpaged. A bevy of hens in awe of the rooster's ability to fly eventually discovers the truth. (Rev: HB 5–6/11; SLJ 3/1/11)

4210 Stower, Adam. *Silly Doggy* (PS–2). Illus. by author. 2012, Scholastic $16.99 (978-054537323-4). 40pp. When young Lily finds a bear in her garden, she mistakes it for a (pretty useless) dog and composes a lost dog poster. (Rev: BL 4/15/12; SLJ 5/1/12)

4211 Sullivan, Mary. *Ball* (PS–3). Illus. by author. 2013, Houghton Mifflin $12.99 (978-0-547-75936-4). 40pp. A funny book about a dog devoted to his ball. ALA Notable Children's Book. (Rev: BL 4/1/13; SLJ 3/13)

4212 Sydor, Colleen. *Camilla Chameleon* (K–2). Illus. by Pascale Constantin. 2005, Kids Can $16.95 (978-1-55337-482-4). A zany story about Camilla, whose ability to blend in with her surroundings stems from her mother's craving for cream-of-chameleon soup when she was pregnant; then her mother gets pregnant again and develops a taste for cream of pterodactyl soup . . . (Rev: SLJ 6/06)

4213 Tashjian, Janet. *Einstein the Class Hamster* (3–5). Illus. by Jake Tashjian. 2013, Henry Holt $12.99 (978-080509610-1). 160pp. In this series starter, Einstein the class hamster and trivia genius wants to help when the class gets a chance to appear on a quiz show — but he can only communicate with Ned; this entertaining story conveys a number of interesting facts. **e** Lexile 750 (Rev: BL 9/1/13)

4214 Taylor, Alastair. *Mr. Blewitt's Nose* (K–2). Illus. by author. 2005, Houghton $16.00 (978-0-618-42353-8). Primrose and her amazingly smelly dog search for the owner of a lost nose in this amusing book. (Rev: SLJ 7/05)

4215 Taylor, Sean. *Robomop* (K–2). Illus. by Edel Rodriguez. 2013, Dial $16.99 (978-080373411-1). 32pp. Poor Robomop is assigned to cleaning a bathroom in the basement; he yearns for freedom and love but only finds this when he is finally consigned to the trash. Lexile 570 (Rev: BL 2/15/13; LMC 8–9/13; SLJ 3/13)

4216 Taylor, Sean. *When a Monster Is Born* (PS–K). Illus. by Nick Sharratt. 2007, Roaring Brook $16.95 (978-1-59643-254-3). 32pp. A humorous look at the various opportunities awaiting a young monster and the life choices that must be made. (Rev: BCCB 10/07; BL 6/1–15/07; HB 7/07; SLJ 6/07)

4217 Teague, Mark. *Dear Mrs. LaRue: Letters from Obedience School* (K–3). Illus. 2002, Scholastic $16.99 (978-0-439-20663-1). Poor Ike LaRue sends pitiful letters home to his owner, complaining about the conditions at doggy school, but the pictures belie his words. (Rev: BL 11/1/02; HBG 3/03; SLJ 9/02)

4218 Teague, Mark. *LaRue Across America: Postcards from the Vacation* (K–4). Illus. by author. 2011, Scholastic $16.99 (978-0-439-91502-1). Unpaged. Ike the dog is forced to shelve his summer cruise plans in exchange for a road trip with his neighbor's detestable felines; he writes letters and postcards from the road. Lexile AD900L (Rev: SLJ 2/1/11)

4219 Teague, Mark. *LaRue for Mayor: Letters from the Campaign* (K–3). Illus. by author. 2008, Scholastic $16.99 (978-0-439-78315-6). 32pp. As in earlier books featuring LaRue the dog, this title uses correspondence and contrasting illustrations to present different perspectives on LaRue's campaign for mayor. (Rev: BL 12/15/07; SLJ 3/08)

4220 Teague, Mark. *The Three Little Pigs and the Somewhat Bad Wolf* (PS–1). Illus. by author. 2013, Scholastic $16.99 (978-0-439-91501-4). 48pp. The hungry wolf finally finds something to eat when he arrives at the third pig's house and is revived by the residents when he hyperventilates. Lexile 520 (Rev: BL 5/1/13; LMC 11–12/13; SLJ 5/13)

4221 Thomas, Jan. *Here Comes the Big, Mean Dust Bunny!* (PS–2). Illus. by author. 2009, Simon & Schuster $12.99 (978-1-4169-9150-2). Unpaged. A big mean dust bunny threatens and teases the others until an incident with a cat inspires a change of heart. (Rev: SLJ 11/1/09)

4222 Thomas, Jan. *Rhyming Dust Bunnies* (PS–2). Illus. by author. 2009, Simon & Schuster $12.99 (978-1-4169-7976-0). 40pp. Happy, oblivious dust bunnies Ed, Ned, and Ted rhyme constantly, correct nervous Bob for not rhyming, and ignore his warnings in this funny book. (Rev: BCCB 1/09; SLJ 2/09)

4223 Thompson, Kay. *Eloise Takes a Bawth* (PS–3). Illus. by Hilary Knight. 2002, Simon & Schuster $17.95 (978-0-689-84288-7). 80pp. The effervescent Eloise ignores Nanny's warnings about her "bawth" and the resulting flood succeeds in making more realistic the Venetian Masked Ball taking place below. (Rev: BL 12/1/02; HB 1/03; HBG 3/03; SLJ 12/02)

4224 Timberlake, Amy. *The Dirty Cowboy* (K–4). Illus. by Adam Rex. 2003, Farrar $16.00 (978-0-374-31791-1). A filthy cowboy is so transformed by his annual bath that his dog, assigned to guard his clothes while he bathed, doesn't recognize him and refuses to surrender the cowpoke's duds. (Rev: SLJ 9/03)

4225 Tobin, Jim. *Sue MacDonald Had a Book* (PS–1). Illus. by Dave Coverly. 2009, Holt $16.95 (978-0-8050-8766-6). 40pp. In this amusing take on the familiar "Old MacDonald Had a Farm," Sue MacDonald must find the vowels *AEIOU* that have escaped from her book. (Rev: BL 7/09; SLJ 6/09)

4226 Tobin, Jim. *The Very Inappropriate Word* (K–2). Illus. by Dave Coverly. 2013, Henry Holt $16.99 (978-0-8050-9474-9). 40pp. Michael loves collecting new words — even bad ones! **e** Lexile AD490 (Rev: BL 10/1/13; LMC 1–2/14; SLJ 7/13)

4227 Trenc, Milan. *Another Night at the Museum* (1–3). Illus. by author. 2013, Henry Holt $16.99 (978-0-8050-8948-6). 32pp. A wacky dream whisks night watchman Larry off on a tour of New York City and marine animals in this followup to *Night at the Museum* (2006). (Rev: BL 3/1/13; LMC 8–9/13; SLJ 2/13)

4228 Urbanovic, Jackie. *Duck and Cover* (PS–2). Illus. by author. 2009, HarperCollins $17.99 (978-0-06-121444-8). 40pp. Irene is surprised when an alligator asks for shelter at her house full of homeless animals. (Rev: BL 11/15/08; SLJ 2/09)

4229 Van Allsburg, Chris. *Probuditi!* (PS–2). 2006, Houghton $18.95 (978-0-618-75502-8). 32pp. Inspired by the performance of a professional magician, young Calvin hypnotizes his sister and then panics when he can't remember the magic word that will undo the spell; eye-catching sepia illustrations full of humor add to the nostalgic atmosphere. (Rev: BL 11/1/06; SLJ 12/06*)

4230 Van Laan, Nancy. *Nit-Pickin'* (PS–K). Illus. by George Booth. 2008, Atheneum $15.99 (978-0-689-83898-9). 32pp. A little girl copes with lice in this bois-

terous romp in verse and cartoon illustrations. (Rev: BL 7/08; SLJ 7/08)

4231 Van Lieshout, Elle, and Erik van Os. *Lovey and Dovey* (K–3). Illus. by Mies van Hout. 2009, Boyds Mills $16.95 (978-1-59078-660-4). Lovey and Dovey, a couple thrown in jail for stealing a pair of socks, find ways to embellish their cell until they are genuinely upset to be released. (Rev: LMC 8/09; SLJ 4/09)

4232 van Mol, Sine. *Meena* (K–2). Illus. by Carianne Wijffels. 2011, Eerdmans $17 (978-0-8028-5394-3). 26pp. Three children convinced that their elderly neighbor is a witch are eventually dissuaded by her granddaughter in this picture book with humorous horror. Lexile AD340L (Rev: BL 10/15/11; SLJ 8/1/11)

4233 Varela, Barry. *Gizmo* (K–2). Illus. by Ed Briant. 2007, Roaring Brook $16.95 (978-1-59643-115-7). 32pp. A zany tale of a professor who invents a perpetual motion machine, the "Gizmo," which becomes a point of controversy in his city. (Rev: BL 5/1/07; LMC 10/07; SLJ 5/07)

4234 Vernick, Audrey. *So You Want to Be a Rock Star* (K–3). Illus. by Kirstie Edmunds. 2012, Walker $16.99 (978-080272092-4); LB $17.89 (978-080272325-3). 40pp. Learn valuable skills in this humorous, reader-friendly guide to strumming an air guitar, sneering, suitable hairstyles, and autograph signing. (Rev: BL 3/1/12)

4235 Waechter, Phillip. *Rosie and the Nightmares* (K–2). Illus. 2005, Handprint $15.95 (978-1-59354-115-6). 32pp. Tormented by monster-filled nightmares, Rosie the bunny seeks help from a dream specialist and visits a Tunnel of Fear. (Rev: BL 12/1/05; SLJ 11/05)

4236 Waldron, Kevin. *Mr. Peek and the Misunderstanding at the Zoo* (PS–K). Illus. by author. 2010, Candlewick $15.99 (978-0-7636-4549-6). 48pp. A group of emotionally fragile zoo animals cope with their shaky self-image when they overhear the zookeeper berating himself for gaining weight. (Rev: BL 4/1/10; LMC 10/10; SLJ 5/1/10)

4237 Walton, Rick. *Mr. President Goes to School* (K–2). Illus. by Brad Sneed. 2010, Peachtree $15.95 (978-1-56145-538-6). 32pp. After a particularly hard day, the President puts on a disguise and spends time finger painting and doing the hokey pokey with elementary school students, learning a lesson about kindness and cooperation in the process. (Rev: BL 9/1/10; SLJ 10/1/10)

4238 Warburton, Tom. *1000 Times No* (PS–1). Illus. by author. 2009, HarperCollins $17.99 (978-0-06-154263-3). 32pp. Noah does not, absolutely not, want to do what his mother says and finds many ways of saying so. (Rev: BL 3/15/09; SLJ 4/09)

4239 Ward, B. J. *Farty Marty* (PS–1). Illus. by Steven Kellogg. 2013, Simon & Schuster $16.99 (978-1-4424-3901-6). 32pp. A funny tale about a cat with an unusual talent. **e** Lexile AD630 (Rev: BL 11/15/13; LMC 5–6/14; SLJ 10/13)

4240 Waterton, Betty. *A Bumblebee Sweater* (K–2). Illus. by Kim LaFave. 2007, Fitzhenry & Whiteside $16.95 (978-1-55455-028-9). 32pp. The sweater that Nellie's grandmother knits for Nellie to wear to her spring concert shrinks with many washings to the point that only the dog can wear it. (Rev: BL 10/15/07; SLJ 11/07)

4241 Watt, Mélanie. *Chester's Masterpiece* (K–2). Illus. by author. 2010, Kids Can $18.95 (978-1-55453-566-8). 32pp. Chester the uppity cat character hides all author Watts' art supplies in this lively story. (Rev: BL 3/1/10; SLJ 4/1/10)

4242 Watt, Mélanie. *Have I Got a Book for You!* (PS–2). Illus. by author. 2009, Kids Can $16.95 (978-1-55453-289-6). 32pp. A wily fox makes a variety of amusing sales pitches to the reader in this entertaining book. (Rev: BL 9/15/09; LMC 11–12/09; SLJ 12/1/09)

4243 Weeks, Sarah. *Mrs. McNosh Hangs Up Her Wash* (PS–K). Illus. by Nadine Bernard Westcott. 1998, HarperCollins $14.99 (978-0-694-01076-9). 24pp. On wash day, Mrs. McNosh gets carried away and begins hanging out such items as the newspaper, the dog, and the phone to dry. (Rev: BCCB 5/98; BL 4/15/98; HBG 10/98; SLJ 7/98)

4244 Weeks, Sarah. *Oh My Gosh, Mrs McNosh!* (PS–1). Illus. by Nadine Bernard Westcott. 2002, HarperCollins LB $15.89 (978-0-06-008858-3). 32pp. Mrs. McNosh suffers a series of misadventures when her dog George breaks free from his leash and she chases him through town. (Rev: BCCB 5/02; BL 5/1/02; HBG 10/02; SLJ 6/02)

4245 Weis, Carol. *When the Cows Got Loose* (PS–2). Illus. by Ard Hoyt. 2006, Simon & Schuster $16.95 (978-0-689-85166-7). 40pp. While Ida Mae is daydreaming about how to get famous, the cows she's been watching wander off, and now she must get busy to round them back up; the illustrations of eccentric cows match the droll tone of the story. (Rev: BL 6/1–15/06; SLJ 8/06)

4246 Weitzman, Jacqueline Preiss. *Superhero Joe* (K–2). Illus. by Ron Barrett. 2011, Simon & Schuster $16.99 (978-1-4169-9157-1). 32pp. Young Joe dons his Cape of Confidence and zooms to the rescue of his parents (reads, gets a mop from the scary cellar so that Mom can wipe up the spilled engine oil). (Rev: BL 9/15/11; SLJ 8/1/11)

4247 Westcott, Nadine Bernard. *Peanut Butter and Jelly: A Play Rhyme* (PS–K). Illus. by author. 1987, Puffin paper $6.99 (978-0-14-054852-5). 32pp. A play rhyme describes the making of this food that is a children's favorite. (Rev: BL 10/1/87; SLJ 9/87)

4248 Whatley, Bruce, and Rosie Smith. *Captain Pajamas* (PS–2). Illus. by Bruce Whatley. 2000, HarperCollins LB $15.89 (978-0-06-026614-1). Late one night Brian believes that aliens have landed, but the sounds he hears are only his dog trying to get into the fridge. (Rev: BCCB 9/00; BL 5/15/00; HBG 10/00; SLJ 6/00)

4249 Wheeler, Lisa. *Bubble Gum, Bubble Gum* (PS–1). Illus. by Laura Huliska-Beith. 2004, Little, Brown $15.95 (978-0-316-98894-0). 32pp. In bouncy rhyming verse and bold illustrations, a number of different animals become snared by a big gob of bubble gum in the middle of the road. (Rev: BL 5/15/04; SLJ 5/04)

4250 White, Linda. *Too Many Pumpkins* (PS–2). Illus. by Megan Lloyd. 1996, Holiday House LB $17.95 (978-0-8234-1245-7). 28pp. Rebecca Estelle, who hates pumpkins, finds she has a bumper crop in her garden. (Rev: BCCB 12/96; BL 9/15/96; SLJ 11/96)

4251 Willems, Mo. *Don't Let the Pigeon Drive the Bus!* (PS). Illus. by author. 2003, Hyperion $12.99 (978-0-7868-1988-1). A pigeon with ambitions, right now to drive the school bus, is shown in attitudes that preschoolers will instantly recognize. Caldecott Honor Book, 2004. (Rev: BL 9/1/03*; HB 7/03; HBG 10/03; SLJ 5/03)

4252 Willems, Mo. *I Am Invited to a Party!* (K–2). Illus. by author. Series: Elephant and Piggie. 2007, Hyperion $8.99 (978-1-4231-0687-6). 64pp. Piggie asks her elephant friend Gerald to help her get ready for her first party. (Rev: BCCB 11/07; HB 1/08; SLJ 10/07)

4253 Willems, Mo. *Knuffle Bunny Too: A Case of Mistaken Identity* (PS–K). Illus. by author. 2007, Hyperion $16.99 (978-1-4231-0299-1). Double trouble begins when lookalike toy bunnies return home from school with the wrong preschool "mommies." Caldecott Honor Book, 2008. (Rev: BCCB 11/07; BL 9/1/07; HB 11/07; SLJ 8/07)

4254 Willems, Mo. *Knuffle Bunny: A Cautionary Tale* (PS–K). Illus. by author. 2004, Hyperion $15.99 (978-0-7868-1870-9). 40pp. Trixie leaves her beloved stuffed animal at the laundromat in this hilarious tale about the difficulties of communicating. Caldecott Honor Book. (Rev: BL 9/15/04*; HB 9/04; SLJ 10/04*)

4255 Willems, Mo. *Leonardo, the Terrible Monster* (PS–K). Illus. 2005, Hyperion $15.99 (978-0-7868-5294-9). 48pp. Leonardo's failure to frighten anyone leads him to formulate a plan to "scare the tuna salad" out of young Sam. (Rev: BL 7/05; SLJ 8/05*) ∩

4256 Willems, Mo. *Naked Mole Rat Gets Dressed* (PS–2). Illus. by author. 2009, Disney $16.99 (978-1-4231-1437-6). 40pp. Wilbur is an unusual naked mole rat — he likes to wear clothes, and fancy clothes at that. Will his colony accept this behavior? (Rev: BCCB 2/09; BL 11/15/08; LMC 5/09; SLJ 2/09)

4257 Willems, Mo. *The Pigeon Has Feelings, Too!* (PS). Illus. by author. 2005, Hyperion $6.99 (978-0-7868-3650-5). The pigeon of *Don't Let the Pigeon Drive the Bus* (2003) is back in this board book, making all sorts of faces to reveal his emotions. (Rev: SLJ 8/05)

4258 Willems, Mo. *The Pigeon Wants a Puppy!* (PS). Illus. by author. 2008, Hyperion $14.99 (978-1-4231-0960-0). 32pp. Pigeon wants a puppy and he wants it now, but when a (huge) puppy does arrive he rapidly changes his mind. (Rev: BL 5/1/08; HB 7/08; SLJ 6/08)

4259 Willems, Mo. *Should I Share My Ice Cream?* (PS–2). Illus. by author. Series: Elephant and Piggie. 2011, Hyperion $8.99 (978-1-4231-4343-7). 64pp. Should Gerald the elephant share his totally yummy ice cream with best friend Piggie??? The decision comes too late. (Rev: BL 10/1/11; SLJ 9/1/11)

4260 Willems, Mo. *There Is a Bird on Your Head!* (K–2). Illus. by author. Series: Elephant and Piggie. 2007, Hyperion $8.99 (978-1-4231-0686-9). 64pp. What could be more entertaining than a bird on your head? Try a whole nest. Gerald the elephant and Piggie figure it out together. (Rev: HB 1/08; SLJ 10/07)

4261 Willems, Mo. *Today I Will Fly!* (PS–1). Illus. by author. Series: Elephant and Piggie. 2007, Hyperion $8.99 (978-1-4231-0295-3). 64pp. Piggie's announcement that he plans to fly is met with skepticism by his pal, Gerald the elephant. (Rev: BCCB 7–8/07; BL 4/1/07; HB 5/07)

4262 Williams, Vera B. *"More More More," Said the Baby: 3 Love Stories* (PS). Illus. 1990, Greenwillow $17.89 (978-0-688-09174-3). 32pp. All the ways that parents and grandparents play with youngsters are portrayed in this humorous picture book. (Rev: BCCB 10/90; BL 10/1/90; HB 11/90; SLJ 10/90*)

4263 Willis, Jeanne. *I Want to Be a Cowgirl* (PS–2). Illus. by Tony Ross. 2002, Holt $14.95 (978-0-8050-6997-6). 24pp. A city girl dreams of forsaking her dolls and tea parties for life as a cowgirl. (Rev: BL 3/15/02; HBG 10/02; SLJ 7/02)

4264 Willis, Jeanne. *I'm Sure I Saw a Dinosaur* (PS–3). Illus. by Adrian Reynolds. 2011, Andersen $16.95 (978-076138093-1). 32pp. A young boy's dinosaur hoax creates a thriving business for his father's ice cream shop in this light, beautifully illustrated story. (Rev: BLO 9/1/11)

4265 Wilson, Karma. *Moose Tracks!* (PS–2). Illus. by Jack E. Davis. 2006, Simon & Schuster $16.95 (978-0-689-83437-0). 32pp. A thoroughly silly story narrated by the owner of a very untidy house who can identify the sources of much of the mess, but not the culprit who left moose tracks all over the place. (Rev: BL 2/15/06; SLJ 4/06)

4266 Wilson, Tony. *The Princess and the Packet of Frozen Peas* (PS–3). Illus. by Sue deGennaro. 2012, Peachtree $16.95 (978-1-56145-635-2). 32pp. Prince Henrik is searching for the girl of his dreams — nothing like his older brother's oversensitive bride — and he finds one who likes both hockey and camping. (Rev: BL 3/15/12; SLJ 4/1/12)

4267 Wing, Natasha. *How to Raise a Dinosaur* (K–2). Illus. by Pablo Bernasconi. 2010, Running Press $16.95 (978-0-7624-3342-1). 24pp. This playful lift-the-flap guide to taking care of a pet dinosaur features practical bits of advice transferable to more ordinary pets. (Rev: BL 11/1/10; SLJ 1/1/11)

4268 Winthrop, Elizabeth. *The Biggest Parade* (K–3). Illus. by Mark Ulriksen. 2006, Holt $16.95 (978-0-8050-7685-1). Chairman of the town's 250th birthday parade, Harvey wants to include everyone, even his basset hound Fred; Fred refuses but, in the end, it seems that Fred has identified the place he is needed most — as a spectator. (Rev: SLJ 10/06)

4269 Winthrop, Elizabeth. *Dancing Granny* (PS–2). Illus. by Salvatore Murdocca. 2003, Marshall Cavendish $16.95 (978-0-7614-5141-9). Granny has a grand time at the party at the zoo, dancing with many animals, including a fetching bear. (Rev: HBG 4/04; SLJ 10/03)

4270 Wood, Audrey. *King Bidgood's in the Bathtub* (PS–2). Illus. by Don Wood. 1985, Harcourt $16.00 (978-0-15-242730-6). 32pp. No one can get the king out of his bathtub, until the young page thinks of pulling the plug. (Rev: BCCB 1/86; BL 10/1/85; SLJ 11/85)

4271 Wood, Audrey. *The Napping House* (PS–2). Illus. by Don Wood. 1984, Harcourt $16.00 (978-0-15-256708-8). 32pp. A cumulative story about all the members of a household taking a nap except for a flea.

4272 Wright, Michael. *Jake Starts School* (1–3). Illus. by author. 2008, Feiwel & Friends $16.95 (978-0-312-36798-5). 32pp. Jake's first day at school is so scary that his parents stay with him. (Rev: BL 5/15/08; LMC 8/08; SLJ 8/08)

4273 Yorinks, Arthur. *The Invisible Man* (PS–1). Illus. by Doug Cushman. 2011, HarperCollins $16.99 (978-0-06-156148-1). 32pp. A Brooklyn fruit merchant has a series of unfortunate experiences when he becomes invisible. (Rev: BL 1/1–15/11*; HB 1–2/11; SLJ 1/1/11)

4274 Young, Amy. *Belinda and the Glass Slipper* (PS–2). 2006, Viking $15.99 (978-0-670-06082-5). 32pp. In this sequel to *Belinda the Ballerina*, Belinda faces competition from a formidable — and underhanded — rival. (Rev: BL 10/1/06; SLJ 10/06)

4275 Ziefert, Harriet. *There Was a Little Girl, She Had a Little Curl* (PS). Illus. by Elliot Kreloff. 2006, Blue Apple $9.95 (978-1-59354-161-3). Preschooler Isabel decides to cut her own hair. (Rev: SLJ 10/06)

NATURE AND SCIENCE

4276 Allan, Nicholas. *Where Willy Went: The Big Story of a Little Sperm!* (PS–1). Illus. 2005, Knopf LB $17.99 (978-0-375-93030-0). 32pp. An unusual and appealing overview of the human reproductive process, in which Willy, a sperm who has spent his life polishing his swimming skills, triumphs over his competitors and fertilizes the egg. (Rev: BL 2/1/05; SLJ 3/05)

4277 Asch, Frank. *The Earth and I* (PS–2). Illus. 1994, Harcourt $15.00 (978-0-15-200443-9). 32pp. A young boy shares many thoughts and activities with his friend the earth. (Rev: BL 1/15/95; HBG 4/04; SLJ 10/94)

4278 Asch, Frank. *Like a Windy Day* (K–2). Illus. by Frank Asch and Devin Asch. 2002, Harcourt $15.00 (978-0-15-216376-1). A little girl thinks about all the neat things the wind can do and imagines herself playing with the personified wind that floats overhead. (Rev: BL 10/1/02; HBG 3/03; SLJ 10/02)

4279 Asch, Frank. *The Sun Is My Favorite Star* (PS–1). Illus. 2000, Harcourt $15.00 (978-0-15-202127-6). 32pp. A little girl sings the praises of the sun and the light that it gives her. (Rev: BL 11/1/00; HBG 3/01; SLJ 10/00)

4280 Aston, Dianna. *An Orange in January* (PS–1). Illus. by Julie Maren. 2007, Dial $16.99 (978-0-8037-3146-2). 32pp. Readers follow the life of an orange from its original blossom through harvest and packing until it finally ends up being shared among a little boy's friends. (Rev: BL 10/15/07; LMC 11/07; SLJ 11/07)

4281 Ayres, Katherine. *Up, Down, and Around* (PS–1). Illus. by Nadine Bernard Westcott. 2007, Candlewick $16.99 (978-0-7636-2378-4). This lively picture book captures the excitement of gardening as two young children help a man plant vegetables, some of which grow up while others grow down. (Rev: BL 3/15/07)

4282 Baines, Becky. *The Bones You Own: A Book About the Human Body* (K–2). Illus. 2009, National Geographic $14.95 (978-1-4263-0410-1). A meaty introduction with a lighthearted approach. (Rev: SLJ 6/09)

4283 Barner, Bob. *Dinosaurs Roar, Butterflies Soar!* (1–3). Illus. by author. 2009, Chronicle $16.99 (978-0-8118-5663-8). 32pp. A fascinating look at the relationship between dinosaurs and butterflies. (Rev: SLJ 6/09)

4284 Base, Graeme. *Uno's Garden* (2–4). Illus. 2006, Abrams $19.95 (978-0-8109-5473-1). Uno builds a home in a beautiful forest, surrounded by Moopaloops, Lumpybums, and Frinklepods, but the colorful setting attracts more and more people until the plants and animals are almost all gone; the attractive illustrations offer opportunities for counting and finding items. (Rev: BL 11/15/06)

4285 Bauer, Marion Dane. *In Like a Lion Out Like a Lamb* (PS–2). Illus. by Emily Arnold McCully. 2011, Holiday House $16.95 (978-0-8234-2238-8). 32pp. A March lion wreaks havoc in a little boy's house until he is finally persuaded to leave and sneezes out a spring lamb to take his place. (Rev: BL 3/1/11; LMC 9–10/11; SLJ 4/11)

4286 Bean, Jonathan. *Big Snow* (PS–K). Illus. by author. 2013, Farrar $17.99 (978-0-374-30696-0). 32pp. Young David's anticipation of a snowstorm causes frustrations until the blizzard finally arrives. **e** Lexile AD470 (Rev: BL 10/1/13; HB 11–12/13; SLJ 9/13)

4287 Berger, Carin. *OK Go* (PS–K). Illus. by author. 2009, HarperCollins $17.99 (978-0-06-157666-9). 32pp. Go green message delivered in recycled material collage. (Rev: BL 6/1–15/09; SLJ 4/09)

4288 Blexbolex. *Seasons* (PS–2). Trans. from French by Claudia Bedrick. Illus. by author. 2010, Enchanted Lion $19.95 (978-1-59270-095-0). Unpaged. A beautiful, thought-provoking exploration of the seasons and how they affect a landscape and the people who live there. (Rev: HB 7–8/10; SLJ 7/1/10*)

4289 Brallier, Jess M. *Tess's Tree* (PS–2). Illus. by Peter H. Reynolds. 2010, HarperCollins $16.99 (978-0-06-168752-5); LB $17.89 (978-0-06-168753-2). Unpaged. A young girl organizes a touching tribute to her 175-year-old maple tree after it's damaged in a storm and must be cut down. (Rev: SLJ 2/1/10)

4290 Buell, Janet. *Sail Away, Little Boat* (PS–3). Illus. by Jui Ishida. 2006, Carolrhoda LB $15.95 (978-1-57505-821-4). From its launching in a brook by a young girl and boy, a plucky toy sailboat heads ever downriver — past fish, deer, and other animals — until it reaches a seashore and is quickly adopted by other children. (Rev: SLJ 4/06)

4291 Bunting, Eve. *Anna's Table* (K–2). Illus. by Taia Morley. 2003, NorthWord $15.95 (978-1-55971-841-7). 32pp. Anna collects treasures that she finds — such as mouse bones, dead butterflies — and keeps them on her nature table. (Rev: BL 3/15/03; SLJ 10/03)

4292 Bunting, Eve. *Butterfly House* (K–2). Illus. by Greg Shed. 1999, Scholastic $17.99 (978-0-590-84884-8). 32pp. A young girl and her grandfather rescue a caterpillar and observe it change into a butterfly. (Rev: BL 6/1–15/99; HBG 10/99; SLJ 4/99)

4293 Bunting, Eve. *Someday a Tree* (PS–3). Illus. by Ronald Himler. 1993, Houghton $16.00 (978-0-395-61309-2). 32pp. In spite of attention from friends, a sick tree continues to die. (Rev: BL 3/1/93; SLJ 5/93)

4294 Bunting, Eve. *Sunflower House* (PS–2). Illus. by Kathryn Hewitt. 1996, Harcourt $15.00 (978-0-15-200483-5). 32pp. A boy plants some sunflower seeds and witnesses the dramatic miracle of plant growth. (Rev: BL 4/1/96; SLJ 5/96)

4295 Carle, Eric. *The Tiny Seed* (K–2). Illus. by author. 1991, Picture Book $16.00 (978-0-88708-015-9). 32pp. A tiny seed travels by the wind, survives all sorts of perils, and grows into a flower. A reissue.

4296 Carlstrom, Nancy White. *Mama, Will It Snow Tonight?* (PS). Illus. by Paul Tong. 2009, Boyds Mills $16.95 (978-1-59078-562-1). 32pp. A little girl and two woodland animals eagerly await the season's first snowfall (Rev: BL 9/15/09; SLJ 11/1/09)

4297 Carr, Jan. *Splish, Splash, Spring* (PS–1). Illus. by Dorothy Donohue. 2001, Holiday House $16.95 (978-0-8234-1578-6). 32pp. It is spring and young playmates and a dog enjoy all its pleasures — playing in the rain, digging for worms, and flying kites. (Rev: BL 4/1/01; HBG 10/01; SLJ 5/01)

4298 Cherry, Lynne. *The Great Kapok Tree: A Tale of the Amazon Rain Forest* (K–3). Illus. 1990, Harcourt $16.00 (978-0-15-200520-7). 32pp. A carefully researched picture book of the Amazon rain forest. (Rev: BL 3/15/90; HB 5/90; SLJ 5/90)

4299 Chin, Jason. *Redwoods* (PS–3). Illus. by author. 2009, Roaring Brook $16.95 (978-1-59643-430-1). A little boy finds a book about redwood trees on a subway platform and his train ride is transformed into a journey of discovery. (Rev: BL 4/1/09; HB 5/09; SLJ 5/09)

4300 Clark, Joan. *Snow* (PS–K). Illus. by Kady M. Denton. 2006, Groundwood $16.95 (978-0-88899-712-8). After a solid month of snow the landscape around Sammy's house is deeply covered, so the young boy climbs to his rooftop to survey the scene and imagine what is going on beneath the blanket of snow. (Rev: SLJ 9/06)

4301 Cole, Henry. *I Took a Walk* (PS–K). Illus. 1998, Greenwillow $16.99 (978-0-688-15115-7). 28pp. A boy narrates his walk through woods and a meadow, by a stream and a pond, as he observes an assortment of animals, plants, and insects. (Rev: BCCB 3/98; BL 5/1/98; HB 5/98; HBG 10/98; SLJ 5/98)

4302 Cole, Henry. *On Meadowview Street* (K–2). Illus. by author. 2007, Greenwillow $16.99 (978-0-06-056481-0). 32pp. A young girl moves with her family to the suburbs and creates a small patch of wilderness within the confines of their otherwise sterile development. (Rev: BL 6/1–15/07; SLJ 9/07)

4303 Cole, Henry. *On the Way to the Beach* (PS–3). Illus. by author. 2003, Greenwillow $16.99 (978-0-688-17515-3). On the fold-out illustrations, readers look for a variety of plant and animal life — a snowy egret, a terrapin, a prickly pear — as they follow a young girl on a walk to the beach. (Rev: BL 5/15//3; HBG 10/03; SLJ 5/03)

4304 Collins, Pat Lowery. *The Deer Watch* (PS–3). Illus. by David Slonim. 2013, Candlewick $15.99 (978-0-7636-4890-9). 32pp. A boy and his father learn a lot about the environment around their house — the dunes, the marsh, the new housing development — and see many animals on their quest to spot a deer. Lexile AD950 (Rev: BL 3/15/13*; LMC 8–9/13; SLJ 3/13)

4305 Crausaz, Anne. *Seasons* (PS–2). Illus. by author. 2011, Kane/Miller $15.99 (978-1-61067-006-7). 48pp. Evocative illustrations accompanied by minimal text takes readers on a colorful tour through the many sensations of the seasons. (Rev: BLO 2/15/11; HB 5–6/11; SLJ 3/1/11)

4306 Crumpacker, Bunny. *Alexander's Pretending Day* (PS–K). Illus. by Dan Andreasen. 2005, Dutton $15.99 (978-0-525-46936-0). 32pp. Alexander plays "what if" and his mother always responds with a reassuring answer. (Rev: BL 2/15/05; SLJ 4/05)

4307 Davick, Linda. *I Love You, Nose! I Love You, Toes!* (PS–1). Illus. by author. 2013, Simon & Schuster $17.99 (978-1-4424-6037-9). 32pp. A rhyming, happy tribute to all the varied parts of the body. (Rev: BLO 4/1/13; HB 3–4/13; LMC 10/13; SLJ 3/13)

4308 Deady, Kathleen W. *All Year Long* (PS–2). Illus. by Linda Bronson. 2004, Carolrhoda $15.95 (978-1-57505-537-4). A young girl explains how changes in her family's activities signal the arrival of a new season. (Rev: BL 4/15/04; SLJ 4/04)

4309 Depalma, Mary Newell. *The Grand Old Tree* (PS–1). Illus. 2005, Scholastic $16.99 (978-0-439-62334-6). 32pp. The life and death of a grand tree is celebrated in an appealing blend of simple text and art. (Rev: BL 11/15/05; SLJ 12/05)

4310 dePaola, Tomie. *The Cloud Book* (K–3). Illus. by author. 1975, Holiday House LB $16.95 (978-0-8234-0259-5); paper $6.95 (978-0-8234-0531-2). 32pp. The 10 most common clouds, along with related myths and sayings.

4311 dePaola, Tomie. *The Quicksand Book* (1–3). Illus. by author. 1977, Holiday House LB $16.95 (978-0-8234-0291-5); paper $6.95 (978-0-8234-0532-9). 32pp. Science is both informative and entertaining in this story of Jungle Girl, who falls into a patch of quicksand.

4312 Dodd, Emma. *I Love Bugs!* (PS–1). Illus. by author. 2010, Holiday House $16.95 (978-0-8234-2280-7).

32pp. Easy-to-read text celebrates the huge variety of insects and spiders in a young child's backyard. (Rev: BL 3/15/10; SLJ 6/1/10)

4313 Ehlert, Lois. *Feathers for Lunch* (PS–2). Illus. 1990, Harcourt $16.00 (978-0-15-230550-5). 32pp. A wide variety of American birds are introduced by way of a cat's stalking activities. (Rev: BCCB 1/91; BL 9/1/90; HB 11/90*; HBG 4/04; SLJ 12/90)

4314 Ehlert, Lois. *In My World* (PS–1). Illus. 2002, Harcourt $15.00 (978-0-15-216269-6). 40pp. Die-cut shapes are used to present various flora and fauna and other phenomena of nature in this impressive picture book. (Rev: BL 5/1/02*; HB 7/02; HBG 10/02; SLJ 5/02)

4315 Ehlert, Lois. *Red Leaf, Yellow Leaf* (PS–2). Illus. 1991, Harcourt $16.00 (978-0-15-266197-7). 32pp. A child tells of buying, planting, and caring for a sugar maple tree. (Rev: BCCB 10/91; BL 10/1/91*; HB 11/91*; SLJ 11/91)

4316 Erdrich, Lise. *Bears Make Rock Soup and Other Stories* (2–4). Illus. by Lisa Fifield. 2002, Children's Book Pr. $16.95 (978-0-89239-172-1). A collection of short stories and art depicting the Native American connection to animals and the earth. (Rev: BCCB 1/03; BL 8/02; HBG 3/03; SLJ 9/02)

4317 Ernst, Lisa Campbell. *Wake Up, It's Spring!* (PS–K). Illus. 2004, HarperCollins LB $17.89 (978-0-06-008986-3). 32pp. The arrival of a warm spring sun is celebrated as plants, animals, and people bask in its rays. (Rev: BL 1/1–15/04; SLJ 2/04)

4318 Fisher, Aileen. *The Story Goes On* (PS–3). Illus. by Mique Moriuchi. 2005, Roaring Brook $16.95 (978-1-59643-037-2). A circular nature tale in which a seed sprouts and grows, a bug finds it appetizing, a frog eats the bug, and so forth through the shooting of a hawk to the final enrichment of the soil. (Rev: HB 9/96; SLJ 6/05)

4319 Fleming, Denise. *The First Day of Winter* (PS–K). Illus. 2005, Holt $15.95 (978-0-8050-7384-3). 32pp. A snowman receives a nice selection of presents in this twist on "The Twelve Days of Christmas." (Rev: BL 12/15/05; SLJ 12/05)

4320 Fleming, Denise. *In the Small, Small Pond* (PS–K). Illus. 1993, Holt $16.95 (978-0-8050-2264-3); paper $6.95 (978-0-8050-5983-0). 30pp. In a series of collages, a frog views a year of changing seasons in a small pond. (Rev: BL 9/1/93; HB 9/93; SLJ 9/93*)

4321 Fletcher, Ralph J. *Hello, Harvest Moon* (K–3). Illus. by Kate Kiesler. 2004, Houghton $16.00 (978-0-618-16451-6). 32pp. The glow of the harvest moon shines over the peaceful neighborhood in this gentle book. (Rev: BL 9/1/03; HBG 4/04; SLJ 9/03)

4322 Fogliano, Julie. *And Then It's Spring* (PS–2). Illus. by Erin E. Stead. 2012, Roaring Brook $16.99 (978-159643624-4). 32pp. After planting seeds, a young boy begins to worry that green shoots will never appear. (Rev: BL 12/15/11*; HB 1–2/12; SLJ 1/12)

4323 Ford, Bernette. *First Snow* (PS). Illus. by Sebastien Braun. 2005, Holiday $16.95 (978-0-8234-1937-1). A bunny and his siblings enjoy exploring their first snow-fall under the light of the moon. (Rev: BL 11/1/05*; HBG 4/06; SLJ 9/05*)

4324 Franco, Betsy. *Bees, Snails, and Peacock Tails: Patterns and Shapes . . . Naturally* (PS–2). Illus. by Steve Jenkins. 2008, Simon & Schuster $16.99 (978-1-4169-0386-4). Poems and collages explore patterns and shapes in nature, with an appendix of scientific facts. (Rev: BL 9/1/08; SLJ 9/08) [811]

4325 Franco, Betsy. *Pond Circle* (PS–1). Illus. by Stefano Vitale. 2009, Simon & Schuster $16.99 (978-1-4169-4021-0). 32pp. Introduction to woodland ecology using a "House that Jack Built" formula. (Rev: BL 6/1–15/09; HB 7/09; SLJ 5/09)

4326 Frasier, Debra. *On the Day You Were Born* (K–2). Illus. 1991, Harcourt $16.00 (978-0-15-257995-1). The wonders of nature and the interdependence of all living things are celebrated in this book that introduces science in a personalized way. (Rev: BL 6/15/91; SLJ 6/91*)

4327 Freedman, Claire. *One Magical Day* (PS–K). Illus. by Tina Macnaughton. 2007, Good Bks. $16.95 (978-1-56148-567-3). A nicely illustrated, simple account of a beautiful day among the flora and fauna of the country. (Rev: SLJ 8/07)

4328 French, Vivian. *Yucky Worms* (PS–2). Illus. by Jessica Ahlberg. 2010, Candlewick $16.99 (978-0-7636-4446-8). 32pp. As they work together in the garden, a grandmother tells her young grandson all about earthworms and the good they do. (Rev: BL 5/1/10; SLJ 6/1/10*)

4329 Geisert, Arthur. *Thunderstorm* (1–3). Illus. by author. 2013, Enchanted Lion $17.95 (978-1-59270-133-9). 32pp. Continuous, visually arresting illustrations accompanied by minimal text follow the course of a thunderstorm in the Midwest. (Rev: BLO 5/1/13; LMC 11–12/13; SLJ 5/13)

4330 George, Jean Craighead. *Luck* (PS–2). Illus. by Wendell Minor. 2006, HarperCollins $16.99 (978-0-06-008201-7). 32pp. Luck is a sandhill crane whose rescue from a plastic six-pack holder, growth, and migration are presented in beautiful artwork and prose in this compelling picture book. (Rev: BL 5/1/06; SLJ 6/06)

4331 George, Kristine O'Connell. *Hummingbird Nest: A Journal of Poems* (K–4). Illus. by Barry Moser. 2004, Harcourt $16.00 (978-0-15-202325-6). 48pp. George conveys the magic of watching a hummingbird raise a family in these short poems partnered by watercolors. (Rev: BL 2/1/04*; SLJ 4/04)

4332 Gibbons, Gail. *The Vegetables We Eat* (K–3). Illus. by author. 2007, Holiday $16.95 (978-0-8234-2001-8). 32pp. A wide-ranging introduction to vegetables and their nutritional benefits. (Rev: BL 9/1/07; SLJ 7/07) [635]

4333 Godkin, Celia. *Wolf Island* (1–3). Illus. by author. 2007, Fitzhenry & Whiteside $17.95 (978-1-55455-007-4); paper $9.95 (978-1-55455-008-1). When a wolf family leaves an island, this sets in motion a chain of events that changes the whole ecology; previously published in

1993, this new edition has more visual appeal. (Rev: BL 2/15/07; SLJ 4/07)

4334 Gomi, Taro. *Spring Is Here / Llegó la primavera* (PS). Illus. by author. 2006, Chronicle $14.50 (978-0-8118-4759-9); paper $6.95 (978-0-8118-4760-5). The changing seasons are artfully illustrated using a calf as the background in this book with text in both English and Spanish. (Rev: SLJ 6/06*)

4335 Griessman, Annette. *Like a Hundred Drums* (PS–K). Illus. by Julie Monks. 2006, Houghton $15.00 (978-0-618-55878-0). 32pp. A summer thunderstorm interrupts a day on a farm in this simple picture book with folk-art illustrations. (Rev: BL 5/1/06; SLJ 6/06)

4336 Hader, Berta, and Elmer Hader. *The Big Snow* (PS–3). Illus. by authors. 1972, Macmillan LB $17.00 (978-0-02-737910-5); paper $6.95 (978-0-689-71757-4). How all the little animals of a country hillside survive a heavy winter storm. Caldecott Medal winner, 1949.

4337 Hall, Zoe. *The Apple Pie Tree* (PS–2). Illus. by Shari Halpern. 1996, Scholastic $16.95 (978-0-590-62382-7). 32pp. The changes that occur to an apple tree during one year are described by two sisters. (Rev: BCCB 12/96; BL 10/1/96; SLJ 12/96)

4338 Haskins, Lori. *Butterfly Fever* (1–3). Illus. by Jerry Smath. Series: Science Solves It! 2004, Kane paper $4.99 (978-1-57565-134-7). 32pp. Fourth-grader Ellie discovers that her new town is a destination for migrating monarch butterflies, and with her classmates she learns all about them. (Rev: BL 2/15/04; SLJ 6/04)

4339 Hayward, Linda. *Monster Bug* (1–2). Illus. by Diane Palmisciano. Series: Science Solves It! 2004, Kane paper $4.99 (978-1-57565-135-4). Scared the day before by the image of a monster bug, Kyle realizes the nature of shadows and plots revenge with an even more frightening sight. (Rev: SLJ 6/04)

4340 Henkes, Kevin. *So Happy!* (1–3). Illus. by Anita Lobel. 2005, Greenwillow LB $16.89 (978-0-06-056484-1). Everything changes for a bored little boy in the Southwest when the rain comes. (Rev: BL 2/1/05; SLJ 3/05)

4341 Hoberman, Mary Ann. *Right Outside My Window* (K–2). Illus. by Nicholas Wilton. 2002, Mondo $15.95 (978-1-59034-194-0). 24pp. Simple two-line rhymes describe the beautiful changing views through the four seasons. (Rev: BL 8/02; HBG 10/02; SLJ 11/02)

4342 Hoberman, Mary Ann. *Whose Garden Is It?* (PS–1). Illus. by Jane Dyer. 2004, Harcourt $16.00 (978-0-15-202631-8). 40pp. The gardener, the plants, the creatures of the garden, and the sun and the rain all come forward to claim credit to the title question as elderly Mrs. McGee and a young child stroll admiringly through it. (Rev: BL 4/15/04; SLJ 5/04)

4343 Hood, Susan. *Rooting for You* (K–2). Illus. by Matthew Cordell. 2014, Disney/Hyperion $16.99 (978-142315230-9). 32pp. A little seed plucks up the courage to send out a shoot and soon discovers that he has many companions. (Rev: BL 3/1/14; LMC 8–9/14; SLJ 3/14)

4344 Horacek, Petr. *Butterfly Butterfly: A Book of Colors* (PS–K). Illus. 2007, Candlewick $12.99 (978-0-7636-3343-1). While waiting for a beautifully butterfly to reappear, a little girl enjoys other insects in this rewarding picture book with die-cut holes and a final pop-up of the returning butterfly. (Rev: BL 4/15/07)

4345 Hubbell, Patricia. *Hurray for Spring!* (PS–K). Illus. by Taia Morley. 2005, North Word $15.95 (978-1-55971-913-1). A little boy describes the many joys of spring in accessible first-person rhyming text. (Rev: BL 5/15/05; SLJ 4/05)

4346 Jackson, Ellen. *Earth Mother* (PS–2). Illus. by Leo Dillon and Diane Dillon. 2005, Walker $16.95 (978-0-8027-8992-1). Earth Mother is presented with conflicting requests from Man, Frog, and Mosquito and declares that all is well; excellent illustrations add to the serenity with beautiful scenery. (Rev: BL 8/05*; SLJ 9/05)

4347 Jarrett, Clare. *Arabella Miller's Tiny Caterpillar* (PS–2). Illus. by author. 2008, Candlewick $16.99 (978-0-7636-3660-9). 32pp. This rhymed story about a little girl who finds a tiny striped caterpillar and cares for it until it becomes a butterfly. (Rev: BL 3/1/08; SLJ 4/08)

4348 Johnston, Tony. *The Whole Green World* (PS–1). Illus. by Elisa Kleven. 2005, Farrar $15.00 (978-0-374-38400-5). A little girl and her dog plant seeds and enjoy the results in this rhyming verse presented within detailed circular illustrations. (Rev: SLJ 4/05)

4349 Karas, G. Brian. *Atlantic* (PS–3). Illus. 2002, Penguin $15.99 (978-0-399-23632-7). 32pp. In this first-person narrative, the Atlantic Ocean tells what and where it is, how people view it, and how it is affected by the moon and sun. (Rev: BCCB 4/02; BL 4/15/02*; HBG 10/02; SLJ 6/02)

4350 Kato, Yukiko. *In the Meadow* (PS). Trans. from Japanese by Yuki Kaneko. Illus. by Komako Sakai. 2011, Enchanted Lion $14.95 (978-1-59270-108-7). Unpaged. A young Asian girl follows a butterfly through a meadow and encounters many other insects on her brief journey. (Rev: HB 7–8/11; LMC 11–12/11; SLJ 7/11)

4351 Keats, Ezra Jack. *The Snowy Day* (PS–1). Illus. by author. 1962, Puffin paper $6.99 (978-0-14-050182-7). 40pp. A young African American boy's delight during his first snowfall. Caldecott Medal winner, 1963.

4352 Knudsen, Michelle. *Bugged!* (1–3). Illus. by Blanche Sims. Series: Science Solves It . 2008, Kane paper $5.95 (978-1-57565-259-7). 32pp. Mosquitoes seem to be very attracted to Riley and he is determined to find out why in this readable title that has lots of bug facts with a scientific approach to research and problem solving. (Rev: BL 2/1/08; SLJ 7/08)

4353 Knudsen, Michelle. *A Moldy Mystery* (1–3). Illus. by Barry Gott. Series: Science Solves It! 2006, Kane paper $4.99 (978-1-57565-167-5). 32pp. Jeff throws out some moldy food containers only to discover that they were part of his older brother's science project and he must work out how to replace them; lots of facts appear in "Did you know?" boxes. (Rev: BL 4/15/06)

4354 Kurtz, Jane, and Christopher Kurtz. *Water Hole Waiting* (PS–3). Illus. by Lee Christiansen. 2002, HarperCollins LB $18.89 (978-0-06-029851-7). 32pp. A picture book about animals taking turns drinking at an African water hole. (Rev: BCCB 6/02; BL 5/15/02; HBG 10/02; SLJ 5/02*)

4355 Lakin, Patricia. *Hurricane!* (1–3). Illus. by Vanessa Lubach. 2000, Millbrook LB $21.90 (978-0-7613-1616-9). 32pp. A girl and her father make preparations to withstand Hurricane Bob and after the storm has passed survey the damage. (Rev: BL 10/15/00; HBG 3/01; SLJ 1/01)

4356 Léger, Diane Carmel. *Who's in Maxine's Tree?* (1–4). Illus. by Darlene Gait. 2006, Orca $17.95 (978-1-55143-346-2). Maxine is thrilled to learn that her favorite tree will be protected from loggers because it is home to an endangered species of bird. (Rev: SLJ 6/06)

4357 Lewis, J. Patrick. *Earth and Me: Our Family Tree* (K–4). Illus. by Christopher Canyon. Series: A Sharing Nature with Children Book. 2002, Dawn $16.95 (978-1-58469-031-3); paper $7.95 (978-1-58469-030-6). Rich artwork and lyric text introduce animals of all kinds — and one boy — appreciating the beauty and bounty of their environment. (Rev: HBG 10/02; SLJ 4/02)

4358 Locker, Thomas. *Walking with Henry: Based on the Life and Works of Henry David Thoreau* (2–4). Illus. 2002, Fulcrum $17.95 (978-1-55591-355-7). 32pp. A fictionalized account of Henry David Thoreau as he hikes through the wilderness, describing his beliefs about man's relationship with nature. (Rev: BL 12/1/02; HBG 3/03; SLJ 1/03) [818]

4359 McCloskey, Robert. *Time of Wonder* (1–4). Illus. by author. 1957, Puffin paper $6.99 (978-0-14-050201-5). 64pp. Full-color watercolors illustrate this poetic text describing a summer on the Maine coast and the hurricane that hits it. Caldecott Medal winner, 1958.

4360 McClure, Nikki. *Apple* (PS–K). Illus. by author. 2012, Abrams/Appleseed $12.95 (978-1-4197-0378-2). 40pp. A single apple's journey from fruit to food to compost to seed to sprout is chronicled in this simple story with minimal text. (Rev: BL 8/12; SLJ 11/12)

4361 McClure, Nikki. *Mama, Is It Summer Yet?* (PS–K). Illus. by author. 2010, Abrams $17.95 (978-0-8109-8468-4). 32pp. A boy longs for summer and watches with his mother as the signs arrive. (Rev: BL 4/15/10; SLJ 4/1/10)

4362 McCue, Lisa. *Quiet Bunny* (PS–1). Illus. by author. 2009, Sterling LB $14.95 (978-1-4027-5719-8). 32pp. A bunny in search of his "voice" drives this lovely story. (Rev: SLJ 6/09)

4363 McGinty, Alice B. *Thank You, World* (PS–1). Illus. by Wendy A. Halperin. 2007, Dial $16.99 (978-0-8037-2705-2). 32pp. Children from eight different nations around the world are shown appreciating all kinds of things — trees, grass, breezes, and so forth. (Rev: BL 10/15/07; SLJ 12/07)

4364 Markle, Sandra. *Butterfly Tree* (K–3). Illus. by Leslie Wu. 2011, Peachtree $16.95 (978-1-56145-539-3).

32pp. Jilly and her mother come across a strange orange cloud over Lake Erie and realize it consists of migrating monarch butterflies; includes a factual author's note. (Rev: BL 12/1/11; LMC 3–4/12; SLJ 10/1/11)

4365 Marlow, Layn. *You Make Me Smile* (PS–2). Illus. by author. 2013, Holiday $16.95 (978-082342922-6). 32pp. As she does every year, a little girl celebrates the arrival of winter by building herself a friend — a snowman. Lexile AD390 (Rev: BLO 9/15/13; SLJ 10/13)

4366 Messner, Kate. *Over and Under the Snow* (PS–3). Illus. by Christopher Silas Neal. 2011, Chronicle $16.99 (978-0-8118-6784-9). 44pp. A girl and her father ski through the woods, discussing the animals that live happily under the snow. (Rev: BL 12/15/11; HB 1–2/12; LMC 3–4/12*; SLJ 12/1/11)

4367 Millard, Glenda. *Isabella's Garden* (PS–2). Illus. by Rebecca Cool. 2012, Candlewick $16.99 (978-0-7636-6016-1). 32pp. Folk-art illustrations accompany lyric rhymed verse in this story of a garden's progress through the seasons. (Rev: BL 5/1/12; SLJ 4/1/12)

4368 Morales, Melita. *Jam and Honey* (PS). Illus. by Laura J. Bryant. 2011, Tricycle $15.99 (978-1-58246-299-8); LB $18.99 (978-1-59246-390-2). 32pp. In this story told alternately from each perspective, a girl and a honeybee learn to leave each other alone and enjoy their garden. (Rev: BL 2/15/11; SLJ 3/1/11)

4369 Nargi, Lela. *The Honeybee Man* (K–3). Illus. by Kyrsten Brooker. 2011, Random House $17.99 (978-0-375-84980-0); LB $20.99 (978-0-375-95695-9). 40pp. In Brooklyn, N.Y., Fred keeps bees on the roof of his apartment building and releases them into the city to gather nectar. e Lexile AD870L (Rev: BL 3/15/11; HB 3–4/11; SLJ 3/1/11)

4370 Neubecker, Robert. *Wow! Ocean!* (PS–2). Illus. by author. 2011, Hyperion/Disney $17.99 (978-1-4231-3113-7). Unpaged. Izzy finds much to wonder at when she and her family arrive at the beach in this eye-catching book. (Rev: HB 7–8/11; SLJ 7/11)

4371 Nidey, Kelli. *When Autumn Falls* (PS–1). Illus. by Susan Swan. 2004, Whitman LB $16.99 (978-0-8075-0490-1). Falling leaves, apples, and temperatures are just some of the features of autumn highlighted. (Rev: SLJ 9/04)

4372 Oberman, Sheldon. *The Wind That Wanted to Rest* (PS–2). Illus. by Neil Waldman. 2012, Boyds Mills $17.95 (978-159078858-5). 32pp. An angry winter wind rejected by many is calmed and befriended by a generous young girl. (Rev: BLO 4/1/12; LMC 11–12/12)

4373 Ochiltree, Dianne. *It's a Firefly Night* (PS–2). Illus. by Betsy Snyder. 2013, Blue Apple $12.99 (978-160905291-1). 32pp. Daddy and his daughter enjoy catching fireflies and then releasing them in this gentle book. (Rev: BLO 6/13)

4374 O'Malley, Kevin. *Straight to the Pole* (PS–3). Illus. by author. 2003, Walker LB $16.85 (978-0-8027-8868-9). A little boy struggles melodramatically through a snowstorm, and just when all hope seems to be lost, two

sled-riding friends appear to tell him that school's been canceled for the day. (Rev: HBG 4/04; SLJ 11/03)

4375 Parker, Michael. *You Are a Star!* (PS–2). Illus. by Judith Rossell. 2012, Walker $16.99 (978-0-8027-2841-8). 40pp. This is a very gentle introduction to the concept of the universe and its origins, presenting a young child who explores the night sky. (Rev: BL 11/15/12; SLJ 9/12)

4376 Paterson, Diane. *Hurricane Wolf* (K–3). Illus. 2006, Albert Whitman $16.99 (978-0-8075-3438-0). 32pp. Together with his parents, young Noah prepares for the arrival of Hurricane Anna and then assesses the damage after the storm has passed. (Rev: BL 3/1/06; SLJ 3/06)

4377 Peet, Bill. *The Wump World* (1–3). Illus. by author. 1981, Houghton $17.00 (978-0-395-19841-4); paper $8.95 (978-0-395-31129-5). An animal parable in which pollution and the waste of natural resources are the main themes.

4378 Perkins, Lynne Rae. *Snow Music* (PS–2). Illus. by author. 2003, Greenwillow LB $16.89 (978-0-06-623958-3). A simple, musical story of a boy searching for his runaway dog in the snow, showing the tracks of deer, rabbits, squirrels. (Rev: BCCB 12/03; BL 9/1/03; HB 11/03; HBG 4/04; LMC 3/04; SLJ 11/03)

4379 Pettenati, Jeanne K. *Galileo's Journal: 1609–1610* (1–3). Illus. by Paolo Rui. 2006, Charlesbridge $16.95 (978-1-57091-879-7); paper $6.95 (978-1-57091-880-3). 32pp. Galileo records in a fictional journal the events of eight key months in his life, a period during which he developed a telescope and made discoveries about the solar system. (Rev: BL 8/06)

4380 Pfister, Marcus. *Ava's Poppy* (PS–2). Illus. by author. 2012, NorthSouth $16.95 (978-073584057-7). 32pp. In this gentle story, a young girl befriends a beautiful poppy flower and is saddened when its petals fall but delighted to meet a new poppy the following spring. Lexile AD500L (Rev: BL 4/15/12; LMC 8–9/12; SLJ 1/12)

4381 Powell, Consie. *The First Day of Winter* (1–3). Illus. 2005, Albert Whitman $16.99 (978-0-8075-2450-3). 32pp. In rhyming text that follows the pattern of "The 12 Days of Christmas," this counting picture book celebrates various aspects of the winter season. (Rev: BL 1/1–15/06; SLJ 1/06)

4382 Raczka, Bob. *Snowy, Blowy Winter* (PS–1). Illus. by Judy Stead. 2008, Albert Whitman $16.99 (978-0-8075-7526-0). 32pp. Simple spare rhymes and color cartoon illustrations feature multicultural families enjoying all the best of the season. (Rev: BLO 10/7/08; SLJ 12/08)

4383 Raschka, Chris. *Little Black Crow* (K–2). Illus. by author. 2010, Atheneum $16.99 (978-0-689-84601-4). 40pp. A little boy speculates about the life of a black crow, wondering whether it questions the universe as he does. e (Rev: BL 6/10; HB 7–8/10; SLJ 7/1/10*)

4384 Ravishankar, Anushka. *Tiger on a Tree* (PS–2). Illus. by Pulak Biswas. 2004, Farrar $15.00 (978-0-374-37555-3). In this impressively illustrated chanting tale from India, villagers capture a tiger and then wonder what they should do with it — in the end, they let it go. (Rev: HB 5/04; SLJ 3/04)

4385 Rawlinson, Julia. *Fletcher and the Springtime Blossoms* (PS–2). Illus. by Tiphanie Beeke. 2009, Greenwillow $17.99 (978-0-06-168855-3). 32pp. Fletcher, a little fox, believes winter has returned when he mistakes blossoms for snowflakes. (Rev: BL 12/1/08; SLJ 4/09)

4386 Reid, Barbara. *Picture a Tree* (PS–1). Illus. by author. 2013, Whitman $16.99 (978-080756526-1). 32pp. A celebration of trees and the varied benefits and opportunities they offer — ranging from sun umbrellas to drawings on the sky. USBBY Outstanding International Book. (Rev: BL 2/15/13*; HB 5-6/13; SLJ 4/13)

4387 Root, Phyllis. *If You Want to See a Caribou* (PS–2). Illus. by Jim Meyer. 2004, Houghton $16.00 (978-0-618-39314-5). 32pp. Set on a wooded island in Lake Superior, this gentle book celebrates the caribou in poetry and woodblock images. (Rev: BL 4/15/04; SLJ 4/04)

4388 Rose, Deborah Lee. *All of the Seasons of the Year* (PS–1). Illus. by Kay Chorao. 2010, Abrams $16.95 (978-081098395-3). 32pp. Celebrates a mother cat's love for her child throughout the year. (Rev: BL 12/1/10; SLJ 10/1/10)

4389 Rosenberry, Vera. *Who Is in the Garden?* (PS–2). Illus. 2001, Holiday House $16.95 (978-0-8234-1529-8). 32pp. A little boy tours a garden and finds such wonders as wrens in a birch tree, a snake in a grape vine, and a turtle under the rhubarb. (Rev: BL 3/1/01; HBG 10/01) [577.5]

4390 Rotner, Shelley. *Senses at the Seashore* (PS–1). Illus. 2006, Millbrook LB $22.60 (978-0-7613-2897-1). This colorful book shows how children can use their five senses to experience all the joys of a day at the beach. (Rev: BL 4/15/06; SLJ 10/06)

4391 Ruiz-Flores, Lupe. *Alicia's Fruity Drinks / Las aguas frescas de Alicia* (K–3). Illus. by Laura Lacámara. 2012, Arte Publico paper $17.99 (978-15588570-5-6). 32pp. Latina Alicia rediscovers her family's tradition of making juice-based sodas in this bilingual story that emphasizes the dangers of diabetes. (Rev: BLO 8/12; LMC 3–4/13; SLJ 9/12)

4392 Ryan, Pam Muñoz. *Hello Ocean* (PS–2). Illus. by Mark Astrella. 2001, Charlesbridge $16.95 (978-0-88106-987-7); paper $6.95 (978-0-88106-988-4). A young girl who is visiting an ocean beach describes how this experience affects her senses. (Rev: BL 3/1/01*; HBG 10/01)

4393 Sabuda, Robert. *Winter's Tale* (K–3). Illus. Series: Classic Collectible Pop-Up. 2005, Simon & Schuster $26.95 (978-0-689-85363-0). 12pp. Spectacular pop-ups celebrate the winter landscape and wildlife. (Rev: BL 9/1/05; SLJ 9/05)

4394 St. Pierre, Stephanie. *What the Sea Saw* (PS–3). Illus. by Beverly Doyle. 2006, Peachtree $16.95 (978-1-56145-359-7). Beautiful paintings accompany simple rhyming text about all there is to see at the seaside. (Rev: SLJ 6/06)

4395 Salas, Laura Purdie. *A Leaf Can Be . . .* (PS–2). Illus. by Violeta Dabija. 2012, Millbrook $17.95 (978-0-7613-6203-6). 32pp. Poetic text communicates the many things leaves can be, including something that captures energy, cleans the air, and is pleasing to look at. **e** (Rev: BL 3/15/12; LMC 10/12; SLJ 3/1/12)

4396 Schaefer, Lola M. *An Island Grows* (PS–2). Illus. by Cathie Felstead. 2006, Greenwillow $16.99 (978-0-06-623930-9). 40pp. The birth of an island (through a volcanic eruption) and its development and habitation by plants, animals, and people are told in simple rhyme; good both for fiction browsers and for science classes. (Rev: BL 7/06; SLJ 7/06)

4397 Schwartz, Amy. *A Beautiful Girl* (PS). 2006, Roaring Brook $16.95 (978-1-59643-165-2). 32pp. On her way to the market Jenna meets four friendly animals, each of which remarks on one of her physical characteristics. (Rev: BL 8/06; SLJ 8/06)

4398 Seuss, Dr. *The Lorax* (K–3). Illus. by author. 1971, Random LB $16.99 (978-0-394-92337-6). 64pp. The Lorax, a little brown creature, has tried in vain to ward off pollution and ecological blight, but Onceler, who wanted the trees for his business, would not heed the warning.

4399 Shelby, Anne. *The Man Who Lived in a Hollow Tree* (K–3). Illus. by Cor Hazelaar. 2009, Atheneum $17.99 (978-0-689-86169-7). 40pp. A carpenter plants two trees for every tree he cuts down. (Rev: BCCB 4/09; BL 6/1–15/09; LMC 8/09; SLJ 2/09)

4400 Sidjanski, Brigitte. *The River* (PS–2). Illus. by Bernadette Watts. 2008, Penguin $16.99 (978-0-698-40077-1). A river's journey to the sea is recorded through the experiences of five little pine cones that fall into a passing brook and join the current. (Rev: BL 2/15/08; LMC 3/08; SLJ 4/08)

4401 Siminovich, Lorena. *I Like Bugs* (PS). Illus. by author. 2010, Candlewick $6.99 (978-076364802-2). 10pp. This sturdy look-and-touch board book uses a variety of textured art effects to present close-up, eye-catching illustrations of familiar insects. (Rev: BL 5/1/10)

4402 Stringer, Lauren. *Winter Is the Warmest Season* (PS–2). Illus. 2006, Harcourt $16.00 (978-0-15-204967-6). 40pp. A young boy lists the many reasons he feels that winter — not summer — is the warmest season of the year. (Rev: BL 9/1/06; HBG 4/07; SLJ 11/06)

4403 Swanson, Susan Marie. *To Be Like the Sun* (PS–1). Illus. by Margaret Chodos-Irvine. 2008, Harcourt $16.00 (978-0-15-205796-1). A young girl plants a sunflower seed and watches it grow into a tall golden bloom. (Rev: BL 4/15/08; LMC 11/08; SLJ 4/08)

4404 Taylor, Joanne. *Full Moon Rising* (1–3). Illus. by Susan Tooke. 2002, Tundra $16.95 (978-0-88776-548-3). An attractive, poetic introduction to the full moons of the year. (Rev: HBG 3/03; SLJ 12/02) [523.3]

4405 Taylor, Theodore. *Hello, Arctic!* (PS–2). Illus. by Margaret Chodos-Irvine. 2002, Harcourt $16.00 (978-0-15-201577-0). 40pp. A simple text and dramatic illustrations show the changing Arctic seasons and the animals and plants found there. (Rev: BL 10/1/02; HBG 3/03; SLJ 11/02)

4406 Udry, Janice May. *A Tree Is Nice* (PS). Illus. by Marc Simont. 1957, HarperCollins LB $18.89 (978-0-06-026156-6); paper $6.99 (978-0-06-443147-7). 32pp. The many delights to be had in, with, or under a tree: picking apples, raking leaves, swinging, or just sitting in the shade. Caldecott Medal winner, 1957.

4407 Walker, Rob D. *Once Upon a Cloud* (K–3). Illus. by Matt Mahurin. 2005, Scholastic $16.95 (978-0-439-68879-6). 40pp. The author explores all the possibilities of what clouds might be, from cotton candy to puffs of pipe smoke, in lighthearted rhyme with imaginative illustrations. (Rev: BL 3/1/05; SLJ 3/05)

4408 Wallace, Nancy Elizabeth. *Leaves! Leaves! Leaves!* (PS–2). Illus. by author. 2003, Marshall Cavendish $16.95 (978-0-7614-5140-2). Buddy Bear and his mother observe the dramatic changes in leaves and trees over the course of the seasons. (Rev: HBG 4/04; SLJ 9/03)

4409 Waring, Geoff. *Oscar and the Frog: A Book About Growing* (PS–2). Illus. by author. Series: Start with Science. 2007, Candlewick $11.99 (978-0-7636-3558-9). 32pp. Oscar, a kitten, asks questions about growth and development that are answered by a knowledgeable frog. (Rev: BL 12/15/07; SLJ 2/08)

4410 Wellington, Monica. *Zinnia's Flower Garden* (K–2). Illus. by author. 2005, Dutton $14.99 (978-0-525-47368-8). An informative tour of gardens and gardening, in the company of Zinnia and her animal friends. (Rev: SLJ 2/05)

4411 Wheeler, Eliza. *Miss Maple's Seeds* (PS–1). Illus. by author. 2013, Penguin $16.99 (978-0-399-25792-6). 32pp. Tiny Miss Maple nurtures "orphan seeds" through the winter, reading them stories and taking them on field trips, before releasing them in spring to root and grow. (Rev: BLO 6/13; SLJ 6/13)

4412 Williams, Karen Lynn. *A Beach Tail* (PS–2). Illus. by Floyd Cooper. 2010, Boyds Mills $17.95 (978-1-59078-712-0). 32pp. Eager to explore the beach but also to obey his father's order not to stray, a little boy makes a very very long tail for the lion he has drawn in the sand. (Rev: BL 4/15/10; LMC 5–6/10; SLJ 3/1/10*)

4413 Yorinks, Arthur. *Happy Bees!* (PS–1). Illus. by Carey Armstrong-Ellis. 2005, Abrams $15.95 (978-0-8109-5866-1). A buzzing group of happy bees enjoy themselves while causing havoc among humans and animals. (Rev: SLJ 4/05)

OTHER TIMES, OTHER PLACES

4414 Addy, Sharon Hart. *Lucky Jake* (PS–2). Illus. by Wade Zahares. 2007, Houghton $17.00 (978-0-618-47286-4). Jake's dad is prospecting for gold, barely scratching out a living, but Jake knows how to take the little they have and use it to make them a better life. (Rev: BL 4/15/07)

4415 Adler, David A. *The Babe and I* (PS–2). Illus. by Terry Widener. 1999, Harcourt $16.00 (978-0-15-201378-3). 32pp. During the Great Depression, the young narrator sells newspapers on the street, and one day Babe Ruth buys a paper from him. (Rev: BCCB 6/99; BL 3/15/99*; HB 3/99; HBG 10/99; SLJ 5/99)

4416 Alakija, Polly. *Catch That Goat!* (PS–2). Illus. by author. 2002, Barefoot Books $16.99 (978-1-84148-908-7). Young Ayoka's goat runs amok in the market in this beautifully illustrated story set in Nigeria. (Rev: HBG 3/03; SLJ 12/02)

4417 Alalou, Elizabeth, and Ali Alalou. *The Butter Man* (K–3). Illus. by Julie Klear Essakalli. 2008, Charlesbridge $14.95 (978-1-58089-127-1). As her father cooks couscous in his special pot, he tells Nora about his childhood in Morocco and the famine that hit the Atlas mountains. (Rev: BCCB 4/08; BL 1/1–15/08; HB 5/08; LMC 10/08; SLJ 2/08)

4418 Alda, Arlene. *Morning Glory Monday* (PS–2). Illus. by Maryann Kovalski. 2003, Tundra $17.95 (978-0-88776-620-6). To lift the spirits of her mother, who is homesick for Italy, a young girl plants morning glory seeds in the window boxes of her family's early-20th-century New York City tenement, and the vines spread to brighten the whole community. (Rev: BL 1/1–15/04; HBG 4/04; SLJ 11/03)

4419 Aliki. *Marianthe's Story: Painted Words / Spoken Memories* (K–3). Illus. by author. 1998, Greenwillow LB $17.89 (978-0-688-15662-6). In this book combining two stories, the first tells how Mari, a young immigrant girl, expresses herself in her paintings; in the second, Mari relates life in her native land. (Rev: BCCB 1/99; HB 9/98; HBG 3/99; SLJ 10/98)

4420 Anaya, Rudolfo. *The First Tortilla: A Bilingual Story* (2–4). Trans. by Enrique R. Lamadrid into Spanish. Illus. by Amy Córdova. 2007, Univ. of New Mexico $16.95 (978-0-8263-4214-0). A traditional Mexican story about a town saved from starvation by the gift of corn from a mountain spirit. In both English and Spanish. (Rev: SLJ 7/07)

4421 Anholt, Laurence. *Camille and the Sunflowers: A Story About Vincent van Gogh* (PS–3). Illus. 1994, Barron's $14.95 (978-0-8120-6409-4). Young Camille befriends the artist van Gogh when he comes to paint in his village in the Netherlands. (Rev: BL 12/1/94; SLJ 2/95)

4422 Anholt, Laurence. *The Magical Garden of Claude Monet* (PS–3). Illus. 2003, Barron's $14.95 (978-0-7641-5574-1). Julie and her dog spend a day with Impressionist painter Claude Monet in this fictionalized look at the artist's later work, with illustrations echoing Monet's style. (Rev: BL 2/15/04; HBG 4/04; SLJ 5/04)

4423 Applegate, Katherine. *The Buffalo Storm* (PS–2). Illus. by Jan Ormerod. 2007, Clarion $16.00 (978-0-618-53597-2). 32pp. As her family travels on a wagon train to a new home in Oregon, Hallie misses her grandmother, whose past words of encouragement not only help Hallie face her fear of storms but also experience the adventures of the journey west. (Rev: BL 12/1/07; HB 1/08; LMC 11/07; SLJ 10/07)

4424 Armand, Glenda. *Love Twelve Miles Long* (2–5). Illus. by Colin Bootman. 2011, Lee & Low $17.95 (978-1-60060-245-0). 32pp. In 1820s Maryland Frederick Douglass's mother describes her thoughts as she walks 12 miles through the night to see her son on a different plantation. (Rev: BL 12/1/11; LMC 5–6/12; SLJ 11/1/11)

4425 Arnold, Marsha Diane. *The Pumpkin Runner* (K–3). Illus. by Brad Sneed. 1998, Dial $16.99 (978-0-8037-2124-1). Based on a true story, this picture book tells of a 61-year-old Australian farmer who eats pumpkins for energy and wins a footrace against younger, better-trained opponents. (Rev: BCCB 11/98; BL 11/1/98; HBG 3/99; SLJ 12/98)

4426 Arrigan, Mary. *Mario's Angels: A Story About the Artist Giotto* (K–3). Illus. by Gillian McClure. 2006, Frances Lincoln $15.95 (978-1-84507-404-3). 32pp. In this appealing picture-book blend of fact and fiction, young Mario suggests that Italian Renaissance artist Giotto include some angels in the fresco that he's painting and offers to pose. (Rev: BL 11/1/06; SLJ 12/06)

4427 Asare, Meshack. *Sosu's Call* (1–4). Illus. by author. 2002, Kane $15.95 (978-1-929132-21-8). 37pp. Sosu, an African boy who is rejected by the villagers because he cannot walk, saves them from a terrible storm with the help of his dog. (Rev: BCCB 5/02; HBG 10/02; SLJ 6/02)

4428 Ashman, Linda. *Come to the Castle!* (1–3). Illus. by S. D. Schindler. 2009, Roaring Brook $16.95 (978-1-59643-155-3). 40pp. A story about the Earl of Daftwood throwing a feast and tournament serves as the framework for a rhyming overview of life in a medieval castle with detailed illustrations. (Rev: BCCB 5/09; BL 3/15/09; HB 5/09; LMC 8/09; SLJ 5/09)

4429 Aston, Dianna Hutts. *Dream Something Big: The Story of the Watts Towers* (K–4). Illus. by Susan L. Roth. 2011, Dial $16.99 (978-0-8037-3245-2). 40pp. Aston uses the voice of a young girl to tell the story of Simon Rodia's painstaking creation of the works of art now known as Los Angeles' Watts Towers. Lexile AD830 (Rev: BL 8/11; LMC 11–12/11; SLJ 10/1/11)

4430 Atkins, Jeannine. *Aani and the Tree Huggers* (2–5). Illus. by Venantius J. Pinto. 1995, Lee & Low $15.95 (978-1-880000-24-3). In this tale set in India, a village woman tries to save a tree from big-city developers by throwing her arms around it. (Rev: SLJ 12/95)

4431 Baasansuren, Bolormaa, and Helen Mixter. *My Little Round House* (K–4). Illus. by Bolormaa Baasansuren. 2009, Groundwood $18.95 (978-0-88899-934-4). A Mongolian child called Jilu describes the first year of his life and the activities of his nomad family. (Rev: BL 5/1/09; SLJ 4/09)

4432 Balit, Christina. *Escape from Pompeii* (1–4). Illus. by author. 2003, Holt $17.95 (978-0-8050-7324-9). This fictionalized account of the fall of the Italian city of Pompeii tells of a young boy and girl who manage to flee to the sea before the eruption of Mount Vesuvius totally destroys the city. (Rev: HBG 4/04; SLJ 11/03)

4433 Bandy, Michael S., and Eric Stein. *White Water* (K–3). Illus. by Shadra Strickland. 2011, Candlewick $16.99 (978-0-7636-3678-4). 40pp. A young black boy growing up in the segregated South sneaks into town to try drinking the water from the "whites only" fountain, only to discover it's no different from the fountain for blacks; based on the author's own experience. (Rev: BL 10/15/11; LMC 3–4/12*; SLJ 9/1/11)

4434 Bania, Michael. *Kumak's House: A Tale of the Far North* (PS–2). Illus. 2002, Alaska Northwest $15.95 (978-0-88240-540-7); paper $8.95 (978-0-88240-541-4). In this story packed with details about Arctic life, Kumak finds his house really feels quite large when all the animals he has taken in finally leave. (Rev: BL 9/1/02; HBG 10/02; SLJ 1/03)

4435 Bania, Michael. *Kumak's River: A Tall Tale from the Far North* (PS–3). 2012, Alaska Northwest $16.99 (978-0-88240-886-6); paper $9.99 (978-0-88240-887-3). 32pp. Kumak and his family find themselves at the mercy of the river when the cracking ice causes the river to flood, but they must work together with the water, not against it, to keep their home safe. (Rev: SLJ 1/13)

4436 Barren, T. A. *High as a Hawk: A Brave Girl's Historic Climb* (1–4). Illus. by Ted Lewin. 2004, Penguin $17.99 (978-0-399-23704-1). In 1905, an 8-year-old girl climbs more than 14,000 feet to the top of Longs Peak in Colorado; panoramic illustrations enhance this story based on truth. (Rev: BL 3/1/04; SLJ 5/04)

4437 Barron, T. A. *The Day the Stones Walked: A Tale of Easter Island* (2–4). Illus. by William Low. 2007, Philomel $16.99 (978-0-399-24263-2). A story about the mysterious Easter Island sculptures coming to the aid of a little boy whose father helped to carve them. (Rev: SLJ 7/07)

4438 Barron, T. A. *Ghost Hands* (K–3). Illus. by William Low. 2011, Philomel $18.99 (978-0-399-25083-5). 40pp. Auki, a young Patagonian hunter, earns a spot in the Cave of the Hands in this novel set thousands of years ago; a foreword provides facts about the cave paintings there. Lexile 510L (Rev: BL 6/1/11; SLJ 8/1/11)

4439 Bartone, Elisa. *Peppe the Lamplighter* (2–4). Illus. by Ted Lewin. 1993, Morrow paper $6.99 (978-0-688-15469-1). The story of an immigrant Italian boy who is a lamplighter in turn-of-the-century New York City. (Rev: BCCB 5/93; BL 4/15/93; SLJ 7/93)

4440 Base, Graeme. *The Jewel Fish of Karnak* (K–3). Illus. by author. 2011, Abrams $19.95 (978-1-4197-0086-6). 40pp. In ancient Egypt two thieves are dispatched by the Cat Pharaoh to retrieve the stolen Jewel Fish of Karnak in this quest story that requires readers to solve puzzles. (Rev: BL 10/15/11; LMC 1–2/12; SLJ 10/1/11)

4441 Bemelmans, Ludwig, and John Bemelmans Marciano. *Madeline in America and Other Holiday Tales* (PS–3). Illus. 1999, Scholastic $19.95 (978-0-590-03910-9). This Madeline tale was completed by the author's grandson. The book also contains a few other short stories, including one about Christmas. (Rev: BL 11/15/99; HBG 10/00; SLJ 2/00)

225

4442 Bildner, Phil. *The Hallelujah Flight* (K–3). Illus. by John Holyfield. 2010, Putnam $16.99 (978-0-399-24789-7). 32pp. This inspiring story of the first African American pilot to fly across the United States is told by Thomas Allen, his young copilot. Lexile AD760L (Rev: BL 2/1/10; LMC 3–4/10; SLJ 2/1/10*)

4443 Bildner, Phil. *Shoeless Joe and Black Betsy* (2–4). Illus. by C. F. Payne. 2002, Simon & Schuster $17.00 (978-0-689-82913-0). 40pp. Mixed-media illustrations complement this tale about Shoeless Joe Jackson and Ol' Charlie, the man who fashioned the bat known as Black Betsy. (Rev: BL 2/15/02; HBG 10/02; SLJ 4/02)

4444 Bildner, Phil. *The Shot Heard 'Round the World* (2–4). Illus. by C. F. Payne. 2005, Simon & Schuster $16.95 (978-0-689-86273-1). The story of the fateful (for baseball fans) summer of 1951, when the Giants beat the Brooklyn Dodgers in a playoff, accompanied by nostalgic artwork. (Rev: BL 3/1/05; SLJ 5/05) [796.357]

4445 Birtha, Becky. *Grandmama's Pride* (K–3). Illus. by Colin Bootman. 2005, Albert Whitman $16.95 (978-0-8075-3028-3). 32pp. In 1956, African American Sarah Marie, with her sister and grandmother, travels by bus to the South and learns about segregation. (Rev: BL 11/1/05; SLJ 11/05)

4446 Birtha, Becky. *Lucky Beans* (1–3). Illus. by Nicole Tadgell. 2010, Whitman $16.99 (978-0-8075-4782-3). 32pp. Young African American Marshall uses math to estimate how many beans there are in a huge jar and win a brand new sewing machine for his mother in this story set in the Great Depression. Lexile 600L (Rev: BL 2/1/10; HB 5–6/10; LMC 5–6/10; SLJ 2/1/10)

4447 Booth, David. *The Dust Bowl* (K–4). Illus. by Karen Reczuch. 1997, Kids Can $16.95 (978-1-55074-295-4). A story about a poor Canadian farm family living in a Western dust bowl during the 1930s. (Rev: BL 9/1/97; SLJ 12/97)

4448 Bouchard, David. *Buddha in the Garden* (4–6). Illus. by Zhong-Yang Huang. 2001, Raincoast $14.95 (978-1-55192-452-6). 32pp. An abandoned baby raised in a monastery learns to tend the garden in this quiet introduction to Buddhism illustrated with evocative water colors. (Rev: BL 1/1–15/02; SLJ 12/01)

4449 Bradby, Marie. *Momma, Where Are You From?* (PS–3). Illus. by Chris K. Soentpiet. 2000, Orchard LB $17.99 (978-0-531-33105-7). 32pp. At her daughter's request, an African American woman describes her life in the rural South during segregation. (Rev: BCCB 3/00; BL 2/15/00; HBG 10/00; SLJ 4/00)

4450 Bradby, Marie. *More Than Anything Else* (K–3). Illus. by Chris K. Soentpiet. 1996, Orchard LB $16.99 (978-0-531-08764-0). 32pp. A fictionalized account of the childhood of Booker T. Washington, told in a picture book format. (Rev: BL 7/95; SLJ 11/95*)

4451 Breen, Steve. *Violet the Pilot* (1–3). Illus. by author. 2008, Dial $16.99 (978-0-8037-3125-7). 32pp. Violet, a mechanical wizard almost since birth, at the age of 8 enters an air show with a plane she's built herself but stops in mid-competition to save Boy Scouts in trouble. (Rev: BL 1/1–15/08; SLJ 2/08)

4452 Brett, Jan. *Daisy Comes Home* (K–3). Illus. 2002, Penguin $16.99 (978-0-399-23618-1). Detailed artwork complements this tale, set in China, of a put-upon chicken named Daisy who is washed down the river, and the resolute young owner who rescues her. (Rev: BCCB 3/02; BL 3/15/02*; HBG 10/02; SLJ 3/02)

4453 Bridges, Shirin Yim. *Ruby's Wish* (K–2). Illus. by Sophie Blackall. 2002, Chronicle $15.95 (978-0-8118-3490-2). 32pp. Ruby is an intelligent girl from a wealthy Chinese family who aspires to go to university at a time when few girls were educated, and to her surprise gets her wish. (Rev: BCCB 10/02; BL 11/15/02; HBG 3/03; SLJ 2/03)

4454 Bridges, Shirin Yim. *The Umbrella Queen* (K–3). Illus. by Taeeun Yoo. 2008, Greenwillow $16.99 (978-0-06-075040-4). In a village in Thailand Noot is now old enough to contribute to her family's umbrella business, but finds the traditional flower and butterfly designs boring and her own elephant paintings finally gain recognition — from the king himself! (Rev: BL 7/08; SLJ 6/08)

4455 Broach, Elise. *Gumption!* (PS–K). Illus. by Richard Egielski. 2010, Atheneum $16.99 (978-1-4169-1628-4). 40pp. Young Peter and his oblivious Uncle Nigel have a thrilling safari in Africa in this clever and funny book in which the illustrations play a key role. (Rev: BL 2/1/10; LMC 5–6/10; SLJ 2/1/10)

4456 Brown, Monica. *Waiting for the Biblioburro* (K–2). Illus. by John Parra. 2011, Tricycle $16.99 (978-1-58246-353-7); LB $19.99 (978-1-58246-398-8). 32pp. A young Colombian girl is inspired to write by the traveling librarian who brings books to her isolated mountain village on his burros Alfa and Beto. Lexile AD880L (Rev: BLO 8/11; HB 7–8/11; SLJ 6/11)

4457 Brown, Ruth. *Gracie the Lighthouse Cat* (K–3). Illus. by author. 2011, Andersen $16.95 (978-0-7613-7454-1). 32pp. Gracie must save her kitten during a terrible storm while the lighthouse keeper's daughter is rescuing shipwrecked passengers; based on real events in 1838, this story uses text for the animals and records the human story mainly in the art. ℮ Lexile AD640L (Rev: BL 2/15/11; SLJ 2/1/11)

4458 Browne, Vee. *The Stone Cutter and the Navajo Maiden: Tsé Yitsidí dóó Ch'ikééh Bitsédaashjéé'* (K–3). Trans. from Navajo by Lorraine Begay Manavi. Illus. by Johnson Yazzie. 2008, Salina Bookshelf $17.95 (978-1-893354-92-0). This tale of a motherless girl's quest to find someone who can repair her grinding stone is presented in both English and Navajo. (Rev: SLJ 9/08)

4459 Browning, Diane. *Signed, Abiah Rose* (1–3). Illus. by author. 2010, Tricycle $15.99 (978-1-58246-311-7). 32pp. In 18th-century America young Abiah Rose, a talented artist, is told not to sign her paintings because she is not a man, and uses a small rose instead. (Rev: BL 2/15/10*; SLJ 4/1/10)

4460 Bryant, Jen. *Call Me Marianne* (K–3). Illus. by David A. Johnson. 2006, Eerdmans $16.00 (978-0-8028-

5242-7). 32pp. In 1940s Brooklyn, young Jonathan encounters poet Marianne Moore at the zoo and the two discuss poetry and the work of poets; a biography of Moore is appended. (Rev: BL 2/15/06; SLJ 3/06)

4461 Buchmann, Stephen, and Diana Cohn. *The Bee Tree* (2–6). Illus. by Paul Mirocha. 2007, Cinco Puntos $17.95 (978-0-938317-98-2). Nizam is thrilled to be part of the annual honey hunt in this story based on traditional practices in Malaysia. Facts on honey collection in Malaysia follow the story. (Rev: LMC 11/07; SLJ 7/07)

4462 Bunting, Eve. *Gleam and Glow* (1–4). Illus. by Peter Sylvada. 2001, Harcourt $16.00 (978-0-15-202596-0). 32pp. A Bosnian mother and children flee their home leaving two precious golden fish in the pond and later return from a refugee camp to find their home ruined but the pond full of golden fish. (Rev: BCCB 12/01; BL 12/15/01; HBG 3/02; SLJ 9/01)

4463 Bunting, Eve. *I Have an Olive Tree* (PS–3). Illus. by Karen Barbour. 1999, HarperCollins LB $15.89 (978-0-06-027574-7). Sophia, a Greek American girl, and her mother go to Greece to revisit their family home and the olive tree that Sophia's grandfather planted before he died. (Rev: BCCB 5/99; BL 5/15/99; HB 7/99; HBG 10/99; SLJ 5/99)

4464 Bunting, Eve. *Pop's Bridge* (K–3). Illus. by C. F. Payne. 2006, Harcourt $17.00 (978-0-15-204773-3). 32pp. Robert and Charlie are proud of their fathers, who are working on the construction of San Francisco's Golden Gate Bridge, but Robert secretly thinks his father's role as a "skywalker" is more important. (Rev: BL 4/15/06; SLJ 6/06)

4465 Bunting, Eve. *So Far from the Sea* (K–4). Illus. by Chris K. Soentpiet. 1998, Clarion $16.00 (978-0-395-72095-0). 32pp. A young Japanese-American girl and her family visit the former internment camp of Manzanar and recall the family's hardships and experiences during their imprisonment from 1942 to the end of World War II. (Rev: BCCB 7–8/98; BL 5/1/98; HB 5/98; HBG 10/98; SLJ 6/98)

4466 Bynum, Eboni, and Roland Jackson. *Jamari's Drum* (K–4). 2004, Groundwood $16.95 (978-0-88899-531-5). Jamari has always loved the sound of the great village drum, but when he takes over its drumming he neglects his duty and disaster nearly ensues. (Rev: HB 1/05; SLJ 11/04)

4467 Campbell, Bebe Moore. *Stompin' at the Savoy* (2–4). Illus. by Richard Yarde. 2006, Philomel $16.99 (978-0-399-24197-0). 40pp. Young Mindy reconsiders her decision to skip an upcoming jazz dance recital after she is magically transported to 1920s Harlem and a night at the Savoy Ballroom. (Rev: BL 8/06; SLJ 3/07)

4468 Campbell, Nicola I. *Shin-chi's Canoe* (3–5). Illus. by Kim LaFave. 2008, Groundwood $18.95 (978-0-88899-857-6). 40pp. A Native American brother and sister are forced into a church boarding school and forbidden to speak to each other. (Rev: BLO 12/30/08; SLJ 3/09)

4469 Capatti, Bérénice. *Klimt and His Cat* (1–3). Illus. by Octavia Monaco. 2005, Eerdmans $18.00 (978-0-8028-5282-3). 40pp. Klimt's cat, Katze, describes his interesting life with the artist in this book full of beautiful illustrations. (Rev: BL 2/1/05)

4470 Carbone, Elisa. *Night Running: How James Escaped with the Help of His Faithful Dog* (2–4). Illus. by E. B. Lewis. 2008, Knopf $16.99 (978-0-375-82247-6). 32pp. Based on fact, this is the remarkable story of a slave boy and his dog who together succeed in escaping to freedom. (Rev: BL 2/1/08; HB 3/08; LMC 1/08; SLJ 1/08)

4471 Casanova, Mary. *The Day Dirk Yeller Came to Town* (PS–2). Illus. by Ard Hoyt. 2011, Farrar $16.99 (978-0-374-31742-3). 40pp. Books prove to be a town's salvation when they soothe the trigger-happy inclinations of an outlaw named Dirk Yeller in this adventure set in the Wild West. (Rev: BL 6/1/11; LMC 10/11; SLJ 7/11)

4472 Castaldo, Nancy F. *Pizza for the Queen* (PS–2). Illus. by Melisande Potter. 2005, Holiday $16.95 (978-0-8234-1865-7). 32pp. This captivating, fact-based tale tells how a Neapolitan pizza maker came up with the recipe for Pizza Margherita — a pie fit for a queen. (Rev: BL 11/15/05; SLJ 9/05)

4473 Castaneda, Omar S. *Abuela's Weave* (K–3). Illus. by Enrique O. Sánchez. 1993, Lee & Low $15.95 (978-1-880000-00-7). 32pp. In Guatemala, a young girl and her grandmother take their handicrafts to sell at a fiesta. (Rev: BL 8/93; SLJ 7/93)

4474 Celenza, Anna Harwell. *Bach's Goldberg Variations* (K–3). Illus. by JoAnn E. Kitchel. 2005, Charlesbridge $19.95 (978-1-57091-510-9). 32pp. This story of the Bach variations that helped a young man win a job as harpsichordist to a count includes a CD of the music. (Rev: BL 5/15/05)

4475 Celenza, Anna Harwell. *The Farewell Symphony* (2–4). Illus. by JoAnn E. Kitchel. 2000, Charlesbridge LB $19.95 (978-1-57091-406-5). A fictional version of the story behind Haydn's "Farewell Symphony" and the effect it had on Prince Nicholas, the composer's sponsor. (Rev: HBG 3/01; SLJ 7/00)

4476 Celenza, Anna Harwell. *The Heroic Symphony* (K–4). Illus. by JoAnn E. Kitchel. 2004, Charlesbridge $19.95 (978-1-57091-509-3). Watercolor illustrations enliven this detailed story of Beethoven's "Eroica" symphony and how he struggled to complete it despite his increasing deafness. (Rev: SLJ 3/04)

4477 Chaconas, Dori. *Pennies in a Jar* (K–2). Illus. by Ted Lewin. 2007, Peachtree $16.95 (978-1-56145-422-8). 32pp. A boy whose father has left to fight in World War II wrestles with his fear of horses as he looks for a gift to send his father. (Rev: BL 10/1/07; SLJ 10/07)

4478 Chall, Marsha Wilson. *Prairie Train* (K–3). Illus. by John Thompson. 2003, HarperCollins LB $16.89 (978-0-688-13434-1). A young girl details her first train trip — a visit to Grandma in St. Paul, Minnesota — and the passing scenery of the early 20th century. (Rev: HBG 4/04; LMC 3/04; SLJ 12/03)

4479 Chamberlin, Mary, and Rich Chamberlin. *Mama Panya's Pancakes: A Village Tale from Kenya* (K–3). Illus. by Julia Cairns. 2005, Barefoot Books $16.99 (978-1-84148-139-5). Mama Panya is worried she won't have enough pancakes for all the people her son Adika has invited, but all the guests bring their own contributions and there is plenty to go round in this story set in Kenya. (Rev: BL 3/1/04; SLJ 5/05)

4480 Chapman, Nancy Kapp. *Tripper's Travels: An International Scrapbook* (K–3). Illus. by Lee Chapman. 2005, Marshall Cavendish $16.95 (978-0-7614-5240-9). Tripper the dog's round-the-world travels are preserved in a scrapbook with maps and factual information. (Rev: SLJ 12/05)

4481 Charles, Veronika M. *The Birdman* (K–3). Illus. by Annouchka Gravel Galouchko. 2006, Tundra $17.95 (978-0-88776-740-1). Deeply shaken by the unexpected death of his wife and children, Nobi the tailor eases his grief by buying caged birds and setting them free; set in Calcutta, this is based on a true story. (Rev: BL 10/1/06; SLJ 12/06)

4482 Chen, Chih-Yuan. *On My Way to Buy Eggs* (PS). Illus. by author. 2003, Kane $15.95 (978-1-929132-49-2). In this import from Taiwan, a little girl on her way to buy eggs finds delights and adventure all around her. (Rev: HBG 4/04; SLJ 10/03)

4483 Cheripko, Jan. *Brother Bartholomew and the Apple Grove* (1–3). Illus. by Kestutis Kasparavicius. 2004, Boyds Mills $15.95 (978-1-59078-096-1). Brother Stephen believes he can do a better job of looking after the orchard than old Brother Bartholomew, but he soon learns the dangers of pride. (Rev: BL 3/1/04; SLJ 4/04)

4484 Choi, Yangsook. *Peach Heaven* (K–2). Illus. 2005, Farrar $16.00 (978-0-374-35761-0). 32pp. A Korean girl and her grandmother rejoice when peaches from a mountaintop orchard rain down on their house during a storm. (Rev: BL 3/15/05)

4485 Cohen, Deborah Bodin. *Nachshon, Who Was Afraid to Swim: A Passover Story* (K–3). Illus. by Jago. 2009, Lerner $17.95 (978-0-8225-8764-4); paper $8.95 (978-0-8225-8765-1). This picture book takes a biblical reference and expands it into a character study of a brave young boy, Nachson, who faces his fear of water by being the first to take the plunge into the sea during the Israelite's exodus from Egypt. (Rev: BLO 2/9/09; SLJ 3/09)

4486 Cohn, Diana. *Dream Carver* (3–6). Illus. by Amy Córdova. 2002, Chronicle $15.95 (978-0-8118-1244-3). 32pp. A simple story based on the career of the artist Manuel Jimenez, about a young sculptor who carves small wooden animals but dreams of creating big, colorful animals. (Rev: BCCB 10/02; BL 6/1–15/02; HBG 10/02; SLJ 7/02)

4487 Collins, Suzanne. *Year of the Jungle* (K–3). Illus. by James Proimos. 2013, Scholastic $17.99 (978-054542516-2). 40pp. Collins, author of The Hunger Games trilogy, draws from her own experiences in this story about war and the deployment of a father in the Vietnam conflict. ℮ Lexile AD450 (Rev: BL 9/1/13*; HB 1–2/14; LMC 3–4/14; SLJ 8/13)

4488 Colon, Edie. *Good-bye, Havana! Hola, New York!* (1–3). Illus. by Raúl Colón. 2011, Simon & Schuster $16.99 (978-1-4424-0674-2). 32pp. Chronicles 6-year-old Gabriella's first year in New York after her parents flee Castro's Cuba. (Rev: BL 9/1/11; SLJ 9/1/11)

4489 Comora, Madeleine. *Rembrandt and Titus: Artist and Son* (4–6). Illus. by Thomas Locker. 2005, Fulcrum $17.95 (978-1-55591-490-5). 32pp. Titus, son of Dutch artist Rembrandt, describes his father's life and vision; the full-page illustrations are based on Rembrandt's paintings or etchings. (Rev: BL 9/1/05; SLJ 10/05)

4490 Compestine, Ying Chang. *The Story of Chopsticks* (K–3). Illus. by YongSheng Xuan. 2001, Holiday House $16.95 (978-0-8234-1526-7). 32pp. An inventive tale of the origin of chopsticks that includes a lesson in table manners and a simple recipe. (Rev: BL 1/1–15/02; HBG 10/02; SLJ 12/01)

4491 Compestine, Ying Chang. *The Story of Kites* (K–3). Illus. by YongSheng Xuan. 2003, Holiday House $16.95 (978-0-8234-1715-5). Those irrepressible Kang brothers try a variety of methods of scaring the birds away from the rice fields before succeeding by inventing kites. (Rev: BL 4/15/03; HBG 10/03; SLJ 5/03)

4492 Compestine, Ying Chang. *The Story of Noodles* (1–3). Illus. by YongSheng Xuan. 2002, Holiday House $16.95 (978-0-8234-1600-4). The inventive Kang brothers of *The Story of Chopsticks* return to help their mother in the emperor's cooking contest. (Rev: BCCB 2/03; BL 11/1/02; HBG 3/03; SLJ 11/02)

4493 Compestine, Ying Chang. *The Story of Paper* (K–3). Illus. by YongSheng Xuan. 2003, Holiday House $16.95 (978-0-8234-1705-6). Disciplined for inattentiveness in class, the resourceful Kang brothers search for a way to redeem themselves and end up inventing paper. (Rev: BL 12/15/03; HBG 4/04; SLJ 11/03)

4494 Connor, Leslie. *Miss Bridie Chose a Shovel* (1–4). Illus. by Mary Azarian. 2004, Houghton $16.00 (978-0-618-30564-3). 32pp. Miss Birdie makes a wise decision when she chooses a shovel rather than a keepsake to take from Ireland to her new life in America in 1856. (Rev: BL 3/1/04*; SLJ 5/04)

4495 Conway, David. *Lila and the Secret of Rain* (PS–2). Illus. by Jude Daly. 2008, Frances Lincoln $16.95 (978-1-84507-407-4). A Kenyan girl succeeds in bringing much-needed rain to her parched village in this beautifully illustrated picture book. (Rev: BL 7/08; SLJ 7/08)

4496 Coombs, Kate. *The Secret-Keeper* (1–4). Illus. by Heather Solomon. 2006, Simon & Schuster $16.95 (978-0-689-83963-4). Keeping the secrets of everyone in the village weighs so heavily on Kalli that she becomes ill, only to recover when she hears some happy news. (Rev: SLJ 7/06)

4497 Cooper, Floyd. *Willie and the All-Stars* (1–3). Illus. by author. 2008, Philomel $16.99 (978-0-399-23340-1). In 1942 10-year-old Willie learns that there really may be a future for black baseball players in this appealing book with sepia illustrations. (Rev: BL 9/1/08)

4498 Cordsen, Carol Foskett. *The Milkman* (PS–2). Illus. by Douglas B. Jones. 2005, Dutton $15.99 (978-0-525-47208-7). 32pp. In a former, easier time, Mr. Plimpton delivers milk and eggs and a great deal more — gifts, cards, and lost puppies, for example. (Rev: BL 5/1/05)

4499 Corey, Shana. *Players in Pigtails* (PS–3). Illus. by Rebecca Gibbon. 2003, Scholastic $16.95 (978-0-439-18305-5). Corey tells the story of a fictional character named Katie Casey who helps start the All-American Girls Professional Baseball League during World War II. (Rev: BL 3/1/04; HBG 10/03; SLJ 4/03)

4500 Corey, Shana. *You Forgot Your Skirt, Amelia Bloomer!* (1–3). Illus. by Chesley McLaren. 2000, Scholastic $18.99 (978-0-439-07819-1). The story of Amelia Bloomer, how she founded a newspaper, worked for women's rights, and started a dress craze. (Rev: BCCB 2/00; BL 2/1/00*; HBG 10/00; SLJ 3/00)

4501 Costanza, Stephen. *Vivaldi and the Invisible Orchestra* (1–3). Illus. by author. 2012, Henry Holt $16.99 (978-080507801-5). 40pp. In 18th-century Venice an orphan named Candida's poems inspire Vivaldi's *The Four Seasons*. (Rev: BL 3/1/12; LMC 8–9/12; SLJ 1/12)

4502 Cotten, Cynthia. *Abbie in Stitches* (K–3). Illus. by Beth Peck. 2006, Farrar $16.00 (978-0-374-30004-3). 32pp. In 19th-century New York State, Abbie resists pressure to do needlework, much preferring to read. (Rev: BL 9/1/06; SLJ 9/06)

4503 Coville, Bruce. *Hans Brinker* (3–5). Illus. by Laurel Long. 2007, Dial $16.99 (978-0-8037-2868-4). A picture-book version of the story about the courageous and generous Dutch boy and his ice-skating race. (Rev: BL 9/15/07; HB 11/07; SLJ 2/08)

4504 Crisp, Marty. *Titanicat* (K–3). Illus. by Robert Papp. 2008, Sleeping Bear $17.95 (978-1-58536-355-1). Based on a true story, this picture book tells the tale of a ship's boy who literally misses the boat when he attempts to return a kitten to its mother. (Rev: BL 8/08; LMC 3/09; SLJ 7/08)

4505 Cullen, Lynn. *Moi and Marie Antoinette* (1–3). Illus. by Amy Young. 2006, Bloomsbury $16.95 (978-1-58234-958-9). 32pp. Marie Antoinette's dog Sebastien chronicles his mistress's life from the age of 13 to becoming queen of France. (Rev: BL 11/1/06)

4506 Cunnane, Kelly. *Chirchir Is Singing* (PS–1). Illus. by Jude Daly. 2011, Random House $17.99 (978-0-375-86198-7). 40pp. A young Kenyan child tries again and again to help with chores such as getting water from the well but becomes discouraged as she fails every time. (Rev: BL 9/1/11; SLJ 9/1/11)

4507 Cunnane, Kelly. *Deep in the Sahara* (K–3). Illus. by Hoda Hadadi. 2013, Random House $17.99 (978-0-3758703-4). 40pp. A young Mauritanian girl named Lalla learns about the significance of the *malafa*,, the veil that she so admires. ALA Notable Children's Book. **e** Lexile AD890 (Rev: BL 11/15/13*; LMC 1–2/14; SLJ 11/13*)

4508 Cunnane, Kelly. *For You Are a Kenyan Child* (PS–K). Illus. by Ana Juan. 2006, Simon & Schuster $16.95 (978-0-689-86194-9). 40pp. A young Kenyan boy is forgiven for his inattention to his cattle in this gentle story that conveys lots of information about rural Africa. (Rev: BL 2/1/06; SLJ 1/06*)

4509 Cutler, Jane. *Guttersnipe* (K–3). Illus. by Emily Arnold McCully. 2009, Farrar $16.95 (978-0-374-32813-9). 32pp. Set in the early 20th century in a Canadian city, this story follows Ben, a 10-year-old Jewish boy who tries to help his immigrant family to make ends meet after the death of his father. (Rev: BL 1/1–15/09)

4510 Daly, Jude. *Sivu's Six Wishes* (1–3). Illus. by author. 2010, Eerdmans $16.99 (978-080285369-1). 32pp. A retelling of a Taoist tale in which an African stone carver with a yen for power discovers that he is happier as a humble artist. (Rev: BL 9/1/10; HB 9–10/10; LMC 11–12/10; SLJ 12/10)

4511 Daly, Niki. *Happy Birthday, Jamela* (PS–K). Series: Jamela. 2006, Farrar $16.00 (978-0-374-32842-9). 32pp. Jamela's mother makes her buy boring, sensible shoes to go with her birthday dress, so Jamela brightens them up with beads in this fourth book about the young South African girl. (Rev: BL 8/06; SLJ 8/06)

4512 Daly, Niki. *The Herd Boy* (PS–3). Illus. by author. 2012, Eerdmans $17 (978-0-8028-5417-9). 32pp. While Malusi looks after his grandfather's herd in South Africa he dreams of becoming president one day. Lexile AD750L (Rev: BL 12/15/12; HB 1–2/13; LMC 5–6/13; SLJ 11/12*)

4513 Daly, Niki. *A Song for Jamela* (PS–2). Illus. by author. 2010, Frances Lincoln $16.95 (978-1-84507-871-3). 36pp. Young Jamela has an exciting day at her aunt's hair salon in South Africa. (Rev: BL 1/1–15/11; SLJ 10/1/10)

4514 Danneberg, Julie. *Cowboy Slim* (PS–2). Illus. by Margot Apple. 2006, Charlesbridge $15.95 (978-1-58089-045-8). 32pp. Slim, a newcomer to the WJ Ranch, wants nothing more than to be a cowboy, but at first his love for poetry seems to get in the way of his dream. (Rev: BL 2/15/06; SLJ 2/06)

4515 Day, Marie. *Quennu and the Cave Bear* (K–3). Illus. by author. 1999, Owl $17.95 (978-1-895688-86-3); paper $6.95 (978-1-895688-87-0). 32pp. A young girl conquers her fear of cave bears and paints one on the wall during a prehistoric ceremony; includes accurate information about cave art. (Rev: HBG 10/99; SLJ 5/99)

4516 Debon, Nicolas. *A Brave Soldier* (2–5). Illus. 2002, Groundwood $15.95 (978-0-88899-481-3). 32pp. This picture book for older children, narrated by a young Canadian soldier, introduces readers to the trenches of World War I. (Rev: BL 11/1/02; HBG 3/03; SLJ 2/03)

4517 Delgado, María Isabel. *Chave's Memories / Los Recuerdos de Chave* (PS–3). Illus. by Yvonne Symank. 1996, Piñata $14.95 (978-1-55885-084-2). A bilingual picture book in which a woman recalls her trips as a child from Brownsville, Texas, to her grandparents' ranch in northern Mexico. (Rev: SLJ 12/96)

4518 Demas, Corinne. *The Boy Who Was Generous with Salt* (K–3). Illus. by Michael Hays. 2002, Marshall Cavendish $15.95 (978-0-7614-5099-3). As cook aboard a fishing vessel in 1850, Ned plots to get home in time for his ninth birthday. (Rev: HBG 10/02; SLJ 5/02)

4519 Demi. *The Greatest Power* (K–3). Illus. 2004, Simon & Schuster $19.95 (978-0-689-84503-1). Ping, introduced in *The Empty Pot* (1990), invites all the children in his empire to consider what might be the greatest power in the world, with interesting results. (Rev: BL 2/1/04; SLJ 3/04)

4520 Demi. *The Magic Pillow* (K–3). Illus. by author. 2008, Simon & Schuster $19.99 (978-1-4169-2470-8). 40pp. A magic pillow cures a poor Chinese boy named Ping of his dreams of wealth and fame; traditional illustrations add atmosphere. (Rev: BL 7/08; HB 7/08; LMC 8/08; SLJ 7/08)

4521 dePaola, Tomie. *Pascual and the Kitchen Angels* (PS–2). Illus. 2004, Penguin $16.99 (978-0-399-24214-4). The patron saint of cooks is introduced in a charming story of a boy who communes with the animals and requires the help of angels when asked to make a meal. (Rev: BL 1/1–15/04; SLJ 2/04)

4522 dePaola, Tomie. *The Song of Francis* (PS–1). Illus. by author. 2009, Putnam $16.99 (978-0-399-25210-5). 32pp. This simple volume distills the essence of St. Francis and his joyful appreciation for and love of nature as he sings about Brother Sun and Sister Moon. (Rev: BL 1/1–15/09; SLJ 1/09)

4523 Diakité, Penda. *I Lost My Tooth in Africa* (PS–2). Illus. by Baba Wague Diakité. 2006, Scholastic $16.99 (978-0-439-66226-0). 32pp. While visiting her extended family in the West African nation of Mali, a young girl loses her tooth and is treated to a visit from the African Tooth Fairy. (Rev: BL 2/1/06; SLJ 1/06)

4524 Dominguez, Angela. *Maria Had a Little Llama/ Maria tenia una llama pequena* (PS–2). Illus. by author. 2013, Henry Holt $16.99 (978-080509333-9). 32pp. The familiar nursery rhyme "Mary Had a Little Lamb" gets a bilingual upgrade in this retelling set in Peru, in which Maria's llama follows her to school, to the delight of her classmates. ALA Notable Children's Book. e (Rev: BLO 9/15/13; HB 11–12/13; LMC 11–12/13)

4525 Dorros, Arthur. *Julio's Magic* (K–2). Illus. by Ann Grifalconi. 2005, HarperCollins LB $17.89 (978-0-06-029005-4). Julio, a young Mexican wood-carver, helps his elderly teacher, Iluminado, to create the winning entry for the annual wood-carving contest. (Rev: BL 1/1–15/05; SLJ 1/05)

4526 Edwards, David. *The Pen That Pa Built* (K–2). Illus. by Ashley Wolff. 2007, Tricycle $14.95 (978-1-58246-153-3). 32pp. Set in the 19th century, this title uses rhyming text and textured illustrations to present the processes of shearing sheep, carding and spinning, dyeing, and so forth, ending with a snuggly blanket. (Rev: BL 11/15/07; LMC 1/08; SLJ 10/07)

4527 Edwards, Pamela Duncan. *Barefoot: Escape on the Underground Railroad* (K–4). Illus. by Henry Cole.

1997, HarperCollins LB $15.89 (978-0-06-027138-1). The birds and other animals in a forest seem to work together to help an escaped slave. (Rev: BL 2/15/97; SLJ 2/97*)

4528 Ellis, Veronica F. *Afro-Bets First Book About Africa* (2–5). Illus. by George Ford. 1990, Just Us Bks. LB $13.95 (978-0-940975-12-5); paper $6.95 (978-0-940975-03-3). 32pp. A classroom of African Americans learns about the history and culture of Africa. (Rev: BL 3/1/90*; SLJ 5/90)

4529 Elvgren, Jennifer Riesmeyer. *Josias, Hold the Book* (1–3). Illus. by Nicole Tadgell. 2006, Boyds Mills $15.95 (978-1-59078-318-4). Living in rural Haiti, Josias must work in the garden instead of going to school until he realizes that book-learning could improve their crops. (Rev: BL 2/15/06; SLJ 3/06)

4530 Ernst, Lisa Campbell. *Sam Johnson and the Blue Ribbon Quilt* (K–3). Illus. by author. 1983, Lothrop LB $17.89 (978-0-688-01517-6); Morrow paper $6.99 (978-0-688-11505-0). 32pp. The men and the women vie for honors in the quilting contest.

4531 Esbaum, Jill. *Ste-e-e-eamboat A-comin'!* (K–4). Illus. by Adam Rex. 2005, Farrar $16.00 (978-0-374-37236-1). The excitement of the arrival of the packet *S. L. Clemens* at sleepy towns on the Mississippi in 1867 is portrayed in rhyming verse and beautiful realistic illustrations. (Rev: SLJ 3/05)

4532 Esbaum, Jill. *To the Big Top* (K–2). Illus. by David Gordon. 2008, Farrar $16.95 (978-0-374-39934-4). In the early 20th century the circus is coming to Willow Grove and Benny and Sam are thrilled to help with setting up the Big Top. (Rev: BL 4/15/08; SLJ 8/08)

4533 Evans, Freddi Williams. *Hush Harbor: Praying in Secret* (K–3). Illus. by Erin Bennett Banks. 2008, Carolrhoda $16.95 (978-0-8225-7965-6). 32pp. Slaves praying at night in their secret "hush harbor" are warned that patrols are on the lookout and quickly return home; an author's note provides history and insight, and evocative paintings add atmosphere. (Rev: BL 10/1/08; SLJ 11/08)

4534 Evans, Shane W. *Underground* (PS–3). Illus. by author. 2011, Roaring Brook $16.99 (978-1-59643-538-4). 32pp. With minimal text and dramatic illustrations, this effective book tells the story of a slave family's escape to the North. Coretta Scott King Illustrator Award. (Rev: BL 2/1/11; HB 1–2/11; LMC 5–6/11; SLJ 1/1/11*)

4535 Evans, Shane W. *We March* (PS–1). Illus. by author. 2012, Roaring Brook $16.99 (978-159643539-1). 32pp. A boy, a girl, and their parents wake early and travel to take part in the 1963 civil rights march on Washington, D.C. (Rev: BL 1/1/12; HB 1–2/12; LMC 3–4/12)

4536 Faulkner, Matt. *The Pirate Meets the Queen* (K–3). Illus. 2005, Philomel $15.99 (978-0-399-24038-6). 32pp. Granny O'Malley, the 16th-century Irish pirate, tells her life story and describes her showdown with Queen Elizabeth I over the capture of Granny's son Toby. (Rev: BL 5/15/05; SLJ 6/05)

4537 Faulkner, Matt. *A Taste of Colored Water* (1–3). Illus. by author. 2008, Simon & Schuster $16.99 (978-1-

4169-1629-1). A segregation story told through the eyes of a white girl, Lulu, who with her cousin Jelly comes face to face with racism in a southern city in the 1960s. (Rev: BL 2/1/08; SLJ 2/08)

4538 Feder, Paula K. *The Feather-Bed Journey* (K–3). Illus. by Stacey Schuett. 1995, Whitman LB $15.95 (978-0-8075-2330-8). 32pp. Grandma tells her grandchildren how her favorite feather pillow was once part of a large feather bed that kept her warm in a Jewish ghetto during World War II. (Rev: BCCB 12/95; BL 10/15/95; SLJ 11/95)

4539 Feeney, Stephanie. *A Is for Aloha* (PS–K). Photos by Jeff Reese. 1985, Univ. of Hawaii $13.95 (978-0-8248-0722-1). A simple introduction to Hawaii and its many cultures.

4540 Fern, Tracey E. *Buffalo Music* (PS–2). Illus. by Lauren Castillo. 2008, Clarion $16.00 (978-0-618-72341-6). 32pp. The story of the near-extinction of the buffalo is told from the point of view of Molly, a woman who in the late 1800s raises two orphan calves; based on the real life of Mary Ann Goodnight. (Rev: BL 4/15/08; SLJ 6/08)

4541 Fern, Tracey E. *Pippo the Fool* (1–3). Illus. by Pau Estrada. 2009, Charlesbridge $15.95 (978-1-57091-655-7). 48pp. A fictionalized account of the life and work of Filippo Brunelleschi, a characterful goldsmith who unexpectedly (in the opinion of others) won the competition to design and build the dome of the Cathedral of Florence. (Rev: BL 1/1–15/09; SLJ 6/09)

4542 Fine, Edith Hope, and Judith Pinkerton. *Armando and the Blue Tarp School* (K–2). Illus. by Hernan Sosa. 2007, Lee & Low $16.95 (978-1-58430-278-0). 48pp. Armando, who lives in Tijuana and helps his father sifting through trash at the dump, gets a chance to attend a school set up on a blue tarp on the ground. (Rev: BL 11/15/07; LMC 1/08; SLJ 10/07)

4543 Fleming, Candace. *Boxes for Katje* (K–3). Illus. by Stacey Dressen-McQueen. 2003, Farrar $16.00 (978-0-374-30922-0). Based on actual events, this is a heartwarming story of an Indiana town's efforts to help Dutch people suffering from severe postwar shortages in 1945. (Rev: HB 9/03; HBG 4/04; SLJ 9/03)

4544 Fleming, Candace. *Papa's Mechanical Fish* (K–2). Illus. by Boris Kulikov. 2013, Farrar $16.99 (978-0-374-39908-5). 40pp. Narrator Virena recounts her Rube Goldberg-style father's often hapless attempts at various inventions including a submarine; based on the life of Lodner Phillips who did create a working submarine in 1851. **e** (Rev: BL 5/1/13; HB 5–6/13; LMC 11–12/13; SLJ 5/13*)

4545 Fletcher, Susan. *Dadblamed Union Army Cow* (K–3). Illus. by Kimberly B. Root. 2007, Candlewick $16.99 (978-0-7636-2263-3). 32pp. The story of a cow that accompanies a Union soldier into battle during the Civil War. (Rev: BL 7/07; LMC 11/07; SLJ 8/07)

4546 Foreman, Michael. *Mia's Story: A Sketchbook of Hopes and Dreams* (1–3). 2006, Candlewick $15.99 (978-0-7636-3063-8). 32pp. Mia, a young resident of a poverty-stricken Chilean village, beautifies her community with the pretty flowers she finds while searching for a missing puppy. (Rev: BL 8/06; SLJ 8/06)

4547 Francis, David "Panama," and Bob Reiser. *David Gets His Drum* (K–2). Illus. by Eric Velasquez. 2002, Marshall Cavendish $16.95 (978-0-7614-5088-7). 32pp. African American jazz musician "Panama" Francis loved music from a young age and here tells the sad story of his first drum. (Rev: BL 11/15/02; HBG 3/03; SLJ 10/02)

4548 Francis, Pauline. *Sam Stars at Shakespeare's Globe* (2–4). Illus. by Jane Tattersfield. 2006, Frances Lincoln $15.95 (978-1-84507-406-7). 32pp. A picture-book account of a boy named Sam who acts in the Globe Theatre and aspires to the role of Juliet. (Rev: BL 11/1/06; SLJ 12/06)

4549 Friedman, Robin. *The Silent Witness: A True Story of The Civil War* (K–3). Illus. by Claire A. Nivola. 2005, Houghton $16.00 (978-0-618-44230-0). A touching story about the young owner of a rag doll that was present at the surrender of the Confederacy in 1865; the girl never saw it after that day but it is now on display in Appomattox. (Rev: BCCB 6/05; HB 5/05; SLJ 6/05)

4550 Fuchs, Bernie. *Ride Like the Wind: A Tale of the Pony Express* (K–4). Illus. by author. 2004, Scholastic $16.95 (978-0-439-26645-1). The fictional adventures of young Pony Express rider Johnny Free and his pony JennySoo are augmented by historical material. (Rev: SLJ 3/04)

4551 Fullerton, Alma. *A Good Trade* (1–3). Illus. by Karen Patkau. 2012, Pajama Press $19.95 (978-0-9869495-9-3). 32pp. A young Ugandan boy named Kato must make a long journey to fetch water for his family every morning, and on one special day is able to trade a white poppy for some precious shoes brought by aid workers. Lexile AD1030 (Rev: LMC 1–2/14*; SLJ 3/13)

4552 Funke, Cornelia. *The Princess Knight* (PS–2). Trans. by Anthea Bell. Illus. by Kerstin Meyer. 2004, Scholastic $15.95 (978-0-439-53630-1). Princess Violetta can joust, ride, and use a sword as well as her older brothers, so when her father wants to give her away as a tournament prize on her 16th birthday, she dons a disguise and takes part in the contest herself. (Rev: BL 2/1/04*; SLJ 3/04)

4553 Garaway, Margaret K. *Ashkii and His Grandfather* (K–3). Illus. by Harry Warren. 1995, Old Hogan $14.95 (978-0-9638851-7-3); paper $8.95 (978-0-9638851-6-6). 33pp. A young Navajo boy helps his grandfather at summer sheep camp. (Rev: BL 3/1/90)

4554 Garay, Luis. *The Kite* (K–2). Illus. 2002, Tundra $14.95 (978-0-88776-503-2). 32pp. Francisco, a Latin American boy who must help support his family after his father's death, dreams of having a kite. (Rev: BL 8/02; HBG 10/02; SLJ 12/02)

4555 Garay, Luis. *Pedrito's Day* (K–3). Illus. 1997, Orchard $14.95 (978-0-531-09522-5). 32pp. Pedrito, a Mexican boy, is heartbroken when he loses the money he had saved to buy a bicycle. (Rev: BL 3/1/97; SLJ 4/97)

4556 Garcia, Cristina. *The Dog Who Loved the Moon* (K–3). Illus. by Sebastia Serra. 2008, Atheneum $15.99 (978-1-4169-1836-3). 32pp. With rich illustrations and rhythmic text, this is an enjoyable story about a Cuban girl named Pilar who loves to dance and her dog, Paco, who won't join her because he's obsessed with the moon. (Rev: BL 4/15/08; SLJ 4/08)

4557 Garland, Sherry. *The Buffalo Soldier* (K–3). Illus. by Ronald Himler. 2006, Pelican $15.95 (978-1-58980-391-6). 32pp. This overview of the "buffalo soldiers" — members of the all-African American cavalry regiments that served after the Civil War — is told from the viewpoint of a fictional recruit who is a former slave; includes eye-catching illustrations and a historical note. (Rev: BL 11/1/06; SLJ 12/06)

4558 Geeslin, Campbell. *Elena's Serenade* (1–3). Illus. by Ana Juan. 2004, Simon & Schuster $16.95 (978-0-689-84908-4). Elena proves her father wrong and succeeds in blowing magnificent pieces of glass in this story set in Mexico. (Rev: BL 3/1/04; SLJ 3/04)

4559 George, Jean Craighead. *Nutik, the Wolf Pup* (PS–3). Illus. by Ted Rand. 2001, HarperCollins LB $17.89 (978-0-06-028165-6). 40pp. Amaroq nurses a wolf pup back to health and then must give him up and return him to the pack. (Rev: BL 2/1/01; HBG 10/01; SLJ 3/01)

4560 Germein, Katrina. *Big Rain Coming* (PS–2). Illus. by Bronwyn Bancroft. 2000, Clarion $16.00 (978-0-618-08344-2). 32pp. In the Australian Outback where it gets very hot, every living creature is waiting for the rain that Old Joseph claims is on its way. (Rev: BL 8/00; HBG 3/01; SLJ 9/00)

4561 Gershator, Phillis. *Sky Sweeper* (K–3). Illus. by Holly Meade. 2007, Farrar $16.00 (978-0-374-37007-7). 40pp. This is the beautifully illustrated, challenging story of Takeboki, who as a boy takes a job tending the gardens at a Zen temple, work he enjoys despite its simplicity. (Rev: BL 3/15/07)

4562 Gerstein, Mordicai. *The First Drawing* (K–2). Illus. by author. 2013, Little, Brown $17 (978-031620478-1). 40pp. A compelling imagination of what spurred the first cave drawing. (Rev: BL 8/13; LMC 3–4/2014*; SLJ 8/13*)

4563 Gerstein, Mordicai. *The Mountains of Tibet* (K–3). Illus. by author. 1989, HarperCollins paper $6.99 (978-0-06-443211-5). 32pp. A woodcutter spends his life in a Tibetan valley in this story of reincarnation. (Rev: BL 11/15/87; HB 11/87; SLJ 11/87)

4564 Gibfried, Diane. *Brother Juniper* (K–2). Illus. by Meilo So. 2006, Clarion $16.00 (978-0-618-54361-8). Brother Juniper, a follower of Father Francis of Assisi, is so generous that he gives away the monks' church, bit by bit, to the poor; for this he is condemned by his brothers but commended by the saint. (Rev: SLJ 5/06)

4565 Gilani-Williams, Fawzia. *Nabeel's New Pants: An Eid Tale* (K–3). Illus. by Proiti Roy. 2010, Marshall Cavendish $15.99 (978-0-7614-5629-2). 24pp. Nabeel's wife, mother, and daughter are too busy cooking for the Eid feast to shorten his new pants in this humorous story set in Turkey. **e** Lexile AD450L (Rev: BL 3/15/10; LMC 8–9/10; SLJ 4/1/10*)

4566 Glaser, Linda. *Hannah's Way* (K–3). Illus. by Adam Gustavson. 2012, Lerner/Kar-Ben paper $7.95 (978-07613513-8-2). 32pp. Uprooted from Minneapolis, a young Jewish girl struggles to make friends in her new rural school in this heartwarming story set during the Great Depression. (Rev: BL 3/15/12; SLJ 4/1/12)

4567 Glass, Andrew. *Bewildered for Three Days: As to Why Daniel Boone Never Wore His Coonskin Cap* (2–3). Illus. 2000, Holiday House $16.95 (978-0-8234-1446-8). 32pp. After several hair-raising adventures including spending a night in a hollow log with a mother raccoon, Daniel Boone swears off wearing his coonskin cap forever. (Rev: BCCB 11/00; BL 9/1/00; HBG 10/01; SLJ 10/00)

4568 Gonzalez, Lucia. *The Storyteller's Candle / La velita de los cuentos* (K–3). Illus. by Lulu Delacre. 2008, Children's Book Pr. $16.95 (978-0-89239-222-3). 32pp. Set in the winter of 1929, this large bilingual picture book tells the story of how New York City's first Puerto Rican librarian, Pura Belpre, influenced the lives of two little Latino girls who very much wanted something to read. (Rev: BL 3/15/08; LMC 11/08; SLJ 4/08)

4569 Gourley, Robbin. *Bring Me Some Apples and I'll Make You a Pie: A Story About Edna Lewis* (K–3). Illus. by author. 2009, Clarion $16.00 (978-0-618-15836-2). 48pp. Recipes and rhymes add atmosphere to this story based on the life of the granddaughter of an emancipated slave who became a famous chef. (Rev: BCCB 1/09; BL 2/1/09; SLJ 2/09) [921]

4570 Graham, Christine. *When Pioneer Wagons Rumbled West* (PS–2). Illus. by Sherry Meidell. 1998, Deseret $14.95 (978-1-57345-272-4). This picture book illustrates the hardships faced by Mormon families and the importance of prayer in their lives as they journeyed to settle land for their new home in Utah. (Rev: BL 9/15/98; SLJ 12/98)

4571 Grant, Shauntay. *Apples and Butterflies* (1–3). Illus. by Tamara Thiebaux-Heikalo. 2013, Nimbus $19.95 (978-155109935-4). 32pp. A young girl describes all the joys of a family vacation on Prince Edward Island in this warm, lyrical narrative. (Rev: BL 3/15/13)

4572 Green, Norma B. *The Hole in the Dike* (K–2). Illus. by Eric Carle. 1975, Scholastic paper $4.95 (978-0-590-46146-7). 32pp. Brilliant illustrations accompany this simple retelling of the Mary Mapes Dodge story of the boy who put his finger in the dike and saved his Dutch town.

4573 Grifalconi, Ann. *Ain't Nobody a Stranger to Me* (PS–3). Illus. by Jerry Pinkney. 2007, Hyperion $16.99 (978-0-7868-1857-0). 32pp. Based on a true story, this book features a grandfather telling his granddaughter how he escaped slavery with the help of courageous strangers on the Underground Railroad. (Rev: BL 5/1/07; SLJ 5/07)

4574 Griffin, Kitty. *The Ride: The Legend of Betsy Dowdy* (1–3). Illus. by Marjorie Priceman. 2010, Atheneum

232

$16.99 (978-1-4169-2816-4). 40pp. In this exciting story of bravery and perseverance, a 16-year-old girl sets off on a 50-mile horseback ride when she learns the Redcoats are on their way to her North Carolina town in 1775. Lexile AD510L (Rev: BL 7/10; LMC 11–12/10; SLJ 8/1/10)

4575 Grigsby, Susan. *In the Garden with Dr. Carver* (1–3). Illus. by Nicole Tadgell. 2010, Whitman $16.99 (978-0-8075-3630-8). 32pp. Dr. George Washington Carver visits a rural elementary school in Alabama and teaches the students about gardening in this picture book with evocative illustrations. Lexile 990L (Rev: BL 9/1/10; LMC 11–12/10; SLJ 10/1/10)

4576 Haddon, Mark. *Footprints on the Moon* (K–3). Illus. by Christian Birmingham. 2009, Candlewick $16.99 (978-0-7636-4440-6). 32pp. A little boy (based on the author) gazes at the moon and dreams about the astronauts landing there. (Rev: LMC 10/09; SLJ 6/09)

4577 Hall, Bruce Edward. *Henry and the Kite Dragon* (PS–2). Illus. by William Low. 2004, Penguin $15.99 (978-0-399-23727-0). 40pp. A cultural clash in 1920s New York City pits kite-flying 8-year-old Henry and his friends from Chinatown against pet pigeon-owning children from nearby Little Italy. (Rev: BL 5/15/04; SLJ 8/04)

4578 Hall, Donald. *Ox-Cart Man* (K–3). Illus. by Barbara Cooney. 1979, Puffin paper $6.99 (978-0-14-050441-5). 40pp. The cycle of production and sale of goods in 19th-century New England is pictured in human terms. Caldecott Medal winner, 1980.

4579 Hanson, Regina. *A Season for Mangoes* (PS–2). Illus. by Eric Velasquez. 2005, Clarion $15.00 (978-0-618-15972-7). 32pp. Sareen, a young Jamaican girl, struggles to find the confidence to address the mourners at her beloved grandmother's wake, or "sit-up." (Rev: BL 2/1/05; SLJ 5/05)

4580 Harris, John. *Jingle Bells: How the Holiday Classic Came to Be* (2–4). Illus. by Adam Gustavson. 2011, Peachtree $16.95 (978-156145590-4). 32pp. Tells the fictionalized story of the composition of the song in 1857, when James Lord Pierpont, then living in Georgia, was homesick for his native New England winters. (Rev: BL 10/1/11; SLJ 10/1/11)

4581 Hartfield, Claire. *Me and Uncle Romie: A Story Inspired by the Life and Art of Romare Bearden* (K–3). Illus. by Jerome Lagarrigue. 2002, Dial $16.99 (978-0-8037-2520-1). James enjoys spending time with his uncle, the Harlem Renaissance artist Romare Bearden, in this picture book with reproductions of the artist's work. (Rev: BL 2/15/03; HBG 3/03; SLJ 12/02)

4582 Harvey, Jeanne Walker. *My Hands Sing the Blues: Romare Bearden's Childhood Journey* (1–3). Illus. by Elizabeth Zunon. 2011, Marshall Cavendish $17.99 (978-0-7614-5810-4). 40pp. A fictionalized first-person narrative recounts the life of the African American collage artist who made his name during the Harlem Renaissance and whose love of the blues was reflected in his work. (Rev: BL 11/1/11; SLJ 10/1/11)

4583 Haseley, Dennis. *Twenty Heartbeats* (2–4). Illus. by Ed Young. 2008, Roaring Brook $16.95 (978-1-59643-238-3). 32pp. A treat for art lovers, this is the story, set in earlier times, of a man who seeks a portrait of his beloved horse. (Rev: BCCB 4/08; BL 5/1/08; LMC 5/08; SLJ 4/08)

4584 Hawes, Louise. *Muti's Necklace: The Oldest Story in the World* (2–4). Illus. by Rebecca Guay. 2006, Houghton $16.00 (978-0-618-53583-5). 32pp. In ancient Egypt, servant Muti risks everything to retrieve her treasured necklace and receives a proposal of marriage from the pharaoh in return; based on an ancient Egyptian story. (Rev: BL 7/06; SLJ 6/06)

4585 Hayes, Joe. *A Spoon for Every Bite / Una cuchara para cada bocado* (1–4). Illus. by Rebecca Leer. 2005, Cinco Puntos paper $8.95 (978-0-938317-93-7). A bilingual version of the story in which a poor couple fools a rich neighbor into spending his fortune on spoons. (Rev: SLJ 10/05)

4586 Haynes, Emily, and Sanjay Patel. *Ganesha's Sweet Tooth* (1–3). Illus. by Sanjay Patel. 2012, Chronicle $16.99 (978-1-4521-0362-4). 40pp. Based on the Hindu myth about the god Ganesha, this nicely illustrated story features Ganesha with an elephant head and body of a child; a super jumbo jawbreaker causes him to break a tusk, but that luckily turns out to be just the instrument that the poet Vyasa needs to write the epic Mahabharata. **e** Lexile AD580L (Rev: BL 10/15/12; LMC 3–4/13; SLJ 10/12)

4587 Hegamin, Tonya Cherie. *Most Loved in All the World* (K–2). Illus. by Cozbi A. Cabrera. 2009, Houghton $17.00 (978-0-618-41903-6). 40pp. Text, quilt art, and primitive paintings tell the story of a slave mother who selflessly pieces together a quilt to guide the people who will help her smuggle her daughter to freedom on the Underground Railroad. (Rev: BCCB 1/09; BL 2/1/09; LMC 10/09; SLJ 1/09)

4588 Heller, Linda. *The Castle on Hester Street* (K–3). Illus. by Boris Kulikov. 2007, Simon & Schuster $15.99 (978-0-689-87434-5). 40pp. With corrections from Grandma, Grandpa tells an elaborate story of their immigration to America to escape the persecution of Jews in Russia. (Rev: BL 12/15/07; SLJ 10/07)

4589 Henson, Heather. *Angel Coming* (PS–2). Illus. by Susan Gaber. 2005, Simon & Schuster $15.95 (978-0-689-85531-3). 40pp. A child living in the Appalachian Mountains in the early 20th century anxiously awaits the arrival of a member of the Frontier Nursing Service — known by locals as "angels on horseback" — who will help the child's mother through childbirth. (Rev: BL 7/05*; SLJ 7/05)

4590 Henson, Heather. *That Book Woman* (2–4). Illus. by David Small. 2008, Atheneum $16.99 (978-1-4169-0812-8). 40pp. Young Cal's desire to read is sparked and later fulfilled when a traveling librarian journeys up to his remote mountain home in this book set in the 1930s. (Rev: BCCB 10/08; BL 9/15/08; HB 11/08; LMC 1/09)

4591 Herbauts, Anne. *Prince Silencio* (1–3). Trans. from French by Zoe Bedrick. 2006, Enchanted Lion $14.95 (978-1-59270-055-4). Prince Silencio ("Silence") teaches his noisy subjects the value of occasional quiet times in this story translated from the French. (Rev: SLJ 6/06)

4592 Hershenhorn, Esther. *Fancy That* (K–3). Illus. by Megan Lloyd. 2003, Holiday House $16.95 (978-0-8234-1605-9). In the 1840s, a young orphan named Pip travels the countryside trying to earn money as a portrait painter, but his realistic style fails to please his customers. (Rev: BL 9/15/03; HBG 4/04; SLJ 11/03)

4593 High, Linda Oatman. *Tenth Avenue Cowboy* (K–2). Illus. by Bill Farnsworth. 2008, Eerdmans $17.00 (978-0-8028-5330-1). A lonely boy named Ben moves from a ranch to crowded New York City in the early 1900s but still makes his cowboy dreams come true — alongside the city's railroad tracks. (Rev: BLO 8/28/08; SLJ 9/08)

4594 Hoberman, Mary Ann. *Mrs. O'Leary's Cow* (K–2). Illus. by Jenny Mattheson. 2007, Little, Brown $16.99 (978-0-316-14840-5). 32pp. With new verses added to the classic song and a transition to a rural environment, this is the humorous story of firefighters' efforts to save the barn after the cow kicks over the lantern. (Rev: BL 4/1/07)

4595 Hoffman, Mary. *Boundless Grace* (PS–3). Illus. by Caroline Binch. 1995, Dial $16.99 (978-0-8037-1715-2). 32pp. Grace's father sends airplane tickets for her to visit him in Gambia and meet his new family. (Rev: BCCB 6/95; BL 4/15/95; HB 7/95; SLJ 5/95*)

4596 Hoffman, Mary. *The Color of Home* (PS–3). Illus. by Karin Littlewood. 2002, Penguin $17.99 (978-0-8037-2841-7). 32pp. A young Somalian boy who has emigrated to America to escape civil war has trouble adjusting to his new life until he is able to paint pictures of his fears and hopes. (Rev: BCCB 10/02; BL 10/15/02; HBG 3/03; SLJ 9/02)

4597 Hofmeyr, Dianne. *The Faraway Island* (PS–3). Illus. by Jude Daly. 2008, Frances Lincoln $16.95 (978-1-84507-644-3). 32pp. This simple story about an unhappy man who chooses to live on a barren island and ends up transforming it into a beautiful haven is based on the experiences of Fernando Lopez, who transformed St. Helena. (Rev: BLO 3/5/09; SLJ 3/09)

4598 Homan, Lynn M., and Thomas Reilly. *The Tuskegee Airmen Story* (K–3). Illus. by Rosalie M. Shepherd. 2002, Pelican $15.95 (978-1-58980-005-2). 32pp. A grandfather tells of his days as a Tuskegee Airman during World War II. (Rev: BL 2/15/03; HBG 3/03)

4599 Hong, Chen Jiang. *Little Eagle* (2–4). Trans. by Claudia Zoe Bedrick. Illus. by author. 2007, Enchanted Lion $16.95 (978-1-59270-071-4). In 15th-century China a kung fu master takes in an orphaned boy and trains him as his disciple, calling him "Little Eagle." (Rev: BL 11/1/07; LMC 1/08; SLJ 11/07)

4600 Hong, Lily T. *The Empress and the Silkworm* (PS–3). Illus. 1995, Whitman LB $16.95 (978-0-8075-2009-3). 32pp. A Chinese empress uses the silk threads she finds when she discovers the cocoons of silkworms to make a robe for the emperor. (Rev: BCCB 12/95; BL 9/15/95; SLJ 11/95)

4601 Hopkinson, Deborah. *Abe Lincoln Crosses a Creek: A Tall, Thin Tale (Introducing His Forgotten Frontier Friend)* (PS–3). Illus. by John Hendrix. 2008, Random $16.99 (978-0-375-83768-5). 40pp. In 1816 7-year-old Abe falls into Knob Creek and is rescued by his friend Austin; commentary by both author and illustrator add to the story. (Rev: BCCB 10/08; BL 9/15/08; HB 9/08; LMC 11/08; SLJ 9/08)

4602 Hopkinson, Deborah. *The Humblebee Hunter: Inspired by the Life and Experiments of Charles Darwin and His Children* (K–2). Illus. by Jen Corace. 2010, Hyperion $16.99 (978-142311356-0). 32pp. Darwin's daughter Henrietta introduces the large family, her father's interest in science, and how they all collaborated in a bee experiment. Lexile AD610L (Rev: BL 1/1/10; LMC 8–9/10; SLJ 4/10)

4603 Hopkinson, Deborah. *Saving Strawberry Farm* (PS–2). Illus. by Rachel Isadora. 2005, Greenwillow LB $18.89 (978-0-688-17401-9). 32pp. During the Depression, young Davy plays a key role in helping Miss Elsie to save her strawberry farm. (Rev: BL 5/1/05)

4604 Hopkinson, Deborah. *Under the Quilt of Night* (K–2). Illus. by James Ransome. 2002, Simon & Schuster $16.00 (978-0-689-82227-8). 40pp. A young slave girl describes her dangerous escape through the Underground Railroad. (Rev: BCCB 2/02; BL 2/15/02; HB 7/02; HBG 10/02; SLJ 1/02*)

4605 Houston, Gloria. *Miss Dorothy and Her Bookmobile* (K–3). Illus. by Susan Condie Lamb. 2011, HarperCollins $16.99 (978-0-06-029155-6). 32pp. Dorothy's work as head of the bookmobile for a rural North Carolina area in the last century is depicted in this inspiring story. Lexile AD1090L (Rev: BL 1/1–15/11; SLJ 1/1/11)

4606 Howard, Ellen. *The Log Cabin Church* (K–3). Illus. by Ronald Himler. 2002, Holiday House $16.95 (978-0-8234-1740-7). 32pp. Elvirey initially questions her Michigan frontier community's desire to build a church in this sequel to *The Log Cabin Quilt* (1996) and *The Log Cabin Christmas* (2000). (Rev: BL 10/1/02; HBG 3/03; SLJ 10/02)

4607 Howard, Ellen. *The Log Cabin Quilt* (K–3). Illus. by Ronald Himler. 1996, Holiday House LB $16.95 (978-0-8234-1247-1). Quilting scraps help chink the holes in a log cabin in this story of Western pioneers. (Rev: BCCB 10/96; BL 12/15/96; SLJ 10/96)

4608 Hubbard, Crystal. *Catching the Moon* (PS–2). Illus. by Randy DuBurke. 2005, Lee & Low $16.95 (978-1-58430-243-8). 32pp. In the 1920s, a young African American girl is determined to become a professional baseball player; based on the life of Toni Stone (1921–1996). (Rev: BL 9/1/05; SLJ 11/05)

4609 Huget, Jennifer LaRue. *Thanks a LOT, Emily Post!* (PS–3). Illus. by Alexandra Boiger. 2009, Random House $16.99 (978-0-375-83853-8); LB $19.99 (978-0-375-93853-5). 40pp. Home life takes a turn for the demanding when children fed up with hearing about their behavior challenge their mother to follow Emily Post's etiquette rules herself; set in the early 1920s. (Rev: BL 9/1/09*; SLJ 10/1/09)

4610 Hughes, Monica. *A Handful of Seeds* (K–3). Illus. by Luis Garay. 1996, Orchard $15.95 (978-0-531-09498-3). 32pp. When Concepcion moves from the country to the city, she brings some seeds with her to start a garden in the barrio. (Rev: BCCB 6/96; BL 4/1/96; SLJ 3/96)

4611 Hunter, Sara H. *The Unbreakable Code* (2–4). Illus. by Julia Miner. 1996, Northland LB $15.95 (978-0-87358-638-2). A Navajo man reassures his grandson that he will adjust successfully to a move off the reservation with his mother and new stepfather. (Rev: SLJ 8/96)

4612 Hurst, Carol Otis. *Rocks in His Head* (K–3). Illus. by James Stevenson. 2001, Greenwillow LB $17.89 (978-0-06-029404-5). 32pp. A man pursues his interest in rock collecting from childhood through raising a family in the Depression until he succeeds in turning a hobby into a career. (Rev: BCCB 12/01; BL 6/1–15/01; HB 7/01; HBG 10/01; SLJ 6/01)

4613 Hurst, Carol Otis. *Terrible Storm* (K–2). Illus. by S. D. Schindler. 2007, Greenwillow $16.99 (978-0-06-009001-2). 32pp. Two grandfathers separately share their memories of the blizzard that hit New England in 1888. (Rev: BL 11/15/06; SLJ 1/07)

4614 Ichikawa, Satomi. *My Father's Shop* (K–2). Illus. 2006, Kane $15.95 (978-1-929132-99-7). 32pp. Mustafa, son of a Moroccan rug seller, doesn't enjoy learning foreign words from his father but in a romp through the local marketplace he attracts the attention of many tourists and brings them back to the rug shop. (Rev: BL 2/15/06)

4615 Iijima, Geneva Cobb. *The Way We Do It in Japan* (K–3). Illus. by Paige Billin-Frye. 2002, Whitman $16.99 (978-0-8075-7822-3). 32pp. When Gregory's family moves to Japan, he learns about the differences between Japanese and American culture. (Rev: BCCB 3/02; BL 5/15/02; HBG 10/02; SLJ 4/02)

4616 Ingalls, Ann, and Maryann Macdonald. *The Little Piano Girl: The Story of Mary Lou Williams, Jazz Legend* (1–5). Illus. by Giselle Potter. 2010, Houghton Mifflin $16 (978-0-618-95974-7). Unpaged. A fictionalized account of the African American jazz great's childhood and youth, and her amazing prowess from as early an age as 3. **e** (Rev: LMC 8–9/10; SLJ 2/1/10)

4617 Isadora, Rachel. *Bring on That Beat* (PS–2). Illus. by author. 2002, Penguin $16.99 (978-0-399-23232-9). 32pp. In this rhyming, rhythmic ode to jazz set in 1930s Harlem, a band plays on a street corner and a crowd gathers to listen. (Rev: BCCB 1/02; BL 2/15/02; HBG 10/02; SLJ 1/02)

4618 Isadora, Rachel. *Luke Goes to Bat* (PS–2). Illus. 2005, Penguin $15.99 (978-0-399-23604-4). In this appealing tale set in 1950s Brooklyn, Luke, a young African American boy who idolizes Jackie Robinson, longs for a chance to play stickball with the older boys in his neighborhood; when he finally gets his chance at bat, he strikes out but realizes that the keys to success are determination and persistence. (Rev: BL 2/1/05; SLJ 2/05)

4619 Jackson, Shelley. *Mimi's Dada Catifesto* (1–4). Illus. by author. 2010, Clarion $17 (978-0-547-12681-4). 48pp. In early 20th-century Switzerland an artistic alley cat named Mimi decides to become Dada's pet; with multimedia illustrations and an author's note. (Rev: BL 6/10*; LMC 10/10; SLJ 6/1/10)

4620 Jacobson, Rick. *The Master's Apprentice* (2–4). Illus. by Laura Fernandez. 2008, Tundra $18.95 (978-0-88776-783-8). 32pp. Marco, young apprentice to the artist Michelangelo and victim of a treacherous older apprentice, appears doomed to disappoint either his father or his master in this intense story about character. (Rev: BL 3/15/08; SLJ 5/08)

4621 Jacobson, Rick. *The Mona Lisa Caper* (2–4). Illus. 2005, Tundra $15.95 (978-0-88776-726-5). 24pp. This fact-based tale chronicles the 1911 theft of Leonardo da Vinci's *Mona Lisa* from the Louvre in Paris. (Rev: BL 7/05; SLJ 8/05)

4622 Jaspersohn, William. *The Scrimshaw Ring* (2–4). Illus. by Vernon Thornblad. 2002, Vermont Folklife Center $15.95 (978-0-916718-19-0). 32pp. In this book set in 1710 New England and based on reality, an amazing thing happens to young William Bateman — one of the pirates plundering his home gives the boy a ring that is then passed down the generations. (Rev: BL 11/15/02; SLJ 12/02)

4623 Jaspersohn, William. *The Two Brothers* (2–4). Illus. Series: Family Heritage. 2000, Vermont Folklife Center $14.95 (978-0-916718-16-9). 32pp. Based on a true story, this novel tells of two German brothers who immigrated separately to the United States in the 1880s and were miraculously reunited. (Rev: BL 11/1/00; SLJ 9/00)

4624 Johnson, Angela. *I Dream of Trains* (PS–2). Illus. by Loren Long. 2003, Simon & Schuster $16.95 (978-0-689-82609-2). A young African American boy working in the cotton fields of the Mississippi Delta dreams of riding away to a better life on a locomotive driven by the legendary Casey Jones. (Rev: HBG 4/04; SLJ 10/03)

4625 Johnson, Angela. *Just Like Josh Gibson* (PS–2). Illus. by Beth Peck. 2004, Simon & Schuster $15.95 (978-0-689-82628-3). 32pp. Negro Leagues legend Josh Gibson is a source of inspiration in this story about an African American girl who finds success at baseball in the 1940s. (Rev: BL 2/15/04; SLJ 3/04)

4626 Johnson, Angela. *The Rolling Store* (K–3). Illus. by Peter Catalanotto. 1997, Orchard LB $16.99 (978-0-531-33015-9). 32pp. A young African American girl tells her friend about the traveling store in a truck that used to visit their community during her grandfather's childhood. (Rev: BCCB 5/97; BL 2/15/97; SLJ 4/97)

4627 Johnson, Angela. *A Sweet Smell of Roses* (K–2). Illus. by Eric Velasquez. 2005, Simon & Schuster $16.95 (978-0-689-83252-9). 32pp. Two African American sisters sneak out of their house to hear a speech by Martin Luther King Jr. (Rev: BL 2/1/05; SLJ 3/05)

4628 Johnson, Angela. *Wind Flyers* (1–3). Illus. by Loren Long. 2007, Simon & Schuster $16.99 (978-0-689-84879-7). 32pp. A young African American boy proudly describes his great-great-uncle's prowess as a flyer and one of the Tuskegee Airmen. (Rev: BL 12/1/06; SLJ 1/07)

4629 Johnston, Tony. *The Harmonica* (3–6). Illus. by Ron Mazellan. 2004, Charlesbridge $15.95 (978-1-57091-547-5). 32pp. This moving tale of a young Jewish boy who plays his harmonica for the concentration camp commandant is based on truth. (Rev: BL 1/1–15/04; SLJ 5/04)

4630 Johnston, Tony. *Levi Strauss Gets a Bright Idea: A Fairly Fabricated Story of a Pair of Pants* (K–3). Illus. by Stacy Innerst. 2011, Harcourt $16.99 (978-0-15-206145-6). 32pp. A tall tale about the California Gold Rush and Levi Strauss's realization that they needed better pants; with a historical note by the author. (Rev: BL 9/15/11; SLJ 8/1/11*)

4631 Jungman, Ann. *The Most Magnificent Mosque* (1–4). Illus. by Shelley Fowles. 2004, Frances Lincoln $15.95 (978-1-84507-012-0). A beautiful mosque in Cordoba, Spain, is saved from destruction through the combined support of three friends — a Christian, a Jew, and a Muslim — who played in its gardens when they were young. (Rev: SLJ 9/04)

4632 Kajikawa, Kimiko. *Tsunami!* (PS–3). Illus. by Ed Young. 2009, Philomel $16.99 (978-0-399-25006-4). An old Japanese man sets his prized rice fields on fire in an attempt to save the villagers from a killer wave. (Rev: BL 11/15/08; SLJ 1/09)

4633 Karim, Roberta. *Kindle Me a Riddle* (K–2). Illus. by Bethanne Andersen. 1999, Greenwillow LB $16.89 (978-0-688-16204-7). 40pp. In frontier America, a family traces the origins of their simple pioneer home and its contents, such as the candles that were once beeswax. (Rev: BL 9/1/99; HBG 3/00; SLJ 1/00)

4634 Kay, Verla. *Covered Wagons, Bumpy Trails* (PS–3). Illus. by S. D. Schindler. 2000, Penguin $16.99 (978-0-399-22928-2). A rhyming tale with excellent paintings that depicts the hardships and triumphs of a pioneer family and their journey to California. (Rev: HB 1/01; HBG 3/01; SLJ 11/00)

4635 Kay, Verla. *Gold Fever* (K–3). Illus. by S. D. Schindler. 1999, Penguin $15.99 (978-0-399-23027-1). A young man encounters many obstacles while traveling to the California Gold Rush but, when he doesn't find gold, must go home disappointed. (Rev: BL 1/1–15/99; HB 3/99; HBG 10/99; SLJ 3/99)

4636 Kay, Verla. *Hornbooks and Inkwells* (PS–3). Illus. by S. D. Schindler. 2011, Putnam $16.99 (978-0-399-23870-3). 32pp. Rhyming text presents the experiences of two brothers attending an 18th-century one-room schoolhouse. (Rev: BL 6/1/11; HB 9–10/11; LMC 11–12/11; SLJ 7/11)

4637 Kay, Verla. *Tattered Sails* (K–3). Illus. by Dan Andreasen. 2001, Penguin $15.99 (978-0-399-23345-6). 32pp. A description of the difficult voyage of three Pilgrim children and their parents on their way to America in search of a better life. (Rev: BL 10/15/01; HBG 3/02; SLJ 9/01)

4638 Kay, Verla. *Whatever Happened to the Pony Express?* (K–3). Illus. by Kimberly Bulcken and Barry Root. 2010, Putnam $16.99 (978-0-399-24483-4). 32pp. Cross-country letters between a brother and sister serve as a framework for a history of the Pony Express and the forms of communication that supplanted it. (Rev: BL 5/1/10; LMC 10/10; SLJ 6/1/10)

4639 Keido, Ippo, retel. *The Butterfly's Dream: Children's Stories from China* (3–6). Illus. by Kazuko Stone. 2003, Tuttle $15.95 (978-0-8048-3480-3). This richly illustrated collection features a number of stories, linked by the flight of a butterfly, based on the ancient Chinese Chuang-Tzu. (Rev: HBG 4/04; SLJ 1/04)

4640 Kellerhals-Stewart, Heather. *Brave Highland Heart* (PS–1). Illus. by Werner Zimmerman. 1999, Stoddart $15.95 (978-0-7737-3099-1). A little Scottish girl fears she will be denied permission to go the ceilidh, a traditional Scottish party that will be held in the family barn, but her father allows her to stay up and enjoy the fun and dancing. (Rev: BL 8/99; SLJ 6/99)

4641 Kessler, Cristina. *The Best Beekeeper of Lalibela: A Tale from Africa* (PS–2). Illus. by Leonard Jenkins. 2006, Holiday $16.95 (978-0-8234-1858-9). 32pp. Almaz, a young Ethiopian girl, is determined to prove the men wrong and succeed at keeping bees and producing honey. (Rev: BL 8/06; SLJ 8/06)

4642 Ketcham, Sallie. *Bach's Big Adventure* (PS–3). Illus. by Timothy Bush. 1999, Orchard LB $17.99 (978-0-531-33140-8). 32pp. Ten-year-old Bach journeys to Hamburg to hear the man who is supposedly the greatest organist in the world. (Rev: BCCB 5/99; BL 4/1/99; HBG 10/99; SLJ 6/99)

4643 Khan, Rukhsana. *King for a Day* (2–4). Illus. by Christiane Krömer. 2013, Lee & Low $17.95 (978-160060659-5). 32pp. Based on the Pakistani spring festival of Basant and depicted through mixed media artwork (yarn, sketches, floss, etc.), *King for a Day* centers on Malik, a young boy confined to a wheelchair, who wins the kite flying contest and defeats the bully next door. Lexile AD600 (Rev: BLO 11/15/13; SLJ 11/13*)

4644 Khan, Rukhsana. *The Roses in My Carpets* (1–4). Illus. by Ronald Himler. 1998, Holiday House $15.95 (978-0-8234-1399-7). 32pp. A young Afghan boy who lives in a refugee camp dreams of freedom and a place without bombs or warfare as he learns to weave carpets. (Rev: BL 11/15/98; HBG 3/99; SLJ 11/98)

4645 Khan, Rukhsana. *Silly Chicken* (PS–2). Illus. by Yunmee Kyong. 2005, Viking $15.99 (978-0-670-05912-6). 32pp. A young Pakistani girl named Rani is jealous of her mother's affection for the family chicken. (Rev: BL 1/1–15/05; SLJ 4/05)

4646 Kimmel, Eric A. *Stormy's Hat: Just Right for a Railroad Man* (PS–2). Illus. by Andrea U'Ren. 2008, Farrar $16.95 (978-0-374-37262-0). 32pp. In the early 1900s, railroad engineer Stormy's long-term search for a suitable hat drives his wife Ida to design one herself, which leads to a successful international business; this story is based on fact, and the hats are still worn today. (Rev: BL 1/1–15/08; SLJ 5/08)

4647 Kimmel, Eric A, adapter. *Joha Makes a Wish: A Middle Eastern Tale* (1–3). Illus. by Omar Rayyan. 2010, Marshall Cavendish $17.99 (978-0-7614-5599-8). 40pp. In this tale based on Middle Eastern folklore, Joha's wishing stick, which he found on the way to Baghdad, causes nothing but trouble. e Lexile AD500L (Rev: HB 5–6/10; LMC 8–9/10; SLJ 4/1/10)

4648 Kimmelman, Leslie. *Everybody Bonjours!* (PS–2). Illus. by Sarah McMenemy. 2008, Knopf $16.99 (978-0-375-84443-0). 40pp. A little girl and her family take a guided tour of Paris in clever rhyme and watercolor art. (Rev: BL 8/08; SLJ 4/08)

4649 Kinsey-Warnock, Natalie. *From Dawn till Dusk* (K–3). Illus. by Mary Azarian. 2002, Houghton $16.00 (978-0-618-18655-6). 40pp. The author describes her childhood on a Vermont farm, contrasting the hard work with the resulting benefits as she details the different activities throughout the year. (Rev: BL 11/15/02; HBG 3/03; SLJ 10/02)

4650 Kinsey-Warnock, Natalie. *Nora's Ark* (K–3). Illus. by Emily Arnold McCully. 2005, HarperCollins LB $17.89 (978-0-06-029517-2). 32pp. The house that Grandpa is building up on the hill proves useful after all when the storms come in this story based on flooding in Vermont in 1927. (Rev: BL 5/15/05)

4651 Kirk, Connie Ann. *Sky Dancers* (1–3). Illus. by Christy Hale. 2004, Lee & Low $16.95 (978-1-58430-162-2). 32pp. John Cloud, a young Mohawk boy, is overwhelmed by New York City and by the skill and daring of his steelworker father, laboring far above the ground on the Empire State Building. (Rev: BL 11/15/04; SLJ 1/05)

4652 Kitamura, Satoshi. *Stone Age Boy* (1–4). Illus. by author. 2007, Candlewick $15.99 (978-0-7636-3474-2). 37pp. Suddenly transported to the Stone Age, a boy meets a girl named Om and learns all about life there, including tools, cave paintings, hunting, and cooking. (Rev: HB 1/08; LMC 3/08; SLJ 1/08)

4653 Knapp, Ruthie. *Who Stole Mona Lisa?* (1–3). Illus. by Jill McElmurry. 2010, Bloomsbury $17.99 (978-1-59990-058-2). 32pp. This account of the Mona Lisa's eventful history, including its theft from the Louvre in 1911, is told from the perspective of the painting. ∩ Lexile AD450L (Rev: BL 11/1/10; LMC 11–12/10; SLJ 12/1/10)

4654 Krebs, Laurie. *We're Riding on a Caravan: An Adventure on the Silk Road* (1–3). Illus. by Helen Cann. 2005, Barefoot Books $16.99 (978-1-84148-343-6). 32pp. This richly illustrated picture book follows a family of silk traders as they travel China's Silk Road. (Rev: BL 11/1/05; SLJ 1/06)

4655 Krensky, Stephen. *Dangerous Crossing: The Revolutionary Voyage of John and John Quincy Adams* (2–4). Illus. by Greg Harlin. 2005, Dutton $16.99 (978-0-525-46966-7). 32pp. This book based on diary accounts and including powerful watercolor paintings brings to life the perilous 1778 voyage of young John Quincy and his father aboard the *Boston.* (Rev: BL 3/1/05; SLJ 2/05)

4656 Krensky, Stephen. *Play Ball, Jackie!* (2–4). Illus. by Joe Morse. 2011, Millbrook $16.95 (978-0-8225-9030-9). 32pp. A father and son attend the opening day baseball game of the Brooklyn Dodgers in 1947 and witness Jackie Robinson's major league debut and the attendant prejudice. e Lexile 480L (Rev: BL 2/1/11; SLJ 3/1/11)

4657 Krensky, Stephen. *Sisters of Scituate Light* (1–3). Illus. by Stacey Schuett. 2008, Dutton $16.99 (978-0-525-47792-1). During the war of 1812 teenage sisters Rebecca and Abbie, alone at the lighthouse their father runs, succeed in scaring off British soldiers who are coming ashore; this exciting tale is based on a true story. (Rev: BL 4/15/08; LMC 10/08; SLJ 6/08)

4658 Krishnaswami, Uma. *Chachaji's Cup* (K–3). Illus. by Soumya Sitaraman. 2003, Children's Book Pr. $16.95 (978-0-89239-178-3). 32pp. Neel, an Indian boy living in the United States, listens to his great-uncle Chachaji's Hindu legends and his stories of the hardships and dangers he faced as a child refugee during the partition of India and Pakistan in 1947. (Rev: BL 3/15/03; HBG 10/03; SLJ 6/03)

4659 Krishnaswami, Uma. *Monsoon* (PS–2). Illus. by Jamel Akib. 2003, Farrar $16.00 (978-0-374-35015-4). A young girl in India and her family await the arrival of the monsoon rains in this attractive picture book full of Indian culture, with informative back matter. (Rev: BCCB 1/04; BL 9/1/03; HBG 4/04; LMC 3/04; SLJ 12/03)

4660 Kroll, Virginia. *Especially Heroes* (3–5). Illus. by Tim Ladwig. 2003, Eerdmans $16.00 (978-0-8028-5221-2). 32pp. The narrator remembers an incident in 1962, when her father reacted to an attack on a black woman in their neighborhood. (Rev: BL 2/1/03; HBG 10/03; SLJ 4/03)

4661 Krull, Kathleen, and Paul Brewer. *Fartiste* (K–3). Illus. by Boris Kulikov. 2008, Simon & Schuster $16.99 (978-1-4169-2828-7). 40pp. Joseph Pujol was a real "fartiste" who in Paris circa 1900 blew the audiences away with his gassy abilities. (Rev: BCCB 6/08; BL 8/08; HB 9/08; LMC 10/08; SLJ 7/08)

4662 Kushner, Tony. *Brundibar* (1–4). Illus. by Maurice Sendak. 2003, Hyperion $19.95 (978-0-7868-0904-2). 56pp. This poignant story, based on a Czech opera originally performed by children at a concentration camp, tells how two children, Pepecik and Anniku, struggle to get milk for their sick mother. (Rev: BL 11/15/03; HBG 4/04; SLJ 12/03)

4663 Kusugak, Michael A. *Arctic Stories* (2–4). Illus. by Vladyana Krykorka. 1998, Annick $18.95 (978-1-55037-452-0); paper $6.95 (978-1-55037-453-7). 40pp. Three stories about an Inuit girl growing up in a village around northern Hudson Bay are simply told with full-page watercolors. (Rev: BL 11/1/98; SLJ 3/99)

4664 Kyuchukov, Hristo. *My Name Was Hussein* (1–3). Illus. by Allan Eitzen. 2004, Boyds Mills $15.95 (978-1-56397-964-4). Based on the author's childhood experiences, this sobering tale looks at persecution of a Roma group in Bulgaria. (Rev: BL 4/15/04; SLJ 4/04)

4665 Lachenmeyer, Nathaniel. *The Origami Master* (PS–2). Illus. by Aki Sogabe. 2008, Albert Whitman $16.99 (978-0-8075-6134-8). 32pp. A Japanese origami master learns important lessons from a little bird; includes directions for folding an origami bird. (Rev: BL 10/1/08; SLJ 10/08)

4666 Lawlor, Laurie. *Old Crump: The True Story of a Trip West* (1–3). Illus. by John Winch. 2002, Holiday House $16.95 (978-0-8234-1608-0). 32pp. The members of a wagon train and their ox, Old Crump, find themselves lost in Death Valley in 1850. (Rev: BL 3/15/02; HBG 10/02; SLJ 6/02)

4667 Lawson, Julie. *Arizona Charlie and the Klondike Kid* (K–3). Illus. by Kasia Charko. 2003, Orca $15.95 (978-1-55143-250-2). Young Ben, an aspiring Gold Rush entertainer, finds the stage more alarming than he expected but shows his mettle when he encounters a thief. (Rev: HBG 10/03; SLJ 9/03)

4668 Lawson, Julie. *The Klondike Cat* (1–3). Illus. by Paul Mombourquette. 2002, Kids Can $15.95 (978-1-55337-013-0). 32pp. Noah doesn't get in trouble for bringing his cat on the journey to the Klondike in 1896 because it turns out that mousers are in great demand. (Rev: BL 11/15/02; HBG 3/03; SLJ 1/03)

4669 Le Tord, Bijou. *A Bird or Two: A Story About Henri Matisse* (K–3). Illus. 1999, Eerdmans $18.00 (978-0-8028-5184-0). 32pp. Using Matisse-like paintings, this picture book tells about the artist and the south of France that he loved. (Rev: BL 11/15/99; HBG 3/00; SLJ 2/00)

4670 Lee-Tai, Amy. *A Place Where Sunflowers Grow / Sabaku Ni Saita Himawari* (1–3). Illus. by Felicia Hoshino. 2006, Children's Book Pr. $16.95 (978-0-89239-215-5). 32pp. In English and Japanese, this is a gentle story of the Japanese internment in World War II, featuring a young Japanese American girl who tries to adjust by painting pictures. (Rev: BL 8/06)

4671 Lee, Huy Voun. *In the Leaves* (K–3). Illus. 2005, Holt $16.95 (978-0-8050-6764-4). On a trip to a farm, Xiao Ming is eager to introduce his friends to the 10 Chinese characters he has learned, and to explain their relationship to the surrounding world; includes effective illustrations and a pronunciation guide. (Rev: BL 8/05; SLJ 8/05)

4672 Lendroth, Susan. *Ocean Wide, Ocean Deep* (PS–2). Illus. by Raul Allen. 2008, Tricycle $15.99 (978-1-58246-232-5). 32pp. Set in 19th-century New England, this title follows a young girl as she yearns in rhymed couplets for the return of her sailor father. (Rev: BLO 12/11/08; SLJ 10/08)

4673 Leonetti, Mike. *Swinging for the Fences: Hank Aaron and Me* (2–4). Illus. by David Kim. 2008, Chronicle $15.99 (978-0-8118-5662-1). Little Leaguer Mark, whose batting leaves something to be desired, is a big fan of Hank Aaron and Aaron's advice helps him to improve his game. (Rev: BL 5/15/08; SLJ 5/08)

4674 Lester, Alison. *Running with the Horses* (2–4). Illus. by author. 2011, NorthSouth $16.95 (978-0-7358-4002-7). Unpaged. In Vienna during World War II, 10-year-old Nina and her father, with the help of an elderly cab horse, rescue four Lipizzaner stallions from the Spanish Riding School. (Rev: LMC 8–9/11; SLJ 4/11)

4675 Levine, Ellen. *Henry's Freedom Box* (1–3). Illus. by Kadir Nelson. 2007, Scholastic $16.99 (978-0-439-77733-9). 40pp. A fictionalized account of the dangerous and exciting story of a young slave who escaped to freedom in a packing crate, traveling by train and by steamboat until he arrived in Philadelphia. Caldecott Honor Book, 2008. (Rev: BL 2/1/07)

4676 Levitin, Sonia. *Junk Man's Daughter* (PS–3). Illus. by Guy Porfirio. Series: Tales of Young America. 2007, Sleeping Bear $17.95 (978-1-58536-315-5). 40pp. When Papa cannot find work in America, Hanna and her brothers help earn money for the family by collecting junk to sell. (Rev: BL 12/1/07; SLJ 4/08)

4677 Lewis, Alan K. *I Grew Up on a Farm* (1–4). Illus. by Bob Fletcher. 2005, Moo Pr. LB $19.95 (978-0-9766805-2-9). 32pp. Simple text and black-and-white family photographs describe growing up on a farm during the 1950s. (Rev: SLJ 2/06)

4678 Lewis, Rose. *I Love You Like Crazy Cakes* (PS–3). Illus. by Jane Dyer. 2000, Little, Brown $14.95 (978-0-316-52538-1). The author, an American, presents a fictional account of her trip to China to adopt a baby girl. (Rev: BL 9/1/00; HBG 10/01; SLJ 10/00)

4679 Lindsey, Kathleen D. *Sweet Potato Pie* (1–3). Illus. by Charlotte Riley-Webb. 2003, Lee & Low $16.95 (978-1-58430-061-8). When foreclosure threatens the farm, Sadie, an 8-year-old African American girl, pitches in with the rest of her family to sell sweet potato pies. (Rev: BL 9/15/03; HBG 4/04; SLJ 12/03)

4680 Lipp, Frederick. *The Caged Birds of Phnom Penh* (PS–3). Illus. by Ronald Himler. 2001, Holiday House $16.95 (978-0-8234-1534-2). 32pp. Ary, an 8-year-old girl living in Cambodia, tests the proverb that says "letting a caged bird go free makes wishes come true." (Rev: BCCB 4/01; BL 4/1/01; HBG 3/02; SLJ 5/01)

4681 Lipp, Frederick. *Running Shoes* (K–2). Illus. by Jason Gaillard. 2008, Charlesbridge $16.95 (978-1-58089-175-2); paper $7.95 (978-1-58089-176-9). 32pp. After she gets a pair of shoes, Sophy, a Cambodian girl, runs 5 miles each way to get to the school where she is the only girl. (Rev: BL 1/1–15/08; LMC 10/08; SLJ 2/08)

4682 Littlesugar, Amy. *Freedom School, Yes!* (PS–3). Illus. by Floyd Cooper. 2001, Penguin $16.99 (978-0-399-23006-6). 40pp. Based on fact, this is the story of volunteers who came South during the civil rights struggle in 1964 and set up "freedom schools." (Rev: BCCB 2/01; BL 2/15/01; HBG 10/01; SLJ 1/01)

4683 Lo, Ginnie. *Auntie Yang's Great Soybean Picnic* (K–2). Illus. by Beth Lo. 2012, Lee & Low $18.95 (978-160060442-3). 32pp. Chinese sisters in Indiana in the

1950s joyously discover a soybean farm and start a tradition of an annual celebration picnic. (Rev: BL 4/15/12*; LMC 11–12/12; SLJ 6/1/12*)

4684 Lodding, Linda Ravin. *A Gift for Mama* (K–2). Illus. by Alison Jay. 2014, Knopf $17.99 (978-038575331-9). 32pp. In 19th-century Vienna young Oskar searches for the perfect gift for his mother, trading one gift for another as he roams the city. **e** (Rev: BL 3/1/14; SLJ 3/14)

4685 Lofthouse, Liz. *Ziba Came on a Boat* (1–3). Illus. by Robert Ingpen. 2007, Kane $15.95 (978-1-933605-52-4). Lofthouse, who has worked with Afghan refugees, tells a simple story of a little girl named Ziba who hopes for a safer life as she travels by sea on a small fishing boat; beautiful illustrations add to the impact. (Rev: BL 11/1/07; LMC 1/08; SLJ 10/07)

4686 Lorbiecki, Marybeth. *Jackie's Bat* (1–3). Illus. by Brian Pinkney. 2006, Simon & Schuster $15.95 (978-0-689-84102-6). 40pp. A young batboy named Joey reveals his prejudice when Jackie Robinson joins the Brooklyn Dodgers and his subsequent growing admiration for the player. (Rev: BL 2/1/06; SLJ 1/06)

4687 Lord, Michelle. *Little Sap and Monsieur Rodin* (2–4). Illus. by Felicia Hoshino. 2006, Lee & Low $16.95 (978-1-58430-248-3). 32pp. Little Sap, a dancer from Cambodia, is flattered to be noticed by the artist Auguste Rodin in this story based on actual events and illustrated with lovely mixed-media paintings. (Rev: BL 5/1/06)

4688 Lowell, Susan. *The Elephant Quilt! Stitch by Stitch to California* (K–3). Illus. by Stacey Dressen-McQueen. 2008, Farrar $16.95 (978-0-374-38223-0). 40pp. With her grandmother, Lily Rose stitches a quilt of her family's journey west by covered wagon in 1859. (Rev: BCCB 5/08; BL 4/15/08; SLJ 7/08)

4689 Lubner, Susan. *A Horse's Tale: A Colonial Williamsburg Adventure* (PS–1). Illus. by Margie Moore. 2008, Abrams $16.95 (978-0-8109-9490-4). In colonial Williamsburg Lancer, Garrick the Gardener's horse, is feeling blue and many of the citizens (animals dressed as humans) have opinions on what ails him; the consensus is that he's lonely and needs a friend. Images introduce the town, and the various jobs are explained. (Rev: BL 5/1/08; SLJ 6/08)

4690 Lunge-Larsen, Lise, and Margi Preus. *The Legend of the Lady Slipper: An Ojibwe Tale* (PS–3). Illus. by Andrea Arroyo. 1999, Houghton $15.00 (978-0-395-90512-8). 32pp. An Ojibwa tale about how a young girl's moccasins are turned into the plant known as lady slippers, as a reward for her saving her village from a plague. (Rev: BCCB 7–8/99; BL 4/15/99; HBG 10/99; SLJ 5/99) [398.2]

4691 Lunn, Janet. *Laura Secord: A Story of Courage* (3–6). Illus. by Maxwell Newhouse. 2002, Tundra $16.95 (978-0-88776-538-4). Lunn's text and the accompanying illustrations give drama to the story of Secord's trek to warn the British during the War of 1812. (Rev: HB 3/02; HBG 10/02; SLJ 4/02)

4692 Lyons, Kelly Starling. *Ellen's Broom* (K–3). Illus. by Daniel Minter. 2012, Putnam $16.99 (978-

039925003-3). 32pp. Two former slaves joyfully legalize their marriage when the state laws are changed in Virginia, bringing with them a symbolic broom reminding them of the "jumping the broom" practice of the past. (Rev: BL 2/1/12; LMC 8–9/12; SLJ 1/12)

4693 McAlister, Caroline. *Holy Molé!* (K–2). Illus. by Stefan Czernecki. 2007, August House $16.95 (978-0-87483-775-9). The author spins a tale about the creation of the first molé in a serendipitous accident in a Mexican monastery's kitchen. (Rev: SLJ 8/07)

4694 McBrier, Page. *Beatrice's Goat* (K–3). Illus. by Lori Lohstoeter. 2001, Simon & Schuster $16.00 (978-0-689-82460-9). 40pp. Beatrice longs to attend school in her Ugandan village, and when her family gets a goat from an aid organization, it provides enough income to send her there. (Rev: BCCB 2/01; BL 2/15/01; HBG 10/01; SLJ 2/01)

4695 McCaughrean, Geraldine. *The Jesse Tree* (2–4). Illus. by Bee Willey. 2005, Eerdmans $20.00 (978-0-8028-5288-5). 96pp. A curious young boy pesters a crotchety old woodcarver into telling him Bible stories about the Old Testament characters who are the spiritual ancestors of Jesus Christ. (Rev: BL 10/1/05; SLJ 1/06)

4696 McClintock, Barbara. *Adele and Simon* (K–3). Illus. 2006, Farrar $16.00 (978-0-374-38044-1). As Adele escorts her little brother home from school through the streets of 1900s Paris, the boy manages to lose something at every stop along the way; endpaper maps add to this view of the City of Light. (Rev: BL 6/1–15/06; HB 9/06; HBG 4/07; LMC 3/07; SLJ 8/06)

4697 McCully, Emily Arnold. *The Escape of Oney Judge: Martha Washington's Slave Finds Freedom* (2–4). Illus. by author. 2007, Farrar $16.00 (978-0-374-32225-0). In this fictionalized account of the escape of one of Martha Washington's slaves, Oney Judge travels with the Washingtons to Philadelphia where she meets free blacks and begins to appreciate the concept of freedom. (Rev: BCCB 6/07; BL 11/15/06; SLJ 2/07)

4698 McCully, Emily Arnold. *Mirette and Bellini Cross Niagara Falls* (PS–3). Illus. 2000, Penguin $15.99 (978-0-399-23348-7). 32pp. A thrilling adventure story in which young Mirette and her guardian, the high-wire-artist, Bellini, come to the States for the ultimate stunt, crossing Niagara Falls on a wire. (Rev: BCCB 1/01; BL 11/15/00; HBG 10/01; SLJ 11/00)

4699 McCully, Emily Arnold. *Mirette on the High Wire* (PS–2). Illus. 1992, Penguin $16.99 (978-0-399-22130-9). 32pp. Set in Paris 100 years ago, this is the story of how a young girl helps a high-wire performer regain his courage. Caldecott Medal winner, 1993. (Rev: BCCB 10/92*; BL 11/15/92; SLJ 10/92)

4700 MacDonald, Maryann. *The Christmas Cat* (K–2). Illus. by Amy June Bates. 2013, Dial $16.99 (978-080373498-2). 32pp. In a stable in Bethlehem a little cat comforts a fractious baby Jesus. (Rev: BLO 11/15/13; HB 11–12/13; SLJ 10/13)

4701 McDonald, Megan. *Saving the Liberty Bell* (K–3). Illus. by Marsha Carrington. 2005, Simon & Schuster

$16.95 (978-0-689-85167-4). In this exciting, fact-based story from the American Revolution, 11-year-old John Jacob Mickley tells how he helped to hide the Liberty Bell from British troops. (Rev: BL 7/05; SLJ 7/05)

4702 McDonnell, Patrick. *Me . . . Jane* (PS–3). Illus. by author. 2011, Little, Brown $15.99 (978-0-316-04546-9). 40pp. With many nice details, this picture book shows Jane Goodall's journey from a young nature-loving child to a brilliant researcher in Africa. (Rev: BL 3/15/11*; HB 3–4/11; LMC 10/11; SLJ 4/11)

4703 McGill, Alice. *Way Up and Over Everything* (2–5). Illus. by Jude Daly. 2008, Houghton $16.00 (978-0-618-38796-0). 32pp. Five recently arrived slaves simply disappear up into the air in this folktale set in the mid-19th century. (Rev: BCCB 7/08; BL 2/1/08; HB 7/08; SLJ 9/08) [398.2]

4704 MacKall, Dandi Daley. *A Girl Named Dan* (1–3). Illus. by Renee Graef. 2008, Sleeping Bear $16.95 (978-1-58536-351-3). 32pp. In 1961 Dandi is excluded from baseball simply because she's a girl. (Rev: BLO 7/30/08; LMC 10/08; SLJ 6/08)

4705 McKissack, Patricia C. *Goin' Someplace Special* (K–3). Illus. by Jerry Pinkney. 2001, Simon & Schuster $16.00 (978-0-689-81885-1). Young Tricia Ann sets off on her first journey by herself and must navigate the South of the 1950s, working out where an African American is allowed to go. (Rev: BCCB 9/01; BL 8/01; HB 11/01; HBG 3/02; SLJ 9/01)

4706 McKissack, Patricia C. *Ma Dear's Aprons* (PS–3). Illus. by Floyd Cooper. 1997, Simon & Schuster $16.00 (978-0-689-81051-0). 32pp. During the early 1900s in Alabama, Ma Dear must support her family by doing domestic work. (Rev: BCCB 6/97; BL 2/15/97; HB 5/97; SLJ 6/97)

4707 McMillan, Bruce. *How the Ladies Stopped the Wind* (K–2). Illus. by Guennella. 2007, Houghton $16.00 (978-0-618-77330-5). 32pp. In windy Iceland, determined women plant trees as a windbreak and try to discourage the sheep from eating them. (Rev: BCCB 10/07; BL 10/1/07; HB 1/08; SLJ 12/07)

4708 McNulty, Faith. *If You Decide to Go to the Moon* (K–3). Illus. by Steven Kellogg. 2005, Scholastic $16.99 (978-0-590-48359-9). 48pp. McNulty describes how it will feel to travel to the moon in this mock guide for prospective travelers. (Rev: BCCB 11/05; BL 11/1/05; HB 9/05; HBG 4/06; LMC 1/06; SLJ 10/05*)

4709 Madrigal, Antonio H. *Erandi's Braids* (PS–3). Illus. by Tomie dePaola. 1999, Penguin $16.99 (978-0-399-23212-1). Erandi, a young member of a poor 1950s Mexican family, reluctantly decides to sell her beautiful hair to help her family. (Rev: BL 1/1–15/99*; HBG 10/99; SLJ 2/99)

4710 Malaspina, Ann. *Finding Lincoln* (2–4). Illus. by Colin Bootman. 2009, Whitman $16.99 (978-080752435-0). 32pp. In segregated Alabama in 1951 a librarian helps young Louis, an African American, to get access to the library and check out books about Abraham Lincoln. (Rev: BL 9/15/09; LMC 11–12/09; SLJ 8/1/09)

4711 Marceau, Fani. *Panorama: A Foldout Book* (1–3). Illus. by Joëlle Jolivet. 2009, Abrams $19.95 (978-0-8109-8332-8). 32pp. An oversize tour of locations around the world with poetic descriptions and dramatic panoramic woodcut illustrations that fold out. (Rev: BL 3/1/09; HB 7/09)

4712 Marciano, John Bemelmans. *Madeline and the Cats of Rome* (PS–1). Illus. by author. 2008, Viking $17.99 (978-0-670-06297-3). 48pp. Sightseeing in Rome, Miss Clavel and the "twelve little girls in two straight lines" have their camera stolen and Madeline and her dog, Genevieve, give chase. (Rev: BL 9/1/08)

4713 Mason, Margaret H. *These Hands* (PS–3). Illus. by Floyd Cooper. 2011, Houghton Harcourt $16.99 (978-0-547-21566-2). 32pp. An African American grandfather tells his grandson about the civil rights movement by relating personal stories of work in a bakery where his skilled hands were not allowed to touch the bread. Lexile AD680L (Rev: BL 2/1/11; LMC 10/11; SLJ 3/1/11)

4714 Medearis, Angela Shelf. *Rum-a-Tum-Tum* (PS–3). Illus. by James Ransome. 1997, Holiday House LB $16.95 (978-0-8234-1143-6). 32pp. All the color, excitement, and sound of a market in the French Quarter of New Orleans at the turn of the century are captured in this picture book. (Rev: BCCB 7–8/97; BL 5/1/97; SLJ 7/97)

4715 Messinger, Carla. *When the Shadbush Blooms* (K–5). Illus. by David Kanietakeron Fadden. 2007, Tricycle $15.95 (978-1-58246-192-2). Traditional Sister and Contemporary Sister describe their Lenni Lenape family traditions in this effective book with endnotes and a pronunciation guide. (Rev: SLJ 11/07)

4716 Meunier, Brian. *Bravo, Tavo!* (K–3). Illus. by Perky Edgerton. 2007, Dutton $16.99 (978-0-525-47478-4). A Mexican boy who loves basketball learns about sacrifice and community spirit in this well-written story. (Rev: BL 5/15/07; SLJ 8/07)

4717 Michelson, Richard. *Busing Brewster* (1–3). Illus. by R. G. Roth. 2010, Knopf $16.99 (978-0-375-83334-2). 32pp. In 1974 Boston two African American brothers are bused across town to a white school and a challenging year. (Rev: BL 3/15/10; LMC 8–9/10; SLJ 6/1/10)

4718 Michelson, Richard. *Happy Feet: The Savoy Ballroom Lindy Hoppers and Me* (K–3). Illus. by E. B. Lewis. 2005, Harcourt $16.00 (978-0-15-205057-3). 32pp. A young African American boy hears the story of the opening of Harlem's Savoy Ballroom on the night he himself was born; this story beautifully evokes the mood of the 1920s. (Rev: BL 11/1/05; SLJ 11/05)

4719 Miller, William. *The Bus Ride* (PS–1). Illus. by John Ward. 1998, Lee & Low $15.95 (978-1-880000-60-1). Set in the segregated South during the 1950s, this picture book tells of the consequences faced by a young girl when she dares to sit in the front of a bus. (Rev: BL 8/98; HBG 3/99; SLJ 10/98)

4720 Miller, William. *The Piano* (K–3). Illus. by Susan Keeter. 2000, Lee & Low $15.95 (978-1-880000-98-4). In the segregated South in the early 1900s, music-loving

Tia is taught to play the piano by the elderly woman for whom she cleans house. (Rev: BCCB 10/00; BL 7/00; HBG 10/00; SLJ 7/00)

4721 Miller, William. *Rent Party Jazz* (1–4). Illus. by Charlotte Riley-Webb. 2001, Lee & Low $16.95 (978-1-58430-025-0). 32pp. A young African American boy named Sonny and an old jazz musician named Smilin' Jack throw a rent party to help Sonny's mother in 1930s New Orleans. (Rev: BL 11/15/01; HBG 3/02; SLJ 11/01)

4722 Miller, William. *Richard Wright and the Library Card* (K–4). Illus. by R. Gregory Christie. 1997, Lee & Low $16.95 (978-1-880000-57-1). In this story based on fact, African American Richard Wright, growing up in the segregated South, borrows books from the all-white library by pretending he is taking them to his white boss. (Rev: BCCB 3/98; BL 12/1/97; HBG 3/98; SLJ 2/98)

4723 Mills, Lauren. *The Rag Coat* (3–5). Illus. 1991, Little, Brown $16.95 (978-0-316-57407-5). 32pp. A picture book that celebrates Appalachia. (Rev: BCCB 1/92; BL 10/15/91; HB 11/91; SLJ 11/91*)

4724 Milway, Katie Smith. *The Good Garden: How One Family Went from Hunger to Having Enough* (2–4). Illus. by Sylvie Daigneault. 2010, Kids Can $18.95 (978-1-55453-488-3). 32pp. Eleven-year-old Maria Luz is put in charge of her Honduran family's garden when her father must leave home to find work. (Rev: BL 11/1/10; SLJ 10/1/10)

4725 Mitchell, Margaree King. *When Grandmama Sings* (2–4). Illus. by James E. Ransome. 2012, HarperCollins $16.99 (978-0-688-17563-4). 40pp. A young African American girl accompanies her talented grandmother on a singing tour through the segregated South of the 1950s in this story that includes many lessons in prejudice and exclusion. (Rev: BL 2/1/12; HB 1–2/12; SLJ 12/1/11)

4726 Miura, Taro. *The Tiny King* (PS–2). Illus. by author. 2013, Candlewick $14.99 (978-076366687-3). 32pp. A tiny king lives in a big palace, with a big bed, big soldiers, and more food than he could ever eat, but he is lonely — until he meets the love of his life, a big princess, and they have an enormous family to fill his big castle. (Rev: BL 11/1/13*; HB 11–12/13; SLJ 11/13)

4727 Mollel, Tololwa M. *My Rows and Piles of Coins* (PS–3). Illus. by E. B. Lewis. 1999, Clarion $16.00 (978-0-395-75186-2). 32pp. Saruni, a Tanzanian boy, scrimps and saves to buy a bicycle, so he can help his mother with her chores. (Rev: BCCB 10/99; BL 8/99; HBG 3/00; SLJ 8/99)

4728 Moore, Inga. *Captain Cat* (PS–3). Illus. by author. 2013, Candlewick $15.99 (978-076366151-9). 48pp. Captain Cat has collected a boatload of cats he loves, and he must make a difficult decision when a young queen offers him riches in exchange for a way to control the rats in her kingdom. Lexile AD960 (Rev: BL 11/1/13; SLJ 10/13)

4729 Mora, Pat. *The Song of Francis and the Animals* (K–3). Illus. by David Frampton. 2005, Eerdmans $16.00 (978-0-8028-5253-3). 32pp. This poetic narrative celebrates the close bonds between Saint Francis and the animals he encountered throughout his life. (Rev: BL 10/15/05; SLJ 10/05)

4730 Morrow, Barbara Olenyik. *A Good Night for Freedom* (K–4). Illus. by Leonard Jenkins. 2004, Holiday House $16.95 (978-0-8234-1709-4). In 1839, young Hallie helps two runaway slave girls despite her father's warnings not to do so. (Rev: BL 3/1/04; SLJ 2/04)

4731 Moser, Lisa. *Kisses on the Wind* (K–3). Illus. by Kathryn Brown. 2009, Candlewick $15.99 (978-0-7636-3110-9). 32pp. Lydia struggles with saying goodbye to Grandma as she and her parents prepare to head west on the Oregon Trail. (Rev: BL 10/1/09; SLJ 12/1/09)

4732 Myers, Tim. *Basho and the Fox* (K–3). Illus. by Oki S. Han. 2000, Marshall Cavendish $15.95 (978-0-7614-5068-9). 32pp. Basho, Japan's famous haiku poet, meets a fox who promises not to eat the poet's cherries if he can produce a poem that the fox thinks is worthy. (Rev: BL 9/15/00; HB 9/00; HBG 3/01; SLJ 10/00)

4733 Naden, Corinne J., and Rose Blue. *Ron's Big Mission* (K–2). Illus. by Don Tate. 2009, Dutton $16.99 (978-0-525-47849-2). 32pp. Nine-year-old Ron McNair, who would later become an astronaut and die in the 1986 *Challenger* explosion, challenges his local library's refusal to give him a library card because he is African American. (Rev: BL 2/1/09; SLJ 2/09)

4734 Namioka, Lensey. *The Laziest Boy in the World* (K–3). Illus. by YongSheng Xuan. 1998, Holiday House $16.95 (978-0-8234-1330-0). 32pp. A humorous story about a Chinese boy who is so lazy he washes alternate sides of his face each day, and the thief who makes him change his ways. (Rev: BL 11/1/98; HBG 3/99; SLJ 10/98)

4735 Napoli, Donna Jo. *The Crossing* (1–3). Illus. by Jim Madsen. 2011, Simon & Schuster $16.99 (978-1-4169-9474-9). Unpaged. Napoli provides a baby's-eye-view of the western Rockies as Sacagawea's son is carried westward in 1805. Lexile AD690L (Rev: LMC 11–12/11; SLJ 7/11)

4736 Napoli, Donna Jo, and Elena Furrow. *Ready to Dream* (K–3). Illus. by Bronwyn Bancroft. 2009, Bloomsbury $16.99 (978-1-59990-049-0). 32pp. Ally, a young artist visiting Australia, meets an Aboriginal woman who mentors the young girl's artistic spirit. (Rev: BL 12/15/08; SLJ 2/09)

4737 Nelson, S. D. *The Star People: A Lakota Story* (PS–2). Illus. by author. 2003, Abrams $14.95 (978-0-8109-4584-5). When two Lakota siblings, Sister Girl and Young Wolf, wander far from home and encounter a multitude of dangers, they are guided to safety by the Star People, the spirits of the Old Ones. (Rev: HBG 4/04; SLJ 9/03)

4738 Nelson, Vaunda Micheaux. *Almost to Freedom* (1–3). Illus. by Colin Bootman. Series: Carolrhoda Picture Books. 2003, Carolrhoda $15.95 (978-1-57505-342-4). This moving story, narrated by the rag doll of a slave child, describes how the child, Lindy, and her family escape to freedom on the Underground Railroad. (Rev: BL 9/15/03; HBG 4/04; SLJ 12/03)

4739 Nez, John Abbott. *Cromwell Dixon's Sky-Cycle* (K–3). Illus. by author. 2009, Putnam $16.99 (978-0-399-25041-5). 32pp. An intriguing fictionalized story set in the early years of the 20th century and describing 14-year-old Cromwell Dixon's determination to pedal into the sky; a one-page biography adds details. (Rev: BL 8/09; LMC 10/09; SLJ 7/09)

4740 Niemann, Christoph. *The Pet Dragon: A Story About Adventure, Friendship, and Chinese Characters* (1–4). Illus. by author. 2008, Greenwillow $16.99 (978-0-06-157776-5). 32pp. An excellent way to introduce Chinese language and characters, this is a story about a young girl, Lin, and her escapee dragon. (Rev: BL 9/1/08; SLJ 9/08)

4741 Nikola-Lisa, W. *Magic in the Margins: A Medieval Tale of Bookmaking* (K–3). Illus. by Bonnie Christensen. 2007, Houghton $17.00 (978-0-618-49642-6). 32pp. Working as an apprentice in a medieval monastery's scriptorium, Simon, a young orphan, dreams of illuminating manuscripts. (Rev: BL 4/1/07)

4742 Noble, Trinka Hakes. *The Legend of the Jersey Devil* (2–4). Illus. by Gerald Kelley. 2013, Sleeping Bear $16.99 (978-1-58536-837-2). 32pp. This spooky picture book tells the story of the legendary creature — part goat, part bat, with horns, a forked tail, and glowing eyes — rumored to haunt the Pine Barrens of New Jersey for hundreds of years. (Rev: BL 7/13; SLJ 8/13)

4743 Noguchi, Rick, and Deneen Jenks. *Flowers from Mariko* (K–3). Illus. by Michelle Reiko Kumata. 2001, Lee & Low $16.95 (978-1-58430-032-8). 32pp. When Mariko's Japanese American family is released from an internment camp after World War II, they must work to rebuild the life they lost. (Rev: BL 11/1/01; HBG 3/02; SLJ 11/01)

4744 Noyes, Deborah. *Hana in the Time of the Tulips* (K–3). Illus. by Bagram Ibatoulline. 2004, Candlewick $16.99 (978-0-7636-1875-9). 40pp. When her father is swept up in the tulip mania gripping 17th-century Holland, young Hana seeks to regain his attention; the illustrations evoke paintings by Rembrandt. (Rev: BL 11/1/04; SLJ 10/04)

4745 Ohi, Ruth. *Kenta and the Big Wave* (PS–3). Illus. by author. 2013, Annick $19.95 (978-155451577-6); paper $9.95 (978-15545157-6-9). 32pp. A Japanese boy named Kenta knows what to do when the tsunami siren goes off; he drops his personalized soccer ball as he runs uphill and is amazed to have it returned eventually by a boy across the ocean. Based on a true story. Lexile AD560 (Rev: BL 11/1/13; LMC 5–6/14*; SLJ 10/13)

4746 Olofsson, Helena. *The Little Jester* (K–3). Illus. 2002, R&S $16.00 (91-29-65499-8). 28pp. French monks reluctantly open the doors of the monastery to a jester, who then performs a miracle. (Rev: BL 3/15/02; HBG 10/02; SLJ 5/02)

4747 Olshan, Matthew. *The Mighty Lalouche* (PS–2). Illus. by Sophie Blackall. 2013, Random House $17.99 (978-0-375-86225-0). 40pp. At the turn of the 20th century a Parisian postman loses his job when an electric automobile is introduced; he decides to become a boxer and finds unexpected success in the ring until the electric cars fail and he returns to his postal route; appealing art and an informative Author's Note enhance this evocative story. ❿ Lexile AD690 (Rev: BL 6/13*; HB 5–6/13; LMC 11–12/13; SLJ 4/13*)

4748 O'Neal, Deborah, and Angela Westengard. *The Trouble with Henry: A Tale of Walden Pond* (PS–2). Illus. by S. D. Schindler. 2005, Candlewick $16.99 (978-0-7636-1828-5). 40pp. A fictional account of Thoreau's efforts to keep Walden Pond free of industry; a note adds biographical information. (Rev: BL 10/15/05; SLJ 10/05)

4749 O'Neill, Alexis. *The Kite That Bridged Two Nations* (2–4). Illus. by Terry Widener. 2013, Boyds Mills/Calkins Creek $16.95 (978-159078938-4). 40pp. Homan Walsh loves kites, and when he hears about the opportunity to create a kite that could span the Niagara between the United States and Canada, he jumps at the chance to create it, even knowing that he faces incredible odds; based on a true story about the 19th century. Lexile 740 (Rev: BL 9/15/13; LMC 1–2/14*; SLJ 10/13)

4750 Oppenheim, Shulamith Levey. *Ali and the Magic Stew* (PS–3). Illus. by Winslow Pels. 2002, Boyds Mills $15.95 (978-1-56397-869-2). 32pp. In this Persian tale, a proud, spoiled merchant's son learns humility when he must beg for coins to save his father's life. (Rev: BCCB 5/02; BL 4/15/02; HBG 10/02; SLJ 4/02)

4751 Ormerod, Jan. *Lizzie Nonsense: A Story of Pioneer Days* (PS–2). Illus. 2005, Clarion $15.00 (978-0-618-57493-3). 32pp. The power of imagination is shown in this beautifully illustrated story of Lizzie and her mother, pioneers living alone on Australia's frontier while Papa goes away to work. (Rev: BL 9/15/05; SLJ 9/05)

4752 Pace, Lorenzo. *Jalani and the Lock* (PS–K). Illus. 2001, Rosen $23.95 (978-0-8239-9700-8). 32pp. A young African boy named Jalani, who spends years as a slave, passes the lock from his chains on to his grandchildren. (Rev: BL 2/15/01)

4753 Panahi, H. L. *Bebop Express* (K–2). Illus. by Steve Johnson. 2005, HarperCollins LB $16.89 (978-0-06-057191-7). 32pp. Rhythm and atmosphere make this a jazzy train trip from New York to New Orleans. (Rev: BL 6/1–15/05)

4754 Park, Frances, and Ginger Park. *Good-Bye, 382 Shin Dang Dong* (1–3). Illus. by Yangsook Choi. 2002, National Geographic $16.95 (978-0-7922-7985-3). Jangmi is sad to leave Korea and her friends and move to Massachusetts. (Rev: HBG 3/03; SLJ 10/02)

4755 Park, Frances, and Ginger Park. *The Royal Bee* (K–3). Illus. by Christopher Zhong-Yuan Zhang. 2000, Boyds Mills $16.95 (978-1-56397-614-8). A simple tale about a poor Korean boy growing up in the the late 19th century and his efforts to get an education so he can lift himself and his mother out of poverty. (Rev: HBG 10/00; SLJ 4/00)

4756 Park, Frances, and Ginger Park. *Where on Earth Is My Bagel?* (K–3). Illus. by Grace Lin. 2001, Lee & Low

$16.00 (978-1-58430-033-5). A Korean boy hungry for a bagel sends a message to New York by pigeon but only receives a recipe in return, which his local baker is happy to make in this book full of bagel shapes. (Rev: HBG 3/02; SLJ 9/01)

4757 Park, Linda Sue. *Bee-bim Bop!* (PS–2). Illus. by Ho Baek Lee. 2005, Clarion $15.00 (978-0-618-26511-4). A hungry Korean girl helps her mother shop for ingredients and then prepare a favorite meal; the recipe is included. (Rev: BL 10/15/05; SLJ 9/05)

4758 Park, Linda Sue. *The Firekeeper's Son* (K–3). Illus. by Julie Downing. 2004, Clarion $16.00 (978-0-618-13337-6). 40pp. In the early 19th-century Korea, a young boy must take his father's place and light the bonfire that is part of the signal system; beautiful watercolor illustrations complement the picture-book story. (Rev: BL 2/1/04; SLJ 5/04)

4759 Pelley, Kathleen T. *Magnus Maximus, A Marvelous Measurer* (K–3). Illus. by S. D. Schindler. 2010, Farrar $16.99 (978-0-374-34725-3). 32pp. In Victorian England, eccentric elderly Magnus Maximus is obsessed with counting and measuring until he learns there's more to life than quantification. (Rev: BL 3/15/10; LMC 5–6/10; SLJ 5/1/10)

4760 Pendziwol, Jean E. *Marja's Skis* (1–3). Illus. by Jirina Marton. 2007, Groundwood $17.95 (978-0-88899-674-9). 32pp. After the death of her father, Marja, a young Finnish immigrant, feels overwhelmed by the difficulties her family faces in the 19th-century Canadian logging town where they live, yet she finds the courage to rescue a man who is in danger. (Rev: BL 12/1/07; SLJ 10/07)

4761 Pendziwol, Jean E. *The Red Sash* (1–3). Illus. by Nicolas Debon. 2005, Groundwood $16.95 (978-0-88899-589-6). 40pp. A young mixed-race boy, son of a voyageur, fur traders who wore red sashes, describes life in and around Lake Huron in the early 19th century. (Rev: BL 12/1/05; SLJ 1/06)

4762 Pennypacker, Sara. *Sparrow Girl* (K–3). Illus. by Yoko Tanaka. 2009, Hyperion $16.99 (978-1-4231-1187-0). 40pp. A little girl called Ming-Li rebels against Chairman Mao's misguided war on sparrows in 1958. (Rev: BCCB 2/09; BL 1/1–15/09; LMC 5/09; SLJ 3/09)

4763 Perlov, Betty Rosenberg. *Rifka Takes a Bow* (PS–1). Illus. by Cosei Kawa. 2013, Lerner/Kar-Ben $17.95 (978-076138127-3). 32pp. Young Rifka, brought up by actors in the Yiddish theater, loves the atmosphere and is thrilled to find herself suddenly at the center of attention. e (Rev: BL 9/15/13; LMC 3–4/14; SLJ 8/13)

4764 Perrin, Clotilde. *At the Same Moment, Around the World* (K–3). Illus. by author. 2014, Chronicle $17.99 (978-145212208-3). 36pp. A trip around the world, starting at the Greenwich meridian and moving east, imagining the activities of children in various countries. e (Rev: BLO 3/1/14; SLJ 3/14)

4765 Phillipps, J. C. *Wink: The Ninja Who Wanted to Be Noticed* (PS–2). Illus. by author. 2009, Viking $15.99 (978-0-670-01092-9). 32pp. Wink's love of self-expres-

sion makes him unsuited to a career as a ninja, but he finds a way to use his training in a circus. (Rev: BCCB 6/09; BL 1/1–15/09; SLJ 2/09)

4766 Polacco, Patricia. *Babushka Baba Yaga* (PS–3). Illus. 1993, Penguin $16.99 (978-0-399-22531-4). In this reversal of the traditional Russian folklore, the witch Baba Yaga is really a kindly grandmother named Babushka. (Rev: BL 8/93)

4767 Polacco, Patricia. *The Blessing Cup* (1–3). Illus. by author. 2013, Simon & Schuster $17.99 (978-1-4424-5047-9). 48pp. In this prequel to *The Keeping Quilt* (1988), Polacco tells the story of a "blessing cup," its difficult journey from czarist Russia to America, and the significance this single tea cup held for generations of a Jewish family. Sydney Taylor Book Award. e Lexile 740 (Rev: BL 10/1/13; LMC 1–2/14; SLJ 8/13)

4768 Polacco, Patricia. *The Butterfly* (K–4). Illus. 2000, Penguin $16.99 (978-0-399-23170-4). Based on a true story, this picture book tells of a little girl growing up in France during World War II who becomes aware that her family is hiding a Jewish family in the cellar. (Rev: BCCB 6/00; BL 4/1/00; HBG 10/00; SLJ 5/00)

4769 Preus, Margi. *The Peace Bell* (1–3). Illus. by Hideko Takahashi. 2008, Holt $16.95 (978-0-8050-7800-8). 32pp. In this fictional memoir based on real events, a Japanese grandmother tells the story of Japanese village life before, during, and after World War II and of "the peace bell" recovered by American sailors. (Rev: BLO 8/28/08; LMC 3/09)

4770 Prince, April Jones. *Twenty-One Elephants and Still Standing* (1–3). Illus. by François Roca. 2005, Houghton $16.00 (978-0-618-44887-6). 32pp. Was this new wonder, the Brooklyn Bridge, safe? P. T. Barnum and his 21 elephants crossed in 1884. (Rev: BL 10/15/05; SLJ 11/05*)

4771 Ramírez, Antonio. *Napí* (PS–2). Illus. by Domi. 2004, Groundwood $15.95 (978-0-88899-610-7). 32pp. This is a very visual portrayal of the importance of nature and colors in the life and dreams of a young Indian girl living in a Mexican village. (Rev: BL 11/15/04; SLJ 9/04)

4772 Ramírez, Antonio. *Napí Goes to the Mountain* (1–3). Trans. from Spanish by Elisa Amado. Illus. by Domi. 2006, Groundwood $18.95 (978-0-88899-713-5). A young Mexican girl and her younger brother go upriver into the jungle in search of their father, and during the course of their search are transformed into deer and meet a series of folkloric creatures; a sequel to *Napí* (2004). (Rev: SLJ 2/07)

4773 Ramsden, Ashley, reteller. *Seven Fathers* (K–3). Illus. by Ed Young. 2011, Roaring Brook $16.99 (978-1-59643-544-5). 32pp. A retelling of a Norwegian tale about a tired traveler seeking shelter for the night who is referred from one old man to his father, and from that older man to an even older one, until he eventually reaches the seventh father and receives a welcome. Lexile AD930L (Rev: BL 3/1/11; LMC 5–6/11; SLJ 3/1/11)

243

4774 Ramsey, Calvin A. *Ruth and the Green Book* (2–5). Illus. by Floyd Cooper. 2010, Carolrhoda $16.95 (978-0-7613-5255-6). 32pp. A young African American girl and her family head south in the 1950s, using "The Green Book" as a guide to places where black people are welcome. Lexile 810L (Rev: BL 11/1/10; LMC 1–2/11; SLJ 11/1/10*)

4775 Ramsey, Calvin A., and Bettye Stroud. *Belle, the Last Mule at Gee's Bend* (K–3). Illus. by John Holyfield. 2011, Candlewick $15.99 (978-0-7636-4058-3). 32pp. One of the mules that pulled Dr. Martin Luther King, Jr.'s casket is given license to eat out of a kindhearted woman's garden in this story full of civil rights history. (Rev: BL 9/15/11; HB 9–10/11; LMC 11–12/11; SLJ 10/1/11)

4776 Rao, Sandhya. *My Mother's Sari* (PS–K). Illus. by Nina Sabnani. 2006, North-South $14.95 (978-0-7358-2101-9). 28pp. A little Indian girl shows the many uses for her mother's sari; the endpapers show how a sari is wrapped. (Rev: BL 8/06)

4777 Rappaport, Doreen, and Lyndall Callan. *Dirt on Their Skirts: The Story of the Young Women Who Won the World Championship* (PS–3). Illus. by E. B. Lewis. 2000, Dial $16.99 (978-0-8037-2042-8). 40pp. A fictionalized account of the 1946 championship game of the All-American Girls Professional Baseball League. (Rev: BCCB 2/00; BL 1/1–15/00; HBG 10/00; SLJ 3/00)

4778 Ravishankar, Anushka. *To Market! To Market* (PS–2). Illus. by Emanuele Scanziani. 2007, Tara $16.95 (978-8-1862-1199-1). In India a girl visits a lively indoor market and looks at all the things she could buy with her few coins; the unusual format allows for illustrations showing a wide expanse. (Rev: BL 7/07)

4779 Rawlings, Marjorie Kinnan. *The Secret River* (PS–3). Illus. by Leo Dillon. 2011, Atheneum $19.99 (978-1-4169-1179-1). 56pp. In this newly illustrated version of a 1956 award winner, young Calpurnia and her dog catch enough fish to feed her poor family and neighbors in this story of magical realism set in Depression-era Florida. Lexile AD720L (Rev: BL 12/15/10; LMC 5–6/11; SLJ 1/1/11*)

4780 Reed, Jennifer B. *The Falling Flowers* (K–3). Illus. by Dick Cole. 2005, Shen's $16.95 (978-1-885008-28-2). Mayumie and her grandmother enjoy viewing Tokyo's cherry blossoms in this book illustrated with beautiful watercolors. (Rev: SLJ 6/06)

4781 Reynolds, Aaron. *Back of the Bus* (1–3). Illus. by Floyd Cooper. 2010, Philomel $16.99 (978-0-399-25091-0). 32pp. A young boy seated at the back of the bus witnesses Rosa Parks's defiance of authority. (Rev: BL 2/1/10; LMC 1–2/10; SLJ 2/1/10)

4782 Reynolds, Marilynn. *The Name of the Child* (1–3). Illus. by Don Kilby. 2002, Orca $16.95 (978-1-55143-221-2). 32pp. Nervous young Lloyd is sent to the country during the 1918 flu epidemic for his safety, but ends up having to take charge in the midst of a storm. (Rev: BL 1/1–15/03; HBG 3/03; SLJ 1/03)

4783 Ringgold, Faith. *Cassie's Word Quilt* (K–3). Illus. 2002, Knopf $13.95 (978-0-375-81200-2). 32pp. This simple wordbook uses a quilt pattern of pictures to introduce the daily life of Cassie, a little girl living in New York City in 1939. (Rev: BL 3/1/02; HBG 10/02; SLJ 2/02)

4784 Rockliff, Mara. *Me and Momma and Big John* (PS–3). Illus. by William Low. 2012, Candlewick $16.99 (978-0-7636-4359-1). 32pp. Three African American children are happy when their mother comes home from her job as a stonecutter working on New York's St. John the Divine cathedral — and awed when they see the place she is working; with historical notes. Lexile AD660L (Rev: BL 11/15/12; LMC 3–4/13; SLJ 9/12)

4785 Rodanas, Kristina. *The Blind Hunter* (K–2). Illus. by author. 2003, Marshall Cavendish $16.95 (978-0-7614-5132-7). Blind Chirobo accompanies Muteye on a hunting trip and proves that there is much that he can "see" with his other senses in this picture book based on a Shona folktale. (Rev: HBG 4/04; SLJ 1/04)

4786 Ross, Stewart. *Egypt in Spectacular Cross-Section* (2–4). Illus. by Stephen Biesty. 2005, Scholastic $18.99 (978-0-439-74537-6). 32pp. Illustrator Biesty's detailed cross-sections provide lots of ways to inform readers of interesting facts within the framework of Ross's story about a trip down the Nile family wedding in the Egypt of Ramses II. (Rev: BL 9/1/05; SLJ 9/05) [932]

4787 Ruelle, Karen Gray. *The Tree* (K–3). Illus. by Deborah Durland DeSaix. 2008, Holiday $16.95 (978-0-8234-1904-3). 32pp. A New York City neighborhood's history comes to life through this story of a single elm tree. (Rev: BL 9/15/08; LMC 3/09)

4788 Rumford, James. *Rain School* (PS–2). Illus. by author. 2010, Houghton Mifflin $16.99 (978-0-547-24307-8). 32pp. Young Thomas is eager to get to school and start learning, unaware that he will first have to help construct the building itself in this story set in Chad. (Rev: BL 9/1/10*; SLJ 10/1/10)

4789 Rumford, James. *Silent Music* (1–3). Illus. by author. 2008, Roaring Brook $17.95 (978-1-59643-276-5). 32pp. A boy named Ali finds comfort in calligraphy during the bombing of Baghdad in 2003. (Rev: BCCB 4/08; BL 4/15/08; HB 3/08; LMC 5/08; SLJ 4/08)

4790 Russell, Margaret Timberlake. *Maggie's Amerikay* (K–3). Illus. by Jim Burke. 2006, Farrar $17.00 (978-0-374-34722-2). 40pp. An African American boy and an Irish American girl befriend each other while enduring hard times in a late-19th-century New Orleans rich in ragtime. (Rev: BL 5/1/06; SLJ 4/06)

4791 Ryan, Pam Muñoz. *Amelia and Eleanor Go for a Ride: Based on a True Story* (2–4). Illus. by Brian Selznick. 1999, Scholastic $17.99 (978-0-590-96075-5). 40pp. An interesting, if exaggerated, variation on the story of Amelia Earhart and Eleanor Roosevelt's shared plane ride. (Rev: BL 10/15/99; HBG 3/00; SLJ 9/99)

4792 Saint-Lot, Katia Novet. *Amadi's Snowman* (PS–1). Illus. by Dimitrea Tokunbo. 2008, Tilbury House $16.95 (978-0-88448-298-7). 32pp. A young Nigerian boy's first glimpse of a snowman prompts a new interest in reading and knowledge. (Rev: BL 7/08; LMC 1/09)

4793 Santore, Charles. *The Silk Princess* (1–3). Illus. by author. 2007, Random $17.99 (978-0-375-83664-0). 32pp. A Chinese princess fascinated by a cocoon sets off on a journey that leads her to a wise man who teaches her how to make silk from the thread. (Rev: BL 11/15/07; LMC 3/08; SLJ 2/08)

4794 Sasso, Sandy Eisenberg. *Butterflies Under Our Hats* (PS–2). Illus. by Joani Keller Rothenberg. 2006, Paraclete $16.95 (978-1-55725-474-0). 32pp. In the town of Chelm — a place famously without luck — a visitor who believes in hope arrives in a cloud of butterflies. (Rev: BL 6/1–15/06; SLJ 8/06)

4795 Say, Allen. *Erika-San* (2–5). Illus. by author. 2009, Houghton $17.00 (978-0-618-88933-4). As a little girl, Erika was enchanted by a painting of a Japanese tea house, and when she grows up she finally finds the place of her dreams far from the madding crowd on a remote island in Japan. (Rev: BL 12/1/08; HB 1/09; LMC 10/09; SLJ 12/08)

4796 Say, Allen. *Kamishibai Man* (1–3). Illus. 2005, Houghton $17.00 (978-0-618-47954-2). 32pp. An elderly Japanese man who once made the rounds selling candy and telling stories to children revisits the magic of a bygone era. (Rev: BCCB 11/05; BL 9/15/05*; HB 11/05; HBG 4/06; LMC 3/06; SLJ 10/05*)

4797 Schick, Eleanor. *Navajo Wedding Day: A Dine Marriage Ceremony* (1–3). Illus. 1999, Marshall Cavendish $15.95 (978-0-7614-5031-3). 40pp. A realistic picture book that describes a marriage ceremony in Navajo country. (Rev: BL 4/15/99; HBG 10/99; SLJ 4/99)

4798 Shank, Ned. *The Sanyasin's First Day* (K–3). Illus. by Catherine Stock. 1999, Marshall Cavendish $15.95 (978-0-7614-5055-9). 32pp. The lives of several people intersect in this story set in modern India about a holy man who begs on the streets and is given alms by a child. (Rev: BL 10/1/99; HBG 3/00; SLJ 11/99)

4799 Shea, Pegi Deitz. *The Carpet Boy's Gift* (2–5). Illus. by Leane Morin. 2003, Tilbury House $16.95 (978-0-88448-248-2). 40pp. This beautifully illustrated fictional picture-book tale of a young Pakistani boy working under dreadful conditions was inspired by the murder of 12-year-old activist Iqbal Masih. (Rev: BL 1/1–15/04; SLJ 2/04)

4800 Shulevitz, Uri. *How I Learned Geography* (K–3). Illus. by author. 2008, Farrar $16.95 (978-0-374-33499-4). A small refugee boy discovers new horizons and forgets his hunger when his father brings home a map of the world; set in 1939, this is based on the author's experiences. Caldecott Honor Book, 2009. (Rev: BL 5/1/08; HB 3/08; SLJ 5/08)

4801 Siebert, Diane. *Rhyolite: The True Story of a Ghost Town* (2–4). Illus. by David Frampton. 2003, Clarion $16.00 (978-0-618-09673-2). 32pp. Woodcut illustrations and simple narrative verse chronicle the brief history of Rhyolite, Nevada, a gold-mining town that enjoyed a brief heyday in the early 1900s. (Rev: BL 4/15/03; HB 7/03; HBG 10/03; SLJ 5/03) [811]

4802 Simon, Norma. *All Kinds of Children* (PS–K). Illus. by Diane Paterson. 1999, Whitman $16.95 (978-0-8075-0281-5). 32pp. This book emphasizes how children around the world have different lifestyles and homes but similar needs. (Rev: BL 3/15/99; HBG 10/99; SLJ 6/99) [305.23]

4803 Simpson, Lesley. *Yuvi's Candy Tree* (1–3). Illus. by Janice Lee Porter. 2011, Lerner/Kar-Ben $17.95 (978-0-7613-5651-6); paper $7.95 (978-0-7613-5652-3). 32pp. Young Yuvi relates her harrowing journey with her Ethiopian Jewish family from war-torn East Africa to Israel, aided by Operation Moses; based on a true story. (Rev: SLJ 7/11)

4804 Skarmeta, Antonio. *The Composition* (3–5). Trans. by Elisa Amado. Illus. 2000, Douglas & McIntyre $14.95 (978-0-88899-390-8). 32pp. Set in a police state in Latin America, this picture book tells of a young boy who is under pressure from the police to betray his parents. (Rev: BL 5/1/00; HB 9/00; HBG 10/00; SLJ 8/00)

4805 Slate, Joseph. *The Great Big Wagon That Rang: How the Liberty Bell Was Saved* (PS–2). Illus. by Craig Spearing. 2002, Marshall Cavendish $16.95 (978-0-7614-5108-2). 32pp. The story of a farmer's role in saving the Liberty Bell from the British. (Rev: BL 11/1/02; HBG 3/03; SLJ 11/02)

4806 Slate, Joseph. *I Want to Be Free* (2–4). Illus. by E. B. Lewis. 2009, Putnam $16.99 (978-0-399-24342-4). A compelling story of a young escaped slave who saves a slave child who eventually frees him from his shackle; based on a tale retold by Rudyard Kipling in *Kim*. (Rev: BCCB 1/09; BL 12/1/08; LMC 5/09; SLJ 1/09)

4807 Smalls, Irene. *Don't Say Ain't* (1–3). Illus. by Colin Bootman. 2003, Charlesbridge $15.95 (978-1-57091-381-5). 32pp. A gifted African American student attending an integrated school in 1957 learns to "speak proper" when appropriate. (Rev: BL 2/15/03; HBG 10/03; SLJ 3/03)

4808 Smith, Lane. *John, Paul, George and Ben* (K–3). Illus. 2006, Hyperion $16.99 (978-0-7868-4893-5). 40pp. A humorous look at the contributions of five of America's founding fathers — John Hancock, Paul Revere, George Washington, Benjamin Franklin, and Thomas Jefferson — with facts appended; best suited to readers who already are familiar with the history. (Rev: BL 2/15/06; SLJ 3/06*) ∩

4809 Spinelli, Eileen. *Do You Have a Cat?* (PS–3). Illus. by Geraldo Valerio. 2010, Eerdmans $15.99 (978-0-8028-5351-6). 26pp. Paintings of cats introduce cat owners through history — from Cleopatra to Scarlatti, Queen Victoria, and Calvin Coolidge — with facts about each person. (Rev: BLO 7/10; SLJ 11/1/10)

4810 Spinelli, Eileen. *Heat Wave* (PS–2). Illus. by Betsy Lewin. 2007, Harcourt $16.00 (978-0-15-216779-0). 32pp. The residents of Lumberville suffer through a hot spell in the days before air conditioning. (Rev: BL 5/1/07; HB 11/07; SLJ 6/07)

4811 Spiotta-Dimare, Loren. *Rockwell: A Boy and His Dog* (1–4). Illus. by Cliff Miller. 2005, Barron's $14.95 (978-0-7641-5790-5). 28pp. A fictional conversation between the painter and his model, Scotty, gives the reader a feel for the artist's inspirations and times. (Rev: SLJ 8/05)

4812 Spivak, Dawnine. *Grass Sandals: The Travels of Basho* (3–5). Illus. by Demi. 1997, Simon & Schuster $16.00 (978-0-689-80776-3). 40pp. An outstanding picture book about the 17th-century poet and his travels around Japan. (Rev: BCCB 7–8/97; BL 5/1/97*; HBG 3/98; SLJ 4/97) [895.6]

4813 Steig, William. *When Everybody Wore a Hat* (K–3). Illus. 2003, HarperCollins LB $18.89 (978-0-06-009701-1). Steig looks back at the Bronx of 1916 — the year he was 8 years old. (Rev: BL 5/1/03; HB 5/03; HBG 10/03; SLJ 5/03) [813.5]

4814 Stengel, Joyce A. *St. Patrick and the Three Brave Mice* (K–3). Illus. by Herb Leonhard. 2009, Pelican $15.95 (978-1-58980-663-4). Ireland's last snake tries to steal St. Patrick's famous bell but is spotted by a little mouse named Tulla; a tense story with Celtic motifs and evocative illustrations. (Rev: BLO 2/9/09; LMC 10/09)

4815 Stewart, Sarah. *The Gardener* (K–3). Illus. by David Small. 1997, Farrar $16.00 (978-0-374-32517-6). 40pp. During the Depression, a little girl is sent off to live with a cold, somber uncle, but gradually she wins him over. (Rev: BL 6/1–15/97; HB 11/97; HBG 3/98; SLJ 8/97*)

4816 Stock, Catherine. *Gugu's House* (1–3). Illus. 2001, Clarion $16.00 (978-0-618-00389-1). Set in Zimbabwe, this is the story of a loving grandmother whose talents include creating paintings and sculptures, as well as telling stories to granddaughter Kukamba. (Rev: BL 2/15/01*; HBG 10/01)

4817 Strohmeier, Lenice. *Mingo* (2–4). Illus. by Bill Farnsworth. 2003, Marshall Cavendish $16.95 (978-0-7614-5111-2). 32pp. The importance of freedom is the main theme in this poignant story of the close relationship between young Olivia and the elderly Robin Mingo, a family slave; historical details about 18th-century Massachusetts are interwoven throughout the picture book. (Rev: BL 6/1–15/03; HBG 10/03; SLJ 6/03)

4818 Stroud, Bettye. *The Patchwork Path: A Quilt Map to Freedom* (K–3). Illus. by Erin Susanne Bennett. 2005, Candlewick $15.99 (978-0-7636-2423-1). On her way with her father to Canada and freedom, 10-year-old slave Hannah thinks of the quilt her mother used to teach her the necessary code. (Rev: BL 2/1/05; SLJ 1/05)

4819 Stryer, Andrea Stenn. *Kami and the Yaks* (K–3). Illus. by Bert Dodson. 2007, Bay Otter $15.95 (978-0-977896-10-3). When a deaf Sherpa boy finds one of his family's herd of yaks in distress in a storm, he must climb all the way down to his village to get help. (Rev: BL 2/1/07; SLJ 4/07)

4820 Stuve-Bodeen, Stephanie. *Babu's Song* (PS–2). Illus. by Aaron Boyd. 2003, Lee & Low $16.95 (978-1-58430-058-8). Set in Tanzania, this heart-warming story tells of the close relationship between Babu and his mute

grandfather and the choices they must make about possessions and expenditures. (Rev: BL 6/1–15/03; HBG 10/03; SLJ 12/03)

4821 Stuve-Bodeen, Stephanie. *Elizabeti's Doll* (PS–1). Illus. by Christy Hale. 1998, Lee & Low $19.95 (978-1-880000-70-0). 32pp. In Tanzania, Elizabeti lacks a doll to copy her mother's activities with her new baby, so the little girl uses a rock instead. (Rev: BL 10/1/98; HB 11/98; HBG 3/99; SLJ 9/98)

4822 Stuve-Bodeen, Stephanie. *Mama Elizabeti* (1–3). Illus. by Christy Hale. 2000, Lee & Low $15.95 (978-1-58430-002-1). Set in contemporary Tanzania, this story involves Elizabeti and her problems caring for her toddler brother. (Rev: BCCB 9/00; BL 8/00; HB 7/00; HBG 10/00; SLJ 7/00)

4823 Sullivan, Sarah. *Passing the Music Down* (K–3). Illus. by Barry Root. 2011, Candlewick $16.99 (978-0-7636-3753-8). 32pp. A boy learns fiddle music from an elderly man, and the two go on to play together in this atmospheric picture book based on the relationship between musicians Melvin Wine and Jake Krack. Lexile AD800 (Rev: BL 4/15/11; HB 5–6/11; SLJ 4/11)

4824 Swain, Gwenyth. *Riding to Washington* (K–3). Illus. by David Geister. 2008, Sleeping Bear $17.95 (978-1-58536-324-7). 40pp. The story of a young girl's bus trip to hear Martin Luther King's historic I Have a Dream speech in August 1963. (Rev: BL 3/1/08; SLJ 6/08)

4825 Sweeney, Joan. *Suzette and the Puppy: A Story About Mary Cassatt* (PS–3). Illus. by Jennifer Heyd Wharton. 2000, Barron's $14.99 (978-0-7641-5294-8). A fictionalized story of a little French girl and how Mary Cassatt came to paint her as the "Little Girl in a Blue Armchair." (Rev: SLJ 1/01)

4826 Tafolla, Carmen. *What Can You Do With a Rebozo?* (K–1). Illus. by Amy Córdova. 2008, Tricycle $14.95 (978-1-58246-220-2). 32pp. A young girl explores the various uses of the traditional Mexican *rebozo* — wearing it as an accessory, making a tunnel with it, framing a cradle for her baby brother, and even seeing it as a superhero's cape. Belpré Honor Book. (Rev: SLJ 1/08)

4827 Tankard, Jeremy. *Me Hungry!* (PS–K). Illus. by author. 2008, Candlewick $15.99 (978-0-7636-3360-8). 40pp. A prehistoric boy is hungry and his parents are busy, so he heads off on a hunt and on the way makes a new friend — a mammoth. (Rev: BCCB 4/08; BL 5/15/08; HB 5/08; SLJ 9/08)

4828 Taulbert, Clifton L. *Little Cliff and the Cold Place* (K–2). Illus. by E. B. Lewis. 2002, Dial $16.99 (978-0-8037-2558-4). Little Cliff lives in Mississippi in the 1950s and longs to go to the Arctic, so his great-grandfather comes up with a compromise — a fishing expedition at the icehouse. (Rev: BL 11/1/02; HBG 3/03; SLJ 9/02)

4829 Taylor, Debbie. *Sweet Music in Harlem* (1–3). Illus. by Frank Morrison. 2004, Lee & Low $16.95 (978-1-58430-165-3). 32pp. A famous 1958 photograph inspired this story about young C.J. scrambling to find his jazz-playing uncle's hat for a photo shoot and in the process attracting some of Harlem's most notable jazzmen, who want to join in. (Rev: BL 5/1/04; SLJ 7/04)

4830 Taylor, Joanne. *Making Room* (1–3). Illus. by Peter Rankin. 2004, Tundra $15.95 (978-0-88776-651-0). In 1800s Nova Scotia, a man gradually adds to his one-room house as his family grows. (Rev: SLJ 11/04)

4831 Thermes, Jennifer. *Sam Bennett's New Shoes* (K–2). 2006, Carolrhoda $15.95 (978-1-57505-822-1). In this story based on an 18th-century custom, Sam Bennett gets new shoes and his father takes the old shoes and hides them in the wall to bring good fortune. (Rev: BL 6/1–15/06; SLJ 3/06)

4832 Thomas, Joyce Carol. *In the Land of Milk and Honey* (PS–3). Illus. by Floyd Cooper. 2012, Amistad $16.99 (978-0-06-025383-7). 32pp. This fictional story remembers the author's move from Oklahoma to California in 1948 and all the wonders of rail travel, the landscape and people they see on the way, and finally the diversity and activity of San Francisco. (Rev: BL 10/15/12; SLJ 9/12)

4833 Thompson, Lauren. *The Forgiveness Garden* (K–3). Illus. by Christy Hale. 2012, Feiwel & Friends $16.99 (978-0-312-62599-3). 32pp. Karune, a Gamte boy, and Sama, a Vayam girl who lives across the river, decide to end the conflict between their villages in this story inspired by the Garden of Forgiveness planted in Beirut in 1990 at the end of the civil war. ⏷ ℮ Lexile 480L (Rev: BL 11/1/12; LMC 3–4/13; SLJ 11/12)

4834 Thong, Roseanne. *Fly Free!* (PS–3). Illus. by Eujin Kim Neilan. 2010, Boyds Mills $17.95 (978-1-59078-550-8). 32pp. Young Mai's compassion for caged sparrows outside a Buddhist temple in Vietnam results in a ripple effect that culminates with the release of the little birds. (Rev: BL 1/1/10; LMC 5–6/10; SLJ 3/1/10)

4835 Thong, Roseanne. *The Wishing Tree* (PS–2). Illus. by Connie McLennan. 2004, Shen's $16.95 (978-1-885008-26-8). 30pp. After years of visits to the Wishing Tree, Ming turns his back on the annual tradition when his grandmother dies. (Rev: BL 2/1/05)

4836 Toews, Marj. *Black-and-White Blanche* (1–3). Illus. by Dianna Bonder. 2006, Fitzhenry & Whiteside $16.95 (978-1-55005-132-2). The Witherspoons, a Victorian family that rigidly adheres to the social ban on colored clothing, are forced to relax their standards when the family's youngest member insists on wearing pink. (Rev: SLJ 8/06)

4837 Tompert, Ann. *The Pied Piper of Peru* (K–2). Illus. by Kestutis Kasparavicius. 2002, Boyds Mills $15.95 (978-1-56397-949-1). A 16th-century Peruvian saint tries to rid the priory of a colony of mice in this story about Saint Martin de Porres. (Rev: BCCB 4/02; BL 3/15/02; HBG 10/02) [270.6]

4838 Tran, Truong. *Going Home, Coming Home / Ve Nha Tham Que Hu'O'Ng* (1–3). Illus. by Ann Phong. 2003, Children's Book Pr. $16.95 (978-0-89239-179-0). 32pp. Eight-year-old Vietnamese American Ami Chi visits the homeland of her parents in this poignant bilingual tale. (Rev: BL 9/1/03; SLJ 9/03)

4839 Turner, Ann. *Drummer Boy: Marching to the Civil War* (3–5). Illus. by Mark Hess. 1998, HarperCollins LB $17.89 (978-0-06-027697-3). 32pp. In this first-person account, a 13-year-old runs away from home to become a drummer boy during the Civil War and later encounters the reality of war and death. (Rev: BCCB 11/98; BL 9/15/98; HBG 3/99; SLJ 11/98)

4840 Uhlberg, Myron. *Dad, Jackie, and Me* (2–5). Illus. by Colin Bootman. 2005, Peachtree $16.95 (978-1-56145-329-0). In Brooklyn in 1947, a boy and his deaf father admire Jackie Robinson's baseball prowess. (Rev: BCCB 5/05; BL 8/05; SLJ 5/05)

4841 Ulmer, Mike. *The Gift of the Inuksuk* (PS–2). Illus. by Melanie Rose. 2004, Sleeping Bear $17.95 (978-1-58536-214-1). This sparely worded, original pourquoi tale offers an explanation for the *Inuksuk*, sculptures of piled stones, that dot the Arctic landscape. (Rev: BL 1/1–15/05; SLJ 4/05)

4842 Uman, Jennifer, and Valerio Vidali. *Jemmy Button* (1–3). Illus. by Jennifer Uman. 2013, Candlewick $16.99 (978-0-7636-6487-9). 48pp. A nicely illustrated picture book based on the true story of Orundellico, a boy taken in the 19th century from remote Tierra del Fuego to Victorian England, where he learns many new things before returning home and adjusting his expectations from life. USBBY Outstanding International Book. (Rev: BL 3/15/13; LMC 10/13; SLJ 3/13)

4843 Ungerer, Tomi. *Otto: The Autobiography of a Teddy Bear* (1–3). Illus. by author. 2010, Phaidon $16.95 (978-0-7148-5766-4). 36pp. An aging teddy bear reminisces on an eventful life lived through 1930s Germany and World War II. (Rev: BL 10/1/10*; HB 11–12/10; SLJ 2/1/11)

4844 Usher, M. D. *Diogenes* (1–3). Illus. by Michael Chesworth. 2009, Farrar $16.95 (978-0-374-31785-0). 32pp. In ancient Greece, a dog named Diogenes is determined to be his own master in this appealing story based on the views of the classical philosopher; with biographical information on Diogenes and his beliefs. (Rev: BLO 5/27/09; SLJ 6/09)

4845 Vander Zee, Ruth. *Always with You* (2–4). Illus. by Ronald Himler. 2008, Eerdmans $17.00 (978-0-8028-5295-3). 32pp. Based on a true story, this picture book follows the story of 4-year-old Kim, orphaned in the Vietnam War. (Rev: BL 2/15/08; SLJ 9/08)

4846 Vaughan, Marcia. *The Secret to Freedom* (K–3). Illus. by Larry Johnson. 2001, Lee & Low $16.95 (978-1-58430-021-2). 32pp. Great Aunt Lucy talks about her days as a slave and the secret quilt code that directed her brother Albert and other slaves on the road to freedom. (Rev: BL 6/1–15/01; HBG 10/01; SLJ 6/01)

4847 Vaughan, Marcia. *Up the Learning Tree* (K–3). Illus. by Derek Blanks. 2003, Lee & Low $16.96 (978-1-58430-049-6). A schoolteacher risks everything to help a brave young slave gain an education. (Rev: BL 11/1/03; HBG 4/04; SLJ 11/03)

4848 Von Ahnen, Katherine. *Charlie Young Bear* (2–3). Illus. by Paulette L. Lambert. Series: Council for Indian

Education. 1994, Roberts Rinehart paper $4.95 (978-1-57098-001-5). 42pp. After the U.S. government agrees on a cash settlement with the Mesquakie Indians in 1955, Charlie Young Bear hopes his share will be a bike. (Rev: SLJ 4/95)

4849 Walker, Sally M. *Freedom Song: The Story of Henry "Box" Brown* (1–3). Illus. by Sean Qualls. 2012, HarperCollins $17.99 (978-0-06-058310-1). 40pp. When slave Henry Brown's wife and children are sold away, he has himself packed in a box and mailed to Pennsylvania in this fictionalized account. (Rev: BL 12/15/11; SLJ 12/1/11)

4850 Wallace, Ian. *Mavis and Merna* (K–3). Illus. 2005, Douglas & McIntyre $16.95 (978-0-88899-647-3). 40pp. Gully's, the general store in her 1960s Canadian town, has always been one of Mavis's favorite places, and when owner Joe Gully dies, Mavis becomes friends with his widow even though the store is closed. (Rev: BL 5/1/05; SLJ 6/05)

4851 Watson, Mary. *The Paper Dragonfly* (K–3). Illus. by author. 2007, Shenanigan $15.95 (978-0-9726614-3-0). 32pp. Instead of learning about growing rice, Kiyoshi makes paper lanterns; however, when the Emperor sees his dragonfly lantern, Kiyoshi's artistic skills are rewarded. (Rev: BL 12/15/07)

4852 Watson, Pete. *The Heart of the Lion* (3–5). Illus. by Mary Watson. 2005, Shenanigan $15.95 (978-0-9726614-1-6). 32pp. A young American boy visits a West African village, meets a new friend, and learns about the region's distinctive culture. (Rev: BL 8/05; SLJ 10/05)

4853 Weatherford, Carole Boston. *Freedom on the Menu: The Greensboro Sit-ins* (1–3). Illus. by Jerome Lararrigue. 2005, Dial $16.99 (978-0-8037-2860-8). 32pp. Seen through the eyes of a young African American girl, this is the story of the 1960 lunch counter sit-ins in North Carolina. (Rev: BL 2/1/05; SLJ 4/05)

4854 Weber, Elka, reteller. *One Little Chicken* (K–2). Illus. by Elisa Kleven. 2011, Tricycle $16.99 (978-1-58246-374-2); LB $19.99 (978-1-58246-401-5). Unpaged. This story about a lost chicken that generates wealth emphasizes the importance of generosity and patience; based on a tale in the Talmud. (Rev: HB 9–10/11; SLJ 7/11)

4855 Weinstein, Muriel Harris. *When Louis Armstrong Taught Me Scat* (PS–2). Illus. by R. Gregory Christie. 2009, Chronicle $16.99 (978-0-8118-5131-2). 32pp. A rhythmic story about a little girl who dreams about singing scat with Louis Armstrong. (Rev: BL 2/1/09; LMC 5/09)

4856 Wells, Rosemary. *The Miraculous Tale of the Two Maries* (K–2). Illus. by Petra Mathers. 2006, Viking $16.99 (978-0-670-05960-7). 32pp. Two teenage girls, both named Marie, drown in the ocean but persuade God to allow them to return to their town to do good deeds; inspired by a story of 19th-century France. (Rev: BL 3/1/06*; HB 3/06; HBG 10/06; SLJ 3/06)

4857 Wenberg, Michael. *Elizabeth's Song* (1–4). Illus. by Cornelius Van Wright. 2002, Beyond Words $15.95 (978-1-58270-069-4). The fictionalized story of African American folk singer Elizabeth Cotton, 11-year-old author of "Freight Train Comin'." (Rev: BL 2/15/03; HBG 10/03)

4858 Weston, Anne. *My Brother Needs a Boa* (2–4). Illus. by Cheryl Nathan. 2005, Star Bright $15.95 (978-1-932065-96-1). To rid his shop of a pesky mouse, Benito heeds his sister's advice and goes in search of a rodent-catching snake. (Rev: SLJ 10/05)

4859 Whelan, Gloria. *The Boy Who Wanted to Cook* (K–3). Illus. by Steve Adams. Series: Tales of the World. 2011, Sleeping Bear $16.95 (978-1-58536-534-0). 32pp. Ten-year-old Pierre is told he is too young to cook in his parents' restaurant in southern France until the day he sneaks some mushrooms into a beef dish and gains a rave review. (Rev: BL 11/1/11; SLJ 10/1/11)

4860 Whelan, Gloria. *Smudge and the Book of Mistakes: A Christmas Story* (1–3). Illus. by Stephen Constanza. 2012, Sleeping Bear $17.95 (978-158536483-1). 48pp. A diminutive 15-year-old named Cuthbert — or Smudge, for his ineptitude when inking letters — is mistakenly given a task illuminating a Christmas story manuscript in this medieval tale of all's-well-that-ends-well. **e** (Rev: BL 11/1/12)

4861 Whelan, Gloria. *Yatandou* (2–4). Illus. by Peter Sylvada. Series: Tales of the World. 2007, Sleeping Bear $17.95 (978-1-58536-211-0). 32pp. This story follows 8-year-old Yatandou as she tries to help others in her traditional West African village. (Rev: BL 10/1/07; SLJ 10/07)

4862 Whelan, Gloria. *Yuki and the One Thousand Carriers* (1–3). Illus. by Yan Nascimbene. Series: Tales of the World. 2008, Sleeping Bear $17.95 (978-1-58536-352-0). 32pp. In 17th-century Japan Yuki, young daughter of a governor, describes in haiku her family's long journey from Kyoto to Edo escorted by more than 1,000 helpers. (Rev: BL 4/15/08; LMC 1/09; SLJ 7/08)

4863 Whitaker, Zai. *Kali and the Rat Snake* (1–3). Illus. by Srividya Natarajan. 2006, Kane $15.95 (978-1-933605-10-4). Kali's classmates are unkind because his father is a snake catcher, but Kali wins their respect and gratitude when he captures a six-foot snake that invades their classroom; with handsome illustrations and endpapers. (Rev: SLJ 10/06)

4864 Wiebe, Rudy. *Hidden Buffalo* (1–3). Illus. by Michael Lonechild. 2004, Red Deer $17.95 (978-0-88995-285-0). 32pp. Based on a traditional tale, this book tells how a dream inspires the starving Cree people to brave dangers and journey to the Badlands in search of buffalo herds. (Rev: BL 3/1/04; SLJ 7/04)

4865 Williams, Karen L. *Painted Dreams* (PS–1). Illus. by Catherine Stock. 1998, Lothrop LB $15.89 (978-0-688-13902-5). 40pp. Set in the slums of Haiti, this picture book tells of little Ti Marie, who finds some discarded paints in an artist's trash and, with his help, cultivates her artistic talent. (Rev: BL 9/15/98; HBG 3/99; SLJ 10/98)

4866 Williams, Karen L. *When Africa Was Home* (PS–2). Illus. by Floyd Cooper. 1991, Orchard LB $16.99 (978-0-531-08525-7). 32pp. A white boy is so at home in Africa with his black friends that he feels lost when he has to go to America. (Rev: BCCB 2/92; BL 1/15/91*; SLJ 4/91)

4867 Williams, Laura E. *Torch Fishing with the Sun* (K–3). Illus. by Fabricio Vandenbroeck. 1999, Boyds Mills $15.95 (978-1-56397-685-8). 32pp. Young Makoa's grandfather tells him that he uses the sun as a torch while he fishes, but the boy has doubts when others claim that the old man actually buys his catch from another fisherman. (Rev: BL 3/15/99; HBG 10/99; SLJ 6/99)

4868 Winch, John. *Fly, Kite, Fly! A Story of Leonardo and a Bird Catcher* (PS–2). Illus. 2009, Trafalgar $15.95 (978-1-921049-81-1). On a mission to catch a red-tailed kite, 10-year-old Giacomo meets Leonardo da Vinci and learns why the elderly artist has been releasing his birds from traps. (Rev: BLO 10/7/08)

4869 Winnick, Karen B. *Mr. Lincoln's Whiskers* (1–3). Illus. 1996, Boyds Mills $16.95 (978-1-56397-485-4). A young girl writes to Lincoln to suggest that he would gain votes if he grew whiskers. (Rev: BL 12/15/96; SLJ 1/97)

4870 Winnick, Karen B. *Sybil's Night Ride* (K–3). Illus. 2000, Boyds Mills $15.95 (978-1-56397-697-1). This picture book re-creates the historic ride of 16-year-old Sybil Ludington who, during the American Revolution, raced on her horse to warn her father's troops that the British were burning Danbury, New York. (Rev: BL 3/1/00; HBG 10/00)

4871 Winter, Jeanette. *Biblioburro: A True Story from Colombia* (PS–2). Illus. by author. 2010, Simon & Schuster $16.99 (978-1-4169-9778-8). 32pp. In the Colombian jungle, a bibliophile shares his collection with those less fortunate by loading his books onto a burro and riding to remote villages where he hosts story hour. (Rev: BL 5/1/10*; LMC 8–9/10; SLJ 6/1/10)

4872 Winter, Jeanette. *Elsina's Clouds* (PS–3). Illus. 2004, Farrar $16.00 (978-0-374-32118-5). 40pp. In Basotho tradition, Elsina paints the outside walls of her house, decorating them with bright colors and scenes of nature. (Rev: BL 3/1/04; HB 3/04; SLJ 4/04)

4873 Winter, Jeanette. *Follow the Drinking Gourd* (K–3). Illus. by author. 1988, Knopf paper $5.99 (978-0-679-81997-4). The story of Peg Leg Pete who helps slaves escape to the North. (Rev: BCCB 1/89; BL 12/15/88; SLJ 5/89)

4874 Winter, Jonah. *The Fabulous Feud of Gilbert and Sullivan* (K–3). Illus. by Richard Egielski. 2009, Scholastic $16.99 (978-0-439-93050-5). 40pp. An entertaining story about the famous musical team and their sometimes troubled collaboration in the Victorian era. (Rev: BL 4/1/09; HB 5/09; SLJ 6/09)

4875 Winter, Jonah. *Steel Town* (1–3). Illus. by Terry Widener. 2008, Atheneum $16.99 (978-1-4169-4081-4). A moving, oversized look at the lives of workers in a 1930s steel town, with rhythmic text, evocative illus-trations, and lots of details on the production process. (Rev: BCCB 7–8/08; BL 4/1/08; HB 7/08; LMC 8/08; SLJ 5/08)

4876 Winters, Kari-Lynn. *Gift Days* (PS–2). Illus. by Stephen Taylor. 2012, Fitzhenry & Whiteside $18.95 (978-155455192-7). 32pp. Eager to learn to read and write, and more, Nassali is thrilled when her brother offers to do her chores for one morning a week so that she can study; set in a Ugandan village. (Rev: BLO 12/15/12; SLJ 5/13)

4877 Wiviott, Meg. *Benno and the Night of Broken Glass* (2–5). Illus. by Josee Bisaillon. 2010, Kar-Ben $17.95 (978-0-8225-9929-6); paper $7.95 (978-0-8225-9-975-3). 32pp. A friendly cat watches as a Jewish Berlin neighborhood is ransacked by the Nazis on Kristallnacht; with an afterword and lists of resources. (Rev: BL 5/1/10; LMC 8–9/10; SLJ 5/1/10*)

4878 Wolff, Ferida, and Harriet May Savitz. *The Story Blanket* (PS–2). Illus. by Elena Odriozola. 2008, Peachtree $16.95 (978-1-56145-466-2). 32pp. Elderly storyteller Babba Zarrah sacrifices wool from her blanket to provide, secretly, needed socks, scarves, mittens, and so forth for the residents of her chilly mountain village; when the villagers work out who has left these gifts they respond in kind. (Rev: BCCB 10/08; BL 10/15/08; LMC 3/09; SLJ 11/08)

4879 Wong, Janet S. *The Trip Back Home* (PS–2). Illus. by Bo Jia. 2000, Harcourt $16.00 (978-0-15-200784-3). 32pp. The food and fun involved when the author visited her grandparents in rural Korea when she was a child are recalled in this tender story of family love. (Rev: BL 11/15/00; HBG 3/01; SLJ 12/00)

4880 Woodruff, Elvira. *The Memory Coat* (K–4). Illus. by Michael Dooling. 1999, Scholastic $16.95 (978-0-590-67717-2). 32pp. This story of a Jewish family's migration from Russia to America focuses on Rachel and her orphaned cousin, Grisha. (Rev: BL 1/1–15/99; HBG 10/99; SLJ 3/99)

4881 Woodruff, Elvira. *Small Beauties: The Journey of Darcy Heart O'Hara* (K–3). Illus. by Adam Rex. 2006, Knopf $15.95 (978-0-375-82686-3). 32pp. Darcy's precious mementoes of her home in Ireland — a pebble, a flower, a chip of stone — give her strength during the family's difficult journey to America. (Rev: BL 8/06)

4882 Woodson, Jacqueline. *Coming on Home Soon* (K–3). Illus. by E. B. Lewis. 2004, Putnam $16.99 (978-0-399-23748-5). Living with her grandmother, young African American Ada Ruth waits for her mother to return from her work in Chicago during World War II. Caldecott Honor Book. (Rev: BL 8/04*; HB 9/04; SLJ 10/04*)

4883 Woodson, Jacqueline. *Show Way* (3–5). Illus. by Hudson Talbott. 2005, Putnam $16.99 (978-0-399-23749-2). 48pp. Woodson looks back in her own family history to tell the story of seven generations of women who pass down secret "Show Way" quilt patterns and a tradition of fighting for freedom. Newbery Honor Book,

2006. (Rev: BCCB 1/06; BL 9/15/05*; HB 11/05; HBG 4/06; SLJ 11/05*)

4884 Wormell, Christopher. *The Wild Girl* (PS–1). Illus. by author. 2006, Eerdmans $17.00 (978-0-8028-5311-0). A young girl who survives a hard and lonely life in a cave with her dog — eating fruit, nuts, and fish — at first tries to chase a bear away, but realizing it has a cub she allows it to come into the cave and they all share what they have. (Rev: SLJ 11/06)

4885 Would, Nick. *The Scarab's Secret* (K–3). Illus. by Christina Balk. 2006, Walker $16.95 (978-0-8027-9561-8). 32pp. A scarab beetle tells how it saved the life of an Egyptian prince and thus secured for itself an important place in the mythology of ancient Egypt. (Rev: BL 3/15/06; SLJ 4/06)

4886 Xiong, Kim. *Little Stone Lion* (PS–2). Illus. 2005, Heryin $13.99 (978-0-9762056-1-6). 32pp. A small stone lion reflects on the people and history of the small Chinese village over which he stands guard. (Rev: BL 11/1/05)

4887 Yang, Belle. *Always Come Home to Me* (PS–2). Illus. by author. 2007, Candlewick $16.99 (978-0-7636-2899-4). Vibrant illustrations add to this story of Chinese twins Mei-Mei and her brother DiDi and their love for their white doves. (Rev: BL 9/1/07; SLJ 11/07)

4888 Yin. *Brothers* (2–4). Illus. by Chris Soentpiet. 2006, Philomel $17.99 (978-0-399-23406-4). Newly arrived in 19th century San Francisco, Ming ignores his older brothers' warnings not to venture outside Chinatown and strikes up a friendship with Patrick, a young Irish immigrant; a sequel to *Coolies* (2000). (Rev: BL 8/06; SLJ 11/06)

4889 Yolen, Jane. *My Uncle Emily* (K–3). Illus. by Nancy Carpenter. 2009, Philomel $17.99 (978-0-399-24005-8). 32pp. A free-verse, fictionalized story about Emily Dickinson's nephew Gib, who calls his aunt an "uncle" and appreciates their close relationship. (Rev: BL 5/1/09; HB 7/09; LMC 10/09; SLJ 6/09)

4890 Yolen, Jane. *Naming Liberty* (1–3). Illus. by Jim Burke. 2008, Philomel $16.99 (978-0-399-24250-2). 32pp. Yolen interweaves the story of the creation of the Statue of Liberty with a Russian Jewish family's journey to America. (Rev: BL 4/15/08; LMC 10/08)

4891 Yong Yi, Hu. *Good Morning China* (PS–2). Illus. by author. 2007, Roaring Brook $16.95 (978-1-59643-240-6). 32pp. In China, people enjoy the morning in the park with activities such as cycling, playing chess, and doing tai chi. (Rev: BL 12/15/07; LMC 3/08; SLJ 1/08)

4892 Young, Ed. *Beyond the Great Mountains: A Visual Poem About China* (4–6). Illus. 2005, Chronicle $17.95 (978-0-8118-4343-0). 36pp. The vastness and beauty of China are celebrated in an appealing but challenging blend of simple poetry and paper collage artwork. (Rev: BL 11/1/05; SLJ 10/05)

PERSONAL PROBLEMS

4893 Ain, Beth. *Starring Jules (as Herself)* (1–3). Illus. by Anne Keenan Higgins. 2013, Scholastic $9.99 (978-0-545-44352-4). 160pp. Jules, 7 going on 8 and upset to lose her best friend, is thrilled to be chosen to appear in a commercial — until she learns she will be promoting a disgusting orange-flavored mouthwash. **e** Lexile 790 (Rev: BLO 3/15/13; HB 3–4/13; LMC 8–9/13; SLJ 5/13)

4894 Allen, Debbie. *Dancing in the Wings* (K–3). Illus. by Kadir Nelson. 2000, Dial $16.99 (978-0-8037-2501-0). 32pp. Sassy is afraid that she is too tall and lanky to become a ballerina, but a Russian ballet master chooses her to dance in a festival. (Rev: BCCB 11/00; BL 11/15/00; HBG 3/01; SLJ 9/00)

4895 Bang, Molly. *When Sophie Gets Angry — Really, Really Angry* (PS–3). Illus. 1999, Scholastic $16.99 (978-0-590-18979-8). 40pp. This book describes in drawings and text what happens to Sophie when she is truly discontented. Caldecott Honor Book, 2000. (Rev: BCCB 4/99; BL 2/1/99; HBG 10/99; SLJ 1/99*)

4896 Beaumont, Karen. *Where's My T-R-U-C-K?* (K–2). Illus. by David Catrow. 2011, Dial $16.99 (978-0-8037-3222-3). 32pp. A little boy hunts everywhere for his lost red truck, his tantrums mounting, until Bowser the dog digs up a hole where he has hidden many treasures. (Rev: BL 11/1/11; SLJ 9/1/11)

4897 Bottner, Barbara. *Bootsie Barker Bites* (PS–3). Illus. by Peggy Rathmann. 1992, Penguin $17.99 (978-0-399-22125-5). 32pp. The young narrator stands just so much from bully Bootsie Barker and finally stands up for herself. (Rev: BCCB 9/92; BL 10/1/92*; HB 3/93; SLJ 2/93*)

4898 Bracken, Beth. *Too Shy for Show-and-Tell* (PS–2). Illus. by Jennifer Bell. 2011, Picture Window LB $22.65 (978-140486654-6). 32pp. Shy Sam (a giraffe) struggles to muster the courage to talk to his class for show-and-tell. (Rev: BLO 12/15/11)

4899 Buehner, Caralyn. *Would I Ever Lie to You?* (K–4). Illus. by Jack E. Davis. 2007, Dial $16.99 (978-0-8037-2793-9). An older cousin is full of scary tales that the narrator must sort out (which are true and which are lies?) in this reassuring story that will help readers deal with teasing. (Rev: SLJ 5/07)

4900 Bunting, Eve. *The Days of Summer* (PS–3). Illus. by William Low. 2001, Harcourt $16.00 (978-0-15-201840-5). 32pp. In this moving picture book, a girl and her younger sister are bewildered when their grandparents divorce. (Rev: BL 4/1/01; HBG 10/01; SLJ 5/01)

4901 Bunting, Eve. *Fly Away Home* (K–3). Illus. by Ronald Himler. 1991, Houghton $16.00 (978-0-395-55962-8). 32pp. The airport serves as a home for two homeless people — a boy and his father. (Rev: BCCB 5/92; BL 4/1/91*; HB 7/91; SLJ 6/91*)

4902 Burnett, Frances Hodgson. *A Little Princess* (K–2). Illus. by Barbara McClintock. 2000, HarperCollins LB $16.89 (978-0-06-029010-8). 32pp. A retelling in a shortened form of Burnett's beloved classic story of a privileged child who turned pauper and back again. (Rev: BL 1/1–15/01; HBG 3/01)

4903 Cadow, Kenneth M. *Alfie Runs Away* (PS–K). Illus. by Lauren Castillo. 2010, Farrar $16.99 (978-0-374-30202-3). 40pp. Alfie is so upset when his mother decides to throw away his favorite too-small shoes, and he decides to leave home; his mother helps him pack and even includes a hug. Lexile AD360L (Rev: BL 6/10; HB 7–8/10; SLJ 6/1/10)

4904 Campbell, Bebe Moore. *I Get So Hungry* (PS–2). Illus. by Amy Bates. 2008, Putnam $16.99 (978-0-399-24311-0). 32pp. Nikki, a young African American girl, learns to control her eating with the help of her teacher, who has herself suffered health problems because of her weight. (Rev: BCCB 6/08; BL 5/1/08; LMC 10/08; SLJ 5/08)

4905 Caraballo, Samuel. *Estrellita Says Good-bye to Her Island / Estrellita se despide de su isla* (3–5). Illus. by Pablo Torrecilla. 2002, Arte Publico $15.95 (978-1-55885-338-6). 32pp. In this bilingual book, a young girl bids good-bye to her island home and all the sights and sounds that are important to her. (Rev: BL 5/1/02)

4906 Carlson, Nancy. *This Morning Sam Went to Mars: A Book about Paying Attention* (K–3). Illus. by author. 2013, Free Spirit $15.99 (978-157542433-0); paper $9.99 (978-15754243-4-7). 32pp. Sam's daydreams about Mars are interrupting his life both at school and at home, and he gets valuable advice on improving his ability to focus. e (Rev: BL 5/1/13; LMC 11–12/13)

4907 Carrick, Carol. *Patrick's Dinosaurs* (PS–3). Illus. by Donald Carrick. 1983, Houghton $16.00 (978-0-89919-189-8); paper $5.95 (978-0-89919-402-8). 32pp. Patrick is frightened when his brother tells him about dinosaurs.

4908 Cave, Kathryn. *You've Got Dragons* (K–3). Illus. by Nick Maland. 2003, Peachtree $16.95 (978-1-56145-284-2). Young Ben explains about the dragons he gets when in stressful situations, and what he does to get rid of them. (Rev: BCCB 11/03; BL 10/15/03; HBG 4/04; SLJ 12/03)

4909 Chapra, Mimi. *Sparky's Bark / El ladrido de Sparky* (PS–2). Illus. by Vivi Escriva. 2006, HarperCollins $16.99 (978-0-06-053172-0). 32pp. A Hispanic girl visiting relatives in Ohio overcomes her culture shock and begins to learn English in this bilingual picture book. (Rev: BL 5/1/06; SLJ 6/06)

4910 Clark, Emma Chichester. *What Shall We Do, Blue Kangaroo?* (PS–1). Illus. by author. 2003, Doubleday LB $17.99 (978-0-385-90866-5). Lily is delighted to realize she doesn't have to depend on adults for things to do, but glad that stuffed toy Blue Kangaroo is still around to help. (Rev: BL 5/15/03; HB 9/03; HBG 4/04; SLJ 7/03)

4911 Cooper, Helen. *Tatty Ratty* (PS–K). Illus. 2002, Farrar $16.00 (978-0-374-37386-3). 32pp. When Molly accidentally leaves her favorite stuffed animal on the bus, she is comforted by thoughts of the grand adventures he is having. (Rev: BL 2/15/02; HBG 10/02; SLJ 4/02)

4912 Cooper, Ilene. *Jake's Best Thumb* (PS–1). Illus. by Claudio Munoz. 2008, Dutton $16.99 (978-0-525-47788-4). Jake's kindergarten classmate Cliff denounces Jake as a thumb-sucker, but does Cliff have his own security need? (Rev: BCCB 9/08; BLO 8/1/08; SLJ 3/09)

4913 Cote, Nancy. *Jackson's Blanket* (PS). Illus. by author. 2008, Putnam $16.99 (978-0-399-24694-4). Jackson won't be parted from his blanket until the day he finds a kitten in the snow and realizes it needs the blanket more than he does. (Rev: BLO 9/24/08)

4914 Cottin, Menena. *The Black Book of Colors* (K–3). Trans. by Elisa Amado. Illus. by Rosana Faria. 2008, Groundwood $17.95 (978-0-88899-873-6). 24pp. This unusual book challenges readers to imagine being blind and to experience colors through touch, as blind people do; with a guide to the Braille alphabet. (Rev: BL 10/1/08; LMC 11/08; SLJ 9/08)

4915 Cowley, Joy. *Big Moon Tortilla* (PS–3). Illus. by Dyanne Strongbow. 1998, Boyds Mills $14.95 (978-1-56397-601-8). When Marta Enos has a bad day at home on the Papago reservation in southern Arizona, her grandmother tells her a traditional tale to help her cope with problems. (Rev: BL 10/15/98; HBG 10/99; SLJ 11/98)

4916 Cox, Judy. *Puppy Power* (2–4). Illus. by Steve Björkman. 2008, Holiday $15.95 (978-0-8234-2073-5). 96pp. Fran, an overbearing 3rd-grader, learns a little about self-control while taking her rambunctious Newfoundland puppy to obedience class. (Rev: BCCB 6/08; BL 5/1/08; LMC 10/08; SLJ 6/08)

4917 Crocker, Nancy. *Betty Lou Blue* (PS–2). Illus. by Boris Kulikov. 2006, Dial $16.99 (978-0-8037-2937-7). 32pp. Poor Betty Lou Blue is taunted mercilessly by classmates because of her large feet, but those appendages come to the rescue when an avalanche traps her tormentors in snowdrifts. (Rev: BL 8/06; SLJ 12/06)

4918 Croza, Laurel. *I Know Here* (PS–2). Illus. by Matt James. 2010, Groundwood $18.95 (978-0-88899-923-8). 40pp. A young girl used to living in a rural setting worries about moving to the big city of Toronto. (Rev: BL 5/15/10; SLJ 10/1/10)

4919 Curtis, Jamie Lee. *Today I Feel Silly: And Other Moods That Make My Day* (PS–2). Illus. by Laura Cornell. 1998, HarperCollins $16.99 (978-0-06-024560-3). 32pp. In this lighthearted picture book, the young narrator describes how she feels on different days and the ways she copes with emotional ups and downs. (Rev: BL 10/15/98; HBG 3/99; SLJ 12/98)

4920 Denise, Anika. *Bella and Stella Come Home* (PS–1). Illus. by Christopher Denise. 2010, Philomel $16.99 (978-0-399-24243-4). 40pp. With some suspicion, Bella explores her new home with her stuffed toy elephant named Stella. (Rev: BL 12/15/10; SLJ 12/1/10)

4921 dePaola, Tomie. *Oliver Button Is a Sissy* (K–3). Illus. by author. 1979, Harcourt $14.00 (978-0-15-257852-7); paper $6.00 (978-0-15-668140-7). 48pp. People think Oliver is a sissy until he shines in a talent show as a fine tap dancer.

4922 Devlin, Jane. *Hattie the Bad* (PS–1). Illus. by Joe Berger. 2010, Dial $16.99 (978-0-8037-3447-0). 32pp. Hattie is just naturally bad and trying to be good just doesn't seem to work for her. (Rev: BL 2/15/10; SLJ 3/1/10)

4923 Dierssen, Andreas. *The Old Red Tractor* (PS–K). Trans. by Marianne Martens. Illus. by Daniel Sohr. 2006, North-South $16.95 (978-0-7358-2088-3). 32pp. Towhead Tony loves his old red tractor until a friend shows up with a brand-new tractor that has a horn. (Rev: BL 9/15/06; SLJ 10/06)

4924 Diggs, Taye. *Chocolate Me!* (PS–2). Illus. by Shane W. Evans. 2011, Feiwel & Friends $16.99 (978-0-312-60326-7). 40pp. With his mother's help, a young African American boy learns to stand up to bullying and take pride in himself and his looks. ℮ (Rev: BL 2/1/12; LMC 1–2/12; SLJ 12/1/11)

4925 DiPucchio, Kelly. *Clink* (PS–1). Illus. by Matthew Myers. 2011, HarperCollins $16.99 (978-0-06-192928-1). 32pp. An outdated robot with low self-esteem despairs of ever being purchased, until a young boy who likes simpler things picks him up and takes him home. ℮ (Rev: BL 4/1/11; HB 5–6/11; SLJ 3/1/11)

4926 Edwards, Becky. *My Brother Sammy* (PS–2). Illus. by David Armitage. 1999, Millbrook LB $23.90 (978-0-7613-1417-2). An older boy has troubles adjusting to the erratic behavior of his autistic younger brother, Sammy. (Rev: HBG 10/99; SLJ 7/99)

4927 Ehrlich, H. M. *Gotcha, Louie!* (PS–K). Illus. by Emily Bolam. 2002, Houghton $15.00 (978-0-618-19549-7). 32pp. Young Louie gets lost in the tall grass close to the beach, but his mother very cleverly finds him. (Rev: BL 4/15/02; HBG 10/02; SLJ 4/02)

4928 Ehrlich, H. M. *Louie's Goose* (PS–3). Illus. by Emily Bolam. 2000, Houghton $15.00 (978-0-618-03023-1). Louie is so attached to his stuffed goose, Rosie, that, although it is falling apart and needs constant repair, he can't part with it. (Rev: BL 3/1/00; HBG 10/00; SLJ 3/00)

4929 Elliott, David. *Finn Throws a Fit!* (PS–1). Illus. by Timothy Basil Ering. 2009, Candlewick $16.99 (978-0-7636-2356-2). 32pp. The emotional roller-coaster of toddler life is depicted in this tale of Finn who definitely does not want his peaches, but after his "fit" subsides he changes his mind. (Rev: BL 7/09; SLJ 9/09)

4930 Ellis, Sarah. *Ben Over Night* (PS–2). Illus. by Kim LaFave. 2005, Fitzhenry & Whiteside $16.95 (978-1-55041-807-1). Peter's house is only across the street, but even though Ben loves to play there, he's scared to stay there overnight. (Rev: BL 5/1/05; SLJ 6/05)

4931 Elya, Susan Middleton. *Home at Last* (K–3). Illus. by Felipe Davalos. 2002, Lee & Low $16.95 (978-1-58430-020-5). 32pp. Ana, who has recently arrived from Mexico with her family, helps persuade her mother to attend English-language classes. (Rev: BCCB 9/02; BL 5/1/02; HBG 10/02; SLJ 7/02)

4932 Figueredo, D. H. *When This World Was New* (PS–3). Illus. by Enrique O. Sánchez. 1999, Lee & Low $15.95 (978-1-880000-86-1). Danilito leaves his warm Caribbean island to migrate with his parents to the U.S., and there he has many unsettling experiences but one outstanding joy — seeing the city transformed by snow. (Rev: BL 6/1–15/99; HBG 10/99; SLJ 7/99)

4933 Fine, Edith Hope. *Under the Lemon Moon* (K–3). Illus. by Rene King Moreno. 1999, Lee & Low $16.95 (978-1-880000-69-4). Young Rosalinda learns to cope with loss when a thief steals all the lemons from her pet tree and damages it as well. (Rev: BL 5/15/99; HBG 10/99; SLJ 4/99)

4934 Fitzpatrick, Marie-Louise. *I Am I* (K–3). Illus. by author. 2006, Roaring Brook $16.95 (978-1-59643-054-9). Two children compete for dominance and their hateful words destroy the landscape around them; they eventually work out that peaceful coexistence is a much better strategy. (Rev: SLJ 6/06*)

4935 Fleming, Virginia. *Be Good to Eddie Lee* (K–3). Illus. by Floyd Cooper. 1993, Penguin $16.99 (978-0-399-21993-1). Eddie Lee, a boy with Down's syndrome, teaches his neighbor, Christy, to look at the world differently. (Rev: BL 1/15/94; SLJ 2/94)

4936 Foreman, Michael. *A Child's Garden: A Story of Hope* (K–3). Illus. by author. 2009, Candlewick $17.99 (978-0-7636-4271-6). 32pp. In a time of conflict, children from opposing sides find hope and joy in a garden. (Rev: BL 5/1/09; SLJ 6/09)

4937 Forler, Nan. *Bird Child* (1–3). Illus. by Francois Thisdale. 2009, Tundra $19.95 (978-0-88776-894-1). 32pp. Eliza, a child who believes in her ability to fly, uses her self-confidence to help new student Lainey, the victim of bullying. (Rev: BL 11/1/09; SLJ 9/1/09)

4938 Fox, Mem. *Harriet, You'll Drive Me Wild!* (PS). Illus. by Marla Frazee. 2000, Harcourt $16.00 (978-0-15-201977-8). 32pp. Harriet is such a pest that her usually patient mother begins to shout at her but then they kiss and make up. (Rev: BCCB 6/00; BL 3/1/00; HB 3/00; HBG 10/00; SLJ 4/00)

4939 Frame, Jeron Ashford. *Yesterday I Had the Blues* (K–2). Illus. by R. Gregory Christie. 2003, Tricycle $14.95 (978-1-58246-084-0). A young African American boy, who's suffered a bout of the blues, ponders the varied moods of his family members and assigns each a color; vibrant illustrations add to the engaging text. (Rev: HBG 4/04; SLJ 10/03)

4940 Freymann, Saxton, and Joost Elffers. *How Are You Peeling? Foods with Moods* (PS–1). Illus. 1999, Scholastic $16.95 (978-0-439-10431-9). 48pp. Collages of fruits and vegetables are used to portray human emotions. (Rev: BL 2/1/00; HBG 3/00; SLJ 1/00) [152.4]

4941 Garland, Sarah. *Azzi in Between* (1–3). Illus. by author. 2013, Frances Lincoln $17.99 (978-184780261-3). 38pp. Azzi and her family must immigrate to another country to escape the war in their homeland, but with the help of new friends and a special teacher, Azzi finds that she might just be able to adjust to her new life. USBBY Outstanding International Book. (Rev: BLO 9/15/13; LMC 5–6/14; SLJ 1/14)

4942 Gifaldi, David. *Ben, King of the River* (K–3). Illus. by Layne Johnson. 2001, Whitman $16.99 (978-0-8075-0635-6). 32pp. An older boy is afraid his disabled brother will spoil the family's first camping trip. (Rev: BL 3/1/01; HBG 10/01)

4943 Gilmore, Rachna. *Grandpa's Clock* (2–4). Illus. by Amy Meissner. 2006, Orca $17.95 (978-1-55143-333-2). Cayley's grandfather promises to make her a special clock, but the project must be put on hold when he has a heart attack and goes to the hospital. (Rev: SLJ 6/06)

4944 Gleeson, Libby. *Clancy and Millie and the Very Fine House* (PS–2). Illus. by Freya Blackwood. 2010, IPG/Little Hare $16.99 (978-1-921541-19-3). 32pp. His new house seems very large and empty, and young Clancy is happy when his new friend Millie comes to play with him, building things with boxes. (Rev: BL 11/1/10; SLJ 1/1/11*)

4945 Golding, Theresa Martin. *Abby's Asthma and the Big Race* (K–3). Illus. by Margeaux Lucas. 2009, Albert Whitman $16.99 (978-0-8075-0465-9). 32pp. Abby is a fast runner but she has asthma, and this book shows just what she goes through to succeed. (Rev: BL 3/15/09; SLJ 4/09)

4946 Gow, Nancy. *Ten Big Toes and a Prince's Nose* (PS–2). Illus. by Stephen Costanza. 2010, Sterling $14.95 (978-1-4027-6396-0). 32pp. An embarrassingly big-footed princess and an awkwardly big-nosed prince meet and fall in love in this reassuring tale. (Rev: BL 10/15/10; LMC 1–2/11; SLJ 11/1/10)

4947 Grant, Karima. *Sofie and the City* (PS–2). Illus. by Janet Montecalvo. 2006, Boyds Mills $15.95 (978-1-59078-273-6). A little girl from Senegal yearns for home but learns to appreciate life in the United States when she makes a friend. (Rev: SLJ 5/06)

4948 Gravett, Emily. *Little Mouse's Big Book of Fears* (2–4). Illus. by author. 2008, Simon & Schuster $17.99 (978-1-4050-8948-7). 32pp. Little Mouse talks about his many fears — which include ablutophobia (fear of bathing) and sciaphobia (fear of shadows) — in this sensitive yet humorous book. (Rev: BL 12/1/08; HB 1/09; LMC 3/09; SLJ 10/08*)

4949 Gregory, Nan. *Pink* (K–2). Illus. by Luc Melanson. 2007, Groundwood $17.95 (978-0-88899-781-4). Vivi works hard to earn enough to buy the pink doll she covets, and is distressed to find it's already been sold. (Rev: BCCB 10/07; BL 10/1/07; SLJ 11/07)

4950 Grimm, Edward. *The Doorman* (K–3). Illus. by Ted Lewin. 2000, Orchard LB $17.99 (978-0-531-33280-1). Residents in a New York City apartment building mourn the death of the doorman who meant so much to them. (Rev: BCCB 7–8/00; BL 7/00; HBG 3/01; SLJ 10/00)

4951 Gunning, Monica. *A Shelter in Our Car* (K–3). Illus. by Elaine Pedlar. 2004, Children's Book Pr. $16.95 (978-0-89239-183-7). 32pp. Jamaican-born Zettie and her mother live in the backseat of their car while they try to make a real life for themselves. (Rev: BL 4/1/04)

4952 Headley, Justina Chen. *The Patch* (PS–2). Illus. by Mitch Vane. 2006, Charlesbridge $15.95 (978-1-58089-049-6). 32pp. Five-year-old Becca, an aspiring ballerina, at first balks at wearing an eye patch to correct her lazy eye but finds a way to turn the patch into a fashion asset. (Rev: BL 2/1/06; SLJ 2/06)

4953 Hobbie, Holly. *Fanny and Annabelle* (PS–3). Illus. by author. 2009, Little, Brown $16.99 (978-0-316-16688-1). 40pp. Life imitates art when Fanny writes a story about a child called Annabelle who needs the money to buy a locket for her aunt's birthday; a sequel to *Fanny* (2008). (Rev: BL 9/15/09; SLJ 12/1/09)

4954 Holmes, Janet A. *Have You Seen Duck?* (PS). Illus. by Jonathan Bentley. 2011, Scholastic $8.99 (978-0-545-22488-8). 24pp. Convinced his stuffed animal friend needs him to be there, always, a young boy embarks on a frantic search when his duck goes missing. (Rev: BL 1/1–15/11; SLJ 2/1/11)

4955 Howard, Arthur. *The Hubbub Above* (K–2). Illus. by author. 2005, Harcourt $16.00 (978-0-15-204592-0). Sydney is very happy living on the 52nd floor of Ivory Towers until elephant neighbors called the Kabooms move in and destroy her peace. (Rev: SLJ 5/05)

4956 Howard, Elizabeth F. *Virgie Goes to School with Us Boys* (K–2). Illus. by E. B. Lewis. 2000, Simon & Schuster $16.00 (978-0-689-80076-4). Virgie, youngest in a family of boys, vows that she will accompany her brothers when they walk the seven miles to school every Monday morning. (Rev: BCCB 2/00; BL 11/1/99*; HBG 10/00; SLJ 3/00)

4957 Isherwood, Shirley. *Flora the Frog* (K–3). Illus. by Anna C. Leplar. 2000, Peachtree $16.95 (978-1-56145-223-1). Flora is so upset at playing a frog in the class play, that she throws away the frog costume that her mother and aunt have made. (Rev: BCCB 11/00; BL 9/15/00; HBG 3/01; SLJ 10/00)

4958 Jenkins, Emily. *The Little Bit Scary People* (PS–2). Illus. by Alexandra Boiger. 2008, Hyperion $16.99 (978-1-4231-0075-1). A little girl discovers that people are less scary if she imagines how they behave in other situations. (Rev: BCCB 11/08; BL 12/15/08; HB 11/08; LMC 1/09; SLJ 9/08)

4959 Jimenez, Francisco. *La Mariposa* (K–3). Illus. by Simon Silva. 1998, Houghton $16.00 (978-0-395-81663-9). 40pp. Francisco becomes adept at drawing butterflies and, as a gesture of reconciliation, offers one of his drawings to the boy who beat him up on the playground. (Rev: BL 3/1/99; HBG 3/99; SLJ 11/98)

4960 Jordan, Deloris, and Roslyn M. Jordan. *Salt in His Shoes: Michael Jordan in Pursuit of a Dream* (K–4). Illus. by Kadir Nelson. 2000, Simon & Schuster $16.95 (978-0-689-83371-7). 32pp. A fictionalized tale about a youthful Michael Jordan whose mother (the author) encourages him to pursue his basketball dreams even though he's the shortest boy on the team. (Rev: BL 2/1/01; HBG 3/01)

4961 Keane, Jerome. *Ellie's Bad Hair Day* (K–2). Illus. by Susana de Dios. 2012, IPG/Pavilion $15.99 (978-1-84365-140-6). 32pp. Ellie and her rabbit friend Oscar set out to find another person — anywhere in the world —

with hair as crazy as hers; but her hair turns out to have a benefit when they get lost and searchers can focus in on her unruly locks. (Rev: BLO 10/15/12; SLJ 11/12)

4962 Kelley, Marty. *Winter Woes* (PS–2). Illus. by author. 2005, Zino $12.95 (978-1-55933-306-1). A little boy imagines in humorous detail the myriad dangers that might befall him should he go out into the snow. (Rev: SLJ 4/05)

4963 Koch, Miriam. *Digby Differs* (PS–2). 2013, Peter Pauper $17.99 (978-144131306-5). 40pp. In this uplifting tale about belonging, Digby is a red and white striped sheep who tries to make friends with similarly striped objects, but it isn't until he finds a place where there is a red and white striped lighthouse and plain white sheep that live on the nearby hill that he is accepted despite his different appearance. (Rev: BLO 10/1/13; SLJ 12/13)

4964 Kolbisen, Irene M. *Wiggle-Butts and Up-Faces* (PS–K). Illus. by Sandy D. Zmolek. 1989, I Think I Can LB $14.95 (978-1-877863-00-4). Ingrid's young brother is afraid of taking beginner swimming lessons. (Rev: BL 12/1/89)

4965 Kostecki-Shaw, Jenny Sue. *My Travelin' Eye* (K–2). Illus. by author. 2008, Holt $16.95 (978-0-8050-8169-5). 40pp. When Jenny Sue's eye problems mean she has to wear a patch, her mother helps her create bright, imaginative eyewear. (Rev: BL 4/1/08; SLJ 6/08)

4966 Krisher, Trudy. *Kathy's Hats: A Story of Hope* (PS–3). Illus. by Nadine Bernard Westcott. 1992, Whitman LB $16.99 (978-0-8075-4116-6). 32pp. When Kathy undergoes chemotherapy for cancer, she finds a new reason to wear her hats. (Rev: BCCB 10/92; BL 10/1/92; SLJ 6/91)

4967 Krishnaswami, Uma. *The Closet Ghosts* (PS–2). Illus. by Shiraaz Bhabha. 2006, Children's Book Pr. $16.95 (978-0-89239-208-7). 32pp. Anu has just moved and is distressed to find ghosts in her closet; with the help of a Hindu god and the friends she finds at her new school, all ends well. (Rev: SLJ 6/06)

4968 Kroll, Virginia. *Brianna Breathes Easy: A Story About Asthma* (1–3). Illus. by Jayoung Cho. 2005, Whitman $16.99 (978-0-8075-0880-0). 32pp. Brianna learns she has asthma and how to control it in this informative story that will ease the fears of children with this condition. (Rev: BL 3/1/05)

4969 Kroll, Virginia. *Ryan Respects* (K–2). Illus. by Paige Billin-Frye. Series: The Way I Act. 2006, Albert Whitman $15.99 (978-0-8075-6946-7). 24pp. After unkindly teasing his friend Doug, young Ryan gets his comeuppance and also learns some lessons about the importance of respecting others' feelings. (Rev: BL 4/15/06; SLJ 3/06)

4970 Lagercrantz, Rose. *My Happy Life* (1–3). Illus. by Eva Eriksson. 2013, Gecko $16.95 (978-1-8775-7935-6). 136pp. Dani is eager to start school, but also apprehensive — will her life remain so happy? With large black-and-white drawings this is a chapter book translated from Swedish about friendship and depression when a friend moves away. ALA Notable Children's

Book. Lexile 500 (Rev: BL 5/1/13*; LMC 11–12/13; SLJ 3/13*)

4971 Lears, Laurie. *Nathan's Wish: A Story About Cerebral Palsy* (1–3). Illus. by Stacey Schuett. 2005, Albert Whitman $16.99 (978-0-8075-7101-9). Nathan, who has cerebral palsy, is encouraged when his neighbor finds a way to help an injured owl. (Rev: SLJ 7/05)

4972 Leonetti, Mike. *The Goalie Mask* (2–4). Illus. by Shayne Letain. Series: Hockey Heroes. 2004, Raincoast $15.95 (978-1-55192-703-9). A young player learns from his grandfather about the invention of the mask that protects players' faces from hockey pucks. (Rev: SLJ 2/05)

4973 Leonetti, Mike. *Gretzky's Game* (1–3). Illus. by Greg Banning. 2006, Raincoast $15.95 (978-1-55192-851-7). 32pp. Ryan, a young hockey player who's small for his age, patterns his playing style after that of his idol, Wayne Gretzky. (Rev: BL 2/15/06)

4974 Levis, Caron. *Stuck with the Blooz* (K–3). Illus. by Jon Davis. 2012, Harcourt $16.99 (978-0-547-74560-2). 40pp. A little girl tries to cope with the blue monster that is making her feel depressed. (Rev: BL 11/1/12; LMC 8–9/12; SLJ 11/12)

4975 Levy, Janice. *Alley Oops* (1–4). Illus. by Cynthia B. Decker. 2005, Flashlight $15.95 (978-0-9729225-4-8). J.J. has been bullying an overweight boy called Patrick, so J.J.'s father sits down with him and tells him a story about his own behavior as a boy. (Rev: SLJ 8/05)

4976 Lewis, Rose. *Orange Peel's Pocket* (PS–2). Illus. by Grace Zong. 2010, Abrams $16.95 (978-0-8109-8394-6). 32pp. An adopted Chinese child turns to the Chinese American community around her to learn about her origins. (Rev: BLO 3/1/10; SLJ 4/1/10)

4977 Liao, Jimmy. *The Sound of Colors: A Journey of the Imagination* (1–5). Adapted by Sarah L. Thomson. Illus. by author. 2005, Little, Brown $16.99 (978-0-316-93992-8). A blind girl imagines a colorful journey over land and sea as she makes her way through the subway. (Rev: SLJ 9/05)

4978 Lichtenheld, Tom. *Bridget's Beret* (K–2). Illus. by author. 2010, Henry Holt $16.99 (978-0-8050-8775-8). 40pp. Bridget gets "artists' block" when her trademark black beret goes missing. (Rev: BL 2/15/10*; SLJ 4/1/10)

4979 Lichtenheld, Tom. *What Are You So Grumpy About?* (K–3). Illus. 2003, Little, Brown $15.95 (978-0-316-59236-9). 32pp. Humorous double-spread cartoons show situations that could provoke a bad temper. (Rev: BL 3/15/03; HBG 10/03; SLJ 4/03)

4980 Look, Lenore. *Polka Dot Penguin Pottery* (1–3). Illus. by Yumi Heo. 2011, Random House $16.99 (978-0-375-86332-5); LB $19.99 (978-0-375-96332-2). 40pp. A young girl struggling with writer's block is taken to a pottery studio by her perceptive grandma; there, she eventually conquers her creative logjam. (Rev: BLO 8/11; SLJ 10/1/11)

4981 Ludwig, Trudy. *Just Kidding* (K–3). Illus. by Adam Gustavson. 2006, Tricycle $15.95 (978-1-58246-163-2).

32pp. D.J. gets help from his father and a teacher when Vince's bullying becomes upsetting; front matter offers advice to adults and back matter provides tips for children. (Rev: BL 4/15/06; SLJ 6/06)

4982 Lyon, George Ella. *The Pirate of Kindergarten* (PS–2). Illus. by Lynne Avril. 2010, Simon & Schuster $16.99 (978-1-4169-5024-0). 40pp. Ginny struggles with double vision until the problem is diagnosed and corrected with a temporary eye patch. ❂ Lexile AD580L (Rev: BL 5/1/10; LMC 8–9/10; SLJ 6/1/10)

4983 McKissack, Patricia C. *The Honest-to-Goodness Truth* (PS–3). Illus. by Giselle Potter. 2000, Simon & Schuster $16.00 (978-0-689-82668-9). 32pp. When Libby tells the honest truth to her friends and classmates, she finds that she can hurt their feelings. (Rev: BCCB 2/00; BL 12/15/99; HBG 10/00; SLJ 1/00)

4984 Manning, Jane. *Millie Fierce* (PS–1). Illus. by author. 2012, Philomel $16.99 (978-0-399-25642-4). 32pp. Millie is tired of being ignored but her initial strategy of causing trouble to gain attention doesn't work out well. (Rev: BLO 9/15/12; SLJ 8/12)

4985 Mayer, Mercer. *There Are Monsters Everywhere* (PS–2). Illus. by author. 2005, Dial $15.99 (978-0-8037-0621-7). Fearful of the monsters that follow him everywhere he goes, a young boy takes karate lessons. (Rev: SLJ 12/05)

4986 Meddaugh, Susan. *Just Teenie* (PS–2). Illus. 2006, Houghton $16.00 (978-0-618-68565-3). 32pp. Justine is totally frustrated by her tininess until an out-of-control plant gives her a different perspective on life. (Rev: BL 4/15/06; SLJ 6/06)

4987 Miller, William. *Night Golf* (1–3). Illus. by Cedric Lucas. 1999, Lee & Low $15.95 (978-1-880000-79-3). This is the story of an African American boy in the late 1950s, the prejudice he encounters when he wants to play golf on an all-white course, and how he perseveres and overcomes this problem. (Rev: HBG 10/99; SLJ 6/99)

4988 Millman, Isaac. *Moses Goes to a Concert* (K–4). Illus. 1998, Farrar $16.00 (978-0-374-35067-3). 40pp. This picture book, written in both English and American Sign Language, portrays the everyday experiences of a deaf child, Moses, and of a special occasion when he and his classmates go to a concert. (Rev: BL 4/15/98*; HBG 10/98; SLJ 4/98)

4989 Millman, Isaac. *Moses Goes to School* (PS–3). Illus. 2000, Farrar $16.00 (978-0-374-35069-7). 32pp. This story, written in both English and sign language, tells how Moses and his friends learn at their special school for the deaf. (Rev: BL 8/00; HBG 3/01; SLJ 8/00)

4990 Millman, Isaac. *Moses Goes to the Circus* (PS–2). Illus. by author. 2003, Farrar $16.00 (978-0-374-35064-2). Moses, who is deaf, and his family go to a circus for vision- and hearing-impaired children. (Rev: BL 4/15/03; HBG 10/03; SLJ 3/03)

4991 Mochizuki, Ken. *Baseball Saved Us* (2–4). Illus. by Dom Lee. 1993, Lee & Low $15.95 (978-1-880000-01-4). A Japanese American boy gains acceptance playing an excellent game of baseball learned while an internee during World War II. (Rev: BCCB 5/93; BL 4/15/93; HB 7/93; SLJ 6/93)

4992 Moore, Genevieve. *Catherine's Story* (PS–3). Illus. by Karin Littlewood. 2010, Frances Lincoln $17.95 (978-1-84507-655-9). 28pp. Catherine's single-parent dad patiently guides the young girl toward realizing her full potential despite her physical and emotional limitations in this tender picture book about disabilities. (Rev: BL 1/1–15/11; SLJ 1/1/11)

4993 Moore, Julianne. *Freckleface Strawberry* (PS–2). Illus. by LeUyen Pham. 2007, Bloomsbury $16.95 (978-1-59990-107-7). 32pp. A 7-year-old girl is unhappy with her many freckles. (Rev: SLJ 10/07)

4994 Moundlic, Charlotte. *The Bathing Costume, or the Worst Vacation of My Life* (1–3). Trans. from French by Claudia Zoe Bedrick. Illus. by Olivier Tallec. 2013, 978-1-59270-141-4 $15.95 (Enchanted Lion). 64pp. On his first vacation without his parents, 8-year-old Myron meets many challenges — a scary dive off a 10-foot board, teasing older cousins, and demanding grandparents. ALA Notable Children's Book; Batchelder Honor Award. (Rev: SLJ 8/13)

4995 Munsch, Robert, and Saoussan Askar. *From Far Away* (K–3). Illus. by Michael Martchenko. 1995, Firefly LB $16.95 (978-1-55037-397-4); paper $5.95 (978-1-55037-396-7). 24pp. Saoussan, a war refugee, has problems adjusting to her new home in Canada. (Rev: BL 1/1–15/96; SLJ 3/96)

4996 Napoli, Donna Jo. *Flamingo Dream* (K–3). Illus. by Cathie Felstead. 2002, HarperCollins LB $16.89 (978-0-688-17863-5). 32pp. A young narrator suffers the loss of her beloved father to cancer. (Rev: BL 4/15/02; HB 7/02; HBG 10/02; SLJ 5/02)

4997 Ness, Evaline. *Sam, Bangs and Moonshine* (K–2). Illus. by author. 1966, Holt $15.95 (978-0-8050-0314-7); paper $6.95 (978-0-8050-0315-4). A little girl learns to distinguish truth from "moonshine" only after her cat and playmate nearly meet tragedy. Caldecott Medal winner, 1967.

4998 Newman, Barbara Johansen. *Glamorous Glasses* (K–2). Illus. by author. 2012, Boyds Mills $16.95 (978-1-59078-878-3). 40pp. Joanie needs glasses but doesn't really like the prospect, while her cousin Bobbie finds the whole idea glamorous; Bobbie comes up with an ingenious swap that doesn't quite work. (Rev: BLO 11/1/12; LMC 3–4/13; SLJ 10/12)

4999 Newman, Lesléa. *Saturday Is Pattyday* (PS–3). Illus. by Annette Hegel. 1993, New Victoria LB $14.95 (978-0-934678-52-0); paper $6.95 (978-0-934678-51-3). 24pp. Frankie is unhappy when his two moms break up and one moves to her own apartment. (Rev: BCCB 11/93; BL 11/1/93)

5000 Newsome, Jill. *Dream Dancer* (PS–2). Illus. by Claudio Munoz. 2002, HarperCollins LB $15.89 (978-0-06-001322-6). 48pp. A ballerina doll given to her by her grandmother helps Lily through her long recovery after an injury leaves her unable to dance. (Rev: BL 1/1–15/02; HBG 10/02; SLJ 3/02)

5001 Niner, Holly L. *I Can't Stop! A Story About Tourette Syndrome* (1–3). Illus. by Meryl Treatner. 2005, Albert Whitman $16.99 (978-0-8075-3620-9). 32pp. Nathan learns to deal with his Tourette syndrome in this realistic story that is bolstered by factual information contributed by a doctor. (Rev: BL 11/15/05)

5002 Nordling, Lee. *The Bramble* (PS–2). Illus. by Bruce Zick. 2013, Carolrhoda $16.95 (978-076135856-5). 32pp. This nearly wordless book focuses on young Cameron, an uncertain boy who gains self-confidence when he meets a kindly, playful monster. **e** (Rev: BL 9/15/13; LMC 3–4/14; SLJ 9/13)

5003 Polacco, Patricia. *Thank You, Mr. Falker* (K–4). Illus. 1998, Penguin $16.99 (978-0-399-23166-7). 40pp. Based on the author's personal experiences, this is the story of Trisha, who was able to draw beautifully but hid the fact that she couldn't read until she got special help in the 5th grade. (Rev: BCCB 6/98; BL 5/1/98; HBG 10/98; SLJ 6/98)

5004 Prats, Joan de Déu. *Sebastian's Roller Skates* (PS–2). Illus. by Francesc Rovira. 2005, Kane $15.95 (978-1-929132-81-2). 40pp. Shy Sebastian finds his self-confidence and ability to express himself growing after he masters roller skating. (Rev: BL 11/1/05; SLJ 10/05)

5005 Primavera, Elise. *Louise the Big Cheese and the La-Di-Da Shoes* (K–2). Illus. by Diane Goode. 2010, Simon & Schuster $16.99 (978-1-4169-7181-8). Unpaged. Louise's desire for fancy shoes evaporates when she realizes how uncomfortable the shiny pumps really are. (Rev: SLJ 2/1/10)

5006 Raschka, Chris. *The Purple Balloon* (1–3). Illus. 2007, Random $16.99 (978-0-375-84146-0). 32pp. Designed primarily for terminally ill children and their friends and family members, this book deals sensitively with the issues that face those who are dying and the people who love them, emphasizing how many people are there to help. (Rev: BL 4/1/07)

5007 Recorvits, Helen. *My Name Is Yoon* (K–2). Illus. by Gabi Swiatkowska. 2003, Farrar $16.00 (978-0-374-35114-4). Yoon, a Korean immigrant child, is unhappy in America until she begins to feel at home in her new and different surroundings. (Rev: BL 3/15/03; HBG 10/03; SLJ 5/03)

5008 Reynolds, Marilynn. *Goodbye to Griffith Street* (K–2). Illus. by Renn Benoit. 2004, Orca $16.95 (978-1-55143-285-4). It snows on John's last day on Griffith Street (his parents are getting divorced and he and his mother must move), and John decides to leave his friends and neighbors with the gift of snow angels and stars. (Rev: SLJ 1/05)

5009 Riggs, Shannon. *Not in Room 204* (1–3). Illus. by Jaime Zollars. 2007, Albert Whitman $16.99 (978-0-8075-5764-8). 32pp. A class about "stranger danger" gives Regina the courage to tell her teacher about her father's inappropriate behavior; a sensitive story that provides no details. (Rev: BL 2/1/07)

5010 Robberecht, Thierry. *Angry Dragon* (PS–2). Illus. by Philippe Goossens. 2004, Clarion $15.00 (978-0-618-47430-1). A little boy pictures himself transformed into a fire-breathing dragon every time his anger gets out of control. (Rev: BL 1/1–15/05)

5011 Robberecht, Thierry. *Sam Is Never Scared* (PS–2). Illus. by Philippe Goossens. 2006, Clarion $12.00 (978-0-618-73278-4). Sam acts brave in public but hides his fears of monsters and ghosts until the day a huge spider lands on his hand; his father reassures him that everyone is afraid of something. (Rev: SLJ 10/06)

5012 Rodriguez, Luis J. *America Is Her Name* (2–4). Illus. by Carlos Vazquez. 1998, Curbstone $15.95 (978-1-880684-40-5). Lonely in her barrio home in Chicago, America Soliz learns to express herself in poetry. (Rev: HBG 10/98; SLJ 9/98)

5013 Rosenberry, Vera. *Vera Runs Away* (PS–3). Illus. 2000, Holt $16.00 (978-0-8050-6267-0). 32pp. Vera feels so underappreciated at home when she receives a straight-A report card that she decides to run away. (Rev: BL 10/15/00; HBG 3/01; SLJ 11/00)

5014 Rosenthal, Amy Krouse. *It's Not Fair!* (PS–3). Illus. by Tom Lichtenheld. 2008, HarperCollins $16.99 (978-0-06-115257-3). 40pp. "Why'd I get the smaller half?" "Why does my team always lose?" Children, but also animals and inanimate objects, air their complaints. (Rev: BCCB 6/08; BL 4/15/08; SLJ 4/08)

5015 Rotner, Shelley, and Sheila Kelly. *Something's Different* (K–3). Illus. 2002, Millbrook LB $22.90 (978-0-7613-1923-8). 32pp. A boy tries to understand his parents' marital problems. (Rev: BL 3/1/02; HBG 10/02; SLJ 8/02)

5016 Say, Allen. *Allison* (PS–3). Illus. 1997, Houghton $17.00 (978-0-395-85895-0). 32pp. Little Allison, an Asian girl, is upset when she learns that she has been adopted by her Caucasian parents. (Rev: BL 12/15/97*; HBG 3/98; SLJ 10/97)

5017 Say, Allen. *Emma's Rug* (PS–3). Illus. 1996, Houghton $16.95 (978-0-395-74294-5). 32pp. Emma is inconsolable when she loses the rug that has been the inspiration for her art. (Rev: BCCB 11/96; BL 10/1/96; HB 9/96; SLJ 9/96)

5018 Say, Allen. *The Favorite Daughter* (1–3). Illus. by author. 2013, Scholastic $17.99 (978-0-545-17662-0). 32pp. Yuriko is distressed by the fact that she is not more American until her father reminds her how special her heritage makes her. Lexile 300 (Rev: BL 6/13; HB 7–8/13; LMC 11–12/13; SLJ 5/13)

5019 Scacco, Linda. *Always My Grandpa: A Story for Children About Alzheimer's Disease* (1–3). Illus. by Nicole Wong. 2006, Magination $14.95 (978-1-59147-311-4); paper $8.95 (978-1-59147-312-1). Daniel is sad to see his grandfather changing during one summer at the beach house, and he is encouraged to discuss his feelings with his family. (Rev: SLJ 6/07)

5020 Schick, Eleanor. *Mama* (K–3). Illus. 2000, Marshall Cavendish $15.95 (978-0-7614-5060-3). 32pp. A mother's death and the ensuing sorrow, acceptance, and cherishing of memories are the subjects of this picture book, seen through a young daughter's eyes. (Rev: BL 2/15/00; HBG 10/00; SLJ 5/00)

5021 Schotter, Roni. *Room for Rabbit* (PS–2). Illus. by Cyd Moore. 2003, Clarion $15.00 (978-0-618-18183-4). Kara finds that her father's new wife is taking up too much space and uses her rabbit as her spokesperson. (Rev: BL 3/1/03; HBG 10/03; SLJ 4/03)

5022 Seeger, Pete, and Paul Dubois Jacobs. *The Deaf Musicians* (K–3). Illus. by R. Gregory Christie. 2006, Putnam $16.99 (978-0-399-24316-5). When jazz pianist Lee loses his hearing, he has to leave the group he's been playing with, but while studying sign language at a school for the deaf he meets Max, a sax player, and together they start up a sign-language band. (Rev: SLJ 11/06*)

5023 Senisi, Ellen B. *All Kinds of Friends, Even Green!* (K–4). Photos by author. 2002, Woodbine $15.95 (978-1-890627-35-5). Wheelchair-bound Zaki chooses a neighbor's iguana for his school assignment, because the plucky animal manages to cope despite missing toes. (Rev: HBG 10/03; SLJ 11/02)

5024 Shange, Ntozake. *White Wash* (PS–2). Illus. by Michael Sporn. 1997, Walker $15.95 (978-0-8027-8490-2). Helene-Angel and her brother are attacked by a group of white thugs who cover her face with white paint and traumatize her so much that she doesn't want to return to school. (Rev: HBG 3/98; SLJ 5/98)

5025 Shannon, David. *A Bad Case of Stripes* (1–3). Illus. 1998, Scholastic $16.99 (978-0-590-92997-4). Camilla's desire to please and be popular causes her some problems. (Rev: BCCB 3/98; BL 1/1–15/98; HBG 10/98; SLJ 3/98)

5026 Shannon, David. *Too Many Toys* (PS–3). Illus. by author. 2008, Scholastic $16.99 (978-0-439-49029-0). 32pp. Spencer's room looks like a Toys R Us aisle and his mom rules that some of them have got to go, forcing Spencer to make some difficult decisions. (Rev: BL 10/1/08; LMC 1/09; SLJ 1/09)

5027 Shavick, Andrea. *You'll Grow Soon, Alex* (PS–1). Illus. by Russell Ayto. 2000, Walker $15.95 (978-0-8027-8736-1). Alex tries everything including diet and exercise to hasten his growth but later decides that being tall has its disadvantages. (Rev: BL 10/15/00; HBG 10/01; SLJ 10/00)

5028 Shin, Sun Yung. *Cooper's Lesson* (PS–3). Trans. by Min Paek. Illus. by Kim Cogan. 2004, Children's Book Pr. $16.95 (978-0-89239-193-6). 32pp. Cooper's mother is Korean and his father is white, resulting in some confusion for the young boy; the story is told in English and Korean. (Rev: BL 3/15/04*; SLJ 5/04)

5029 Shreeve, Elizabeth. *Oliver at the Window* (PS–K). Illus. by Candice Hartsough McDonald. 2009, Front St $16.95 (978-1-59078-548-5). 32pp. Oliver is sad and reclusive after his parents' divorce until an unhappy new student at preschool gives him a reason to reach out. (Rev: BL 11/1/09; SLJ 10/1/09)

5030 Singer, Marilyn. *Tallulah's Tutu* (PS–2). Illus. by Alexandra Boiger. 2011, Clarion $16.99 (978-0-547-17353-5). 40pp. Devoted to the idea of having a tutu, Tallulah finds learning the basics of ballet — and the leotard — disappointing. (Rev: BL 2/15/11; SLJ 3/1/11)

5031 Smothers, Ethel Footman. *The Hard-Times Jar* (1–3). Illus. by John Holyfield. 2003, Farrar $16.00 (978-0-374-32852-8). 32pp. Emma, the dark-skinned daughter of migrant workers, finds the strength to face her new 3rd-grade classroom in Pennsylvania, and learns to appreciate reading and books. (Rev: BL 8/03; HBG 4/04; SLJ 10/03)

5032 Snicket, Lemony. *The Dark* (PS–2). Illus. by Jon Klassen. 2013, Little, Brown $16.99 (978-0-316-18748-0). 40pp. Young Laszlo is afraid of "the dark" that comes out at night, but is forced to confront his fears when his night-light burns out — and is amazed to find that "the dark" helps him. ALA Notable Children's Book. Lexile AD660 (Rev: BL 3/1/13*; HB 3–4/13; LMC 10/13*; SLJ 4/13*)

5033 Soman, David, and Jacky Davis. *Ladybug Girl at the Beach* (K–1). Illus. by David Soman. 2010, Dial $16.99 (978-0-8037-3416-6). Unpaged. Lulu (aka Ladybug Girl) and her dog spend a day at the beach and find that some aspects are quite frightening. (Rev: SLJ 6/1/10)

5034 Spalding, Andrea, and Janet Wilson. *Me and Mr. Mah* (PS–2). Illus. 2000, Orca $14.95 (978-1-55143-168-0). Ian misses his father after his parents divorce but finds a friend and kindred spirit in Mr. Mah, a neighbor who misses his family in China. (Rev: BL 3/1/03; HBG 9/00; SLJ 3/00)

5035 Spelman, Cornelia Maude. *When I Feel Jealous* (PS–1). Illus. by Kathy Parkinson. Series: The Way I Feel. 2003, Whitman LB $15.99 (978-0-8075-8886-4). A little bear talks about the sorts of things that make her jealous and what she does to cope with such feelings. (Rev: HBG 4/04; SLJ 10/03)

5036 Spelman, Cornelia Maude. *When I Feel Worried* (PS–1). Illus. by Kathy Parkinson. Series: The Way I Feel. 2013, Whitman $15.99 (978-080758893-2). 24pp. Worrying is the subject of this children's story and a little guinea pig is the narrator, explaining the things that make her feel worried and how she combats this feeling. (Rev: BL 9/15/13; SLJ 8/13)

5037 Spinelli, Eileen. *Wanda's Monster* (K–2). Illus. by Nancy Hayashi. 2002, Whitman $15.95 (978-0-8075-8656-3). 32pp. Granny is the only one who believes there's a monster in Wanda's closet, but points out that it can't be much fun for the monster. (Rev: BL 12/1/02; HB 1/03; HBG 3/03; SLJ 10/02)

5038 Spinelli, Eileen. *When No One Is Watching* (PS–2). Illus. by David A. Johnson. 2013, Eerdmans $16 (978-0-8028-5303-5). 26pp. A young girl has great fun when she's by herself — dancing and singing; but when others are around (apart from her shy friend Loretta) she is quiet and withdrawn. Lexile AD440 (Rev: BL 3/1/13; LMC 10/13; SLJ 3/13*)

5039 Steig, William. *Spinky Sulks* (K–3). Illus. 1988, Farrar paper $4.95 (978-0-374-46990-0). 32pp. Spinky is a first-class sulker but is forced to reconsider his position. (Rev: BCCB 12/88; BL 1/15/89; HB 3/89)

5040 Stein, Sara Bonnett. *About Dying* (1–3). Illus. by author. 1974, Walker $10.95 (978-0-8027-6172-9); paper $8.95 (978-0-8027-7223-7). 48pp. Sensitive portrayal of the death of a bird and of a grandfather. Also use: *About Handicaps* (1974); *Making Babies* (1974); *About Phobias; The Adopted One; On Divorce* (all 1979).

5041 Stier, Catherine. *Bugs in My Hair?!* (K–3). Illus. by Tammie Lyon. 2008, Albert Whitman $16.99 (978-0-8075-0908-1). Third-grader Ellie, who's a bit of a perfectionist, is devastated to find she has lice in her hair, but once she's accepted the fact decides to take steps to help others. (Rev: BL 7/08; SLJ 5/08)

5042 Stolz, Mary. *Storm in the Night* (K–3). Illus. by Pat Cummings. 1988, HarperCollins paper $6.99 (978-0-06-443256-6). 32pp. Grandfather tells Thomas, a young African American boy, of a time when he was afraid, in order to calm the child's fears about a dark, stormy night. (Rev: BL 2/1/88; HB 7/88; SLJ 3/88)

5043 Sylvester, Kevin. *Splinters* (K–3). Illus. by author. 2010, Tundra $17.95 (978-0-88776-944-3). 40pp. Hockey team outcast Cindy receives a visit from a "fairy goaltender" in this twist on the Cinderella story that features two evil sisters, their mother (the coach), and a golden skate; a sports story with a fairy tale feel. (Rev: BL 9/1/10; SLJ 9/1/10)

5044 Taback, Simms. *I Miss You Every Day* (PS–1). Illus. by author. 2007, Viking $16.99 (978-0-670-06192-1). In this picture book with rhyming lines, a young girl wraps herself up and mails herself to a far-away loved one. (Rev: BL 9/1/07; SLJ 8/07)

5045 Tarpley, Natasha Anastasia. *Joe-Joe's First Flight* (PS–2). Illus. by E. B. Lewis. 2003, Knopf $15.95 (978-0-375-81053-4). In the 1920s, young Joe-Joe dreams of flying a plane but fears that, as an African American, he won't be allowed to. (Rev: BL 2/15/04; HBG 10/03; SLJ 7/03)

5046 Tinkham, Kelly A. *Hair for Mama* (K–3). Illus. by Amy June Bates. 2007, Dial $16.99 (978-0-8037-2955-1). Marcus tries to help out when his mother is reluctant to have her picture taken after losing her hair to cancer treatment. (Rev: HB 7/07; SLJ 7/07)

5047 Vail, Rachel. *Sometimes I'm Bombaloo* (PS–2). Illus. by Yumi Heo. 2002, Scholastic $16.95 (978-0-439-08755-1). Katie is a mostly-good kid who sometimes turns into an angry "Bombaloo." (Rev: BCCB 4/02; BL 2/1/02; HBG 10/02; SLJ 3/02)

5048 Vettiger, Susanne. *Basghetti Spaghetti* (K–2). Illus. by Marie-Anne Räber. 2005, North-South LB $16.50 (978-0-7358-1992-4). Oscar, a crab, has some trouble pronouncing words correctly when he's nervous but improves after visiting Doctor Octopus. (Rev: SLJ 8/05)

5049 Villeneuve, Anne. *Loula Is Leaving for Africa* (PS–2). Illus. by author. 2013, Kids Can $16.95 (978-155453941-3). 32pp. Loula is fed up with her younger brothers and decides to run away to Africa, and with a little imagination (and a very helpful chauffeur), has an unforgettable day watching imaginary monkeys, drinking imaginary tea, and eating imaginary ostrich-egg souffle. Lexile AD400 (Rev: BLO 9/15/13; SLJ 9/13)

5050 Viorst, Judith. *The Tenth Good Thing About Barney* (K–2). Illus. by Erik Blegvad. 1971, Macmillan $14.00 (978-0-689-20688-7); paper $4.99 (978-0-689-71203-6). 32pp. At a backyard funeral, a little boy tries to think of 10 good things to say about his cat, Barney — but can come up with only nine.

5051 Waber, Bernard. *Ira Sleeps Over* (PS–2). Illus. by author. 1973, Houghton $16.00 (978-0-395-13893-9); paper $6.95 (978-0-395-20503-7). 48pp. When Ira is invited to sleep overnight at Reggie's house, he wants to go, but should he or shouldn't he take along his teddy bear?

5052 Wagner, Anke. *Tim's Big Move* (PS–1). Illus. by Eva Eriksson. 2012, NorthSouth $17.95 (978-0-7358-4090-4). 32pp. Tim doesn't mind the idea of moving to Calabash, but his stuffed animal Pico is very nervous about it. (Rev: BL 10/15/12; HB 11–12/12; LMC 5–6/13; SLJ 11/12)

5053 Wahl, Jan. *Candy Shop* (K–3). Illus. by Nicole Wong. 2004, Charlesbridge $15.95 (978-1-57091-508-6). 32pp. Daniel, a young African American boy, not only dresses as a cowboy but also tries to act like one, and he takes action when hateful words are written in front of his favorite candy store. (Rev: BL 4/15/04; SLJ 3/04)

5054 Watts, Jeri Hanel. *Keepers* (K–3). Illus. by Felicia Marshall. 1997, Lee & Low $15.95 (978-1-880000-58-8). 32pp. Kenyon feels guilty because he has bought a baseball glove with the money intended for Grandmother's 90th birthday present. (Rev: BL 1/1–15/98; HBG 3/98; SLJ 1/98)

5055 Weigelt, Udo. *Becky the Borrower* (PS–2). Illus. by Astrid Henn. 2008, North-South $16.95 (978-0-7358-2205-4). Becky borrows and borrows from her kindergarten classmates until she does not know what is whose any more. (Rev: BLO 12/30/08; LMC 5/09; SLJ 9/08)

5056 Willems, Mo. *Knuffle Bunny Free: An Unexpected Diversion* (PS–1). Illus. by author. 2010, HarperCollins $17.99 (978-0-0619-2957-1). 52pp. Knuffle Bunny gets left behind on an airplane to Holland in this poignant conclusion to the series. (Rev: BL 7/10; HB 9–10/10; SLJ 10/1/10*)

5057 Willis, Jeanne. *Susan Laughs* (PS–K). Illus. 2000, Holt $15.00 (978-0-8050-6501-5). 32pp. Susan is presented in a series of activities — laughing, singing, and swimming, for example — and on the last page is shown in her wheelchair. (Rev: BCCB 10/00; BL 8/00; HBG 3/01; SLJ 11/00)

5058 Winter, Jeanette. *Angelina's Island* (PS–2). 2007, Farrar $16.00 (978-0-374-30349-5). 320pp. Living in New York City with her parents, Angelina longs for the sun, food, and friends of her former home in Jamaica. (Rev: BL 2/1/07)

5059 Wishinsky, Frieda. *Each One Special* (PS–2). Illus. by H. Werner Zimmermann. 1999, Orca $14.95 (978-1-55143-122-2). 32pp. When a creative cake decorator is fired from his job, he takes up a related field — sculpting. (Rev: BL 1/1–15/99; HBG 10/99; SLJ 7/99)

5060 Yolen, Jane. *How Do Dinosaurs Say I'm Mad?* (PS–1). Illus. by Mark Teague. 2013, Scholastic $16.99 (978-054514315-8). 40pp. Dinosaurs get mad just like humans, and this is depicted in a multitude of ways in rhyming text and illustrations about handling your anger. (Rev: BLO 9/15/13; SLJ 10/13)

5061 Zolotow, Charlotte. *The Three Funny Friends* (PS–2). Illus. by Linda Bronson. 2003, Running Pr. $15.95 (978-0-7624-1553-3). A lonely young girl, who has just moved to a new town, comforts herself with three imaginary friends — Guy-Guy, Bickerina, and Mr. Dobie — until a real-life friend comes along. (Rev: SLJ 12/03)

REAL AND ALMOST REAL ANIMALS

5062 Abley, Mark. *Ghost Cat* (PS–K). Illus. by Karen Reczuch. 2001, Groundwood $16.95 (978-0-88899-433-2). 32pp. Elderly Miss Wilkinson depends on her cat for companionship and is bereft when he becomes ill and dies, but comforted when the rose bush she plants on his grave blooms. (Rev: HBG 3/02; SLJ 9/01)

5063 Agee, Jon. *My Rhinoceros* (PS–2). Illus. by author. 2011, Scholastic $16.95 (978-0-545-29441-6). 32pp. A young boy is disappointed with his pet rhinoceros's limited talents, until he finds himself in a situation where only the rhino can save the day. This funny story is also available in Spanish. Lexile AD310L (Rev: BL 10/15/11; HB 11–12/11; LMC 1–2/12; SLJ 10/1/11)

5064 Alborough, Jez. *Six Little Chicks* (PS). Illus. by author. 2013, Barron's $6.99 (978-143800181-4). 32pp. A mother hen must protect her five chicks and a sixth egg from a big bad fox. Lexile AD860 (Rev: BLO 4/1/13; SLJ 4/13)

5065 Alsenas, Linas. *Peanut* (PS–1). Illus. by author. 2007, Scholastic $16.99 (978-0-439-77980-7). 32pp. A lonely old woman named Mildred adopts a stray "puppy" (actually an elephant) and names him Peanut; when a man from the circus finally comes to take him away, she is sad until she spots a stray "kitten" (actually a camel). (Rev: LMC 10/07*; SLJ 12/07)

5066 Anderson, Sara. *Octopus Oyster Hermit Crab Snail: A Poem of the Sea* (1–3). Illus. by author. 2005, Handprint $16.95 (978-1-59354-079-1). Eye-catching illustrations and rhyming text introduce a variety of marine creatures. (Rev: HBG 4/06; SLJ 12/05)

5067 Antle, Bhagavan, and Thea Feldman. *Suryia and Roscoe: The True Story of an Unlikely Friendship* (PS–1). Illus. by Barry Bland. 2011, Henry Holt $16.99 (978-0-8050-9316-2). 32pp. This photoessay shares the inspiring story of an orangutan and a dog that become friends. (Rev: BL 4/15/11; SLJ 5/1/11)

5068 Appelt, Kathi. *Where, Where Is Swamp Bear?* (PS–1). Illus. by Megan Halsey. 2002, HarperCollins LB $15.89 (978-0-688-17103-2). 32pp. A young Louisi-ana boy called Pierre goes fishing with his Granpere, but the boy's main preoccupation is looking for the elusive Swamp Bear and learning about the bear's life. (Rev: BL 2/15/02; HBG 10/02; SLJ 1/02*)

5069 Araki, Mie. *Kitten's Big Adventure* (PS). Illus. 2005, Harcourt $15.00 (978-0-15-216738-7). 40pp. A small kitten enjoys chasing a butterfly but is quick to hurry back to its mother's side. (Rev: BL 5/1/05; SLJ 6/05)

5070 Arnosky, Jim. *At This Very Moment* (PS–3). Illus. by author. 2011, Dutton $16.99 (978-0-525-42252-5). 32pp. Young readers are invited to consider what wild animals are doing at various times throughout the day, juxtaposed against everyday human activities. (Rev: BL 5/1/11; SLJ 6/11)

5071 Arnosky, Jim. *Babies in the Bayou* (PS–2). Illus. by author. 2007, Putnam $16.99 (978-0-399-22653-3). 32pp. A look at the young animals of the bayou and their mothers, with simple text and lush illustrations. (Rev: BL 12/1/06; SLJ 1/07)

5072 Arnosky, Jim. *Dolphins on the Sand* (PS–2). Illus. by author. 2008, Putnam $16.99 (978-0-399-24606-7). 32pp. A young boy is among the rescuers who work through a night to save dolphins stranded on a sandbar; this moving story also delivers a message about nature and the environment. (Rev: BL 7/08; SLJ 9/08)

5073 Arnosky, Jim. *Gobble It Up! A Fun Song About Eating!* (PS). Illus. by author. 2008, Scholastic $16.99 (978-0-439-90362-2). 32pp. This simple rhyming picture book introduces a variety of animals and their eating habits; an accompanying CD holds a catchy song sung by the author. (Rev: BL 9/1/08; SLJ 9/08)

5074 Arnosky, Jim. *Grandfather Buffalo* (PS–2). Illus. 2006, Putnam $16.99 (978-0-399-24169-7). 32pp. A heartwarming story about an aging buffalo, unable to keep up with the herd, that finds renewed interest in life when he saves a newborn calf in a dust storm. (Rev: BL 2/1/06; HBG 10/06; SLJ 2/06*)

5075 Arnosky, Jim. *Turtle in the Sea* (PS–2). Illus. 2002, Penguin $16.99 (978-0-399-22757-8). 32pp. A sea turtle survives the dangers surrounding her in the ocean. (Rev: BL 9/1/02; HBG 3/03; SLJ 8/02)

5076 Aruego, Jose, and Ariane Dewey. *The Last Laugh* (PS). Illus. 2006, Dial $12.99 (978-0-8037-3093-9). 24pp. A bullying snake gets his comeuppance from a clever duck in this nearly wordless humorous story. (Rev: BCCB 5/06; BL 2/1/06; HBG 10/06; SLJ 3/06)

5077 Ashman, Linda. *Stella, Unleashed: Notes from the Doghouse* (PS–K). Illus. by Paul Meisel. 2008, Sterling $14.95 (978-1-4027-3987-3). 40pp. In a series of poems a mongrel named Stella describes the joys (and puzzles) of life with the human family that has adopted her. (Rev: BL 5/1/08; SLJ 4/08)

5078 Austin, Patricia. *The Cat Who Loved Mozart* (1–3). Illus. by Henri Sorenson. 2001, Holiday House $16.95 (978-0-8234-1535-9). 32pp. Nine-year-old Jennifer adopts a stray cat that resists her affection until it hears her practicing for a piano recital. (Rev: BL 5/1/01; HBG 10/01; SLJ 6/01)

5079 Bailey, Linda. *Stanley at Sea* (PS–2). Illus. by Bill Slavin. 2008, Kids Can $16.95 (978-1-55453-193-6). 32pp. The appealing Stanley and his pack of hungry doggy friends return for another adventure as they set off to sea in a rowboat. (Rev: SLJ 4/08)

5080 Bailey, Linda. *Stanley's Party* (PS–3). Illus. by Bill Slavin. 2003, Kids Can $14.95 (978-1-55337-382-7). Stanley the dog samples forbidden pleasures while his owners are out. (Rev: HBG 10/03; SLJ 7/03)

5081 Bailey, Linda. *Stanley's Wild Ride* (PS–2). Illus. by Bill Slavin. 2006, Kids Can $14.95 (978-1-55337-960-7). 32pp. Stanley the dog escapes from his backyard and liberates his canine friends for a wild time on the town. (Rev: BL 3/1/06; SLJ 6/06)

5082 Balouch, Kristen. *The Little Little Girl with the Big Big Voice* (PS–2). Illus. by author. 2011, Simon & Schuster $12.99 (978-1-4424-0808-1). 32pp. A loud-mouthed little girl scares away most large animals until she comes across a lion in this lively story with vibrant illustrations. (Rev: BL 6/1/11; HB 7–8/11; SLJ 6/11)

5083 Banks, Kate. *The Cat Who Walked Across France* (PS–2). Illus. by Georg Hallensleben. 2004, Farrar $16.00 (978-0-374-39968-9). 40pp. A French cat who has been uprooted after the death of his owner decides to head back to the house he loves; beautiful paintings document his long and difficult journey. (Rev: BL 3/15/04; HB 3/04; SLJ 3/04)

5084 Bardoe, Cheryl. *The Ugly Duckling Dinosaur: A Prehistoric Tale* (PS–2). Illus. by Doug Kennedy. 2011, Abrams $16.95 (978-0-8109-9739-4). 32pp. A young T. rex rejected by a duck family heads into the forest and eventually finds a home. (Rev: BL 5/1/11; SLJ 4/11)

5085 Base, Graeme. *The Water Hole* (PS–1). Illus. 2001, Abrams $18.95 (978-0-8109-4568-5). 30pp. Part counting book, part introduction to animal species, and part overview of the water cycle, this richly illustrated picture book shows various animals — from 1 rhino to 10 kangaroos — gathering at a water hole. (Rev: BL 10/1/01; HBG 3/02; SLJ 12/01)

5086 Beames, Margaret. *Night Cat* (K–4). Illus. by Sue Hitchcock. 2003, Scholastic $15.95 (978-0-439-38576-3). Menacing creatures and a shower of rain persuade Oliver the cat of the benefits of home. (Rev: HBG 4/04; SLJ 9/03)

5087 Beard, Alex. *Crocodile's Tears* (2–4). Illus. by author. 2012, Abrams $17.95 (978-1-4197-0008-8). Unpaged. A rhino is curious about his friend crocodile's tears, and goes around to other endangered animals seeking an explanation; includes information on the threats the animals face. (Rev: LMC 8–9/12; SLJ 12/1/11)

5088 Beck, Carolyn. *Dog Breath* (PS–2). Illus. by Brooke Kerrigan. 2011, Fitzhenry & Whiteside $18.95 (978-155455180-4). 32pp. A young boy remembers all the good times he shared with his dog in this gentle story about loss of a pet. (Rev: BL 2/15/12; LMC 10/12)

5089 Belton, Robyn. *Herbert: The True Story of a Brave Sea Dog* (PS–2). Illus. by author. 2010, Candlewick $15.99 (978-0-7636-4741-4). 40pp. A small dog named Herbert falls overboard in a storm off New Zealand and his 12-year-old master spends the night searching, finding him after he had been in the water for 30 hours; based on a true story. (Rev: BL 5/1/10; LMC 10/10; SLJ 7/1/10)

5090 Bennett, Dean. *Finding a Friend in the Forest: A True Story* (PS–3). Illus. by author. 2005, Down East $15.95 (978-0-89272-662-2). A beagle and a doe become fast friends in this appealing picture book set in northern Maine. (Rev: SLJ 1/06)

5091 Bennett, Kelly. *Not Norman: A Goldfish Story* (K–3). Illus. by Noah Z. Jones. 2005, Candlewick $15.99 (978-0-7636-2384-5). 32pp. A goldfish isn't the kind of pet the narrator initially wants in this entertaining and eye-catching story. (Rev: BL 2/15/05; SLJ 3/05)

5092 Berenzy, Alix. *Sammy: The Classroom Guinea Pig* (PS–2). Illus. 2005, Holt $16.95 (978-0-8050-4024-1). Lots of information about guinea pigs is conveyed as Ms. B.'s class investigates why Sammy is making so much noise. (Rev: BL 5/15/05)

5093 Berger, Lou. *Dream Dog* (K–3). Illus. by David J. Catrow. 2013, Random House $17.99 (978-037586655-5). 40pp. Harry can't have a real dog because of his father's allergies, so he does the next best thing: he dreams up a big blue dog named Waffle — but when his father transfers jobs and the allergies evaporate, Harry gets a wonderful surprise. **e** Lexile AD710 (Rev: BL 11/1/13; SLJ 1/1/14)

5094 Bergman, Mara. *Yum, Yum! What Fun!* (PS–2). Illus. by Nick Maland. 2009, Greenwillow $17.99 (978-0-06-168860-7). 32pp. When young Katie and James bake bread, the smell attracts a menagerie of unexpected visitors from the zoo next door. (Rev: BL 2/1/09; SLJ 4/09)

5095 Berkes, Marianne. *Marsh Morning* (2–4). Illus. by Robert Noreika. 2003, Millbrook LB $22.90 (978-0-7613-2568-0). 32pp. Watercolor illustrations and short rhymes tell the stories of 15 species of birds and their morning songs. (Rev: BL 3/15/03; HBG 10/03; SLJ 4/03)

5096 Best, Cari. *Ava and the Real Lucille* (PS–3). Illus. by Madeline Valentine. 2012, Farrar $16.99 (978-037439903-0). 32pp. Ava and her sister Arlie expect to win a dog in the poetry competition and are disappointed when they receive a bird instead. (Rev: BL 11/1/12; LMC 1–2/13)

5097 Best, Cari. *Goose's Story* (PS–3). Illus. by Holly Meade. 2002, Farrar $16.00 (978-0-374-32750-7). 32pp. A young girl witnesses how an injured goose copes with his disability and tries to survive though left behind by the flock. (Rev: BCCB 9/02; BL 5/1/02*; HB 5/02; HBG 10/02; SLJ 7/02)

5098 Bevis, Mary. *Wolf Song* (K–3). Illus. by Consie Powell. 2007, Raven $18.95 (978-0-9794202-0-7); paper $12.95 (978-0-9794202-1-4). Young Nell and her uncle go into the north woods and enjoy the song of the wolves; with facts about wolves and about howling expeditions. (Rev: SLJ 12/07)

5099 Blackford, Harriet. *Elephant's Story* (PS–2). Illus. by Manja Stojic. 2008, Sterling $14.95 (978-1-905417-75-9). 32pp. Large text, effective illustrations, and a factual note at the end introduce elephants through the fictional story of one baby elephant on the African savanna. (Rev: BCCB 5/08; BL 4/1/08; SLJ 10/08)

5100 Blackstone, Stella. *I Dreamt I Was a Dinosaur* (PS–2). Illus. by Clare Beaton. 2005, Barefoot Books $15.99 (978-1-84148-238-5). A child dreams of being a dinosaur and cavorting with all sorts of prehistoric creatures; factual information is appended. (Rev: SLJ 1/06)

5101 Blackstone, Stella. *Secret Seahorse* (PS–2). Illus. by Clare Beaton. 2004, Barefoot Books $15.99 (978-1-84148-704-5). 32pp. A fast-moving seahorse weaves in and out of sight through the coral reefs and caves beneath the sea. (Rev: BL 4/15/04; SLJ 1/05)

5102 Blackstone, Stella. *Who Are You, Baby Kangaroo?* (PS–K). Illus. by Clare Beaton. 2004, Barefoot Books $14.99 (978-1-84148-217-0). A puppy determined to find out the word for a baby kangaroo travels far and wide asking other animals. (Rev: SLJ 11/04)

5103 Blake, Robert J. *Akiak: A Tale from the Iditarod* (PS–3). Illus. 1997, Penguin $16.99 (978-0-399-22798-1). An aging sled dog named Akiak participates in the Iditarod sled race for the last time. (Rev: BL 9/1/97; HBG 3/98; SLJ 9/97*)

5104 Blake, Robert J. *Little Devils* (K–3). Illus. by author. 2009, Philomel $16.99 (978-0-399-24322-6). 40pp. When their mother disappears, three Tasmanian Devil pups leave their den to find food and in the process find their mother and rescue her from a cage. (Rev: BL 11/15/09; SLJ 10/1/09)

5105 Blake, Robert J. *Painter and Ugly* (K–3). Illus. by author. 2011, Philomel $16.99 (978-0-399-24323-3). 48pp. Fast-running sled dogs Painter and Ugly are inseparable until they are sold to different owners; lonely by themselves, they find each other again during the Junior Iditarod and find a way to compete and yet be together. Lexile AD880L (Rev: BL 2/1/11; LMC 5–6/11*; SLJ 2/1/11)

5106 Blake, Robert J. *Togo* (2–4). Illus. 2002, Penguin $16.99 (978-0-399-23381-4). Blake's brilliantly illustrated story is a gripping tribute to Togo, the dog that should have got credit for the famous serum run during the diphtheria epidemic in Nome in 1925. (Rev: BL 9/15/02; HBG 3/03; SLJ 9/02*)

5107 Bliss, Harry. *Bailey at the Museum* (PS–2). Illus. by author. 2012, Scholastic $16.99 (978-0-545-23345-3). 32pp. Bailey, the dog first met in an adventure published in 2011 (*Bailey*), now joins his human classmates on a fun-filled trip to the Museum of Natural History. (Rev: BLO 9/1/12; LMC 3–4/13; SLJ 10/12)

5108 Bloom, Suzanne. *No Place for a Pig* (K–3). Illus. by author. 2003, Boyds Mills $15.95 (978-1-59078-047-3). When her apartment becomes too small for her rapidly growing pig, Ms. Taffy's neighbors come to the rescue. (Rev: BL 1/1–15/04; HBG 4/04; SLJ 11/03)

5109 Bloxam, Frances. *Little Tom Turkey* (PS–2). Illus. by Jim Sollers. 2005, Down East $15.95 (978-0-89272-671-4). In rhyming verse with dollops of humor and fact, Bloxam tells the story of an appealing and ambitious young wild turkey. (Rev: SLJ 6/05)

5110 Blumenthal, Deborah. *Black Diamond and Blake* (1–3). Illus. by Miles Hyman. 2009, Knopf $16.99 (978-0-375-84003-6). 40pp. This picture-book story is told from the point of view of a racehorse who, after an injury, finds himself in a prison rehabilitation program, where he eventually finds happiness. (Rev: BL 12/15/08; LMC 5/09; SLJ 2/09)

5111 Blumenthal, Deborah. *The Blue House Dog* (K–3). Illus. by Adam Gustavson. 2010, Peachtree $15.95 (978-1-56145-537-9). 32pp. Remembering his own dog's death, young Cody sets about befriending a stray dog he calls Blue. (Rev: BL 7/10; LMC 1–2/11; SLJ 8/1/10)

5112 Boelts, Maribeth. *Before You Were Mine* (PS–2). Illus. by David Walker. 2007, Putnam $15.99 (978-0-399-24526-8). 32pp. A young boy wonders about the life his new dog may have led before the boy and his family chose the dog from an animal shelter. (Rev: BCCB 12/07; BL 12/1/07; SLJ 10/07)

5113 Bowman, Patty. *The Amazing Hamweenie* (PS–1). Illus. by author. 2012, Philomel $16.99 (978-0-399-25688-2). 32pp. Hamweenie, a cat with an active imagination and a less-than-satisfactory (but actually luxurious) life, stars in this humorous story of inflated expectations. (Rev: BL 10/1/12; SLJ 9/12)

5114 Boyer, Cecile. *Run, Dog!* (PS–K). Illus. 2013, Chronicle $16.99 (978-145212708-8). 48pp. A story with minimal text and plenty of flaps featuring a dog chasing a ball hither and thither. (Rev: BLO 3/1/14; SLJ 3/14)

5115 Bradford, Karleen. *You Can't Rush a Cat* (2–3). Illus. by Leslie Elizabeth Watts. 2003, Orca $16.95 (978-1-55143-247-2). 32pp. Jessica helps her grandfather coax a shy stray kitten out of the bushes in this charming story. (Rev: BL 2/1/04; HBG 4/04; SLJ 2/04)

5116 Bradley, Kimberly Brubaker. *The Perfect Pony* (K–2). Illus. by Shelagh McNicholas. 2007, Dial $16.99 (978-0-8037-2851-6). 32pp. A young girl talks about learning to ride and her search for just the right pony. (Rev: BL 4/1/07)

5117 Braeuner, Shellie. *The Great Dog Wash* (PS–K). Illus. by Robert Neubecker. 2009, Simon & Schuster $15.99 (978-1-4169-7116-0). 32pp. A dog wash bubbles out of control when a cat strolls by. (Rev: BL 5/15/09)

5118 Brendler, Carol. *Winnie Finn, Worm Farmer* (PS–2). Illus. by Ard Hoyt. 2009, Farrar $15.99 (978-0-374-38440-1). Unpaged. Hoping to enter her prize earthworms in the county fair, young Winnie constructs a simple worm farm to show them off, helping her neighbors in the meantime. (Rev: LMC 11–12/09; SLJ 9/1/09)

5119 Brett, Jan. *Mossy* (PS–1). Illus. by author. 2012, Putnam $17.99 (978-0-399-25782-7). 32pp. In this beautifully illustrated book set in the Edwardian era, a turtle who has sprouted amazing plants on her shell is exhibited at a museum until thoughtful children point out how unhappy she is. Lexile 770 (Rev: BL 8/12; LMC 5–6/13; SLJ 8/12)

5120 Broach, Elise. *Wet Dog!* (PS–2). Illus. by David Catrow. 2005, Dial $16.99 (978-0-8037-2809-7). After he is turned away from nearly every source of water in town, a very hot dog interrupts a wedding party by a cool lake. (Rev: SLJ 7/05)

5121 Broome, Errol. *Drusilla the Lucky Duck* (3–4). Illus. by Sharon Thompson. 2003, Annick $16.95 (978-1-55037-799-6); paper $4.95 (978-1-55037-798-9). 72pp. The story of young Carrie and her pet duckling Drusilla, and how Carrie races to save Drusilla from becoming someone's dinner. (Rev: SLJ 3/04)

5122 Brown, Alison. *Eddie and Dog* (PS–1). Illus. by author. 2014, Capstone paper $14.95 (978-16237011-4-7). 32pp. An imaginative young boy named Eddie and a determined dog named Dog have happy adventures together despite the disapproval of Eddie's mother. (Rev: BLO 3/1/14; LMC 10/14; SLJ 3/14)

5123 Brown, Margaret Wise. *Big Red Barn* (PS–1). Illus. by Felicia Bond. 1989, HarperCollins LB $17.89 (978-0-06-020749-6). 32pp. The big red barn contains lots and lots of animals and their offspring. (Rev: BL 3/1/89; SLJ 6/89)

5124 Brown, Ruth. *The Tale of Two Mice: A Cat-and-Mouse Tale* (PS–3). Illus. by author. 2008, Candlewick $16.99 (978-0-7636-4015-6). 32pp. Two very hungry little mice mount an assault on a human kitchen all the while on the lookout for the cat; lift-up flaps add to the fun. (Rev: BL 12/15/08; SLJ 1/09)

5125 Brown, Tricia. *Groucho's Eyebrows* (K–2). Illus. by Barbara Lavallee. 2003, Alaska Northwest $15.95 (978-0-88240-556-8). Enticing illustrations grace this story of an Alaskan girl named Kristie and her white cat with magnificent black eyebrows. (Rev: HBG 4/04; SLJ 6/04)

5126 Bruel, Nick. *Little Red Bird* (PS–2). Illus. by author. 2008, Roaring Brook $16.95 (978-1-59643-339-7). 32pp. After a day free from her cage, Little Red Bird must decide whether to continue exploring or return to the comforts of home. (Rev: BL 4/15/08; LMC 5/08; SLJ 6/08)

5127 Bruel, Robert O. *Bob and Otto* (PS–K). Illus. by Nick Bruel. 2007, Roaring Brook $15.95 (978-1-59643-203-1). In their early years, worms Bob and Otto are inseparable, but the two must part ways when Bob's metamorphosis into a butterfly approaches. (Rev: BL 4/1/07)

5128 Bunting, Eve. *Emma's Turtle* (PS–2). Illus. by Marsha Winborn. 2007, Boyds Mills $15.95 (978-1-59078-350-4). Emma's turtle has a yen for foreign travel and imagines himself in Africa, Australia, and India when he escapes from his pen. (Rev: BL 10/1/07; SLJ 9/07)

5129 Bunting, Eve. *My Dog Jack Is Fat* (PS–1). Illus. by Michael Rex. 2011, Marshall Cavendish $16.99 (978-0-7614-5809-8). 32pp. A young boy helps his overweight dog to get fit in this lighthearted take on diet and exercise. (Rev: BL 4/15/11; SLJ 5/1/11)

5130 Bunting, Eve. *Whales Passing* (PS–2). Illus. by Lambert Davis. 2003, Scholastic $15.95 (978-0-590-60358-4). A gentle — and fact-filled — story of a boy being introduced by his father to the wonders of orcas and nature in general. (Rev: HBG 10/03; SLJ 6/03)

5131 Burke, Tina. *Fly, Little Bird* (PS–K). Illus. by author. 2006, Kane $14.95 (978-1-933605-02-9). 32pp. A nearly wordless book that depicts a little girl, accompanied by her puppy, capturing and then setting free a baby wild parrot. (Rev: BL 5/15/06)

5132 Burleigh, Robert. *Good-bye, Sheepie* (K–2). Illus. by Peter Catalanotto. 2010, Marshall Cavendish $16.99 (978-0-7614-5598-1). 32pp. A young boy grieves over and eventually accepts the death of his beloved dog. (Rev: BL 3/15/10; SLJ 4/1/10)

5133 Butler, John. *Pi-Shu, the Little Panda* (K–2). Illus. 2001, Peachtree $15.95 (978-1-56145-242-2). 32pp. The daily activities of a baby panda named Pi-shu are recounted in this picture book that also gives information on why this is an endangered species. (Rev: BL 3/15/01; HBG 10/01)

5134 Buxton, Jane. *The Littlest Llama* (PS–2). Illus. by Jenny Cooper. 2008, Sterling $9.95 (978-1-4027-5277-3). 32pp. Rhyming couplets tell the story of a little llama who has nobody to play with; the detailed illustrations show typical llama behaviors. (Rev: BL 4/15/08; SLJ 4/08)

5135 Buzzeo, Toni. *Little Loon and Papa* (PS–2). Illus. by Margaret Spengler. 2004, Dial $16.99 (978-0-8037-2958-2). Despite his father's patient advice, Little Loon is having trouble learning to dive until outside pressures force him to take the plunge. (Rev: SLJ 6/04)

5136 Buzzeo, Toni. *Stay Close to Mama* (PS–K). Illus. by Mike Wohnoutka. 2012, Hyperion $15.99 (978-142313482-4). 32pp. An adventurous baby giraffe repeatedly risks danger as he seeks to explore his world. (Rev: BL 3/15/12; LMC 5–6/12; SLJ 1/12)

5137 Byars, Betsy, and Betsy Duffey. *Dog Diaries: Secret Writings of the WOOF Society* (3–4). Illus. by Erik Brooks. 2007, Holt $15.95 (978-0-8050-7657-9). 72pp. Eleven stories by dogs are presented at a book club for dogs called the WOOF Society. Dog-lovers will enjoy reading these brief, varied tales by dogs in all sorts of situations. (Rev: SLJ 6/07)

5138 Campbell, Eileen, and Judy Rand. *Charlie and Kiwi: An Evolutionary Adventure* (K–3). Illus. by Peter H. Reynolds. 2011, Atheneum $16.99 (978-1-4424-2112-7). 48pp. Charlie explores the history of the kiwi and evolution of birds in this book that blends science, history, and a bit of time travel. **e** Lexile AD480L (Rev: BL 6/1/11; HB 7–8/11; LMC 11–12/11; SLJ 7/11)

5139 Campbell, Rod. *Dear Zoo* (PS). Illus. by author. 1983, Puffin paper $4.95 (978-0-317-62180-8). 22pp. A youngster keeps sending back the pets requested from a zoo until a puppy arrives.

5140 Cantrell, Charlie, and Rachel Wagner. *A Friend for Einstein: The Smallest Stallion* (PS–2). 2011, Hyperion/Disney $16.99 (978-1-4231-4563-9). 40pp. A tiny miniature horse, lonely because of his strange size, finds the perfect playmate in a boxer dog named Lilly. Lexile AD780L (Rev: BL 7/11; SLJ 8/1/11)

5141 Carle, Eric. *Does a Kangaroo Have a Mother, Too?* (PS–1). Illus. 2000, HarperCollins LB $17.89 (978-0-06-028767-2). 32pp. In this simple book about wildlife, 12 young animals are presented along with their mothers. (Rev: BCCB 4/00; BL 1/1–15/00; HBG 10/00; SLJ 4/00) [591.3]

5142 Carle, Eric. *Have You Seen My Cat?* (PS–2). Illus. by author. 1991, Picture Book $16.00 (978-0-88708-054-8). A small boy loses his cat, sees many other felines, and returns home to find that his cat has had kittens. A reissue of a 1973 title.

5143 Carle, Eric. *Mister Seahorse* (PS–3). Illus. 2004, Penguin $17.99 (978-0-399-24269-4). Imaginative tissue-paper collages with occasional overlays show Mr. Seahorse as he keeps vigil over Mrs. Seahorse's eggs in his pouch and encounters other marine fathers who play a role in caring for their young. (Rev: BL 4/1/04*; SLJ 5/04)

5144 Carnesi, Monica. *Little Dog Lost: The True Story of a Brave Dog Named Baltic* (K–2). Illus. by author. 2012, Penguin $15.99 (978-039925666-0). 32pp. Based on a true story, this is a dramatic tale about a dog found floating on an iceberg toward and ultimately into the Baltic Sea. (Rev: BL 1/1/12; HB 1–2/12; SLJ 1/12)

5145 Carrick, Carol. *The Polar Bears Are Hungry* (PS–2). Illus. by Paul Carrick. 2002, Clarion $14.00 (978-0-618-15962-8). 32pp. A polar bear mother finds it more and more difficult to feed her cubs as spring and summer arrive, in this fictional presentation that will prompt discussion of human impact on animals. (Rev: BL 10/15/02; HBG 3/03; SLJ 11/02)

5146 Cartwright, Reg. *What We Do* (PS–1). Illus. by author. 2005, Holt $7.95 (978-0-8050-7671-4). In rhyming text and bright illustrations, a variety of animals explain the way they move and behave. (Rev: SLJ 10/05)

5147 Casanova, Mary. *Utterly Otterly Day* (PS–1). Illus. by Ard Hoyt. 2008, Simon & Schuster $16.99 (978-1-4169-0868-5). 40pp. Brave Little Otter has some scary adventures when he spends a day by himself. (Rev: BL 5/15/08; SLJ 6/08)

5148 Casanova, Mary. *Utterly Otterly Night* (PS–2). Illus. by Ard Hoyt. 2011, Simon & Schuster $16.99 (978-1-4169-7562-5). Unpaged. A young otter heads out at night for some snowy fun and shows that he knows what to do when danger is near. (Rev: SLJ 11/1/11)

5149 Castillo, Lauren. *Melvin and the Boy* (PS–1). Illus. by author. 2011, Henry Holt $16.99 (978-0-8050-8929-5). 40pp. Desperate for a pet, a young boy brings home a turtle, but soon realizes the turtle is unhappy in a house and releases him back in the park. (Rev: BL 5/1/11; SLJ 7/11)

5150 Cate, Annette LeBlanc. *The Magic Rabbit* (K–3). Illus. by author. 2007, Candlewick $15.99 (978-0-7636-2672-3). 32pp. Street magician Ray and his sidekick, a white rabbit called Bunny, become separated in an ac-

cident and spend the day searching for each other. (Rev: BL 9/15/07; SLJ 9/07)

5151 Chamberlain, Margaret. *Please Don't Tease Tootsie* (PS–2). Illus. by author. 2008, Dutton $16.99 (978-0-525-47982-6). 32pp. This playful story told in verse focuses on the proper care of pets and is illustrated with bright artwork. (Rev: BLO 8/28/08; SLJ 8/08)

5152 Chess, Victoria. *The Costume Party* (K–2). Illus. 2005, Kane $15.95 (978-1-929132-87-4). Trapped indoors by several days of bad weather, Madame Coco throws a costume party to entertain her five pet dogs. (Rev: BL 10/15/05; SLJ 9/05)

5153 Chitwood, Suzanne Tanner. *Wake Up, Big Barn!* (PS–1). Illus. 2002, Scholastic $15.95 (978-0-439-26627-7). 40pp. Farm animals are introduced in lively collages in this rhythmic book for preschoolers. (Rev: BL 2/1/02; HBG 10/02; SLJ 4/02)

5154 Clark, Emma Chichester. *Will and Squill* (PS–2). Illus. 2006, Carolrhoda $15.95 (978-1-57505-936-5). 32pp. A boy named Will and a squirrel called Squill are great friends despite their mothers' disapproval. (Rev: BL 3/1/06; SLJ 3/06)

5155 Clarke, Jane. *Only Tadpoles Have Tails* (PS–2). Illus. by Jane Gray. Series: Flying Foxes. 2004, Crabtree LB $22.60 (978-0-7787-1484-2); paper $4.95 (978-0-7787-1530-6). 46pp. Kicky the frog is embarrassed about his tadpole tail until it helps him swim fast enough to escape piranhas. (Rev: SLJ 8/04)

5156 Clarke, Jane. *Stuck in the Mud* (PS–1). Illus. by Garry Parsons. 2008, Walker $16.95 (978-0-8027-9758-2). 32pp. A cumulative tale in which Hen discovers that one of her chicks is stuck in the mud and is helped by a succession of animals that all become stuck too; a final gatefold brings a surprise. (Rev: BL 2/15/08; SLJ 2/08)

5157 Clayton, Elaine. *A Blue Ribbon for Sugar* (K–2). 2006, Roaring Brook $16.95 (978-1-59643-157-7). 32pp. When Bonnie's beloved rocking horse breaks, she's treated to riding lessons on a real pony and eventually wins a blue ribbon at a horse show. (Rev: BL 6/1–15/06; SLJ 5/06)

5158 Clements, Andrew. *Naptime for Slippers* (PS–1). Illus. by Janie Bynum. 2005, Dutton $12.99 (978-0-525-47287-2). 32pp. Slippers the puppy is active and interested in everything going on around him, so much so that he misses naptime and is exhausted when it's time for a walk. (Rev: BL 2/1/05; SLJ 2/05)

5159 Cochran, Bill. *The Forever Dog* (PS–2). Illus. by Dan Andreasen. 2007, HarperCollins $16.99 (978-0-06-053939-9). 32pp. A young boy tries to forgive his dead dog for deserting him. (Rev: BL 4/1/07; SLJ 3/07)

5160 Cohen, Barbara S. *Forever Friends* (PS–2). Illus. by Dorothy Louise Hall. 2002, Tallfellow/Smallfellow $16.95 (978-1-931290-12-8). 32pp. Petey the dog describes all he does for his owner, Skip, in this playful picture book. (Rev: BL 7/02)

5161 Cole, Henry. *Trudy* (PS–1). Illus. by author. 2009, Greenwillow $17.99 (978-0-06-154267-1). Esme's goat

Trudy seems to have an unusual talent — she can predict snow? (Rev: BL 12/1/08; SLJ 12/08)

5162 Cooper, Elisha. *Homer* (PS–2). Illus. by author. 2012, Greenwillow $16.99 (978-0-06-201248-7). 32pp. An aging dog named Homer is content to spend his time on the porch — with food and favorite armchair — while children and younger dogs rush and play. (Rev: BL 4/15/12*; SLJ 10/12)

5163 Cooper, Elisha. *Magic Thinks Big* (PS–1). Illus. 2004, Greenwillow LB $15.89 (978-0-06-058165-7). 32pp. Readers are invited into the musings of an imaginative but idle tabby cat named Magic. (Rev: BL 5/15/04; HB 5/04; SLJ 4/04)

5164 Cousins, Lucy. *Peck, Peck, Peck* (PS–K). Illus. by author. 2013, Candlewick $15.99 (978-0-7636-6621-7). 32pp. A baby woodpecker pecks holes in all sorts of unsuitable things in this exuberant picture book. (Rev: BL 7/13*; SLJ 8/13*)

5165 Cowen-Fletcher, Jane. *Hello, Puppy!* (PS–K). Illus. by author. 2010, Candlewick $12.99 (978-0-7636-4303-4). 32pp. A child spends time exploring her new puppy's behavior. (Rev: BL 8/10; SLJ 5/1/10)

5166 Craig, Lindsey. *Farmyard Beat* (PS). Illus. by Marc Brown. 2011, Knopf $15.99 (978-0-375-86455-1); LB $18.99 (978-0-375-96455-8). 32pp. This rhythmic and repetitive celebration of barnyard sounds features paper collage artwork. (Rev: BL 6/1/11; SLJ 7/11)

5167 Crosby, Jeff. *Wiener Wolf* (PS–2). Illus. by author. 2011, Hyperion/Disney $15.99 (978-1-4231-3983-6). Unpaged. A bored lap dog joins a pack of wolves in order to satisfy a longing for adventure and finds he has bitten off more than he can chew. (Rev: LMC 11–12/11; SLJ 6/11)

5168 Crum, Shutta. *Click!* (K–2). Illus. by John Beder. 2003, Fitzhenry & Whiteside $14.95 (978-1-55005-074-5). 24pp. A nicely illustrated story told in parallel about a boy and his mother (who are wildlife photographers) and a bear and her cub. (Rev: BL 2/15/04; SLJ 2/04)

5169 Crum, Shutta. *A Family for Old Mill Farm* (1–3). Illus. by Niki Daly. 2007, Clarion $16.00 (978-0-618-42846-5). 32pp. A house-hunting family rejects one house after another, finally selecting on an old farm that many animal families call home as well. (Rev: SLJ 6/07)

5170 Cyrus, Kurt. *Big Rig Bugs* (PS–1). Illus. by author. 2010, Walker $16.99 (978-0-8027-8674-6). 32pp. Giant, digitally enhanced illustrations show a variety of bugs devouring a sandwich discarded at a construction site. (Rev: BL 5/15/10; LMC 8–9/10; SLJ 4/1/10)

5171 Cyrus, Kurt. *The Voyage of Turtle Rex* (PS–2). Illus. by author. 2011, Houghton Harcourt $16.99 (978-0-547-42924-3). Unpaged. Follows the life of a giant prehistoric sea turtle, showing the dangers it faces and explaining its habitat. Lexile AD580L (Rev: LMC 10/11; SLJ 5/1/11*)

5172 Daly, Cathleen. *Prudence Wants a Pet* (PS–2). Illus. by Stephen Michael King. 2011, Roaring Brook $16.99 (978-1-59643-468-4). 32pp. A young girl desperate for a pet tries some novel alternatives — a car tire, a tree

branch — before finally getting what she really wants. (Rev: BL 6/1/11; HB 7–8/11; SLJ 5/1/11)

5173 Davies, Nicola. *White Owl, Barn Owl* (K–3). Illus. by Michael Foreman. 2007, Candlewick $16.99 (978-0-7636-3364-6). 32pp. A story about a barn owl who nests in a child's homemade box includes basic facts about the bird and its characteristics. (Rev: BL 5/15/07; SLJ 7/07*)

5174 Davis, Anne. *No Dogs Allowed!* (PS–2). Illus. by author. 2011, HarperCollins $16.99 (978-0-06-075353-5). 32pp. Bud the cat is unhappy when his feline friend Gabby is welcoming toward a dog that turns up at their door. (Rev: BL 4/1/11; HB 7–8/11; SLJ 4/11)

5175 Day, Alexandra. *Carl's Summer Vacation* (PS–K). Illus. by author. 2008, Farrar $12.95 (978-0-374-31085-1). Madeleine and Carl the rottweiler have an enjoyable afternoon exploring around the summer cottage while they are supposed to be napping. (Rev: BL 8/08; HB 7/08; SLJ 5/08)

5176 De Cock, Nicole. *The Girl and the Elephant* (K–2). Illus. by author. 2004, Tricycle $15.95 (978-1-58246-133-5). A girl misses the elephant when he leaves the zoo and decides to go to Africa in pursuit. (Rev: SLJ 11/04)

5177 Delaney, Michael. *Obi, Gerbil on the Loose!* (2–4). Illus. by author. 2008, Dutton $15.99 (978-0-525-47890-4). Obi the gerbil has a scary time when her family goes away and the neighbor looking after the pets seems to be unaware of her existence. (Rev: BL 6/1–15/08; SLJ 11/08)

5178 Demas, Corinne. *Always in Trouble* (K–2). Illus. by Noah Z. Jones. 2009, Scholastic $16.99 (978-0-545-02453-2). 40pp. Toby, a bouncy unruly dog who belongs to an African American family, goes to obedience school not just once but twice. (Rev: BCCB 1/09; BL 1/1–15/09; SLJ 1/09)

5179 Denslow, Sharon Phillips. *In the Snow* (PS–K). Illus. by Nancy Tafuri. 2005, Greenwillow $15.99 (978-0-06-059683-5). 40pp. A young child puts out seeds to feed hungry woodland animals in this gentle story that introduces animals and the idea of animal footprints. (Rev: BL 10/15/05; SLJ 3/06)

5180 Díaz, Katacha. *Badger at Sandy Ridge Road* (K–3). Illus. by Kristin Kest. Series: Smithsonian's Backyard. 2005, Soundprints $15.95 (978-1-59249-420-0). 31pp. The story of a desert badger looking for a place to give birth is followed by facts about the North American badger. (Rev: SLJ 7/05)

5181 Dicmas, Courtney. *Harold Finds a Voice* (PS–2). Illus. by author. 2013, Child's Play $16.99 (978-1-84643-550-8). 32pp. A Parisian parrot tires of mimicking the noises in his apartment and ventures out into the world. (Rev: BL 7/13; SLJ 7/13)

5182 Diehl, Jean Heilprin. *Loon Chase* (1–3). Illus. by Kathryn Freeman. 2006, Sylvan Dell $15.95 (978-0-9764943-8-6). When their bird dog's hunting instincts send it in pursuit of a mother loon and her babies, a boy and his mother worry that their pet will hurt the endangered birds. (Rev: SLJ 4/06)

5183 DiTerlizzi, Angela. *Say What?* (PS–1). Illus. by Joey Chou. 2011, Simon & Schuster $15.99 (978-1-4169-8694-2). 32pp. A little boy wonders about the noises animals make and what they really mean. **e** (Rev: SLJ 6/11)

5184 Dixon, Ann. *Blueberry Shoe* (PS–3). Illus. by Evon Zerbetz. 1999, Alaska Northwest $22.95 (978-0-88240-518-6); paper $8.95 (978-0-88240-519-3). 32pp. Several Alaskan animals are introduced in this story of a lost red sneaker and how each of the animals that finds it changes it. (Rev: BL 10/15/99; HBG 3/00; SLJ 12/99)

5185 Dockray, Tracy. *The Lost and Found Pony* (PS–2). Illus. by author. 2011, Feiwel & Friends $16.99 (978-0-312-59259-2). 48pp. A little pony has several careers but never forgets his years belonging to a young girl; eventually the young girl, now an adult, finds him and the two are reunited. Lexile 660L (Rev: BL 6/1/11; LMC 11–12/11; SLJ 8/1/11)

5186 Dodd, Emma. *I Don't Want a Cool Cat!* (PS–1). Illus. by author. 2010, Little, Brown $15.99 (978-031603674-0). 32pp. In this funny book, a young girl enumerates the types of cats she definitely does not want — stuffy, greedy, and so forth — before settling on a playful kitten. (Rev: BL 6/10*; SLJ 7/10)

5187 Dodd, Emma. *I Don't Want a Posh Dog* (PS–1). Illus. by author. 2009, Little, Brown $15.99 (978-0-316-03390-9). 32pp. In simple verses accompanied by colorful art, a young girl surveys a number of dog options and finally identifies the kind of dog she wants. (Rev: BL 4/15/09; SLJ 6/09)

5188 Dodd, Emma. *What Pet to Get?* (PS–2). Illus. by author. 2008, Scholastic $16.99 (978-0-545-03570-5). 32pp. Jack needs a pet and after considering everything from an elephant (too big) to a Tyrannosaurus rex (too extinct), he finally decides a dog will do just fine. (Rev: BL 3/1/08; SLJ 3/08)

5189 Dominguez, Angela. *Santiago Stays* (PS). Illus. by author. 2013, Abrams/Appleseed $12.95 (978-141970821-3). 32pp. Despite treats, pleading, and bribes, French bulldog Santiago will not come when his young owner calls him; however, when a baby cries Santiago rushes to help. (Rev: BL 9/1/13; SLJ 10/13)

5190 Don, Lari. *The Tortoise's Gift: A Story from Zambia* (1–3). Illus. by Melanie Williamson. 2012, Barefoot paper $7.99 (978-1-84686-774-3). 48pp. Tortoise may be slow but he's steady and motivated, and he solves the problem of how to get much-needed fruit from a magical tree; an easy-reader chapter book. Lexile 530L (Rev: BLO 9/1/12; SLJ 2/13)

5191 Donaldson, Julia. *Tabby McTat, the Musical Cat* (PS–2). Illus. by Axel Scheffler. 2012, Scholastic $16.99 (978-0-545-45168-0). 32pp. Street musician Fred and his cat Tabby are separated in an accident; each goes on to a different life but they both wonder about their former companions. Lexile 810L (Rev: BL 12/1/12; SLJ 11/12)

5192 Dowson, Nick. *Tracks of a Panda* (PS–2). Illus. by Yu Rong. 2007, Candlewick $16.99 (978-0-7636-3146-8). 32pp. Facts about pandas are interwoven into a story about a mother panda rearing her cub in the face of humans taking over their habitat. (Rev: BL 10/15/07; HB 11/07; SLJ 2/08)

5193 Doyle, Malachy. *Horse* (K–2). Illus. by Angelo Rinaldi. 2008, Simon & Schuster $16.99 (978-1-4169-2467-8). 32pp. This companion to *Cow* (2002) follows a foal from birth through the first year of life, featuring realistic paintings and a simple text. (Rev: BCCB 7–8/08; BL 6/1–15/08; SLJ 7/08)

5194 Drachman, Eric. *A Frog Thing* (PS–2). Illus. by James Muscarello. 2006, Kidwick $18.95 (978-0-9703809-3-7). A frog named Frank who longs to fly finally gets his chance but comes to recognize that flying really isn't a frog thing; with beautiful illustrations and CD. (Rev: SLJ 6/06)

5195 Drummond, Ree. *Charlie the Ranch Dog* (PS–2). Illus. by Diane deGroat. 2011, HarperCollins $16.99 (978-0-06-199655-9). 40pp. Ranch dog Charlie, a lazy basset hound, describes his busy life even as his friend Suzie, a lively Jack Russell puppy, actually does all the work. Lexile AD440L (Rev: BL 4/1/11; LMC 10/11; SLJ 5/1/11)

5196 Dunbar, Joyce. *Four Fierce Kittens* (PS–K). Illus. by Jakki Wood. 1992, Scholastic $13.95 (978-0-590-45535-0). 32pp. Four kittens think they are fierce but cannot frighten the other farm animals. (Rev: BL 6/1/92; SLJ 4/92)

5197 Edwards, Pamela Duncan. *Muldoon* (PS–K). Illus. by Henry Cole. 2002, Hyperion $14.99 (978-0-7868-0360-6). 32pp. Muldoon, a dog, is convinced that he "works" for the West family — but he's actually a much-loved pet. (Rev: BL 2/15/03; HBG 3/03; SLJ 12/02)

5198 Ehlert, Lois. *Oodles of Animals* (PS–1). Illus. by author. 2008, Harcourt $17.00 (978-0-15-206274-3). 56pp. Inventive illustrations of animals are paired with brief, humorous poems. (Rev: BCCB 5/08; BL 7/08; LMC 10/08; SLJ 5/08)

5199 Ehlert, Lois. *RRRalph* (PS–3). Illus. by author. 2011, Simon & Schuster $17.99 (978-1-4424-1305-4). 40pp. A talking dog provides answers to a variety of questions using words such as "roof," "bark," and "rough;" along with guessing the words the dog will use, children will enjoy the inventive artwork. (Rev: BL 2/15/11*; SLJ 5/1/11)

5200 Ehlert, Lois. *Wag a Tail* (PS–2). 2007, Harcourt $16.00 (978-0-15-205843-2). 40pp. Ehlert's colorful paper collages portray happy dogs as they first visit a farmer's market with their humans, then cavort leash-free at a dog park. (Rev: BL 1/1–15/07)

5201 Engle, Margarita. *When You Wander: A Search-and-Rescue Dog Story* (PS–2). Illus. by Mary Morgan. 2013, Henry Holt $16.99 (978-0-8050-9312-4). 32pp. A dog that has graduated from "sniffing school" explains what a small child should do when he or she is lost; includes information on dog noses. **e** (Rev: BLO 6/13; LMC 10/13; SLJ 4/13)

5202 Esbaum, Jill. *Tom's Tweet* (K–2). Illus. by Dan Santat. 2011, Knopf $16.99 (978-0-375-85171-1); LB $19.99 (978-0-375-95171-8). Unpaged. Tom, a fat and hungry cat, ends up taking pity on a fallen baby bird called Tweet and the two become fast friends; a funny read full of wordplay. (Rev: SLJ 11/1/11)

5203 Falwell, Cathryn. *Gobble Gobble* (1–3). Illus. by author. 2011, Dawn $16.95 (978-158469-148-8;); paper $8.95 (978-1-58469-149-5). 32pp. Jenny introduces readers in rhyme to the wild turkeys that she sees around her rural home, and documents facts about the birds in a journal. Lexile 500L (Rev: BL 10/15/11; LMC 1–2/12; SLJ 12/1/11)

5204 Falwell, Cathryn. *Pond Babies* (PS–K). Illus. by author. 2011, Down East $15.95 (978-0-89272-920-3). 32pp. A mother and her young son watch the various animal babies at the local pond — a duck, a turtle, a frog, and so forth — in this book that presents questions on one page and answers on the next. (Rev: BLO 9/1/11; SLJ 8/1/11)

5205 Falwell, Cathryn. *Scoot!* (PS). Illus. by author. 2008, Greenwillow $16.99 (978-0-06-128882-1). As all manner of animals frolic around a pond, the six turtles on a log remain still and silent — until a strong wind comes up; end matter includes additional information and advice on making painted textures on paper. (Rev: BL 1/1–15/08; SLJ 1/08)

5206 Feder, Jane. *A Little Puppy* (PS). Illus. by Amy Schwartz. 2009, Candlewick $4.99 (978-0-7636-2651-8). 14pp. A simple board-book story about a little puppy exploring its surroundings. (Rev: BL 5/1/09)

5207 Fischer, Scott M. *Jump!* (PS–K). Illus. by author. 2010, Simon & Schuster $14.99 (978-1-4169-7884-8). 32pp. This lively book features short rhythmic verses that depict smaller animals leaping out of the range of bigger ones — usually just in the nick of time. (Rev: BL 1/1/10; LMC 5–6/10; SLJ 2/1/10)

5208 Fleming, Candace. *Seven Hungry Babies* (PS–1). Illus. by Eugene Yelchin. 2010, Atheneum $16.99 (978-1-4169-5402-6). 40pp. The suspense builds as a frenzied mama bird returns to feed ravenous nestling after nestling in this infectious story. (Rev: BL 1/1/10; SLJ 2/1/10)

5209 Fleming, Denise. *Barnyard Banter* (PS–1). Illus. 1994, Holt $16.95 (978-0-8050-1957-5). 32pp. All the farm animals greet Goose with their appropriate sounds as she tours the farmyard. (Rev: BCCB 5/94; BL 5/1/94; HB 5/94; SLJ 5/94*)

5210 Fleming, Denise. *Buster* (PS–1). Illus. by author. 2003, Holt $15.95 (978-0-8050-6279-3). The idyllic life of Buster the dog is threatened by the arrival of Betty the kitten, but when he runs away and gets lost, it's Betty who comes to the rescue. (Rev: HB 9/03; HBG 4/04; SLJ 9/03)

5211 Fleming, Denise. *Buster Goes to Cowboy Camp* (PS–3). Illus. by author. 2008, Holt $8.95 (978-0-8050-

7892-3). 40pp. Buster the dog (last seen in *Buster*, 2003) has a great time at "camp" in this story with a Wild West flavor. (Rev: BCCB 7–8/08; BL 5/15/08; SLJ 7/08)

5212 Fleming, Denise. *In the Tall, Tall Grass* (PS–1). Illus. 1991, Holt $16.95 (978-0-8050-1635-2). 32pp. An excellent story-hour book in which a caterpillar munches through the tall, tall grass, watching nature along the way. (Rev: BL 10/1/91*; HB 1/92*; SLJ 9/91*)

5213 Fleming, Denise. *Underground* (PS–K). Illus. by author. 2012, Simon & Schuster $17.99 (978-1-4424-5882-6). 40pp. Fleming uses her signature illustrations to reveal creatures that burrow into the ground, with rhythmic text, touches of humor, and an informative "Creature Identification" index. **e** (Rev: BL 12/15/12; SLJ 8/12)

5214 Fletcher, Ashlee. *My Dog, My Cat* (PS–K). Illus. by author. 2011, Tanglewood $13.95 (978-1-933718-22-4). 32pp. A little boy contrasts behaviors and physical traits of his dog and his cat. (Rev: BL 9/1/11; SLJ 7/11)

5215 Fogliano, Julie. *If You Want to See a Whale* (PS–2). Illus. by Erin E. Stead. 2013, Roaring Brook $16.99 (978-1-59643-731-9). 32pp. What do you need to concentrate on if you want to see a whale? A boy and his dog learn about patience and surveying their surroundings in this nicely illustrated, simple book. Booklist Editors' Choice: Books for Youth. (Rev: BL 4/1/13*; HB 5–6/13; LMC 11–12/13; SLJ 6/13*)

5216 Fox, Mem. *Two Little Monkeys* (PS). Illus. by Jill Barton. 2012, Simon & Schuster $16.99 (978-141698687-4). 32pp. Two lively monkeys' escape from a hungry leopard is narrated in bouncy rhyme with a catchy refrain. **e** (Rev: BL 3/15/12; HB 7–8/12; LMC 5–6/12; SLJ 6/1/12)

5217 Frasier, Debra. *Spike: Ugliest Dog in the Universe* (K–2). Illus. by author. 2013, Simon & Schuster $16.99 (978-144241452-5). 40pp. Spike may not be beautiful but his courage in rescuing a cat named Evangeline earns him a home outside the pound. **e** Lexile AD380 (Rev: BL 11/1/13; LMC 3–4/14; SLJ 9/13)

5218 Frazee, Marla. *Boot and Shoe* (PS–3). Illus. by author. 2012, Simon & Schuster $16.99 (978-1-4424-2247-6). 40pp. Dog brothers Boot and Shoe become separated when they get sidetracked by a pesky squirrel; fortunately, reunion is sweet. Booklist Editors' Choice: Books for Youth, 2012. ∩ Lexile 470 (Rev: BL 8/12*; HB 9–10/12; LMC 1–2/13; SLJ 8/12*)

5219 Frazier, Craig. *Hank Finds Inspiration* (K–3). Illus. by author. 2008, Roaring Brook $16.95 (978-1-59643-358-8). 32pp. Unhappy with their "flat and boring yard," Stanley the boy and Hank the snake seek inspiration in the big city. (Rev: BLO 9/24/08; SLJ 9/08)

5220 Freedman, Claire. *Gooseberry Goose* (PS–2). Illus. by Vanessa Cabban. 2003, Tiger Tales $15.95 (978-1-58925-030-7). Gooseberry the gosling practices his flying techniques in preparation for migration south, while animals are busy getting ready for the coming of winter. (Rev: SLJ 12/03)

5221 Freedman, Claire. *One Magical Morning* (PS). Illus. by Louise Ho. 2005, Good Bks. $16.00 (978-1-56148-472-0). A mother bear and her baby watch morning arrive and the animals waking up. (Rev: SLJ 5/05)

5222 French, Vivian. *Caribou Journey* (1–3). Illus. by Lisa Flather. Series: Fantastic Journeys. 2001, Zero to Ten $15.95 (978-1-84089-216-1). Animal migration is explored in this story about a pregnant caribou, Ragged Ear, and the herd's annual march to the calving grounds. (Rev: BL 4/1/02; SLJ 12/01)

5223 Gal, Susan. *Please Take Me for a Walk* (PS–2). Illus. by author. 2010, Knopf $15.99 (978-0-375-85863-5); LB $18.99 (978-0-375-95863-2). Unpaged. A little white terrier begs over and over for a walk, listing the things he will enjoy. (Rev: BL 4/1/10; LMC 8–9/10; SLJ 5/1/10)

5224 Gannij, Joan. *Elusive Moose* (PS–2). Illus. by Clare Beaton. 2006, Barefoot Books $15.99 (978-1-905236-75-6). 32pp. An invisible narrator lists all the animals he has seen in the north woods, except for the moose that's hiding in each scene. (Rev: BL 11/15/06; SLJ 11/06)

5225 Gannij, Joan. *Hidden Hippo* (PS–2). Illus. by Clare Beaton. 2008, Barefoot Books $15.99 (978-1-84686-170-3). 32pp. A young, unseen narrator searches an African plain for a hippo but only finds other animals — elephants, lions, leopards; readers will spot the hippo hidden on each spread and will appreciate the information on endangered species at the end. (Rev: BLO 9/24/08; LMC 3/09) [590]

5226 George, Jean Craighead. *Frightful's Daughter* (1–3). Illus. by Daniel San Souci. 2002, Dutton $16.99 (978-0-525-46907-0). 32pp. Sam Gribley (of *My Side of the Mountain* and its sequels) must rescue a chick of the falcon he calls Frightful. (Rev: BL 9/1/02; HBG 3/03; SLJ 9/02)

5227 George, Jean Craighead. *Frightful's Daughter Meets the Baron Weasel* (2–4). Illus. by Daniel San Souci. 2007, Dutton $16.99 (978-0-525-47202-5). 48pp. A predatory weasel has its eye on the chicks of peregrine falcon Oksi in this sequel to *Frightful's Daughter* (2002). (Rev: BL 9/1/07)

5228 George, Lindsay Barrett. *In the Garden: Who's Been Here?* (PS–2). Illus. 2006, Greenwillow $16.99 (978-0-06-078762-2). 48pp. While picking vegetables in the garden, Christina and Jeremy wonder about the animals that got there first. (Rev: BL 4/15/06; SLJ 5/06)

5229 George, Lindsay Barrett. *Maggie's Ball* (PS). Illus. by author. 2010, Greenwillow $16.99 (978-0-06-172166-3); LB $17.89 (978-0-06-172170-0). 32pp. Maggie the dog searches all over the town for her ball in this oversize book with illustrations that show lots of potential balls for children to spot. (Rev: BL 2/15/10; SLJ 3/1/10)

5230 George, Lindsay Barrett. *That Pup!* (PS–1). Illus. by author. 2011, Greenwillow $16.99 (978-0-06-200413-0). 32pp. A puppy has fun digging up a squirrel's acorns until it meets up with the squirrel itself and the two decide to rebury them together. (Rev: BL 10/1/11; SLJ 11/1/11)

5231 George, Twig C. *Seahorses* (K–3). 2003, Millbrook LB $24.90 (978-0-7613-2869-8). 32pp. Seahorses and their lives are presented in eye-catching illustrations and poetic but informative text. (Rev: HBG 4/04; SLJ 4/04) [597]

5232 Gershator, Phillis. *Who's in the Farmyard?* (PS). Illus. by Jill McDonald. 2012, Barefoot $14.99 (978-184686574-9). 24pp. Starting with the rooster, readers meet the diverse animals of the farmyard. (Rev: BL 3/1/12; SLJ 2/12)

5233 Giff, Patricia Reilly. *The Sneaky Snow Fox* (K–2). Illus. by Diane Palmisciano. Series: Fiercely and Friends. 2012, Scholastic $16.99 (978-054543378-5); paper $6.99 (978-05452445-8-9). 40pp. Jilli is convinced she has seen a fox outside, and she and her friend Jim chase her dog Fiercely out into the snow, determined to save him from danger. Lexile 270L (Rev: BL 11/1/12)

5234 Gill, Shelley. *Big Blue* (1–3). Illus. by Ann Barrow. 2003, Charlesbridge LB $15.95 (978-1-57091-352-5). In this delightful tale based on a real-life experience of the author, a young girl's dream of swimming with a blue whale is fulfilled when her mother takes her on a trip to Baja California in Mexico. (Rev: HBG 4/04; SLJ 8/03)

5235 Godwin, Laura. *One Moon, Two Cats* (PS–2). Illus. by Yoko Tanaka. 2011, Atheneum $16.99 (978-1-4424-1202-6). 32pp. Paired illustrated spreads show a city cat and a country cat going about their nightly activities in very different and richly detailed settings. e (Rev: BL 10/15/11; HB 11–12/11; SLJ 8/1/11)

5236 Goldfinger, Jennifer P. *My Dog Lyle* (K–2). Illus. by author. 2007, Clarion $16.00 (978-0-618-63983-0). 32pp. An amusing child's view of why her beloved pet dog is so special. (Rev: BCCB 9/07; BL 6/1–15/07; SLJ 6/07)

5237 Golson, Terry. *Tillie Lays an Egg* (PS–2). Illus. by Ben Fink. 2009, Scholastic $14.99 (978-0-545-00537-1). Tillie the hen likes to lay her eggs in inventive places in this I-spy story that also provides basic information about chickens plus opportunities for counting and reviewing days of the week. (Rev: BCCB 1/09; BL 1/1–15/09; SLJ 1/09)

5238 Goodrich, Carter. *Say Hello to Zorro!* (PS–1). Illus. by author. 2011, Simon & Schuster $15.99 (978-1-4169-3893-4). Unpaged. Mr. Bud the dog does not welcome new pup Zorro to his house but the two gradually come to realize they share priorities. (Rev: SLJ 3/1/11*)

5239 Goodrich, Carter. *Zorro Gets an Outfit* (PS–1). Illus. by author. 2012, Simon & Schuster $15.99 (978-1-4424-3535-3). 48pp. Initially aghast at the prospect of wearing a costume, Zorro the pug comes around when he sees another dressed-up dog at the park. (Rev: BL 5/1/12; SLJ 4/1/12)

5240 Gorbachev, Valeri. *The Best Cat* (PS–1). Illus. by author. 2010, Candlewick $15.99 (978-0-7636-3675-3). 32pp. Siblings Jeff and Ginny have differing opinions on the family cat's diverse talents, but both agree she's the best cat there is; the illustrations add to the humor. Lexile 820 (Rev: BL 1/1/10; SLJ 3/1/10)

5241 Gore, Leonid. *Danny's First Snow* (PS–K). Illus. by author. 2007, Atheneum $16.99 (978-1-4169-1330-6). 32pp. A little bunny wakes up to find his world transformed by a snowfall. (Rev: BL 10/1/07; SLJ 12/07)

5242 Gore, Leonid. *Worms for Lunch?* (PS–1). Illus. by author. 2011, Scholastic $16.99 (978-0-545-24338-4). 32pp. Animals of various kinds reveal what they like to eat in simple text and illustrations with die-cuts and flaps. (Rev: BL 3/1/11; HB 3–4/11; SLJ 3/1/11)

5243 Graber, Janet. *Muktar and the Camels* (PS–3). Illus. by Scott Mack. 2009, Holt $16.99 (978-0-8050-7834-3). 32pp. Muktar, an 11-year-old orphan on Kenya's border with Somalia who remembers his librarian father delivering books by camel, tends an injured camel and wins himself a job. (Rev: BL 6/1–15/09; LMC 10/09; SLJ 8/09)

5244 Graham-Barber, Lynda. *KokoCat, Inside and Out* (K–2). Illus. by Nancy Lane. 2012, Gryphon $16.95 (978-094071912-5). 24pp. A contented indoor cat has a scary adventure in the outdoors in this story that includes notes for adults on keeping cats safe. e (Rev: BLO 3/1/12)

5245 Graham, Bob. *How to Heal a Broken Wing* (PS–1). Illus. by author. 2008, Candlewick $16.99 (978-0-7636-3903-7). 40pp. A kind boy rescues an injured bird on a busy city street and nurses it back to health; the illustrations extend and highlight the poignant moments. (Rev: BCCB 10/08; BL 9/15/08*; SLJ 10/08*)

5246 Graham, Bob. *"The Trouble with Dogs . . ." Said Dad* (PS–2). Illus. by author. 2007, Candlewick $12.99 (978-0-7636-3316-5). 32pp. Kate's family sends hyper dog Dave to a trainer, but has he learned obedience at the expense of his fun personality? A sequel to 2001's *"Let's Get a Pup!" Said Kate.* (Rev: BCCB 9/07; BL 7/07; HB 9/07; SLJ 10/07)

5247 Gravett, Emily. *Dogs* (PS–K). Illus. by author. 2010, Simon & Schuster $15.99 (978-1-4169-8703-1). 32pp. Looks at all kinds of dogs — big, small, spotty, shabby, wrinkly — and why we love them. (Rev: BL 3/15/10; LMC 8–9/10; SLJ 3/1/10*)

5248 Gravett, Emily. *Matilda's Cat* (PS–1). Illus. by author. 2014, Simon & Schuster $16.99 (978-144247527-4). 32pp. Matilda tries to learn what her cat enjoys doing but has little success until she finally hits on the right answer — the cat likes Matilda herself! e Lexile NC1090 (Rev: BL 3/1/14; LMC 8–9/14; SLJ 4/14)

5249 Greene, Stephanie. *Princess Posey and the Next-Door Dog* (K–2). Illus. by Stephanie Roth Sisson. 2011, Putnam $12.99 (978-039925463-5); paper $4.99 (978-01424193-9-7). 96pp. Six-year-old Posey's princess wand gives her the courage to help the big dog next door when his paw gets stuck in the fence; a beginning chapter book. e (Rev: BLO 11/15/11)

5250 Griffin, Molly Beth. *Loon Baby* (PS–2). Illus. by Anne Hunter. 2011, Houghton Mifflin $16.99 (978-0-

547-25487-6). 32pp. A baby loon learns to dive during a brief panic when his mother seems to be underwater too long. (Rev: BL 2/15/11; SLJ 5/1/11)

5251 Grimes, Nikki. *When Gorilla Goes Walking* (PS–2). Illus. by Shane Evans. 2007, Scholastic $16.99 (978-0-439-31770-2). 32pp. Cecelia, a young African American girl, describes in interconnected poems the exploits of her assertive cat called Gorilla. (Rev: BL 4/15/07; HBG 10/07)

5252 Grindley, Sally. *Little Sibu: An Orangutan Tale* (PS–2). Illus. by John Butler. 1999, Peachtree $15.95 (978-1-56145-196-8). Little Sibu is now 7 and his mother must force him to leave her and live on his own as other male orangutans do. (Rev: HBG 10/99; SLJ 5/99)

5253 Grogan, John. *Bad Dog, Marley!* (PS–2). Illus. by Richard Cowdrey. 2007, HarperCollins $16.99 (978-0-06-117114-7). A yellow lab gets into all kinds of trouble but proves himself an important member of the family in this adaptation of the author's adult novel *Marley & Me.* (Rev: SLJ 8/07)

5254 Gudeon, Adam. *Me and Meow* (PS–K). Illus. by author. 2011, HarperCollins $12.99 (978-0-06-199821-8). Unpaged. A young girl and her constant companion Meow have a fun-filled day outside in this story full of repetition. (Rev: SLJ 8/1/11)

5255 Haas, Jessie. *Bramble and Maggie: Horse Meets Girl* (1–3). Illus. by Alison Friend. 2012, Candlewick $14.99 (978-076364955-5). 48pp. A horse bored with giving riding lessons chooses a new home with a little girl named Maggie, who seems to understand. (Rev: BL 4/1/13; HB 3–4/12; SLJ 3/1/12)

5256 Halfmann, Janet. *Little Skink's Tail* (2–4). Illus. by Laurie Allen Klein. 2007, Sylvan Dell $15.95 (978-0-9768823-8-1); paper $8.95 (978-1-934359-20-4). Little Skink quickly jettisons her tail when attacked by a crow and then tries on some other ones for size; this humorous story also offers information about animals and their appendages. (Rev: LMC 1/08; SLJ 1/08)

5257 Hammerle, Susa. *Let's Try Horseback Riding* (PS–2). Trans. by Marisa Miller. Illus. by Kyrima Trapp. 2006, North-South $12.95 (978-0-7358-2093-7). 24pp. Rebecca is thrilled to receive riding lessons for her birthday, and learns all about caring for horses, horseback riding, and equine behavior. (Rev: BL 9/15/06; SLJ 11/06)

5258 Harper, Isabelle. *My Cats Nick and Nora* (PS–1). Illus. by Barry Moser. 1995, Scholastic $14.95 (978-0-590-47620-1). Isabelle and cousin Emmie spend every Sunday taking care of the family pets, Nick and Nora. A sequel to *My Dog Rosie* (1994). (Rev: BL 10/1/95; SLJ 10/95)

5259 Harrington, Janice N. *Busy-Busy Little Chick* (PS–1). Illus. by Brian Pinkney. 2013, Farrar $15.99 (978-0-374-34746-8). 32pp. A Central African folktale about Mama Nsoso and her family of chicks; Mama knows that they need a new home but each day they are distracted by worms, crickets, and other treats, so Little Chick takes it on himself to gather the necessary materials for a nice warm nest. **e** (Rev: BL 3/1/13; HB 3–4/13; LMC 8–9/13; SLJ 2/13)

5260 Harris, Trudy. *Say Something, Perico* (PS–2). Illus. by Cecilia Rebora. 2011, Millbrook $16.95 (978-0-7613-5231-0). 32pp. A Spanish-speaking parrot keeps being returned to the pet store by his English-speaking new owners and begins to despair of ever finding a permanent home; includes a glossary of Spanish words. Lexile AD570L (Rev: BL 12/1/11; LMC 1–2/12; SLJ 12/1/11)

5261 Harshman, Terry Webb. *Bessie's Bed* (PS–2). Illus. by Sharon Hawkins Vargo. Series: Silly Millies. 2003, Millbrook LB $17.90 (978-0-7613-2742-4). In this cumulative tale for beginning readers, a variety of creatures climb into Bessie's bed on a stormy night, but they all make too much noise for sleep. (Rev: HBG 4/04; SLJ 3/04)

5262 Hassett, John, and Ann Hassett. *The Nine Lives of Dudley Dog* (PS–2). Illus. by John Hassett. 2008, Houghton $16.00 (978-0-618-81153-3). 32pp. A little girl who wants a cat instead finds herself the owner of a dog that will chase cats over hill and dale, through thick and thin. (Rev: BL 6/1–15/08)

5263 Havill, Juanita. *Call the Horse Lucky* (K–3). Illus. by Nancy Lane. 2010, Gryphon $15.95 (978-0-940719-10-1). Unpaged. A young girl is instrumental in helping a neglected horse find a new, safe home. (Rev: SLJ 2/1/11)

5264 Hawkins, Emily. *Little Snow Goose* (PS). Illus. by Maggie Kneen. 2009, Dutton $16.99 (978-0-525-42166-5). 28pp. When a little fox scares a mother goose from her nest, he takes responsibility for raising her chick. (Rev: BL 11/1/09; SLJ 10/1/09)

5265 Heiligman, Deborah. *Cool Dog, School Dog* (PS–2). Illus. by Tim Bowers. 2009, Marshall Cavendish $15.99 (978-0-7614-5561-5). Unpaged. A golden retriever follows her boy to school and, despite the teacher's displeasure, soon finds a role for herself. (Rev: SLJ 9/1/09)

5266 Heiligman, Deborah. *Fun Dog, Sun Dog* (K–3). Illus. by Tim Bowers. 2005, Marshall Cavendish $14.95 (978-0-7614-5162-4). Tinka, an energetic golden retriever, and her boy enjoy a day at the beach, described in catchy rhymes. (Rev: BL 5/1/05; SLJ 5/05)

5267 Heiligman, Deborah. *Snow Dog, Go Dog* (PS–2). Illus. by Tim Bowers. 2013, Amazon/Two Lions $15.99 (978-147781724-7). Illustrated with textured acrylics and written in light, rhyming prose, *Snow Dog, Go Dog* centers on Tinka, a golden retriever who briefly gets lost in the snow before finding her way back to her owner and settling down in the cozy house for the night. Lexile AD360 (Rev: BL 10/1/13; SLJ 3/14)

5268 Henderson, Kathy. *Dog Story* (PS–K). Illus. 2005, Bloomsbury $16.99 (978-0-7475-5071-6). 32pp. Jo eventually gets the dog she wants, but only after she has been offered various substitutes — a mouse, a cat, a brother, and so forth. (Rev: BL 2/15/05; SLJ 4/05)

5269 Henkes, Kevin. *Birds* (PS–K). Illus. by Laura Dronzek. 2009, Greenwillow $17.99 (978-0-06-136304-

7). 32pp. A little girl is fascinated by birds — their colors, shapes, sizes, movements, and so forth. (Rev: BL 1/1–15/09; SLJ 2/09)

5270 Henkes, Kevin. *A Good Day* (PS–K). Illus. by author. 2007, Greenwillow $16.99 (978-0-06-114018-1). Four animals start off having a bad day, but luckily things turn around before the day is over. (Rev: BL 12/15/06; SLJ 3/07*)

5271 Henkes, Kevin. *Little White Rabbit* (PS–1). Illus. by author. 2011, Greenwillow $16.99 (978-0-06-200642-4). 40pp. An imaginative little rabbit is transformed into all the things he thinks about as he hops through the forest in this simple story with humor and appealing illustrations. (Rev: BL 11/15/10; HB 1–2/11; SLJ 2/1/11*)

5272 Henkes, Kevin. *Old Bear* (PS). Illus. by author. 2008, Greenwillow $17.99 (978-0-06-155205-2). 32pp. Throughout his long hibernation Old Bear dreams that he is a young cub enjoying the changing seasons. (Rev: BCCB 11/08; BL 6/1–15/08; HB 11/08; SLJ 9/08)

5273 Henrichs, Wendy. *When Anju Loved Being an Elephant* (1–3). Illus. by John Butler. 2011, Sleeping Bear $16.95 (978-1-58536-533-3). 32pp. A former circus elephant recalls the happier days of her youth living in the wild as she's moved to an elephant sanctuary. (Rev: BLO 11/15/11; SLJ 10/1/11)

5274 Hest, Amy. *Charley's First Night* (PS–1). Illus. by Helen Oxenbury. 2012, Candlewick $15.99 (978-0-7636-4055-2). 32pp. Henry's parents lose the battle to have the new puppy, Charley, sleep in the kitchen in this nicely illustrated gentle story. ALA Notable Children's Book. **e** Lexile AD940L (Rev: BL 11/15/12*; HB 1–2/13; LMC 3–4/13; SLJ 10/12)

5275 Hest, Amy. *The Dog Who Belonged to No One* (PS–1). Illus. by Amy Bates. 2008, Abrams $15.95 (978-0-8109-9483-6). 32pp. A lonely girl named Lia and a stray dog caught out in a storm find happiness and friendship. (Rev: BL 8/08; SLJ 8/08)

5276 Himler, Ronald. *Six Is So Much Less Than Seven* (K–2). Illus. by author. 2002, Star Bright $16.95 (978-1-887734-91-2). An old man mourns the death of his cat, which leaves him with only six. (Rev: HBG 10/02; SLJ 12/02)

5277 Himmelman, John. *Katie and the Puppy Next Door* (PS–K). Illus. by author. 2013, Henry Holt $16.99 (978-0-8050-9484-8). 32pp. Despite a bad start to their relationship, Katie the dog finally learns to play and share with new neighbor Ruby the dachshund. (Rev: BL 4/1/13; SLJ 2/13)

5278 Himmelman, John. *Katie Loves the Kittens* (PS–2). Illus. by author. 2008, Holt $14.95 (978-0-8050-8682-9). 32pp. Katie the dog is much too rambunctious for the three new kittens until she learns that her joy is scaring them. (Rev: BLO 8/28/08; SLJ 9/08)

5279 Hobbie, Holly. *Everything but the Horse* (PS–3). Illus. by author. 2010, Little, Brown $16.99 (978-0-316-07019-5). 32pp. Holly longs for a horse when her family moves from the city to a farm; based on the author's childhood. (Rev: BL 12/15/10; SLJ 12/1/10*)

269

5280 Hobbs, Leigh. *Old Tom, Man of Mystery* (K–2). Illus. by author. 2005, Peachtree $16.95 (978-1-56145-346-7). Angry when his mistress assigns him a number of chores, Old Tom the cat decides to play a trick on her; a sequel to *Old Tom's Holiday* (2004). (Rev: SLJ 12/05)

5281 Hobbs, Leigh. *Old Tom's Holiday* (K–3). Illus. by author. 2004, Peachtree $16.95 (978-1-56145-316-0). Angela Throgmorton believes she left her cat at home but she is lonely on holiday and is thrilled to find out that he came along after all. (Rev: SLJ 11/04)

5282 Hodgkins, Fran. *The Cat of Strawberry Hill: A True Story* (PS–2). Illus. by Lesia Sochor. 2005, Down East $15.95 (978-0-89272-684-4). A playful kitten that goes astray from its owners at a highway rest stop is adopted by innkeepers and has a satisfying life thereafter. (Rev: BL 12/15/05; SLJ 3/06)

5283 Hodgkins, Fran. *Who's Been Here? A Tale in Tracks* (PS–2). Illus. by Karel Hayes. 2008, Down East $15.95 (978-0-89272-714-8). Three siblings follow their dog on a winter's day and inspect the various tracks left in the snow. (Rev: SLJ 12/08)

5284 Hodgkinson, Leigh. *Boris and the Snoozebox* (PS–2). Illus. by author. 2008, Tiger Tales $15.95 (978-1-58925-071-0). 32pp. When Boris the cat is tired he climbs into a cardboard box for a nap, only to find himself being shipped overseas. (Rev: BL 4/1/08; SLJ 7/08)

5285 Holmes, Mary Tavener, and John Harris. *A Giraffe Goes to Paris* (1–3). Illus. by Jon Cannell. 2010, Marshall Cavendish $17.99 (978-0-7614-5595-0). 32pp. Belle the giraffe's 1826 journey to Paris from Egypt is the subject of this handsomely illustrated novel, which contains many factual details. (Rev: BL 4/1/10; LMC 8–9/10; SLJ 4/1/10)

5286 Holtei, Christa. *Nanuk Flies Home* (K–2). Illus. by Astrid Vohwinkel. 2008, Eerdmans $16.00 (978-0-8028-5342-4). A baby polar bear's dream of flying comes true in a most unusual way. (Rev: SLJ 9/08)

5287 Hornsey, Chris. *Why Do I Have to Eat off the Floor?* (PS–1). Illus. by Gwyn Perkins. 2007, Walker $15.95 (978-0-8027-9617-2). 24pp. Murphy, a fun-loving beagle, poses all sorts of questions about his life to his young owner. (Rev: BL 4/1/07; SLJ 3/07)

5288 Hosta, Dar. *Doggie Do!* (PS–1). Illus. by author. 2009, Brown Dog $17.95 (978-097219674-1). 32pp. This lively picture book follows a group of playful dogs through the day, from eating and fetching to taking a snooze. (Rev: BLO 11/15/09)

5289 Houran, Lori Haskins. *I Will Keep You Safe and Sound* (PS–K). Illus. by Petra Brown. 2013, Scholastic $16.99 (978-0-545-19751-9). 32pp. A gentle, rhyming story about young animals finding safety with their parents. Lexile AD680 (Rev: BL 3/15/13; SLJ 3/13)

5290 Hubbell, Patricia. *Bouncing Time* (PS). Illus. by Melissa Sweet. 2000, HarperCollins LB $15.89 (978-0-688-17377-7). 32pp. A delightful rhyming poem about a mother with a child in a backpack who visit a zoo and watch the animals at play. (Rev: BCCB 5/00; BL 4/1/00; HBG 10/00; SLJ 7/00)

5291 Hubbell, Patricia. *Horses: Trotting! Prancing! Racing!* (PS–1). Illus. by Joe Mathieu. 2011, Marshall Cavendish $17.99 (978-0-7614-5949-1). 32pp. Rhyming text introduces a wide variety of horses and their occupations, showing how we feed them and care for them. ⊖ (Rev: BLO 12/15/11; SLJ 9/1/11)

5292 Hucke, Johannes. *Pip in the Grand Hotel* (PS–2). Illus. by Daniel Muller. 2009, North-South $16.95 (978-0-7358-2225-2). 32pp. A pet mouse named Pip's escape prompts a boisterous chase through an exclusive hotel; detailed illustrations add to the fun. (Rev: BL 3/1/09; SLJ 5/09)

5293 Huneck, Stephen. *Sally Gets a Job* (PS–2). Illus. by author. 2008, Abrams $16.95 (978-0-8109-9493-5). 32pp. Sally the black lab imagines herself in a variety of jobs — teacher, archaeologist, hip hop star, chef, and so forth. (Rev: BL 4/1/08; SLJ 4/08)

5294 Huneck, Stephen. *Sally Goes to the Beach* (K–3). Illus. 2000, Abrams $17.95 (978-0-8109-4186-1). Simple color woodcuts are used to illustrate this dog's-eye view of a day at the beach. (Rev: BCCB 11/00; BL 5/15/00; HBG 10/00; SLJ 6/00)

5295 Huneck, Stephen. *Sally's Great Balloon Adventure* (PS–2). Illus. by author. 2010, Abrams $16.95 (978-0-8109-8331-1). 32pp. Enticed by the smell of fried chicken, Sally the lab ends up taking a solo ride in a hot air balloon. (Rev: BLO 2/1/10; SLJ 4/1/10)

5296 Huneck, Stephen. *Sally's Snow Adventure* (PS–2). 2006, Abrams $15.95 (978-0-8109-7061-8). 32pp. While on a ski trip to a dog-friendly resort, Sally the black Labrador retriever gets lost but is finally saved by a pair of rescue dogs that she befriended earlier. (Rev: BL 9/1/06; SLJ 10/06)

5297 Imai, Ayano. *Chester* (PS–1). Illus. by author. 2007, Penguin $16.99 (978-0-698-40062-7). 32pp. Chester the dog runs away because he feels neglected by his human family, and his fruitless quest for a new home makes him appreciate his owners, who had never stopped searching for him. (Rev: BL 6/1–15/07; SLJ 12/07)

5298 Isadora, Rachael. *A South African Night* (PS–K). Illus. 1998, Greenwillow $14.89 (978-0-688-11390-2). 24pp. As the people of Johannesburg go home after a day's work and prepare for bed, many of the animals in the Kruger National Park begin their nocturnal activities. (Rev: BCCB 4/98; BL 2/15/98; HBG 10/98; SLJ 8/98)

5299 Isop, Laurie. *How Do You Hug a Porcupine?* (PS–1). Illus. by Gwen Millward. 2011, Simon & Schuster $15.99 (978-1-4424-1291-0). 32pp. A little boy interested in cuddling animals carefully considers how one would go about hugging a porcupine. (Rev: BL 7/11; SLJ 8/1/11)

5300 Jagtenberg, Yvonne. *Jack's Rabbit* (PS–1). Illus. 2003, Millbrook $15.95 (978-0-7613-1544-5). 32pp. Jack's rabbit escapes while Jack is trying to draw him and Jack hunts for him all over the place. (Rev: BL 3/1/03)

5301 James, Simon. *George Flies South* (PS–2). Illus. by author. 2011, Candlewick $16.99 (978-0-7636-5724-6).

Unpaged. Young bird George has been unwillingly to leave his nest and learn to fly, but a gust of wind carries his nest out of the tree and he is forced to take action. (Rev: HB 11–12/11; SLJ 10/1/11)

5302 Janisch, Heinz. *Heave Ho!* (PS–K). Illus. by Carola Holland. 2006, North-South $16.95 (978-0-7358-2091-3). In only 12 sentences, this entertaining tale shows a dog, a cat, and a few mice banding together to raid the refrigerator. (Rev: SLJ 11/06)

5303 Jeffers, Oliver. *This Moose Belongs to Me* (PS–3). Illus. by author. 2012, Philomel $16.99 (978-0-399-16103-2). 32pp. Delighted at first to claim a moose as his pet, Wilfred is disappointed to discover that these animals do not really understand the rules. ALA Notable Children's Book. Lexile AD560L (Rev: BL 12/1/12*; SLJ 1/13*)

5304 Jeffers, Susan. *My Chincoteague Pony* (PS–3). Illus. by author. 2008, Hyperion $16.99 (978-1-4231-0023-2). 40pp. Young Julie, a fan of *Misty of Chincoteague*, is desperate to get a pony and finally succeeds through the generosity of others. (Rev: BCCB 7–8/08; BL 4/15/08; HB 7/08; LMC 3/08; SLJ 6/08)

5305 Jenkins, Emily. *Skunkdog* (PS–2). Illus. by Pierre Pratt. 2008, Farrar $16.95 (978-0-374-37009-1). Dumpling is a lonely dog because she's different — she has no sense of smell — and to her family's dismay she makes friends with a skunk. (Rev: BL 5/1/08; SLJ 4/08)

5306 Jenkins, Emily. *Sugar Would Not Eat It* (PS–2). Illus. by Giselle Potter. 2009, Random $16.99 (978-0-375-83603-9). 40pp. Leo has adopted a stray cat he calls Sugar and he cannot understand why it won't eat a piece of his birthday cake. (Rev: BCCB 7–8/09; BL 3/15/09; SLJ 5/09)

5307 Jennings, Linda. *Little Puppy Lost* (PS–K). Illus. by Alison Edgson. 2008, Good Bks. $16.95 (978-1-56148-635-9). 32pp. Ollie, a little golden puppy, finds himself lost and alone in a snowy field and must bravely try to find his way home. (Rev: BL 12/1/08; SLJ 12/08)

5308 Jennings, Sharon. *Bearcub and Mama* (PS). Illus. by Melanie Watt. 2005, Kids Can $15.95 (978-1-55337-556-2). 32pp. Bearcub has learned well from his mother, and when he is separated from her in a storm, he knows what to do. (Rev: BL 2/15/05)

5309 Jonas, Ann. *Bird Talk* (K–2). Illus. 1999, Greenwillow LB $14.89 (978-0-688-14173-8). 32pp. About 65 different species of birds comment on a garden being seeded, with each bird identified by name at the back of this imaginative nature book. (Rev: BCCB 5/99; BL 6/1–15/99; HBG 10/99; SLJ 4/99)

5310 Jones, Jolie. *Little Kisses* (K–2). Illus. by Julie Downing. Series: The Julie Andrews Collection. 2005, HarperCollins LB $16.89 (978-0-06-058699-7). Bejinhos the dog and Jolie enjoy each other's company and know the rules, but Bejinhos gets into trouble while his mistress is at school; appealing illustrations enhance the meandering text. (Rev: SLJ 1/06)

5311 Joosse, Barbara M. *Bad Dog School* (K–3). Illus. by Jennifer Plecas. 2004, Clarion $15.00 (978-0-618-

13331-4). After going to obedience school, formerly over-zesty puppy Zippy becomes too restrained and his family decides to untrain him a bit. (Rev: SLJ 9/04)

5312 Joosse, Barbara M. *Wind-Wild Dog* (1–3). Illus. by Kate Kiesler. 2006, Holt $16.95 (978-0-8050-7053-8). 32pp. Sled-dog Ziva faces a difficult choice between remaining with the man who has shown his faith in her and running free with the wolves she hears at night. (Rev: BL 10/1/06; SLJ 11/06)

5313 Judge, Lita. *Red Hat* (PS). Illus. by author. 2013, Atheneum $16.99 (978-1-4424-4232-0). 40pp. In this almost wordless companion to *Red Sled* (2011), a series of young animals play with the little boy's red hat, and it unravels gradually to a single piece of string. ❤ (Rev: BL 3/1/13; SLJ 2/13)

5314 Kasza, Keiko. *The Dog Who Cried Wolf* (PS–2). Illus. 2005, Putnam $15.99 (978-0-399-24247-2). 32pp. When his owner reads him a book about wolves, Moka the dog decides to run away to the wilds and live free, but eventually discovers a wolf's life is not quite what he expected. (Rev: BL 9/1/05; SLJ 12/05*)

5315 Keenan, Sheila. *As the Crow Flies* (PS–1). Illus. by Kevin Duggan. 2012, Feiwel & Friends $16.99 (978-0-312-62156-8). 40pp. A nicely illustrated, rhyming introduction to crows and their interesting behaviors. 🎧 ❤ Lexile AD500L (Rev: BL 12/1/12; LMC 1–2/13; SLJ 8/12)

5316 Keller, John G. *The Rubber-Legged Ducky* (K–2). Illus. by Henry Cole. 2008, Harcourt $16.00 (978-0-15-205289-8). 32pp. Five the duckling was born with a rubber leg (his mother accidentally swallowed a rubber band) and says "bing-boing" instead of quacking; but his strange physique proves useful when a fox comes prowling. (Rev: BL 5/15/08; SLJ 4/08)

5317 Kelly, Irene. *A Small Dog's Big Life: Around the World with Owney* (PS–2). Illus. 2005, Holiday $16.95 (978-0-8234-1863-3). 32pp. This engaging picture book chronicles in fictionalized letters and newspaper accounts the story of Owney, a stray dog that became a post office mascot in the late 19th century and traveled around the world. (Rev: BL 7/05; SLJ 8/05)

5318 Kenah, Katharine. *Ferry Tail* (PS–2). Illus. by Nicole Wong. 2014, Sleeping Bear $16.99 (978-158536829-7). 32pp. A cat called Cupcake is the only thorn in Walter the dog's side, making him question his life aboard a ferry. Lexile AD480 (Rev: BL 3/1/14; SLJ 4/14)

5319 Kerby, Mona. *Owney, the Mail-Pouch Pooch* (K–3). Illus. by Lynne Barasch. 2008, Farrar $16.95 (978-0-374-35685-9). 40pp. A stray dog called Owney finds a home at the post office, traveling all the way across the country and even further afield as he guards the mail; based on the true story of a late 19th-century dog whose body is preserved at the Smithsonian. (Rev: BCCB 6/08; BL 4/1/08; HB 7/08; SLJ 4/08)

5320 Kerr, Judith. *Goodbye Mog* (K–3). Illus. by author. 2003, HarperCollins $17.95 (978-0-00-714968-1). Mog the cat dies early in this book but lingers around in spirit to watch over her family's recovery and acceptance of a new kitten. (Rev: SLJ 4/03)

5321 Kerr, Judith. *Goose in a Hole* (PS–2). Illus. by author. 2006, Collins $15.99 (978-0-00-720793-0). In search of the water that has mysteriously gone missing from the village pond, Katerina the goose fearlessly sets off down a hole, family in tow. (Rev: SLJ 7/06)

5322 Kimmel, Haven. *Orville: A Dog Story* (K–3). Illus. by Robert Andrew Parker. 2003, Clarion $15.00 (978-0-618-15955-0). 32pp. A moving story about a stray dog trying to find a comfortable home. (Rev: BCCB 11/03; BL 9/15/03; HBG 4/04; LMC 1/04; SLJ 11/03)

5323 King, Stephen Michael. *Mutt Dog!* (PS–2). Illus. 2005, Harcourt $16.00 (978-0-15-205561-5). 32pp. Mutt Dog struggles to survive on the city streets until he is adopted by a worker at the local homeless shelter. (Rev: BL 10/1/05; SLJ 11/05)

5324 Kirk, David. *Little Bunny, Biddle Bunny* (PS). Illus. by author. 2002, Scholastic $9.95 (978-0-439-33819-6). A gentle story of a little rabbit's adventures in sunny meadows. (Rev: HBG 10/02; SLJ 4/02)

5325 Kirk, Katie. *Eli, No!* (PS–K). Illus. by author. 2011, Abrams $14.95 (978-0-8109-8964-1). 32pp. An energetic, good-natured black Lab endures many a rebuke from his human family, knowing in the end that they love him despite the mischief he creates. (Rev: BL 11/15/11; LMC 1–2/12; SLJ 11/1/11)

5326 Kotzwinkle, William, and Glenn Murray. *Walter the Farting Dog* (K–3). Illus. by Audrey Colman. 2001, Frog $14.95 (978-1-58394-053-2). 32pp. Poor Walter's flatulence almost causes his new family to return him to the pound, until he uses his unique "gift" to save them from burglars. (Rev: BL 2/15/02)

5327 Kotzwinkle, William, and Glenn Murray. *Walter the Farting Dog: Trouble at the Yard Sale* (K–3). Illus. by Audrey Colman. 2004, Dutton $16.99 (978-0-525-47217-9). 32pp. Walter proves himself a hero in this grossly amusing second book about his flatulent tendencies. (Rev: BL 4/15/04; SLJ 4/04)

5328 Krebs, Laurie. *We're Sailing to Galapagos: A Week in the Pacific* (PS–3). Illus. by Grazia Restelli. 2005, Barefoot Books $16.99 (978-1-84148-902-5). During a visit to the Galapagos, readers are introduced to the various animals found there, with informative text following a rhyming story. (Rev: SLJ 5/05)

5329 Krilanovich, Nadia. *Chicken, Chicken, Duck!* (PS). Illus. by author. 2011, Tricycle $14.99 (978-1-58246-385-8); LB $17.99 (978-1-58246-389-6). 32pp. A bunch of barnyard animals pile into a boisterous pyramid of shapes, colors, and noises. (Rev: BL 3/1/11; SLJ 3/1/11)

5330 Kroll, Steven. *Patches Lost and Found* (K–3). Illus. by Barry Gott. 2001, Winslow $15.95 (978-1-890817-53-4). Jenny loves to draw pictures but can't write stories, so she draws pictures of her pet hamster and fills in the words of a story afterward. (Rev: BL 3/1/01*; HBG 10/01)

5331 Kroll, Steven. *A Tale of Two Dogs* (PS–1). Illus. by Mike Reed. 2004, Marshall Cavendish $16.95 (978-0-

7614-5161-7). 32pp. When the Morrisons return puppy Morgan to the pound and come home with a less unruly dog, are they really further ahead? (Rev: BL 4/15/04; SLJ 7/04)

5332 Kulling, Monica. *Lumpito and the Painter from Spain* (K–3). Illus. by Dean Griffiths. 2013, Pajama $19.95 (978-1-927485-00-2). 32pp. A beautifully illustrated fictionalized story about a dachshund adopted by Picasso and included in several of his paintings. Lexile AD620 (Rev: BL 5/1/13; LMC 1–2/14; SLJ 4/13)

5333 Kumin, Maxine. *Oh, Harry!* (K–2). Illus. by Barry Moser. 2011, Roaring Brook $16.99 (978-1-59643-439-4). 32pp. Harry the horse has various talents including opening doors, which comes in handy when pesky 6-year-old Algernon gets locked in a grain bin and is rescued, albeit not immediately. (Rev: BL 5/1/11; SLJ 5/1/11)

5334 Kuskin, Karla. *So, What's It Like to Be a Cat?* (PS–2). Illus. by Betsy Lewin. 2005, Simon & Schuster $15.95 (978-0-689-84733-2). 32pp. A self-confident cat happily answers in graceful lyrics the questions posed by a young interviewer. (Rev: BL 5/1/05)

5335 Kutner, Merrily. *Down on the Farm* (PS). Illus. by Will Hillenbrand. 2004, Holiday House $16.95 (978-0-8234-1721-6). Barnyard animals are introduced in bouncy rhymes and lots of caws, honks, and oinks. (Rev: SLJ 3/04)

5336 Kwon, Yoon-duck. *My Cat Copies Me* (K–3). Illus. 2007, Kane $15.95 (978-1-933605-26-5). 32pp. A young girl and her cat have fun together, copying each other's movements at play. (Rev: BL 4/15/07)

5337 Lacombe, Benjamin. *Cherry and Olive* (PS–2). Illus. by author. 2007, Walker $16.95 (978-0-8027-9707-0). 32pp. In desperate need of a friend, lonely Cherry falls in love with a wrinkly dog at the animal shelter where her father works. (Rev: BL 11/1/07; SLJ 12/07)

5338 Laminack, Lester L. *Three Hens and a Peacock* (PS–2). Illus. by Henry Cole. 2011, Peachtree $15.95 (978-1-56145-564-5). 32pp. The unexpected arrival of a rogue peacock creates jealousy amongst the other feathered creatures on a farm. Lexile AD590L (Rev: BL 4/1/11; LMC 10/11; SLJ 4/11)

5339 Lamstein, Sarah. *Big Night for Salamanders* (K–3). Illus. by Carol Benioff. 2010, Boyds Mills $17.95 (978-1-932425-98-7). 32pp. On a warm, rainy spring night, a young boy and his parents help spotted salamanders cross a dangerous road. (Rev: BL 2/15/10; LMC 8–9/10; SLJ 3/1/10)

5340 Lang, Glenna. *Looking Out for Sarah* (PS–3). Illus. 2001, Charlesbridge $15.95 (978-0-88106-647-0). 32pp. Based on a true story, this book presents a typical day in the life of a blind woman through the eyes of her guide dog, Perry. (Rev: BL 11/1/01; HB 9/01; HBG 3/02; SLJ 9/01)

5341 Lange, Willem. *John and Tom* (K–3). Illus. by Burt Dodson. Series: Family Heritage. 2001, Vermont Folklife Center $14.95 (978-0-916718-17-6). 32pp. A young logger named John is pinned beneath a tree and is rescued by his horse in this based-in-truth tale set in 1950s Vermont. (Rev: BL 11/1/01; SLJ 12/01)

5342 Lareau, Kara. *Ugly Fish* (1–4). Illus. by Scott Magoon. 2006, Harcourt $16.00 (978-0-15-205082-5). Ugly Fish, who would rather eat other fish than make friends, gets his comeuppance when Shiny Fish is introduced into his tank. (Rev: SLJ 7/06) ⌒

5343 Lears, Laurie. *Stay Away from Rat Boy!* (PS–3). Illus. by Red Hansen. 2009, Albert Whitman $16.99 (978-0-8075-6789-0). 32pp. A bully reforms through his close connection to the class rat. (Rev: BL 4/1/09; SLJ 4/09)

5344 Lechner, John. *A Froggy Fable* (PS–2). Illus. 2005, Candlewick $14.99 (978-0-7636-2123-0). 32pp. Accepting change is the message of this fable about a frog who is dismayed when his cozy home under a rock is disturbed. (Rev: BL 6/1–15/05; SLJ 5/05)

5345 Lee, Spike, and Tonya Lewis Lee. *Please, Puppy, Please* (PS–1). Illus. by Kadir Nelson. 2005, Simon & Schuster $16.95 (978-0-689-86804-7). 32pp. Two African American children give their high-energy puppy lots of instructions he fails to heed. (Rev: BL 11/1/05; SLJ 11/05)

5346 Leedy, Loreen. *Mapping Penny's World* (PS–2). Illus. 2000, Holt $17.00 (978-0-8050-6178-9). 32pp. Using her newly learned map skills, Penny draws maps of the territory covered by her pet boxer, Lisa. (Rev: BCCB 9/00; BL 7/00; HBG 3/01; SLJ 9/00)

5347 Lerner, Sharon. *Black Beauty* (K–2). Illus. by Susan Jeffers. 2009, Random $16.99 (978-0-375-85892-5). 40pp. This adaptation of the classic story excludes many details yet still retains the plot to create a shorter yet gratifying read with fine illustrations. (Rev: BLO 6/17/09; LMC 11/09)

5348 Lester, Alison. *Noni the Pony* (PS–K). Illus. by author. 2012, Simon & Schuster $15.99 (978-1-4424-5959-5). 32pp. A bouncy, rhyming story about an active pony who frisks with other animals on her farm, including Dave Dog and Coco the Cat. e Lexile AD930L (Rev: BL 10/15/12; SLJ 10/12)

5349 Levine, Ellen. *Seababy* (PS–3). Illus. by Jon Van Zyle. 2012, Walker $16.99 (978-080279808-4). 32pp. A baby sea otter separated from his mother during a storm is cared for at a rehabilitation center and taught how to look after himself before being released into the wild. (Rev: BL 4/15/12)

5350 Lewin, Betsy. *Where Is Tippy Toes?* (PS–K). Illus. by author. 2010, Simon & Schuster $16.99 (978-1-4169-3808-8). Unpaged. Where does Tippy Toes the cat spend his time? Readers lift the flaps to follow his adventures. (Rev: LMC 11–12/10; SLJ 9/1/10)

5351 Lewin, Ted. *Nilo and the Tortoise* (K–3). Illus. by author. 1999, Scholastic $16.95 (978-0-590-69004-1). Young Nilo is stranded overnight on one of the Galapagos Islands and shares sleeping quarters with a giant tortoise. (Rev: BL 8/99; SLJ 4/99)

5352 Lewis, J. Patrick. *The Good Ship Crocodile* (PS–1). Illus. by Monique Felix. 2013, Creative Editions $17.99 (978-156846238-7). 32pp. With lovely watercolor illustrations, this picture book tells the story of a crocodile who helps fireflies, frogs, and other small creatures cross a stormy river, and whose kindness is reciprocated when the fireflies light his way back home after the river dries up and he loses his way. (Rev: BLO 11/15/13; SLJ 1/1/14)

5353 Lewis, Kim. *A Puppy for Annie* (PS–2). Illus. by author. 2006, Candlewick $15.99 (978-0-7636-3200-7). Annie loves her Border collie Bess and gradually learns to understand what Bess is trying to convey as the two roam together in the English countryside. (Rev: BL 11/15/06; SLJ 2/07)

5354 Lewis, Wendy A. *In Abby's Hands* (1–4). Illus. by Marilyn Mets and Peter Ledwon. 2004, Red Deer $17.95 (978-0-88995-282-9). Abby is home alone when her Labrador retriever goes into labor, and she gains confidence as she offers the dog comfort and aid. (Rev: SLJ 3/04)

5355 Lindbergh, Reeve. *Homer the Library Cat* (PS–1). Illus. by Anne Wilsdorf. 2011, Candlewick $15.99 (978-0-7636-3448-3). 32pp. A cat used to the quiet life falls out a window and goes searching for a calm place to hang out; the perfect spot turns out to be the library. (Rev: BL 10/1/11; SLJ 12/1/11)

5356 Lindgren, Barbro. *Julia Wants a Pet* (K–2). Trans. from Swedish by Elisabeth Kallick Dyssegaard. Illus. by Eva Eriksson. 2003, R&S $15.00 (91-29-65940-X). Seven-year-old Julia travels far and wide in her search for the perfect pet. (Rev: HB 9/03; HBG 4/04; SLJ 11/03)

5357 Liwska, Renata. *Little Panda* (PS–2). Illus. by author. 2008, Houghton $12.95 (978-0-618-96627-1). Alone for a time — and despite warnings from his mother and grandfather — little panda Bao Bao finds himself facing a hungry tiger in this charming picture book. (Rev: BL 12/1/08; HB 1/09; SLJ 11/08)

5358 Lobel, Anita. *Hello, Day!* (PS). Illus. by author. 2008, Greenwillow $16.99 (978-0-06-078765-3). 32pp. The animals of the farmyard greet the sun with various noises but only the owl signals its departure with a "Whoo-ooo." (Rev: BCCB 7–8/08; BL 4/1/08; HB 3/08; SLJ 3/08)

5359 Lobel, Anita. *Nini Here and There* (PS–K). Illus. 2007, Greenwillow $16.99 (978-0-06-078767-7). 32pp. Watching her family pack, Nini the cat fears she will be left behind but instead finds herself in a new and wonderful place. (Rev: BCCB 9/07; BL 5/1/07; SLJ 6/07)

5360 Lobel, Anita. *Nini Lost and Found* (PS–1). Illus. by author. 2010, Knopf $15.99 (978-0-375-85880-2). 40pp. Overly adventurous tabby cat Nini goes exploring and finds the night world scarier than she expected. (Rev: BL 8/10*; HB 11–12/10; SLJ 9/1/10)

5361 Lobel, Gillian. *Moonshadow's Journey* (K–1). Illus. by Karin Littlewood. 2009, Whitman $16.99 (978-080755273-5). 32pp. A young swan learns about the dangers of migration in this story of family support and survival. (Rev: BLO 11/15/09; SLJ 8/1/09)

5362 London, Jonathan. *Baby Whale's Journey* (1–3). Illus. by Jon Van Zyle. 1999, Chronicle $14.95 (978-0-

8118-2496-5). 35pp. A poetic introduction to the life of a sperm whale from its birth through weaning to final acceptance by the pod as they feed on a giant squid. (Rev: BL 11/1/99; HBG 3/00; SLJ 1/00)

5363 London, Jonathan. *Little Swan* (PS–3). Illus. by Kristina Rodanas. 2009, Marshall Cavendish $17.99 (978-0-7614-5523-3). 32pp. London follows a trumpeter swan's development from breaking out of its shell to its first migration. (Rev: BL 5/1/09; SLJ 4/09)

5364 Long, Ethan. *Bird and Birdie in a Fine Day* (PS–1). Illus. by author. 2010, Tricycle $14.99 (978-1-58246-321-6). Unpaged. Cartoon characters Bird and Birdie enjoy a beautiful morning, a wonderful afternoon, and a marvelous evening together. (Rev: BL 3/1/10; SLJ 4/1/10)

5365 Lord, Janet. *Where Is Catkin?* (PS). Illus. by Julie Paschkis. 2010, Peachtree $16.95 (978-1-56145-523-2). 32pp. Folk-style artwork full of hidden details will engage readers in this story of a cat hunting for other animals. (Rev: BL 2/15/10; SLJ 4/1/10)

5366 Love, Donna. *Henry the Impatient Heron* (PS–3). Illus. by Christina Wald. 2009, Sylvan Dell $16.95 (978-1-934359-90-7); paper $8.95 (978-1-607180-35-7). 32pp. A simple story with happy illustrations tell this heron's tale; fact boxes and lesson plans. (Rev: SLJ 6/09)

5367 Lujan, Jorge. *Stephen and the Beetle* (K–2). Illus. by Chiara Carrer. 2012, Groundwood $18.95 (978-1-55498-192-2). 36pp. Young Stephen decides to spare a beetle's life in this simple, gentle story with eye-catching illustrations. Lexile AD780L (Rev: BL 9/1/12; SLJ 11/12)

5368 Luthardt, Kevin. *Peep!* (PS–2). Illus. by author. 2003, Peachtree $15.95 (978-1-56145-046-6). A young boy and a hatchling duck become fast friends; when the bird eventually flies away, the youngster is sad until one day, on a walk, he hears a "mew." (Rev: BL 5/03; HB 7/03; HBG 10/03; SLJ 5/03)

5369 Luxbacher, Irene. *Mattoo, Let's Play!* (PS–2). Illus. by author. 2010, Kids Can $16.95 (978-1-55453-424-1). 32pp. Young Ruby is too rough for her cat Mattoo, and it is only when she pretends to tame him in the jungle that she discovers how cuddly he can be. (Rev: BLO 4/15/10; SLJ 5/1/10)

5370 Lyon, George E. *A Traveling Cat* (PS–1). Illus. by Paul Johnson. 1998, Orchard $15.95 (978-0-531-30102-9). 32pp. A little girl cares for a stray cat and tends to her litter. When the cat later disappears, the girl realizes that she is a born traveler. (Rev: BL 11/15/98; HB 11/98; HBG 3/99; SLJ 9/98)

5371 Lyon, Tammie. *Olive and Snowflake* (PS–1). Illus. by author. 2011, Marshall Cavendish $16.99 (978-0-7614-5955-2). Unpaged. When her parents say Snowflake must go to obedience school, Olive worries that — like her dog — she will have to sit, stay, and generally learn to behave. ℮ (Rev: LMC 3–4/12; SLJ 9/1/11)

5372 McAllister, Angela. *Little Mist* (PS–1). Illus. by Sarah Fox-Davies. 2011, Knopf $16.99 (978-0-375-86788-0); LB $19.99 (978-0-375-96788-7). 32pp. A

young snow leopard feels very small when he follows his mama out of their cave for the first time. (Rev: BL 4/1/11; SLJ 3/1/11)

5373 Macaulay, David. *Angelo* (K–3). Illus. 2002, Houghton $16.00 (978-0-618-16826-2). 48pp. An Italian artist and a wounded pigeon share an unlikely friendship in this beautifully illustrated picture book that gives a bird's-eye view of Rome. (Rev: BCCB 6/02; BL 7/02; HB 5/02; HBG 10/02; SLJ 5/02)

5374 McBratney, Sam. *I Love It When You Smile* (PS–1). Illus. by Charles Fuge. 2006, HarperCollins $15.99 (978-0-06-084245-1). Lively illustrations incorporating an onlooking mouse and duck add to the simple text about a mother kangaroo trying to cheer up her grumpy child. (Rev: SLJ 5/06)

5375 MacCarthy, Patricia. *Moon Forest* (K–3). Illus. by author. 2013, Frances Lincoln $17.99 (978-184780283-5). 32pp. At night a fox prowls through a forest full of other animals also hunting for food. (Rev: BLO 11/15/13; LMC 5–6/14; SLJ 12/13)

5376 McCarty, Peter. *Fabian Escapes* (PS–K). Illus. 2007, Holt $16.95 (978-0-8050-7713-1). In this colorful sequel to *Hondo and Fabian* (2002), Fabian the cat leads a canine trio on a merry chase while Hondo the dog is stuck at home playing with the toddler. (Rev: BL 3/15/07)

5377 McCarty, Peter. *Hondo and Fabian* (PS–K). Illus. 2002, Holt $16.95 (978-0-8050-6352-3). 32pp. Captivating illustrations and simple text portray a day in the life of two family pets, Hondo the dog and Fabian the cat. Caldecott Honor Book, 2003. (Rev: BL 2/15/02; HBG 10/02; SLJ 6/02)

5378 McClure, Nikki. *How to Be a Cat* (PS–K). Illus. by author. 2013, Abrams/Appleseed $16.95 (978-1-4197-0528-1). 40pp. In nice cut-paper illustrations, a kitten learns the basics of cat behavior from an adult cat — stretching, cleaning, pouncing, and so forth. (Rev: BLO 4/1/13; SLJ 4/13*)

5379 McCully, Emily Arnold. *Wonder Horse: The True Story of the World's Smartest Horse* (PS–2). Illus. by author. 2010, Henry Holt $16.99 (978-0-8050-8793-2). 32pp. This fascinating novel is based on the true story of a former slave, Bill "Doc" Key, who became a veterinarian after the Civil War and taught a very clever horse the alphabet, colors, and counting. (Rev: BL 4/15/10*; LMC 8–9/10; SLJ 6/1/10*)

5380 McDonnell, Christine. *Dog Wants to Play* (PS–K). Illus. by Jeff Mack. 2009, Viking $15.99 (978-0-670-01126-1). 32pp. When one barnyard animal after another turns down a puppy's invitation to play, he finally finds the perfect companion: a little boy. (Rev: BL 11/1/09; SLJ 9/1/09)

5381 McFarland, Lyn Rossiter. *Widget* (PS–1). Illus. by Jim McFarland. 2001, Farrar $16.00 (978-0-374-38428-9). 32pp. Preschoolers will love the charming illustrations and humorous story about a stray dog who pretends to be a cat in order to fit in at his new home. (Rev: BL 11/1/01; HBG 3/02; SLJ 8/01*)

5382 McFarland, Lyn Rossiter. *Widget and the Puppy* (PS–2). Illus. by Jim McFarland. 2004, Farrar $16.00 (978-0-374-38429-6). Widget the dog falls asleep while babysitting a puppy and it is the six cats of the household that save the day, although they get none of the praise. (Rev: SLJ 9/04)

5383 McFarlane, Sheryl. *This Is the Dog* (PS–2). Illus. by Chrissie Wysotski. 2003, Fitzhenry & Whiteside $15.95 (978-1-55041-551-3). Rhythmic text and striking illustrations highlight this story of a wayward golden retriever puppy. (Rev: SLJ 10/03)

5384 McGhee, Alison. *Always* (PS–1). Illus. by Pascal LeMaitre. 2009, Simon & Schuster $15.99 (978-1-4169-7481-9). 40pp. A lovable dog explains, through words and sweet illustrations, the many ways he will keep the "castle" safe because he loves his young owner so much. (Rev: LMC 10/09; SLJ 5/09)

5385 McGrory, Anik. *Kidogo* (PS–1). Illus. by author. 2005, Bloomsbury $15.95 (978-1-58234-974-9). Kidogo, a young elephant, is feeling very small until he encounters a colony of ants. (Rev: SLJ 9/05*)

5386 McHenry, E. B. *Has Anyone Seen Winnie and Jean?* (PS–1). Illus. by author. 2007, Bloomsbury $16.95 (978-1-58234-999-2). 32pp. Corgis Winnie and Jean escape from their yard and have a great deal of fun before being captured. (Rev: BL 6/1–15/07; SLJ 7/07)

5387 McHenry, E. B. *Poodlena* (PS–1). Illus. 2004, Bloomsbury $16.95 (978-1-58234-824-7). 32pp. Poodlena, a pampered pink poodle, takes pains to preserve her pristine appearance until an encounter with a playful canine persuades her that she's been missing out on a lot of fun. (Rev: BL 5/1/04; SLJ 11/04)

5388 McKay, Hilary. *Lulu and the Duck in the Park* (2–4). Illus. by Priscilla Lamont. 2012, Whitman $13.99 (978-0-8075-4808-0). 104pp. Lulu, an animal lover, is banned from bringing any more to school but cannot resist the lure of an abandoned duck egg, with humorous results. ALA Notable Children's Book. e Lexile 740L (Rev: BL 10/1/12*; HB 9–10/12; LMC 3–4/13; SLJ 11/12*)

5389 McKinlay, Meg. *Duck for a Day* (2–4). Illus. by Leila Rudge. 2012, Candlewick $12.99 (978-0-7636-5784-0). 96pp. Neighbors Abby and Noah quibble over who will be allowed to bring their teacher's pet duck home for a night; when the duck escapes it takes teamwork to bring him home. (Rev: BL 4/15/12; HB 5–6/12; SLJ 8/12)

5390 McKinlay, Penny. *Flabby Tabby* (PS–1). Illus. by Britta Teckentrup. 2006, Frances Lincoln $15.95 (978-1-84507-090-8). 32pp. Tabby, an overweight cat, embarks on a secret fitness program when a new kitten arrives in the house and keeps beating her to the food bowl. (Rev: BL 1/1–15/06; SLJ 2/06)

5391 McLellan, Stephanie Simpson. *Leon's Song* (PS–3). Illus. by Dianna Bonder. 2004, Fitzhenry & Whiteside $15.95 (978-1-55041-813-2). Leon, a 40-year-old frog who lacks a sense of fulfillment, comes into his own when he alerts the pond creatures to the presence of danger. (Rev: SLJ 1/05)

5392 McPhail, David. *The Searcher and Old Tree* (PS–K). Illus. by author. 2008, Charlesbridge $15.95 (978-1-58089-223-0). 32pp. After a night of searching for food, a raccoon climbs into his usual old tree and manages to sleep through a raging thunderstorm. (Rev: BL 2/15/08; LMC 10/08; SLJ 2/08)

5393 Mader, C. Roger. *Lost Cat* (PS–2). Illus. by author. 2013, Houghton Mifflin $17.99 (978-054797458-3). 32pp. A sweet story in which Slipper the cat is accidentally left behind when her elderly owner moves, and searches unsuccessfully for a suitable new home until a serendipitous meeting solves the problem. Lexile AD770 (Rev: BL 11/1/13; SLJ 8/13)

5394 Madison, Alan. *Velma Gratch and the Way Cool Butterfly* (PS–2). Illus. by Kevin Hawkes. 2007, Schwartz & Wade $16.99 (978-0-375-83597-1). A monarch butterfly rescues 1st-grader Velma from the long shadows cast by her talented older sisters in this story full of butterfly facts. (Rev: BL 10/15/07; SLJ 12/07)

5395 Mahy, Margaret. *Dashing Dog!* (PS–2). Illus. by Sarah Garland. 2002, HarperCollins LB $15.89 (978-0-06-000457-6). 32pp. Rhyming verse and lively illustrations present a poodle's day at the beach, during which the rambunctious pup ruins his nice hairdo, chases birds and Frisbees . . . and rescues the baby. (Rev: BL 10/1/02; HBG 3/03; SLJ 9/02)

5396 Maltbie, P. I. *Picasso and Minou* (PS–2). Illus. by Pau Estrada. 2005, Charlesbridge $15.95 (978-1-57091-620-5). 32pp. Minou, a cat of strong artistic tastes who lives with Picasso, is pleased when the artist leaves his Blue Period in this beautifully illustrated picture book that blends fact and fiction. (Rev: BL 2/15/05; SLJ 4/05)

5397 Manning, Mick. *Cock-a-Doodle-Hooooooo!* (PS–2). Illus. by Brita Granström. 2007, Good Bks. $16.95 (978-1-56148-568-0). An owl makes himself at home on a farm that needs a rooster and finds that his talent for rodent-catching comes in handy. (Rev: SLJ 5/07)

5398 Mansfield, Howard. *Hogwood Steps Out: A Good, Good Pig Story* (K–2). Illus. by Barry Moser. 2008, Roaring Brook $16.95 (978-1-59643-269-7). 32pp. A huge pig named Christopher Hogwood narrates his adventures as he unlocks the gate and heads off into an exciting spring day. (Rev: BL 3/1/08; LMC 3/08; SLJ 6/08)

5399 Markle, Sandra. *Little Lost Bat* (2–4). Illus. by Allan Marks. 2006, Charlesbridge $15.95 (978-1-57091-656-4). This picture-book tale about a newborn bat left to fend for itself after its mother is killed by a predator is full of bat facts and lore. (Rev: BL 6/1–15/06; HB 7/07; HBG 4/07; LMC 1/07; SLJ 8/06*)

5400 Markle, Sandra. *Race the Wild Wind: A Story of the Sable Island Horses* (K–3). Illus. by Layne Johnson. 2011, Walker $17.99 (978-0-8027-9766-7). 32pp. Markle tells the story of the wild horses that live on Nova Scotia's Sable Island, focusing on a leading stallion that learns how to survive in the harsh climate. (Rev: BL 7/11; LMC 10/11; SLJ 7/11)

5401 Martin, Bill. *Ten Little Caterpillars* (PS–K). Illus. by Lois Ehlert. 2011, Simon & Schuster $17.99 (978-

1-4424-3385-4). 40pp. Brightly hued botanical illustrations — complete with labels — add appeal to the simple, rhymed story of ten caterpillars' adventures in a field of flowers and the process of metamorphosis. (Rev: BL 7/11; SLJ 8/1/11)

5402 Martin, Bill, Jr. *Baby Bear, Baby Bear, What Do You See?* (PS–K). Illus. by Eric Carle. 2007, Holt $16.95 (978-0-8050-8336-1). Searching for his mother, a baby bear meets many native American animals. (Rev: BL 6/1–15/07; SLJ 8/07)

5403 Martin, Bill, Jr. *Panda Bear, Panda Bear, What Do You See?* (PS–2). Illus. by Eric Carle. 2003, Holt $15.95 (978-0-8050-1758-8). Ten endangered animals — including the bald eagle, red wolf, and black panther — are introduced in Martin and Carle's familiar format. (Rev: HBG 4/04; SLJ 8/03)

5404 Martin, Bill, Jr. *Polar Bear, Polar Bear, What Do You Hear?* (PS–K). Illus. by Eric Carle. 1991, Holt $15.95 (978-0-8050-1759-5). 32pp. Animal sounds from 10 different animals are featured in this picture book. (Rev: BCCB 12/91; BL 11/15/91; HB 1/92; SLJ 11/91*)

5405 Marzollo, Jean. *Mama Mama* (PS). Illus. by Laura Regan. Series: Harper Growing Tree. 1999, HarperCollins $6.99 (978-0-694-01245-9). This board book celebrates the tender mother-child relations that exist with such animals as a lioness, leopard, chimpanzee, panda, elephant, and sea otter. (Rev: SLJ 11/99)

5406 Masurel, Claire. *¡No, Tito, no! / No, No, Titus!* (K–2). Trans. by Diego Lasconi. Illus. by Shari Halpern. 2006, North-South LB $16.50 (978-0-7358-2074-6); paper $6.95 (978-0-7358-2075-3). An endearing puppy, newly adopted by a farm family, tries to figure out where he fits in the overall scheme of things. (Rev: SLJ 10/06)

5407 Masurel, Eric. *Un gato y un perro / A Cat and a Dog* (PS–1). Trans. by Andres Antreasyan. Illus. by Bob Kolar. 2003, North-South paper $6.95 (978-0-7358-1784-5). A cat and dog, normally antagonistic toward each other, decide to band together to solve each other's problems in this bilingual tale. (Rev: BL 3/1/04)

5408 Meade, Holly. *If I Never Forever Endeavor* (PS–2). Illus. by author. 2011, Candlewick $15.99 (978-0-7636-4071-2). 32pp. A little bird mulls over the pros and cons of leaving the nest and testing its flying abilities in this beautifully illustrated book. (Rev: BL 4/15/11; LMC 5–6/11; SLJ 5/1/11)

5409 Meade, Holly. *A Place to Sleep* (PS–2). Illus. 2001, Marshall Cavendish $15.95 (978-0-7614-5096-2). 32pp. Facts about where and how different animals sleep, playfully conveyed through colorful illustrations and amusing text. (Rev: BCCB 12/01; BL 9/1/01; HBG 3/02; SLJ 9/01)

5410 Meadows, Michelle. *Itsy-Bitsy Baby Mouse* (PS–1). Illus. by Matthew Cordell. 2012, Simon & Schuster $15.99 (978-1-4169-3786-9). 40pp. A tiny baby mouse gets lost and has a scary time before finding his way home with the help of an older mouse. (Rev: BL 3/15/12; SLJ 2/1/12)

5411 Meister, Cari. *My Pony Jack at Riding Lessons* (PS–K). Illus. by Amy Young. Series: Viking Easy-to-Read. 2005, Viking $13.99 (978-0-670-05918-8). 32pp. In this sequel to *My Pony Jack* (2005) suitable for beginning readers, Lacy takes riding lessons. (Rev: BL 10/15/05; SLJ 10/05)

5412 Meister, Cari. *My Pony Jack at the Horse Show* (PS–2). Illus. by Amy Young. Series: Viking Easy-to-Read. 2006, Viking $13.99 (978-0-670-05919-5). 32pp. Lacy gets her pony Jack ready for a show, suffers some nerves when she arrives at the ring, and comes home with second prize; for beginning readers. (Rev: SLJ 8/06)

5413 Meister, Cari. *Tiny on the Farm* (K–1). Illus. by Rich Davis. 2008, Viking $16.99 (978-0-670-06246-1). Tiny, the gigantic dog, helps to find kittens in this simple picture-book story that will have readers searching the images. (Rev: SLJ 5/08)

5414 Meyers, Susan. *Kittens! Kittens! Kittens!* (PS–K). Illus. by David Walker. 2007, Abrams $15.95 (978-0-8109-1218-2). 32pp. Rhyming text and cheerful pictures track kittens as they play, explore, and grow. (Rev: BL 1/1–15/07)

5415 Miles, Victoria. *Old Mother Bear* (PS–3). Illus. by Molly Bang. 2007, Chronicle $16.95 (978-0-8118-5033-9). 32pp. This strikingly illustrated picture book based on true events follows an aging female grizzly bear as she guides her final set of cubs along the path to adulthood. (Rev: BL 4/15/07)

5416 Minor, Florence. *If You Were a Penguin* (PS). Illus. by Wendell Minor. 2009, HarperCollins $17.99 (978-0-06-113097-7). 32pp. Rhyming text presents all the things you could do if you were a penguin in this happy, fact-filled volume. (Rev: BL 1/1–15/09; SLJ 4/09)

5417 Minor, Wendell. *My Farm Friends* (PS–K). Illus. by author. 2011, Putnam $16.99 (978-0-399-24477-3). 32pp. Barnyard animals are portrayed through sweetly quirky rhymes and lively, comic illustrations. (Rev: BL 1/1–15/11; SLJ 2/1/11)

5418 Minshull, Evelyn. *Eaglet's World* (PS–2). Illus. by Andrea Gabriel. 2002, Whitman $16.95 (978-0-8075-8929-8). 32pp. An eaglet ventures first from his egg and then from his nest in this story about growth and independence. (Rev: BL 3/1/02; HBG 10/02; SLJ 5/02)

5419 Mitchell, Adrian, and Daniel Pudles. *Twice My Size* (PS–1). Illus. 1999, Millbrook LB $22.90 (978-0-7613-1423-3). 32pp. A series of animals each introduces another animal friend that is bigger than it is. (Rev: BL 4/15/99; HBG 10/99; SLJ 6/99)

5420 Mitton, Tony. *All Afloat on Noah's Boat!* (PS–2). Illus. by Guy Parker-Rees. 2007, Scholastic $16.99 (978-0-439-87397-0). During the animal talent show on the ark, the two caterpillars on board are busy in their cocoons. They display their special "talent" at the end of this rhyming story, when they turn into butterflies. (Rev: SLJ 5/07)

5421 Mockford, Caroline. *Cleo the Cat* (PS). Illus. by author. 2000, Barefoot Books $14.99 (978-1-84148-259-

0). A charming story about a cat named Cleo who finds a home and a friend. (Rev: HBG 3/01; SLJ 12/00)

5422 Mockford, Caroline. *Come Here, Cleo!* (PS–1). Illus. by author. 2001, Barefoot Books $14.99 (978-1-84148-329-0). A cat has simple adventures such as climbing a tree and chasing a butterfly. (Rev: HBG 10/01; SLJ 4/01)

5423 Molski, Carol. *Swimming Sal* (K–2). Illus. by Mary Newell Depalma. 2009, Eerdmans $17.00 (978-0-8028-5327-1). A Portuguese water dog with ambition finally gets to display her swimming skills. (Rev: BL 4/15/09; SLJ 3/09)

5424 Montenegro, Laura Nyman. *A Poet's Bird Garden* (PS–3). Illus. by author. 2007, Farrar $16.00 (978-0-374-36038-2). 32pp. Natalie's pet bird has escaped, and even some local poets can't find the words to coax the bird out of a tree. (Rev: BL 7/07; SLJ 12/07)

5425 Moss, Miriam. *Jungle Song* (PS–2). Illus. by Adrienne Kennaway. 2004, Lincoln $15.95 (978-1-84507-039-7). 32pp. A young tapir is lured away from his mother by a spider and explores the lush and busy South American rain forest. (Rev: BL 10/1/04; SLJ 10/04)

5426 Murphy, Yannick. *Ahwooooooooo!* (PS–2). 2006, Clarion $16.00 (978-0-618-11762-8). 32pp. Little Wolf's parents are too busy to teach him how to howl, so he turns to his grandfather for help. (Rev: BL 8/06; SLJ 6/06)

5427 Murphy, Yannick. *Baby Polar* (PS–K). Illus. by Kristen Balouch. 2009, Clarion $16 (978-0-618-99850-0). 32pp. A baby polar bear lost in a snowstorm mistakes his mother for a warm snow cave. (Rev: BL 11/15/09; SLJ 11/1/09)

5428 Myers, Christopher. *Black Cat* (3–8). Illus. 1999, Scholastic $16.95 (978-0-590-03375-6). 40pp. An intriguing picture book with rap rhythm that tells of a black cat's progress walking through a city's streets. (Rev: BCCB 2/99; BL 4/15/99; HB 3/99; HBG 10/99; SLJ 3/99)

5429 Na, Il Sung. *A Book of Babies* (PS–1). Illus. by author. 2014, Knopf $15.99 (978-038575290-9). 32pp. Using computer enhanced graphics that add color and texture, a duck takes children on a brief, but engaging trek through different parts of the world to demonstrate how the experiences of newborn animals vary depending on their species. (Rev: BL 11/15/13; SLJ 12/13)

5430 Na, Il Sung. *A Book of Sleep* (K–2). Illus. by author. 2009, Knopf $15.99 (978-0-375-86223-6); LB $18.99 (978-0-375-96223-3). 24pp. A watchful owl oversees a forest filled with animals at rest in this evocative tale. (Rev: BL 11/1/09*; SLJ 11/1/09*)

5431 Na, Il Sung. *Snow Rabbit, Spring Rabbit: A Book of Changing Seasons* (PS–K). Illus. by author. 2011, Knopf $15.99 (978-0-375-86786-6); LB $18.99 (978-0-375-96786-3). 24pp. A rabbit, her coat white for winter, watches other animals' preparations for and behavior during winter, before welcoming the spring as her own coat changes color. ℮ Lexile 450L (Rev: BL 1/1–15/11; SLJ 2/1/11*)

5432 Nelson, Jessie, and Karen Leigh Hopkins. *Labracadabra* (K–2). Illus. by Deborah Melmon. 2011, Viking $14.99 (978-0-670-01251-0). 36pp. Zach is kind of disappointed with his new (rescued) dog Larry until Larry's tail seems to exhibit magical abilities. (Rev: SLJ 8/1/11)

5433 Nelson, Marilyn. *Ostrich and Lark* (K–3). Illus. 2012, Boyds Mills $16.95 (978-1-59078-702-1). 32pp. In a brightly portrayed African desert Lark and other birds sing happily while Ostrich has no voice until rains end a drought; the illustrations are done by members of the San artists of the Kuru Project of Botswana. (Rev: BL 12/1/12; LMC 5–6/13; SLJ 9/12)

5434 Nelson, Marilyn. *Snook Alone* (K–3). Illus. by Timothy Basil Ering. 2010, Candlewick $16.99 (978-0-7636-2667-9). 48pp. A monk, Abba Jacob, and his loyal and devoted terrier Snook become separated during a storm in this emotive story. Lexile AD890L (Rev: BL 6/10*; HB 1–2/11; LMC 11–12/10; SLJ 10/1/10*)

5435 Newman, Lesléa. *The Best Cat in the World* (PS–2). Illus. by Ronald Himler. 2004, Eerdmans $16.00 (978-0-8028-5252-6). 32pp. Mourning for his dead cat Charlie, Victor is reluctant to bring a new kitten into his life. (Rev: BL 1/1–15/04; SLJ 2/04)

5436 Newton, Jill. *Crash Bang Donkey!* (PS–2). Illus. by author. 2010, Whitman $16.99 (978-0-8075-1330-9). 32pp. Farmer Gruff is wakened from his badly needed slumber by a rambunctious musical donkey in this rhythmic story in which the pair finally find mutual benefits in a life together. (Rev: BL 2/1/10; SLJ 2/1/10)

5437 Niland, Deborah. *Annie's Chair* (PS–K). Illus. by author. 2006, Walker $16.95 (978-0-8027-8082-9). Annie initially has a very big problem when she finds the dog sitting in her special chair, but a kindly lick reminds her how to share. (Rev: SLJ 6/06)

5438 Nodset, Joan L. *Come Back, Cat* (PS–2). Illus. by Steven Kellogg. 2008, HarperCollins $16.99 (978-0-06-028081-9). 40pp. It takes some doing, but a little girl finally succeeds in making friends with a jumpy cat; originally published in 1973, this edition has new mixed-media illustrations. (Rev: BLO 8/28/08)

5439 Nolan, Lucy. *Bad to the Bone* (1–3). Illus. by Mike Reed. Series: Down Girl and Sit. 2008, Marshall Cavendish $14.99 (978-0-7614-5439-7). 64pp. A funny dog's-eye view of life, featuring Down Girl, her best friend Sit, and their efforts to train their humans. (Rev: BL 11/15/08; SLJ 1/09)

5440 North, Sherry. *Champ's Story: Dogs Get Cancer Too!* (1–3). Illus. by Kathleen Rietz. 2010, Sylvan Dell $16.95 (978-1-60718-077-7); paper $8.95 (978-1-60718-088-3). 32pp. Cody sees his dog through treatment for cancer, and then Champ in turn provides care and comfort to Cody after he hurts his ankle. ℮ (Rev: LMC 1–2/11; SLJ 10/1/10)

5441 Noullet, Georgette. *Bed Hog* (PS–1). Illus. by David Slonim. 2011, Marshall Cavendish $12.99 (978-0-7614-5823-4). 24pp. A sweet-eyed beagle goes padding from one bed to another, looking for space to settle down;

eventually he finds it in a young boy's room. (Rev: BL 4/15/11; SLJ 4/11)

5442 Numeroff, Laura. *What Puppies Do Best* (PS–2). Illus. by Lynn Munsinger. 2011, Chronicle $14.99 (978-0-8118-6601-9). Unpaged. This simple book showcases life as a puppy — chasing balls, digging holes, learning to sit, giving and getting kisses. (Rev: SLJ 10/1/11)

5443 Oates, Joyce Carol. *Naughty Chérie!* (PS–K). Illus. by Mark Graham. 2008, HarperCollins $16.99 (978-0-06-074358-1). After a visit to an animal "kinder-care," Little Chérie, a naughty kitten, learns to be better behaved and returns to her happy family. (Rev: BL 12/15/07; SLJ 1/08)

5444 Ochiltree, Dianne. *Pillow Pup* (PS–1). Illus. by Mireille D'Allance. 2002, Simon & Schuster $14.95 (978-0-689-83408-0). 32pp. Puppy Maggie and her owner enjoy a friendly pillow fight. (Rev: BL 5/15/02; HBG 10/02)

5445 O'Connell, Caitlin. *A Baby Elephant in the Wild* (K–3). Illus. by author. 2014, Houghton Mifflin $16.99 (978-054414944-1). 40pp. A lovely photo-essay about elephants in the Namibian desert, focusing on a baby called Liza. (Rev: BL 3/1/14; HB 3–4/14; LMC 8–9/14; SLJ 3/14) [599.67]

5446 O'Connor, Jane, and Jessie Hartland. *The Perfect Puppy for Me!* (1–3). Illus. by Jessie Hartland. 2003, Viking $15.99 (978-0-670-03614-1). A young boy who loves dogs researches the breeds that will be available on his birthday, conveying lots of information along with the endearing story. (Rev: BL 5/15/03; HBG 10/03; SLJ 7/03)

5447 O'Connor, Sandra Day. *Finding Susie* (PS–2). Illus. by Tom Pohrt. 2009, Knopf $16.99 (978-0-375-84103-3). 40pp. Longing for a pet, Sandra takes in a number of wild animals and then sets them free before deciding that what she needs is a dog; based on the childhood of the Supreme Court justice. (Rev: BLO 6/23/09; SLJ 5/09)

5448 O'Hair, Margaret. *My Kitten* (K–2). Illus. by Tammie Lyon. 2011, Marshall Cavendish $15.99 (978-0-7614-5811-1). 32pp. A little girl describes and sometimes imitates her kitten's behavior in this well-illustrated book. (Rev: BL 5/1/11; SLJ 5/1/11)

5449 O'Hair, Margaret. *My Pup* (PS). Illus. by Tammie Lyon. 2008, Marshall Cavendish $14.99 (978-0-7614-5389-5). 32pp. A little girl and her puppy pass a happy day together in this simple read-aloud with lots of repetition. (Rev: BL 4/1/08; SLJ 6/08)

5450 Ohora, Zachariah. *Stop Snoring, Bernard!* (PS–2). Illus. by author. 2011, Henry Holt $16.99 (978-0-8050-9002-4). 32pp. An otter with a snoring problem is banished by his peers at the zoo and tries unsuccessfully to find somewhere else to sleep; eventually the other otters realize they miss him and welcome him back. Lexile AD370L (Rev: BL 4/1/11; LMC 5–6/11; SLJ 3/1/11)

5451 Oliver, Narelle. *Twilight Hunt: A Seek-and-Find Book* (PS–K). Illus. by author. 2007, Star Bright $16.95 (978-1-59572-107-5). 33pp. As a mother screech owl sets out on her evening hunt to feed her babies, the il-

lustrations clearly show the challenges she faces. (Rev: SLJ 12/07)

5452 Page, Gail. *How to Be a Good Dog* (PS–2). Illus. by author. 2006, Bloomsbury $15.95 (978-1-58234-683-0). Bobo wants to be a good dog, so the cat teaches him how to behave, with mixed results. (Rev: SLJ 6/06)

5453 Park, Linda Sue. *Mung-Mung: A Foldout Book of Animal Sounds* (PS). Illus. by Diane Bigda. 2004, Charlesbridge $9.95 (978-1-57091-486-7). This guessing game for preschoolers involves animal sounds in several languages — first the onomatopoeic sound in lettering, then, overleaf, a drawing of the animal who makes it. (Rev: SLJ 6/04) [418]

5454 Parker, Marjorie Blain. *Jasper's Day* (1–3). Illus. by Janet Wilson. 2002, Kids Can $15.95 (978-1-55074-957-1). A touching but realistic story of a family's last day with their pet dog, before he is put to sleep. (Rev: BL 12/15/02; HBG 3/03; SLJ 1/03)

5455 Partridge, Elizabeth. *Big Cat Pepper* (K–3). Illus. by Lauren Castillo. 2009, Bloomsbury $16.99 (978-1-59990-024-7). 32pp. Pepper the cat becomes ill and dies in this story about loss. (Rev: BL 4/15/09; SLJ 6/09)

5456 Pelley, Kathleen T. *Raj the Bookstore Tiger* (K–3). Illus. by Paige Keiser. 2011, Charlesbridge $15.95 (978-1-58089-230-8). 32pp. Raj, a bookstore cat who thinks he's a tiger, copes with injured self-esteem when a new employee's pet insists he's a "plain old kitty cat." Lexile AD740L (Rev: BL 2/15/11; SLJ 3/1/11)

5457 Perrow, Angeli. *Lighthouse Dog to the Rescue* (K–3). Illus. by Emily Harris. 2000, Down East $14.95 (978-0-89272-487-1). Based on a real incident in Maine during the 1930s, a dog that lives in a lighthouse brings a mail boat's captain safely home during a terrible blizzard. (Rev: BL 3/1/01; HBG 10/01)

5458 Peters, Lisa Westberg. *Frankie Works the Night Shift* (PS–K). Illus. by Jennifer Taylor. 2010, Greenwillow $16.99 (978-0-06-009095-1). 32pp. Frankie the cat chases mice for a living in this funny story with a strong counting component. (Rev: BL 4/15/10; SLJ 2/1/10)

5459 Pfeffer, Wendy. *Mallard Duck at Meadow View Pond* (PS–3). Illus. by Taylor Oughton. Series: Smithsonian Backyard. 2001, Smithsonian Institution $15.95 (978-1-56899-956-2). 32pp. This fictional story about a duck focuses on true facts about the animal's life and habitat. (Rev: BL 2/1/02)

5460 Pichon, Liz. *Penguins* (PS–K). Illus. by author. 2008, Scholastic $12.99 (978-0-545-02215-6). 24pp. Penguins at the zoo find a camera and have a wonderful time mugging for it. (Rev: BL 9/1/08)

5461 Pierce, Terry. *Blackberry Banquet* (K–3). Illus. by Lisa Downey. 2008, Sylvan Dell $16.95 (978-1-934359-70-9); paper $8.95 (978-1-934359-28-0). 32pp. Forest animals feast on wild blackberries — until the bear comes; a "For Creative Minds" section features interesting facts. (Rev: LMC 11/08; SLJ 9/08)

5462 Pilkey, Dav. *Dogzilla* (K–3). Illus. 1993, Harcourt paper $7.00 (978-0-15-223945-9). 32pp. Using retouched photos of the author's pets as illustrations, this zany story tells of Dreadful Dogzilla, whose breath could send everyone running. Also use *Kat Kong* (1993). (Rev: BL 9/1/93; SLJ 12/93)

5463 Pinfold, Levi. *Black Dog* (K–2). Illus. by author. 2012, Candlewick $15.99 (978-0-7636-6097-0). 32pp. A gigantic black dog terrorizes the members of a timid family, except for the youngest child, in whose fearless presence it shrinks to a normal size and is invited inside. Boston Globe–Horn Book Honor 2013; ALA Notable Children's Book. Lexile AD530L (Rev: BL 11/1/12*; HB 9–10/12; LMC 1–2/13; SLJ 9/12)

5464 Pitzer, Susanna. *Not Afraid of Dogs* (PS–2). Illus. by Larry Day. 2006, Walker $16.95 (978-0-8027-8067-6). 32pp. Daniel is not scared of dogs although he does everything he can to avoid them, but when he finds his visiting aunt's dog cowering in the bathroom during a thunderstorm, he can't resist offering comfort. (Rev: BL 6/1–15/06; SLJ 7/06*)

5465 Poppenhäger, Nicole. *Snow Leopards* (K–3). Trans. from German by J. Alison James. Illus. by Ivan Gantschev. 2006, North-South $15.95 (978-0-7358-2087-6). Two young snow leopards separated by an avalanche search for each other and are eventually reunited; a moving story with dramatic artwork. (Rev: SLJ 11/06)

5466 Postgate, Daniel. *Smelly Bill* (PS–2). Illus. by author. 2007, North-South $16.95 (978-0-7358-2135-4). Great Aunt Bleach manages to catch and bathe a very dirty dog named Bill, but only after a messy battle described in humorous rhyme. (Rev: SLJ 8/07)

5467 Prince, Joshua. *I Saw an Ant on the Railroad Track* (PS–1). Illus. by Macky Pamintuan. 2006, Sterling $14.95 (978-1-4027-2183-0). 24pp. Jack, a brawny switchman, tries to avoid a collision between an oncoming train and an ant that's on the tracks. (Rev: BL 2/1/06; SLJ 7/06)

5468 Prosek, James. *Bird, Butterfly, Eel* (K–3). Illus. by author. 2009, Simon & Schuster $16.99 (978-0-689-86829-0). 40pp. This nicely illustrated volume follows the long migratory journeys of a monarch butterfly, a barn swallow, and an eel. (Rev: BL 1/1–15/09; SLJ 2/09)

5469 Provensen, Alice. *A Day in the Life of Murphy* (PS–2). Illus. by author. 2003, Simon & Schuster $16.95 (978-0-689-84884-1). Murphy, a fun-loving terrier who lives on a farm, describes a typical day in his life. (Rev: BL 5/15/03; HB 7/03; HBG 10/03; SLJ 7/03)

5470 Radunsky, Vladimir. *You?* (PS–2). Illus. by author. 2009, Harcourt $16.00 (978-0-15-205177-8). 40pp. A little girl who wants a dog meets a little dog who wants a girl. (Rev: BL 5/15/09; SLJ 6/09)

5471 Raff, Courtney Granet. *Giant of the Sea: A Story of a Sperm Whale* (PS–2). Illus. by Shawn Gould. 2002, Soundprints $4.95 (978-1-931465-72-4); paper $6.95 (978-1-931465-80-9). 32pp. A fictional look at the behavior, diet, and habitat of a mother sperm whale and her young, with attractive illustrations that often show the animal's perspective. (Rev: BL 2/1/03)

5472 Rammell, S. Kelly. *City Beats: A Hip-Hoppy Pigeon Poem* (PS–2). Illus. by Jeanette Canyon. 2006,

Dawn $16.95 (978-1-58469-076-4); paper $8.95 (978-1-58469-077-1). A hip-hop-style poem describes a city pigeon's life from dawn to dusk. (Rev: SLJ 8/06)

5473 Rand, Gloria. *Little Flower* (PS–1). Illus. by R. W. Alley. 2002, Holt $16.95 (978-0-8050-6480-3). 32pp. Miss Pearl takes a fall and is saved in a unique way by her potbellied pig, Little Flower. (Rev: BL 3/15/02; HBG 10/02; SLJ 8/02)

5474 Rand, Gloria. *Mary Was a Little Lamb* (PS–1). Illus. by Ted Rand. 2004, Holt $16.95 (978-0-8050-6816-0). 32pp. Based on truth, this is the story of a lovable lamb named Mary who becomes such a distraction that she is banished to a petting zoo. (Rev: BL 4/15/04; SLJ 6/04)

5475 Rankin, Laura. *Fluffy and Baron* (PS–1). Illus. by author. 2006, Dial $16.99 (978-0-8037-2953-7). The story of an unlikely friendship between a large dog and a wild duck, with beautiful illustrations. (Rev: SLJ 7/06)

5476 Raschka, Chris. *Hip Hop Dog* (PS–2). Illus. by Vladimir Radunsky. 2010, HarperCollins $16.99 (978-0-06-123963-2). 32pp. An unwanted urban dog turns street-smart and learns to rap in this positive, colorful book about making the best of a bad situation. (Rev: BL 1/1/10; HB 3–4/10; SLJ 3/1/10)

5477 Rathmann, Peggy. *Officer Buckle and Gloria* (PS–2). Illus. 1995, Penguin $16.99 (978-0-399-22616-8). 32pp. A police dog named Gloria steals the show when Officer Buckle gives a presentation on safety to local school children. Caldecott Medal winner, 1996. (Rev: BCCB 10/95; BL 11/1/95*; HB 11/95; HBG 4/04; SLJ 9/95*)

5478 Ravishankar, Anushka. *Elephants Never Forget!* (PS–K). Illus. by Christiane Pieper. 2008, Houghton $16.00 (978-8-1862-1104-5). 32pp. A young elephant is separated from his family in a storm and finds a new home with a herd of water buffalo but later must make a difficult decision. (Rev: BL 6/1–15/08; HB 3/08)

5479 Raye, Rebekah. *Bear-ly There* (1–3). Illus. by author. 2009, Tilbury $16.95 (978-0-88448-314-4). 32pp. Young Charlie and his family work together to discourage a bear from invading their territory in this well-illustrated novel. (Rev: BL 1/1/10; SLJ 2/1/10)

5480 Raye, Rebekah. *The Very Best Bed* (PS–2). Illus. by author. 2006, Tilbury House $16.95 (978-0-88448-284-0). A squirrel searching for the perfect place to sleep tries out various other animals' solutions. (Rev: SLJ 1/07)

5481 Rayner, Catherine. *Harris Finds His Feet* (PS–2). Illus. by author. 2008, Good Bks. $16.95 (978-1-56148-616-8). 28pp. Worried about his large feet, young hare Harris consults his grandfather and learns all the advantages of these appendages. (Rev: BL 6/1–15/08; SLJ 8/08)

5482 Reed, Lynn Rowe. *Basil's Birds* (PS–1). Illus. by author. 2010, Marshall Cavendish $17.99 (978-0-7614-5627-8). 32pp. Birds build a nest on school janitor Basil's head, and he becomes quite devoted to the little hatchlings. (Rev: BL 5/15/10; SLJ 3/1/10)

5483 Reed, Lynn Rowe. *Roscoe and the Pelican Rescue* (PS–2). Illus. by author. 2011, Holiday House $14.95

(978-0-8234-2352-1). 32pp. A young boy's trip to the beach is spoiled by the Deepwater Horizon drilling disaster but his work rescuing oil-covered pelicans and other creatures is rewarding. Lexile AD810L (Rev: BL 6/1/11; LMC 11–12/11; SLJ 7/11)

5484 Reynolds, Cynthia Furlong. *The Far-Flung Adventures of Homer the Hummer* (1–3). Illus. by Catherine McClung. 2005, Mitten $17.95 (978-1-58726-269-2). 32pp. In the spring a ruby-throated hummingbird called Homer leaves the jungles of Costa Rica on a long and dangerous journey north to the United States, where he meets a female called Ruby in an artist's garden. (Rev: BL 9/1/05; SLJ 12/05)

5485 Richardson, Justin, and Peter Parnell. *And Tango Makes Three* (PS–2). Illus. by Henry Cole. 2005, Simon & Schuster $14.95 (978-0-689-87845-9). 32pp. This warm story of two male penguins who prefer each other's company to that of females and who together raise a chick called Tango is based on a true story. (Rev: BL 5/15/05)

5486 Richardson, Justin, and Peter Parnell. *Christian, the Hugging Lion* (K–3). Illus. by Amy June Bates. 2010, Simon & Schuster $16.99 (978-1-4169-8662-1). Unpaged. Tells the story of Ace and John, who buy a lion at Harrods department store in London and raise it in an apartment until it becomes too big and must be moved to Kenya; based on a true story. (Rev: LMC 8–9/10; SLJ 6/1/10)

5487 Ritz, Karen. *Windows with Birds* (PS–2). Illus. by author. 2010, Boyds Mills $16.95 (978-1-59078-656-7). 32pp. A cat learns to adjust to his new surroundings when his family moves from a large house to an apartment. (Rev: BL 2/15/10; LMC 8–9/10; SLJ 3/1/10)

5488 Roberton, Fiona. *Wanted: The Perfect Pet* (PS–3). Illus. by author. 2010, Putnam $16.99 (978-0-399-25461-1). 32pp. A lonely duck answers a little boy's ad seeking canine companionship, and the two manage to get on surprisingly well. (Rev: BL 7/10; LMC 10/10; SLJ 7/1/10)

5489 Robey, Katharine Crawford. *Where's the Party?* (PS–2). Illus. by Kate Endle. 2011, Charlesbridge $15.95 (978-1-58089-268-1); paper $6.95 (978-1-58089-269-8). 32pp. Kate wakes to birdsong announcing a "Par-ty!" and follows the sounds to a brook where there are new ducklings; includes information on the 10 birds featured. (Rev: BLO 8/11; SLJ 6/11)

5490 Rockwell, Anne. *Backyard Bear* (PS–2). Illus. by Megan Halsey. 2006, Walker $15.95 (978-0-8027-9573-1). A young bear finds itself roaming through a human neighborhood in this realistic story about the effects of development on animal habitats. (Rev: BL 10/15/06; SLJ 10/06)

5491 Root, Phyllis. *Flip, Flap, Fly!* (PS). Illus. by David Walker. 2009, Candlewick $14.99 (978-0-7636-3109-3). 32pp. A procession of baby animals demonstrate how they move as they spot other baby animals all around. (Rev: BL 4/15/09; HB 5/09; SLJ 5/09)

5492 Root, Phyllis. *Looking for a Moose* (PS–K). Illus. by Randy Cecil. 2006, Candlewick $15.99 (978-0-7636-2005-9). 32pp. Bouncy text and appealing hide-and-seek illustrations follow a group of children on an adventurous search for an elusive moose. (Rev: BL 10/1/06; SLJ 10/06)

5493 Root, Phyllis. *Scrawny Cat* (PS–2). Illus. by Alison Friend. 2011, Candlewick $16.99 (978-0-7636-4164-1). Unpaged. A scared and lonely stray cat finds a new home with a woman who is also lonely. (Rev: HB 11–12/11; SLJ 12/1/11)

5494 Rosenthal, Eileen. *I'll Save You Bobo!* (PS–1). Illus. by Marc Rosenthal. 2012, Atheneum $14.99 (978-1-4424-0378-9). 40pp. Willy (a boy) is fed up with his pesky cat Earl and writes a jungle story featuring his stuffed monkey Bobo facing many dangers, but this exercise proves salutary and the two come to an understanding. **e** (Rev: BLO 2/15/12; SLJ 4/1/12*)

5495 Rostoker-Gruber, Karen. *Bandit* (PS–1). Illus. by Vincent Nguyen. 2008, Marshall Cavendish $15.99 (978-0-7614-5382-6). 40pp. Moved against his will to a new house, Bandit the cat returns immediately to the old one only to find that new people are living there; all turns out well in this humorous and well illustrated story. (Rev: BL 5/15/08; SLJ 5/08)

5496 Rostoker-Gruber, Karen. *Bandit's Surprise* (PS–1). Illus. by Vincent Nguyen. 2010, Marshall Cavendish $16.99 (978-0-7614-5623-0). 32pp. Bandit the cat copes with change when his owner brings home a fuzzy gray kitten. (Rev: BL 4/1/10; SLJ 3/1/10*)

5497 Rostoker-Gruber, Karen. *Ferret Fun* (PS–1). Illus. by Paul Rátz de Tagyos. 2011, Marshall Cavendish $17.99 (978-0-7614-5817-3). 32pp. Two ferrets, Fudge and Einstein, are frightened of a visiting house cat, but Marvel turns out to be OK and even has useful talents. (Rev: BL 3/15/11; LMC 8–9/11; SLJ 4/11*)

5498 Rostoker-Gruber, Karen. *Rooster Can't Cock-a-Doodle-Doo* (PS–2). Illus. by Paul Rátz de Tagyos. 2004, Dial $15.99 (978-0-8037-2877-6). All the animals band together to wake Farmer Ted when the rooster has a sore throat. (Rev: HB 7/04; SLJ 7/04)

5499 Ruelle, Karen Gray. *Bark Park* (PS–2). Illus. by author. 2008, Peachtree $15.95 (978-1-56145-434-1). Dogs of all kinds congregate at the dog park, described in simple rhymes and bright collages. (Rev: BL 4/1/08; SLJ 5/08)

5500 Ruepp, Krista. *Anna's Prince* (K–3). Trans. from German by J. Alison James. Illus. by Ulrike Heyne. 2006, North-South $15.95 (978-0-7358-2081-4). Young Anna trains her beloved pony, Prince, to carry a rider in this sequel, set in Iceland, to *Winter Pony* (2002) and *Runaway Pony* (2005). (Rev: SLJ 11/06)

5501 Ruepp, Krista. *Runaway Pony* (PS–2). Illus. by Ulrike Heyne. 2005, North-South $15.95 (978-0-7358-1985-6). 32pp. Anna's pony, Prince, is back home from the herd, but Anna must work to regain his trust when he is spooked by a loud tractor in this sequel to *The Winter Pony* (2002). (Rev: BL 6/1–15/05)

5502 Ruiz, Emilio. *Waluk* (2–4). Illus. by Ana Miralles. 2013, Lerner LB $26.65 (978-146771598-0); paper $7.95 (9781467716062). 56pp. Waluk, an abandoned polar bear cub, learns about the effects of global warming and the dangers of humans from his mentor, Manitok, an older polar bear who one day gets caught in a human trap, leaving Waluk to find a way to rescue him. ALA Notable Children's Book. **e** (Rev: BL 11/15/13; LMC 5–6/14)

5503 Rumford, James. *Chee-Lin: A Giraffe's Journey* (1–3). Illus. by author. 2008, Houghton $17.00 (978-0-618-71720-0). 40pp. This vividly imagined story follows an East African giraffe who survives a dangerous trip to China and finally lands in the emperor's palace; inspired by a 15th-century Chinese painting. (Rev: BL 9/15/08)

5504 Rylant, Cynthia. *The Bookshop Dog* (PS–K). Illus. 1996, Scholastic $17.99 (978-0-590-54331-6). 40pp. A dog named Martha Jane becomes the mascot at her owner's bookshop. (Rev: BL 9/1/96; SLJ 9/96)

5505 Rylant, Cynthia. *Cat Heaven* (PS–3). Illus. 1997, Scholastic $16.95 (978-0-590-10054-0). 40pp. A picture book about activities in cat heaven. (Rev: BL 9/1/97; HBG 3/98; SLJ 10/97)

5506 Sabates, Berta Garcia, and Merce Segarra. *Let's Take Care of Our New Hamster* (PS–2). Trans. by Sally-Ann Hopwood. Illus. by Rosa M. Curto. Series: Let's Take Care of. 2008, Barron's paper $6.99 (978-0-7641-3872-0). 32pp. A family brings home a new hamster in this fictional story that provides plenty of useful information on the care of these pets. (Rev: BL 4/15/08; SLJ 7/08)

5507 Sáez Castán, Javier. *The Three Hedgehogs* (K–3). Illus. by Javier Saez Caston. 2004, Groundwood $15.95 (978-0-88899-595-7). 32pp. In this colorfully illustrated tale told in two acts, three hungry hedgehogs steal apples from an orchard and must undergo a trial. (Rev: SLJ 7/04)

5508 Salerno, Steven. *Little Tumbo* (PS–2). Illus. by author. 2003, Marshall Cavendish $14.95 (978-0-7614-5136-5). Little Tumbo is a very small elephant and his squeaks initially fail to raise an alarm, but when he is captured for a second time he manages a full-blown trumpet. (Rev: HBG 4/04; SLJ 12/03)

5509 Saltzberg, Barney. *I Love Cats* (PS). Illus. by author. 2005, Candlewick $8.99 (978-0-7636-2588-7). Good reasons to love cats, in rhyming text with sweet illustrations. (Rev: SLJ 8/05)

5510 Saltzberg, Barney. *I Love Dogs* (PS). Illus. by author. 2005, Candlewick $8.99 (978-0-7636-2587-0). Good reasons to love dogs, in rhyming text with sweet illustrations. (Rev: SLJ 8/05)

5511 Samuels, Barbara. *The Trucker* (PS–K). Illus. by author. 2010, Farrar $16.99 (978-0-374-37804-2). 40pp. Disappointed to receive a cat instead of the toy truck he wants, vehicle-obsessed Leo quickly discovers his new pet is actually the best play companion ever. (Rev: BL 4/15/10; SLJ 5/1/10*)

5512 Sayre, April Pulley. *Eat like a Bear* (PS–3). Illus. by Steve Jenkins. 2013, Henry Holt $16.99 (978-080509039-0). 32pp. A grizzly bear wakes from hibernation, spends months eating to build up her strength, and in November heads back to her den and the birth of two cubs. ALA Notable Children's Book. **e** (Rev: BL 11/1/13; HB 11–12/13; LMC 1–2/14*; SLJ 10/13)

5513 Sayre, April Pulley. *If You're Hoppy* (PS–1). Illus. by Jackie Urbanovic. 2011, Greenwillow $16.99 (978-0-06-156634-9). 40pp. A rhyming twist on "If You're Happy and You Know It," presenting animals that are hoppy, floppy, flappy, slimy, and so forth. (Rev: BL 3/1/11; SLJ 1/1/11)

5514 Scamell, Ragnhild. *Wish Come True Cat* (K–2). Illus. by Gaby Hansen. 2001, Barron's $13.95 (978-0-7641-5392-1). A little girl comes to love a scruffy cat who turns up after she had wished for a cute kitten. (Rev: HBG 3/02; SLJ 1/02)

5515 Schachner, Judy. *Skippyjon Jones* (K–3). Illus. by author. 2003, Dutton $15.99 (978-0-525-47134-9). Young readers will fall in love with Skippyjon Jones, a rambunctious Siamese kitten who would rather play at being a bird or dog than accept his true identity as a cat. (Rev: HBG 4/04; SLJ 1/04)

5516 Schaefer, Lola M. *Arrowhawk* (2–3). Illus. by Gabi Swiatkowska. 2004, Holt $16.95 (978-0-8050-6371-4). Based on real events, this is a beautifully illustrated story, told from the bird's point of view, of a young red-tailed hawk that was nursed back to health after being shot by an arrow. (Rev: BL 5/15/04; SLJ 5/04)

5517 Schertle, Alice. *Very Hairy Bear* (PS–K). Illus. by Matt Phelan. 2007, Harcourt $16.00 (978-0-15-216568-0). 32pp. A big, brown, hairy bear (apart from his nose) frolics through the seasons before settling down for the winter. (Rev: BCCB 12/07; BL 10/1/07; SLJ 12/07)

5518 Schmid, Paul. *A Pet for Petunia* (PS–2). Illus. by author. 2011, HarperCollins $12.99 (978-0-06-196331-5). 40pp. Petunia is obsessed with her stuffed toy skunk and determined to have a real one, despite her parents' adamant refusals. (Rev: BL 5/1/11; SLJ 5/1/11*)

5519 Schmidt, Karen Lee. *Carl's Nose* (PS–2). Illus. by author. 2006, Harcourt $16.00 (978-0-15-205049-8). Carl the dog has a nose for bad weather and provides reliable forecasts to the citizens of Grimsville until the climate suddenly turns sunny and he must seek a new occupation, now using his nose to search for lost souls. (Rev: SLJ 11/06)

5520 Schoenherr, Ian. *Cat and Mouse* (PS–2). Illus. by author. 2008, HarperCollins $16.99 (978-0-06-136313-9). 40pp. A friendship between Cat and Mouse explodes into animated cat and mouse play. (Rev: SLJ 9/08)

5521 Schulman, Janet. *A Bunny for All Seasons* (PS–K). Illus. by Meilo So. 2003, Knopf $9.95 (978-0-375-82256-8). 32pp. A gentle story of a bunny enjoying a wonderful garden full of food, meeting another rabbit, getting cozy for the winter, and the pair returning to the garden with their young in the spring. (Rev: BL 3/1/03; HBG 10/03; SLJ 2/03)

5522 Scillian, Devin. *Memoirs of a Hamster* (K–3). Illus. by Tim Bowers. 2013, Sleeping Bear $15.99 (978-1-58536-831-0). 32pp. A hamster named Seymour tempted out of his cage by an evil cat is glad to escape with his life and be ensconced back in his home. (Rev: BLO 6/13; SLJ 7/13)

5523 Seeger, Laura Vaccaro. *Dog and Bear* (PS–K). Illus. 2007, Roaring Brook $12.95 (978-1-59643-053-2). 32pp. Three simple stories with minimal text depict the friendship between Dog, a fun-loving dachshund, and Bear, a stuffed animal. (Rev: BCCB 6/07; BL 3/15/07; HB 5/07; HBG 10/07; LMC 8/07)

5524 Segal, John. *The Lonely Moose* (PS–2). Illus. by author. 2007, Hyperion $15.99 (978-1-4231-0173-4). Used to a life by himself, Moose helps Bird, who has fallen into the lake, and the two learn to enjoy each other's friendship. (Rev: BL 11/1/07; LMC 11/07; SLJ 10/07)

5525 Seymour, Tres. *Hunting the White Cow* (PS–3). Illus. by Wendy A. Halperin. 1993, Orchard LB $17.99 (978-0-531-08646-9). 32pp. After a white cow has escaped from the farm, several people try unsuccessfully to catch her. (Rev: BCCB 10/93; BL 9/1/93; HB 11/93; SLJ 12/93*)

5526 Shannon, David. *Good Boy, Fergus!* (K–2). Illus. 2006, Scholastic $15.99 (978-0-439-49027-6). 40pp. West Highland terrier Fergus has a great day, encouraged in his chasing and scratching and munching by his young master. (Rev: BL 1/1–15/06; SLJ 3/06)

5527 Shaw, Nancy. *Raccoon Tune* (PS–2). Illus. by Howard Fine. 2003, Holt $15.95 (978-0-8050-6544-2). A family of raccoons have a splendid (and noisy) time raiding trash cans and feasting on a surprise haul of trout. (Rev: HBG 10/03; SLJ 7/03)

5528 Sherry, Kevin. *Acorns Everywhere!* (PS). Illus. by author. 2009, Dial $16.99 (978-0-8037-3256-8). 32pp. A manic squirrel feverishly gathers and buries acorns, and then has trouble remembering where he hid them. (Rev: BL 9/15/09; SLJ 10/1/09)

5529 Shields, Gillian. *DogFish* (PS–2). Illus. by Dan Taylor. 2008, Atheneum $16.99 (978-1-4169-7127-6). 32pp. A little boy who really wants a dog learns to make the most out of his goldfish. (Rev: BL 11/15/08; SLJ 12/08)

5530 Sillifant, Alec. *Farmer Ham* (K–3). Illus. by Mike Spoor. 2007, North-South $15.95 (978-0-7358-2134-7). 24pp. This farmer is not as silly as the crows think he is. (Rev: SLJ 10/07)

5531 Simmons, Jane. *Ebb and Flo and the Baby Seal* (PS–2). Illus. 2002, Simon & Schuster $16.00 (978-0-689-84368-6). 32pp. A dog named Ebb helps reunite a baby seal with its mother. (Rev: BL 1/1–15/02; HBG 10/02; SLJ 3/02*)

5532 Simont, Marc. *The Stray Dog* (PS–3). Illus. 2001, HarperCollins LB $17.89 (978-0-06-028934-8). 32pp. A family goes back to a picnic ground to bring home the stray dog they saw the week before in this tender animal story. Caldecott Honor Book, 2002. (Rev: BCCB 3/01; BL 1/1–15/01; HBG 10/01; SLJ 2/01)

5533 Singer, Marilyn. *What Is Your Dog Doing?* (PS–1). Illus. by Kathleen Habbley. 2011, Atheneum $12.99 (978-1-4169-7931-9). 32pp. Simple wordplay and rhymed text add appeal to this book depicting dogs of all different walks of life. ℮ (Rev: BL 7/11; SLJ 6/11)

5534 Siomades, Lorianne. *Katy Did It!* (PS–2). Illus. by author. 2009, Boyds Mills $16.95 (978-1-59078-602-4). An overly energetic katydid named Katy has an annoying little brother who blames everything on her, but his cry of "Katy did it!" is finally appropriately pleasing. (Rev: BLO 5/15/09; SLJ 3/09)

5535 Sloat, Teri. *I'm a Duck!* (PS–2). Illus. 2006, Putnam $15.99 (978-0-399-24274-8). 32pp. A happy duck celebrates its duck-ness and in the process introduces readers to its life cycle. (Rev: BL 3/1/06; SLJ 2/06)

5536 Slonim, David. *Patch* (PS–2). Illus. by author. 2013, Roaring Brook $15.99 (978-1-59643-643-5). 32pp. Rabbits, fleas, and a pet contest are featured in three vignettes about a boy and his dog. (Rev: BL 7/13; SLJ 7/13)

5537 Smath, Jerry. *Sammy Salami* (PS–2). Illus. by author. 2007, Abrams $18.95 (978-0-8109-9350-1). A story about a salami-loving cat and his adventures in pursuit of his owner Pete, who has departed on vacation. (Rev: BL 1/1–15/08; SLJ 10/07)

5538 Smith, Linda. *Mrs. Crump's Cat* (2–4). Illus. by David Roberts. 2006, HarperCollins $16.99 (978-0-06-028302-5). When a stray cat shows up on her porch, the life of cranky Mrs. Crump takes a turn for the better. (Rev: SLJ 4/06)

5539 Smith, Maggie. *Desser the Best Ever Cat* (PS–1). Illus. 2001, Knopf $14.95 (978-0-375-81056-5). 32pp. An engaging picture book arranged like a scrapbook of memories that tells the life story of a family's beloved cat from the day he was adopted as a stray. (Rev: BL 2/15/01; HBG 10/01)

5540 Spinelli, Eileen. *Do You Have a Dog?* (K–2). Illus. by Geraldo Valerio. 2011, Eerdmans $16 (978-0-8028-5387-5). 26pp. Eleven historical figures and their dogs are portrayed in this light blend of history and canine affection told in rhyme. (Rev: BLO 10/15/11; LMC 3–4/12; SLJ 11/1/11)

5541 Spinelli, Eileen. *Hero Cat* (PS–2). Illus. by Jo Ellen McAllister Stammen. 2006, Marshall Cavendish $16.95 (978-0-7614-5223-2). 32pp. A mother cat rescues her kittens from a fire in this story based on truth. (Rev: BL 3/1/06; SLJ 4/06)

5542 Spirin, Gennady. *Martha* (PS–K). Illus. by author. 2005, Philomel $15.99 (978-0-399-23980-9). Spirin's son brings to their home in Moscow a crow with a broken wing and insists that they keep it alive. (Rev: BCCB 4/05; BL 7/05; SLJ 4/05)

5543 Springett, Martin. *Kate and Pippin: An Unlikely Love Story* (PS–2). Illus. by Isobel Springett. 2012, Henry Holt $16.99 (978-080509487-9). 32pp. This moving true story documents with appealing photographs the relationship between a Great Dane named Kate and an abandoned fawn. ℮ Lexile AD830L (Rev: BL 9/1/12; SLJ 4/12)

5544 Stainton, Sue. *I Love Cats* (PS–1). Illus. by Anne Mortimer. 2007, HarperCollins $15.99 (978-0-06-085154-5). 24pp. A colorful celebration of cats of all kinds. (Rev: BL 3/15/07; SLJ 3/07)

5545 Stanley, Mandy. *What Do You Do?* (PS). Illus. by author. 2005, Simon & Schuster $7.99 (978-1-4169-0499-1). A number of animals answer the title's question in this book, which is similar to the author's *What Do You Say?* (2003). (Rev: SLJ 7/05)

5546 Stein, David Ezra. *Leaves* (PS–1). Illus. by author. 2007, Putnam $15.99 (978-0-399-24636-4). What's a young bear to think when the leaves start falling off the trees? Simple text and lovely illustrations follow him through the changes of season. (Rev: BL 9/1/07; SLJ 8/07)

5547 Stein, David Ezra. *Ned's New Friend* (PS–2). Illus. by author. 2007, Simon & Schuster $14.99 (978-1-4169-2490-6). 32pp. Jealous at first of Cowboy Ned's new lady friend, Andy the horse soon realizes that he and Ned will always be friends. (Rev: BL 6/1–15/07; SLJ 11/07)

5548 Stein, David Ezra. *Pouch!* (PS–K). Illus. by author. 2009, Putnam $15.99 (978-0-399-25051-4). 32pp. A young kangaroo has his first alarming adventure outside his mother's pouch. (Rev: BL 9/15/09*; HB 11–12/09; SLJ 9/1/09)

5549 Stephens, Helen. *Fleabag* (PS–1). Illus. by author. 2010, Henry Holt $16.99 (978-0-8050-7975-2). 32pp. A flea-ridden stray dog makes a new friend in this story about loyal friends. (Rev: BL 4/15/10; SLJ 7/1/10)

5550 Stevens, Janet, and Susan Stevens Crummel. *Find a Cow Now!* (K–3). Illus. by Janet Stevens. 2012, Holiday $16.95 (978-0-8234-2218-0). 32pp. Bossy Bird is tired of Dog's rambunctious shenanigans and sends him off to find a cow, which proves surprisingly difficult. Lexile AD140L (Rev: BL 11/1/12; HB 1–2/13; SLJ 10/12)

5551 Stevens, Janet, and Susan Stevens Crummel. *The Great Fuzz Frenzy* (PS–2). Illus. 2005, Harcourt $17.00 (978-0-15-204626-2). 56pp. Chaos erupts when a green tennis ball drops into a prairie dog burrow; an exciting read with inventive illustrations enhanced by the oversize format. (Rev: BL 9/1/05; SLJ 9/05*)

5552 Stewart, Paul. *In the Dark of the Night* (1–3). Illus. by Tim Vyner. 2009, Frances Lincoln $17.95 (978-1-84507-764-8). Unpaged. A wolf cub, Cub-of-Mine, accompanies his father out into the night and learns all about the importance of the moon and the wolf song. (Rev: LMC 3–4/10; SLJ 12/1/09)

5553 Stohner, Anu. *Brave Charlotte* (PS–2). Illus. by Henrike Wilson. 2005, Bloomsbury $16.95 (978-1-58234-690-8). 32pp. Charlotte, an adventurous sheep, comes to the rescue when the shepherd breaks his leg in this picture book featuring excellent illustrations. (Rev: BL 8/05; SLJ 1/06)

5554 Surovec, Yasmine. *I See Kitty* (PS–K). Illus. by author. 2013, Roaring Brook $15.99 (978-159643862-0). 40pp. Young Chloe wants a kitten so badly that she sees them everywhere she goes in this sweet story that ends happily. ℮ (Rev: BL 9/1/13; SLJ 9/13)

5555 Sutherland, T. T. *Runaway Retriever* (4–6). Series: Pet Trouble. 2009, Scholastic paper $5.99 (978-0-545-10241-4). Merlin the golden retriever, a real escape artist, is devoted to Parker and breaks out to be with him wherever he goes. (Rev: BLO 5/15/09)

5556 Swaim, Jessica. *The Hound from the Pound* (K–2). Illus. by Jill McElmurry. 2007, Candlewick $15.99 (978-0-7636-2330-2). 32pp. Adopting a naughty basset hound changes life for lonely Miss Mary in this lively book full of humor and wordplay. (Rev: BL 10/1/07; HB 1/08; SLJ 10/07) [811]

5557 Sweet, Melissa. *Tupelo Rides the Rails* (K–3). Illus. by author. 2008, Houghton $17.00 (978-0-618-71714-9). 40pp. After being dumped by the wayside, courageous dog Tupelo meets up with other strays and finds herself on a train to a new life in this story full of doggy lore. (Rev: BL 1/1–15/08; SLJ 3/08)

5558 Taback, Simms. *Simms Taback's City Animals* (PS). Illus. by author. 2009, Blue Apple $12.99 (978-1-934706-52-7). 20pp. This board book neatly unfolds to reveal six animals clue by clue. (Rev: BLO 5/15/09; SLJ 6/09)

5559 Tafuri, Nancy. *Five Little Chicks* (PS). Illus. 2006, Simon & Schuster $14.95 (978-0-689-87342-3). 32pp. A mother hen teaches her five newborn chicks where to find a good meal. (Rev: BL 12/15/05; SLJ 2/06)

5560 Tafuri, Nancy. *Whose Chick Are You?* (PS–K). Illus. by author. 2007, HarperCollins $16.99 (978-0-06-082514-0). When a baby swan hatches, nobody seems to know who it belongs to. (Rev: BL 12/15/06; SLJ 2/07)

5561 Talbott, Hudson. *It's All about Me-ow* (K–2). Illus. by author. 2012, Penguin $16.99 (978-0-399-25403-1). 32pp. An adult cat, Buddy, advises three kittens on dealing with humans, using charts, diagrams, and demonstrations — and conveying (with humor) a fair amount of information on cats and their behavior. Lexile AD460L (Rev: BL 9/15/12*; SLJ 8/12*)

5562 Teckentrup, Britta. *Grumpy Cat* (PS–K). Illus. by author. 2008, Boxer $14.95 (978-1-905417-69-8). 32pp. A lovable kitten manages to break through Grumpy Cat's defenses and the two become fast friends. (Rev: BL 4/1/08; SLJ 5/08)

5563 Thompson, Lauren. *Little Quack* (PS–K). Illus. by Derek Anderson. 2003, Simon & Schuster $14.95 (978-0-689-84723-3). 32pp. Five little ducklings follow their mother — the last very reluctantly — into the pond in this charming picture book. (Rev: BL 2/1/03; HBG 10/03; SLJ 6/03)

5564 Thompson, Lauren. *Polar Bear Morning* (PS–K). Illus. by Stephen Savage. 2013, Scholastic $16.99 (978-0-439-69885-6). 32pp. A little polar bear leaves her mother's den and meets another cub, followed by a lot of polar bear fun. Lexile 600L (Rev: BL 12/15/12; SLJ 2/13)

5565 Thompson, Lauren. *Wee Little Bunny* (PS–1). Illus. by John Butler. Series: Wee Little. 2010, Simon & Schuster $14.99 (978-1-4169-7937-1). 32pp. A baby bunny has some brave adventures in the big woods: chasing a dragonfly, encountering a grumpy porcupine, and eventually returning home to tell his mom all about it. (Rev: BL 1/1/10; SLJ 2/1/10)

5566 Thomson, Sarah L. *Cub's Big World* (PS–K). Illus. by Joe Cepeda. 2013, Harcourt $16.99 (978-054405739-5). 32pp. A polar bear cub bravely explores the world outside its cave, hoping Mom is keeping a close eye; a beautifully illustrated story about first adventures. (Rev: BL 11/15/13; HB 11–12/13; SLJ 11/13)

5567 Tildes, Phyllis L. *Animals: Black and White* (PS–2). Illus. by author. 1996, Charlesbridge paper $6.95 (978-0-88106-959-4). This picture puzzle book consists of guessing games in which several black-and-white animals describe themselves and show parts of their bodies before their identities are revealed. (Rev: SLJ 1/97)

5568 Tildes, Phyllis L. *Calico's Curious Kittens* (PS). Illus. 2003, Charlesbridge $16.95 (978-1-57091-511-6); paper $6.95 (978-1-57091-512-3). 32pp. Calico's kittens are full of mischief, but as cute as can be. (Rev: BL 2/1/03; HBG 10/03; SLJ 2/03)

5569 Tillman, Nancy. *Tumford's Rude Noises* (PS–2). Illus. by author. 2012, Feiwel & Friends $16.99 (978-0-312-36841-8). 32pp. Tumford the cat is reprimanded for making rude noises but reassured that his owners love him despite his naughtiness. **e** (Rev: BL 9/1/12; SLJ 9/12)

5570 Townsend, Una Belle. *Grady's in the Silo* (1–4). Illus. by Bob Artley. 2003, Pelican $15.95 (978-1-58980-098-4). Based on a real-life event, this is an entertaining story about Grady, a cow that gets stuck in a silo while trying to avoid an injection. (Rev: HBG 10/03; SLJ 5/03)

5571 Tsubakiyama, Margaret. *Mei-Mei Loves the Morning* (PS–3). Illus. by Cornelius Van Wright and Ying-Hwa Hu. 1999, Whitman $15.95 (978-0-8075-5039-7). In modern, urban China, Mei-Mei and her grandfather participate in the family's daily routines, such as feeding the bird, eating breakfast, going to the park, and shopping at the market. (Rev: BCCB 5/99; BL 3/15/99; HBG 10/99; SLJ 5/99)

5572 Turner, Sandy. *Cool Cat, Hot Dog* (PS–2). Illus. by author. 2005, Simon & Schuster $16.95 (978-0-689-84946-6). Imaginative torn-paper artwork is the highlight of this discussion — between a dog and cat — of their different characteristics. (Rev: SLJ 8/05)

5573 Umansky, Kaye. *I Don't Like Gloria!* (PS–1). Illus. by Margaret Chamberlain. 2007, Candlewick $15.99 (978-0-7636-3202-1). Calvin, a dog, is not at all fond of Gloria, the new cat in the house, and both of them are distraught when a third pet comes on the scene. (Rev: SLJ 5/07)

5574 Underwood, Deborah. *Granny Gomez and Jigsaw* (PS–2). Illus. by Scott Magoon. 2010, Hyperion $16.99 (978-078685216-1). 40pp. When Granny Gomez's spirited pet pig outgrows her house, she builds him a barn, missing his companionship until she breaks out her camping gear and joins him there; this quirky, offbeat story features bright illustrations. (Rev: BL 1/1/10; LMC 8–9/10)

5575 Vernick, Audrey Glassman, and Ellen Glassman Gidaro. *Bark and Tim: A True Story of Friendship Based on the Paintings of Tim Brown* (K–3). Illus. by Tim Brown. 2003, Overmountain $14.95 (978-1-57072-271-4). This charming story, based on the Mississippi childhood of African American folk artist Tim Brown, tells about a young boy's loving relationship with a dog named Bark. (Rev: HBG 4/04; SLJ 1/04)

5576 Viau, Nancy. *Look What I Can Do!* (PS). Illus. by Anna Vojtech. 2013, Abrams $16.95 (978-1-4197-0529-8). 32pp. Young animals display their amazing new talents in this nicely illustrated, rhythmic book. (Rev: BLO 6/13; SLJ 4/13)

5577 Vischer, Frans. *Fuddles* (PS–2). Illus. by author. 2011, Aladdin $15.99 (978-1-4169-9155-7). 32pp. Bored with his everyday routine, Fuddles the cat escapes into the wide world only to find that it is a pretty scary place. **e** Lexile 500L (Rev: BL 4/1/11; LMC 8–9/11; SLJ 4/11)

5578 Voake, Charlotte. *Ginger and the Mystery Visitor* (PS–2). Illus. by author. 2010, Candlewick $15.99 (978-0-7636-4865-7). 40pp. Ginger and the kitten are outraged when a neighborhood cat decides to invade their house, especially at mealtimes. (Rev: HB 11–12/10; SLJ 10/1/10)

5579 Von Buhler, Cynthia. *The Cat Who Wouldn't Come Inside: Based on a True Story* (PS–2). Photos by author. Illus. by author. 2006, Houghton $16.00 (978-0-618-56314-2). In an effort to convince a stray cat to stay, a woman adds more and more attractions to her front porch, until it's just as nice outside as inside. (Rev: SLJ 11/06)

5580 Votaw, Carol. *Good Morning, Little Polar Bear* (PS–2). Illus. by Susan Banta. 2005, NorthWord $15.95 (978-1-55971-932-2). In this appealing picture book, a young Inuit child celebrates the arrival of summer by making the rounds of the creatures that call the Arctic home. (Rev: SLJ 11/05)

5581 Waddell, Martin. *It's Quacking Time!* (PS–K). Illus. by Jill Barton. 2005, Candlewick $15.99 (978-0-7636-2738-6). 32pp. Young Duckling learns a lot about nature as his family waits for a new egg to hatch. (Rev: BL 2/1/05; SLJ 4/05)

5582 Wahman, Wendy. *A Cat Like That* (PS–1). Illus. by author. 2011, Henry Holt $16.99 (978-0-8050-8942-4). 32pp. A condescending cat explains all the bad things humans do and what it takes to be a cat's best friend. (Rev: BL 5/1/11; SLJ 6/11)

5583 Waldron, Kathleen Cook. *Roundup at the Palace* (K–3). Illus. by Alan Daniel and Lea Daniel. 2006, Red Deer $17.95 (978-0-88995-319-2). A bull escapes from a truck on the way to a stock show in Denver, and Zack and Alice must coax him back to safety in this story based on an actual event. (Rev: SLJ 7/06)

5584 Walsh, Barbara. *Sammy in the Sky* (K–3). Illus. by Jamie Wyeth. 2011, Candlewick $16.99 (978-0-7636-4927-2). 32pp. A young girl's family helps her to cope when the family dog passes away. Lexile AD740L (Rev: BL 8/11; LMC 11–12/11; SLJ 8/1/11*)

5585 Walsh, Melanie. *Do Lions Live on Lily Pads?* (PS). 2006, Houghton $15.00 (978-0-618-47300-7). 32pp. Using questions and answers, this simple picture book reveals the distinctive habitats of animals including lions, parakeets, giraffes, and crocodiles. (Rev: BL 6/1–15/06; SLJ 7/06)

5586 Wardlaw, Lee. *Won Ton: A Cat Tale Told in Haiku* (K–3). Illus. by Eugene Yelchin. 2011, Henry Holt $16.99 (978-0-8050-8995-0). 40pp. A cynical and feisty stray cat gets adopted, and slowly learns to love his new home in this story told from the cat's perspective in a series of senryu poems — similar to haiku but reflective of personality and behavior rather than the natural world. ALSC Notable Children's Book, 2012. 🎧 (Rev: BL 2/1/11*; HB 3–4/11; LMC 5–6/11*; SLJ 2/1/11*)

5587 Warhola, James. *Uncle Andy's Cats* (PS–1). Illus. by author. 2009, Putnam $16.99 (978-0-399-25180-1). An amusingly illustrated story of Andy Warhol's 25 cats, written by his nephew, who visited the house and the cats frequently. (Rev: BL 7/09)

5588 Waring, Geoff. *Oscar and the Bat: A Book About Sound* (PS–2). Illus. by author. Series: Start with Science. 2008, Candlewick $14.99 (978-0-7636-4025-5). 32pp. In this fiction and science hybrid title, a cat named Oscar and his bat friend explore how animals make sounds and how we hear them. (Rev: BL 12/1/08; SLJ 12/08)

5589 Warnes, Tim. *Mommy Mine* (PS). Illus. by Jane Chapman. 2005, HarperCollins $16.99 (978-0-06-058947-9). 32pp. Contrasting mothers and their babies — mice and elephants, for example — are juxtaposed in bright pictures with a simple rhyme. (Rev: BL 5/15/05)

5590 Warrick, Karen Clemens. *If I Had a Tail* (PS–2). Illus. by Sherry Neidigh. 2001, Rising Moon LB $15.95 (978-0-87358-781-5). 32pp. An amusing picture book in which the tails of various animals and their uses are explored. (Rev: BL 4/1/01; HBG 10/01; SLJ 6/01)

5591 Weaver, Tess. *Cat Jumped In!* (PS–2). Illus. by Emily Arnold McCully. 2007, Clarion $16.00 (978-0-618-61488-2). 32pp. A lively and curious cat creates havoc as it moves through an artist's house. (Rev: BL 12/15/07; SLJ 12/07)

5592 Weller, Frances W. *The Day the Animals Came: A Story of Saint Francis Day* (PS–2). Illus. by Loren Long. 2003, Philomel $16.99 (978-0-399-23630-3). The blessing of the animals at the Cathedral of St. John the Divine in New York City makes a young Caribbean girl named Ria feel more at home. (Rev: BL 10/1/03; HBG 4/04; SLJ 11/03)

5593 West, Jim, and Marshall Izen. *The Dog Who Sang at the Opera* (1–3). Illus. by Erika Oller. 2004, Abrams $16.95 (978-0-8109-4928-7). 32pp. A Russian wolfhound's operatic debut ends ignominiously in this story based on a real incident. (Rev: BL 1/1–15/05; SLJ 2/05)

5594 Wheeler, Lisa. *The Pet Project: Cute and Cuddly Vicious Verses* (K–3). Illus. by Zachariah OHora. 2013, Atheneum $16.99 (978-141697595-3). 40pp. A daughter of scientists researches potential pets and records her findings in poems. (Rev: BL 4/1/13; SLJ 3/13)

5595 Wheeler, Lisa. *Sixteen Cows* (PS–2). Illus. by Kurt Cyrus. 2002, Harcourt $16.00 (978-0-15-202676-9). 32pp. After their herds of cows mingle when a dividing fence is blown down, Cowboy Gene and Cowgirl Sue decide they should also, and so they get married. (Rev: BL 6/1–15/02; HBG 10/02; SLJ 4/02)

5596 White, Amanda. *Rip and Rap* (PS). Illus. by Debbie Harter. 2002, Barefoot Books $14.99 (978-1-84148-944-5). Sheepdog puppies Rip and Rap become indistinguishable when Rap gets covered in mud. (Rev: HBG 3/03; SLJ 1/03)

5597 White, Kathryn. *The Nutty Nut Chase* (PS–3). Illus. by Vanessa Cabban. 2004, Good Bks. $16.00 (978-1-56148-446-1). Two quarrelsome squirrels are among the animals much surprised by a disappearing nut. (Rev: SLJ 1/05)

5598 Wild, Margaret. *Harry and Hopper* (PS–2). Illus. by Freya Blackwood. 2011, Feiwel & Friends $16.99 (978-0-312-64261-7). 32pp. Young Harry slowly learns to accept the fact that his dog Hopper was killed in an accident in this touching story about grief. Lexile AD690L (Rev: BL 2/1/11*; HB 1–2/11; SLJ 4/11*)

5599 Wild, Margaret. *Puffling* (PS–2). Illus. by Julie Vivas. 2009, Feiwel & Friends $16.99 (978-0-312-56570-1). 32pp. A baby puffin hatches and grows under the care of his loving parents, eager to grow strong enough to leave his parents and start his own life; the lovely illustrations show the puffling's progress. (Rev: BL 9/15/09*; LMC 10/09; SLJ 12/1/09)

5600 Wildsmith, Brian, and Rebecca Wildsmith. *Wake Up, Wake Up!* (PS–1). Illus. 1993, Harcourt $6.95 (978-0-15-200685-3). 16pp. One by one, the animals wake up until, finally, the farmer also wakes up to feed them. (Rev: BL 3/15/93)

5601 Willems, Mo. *City Dog, Country Frog* (PS–2). Illus. by Jon J Muth. 2010, Hyperion $17.99 (978-1-4231-0300-4). 64pp. In spring City Dog gets to go to the country and makes friends with a frog; the two play together over successive visits, but come winter Country Frog is gone and a lonely City Dog must wait for the next spring to make a new friend. ALSC Notable Children's Book, 2011. Lexile AD490L (Rev: BL 3/15/10*; HB 7–8/10; SLJ 5/1/10*)

5602 Willis, Nancy Carol. *Raccoon Moon* (PS–2). Illus. 2002, Birdsong $15.95 (978-0-9662761-2-1); paper $6.95 (978-0-9662761-3-8). 32pp. Three raccoon cubs are born and grow up in this wonderfully illustrated introduction to a raccoon's lifecycle. (Rev: BL 12/15/02; SLJ 1/03)

5603 Wilson, Karma. *What's in the Egg, Little Pip?* (K–2). Illus. by Jane Chapman. 2010, Simon & Schuster $16.99 (978-1-4169-4204-7). 40pp. Penguin Little Pip is jealous of the egg her parents are protecting so carefully in this third book in the series that features warm, realistic illustrations. **e** (Rev: BL 2/1/11; SLJ 2/1/11)

5604 Wilson, Sarah. *A Nap in a Lap* (PS). Illus. by Akemi Gutierrez. 2003, Holt $15.95 (978-0-8050-6973-0). A little girl and her dog observe the diverse places and ways in which various animals nap before heading home where, the child herself takes a nap on her mother's lap. (Rev: BL 1/1–15/04; SLJ 1/04)

5605 Winstead, Rosie. *Ruby and Bubbles* (K–2). Illus. by author. 2006, Dial $15.99 (978-0-8037-3024-3). Ruby's love for her pet bird Bubbles is shaken when bullies mock the bird and its inability to fly. (Rev: SLJ 2/06)

5606 Wood, Audrey. *A Dog Needs a Bone!* (PS–2). Illus. by author. 2007, Scholastic $16.99 (978-0-545-00005-5). 32pp. A dog who desperately wants a bone has a mistress who loves to tease. (Rev: BL 10/15/07; SLJ 9/07)

5607 Wood, Audrey. *It's Duffy Time!* (PS–1). Illus. by Don Wood. 2012, Scholastic $16.99 (978-0-545-22089-7). 40pp. Duffy the dog enjoys a luxurious life that is punctuated by many naps in this nicely illustrated light book. Lexile 600L (Rev: BL 10/1/12; SLJ 11/12)

5608 Woodson, Jacqueline. *This Is the Rope: A Story from the Great Migration* (1–3). Illus. by James Ransome. 2013, Penguin $16.99 (978-0-399-23986-1). 32pp. This lyrical story follows an African American family's continuing use (in different ways — for skipping, for tying belongings to the roof of the car) of a rope over three generations of movement and growth. Lexile AD1090 (Rev: BL 6/13; HB 7–8/13; LMC 1–2/14*; SLJ 7/13*)

5609 Wright, Cliff. *Bear and Ball* (PS). Illus. by author. 2005, Chronicle $5.95 (978-0-8118-4819-0). A simple board book rhyming story about two bear cubs playing with a ball. Also use *Bear and Kite* (2005). (Rev: SLJ 7/05)

5610 Wright, Johanna. *Bandits* (PS–1). Illus. by author. 2011, Roaring Brook $16.99 (978-1-59643-583-4). 32pp. Expressive illustrations add appeal to this story of "bandits" — raccoons — roaming a neighborhood after dark. (Rev: BL 9/1/11*; SLJ 8/1/11)

5611 Yang, James. *Joey and Jet* (PS–2). Illus. 2004, Simon & Schuster $15.95 (978-0-689-86926-6). 32pp. A boy and a dog have fun with a ball in this attractive volume that highlights the use of prepositions. (Rev: BL 1/1–15/05)

5612 Yolen, Jane. *The Day Tiger Rose Said Goodbye* (PS–3). Illus. by Jim LaMarche. 2011, Random House $16.99 (978-0-375-86663-0); LB $19.99 (978-0-375-96663-7). 32pp. An old cat's last day on earth is documented in this sensitive story. **e** (Rev: BL 7/11; LMC 1–2/12*; SLJ 8/1/11)

5613 Yolen, Jane. *Hoptoad* (PS–K). Illus. by Karen Lee Schmidt. 2003, Harcourt $16.00 (978-0-15-216352-5). In this simple, appealing tale told in rhyming text, a man and his son stop their camper to rescue a toad from a dangerous trip across the road. (Rev: BL 5/15/03; HBG 10/03; SLJ 6/03)

5614 Yolen, Jane. *Owl Moon* (PS–2). Illus. by John Schoenherr. 1987, Penguin $16.99 (978-0-399-21457-8). 32pp. Winner of the 1988 Caldecott Medal, this is the poetic story of a little girl and her father on an owl adventure in winter. (Rev: BL 12/15/87; SLJ 12/87)

5615 Young, Judy. *A Pet for Miss Wright* (PS–3). Illus. by Andrea Wesson. 2011, Sleeping Bear $15.95 (978-1-58536-509-8). 32pp. A lonely writer tries one pet after another, eventually settling on a dog who watches, listens, and learns to retrieve the dictionary and thesaurus. (Rev: BL 4/1/11; SLJ 5/1/11)

5616 Zarins, Kim. *The Helpful Puppy* (PS–1). Illus. by Emily Arnold McCully. 2012, Holiday $16.95 (978-0-8234-2318-7). 32pp. A puppy with aspirations finally figures out what he's suited to — being a companion for his boy. Lexile AD400 (Rev: BL 8/12; SLJ 10/12)

5617 Ziefert, Harriet. *Beach Party!* (PS). Illus. by Simms Taback. 2005, Blue Apple $8.95 (978-1-59354-067-8). A board book featuring adorable sea animals on their way to the ocean for a swim. (Rev: SLJ 8/05)

5618 Ziefert, Harriet. *Birdhouse for Rent* (PS–K). Illus. by Donald Dreifuss. 2001, Houghton $16.00 (978-0-618-04881-6). A birdhouse is used by bees and chipmunks before Mrs. Chickadee moves in, lays her eggs, and sees her chicks hatch. (Rev: HBG 3/02; SLJ 9/01)

5619 Ziefert, Harriet. *Murphy Jumps a Hurdle* (K–3). Illus. by Emily Bolam. 2006, Blue Apple $15.95 (978-1-59354-174-3). 40pp. Murphy the yellow Lab and his owner Cheryl tackle agility training in this entertaining book with cartoonlike illustrations. (Rev: BL 11/1/06)

5620 Ziefert, Harriet. *My Dog Thinks I'm a Genius* (PS–2). Illus. by Barroux. 2011, Blue Apple $16.99 (978-1-60905-059-7). Unpaged. A boy who loves making paintings of his dog discovers that the dog has artistic abilities all his own. (Rev: SLJ 9/1/11)

5621 Ziefert, Harriet. *One Smart Skunk* (PS–3). Illus. by Santiago Cohen. 2004, Blue Apple $15.95 (978-1-59354-064-7). Rebecca the skunk's life under the deck becomes unbearable as she suffers from a combination of moth balls and rap music. (Rev: SLJ 1/05)

5622 Zoboli, Giovanna. *I Wish I Had . . .* (PS–3). Illus. by Simona Mulazzani. 2013, Eerdmans $16.00 (978-0-8028-5415-5). 27pp. A beautifully illustrated contemplation of the attributes of various animals. Lexile AD800 (Rev: BL 5/1/13*; HB 5–6/13; SLJ 5/13)

SCHOOL STORIES

5623 Abercrombie, Barbara. *The Show-and-Tell Lion* (K–2). Illus. by Lynne Avril Cravath. 2006, Simon & Schuster $16.95 (978-0-689-86408-7). 32pp. Unprepared for show-and-tell, young Matthew makes up a story about having a lion but faces a real dilemma when his classmates want to see it. (Rev: BL 9/15/06; HBG 4/07; SLJ 7/06)

5624 Adams, Diane. *I Want to Help!* (K–2). Illus. by Nancy Hayashi. 2012, Peachtree $15.95 (978-1-56145-630-7). 32pp. Emily Pearl is perhaps overly enthusiastic, independent, and eager to please, but when her father is late to pick her up that confidence ebbs. Lexile AD600L (Rev: BLO 10/1/12; SLJ 8/12)

5625 Alexander, Martha, and James Rumford. *Max and the Dumb Flower Picture* (PS–K). Illus. by Martha Alexander. 2009, Charlesbridge $9.95 (978-1-58089-156-1). Max refuses to cooperate with his teacher by coloring in the lines and instead creates an original work of art. (Rev: BL 7/09)

5626 Aliki. *A Play's the Thing* (2–4). Illus. 2005, HarperCollins $16.99 (978-0-06-074355-0). 32pp. José is less than thrilled when his teacher, Miss Brilliant, decides the class will put on a dramatization of "Mary Had a Little Lamb"; cartoon panels and a running narrative tell the story. (Rev: BL 10/15/05; HB 9–1/05; HBG 4/06; LMC 5/06; SLJ 8/05*)

5627 Allard, Harry. *Miss Nelson Has a Field Day* (1–3). Illus. by James Marshall. 1985, Houghton $16.00 (978-0-395-36690-5); paper $5.95 (978-0-395-48654-2). 32pp. The plucky Miss Nelson gets a losing football team into shape. (Rev: BCCB 7–8/85; BL 5/15/85; HB 5/85)

5628 Allard, Harry. *Miss Nelson Is Missing!* (K–2). Illus. by James Marshall. 1985, Houghton $16.00 (978-0-395-25296-3); paper $6.99 (978-0-395-40146-0). When Miss Nelson's students in Room 207 misbehave, she disappears and is replaced by a martinet. A sequel is: *Miss Nelson Is Back* (1985).

5629 Aston, Dianna. *Not So Tall for Six* (1–2). Illus. by Frank W. Dormer. 2008, Charlesbridge $14.95 (978-1-57091-705-9). 32pp. Kylie Bell, in 1st grade, may not be tall in stature but she's big on courage when she's being bullied. (Rev: BCCB 4/08; SLJ 4/08)

5630 Barnes, Derrick. *Ruby and the Booker Boys: Brand New School, Brand New Ruby* (2–4). Illus. by Vanessa Brantley Newton. 2008, Scholastic paper $4.99 (978-0-545-01760-2). 144pp. About to start 3rd grade at her new school, which her three brothers already attend, African American Ruby Booker aims to make her own mark. (Rev: BLO 3/19/09)

5631 Beaty, Andrea. *Iggy Peck, Architect* (K–2). Illus. by David Roberts. 2007, Abrams $16.95 (978-0-8109-1106-2). 32pp. Iggy's teacher doesn't appreciate the 2nd-grader's precocious talent for building until the class needs an emergency suspension bridge. (Rev: LMC 1/08; SLJ 11/07)

5632 Bergman, Mara. *Lively Elizabeth! What Happens When You Push* (PS–1). Illus. by Cassia Thomas. 2010, Whitman $16.99 (978-0-8075-4702-1). 32pp. One child's push leads to a disastrous domino effect, lots of blame, and plenty of regret. (Rev: BL 10/1/10; SLJ 9/1/10)

5633 Best, Cari. *Shrinking Violet* (K–3). Illus. by Giselle Potter. 2001, Farrar $16.00 (978-0-374-36882-1). Shy Violet has her moment in the limelight when she's cast in an offstage speaking role. (Rev: BCCB 10/01; BL 8/01; HB 9/01; HBG 3/02; SLJ 8/01*)

5634 Blake, Stephanie. *I Don't Want to Go to School!* (PS–1). Illus. by author. 2009, Random $12.99 (978-0-375-85688-4). Simon is certain that he doesn't want to go to school, but after a day of learning and playing he changes his mind. (Rev: BL 7/09)

5635 Boelts, Maribeth. *When It's the Last Day of School* (K–2). Illus. by Hanako Wakiyama. 2004, Penguin $15.99 (978-0-399-23498-9). 32pp. Full of anticipation about summer vacation, James vows to be on his best behavior on the very last day of school. (Rev: BL 4/15/04; SLJ 4/04)

5636 Borden, Louise. *The John Hancock Club* (2–4). Illus. by Adam Gustavson. 2007, Simon & Schuster $16.99 (978-1-4169-1813-4). Sean is not looking forward to learning cursive writing but his 3rd-grade teacher provides motivation. (Rev: BL 5/1/07; LMC 10/07; SLJ 6/07)

5637 Borden, Louise. *The Last Day of School* (1–3). Illus. by Adam Gustavson. 2006, Simon & Schuster $15.95 (978-0-689-86869-6). 40pp. It's the last day of school, and one of Mrs. Mallory's 3rd-grade students has a special surprise for her. (Rev: BL 2/1/06; SLJ 3/06)

5638 Bowen, Anne. *The Great Math Tattle Battle* (1–3). Illus. by Jaime Zollars. 2006, Albert Whitman $15.99 (978-0-8075-3163-1). Math whiz Harley Harrison is the scourge of his 2nd-grade class, constantly tattling on his classmates until a newcomer called Emma Jean turns the tables on him. (Rev: BL 4/15/06; SLJ 6/06)

5639 Brisson, Pat. *I Remember Miss Perry* (K–3). Illus. by Stephanie Jorisch. 2006, Dial $16.99 (978-0-8037-2981-0). 32pp. Stevie fondly remembers Miss Perry — his first teacher — when she is killed in a car accident. (Rev: BL 2/1/06; SLJ 3/06)

5640 Brown, Marc. *D.W.'s Guide to Preschool* (PS). Illus. by author. 2003, Little, Brown $15.95 (978-0-316-12069-2). D. W., Arthur's little sister, offers advice on virtually every aspect of preschool life, covering such important topics as bathroom breaks, circle time, and snack time. (Rev: HBG 4/04; SLJ 12/03)

5641 Bunting, Eve. *My Special Day at Third Street School* (K–3). Illus. by Suzanne Bloom. 2004, Boyds Mills $15.95 (978-1-59078-075-6). 32pp. A boy explains in engaging detail the class preparations for an author visit by Amanda Drake — and the successes of the day itself. (Rev: BL 3/15/04*; SLJ 3/04)

5642 Bunting, Eve. *Our Teacher's Having a Baby* (K–2). Illus. by Diane deGroat. 1992, Houghton $15.00 (978-0-395-60470-0). 32pp. Mrs. Neal explains to her class that she is going to have a baby, and together they prepare for the event. (Rev: BL 9/15/92; HB 5/04; SLJ 3/93)

5643 Bush, Laura, and Jenna Bush. *Read All About It!* (K–3). Illus. by Denise Brunkus. 2008, HarperCollins $17.99 (978-0-06-156075-0). 32pp. Tyrone is popular and enjoys school except for reading until he finally listens to a story and discovers a whole new world. (Rev: BL 5/1/08; SLJ 6/08)

5644 Buzzeo, Toni. *Adventure Annie Goes to Kindergarten* (PS–K). Illus. by Amy Wummer. 2010, Dial $16.99 (978-0-8037-3358-9). 32pp. Plucky Annie may have difficulty following the kindergarten rules but when two students get lost she is the one who leaps to the rescue. (Rev: BL 5/1/10; LMC 8–9/10; SLJ 5/1/10)

5645 Buzzeo, Toni. *The Library Doors* (PS–1). Illus. by Nadine Bernard Westcott. 2008, Upstart $17.95 (978-1-60213-037-1). Using the well-known children's song "The Wheels on the Bus" as a framework, this is a rhythmic introduction to various activities at the library. (Rev: BLO 1/7/09)

5646 Buzzeo, Toni. *Our Librarian Won't Tell Us Anything!* (2–5). Illus. by Sachiko Yoshikawa. 2006, Upstart $17.95 (978-1-932146-73-8). Robert, a new student at Liberty Elementary, discovers that the conventional wisdom is awry and the librarian is in fact very helpful. (Rev: SLJ 2/07)

5647 Calmenson, Stephanie. *Late for School!* (K–2). Illus. by Sachiko Yoshikawa. 2008, Carolrhoda $16.95 (978-1-57505-935-8). 32pp. Mr. Bungles, the teacher, is late for school and tries many options in his zeal to get there; illustrations full of motion add to the fun. (Rev: BL 8/08; LMC 1/09; SLJ 9/08)

5648 Calmenson, Stephanie. *Ollie's School Day: A Yes-and-No Book* (PS–K). Illus. by Abby Carter. 2012, Holiday $15.95 (978-0-8234-2377-4). 24pp. Readers share the various, often funny, choices a little boy must make while getting ready for school. (Rev: BLO 8/12; SLJ 10/12)

5649 Carlson, Nancy. *Hooray for Grandparents' Day!* (PS–2). Illus. 2000, Viking $15.99 (978-0-670-88876-4). Arnie has no grandparents to bring to school on Grandparents' Day and he feels left out. (Rev: BL 6/1–15/00; HBG 3/01; SLJ 8/00)

5650 Carlson, Nancy. *Look Out Kindergarten, Here I Come!* (PS–K). Illus. 1999, Viking $15.99 (978-0-670-88378-3). 32pp. Henry is excited about his first day in kindergarten, particularly after he makes a new friend. (Rev: BL 6/1–15/99; HBG 10/99; SLJ 7/99)

5651 Carson, Jana. *Stop Teasing Taylor!* (K–2). Illus. by Meryl Treatner. Series: We Both Read. 2005, Treasure Bay $7.99 (978-1-891327-61-2); paper $3.99 (978-1-891327-62-9). Designed to be read in tandem by a beginning reader and one who's more advanced, this is a simple story about a young boy's first day at school. (Rev: SLJ 4/06)

5652 Chapra, Mimi. *Amelia's Show-and-Tell Fiesta / Amelia y la fiesta de "muestra y cuenta"* (K–2). 2004, HarperCollins LB $17.89 (978-0-06-050256-0). When she gets to school, Amelia worries that her Cuban fiesta dresses are not suitable for show-and-tell in this book with lively English text and a more pedestrian Spanish translation. (Rev: SLJ 9/04)

5653 Choldenko, Gennifer. *How to Make Friends with a Giant* (K–2). Illus. by Amy Walrod. 2006, Putnam $16.99 (978-0-399-23779-9). Tiny Jake and giant Ja-

como become unlikely friends in this story about the advantages of being different. (Rev: SLJ 7/06)

5654 Cocca-Leffler, Maryann. *Jack's Talent* (PS–2). Illus. by author. 2007, Farrar $16.00 (978-0-374-33681-3). 32pp. In this reassuring book, Jack overcomes his insecurity on the first day of school as he discovers a talent for remembering names and facts. (Rev: BL 6/1–15/07; HB 9/07; SLJ 11/07)

5655 Cocca-Leffler, Maryann. *Mr. Tanen's Tie Trouble* (K–3). Illus. by author. 2003, Whitman LB $16.99 (978-0-8075-5305-3). Mr. Tanen the school principal puts his collection of wondrous ties up for auction when he discovers the playground has no funds. (Rev: BL 6/03; SLJ 5/03)

5656 Cocca-Leffler, Maryann. *Mr. Tanen's Ties* (PS–2). Illus. 1999, Whitman LB $16.99 (978-0-8075-5301-5). 32pp. Mr. Tanen wears different ties to school each day to mark various occasions, but Mr. Apple, the superintendent of schools, doesn't like it. (Rev: BL 5/15/99; HBG 10/99; SLJ 3/99)

5657 Cohen, Miriam. *First Grade Takes a Test* (K–1). Illus. by Ronald Himler. 2006, Star Bright $15.95 (978-1-59572-054-2); paper $5.95 (978-1-59572-055-9). 32pp. A newly illustrated version of Cohen's story about a 1st-grade class and what they learn about aptitude when they take an intelligence test. (Rev: BL 11/15/06)

5658 Cohen, Miriam. *Will I Have a Friend?* (PS–2). Illus. by Ronald Himler. 2009, Star Bright $15.95 (978-1-59572-069-6). 32pp. Jim worries about making friends on his first day of school in this updated version of a classic story with new illustrations. (Rev: BL 4/1/09)

5659 Cook, Lisa Broadie. *Peanut Butter and Homework Sandwiches* (K–2). Illus. by Jack E. Davis. 2011, Putnam $16.99 (978-0-399-24533-6). 32pp. Martin has a difficult week at school when a substitute teacher replaces the cool Mr. Elliot. (Rev: BL 8/11; LMC 11–12/11; SLJ 7/11)

5660 Corey, Shana. *First Graders from Mars: Episode 1 — Horus's Horrible Day* (K–2). Illus. by Mark Teague. 2001, Scholastic $14.95 (978-0-439-26220-0). 32pp. Horus, a Martian lad, is having a horrible time getting used to 1st grade until he meets another scared student. (Rev: BL 8/01; HBG 3/02; SLJ 9/01)

5661 Couric, Katie. *The Brand New Kid* (K–2). Illus. by Marjorie Priceman. 2000, Doubleday $15.95 (978-0-385-50030-2). Lazlo S. Gasky is unhappy and friendless at his new school, until a classmate decides to help him. (Rev: SLJ 2/01)

5662 Cox, Judy. *Don't Be Silly, Mrs. Millie!* (PS–K). Illus. by Joe Mathieu. 2005, Marshall Cavendish $14.95 (978-0-7614-5166-2). 32pp. Kindergarten teacher Mrs. Millie is prone to confusing her words — "coats" become "goats" — and the illustrations add to the general zaniness. (Rev: BL 8/05; SLJ 10/05)

5663 Creech, Sharon. *A Fine, Fine School* (K–3). Illus. by Harry Bliss. 2001, HarperCollins LB $17.89 (978-0-06-027737-6). 32pp. A wonderfully illustrated, very funny story about a school principal who just doesn't know when to quit. (Rev: BL 8/01; HBG 3/02; SLJ 8/01)

5664 Cuyler, Margery. *Bullies Never Win* (PS–2). Illus. by Arthur Howard. 2009, Simon & Schuster $16.99 (978-0-689-86187-1). In 1st grade, Jessica is bulled by classmate Brenda until Jessica finally tells her mother, who helps her deal with the problem. (Rev: BL 7/09; SLJ 6/09)

5665 Cuyler, Margery. *Hooray for Reading Day!* (PS–1). Illus. by Arthur Howard. Series: Jessica Worries. 2008, Simon & Schuster $15.99 (978-0-689-86188-8). 32pp. First-grader Jessica is terrified of reading aloud on Reading Theater Day and practices with her dog Wiggles. (Rev: BL 8/08; LMC 11/08; SLJ 8/08)

5666 Cuyler, Margery. *Stop, Drop, and Roll* (K–3). Illus. by Arthur Howard. 2001, Simon & Schuster $16.00 (978-0-689-84355-6). 32pp. Jessica agonizes over her role in a play for Fire Prevention Week. (Rev: BCCB 11/01; BL 9/15/01; HBG 3/02; SLJ 10/01)

5667 Cuyler, Margery. *We're Going on a Lion Hunt* (PS–2). Illus. by Joe Mathieu. 2008, Marshall Cavendish $14.99 (978-0-7614-5454-0). 32pp. An intrepid teacher and students set off on a make-believe safari and meet a variety of animals before they come across one with a cold nose and sharp teeth. (Rev: BL 9/1/08)

5668 Danneberg, Julie. *First Year Letters* (K–3). Illus. by Judy Love. 2003, Charlesbridge $16.95 (978-1-58089-084-7); paper $6.95 (978-1-58089-085-4). Letters exchanged by a fictional new teacher and her students reveal how they learn together during the course of a school year. (Rev: BL 2/1/03; HBG 10/03; SLJ 4/03)

5669 Danneberg, Julie. *Last Day Blues* (K–2). Illus. by Judy Love. 2006, Charlesbridge $16.95 (978-1-58089-046-5); paper $6.95 (978-1-58089-104-2). 32pp. Mrs. Hartwell's class worries that she will be lonely during the summer and tries to think of a suitable gift; meanwhile, Mrs. Hartwell can be seen celebrating the end of school with other teachers. (Rev: BL 1/1–15/06; SLJ 2/06)

5670 Davis, Katie. *Kindergarten Rocks!* (PS–K). Illus. by author. 2005, Harcourt $15.00 (978-0-15-204932-4). Dexter isn't nervous at all during his first day of kindergarten, but his stuffed dog Rufus is quite apprehensive. (Rev: SLJ 9/05)

5671 dePaola, Tomie. *The Art Lesson* (K–3). Illus. by author. 1989, Penguin $16.99 (978-0-399-21688-6). 32pp. Tommy just keeps on drawing and drawing and drawing. (Rev: BCCB 3/89; BL 3/1/89; SLJ 4/89)

5672 dePaola, Tomie. *Stagestruck* (PS–2). Illus. 2005, Penguin $16.99 (978-0-399-24338-7). 32pp. When Tommy fails to win the starring role in his kindergarten production of Peter Rabbit, he decides to steal the show anyway, and ends up apologizing. (Rev: BL 1/1–15/05; SLJ 1/05)

5673 Derby, Sally. *The Wacky Substitute* (K–3). Illus. by Jennifer Herbert. 2005, Marshall Cavendish $14.95 (978-0-7614-5219-5). When substitute teacher Mr.

Wuerst loses his eyeglasses, it sets the stage for some entertaining mishaps in the classroom. (Rev: SLJ 10/05)

5674 Diesen, Deborah. *Picture Day Perfection* (K–2). Illus. by Dan Santat. 2013, Abrams $16.95 (978-141970844-2). 32pp. A funny tale about a young boy's preparations for his school picture — not exactly what his mother expected, but not quite what he planned either. Lexile 570 (Rev: BL 9/1/13; SLJ 10/13)

5675 DiPucchio, Kelly. *Grace for President* (1–3). Illus. by LeUyen Pham. 2008, Hyperion $15.99 (978-0-7868-3919-3). 40pp. African American Grace runs for president of the elementary school in this appealing novel that explains much about the American election process. (Rev: BL 2/15/08; SLJ 2/08)

5676 DiPucchio, Kelly S. *Mrs. McBloom, Clean Up Your Room!* (K–2). Illus. by Guy Francis. 2005, Hyperion $15.99 (978-0-7868-0932-5). 32pp. Mrs. McBloom is retiring after a half century of teaching, and her students help to clean up the amazingly diverse clutter in her classroom. (Rev: BL 8/05; SLJ 9/05)

5677 Dodds, Dayle Ann. *Teacher's Pets* (PS–2). Illus. by Marylin Hafner. 2006, Candlewick $15.99 (978-0-7636-2252-7). 40pp. Miss Fry's classroom becomes home to her students' pets in this story of a happy menagerie. (Rev: BL 5/15/06; SLJ 5/06)

5678 Driscoll, Laura. *Lila the Fair* (1–3). Illus. by Blanche Sims. 2005, Kane paper $4.99 (978-1-57565-148-4). Lila calls herself "fair" because of her abilities as a peacemaker, which she exercises often as a middle child. (Rev: BL 3/1/05)

5679 Dubosarsky, Ursula. *Rex* (K–2). Illus. by David Mackintosh. 2006, Roaring Brook $16.95 (978-1-59643-186-7). 32pp. In words and art, various students describe what happened when they took Rex the class chameleon home for the night. (Rev: BL 11/15/06; SLJ 9/06)

5680 Edwards, Becky. *My First Day at Nursery School* (PS–1). Illus. by Anthony Flintoft. 2002, Bloomsbury $15.95 (978-1-58234-761-5). 32pp. A reassuring tale of a child's first day at nursery school. (Rev: BL 8/02; SLJ 8/02)

5681 Elschner, Géraldine. *Max's Magic Seeds* (PS–1). Illus. by Jean Pierre Corderoch. 2007, Penguin $16.99 (978-0-698-40059-7). 32pp. Detailed drawings of European village life will attract readers to this story of a boy who plants flowers along his daily walk to school. (Rev: BL 5/15/07; SLJ 7/07)

5682 Ely, Lesley. *Looking After Louis* (1–3). Illus. by Polly Dunbar. 2004, Whitman $16.99 (978-0-8075-4746-5). 32pp. Through the eyes of a little girl, this story looks at the experiences of an autistic boy and his treatment by his classmates. (Rev: BL 4/15/04; SLJ 4/04)

5683 Esham, Barbara. *Last to Finish: A Story About the Smartest Boy in Math Class* (1–3). Illus. by Mike Gordon. Series: The Adventures of Everyday Geniuses. 2008, Mainstream $16.99 (978-1-60336-456-0). 32pp. Max's enjoyment of math is jeopardized when the teacher starts timing tests. (Rev: BL 7/08)

5684 Esham, Barbara. *Stacey Coolidge's Fancy-Smancy Cursive Handwriting* (1–3). Illus. by Mike Gordon. Series: Adventures of Everyday Geniuses. 2008, Mainstream $16.95 (978-1-60336-462-1). Carolyn enjoys 2nd grade until they start cursive writing. (Rev: BL 6/1–15/08)

5685 Fain, Moira. *Snow Day* (K–3). Illus. 1996, Walker LB $16.85 (978-0-8027-8410-0). 32pp. Maggie Murphy escapes a school punishment when a snow day is declared the following day. (Rev: BCCB 10/96; BL 10/15/96; SLJ 10/96*)

5686 Falwell, Cathryn. *David's Drawings* (PS–2). Illus. 2001, Lee & Low $16.00 (978-1-58430-031-1). Collages of cut-paper and fabric illustrate this story of how one boy's drawing of a bare tree becomes a classroom's cooperative masterpiece. (Rev: BL 11/15/01; HBG 10/02; SLJ 10/01)

5687 Finchler, Judy. *Testing Miss Malarkey* (1–4). Illus. by Kevin O'Malley. 2000, Walker LB $16.85 (978-0-8027-8737-8). 32pp. A humorous story in which kids are being prepared for standardized tests that they eventually pass with flying colors. (Rev: BL 10/1/00)

5688 Finchler, Judy, and Kevin O'Malley. *Miss Malarkey Leaves No Reader Behind* (1–3). Series: Miss Malarkey. 2006, Walker $16.95 (978-0-8027-8084-3). 32pp. Miss Malarkey finally finds a book that's just right for a guy who's not too fond of reading. (Rev: BL 7/06; SLJ 8/06)

5689 Frasier, Debra. *Miss Alaineus: A Vocabulary Disaster* (3–5). Illus. 2000, Harcourt $16.00 (978-0-15-202163-4). Fifth-grader Sage mistakes the word *miscellaneous* for *Miss Alaineus* but turns this embarrassment into a triumph. (Rev: BL 9/15/00; HBG 3/01; SLJ 9/00)

5690 French, Simon. *Guess the Baby* (PS–1). Illus. by Donna Rawlins. 2002, Clarion $14.00 (978-0-618-25989-2). 32pp. Classmates bring in their baby pictures and try to guess who's who. (Rev: BL 12/15/02; HBG 3/03; SLJ 12/02)

5691 Gall, Chris. *Substitute Creacher* (K–2). Illus. by author. 2011, Little, Brown $16.99 (978-0-316-08915-9). 40pp. A classroom of rambunctious kids is faced with a slimy, tentacled substitute teacher, who spins terrifying tales about previous students who misbehaved. (Rev: BL 6/1/11; LMC 10/11; SLJ 7/11)

5692 Grandits, John. *Ten Rules You Absolutely Must Not Break If You Want to Survive the School Bus* (K–3). Illus. by Michael Allen Austin. 2011, Clarion $16.99 (978-0-618-78822-4). 32pp. This tongue-in-cheek book features a big brother laying down 10 school bus survival rules for his younger brother, who manages to break all of them in one day and live to tell the tale. (Rev: BL 7/11; LMC 10/11*; SLJ 7/11*)

5693 Greene, Stephanie. *Princess Posey and the Tiny Treasure* (1–2). Illus. by Stephanie Roth Sisson. 2013, Putnam $12.99 (978-039925711-7). 96pp. When Posey takes her new pink pig to school, the toy is confiscated and put in the Consequences drawer. ℮ (Rev: BL 12/15/12)

5694 Grigsby, Susan. *First Peas to the Table* (1–3). Illus. by Nicole Tadgell. 2012, Whitman $16.99 (978-0-8075-2452-7). 32pp. A teacher successfully uses a vegetable garden as an opportunity to discuss the life and accomplishments of Thomas Jefferson. (Rev: BL 3/15/12; LMC 8–9/12; SLJ 2/1/12)

5695 Grindley, Sally. *It's My School* (PS–2). Illus. by Margaret Chamberlain. 2006, Walker $15.95 (978-0-8027-8086-7). 32pp. Tom is not pleased when his little sister starts school but is quick to protect her when necessary. (Rev: BL 8/06; SLJ 7/06*)

5696 Gutman, Dan. *Miss Child Has Gone Wild!* (1–3). Illus. by Jim Paillot. Series: My Weirder School. 2011, HarperCollins LB $15.89 (978-006196917-1); paper $3.99 (978-006196916-4). 112pp. A.J. and his friends — now in 3rd grade at Ella Mentry School — enjoy a field trip to the zoo in this first volume in a new series. Lexile 600L (Rev: BLO 11/15/11)

5697 Gutman, Dan. *Mr. Klutz Is Nuts!* (2–3). Illus. by Jim Paillot. Series: My Weird School. 2004, HarperCollins LB $15.89 (978-0-06-050703-9); paper $3.99 (978-0-06-050702-2). 96pp. The school principal is an eccentric character who uses unusual incentives in this humorous easy chapter book that will appeal to reluctant readers. (Rev: SLJ 11/04)

5698 Harley, Bill. *Lost and Found* (K–3). Illus. by Adam Gustavson. 2012, Peachtree $16.95 (978-1-56145-628-4). 32pp. Justin's grandmother is coming to visit and he has lost the hat she made; can he find the courage to ask the scary janitor, Mr. Rumkowsky, if it's in the lost and found box? Lexile AD390L (Rev: BL 11/1/12; LMC 5–6/13; SLJ 2/13)

5699 Harper, Jessica. *A Place Called Kindergarten* (PS–K). Illus. by G. Brian Karas. 2006, Putnam $15.99 (978-0-399-24226-7). 32pp. The barnyard animals worry when Tommy doesn't turn up as usual, but he has only gone to kindergarten and returns to tell them all about it. (Rev: BL 8/06; SLJ 8/06)

5700 Harris, Robie H. *I Am Not Going to School Today!* (PS–K). Illus. by Jan Ormerod. 2003, Simon & Schuster $16.95 (978-0-689-83913-9). All the worries of the first day of school are captured in this story that ends happily. (Rev: HBG 4/04; SLJ 7/03)

5701 Hartt-Sussman, Heather. *Noni Is Nervous* (PS–K). Illus. by Genevieve Cote. 2013, Tundra $17.95 (978-1-77049-323-0). 24pp. Noni's first day at school is a nerve-wracking experience for the whole family — but it all turns out OK. (Rev: BL 7/13; SLJ 8/13)

5702 Hays, Anna Jane. *Ready, Set, Preschool!* (PS). Illus. by True Kelley. 2005, Knopf $16.95 (978-0-375-82519-4). This collection of rhymes, stories, and interactive games offers lots of concepts and ideas for preschoolers and their parents. (Rev: BL 8/05; SLJ 9/05)

5703 Heck, Ed. *Monkey Lost* (PS–2). Illus. by author. 2005, Milk & Cookies $15.95 (978-0-689-04633-9). Eric's teacher and classmates pitch in to help find the monkey he brought to school for show-and-tell, unaware that it is only a stuffed animal. (Rev: SLJ 11/05)

5704 Henkes, Kevin. *Lilly's Purple Plastic Purse* (PS–K). Illus. 1996, Greenwillow $17.89 (978-0-688-12898-2). 32pp. Lilly runs afoul of her teacher, Mr. Slinger, whom she adores. A sequel to *Julius, the Baby of the World* (1990). (Rev: BCCB 10/96; BL 8/96*; HB 9/96; SLJ 8/96*)

5705 Hennessy, B. G. *Mr. Ouchy's First Day* (K–2). Illus. by Paul Meisel. 2006, Putnam $15.99 (978-0-399-24248-9). 32pp. Mr. Ouchy is nervous about his first day as a teacher until he actually interacts with the class. (Rev: BL 8/06; SLJ 7/06)

5706 Herrera, Juan Felipe. *The Upside Down Boy / El niño de cabeza* (2–5). Illus. by Elizabeth Gomez. 2000, Children's Book Pr. $15.95 (978-0-89239-162-2). 31pp. Juanito, a young Hispanic American, is afraid that he won't fit into his new Anglo school, but he is pleasantly surprised. (Rev: BCCB 4/00; HB 9/00; HBG 10/00; SLJ 3/00)

5707 Hobbie, Nathaniel. *Priscilla Superstar!* (1–3). Illus. by Jocelyn Hobbie. 2006, Little, Brown $16.99 (978-0-316-01386-4). Even though Priscilla doesn't get the lead in her roller-skating school's play she still shows off her talent and learns what it means to be a real star. (Rev: BL 2/1/07; SLJ 10/06)

5708 Hoffman, Mary. *Princess Grace* (K–3). Illus. by Cornelius Van Wright. 2008, Dial $16.99 (978-0-8037-3260-5). 32pp. On parade day, Grace and her classmates portray royalty from different cultures, Grace in West African Kente robes. (Rev: BL 2/15/08; HB 3/08; SLJ 1/08)

5709 Hole, Stian. *Garmann's Summer* (1–3). Trans. by Don Bartlett. Illus. by author. 2008, Eerdmans $17.50 (978-0-8028-5339-4). Fall is coming and with it the beginning of 1st grade, which Garmann, a thoughtful boy, views with some trepidation; but discussions with various adults make it clear that everyone has to deal with fears. (Rev: BL 5/1/08; SLJ 6/08)

5710 Hurwitz, Johanna. *Mostly Monty* (1–3). Illus. by Anik McGrory. 2007, Candlewick $15.99 (978-0-7636-2831-4). Monty is a 1st-grader with asthma who learns to overcome his physical limits by discovering his many unique talents and sharing them with others. Also use *Mighty Monty* (2008). (Rev: BCCB 9/07; BL 6/1–15/07; LMC 11/07; SLJ 7/07)

5711 Husband, Amy. *Dear Teacher* (K–2). Illus. by author. 2010, Sourcebooks paper $8.99 (978-1-4022-4-268-7). 24pp. Young Michael composes a series of extravagantly inventive excuses for his absence on the first day back at school. (Rev: BL 8/10; LMC 11–12/10; SLJ 8/1/10)

5712 Jacobson, Jennifer. *Andy Shane and the Queen of Egypt* (K–2). Illus. by Abby Cater. Series: Andy Shane. 2008, Candlewick $13.99 (978-0-7636-3211-3). 64pp. Andy must make a choice when both he and the bossy Dolores want Egypt for their African country project; will he decide to work with her? (Rev: BL 4/1/08; SLJ 7/08)

5713 Johnson, Dolores. *My Mom Is My Show-and-Tell* (K–3). Illus. 1999, Marshall Cavendish $15.95 (978-0-7614-5041-2). 32pp. Brian, an African American boy who is the class clown, is anxious about his mother's visit on Parents' Day. (Rev: BL 4/15/99; HBG 10/99; SLJ 5/99)

5714 Johnson, Doug. *Substitute Teacher Plans* (1–3). Illus. by Tammy Smith. 2002, Holt $16.95 (978-0-8050-6520-6). 32pp. An exhausted teacher mixes up the instructions for her substitute with her list of things to do on her day off, sending her students on an adventure. (Rev: BL 9/15/02; HBG 3/03; SLJ 8/02)

5715 Jules, Jacqueline. *No English* (PS–2). Illus. by Amy Huntington. 2007, Mitten $17.95 (978-1-58726-474-0). 32pp. Second-grader Diane befriends a new student, Blanca, when she discovers that she cannot speak English, and they use drawings to get to know one another. (Rev: BL 11/1/07; LMC 1/08; SLJ 1/08)

5716 Karas, G. Brian. *The Class Artist* (K–3). Illus. 2001, Greenwillow LB $15.89 (978-0-688-17815-4). A boy struggles with an art assignment until his teacher suggests that he draw a picture of how he feels. (Rev: BCCB 9/01; BL 11/15/01; HBG 3/02; SLJ 9/01)

5717 Kelley, True. *School Lunch* (K–2). Illus. 2005, Holiday $16.95 (978-0-8234-1894-7). 32pp. When Harriet, the school cook, takes a vacation, students and faculty are disappointed in her replacements and write letters begging her to return. (Rev: BL 9/15/05; SLJ 11/05)

5718 Kirk, Daniel. *Keisha Ann Can!* (PS–1). Illus. by author. 2008, Putnam $15.99 (978-0-399-24179-6). 32pp. African American Keisha Ann loves everything about school and is proud of her achievements in this brightly illustrated story with rhyming text. (Rev: BL 6/1–15/08; SLJ 7/08)

5719 Koster, Gloria. *The Peanut-Free Café* (K–2). Illus. by Maryann Cocca-Leffler. 2006, Albert Whitman $16.99 (978-0-8075-6386-1). Food allergies take center stage in this story about the steps a classmate takes to make life more comfortable for a student with a peanut allergy. (Rev: BL 2/1/06; SLJ 9/06)

5720 Krishnaswami, Uma. *The Happiest Tree: A Yoga Story* (PS–2). Illus. by Ruth Jeyaveeran. 2005, Lee & Low $16.95 (978-1-58430-237-7). 32pp. Meena signs up for a children's yoga class that she hopes will help her to overcome her clumsiness. (Rev: BL 10/1/05; SLJ 11/05)

5721 Laminack, Lester L. *Jake's 100th Day of School* (1–3). Illus. by Judy Love. 2006, Peachtree $16.95 (978-1-56145-355-9). 32pp. Jake has prepared 100 family photographs for the 100th day of school but leaves them at home in his excitement; his principal and a 100-year-old woman rescue the day. (Rev: BL 2/1/06; SLJ 3/06)

5722 Laminack, Lester L. *Snow Day!* (K–2). Illus. by Adam Gustavson. 2007, Peachtree $16.95 (978-1-56145-418-1). A narrator gleefully fantasizes about the various ways to spend a snow day — from snuggling on the sofa to building a snow fort — and the reader is surprised at the end to learn the narrator is in fact the father, a teacher. (Rev: BL 10/1/07; SLJ 10/07)

5723 Larsen, Andrew. *Bella and the Bunny* (PS–K). Illus. by Kate Endle. 2007, Kids Can $14.95 (978-1-55337-970-6). Bella loses her favorite grandma-made sweater at preschool, but is happy to find it again. (Rev: SLJ 5/07)

5724 Larsen, Kirsten. *The Ghost Town Mystery* (K–3). Illus. by Jerry Smath. 2008, Kane paper $5.95 (978-1-57565-257-3). 32pp. On a field trip to a ghost town, Max learns American history, solves a mystery and successfully faces down his fear. (Rev: BLO 2/8/08; SLJ 7/08)

5725 Lee, Hyun Young. *Something for School* (PS–1). Illus. by author. 2008, Kane $15.95 (978-1-933605-85-2). 40pp. It's the first day of kindergarten and everyone thinks Yoon is a boy. (Rev: SLJ 9/08)

5726 Levert, Mireille. *Eddie Longpants* (K–1). Illus. by author. 2005, Groundwood $16.95 (978-0-88899-671-8). Teased by his classmates about being so tall, Eddie Longpants must decide whether to retaliate in kind or show his tormentors that he knows a better way to behave. (Rev: SLJ 10/05)

5727 Lin, Grace. *Lissy's Friends* (PS–2). Illus. by author. 2007, Viking $15.99 (978-0-670-06072-6). 32pp. Lonely at her new school, Lissy makes origami friends that lead to a real-life friendship. (Rev: BL 5/15/07; SLJ 7/07)

5728 Loewen, Nancy. *The Last Day of Kindergarten* (PS–K). Illus. by Sachiko Yoshikawa. 2011, Marshall Cavendish $16.99 (978-0-7614-5807-7). Unpaged. A young girl reflects on her year in kindergarten and her forthcoming graduation. (Rev: SLJ 3/1/11)

5729 Lorenz, Albert. *The Exceptionally, Extraordinarily Ordinary First Day of School* (2–4). Illus. by author. 2010, Abrams $15.95 (978-0-8109-8960-3). Unpaged. An imaginative young boy eager for an ordinary, unremarkable school describes his old one — full of quirky characters, animals everywhere, crazy field trips — with much detail and aplomb in this surreal story full of humor. (Rev: SLJ 11/1/10)

5730 Lovell, Patty. *Stand Tall, Molly Lou Melon* (K–3). Illus. by David Catrow. 2001, Penguin $15.99 (978-0-399-23416-3). First-grader Molly Lou's grandmother has told her to believe in herself, and Molly Lou puts this successfully into action when she moves to a new school and must deal with the bully. (Rev: BCCB 10/01; HBG 3/02; SLJ 10/01)

5731 Ludwig, Trudy. *The Invisible Boy* (PS–2). Illus. by Patrice Barton. 2013, Knopf $16.99 (978-158246450-3). 40pp. It takes the arrival of a new boy at school to make Brian visible to his teacher and classmates — and to find appreciation for his wonderful artwork, which morphs from gray and white to glorious color. Lexile AD680 (Rev: BL 11/1/13; SLJ 9/13*)

5732 McCain, Becky Ray. *Nobody Knew What to Do: A Story About Bullying* (K–3). Illus. by Todd Leonardo. 2001, Whitman $16.99 (978-0-8075-5711-2). 32pp. When a boy sees bullies bothering one of his classmates,

he decides to ask the teacher for help. (Rev: BL 5/15/01; HBG 10/01; SLJ 5/01)

5733 McCourt, Lisa. *Ready for Kindergarten, Stinky Face?* (PS–K). Illus. by Cyd Moore. 2010, Scholastic paper $3.99 (978-0-545-11-518-6). 32pp. A young boy's wild anxieties about the first day of school are calmly put to rest by his patient mother in this reassuring story. (Rev: BL 8/10; SLJ 9/1/10)

5734 McGhee, Alison. *Countdown to Kindergarten* (PS–K). Illus. by Harry Bliss. 2002, Harcourt $16.00 (978-0-15-202516-8). 32pp. A soon-to-be kindergartner fears starting school because she's heard that, among other things, you must be able to tie your shoes. (Rev: BCCB 10/02; BL 8/02; HBG 3/03; SLJ 9/02)

5735 McGhee, Alison. *Mrs. Watson Wants Your Teeth* (K–2). Illus. by Harry Bliss. 2004, Harcourt $16.00 (978-0-15-204931-7). A rumor that her teacher is a 300-year-old alien with a purple tongue and a liking for baby teeth scares a 1st-grader on her first day of school. (Rev: SLJ 9/04)

5736 MacKall, Dandi Daley. *First Day* (PS–K). Illus. by Tiphanie Beeke. 2003, Harcourt $16.00 (978-0-15-216577-2). Told in rhyming text, this story of a little girl's first day of school is a good choice for children facing the transition from family room to classroom. (Rev: HBG 4/04; SLJ 9/03)

5737 McNamara, Margaret. *How Many Seeds in a Pumpkin?* (K–3). Illus. by G. Brian Karas. 2007, Random $14.99 (978-0-375-84014-2). 40pp. The smallest boy in the class gains confidence by correctly guessing the number of seeds in three pumpkins, and everyone learns some basic math and science concepts in the process. (Rev: BL 6/1–15/07; SLJ 7/07)

5738 McNamara, Margaret. *Martin Luther King Jr. Day* (K–1). Illus. by Mike Gordon. Series: Robin Hill School. Ready-to-Read. 2007, Simon & Schuster LB $13.89 (978-1-4169-3495-0); paper $3.99 (978-1-4169-3494-3). 32pp. On a trip to a museum, 1st-graders learn about Dr. King and his importance. (Rev: SLJ 4/08)

5739 McNaughton, Colin. *When I Grow Up* (PS–1). Illus. by author. 2005, Candlewick $12.99 (978-0-7636-2675-4). Children putting on a school play tell what they want to be one day — except for one little boy, who is reassured when he says he doesn't want to grow up. (Rev: SLJ 7/05)

5740 Mahoney, Daniel J. *Monstergarten* (PS–1). Illus. by Jef Kaminsky. 2013, Feiwel & Friends $16.99 (978-125001441-2). 40pp. Monster Patrick is worried about the first day of kindergarten because he just doesn't think he's scary enough. Will he fit in? Lexile AD360 (Rev: BLO 9/15/13; SLJ 11/13)

5741 Mills, Claudia. *Ziggy's Blue-Ribbon Day* (K–3). Illus. by R. W. Alley. 2005, Farrar $16.00 (978-0-374-32352-3). 32pp. Ziggy's artistic talent makes up for his lack of athletic ability at the track-and-field meet. (Rev: BL 9/1/05; SLJ 11/05)

5742 Milord, Susan. *Happy 100th Day* (K–2). Illus. by Mary Newell DePalma. 2011, Scholastic $16.99 (978-

0-439-88281-1). 40pp. Graham dreads the 100th Day of School, which coincides with his birthday, when he learns he must read 100 books by then. Lexile AD650L (Rev: BLO 1/1–15/11; SLJ 2/1/11)

5743 Milord, Susan. *Happy School Year!* (PS–1). Illus. by Mary Newell Depalma. 2008, Scholastic $15.99 (978-0-439-88280-4). All over town a great variety of multi-cultural children prepare for their first day of school in a variety of different ways. (Rev: BL 8/08; LMC 10/08; SLJ 7/08)

5744 Mochizuki, Ken. *Heroes* (2–4). Illus. by Dom Lee. 1995, Lee & Low $15.95 (978-1-880000-16-8). 32pp. During the Vietnam War, a Japanese American child becomes the butt of other children's bullying. (Rev: BL 3/15/95; HB 5/95; SLJ 7/95)

5745 Moon, Nicola. *Something Special* (K–2). Illus. by Alex Ayliffe. 1997, Peachtree $14.95 (978-1-56145-137-1). Charlie decides to bring his new baby sister to school for a special show-and-tell. (Rev: BL 6/1–15/97; SLJ 6/97)

5746 Moore-Mallinos, Jennifer. *My Brother Is Autistic* (1–3). Illus. by Marta Fàbrega. 2008, Barron's paper $6.99 (978-0-7641-4044-0). 32pp. A young boy is ashamed of his autistic brother's behavior at school until an observant teacher steps in. (Rev: SLJ 6/09)

5747 Moreillon, Judi. *Ready and Waiting for You* (PS–2). Illus. by Catherine Stock. 2013, Eerdmans $17 (978-080285355-4). 32pp. Bright collage artwork and repetition on gatefold pages fill this warm picture book that welcomes a new student (never pictured, thus representing the reader) onto the school bus, into the new school, and finally into a cheerful new classroom. (Rev: BL 9/1/13)

5748 Morton, Carlene. *The Library Pages* (K–3). Illus. by Valeria Docampo. 2010, Upstart $17.95 (978-1-60213-045-6). Unpaged. While out on maternity leave, the school librarian receives a DVD showing her students "helping" around the library by reshelving everything and making repairs with glitter tape; the librarian is horrified until everyone yells "April Fool!" (Rev: LMC 11–12/10; SLJ 9/1/10)

5749 Munsch, Robert. *We Share Everything!* (PS–1). Illus. by Michael Martchenko. 1999, Scholastic $11.95 (978-0-590-89600-9). 32pp. In kindergarten, the high jinks of Amanda and Jeremiah prove to be too much for their long-suffering teacher. (Rev: BCCB 11/99; BL 9/1/99; HBG 3/00; SLJ 9/99)

5750 Northway, Jennifer. *See You Later, Mom!* (PS). Illus. by author. 2006, Frances Lincoln $15.95 (978-1-84507-537-8). William takes his time separating from Mom and making friends at preschool. (Rev: SLJ 6/06)

5751 O'Connor, Jane. *Fancy Nancy: Poet Extraordinaire!* (1–3). Illus. by Robin Preiss Glasser. Series: Fancy Nancy. 2010, HarperCollins $12.99 (978-006189643-9). 32pp. Fancy Nancy is inspired by her class poetry unit but finds herself unable to get started writing. (Rev: BL 4/15/10)

5752 O'Neill, Alexis. *The Recess Queen* (PS–1). Illus. by Laura Huliska-Beith. 2002, Scholastic $16.99 (978-0-439-20637-2). 32pp. Mean Jean, the recess queen, has a change in attitude when the new girl at school asks her to play in this brightly illustrated, energetic tale. (Rev: BCCB 3/02; BL 3/1/02; HBG 10/02; SLJ 3/02)

5753 O'Neill, Alexis. *The Worst Best Friend* (PS–K). Illus. by Laura Huliska-Beith. 2008, Scholastic $16.99 (978-0-545-01023-8). 32pp. A tale of preschool friendship, betrayal, and making up that children will recognize. (Rev: BL 9/1/08)

5754 Pak, Soyung. *Sumi's First Day of School Ever* (PS–1). Illus. by Joung Un Kim. 2003, Viking $15.99 (978-0-670-03522-9). Sumi, a little Korean girl, is afraid on her first day of school, but the kindness of a teacher and friendliness of a classmate make her feel more comfortable. (Rev: HB 7/03; HBG 4/04; SLJ 8/03)

5755 Pattison, Darcy. *19 Girls and Me* (PS–2). Illus. by Steven Salerno. 2006, Philomel $16.99 (978-0-399-24336-3). John Hercules is dismayed to learn he is the only boy in his kindergarten class, but soon sets aside his assumptions about girls and thinks of his 19 classmates as friends. (Rev: SLJ 7/06)

5756 Pérez, L. King. *First Day in Grapes* (1–3). Illus. by Robert Casilla. 2002, Lee & Low $16.95 (978-1-58430-045-8). 32pp. Chico, the son of migrant workers, starts 3rd grade in yet another school with trepidation, but his first day goes well despite bullies and a surly bus driver. (Rev: BL 11/15/02; HBG 3/03; SLJ 10/02)

5757 Plourde, Lynn. *Book Fair Day* (1–3). Illus. by Thor Wickstrom. 2006, Dutton $16.99 (978-0-525-47696-2). 40pp. It's Book Fair Day in the school library, and Dewey Booker is worried that all the good books will be gone by the time his class gets its turn. (Rev: BL 8/06; SLJ 7/06)

5758 Plourde, Lynn. *Pajama Day* (PS–2). Illus. by Thor Wickstrom. 2005, Dutton $16.99 (978-0-525-47355-8). 40pp. Drew A. Blank shows his inventiveness when he arrives at school unprepared for Pajama Day. (Rev: BL 1/1–15/05; SLJ 2/05)

5759 Plourde, Lynn. *School Picture Day* (K–2). Illus. by Thor Wickstrom. 2002, Dutton $16.99 (978-0-525-46886-8). 40pp. Josephina Caroleena Wattasheena's curious nature causes a calamity at her school on picture day. (Rev: BL 8/02; HBG 3/03; SLJ 7/02)

5760 Plourde, Lynn. *Science Fair Day* (PS–3). Illus. by Thor Wickstrom. 2008, Dutton $16.99 (978-0-525-47878-2). 40pp. On the final day of science fair preparations Ima Kindanozee creates havoc as she investigates her fellow students' projects. (Rev: BL 11/15/07; SLJ 3/08)

5761 Polacco, Patricia. *Mr. Lincoln's Way* (K–3). Illus. 2001, Penguin $16.99 (978-0-399-23754-6). 40pp. A school principal uses a bully's interest in birds to teach him about tolerance and kindness. (Rev: BL 9/1/01; HBG 3/02; SLJ 8/01)

5762 Portis, Antoinette. *Kindergarten Diary* (PS–1). Illus. by author. 2010, HarperCollins $12.99 (978-0-

06-145691-6). 32pp. Annalina confides her early fears about kindergarten and how it took only a month before she realized she was enjoying herself. (Rev: BL 5/15/10; HB 7–8/10; SLJ 7/1/10)

5763 Poydar, Nancy. *The Bad-News Report Card* (K–3). Illus. 2006, Holiday $16.95 (978-0-8234-1992-0). 32pp. Stricken by an attack of report card anxiety, Isabel hides the card away and tries to forget about it; when she finally checks it out, she discovers that all her worries were unwarranted. (Rev: BL 9/1/06)

5764 Poydar, Nancy. *The Biggest Test in the Universe* (1–3). Illus. by author. 2005, Holiday House $16.95 (978-0-8234-1944-9). Sam is apprehensive about taking the "big test" after hearing horror stories about it from the older kids, but he discovers these stories are exaggerated. (Rev: SLJ 9/05)

5765 Poydar, Nancy. *Bunny Business* (PS–3). Illus. by author. 2003, Holiday House $16.95 (978-0-8234-1771-1). Harry turns out to be a good listener despite his fellow students' low opinion. (Rev: HBG 10/03; SLJ 4/03)

5766 Poydar, Nancy. *Fish School* (1–3). Illus. by author. 2009, Holiday $16.95 (978-0-8234-2140-4). Charlie hopes to educate his treasured pet goldfish on a class trip to the aquarium; however, when Charlie's backpack and the bag containing his goldfish goes missing, it is Charlie who learns a lesson; includes information on caring for goldfish. (Rev: BL 7/09; SLJ 8/09)

5767 Poydar, Nancy. *No Fair Science Fair* (K–3). Illus. by author. 2011, Holiday House $14.95 (978-0-8234-2269-2). 32pp. Otis's efforts at attracting birds earn a "Stick-withit-Prize" from the science fair judges. Lexile AD420L (Rev: BL 3/1/11; SLJ 3/1/11)

5768 Poydar, Nancy. *Zip, Zip . . . Homework* (PS–2). Illus. by author. 2008, Holiday $16.95 (978-0-8234-2090-2). 32pp. Violet is so absorbed in the organization of her efficient new backpack that she leaves her assignment at school and finds herself weaving a tangled web. (Rev: BL 9/1/08; SLJ 9/08)

5769 Preller, James. *A Pirate's Guide to First Grade* (PS–1). Illus. by Greg Ruth. 2010, Feiwel & Friends $16.99 (978-0-312-36928-6). 48pp. An imaginative young boy narrates his first day in 1st grade using dynamic pirate lingo. e Lexile AD690L (Rev: BL 8/10; LMC 8–9/10; SLJ 8/1/10*)

5770 Primavera, Elise. *Louise the Big Cheese and the Back-to-School Smarty-Pants* (K–2). Illus. by Diane Goode. 2011, Simon & Schuster $16.99 (978-1-4424-0600-1). Unpaged. Louise enters 2nd grade determined to make straight A's, but things don't work out as planned. (Rev: SLJ 6/11*)

5771 Pulver, Robin. *Author Day for Room 3T* (K–3). Illus. by Chuck Richards. 2005, Clarion $16.00 (978-0-618-35406-1). It's Author Day and the class has been eagerly anticipating someone "new and different," so when a chimp turns up (the librarian is very near-sighted), they are not taken aback. (Rev: BL 5/1/05; SLJ 4/05)

5772 Pulver, Robin. *The Case of the Incapacitated Capitals* (PS–3). Illus. by Lynn Rowe Reed. 2012, Holiday $16.95 (978-0-8234-2402-3). 32pp. The students in Mr. Wright's class are not using their capital letters, and this has led to a serious problem. (Rev: BL 10/1/12*; HB 11–12/12; SLJ 10/12)

5773 Pulver, Robin. *Thank You, Miss Doover* (1–3). Illus. by Stephanie Roth Sisson. 2010, Holiday House $16.95 (978-0-8234-2046-9). 32pp. Young Jack struggles to learn how to write a thank-you letter in this funny book with cartoonlike illustrations. Lexile GN540L (Rev: BL 11/15/10; LMC 3–4/11; SLJ 10/1/10)

5774 Quackenbush, Robert. *First Grade Jitters* (K–1). Illus. by Yan Nascimbene. 2010, HarperCollins $16.99 (978-0-06-077632-9). 32pp. A boy needs reassurance from his friends before starting 1st grade in this updated version of the 1982 classic. e (Rev: BLO 7/10; SLJ 7/1/10)

5775 Radabaugh, Melinda. *Going to School* (PS–1). Series: First Time. 2003, Heinemann LB $18.50 (978-1-4034-0227-1). A reassuring, simple introduction to what happens during a typical day at school. (Rev: HBG 10/03; SLJ 6/03) [372.12]

5776 Reiser, Lynn. *Earthdance* (PS–3). Illus. 1999, Greenwillow LB $15.89 (978-0-688-16327-3). 32pp. While Terra is at school preparing for a show, her astronaut mother is traveling to the end of the universe. (Rev: BL 12/1/99; HBG 3/00; SLJ 10/99)

5777 Reynolds, Peter H. *The Dot* (K–2). Illus. by author. 2003, Candlewick $14.00 (978-0-7636-1961-9). A young girl who is sure she can't draw finds success when she heeds her teacher's advice to "make a mark and see where it takes you." (Rev: HBG 4/04; SLJ 11/03)

5778 Rockwell, Anne. *Career Day* (PS–K). Illus. by Lizzy Rockwell. 2000, HarperCollins $16.99 (978-0-06-027565-5). 32pp. During Mrs. Madoff's classroom Career Day presentations, 10 children introduce a parent or grandparent who talks about his or her occupation. (Rev: BL 5/1/00; HBG 10/00; SLJ 7/00)

5779 Rockwell, Anne. *First Day of School* (K–2). Illus. by Lizzy Rockwell. 2011, HarperCollins $16.99 (978-0-06-050191-4). 40pp. A diverse group of kids prepare for their first day of school by recalling how they got through last year's first day. (Rev: BL 8/11; SLJ 9/1/11)

5780 Rockwell, Anne. *My Preschool* (PS). Illus. by author. 2008, Holt $16.95 (978-0-8050-7955-5). 32pp. This picture book follows little Fred's day at preschool, looking at both the fun and the difficult parts. (Rev: BL 8/08; SLJ 4/08)

5781 Rodman, Mary Ann. *First Grade Stinks!* (PS–1). Illus. by Beth Spiegel. 2006, Peachtree $15.95 (978-1-56145-377-1). Haley pretty quickly decides that 1st grade is no fun in comparison with kindergarten. (Rev: BL 8/06; SLJ 8/06)

5782 Rogers, Jacqueline. *Tiptoe into Kindergarten* (PS–1). Illus. 1999, Scholastic $10.95 (978-0-590-46653-0). 32pp. A preschooler steals into her brother's kindergarten class and soon becomes part of the activities. (Rev: BL 8/99; HBG 3/00; SLJ 9/99)

5783 Rosen, Michael. *Totally Wonderful Miss Plumberry* (PS–K). Illus. by Chinlun Lee. 2006, Candlewick $15.99 (978-0-7636-2744-7). 40pp. Molly's teacher recognizes Molly's huge disappointment when Russell's stegosaurus seems to be stealing the show and she refocuses the class on Molly's crystal. (Rev: BL 8/06)

5784 Rousaki, Maria. *Unique Monique* (PS–2). Illus. by Polina Papanikolaou. 2003, Kane $15.95 (978-1-929132-51-5). Monique experiments with various ways to enhance her drab school uniform, but they all meet with the principal's disapproval until she thinks of her teeth. (Rev: HBG 4/04; SLJ 11/03)

5785 Schaefer, Carole Lexa. *Kids Like Us* (PS). Illus. by Pierr Morgan. 2008, Viking $15.99 (978-0-670-06290-4). On a gray and rainy day, children in a classroom use their imaginations to fuel their play. (Rev: BL 5/1/08; SLJ 5/08)

5786 Scieszka, Jon. *Math Curse* (1–4). Illus. by Lane Smith. 1995, Viking $17.99 (978-0-670-86194-1). All sorts of math problems and riddles, from the practical to the absurd are presented in this school story. (Rev: BCCB 10/95; BL 11/1/95*; HB 11/95; SLJ 9/95*)

5787 Senisi, Ellen B. *Kindergarten Kids* (PS–K). Illus. 1994, Scholastic paper $3.25 (978-0-590-47614-0). 32pp. A photo-essay that describes a typical day in a kindergarten class in Schenectady, New York. (Rev: BL 11/1/94) [372.21]

5788 Shannon, David. *David Goes to School* (PS–K). Illus. 1999, Scholastic $16.99 (978-0-590-48087-1). David, an imaginative nonconformist, has difficulty doing the right thing when he begins school. (Rev: BCCB 1/00; BL 8/99*; HBG 3/00; SLJ 9/99)

5789 Slate, Joseph. *Miss Bindergarten Celebrates the Last Day of Kindergarten* (PS–K). Illus. by Ashley Wolff. 2006, Button $16.99 (978-0-525-47744-0). 48pp. The school year comes to an end for Miss Bindergarten and her 26 alphabetical kindergarten students. (Rev: BL 2/15/06; SLJ 3/06)

5790 Slate, Joseph. *Miss Bindergarten Takes a Field Trip* (PS–K). Illus. by Ashley Wolff. 2001, Dutton $16.99 (978-0-525-46710-6). 32pp. Miss Bindergarten takes her kindergartners on an interesting field trip that subtly introduces all sorts of shapes. (Rev: BL 10/1/01; HBG 3/02; SLJ 9/01)

5791 Stampler, Ann R. *Go Home, Mrs. Beekman!* (PS). Illus. by Marsha Carrington. 2008, Dutton $16.99 (978-0-525-46933-9). 32pp. Emily asks her mother to stay with her when she gets to preschool but then finds that her mother won't leave. (Rev: BL 8/08; LMC 11/08)

5792 Stoeke, Janet Morgan. *The Bus Stop* (PS–1). Illus. by author. 2007, Dutton $12.99 (978-0-525-47805-8). 24pp. This charming, reassuring picture book focuses on three young children as they prepare to ride the school bus for the very first time. (Rev: BL 5/15/07; SLJ 7/07)

5793 Stoeke, Janet Morgan. *It's Library Day* (K–2). Illus. by author. 2008, Dutton $12.99 (978-0-525-47944-4). A multicultural group of children enjoy visiting the school library and finding just the right books to read. (Rev: BL 7/08; SLJ 7/08)

5794 Stuve-Bodeen, Stephanie. *Elizabeti's School* (PS–1). Illus. by Christy Hale. 2002, Lee & Low $16.95 (978-1-58430-043-4). Elizabeti tackles her first day at school and comes home to tell her loving family all about it in this story set in Tanzania. (Rev: BCCB 12/02; BL 9/15/02; HB 11/02; HBG 3/03; SLJ 9/02)

5795 Trice, Linda. *Kenya's Word* (1–3). Illus. by Pamela Johnson. 2006, Charlesbridge $16.95 (978-1-57091-887-2); paper $6.95 (978-1-57091-888-9). 32pp. After a series of homework assignments that went awry, Kenya is determined to impress her teacher and classmates with her "favorite describing word." (Rev: BL 2/1/06; SLJ 3/06)

5796 Uegaki, Chieri. *Suki's Kimono* (K–3). Illus. by Stephane Jorisch. 2003, Kids Can $15.95 (978-1-55337-084-0). Undeterred by her older sisters' opposition, young Suki proudly wears her favorite garment — a kimono — on the first day of school. (Rev: HBG 4/04; SLJ 12/03)

5797 Urdahl, Catherine. *Polka-Dot Fixes Kindergarten* (PS–K). Illus. by Mai S. Kemble. 2011, Charlesbridge $16.95 (978-1-57091-737-0); paper $7.95 (978-1-57091-738-7). 32pp. Starting kindergarten is stressful for Polka-Dot, and even Grandpa's emergency kit doesn't help her cope with classmate Liz; Polka-Dot finds her own solution in the end. (Rev: BL 8/11; SLJ 7/11)

5798 Veldkamp, Tjibbe. *The School Trip* (PS–3). Illus. by Philip Hopman. 2001, Front St $15.95 (978-1-886910-70-6). 32pp. Afraid of attending school, Davy opts to build his own, and when he adds wheels the fun really starts. (Rev: BL 8/01; HBG 10/01; SLJ 7/01)

5799 Vernick, Audrey. *Is Your Buffalo Ready for Kindergarten?* (PS–K). Illus. by Daniel Jennewein. 2010, HarperCollins $16.99 (978-0-06-176275-8). 32pp. A young buffalo does his best to behave in a kindergarten class full of children also learning the rules in this funny story. (Rev: BL 8/10; SLJ 6/1/10)

5800 Wells, Rosemary. *Hands Off, Harry!* (PS–K). Illus. by author. 2011, HarperCollins $14.99 (978-0-06-192112-4). 40pp. A young boy having a hard time respecting others' personal space learns a different way of behaving. (Rev: BL 5/1/11; SLJ 7/11)

5801 Winters, Kay. *This School Year Will Be the Best!* (K–2). Illus. by Renee Andriani. 2010, Dutton $16.99 (978-0-525-42775-4). 32pp. When a teacher asks her young students to share their hopes for the coming year, the responses are satisfyingly diverse. (Rev: BL 5/1/10; SLJ 8/1/10)

5802 Woodson, Jacqueline. *Each Kindness* (K–3). Illus. by E. B. Lewis. 2012, Penguin $16.99 (978-0-399-24652-4). 32pp. In this story told from the bully's perspective, mean African American Chloe never gets a chance to make things right with a white girl she tormented. Jane Addams Book Award; ALA Notable Children's Book; Charlotte Zolotow Award. ⌒ Lexile AD640 (Rev: BL 8/12*; HB 1–2/13; LMC 1–2/13; SLJ 9/12*)

5803 Wortche, Allison. *Rosie Sprout's Time to Shine* (PS–1). Illus. by Patrice Barton. 2011, Knopf $17.99 (978-037586721-7); LB $20.99 (978-037596721-4). 40pp. Rosie has always been jealous of overly confident and successful Violet, but she discovers she herself can shine when a gardening project — and a chance to be generous — comes along. (Rev: BLO 12/15/11; LMC 3–4/12; SLJ 1/12)

5804 Yashima, Taro. *Crow Boy* (K–3). Illus. by author. 1955, Puffin paper $6.99 (978-0-14-050172-8). 40pp. Distinguished picture book about a shy little Japanese boy who feels like an outsider at school.

5805 Zemach, Kaethe. *Ms. McCaw Learns to Draw* (K–3). Illus. by author. 2008, Scholastic $16.99 (978-0-439-82914-4). Dudley's teacher, Ms. McCaw, is patient with his learning disabilities and Dudley happily comes to her rescue with his artistic talent. (Rev: BL 2/1/08; LMC 1/08; SLJ 1/08)

5806 Ziefert, Harriet. *Schools Have Learn* (PS–2). Illus. by Amanda Haley. 2004, Blue Apple $15.95 (978-1-59354-056-2). Inventive wordplay — "good-byes have hugs, backpacks have lugs" — accompanies children through a typical day. (Rev: BCCB 12/04; SLJ 2/05)

TRANSPORTATION AND MACHINES

5807 Bee, William. *And the Train Goes . . . .* (PS–K). Illus. by author. 2007, Candlewick $15.99 (978-0-7636-3248-9). There's a lot going on in this train. People off to various destinations are portrayed in lovely illustrations and described in entertaining text. (Rev: SLJ 6/07)

5808 Bell, Babs. *The Bridge Is Up!* (PS). Illus. by Rob Hefferan. 2004, HarperCollins LB $13.89 (978-0-06-053794-4). A colorfully illustrated cumulative tale about a long line of vehicles (driven by various animals) all waiting to cross a drawbridge. (Rev: SLJ 3/04)

5809 Biggs, Brian. *Everything Goes in the Air* (PS–2). Illus. by author. 2012, HarperCollins $14.99 (978-006195810-6). 56pp. This colorful cartoon-style book follows Henry and his parents as they arrive at the airport, ride the bus from long-term parking, go through security, board their plane, and take off; includes cutaways of planes, seek-and-find activities, and interactive features. (Rev: BLO 10/15/12; HB 11–12/12)

5810 Biggs, Brian. *Everything Goes: On Land* (K–2). Illus. by author. 2011, HarperCollins $14.99 (978-0-06-195809-0). 56pp. A busy look at city streets crowded with vehicles of all kinds, as Dad answers young Henry's many questions about modes of transportation. (Rev: BL 11/1/11; SLJ 11/1/11)

5811 Brown, Margaret Wise. *Two Little Trains* (PS–K). Illus. by Diane Dillon. 2001, HarperCollins $16.99 (978-0-06-028376-6). 40pp. Using double-page spreads, this book shows two parallel journeys, one by a streamlined diesel train as it travels across the country and the other by a toy train as it moves around a house. (Rev: BL 4/15/01*; HB 5/01*; HBG 10/01; SLJ 5/01)

5812 Burton, Virginia Lee. *Mike Mulligan and His Steam Shovel* (1–3). Illus. by author. 1939, Houghton LB $11.95 (978-0-395-06681-2); paper $7.99 (978-0-395-25939-9). A thrilling race against time as Mike Mulligan and his steam shovel dig a cellar in one day. Also use: *Katy and the Big Snow* (1973).

5813 Clement, Nathan. *Job Site* (PS–1). Illus. by author. 2011, Boyds Mills $16.95 (978-1-59078-769-4). Unpaged. A community park takes shape as a bulldozer, excavator, loader, and other heavy machinery work according to the instructions of the boss. (Rev: SLJ 5/11)

5814 Cohen, Deborah Bodin. *Engineer Ari and the Rosh Hashanah Ride* (K–3). Illus. by Shahar Kober. 2008, Lerner $17.95 (978-0-8225-8648-7); paper $7.95 (978-0-8225-8650-0). 32pp. In 1892 Israel's first train makes its way — on Rosh Hashanah, the Jewish New Year — from Jaffa to Jerusalem with Engineer Ari at the wheel, a boastful man who takes time on this holy day to reconsider his treatment of his friends. (Rev: BL 9/1/08; SLJ 9/08)

5815 Cooper, Elisha. *Train* (K–3). Illus. by author. 2013, Scholastic $17.99 (978-0-545-38495-7). 40pp. Blending fiction and fact, this picture book introduces the daily routines of a variety of trains and the people who travel and work on them; includes a useful glossary. Booklist Editors' Choice: Books for Youth. (Rev: BL 7/13*; HB 1–2/14; LMC 1–2/14; SLJ 8/13*)

5816 Cowley, Joy. *The Rusty, Trusty Tractor* (K–2). Illus. by Olivier Dunrea. 1999, Boyds Mills $15.95 (978-1-56397-565-3). 40pp. In spite of a tractor salesman's dire predictions, Micah's grandfather's 50-year-old tractor takes the old man through another season on the farm. (Rev: BCCB 3/99; BL 3/15/99; HBG 10/99; SLJ 5/99)

5817 Crews, Donald. *Flying* (PS). Illus. by author. 1986, Greenwillow $17.89 (978-0-688-04319-3); Morrow paper $6.99 (978-0-688-09235-1). Brief text and full-color art highlight this study in movement as a plane takes off, flies over different landscapes, and lands. (Rev: BL 9/1/86; SLJ 10/86)

5818 Crews, Donald. *Freight Train / Tren de carga* (PS–2). Trans. by M. J. Infante. Illus. by author. 2003, Greenwillow $16.99 (978-0-06-056202-1). A lively bilingual book version of the 1979 Caldecott Honor Book showing a multicolored freight train as it makes its journey through tunnels, over bridges, and around big cities. (Rev: HBG 4/04; SLJ 12/03)

5819 Crews, Donald. *Inside Freight Train* (PS). Illus. 2001, HarperCollins $9.99 (978-0-688-17087-5). 12pp. A well-designed board book that makes Crews's famous 1978 book interactive by using split pages that slip sideways to reveal smaller pages. (Rev: BL 12/15/00*; HBG 10/01)

5820 Crews, Donald. *School Bus* (PS–1). Illus. by author. 1984, Greenwillow $17.89 (978-0-688-02808-4); Morrow paper $6.99 (978-0-688-12267-6). 32pp. Many kinds of school buses pick up children for school.

5821 Cuyler, Margery. *The Little Dump Truck* (PS–1). Illus. by Bob Kolar. 2009, Henry Holt $12.99 (978-0-8050-8281-4). 32pp. A contented dump truck and its driver, Hard Hat Pete, are busy at a construction site in this rhyming story with digital art. (Rev: BL 9/15/09; SLJ 11/1/09)

5822 de Roo, Elena. *The Rain Train* (PS–1). Illus. by Brian Lovelock. 2011, Candlewick $15.99 (978-0-7636-5313-2). 32pp. A little boy enjoys a trip on a train through a rainy night — that all turns out to be a dream. (Rev: BL 5/1/11; SLJ 6/11)

5823 Delafosse, Claude. *Tools* (PS–1). Trans. from French by Wendy Barish. Illus. by Daniel Moignot. Series: First Discovery. 1999, Scholastic $12.95 (978-0-439-04404-2). This book covers such common tools as pliers, wall anchors, saws, and hammers. (Rev: HBG 3/00; SLJ 1/00)

5824 Frazee, Marla. *Roller Coaster* (PS–1). Illus. by author. 2003, Harcourt $16.00 (978-0-15-204554-8). A young boy who is just tall enough to ride the giant coaster for the first time has a breath-taking experience. (Rev: HB 5/03; HBG 10/03; SLJ 7/03)

5825 Freymann, Saxton, and Joost Elffers. *Fast Food* (PS–2). Illus. by Saxton Freymann. 2006, Scholastic $12.99 (978-0-439-11019-8). 32pp. In this volume, Freymann and Effers turn their ordinary fruits and vegetables into a variety of modes of transportation. (Rev: BL 2/1/06*; LMC 5/06; SLJ 4/06) [641.8]

5826 Gall, Chris. *Dinotrux* (PS–1). Illus. by author. 2009, Little, Brown $16.99 (978-0-316-02777-9). 32pp. A funny tale of ferocious prehistoric trucks — Craneosaurus, Dumploducus — that roamed with the dinosaurs. (Rev: BL 7/09; SLJ 6/09)

5827 Garcia, Emma. *Tip Tip Dig Dig* (PS–K). Illus. by author. 2007, Sterling $14.95 (978-1-905417-58-2). 32pp. From hole in the ground to finished playground, a variety of construction vehicles are called into action. (Rev: SLJ 11/07)

5828 Garland, Michael. *Car Goes Far* (PS–2). Illus. by author. 2013, Holiday $14.95 (978-0-8234-2598-3). 32pp. A simple story about a car that has various adventures and winds up extremely dirty, in dire need of a visit to the car wash. (Rev: BL 6/13; SLJ 4/13)

5829 Gibbons, Faye. *Full Steam Ahead* (K–3). Illus. by Sherry Meidell. 2002, Boyds Mills $15.95 (978-1-56397-858-6). 32pp. Sammy and his family experience the excitement of seeing the first train to roll through their home town in Georgia. (Rev: BL 4/1/02; HBG 10/02; SLJ 7/02)

5830 Gramatky, Hardie. *Little Toot* (K–3). Illus. by author. 1939, Penguin paper $7.99 (978-0-698-11576-7). 96pp. Little Toot, son of the mightiest tug in the harbor, had no ambition until he became a hero during a raging storm.

5831 Hamilton, Kersten. *Red Truck* (PS–K). Illus. by Valeria Petrone. 2008, Viking $15.99 (978-0-670-06275-1). Can the little red tow truck make it through the mud to rescue the children on the school bus? We think he can. (Rev: BL 1/1–15/08; SLJ 4/08)

5832 Hill, Lee S. *Earthmovers* (2–3). Illus. Series: Pull Ahead Books. 2002, Lerner LB $22.60 (978-0-8225-0689-8); paper $5.95 (978-0-8225-0603-4). A small-

format book for younger readers about how earthmovers and their drivers accomplish their tasks. Also use *Trains* (2002). (Rev: BL 8/02; HBG 3/03; SLJ 10/02)

5833 Hoban, Tana. *Construction Zone* (PS–1). Illus. 1997, Greenwillow $15.89 (978-0-688-12285-0). 32pp. Thirteen construction machines like the bulldozer, backhoe, and forklift are introduced in pictures and a simple text. (Rev: BCCB 4/97; BL 4/1/97; SLJ 3/97) [624]

5834 Holub, Joan. *Dig, Scoop, Ka-boom!* (PS–1). Illus. by David Gordon. 2013, Random House paper $3.99 (978-03758691-0-5). 24pp. Six construction vehicles work together at a site that eventually reveals it to be a children's sandbox. (Rev: BL 6/13)

5835 Horacek, Petr. *Choo Choo* (PS). Illus. by author. 2008, Candlewick $5.99 (978-0-7636-3477-3). 16pp. A trainful of children head for the beach in this bright and rhythmic board book. (Rev: BL 7/08)

5836 Hubbell, Patricia. *Airplanes: Soaring! Diving! Turning!* (PS–2). Illus. by Megan Halsey. Series: Things That Go! 2008, Marshall Cavendish $16.99 (978-0-7614-5388-8). 32pp. Paired with simple rhyming text, planes of all kinds — cargo, military, modern, vintage — fly across the pages of this attractive book. (Rev: BL 4/1/08; SLJ 7/08)

5837 Hubbell, Patricia. *My First Airplane Ride* (PS–1). Illus. by Nancy Speir. 2008, Marshall Cavendish $16.99 (978-0-7614-5436-6). 40pp. A boy's first trip by plane is chronicled in rhyming text and detailed illustrations of pre-departure procedures such as getting boarding passes and clearing security. (Rev: BL 9/1/08)

5838 Hubbell, Patricia. *Trains: Huffing! Puffing! Pulling!* (1–3). 2005, Marshall Cavendish $14.95 (978-0-7614-5194-5). 32pp. With an appealing blend of rhyming text and intricate collage illustrations, this picture book introduces young readers to different types of trains. (Rev: BL 10/1/05; SLJ 9/05)

5839 Hundal, Nancy. *Number 21* (PS–3). Illus. by Brian Denes. 2001, Fitzhenry & Whiteside $16.95 (978-1-55041-543-8). 32pp. Three children are excited to see Dad's new dump truck, especially when he fills the dump box with water to make an instant swimming pool. (Rev: BL 8/01; SLJ 4/01)

5840 Jorgensen, Norman. *The Call of the Osprey* (K–3). Illus. by Brian Harrison-Lever. 2004, Fremantle Arts Centre $22.50 (978-1-920731-85-4). A young boy named Tom and a retired sea captain lovingly restore a steamboat, which Tom then inherits, in a simple story full of sea lore. (Rev: SLJ 2/05)

5841 Kuklin, Susan. *All Aboard! A True Train Story* (PS–1). Illus. 2003, Scholastic $16.99 (978-0-439-45583-1). An eye-catching visit to the Durango & Silverton narrow-gauge steam railway in Colorado, with minimal text. (Rev: BL 2/1/04; HBG 4/04; SLJ 12/03)

5842 Liebman, Dan. *I Want to Be a Mechanic* (K–2). Series: I Want to Be. 2003, Firefly LB $14.95 (978-1-55297-695-1); paper $3.99 (978-1-55297-693-7). A photo-filled inside look at a day in the life of an auto mechanic. (Rev: SLJ 8/03) [629.28]

5843 London, Jonathan. *My Big Rig* (PS–K). Illus. by Viviana Garofoli. 2007, Marshall Cavendish $14.99 (978-0-7614-5346-8). 32pp. Inspired by his toy truck, a young boy imagines a cross-country trip at the wheel of a tractor-trailer. (Rev: BL 4/15/07)

5844 London, Jonathan. *A Plane Goes Ka-Zoom!* (PS). Illus. by Denis Roche. 2010, Henry Holt $15.99 (978-0-8050-8970-7). 32pp. A family visits an air show, watches activities at an airport, and then takes a ride in a plane. (Rev: BL 9/1/10; SLJ 11/1/10)

5845 London, Jonathan. *A Train Goes Clickety-Clack* (PS–K). Illus. by Denis Roche. 2007, Holt $15.95 (978-0-8050-7972-2). 32pp. This choo-choo title is right on track with its rhythmic and colorful look at trains old and new. (Rev: SLJ 10/07)

5846 London, Jonathan. *A Truck Goes Rattley-Bumpa* (PS). Illus. by Denis Roche. 2005, Holt $14.95 (978-0-8050-7233-4). Trucks of all shapes and sizes performing different tasks are shown in simple illustrations with short rhyming couplets. (Rev: BL 10/1/05; SLJ 9/05)

5847 Lyon, George E. *Trucks Roll!* (PS). Illus. by Craig Frazier. 2007, Atheneum $14.99 (978-1-4169-2435-7). 40pp. Rhyming verses and eye-catching illustrations show how trucks carry many different cargos. (Rev: BL 5/1/07; HB 7/07; SLJ 9/07)

5848 Lyon, George Ella. *Planes Fly!* (PS–2). Illus. by Mick Wiggins. 2013, Atheneum $17.99 (978-144245025-7). 40pp. A picture-book celebration of different kinds of planes, their characteristics and abilities, and the passengers that fly in them. **℮** (Rev: BL 9/15/13*; HB 9–10/13; LMC 1–2/14; SLJ 7/13)

5849 McCarty, Peter. *Moon Plane* (PS–K). 2006, Holt $16.95 (978-0-8050-7943-2). 32pp. Gazing up at a plane in the sky, a young boy imagines what it would be like to board such an aircraft and fly all the way to the moon; the simple, effective text and illustrations encourage imagination. (Rev: BL 9/1/06; HBG 4/07)

5850 McMullan, Kate. *I'm Fast!* (PS–1). Illus. by Jim McMullan. 2012, HarperCollins $16.99 (978-006192085-1). 40pp. A train and a red sports car engage in a (not too) exciting battle of speed. (Rev: BL 12/15/11; HB 1–2/12; SLJ 1/12)

5851 McMullen, Kate. *I'm Dirty!* (PS–2). Illus. by Jim McMullen. 2006, HarperCollins $16.99 (978-0-06-009293-1). A spirited backhoe loader groans aloud as it works, counting the items it is moving and generally enjoying getting good and dirty. (Rev: BCCB 10/06; BL 9/15/06; HB 11/06; HBG 4/07)

5852 Mandel, Peter. *Jackhammer Sam* (K–2). Illus. by David Catrow. 2011, Roaring Brook $16.99 (978-1-59643-034-1). 40pp. Sam is proud of his jackhammer's vibrations and bounces along to the rhythm as he sends people flying. (Rev: BL 11/15/11; HB 11–12/11; SLJ 11/1/11)

5853 Mayo, Margaret. *Emergency!* (PS–1). Illus. by Alex Ayliffe. 2002, Carolrhoda $14.95 (978-0-87614-922-5). 32pp. Arresting artwork details emergency vehicles and their uses in this exciting, large-format picture book. (Rev: BL 8/02; HBG 3/03; SLJ 10/02)

5854 Meltzer, Lynn. *The Construction Crew* (PS–K). Illus. by Carrie Eko-Burgess. 2011, Henry Holt $12.99 (978-0-8050-8884-7). 40pp. A construction crew demolishes an old building and builds a house in this simple story with rhyming text and colorful illustrations. (Rev: BL 12/1/11; SLJ 12/1/11)

5855 Milusich, Janice. *Off Go Their Engines, Off Go Their Lights* (K–1). Illus. by David Gordon. 2008, Dutton $15.99 (978-0-525-47940-6). 32pp. On their way home in a yellow taxi, a mother and son watch vehicles of all kinds parking at the end of their working day. (Rev: BL 6/1–15/08; SLJ 8/08)

5856 Moore, Patrick. *The Mighty Street Sweeper* (PS). Illus. 2006, Holt $15.95 (978-0-8050-7789-6). 32pp. A colorful celebration of the street sweeper, a little truck with a very big responsibility. (Rev: BL 10/15/06; SLJ 10/06)

5857 Mortensen, Denise Dowling. *Wake Up Engines* (PS–K). Illus. by Melissa Iwai. 2007, Clarion $16.00 (978-0-618-51736-7). 32pp. Morning traffic outside parallels the activities of a little boy playing with his toys inside. (Rev: BL 7/07; SLJ 7/07)

5858 Munro, Roxie. *Go! Go! Go!* (PS–2). Illus. by author. 2009, Sterling LB $15.95 (978-1-4027-3773-2). 24pp. With folds, flaps, and lots of energy, Munro presents many people on the go — firemen heading to an emergency, riders on horseback, race car pit crews, and so forth. (Rev: HB 7/09; SLJ 6/09)

5859 Neitzel, Shirley. *I'm Taking a Trip on My Train* (PS–1). Illus. by Nancy W. Parker. 1999, Greenwillow LB $14.89 (978-0-688-15834-7). 32pp. A boy pretends he is an engineer on his toy train in this picture book, which uses rebus drawings to introduce parts of a train and a freight yard. (Rev: BL 4/15/99; HBG 10/99; SLJ 3/99)

5860 Niemann, Christoph. *That's How!* (PS–1). Illus. by author. 2011, HarperCollins $16.99 (978-0-06-201963-9). Unpaged. An imaginative little boy pictures the mysterious mechanisms — which usually involve animals — behind various construction machines and vehicles. (Rev: BL 7/1/11; SLJ 5/1/11)

5861 Parker, Neal Evan. *Captain Annabel* (PS–4). Illus. by Emily Harris. 2005, Down East $15.95 (978-0-89272-653-0). Encouraged by her father, Annabel has always loved sailing, and she grows up to be a tugboat captain. (Rev: SLJ 5/05)

5862 Piper, Watty. *The Little Engine That Could* (PS–1). Illus. by Loren Long. 2005, Philomel $17.99 (978-0-399-24467-4). This new edition of the beloved children's classic, originally published in 1930, about a diminutive but determined train engine is beautifully illustrated in rich, warm colors. (Rev: BL 9/1/05; SLJ 9/05)

5863 Pulver, Robin. *Axle Annie and the Speed Grump* (K–3). Illus. 2005, Dial $16.99 (978-0-8037-2787-8). 32pp. Axle Annie, Burskyville's beloved and very skilled school bus driver, saves the life of dangerous driver Rush Hotfoot with the help of her passengers. (Rev: BL 11/1/05; SLJ 12/05)

5864 Ransom, Candice F. *The Old Blue Pickup Truck* (PS–1). Illus. by Jenny Mattheson. 2009, Walker $16.99 (978-0-8027-9591-5). 32pp. A daughter notices how many different uses the pickup has as she and her father run several errands together. (Rev: BL 7/09; SLJ 5/09)

5865 Ransom, Candice F. *Tractor Day* (PS). Illus. by Laura J. Bryant. 2007, Walker $16.95 (978-0-8027-8090-4). This cozy, rhyming tribute to farming depicts a cheerful family hard at work, with dad and daughter riding the big red tractor all day. (Rev: BL 1/1–15/07; SLJ 3/07)

5866 Rex, Michael. *My Race Car* (PS–2). Illus. 2000, Holt $15.95 (978-0-8050-6101-7). 32pp. In this fantasy, a young boy imagines being on a racetrack in his car and, after checking the car, participating in an exciting race at top speed. (Rev: BCCB 9/00; BL 5/1/00; HBG 10/00; SLJ 7/00) [629.228]

5867 Richards, Laura E. *Jiggle Joggle Jee!* (PS). Illus. by Sam Williams. 2001, HarperCollins LB $15.89 (978-0-688-17833-8). 32pp. A newly illustrated version of an early-20th-century fantasy poem about a train. (Rev: BL 7/01; HBG 10/01; SLJ 5/01)

5868 Sarcone-Roach, Julia. *Subway Story* (1–3). Illus. by author. 2011, Knopf $16.99 (978-0-375-85859-8). Unpaged. A fascinating story of a New York City subway car named Jessie, who works for decades before being recycled as part of an artificial reef in the Atlantic. (Rev: HB 11–12/11*; LMC 11–12/11; SLJ 9/1/11)

5869 Savage, Stephen. *Little Tug* (PS–K). Illus. by author. 2012, Roaring Brook $12.99 (978-1-59643-648-0). 32pp. Little Tug may not be an impressive sight but he comes to the aid of all the other boats whenever he is needed. ♫ ❧ Lexile AD410L (Rev: BL 10/1/12; HB 11–12/12; SLJ 11/12)

5870 Scieszka, Jon. *Melvin Might?* (PS–K). Illus. by Juan Pablo Navas. Series: Trucktown. 2008, Simon & Schuster $16.99 (978-1-4169-4134-7). 44pp. Melvin the cement mixer is not at all brave, even in front of Payloader Pete and Jack Truck, but finds unexpected courage when Rescue Rita is in trouble. (Rev: BL 8/08)

5871 Siebert, Diane. *Train Song* (PS–2). Illus. by Mike Wimmer. 1990, HarperCollins LB $16.89 (978-0-690-04728-8). 32pp. This poem portrays trains as they travel across America. (Rev: BCCB 12/90; BL 10/1/90; SLJ 9/90*)

5872 Singer, Marilyn. *I'm Your Bus* (PS–K). Illus. by Evan Polenghi. 2009, Scholastic $16.99 (978-0-545-08918-0). 32pp. A rhythmic romp with a friendly school bus explains the ins and outs of a bus's day. (Rev: BL 7/09)

5873 Sís, Peter. *Trucks Trucks Trucks* (PS). Illus. 1999, Greenwillow $16.99 (978-0-688-16276-4). Matt enters an imaginary world where he operates a number of massive trucks and oversees their many operations. (Rev: BCCB 5/99; BL 6/1–15/99; HB 5/99; HBG 10/99; SLJ 5/99)

5874 Steggall, Susan. *The Diggers Are Coming!* (K–3). Illus. by author. 2013, Frances Lincoln $17.99 (978-184780288-0). 32pp. Young construction fans are the target audience for this rhyming book, which details how a neighborhood is made with construction vehicles, finally finishing with a furniture moving crew. (Rev: BL 9/15/13; SLJ 12/13*)

5875 Stein, Peter. *Cars Galore* (PS–1). Illus. by Bob Staake. 2011, Candlewick $15.99 (978-0-7636-4743-8). 32pp. Using illustrations and rhyming text, Stein presents a variety of cars of different shapes, sizes, and characteristics, including one that runs on air. (Rev: BL 3/1/11; HB 3–4/11; SLJ 2/1/11)

5876 Suen, Anastasia. *Red Light, Green Light* (PS). Illus. by Ken Wilson-Max. 2005, Harcourt $16.00 (978-0-15-202582-3). 40pp. Minimal text and bold illustrations blend to depict a toddler deploying his toy vehicles on a busy traffic grid. (Rev: BL 11/15/05; SLJ 10/05)

5877 Suen, Anastasia. *Road Work Ahead* (PS–K). Illus. by Jannie Ho. 2011, Viking $15.99 (978-0-670-01288-6). 32pp. A boy, his mother, and their dog have a delay-filled journey to Grandma's house, allowing them to enjoy all the details of construction work. (Rev: BL 9/15/11; SLJ 10/1/11)

5878 Sutton, Sally. *Demolition* (PS–2). Illus. by Brian Lovelock. 2012, Candlewick $15.99 (978-076365830-4). 32pp. A team of construction and demolition machines tear down an old parking garage and create an attractive city park. (Rev: BL 2/15/12; SLJ 6/1/12*)

5879 Sutton, Sally. *Roadwork* (PS–1). Illus. by Brian Lovelock. 2008, Candlewick $15.99 (978-0-7636-3912-9). 32pp. A boisterous, rhyming look at all the machines and people involved in building a new road. (Rev: BL 6/1–15/08; SLJ 8/08)

5880 Vetter, Jennifer Riggs. *Down by the Station* (PS–K). Illus. by Frank Remkiewicz. 2009, Ten Speed $15.99 (978-1-58246-243-1). All sorts of modes of transportation are included in this expanded version of the traditional children's song with energetic illustrations. (Rev: BL 4/1/09; SLJ 4/09)

5881 Viva, Frank. *Along a Long Road* (PS–1). Illus. by author. 2011, Little, Brown $16.99 (978-0-316-12925-1). 40pp. Spare text accompanies continuous woodcut-style illustrations in this paean to cycling. (Rev: BL 5/1/11; SLJ 6/11*)

5882 Weatherby, Brenda. *The Trucker* (PS–2). Illus. by Mark Alan Weatherby. 2004, Scholastic $15.95 (978-0-439-39877-0). 32pp. A little boy dreams he's driving a tractor-trailer in this well-illustrated book, and wakes to find that he's been riding along in his father's big rig. (Rev: BL 2/15/04; SLJ 4/04)

5883 *Wheels on the Go!* (PS). Illus. by La Coccinella. Series: Look and See. 2008, Sterling $6.95 (978-1-4027-5826-3). 26pp. A rhyming riddle introduces the vehicles featured in this rugged board book with die-cut holes. (Rev: BL 9/1/08)

5884 Wickberg, Susan. *Hey Mr. Choo-Choo, Where Are You Going?* (PS–K). Illus. by Yumi Heo. 2008, Putnam

$16.99 (978-0-399-23993-9). 32pp. Mister Choo-choo travels far and wide to reach the bright blue sea; children will want to chant along to the rhythmic narrative. (Rev: SLJ 4/08)

5885 Willems, Mo. *The Pigeon Loves Things That Go!* (PS). Illus. by author. 2005, Hyperion $6.99 (978-0-7868-3651-2). A board book featuring the beloved pigeon from *Don't Let the Pigeon Drive the Bus* (2003) and another children's favorite: things that move. (Rev: SLJ 8/05)

5886 Williams, Treat. *Air Show!* (PS-2). Illus. by Robert Neubecker. 2010, Hyperion $16.99 (978-1-4231-1185-6). 40pp. Their father flies young Ellie and Gill to an air show where they see all kinds of aircraft. (Rev: BL 6/10; HB 9–10/10; SLJ 7/1/10)

5887 Wolf, Sallie. *Truck Stuck* (PS). Illus. by Andy Robert Davies. 2008, Charlesbridge $14.95 (978-1-58089-119-6). 32pp. An 18-wheeler gets stuck under a viaduct, and the ensuing traffic jam boosts sales at lemonade stand. (Rev: BL 3/1/08; SLJ 2/08)

5888 Ziefert, Harriet. *Train Song* (PS). Illus. by Donald Saaf. 2000, Orchard $14.95 (978-0-531-30204-0). 32pp. A little boy watches a freight train go by and sees the contents of all the cars: logs, pigs, ducks, cows, and so on. (Rev: BL 4/1/00; HBG 10/00; SLJ 4/00)

5889 Zimmerman, Andrea. *Train Man* (PS–K). Illus. by David Clemesha. 2012, Henry Holt $14.99 (978-080507991-3). 32pp. Two young boys who enjoy playing with a toy train set are taken on a fun ride on a zoo train. (Rev: BL 3/1/12; SLJ 5/1/12)

5890 Zimmerman, Andrea, and David Clemesha. *Dig!* (PS–K). Illus. by Marc Rosenthal. 2004, Harcourt $16.00 (978-0-15-216785-1). Mr. Rally and his dog, Lightning, really enjoy digging — with a backhoe or without. (Rev: BL 5/15/04; SLJ 7/04)

5891 Zullo, Germano. *Line 135* (K–3). Illus. by Albertine. 2013, Chronicle $18.95 (978-1-4521-1934-2). 44pp. With interesting line illustrations and a brightly colored train, this unusual picture book follows a little girl's train journey from the city to the country. ℮ (Rev: BLO 7/13; SLJ 6/13)

Stories About Holidays and Holy Days

GENERAL AND MISCELLANEOUS

5892 Alko, Selina. *Daddy Christmas and Hanukkah Mama* (PS–1). Illus. by author. 2012, Knopf $16.99 (978-037586093-5). 32pp. Sadie describes how her family celebrates both Hanukkah and Christmas; a nicely illustrated story of a blended family that enjoys two traditions. ℮ (Rev: BL 11/15/12; HB 11–12/12; SLJ 10/12)

5893 Alvarez, Julia. *A Gift of Gracias* (1–3). Illus. by Beatriz Vidal. 2005, Knopf $15.95 (978-0-375-82425-8). 40pp. The patron saint of the Dominican Republic — Nuestra Señora de la Altagracia — features in this story of a family facing a devastating crop failure. (Rev: BL 9/15/05; HBG 4/06; LMC 1/06; SLJ 11/05)

5894 Bouchard, David. *The Dragon New Year: A Chinese Legend* (PS–3). Illus. by Zhong-Yang Huang. 1999, Peachtree $16.95 (978-1-56145-210-1). A Chinese grandmother explains to her frightened grandchild the origin of the noisy Dragon Dance at New Year's and how it was intended to frighten a real dragon who lived at the bottom of the sea. (Rev: BL 9/1/99; HBG 3/00; SLJ 11/99)

5895 Brown, Marc. *Arthur's April Fool* (PS–2). Illus. by author. 1985, Little, Brown paper $5.95 (978-0-316-11234-5). 32pp. Arthur is afraid he will forget his magic tricks prepared for the April Fools' Day show.

5896 Bunting, Eve. *The Mother's Day Mice* (PS–1). Illus. by Jan Brett. 1986, Houghton $15.00 (978-0-89919-387-8); paper $5.95 (978-0-89919-702-9). Three little mice go out to seek presents for Mother's Day; the smallest one brings home a song he heard a human sing. (Rev: BCCB 4/86; BL 4/1/86; SLJ 3/86)

5897 Bunting, Eve. *A Perfect Father's Day* (PS–1). Illus. by Susan Meddaugh. 1993, Houghton paper $5.95 (978-0-395-66416-2). 32pp. Susie plans a perfect time for her father on Father's Day. (Rev: BL 4/15/91; SLJ 5/91)

5898 Bunting, Eve. *St. Patrick's Day in the Morning* (PS–2). Illus. by Jan Brett. 1983, Houghton $16.00 (978-0-395-29098-9); paper $5.95 (978-0-89919-162-1). Jamie is too small to parade to the top of the hill with the rest of his family, so he rises early and has a St. Patrick's Day adventure of his own.

5899 Callahan, Sean. *The Leprechaun Who Lost His Rainbow* (K–3). Illus. by Nancy Cote. 2009, Whitman $16.99 (978-0-8075-4454-9). Unpaged. A charming leprechaun named Roy G. Biv asks for Colleen's help in bringing an end to the St. Patrick's Day rain. (Rev: SLJ 11/1/09)

5900 Compestine, Ying Chang. *The Runaway Rice Cake* (PS–3). Illus. by Tungwai Chau. 2001, Simon & Schuster $16.95 (978-0-689-82972-7). 40pp. As part of the Chinese New Year's Eve celebration, Mooma Chang cooks a rice cake that comes to life and runs away. (Rev: BL 2/1/01; HBG 3/02; SLJ 2/01)

5901 Compestine, Ying Chang. *The Runaway Wok: A Chinese New Year Tale* (K–3). Illus. by Sebastià Serra. 2011, Dutton $16.99 (978-0-525-42068-2). 32pp. A desperately poor Chinese family comes upon a magical wok that allows them to share their good luck with their neighbors on Chinese New Year. ℮ (Rev: BL 1/1–15/11; SLJ 2/1/11)

5902 Cox, Judy. *Cinco de Mouse-O!* (K–2). Illus. by Jeffrey Ebbeler. 2010, Holiday House $16.95 (978-0-8234-2194-7). 32pp. Mouse enjoys the festivities on Cinco de Mayo despite the relentless Cat and the dangers from exuberant humans. (Rev: BL 2/15/10; LMC 8–9/10; SLJ 4/1/10)

5903 deGroat, Diane. *April Fool! Watch Out at School!* (PS–2). Illus. by author. Series: Gilbert and Friends. 2009, HarperCollins $17.99 (978-0-06-143042-8). 32pp. Gilbert the possum is annoyed to be fooled so many times and plots revenge on the much-disliked Lewis. (Rev: BL 12/1/08; SLJ 5/09)

5904 deGroat, Diane. *Mother, You're the Best (But Sister, You're a Pest!)* (PS–2). Illus. by author. 2008, Harper-Collins $16.99 (978-0-06-123899-4). On Mother's Day, Gilbert the possum entertains his little sister, thereby giving mom some much-appreciated time to herself. (Rev: BL 2/15/08; SLJ 3/08)

5905 dePaola, Tomie. *The Lady of Guadalupe* (K–3). Illus. by author. 1980, Holiday House LB $18.95 (978-0-8234-0373-8); paper $8.95 (978-0-8234-0403-2). 48pp. The legend of the patron saint of Mexico is retold in this excellent picture book.

5906 English, Karen. *Nadia's Hands* (K–4). Illus. by Jonathan Weiner. 1999, Boyds Mills $16.95 (978-1-56397-667-4). A Pakistani American girl learns to appreciate the rich traditions of marriage in her faith when she is asked to be a flower girl at her aunt's wedding. (Rev: BCCB 4/99; BL 3/1/99; HBG 10/99; SLJ 4/99)

5907 Ford, Juwanda G. *K Is for Kwanzaa: A Kwanzaa Alphabet Book* (K–3). Illus. by Ken Wilson-Max. 1997, Scholastic $10.95 (978-0-590-92200-5). 32pp. Various objects, customs, and rituals connected with Kwanzaa are introduced in alphabetical order. (Rev: BL 9/1/97; HBG 3/98; SLJ 10/97) [394.261]

5908 Garcia, Aurora Colon. *Cinco de Mayo* (1–3). Series: Holiday Histories. 2003, Heinemann LB $22.79 (978-1-4034-3501-9). 32pp. The annual celebration marking Mexico's battlefield victory over French forces on May 5, 1862, is explained for younger readers in this well-illustrated book. (Rev: SLJ 5/04) [394.262]

5909 Gerstein, Mordicai. *The White Ram: A Story of Abraham and Isaac* (3–5). 2006, Holiday $16.95 (978-0-8234-1897-8). 32pp. This beautifully illustrated retelling of the Old Testament story of Abraham and Isaac focuses on the white ram that ultimately takes the place of Isaac on the sacrificial altar. (Rev: BL 10/1/06; SLJ 9/06*)

5910 Gower, Catherine. *Long-Long's New Year* (K–3). Illus. by He Zhihong. 2005, Tuttle $16.95 (978-0-8048-3666-1). Long-Long and his grandfather sell cabbages at the market to raise money for the upcoming Spring Festival, also known as Chinese New Year. (Rev: BL 2/15/05; SLJ 6/05)

5911 Holub, Joan. *Groundhog Weather School* (PS–3). Illus. by Kristin Sorra. 2009, Putnam $16.99 (978-0-399-24659-3). 32pp. Groundhog realizes the importance of correct weather prediction and opens a school. (Rev: BL 11/15/09; SLJ 11/1/09)

5912 Jalali, Reza. *Moon Watchers: Shirin's Ramadan Miracle* (2–4). Illus. by Anne Sibley O'Brien. 2010, Tilbury $16.95 (978-0-88448-321-2). 32pp. Disappointed because she is too young to fast, 9-year-old Shirin instead focuses on learning about Ramadan and doing good deeds. (Rev: BL 6/10; LMC 11–12/10; SLJ 9/1/10)

5913 Katz, Karen. *My First Kwanzaa* (PS). Illus. by author. 2003, Holt $14.95 (978-0-8050-7077-4). Double-page spreads with colorful illustrations introduce the

seven days of Kwanzaa and the associated traditions. (Rev: HBG 4/04; SLJ 10/03) [394.2]

5914 Keep, Richard. *Clatter Bash! A Day of the Dead Celebration* (K–3). Illus. by author. 2004, Peachtree $15.95 (978-1-56145-322-1). After the people leave the graveyards, the skeletons emerge and have a party, enjoying the food left behind for them. (Rev: SLJ 2/05)

5915 Khan, Hena. *Night of the Moon: A Muslim Holiday Story* (K–2). Illus. by Julie Paschkis. 2008, Chronicle $16.99 (978-0-8118-6062-8). 32pp. Seven-year-old Pakistani American Yasmeen and her family celebrate the month of Ramadan, ending with the "night of the moon." (Rev: BL 10/1/08; LMC 5/09; SLJ 9/08)

5916 Kimmelman, Leslie. *Happy 4th of July, Jenny Sweeney!* (PS–1). Illus. by Nancy Cote. 2003, Whitman LB $16.99 (978-0-8075-3152-5). Young Jenny observes the Fourth of July celebrations of her ethnically diverse community. (Rev: BL 5/15/03; HBG 10/03; SLJ 7/03)

5917 Klein, Adria F. *Max Celebrates Chinese New Year* (K–2). Illus. by Mernie Gallagher-Cole. Series: Max. 2007, Picture Window LB $19.93 (978-1-4048-3147-6). 24pp. Max celebrates Chinese New Year with his friend Lily in this easy reader. (Rev: SLJ 7/07)

5918 Levy, Janice. *The Spirit of Tio Fernando: A Day of the Dead Story/El Espiritu de Tio Fernando: Una Historia del Dia de los Muertos* (1–3). Trans. by Teresa Mlawer. Illus. by Morella Fuenmayor. 1995, Whitman $14.95 (978-0-8075-7585-7); paper $6.95 (978-0-8075-7586-4). On the Day of the Dead, Nando remembers his Uncle Fernando, who died six months before. (Rev: BL 11/15/95; SLJ 11/95)

5919 Lin, Grace. *Bringing in the New Year* (PS–1). Illus. by author. 2008, Knopf $15.99 (978-0-375-83745-6). 32pp. A Chinese family prepares to celebrate the Chinese New Year in this colorful and informative picture book. (Rev: BL 12/15/07; SLJ 3/08)

5920 Lin, Grace. *Thanking the Moon: Celebrating the Mid-Autumn Moon Festival* (PS–3). Illus. by author. 2010, Knopf $16.99 (978-0-375-86101-7). 32pp. A Chinese American family celebrates the traditional festival of the mid-autumn moon in this nicely illustrated book with cultural information. **e** (Rev: BL 9/15/10; LMC 1–2/11; SLJ 9/1/10)

5921 Luenn, Nancy. *A Gift for Abuelita: Celebrating the Day of the Dead / Un regalo para Abuelita: En celebración del Día de los Muertos* (K–3). Illus. by Robert Chapman. 1998, Rising Moon $15.95 (978-0-87358-688-7). 32pp. Told in English and Spanish, this picture book relates Rosita's tribute to her grandmother on the Day of the Dead. (Rev: BCCB 1/99; BL 3/15/99; HBG 3/99; SLJ 3/99)

5922 May, Eleanor. *The Best Mother's Day Ever* (K–2). Illus. by M. H. Pilz. 2010, Kane paper $5.95 (978-1-57565-299-3). 32pp. Lucy, who has a bad record with efforts to please her mother, asks her friend Diego to help and they plan a Mexican Mother's Day, with predictable results but a happy ending. (Rev: BL 2/15/10; SLJ 3/1/10)

5923 Medearis, Angela Shelf. *Seven Spools of Thread: A Kwanzaa Story* (K–3). Illus. by Daniel Minter. 2000, Whitman $15.95 (978-0-8075-7315-0). 40pp. An original folktale that takes place in a Ghanaian village and effectively introduces the seven principles of Kwanzaa. (Rev: BL 9/15/00; HBG 3/01)

5924 Miller, Pat. *Squirrel's New Year's Resolution* (PS–1). Illus. by Kathi Ember. 2010, Whitman $16.99 (978-0-8075-7591-8). 32pp. Squirrel learns what resolutions are but can't immediately think of one worth making. (Rev: BL 10/15/10; LMC 11–12/10; SLJ 10/1/10)

5925 Mobin-Uddin, Asma. *A Party in Ramadan* (1–3). Illus. by Laura Jacobsen. 2009, Boyds Mills $16.95 (978-1-59078-604-8). 32pp. It's Ramadan, and Leena is invited to a party on the day she plans to fast. Will she be able to resist the chocolate cake? (Rev: BCCB 5/09; BL 3/15/09; SLJ 4/09)

5926 Mora, Pat. *Book Fiesta! Celebrate Children's Book Day/Book Day / Celebremos El día de los niños/El día de los libros* (PS–2). Illus. by Rafael Lopez. 2009, HarperCollins $17.99 (978-0-06-128877-7). 40pp. Written in Spanish and English, this brightly illustrated book about Children's Day/Book Day features multicultural children playing, reading, and listening to stories; written by the founder of this holiday. (Rev: BL 1/1–15/09; SLJ 2/09)

5927 Murray, Julie. *Groundhog Day* (PS–2). Illus. 2014, ABDO LB $17.95 (978-162403185-4). 24pp. A wide-ranging overview of the holiday and its origins, with facts about groundhogs and about the seasons, plus information on contemporary traditions and famous groundhogs. Also use *Earth Day, Diwali,* and *Day of the Dead* (all 2014). (Rev: BL 3/1/14) [394.261]

5928 Nielsen, Laura. *Mrs. Muddle's Holidays* (PS–2). Illus. by Thomas Yezerski. 2008, Farrar $16.95 (978-0-374-35094-9). 32pp. Maple Street's diverse residents already celebrate a bunch of holidays, but when Mrs. Muddle moves in they discover more — First Robin Day, Earthworm Appreciation Day, and so forth. (Rev: BL 5/1/08; SLJ 4/08)

5929 Nolan, Janet. *The St. Patrick's Day Shillelagh* (2–4). Illus. by Ben F. Stahl. 2002, Whitman $16.95 (978-0-8075-7344-0). 32pp. On his trip from Ireland to America during the potato famine, Fergus carved a beautiful shillelagh that is passed from generation to generation. (Rev: BL 1/1–15/03; HBG 3/03; SLJ 12/02)

5930 Patrick, Diane. *Family Celebrations* (2–5). Illus. by Michael Bryant. 1993, Silver Moon LB $14.95 (978-1-881889-04-5). 62pp. Portrays a variety of family gatherings that are associated with such occasions as birth, marriage, and death as they are observed in many cultures. (Rev: BL 6/1–15/93) [392]

5931 Piernas-Davenport, Gail. *Shante Keys and the New Year's Peas* (K–2). Illus. by Marion Eldridge. 2007, Albert Whitman $16.95 (978-0-8075-7330-3). 32pp. When Grandma discovers there are no black-eyed peas, Shanté is sent in search of the ingredient that will bring her African American family luck and in her diverse neighborhood encounters a Chinese lady, a Scottish grocer, a Mexican restaurant keeper, and a Hindu family. (Rev: BL 11/15/07; SLJ 1/08)

5932 Rahaman, Vashanti. *Divali Rose* (K–3). Illus. by Jamel Akib. 2008, Boyds Mills $16.95 (978-1-59078-524-9). 32pp. In Trinidad Ricki's family is preparing for the Hindu festival of lights when Ricki accidentally snaps a rosebud off a bush; his grandfather blames their new neighbors from India and Ricki must decide whether to confess. (Rev: BL 10/1/08; LMC 11/09; SLJ 9/08)

5933 Robert, Na'ima B. *Ramadan Moon* (K–3). Illus. by Shirin Adl. 2009, Frances Lincoln $17.95 (978-1-84507-922-2). 32pp. This book about the Islamic holiday follows a Muslim family through the rituals of the month. (Rev: BL 11/15/09; SLJ 12/1/09)

5934 Roberts, Bethany. *Fourth of July Mice!* (PS–1). Illus. by Doug Cushman. Series: Holiday Mice. 2004, Clarion $13.00 (978-0-618-31367-9). 32pp. The family of mice featured in other holiday titles celebrate Independence Day in fine style. (Rev: BL 5/15/04)

5935 Rockwell, Anne. *Mother's Day* (PS–1). Illus. by Lizzy Rockwell. 2004, HarperCollins $16.99 (978-0-06-051374-0). 40pp. Looking forward to Mother's Day, the children in Mrs. Madoff's classroom explain how they will celebrate the occasion. (Rev: BL 2/15/04; SLJ 3/04)

5936 Rockwell, Anne. *President's Day* (K–2). Illus. by Lizzy Rockwell. 2008, HarperCollins $16.99 (978-0-06-050194-5). 40pp. It's Presidents' Day, and Mrs. Madoff's class learns about Washington and Lincoln plus Jefferson and Teddy Roosevelt for good measure. (Rev: BL 2/15/08; SLJ 1/08)

5937 Schnetzler, Pattie. *Earth Day Birthday* (PS–4). Illus. by Chad Wallace. Series: Sharing Nature with Children. 2004, Dawn $16.95 (978-1-58469-053-5); paper $8.95 (978-1-58469-054-2). Set to the melody of "The Twelve Days of Christmas," the lyrics in this attractively illustrated song showcase 12 animal species from different parts of the world; information on Earth Day follows the text. (Rev: SLJ 7/04) [782.42]

5938 Shragg, Karen I. *A Solstice Tree for Jenny* (K–3). Illus. by Heidi Schwabacher. 2001, Prometheus paper $13.98 (978-1-57392-930-1). Jenny wants to know why her family doesn't celebrate any religious holidays. (Rev: BL 12/15/01)

5939 Washington, Donna L. *Li'l Rabbit's Kwanzaa* (PS–K). Illus. by Shane W. Evans. 2010, HarperCollins paper $12.99 (978-00607281-6-8). 32pp. A young rabbit rallies the family's animal friends to help his sick Granna celebrate the holiday; includes "The Nguzo Saba — The Seven Principles of Kwanzaa." (Rev: BL 11/1/10; HB 11–12/10; SLJ 10/10)

5940 Weatherford, Carole Boston. *Juneteenth Jamboree* (2–4). Illus. by Yvonne Buchanan. 1995, Lee & Low $15.95 (978-1-880000-18-2). Two youngsters, new to Texas, celebrate Juneteenth, which commemorates the day Texas slaves learned that the Emancipation Proclamation freed them. (Rev: SLJ 1/96)

5941 Whitehead, Kathy. *Looking for Uncle Louie on the 4th of July* (K–3). Illus. by Pablo Torrecilla. 2005, Boyds Mills $15.95 (978-1-59078-061-9). 32pp. On the 4th of July in Texas, young Joe watches the parade, waiting with bated breath for the arrival of his Uncle Louie's spectacular car. (Rev: BL 5/15/05; SLJ 5/05)

5942 Wong, Janet S. *Apple Pie Fourth of July* (PS–2). Illus. by Margaret Chodos-Irvine. 2002, Harcourt $16.00 (978-0-15-202543-4). A young Chinese American girl working in her parents' grocery is convinced no one will want to eat their Chinese food on the Fourth of July. (Rev: BL 8/02; HBG 10/02; SLJ 5/02)

5943 Wong, Janet S. *This Next New Year* (PS–3). Illus. by Yangsook Choi. 2000, Farrar $16.00 (978-0-374-35503-6). 32pp. A little boy who is half Korean prepares to celebrate Chinese New Year and describes the traditional and modern customs involved. (Rev: BCCB 9/00; BL 9/15/00; HB 11/00; HBG 3/01; SLJ 10/00)

BIRTHDAYS

5944 Avraham, Kate Aver. *What Will You Be, Sara Mee?* (PS–3). Illus. by Anne Sibley O'Brien. 2010, Charlesbridge $16.95 (978-1-58089-210-0); paper $7.95 (978-1-58089-211-7). 32pp. This story of a Korean American girl's lively first birthday party is narrated by her older brother, Chong. (Rev: BL 2/1/10; SLJ 2/1/10)

5945 Bailey, Debbie. *Happy Birthday* (PS). Photos by Susan Huszar. Series: Talk-About-Books. 1999, Annick $5.95 (978-1-55037-559-6). In this board book, full-color illustrations are used to show different ways of celebrating children's birthdays. (Rev: SLJ 9/99)

5946 Beck, Andrea. *Elliot Bakes a Cake* (PS–1). Illus. 1999, Kids Can $12.95 (978-1-55074-443-9). 32pp. Elliot Moose and his stuffed toy friends converge on the kitchen to bake a birthday cake for their pal Lionel Lion. (Rev: BL 10/1/99; HBG 3/00; SLJ 12/99)

5947 Bertrand, Diane Gonzales. *The Last Doll / La Ultima Muneca* (PS–3). Illus. by Anthony Accardo. 2001, Arte Publico $14.95 (978-1-55885-290-7). 32pp. A special doll dressed in white lace is chosen to be a gift for Teresa at her *quinceanera* coming-of-age party. (Rev: BL 10/1/01; SLJ 4/01)

5948 Brown, Marc. *Arthur's Birthday* (K–2). Illus. 1989, Little, Brown $15.95 (978-0-316-11073-0); paper $5.95 (978-0-316-11074-7). Muffy is upset to learn that Arthur's birthday is the same day as hers. (Rev: BL 4/15/89; HB 5/89)

5949 Capucilli, Alyssa Satin. *Happy Birthday, Biscuit!* (PS). Illus. by Pat Schories. Series: I Can Read. 1999, HarperCollins LB $16.89 (978-0-06-028361-2). 24pp. A frisky puppy named Biscuit enjoys a birthday romp with his friends in this book for beginning readers. (Rev: BL 6/1–15/99; HBG 10/99; SLJ 6/99)

5950 Carle, Eric. *The Secret Birthday Message* (PS–1). Illus. by author. 1972, HarperCollins LB $17.89 (978-0-690-72348-9); paper $6.99 (978-0-06-443099-9). 26pp. In a brightly illustrated picture book with intriguing cut-

outs, a little boy has to decipher the coded message to find his birthday present.

5951 Chavarria-Chairez, Becky. *Magda's Pinata Magic / Magda y el Piñata Magica* (K–3). Trans. by Gabriela Baeza Ventura. Illus. by Anne Vega. 2001, Arte Publico $14.95 (978-1-55885-320-1). Gabriel is upset by the idea of destroying his birthday pinata, so his sister Magda comes up with a solution in this bilingual picture book. (Rev: BL 10/15/01; SLJ 1/02)

5952 Chavarria-Chairez, Becky. *Magda's Tortillas / Las tortillas de Magda* (K–2). Trans. by Julia Mercedes Castilla. Illus. by Anne Vega. 2000, Piñata $14.95 (978-1-55885-286-0). On her birthday, Magda produces tortillas in different shapes in this bilingual book. (Rev: SLJ 10/00)

5953 Corderoy, Tracey. *Whizz! Pop! Granny, Stop!* (PS–2). Illus. by Joe Berger. 2013, Candlewick $14.99 (978-0-7636-6551-7). 32pp. With rhyming prose and brush-pen cartoons, Corderoy tells the story of a grandmother and her granddaughter, both magically inclined, who decide not to use magic for the granddaughter's birthday party, resulting a series of comical mishaps. (Rev: BLO 10/1/13; SLJ 8/13)

5954 Dale, Penny. *Dinosaur Zoom!* (PS–1). Illus. by author. 2012, Candlewick $15.99 (978-0-7636-6448-0). 32pp. In varied vehicles, ten dinosaurs rush to get ready for a surprise birthday party. (Rev: BLO 12/15/12; SLJ 3/13)

5955 Day, Alexandra. *Carl's Birthday* (PS–2). Illus. 1995, Farrar $12.95 (978-0-374-31144-5). 32pp. In this almost wordless picture book, Madeline and her beloved Rottweiler, Carl, secretly help prepare a surprise birthday party for the dog. (Rev: BL 1/1–15/96; SLJ 12/95)

5956 Dokas, Dara Sanders. *Muriel's Red Sweater* (PS–K). Illus. by Bernadette Pons. 2009, Dutton $16.99 (978-0-525-47962-8). 32pp. Unbeknownst to Muriel, her red sweater slowly comes apart as she visits her friends' houses with birthday party invitations, but her resourceful friends use the red yarn in many ways including a bow for her gift — a new sweater! (Rev: SLJ 2/09)

5957 Dominguez, Kelli Kyle. *The Perfect Pinata / La Piñata Perfecta* (PS–2). Trans. by Teresa Mlawer. Illus. by Diane Patterson. 2002, Whitman $16.99 (978-0-8075-6495-0). 32pp. This bilingual text describes Marisa's reluctance to break her beautiful sixth-birthday pinata and her parents' happy solution. (Rev: BL 4/15/02; HBG 10/02)

5958 Edmiston, Jim. *The Emperor Who Forgot His Birthday* (PS–1). Illus. by author. Series: A Barefoot Beginner Book. 1999, Barefoot Books $14.95 (978-1-84148-015-2). An emperor wakes up and finds that his cat, family, and servants are all missing, little knowing that they are preparing a surprise birthday party for him. (Rev: SLJ 12/99)

5959 Falwell, Cathryn. *Butterflies for Kiri* (K–3). Illus. by author. 2003, Lee & Low $16.95 (978-1-58430-100-4). Kiri, a young Japanese-American girl, overcomes her initial frustrations as she struggles to make sense of the origami kit she's received as a birthday gift. (Rev: BL 5/15/03; HBG 10/03; SLJ 5/03)

5960 Fox, Mem. *Night Noises* (PS–2). Illus. by Terry Denton. 1989, Harcourt $16.00 (978-0-15-200543-6); paper $4.95 (978-0-15-257421-5). 32pp. An old lady's dog becomes agitated at the commotion he hears outside while the woman sleeps, which turns out to be relatives arriving for a surprise ninetieth birthday party. (Rev: BL 11/15/89; HB 11/89*; SLJ 9/89*)

5961 Geras, Adele. *Little Ballet Star* (PS–2). Illus. by Shelagh McNicholas. 2008, Dial $16.99 (978-0-8037-3237-7). 32pp. Aunt Gina, a ballerina, takes Tilly backstage to see the dancers warming up for their roles and then — as a birthday surprise — invites her onstage to dance. (Rev: BL 3/1/08; SLJ 3/08)

5962 Graham, Bob. *Oscar's Half Birthday* (PS–K). Illus. 2005, Candlewick $16.99 (978-0-7636-2699-0). 32pp. A happy interracial family goes to the park to celebrate little Oscar's birthday. (Rev: BL 5/1/05)

5963 Hobbie, Holly. *Toot and Puddle: A Present for Toot* (PS–1). Illus. 1998, Little, Brown $12.95 (978-0-316-36556-7). 32pp. Puddle, a pig, is in a quandary about buying a birthday present for friend Toot, another pig. (Rev: BL 11/1/98; HBG 3/99; SLJ 10/98)

5964 Hutchins, Pat. *Happy Birthday, Sam* (1–3). Illus. by author. 1978, Morrow paper $6.99 (978-0-688-10482-5). 32pp. Sam is disappointed on his birthday morning to discover that he hasn't grown at all.

5965 Hutchins, Pat. *It's My Birthday* (PS–2). 1999, Greenwillow LB $14.89 (978-0-688-09664-9). 32pp. Monster Billy acts so selfishly about his birthday presents that he finds it difficult to get anyone to play with him. (Rev: BL 6/1–15/99; HBG 10/99; SLJ 3/99)

5966 Janni, Rebecca. *Every Cowgirl Needs a Horse* (K–2). Illus. by Lynne Avril. 2010, Dutton $16.99 (978-0-525-42164-1). 32pp. Wannabe cowgirl Nellie Sue makes the best of disappointment when she receives a bike — not the horse she wanted — for her birthday. Lexile AD650L (Rev: BL 2/1/10; LMC 3–4/10; SLJ 2/1/10)

5967 Javernick, Ellen. *The Birthday Pet* (PS–2). Illus. by Kevin O'Malley. 2009, Marshall Cavendish $16.99 (978-0-7614-5522-6). 32pp. Danny's birthday wish is to have a pet turtle and he persists despite suggestions that he consider a dog, a cat, a rat, a bird. (Rev: BL 4/1/09; SLJ 3/09)

5968 Kasza, Keiko. *My Lucky Birthday* (PS–1). Illus. by author. 2013, Penguin $16.99 (978-0-399-25763-6). 32pp. A canny piglet manages to share in Alligator Al's birthday party without getting eaten himself. (Rev: BLO 6/13; SLJ 7/13)

5969 Kromhout, Rindert. *Little Donkey and the Birthday Present* (K–2). Trans. from Dutch by Marianne Martens. Illus. by Annemarie van Haeringen. 2007, North-South $15.95 (978-0-7358-2132-3). Little Donkey chooses a beautiful kite as a present for his friend Jackie the yak, but then decides he wants to keep it himself. (Rev: SLJ 4/07)

5970 Lewis, Rose. *Every Year on Your Birthday* (PS–K). Illus. by Jane Dyer. 2007, Little, Brown $16.99 (978-0-316-52552-7). 32pp. A single mother shares with her adopted Asian daughter why her birthday is so special, and recounts the many fun experiences they share together each year on that day. (Rev: BL 6/1–15/07; SLJ 6/07)

5971 Look, Lenore. *Henry's First-Moon Birthday* (PS–3). Illus. by Yumi Heo. 2001, Simon & Schuster $16.00 (978-0-689-82294-0). 40pp. Young Jen, a Chinese American girl, helps her grandmother in the preparation of her young brother's first-moon birthday party. (Rev: BCCB 3/01; BL 4/1/01*; HBG 10/01; SLJ 6/01*)

5972 Lopez, Loretta. *The Birthday Swap* (PS–3). Illus. 1997, Lee & Low $15.95 (978-1-880000-47-2). 32pp. A young Mexican American girl enjoys the annual reunion of family from both sides of the border, when everyone comes to celebrate her older sister's birthday. (Rev: BCCB 6/97; BL 5/1/97; SLJ 6/97)

5973 McClatchy, Lisa. *Dear Tyrannosaurus Rex* (K–2). Illus. by John Manders. 2010, Random House $16.99 (978-0-375-85608-2); LB $19.99 (978-0-375-95608-9). 40pp. Erin attempts to entice a local museum's T-rex to her 6th birthday party by explaining all the treats in store — including the hokey pokey, the trampoline, and pin-the-tail-on-the-dinosaur. e (Rev: BLO 8/10; SLJ 12/1/10)

5974 McLarey, Kristina Thermaenius, and Myra McLarey. *When You Take a Pig to a Party* (PS–3). Illus. by Marjory Wunsch. 2000, Orchard LB $16.99 (978-0-531-33257-3). 32pp. When Adelaide is invited to Ethan's birthday party she makes the mistake of bringing her pet pig, Sherman, along. (Rev: BL 4/15/00; HBG 10/00; SLJ 4/00)

5975 McNamara, Margaret. *George Washington's Birthday: A Mostly True Tale* (K–3). Illus. by Barry Blitt. 2012, Random House $17.99 (978-037584499-7). 40pp. Wry illustrations add appeal to this story of 7-year-old George, who ends up spending his birthday chopping down a cherry tree, throwing rocks across the Rappahannock, and more, while believing his family has forgotten the celebration. e (Rev: BL 2/1/12; HB 1–2/12; LMC 5–6/12; SLJ 1/12)

5976 McPhail, David. *Big Brown Bear's Birthday Surprise* (K–2). Illus. 2007, Harcourt $16.00 (978-0-15-206098-5). 32pp. Although he's forgotten this, it's Bear's birthday — and more surprises are to come during this day he shares with Rat. (Rev: BL 5/1/07; SLJ 6/07)

5977 Moon, Nicola. *Happy Birthday, Amelia* (K–2). Illus. by Jenny Jones. 2000, Pavilion $17.95 (978-1-86205-208-6). 32pp. On her birthday, Amelia follows clues that take her around her farmyard home and eventually to the orchard where everyone is waiting for her party to begin. (Rev: BL 7/00)

5978 Nakagawa, Chihiro. *Who Made This Cake?* (PS–1). Trans. by Chihiro Nakagawa. Illus. by Junji Koyose. 2008, Front St. $16.95 (978-1-59078-595-9). 32pp. A birthday cake is made by a crew of tiny yet happy people who must use dump trucks, cranes, and other equipment. (Rev: BL 9/1/08; HB 1/09)

5979 Patricelli, Leslie. *The Birthday Box* (PS). Illus. by author. 2007, Candlewick $15.99 (978-0-7636-2825-3). A young child is just as thrilled with the box that holds a birthday present as he is with what's inside in this picture book that encourages imaginative play. (Rev: SLJ 5/07)

5980 Rempt, Fiona. *Snail's Birthday Wish* (PS–1). Illus. by Noëlle Smit. 2007, Sterling LB $14.95 (978-1-905417-52-0). 32pp. Snail's friends, sensitive to his dream of moving faster, bring him puzzling presents that fit together for a surprise ending — a car. (Rev: SLJ 11/07)

5981 Rose, Deborah L. *Birthday Zoo* (PS–2). Illus. by Lynn Munsinger. 2002, Whitman $15.95 (978-0-8075-0776-6). 32pp. A little boy is treated to a rollicking birthday party hosted by the animals at the zoo in this rhyming picture book. (Rev: BL 9/15/02; HB 11/02; HBG 3/03; SLJ 10/02)

5982 Ross, Tony. *I Want Two Birthdays!* (PS–2). Illus. by author. 2010, Andersen $16.95 (978-0-7613-5495-6). 32pp. Little Princess becomes too greedy about birthdays and it takes an "unbirthday" to make the day special again. Lexile AD590L (Rev: BL 2/1/10; LMC 8–9/10; SLJ 3/1/10)

5983 Roth, Susan L. *Happy Birthday Mr. Kang* (2–4). Illus. 2001, National Geographic $16.95 (978-0-7922-7723-1). When Mr. Kang's grandson Sam asks if the old man's hua mei bird wants its freedom, Mr. Kang releases it with surprising results in this birthday story. (Rev: BL 1/1–15/01; HBG 10/01; SLJ 2/01)

5984 Scamell, Ragnhild. *Toby's Doll's House* (PS–3). Illus. by Adrian Reynolds. 1999, Levinson $14.95 (978-1-86233-026-9). Toby takes all the boxes in which his birthday gifts were packed and turns them into the doll's house that he really wanted. (Rev: SLJ 9/99)

5985 Scanlon, Liz Garton. *Happy Birthday, Bunny!* (PS–K). Illus. by Stephanie Graegin. 2013, Simon & Schuster $16.99 (978-1-4424-0287-4). 32pp. Readers follow a little bunny through the excitement of a birthday portrayed in rhyming text and welcoming pencil and watercolor illustrations. e (Rev: BL 12/15/12; SLJ 2/13)

5986 Schaefer, Carole Lexa. *Dragon Dancing* (PS–1). Illus. by Pierr Morgan. 2007, Viking $16.99 (978-0-670-06084-9). For Mei Lin's birthday, the class decorates dragons and enjoys a boisterous and colorful dragon dance. (Rev: BL 1/1–15/07; SLJ 3/07*)

5987 Schoenherr, Ian. *Don't Spill the Beans!* (PS). Illus. by author. 2010, Greenwillow $16.99 (978-0-06-172457-2); LB $17.89 (978-0-06-172458-9). 32pp. Bear has a difficult time hiding the fact that it's his birthday from his animal friends. (Rev: BL 2/1/10; SLJ 1/1/10*)

5988 Scieszka, Jon, and Mac Barnett. *Battle Bunny* (K–5). Illus. by Matthew Myers. 2013, Simon & Schuster $14.99 (978-144244673-1). 32pp. It's Alex's birthday and the little boy takes a blah story about a Birthday Bunny and transforms it with his No. 2 pencil into a

much more exciting tale featuring rockets, bombs, and adventure. ALA Notable Children's Book. e (Rev: BL 10/1/13*; HB 11–12/13; LMC 3–4/14; SLJ 11/13*)

5989 Segal, Lore. *Morris the Artist* (PS–2). Illus. by Boris Kulikov. 2003, Farrar $16.00 (978-0-374-35063-5). Morris, an aspiring artist, takes a gift of a paint set to Benjamin's birthday party but finds he cannot part with it and eventually opens it up himself. (Rev: HBG 4/04; SLJ 6/03)

5990 Shaw, Nancy. *Sheep in a Shop* (PS–1). Illus. by Margot Apple. 1991, Houghton $15.00 (978-0-395-53681-0). 32pp. Five sheep are a little short of cash when they shop for a present for a friend. (Rev: HB 5/91*; SLJ 2/91)

5991 Soto, Gary. *Chato and the Party Animals* (PS–3). Illus. by Susan Guevara. 2000, Penguin $16.99 (978-0-399-23159-9). 32pp. Because he is from a pound, Novio Boy doesn't know his birthday, so Chato the Cat organizes a special surprise birthday party for him. (Rev: BL 8/00; HBG 3/01; SLJ 7/00)

5992 Sperring, Mark. *The Fairytale Cake* (PS–K). Illus. by Jonathan Langley. 2005, Scholastic $15.95 (978-0-439-68329-6). 32pp. Detailed drawings add to the fun in this story of a parade of nursery rhyme and fairy tale characters delivering a little boy's birthday cake. (Rev: BL 7/05; SLJ 9/05)

5993 Spinelli, Eileen. *In My New Yellow Shirt* (PS). Illus. by Hideko Takahashi. 2001, Holt $15.95 (978-0-8050-6242-7). 32pp. A birthday boy sees lots of potential in his new yellow shirt, despite his friend's dismissal of the gift. (Rev: BCCB 9/01; BL 6/1–15/01; HBG 3/02; SLJ 8/01)

5994 Starr, Meg. *Alicia's Happy Day* (PS–1). Illus. by Ying-Hwa Hu. 2003, Star Bright $15.95 (978-1-887724-85-2). 32pp. Alicia's birthday is a happy, special day thanks to her friends, neighbors, and family. (Rev: BL 2/1/03)

5995 Stein, David Ezra. *Cowboy Ned and Andy* (PS–2). Illus. by author. 2006, Simon & Schuster $14.95 (978-1-4169-0041-2). Andy, a horse, wants to get Cowboy Ned a cake for his birthday, but when he can't find one in the desert, he gives Ned a hug instead. (Rev: SLJ 7/06)

5996 Wallace, John. *Tiny Rabbit Goes to a Birthday Party* (PS–K). Illus. 2000, Holiday House $16.95 (978-0-8234-1489-5). 32pp. Tiny Rabbit is worried about going to his first birthday party but, when he has a good time, he starts to make plans for his own party. (Rev: BL 2/1/00; HBG 10/00; SLJ 4/00)

5997 Wallace, Nancy Elizabeth. *Tell-A-Bunny* (PS–1). Illus. 2000, Winslow $15.95 (978-1-890817-29-9). 32pp. When bunnies phone each other about a surprise birthday party, the message gets garbled as it is passed from one bunny to another. (Rev: BL 5/15/00; HBG 10/00; SLJ 5/00)

5998 Wilson, Karma. *Whopper Cake* (PS–2). Illus. by Will Hillenbrand. 2007, Simon & Schuster $16.99 (978-0-689-83844-6). 40pp. Exaggerated illustrations complement this funny, larger-than-life story about Grandpa, who decides to make a birthday cake as big as a house for his wife, Grandma. (Rev: BL 6/1–15/07; SLJ 7/07)

5999 Wright, Betty R. *The Blizzard* (PS–2). Illus. by Ronald Himler. 2003, Holiday House $16.95 (978-0-8234-1656-1). It's Billy's birthday and a snowstorm means his cousins can't come to celebrate, but his disappointment disappears when a full-blown blizzard means his whole class must spend the night at his house. (Rev: BL 7/03*; HBG 4/04; SLJ 10/03)

CHRISTMAS

6000 Agee, Jon. *Little Santa* (PS–K). Illus. by author. 2013, Dial $17.99 (978-080373906-2). 40pp. Mr. and Mrs. Claus and the rest of the family are thinking it's time for a move to Florida when they get snowed in at the North Pole, and it's up to little Santa, the only one who truly loves the the snow, to save the day — in true Christmas fashion! ALA Notable Children's Book. Lexile 500 (Rev: BL 9/15/13*; HB 11–12/13; SLJ 10/13)

6001 Aliki. *Christmas Tree Memories* (PS–2). Illus. 1991, HarperCollins LB $14.89 (978-0-06-020008-4). This is a remembrance of Christmases past and the activities associated with celebrations years ago. (Rev: BL 7/91; HB 11/91)

6002 Alsenas, Linas. *Mrs. Claus Takes a Vacation* (K–3). Illus. by author. 2006, Scholastic $16.99 (978-0-439-77978-4). Feeling restricted, Mrs. Claus decides to take a world tour of her own, leaving Mr. Claus at home to worry about her. (Rev: HB 11/06; HBG 4/07; SLJ 10/06)

6003 Appelt, Kathi. *Merry Christmas, Merry Crow* (PS–2). Illus. by Jon Goodell. 2005, Harcourt $16.00 (978-0-15-202651-6). 32pp. In this charming rhyming Christmas tale, a clever crow flies around town collecting odds and ends with which to decorate a Christmas tree. (Rev: BL 10/15/05; HBG 4/06; SLJ 10/05)

6004 Arnold, Katya. *The Adventures of Snowwoman* (PS–3). Illus. 1998, Holiday House $15.95 (978-0-8234-1390-4). Children build Snowwoman to take a message to Santa to bring them a tree. (Rev: BL 12/1/98; HBG 3/99; SLJ 3/99)

6005 Auch, Mary Jane. *The Nutquacker* (K–3). Illus. 1999, Holiday House $17.95 (978-0-8234-1524-3). 32pp. Clara the duck wanders off to find something called "Christmas," which she hears is on its way, only to find that Christmas is a time for being with people who love you. (Rev: BL 11/1/99; HBG 3/00; SLJ 10/99)

6006 Barrett, Judi. *Santa from Cincinnati* (K–3). Illus. by Kevin Hawkes. 2012, Atheneum $16.99 (978-144242993-2). 48pp. Here is Santa's memoir, describing his childhood in a home full of toys, his school and college days — including playing in a rock band, his meeting the future Mrs. Claus, and his efforts to keep up with technology; the illustrations extend the fun. **e** Lexile AD800L (Rev: BL 11/1/12*; HB 11–12/12; SLJ 10/12)

6007 Barry, Robert. *Mr. Willowby's Christmas Tree* (PS–2). Illus. 2000, Doubleday $15.95 (978-0-385-32721-3). 32pp. A Christmas tree makes the rounds of seven different homes. In each case it is chopped down a little to

fit the house, until the last part is so small that three little mice find it just right. (Rev: BL 9/1/00; HBG 10/01)

6008 Bauer, Marion Dane. *Christmas Lights* (PS–1). Illus. by Susan Mitchell. 2006, Simon & Schuster $14.95 (978-0-689-86942-6). This colorful light-up book celebrates the joys of Christmas. (Rev: SLJ 10/06)

6009 Bauer, Sepp. *The Christmas Rose* (1–4). Illus. by Else Wenz-Vietor. 2008, Charlesbridge $12.95 (978-1-58089-232-2). 48pp. Arranged in parts like an Advent calendar, this story about children Fritz and Gretel, who ask Saint Nikolaus for help in healing their sick father, can be read a day at a time. (Rev: BLO 8/28/08)

6010 Beck, Andrea. *Elliot's Christmas Surprise* (PS–1). Illus. by author. Series: An Elliot Moose Story. 2003, Kids Can $12.95 (978-1-55337-474-9); paper $5.95 (978-1-55337-661-3). Elliot, the stuffed moose, scrambles to get Christmas gifts for all his friends after he receives a big red box. (Rev: HBG 4/04; SLJ 10/03)

6011 Bond, Michael. *Paddington Bear and the Christmas Surprise* (K–2). Illus. by R. W. Alley. 1997, HarperCollins $11.95 (978-0-694-00897-1). Paddington's visit with his family to a department store at Christmas is not the joyful occasion he had hoped for. (Rev: BL 9/15/97; SLJ 10/97)

6012 Bowen, Anne. *Christmas Is Coming* (PS–2). Illus. by Tomek Bogacki. 2007, Carolrhoda $16.95 (978-1-57505-934-1). A little girl tells her baby brother that Christmas is coming and describes the family traditions. (Rev: BL 9/15/07)

6013 Boynton, Sandra. *Bob: And 6 More Christmas Stories* (PS–K). Illus. by author. 1999, Simon & Schuster $7.99 (978-0-689-82568-2). A humorous book that consists of seven double-page stories about animals celebrating Christmas. (Rev: SLJ 10/99)

6014 Boynton, Sandra. *Christmas Parade* (PS–K). Illus. by author. 2012, Simon & Schuster $14.99 (978-144246813-9). 32pp. An animal band — an elephant, a rhino, cows, mice, ducks, and chickens with a variety of instruments — leads the Christmas parade in this bouncy story. **e** (Rev: BL 12/1/12; HB 11–12/12; SLJ 10/12)

6015 Brett, Jan. *Christmas Trolls* (K–3). Illus. 1993, Penguin LB $16.99 (978-0-399-22507-9). 32pp. Treva discovers that the mysterious disappearance of objects from her house is the work of trolls. (Rev: BL 7/93)

6016 Brett, Jan. *Home for Christmas* (K–3). Illus. by author. 2011, Putnam $17.99 (978-039925653-0). 32pp. A young troll runs away from his family seeking a less demanding place to live but finds, just in time for Christmas, that home is best. (Rev: BL 10/15/11; SLJ 10/1/11)

6017 Brett, Jan. *The Wild Christmas Reindeer* (K–2). Illus. 1990, Penguin $17.99 (978-0-399-22192-7). 32pp. Santa has a whole new crew of wild reindeer that might not want to work on Christmas Eve. (Rev: BL 9/15/90*)

6018 Brown, Elizabeth Ferguson. *Coal Country Christmas* (PS–2). Illus. by Harvey Stevenson. 2003, Boyds Mills $15.95 (978-1-59078-020-6). A bittersweet Christmas story about a young girl visiting her grandmother's home in Pennsylvania's depressed coal country. (Rev: HBG 4/04; SLJ 10/03)

6019 Brown, Marc. *Arthur's Christmas* (K–2). Illus. by author. 1984, Little, Brown $15.95 (978-0-316-11180-5). Arthur, an anteater, has a series of Christmas adventures.

6020 Brown, Margaret Wise. *The Little Fir Tree* (K–2). Illus. by Jim LaMarche. 2005, HarperCollins $15.99 (978-0-06-028189-2). 32pp. LaMarche's art breathes new life into the classic tale, first published in 1954, of a little fir tree and how it helped to brighten Christmas for a lame boy. (Rev: BL 9/15/05; SLJ 10/05)

6021 Brown, Rachel W.N. *Small Camel Follows the Star* (PS–2). Illus. by Giuliano Ferri. 2007, Albert Whitman $16.95 (978-0-8075-7453-9). 32pp. Small Camel tells the Nativity story from his perspective as the animal who carries precious gifts for the baby Jesus. (Rev: BL 9/15/07)

6022 Buck, Nola. *A Christmas Goodnight* (PS–K). Illus. by Sarah Jane Wright. 2011, HarperCollins $12.99 (978-006166491-5). 24pp. A Christmas bedtime book in which a young boy bids goodnight to all the characters in a manger scene. (Rev: BL 10/15/11; HB 11–12/11; SLJ 10/1/11)

6023 Buehner, Caralyn. *Snowmen at Christmas* (PS–K). Illus. by Mark Buehner. 2005, Dial $16.99 (978-0-8037-2995-7). 32pp. First seen in *Snowmen at Night* (2002), these jolly characters return to show how snow families celebrate Christmas. (Rev: BL 9/1/05; SLJ 10/05)

6024 Bunting, Eve. *Christmas Cricket* (PS–2). Illus. by Timothy Bush. 2002, Clarion $15.00 (978-0-618-06554-7). 32pp. A cricket perched among the branches of a Christmas tree is heartened to hear his chirping described as an angel's song. (Rev: BL 9/15/02; HBG 3/03; SLJ 10/02)

6025 Bunting, Eve. *December* (K–3). Illus. by David Diaz. 1997, Harcourt $16.00 (978-0-15-201434-6). 40pp. A miracle occurs when a homeless mother and her son allow an old lady to sleep in their cardboard home at Christmas time. (Rev: BL 9/1/97*; HBG 3/98; SLJ 10/97*)

6026 Bunting, Eve. *We Were There: A Nativity Story* (PS–3). Illus. by Wendell Minor. 2001, Clarion $16.00 (978-0-395-82265-4). A variety of creatures including the rat, spider, toad, and snake claim they too were present at Jesus' birth. (Rev: BL 9/1/01; HBG 3/02; SLJ 10/01)

6027 Carle, Eric. *Dream Snow* (PS–1). Illus. 2000, Philomel $21.99 (978-0-399-23579-5). 32pp. In this counting book set at Christmastime, a farmer dreams that a gentle snow covers all his animals. (Rev: BCCB 10/00; BL 9/1/00; HBG 3/01)

6028 Carlson, Lori M. *Hurray for Three Kings' Day!* (PS–3). Illus. by Ed Martinez. 1999, Morrow LB $15.89 (978-0-688-16240-5). 32pp. The traditional Latin American holiday is the setting for this story about Anita and her older brothers, who dress as the Christmas kings and carry make-believe gifts around the town. (Rev: BL 9/1/99; HBG 3/00; SLJ 10/99)

6029 Carlson, Nancy. *Harriet and George's Christmas Treat* (PS–2). Illus. 2001, Carolrhoda $15.95 (978-1-57505-506-0). 32pp. Harriet and George try unsuccessfully to avoid eating Mrs. Hoozit's Christmas fruitcake. (Rev: BL 10/1/01; HBG 3/02; SLJ 10/01)

6030 Catalano, Dominic. *Santa and the Three Bears* (PS–K). Illus. 2000, Boyds Mills $15.95 (978-1-56397-864-7). 32pp. Mama, Papa, and Baby Bear seek shelter in Santa's house while he is out delivering gifts and the three intruders wreak mayhem before falling asleep. (Rev: BL 9/1/00; HBG 3/01)

6031 Caudill, Rebecca. *A Certain Small Shepherd* (3–6). Illus. by William Pene du Bois. 1997, Holt paper $6.95 (978-0-8050-5392-0). A mute boy gets an opportunity to play one of the shepherds in a Christmas pageant.

6032 Chaconas, Dori. *Christmas Mouseling* (PS–2). Illus. by Susan Kathleen Hartung. 2005, Viking $15.99 (978-0-670-05984-3). 32pp. When a wintry wind destroys their nest, a mother mouse finds shelter for her newborn in the manger in which Jesus Christ was just born. (Rev: BL 10/15/05; SLJ 10/05)

6033 Chaconas, Dori. *When Cows Come Home for Christmas* (PS–2). Illus. by Lynne Chapman. 2005, Albert Whitman $15.95 (978-0-8075-8877-2). 32pp. In this romp of a Christmas tale, members of an extended bovine family try to squeeze together in a small house to celebrate the holiday. (Rev: BL 10/15/05; SLJ 10/05)

6034 Chen, Chih-Yuan. *The Best Christmas Ever* (PS–2). Illus. 2005, Heryin $13.99 (978-0-9762056-2-3). In this gentle Christmas tale, Little Bear works behind the scenes to ensure that the holiday is a happy one for everyone in his family despite the lack of money. (Rev: BL 12/1/05)

6035 Chen, Pauline. *Peiling and the Chicken-Fried Christmas* (4–6). 2007, Bloomsbury $15.95 (978-1-59990-122-0). 142pp. Eleven-year-old Peiling and her family, immigrants from Taiwan, experiment with celebrating Christmas. (Rev: BL 10/15/07; HB 11/07; LMC 11/07)

6036 Chorao, Kay. *The Christmas Story* (PS–3). Illus. 1996, Holiday House LB $16.95 (978-0-8234-1251-8). 28pp. The biblical account of Christmas from the King James version is illustrated in Renaissance-like paintings. (Rev: BL 9/1/96)

6037 *A Christmas Treasury: Very Merry Stories and Poems* (2–5). Illus. by Kevin Hawkes. 2001, HarperCollins LB $16.89 (978-0-688-12040-5). 48pp. This combination of Christmas stories, carols, and poems is enhanced by Hawkes's detailed, full-color art. (Rev: BL 9/1/01; HBG 3/02; SLJ 10/01)

6038 Clark, Mary Higgins. *The Magical Christmas Horse* (PS–1). Illus. by Wendell Minor. 2011, Simon & Schuster $17.99 (978-141699478-7). 40pp. A young Arizona boy reminisces about the wonderful Christmas he shared with his Connecticut grandparents, and wishes his younger brother could experience one like it. (Rev: BL 10/1/11; SLJ 10/1/11)

6039 Coffey, Tim. *Christmas at the Top of the World* (PS). Illus. by author. 2003, Whitman LB $16.95 (978-0-8075-5762-4). Little Reindeer, joined by his mother and other animals, travels to the North Pole to find his father and see the wonders "at the top of the world." (Rev: HBG 4/04; SLJ 10/03)

6040 Cole, Brock. *The Money We'll Save* (1–3). Illus. by author. 2011, Farrar $16.99 (978-037435011-6). 40pp. Penny-pinching Pa's plan to raise a turkey to eat for Christmas dinner goes spectacularly awry in this comic story set in 19th-century New York City. (Rev: BL 12/1/11; HB 11–12/11; SLJ 10/1/11)

6041 Conover, Chris. *The Christmas Bears* (PS–2). Illus. by author. 2008, Farrar $16.95 (978-0-374-33275-4). A happy and beautifully illustrated Christmas story featuring a father (Santa Bear) and seven little cubs who make cookies, decorate a tree, and anticipate. (Rev: BL 10/1/08; HB 11/08; SLJ 10/08)

6042 Cotten, Cynthia. *This Is the Stable* (PS–2). Illus. by Delana Bettoli. 2006, Holt $16.95 (978-0-8050-7556-4). Using a "This Is the House that Jack Built" style, this rhyming retelling of the Nativity story is a good choice for read-alouds. (Rev: BL 11/1/06; SLJ 10/06)

6043 Cowley, Joy. *Mrs. Wishy-Washy's Christmas* (PS–1). Illus. by Elizabeth Fuller. 2005, Philomel $15.99 (978-0-399-24344-8). 32pp. When Mrs. Wishy-Washy orders the farm animals to get cleaned up for Christmas, the creatures balk at using the icy tub in the barnyard and instead go inside to use her tub. (Rev: BL 9/15/05; SLJ 10/05)

6044 Crisp, Marty. *The Most Precious Gift: A Story of the Nativity* (PS–2). 2006, Philomel $16.99 (978-0-399-24296-0). 32pp. A poor boy named Ameer joins a caravan to go see the baby Jesus and must decide what gift he can offer the newborn king. (Rev: BL 11/15/06; SLJ 10/06)

6045 Dealey, Erin. *Deck the Walls! A Wacky Christmas Carol* (K–2). Illus. by Nick Ward. 2013, Sleeping Bear $14.99 (978-158536857-0). 32pp. A traditional carol gets a whacky update that will get children singing. ℮ (Rev: BLO 9/15/13)

6046 Demas, Corinne. *Two Christmas Mice* (PS–2). Illus. by Stephanie Roth. 2005, Holiday $16.95 (978-0-8234-1785-8). 32pp. Neighbors Annamouse and Willamouse join forces to celebrate Christmas. (Rev: BL 10/15/05; SLJ 10/05)

6047 dePaola, Tomie. *The Birds of Bethlehem* (PS–1). Illus. by author. 2012, Penguin $16.99 (978-039925780-3). 40pp. On the morning after the first Christmas, the birds of Bethlehem discuss the events of the previous night and fly together to visit the stable. ℮ Lexile AD790L (Rev: BL 11/1/12; HB 11–12/12; SLJ 10/12)

6048 dePaola, Tomie. *An Early American Christmas* (K–2). Illus. by author. 1987, Holiday House $17.95 (978-0-8234-0617-3); paper $6.95 (978-0-8234-0979-2). 32pp. What it might have been like for a German family of long ago to move to a New England village where most of the people did not celebrate Christmas. (Rev: BCCB 11/87; BL 9/1/87)

6049 dePaola, Tomie. *Merry Christmas, Strega Nona* (PS–3). Illus. by author. 1986, Harcourt paper $7.00 (978-0-15-253184-3). 32pp. Strega Nona is worried because her helper Big Anthony doesn't seem to be helping her to prepare for Christmas at all. (Rev: BL 11/1/86; HB 11/86)

6050 dePaola, Tomie. *The Night of Las Posadas* (K–4). Illus. 1999, Penguin $16.99 (978-0-399-23400-2). 32pp. During the festival of Las Posadas, a Spanish custom that celebrates the search for shelter by Joseph and Mary, a miracle occurs in this fantasy set in Santa Fe, New Mexico. (Rev: BL 9/1/99; HBG 3/00; SLJ 10/99)

6051 dePaola, Tomie. *Strega Nona's Gift* (K–2). Illus. by author. 2011, Penguin $16.99 (978-039925649-3). 32pp. At Christmas time, Big Anthony finds himself so enticed by Strega Nona's cooking that he eats a pot of turnips intended for the goat, and the goat retaliates by eating his blanket; meantime Strega Nona sends out nighttime gifts. ∩ ℮ (Rev: BL 12/15/11; HB 11–12/11; SLJ 10/1/11)

6052 dePaola, Tomie, retel. *The Legend of Old Befana* (PS–3). Illus. by Tomie dePaola. 1980, Harcourt $16.00 (978-0-15-243816-6); paper $6.00 (978-0-15-243817-3). 32pp. The legend of the old lady who is still searching for the Christ child.

6053 DiCamillo, Kate. *Great Joy* (PS–2). Illus. by Bagram Ibatoulline. 2007, Candlewick $16.99 (978-0-7636-2920-5). 32pp. With illustrations that evoke the 1940s, this is a gentle Christmas story about a young girl, Frances, who is distressed by the thought that an organ grinder and his monkey have no home to go to. (Rev: BCCB 12/07; BL 10/15/07; LMC 3/08)

6054 Dooley, Norah. *Everybody Serves Soup* (2–4). Illus. by Peter J. Thornton. 2000, Carolrhoda $15.95 (978-1-57505-422-3). 40pp. When Carrie tastes her neighbors' soups, she gets an idea for a unique Christmas present for her mother. (Rev: BL 1/1–15/01; HBG 3/01)

6055 Dunbar, Joyce. *This Is the Star* (K–3). Illus. by Gary Blythe. 1996, Harcourt $16.00 (978-0-15-200851-2). 36pp. A cumulative tale using the story of the Nativity as a framework. (Rev: BL 9/1/96; HBG 4/04; SLJ 4/04)

6056 Dunrea, Olivier. *A Christmas Tree for Pyn* (PS–2). Illus. by author. 2011, Philomel $16.99 (978-039924506-0). 32pp. A young girl pining for her own Christmas tree finally breaks through to her distant father when she gets lost in the snowy woods; in the end, she receives both a tree and the affection she craves. Lexile AD700L (Rev: BL 10/15/11; HB 11–12/11; SLJ 10/1/11*)

6057 Duval, Kathy. *The Three Bears' Christmas* (PS–K). Illus. by Paul Meisel. 2005, Holiday $16.95 (978-0-8234-1871-8). 32pp. The three bears return from a Christmas Eve walk to find that someone has been in their house — even tried out the beds — and left a red coat and presents under the tree. (Rev: BL 9/1/05*; HB 11/05; HBG 4/06; SLJ 10/05)

6058 Elschner, Géraldine. *Pashmina the Little Christmas Goat* (PS–2). Illus. by Angela Kehlenbeck. 2006, Penguin $16.99 (978-0-698-40046-7). 32pp. When father brings home a small white goat to eat for Christmas dinner the family decides instead to keep it and raise it, and the rewards continue year after year; rich illustrations add to the warmth of the story. (Rev: BL 12/1/06; SLJ 10/06)

6059 Emmett, Jonathan. *The Santa Trap* (2–4). Illus. by Poly Bernatene. 2012, Peachtree $15.95 (978-1-56145670-3). 32pp. A darkly humorous book about a bad boy — Bradley Bartleby — who plots to trap Santa, who has been giving him socks for Christmas for years. Lexile AD850L (Rev: BLO 10/1/12; HB 11–12/12; SLJ 10/12)

6060 Evans, Richard Paul. *The Christmas Candle* (3–6). Illus. by Jacob Collins. 2007, Simon & Schuster $9.99 (978-1-4169-5047-9). 32pp. A magical candle he buys on Christmas morning allows Thomas to see strangers in a new, charitable light. (Rev: BL 9/15/07)

6061 Evans, Richard Paul. *The Light of Christmas* (K–2). Illus. by Daniel Craig. 2002, Simon & Schuster $16.95 (978-0-689-83468-4). A boy called Alexander does a good deed and is rewarded with the special right to light the flame on Christmas Eve. (Rev: BL 10/1/02; HBG 3/03; SLJ 10/02)

6062 Fackelmayer, Regina. *The Gifts* (PS–3). Illus. by Christa Unzner. 2009, NorthSouth $16.95 (978-073582265-8). 32pp. In this quiet story, a generous young girl is rewarded for her good deeds when a kind-hearted man and a boy decorate her Christmas tree for her. (Rev: BL 11/1/09; HB 11–12/09)

6063 Falconer, Ian. *Olivia Helps with Christmas* (PS–1). Illus. by author. 2007, Atheneum $18.99 (978-1-4169-0786-2). 58pp. Little pig Olivia tries — really! — to help with Christmas preparations. (Rev: BL 9/15/07; HB 11/07) ∩

6064 *The Family Christmas Treasury: Tales of Anticipation, Celebration, and Joy* (PS–3). Illus. 2013, Houghton Mifflin $18.99 (978-054409249-5). 288pp. Multiple Christmas books are included in this treasury, and after each story, there is a Christmas carol for children to sing. (Rev: BLO 9/15/13; HB 11–12/13; SLJ 10/13)

6065 Fine, Edith Hope. *Cricket at the Manger* (PS–2). Illus. by Winslow Pels. 2005, Boyds Mills $15.95 (978-1-56397-993-4). Awakened by strange noises, an initially grouchy cricket witnesses the birth of Jesus in a manger. (Rev: BL 9/1/05; SLJ 10/05)

6066 Foreman, Michael. *Cat in the Manger* (PS–3). Illus. 2001, Holt $16.95 (978-0-8050-6677-7). 24pp. A cat is displaced from his bed to make room for a baby in the manger. (Rev: BCCB 11/01; BL 9/15/01; HBG 3/02; SLJ 10/01)

6067 Frazee, Marla. *Santa Claus: The World's Number One Toy Expert* (PS–K). Illus. 2005, Harcourt $16.00 (978-0-15-204970-6). 40pp. A portrait of Santa hard at work, taking requests and testing toys. (Rev: BCCB 12/05; BL 11/1/05*; HB 11/05; HBG 4/06; SLJ 10/05*)

6068 Freeman, Martha. *Who Is Stealing the 12 Days of Christmas?* (4–6). 2003, Holiday House $16.95 (978-0-8234-1788-9). 200pp. When Christmas displays at the 12 houses on Chickadee Court — each decorated for a different stanza of "The 12 Days of Christmas" — begin disappearing, Alex Parakeet and his best friend Yasmeen try to find out who — or what — is responsible. (Rev: HB 11/03; HBG 4/04; SLJ 10/03)

6069 Gammell, Stephen. *Wake Up, Bear . . . It's Christmas!* (PS–1). Illus. by author. 1981, Morrow paper $4.95 (978-0-688-09934-3). 32pp. A bear is afraid he will sleep through Christmas.

6070 Gantos, Jack. *Rotten Ralph's Rotten Christmas* (K–2). Illus. by Nicole Rubel. 1984, Houghton $16.00 (978-0-395-35380-6); paper $7.95 (978-0-395-45685-9). 32pp. This miserable cat is determined that Sarah's Christmas will also be miserable.

6071 Garland, Michael. *Christmas Magic* (PS–3). Illus. 2001, Dutton $16.99 (978-0-525-46797-7). 32pp. Arresting artwork shows how Emily's Christmas Eve was a night of real enchantment. (Rev: BCCB 11/01; BL 9/1/01; HBG 3/02; SLJ 10/01)

6072 Ghigna, Charles. *I See Winter* (PS). Illus. by Ag Jatkowska. 2011, Picture Window $21.32 (978-140486588-4); paper $4.95 (978-14048685-0-2). 24pp. From subtle changes in the weather and landscape to preparations for Christmas, this book celebrates winter in simple, poetic text. (Rev: BLO 11/15/11)

6073 Gillmor, Don. *The Christmas Orange* (K–2). Illus. by Marie-Louise Gay. 1999, Stoddart $15.95 (978-0-7737-3100-4). When Anton receives only an orange for Christmas, he sues Santa for breach of promise. (Rev: BL 1/1–15/00)

6074 Gliori, Debi. *What Can I Give Him?* (PS–3). Illus. 1998, Holiday House $15.95 (978-0-8234-1392-8). 32pp. Using double-page spreads — one depicting a contemporary girl with her loving family at Christmastime and the other a poor servant girl in the stable where Jesus was born — this book explores the question of what one should give as a loving present. (Rev: BL 9/1/98; HBG 3/99; SLJ 10/98)

6075 Greene, Stephanie. *Princess Posey and the Christmas Magic* (1–2). Illus. by Stephanie Roth Sisson. 2013, Putnam $13.99 (978-039916363-0). 96pp. Posey wants a magic wand for Christmas more than anything, but she's sure that Santa knows that she's done some things she shouldn't have; luckily Gramps and Mom know just how to help Posey. ℮ Lexile 340 (Rev: BLO 9/15/13)

6076 Gutman, Anne. *Gaspard and Lisa's Christmas Surprise* (PS–K). Illus. by Georg Hallensleben. Series: The Misadventures of Gaspard and Lisa. 2002, Knopf $9.95 (978-0-375-82229-2). Gaspard and Lisa, young animals, set out to make a raincoat for their teacher. (Rev: HBG 3/03; SLJ 10/02)

6077 Harley, Bill. *Dear Santa: The Letters of James B. Dobbins* (PS–2). Illus. by R. W. Alley. 2005, HarperCollins $15.99 (978-0-06-623778-7). 32pp. In a series of letters to Santa Claus, Jimmy Dobbins places orders for some pretty outrageous Christmas gifts and also offers explanations for some of his lapses in behavior over the past year. (Rev: BL 10/1/05; SLJ 10/05)

6078 Hassett, Ann, and John Hassett. *The Finest Christmas Tree* (K–2). Illus. 2005, Houghton $16.00 (978-0-618-50901-0). 32pp. Things look bleak for Farmer Tuttle when the demand for his Christmas trees drops as more and more of his customers opt for the artificial variety. (Rev: BL 11/1/05; SLJ 10/05)

6079 Helmer, Marilyn. *One Splendid Tree* (K–2). Illus. by Dianne Eastman. 2005, Kids Can $15.95 (978-1-55337-683-5). With their father off fighting in World War II, siblings Junior and Hattie try to give their tiny apartment a bit of Christmas spirit by decorating a discarded plant; the illustrations offer lots of period details. (Rev: SLJ 10/05)

6080 High, Linda Oatman. *The Last Chimney of Christmas Eve* (PS–2). Illus. by Kestutis Kasparavicius. 2001, Boyds Mills $15.95 (978-1-56397-804-3). 32pp. Nicholas, a chimney sweep, repays a kind stranger by growing up to be Santa Claus. (Rev: BL 9/15/01; HBG 3/02; SLJ 10/01)

6081 Hoban, Lillian. *Arthur's Christmas Cookies* (1–2). Illus. by author. 1972, HarperCollins paper $3.99 (978-0-06-444055-4). What can Arthur give his parents for Christmas? Christmas cookies such as he learned to bake in Cub Scouts are the answer, but a hilarious mix-up occurs when salt is used instead of sugar.

6082 Holland, Trish, and Christine Ford. *The Soldiers' Night Before Christmas* (K–3). Illus. by John Manders. 2006, Random $8.99 (978-0-375-83795-1). Using the structure of Clement Moore's classic Christmas poem, this story in rhyme is set on a U.S. Army base in the desert, and the gifts arrive not in a sleigh but by Humvee. (Rev: SLJ 10/06)

6083 Hooks, William H. *The Legend of the Christmas Rose* (K–4). Illus. by Richard A. Williams. 1999, HarperCollins LB $14.89 (978-0-06-027103-9). 32pp. Dorothy has no presents to offer the infant Jesus, but an angel provides her with the flower now known as the Christmas Rose. (Rev: BL 9/1/99; HBG 3/00)

6084 Hooper, Maureen Brett. *Silent Night: A Christmas Carol Is Born* (1–3). Illus. by Kasi Kubiak. 2001, Boyds Mills $15.95 (978-1-56397-782-4). The fictionalized story behind the carol "Silent Night." (Rev: BL 9/15/01; HBG 3/02; SLJ 10/01)

6085 Horn, Sandra Ann. *Babushka* (K–3). Illus. by Sophie Fatus. 2002, Barefoot Books $16.99 (978-1-84148-353-5). 32pp. In this version of a Russian tale, Babushka travels to visit the newly born Christ child, but gives away the gifts she brought to needy people along the way. (Rev: BL 12/15/02; HBG 3/03; SLJ 10/02)

6086 Horse, Harry. *Little Rabbit's Christmas* (PS–1). Illus. by author. 2007, Peachtree $15.95 (978-1-56145-419-8). 32pp. Little Rabbit learns a lesson on Christmas morning when his friends help him fix the little red sled he refused to share. (Rev: BL 9/15/07; HB 11/07)

6087 Howard, Ellen. *The Log Cabin Christmas* (K–3). Illus. by Ronald Himler. 2000, Holiday House $16.95 (978-0-8234-1381-2). 32pp. Set in Michigan during pioneer times, Elvirey and her family are afraid there will be no Christmas now that Mam's dead, but the young girl decides she can save the day. (Rev: BCCB 11/00; BL 11/15/00; HBG 3/01)

6088 Hudson, Cheryl W. *Hold Christmas in Your Heart: African-American Songs, Poems, and Stories for the Holidays* (K–2). Illus. 1995, Scholastic $10.95 (978-0-590-48024-6). 32pp. Poems, stories, and songs from African American authors are found in this fine anthology. (Rev: BL 9/15/95)

6089 Hughes, Langston. *Carol of the Brown King* (PS–3). Illus. by Ashley Bryan. 1998, Simon & Schuster $16.00 (978-0-689-81877-6). 32pp. A colorful picture book that presents six short poems about Christmas — five by Langston Hughes plus one poem he translated from a Puerto Rican Christmas card. (Rev: BL 9/1/98; HB 9/98; HBG 3/99; SLJ 10/98) [811]

6090 Jay, Alison. *Christmastime* (PS–1). Illus. by author. 2012, Dial $16.99 (978-080373804-1). 32pp. Two children journey to the North Pole in this nicely illustrated almost-wordless story that simply presents various aspects of Christmas and contains hidden surprises. (Rev: BL 11/1/12*; HB 11–12/12; SLJ 10/12)

6091 Jay, Alison. *The Nutcracker* (K–3). Illus. by author. 2010, Dial $16.99 (978-080373285-8). 40pp. Nostalgic illustrations grace this retelling of the classic story about the nutcracker soldier who becomes a prince. (Rev: BL 10/15/10; HB 11–12/10)

6092 Jeffers, Susan. *The Twelve Days of Christmas* (PS–2). Illus. by author. 2013, HarperCollins $17.99 (978-006206615-2). 40pp. A little girl drops a snow globe, setting off a series of dream-like events in which she is transported to the North Pole, where she sees common events from the popular carol and Santa repairs the broken snow globe. Lexile AD650 (Rev: BLO 9/15/13; HB 11–12/13; SLJ 10/13)

6093 Jeffs, Stephanie. *Christopher Bear's First Christmas* (PS–K). Illus. by Jacqui Thomas. Series: Christopher Bear. 2002, Augsburg $5.99 (978-0-8066-4349-6). 29pp. Joe and his bear participate in the preschool's presentation of the first Christmas. (Rev: SLJ 10/02)

6094 Jimenez, Francisco. *The Christmas Gift: El regalo de Navidad* (K–4). Illus. by Claire B. Cotts. 2000, Houghton $16.00 (978-0-395-92869-1). In this bilingual book, Panchito is disappointed because there is no money to buy him the red ball he wants for Christmas. (Rev: BCCB 12/00; BL 9/1/00; HBG 3/01)

6095 Johnston, Tony. *A Kenya Christmas* (K–2). Illus. by Leonard Jenkins. 2003, Holiday House $16.95 (978-0-8234-1623-3). A Kenyan man tells his grandchildren about a wondrous Christmas from his past, involving snow made from chicken feathers and a Santa carried on an elephant. (Rev: HBG 4/04; SLJ 10/03)

6096 Katz, Karen. *Counting Christmas* (PS). Illus. by author. 2003, Simon & Schuster $14.95 (978-0-689-

84925-1). Counting from 10 down to one, this holiday book features double-page spreads full of Christmas details. (Rev: HBG 4/04; SLJ 10/03)

6097 Kimmel, Eric A. *The Spider's Gift: A Ukrainian Christmas Story* (K–2). Illus. by Katya Krenina. 2010, Holiday House $16.95 (978-082341743-8). 32pp. Katrusya's impoverished family cuts down a small pine tree for Christmas and decorates it with buttons, but spiders nesting in the tree give them an unexpected present. Lexile AD500L (Rev: BL 8/10; SLJ 10/1/10)

6098 Kladstrup, Kristin. *The Gingerbread Pirates* (PS–2). Illus. by Matt Tavares. 2009, Candlewick $16.99 (978-076363223-6). 32pp. A group of pirate-shaped gingerbread cookies come to life in a daring attempt to save themselves from being eaten by Santa. (Rev: BL 9/15/09; HB 11–12/09; SLJ 10/09)

6099 Knott, Anthony. *An Angel Came to Nazareth: A Story of the First Christmas* (K–5). Illus. by Maggie Kneen. 2005, Chronicle $15.95 (978-0-8118-4798-8). An angel offers four beasts of burden — horse, donkey, camel, and ox — the option of choosing their riders for a trip from Nazareth to Bethlehem; a simple story with lush illustrations. (Rev: SLJ 10/05)

6100 Kroll, Steven. *Pooch on the Loose: A Christmas Adventure* (PS–1). Illus. by Michael Garland. 2005, Marshall Cavendish $14.95 (978-0-7614-5239-3). 32pp. Bart the dog escapes from his master and visits the sights of New York City; Photoshop art gives a realistic view of the city and Christmas. (Rev: BL 9/1/05; SLJ 10/05)

6101 Kroll, Virginia. *Uno, Dos, Tres, Posada! Let's Celebrate Christmas* (PS–2). Illus. by Loretta Lopez. 2006, Viking $17.99 (978-0-670-05923-2). Readers learn vocabulary and numbers in Spanish as a little girl introduces each step of a posada, a Hispanic holiday tradition celebrated on the nine nights before Christmas. (Rev: SLJ 10/06)

6102 Krupinski, Loretta. *Christmas in the City* (PS–2). Illus. 2002, Hyperion $15.99 (978-0-7868-0834-2). 40pp. This beautifully illustrated book tells the tale of Mr. and Mrs. Mouse and their Christmas trip to New York during which they explore the city and Mrs. Mouse gives birth in a manger. (Rev: BL 9/15/02; HBG 3/03; SLJ 10/02)

6103 Krykorka, Ian. *Carl, the Christmas Carp* (K–3). Illus. by Vladyana Krykorka. 2006, Orca $17.95 (978-1-55143-329-5). 32pp. Radim's Czech family usually eats carp for Christmas but when he feels sorry for the fish and releases it into the river, his family learns a new tradition for the holiday. (Rev: BL 11/15/06)

6104 Landa, Norbert. *Little Bear's Christmas* (PS–K). Illus. by Marlis Scharff-Kniemeyer. 1999, Little Tiger $14.95 (978-1-888444-60-5). 32pp. Little Bear sets the alarm clock so he will not hibernate through Christmas and miss seeing Santa Claus. (Rev: BL 10/1/99; HBG 3/00; SLJ 10/99)

6105 Lester, Helen. *Tacky's Christmas* (PS–2). Illus. by Lynn Munsinger. 2010, Houghton Mifflin $16.95 (978-054717208-8). 32pp. Tacky's Santa costume convinces penguin hunters to put down their guns and spare his friends. (Rev: BL 10/15/10; HB 11–12/10; SLJ 10/10)

6106 Leuck, Laura. *Santa Claws* (1–4). Illus. by Gris Grimly. 2006, Chronicle $16.95 (978-0-8118-4992-0). In this offbeat Christmas tale, Mack and Zack, two young monsters, prepare for the arrival of Santa Claws. (Rev: SLJ 10/06)

6107 Lewis, Anne Margaret. *What Am I? Christmas* (PS–K). Illus. by Tom Mills. Series: My Look and See Holiday Book. 2011, Whitman $9.99 (978-080758958-8). 24pp. This Christmas flap-book with rhyming text presents readers with a series of short, guessable, what am I queries. (Rev: BL 11/1/11; SLJ 10/1/11)

6108 Lewis, J. Patrick. *The Snowflake Sisters* (PS–2). Illus. by Lisa Desimini. 2003, Simon & Schuster $16.95 (978-0-689-85029-5). Crystal and Ivory, two snowflake siblings, find themselves in New York and settle on a snowman in Central Park in this Christmas-related story with wonderful collage illustrations. (Rev: HBG 4/04; SLJ 10/03)

6109 Light, Steve. *The Christmas Giant* (PS–1). Illus. by author. 2010, Candlewick $15.99 (978-076364692-9). 32pp. A giant and an elf collaborate to grow the perfect Christmas tree in this story with brief text but detailed illustrations. (Rev: BL 10/15/10; HB 11–12/10)

6110 Lloyd-Jones, Sally. *Song of the Stars: A Christmas Story* (PS–1). Illus. by Alison Jay. 2011, Zondervan $15.99 (978-031072291-5). 32pp. Nature and the animals welcome the birth of the baby Jesus in this alliterative text with rich illustrations and spare, poetic language. (Rev: BL 11/1/11; SLJ 10/1/11)

6111 Love, Maryann Cusimano. *You Are My Miracle* (PS–K). Illus. by Satomi Ichikawa. 2005, Philomel $15.99 (978-0-399-24037-9). A mother bear and her child celebrate Christmas in rhyming text that emphasizes togetherness. (Rev: SLJ 10/05)

6112 Lucas, David. *Christmas at the Toy Museum* (PS–1). Illus. by author. 2012, Candlewick $15.99 (978-076365868-7). 32pp. Distressed by the lack of presents around their tree, the 22 toys at the museum decide to wrap themselves up and become each other's gifts. (Rev: BL 12/1/12; HB 11–12/12)

6113 McAnulty, Stacy. *Dear Santasaurus* (K–3). Illus. by Jef Kaminsky. 2013, Boyds Mills $15.95 (978-159078876-9). 32pp. Ernest the spinosaurus is a very good dino — and sends multiple letters to Santasaurus explaining his achievements and his Christmas, well - yearlong, needs. (Rev: BLO 9/15/13)

6114 McCaughrean, Geraldine. *How the Reindeer Got Their Antlers* (1–3). Illus. by Heather Holland. 2000, Holiday House $16.95 (978-0-8234-1562-5). 32pp. The reindeer is ashamed of its twisted antlers, until Santa uses them to save the day when his sleigh slips on ice. (Rev: BL 9/1/00; HBG 3/01)

6115 McCourt, Frank. *Angela and the Baby Jesus* (K–3). Illus. by Raúl Colón. 2007, Simon & Schuster $17.99 (978-1-4169-3789-0). 32pp. Warm illustrations enhance this story about 6-year-old Angela's misguided effort to keep the baby Jesus in the church creche warm. (Rev: BCCB 12/07; BL 9/15/07)

6116 McCutcheon, John. *Christmas in the Trenches* (2–4). Illus. by Henri Sorenson. 2006, Peachtree $18.95 (978-1-56145-374-0). 32pp. On Christmas Day, a World War I veteran tells his grandchildren about the incredible Christmas truce of 1914; McCutcheon's song by the same name is printed at the end. (Rev: BL 8/06; SLJ 10/06)

6117 McGinley, Phyllis. *The Year Without a Santa Claus* (K–3). Illus. by John Manders. 2010, Marshall Cavendish $16.99 (978-076145799-2). 40pp. New illustrations grace this update of McGinley's rhyming story, originally published in 1957, about how children react when Santa decides to take a vacation. Lexile AD810L (Rev: BLO 11/15/10; HB 11–12/10; SLJ 10/10)

6118 McGovern, Ann. *The Lady in the Box* (K–3). Illus. by Marni Backer. 1997, Turtle $14.95 (978-1-890515-01-0). 32pp. At Christmas time, two youngsters help a homeless woman who is living over a hot-air vent. (Rev: BL 9/1/97; SLJ 10/97)

6119 McKissack, Patricia C. *The All-I'll-Ever-Want Christmas Doll* (K–3). Illus. by Jerry Pinkney. 2007, Random $16.99 (978-0-375-83759-3). 40pp. During the depression, Nella and her African American sisters must share a single Christmas doll. (Rev: BCCB 12/07; BL 9/15/07; HB 11/07; LMC 11/07)

6120 Major, Kevin. *Aunt Olga's Christmas Postcards* (K–3). Illus. by Bruce Roberts. 2005, Groundwood $18.95 (978-0-88899-593-3). 40pp. Anna and her 95-year-old great-great-Aunt Olga write Christmas verses together and share historic postcards and memories. (Rev: BL 11/1/05; SLJ 10/05)

6121 Martín, Hugo C. *Pablo's Christmas* (K–4). Illus. by Lee Chapman. 2006, Sterling LB $14.95 (978-1-4027-2560-9). Left behind to watch over his expectant mother when his father leaves Mexico to find work in the United States, Pablo does his best to prepare for Christmas. (Rev: SLJ 10/06)

6122 Martin, Ruth. *Santa's on His Way* (PS–K). Illus. by Sophy Williams. 2011, Candlewick $12.99 (978-076365555-6). 14pp. Santa, the elves, and the reindeer rush around getting ready for Christmas Eve in this story with "changing pictures" that involve lifting flaps. (Rev: BLO 10/15/11; SLJ 10/1/11)

6123 Marzollo, Jean. *I Spy Christmas: A Book of Picture Riddles* (PS–3). Illus. by Walter Wick. 1992, Scholastic $13.99 (978-0-590-45846-7). 40pp. Full-color photos illustrate 13 scenes of Christmas. (Rev: BCCB 11/92; BL 11/1/92) [793.73]

6124 May, Robert L. *Rudolph the Red-Nosed Reindeer: The Original Story of Rudolph* (K–3). Illus. by David Wenzel. 2001, Grosset $9.99 (978-0-448-42534-4). The original text of Rudolph is presented with new illustrations that convey a warm, nostalgic feeling. (Rev: HBG 3/02; SLJ 10/01)

6125 Mayer, Mercer. *The Little Drummer Mouse* (K–3). Illus. by author. 2006, Dial $16.99 (978-0-8037-3147-

9). A little mouse, playing on his acorn drum, helps to celebrate the birth of Jesus Christ. (Rev: SLJ 10/06)

6126 Medearis, Angela Shelf. *Poppa's Itchy Christmas* (PS–1). Illus. by John Ward. 1998, Holiday House $15.95 (978-0-8234-1298-3). 32pp. George, an African American youngster, is not happy with the scarf and red long underwear he receives for Christmas, but when he falls through the ice while trying out his new skates, they are the two items that help save his life. (Rev: BL 9/1/98; HBG 10/99; SLJ 10/98)

6127 Milgrim, David. *Santa Duck and His Merry Helpers* (PS–1). Illus. by author. 2010, Putnam $12.99 (978-039925473-4). 32pp. Nicholas Duck ponders on the real meaning of Christmas when his siblings try to help him with his duties for Santa. (Rev: BL 12/1/10; HB 11–12/10; SLJ 10/10*)

6128 Minor, Wendell, and Florence Minor. *Christmas Tree!* (PS–2). Illus. by authors. 2005, HarperCollins $16.99 (978-0-06-056034-8). Christmas trees of all kinds and sizes are celebrated in rhyming text and colorful illustrations. (Rev: SLJ 10/05)

6129 Modugno, Maria. *Santa Claus and the Three Bears* (PS–1). Illus. by Jane Dyer. 2013, HarperCollins $17.99 (978-006170023-1). 40pp. Santa takes the place of Goldilocks in this retelling of Goldilocks and the Three Bears, offering a Christmas twist to the well-known tale. Lexile AD830 (Rev: BLO 9/15/13)

6130 Moore, Clement C., and Carter Goodrich. *A Creature Was Stirring: One Boy's Night Before Christmas* (PS–2). Illus. by Carter Goodrich. 2006, Simon & Schuster $16.95 (978-0-689-86399-8). 40pp. Moore's classic Christmas poem is presented here along with a young boy's account of what he did that night when he could not sleep. (Rev: BL 11/15/06; SLJ 10/06)

6131 Morpurgo, Michael. *On Angel Wings* (K–2). Illus. by Quentin Blake. 2007, Candlewick paper $8.99 (978-0-7636-3466-7). 48pp. The Angel Gabriel makes it possible for a young shepherd to see the newborn Christ in this small-format Nativity story. (Rev: BL 10/15/07; HB 11/07)

6132 Morrissey, Dean. *The Christmas Ship* (K–4). Illus. 2000, HarperCollins LB $16.89 (978-0-06-028576-0). 40pp. On Christmas Eve, toy maker Sam Thatcher helps Santa by delivering toys from his boat, which soars through the night sky. (Rev: BL 10/1/00; HBG 3/01)

6133 Moulton, Mark Kimball. *Reindeer Christmas* (PS–2). Illus. by Karen Hillard Good. 2008, Simon & Schuster $15.99 (978-1-4169-6108-6). 40pp. A warm, rhyming tale about a family that cares for an injured reindeer and later discovers that it was Donner; Santa is grateful. (Rev: BL 9/1/08)

6134 Noble, Trinka Hakes. *A Christmas Spider's Miracle* (K–3). Illus. by Stephen Costanza. 2011, Sleeping Bear $16.95 (978-158536602-6). 32pp. Sensing the dire state of a poor family's Christmas, a kind spider covers their spare Christmas tree with shimmering, woven designs; based on a Ukrainian legend. (Rev: BLO 11/15/11; SLJ 10/1/11)

6135 Oppenheim, Joanne. *The Miracle of the First Poinsettia: A Mexican Christmas Story* (K–2). Illus. by Fabian Negrin. 2003, Barefoot Books $16.99 (978-1-84148-245-3). Young Juanita has no money to give to the church so she follows the advice of a stone angel and gathers weeds, which are miraculously transformed into the beautiful scarlet blossoms of a poinsettia. (Rev: HBG 4/04; SLJ 10/03)

6136 Palatini, Margie. *Moosletoe* (PS–1). Illus. by Henry Cole. 2000, Hyperion $15.99 (978-0-7868-0567-9). 32pp. The moose with the remarkable mustache allows it to be decked with ornaments to preserve the spirit of the Christmas season. (Rev: BL 9/1/00; HBG 3/01)

6137 Pallotta, Jerry. *Who Will Guide My Sleigh Tonight?* (PS–2). Illus. by David Biedrzycki. 2006, Scholastic paper $5.99 (978-0-439-85369-9). Santa Claus, searching for animals to pull his gift-laden sleigh, considers a wide array of possibilities — from skunks and giraffes to kangaroos and snakes — before finally settling on reindeer. (Rev: SLJ 10/06)

6138 Papineau, Lucie. *Christmas Eve Magic* (2–5). Trans. from French by Brigitte Shapiro. Illus. by Stéphane Poulin. 2006, Kids Can $16.95 (978-1-55337-953-9). In this story inspired by Dickens's *A Christmas Carol*, animals take the leading roles, led by a greedy pig called Barton. (Rev: SLJ 10/06)

6139 Parish, Peggy. *Merry Christmas, Amelia Bedelia* (1–2). Illus. by Lynn Sweat. Series: Amelia Bedelia. 1986, Greenwillow $17.89 (978-0-688-06102-9); Avon paper $3.99 (978-0-380-70325-8). 64pp. Christmas fun with silly Amelia Bedelia, the maid with nonsensical assumptions. (Rev: BCCB 10/86; BL 10/1/86)

6140 Park, Linda Sue. *The Third Gift* (K–2). Illus. by Bagram Ibatoulline. 2011, Clarion $16.99 (978-054720195-5). 32pp. A boy and his father wander the landscape, collecting precious sap — myrrh — to be sold to the Wise Men, who have a special birth to attend. (Rev: BL 10/15/11; SLJ 10/1/11)

6141 Parker, Toni Trent. *Snowflake Kisses and Gingerbread Smiles* (PS–2). Photos by Earl Anderson. 2002, Scholastic $6.95 (978-0-439-33872-1). Photographs of seasonal items and African American children emphasize the delights of Christmas. (Rev: HBG 3/03; SLJ 10/02)

6142 Pfister, Marcus. *Snow Puppy* (PS–1). Trans. by NordSud Verlag. Illus. by author. 2011, NorthSouth $16.95 (978-0-7358-4031-7). 32pp. A kindhearted man who returns a puppy lost in the snow is invited to share Christmas with the pup's family. (Rev: BL 10/1/11; SLJ 11/1/11)

6143 Polacco, Patricia. *Welcome Comfort* (K–3). Illus. by author. 1999, Philomel LB $16.99 (978-0-399-23169-8). Welcome Comfort, an overweight foster child, gets a special surprise at Christmas. (Rev: BCCB 11/99; HBG 3/00; SLJ 10/99)

6144 Primavera, Elise. *Auntie Claus* (PS–2). Illus. 1999, Harcourt $16.00 (978-0-15-201909-9). 40pp. Sophie Crinkle follows her Aunt Claus to a snowy land and there discovers that her relative is the real force behind Christmas. (Rev: BCCB 12/99; BL 9/1/99; HBG 3/00; SLJ 10/99)

6145 Pulver, Robin. *Christmas for a Kitten* (PS–2). Illus. by Layne Johnson. 2003, Whitman LB $16.95 (978-0-8075-1151-0). Santa adopts a tiny abandoned kitten that has been having a tough time. (Rev: HBG 4/04; SLJ 10/03)

6146 Pulver, Robin. *Christmas Kitten, Home at Last* (PS–2). Illus. by Layne Johnson. 2010, Whitman $16.99 (978-080751157-2). 32pp. Santa, who apparently is allergic to cats, matches a stray kitten picked up on Christmas Eve with a little girl who will love him. (Rev: BL 10/15/10)

6147 Rahaman, Vashanti. *O Christmas Tree* (K–3). Illus. by Frane Lessac. 1996, Boyds Mills $14.95 (978-1-56397-237-9). 26pp. Anslem has problems believing in a traditional Christmas with snow and Christmas trees in his Caribbean home. (Rev: BCCB 11/96; BL 9/1/96*)

6148 Ransom, Candice F. *The Christmas Dolls* (K–3). Illus. by Moira Fain. 1998, Walker LB $16.85 (978-0-8027-8661-6). 32pp. Claire is sad because her father will be absent for Christmas. She is comforted by helping her mother repair dolls to give to poor children and by making a rag doll that she will give her mother on Christmas morning. (Rev: BL 9/1/98; HBG 3/99; SLJ 10/98)

6149 Rawlinson, Julia. *Fletcher and the Snowflake Christmas* (PS–1). Illus. by Tiphanie Beeke. Series: Fletcher. 2010, Greenwillow $16.99 (978-006199033-5). 32pp. Fletcher the fox and his animal friends worry that Santa won't be able to find the rabbits' new burrow. Lexile AD810L (Rev: BL 12/1/10; HB 11–12/10; SLJ 10/10)

6150 Recorvits, Helen. *Yoon and the Christmas Mitten* (PS–2). Illus. by Gabi Swiatkowska. 2006, Farrar $16.00 (978-0-374-38688-7). 32pp. Yoon, a young Korean American girl, learns about the Christmas holiday in her American school and tries to persuade her family that they can celebrate the holiday and still be true to their Korean customs; a sequel to *My Name Is Yoon* (2003). (Rev: BL 12/1/06; SLJ 10/06)

6151 Rees, Douglas. *Jeannette Claus Saves Christmas* (PS–2). Illus. by Olivier Latyk. 2010, Simon & Schuster $16.99 (978-141692686-3). 40pp. Santa's hip daughter Jeanette saves the day when a few ne'er-do-well reindeer escape their harness on Christmas Eve. (Rev: BL 11/15/10; HB 11–12/10; SLJ 10/10)

6152 Reiss, Mike. *Merry Un-Christmas* (1–3). Illus. by David Catrow. 2006, HarperCollins $15.99 (978-0-06-059126-7). Noelle and her family live in Texmas, where it's Christmas 364 days of the year and the one day they look forward to eagerly is Un-Christmas, when there are no gifts and the kids can go to school. (Rev: SLJ 10/06)

6153 Reiss, Mike. *Santa Claustrophobia* (2–5). Illus. by David Catrow. 2002, Price Stern Sloan $10.99 (978-0-8431-7756-5). Santa is suffering from claustrophobia and Doc Holiday recommends some time off. (Rev: BCCB 12/02; HBG 3/03; SLJ 10/02)

6154 Repchuk, Caroline. *The Snow Tree* (PS–1). Illus. by Josephine Martin. 1997, Dutton $15.99 (978-0-525-45903-3). 32pp. Animals offer to a little bear many colorful objects to decorate his Christmas tree. (Rev: BL 9/1/97; HBG 3/98)

6155 Reynolds, Peter H. *The Smallest Gift of Christmas* (PS–1). Illus. by Peter H. Reynolds. 2013, Candlewick $14 (978-076366103-8). 40pp. Roland is just sure he's going to get the biggest gift ever for Christmas, so he's disappointed when he actually gets the smallest gift of all; but after considering a dream present he realizes that size isn't everything. ∩ (Rev: BLO 9/15/13; HB 11–12/13; SLJ 10/13)

6156 Roberts, Bethany. *Cookie Angel* (PS–2). Illus. by Vladimir Vagin. 2007, Holt $16.95 (978-0-8050-6974-7). 32pp. When the clock strikes midnight on Christmas Eve, a cookie angel atop the tree and toys arrayed around the bottom come alive and have a wild time. (Rev: BL 9/15/07)

6157 Rox, John. *I Want a Hippopotamus for Christmas* (K–3). Illus. by Bruce Whatley. 2005, HarperCollins $17.99 (978-0-06-052942-0). A girl's Christmas wish is granted when a hippo arrives at her house in this funny version of a 1953 song. (Rev: SLJ 10/05)

6158 Rylant, Cynthia. *Christmas in the Country* (K–2). Illus. by Diane Goode. 2002, Scholastic $15.95 (978-0-439-07334-9). 32pp. A story of a loving family's beautiful white Christmas, full of tradition and celebration. (Rev: BL 9/15/02; HB 11/02; HBG 3/03; SLJ 10/02)

6159 Rylant, Cynthia. *Mr. Putter and Tabby Bake the Cake* (1–3). Illus. by Arthur Howard. 1994, Harcourt $13.00 (978-0-15-200205-3); paper $6.00 (978-0-15-200214-5). 44pp. Mr. Putter bakes a Christmas cake for his neighbor, Mrs. Teaberry, in this easily read book. (Rev: BL 10/15/94; HB 9/94; SLJ 12/94)

6160 Rylant, Cynthia. *Silver Packages: An Appalachian Christmas Story* (K–3). Illus. by Chris K. Soentpiet. 1997, Orchard LB $17.99 (978-0-531-33051-7). 32pp. At Christmas time, a young doctor tries to repay an Appalachian community for the gifts that were given to him in the past. (Rev: BL 9/1/97; HBG 3/98; SLJ 10/97)

6161 Sacre, Antonio. *La Noche Buena: A Christmas Story* (2–4). Illus. by Angela Dominguez. 2010, Abrams $16.95 (978-081098967-2). 32pp. Visiting her grandmother in Miami's Little Havana, young New Englander Nina learns to appreciate new Christmas traditions. (Rev: BL 10/15/10; HB 11–12/10)

6162 Sanders, Rob. *Cowboy Christmas* (PS–1). Illus. by John Manders. 2012, Random House $10.99 (978-037586985-3). 32pp. Stuck out on the range at Christmas, a group of cowboys do their best to perk up their celebrations and are mighty surprised when who should turn up but Santa — and isn't it a shame that the cook has gone off somewhere? e (Rev: BL 8/12; SLJ 10/12)

6163 Santiago, Esmeralda. *A Doll for Navidades* (K–2). Illus. by Enrique O. Sánchez. 2005, Scholastic $16.99 (978-0-439-55398-8). 32pp. Seven-year-old Esmeralda desperately wants a doll for Three Kings' Day and she

is deeply disappointed when her younger sister receives one instead in this picture book set in Puerto Rico. (Rev: BL 11/1/05; SLJ 10/05)

6164 Say, Allen. *Tree of Cranes* (PS–3). Illus. 1991, Houghton $17.95 (978-0-395-52024-6). 32pp. A Japanese woman brings a tree indoors because it reminds her of the Christmas she spent years ago in California. (Rev: BCCB 9/91*; BL 9/15/91; HB 11/91*)

6165 Schneider, Antonie. *Advent Storybook: 24 Stories to Share Before Christmas* (K–3). Trans. by Marisa Miller. Illus. by Maja Dusikova. 2005, North-South $17.95 (978-0-7358-1963-4). Benjamin Bear's mother tells him a Christmas-related story for each of the 24 days in the little bear's Advent calendar; each parable features Little Bear and ends with a moral. (Rev: SLJ 10/05)

6166 Shannon, David. *It's Christmas, David!* (PS–1). Illus. by author. 2010, Scholastic $16.99 (978-054514311-0). 32pp. Christmas is coming and seems to bring equal amounts of joy and misery for rambunctious young David. (Rev: BL 9/15/10; HB 11–12/10; SLJ 10/10)

6167 Sharkey, Niamh. *Santasaurus* (PS–2). Illus. by author. 2005, Candlewick $15.99 (978-0-7636-2671-6). Full of Christmas spirit, dinosaur siblings Milo, Mollie, and Ollie eagerly await the arrival of Santasaurus. (Rev: SLJ 10/05)

6168 Shea, Bob. *Dinosaur vs. Santa* (PS). Illus. by author. 2012, Disney/Hyperion $15.99 (978-1-42316806-5). 40pp. Little Dinosaur writes a letter to Santa, puts up decorations, and makes gifts in this sequel to *Dinosaur vs. the Potty* (2010). (Rev: BLO 9/1/12; HB 11–12/12; SLJ 10/12)

6169 Slate, Joseph. *The Secret Stars* (PS–2). Illus. by Felipe Davalos. 1998, Marshall Cavendish $15.95 (978-0-7614-5027-6). 32pp. On the Night of the Three Kings holiday, the weather in New Mexico is so bad that Pepe and Sila worry that the kings will not be able to deliver their presents. (Rev: BL 9/15/98; HBG 3/99; SLJ 10/98)

6170 Slegers, Liesbet. *The Child in the Manger* (PS–2). Illus. by author. 2010, Clavis $15.95 (978-160537084-2). 32pp. Simple text and illustrations tell the story of Christ's birth. (Rev: BL 10/15/10; SLJ 10/10)

6171 Smith, Cynthia Leitich, and Greg Leitich Smith. *Santa Knows* (K–3). Illus. by Steve Björkman. 2006, Dutton $16.99 (978-0-525-47757-0). Alfie F. Snorklepuss is convinced there's no Santa, so it's an eye-opening experience for this Santa-doubter when the man himself shows up to take Alfie on a trip to the North Pole. (Rev: SLJ 10/06)

6172 Smith, Maggie. *Christmas with the Mousekins: A Story with Crafts, Recipes, Poems and More!* (K–3). Illus. by author. 2010, Knopf $15.99 (978-037583330-4). 40pp. A quaint mouse family busies itself getting ready for Christmas in this activity book with charming illustrations, recipes, and directions for crafts. e (Rev: BL 9/15/10; HB 11–12/10)

6173 Snow, Alan. *How Santa Really Works* (2–4). 2004, Simon & Schuster $15.95 (978-0-689-85817-8). 48pp. Is there a Santa? The answers in this picture book may be implausible but they will keep young readers highly entertained. (Rev: BL 11/15/04; SLJ 10/04)

6174 Soto, Gary. *Too Many Tamales* (PS–1). Illus. by Ed Martinez. 1993, Penguin $16.99 (978-0-399-22146-0). 32pp. A Hispanic child enthusiastically enters into the cooking and other rituals that surround her family's celebration of Christmas. (Rev: BCCB 10/93; BL 9/15/93; HB 11/93)

6175 Speirs, John. *The Little Boy's Christmas Gift* (PS–3). Illus. 2001, Abrams $16.95 (978-0-8109-4399-5). 32pp. A boy's gift to the Holy Family is a decorated tree in this lavishly illustrated picture book. (Rev: BL 10/15/01; HBG 3/02)

6176 Spinelli, Eileen. *Together at Christmas* (PS–2). Illus. by Bin Lee. 2012, Whitman $15.99 (978-080758010-3). 24pp. On a cold Christmas Eve, 10 shivering mice — one by one — go off to find a warm place to sleep until they all realize that they want to be together on this special night. (Rev: BLO 10/15/12; SLJ 10/12)

6177 Stoeke, Janet Morgan. *Minerva Louise on Christmas Eve* (PS–2). Illus. by author. 2007, Dutton $15.99 (978-0-525-47857-7). 32pp. Chicken Minerva Louise comes to her usual strange conclusions while following Santa down a chimney on Christmas Eve. (Rev: BL 9/15/07; HB 11/07)

6178 Tafuri, Nancy. *The Donkey's Christmas Song* (PS). Illus. 2002, Scholastic $16.95 (978-0-439-27313-8). 32pp. A donkey is reluctant to add his braying to the manger lullaby. (Rev: BL 9/15/02; HBG 3/03; SLJ 10/02)

6179 Tews, Susan. *The Gingerbread Doll* (K–3). Illus. by Megan Lloyd. 1993, Clarion $16.00 (978-0-395-56438-7). 32pp. Starting as a poor youngster during the Great Depression when she gets a gingerbread doll, Rebecca finds that her Christmas presents change as her family gets more prosperous. (Rev: BL 9/1/93)

6180 Thompson, Kay. *Eloise at Christmastime* (PS–3). Illus. by Hilary Knight. 1999, Simon & Schuster $17.50 (978-0-689-83039-6). A reissue of the book about the little girl who lives in the Plaza Hotel in New York City and her adventures at Christmas. (Rev: BL 11/15/99; HBG 3/00)

6181 Thompson, Lauren. *The Christmas Magic* (PS–1). Illus. by Jon J Muth. 2009, Scholastic $16.99 (978-043977497-0). 40pp. A lonely, rather scrawny Santa readies his sleigh, gifts, and reindeer, waiting for the magic to arrive before setting out to bring joy to children around the world. (Rev: BL 11/1/09; HB 11–12/09; SLJ 10/09)

6182 Thompson, Lauren. *One Starry Night* (PS–1). Illus. by Jonathan Bean. 2011, Simon & Schuster $16.99 (978-068982851-5). 32pp. Parent-child animal pairs make their way to the manger to behold baby Jesus in this serene retelling of the story. (Rev: BL 11/15/11; HB 11–12/11; SLJ 10/1/11*)

6183 Trumbauer, Lisa. *The Great Reindeer Rebellion* (PS–2). Illus. by Jannie Ho. 2009, Sterling $14.95 (978-140274462-4). 28pp. When the reindeer go on strike,

Santa struggles to fill his sled-team with other animals. (Rev: BL 11/15/09; SLJ 10/09)

6184 Tudor, Tasha. *Corgiville Christmas* (K–2). Illus. by author. 2003, Front St. $15.95 (978-1-932425-00-0). Corgiville, a 1920s New England village populated by corgis, cats, rabbits, and other animals, is buzzing with activity as its residents prepare for the Christmas holiday. (Rev: HBG 4/04; SLJ 10/03)

6185 Underwood, Deborah. *The Christmas Quiet Book* (PS–K). Illus. by Renata Liwska. 2012, Houghton Mifflin $12.99 (978-054755863-9). 32pp. Appealing animal characters participate in quiet events associated with Christmas in this companion to *The Quiet Book* (2010) and *The Loud Book!* (2011). (Rev: BL 10/1/12; HB 11–12/12; SLJ 10/12)

6186 Van Allsburg, Chris. *The Polar Express* (K–2). Illus. by author. 1985, Houghton $18.95 (978-0-395-38949-2). 32pp. Whisked aboard the Polar Express to the North Pole on Christmas Eve, a young boy gets to receive the first gift of Christmas. Caldecott Medal winner, 1986. (Rev: BCCB 10/85; BL 10/1/85; SLJ 10/85)

6187 Van Steenwyk, Elizabeth. *Prairie Christmas* (K–3). Illus. by Ronald Himler. 2006, Eerdmans $17.00 (978-0-8028-5280-9). 32pp. In 1880s Nebraska, 11-year-old Emma experiences a very special Christmas on a trip with her mother to deliver a new baby. (Rev: BL 9/15/06; SLJ 10/06)

6188 Vischer, Frans. *A Very Fuddles Christmas* (PS–2). Illus. by author. 2013, Aladdin $15.99 (978-141699156-4). 32pp. Fuddles is thrilled when his family gives him gifts and a beautiful tree to climb. (Rev: BLO 9/15/13; HB 11–12/13)

6189 Wallace, Ian. *The Man Who Walked the Earth* (3–5). Illus. by author. 2003, Groundwood $16.95 (978-0-88899-545-2). On a prairie farm in the 1930s, a mother, daughter, and son wait for the return of their long-absent husband and father — and on Christmas Day a mysterious stranger arrives. (Rev: HBG 4/04; SLJ 10/03)

6190 Wallner, Alexandra. *An Alcott Family Christmas* (K–2). Illus. 1996, Holiday House LB $15.95 (978-0-8234-1265-5). 30pp. A fictionalized account of how Louisa May Alcott's family might have observed Christmas as the March family did in *Little Women*. (Rev: BL 9/1/96)

6191 Walsh, Vivian, and J. Otto Seibold. *Olive, the Other Reindeer* (1–3). Illus. 1997, Chronicle $13.95 (978-0-8118-1807-0). 32pp. A little dog believes that she is really a reindeer and heads to the North Pole to give Santa a hand. (Rev: BL 10/15/97; HBG 3/98)

6192 Ward, Helen. *The Animals' Christmas Carol* (PS–3). Illus. 2001, Millbrook LB $24.90 (978-0-7613-2408-9). 40pp. A beautifully illustrated book based on the Christmas carol "The Friendly Beasts," in which animals bring gifts to baby Jesus in the manger. (Rev: BCCB 11/01; BL 9/15/01; HBG 3/02)

6193 Watt, Mélanie. *Scaredy Squirrel Prepares for Christmas: A Safety Guide for Scaredies* (1–3). 2012, Kids Can $17.95 (978-155453469-2). 80pp. Poor Scaredy

Squirrel, he has many difficult decisions to make before Christmas — and many inventive ideas. Lexile AD680L (Rev: BL 12/15/12; SLJ 10/12)

6194 Weigelt, Udo. *Little Donkey's Wish* (K–2). Trans. by Marianne Martens. Illus. by Pirkko Vainio. 2005, North-South $15.95 (978-0-7358-2031-9). A shy donkey gets her Christmas wish when Santa chooses her to fill in for one of his reindeer. (Rev: SLJ 10/05)

6195 Westerlund, Kate. *Sharing Christmas* (PS–2). Illus. by Eve Tharlet. 2007, Penguin $16.99 (978-0-698-40074-0). 32pp. A wish upon a star and the sound of bells lead the young deer Clara, her mother, and a variety of forest creatures to the farm for a joyous Christmas. (Rev: BL 9/15/07)

6196 Willey, Margaret. *A Clever Beatrice Christmas* (PS–2). Illus. by Heather Solomon. 2006, Simon & Schuster $16.95 (978-0-689-87017-0). 40pp. To prove the existence of Père Noël to some skeptical friends, clever Beatrice promises to bring some irrefutable evidence, such as a clipping from his beard or a bell from his sleigh. (Rev: BL 10/15/06; SLJ 10/06)

6197 Wilson, Karma. *Mortimer's Christmas Manger* (PS–2). Illus. by Jane Chapman. 2005, Simon & Schuster $15.95 (978-0-689-85511-5). Tired of his home in a dark hole under the stairs, Mortimer the mouse takes up residence in a Nativity scene. (Rev: SLJ 10/05)

6198 Winthrop, Elizabeth. *The First Christmas Stocking* (2–4). Illus. by Bagram Ibatoulline. 2006, Random $15.95 (978-0-385-32804-3). 40pp. On Christmas Eve, Claire gives the stockings she's knitted to a poor boy on the street instead of to the rich customer who ordered them, and wakes up on Christmas morning to find a miracle of her own. (Rev: BL 11/15/06)

6199 Wolfe, Frances. *The Little Toy Shop* (PS–2). Illus. by author. 2008, Tundra $19.95 (978-0-88776-865-1). When a little stuffed bunny is accidentally sold from the toy shop, it takes a Christmas miracle to restore him to good health and get him to his intended child. (Rev: BLO 10/7/08; SLJ 10/08)

6200 Wolff, Patricia Rae. *A New Improved Santa* (K–3). Illus. by Lynne W. Cravath. 2002, Scholastic $15.95 (978-0-439-35249-9). Santa spends the year on self-improvement — diet, exercise, new hairstyle — only to find the children prefer him the old way. (Rev: BCCB 11/02; HBG 3/03; SLJ 10/02)

6201 Wood, Audrey. *The Christmas Adventure of Space Elf Sam* (PS–3). Illus. by Bruce Robert Wood. 1998, Scholastic $15.95 (978-0-590-03143-1). When families from Earth colonize outer space, Santa Claus needs help to perform his Christmas Eve duties. (Rev: BL 9/1/98; HBG 3/99; SLJ 10/98)

6202 Wood, Don, and Audrey Wood. *Merry Christmas, Big Hungry Bear!* (PS–2). Illus. 2002, Scholastic $16.99 (978-0-439-32092-4). Little Mouse decides to share his Christmas with Big Hungry Bear, who never gets any presents. (Rev: BCCB 11/02; BL 9/15/02; HBG 3/03; SLJ 10/02)

6203 Yin. *Dear Santa, Please Come to the 19th Floor* (1–3). Illus. by Chris Soentpiet. 2002, Philomel $17.99 (978-0-399-23636-5). Willy asks Santa for a special present for his friend Carlos, who is in a wheelchair and living in poverty. (Rev: HBG 3/03; SLJ 10/02)

6204 Young, Ned. *Zoomer's Out-of-This-World Christmas* (PS–2). Illus. by author. 2013, HarperCollins $17.99 (978-006199959-8). 32pp. Zoomer and the other beagles are watching for Santa, but they are instead surprised by a crew of aliens who have crash-landed in their backyard, and it is up to Zoomer to save the day. Lexile 680 (Rev: BLO 9/15/13)

6205 Zagwyn, Deborah Turney. *The Winter Gift* (K–3). Illus. 2000, Tricycle $15.95 (978-1-883672-93-5). 32pp. Grandma is selling all her furniture before moving into an apartment, but she gives her piano to her grandchildren to continue the tradition of playing it at Christmas. (Rev: BL 9/1/00*; HBG 3/01)

6206 Ziefert, Harriet. *Home for Navidad* (PS–3). Illus. by Santiago Cohen. 2003, Houghton $15.00 (978-0-618-34976-0). Ten-year-old Rosa, who lives with her grandmother and uncle in Mexico, hopes her mother will finally make it back from New York to spend Christmas with them. (Rev: HB 9/03; HBG 4/04; SLJ 10/03)

EASTER

6207 Bergren, Lisa Tawn. *God Gave Us Easter* (PS–1). Illus. by Laura J. Bryant. 2013, WaterBrook $10.99 (978-030773072-5). 40pp. Little Cub, a polar bear, learns from her father about Easter and its roots. **e** Lexile AD500L (Rev: BLO 12/15/12)

6208 Berlin, Irving. *Easter Parade* (PS–1). Illus. by Lisa McCue. 2003, HarperCollins LB $16.89 (978-0-06-029126-6). 32pp. Father Rabbit and his behatted young daughter parade down the street with all the other finely dressed animals in this cheerful rendition of the famous Irving Berlin song. (Rev: BL 3/15/03; HBG 4/04; SLJ 2/03) [782.42164]

6209 Bostrom, Kathleen Long. *Sunrise Hill: An Easter Story of Faith, Inspiration, and Courage* (K–3). Illus. by Rick Johnson. 2004, Zondervan $14.99 (978-0-310-70508-6). 32pp. Despite the loss of their church, the people of a 19th-century farming community celebrate a special Easter service on Sunrise Hill, affirming their faith in rebirth. (Rev: BL 3/1/04)

6210 Brett, Jan. *The Easter Egg* (PS–K). Illus. by author. 2010, Putnam $17.99 (978-0-399-25238-9). 32pp. Hoppi the rabbit's hopes of winning the Easter egg competition are derailed when he heeds a mother robin's cry for help; in the end, his generosity is commended. (Rev: BL 12/1/09; LMC 1–2/10; SLJ 2/1/10)

6211 deGroat, Diane. *Last One in Is a Rotten Egg!* (PS–2). Illus. by author. Series: Gilbert. 2007, HarperCollins $15.99 (978-0-06-089294-4). A much-anticipated visit from their cousin turns out to be far less fun than expected for Gilbert the opossum and his sister. (Rev: BL 1/1–15/07; SLJ 2/07)

6212 Elschner, Géraldine. *The Easter Chick* (PS–2). Trans. by Marianne Martens. Illus. by Alexandra Junge. 2004, North-South $15.95 (978-0-7358-1855-2). 32pp. The fact that Easter is a movable feast is underlined in this story in which an owl helps a mother hen to schedule the hatching of her chick. (Rev: BL 3/1/04; SLJ 5/04)

6213 Engelbreit, Mary. *Queen of Easter* (PS–K). Illus. by author. Series: Ann Estelle Stories. 2006, HarperCollins $15.99 (978-0-06-008184-3). Disappointed with the plain straw hat she is given for the Easter parade, Ann Estelle leaves it outside, where robins adopt it as a nest; Ann Estelle enjoys redecorating last year's hat and the new family in this year's. (Rev: SLJ 2/06)

6214 Friedrich, Priscilla, and Otto Friedrich. *The Easter Bunny That Overslept* (PS–2). Illus. by Donald Saaf. 2002, HarperCollins LB $17.89 (978-0-06-029646-9). 32pp. In this bright new version of a 1950s classic, the Easter Bunny oversleeps and discovers that no one wants Easter eggs on the Fourth of July or Halloween. (Rev: BL 2/15/02; HBG 10/02; SLJ 1/02)

6215 Gibbons, Gail. *Easter* (PS–2). Illus. by author. 1989, Holiday House LB $17.95 (978-0-8234-0737-8); paper $6.95 (978-0-8234-0866-5). 32pp. Biblical, pagan, and modern aspects of the holiday are described. (Rev: BL 4/1/89; SLJ 3/89)

6216 Heyward, DuBose. *The Country Bunny and the Little Gold Shoes* (K–3). Illus. by Marjorie Flack. 1939, Houghton $15.00 (978-0-395-15990-3); paper $6.95 (978-0-395-18557-5). 48pp. Cottontail, the mother of 21 bunnies, finally realizes her great ambition to be an Easter Bunny.

6217 Mackall, Dandi Daley. *The Story of the Easter Robin* (PS–2). Illus. by Anna Vojtech. 2010, Zondervan $15.99 (978-031071331-9). 24pp. Two Easter stories are intertwined in this warm novel — that of Tressa, who worries about the robin's eggs on the window ledge, and that of a small brown robin that pulled a thorn from Jesus's crown. (Rev: BL 2/15/10)

6218 Mortimer, Anne. *Bunny's Easter Egg* (PS–K). Illus. by author. 2010, HarperCollins $12.99 (978-0-06-126664-2). 32pp. Busy Bunny is exhausted after hiding all but one of her Easter eggs and takes it into her basket while she has a rest; and overnight it hatches into a downy little duckling. (Rev: BL 3/15/10; SLJ 1/1/10)

6219 Polacco, Patricia. *Chicken Sunday* (PS–3). Illus. 1992, Penguin $16.99 (978-0-399-22133-0). 32pp. Three youngsters of different races and religions unite to help Miss Eula have a good Easter. (Rev: BCCB 7–8/92; BL 3/15/92*; SLJ 5/92*)

6220 Stoeke, Janet Morgan. *Minerva Louise and the Colorful Eggs* (PS–2). 2006, Dutton $15.99 (978-0-525-47633-7). It's spring, but Minerva Louise the chicken doesn't know what to make of the brightly colored eggs she discovers hidden in odd places around the farmyard. (Rev: BL 2/1/06; SLJ 2/06)

6221 Tegen, Katherine. *The Story of the Easter Bunny* (PS–1). Illus. by Sally Anne Lambert. 2005, HarperCollins LB $14.89 (978-0-06-050712-1). A pet white rabbit takes over the Easter preparations — basket weaving, candy making, and egg coloring — when the elderly couple who own him become too old to continue. (Rev: BL 2/1/05; SLJ 2/05)

6222 Thomas, Jan. *The Easter Bunny's Assistant* (PS–K). Illus. by author. 2012, HarperCollins $12.99 (978-006169286-4). 40pp. Skunk gets so excited about dyeing Easter eggs with his bunny friend that he loses control of his stink in this funny book with directions for making colored eggs. (Rev: BL 1/1/12; SLJ 1/12)

6223 Vail, Rachel. *Piggy Bunny* (PS–2). Illus. by Jeremy Tankard. 2012, Feiwel & Friends $14.99 (978-031264988-3). 32pp. A little pig determined to be the Easter Bunny gets a lift from a creative grandma who orders him a costume. (Rev: BL 1/1/12; SLJ 1/12)

6224 Vainio, Pirkko. *Who Hid the Easter Eggs?* (PS–1). Illus. by author. 2011, NorthSouth $16.95 (978-0-7358-2304-4). 32pp. A squirrel named Harry persuades a jackdaw to try to replace the Easter eggs he has stolen, and reassures Jack that he will soon have his own eggs to look after. Lexile AD580L (Rev: BLO 1/1–15/11; SLJ 5/1/11)

6225 Wells, Rosemary. *Max Counts His Chickens* (PS–K). Illus. 2007, Viking $15.99 (978-0-670-06222-5). 32pp. Combining a counting lesson with Max and Ruby's familiar sibling tussles, this charming tale features a marshmallow chick hunt and a special delivery from the Easter bunny. (Rev: BL 1/1–15/07)

6226 Zolotow, Charlotte. *The Bunny Who Found Easter* (PS–2). Illus. by Helen Craig. 1998, Houghton $16.00 (978-0-395-86265-0). 32pp. A new edition of the story about a bunny who wanders through a year searching for Easter so he can enjoy the company of other bunnies. The 1959 edition is illustrated by Betty Peterson. (Rev: BL 3/1/98; HBG 3/99; SLJ 9/98)

HALLOWEEN

6227 Atwell, Debby. *The Warthog's Tail* (K–3). 2005, Houghton $16.00 (978-0-618-50781-8). 32pp. When a young witch is unable to conjure up a spell powerful enough to remove a sleeping warthog from her path, she decides instead to try her powers of persuasion. (Rev: BL 10/1/05; SLJ 11/05)

6228 Axelrod, Amy. *Pigs Go to Market: Halloween Fun with Math and Shopping* (2–4). Illus. by Sharon McGinley-Nally. 1997, Simon & Schuster paper $14.00 (978-0-689-81069-5). At Halloween, the Pig family eats all the candy before the guests arrive. (Rev: HBG 3/98; SLJ 9/97)

6229 Bauer, Marion Dane. *Halloween Forest* (K–2). Illus. by John Shelley. 2012, Holiday $16.95 (978-0-8234-2324-8). 32pp. A spooky tale featuring a young boy who ventures into the forest on Halloween to find that it's made of bones. (Rev: BL 9/1/12; SLJ 9/12)

6230 Bauer, Marion Dane. *I'm Not Afraid of Halloween! A Pop-up and Flap Book* (PS–K). Illus. by Rusty Fletcher. 2006, Simon & Schuster $7.99 (978-0-689-85050-9). This colorful pop-up book, which includes lift-the-flap features, showcases a host of costumed trick-or-treaters who come calling at a young vampire's door on Halloween night. (Rev: SLJ 9/06)

6231 Behn, Harry. *Halloween* (2–3). 2003, Cheshire Studio Bks. $15.95 (978-0-7358-1609-1). Three children costumed as a devil, skeleton, and witch find trick-or-treating can become very spooky as the evening progresses. (Rev: BL 9/1/03; HBG 4/04; SLJ 8/03)

6232 Bollinger, Peter. *Algernon Graeves Is Scary Enough* (K–2). Illus. by author. 2005, HarperCollins LB $15.89 (978-0-06-052269-8). Algernon can't decide between spooky costumes for Halloween and decides to combine them all. (Rev: SLJ 8/05)

6233 Bridwell, Norman. *Clifford's Halloween* (PS–1). Illus. by author. 1970, Scholastic paper $3.99 (978-0-590-44287-9). 32pp. Halloween adventures of a big red dog.

6234 Broyles, Anne. *Shy Mama's Halloween* (2–4). Illus. by Leane Morin. 2000, Tilbury House $16.95 (978-0-88448-218-5). 40pp. Recently arrived from Russia, Anya and her siblings are taken out on Halloween by their mother and suddenly feel more at home in their new country. (Rev: BL 11/15/00; HBG 3/01; SLJ 1/01)

6235 Bullard, Lisa. *Trick-or-Treat on Milton Street* (K–2). Illus. by Joni Oeltjenbruns. 2001, Carolrhoda LB $15.95 (978-1-57505-158-1). Charley gets a big surprise on Halloween that makes him look at his new neighborhood in quite a different way. (Rev: HBG 3/02; SLJ 9/01)

6236 Bunting, Eve. *Scary, Scary Halloween* (PS–1). Illus. by Jan Brett. 1986, Houghton $16.00 (978-0-89919-414-1); paper $6.95 (978-0-89919-799-9). 32pp. A scary poem tells of a parade of creatures on Halloween night. (Rev: BCCB 9/86; BL 9/1/86; HB 11/86)

6237 Cazet, Denys. *The Perfect Pumpkin Pie* (PS–2). Illus. 2005, Simon & Schuster $15.95 (978-0-689-86467-4). In this lively Halloween tale, a boy and his grandmother are visited by a ghost who's searching for some pumpkin pie. (Rev: BL 10/15/05; SLJ 10/05)

6238 Choi, Yangsook. *Behind the Mask* (K–3). Illus. 2006, Farrar $16.00 (978-0-374-30522-2). 40pp. A young Korean American boy, still grieving over his grandfather's death, gains cachet among his classmates when he wears his grandfather's scary mask dance costume for Halloween. (Rev: BL 10/15/06; SLJ 12/06)

6239 Cox, Judy. *Haunted House, Haunted Mouse* (K–2). Illus. by Jeffrey Ebbeler. 2011, Holiday House $16.95 (978-0-8234-2315-6). 32pp. Mouse ends up in a pickle when he dives into a trick-or-treater's goody bag and gets carried along to a haunted house. Lexile AD460L (Rev: BL 10/15/11; SLJ 10/1/11)

6240 Crimi, Carolyn. *Boris and Bella* (K–2). Illus. by Gris Grimly. 2004, Harcourt $15.00 (978-0-15-202528-1). Messy monster Bella Lagrossi and her fastidious neighbor Boris Kleanitoff find they have something in common in this entertaining Halloween tale full of wordplay. (Rev: BL 1/1–15/05; SLJ 9/04)

6241 Cronin, Doreen. *Click, Clack, Boo! A Tricky Treat* (PS–2). Illus. by Betsy Lewin. 2013, Atheneum $16.99 (978-1-4424-6553-4). 40pp. In defiance of Farmer

Brown, his animals hold a festive Halloween party at the barn. Lexile AD640 (Rev: BL 6/13; HB 9–10/13; SLJ 6/13)

6242 Cuyler, Margery. *The Bumpy Little Pumpkin* (PS–2). Illus. by Will Hillenbrand. 2005, Scholastic $15.95 (978-0-439-52835-1). Her older siblings scoff when Little Nell (first seen in *The Biggest, Best Snowman*, published in 1998) selects an ugly little pumpkin at harvest time, but the girl manages to transform the gourd into a nice-looking jack-o'-lantern with the help of a few animal friends. (Rev: BL 9/1/05; SLJ 8/05)

6243 deGroat, Diane. *Trick or Treat, Smell My Feet* (PS–3). Illus. Series: Gilbert. 1998, Morrow LB $14.89 (978-0-688-15767-8). 32pp. Gilbert takes his sister's Halloween costume to the school parade instead of his own by mistake and finds that he has to dress as a ballerina instead of a Martian space pilot. (Rev: BL 9/1/98; HBG 3/99; SLJ 10/98)

6244 Demas, Corinne. *Halloween Surprise* (PS–1). Illus. by R. W. Alley. 2011, Walker $12.99 (978-0-8027-8612-8). 32pp. A young girl's two cats watch and react as she tries out many different Halloween costume possibilities before hitting on a perfect, creative solution. (Rev: BLO 7/11; SLJ 8/1/11)

6245 Desimini, Lisa. *Trick-or-Treat, Smell My Feet!* (PS–2). Illus. 2005, Scholastic $16.95 (978-0-439-23323-1). Delia and Ophelia, twin witches, cast a spell over the neighborhood trick-or-treaters. (Rev: BL 9/15/05; SLJ 8/05)

6246 Druce, Arden. *Halloween Night* (PS–K). Illus. by David Wenzel. 2001, Rising Moon $14.95 (978-0-87358-797-6); paper $6.95 (978-0-87358-762-4). Rhyming riddles about a spooky Halloween night are accompanied by illustrations that suit the mood and contain clues. (Rev: BCCB 9/01; BL 9/1/01; HBG 3/02; SLJ 9/01)

6247 Egan, Tim. *The Experiments of Doctor Vermin* (K–3). Illus. 2002, Houghton $15.00 (978-0-618-13224-9). 32pp. Sheldon the pig stumbles into Dr. Vermin's spooky mansion on Halloween night, but finds refuge with the wolves next door in this amusing story. (Rev: BL 9/1/02; HBG 3/03; SLJ 10/02)

6248 *Five Little Pumpkins* (PS). Illus. by Dan Yaccarino. 1998, HarperCollins $5.99 (978-0-694-01177-3). 16pp. A board book that illustrates the old rhyme about five little pumpkins sitting on a gate. (Rev: BL 12/15/98; HBG 3/99; SLJ 2/99)

6249 Fleming, Denise. *Pumpkin Eye* (1–3). Illus. 2001, Holt $15.95 (978-0-8050-6681-4). Lightly scary Halloween excitement is captured in rhyming text and inventive artwork. (Rev: BCCB 10/01; BL 9/15/01; HBG 3/02; SLJ 9/01)

6250 Fraser, Mary Ann. *Heebie-Jeebie Jamboree* (PS–2). Illus. by author. 2011, Boyds Mills $15.95 (978-1-59078-857-8). 32pp. At Halloween Sam and his sister Daphne, dressed as a ghost and a witch, attend the festivities at the cemetery. (Rev: BL 9/1/11; SLJ 9/1/11)

6251 Friedman, Laurie. *I'm Not Afraid of This Haunted House* (K–2). Illus. by Teresa Murfin. 2005, Carolrhoda $15.95 (978-1-57505-751-4). In this spine-tingling Halloween tale, told in rhyming couplets, young Simon Lester Henry Strauss takes friends on a tour of a haunted house. (Rev: BL 9/1/05; SLJ 9/05)

6252 Grambling, Lois G. *T. Rex Trick-or-Treats* (K–2). Illus. by Jack E. Davis. 2005, HarperCollins $12.99 (978-0-06-050252-2). 32pp. T. Rex can't decide what he wants to wear when he goes trick-or-treating. (Rev: BL 9/1/05; SLJ 8/05)

6253 Greene, Stephanie. *Princess Posey and the Monster Stew* (1–2). Illus. by Stephanie Roth Sisson. 2012, Putnam $12.99 (978-0-399-25464-2). 96pp. Posey looks forward to Halloween and Miss Lee's "monster stew" with a mixture of trepidation and happy anticipation; suitable for young readers moving from beginning readers to chapter books. e (Rev: BLO 9/15/12; SLJ 8/12)

6254 Hall, Zoe. *It's Pumpkin Time!* (K–3). Illus. by Shari Halpern. 1994, Scholastic $13.95 (978-0-590-47833-5). This picture book describes how two children plant a pumpkin seed and care for it so that it will be useful at Halloween. (Rev: SLJ 11/94)

6255 Hatch, Elizabeth. *Halloween Night* (PS–1). Illus. by Jimmy Pickering. 2005, Doubleday $15.95 (978-0-385-74622-9). A cumulative, mildly scary story in which a timid little mouse winds up with the treats. (Rev: SLJ 8/05)

6256 Heidbreder, Robert. *Black and Bittern Was Night* (K–2). Illus. by John Martz. 2013, Kids Can $16.95 (978-1-55453-302-2). 32pp. In this rhyming nonsense story, the children of a town must save Halloween from the invading skul-a-mug-mugs. Lexile AD570 (Rev: BL 11/15/13; SLJ 9/13)

6257 Hood, Susan. *Just Say Boo!* (PS–1). Illus. by Jed Henry. 2012, HarperCollins $12.99 (978-0-06-201029-2). 32pp. What should young trick-or-treaters say when they meet various situations on Halloween? This rhyming story provides the answers. (Rev: BL 9/1/12; SLJ 8/12)

6258 Horowitz, Dave. *The Ugly Pumpkin* (K–2). Illus. by author. 2005, Putnam $16.99 (978-0-399-24267-0). A misshapen pumpkin feels out of place as Halloween nears. (Rev: SLJ 8/05)

6259 Hubbard, Patricia. *Trick or Treat Countdown* (PS). Illus. by Michael Letzig. 1999, Holiday House $16.95 (978-0-8234-1367-6). A simple counting rhyme goes from one to 12 and back again, using Halloween symbols and general spookiness. (Rev: BCCB 10/99; BL 9/1/99; HBG 3/00; SLJ 9/99)

6260 Hubbell, Patricia. *Boo! Halloween Poems and Limericks* (K–4). Illus. by Jeff Spackman. 1998, Marshall Cavendish $15.95 (978-0-7614-5023-8). 32pp. Witty original poems and limericks about Halloween are presented with suitably lurid illustrations. (Rev: BL 9/1/98; HBG 3/99; SLJ 9/98) [811]

6261 Hulme, Joy N. *Eerie Feary Feeling: A Hairy Scary Pop-Up Book* (K–2). Illus. by Paul Ely. 1998, Orchard $13.95 (978-0-531-30086-2). Cats, bats, witches, ghosts, and ghouls are all featured in this interactive pop-up book. (Rev: SLJ 12/98)

6262 Hutchins, Pat. *Which Witch Is Which?* (PS–K). Illus. 1989, Greenwillow $17.89 (978-0-688-06358-0). 24pp. Identical twins dress as witches on Halloween. (Rev: BL 9/1/89; SLJ 8/89*)

6263 Johnston, Tony. *The Vanishing Pumpkin* (PS–2). Illus. by Tomie dePaola. 1996, Penguin paper $6.99 (978-0-698-11414-2). 32pp. An old man and an old woman set out on Halloween to find their pumpkin.

6264 Kimball, Linda Hoffman. *Come with Me on Halloween* (PS–1). Illus. by Mike Reed. 2005, Albert Whitman $16.95 (978-0-8075-3132-7). The father-son relationship is reversed as the two meet fearsome characters while trick-or-treating. (Rev: SLJ 10/05)

6265 Kovalski, Maryann. *Omar's Halloween* (PS–K). 2006, Fitzhenry & Whiteside $16.95 (978-1-55041-559-9). 32pp. As Halloween nears, Omar the bear has terrible trouble with costume selection, but on the day his ghost outfit finally comes into its own. (Rev: BL 9/1/06; SLJ 9/06)

6266 Krieb, Mr. *We're Off to Find the Witch's House* (PS–2). Illus. by R. W. Alley. 2005, Dutton $14.99 (978-0-525-47003-8). 32pp. In this fun-filled Halloween tale told in rhyming text, four trick-or-treaters encounter all sorts of frightening ghosts and ghouls when they set off in search of a witch's house. (Rev: BL 9/15/05; SLJ 8/05)

6267 Kroll, Steven. *The Biggest Pumpkin Ever* (PS–2). Illus. by Jeni Bassett. 1984, Holiday House LB $17.95 (978-0-8234-0505-3); Scholastic paper $2.50 (978-0-590-41113-4). Two mice hope to grow the largest pumpkin ever for Halloween.

6268 Krosoczka, Jarrett J. *Annie Was Warned* (PS–3). Illus. by author. 2003, Knopf LB $17.99 (978-0-375-91567-3). By turns suspenseful and amusing, this engaging story tells what happens when Annie, acting on a dare, disregards her parents' warnings and visits a creepy neighborhood mansion on Halloween night. (Rev: HBG 4/04; SLJ 9/03)

6269 Landry, Leo. *Trick or Treat* (K–1). Illus. by author. 2012, Houghton Mifflin $12.99 (978-0-547-24969-8). 32pp. Oliver the ghost has some unexpected guests at his Halloween party. (Rev: BL 9/1/12; HB 9–10/12; LMC 10/12; SLJ 9/12)

6270 Lattimore, Deborah N. *Cinderhazel: The Cinderella of Halloween* (PS–2). Illus. 1997, Scholastic $15.95 (978-0-590-20232-9). 32pp. A parody on the famous fairy tale, with a feminist twist and a Halloween setting. (Rev: BL 9/1/97; HBG 3/98; SLJ 10/97)

6271 Leedy, Loreen. *2 x 2=Boo! A Set of Spooky Multiplication Stories* (1–4). Illus. 1995, Holiday House LB $17.95 (978-0-8234-1190-0). 32pp. Halloween creatures and objects are used in a series of scary stories to demonstrate the principles of multiplication. (Rev: BL 9/15/95; SLJ 11/95)

6272 Lewis, Kevin. *The Runaway Pumpkin* (PS–2). Illus. by S. D. Schindler. 2003, Scholastic $15.95 (978-0-439-43974-9). A giant pumpkin on the rampage is finally brought under control in this Halloween story with a repetitive chorus. (Rev: HBG 4/04; SLJ 10/03)

6273 McGhee, Alison. *Only a Witch Can Fly* (K–2). Illus. by Taeeun Yoo. 2009, Feiwel & Friends $16.99 (978-0-312-37503-4). On Halloween, a young witch finally masters her broom. (Rev: BL 5/1/09; HB 9/09)

6274 McGhee, Alison. *A Very Brave Witch* (K–2). Illus. by Harry Bliss. 2006, Simon & Schuster $12.95 (978-0-689-86730-9). On Halloween night, a young witch has an eye-opening encounter with some colorfully costumed trick-or-treaters. (Rev: SLJ 8/06)

6275 McGrath, Barbara Barbieri. *The Little Green Witch* (K–2). Illus. by Martha Alexander. 2005, Charlesbridge $14.95 (978-1-58089-042-7). In a Halloween twist on "The Little Red Hen," a little witch grows a pumpkin and no one wants to help her until it's time to eat pumpkin pie. (Rev: SLJ 8/05)

6276 Mayr, Diane. *Littlebat's Halloween Story* (PS–1). Illus. by Gideon Kendall. 2001, Whitman $16.99 (978-0-8075-7629-8). 32pp. Littlebat loves story time but his mother tells him he must remain hidden until he can make an appearance without scaring the children. (Rev: BL 9/1/01; HBG 3/02; SLJ 9/01)

6277 Mills, Claudia. *Gus and Grandpa and the Halloween Costume* (2–3). Illus. by Catherine Stock. Series: Gus and Grandpa. 2002, Farrar $15.00 (978-0-374-32816-0). 48pp. It's Grandpa who solves Gus's Halloween costume crisis, producing a Mounties uniform that Gus's father wore when he was a boy. (Rev: BL 9/1/02; HBG 3/03)

6278 Mitton, Tony. *Spooky Hour* (PS–2). Illus. by Guy Parker-Rees. 2004, Scholastic $16.95 (978-0-439-60373-7). A bouncy Halloween book featuring witches, ghosts, skeletons, and other characters on their way to a great feast. (Rev: SLJ 8/04)

6279 Montes, Marisa. *Los Gatos Black on Halloween* (K–2). Illus. by Yuri Morales. 2006, Holt $16.95 (978-0-8050-7429-1). There's a Monster's Ball at Haunted Hall and a rhythmic English/Spanish text describes the antics of los gatos, los muertos, las brujas, and their friends, all enjoying themselves until the arrival of the scary trick-or-treaters. (Rev: BL 8/06)

6280 Montijo, Rhode. *The Halloween Kid* (PS–2). Illus. by author. 2010, Simon & Schuster $12.99 (978-1-4169-3575-9). 32pp. When Goodie Goblins arrive in town to steal candy, the courageous Halloween Kid saves the day. e (Rev: BL 9/1/10; LMC 10/10; SLJ 7/1/10)

6281 Neitzel, Shirley. *Who Will I Be? A Halloween Rebus Story* (PS–2). Illus. by Nancy W. Parker. 2005, Greenwillow LB $13.89 (978-0-06-056068-3). 32pp. In this engaging rebus tale, a young girl tries to decide what sort of costume to wear for Halloween. (Rev: BL 8/05; SLJ 9/05)

6282 Nikola-Lisa, W. *Shake Dem Halloween Bones* (PS–2). Illus. by Mike Reed. 1997, Houghton $16.00 (978-0-395-73095-9). 32pp. Fairy tale characters shake, rattle, and roll at a super Halloween party. (Rev: BL 10/1/97; HBG 3/98)

6283 O'Connell, Jennifer. *It's Halloween Night!* (PS–K). Illus. by Jennifer Morris. 2012, Scholastic paper $6.99 (978-0-545-40-283-5). 32pp. Five children prepare to go trick-or-treating in this simple rhyming story with lots of details in the illustrations. (Rev: BLO 10/15/12; SLJ 8/12)

6284 Pamintuan, Macky. *Twelve Haunted Rooms of Halloween* (PS–2). Illus. by author. 2011, Sterling $14.95 (978-1-4027-7935-0). Unpaged. This Halloween take on "The Twelve Days of Christmas" involving a bear's visit to a haunted house features detailed illustrations with an "I Spy" element that will keep readers occupied. (Rev: SLJ 9/1/11)

6285 Parish, Herman. *Happy Haunting, Amelia Bedelia* (K–2). Illus. by Lynn Sweat. Series: Amelia Bedelia. 2004, Greenwillow LB $16.89 (978-0-06-051894-3). 64pp. Amelia Bedelia is supposed to be helping Mr. and Mrs. Rogers with their Halloween party. (Rev: SLJ 8/04)

6286 Passen, Lisa. *Attack of the 50-Foot Teacher* (K–3). Illus. 2000, Holt $16.00 (978-0-8050-6100-0). 32pp. Miss Birmbaum assigns homework on Halloween but, after an encounter with space aliens and a visit with her principal, she realizes that nobody gives homework on a holiday like this. (Rev: BL 11/15/00; HBG 3/01; SLJ 12/00)

6287 Pilkey, Dav. *The Hallo-Wiener* (PS–2). Illus. 1995, Scholastic $16.95 (978-0-590-41703-7). 32pp. At Halloween, Oscar the dachshund earns a change in his nickname from Wiener Dog to Hero Sandwich. (Rev: BCCB 10/95; BL 9/15/95; SLJ 10/95*)

6288 Polacco, Patricia. *Picnic at Mudsock Meadow* (K–3). Illus. 1992, Penguin $16.99 (978-0-399-21811-8). 32pp. During the Halloween festivities, William is a failure until he has courage enough to investigate a scary swamp. (Rev: BL 11/15/92; HB 11/92; SLJ 10/92)

6289 Poydar, Nancy. *The Perfectly Horrible Halloween* (PS–3). Illus. 2001, Holiday House $16.95 (978-0-8234-1592-2). 32pp. Arnold successfully improvises for the Halloween contest after forgetting his costume. (Rev: BL 9/1/01; HBG 3/02; SLJ 9/01)

6290 Reiner, Carl. *Tell Me a Scary Story . . . But Not Too Scary!* (PS–2). Illus. by James Bennett. 2003, Little, Brown $18.95 (978-0-316-83329-5). In this suspenseful Halloween tale, a curious boy finds more than he bargained for when he goes exploring in the basement of a mysterious neighbor. (Rev: HBG 4/04; SLJ 10/03)

6291 Roberts, Bethany. *Halloween Mice!* (PS–1). Illus. by Doug Cushman. 1995, Clarion $13.00 (978-0-395-67064-4). At Halloween, a group of mice turn the tables and frighten a cat. (Rev: BL 9/15/95; SLJ 9/95)

6292 Rohmann, Eric. *Bone Dog* (PS–2). Illus. by author. 2011, Roaring Brook $16.99 (978-1-59643-150-8). 32pp. A boy's beloved dog passes away but is reanimated as a bone dog on Halloween, just in time to save him from a graveyard full of skeletons. (Rev: BL 11/15/11; SLJ 7/11*)

6293 Rosenberry, Vera. *Vera's Halloween* (K–2). Illus. by author. 2008, Holt $16.95 (978-0-8050-8144-2). 32pp. Vera's Halloween starts out well with her toilet-paper mummy costume, but when she stops to adjust a bandage she finds herself alone. (Rev: BL 9/1/08)

6294 Ross, Eileen. *The Halloween Showdown* (K–2). Illus. by Lynn Rowe Reed. 1999, Holiday House $15.95 (978-0-8234-1395-9). At Halloween, Grandmother Katt enlists the help of her animal friends to save a kitty that has been stolen by a witch named Grizzorka. (Rev: BCCB 10/99; HBG 3/00; SLJ 9/99)

6295 Ruelle, Karen Gray. *Spookier Than a Ghost* (1–2). Illus. 2001, Holiday House $14.95 (978-0-8234-1667-7). 32pp. Kitten Emily's Halloween costume doesn't turn out quite as she had hoped, but she and brother Harry still have fun trick-or-treating in this easy reader. (Rev: BL 9/15/01; HBG 3/02; SLJ 9/01)

6296 Rylant, Cynthia. *Moonlight: The Halloween Cat* (PS–K). Illus. by Melissa Sweet. 2003, HarperCollins LB $17.89 (978-0-06-029712-1). Moonlight the black cat serves as tour guide for this non-spooky celebration of Halloween. (Rev: HBG 4/04; SLJ 9/03)

6297 Sharratt, Nick. *What's in the Witch's Kitchen?* (1–3). Illus. by author. 2011, Candlewick $12.99 (978-0-7636-5224-1). Unpaged. This appealing flap book full of choices takes readers on a tour through a witch's kitchen and some of the favorite ingredients; the illustrations are full of Halloween images. (Rev: SLJ 8/1/11)

6298 Shaw, Nancy. *Sheep Trick or Treat* (PS–1). Illus. by Margot Apple. 1997, Houghton $14.00 (978-0-395-84168-6). 32pp. Sheep in costumes go trick-or-treating at Halloween and have unexpected adventures. (Rev: BL 9/1/97; HB 9/97; HBG 3/98; SLJ 9/97)

6299 Spurr, Elizabeth. *Halloween Sky Ride* (PS–3). Illus. by Ethan Long. 2005, Holiday House $16.95 (978-0-8234-1870-1). A not-too-scary witch takes too many friends on a broom ride to a Halloween party. (Rev: SLJ 8/05)

6300 Spurr, Elizabeth. *Pumpkin Hill* (PS–2). Illus. by Whitney Martin. 2006, Holiday House $16.95 (978-0-8234-1869-5). There's an orange avalanche in this rollicking Halloween tale as hundreds of plump pumpkins roll down a hill into town, causing confusion at first but paving the way for festive holiday decorations. (Rev: SLJ 10/06)

6301 Thomas, Jan. *Pumpkin Trouble* (PS–K). Illus. by author. 2011, HarperCollins $9.99 (978-0-06-169284-0). 40pp. Duck ends up trapped inside the jack-o-lantern he carved to surprise his friends Pig and Mouse. (Rev: BL 9/1/11; SLJ 6/11)

6302 Thompson, Lauren. *Mouse's First Halloween* (PS–K). Illus. by Buket Erdogan. 2000, Simon & Schuster $12.95 (978-0-689-83176-8). 32pp. On his first Halloween, Mouse has a few scary adventures. (Rev: BL 9/1/00; HBG 3/01; SLJ 8/00)

6303 Vaughan, Marcia. *We're Going on a Ghost Hunt* (PS–3). Illus. by Ann Schweninger. 2001, Harcourt $15.00 (978-0-15-202353-9). 32pp. A lighthearted rhyming Halloween story of two children who go out hunting for a ghost, only to become frightened and run home. (Rev: BL 9/15/01; HBG 3/02; SLJ 9/01)

6304 Walker, Sally M. *Druscilla's Halloween* (PS–3). Illus. by Lee White. 2009, Carolrhoda LB $16.95 (978-0-8225-8941-9). 32pp. Before the days of brooms, witches used to sneak up and frighten children on Halloween; elderly Drusilla's knees creak too loudly and she seeks a silent form of transportation. (Rev: BL 9/15/09; SLJ 9/1/09)

6305 Walton, Rick. *Mrs. McMurphy's Pumpkin* (PS–3). Illus. by Delana Bettoli. 2004, HarperCollins $8.99 (978-0-06-053409-7). An uppity pumpkin challenges an unafraid Mrs. Murphy. (Rev: SLJ 8/04)

6306 Watt, Mélanie. *Scaredy Squirrel Prepares for Halloween* (1–3). Illus. by author. 2013, Kids Can $17.95 (978-189478687-4). 64pp. Scaredy Squirrel must prepare for Halloween, one of the scariest holidays of the year, and he does so with his typical eye for detail, offering safety tips and explaining which costumes are too scary to be worn. Lexile AD670 (Rev: BLO 9/15/13; SLJ 12/13)

6307 Weston, Martha. *Tuck's Haunted House* (PS–2). Illus. 2002, Clarion $14.00 (978-0-618-15966-6). 32pp. Tuck the pig stages a haunted house for his friends, and his little sister Bunny adds to the scariness of Halloween. (Rev: BL 9/1/02; HBG 3/03; SLJ 10/02)

6308 Winters, Kay. *The Teeny Tiny Ghost* (PS–1). Illus. by Lynn Munsinger. 1997, HarperCollins LB $14.89 (978-0-06-025684-5). 32pp. A tiny ghost passes the test of not being frightened on Halloween. (Rev: BL 9/1/97; HBG 3/98; SLJ 11/97)

6309 Winters, Kay. *Whooo's Haunting the Teeny Tiny Ghost?* (PS–1). Illus. by Lynn Munsinger. 1999, HarperCollins $14.95 (978-0-06-027358-3). 32pp. The teeny tiny ghost finds that someone is haunting his house and later discovers that it is his cousin practicing his haunting techniques. (Rev: BL 9/1/99; HBG 3/00; SLJ 9/99)

6310 Yee, Wong H. *Mouse and Mole, a Perfect Halloween* (K–2). Illus. by author. Series: Mouse and Mole. 2011, Houghton Mifflin $14.99 (978-0-547-55152-4). Unpaged. Friends Mouse and Mole prepare for Halloween and explore their fears about the holiday. (Rev: SLJ 9/1/11)

6311 Ziefert, Harriet. *On Halloween Night* (PS–2). Illus. by Renée Andriani. 2001, Puffin paper $5.99 (978-0-14-056820-2). Emily's costume grows in "The House That Jack Built" fashion as her whole family pitches in to help. (Rev: SLJ 9/01)

JEWISH HOLY DAYS

6312 Adler, Tzivia. *The Sefer Torah Parade* (PS). Illus. by Ito Esther Perez. 2005, Hachai $11.95 (978-1-929628-26-1). A Jewish girl describes the festivities as a new

Torah is brought into her family's temple. (Rev: HBG 4/06; SLJ 9/05)

6313 Biers-Ariel, Matt. *Solomon and the Trees* (K–3). Illus. by Esti Silverberg-Kiss. 2001, UAHC $13.95 (978-0-8074-0749-3). 32pp. King Solomon rues the day that he inadvertently allowed his forest to be cut down to build the Temple, in the legend said to have inspired the Jewish holiday of Tu Bish'vat. (Rev: BL 8/01)

6314 Brown, Barbara. *Hanukkah in Alaska* (PS–2). Illus. by Stacey Shuett. 2013, Henry Holt $16.99 (978-080509748-1). 32pp. When there's a moose who simply won't leave a young girl's backyard in Alaska, she discovers that the way to get him to leave her favorite swing alone is to give him a true taste of Hanukkah — latkes! **e** (Rev: BLO 9/15/13; HB 11–12/13; LMC 1–2/14; SLJ 10/13)

6315 Carter, David A. *Chanukah Bugs: A Pop-Up Celebration* (PS–K). Illus. by author. 2002, Simon & Schuster $10.95 (978-0-689-81860-8). Flaps that resemble gift boxes open to reveal the "Shammash Bug," the "Dizzy Dreidel Bug," and so forth, one for each of the eight nights. (Rev: SLJ 10/02)

6316 Cleary, Brian P. *Eight Wild Nights: A Family Hanukkah Tale* (K–3). Illus. by David Udovic. 2006, Lerner LB $16.95 (978-1-58013-152-0). The members of an extended and rambunctious family gather for Festival of Lights. (Rev: SLJ 10/06)

6317 Da Costa, Deborah. *Hanukkah Moon* (K–3). Illus. by Gosia Mosz. 2007, Kar-Ben $17.95 (978-1-58013-244-2); paper $7.95 (978-1-58013-245-9). 32pp. Isobel spends Hanukkah with her Aunt Luisa and learns that the holiday can be celebrated in various different ways. (Rev: BCCB 10/07; BL 9/15/07)

6318 Glaser, Linda. *Hoppy Passover!* (PS–K). Illus. by Daniel Howarth. 2011, Whitman $15.99 (978-0-8075-3380-2). 24pp. Bunnies Violet and Simon celebrate Passover with their family in this warm family story, a sequel to *Hoppy Hanukkah!* (2009). (Rev: BL 2/1/11; SLJ 2/1/11)

6319 Gold-Vukson, Marji. *The Colors of My Jewish Year* (PS). Illus. by Madeline Wikler. 1998, Kar-Ben $4.95 (978-1-58013-011-0). This concept book introduces the colors of the rainbow (plus a few others) while describing the Jewish holidays associated with each. (Rev: SLJ 11/98)

6320 Goldin, Barbara D. *The World's Birthday: A Rosh Hashanah Story* (PS–3). Illus. by Jeanette Winter. 1990, Harcourt $13.95 (978-0-15-299648-2). 32pp. On Rosh Hashanah, the celebration of the birth of the world, Daniel wants to invite the world over to its birthday party. (Rev: BL 9/1/90; HB 11/90; SLJ 2/91)

6321 Goldin, Barbara Diamond. *Cakes and Miracles: A Purim Tale* (PS–3). Illus. by Jaime Zollars. 2010, Marshall Cavendish $17.99 (978-0-7614-5701-5). Unpaged. A newly edited and illustrated edition of the 1991 publication about young, blind Hershel who discovers new abilities during the Jewish holiday of Purim. (Rev: SLJ 10/1/10)

6322 Groner, Judye, and Madeline Wikler. *All About Hanukkah: In Story and Song. Rev. ed.* (K–3). Illus. by Kinny Kreiswirth. 1999, Kar-Ben paper $12.95 (978-1-58013-057-8). 32pp. This story on the origins of Hanukkah tells of struggles of the Jewish people of 2000 years ago to regain their religious freedom by opposing the power of a Syrian king. (Rev: SLJ 10/99) [286]

6323 Hanft, Josh. *The Miracles of Passover* (K–3). Illus. by Seymour Chwast. 2007, Blue Apple $15.95 (978-1-59354-600-7). This is an attractive book that explains Passover traditions in engaging text and imaginative lift-the-flaps. (Rev: SLJ 4/07) [296.4]

6324 Howland, Naomi. *Latkes, Latkes, Good to Eat: A Chanukah Story* (PS–1). Illus. 1999, Clarion $16.00 (978-0-395-89903-8). 32pp. As a reward for helping an old lady, Sadie is given a magic frying pan, which will produce as many latkes at Hanukkah as she wants. (Rev: BL 9/1/99; HBG 3/00; SLJ 10/99)

6325 Howland, Naomi. *The Matzah Man: A Passover Story* (PS–1). Illus. 2002, Clarion $16.00 (978-0-618-11750-5). 32pp. Matzah Man attempts to escape the Passover seder in this version of the story of the gingerbread boy filled with familiar Jewish references. (Rev: BL 2/15/02; HBG 10/02; SLJ 3/02)

6326 Hyde, Heidi Smith. *Emanuel and the Hanukkah Rescue* (K–3). Illus. by Jamel Akib. 2012, Lerner/Kar-Ben $17.95 (978-076136625-6); paper $7.95 (978-07613662-7-0). 32pp. In 18th-century Massachusetts, 9-year-old Emanuel shows his Jewish community the importance of openness about their religion. **e** (Rev: BL 11/15/12; SLJ 10/12)

6327 Jacobs, Laurie A. *A Box of Candles* (2–4). Illus. by Shelly Schonebaum Ephraim. 2005, Boyds Mills $17.95 (978-1-59078-169-2). 40pp. Given a silver candlestick and a year's worth of candles for her birthday, 7-year-old Ruthie faithfully observes Shabbat and other Jewish holidays as she struggles to adjust to changes in her family life. (Rev: BL 10/15/05; SLJ 9/05)

6328 Jules, Jacqueline. *Clap and Count! Action Rhymes for the Jewish New Year* (PS). Illus. by Sally Springer. 2001, Kar-Ben $17.95 (978-1-58013-067-7). 56pp. Nursery rhymes and finger plays with a Jewish twist take children through the holidays and holy days of the Jewish year. (Rev: BL 11/1/01)

6329 Kimmel, Eric A. *Asher and the Capmakers: A Hanukkah Story* (K–3). Illus. by Will Hillenbrand. 1993, Holiday House LB $16.95 (978-0-8234-1031-6). 32pp. Asher has many adventures when he sets out to borrow an egg for the family's latkes. (Rev: BL 7/93)

6330 Kimmel, Eric A. *The Chanukkah Guest* (PS–2). Illus. by Giora Carmi. 1990, Holiday House LB $17.95 (978-0-8234-0788-0); paper $6.95 (978-0-8234-0978-5). 32pp. Bubba Brayna is making potato latkes for the rabbi. (Rev: BCCB 12/90; BL 9/15/90*)

6331 Kimmel, Eric A. *Hanukkah Bear* (K–3). Illus. by Mike Wohnoutka. 2013, Holiday $16.95 (978-082342855-7). 32pp. Old Bear is enticed inside by Bubba Brayna's wonderful latkes, but he quickly realizes that she has mistaken him for the rabbi. National Jewish Book Award. Lexile AD370 (Rev: BLO 9/15/13)

6332 Kimmel, Eric A. *Hershel and the Hanukkah Goblins* (K–3). Illus. by Trina S. Hyman. 1989, Holiday House LB $17.95 (978-0-8234-0769-9). 32pp. In this tale set in Eastern Europe, Hershel is looking forward to Hanukkah until he finds that the synagogue is haunted by goblins. (Rev: BCCB 10/89; BL 9/1/89; HB 1/90)

6333 Kimmel, Eric A. *The Magic Dreidels: A Hanukkah Story* (PS–3). Illus. by Katya Krenina. 1996, Holiday House LB $16.95 (978-0-8234-1256-3). 28pp. In this Hanukkah story, Jacob receives a magic dreidel from a goblin. (Rev: BCCB 11/96; BL 9/1/96)

6334 Kimmel, Eric A. *Zigazak! A Magical Hanukkah Night* (PS–4). Illus. by Jon Goodell. 2001, Doubleday $15.95 (978-0-385-32652-0). 32pp. A rabbi outwits two playful devils who are disrupting a small town's Hanukkah celebration. (Rev: BCCB 10/01; BL 10/1/01; HBG 3/02; SLJ 10/01)

6335 Kimmelman, Leslie. *The Runaway Latkes* (PS). Illus. by Paul Yalowitz. 2000, Whitman $15.95 (978-0-8075-7176-7). 32pp. In this humorous Hanukkah version of "The Gingerbread Man," three latkes jump out of the pan and roll off to see the town. (Rev: BL 9/1/00; HBG 3/01)

6336 Kimmelman, Leslie. *Sound the Shofar! A Story for Rosh Hashanah and Yom Kippur* (PS–1). Illus. by John Himmelman. 1998, HarperCollins $15.99 (978-0-06-027501-3). 32pp. A young girl describes the family's activities during Rosh Hashanah and Yom Kippur while her uncle blows the ram's horn, known as the shofar. (Rev: BL 10/1/98; HBG 3/99; SLJ 1/99)

6337 Korngold, Jamie. *Sadie's Almost Marvelous Menorah* (PS–1). Illus. by Julie Fortenberry. 2013, Lerner/Kar-Ben $17.95 (978-076136493-1); paper $7.95 (978-07613649-5-5). 24pp. Sadie drops her lovely menorah but despite the damage her mother finds a way to use it in the Hanukkah celebrations. (Rev: BLO 9/15/13; HB 11–12/13)

6338 Krensky, Stephen. *Hanukkah at Valley Forge* (2–4). Illus. by Greg Harlin. 2006, Dutton $17.99 (978-0-525-47738-9). 32pp. In this fact-based historical tale, a young Jewish soldier explains to General George Washington the meaning of the Hanukkah celebration. (Rev: BL 9/1/06; SLJ 10/06)

6339 Kroll, Steven. *The Hanukkah Mice* (PS–2). Illus. by Michelle Shapiro. 2008, Marshall Cavendish $14.99 (978-0-7614-5428-1). A family of mice enjoys Rachel's Hanukkah dollhouse and celebrates the holiday along with her. (Rev: BL 9/1/08)

6340 Kropf, Latifa Berry. *Happy Birthday, World: A Rosh Hashanah Celebration* (PS). Illus. by Lisa Carlson. 2005, Lerner $5.95 (978-0-929371-32-0). This attractive board book introduces young readers to Rosh Hashanah by comparing the rituals of the Jewish holiday to those of a child's birthday. (Rev: SLJ 11/05)

6341 Lamstein, Sarah Marwil. *Letter on the Wind* (K–3). Illus. by Neil Waldman. 2007, Boyds Mills $16.95 (978-

1-932425-74-1). Hayim asks the Almighty for help when his village has no oil for the Hanukkah lights; based on a folktale. (Rev: BL 9/15/07; LMC 11/07)

6342 Lanton, Sandy. *Lots of Latkes: A Hanukkah Story* (K–3). Illus. by Vicki Jo Redenbaugh. 2003, Lerner $14.95 (978-1-58013-091-2); paper $6.95 (978-1-58013-061-5). Despite the fact that everyone brought latkes instead of the varied spread that had been planned, the guests at Rivka Leah's Hanukkah party have a wonderful time. (Rev: HBG 4/04; SLJ 10/03)

6343 Levine, Abby. *This Is the Dreidel* (PS–2). Illus. by Paige Billin-Frye. 2003, Whitman LB $16.99 (978-0-8075-7884-1). Simple rhyming couplets and bright illustrations show Max and his younger sister Ruth preparing for and participating in the fun of Hanukkah. (Rev: HBG 4/04; SLJ 10/03)

6344 Levine, Abby. *This Is the Matzah* (PS–2). Illus. by Paige Billin-Frye. 2005, Whitman $16.99 (978-0-8075-7885-8). 32pp. Max and his sister Ruth help their parents prepare for the Seder celebration in this introduction to the traditions of Passover told in rhyming couplets. (Rev: BL 2/15/05; SLJ 5/05)

6345 Manushkin, Fran. *The Matzah That Papa Brought Home* (PS–1). Illus. by Ned Bittinger. 1995, Scholastic $14.95 (978-0-590-47146-6). 32pp. A cumulative tale that introduces symbols associated with Passover. (Rev: BL 1/15/95; SLJ 2/95)

6346 Marshall, Linda Elovitz. *The Passover Lamb* (K–3). Illus. by Tatjana Mai-Wyss. 2013, Random House $17.99 (978-0-307-93177-1). 32pp. The arrival of a new lamb that is neglected by its mother jeopardizes Miriam's chance to shine at the Passover seder until she decides to take the little one along. **e** (Rev: BL 12/15/12; LMC 5–6/13; SLJ 1/13)

6347 Medoff, Francine. *The Mouse in the Matzah Factory* (K–3). Illus. by Nicole In den Bosch. 2003, Kar-Ben paper $6.95 (978-1-58013-048-6). 32pp. A curious mouse follows a harvest of wheat from field to mill to bakery, where it is made into matzohs for Passover. (Rev: BL 3/15/03; SLJ 10/03)

6348 Melmed, Laura K. *Moishe's Miracle: A Hanukkah Story* (K–3). Illus. by David Slonim. 2000, HarperCollins LB $15.89 (978-0-688-14683-2). 32pp. Moishe's generosity at Hanukkah results in a gift of a magical pan that makes pancakes for all. (Rev: BL 9/1/00; HB 9/00; HBG 3/01)

6349 Michelson, Richard. *Grandpa's Gamble* (PS–4). Illus. by Barry Moser. 1999, Marshall Cavendish $15.95 (978-0-7614-5034-4). At Passover, Grandpa, a Jewish immigrant of many years ago, regrets that he lied and cheated to get ahead and tells how he changed his wicked ways. (Rev: BCCB 4/99; BL 3/15/99; HBG 10/99; SLJ 6/99)

6350 Modesitt, Jeanne. *It's Hanukkah!* (PS–1). Illus. by Robin Spowart. 1999, Holiday House $15.95 (978-0-8234-1451-2). A family of mice enjoy all the activities associated with Hanukkah, including lighting the Menorah and eating latkes. (Rev: HBG 3/00; SLJ 10/99)

6351 Newman, Lesléa. *The Eight Nights of Chanukah* (K–2). Illus. by Elivia Savadier. 2005, Abrams $12.95 (978-0-8109-5785-5). 24pp. Newman gives "The Twelve Days of Christmas" a new twist with a version that celebrates Hanukkah; a note and a glossary follow the text. (Rev: BL 10/15/05; SLJ 10/05)

6352 Newman, Lesléa. *Matzo Ball Moon* (PS–3). Illus. by Elaine Greenstein. 1998, Clarion $15.00 (978-0-395-71530-7). 32pp. At Passover, all of Eleanor's family enjoy the matzo balls of her grandmother, Bubbe, and when Eleanor opens the door to welcome the prophet Elijah, she sees a full moon and imagines it to be another of Bubbe's yummy creations. (Rev: BL 4/1/98; HBG 10/98; SLJ 6/98)

6353 Newman, Lesléa. *Runaway Dreidel!* (PS–2). Illus. by Kyrsten Brooker. 2002, Holt $17.95 (978-0-8050-6237-3). 32pp. A rhyming fantasy about a dreidel that takes off, zooming into space to become a star. (Rev: BCCB 11/02; BL 9/1/02; HBG 3/03; SLJ 10/02)

6354 Newman, Lesléa. *A Sweet Passover* (K–3). Illus. by David Slonim. 2012, Abrams $16.95 (978-1-8109-9737-0). 40pp. Miriam loves Passover at Grandma and Grandpa's house but by the eighth day she is sick of eating matzah; includes a recipe for matzah brei and a glossary. (Rev: BL 2/15/12; SLJ 4/1/12)

6355 Oberman, Sheldon. *By the Hanukkah Light* (1–4). Illus. by Neil Waldman. 1997, Boyds Mills $15.95 (978-1-56397-658-2). 32pp. As Rachel and her grandfather polish the menorah at Hanukkah, he tells her about the Holocaust and its meaning for the Jewish people. (Rev: BL 9/1/97*; HBG 3/98; SLJ 10/97)

6356 Olswanger, Anna. *Shlemiel Crooks* (2–4). Illus. by Paula Goodman Koz. 2005, NewSouth paper $14.95 (978-1-58838-165-1). Based on a true incident, this humorous story tells of the hapless thieves who plan to steal Reb Elias's special Passover wine. (Rev: BL 5/15/05; SLJ 6/05)

6357 Pushker, Gloria Teles. *Toby Belfer and the High Holy Days* (K–3). Illus. by Judith Hierstein. Series: Toby Belfer. 2001, Pelican $15.95 (978-1-56554-765-0). 32pp. Toby explains the meaning of the Jewish holidays of Rosh Hashanah and Yom Kippur to her friend Donna. (Rev: BL 10/1/01; HBG 3/02; SLJ 1/02)

6358 Rauchwerger, Diane Levin. *Dinosaur on Passover* (PS–K). Illus. by Jason Wolff. 2006, Lerner LB $15.95 (978-1-58013-156-8); paper $6.95 (978-1-58013-161-2). A dinosaur joins in the Passover seder in this story with rhyming text that covers all the usual rituals. (Rev: SLJ 4/06)

6359 Rosen, Michael J. *Our Eight Nights of Hanukkah* (K–3). Illus. by DyAnne DiSalvo-Ryan. 2000, Holiday House $16.95 (978-0-8234-1476-5). 32pp. The activities of a Jewish family are chronicled as they celebrate the eight nights of Hanukkah. (Rev: BL 9/1/00; HBG 3/01)

6360 Rosenberg, Madelyn. *Happy Birthday, Tree! A Tu B'Shevat Story* (PS–2). Illus. by Jana Christy. 2012, Whitman $15.99 (978-0-8075-3151-8). 24pp. Joni and her neighbor Nate celebrate a tree in her front yard in honor of the Jewish New Year for Trees. (Rev: BLO 10/15/12; LMC 1–2/13; SLJ 9/12)

6361 Rouss, Sylvia. *Sammy Spider's First Passover* (PS–K). Illus. by Katherine J. Kahn. 1995, Kar-Ben paper $7.95 (978-0-929371-82-5). A pleasant story about a little spider that watches the Shapiro family make preparations for Passover. (Rev: SLJ 7/95)

6362 Rouss, Sylvia. *Sammy Spider's First Rosh Hashanah* (PS–1). Illus. by Katherine J. Kahn. 1996, Kar-Ben paper $7.95 (978-0-929371-99-3). Mother Spider explains to her son Sammy the holiday customs and symbols associated with the Jewish New Year. (Rev: SLJ 5/97)

6363 Rouss, Sylvia. *Sammy Spider's First Shabbat* (K–2). Illus. by Katherine J. Kahn. 1998, Kar-Ben $14.95 (978-1-58013-007-3); paper $7.95 (978-1-58013-006-6). Sammy Spider observes the Shapiro family's preparations for the Shabbat, including braiding the challah. (Rev: SLJ 6/98)

6364 Schotter, Roni. *Passover!* (PS–1). Illus. by Erin Eitter Kono. 2006, Little, Brown $12.99 (978-0-316-93991-1). A Jewish family's preparations for Passover are described in rhyming text with cartoon illustrations. (Rev: BL 2/15/06; SLJ 4/06)

6365 Shulman, Goldie. *Way Too Much Challah Dough* (PS–2). Illus. by Vitaliy Romanenko. 2006, Hachai $12.95 (978-1-929628-23-0). 32pp. When Mindy uses too much yeast, her challah dough grows out of control and her grandmother must come to the rescue. (Rev: BL 10/1/06)

6366 Simpson, Lesley. *The Shabbat Box* (PS–1). Illus. by Nicole In den Bosch. 2001, Kar-Ben paper $6.95 (978-1-58013-027-1). Ira must come up with a solution when he loses the treasured class Shabbat box on his way home from school. (Rev: BL 10/1/01; SLJ 12/01)

6367 Spinner, Stephanie. *It's a Miracle: A Hanukkah Storybook* (K–2). Illus. by Jill McElmurry. 2003, Simon & Schuster $16.95 (978-0-689-84493-5). Owen lights the candles each night of the holiday and his Grandma Karen tells a story of Jewish family life. (Rev: HBG 4/04; SLJ 10/03)

6368 Stillerman, Marci. *Nine Spoons: A Chanukah Story* (K–2). Illus. by Pesach Gerber. 1998, Hachai $12.95 (978-0-922613-84-7). In a Nazi concentration camp, Raizel shows her ingenuity by fashioning a menorah out of nine spoons so that Hanukkah can be celebrated. (Rev: HB 1/99; HBG 3/99; SLJ 10/98)

6369 Terwilliger, Kelly. *Bubbe Isabella and the Sukkot Cake* (PS–K). Illus. by Phyllis Hornung. 2005, Kar-Ben $15.95 (978-1-58013-187-2); paper $6.95 (978-1-58013-128-5). 24pp. A Jewish grandmother makes a lemon cake and a beautiful sukkah for the Sukkot holiday, but at first the only guests are animals that prefer the decoration to the cake. (Rev: BL 9/1/05; SLJ 10/05)

6370 Topek, Susan Remick. *Shalom Shabbat: A Book for Havdalah* (PS). Illus. by Shelly Schonebaum Ephraim. 1998, Kar-Ben $5.95 (978-1-58013-010-3). This simple board book celebrates the ceremony of Havdalah that takes place at the end of the Jewish Sabbath. (Rev: SLJ 2/99)

6371 Ungar, Richard. *Rachel's Gift* (K–3). Illus. 2003, Tundra $16.95 (978-0-88776-616-9). 32pp. With humor and style, Ungar describes a Chelm family's preparations for its Passover seder. (Rev: BL 5/1/03; HBG 10/03; SLJ 5/03)

6372 Vorst, Rochel Groner. *The Sukkah That I Built* (PS–2). Illus. by Elizabeth Victor-Elsby. 2002, Hachai $10.95 (978-1-929628-07-0). 26pp. A young boy (with help from his family) builds a sukkah — a temporary structure used in the celebration of Sukkot — to the refrain of "The House that Jack Built." (Rev: BL 10/1/02; HBG 3/03)

6373 Wayland, April Halprin. *New Year at the Pier: A Rosh Hashanah Story* (PS–3). Illus. by Stephane Jorisch. 2009, Dial $16.99 (978-0-8037-3279-7). 32pp. Izzy and his parents prepare to make amends for mistakes during the Jewish New Year tradition of Tashlich. (Rev: BL 6/1–15/09; SLJ 7/09)

6374 Weber, Elka. *The Yankee at the Seder* (1–3). Illus. by Adam Gustavson. 2009, Tricycle $16.99 (978-1-58246-256-1). Loosely based on a true event detailed in the endnote, this unusual story tells how a Confederate family shares a Seder dinner with a Jewish Yankee soldier. (Rev: BCCB 5/09; BLO 1/7/09; SLJ 1/09)

6375 Wilkowski, Susan. *Baby's Bris* (PS–1). Illus. by Judith Friedman. 1999, Karben $16.95 (978-1-58013-052-3); paper $6.95 (978-1-58013-053-0). 32pp. A young girl grows to love her baby brother particularly through an understanding of the bris ceremony when the boy is circumcised. (Rev: BL 1/1–15/00; HBG 3/00; SLJ 1/00)

6376 Wohl, Lauren L. *The Eighth Menorah* (PS–1). Illus. by Laura Hughes. 2013, Whitman $16.99 (978-080751892-2). 32pp. Sam's class is making menorahs to take home for the holidays, but his parents already have seven menorahs — what is he to do? Lexile AD530 (Rev: BL 9/15/13; LMC 1–2/14)

6377 Yolen, Jane. *How Do Dinosaurs Say Happy Chanukah?* (PS–1). Illus. by Mark Teague. 2012, Scholastic $16.99 (978-054541677-1). 40pp. With the signature amusing illustrations and rhyming text, this book shows how young dinosaurs should behave during the Festival of Lights. (Rev: BL 9/1/12; HB 11–12/12; SLJ 10/12)

6378 Zalben, Jane Breskin. *Pearl's Passover: A Family Celebration Through Stories, Recipes, Crafts, and Songs* (K–3). Illus. 2002, Simon & Schuster $16.00 (978-0-689-81487-7). 48pp. A lamb named Pearl and her family prepare for Passover in this volume that interweaves fictional characters with recipes, crafts, and basic information about the holiday. (Rev: BL 2/15/02; HB 3/02; HBG 10/02; SLJ 2/02)

6379 Zolkower, Edie Stoltz. *Too Many Cooks: A Passover Parable* (PS–2). Illus. by Shauna Mooney Kawasaki. 2000, Kar-Ben paper $5.95 (978-1-58013-063-9). At Passover, everyone in the family decides to add a spe-

cial ingredient to Bubbie's charoses for the seder. (Rev: SLJ 12/00)

THANKSGIVING

6380 Alcott, Louisa May. *An Old Fashioned Thanksgiving* (4–5). Illus. by Jody Wheeler. 1990, Applewood paper $5.95 (978-1-55709-135-2). 40pp. The happenings in a New Hampshire farm family in the 1820s, first published in 1881. (Rev: BL 10/1/89; SLJ 10/89)

6381 Anderson, Derek. *Over the River: A Turkey's Tale* (PS–K). Illus. 2005, Simon & Schuster $14.95 (978-0-689-87635-6). 40pp. The popular Thanksgiving song is given a new twist in this tale of a turkey family on its way to celebrate the holiday with Grandma. (Rev: BL 9/15/05; HBG 4/06; SLJ 10/05)

6382 Archer, Peggy. *Turkey Surprise* (PS–K). Illus. by Thor Wickstrom. 2005, Dial $10.99 (978-0-8037-2969-8). 32pp. A turkey succeeds in eluding two Pilgrim brothers, who settle for a vegetarian Thanksgiving feast. (Rev: BL 9/1/05; HBG 4/06)

6383 Auch, Mary Jane, and Herm Auch. *Beauty and the Beaks: A Turkey's Cautionary Tale* (K–3). Illus. by Mary Jane Auch. 2007, Holiday $16.95 (978-0-8234-1990-6). 32pp. "Wattle I do?" asks pretentious turkey Lance when he discovers he's been invited to be the main dish in this funny story full of wordplay. (Rev: BL 9/15/07; SLJ 9/07)

6384 Bateman, Teresa. *Gus, the Pilgrim Turkey* (PS–2). Illus. by Ellen Sasaki. 2008, Albert Whitman $16.99 (978-0-8075-1266-1). Gus is a happy young turkey until he learns that his life might be in danger toward Thanksgiving, and he sets off for points south. (Rev: BL 9/15/08; SLJ 9/08)

6385 Bateman, Teresa. *A Plump and Perky Turkey* (PS–2). Illus. by Jeff Shelly. 2001, Winslow $15.95 (978-1-890817-91-6). 40pp. Pete the turkey cleverly escapes hungry townspeople on Thanksgiving. (Rev: BCCB 11/01; BL 9/1/01; HBG 3/02; SLJ 9/01)

6386 Bildner, Phil. *Turkey Bowl* (1–3). Illus. by C. F. Payne. 2008, Simon & Schuster $15.99 (978-0-689-87896-1). Ethan's dream of playing in his family's annual Thanksgiving football game melts away when a big snowstorm comes. (Rev: BL 9/15/08)

6387 Brown, Marc. *Arthur's Thanksgiving* (K–3). Illus. by author. 1983, Little, Brown paper $5.95 (978-0-316-11232-1). Arthur is made director of his class Thanksgiving play.

6388 Bunting, Eve. *How Many Days to America? A Thanksgiving Story* (2–4). Illus. by Beth Peck. 1988, Houghton $16.00 (978-0-89919-521-6); paper $6.95 (978-0-395-54777-9). 32pp. A family flees oppression on a Caribbean island and heads for the United States. (Rev: BL 11/1/88; SLJ 10/88)

6389 Bunting, Eve. *A Turkey for Thanksgiving* (PS–1). Illus. by Diane deGroat. 1991, Houghton $16.00 (978-0-89919-793-0). 32pp. After bringing a live turkey home at Thanksgiving, Mr. and Mrs. Moose decide to have a vegetarian meal. (Rev: BCCB 9/91; BL 10/1/91; SLJ 9/91)

6390 Capucilli, Alyssa Satin. *Happy Thanksgiving, Biscuit!* (PS). Illus. by Pat Schories. 1999, HarperCollins paper $6.99 (978-0-694-01221-3). In this flap book, Biscuit, an endearing puppy, enjoys the fuss surrounding Thanksgiving. (Rev: SLJ 12/99)

6391 Cazet, Denys. *Minnie and Moo and the Thanksgiving Tree* (1–2). Illus. 2000, DK $12.99 (978-0-7894-2654-3); paper $3.99 (978-0-7894-2655-0). 418pp. At Thanksgiving, Minnie and Moo help the animals (starting with the turkeys) escape by hiding them in a tree only to discover that the farmer and his family are vegetarians. (Rev: BL 9/1/00; HB 9/00; HBG 3/01; SLJ 9/00)

6392 Cowley, Joy. *Gracias, the Thanksgiving Turkey* (PS–2). Illus. by Joe Cepeda. 1996, Scholastic $15.95 (978-0-590-46976-0). 32pp. A New York City boy dreads Thanksgiving, when his pet turkey, Gracias, will be killed. (Rev: BCCB 11/96; BL 9/1/96; SLJ 12/96)

6393 Cox, Judy. *One Is a Feast for Mouse: A Thanksgiving Tale* (PS–2). Illus. by Jeffrey Ebbeler. 2008, Holiday $16.95 (978-0-8234-1977-7). 32pp. A little mouse who has amassed a feast from the Thanksgiving leftovers loses almost all of it when the cat pounces — but one luscious pea remains. (Rev: BL 10/1/08; HB 11/08; SLJ 9/08)

6394 deGroat, Diane. *We Gather Together . . . Now Please Get Lost!* (PS–2). Illus. Series: Gilbert. 2001, North-South LB $15.88 (978-1-58717-096-6). 32pp. Gilbert and his animal classmates take an entertaining, mishap-filled field trip to Pilgrim Town. (Rev: BL 9/1/01; HBG 3/02; SLJ 8/01)

6395 Elliott, Laura Malone. *Thanksgiving Day Thanks* (PS–2). Illus. by Lynn Munsinger. 2013, HarperCollins $17.99 (978-006000236-7). 32pp. A bear cub named Sam has trouble coming up with a special thing for which he is grateful. (Rev: BL 9/1/13; SLJ 8/13)

6396 Gibbons, Gail. *Thanksgiving Is . . .* (PS–2). Illus. by author. 2004, Holiday House $17.95 (978-0-8234-1849-7). Brief text introduces the holiday and its relation to harvest time, Pilgrims, and Native Americans. (Rev: SLJ 9/04) [394.2]

6397 Goode, Diane. *Thanksgiving Is Here!* (PS–2). Illus. by author. 2003, HarperCollins LB $16.89 (978-0-06-051589-8). An appealing portrait of an extended family gathering for its annual Thanksgiving feast. (Rev: HBG 4/04; SLJ 9/03)

6398 Jackson, Alison. *I Know an Old Lady Who Swallowed a Pie* (PS–2). Illus. by Judith Byron Schachner. 1997, Dutton $15.99 (978-0-525-45645-2). 32pp. This favorite folk song is given a new twist by using foods associated with Thanksgiving. (Rev: BL 9/1/97; HBG 3/98; SLJ 11/97)

6399 Jennings, Sharon. *Franklin's Thanksgiving* (PS–1). Illus. by Brenda Clark. Series: Franklin. 2001, Kids Can $10.95 (978-1-55074-798-0). 32pp. Franklin the turtle's family Thanksgiving dinner becomes so overcrowded

that the feast is moved outdoors. (Rev: BL 9/15/01; HBG 3/02; SLJ 9/01)

6400 Kroll, Steven. *Oh, What a Thanksgiving!* (K–2). Illus. by S. D. Schindler. 1988, Scholastic paper $3.95 (978-0-590-40616-1). David imagines himself at Plymouth in 1620. (Rev: BL 9/15/88; SLJ 9/88)

6401 Kroll, Virginia. *The Thanksgiving Bowl* (PS–2). Illus. by Philomena O'Neill. 2007, Pelican $15.95 (978-1-58980-365-7). 32pp. Grandma Grace's yellow plastic gratitude bowl is the central image in this Thanksgiving story. (Rev: BL 10/1/07)

6402 Manushkin, Fran. *Katie Saves Thanksgiving* (K–2). Illus. by Tammie Lyon. Series: Katie Woo. 2010, Picture Window LB $19.99 (978-1-4048-5988-3); paper $3.95 (978-1-4048-6367-5). 32pp. Katie is able to save her family's Thanksgiving through thoughtfulness, generosity, and neighborliness. (Rev: SLJ 3/1/11)

6403 Mayr, Diane. *Run, Turkey, Run!* (PS–2). Illus. by Laura Rader. 2007, Walker $15.95 (978-0-8027-9630-1). Turkey's frantic attempts to avoid becoming Thanksgiving dinner end in success when the family eats grilled cheese sandwiches. (Rev: BL 9/15/07; LMC 11/07; SLJ 10/07)

6404 Milgrim, David. *Thank You, Thanksgiving* (PS–K). Illus. by author. 2003, Clarion $9.95 (978-0-618-27466-6). 32pp. A little girl walks through town expressing in simple words her thanks to all the animals and objects that enrich her life. (Rev: HBG 4/04; SLJ 9/03)

6405 Parish, Herman. *Amelia Bedelia Talks Turkey* (1–3). Illus. by Lynn Sweat. 2008, HarperCollins $16.99 (978-0-06-084352-6). 64pp. Wordplay and hilarity abound when Amelia Bedelia is put in charge of the 3rd-grade Thanksgiving play. (Rev: SLJ 3/09)

6406 Pomeranc, Marion Hess. *The Can-Do Thanksgiving* (K–2). Illus. by Nancy Cote. 1998, Whitman $16.99 (978-0-8075-1054-4). Through a school food drive and a contribution of a can of peas, Dee is chosen to help serve a Thanksgiving meal and, there, meets a new friend. (Rev: BL 11/1/98; HBG 3/99; SLJ 9/98)

6407 Reed, Lynn Rowe. *Thelonius Turkey Lives!* (PS–2). Illus. by author. 2005, Knopf $15.95 (978-0-375-83126-3). The other farm animals gang up on their keeper when Thelonious becomes convinced she wants to eat him for Thanksgiving. (Rev: SLJ 8/05)

6408 Roberts, Bethany. *Thanksgiving Mice!* (PS–1). Illus. by Doug Cushman. 2001, Clarion $13.00 (978-0-618-12040-6). 32pp. Mice put on a play about the trials of the Pilgrims and the first Thanksgiving. (Rev: BL 9/1/01; HBG 3/02; SLJ 9/01)

6409 Ruelle, Karen G. *The Thanksgiving Beast Feast* (1–2). Illus. 1999, Holiday House $15.95 (978-0-8234-1511-3). 32pp. At Thanksgiving, Harry Cat and his sister, Emily, decide to show their thanks by preparing food for the birds, squirrels, and chipmunks in their neighborhood. (Rev: BL 9/1/99; HB 9/99; HBG 3/00; SLJ 9/99)

6410 Scheer, Julian. *A Thanksgiving Turkey* (PS–3). Illus. by Ronald Himler. 2001, Holiday House $16.95 (978-0-8234-1674-5). 32pp. A boy learns to know his grandfather and Virginia farm life in a beautifully illustrated and sensitive story that culminates with the capture and release of a wild turkey. (Rev: BCCB 10/01; BL 9/1/01; HBG 3/02; SLJ 9/01)

6411 Shore, Diane Z. *This Is the Feast* (PS–2). Illus. by Megan Lloyd. 2008, HarperCollins $16.99 (978-0-06-623794-7). 32pp. The story of the Pilgrims' voyage, arrival in America, and the first celebratory Thanksgiving feast is told in poetic text and bright illustrations. (Rev: BL 9/15/08)

6412 Spinelli, Eileen. *The Perfect Thanksgiving* (PS–2). Illus. by JoAnn Adinolfi. 2003, Holt $15.95 (978-0-8050-6531-2). Rhyming text and lively illustrations enhance this amusing comparison of the very different Thanksgiving experiences of two families. (Rev: HBG 4/04; SLJ 9/03)

6413 Spirn, Michele. *The Know-Nothings Talk Turkey* (1–2). Illus. Series: I Can Read. 2000, HarperCollins $14.95 (978-0-06-028183-0). 48pp. In his easy-to-read book, four friends and their dog Floris decide to serve a turkey at Thanksgiving so they invite one to their dinner. (Rev: BL 9/1/00; HBG 3/01; SLJ 10/00)

6414 Willey, Margaret. *Thanksgiving with Me* (PS–2). Illus. by Lloyd Bloom. 1998, HarperCollins $15.95 (978-0-06-027113-8). 32pp. While her mother describes each of her six brothers, a little girl waits with great anticipation for the arrival of her uncles at Thanksgiving time. (Rev: BCCB 11/98; BL 9/1/98; HBG 3/99; SLJ 9/98)

6415 Wilson, Karma. *Give Thanks to the Lord: Celebrating Psalm 92* (PS–2). Illus. by Amy June Bates. 2007, Zondervan $14.99 (978-0-310-71118-6). 32pp. A young boy gives thanks for the wonders of Thanksgiving Day. (Rev: BL 10/1/07) [242]

VALENTINE'S DAY

6416 Bond, Felicia. *The Day It Rained Hearts* (PS–K). 2001, HarperCollins LB $17.89 (978-0-06-001078-2). 63pp. When it rains hearts, Cornelia catches them and makes unique, individualized valentines for her friends. (Rev: BL 12/1/01; HBG 3/02)

6417 Bunting, Eve. *The Valentine Bears* (K–3). Illus. by Jan Brett. 1983, Houghton $16.00 (978-0-89919-138-6); paper $5.95 (978-0-89919-313-7). 32pp. Mr. and Mrs. Bear decide not to sleep through Valentine's Day this year.

6418 Capucilli, Alyssa Satin. *Biscuit's Valentine's Day* (PS). Illus. by Pat Schories. 2000, HarperCollins $6.99 (978-0-694-01222-0). 20pp. While his young owner is preparing for Valentine's Day, Biscuit the dog is engaged in all sorts of activities that are revealed when the reader lifts the flaps in this interactive book. (Rev: BL 2/15/01)

6419 Carlson, Nancy. *Henry and the Valentine Surprise* (PS–1). Illus. by author. 2008, Viking $15.99 (978-0-670-06267-6). 32pp. Does Henry the mouse's teacher have a girlfriend? Henry and his classmates investigate. (Rev: BL 2/1/09; SLJ 12/08)

6420 Carr, Jan. *Sweet Hearts* (PS–2). Illus. by Dorothy Donohue. 2002, Holiday House $16.95 (978-0-8234-1732-2). 32pp. Elaborately constructed collage valentines star in this story in which a little panda creates and decorates paper hearts for his parents. (Rev: BL 12/1/02; HBG 3/03; SLJ 11/02)

6421 Choldenko, Gennifer. *A Giant Crush* (K–3). Illus. by Melissa Sweet. 2011, Putnam $16.99 (978-0-399-24352-3). 32pp. A young bunny too shy to declare his affection hides little presents for Cami to find, until a friend tells him he must speak up. (Rev: BL 12/1/11; SLJ 11/1/11)

6422 Demas, Corinne. *Valentine Surprise* (PS–1). Illus. by R. W. Alley. 2008, Walker $12.95 (978-0-8027-9664-6). 32pp. Lily's disappointment with her efforts to make a perfect heart-shaped Valentine for her mother leads her to a lovely solution. (Rev: BL 1/1–15/08; SLJ 3/08)

6423 Elliot, Laura Malone. *A String of Hearts* (K–3). Illus. by Lynn Munsinger. 2010, HarperCollins $16.99 (978-0-06-000085-1). 32pp. Mary Ann, a young squirrel, helps her bear friend Sam come up with the perfect things to write on Tiffany's valentine and Sam comes to realize Mary Ann's true value. Lexile AD510L (Rev: BLO 12/1/10; SLJ 1/1/11)

6424 Friedman, Laurie. *Love, Ruby Valentine* (K–4). Illus. by Lynne Avril Cravath. 2006, Carolrhoda $15.95 (978-1-57505-899-3). Ruby Valentine works so hard to prepare for Valentine's Day that when the big day comes, she sleeps through it and must deliver her gifts a day late. (Rev: SLJ 11/06)

6425 Friedman, Laurie. *Ruby Valentine Saves the Day* (PS–1). Illus. by Lynne Avril. 2010, Carolrhoda $16.95 (978-0-7613-4213-7). 32pp. Ruby Valentine and her cockatoo move their Valentine's Day party to town when snow prevents their guests from attending. ℮ Lexile AD540L (Rev: BL 1/1–15/11; SLJ 12/1/10)

6426 Hoban, Lillian. *Silly Tilly's Valentine* (K–2). Illus. by author. Series: I Can Read. 1998, HarperCollins LB $16.89 (978-0-06-027401-6). 47pp. Tilly the mole is so excited about a snowfall that she forgets it is Valentine's Day. (Rev: HBG 10/98; SLJ 2/98)

6427 Manushkin, Fran. *No Valentines for Katie* (K–2). Illus. by Tammie Lyon. Series: Katie Woo. 2010, Picture Window LB $19.99 (978-1-4048-5986-9); paper $3.95 (978-1-4048-6365-1). 32pp. Katie is so involved in making a valentine that she forgets to put her name in the box. (Rev: SLJ 3/1/11)

6428 Petersen, David. *Snowy Valentine* (PS–1). Illus. by author. 2011, HarperCollins $14.99 (978-0-06-146378-5). 32pp. In hopes of finding an ideal gift for his wife Lily, Jasper Bunny spends Valentine's Day visiting friends and seeking advice — and ends up with a perfect but unintended present. (Rev: BL 12/15/11; SLJ 11/1/11)

6429 Poydar, Nancy. *Rhyme Time Valentine* (PS–3). Illus. 2002, Holiday House $16.95 (978-0-8234-1684-4). Poor little Ruby is dismayed when the valentines she made are blown away by a strong wind. (Rev: BL 1/1–15/03; HBG 3/03; SLJ 11/02)

6430 Roberts, Bethany. *Valentine Mice!* (PS–K). Illus. by Doug Cushman. 1998, Clarion $13.00 (978-0-395-77518-9). 32pp. A group of mice are so busy delivering valentines in a snowy forest that they don't realize the smallest one of them is missing. (Rev: BL 12/15/97; HBG 10/98; SLJ 1/98)

6431 Roop, Peter, and Connie Roop. *Let's Celebrate Valentine's Day* (2–4). Illus. by Katy K. Arnsteen. Series: Let's Celebrate. 1999, Millbrook LB $22.90 (978-0-7613-0972-7); paper $5.95 (978-0-7913-0428-0). 32pp. Discusses the origins of Valentine's Day, describes how it is celebrated, and includes many related jokes and riddles. (Rev: BL 2/15/99; HBG 10/99; SLJ 4/99) [394.2618]

6432 Ruelle, Karen G. *Snow Valentines* (1–2). Illus. Series: Holiday House Reader. 2000, Holiday House $15.95 (978-0-8234-1533-5). 32pp. A book for beginning readers that describes how two little cats solve the problem of what to get their parents for Valentine's Day. (Rev: BL 7/00; HBG 10/01; SLJ 9/00)

6433 Weeks, Sarah. *Be Mine, Be Mine, Sweet Valentine* (PS–K). Illus. by Fumi Kosaka. 2005, HarperCollins $9.99 (978-0-694-01514-6). A rhyming guessing game in which the reader must supply the name of the Valentine's Day gift. (Rev: SLJ 1/06)

Books for Beginning Readers

6434 Adler, David A. *Bones and the Birthday Mystery* (K–2). Illus. by Barbara Johansen Newman. Series: Jeffrey Bones. 2007, Viking $13.99 (978-0-670-06164-8). 32pp. Bones solves the mystery of a missing card in this funny, accessible fifth volume in the series. Other installments include *Bones and the Cupcake Mystery, Bones and the Dinosaur Mystery* (2005), and *Bones and the Math Test Mystery* (2008). (Rev: BL 5/1/07; SLJ 5/07)

6435 Adler, David A. *Young Cam Jansen and the 100th Day of School Mystery* (1–2). Illus. by Susanna Natti. Series: Viking Easy-to-Read. 2009, Viking $13.99 (978-0-670-06172-3). 32pp. Cam Jansen is back, working on a case involving pizzas missing from the class's "Letter P" party. Earlier volumes in the series include *Young Cam Jansen and the Dinosaur Game* (1996), *Young Cam Jansen and the Baseball Mystery* (1999), *Young Cam Jansen and the Library Mystery* (2001), *Young Cam Jansen and the Double Beach Mystery* (2002), *Young Cam Jansen and the New Girl Mystery* (2004), *Young Cam Jansen and the Substitute Mystery* (2005), *Young Cam Jansen and the Lions' Lunch Mystery* (2007), and *Young Cam Jansen and the Molly Shoe Mystery* (2008). (Rev: BL 7/09)

6436 Alphin, Elaine M. *Dinosaur Hunter* (1–2). Illus. by Don Bolognese. Series: I Can Read Book. 2003, HarperCollins LB $16.89 (978-0-06-028304-9). 48pp. After discovering dinosaur bones on his family's Wyoming ranch in the late 19th century, Ned foils the attempts of a fossil hunter to swindle him out of them. (Rev: BL 9/1/03; HBG 4/04; SLJ 12/03)

6437 Armstrong, Jennifer. *Sunshine, Moonshine* (1–2). Illus. by Lucia Washburn. 1997, Random paper $3.99 (978-0-679-86442-4). A busy day in the life of a young boy is chronicled in this easy-to-read book. (Rev: BL 5/1/97; SLJ 8/97)

6438 Arnold, Caroline. *Wiggle and Waggle* (K–2). Illus. by Mary Peterson. 2007, Charlesbridge $12.95 (978-1-58089-306-0). 48pp. Two worm friends have amusing adventures in this well-designed easy-reader that conveys some information about worms. (Rev: BL 7/07; LMC 1/08; SLJ 11/07)

6439 Arnold, Tedd. *Buzz Boy and Fly Guy* (PS–2). Illus. by author. Series: Fly Guy. 2010, Scholastic paper $5.99 (978-05452227-4-7). 32pp. Buzz creates a book in which his pet fly is now the size of a man and can speak, having adventures with a dragon and pirates. (Rev: BL 9/1/10; SLJ 10/10)

6440 Arnold, Tedd. *Fly Guy and the Frankenfly* (K–2). Illus. by author. 2013, Scholastic $6.99 (978-054549328-4). 32pp. Buzz dreams that Fly Guy has created a scary monster called Frankenfly. Lexile 300 (Rev: BL 7/13)

6441 Arnold, Tedd. *Fly Guy Meets Fly Girl!* (K–2). Illus. by author. Series: Fly Guy. 2010, Scholastic $5.99 (978-0-545-11029-7). 30pp. Fly Guy meets Fly Girl in this offbeat love story; but can they leave Buzz and Liz? (Rev: SLJ 6/1/10)

6442 Arnold, Tedd. *Fly Guy vs. the Fly Swatter!* (PS–2). Series: Fly Guy. 2011, Scholastic $6.99 (978-0-545-31286-8). 30pp. Fly Guy accidentally gets taken along on a school trip to a fly swatter factory in this 10th book in the series. (Rev: SLJ 9/1/11)

6443 Arnold, Tedd. *Hi! Fly Guy!* (K–2). Illus. by author. 2005, Scholastic $5.99 (978-0-439-63903-3). 30pp. Buzz enters a fly in a pet competition, and the gifted insect impresses everyone with its multiple talents. Theodor Seuss Geisel Honor Book. The insect's subsequent feats are recorded in *Shoo, Fly Guy!* and *Super Fly Guy* (2006), *There Was an Old Lady Who Swallowed Fly Guy* (2007), and *Hooray for Fly Guy!* and *Fly High, Fly Guy!* (2008). (Rev: BCCB 10/05; HBG 4/06; LMC 1/06; SLJ 2/06) ∩

6444 Arnold, Tedd. *I Spy Fly Guy!* (1–3). Illus. by author. Series: Fly Guy. 2009, Scholastic $5.99 (978-0-545-11028-0). 32pp. Fly Guy has a narrow escape when he hides in the garbage can during a game of hide-and-seek. ∩ (Rev: BLO 11/1/09; SLJ 12/1/09)

6445 Arnold, Tedd. *Ride, Fly Guy, Ride!* (PS–2). Illus. by author. Series: Fly Guy. 2012, Scholastic paper $6.99 (978-05452227-6-1). 32pp. Fly Guy has a wild time when he is blown out the car window and into a passing truck — then a boat, a train, and an airplane — with Buzz and his dad in hot pursuit. (Rev: BL 3/1/12)

6446 Avi. *Abigail Takes the Wheel* (2–4). Illus. by Don Bolognese. Series: I Can Read. 1999, HarperCollins LB $17.89 (978-0-06-027663-8). 64pp. In this easily read story set in the 1880s, young Abigail steers a freight boat up the Hudson after the mate gets sick. (Rev: BCCB 6/99; BL 4/1/99; HB 3/99; HBG 10/99; SLJ 5/99)

6447 Bader, Bonnie. *Benny the Big Shot Goes to Camp* (1–2). Illus. by Shari Warren. Series: All Aboard Reading. 2003, Grosset paper $3.99 (978-0-448-42894-9). 48pp. Benny's bragging fails to impress his campmates and they steal his "blankie." (Rev: BL 5/15/03; HBG 10/03)

6448 Baker, Keith. *Little Green* (PS–1). Illus. 2001, Harcourt $16.00 (978-0-15-292859-9). 32pp. In this easy reader, a boy is fascinated by the behavior of a hummingbird. (Rev: BCCB 4/01; BL 4/15/01; HBG 10/01; SLJ 4/01)

6449 Baker, Keith. *Lucky Days with Mr. and Mrs. Green* (K–2). Illus. by author. 2005, Harcourt $16.00 (978-0-15-216500-0). 72pp. Mr. Green looks for his wife's lost pearls, guesses the number of gumballs in a jar, and enters a singing contest in the three stories in this chapter book. (Rev: BCCB 4/05; HB 5/05; SLJ 3/05)

6450 Baker, Keith. *On the Go with Mr. and Mrs. Green* (PS–2). Series: Mr. and Mrs. Green. 2006, Harcourt $16.00 (978-0-15-205762-6). 72pp. The further adventures of the affectionate alligators include magic tricks and high technology. (Rev: BL 5/1/06; SLJ 6/06)

6451 Bang-Campbell, Monika. *Little Rat Rides* (2–4). Illus. by Molly Bang. 2004, Harcourt $15.00 (978-0-15-204667-5). 48pp. Although she has long dreamed of riding a horse, just as her father once did, Little Rat is consumed by misgivings when the opportunity to ride finally arrives. Little Rat struggles with learning the violin in a sequel, *Little Rat Makes Music* (2007). (Rev: BL 5/1/04; HB 5/04; SLJ 5/04)

6452 Banks, Kate. *Monkeys and the Universe* (PS–2). Illus. by Tomek Bogacki. 2009, Farrar $14.95 (978-0-374-35028-4). With some mutual disagreement, Max the monkey and his big brother Pete learn about the solar system and the stars; for beginning readers. (Rev: BL 4/1/09; HB 7/09; SLJ 3/09)

6453 Bauer, Marion Dane. *Bear's Hiccups* (1–2). Illus. by Diane D. Hearn. Series: Holiday House Reader. 1998, Holiday House $15.95 (978-0-8234-1339-3). 48pp. A group of animals demands to know if Bear, a grouch who wants to dominate the forest pond, is responsible for the disappearance of Frog. (Rev: BCCB 6/98; BL 5/1/98; HBG 10/98; SLJ 6/98)

6454 Bauer, Marion Dane. *Turtle Dreams* (1–2). Illus. by Diane D. Hearn. Series: Holiday House Reader. 1997, Holiday House LB $14.95 (978-0-8234-1322-5). 48pp. In this easy reader, Turtle goes to sleep for the winter and finds that he has wonderful dreams. (Rev: BL 2/1/98; HBG 3/98; SLJ 1/98)

6455 Bell, Cece. *Rabbit and Robot: The Sleepover* (K–3). Illus. by author. 2012, Candlewick $14.99 (978-0-7636-5475-7). 56pp. Rabbit and his pal Robot have a

fun sleepover together in this sweet story full of light humor. ALA Notable Children's Book. Lexile 360 (Rev: BL 8/12; SLJ 9/12)

6456 Benjamin, A. H. *Jumping Jack* (1–2). Illus. by Garry Parsons. Series: I Am Reading. 2009, Kingfisher paper $3.99 (978-0-7534-6-297-3). 48pp. When Jack's grandmother cooks him a breakfast of jumping beans, suddenly he's bouncing and flying everywhere he goes until his clever grandma solves the problem by baking him leaden brownies. (Rev: BLO 11/15/09; LMC 5–6/10; SLJ 2/1/10)

6457 Björkman, Steve. *Dinosaurs Don't, Dinosaurs Do* (PS–1). Illus. by author. Series: I Like to Read. 2011, Holiday House $14.95 (978-0-8234-2355-2). Unpaged. Simple text and humorous illustrations introduce some basics of good behavior. (Rev: SLJ 11/1/11)

6458 Black, Sonia. *Hanging Out with Mom* (1–2). Illus. by George Ford. 2000, Scholastic paper $3.99 (978-0-590-86636-1). A beginning reader about a day that an African American boy and his mother spend in the park. (Rev: BL 10/1/00)

6459 Blackaby, Susan. *Brownie Groundhog and the February Fox* (1–3). Illus. by Carmen Segovia. 2011, Sterling $14.95 (978-1-4027-4336-8). 24pp. A hungry fox and a clever groundhog become unlikely friends when they discover what they have in common: a longing for spring. (Rev: BLO 12/15/10; LMC 3–4/11; SLJ 2/1/11*)

6460 Blackwood, Gary L. *The Just-So-Woman* (1–3). Illus. by Jane Manning. 2006, HarperCollins $15.99 (978-0-06-057727-8). 48pp. Once upon a time in the days before electricity, the Just-So Woman ran out of soap, butter, and other farm essentials and asked her neighbor, the Any-Way Man, for help, learning an important lesson in the process; a funny book for beginning readers. (Rev: BL 12/1/06; SLJ 11/06)

6461 Blair, Eric, retel. *Belling the Cat: A Retelling of Aesop's Fable* (K–3). Illus. by Dianne Silverman. Series: Read-It! Readers Fairy Tales. 2004, Picture Window LB $19.93 (978-1-4048-0321-3). 24pp. A simple retelling for beginning readers, with brief material on Aesop and on the nature of a fable. Also use *The Shoemaker and His Elves: A Retelling of the Grimms' Fairy Tale*. (Rev: SLJ 8/04)

6462 Bonsall, Crosby. *Mine's the Best* (1–2). Illus. by author. 1997, HarperCollins paper $3.99 (978-0-06-444213-8). 32pp. Two small boys discover they have identical balloons, and then begins the argument — whose is the best?

6463 Bonsall, Crosby. *Piggle* (1–2). Illus. by author. 1973, HarperCollins LB $15.89 (978-0-06-020580-5). 64pp. Homer goes in search of someone to play games with and finds Bear, who enjoys "Piggle" with him. This rhyming spree of nonsense words will please beginning readers. (Rev: HBG 10/02)

6464 Bonsall, Crosby. *Who's a Pest?* (1–3). Illus. by author. 1962, HarperCollins paper $3.99 (978-0-06-444099-8). 64pp. Even though his four sisters, a lizard, a rabbit, and a chipmunk insist that he's a pest, Homer refuses to believe it. (Rev: HBG 10/02)

6465 Bonsall, Crosby. *Who's Afraid of the Dark?* (1–3). Illus. by author. 1980, HarperCollins paper $3.99 (978-0-06-444071-4). A little boy talks about how Stella, his dog, is afraid of the dark. (Rev: HBG 10/02)

6466 Bottner, Barbara. *Bootsie Barker Ballerina* (1–2). Illus. by G. Brian Karas. 1997, HarperCollins LB $15.89 (978-0-06-027101-5). 40pp. Bootsie Barker gets her comeuppance when she tries to bully everyone in her ballet class, including the teacher. (Rev: BL 5/1/97; SLJ 6/97)

6467 Bottner, Barbara. *Two Messy Friends* (K–2). Illus. by author. Series: Hello Reader! 1999, Scholastic paper $3.50 (978-0-590-63285-0). In this beginning reader, two very different friends accommodate their differences because they value their friendship. (Rev: SLJ 8/99)

6468 Bottner, Barbara, and Gerald Kruglik. *Pish and Posh Wish for Fairy Wings* (K–2). Illus. by Barbara Bottner. 2006, HarperCollins $15.99 (978-0-06-051419-8). 48pp. Trainee fairies Pish and Posh learn to cooperate (with a little help from the Monster Under the Bed) in order to make a wise wish and earn their fairy wings. (Rev: BL 12/1/06)

6469 Brenner, Barbara. *Wagon Wheels* (1–3). Illus. by Don Bolognese. 1993, HarperCollins paper $3.99 (978-0-06-444052-3). 64pp. The adventures of an African American family in Kansas in the 1870s.

6470 Bridwell, Norman. *Clifford Makes a Friend* (1). Illus. Series: Hello Reader! 1998, Scholastic paper $3.99 (978-0-590-37930-4). Clifford, the beloved shaggy dog, meets a boy and, after copying his actions, becomes his friend. (Rev: BL 3/15/99)

6471 Brill, Marlene T. *Allen Jay and the Underground Railroad* (1–2). Illus. by Janice L. Porter. Series: On My Own. 1993, Carolrhoda LB $23.93 (978-0-87614-776-4); paper $5.95 (978-0-87614-605-7). 48pp. This story, which is based on fact, tells how a young Quaker child helped a slave to freedom. (Rev: BL 7/93; SLJ 8/93)

6472 Brimner, Larry Dane. *Cats!* (1). Illus. by Tom Payne. Series: Rookie Readers. 2000, Children's Book Pr. paper $4.95 (978-0-516-27075-3). 24pp. After a little girl lets nine cats into her room, they oblige by playing with her in this book for beginning readers. (Rev: BL 2/15/01)

6473 Brimner, Larry Dane. *Twelve Plump Cookies* (1–2). Illus. by Sharon L. Holm. Series: Magic Door to Learning. 2005, The Child's World LB $21.36 (978-1-59296-523-6). 24pp. A young boy bakes a dozen cookies for guests, but when more people than expected show up, he must use his ingenuity to see that everyone gets at least part of a cookie. (Rev: SLJ 12/05)

6474 Brisson, Pat. *Little Sister, Big Sister* (2–3). Illus. 1999, Holt $15.95 (978-0-8050-5887-1). Two sisters, Zelda and Ivy, are sometimes friends and sometimes enemies in these four stories for beginning readers. (Rev: BCCB 3/99; BL 4/15/99; HBG 10/99; SLJ 7/99)

6475 Brown, Charlotte Lewis. *Beyond the Dinosaurs: Monsters of the Air and Sea* (K–3). Illus. by Phil Wilson. 2007, HarperCollins $15.99 (978-0-06-053056-3). 32pp. Prehistoric creatures are featured in this simple illustrated book for beginning readers. (Rev: SLJ 6/07)

6476 Brown, Margaret Wise. *I Like Stars* (1). Illus. by Joan Paley. Series: Road to Reading. 1998, Golden paper $3.99 (978-0-307-26105-2). 32pp. A little rabbit leaves his bed and joins in play with a frog, a bird, and a mouse in this easy-to-read book. (Rev: BL 3/15/99)

6477 Brust, Beth Wagener. *The Great Tulip Trade* (K–2). Illus. by Jenny Mattheson. Series: Step into Reading. 2005, Random LB $11.99 (978-0-375-92573-3); paper $3.99 (978-0-375-82573-6). 48pp. In tulip-crazy 1636 Holland, Anna refuses to trade her most cherished bloom even in exchange for gold and diamonds. (Rev: BL 6/1–15/05)

6478 Buck, Nola. *Sid and Sam* (PS–K). Illus. Series: My First I Can Read Book. 1996, HarperCollins LB $14.89 (978-0-06-025372-1). Sid's song is so long that his friend Sam says, "So long." (Rev: BCCB 7–8/96; BL 8/96; SLJ 6/96)

6479 Bunting, Eve. *Frog and Friends* (1–2). Illus. by Josée Masse. Series: I Am a Reader! 2011, Sleeping Bear $9.95 (978-1-58536-548-7); paper $3.99 (978-1-58536-689-7). 37pp. In three chapters about Frog and his friends a strange round object appears on the pond and causes some consternation; regifting gains acceptance; and an uninvited hippo visits. (Rev: SLJ 10/1/11)

6480 Bunting, Eve. *Frog and Friends: Best Summer Ever* (1–3). Illus. by Josée Masse. Series: I Am a Reader! 2012, Sleeping Bear $9.95 (978-1-58536-550-0); paper $3.99 (978-1-58536-691-0). 48pp. In three simple stories, Frog compares himself to a bat, goes on vacation with more friends than expected, and learns about the stars. (Rev: BLO 5/15/12; SLJ 11/12)

6481 Byars, Betsy. *Boo's Dinosaur* (1–3). Illus. by Erik Brooks. 2006, Holt $15.95 (978-0-8050-7958-6). 41pp. Boo convinces her older brother to join in the fun as she entertains a dinosaur that only she can see in this appealing early chapter book. (Rev: SLJ 9/06)

6482 Cameron, Ann. *Julian, Dream Doctor* (2–4). Illus. by Ann Strugnell. Series: Stepping Stone. 1990, Random LB $11.99 (978-0-679-90524-0); paper $3.99 (978-0-679-80524-3). 40pp. In this warm story of an African American family, Julian wants to discover Dad's idea of a dream birthday present. (Rev: BCCB 3/90; BL 5/15/90; HB 9/90; SLJ 7/90)

6483 Cameron, Ann. *Julian's Glorious Summer* (2–3). Illus. by Dora Leder. 1987, Random paper $3.99 (978-0-394-89117-0). 64pp. Troubles begin for Julian when he lies because he is afraid to ride a bike. Also use two other stories about the ups and downs of this warm African American family: *More Stories Julian Tells* (Knopf 1986); *Julian, Secret Agent* (Random 1988). (Rev: BCCB 12/87; BL 12/15/87; SLJ 12/87)

6484 *Can You Play?* (PS–1). Illus. by Emily Bolam. Series: I'm Going to Read! 2005, Sterling paper $3.95

(978-1-4027-2094-9). Stella and her dog romp through the pages of this curriculum-oriented beginning reader. (Rev: SLJ 9/05)

6485 Caple, Kathy. *Worm Gets a Job* (PS–2). Illus. by author. 2004, Candlewick $15.99 (978-0-7636-1694-6). Worm's efforts to earn money for painting supplies have unexpected consequences. (Rev: SLJ 7/04)

6486 Capucilli, Alyssa Satin. *Bathtime for Biscuit* (1). Illus. by Pat Schories. 1998, HarperCollins LB $17.89 (978-0-06-027938-7). 32pp. A simple story about the problems a little boy has getting his little dog, Biscuit, into the bath. (Rev: BL 11/1/98; HBG 3/99; SLJ 10/98)

6487 Capucilli, Alyssa Satin. *Biscuit* (K–1). Illus. 1996, HarperCollins LB $17.89 (978-0-06-026198-6). 32pp. A dog named Biscuit tries to make his wants known. Also use *Biscuit Finds a Friend* (1997), *Biscuit's New Trick* (2000), *Biscuit Wants to Play* (2001), *Biscuit Goes to School* (2002), and *Biscuit Takes a Walk* (2009). (Rev: BL 8/96; SLJ 7/96)

6488 Capucilli, Alyssa Satin. *Biscuit in the Garden* (PS–K). Illus. by Pat Schories. Series: I Can Read! 2013, HarperCollins $16.99 (978-006193505-3); paper $3.99 (978-00619350-4-6). 32pp. Biscuit the dog is enjoying time outside with a young girl in this story full of nature and animal noises. Lexile AD170 (Rev: BL 5/1/13)

6489 Capucilli, Alyssa Satin. *Inside a Zoo in the City: A Rebus Read-Along Story* (PS–K). Illus. by Tedd Arnold. 2000, Scholastic $11.95 (978-0-590-99715-7). 32pp. Told with pictures that substitute for the names of various animals, this simple rebus book tells how the animals in a zoo actually live in apartments and have to get up in the morning and go to work like other people. (Rev: BL 12/15/00; HBG 10/01; SLJ 3/01)

6490 Capucilli, Alyssa Satin. *Scat, Cat!* (K–1). Illus. by Paul Meisel. 2010, HarperCollins $16.99 (978-0-06-117754-5). 32pp. In this simple book for beginning readers, a lost cat who is shooed away all day eventually finds a porch to curl up on — and is welcomed inside by a young boy in the morning. **℮** (Rev: BL 12/15/10; SLJ 10/1/10)

6491 Carris, Joan. *Welcome to the Bed and Biscuit* (1–3). Illus. by Noah Z. Jones. 2006, Candlewick $15.99 (978-0-7636-2151-3). 128pp. Grandpa Bender runs an animal boardinghouse but his personal pets — a mynah, a cat, and a small pig — have extra privileges and are miffed when Grandpa brings home a tiny puppy. (Rev: BL 10/1/06; SLJ 10/06)

6492 Carter, Candace. *Sid's Surprise* (PS–K). Illus. by Joung Un Kim. Series: Green Light Reader. 2005, Harcourt $12.95 (978-0-15-205183-9); paper $3.95 (978-0-15-205182-2). 32pp. This easy chapter book features a little snake who is thrilled to finally have a rattle — just like the big snakes. (Rev: BL 3/1/05)

6493 Catalanotto, Peter, and Pamela Schembri. *The Veterans Day Visitor* (1–2). Illus. by Peter Catalanotto. Series: 2nd-Grade Friends. 2008, Holt $15.95 (978-0-8050-7840-4). This beginning chapter book touches on both Veterans Day and narcolepsy as Emily worries

that her grandfather will fall asleep in front of her class. (Rev: BLO 7/31/08; HB 9/08)

6494 Cazet, Denys. *The Case of the Missing Jelly Donut* (1–3). Illus. Series: An I Can Read Book. 2005, HarperCollins $15.99 (978-0-06-073007-9). 48pp. Minnie and Moo, bovine detectives, go undercover to track down a suspected donut thief in this entertaining easy chapter book. (Rev: BL 9/1/05; SLJ 10/05)

6495 Cazet, Denys. *Minnie and Moo and the Seven Wonders of the World* (2–4). Illus. by author. 2003, Simon & Schuster $16.95 (978-0-689-85330-2). 134pp. A chapter book in which bovine friends Minnie and Moo seek to save the farm by conducting tours of the "Seven Wonders of the World." (Rev: HBG 4/04; SLJ 11/03)

6496 Cazet, Denys. *Minnie and Moo: The Night of the Living Bed* (1–2). Illus. by author. Series: I Can Read Book. 2003, HarperCollins LB $16.99 (978-0-06-000503-0). 48pp. It's Halloween, and cows Minnie and Moo team up to collect as much chocolate as possible in this book for beginning readers. (Rev: BL 9/1/03; HBG 4/04; SLJ 9/03)

6497 Cazet, Denys. *Minnie and Moo: Wanted Dead or Alive* (K–2). Series: I Can Read. 2006, HarperCollins $15.99 (978-0-06-073010-9). 48pp. Cows Minnie and Moo go to the bank to try to arrange a loan for Mr. Farmer but are mistaken for notorious bank robbers. Also recommended are *Minnie and Moo Go Dancing* and *Minnie and Moo Go to the Moon* (both 1998), *Minnie and Moo Go to Paris* and *Minnie and Moo Save the Earth* (both 1999), *Minnie and Moo and the Musk of Zorro* (2000), and *Minnie and Moo Meet Frankenswine* (2001). (Rev: BL 8/06; SLJ 8/06)

6498 Cazet, Denys. *The Octopus* (1–3). Illus. Series: I Can Read. 2005, HarperCollins LB $16.89 (978-0-06-051089-3). 48pp. Barney the puppy is miserable with chicken pox, so Grandpa tells him an elaborate tall tale about his triumph over an octopus. (Rev: BL 1/1–15/05; SLJ 1/05)

6499 Cazet, Denys. *A Snout for Chocolate* (K–2). Illus. by author. Series: Grandpa Spanielson's Chicken Pox Stories. 2006, HarperCollins $15.99 (978-0-06-051093-0). 48pp. To distract his grandson from a continuing itchy case of chicken pox, Grandpa Spanielson tells the boy how he saved Mrs. Piggerman's life when he was fire chief. Also use *The Shrunken Head* (2007). (Rev: SLJ 1/06)

6500 Chaconas, Dori. *The Collectors* (K–2). Illus. by Lisa McCue. 2008, Viking $13.99 (978-0-670-06286-7). 32pp. When possum Fuzz's "stones" hatch into ducklings, mother duck pushes him into her nest and sits on him and Cork, the muskrat, must come to the rescue. (Rev: BL 3/1/08; SLJ 3/08)

6501 Chaconas, Dori. *Cork and Fuzz* (K–2). Illus. by Lisa McCue. 2005, Viking $13.99 (978-0-670-03602-8). 32pp. Cork and Fuzz, a muskrat and a possum, both bored and lonely, try to overlook their differences and find a common interest. (Rev: SLJ 5/05)

6502 Chaconas, Dori. *Cork and Fuzz: Finders Keepers* (PS–2). Illus. by Lisa McCue. Series: Viking Easy-to-Read. 2009, Viking $13.99 (978-0-670-01113-1). This friendship story has the short muskrat and the tall possum arguing over a green stone, but harmony is soon restored. (Rev: BL 2/1/09; SLJ 1/09)

6503 Chaconas, Dori. *Cork and Fuzz: Short and Tall* (PS–2). Illus. by Lisa McCue. Series: Viking Easy-to-Read. 2006, Viking $13.99 (978-0-670-05985-0). 32pp. The friendship between Cork the muskrat and Fuzz the possum is tested over their differences in size. Also use *Cork and Fuzz: Good Sports* (2007). (Rev: BL 1/1–15/06; SLJ 4/06)

6504 Charles, Veronika M. *Don't Go into the Forest!* (2–3). Illus. by Leanne Franson. Series: Easy-to-Read Spooky Tales. 2001, Stoddart paper $5.95 (978-0-7737-6190-2). 56pp. Young boys tell each other scary stories while they contemplate entering a forest at night. (Rev: SLJ 1/02)

6505 Charles, Veronika M. *Don't Open the Door!* (2–3). Illus. by Leanne Franson. 2001, Stoddart paper $5.95 (978-0-7737-6137-7). 56pp. During a sleepover at the narrator's house, the guests enjoy telling each other scary stories. (Rev: BL 4/15/01; SLJ 9/01)

6506 Chocolate, Deborah N. *Pigs Can Fly* (2–4). Illus. by Leslie Tryon. 2004, Cricket $15.95 (978-0-8126-2706-0). 64pp. In this engaging collection of four stories, Harriet the potbellied pig realizes her dream of flying, helps a friend overcome her fear of heights, competes in a swimming contest, and nearly kills Homer Mouse with kindness. (Rev: BL 5/1/04; SLJ 5/04)

6507 *A Class Play with Ms. Vanilla* (PS–2). Illus. by Martha Gradisher. Series: I'm Going to Read! 2005, Sterling LB $11.95 (978-1-4027-2087-1); paper $3.95 (978-1-4027-2108-3). A class production of Little Red Riding Hood doesn't turn out quite as the students expected in this easy reader. (Rev: SLJ 9/05)

6508 Cleary, Beverly. *Muggie Maggie* (2–3). Illus. by Kay Life. 1990, Avon paper $5.99 (978-0-380-71087-4). Third-grader Maggie decides that learning to write is not necessary for a girl who can use a computer. (Rev: BCCB 6/90; BL 3/15/90; HB 11/90; SLJ 6/90)

6509 Clements, Andrew. *Dolores and the Big Fire: A True Story* (1–2). Illus. by Ellen Beier. Series: Pets to the Rescue. 2002, Simon & Schuster $15.00 (978-0-689-82916-1). Dolores, a cat who is afraid of the dark, manages to save her master when their house catches fire. (Rev: BL 6/1–15/02; HBG 10/02; SLJ 5/02)

6510 Coerr, Eleanor. *Buffalo Bill and the Pony Express* (2–4). Illus. by Don Bolognese. 1995, HarperCollins LB $15.89 (978-0-06-023373-0). 64pp. Billy outsmarts some Indians and scares off a pack of wolves in this easily read adventure. (Rev: BCCB 4/95; BL 4/15/95; HB 7/95; SLJ 5/95)

6511 Coerr, Eleanor. *The Josefina Story Quilt* (1–3). Illus. by Bruce Degen. 1986, HarperCollins LB $16.89 (978-0-06-021349-7); paper $3.99 (978-0-06-444129-2). 64pp. Faith's sorrow at the death of her pet hen during their trip west to California is softened by the quilt she sews in remembrance. (Rev: BCCB 5/86; BL 3/15/86; SLJ 5/86)

6512 Cohen, Caron L. *How Many Fish?* (1–2). Illus. by S. D. Schindler. Series: My First I Can Read Book. 1998, HarperCollins paper $12.95 (978-0-06-027713-0). 32pp. A fish is trapped under a child's upside-down pail, but later it is freed in this easy-to-read adventure. (Rev: BL 2/1/98; HBG 10/98; SLJ 2/98)

6513 Cole, Joanna. *The Missing Tooth* (1–3). Illus. by Marylin Hafner. 1989, Random paper $3.99 (978-0-394-89279-5). 48pp. Arlo is upset when best friend Robby loses a second tooth and he doesn't. (Rev: BL 3/1/89; SLJ 5/89)

6514 Cole, Joanna. *Norma Jean, Jumping Bean* (1–3). Illus. 1987, Random paper $3.99 (978-0-394-88668-8). 48pp. Norma Jean, a kangaroo child, stops jumping when her feelings are ruffled, until field day at school. (Rev: BCCB 6/87; BL 6/1/87; SLJ 6–7/87)

6515 Collicott, Sharleen. *Mildred and Sam and Their Babies* (PS–2). Illus. Series: I Can Read! 2005, HarperCollins LB $16.89 (978-0-06-058112-1). For beginning readers, this is a simple story about eight baby mice growing up in a safe and loving home. (Rev: BL 5/15/05)

6516 Cooper, Ilene. *Absolutely Lucy* (2–4). Illus. Series: Read to Reading. 2000, Golden LB $10.99 (978-0-307-48502-1); paper $3.99 (978-0-307-26502-9). 76pp. An easy chapter book about a boy whose beagle puppy helps him conquer his shyness. (Rev: BCCB 5/00; BL 3/15/00; SLJ 3/01)

6517 Cooper, Ilene. *The Annoying Team* (2–4). Illus. by Colin Paine. Series: Road to Reading. 2002, Random LB $11.99 (978-0-307-46512-2); paper $3.99 (978-0-307-26512-8). 80pp. In this beginning chapter book, Tim tries a new approach to combat the bullying of Big Jon Ferguson. (Rev: BL 6/1–15/02; HBG 10/02)

6518 Cooper, Susan. *The Magician's Boy* (2–4). Illus. by Serena Riglietti. 2005, Simon & Schuster $15.95 (978-0-689-87622-6). 112pp. The Boy, apprenticed to a master magician, is dispatched to find a missing puppet and in the course of his search ends up in a land filled with characters from familiar fairy tales and nursery rhymes. (Rev: BL 1/1–15/05; SLJ 3/05)

6519 Cornwell, Nicki. *Christophe's Story* (2–4). Illus. by Karin Littlewood. 2007, Frances Lincoln $14.95 (978-1-84507-765-5). 96pp. Cristophe, a Rwandan refugee living in England, tells his new classmates about his family's escape, including the death of his baby brother. (Rev: BL 12/15/07)

6520 Cosby, Bill. *The Best Way to Play* (2–4). Illus. 1997, Scholastic $13.95 (978-0-590-13756-0); paper $3.99 (978-0-590-95617-8). 40pp. Little Bill wants a $50 video game but finds that he can have more fun making up a game with his friends. Also use *The Meanest Thing To Say* and *The Treasure Hunt* (both 1997). (Rev: BL 2/15/98; HBG 3/98; SLJ 12/97)

6521 Cosby, Bill. *My Big Lie* (2–4). Illus. 1999, Scholastic $15.95 (978-0-590-52160-4); paper $3.99 (978-

0-590-52161-1). Late for dinner because of a baseball game, Little Bill tells a lie to protect himself and only gets into worse trouble. (Rev: BL 10/15/99; HBG 10/99; SLJ 8/99)

6522 Cosby, Bill. *One Dark and Scary Night* (K–2). Illus. by Varnette P. Honeywood. Series: Little Bill. 1999, Scholastic $13.95 (978-0-590-51475-0); paper $3.99 (978-0-590-51476-7). In this beginning reader, Little Bill learns to conquer his fears concerning noises he hears in the night. (Rev: HBG 10/99; SLJ 7/99)

6523 Cosby, Bill. *Shipwreck Saturday* (2–4). Illus. Series: Little Bill. 1998, Scholastic $13.95 (978-0-590-16400-9); paper $3.99 (978-0-590-95620-8). 40pp. Although Little Bill's boat is destroyed on its first voyage, a friend uses its parts for a kite. (Rev: BL 5/15/98; SLJ 6/98)

6524 Cosby, Bill. *Super-Fine Valentine* (2–4). Illus. Series: Little Bill. 1998, Scholastic $13.95 (978-0-590-16401-6). 40pp. Using eye-catching artwork, this is the simple story of Little Bill who is reluctant to give his friend Mia a Valentine until some of his other friends give her one first. (Rev: BL 5/15/98; SLJ 6/98)

6525 Cottringer, Anne. *Movie Magic: A Star Is Born* (2–4). Illus. by Roger Stewart. Series: Eyewitness Reader. 1999, DK $12.99 (978-0-7894-4009-9); paper $3.99 (978-0-7894-4008-2). 48pp. In this easy reader, which uses color photos to show the movie-making process, a young African American girl gets a part in a science fiction movie. (Rev: SLJ 8/99)

6526 Coxe, Molly. *Big Egg* (1–2). Illus. 1997, Random LB $11.99 (978-0-679-98126-8); paper $3.99 (978-0-679-88126-1). For the beginning reader, this story tells what happens after Hen finds a huge egg among her little ones. (Rev: BL 5/1/97)

6527 Cristaldi, Kathryn. *Baseball Ballerina* (1–3). Illus. by Abby Carter. Series: Step into Reading. 1992, Random paper $3.99 (978-0-679-81734-5). 48pp. A young girl who loves baseball is afraid that her friends will find out she is taking ballet lessons. (Rev: BCCB 6/92; BL 6/1/92; SLJ 9/92)

6528 Cristaldi, Kathryn. *Princess Lulu Goes to Camp* (1–2). Illus. by Heather H. Maione. 1997, Penguin paper $3.99 (978-0-448-41125-5). 48pp. An easy reader about the obnoxious Princess Lulu at a summer camp. (Rev: BL 8/97; SLJ 12/97)

6529 Cushman, Doug. *Dirk Bones and the Mystery of the Haunted House* (K–2). Series: I Can Read! 2006, HarperCollins $16.99 (978-0-06-073764-1). Dirk Bones, a skeleton reporter for the "Ghostly Tombs," investigates a haunted house whose ghostly residents are spooked by unexplained noises. (Rev: BL 8/06; SLJ 7/06)

6530 Cushman, Doug. *Dirk Bones and the Mystery of the Missing Books* (K–2). Illus. by author. Series: I Can Read. 2009, HarperCollins $16.99 (978-0-06-073768-9). 32pp. Dirk, the skeleton detective, is looking into the case of a missing manuscript when he discovers that even more books have disappeared and there is a suspicious plant in the area. (Rev: BL 5/1/09; SLJ 5/09)

6531 Cushman, Doug. *Inspector Hopper's Mystery Year* (1–3). Illus. by author. Series: I Can Read. 2003, HarperCollins LB $16.89 (978-0-06-008963-4). Grasshopper Inspector Hopper and his assistant, McBugg, are kept busy throughout the year with seasonal mysteries to solve. (Rev: HBG 10/03; SLJ 5/03)

6532 Cutler, Jane. *Rose and Riley Come and Go* (K–2). Illus. by Thomas F. Yezerski. 2005, Farrar $15.00 (978-0-374-36341-3). 48pp. Friends Rose, a tiny vole, and Riley, a lively groundhog, make discoveries about nature in three episodic stories for beginning readers that feature silly wordplay and detailed illustrations. (Rev: BL 6/1–15/05)

6533 Cuyler, Margery. *Tick Tock Clock* (PS–K). Illus. by Robert Neubecker. Series: I Can Read. 2012, HarperCollins $16.99 (978-006136309-2). 32pp. Children can reinforce their time-telling skills with this simple account of twins' activities at various times during the day. (Rev: BL 1/1/12; SLJ 1/12)

6534 Dahl, Michael. *The Tall, Tall Slide* (K–2). Illus. by Sara Gray. Series: Read It! Readers. 2006, Picture Window LB $19.93 (978-1-4048-1186-7). 32pp. On a hot summer day, new friends help Tina to overcome her fears of the tall slide at the local swimming pool. (Rev: BL 3/1/06)

6535 Danziger, Paula. *Get Ready for Second Grade, Amber Brown* (1–3). Illus. by Tony Ross. 2002, Penguin $13.99 (978-0-399-23607-5). 48pp. Amber's concerns about the new 2nd-grade teacher turn out to be unfounded in this prequel for beginning readers. (Rev: BL 11/1/02; HBG 10/02; SLJ 7/02)

6536 Danziger, Paula. *It's a Fair Day, Amber Brown* (1–3). Illus. by Tony Ross. 2002, Penguin $14.99 (978-0-399-23606-8). 48pp. Amber and her family spend an enjoyable day at the fair despite some arguments and Amber getting lost. (Rev: BL 11/1/02; HBG 10/02; SLJ 7/02)

6537 Danziger, Paula. *It's Justin Time, Amber Brown* (1–3). Illus. by Tony Ross. 2001, Penguin $13.99 (978-0-399-23470-5). 48pp. In this beginning reader, Amber Brown, age 7, gets her wish of a watch for her birthday now that she has learned to tell the time. (Rev: HBG 10/01; SLJ 3/01)

6538 Danziger, Paula. *Orange You Glad It's Halloween, Amber Brown?* (1–3). Illus. by Tony Ross. 2005, Penguin $13.99 (978-0-399-23471-2). 48pp. In addition to planning for Halloween, Amber has concerns about school and family life in this easy-reader that also features her best friend Justin. (Rev: BL 5/15/05)

6539 Danziger, Paula. *What a Trip, Amber Brown* (K–3). Illus. by Tony Ross. Series: A Is for Amber. 2001, Penguin $13.99 (978-0-399-23469-9). 48pp. Amber and Justin enjoy an on-again off-again friendship on a vacation in the "Poke a nose." (Rev: HBG 10/01; SLJ 4/01)

6540 Day, Alexandra. *Carl and the Baby Duck* (PS–1). Illus. by author. Series: My Readers. 2011, Macmillan $15.99 (978-0-312-62484-2); paper $3.99 (978-0-312-62-485-9). 32pp. Friendly rottweiler Carl helps Mama

Duck search for her missing offspring. (Rev: BL 6/1/11; SLJ 5/1/11)

6541 Dean, James. *Pete the Cat: Pete's Big Lunch* (PS–1). Illus. by author. Series: I Can Read. 2013, HarperCollins $16.99 (978-0-06-211070-1). 32pp. A simple story for beginning readers about Pete the cat's overly ambitious sandwich. (Rev: BL 4/1/13; SLJ 7/13)

6542 Dean, James. *Pete the Cat: Play Ball!* (PS–K). Illus. by author. Series: I Can Read. 2013, HarperCollins $16.99 (978-0-06-211067-1); paper $3.99 (978-0-06-211-066-4). 32pp. The Rocks are playing the Rolls in a big game, and Pete the Cat does his best although he doesn't excel. (Rev: BLO 6/13; SLJ 7/13)

6543 deGroat, Diane. *Gilbert, the Surfer Dude* (K–2). Illus. by author. Series: I Can Read Book: Gilbert and Friends. 2009, HarperCollins $16.99 (978-0-06-125211-2). 32pp. Gilbert the possum has forgotten his bathing suit and buys some too-large "Surfer Dude" trunks only to discover that oversize trunks and surfing don't mix well. (Rev: BL 3/15/09; SLJ 6/09)

6544 Denton, Kady M. *Watch Out, William!* (K–2). Series: I Am Reading. 2006, Kingfisher paper $3.95 (978-0-7534-5960-7). 48pp. Three short chapters recount everyday adventures of William and his little sister Jane. (Rev: BL 5/1/06; SLJ 8/06)

6545 dePaola, Tomie. *Hide-and-Seek All Week* (1–2). Illus. Series: The Barkers. 2001, Penguin paper $3.99 (978-0-448-42545-0). 32pp. Moffie and Morgie and friends decide they want to play hide-and-seek during recess, but can't decide on the rules. (Rev: BL 2/1/02; HBG 3/02; SLJ 2/02)

6546 dePaola, Tomie. *Kit and Kat* (1–2). Illus. 1994, Penguin paper $3.99 (978-0-448-40748-7). 32pp. Three easily read stories about the everyday adventures of Kit and Kat, the Kitten Kids. (Rev: BL 1/1/95)

6547 deRubertis, Barbara. *Deena's Lucky Penny* (1–2). Illus. by Joan Holub and Cynthia Fisher. Series: Math Matters. 1999, Kane paper $4.95 (978-1-57565-091-3). 32pp. This easy reader introduces the simple arithmetic of counting money, through the story of a young girl who saves to buy her mother a birthday present. (Rev: BL 12/1/99)

6548 DiCamillo, Kate. *Mercy Watson Fights Crime* (PS–2). Illus. by Chris Van Dusen. 2006, Candlewick $12.99 (978-0-7636-2590-0). 70pp. Mercy Watson, the crime-fighting pig, nabs a toaster thief red-handed. (Rev: SLJ 11/06*)

6549 DiCamillo, Kate. *Mercy Watson Princess in Disguise* (PS–2). Illus. by Chris Van Dusen. 2007, Candlewick $12.99 (978-0-7636-3014-0). 80pp. Mercy the pig is up to her old shenanigans as she pursues the promise of goodies while trick-or-treating in her Halloween princess costume. (Rev: BL 7/07; SLJ 8/07)

6550 DiCamillo, Kate. *Mercy Watson to the Rescue* (PS–2). Illus. by Chris Van Dusen. 2005, Candlewick $12.99 (978-0-7636-2270-1). The Watsons love Mercy, their pig, so much that they invite her to share their bed, a decision with disastrous consequences; the first in a

new series of chapter books for beginning readers. (Rev: BCCB 12/05; BL 8/05*; HBG 4/06; LMC 1/06; SLJ 10/05)

6551 Donahue, Jill L. *Benny and the Birthday Gift* (1–2). Illus. by Burak Senturk. 2007, Picture Window LB $19.93 (978-1-4048-3164-3). 24pp. Beginning readers will build their confidence with this simple story about Benny's search for a friend's birthday gift. (Rev: SLJ 7/07)

6552 Donnelly, Judy. *The Titanic: Lost . . . and Found* (2–4). Illus. by Keith Kohler. 1987, Random paper $3.99 (978-0-394-88669-5). 48pp. In a simple account the author describes the sinking of the *Titanic* and its rediscovery. (Rev: BCCB 6/87; BL 6/1/87; SLJ 6–7/87)

6553 Donnelly, Judy. *Tut's Mummy: Lost . . . and Found* (2–3). Illus. by James Watling. 1988, Random paper $3.99 (978-0-394-89189-7). 48pp. The story of the 20th-century discovery of King Tut's tomb. (Rev: BL 10/1/88; SLJ 10/88)

6554 Dotlich, Rebecca. *Away We Go!* (PS). Illus. by Dan Yaccarino. Series: Growing Tree. 2000, HarperCollins $9.95 (978-0-694-01393-7). 24pp. All kinds of vehicles — from a school bus and jumbo jet to a wheelchair and sled — are pictured along with people in motion in this easy-to-read book. (Rev: BL 9/1/00; HBG 3/01; SLJ 11/00)

6555 Dotlich, Rebecca Kai. *Peanut and Pearl's Picnic Adventure* (PS–1). Illus. by R. W. Alley. Series: I Can Read. 2007, HarperCollins $15.99 (978-0-06-054920-6). 32pp. Peanut and Pearl set off on a picnic but then become separated and cannot find each other. (Rev: BL 5/1/07; SLJ 10/07)

6556 Duey, Kathleen. *Moonsilver: The Unicorn's Secret #1* (2–4). Illus. by Omar Rayyan. 2001, Simon & Schuster paper $3.99 (978-0-689-84269-6). 80pp. This alluring fantasy tale for younger readers introduces a young girl who finds a mysterious white mare with a scar on its forehead. (Rev: BL 1/1–15/02; SLJ 12/01)

6557 Duey, Kathleen. *The Mountains of the Moon* (2–4). Illus. by Omar Rayyan. Series: Ready-for-Chapters Unicorn's Secret. 2002, Simon & Schuster paper $3.99 (978-0-689-84272-6). 80pp. The fourth episode in the continuing magical story of Heart and her unicorns, for beginning readers. Also use the third book in the series, *The Silver Bracelet* (2002). (Rev: BL 9/1/02; HBG 3/03)

6558 Duey, Kathleen. *The Sunset Gates* (2–4). Illus. by Omar Rayyan. Series: Unicorn's Secret. 2002, Simon & Schuster paper $3.99 (978-0-689-85346-3). 80pp. The adventures of Heart Avamir, who is on the run in an effort to save two unicorns, continue in this easy-reader as she travels with gypsies and learns to read. Also use *True Heart* (2003). (Rev: BL 3/1/03; HBG 10/03)

6559 Durant, Alan. *Brown Bear Gets in Shape* (K–2). Illus. by Annabel Hudson. Series: I Am Reading. 2004, Kingfisher paper $3.95 (978-0-7534-5797-9). 45pp. Brown Bear is determined to get in shape, and tries copying Bunny and Chimp's diet and exercise regimens. (Rev: SLJ 8/04)

6560 Dussling, Jennifer. *Fair Is Fair!* (1–2). Illus. by Diane Palmisciano. Series: Math Matters. 2003, Kane paper $4.99 (978-1-57565-131-6). 32pp. Marco's skill with bar graphs helps him persuade his father to raise his allowance. (Rev: SLJ 2/04)

6561 Eastman, P. D. *Are You My Mother?* (1–3). Illus. by author. 1960, Random LB $13.99 (978-0-394-90018-6). 64pp. A bird falls from the nest and looks for its mother.

6562 Eastman, Peter. *Fred and Ted Go Camping* (PS–2). Illus. by author. Series: Beginner Books. 2005, Random $8.99 (978-0-375-82965-9). Two dog friends enjoy each other's company on a camping trip in this book for beginning readers. (Rev: SLJ 7/05)

6563 Eaton, Deborah. *My Wild Woolly* (K–2). Illus. by G. Brian Karas. Series: Green Light Readers. 2005, Harcourt $12.95 (978-0-15-205148-8). 24pp. A young boy spends an entertaining afternoon playing in his backyard with a "wild woolly," a creature the boy's mother claims does not exist. (Rev: BL 11/1/05)

6564 Egan, Tim. *Dodsworth in London* (K–2). Illus. by author. Series: Dodsworth. 2009, Houghton Mifflin $15 (978-0-547-13816-9). Unpaged. Dodsworth and his duck friend become separated on a trip to London when there is some confusion with the Queen's duck. Lexile 260L (Rev: HB 11–12/09; SLJ 1/1/10)

6565 Egan, Tim. *Dodsworth in New York* (1–2). Illus. by author. 2007, Houghton $15.00 (978-0-618-77708-2). 48pp. Dodsworth the mouse sets off for New York only to find that his friend Hodges's duck has come along for the ride. (Rev: BCCB 10/07; BL 10/15/07; HB 9/07; SLJ 11/07)

6566 Egan, Tim. *Dodsworth in Rome* (K–2). Illus. by author. Series: Dodsworth. 2011, Houghton Mifflin $14.99 (978-0-547-39006-2). Unpaged. Dodsworth and his bouncy, wayward duck take a trip to Rome to see the Sistine Chapel, eat pizza, and take coins from the Trevi Fountain. (Rev: HB 5–6/11; SLJ 4/11)

6567 Egan, Tim. *Dodsworth in Tokyo* (K–3). Illus. by author. Series: Dodsworth. 2013, Houghton Mifflin $14.99 (978-0-547-87745-7). 48pp. Taking his accident-prone duck to Tokyo is a risky idea, but Dodsworth is pleased when the duck mainly stays out of trouble. Lexile 360 (Rev: BL 5/1/13; HB 3–4/13; LMC 8–9/13; SLJ 3/13)

6568 Ehrlich, Amy. *Bravo, Kazam!* (PS–K). Illus. by Barney Saltzberg. Series: Brand New Readers. 2002, Candlewick paper $4.99 (978-0-7636-1316-7). 40pp. In this beginning reader illustrated with cartoons, a rabbit is chased by a pack of magical cards. (Rev: BL 4/15/02)

6569 Emberley, Rebecca, and Ed Emberley. *Mice on Ice* (PS–1). Illus. by Rebecca Emberley. Series: I Like to Read. 2012, Holiday $14.95 (978-0-8234-2576-1). 32pp. Beginning readers will enjoy this day skating on the ice with mice and a friendly cat. (Rev: BL 10/15/12; SLJ 8/12)

6570 Emerson, Carl. *The Autumn Leaf* (K–2). Illus. by Cori Doerrfeld. Series: Read-It! Readers: Science. 2008, Picture Window LB $19.93 (978-1-4048-2624-3); paper $3.95 (978-1-4048-4755-2). 32pp. Owen and Emma ex-

plore how a change of weather changes a tree in this book for beginning readers. Also use *The Busy Spring, The Cold Winter Day,* and *The Summer Playground* (all 2008). (Rev: SLJ 12/08)

6571 Erickson, John R. *Hank the Cowdog: The Case of the Haystack Kitties* (2–3). Illus. by Gerald L. Holmes. Series: Hank the Cowdog. 1998, Gulf $14.95 (978-0-87719-338-8). 113pp. Hank's many adventures on the ranch include being threatened by a bull and saving a family of kittens. (Rev: SLJ 11/98)

6572 Farley, Robin. *Mia and the Big Sister Ballet* (PS–1). Illus. by Olga Ivanov. Series: I Can Read. 2012, HarperCollins paper $3.99 (978-00617330-7-9). 32pp. Aspiring feline ballerina Mia is conflicted when she watches her big sister perform on stage. (Rev: BL 8/12)

6573 Farley, Robin. *Mia and the Too Big Tutu* (PS–1). Illus. by Aleksey Ivanov and Olga Ivanov. Series: I Can Read!: My First Shared Reading. 2010, HarperCollins $16.99 (978-0-06-173302-4); LB $3.99 (978-0-06-173301-7). 32pp. Mia the cat is so excited about going to dance class that she accidentally takes her older sister's tutu. (Rev: SLJ 10/1/10)

6574 Feldman, Thea. *Harry Cat and Tucker Mouse: Tucker's Beetle Band* (1–3). Illus. by Olga Ivanov and Aleksey Ivanov. Series: My Readers. 2011, Square Fish $15.99 (978-0-312-62575-7); paper $3.99 (978-0-312-62576-4). 32pp. Chester the Cricket is called in to play drums for a beetle band that's been disturbing his friends' slumber. **e** Lexile 500L (Rev: SLJ 5/1/11)

6575 Finch, Margo. *The Lunch Bunch* (K–2). Photos by Dorothy Handelman. Series: Real Kids Readers. 1998, Millbrook LB $16.90 (978-0-7613-2005-0); paper $4.99 (978-0-7613-2030-2). 32pp. A new girl at school searches for friends in this enjoyable beginning reader. (Rev: SLJ 7/98)

6576 Fine, Anne. *The Jamie and Angus Stories* (2–4). Illus. by Penny Dale. 2002, Candlewick $15.99 (978-0-7636-1862-9). 112pp. Jamie and toy bull Angus have a variety of gentle adventures in these six stories for beginning chapter-book readers. (Rev: BCCB 10/02; BL 11/15/02; HB 1/03*; HBG 3/03; SLJ 9/02)

6577 Fine, Annie. *Jamie and Angus Together* (PS–2). Illus. by Penny Dale. 2007, Candlewick $15.99 (978-0-7636-3374-5). 112pp. The six short stories in this engaging chapter book follow Jamie as he plays with his beloved stuffed animal Angus; a sequel to *The Jamie and Angus Stories* (2002). (Rev: BL 6/1–15/07; SLJ 8/07)

6578 Florie, Christine. *Lara Ladybug* (PS–1). Illus. by Danny Brooks Dalby. Series: Rookie Reader. 2005, Children's Pr. LB $19.50 (978-0-516-25137-0); paper $4.95 (978-0-516-25281-0). 23pp. Lara has lost her spots in this book for beginning readers illustrated with collages. (Rev: SLJ 7/05)

6579 Floyd, Lucy. *A Place for Nicholas* (PS–2). Illus. by David McPhail. Series: Green Light Reader. 2005, Harcourt paper $3.95 (978-0-15-205149-5). 24pp. Nicholas longs for a space of his own in this reprint of a 1997 title. (Rev: BL 2/15/05)

6580 Ford, Bernette. *Don't Hit Me!* (K–1). Illus. by Gary Grier. Series: Just for You! 2004, Scholastic paper $3.99 (978-0-439-56860-9). 32pp. A simple easy-reader story about friends agreeing to disagree, featuring African Americans. Also use *Hurry Up!!* (2004). (Rev: SLJ 1/05)

6581 Ford, Juwanda G. *Shop Talk* (K–3). Illus. by Jim Hoston. Series: Just for You! 2004, Scholastic paper $3.99 (978-0-439-56873-9). 32pp. A simple easy-reader story about a visit to the barbershop, featuring African Americans. (Rev: SLJ 1/05)

6582 Ford, Juwanda G. *Sunday Best* (K–3). Illus. by Colin Bootman. Series: Just for You! 2004, Scholastic paper $3.99 (978-0-439-56854-8). 32pp. An African American family enjoys a weekend together. (Rev: SLJ 1/05)

6583 Freeman, Martha. *Mrs. Wow Never Wanted a Cow* (K–2). Illus. by Steven Salerno. 2006, Random $8.99 (978-0-375-83418-9). Mrs. Wow's pets change their ways when a cow becomes a member of the family in this humorous brightly illustrated book for beginning readers. (Rev: SLJ 6/06)

6584 Galan, Ana. *Who Wears Glasses?* (K–2). Illus. by Seb Burnett. 2010, Scholastic paper $3.99 (978-0-545-21020-1). Unpaged. Rhyming text and illustrations reveal animals wearing all kinds of glasses. (Rev: SLJ 9/1/10)

6585 Gantos, Jack. *Rotten Ralph Helps Out* (1–2). Illus. by Nicole Rubel. Series: Rotten Ralph Rotten Reader. 2001, Farrar $14.00 (978-0-374-36355-0). 48pp. Ralph the rotten cat helps — or rather hinders — Sarah with her project on ancient Egypt. Also use *Practice Makes Perfect for Rotten Ralph* (2002) and *Best in Show for Rotten Ralph* (2005). (Rev: BL 7/01; HB 9/01; HBG 3/02; SLJ 8/01)

6586 Gauthier, Gail. *A Girl, a Boy, and Three Robbers* (2–4). Illus. by Joe Cepeda. 2008, Putnam $14.99 (978-0-399-24690-6). 87pp. Imaginative Hannah forces Brandon, who would prefer to watch television, to go along with her ideas; but then her wild stories about the children next door seem to come true and Hannah's cat must be rescued. (Rev: HB 9/08; LMC 11/08; SLJ 11/08)

6587 George, Jean Craighead. *Goose and Duck* (PS–2). Illus. by Priscilla Lamont. 2008, HarperCollins $16.99 (978-0-06-117076-8). 48pp. In this humorous book for beginning readers, a goose imitates the actions of a boy while a duck follows the behavior of the goose. (Rev: BCCB 2/08; BL 12/1/07; SLJ 2/08)

6588 George, Kallie. *Spark* (K–3). Illus. by Genevieve Cote. Series: Tiny Tails. 2013, Simply Read $12.95 (978-192701824-8). 44pp. Spark may be a little dragon, but he has a huge flame — and he just can't seem to control it. (Rev: BL 11/1/13; SLJ 12/13)

6589 George, Olivia. *My Birthday Cake* (K–2). Illus. by Martha Aviles. Series: My First Reader. 2005, Children's Pr. LB $18.50 (978-0-516-25178-3). 31pp. A birthday girl tries to make her own cake, covering it with blue icing, in this book for beginning readers with a list of words. (Rev: SLJ 5/05)

6590 Ghigna, Charles. *Mice Are Nice* (1). Illus. by Jon Goodell. Series: Step into Reading. 1999, Random paper $3.99 (978-0-679-88929-8). 32pp. In a pet store, a small mouse tells a little girl why mice make the best pets compared with other animals. (Rev: BL 10/1/99; HBG 3/00)

6591 Gibala-Broxholm, Scott. *Scary Fright, Are You All Right?* (K–3). Illus. 2002, Dial $14.99 (978-0-8037-2588-1). Scary Fright, a little monster, alarms her parents by acting too much like a human girl. (Rev: BL 9/15/02; HBG 3/03; SLJ 8/02)

6592 Giff, Patricia Reilly. *In the Dinosaur's Paw* (2–4). Illus. by Blanche Sims. 1985, Dell paper $3.99 (978-0-440-44150-2). 80pp. The Polk Street School kids in the month of February. Also use: *The Candy Corn Contest* (1984); *December Secrets* (1984); *The Valentine Star* (1985); *All about Stacy* (1988). (Rev: BL 4/15/85)

6593 Giff, Patricia Reilly. *Next Stop, New York City! The Polk Street Kids on Tour* (2–4). Illus. by Blanche Sims. Series: Polk Street Special. 1997, Dell paper $3.99 (978-0-440-41362-2). 119pp. When Ms. Rooney and the Polk Street crowd visit New York City, Emily Arrow is upset because she has been dubbed an expert on the Big Apple, but she really knows nothing about it. (Rev: SLJ 10/97)

6594 Giff, Patricia Reilly. *Sunny-Side Up* (1–3). Illus. by Blanche Sims. 1986, Dell paper $3.99 (978-0-440-48406-6). 74pp. The Polk Street School kids are in summer school and have to deal with Matthew's announcement that he is moving away. Another in this series is: *Spectacular Stone Soup* (1989). (Rev: BL 10/1/86; SLJ 3/87)

6595 Gikow, Louise A. *A Day with Daddy* (PS–2). Illus. by Gustavo Mazali. Series: My First Reader. 2004, Children's Pr. LB $18.50 (978-0-516-24410-5). 31pp. Daddy is the one exhausted by a day out in this rhyming book for beginning readers with cartoon illustrations and a word list. (Rev: SLJ 7/04)

6596 Gilman, Grace. *Dixie* (K–1). Illus. by Sarah McConnell. Series: I Can Read! 2011, HarperCollins $16.99 (978-0-06-171914-1); paper $3.99 (978-0-06-171-913-4). 32pp. A loving little dog tries to derail her owner's involvement in the school play. (Rev: BL 6/1/11; SLJ 6/11)

6597 Gilman, Grace. *Dixie and the School Trip* (K–1). Illus. by Sarah McConnell. Series: I Can Read. 2012, HarperCollins $16.99 (978-0-06-208609-9). 32pp. Dixie the pup creates havoc when she tags along on Emma's school trip to the dinosaur museum. Lexile 330 (Rev: BL 8/12; SLJ 11/12)

6598 *Go Away, Crows!* (PS–2). Illus. by Santiago Cohen. Series: I'm Going to Read! 2005, Sterling LB $11.95 (978-1-4027-2080-2); paper $3.95 (978-1-4027-2103-8). A brother and sister find a way to scare the crows away from their garden in this easy reader. (Rev: SLJ 9/05)

6599 Gorbachev, Valeri. *Me Too!* (PS–1). Illus. by author. Series: I Like to Read. 2013, Holiday $14.95 (978-082342744-4). 32pp. Bear and his always affable friend

Chipmunk have tons of fun building snowmen, skating, and simply enjoying the winter season together. Lexile 90 (Rev: BL 9/15/13; SLJ 10/13*)

6600 Gorbachev, Valeri. *Ms. Turtle the Babysitter* (K–1). Illus. by author. 2005, HarperCollins $15.99 (978-0-06-058073-5). 64pp. Simple chapters describe the ways three little frogs try their turtle babysitter's patience. (Rev: SLJ 8/05)

6601 Graham, Bob. *Tales from the Waterhole* (K–3). Illus. by author. 2004, Candlewick $16.99 (978-0-7636-2324-1). The animals of the savannah enjoy playing around the waterhole — soccer, skateboarding, and so forth — in this series of five short stories for beginning readers. (Rev: SLJ 7/04)

6602 Grant, Judyann Ackerman. *Chicken Said, "Cluck!"* (K–2). Illus. by Sue Truesdell. Series: I Can Read! 2008, HarperCollins $16.99 (978-0-06-028723-8). 32pp. Earl and Pearl banish the pesky Chicken when they plant a pumpkin patch, but Chicken proves very useful when the grasshoppers turn up. (Rev: HB 1/09; SLJ 11/08)

6603 Greco, Francesca. *Gideon* (2–4). Illus. by author. 2003, Star Bright $16.95 (978-1-932065-02-2). Poor Gideon the chameleon — always invisible to his jungle neighbors — comes into his own when he warns them of an approaching tiger. (Rev: HBG 10/03; SLJ 5/03)

6604 Green, Jessica. *Scratch Kitten Goes to Sea* (2–4). Illus. by Mitch Vane. 2010, IPG/Little Hare paper $6.99 (978-19212724-4-8). 81pp. A kitten named Scratch hopes to make a life aboard a sailing ship, but his adventures with mice bring his downfall; the first in a series of beginning chapter books. Lexile 600L (Rev: BL 1/1/10)

6605 Greenburg, Dan. *Dude, Where's My Spaceship?* (2–3). Illus. by Dave Calver. Series: Weird Planet. 2006, Random LB $11.99 (978-0-375-93344-8); paper $3.99 (978-0-375-83344-1). After crashing their spaceship on Earth, alien Klatu and his brother Lek try to rescue their sister Ploo, who's been taken captive by a band of earthlings; humor and large print make this suitable for emerging readers. (Rev: SLJ 3/06)

6606 Greene, Stephanie. *Moose Crossing* (1–3). Illus. by Joe Mathieu. Series: Moose and Hildy. 2005, Marshall Cavendish $14.95 (978-0-7614-5233-1). In this easy-reader chapter book, Moose finds that celebrity is not as much fun as he expected. (Rev: SLJ 3/06)

6607 Greene, Stephanie. *Moose's Big Idea* (1–3). Illus. by Joe Mathieu. Series: Moose and Hildy. 2005, Marshall Cavendish $14.95 (978-0-7614-5212-6). 51pp. In this easy-reader chapter book, Moose bemoans his lost antlers, draws pictures at home during hunting season, and later sells puts on a disguise and sells doughnuts, coffee, and original artwork to unsuspecting hunters; all this in the company of his pig friend Hildy. (Rev: SLJ 10/05)

6608 Greene, Stephanie. *The Show-Off* (1–3). Illus. by Joe Mathieu. Series: Moose and Hildy. 2007, Marshall Cavendish $14.99 (978-0-7614-5374-1). Hildy the pig and her friend Moose help boring cousin Vincent learn how to behave; a short chapter book for transitional readers. (Rev: SLJ 10/07)

6609 Gregorich, Barbara. *Waltur Buys a Pig in a Poke and Other Stories* (2–4). Illus. by Kristin Sorra. 2006, Houghton $15.00 (978-0-618-47306-9). 64pp. In this easy-reader chapter book full of wordplay, Waltur the bear learns the truth behind three widely held maxims. (Rev: BL 6/1–15/06; SLJ 7/06)

6610 Gregorich, Barbara. *Waltur Paints Himself into a Corner and Other Stories* (K–3). Illus. by Kristin Sorra. 2007, Houghton $15.00 (978-0-618-74796-2). 48pp. Each story in this humorous easy-reader features Waltur the bear learning the meaning of a different idiom, such as "putting the cart before the horse." (Rev: BL 12/1/07; SLJ 10/07)

6611 Griffiths, Andy. *The Big Fat Cow That Goes Kapow* (2–3). Illus. by Terry Denton. 2009, Feiwel & Friends $14.99 (978-0-312-36788-6). 123pp. Ten zany short stories featuring Seuss-like rhymes and cheeky illustrations are collected in this book for beginning readers. Lexile 380L (Rev: SLJ 1/1/10*)

6612 Griffiths, Andy. *The Cat on the Mat Is Flat* (2–4). Illus. by Terry Denton. 2007, Feiwel & Friends paper $9.95 (978-0-312-36787-9). 176pp. Nine action-packed rhyming stories are full of fun and wordplay. (Rev: SLJ 1/08)

6613 Grimes, Nikki. *A Day With Daddy* (K–2). Illus. by Nicole Tadgell. Series: Just for You! 2004, Scholastic paper $3.99 (978-0-439-56850-0). 32pp. An African American child who lives with his mother looks forward to an outing with his father in this easy-reader. (Rev: BL 10/15/04; SLJ 2/05)

6614 Grimes, Nikki. *Wild, Wild Hair* (1–2). Illus. by George Ford. Series: Hello Reader! 1997, Scholastic $3.99 (978-0-590-26590-4). A young African American girl dreads Monday, when her hair is braided, in this easy-to-read book. (Rev: BL 5/1/97; SLJ 4/97)

6615 Grindley, Sally. *Poppy and Max and the Fashion Show* (K–2). Illus. by Lindsey Gardiner. Series: Poppy and Max. 2009, Orchard paper $6.95 (978-1-84362-393-9). 32pp. Amiable Poppy and her talking dog Max have a chance to be in a fashion show and while Poppy is excited to volunteer, Max is hesitant at first. (Rev: SLJ 5/09)

6616 Grindley, Sally. *Poppy and Max and the Lost Puppy* (K–2). Illus. by Lindsey Gardiner. Series: Poppy and Max. 2009, Orchard paper $6.95 (978-1-84362-394-6). 32pp. Poppy's talking dog Max must deal with some jealousy when Poppy finds a lost puppy. Also use *Poppy and Max and the River Picnic*, *Poppy and Max and the Noisy Night*, and *Poppy and Max and the Snow Dog* (all 2009). (Rev: SLJ 5/09)

6617 Guest, Elissa Haden. *Iris and Walter and the Birthday Party* (1–3). Illus. by Christine Davenier. Series: Iris and Walter. 2006, Harcourt $15.00 (978-0-15-205015-3). 44pp. Walter and Iris's friends will get to ride Walter's horse on his birthday, but there is a surprise — a foal — awaiting them. (Rev: BL 2/1/06; SLJ 3/06)

6618 Guest, Elissa Haden. *Iris and Walter and the Field Trip* (1–3). Illus. by Christine Davenier. 2005, Harcourt $15.00 (978-0-15-205014-6). 44pp. Despite his teacher's warnings to stay together, Walter is so entranced by the coral reef exhibit at the aquarium that the class has to go back to get him. (Rev: BL 5/15/05; SLJ 6/05)

6619 Guest, Elissa Haden. *Iris and Walter: The School Play* (K–2). Illus. by Christine Davenier. Series: Iris and Walter. 2003, Harcourt $15.00 (978-0-15-216481-2). 44pp. Iris and Walter are excited to have roles in the school play, but when the big day finally arrives, Iris is sick. Also use *Iris and Walter: Lost and Found* (2004). (Rev: HB 5/03; HBG 10/03; SLJ 4/03)

6620 Guilfoile, Elizabeth. *Nobody Listens to Andrew* (1–3). Illus. by Mary Stevens. 1957, Modern Curriculum paper $7.50 (978-0-8136-5959-6). The reaction of Andrew's elders when he tells them there is a bear in his bed.

6621 Gunderson, Jessica. *The Emperor's Painting: A Story of Ancient China* (2–5). Illus. by Caroline Hu. Series: Read-it! Chapter Books: Historical Tales. 2008, Picture Window LB $21.26 (978-1-4048-4734-7). 64pp. Eye-catching illustrations add appeal to this historical fiction chapter book for newly independent readers about an artist's apprentice who learns a valuable lesson along with the art of scroll painting. (Rev: SLJ 2/09)

6622 Gunderson, Jessica. *The Jade Dragon: A Story of Ancient China* (2–5). Illus. by Caroline Hu. Series: Read-it! Chapter Books: Historical Tales. 2008, Picture Window LB $21.26 (978-1-4048-4735-4). A young boy's fortune changes when he finds a jade dragon and learns an important lesson about luck. Also use *Stranger on the Silk Road* and *The Terracotta Girl* (both 2008). (Rev: SLJ 2/09)

6623 Gutierrez, Akemi. *The Mummy and Other Adventures of Sam and Alice* (K–2). Illus. by author. 2005, Houghton $16.00 (978-0-618-50761-0). Siblings Sam and Alice show — in three short stories — how the power of imagination can turn a humdrum day into a fascinating adventure. (Rev: SLJ 11/05)

6624 Haas, Jessie. *Bramble and Maggie: Give and Take* (1–3). Illus. by Alison Friend. 2013, Candlewick $14.99 (978-076365021-6). 48pp. Bramble the horse is bored when Maggie her owner is at school and decides to trim the neighbor's roses, in the process meeting a helpful hen. Lexile 290 (Rev: BL 4/1/13; HB 3–4/13; SLJ 6/13)

6625 Haddix, Margaret P. *Say What?* (2–4). Illus. by James Bernardin. 2004, Simon & Schuster $12.95 (978-0-689-86255-7). 96pp. Sukie is much confused when her parents start talking nonsense, and she and her siblings retaliate in kind when they discover their parents' real motive. (Rev: BL 2/15/04; SLJ 2/04)

6626 Hapka, Catherine. *The New Pony* (1–3). Illus. by Anne Kennedy. Series: Pony Scouts I Can Read. 2013, HarperCollins $16.99 (978-006208674-7). 32pp. Jill gets to help train a difficult new palomino pony named Taffy in this 7th installment in the series. (Rev: BLO 4/1/13)

6627 Hapka, Catherine. *Pony Scouts: Back in the Saddle* (PS–2). Illus. by Anne Kennedy. Series: I Can Read! 2011, HarperCollins $16.99 (978-0-06-125539-7); paper $3.99 (978-0-06-125541-0). 32pp. After falling off her pony during a riding lesson, Annie must decide whether or not to get back on in this simple book for beginning readers. (Rev: SLJ 9/1/11)

6628 Hapka, Catherine. *Runaway Ponies!* (K–2). Illus. by Anne Kennedy. Series: Pony Scouts I Can Read. 2012, HarperCollins $16.99 (978-006208669-3); paper $3.99 (978-00620866-7-9). 32pp. Meg is spending the weekend at Jill's and her absentmindedness results in all five ponies getting out of the stable, posing the girls a challenge. ∩ (Rev: BL 4/1/12)

6629 Hapka, Cathy, and Ellen Titlebaum. *How Not to Babysit Your Brother* (K–3). Illus. by Debbie Palen. Series: Step into Reading. 2005, Random LB $11.99 (978-0-375-92856-7); paper $3.99 (978-0-375-82856-0). 48pp. A humorous early chapter book about two brothers who create quite a stir while their grandmother is sleeping. (Rev: SLJ 8/05)

6630 Hapka, Cathy, and Ellen Titlebaum. *How Not to Start Third Grade* (1–3). Illus. by Debbie Palen. 2007, Random LB $11.99 (978-0-375-93904-4); paper $3.99 (978-0-375-83904-7). 48pp. Will's first day of 3rd grade is seriously disrupted by the antics of his little brother Steve, who is starting kindergarten. (Rev: BL 9/1/07; SLJ 7/07)

6631 Harrison, David L. *Johnny Appleseed: My Story* (1–2). Illus. by Mike Wohnoutka. Series: Step into Reading. 2001, Random paper $3.99 (978-0-375-81247-7). 48pp. Johnny Appleseed tells the story of his life to a pioneer family. (Rev: BL 2/1/02; HBG 3/02) [634]

6632 *Harry's Bath* (K–1). Illus. by Seymour Chwast. Series: I'm Going to Read! 2005, Sterling paper $3.95 (978-1-4027-2100-7). Harry claims he can't get in the tub because it's already full of animals in this beginning reader. (Rev: SLJ 9/05)

6633 Hartnett, Sonya. *Sadie and Ratz* (K–3). Illus. by Ann James. 2012, Candlewick $14.99 (978-0-7636-5315-6). 64pp. Clever Hannah blames her hands, which she's named Sadie and Ratz, whenever she does something wrong, which happens regularly when she's near her irritating younger brother. (Rev: BL 5/1/12; SLJ 4/1/12*)

6634 Hay, Samantha. *Hocus-Pocus Hound* (1–3). Illus. by Nathan Reed. Series: I Am Reading. 2006, Kingfisher paper $3.95 (978-0-7534-5957-7). 48pp. A scruffy-looking hound becomes an unexpectedly helpful assistant to Marvo the Magician. (Rev: SLJ 1/07)

6635 Hayes, Geoffrey. *Benny and Penny: In Just Pretend* (PS–1). Illus. by author. 2008, Raw Junior/TOON $12.95 (978-0-9799238-0-7). 32pp. An easy-reader graphic novel in which Benny the pirate mouse has a falling-out with his sister followed by a change of heart at the end. (Rev: BL 3/15/08; SLJ 5/08)

6636 Hayes, Geoffrey. *A Poor Excuse for a Dragon* (PS–2). Illus. by author. Series: Step into Reading. 2011, Random House $12.99 (978-0-375-87180-1); paper

$3.99 (978-0-375-86867-2). 48pp. A kind young dragon struggling with ferocity is awarded a job guarding a castle. ℮ (Rev: BL 8/11; LMC 11–12/11; SLJ 6/11)

6637 Hays, Anna Jane. *The Secret of the Circle-K Cave* (2–4). Illus. by Jerry Smath. Series: Science Solves It. 2006, Kane paper $4.99 (978-1-57565-189-7). 32pp. While visiting his aunt and uncle in New Mexico, Rick and his cousins explore a cave where they discover clues to an unsolved 19th-century robbery; scientific aspects are covered in sidebars. (Rev: BL 8/06)

6638 Hays, Anna Jane. *Smarty Sara* (1–2). Illus. by Sylvie Wickstrom. Series: Step into Reading. 2008, Random LB $11.99 (978-0-375-95054-4); paper $3.99 (978-0-375-83512-4). Sara enjoys reading and writing as well as planning entertainment for her friends. (Rev: BL 7/08)

6639 Hays, Anna Jane. *Spring Surprises* (PS–1). Illus. by Hala Wittwer Swearingen. Series: Step Into Reading. 2010, Random House paper $3.99 (978-03758548-0-6). 24pp. Celebrates the arrival of spring in rhyming text suitable for beginning readers. (Rev: BL 2/1/10)

6640 Hayward, Linda. *What Homework?* (1–3). Illus. by Page Eastburn O'Rourke. 2002, Kane paper $4.99 (978-1-57565-116-3). 32pp. Andy succeeds in completing his assignment in the nick of time. (Rev: SLJ 11/02)

6641 Hazen, Lynn E. *Cinder Rabbit* (K–2). Illus. by Elyse Pastel. 2008, Holt $15.95 (978-0-8050-8194-7). 64pp. A little bunny who's lost her hop must face her fears when she is chosen for the role of Cinder Rabbit in the class play. (Rev: BL 6/1/08; SLJ 3/08)

6642 Head, Judith. *Mud Soup* (1–2). Series: Step into Reading. 2003, Random LB $11.99 (978-0-375-81087-9). 48pp. In this charming cross-cultural tale for beginning readers, Josh learns from a Latina friend that different doesn't mean bad. (Rev: BL 8/03; HBG 4/04)

6643 Henkes, Kevin. *Penny and Her Doll* (K–2). Illus. by author. 2012, Greenwillow $12.99 (978-0-06-208199-5). 32pp. Penny, a mouse, loves the doll she gets from her grandmother but has trouble coming up with a suitable name in this beginning-reader sequel to *Penny and Her Song* (2011). ALA Notable Children's Book. ∩ ℮ Lexile AD200L (Rev: BL 9/1/12; HB 8–9/12; SLJ 10/12*)

6644 Henkes, Kevin. *Penny and Her Marble* (PS–3). Illus. by author. 2013, Greenwillow $12.99 (978-0-06-208203-9). 48pp. Penny the mouse feels guilty after taking a beautiful blue marble from a neighbor's lawn, so she decides to return it only to be told that Mrs. Goodwin had hoped somebody would find it and enjoy it; suitable for beginning readers. ALA Notable Children's Book. ℮ Lexile 350L (Rev: BL 12/15/12*; HB 3–4/13; SLJ 2/13*)

6645 Henry, Steve. *Happy Cat* (PS–1). Illus. by author. Series: I Like to Read. 2013, Holiday $14.95 (978-0-8234-2659-1). 32pp. Illustrated in ink, watercolor, and gouache, this easy reader tells the story of a cold and homeless cat who finds a new home in the attic of a house full of kind animals. (Rev: BL 10/1/13; SLJ 8/13)

6646 Hicks, Betty. *Basketball Bats* (2–4). Illus. by Adam McCauley. Series: Gym Shorts. 2008, Roaring Brook $14.95 (978-1-59643-243-7). 64pp. Henry has trouble sharing the ball when his team is challenged by the rival Tigers. (Rev: BL 6/1–15/08; HB 7/08; LMC 5/08; SLJ 7/08)

6647 Hicks, Betty. *Goof-off Goalie* (2–4). Illus. by Adam McCauley. Series: Gym Shorts. 2008, Roaring Brook $14.95 (978-1-59643-244-4). Goose must overcome his reputation as a dreamer and convince the soccer coach that he's a good candidate for goalie. (Rev: BLO 7/31/08; HB 7/08; LMC 5/08; SLJ 7/08)

6648 Hicks, Betty. *Swimming with Sharks* (1–3). Illus. by Adam McCauley. Series: Gym Shorts. 2008, Roaring Brook $15.95 (978-1-59643-245-1). Rita is disappointed when she can't join her friends on the Sharks swimming team. (Rev: BL 9/15/08; HB 9/08)

6649 Hill, Susan. *Black Beauty and the Thunderstorm* (1–3). Illus. by Bill Farnsworth. Series: My Readers. 2011, Square Fish $15.99 (978-0-312-64705-6); paper $3.99 (978-0-312-64721-6). 48pp. Black Beauty tells some of the events of his life, including when he rescued his owner's daughter's cat during a thunderstorm. (Rev: SLJ 6/11)

6650 Hill, Susan. *Ruby Bakes a Cake* (K–3). Illus. by Margie Moore. Series: An I Can Read Book. 2004, HarperCollins LB $16.89 (978-0-06-008976-4). Ruby, a raccoon, consults her friends before making a cake and includes all the ingredients they suggest. (Rev: SLJ 6/04)

6651 Hill, Susan. *Ruby's Perfect Day* (PS–K). Illus. by Margie Moore. 2006, HarperCollins $15.99 (978-0-06-008982-5). 32pp. Ruby Raccoon learns that playing by herself can be just as much fun as playing with all her woodland friends. (Rev: BL 12/1/06; SLJ 10/06)

6652 Himmelman, John. *The Animal Rescue Club* (1–3). Illus. by author. Series: An I Can Read Book. 1998, HarperCollins LB $15.89 (978-0-06-027409-2). 46pp. In this easy reader, members of the Animal Rescue Club take a number of creatures in distress to a hospital and later return them to their natural habitats. (Rev: HBG 10/98; SLJ 6/98)

6653 Hindley, Judy. *Princess Rosa's Winter* (1–2). Illus. by Margaret Chamberlain. Series: I Am Reading. 2005, Kingfisher paper $3.95 (978-0-7534-5859-4). Princess Rosa and her family remember what they enjoy about winter when Hoda the jester entertains them in their castle. (Rev: BL 3/15/05)

6654 Hoban, Lillian. *Arthur's Birthday Party* (1–2). Illus. 1999, HarperCollins $14.95 (978-0-06-027798-7). 64pp. As expected at Arthur's birthday party, all his friends perform amazing gymnastic tricks, but Arthur wins the best all-round gymnast award. (Rev: BL 3/15/99; HB 1/99; HBG 10/99; SLJ 2/99)

6655 Hoban, Lillian. *Arthur's Loose Tooth* (1–3). Illus. by author. 1985, HarperCollins LB $17.89 (978-0-06-022354-0); paper $3.99 (978-0-06-444093-6). 64pp. Brave Arthur the chimp is afraid of blood, so how does he get rid of his loose tooth in order to eat taffy apples? (Rev: BL 10/15/85; HB 11/85; SLJ 12/85)

6656 Hoban, Russell. *Bedtime for Frances* (1–2). Illus. by Garth Williams. 1960, HarperCollins LB $13.89 (978-0-06-022351-9); paper $6.99 (978-0-06-443451-5). 32pp. Frances, a badger, tries every familiar trick to tease her way past bedtime. Others in the series: *Bread and Jam for Frances* (1965); *A Bargain for Frances* (1970).

6657 Hoban, Russell. *Best Friends for Frances* (1–2). Illus. by Lillian Hoban. 1969, HarperCollins LB $17.89 (978-0-06-022328-1); paper $6.99 (978-0-06-443008-1). When friend Albert decides that he must exclude girls from his "wondering day" and baseball game, Frances chooses younger sister Gloria as a companion. Also use: *A Baby Sister for Frances* (1964).

6658 Hoff, Syd. *Barney's Horse* (1–3). Illus. by author. 1987, HarperCollins LB $16.89 (978-0-06-022450-9); paper $3.99 (978-0-06-444142-1). Barney the peddler and his horse delight children, but elevated trains soon begin to rumble overhead. (Rev: BCCB 11/87; BL 10/1/87)

6659 Hoff, Syd. *Danny and the Dinosaur* (K–2). Illus. by author. 1958, HarperCollins LB $17.89 (978-0-06-022466-0); paper $3.99 (978-0-06-444002-8). 64pp. Danny wanted to play and so did the dinosaur. What could have been more natural than for them to leave the museum together? Also from the same author and publisher: *Sammy the Seal* (1959).

6660 Hoff, Syd. *Danny and the Dinosaur Go to Camp* (1–3). Illus. 1996, HarperCollins LB $17.89 (978-0-06-026440-6). 32pp. At summer camp, a dinosaur provides transportation for tired boys and girls. (Rev: BL 8/96; SLJ 6/96)

6661 Hoff, Syd. *Mrs. Brice's Mice* (PS–2). Illus. by author. 1988, HarperCollins paper $3.99 (978-0-06-444145-2). 32pp. Mrs. Brice has 25 mice — one is an individualist. (Rev: BCCB 12/88; BL 12/1/88; SLJ 4/89)

6662 Hoff, Syd. *Stanley* (1–3). Illus. by author. 1992, HarperCollins paper $3.99 (978-0-06-444010-3). 64pp. A caveman finds a new home in this inventive tale.

6663 Hood, Susan. *Pup and Hound Hatch an Egg* (PS–1). Illus. by Linda Hendry. Series: Pup and Hound. 2007, Kids Can $14.95 (978-1-55337-974-4); paper $3.95 (978-1-55337-975-1). Whose egg have Pup and Hound found? Readers will be surprised when a baby turtle emerges, ready for fun with the two friends. Also use *Pup and Hound Stay Up Late* and *Pup and Hound in Trouble* (both 2005) and *Pup and Hound Catch a Thief* (2007). (Rev: SLJ 6/07)

6664 Hooks, Gwendolyn. *The Mystery of the Missing Dog* (K–3). Illus. by Nancy Devard. Series: Just for You! 2004, Scholastic paper $3.99 (978-0-439-56864-7). 32pp. Alex, an African American boy, searches his apartment looking for his dog in this easy-reader. Also use *Three's a Crowd* (2004), about jealousy. (Rev: SLJ 1/05)

6665 Hooks, Gwendolyn. *Nice Wheels* (K–2). Illus. by Renée Andriani. Series: My First Reader. 2005, Children's Pr. LB $18.50 (978-0-516-25179-0). 31pp. The

new boy in class has a wheelchair in this book for beginning readers with a list of words. (Rev: SLJ 5/05)

6666 Hopkinson, Deborah. *Billy and the Rebel* (1–3). Illus. by Brian Floca. Series: Ready-to-Read. 2005, Simon & Schuster $14.95 (978-0-689-83964-1). A young boy and his mother give sanctuary to a Confederate deserter at their farm near Gettysburg in this story based on a real incident. (Rev: BL 2/1/05; SLJ 4/05)

6667 Hopkinson, Deborah. *From Slave to Soldier: Based on a True Civil War Story* (2–4). Illus. by Brian Floca. Series: Ready-to-Read. 2005, Simon & Schuster $14.95 (978-0-689-83965-8). 48pp. Inspired by real events, this book for beginning readers chronicles the experiences of a slave boy who runs off to join the Union army and works as a mule driver; an afterword adds context. (Rev: BL 1/1–15/06; SLJ 10/05)

6668 Horowitz, Ruth. *Big Surprise in the Bug Tank* (1–3). Illus. by Joan Holub. Series: Dial Easy-to-Read. 2005, Dial $14.99 (978-0-8037-2874-5). 46pp. The two boys first seen in *Breakout at the Bug Lab* (2001) adopt two giant cockroaches from the mother's lab and, of course, the population soon expands from two. (Rev: BCCB 1/05; HB 5/05; SLJ 2/05)

6669 Howe, James. *Houndsley and Catina and the Birthday Surprise* (PS–2). Illus. by Marie-Louise Gay. 2006, Candlewick $14.99 (978-0-7636-2405-7). 48pp. Houndsley the dog and Catina the cat are sad that they do not know their birthdays but they find a creative way to get around this; an easy-reader sequel to *Houndsley and Catina* (2006). (Rev: BL 10/1/06; SLJ 11/06)

6670 Howe, James. *Houndsley and Catina: Plink and Plunk* (PS–2). Illus. by Marie-Louise Gay. 2009, Candlewick $15.99 (978-0-7636-3385-1). Catina the cat teaches Houndsley the dog to ride a bike and he teaches her to swim in this easy reader about conquering fears. (Rev: BL 5/1/09)

6671 Howe, James. *Pinky and Rex and the New Baby* (K–3). Illus. by Melissa Sweet. 1994, Avon paper $3.99 (978-0-380-12083-3). 48pp. Rex and her best friend are nervous about the new baby Rex's parents are planning to adopt. (Rev: BL 3/1/93; SLJ 6/93)

6672 Howe, James. *The Vampire Bunny* (1–3). Illus. by Jeff Mack. 2004, Simon & Schuster $14.95 (978-0-689-85724-9). 41pp. Chester the cat and Harold the dog disagree over whether the baby bunny they have found is a vampire in this adaptation for beginning readers. (Rev: SLJ 6/04)

6673 Hsu, Stacey W. *Old Mo* (PS–1). Illus. by Adam Ritter. Series: Rookie Reader. 2006, Children's Pr. LB $19.50 (978-0-516-24981-0). 32pp. A boy and his beloved pet cat enjoy each other's company throughout the day in this easy reader. (Rev: SLJ 6/06)

6674 Hudson, Wade. *Jamal's Busy Day* (PS–1). Illus. by George Ford. 1991, Just Us Bks. LB $12.95 (978-0-940975-21-7); paper $6.95 (978-0-940975-24-8). Jamal, an African American boy, prepares with his parents for a busy day — he will spend his at school and they at work. (Rev: SLJ 2/92)

6675 Hudson, Wade. *The Two Tyrones* (K–3). Illus. by Mark Page. 2004, Scholastic paper $3.99 (978-0-439-56866-1). School is starting and it turns out there will be two Tyrones this year. (Rev: SLJ 1/05)

6676 Hulme, Joy N. *Mary Clare Likes to Share: A Math Reader* (K–1). Illus. by Lizzy Rockwell. Series: Step into Reading. 2006, Random LB $11.99 (978-0-375-93421-6); paper $3.99 (978-0-375-83421-9). 32pp. A humorous, rhyming easy-reader that uses Mary Clare's sharing of food to introduce fractions. (Rev: SLJ 2/07)

6677 Hutchins, Hazel. *Robyn's Art Attack* (K–3). Illus. by Yvonne Cathcart. Series: First Novels. 2002, Formac paper $3.99 (978-0-88780-564-6). 59pp. Robyn's classmates expect a boring day when she chooses an art gallery for their field trip. (Rev: SLJ 1/03)

6678 *I Am Sick* (K–2). Illus. by Johanna Hantel. Series: My First Reader. 2005, Children's Pr. LB $18.50 (978-0-516-24878-3); paper $3.95 (978-0-516-24970-4). A young girl is nervous about going to the doctor, but her father goes with her and the doctor is kind, giving her medicine that makes her headache and sore throat better; for beginning readers. (Rev: SLJ 1/06)

6679 Inches, Alison. *Corduroy Writes a Letter* (K–2). Illus. by Allan Eitzen. Series: Viking Easy-to-Read. 2002, Viking $13.99 (978-0-670-03548-9). 32pp. Corduroy the teddy bear and Lisa, an African American girl, find out how much they can accomplish by writing letters. Also use *Corduroy's Garden* (2002). (Rev: BL 1/1–15/03; HBG 3/03)

6680 Jacobson, Jennifer. *Andy Shane and the Pumpkin Trick* (1–3). Illus. by Abby Carter. 2006, Candlewick $13.99 (978-0-7636-2605-1). Andy is reluctant to spend so much time on bossy Dolores's birthday party, especially as it's on Halloween, but in the end he saves the day, confounding pranksters. (Rev: BL 9/1/06; SLJ 10/06)

6681 Jane, Pamela. *Milo and the Flapjack Fiasco* (K–3). Illus. by Meredith Johnson. 2004, Mondo $13.95 (978-1-59336-113-6). 32pp. Milo and his sister Sam try to make flapjacks for the visiting teacher in this easy-reader. (Rev: SLJ 6/04)

6682 Jarman, Julia. *The Magic Backpack* (PS–2). Illus. by Adriano Gon. Series: Flying Foxes. 2004, Crabtree LB $22.60 (978-0-7787-1487-3); paper $4.95 (978-0-7787-1533-7). 48pp. Josh forgets to bring a key ingredient for the class cake, but fortunately his magic backpack flies him to a cocoa plantation in Ghana. (Rev: SLJ 8/04)

6683 Jennings, Patrick. *The Tornado Watches: An Ike and Mem Story* (2–5). Illus. by Anna Alter. 2002, Holiday House $15.95 (978-0-8234-1672-1). A young boy named Ike fears his family is in danger after a tornado warning causes them to spend the night in their basement. (Rev: BL 8/02; HB 1/03; HBG 3/03; SLJ 12/02)

6684 Jennings, Patrick. *The Weeping Willow* (2–4). Illus. by Anna Alter. 2002, Holiday House $15.95 (978-0-8234-1671-4). Friends Ike and Buzzy decide to build a tree house, only to find themselves embroiled in argu-

ments. (Rev: BL 12/15/02; HB 1/03*; HBG 3/03; SLJ 2/03)

6685 Jinkins, Jim. *Pinky Dinky Doo: Back to School Is Cool* (K–3). Illus. by author. Series: Step into Reading. 2005, Random $12.95 (978-0-375-83236-9); paper $3.99 (978-0-375-83237-6). 48pp. Pinky makes up a funny story about picture day at school to tell to her little brother. (Rev: SLJ 9/05)

6686 Johansen, K. V. *Pippin and the Bones* (PS–2). Illus. by Bernice Lum. 2000, Kids Can $12.95 (978-1-55074-629-7). 32pp. For beginning readers, this is the story of a dog named Pippin who digs up some huge bones that his master gives to the museum. (Rev: BL 8/00; HBG 10/00; SLJ 8/00)

6687 Johnson, Crockett. *Harold and the Purple Crayon* (K–2). Illus. by author. 1958, HarperCollins paper $6.99 (978-0-06-443022-7). 64pp. A little boy draws all of the things necessary for him to go for a walk. Three sequels are: *Harold's Trip to the Sky* (1957); *Harold's Circus* (1959); *A Picture for Harold's Room* (1960).

6688 Jones, Christianne C. *Emma's New Look* (1–2). Illus. by Necdet Yilmaz. 2007, Picture Window LB $19.93 (978-1-4048-3138-4). This easy reader with a simple story and fun illustrations will help build skills. (Rev: SLJ 7/07)

6689 Joyner, Andrew. *Boris on the Move* (K–2). Illus. by author. 2013, Scholastic $15.99 (978-054548442-8); paper $4.99 (978-0-545-48443-5). 80pp. Boris is an enthusiastic pig who longs for adventure in this easy-reader with large illustrations. Lexile 230 (Rev: BLO 6/13; LMC 11–12/13; SLJ 7/13)

6690 Kann, Victoria. *Pinkalicious: Pink Around the Rink* (PS–2). Illus. by author. Series: I Can Read! 2010, HarperCollins $16.99 (978-0-06-192880-2); paper $3.99 (978-0-06-192879-6). 32pp. Pinkalicious brightens her new white ice skates with a pink magic marker, that unfortunately bleeds onto the ice, highlighting all the places she has fallen. (Rev: SLJ 1/1/11)

6691 Kann, Victoria. *Puptastic!* (K–2). Illus. by author. Series: Pinkalicious. 2013, HarperCollins $16.99 (978-006218786-4). 32pp. Pinkalicious looks forward eagerly to the arrival of a little white poodle named Pinky, who they will be dog-sitting; but things don't go as expected at first. (Rev: BL 5/1/13)

6692 Kenah, Katharine. *The Best Chef in Second Grade* (K–2). Illus. by Abby Carter. 2007, HarperCollins $15.99 (978-0-06-053561-2). 48pp. Ollie jumps at the opportunity to showcase his hidden cooking talents when a TV chef visits Mr. Hopper's class; for beginning readers. (Rev: BCCB 1/08; BL 11/1/07; SLJ 12/07)

6693 Kenah, Katharine. *The Best Seat in Second Grade* (K–2). Illus. by Abby Carter. Series: I Can Read! 2005, HarperCollins $16.99 (978-0-06-000734-8). 64pp. Sam, a 2nd-grader, gets more than he bargained for when he takes the class hamster along on a school field trip. (Rev: BL 8/05; SLJ 7/05)

6694 Kenah, Katharine. *The Best Teacher in Second Grade* (K–2). Illus. by Abby Carter. Series: I Can Read!

2006, HarperCollins $16.99 (978-0-06-053564-3). 48pp. Luna's teacher supports the new girl's idea for a special night sky program even though her classmates are cool to the suggestion. (Rev: BL 6/1–15/06; SLJ 7/06)

6695 Kerrin, Jessica Scott. *Martin Bridge on the Lookout!* (2–4). Illus. by Joseph Kelly. 2005, Kids Can $14.95 (978-1-55337-689-7); paper $4.95 (978-1-55337-773-3). 142pp. In this beginning chapter book, Martin Bridge returns in a trio of short stories about minor misadventures that turn out well. (Rev: SLJ 11/05)

6696 Kerrin, Jessica Scott. *Martin Bridge, Ready for Takeoff!* (2–4). Illus. by Joseph Kelly. 2005, Kids Can $14.95 (978-1-55337-688-0). 120pp. Martin must deal with typical 3rd-grade dilemmas in this three-chapter book with pencil illustrations. (Rev: BL 3/15/05; SLJ 5/05)

6697 Kertell, Lynn Maslen. *Cupcake Surprise!* (PS–1). Illus. by Sue Hendra. Series: Scholastic Reader. 2012, Scholastic paper $3.99 (978-05453826-9-4). 32pp. Siblings Jack and Anna bake cupcakes for their dad's birthday and have several surprises in the process. (Rev: BLO 2/27/12)

6698 Kessler, Leonard. *Here Comes the Strikeout* (1–2). Illus. by author. 1992, HarperCollins paper $3.99 (978-0-06-444011-0). 64pp. Bobby always strikes out at bat until his friend Willie helps him to improve his game. Two other sports stories by the same author and publisher are: *Kick, Pass and Run* (1966); *Last One in Is a Rotten Egg* (1969). (Rev: BL 12/1/92)

6699 Kimmelman, Leslie. *In the Doghouse* (K–2). Illus. by True Kelley. Series: Holiday House Reader. 2006, Holiday $14.95 (978-0-8234-1882-4). Emma's dog Bo disappears after she is angry with him, causing much anguish but ending in a joyous reunion in this well-rounded book for beginning readers. (Rev: BL 4/15/06; SLJ 5/06)

6700 King-Smith, Dick. *The Twin Giants* (1–3). Illus. by Mini Grey. 2008, Candlewick $16.99 (978-0-7636-3529-9). 80pp. Identical twin giants Normous and Lottavim have an enjoyable childhood and adolescence and decide at the age of 20 that they each need a wife, a task that poses challenges; attractive illustrations add to the humor. (Rev: BL 7/08; SLJ 7/08)

6701 Klein, Adria F. *Max Goes to School* (PS–1). Illus. by Mernie Gallagher-Cole. Series: Read-it! Readers. 2005, Picture Window LB $19.93 (978-1-4048-1179-9). 24pp. Max, a young African American boy, spends an enjoyable first day at school in this simple easy reader. Also use *Max Goes to the Barber* and *Max Goes to the Dentist* (both 2005), *Max and the Adoption Day Party* and *Max Learns Sign Language* (both 2007), and *Max Goes to the Farmers' Market* (2009). (Rev: SLJ 1/06)

6702 Klimo, Kate. *Twinky the Dinky Dog* (1–3). Illus. by Michael Fleming. 2013, Random House paper $3.99 (978-03079766-7-3). 46pp. Twinky may be a small dog but he thinks big, and when he makes a visit to the dog park he learns lessons that help him gain some freedom from his over-cosseting owner. ℮ (Rev: BL 5/1/13)

6703 Kline, Suzy. *Herbie Jones Sails into Second Grade* (1–3). Illus. by Sami Sweeten. 2006, Putnam $14.99 (978-0-399-22665-6). 64pp. On his first day of 2nd grade, Herbie Jones meets a new friend and learns that his teacher is a man who has a sense of humor. (Rev: BL 8/06)

6704 Kline, Suzy. *Horrible Harry and the Dragon War* (1–3). Illus. by Frank Remkiewicz. 2002, Viking $13.99 (978-0-670-03559-5). 64pp. Harry and classmate Song Lee quarrel over a school project on dragons but finally become friends again. (Rev: BL 6/1–15/02; HBG 3/03; SLJ 8/02)

6705 Kline, Suzy. *Horrible Harry and the Locked Closet* (2–4). Illus. by Frank Remkiewicz. 2004, Viking $13.99 (978-0-670-05944-7). 80pp. Bored after four days of indoor recess and not completely diverted by their study of volcanoes, Horrible Harry and other students in Miss Mackle's class investigate what's behind a locked closet door. (Rev: BL 5/1/04; SLJ 11/04)

6706 Kline, Suzy. *Horrible Harry and the Mud Gremlins* (2–4). Illus. by Frank Remkiewicz. Series: Horrible Harry. 2003, Viking $13.99 (978-0-670-03617-2). 64pp. Horrible Harry encourages his classmates to break a school rule and go under the playground fence to see fungi with his mini-microscope. (Rev: BL 3/15/03; HBG 10/03)

6707 Kline, Suzy. *Horrible Harry Bugs the Three Bears* (2–4). Illus. by Frank Remkiewicz. 2008, Viking $13.99 (978-0-670-06293-5). 80pp. Horrible Harry gives Edward the earwig a proper burial and along with his classmates performs "Goldilocks and the Three Bugs." (Rev: BL 2/1/08)

6708 Kline, Suzy. *Horrible Harry Goes to the Moon* (2–3). Illus. by Frank Remkiewicz. 2000, Viking $13.99 (978-0-670-88764-4). In this story about Horrible Harry, Miss Mackle's 3rd-grade class decides to hold a bake sale to buy a used telescope. (Rev: HBG 10/00; SLJ 2/00)

6709 Kline, Suzy. *Horrible Harry Takes the Cake* (1–3). Illus. by Frank Remkiewicz. Series: Horrible Harry. 2006, Viking $13.99 (978-0-670-06075-7). 64pp. Harry tries to find out who their teacher is marrying; the nineteenth book in this humorous series. (Rev: BL 2/1/06; SLJ 5/06)

6710 Knudsen, Michelle. *Fish and Frog* (PS). Illus. by Valeria Petrone. Series: Brand New Readers. 2005, Candlewick paper $5.99 (978-0-7636-2457-6). 40pp. An enjoyable beginning reader with a simple story line and bright illustrations portraying a fish and frog that live in the same pond. (Rev: SLJ 8/05)

6711 Konrad, Marla Stewart. *Mom and Me* (PS–K). Illus. Series: World Vision Early Reader. 2009, Tundra $12.95 (978-0-88776-866-8). 24pp. Accompanied by minimal text, color photographs show mothers and children around the world in everyday activities. (Rev: BL 5/1/09; SLJ 5/09)

6712 Kramer, Sydelle. *Wagon Train* (2–4). Illus. by Deborah Kogan Ray. Series: All Aboard Reading. 1997,

Penguin paper $3.99 (978-0-448-41334-1). This easy-to-read book follows a family as it crosses the United States wagon in 1848. (Rev: BL 2/1/98)

6713 Krensky, Stephen. *Buster's Dino Dilemma* (1–3). Illus. by Marc Brown. Series: A Marc Brown Arthur Chapter Book. 1998, Little, Brown paper $3.95 (978-0-316-11560-5). 58pp. Based on scripts used in the PBS series, this easy chapter book involves Arthur and a fossil he has found during a school field trip. Also use *Locked in the Library!* (1998). (Rev: HBG 10/98; SLJ 11/98)

6714 Krensky, Stephen. *Lionel's Birthday* (1–3). Illus. by Susanna Natti. Series: Dial Easy-to-Read. 2003, Penguin $13.99 (978-0-8037-2752-6). 48pp. In this ninth easy-reader about Lionel, he prepares for an upcoming birthday and buries a time capsule. (Rev: BL 7/03; HBG 4/04; SLJ 10/03)

6715 Krensky, Stephen. *We Just Moved!* (1–2). Illus. by Larry DiFiori. Series: Hello Reader! 1998, Scholastic paper $3.99 (978-0-590-33127-2). 32pp. Set during the Middle Ages, this humorous story tells of a young boy's move to a new castle and how this compares with a change of homes in modern times. (Rev: BL 7/98)

6716 Kroll, Virginia. *Honest Ashley* (K–3). Illus. by Nancy Cote. Series: The Way I Act. 2005, Albert Whitman $15.99 (978-0-8075-3371-0). 32pp. The virtues of honesty are explored in this tale of a girl trying to decide whether to copy an old essay of her brother's or to do the school assignment on her own. (Rev: BL 6/1–15/06; SLJ 3/06)

6717 Kuenzler, Lou. *The Ugly Egg* (1–3). Illus. by David Hitch. Series: I Am Reading. 2009, Kingfisher paper $3.99 (978-0-7534-6-284-3). 48pp. When a kindhearted puffin longing for offspring finds and hatches a dragon egg, the other birds are scornful — until the dragon's nest-warming skills are realized and embraced. (Rev: BLO 11/15/09; SLJ 2/1/10)

6718 Kvasnosky, Laura McGee. *Zelda and Ivy: The Big Picture* (1–3). Illus. by author. 2010, Candlewick $14.99 (978-0-7636-4180-1). 48pp. A movie starring Secret Agent Fox inspires the fox siblings to do some sleuthing of their own in this episodic book for beginning readers. (Rev: HB 9–10/10; SLJ 9/1/10)

6719 Kvasnosky, Laura McGee. *Zelda and Ivy: The Runaways* (K–3). 2006, Candlewick $14.99 (978-0-7636-2689-1). Fox sisters Zelda and Ivy decide to run away from home, bury a time capsule, and experiment with a creative juice. (Rev: BL 6/1–15/06; SLJ 7/06*)

6720 Labatt, Mary. *A Parade for Sam* (PS–2). Illus. by Marisol Sarrazin. Series: Kids Can Read. 2005, Kids Can $14.95 (978-1-55337-787-0); paper $3.95 (978-1-55337-788-7). 32pp. Not content to watch the carnival parade from the sidelines, Sam, a fluffy puppy, wants to be a part of it; suitable for beginning readers. (Rev: BL 10/15/05)

6721 Labatt, Mary. *Pizza for Sam* (PS–1). Illus. by Marisol Sarrazin. Series: Kids Can Read. 2003, Kids Can $14.95 (978-1-55337-329-2); paper $3.95 (978-

1-55337-331-5). 32pp. Sam does not want to eat dog food and greets a pizza with joy. (Rev: BL 3/1/03; HBG 10/03; SLJ 5/03)

6722 Labatt, Mary. *Sam at the Seaside* (PS–2). Illus. by Marisol Sarrazin. Series: Kids Can Read. 2006, Kids Can $14.95 (978-1-55337-876-1). On a visit to the seashore with her owners, Sam the puppy's exuberance gets her into all sorts of problems. Also use *Sam Goes Next Door* (2006). (Rev: SLJ 11/06)

6723 Labatt, Mary. *Sam Finds a Monster* (PS–2). Illus. by Marisol Sarrazin. Series: Kids Can Read. 2003, Kids Can $14.95 (978-1-55337-351-3); paper $3.95 (978-1-55337-352-0). 32pp. A lovable puppy named Sam tries to track down a monster she believes has escaped from the television into her owners' house. (Rev: HBG 10/03; SLJ 5/03)

6724 Laurence, Daniel. *Captain and Matey Set Sail* (K–2). Illus. by Claudio Munoz. Series: An I Can Read Book. 2001, HarperCollins LB $15.89 (978-0-06-028957-7). 64pp. Two pirates bicker constantly about everything — what to call their parrot, what to do with the treasure if they ever find it, which song to sing while scrubbing the deck, and so forth. (Rev: BCCB 9/01; BL 7/01; HB 1/02; HBG 3/02; SLJ 11/01)

6725 Lavis, Steve. *Little Mouse Has a Busy Day* (PS–K). Illus. by author. 2000, Ragged Bear $6.95 (978-1-929766-10-9). This book for beginning readers traces the hour-by-hour activities of Little Mouse from getting up at 8 A.M. to bedtime at 6. Also use *Little Mouse Has an Adventure*. (Rev: SLJ 1/01)

6726 Le Sieg, Theo. *Ten Apples Up on Top* (K–2). Illus. 1961, Random LB $11.99 (978-0-394-90019-3). 72pp. Three bears try to pile apples on their heads in this nonsense story. Also from the same author and publisher: *I Wish That I Had Duck Feet* (1965); *Eye Book* (1968).

6727 Leonard, Marcia. *Best Friends* (PS–1). Photos by Dorothy Handelman. Series: Real Kids Readers. 1999, Millbrook LB $18.90 (978-0-7613-2064-7); paper $4.99 (978-0-7613-2089-0). 30pp. In this simple story for very beginning readers that is illustrated with photographs, two girls describe their similarities and differences. (Rev: SLJ 1/00)

6728 Leonard, Marcia. *Get the Ball, Slim* (1). Illus. by Dorothy Handelman. Series: Real Kids Readers. 1998, Millbrook LB $18.90 (978-0-7613-2000-5); paper $4.99 (978-0-7613-2025-8). 32pp. Using photographs for illustrations, this simple reader tells about African American twins Tim and Jim and their dog Slim. (Rev: BL 5/1/98; HBG 10/98; SLJ 6/98)

6729 Leonard, Marcia. *I Like Mess* (1). Illus. by Dorothy Handelman. Series: Real Kids Readers. 1998, Millbrook LB $18.90 (978-0-7613-2002-9); paper $4.99 (978-0-7613-2027-2). 32pp. In this simple reader illustrated with photographs, a young girl tries to please her mother by cleaning up the mess she has created. (Rev: BL 5/1/98; SLJ 6/98)

6730 Leonard, Marcia. *My Pal Al* (PS–1). Photos by Dorothy Handelman. Series: Real Kids Readers. 1998,

Millbrook LB $18.90 (978-0-7613-2001-2); paper $4.99 (978-0-7613-2026-5). 31pp. A beginning reader that describes how a little African American girl loves her favorite toy. (Rev: SLJ 6/98)

6731 Leonard, Marcia. *No New Pants!* (1). Illus. by Dorothy Handelman. Series: Real Kids Readers. 1999, Millbrook LB $18.90 (978-0-7613-2063-0); paper $4.99 (978-0-7613-2088-3). 32pp. A young African American child doesn't want to go shopping for pants with his mother, but he enjoys getting a pair of hand-me-downs from his brother. (Rev: BL 12/1/99; HBG 3/00)

6732 Levinson, Nancy S. *Clara and the Bookwagon* (1–2). Illus. by Carolyn Croll. 1988, HarperCollins LB $15.89 (978-0-06-023838-4); paper $3.99 (978-0-06-444134-6). 64pp. A real-life story about a young girl who wants to read despite her father's objections. (Rev: BL 4/1/88; SLJ 7/88)

6733 Levinson, Nancy S. *Prairie Friends* (2–4). Illus. by Stacey Schuett. Series: An I Can Read Book. 2003, HarperCollins LB $16.89 (978-0-06-028002-4). Betsy is thrilled when a girl her age moves into the neighborhood, but the city girl takes time to adapt to her new surroundings in this story that includes lots of interesting facts about prairie life in the middle 1800s. (Rev: BL 1/1–15/03; HBG 10/03; SLJ 3/03)

6734 Levy, Elizabeth. *A Hare-Raising Tail* (2–5). Illus. by Mordicai Gerstein. Series: Ready-for-Chapters. 2002, Simon & Schuster paper $3.99 (978-0-689-84626-7). 64pp. Fletcher the basset hound finds a new home with Jill, and all goes well until Jill takes him to school for show-and-tell. (Rev: BL 9/1/02; HBG 10/02; SLJ 1/03)

6735 Lewin, Betsy. *You Can Do It!* (PS). Illus. by author. Series: I Like to Read. 2013, Holiday $14.95 (978-0-8234-2522-8). 32pp. A simple story about two alligators preparing for a big race. (Rev: BL 5/1/13; SLJ 4/13)

6736 Lewin, Ted. *Look!* (PS–1). Illus. by author. Series: I Like to Read. 2013, Holiday $14.95 (978-0-8234-2607-2). 32pp. Emergent readers are introduced to African animals — an elephant eating, zebras running, giraffes drinking water — followed by a boy playing, reading, and dreaming, surrounded by toy animals. (Rev: BLO 4/1/13; SLJ 4/13)

6737 Lewis, J. Patrick. *Tugg and Teeny* (K–2). Illus. by Christopher Denise. 2011, Sleeping Bear $9.95 (978-1-58536-514-2); paper $3.99 (978-1-58536-685-9). 40pp. Tugg the gorilla and Teeny the monkey share three simple adventures in which they explore music, art, and poetry. (Rev: BL 3/15/11; SLJ 5/1/11)

6738 Lin, Grace. *Ling and Ting Share a Birthday* (K–2). Illus. by author. 2013, Little, Brown $15 (978-0-316-18405-2). 48pp. The 6-year-old twins have various birthday experiences in six linked chapters that will please beginning readers. Lexile 380 (Rev: BLO 7/13; SLJ 8/13)

6739 Lin, Grace. *Ling and Ting: Not Exactly the Same!* (1–2). Illus. by author. 2010, Little, Brown $14.99 (978-0-316-02452-5). 48pp. Twin sisters Ling and Ting may look alike but they prove in these six short chapters that

they are in fact quite different. Lexile 390L (Rev: BL 5/1/10*; LMC 8–9/10; SLJ 7/1/10*)

6740 Lindeen, Mary. *Ships* (PS–3). Series: Mighty Machines. 2007, Children's Pr. LB $18.50 (978-1-60014-060-0). 24pp. The basics about ships for young readers, clearly presented and accompanied by engaging photographs. (Rev: SLJ 7/07)

6741 Little, Jean. *Emma's Magic Winter* (1–2). Illus. by Jennifer Plecas. 1998, HarperCollins $15.95 (978-0-06-025389-9). 64pp. Though Emma is basically very shy, she is brave enough to make a good friend of Sally, the new girl next door. (Rev: BCCB 10/98; BL 11/1/98; HB 9/98*; HBG 3/99; SLJ 10/98)

6742 Lloyd, Jennifer. *Murilla Gorilla: Jungle Detective* (K–3). Illus. by Jacqui Lee. 2013, Simply Read $9.95 (978-1-927018-15-6). 40pp. Who stole Mrs. Chimpanzee's banana muffins? Murilla investigates in this nicely illustrated early reader. (Rev: BL 5/1/13; LMC 11–12/13; SLJ 5/13)

6743 Lobel, Arnold. *Frog and Toad Are Friends* (K–2). Illus. by author. 1970, HarperCollins LB $17.89 (978-0-06-023958-9); paper $3.99 (978-0-06-444020-2). 64pp. Two new friends for the independent reader. Three sequels are: *Frog and Toad Together* (1972); *Frog and Toad All Year* (1976); *Days with Frog and Toad* (1979).

6744 Lobel, Arnold. *Mouse Soup* (1–2). Illus. by author. 1977, HarperCollins LB $17.89 (978-0-06-023968-8); paper $3.99 (978-0-06-444041-7). 64pp. When Mouse is caught by Weasel, who plans to use him for soup, he convinces his captor that "mouse soup must be mixed with stones to make it taste really good."

6745 Lobel, Arnold. *Mouse Tales* (1–2). Illus. by author. 1972, HarperCollins LB $17.89 (978-0-06-023942-8); paper $3.99 (978-0-06-444013-4). Seven bedtime stories told by Papa Mouse to his seven sons. Lively little drawings add to the humor.

6746 Lobel, Arnold. *Owl at Home* (1–2). Illus. by author. 1975, HarperCollins LB $17.89 (978-0-06-023949-7); paper $3.99 (978-0-06-444034-9). 64pp. Five stories dealing with the humorous and bungling attempts of Owl to be helpful.

6747 Lobel, Arnold. *Small Pig* (K–2). Illus. by author. 1969, HarperCollins LB $17.89 (978-0-06-023932-9); paper $3.99 (978-0-06-444120-9). 64pp. A dirty little pig in a search for mud ends up in cement.

6748 Lodge, Bernard. *Custard Surprise* (K–2). Illus. by Tim Bowers. 2007, HarperCollins $15.99 (978-0-06-073687-3). 48pp. Dinah and Rufus, two chickens, serve up tasty meals for animal customers in their diner but refuse to give a fox what he wants — a chicken dinner. (Rev: SLJ 8/07)

6749 Loehr, Mallory. *Dragon Egg* (PS–K). Illus. by Hala Wittwer. 2007, Random LB $11.99 (978-0-375-94350-8); paper $3.99 (978-0-375-84350-1). A cumulative story about a dragon egg that is chased by a trail of characters as it rolls down a hill, only to have the procession reversed when the newborn heads back home. (Rev: BL 9/1/07)

6750 Lofting, Hugh. *Doctor Dolittle's Great Adventure* (1–2). Adapted by Diane Namm. Illus. by John Kanzler. Series: The Story of Doctor Dolittle. 2007, Sterling paper $3.95 (978-1-4027-4122-7). 32pp. In this third installment, the doctor and his friends are trying to take Circus Crocodile home when they are shipwrecked and then imprisoned, but in the end, of course, they do succeed. Also use *Doctor Dolittle's Magical Cure* (2007), the fourth book in the series. (Rev: SLJ 1/08)

6751 Low, Alice. *The Witch Who Was Afraid of Witches* (2–4). Illus. Series: I Can Read. 1999, HarperCollins LB $14.89 (978-0-06-028306-3). 48pp. In this easy chapter book, Wendy, a witch who doubts her own powers, gains confidence one Halloween night. (Rev: BL 9/1/99; HBG 3/00; SLJ 12/99)

6752 Lowry, Lois. *Gooney Bird Is So Absurd* (2–4). Illus. by Middy Thomas. 2009, Houghton $15.00 (978-0-547-11967-0). 112pp. Gooney Bird Greene and her 2nd-grade classmates try to comfort their poetry teacher when her mother dies in this story full of humor, poems, and poignancy. (Rev: BL 2/1/09; HB 5/09; SLJ 3/09) ∩

6753 Lucas, Sally. *Dancing Dinos Go to School* (PS–K). Illus. by Margeaux Lucas. Series: Step into Reading. 2006, Random LB $11.99 (978-0-375-93241-0); paper $Random,.00 (978-0-375-83241-3). 32pp. A group of dinosaurs leap from the pages of a book and spend a wild day disrupting the school. (Rev: BL 8/06; SLJ 10/06)

6754 Maccarone, Grace. *My Tooth Is About to Fall Out* (1–2). Illus. by Betsy Lewin. 1995, Scholastic $3.99 (978-0-590-48376-6). 32pp. An easy-to-read book about the problems of having a loose tooth. (Rev: BL 7/95)

6755 McCully, Emily Arnold. *The Grandma Mix-Up* (1–3). Illus. by author. 1988, HarperCollins LB $15.89 (978-0-06-024202-2); paper $3.99 (978-0-06-444150-6). 64pp. Two grandmothers with very different ways arrive to baby-sit. (Rev: BL 12/1/89; SLJ 3/89)

6756 McCully, Emily Arnold. *Grandmas at Bat* (1–2). Illus. 1993, HarperCollins paper $3.99 (978-0-06-444193-3). 64pp. Pip's two grandmothers, last-minute replacements, coach his baseball team. (Rev: BL 3/1/93; HB 7/93; SLJ 6/93)

6757 McCully, Emily Arnold. *Late Nate in a Race* (PS–1). Illus. by author. Series: I Like to Read. 2012, Holiday House $14.95 (978-0-8234-2421-4). 24pp. Nate is a mouse who is chronically slow but surprises everybody, including himself, on race day. (Rev: BL 2/15/12; SLJ 4/1/12)

6758 McCully, Emily Arnold. *Little Ducks Go* (PS–K). Illus. by author. Series: I Like to Read. 2014, Holiday $14.95 (978-082342941-7). 32pp. A mother duck struggles to rescue her six ducklings when they are swept into a storm drain. (Rev: BL 3/1/14; SLJ 3/14)

6759 McCully, Emily Arnold. *Pete Won't Eat* (PS–3). Illus. by author. Series: I Like to Read. 2013, Holiday $14.95 (978-082342853-3). 32pp. Pete the pig initially rejects the green slop his mother has made for dinner, but

is surprised how good it is when he's persuaded to give it a try. Lexile AD200 (Rev: BLO 9/15/13; SLJ 10/13*)

6760 McDonald, Megan. *Ant and Honey Bee: A Pair of Friends in Winter* (K–2). Illus. by G. Brian Karas. 2013, Candlewick $14.99 (978-076365712-3). 64pp. Ant is getting ready for her winter hibernation, but before she can settle in, she has to see her friend Honey Bee — but Honey Bee is in a bad mood, and it's up to Ant to cheer up her friend. Lexile 640 (Rev: BLO 9/15/13; LMC 5–6/14; SLJ 9/13)

6761 McDonald, Megan. *Beezy and Funnybone* (1–2). Illus. by Nancy Poydar. Series: Beezy. 2000, Orchard LB $15.99 (978-0-531-33211-5); paper $4.95 (978-0-531-07161-8). 48pp. A book for beginning readers that contains three simple stories about a little girl and her dog Funnybone. (Rev: BL 7/00; HBG 10/00; SLJ 9/00)

6762 McDonald, Megan. *Beezy at Bat* (1–2). Illus. by Nancy Poydar. 1998, Orchard LB $14.99 (978-0-531-33085-2). 48pp. In this, the third book about Beezy, she plays baseball, exchanges riddles with Gran, and scares a friend with a snake. (Rev: BL 11/1/98; HBG 3/99; SLJ 9/98)

6763 McDonald, Megan. *Stink and the Great Guinea Pig Express* (2–4). Illus. by Peter H. Reynolds. 2008, Candlewick $12.99 (978-0-7636-2835-2). 128pp. Stink, Sophie, and Webster are on a mission to find homes for 101 rescued guinea pigs in this easy-to-read chapter book. (Rev: BL 3/1/08; SLJ 3/08)

6764 McDonald, Megan. *Stink: The Incredible Shrinking Kid* (2–4). Illus. by Peter H. Reynolds. Series: Judy Moody. 2005, Candlewick $12.99 (978-0-7636-2025-7). 112pp. Stink, Judy Moody's younger brother, is convinced he's shrinking and decides to make the best of it in this beginning chapter book. (Rev: BL 3/1/05; SLJ 4/05)

6765 McEwan, Jamie. *Whitewater Scrubs* (K–2). Illus. by John Margeson. 2005, Darby Creek $14.99 (978-1-58196-038-9). 64pp. Accustomed to athletic success, Clara must conquer her fears when she joins Willie and the football scrubs for a kayaking class; suitable for beginning chapter-book readers. (Rev: BL 9/1/05; SLJ 11/05)

6766 McKay, Sindy. *Ben and Becky in the Haunted House* (1–3). Illus. by Meredith Johnson. Series: We Both Read. 1999, Treasure Bay $7.99 (978-1-891327-14-8); paper $3.99 (978-1-891327-18-6). The story of two children who are forced to spend a night in a haunted house is told with two texts, one for adults and the other for beginning readers. (Rev: SLJ 11/99)

6767 McKenna, Colleen O'Shaughnessy. *Doggone . . . Third Grade!* (2–3). Illus. by Stephanie Roth. 2002, Holiday House $15.95 (978-0-8234-1696-7). 80pp. Third-grader Gordie comes up with a trick for his dog to perform in the class talent show. (Rev: BL 7/02; HBG 10/02; SLJ 7/02)

6768 McKenna, Colleen O'Shaughnessy. *Third Grade Ghouls* (2–4). Illus. by Stephanie Roth. 2001, Holiday House $15.95 (978-0-8234-1652-3). 80pp. This simple beginning chapter book finds 3rd-grader Gordie searching for the perfect costume to wear for the Halloween parade. (Rev: BL 1/1–15/02; HBG 10/02; SLJ 2/02)

6769 McKenna, Colleen O'Shaughnessy. *Third Grade Wedding Bells* (2–4). Illus. by Stephanie Roth. Series: Third Grade. 2006, Holiday $15.95 (978-0-8234-1943-2). 160pp. Gordie, Lucy, and Lamont are distressed to hear their teacher is getting married — will they lose her? (Rev: BL 5/1/06; SLJ 4/06)

6770 McKissack, Patricia C. *Tippy Lemmey* (2–4). Illus. by Susan Keeter. Series: Ready-for-Chapters. 2003, Simon & Schuster paper $3.99 (978-0-689-85019-6). 64pp. Mischievous Tippy the dog is a source of annoyance to Leandra and her friends, but when the pup is kidnapped, they come to his rescue in this story set in Tennessee in 1951. (Rev: BCCB 3/03; BL 1/1–15/03; HB 3/03; HBG 10/03; SLJ 1/03)

6771 McKissack, Patricia C., and Fredrick McKissack. *Messy Bessey's Family Reunion* (K–1). Illus. by Dana Regan. Series: Rookie Readers. 2000, Children's Book Pr. LB $19.50 (978-0-516-20830-5); paper $4.95 (978-0-516-26552-0). 32pp. In this easy reader, Messy Bessey is so upset at the mess she and her relatives have made at an outdoor picnic that she organizes them into a clean-up squad. (Rev: BL 12/1/00)

6772 McKissack, Patricia C., and Fredrick McKissack. *Messy Bessey's Holidays* (PS–2). Illus. by Dana Regan. Series: Rookie Readers. 1999, Children's Book Pr. LB $19.50 (978-0-516-20829-9). 30pp. In this beginning reader, a child bakes cookies for her friends for Hanukkah, Christmas, and Kwanzaa. (Rev: HBG 10/99; SLJ 8/99)

6773 McKissack, Patricia C., and Fredrick McKissack. *Miami Makes the Play* (2–4). Illus. Series: Road to Reading. 2001, Golden paper $3.99 (978-0-307-26505-0). 92pp. Miami and friends head for baseball camp for a summer of fun and play but must make some decisions, such as whether to support a coed team. (Rev: BL 5/1/01; HBG 10/01)

6774 MacLachlan, Patricia. *White Fur Flying* (2–4). 2013, Simon & Schuster $15.99 (978-1-4424-2171-4). 128pp. When he moves next-door to a family that rescues Great Pyrenees dogs, young Phillip comes out of his shell and starts to talk. **e** Lexile 450L (Rev: BL 12/1/12; LMC 8–9/13; SLJ 3/13)

6775 McMullan, Kate. *Pearl and Wagner: Five Days Till Summer* (1–3). Illus. by R. W. Alley. 2012, Dial $14.99 (978-080373589-7). 40pp. Pearl, a rabbit, and Wagner, a mouse, speculate about whether next year's teacher will be mean or nice. Lexile AD420 (Rev: BL 8/12; HB 7–8/12; SLJ 6/1/12)

6776 McMullan, Kate. *Pearl and Wagner: Four Eyes* (K–2). Illus. by R. W. Alley. 2010, Dial $15.99 (978-0-8037-3086-1). 40pp. Friends and a teacher help Wagner the mouse adjust to the fact that he needs to wear glasses. (Rev: HB 9–10/10; LMC 1–2/11; SLJ 9/1/10)

6777 McMullan, Kate. *Pearl and Wagner: One Funny Day* (K–2). Illus. by R. W. Alley. 2009, Dial $14.99 (978-0-8037-3085-4). An easy-reader featuring Wagner and Pearl on April Fools' day. (Rev: BCCB 6/09; BL 11/15/08; HB 3/09; SLJ 3/09)

6778 McNamara, Margaret. *The Counting Race* (PS–1). Illus. by Mike Gordon. Series: Ready-to-Read. 2003, Simon & Schuster paper $3.99 (978-0-689-85539-9). 31pp. The concept of counting by twos is introduced in this easy-reader story about 1st-graders at Robin Hill School. (Rev: HBG 4/04; SLJ 7/03)

6779 McNamara, Margaret. *Fall Leaf Project* (PS–K). Illus. by Mike Gordon. Series: Ready-to-Read. 2006, Simon & Schuster paper $3.99 (978-1-4169-1537-9). 32pp. Mrs. Connor's class collects leaves in a variety of fall colors and sends them to a 1st-grade class in the Southwest. (Rev: BL 1/1–15/07)

6780 McNamara, Margaret. *The First Day of School* (K–2). Illus. by Mike Gordon. Series: Ready-to-Read. 2005, Aladdin LB $11.89 (978-0-689-86915-0); paper $3.99 (978-0-689-86914-3). 32pp. Michael can't wait to start 1st grade until he learns that he won't be able to take his dog to class; suitable for beginning readers. (Rev: BL 8/05; SLJ 8/05)

6781 McNamara, Margaret. *The Garden Project* (PS–1). Illus. by Mike Gordon. 2010, Aladdin paper $3.99 (978-14169917-1-7). 32pp. A class of 1st-graders plants and tends a small vegetable garden in this story for beginning readers. (Rev: BLO 7/10)

6782 McNamara, Margaret. *One Hundred Days (Plus One)* (K–3). Illus. by Mike Gordon. Series: Robin Hill School. 2003, Simon & Schuster paper $3.99 (978-0-689-85535-1). Hannah is miserable when she misses the 100th day of school, for which she has been collecting buttons, but gets a happy surprise when she returns to class. (Rev: HBG 10/03; SLJ 4/03)

6783 McNamara, Margaret. *Summer Treasure* (PS–1). Illus. by Mike Gordon. Series: Robin Hill School. 2012, Simon & Schuster $15.99 (978-1-44243646-6). 32pp. Hannah is shocked to see her teacher lying on the beach in this funny early reader. Lexile AD240 (Rev: BL 8/12)

6784 McPhail, David. *Boy, Bird, and Dog* (PS–1). Illus. by author. Series: I Like to Read. 2011, Holiday House $14.95 (978-0-8234-2346-0). Unpaged. Simple text and humorous illustrations introduce the concept of up and down as a boy, a bird, and a dog, enjoy a tree house. (Rev: SLJ 11/1/11)

6785 McPhail, David. *A Bug, a Bear, and a Boy* (1–2). Illus. 1998, Scholastic paper $3.99 (978-0-590-14904-4). A young boy spends an enjoyable day with his two companions, a bear and a bug. (Rev: BL 11/1/98)

6786 McPhail, David. *The Day the Sheep Showed Up* (1–2). Illus. Series: Hello Reader! 1998, Scholastic paper $3.99 (978-0-590-84910-4). An uproarious farce in which the other animals try to find out what sort of being is a sheep after it unexpectedly joins the farm community. (Rev: BL 5/1/98)

6787 McPhail, David. *The Great Race* (1–2). Illus. Series: Hello Reader! 1998, Scholastic paper $3.99 (978-0-590-84909-8). 32pp. In this humorous easy reader, the animals have a race and, in spite of many mistakes, end together — each one a winner! (Rev: BL 5/1/98)

6788 McPhail, David. *Rick Is Sick* (PS–1). Illus. Series: Green Light Reader. 2004, Harcourt $11.95 (978-0-15-205091-7). 24pp. Bunny Jack finds Rick the bear sick in bed and does what he can to help in this simple story for very early readers. (Rev: BL 3/15/04; SLJ 5/04)

6789 McPhail, David. *Sick Day* (K–1). Illus. by author. Series: I Like to Read. 2012, Holiday $14.95 (978-0-8234-2424-5). 32pp. Sick in bed, Boy rejects a bone from Dog and pizza from Bird but accepts soup from Mom; sensibly, as it turns out, because Dog and Bird don't feel so good after they eat their own offerings. (Rev: BL 10/1/12; SLJ 8/12)

6790 Manushkin, Fran. *Katie in the Kitchen* (K–2). Illus. by Tammie Lyon. 2010, Capstone LB $19.99 (978-1-4048-5724-7). 32pp. Frustrated that no one will let her help with household jobs, young Katie Woo decides to cook dinner — with predictably chaotic results. Lexile 380L (Rev: BLO 7/10; SLJ 5/1/10)

6791 Manushkin, Fran. *Katie Woo Has the Flu* (K–2). Illus. by Tammie Lyon. 2011, Capstone $19.99 (978-140486518-1); paper $3.95 (978-14048685-4-0). 32pp. Sick with the flu, Katie misses the fun and friends she enjoys at school. (Rev: BLO 12/15/11)

6792 Marshall, Edward. *Three by the Sea* (1–3). Illus. by James Marshall. 1981, Puffin paper $3.99 (978-0-14-037004-1). Three friends, Lolly, Spider, and Sam, tell stories by the seashore.

6793 Marshall, James. *Fox Outfoxed* (2–3). Illus. 1992, Viking paper $3.99 (978-0-14-038113-9). 48pp. Three easily read stories about Fox and how his careful plans misfire. (Rev: BCCB 4/92; BL 4/1/92; HB 7/92; SLJ 5/92*)

6794 Marzollo, Jean. *I Am an Apple* (PS–1). Illus. by Judith Moffatt. Series: Hello Reader! 1997, Scholastic $3.99 (978-0-590-37223-7). A beginning reader that details the life of an apple from flower to fruit to market to table. (Rev: SLJ 1/98)

6795 Marzollo, Jean. *I'm a Caterpillar* (K–2). Illus. by Judith Moffatt. Series: Hello Reader! 1997, Scholastic $3.99 (978-0-590-84779-7). A beginning reader that presents, in story form, the life cycle of a caterpillar. (Rev: SLJ 11/97)

6796 Marzollo, Jean. *Once Upon a Springtime* (1–2). Illus. by Jacqueline Rogers. Series: Hello Reader! 1998, Scholastic paper $3.99 (978-0-590-46017-0). 30pp. A fawn and its mother stay together during the first year of its life and observe humans and their comparable annual activities. (Rev: BL 5/1/98)

6797 Marzollo, Jean, et al. *Football Friends* (1–2). Illus. by True Kelley. Series: Hello Reader! 1997, Scholastic $3.99 (978-0-590-38395-0). 32pp. Freddy becomes so angry with his friend Mark when they choose teams for playing football that he begins using his fists and feet in this easy-to-read sports book. (Rev: BL 2/1/98; SLJ 3/98)

6798 Masters, Anthony. *Ricky's Rat Gang* (1–3). Illus. by Chris Fisher. Series: I Am Reading. 2004, Kingfisher paper $3.95 (978-0-7534-5800-6). 41pp. Three mice plot to drive bullying rats from the supermarket storeroom in this book for beginning readers. (Rev: SLJ 9/04)

6799 Masurel, Claire. *That Bad, Bad Cat* (1). Illus. by True Kelley. Series: All Aboard Reading. 2002, Penguin paper $3.99 (978-0-448-42622-8). 32pp. The family cat is always misbehaving, but when he fails to show up for dinner everyone misses him. (Rev: BL 6/1–15/02; HBG 10/02)

6800 Mayfield, Sue. *Shoot!* (1–2). Illus. by Ken Cox. Series: Blue Bananas. 2001, Crabtree LB $22.60 (978-0-7787-0847-6). 48pp. Shoot the dog, the team mascot, helps Jamie and his friends win the soccer game. (Rev: SLJ 7/02)

6801 Medearis, Angela Shelf. *On the Way to the Pond* (K–2). Illus. by Lorinda Bryan Cauley. 2006, Harcourt $12.95 (978-0-15-205599-8); paper $3.95 (978-0-15-205623-0). Tess Tiger and Herbert Hippo have a picnic by a cool pond in this easy reader. (Rev: SLJ 6/06)

6802 Medearis, Angela Shelf. *Singing for Dr. King* (K–3). Illus. by Cornelius Van Wright and Ying-Hwa Hu. Series: Just for You! 2004, Scholastic paper $3.99 (978-0-439-56855-5). 32pp. An African American 3rd-grader becomes involved in civil rights in this easy-reader. (Rev: SLJ 1/05)

6803 Meisel, Paul. *See Me Dig* (PS–K). Illus. by author. Series: I Like to Read. 2013, Holiday $14.95 (978-0-8234-2743-7). 32pp. The dogs from *See Me Run* (2011) are on a digging tear in this entertaining offering for beginning readers. (Rev: BL 5/1/13; SLJ 3/13)

6804 Meisel, Paul. *See Me Run* (PS–1). Illus. by author. Series: I Like to Read. 2011, Holiday House $14.95 (978-0-8234-2349-1). Unpaged. Simple text and humorous illustrations describe dogs having a wonderful time at the dog park. (Rev: SLJ 11/1/11)

6805 Meister, Cari. *My Pony Jack* (PS–K). Illus. by Amy Young. Series: Viking Easy-to-Read. 2005, Viking $13.99 (978-0-670-05917-1). In simple rhyming couplets suitable for beginning readers, Lacy talks about her pony and how she grooms him. (Rev: BL 5/1/05)

6806 Meister, Cari. *Skinny and Fats, Best Friends* (K–2). Illus. by Steve Björkman. Series: Holiday House Reader. 2002, Holiday House $14.95 (978-0-8234-1692-9). 32pp. Skinny, a rabbit, and Fats, a pig, enjoy spending time fishing, making marshmallows, and building rockets. (Rev: HBG 3/03; SLJ 10/02)

6807 Meister, Cari. *Tiny Goes Camping* (PS). Illus. by Rich Davis. Series: Viking Easy-to-Read. 2006, Viking $13.99 (978-0-670-89250-1). A boy and his huge dog ("Tiny" of the title) plan to camp out in their back yard in this easy reader. (Rev: BL 5/1/06; SLJ 6/06)

6808 Michalak, Jamie. *Joe and Sparky Get New Wheels* (1–3). Illus. by Frank Remkiewicz. 2009, Candlewick $15.99 (978-0-7636-3387-5). 48pp. Unlikely friends Joe the giraffe and Sparky the turtle enjoy a day out of the zoo. (Rev: BCCB 4/09; SLJ 4/09)

6809 Miller, Sara S. *Cat in the Bag* (1). Illus. by Benton Mahan. Series: Rookie Readers. 2001, Children's Book Pr. $19.50 (978-0-516-22014-7). 32pp. While trying to pack, a little girl must keep chasing her cat out of her suitcase in this easy reader. (Rev: BL 11/1/01)

6810 Miller, Sara S. *Three More Stories You Can Read to Your Cat* (1–3). Illus. by True Kelley. 2002, Houghton $15.00 (978-0-618-11035-3). 48pp. These simple, playful stories are about cats who face such problems as wanting to come inside during a snow storm and finding entertainment on a particularly boring birthday. (Rev: BL 4/15/02; HBG 10/02; SLJ 5/02)

6811 Miller, Sara S. *Three More Stories You Can Read to Your Dog* (2–3). Illus. 2000, Houghton $15.00 (978-0-395-92293-4). Three amusing easy-to-read stories that will amuse children, even if they don't have a dog. (Rev: BL 3/15/00; HBG 10/00; SLJ 4/00)

6812 Miller, Sara S. *Three Stories You Can Read to Your Teddy Bear* (1–3). Illus. by True Kelley. 2004, Houghton $15.00 (978-0-618-30397-7). 48pp. In this companion to *Three Stories You Can Read to Your Cat* (1993) and *Three Stories You Can Read to Your Dog* (1995), three entertaining stories are designed to be read to a teddy bear. (Rev: BL 3/1/04; SLJ 6/04)

6813 Mills, Claudia. *Gus and Grandpa Go Fishing* (1–3). Illus. by Catherine Stock. Series: Gus and Grandpa. 2003, Farrar $15.00 (978-0-374-32815-3). 48pp. Grandpa shows Gus how to fish in this installment in the long-running series. (Rev: BL 9/1/03; HBG 4/04; SLJ 10/03)

6814 Minarik, Else Holmelund. *Little Bear* (K–2). Illus. by Maurice Sendak. 1957, HarperCollins LB $16.89 (978-0-06-024241-1); paper $3.95 (978-0-06-444004-2). 64pp. Humorous adventure stories of Mother Bear and Little Bear. Others in the series: *Little Bear's Friend* (1960); *Little Bear's Visit* (1961); *A Kiss for Little Bear* (1968).

6815 Minarik, Else Holmelund. *Little Bear and the Marco Polo* (K–1). Illus. by Dorothy Doubleday. Series: I Can Read. 2010, HarperCollins $16.99 (978-0-06-085485-0); paper $3.99 (978-0-06-085487-4). 32pp. Little Bear learns about his grandfather's seafaring life and the fact that there are bears of different kinds around the world. (Rev: HB 9–10/10; SLJ 8/1/10)

6816 Minarik, Else Holmelund. *No Fighting, No Biting!* (PS–3). Illus. by Maurice Sendak. 1958, HarperCollins LB $17.89 (978-0-06-024291-6); paper $3.95 (978-0-06-444015-8). 64pp. Light-foot and Quick-foot, two little alligators, teach Rosa and Willy a lesson.

6817 Morris, Jennifer E. *May I Please Have a Cookie?* (K–1). Illus. Series: Scholastic Reader. 2005, Scholastic paper $3.99 (978-0-439-73819-4). A young alligator learns the right way to get a cookie from his mother in this beginning reader. (Rev: BL 1/1–15/06)

6818 Morris, Jennifer E. *Please Write Back!* (PS–1). Illus. by author. 2010, Scholastic paper $3.99 (978-0-545-11506-3). Unpaged. A young crocodile sends his grandma a simple letter, and eagerly awaits her response. (Rev: SLJ 4/1/10)

6819 Morris, Kim. *Molly in the Middle* (2–3). Illus. by Dorothy Handelman. Series: Real Kids Readers. 1999, Millbrook LB $18.90 (978-0-7613-2059-3); paper $4.99 (978-0-7613-2084-5). 48pp. Molly, a middle child, decides that if she can't be the youngest or oldest, she will be the "est" in some other way, such as being the loudest or funniest. (Rev: BL 5/15/99; SLJ 8/99)

6820 Mould, Chris. *Pip and the Wood Witch Curse* (3–6). Illus. by author. Series: Spindlewood Tales. 2012, Whitman $12.99 (978-0-8075-6548-3). 176pp. After escaping from an orphanage, young Pip faces scary urban and forest adventures in this suspenseful tale that draws on *Great Expectations*; the first installment in a series. e Lexile 810L (Rev: BL 12/1/12; LMC 1–2/13; SLJ 3/13)

6821 Nagda, Ann Whitehead. *The Valentine Cat* (2–4). Illus. by Stephanie Roth. 2008, Holiday $16.95 (978-0-8234-2123-7). 128pp. Jenny's brother develops asthma and she must find a new home for her cat Munchkin; keeping at school seems to be a good option. (Rev: BLO 12/18/08; SLJ 2/09)

6822 Namm, Diane. *Guess Who?* (PS–2). Illus. by David Sheldon. Series: My First Reader. 2004, Children's Pr. LB $18.50 (978-0-516-24412-9). 31pp. Potential visitors are the subject of this rhyming book for beginning readers with cartoon illustrations and a word list. (Rev: SLJ 7/04)

6823 Napoli, Donna Jo, and Robert Furrow. *Sly the Sleuth and the Food Mysteries* (2–4). Illus. by Heather Maione. 2007, Dial $16.99 (978-0-8037-3119-6). 144pp. Sly and her friends explore three food-related mysteries presented in short sentences and basic vocabulary. (Rev: BL 5/1/07; SLJ 6/07)

6824 Napoli, Donna Jo, and Robert Furrow. *Sly the Sleuth and the Pet Mysteries* (2–4). Illus. by Heather Maione. Series: Sly the Sleuth. 2005, Dial $15.99 (978-0-8037-2993-3). 96pp. Sylvia (a.k.a. "Sly the Sleuth") solves her friends' pet mysteries in this illustrated easy reader, the first in a series. (Rev: BL 3/1/05)

6825 Nelson, Vaunda Micheaux. *Ready? Set. Raymond!* (K–1). Illus. by Derek Anderson. Series: Step into Reading. 2002, Random LB $11.99 (978-0-375-91363-1); paper $3.99 (978-0-375-81363-4). Raymond, an appealing African American boy, "does things fast," including making a friend and running a race, in this collection of three short, nicely illustrated stories. (Rev: BL 9/15/02; HBG 3/03; SLJ 12/02)

6826 O'Connor, Jane. *Every Day Is Earth Day* (K–2). Illus. by Robin Preiss Glasser. Series: Fancy Nancy. 2010, HarperCollins $16.99 (978-006187327-0); paper $3.99 (978-00618732-6-3). 32pp. Fancy Nancy learns to balance her newfound environmental zeal with tolerance when her family resists her new rules. e (Rev: BLO 6/10)

6827 O'Connor, Jane. *Fancy Nancy: Apples Galore!* (K–2). Illus. by Robin Preiss Glasser. Series: I Can Read! 2013, HarperCollins $16.99 (978-006208311-1); paper $3.99 (978-00620831-0-4). 32pp. Nancy and her school friends enjoy a trip to an apple orchard in this funny blend of clever vocabulary and bright illustrations. (Rev: BLO 9/1/13)

6828 O'Connor, Jane. *Fancy Nancy and the Fabulous Fashion Boutique* (1–3). Illus. by Robin Preiss Glasser. Series: Fancy Nancy. 2010, HarperCollins $17.99 (978-006123592-4). 32pp. Fancy Nancy grapples with kindness, instant gratification, and generosity as she has a fashion yard sale and plans for her little sister's birthday party. 🎧 (Rev: BL 11/15/10)

6829 O'Connor, Jane. *Kate Skates* (PS–1). Illus. by DyAnne DiSalvo. 1995, Penguin paper $3.99 (978-0-448-40935-1). Tiny Jen easily learns to skate on her double blades, but older sister Kate has problems with her grownup single blades. (Rev: BL 1/1–15/96; SLJ 5/96)

6830 O'Connor, Jane. *Nina, Nina Ballerina* (PS–1). Illus. by DyAnne DiSalvo. 1993, Penguin paper $3.99 (978-0-448-40511-7). 32pp. When Nina breaks her arm, she worries that she will not be able to perform in her ballet class show. (Rev: BL 7/93; SLJ 8/93)

6831 O'Connor, Jane. *Poison Ivy Expert* (K–2). Illus. by Ted Enik. Series: Fancy Nancy. I Can Read! 2009, HarperCollins $16.99 (978-0-06-123614-3); paper $3.99 (978-0-06-123613-6). 32pp. Nancy thinks she can recognize poison ivy, but gathering wildflowers for her teacher proves otherwise; for beginning readers. (Rev: SLJ 3/09)

6832 Ormerod, Jan. *The Newest Dancer* (PS–1). Illus. by author. Series: Ballet Sisters. 2008, Scholastic paper $5.99 (978-0-439-82282-4). Bonnie's little sister Sylvie has her first ballet class. (Rev: BL 2/15/08; SLJ 5/08)

6833 Osborne, Mary Pope. *Dinosaurs Before Dark* (1–2). Illus. by Sal Murdocca. 1992, Random LB $11.99 (978-0-679-92411-1). Jack and his sister time-travel to the days of the dinosaurs. (Rev: BL 10/1/92; SLJ 9/92)

6834 Osborne, Mary Pope. *Mummies in the Morning* (1–4). Illus. Series: Magic Tree House. 1993, Random LB $11.99 (978-0-679-92424-1); paper $3.99 (978-0-679-82424-4). Jack and Annie time-travel to ancient Egypt to help a queen find a copy of the Book of the Dead. (Rev: BL 4/1/94)

6835 Packard, Mary. *The Very Bad Day* (PS–2). Illus. by Joy Allen. 2004, Children's Pr. LB $18.50 (978-0-516-24415-0). 31pp. Things do not start off well for the young heroine of this rhyming book for beginning readers, with cartoon illustrations and a word list. (Rev: SLJ 7/04)

6836 Parish, Herman. *Amelia Bedelia Bakes Off* (1–3). Illus. by Lynn Sweat. 2010, Greenwillow $17.99 (978-0-06-084358-8); LB $18.89 (978-0-06-084359-5). 64pp. Amelia Bedelia sets out to enter her famed baked goods in a bake-off, but her literal interpretations nearly get her in trouble. (Rev: SLJ 2/1/11)

6837 Parish, Herman. *Amelia Bedelia Road Trip!* (2–4). Illus. by Lynne Avril. 2013, Greenwillow $15.99 (978-006209503-9); paper $4.99 (978-00620950-2-2). 160pp. Amelia Bedelia is taking a vacation, but unfortunately not quite where she had hoped; however, she still finds a way to have fun. (Rev: BLO 9/15/13)

6838 Parish, Herman. *Amelia Bedelia, Cub Reporter* (1–3). Illus. by Lynn Sweat. 2012, Greenwillow $16.99 (978-0-06-209510-7). 64pp. Amelia has fun writing headlines for the school newspaper. Lexile 460 (Rev: BL 8/12; SLJ 9/12)

6839 Parish, Herman. *Amelia Bedelia's First Apple Pie* (PS–2). Illus. by Lynne Avril. 2010, Greenwillow $16.99 (978-0-06-196409-1); LB $17.89 (978-0-06-196410-7). Unpaged. With her usual over-literal interpretations, Amelia accompanies her grandmother to the farmer's market to buy ingredients for a pie. (Rev: SLJ 12/1/10)

6840 Parish, Herman. *Amelia Bedelia's First Day of School* (K–2). Illus. by Lynne Avril. 2009, Greenwillow $16.99 (978-0-06-154455-2); LB $17.89 (978-0-06-154456-9). 32pp. Amelia's first day of school is full of funny misunderstandings. (Rev: BL 9/15/09; SLJ 11/1/09)

6841 Parish, Herman. *Amelia Bedelia's First Field Trip* (1–3). Illus. by Lynne Avril. 2011, Greenwillow $16.99 (978-0-06-196413-8); LB $17.89 (978-0-06-196414-5). 32pp. Comic literalist Amelia Bedelia enjoys a class trip to a farm, where she "tosses salad," "shakes a leg," and looks forward to a swim in the "car pool" on the way home. (Rev: SLJ 9/1/11)

6842 Parish, Herman. *Amelia Bedelia's Masterpiece* (1–3). Illus. by Lynn Sweat. Series: Amelia Bedelia. 2007, Greenwillow $15.99 (978-0-06-084355-7). 64pp. The literal-minded housekeeper visits an art museum and suffers many misinterpretations. Other recent titles in this funny, long-running series include *Calling Doctor Amelia Bedelia* (2002), *Amelia Bedelia, Rocket Scientist?* (2005), *Amelia Bedelia Under Construction* (2006), and *Amelia Bedelia's Masterpiece* (2007). (Rev: BL 6/1–15/07)

6843 Parish, Peggy. *No More Monsters for Me!* (K–3). Illus. by Marc Simont. 1981, HarperCollins LB $17.89 (978-0-06-024658-7); paper $3.99 (978-0-06-444109-4). A young girl wants to keep a monster for a pet.

6844 Parish, Peggy. *Scruffy* (1–2). Illus. by Kelly Oechsli. 1988, HarperCollins paper $3.99 (978-0-06-444137-7). 64pp. A small boy learns how to choose and care for his first pet — a kitten. (Rev: BL 2/1/88; SLJ 7/88)

6845 Park, Barbara. *Junie B. Jones Has a Monster Under Her Bed* (2–3). Illus. by Denise Brunkus. Series: Stepping Stone. 1997, Random $11.99 (978-0-679-96697-5). 80pp. An easy reader in which little Junie is convinced that an invisible monster lives under her bed. Also use *Junie B. Jones Is Not a Crook* (1997). (Rev: HB 7/97; SLJ 11/97)

6846 Park, Barbara. *Junie B., First Grader (at Last!)* (2–3). Illus. by Denise Brunkus. 2001, Random LB $13.99 (978-0-375-81516-4). When her best friend deserts her and she finds out she needs glasses, Junie B. Jones discovers that 1st grade is not what she expected. (Rev: BL 11/15/01; HBG 3/02; SLJ 1/02)

6847 Park, Barbara. *Junie B., First Grader: One Man Band* (1–3). Illus. by Denise Brunkus. Series: Junie B. Jones. 2003, Random LB $13.99 (978-0-375-92522-1).

Junie B. debuts as a cheerleader in this entry in the popular series. Also use *Shipwrecked* (2004). (Rev: HBG 4/04; SLJ 3/04)

6848 Parker, Marjorie Blain. *Hello, Freight Train!* (PS–K). Illus. by Bob Kolar. Series: Scholastic Reader. 2005, Scholastic paper $3.99 (978-0-439-59891-0). 32pp. A dog tells his puppy about the different types of wagons on the passing freight train. (Rev: BL 5/15/05)

6849 Paul, Ann Whitford. *Hop! Hop! Hop!* (PS–K). Illus. by Jan Gerardi. Series: Step into Reading. 2005, Random LB $11.99 (978-0-375-92857-4); paper $3.99 (978-0-375-82857-7). 32pp. An early reader featuring Little Rabbit, who tries to do what Big Rabbit does but can't always keep up. (Rev: SLJ 8/05)

6850 Paul, Ann Whitford. *Snail's Good Night* (PS–1). Illus. by Rosanne Litzinger. 2008, Holiday $14.95 (978-0-8234-1912-8). 32pp. Snail slides — very slowly — from friend to friend to bid them each good night, usually arriving far too late. (Rev: BL 3/1/08; SLJ 2/08)

6851 Pearson, Susan. *Eagle-Eye Ernie Comes to Town* (2–3). Illus. by Gioia Fiammenghi. 1990, Simon & Schuster paper $11.95 (978-0-671-70564-0). 70pp. Ernestine earns the admiration of her classmates when she solves the mystery of items missing from lunch bags. (Rev: BCCB 12/92; BL 10/1/90; SLJ 4/91)

6852 Pennypacker, Sara. *Clementine's Letter* (2–4). Illus. by Marla Frazee. 2008, Hyperion $14.99 (978-0-7868-3884-4). Third-grader Clementine is not happy that she may lose her beloved teacher and is not inclined to write a letter supporting his nomination for the program that will take him away. (Rev: BL 4/1/08; HB 7/08; SLJ 7/08) ∩

6853 *Pet Stories: You Don't Have to Walk* (1–2). Illus. 2000, North-South LB $14.88 (978-1-58717-032-4). A book for beginning readers that features stories and excerpts from well-known easy-to-read books like Cynthia Rylant's Henry and Mudge stories. A companion book is *School Stories: Your Dog Didn't Eat* (2000). (Rev: BL 7/00; HBG 3/01)

6854 Pierce, Terry. *Tae Kwon Do!* (PS–K). Illus. by Todd Bonita. Series: Step into Reading. 2006, Random $3.99 (978-0-375-83448-6). 32pp. For beginning readers, this is a simple rhyming account of a brother and sister's tae kwon do class. (Rev: SLJ 5/06)

6855 Pilkey, Dav. *Big Dog and Little Dog Making a Mistake* (PS–K). Illus. by author. Series: A Big Dog and Little Dog Book. 1999, Harcourt $5.95 (978-0-15-200354-8). This board book for beginning readers tells what happens when two doggy friends mistake a skunk for a kitten. (Rev: SLJ 6/99)

6856 Pinkwater, Daniel. *Mush's Jazz Adventure* (2–4). Illus. by Jill Pinkwater. Series: Ready-for-Chapters. 2002, Simon & Schuster paper $3.99 (978-0-689-84572-7). 37pp. Mush, an alien dog, tells the story of her arrival on Earth and how she and three other animals saved a dance hall owner from robbers in this entertaining and improbable beginning chapter book. (Rev: HBG 3/03; SLJ 2/03)

6857 Platt, Kin. *Big Max and the Mystery of the Missing Giraffe* (K–2). Illus. by Lynne Cravath. Series: I Can Read. 2005, HarperCollins $15.99 (978-0-06-009918-3). 64pp. Big Max continues his detective work in this entertaining mystery for beginning readers. (Rev: SLJ 7/05)

6858 Pomerantz, Charlotte. *The Outside Dog* (1–3). Illus. by Jennifer Plecas. 1993, HarperCollins LB $15.89 (978-0-06-024783-6). 64pp. An easy-reader that tells how Marisol gradually breaks down her grandfather's opposition to having a dog as a pet. (Rev: BCCB 10/93; BL 9/15/93*; SLJ 11/93*)

6859 *The Prince Has a Boo-Boo!* (K–1). Illus. by R. W. Alley. Series: I'm Going to Read. 2005, Sterling paper $3.95 (978-1-4027-2089-5). 28pp. This beginning reader featuring a cumulative story about a prince in need of a bandage introduces 50 basic vocabulary words. (Rev: BL 9/1/05; SLJ 9/05)

6860 Proimos, James. *Mutton Soup: More Adventures of Johnny Mutton* (2–4). Illus. 2004, Harcourt $16.00 (978-0-15-216772-1). In these five graphic-novel-style stories, Johnny Mutton — the lamb adopted by humans — gets etiquette lessons, goes on the rollercoast, and has other adventures. (Rev: BL 3/1/04; HB 3/04; SLJ 4/04)

6861 Proimos, James, and Andy Rheingold. *When Guinea Pigs Fly!* (2–5). Illus. by James Proimos. 2005, Scholastic paper $3.99 (978-0-439-51902-1). Brooks the guinea pig dreams of freedom from his pet shop, so he is initially ecstatic when he and friends Leone and Allen are accidentally set free in a park; a beginning chapter book with black-and-white cartoon drawings. (Rev: SLJ 11/05)

6862 Ransom, Candice F. *Danger at Sand Cave* (1–3). Illus. by Den Schofield. Series: On My Own History. 2000, Carolrhoda LB $21.27 (978-1-57505-379-0); paper $23.93 (978-1-57505-454-4). A fictitious 10-year-old boy helps in the unsuccessful efforts to rescue Floyd Collins from a cave in 1925. (Rev: HB 7/00; HBG 10/00; SLJ 8/00)

6863 Rau, Dana Meachen. *Chilly Charlie* (K–1). Illus. by Martin Lemelman. Series: Rookie Readers. 2001, Children's Book Pr. paper $4.95 (978-0-516-27288-7). 24pp. Charlie feels that he is getting cold and needs a hug to keep him warm. (Rev: BL 4/15/01)

6864 Rau, Dana Meachen. *In the Yard* (K–1). Illus. by Elizabeth Wolf. Series: Compass Point Early Reader. 2001, Compass Point LB $14.95 (978-0-7565-0116-7). 24pp. A brief, simple text and bold illustrations depict an African American family enjoying their backyard. (Rev: SLJ 2/02)

6865 Rau, Dana Meachen. *Robot, Go Bot!* (PS–1). Illus. by Wook Jin Jung. Series: Step into Reading Comic Readers. 2013, Random House paper $3.99 (978-03758708-3-5). 32pp. Tired of his little girl's demands, her robot runs away; the comic book format is suitable for beginning readers. ALA Notable Children's Book. (Rev: BL 7/13)

6866 Rau, Dana Meachen. *Shoo, Crow! Shoo!* (1). Illus. by Mary Galan Rojas. Series: Compass Point Early Reader. 2001, Compass Point LB $14.95 (978-0-7565-0072-6). 24pp. Two children make a scarecrow from old clothes, hay, and a pumpkin. (Rev: BL 7/01; SLJ 8/01)

6867 Reggier, DeMar. *Gooci Food* (K–2). Illus. by David Austin Clar. Series: My First Reader. 2005, Children's Pr. LB $18.50 (978-0-516-24879-0); paper $3.95 (978-0-516-24969-8). 32pp. In this easy-reader, a young boy accompanies his father to the grocery store where they buy ingredients for a special meal for Mom. (Rev: SLJ 1/06)

6868 Ries, Lori. *Aggie and Ben: Three Stories* (K–2). Illus. by Frank W. Dormer. 2006, Charlesbridge $12.95 (978-1-57091-594-9). 48pp. A beginning chapter book in which Ben takes home a new pet dog, Aggie, and the two get to know each other. (Rev: SLJ 7/06)

6869 Ries, Lori. *Aggie Gets Lost* (K–2). Illus. by Frank W. Dormer. 2011, Charlesbridge $12.95 (978-1-57091-633-5). 48pp. After a boy and his family have tried everything to find their dog, their blind neighbor suggests a different approach. (Rev: SLJ 8/1/11)

6870 Ries, Lori. *Aggie the Brave* (1–3). Illus. by Frank W. Dormer. 2010, Charlesbridge $12.95 (978-1-57091-635-9). 48pp. Ben worries about his dog Aggie while she is being spayed, and looks after her when she comes home. Lexile AD230L (Rev: BLO 11/15/10; HB 9–10/10; LMC 1–2/11; SLJ 8/1/10*)

6871 Ries, Lori. *Good Dog, Aggie* (1–3). Illus. by Frank W. Dormer. 2009, Charlesbridge $12.95 (978-1-57091-645-8). 48pp. When Ben's dog Aggie gets kicked out of obedience school, Ben teaches her with help from a friendly neighbor. (Rev: BCCB 3/09; BLO 5/27/09; SLJ 5/09)

6872 Ritchie, Alison. *Horrible Haircut* (1–2). Illus. by Ian Newsham. Series: Blue Bananas. 2001, Crabtree LB $22.60 (978-0-7787-0844-5); paper $4.95 (978-0-7787-0890-2). 45pp. Lucy and her mother make a deal — if Lucy doesn't like the cut her mother gives her, she gets to cut her mother's hair — in this book for fluent beginning readers. (Rev: SLJ 7/02)

6873 Rocklin, Joanne. *This Book Is Haunted* (K–2). Illus. by JoAnn Adinolfi. 2002, HarperCollins LB $17.89 (978-0-06-028457-2). 46pp. A selection of not-very-frightening Halloween stories for beginning readers. (Rev: BCCB 10/02; HBG 3/03; SLJ 9/02)

6874 Roy, Ron. *Kidnapped at the Capital* (2–4). Illus. by Liza Woodruff. Series: Capital Mysteries. 2002, Golden paper $3.99 (978-0-307-26514-2). 80pp. A mystery takes K.C. Corcoran and Marshall Li on a lively hunt through Washington, D.C. (Rev: BL 9/1/02)

6875 Ruelle, Karen Gray. *April Fool!* (1–2). Series: Holiday House Reader. 2002, Holiday House $14.95 (978-0-8234-1686-8). 32pp. Two little kittens try to come up with April Fool's jokes to play on their parents and each other. (Rev: BL 2/1/02; HBG 10/02; SLJ 6/02)

6876 Ruelle, Karen Gray. *The Crunchy, Munchy Christmas Tree* (1–2). Illus. by author. Series: Holiday House

Reader. 2004, Holiday House $14.95 (978-0-8234-1787-2). 32pp. Kitten siblings Harry and Emily's find a way to entertain themselves when their Christmas plans are disrupted by a snowstorm. (Rev: BL 9/1/03; HBG 4/04; SLJ 10/03)

6877 Ruelle, Karen Gray. *Easter Egg Disaster* (1–2). Illus. Series: Holiday House Reader. 2004, Holiday House $14.95 (978-0-8234-1806-0). 32pp. In four short chapters suitable for beginning readers, kittens Harry and Emily have various misadventures with eggs. (Rev: BL 3/15/04; SLJ 4/04)

6878 Ruelle, Karen Gray. *Easy as Apple Pie: A Harry and Emily Adventure* (K–2). Illus. by author. Series: Holiday House Reader. 2002, Holiday House $14.95 (978-0-8234-1759-9). 32pp. Kittens Harry and Emily have different reactions when invited to pick apples with their grandparents. (Rev: BL 8/02; HBG 3/03; SLJ 10/02)

6879 Rylant, Cynthia. *Annie and Snowball and the Cozy Nest* (PS–2). Illus. by Sucie Stevenson. Series: Annie and Snowball Ready-to-Read. 2009, Simon & Schuster $15.99 (978-1-4169-3943-6). 40pp. Annie and her bunny and other friends watch a mother robin sitting on her eggs and eventually hear the sound of baby birds. (Rev: BL 4/1/09)

6880 Rylant, Cynthia. *Annie and Snowball and the Dress-up Birthday* (K–2). Illus. by Sucie Stevenson. Series: Ready-to-Read. 2007, Simon & Schuster $14.99 (978-1-4169-0938-5). 40pp. Annie (cousin of Henry of Henry and Mudge) likes wearing nice ribbons and bows, so she and her pet rabbit Snowball invite Henry and Mudge to a "Dress-up Birthday," but that term can be misinterpreted . . . (Rev: SLJ 4/07)

6881 Rylant, Cynthia. *Annie and Snowball and the Surprise Day* (K–2). Illus. by Sucie Stevenson. 2012, Simon & Schuster $15.99 (978-141693944-3). 40pp. Annie, her pet rabbit, and her dad share a pleasant day in the country. (Rev: BLO 4/1/12)

6882 Rylant, Cynthia. *Brownie and Pearl Get Dolled Up* (PS). Illus. by Brian Biggs. Series: Brownie and Pearl. 2010, Simon & Schuster $13.99 (978-1-4169-8631-7). 24pp. Brownie and her cat Pearl have a great time dressing to the nines. (Rev: BLO 4/15/10; SLJ 4/1/10)

6883 Rylant, Cynthia. *Brownie and Pearl Grab a Bite* (PS–1). Illus. by Brian Biggs. Series: Brownie and Pearl. 2011, Simon & Schuster $13.99 (978-1-4169-8634-8). 24pp. Brownie and her cat Pearl forage in the refrigerator and pantry to assemble a tasty snack for themselves. (Rev: BL 9/1/11; SLJ 8/1/11)

6884 Rylant, Cynthia. *Brownie and Pearl Hit the Hay* (PS–1). Illus. by Brian Biggs. Series: Brownie and Pearl. 2011, Simon & Schuster $13.99 (978-1-4169-8635-5). Unpaged. Brownie and her cat Pearl enjoy a bath, snack, and story before heading off to bed together. e (Rev: SLJ 9/1/11)

6885 Rylant, Cynthia. *Brownie and Pearl Step Out* (PS–K). Illus. by Brian Biggs. Series: Brownie and Pearl. 2010, Simon & Schuster $12.99 (978-1-4169-8632-4). 24pp. Suffering a moment of shyness when arriving at a friend's party, Brownie relies on her gregarious cat Pearl to lead the way. Also use *Brownie and Pearl See the Sights* (2010). (Rev: BL 12/1/09; SLJ 2/1/10)

6886 Rylant, Cynthia. *The Case of the Desperate Duck* (1–3). Illus. by G. Brian Karas. Series: The High-Rise Private Eyes. 2005, HarperCollins $14.99 (978-0-06-053451-6). 48pp. A rabbit and a raccoon solve the mystery of the missing sugar cubes in this easy-reader. (Rev: SLJ 8/05)

6887 Rylant, Cynthia. *Henry and Mudge and the Big Sleepover* (K–2). Illus. by Sucie Stevenson. 2006, Simon & Schuster $14.95 (978-0-689-81171-5). 40pp. Henry and his dog Mudge enjoy a variety of typical sleepover activities at Patrick's house. (Rev: BL 8/06; SLJ 7/06)

6888 Rylant, Cynthia. *Henry and Mudge and the Great Grandpas* (K–2). Illus. by Sucie Stevenson. Series: Ready-to-Read. 2005, Simon & Schuster $14.95 (978-0-689-81170-8). 40pp. Henry and Mudge the dog visit Great Grandpa Bill, and all the other grandpas who live there too. (Rev: BL 5/1/05) ∩

6889 Rylant, Cynthia. *The High-Rise Private Eyes: The Case of the Puzzling Possum* (2–4). Illus. by G. Brian Karas. 2001, Greenwillow $16.99 (978-0-688-16308-2). 48pp. In this beginning chapter book, the mystery of why a trombone is continually stolen and returned is solved by detective Bunny Brown and her bumbling sidekick, the raccoon named Jack. (Rev: BL 12/1/00; HB 3/01; HBG 10/01)

6890 Rylant, Cynthia. *The High-Rise Private Eyes: The Case of the Troublesome Turtle* (2–4). Illus. 2001, Greenwillow LB $14.89 (978-0-688-16311-2). 48pp. Bunny Brown and her partner Jack Jones, a raccoon, investigate the disappearance of some balloons. (Rev: BL 5/15/01; HB 5/01; HBG 10/01; SLJ 7/01)

6891 Rylant, Cynthia. *Mr. Putter and Tabby Clear the Decks* (K–2). Illus. by Arthur Howard. Series: Mr. Putter and Tabby. 2010, Harcourt $15 (978-0-15-206715-1). Unpaged. On a hot summer day Mr. Putter and his cat Tabby join Mrs. Teaberry and her mischievous dog Zeke on a sightseeing boat cruise. (Rev: SLJ 10/1/10)

6892 Rylant, Cynthia. *Mr. Putter and Tabby Dance the Dance* (K–2). Illus. by Arthur Howard. 2012, Harcourt $14.99 (978-015206415-0). 40pp. Mr. Putter reluctantly agrees to go ballroom dancing with Mrs. Teaberry along with Tabby the cat and Zeke the dog. ∩ Lexile AD390L (Rev: BL 10/1/12; HB 9–10/12)

6893 Rylant, Cynthia. *Mr. Putter and Tabby Drop the Ball* (K–2). Illus. by Arthur Howard. 2013, Harcourt $14.99 (978-015205072-6). 44pp. Mr. Putter has joined Mrs. Teaberry's baseball team and Tabby is happy to come along and watch — but Zeke, Mrs. Teaberry's dog, would rather play than sit on the sidelines. Lexile 410 (Rev: BLO 9/15/13; SLJ 7/13)

6894 Rylant, Cynthia. *Mr. Putter and Tabby Ring the Bell* (K–2). Illus. by Arthur Howard. Series: Mr. Putter and Tabby. 2011, Harcourt $14.99 (978-0-15-205071-9). 44pp. It's fall and Mr. Putter thinks back to his happy days at school, inspiring him and Mrs. Teaberry to take their pets to an unexpectedly unruly "show-and-tell." (Rev: BL 10/1/11; SLJ 8/1/11)

6895 Rylant, Cynthia. *Mr. Putter and Tabby Run the Race* (K–2). Illus. by Arthur Howard. 2008, Harcourt $15.00 (978-0-15-206069-5). 44pp. Mr. Putter agrees to run in a senior marathon when he learns that one of the prizes is a train set. Earlier installments in this long-running series featuring Tabby the cat and neighbor Mrs. Teaberry and her dog Zeke include *Mr. Putter and Tabby Paint the Porch* (2000), *Mr. Putter and Tabby Stir the Soup* (2003), *Mr. Putter and Tabby Make a Wish* (2005), and *Mr. Putter and Tabby Spin the Yarn* (2006). (Rev: BL 4/1/08; SLJ 2/08) ∩

6896 Rylant, Cynthia. *Mr. Putter and Tabby Spill the Beans* (K–2). Illus. by Arthur Howard. 2009, Harcourt $15 (978-0-15-205070-2). 44pp. Mr. Putter is in for more fun than he expected when he goes to a bean cookery class with Mrs. Teaberry. (Rev: BL 8/09; SLJ 12/1/09)

6897 Rylant, Cynthia. *Poppleton Everyday* (PS–2). Illus. by Mark Teague. 1998, Scholastic $15.95 (978-0-590-84845-9). 48pp. A beginning reader that presents Poppleton the pig in three humorous stories about his misadventures. (Rev: BCCB 4/98; HBG 10/98; SLJ 5/98)

6898 Rylant, Cynthia. *Poppleton in Fall* (1–2). Illus. by Mark Teague. 1999, Scholastic $14.95 (978-0-590-84789-6). 56pp. In these three episodes, Poppleton Pig is always helped out of troubling situations by his dear friend Cherry Sue, the llama. (Rev: BL 10/15/99; HBG 3/00; SLJ 9/99)

6899 Rylant, Cynthia. *Puppy Mudge Wants to Play* (PS–K). Illus. by Suçie Stevenston. Series: Ready-to-Read Puppy Mudge. 2005, Simon & Schuster $14.95 (978-0-689-83984-9). 32pp. Puppy Mudge finally succeeds in distracting Henry from his book and getting him to play. (Rev: BL 5/15/05)

6900 Rylant, Cynthia. *The Whale* (2–4). Illus. by Preston McDaniels. Series: The Lighthouse Family. 2003, Simon & Schuster $14.95 (978-0-689-84881-0). 64pp. In this sequel to *The Lighthouse Family: The Storm*, mouse children Lila and Whistler, with the help of a grumpy cormorant, seek to reunite a lost baby whale with his mother. (Rev: BL 9/1/03; HBG 4/04; SLJ 11/03)

6901 Sachar, Louis. *Marvin Redpost: Kidnapped at Birth?* (1–3). Illus. by Neal Hughes. Series: Stepping Stone. 1992, Random LB $11.99 (978-0-679-91946-9); paper $3.99 (978-0-679-81946-2). 68pp. Marvin Redpost secretly believes that he is the kidnapped son of the king. (Rev: BCCB 10/92; BL 12/1/92; SLJ 3/93)

6902 Scarry, Richard. *Mr. Fixit's Magnet Machine* (1–2). Illus. Series: Ready-to-Read. 1998, Simon & Schuster paper $3.99 (978-0-671-81624-7). 32pp. When Huckle, Lowly, and Mr. Frumble notice metal objects flying into the air, they trace this phenomenon to Mr. Fixit's new magnet machine. (Rev: BL 7/98)

6903 Schaefer, Carole Lexa. *Monkey and Elephant Get Better* (K–3). Illus. by Galia Bernstein. 2013, Candlewick $14.99 (978-0-7636-4841-1). 48pp. Monkey and

Elephant try to make each other feel better as each in succession comes down with a cold. (Rev: BL 3/15/13; SLJ 3/13)

6904 Schaefer, Lola M. *Follow Me, Mittens* (PS–2). Illus. by Susan Kathleen Hartung. Series: My First I Can Read. 2007, HarperCollins $15.99 (978-0-06-054665-6). 25pp. A companion to *What's That, Mittens?*, this simple story of Nick and Mittens on a walk will build the confidence of young readers. (Rev: SLJ 7/07)

6905 Schaefer, Lola M. *Mittens* (PS–K). Illus. by Susan Kathleen Hartung. Series: My First I Can Read. 2006, HarperCollins $14.99 (978-0-06-054659-5). 32pp. A simple book for beginning readers about Mittens the kitten's fears about his new home. (Rev: BL 4/15/06; SLJ 6/06)

6906 Schmauss, Judy Kentor. *Parade Day* (K–1). Illus. by Randy Chewning. Series: Reader's Clubhouse. 2006, Barron's paper $3.99 (978-0-7641-3293-3). 24pp. This simple tale of friends gathering for a parade is designed to help children practice their phonics skills, focusing in this title on the long "a" sound. Part of a series that includes *Too, Too Hot!* and *Luke's Mule* (both 2006). (Rev: SLJ 11/06)

6907 Schneider, Josh. *Tales for Very Picky Eaters* (K–3). Illus. by author. 2011, Clarion $14.99 (978-0-547-14956-1). 48pp. An inventive Dad tries everything imaginable to get his very picky son to eat, weaving complex, giggle-inducing fantasies; an easy-reading chapter book. (Rev: BL 5/1/11; SLJ 6/11)

6908 Schulte, Mary. *Who Do I Look Like?* (PS–1). Illus. by Maryn Roos. Series: A Rookie Reader. 2006, Children's Pr. LB $19.50 (978-0-516-24978-0). 32pp. An easy reader that features a child in a racially mixed family wondering whom he most resembles. (Rev: SLJ 6/06)

6909 Schwartz, Alvin. *Ghosts! Ghostly Tales from Folklore* (K–2). Illus. by Victoria Chess. 1991, HarperCollins LB $17.89 (978-0-06-021797-6); paper $3.99 (978-0-06-444170-4). Contains a number of suspenseful ghost stories written for the beginning reader. (Rev: BCCB 9/91; BL 9/15/91; HB 9/91; SLJ 9/91)

6910 Schwartz, Alvin. *I Saw You in the Bathtub and Other Folk Rhymes* (1–3). Illus. by Syd Hoff. 1989, HarperCollins paper $3.99 (978-0-06-444151-3). 64pp. An amusing assortment of folk rhymes. Also use: *All of Our Noses Are Here and Other Noodle Tales* (1985). (Rev: BCCB 4/89; BL 3/1/89; SLJ 5/89)

6911 Scieszka, Jon. *The Spooky Tire* (K–2). Illus. by David Shannon and Loren Long. Series: Jon Scieszka's Trucktown. Ready-to-Roll. 2009, Simon & Schuster LB $13.89 (978-1-4169-4153-8); paper $3.99 (978-1-4169-4142-2). Unpaged. A cement truck rummaging through a junkyard for a new tire on a dark and stormy night gets spooked by an ominous voice. (Rev: SLJ 11/1/09)

6912 Seeger, Laura Vaccaro. *Two's Company* (PS–1). Illus. by author. 2008, Roaring Brook $12.95 (978-1-59643-273-4). The teddy bear and dachshund friends first seen in *Dog and Bear* (2007) return in three brief

stories paired with simple paintings. (Rev: BCCB 4/08; BL 4/1/08; HB 3/08; LMC 8/08; SLJ 4/08)

6913 Seuss, Dr. *The Cat in the Hat* (1–3). Illus. by author. 1957, Random LB $11.99 (978-0-394-90001-8). 72pp. The story of the fabulous cat that came to visit one rainy day when Mother was away. Also from the same author and publisher: *The Cat in the Hat Comes Back!* (1958); *Foot Book* (1968).

6914 Seuss, Dr. *Green Eggs and Ham* (K–3). Illus. by author. 1960, Random $11.99 (978-0-394-90016-2). 72pp. A charming nonsense book.

6915 Seuss, Dr. *Hop on Pop* (1–2). Illus. by author. 1963, Random LB $11.99 (978-0-394-90029-2). 72pp. One of the many entertaining, controlled vocabulary stories of Dr. Seuss. Also use: *One Fish, Two Fish, Red Fish, Blue Fish* (1960); *Fox in Socks* (1965).

6916 Seuss, Dr. *I Can Lick Thirty Tigers Today and Other Stories* (K–3). Illus. by author. 1969, Random $14.95 (978-0-394-80094-3). The Cat in the Hat tells three zany stories.

6917 Seuss, Dr. *I Can Read with My Eyes Shut!* (1–2). Illus. by author. 1978, Random LB $11.99 (978-0-394-93912-4). The Cat in the Hat tells us of all the joys of reading.

6918 Seuss, Dr. *Oh Say Can You Say?* (1–3). Illus. by author. 1979, Random LB $11.99 (978-0-394-94255-1). Tongue-twisting verses presented by a variety of imaginative creatures.

6919 Sharmat, Marjorie W. *Nate the Great* (1–3). Illus. by Marc Simont. 1986, Dell paper $4.50 (978-0-440-46126-5). 48pp. Nate, a boy detective, puts on his Sherlock Holmes outfit and sets out confidently to solve the mystery of the missing painting. Other titles in the series: *Nate the Great Goes Undercover* (1977); *Nate the Great and the Lost List* (1976); *Nate the Great and the Phony Clue* (1981); *Nate the Great and the Sticky Case* (1981); *Nate the Great and the Missing Key* (1981); *Nate the Great and the Snowy Trail* (1982).

6920 Sharmat, Marjorie W., and Mitchell Sharmat. *Nate the Great Talks Turkey* (K–2). Illus. by Jody Wheeler. 2006, Delacorte $11.95 (978-0-385-73336-6). 80pp. Boy detective Nate the Great decides to pass on the case of the missing turkey until he uncovers a clue that just cannot be ignored; his cousin Olivia meanwhile is doing her own sleuthing. (Rev: BL 10/15/06; SLJ 10/06)

6921 Shaw, Nancy. *Sheep in a Jeep* (K–2). Illus. by Margot Apple. 1986, Houghton $15.00 (978-0-395-41105-6); paper $5.95 (978-0-395-47030-5). 32pp. Silly sheep in a silly tale; they fall down, Jeep and all, and land in a muddy pool. Also use: *Sheep on a Ship* (1989). (Rev: BL 9/15/86; HB 11/86)

6922 Shaw, Nancy. *Sheep Out to Eat* (PS–1). Illus. by Margot Apple. 1992, Houghton $15.00 (978-0-395-61128-9). 32pp. Several sheep are asked to leave a tea shop after they misbehave in this amusing story in rhyme. (Rev: BL 9/15/92; SLJ 9/92)

6923 Shea, George. *First Flight: The Story of Tom Tate and the Wright Brothers* (2–3). Illus. by Don Bolognese.

Series: I Can Read. 1997, HarperCollins LB $15.89 (978-0-06-024504-7). 48pp. A fictional account of a boy who is a friend of Orville and Wilbur Wright and participates in their flights. (Rev: BL 11/15/96; HB 3/97; SLJ 1/97)

6924 Shreeve, Elizabeth. *Hector Springs Loose* (2–4). Illus. by Pamela Levy. Series: The Adventures of Hector Fuller. 2004, Simon & Schuster paper $3.99 (978-0-689-86414-8). 67pp. Hector the wumblebug loses his home to a flea circus and goes off in search of a new one in this work for new chapter-book readers. (Rev: SLJ 3/04)

6925 Sias, Ryan. *Zoe and Robot: Let's Pretend* (PS–2). Illus. by author. 2011, Blue Apple $10.99 (978-160905063-4). 40pp. A young girl tries in vain to get a robot to understand imaginative play in this graphic novel for beginning readers. (Rev: BL 6/1/11)

6926 Silverman, Erica. *Cowgirl Kate and Cocoa* (PS–2). Illus. by Betsy Lewin. 2005, Harcourt $15.00 (978-0-15-202124-5). 48pp. Four easy-to-read chapters about the fun-filled friendship between a cowgirl and her talking horse. (Rev: BL 3/1/05; SLJ 3/05)

6927 Silverman, Erica. *Partners* (1–3). Illus. by Betsy Lewin. 2006, Harcourt $15.00 (978-0-15-202125-2). 44pp. Kate and her faithful horse Cocoa continue their happy friendship in four new episodes; a sequel to *Cowboy Kate and Cocoa* (2005). (Rev: BL 2/15/06; SLJ 8/06)

6928 Silverman, Erica. *Rain or Shine* (PS–2). Illus. by Betsy Lewin. Series: Cowgirl Kate and Cocoa. 2008, Harcourt $15.00 (978-0-15-205384-0). 44pp. The affectionate relationship between Cowgirl Kate and her horse Cocoa continues through four more adventures — mainly in the rain. (Rev: BL 4/15/08; SLJ 4/08)

6929 Silverman, Erica. *School Days* (PS–2). Illus. by Betsy Lewin. Series: Cowgirl Kate and Cocoa. 2007, Harcourt $15.00 (978-0-15-205378-9). 48pp. Cocoa the horse suffers separation anxiety when Kate starts school and seems to be preoccupied with homework and her new friend. (Rev: BL 3/15/07)

6930 Silverman, Erica. *Spring Babies* (K–2). Illus. by Betsy Lewin. Series: Cowgirl Kate and Cocoa. 2010, Houghton Harcourt $15 (978-0-15-205396-3). 40pp. Cowgirl Kate and her talking horse help with the arrival of a new calf, and Cocoa learns to accept a new puppy. ♫ Lexile 360L (Rev: BL 1/1/10; HB 5–6/10; SLJ 6/1/10)

6931 Simon, Charnan. *I Like to Win!* (PS–1). Photos by Dorothy Handelman. Series: Real Kids Readers. 1999, Millbrook LB $16.90 (978-0-7613-2062-3); paper $4.99 (978-0-7613-2087-6). 31pp. An African American girl and boy resolve their differences about winning at board games in this book for the very beginning reader. (Rev: SLJ 1/00)

6932 Simon, Charnan. *Mud!* (1). Illus. by Dorothy Handelman. Series: Real Kids Readers. 1999, Millbrook LB $18.90 (978-0-7613-2051-7); paper $4.99 (978-0-7613-2076-0). 32pp. Color photographs are used to illustrate this easy-to-read story about three boys playing in the mud. (Rev: BL 5/15/99)

6933 Simon, Francesca. *Horrid Henry* (1–3). Illus. by Tony Ross. 2009, Sourcebooks paper $4.99 (978-1-4022-1775-3). 112pp. In four short and funny chapters, Horrid Henry unsettles his brother Perfect Peter, disrupts a dance recital, spars with his neighbor Moody Margaret, and ruins a camping trip. (Rev: BCCB 6/09; BL 5/15/09; SLJ 4/09)

6934 Smith, Charles R., Jr. *Let's Play Baseball!* (PS–1). Illus. by Terry Widener. 2006, Candlewick $8.99 (978-0-7636-1646-5). A little boy can't resist the call of a baseball wanting to play. (Rev: SLJ 7/06)

6935 Spinner, Stephanie. *Paddywack* (K–3). Illus. by Daniel Howarth. Series: Step into Reading. 2010, Random House paper $3.99 (978-0-375-86186-4). 48pp. Paddywack the horse and Jane come to a better understanding when she learns the importance of rewarding him with treats. (Rev: SLJ 6/1/10)

6936 Spohn, Kate. *Turtle and Snake's Spooky Halloween* (PS–1). Illus. by author. 2002, Viking $13.99 (978-0-670-03560-1). Turtle and Snake plan a really good Halloween party and follow their checklist. (Rev: HBG 3/03; SLJ 9/02)

6937 Stamper, Judith B. *Five Goofy Ghosts* (2–3). Illus. by Tim Raglin. Series: Hello Reader! 1997, Scholastic $3.99 (978-0-590-92152-7). 32pp. Five horror stories that are also humorous are contained in this simple beginning reader. (Rev: BL 2/1/98)

6938 Stamper, Judith B. *The Wild Leaf Ride* (PS–2). Illus. by Carolyn Bracken. Series: Scholastic Reader. 2004, Scholastic paper $3.99 (978-0-439-56998-9). Ms. Frizzle's students have an exciting time on the Magic School Bus as they set off in search of a leaf in this book for beginning readers. (Rev: SLJ 3/05)

6939 Standford, Natalie. *The Bravest Dog Ever: The True Story of Balto* (1–3). Illus. by Donald Cook. 1989, Random paper $3.99 (978-0-394-89695-3). 48pp. In easy-to-read format, this is the true story of an amazing dog who guided a sled team carrying medicine to Nome, Alaska. (Rev: BCCB 1/90; BL 2/1/90; SLJ 2/90) [636.7]

6940 Stanley, George E. *Ghost Horse* (1–3). Illus. by Ann Barrow. Series: Road to Reading. 2000, Golden paper $3.99 (978-0-307-26500-5). 69pp. With the help of a new friend, Emily solves the mystery of a ghost horse she spies from her bedroom window. (Rev: SLJ 3/01)

6941 Stanley, George E. *Snake Camp* (1–2). Illus. by Jared Lee. Series: Road to Reading. 2000, Golden $10.99 (978-0-307-46406-4); paper $3.99 (978-0-307-26406-0). 32pp. In this easy-reader, Stevie mistakenly is sent to a snake camp instead of a computer camp and, unfortunately, Stevie is terrified of snakes. (Rev: BL 12/1/00; HBG 3/01)

6942 Stauffacher, Sue. *Bessie Smith and the Night Riders* (2–4). Illus. by John Holyfield. 2006, Putnam $16.99 (978-0-399-24237-3). 32pp. A fictionalized, dramatically illustrated account of a real-life confrontation between singer Bessie Smith and Ku Klux Klan members in 1927. (Rev: BL 2/1/06; SLJ 1/06)

6943 Stevenson, James. *Mud Flat April Fool* (1–3). Illus. 1998, Greenwillow $15.89 (978-0-688-15164-5). 48pp. A humorous book for beginning readers in which the animal residents of Mud Flat have fun playing jokes on April Fools' Day. (Rev: BL 2/15/98; HB 5/98; HBG 10/98; SLJ 3/98)

6944 Suen, Anastasia. *Willie's Birthday* (K–2). Illus. by Allan Eitzen. 2001, Viking $13.99 (978-0-670-88943-3). 32pp. A beginning reader in which mayhem results when Peter invites his friends and their pets to help celebrate the birthday of his dachshund, Willie. (Rev: HBG 10/01; SLJ 3/01)

6945 Suen, Anastasia, and Ezra Jack Keats. *The Clubhouse* (K–2). Illus. by Allan Eitzen. Series: Viking Easy-to-Read. 2002, Viking $13.99 (978-0-670-03537-3). 32pp. Peter, an African American boy, and his friends find a pile of wood and build a place to play. (Rev: BL 4/15/02; HBG 10/02; SLJ 8/02)

6946 Sullivan, Paula. *Todd's Box* (PS–1). Illus. by Nadine Bernard Westcott. Series: Green Light Reader. 2004, Harcourt $11.95 (978-0-15-205093-1). Todd ignores his mother's scolding and continues to pick up items of interest, presenting them all to her once they are on the bus. (Rev: BL 3/15/04; SLJ 5/04)

6947 Surgal, Jon. *Have You Seen My Dinosaur?* (PS–2). Illus. by Joe Mathieu. Series: Beginner Books. 2010, Random House $8.99 (978-0-375-85639-6); LB $12.99 (978-0-375-95639-3). Unpaged. A young boy searches high and low for his beloved dinosaur, not realizing that his pet is following him the whole way. (Rev: SLJ 5/1/10)

6948 Tafuri, Nancy. *Will You Be My Friend?* (PS–K). Illus. 2000, Scholastic $16.95 (978-0-590-63782-4). In this easy reader, a young bunny and his friends help Bird rebuild his home when his nest is ruined in a rainstorm. (Rev: BL 1/1–15/00; HBG 10/00; SLJ 3/00)

6949 Tate, Lindsey. *Kate Larkin, the Bone Expert* (1–4). Illus. by Diane Palmisciano. 2008, Holt $16.95 (978-0-8050-7901-2). 80pp. Eight-year-old Kate tells the story of her broken arm and how it healed in this book for beginning readers with large type, many illustrations, and two activities. (Rev: LMC 3/09; SLJ 4/08)

6950 Taylor-Butler, Christine. *Ah-Choo* (K–2). Illus. by Carol Koeller. Series: My First Reader. 2005, Children's Pr. LB $18.50 (978-0-516-25175-2). 31pp. A girl at home with a cold finds ways to amuse herself in this book for beginning readers with a list of words. (Rev: SLJ 5/05)

6951 Taylor-Butler, Christine. *Step-by-Step* (K–2). Illus. by Susan Miller. Series: My First Reader. 2005, Children's Pr. LB $18.50 (978-0-516-24875-2); paper $3.95 (978-0-516-24974-2). 32pp. A young boy makes a beautiful bouquet for his grandmother by dyeing white flowers using bright colors. (Rev: SLJ 1/06)

6952 Taylor-Butler, Christine. *Who Needs Friends?* (PS–1). Illus. by Susan Havice. Series: A Rookie Reader. 2006, Children's Pr. LB $19.50 (978-0-516-24979-7). 32pp. A young boy decides to throw himself a birthday

party when it seems no one has remembered the special day. (Rev: SLJ 6/06)

6953 Taylor, Sean. *Small Bad Wolf* (K–2). Illus. by Jan Lewis. Series: I Am Reading. 2004, Kingfisher paper $3.95 (978-0-7534-5801-3). 45pp. Small Bad Wolf wants to emulate his father, but his father's lessons leave something to be desired. (Rev: SLJ 8/04)

6954 Thiesing, Lisa. *A Dark and Noisy Night* (PS–1). Illus. Series: Dutton Easy Reader. 2005, Dutton $13.99 (978-0-525-47388-6). 32pp. Peggy the Pig cannot fall asleep because of the scary noises that seem to be everywhere. (Rev: BL 9/15/05; SLJ 1/06)

6955 Thomas, Shelley Moore. *Get Well, Good Knight* (K–2). Illus. by Jennifer Plecas. Series: Dutton Easy Reader. 2002, Dutton $13.99 (978-0-525-46914-8). 48pp. The Good Knight rides off on a quest to cure three little dragons with horrible colds, in this appealing easy reader. (Rev: BCCB 12/02; BL 1/1–15/03; HB 9/02; HBG 3/03; SLJ 11/02)

6956 Thomas, Shelley Moore. *Good Night, Good Knight* (1–3). Illus. by Jennifer Plecas. Series: Dutton Easy Reader. 2000, Dutton $13.99 (978-0-525-46326-9). 48pp. A gentle knight discovers three young dragons who want to be tucked in for the night in this charming bedtime book for beginning readers. (Rev: BCCB 2/00; BL 2/15/00; HBG 10/00; SLJ 3/00)

6957 Thomas, Shelley Moore. *Happy Birthday, Good Knight* (K–2). Illus. by Jennifer Plecas. Series: Dutton Easy Reader. 2006, Dutton $13.99 (978-0-525-47184-4). Things go badly when the Good Knight's three little dragon friends try to create a birthday gift. (Rev: BL 1/1–15/06; SLJ 3/06)

6958 Thomson, Melissa. *Keena Ford and the Second-Grade Mix-Up* (2–4). Illus. by Frank Morrison. 2008, Dial $14.99 (978-0-8037-3263-6). 112pp. In Washington, D.C., a 2nd-grade African American girl records in her diary her problems at school, where she seems to invite problems. (Rev: BCCB 7–8/08; BLO 12/30/08; LMC 1/09; SLJ 10/08)

6959 Tidd, Louise Vitellaro. *I'll Do It Later* (1–2). Illus. by Dorothy Handelman. Series: Real Kids Readers. 1999, Millbrook LB $18.90 (978-0-7613-2066-1); paper $4.99 (978-0-7613-2091-3). 32pp. In this easy reader, a snow day provides a lazy boy with a reprieve from submitting a school assignment. (Rev: BL 12/1/99; SLJ 11/99)

6960 Tidd, Louise Vitellaro. *Let Me Help!* (1–2). Illus. by Dorothy Handelman. Series: Real Kids Readers. 1999, Millbrook LB $18.90 (978-0-7613-2067-8); paper $4.99 (978-0-7613-2092-0). 32pp. In spite of Tara's good intentions, her efforts to help her father always end disastrously. (Rev: BL 10/1/99; HBG 3/00)

6961 Torrey, Richard. *Beans Baker's Best Shot* (1–3). Series: Step into Reading. 2006, Random LB $11.99 (978-0-375-92839-0); paper $3.99 (978-0-375-82839-3). 48pp. An injury sidelines Beans Baker from his soccer team's championship game, but he tries to do his part by cheering on his teammates. (Rev: BL 8/06; SLJ 10/06)

6962 Umansky, Kaye. *Alien Alby* (1–2). Illus. by Sophie Rohrbach. Series: I Am Reading. 2010, Kingfisher paper $3.99 (978-07534300-5-7). 48pp. In this wacky book for beginning readers full of wordplay, a young alien misses his pet Squee, who's been banished from the bed after refusing to wipe his paws. (Rev: BL 8/10)

6963 Underwood, Deborah. *Pirate Mom* (PS–2). Illus. by Stephen Gilpin. Series: Step into Reading. 2006, Random LB $11.99 (978-0-375-93323-3); paper $3.99 (978-0-375-83323-6). 48pp. When Pete's mother is hypnotized into thinking she is a pirate, it's up to Pete to try to stop her zany behavior. (Rev: BL 5/1/06)

6964 Urbanovic, Jackie. *Ducks in a Row* (K–2). Illus. by author and Joe Mathieu. Series: I Can Read! 2011, HarperCollins $16.99 (978-0-06-186438-4); paper $3.99 (978-0-06-186437-7). 32pp. Max the Duck feels unwanted until his demanding aunts stop in on their way south, and soon he longs to get back to his relaxing life. (Rev: SLJ 3/1/11)

6965 Vail, Rachel. *Mama Rex and T: Homework Trouble* (2–4). Illus. by Steve Björkman. 2002, Scholastic $14.95 (978-0-439-40628-4). Mama Rex and T, a young dinosaur, finish the project he's neglected in this challenging beginning chapter book. Also use *Mama Rex and T: The Horrible Play Date* (2002), about friendship. (Rev: HBG 3/03; SLJ 10/02)

6966 Vail, Rachel. *Mama Rex and T: The Reading Champion* (1–3). Illus. by Steve Bjarkman. 2004, Scholastic paper $3.99 (978-0-439-57822-6). A young dinosaur initially has trouble reading in this appealing easy-reader. (Rev: SLJ 8/04)

6967 Van Leeuwen, Jean. *Amanda Pig and the Really Hot Day* (K–2). Illus. by Ann Schweninger. Series: Dial Easy-to-Read. 2005, Dial $14.99 (978-0-8037-2887-5). 48pp. Four episodic easy-reader stories show Amanda Pig and her family coping with hot weather. (Rev: BL 6/1–15/05)

6968 Van Leeuwen, Jean. *Amanda Pig and the Wiggly Tooth* (K–2). Illus. by Ann Schweninger. Series: Oliver and Amanda. 2008, Dial $14.99 (978-0-8037-3104-2). 40pp. Amanda Pig won't let her father pull out her wiggly tooth, but then it falls out by itself and she loses it! (Rev: BL 5/15/08; SLJ 4/08)

6969 Van Leeuwen, Jean. *Oliver Pig and the Best Fort Ever* (K–2). Illus. by Ann Schweninger. Series: Dial Easy-to-Read. 2006, Dial $15.99 (978-0-8037-2888-2). 40pp. Oliver Pig calls on his friends to help him build "the best fort ever" in four chapters suited to beginning readers. (Rev: BL 4/15/06; SLJ 7/06)

6970 Van Leeuwen, Jean. *Oliver the Mighty Pig* (PS–2). Illus. by Ann Schweninger. Series: Dial Easy-to-Read. 2004, Dial $14.99 (978-0-8037-2886-8). 48pp. Oliver really enjoys the superhero powers imparted by his Mighty Pig cape, and feels very weak while it's in the wash in this easy-reader. (Rev: BL 3/1/04; SLJ 3/04)

6971 Viorst, Judith. *Alexander, Who Used to Be Rich Last Sunday* (K–2). Illus. by Ray Cruz. 1978, Macmillan LB $16.00 (978-0-689-30602-0); paper $4.99 (978-0-689-

71199-2). 32pp. Alexander spends his dollar gift foolishly penny by penny. (Rev: SLJ 6/04)

6972 Walker, Sally M. *The 18 Penny Goose* (2–4). Illus. by Ellen Beier. Series: I Can Read. 1998, HarperCollins LB $15.89 (978-0-06-027557-0). 64pp. In this easy reader based on fact, a little girl is afraid that the British army raiders will eat her pet goose during the Revolutionary War. (Rev: BL 2/1/98; HB 5/98; HBG 10/98; SLJ 3/98)

6973 Wallace, Carol. *Easter Bunny Blues* (1–2). Illus. by Steve Björkman. 2009, Holiday $15.95 (978-0-8234-2162-6). 32pp. The Easter Bunny is sick and two dogs enlist an engaging assemblage of kindly animals to collect eggs, paint them, and distribute Easter baskets. (Rev: BLO 2/9/09; SLJ 2/09)

6974 Wallace, Carol. *One Nosy Pup* (PS–2). Illus. by Steve Björkman. Series: Holiday House Reader. 2005, Holiday House $15.95 (978-0-8234-1917-3). 40pp. A beagle puppy discovers a new friend, Charlie the hamster, in the kitchen of his owners' new house. (Rev: BL 3/1/05; SLJ 4/05)

6975 Wallace, Carol. *Turkeys Together* (K–2). Illus. by Jacqueline Rogers. Series: Holiday House Reader. 2005, Holiday House $15.95 (978-0-8234-1895-4). A hunting dog befriends two mother turkeys in this easy-reader. (Rev: SLJ 8/05)

6976 Wallace, Rich. *Benched* (2–4). Illus. by Jimmy Holder. Series: Kickers. 2010, Knopf $12.99 (978-037585756-0); LB $15.99 (978-037595756-7). 128pp. Ben's behavior at school deteriorates as he faces problems at home, and he finds himself in trouble on the soccer field; with soccer tips. ℮ (Rev: BL 1/1–15/11)

6977 Walsh, Vivian. *Gluey: A Snail Tale* (K–3). Illus. by J. Otto Seibold. 2002, Harcourt $15.00 (978-0-15-216620-5). 48pp. Celerina the rabbit moves into Gluey the snail's home, believing it to be abandoned, and hosts a disastrous party in this complex tale for beginning readers. (Rev: BL 10/15/02; HBG 3/03; SLJ 12/02)

6978 Warner, Sally. *Excellent Emma* (2–4). Illus. by Jamie Harper. 2009, Viking $14.99 (978-0-670-06310-9). 144pp. Third-grader Emma tries to get her father's attention by entering a school sports competition in this lively story about divorce and school life. (Rev: BLO 2/9/09; SLJ 3/09)

6979 Watts, Frances. *The Greatest Sheep in History* (2–4). Illus. by Judy Watson. Series: Ernie & Maud. 2011, Eerdmans paper $5.99 (978-0-8028-5-374-5). 86pp. Superhero-in-training Ernie and his sheep sidekick Maud attend a superhero convention that turns out to pose superhero challenges. Lexile 910L (Rev: BL 7/11; SLJ 7/11)

6980 Weeks, Sarah. *Mac and Cheese* (K–2). Illus. by Jane Manning. Series: I Can Read. 2010, HarperCollins $16.99 (978-0-06-117079-9). 32pp. Two feline friends who couldn't be more different share an adventure when the wind blows away Macaroni's hat in this book for beginning readers. ℮ Lexile 510L (Rev: BL 12/15/10; SLJ 9/1/10)

6981 Weeks, Sarah. *Pip Squeak* (PS–2). Illus. by Jane Manning. 2007, HarperCollins $15.99 (978-0-06-075635-2). 32pp. Pip Squeak the mouse (first seen in the 2000 publication *Drip, Drop*) busies himself cleaning for his friend Max only to find that Max is one of the messiest people ever. (Rev: HB 7/07; SLJ 2/08)

6982 Weiss, Ellen, and Mel Friedman. *Porky and Bess* (K–3). Illus. by Marsha Winborn. Series: Step into Reading. 2010, Random House $12.99 (978-0-375-85458-3); paper $3.99 (978-0-375-96113-7). 48pp. A slovenly bachelor pig and a tidy cat with three kittens become friends despite their differences in this whimsical book for beginning readers. Lexile 410L (Rev: BL 1/1/10; LMC 5–6/10; SLJ 1/1/10)

6983 Weiss, Ellen, and Mel Friedman. *The Stinky Giant* (K–3). Illus. by Alessia Girasole. Series: Step into Reading. 2012, Random House LB $12.99 (978-037596743-6); paper $3.99 (9780375867439). 48pp. Courageous Pepper and Jake seek to stop a giant whose laundry tub floods their village every week. **e** (Rev: BL 8/12)

6984 West, Colin. *Moose and Mouse* (K–2). Illus. by author. Series: I Am Reading. 2004, Kingfisher paper $3.95 (978-0-7534-5715-3). 45pp. Moose and mouse are friends despite their differences. (Rev: SLJ 8/04)

6985 Westera, Marleen. *Sheep and Goat* (1–3). Illus. by Sylvia van Ommen. 2006, Front St. $16.95 (978-1-932425-81-9). 99pp. Sheep and Goat are very fond of each other despite their differences in these 18 short stories in an early-chapter-book format. (Rev: BL 2/1/07; SLJ 11/06)

6986 Weston, Martha. *Jack and Jill and Big Dog Bill: A Phonics Reader* (1). Illus. Series: Early Step into Reading. 2002, Random paper $3.99 (978-0-375-81248-4). Two small children, Jack and Jill, along with their dog, try to slide down a snow-covered hillside on their sled with amusing results in this easy reader. (Rev: BL 4/15/02; HBG 10/02; SLJ 7/02)

6987 Weston, Martha. *Space Guys* (K–1). Illus. Series: Holiday House Reader. 2000, Holiday House $14.95 (978-0-8234-1487-1). A group of space travelers spend a riotous night in an average American home in this science fiction easy-reader. (Rev: BL 4/15/00; HBG 10/00; SLJ 5/00)

6988 Wheeler, Lisa. *Who's Afraid of Granny Wolf?* (1–2). Illus. by Frank Ansley. 2004, Simon & Schuster $14.95 (978-0-689-84952-7). 47pp. Traditional enemies — the wolf and the pig — are best of friends in this humorous original story. (Rev: SLJ 8/04)

6989 Wilhelm, Hans. *I Lost My Tooth!* (PS–1). Illus. by author. Series: Hello Reader! 1999, Scholastic paper $3.99 (978-0-590-64230-9). A little puppy plans to leave his loose tooth for the Tooth Fairy when it falls out, but he accidentally swallows it. (Rev: SLJ 9/99)

6990 Wilhelm, Hans. *It's Too Windy!* (1). 2000, Scholastic paper $3.99 (978-0-439-10849-2). 32pp. An easy-to-read book about a shaggy white dog who saves a baby when its stroller rolls away. (Rev: BL 7/00)

6991 Willems, Mo. *Are You Ready to Play Outside?* (PS–2). Illus. by author. 2008, Hyperion $8.99 (978-1-4231-1347-8). 64pp. Rain dampens Piggie's happy disposition until Gerald the elephant lends her an ear. (Rev: BL 11/15/08; SLJ 12/08)

6992 Willems, Mo. *Let's Say Hi to Friends Who Fly!* (PS–1). Illus. by author. 2010, HarperCollins $12.99 (978-0-06-172842-6); LB $14.89 (978-0-06-172846-4). 32pp. In this bright book for beginning readers, Cat the Cat and her similarly named animal friends have high-flying adventures in the sky. (Rev: BL 1/1/10; HB 5–6/10; SLJ 2/1/10)

6993 Willis, Jeanne. *Be Quiet, Parrot!* (1–2). Illus. by Mark Birchall. 2000, Carolrhoda $7.25 (978-1-57505-492-6). 32pp. In this beginning reader, a noisy parrot interrupts everyone and everything with his constant talking. Also use *Take Turns, Penguin!* (2000), an additional story about sharing and selfishness. (Rev: BL 12/1/00; HBG 3/01; SLJ 1/01)

6994 Wiseman, Bernard. *Morris and Boris at the Circus* (1–2). Illus. by author. 1988, HarperCollins paper $3.99 (978-0-06-444143-8). 64pp. Two friends, a moose and a bear, attend the circus. Also use: *Morris Goes to School* (1983). (Rev: BL 12/1/88; SLJ 2/89)

6995 Wishinsky, Frieda. *A Bee in Your Ear* (2–4). Illus. by Louise-Andree Laliberte. 2005, Orca paper $4.99 (978-1-55143-324-0). 64pp. Kate must contend with spelling-bee pressure, a bully named Violet, and problems with her friend Jake in this beginning chapter book. (Rev: BL 3/15/05)

6996 Wishinsky, Frieda. *Just Mabel* (1–3). Illus. by Sue Heap. Series: I Am Reading. 2004, Kingfisher paper $3.95 (978-0-7534-5742-9). 45pp. Mabel finds a way to stop the teasing about her name and her clothes in this book for beginning readers. (Rev: SLJ 9/04)

6997 Yorinks, Arthur. *Flappy and Scrappy* (K–2). Illus. by Aleksey Ivanov and Olga Ivanov. Series: I Can Read! 2011, HarperCollins $16.99 (978-0-06-205117-2). 48pp. In this book for beginning readers, dogs Flappy and Scrappy are always there for each other. (Rev: SLJ 3/1/11)

6998 Ziefert, Harriet. *Sometimes I Share* (PS–1). Illus. by Carol Nicklaus. Series: I'm Going to Read! 2005, Sterling $11.95 (978-1-4027-2068-0); paper $3.95 (978-1-4027-2090-1). Simple first-person text chronicles the ups and downs of a girl's relationship with her little brother; suitable for early beginning readers. (Rev: BL 8/05)

6999 Ziefert, Harriet. *Toes Have Wiggles Kids Have Giggles* (K–3). Illus. by Rebecca Doughty. 2002, Penguin $13.99 (978-0-399-23617-4). Clever wordplays and amusing rhymes introduce readers to what words can do. (Rev: BL 6/1–15/02)

Graphic Novels

7000 Aguirre, Jorge. *Giants Beware!* (2–5). Illus. by Rafael Rosado. 2012, First Second paper $14.99 (978-15964358-2-7). 208pp. Young tomboy Claudette is determined to do her civil duty and slay a giant, but this proves to be more problematic than she expected. (Rev: BL 3/15/12; HB 9–10/12; LMC 10/12; SLJ 5/1/12*)

7001 Akimoto, Nami. *Ultra Cute, Vol. 1* (5–8). Trans. from Japanese by Emi Onishi. Illus. by author. 2006, TokyoPop paper $9.99 (978-1-59532-956-1). Ami and Noa, more rivals than friends, compete with each other over two guys who are not as nice as they seem. (Rev: SLJ 7/06)

7002 Alley, Zoe B. *There's a Princess in the Palace* (3–5). Illus. by R. W. Alley. 2010, Roaring Brook $19.99 (978-159643471-4). 40pp. Cinderella, Sleeping Beauty, Snow White, the frog prince, and the princess and the pea all are featured in this fractured, comic book retelling. (Rev: BL 8/10; HB 9–10/10; LMC 11–12/10; SLJ 9/10)

7003 *The Amazing Spider-Man* (3–6). Illus. by Andy Mansfield. Series: Marvel Comics True Believers Retro Character Collection. 2007, Candlewick $24.99 (978-0-7636-3263-2). Pop-ups and pull tabs introduce young readers to the world of the classic superhero and his enemies. (Rev: SLJ 5/07)

7004 Arni, Samhita. *Sita's Ramayana* (5–12). Illus. by Moyna Chitrakar. 2011, Groundwood $24.95 (978-155498145-8). 152pp. With Patua scroll paintings, this graphic-novel retelling has Rama's beautiful wife as its main focus. ALA Notable Children's Book 2012. (Rev: BL 9/15/11*; LMC 1–2/12*; SLJ 9/1/11*)

7005 Baltazar, Art, and Franco. *Billy Batson and the Magic of Shazam: Mr. Mind over Matter* (3–5). Illus. by Byron Vaughns. 2011, DC Comics paper $12.99 (978-14012299-3-1). 144pp. Witty text and unified themes add cross-generational appeal to this updated take on Captain Marvel. (Rev: BL 6/1/11)

7006 Baltazar, Art, and Franco. *Superman Family Adventures, v.1* (K–3). Illus. by Art Baltazar. 2013, DC Comics paper $12.99 (978-14012405-0-9). 128pp. Superman's not the only hero in this story, which includes Supergirl and Superboy, cousins of the main man, who aid Superman in taking down well-known villains such as Lex Luthor and BIzarro in true fast-paced cartoon style. (Rev: BL 9/15/13*)

7007 Baltazar, Art, and Franco Aureliani. *Patrick the Wolf Boy, Vol. 1* (4–7). Illus. by Art Baltazar. 2005, DDP paper $10.95 (978-1-932796-27-8). A graphic novel about the hilarious adventures of a young werewolf. (Rev: SLJ 7/05)

7008 Bar-el, Dan. *That One Spooky Night* (3–5). Illus. by David Huyck. 2012, Kids Can $16.95 (978-1-55453751-8); paper $8.95 (978-15545375-2-5). 80pp. Three graphic-novel tales that meld spookiness and humor feature a broom that carries a young trick-or-treater off into the sky, a strange underwater world in a bathtub, and a session in Dracula's mansion. Lexile GN130L (Rev: BL 10/15/12; HB 5–6/13; SLJ 1/13)

7009 Barba, Corey. *Yam: Bite-Size Chunks* (K–3). Illus. by author. 2008, Top Shelf paper $10.00 (978-1-60309-014-8). 88pp. This wordless graphic novel follows a young boy who lives on a remote island through a series of magical adventures. (Rev: BLO 9/17/08)

7010 Barker, Henry, and Shannon Lowry, adapts. *Historical Adventure* (4–8). Illus. by Dan Spiegle. Series: Bank Street Graphic Novels. 2007, World Almanac LB $29.27 (978-0-8368-7927-8). 56pp. Versions of *A Connecticut Yankee in King Arthur's Court*, *Around the World in Eighty Days*, and *The Prisoner of Zenda* are included here and act as good introductions to the classic stories. (Rev: SLJ 7/07)

7011 Barnett, Mac. *Oh No! (Or How My Science Project Destroyed the World)* (K–3). Illus. by Dan Santat. 2010, Hyperion/Disney $16.99 (978-1-4231-2312-5). Unpaged. Things get out of control when a girl builds a robot for the science fair in this fast-paced graphic novel. (Rev: LMC 11–12/10; SLJ 7/1/10)

7012 Baum, L. Frank. *The Wizard of Oz* (3–5). Adapted by Michael Cavallero. 2005, Puffin paper $10.99 (978-

0-14-240471-3). 152pp. In this graphic adaptation that retains original dialogue, Dorothy wears jeans, the Good Witch of the North sports sunglasses, and the Tin Woodman has traded his ax for a buzz saw. (Rev: SLJ 11/05)

7013 Beka. *Dance Class: So, You Think You Can Hip-Hop?* (4–8). Illus. by Crip. 2012, Papercutz $9.99 (978-159707254-0). 48pp. A graphic novel in which dance students compete for the lead role in *Sleeping Beauty* while at the same time swooning over KT, the hip-hop teacher. (Rev: BL 3/15/12; LMC 10/12)

7014 Blackman, Haden. *Clone Wars Adventures* (4–7). Series: Star Wars Clone Wars Adventures. 2006, Dark Horse paper $6.95 (978-1-59307-483-8). This fifth volume of the fantasy series, based on the TV cartoon show, includes four fast-paced stories of graphic novel action and adventure. (Rev: BL 6/1–15/06)

7015 Bliss, Harry. *Luke on the Loose* (PS–2). Illus. by author. 2009, Raw Junior/TOON $12.95 (978-1-935179-00-9). 32pp. An African American boy called Luke chases a pigeon all around New York City; the simple text makes this graphic novel suitable for beginning readers. (Rev: BCCB 6/09; BL 3/1/09; LMC 5/09)

7016 Bolton, Chris A. *Smash, Book 1: Trial by Fire* (5–8). Illus. by Kyle Bolton. 2013, Candlewick $18.99 (978-076365596-9). 160pp. Superpowers are not the only attributes of superheroes, as 5th-grader Andrew finds out when his idol, Defender, dies and Andrew inherits his abilities — only to find himself doubting his role. (Rev: BL 3/1/14; LMC 3–4/2014*; SLJ 9/13) [340]

7017 Brennan, Michael. *Electric Girl, Vol. 2* (5–8). 2002, Mighty Gremlin paper $13.95 (978-0-9703555-1-5). In this graphic novel, Virginia, who can release bursts of electricity at will, locks horns with evil gremlin Oogleeoog. (Rev: BL 5/1/02; SLJ 5/02)

7018 Brown, Jeffrey. *Star Wars: Jedi Academy* (3–7). Illus. by author. 2013, Scholastic $12.99 (978-054550517-8). 160pp. Roan is devastated when he learns that he's going to Coruscant Jedi Academy instead of Pilot Academy like his brother and father, but he slowly finds a way to fit in with the help of his ability to draw. YALSA Quick Pick for Reluctant Readers. **e** (Rev: BL 9/15/13*; SLJ 1/14)

7019 Cali, Davide, and Vincent Pianina. *10 Little Insects* (4–7). Illus. by Davide Cali. 2013, IPG/Wilkins Farago $19.99 (978-098710991-0). 80pp. Ten insects are invited to a remote island where find themselves confronted with mysterious deaths; a send-up of an Agatha Christie classic. (Rev: BL 6/13; SLJ 1/14)

7020 Cammuso, Frank. *The Battling Bands* (3–5). Illus. by author. Series: Knights of the Lunch Table. 2011, Scholastic paper $10.99 (978-04399031-8-9). 128pp. Artie and his friends want to start a rock band but first have to find the Singing Sword. Lexile GN260L (Rev: BL 10/15/11)

7021 Cammuso, Frank. *The Dodgeball Chronicles* (2–4). Illus. by author. 2008, Scholastic paper $9.99 (978-0-439-90322-6). 142pp. In this humorous graphic novel with an Arthurian flavor, our middle-school hero Artie

King fights bullies and bad lunches. (Rev: BL 3/15/08; LMC 11/08; SLJ 7/08)

7022 Cammuso, Frank. *The Dragon Players* (2–4). Illus. by author. Series: Knights of the Lunch Table. 2009, Scholastic paper $9.99 (978-04399032-3-3). 128pp. Artie and his Camelot Middle School friends enter a robot contest, vying against the bully called Horde; Merlin offers advice and the Ladies of the Lunch stir a boiling pot. (Rev: BL 11/15/09; SLJ 1/10)

7023 Cammuso, Frank. *The Misadventures of Salem Hyde: Big Birthday Bash* (3–5). Illus. by author. 2014, Abrams/Amulet $14.95 (978-141971025-4); paper $6.95 (978-14197102-6-1). 96pp. In this second installment in the slapstick series, Salem's witch skills are still causing problems as she prepares for Edgar's birthday party. (Rev: BL 3/1/14; SLJ 5/14)

7024 Cammuso, Frank, and Jay Lynch. *Otto's Orange Day* (K–2). Illus. by Frank Cammuso. 2008, Raw Junior/TOON $12.95 (978-0-9799238-2-1). Granting Otto's wish, a genie turns the world orange, which turns out not to have been the best choice of colors. (Rev: BL 3/15/08; HB 7/08; LMC 3/08; SLJ 5/08)

7025 Castellucci, Cecil. *Odd Duck* (2–4). Illus. by Sara Varon. 2013, First Second paper $15.99 (978-15964355-7-5). 96pp. Theodora, a duck with some eccentricities (she stays north for the winter and swims with a teacup balanced on her head), regards newcomer Chad's habits with suspicion; but which one is really the "odd duck"? Lexile AD540L (Rev: BL 3/1/13; HB 5–6/13; LMC 11–12/13; SLJ 5/13*)

7026 Chabot, Jacob, et al. *Hello Kitty: Delicious!* (K–2). Illus. by author. 2014, VIZ Media paper $7.99 (978-14215587-9-0). 64pp. A collection of Kitty adventures involving food. (Rev: BL 3/1/14)

7027 Chad, Jon. *Leo Geo and His Miraculous Journey Through the Center of the Earth* (3–6). Illus. by author. 2012, Roaring Brook $15.99 (978-159643661-9). 40pp. This squat but wide graphic novel offers narrator Leo Geo a chance to illustrate his adventures as he tunnels through the Earth and delivers facts about geology (and the occasional monster and other surprises). (Rev: BL 2/15/12; LMC 5–6/12; SLJ 2/12*)

7028 Chantler, Scott. *The Captive Prince* (3–5). Illus. by author. Series: Three Thieves. 2012, Kids Can $17.95 (978-1-55453776-1); paper $8.95 (978-15545377-7-8). 116pp. The three circus friends are still running from the Queen's Dragons in this third installment when tightrope-walker Dessa inadvertently rescues a prince and sets further adventures in motion. (Rev: BLO 9/15/12)

7029 Chantler, Scott. *The King's Dragon* (4–6). Illus. by author. Series: Three Thieves. 2014, Kids Can $17.95 (978-155453778-5). 112pp. Captain Drake is at the center of this fourth installment as he searches for Desa, Topper, and Fisk and in the process reviews his past. (Rev: BL 3/1/14; SLJ 5/14)

7030 Chantler, Scott. *The Sign of the Black Rock* (4–7). Illus. by author. Series: Three Thieves. 2011, Kids Can $17.95 (978-155453416-6); paper $8.95 (978-

15545341-7-3). 112pp. Dessa and her fugitive friends spend a rainy night at the Black Rock Inn, evading detection by the Queen's soldiers, also guests at the inn, who've been sent to capture her; this second installment in the series focuses in part on the innkeeper and his shady activities. Lexile GN510L (Rev: BL 10/15/11; SLJ 11/1/11)

7031 Cibos, Lindsay, and Jared Hodges. *Peach Fuzz, Vol. 1* (3–5). Illus. by authors. 2005, TokyoPop paper $9.99 (978-1-59532-599-0). The story of a girl and her pet ferret, told from both pet's and owner's point of view. (Rev: SLJ 7/05)

7032 Clamp. *Cardcaptor Sakura, vol. 1* (3–8). Illus. by author. 2010, Dark Horse paper $19.99 (978-15958252-2-3). 576pp. Three previously published volumes in the series about 4th-grader Sakura and her efforts to save the universe are collected in this remastered and newly translated volume. (Rev: BLO 1/1–15/11)

7033 Clugston, Chynna. *Queen Bee* (5–8). 2005, Scholastic paper $8.99 (978-0-439-70987-3). In this humorous graphic novel about school cliques, Haley and Alexa, two middle school students with psychokinetic powers, battle each other to become the school's most popular girl. (Rev: BL 9/15/05; SLJ 1/06; VOYA 12/05)

7034 Colfer, Eoin, and Andrew Donkin. *Artemis Fowl: The Graphic Novel* (5–7). Illus. by Giovanni Rigano. 2007, Hyperion $18.99 (978-0-7868-4881-2); paper $9.99 (978-0-7868-4882-9). A well-illustrated graphic novel rendering of the 2001 novel about the 12-year-old genius and adventurous criminal entrepreneur Artemis Fowl. (Rev: BL 11/15/07; LMC 2/08; SLJ 1/08)

7035 Conway, Gerry. *Crawling with Zombies* (3–6). Illus. by Paulo Henrique. 2010, Papercutz $10.99 (978-159707220-5); paper $6.99 (978-15970721-9-9). 64pp. This graphic novel brings the Hardy Boys detectives of the 1950s up-to-date with a story of zombie-like behavior among the teenagers of Bayport. (Rev: BLO 2/15/11; SLJ 5/1/11)

7036 Cosentino, Ralph. *Batman: The Story of the Dark Knight* (1–3). Illus. by author. 2008, Viking $15.99 (978-0-670-06255-3). 40pp. A well-designed picture-book/comic-book introduction to the superhero's life, told in simple first-person text. (Rev: BL 7/08; SLJ 9/08) [741.5]

7037 Cosentino, Ralph. *Superman: The Story of the Man of Steel* (1–3). Illus. by author. 2010, Viking $16.99 (978-0-670-06285-0). 40pp. This action-packed book serves as a fine introduction to the superhero and his origins; includes retro cartoon art in bold primary colors. Lexile 1430 (Rev: BL 1/1/10; SLJ 5/10)

7038 Cosentino, Ralph. *Wonder Woman: The Story of the Amazon Princess* (1–3). Illus. by author. 2011, Viking $16.99 (978-067006256-0). 40pp. Tells the story of Wonder Woman's origins and transformation into a superhero capable of destroying villains. (Rev: BLO 3/14/11; SLJ 5/1/11)

7039 Coudray, Philippe. *Benjamin Bear in Bright Ideas!* (K–2). Illus. by author. 2013, TOON $12.95 (978-

193517922-1). 32pp. A collection of funny cartoon vignettes featuring a clever bear and his various animal friends. ALA Notable Children's Book. (Rev: BL 3/1/13*; HB 3–4/13; SLJ 5/13*)

7040 Coudray, Philippe. *Benjamin Bear in Fuzzy Thinking* (K–2). Trans. by Leigh Stein. Illus. by author. 2011, TOON $12.95 (978-193517912-2). 32pp. Funny comic strip stories for emerging readers feature a bear with unusual thought processes. Lexile GN20L (Rev: BL 10/15/11; HB 11–12/11; LMC 1–2/12; SLJ 11/1/11)

7041 Craddock, Erik. *Stone Rabbit: BC Mambo* (3–5). Illus. by author. 2009, Random LB $11.99 (978-0-375-93922-8); paper $5.99 (978-0-375-84360-0). 96pp. A young rabbit finds himself transported first into a prehistoric world where he is seen as a god and then pursued for his barbecue sauce. (Rev: BL 11/15/08; LMC 5/09)

7042 *Creepy Creatures* (3–5). Illus. by Gabriel Hernandez, et al. Series: Goosebumps Graphix. 2006, Scholastic $16.99 (978-0-439-84124-5); paper $8.99 (978-0-439-84125-2). 144pp. Three Goosebumps stories — "The Werewolf of Fever Swamp," "The Scarecrow Walks at Midnight," and "The Abominable Snowman of Pasadena" — are presented in black-and-white graphic-novel format. (Rev: BL 10/1/06; SLJ 11/06)

7043 Crilley, Mark. *Akiko and the Journey to Toog* (3–5). Illus. by author. 2003, Delacorte $9.95 (978-0-385-73042-6). 164pp. In this comic-style intergalactic fantasy, fifth grader Akiko and a number of her friends journey to the planet Toog on a rescue mission. (Rev: HBG 4/04; SLJ 12/03)

7044 Crilley, Mark. *Spring* (4–7). Series: Miki Falls. 2007, HarperTempest paper $7.99 (978-0-06-084616-9). In this manga-style romance novel, high school senior Miki is determined to break through the defenses of the gorgeous but secretive new boy called Hiro. (Rev: BL 3/15/07; SLJ 7/07)

7045 Dahl, Michael. *The Man Behind the Mask* (3–5). Illus. by Dan Schoening. Series: DC Super Heroes: Batman. 2009, Stone Arch LB $25.32 (978-1-4342-1563-5); paper $5.95 (978-1-4342-1730-1). 56pp. Batman faces the villain responsible for his parents' deaths in this fast-moving graphic novel. Also use *My Frozen Valentine* (2009). (Rev: SLJ 1/1/10)

7046 Dauvillier, Loic. *Hidden: A Child's Story of the Holocaust* (K–3). Illus. by Marc Lizano. 2014, First Second $16.99 (978-159643873-6). 80pp. A grandmother tells her young granddaughter the basics about her experiences during the Holocaust. (Rev: BL 3/1/14; HB 7–8/14; SLJ 3/14)

7047 Davila, Claudia. *Luz Makes a Splash* (4–7). Illus. by author. Series: Future According to Luz. 2012, Kids Can $16.95 (978-155453762-4). 96pp. Luz and her friends set out to solve problems associated with a drought and a company draining water from the local swimming hole. (Rev: BLO 10/15/12; LMC 5–6/13; SLJ 1/13)

7048 Davis, Eleanor. *The Secret Science Alliance and the Copycat Crook* (4–6). Illus. by author. 2009, Bloomsbury $18.99 (978-1-59990-142-8); paper $10.99 (978-

1-59990-396-5). 160pp. The technology — some gadget instructions are included — will fascinate readers of this story about 10-year-old Julian Calendar who enters a new school hoping to create a new, popular personality for himself but finds that his scientific skills are actually appreciated. (Rev: BCCB 11/09; BL 7/09; LMC 11/09; SLJ 9/09)

7049 Davis, Eleanor. *Stinky* (K–2). Illus. by author. 2008, Raw Junior/TOON $12.95 (978-0-9799238-4-5). 40pp. Stinky the swamp monster becomes friends with a much-too-clean little boy in this graphic novel full of repetition. (Rev: BL 9/1/08; SLJ 9/08)

7050 Davis, Jim. *The Curse of the Cat People* (2–5). Illus. by author. Series: Garfield & Co. 2011, Papercutz $7.99 (978-1-59707-267-0). 32pp. Garfield finds himself in ancient Egypt and meets Neferkitty and some cats that want him to be their new pharaoh. Also use *Fish to Fry* (2011), in which Garfield is in court for crimes against fishkind. (Rev: SLJ 7/1/11)

7051 Davis, Jim. *Garfield: 30 Years of Laughs and Lasagna* (5–10). Illus. by author. 2008, Ballantine $35.00 (978-0-345-50379-4). 288pp. A collection of the popular comic strip that centers on a grumpy, overweight cat. (Rev: BL 10/15/08; SLJ 1/09)

7052 de Campi, Alex. *Kat and Mouse: Tripped* (3–5). Illus. by Federica Manfredi. 2007, TokyoPop paper $5.99 (978-1-59816-549-4). In this second installment in the manga mystery series, Kat and Mouse are on a field trip to the art museum when a famous painting is stolen. (Rev: BL 3/15/07)

7053 de Saint-Exupéry, Antoine, and Joann Sfar. *The Little Prince* (5–9). Illus. by Joann Sfar. 2010, Houghton Mifflin $19.99 (978-054733802-6). 112pp. A respectful graphic-novel retelling of Saint-Exupery's classic about a stranded pilot and a little boy who discuss matters of life and love. **e** (Rev: BL 9/15/10*; SLJ 11/10; VOYA 12/10)

7054 Denton, Terry. *Storymaze 1: The Ultimate Wave* (3–6). Illus. 2003, Allen & Unwin paper $5.95 (978-1-86508-378-0). 144pp. An imaginative visit to a parallel universe, very similar to ours, where there is an ongoing battle between good and evil; a decoder glossary allows translation of digital speech. A recommended sequel is *Storymaze 2: The Eye of Ulam* (2003). (Rev: BL 5/15/03)

7055 Despeyroux, Denise. *Dark Graphic Tales by Edgar Allan Poe* (4–7). Illus. by Miquel Serratosa. Series: Dark Graphic Novels. 2012, Enslow LB $30.60 (978-076604086-1). 96pp. Three Poe stories — "The Gold Bug," "The System of Doctor Tarr and Professor Fether," and "The Fall of the House of Usher" — are given effective graphic-novel treatment. (Rev: BL 11/15/12; LMC 3–4/13; SLJ 7/1/12; VOYA 10/12)

7056 Deutsch, Barry. *Hereville: How Mirka Got Her Sword* (3–6). Illus. by author. 2010, Abrams $15.95 (978-081098422-6). 144pp. Mirka, an 11-year-old Orthodox Jewish girl with a longing for adventure, is challenged when a talking pig arrives in the village. (Rev: BL 10/15/10; HB 11–12/10; LMC 1–2/11)

7057 Deutsch, Barry. *Hereville: How Mirka Met a Meteorite* (4–7). Illus. by author. 2012, Abrams/Amulet $16.95 (978-141970398-0). 128pp. In this sequel to *How Mirka Got Her Sword* (2010), the plucky 11-year-old Orthodox Jew must deal with a meteorite that is turned into a clone of herself. Sydney Taylor Book Award. **e** Lexile GN300L (Rev: BL 11/15/12; HB 11–12/12; SLJ 11/12*)

7058 Dezago, Todd. *Spider-Man: The Terrible Threat of the Living Brain!* (5–8). Illus. by Jonboy Meyers, et al. Series: Spider-Man. 2006, ABDO LB $21.35 (978-1-59961-008-5). Spider-Man, with a little help from Flash, foils the theft of the Living Brain, a powerful robot-like computer. (Rev: SLJ 11/06)

7059 Dezago, Todd. *Spider-Man and Captain America: Stars, Stripes, and Spiders!* (5–8). Series: Spider-Man Team Up. 2006, ABDO LB $21.35 (978-1-59961-001-6). In this action-packed comic-book fantasy, superheroes Spider-Man and Captain America team up to battle the Grey Gargoyle. (Rev: SLJ 11/06)

7060 Di Fiori, Larry. *Jackie and the Shadow Snatcher* (K–2). Illus. 2006, Knopf $15.95 (978-0-375-87515-1). With the help of his dog Baxter and elderly friend Mr. Socrates, young Jackie hopes to recover his shadow from the villainous Shadow Snatcher in this picture-book-sized graphic novel set in the first half of the 20th century with detailed black-and-white illustrations. (Rev: BL 4/15/06; SLJ 7/06)

7061 Dillard, Sarah. *Extraordinary Warren: A Super Chicken* (2–4). Illus. by author. 2014, Aladdin $12.99 (978-144245340-1). 64pp. Bored with life Warren explores a wider world and discovers he can play an important role. **e** (Rev: BL 3/1/14; LMC 8–9/14)

7062 Duffy, Chris, ed. *Fairy Tale Comics: Classic Tales Told by Extraordinary Cartoonists* (PS–2). Illus. 2013, First Second $19.99 (978-159643823-1). 128pp. Seventeen stories, some very familiar and others less so, are presented in graphic form by different authors/illustrators. **e** (Rev: BL 6/13*; LMC 3–4/14; SLJ 9/13)

7063 Dunklee, Annika. *My Name Is Elizabeth!* (PS–1). Illus. by Matthew Forsythe. 2011, Kids Can $14.95 (978-1-55453-560-6). Unpaged. A young girl fed up with nicknames shouts out her name preference — Elizabeth! (Rev: LMC 1–2/12; SLJ 10/1/11)

7064 DuPrau, Jeanne, and Dallas Middaugh. *The City of Ember* (4–7). Illus. by Niklas Asker. 2012, Random House $18.99 (978-037586821-4); LB $21.99 (978-037596821-1). 144pp. A graphic novel version of the first book in the successful Books of Ember series, in which Lina and Doon work to find a way out of their isolated and decaying city, where the population is beginning to panic. (Rev: BL 10/15/12; SLJ 11/12*)

7065 Eaton, Maxwell. *The Flying Beaver Brothers and the Evil Penguin Plan* (2–4). Illus. by author. 2012, Knopf LB $12.99 (978-037596447-3); paper $6.99 (978-037586447-6). 96pp. Two beavers must stop penguins from an evil plot to destroy their island by turning it into a frosty resort. (Rev: BL 1/12; LMC 3–4/12; SLJ 3/1/12)

7066 Eaton, Maxwell. *The Flying Beaver Brothers and the Mud-Slinging Moles* (2–4). Illus. by author. 2013, Knopf $12.99 (978-044981020-0); paper $6.99 (978-04498101-9-4). 96pp. Beavers Ace and Bub must defend their forest island from a group of marauding moles trying to steal their dirt; the cartoon artwork adds to the slapstick humor. (Rev: BLO 7/13; SLJ 7/13)

7067 Eisner, Will. *The Princess and the Frog: By the Grimm Brothers* (4–7). 1999, NBM $15.95 (978-1-56163-244-2). A retelling of the familiar fairy tale in graphic novel style. (Rev: BL 12/15/99; HBG 3/00) [398.2]

7068 Emerson, Sharon. *Zebrafish* (5–8). Illus. by Renee Kurilla. 2010, Simon & Schuster $16.99 (978-1-4169-9525-8). 128pp. Led by purple-haired Vita — the only one with any musical abilities — the members of a middle-school rock band prepare for a performance that will bring donations for the fight against cancer. (Rev: BL 3/15/10; LMC 10/10; SLJ 5/10)

7069 Everheart, Chris. *Shadow Cell Scam* (4–8). Illus. by Arcana Studio. Series: The Recon Academy. 2009, Stone Arch $25.32 (978-1-4342-1166-8). 64pp. Working together, four superpower-endowed teens confront danger and adversity when they're sent to protect the launch of a Navy spy satellite in this thrilling graphic novel. (Rev: LMC 10/09; SLJ 9/09)

7070 *Fairy Tales of Oscar Wilde* (5–8). Illus. by P. Craig Russell. 1992, Nantier $15.95 (978-1-56163-056-1). Graphic novel treatment enlivens this retelling of two of Wilde's short stories. (Rev: BL 1/15/93)

7071 Faller, Regis. *The Adventures of Polo* (PS–2). Illus. 2006, Roaring Brook $16.95 (978-1-59643-160-7). 80pp. In this wordless graphic novel, Polo the dog sets off in a tiny boat on a series of magical adventures. (Rev: BL 3/15/06; SLJ 6/06*)

7072 Faller, Regis. *Polo and the Magic Flute* (PS–2). Illus. by author. 2009, Roaring Brook $9.95 (978-1-59643-495-0). 32pp. Polo the dog's fishing trip turns into a magical adventure in this wordless book. (Rev: BL 3/1/09; SLJ 7/09)

7073 Farshtey, Greg. *The Rise of the Toa Nuva* (3–6). Illus. by Carlos D'Anda. 2008, Papercutz $12.95 (978-1-59707-110-9). 112pp. Cyborgs defend a tropical island in this complex graphic novel based on a Lego game. (Rev: BL 8/08)

7074 Fearing, Mark. *Earthling!* (3–6). Illus. by author. 2012, Chronicle $22.99 (978-081187106-8); paper $12.99 (978-14521090-6-0). 248pp. Bud accidentally gets on the wrong bus and ends up in an intergalactic school, where he must hide his earthling status or risk arousing suspicion. (Rev: BL 3/15/12; LMC 8–9/12; SLJ 9/12; VOYA 6/12)

7075 Fisher, Jane Smith. *WJHC: Hold Tight* (4–7). 2005, Wilson Place paper $11.95 (978-0-9744235-1-7). This graphic-novel sequel to *WJHC: On the Air* (2003) con-

tinues the adventures of six diverse teenage friends who launched a high school radio station, following them through a reality TV show, a celebrity fashion show, and a trip to a rock concert. (Rev: BL 11/1/05; SLJ 1/06)

7076 Fisher, Jane Smith. *WJHC: On the Air!* (4–8). 2003, Wilson Place paper $11.95 (978-0-9744235-0-0). Six episodes catalog the entertaining misadventures of a diverse band of teens who launch a high school radio station. (Rev: BL 2/1/04; VOYA 12/03)

7077 Ford, Christopher. *Stickman Odyssey, Vol. 1: An Epic Doodle* (5–8). Illus. by author. 2011, Philomel $12.99 (978-039925426-0). 208pp. Banished by his evil stepmother, Zozimos has many adventures as he journeys home to reclaim his throne in this graphic-novel take on the *Odyssey*. (Rev: BL 6/1/11; SLJ 9/1/11)

7078 Frampton, Otis. *Oddly Normal, Vol. 1* (4–7). 2006, Viper paper $11.95 (978-0-9777883-0-9). Half-human and half-witch, unhappy 10-year-old Oddly Normal struggles to find a place where she fits in; a collection of four issues of a mini-series published by Viper Comics. Also use *Family Reunion* (2007). (Rev: BL 11/1/06)

7079 French, Renee. *Barry's Best Buddy* (PS–1). Illus. by author. 2013, TOON $12.95 (978-193517921-4). 32pp. Polarhog tries to brighten his bird friend Barry's life in this funny story that will suit beginning readers. (Rev: BL 3/1/13; LMC 10/13; SLJ 5/13)

7080 Friesen, Ray. *A Cheese Related Mishap and Other Stories* (5–8). 2005, Don't Eat Any Bugs paper $8.95 (978-0-9728177-6-9). This collection of zany tales full of entertaining characters and situations was created by a teenage author/illustrator. (Rev: BL 11/15/05; SLJ 3/06)

7081 Friesen, Ray. *Cupcakes of Doom: A Collection of YARG! Piratey Comics* (4–6). Illus. by author. 2009, Don't Eat Any Bugs paper $12.95 (978-0-9802314-1-0). 100pp. Swashbuckling pirates are marooned on an island with a single Pirate Cookie at the beginning of this boisterous adventure full of wordplay. (Rev: BL 3/1/09)

7082 Friesen, Ray. *Piranha Pancakes* (3–5). Illus. by author. 2010, Don't Eat Any Bugs paper $9.95 (978-09802314-3-4). 100pp. Melville and Tbyrd are back in another volume of zany stories full of wordplay and bold illustrations. (Rev: BL 4/15/11)

7083 Friesen, Ray. *Yarg!* (3–5). Illus. Series: Lookit! 2007, Don't Eat Any Bugs paper $11.95 (978-0-972817-79-0). 102pp. Back for a new round of adventures in this madcap sequel to *A Cheese Related Mishap* (2005), Melville the penguin and his friends scramble for gold in an effort to pay the back rent on the castle of Pellmellia. (Rev: BL 3/15/07)

7084 Fuji, Machiko. *The Big Adventures of Majoko* (3–6). Illus. by Tomomi Mizuna. Series: Manga for Kids. 2009, Udon paper $7.99 (978-1-897376-81-2). 200pp. A young witch named Majoko and a shy girl named Nana team up in this magical adventure manga. (Rev: BL 4/1/09)

7085 Fujino, Moyamu. *The First King Adventure, Vol. 1* (4–8). Trans. from Japanese by Kay Bertrand. Illus. by author. 2004, ADV paper $9.99 (978-1-4139-0194-8). Prince Tiltu cannot succeed his father as king until he's made contracts with all of the spirit masters that inhabit the kingdom. (Rev: SLJ 7/05)

7086 Gaiman, Neil. *Coraline* (4–7). Illus. by P. Craig Russell. 2008, HarperCollins LB $19.89 (978-0-06-082544-7); paper $18.99 (978-0-06-082543-0). 192pp. This adaptation of the 2002 novel by the same name graphically captures Coraline's horror as her nightmares become real behind a strange door. (Rev: BL 3/15/08; SLJ 7/08)

7087 Gallardo, Adam. *Gear School* (4–7). Illus. by Nuria Peris. 2007, Dark Horse paper $7.95 (978-1-59307-854-6). Teresa, 13, is being trained to operate huge robotic attack machines called Gear when aliens attack and she and her classmates must defend themselves. (Rev: BL 11/15/07)

7088 Geary, Rick. *Great Expectations. Rev. ed.* (4–7). Illus. by author. Series: Classics Illustrated. 2008, Papercutz $9.95 (978-1-59707-097-3). The Dickens classic is retold in graphic novel format with illustrations that highlight the key parts of the story. (Rev: BL 3/15/08)

7089 Giarrusso, Chris. *G-Man: Learning to Fly* (3–5). Illus. by author. 2010, Image paper $9.99 (978-16070627-0-7). 96pp. A spirited young boy commandeers his family's magic blanket for a bit of lively fun in this superpowered collection of funny adventures. (Rev: BL 12/15/10)

7090 Goodwin, Vincent. *The Adventure of the Blue Carbuncle* (2–4). Illus. by Ben Dunn. Series: Graphic Novel Adventures of Sherlock Holmes. 2012, ABDO LB $29.93 (978-161641891-5). 48pp. A retelling in graphic-novel form of a classic Christmas mystery about a mysterious blue gem found inside a carved goose. Lexile 500 (Rev: BL 8/12)

7091 Gownley, Jimmy. *Amelia Rules! The Whole World's Crazy* (3–5). Illus. 2003, iBooks paper $14.95 (978-0-7434-7503-7). 160pp. This is a compilation of previously self-published comic-book episodes about the entertaining exploits, triumphs, and disappointments of fourth-grade Amelia. (Rev: BL 2/1/04)

7092 Gownley, Jimmy. *Her Permanent Record* (4–6). Illus. by author. Series: Amelia Rules! 2012, Atheneum $19.99 (978-1-41698615-7); paper $10.99 (978-14169861-4-0). 160pp. Now 11, Amelia, Ronda, and Kyle are back as they board a bus to search for Amelia's missing Aunt Tanner; the 8th and final book in the series. Lexile GN380L (Rev: BLO 9/15/12; SLJ 1/13)

7093 Gownley, Jimmy. *The Meaning of Life . . . and Other Stuff* (3–7). Illus. by author. Series: Amelia Rules! 2011, Atheneum paper $10.99 (978-14169861-2-6). 160pp. This seventh book in the Amelia Rules series finds the protagonist on the verge of puberty and yearning for simpler times. (Rev: BL 9/15/11)

7094 Gownley, Jimmy. *Superheroes* (4–7). Illus. by author. Series: Amelia Rules! 2007, Renaissance paper $14.95 (978-0-9712169-6-9). Amelia's life is a blend of comedy and angst as she faces life after her parents' divorce, a new neighborhood, and new friends. (Rev: BL 9/1/07)

7095 Gownley, Jimmy. *True Things (Adults Don't Want Kids to Know)* (3–7). Illus. by author. Series: Amelia Rules! 2010, Atheneum paper $10.99 (978-14169860-9-6). 176pp. In this sixth Amelia offering, Amelia contends with a powerful crush, her aunt dating her teacher, and increasing tension between her family and friends. (Rev: BL 10/15/10; SLJ 1/1/11)

7096 Gownley, Jimmy. *The Tweenage Guide to Not Being Unpopular* (3–7). Illus. by author. Series: Amelia Rules! 2010, Atheneum paper $10.99 (978-14169860-8-9). 192pp. Amelia and her friend Rhonda are determined to avoid unpopularity in middle school, though their popularity crusade hits some obstacles. (Rev: BL 3/15/10; SLJ 5/10)

7097 Grant, Alan. *Kidnapped: The Graphic Novel* (5–8). Illus. by Cam Kennedy. 2007, Tundra paper $11.95 (978-0-88776-843-9). A graphic novel adaptation of the story by Robert Louis Stevenson that captures the spirit of the original. (Rev: BL 10/1/07; SLJ 1/08)

7098 Grayson, Devin. *X-Men: Evolution: Hearing Things* (5–8). Illus. by UDON, et al. Series: X-Men Evolution. 2006, ABDO LB $21.35 (978-1-59961-053-5). In this comic-book adventure from the early years of the X-Men series, Jean Grey comes to grips with her telepathic and telekinetic powers. (Rev: SLJ 11/06)

7099 *Green Lantern* (4–10). Series: Showcase Presents. 2005, DC Comics paper $9.99 (978-1-4012-0759-5). A collection of black-and-white reprints of the early comics about the handsome crime fighter. (Rev: SLJ 5/06)

7100 Guibert, Emmanuel. *Ariol: Just a Donkey Like You and Me* (2–4). Illus. by Marc Boutavant. Series: Ariol. 2013, Papercutz paper $12.99 (978-15970739-9-8). 124pp. This charming and funny graphic novel includes 10 stories about the adventures of a tween donkey and his anthropomorphic animal friends; the first in a series first published in France. ℮ (Rev: BL 3/1/13; LMC 1–2/14; SLJ 7/13)

7101 Guibert, Emmanuel. *A Beautiful Cow* (2–5). Illus. by Marc Boutavant. Series: Ariol. 2014, Papercutz paper $12.99 (978-15970751-3-8). 124pp. The little donkey called Ariol has a crush on a beautiful cow named Petula, but has trouble screwing up courage to tell her; the fourth volume in a French series that can be read out of order. (Rev: BL 3/1/14*; SLJ 7/14)

7102 Guibert, Emmanuel. *Sardine in Outer Space* (3–5). Trans. by Sasha Watson. Illus. by Joann Sfar. Series: Sardine in Outer Space. 2006, Roaring Brook paper $12.95 (978-1-59643-126-3). 128pp. In this comic book space fantasy, an import from France, a young girl named Sardine enlists the help of her cousin and uncle to foil the villainous plans of Supermuscleman. (Rev: BL 3/15/06; SLJ 7/06)

7103 Guibert, Emmanuel. *Sardine in Outer Space 2* (4–6). Illus. by Joann Sfar. Series: Sardine in Outer Space. 2006, Roaring Brook paper $12.95 (978-1-59643-127-0). 128pp. In the second volume of this graphic novel series, the redheaded Sardine and her fellow space pirates duel once again with the villainous — but slow-witted — Supermuscleman. (Rev: BL 9/1/06; SLJ 11/06)

7104 Hakamada, Mera. *Fairy Idol Kanon, Vol. 1* (2–5). Illus. by author. Series: Manga for Kids. 2009, Udon paper $7.99 (978-1-897376-89-8). 200pp. Kanon, a 4th-grader who loves to sing, meets a fairy who may make her a star in this manga for young readers. (Rev: BLO 4/30/09; LMC 10/09)

7105 Hale, Nathan. *One Dead Spy* (3–6). Illus. by author. Series: Nathan Hale's Hazardous Tales. 2012, Abrams/Amulet $12.95 (978-1-41970396-6). 128pp. A colorful tale in which spy Nathan Hale is whisked away on a time travel adventure, which enables him to foretell the future from the gallows, imparting some history along the way. (Rev: BL 8/12; HB 9–10/12; VOYA 8/12)

7106 Hale, Shannon, and Dean Hale. *Rapunzel's Revenge* (5–8). Illus. by Nathan Hale. 2008, Bloomsbury $18.99 (978-1-59990-070-4). 144pp. In the Wild West, a girl called Rapunzel eventually escapes from a prison in a magic tree and uses her hair to gain revenge against the woman who kept her real mother a slave. ALA Notable Children's Book 2009. (Rev: BL 9/1/08; HB 11–12/08; LMC 11–12/08*; SLJ 9/08)

7107 Harper, Charise Mericle. *Fashion Kitty Versus the Fashion Queen* (4–7). Illus. by author. 2007, Hyperion paper $8.99 (978-0-7868-3726-7). Superhero Fashion Kitty (Kiki Kittie's alter ego) continues to rescue victims of fashion emergencies in this funny sequel to *Fashion Kitty* (2005). (Rev: BCCB 7–8/07; SLJ 11/07)

7108 Hatke, Ben. *Legends of Zita the Spacegirl* (3–6). Illus. by author. 2012, First Second $18.99 (978-1-59643806-4); paper $12.99 (978-15964344-7-9). 224pp. In this second funny and fast-paced volume about her exploits, Zita faces many challenges while she tries to get back home — including dealing with her new role as a superstar. ALA Notable Children's Book. Lexile 250 (Rev: BL 8/12*; SLJ 9/12*)

7109 Hatke, Ben. *The Return of Zita the Spacegirl* (3–6). Illus. by author. 2014, First Second $18.99 (978-162672058-9); paper $12.99 (978-15964387-6-7). 240pp. Even though she is sentenced to a dungeon for her "crimes," Zita still manages to escape and eventually frustrate the plans of evil forces; the final volume in the trilogy. Lexile 280 (Rev: BL 3/1/14*; SLJ 5/14)

7110 Hatke, Ben. *Zita the Spacegirl* (3–6). Illus. by author. 2011, Roaring Brook $17.99 (978-159643695-4); paper $10.99 (978-15964344-6-2). 188pp. Joseph is abducted when he and Zita open a portal to an alien dimension, and Zita must follow and rescue him, experiencing many adventures. (Rev: BL 12/15/10; LMC 3–4/11; SLJ 1/1/11)

7111 Hayes, Geoffrey. *Benny and Penny in Lights Out!* (PS–1). Illus. by author. 2012, TOON $12.95 (978-193517920-7). 32pp. Mouse siblings Benny and Penny prepare for the night with stories and mildly scary adventures in this 4th book in the series for beginning readers. Lexile GN170L (Rev: BL 10/15/12; SLJ 10/12)

7112 Hayes, Geoffrey. *Benny and Penny in the Big No-No!* (K–1). Illus. by author. 2009, Raw Junior/TOON $12.95 (978-0-9799238-9-0). 32pp. Is their new neighbor a thief? Mice Benny and Penny bravely investigate and discover they totally misjudged her. (Rev: BL 3/1/09)

7113 Hayes, Geoffrey. *Benny and Penny in the Toy Breaker* (PS–2). Illus. by author. 2010, Raw Junior/TOON $12.95 (978-1-935179-07-8). 32pp. Mouse siblings Benny and Penny unite to protect their toys from their boisterous cousin Bo when he comes to visit; the cartoon illustrations will attract new readers. (Rev: BL 3/15/10; SLJ 7/1/10)

7114 Hayes, Geoffrey. *Patrick in a Teddy Bear's Picnic and Other Stories* (K–2). Illus. by author. 2011, TOON $12.95 (978-193517909-2). 32pp. Patrick the bear has a variety of adventures in this comic book full of lovable, dynamic illustrations; suitable for beginning readers. (Rev: BL 4/15/11; SLJ 7/1/11)

7115 Hicks, Faith Erin. *The War at Ellsmere* (5–8). Illus. by author. 2008, SLG paper $12.95 (978-1-59362-140-7). 156pp. The war is between wealthy snobs and a scholarship student at a classy boarding school, with a legendary unicorn thrown into this readable mix. (Rev: BL 3/1/09)

7116 Hoena, Blake A. *Eek and Ack vs. the Wolfman* (1–3). Illus. by Steve Harpster. Series: Graphic Sparks. 2009, Stone Arch LB $16.99 (978-1-4342-1189-7). 40pp. Aliens Eek and Ack arrive on Earth on Halloween and find themselves facing a werewolf. (Rev: BL 3/1/09)

7117 Hoena, Blake A. *Jack and the Beanstalk* (K–2). Illus. by Ricardo Tercio. 2008, Stone Arch $15.95 (978-1-4342-0766-1). A snappy new graphic novel version of the suspenseful classic. (Rev: BLO 9/17/08; LMC 5/09)

7118 Holm, Jennifer. *Skater Girl* (3–5). Illus. by Matthew Holm. Series: Babymouse. 2007, Random LB $12.99 (978-0-375-93989-1); paper $5.99 (978-0-375-83989-4). Babymouse is good at skating but does she have the determination to make it big on the ice? This 7th installment in the series will also attract reluctant readers. (Rev: BL 9/1/07; HB 11/07)

7119 Holm, Jennifer L., and Matthew Holm. *Babymouse: Mad Scientist* (3–5). Illus. by Jennifer L. Holm. Series: Babymouse. 2011, Random House LB $12.99 (978-037596574-6); paper $6.99 (978-037586574-9). 96pp. Babymouse discovers an amoeba named Squish while working on her science fair project. (Rev: BL 9/15/11)

7120 Holm, Jennifer L., and Matthew Holm. *Babymouse Burns Rubber* (4–6). Illus. by Jennifer L. Holm. Series: Babymouse. 2010, Random House LB $12.99 (978-037595713-0); paper $5.99 (978-037585713-3). 96pp. Babymouse's dreams of driving a race car come true when her friend Wilson helps her build a soapbox derby car. (Rev: BL 1/1/10)

7121 Holm, Jennifer L., and Matthew Holm. *Cupcake Tycoon* (4–6). Illus. by Jennifer L. Holm. Series: Babymouse. 2010, Random House LB $12.99 (978-037596573-9); paper $6.99 (978-037586573-2). 96pp.

Babymouse participates in a library fundraiser after she accidentally sets off the sprinkler system and ruins some books; the 13th installment in the series. (Rev: BL 10/15/10)

7122 Holm, Jennifer L., and Matthew Holm. *Super Amoeba* (3–5). Illus. by Jennifer L. Holm. Series: Squish. 2011, Random House LB $12.99 (978-037593783-5); paper $6.99 (978-037584389-1). 96pp. The first volume in a new humorous series about an amoeba named Squish who imitates his favorite superhero in an effort to stop bullies from tormenting his friends. (Rev: BL 3/15/11; LMC 10/11; SLJ 7/1/11)

7123 Holm, Jennifer L., and Matthew Holm. *A Very Babymouse Christmas* (3–5). Illus. by Jennifer L. Holm. Series: Babymouse. 2011, Random House LB $12.99 (978-037596779-5); paper $6.99 (978-037586779-8). 96pp. Babymouse is determined to get the new Whiz Bang, an electronic gadget, for Christmas and is willing to take on Santa to get it. **e** (Rev: BLO 12/15/11; HB 11–12/11; SLJ 10/1/11)

7124 Holm, Jennifer, and Matthew Holm. *Babymouse: Beach Babe* (4–6). Illus. Series: Babymouse. 2006, Random LB $12.99 (978-0-375-93231-1); paper $5.95 (978-0-375-83231-4). School is over for the year, and the lively Babymouse is headed to the beach for a summer of fun and adventure. (Rev: BL 3/15/06; SLJ 7/06)

7125 Holm, Jennifer, and Matthew Holm. *Babymouse: Monster Mash* (4–6). Illus. by Jennifer Holm. 2008, Random LB $11.99 (978-0-375-93789-7); paper $5.99 (978-0-375-84387-7). 96pp. Orange replaces pink as the dominant color in this Halloween-themed installment in the series about the young mouse. (Rev: BLO 7/22/08; HB 9/08)

7126 Holm, Jennifer, and Matthew Holm. *Babymouse: Our Hero* (4–6). Illus. 2005, Random LB $12.99 (978-0-375-93230-4); paper $5.95 (978-0-375-83230-7). 96pp. Babymouse dreads competing in her class's annual dodgeball tournament, but when her best friend is threatened she surprises herself and saves the day for her team. (Rev: BL 12/1/05; SLJ 3/06)

7127 Holm, Jennifer, and Matthew Holm. *Babymouse: Queen of the World* (4–6). Illus. 2005, Random LB $12.99 (978-0-375-93229-8); paper $5.95 (978-0-375-83229-1). Babymouse learns some important lessons about the true meaning of friendship after she slights Wilson Weasel to win an invitation to Felicia Furrypaws' slumber party. (Rev: BL 12/1/05; SLJ 3/06)

7128 Holm, Jennifer, and Matthew Holm. *Babymouse: Rock Star* (2–4). 2006, Random LB $12.99 (978-0-375-93232-8); paper $5.95 (978-0-375-83232-1). Babymouse may play the flute at school but in her dreams she's a wildly popular rock star. (Rev: SLJ 9/06)

7129 Holm, Jennifer, and Matthew Holm. *Babymouse: The Musical* (4–6). Illus. by Jennifer Holm. 2009, Random LB $11.99 (978-0-375-93791-0); paper $5.99 (978-0-375-84388-4). It's school musical time, and — despite her shortcomings on stage — Babymouse tries out for

a role on the urging of a new student, British hedgehog Henry Higgins. (Rev: BL 3/1/09)

7130 Hosler, Jay. *Clan Apis* (5–7). 2001, Active Synapse paper $15.00 (978-0-9677255-0-5). Nyuki, a honeybee, describes his hive's history and migration to a new location in a text presented in graphic novel style that includes information about bees and their environment. (Rev: BL 7/01)

7131 Huey, Debbie. *Bumperboy and the Loud, Loud Mountain* (2–4). 2006, AdHouse paper $8.95 (978-0-9766610-1-6). 128pp. Bumperboy and his faithful canine sidekick try to unravel the mysteries surrounding the disappearance of the Grums and an endangered talking mountain called Jumbra; the second installment in a graphic-novel series. (Rev: BL 8/06)

7132 Hugo, Victor. *The Hunchback of Notre Dame* (5–12). Retold by Michael Ford. Illus. by Penko Gelev. Series: Graphic Classics. 2007, Barron's $15.99 (978-0-7641-5979-4). The classic story about the misshapen bell ringer is presented in graphic-novel format. (Rev: SLJ 5/07)

7133 Hunter, Erin, and Dan Jolley. *The Lost Warrior, Vol. 1* (4–6). Illus. by James L. Barry. Series: Warriors. 2007, paper $6.99 (978-0-06-124020-1). Graystripe resents his capture and domestication in this adaptation of the author's series of novels. Also use *Warrior's Refuge, The Rise of Scourge,* and *Escape from the Forest,* in the Warriors: Tigerstar and Sasha series (all 2007). (Rev: LMC 11/07; SLJ 7/07)

7134 Ikezawa, Satomi. *Guru Guru Pon-Chan, Vol. 1* (5–12). Trans. from Japanese by Douglas Varenas. Illus. by author. 2005, Del Rey paper $10.95 (978-0-345-48095-8). In this whimsical shape-changing story, Ponta, a Labrador retriever puppy, nibbles on a newly invented "chit-chat" bone and turns into a human girl who comically retains doggy behavior. (Rev: SLJ 11/05)

7135 Ikumi, Mia. *Tokyo Mew Mew a la Mode, Vol. 1* (5–8). Trans. from Japanese by Yoohae Yang. Illus. by author. 2005, TokyoPop paper $9.99 (978-1-59532-789-5). In the opening volume of the Tokyo Mew Mew a la Mode series, 12-year-old Berry Shirayuki is shanghaied into a team of girl superheroes and soon finds herself doing battle with dragons and the evil Saint Rose Crusaders. (Rev: SLJ 11/05)

7136 Irwin, Jane, and Jeff Berndt. *Vogelein: Clockwork Faerie* (5–12). 2003, Fiery Studios paper $12.95 (978-0-9743110-0-5). A beautiful 17th-century mechanical fairy who is immortal but depends on others to wind her up stars in this graphic novel. (Rev: BL 11/1/03)

7137 Jacques, Brian. *Redwall: The Graphic Novel* (4–7). Illus. by Bret Blevins. Series: Redwall. 2007, Philomel paper $12.99 (978-0-399-24481-0). Redwall makes an effective transition to the graphic novel format with this spirited adaptation. (Rev: BL 9/1/07; SLJ 9/07)

7138 Jansson, Tove. *Moomin's Winter Follies* (2–4). Illus. by author. 2012, Enfant paper $9.95 (978-17704609-8-0). 48pp. The Moomins decide against hibernation and

365

instead participate in Mr. Brisk's winter sports, with mixed results; a reissue in color. (Rev: BL 12/15/12)

7139 Johns, Geoff. *Teen Titans: The Future Is Now* (5–8). Series: Teen Titans. 2005, DC Comics paper $9.99 (978-1-4012-0475-4). In volume four of the series, the title characters return from a mission into the future to learn that Robin's father died while they were away. (Rev: BL 3/15/06)

7140 Johnson, R. Kikuo. *The Shark King* (2–4). Illus. by author. 2012, TOON $12.95 (978-193517916-0). 40pp. The shape-shifting shark god Kamohoalii has a child with a young human woman, and the child has trouble fitting in with the people of his village; a graphic novel for early readers. (Rev: BL 3/15/12*; HB 7–8/12; LMC 10/12; SLJ 5/1/12)

7141 Jolley, Dan. *The Hero Twins: Against the Lords of Death* (3–5). Illus. by David Witt. Series: Graphic Myths and Legends. 2008, Lerner LB $26.60 (978-0-8225-7495-8). 48pp. An action-packed myth about two Mayan twins who anger the Lords of Death. (Rev: BLO 3/3/08; SLJ 7/08) [741.5]

7142 Jolley, Dan. *The Time Travel Trap* (4–8). Illus. by Matt Wendt. Series: Twisted Journeys. 2008, Lerner LB $27.93 (978-0-7613-9472-3); paper $7.95 (978-0-8225-8874-0). 112pp. Readers can choose which way the plot will go in this time-travel adventure story. (Rev: SLJ 5/08)

7143 Kibuishi, Kazu. *Copper* (5–8). 2010, Graphix paper $12.99 (978-0-545-09893-9). 96pp. A collection of funny short stories, in graphic novel format, featuring a boy named Copper and his fraidy-cat talking dog Fred; with author comments on how he creates comic strips. (Rev: BL 12/1/09; LMC 3–4/10; SLJ 5/10)

7144 Kibuishi, Kazu. *The Last Council* (4–7). Illus. by author. Series: Amulet. 2011, Scholastic paper $10.99 (978-05452088-7-1). 224pp. Emily and her friends arrive in the cloud city of Cielis and find themselves in a contest for a seat on the Guardian Council. Lexile GN400L (Rev: BL 10/15/11)

7145 Kibuishi, Kazu. *Prince of the Elves* (4–7). Illus. by author. Series: Amulet. 2012, Scholastic paper $12.99 (978-05452088-9-5). 208pp. In the fifth book in the series, war is looming over the city of Cielis and Emily and her friends must meet the Elf King. Lexile 400L (Rev: BLO 9/15/12; SLJ 9/12)

7146 Kibuishi, Kazu. *The Stonekeeper* (4–7). Illus. by author. Series: Amulet. 2008, Scholastic $21.99 (978-0-439-84680-6); paper $9.99 (978-0-439-84681-3). Emily's father is killed in a car crash and her mother swallowed by a monster after opening a doorway to another world in this first volume in the series. (Rev: BL 12/1/07; LMC 2/08; SLJ 1/08)

7147 Kibuishi, Kazu. *The Stonekeeper's Curse* (4–7). Series: Amulet. 2009, Graphix $21.99 (978-0-439-84682-0). 224pp. This sequel to *The Stonekeeper* (2007) has Emily and Navin searching for a remedy that will save their mother from poison, even as the evil Elf King is in pursuit. (Rev: BL 10/15/09; LMC 1–2/10; SLJ 11/09)

7148 Kibuishi, Kazu, ed. *Flight Explorer, Vol. 1* (4–6). Illus. by Kazu Kibuishi. 2008, Villard paper $10.00 (978-0-345-50313-8). 112pp. A collection of 10 pieces of graphic fiction that showcases the genre's variety of artistic styles and subject and story strategies. (Rev: BL 3/15/08; SLJ 5/08)

7149 Kibuishi, Kazu, ed. *The Lost Islands* (4–8). Illus. 2013, Abrams/Amulet $19.95 (978-141970881-7); paper $10.95 (978-14197088-3-1). 128pp. An island themed compilation of stories written and drawn by seven well-known graphic novelists. (Rev: BL 11/15/13; LMC 5–6/14; SLJ 11/13*)

7150 Kim, Susan, and Laurence Klavan. *City of Spies* (4–7). Illus. by Pascal Dizin. 2010, First Second paper $16.99 (978-1-59643-262-8). 176pp. Evelyn and her friend Tony expose Nazi spies in this story set in New York in 1942. (Rev: BL 3/15/10*; LMC 8–9/10; SLJ 5/10)

7151 Kipling, Rudyard, and Lewis Helfand. *Kim* (5–8). Illus. by Rakesh Kumar. 2011, Campfire paper $9.99 (978-93800284-2-2). 72pp. The classic story of the boy who becomes a spy is presented in graphic-novel format with accessible text and colorful illustrations. (Rev: BL 1/1–15/11; LMC 5–6/11)

7152 Knight, Hilary, and Steven Kroll. *Nina in That Makes Me Mad!* (PS–2). Illus. by Hilary Knight. 2011, TOON $12.95 (978-193517910-8). 32pp. On one side of each two-page spread, expressive young Nina exclaims about a variety of different things that make her mad; the opposite side is a funny comic strip illustrating the girl's complaint. Lexile GN160L (Rev: BL 10/15/11; LMC 1–2/12; SLJ 11/1/11)

7153 Kobayashi, Makoto. *Planet of the Cats* (5–8). Series: What's Michael? 2006, Dark Horse paper $9.95 (978-1-59307-525-5). In this 11th, concluding volume of the graphic novel series first published in Japan, Hanako, a human exobiologist, and her spaceship crew find themselves stranded on a planet ruled by house cats. (Rev: BL 9/1/06)

7154 Kobayashi, Makoto. *Sleepless Nights* (5–8). Series: What's Michael? 2005, Dark Horse paper $8.95 (978-1-59307-337-4). Volume ten of the continuing adventures of the house cat who has been described as "Japan's version of Garfield, Heathcliff, and Krazy Kat all rolled into one." (Rev: BL 9/1/05)

7155 Kochalka, James. *The Glorkian Warrior Delivers a Pizza* (K–3). Illus. by author. 2014, First Second $17.99 (978-162672103-6); paper $12.99 (978-15964391-7-7). 112pp. An intergalactic traveler seeks to deliver a peanut-butter-and-clam pizza with the help of his talking super backpack. Lexile 190 (Rev: BL 3/1/14; SLJ 3/14)

7156 Kochalka, James. *Johnny Boo and the Happy Apples* (K–3). Illus. by author. 2009, Top Shelf $9.95 (978-160309041-4). 40pp. Little ghost Johnny Boo wants big muscles and hears that Happy Apples will supply these, but the apples are hard to acquire. The fourth adventure in this series is *Johnny Boo and the Mean Little Boy* (2010). (Rev: BL 10/15/09)

7157 Kochalka, James. *Johnny Boo: The Best Little Ghost in the World!* (K–3). Illus. by author. 2008, Top Shelf paper $9.95 (978-1-60309-013-1). Johnny is a good little ghost and proud of his "boo" but this doesn't stop him being afraid of the Ice Cream Monster. (Rev: BL 3/15/08; LMC 5/09)

7158 Kochalka, James. *Johnny Boo: Twinkle Power* (K–3). Illus. by author. 2008, Top Shelf paper $9.95 (978-1-60309-015-5). 40pp. A silly adventure in which ghost Johnny Boo and his sidekick Squiggle consider the potential of stars' Twinkle Power, then wonder about wiggle power, and find some fun in Johnny Boo's hair. (Rev: BL 3/1/09)

7159 Kovac, Tommy. *Wonderland* (4–8). Illus. by Sonny Liew. 2009, Disney $19.99 (978-1-4231-0451-3). 160pp. A chaotic graphic Alice in Wonderland novel from the point of view of the terribly tidy maid, Mary Ann. (Rev: BCCB 6/09; BL 5/15/09; SLJ 5/09)

7160 Krosoczka, Jarrett J. *Lunch Lady and the Bake Sale Bandit* (2–4). Illus. by author. 2010, Knopf LB $12.99 (978-037596729-0); paper $6.99 (978-037586729-3). 96pp. Who is stealing bake sale goods? The Lunch Lady, Dee, Hector, and Terrence go head-to-head with a notorious bandit. (Rev: BL 2/15/11)

7161 Krosoczka, Jarrett J. *Lunch Lady and the Cyborg Substitute* (2–4). Illus. by author. 2009, Knopf LB $11.99 (978-0-375-94683-7); paper $5.99 (978-0-375-84683-0). 96pp. Lunch Lady, an undercover crime fighter, with her assistant Betty and three students investigates a cyborg plot to replace teachers with robots. (Rev: BL 3/1/09)

7162 Krosoczka, Jarrett J. *Lunch Lady and the Summer Camp Shakedown* (3–5). Illus. by author. 2010, Knopf LB $12.99 (978-0-375-96095-6); paper $6.99 (978-0-375-86095-9). 96pp. Lunch Lady is working as cook at the summer camp Hector, Dee, and Terrence are attending, and together they tackle the mysterious Scum Monster. ⊖ Lexile GN390L (Rev: BLO 6/10; SLJ 7/10)

7163 Labatt, Mary. *Dracula Madness* (2–4). Illus. by Jo Rioux. Series: Sam and Friends Mystery. 2009, Kids Can $16.95 (978-1-55453-418-0); paper $7.95 (978-1-55337-303-2). 96pp. Based on *Spying on Dracula* (1999), this graphic novel features Sam the independent-minded sheepdog detective and 10-year-old Jennie, who can hear Sam's thoughts, as they investigate a neighbor's suspicious behavior. (Rev: BL 3/1/09)

7164 Labatt, Mary. *Witches' Brew* (2–4). Illus. by Jo Rioux. Series: Sam and Friends. 2011, Kids Can $16.95 (978-155453472-2); paper $7.95 (978-15545347-3-9). 96pp. Three strange women move into the neighborhood with pets including toads and a black cat. Could they be witches? Sam the sheepdog detective and his human friends investigate. (Rev: BL 5/1/11)

7165 Langridge, Roger. *The Muppet Show Comic Book: Family Reunion* (3–6). Illus. by Amy Mebberson. 2010, Boom! paper $9.99 (978-16088658-7-1). 112pp. This deftly illustrated book captures all the distinct personalities of the Muppets, and reworks some favorite sketches. (Rev: BL 11/15/10)

7166 Langridge, Roger. *The Muppets: The Four Seasons* (3–6). Illus. by author. 2012, Marvel paper $14.99 (978-07851653-8-5). 96pp. The Muppets celebrate the four seasons with shows at the Muppet Theater. (Rev: BL 3/1/13)

7167 Lawrie, Robin, and Chris Lawrie. *Cheat Challenge* (2–6). Illus. by Robin Lawrie. Series: Ridge Riders. 2007, Stone Arch LB $21.26 (978-1-59889-347-2). 32pp. Should Slam reveal the location of a secret mountain-bike racecourse to his fellow Ridge Riders? Another action-packed installment in the series that emphasizes good character and also includes *Fear 3.1, Snow Bored,* and *White Lightning* (all 2007). (Rev: LMC 10/07; SLJ 9/07)

7168 Le Gall, Frank. *Freedom!* (2–4). Trans. by Carol Klio Burrell. Illus. by Flore Balthazar. 2012, Lerner LB $29.27 (978-076137884-6); paper $6.95 (978-076138546-2). 48pp. A bored kitten named Miss Annie has gentle adventures, including venturing out of an open window, in this simple graphic novel. ⊖ (Rev: BL 2/15/12; LMC 5–6/12; SLJ 5/1/12)

7169 Lechner, John. *Sticky Burr: The Prickly Peril* (K–3). Illus. by author. 2009, Candlewick $15.99 (978-076364145-0); paper $6.99 (978-07636458-0-9). 56pp. Scurvy Burr, irritated by the general acceptance of the nicer Spiny Burr, decides to take over Burr Village with the help of exiled Burweena. (Rev: BL 11/15/09; SLJ 11/09)

7170 Lee, Stan. *The Fantastic Four, Vol. 1* (5–10). Illus. by Jack Kirby. 2009, Marvel paper $24.99 (978-0-7851-3710-8). 272pp. This volume collects the first 10 stories about the four who returned to Earth with superhuman abilities after being exposed to cosmic rays. (Rev: BLO 4/30/09)

7171 Lindgren, Astrid. *Pippi Fixes Everything* (K–2). Trans. by Tiina Nunnally. Illus. by Ingrid Vang Nyman. 2013, Drawn & Quarterly $14.95 (978-177046131-4). 56pp. Following on the heels of *Pippi Moves In* (2012), this collection of vintage Pippi comics brings her exuberance to a new generation. (Rev: BL 11/15/13; SLJ 3/14)

7172 Lindgren, Astrid. *Pippi Moves In!* (2–4). Trans. by Tiina Nunnally. Illus. by Ingrid Vang Nyman. Series: Pippi Longstocking Comics. 2012, Drawn & Quarterly $14.95 (978-177046099-7). 56pp. In English for the first time, this collection of comics about Pippi's life with her horse and donkey dates back to 1957. (Rev: BLO 12/15/12; SLJ 3/13)

7173 Liniers, Ricardo. *The Big Wet Balloon* (K–3). Illus. by author. 2013, TOON $12.95 (978-193517932-0). 32pp. Clemmie isn't sure that her older sister is right about playing in the rain, but Matilda soon shows Clemmie that rainy days can be just as fun as sunny ones, complete with rainbows. Lexile 190 (Rev: BL 9/15/13; LMC 3–4/14; SLJ 9/13)

7174 Lobdell, Scott. *The Ocean of Osyria* (4–6). Illus. by Lea Hernandez. 2005, Papercutz paper $7.95 (978-1-59707-001-0). 96pp. Joe and Frank Hardy appear in a fast-paced graphic novel full of high-tech features — the first in a new series — and attempt to rescue their best friend, who has been implicated in an important theft. (Rev: BL 5/15/05)

7175 Long, Ethan. *Rick and Rack and the Great Outdoors* (1–3). Illus. by author. 2010, Blue Apple $10.99 (978-160905034-4). 40pp. This lively graphic novel for beginning readers comprises three short, comic stories about a raccoon and moose and their adventures in the forest. (Rev: BL 10/15/10)

7176 Loux, Matthew. *Salt Water Taffy: The Seaside Adventures of Jack and Benny* (2–4). Illus. by author. 2008, Oni paper $5.95 (978-1-932664-94-2). 96pp. Brothers Jack, 11, and Benny, 8, are dreading a vacation on the coast of Maine but soon find lots of exciting adventures there. (Rev: BL 7/08; SLJ 11/08)

7177 Loux, Matthew. *The Truth About Dr. True* (3–6). Illus. by author. Series: Salt Water Taffy. 2009, Oni paper $5.95 (978-19349640-4-0). 96pp. Adventure and mystery — involving a 19th-century murder and an unusual ghost — await Jack and Benny when they spend the summer in a small Maine seaside town. The fourth volume in the series is *Caldera's Revenge* (2011). (Rev: BL 1/1/10)

7178 Lowry, Shannon, and Suzette Haden Elgin, adapts. *Murder and Mystery* (4–8). Illus. by Mike Vosburg and Dan Spiegle. Series: Bank Street Graphic Novels. 2007, World Almanac LB $29.27 (978-0-8368-7928-5). 56pp. Well-drawn graphic versions *The Hound of the Baskervilles*, *Macbeth*, and *The Legend of Sleepy Hollow* are included here. (Rev: SLJ 7/07)

7179 Luciani, Brigitte. *A Hubbub* (K–3). Trans. by Edward Gauvin. Illus. by Eve Tharlet. Series: Mr. Badger and Mrs. Fox. 2010, Lerner $25.26 (978-076135626-4); paper $6.95 (978-07613563-2-5). 32pp. The Badger and Fox families introduced in *The Meeting* (2010) have blended together, although Ginger Fox has trouble adjusting to her badger stepbrothers. (Rev: BL 12/15/10; SLJ 11/10)

7180 Luciani, Brigitte. *The Meeting* (K–3). Trans. by Carol Klio Burrell. Illus. by Eve Tharlet. Series: Mr. Badger and Mrs. Fox. 2010, Lerner LB $25.26 (978-0-7613-5625-7); paper $6.95 (978-0-7613-5631-8). 32pp. Two families — foxes and badgers — share the same burrow, with some opposition from the children. Also use *What a Team!* (2011). (Rev: BL 3/15/10*; LMC 8–9/10; SLJ 5/10)

7181 Lynch, Jay. *Mo and Jo: Fighting Together Forever* (K–2). Illus. by Dean Haspiel. 2008, Raw Junior/TOON LB $12.95 (978-0-9799238-5-2). 40pp. Twins Mona and Joey, usually at odds with one another, learn to cooperate when they acquire superhero powers. (Rev: BL 9/15/08; LMC 1/09; SLJ 9/08)

7182 McCranie, Stephen. *Belly Flop!* (2–5). Illus. by author. Series: Mal and Chad. 2012, Philomel paper $9.99

(978-03992565-8-5). 224pp. A funny, fast-paced adventure in which Mal hopes to impress his crush Megan but meets constant obstacles. (Rev: BLO 10/15/12; SLJ 3/13)

7183 McCranie, Stephen. *Mal and Chad: The Biggest, Bestest Time Ever!* (2–5). Illus. by author. 2011, Philomel paper $9.99 (978-03992522-1-1). 224pp. Child genius Mal and his dog Chad have a variety of shape-shifting, time-travel adventures even as Mal tackles the usual concerns of a 4th-grader. (Rev: BL 5/1/11; SLJ 7/1/11)

7184 McGuiness, Dan. *Pilot and Huxley: The First Adventure* (2–4). Illus. by author. 2010, Scholastic paper $7.99 (978-05452650-4-1). 64pp. Pilot and Huxley have a series of daring and zany adventures in this funny graphic novel. Lexile GN400L (Rev: BL 12/15/10; LMC 5–6/11; SLJ 3/1/11)

7185 McGuiness, Dan. *Pilot and Huxley: The Next Adventure* (1–3). Illus. by author. 2011, Scholastic paper $8.99 (978-05452684-5-5). 64pp. Pilot and Huxley find themselves in an alternate holiday universe where Santa Claus is evil and zombies are friendly. (Rev: BL 10/15/11; SLJ 11/1/11)

7186 Mack, Stan, and Susan Champlin. *Road to Revolution!* (4–6). Illus. by Stan Mack. Series: The Cartoon Chronicles of America. 2009, Bloomsbury $16.99 (978-1-59990-013-1); paper $9.99 (978-1-59990-371-2). 128pp. In 1775, Penny and Nick help the revolutionary cause and meet many important personalities, such as Samuel Adams and Paul Revere. (Rev: BL 6/1–15/09; SLJ 7/09)

7187 McKeever, Sean. *The Loyalty Thing* (5–8). Illus. by Takeshi Miyazawa and Norman Lee. Series: Mary Jane. 2006, ABDO LB $21.35 (978-1-59961-037-5). All about Spider-Man's girlfriend before Spidey enters her life. (Rev: SLJ 5/07)

7188 McKeever, Sean. *Marvel Adventures Spider-Man: Power Struggle* (4–6). Illus. by Patrick Scherberger. 2006, Marvel paper $6.99 (978-0-7851-1903-6). A Spider-Man for modern readers, well-drawn and lots of fun for fans of superheroes. (Rev: SLJ 7/06)

7189 McKeever, Sean. *The Money Thing* (5–8). Illus. by Takeshi Miyazawa and Norman Lee. Series: Mary Jane. 2006, ABDO LB $21.35 (978-1-59961-038-2). All about Spider-Man's girlfriend before Spidey enters her life and written in a contemporary style, this will appeal to girls who want the other side of the story. (Rev: SLJ 5/07)

7190 Maeda, Shunshin. *Ninja Baseball Kyuma, Vol. 1* (2–4). Illus. by author. 2009, Udon paper $7.99 (978-1-897376-86-7). 200pp. Kyuma, a ninja who has been living alone on a mountain with his dog, finds himself drawn suddenly into the world of baseball, which he totally misunderstands; an action-filled manga. (Rev: BLO 3/11/09)

7191 Martin, Ann M., and Raina Telgemeier. *Kristy's Great Idea* (4–6). Illus. by Raina Telgemeier. Series: Baby-Sitters Club. 2006, Scholastic paper $16.99 (978-

0-439-80241-3). 192pp. The first volume in the popular Baby-Sitters Club series returns in graphic-novel format. Also in this series: *The Truth About Stacey* (2006). (Rev: BL 3/15/06; SLJ 7/06)

7192 Marunas, Nathaniel. *Manga Claus: The Blade of Kringle* (5–8). Illus. by Erik Craddock. 2006, Penguin $12.99 (978-1-59514-134-7). In this graphic novel Christmas tale, a disgruntled elf triggers a series of events that wrecks Santa's North Pole workshop and threatens to ruin Christmas for millions of children around the world. (Rev: BL 10/15/06; SLJ 10/06)

7193 Masters, Anthony. *Joker* (2–4). Illus. by Michael Reid. Series: Graphic Trax. 2006, Stone Arch LB $21.26 (978-1-59889-024-2). 66pp. In this easy-to-read graphic novel, Mel's magic performances in the classroom have fallen flat, but the boy comes to the rescue when his dad — a bank manager — is seized by would-be robbers. (Rev: SLJ 9/06)

7194 Mazan, and Cecile Chicault. *Tales from the Brothers Grimm* (3–5). Trans. by Joe Johnson. Illus. Series: Classics Illustrated Deluxe. 2008, Papercutz LB $17.95 (978-1-59707-101-7); paper $13.95 (978-1-59707-100-0). 130pp. "Hansel and Gretel," "The Valiant Little Tailor," "Learning to Shudder," and "The Devil and the Three Golden Hairs" are the four tales included in this comic-book adaptation. (Rev: BLO 7/30/08; LMC 11/08)

7195 Melville, Herman. *Moby Dick* (5–12). Retold by Sophie Furse. Illus. by Penko Gelev. Series: Graphic Classics. 2007, Barron's $15.99 (978-0-7641-5977-0). The classic story about the giant white whale is presented in graphic novel format. (Rev: SLJ 5/07)

7196 Mendes, Melissa. *Freddy Stories* (2–4). Illus. by author. 2011, Hand Thumb paper $10 (978-09835942-1-5). 112pp. A hoodie-wearing girl named Freddy stars in a series of short stories featuring her everyday adventures with her dog, her fractured but loving family, and her imagination. (Rev: BLO 2/28/12)

7197 Miller, Frank. *Batman: Year One* (4–8). Illus. by David Mazzucchelli and Richmond Lewis. 2007, DC Comics paper $19.99 (978-1-4012-0752-6). 96pp. This collection of four comic originally produced in 1988 emphasizes Batman's dark early days and the shady characters he had to deal with. (Rev: SLJ 5/07)

7198 Misako Rocks!. *Biker Girl* (5–8). Illus. by author. 2006, Hyperion paper $7.99 (978-0-7868-3676-5). Aki, a shy, bookish girl, is transformed into a superhero after finding a discarded bicycle in her grandfather's garage. (Rev: BL 3/15/06; SLJ 9/06)

7199 Modan, Rutu. *Maya Makes a Mess* (PS–2). Illus. by author. 2012, TOON $12.95 (978-193517917-7). 32pp. Maya's terrible table manners do not faze the queen in this funny graphic novel for early readers. Lexile GN240L (Rev: BL 10/15/12; LMC 3–4/13; SLJ 11/12)

7200 Morse, Scott. *Magic Pickle* (2–4). Illus. by author. 2008, Scholastic paper $9.99 (978-0-439-87995-8). 64pp. A superhero pickle — Weapon Kosher — explodes into grade-schooler Jojo's life. Will she become the pickle's sidekick and enjoy more wacky adventures? (Rev: BL 3/15/08; SLJ 7/08)

7201 Mucci, Tim. *The Odyssey* (5–8). Illus. by Emanuel Tenderini. 2010, Sterling paper $7.95 (978-1-4027-3155-6). 128pp. This graphic novel emphasizes Odysseus's various adventures on his journey home — with Circe, Calypso, the cyclops, the sirens, and so forth. (Rev: BL 4/15/10*; LMC 10/10; SLJ 7/10)

7202 Nagda, Ann Whitehead. *The Perfect Cat-Sitter* (3–5). Illus. by Stephanie Roth. 2007, Holiday $15.95 (978-0-8234-2112-1). Susan faces many challenges as she pet-sits for Rana and her family while they are in India. (Rev: BCCB 1/08; BL 12/1/07; SLJ 4/08)

7203 Neel, Julien. *Secret Diary* (4–7). Trans. by Carol Klio Burrell. Illus. by author. 2012, Lerner LB $27.93 (978-076138776-3); paper $8.95 (978-076138868-5). 48pp. Lou, 12, contends with her shiftless single mom, the mean girls at school, and her timidity about dating in this appealing graphic novel. e (Rev: BL 3/15/12; LMC 11–12/12; SLJ 7/1/12)

7204 Nickel, Scott. *The Incredible Rockhead vs. Papercut* (2–4). Illus. by C. S. Jennings. Series: Graphic Sparks. 2010, Stone Arch LB $22.65 (978-143421976-3). 40pp. In this quirky superhero comic, Chip Stone (a rock) faces off against the dangerous and unpredictable Papercut. Lexile GN240L (Rev: BLO 9/1/10)

7205 Nykko. *The Master of Shadows* (4–7). Trans. by Carol Kilo Burrell. Illus. by Bannister. Series: Else-Where Chronicles. 2009, Graphic Universe LB $27.93 (978-076134461-2); paper $6.95 (978-076134744-6). 48pp. Max, Rebecca, Theo, and Noah must tackle the Master of Shadows in their continuing search for a way to escape the strange world of ElseWhere. (Rev: BL 4/15/09; LMC 10/09; SLJ 5/09) [741.5]

7206 Nykko. *The Shadow Spies. Bk. 2* (4–8). Illus. by Bannister. Series: The ElseWhere Chronicles. 2009, Lerner LB $27.93 (978-0-7613-4460-5); paper $6.95 (978-0-7613-3964-9). 48pp. Max, Theo, Noah, and Rebecca enter a strange world called ElseWhere and must evade the Shadow Spies to get back home. (Rev: LMC 10/09; SLJ 5/09)

7207 Nytra, David. *The Secret of the Stone Frog* (2–4). Illus. by author. 2012, TOON $14.95 (978-1-93517918-4). 80pp. Leah and her brother head down a path indicated by a stone frog, and discover a variety of mystical creatures in this dreamlike graphic novel. Lexile 220 (Rev: BL 8/12*; LMC 5–6/13; SLJ 9/1/12)

7208 O'Brien, Anne S. *The Legend of Hong Kil Dong: The Robin Hood of Korea* (3–5). 2006, Charlesbridge $14.95 (978-1-58089-302-2). 48pp. In graphic novel format, this is a Korean tale — perhaps the first novel written in the Korean alphabet — that features a strong character seeking to undo injustices. (Rev: BL 7/06; SLJ 9/06)

7209 O'Connor, George. *Athena: Grey-Eyed Goddess* (5–9). Illus. by author. 2010, Roaring Brook $16.99 (978-159643649-7); paper $9.99 (978-15964343-2-5). 80pp. A graphic-novel retelling of the myths involving

Athena, the Greek goddess of wisdom and war. (Rev: BL 5/1/10; SLJ 5/10)

7210 O'Donnell, Liam. *Blackbeard's Sword: The Pirate King of the Carolinas* (3–5). Illus. by Mike Spoor. Series: Graphic Flash. 2007, Stone Arch LB $23.93 (978-1-59889-309-0). 48pp. History and fiction combine in this graphic story of a boy who wrongly admires Blackbeard. (Rev: LMC 10/07; SLJ 8/07)

7211 O'Donnell, Liam. *Max Finder Mystery: Collected Casebook, Vol. 1* (4–7). Illus. by Michael Cho. 2009, Owlkids paper $9.95 (978-2-8957-9116-4). 96pp. First published in *Owl Magazine*, this graphic novel collection includes 10 mysteries starring 7th-graders Max Finder and Alison Santos that invite the reader to help solve the case — answers and puzzles are included. Also use volumes 2 and 3. (Rev: BL 7/09)

7212 O'Donnell, Liam. *Ramp Rats* (4–6). Illus. by Mike Deas. Series: Graphic Guide Adventure. 2008, Orca paper $9.95 (978-1-55143-880-1). This graphic novel about Bounce, an avid skateboarder, also features bullies and a motorcycle gang as well as skateboarding tips. (Rev: BL 9/15/08)

7213 O'Donnell, Liam. *Soccer Sabotage* (4–7). Illus. by Mike Deas. Series: Graphic Guide Adventure. 2009, Orca paper $9.95 (978-1-55143-884-9). 56pp. Why is their soccer team experiencing so many problems in the national under-18 tournament? Nadia and Devin investigate in this mystery full of soccer tips. (Rev: BL 3/1/09; SLJ 9/09)

7214 O'Donnell, Liam. *Wild Ride* (4–6). Illus. by Mike Deas. Series: Graphic Guide Adventure. 2007, Orca paper $8.95 (978-1-55143-756-9). 64pp. Reluctant readers will enjoy this adventure in which three young people must rely on their survival skills after their plane crashes in the Canadian woods. (Rev: BL 1/1–15/08; LMC 3/08; SLJ 7/08; VOYA 2/08)

7215 O'Malley, Kevin. *Desk Stories* (1–3). Illus. by author. 2011, Whitman $16.99 (978-0-8075-1562-4). 32pp. Six short graphic-novel stories depict richly imagined comic scenarios involving school desks. (Rev: BL 8/11; LMC 1–2/12; SLJ 8/1/11)

7216 Orme, David. *Ice Caves of Pluto* (2–4). Illus. by Peter Richardson. Series: Billy Blaster. 2009, Stone Arch LB $22.65 (978-1-4342-1275-7). 40pp. Billy and Wu Hoo travel to icy Pluto in this sleek, manga-style story that relies more on art than on dialogue. Also use *Mind Thief* (2009). (Rev: LMC 10/09; SLJ 5/09)

7217 Parker, Jake. *Rescue on Tankium3* (3–6). Illus. by author. 2011, Scholastic $21.99 (978-054511716-6); paper $10.99 (978-05451171-7-3). 146pp. Galactic Security Agent Missile Mouse battles an evil king on a distant galaxy, dodging peril at every turn in this lively graphic novel. (Rev: BL 4/15/11; LMC 10/11; SLJ 3/11)

7218 Patterson, James, and Leopold Gout. *Alien Hunter* (5–8). Illus. by Klaus Lyngeled. 2008, Little, Brown paper $9.99 (978-0-316-00425-1). This action-packed graphic novel follows the exploits of Daniel, an orphaned alien who hunts evil extraterrestrials on Earth. (Rev: BL 10/1/08; SLJ 11/08; VOYA 6/08)

7219 Pearson, Luke. *Hilda and the Bird Parade* (2–5). Illus. by author. 2013, Flying Eye $24 (978-190926306-2). 44pp. In this 3rd installment in the series that started with *Hildafolk* (2010) and *Hilda and the Midnight Giant* (2012), the plucky girl must adapt to life in a city and its strange inhabitants. Booklist Editors' Choice: Books for Youth. (Rev: BL 3/1/13*)

7220 Peters, Stephanie. *Rapunzel* (2–4). Illus. by Jeffrey Stewart Timmins. Series: Graphic Spin. 2009, Stone Arch LB $16.99 (978-1-4342-1194-1). This graphic-novel adaptation offers arresting artwork. (Rev: BL 3/1/09)

7221 Petrucha, Stefan. *Beowulf* (4–10). Illus. by Kody Chamberlain. 2007, HarperTrophy paper $8.99 (978-0-06-134390-2). A graphic novel version of the epic story. (Rev: SLJ 1/08; VOYA 2/08)

7222 Petrucha, Stefan. *Nancy Drew: The Demon of River Heights* (4–9). Series: Nancy Drew, Girl Detective. 2005, Papercutz $12.95 (978-1-59707-004-1). The familiar heroine returns in graphic-novel format with this story in which Nancy, Bess, George discover the secret behind a legendary monster. (Rev: SLJ 8/05)

7223 Peyo. *The Red Taxis* (4–7). Illus. by author. Series: Benny Breakiron. 2013, Papercutz $11.99 (978-159707409-4). 64pp. Eight-year-old Benny Breakiron has superhuman strength and amazing speed, but since he's only 8 years old, the police don't believe him when he tells them of the evil Red Taxi Company, so he must find a way to implicate Mr. Hairynose and the taxis on his own and save his friend Mr. Dussiflard. (Rev: BL 9/15/13; LMC 3–4/14)

7224 Phelan, Matt. *Bluffton: My Summers with Buster* (4–7). Illus. by author. 2013, Candlewick $22.99 (978-076365079-7). 240pp. An engaging story about a boy named Henry who becomes friends with the young Buster Keaton, and the differences between small-town life and show business glamor. ALA Notable Children's Book. Lexile 370 (Rev: BL 9/15/13*; LMC 3–4/14; SLJ 7/13*)

7225 Phelan, Matt. *The Storm in the Barn* (5–8). 2009, Candlewick $24.99 (978-0-7636-3618-0). 208pp. In 1937 Kansas 11-year-old Jack faces many challenges — bullies, a sister with problems, and above all the hardships of the Dust Bowl — to which he may have a solution. ALA Notable Children's Book 2010. (Rev: BL 8/09*; LMC 11–12/09; SLJ 9/09)

7226 Pilkey, Dav. *The Adventures of Ook and Gluk, Kung-Fu Cavemen from the Future* (2–4). Illus. by author. 2010, Scholastic $9.99 (978-054517530-2). 176pp. In this wacky graphic novel, two young Stone Age cavemen travel to the year 2222 and learn kung fu in order to save their own time from an evil corporation. ℮ Lexile GN420L (Rev: BL 9/15/10; LMC 1–2/11; SLJ 11/10)

7227 Pilkey, Dav. *Super Diaper Baby 2: The Invasion of the Potty Snatchers* (1–3). Illus. by author. 2011, Scholastic $9.99 (978-054517532-6). 192pp. George and

Harold, in trouble because of their earlier comic book about poop, decided to do a book about pee. (Rev: BL 9/15/11; SLJ 1/12)

7228 Plessix, Michel. *The Wind in the Willows. Rev. ed.* (4–7). Illus. by author. Series: Classics Illustrated Deluxe. 2008, Papercutz $17.95 (978-1-59707-095-9); paper $13.95 (978-1-59707-096-6). The classic animal story, presented in a graphic format with beautiful illustrations. (Rev: BL 3/18/08)

7229 Poe, Marshall. *A House Divided* (4–6). Illus. by Leland Purvis. Series: Turning Points. 2009, Aladdin paper $8.99 (978-1-4169-5057-8). 128pp. Black-and-white art illustrates the story of brothers Owen and Amos Bennington, who choose different directions after their abolitionist parents are murdered in 1856, one opting for peaceful action and the other for more aggressive means. (Rev: BLO 2/9/09; SLJ 3/09)

7230 Poe, Marshall. *Sons of Liberty* (3–7). Illus. by Leland Purvis. Series: Turning Points. 2008, Simon & Schuster paper $7.99 (978-1-4169-5067-7). 120pp. Young Nathaniel joins the cause of the American Revolution and even meets Samuel Adams and Paul Revere as he fights for the young nation. (Rev: LMC 1/09; SLJ 7/08)

7231 Poon, Janice. *Claire and the Water Wish* (2–4). Illus. by author. 2009, Kids Can $15.95 (978-1-55453-381-7); paper $7.95 (978-1-55453-382-4). Mystery, environmental concerns, and photography are interwoven in this graphic novel about Claire and her new friends Jet and Sky, who investigate toxic waste in a lake; includes craft ideas. (Rev: BL 4/15/09; SLJ 9/09)

7232 Pope, Paul. *Battling Boy* (5–8). Illus. by author. 2013, First Second $24.99 (978-159643805-7); paper $15.99 (978-15964314-5-4). 208pp. Twelve-year-old demigod Battling Boy is sent to deal with unrest and monsters in the city of Arcopolis. ALA Notable Children's Book; YALSA Great Graphic Novels for Teens. ℮ Lexile 390 (Rev: BL 9/15/13*; LMC 1–2/14)

7233 Raicht, Mike. *Spider-Man: Kraven the Hunter* (5–8). Illus. by Jamal Igle, et al. Series: Spider-Man. 2006, ABDO LB $21.35 (978-1-59961-009-2). Spider-Man once again does battle with Kraven the Hunter, one of his oldest enemies. (Rev: SLJ 11/06)

7234 Reit, Seymour. *Science Fiction and Fantasy* (4–6). Illus. by Ernie Colon. Series: Bank Street Graphic Novels. 2007, World Almanac LB $29.27 (978-0-8368-7929-2). 56pp. *Frankenstein*, *The War of the Worlds*, and *20,000 Leagues Under the Sea* are presented here in condensed, graphic-novel form to appeal to reluctant readers and comic-book fans. (Rev: SLJ 7/07)

7235 Reit, Seymour, adapt. *Great Heroes* (4–6). Illus. by Ernie Colon. 2007, World Almanac LB $29.27 (978-0-8368-7925-4). Stories of King Arthur, Don Quixote, and Sherlock Holmes are presented here in condensed, graphic-novel form to appeal to reluctant readers and comic-book fans. (Rev: SLJ 7/07)

7236 Reit, Seymour, adapt. *Travel and Adventure* (4–8). Illus. by Ernie Colon and Richard Rockwell. Series:

Bank Street Graphic Novels. 2007, World Almanac LB $29.27 (978-0-8368-7930-8). 56pp. *The Travels of Marco Polo*, *Moby-Dick*, and *Gulliver's Travels* are transformed into graphic novels. (Rev: SLJ 7/07)

7237 Renier, Aaron. *Spiral Bound: Top Secret Summer* (4–7). 2005, Top Shelf paper $14.95 (978-1-891830-50-1). This delightful graphic novel chronicles the summer adventures of the animal residents of the Town, a community with a monster in its pond. (Rev: BL 11/1/05)

7238 Renier, Aaron. *The Unsinkable Walker Bean* (5–8). Illus. by author. 2010, First Second paper $13.99 (978-159643453-0). 208pp. Exciting action rules in this imaginative story of courageous young Walter's dangerous quest to return a pearl skull to the witches on the Mango Islands. (Rev: BL 6/1/10*; LMC 3–4/11; SLJ 9/10; VOYA 6/10)

7239 Reynolds, Aaron. *Big Hairy Drama* (3–5). Illus. by Neil Numberman. Series: Joey Fly, Private Eye. 2010, Henry Holt $16.99 (978-080508243-2); paper $9.99 (978-08050911-0-6). 128pp. Joey Fly and his sidekick Sammy Stingtail (a scorpion) investigate the disappearance of stage star Greta Divawing, a butterfly. (Rev: BL 12/15/10; SLJ 1/11)

7240 Reynolds, Aaron. *Creepy Crawly Crime* (3–5). Illus. by Neil Numberman. 2009, Holt $16.95 (978-0-8050-8242-5). 96pp. Crime fighter Joey Fly and his sidekick Sammy Stingtail investigate the case of a missing diamond pencil box in this hardboiled graphic novel. (Rev: BCCB 5/09; BL 3/1/09)

7241 Rioux, Jo. *The Golden Twine* (4–7). Illus. by author. 2012, Kids Can $17.95 (978-155453636-8); paper $9.95 (978-15545363-7-5). 112pp. Suri, an orphan living in a traveling caravan, is determined to prove herself a monster tamer. Lexile 260L (Rev: BL 8/12; LMC 5–6/13; SLJ 11/12)

7242 Robbins, Trina. *The Drained Brains Caper* (4–7). Illus. by Tyler Page. Series: Chicagoland Detective Agency. 2010, Lerner LB $29.27 (978-076134601-2); paper $6.95 (978-076135635-6). 64pp. New to summer school, Megan, 13, soon becomes suspicious about the principal's motives and seeks help from computer genius Raf. The second volume is *The Maltese Mummy* (2011). Lexile GN390L (Rev: BL 9/15/10; LMC 1–2/11; SLJ 11/10)

7243 Robbins, Trina. *The Time Team* (3–6). Illus. by Anne Timmons. Series: Go Girl! 2004, Dark Horse paper $5.95 (978-1-59307-230-8). 96pp. Three high school girls find themselves stuck in the days of the dinosaurs. (Rev: BL 1/1–15/05)

7244 Robinson, Fiona. *The 3-2-3 Detective Agency: The Disappearance of Dave Warthog* (2–4). Illus. by author. 2009, Abrams $17.95 (978-0-8109-8489-9); paper $9.95 (978-0-8109-7094-6). 80pp. An entertaining ensemble of animal detectives investigate disappearances in Whiska City. (Rev: BL 7/09; SLJ 9/09)

7245 Rodi, Rob. *Crossovers* (5–12). 2003, CrossGeneration paper $15.95 (978-1-931484-85-5). This graphic novel is an entertaining look at a suburban family whose members possess a unique power. (Rev: BL 2/1/04)

7246 Roman, Dave. *Astronaut Academy: Re-entry* (4–6). Illus. by author. 2013, First Second paper $9.99 (978-15964362-1-3). In this funny, fast-paced and romance-filled second installment in the series, Hakata Soy discovers that a strange creature is stalking Astronaut Academy and stealing students' hearts. (Rev: BL 6/13; SLJ 7/13)

7247 Roman, Dave. *Astronaut Academy: Zero Gravity* (5–8). Illus. by author. 2011, First Second paper $9.99 (978-1-59643-620-6). 187pp. Child space hero Hakata Soy enrolls in Astronaut Academy and meets danger in his first term when a robot doppelganger is sent to kill him. (Rev: BL 6/11; LMC 8–9/11; SLJ 5/1/11)

7248 Rosa, Don. *The Life and Times of Scrooge McDuck* (5–8). Illus. by author. 2010, Boom! $24.99 (978-1-60886-538-3). 127pp. Rosa tells the story of Scrooge McDuck's origins in Scotland, exploits in America, and success in Africa, rendering him the world's richest duck and introducing many famous characters along the way. (Rev: BL 3/15/10*; SLJ 5/10)

7249 Rosenstiehl, Agnes. *Silly Lilly* (PS). Illus. by author. 2008, Raw Junior/TOON $12.95 (978-0-9799238-1-4). For beginning readers, this graphic novel follows bright and imaginative young Lilly as she moves through familiar seasonal activities from spring through winter and back again. (Rev: BL 3/15/08; HB 7/08; SLJ 5/08)

7250 Ross, Stewart. *Instruments of Death* (3–6). Illus. by Inklink. 2007, DK $14.99 (978-0-7566-2566-5); paper $3.99 (978-0-7566-2565-8). 48pp. Eleven-year-old Shen is called to the emperor's court and encounters a mystery in this story set in ancient China. The graphic-novel format will interest young readers. (Rev: SLJ 5/07)

7251 Ross, Stewart. *The Price of Victory* (3–6). Illus. by Inklink. 2007, DK $14.99 (978-0-7566-2568-9); paper $3.99 (978-0-7566-2567-2). 48pp. Eleven-year-old Pylades tries to find out who is trying to keep his brother from competing in the Olympics in this story set in ancient Greece. (Rev: SLJ 5/07)

7252 Ross, Stewart. *The Terror Trail* (3–6). Illus. by Inklink. 2007, DK $14.99 (978-0-7566-2570-2); paper $3.99 (978-0-7566-2569-6). 48pp. Sabina and Publius, two children living in North Africa in A.D. 145, fear for their father, who is nearly condemned to death in the Colosseum. (Rev: SLJ 5/07)

7253 Runton, Andy. *Flying Lessons* (3–5). Illus. Series: Owly. 2005, Top Shelf paper $10.00 (978-1-891830-76-1). A flying squirrel at first resists Owly's overtures of friendship but later offers to teach the young bird to fly. Also use *A Time to Be Brave* (2007). (Rev: BL 3/15/06)

7254 Runton, Andy. *Owly: Just a Little Blue* (3–5). Illus. Series: Owly. 2005, Top Shelf paper $10.00 (978-1-891830-64-8). 128pp. Owly and his friend Wormy try to help a bluebird whose habitat is endangered, but their overtures of friendship are at first rebuffed. (Rev: BL 7/05; SLJ 3/06)

7255 Runton, Andy. *Owly: The Way Home and the Bittersweet Summer* (3–5). Illus. 2004, Top Shelf paper $10.00 (978-1-891830-62-4). Two sweet and simple graphic novellas feature lonely Owly the Owl and her new friend Wormy. (Rev: BL 2/1/05)

7256 Russell, P. Craig. *The Birthday of the Infanta: Fairy Tales of Oscar Wilde, Vol. 3* (5–8). 1998, NBM $15.95 (978-1-56163-213-8). A graphic novel version of Wilde's fairy tale about the misshapen dwarf who dies of a broken heart. (Rev: BL 4/1/99)

7257 Russell, P. Craig. *The Fairy Tales of Oscar Wilde: The Devoted Friend, The Nightingale and the Rose* (5–8). Illus. by author. 2004, NBM $15.95 (978-1-56163-391-3). Two of Oscar Wilde's fairy tales — "The Devoted Friend" and "The Nightingale and the Rose" — are presented in a rich, picture-book-size graphic novel format. (Rev: BL 8/04; SLJ 11/04)

7258 Santat, Dan. *Sidekicks* (3–6). Illus. by author. 2011, Scholastic $24.99 (978-0-439-29811-7); paper $12.99 (978-0-439-29819-3). 224pp. Middle-aged superhero Captain Amazing is looking for a new sidekick, and his pets Roscoe and Fluffy both seek the job — leading to new adventures. (Rev: BL 4/15/11; HB 7–8/11; LMC 10–11/11*; SLJ 7/1/11)

7259 Sava, Scott Christian. *Hyperactive* (2–6). Illus. by Joseph Bergin. 2008, IDW paper $12.99 (978-1-60010-313-1). A zippy, funny story about Joey Johnson, whose innate speediness accelerates to superhero proportions and brings him joy and angst. (Rev: BL 3/1/09)

7260 Schmitt, Michel-Yves. *Your Pajamas Are Showing!* (1–3). Illus. by Vincent Caut. Series: Where's Leopold? 2013, Lerner LB $25.26 (978-146770769-5); paper $6.95 (9781467708715). 40pp. Annoying younger brother Leopold discovers he can become invisible, resulting in many tricks on older sister Celine and others. ℮ (Rev: BL 3/1/13; LMC 10/13)

7261 Schulz, Charles M. *Snoopy: Cowabunga!* (2–7). Illus. by Charles M. Schulz. 2013, Andrews and McMeel paper $9.99 (978-14494507-9-3). 224pp. Although Charlie Brown was the main character in the Peanuts comic strip, Snoopy became a star in his own right, and this book is devoted to multiple popular strips featuring Snoopy having daring adventures. (Rev: BL 9/15/13; LMC 3–4/14)

7262 Schwarz, Viviane. *The Sleepwalkers* (2–5). Illus. by author. 2013, Candlewick paper $9.99 (978-07636623-0-1). 96pp. The three sheep known as the Sleepwalkers are ready to retire and set out to train their replacements, who will save children from nightmares. (Rev: BL 4/15/13*; LMC 1–2/14; SLJ 7/13)

7263 Schweizer, Chris. *Tricky Coyote Tales* (2–4). Illus. by Chad Thomas. Series: Tricky Journeys. 2011, Lerner LB $27.93 (978-076136601-0); paper $6.95 (978-076137859-4). 64pp. In this book that blends graphic novel format with running text, readers help a hungry coyote decide how to react to a variety of animals. ℮ (Rev: BL 10/15/11; LMC 1–2/12)

7264 Scieszka, Jon. *Nightmare on Joe's Street* (2–4). Ed. by Zachary Rau. Illus. by Peter K. Hirsch. Series: Time Warp Trio. 2006, paper $6.99 (978-0-06-111639-1). In the opening volume of this graphic-novel adaptation of the Time Warp Trio television series, Joe and Sam transport Frankenstein's monster back in time so that he can reconcile his differences with his creator, Mary Shelley. (Rev: BL 10/1/06; SLJ 1/07)

7265 Sewell, Anna. *Anna Sewell's Black Beauty: The Graphic Novel* (4–6). Ed. and illus. by June Brigman and Roy Richardson. Series: Puffin Graphics. 2005, Puffin $10.99 (978-0-14-240408-9). 176pp. A graphic-novel version of the classic Victorian story about an impressive horse's complex life. (Rev: BL 5/1/05) [741.5]

7266 Sfar, Joann, and Lewis Trondheim. *Zenith: Back in Style, Vol. 3* (5–9). Trans. from French by Joe Johnson. Illus. by Boulet. Series: Dungeon. 2009, NBM paper $14.95 (978-1-56163-550-4). A story in an animal-inhabited fantasy land based on Dungeons and Dragons and full of romance, danger, and humor. (Rev: SLJ 7/09)

7267 Shanower, Eric. *Adventures in Oz* (4–7). Illus. by author. 2007, IDW $75.00 (978-1-60010-071-0); paper $39.99 (978-1-933239-61-3). Dorothy and her friends from Oz return in this beautifully drawn collection of five graphic novel adventures. (Rev: BL 3/15/07; SLJ 3/07; VOYA 4/07)

7268 Shaw, Murray, and M. J. Cosson. *Sherlock Holmes and a Scandal in Bohemia* (4–6). Illus. by Sophie Rohrbach. Series: On the Case with Holmes and Watson. 2010, Lerner LB $26.60 (978-076136185-5); paper $6.95 (978-076136197-8). 48pp. This engaging graphic novel adaptation of the classic tale involving a blackmail plot against the king of Bohemia includes a section explaining Holmes's reasoning; the first in a series. Lexile GN600L (Rev: BL 11/15/10)

7269 Shiga, Jason. *Meanwhile* (4–9). Illus. by author. 2010, Abrams $15.95 (978-0-8109-8423-3). Unpaged. A mad scientist asks a boy to test one of three inventions in this choose-your-own-adventure graphic novel. ALA Notable Children's Book 2011; YALSA Great Graphic Novels Top Ten 2011. (Rev: BL 1/1/10*; SLJ 3/10)

7270 Shone, Rob. *Greek Myths* (5–9). Illus. by author. Series: Graphic Mythology. 2006, Rosen LB $29.25 (978-1-4042-0801-8). "Jason and the Golden Fleece," "Icarus," and "The Labors of Hercules" are the three tales presented here in graphic novel format. (Rev: SLJ 9/06) [292.1]

7271 *Showcase Presents Superman, Vol. 1* (3–8). 2005, DC Comics paper $9.99 (978-1-4012-0758-8). 560pp. This impressive volume collects 29 Superman comics published between 1959 and 1963. (Rev: SLJ 1/06)

7272 *Showcase Presents the House of Mystery, Vol. 1* (5–9). 2006, DC Comics paper $16.99 (978-1-4012-0786-1). A collection of relatively tame horror comics that first appeared in the 1960s, in black and white. (Rev: SLJ 7/06)

7273 Slade, Christian. *Korgi. Bk. 1* (2–5). Illus. by author. 2007, Top Shelf paper $10.00 (978-1-891830-90-7).

84pp. A young girl and her dog have adventures in the woods of Korgi in this beautifully drawn, almost wordless book that features a fairy people and beasts including giant spiders. (Rev: LMC 1/08; SLJ 3/08)

7274 Slavin, Bill. *Big Top Otto* (2–4). Illus. by author. Series: Elephants Never Forget. 2013, Kids Can $16.95 (978-155453806-5); paper $7.95 (978-15545380-7-2). 90pp. Otto the elephant and Crackers the parrot are still searching for chimpanzee Georgie in this second installment in the funny series full of misadventures. Lexile 330 (Rev: BL 3/1/13; LMC 6/15/13; SLJ 11/13)

7275 Smith, Jeff. *Eyes of the Storm, Vol. 3* (4–8). Illus. by author. Series: Bone. 2006, Scholastic $19.99 (978-0-439-70625-4); paper $9.99 (978-0-439-70638-4). The final book in the first Bone trilogy, this comic-book fantasy has funny moments, suspense and dream sequences that fans will love. (Rev: SLJ 7/06)

7276 Smith, Jeff. *Little Mouse Gets Ready* (PS–K). Illus. by author. 2009, Raw Junior/TOON $12.95 (978-193517901-6). 32pp. A little mouse gets dressed to go to the barn with his mother, struggling with buttonholes and tucking in tags in this funny graphic novel. (Rev: BL 8/09; LMC 11–12/09; SLJ 11/09)

7277 Smith, Jeff. *Old Man's Cave* (5–12). Illus. by author. Series: Bone. 2007, Scholastic $18.99 (978-0-439-70628-5); paper $9.99 (978-0-439-70635-3). Episode six of this series that combines goofy-looking characters with dramatic fantasy plots finds Phoney Bone and Thorn in grave danger. (Rev: BL 11/1/07)

7278 Sonneborn, Scott. *Shell Shocker* (2–4). Illus. by Dan Schoening. Series: DC Super Heroes. 2011, Stone Arch LB $25.32 (978-1-4342-2615-0); paper $5.95 (978-1-4342-3092-8). 56pp. The Flash (aka police scientist Barry Allen) prevents a series of catastrophes in this fast-paced chapter book. (Rev: BL 7/11; SLJ 6/11)

7279 Soo, Kean. *Jellaby* (4–7). Illus. by author. 2008, Hyperion $18.99 (978-1-4231-0337-0); paper $9.99 (978-1-4231-0303-5). A gentle purple monster changes the lives of 10-year-old Portia and her friend Jason. (Rev: BL 3/15/08; SLJ 1/08)

7280 Spiegelman, Art. *Jack and the Box* (K–1). Illus. by author. 2008, Raw Junior/TOON $12.95 (978-0-9799238-3-8). 32pp. A young bunny wrestles with a jack-in-the-box that seems to have a mind of its own in this bouncy graphic novel. (Rev: BL 9/1/08; HB 11/08)

7281 Spiegelman, Art. *Little Lit: Folklore and Fairy Tale Funnies* (4–9). 2000, HarperCollins $19.95 (978-0-06-028624-8). In this presentation in graphic novel format, 15 different artists create brilliant variations on standard fairy and folk tales. (Rev: BL 1/1–15/01*; HB 9–10/00; HBG 3/01; SLJ 12/00) [398.2]

7282 Spiegelman, Art, and Francoise Mouly, eds. *Little Lit: It Was a Dark and Silly Night* (2–5). Illus. Series: Little Lit. 2003, HarperCollins $19.99 (978-0-06-028628-6). 48pp. Fifteen authors and artists each offer a cartoon story that begins with the line "It was a dark and silly night . . ." (Rev: HBG 4/04; SLJ 9/03)

373

7283 Spiegelman, Art, and Francoise Mouly, eds. *The TOON Treasury of Classic Children's Comics* (3–6). Illus. 2009, Abrams ComicArts $40 (978-081095730-5). 352pp. A collection of comics from the 1930s through the early 1960s, including Captain Marvel, Pogo, Donald Duck, and Dennis the Menace. (Rev: BL 10/1/09*; SLJ 11/09)

7284 Spiegelman, Nadja. *Zig and Wikki in Something Ate My Homework* (K–2). Illus. by Trade Loeffler. 2010, Raw Junior/TOON $12.95 (978-193517902-3). 40pp. Aliens Zig and Wikki are dispatched to Earth in search of specimens for their class zoo in this zany, science-infused story. (Rev: BL 3/15/10; SLJ 7/10)

7285 Spiegelman, Nadja. *Zig and Wikki in The Cow* (1–3). Illus. by Trade Loeffler. 2012, TOON $12.95 (978-193517915-3). 40pp. Aliens Zig and Wikki must get eaten by a cow in order to reclaim their missing spaceship in this sequel to 2010's *Zig and Wikki in Something Ate My Homework*. (Rev: BL 3/15/12; LMC 10/12; SLJ 5/1/12)

7286 Spires, Ashley. *Binky Takes Charge* (2–4). Illus. by author. 2012, Kids Can $16.95 (978-1-55453703-7); paper $8.95 (978-15545376-8-6). 64pp. Binky, now a lieutenant, is responsible for training new space cats but the current recruit makes him nervous; the fourth book in the series. Lexile 560L (Rev: BLO 9/15/12; SLJ 9/12)

7287 Spires, Ashley. *Binky the Space Cat* (2–4). Illus. by author. 2009, Kids Can $16.95 (978-155453309-1). 64pp. A humorous story about Binky the cat's adventurous spirit and conflicting love for his humans. (Rev: BL 8/09; LMC 10/09; SLJ 11/09)

7288 Spires, Ashley. *Binky to the Rescue* (2–4). Illus. by author. 2010, Kids Can $16.95 (978-155453502-6). 64pp. A zany graphic novel about a house cat who imagines himself in a space station. (Rev: BL 10/15/10; SLJ 11/10)

7289 Spires, Ashley. *Binky Under Pressure* (2–4). Illus. by author. 2011, Kids Can $16.95 (978-155453504-0); paper $8.95 (978-15545376-7-9). 64pp. Binky, an imaginative cat with aspirations to living in a space station, is not pleased when a new cat named Gracie arrives in his abode. (Rev: BL 9/15/11; SLJ 11/1/11)

7290 Steinberg, D. J. *Game On!* (3–5). Illus. by Brian Smith. 2009, Grosset paper $5.99 (978-0-448-44700-1). Loud Boy and his friends must stop an evil plot to turn all the children in the world into a video game. (Rev: BL 6/1–15/09)

7291 Steinberg, D. J. *Sound Off! The Adventures of Daniel Boom aka Loud Boy* (3–5). Illus. by Brian Smith. 2008, Grosset paper $5.99 (978-0-448-44698-1). This well-paced title with nice tension and great puns follows Daniel, an almost-10-year-old with a voice that shatters glass, to a special school where his "problem" is unveiled as a superpower. (Rev: BL 3/15/08; SLJ 11/08)

7292 Stevens, Eric. *The Revenge of Clayface* (2–5). Illus. by Gregg Schigiel and Lee Loughridge. Series: DC Super Heroes: Batman. 2009, Stone Arch LB $25.32 (978-1-4342-1149-1); paper $5.95 (978-1-4342-1369-3).

56pp. A highly illustrated chapter book in which Batman faces Clayface and the Joker. (Rev: SLJ 6/09)

7293 Stevenson, Robert Louis. *Kidnapped* (4–8). Illus. by Penko Gelev. Series: Graphic Classics. 2007, Barron's LB $15.99 (978-0-7641-5980-0); paper $8.99 (978-0-7641-3494-4). 48pp. The dramatic artwork will draw readers into this story; information on Stevenson gives background and historical context. (Rev: SLJ 11/07)

7294 Stevenson, Robert Louis. *Treasure Island* (5–9). Illus. by Tim Hamilton. Series: Puffin Graphics. 2005, Puffin paper $10.99 (978-0-14-240470-6). Robert Louis Stevenson's adventure classic springs to life in this striking graphic novel adaptation that remains faithful to the original text. (Rev: SLJ 11/05)

7295 Stine, R. L. *Terror Trips* (3–7). Adapted by Jill Thompson, Jamie Tolagson, & Amy Kim Thompson. Illus. by Jill Thompson, et al. Series: Goosebumps Graphix. 2007, Scholastic $16.99 (978-0-439-85777-2); paper $8.99 (978-0-439-85780-2). 139pp. *One Day at Horrorland, A Shocker on Shock Street,* and *Deep Trouble,* all originally full-length Goosebumps novels, are presented here as action-packed black-and-white graphic novels. (Rev: SLJ 5/07)

7296 Storrie, Paul D. *Nightmare on Zombie Island* (4–8). Illus. by David Witt. Series: Twisted Journeys. 2008, Lerner LB $27.93 (978-0-8225-6198-9); paper $7.95 (978-0-8225-6200-9). 112pp. Readers can choose which way the plot will go in this horror story. (Rev: SLJ 5/08)

7297 Storrie, Paul D. *Yu the Great: Conquering the Flood* (4–7). Illus. by Sandy Carruthers. Series: Graphic Myths and Legends. 2007, Lerner LB $26.60 (978-0-8225-3088-6). In this graphic novel adaptation of an ancient Chinese folk tale, the emperor Shun asks Yu to save China and its people from the floods that are ravaging the land. (Rev: BL 3/15/07; SLJ 5/07) [398.2]

7298 Sturm, James, and Andrew Arnold. *Adventures in Cartooning: How to Turn Your Doodles into Comics* (PS–5). Illus. by James Sturm. 2009, Roaring Brook paper $12.95 (978-1-59643-369-4). An adventure featuring a princess, a knight, an elf, and a dragon serves as the backdrop for instruction in the art of cartooning. (Rev: BL 3/1/09; SLJ 4/09)

7299 Sturm, James, and Andrew Arnold, et al. *Adventures in Cartooning: Christmas Special* (PS–3). Illus. by James Sturm. 2012, First Second paper $9.99 (978-15964373-0-2). 64pp. An elf and a knight team up to create a comic that will distract children from their electronics; includes information about story elements, rhyming text, and creating comic strips. (Rev: BLO 10/15/12; HB 11–12/12; SLJ 10/12)

7300 Taniguchi, Tomoko. *Call Me Princess* (5–8). Trans. from Japanese by Mutsumi Masuda and C. B. Cebulski. Illus. by author. 2003, CPM Manga paper $9.99 (978-1-58664-898-5). This graphic novel, set in Japan, centers on the young heroine's romantic attachments but gets a "G" rating. (Rev: SLJ 3/04)

7301 Tatsuyama, Sayuri. *Happy Happy Clover, Vol. 1* (3–6). Illus. by author. 2009, VIZ Media paper $7.99

(978-1-4215-2656-0). 200pp. Clover and her young rabbit friends explore Crescent Forest and the world outside it in this manga offering. (Rev: BL 3/1/09)

7302 Team, Marathon. *The O. P.* (3–5). Illus. 2006, Papercutz paper $7.95 (978-1-59707-043-0). 96pp. Based on the Cartoon Network's "Totally Spies" series, this slight but enjoyable graphic novel features teen girls who spy for the World Organization of Human Protection. (Rev: BL 1/1–15/07)

7303 *Teen Titans: Jam Packed Action!* (4–8). 2005, DC Comics paper $7.99 (978-1-4012-0902-5). Two exciting technology-oriented stories are drawn from the Cartoon Network show. (Rev: SLJ 5/06)

7304 Telgemeier, Raina. *Claudia and Mean Janine* (3–5). Illus. by author. Series: Baby-Sitters Club. 2008, Scholastic paper $8.99 (978-0-439-88517-1). A graphic-novel adaptation of the book about two different sisters and their way of coping with their grandmother after she has a stroke. (Rev: BL 3/1/09)

7305 Telgemeier, Raina. *Mary Anne Saves the Day* (4–6). Illus. by author. Series: Baby-sitters' Club. 2007, Scholastic paper $8.99 (978-0-439-88516-4). Twelve-year-old Mary Anne copes with feuding club members feud as well as an overly strict father while she manages to overcome shyness and make a new friend. (Rev: BL 11/1/07)

7306 TenNapel, Doug. *Cardboard* (5–8). Illus. by author. 2012, Scholastic $24.99 (978-054541872-0); paper $12.99 (978-05454187-3-7). 288pp. A jobless father's meager birthday gift — a cardboard box that the two fashion into a boxer — comes alive for his son and mayhem ensues. (Rev: BL 3/15/12; HB 7–8/12; LMC 11–12/12; SLJ 9/12*; VOYA 6/12)

7307 TenNapel, Doug. *Ghostopolis* (5–8). Illus. by author. 2010, Scholastic $24.99 (978-0-545-21027-0); paper $14.99 (978-0-545-21-028-7). 288pp. When Frank Gallows of the Supernatural Immigration Task Force accidentally transports him to the afterlife, young Garth Hale discovers he has hitherto unknown powers and is in danger from the sinister ruler of Ghostopolis. YALSA Quick Picks for Reluctant Young Adult Readers 2012; YALSA Great Graphic Novels Top Ten 2011. Lexile GN300L (Rev: BL 3/15/10; SLJ 7/10; VOYA 2/10)

7308 Thompson, Jill. *Magic Trixie* (3–5). Illus. by author. 2008, HarperCollins paper $7.99 (978-0-06-117045-4). This graphic novel tells the story of Magic Trixie, a little witch who has used everything in her bag of tricks for show-and-tell and has just one more spell left: making something disappear, which might just be the new baby. (Rev: BL 9/1/08)

7309 Tolkien, J. R. R. *The Hobbit; or, There and Back Again* (5–10). Adapted by Charles Dixon. 1990, Eclipse Books paper $12.95 (978-0-345-36858-4). The classic story of Bilbo Baggins and his companions is introduced to reluctant readers in this full-color graphic novel. (Rev: BL 9/1/91)

7310 Torres, J. *Bigfoot Boy, v.1: Into the Woods* (3–5). Illus. by Faith Erin Hicks. 2012, Kids Can $17.95 (978-1-55453711-2); paper $9.95 (978-15545371-2-9). 100pp. Bored at his grandmother's house, Rufus heads into the woods and there finds a strange totem that changes him into Bigfoot Boy, bringing new powers and adventures. Lexile GN190L (Rev: BL 9/15/12; LMC 5–6/13; SLJ 11/12)

7311 Townsend, Michael. *Billy Tartle in Say Cheese!* (1–3). Illus. by author. 2007, Knopf $15.99 (978-0-375-83932-0). Billy adds some color to class picture day in this comic-book style story with zany-looking characters. (Rev: BCCB 9/07; LMC 11/07; SLJ 7/07)

7312 Trondheim, Lewis. *Mister O* (4–8). Illus. by author. 2004, NBM $13.95 (978-1-56163-382-1). Mister O, portrayed in wordless rectangular cartoons, is a round caricature who — à la Wile E. Coyote — can't seem conquer a chasm, no matter how many successful crossings he views. (Rev: SLJ 9/04)

7313 Trondheim, Lewis. *Tiny Tyrant* (4–7). Illus. by Fabrice Parme. 2007, Roaring Brook paper $12.95 (978-1-59643-094-5). Ethelbert, the diminutive and willful 6-year-old child-king of Portocristo, is used to getting his own way in this series of funny episodes. (Rev: BL 3/15/07; SLJ 9/07)

7314 Tukel, Onur. *Little Friends* (K–2). Illus. by author. 2012, Marshall Cavendish $14.99 (978-076146260-6). 64pp. Friends Louisa and Sara have an on-again off-again relationship with a neighboring boy named Barry. (Rev: BL 4/15/12; LMC 11–12/12; SLJ 6/1/12)

7315 Twain, Mark, and Jean David Morvan, et al. *The Adventures of Tom Sawyer* (5–8). Illus. by Severine Lefebvre. Series: Papercutz' Classics Illustrated Deluxe. 2009, Papercutz $17.95 (978-159707152-9); paper $13.95 (978-15970715-3-6). Bold manga-style illustrations enhance this adaptation that preserves the plot twists and tenor of the original story. (Rev: BL 1/1/10; SLJ 1/10)

7316 Uderzo, Albert. *Asterix and the Actress* (4–7). Trans. by Anthea Bell and Derek Hockridge. 2001, Sterling $12.95 (978-0-7528-4657-6). These pun-filled, graphic novel exploits of Asterix the Gaul include a boisterous shared birthday with the rotund Obelix and a daring rescue of prisoners in a Roman jail. (Rev: BL 8/01)

7317 Varon, Sara. *Bake Sale* (5–8). Illus. by author. 2011, First Second $19.99 (978-159643740-1); paper $16.99 (978-15964341-9-6). 160pp. Cupcake, who runs a bakery and plays in a band, is thrilled when his friend Eggplant invites him to go to Istanbul and meet his idol, Turkish Delight. (Rev: BL 9/15/11; LMC 1–2/12; SLJ 11/1/11)

7318 Venable, Colleen. *And Then There Were Gnomes* (2–4). Illus. by Stephanie Yue. Series: Guinea Pig, Pet Shop Private Eye. 2010, Lerner LB $27.93 (978-076134599-2); paper $6.95 (978-076135480-2). 48pp. Sasspants the detective guinea pig and her wannabe assistant Hamisher the Hamster believe a ghost is the culprit in the case of the missing pet shop mice. This volume is followed by *The Ferret's a Foot* and *Fish You Were Here* (both 2011). Lexile GN220L (Rev: BLO 6/10)

7319 Venable, Colleen. *Hamster and Cheese* (1–3). Illus. by Stephanie Yue. Series: Guinea Pig, Pet Shop Private Eye. 2010, Lerner LB $27.93 (978-0-7613-4598-5); paper $6.95 (978-0-7613-5479-6). 48pp. Guinea pig Sasspants and other animals at the pet shop investigate the theft of Mr. Venezi's sandwiches. (Rev: BL 3/15/10; LMC 10/10; SLJ 5/10)

7320 Verne, Jules. *Journey to the Center of the Earth* (4–8). Illus. by Penko Gelev. Series: Graphic Classics. 2007, Barron's LB $15.99 (978-0-7641-5982-4); paper $8.99 (978-0-7641-3495-1). The dramatic artwork will draw readers into this story; information on Verne gives background and historical context. (Rev: SLJ 11/07)

7321 Vernon, Ursula. *Dragonbreath* (3–5). Illus. by author. 2009, Dial $12.99 (978-0-8037-3363-3). 144pp. After he gets a failing grade on his ocean report, Danny the dragon goes on an undersea adventure. (Rev: BCCB 9/09; BL 5/15/09)

7322 Viva, Frank. *A Trip to the Bottom of the World with Mouse* (PS–1). Illus. by author. 2012, TOON $12.95 (978-1-935179-19-1). 40pp. A mouse and a boy journey to Antarctica aboard a ship in this beautifully illustrated graphic novel that will appeal to beginning readers. (Rev: BL 11/15/12; HB 11–12/12; SLJ 1/13*)

7323 Wagner, Josh. *Sky Pirates of Neo Terra* (4–7). Illus. by Camilla D'Errico. 2010, Image paper $17.99 (978-16070632-4-7). 128pp. Billy sets out to thwart the Witch Queen's evil plans by rescuing her mechanic — his friend Ricket's dad. (Rev: BLO 1/1–15/11)

7324 Watts, Irene N. *Good-Bye Marianne* (3–7). Illus. by Kathryn E. Shoemaker. 2008, Tundra paper $12.95 (978-0-88776-830-9). 128pp. Marianne, an 11-year-old Jewish girl first seen in *Remember Me* (2000), deals with various problems as the Nazis take over in 1937 Berlin in this affecting graphic novel. (Rev: BLO 9/24/08)

7325 Weigel, Jeff. *Thunder from the Sea: Adventure on Board the HMS Defender* (3–5). Illus. by author. 2010,

Putnam $17.99 (978-0-399-25089-7). 48pp. Twelve-year-old Jack Hoyton enlists in the Royal Navy during the time of the Napoleonic Wars in this exciting graphic novel. e (Rev: BL 4/15/10; LMC 10/10; SLJ 8/1/10)

7326 West, David. *Mesoamerican Myths* (5–9). Illus. by Mike Taylor. Series: Graphic Mythology. 2006, Rosen LB $29.25 (978-1-4042-0802-5). Presented in graphic novel format are three tales from the mythology of Mexico and Central America — two creation stories and a hero tale. (Rev: SLJ 9/06) [398.2]

7327 Wilson, Bob. *Fearless Dave* (2–6). Illus. by author. 2006, Frances Lincoln $15.95 (978-1-84507-496-8). This is an enjoyably silly story about a reluctant knight named Dave whose mother succeeds in bringing him glory — and the princess. (Rev: SLJ 12/06)

7328 Wood, Don. *Into the Volcano* (4–7). Illus. by author. 2008, Scholastic $18.99 (978-0-439-72671-9). 176pp. An action-packed graphic-novel thriller in which two brothers, Duffy and Sumo, find themselves inside an erupting volcano. (Rev: BCCB 11/08; BL 11/15/08; HB 9/08; LMC 1/09; SLJ 9/08)

7329 Young, Frank. *Oregon Trail: The Road to Destiny* (3–6). Illus. by David Lasky. 2011, Sasquatch paper $14.95 (978-15706164-9-5). 128pp. Rebecca, 11, chronicles her family's journey along the Oregon Trail in this historical graphic novel that includes lots of discomforts and hardships and the occasional tragedy. (Rev: BLO 11/15/11; SLJ 1/12)

7330 Zirkel, Huddleston. *A Bit Haywire* (4–7). 2006, Viper paper $11.95 (978-0-977788-35-4). Owen has many extraordinary powers, but he's having trouble figuring out how to control them. (Rev: BL 3/15/07)

7331 Zornow, Jeff. *The Legend of Sleepy Hollow* (5–7). Illus. by author. Series: Graphic Planet: Graphic Horror. 2008, ABDO LB $18.95 (978-1-60270-060-4). A graphic adaptation of the classic story with satisfyingly creepy illustrations. (Rev: BL 3/15/08; SLJ 5/08)

Fiction for Older Readers

General

7332 Abrahams, Peter. *Giving to the Poor* (5–8). Series: The Outlaws of Sherwood Street. 2013, Philomel $16.99 (978-039925503-8). 304pp. Robbie and her friends, with the help of their silver charm, protect an Indian burial ground from aggressive urban developers in this exciting, multilayered second book in the series. Lexile 690 (Rev: BL 6/13; SLJ 6/13)

7333 Abrahams, Peter. *Robbie Forester and the Outlaws of Sherwood Street* (5–8). Series: The Outlaws of Sherwood Street. 2012, Philomel $16.99 (978-039925502-1). 320pp. Robyn, a 7th-grader, receives a charm bracelet as thanks for a good deed and finds that she has special powers that help in her mission to fight injustice in her Brooklyn neighborhood. ℮ (Rev: BL 2/1/12; LMC 8–9/12; SLJ 2/12)

7334 Ada, Alma Flor, and Gabriel M. Zubizarreta. *Love, Amalia* (3–6). 2012, Atheneum $15.99 (978-1-4424-2402-9). 144pp. Sixth-grader Amalia is rocked by the death of her abuelita and her best friend moving away, but eventually figures out a way to cope with each situation. ℮ Lexile 940 (Rev: BL 8/12; HB 7–8/12; LMC 1–2/13; SLJ 8/12)

7335 Adler, C. S. *Always and Forever Friends* (5–7). 1990, Avon paper $3.99 (978-0-380-70687-7). Wendy, at 11, is having a painful struggle making new friends after Meg moves away until she meets Honor, who is African American and very hesitant about accepting Wendy. (Rev: BCCB 4/88; BL 4/1/88; SLJ 4/88)

7336 Adler, C. S. *The Magic of the Glits* (5–7). Illus. by Ati Forberg. 1987, Avon paper $2.50 (978-0-380-70403-3). Jeremy, age 12, takes care of 7-year-old Lynette for the summer. A reissue of the 1979 edition. Also use *Some Other Summer* (1988).

7337 Almond, David. *My Name Is Mina* (4–7). 2011, Delacorte $15.99 (978-0-385-74073-9); LB $18.99 (978-0-375-98964-3). 304pp. This prequel to *Skellig* (1998) explores the life of homeschooled Mina, who lives next door to Michael, and her imaginative fascination with language and nature. (Rev: BL 9/15/11*; SLJ 11/1/11)

7338 Amesse, Susan. *Kissing Brendan Callahan* (4–6). 2005, Roaring Brook $15.95 (978-1-59643-015-0). 160pp. Twelve-year-old Sarah, an aspiring romance writer, is devastated when her mother won't let her enter a writing contest to be judged by the girl's favorite author; meanwhile kissable Brendan offers a questionable alternative. (Rev: BL 11/15/05; HBG 4/06; SLJ 12/05; VOYA 12/05)

7339 Anderson, M. T. *Me, All Alone, at the End of the World* (4–6). Illus. by Kevin Hawkes. 2005, Candlewick $16.99 (978-0-7636-1586-4). A boy's solitary but idyllic life at the End of the World is threatened by the arrival of an elderly entrepreneur who proposes to turn the area into a massive theme park. (Rev: BL 11/15/05; HBG 4/06; LMC 1/06; SLJ 12/05)

7340 Anderson, M. T. *The Serpent Came to Gloucester* (2–4). Illus. by Bagram Ibatoulline. 2005, Candlewick $16.99 (978-0-7636-2038-7). 40pp. In poetic narrative, Anderson tells, from the point of view of a young boy, the story of continued sightings of a supposed sea serpent on the coast of Massachusetts in 1817. (Rev: BL 6/1–15/05; SLJ 6/05)

7341 Appelt, Kathi. *Keeper* (4–7). Illus. by August Hall. 2010, Simon & Schuster $16.99 (978-1-4169-5060-8). 399pp. Ten-year-old Keeper believes her absent mother is a mermaid and sets off in a boat, in the company of her dog and a seagull, to find her. ☊ Lexile 770L (Rev: BL 6/10; HB 9–10/10; LMC 10/10; SLJ 7/10)

7342 Appelt, Kathi. *The True Blue Scouts of Sugar Man Swamp* (5–8). Illus. by Jennifer Bricking. 2013, Atheneum $16.99 (978-1-44242105-9). 384pp. This multilayered story about a Texas swamp is full of quirky Bayou characters and exotic wild animals. ALA Notable Children's Book. ℮ Lexile 810 (Rev: BL 5/1/13*; LMC 11–12/13; SLJ 7/13*)

7343 Applegate, Katherine. *Home of the Brave* (5–8). 2007, Feiwel & Friends $16.95 (978-0-312-36765-7). Young refugee Kek, who barely escaped death in Sudan, where his brother and father were murdered, finds a new home — and culture shock — in Minnesota. ∩ (Rev: BCCB 2/08; BL 7/07; HB 11–12/07; SLJ 10/07)

7344 Auch, Mary Jane. *One Plus One Equals Blue* (5–8). 2013, Henry Holt $16.99 (978-0-8050-9405-3). 272pp. Basil's new friend Tenzie helps him cope with the unexpected reappearance of his estranged mother even as the two 7th-graders explore their shared synesthesia. Lexile 690 (Rev: BL 3/15/13; SLJ 4/13)

7345 Babbitt, Natalie. *The Moon Over High Street* (3–5). 2012, Scholastic $15.95 (978-054537636-5). 160pp. Joe, 12 and an aspiring astronomer, goes to live with his aunt in a small Ohio town, where the richest man in town sees promise in the orphan and offers him a promising future as a businessman. (Rev: BL 3/15/12; HB 5–6/12; LMC 8–9/12; SLJ 4/12; VOYA 6/12)

7346 Bacigalupi, Paolo. *Zombie Baseball Beatdown* (4–7). 2013, Little, Brown $16.99 (978-031622078-1). 304pp. Zombie burgers? Yup. While playing baseball and dealing with bullies and other problems, middle-school friends Rabi, Miguel, and Joe discover a heinous plot at an Iowa meat-packing plant. ℮ Lexile 650 (Rev: BL 7/13; LMC 3–4/14; SLJ 8/13)

7347 Bair, Sheila. *Rock, Brock, and the Savings Shock* (3–5). Illus. by Barry Gott. 2006, Albert Whitman $16.99 (978-0-8075-7094-4). While Brock saves his money, his twin brother Rock squanders it, and learns a lesson about the value of a dollar; saving tips and a brief math lesson at the end explain the underlying concepts. (Rev: SLJ 7/06)

7348 Banerjee, Anjali. *Seaglass Summer* (4–6). 2010, Random House $15.99 (978-038573567-4); LB $18.99 (978-038590555-8). 176pp. Aspiring veterinarian Poppy, 11, learns some important lessons while helping her uncle Sanjay at his vet practice. ℮ Lexile 590L (Rev: BL 3/1/10; LMC 8–9/10; SLJ 6/10)

7349 Baskin, Nora Raleigh. *The Truth about My Bat Mitzvah* (5–8). 2008, Simon & Schuster $15.99 (978-1-4169-3558-2). Caroline, daughter of a Jewish mother and Christian father, has never been a practicing Jew but when her grandmother dies and leaves her a Star of David necklace — and her best friend Rachel is preparing for her bat mitzvah at the same time — she begins to acknowledge this part of her identity. (Rev: BL 3/15/08; SLJ 4/08)

7350 Bateson, Catherine. *Stranded in Boringsville* (5–8). 2005, Holiday House $16.95 (978-0-8234-1969-2). Twelve-year-old Rain's life is turned upside down when she and her mother move from cosmopolitan Melbourne to a small Australian town in the middle of nowhere; but she finds a good friend in her neighbor Daniel. (Rev: BL 12/1/05; SLJ 2/06; VOYA 2/06)

7351 Bauer, Marion Dane. *On My Honor* (5–7). 1986, Houghton Mifflin $15.00 (978-0-89919-439-4); paper $4.99 (978-0-440-46633-8). A powerful story in which

12-year-old Joel faces telling his parents that his friend Tony has drowned in the river they promised never to swim. (Rev: BCCB 10/86; BL 9/1/86; SLJ 11/86)

7352 Beard, Darleen Bailey. *Annie Glover Is Not a Tree Lover* (3–6). Illus. by Heather Maione. 2009, Farrar $15.99 (978-0-374-30351-8). 120pp. Despite her initial mortification at her grandmother's histrionic behavior, 9-year-old Annie, her best friend, and her grandma rally their town together to save a historic elm tree. (Rev: LMC 1–2/10; SLJ 11/09)

7353 Beaty, Andrea. *Dorko the Magnificent* (4–6). 2013, Abrams/Amulet $16.95 (978-141970638-7). 192pp. Robbie Darko, a 5th-grader obsessed with magic but not particularly skilled yet, learns a lot when his grumpy grandmother moves into his bedroom. ℮ Lexile 740 (Rev: BLO 4/15/13; LMC 11–12/13; SLJ 6/13*)

7354 Bell, Alison. *Zibby Payne and the Party Problem* (3–6). 2008, Lobster paper $6.95 (978-1-897073-69-8). 95pp. Sixth-grader Zibby wants to have an inclusive party — unlike the exclusive party her friend Amber is having — but realizes she'll have to invite the losers too. (Rev: BL 4/15/08)

7355 Bell, Alison. *Zibby Payne and the Wonderful, Terrible Tomboy Experiment* (3–5). Series: Zibby Payne. 2006, Lobster paper $6.95 (978-1-897073-39-1). When her longtime friend Sarah shows more interest in fashion and boy-watching than sports, 6th-grader Zibby reacts by becoming a total tomboy. (Rev: SLJ 12/06)

7356 Bell, Joanne. *Breaking Trail* (5–7). 2005, Groundwood $15.95 (978-0-88899-630-5); paper $6.95 (978-0-88899-662-6). Becky's dreams of training a dog team to participate in the Junior Quest fade when her father grows increasingly depressed, but a sled trip back to the family's cabin offers a chance to make those dreams come true. (Rev: SLJ 10/05)

7357 Bell, Juliet. *Kepler's Dream* (5–7). 2012, Putnam $16.99 (978-039925645-5). 256pp. Ella goes to live with her estranged grandmother in Albuquerque while her mother is being treated for cancer and finds herself learning about family history and investigating a mystery. (Rev: BL 5/15/12*; LMC 11–12/12; SLJ 5/1/12)

7358 Belton, Sandra. *The Tallest Tree* (3–5). 2008, Greenwillow $16.99 (978-0-06-052749-5). 160pp. Paul Robeson serves as a source of inspiration for African Americans young and old in a depressed neighborhood. (Rev: BL 2/1/08; SLJ 3/08)

7359 Bennet, Olivia. *The Allegra Biscotti Collection* (5–8). Illus. 2010, Sourcebooks paper $8.99 (978-1-4022-4391-2). 256pp. Eighth-grader Emma adopts an alter ego, Allegra Biscotti, to represent her fashion designs for the likes of *Vogue* in this entertaining book full of Emma's sketches. (Rev: BL 12/15/10; SLJ 12/1/10)

7360 Berlin, Eric. *The Puzzler's Mansion* (4–7). Series: Puzzling World of Winston Breen. 2012, Putnam $16.99 (978-039925697-4). 288pp. Winston and other puzzle fiends journey to a mansion owned by a man offering rewards for the solvers of word, number, logic, and grouping puzzles in this third volume in the series. **e** (Rev: BLO 7/12)

7361 Bernard, Virginia. *Eliza Down Under: Going to Sydney* (5–8). Series: Going To. 2000, Four Corners paper $7.95 (978-1-893577-02-2). This novel deals with Eliza's adventures in Australia when she accompanies her mother to the 2000 Olympic Games in Sydney. (Rev: SLJ 3/00)

7362 Blatchford, Claire H. *Nick's Secret* (5–7). 2000, Lerner LB $14.95 (978-0-8225-0743-7). When 13-year-old Nick, who is deaf, is summoned to a motel by Darryl Smythe and his gang of vandals, the boy knows he is in for trouble. (Rev: BL 9/15/00; HBG 3/01; SLJ 12/00; VOYA 2/01)

7363 Blexbolex. *People* (4–12). Trans. from French by Claudia Bedrick. Illus. by author. 2011, Enchanted Lion $19.95 (978-1-59270-110-0). Unpaged. A stimulating look at the similarities and differences in our lives, pairing, for example, a contortionist and a plumber, a bystander and a rescuer, a partygoer and a hermit. (Rev: HB 9–10/11; SLJ 9/1/11)

7364 Boles, Philana Marie. *Little Divas* (5–8). 2006, HarperCollins LB $16.89 (978-0-06-073300-1). Twelve-year-old Cass is facing a lot of change in her life: her parents' divorce, living with her father, a new friend, a first kiss, and perhaps a new school. (Rev: BL 4/1/06; SLJ 1/06)

7365 Boyce, Frank Cottrell. *The Unforgotten Coat* (3–6). Illus. by Carl Hunter. 2011, Candlewick $15.99 (978-0-7636-5729-1). 112pp. Two Mongolian immigrant boys turn to kindhearted Julie, 12, for help in navigating the culture in their new home near Liverpool, England. (Rev: BL 9/1/11; SLJ 11/1/11)

7366 Brahmachari, Sita. *Mira in the Present Tense* (5–8). 2013, Whitman $16.99 (978-080755149-3). 336pp. This novel about grief, growth, young romance, and the value of honest journal keeping focuses on 12-year-old Mira Levenson, half Jewish and half Indian and living in London. USBBY Outstanding International Book. Lexile 870 (Rev: BL 9/1/13; LMC 3–4/2014*; SLJ 10/13; VOYA 10/13)

7367 Branford, Anna. *Violet Mackerel's Brilliant Plot* (2–4). Illus. by Elanna Allen. 2012, Atheneum $14.99 (978-1-4424-3585-8); paper $5.99 (978-1-4424-3586-5). 112pp. Seven-year-old Violet comes up with a winning strategy to get the $10 she needs to acquire the blue china bird she has seen in the Saturday market. **e** (Rev: BLO 9/1/12; LMC 3–4/13; SLJ 12/12)

7368 Bredsdorff, Bodil. *Alek* (4–7). Trans. from Danish by Elisabeth Kallick Dyssegaard. Series: Children of Crow Cove. 2012, Farrar $16.99 (978-0-374-31269-5). 134pp. In this final book in the series, Doup adopts his real name of Alek and travels to Last Harbor to be with his lovesick brother Ravnar; there he works at an inn, uncovers shipwreckers, and rescues a girl. **e** Lexile 830L (Rev: BL 6/12; HB 7–8/12; SLJ 8/1/12)

7369 Brooks, Bruce. *Everywhere* (5–8). 1990, HarperCollins LB $16.89 (978-0-06-020729-8). Eleven-year-old Dooley, who is African American, helps a 10-year-old white boy live through the emotional trauma of waiting to see if his beloved grandfather will recover from a heart attack. (Rev: BCCB 10/90; BL 10/15/90*; SLJ 9/90*)

7370 Brown, Jason Robert, and Dan Elish. *13* (5–7). 2008, HarperCollins $15.99 (978-006078749-3); LB $16.89 (978-006078750-9). 208pp. In this humorous coming-of-age story, Evan finds himself relocated halfway across the country — from comfortable New York City to the middle of Indiana — and grappling with the social terrain of his new school and preparations for his bar mitzvah speech. (Rev: BL 9/1/08)

7371 Butcher, Kristin. *The Runaways* (5–8). 1998, Kids Can $16.95 (978-1-55074-413-2). During an unsuccessful attempt to run away from home, young Nick Battle meets Luther, a homeless man, and through this friendship gains insights into poverty in America. (Rev: BL 4/15/98; HBG 10/98; SLJ 4/98)

7372 Butler, Don Hillestad. *Tank Talbott's Guide to Girls* (4–6). 2006, Albert Whitman $15.99 (978-0-8075-7761-5). 178pp. As part of his effort to move on to 6th grade, Tank Talbott writes a guide to girls, filled with advice he'll need himself if he's to survive a summer-long visit from his stepsisters; a sequel to *Trading Places with Tank Talbott* (2003). (Rev: BL 4/15/06; SLJ 5/06)

7373 Butler, Dori Hillestad. *The Truth about Truman School* (5–8). 2008, Whitman $15.95 (978-0-8075-8095-0). Zebby and Amr start an alternative, online school newspaper and soon learn that not all postings are fit to print in this story told from many characters' points of view. (Rev: BL 3/15/08; SLJ 5/08)

7374 Byars, Betsy. *The Pinballs* (5–7). 1977, HarperCollins LB $16.89 (978-0-06-020918-6). Three misfits in a foster home band together to help lessen their problems.

7375 Byrd, Sandra. *Island Girl* (5–8). Series: Friends for a Season. 2005, Bethany House paper $9.99 (978-0-7642-0020-5). Confused by changes in her family situation, 13-year-old Meg spends a summer with her grandparents on an Oregon island where she meets and befriends Tia. (Rev: BL 10/1/05)

7376 Cabot, Meg. *Allie Finkle's Rules for Girls: Moving Day* (3–5). 2008, Scholastic $15.99 (978-0-545-03947-5). 240pp. Nine-year-old Allie, whose rules usually result from her somewhat reckless behavior ("Don't Stick a Spatula Down Your Best Friend's Throat"), now faces moving to a new neighborhood and school. (Rev: BL 6/1–15/08; SLJ 6/08) ∩

7377 Cabot, Meg. *Blast from the Past* (3–5). Series: Allie Finkle's Rules for Girls. 2010, Scholastic $15.99 (978-054504048-8). 240pp. When her school field trip group merges with people from her old school, Allie contends with their meanness by being true to herself. ∩ **e** Lexile 840L (Rev: BLO 10/15/10)

7378 Calhoun, Dia. *After the River the Sun* (4–6). 2013, Atheneum $16.99 (978-144243985-6). 368pp. With the help of his new friend Eva, 13-year-old orphan Eckhart Lyon struggles to accept a trial visit to his Uncle Al in this stand-alone novel-in-verse companion to *Eva of the Farm* (2012). Lexile 720 (Rev: BLO 7/13; SLJ 8/13)

7379 Calhoun, Dia. *Eva of the Farm* (5–7). Illus. by Kate Slater. 2012, Simon & Schuster $16.99 (978-1-4424-1700-7). 236pp. Twelve-year-old Eva's family farm in Washington state is endangered when their crops fail and her younger brother gets sick, and she tries selling her poems to help make ends meet. ℮ Lexile 840L (Rev: LMC 1–2/13; SLJ 8/1/12)

7380 Carlson, Ron. *The Speed of Light* (4–7). 2003, HarperTempest LB $16.89 (978-0-06-029825-8). Baseball, science experiments, and the mysteries of the universe occupy Larry and his two best friends during the summer before junior high. (Rev: BL 8/03; HBG 4/04; SLJ 7/03; VOYA 10/03)

7381 Carlyle, Carolyn. *Mercy Hospital: Crisis!* (5–8). 1993, Avon paper $3.50 (978-0-380-76846-2). Three friends volunteer at a local hospital. (Rev: SLJ 7/93)

7382 Caseley, Judith. *The Kissing Diary* (5–8). 2007, Farrar $16.00 (978-0-374-36346-8). After her parents' divorce, 12-year-old Rosie keeps a diary in which she describes problems at home and at school and her crush on Robbie Romano. (Rev: BL 8/07; SLJ 11/07)

7383 Cheng, Andrea. *Honeysuckle House* (4–7). 2004, Front St $16.95 (978-1-886910-99-7). The problems of immigration and adjustment to new cultures are shown in this story of two girls of Chinese heritage, told in the girls' alternating voices. (Rev: BL 4/1/04; HB 7–8/04; SLJ 6/04)

7384 Cheng, Andrea. *Where Do You Stay?* (4–7). 2011, Boyds Mills $17.95 (978-1-59078-707-6). 136pp. After Jerome's mother dies, the 11-year-old goes to live with an aunt and cousins, struggling to adjust to his new setting with the help of a homeless man who shares his love of music. Lexile 590L (Rev: BL 3/15/11; SLJ 5/11)

7385 Chocolate, Deborah M. *NEATE to the Rescue!* (4–7). Series: NEATE. 1992, Just Us paper $3.95 (978-0-940975-42-2). A 13-year-old African American girl and her friends help out when her mother's seat on the local council is put in doubt by a racist. (Rev: BCCB 3/93; BL 3/15/93)

7386 Choyce, Lesley. *Rat* (5–8). Series: Orca Soundings. 2012, Orca LB $16.95 (978-145980301-5); paper $9.95 (9781459803008). 128pp. Colin finally rebels against the bullying at school in this novel suitable for reluctant readers. ℮ Lexile 580L (Rev: BLO 9/15/12; LMC 5–6/13)

7387 Christopher, Lucy. *Flyaway* (5–8). 2011, Scholastic $16.99 (978-0-545-31771-9). 336pp. Thirteen-year-old Isla's deep connection with birds and nature helps her when her father is in the hospital and she befriends a boy with leukemia. ALA Notable Children's Book 2012. ⌒ ℮ Lexile HL580L (Rev: BL 8/11*; SLJ 12/1/11*; VOYA 8/11)

7388 Clark, Catherine. *How Not to Run for President* (5–8). 2012, Egmont $15.99 (978-160684101-3). 192pp. After he saves a candidate's life, Aidan is brought along on the campaign trail, where he learns firsthand how the fickle media game works. ℮ Lexile 600L (Rev: BL 2/1/12; LMC 3–4/12; SLJ 1/12)

7389 Clements, Andrew. *The Report Card* (4–7). 2004, Simon & Schuster $15.95 (978-0-689-84515-4). Nora, a bright 5th-grader, deliberately gets low grades in a bid to boost her friend Stephen's self-esteem, but her plans backfire. (Rev: BL 2/15/04; SLJ 3/04)

7390 Clements, Andrew. *The School Story* (4–7). 2001, Simon & Schuster $16.00 (978-0-689-82594-1). Two 12-year-old girls tackle the task of getting a book by a new author published. (Rev: BCCB 7–8/01; BL 6/1–15/01; HB 7–8/01; HBG 10/01; SLJ 6/01)

7391 Clements, Andrew. *A Week in the Woods* (4–8). 2002, Simon & Schuster $16.95 (978-0-689-82596-5). Mark, a lonely 5th-grader, and a forceful teacher test each other — and Mark's survival skills — on a week-long camping trip. (Rev: BCCB 1/03; BL 10/1/02; HBG 3/03; SLJ 11/02)

7392 Codell, Esmé Raji. *Vive la Paris* (4–6). 2006, Hyperion $15.99 (978-0-7868-5124-9). 192pp. Paris McCray, an African American fifth grader, develops a very special relationship with her piano teacher, a Holocaust survivor; a companion to *Sahara Special* (2003). (Rev: BL 9/15/06; SLJ 10/06)

7393 Cohen, Tish. *The Invisible Rules of the Zoe Lama* (4–7). 2007, Dutton $15.99 (978-0-525-47810-2). This playfully illustrated story about 7th-grader Zoë describes her busy life at home and at school, offering advice and organizing projects and lives. (Rev: BL 10/1/07; SLJ 8/07)

7394 Cole, Sheila. *The Canyon* (4–6). 2002, HarperCollins LB $15.89 (978-0-06-029496-0). 144pp. A California sixth-grader named Zach fights to preserve the canyon near his home when he discovers it is targeted for development. (Rev: BL 8/02; HBG 10/02; SLJ 6/02)

7395 Colfer, Eoin. *Benny and Omar* (5–8). 2001, O'Brien paper $7.95 (978-0-86278-567-3). Benny, a young Irish lad, has trouble adjusting to his new life in Tunisia until he befriends Omar, a local orphan without a home, and the two have some exciting and amusing adventures. (Rev: BL 8/01; SLJ 12/01)

7396 Conrad, Pam. *Our House: The Stories of Levittown* (4–7). Illus. by Brian Selznick. 1995, Scholastic paper $14.95 (978-0-590-46523-6). A series of fictional vignettes trace the history of the middle-class community of Levittown, New York. (Rev: BCCB 12/95; BL 1/1–15/96; HB 11–12/95; SLJ 11/95)

7397 Cooper, Ilene. *Angel in My Pocket* (5–8). 2011, Feiwel & Friends $16.99 (978-0-312-37014-5). 288pp. A magical coin travels from middle-schooler Bette to three classmates who also are suffering a variety of problems in this novel about friendship, magic, and transformation. Lexile 810L (Rev: BLO 2/15/11; LMC 5–6/11; SLJ 3/1/11; VOYA 6/11)

7398 Creech, Sharon. *Granny Torrelli Makes Soup* (4–6). Illus. by Chris Raschka. 2003, HarperCollins LB $16.89 (978-0-06-029291-1). Food, warmth, and wisdom blend as 12-year-old Rosie spends time with her grandmother and talks about her blind friend Bailey and other life experiences. (Rev: BL 9/1/03*; HB 11/03; HBG 4/04; SLJ 8/03*)

7399 Cuevas, Michelle. *The Masterwork of a Painting Elephant* (3–7). Illus. by Ed Young. 2011, Farrar $15.99 (978-0-374-34854-0). 144pp. An artistic elephant named Birch and a boy abandoned as a baby, Pigeon Jones, become fast friends and travel together in search of their loved ones. (Rev: BL 9/1/11; SLJ 12/1/11)

7400 Cummings, Mary. *Three Names of Me* (2–5). Illus. by Lin Wang. 2006, Albert Whitman $15.95 (978-0-8075-7903-9). A young Chinese American girl tells the story behind her three names — one from her birth mother, another she received at the orphanage, and a third given by her adoptive parents. (Rev: SLJ 10/06)

7401 Danziger, Paula, and Ann M. Martin. *P. S. Longer Letter Later* (5–8). 1998, Scholastic paper $16.95 (978-0-590-21310-3). This novel consists of letters between two recently separated girlfriends — one who is adjusting well and the other who is facing family problems after her father loses his job and the family must change its lifestyle. (Rev: BL 6/1–15/98; HBG 10/98; SLJ 5/98; VOYA 8/98)

7402 Davies, Jacqueline. *The Lemonade Crime* (3–5). 2011, Houghton Mifflin $15.99 (978-0-547-27967-1). 160pp. Siblings Jessie and Evan (of 2007's *The Lemonade War*) are now in the same 4th-grade class and bond over a trial seeking justice about the missing proceeds from the lemonade stand. (Rev: BL 5/1/11; SLJ 8/11)

7403 Davies, Jacqueline. *The Lemonade War* (3–5). 2007, Houghton $16.00 (978-0-618-75043-6). 192pp. Evan and his younger sister Jessie — who has just skipped third grade and will be in Evan's class next year — now find themselves in constant conflict, even over their money-raising activities; includes tips for running a lemonade stand. (Rev: BL 3/15/07)

7404 DeFelice, Cynthia. *The Light on Hogback Hill* (4–8). 1993, Macmillan paper $15.00 (978-0-02-726453-1). When 11-year-olds Hadley and Josh discover that the Witch Woman of Hogback Hill is really a shy, deformed woman, they help her find the courage to return to town. (Rev: BCCB 12/93; BL 11/1/93; SLJ 11/93)

7405 Denman, K. L. *Mirror Image* (5–8). Series: Currents. 2007, Orca $14.95 (978-1-55143-667-8); paper $8.95 (978-1-55143-667-4). Popular Lacey and Sable, an immigrant to Canada from Bosnia who is a loner, could not be more different, and the girls are initially disappointed to be paired for an art project. (Rev: BL 3/15/07)

7406 Dionne, Erin. *Notes from an Accidental Band Geek* (5–8). 2011, Dial $16.99 (978-0-8037-3564-4). 304pp. Ambitious 9th-grader Elsie has her heart set on becoming a French horn player in an orchestra and is surprised to find that she actually enjoys playing the melliphone in the school's marching band despite her initial resistance. (Rev: BL 11/1/11; SLJ 10/1/11)

7407 Dionne, Erin. *The Total Tragedy of a Girl Named Hamlet* (4–7). 2010, Dial $16.99 (978-0-803-73298-8).

304pp. It's not easy for socially uncertain 8th-grader Hamlet when her genius 7-year-old sister Desdemona starts attending her middle school; however an audition for *A Midsummer Night's Dream* reveals Hamlet's acting abilities. e Lexile 750L (Rev: BL 1/1/10; LMC 5–6/10; SLJ 2/10)

7408 Draper, Sharon M. *The Space Mission Adventure* (3–6). Illus. by Jesse Joshua Watson. Series: Ziggy and the Black Dinosaurs. 2006, Simon & Schuster paper $4.99 (978-0-689-87914-2). 121pp. While attending Space Camp in Huntsville, Alabama, Ziggy and his friends (African American boys from Ohio) cooperate with other campers and experience the weightlessness of space travel during a simulated shuttle mission; lots of scientific information is interwoven. (Rev: SLJ 1/07)

7409 Dunlop, Eileen. *Finn's Search* (4–7). 1994, Holiday $14.95 (978-0-8234-1099-6). Two Scottish boys try to save a gravel pit from local developers. (Rev: BCCB 12/94; BL 10/1/94; SLJ 10/94)

7410 Dutton, Sandra. *Mary Mae and the Gospel Truth* (4–6). 2010, Houghton Mifflin $15 (978-0-547-24966-7). 144pp. Ten-year-old Mary Mae touches off a family debate over science versus religion when her interest in fossils worries her devout mother. e Lexile 680L (Rev: BL 6/10; SLJ 7/10)

7411 Edgar, Elsbeth. *The Visconti House* (4–7). 2011, Candlewick $16.99 (978-0-7636-5019-3). 304pp. Laura, who wants to fit in in her 8th-grade class, and Leon, a new student, become friends as they work together to unravel the history of Laura's supposedly haunted house; set in Australia. e Lexile 650L (Rev: BL 2/1/11; SLJ 2/1/11; VOYA 4/11)

7412 Eduar, Gilles. *Gigi and Zachary's Around-the-World Adventure: A Seek-and-Find Game* (2–4). Illus. by author. 2003, Chronicle $16.95 (978-0-8118-3909-9). Young readers follow Gigi the giraffe and Zachary the zebra on a trip to far-flung countries, learning about exotic destinations and searching for specific items in the accompanying illustrations. (Rev: HBG 10/03; SLJ 6/03)

7413 Ekeland, Ivar. *The Cat in Numberland* (3–5). Illus. by John O'Brien. 2006, Cricket $19.95 (978-0-8126-2744-2). 59pp. Is zero a number? What is infinity? The answers are found at Hotel Infinity, where there is always room . . . even though all the rooms are full; a clever book introducing complex ideas. (Rev: SLJ 7/06)

7414 Ellerbee, Linda. *Girl Reporter Blows Lid Off Town!* (4–7). Series: Get Real. 2000, HarperCollins LB $14.89 (978-0-06-028245-5). Casey Smith, a 6th-grade reporter, discovers the thrill of tracking down stories and getting at the truth in this lighthearted story set in a small town in the Berkshires. Also use *Girl Reporter Sinks School!* (Rev: BL 3/1/00; HBG 10/00; SLJ 6/00)

7415 Ellison, James Whitfield. *Akeelah and the Bee* (4–6). 2006, Newmarket paper $6.95 (978-1-55704-729-8). 186pp. A novelization of the movie about Akeelah, an 11-year-old student at a middle school in South Central Los Angeles, who is pushed into participating in her school's spelling bee and wins, qualifying her for the district competition. (Rev: SLJ 11/06)

7416 Emerson, Kevin. *Carlos Is Gonna Get It* (4–7). 2008, Scholastic $16.99 (978-0-439-93525-8). 291pp. A group of 7th-graders plan a prank on their special-needs classmate during a wilderness trip, but their plan backfires when they become lost in the forest during a lightning storm. (Rev: BCCB 11/08; BL 10/1/08; SLJ 12/08)

7417 Farrar, Josh. *A Song for Bijou* (4–8). 2013, Walker $16.99 (978-0-8027-3394-8). 324pp. A beautiful Haitian girl who moved to Brooklyn after the earthquake instantly wins 7th-grader Alex's heart, but he must learn about her family's strict dating rules and together they face bullies and misunderstandings. e Lexile 750L (Rev: BLO 7/13; LMC 5–6/13; SLJ 2/13; VOYA 12/12)

7418 Federle, Tim. *Better Nate Than Ever* (5–8). 2013, Simon & Schuster $16.99 (978-144244689-2). 288pp. Thirteen-year-old Nate Foster leaves his hometown of Jankburg, Pennsylvania, and travels to New York City to audition for a role in "E.T.: The Musical"; full of humor and suspense, this is a multilayered novel. ALA Notable Children's Book; YALSA Best Fiction; Golden Kite Award. e Lexile 930 (Rev: BL 2/15/13; LMC 8–9/13; SLJ 3/13)

7419 Feldman, Jody. *The Gollywhopper Games* (4–7). Illus. by Victoria Jamieson. 2008, Greenwillow $16.99 (978-0-06-121450-9). Gil Goodson is determined to win the Gollywhopper Games, sponsored by the Golly Toy and Game Company, in this engaging novel that includes the puzzles that Gil must solve to be victorious. (Rev: BL 12/1/07; SLJ 3/08)

7420 Fellowes, Julian. *The Curious Adventures of the Abandoned Toys* (3–5). Illus. by S. D. Schindler. 2007, Holt $17.95 (978-0-8050-7526-7). 64pp. Replaced by newer toys at the children's hospital, a teddy bear named Doc finds himself in the junkyard but soon makes a new life with new rewards. (Rev: BL 10/1/07; SLJ 1/08)

7421 Fleischman, Paul. *Seedfolks* (4–8). 1997, HarperCollins LB $15.89 (978-0-06-027472-6). Thirteen people from many cultures explain why they have planted gardens in a vacant lot in Cleveland, Ohio. (Rev: BCCB 7–8/97; BL 5/15/97; HB 5–6/97; SLJ 5/97*; VOYA 6/97)

7422 Fletcher, Ralph. *Flying Solo* (5–8). 1998, Clarion $16.00 (978-0-395-87323-6). This novel answers the question, "What would a 6th-grade class do if their substitute teacher fails to appear and they are left alone for a whole day?" (Rev: BCCB 9/98; BL 8/98*; HB 11–12/98; HBG 3/99; SLJ 10/98)

7423 Frank, Lucy. *Lucky Stars* (4–7). 2005, Simon & Schuster $16.95 (978-0-689-85933-5). Kira, a talented singer with a feisty character, arrives in New York City to find that her father has plans that don't fit in with her own. (Rev: BL 5/15/05; SLJ 7/05)

7424 Fraustino, Lisa Rowe. *The Hole in the Wall* (5–8). 2010, Milkweed $16.95 (978-157131696-7). 280pp. Strip mining has ruined their environment and 11-year-old twins Sebby and Barbara wonder if some of the strange things they are seeing are real in this novel that blends ecology and science fiction. (Rev: BL 12/15/10; LMC 3–4/11)

7425 Frazier, Sundee T. *Brendan Buckley's Sixth-Grade Experiment* (4–6). 2012, Delacorte $16.99 (978-038574050-0); LB $19.99 (978-037598949-0). 288pp. Biracial, science-savvy Brendan is now in middle school and dealing with his growing feelings for new girl Morgan, his changing friendship with Khal, and problems with his African American father. ⌒ e (Rev: BLO 2/1/12; LMC 3–4/12; SLJ 1/12)

7426 Frederick, Heather Vogel. *The Mother-Daughter Book Club* (4–7). 2007, Simon & Schuster $15.99 (978-0-689-86412-4). Four very different 6th-grade girls join a book club where they will read *Little Women* with their mothers. (Rev: BL 6/1–15/07; SLJ 8/07)

7427 Frederick, Heather Vogel. *Much Ado About Anne* (5–8). 2008, Simon & Schuster $15.99 (978-0-689-85566-5). 324pp. Seventh-graders Cassidy, Megan, Jess, and Emma are reading books by Lucy Maud Montgomery with their mothers and using insights gained there in dealing with various problems; a sequel to *The Mother-Daughter Book Club* (2007). (Rev: SLJ 11/08)

7428 Fredericks, Mariah. *Fame* (5–8). Illus. by Liselotte Watkins. Series: In the Cards. 2008, Atheneum $15.99 (978-0-689-87656-1). Eve tries out for the 8th-grade play only after the tarot cards tell her it could lead to fame in this sequel to *In the Cards: Love* (2007). (Rev: BL 1/1–15/08; SLJ 8/08)

7429 Fredericks, Mariah. *Life* (5–8). Series: In the Cards. 2008, Simon & Schuster $16.99 (978-068987658-5). 262pp. Syd narrates this well-written stand-alone volume in a tarot-reading series as the three best friends seek answers about their daily lives. Lexile NC560L (Rev: BL 9/1/08; SLJ 8/08)

7430 French, S. Terrell. *Operation Redwood* (5–7). 2009, Abrams $16.95 (978-0-8109-8354-0). 368pp. Twelve-year-old Julian tries to save historic redwoods with a little help from his friends. (Rev: BLO 5/28/09; HB 7/09; SLJ 7/09)

7431 Friedman, Laurie. *Heart to Heart with Mallory* (2–4). Illus. by Barbara Pollak. 2006, Carolrhoda LB $15.95 (978-1-57505-932-7). 159pp. In diary format, Mallory worries that Joey's father and Mary Ann's mother will get married, and that Joey and Mary Ann will forget about Mallory. (Rev: SLJ 1/07)

7432 Friedman, Laurie. *Mallory's Super Sleepover* (3–5). Illus. by Jennifer Kalis. Series: Mallory. 2011, Darby Creek $15.95 (978-082258887-0). 160pp. Mallory struggles to plan a 10th birthday sleepover that will please both her friends and her parents. (Rev: BL 12/15/11)

7433 Friedman, Laurie. *Red, White and True Blue Mallory* (2–4). Illus. by Jennifer Kalis. 2009, Carolrhoda $15.95 (978-0-8225-8882-5). 184pp. Fourth-grader Mallory journals her way through a class trip to Washington, D.C., describing the things she sees and her relationships with her classmates. (Rev: BL 4/1/09; SLJ 9/09)

7434 Friend, Catherine. *Barn Boot Blues* (4–7). 2011, Marshall Cavendish $16.99 (978-0-7614-5930-9). 144pp. Twelve-year-old Taylor is miserable when her family moves from Minneapolis to a rural farm, but her innate sense of humor helps her make new friends at school. e (Rev: HB 11–12/11; LMC 1–2/12; SLJ 12/1/11)

7435 Friesen, Jonathan. *The Last Martin* (5–7). 2011, Zondervan $14.99 (978-0-310-72080-5). 264pp. Convinced that he is about to die because of a family curse, 13-year-old Martin starts to exhibit increasingly reckless behavior but also finds himself making new friends who try to help him; a story full of humor. e (Rev: SLJ 5/11*)

7436 Gallagher, Diana G. *Guilty! The Complicated Life of Claudia Cristina Cortez* (4–7). Illus. by Brann Garvey. Series: Claudia Cristina Cortez. 2008, Stone Arch LB $23.93 (978-1-59889-838-5); paper $5.95 (978-1-59889-881-1). Claudia and are friend Monica are accused of stealing $10 in this novel that will attract reluctant readers. Also use *Whatever!* (2008), in which the girls in Claudia's club must decide whether a boy can join and *Camp Can't* (2008), about Claudia's efforts to become a junior counselor. (Rev: SLJ 1/08)

7437 Gantos, Jack. *Heads or Tails: Stories from the Sixth Grade* (5–8). 1994, Farrar $16.00 (978-0-374-32909-9). A collection of eight unusual short stories about 6th-grader Jack, a born survivor who overcomes amazing obstacles in this book set in Fort Lauderdale. (Rev: BCCB 7–8/94; HB 7–8/94; SLJ 6/94*)

7438 Gantos, Jack. *Jack on the Tracks: Four Seasons of Fifth Grade* (5–7). 1999, Farrar $16.00 (978-0-374-33665-3). An episodic novel (the fourth about Jack Henry) in which Jack, a preadolescent, has several innocent adventures while growing up. (Rev: BCCB 9/99; BL 9/1/99; HB 11–12/99; HBG 3/00; SLJ 10/99; VOYA 2/00)

7439 German, Carol. *A Midsummer Night's Dork* (4–7). 2004, HarperCollins $15.99 (978-0-06-050718-3). In this sequel to *Dork on the Run* (2002), 6th-grader Jerry's class puts on an Elizabethan fair and Jerry has to stand up to another bully, even if it means making a fool of himself. (Rev: BL 2/1/04; SLJ 3/04)

7440 Gibson, Sarah. *The Truth About Horses, Friends, and My Life as a Coward* (2–5). Illus. by Glin Dibley. 2008, Marshall Cavendish $15.99 (978-0-7614-5459-5). 160pp. Living on an island in Maine, Sophie acquires some true friends as she struggles to overcome her fear of the horses her family owns. (Rev: BLO 8/28/08; LMC 3/09)

7441 Gidwitz, Adam. *A Tale Dark and Grimm* (4–7). 2010, Dutton $16.99 (978-0-525-42334-8). 256pp. Capitalizing on the gruesome nature of many of the Grimm tales, Gidwitz puts long-suffering Hansel and Gretel through a series of torturous scenarios en route to their happy ending. ALA Notable Children's Book

2011. (Rev: BL 11/15/10; HB 1–2/11; LMC 1–2/11; SLJ 11/1/10*)

7442 Gilson, Jamie. *Thirteen Ways to Sink a Sub* (4–7). Illus. by Linda Strauss Edwards. 1982, Lothrop $15.95 (978-0-688-01304-2). The girls in Room 4A challenge the boys to see who can first make their substitute teacher cry. A sequel is *4B Goes Wild* (1983).

7443 Givner, Joan. *Ellen Fremedon* (5–7). 2004, Groundwood $15.95 (978-0-88899-557-5). When her family seeks to block a proposed housing development, 12-year-old Ellen Fremedon, an aspiring novelist, must set aside her summer project to cope with the repercussions. (Rev: BL 11/15/04)

7444 Givner, Joan. *Ellen Fremedon, Journalist* (5–7). 2005, Groundwood $15.95 (978-0-88899-668-8). In this appealing sequel to *Ellen Fremedon* (2004), young Ellen uncovers some shocking stories when she starts a newspaper in quiet Partridge Cove. (Rev: BL 11/1/05; SLJ 2/06)

7445 Givner, Joan. *Ellen's Book of Life* (5–8). 2008, Groundwood $17.95 (978-088899853-8). 208pp. When Ellen's mother dies, Ellen seeks out her birth mother and is introduced to Judaism in this multilayered first-person narrative, the third in a series. (Rev: BL 10/15/08; SLJ 1/1/09)

7446 Goldberg, Whoopi, and Deborah Underwood. *Plum Fantastic: Sugar Plum Ballerinas* (3–5). Illus. by Maryn Roos. 2008, Hyperion paper $4.99 (978-0-7868-5260-4). Alexandrea's recent move to Harlem is stressing her enough without her mother's dream that she become a ballet dancer (instead of the speed skater Alex would like to be). (Rev: BL 1/1–15/09; SLJ 12/08)

7447 Golds, Cassandra. *The Museum of Mary Child* (5–8). 2009, Kane/Miller $16.99 (978-1-935279-13-6). 329pp. Sad teen Heloise, who longs for love, finds a doll under the floorboards of her bedroom and runs away from home when her unloving godmother threatens it. Lexile 840L (Rev: BLO 8/09; LMC 1–2/10; SLJ 12/09)

7448 Graff, Lisa. *Double Dog Dare* (3–5). 2012, Philomel $16.99 (978-0-399-25516-8). 304pp. Two 4th-graders vying for news anchor position in the media club enter a school-sanctioned dare contest, only to discover that their troubled family lives mean they'd be better off as friends than rivals. (Rev: BL 3/15/12; LMC 10/12; SLJ 4/1/12)

7449 Grant, Vicki. *Nine Doors* (5–9). Series: Orca Currents. 2009, Orca LB $16.95 (978-1-55469-074-9); paper $9.95 (978-1-55469-073-2). 96pp. When Emery and Richard play pranks on their neighbors, they get more than they bargained for and end up in serious trouble; for reluctant readers. Lexile HL470L (Rev: BL 5/15/09; SLJ 8/09)

7450 Greene, Constance C. *A Girl Called Al* (5–7). Illus. by Byron Barton. 1991, Puffin paper $5.99 (978-0-14-034786-9). The friendship between two 7th-graders and their apartment building superintendent is humorously and deftly recounted.

7451 Greene, Stephanie. *Happy Birthday, Sophie Hartley* (3–5). 2010, Clarion $16 (978-0-547-25128-8). 128pp. Eager for attention, Sophie grandly tells her friends that she will be getting a baby gorilla for her 10th birthday — and then must face the consequences. (Rev: BLO 5/15/10; SLJ 7/1/10)

7452 Greenwald, Lisa. *My Life in Pink and Green* (4–7). 2009, Abrams $16.95 (978-0-8109-8352-6). 272pp. Twelve-year-old Lucy's family's pharmacy is in serious financial trouble until Lucy has the idea to turn part of it into an eco-spa. **e** Lexile 680L (Rev: BL 2/15/09; SLJ 4/1/09)

7453 Greenwald, Sheila. *Rosy Cole's Worst Ever, Best Yet Tour of New York City* (3–5). 2003, Farrar $16.00 (978-0-374-36349-9). 128pp. Rosy takes her cousin on a tour of New York City and, despite her plans constantly going awry, the two have wonderful adventures. (Rev: BL 7/03; HB 7/03; HBG 4/04; SLJ 11/03)

7454 Greenwald, Sheila. *Watch Out, World — Rosy Cole Is Going Green!* (3–5). Illus. by author. 2010, Farrar $15.99 (978-0-371-36280-5). 112pp. Rosy's efforts for the school's "Keep It Green" fair involve keeping 2,000 worms in a dresser drawer. Lexile 760L (Rev: BL 2/15/10; LMC 5–6/10; SLJ 4/1/10)

7455 Gregory, Deborah. *Wishing on a Star* (5–8). Series: The Cheetah Girls. 1999, Hyperion paper $3.99 (978-0-7868-1384-1). A light novel about five girls in New York City who form a singing group, the Cheetah Girls, and are soon signed up for an important gig. (Rev: SLJ 1/00)

7456 Grimes, Nikki. *Almost Zero* (2–4). Illus. by R. Gregory Christie. 2010, Putnam $10.99 (978-0-399-25177-1). 128pp. Dyamonde is annoyed when her mother refuses to buy her a new pair of shoes, but when a classmate's apartment is destroyed she is determined to help. Lexile 630L (Rev: BLO 11/1/10; HB 11–12/10; SLJ 1/1/11)

7457 Grimes, Nikki. *The Road to Paris* (4–7). 2006, Putnam $15.99 (978-0-399-24537-4). Half-white and half-black, 9-year-old Paris suddenly finds herself separated from her older brother Malcolm and living with a foster family in a mostly white neighborhood. Coretta Scott King Author Honor. ∩ (Rev: BL 8/06; SLJ 12/06)

7458 Grunwell, Jeanne Marie. *Mind Games* (5–8). 2003, Houghton Mifflin $15.00 (978-0-618-17672-4). Six very different 7th-graders get to know each other as they collaborate on a science fair project in this inventive novel sprinkled with press clippings and project notes. (Rev: BL 5/15/03; HB 5–6/03; HBG 10/03; LMC 10/03; SLJ 5/03)

7459 Gutman, Dan. *Nightmare at the Book Fair* (4–6). 2008, Simon & Schuster $15.99 (978-1-4169-2438-6). 230pp. A bang on the head sends 5th-grader Trip Dinkleman into a totally unexpected world of literary adventures, and he discovers that reading might not be so bad after all. (Rev: LMC 11/08; SLJ 9/08)

7460 Gutman, Dan. *The Talent Show* (4–7). 2010, Simon & Schuster $15.99 (978-1-4169-9003-1). 211pp. A small Kansas town decides to hold a talent show to renew their spirits after a destructive tornado; however, even as the show takes place and the students have picked a favorite another tornado affects the outcome. **e** Lexile 800L (Rev: BL 6/10; LMC 11–12/10; SLJ 8/10)

7461 Hächler, Bruno. *Hubert and the Apple Tree* (2–4). Trans. by Rosemary Lanning. Illus. by Albrecht Rissler. 2006, North-South $15.95 (978-0-7358-2044-9). 32pp. Hubert loves the apple tree he has grown up with, and is distressed when it is hit by lightning; a challenging, beautifully illustrated, picture book for older children. (Rev: BL 4/15/06)

7462 Haddix, Margaret P. *Dexter the Tough* (2–5). Illus. by Mark Elliott. 2007, Simon & Schuster $15.99 (978-1-4169-1159-3). 139pp. After getting off on the wrong foot at his new school, Dexter puts on a tough exterior to hide his anxieties, but a persistent teacher and a would-be friend manage to break through to the uncertain young boy inside. (Rev: SLJ 1/07)

7463 Hahn, Mary Downing. *Janey and the Famous Author* (2–4). Illus. by Timothy Bush. 2005, Clarion $15.00 (978-0-618-35408-5). 48pp. Devastated when she gets separated from her class and misses an opportunity to meet her favorite author at a literary festival, Janey is comforted by a kindly older woman. (Rev: BL 12/1/05)

7464 Hall, Katy, and Lisa Eisenberg. *The Paxton Cheerleaders: Go for It, Patti!* (4–7). 1994, Simon & Schuster paper $3.50 (978-0-671-89490-0). Four 7th-grade girls from different backgrounds make the cheerleading team in their junior high school. (Rev: BL 2/1/95)

7465 Han, Jenny. *Shug* (5–8). 2006, Simon & Schuster $14.95 (978-1-4169-0942-2). Annemarie Wilcox, a 7th-grader better known as Shug, faces numerous challenges in addition to the usual middle-school problems: a gorgeous older sister, squabbling parents, a fight with her best friend, and a crush on Mark that doesn't seem to be reciprocated. (Rev: BL 2/15/06; SLJ 5/06)

7466 Harkrader, Lisa. *The Adventures of Beanboy* (4–7). Illus. by author. 2012, Houghton Mifflin $9.99 (978-054755078-7). 240pp. Thirteen-year-old Tucker's creation of a superhero sidekick for a comic book competition leads to a big boost in his own confidence in and out of school. **e** Lexile 670L (Rev: BL 3/1/12; SLJ 2/12*)

7467 Harley, Bill. *The Amazing Flight of Darius Frobisher* (4–6). 2006, Peachtree $14.95 (978-1-56145-381-8). 160pp. When his father disappears on a hot-air balloon trip and is presumed dead, 11-year-old Darius Frobisher is sent to live with his cranky Aunt Inga, a situation lightened when he meets a man who may have built a bicycle that will fly. (Rev: SLJ 12/06)

7468 Harper, Charise Mericle. *Dreamer, Wisher, Liar* (4–6). 2014, HarperCollins $16.99 (978-006202675-0). 408pp. A jar full of wishes and a little magic help Ashley get through a difficult summer without her best friend. (Rev: BL 3/1/14; SLJ 4/14; VOYA 2/14)

7469 Harrington, Jane. *Four Things My Geeky-Jock-of-a-Best-Friend Must Do in Europe* (5–8). 2006, Darby Creek LB $15.95 (978-1-58196-041-9). From the European cruise she is taking with her mother, 13-year-old

Brady reports via letter on her progress in meeting her must-dos — which include wearing a revealing bikini and meeting a "code-red Euro-hottie." (Rev: SLJ 6/06)

7470 Harrison, Paula. *The Secret Promise* (2–4). Illus. by Artful Doodlers. Series: The Rescue Princesses. 2013, Scholastic paper $4.99 (978-05455091-3-8). 128pp. Four 9-year-old princesses — Emily, Clarabel, Lulu, and Jaminta — are more interested in animal rescue than in etiquette. ℯ Lexile 690 (Rev: BL 6/13)

7471 Hathaway, Barbara. *Missy Violet and Me* (3–5). 2004, Houghton $15.00 (978-0-618-37163-1). Stories of growing up in a southern town in the 1930s are told from the viewpoint of an 11-year-old girl. (Rev: BL 2/15/04; SLJ 5/04)

7472 Havill, Juanita. *Grow: A Novel in Verse* (2–5). Illus. by Stanislawa Kodman. 2008, Peachtree $14.95 (978-1-56145-441-9). 160pp. A community garden in Minneapolis brings together a diverse group, including unhappy 12-year-old Kate. (Rev: BL 6/1–15/08; SLJ 5/08)

7473 Hawking, Lucy, and Stephen Hawking. *George's Secret Key to the Universe* (3–6). Illus. by Garry Parsons. 2007, Simon & Schuster $17.99 (978-1-4169-5220-6). 304pp. Stephen Hawking and his daughter weave scientific information into this fictional story of George's adventures traveling through a computer portal and learning about the universe. (Rev: BL 12/1/07; LMC 5/08)

7474 Hawkins, Aaron R. *The Year Money Grew on Trees* (5–8). 2010, Houghton Mifflin $16 (978-0-547-27977-0). 304pp. Fourteen-year-old Jackson learns a lot about farming — and about himself — when his manipulative neighbor promises him the deed to her son's apple orchard — if he can sell $8,000 worth of fruit in the first year. ℯ Lexile 810L (Rev: BL 9/15/10; LMC 3–4/11; SLJ 10/1/10)

7475 Haworth, Danette. *A Whole Lot of Lucky* (4–7). 2012, Walker $16.99 (978-0-8027-2393-2). 240pp. Hailee has a difficult time adjusting when her family wins millions in the lottery and her lifestyle moves from embarrassing to uncertain. ℯ Lexile 730L (Rev: BL 9/15/12; SLJ 12/12)

7476 Heldring, Thatcher. *The League* (5–8). 2013, Delacorte $15.99 (978-038574181-1). 240pp. Football, family, bullies, a first crush, friendship, and deceit all feature in this story of Wyatt Parker and his efforts to navigate the summer between middle school and high school. ℯ Lexile 610 (Rev: BL 9/1/13; SLJ 9/13)

7477 Hemingway, Edith M. *Road to Tater Hill* (5–8). 2009, Delacorte $16.99 (978-0-385-73677-0). 224pp. In the mountains of North Carolina in 1963, 10-year-old Annie must deal with her baby sister's death, her mother who is silent and absent with grief, and her father who is overseas. (Rev: BCCB 10/09; BL 7/09; SLJ 12/09)

7478 Henkes, Kevin. *Bird Lake Moon* (5–7). 2008, Greenwillow $15.99 (978-0-06-147076-9). Unsettled because his parents are divorcing, Mitch hopes to move into the empty house next door and is annoyed when the family who owns it turns up; he decides to trick them

into thinking their dead son is haunting them, a choice that has consequences when he becomes friends with the son. ⋒ (Rev: BL 3/15/08; SLJ 3/08)

7479 Henkes, Kevin. *Olive's Ocean* (5–8). 2003, Greenwillow LB $16.89 (978-0-06-053544-5). During a summer at the beach, Martha, an aspiring writer, wrestles with a classmate's sudden death, has her first whiff of romance, and gets to know her family and herself better. Newbery Honor 2004. (Rev: BL 9/1/03*; HB 11–12/03*; HBG 4/04; SLJ 8/03*)

7480 Henkes, Kevin. *The Year of Billy Miller* (3–7). Illus. by author. 2013, Greenwillow $16.99 (978-0-06-226812-9). 240pp. Second grade isn't as bad as Billy Miller feared and he learns many lessons at home too. Newbery Honor; ALA Notable Children's Book. Lexile 620 (Rev: BL 7/13; SLJ 7/13*)

7481 Henson, Heather. *Dream of Night* (4–8). 2010, Simon & Schuster $15.99 (978-1-4169-4899-5). 224pp. Twelve-year-old Shiloh slowly learns to trust others with the help of her foster mother and Dream of Night, a horse that has also suffered and that offers its own perspective. ℯ Lexile 470L (Rev: BLO 4/15/10; LMC 8–9/10; SLJ 4/10)

7482 Hermes, Patricia. *Emma Dilemma, the Nanny, and the Best Horse Ever* (3–5). 2011, Marshall Cavendish $15.99 (978-0-7614-5905-7). 144pp. Emma's favorite horse is to be sold, and her best friend, Luisa, is moving away. What else can go wrong? ℯ Lexile 550L (Rev: BL 4/1/11; SLJ 3/1/11)

7483 Hershey, Mary. *Love and Pollywogs from Camp Calamity* (3–5). 2010, Random House $15.99 (978-0-385-73744-9); LB $18.99 (978-0-385-90666-1). 224pp. Fourth-grader Effie's much-awaited week at Camp Wickitawa doesn't go according to plan when she discovers her older sister will be there too, and that she suffers totally unexpected homesickness. (Rev: SLJ 6/1/10)

7484 Hiaasen, Carl. *Chomp* (5–8). 2012, Knopf $16.99 (978-037586842-9); LB $19.99 (978-037596842-6). 304pp. A reality TV show called "Expedition Survival" sparks an exciting environmental adventure when the star disappears in the Everglades. ⋒ ℯ Lexile 800L (Rev: BL 11/15/11; HB 3–4/12; LMC 5–6/12*; SLJ 3/12*)

7485 Hiaasen, Carl. *Flush* (5–8). 2005, Knopf LB $18.99 (978-0-375-92182-7). Noah Underwood and his younger sister Abbey set out to prove their father was justified in sinking a floating casino because it was polluting. (Rev: BL 8/05; SLJ 9/05)

7486 Hicks, Betty. *The Worm Whisperer* (3–5). Illus. by Ben Hatke. 2013, Roaring Brook $15.99 (978-159643490-5). 192pp. Ellis decides to help his struggling family by entering a caterpillar in the annual Woolly Worm Race, which offers a prize of $1,000. ℯ Lexile 560L (Rev: BL 12/15/12; HB 1–2/13; LMC 8–9/13; SLJ 2/13)

7487 Hirsch, Odo. *Have Courage, Hazel Green!* (4–7). 2006, Bloomsbury $15.95 (978-1-58234-659-5). Independent-minded Hazel Green and her friends must mend some fences when her plan to shame a neighbor into apologizing for a blatant act of ethnic prejudice backfires. (Rev: BL 6/1–15/06; SLJ 8/06)

7488 Hirsch, Odo. *Hazel Green* (3–6). 2003, Bloomsbury $15.95 (978-1-58234-820-9). 188pp. The title character in this appealing tale takes on the adult establishment in her community as she fights for the right of children to march in the annual Frogg Day parade. (Rev: BL 6/1–15/03; HBG 10/03; SLJ 6/03)

7489 Hobbs, Valerie. *Defiance* (4–7). 2005, Farrar $16.00 (978-0-374-30847-6). An elderly neighbor named Pearl — and her cow — become valuable friends to 11-year-old Toby, who does not want to tell his parents that his cancer is back. (Rev: BL 8/05; SLJ 9/05)

7490 Holm, Jennifer L. *Eighth Grade Is Making Me Sick: Ginny Davis's Year in Stuff* (5–8). Illus. by Elicia Castaldi. 2012, Random House $15.99 (978-0-375-86851-1); LB $18.99 (978-0-375-96851-8). 128pp. In this moving and funny sequel to *Middle School Is Worse Than Meatloaf* (2007), Ginny relates through a variety of formats — notes, poems, emails, and other ephemera — her ambitions for the year and the problems that arise when her stepfather loses his job, her brother Henry gets in trouble, and a new baby is on the way. (Rev: BL 9/1/12; SLJ 10/12)

7491 Holm, Jennifer L. *Middle School Is Worse Than Meatloaf: A Year Told through Stuff* (5–8). Illus. by Elicia Castaldi. 2007, Atheneum $12.99 (978-0-689-85281-7). Receipts, notes, cards, magazine clippings, and other "stuff" tell of an eventful year in Ginny's life that includes bad hair days, iffy report cards, her mother's remarriage, and other tragedies. (Rev: BL 10/15/07; SLJ 9/07)

7492 Holmes, Elizabeth. *The Normal Kid* (5–7). 2012, Carolrhoda $17.95 (978-0-7613-8085-6). 248pp. In alternating first-person narratives, 5th-graders Sylvan and Charity describe their efforts to be accepted and recognize that the other students feel the same way. 📖 Lexile 780L (Rev: BL 11/1/12; LMC 3–4/13; SLJ 9/12)

7493 Holt, Kimberly Willis. *Piper Reed, Campfire Girl* (3–5). Illus. by Christine Davenier. 2010, Henry Holt $15.99 (978-080509006-2). 160pp. Fifth-grader Piper takes pity on a classmate after he embarrasses himself on a weekend camping trip; the fourth installment in this chapter book series. 📖 Lexile 530L (Rev: BL 1/1–15/11)

7494 Holt, Kimberly Willis. *Piper Reed, Forever Friend* (3–5). Illus. by Christine Davenier. 2012, Henry Holt $15.99 (978-080509008-6). 160pp. Piper's Navy father is assigned to Norfolk and she must make new friends and reconnect with old ones. 📖 (Rev: BLO 11/1/12)

7495 Holt, Kimberly Willis. *When Zachary Beaver Came to Town* (5–9). 1999, Henry Holt $16.95 (978-0-8050-6116-1). Thirteen-year-old Toby Wilson learns the value of love and friendship when he gets to know Zachary Beaver, a 643-pound teen who has been abandoned by his guardian. (Rev: BCCB 12/99; BL 9/15/99; HB 11–12/99; HBG 3/00; SLJ 11/99*; VOYA 12/99)

7496 Honeycutt, Natalie. *Josie's Beau* (5–7). 1988, Avon paper $2.95 (978-0-380-70524-5). Beau's mother doesn't want him fighting, so Josie offers to say she's the one who fights — but the lie backfires. (Rev: BCCB 12/87; BL 12/1/87; SLJ 12/87)

7497 Horvath, Polly. *My One Hundred Adventures* (4–6). 2008, Random $16.99 (978-0-375-84582-6). 272pp. Twelve-year-old Jane lives at the beach with her mother and younger siblings, and longs for adventures; although she does not reach the desired 100, she does indeed have a busy summer with many new experiences. (Rev: BCCB 10/08; BL 6/1–15/08; HB 9/08; LMC 11/08; SLJ 9/08) 🎧

7498 Horvath, Polly. *Northward to the Moon* (5–8). 2010, Random House LB $20.99 (978-0-375-96110-6). 256pp. Jane recounts her family's varied experiences as, after their stepfather is fired from his teaching job, they travel back from Saskatchewan to Massachusetts in this sequel to *My One Hundred Adventures* (2008). 🎧 📖 Lexile 750L (Rev: BL 11/15/09; HB 1–2/10; LMC 3–4/10; SLJ 2/10)

7499 Horvath, Polly. *One Year in Coal Harbor* (5–7). 2012, Random House $16.99 (978-037586970-9); LB $19.99 (978-037596970-6). 224pp. Primrose Squarp works to make a match for her Uncle Jack, befriends foster child Ked, and writes a cookbook with Ked's help in this sequel to *Everything on a Waffle* (2001). 🎧 📖 Lexile 880L (Rev: BL 7/12; HB 9–10/12; LMC 11–12/12; SLJ 8/12)

7500 Hossack, Sylvie. *Green Mango Magic* (4–7). 1999, Avon $14.00 (978-0-380-97613-3). Maile, who lives alone with her grandmother in Hawaii since her father abandoned her, finds a friend in Brooke, from Seattle, who is a recovering cancer patient. (Rev: BCCB 12/98; BL 5/1/99; HBG 10/99; SLJ 2/99; VOYA 8/99)

7501 Howe, James. *The Misfits* (5–8). 2001, Simon & Schuster $16.00 (978-0-689-83955-9). A group of 7th-grade social misfits challenge the so-called norms at their school by running for student council and instituting a no-names-calling day. (Rev: BCCB 1/02; BL 11/15/01; HB 11–12/01; HBG 3/02; SLJ 11/01; VOYA 12/01)

7502 Hudson, Wade. *Anthony's Big Surprise* (5–7). Series: NEATE. 1998, Just Us paper $3.95 (978-0940975736). Interracial tensions erupt in junior high school when some African American students are suspended and Anthony, who is also trying to cope with a family crisis, must deal with both problems. (Rev: SLJ 6/99)

7503 Hughes, Alison. *Poser* (5–8). 2013, Orca paper $9.95 (978-14598014-7-9). 168pp. Luke, 12, is being pushed into modeling jobs by his agent aunt when all he wants to do is attend school and hang out with his friends; the lies he tells to cover his absences eventually spiral out of control but with a humorous rather than tragic twist. Lexile 670 (Rev: BLO 6/13; LMC 10/13; SLJ 7/13)

7504 Hyde, Natalie. *Saving Arm Pit* (3–6). 2011, Fitzhenry & Whiteside paper $9.95 (978-1-55455-151-4). 136pp. A baseball team in a challenged town called Harmony Point starts a feverish letter-writing campaign in hopes of keeping their beloved postmaster coach on the job. (Rev: LMC 1–2/12; SLJ 10/1/11*)

7505 Ignatow, Amy. *The Long-Distance Dispatch Between Lydia Goldblatt and Julie Graham-Chang* (4–6). Illus. by author. Series: The Popularity Papers. 2011, Abrams $15.95 (978-0-8109-9724-0). 208pp. Julie copes with making her own way in junior high when Lydia's mother gets a job in London in this believable story told through shared letters and e-mails. (Rev: BL 4/15/11; SLJ 7/11)

7506 Ignatow, Amy. *Research for the Social Improvement and General Betterment of Lydia Goldblatt and Julie Graham-Chang* (3–6). Illus. by author. Series: The Popularity Papers. 2010, Abrams $15.95 (978-0-8109-8421-9). 208pp. Fifth-graders Lydia and Julie decide to launch a social investigation into the lives of their school's popular girls so they will be more prepared for junior high. (Rev: BL 3/1/10; SLJ 4/10; VOYA 8/10)

7507 Ignatow, Amy. *Words of (Questionable) Wisdom from Lydia Goldblatt and Julie Graham-Chang* (3–6). Illus. by author. Series: The Popularity Papers. 2011, Abrams $15.95 (978-141970063-7). 208pp. Twelve-year-old best friends Lydia and Julie record their lives as they deal with challenges ranging from plagiarism to a friend's mother's death. (Rev: BLO 11/15/11; SLJ 4/10)

7508 Jennings, Patrick. *The Beastly Arms* (5–7). 2001, Scholastic paper $16.95 (978-0-439-16589-1). A dreamy 6th-grader who pictures animals in everything he sees, discovers a world of real beasts when he and his mother move to the Beastly Arms. (Rev: BCCB 10/01; BL 5/1/01; HB 7–8/01; HBG 10/01; SLJ 4/01)

7509 Jennings, Richard W. *The Great Whale of Kansas* (5–9). 2001, Houghton Mifflin $15.00 (978-0-618-10228-0). When a boy finds a prehistoric whale fossil in his backyard, the discovery brings unexpected consequences. (Rev: HB 9–10/01; HBG 3/02; SLJ 8/01; VOYA 2/02)

7510 Jennings, Richard W. *Stink City* (5–8). 2006, Houghton Mifflin $16.00 (978-0-618-55248-1). Cade Carlsen, heir to his family's successful — but smelly — catfish bait business, becomes an anti-fishing activist. (Rev: BL 10/15/06)

7511 Johnson, Peter. *The Amazing Adventures of John Smith, Jr. AKA Houdini* (5–7). 2012, HarperCollins $15.99 (978-006198890-5). 176pp. Thirteen-year-old John "Houdini" Smith writes a novel that describes his life in Providence, Rhode Island, his family problems, and his efforts to make money raking leaves. ℮ Lexile 950L (Rev: BL 1/12; SLJ 4/12*)

7512 Jukes, Mavis. *Getting Even* (5–7). 1988, Knopf paper $4.50 (978-0-679-86570-4). Maggie seems unable to stop the nasty pranks of classmate Corky, and receives differing advice from her divorced parents. (Rev: BCCB 5/88; BL 4/1/88; SLJ 5/88)

7513 Jukes, Mavis. *The New Kid* (2–5). 2011, Knopf $14.99 (978-0-375-85879-6); LB $17.99 (978-0-375-95879-3). 288pp. Carson Blum, an adopted child and nearly 9 years old, moves with his dad to California and must deal with missing his grandparents and friends along with meeting students at his new public school. (Rev: BL 12/15/11; HB 1–2/12; SLJ 12/1/11)

7514 Kain, P. G. *Picture Perfect* (5–8). Series: Commercial Breaks. 2012, Aladdin paper $6.99 (978-14169978-7-0). 288pp. Teen actress Cassie recognizes that the "picture perfect" commercials she appears in are far from the reality of her home life. ℮ Lexile 1240L (Rev: BLO 6/12; SLJ 1/13; VOYA 12/12)

7515 Kehret, Peg. *Trapped* (4–6). 2006, Dutton $17.99 (978-0-525-47728-0). 192pp. A cat called Pete participates in this exciting story about efforts to track down the man who's setting illegal traps. (Rev: BL 12/1/06; SLJ 11/06)

7516 Kelley, Jane. *Nature Girl* (4–6). 2010, Random House $16.99 (978-0-375-85634-1); LB $19.99 (978-0-375-95634-8). 256pp. Unsettled by spending a technology-free summer in Vermont and missing her best friend Lucy, 12-year-old urban girl Megan takes off on the Appalachian Trail with only her dog for company. ℮ Lexile 590L (Rev: BL 4/1/10; SLJ 3/10)

7517 Kelsey, Marybeth. *Tracking Daddy Down* (4–7). 2008, HarperCollins $16.99 (978-0-06-128842-5). 292pp. Eleven-year-old Billie knows her father and uncle have robbed a bank and she hopes to persuade them to surrender. (Rev: LMC 3/09; SLJ 12/08)

7518 Kerrin, Jessica Scott. *Martin Bridge Blazing Ahead!* (2–4). Illus. by Joseph Kelly. 2006, Kids Can $14.95 (978-1-55337-961-4); paper $4.95 (978-1-55337-962-1). Martin Bridge is back in a funny early chapter book with two new slice-of-life tales: an overnight camping trip with the Junior Badgers and a lawnmower repair session with his dad. (Rev: SLJ 11/06)

7519 Kerrin, Jessica Scott. *Martin Bridge: Onwards and Upwards!* (2–4). Illus. by Joseph Kelly. 2009, Kids Can $16.95 (978-1-55453-160-8). 112pp. Martin's mother takes up the electronic keyboard in the first of these two stories; in the second, Laila wants to join the boys' Junior Badgers club but meets resistance. (Rev: BL 5/1/09)

7520 Key, Watt. *Fourmile* (5–6). 2012, Farrar $16.99 (978-0-374-35095-6). 240pp. Twelve-year-old Foster is suffering from his father's death, the violent behavior of his mother's boyfriend, and a deteriorating relationship with his mother when a stranger arrives at their Alabama farm bringing a new set of problems. ℮ Lexile 580L (Rev: BLO 11/1/12; HB 11–12/12; LMC 3–4/13*; SLJ 11/12*)

7521 Kherdian, David. *The Revelations of Alvin Tolliver* (5–7). 2001, Hampton Roads paper $7.95 (978-1-57174-255-1). Twelve-year-old Alvin is fascinated with nature and the great outdoors, and finds some unusual adult friends who introduce him to nature's charms. (Rev: BL 12/1/01; SLJ 3/02)

7522 Kimmel, Elizabeth Cody. *Lily B. on the Brink of Paris* (5–8). 2006, HarperCollins $16.99 (978-0-06-083948-2). Lily B.'s latest diary entries record the cultural sights of Paris, where the 13-year-old travels with her French class. (Rev: BL 1/1–15/07; SLJ 1/07)

7523 King-Smith, Dick. *The Catlady* (3–5). Illus. by John Eastwood. 2006, Knopf LB $17.99 (978-0-375-92985-4). In 1901 England, Muriel Ponsonby has a house full of cats, many of whom she believes are reincarnated — including Queen Victoria. (Rev: BL 1/1–15/06; SLJ 1/06)

7524 King, Daren. *Mouse Noses on Toast* (2–4). Illus. by David Roberts. 2008, Putnam $15.99 (978-0-399-25037-8). 128pp. When Paul Mouse discovers that a restaurant is serving mouse noses on toast, he and his friends campaign to change the menu. (Rev: BL 12/1/07)

7525 Kline, Lisa Williams. *The Princesses of Atlantis* (5–7). 2002, Cricket $16.95 (978-0-8126-2855-5). Twelve-year-old Arlene experiences ups and downs in her friendship with Carly, with whom she is writing a novel about two princesses. (Rev: BL 4/15/02; HBG 10/02; SLJ 7/02)

7526 Koertge, Ron. *The Heart of the City* (5–7). 1998, Orchard LB $16.99 (978-0-531-33078-4). Apprehensive about moving to the big city of Los Angeles, 10-year-old Joy soon finds a friend in a young African American girl and together they fight the takeover of an abandoned house by hoods. (Rev: BCCB 4/98; BL 4/1/98; HBG 10/98)

7527 Kompaneyets, Marc. *The Squishiness of Things* (2–5). Illus. 2005, Knopf $15.95 (978-0-375-82750-1). Hieronymus, an eccentric scholar, embarks on an epic journey to discover the origin of a single strand of hair that appears one morning on his desktop. (Rev: BL 7/05; SLJ 8/05)

7528 Konigsburg, E. L. *The Mysterious Edge of the Heroic World* (5–7). 2007, Simon & Schuster $16.99 (978-1-4169-4972-5). Amedeo Kaplan hopes to make a name for himself by discovering something important; could he have the opportunity as he and his new friend William help to clean out the home of Mrs. Aida Zender, a former opera singer? Blending humor and mystery, this story has an added layer of Holocaust history. ⌒ (Rev: BL 9/15/07; SLJ 9/07)

7529 Konigsburg, E. L. *The Outcasts of 19 Schuyler Place* (4–8). 2004, Simon & Schuster $16.95 (978-0-689-86636-4). Rescued from summer camp by aging uncles, Margaret is dismayed to find that their prized garden sculptures are endangered in this absorbing, amusing, and thought-provoking novel. (Rev: BL 12/15/03*; HB 3–4/04; SLJ 1/04*)

7530 Konigsburg, E. L. *The View from Saturday* (5–7). 1996, Simon & Schuster $16.00 (978-0-689-80993-4). A complicated tale about four 6th-graders who are contestants in an Academic Bowl competition. Newbery Medal 1997. (Rev: BCCB 11/96; BL 10/15/96; SLJ 9/96*)

7531 Korman, Gordon. *The Twinkie Squad* (5–7). 1992, Scholastic paper $13.95 (978-0-590-45249-6). A bossy, insecure 6th-grader and a defender of weaker kids are sentenced to the school's Special Discussion Group. (Rev: BCCB 11/92; BL 9/15/92; SLJ 9/92)

7532 Koss, Amy Goldman. *The Not-So-Great Depression* (5–7). 2010, Roaring Brook paper $9.99 (978-1-59643-613-8). 272pp. When her divorced mother is laid off, 14-year-old Jacki and her siblings face losing their privileged private-school life; the subtitle, *In Which the Economy Crashes, My Sister's Plans Are Ruined, My Mom Goes Broke, My Dad Grows Vegetables, and I Do Not Get a Hamster,* fills in some of the rest of the story. ⓔ Lexile 810L (Rev: BL 3/15/10; HB 5–6/10; LMC 5–6/10; SLJ 5/10)

7533 Kowitt, H. N. *The Loser List* (4–7). Illus. by author. 2011, Scholastic $9.99 (978-0-545-24004-8). 224pp. Seventh-grader Danny Shine finds himself in trouble when he ends up on the Loser List in the girls' bathroom, and then befriends a bully in detention. Lexile 480L (Rev: BL 3/15/11; LMC 10/11; SLJ 4/11)

7534 Kowitt, H. N. *Revenge of the Loser* (4–7). Illus. by author. 2012, Scholastic paper $9.99 (978-05453992-6-5). 240pp. Jealous 7th-grader Danny finally finds a flaw in seemingly perfect new kid Ty but his attempts to exploit it go off track; the diary-style narrative is peppered with cartoons. (Rev: BLO 5/15/12; SLJ 6/12)

7535 Krishnaswami, Uma. *The Problem with Being Slightly Heroic* (4–6). Illus. by Abigail Halpin. 2013, Atheneum $16.99 (978-144242328-2). 288pp. A whirlwind tale in which 11-year-old best friends Dini and Maddie attempt to help Bollywood movie star Dolly prepare for a U.S. film premiere. Lexile 680 (Rev: BLO 7/13; LMC 1–2/14; SLJ 9/13)

7536 Kurtz, Jane. *Lanie* (3–5). Illus. by Robert Papp. 2010, American Girl paper $6.95 (978-1-59369-682-5). 108pp. Outdoorsy, scientifically inclined Lanie, 10, misses her friend Dakota, who is away in Indonesia, but enjoys exploring her backyard with her favorite aunt. The second book in the series is *Lanie's Real Adventures* (2010), in which her environmental gardening methods are challenged. (Rev: SLJ 7/1/10)

7537 Lainez, Rene Colato. *My Shoes and I* (2–4). Illus. by Fabrico Vanden Broeck. 2010, Boyds Mills $16.95 (978-1-59078-385-6). 32pp. Mario gains strength and inspiration from a new pair of shoes as he and his papa undertake a long, challenging journey to join his mother in the United States. Lexile AD330L (Rev: BL 2/1/10; LMC 5–6/10; SLJ 3/1/10)

7538 Lantz, Francess. *The Day Joanie Frankenhauser Became a Boy* (4–6). 2005, Dutton $16.99 (978-0-525-47437-1). When she moves to a new school and finds her name has been listed as John, Joanie decides to try life as a boy. (Rev: BL 6/1–15/05)

7539 Lasky, Kathryn. *Georgia Rises* (2–4). Illus. by Ora Eitan. 2009, Farrar $16.95 (978-0-374-32529-9). 40pp. This narrative follows artist Georgia O'Keeffe through a

388

day of painting in her later life on a ranch in New Mexico. (Rev: BCCB 9/09; BL 5/15/09; SLJ 6/09)

7540 Lean, Sarah. *A Hundred Horses* (4–7). 2014, HarperCollins $16.99 (978-006212229-2). 224pp. Sent to the country to visit her aunt and cousins, 11-year-old Nell meets Angel, a runaway girl her own age with a foal and a mysterious past. ⋒ ℮ (Rev: BL 11/1/13*; SLJ 1/1/14)

7541 Leavitt, Lindsey. *Princess for Hire* (5–8). 2010, Hyperion $16.99 (978-142312192-3). 256pp. Fifteen-year-old Desi is offered a chance to escape her humdrum life — to "sub" for real princesses — but soon learns this is harder than it seems. Lexile 670L (Rev: BLO 3/1/10; SLJ 5/10)

7542 Lee, Milly. *Landed* (3–5). Illus. by Yangsook Choi. 2006, Farrar $16.00 (978-0-374-34314-9). 40pp. Twelve-year-old Sun must study hard to prepare for the tests he will face from American immigration officials. (Rev: BCCB 5/06; BL 1/1–15/06*; HBG 10/06; LMC 11/06; SLJ 2/06)

7543 Lewis, Maggie. *Morgy Coast to Coast* (3–5). Illus. by Michael Chesworth. 2005, Houghton $15.00 (978-0-618-44896-8). 80pp. Morgy describes life at school and at home — hockey, the trumpet, and a retired greyhound figure large — through narrative and emails to his friend in California in this sequel to *Morgy Makes His Move* (2002). (Rev: BL 6/1–15/05; SLJ 5/05)

7544 Lewis, Maggie. *Morgy's Musical Summer* (3–5). Illus. by Michael Chesworth. 2008, Houghton $15.00 (978-0-618-77707-5). 112pp. Morgy goes to summer music camp in this third installment in the chapter book series. (Rev: BL 4/1/08; SLJ 5/08)

7545 Lichtman, Wendy. *Do the Math: Secrets, Lies, and Algebra* (5–9). 2007, HarperCollins $16.99 (978-0-06-122955-8). Tess, 13, applies mathematical principles to all situations in her life including a cheating classmate, untrustworthy friends, and a potential murder. (Rev: BCCB 9/07; SLJ 12/07)

7546 Lieb, Josh. *I Am a Genius of Unspeakable Evil and I Want to Be Your Class President* (5–7). 2009, Penguin $15.99 (978-1-59514-240-5). 304pp. Overweight, apparently slow but secretly genius 7th-grader Oliver Watson takes on his arch nemesis — his father — by running for class president, a move secretly motivated by a desire for Dad's affection. ⋒ ℮ Lexile 780L (Rev: BL 10/15/09; SLJ 10/09; VOYA 12/09)

7547 Lindo, Elvira. *Manolito Four-Eyes* (4–6). Trans. by Joanne Moriarity. Illus. by Emilio Urberuaga. 2008, Marshall Cavendish $15.99 (978-0-7614-5303-1). Ten-year-old Manolito, who is unfazed by his thick glasses and happy with the nickname "Four Eyes," shares with humor the activities of his life in a Madrid suburb. (Rev: BL 5/1/08; LMC 10/08; SLJ 7/08)

7548 Look, Lenore. *Alvin Ho: Allergic to Dead Bodies, Funerals, and Other Fatal Circumstances* (2–4). Illus. by LeUyen Pham. 2011, Random House $15.99 (978-037586831-3); LB $18.99 (978-037596831-0). 176pp. Perennially worried Chinese American 2nd-grader Alvin prepares himself to attend his grandfather's best friend's funeral in this humorous take on death and funerals. ⋒ ℮ Lexile 600L (Rev: BL 10/15/11; HB 9–10/11)

7549 Look, Lenore. *Ruby Lu, Star of the Show* (2–4). Illus. by Stef Choi. 2011, Simon & Schuster $15.99 (978-1-4169-1775-5). 144pp. Ruby's father loses his job just as she is starting 3rd grade, causing many changes in her life. ℮ Lexile 620L (Rev: BL 2/1/11; HB 3–4/11; SLJ 3/1/11)

7550 Lopez, Diana. *Ask My Mood Ring How I Feel* (5–8). 2013, Little, Brown $16.99 (978-031620996-0). 326pp. Middle-schooler Erica "Chia" Montenegro's life is upended when her mother is diagnosed with breast cancer. Lexile 700 (Rev: BLO 7/13; LMC 3–4/14; SLJ 11/13)

7551 Lord, Cynthia. *Rules* (4–7). 2006, Scholastic $15.99 (978-0-439-44382-1). Catherine is a likable 12-year-old struggling to cope with the family challenges posed by her younger autistic brother. Newbery Honor 2007. (Rev: BL 2/15/06; SLJ 4/06)

7552 Lord, Cynthia. *Touch Blue* (4–7). 2010, Scholastic $16.99 (978-0-545-03531-6). 192pp. When the state of Maine threatens to close an island school for lack of pupils, the families take in foster children, and 11-year-old Tess must adjust to the arrival of 13-year-old Aaron. ⋒ Lexile 750L (Rev: BL 8/10; HB 11–12/10; SLJ 9/1/10)

7553 Lubar, David. *Hidden Talents* (5–9). 1999, Tor $16.95 (978-0-312-86646-4). Five misfits, who are attending the last-resort Edgeview Alternative School, become friends and discover extrasensory talents they can use against the school bully. (Rev: BL 9/15/99; HBG 10/99; SLJ 11/99; VOYA 10/99)

7554 Luddy, Karon. *Spelldown: The Big-Time Dreams of a Small-Town Word Whiz* (5–8). 2007, Simon & Schuster $15.99 (978-1-4169-1610-9). Mentored by her Latin teacher, 13-year-old Karlene manages to win the spelling championship in her rural South Carolina county and moves on to competitions at the state and national levels. (Rev: BL 1/1–15/07; LMC 8–9/07; SLJ 2/07)

7555 Lyons, Kelly Starling. *Eddie's Ordeal* (5–8). 2004, Just Us paper $3.95 (978-0-940975-16-3). When Eddie's grades slip, his father makes him quit baseball. (Rev: BL 2/1/05)

7556 MacDonald, Amy. *Too Much Flapdoodle!* (5–8). Illus. by Cat B. Smith. 2008, Farrar $16.95 (978-0-374-37671-0). 192pp. Parker, 12, suffers a severe shock to his urban self when he goes to spend the summer on a ramshackle farm without Internet and cell service and nothing to do but chores. (Rev: BL 12/15/08; SLJ 11/08)

7557 MacDonald, Anne Louise. *Seeing Red* (5–8). 2009, Kids Can $17.95 (978-1-55453-291-9); paper $8.95 (978-1-55453-292-6). 224pp. Thirteen-year-old Frankie wonders if he has supernatural powers as he discovers new talents — for working with horses and disabled children, helping injured birds, and making friends. (Rev: BL 3/1/09; LMC 10/09; SLJ 8/09)

7558 McDonald, Megan. *Judy Moody Declares Independence* (2–4). Illus. by Peter Reynolds. 2005, Candlewick $15.99 (978-0-7636-2361-6). 150pp. A visit to historic sites in Boston provokes a spirited uprising against various parental rules and requirements. (Rev: BL 6/1–15/05)

7559 McGhee, Alison. *Julia Gillian (and the Art of Knowing)* (3–5). Illus. by Drazen Kozjan. 2008, Scholastic $15.99 (978-0-545-03348-0). 281pp. Over the summer, 9-year-old Julia explores her Minneapolis neighborhood with her dog, reflects on changes in her life, and resists finishing a book that may have an unhappy ending. (Rev: BL 8/08; HB 7/08; LMC 11/08; SLJ 7/08)

7560 McGhee, Alison. *Julia Gillian (and the Dream of the Dog)* (4–6). Illus. by Drazen Kozjan. 2010, Scholastic $16.99 (978-0-545-03351-0). 327pp. While dealing with the myriad problems of middle school, Julia also must face the fact that her aging dog is reaching the end of his life. Lexile 810L (Rev: HB 9–10/10; SLJ 8/10)

7561 McKinlay, Meg. *Below* (5–7). 2013, Candlewick $15.99 (978-076366126-7). 224pp. Cassie has grown up in New Lower Grange, a town that replaced Old Lower Grange when it was flooded with a man-made lake; now 12 years old she finds herself drawn to the forbidden waters. e (Rev: BLO 6/13; LMC 8–9/13; SLJ 5/13)

7562 McLean, Dirk. *Curtain Up!* (1–4). Illus. by France Brassard. 2010, Tundra $17.95 (978-0-88776-899-6). 40pp. McLean provides many details of a musical production through the eyes of Amaya, a young girl who lands a role. (Rev: BL 11/1/10; SLJ 10/1/10)

7563 MacLean, Jill. *The Nine Lives of Travis Keating* (5–8). 2008, Fitzhenry & Whiteside paper $11.95 (978-1-55455-104-0). 215pp. Eleven-year-old Travis misses his mother and his old life but soon finds new purpose when he finds a tribe of feral cats who need care and protection. (Rev: BLO 11/19/08; SLJ 3/09)

7564 MacLean, Jill. *The Present Tense of Prinny Murphy* (5–8). 2010, Fitzhenry & Whiteside paper $11.95 (978-1-55455-145-3). 192pp. In Fiddler's Cove, Newfoundland, Prinny Murphy faces many challenges — an alcoholic mother who no longer lives at home, a distant father, loss of her best friend, bullying — but when she reads Virginia Euwer Wolff's *Make Lemonade* she recognizes a kindred spirit and resolves to conquer her problems. Lexile 700L (Rev: BL 12/15/10; LMC 11–12/10; SLJ 7/10; VOYA 8/10)

7565 Mankell, Henning. *When the Snow Fell* (5–8). Trans. from Swedish by Laurie Thompson. 2009, Delacorte $15.99 (978-0-385-73497-4); LB $18.99 (978-0-385-90491-9). 247pp. Now almost 14, Joel becomes a hero when he rescues an old man from freezing to death in this third volume about the appealing young Swede. (Rev: BL 10/1/09*; SLJ 12/09)

7566 Margolis, Leslie. *Boys Are Dogs* (4–7). 2008, Bloomsbury $15.99 (978-1-59990-221-0). 208pp. Sixth-grader Annabelle is struggling to cope at her new school and discovers that the training manual that came with her new, rambunctious puppy offers useful advice. ∩ (Rev: BCCB 11/08; SLJ 11/08)

7567 Marino, Nan. *Hiding Out at the Pancake Palace* (3–6). 2013, Roaring Brook $16.99 (978-159643753-1). 256pp. Eleven-year-old Elvis Ruby is mortified when he

gets stage fright on live TV; he retires to the Pinelands of New Jersey, dyes his hair, and changes his name to Aaron but discovers that he cannot escape his musical destiny. e Lexile 580 (Rev: BL 4/15/13; LMC 10/13; SLJ 5/13*)

7568 Marsden, Carolyn, and Virginia Shin-Mui Loh. *The Jade Dragon* (2–4). 2006, Candlewick $15.99 (978-0-7636-3012-6). 176pp. Ginny, a young Chinese American girl, and Stephanie, adopted by a Caucasian American couple, become friends after a few false starts. (Rev: BL 11/1/06; SLJ 11/06)

7569 Martin, Ann M. *Ten Good and Bad Things About My Life (So Far)* (3–6). 2012, Feiwel & Friends $16.99 (978-0-312-64299-0). 272pp. Pearl is starting 5th grade and writes an essay about her summer vacation — during which her father loses his job, she has to go to a camp where her older sister is a counselor, and she has a big fight with her friend James Brubaker III; a sequel to *Ten Rules for Living with My Sister* (2011). e (Rev: BL 10/15/12; HB 11–12/12; SLJ 10/12)

7570 Mason, Jane. *Bella Baxter Inn Trouble* (2–4). Illus. by John Shelley. 2005, Simon & Schuster paper $3.99 (978-0-689-86280-9). 80pp. Seven-year-old Bella is proud to be able to contribute when her family buys an old house, planning to turn it into an inn. (Rev: BL 5/15/05)

7571 Mason, Jane B., and Sarah Hines Stephens. *Bella Baxter and the Itchy Disaster* (2–4). Illus. by John Shelley. 2005, Simon & Schuster paper $3.95 (978-0-689-86281-6). 80pp. Bella Baxter's special preparations for the arrival of a visiting botanist at the Sea Inn take a dangerous turn. (Rev: BL 12/15/05)

7572 Mass, Wendy. *Every Soul a Star* (5–8). 2008, Little, Brown $16.99 (978-0-316-00256-1). Three quite different young teens meet at a wilderness camp to view a spectacular solar eclipse and find themselves much changed by the experience. ∩ (Rev: BL 12/1/08; HB 11/08; LMC 5/09; SLJ 11/08)

7573 Mass, Wendy. *Finally* (4–7). 2010, Scholastic $16.99 (978-0-545-05242-9). 304pp. Rory's long-nurtured dreams about what she'll do when she turns 12 turn out to be full of pitfalls in this light, funny story about confidence and insecurity. ∩ (Rev: BL 2/1/10; SLJ 7/10)

7574 Mass, Wendy. *Thirteen Gifts* (4–7). 2011, Scholastic $16.99 (978-0-545-31003-1). 352pp. This story of Tara's summer in Willow Falls combines magic, mystery, and quirky characters. ∩ e Lexile 720L (Rev: BL 8/11; SLJ 9/1/11*)

7575 Mazer, Norma Fox. *10 Ways to Make My Sister Disappear* (3–5). 2007, Scholastic $16.99 (978-0-439-83983-9). 143pp. Ten-year-old Sprig must cope with her 12-year-old sister Dakota, unsettled friendships, boys, and a father who is away in Afghanistan. (Rev: BCCB 10/07; BL 9/1/07; HB 11/07; SLJ 11/07)

7576 Messner, Kate. *The Brilliant Fall of Gianna Z* (4–7). 2009, Bloomsbury $16.99 (978-0-8027-9842-8). 198pp. Seventh-grader Gianna must complete a science assignment in order to compete in the cross-country running sectionals but life keeps interfering. (Rev: BL 8/09; SLJ 12/09)

7577 Mills, Claudia. *How Oliver Olson Changed the World* (2–4). Illus. by Heather Maione. 2009, Farrar $15.95 (978-0-374-32487-1). Oliver is worried that his hovering parents will nix the 3rd-grade space sleepover, but his diorama partner Crystal helps him find a way to display some independence. (Rev: BL 2/15/09; HB 3/09; SLJ 3/09)

7578 Mills, Claudia. *The Totally Made-up Civil War Diary of Amanda MacLeish* (3–5). 2008, Farrar $16.00 (978-0-374-37696-3). 208pp. Amanda's fictional Civil War diary, a history project, begins to resemble her home life as her parents separate and she and her best friend grow apart. (Rev: BL 1/1–15/08; SLJ 5/08)

7579 Mitton, Tony. *The Storyteller's Secrets* (4–6). Illus. by Peter Bailey. 2010, Random House $15.99 (978-0-385-75190-2); LB $18.99 (978-0-385-75191-9). 128pp. Twins Toby and Tess are fascinated by the verse adaptations of European folklore told by a mysterious old man in this richly illustrated book. (Rev: BL 6/10; LMC 10/10; SLJ 6/10)

7580 Moranville, Sharelle Byars. *The Hop* (4–6). Illus. by Niki Daly. 2012, Hyperion $16.99 (978-142313736-8). 288pp. A timid toad and a nature-loving girl work together in different ways to save a patch of woods from destruction in this contemporary novel with an element of fantasy. (Rev: BL 3/15/12; LMC 5–6/12; SLJ 3/12)

7581 Morgan, Melissa J. *Natalie's Secret* (4–6). Series: Camp Confidential. 2005, Grosset paper $4.99 (978-0-448-43737-8). 160pp. Eleven-year-old Natalie is a city girl and finds adjusting to camp challenging, especially when her famous father is arriving and she will have to tell her new friends the truth. (Rev: SLJ 4/05)

7582 Morpurgo, Michael. *I Believe in Unicorns* (3–5). Illus. by Gary Blythe. 2006, Candlewick $12.99 (978-0-7636-3050-8). 80pp. A moving story about a boy's love of books and storytelling and his and others' efforts to save the contents of the library when war arrives. (Rev: BL 12/1/06; SLJ 12/06)

7583 Morris, Taylor. *Class Favorite* (5–8). 2007, Simon & Schuster paper $5.99 (978-1-4169-3598-8). It's hard enough being an 8th-grader, but Sara has to endure countless public embarrassments at her school — still, this hilarious book shows how this unflappable girl keeps trying to climb the social ladder in spite of it all. (Rev: SLJ 3/08)

7584 Moskowitz, Hannah. *Marco Impossible* (5–8). 2013, Roaring Brook $15.99 (978-1-59643-721-0). 144pp. Gay friends Stephen and Marco will be separated when they head to different high schools and plan a couple of final detective and personal missions. Lexile 660 (Rev: BL 3/1/13; LMC 10/13; SLJ 3/13)

7585 Moss, Marissa. *Vote 4 Amelia* (4–7). Illus. by author. 2007, Simon & Schuster $9.99 (978-1-4169-2789-1). Amelia is running for secretary and her friend Carly for president; they didn't expect the campaign to be so

intense and Amelia's diary entries are — as always — humorous and revealing. (Rev: SLJ 9/07)

7586 Murphy, Pat. *The Wild Girls* (5–8). 2007, Viking $16.99 (978-0-670-06226-3). Joan and best friend Sarah (who calls herself Fox) love to explore in the woods and to write — a pastime that wins them spots at a writing camp and an outlet for their frustrations with their family lives. ♪ (Rev: BL 10/1/07; SLJ 11/07)

7587 Myers, Walter Dean. *Amiri and Odette* (4–8). Illus. by Javaka Steptoe. 2009, Scholastic $17.99 (978-059068041-7). 40pp. Overtones of urban youth, hip-hop, and Shakespeare abound in this colorfully illustrated, modern-day version in verse of the ballet Swan Lake. (Rev: BL 12/1/08; LMC 5–6/09; SLJ 1/1/09; VOYA 10/09)

7588 Myers, Walter Dean. *Checkmate* (5–8). 2011, Scholastic $16.99 (978-0-439-91627-1). 144pp. Zander and his middle-school friends in Harlem intervene when their chess-star classmate Sidney is caught trying to buy drugs. (Rev: BL 9/1/11; SLJ 10/1/11)

7589 Myers, Walter Dean. *The Dream Bearer* (5–8). 2003, HarperCollins LB $24.00 (978-0-06-054277-1). David, 12 and living in Harlem, gains valuable insights about his heritage and his ambitions when he gets to know an old man who calls himself a "dream bearer." (Rev: BL 7/03; HBG 4/04; SLJ 6/03; VOYA 6/03)

7590 Myers, Walter Dean. *145th Street: Stories* (5–9). 2000, Delacorte $15.95 (978-0-385-32137-2). A Harlem neighborhood is the setting for this collection of short stories dealing with a wide range of human emotions. (Rev: BL 12/15/99; HB 3–4/00; HBG 10/00; SLJ 4/00)

7591 Myracle, Lauren. *Eleven* (4–7). 2004, Dutton $16.99 (978-0-525-47165-3). Covering Winnie's life from her 11th birthday to her 12th, this novel reveals typical friendship and family tensions. (Rev: BL 4/15/04; SLJ 2/04)

7592 Myracle, Lauren. *The Fashion Disaster That Changed My Life* (5–8). 2005, Dutton $15.99 (978-0-525-47222-3). Through her diary and instant messages, Allison relates the turmoil of 7th grade, from her humiliating first-day arrival with her mother's underwear clinging to her pants to her problems making and keeping friends. (Rev: BL 9/15/05; SLJ 7/05)

7593 Myracle, Lauren. *Penguin Problems* (2–4). Illus. by Jed Henry. Series: Life of Ty. 2013, Dutton $12.99 (978-0-525-42264-8). 128pp. Second-grader Ty is already having problems (a new baby in the house, a troublesome cat, friends at school) when he decides to "rescue" a baby penguin from the aquarium; a spinoff from the Winnie Years series. Lexile 540 (Rev: BL 5/1/13; LMC 1–2/14; SLJ 7/13)

7594 Naylor, Phyllis Reynolds. *All But Alice* (5–8). 1992, Macmillan $15.95 (978-0-689-31773-6). Alice, now a 7th grader and still motherless, deals with the challenges of friendship and popularity. (Rev: BCCB 5/92; BL 3/1/92; HB 7–8/92; SLJ 5/92*)

7595 Naylor, Phyllis Reynolds. *Anyone Can Eat Squid!* (2–4). Illus. by Marcy Ramsey. Series: Simply Sarah.

2005, Marshall Cavendish $14.95 (978-0-7614-5182-2). 76pp. Sarah, hoping to be recognized as "special," tries to help a classmate whose parents own a Chinese restaurant. (Rev: SLJ 7/05)

7596 Naylor, Phyllis Reynolds. *Faith, Hope, and Ivy June* (5–8). 2009, Delacorte $16.99 (978-0-385-73615-2). 288pp. Seventh-graders Ivy June and Catherine trade lives for two weeks — Kentucky mountain vs. modern suburb — and track their experiences in journals. ∩ (Rev: BCCB 9/09; BL 5/15/09; HB 9/09; LMC 10/09; SLJ 10/09; VOYA 8/09)

7597 Naylor, Phyllis Reynolds. *Patches and Scratches* (2–4). Illus. by Marcy Ramsey. Series: Simply Sarah. 2007, Marshall Cavendish $14.99 (978-0-7614-5347-5). 77pp. Sarah helps out her friend Peter when his grandmother says Peter can't keep a pet in their apartment. (Rev: SLJ 6/07)

7598 Naylor, Phyllis Reynolds. *Roxie and the Hooligans* (3–5). Illus. by Alexandra Boiger. 2006, Simon & Schuster $15.95 (978-1-4169-0243-0). 128pp. Fantasy and reality become blurred in this multilayered story about 9-year-old Roxie Warbler, who applies her book-learned knowledge to survive and conquer when stranded on a desert island with bullies and robbers. (Rev: BL 2/15/06; SLJ 4/06)

7599 Neri, G. *Ghetto Cowboy* (5–8). Illus. by Jesse Joshua Watson. 2011, Candlewick $15.99 (978-0-7636-4922-7). 224pp. African American Cole, 12, finally pushes his mother over the edge and she drives him from Detroit to Philadelphia where he will live with the father he has never met — who turns out to be an inner city cowboy. Odyssey Honor Recording 2012. ∩ ℮ Lexile 660L (Rev: BL 9/15/11; LMC 11–12/11; SLJ 10/1/11)

7600 Nuzum, K. A. *The Leanin' Dog* (4–7). 2008, HarperCollins $15.99 (978-0-06-113934-5). 176pp. A starving dog appears at the door of an unhappy 11-year-old girl's wilderness home. ∩ (Rev: BCCB 11/08; BL 11/15/08; SLJ 10/08)

7601 Obed, Ellen Bryan. *Twelve Kinds of Ice* (4–7). Illus. by Barbara McClintock. 2012, Houghton Mifflin $16.99 (978-0-618-89129-0). 64pp. A family in Maine celebrates the different kinds of ice that take them through the winter. ALA Notable Children's Book; Booklist Editors' Choice: Books for Youth. Lexile 870L (Rev: BL 10/1/12*; HB 11–12/12; LMC 10/12; SLJ 12/12*)

7602 O'Connor, Barbara. *Greetings from Nowhere* (4–6). 2008, Farrar $16.00 (978-0-374-39937-5). 208pp. Set in a motel in the Smoky Mountains, this appealing novel interweaves the stories of four groups of individuals looking for change in their lives. (Rev: BL 1/1–15/08; SLJ 3/08)

7603 O'Connor, Barbara. *On the Road to Mr. Mineo's* (4–6). 2012, Farrar $16.99 (978-0-374-38002-1). 192pp. A one-legged pigeon attracts a great deal of attention in this story set in a peaceful South Carolina town and told from a variety of perspectives. ∩ ℮ Lexile 830L (Rev: BL 10/15/12; HB 11–12/12; LMC 3–4/13; SLJ 11/12*)

7604 Olander, Johan. *My Robots: The Robotic Genius of Lady Regina Bonquers III* (4–6). Illus. 2012, Amazon Children's $16.99 (978-0-7614-6173-9). 64pp. Lady Regina Bonquers III's imaginative robotic inventions are documented here with details of designs, correspondence, reviews, etc., and fascinating illustrations and ephemera. ℮ (Rev: BL 12/1/12; SLJ 1/13)

7605 Orlev, Uri. *The Song of the Whales* (5–8). Trans. by Hillel Halkin. 2010, Houghton Mifflin $16 (978-054725752-5). 112pp. Living in Jerusalem, Mikha'el becomes close to his grandfather and joins him on nightly dream journeys; as the old man's health fails he passes his ability as a dream master on to his grandson. (Rev: BL 3/1/10*; SLJ 5/10)

7606 Palmer, Robin. *Yours Truly, Lucy B. Parker: Girl vs. Superstar* (5–7). 2010, Putnam $15.99 (978-0-399-25489-5). 224pp. Plagued by family, friendship, and puberty problems, 12-year-old Lucy writes to Dr. Maude, a famous psychologist, for advice about handling her complicated life. Lexile 1080L (Rev: BL 6/10; LMC 8–9/10; SLJ 4/10)

7607 Papademetriou, Lisa. *Sugar and Spice* (4–7). Series: Confectionately Yours. 2013, Scholastic paper $5.99 (978-05452223-0-3). 224pp. Friendship is at the center of this third installment in the series as Hayley also copes with the aftermath of her parents' divorce. Lexile 690 (Rev: BLO 3/15/13)

7608 Paratore, Coleen Murtagh. *The Cupid Chronicles* (5–9). 2006, Simon & Schuster $15.95 (978-1-4169-0867-8). Now that her mother is married, Willa puts her considerable energies into the campaign to save the town library, and somehow romance keeps intruding; a sequel to *The Wedding Planner's Daughter* (2005). ∩ (Rev: SLJ 4/07)

7609 Paratore, Coleen Murtagh. *Sweet and Sunny* (3–4). 2010, Scholastic $16.99 (978-0-545-07582-4). 178pp. Plucky African American Sunny copes with many problems as she continues her quest to create a national Kid's Day. (Rev: SLJ 5/1/10)

7610 Parkinson, Siobhan. *Something Invisible* (4–7). 2006, Roaring Brook $16.95 (978-1-59643-123-2). Jake, a self-absorbed 11-year-old, learns a lot about family and friendship over a summer that involves tragedy. (Rev: BL 3/1/06; SLJ 4/06; VOYA 6/06)

7611 Parry, Rosanne. *Heart of a Shepherd* (4–7). 2009, Random House $15.99 (978-0-375-84802-5); LB $18.99 (978-0-375-94802-2). 176pp. In this heartwarming faith-based coming-of-age story, 11-year-old Brother learns a lot about ranching in eastern Oregon — and himself — when his courageous father is deployed to Iraq. ∩ ℮ (Rev: BL 2/15/09; HB 5–6/09*; SLJ 3/1/09)

7612 Patron, Susan. *Lucky Breaks* (3–6). Illus. by Matt Phelan. 2009, Atheneum $16.99 (978-1-4169-3998-6). 192pp. In this sequel to *The Higher Power of Lucky* (2006), Lucky and her mother have found a home in the desert community of Hard Pan (population 43) and Lucky is busy learning how to make a best friend, figuring out if she might almost be in love, and getting herself into a very deep hole. (Rev: BCCB 5/09; BL 1/1–15/09; HB 9/09; SLJ 3/09) ∩

7613 Patterson, Nancy Ruth. *The Winner's Walk* (3–5). Illus. by Thomas F. Yezerski. 2006, Farrar $16.00 (978-0-374-38445-6). 128pp. Nine-year-old Case Callahan, fearful he'll be a loser all his life, takes in a stray dog so talented that it makes the boy look good, but Case soon discovers that the dog's rightful owner is a disabled girl. (Rev: BL 8/06; SLJ 10/06)

7614 Paulsen, Gary. *Notes from the Dog* (4–7). 2009, Random House $15.99 (978-0-385-73845-3); LB $18.99 (978-0-385-90730-9). 133pp. Fourteen-year-old Finn overcomes his shyness as he befriends his new neighbor, 24-year-old breast cancer survivor Johanna, who inspires him with her enthusiasm for life. ℮ Lexile 760L (Rev: BL 8/09; LMC 11–12/09; SLJ 9/09; VOYA 10/09)

7615 Paulsen, Gary, and Jim Paulsen. *Road Trip* (3–7). 2013, Random House $12.99 (978-038574191-0); LB $15.99 (978-037599031-1). 128pp. Fourteen-year-old Ben and his father — along with the family dog Atticus — have many adventures on a trip to adopt a rescued dog from a shelter; written by Paulsen and his son, this book is narrated in part by Atticus. ∩ ℮ Lexile 700L (Rev: BL 12/15/12; LMC 8–9/13; SLJ 2/13; VOYA 2/13)

7616 Pavlicin, Karen. *Perch, Mrs. Sackets, and Crow's Nest* (4–7). 2007, Alma Little $16.95 (978-1-934617-00-7). Ten-year-old Andy Parker dreads the idea of a summer in the country but in the end finds he really enjoys it. (Rev: SLJ 12/07)

7617 Payne, C. C. *Lula Bell on Geekdom, Freakdom, and the Challenges of Bad Hair* (3–5). 2012, Amazon Children's $16.99 (978-0-7614-6225-5). 272pp. Lula Bell, a 5th grader, has relied on her grandmother to support her through bullying and other crises, so when Grandma dies she must draw on her own resources and face the talent show alone. ∩ ℮ (Rev: BL 11/15/12; SLJ 12/12)

7618 Payne, C. C. *Something to Sing About* (4–6). 2008, Eerdmans paper $8.50 (978-0-8028-5344-8). 176pp. Ten-year-old Jamie Jo, who lives in Kentucky, is capital-T-terrified of bees but must confront her fear when the possibility of a puppy arises, in this novel that includes Christian themes. (Rev: BL 10/1/08; SLJ 3/09)

7619 Peacock, Carol Antoinette. *Red Thread Sisters* (3–5). 2012, Viking $15.99 (978-0-670-01386-9). 224pp. When 11-year-old Wen is adopted from a Chinese orphanage, she is determined to find an American home for her best friend, Shu Ling, who unfortunately has a clubfoot and is growing too old for the orphanage. ℮ Lexile 700L (Rev: BL 11/1/12; LMC 1–2/13; SLJ 10/12)

7620 Pearsall, Shelley. *All of the Above* (5–8). 2006, Little, Brown $15.99 (978-0-316-11524-7). In this inspiring, fact-based novel, a 7th-grade math teacher challenges his students to build the world's largest tetrahedron and ends up involving the whole community; alternating chapters are narrated by the teacher and four of the students. (Rev: BL 9/1/06; SLJ 9/06)

7621 Peirce, Lincoln. *Big Nate on a Roll* (3–6). Illus. by author. Series: Big Nate. 2011, HarperCollins $12.99 (978-0-06-194438-3); LB $14.89 (978-0-06-194439-0). 216pp. Sixth-grader Nate aims to beat newcomer Artur — Mr. Perfect — and win the scouts' fundraising drive and the accompanying prize of a skateboard. (Rev: HB 9–10/11; SLJ 10/1/11)

7622 Perkins, Lynne Rae. *All Alone in the Universe* (5–8). 1999, Greenwillow $16.99 (978-0-688-16881-0). Debbie is crushed when her friend of many years drops her for another, but she has the courage to adjust and reach out to others. (Rev: BCCB 10/99; BL 9/1/99*; HB 9–10/99; HBG 3/00; SLJ 10/99)

7623 Perl, Erica S. *When Life Gives You O.J.* (4–6). 2011, Knopf $15.99 (978-0-375-85924-3); LB $18.99 (978-0-375-95924-0). 208pp. Ten-year-old Zelly agrees to look after a practice dog — an orange juice container — while she waits for the real thing. ℮ (Rev: BL 6/1/11; SLJ 9/1/11)

7624 Phillips, Gin. *The Hidden Summer* (5–8). 2013, Dial $16.99 (978-080373836-2). 208pp. When their mothers quarrel, 6th-graders Lydia and Nell concoct stories that allow them to spend summer days together at an abandoned golf course — but all does not go well there either. Lexile 750 (Rev: BLO 7/13; SLJ 7/13)

7625 Potter, Ellen. *The Humming Room* (4–7). 2012, Feiwel & Friends $16.99 (978-031264438-3). 192pp. Sent to live with an estranged uncle on a remote island, 12-year-old orphan Roo finds a frail cousin named Phillip, a wild boy, and a walled-off and abandoned garden; inspired by Frances Hodgson Burnett's *The Secret Garden*. ℮ Lexile 800L (Rev: BL 2/1/12*; LMC 8–9/12; SLJ 5/1/12)

7626 Potter, Ellen. *Slob* (4–7). 2009, Philomel $16.99 (978-0-399-24705-7). 208pp. Twelve-year-old Owen is smart and fat and carries around a tragic memory. (Rev: BCCB 9/09; BL 6/1–15/09; SLJ 7/09*)

7627 Preller, James. *Justin Fisher Declares War!* (3–5). 2010, Scholastic $15.99 (978-054503301-5). 144pp. Snarky middle-school class clown Justin learns how to go for laughs without alienating his peers in this coming-of-age story. (Rev: BLO 10/15/10; SLJ 12/1/10)

7628 Railsback, Lisa. *Noonie's Masterpiece* (3–5). Illus. by Sarajo Frieden. 2010, Chronicle $18.99 (978-08118-6654-5). 208pp. Fourth-grade artist Noonie has been through a "blue period" since her mother's death but now hopes that a "purple period" will bring her archaeologist father home — especially if she wins the art contest. Lexile 660L (Rev: BL 5/1/10; LMC 8–9/10; SLJ 7/10)

7629 Ray, Delia. *Here Lies Linc* (5–8). 2011, Knopf $16.99 (978-0-375-86757-6); LB $19.99 (978-0-375-96756-6). 304pp. Eager to impress his new classmates, formerly home-schooled 12-year-old Linc throws himself into the Adopt-a-Grave project and finds out some unexpected facts about his own family. (Rev: BL 9/1/11; SLJ 9/1/11)

393

7630 Rayban, Chloe. *Hollywood Bliss: My Life So Far* (5–8). Series: Hollywood Bliss. 2007, Bloomsbury $16.95 (978-1-59990-093-3). Hollywood's famous and super-rich mom is getting married in an over-the-top ceremony — and Hollywood is gaining a new stepbrother in this glamorous and funny sequel to *Hollywood Bliss: My Life Starring Mum* (2006). (Rev: BL 7/07; SLJ 2/08)

7631 Rayburn, Tricia. *Ruby's Slippers* (4–7). 2010, Aladdin paper $6.99 (978-1-4169-8701-7). 352pp. A Wizard of Oz-inspired tale in which 7th-grader Ruby is swept from her rural Kansas home to a new life in Florida filled with new electronics and culture, a grandmother, and typical middle school politics. **e** Lexile 790L (Rev: BL 6/10; LMC 11–12/10)

7632 Reedy, Trent. *Stealing Air* (4–6). 2012, Scholastic $16.99 (978-0-545-38307-3). 288pp. A move to Iowa puts 6th-grader Brian in position to be picked on by a bully but also to find friendship and the chance to help building a secret airplane. ⌂ **e** Lexile 650L (Rev: BL 11/1/12; LMC 1–2/13; SLJ 12/12)

7633 Regan, Dian C. *The World According to Kaley* (3–5). 2005, Darby Creek $14.99 (978-1-58196-039-6). 112pp. Kaley's fourth-grade World History assignments include a lot of commentary about her personal life, plus some rather hazy understanding of world history with an emphasis on interpretation. (Rev: BL 11/1/05)

7634 Resau, Laura. *Star in the Forest* (4–8). 2010, Delacorte $14.99 (978-0-385-73792-0). 160pp. After her father is deported to Mexico as an illegal immigrant, 11-year-old Zitlally turns to her trailer-park neighbor Crystal and the two girls care for an abandoned dog that Zitlally believes holds the key to her father's return. **e** Lexile 780L (Rev: BL 2/1/10*; HB 3–4/11; LMC 5–6/10; SLJ 2/10)

7635 Rhodes, Jewell Parker. *Ninth Ward* (5–8). 2010, Little, Brown $15.99 (978-0-316-04307-6). 160pp. Plucky 12-year-old Lanesha, who lives in New Orleans's Ninth Ward, draws on her special gifts when Hurricane Katrina arrives. Coretta Scott King Author Honor 2011; ALA Notable Children's Book 2011. ⌂ (Rev: BL 5/1/10; LMC 10/10; SLJ 8/10)

7636 Rising, Janet. *The Word on the Yard* (4–6). Series: The Pony Whisperer. 2010, Sourcebooks paper $6.99 (978-1-4022-3952-6). 208pp. Teenager Pia navigates her new school and tension with her dad's girlfriend by spending time with her horse; in a supernatural twist, she discovers a mysterious statue that allows her to hear her horse's thoughts. The first volume in a series. (Rev: BL 6/10; SLJ 9/1/10)

7637 Roberts, Diane. *Puppet Pandemonium* (3–5). 2006, Delacorte $15.95 (978-0-385-73309-0). 115pp. Still recovering from the trauma of moving from Seattle to small-town Texas, fifth-grader Baker gains recognition with his ventriloquist skills. (Rev: SLJ 12/06)

7638 Robinson, Sharon. *Safe at Home* (4–7). 2006, Scholastic $16.99 (978-0-439-67197-2). Still shaken by the sudden death of his father, 10-year-old Elijah Breeze must cope with culture shock when his mother moves

him from suburban Connecticut to New York City's Harlem and he attends a coed summer baseball camp. (Rev: SLJ 10/06)

7639 Rocklin, Joanne. *One Day and One Amazing Morning on Orange Street* (3–6). 2011, Abrams $16.95 (978-0-8109-9719-6). 224pp. The last remaining orange tree on an empty lot is precious to the residents of its Southern California neighborhood, and when it is threatened they come together to face their myriad problems. **e** Lexile 830L (Rev: BL 3/15/11; HB 7–8/11; SLJ 5/11*)

7640 Romain, Trevor. *Under the Big Sky* (4–7). 2001, HarperCollins LB $14.89 (978-0-06-029495-3). Encouraged by his grandfather, a young boy searches far and wide for the secret of life. (Rev: BL 8/01; HBG 10/01; SLJ 8/01)

7641 Rupp, Rebecca. *After Eli* (5–8). 2012, Candlewick $15.99 (978-0-7636-5810-6). 256pp. Three years after his older brother's death in Iraq, 14-year-old Daniel finally finds some solace. ⌂ **e** Lexile 1020L (Rev: BL 9/15/12*; HB 11–12/12; SLJ 9/12)

7642 Rylant, Cynthia. *God Went to Beauty School* (4–8). 2003, HarperCollins LB $15.89 (978-0-06-009434-8). God indulges in a lot of mortal activities, some fairly wacky, in this collection of thought-provoking poems. (Rev: BL 8/03; HB 7–8/03*; HBG 10/03; SLJ 6/03; VOYA 8/03)

7643 Sachs, Marilyn. *The Bears' House* (4–7). Illus. by Louis Glanzman. 1987, Avon paper $2.99 (978-0-380-70582-5). A poor girl escapes from reality by living in a fantasy in her classroom. A reissue of the 1971 edition.

7644 Salisbury, Graham. *Calvin Coconut: Trouble Magnet* (3–5). Illus. by Jacqueline Rogers. 2009, Random $12.99 (978-0-385-73701-2). 160pp. Calvin leaves the Hawaiian beach behind and starts 4th grade — walking right into the arms of bullies, tough teachers, new girls, and family troubles. (Rev: BCCB 4/09; BL 1/1–15/09; SLJ 5/09)

7645 Salisbury, Graham. *Extra Famous* (3–5). Illus. by Jacqueline Rogers. Series: Calvin Coconut. 2013, Random House $12.99 (978-038574220-7); LB $15.99 (978-037599047-2). 176pp. In this 9th installment in the series, Calvin and his friends get to appear as extras in a zombie movie. (Rev: BL 4/1/13)

7646 Samworth, Kate. *Aviary Wonders Inc: Spring Catalog and Instruction Manual* (4–6). Illus. by author. 2014, Clarion $17.99 (978-0547978-99-4). 32pp. A quirky pictorial guide to a future service offering replacement parts for birds that have become extinct, along with instructions on how to assemble them and how to teach these birds to fly and to sing; a thought-provoking, visually arresting title enhanced by the advertising lingo. **e** (Rev: BL 3/1/14*; LMC 8–9/14; SLJ 1/14)

7647 San Souci, Daniel. *Space Station Mars* (1–4). Illus. by author. Series: A Clubhouse Book. 2005, Tricycle $15.95 (978-1-58246-142-7). When they find a strange-looking rock in their neighbor's yard, the San Souci brothers and their friends become convinced that it's a meteor from Mars; a sequel to *The Dangerous Snake and Reptile Club* (2004). (Rev: SLJ 10/05)

7648 Schaefer, Laura. *The Secret Ingredient* (4–7). Illus. 2011, Simon & Schuster $15.99 (978-1-4424-1959-9). 240pp. Annie, 14 and in her last summer before high school, gets her friends to help her compete in a scone baking contest to win a vacation in London; a sequel to *The Teashop Girls* (2008). **e** Lexile 710L (Rev: BL 6/1/11; SLJ 8/11)

7649 Schaefer, Laura. *The Teashop Girls* (5–8). Illus. by Sujean Rim. 2008, Simon & Schuster $15.99 (978-1-4169-6793-4). 256pp. Annie and her friends try a variety of business strategies to help save Annie's grandmother's teashop in this book full of tea trivia. (Rev: BL 12/1/08)

7650 Schroeder, Lisa. *It's Raining Cupcakes* (4–7). 2010, Simon & Schuster $15.99 (978-1-4169-9084-0). 224pp. As her mother opens a cupcake shop, 12-year-old Isabel longs to travel and pins her hopes on a baking contest; with recipes. **e** Lexile 640L (Rev: BLO 2/15/10; SLJ 2/10)

7651 Schroeder, Lisa. *Sprinkles and Secrets* (4–7). 2011, Simon & Schuster $15.99 (978-1-4424-2263-6). 224pp. Sophie's dreams of becoming an actress are on the verge of coming true, but can she appear in a commercial advertising the competitor to her best friend Isabel's shop? A sequel to *It's Raining Cupcakes* (2010). (Rev: SLJ 10/1/11)

7652 Schwartz, Ellen. *Stealing Home* (4–7). 2006, Tundra $8.95 (978-0-88776-765-4). Joey, a biracial 9-year-old baseball fan living in the Bronx, is orphaned with his mother's death and moved to live with his Jewish maternal grandparents in Brooklyn, where he must cope with a startlingly different world. (Rev: BL 9/1/06; SLJ 10/06)

7653 Scotto, Michael. *Latasha and the Kidd on Keys* (4–6). Illus. by Evette Gabriel. 2013, Midlandia paper $10.99 (978-09837243-9-1). 254pp. Latasha hopes to reconnect with her father as she also faces challenges at school and in friendship. (Rev: BL 4/1/13)

7654 Senzai, N. H. *Shooting Kabul* (4–7). 2010, Simon & Schuster $16.99 (978-1-4424-0194-5). 272pp. Fadi's little sister Mariam is lost when the family flees Afghanistan in July 2001, and they continue to search for her even as they deal with a new life in the United States and the backlash after September 11. **e** Lexile 800L (Rev: BL 6/10; LMC 10/10; SLJ 6/10; VOYA 8/10)

7655 Shura, Mary Francis. *The Josie Gambit* (5–7). 1986, Avon paper $2.50 (978-0-380-70497-2). Josie's friend Tory behaves in an inexplicable way to his new friend Greg. (Rev: BCCB 5/86; SLJ 9/86)

7656 Silberberg, Alan. *Milo: Sticky Notes and Brain Freeze* (5–8). Illus. by author. 2010, Simon & Schuster $15.99 (978-1-4169-9430-5). 288pp. The death of 12-year-old Milo's mother overshadows all the normal trials and tribulations of middle school in this novel that interweaves humor and pain. **e** (Rev: HB 11–12/10; LMC 11–12/11; SLJ 9/1/10*)

7657 Simon, Coco. *Alexis and the Perfect Recipe* (4–6). Series: Cupcake Diaries. 2011, Simon & Schuster paper $5.99 (978-14424290-1-7). 160pp. Alexis, who loves organization and planning, gets a little haphazard when she develops a major crush on Emma's brother Matt. (Rev: BL 1/1/12)

7658 Smith, Anne Warren. *Tails of Spring Break* (4–6). 2005, Whitman $15.99 (978-0-8075-6358-8). 128pp. Things don't go well for Katie and her little brother when they decide to start a pet-sitting business. (Rev: BL 5/15/05; SLJ 5/05)

7659 Snyder, Zilpha Keatley. *The Egypt Game* (5–7). Illus. by Alton Raible. 1967, Dell paper $5.99 (978-0-440-42225-9). Humor and suspense mark an outstanding story of city children whose safety, while playing at an unsupervised re-creation of an Egyptian ritual, is threatened by a violent lunatic.

7660 Sonnenblick, Jordan. *Zen and the Art of Faking It* (5–8). 2007, Scholastic $16.99 (978-0-439-83707-1). Adopted from China as a child and tired of moving to new schools, 8th-grader San Lee decides to play the role of a Zen master when he arrives in Pennsylvania. (Rev: BL 10/1/07; HB 11–12/07; LMC 1/08; SLJ 10/07)

7661 Soto, Gary. *Facts of Life* (5–8). 2008, Harcourt $16.00 (978-0-15-206181-4). Soto offers 10 new stories about important events in the lives of Latino tweens and teens living in California. (Rev: BL 3/1/08; SLJ 7/08)

7662 Soto, Gary. *Local News* (4–7). 1993, Harcourt $14.00 (978-0-15-248117-9). This collection of 13 short stories deals with a number of Mexican American youngsters at home, school, and play. (Rev: BL 4/15/93; HB 7–8/93*)

7663 Soto, Gary. *Petty Crimes* (5–8). 1998, Harcourt $17.00 (978-0-15-201658-6). Ten short stories about Mexican American teenagers in California's Central Valley deal with some humorous situations but more often with gangs, violence, and poverty. (Rev: BL 3/15/98; HBG 10/98; SLJ 5/98)

7664 Spinelli, Jerry. *Maniac Magee* (5–7). 1990, Little, Brown $15.95 (978-0-316-80722-7). This thought-provoking Newbery Medal winner (1991) tells the story of an amazing white boy who runs away from home and suddenly becomes aware of the racism in his town. (Rev: BL 6/1/90*; SLJ 6/90)

7665 Springstubb, Tricia. *What Happened on Fox Street* (4–7). 2010, HarperCollins $15.99 (978-0-06-198635-2). 224pp. Although she still misses her dead mother, 10-year-old Mo is fairly happy with life on Fox Street until the summer her friend Mercedes seems to change and her father receives an interesting offer for their house. ☊ **e** (Rev: BL 9/1/10*; HB 9–10/10; SLJ 9/1/10)

7666 Stead, Rebecca. *Liar and Spy* (5–7). 2012, Random House $15.99 (978-0-385-73743-2); LB $18.99 (978-0-385-90665-4). 208pp. Coping with his father's job loss, his mother's double shifts at work, and bullies at school, 7th-grader Georges is pleased to meet a neighbor boy who wants his help investigating a mystery. ☊ **e** Lexile

670L (Rev: BL 6/12; HB 9–10/12; LMC 3–4/13*; SLJ 9/12*; VOYA 10/12)

7667 Stolz, Mary. *The Bully of Barkham Street* (4–8). Illus. by Leonard Shortall. 1963, HarperCollins paper $6.99 (978-0-06-440159-3). Eleven-year-old Martin goes through a typical phase of growing up — feeling misunderstood. Also use *A Dog on Barkham Street* (1960).

7668 Stout, Shawn K. *Penelope Crumb Finds Her Luck* (3–5). Illus. by Valeria Docampo. 2013, Philomel $14.99 (978-039916254-1). 218pp. Fourth grader Penelope learns important lessons about her need to always be people's favorite and the redeeming power of love and forgiveness after she alienates all her friends and family in this third installment of the series. e Lexile 760 (Rev: BLO 9/1/13; SLJ 8/13)

7669 Talbott, Hudson. *Safari Journal* (3–6). Illus. by author. 2003, Harcourt $18.00 (978-0-15-216393-8). 64pp. Twelve-year-old Carey is not happy when his aunt drags him off for a two-week safari in East Africa, but once he arrives he is enchanted by the new people, customs, and sights and records them all in his diary. (Rev: HBG 10/03; SLJ 4/03)

7670 Tarshis, Lauren. *Emma-Jean Lazarus Fell in Love* (5–7). 2009, Dial $16.99 (978-0-8037-3321-3). 176pp. Emma-Jean is a bright 7th-grader who applies logic even to matters of the heart. (Rev: BL 5/15/09; SLJ 7/09)

7671 Tashjian, Janet. *My Life as a Book* (4–7). Illus. by Jake Tashjian. 2010, Henry Holt $16.99 (978-0-8050-8903-5). 224pp. Derek spends a summer at reading camp and, to his surprise, learns to love books. A sequel is *My Life As a Cartoonist* (2013), in which Derek and fellow cartoonist Umberto have a difficult relationship. (Rev: BL 8/10*; LMC 8–9/10; SLJ 8/10)

7672 Thomas, Frances. *Polly's Absolutely Worst Birthday Ever* (2–4). 2003, Delacorte $14.95 (978-0-385-73025-9). 96pp. In her diary, 9-year-old Polly confides in detail the disappointments and triumphs of her life. (Rev: BL 7/03; HBG 10/03; SLJ 11/03)

7673 Timberlake, Amy. *That Girl Lucy Moon* (5–8). 2006, Hyperion $15.99 (978-0-7868-5298-7). When her mother takes off on an extended photography assignment, Lucy Moon is left without her biggest ally in her campaigns for animal rights, social justice, and, now, for the liberation of a sledding hill. (Rev: SLJ 9/06)

7674 Tolan, Stephanie S. *Applewhites at Wit's End* (5–8). 2012, HarperCollins $15.99 (978-006057938-8). 272pp. Facing foreclosure, the eccentric Applewhites decide to turn their rambling property into a retreat for fellow artists; humor and mystery are blended with bouncy action. e Lexile 840L (Rev: BL 5/1/12; SLJ 6/12)

7675 Trueit, Trudi. *Julep O'Toole: What I Really Want to Do Is Direct* (5–7). 2007, Dutton $16.99 (978-0-525-47781-5). Julep auditions for the school play to earn extra English credit but ends up as assistant director in this enjoyable third installment in the series. (Rev: SLJ 6/07)

7676 Tulloch, Richard. *Freaky Stuff* (5–8). Illus. by Shane Nagle. 2007, Walker $16.95 (978-0-8027-9623-3).

Funny illustrations are included in this sequel to *Weird Stuff* (2006), in which Brian is unhappy with a TV series based on his favorite books and the effect the show has on his little brother. (Rev: SLJ 6/07)

7677 Turetsky, Bianca. *The Time-Traveling Fashionista* (5–8). Illus. by Sandra Suy. 2011, Little, Brown $17.99 (978-0-316-10542-2). 260pp. Seventh-grader Louise tries on a vintage dress for the school dance and finds herself whisked back in time — to a glamorous life on the *Titanic*; this first volume in a series includes full-color illustrations of elegant gowns. e Lexile 860L (Rev: BL 4/1/11; HB 3–4/12; SLJ 4/11; VOYA 6/11)

7678 Urban, Linda. *A Crooked Kind of Perfect* (3–5). 2007, Harcourt $16.00 (978-0-15-206007-7). 224pp. Zoe, 10, dreams of becoming a classical pianist and performing at Carnegie Hall, but she settles for the Perfectone D-60 electric organ her father gives her and sets out to succeed on this instrument. (Rev: BCCB 2/08; BL 11/15/07; HB 1/08; SLJ 9/07)

7679 Vail, Rachel. *If You Only Knew* (4–7). Series: Friendship Ring. 1998, Scholastic paper $14.95 (978-0-590-03370-1). In this book shaped like a CD, Zoe Grandon, a 7th grader, gives up a boy she likes to pursue a friendship. (Rev: BCCB 10/98; BL 10/15/98; HBG 3/99; SLJ 10/98; VOYA 6/99)

7680 Vail, Rachel. *Justin Case: School, Drool, and Other Daily Disasters* (3–5). Illus. by Matthew Cordell. 2010, Feiwel & Friends $16.99 (978-0-312-53290-1). 256pp. Third-grader Justin shares in his diary his worries about coping at school and at home (making friends, gym class, his self-confident younger sister, his beloved stuffed animal). (Rev: BL 3/1/10; LMC 5–6/10; SLJ 5/1/10)

7681 Vail, Rachel. *Not That I Care* (4–7). Series: Friendship Ring. 1998, Scholastic paper $14.95 (978-0-590-03476-0). For a classroom presentation on 10 items that reveal who you are, Morgan Miller remembers crucial incidents in her life but, in her final report, glosses over the truth. (Rev: BCCB 12/98; BL 11/15/98; HBG 3/99; SLJ 12/98; VOYA 6/99)

7682 Vail, Rachel. *Please, Please, Please* (4–7). Series: Friendship Ring. 1998, Scholastic paper $14.95 (978-0-590-00327-8). CJ Hurley has to overcome a controlling mother in order to hang out with her friends in this book shaped like a CD. (Rev: BCCB 10/98; BL 10/15/98; HBG 3/99; SLJ 12/98; VOYA 6/99)

7683 Van Draanen, Wendelin. *Flipped* (5–8). 2001, Knopf $14.95 (978-0-375-81174-6). In 2nd grade Julianna was infatuated with Bryce, but now, six years later, the situation is reversed in this story told from each viewpoint in alternating chapters. (Rev: BCCB 1/02; BL 12/15/01; HBG 3/02; SLJ 11/01*; VOYA 12/01)

7684 Van Tol, Alex. *Oracle* (5–8). Series: Orca Currents. 2012, Orca LB $16.95 (978-1-4598-0133-2); paper $9.95 (978-1-4598-0132-5). 128pp. Fourteen-year-old Owen is upset that Kamryn has a crush on his older brother, and sets out to win her himself with the aid of an advice Web site he creates; for reluctant readers. e Lexile 410L (Rev: BLO 10/15/12; SLJ 3/13; VOYA 2/13)

7685 Vaupel, Robin. *My Contract with Henry* (5–8). 2003, Holiday $16.95 (978-0-8234-1701-8). An 8th-grade Thoreau project brings a group of outsider students together as they learn about the environment, the simple life, and each other. (Rev: BL 7/03; HBG 10/03; SLJ 7/03; VOYA 10/03)

7686 Vernick, Audrey. *Water Balloon* (4–7). 2011, Clarion $16.99 (978-0-547-59554-2). 310pp. Thirteen-year-old Marley is having a tough summer — her parents have separated and she must move into her father's home; her friends seem to have changed — until she meets a new boy who offers friendship and maybe more. **e** Lexile 630L (Rev: SLJ 10/1/11*; VOYA 10/11)

7687 Viau, Nancy. *Samantha Hansen Has Rocks in Her Head* (3–6). Illus. by LeUyen Pham. 2008, Abrams $15.95 (978-0-8109-7299-5). 178pp. Samantha, a 10-year-old with a passion for science and rocks in particular, struggles to master her temper so that her mother will take her on a trip to the Grand Canyon. (Rev: LMC 3/09; SLJ 3/09)

7688 Wallace, Karen. *Something Slimy on Primrose Drive* (2–4). Illus. by Helen Flook. 2006, Stone Arch LB $22.60 (978-1-59889-113-3). 65pp. Pearl Wolfbane hopes life will become more normal when her Munsters-like family moves to Primrose Drive, but her new, conservative neighbors surprise her when they all join forces to track down a thief. (Rev: BL 11/15/06)

7689 Walters, Eric. *Tagged* (4–6). 2013, Orca LB $16.95 (978-145980168-4); paper $9.95 (9781459801677). 136pp. A high-interest/low-reading-level tale about teen street artists in conflict with the town fathers. **e** Lexile 650 (Rev: BL 6/13; LMC 10/13)

7690 Warner, Sally. *It's Only Temporary* (5–7). Illus. by author. 2008, Viking $15.99 (978-0-670-06111-2). With sketches and lists, 12-year-old Skye reviews her problems in her journal when she is sent to live with her grandmother after her brother has a bad accident. (Rev: BL 6/1–15/08; SLJ 8/08)

7691 Watson, Stephanie. *Elvis and Olive* (3–5). 2008, Scholastic $15.99 (978-0-545-03183-7). 205pp. Dependable Natalie, 10, and an unruly new girl called Annie become friends despite their differences, rename themselves Olive and Elvis, and spend the summer spying on their neighbors with predictably unhappy results. (Rev: BL 4/1/08; SLJ 4/08)

7692 Waysman, Dvora. *Back of Beyond: A Bar Mitzvah Journey* (5–7). 1996, Pitspopany paper $4.95 (978-0-943706-54-2). On a trip to Australia, a 12-year-old Jewish boy becomes involved in the Aborigine culture and witnesses a ritual of manhood similar to a bar mitzvah. (Rev: SLJ 5/96)

7693 Weatherford, Carole Boston. *Princeville: The 500-Year Flood* (3–5). Illus. by Douglas Alvord. 2001, Coastal Carolina LB $14.95 (978-1-928556-32-9). 32pp. An African American family in North Carolina is forced to leave home as the waters caused by Hurricane Floyd rise. (Rev: BL 2/15/02)

7694 Wedekind, Annie. *A Horse of Her Own* (5–7). 2008, Feiwel & Friends $16.95 (978-0-312-36927-9). At horse camp, Jane is surrounded by girls who come from wealthy families and who have horses of their own, a fact that bothers her until she wins an important competition. (Rev: BL 5/15/08; SLJ 8/08)

7695 Wells, Rosemary, and Secundino Fernandez. *My Havana: Memories of a Cuban Boyhood* (3–5). Illus. by Peter Ferguson. 2010, Candlewick $17.99 (978-0-7636-4305-8). 72pp. This fictionalized account of the life of Cuban architect Secundino Fernandez captures the uncertainty and upheaval he faced as he moved from Cuba to Spain, back to Cuba, and then — fleeing the Castro regime in the late 1950s — to New York. (Rev: BL 8/10; SLJ 9/1/10)

7696 Wells, Tina. *The Secret Crush* (4–8). Illus. by Michael Segawa. Series: Mackenzie Blue. 2010, HarperCollins $10.99 (978-0-06-158311-7). 226pp. Seventh-grader Mackenzie Blue hopes to catch the attention of cute Landon, and the school's forthcoming rock-and-roll musical seems a good opportunity. **e** (Rev: SLJ 5/10)

7697 Weston, Carol. *Ava and Pip* (4–6). 2014, Sourcebooks/Jabberwocky $15.99 (978-140228870-8). 224pp. Ava and Pip both love words, but Ava's word skills — used in an effort to protect shy Pip — end up getting her into trouble. **e** Lexile 720 (Rev: BL 3/1/14; LMC 10/14; SLJ 3/14)

7698 Weston, Carol. *Melanie in Manhattan* (3–6). 2005, Knopf LB $17.99 (978-0-375-93028-7). 266pp. Romance — with Miguel, who is coming from Spain to visit — and friendship with Cecily preoccupy the thoughts of fifth grader Melanie. (Rev: SLJ 1/05)

7699 Weyn, Suzanne. *Empty* (5–8). 2010, Scholastic $17.99 (978-054517278-3). 192pp. In this dystopian story, three teens struggle to survive in a world thrown into chaos by global warming and lack of petroleum. (Rev: BL 10/15/10; LMC 3–4/11; SLJ 1/1/11)

7700 Wight, Eric. *Frankie Pickle and the Pine Run 3000* (2–4). Illus. by author. 2010, Simon & Schuster $9.99 (978-1-4169-6485-8). 112pp. When Frankie doesn't do well enough at knot-tying to qualify for the Possum Scout badge, he tries his hand at model car racing instead. Lexile 600L (Rev: BL 2/1/10; SLJ 2/1/10)

7701 Wiles, Deborah. *The Aurora County All-Stars* (4–6). 2007, Harcourt $16.00 (978-0-15-206068-8). 272pp. Among other worries, 12-year-old House Jackson, captain of the Aurora County All-Stars, faces a conflict between his big game and a July 4th pageant in this humorous novel set in the same small Mississippi town as *Love, Ruby Lavender* (2001) and *Each Little Bird That Sings* (2005). (Rev: BCCB 12/07; BL 9/1/07; HB 9/07; SLJ 10/07) ∩

7702 Williams, Maiya. *The Fizzy Whiz Kid* (5–8). 2010, Abrams $16.95 (978-081098347-2). 288pp. Suddenly plunked down among the children of movie stars, producers, and makeup artists, midwesterner Mitchell wins over his new classmates when he lands a spot in a TV commercial. **e** (Rev: BL 3/1/10; SLJ 5/10)

7703 Wilson, Jacqueline. *Candyfloss* (4–7). Illus. by Nick Sharratt. 2007, Roaring Brook $14.95 (978-1-59643-241-3). Flossie, busy helping her divorced dad at his restaurant while her mother and stepfather are in Australia, must also deal with old and new friends at school in this story set in England. (Rev: BL 10/1/07; HB 9–10/07; LMC 11/07; SLJ 9/07)

7704 Winerip, Michael. *Adam Canfield of the Slash* (4–7). 2005, Candlewick $15.99 (978-0-7636-2340-1). As editors of the *Slash*, the Harris Elementary/Middle School student newspaper, Adam and Jennifer chase scoops and tackle ethical questions. (Rev: BL 5/1/05; SLJ 3/05)

7705 Winerip, Michael. *Adam Canfield, Watch Your Back!* (5–8). Series: Adam Canfield. 2007, Candlewick $15.99 (978-0-7636-2341-8). Adam of *Adam Canfield of the Slash* has even more on his plate in this sequel: writing for the school newspaper, exposing an unfair science fair, and even facing down high school muggers. (Rev: BL 4/1/08; SLJ 12/07)

7706 Winston, Sherri. *The Kayla Chronicles* (5–9). 2008, Little, Brown $16.99 (978-0-316-11430-1). African American Kayla alienates her friend Rosalie when she joins her Florida high school's hip-hop dance team. (Rev: BL 2/1/08; SLJ 4/08)

7707 Winters, Ben H. *The Secret Life of Ms. Finkleman* (5–8). 2010, HarperCollins $16.99 (978-0-06-196541-8). 256pp. Brainy 7th-grader Bethesda investigates her music teacher and uncovers an unsuspected past as a punk rocker, resulting in an unusual school concert. Lexile 910L (Rev: BL 11/15/10; LMC 3–4/11; SLJ 11/1/10)

7708 Wise, Rachel. *Read All About It!* (5–7). Series: Dear Know-It-All. 2012, Simon & Schuster paper $5.99 (978-14424440-2-7). 176pp. Seventh-grade Samantha is thrilled to be named the school newspaper's advice columnist but less happy to realize that her best friend Hailey is crushing on Sam's own romantic target. ❧ (Rev: BLO 6/12; LMC 1–2/13)

7709 Wittlinger, Ellen. *Gracie's Girl* (4–7). 2000, Simon & Schuster $16.95 (978-0-689-82249-0). Bess and her best friend Ethan, both middle schoolers, get involved with a homeless old lady. (Rev: BCCB 2/01; BL 9/15/00; HBG 3/01; SLJ 11/00; VOYA 10/01)

7710 Wolitzer, Meg. *The Fingertips of Duncan Dorfman* (5–8). 2011, Dutton $16.99 (978-0-525-42304-1). 256pp. Three middle-school students learn about themselves as they spend time at the Youth Scrabble Tournament. ALA Notable Children's Book 2012. ❧ (Rev: BL 9/15/11; LMC 1–2–12; SLJ 9/1/11)

7711 Woods, Brenda. *Saint Louis Armstrong Beach* (4–7). 2011, Penguin $16.99 (978-0-399-25507-6). 144pp. When Hurricane Katrina arrives, 12-year-old clarinet-playing Saint Louis Armstrong Beach makes plans to get the dog he loves, Shadow, to safety. ❧ Lexile 660L (Rev: BL 11/15/11; HB 11–12/11; LMC 1–2/12*; SLJ 10/1/11*)

7712 Woodson, Jacqueline. *Feathers* (4–6). 2007, Putnam $15.99 (978-0-399-23989-2). 118pp. When a white boy joins Frannie's 1971 sixth-grade class, and is sometimes

called the "Jesus Boy," Frannie examines her own faith and the problems in her home. Newbery Medal, 2008. (Rev: BL 11/15/06; SLJ 4/07*)

7713 Wynne-Jones, Tim. *Rex Zero, King of Nothing* (4–6). 2008, Farrar $16.95 (978-0-374-36259-1). In early 1960s Ottawa, 6th-grader Rex struggles with a mean teacher, a father with postwar terrors, and several puzzling mysteries. (Rev: BL 3/15/08; HB 3/08; SLJ 5/08)

7714 Wynne-Jones, Tim. *Rex Zero: The Great Pretender* (4–7). Series: Rex Zero. 2010, Farrar $16.99 (978-0-374-36260-7). 224pp. Rex, now 12, is unhappy that his family has moved across town yet determined to start middle school with his old friends, however difficult that may be; set in 1963 Ottawa against a backdrop of civil rights turmoil. ❧ Lexile 610L (Rev: BL 12/1/10; HB 11–12/10; SLJ 10/1/10)

7715 Yee, Lisa. *Warp Speed* (4–7). 2011, Scholastic $16.99 (978-0-545-12276-4). 320pp. Marley, a shy wallflower geek who loves Star Trek and suffers bullying, must chart a new course for himself when his speed and agility catch the coach's eye and Marley becomes a star athlete. Lexile HL620L (Rev: BL 2/15/11; HB 3–4/11; SLJ 5/11)

Adventure and Mystery

7716 Abela, Deborah. *Mission: The Nightmare Vortex* (4–6). Illus. by George O'Connor. Series: Spy Force. 2005, Simon & Schuster $9.95 (978-0-689-87359-1). Eleven-year-old Max Remy and her best friend Linden, Spy Force agents, spring into action to foil the evil plans of Mr. Blue to activate a dormant volcano and destroy all the spies at a secret awards ceremony. (Rev: HBG 4/06; SLJ 4/06)

7717 Abrahams, Peter. *Into the Dark* (5–12). Series: Echo Falls. 2008, HarperCollins $15.99 (978-0-06-073708-5). Ingrid's grandfather, a World War II veteran, is a suspect in a murder committed using a World War II-era rifle. Can Ingrid solve the mystery and clear her grandfather's name? (Rev: BL 5/1/08; SLJ 3/08)

7718 Adam, Paul. *Max Cassidy: Escape from Shadow Island* (5–9). 2009, HarperCollins $16.99 (978-0-06-186323-3). 295pp. Max Cassidy, a British 14-year-old escape artist who still performs despite the fact that his mother is accused of murdering his father; sets out to prove her innocence in this fast-paced novel full of tension. (Rev: SLJ 4/10; VOYA 4/10)

7719 Adams, W. Royce. *Me and Jay* (5–8). 2001, Rairarubia paper $10.99 (978-1-58832-021-6). Two 13-year-olds meet with trouble at every turn when they venture into forbidden territory in search of a hidden pond. (Rev: BL 1/1–15/02)

7720 Adler, David A. *Andy Russell, NOT Wanted by the Police* (3–5). Illus. by Leanne Franson. 2001, Harcourt $14.00 (978-0-15-216474-4). Andy and Tamika solve the mystery of an intruder at a neighbor's house in this beginning chapter book. (Rev: BL 1/1–15/02; HBG 3/02; SLJ 1/02)

7721 Adler, David A. *Cam Jansen and the Birthday Mystery* (2–4). Illus. 2000, Viking $13.99 (978-0-670-88877-1). In this beginning chapter book, Cam, with her photographic memory, solves the mystery of who stole her grandparents' luggage at the airport. (Rev: BL 11/1/00; HBG 3/01; SLJ 1/01)

7722 Adler, David A. *Cam Jansen and the First Day of School Mystery* (2–4). Illus. by Susanna Natti. 2002, Viking $13.99 (978-0-670-03575-5). 64pp. Cam's great memory comes into play when her teacher is arrested and taken away on the first day of school. (Rev: BL 12/1/02; HBG 3/03; SLJ 1/03)

7723 Adler, David A. *Cam Jansen and the School Play Mystery* (2–4). Illus. 2001, Viking $14.99 (978-0-670-89280-8). 64pp. Readers already familiar with Cam's exploits will enjoy this story in which Cam uses her photographic memory to solve the mystery of the missing admission money while her friends act onstage in a play about Honest Abe. (Rev: BL 8/01; HBG 3/02; SLJ 1/02)

7724 Adler, David A. *Cam Jansen and the Secret Service Mystery* (2–4). Illus. by Susanna Natti. 2006, Viking $13.99 (978-0-670-06092-4). When the pearls belonging to a school donor are stolen, Cam Jansen, girl detective, teams up with the Secret Service to try to track them down. (Rev: BL 10/15/06; HBG 4/07)

7725 Adler, David A. *Cam Jansen and the Tennis Trophy Mystery* (2–4). Illus. by Susanna Natti. Series: Cam Jansen. 2003, Viking $13.99 (978-0-670-03643-1). In this 23rd adventure for young detective Cam Jansen, a teacher falls under suspicion in the theft of a tennis trophy. (Rev: HBG 4/04; SLJ 3/04)

7726 Adler, David A. *Cam Jansen and the Valentine Baby Mystery* (2–4). Illus. by Susanna Natti. Series: Cam Jansen. 2005, Viking $13.99 (978-0-670-06009-2). 80pp. Girl detective Cam Jansen and her friend Eric investigate the disappearance of Eric's mother's purse from a hospital waiting room; the 25th installment in this popular series. (Rev: BL 1/1–15/06; HBG 4/06)

7727 Adler, David A. *Cam Jansen: The Summer Camp Mysteries* (3–5). Illus. by Joy Allen. 2007, Viking $13.99 (978-0-670-06218-8); Penguin paper $4.99 (978-0-14-240742-4). Cam sleuthes her way through three separate summer camp cases, including the mystery of the missing snack money. (Rev: BL 5/15/07)

7728 Aguiar, Nadia. *Secrets of Tamarind* (5–8). 2011, Feiwel & Friends $16.99 (978-0-312-38030-4). 384pp. The Nelson children first seen in *The Lost Island of Tamarind* (2008) return to the magical island to save it from environmental disaster in this blend of adventure and fantasy. e Lexile 860L (Rev: BL 7/11; SLJ 9/1/11)

7729 Aiken, Joan. *Midwinter Nightingale* (5–8). Series: Wolves Chronicles. 2003, Delacorte $15.95 (978-0-385-73081-5). Dido Twite and Simon, Duke of Battersea, continue their adventures in this eighth installment in the series, protecting a dying king, searching for a miss-

ing coronet, and defeating an evil baron. (Rev: BL 6/1–15/03; HBG 10/03; SLJ 6/03)

7730 Alexander, Lloyd. *The Golden Dreams of Carlo Chuchio* (5–8). 2007, Henry Holt $17.95 (978-0-8050-8333-0). The final book by the late Alexander takes Carlo along the Road of Golden Dreams in search of treasure. (Rev: BCCB 10/07; BL 7/07; HB 9–10/07; LMC 2/08; SLJ 8/07)

7731 Alexander, Lloyd. *The Xanadu Adventure* (5–8). 2005, Button $16.99 (978-0-525-47371-8). Vesper Holly, accompanied by friends and guardians, sets off for Asia Minor to search for an artifact in the ancient city of Troy but soon finds herself in the clutches of her nemesis, Dr. Desmond Helvitius. (Rev: BL 2/1/05*; SLJ 2/05)

7732 Allison, Jennifer. *The Bones of the Holy* (5–8). Series: Gilda Joyce Psychic Investigator. 2011, Dutton $16.99 (978-052542212-9). 288pp. Teen sleuth Gilda uses her perceptive powers to investigate a spooky and sinister past her mother's prospective new husband seems to be hiding. ∩ (Rev: BL 5/1/11; SLJ 6/12)

7733 Allison, Jennifer. *Gilda Joyce: Psychic Investigator* (5–7). 2005, Dutton $13.99 (978-0-525-47375-6). Thirteen-year-old Gilda Joyce and a new friend, Juliet, look into the suicide of Juliet's aunt in this richly layered mystery. (Rev: BL 5/1/05*; SLJ 7/05*)

7734 Allison, Jennifer. *Gilda Joyce: The Ghost Sonata* (5–8). 2007, Dutton $15.99 (978-0-525-47808-9). Gilda's psychic abilities come in handy as she accompanies her friend Wendy to a piano competition in England and discovers that Wendy is being haunted. ∩ (Rev: SLJ 8/07)

7735 Allison, Jennifer. *Gilda Joyce: The Ladies of the Lake* (5–8). 2006, Dutton $16.99 (978-0-525-47693-1). Thirteen-year-old Gilda Joyce — introduced in *Gilda Joyce: Psychic Investigator* (2005) — uses all her psychic abilities to unravel the mystery surrounding a drowning death at her school. (Rev: BL 10/15/06; HBG 4/07; SLJ 9/06)

7736 Almond, David. *The Boy Who Swam with Piranhas* (4–6). Illus. by Oliver Jeffers. 2013, Candlewick $15.99 (978-076366169-4). 256pp. Orphaned Stanley Potts runs away to the circus where Pancho Pirelli, the man who swims with piranhas, takes him under his wing and tries to introduce him to new ideas. Lexile 550 (Rev: BL 10/1/13*; HB 9–10/13; LMC 3–4/14; SLJ 10/13)

7737 Anastasio, Dina. *The Case of the Glacier Park Swallow* (4–7). 1994, Roberts Rinehart paper $6.95 (978-1-879373-85-3). Juliet, who wants to be a veterinarian, stumbles upon a drug-smuggling ring in this tightly knit mystery. (Rev: BL 12/1/94; SLJ 10/94)

7738 Anastasio, Dina. *The Case of the Grand Canyon Eagle* (5–8). Series: Juliet Stone Environmental Mystery. 1994, Roberts Rinehart paper $6.95 (978-1-879373-84-6). In this ecological mystery, 17-year-old Juliet Stone investigates the disappearance of eagle eggs. (Rev: SLJ 10/94)

7739 Anderson, M. T. *The Clue of the Linoleum Lederhosen: M. T. Anderson's Thrilling Tales* (4–7). Illus. by

Kurt Cyrus. 2006, Harcourt $15.00 (978-0-15-205352-9). Jasper Dash, Boy Technonaut, Katie, and Lily are caught up in an exciting mystery at Moose Tongue Lodge in this zany sequel to *Whales on Stilts* (2005). ∩ (Rev: BCCB 7–8/06; BL 5/1/06*; HB 5–6/06; HBG 10/06; SLJ 6/06; VOYA 6/06)

7740 Anderson, M. T. *Whales on Stilts!* (5–7). 2005, Harcourt $15.00 (978-0-15-205340-6). Twelve-year-old Lily Gefelty enlists the help of two friends to foil a plan to take over the world using an army of mind-controlled whales on stilts; a fast-paced adventure full of tongue-in-cheek fun. (Rev: BL 2/15/05*; SLJ 5/05)

7741 Andrews, Jan. *When Apples Grew Noses and White Horses Flew: Tales of Ti-Jean* (2–6). Illus. by Dusan Petricic. 2011, Groundwood $16.95 (978-0-88899-952-8). 70pp. Canadian folk hero Ti-Jean is featured in three comic tales of trickery, valor, and disguise. (Rev: HB 7–8/11; LMC 10/11; SLJ 8/11)

7742 Angleberger, Tom. *Horton Halfpott, or, The Fiendish Mystery of Smugwick Manor, or, The Loosening of M'Lady Luggertuck's Corset* (3–6). Illus. by author. 2011, Abrams $14.95 (978-0-8109-9715-8). 224pp. In 19th-century England a kitchen boy named Horton becomes embroiled in romance and mystery when a diamond is stolen at Smugwick Manor. ∩ ℮ (Rev: BL 5/1/11; LMC 8–9/11; SLJ 6/11)

7743 Arrigan, Mary. *Rabbit Girl* (4–6). 2011, Frances Lincoln paper $8.95 (978-18478015-6-2). 224pp. A mysterious portrait ties Mallie Kelly to the era in which it was drawn — London during the blitz — in this quirky novel that brings past and present together. (Rev: BL 1/1/12; SLJ 2/12)

7744 Avi. *Captain Grey* (5–8). 1993, Morrow paper $4.95 (978-0-688-12234-8). In 1783, young Kevin is captured by pirates. A reissue.

7745 Avi. *Murder at Midnight* (5–8). 2009, Scholastic $17.99 (978-0-545-08090-3). 272pp. In this compelling companion to *Midnight Magic* (2009) set in Italy in 1490, Mangus the magician and his young servant Fabrizio race against the clock as they strive to uncover a traitor. ∩ (Rev: BL 8/09; LMC 1–2/10; SLJ 10/09)

7746 Avi. *Who Stole the Wizard of Oz?* (4–6). Illus. by Derek James. 1990, McKay paper $4.99 (978-0-394-84992-8). 128pp. Several books disappear from the Chickertown Library book sale.

7747 Avi. *Windcatcher* (4–7). 1991, Avon paper $4.99 (978-0-380-71805-4). Eleven-year-old Tony dreads a summer by the sea, but ends up finding a sailing adventure. (Rev: BCCB 5/91; BL 3/1/91; HB 5–6/91; SLJ 4/91)

7748 Baccalario, Pierdomenico. *The Door to Time* (4–6). Illus. by Iacopo Bruno. Series: Ulysses Moore. 2006, Scholastic $12.99 (978-0-439-77438-3). 240pp. After moving to a home on the English coast, Jason and Julia, 11-year-old twins, along with a new friend, try to unravel the mysteries surrounding their new house. (Rev: BL 12/15/05; SLJ 1/06)

7749 Baccalario, Pierdomenico. *Star of Stone* (5–9). Trans. from Italian by Leah D. Janeczko. Series: Century Quartet. 2010, Random House $16.99 (978-0-375-85896-3); LB $19.99 (978-0-375-95896-0). 304pp. Harvey, Elettra, Mistral, and Sheng are led all around Manhattan by tricky clues left by an eccentric professor in this action-packed sequel to *Ring of Fire* (2009). Also use *City of Wind* (2011). ∩ ℮ (Rev: SLJ 11/1/10)

7750 Balliett, Blue. *Chasing Vermeer* (5–8). Illus. by Brett Helquist. 2004, Scholastic $16.95 (978-0-439-37294-7). Petra and Calder, brainy 12-year-old classmates at the University of Chicago Lab School, join forces to find out what happened to a missing Vermeer painting. (Rev: BL 4/1/04*; HB 7–8/04; SLJ 7/04)

7751 Balliett, Blue. *The Danger Box* (5–7). 2010, Scholastic $16.99 (978-0-439-85209-8). 320pp. When isolated, myopic Zoomy, 12, receives a mysterious box of "treasures" from his alcoholic father, curious things begin to happen. ∩ ℮ Lexile 750L (Rev: BL 10/1/10; LMC 3–4/11; SLJ 9/1/10*)

7752 Balliett, Blue. *Hold Fast* (4–7). 2013, Scholastic $17.99 (978-0-545-29988-6). 288pp. When her father disappears, 11-year-old Early, her mother, and her younger brother can no longer afford their South Side Chicago one-room apartment and must move to a homeless shelter while Early investigates the mystery. ∩ ℮ Lexile 780L (Rev: BL 1/13*; LMC 10/13; SLJ 4/13*)

7753 Bancks, Tristan. *Mac Slater vs. the City* (5–8). 2011, Simon & Schuster $15.99 (978-1-4169-8576-1). 192pp. Eighth-grader Mac and his friend Paul are excited to travel to New York City to compete in a Coolhunter competition but find more challenges than expected. (Rev: BLO 3/25/11; SLJ 4/11)

7754 Barnett, Mac. *The Case of the Case of Mistaken Identity* (4–6). Illus. by Adam Rex. Series: Brixton Brothers. 2009, Simon & Schuster $14.99 (978-1-4169-7815-2). 192pp. Twelve-year-old gumshoe Steve Brixton gets mixed up with a ring of undercover crime-fighting librarians as he hunts for an invaluable quilt in this funny series opener. ∩ Lexile 590L (Rev: BL 10/15/09; LMC 11–12/09; SLJ 3/10)

7755 Barnett, Mac. *Danger Goes Berserk* (4–6). Illus. by Matthew Myers. Series: Brixton Brothers. 2012, Simon & Schuster $14.99 (978-144243977-1). 256pp. A humorous mystery featuring 12-year-old Steve Brixton and his friend Dana as they struggle to resolve several cases. ℮ Lexile 620L (Rev: BL 11/1/12)

7756 Barnett, Mac. *The Ghostwriter Secret* (3–6). Illus. by Adam Rex. Series: Brixton Brothers. 2010, Simon & Schuster $14.99 (978-1-4169-7817-6). 240pp. Detective agency operator Steve Brixton, 12, becomes embroiled in a kidnapping scheme when he sets out in search of his hero, mystery author MacArthur Bart. ∩ ℮ Lexile 690L (Rev: SLJ 12/1/10)

7757 Barnett, Mac. *It Happened on a Train* (4–6). Illus. by Adam Rex. Series: Brixton Brothers. 2011, Simon & Schuster $15.99 (978-141697819-0). 288pp. Seventh-grader Steve Brixton's short-lived retirement from sleuthing is interrupted when he discovers a mystery on a train trip through California. (Rev: BL 11/1/11)

7758 Barrett, Tracy. *The Beast of Blackslope* (4–6). Series: Sherlock Files. 2009, Holt $15.95 (978-0-8050-8341-5). 160pp. Xander and Xena Holmes are in England and investigate a mysterious beast in the woods, with some help from their ancestor Sherlock's files. (Rev: BLO 4/23/09; SLJ 6/09)

7759 Barrett, Tracy. *The Case That Time Forgot* (4–6). Series: Sherlock Files. 2010, Henry Holt $15.99 (978-0-8050-8046-9). 160pp. Xena and Xander, descendants of Sherlock himself, help a classmate called Karim to find an ancient Egyptian amulet in this story full of modern technology and old-fashioned codes and sleuthing. ∩ ℮ Lexile 700L (Rev: BL 5/1/10; SLJ 7/10)

7760 Barrett, Tracy. *The 100-Year-Old Secret* (4–6). Series: Sherlock Files. 2008, Holt $15.95 (978-0-8050-8340-8). 160pp. Arriving in London from Florida, 12-year-old Xena Holmes and her younger brother Xander discover they are descendants of Sherlock Holmes and receive his notebook of unsolved cases. (Rev: BL 5/1/08; LMC 3/09; SLJ 6/08)

7761 Base, Graeme. *Enigma: A Magical Mystery* (2–4). Illus. by author. 2008, Abrams $19.95 (978-0-8109-7245-2). 48pp. A retirement home for magicians is the setting for this mystery story that asks readers to participate as Bertie Badger sets off to find stolen magic props; a fold-out decoder appears in the back of the book. (Rev: BL 10/1/08; SLJ 11/08)

7762 Beauregard, Lynda. *In Search of the Fog Zombie: A Mystery About Matter* (3–5). Illus. by Der-shing Helmer. Series: Summer Camp Science Mysteries. 2012, Lerner LB $29.27 (978-076135689-9); paper $6.95 (978-076138544-8). 48pp. Science and mystery are combined in this graphic novel set in a summer camp (with a rumored zombie) and including information about solids, liquids, gases, and so forth. ℮ (Rev: BL 3/15/12; SLJ 5/1/12)

7763 Beil, Michael D. *The Mistaken Masterpiece* (5–8). Series: The Red Blazer Girls. 2011, Knopf $16.99 (978-0-375-86740-8); LB $19.99 (978-0-375-96740-5). 320pp. The Red Blazer Girls are asked to investigate the ownership of a family heirloom, and discover more than they bargained for. ∩ ℮ (Rev: BL 5/1/11; SLJ 8/11)

7764 Beil, Michael D. *The Red Blazer Girls: The Ring of Rocamadour* (5–8). 2009, Knopf $15.99 (978-0-375-84814-8). 304pp. In this snappy title, a quirky bunch of schoolgirls from St. Veronica's in Manhattan attempt to solve a mystery while also dealing with almost-boyfriends and other daily challenges. (Rev: BL 1/1–15/09*; SLJ 6/09)

7765 Beil, Michael D. *Summer at Forsaken Lake* (4–6). 2012, Knopf $16.99 (978-037586742-2); LB $19.99 (978-037596742-9). 256pp. While spending a summer at the cabin his dad vacationed at as a kid, Nicholas, 12, learns to sail and uncovers some mysterious happenings with his twin sisters and a cute new friend called Charlie. ∩ Lexile 770 (Rev: BL 8/12; SLJ 6/12; VOYA 4/12)

7766 Beil, Michael D. *The Vanishing Violin* (5–8). Series: The Red Blazer Girls. 2010, Knopf $16.99 (978-0-375-86103-1); LB $19.99 (978-0-375-96103-8). 336pp. The four Red Blazer Girls — Sophie, Margaret, Becca, and Leigh Ann — must solve various violin-related mysteries at St. Veronica's School. ∩ ℮ (Rev: BL 7/10; SLJ 8/10)

7767 Berlin, Eric. *The Potato Chip Puzzles* (4–7). Series: The Puzzling World of Winston Breen. 2009, Putnam $16.99 (978-0-399-25198-6). 244pp. Winston and his friends compete to win $50,000 for their school by solving puzzles. Brainteasers throughout the story will entertain readers. (Rev: BL 5/1/09; SLJ 8/09)

7768 Berlin, Eric. *The Puzzling World of Winston Breen* (4–6). 2007, Putnam $16.99 (978-0-399-24693-7). 224pp. Puzzle fan Winston Breen, 12, and his younger sister Kate find themselves embroiled in a group treasure hunt in this mystery story full of brainteasers to solve along the way. (Rev: BCCB 11/07; BL 11/15/07; LMC 11/07; SLJ 11/07)

7769 Biedrzycki, David. *Ace Lacewing: Bug Detective* (2–4). Illus. 2005, Charlesbridge $15.95 (978-1-57091-569-7). 40pp. Full of funny wordplay and cartoon-style art, this is the story of bug detective Ace Lacewing's efforts to find the missing Queenie Bee. Also use *Bad Bugs Are My Business* (2009). (Rev: BL 9/1/05; SLJ 8/05)

7770 Black, Holly. *Doll Bones* (5–8). Illus. by Eliza Wheeler. 2013, Simon & Schuster $16.99 (978-141696398-1). 256pp. Friends Poppy, Alice, and Zach, who have long enjoyed playing together with dolls and action figures, find themselves on a real-life mission to bury a doll that contains a girl's bones. Newbery Honor 2014; Booklist Editors' Choice: Books for Youth; ALA Notable Children's Book. ∩ ℮ Lexile 840L (Rev: BL 3/1/13*; HB 7–8/13; LMC 10/13*; SLJ 6/13*)

7771 Bledsoe, Lucy Jane. *The Antarctic Scoop* (4–7). 2003, Holiday House $16.95 (978-0-8234-1792-6). In this fast-paced adventure story, 12-year-old Victoria, a shy girl with ambitious dreams, wins a trip to Antarctica but discovers during her travels that the real goal of the contest sponsor is to develop and exploit the icy continent. (Rev: BL 1/1–15/04; SLJ 1/04)

7772 Bloor, Edward. *Taken* (5–8). 2007, Knopf $16.99 (978-0-375-83636-7). In Florida in the year 2035, where kidnapping has become a common crime with recognized procedures, 13-year-old Charity must find a way to escape and survive when her wealthy family's payoff to the kidnappers goes wrong. (Rev: BL 9/1/07; SLJ 12/07)

7773 Bodett, Tom. *Williwaw* (5–8). 1999, Random House paper $5.50 (978-0-375-80687-2). The story of two youngsters — 13-year-old September Crane and her 12-year-old brother Ivan — and their life in the wilds of Alaska, where they are often left alone by their fisherman father. (Rev: BCCB 6/99; BL 4/1/99; HBG 10/99; SLJ 5/99)

7774 Boie, Kirsten. *The Princess Plot* (4–8). 2009, Scholastic $17.99 (978-0-545-03220-9). 384pp. Fourteen-year-old Jenna soon realizes her "acting test" assignment — impersonating the princess of a government in dangerous turmoil — involves more than she was told. ∩ (Rev: BCCB 9/09; BLO 5/28/09; SLJ 10/09; VOYA 10/09)

7775 Bonk, John J. *Madhattan Mystery* (5–8). 2012, Walker $16.99 (978-080272349-9). 304pp. Twelve-year-old Lexi and her younger brother Kevin overhear details about stolen jewels while staying in New York City with their aunt; a wild chase through subway tunnels and parks ensues. ⅇ Lexile 790L (Rev: BL 5/1/12*; LMC 10/12; SLJ 5/1/12)

7776 Bosch, Pseudonymous. *The Name of This Book Is Secret* (4–7). 2007, Little, Brown $16.99 (978-0-316-11366-3). What's inside this book is secret, too, and only after much cautioning does the narrator begin to tell the story of a group trying to discover the key to immortality. ∩ (Rev: BL 7/07; SLJ 1/08)

7777 Boyce, Frank Cottrell. *Chitty Chitty Bang Bang Flies Again* (3–6). Illus. by Joe Berger. 2012, Candlewick $15.99 (978-076365957-8). 192pp. In this funny sequel to the original Ian Fleming (1964) story, the 21st-century British Tooting family find themselves owning an aging camper van that suddenly sprouts wings and carries them off to adventure. ⅇ Lexile 710L (Rev: BL 2/1/12; LMC 8–9/12; SLJ 3/12*)

7778 Bracegirdle, P. J. *Fiendish Deeds* (5–7). Series: The Joy of Spooking. 2008, Simon & Schuster $15.99 (978-1-4169-3416-5). 215pp. When 11-year-old Joy learns that there are plans to build a water park on Spooking's bog — where she believes a monster resides — the young fan of horror stories sets out to stop this; the spooky setting and dark humor add to the appeal. (Rev: LMC 3/09; SLJ 3/09)

7779 Bransford, Nathan. *Jacob Wonderbar for President of the Universe* (4–6). Illus. by C. S. Jennings. 2012, Dial $15.99 (978-080373538-5). 224pp. Jacob Wonderbar's bid to be elected president of the universe meets various obstacles including dirty politics and threats to Earth's survival. (Rev: BL 3/15/12; SLJ 6/12)

7780 Brezenoff, Steve. *The Burglar Who Bit the Big Apple* (3–6). Illus. by C. B. Canga. Series: Field Trip Mysteries. 2010, Stone Arch LB $23.99 (978-1-4342-2139-1); paper $5.95 (978-1-4342-2771-3). 88pp. Sixth-grade friends Cat, Sam, Egg, and Gum solve a satisfying mystery while on a class trip to New York City. Also use *The Zombie Who Visited New Orleans* (2010). Lexile 500L (Rev: SLJ 1/1/11)

7781 Brezenoff, Steve. *The Zoo with the Empty Cage* (3–6). Illus. by C. B. Canga. Series: Field Trip Mysteries. 2009, Stone Arch LB $23.99 (978-1-4342-1610-6). 88pp. Edward G. Garrison (Egg) and his friends in the Science Club search for the rare and endangered Island Foxes that have gone missing from the zoo. Also use *The Painting That Wasn't There* (2009). (Rev: LMC 1–2/10; SLJ 2/1/10)

7782 Broach, Elise. *Masterpiece* (3–6). Illus. by Kelly Murphy. 2008, Holt $16.95 (978-0-8050-8270-8).

304pp. A lonely artistic boy and an overprotected artistic beetle become unlikely friends and solve a mystery. (Rev: BL 9/15/08; HB 11/08; LMC 5/09)

7783 Broach, Elise. *Missing on Superstition Mountain* (3–5). Illus. by Antonio Caparo. Series: Superstition Mountain. 2011, Henry Holt $15.99 (978-0-8050-9047-5). 272pp. Fascinated by Superstition Mountain, three young brothers new to Arizona ignore their parents' warnings and investigate; the first volume in a series. (Rev: BL 5/1/11; SLJ 7/11)

7784 Broach, Elise. *Treasure on Superstition Mountain* (3–6). Series: Superstition Mountain. 2012, Henry Holt $15.99 (978-080507763-6). 224pp. This second book in the series finds the Barker brothers and their friend Delilah in danger as they search for gold. ⅇ Lexile 670L (Rev: BLO 11/15/12)

7785 Broad, Michael. *Ghost Diamond!* (2–4). Illus. by author. Series: Agent Amelia. 2011, Darby Creek $22.60 (978-0-7613-8056-6); paper $5.95 (978-0-7613-8060-3). 143pp. Elementary school mastermind Amelia solves three short cases using ingenious gadgetry and always staying one step ahead of her too-curious mother. Also use *Zombie Cows!* (2011). ⅇ (Rev: LMC 3–4/12; SLJ 8/1/11)

7786 Brodien-Jones, Christine. *The Scorpions of Zahir* (5–8). Illus. by Kelly Murphy. 2012, Delacorte $17.99 (978-0-385-73933-7); LB $20.99 (978-0-385-90783-5). 256pp. Archaeologist's daughter Zagora, 11, employs an ancient stone to help restore the ruined city of Zahir, Morocco, in this exciting mix of fantasy and adventure. ⅇ (Rev: BL 8/12; LMC 1–2/13; SLJ 10/12; VOYA 8/12)

7787 Bruchac, Joseph. *Bearwalker* (5–8). Illus. by Sally Wern Comport. 2007, HarperCollins $15.99 (978-0-06-112309-2). Thirteen-year-old Baron, Native American and not as tall as he would like, comes into his own on a class trip to the Adirondacks as he draws on strengths that were not apparent to his classmates. (Rev: BL 9/15/07; SLJ 8/07)

7788 Bruchac, Joseph. *Night Wings* (5–8). Illus. by Sally Wern Comport. 2009, HarperCollins $15.99 (978-0-06-112318-4). 208pp. Indian lore gives this thriller an additional layer of meaning. (Rev: BL 6/1–15/09; SLJ 7/09)

7789 Bruchac, Joseph. *The Return of Skeleton Man* (5–8). Illus. by Sally Wern Comport. 2006, HarperCollins $15.99 (978-0-06-058090-2). Molly, the Mohawk teen who survived a terrifying kidnapping in *Skeleton Man* (2001), discovers her nemesis is back. (Rev: BL 9/15/06; SLJ 8/06)

7790 Buckey, Sarah Masters. *The Stolen Sapphire: A Samantha Mystery* (2–4). Series: American Girl Mysteries. 2006, American Girl paper $6.95 (978-1-59369-099-1). Traveling to Europe on an ocean liner in the early 1900s, Samantha and her adopted sister Nellie try to prove the innocence of their French tutor, who's been accused of stealing a valuable gem. (Rev: SLJ 4/06)

7791 Buckley, Michael. *M Is for Mama's Boy* (4–7). Illus. by Ethen Beavers. Series: NERDS. 2010, Abrams $14.95 (978-0-8109-8986-3). 288pp. The 5th-grade

NERDS team is back to deal with more outrageous behavior by supervillain Simon. 🎧 Lexile 780L (Rev: BL 9/15/10; LMC 1–2/11; SLJ 12/1/10)

7792 Buckley, Michael. *NERDS: National Espionage, Rescue, and Defense Society* (4–7). Illus. by Ethen Beavers. Series: NERDS. 2009, Abrams $14.95 (978-0-8109-4324-7). 306pp. Former cool kid Jackson Jones now finds himself among the school's nerd population, but he soon learns that the unassuming geeks whom he so recently delighted in tormenting are actually members of a top-secret spy ring that is attempting to stop the insidious Dr. Jigsaw from destroying the world. The second and third volumes in the series are *M Is for Mama's Boy* (2010) and *The Cheerleaders of Doom* (2011). 🎧 Lexile 760L (Rev: BL 10/15/09; LMC 1–2/11; SLJ 12/09)

7793 Buckley, Michael. *The Unusual Suspects* (4–6). Illus. by Peter Ferguson. Series: Sisters Grimm. 2005, Abrams $14.95 (978-0-8109-5926-2). 290pp. Sabrina and Daphne Grimm, descendants of Wilhelm and living in a community full of fairy-tale figures, investigate the mysterious death of Sabrina's teacher; a multilayered, fast-paced second installment in the series. Also use *Magic and Other Misdemeanors* (2007). (Rev: SLJ 1/06; VOYA 8/06)

7794 Bullard, Lisa. *Turn Left at the Cow* (4–7). 2013, Harcourt $16.99 (978-054402900-2). 304pp. Thirteen-year-old Travis lives with his mother and stepfather but is curious about his father; he runs away from home and is drawn into a mystery about his father and a bank heist. 🕮 Lexile 850 (Rev: BL 11/1/13; LMC 3–4/14; SLJ 11/13)

7795 Bunting, Eve. *Someone Is Hiding on Alcatraz Island* (5–8). 1986, Berkley paper $5.99 (978-0-425-10294-7). A boy and a young woman ranger are trapped by a gang of thugs on Alcatraz. (Rev: BL 7/88)

7796 Burchette, Jan. *Avalanche Alert* (2–4). Illus. Series: Wild Rescue. 2012, Capstone $23.99 (978-143423772-9). 152pp. In this 7th volume in the series twins Ben and Zoe must reunite a family of snow leopards in the Himalayas. Lexile 650L (Rev: BLO 11/15/12)

7797 Butler, Dori Hillestad. *The Case of the Fire Alarm* (2–4). Illus. by Jeremy Tugeau. Series: The Buddy Files. 2010, Whitman $14.99 (978-080750913-5); paper $4.99 (978-08075093-5-7). 128pp. Buddy happily takes a break from being a therapy dog to solve a mystery in this satisfying story. Also use *The Case of the Missing Family* (2010). 🕮 Lexile 480L (Rev: BL 1/1–15/11)

7798 Butler, Dori Hillestad. *The Case of the Library Monster* (1–3). Illus. by Jeremy Tugeau. Series: The Buddy Files. 2011, Whitman $14.99 (978-080750914-2). 128pp. Buddy the dog detective decides to investigate the case of the blue skink that's been skulking around the school library. (Rev: BLO 3/25/11)

7799 Butler, Dori Hillestad. *The Case of the Lost Boy* (1–3). Illus. by Jeremy Tugeau. Series: The Buddy Files. 2010, Whitman $14.99 (978-0-8075-0910-4). 128pp. After being adopted from the dog pound, golden retriever Buddy — formerly known as King — works to solve the mystery of why his old family gave him up. 🕮 Lexile 450L (Rev: BL 1/1/10; LMC 5–6/10; SLJ 2/1/10)

7800 Butler, Dori Hillestad. *Do You Know the Monkey Man?* (5–7). 2005, Peachtree $14.95 (978-1-56145-340-5). After a psychic says that her twin sister — believed drowned 10 years before — is not dead at all, 13-year-old Samantha sets off with a friend to investigate. (Rev: BL 5/1/05; SLJ 6/05)

7801 Byars, Betsy. *The Black Tower* (4–6). 2006, Viking $12.99 (978-0-670-06174-7). 144pp. Herculeah Jones tries to unravel the suspenseful mystery surrounding the dark past of a neighborhood mansion. (Rev: BL 10/15/06; SLJ 12/06)

7802 Byars, Betsy. *King of Murder* (4–6). Series: A Herculeah Jones Mystery. 2006, Sleuth $10.99 (978-0-670-06065-8). 115pp. Herculeah finds herself in grave danger as she tries to unmask suspected murderer Mathias King. (Rev: SLJ 6/06)

7803 Cadenhead, MacKenzie. *Sally's Bones* (4–6). Illus. by T. S. Spookytooth. 2011, Sourcebooks paper $6.99 (978-1-4022-5-943-2). 176pp. Sally Simplesmith, 11 and still mourning for her mother, is adopted by a lovable skeleton dog that she must then protect from false accusations. (Rev: BL 9/15/11; SLJ 12/1/11)

7804 Capeci, Anne. *Danger: Dynamite!* (3–6). Illus. by Paul Casale. Series: Cascade Mountain Railroad Mysteries. 2003, Peachtree $12.95 (978-1-56145-288-0). 127pp. In this engaging mystery tale set in the 1920s, 10-year-old Billy and his best friend Finn investigate the mysterious disappearance of a crate of dynamite. (Rev: HBG 4/04; SLJ 1/04)

7805 Capeci, Anne. *Ghost Train* (3–5). Illus. by author. Series: Cascade Mountain Railroad Mysteries. 2004, Peachtree $12.95 (978-1-56145-324-5). 144pp. Billy, Finn, and Dannie are instrumental in preventing a train robbery in this fast-paced mystery full of historical detail. (Rev: SLJ 1/05)

7806 Carman, Patrick. *Floors* (4–7). 2011, Scholastic $16.99 (978-0-545-25519-6). 272pp. Charged with taking care of the magical Whippet Hotel, Leo and his dad must protect the place from a foreboding future hinted at by mysterious clues. 🕮 Lexile 870L (Rev: BL 10/15/11; SLJ 11/1/11)

7807 Catanese, P. W. *The Thief and the Beanstalk* (4–6). 2005, Simon & Schuster paper $4.99 (978-0-689-87173-3). 272pp. An exciting adventure in which Nick, with greed in his heart, climbs a giant beanstalk and finds at the top the giant's wife and her evil sons — and a moral dilemma. (Rev: SLJ 7/05)

7808 Cavanagh, Helen. *Panther Glade* (5–8). 1993, Simon & Schuster paper $16.00 (978-0-671-75617-8). Bill spends a summer in Florida with his great-aunt Cait. He's afraid of the Everglades and alligators, but he comes to appreciate Indian history and crafts. (Rev: BL 6/1–15/93; SLJ 6/93; VOYA 10/93)

7809 Chari, Sheela. *Vanished* (4–7). 2011, Hyperion/Disney $16.99 (978-1-4231-3163-2). 240pp. East Indian

American Neela, 11, gets embroiled in a mystery when her grandmother's prized veena (a traditional Indian instrument) is stolen. (Rev: BL 9/1/11; SLJ 12/1/11)

7810 Cheshire, Simon. *The Curse of the Ancient Mask and Other Case Files* (3–5). Illus. by R. W. Alley. 2009, Roaring Brook $13.95 (978-1-59643-474-5). 176pp. Saxby Smart, 10, has his Crime Headquarters in a shed in his backyard and from there conducts three investigations. (Rev: BL 5/1/09; LMC 10/09; SLJ 6/09)

7811 Cheshire, Simon. *Treasure of Dead Man's Lane and Other Case Files* (4–7). Illus. by R. W. Alley. Series: Saxby Smart, Private Detective. 2010, Roaring Brook $16.99 (978-159643475-2). 208pp. Schoolboy sleuth Saxby solves three challenging mysteries with the help of his sidekicks in this book that underlines the clues. **e** (Rev: BL 5/15/10*; SLJ 7/10)

7812 Child, Lauren. *Ruby Redfort: Look into My Eyes* (5–8). Illus. 2012, Candlewick $16.99 (978-076365120-6). 400pp. Brilliant 13-year-old Ruby is hired to crack codes for a secret crime-fighting organization in this multilayered, fast-paced novel. ∩ **e** Lexile 800L (Rev: BL 2/15/12; LMC 8–9/12; SLJ 4/12; VOYA 4/12)

7813 Choldenko, Gennifer. *Al Capone Does My Homework* (5–8). 2013, Dial $17.99 (978-080373472-2). 224pp. Moose must investigate a mysterious fire while caring as usual for his sister in this conclusion to the trilogy in which Moose's father is promoted to assistant warden of Alcatraz. ∩ Lexile 570 (Rev: BL 6/13*; HB 7–8/13; SLJ 6/13; VOYA 10/13)

7814 Cirrone, Dorian. *The Missing Silver Dollar* (2–4). Illus. by Liza Woodruff. Series: Lindy Blues. 2006, Marshall Cavendish $14.95 (978-0-7614-5284-3). 74pp. Lindy Blues, a fourth grader and self-appointed investigative reporter for her neighborhood, tracks down a neighbor's missing silver dollar. (Rev: SLJ 9/06)

7815 Clements, Andrew. *Fear Itself* (4–6). Illus. by Adam Stower. Series: Benjamin Pratt and the Keepers of the School. 2011, Atheneum $14.99 (978-141693887-3). 224pp. In this followup to 2010's *We the Children*, sleuths Ben and Jill befriend a retired janitor and solve some maritime clues that help them in their desperate fight to save their school. ∩ **e** Lexile 800L (Rev: BL 9/15/10; SLJ 9/1/10)

7816 Clements, Andrew. *Room One* (3–5). Illus. by Chris Blair. 2006, Simon & Schuster $15.95 (978-0-689-86686-9). 176pp. Ted, the only 6th grader in his one-room school, discovers a mystery while delivering papers one morning in this story set in rural Nebraska. (Rev: BL 5/1/06; SLJ 7/06) ∩

7817 Clements, Andrew. *We the Children* (4–6). Illus. by Adam Stower. Series: Benjamin Pratt and the Keepers of the School. 2010, Atheneum $14.99 (978-141693886-6). 160pp. Sixth-grader Benjamin is adjusting to his parents' separation when he and his friend Jill uncover a string of clues in their quest to save their historic school from nefarious developers. (Rev: BL 3/15/10; HB 5–6/10; LMC 10/10; SLJ 5/10)

7818 Clifford, Eth. *Help! I'm a Prisoner in the Library* (3–5). Illus. by George Hughes. 1979, Houghton $16.00 (978-0-395-28478-0); Scholastic paper $5.99 (978-0-590-44351-7). 112pp. Two youngsters are locked in a library after it closes. Two sequels are: *The Dastardly Murder of Dirty Pete* (1981); *Just Tell Me When We're Dead!* (1983).

7819 Colfer, Eoin. *Half Moon Investigations* (4–6). 2006, Hyperion $16.95 (978-0-7868-4957-4). Fletcher ("Half") Moon, an aspiring private investigator, finds himself in all sorts of trouble when pretty April Devereux asks him to nab a thief in their Irish town; this story is full of jargon and humor. (Rev: BL 5/1/06; SLJ 4/06) ∩

7820 Collard, Sneed B. *Double Eagle* (5–8). 2009, Peachtree $15.95 (978-1-56145-480-8). 245pp. In 1973, 13-year-old Mike and a friend find a rare coin and rush to see if there are more before an approaching hurricane arrives. (Rev: BL 5/1/09; SLJ 12/09)

7821 Collard, Sneed B. *The Governor's Dog Is Missing!* (4–7). Series: Slate Stephens Mysteries. 2011, Bucking Horse $16 (978-0-9844460-1-8). 176pp. Slate and Daphne, both 12, investigate the disappearance of Cat, the governor of Minnesota's dog. (Rev: BL 5/1/11; SLJ 6/11)

7822 Collard, Sneed B. *Hangman's Gold* (4–7). Series: Slate Stephens Mysteries. 2011, Bucking Horse $16 (978-098444602-5). 208pp. Crime-solving duo Slate and Daphne return with a Wild West mystery involving cowboy art and missing gold. (Rev: BL 1/1/12; SLJ 1/12)

7823 Collier, James Lincoln. *The Dreadful Revenge of Ernest Gallen* (5–8). 2008, Bloomsbury $16.95 (978-1-59990-220-3). Gene, the main character in this Depression-era mystery, is haunted by a ghost looking for revenge and searches for the role his family and neighbors played in a horrible crime. (Rev: BL 8/08; SLJ 9/08)

7824 Comino, Sandra. *The Little Blue House* (4–7). 2003, Douglas & McIntyre $15.95 (978-0-88899-504-9). Young Cintia and her friend Bruno investigate why an abandoned house in their small town in Argentina turns blue for one day each year in this suspenseful novel that contains some violence. (Rev: BL 2/15/04)

7825 Conly, Jane Leslie. *Murder Afloat* (5–8). 2010, Hyperion/Disney $17.99 (978-142310416-2). 176pp. In the 1870s privileged 14-year-old Benjamin is kidnapped and put to work aboard an oyster ship in this suspenseful high seas adventure. (Rev: BL 12/1/10; HB 11–12/10; LMC 1–2/11; SLJ 3/1/11)

7826 Copeland, Mark. *The Bundle at Blackthorpe Heath* (4–7). 2006, Houghton Mifflin $15.00 (978-0-618-56302-9). With the help of a spyglass he receives as a birthday present, 12-year-old Arthur Piper uncovers a conspiracy to undermine his grandfather's traveling insect circus. (Rev: BL 6/1–15/06; SLJ 7/06)

7827 Corriveau, Art. *Thirteen Hangmen* (5–7). 2012, Abrams $16.95 (978-1-4197-0159-7). 352pp. Transported during the night on his 13th birthday, Tony finds himself in the company of 13-year-old boys from throughout Boston's history, tasked with solving a dynamic mystery. (Rev: BL 5/1/12; LMC 11–12/12; SLJ 9/12)

7828 Couloumbis, Audrey. *Maude March on the Run! or, Trouble Is Her Middle Name* (5–7). 2007, Random House $15.99 (978-0-375-83246-8). In this action-packed sequel to *The Misadventures of Maude March*, 16-year-old Maude and her 12-year-old sister, both orphans, are pursued by the law after Maude is unjustly accused of multiple crimes. (Rev: SLJ 1/07)

7829 Coven, Wanda. *Heidi Heckelbeck Has a Secret* (1–3). Illus. by Priscilla Burris. 2012, Simon & Schuster $14.99 (978-144244087-6); paper $4.99 (978-14424356-5-0). 128pp. After being home-schooled, Heidi starts 2nd grade at a public school and meets with trouble on her very first day; for new chapter-book readers. (Rev: BL 2/15/12; SLJ 6/1/12)

7830 Cox, Judy. *The Case of the Purloined Professor* (4–7). Illus. by Omar Rayyan. 2009, Marshall Cavendish $16.99 (978-076145544-8). 256pp. Rat brothers Ishbu and Frederick team up to find a missing scientist in this adventure-filled story. Lexile 710L (Rev: BL 9/15/09; LMC 11–12/09; SLJ 11/09)

7831 Cray, Jordan. *Dead Man's Hand* (5–9). Series: danger.com. 1998, Simon & Schuster paper $3.99 (978-0-689-82383-1). In this light read, Nick Annunciato and his stepsister, Annie Hanley, use their brains and a computer to solve a murder and escape a biological-weapons smuggling ring. (Rev: SLJ 2/99)

7832 Cray, Jordan. *Shiver* (5–8). Series: danger.com. 1998, Simon & Schuster paper $3.99 (978-0-689-82384-8). Six drama students are spending a weekend in the Green Mountains of Vermont, when one of the group is murdered. (Rev: SLJ 2/99)

7833 Creech, Sharon. *The Wanderer* (5–9). Illus. by David Diaz. 2000, HarperCollins LB $17.89 (978-0-06-027731-4). In this Newbery Honor Book, 13-year-old Sophie, her two cousins, and three uncles sail across the Atlantic to England in a 45-foot yacht. (Rev: BCCB 4/00*; BL 4/1/00; HB 5–6/00; HBG 10/00; SLJ 4/00*)

7834 Crocker, Carter. *Last of the Gullivers* (5–7). 2012, Philomel $16.99 (978-039924231-1). 240pp. Twelve-year-old orphan Michael is a boy headed for trouble until he finds purpose when he discovers a village full of Lilliputians and is entrusted with their care. e Lexile 750L (Rev: BL 2/1/12; HB 9–10/12; SLJ 2/12)

7835 Cronin, Doreen. *The Trouble with Chickens* (3–5). Illus. by Kevin Cornell. Series: J. J. Tully Mysteries. 2011, HarperCollins $14.99 (978-0-06-121532-2); LB $15.89 (978-0-06-121533-9). 128pp. J. J. Tully, retired search-and-rescue dog, undertakes a search for two missing chickens and meets unexpected challenges in this funny whodunit. e Lexile 570L (Rev: BL 2/1/11; HB 3–4/11; SLJ 2/1/11)

7836 Crossman, David A. *The Mystery of the Black Moriah* (5–8). Series: A Bean and Ab Mystery. 2002, Down East $16.95 (978-0-89272-536-6). The ever-curious Bean and Ab become caught up in a mystery adventure involving pirates, kidnappers, and a legendary ghost. (Rev: HBG 3/03; SLJ 12/02)

7837 Crossman, David A. *The Secret of the Missing Grave* (5–8). Series: A Bean and Ab Mystery. 1999, Down East $16.95 (978-0-89272-456-7). Two girls investigate a haunted house and become involved in a mystery concerning a missing treasure and stolen paintings in this fast-paced novel set in Maine. (Rev: HBG 3/00; SLJ 1/00)

7838 Crowder, Melanie. *Parched* (4–8). 2013, Harcourt $15.99 (978-054797651-8). 160pp. In a country plagued by drought and strife, Sarel — accompanied by her dog Nandi — flees after her parents are murdered; she is joined by Musa, a boy who has escaped from slavery; a harrowing, exciting story told from the perspectives of the two young people and the dog. Lexile 890 (Rev: BL 6/13; LMC 8–9/13; SLJ 5/13)

7839 Curtis, Christopher Paul. *Mr. Chickee's Funny Money* (4–6). Series: Flint Future Detectives. 2005, Random $15.95 (978-0-385-32772-5). 160pp. Nine-year-old Steven and his friends try to find out if the quadrillion dollar bill he was given by his blind neighbor is the real thing in this fast-paced and humorous mystery. A sequel is *Mr. Chickee's Messy Mission* (2007). (Rev: BL 8/05; SLJ 10/05*)

7840 Dahl, Michael. *Hocus Pocus Hotel* (4–6). Illus. by Lisa K. Weber. 2012, Stone Arch $10.95 (978-1-4342-4253-2). 216pp. Budding sleuth Charlie is asked to get to the bottom of two mysteries at the Abracadabra Hotel, which is home to professional magicians. The two stories are also available separately as *Out the Rear Window* and *To Catch a Ghost* (both 2012). (Rev: BL 8/12; LMC 1–2/13; SLJ 8/12)

7841 DeFelice, Cynthia. *Lostman's River* (5–7). 1994, Macmillan LB $15.00 (978-0-02-726466-1). Tyler's trust is betrayed when he takes an eccentric scientist to a secret rookery in the Everglades and the man reveals himself to be an unscrupulous plume hunter. (Rev: BCCB 6/94; BL 5/15/94; HB 9–10/94; SLJ 7/94)

7842 DeFelice, Cynthia. *The Missing Manatee* (5–8). 2005, Farrar $16.00 (978-0-374-31257-2). Skeet Waters sets out to solve the mystery of a murdered manatee he finds near his Florida home. (Rev: BL 3/1/05; SLJ 6/05)

7843 Delaney, Mark. *The Protester's Song* (5–9). Series: Misfits, Inc. 2001, Peachtree paper $5.95 (978-1-56145-244-6). Four teens keep themselves busy investigating an incident that occurred during riots in Ohio in 1970 and, in a subplot, try to stop the new principal from removing books from the library. (Rev: SLJ 8/01)

7844 Delaney, Mark. *The Vanishing Chip* (5–8). Series: Misfits, Inc. 1998, Peachtree paper $5.95 (978-1-56145-176-0). Four teens who don't fit in at school investigate the disappearance of the world's most powerful computer chip. (Rev: BL 12/15/98; SLJ 2/99)

7845 Demers, Barbara. *Willa's New World* (5–8). 2000, Coteau paper $6.95 (978-1-55050-150-6). An adventure story set in Canada around 1800 in which 15-year-old

Willa is sent to a trading post on Hudson's Bay. (Rev: BL 9/15/00; SLJ 9/00)

7846 Dionne, Erin. *Moxie and the Art of Rule Breaking* (5–8). 2013, Dial $16.99 (978-080373871-3). 256pp. Moxie, 13, and her friend Ollie have 14 days to find artwork stolen in Boston in a heist in which her grandfather was involved; this story, which requires some suspension of disbelief, is based on an art theft in 1990 and information on this is appended. ∩ e Lexile 760 (Rev: BL 5/1/13; LMC 11–12/13; SLJ 6/13; VOYA 8/13)

7847 Doder, Joshua. *A Dog Called Grk* (5–8). 2007, Delacorte $14.99 (978-0-385-73359-5). In this fast-paced adventure, 12-year-old Londoner Tim, trying to help the Stanislavian ambassador's family — and dog — becomes enmeshed in international political intrigue. A sequel is *Grk and the Pelotti Gang* (2007). (Rev: BL 1/1–15/07; SLJ 3/07)

7848 Doder, Joshua. *Operation Tortoise* (5–8). Series: The Grk Books. 2009, Random $15.99 (978-0-385-73362-5). 240pp. Tim, 12, and his dog Grk are in the Seychelles and find themselves investigating a sinister laboratory in this fast-paced suspense story. (Rev: BL 3/1/09)

7849 Dowd, Siobhan. *The London Eye Mystery* (5–8). 2008, Random House $15.99 (978-0-375-84976-3). Ted and Kat's cousin Salim disappears after entering a ride called the London Eye, and Ted relies on his unusual intellectual abilities to try to find him. (Rev: BL 1/1–15/08; HB 5–6/08; LMC 3/08; SLJ 2/08)

7850 Doyle, Bill, and David Borgenicht. *Everest* (4–8). Illus. by Yancey Labat. Series: Worst-Case Scenario Ultimate Adventure. 2011, Chronicle $12.99 (978-0-8118-7123-5). 204pp. Readers are invited to participate in the decision-making process in this choose-your-own-adventure style story of a team trying to summit Mount Everest. e (Rev: SLJ 6/11)

7851 Doyle, Roddy. *Wilderness* (5–7). 2007, Scholastic $16.99 (978-0-439-02356-6). Johnny and Tom must find their mother in frozen Lapland when her dogsled team is lost; meanwhile the boys' half sister is reunited with her own mother, who left her family long ago. (Rev: BL 11/15/07; HB 1–2/08; SLJ 11/07)

7852 Draper, Penny. *Terror at Turtle Mountain* (4–7). 2006, Coteau paper $7.95 (978-1-55050-343-2). In Canada's Northwest Territory in 1903, a 13-year-old girl participates in frantic efforts to rescue victims of a rock slide; an action-packed novel based on a real-life incident. (Rev: SLJ 10/06)

7853 Draper, Sharon M. *Lost in the Tunnel of Time* (3–6). Illus. by Michael Bryant. Series: Ziggy and the Black Dinosaurs. 1996, Just Us Bks. paper $6.00 (978-0-940975-63-7). 96pp. While exploring tunnels used by the Underground Railroad, boys are trapped underground when one of the tunnels collapses. (Rev: SLJ 8/96)

7854 Draper, Sharon M. *Shadows of Caesar's Creek* (3–5). Series: Ziggy and the Black Dinosaurs. 1997, Just Us Bks. paper $6.00 (978-0-940975-76-7). 91pp. A group of African American kids get lost in a state park and are rescued by a Shawnee chief. (Rev: SLJ 6/98)

7855 Duncan, Lois. *News for Dogs* (3–5). 2009, Scholastic $16.99 (978-0-545-10853-9). 224pp. Andi and her older, middle-school brother Bruce start a newspaper for dogs and take on a dog-napping case. (Rev: BL 4/1/09) ∩

7856 Eames, Brian. *The Dagger Quick* (4–7). 2011, Simon & Schuster $15.99 (978-1-4424-2311-4). 320pp. Kitto, a 12-year-old with a clubfoot, finds himself setting out to sea with his long-lost pirate uncle in this fast-paced adventure set in the 17th century. e Lexile 690L (Rev: LMC 11–12/11; SLJ 8/11)

7857 Eden, Alexandra. *Holy Smoke: A Bones and Duchess Mystery* (5–7). 2004, Alien A. Knoll $16.00 (978-1-888310-46-7). Ex-cop Bones Fatzinger and Verity Buscador, a 12-year-old girl with Asperger's syndrome, work together to track down the person responsible for setting fire to a local church. (Rev: BL 5/1/04)

7858 Elish, Dan. *The School for the Insanely Gifted* (4–6). 2011, HarperCollins $15.99 (978-0-06-113873-7). 304pp. Eleven-year-old Daphna, student at a school for geniuses, sets off with her friends to find her missing mother. (Rev: BL 9/15/11; SLJ 8/11)

7859 Ellis, Mary. *Lily Dragon* (3–5). Illus. by Rachael Phillips. 2001, HarperCollins paper $7.50 (978-0-00-675458-9). 139pp. Lily sets off on a trip to visit her mother's family in China, determined to hunt for the hidden treasure she's heard about so often. (Rev: SLJ 8/01)

7860 Elmer, Robert. *Far from the Storm* (4–7). Series: Young Underground. 1995, Bethany House paper $5.99 (978-0-556-61377-0). At the end of World War II, Danish twins Peter and Elise set out to find the culprit who set their uncle's boat on fire. (Rev: BL 2/15/96)

7861 Emerson, Kathy L. *The Mystery of the Missing Bagpipes* (5–7). 1991, Avon paper $2.95 (978-0-380-76138-8). Kim tries to find the real culprit when a young boy is wrongfully accused of stealing a set of ancient bagpipes and some precious daggers. (Rev: BL 9/15/91)

7862 Emerson, Scott. *The Case of the Cat with the Missing Ear: From the Notebooks of Edward R. Smithfield, D.V.M.* (5–7). 2003, Simon & Schuster LB $15.95 (978-0-689-85861-1). This canine takeoff of the Sherlock Holmes format features Yorkshire terrier Samuel Blackthorne and his sidekick and chronicler Dr. Edward Smithfield, who investigate mysteries with humor and deductive prowess. (Rev: BCCB 10/02; BL 12/1/03; HBG 4/04; SLJ 3/04)

7863 Erickson, John R. *Discovery at Flint Springs* (5–8). 2004, Viking $16.99 (978-0-670-05946-1). In 1927, 14-year-old Riley and his younger brother Coy join in an exciting search for archaeological sites on their Texas ranch. (Rev: BL 2/1/05; SLJ 12/04)

7864 Ernst, Kathleen. *Midnight in Lonesome Hollow* (4–6). 2007, Pleasant $10.95 (978-1-59369-161-5); paper $6.95 (978-1-59369-160-8). 180pp. In rural Kentucky during the Depression, Kit investigates threats to a professor researching local traditions and worried about her friend Fern, who may end up in an orphanage. (Rev: BL 5/15/07; SLJ 5/07)

7865 Ernst, Kathleen. *Secrets in the Hills: A Josefina Mystery* (4–7). Series: American Girl Mystery. 2006, Pleasant paper $6.95 (978-1-59369-097-7). In 1820s New Mexico, Josefina decides to investigate the possibility that there is treasure buried near her home. (Rev: BL 5/15/06; SLJ 4/06)

7866 Evans, Lissa. *Horten's Miraculous Mechanisms* (4–7). 2012, Sterling $14.95 (978-140279806-1). 272pp. Diminutive 10-year-old Stuart Horten has moved with his family to his father's hometown, and soon discovers mysterious old coins that offer clues to the disappearance long ago of his great-uncle Tony, a magician. (Rev: BL 4/1/12; SLJ 5/1/12)

7867 Ewing, Lynne. *Drive-By* (5–8). 1996, HarperCollins paper $4.99 (978-0-06-440649-9). When Tito's brother is killed in a gang-related shooting, he is bullied and threatened by the gang to reveal where his brother hid a cache of stolen money. (Rev: SLJ 8/96)

7868 Fagan, Deva. *Fortune's Folly* (5–7). 2009, Holt $17.95 (978-0-8050-8742-0). 272pp. Seventeen-year-old Fortunata becomes a fortune teller to support herself and her father and finds herself in a pickle when her predictions threaten her father's life. (Rev: BCCB 9/09; BL 4/1/09; SLJ 7/09)

7869 Fairlie, Emily. *The Lost Treasure of Tuckernuck* (4–6). 2012, HarperCollins $16.99 (978-0-06-211890-5). 304pp. Sixth-graders Laurie and Bud hunt for a treasure hidden for 80 years in their school, Tuckernuck Hall, which is in danger of being torn down; this mystery is full of clever clues. **e** (Rev: BLO 10/15/12; SLJ 12/12)

7870 Fairlie, Emily. *The Magician's Bird* (4–6). 2013, HarperCollins $16.99 (978-006211893-6). 288pp. Laurie and Bud are 7th-graders at Tuckernuck Hall, and when they start digging around their school to create a scavenger hunt, they find that their school's founder might have some skeletons in her closet — literally. **e** Lexile 600 (Rev: BLO 9/15/13; SLJ 12/13)

7871 Falcone, L. M. *The Mysterious Mummer* (5–7). 2003, Kids Can $16.95 (978-1-55337-376-6). When Joey, 13, arrives in Newfoundland to spend Christmas with his aunt, he finds some very mysterious goings-on. (Rev: HBG 4/04; SLJ 10/03)

7872 Fama, Elizabeth. *Overboard* (4–8). 2002, Cricket $15.95 (978-0-8126-2652-0). Fourteen-year-old Emily struggles to save her own life and that of a boy named Isman when a ferry sinks off the coast of Sumatra. (Rev: BCCB 6/02; BL 7/02; HBG 10/02; SLJ 7/02)

7873 Farber, E. S. *Seagulls Don't Eat Pickles* (3–6). Illus. by Jason Beene. Series: Fish Finelli. 2013, Chronicle $15.99 (978-1-4521-0820-9). 160pp. Humor and clues abound in this scientific-minded story about Fish Finelli and his search for Captain Kidd's lost treasure. (Rev: BLO 4/1/13; LMC 10/13; SLJ 6/13)

7874 Fardell, John. *The Flight of the Silver Turtle* (5–8). 2006, Putnam $15.99 (978-0-399-24382-0). The same crew from *The 7 Professors of the Far North* (2005)

must find an antigravity machine before the villains discover it, in an exciting chase around Europe. (Rev: BL 12/15/06; SLJ 10/06)

7875 Feinstein, John. *Change-Up: Mystery at the World Series* (5–8). 2009, Knopf $16.99 (978-0-375-85636-5); LB $19.99 (978-0-375-95636-2). 336pp. What is Nationals pitcher Norbert Doyle hiding? Teen sports reporters Stevie and Susan Carol investigate. ⌕ Lexile 770L (Rev: BL 9/1/09; SLJ 9/09; VOYA 6/09)

7876 Ferguson, Dwayne J. *Kid Caramel, Private Investigator: The Werewolf of PS 40* (3–5). Series: Kid Caramel. 1998, Just Us Bks. paper $4.50 (978-0-940975-82-8). 68pp. When animals begin to disappear from his town, Kid Caramel and his sidekick, Earnie, set out to find the culprit. (Rev: SLJ 3/99)

7877 Ferraiolo, Jack D. *The Big Splash* (5–7). 2008, Abrams $15.95 (978-0-8109-7067-0). 288pp. Matt Stevens, an average middle-schooler with a glib tongue and a knack for solving crimes, uncovers a mystery while working with "the organization," a mafia-like syndicate run by 7th-grader Vincent "Mr. Biggs" Biggio, and specializing in forged hall passes, test-copying rings, black market candy selling, and so forth. ⌕ (Rev: BCCB 11/08; BLO 10/7/08; LMC 3/09; SLJ 11/08; VOYA 10/08)

7878 Fields, T. S. *Danger in the Desert* (5–7). 1997, Rising Moon $12.95 (978-0-87358-666-5); paper $6.95 (978-0-87358-664-1). A survival story about two boys who endure great hardships when they are left without food or supplies in the desert. (Rev: HBG 3/98; SLJ 11/97)

7879 Fienberg, Anna. *Horrendo's Curse* (3–6). Illus. by Kim Gamble. 2002, Annick $18.95 (978-1-55037-773-6); paper $6.95 (978-1-55037-772-9). 160pp. Twelve-year-old Horrendo, whose curse is an inability to say anything cruel although surrounded by rude foulmouths, manages to persuade his pirate kidnappers that politeness is the best policy. (Rev: BL 12/1/02; HBG 10/03; SLJ 2/03)

7880 Figley, Marty Rhodes. *The Schoolchildren's Blizzard* (1–3). Illus. by Shelly O. Haas. Series: On My Own History. 2004, Carolrhoda LB $27.93 (978-1-57505-586-2). 48pp. A teacher rescues 16 students after the roof of the school is blown off during a severe blizzard in 1888 in this story based on a Nebraska storm. (Rev: BL 3/1/04)

7881 Finney, Patricia. *Feud* (4–7). Series: Lady Grace Mysteries. 2006, Delacorte $7.95 (978-0-385-73323-6); paper $9.99 (978-0-385-90342-4). Lady Grace, maid of honor to Queen Elizabeth I, attempts to unravel the mystery surrounding the poisoning of another maid of honor. (Rev: BL 10/15/06)

7882 Flanagan, John. *The Hunters* (4–8). Series: Brotherband Chronicles. 2012, Philomel $18.99 (978-039925621-9). 432pp. In this sequel to 2012's *The Invaders*, Hal realizes he must engage in a one-on-one fight with Zavac in order to defeat the villainous pirate. ⌕ **e** Lexile 780L (Rev: BL 10/15/12)

7883 Fleck, Earl. *Chasing Bears: A Canoe-Country Adventure* (5–8). Illus. by author. 1999, Holy Cow paper $12.95 (978-0-930100-90-2). An adventure story set near the Minnesota-Canada border that involves Danny, a 12-year-old who is on a canoe trip with his father and older brother. (Rev: SLJ 12/99)

7884 Fleischman, Paul. *The Half-a-Moon Inn* (5–7). Illus. by Kathryn Jacobi. 1991, HarperCollins paper $5.99 (978-0-06-440364-1). A young mute boy sets out to find his mother in a violent snowstorm.

7885 Fleischman, Sid. *The Ghost in the Noonday Sun* (5–7). Illus. by Warren Chappell. 1989, Scholastic paper $3.50 (978-0-590-43662-5). This pirate story features all the standard ingredients — a shanghaied boy, a villainous captain, and buried treasure. (Rev: VOYA 8/89)

7886 Fleischman, Sid. *The Giant Rat of Sumatra or Pirates Galore* (4–6). Illus. by John Hendrix. 2005, Greenwillow LB $16.89 (978-0-06-074239-3). 208pp. In a fast-paced adventure, 12-year-old cabin boy Edmund Amos Peters, who's been shipwrecked and captured by pirates, arrives in mid-19th-century San Diego to find his adventures are not over. (Rev: BL 2/1/05; SLJ 1/05)

7887 Fleischman, Sid. *The Whipping Boy* (5–7). 1986, Greenwillow $16.99 (978-0-688-06216-3). Prince Brat and his whipping boy, Jemmy, who takes the blame for all the bad things the prince does, find their roles reversed when they meet up with CutWater and Hold-Your-Nose Billy. Newbery Medal 1987. (Rev: BCCB 3/86; BL 3/1/86; SLJ 5/86)

7888 Flower, Amanda. *Andi Unexpected* (5–7). Series: Andi Boggs. 2013, Zonderkidz $10.99 (978-031073701-8). 224pp. Orphaned 12-year-old Andi Boggs and her sister Bethany move to Killdeer, Ohio, to live with their Aunt Amelia, an English professor, where Andi discovers a 1930 photograph of a mysterious girl with the same name and plunges into investigation of the circumstances. e (Rev: BL 10/1/13; SLJ 1/14)

7889 Fontes, Justine, and Ron Fontes. *Captured by Pirates* (4–6). Illus. by David Witt. Series: Twisted Journey. 2007, Lerner $27.93 (978-0-8225-6201-6); paper $7.95 (978-0-8225-6202-3). 112pp. Will you be captured by pirates? Set sail from England as a boy in 1635 and make your own choices in this part-text part-graphic novel book. (Rev: BL 10/1/07; SLJ 9/07)

7890 Frazier, Angie. *The Mastermind Plot* (4–7). 2012, Scholastic $16.99 (978-054520864-2). 240pp. Zanna hopes to get closer to her detective uncle while in Boston, and fulfill her dream of becoming a real sleuth in this mystery set in 1904; a sequel to *The Midnight Tunnel* (2011). (Rev: BL 5/1/12; SLJ 2/12)

7891 Frazier, Angie. *The Midnight Tunnel* (4–7). 2011, Scholastic $16.99 (978-0-545-20862-8). 288pp. In New Brunswick at the turn of the 20th century, 11-year-old Suzanna (Zanna) Snow prefers sleuthing to working at her family's inn; however, her famous detective uncle's efforts to solve a mysterious disappearance disappoint her. e Lexile 800L (Rev: BL 2/1/11; LMC 5–6/11; SLJ 4/11)

7892 Freeman, Martha. *The Case of the Diamond Dog Collar* (2–4). Series: First Kids Mystery. 2011, Holiday House $16.95 (978-082342337-8). 144pp. The president's dog has a fancy new collar and one of the gems is missing. Could it be a diamond? First Daughters Cammie, 10, and Tessa, 7, investigate. Lexile 630L (Rev: BL 10/15/11; LMC 3–4/12)

7893 Freeman, Martha. *The Case of the Rock 'n' Roll Dog* (2–4). Series: First Kids Mystery. 2010, Holiday House $16.95 (978-0-8234-2267-8). 128pp. First Daughter Cammie, 10, and her younger sister Tessa investigate when items go missing from the White House. Lexile 580L (Rev: BL 11/1/10; SLJ 11/1/10)

7894 Freeman, Martha. *The Case of the Ruby Slippers* (2–4). Series: First Kids Mystery. 2012, Holiday House $16.95 (978-082342409-2). 124pp. First daughters Tessa and Cammie swing into action when Dorothy's real ruby slippers disappear from the Smithsonian. (Rev: BL 5/1/12; SLJ 5/1/12)

7895 Freeman, Martha. *Who Stole Grandma's Million-Dollar Pumpkin Pie?* (3–6). Series: Chickadee Court Mystery. 2009, Holiday House $16.95 (978-0-8234-2215-9). 209pp. Alex and Yasmeen, 11, are hot on the trail of their grandma's secret, prizewinning pumpkin pie recipe in this lively mystery. Lexile 760L (Rev: SLJ 1/1/10)

7896 Freeman, Martha. *Who Stole Halloween?* (4–6). 2005, Holiday $16.95 (978-0-8234-1962-3). 232pp. Alex, boy detective, asks his friend Yasmeen to help him track down a missing cat named Halloween. (Rev: BL 8/05; SLJ 10/05)

7897 Freeman, Martha. *Who Stole Uncle Sam?* (4–6). 2008, Holiday $16.95 (978-0-8234-2091-9). 256pp. Alex and his friend Yasmeen investigate the disappearance of a baseball coach/Uncle Sam impersonator; a humorous read with lots of background information. (Rev: BLO 8/28/08)

7898 Fusilli, Jim. *Marley Z. and the Bloodstained Violin* (5–8). 2008, Dutton $16.99 (978-0-525-47907-9). Marley's musician friend Marisol is accused of stealing a valuable violin, and Marley is determined to prove her innocence in this mystery set in New York City. (Rev: BL 5/1/08; SLJ 9/08)

7899 Gaetz, Dayle Campbell. *Alberta Alibi* (4–6). 2005, Orca paper $6.95 (978-1-55143-404-9). When Sheila's divorced father is accused of sabotaging a housing development near his Canadian ranch, the 12-year-old and her friends Katie and Rusty try to prove him innocent and identify the real culprits; the third installment in a series. (Rev: SLJ 4/06; VOYA 4/06)

7900 Garden, Nancy. *The Case of the Stolen Scarab* (4–6). Illus. by Danamarie Hosler. Series: Candlestone Inn Mystery. 2004, Two Lives paper $8.95 (978-0-9674468-7-5). 205pp. Nikki and Travis, with their mothers, have only just arrived at their new inn when a mystery presents itself — a scarab has been stolen and the thief may be in the area. (Rev: SLJ 3/05)

7901 Garland, Sherry. *The Silent Storm* (4–7). 1993, Harcourt $14.95 (978-0-15-274170-9). Alyssa, who has lost both of her parents in a violent storm and has become mute because of the trauma, hears that another hurricane is approaching. (Rev: BCCB 4/93; BL 6/1–15/93; SLJ 7/04)

7902 Garretson, Dee. *Wildfire Run* (4–7). Series: Danger's Edge. 2010, HarperCollins $16.99 (978-006195347-7). 272pp. In this action-packed story, the president's son and two friends are marooned at Camp David when a series of natural disasters overwhelms the security system. (Rev: BL 10/15/10; SLJ 9/1/10)

7903 George, Jean Craighead. *Julie of the Wolves* (5–8). Illus. by John Schoenherr. 1974, HarperCollins LB $16.89 (978-0-06-021944-4); paper $5.99 (978-0-06-440058-9). Julie (Inuit name, Miyax) begins a trek across frozen Alaska and is saved only by the friendship of a pack of wolves. Newbery Medal 1973.

7904 George, Jean Craighead. *Julie's Wolf Pack* (5–7). Series: Julie of the Wolves. 1997, HarperCollins LB $18.89 (978-0-06-027407-8). Kapu, leader of the pack, is captured by researchers in this continuing story of Julie and her wolf friends. (Rev: BL 9/1/97; HBG 3/98; SLJ 9/97; VOYA 6/98)

7905 Gerson, Corinne. *My Grandfather the Spy* (5–7). 1990, Walker $14.95 (978-0-8027-6955-8). When a man arrives on the family farm in Vermont with a briefcase full of money, Danny suspects his grandfather is a spy. (Rev: BL 6/15/90; SLJ 8/90)

7906 Gibbs, Stuart. *Belly Up* (5–7). 2010, Simon & Schuster $15.99 (978-1-4169-8731-4). 304pp. Who is responsible for the death of the zoo's star hippo? Twelve-year-old Teddy and Summer, daughter of the zoo owner, investigate in this fast-paced story full of humor and animal facts. e Lexile 820L (Rev: BL 5/1/10; LMC 10/10; SLJ 5/10)

7907 Gibbs, Stuart. *Spy School* (4–7). 2012, Simon & Schuster $15.99 (978-144242182-0). 304pp. Twelve-year-old Ben achieves his lifelong wish when he leaves his middle school for the CIA's secretive Academy of Espionage — only to find that a life of spying isn't all it's cracked up to be. (Rev: BL 3/15/12; SLJ 2/12)

7908 Giff, Patricia Reilly. *Eleven* (3–6). 2008, Random $15.99 (978-0-385-73069-3). 144pp. Sam, 10, finds a newspaper article with his picture and the word "missing" and, with the help of a new classmate, Caroline, he begins to uncover the complex mystery of his past. (Rev: BL 12/1/07; HB 9/08; LMC 1/08; SLJ 1/08) ∩

7909 Giff, Patricia Reilly. *Hunter Moran Hangs Out* (4–6). 2013, Holiday $16.95 (978-082342859-5). 144pp. Hunter and Zack, twins in the six (soon to be seven) sibling Moran family, have a lot to deal with right now: they've got to write three book reports in four days, and their brother might just be the target of a kidnapper; a humorous mystery. e Lexile 490 (Rev: BL 9/15/13; LMC 3–4/14; SLJ 9/13)

7910 Giles, Stephen M. *The Body Thief* (5–7). Series: The Death (and Further Adventures) of Silas Winterbottom.

2010, Sourcebooks $12.99 (978-1-4022-4090-4). 240pp. When rich, elderly Uncle Silas invites three 12-year-old prospective heirs to his estate, the three very different cousins — Adele, Milo, and Isabella — become closer as they recognize that his intentions are far from benign. e Lexile 830L (Rev: BL 9/15/10; LMC 11–12/10)

7911 Givner, Joan. *Ellen Fremedon, Volunteer* (4–6). 2007, Groundwood $16.95 (978-0-88899-743-2). 184pp. Thirteen-year-old Ellen, at loose ends with her best friend away at summer camp, volunteers to help out a local retirement center and gets drawn into the mystery surrounding the disappearance of a new friend's mother. (Rev: BL 4/1/07)

7912 Golding, Julia. *Cat O'Nine Tails* (5–8). Series: Cat Royal Adventures. 2009, Roaring Brook $16.99 (978-159643445-5). 400pp. Cat and her friends are kidnapped and pressed into service in the British Navy and must use guile and courage to survive as they travel to the New World, where Cat becomes engaged to a Creek Indian. Lexile 760L (Rev: BL 11/1/09; SLJ 11/09; VOYA 2/10)

7913 Gordon, Amy. *Return to Gill Park* (5–8). Series: Gill Park. 2006, Holiday $16.95 (978-0-8234-1998-2). This oddball sequel to *The Gorillas of Gill Park* (2006) finds Willy Wilson on the trail of vandals determined to destroy the beauty of the park he now owns. (Rev: BL 5/15/06; SLJ 4/06)

7914 Gordon, Amy. *Twenty Gold Falcons* (4–7). 2010, Holiday House $16.95 (978-0-8234-2252-4). 240pp. Aiden's finding it hard to adjust to her new life in the city of Gloria until she learns about 20 missing gold coins and sets out to find them with some newly made friends. Lexile 710L (Rev: BL 5/1/10; LMC 11–12/10; SLJ 8/10)

7915 Gourley, Catherine, ed. *Read for Your Life: Tales of Survival from the Editors of Read Magazine* (5–8). Series: Best of Read. 1998, Millbrook paper $5.95 (978-0-7613-0344-2). This is a collection of excellent survival stories from 50 years of *Read,* a literary magazine for middle and high school students. (Rev: BL 8/98)

7916 Grabenstein, Chris. *Escape from Mr. Lemoncello's Library* (4–7). 2013, Random House $16.99 (978-037587089-7); LB $19.99 (978-037597089-4). 304pp. A dozen 12-year-olds enjoy an overnight stay at the newly designed library, but wake to find they must solve a series of puzzles in order to leave the building. ALA Notable Children's Book. e Lexile 720 (Rev: BL 6/13*; LMC 11–12/13; SLJ 6/13)

7917 Grabenstein, Chris. *The Smoky Corridor* (5–8). Series: Haunted Places Mystery. 2010, Random House $16.99 (978-0-375-86511-4); LB $19.99 (978-0-375-96511-1). 336pp. Zach Jennings, the boy who can communicate with ghosts, starts 6th grade at a new school and discovers that its many challenges include a brain-eating zombie and a host of ghosts guarding a cemetery. e Lexile 690L (Rev: BLO 12/1/10; SLJ 7/10)

7918 Graf, Mike. *Bryce and Zion: Danger in the Narrows* (5–8). Illus. by Marjorie Leggitt. Series: Adventures with the Parkers. 2006, Fulcrum paper $9.95 (978-1-55591-

532-2). On a vacation in the national parks of southern Utah, 10-year-old twins James and Morgan Parker learn about the delicate ecology of the area, rescue an injured hiker, and come to the aid of their father when he slips and falls in the Narrows; a fact-filled adventure story with full-color photographs and nature sketches. (Rev: SLJ 12/06)

7919 Grant, Katy. *Hide and Seek* (5–8). 2010, Peachtree $15.95 (978-1-56145542-3). 240pp. Chase, 14, enjoys geocaching (using a GPS to locate hidden items) and exploring in the Arizona mountains with his dog; one day he stumbles on two abducted boys and becomes embroiled in their plight. Lexile 700L (Rev: BL 10/1/10; LMC 11–12/10; SLJ 9/1/10)

7920 Grant, Michael. *The Key* (5–8). Series: Magnificent 12. 2012, HarperCollins $16.99 (978-006183370-0). 288pp. In this third volume in the action-packed series, 12-year-old Mack continues his mission to find a dozen 12-year-olds with special powers, at the same time encountering danger, challenges — and achievement; a sequel to *The Call* (2010) and *The Trap* (2011). e Lexile 750L (Rev: BL 10/1/12; SLJ 9/12)

7921 Graves, Keith. *The Orphan of Awkward Falls* (5–8). Illus. by author. 2011, Chronicle $16.99 (978-0-8118-7814-2). 338pp. When 12-year-old Josephine Cravitz and her family move to Awkward Falls, she becomes the target of a mad cannibal escaped from the town's Asylum for the Dangerously Insane; a complex, suspenseful story with light humor and horror. (Rev: BLO 11/15/11; LMC 1–2/12; SLJ 10/1/11)

7922 Greenburg, Dan. *Treachery and Betrayal at Jolly Days* (4–6). Illus. by Scott M. Fischer. Series: Secrets of the Dripping Fang. 2006, Harcourt $11.95 (978-0-15-205463-2). 144pp. Once again fleeing the evil Mandible sisters, the Schluffmuffin twins find themselves in a swamp and encounter a zombie who just might be their long-lost father. (Rev: BL 2/15/06; SLJ 6/06)

7923 Gregory, Kristiana. *The Secret of Robber's Cave* (3–5). Illus. by Patrick Faricy. Series: Cabin Creek Mysteries. 2008, Scholastic paper $4.99 (978-0-439-92950-9). 176pp. A fast-moving mystery adventure about two brothers who set off for Lost Island to solve a mystery from the 1880s. (Rev: BLO 3/3/08; SLJ 3/08)

7924 Grover, Wayne. *Dolphin Freedom* (3–5). Illus. 1999, Greenwillow $15.00 (978-0-688-16010-4). Diver Wayne Grover tries to save dolphins that are the target of a poaching ring working off the coast of Florida. (Rev: BL 5/15/99; HBG 10/99; SLJ 6/99)

7925 Gustafson, Scott. *Eddie: The Lost Youth of Edgar Allan Poe* (3–6). Illus. by author. 2011, Simon & Schuster $15.99 (978-1-4169-9764-1). 208pp. Gustafson imagines an episode in young Poe's childhood, in which he relies on the help of animals — including a raven — to clear his name after being falsely accused of property destruction. (Rev: BL 9/1/11; SLJ 12/1/11)

7926 Gutman, Dan. *Getting Air* (5–8). 2007, Simon & Schuster $15.99 (978-0-689-87680-6). Thirteen-year-old Jimmy and five others prevent a hijacking, survive a plane crash, and find themselves faced with surviving in a Canadian forest; girl scout lore comes to their aid and they even find time to build a half-pipe for skateboarding. (Rev: BL 7/07; SLJ 6/07)

7927 Gutman, Dan. *Mission Unstoppable* (5–8). Illus. Series: The Genius Files. 2011, HarperCollins $16.99 (978-0-06-182764-8); LB $17.89 (978-0-06-182765-5). 256pp. Twin geniuses Coke and Pepsi McDonald, 12, are pursued by nefarious government agents while on a cross-country road trip with their parents. The second and third books in the series are *Never Say Genius* (2012) and *You Only Die Twice* (2013). e (Rev: BL 12/1/10; LMC 8–9/11; SLJ 3/1/11)

7928 Gutman, Dan. *Shoeless Joe and Me* (4–7). Series: Baseball Card Adventure. 2002, HarperCollins LB $17.89 (978-0-06-029254-6). Thirteen-year-old Joe travels back in time to remedy the 1919 Black Sox scandal and save Shoeless Joe's reputation. (Rev: BL 1/1–15/02; HBG 10/02; SLJ 3/02)

7929 Hahn, Mary Downing. *Closed for the Season: A Mystery Story* (5–8). 2009, Clarion $16 (978-0-547-08451-0). 182pp. Thirteen-year-old Logan's search for a murderer leads him and his new friend Arthur to an eerie, abandoned amusement park in this well-executed mystery. ⌒ e Lexile 670L (Rev: LMC 10/09; SLJ 9/09; VOYA 10/09)

7930 Hahn, Mary Downing. *The Ghost of Crutchfield Hall* (4–7). 2010, Clarion $17 (978-0-547-38560-0). 160pp. Florence goes to live at her great-aunt's house, realizing too late that the house is haunted by the malicious ghost of her cousin Sophia, who died suspiciously. ⌒ e Lexile 680L (Rev: BL 10/1/10; LMC 1–2/11; SLJ 8/10)

7931 Hale, Bruce. *From Russia with Lunch* (3–5). Illus. by author. Series: Chet Gecko Mystery. 2009, Houghton $15.00 (978-0-15-205488-5). 144pp. The wisecracking and very punny Chet Gecko leaps to solve a new mystery at school in this 14th volume in the series. (Rev: BL 2/1/09)

7932 Harlow, Joan Hiatt. *Star in the Storm* (4–7). 2000, Simon & Schuster $16.00 (978-0-689-82905-5). This novel, set in Newfoundland in 1912, tells how a girl and her dog save a ship full of stranded passengers. (Rev: BCCB 3/00; BL 1/1–15/00; HB 3–4/00; HBG 10/00; SLJ 4/00)

7933 Harrington, Kim. *Framed and Dangerous* (4–7). Series: Sleuth or Dare. 2012, Scholastic paper $5.99 (978-05453896-6-2). 192pp. Despite an earlier difference of opinion 7th-graders Norah and Darcy work together to clear Zane of a crime he did not commit. Lexile 580 (Rev: BL 8/12)

7934 Harrington, Kim. *Partners in Crime* (4–7). Series: Sleuth or Dare. 2012, Scholastic paper $5.99 (978-05453896-4-8). 192pp. Best friend 7th-graders Darcy and Norah create a detective website for a school project and uncover a real mystery in this light story. e Lexile 580L (Rev: BL 5/1/12; LMC 8–9/12)

7935 Harvey, Jacqueline. *Alice-Miranda at School* (2–4). 2011, Delacorte $14.99 (978-0-385-73993-1); LB $17.99 (978-0-385-90811-5). 272pp. Alice-Miranda, seven and a quarter years old, starts at her posh new prep school and immediately sets about solving all manner of mysteries large and small. (Rev: LMC 10/11; SLJ 4/11)

7936 Haugaard, Erik C. *Under the Black Flag* (5–7). 1994, Roberts Rinehart paper $8.95 (978-1-879373-63-1). Fourteen-year-old William is captured by the pirate Blackbeard and held for ransom in this 18th-century yarn. (Rev: BL 4/1/94; HB 9–10/94; SLJ 5/94)

7937 Haven, Paul. *The Seven Keys of Balabad* (5–8). Illus. by Mark Zug. 2009, Random $16.99 (978-0-375-83350-2). 288pp. Twelve-year-old Oliver, whose father is a foreign correspondent assigned to Balabad, finds himself pulled out of Manhattan and into the middle of an exotic and dangerous mystery surrounding a 500-year-old sacred carpet. (Rev: BCCB 2/09; BL 1/1–15/09; SLJ 4/09)

7938 Hawks, Robert. *The Richest Kid in the World* (4–8). 1992, Avon paper $2.99 (978-0-380-76241-5). Josh is kidnapped and taken to the estate of billionaire Grizzle Welch. (Rev: SLJ 5/92)

7939 Hayes, Daniel. *The Trouble with Lemons* (5–8). 1991, Random House paper $5.99 (978-0-449-70416-5). Tyler, 14, has all kinds of problems — allergies, asthma, and nightmares — and then he finds a dead body. (Rev: BL 5/1/91; SLJ 6/91)

7940 Hearne, Betsy. *Who's in the Hall? A Mystery in Four Chapters* (2–4). Illus. 2000, Greenwillow LB $16.89 (978-0-688-16262-7). 32pp. Three different sets of kids in the same apartment building are troubled by a stranger who knocks at their doors asking to be let in. (Rev: BCCB 1/01; BL 9/15/00; HBG 3/01; SLJ 8/00)

7941 Henderson, Aileen K. *The Summer of the Bonepile Monster* (3–5). Illus. 1995, Milkweed paper $6.95 (978-1-57131-602-8). 140pp. Hollis changes into a self-reliant young man during a summer spent in the country during which he solves a community mystery. (Rev: BCCB 7–8/95; BL 5/1/95; SLJ 7/95)

7942 Hesse, Karen. *Stowaway* (5–8). 2000, Simon & Schuster $17.95 (978-0-689-83987-0). Told by an 11-year-old stowaway, this adventurous sea story tells of Captain Cook's two-and-a-half-year voyage around the world beginning in 1768. (Rev: BL 12/15/00; HB 1–2/01; HBG 3/01; SLJ 11/00; VOYA 4/01)

7943 Heyes, Eileen. *O'Dwyer and Grady Starring in Tough Act to Follow* (4–7). Illus. by Eric Bowman. Series: O'Dwyer and Grady. 2003, Simon & Schuster paper $4.99 (978-0-689-84920-6). Young actors Billy and Virginia stumble into a mystery while searching for props for a show in this action-packed story set in the 1930s. (Rev: BL 5/15/03; SLJ 7/03)

7944 Heyman, Alissa, adapt. *The Big Book of Adventure* (3–6). Illus. by Pedro Rodriguez. 2008, Sterling LB $12.95 (978-1-4027-5156-1). A collection of classic adventure stories — some well-known, others less familiar — prefaced with author biographies and integrated with cartoon graphics. (Rev: SLJ 9/08)

7945 Hiaasen, Carl. *Scat* (5–8). 2009, Knopf $16.99 (978-037583486-8); LB $19.99 (978-037593486-5). 384pp. Nick and Marta team up to solve the real cause of their high school biology teacher's disappearance in this well-paced, conservation-themed read set in the Florida Everglades. ⋒ Lexile 810L (Rev: BL 11/1/08; HB 1–2/09; SLJ 1/1/09*)

7946 Hicks, Deron R. *Secrets of Shakespeare's Grave* (4–6). Illus. by Mark E. Geyer. Series: The Letterford Mysteries. 2012, Houghton Mifflin $16.99 (978-0-547-84034-5). 304pp. Colophon Letterford, 12, is determined to find an elusive family treasure and rescue her family's 400-year-old publishing business. ℮ Lexile 720L (Rev: BL 10/15/12; LMC 5–6/13; SLJ 9/12)

7947 Hicks, Deron R. *Tower of the Five Orders* (4–6). Series: Shakespeare Mysteries. 2013, Houghton Mifflin $16.99 (978-054783953-0). 320pp. Colophon Letterford continues her efforts to save her family's publishing house, following clues that lead this time to Christopher Marlowe. ℮ Lexile 680 (Rev: BLO 9/15/13; SLJ 11/13)

7948 Higgins, F. E. *The Black Book of Secrets* (5–7). 2007, Feiwel & Friends $14.95 (978-0-312-36844-9). Joe Zabbidou takes the confessions of everyone in the remote village of Pagus Parvus, collecting them in a black book. Ludlow Fitch, a desperate boy on the run from cruel parents, acts as Joe's scribe, a dangerous position in a dangerous world. (Rev: BL 10/15/07; HB 1–2/08; LMC 4–5/08; SLJ 4/08)

7949 Higgins, Jack, and Justin Richards. *Death Run* (5–8). Series: Rich and Jade. 2008, Putnam $16.99 (978-039925081-1). 272pp. Teenage twins Rich and Jade travel around the world with their secret-agent dad in this action-packed, fast-paced sequel to 2007's *Sure Fire*. ℮ Lexile HL660L (Rev: BL 9/1/08; SLJ 12/08; VOYA 8/08)

7950 Higgins, Jack, and Justin Richards. *First Strike* (5–8). Series: Rich and Jade. 2010, Putnam $16.99 (978-039925240-2). 240pp. When two disparate sets of villains invade the White House with designs on stealing nuclear launch codes, the British twins Rich and Jade and their secret-agent father again save the day. (Rev: BLO 6/10; VOYA 8/10)

7951 Higgins, Jack, and Justin Richards. *Sharp Shot* (5–8). Series: Rich and Jade. 2009, Putnam $16.99 (978-0-399-25239-6). 240pp. In this action-packed volume, the third in a series, twins Jade and Rich find themselves on a dangerous mission to thwart an evil plot after they're attacked by one of their secret agent dad's old enemies. Lexile HL730L (Rev: BLO 11/1/09; SLJ 3/10)

7952 Higgins, Simon. *Moonshadow: Rise of the Ninja* (4–7). 2010, Little, Brown $15.99 (978-0-316-05531-4). 336pp. Moonshadow is forced to test his skills as a ninja when Silver Wolf's warriors attack in this story set in Japan in the time of the samurai. Lexile 840L (Rev: BL 6/10; LMC 8–9/10; SLJ 8/10)

7953 Higson, Charlie. *Blood Fever: A James Bond Adventure* (5–8). Series: Young Bond. 2006, Hyperion $16.95 (978-0-7868-3662-8). Even at 13, Bond is having adventures: this one finds him on the island of Sardinia, caught up in an art-theft mystery and rescuing a girl in peril. (Rev: SLJ 6/06)

7954 Hilgartner, Beth. *A Murder for Her Majesty* (5–8). 1986, Houghton Mifflin paper $6.95 (978-0-395-61619-2). Alice disguises herself as a boy to escape her father's murderers. (Rev: BCCB 9/86; SLJ 10/86)

7955 Hill, David. *Running Hot* (5–8). 2007, Simply Read paper $9.95 (978-1-894965-52-1). A group of students clearing forest trees in rural New Zealand suddenly find themselves threatened by a raging fire. (Rev: SLJ 4/07)

7956 Hobbs, Will. *Jackie's Wild Seattle* (5–8). 2003, HarperCollins LB $16.89 (978-0-06-051631-4). In the aftermath of September 11, 2001, Shannon, 14, and her younger brother spend an exciting and healing summer in Seattle with their animal rescuer uncle. (Rev: BL 6/1–15/03; HBG 4/04; SLJ 5/03; VOYA 8/03)

7957 Hobbs, Will. *Jason's Gold* (5–9). 1999, Morrow $17.99 (978-0-688-15093-8). In this sharply realistic novel, 15-year-old Jason leaves Seattle in 1897 and, with a dog he has saved, heads for the Klondike and gold. (Rev: BL 8/99; HB 9–10/99; HBG 3/00; SLJ 11/99)

7958 Holm, Jennifer, and Jonathan Hamel. *You Only Have Nine Lives* (3–5). Illus. by Brad Weinman. Series: The Stink Files. 2005, HarperCollins $14.99 (978-0-06-052985-7). 128pp. Traveling to France as the winner of a cat food competition, cat sleuth Mr. Stink is mistaken as a prince and uncovers secrets about his own origins. (Rev: SLJ 12/05)

7959 Holman, Felice. *Slake's Limbo* (5–9). 1974, Macmillan paper $4.99 (978-0-689-71066-7). Thirteen-year-old Artemis Slake finds an ideal hideaway for four months in the labyrinth of the New York City subway. (Rev: BL 6/1/88)

7960 Hopper, Nancy J. *Ape Ears and Beaky* (4–7). 1987, Avon paper $2.50 (978-0-380-70270-1). Scott and Beaky solve the mystery of the robberies in a condominium.

7961 Horowitz, Anthony. *Alex Rider: The Gadgets* (5–8). Illus. by John Lawson. 2006, Philomel $15.99 (978-0-399-24486-5). A look at all the gadgets used in the first five Alex Rider mysteries — including such wonders as a radio mouth brace, exploding ear stud, and pizza delivery assassin kit — with diagrams and details of how they were used. (Rev: BL 4/1/06; SLJ 4/06)

7962 Horowitz, Anthony. *The Greek Who Stole Christmas* (4–7). Series: A Diamond Brothers Mystery. 2008, Penguin paper $7.99 (978-01424037-5-4). 144pp. Amid the Christmas noise and bustle, Diamond brothers Nick and Tim bumble their way through protecting a dazzling young pop star who has received death threats. **e** Lexile 630L (Rev: BL 11/1/08; SLJ 8/09)

7963 Horowitz, Anthony. *South by Southeast* (4–7). Series: Diamond Brothers. 2005, Philomel $16.99 (978-0-399-24155-0); paper $5.99 (978-0-14-240374-7). Hapless private eye Tim Diamond and his brother Nick find themselves drawn into a labyrinthine mystery after a visit from a stranger. (Rev: BL 12/1/05; SLJ 12/05)

7964 Horowitz, Anthony. *Stormbreaker* (5–9). Series: Alex Rider. 2001, Philomel $17.99 (978-0-399-23620-4). Fourteen-year-old Alex becomes embroiled in dangerous undercover exploits when his MI6 uncle is murdered. (Rev: BCCB 9/01; BL 9/1/01; HBG 10/01; SLJ 6/01; VOYA 8/01)

7965 Horowitz, Anthony. *Three of Diamonds* (5–8). Series: Diamond Brothers. 2005, Philomel $16.99 (978-0-399-24157-4). Tim and Nick succeed in solving crimes despite Tim's blunderings in these three fast-paced and entertaining mystery stories full of wordplay. (Rev: BL 5/15/05; SLJ 5/05)

7966 Horse, Harry. *The Last Castaways* (2–5). Illus. by author. 2009, Peachtree $12.95 (978-1-56145-439-6). 128pp. Letters, logs, and diaries tell the story of Grandfather's adventures at sea — and marooned on land — with his dog Roo. (Rev: BL 4/1/09)

7967 Horse, Harry. *The Last Gold Diggers* (2–4). Illus. by author. 2008, Peachtree $12.95 (978-1-56145-435-8). 136pp. In letters and journal entries Grandfather describes a series of zany adventures in Australia with his talented dog Roo as they search for Grandfather's missing brother. (Rev: BL 4/15/08)

7968 Horvath, Polly. *Mr. and Mrs. Bunny — Detectives Extraordinaire!* (3–6). Illus. by Sophie Blackall. 2012, Random House $16.99 (978-0-375-86755-2); LB $19.99 (978-0-375-96755-9). 256pp. When Madeline's hopelessly anachronistic parents go missing, the dutiful 5th-grader who can communicate with animals enlists the help of neighboring detectives Mr. and Mrs. Bunny to bring them home. ⋒ **e** Lexile 730L (Rev: BL 2/15/12*; HB 1–2/12; LMC 5–6/12; SLJ 2/1/12)

7969 Hunt, L. J. *The Abernathy Boys* (5–7). 2004, HarperCollins LB $16.89 (978-0-06-029259-1). Young Bud and Temple Abernathy survive an eventful journey through the desert in this fictionalized version of a real expedition in the early 20th century. (Rev: BL 1/1–15/04; SLJ 3/04)

7970 Hyde, Dayton O. *Mr. Beans* (5–7). 2000, Boyds Mills $14.95 (978-1-56397-866-1). In a small town in Oregon in the early 1940s, bully Mugsy wrongfully accuses a tame bear of attacking him, and timid Chirp frees the bear and takes off with him on a wilderness journey. (Rev: BL 11/15/00; HBG 10/01; SLJ 1/01; VOYA 4/01)

7971 Hyland, Hilary. *The Wreck of the Ethie* (4–7). Illus. by Paul Bachem. 1999, Peachtree paper $7.95 (978-1-56145-198-2). Told through the eyes of two youngsters, this is a novelization of a true incident in which a dog saved passengers after their ship sank off the coast of Newfoundland. (Rev: SLJ 4/00)

7972 Jackson, Melanie. *The Big Dip* (4–7). 2009, Orca paper $9.95 (978-1-55469-178-4). 112pp. Fifteen-year-old Joe's little sister is kidnapped soon after Joe witnessed a man shot to death at an amusement park; Joe investigates in this suspenseful novel suitable for reluctant readers. (Rev: BL 2/1/10; LMC 5–6/10; SLJ 11/09)

7973 Jackson, Melanie. *Queen of Disguises* (4–6). 2009, Orca paper $9.95 (978-1-55469-037-4). A funny mystery in which young sleuth and singer Dinah Galloway is threatened by a vengeful actress. (Rev: BL 5/1/09)

7974 Jacobson, Jennifer Richard. *Small as an Elephant* (4–7). 2011, Candlewick $15.99 (978-0-7636-4155-9). 288pp. Abandoned in Maine by his bipolar mother, 11-year-old Jack sets out for his Boston home determined to escape detection by adults. ∩ **e** Lexile 790L (Rev: BL 6/1/11; HB 3–4/11; SLJ 4/11; VOYA 2/11)

7975 Jam, Teddy. *ttuM* (2–4). Illus. by Harvey Chan. Series: A Charlotte Novel. 1999, Groundwood $14.95 (978-0-88899-373-1); paper $5.95 (978-0-88899-374-8). 109pp. In this beginning chapter book, a little girl who speaks to her dog, ttuM, in reverse, solves a mystery about a strange person in black seen canoeing on the village lake. (Rev: SLJ 3/00)

7976 Jaramillo, Ann. *La Línea* (5–8). 2006, Roaring Brook $16.95 (978-1-59643-154-6). Miguel, 15, and his sister Elena, 13, survive a terrifying journey across the border (la linea) from Mexico to California to join their parents. (Rev: BCCB 5/06; BL 3/15/06*; HBG 10/06; LMC 10/06; SLJ 4/06; VOYA 4/06)

7977 Jennings, Patrick. *The Bird Shadow: An Ike and Mem Story* (2–4). Illus. by Anna Alter. 2001, Holiday House $15.95 (978-0-8234-1670-7). 55pp. Ike and little sister Mem end up making a new friend when they dare to investigate a spooky old house. (Rev: HBG 10/02; SLJ 3/02)

7978 Jennings, Richard W. *The Pirates of Turtle Rock* (5–8). 2008, Houghton Mifflin $16.00 (978-0-618-98793-1). A modern-day Florida girl falls for a young pirate and the two embark on a treasure hunt for an ancient Caribbean artifact; a novel full of humor and adventure. (Rev: BL 4/15/08; SLJ 8/08)

7979 Johns, Linda. *Hannah West in Deep Water* (5–8). Series: Hannah West. 2006, Puffin paper $5.99 (978-0-14-240700-4). Hannah investigates environmental shenanigans while she and her mother are house-sitting a houseboat and a dog. (Rev: BL 12/15/06)

7980 Johns, Linda. *Hannah West in the Belltown Towers: A Mystery* (5–8). Series: Hannah West. 2006, Sleuth paper $5.99 (978-0-14-240637-3). Hannah, an adopted Chinese girl with lots of nerve and curiosity, moves with her mother to Seattle and soon finds herself embroiled in an art theft. (Rev: BL 5/1/06)

7981 Johns, Linda. *Hannah West on Millionaire's Row* (5–8). Series: Hannah West. 2007, Puffin paper $5.99 (978-0-14-240824-7). Girl sleuth Hannah West, who was adopted from China, solves a mystery involving feng shui, antiques, and old mansions in this fourth installment in the series. (Rev: BL 10/1/07)

7982 Johnson, Annabel, and Edgar Johnson. *The Grizzly* (5–7). Illus. by Gilbert Riswold. 1964, HarperCollins paper $4.95 (978-0-06-440036-7). A perceptive story of a father-son relationship in which David, on a camping trip, saves his father's life when a grizzly bear attacks.

7983 Johnson, Henry, and Paul Hoppe. *Travis and Freddy's Adventures in Vegas* (5–8). 2006, Dutton $15.99 (978-0-525-47646-7). A lighthearted, fast-paced adventure in which preteens Travis and Freddy head to Las Vegas to win enough money to save Travis's home; there they win big but soon find they have the mob at their heels. (Rev: BL 2/15/06; SLJ 4/06; VOYA 4/06)

7984 Johnson, Rodney. *The Secret of Dead Man's Mine* (5–7). Illus. by Jill Thompson. Series: Rinnah Two Feathers Mystery. 2001, Uglytown paper $12.00 (978-0-9663473-3-3). Rinnah Two Feathers and two friends set out to solve the mystery of a suspicious stranger and find themselves in danger. (Rev: SLJ 9/01)

7985 Jones, Elizabeth McDavid. *Traitor in Williamsburg* (3–5). Series: Felicity Mystery. 2008, American Girl paper $6.95 (978-1-59369-296-4). In 1776 Williamsburg, Felicity and Elizabeth investigate mysterious anonymous notices accusing Felicity's father, among others, of helping the British. (Rev: BL 4/15/08)

7986 Joosse, Barbara M. *Dead Guys Talk: A Wild Willie Mystery* (3–5). Illus. by Abby Carter. 2006, Clarion $15.00 (978-0-618-30666-4). A puzzle at the cemetery tasks the nerve and sleuthing skills of Scarface Detectives Willie, Lucy, and Kyle. (Rev: BL 5/1/06; SLJ 9/06)

7987 Joosse, Barbara M. *Ghost Trap: A Wild Willie Mystery* (3–5). Illus. 1998, Clarion $15.00 (978-0-395-66587-9). 69pp. An easily read mystery about three friends, Willie, Kyle, and Lucy, and mysterious happenings that occur in a house formerly owned by an amateur detective and now the home of Kyle and his family. (Rev: BCCB 7–8/98; BL 6/1–15/98; HB 7/98; HBG 10/98; SLJ 6/98)

7988 Jung, Mike. *Geeks, Girls, and Secret Identities* (4–7). Illus. by Mike Maihack. 2012, Scholastic $16.99 (978-0-545-33548-5). 320pp. Vincent, 12, contends with the realization that his superhero idol Captain Stupendous and his crush Polly are the same person even as they work to save Vincent's kidnapped mother. **e** Lexile 790L (Rev: BL 10/15/12; LMC 1–2/13; SLJ 12/12)

7989 Keane, Dave. *The Haunted Toolshed* (2–5). Illus. by author. Series: Joe Sherlock, Kid Detective. 2006, HarperCollins paper $3.99 (978-0-06-076188-2). 120pp. Goofy boy detective Joe Sherlock gets to the bottom of a tricky mystery in this first installment in a series that will entertain the flatulence gang. (Rev: SLJ 7/06)

7990 Keaney, Brian. *The Haunting of Nathaniel Wolfe* (4–7). 2012, IPG/Hodder paper $8.99 (978-18461652-0-7). 240pp. Scam medium's son Nathaniel discovers an unexpected entrance into the spirit world, where he and a friend are tasked with solving a spine-chilling murder in this mystery set in Victorian-era London. **e** (Rev: BL 5/1/12)

7991 Keene, Carolyn. *Where's Nancy?* (4–7). Series: Nancy Drew Super Mystery. 2005, Simon & Schuster paper $4.99 (978-0-416-90034-7). Nancy herself is missing in this first installment of a new series. (Rev: BL 5/1/05)

7992 Kehret, Peg. *Earthquake Terror* (4–7). 1998, Puffin paper $5.99 (978-0-14-038343-0). A violent earthquake strikes the small island on which 12-year-old Jonathan is alone with his younger sister, Abby. (Rev: BCCB 3/96; BL 1/1–15/96; SLJ 2/96)

7993 Kehret, Peg. *Stolen Children* (4–7). 2008, Dutton $16.99 (978-0-525-47835-5). 208pp. Fourteen-year-old Amy is babysitting for a wealthy family when she and 3-year-old Kendra are kidnapped in this fast-paced, dramatic story. (Rev: BL 12/15/08; SLJ 12/08)

7994 Kehret, Peg. *The Stranger Next Door* (4–6). 2002, Dutton $15.99 (978-0-525-46829-5). 160pp. Twelve-year-old Alex discovers who's behind a spate of vandalism and arson in his new neighborhood, with the help of his feline friend Pete. (Rev: BL 2/1/02; HBG 10/02; SLJ 3/02)

7995 Kelly, Katy. *Melonhead and the Undercover Operation* (3–5). Illus. by Gillian Johnson. 2011, Delacorte $12.99 (978-0-385-73659-6); LB $15.99 (978-0-385-90618-0). 256pp. Melonhead and his fellow FBI Junior Special Agent Sam investigate whether a neighbor is one of the Ten Most Wanted criminals. (Rev: BL 11/1/11; SLJ 11/1/11)

7996 Kelsey, Marybeth. *A Recipe 4 Robbery* (4–6). 2009, HarperCollins $16.99 (978-0-06-128843-2). 288pp. Sixth-grader Lindy finds a stolen locket and, with her friends Margaret and Gus, sets out to find the robber and clear all suspicion from Granny Goose. (Rev: BL 5/1/09; SLJ 7/09)

7997 Kennedy, Emma. *The Case of the Fatal Phantom* (5–8). 2012, Dial $16.99 (978-080373542-2). 272pp. In this third installment in the humorous mystery series with complex plots, Wilma and her beagle look for a treasure supposedly guarded by a dangerous ghost. **e** (Rev: BLO 7/12)

7998 Kennedy, Emma. *The Case of the Frozen Hearts* (4–7). Series: Wilma Tenderfoot. 2011, Dial $16.99 (978-0-8037-3540-8). 352pp. Wilma Tenderfoot, a 10-year-old orphan servant, finally gets the chance to try her sleuthing skills when she meets a famous detective. **e** (Rev: BL 11/15/11; LMC 1–2/12; SLJ 10/1/11)

7999 Kidd, Ronald. *The Year of the Bomb* (4–7). 2009, Simon & Schuster $15.99 (978-1-4169-5892-5). 208pp. In 1955 California as *Invasion of the Body Snatchers* is being filmed, four 7th-grade boys face danger as they learn about Cold War tensions and spies. (Rev: BL 5/1/09; LMC 10/09; SLJ 7/09; VOYA 10/09)

8000 King-Smith, Dick. *Harry's Mad* (4–6). Illus. 1990, Macmillan $15.95 (978-0-7451-1101-8); Knopf paper $4.99 (978-0-679-88688-4). Mad the talking parrot is stolen, but the sharp-witted bird finally makes it back home. (Rev: BCCB 5/87; BL 7/87; SLJ 5/87)

8001 King, Wesley. *The Vindico* (5–8). 2012, Putnam $16.99 (978-0-399-25654-7). 298pp. A troupe of aging supervillains kidnaps five teens to train as their successors, but James, Lana, Hayden, Emily, and Sam resist their fates when they see the destruction they will be creating. **e** Lexile 700L (Rev: BL 5/15/12; HB 7–8/12; SLJ 8/1/12)

8002 Kittscher, Kristen. *The Wig in the Window* (5–7). Series: Sophie Young and Grace Yang Mysteries. 2013, HarperCollins $16.99 (978-006211050-3). 368pp. Pre-teen sleuths Grace and Sophie conduct midnight spy missions in hopes of catching criminals, and the results strain their relationship; the first volume in a series. (Rev: BL 5/1/13; SLJ 8/13*)

8003 Klise, Kate. *Till Death Do Us Bark* (3–6). Illus. by M. Sarah Klise. Series: 43 Old Cemetery Road. 2011, Harcourt $15 (978-054740036-5). 144pp. In this third installment in the humorous mystery series, Seymour's newly adopted, barking wolfhound leads him into a puzzle involving an inheritance. **e** Lexile 710L (Rev: BL 1/1–15/11)

8004 Klise, Kate. *Trial by Jury Journal* (5–8). Illus. by M. Sarah Klise. 2001, HarperCollins LB $16.89 (978-0-06-029541-7). When she is given the opportunity to serve as her state's first juvenile juror, 12-year-old Lily's sleuthing skills solve a murder mystery and save the day. (Rev: BCCB 4/01; BL 9/1/01; HB 5–6/01; HBG 10/01; SLJ 6/01)

8005 Konigsburg, E. L. *From the Mixed-Up Files of Mrs. Basil E. Frankweiler* (5–7). Illus. by author. 1967, Macmillan $17.00 (978-0-689-20586-6). Adventure, suspense, detection, and humor are involved when 12-year-old Claudia and her younger brother elude the security guards and live for a week in New York's Metropolitan Museum of Art. Newbery Medal winner, 1968.

8006 Konigsburg, E. L. *Silent to the Bone* (5–9). 2000, Simon & Schuster $16.00 (978-0-689-83601-5). A mystery story filled with suspense about a baby who's been dropped and a 13-year-old suspect who has lost his ability to speak. (Rev: BL 8/00*; HB 11–12/00; HBG 3/01; SLJ 9/00; VOYA 12/00)

8007 Korman, Gordon. *The Abduction* (4–7). Series: Kidnapped. 2006, Scholastic paper $4.99 (978-0-439-84777-3). A fast-paced thriller, the opening volume of a new series, in which 15-year-old Aiden works with the FBI to rescue his 11-year-old sister Meg, who was abducted while on her way home from school and is meanwhile resisting her captors. The second volume is *The Search* (2006). (Rev: BL 8/06; SLJ 9/06)

8008 Korman, Gordon. *Chasing the Falconers* (4–7). 2005, Scholastic paper $4.99 (978-0-439-65136-3). In this fast-paced adventure, Aiden and Meg Falconer must evade pursuers as they work to gather evidence that will prove their parents' innocence of treason. (Rev: BL 5/15/05; SLJ 8/05)

8009 Korman, Gordon. *Framed* (5–7). 2010, Scholastic $16.99 (978-0-545-17849-5). 240pp. A Super Bowl ring has gone missing and Griffin's retainer is found in its place. He and his friends try to clear his name in this follow-up to *Swindle* (2008) and *Zoobreak* (2009). 🎧 Lexile 730L (Rev: LMC 11–12/10; SLJ 9/1/10)

8010 Korman, Gordon. *The Hypnotists* (4–7). 2013, Scholastic $16.99 (978-054550322-8). 240pp. Jackson Opus seems like the luckiest guy ever: he always gets the girl, he's a star student and a great athlete, but it turns out that it's not just luck; he's a hypnotist, and the people who say they want to help him hone his gift may not really want to help him at all. ❤ (Rev: BLO 9/15/13; LMC 1–2/14; SLJ 9/13)

8011 Korman, Gordon. *Jackpot* (3–6). Series: Swindle. 2014, Scholastic $16.99 (978-054556146-4). 208pp. Mr. Fielder's winning lottery ticket is missing and Griffin Bing and his friends set out to find it with the help of Griffin's father's latest invention. ❤ Lexile 760 (Rev: BLO 3/1/14)

8012 Korman, Gordon. *One False Note* (4–8). Series: The 39 Clues. 2008, Scholastic $12.99 (978-0-545-06042-4). 176pp. Amy and Dan Cahill's arguments continue as they race to stay ahead of their cousins in hunting down the next clue that will solve their family mystery; a sequel to Rick Riordan's *The Maze of Bones* (2008). ∩ (Rev: BL 2/1/09; SLJ 7/09; VOYA 4/09)

8013 Korman, Gordon. *Swindle* (3–6). 2008, Scholastic $16.99 (978-0-439-90344-8). 252pp. Griffin Bings organizes a 6th-grade effort to rescue a rare baseball card and save the family business. (Rev: BL 1/1–15/08; SLJ 2/08)

8014 Korman, Gordon. *Zoobreak* (4–7). Series: Swindle. 2009, Scholastic $16.99 (978-054512499-7). 240pp. When Savannah finds her missing pet monkey Cleo at a floating animal zoo, she and her friends plan a rescue mission; a sequel to *Swindle* (2008). ∩ ❤ Lexile 700L (Rev: BL 11/1/09; LMC 11–12/09; SLJ 11/09; VOYA 10/09)

8015 Krieg, Jim. *Griff Carver, Hallway Patrol* (4–7). 2010, Penguin $15.99 (978-1-59514-276-4). 272pp. Thirteen-year-old Griff Carver fights crime as part of the Safety Patrol at Rampart Middle School, disciplining everyone from the principal on down in this humorous spoof of a police procedural that includes a hall-pass counterfeiting ring. ∩ ❤ Lexile 710L (Rev: BL 5/1/10*; HB 5–6/10; LMC 3–4/10; SLJ 3/10)

8016 Kuhlman, Evan. *Brother from a Box* (4–6). Illus. by Iacopo Bruno. 2012, Atheneum $16.99 (978-144242658-0). 304pp. Matthew's computer-genius father creates a robotic twin brother for him that proves such a success that unsavory characters seek to steal him; this multilayered story is full of action and humor. ❤ (Rev: BLO 4/1/12; LMC 8–9/12; SLJ 6/12)

8017 Lacey, Josh. *Island of Thieves* (4–7). 2012, Houghton Mifflin $15.99 (978-054776327-9). 240pp. Tom and his shifty Uncle Harvey hunt for lost treasure in Peru and find themselves almost immediately in danger in this exciting, fast-paced story. ∩ ❤ Lexile 640L (Rev: BL 5/1/12*; LMC 8–9/12; SLJ 6/12)

8018 Lacey, Josh. *The Sultan's Tigers* (4–7). 2013, Houghton Mifflin $16.99 (978-054409645-5). 304pp. Off on another dubious adventure with his Uncle Harvey, Tom heads to southern India in search of a jeweled tiger statue hidden centuries ago by a relative, and learns about a new culture. ❤ Lexile 640 (Rev: BL 11/1/13; SLJ 2/14)

8019 Lachtman, Ofelia Dumas. *Call Me Consuelo* (4–6). 1997, Arte Publico paper $9.95 (978-1-55885-187-0). 147pp. Consuelo, a recent arrival in Los Angeles, be-

comes involved in finding the criminals who are committing mysterious local robberies. (Rev: SLJ 7/97)

8020 LaFevers, R. L. *The Basilisk's Lair* (2–5). Illus. by Kelly Murphy. Series: Nathaniel Fludd, Beastologist. 2010, Houghton Mifflin $15 (978-0-547-23867-8). 160pp. Young Nate's beastology skills are tested when he goes off to West Africa with his Aunt Phil in pursuit of a highly dangerous escaped basilisk. (Rev: BL 5/15/10; SLJ 7/1/10)

8021 Lafevers, R. L. *The Flight of the Phoenix* (2–5). Illus. by Kelly Murphy. Series: Nathaniel Fludd, Beastologist. 2009, Houghton Mifflin $16 (978-0-547-23865-4). 144pp. Nathaniel's parents are declared lost at sea in 1926 and he goes to live with his father's cousin, finding himself in training as a beastologist. ∩ (Rev: BL 10/1/09; LMC 1–2/10; SLJ 9/1/09)

8022 LaFevers, R. L. *Theodosia and the Eyes of Horus* (5–8). Illus. by Yoko Tanaka. Series: Theodosia. 2010, Houghton Mifflin $16 (978-0-547-22592-0). 384pp. Supernaturally talented Theodosia, 11, copes with her difficult family while using her knowledge of Egyptian lore to stymie the evil powers of the Arcane Order of the Black Sun. (Rev: BLO 2/1/10; SLJ 7/10)

8023 LaFevers, R. L. *Theodosia and the Last Pharaoh* (5–8). Illus. by Yoko Tanaka. Series: Theodosia. 2011, Houghton Mifflin $16.99 (978-054739018-5). 400pp. Endeavoring to return a priceless Egyptian artifact, 11-year-old Theodosia and her cat Isis arouse interest as soon as they arrive in Cairo. (Rev: BL 5/1/11)

8024 Lafevers, R. L. *Theodosia and the Serpents of Chaos* (5–8). Illus. by Yoko Tanaka. 2007, Houghton Mifflin $16.00 (978-0-618-75638-4). In the early 20th century, precocious 11-year-old Theodosia finds herself embroiled in a supernatural mystery involving Egyptian artifacts. (Rev: BL 5/1/07*; SLJ 4/07)

8025 LaFevers, R. L. *Theodosia and the Staff of Osiris* (5–8). 2008, Houghton Mifflin $16 (978-061892764-7). 400pp. Brainy 11-year-old Theodosia solves the puzzles of misplaced mummies and ancient curses — all the while coping with a conniving grandmother and a father in prison — in this witty first-person tale set in Edwardian England. ∩ ❤ Lexile 750L (Rev: BL 11/15/08; SLJ 12/08)

8026 LaFevers, R. L. *The Unicorn's Tale* (2–5). Illus. by Kelly Murphy. Series: Nathaniel Fludd, Beastologist. 2011, Houghton Mifflin $14.99 (978-054748277-4). 160pp. Nate and Aunt Phil nurse a sick unicorn and continue the search for information about Nate's parents. Lexile 730L (Rev: BL 4/1/11)

8027 Lalicki, Tom. *Danger in the Dark: A Houdini and Nate Mystery* (3–6). 2006, Farrar $14.95 (978-0-374-31680-8). 192pp. With the help of Harry Houdini, 12-year-old Nate plans to uncover suspected swindling by the strange man who's been holding séances with Nate's rich great-aunt in this historical mystery set in 1911 Manhattan. (Rev: BL 11/15/06; SLJ 10/06)

8028 Lalicki, Tom. *Shots at Sea: A Houdini and Nate Mystery* (4–7). Series: Houdini and Nate. 2007, Farrar

$15.95 (978-0-374-31679-2). In the second book in the series, Nate, 13, is aboard the *Lusitania* and finds among his fellow-passengers both Harry Houdini and Teddy Roosevelt; Nate and the former rescue the latter from an assassination attempt. (Rev: BL 1/1–15/08; SLJ 11/07)

8029 Lane, Andrew. *Fire Storm* (5–8). Series: Sherlock Holmes: The Legend Begins. 2013, Farrar $17.99 (978-037432311-0). 352pp. Young Sherlock travels to Scotland in search of his former tutor and his daughter. e Lexile 880 (Rev: BLO 3/1/14)

8030 Lane, Kathleen. *Nana Cracks the Case!* (2–4). Illus. by Sarah Horne. 2009, Chronicle $14.99 (978-0-8118-6258-5). 120pp. Feisty Nana and her lively grandchildren Eufala and Bog investigate missing candy in this funny mystery loaded with visual jokes. (Rev: LMC 8/09; SLJ 6/09)

8031 Lasky, Kathryn. *Born to Rule* (3–6). Series: Camp Princess. 2006, HarperCollins $15.99 (978-0-06-058761-1). This first book in the Camp Princess series has Princess Alicia of All the Belgravias reluctantly attending princess training camp and stumbling upon a ghost story. (Rev: SLJ 5/06)

8032 Latta, Sara. *Stella Brite and the Dark Matter Mystery* (2–4). Illus. by Meredith Johnson. 2006, Charlesbridge paper $6.95 (978-1-57091-884-1). To give their fledgling detective agency a higher profile, Stella Brite and her brother Max try to unravel the mystery of invisible dark matter in the universe. (Rev: SLJ 4/06)

8033 Lawrence, Caroline. *The Case of the Deadly Desperados* (4–6). Series: Western Mysteries. 2012, Putnam $16.99 (978-039925633-2). 272pp. In 1862 Nevada Territory 12-year-old Pinky Pinkerton finds his foster parents scalped in their cabin, and flees to the silver mining town of Virginia City pursued by a trio of baddies who want a mysterious legacy from his father. ⌒ e (Rev: BL 2/15/12*; HB 5–6/12; SLJ 3/12; VOYA 4/12)

8034 Lawrence, Caroline. *P. K. Pinkerton and the Petrified Man* (4–6). Series: Western Mysteries. 2013, Putnam $16.99 (978-039925634-9). 288pp. Young P. K. Pinkerton sets up his own detective agency in Nevada in 1862 and tackles a case involving a murder and subsequent disappearance in this compelling story. ⌒ Lexile 750 (Rev: BL 3/15/13*; LMC 10/13; SLJ 5/13)

8035 Lawrence, Iain. *The Séance* (5–7). 2008, Delacorte $15.99 (978-0-385-73375-5). Scooter, whose spiritualist mother performs fake séances, is caught up in a murder mystery involving his idol, Houdini, in this novel that captures the tone of 1920s New York City. (Rev: BL 5/1/08; SLJ 8/08)

8036 Leach, Sara. *Count Me In* (4–6). 2011, Orca paper $9.95 (978-1-55469-404-4). 164pp. Tabitha, her three hateful cousins, and her aunt find themselves stranded in the woods with a hungry bear and a raging river in this survival story suitable for reluctant readers. e Lexile 560L (Rev: SLJ 11/1/11)

8037 Leavey, Peggy Dymond. *The Deep End Gang* (3–7). 2003, Napoleon paper $7.95 (978-0-929141-89-3). 125pp. Twelve-year-old Martin joins forces with two friends to investigate suspicious events at a deserted house in his neighborhood. (Rev: SLJ 9/03)

8038 Lee, Norman. *Camel Rider* (5–7). 2007, Charlesbridge $15.95 (978-1-58089-314-5). Two boys — a 12-year-old Australian named Adam and Walid, a camel driver from Bangladesh — find themselves alone in the desert during a Middle Eastern war and must struggle to survive; told in alternating first-person narratives, this is an exciting story that also shows how people with no common language can learn to communicate. (Rev: BL 9/1/07; SLJ 7/07)

8039 Levy, Elizabeth. *Diamonds and Danger: A Mystery at Sea* (4–6). Illus. by Mordicai Gerstein. 2010, Roaring Brook $16.99 (978-159643462-2). 160pp. Eleven-year-old mystery lover Philippa and her parents live on a large cruise ship, and Philippa investigates questions surrounding the new captain and his son Philip; includes lots of details of life at sea. (Rev: BL 11/1/10; LMC 1–2/11; SLJ 11/1/10)

8040 Lewman, David. *The Case of the Mystery Meat Loaf* (4–7). Series: Club CSI. 2012, Simon & Schuster $15.99 (978-144244646-5); paper $5.99 (978-14424339-4-6). 160pp. When the whole school swim team comes down with food poisoning, three middle-grade sleuths kick into action to figure out the cause and the culprit. e (Rev: BLO 4/1/12; SLJ 4/12)

8041 Little, Kimberley Griffiths. *Enchanted Runner* (5–7). 1999, Avon $15.00 (978-0-380-97623-2). Twelve-year-old Kendall, who is half Native American, hopes to excel in running as his ancestors did, and is given an unusual opportunity to test himself. (Rev: BCCB 9/99; BL 9/1/99; HBG 3/00; SLJ 12/99)

8042 Lloyd Jones, Rob. *Wild Boy* (5–8). 2013, Candlewick $16.99 (978-076366252-3). 304pp. In Victorian England, a circus freak and his acrobat friend Clarissa investigate a murder and a machine that might cure "Wild Boy" of his excessively hairy body. ⌒ e Lexile 660 (Rev: BL 9/1/13; LMC 3–4/14; SLJ 10/13)

8043 London, C. Alexander. *We Are Not Eaten by Yaks* (5–8). Series: An Accidental Adventure. 2011, Philomel $12.99 (978-0-399-25487-1). 240pp. When their mother goes missing, 11-year-old twins Oliver and Celia journey with their father to Tibet, where they encounter many dangerous adventures. Also use *We Dine with Cannibals* (2011). ⌒ Lexile 760L (Rev: BL 1/1–15/11; SLJ 4/11)

8044 London, C. Alexander. *We Dine with Cannibals* (5–8). Illus. by Jonny Duddle. Series: An Accidental Adventure. 2011, Philomel $12.99 (978-039925488-8). 368pp. Their explorer father drags 11-year-old twins Celia and Oliver deep into the Amazon in search of El Dorado and their mother in this humorous sequel to *We Are Not Eaten by Yaks* (2011). e Lexile 700L (Rev: BL 11/1/11; SLJ 1/12)

8045 Lourie, Peter. *The Lost Treasure of Captain Kidd* (5–8). 1996, Shawangunk paper $10.95 (978-1-885482-03-7). Friends Killian and Alex set out to discover Captain Kidd's treasure buried on the banks of the Hudson River centuries ago. (Rev: BL 2/15/96; SLJ 6/96)

8046 Low, Dene. *The Entomological Tales of Augustus T. Percival: Petronella Saves Nearly Everyone* (5–8). Illus. by Jen Corace. 2009, Houghton $16.00 (978-0-547-15250-9). 196pp. In Victorian London, 16-year-old Petronella must deal with her embarrassing, bug-eating uncle and save an international dignitary who has been kidnapped. (Rev: BL 7/09; SLJ 10/09)

8047 Mac. *Anna Smudge: Professional Shrink* (4–6). Illus. by Glenn Fabry. 2008, Toasted Coconut paper $9.99 (978-1-934906-00-2). 256pp. While dealing with the usual problems of her age, Anna, an 11-year-old who is good at listening, sets herself up as a psychologist and soon finds herself drawn into a complex mystery. (Rev: BL 6/1–15/08; SLJ 6/08)

8048 McCall Smith, Alexander. *The Cowgirl Aunt of Harriet Bean* (2–4). Illus. by Laura Rankin. 2006, Bloomsbury $9.95 (978-1-58234-977-0). 67pp. Out West to meet her Aunt Formica for the first time, girl detective Harriet Bean, accompanied by Aunts Thessalonika and Japonica, uses her sleuthing skills to help track down some cattle rustlers. (Rev: SLJ 1/07)

8049 McCall Smith, Alexander. *Max and Maddy and the Chocolate Money Mystery* (2–4). Illus. by Macky Pamintuan. 2007, Bloomsbury $9.95 (978-1-59990-036-0). 80pp. Child detectives Max and Maddy solve the mystery of why dogs are robbing Swiss banks. (Rev: BL 7/07; LMC 5/07)

8050 McCall Smith, Alexander. *The Mystery of Meerkat Hill: A Precious Ramotswe Mystery for Young Readers* (3–6). Illus. by Iain McIntosh. Series: Precious Ramotswe's First Cases. 2013, Anchor paper $6.99 (978-03458044-6-4). 112pp. A young Precious Ramotswe makes new friends at her Botswana school and helps them find their missing cow. (Rev: BL 10/1/13*; SLJ 12/13)

8051 McCaughrean, Geraldine. *The Death-Defying Pepper Roux* (5–8). 2010, HarperCollins LB $17.89 (978-0-06-183666-4). 336pp. Believing his aunt's prediction that he will die at the age of 14, young Pepper Roux first runs away to sea and then has a series of exciting adventures; set in France. ⌒ Lexile 920L (Rev: BL 11/1/09*; HB 1–2/10; LMC 5–6/10; SLJ 1/10)

8052 McClintock, Norah. *Shadow of Doubt* (5–8). Series: Robyn Hunter Mysteries. 2012, Lerner LB $27.93 (978-076138315-4); paper $8.95 (9780761393979). 232pp. Robyn investigates a strange package delivered to her favorite new teacher in this fifth installment in the series that also follows her family and romantic life. ℮ Lexile HL580L (Rev: BL 9/1/12)

8053 MacDonald, Bailey. *The Secret of the Sealed Room: A Mystery of Young Benjamin Franklin* (5–8). 2010, Simon & Schuster $16.99 (978-1-4169-9760-3). 208pp. A young Benjamin Franklin helps 14-year-old Patience, a runaway indentured servant who is suspected of murder. ℮ Lexile 1050L (Rev: BL 12/1/10; SLJ 1/1/11)

8054 MacDonald, Bailey. *Wicked Will: A Mystery of Young William Shakespeare* (4–7). 2009, Aladdin $16.99 (978-1-4169-8660-7). 208pp. In Stratford in the 16th century, Viola, an actress disguised as a boy, meets 12-year-old Will Shakespeare and together they try to trap a murderer. (Rev: BL 5/1/09; LMC 10/09; SLJ 8/09)

8055 McDonald, Megan. *Judy Moody, Girl Detective* (3–5). Illus. by Peter H. Reynolds. 2010, Candlewick $15.99 (978-0-7636-3450-6). 192pp. Ardent Nancy Drew fan Judy Moody, a 3rd-grader, investigates the mystery of the missing police dog. ⌒ ℮ Lexile 570L (Rev: BL 9/1/10; SLJ 8/1/10)

8056 McDonald, Megan. *Judy Moody's Mini-Mysteries and Other Sneaky Stuff for Super-Sleuths* (3–5). Illus. by Peter H. Reynolds. Series: Judy Moody. 2012, Candlewick paper $4.99 (978-07636594-1-7). 128pp. A collection of six short mystery stories full of clues, codes, and opportunities to use your own deductions. ℮ Lexile 640L (Rev: BLO 9/15/12)

8057 McFadden, Deanna. *Robinson Crusoe: Retold from the Daniel Defoe Original* (4–7). Illus. by Jamel Akib. Series: Classic Starts. 2006, Sterling $4.95 (978-1-4027-2664-4). The 1719 original text is retold in brief, accessible sentences that portray Crusoe and Friday as equals. (Rev: BL 2/15/06)

8058 Machado, Ana Maria. *From Another World* (4–7). Illus. by Lucia Brandao. 2005, Douglas & McIntyre $15.95 (978-0-88899-597-1). Spending a night in an outbuilding of an old farmhouse, Mariano and his three friends meet the ghost of a 19th-century slave girl and promise to help in this story set in Brazil. (Rev: BL 5/1/05; SLJ 6/05)

8059 Mack, Jeff. *Clueless McGee* (4–6). Illus. by author. 2012, Philomel $12.99 (978-0-399-25749-0). 244pp. Who stole the macaroni and cheese from the cafeteria? Ten-year-old P.J. McGee tells his absent father about his investigations and other adventures in a series of letters. ℮ Lexile 530L (Rev: BLO 9/1/12; LMC 3–4/13; SLJ 8/12)

8060 Mack, Tracy, and Michael Citrin. *The Fall of the Amazing Zalindas* (4–7). Illus. by Greg Ruth. Series: Sherlock Holmes and the Baker Street Irregulars. 2006, Scholastic $16.99 (978-0-439-82836-9). Sherlock Holmes calls on a gang of street children to help him investigate the mysterious deaths of a family of trapeze artists. (Rev: BL 11/1/06; SLJ 1/07)

8061 Mack, Tracy, and Michael Citrin. *The Mystery of the Conjured Man* (5–7). Series: Sherlock Holmes and the Baker Street Irregulars. 2009, Scholastic paper $6.99 (978-0-439-83667-8). 208pp. This second fast-paced installment in the series contains séances, death, hidden passages, fraud, and a twist at the end. (Rev: BLO 6/16/09; SLJ 6/09)

8062 Maddox, Jake. *Blizzard!* (5–9). Illus. by Sean Tiffany. Series: A Jake Maddox Sports Story. 2009, Stone Arch LB $23.99 (978-1-4342-1206-1). 72pp. Two teen boys are on their way to an awards dinner when a catastrophic blizzard challenges their survival skills; suitable for reluctant readers, this easy-reading novel includes large black-and-white illustrations. (Rev: SLJ 6/1/09)

8063 Maddox, Jake. *Shipwreck!* (5–9). Illus. by Sean Tiffany. Series: A Jake Maddox Sports Story. 2009, Stone Arch LB $23.99 (978-1-4342-1207-8). 72pp. When their whale-watching boat sinks, three teens must use their wits to survive sweltering heat, storms, and even a shark attack; suitable for reluctant readers, this easy-reading novel includes large black-and-white illustrations. (Rev: SLJ 6/1/09)

8064 Madormo, John. *The Homemade Stuffing Caper: Charlie Collier, Snoop for Hire* (4–7). 2012, Philomel $15.99 (978-039925543-4). 256pp. An exciting mystery in which Charlie and his friend Henry investigate missing pet birds. ❤ (Rev: BL 5/1/12; LMC 11–12/12; SLJ 6/12)

8065 Malaghan, Michael. *Greek Ransom* (4–7). 2010, Andersen paper $9.99 (978-1-84270-786-9). 264pp. When their archaeologist parents are kidnapped on a Greek island, Nick and Callie must rescue them in an action-packed adventure that includes hidden treasure, exciting chases, and even an earthquake and a monster. (Rev: BL 4/15/10; SLJ 2/10)

8066 Margolin, Phillip, and Ami Margolin Rome. *Vanishing Acts* (4–7). 2011, HarperCollins $16.99 (978-006188556-3). 176pp. Nancy Drew protégée Madison Kincaid, 12, solves two missing-person cases — one in collaboration with her attorney father — while coping with junior high in Portland, Oregon. (Rev: BL 5/1/11; SLJ 2/12)

8067 Margolis, Leslie. *Girl's Best Friend: A Maggie Brooklyn Mystery* (5–8). 2010, Bloomsbury $14.99 (978-1-59990-525-9). 272pp. Twelve-year-old Maggie, a Nancy Drew fan, solves the mystery of disappearing dogs in Park Slope, Brooklyn, and then tackles missing money in this lighthearted novel. ❤ Lexile 620L (Rev: HB 9–10/10; LMC 10/10; SLJ 12/1/10)

8068 Martin, Terri. *A Family Trait* (5–7). 1999, Holiday $15.95 (978-0-8234-1467-3). In this fast-paced story, Iris, 11 years old and incurably curious, has a number of mysteries to solve while trying to finish a book report. (Rev: BL 10/1/99; HBG 3/00; SLJ 10/99)

8069 Mason, Jane B., and Sarah Hines Stephens. *Bella Baxter and the Lighthouse Mystery* (2–4). Illus. by John Shelley. Series: Bella Baxter. 2006, Simon & Schuster paper $3.99 (978-0-689-86282-3). 80pp. Bella Baxter, excited when a popular filmmaker pays a visit to her family's inn, volunteers to guide him to a local lighthouse that may be haunted. (Rev: BL 2/15/06)

8070 Mass, Wendy. *The Candymakers* (4–6). 2010, Little, Brown $16.99 (978-0-316-00258-5). 464pp. Four children gather at a candy factory in a contest to create a new candy sensation in this character-driven mystery with echoes of *Charlie and the Chocolate Factory.* ⌒ ❤ Lexile 740L (Rev: BL 11/15/10; HB 11–12/10; SLJ 11/1/10)

8071 Mass, Wendy. *Jeremy Fink and the Meaning of Life* (5–8). 2006, Little, Brown $15.99 (978-0-316-05829-2). Just before his 13th birthday, Jeremy Fink receives a package from his dead father containing a locked box but no keys; Jeremy and Liz set off on a tour of New York City in search of the keys and meet a number of characters with different views on the meaning of life. (Rev: BL 12/15/06; SLJ 12/06)

8072 Mazer, Harry. *Snow Bound* (5–7). 1987, Dell $21.50 (978-0-8446-6240-4); paper $5.50 (978-0-440-96134-5). Tony and Cindy survive for several days after being trapped in a snow storm. (Rev: BL 9/1/89)

8073 Medearis, Angela Shelf. *The Spray-Paint Mystery* (3–5). 1996, Scholastic paper $2.99 (978-0-590-48474-9). 102pp. A young African American third-grader sets out to find the culprit who is spray-painting a wall in his school. (Rev: BL 2/15/97; SLJ 4/97)

8074 Messner, Kate. *Capture the Flag* (5–7). 2012, Scholastic $16.99 (978-0-545-39539-7). 240pp. Seventh-graders Anne, José, and Henry discover that they are all descendants of the Silver Jaguar Society as they investigate the theft of the original Star Spangled Banner. ❤ Lexile 700L (Rev: BLO 8/12; LMC 1–2/13; SLJ 10/12)

8075 Miller, Ashley Edward, and Zack Stentz. *Colin Fischer* (5–8). 2012, Penguin $17.99 (978-159514578-9). 256pp. Colin, a 14-year-old with Asperger's and few friends, is nonetheless a good observer and sets out to solve a shooting and absolve the bully who is initially presumed to be responsible. ❤ Lexile 870L (Rev: BL 11/1/12; HB 1–2/13; LMC 5–6/13*; SLJ 1/13)

8076 Miller, Kirsten. *Kiki Strike: Inside the Shadow City* (5–8). 2006, Bloomsbury $16.95 (978-1-58234-960-2). A complex story featuring adventurous and multitalented 12-year-old girls exploring the subterranean levels of New York City. (Rev: BL 7/06; HBG 10/06; LMC 10/06; SLJ 6/06; VOYA 8/06)

8077 Miller, Kirsten. *Kiki Strike: The Darkness Dwellers* (5–8). 2013, Bloomsbury $17.99 (978-159990736-9). 416pp. In Paris Betty Bent rescues Kiki Strike from her evil aunt and the two become involved in a subterranean adventure. ❤ (Rev: BL 12/15/12; SLJ 2/13)

8078 Miller, Kirsten. *Kiki Strike: The Empress's Tomb* (5–8). 2007, Bloomsbury $16.95 (978-1-59990-047-6). Kiki and the Irregulars tackle assorted bad guys in this sequel to *Kiki Strike: Inside the Shadow City,* again set in the world under New York City. (Rev: SLJ 12/07)

8079 Milway, Alex. *The Curse of Mousebeard* (4–7). Series: Mousehunter Trilogy. 2010, Little, Brown $15.99 (978-0-316-07744-6). 368pp. In this followup to 2009's *The Mousehunter,* Emiline and her friends find themselves in the lost land of mice known as Norgammon as they seek a way to free Mousebeard from his curse. ❤ (Rev: BLO 5/15/10; SLJ 6/10)

8080 Milway, Alex. *The Mousehunter* (4–7). Illus. by author. 2009, Little, Brown $15.99 (978-0-316-02454-9). 422pp. Twelve-year-old Emiline is a mousekeeper in a world where many breeds of mice are prized, and she bravely sets out to defeat a pirate named Mousebeard. (Rev: BL 12/15/08; SLJ 3/09)

8081 Mitchelhill, Barbara. *The Graffiti Mystery* (2–4). Illus. by Tony Ross. Series: Damian Drooth Supersleuth. 2009, Stone Arch $17.99 (978-1-4342-1215-3). 72pp. A misspelling in the graffiti in the boys' bathroom leads

Damian to hold a contest that will reveal the culprit; a funny, light story. (Rev: BL 5/1/09; LMC 10/09; SLJ 6/09)

8082 Mitchelhill, Barbara. *Storm Runners* (4–8). 2008, Andersen paper $9.95 (978-18427064-0-4). 217pp. In this thrilling read, global warming turns out to be a conspiracy masterminded by villains, and it's up to 10-year-old Ally and her older sister to save the next city on the bad guys' "hit list"— Edinburgh, Scotland. Lexile 630L (Rev: BL 11/1/08)

8083 Mitchell, Marianne. *Finding Zola* (5–8). 2003, Boyds Mills $16.95 (978-1-59078-070-1). A 13-year-old girl in a wheelchair investigates the disappearance of an elderly woman who has been staying with her. (Rev: BL 5/15/03; HBG 10/03; SLJ 2/03; VOYA 10/03)

8084 Mitchell, Marianne. *Firebug* (5–8). 2004, Boyds Mills $16.95 (978-1-59078-170-8). Twelve-year-old Haley investigates a suspicious fire at her Uncle Jake's Arizona ranch. (Rev: BL 3/15/04; SLJ 2/04)

8085 Mitchell, Nancy. *Global Warning: Attack on the Pacific Rim!* (5–8). Illus. by Darren Wiebe and Ryan T. Fong. Series: The Changing Earth Trilogy. 1999, Lightstream paper $5.95 (978-1-892713-02-5). A thrilling adventure story about Jenny Powers, a wheelchair-bound youngster, who must warn the authorities of an impending biological disaster at her school. (Rev: SLJ 10/99)

8086 Mone, Gregory. *Fish* (3–5). 2010, Scholastic $16.99 (978-0-545-11632-9). 256pp. A young boy named Fish reluctantly trades his Irish farm life for a trip aboard a pirate ship and becomes embroiled in adventure and mystery. (Rev: BL 7/10; LMC 11–12/10; SLJ 9/1/10)

8087 Montgomery, Lewis B. *The Case of the Diamonds in the Desk* (1–3). Illus. by Amy Wummer. Series: Milo and Jazz Mysteries. 2012, Kane LB $22.60 (978-157565392-1); paper $6.95 (978-157565391-4). 96pp. Milo finds diamonds in his school desk, and he and Jazz swing into investigative mode. e (Rev: BL 2/15/12)

8088 Montgomery, Lewis B. *The Case of the Missing Moose* (2–4). Illus. by Amy Wummer. Series: Milo and Jazz Mysteries. 2011, Kane $22.60 (978-157565331-0); paper $6.95 (978-15756532-2-8). 96pp. Away at summer camp, Milo is able to solve a sports mystery with the help of Jazz, who is staying at a girls' camp on the same lake and shows up in the nick of time. Also use *The Case of the July 4th Jinx* (2010). (Rev: BL 5/1/11)

8089 Montgomery, Lewis B. *The Case of the Poisoned Pig. Bk. 2* (1–4). Illus. by Amy Wummer. Series: Milo and Jazz Mysteries. 2009, Kane LB $22.60 (978-1-57565-289-4); paper $6.95 (978-1-57565-286-3). 96pp. Jazz's pig is sick and the veterinarian suspects poisoning; Milo and Jazz investigate. (Rev: SLJ 7/09)

8090 Montgomery, Lewis B. *The Case of the Stinky Socks* (2–4). Illus. by Amy Wummer. Series: Milo and Jazz Mysteries. 2009, Kane $22.60 (978-1-57565-288-7); paper $6.95 (978-1-57565-285-6). 96pp. Where are Jazz's brother's lucky socks? Milo and Jazz investigate in this first volume in a new early chapter-book series. (Rev: BL 5/1/09; SLJ 7/09)

8091 Moodie, Craig. *Into the Trap* (4–8). 2011, Roaring Brook $15.99 (978-1-59643-585-8). 208pp. An action-packed story set off the coast of Maine and featuring 12-year-old Eddie, who enlists a summer visitor to help in catching the person who has been stealing his family's lobsters. e Lexile 600L (Rev: BL 7/11; SLJ 8/11)

8092 Morpurgo, Michael. *Kensuke's Kingdom* (4–7). 2003, Scholastic paper $16.95 (978-0-439-38202-1). A boy washed onto a seemingly deserted island finds a friend in a Japanese soldier who has lived there since World War II. (Rev: BL 2/15/03; HB 5–6/03; HBG 10/03; SLJ 3/03; VOYA 6/03)

8093 Moulton, Erin E. *Flutter: The Story of Four Sisters and One Incredible Journey* (4–7). 2011, Philomel $16.99 (978-0-399-25515-1). 208pp. Guided by Vermont folklore, Maple, 9, and her sister Dawn undertake a daring trek into the heart of the mountains to gather water from a mysterious well, hoping to save their premature baby sister's life. (Rev: BLO 5/1/11; SLJ 7/11)

8094 Muller, Rachel Dunstan. *Squeeze* (5–8). Series: Orca Sports. 2010, Orca paper $9.95 (978-1-55469-324-5). 166pp. Four teens embark on a caving expedition with disastrous results in this suspenseful story full of betrayal and teen drama. e Lexile HL640L (Rev: BL 11/1/10; SLJ 10/1/10)

8095 Mundis, Hester. *My Chimp Friday* (4–7). 2002, Simon & Schuster $16.00 (978-0-689-83837-8). Rachel and her family grow to love their new pet, a chimp named Friday, but when kidnappers try to steal Friday, Rachel realizes he is not an ordinary chimp. (Rev: BL 6/1–15/02; HBG 10/02; SLJ 6/02)

8096 Murphy, T. M. *The Secrets of Code Z* (4–8). Series: A Belltown Mystery. 2001, J. N. Townsend paper $9.95 (978-1-880158-33-3). Orville Jacques becomes embroiled in a fast-paced mystery involving CIA cover-ups, a death powder, and an evil Russian. (Rev: BL 5/15/01; SLJ 7/01)

8097 Napoli, Donna Jo. *North* (4–7). 2004, Greenwillow $16.99 (978-0-06-057987-6). Twelve-year-old Alvin, an African American boy fascinated by explorer Matthew Henson, sets off for the Arctic and, with the help of several adults along the way, makes the long and complex journey safely. (Rev: BL 3/1/04; SLJ 5/04)

8098 Naylor, Phyllis Reynolds. *Bernie Magruder and the Bats in the Belfry* (4–7). 2003, Simon & Schuster $16.95 (978-0-689-85066-0). Bernie is investigating a bat with a fatal bite; could it be connected to the fact that the bells in the belfry are annoyingly stuck on the same tune? (Rev: BL 1/1–15/03; HBG 10/03; SLJ 4/03)

8099 Newsome, Richard. *The Billionaire's Curse* (4–6). Illus. by Jonny Duddle. Series: The Archer Legacy. 2010, HarperCollins $16.99 (978-0-06-194490-1). 352pp. In this action-packed story, 13-year-old Gerald, an Australian, inherits money from an English great-aunt — along with a letter charging him with solving the mystery of her death. e Lexile 730L (Rev: BL 5/1/10; LMC 11–12/10; SLJ 7/10)

419

8100 Newsome, Richard. *The Emerald Casket* (4–6). Illus. by Jonny Duddle. Series: The Archer Legacy. 2011, HarperCollins $16.99 (978-0-06-194492-5). 368pp. Gerald, a 13-year-old Australian billionaire, and his friends Ruby and Sam visit India to seek a casket full of gems in this fast-paced second installment in the series that features the evil Mason Green. e Lexile 660L (Rev: BL 4/1/11; SLJ 8/11)

8101 Nickerson, Sara. *How to Disappear Completely and Never Be Found* (4–8). Illus. by Sally Wern Comport. 2002, HarperCollins LB $17.89 (978-0-06-029772-5). Two youngsters with problems, 12-year-old Margaret and her friend Boyd, explore a deserted mansion and solve the mystery of the supernatural terrors it supposedly contains. (Rev: BCCB 5/02; BL 4/1/02; HB 7–8/02; HBG 10/02; SLJ 4/02)

8102 Nolan, Peggy. *The Spy Who Came in from the Sea* (4–8). 1999, Pineapple $14.95 (978-1-56164-186-4). In this adventure story set in World War II Florida, 14-year-old Frank, who has a reputation for lying, is not believed when he claims to have seen a German sub off the coast. (Rev: HBG 3/00; SLJ 1/00)

8103 Nordin, Sofia. *In the Wild* (4–7). Trans. from Swedish by Maria Lundin. 2005, Groundwood $15.95 (978-0-88899-648-0). Set in Sweden, this is an adventure story featuring 6th-grade outcast Amanda and bully Philip, who become lost and must rely on their own resources to survive. (Rev: SLJ 10/05)

8104 Nowra, Louis. *Into That Forest* (5–8). 2013, Amazon/Skyscape $16.99 (978-147781725-4). 160pp. Hannah, 76, recounts an episode from her childhood in Tasmania, when she and a friend were rescued from a flood by tigers and raised by them until they were finally discovered and returned to civilization, forcing a difficult time of adjustment. Notable Australian Children's Book. ∩ e (Rev: BL 9/1/13; LMC 3–4/14; SLJ 11/13)

8105 Obrist, Jürg. *Case Closed?! 40 Mini-Mysteries for You to Solve* (2–5). Illus. 2003, Millbrook LB $22.90 (978-0-7613-2739-4). Readers help young detectives Daisy and Ridley solve mysteries involving puzzles, codes, and other challenges. (Rev: BL 2/15/04; HBG 4/04; SLJ 2/04)

8106 Obrist, Jürg. *Complex Cases: Three Major Mysteries for You to Solve* (3–6). Illus. by author. Series: Mini-Mysteries. 2006, Millbrook LB $23.93 (978-0-7613-3419-4); paper $6.95 (978-0-8225-5975-7). 93pp. This new volume in the series presents three longer mysteries, challenging readers to solve them using deduction and the clues in the many illustrations. (Rev: SLJ 6/06)

8107 O'Connor, Barbara. *The Fantastic Secret of Owen Jester* (4–6). 2010, Farrar $15.99 (978-0-374-36850-0). 176pp. Mischievous Owen contends with his rival Viola's distaste for his pet frog — and struggles to keep his fantastic two-passenger submarine a secret from her. e Lexile 770L (Rev: BL 9/15/10; HB 11–12/10; LMC 1–2/11; SLJ 10/1/10*)

8108 O'Connor, Jane. *Nancy Clancy Sees the Future* (2–4). Illus. by Robin Preiss Glasser. 2013, HarperCollins $9.99 (978-006208297-8). 128pp. Nancy Clancy finds fortune-telling more complicated than she anticipated in this third mystery in the series. e Lexile 480 (Rev: BLO 11/15/13)

8109 O'Connor, Jane. *Nancy Clancy, Secret Admirer* (2–4). Illus. by Robin Preiss Glasser. Series: Nancy Clancy. 2013, HarperCollins $9.99 (978-006208295-4). 128pp. Nancy Clancy decides to engineer a match between her guitar teacher, Andy, and her babysitter, Annie, in this engaging chapter book with a focus more on romance and Valentine's Day than on mystery. e Lexile 470L (Rev: BL 12/15/12)

8110 O'Dell, Scott. *Black Star, Bright Dawn* (5–8). 1988, Houghton Mifflin $18.00 (978-0-395-47778-6). An Inuit girl decides to run the 1,197-mile sled dog race called the Iditarod. (Rev: BCCB 6/88; BL 4/1/88; SLJ 5/88; VOYA 6/88)

8111 O'Dell, Scott. *Island of the Blue Dolphins* (5–8). 1960, Houghton Mifflin $16.00 (978-0-395-06962-2); paper $6.50 (978-0-440-43988-2). An Indian girl spends 18 years alone on an island off the coast of California in the 1800s. A sequel is *Zia* (1976). Newbery Medal 1961. (Rev: BL 3/1/88)

8112 Odyssey, Shawn Thomas. *The Wizard of Dark Street* (4–7). 2011, Egmont $16.99 (978-1-60684-143-3). 352pp. Blending fantasy and mystery, this book set in 1877 New York City follows 12-year-old Oona, who has decided to become a detective rather than follow in her wizard family's footsteps — until her wizard uncle is attacked. Lexile 890L (Rev: BL 7/11; SLJ 9/1/11)

8113 Oliver, Andrew. *If Photos Could Talk* (4–7). Series: A Sam and Stephanie Mystery. 2005, Adams-Pomeroy paper $12.95 (978-0-9661009-6-9). Twelve-year-olds Sam and Stephanie investigate the disappearance of an elderly man in their small Wisconsin town in this well-plotted novel. (Rev: SLJ 1/06)

8114 Orr, Wendy. *Nim at Sea* (3–6). Illus. by Kerry Millard. 2008, Knopf LB $15.99 (978-0-385-90535-0). 128pp. When a dastardly poacher kidnaps her sea lion friend, Selkie, Nim and her family members each set out on individual rescue adventures. (Rev: BL 3/1/08; SLJ 5/08)

8115 Park, Linda Sue. *Trust No One* (5–8). Series: 39 Clues: Cahills versus Vespers. 2012, Scholastic $12.99 (978-054529843-8). 192pp. In this 5th installment of the series written by multiple authors, Amy and Dan Cahill discover a mole in the organization and learn more about the real motives of the Vespers. Lexile 640 (Rev: BLO 3/15/13)

8116 Parkinson, Curtis. *Storm-Blast* (4–8). 2003, Tundra paper $7.95 (978-0-88776-630-5). On a sailing trip in the Caribbean, three teens become stranded in a small dinghy and must use their resources to survive. (Rev: SLJ 10/03; VOYA 8/03)

8117 Patneaude, David. *The Last Man's Reward* (5–8). 1996, Whitman LB $15.99 (978-0-8075-4370-2). In this adventure, a group of boys agree to a pact rewarding the last to leave the neighborhood. (Rev: BL 6/1–15/96; SLJ 7/96)

8118 Patneaude, David. *A Piece of the Sky* (5–8). 2007, Whitman $15.95 (978-0-8075-6536-0). In Oregon to help his grandfather settle into an assisted-living residence, 14-year-old Russell and his new friend Phoebe, pursued by a sinister character, set off on an unexpectedly dangerous meteorite search. (Rev: SLJ 5/07)

8119 Patterson, James. *Treasure Hunters* (4–6). Illus. by Juliana Neufeld. 2013, Little, Brown $14.99 (978-031620756-0). 450pp. After their parents disappear, 12-year-old twins Bickford and Rebecca, along with their two siblings, decide to continue the family's treasure-hunting business despite the obvious dangers. ∩ e Lexile 750 (Rev: BL 10/1/13)

8120 Paulsen, Gary. *Brian's Winter* (5–9). 1996, Delacorte $15.95 (978-0-385-32198-3). In a reworking of the ending of *Hatchet,* in which Brian Robeson is rescued after surviving a plane crash, this novel tells what would have happened had Brian had to survive a harsh winter in the wilderness. (Rev: BL 12/15/95; SLJ 2/96; VOYA 2/97)

8121 Paulsen, Gary. *Escape from Fire Mountain* (4–6). Series: Culpepper Adventure. 1995, Dell paper $3.99 (978-0-440-41025-6). 67pp. An adventure story in which a young girl faces incredible challenges to rescue two lost children. (Rev: SLJ 7/95)

8122 Paulsen, Gary. *The River* (5–10). 1991, Delacorte $15.95 (978-0-385-30388-0). In this sequel to *Hatchet,* Paulsen takes the wilderness adventure beyond self-preservation and makes teen Brian responsible for saving someone else. (Rev: BL 5/15/91)

8123 Paver, Michelle. *Gods and Warriors* (5–8). 2012, Dial $16.99 (978-0-8037-3877-5). 288pp. A bronze dagger is at the heart of this tale of adventure featuring 12-year-old Hylas and his journeys around the Mediterranean in the Bronze Age. e Lexile 680L (Rev: BL 8/12; LMC 3–4/13; SLJ 10/12; VOYA 12/12)

8124 Pearson, Ridley. *The Challenge* (5–8). 2008, Disney $16.99 (978-1-4231-0640-1). Steve is caught up in a terrorist kidnapping plot when he looks inside an abandoned briefcase in this fast-paced adventure. (Rev: BL 1/1–15/08; LMC 4–5/08)

8125 Penn, Audrey. *Mystery at Blackbeard's Cove* (5–8). Illus. by Joshua Miller. 2004, Tanglewood $14.95 (978-0-9749303-1-2). The death of Mrs. McNemmish, a descendant of Blackbeard the pirate, sets in motion a series of adventures for four young residents of Okracoke Island. (Rev: BL 1/1–15/05)

8126 Peterson, P. J. *Wild River* (4–7). 2009, Delacorte $14.99 (978-0-385-73724-1); LB $17.99 (978-0-385-90656-2). 120pp. When a kayaking trip with his older brother turns dangerous, 12-year-old Ryan must make life-or-death decisions in this exciting, harrowing tale. e Lexile 420L (Rev: BL 8/09; SLJ 9/09)

8127 Philbrick, Rodman. *The Young Man and the Sea* (5–6). 2004, Scholastic $16.95 (978-0-439-36829-2). 192pp. With a nod to Hemingway, this is the story of Skiff, a 12-year-old boy living in Maine, who seeks to solve his problems by catching a giant bluefin tuna. (Rev: BL 1/1–15/04; HB 3/04; SLJ 2/04)

8128 Phillips, Helen. *Here Where the Sunbeams Are Green* (4–7). 2012, Delacorte $17.99 (978-038574236-8); LB $20.99 (978-037599056-4). 304pp. Sisters Madeline and Ruby travel to a Central American jungle to join their father, an ornithologist, only to find themselves embroiled in ecological intrigue. e Lexile 940L (Rev: BLO 12/15/12; LMC 3–4/13; SLJ 1/13)

8129 Pierpoint, Eric. *The Last Ride of Caleb O'Toole* (4–6). 2013, Sourcebooks/Jabberwocky paper $7.99 (978-14022817-1-6). 288pp. In this exciting and action-packed novel about traveling the Oregon Trail in 1877, 12-year-old Caleb O'Toole and his two sisters are orphaned and must get to their Aunt Sarah's home in Montana without getting killed by Indians, murderous sheriffs, floods, tornados, or the Blackstone Gang, who are in pursuit of Caleb because he inadvertently witnessed a murder. e Lexile 770 (Rev: BL 10/1/13; LMC 3–4/14; SLJ 9/13)

8130 Pilling, Ann. *The Year of the Worm* (5–7). 2000, Lion paper $7.50 (978-0-7459-4294-0). Lonely Peter Wrigley, who is mourning his father's death, gets his chance to become a hero when he uncovers a group of birds'-nest poachers in this English novel set in the Lake District. (Rev: SLJ 3/01)

8131 Potter, Ellen. *The Kneebone Boy* (4–8). 2010, Feiwel & Friends $16.99 (978-0-312-37772-4). 288pp. Otto, Lucia, and Max Hardscrabble, three idiosyncratic children, have many adventures while looking for their long-absent mother in a British seaside town. e Lexile 850L (Rev: BL 9/15/10; HB 9–10/10; LMC 11–12/10; SLJ 9/1/10)

8132 Potter, Ellen. *Pish Posh* (4–6). 2006, Philomel $15.99 (978-0-399-23995-3). 240pp. Eleven-year-old Clara Frankofile is a horrible snob who rules the roost at her parents' posh New York City restaurant, but she finds herself in new territory when she investigates a mystery about the soup chef. (Rev: BL 2/1/06; SLJ 4/06)

8133 Promitzer, Rebecca. *The Pickle King* (5–8). 2010, Scholastic $17.99 (978-0-545-17087-1). 416pp. A complex, multilayered novel in which 11-year-old Bea and her friends investigate a mystery involving a ghost. ∩ Lexile 880L (Rev: BL 2/1/10; LMC 3–4/10; SLJ 6/10)

8134 Pullman, Philip. *The Scarecrow and His Servant* (4–6). Illus. by Peter Bailey. 2005, Knopf $15.95 (978-0-375-81531-7). 240pp. A multilayered tale in which a scarecrow and his orphan-boy servant embark on a series of adventures. (Rev: BCCB 9/05; BL 9/1/05*; HB 9/05; LMC 1/06; SLJ 9/05)

8135 Pullman, Philip. *Two Crafty Criminals! And How They Were Captured by the Daring Detectives of the New Cut Gang* (3–6). Illus. by Martin Brown. 2012, Knopf $16.99 (978-037587029-3); LB $19.99 (978-037597029-0). 320pp. In Victorian London, the New Cut Gang, led by 11-year-old Benny Kaminsky, solves two mysteries involving counterfeiting and theft. ∩ ℓ (Rev: BL 4/1/12; HB 5–6/12; LMC 10/12; SLJ 5/1/12*)

8136 Quattlebaum, Mary. *Jackson Jones and the Curse of the Outlaw Rose* (3–5). 2006, Delacorte $14.95 (978-0-385-73349-6). 112pp. Jackson and friends, who garden in an inner-city community patch, tussle with mystery when a rose twig, removed from an old cemetery, seems to bring bad luck; the third installment in the series. (Rev: BL 1/1–15/07; SLJ 11/06)

8137 Quimby, Laura. *The Icarus Project* (4–7). 2012, Abrams/Amulet $16.95 (978-1-4197-0402-4). 304pp. On an expedition to the Arctic with her father, 13-year-old Maya discovers a strange creature preserved in ice. ℓ (Rev: BL 12/1/12; SLJ 12/12)

8138 Ransome, Arthur. *Swallows and Amazons* (4–7). Illus. by author. 1985, Godine paper $14.95 (978-0-87923-573-4). These adventures of the four Walker children have been read for many years. A reissue. Others in the series *Swallowdale* (1985); *Peter Duck* (1987).

8139 Ransome, Arthur. *Winter Holiday* (4–7). Illus. by author. 1989, Godine paper $14.95 (978-0-87923-661-8). Further adventures of the Swallows and Amazons. A reissue. A sequel is *Coot Club*.

8140 Reiss, Kathryn. *A Bundle of Trouble* (4–7). Illus. by Sergio Giovine. 2011, American Girl $10.95 (978-159369753-2); paper $6.95 (978-15936975-4-9). 165pp. In early 20th-century New York during a rash of kidnappings, Rebecca becomes suspicious of some of the people she meets in her neighborhood. (Rev: BL 5/1/11)

8141 Repp, Gloria. *Mik-Shrok* (4–8). Illus. by Jim Brooks. 1998, Bob Jones Univ. paper $7.49 (978-1-57924-069-1). A married missionary couple journey to a remote Alaska village in 1950, where they begin their work and, in time, acquire a dog team led by Mik-Shrok. (Rev: BL 3/1/99)

8142 Richards, Justin. *Thunder Raker* (3–5). Illus. by Jim Hansen. Series: Agent Alfie. 2010, HarperCollins paper $6.99 (978-00072735-7-7). 112pp. Mistakenly enrolled in spy school. Alfie ends up triumphing over tough assignments and quirky teachers to save the day. (Rev: BL 1/1–15/11)

8143 Richardson, V. A. *The Moneylender's Daughter* (5–8). 2006, Bloomsbury $17.95 (978-1-58234-885-8). In this exciting sequel to *The House of Windjammer* (2003), Adam Windjammer sets sail for America, finds himself burdened with more responsibility on the death of his uncle, and is preoccupied with thoughts of Jade van Helsen, daughter of the man who brought his family to the brink of ruin. (Rev: BL 6/1–15/06; SLJ 9/06)

8144 Riel, Jorn. *The Shipwreck* (4–6). Illus. by Helen Cann. Series: Inuk Quartet. 2011, Barefoot paper $12.99 (978-1-84686-335-6). 112pp. A young Viking boy, Leiv, is shipwrecked off the coast of Greenland and finds a new home with an Inuit community, discovering a liking for their rejection of violence. (Rev: BLO 11/15/11; SLJ 11/1/11)

8145 Ringwald, Whitaker. *The Secret Box* (4–7). 2014, HarperCollins $16.99 (978-006221614-4). 304pp. A

mysterious birthday present sets 12-year-old Jax off on a quest that mixes Greek mythology, adventure, and a little magic. ℓ Lexile 580 (Rev: BL 3/1/14; SLJ 4/14)

8146 Riordan, Rick. *The Maze of Bones* (4–8). Series: The 39 Clues. 2008, Scholastic $12.99 (978-054506039-4); LB $12.99 (978-054509054-4). 224pp. Part adventure story, part online gaming platform, this book kicks off a ten-title series with the story of orphans Amy and Dan, who decipher clues and puzzles in their round-the-world quest. ∩ ℓ Lexile 610L (Rev: BL 10/15/08; LMC 5–6/09; SLJ 11/1/08*)

8147 Roberts, Willo Davis. *Baby-Sitting Is a Dangerous Job* (5–7). 1987, Fawcett paper $6.50 (978-0-449-70177-5). Darcy tries to cope with three bratty children, but a kidnapping puts her and her charges in the hands of three dangerous men. (Rev: BCCB 3/85; BL 5/1/85; SLJ 5/85)

8148 Roberts, Willo Davis. *The One Left Behind* (4–7). 2006, Simon & Schuster $16.95 (978-0-689-85075-2). Mandy, an 11-year-old mourning her dead twin sister, is accidentally left home alone for the weekend and pluckily investigates when there's a break-in downstairs. (Rev: BL 4/1/06; SLJ 5/06)

8149 Rogan, S. Jones. *The Daring Adventures of Penhaligon Brush* (3–5). Illus. by Christian Slade. 2007, Knopf $15.99 (978-0-375-84344-0). 224pp. Heroic fox Penhaligon Brush finds himself on a mission to rescue his brother and an entire village from the evil paws of the feline Sir Derek in this humorous adventure with elements of mystery and romance. (Rev: BCCB 12/07; BL 11/15/07; LMC 11/07; SLJ 11/07)

8150 Rollins, James. *Jake Ransom and the Howling Sphinx* (5–8). 2011, HarperCollins $16.99 (978-0-06-147382-1). 370pp. An evil mummified creature delivers an ominous message to siblings Jake and Kady, who must fight for their lives in this fast-paced archaeological time-travel thriller. ∩ ℓ Lexile 700L (Rev: LMC 11–12/11; SLJ 10/1/11; VOYA 8/11)

8151 Rose, Malcolm. *Blood Brother* (4–7). Series: Traces. 2008, Kingfisher paper $5.95 (978-0-7534-6170-9). Luke and his robot sidekick are investigating 26 mysterious deaths at York Hospital; could Luke's doctor father, the principal investigator on a clinical trial at the hospital, somehow be responsible? (Rev: BL 11/15/07)

8152 Ross, Jeff. *Dawn Patrol* (5–12). Series: Orca Sports. 2012, Orca paper $9.95 (978-1-4598-0062-5). 160pp. Luca and Esme travel to Panama in search of their missing friend Kevin in this story for reluctant readers that features surfing and mystery. ℓ Lexile HL530L (Rev: LMC 11–12/12; SLJ 6/12)

8153 Rossell, Judith. *Jack Jones and the Pirate Curse* (4–7). 2007, Walker $15.95 (978-0-8027-9661-5). Jack inherits the family curse and finds himself suddenly facing a band of vengeful pirates he knows he must fight with brain rather than brawn. (Rev: BL 4/1/07; SLJ 6/07)

8154 Roy, Ron. *The Deadly Dungeon* (2–4). Illus. by John S. Gurney. Series: A to Z Mysteries. 1998, Random LB $11.99 (978-0-679-98755-0); paper $3.99 (978-0-

679-88755-3). 86pp. Dink, Josh, and Ruth Rose uncover a mystery when they travel to Maine to visit a castle. (Rev: SLJ 10/98)

8155 Roy, Ron. *The Goose's Gold* (2–4). Illus. by John S. Gurney. Series: Stepping Stone. 1999, Random paper $3.99 (978-0-679-89078-2). 86pp. An easy chapter book mystery in which three young sleuths overhear a man planning a robbery and set out to foil his plot. (Rev: BL 10/15/99; HBG 10/99; SLJ 7/99)

8156 Roy, Ron. *January Joker* (1–3). Illus. by John Steven Gurney. Series: Calendar Mysteries. 2009, Random House LB $11.99 (978-0-375-95661-4); paper $4.99 (978-0-375-85661-7). 96pp. Seven-year-old twins Bradley and Brian and friends Nate and Lucy (younger siblings and cousins of the characters in the A to Z Mystery series) investigate strange lights in the backyard and decided that aliens have landed. (Rev: LMC 11–12/09; SLJ 12/1/09)

8157 Ruckman, Ivy. *Night of the Twisters* (4–6). 1984, HarperCollins LB $16.89 (978-0-690-04409-6); paper $5.99 (978-0-06-440176-0). 160pp. An 11-year-old boy witnesses a series of tornadoes that destroy his Nebraska town.

8158 Ruckman, Ivy. *Spell It M-U-R-D-E-R* (4–6). 1994, Bantam paper $3.50 (978-0-553-48175-4). Two girls stumble upon a murderer when they try to escape from a summer camp they detest. (Rev: BL 7/94; SLJ 8/94)

8159 Runholt, Susan. *Adventure at Simba Hill* (5–8). 2011, Viking $16.99 (978-0-670-01201-5). 288pp. Fourteen-year-old friends Kari and Lucas accompany Kari's archaeologist uncle to Kenya, where they solve a mystery involving disappearing artifacts. ℮ Lexile 870L (Rev: BL 5/1/11; SLJ 7/11)

8160 Runholt, Susan. *Rescuing Seneca Crane* (5–8).

8161 St. George, Judith. *The Ghost, The White House, and Me* (3–6). 2007, Holiday House $16.95 (978-0-8234-2045-2). 160pp. First daughters KayKay and Annie do their best to adapt to life in the less-than-homey White House and investigate some ghostly suspicions in the Lincoln bedroom while their mother is occupied with her presidential duties. (Rev: BCCB 2/08; BL 11/1/07; LMC 1/08; SLJ 11/07)

8162 Salane, Jeffrey. *Lawless* (5–8). 2013, Scholastic $16.99 (978-054545029-4). 336pp. M Freeman, a 12-year-old named for her master criminal father, finds herself enrolled in Lawless School, where she excels even as she suspects the motives of the people around her. Lexile 850 (Rev: BLO 6/13; LMC 11–12/13; SLJ 8/13)

8163 Salisbury, Graham. *Night of the Howling Dogs* (5–8). 2007, Random House $16.99 (978-0-385-73122-5). Dylan, an 8th-grader from Hilo, Hawaii, goes on a trip to the coast with his scout troop to camp in the shadow of a volcano and faces a bully and natural disasters. ∩ (Rev: BL 8/07; HB 9–10/07; SLJ 8/07)

8164 Santopolo, Jill. *The Nina, the Pinta, and the Vanishing Treasure* (3–5). Illus. by C. B. Canga. Series: Alec Flint. 2008, Scholastic $15.99 (978-0-439-90352-3).

208pp. With classmate Gina Rossi, 4th-grader Alec Flint investigates the disappearances of a Christopher Columbus exhibit and of the art teacher. (Rev: BL 5/1/08; LMC 10/08)

8165 Schade, Susan. *Faradawn* (3–5). Illus. by Jon Buller. Series: Fog Mound. 2007, Simon & Schuster $15.99 (978-0-689-87686-8). 208pp. Thelonious Chipmunk and his animal friends leave Fog Mound to explore further afield and perhaps find out what happened to the humans. (Rev: BL 9/15/07)

8166 Scieszka, Jon. *Knights of the Kitchen Table* (3–5). Illus. by Lane Smith. 1991, Viking $15.99 (978-0-670-83622-2). 64pp. The Time Warp Trio hangs out with Lancelot and his pals. Also use: *The Not-So-Jolly Roger* (1991). (Rev: BCCB 7–8/91; BL 5/1/91; SLJ 8/91*)

8167 Selfors, Suzanne. *Smells Like Treasure* (4–7). 2011, Little, Brown $15.99 (978-0-316-04399-1). 416pp. Homer Winslow Pudding, 12, faces a challenger for his uncle's place in the society of Legends, Objects, Secrets, and Treasures (LOST) and hopes his basset hound, Dog, will help him prevail. A sequel to *Smells Like Dog* (2010). (Rev: BL 5/1/11; SLJ 9/1/11*)

8168 Selznick, Brian. *The Invention of Hugo Cabret* (4–9). Illus. by author. 2007, Scholastic $22.99 (978-0-439-81378-5). In 1930s Paris a young apprentice clock keeper, an orphan who struggles to make his way in life, finds himself drawn into a complex mystery that threatens the anonymity he treasures; part graphic novel, part flip book, the design is as compelling as the story. Caldecott Medal 2008; ALA Notable Children's Book 2008. (Rev: BL 1/1–15/07; SLJ 3/07*)

8169 Shahan, Sherry. *Death Mountain* (5–8). 2005, Peachtree $15.95 (978-1-56145-353-5). In this gripping thriller, 14-year-old Erin uses her survival skills to rescue her new friend Mae and navigate their way through a mountain wilderness to safety. (Rev: SLJ 11/05; VOYA 2/06)

8170 Shahan, Sherry. *Ice Island* (4–7). 2012, Delacorte $15.99 (978-038574154-5); LB $18.99 (978-037599009-0). 176pp. Thirteen-year-old Tatum finds herself on a scary dogsled trip in this survival story full of facts about Alaska. ℮ (Rev: BL 3/1/12; LMC 5–6/12; SLJ 1/12)

8171 Shearer, Alex. *Sea Legs* (4–6). 2005, Simon & Schuster $15.95 (978-0-689-87143-6). 320pp. Twins Clive and Eric stow away on the cruise sip where their father works and end up fighting pirates in this entertaining story. (Rev: BL 3/15/05; SLJ 3/05)

8172 Shelton, Dave. *A Boy and a Bear in a Boat* (3–5). Illus. by author. 2012, Random House $16.99 (978-038575248-0); LB $19.99 (978-038575249-7). 304pp. A boy and a bear aboard a small boat in the middle of a very large sea experience boredom, bickering, and fear. (Rev: BL 5/15/12*; LMC 10/12)

8173 Sherry, Maureen. *Walls Within Walls* (4–7). Illus. by Adam Stower. 2010, HarperCollins $16.99 (978-0-06-176700-5). 348pp. When three young siblings move into a luxurious Manhattan apartment, they discover that their new home is full of clues that may reveal a treasure. ℮ Lexile 770L (Rev: BL 9/15/10; LMC 3–4/11; SLJ 10/1/10)

8174 Simner, Janni Lee. *Secret of the Three Treasures* (3–5). 2006, Holiday $16.95 (978-0-8234-1914-2). 134pp. The irrepressible Tiernay, emulating her novelist father's heroes, sets out with her mother's boyfriend's son in search of buried treasure and finds herself in real danger; a humorous multilayered story that also tackles bullying and genealogy. (Rev: BL 5/1/06; SLJ 8/06)

8175 Singh, Vandana. *Younguncle Comes to Town* (3–5). Illus. by B. M. Kamath. 2006, Viking $14.99 (978-0-670-06051-1). Three siblings in northern India are captivated by the real-life adventures of Younguncle, their father's youngest brother. (Rev: BL 4/1/06; SLJ 5/06)

8176 Skurzynski, Gloria, and Alane Ferguson. *Buried Alive* (4–7). Series: Mysteries in Our National Parks. 2003, National Geographic $15.95 (978-0-7922-6966-3). A hit man and an avalanche are only two of the challenges Jack and Ashley face while on vacation with their parents in Denali National Park. (Rev: HBG 10/03; SLJ 12/03)

8177 Skurzynski, Gloria, and Alane Ferguson. *Cliff-Hanger* (4–7). Series: Mysteries in Our National Parks. 1999, National Geographic $15.95 (978-0-7922-7036-2). In Mesa Verde National Park, the Landon family encounters two problems — a foster care girl named Lucky, who is deceitful, and a rampaging cougar. (Rev: BL 4/15/99; HBG 10/99; SLJ 5/99)

8178 Skurzynski, Gloria, and Alane Ferguson. *Deadly Waters* (4–7). Series: Mysteries in Our National Parks. 1999, National Geographic $15.95 (978-0-7922-7037-9). The Landon kids — Jack, Ashley, and foster brother, Bridger — travel to the Florida Everglades where their parents are investigating the mysterious deaths of some manatees. (Rev: BL 10/15/99; HBG 3/00; SLJ 10/99)

8179 Skurzynski, Gloria, and Alane Ferguson. *Ghost Horses* (4–6). Illus. Series: National Parks Mystery. 2000, National Geographic $15.95 (978-0-7922-7055-3). 152pp. Horses that are behaving strangely, a flash flood, and interpersonal conflicts are three of the elements in this mystery story set in Utah's Zion National Park. (Rev: BL 12/15/00; HBG 3/01; SLJ 11/00)

8180 Skurzynski, Gloria, and Alane Ferguson. *The Hunted* (5–8). Series: Mysteries in Our National Parks. 2000, National Geographic $15.95 (978-0-7922-7053-9). The Landon family sets out to discover why young grizzly bears are disappearing from Glacier National Park. (Rev: BL 6/1–15/00; HBG 10/00; SLJ 8/00)

8181 Skurzynski, Gloria, and Alane Ferguson. *Wolf Stalker* (5–8). Series: Mysteries in Our National Parks. 1997, National Geographic $15.00 (978-0-7922-7034-8). Three youngsters solve the mystery of who is killing the wolves of Yellowstone Park. (Rev: HBG 3/98; SLJ 1/98)

8182 Smith, Roland. *Cryptid Hunters* (5–8). 2005, Hyperion $15.99 (978-0-7868-5161-4). Thirteen-year-old twins Marty and Grace find themselves in an action-packed adventure in the Congo. (Rev: BL 2/1/05; SLJ 5/05)

8183 Smith, Roland. *Eruption* (5–8). Series: Storm Runners. 2012, Scholastic $16.99 (978-054508174-0). 160pp. While in Mexico pursuing a missing circus act, Chase and his dad end up a hair too close to an erupting volcano and a few wild animals. (Rev: BL 3/15/12)

8184 Smith, Roland. *I, Q* (5–8). Series: I, Q. 2008, Sleeping Bear paper $8.95 (978-15853632-5-4). 293pp. Q and Angela's musician parents have recently married, sentencing the two teens to a yearlong band tour enlivened by mysterious stalkers who may be related to Angela's dead mother, who worked for the Secret Service. Lexile HL660L (Rev: BL 10/15/08; SLJ 12/08)

8185 Smith, Roland. *Jack's Run* (5–8). 2005, Hyperion $15.99 (978-0-7868-5592-6). Last seen adapting to being in the witness protection program in *Zach's Lie* (2001), Jack and Joanne are now in danger after Joanne has blown their cover in this fast-paced, suspenseful story. (Rev: BL 8/05; SLJ 12/05; VOYA 10/05)

8186 Smith, Roland. *Storm Runners* (5–8). Series: Storm Runners. 2011, Scholastic $16.99 (978-0-545-08175-7). 160pp. Chase, 13, is well prepared for the challenges posed by a hurricane, a bus accident, and escaped zoo animals in this exciting, fast read. (Rev: BL 4/15/11; SLJ 4/11)

8187 Snicket, Lemony. *The Ersatz Elevator* (3–6). Illus. Series: A Series of Unfortunate Events. 2001, HarperCollins LB $15.89 (978-0-06-028889-1). Count Olaf soon finds the Baudelaire orphans at their new home, chez Mr. and Mrs. Squalor. (Rev: BL 8/01; HBG 10/01; SLJ 8/01)

8188 Snicket, Lemony. *The Hostile Hospital* (4–6). Illus. by Brett Helquist. Series: A Series of Unfortunate Events. 2001, HarperCollins LB $15.89 (978-0-06-028891-4). The Baudelaire children face danger and intrigue in their quest to find out more about their dead parents. (Rev: BL 10/15/01; HBG 3/02; SLJ 11/01)

8189 Snicket, Lemony. *The Miserable Mill* (4–6). Series: A Series of Unfortunate Events. 2000, HarperCollins LB $15.89 (978-0-06-028315-5). 128pp. The unfortunate Baudelaire orphans are forced to work in a lumber mill in this entertaining segment of the ongoing melodrama set in mock-Victorian times. (Rev: BL 5/1/00; HBG 10/00; SLJ 7/00)

8190 Snicket, Lemony. *The Slippery Slope* (3–5). Illus. by Brett Helquist. 2003, HarperCollins LB $15.89 (978-0-06-029641-4). In this episode in the continuing saga, Violet and Klaus get help from a stranger as they seek to free Sunny from the clutches of Count Olaf and find the "last safe place." (Rev: BL 1/1–15/04; HBG 4/04; SLJ 1/04)

8191 Snicket, Lemony. *The Vile Village* (3–6). Illus. Series: A Series of Unfortunate Events. 2001, HarperCollins LB $15.89 (978-0-06-028890-7). 272pp. Aphorisms abound as a village decides to raise three children and takes on the Baudelaire orphans. (Rev: BL 8/01; HBG 3/02; SLJ 8/01)

8192 Snicket, Lemony. *When Did You See Her Last?* (4–7). Illus. Series: All the Wrong Questions. 2013, Little, Brown $15.99 (978-031612305-1). 288pp. Lemony, 12, initially asks all the wrong questions when investigating the disappearance of Miss Cleo Knight in this fast-paced, suspenseful installment. ◯ ℯ (Rev: BL 7/13; SLJ 9/13)

8193 Snicket, Lemony. *Who Could That Be at This Hour?* (4–7). Illus. by Seth. Series: All the Wrong Questions. 2012, Little, Brown $15.99 (978-0-316-12308-2). 272pp. Thirteen-year-old Lemony Snicket, an apprentice to S. Theodora Markson, helps investigate the theft of a statue in this fast-paced "autobiographical" romp. ◯ ℯ Lexile 870L (Rev: BL 9/15/12; LMC 5–6/13; SLJ 12/12*)

8194 Snyder, Zilpha Keatley. *The Treasures of Weatherby* (4–6). 2007, Simon & Schuster $15.95 (978-1-4169-1398-6). 213pp. Harleigh J. Weatherby, IV, an undersized 12-year-old, makes friends with Allegra, a mysterious stranger, and together they set out to foil a plot to steal the long-lost Weatherby treasure. (Rev: SLJ 2/07)

8195 Sobol, Donald J. *Encyclopedia Brown and the Case of the Jumping Frogs* (4–6). Illus. 2003, Delacorte $14.95 (978-0-385-72931-4). The 10-year-old sleuth cracks another bunch of not-so-easy cases in this new entry in a long series. (Rev: BL 2/1/04; HBG 4/04)

8196 Sobol, Donald J. *Encyclopedia Brown and the Case of the Mysterious Handprints* (3–5). Illus. 1985, Morrow $15.99 (978-0-688-04626-2). 96pp. Matching wits with the 10-year-old sleuth in ten more crime cases. Also use: *Encyclopedia Brown and the Case of the Secret Pitch* (1978, Bantam); *Encyclopedia Brown Lends a Hand* (1979, Dutton); *Encyclopedia Brown and the Case of the Treasure Hunt* (1988). (Rev: BL 11/15/85; SLJ 2/86)

8197 Sobol, Donald J. *Encyclopedia Brown, Super Sleuth* (3–6). Illus. by James Bernardin. 2009, Dutton $15.99 (978-052542100-9). 96pp. Ten short mysteries engage venerable sleuth Encyclopedia Brown in this new collection; the solutions are in the back of the book. (Rev: BLO 11/15/09)

8198 Soto, Gary. *Crazy Weekend* (4–7). 1994, Scholastic paper $13.95 (978-0-590-47814-4). Two boys are being pursued by some crooks in this fast-moving adventure story. (Rev: BCCB 7–8/94; SLJ 3/94)

8199 Soup, Cuthbert. *A Whole Nother Story* (3–6). Illus. by Jeffrey Stewart Timmins. 2010, Bloomsbury $16.99 (978-159990435-1). 272pp. A scientist and his three children and psychic dog are on the run from spies and government agents who want to steal their time machine in this adventure laced with humor. (Rev: BL 11/15/09; LMC 3–4/10; SLJ 1/10)

8200 Spencer, Octavia. *The Case of the Time-Capsule Bandit* (4–6). 2013, Simon & Schuster $16.99 (978-144247681-3). 224pp. Twelve-year-old Randi has lost her mother and must move from Brooklyn to tiny Deer Creek, Tennessee, where she is worried she will not be able to solve crimes any more, but when the town's time capsule disappears, she befriends two other children

who are new in town and gets to work solving a crime that could literally save her new city. ℯ Lexile 680 (Rev: BL 11/1/13; LMC 3–4/14; SLJ 11/13)

8201 Sperry, Armstrong. *Call It Courage* (5–8). Illus. by author. 1968, Macmillan $16.95 (978-0-02-786030-6); paper $4.99 (978-0-689-71391-0). The "Crusoe" theme is interwoven with this story of a Polynesian boy's courage in facing the sea he feared. Newbery Medal 1941.

8202 Spirn, Michele. *The Bridges in London: Going to London* (5–7). Series: Going To. 2000, Four Corners paper $7.95 (978-1-893577-00-8). When two sisters fly to London with their parents, they become involved in a mystery when they find a suitcase full of knives. (Rev: SLJ 3/00)

8203 Spizman, Robyn Freedman, and Mark Johnston. *The Secret Agents Strike Back* (5–8). 2007, Simon & Schuster $16.99 (978-1-4169-0086-3). Information about a possible cure for cancer is stolen and Kyle and his friends chase clues all over New York City in this entertaining mystery. (Rev: SLJ 6/07)

8204 Springer, Nancy. *The Case of the Cryptic Crinoline* (5–8). Series: Enola Holmes Mystery. 2009, Philomel $14.99 (978-0-399-24781-1). Florence Nightingale may be able to help Sherlock's younger sister Enola Holmes as she investigates the disappearance of her landlady. (Rev: BLO 4/23/09; SLJ 7/09)

8205 Springer, Nancy. *The Case of the Missing Marquess: An Enola Holmes Mystery* (5–8). Series: Enola Holmes. 2006, Philomel paper $10.99 (978-0-399-24304-2). Enola Holmes, the much younger sister of Sherlock and Mycroft, embarks on a search for her mother, who disappears on Enola's 14th birthday. (Rev: BCCB 2/06; BL 12/1/05*; HBG 10/06; SLJ 2/06*)

8206 Springer, Nancy. *Lionclaw* (5–8). Series: Tales of Rowan Hood. 2002, Putnam $16.99 (978-0-399-23716-4). Gentle, music-loving Lionel abandons his timidity when Rowan Hood is captured, but, despite his newfound courage, his father still refuses to accept him in this sequel to *Rowan Hood: Outlaw Girl of Sherwood Forest* (2001). (Rev: BL 10/1/02; HBG 10/03; SLJ 10/02; VOYA 12/02)

8207 Springer, Nancy. *My Sister's Stalker* (5–8). 2012, Holiday House $16.95 (978-082342358-3). 194pp. Rig, 16, discovers his college-age sister is being stalked and pursues him with the help of his father in this taut novel that will appeal to reluctant readers. ◯ Lexile 770L (Rev: BL 5/1/12; SLJ 5/1/12)

8208 Springer, Nancy. *Outlaw Princess of Sherwood* (4–7). Series: Tales of Rowan Hood. 2003, Putnam $16.99 (978-0-399-23721-8). The third installment of this series features Princess Ettarde, whose father has hatched a dastardly plot to lure Etty away from Sherwood Forest. (Rev: BL 12/1/03; HBG 4/04; SLJ 9/03)

8209 Standiford, Natalie. *The Secret Tree* (4–7). 2012, Scholastic $16.99 (978-0-545-33479-2). 256pp. Minty discovers a tree with a hole in its trunk where people have placed notes about their aspirations and secrets; she and her new friend Raymond start spying on the neighbors to match them with the notes. **e** Lexile 510L (Rev: BL 5/1/12; LMC 8–9/12; SLJ 7/12)

8210 Stanley, Diane. *The Mysterious Case of the Allbright Academy* (4–7). 2008, HarperCollins $15.99 (978-0-06-085817-9). What's going on at Allbright Academy? Frannie suspects that her "perfect" classmates are being brainwashed and placed into positions of authority in the U.S. government, and she sets out to foil the plot. (Rev: BL 11/15/07; SLJ 3/08)

8211 Stanley, George E. *The Clue of the Left-Handed Envelope* (2–3). Illus. by Sal Murdocca. Series: Third-Grade Detectives. 2000, Simon & Schuster paper $3.99 (978-0-689-82194-3). 80pp. Noelle and Todd together with the other third graders and their teacher, Mr. Merlin, unmask the identity of the person who has sent Amber Lee a secret-admirer letter. (Rev: BCCB 12/00; SLJ 2/01)

8212 Stanley, John P. *Mickey Price: Journey to Oblivion* (4–6). 2013, Tanglewood $15.99 (978-193371888-0). 308pp. In this exciting tale that strains credulity, three preteen boys are invited by NASA to take part in a mission that cannot be conducted by adults. Lexile 770 (Rev: BL 10/1/13; LMC 5–6/14; SLJ 11/13)

8213 Stead, Rebecca. *When You Reach Me* (4–7). 2009, Random $15.99 (978-0-385-73742-5). 208pp. Sixth-grader Miranda receives notes from someone she believes knows the future. Newbery Medal 2010; Boston Globe–Horn Book Fiction; ALA Notable Children's Book. ∩ **e** (Rev: BCCB 9/09; BL 6/1–15/09*; HB 7/09; LMC 10/09; SLJ 7/09*)

8214 Steer, Dugald, ed. *Pirateology: The Sea Journal of Captain William Lubber* (4–7). Illus. by Yvonne Gilbert. 2006, Candlewick $19.99 (978-0-7636-3143-7). An authentic-looking large-format scrapbook chronicling the pirate-chasing adventures of a sea captain of old, complete with treasure maps and a working compass. (Rev: BL 7/06; SLJ 12/06)

8215 Steiner, Barbara. *Foghorn Flattery and the Dancing Horses* (4–6). 1991, Avon paper $2.95 (978-0-380-76147-0). 108pp. Carly and brother Foghorn travel to Vienna and encounter a mystery. (Rev: BL 6/15/91)

8216 Stem, Jacqueline. *The Cellar in the Woods* (4–6). 1997, Eakin $14.95 (978-1-57168-115-7). 145pp. In East Texas, three cousins explore a deserted house and encounter danger. (Rev: SLJ 1/98)

8217 Stengel, Joyce A. *Mystery of the Island Jewels* (5–8). 2002, Simon & Schuster paper $4.99 (978-0-689-85049-3). On a cruise to Martinique with her father and new stepfamily, 14-year-old Cassie and new friend Charles uncover a mystery. (Rev: SLJ 6/02)

8218 Stenhouse, Ted. *Murder on the Ridge* (5–8). 2006, Kids Can $16.95 (978-1-55337-892-1); paper $6.95 (978-1-55337-893-8). Will and Arthur, a white boy and an Indian boy who are friends despite the prejudices of 1950s Canada, investigate a World War I mystery in the latest installment in the series that started with *Across the Steel River* (2001) and *A Dirty Deed* (2003). (Rev: BL 5/15/06)

8219 Stevenson, Robert Louis. *Treasure Island* (5–9). Illus. by N. C. Wyeth. Series: Scribner Storybook Classic. 2003, Simon & Schuster $18.95 (978-0-689-85468-2). This picture-book adaptation of the classic story features beautiful paintings by N. C. Wyeth. (Rev: BL 8/03; HBG 4/04)

8220 Stevenson, Robin. *Dead in the Water* (5–8). Series: Orca Sports. 2008, Orca paper $9.95 (978-1-55143-962-4). While at sea as part of a sailing camp, Simon ends up a captive on a boat full of poachers in this thriller for reluctant readers. (Rev: BL 3/15/08)

8221 Stewart, Trenton Lee. *The Extraordinary Education of Nicholas Benedict* (4–6). Illus. by Diana Sudyka. 2012, Little, Brown $17.99 (978-031617619-4). 480pp. At his new orphanage 9-year-old Nicholas, who has an ugly nose and narcolepsy, learns to avoid the vicious bullies known as the Spiders and discovers a mystery that may change his life. ∩ **e** Lexile 900L (Rev: BL 2/1/12*; HB 3–4/12; LMC 8–9/12; SLJ 4/12; VOYA 4/12)

8222 Stewart, Trenton Lee. *The Mysterious Benedict Society and the Perilous Journey* (4–7). Illus. by Diana Sudyka. Series: The Mysterious Benedict Society. 2008, Little, Brown $16.99 (978-0-316-05780-6). Reynie, Kate, Sticky, and Constance have many adventures as they travel to rescue Mr. Benedict from the evil Mr. Curtain in this action-packed sequel to *The Mysterious Benedict Society* (2007). (Rev: BL 3/15/08; SLJ 5/08)

8223 Stine, R. L. *The Wrong Number* (5–9). 1990, Pocket paper $4.99 (978-0-671-69411-1). While making a crank telephone call, a teenager hears a murder being committed. (Rev: SLJ 6/90)

8224 Stolz, Mary. *Casebook of a Private (Cat's) Eye* (3–5). Illus. 1999, Front St. $14.95 (978-0-8126-2650-6). 128pp. Eileen O'Kelly, a cat detective from Boston, solves a number of short mysteries in this novel set in 1912. (Rev: BCCB 6/99; BL 4/15/99; HBG 10/99; SLJ 6/99)

8225 Strickland, Brad. *The House Where Nobody Lived* (5–8). Series: Lewis Barnavelt. 2006, Dial $16.99 (978-0-8037-3148-6). Lewis befriends David, whose family has moved into a creepy, long-abandoned house, which may be haunted; with help from Uncle Jonathan and a neighborhood witch, Lewis confronts magic and danger. (Rev: BL 1/1–15/07; SLJ 1/07)

8226 Sukach, Jim. *Clever Quicksolve Whodunit Puzzles* (4–7). Illus. by Lucy Corvino. Series: Mini-Mysteries for You to Solve. 1999, Sterling $14.95 (978-0-8069-6569-7). Thirty-five mini-mysteries are presented with answers appended. (Rev: SLJ 1/00)

8227 Suma, Nova Ren. *Dani Noir* (5–8). 2009, Simon & Schuster $15.99 (978-1-4169-7564-9). 266pp. Thirteen-year-old Dani's main enjoyment is watching noir films at the local art theater, and these fuel her imagination to the point that she suspects an older teen, Jackson, of two-timing his girlfriend. Her resulting investigation teaches her about life and herself. (Rev: BL 11/1/09; LMC 11–12/09; SLJ 12/09)

8228 Sylvester, Kevin. *Neil Flambé and the Marco Polo Murders* (4–8). Illus. by author. 2012, Simon & Schuster $12.99 (978-144244604-5). 304pp. Fourteen-year-old Neil Flambé's ultrasensitive nose serves him well in the kitchen but also while investigating crimes, in this case the murders of chefs that are somehow linked to exotic spices; first published in Canada in 2010. (Rev: BL 4/15/12; LMC 10/12; SLJ 4/10)

8229 Tate, Nikki. *Venom* (5–8). 2009, Orca paper $9.95 (978-1-55469-071-8). 176pp. For reluctant readers, this suspenseful story set in the world of horse racing features 16-year-old Spencer, who challenges dangerous forces when he suspects the use of illegal drugs. (Rev: BL 5/1/09)

8230 Taylor, Cora. *Murder in Mexico* (4–7). Series: The Spy Who Wasn't There. 2007, Coteau paper $7.95 (978-1-55050-353-1). In this second, fast-paced installment in the mystery series, twins Jennifer and Maggie are visiting ruins in the Yucatan when Jennifer must use her ability to become invisible to solve a crime. (Rev: SLJ 4/07)

8231 Taylor, Theodore. *The Cay* (5–8). 1987, Doubleday $16.95 (978-0-385-07906-8); paper $4.95 (978-0-380-00142-2). A blind boy and an old black sailor are shipwrecked on a coral island. (Rev: BL 9/1/89)

8232 Taylor, Theodore. *Ice Drift* (4–7). 2005, Harcourt $16.00 (978-0-15-205081-8). Inuit brothers Alika, 14, and Sulu, 10, struggle to survive over the months that they are trapped on an ice floe that is slowly floating south in the Greenland Strait. (Rev: BL 2/1/05; SLJ 1/05)

8233 Thomas, Jane Resh. *Blind Mountain* (4–7). 2006, Clarion $15.00 (978-0-618-64872-6). Forced to go on a hiking trip with his bossy father in the mountainous Montana wilderness, 12-year-old Sam finds himself in charge of their survival when his father is temporarily blinded by a branch. (Rev: BL 12/1/06; SLJ 12/06)

8234 Thomas, Jane Resh. *Courage at Indian Deep* (5–7). 1984, Houghton Mifflin paper $6.95 (978-0-395-55699-3). A young boy must help save a ship caught in a sudden storm.

8235 Thompson, J. E. *The Girl from Felony Bay* (4–6). Series: Felony Bay Mysteries. 2013, HarperCollins $16.99 (978-006210446-5). 384pp. Living in South Carolina with a disinterested aunt and uncle, 12-year-old Abbey is determined to prove her father's innocence of theft, and finds a new African American friend who helps her investigate. ℮ (Rev: BLO 7/13; LMC 10/13; SLJ 6/13)

8236 Thompson, Kate. *Highway Robbery* (4–7). Illus. by Robert Dress. 2009, HarperCollins $15.99 (978-0-06-173034-4). 128pp. A young boy suffers through a long cold night looking after a stranger's horse only to learn that the stranger might have been Dick Turpin and the horse his famous Black Bess. (Rev: BCCB 7–8/09; BL 6/1–15/09; HB 7/09; SLJ 6/09)

8237 Torrey, Michele. *The Case of the Mossy Lake Monster and Other Super-Scientific Cases* (3–5). Illus. by Barbara Johansen Newman. Series: Doyle and Fossey,

Science Detectives. 2002, Dutton $14.99 (978-0-525-46815-8). 112pp. Fifth-graders Drake Doyle and Nell Fossey solve a string of mysteries using scientific reasoning in this easy-to-read second book in the series. (Rev: BL 1/1–15/02; HBG 10/02; SLJ 2/02)

8238 Torrey, Michele. *Voyage of Ice* (4–7). Series: Chronicle of Courage. 2004, Knopf LB $17.99 (978-0-375-92381-4). In 1851, 15-year-old Nick signs on as a hand aboard the whaler *Sea Hawk* and soon discovers unexpected hardships, including struggling to survive in the Arctic. (Rev: BL 5/15/04; SLJ 7/04)

8239 Trembath, Don. *Emville Confidential* (5–8). 2007, Orca paper $8.95 (978-1-55143-671-5). A tongue-in-cheek hard-boiled detective novel featuring 7th-graders Baron, Myles, and Rebecca. (Rev: BL 11/1/07; SLJ 2/08)

8240 Trout, Richard E. *Czar of Alaska: The Cross of Charlemagne* (5–8). Series: MacGregor Family Adventure. 2005, Pelican $15.95 (978-1-58980-328-2). In volume four of the series, the five MacGregors travel to Alaska to assess the environmental impact of drilling for oil and become entangled with ecoterrorists and priests seeking an ancient cross. (Rev: SLJ 12/05)

8241 Turnage, Sheila. *The Ghosts of Tupelo Landing* (4–6). 2014, Penguin $16.99 (978-080373671-9). 368pp. A 6th-grade class assignment sends Mo and her friend Dale (the Desperado Detective Agency) to interview a ghost that haunts the Old Tupelo Inn; a sequel to *Three Times Lucky* (2012). Lexile 550 (Rev: BL 12/15/13*; SLJ 1/14*)

8242 Turnage, Sheila. *Three Times Lucky* (4–6). 2012, Dial $16.99 (978-080373670-2). 320pp. A murder, a kidnapping, and lots of unanswered questions about family histories set the scene for this satisfying mystery featuring 11-year-old protagonist Mo. ᗡ ℮ Lexile 560L (Rev: BL 5/1/12*; HB 7–8/12; LMC 11–12/12; SLJ 6/12; VOYA 8/12)

8243 Twain, Mark. *The Stolen White Elephant* (4–8). 1882, Ayer $19.95 (978-0-8369-3486-1). The tale of the elephant's guardian who naively is impressed by a corrupt police detective. (Rev: BL 5/1/88; SLJ 2/88)

8244 Umansky, Kaye. *Solomon Snow and the Stolen Jewel* (4–7). 2007, Candlewick $12.99 (978-0-7636-2793-5). In this sequel to *Solomon Snow and the Silver Spoon* (2005), Solomon and Prudence set out to help Prudence's father escape from a prison ship and become caught up in a plot to steal a cursed ruby. (Rev: BL 4/15/07; SLJ 7/07)

8245 Valgardson, W. D. *Winter Rescue* (4–6). Illus. by Ange Zhang. 1995, Simon & Schuster paper $15.00 (978-0-689-80094-8). An adventure story that involves a young boy and the Icelandic-Canadian fishermen around Lake Winnipeg. (Rev: BCCB 12/95; SLJ 11/95)

8246 Van Draanen, Wendelin. *The Greatest Power* (3–5). Illus. by Stephen Gilpin. 2009, Knopf $12.99 (978-0-375-84377-8). 208pp. Dave, 13, and his sidekick gecko Sticky investigate a bank robbery by the evil Damien Black. (Rev: BL 5/1/09; LMC 10/09; SLJ 4/09)

8247 Van Draanen, Wendelin. *Sammy Keyes and the Art of Deception* (5–8). Series: Sammy Keyes. 2003, Knopf $15.95 (978-0-375-81176-0). Sammy (with some help from Grams) solves a mystery involving an art thief. (Rev: BL 2/1/03; HBG 10/03; SLJ 3/03; VOYA 8/03)

8248 Van Draanen, Wendelin. *Sammy Keyes and the Dead Giveaway* (5–8). 2005, Knopf LB $17.99 (978-0-375-92350-0). Seventh-grade sleuth Sammy tackles personal problems — should she make a confession that would exonerate her archenemy? — and community ones as she investigates abuse of eminent domain. (Rev: BL 9/1/05; SLJ 11/05)

8249 Van Draanen, Wendelin. *Sammy Keyes and the Night of Skulls* (5–8). 2011, Knopf $15.99 (978-037586108-6); LB $18.99 (978-037596108-3). 272pp. Junior high sleuth Sammy and her friends find themselves in the midst of a mystery in a graveyard on Halloween night. (Rev: BL 10/1/11)

8250 Van Draanen, Wendelin. *Sammy Keyes and the Power of Justice Jack* (5–8). 2012, Knopf $16.99 (978-037587052-1); LB $19.99 (978-037597052-8). 288pp. Sammy contends with a growing tangle of complications: a new superhero wannabe in town, her friend Billy angling to be the guy's sidekick, a missing woman, and a City Hall statue that has disappeared. **e** (Rev: BL 5/1/12)

8251 Van Draanen, Wendelin. *Sammy Keyes and the Skeleton Man* (5–8). 1998, Knopf paper $4.99 (978-0-375-80054-2). Sammy, the youthful sleuth, is challenged when she tries to solve the mystery of a man dressed in a skeleton costume. (Rev: BL 9/1/98; HBG 3/99; SLJ 9/98)

8252 Van Draanen, Wendelin. *Sammy Keyes and the Wedding Crasher* (5–8). 2010, Knopf $16.99 (978-037586107-9); LB $19.99 (978-037596107-6). 304pp. Starting 8th grade Sammy is shocked to find herself suspected of making threats against her history teacher; she also must cope with her nemesis Heather and her duties as a reluctant bridesmaid. ∩ **e** Lexile 750L (Rev: BL 12/15/10; VOYA 2/11)

8253 Van Draanen, Wendelin. *Shredderman: Meet the Gecko* (3–5). 2005, Knopf LB $14.99 (978-0-375-92353-1). Nerdy Nolan Byrd assumes his Shredderman superhero persona to help a young TV star chase off a pesky reporter. (Rev: BL 2/1/05; SLJ 1/05)

8254 Van Draanen, Wendelin. *Sinister Substitute* (3–5). Illus. by Stephen Gilpin. Series: The Gecko and Sticky. 2010, Knopf $12.99 (978-037584378-5); LB $15.99 (978-037594572-4). 208pp. Middle school superhero Dave, aka the Gecko, and his sidekick Sticky — an actual gecko — set out to thwart a sinister bad guy who's disguised himself as a substitute teacher in this energetic adventure story. ∩ Lexile 860L (Rev: BL 1/1/10)

8255 Van Tol, Alex. *Gravity Check* (4–6). Series: Orca Sports. 2011, Orca paper $9.95 (978-15546934-9-8). 176pp. Five riders on a British Columbia bike trail discover a clandestine pot farm in this tense thriller for reluctant readers. (Rev: BL 9/1/11)

8256 Vazquez, Diana. *Lost in Sierra* (4–6). Illus. by German Jaramillo. 2002, Coteau paper $7.95 (978-1-55050-184-1). On a visit to Spain, 13-year-old Ana discovers why her grandmother's brother never came back from Spain's civil war. (Rev: SLJ 8/02)

8257 Voelkel, Jon, and Pamela Voelkel. *The End of the World Club* (4–6). Series: Jaguar Stones. 2010, Egmont $16.99 (978-1-60684-072-6). 416pp. Max and Lola travel to Spain to retrieve a magical stone needed to save Max's parents from the Maya Lords of Death. ∩ **e** Lexile 760L (Rev: BL 2/1/11; LMC 5–6/11; SLJ 1/1/11)

8258 Voigt, Cynthia. *The Book of Lost Things* (4–6). Illus. by Iacopo Bruno. Series: Mister Max. 2013, Knopf $16.99 (978-030797681-9). 384pp. When his parents desert him in the early 1900s, 12-year-old Max discovers he can support himself solving mysteries. ∩ **e** Lexile 890 (Rev: BLO 7/13; SLJ 7/13)

8259 Wade, Rebecca. *The Whispering House* (5–8). 2012, HarperCollins $16.99 (978-006077497-4). 272pp. When 14-year-old Hannah's family moves into Cowleigh Lodge, she discovers that a young girl was probably murdered there in 1877; a sequel to *The Theft and the Miracle* (2007). **e** Lexile 830L (Rev: BL 5/1/12; SLJ 6/12)

8260 Walden, Mark. *Dreadnought* (5–8). Series: H.I.V.E. 2011, Simon & Schuster $16.99 (978-144242186-8). 304pp. When an especially villainous classmate hijacks the villain school's airborne defense platform, Otto and his friends come to the rescue. **e** Lexile 1000L (Rev: BL 4/15/11)

8261 Walden, Mark. *Escape Velocity* (5–8). Series: H.I.V.E. 2011, Simon & Schuster $16.99 (978-144242185-1). 352pp. Otto, who is still learning to use his newfound abilities, must break into MI6 in order to rescue Dr. Nero from H.O.P.E. — the Hostile Operative Prosecution Executive. Also use *Rogue* (2011). **e** Lexile 990L (Rev: BL 6/1/11)

8262 Walden, Mark. *H.I.V.E: The Higher Institute of Villainous Education* (5–8). Series: H.I.V.E. 2007, Simon & Schuster $15.99 (978-1-4169-3571-1). Kidnapped along with three of his friends and enrolled in an academy that grooms students in the villainous arts, 13-year-old brilliant orphan Otto maps a plan to escape, a feat never before accomplished. (Rev: BL 4/1/07; SLJ 6/07)

8263 Walden, Mark. *The Overlord Protocol* (5–8). Series: H.I.V.E. 2008, Simon & Schuster $15.99 (978-1-4169-6016-4). 384pp. Wing and Otto, students at the Higher Institute of Villainous Education (H.I.V.E.), travel to Japan for Wing's father's funeral and realize they have fallen into an evil trap. (Rev: BL 3/1/08)

8264 Wallace, Bill. *Blackwater Swamp* (4–6). Illus. 1994, Holiday House $16.95 (978-0-8234-1120-7). 185pp. A woman, known by all to be a witch, helps Ted catch a group of crooks responsible for some local robberies. (Rev: BCCB 5/94; BL 6/1–15/94; SLJ 4/94)

8265 Wallace, Bill. *Danger in Quicksand Swamp* (4–7). 1989, Holiday $16.95 (978-0-8234-0786-6). While searching for buried treasure, Ben and Jake become stranded on an island near Quicksand Swamp. (Rev: BL 1/1/90; SLJ 10/89)

8266 Wallace, Bill. *Trapped in Death Cave* (5–8). 1984, Holiday $16.95 (978-0-8234-0516-9). Gary is convinced his grandpa was murdered to secure a map indicating where gold is buried.

8267 Wallace, Karen. *The Secret of the Crocodiles* (4–6). Series: Lady Violet's Casebook. 2008, Simon & Schuster paper $9.95 (978-0-689-87483-3). 236pp. Lady Violet is a teen at the turn of the 20th century and in this volume travels with her family, governess, and pet monkey to Egypt, where they become entangled in intrigues and Violet longs for more freedom. (Rev: BL 7/08)

8268 Walters, Eric. *Northern Exposures* (5–8). 2008, Fitzhenry & Whiteside paper $11.95 (978-1-55455-107-1). In this fast-paced novel, a 13-year-old boy finds himself on an adventure when he wins a trip to photograph polar bears and gets involved with poachers; this will appeal to reluctant readers. (Rev: SLJ 2/09)

8269 Warner, Gertrude Chandler. *The Clue in the Recycling Bin* (2–4). Illus. by Robert Papp. Series: Boxcar Children. 2011, Whitman $14.99 (978-080751208-1). 128pp. Volunteering at a recycling center, the Alden children stumble upon a string of break-ins involving reclaimed metal. (Rev: BL 5/1/11)

8270 Warner, Gertrude Chandler. *The Dog-Gone Mystery* (2–5). Illus. by Robert Papp. Series: Boxcar Children. 2009, Whitman LB $14.99 (978-0-8075-1658-4); paper $4.99 (978-0-8075-1657-7). 120pp. When two dogs disappear from their dog Watch's obedience class, the four Alden children swing into action. (Rev: SLJ 12/1/09)

8271 Warner, Gertrude Chandler. *The Pumpkin Head Mystery* (2–4). Illus. by Robert Papp. Series: Boxcar Children. 2010, Whitman $14.99 (978-080756668-8); paper $4.99 (978-08075666-9-5). 128pp. The Boxcar Children attempt to dispel the bad luck stalking their grandparents' friends' farm. **e** Lexile 430L (Rev: BL 1/1–15/11)

8272 Warner, Gertrude Chandler. *The Spy in the Bleachers* (2–5). Illus. by Robert Papp. Series: Boxcar Children. 2010, Whitman $14.99 (978-080757606-9); paper $4.99 (978-08075760-7-6). 128pp. The four siblings investigate when it seems someone is stealing players' signals and relaying them to the other team. (Rev: BL 5/1/10)

8273 Watson, Geoff. *Edison's Gold* (4–7). 2010, Egmont $15.99 (978-160684094-8). 320pp. Tom Edison IV, the great-great-grandson of the esteemed inventor, hatches a plan to restore his family's fortune by creating gold in this action-filled mystery involving a secret society and a descendant of Nikola Tesla. Lexile 880L (Rev: BL 11/1/10; LMC 1–2/11; SLJ 1/1/11)

8274 Watson, Jude. *In Too Deep* (4–7). Series: 39 Clues. 2009, Scholastic $12.99 (978-054506046-2); LB $12.99 (978-054509064-3). 208pp. Amy and Dan travel to Australia searching for clues to their parents' disappearance while battling threats from humans and animals in this

sixth installment in the series. ∩ **e** Lexile 550L (Rev: BL 1/1/10)

8275 Watson, Stephanie. *Elvis and Olive: Super Detectives* (3–6). Series: Elvis & Olive. 2010, Scholastic $15.99 (978-054515148-1). 240pp. The quite different preteen friends Natalie and Annie (the series uses their code names) start a successful detective agency. (Rev: BLO 11/1/10; LMC 8–9/10; SLJ 8/10)

8276 Weeks, Sarah. *Pie* (3–6). 2011, Scholastic $16.99 (978-0-545-27011-3). 192pp. After her beloved aunt Polly's death, 10-year-old Alice and her friend Charlie investigate the disappearance of Polly's cat and the destruction of her famous bakery; a chapter book set in 1955. (Rev: BL 9/1/11; SLJ 9/1/11*)

8277 Weir, Joan. *The Mysterious Visitor* (5–7). Series: Lion and Bobbi. 2002, Raincoast paper $6.99 (978-1-55192-404-5). Two Canadian youngsters, Lion and sister Bobbi, try to solve the mystery of strange events occurring on a friend's land. (Rev: BL 5/1/02)

8278 Weltman, June. *Mystery of the Missing Candlestick* (5–8). 2004, Mayhaven $23.95 (978-1-878044-98-3). Miranda, 17, and her friends Leila and Rebecca join forces to solve the mystery of a valuable antique candlestick that has been stolen from Rebecca's grandfather. (Rev: BL 5/1/04)

8279 White, Ruth. *The Search for Belle Prater* (4–7). 2005, Farrar $16.00 (978-0-374-30853-7). In this sequel to *Belle Prater's Boy,* 13-year-old Woodrow and his cousin Gypsy continue to search for Woodrow's missing mother against the backdrop of mid-1950s segregation. (Rev: BL 2/15/05*; SLJ 4/05)

8280 Whitehouse, Howard. *The Faceless Fiend: Being the Tale of a Criminal Mastermind, His Masked Minions and a Princess with a Butter Knife, Involving Explosives and a Certain Amount of Pushing and Shoving* (4–7). Illus. by Bill Slavin. 2007, Kids Can $16.95 (978-1-55453-130-1); paper $7.95 (978-1-55453-180-6). In this sequel to *The Strictest School in the World* (2006), Emmaline and her friend Princess Purnah escape from St. Grimelda's School for Young Ladies and — with a motley crew of supporters and many comical mishaps along the way — manage to foil a kidnapping. (Rev: LMC 1/08; SLJ 11/07)

8281 Wildavsky, Rachel. *The Secret of Rover* (4–7). 2011, Abrams $16.95 (978-0-8109-9710-3). 368pp. Katie and David, 12-year-old twins whose parents invented a secret spying device, find themselves embroiled in political intrigue. (Rev: BL 5/1/11; SLJ 4/11*)

8282 Wilkins, Kay. *A Scaly Tale* (4–7). Illus. by Ailin Chambers. Series: Ripley's Bureau of Investigation. 2010, Ripley paper $4.99 (978-18939515-2-5). 128pp. After a half-man, half-reptile creature is spotted in the Florida Everglades, Ripley's Bureau of Investigation sends a team with special powers to look into the matter. **e** Lexile 820L (Rev: BL 9/1/10)

8283 Wilson, Barbara. *A Clear Spring* (4–6). 2002, Feminist paper $12.50 (978-1-55861-277-8). 176pp. While working at a nature center with her aunt's lesbian partner, Willa teams up with her cousins to track down polluters. (Rev: BL 7/02; HBG 10/02)

8284 Wilson, Eric. *Murder on the Canadian: A Tom Austen Mystery* (4–8). Illus. by Richard Row. 2000, Orca paper $4.99 (978-1-55143-151-2). A fast-moving mystery starring an intrepid hero who is also featured in *Vancouver Nightmare: A Tom Austen Mystery* (2000). (Rev: SLJ 1/01)

8285 Wilson, N. D. *Leepike Ridge* (4–7). 2007, Random House $15.99 (978-0-375-83873-6). Eleven-year-old Tom must use his survival skills when he finds himself trapped in a series of caves where he meets Reg, who's been trapped for three years, and discovers mysterious carvings on the wall. (Rev: BL 5/15/07; HB 5–6/07; LMC 10/07; SLJ 5/07)

8286 Winters, Ben H. *The Mystery of the Missing Everything* (5–8). 2011, HarperCollins $16.99 (978-0-06-196544-9). 272pp. Eighth-grader Bethesda Fielding investigates a missing sports trophy in this sequel to *The Secret Life of Ms. Finkleman* (2010). (Rev: BL 10/1/11; SLJ 10/1/11)

8287 Wright, Betty R. *The Dollhouse Murders* (4–7). 1983, Holiday $16.95 (978-0-8234-0497-1). Dolls in a dollhouse come to life in this mystery about long-ago murders.

8288 Wright, Betty R. *Princess for a Week* (3–5). Illus. by Jacqueline Rogers. 2006, Holiday $16.95 (978-0-8234-1945-6). 105pp. Roddy is already stressed when an overbearing girl called Princess comes to stay; she persuades him to investigate the goings-on at an abandoned house nearby. (Rev: BL 5/1/06; SLJ 5/06)

8289 Yep, Laurence. *The Case of the Firecrackers* (4–7). 1999, HarperCollins LB $15.89 (978-0-06-024452-1). In this Chinatown mystery, Tiger Lil and her great-niece Lily are on the trail of the murderer who killed the star of the television show in which they were extras. (Rev: BL 9/15/99; HBG 3/00; SLJ 9/99)

8290 Yep, Laurence. *The Case of the Lion Dance* (4–6). Series: Chinatown Mystery. 1998, HarperCollins LB $15.89 (978-0-06-024448-4). Lily and her great aunt Tiger Lil, a public relations expert, try to find out who is responsible for ruining the opening of a new restaurant and stealing money meant for a charity. (Rev: BL 10/15/98; HBG 3/99; SLJ 11/98)

8291 Young, E. L. *The Black Sphere* (5–8). Illus. Series: STORM. 2009, Dial $16.99 (978-0-8037-3268-1). Three 14-year-olds — Andrew, Will, and Gaia — save the day in this thriller featuring high-tech intrigue and budding romance. (Rev: BL 2/1/09; SLJ 9/09; VOYA 3/09)

8292 Young, E. L. *The Infinity Code* (5–8). 2008, Dial $16.99 (978-0-8037-3265-0). Young computer whizzes Andrew, Will, Gaia, and Caspian make up the group STORM ("Science and Technology to Over-Rule Misery") and find themselves in a tech-driven battle against a group that has kidnapped Caspian's father. (Rev: BL 3/1/08; SLJ 5/08)

8293 Zambreno, Mary F. *Journeyman Wizard* (4–7). 1994, Harcourt $16.95 (978-0-15-200022-6). Student

wizard Jeremy is studying the casting of spells with Lady Allons when an unfortunate death occurs and he is accused of murder. (Rev: BL 5/1/94; SLJ 6/94)

Animal Stories

8294 Adler, C. S. *More Than a Horse* (5–7). 1997, Clarion $15.00 (978-0-395-79769-3). Leeann and her mother move to a dude ranch in Arizona, where the young girl develops a love of horses. (Rev: BCCB 3/97; BL 3/15/97; SLJ 4/97)

8295 Adler, C. S. *One Unhappy Horse* (5–7). 2001, Clarion $16.00 (978-0-618-04912-7). Set on a small ranch near Tucson, this novel features 12-year-old Jan, her horse, Dove, an old lady in a retirement home, and Jan's new friend, Lisa. (Rev: BL 3/1/01; HBG 10/01; SLJ 4/01)

8296 Ahlberg, Allan. *Half a Pig* (3–5). Trans. by Allan Ahlberg and Jessica Ahlberg. Illus. by Jessica Ahlberg. 2004, Candlewick $16.99 (978-0-7636-2373-9). 40pp. An amusing story of a married couple's conflict over the fate of their jointly owned pig, Esmeralda, also serves as the basis for tips on language and use of words. (Rev: BL 8/04; HB 7/04; SLJ 8/04)

8297 Altbacker, E. J. *Shark Wars* (4–6). 2011, Penguin $12.99 (978-1-59514-376-1). 256pp. Young reef shark Gray is banished from his clan, or shiver, and must find a new home and battle to protect it. ⌒ ℮ (Rev: LMC 10/11; SLJ 8/11)

8298 Alter, Judith. *Callie Shaw, Stable Boy* (5–8). 1996, Eakin $16.95 (978-1-57168-092-1). During the Great Depression, Callie, disguised as a boy, works in a stable and uncovers a race-fixing racket. (Rev: BL 2/1/97; SLJ 8/97)

8299 Alter, Judith. *Maggie and a Horse Named Devildust* (5–7). 1989, Ellen C. Temple paper $5.95 (978-0-936650-08-1). Maggie is determined to ride her spirited horse in the Wild West show in this historical horse story. (Rev: BL 4/15/89)

8300 Alter, Judith. *Maggie and the Search for Devildust* (5–7). 1989, Ellen C. Temple paper $5.95 (978-0-936650-09-8). Maggie, a gorgeous girl of the Old West, sets out to find her horse, which has been stolen. (Rev: BL 10/1/89)

8301 Appelt, Kathi. *The Underneath* (4–8). Illus. by David Small. 2008, Atheneum $16.99 (978-1-4169-5058-5). Newborn kittens, a bloodhound named Ranger, and a water snake find safety together in this story set in the mysterious bayous of East Texas. Newbery Honor 2009. (Rev: BL 5/15/08; SLJ 6/08)

8302 Applegate, Katherine. *The One and Only Ivan* (3–6). Illus. by Patricia Castelao. 2012, HarperCollins $16.99 (978-006199225-4). 320pp. A bored gorilla named Ivan makes his elephant friend Stella an improbable promise in this first-person story based on real life. ℮ (Rev: BL 2/15/12; HB 1–2/12; SLJ 1/12)

8303 Arnosky, Jim. *Slow Down for Manatees* (1–3). Illus. by author. 2010, Putnam $16.99 (978-0-399-24170-3). 32pp. A pregnant manatee injured by a motorboat is rehabilitated at an aquarium in this touching story that examines the real threats boaters pose to the animals. Lexile AD860L (Rev: BL 3/1/10; HB 5–6/10; LMC 3–4/10; SLJ 2/1/10)

8304 Avi. *The Good Dog* (3–6). 2001, Simon & Schuster $16.00 (978-0-689-83824-8). 256pp. A malamute dog reconsiders his position as a pet when a wolf comes to town. (Rev: BL 9/1/01; HB 1/02; HBG 3/02; SLJ 12/01)

8305 Bagnold, Enid. *National Velvet* (5–8). Illus. by Ted Lewin. 1985, Avon paper $4.99 (978-0-380-71235-9). The now-classic story of Heather Brown and her struggle to ride in the Grand National. A reissue. (Rev: BL 12/15/85)

8306 Bastedo, Jamie. *Tracking Triple Seven* (5–7). 2001, Red Deer paper $9.95 (978-0-88995-238-6). Benji, a teenage boy grieving his mother's death, becomes involved with biologists tracking grizzly bears near his father's mine in Canada. (Rev: BL 2/1/02)

8307 Bauer, Marion Dane. *Runt* (3–6). 2002, Clarion $14.00 (978-0-618-21261-3). 144pp. A tale of a wolf born the runt of the litter and his struggle to improve his position in the pack and earn his father's approval. (Rev: BL 10/15/02; SLJ 9/02)

8308 Bauer, Michael Gerard. *Just A Dog* (4–6). 2012, Scholastic $15.99 (978-0-545-37452-1). 144pp. After the death of the family dog, Mister Mosely, young Corey tells funny and moving stories about his exploits. Lexile 940L (Rev: BL 12/15/12; HB 1–2/13; LMC 1–2/13; SLJ 12/12)

8309 Baylor, Byrd. *Hawk, I'm Your Brother* (3–5). Illus. by Peter Parnall. 1976, Macmillan paper $5.99 (978-0-689-71102-2). 48pp. A desert boy captures a young hawk, hoping it will teach him how to fly.

8310 Bechtold, Lisze. *Buster and Phoebe: The Great Bone Game* (1–4). Illus. by author. 2003, Houghton $15.00 (978-0-618-20862-3). Phoebe, the resident dog, greets newcomer Buster with skepticism, but the two soon come to terms in this beginning chapter book. (Rev: HB 9/03; HBG 4/04; SLJ 7/03)

8311 Beha, Eileen. *Tango: The Tale of an Island Dog* (4–6). 2009, Bloomsbury $15.99 (978-1-59990-262-1). A little Yorkie used to living in the lap of luxury suddenly finds himself washed up on Prince Edward Island where he must adapt to a new lifestyle. (Rev: SLJ 7/09) ∩

8312 Behrens, Andy. *The Fast and the Furriest* (2–5). 2010, Knopf $15.99 (978-0-375-85922-9); LB $18.99 (978-0-375-95922-6). 224pp. A funny story about 12-year-old Kevin's sudden interest in competition when his dog shows skill in agility courses. ∩ **e** Lexile 660L (Rev: BL 2/1/10; SLJ 3/10)

8313 Blom, Jen J. *Possum Summer* (4–7). Illus. by Omar Rayyan. 2011, Holiday House $17.95 (978-0-8234-2331-6). 160pp. Eleven-year-old Princess ("P") misses her father when he is stationed in Iraq, and ignoring his advice about wild animals she rescues a baby possum on their Oklahoma ranch. (Rev: BL 5/1/11; SLJ 6/11)

8314 Briggs-Bunting, Jane. *Laddie of the Light* (4–6). Illus. 1997, Black River Trading $17.00 (978-0-9649083-1-4). Jessie adjusts to her parents' approaching divorce with the help of two dogs, one real and the other a fictitious one that her grandfather tells her about. (Rev: BL 7/97)

8315 Brooke, Lauren. *Heartland: Coming Home* (4–7). 2000, Scholastic paper $4.99 (978-0-439-13020-2). When her mother dies, Amy works through her grief by helping horses with behavioral problems in this novel set on a Virginia horse farm. (Rev: BL 9/15/00)

8316 Bunting, Eve. *Reggie* (1–3). Illus. by D. Brent Burkett. 2006, Cricket $16.95 (978-0-8126-2746-6). 112pp. Alex keeps a toy mouse he finds even though he knows another child is looking for it, but when his own dog Patch disappears, he questions his decision. (Rev: BL 10/1/06; SLJ 11/06)

8317 Burgess, Melvin. *The Cry of the Wolf* (5–8). 1994, Morrow $17.99 (978-0-397-30693-0). Young Ben Tilley insists that wolves run past his farm in rural Surrey, even though they have supposedly been gone from England for 500 years. (Rev: BL 10/15/92; SLJ 9/92)

8318 Byars, Betsy. *The Midnight Fox* (4–6). Illus. by Ann Grifalconi. 1968, Puffin paper $5.99 (978-0-14-031450-2). 160pp. When Tom spends two months on a farm with his aunt and uncle, he never expects that a black fox will become the focus of his life.

8319 Byars, Betsy. *Tornado* (3–5). Illus. 1996, HarperCollins LB $15.89 (978-0-06-026452-9). 64pp. To pass the time during a tornado watch, Pete, a farmhand, tells about another Tornado, an unusual dog. (Rev: BCCB 11/96; BL 9/15/96; HB 11/96; SLJ 11/96)

8320 Byars, Betsy, et al. *My Dog, My Hero* (3–6). Illus. 2000, Holt $16.00 (978-0-8050-6327-1). Author Byars and her two daughters collaborated on this collection of eight stories about heroic dogs. (Rev: BL 1/1–15/01; HBG 3/01; SLJ 1/01)

8321 Carlson, Nolan. *Summer and Shiner* (5–8). 1992, Hearth paper $6.95 (978-0-9627947-4-2). In a small Kansas town in the 1940s, 12-year-old Carley adopts a raccoon called Shiner. (Rev: BL 9/15/92)

8322 Cleary, Beverly. *Strider* (5–9). 1991, Morrow LB $17.89 (978-0-688-09901-5). In this sequel to the 1984 Newbery winner *Dear Mr. Henshaw*, Leigh Botts is beginning high school and still writing in his diary, with his beloved dog, Strider, by his side. (Rev: BCCB 10/91; BL 7/91*; HB 9–10/91; SLJ 9/91)

8323 Cole, Henry. *A Nest for Celeste: A Story About Art, Inspiration, and the Meaning of Home* (2–5). Illus. by author. 2010, HarperCollins $16.99 (978-0-06-170410-9); LB $17.89 (978-0-06-170411-6). 352pp. In this story set in 1821 Louisiana, Celeste the mouse's life improves when John James Audubon and his assistant move into her house, offering her protection from rats and other dangers. (Rev: BL 2/15/10; LMC 3–4/10; SLJ 3/1/10)

8324 Cole, Joanna, and Stephanie Calmenson, eds. *Give a Dog a Bone: Stories, Poems, Jokes, and Riddles About Dogs* (2–3). Illus. 1996, Scholastic $16.95 (978-0-590-46374-4). An anthology of writings, anecdotes, and jokes about dogs. (Rev: BL 2/1/96; SLJ 3/96)

8325 Cuffe-Perez, Mary. *Skylar* (3–5). Illus. by Renata Liwska. 2008, Philomel $14.99 (978-0-399-24543-5). 144pp. Answering a plea for help from an injured heron, five out-of-shape pond geese set off on their first migration and meet many challenges, learning to work together and fly above their fears. (Rev: BL 1/1–15/08; SLJ 7/08)

8326 DeJong, Meindert. *Along Came a Dog* (4–7). Illus. by Maurice Sendak. 1958, HarperCollins paper $5.95 (978-0-06-440114-2). The friendship of a timid, lonely dog and a toeless little red hen is the basis for a very moving story, full of suspense.

8327 Duncan, Lois. *Movie for Dogs* (4–6). 2010, Scholastic $16.99 (978-054510854-6). 208pp. Andi and her brother Bruce collaborate on a dog-themed movie; do they have a chance at Hollywood? ∩ (Rev: BLO 5/15/10; VOYA 6/10)

8328 Edwards, Julie Andrews. *Little Bo in London: The Ultimate Adventure of Bonnie Boadicea* (1–3). Illus. by Henry Cole. 2012, HarperCollins $19.99 (978-0-06-008911-5). 112pp. Cruising in the Mediterranean, Little Bo the cat and her master find themselves facing down kidnappers before returning to England with the rescued shipowner; the final adventure in the nicely illustrated series. Lexile 860L (Rev: BL 11/1/12; SLJ 1/13)

8329 Edwards, Julie Andrews, and Emma Walton Hamilton. *Little Bo in Italy: The Continued Adventures of Bonnie Boadicea* (1–3). Illus. by Henry Cole. 2010, HarperCollins $19.99 (978-006008908-5). 112pp. Little Bo the cat and her master Billy have a European adventure when the yacht they're working on visits Rome and Pisa. (Rev: BL 2/1/11)

8330 Erickson, John R. *The Case of the Vanishing Fishhook* (3–6). Illus. by Gerald L. Holmes. Series: Hank the Cowdog. 1999, Viking $14.99 (978-0-670-88438-4); paper $4.99 (978-0-14-130356-7). 144pp. When Hank, a lovable dog, eats the liver that his young owner is using for fish bait, he realizes that he has also eaten a fish hook. (Rev: HBG 10/99; SLJ 4/99)

8331 Farley, Terri. *The Wild One* (4–6). 2002, Avon paper $4.99 (978-0-06-441085-4). Sam is determined to find her stallion, Blackie, who ran away after she fell off and hit her head. (Rev: BL 9/1/02; SLJ 12/02)

8332 Feiffer, Jules. *A Room with a Zoo* (3–5). Illus. 2005, Hyperion $16.95 (978-0-7868-3702-1). Julie (daughter of author and cartoonist Feiffer) wants a dog, and the procession of intervening pets do not assuage this need. (Rev: BL 9/15/05; SLJ 11/05)

8333 Feldman, Eve B. *That Cat!* (2–4). Illus. 1994, Morrow $14.00 (978-0-688-13310-8). 112pp. Molly is devastated when her cat disappears, and she tries many tactics to get him home. (Rev: BL 10/1/94; SLJ 9/94)

8334 Fine, Anne. *The Diary of a Killer Cat* (2–4). Illus. by Steve Cox. 2006, Farrar $15.00 (978-0-374-31779-9). 64pp. Tuffy the cat cannot understand the reactions of his humans to what he views as totally normal feline behavior. (Rev: BL 1/1–15/06; SLJ 2/06)

8335 Fine, Anne. *Notso Hotso* (2–4). Illus. by Tony Ross. 2006, Farrar $15.00 (978-0-374-35550-0). 96pp. Anthony, a British dog with a sense of dignity but a bad skin condition, is initially mortified when his fur is shaved off, but then decides he looks like a lion; an easy chapter book that will appeal to reluctant readers. (Rev: BL 1/1–15/06; SLJ 3/06)

8336 Fine, Anne. *The Return of the Killer Cat* (3–5). Illus. by Steve Cox. 2007, Farrar $16.00 (978-0-374-36248-5). 74pp. In this sequel to *The Diary of a Killer Cat* (2006), Tuffy plans to do as he pleases while his family vacations, but his hopes are dashed when he learns that the vicar is coming to cat-sit him. (Rev: BL 3/15/07; SLJ 2/07)

8337 Gallaz, Christophe. *The Wolf Who Loved Music* (3–6). Illus. by Marshall Arisman. 2003, Creative Editions $17.95 (978-1-56846-178-6). 32pp. In this bittersweet tale set in Switzerland, Anne is devastated when townspeople hunt down and kill a wolf that may have been attracted by the young's girl violin playing. (Rev: HBG 4/04; SLJ 12/03)

8338 Ganny, Charlee. *Chihuawolf: A Tail of Mystery and Horror* (3–6). Illus. by Nicola Slater. 2011, Sourcebooks paper $6.99 (978-1-4022-5-940-1). 144pp. A privileged Chihuahua named Paco has everything he needs in life except romance, and sets his sights on a beautiful Afghan hound named Natasha, which poses many challenges. (Rev: BL 10/1/11; LMC 1–2/12; SLJ 9/1/11)

8339 George, Jean Craighead. *The Cats of Roxville Station* (4–6). Illus. by Tom Pohrt. 2009, Dutton $16.99 (978-0-525-42140-5). 192pp. A young cat named Ratchet, throw into a river by her owner, must learn to survive in the wild. (Rev: BL 3/15/09; HB 7/09; SLJ 6/09)

8340 George, Jean Craighead. *The Cry of the Crow* (5–7). 1980, HarperCollins paper $5.99 (978-0-06-440131-9). Mandy finds a helpless baby crow in the woods and tames it.

8341 George, Jean Craighead. *Frightful's Mountain* (5–8). 1999, Dutton $18.99 (978-0-525-46166-1). Frightful, the falcon in *My Side of the Mountain,* is the central character in this novel in which she has difficult and enjoyable adventures in the wild. (Rev: BL 9/1/99; HBG 3/00; SLJ 9/99; VOYA 6/00)

8342 Ghent, Natale. *No Small Thing* (5–8). 2005, Candlewick $15.00 (978-0-7636-2422-4). Nathaniel and his siblings struggle to keep their horse while their single mother struggles to keep her family afloat. (Rev: BL 3/1/05; SLJ 4/05)

8343 Ghent, Natale. *Piper* (5–7). 2001, Orca paper $6.95 (978-1-55143-167-3). The love and attention young Wesley showers on a tiny Australian shepherd puppy helps her recover from the death of her father. (Rev: BL 3/1/01)

8344 Giff, Patricia Reilly. *Wild Girl* (3–6). 2009, Random $15.99 (978-0-375-83890-3). 160pp. After a long separation, 12-year-old Lydie is reunited with her father and brother only to find it hard going until she comes upon a horse who helps her through. (Rev: BL 6/1–15/09; HB 9/09)

8345 Haas, Jessie. *Jigsaw Pony* (2–4). Illus. by Ying-Hwa Hu. 2005, Greenwillow $15.99 (978-0-06-078245-0). 112pp. Sharing isn't easy for twins Fran and Kiera, but they eventually come together over their adopted pony Jigsaw. (Rev: BL 9/1/05; SLJ 12/05)

8346 Hall, Elizabeth. *Child of the Wolves* (4–7). 1996, Houghton Mifflin $16.00 (978-0-395-76502-9). Granite, a Siberian husky pup, must survive in the wilderness when he is separated from his family. (Rev: BCCB 3/96; BL 4/1/96; VOYA 6/96)

8347 Hall, Lynn. *The Soul of the Silver Dog* (5–8). 1992, Harcourt $16.95 (978-0-15-277196-6). A handicapped dog bonds with his new teenage owner living in a troubled family. (Rev: BL 4/15/92; SLJ 6/92)

8348 Heinz, Brian. *Cheyenne Medicine Hat* (4–8). Illus. by Gregory Manchess. 2006, Creative Editions $18.95 (978-1-56846-181-6). The story of a summer in the life of a wild mustang mare as she tries to keep her band safe from predators — both animal and human. (Rev: SLJ 11/06)

8349 Henkes, Kevin. *Protecting Marie* (5–7). 1995, Greenwillow $19.99 (978-0-688-13958-2). Fanny is afraid that she will lose her pet dog if her temperamental father decides the dog must go. (Rev: BCCB 3/95; BL 3/15/95; HB 7–8/95; SLJ 5/95*)

8350 Henry, Marguerite. *King of the Wind* (5–8). Illus. by Wesley Dennis. 1990, Macmillan $17.95 (978-0-02-743629-7). The story of the famous stallion Godolphin Arabian, ancestor of Man O'War and founder of the Thoroughbred breed. Also use *Black Gold* and *Born to Trot* (both 1987). Newbery Medal 1949.

8351 Henry, Marguerite. *San Domingo: The Medicine Hat Stallion* (4–6). Illus. by Robert Lougheed. 1992, Macmillan paper $4.99 (978-0-689-71631-7). 240pp. Set in the West during the mid-19th century, this is the story of a young man who rights a wrong inflicted on his father. Also from the same author and publisher: *Brighty of the Grand Canyon; Justin Morgan Had a Horse* (both 1991).

8352 Hesse, Karen. *Sable* (2–4). Illus. by Marcia Sewall. 1994, Holt $15.95 (978-0-8050-2416-6). 60pp. Tate is sure that her dog, Sable, who has been given away for misbehaving, will return. (Rev: BCCB 5/94; BL 6/1–15/94; HB 7/94; SLJ 5/94*)

8353 Hiaasen, Carl. *Hoot* (5–8). 2002, Knopf $15.95 (978-0-375-82181-3). Roy Eberhart, the new kid in Coconut Cove, finds himself embroiled in a battle to save some owls. Newbery Honor. (Rev: BCCB 11/02; BL 10/15/02; HB 11–12/02; HBG 3/03; SLJ 8/02)

8354 High, Linda O. *Hound Heaven* (5–8). 1995, Holiday $15.95 (978-0-8234-1195-5). More than anything in the world, Silver Iris wants a dog, but her grandfather won't allow it. (Rev: BCCB 12/95; SLJ 11/95; VOYA 2/96)

8355 Hobbs, Valerie. *Sheep* (4–6). 2006, Farrar $16.00 (978-0-374-36777-0). 128pp. A poignant tale of a smart and sensitive border collie desperately searching for a home and the chance to herd sheep. (Rev: BL 2/1/06; SLJ 3/06)

8356 Hobbs, Valerie. *Wolf* (3–6). 2013, Farrar $15.99 (978-037431575-7). 128pp. Jack is a hard-working, aging border collie who protects his sheep and his boy and must now find the strength to face down a rabid wolf. **e** Lexile 640 (Rev: BLO 9/15/13; LMC 3–4/14; SLJ 10/13)

8357 Holt, Christopher. *The Vanishing* (5–8). Illus. by Greg Call. Series: The Lost Dogs. 2012, Little, Brown $16.99 (978-031620005-9). 368pp. A Labrador named Max and a dachshund called Rocky face many challenges as they struggle to survive in a dystopian world without humans; the 1st volume in a series. ⌒ **e** (Rev: BL 10/1/12; SLJ 5/13)

8358 Hucklesby, Jill. *Samphire Song* (4–8). 2013, Whitman $16.99 (978-0-8075-7224-5). 304pp. Jodie, 14 and struggling with family concerns including her younger brother's ill health, is willing to sell her much-loved horse when it becomes necessary, but searches for him as soon as the family's finances improve. Lexile 850 (Rev: BL 3/15/13; LMC 1–2/14; SLJ 4/13; VOYA 6/13)

8359 Hunter, Erin. *Seekers: The Quest Begins* (5–8). Series: Seekers. 2008, HarperCollins $16.99 (978-0-06-087122-2). Readers are introduced to three bear cubs — a polar bear, a black bear, and a grizzly — in this first installment in a series about survival and the realities of bear life in the wild and in captivity. (Rev: BL 5/15/08)

8360 Hurwitz, Johanna. *One Small Dog* (3–5). 2000, HarperCollins LB $15.89 (978-0-06-029220-1). Curtis has always wanted a dog and finally gets one, but the small cocker spaniel causes enormous problems. (Rev: BCCB 9/00; BL 10/15/00; HB 9/00; HBG 3/01; SLJ 11/00)

8361 Hutchins, Hazel. *T J and the Cats* (2–4). 2002, Orca paper $5.95 (978-1-55143-205-2). 112pp. A beginning chapter book about a boy who doesn't like cats, but agrees to care for his grandmother's four while she's on vacation and slowly changes his mind. (Rev: BL 12/15/02; SLJ 2/03)

8362 Ibbotson, Eva. *One Dog and His Boy* (3–6). 2012, Scholastic $16.99 (978-054535196-6). 288pp. Ten-year-old Hal is overjoyed when his wealthy parents finally agree to get him a dog — until he discovers that it is merely a weekend rental. ⌒ (Rev: BL 3/1/12; HB 5–6/12; LMC 5–6/12; SLJ 3/12)

8363 Jennings, Patrick. *Guinea Dog* (3–5). 2010, Egmont $15.99 (978-1-60684-053-5). 192pp. Fifth-grader Rufus is disappointed when his mother brings him a guinea pig rather than a dog, but he names him Fido and is surprised by the rodent's doglike talents. Lexile 600L (Rev: BL 6/10; LMC 10/10; SLJ 9/1/10)

8364 Jimenez, Juan Ramon. *Platero y Yo / Platero and I* (5–7). Trans. by Myra Cohn Livingston and Joseph F. Dominguez. Illus. by Antonio Frasconi. 1994, Clarion $16.00 (978-0-395-62365-7). Using both Spanish and English texts, this book contains excerpts from the prose poem about a writer and his donkey. (Rev: BL 6/1–15/94) [863]

8365 Kehret, Peg. *Ghost Dog Secrets* (5–7). 2010, Dutton $16.99 (978-0-525-42178-8). 192pp. The ghost of an abused dog helps 6th-grader Rusty locate and save other abused dogs in this slightly creepy story with a strong, believable protagonist. Lexile 730L (Rev: BL 10/1/10; LMC 1–2/11; SLJ 9/1/10; VOYA 8/10)

8366 Kehret, Peg. *Saving Lilly* (3–6). 2001, Pocket $16.00 (978-0-671-03422-1). Two sixth-graders boycott a class trip to the circus because of animal cruelty and persuade the class to raise funds to send performer Lilly to an elephant sanctuary. (Rev: BL 12/1/01; HBG 10/02; SLJ 11/01)

8367 Kimmel, Eric A. *Hiss-s-s-s!* (4–6). 2012, Holiday $16.95 (978-0-8234-2415-3). 160pp. Young Muslim American Omar promises his phobic mother that his pet snake will be kept out of her sight; what is he to do when the snake escapes? e Lexile 540L (Rev: BLO 10/1/12; SLJ 10/12)

8368 King-Smith, Dick. *The Cuckoo Child* (3–6). Illus. by Leslie Bowman. 1995, Hyperion paper $3.95 (978-0-7868-1001-7). 128pp. Jack oversees the hatching of an ostrich egg and tends the offspring, Oliver, for two years in this humorous story. (Rev: BL 4/15/93; SLJ 4/93*)

8369 King-Smith, Dick. *Dinosaur Trouble* (2–4). Illus. by Nick Bruel. 2008, Roaring Brook $14.95 (978-1-59643-324-3). 128pp. Two young dinosaurs from opposing families join forces to end the Tyrannosaurus rex's reign of terror. (Rev: BL 3/1/08; LMC 3/08; SLJ 3/08)

8370 King-Smith, Dick. *Hairy Hezekiah* (2–4). Illus. by Nick Bruel. 2007, Roaring Brook $12.95 (978-1-59643-318-2). 89pp. A lonely zoo camel figures out how to unlock his gate and ambles off on an adventure. (Rev: BCCB 10/07; SLJ 10/07)

8371 King-Smith, Dick. *The Invisible Dog* (2–4). Illus. by Roger Roth. 1995, Random paper $4.99 (978-0-679-87041-8). Janie can't have a pet dog so she invents one. (Rev: BCCB 4/93; BL 3/1/93; HB 5/93; SLJ 5/93)

8372 Kipling, Rudyard. *The Jungle Book: Mowgli's Story* (2–4). Illus. by Nicola Bayley. 2005, Candlewick $19.99 (978-0-7636-2317-3). 160pp. An appealing presentation of unabridged Mowgli adventures. (Rev: BL 5/1/05; SLJ 6/05)

8373 Kipling, Rudyard. *The Jungle Book: The Mowgli Stories* (4–7). Illus. by Jerry Pinkney. 1995, Morrow $25.99 (978-0-688-09979-4). Eight stories about Mowgli are reprinted with 18 handsome watercolors. (Rev: BCCB 6/96; BL 10/15/95; SLJ 11/95)

8374 Kipling, Rudyard. *Just So Stories* (4–6). Illus. by Barry Moser. 1996, Morrow $24.99 (978-0-688-13957-5). 160pp. Twelve classic stories are featured in this well-illustrated edition of Kipling favorites. (Rev: BL 11/1/96)

8375 Korman, Gordon. *Showoff* (3–6). Series: Swindle. 2012, Scholastic $16.99 (978-054532059-7). 256pp. Luthor the clumsy Doberman wreaks havoc at a Dog Show, before Griffin Bing — the Man with the Plan — intervenes and succeeds in transforming him into a success. ∩ e Lexile 740L (Rev: BL 1/1/12; SLJ 5/1/12)

8376 Kurtz, Chris. *The Pup Who Cried Wolf* (3–5). Illus. by Guy Francis. 2010, Bloomsbury $15.99 (978-1-59990-497-9); paper $5.99 (978-1-59990-492-4). 160pp. Lobo, a New York City Chihuahua who longs to run wild with wolves, gets a reality check when he gets to Yellowstone. Lexile 630L (Rev: BL 5/15/10; LMC 10/10; SLJ 9/1/10)

8377 Lester, Alison. *The Circus Horse* (1–3). Illus. by Roland Harvey. Series: Horse Crazy. 2009, Chronicle paper $4.99 (978-0-8118-6656-9). 64pp. For horse lovers who are graduating from easy readers, this tale set in Australia is a satisfying story about trick riding. (Rev: BL 3/15/09; LMC 8/09; SLJ 7/09)

8378 Lester, Alison. *The Sea Rescue* (2–4). Illus. by Roland Harvey. Series: Horse Crazy. 2009, Chronicle paper $4.99 (978-0-8118-6940-9). 64pp. Horseback-riding friends Bonnie and Sam get caught in a storm and aid in the rescue of drowning men in this chapter book set in the Australian bush. Also use *The Royal Show* (2009). (Rev: SLJ 1/1/10)

8379 Levin, Betty. *Look Back, Moss* (5–8). 1998, Greenwillow $15.00 (978-0-688-15696-1). Young Moss, disturbed by his mother's lack of attention and his own weight problems, welcomes an injured sheepdog into the family. (Rev: BCCB 10/98; BL 8/98; HB 1–2/99; HBG 3/99; SLJ 11/98)

8380 Levin, Betty. *That'll Do, Moss* (4–6). 2002, HarperCollins LB $15.89 (978-0-06-000532-0). 128pp. Moss the Border collie and a girl named Diane, who works at the farm where Moss lives, rescue one of the farmer's sons who has run away. (Rev: BL 8/02; HBG 10/02; SLJ 10/02)

8381 Loizeaux, William. *Wings* (4–6). Illus. by Leslie Bowman. 2006, Farrar $16.00 (978-0-374-34802-1). In 1960, 10-year-old Nick finds a baby mockingbird that's been abandoned by its mother and nurses it back to health. (Rev: BL 9/1/06; SLJ 9/06)

8382 Lowry, Lois. *Bless This Mouse* (3–6). Illus. by Eric Rohmann. 2011, Houghton Harcourt $15.99 (978-0-547-39009-3). 160pp. A colony of church mice, led by Mouse Mistress Hildegarde, face challenges from an exterminator and from the cats and other pets expected to attend the Blessing of the Animals. ∩ e Lexile 690L (Rev: BL 3/1/11; SLJ 3/1/11)

8383 Lowry, Lois. *Stay! Keeper's Story* (5–8). 1997, Houghton Mifflin $16.00 (978-0-395-87048-8). A dog named Keeper narrates this story about his puppyhood and the three different masters he has had. (Rev: BL 11/1/97; HBG 3/98; SLJ 10/97)

8384 Lubar, David. *Dog Days* (3–6). 2004, Darby Creek $15.95 (978-1-58196-013-6). 112pp. Larry Haskins passes his summer playing baseball and taking care of three stray dogs; his worries about the rising price of dog food are resolved when he finds the solution to a mysterious stain. (Rev: BL 4/1/04; SLJ 5/04)

8385 McKay, Hilary. *Lulu and the Dog from the Sea* (2–4). Illus. by Priscilla Lamont. 2013, Whitman $13.99 (978-0-8075-4820-2). 112pp. On vacation at the seaside, cousins Lulu and Mellie learn to love a bouncy stray dog that lives in the dunes. ALA Notable Children's Book. Lexile 770 (Rev: BL 3/1/13; HB 3–4/13; SLJ 3/13*)

8386 Malterre, Elona. *The Last Wolf of Ireland* (5–7). 1990, Houghton Mifflin $15.00 (978-0-395-54381-8). Devin and his friend Katey hide wolf pups when the pups are threatened. (Rev: BCCB 10/90; BL 9/15/90*; SLJ 10/90)

8387 Martin, Ann M. *A Dog's Life: The Autobiography of a Stray* (4–6). 2005, Scholastic $16.99 (978-0-439-71559-1). Squirrel the dog looks back on the difficult years she spent as a stray before she was finally adopted by a loving human family. (Rev: BL 12/1/05; SLJ 11/05; VOYA 12/05)

8388 Martin, Ann M. *Everything for a Dog* (5–8). 2009, Feiwel & Friends $16.99 (978-0-312-38651-1). Three separate story lines introduce Bone, a dog who has suffered through losing more than one home; Sunny, a dog who comforts her young master after his brother's death; and a boy named Henry who longs to have a dog. (Rev: BL 6/1–15/09)

8389 Michaels, Vaughn. *Dodi's Prince* (3–5). Illus. by Jacqueline Rogers. 2003, Dutton $15.99 (978-0-525-47034-2). 96pp. Life in a trailer park in a remote Texas town is lonely for 8-year-old Dodi until a stray dog appears. (Rev: BL 3/15/03; HBG 10/03; SLJ 3/03)

8390 Mills, Claudia. *Mason Dixon: Pet Disasters* (3–6). Illus. by Guy Francis. 2011, Knopf $12.99 (978-0-375-86873-3); LB $15.99 (978-0-375-96873-0). 176pp. Mason, 9, resists all attempts to get him to bond with a pet until his friend Brody introduces him to a three-legged dog. Lexile 780L (Rev: SLJ 11/1/11)

8391 Moeyaert, Bart. *Bare Hands* (3–7). Trans. by David Colmer. 1999, Front St. $14.95 (978-1-886910-32-4). 112pp. In this translation of a powerful novel from the Netherlands, Young Ward seeks revenge when the village loner, who is also his mother's suitor, kills his dog. (Rev: BL 12/15/98*; HBG 10/99; SLJ 2/99)

8392 Morey, Walt. *Gentle Ben* (5–8). 1991, Puffin paper $6.99 (978-0-14-036035-6). A warm story of deep trust and friendship between a boy and an Alaskan bear.

8393 Morey, Walt. *Scrub Dog of Alaska* (4–8). 1989, Blue Heron paper $7.95 (978-0-936085-13-5). A pup, abandoned because of his small size, turns out to be a winner. Also use *Kavik the Wolf Dog* (1977).

8394 Morey, Walt. *Year of the Black Pony* (5–8). Illus. by Fredrika Spillman. 1989, Blue Heron paper $6.95 (978-0-936085-14-2). A family story about a boy's love for his pony in rural Oregon at the turn of the 20th century.

8395 Morgan, Clay. *The Boy Who Spoke Dog* (5–8). 2003, Dutton $15.99 (978-0-525-47159-2). Marooned on an island dominated by two warring dog packs, Jack, a young cabin boy, feels very much alone until he develops a friendship with a border collie named Moxie. (Rev: BL 1/1–15/04; SLJ 1/04; VOYA 6/04)

8396 Mowat, Farley. *The Dog Who Wouldn't Be* (4–7). Illus. by Paul Galdone. 1957, Bantam paper $4.99 (978-0-553-27928-3). The humorous story of Mutt, a dog of character and personality, and his boy.

8397 Mukerji, Dhan Gopal. *Gay-Neck: The Story of a Pigeon* (4–8). Illus. by Boris Artzybasheff. 1968, Dutton $16.99 (978-0-525-30400-5). A boy from India's brave carrier pigeon is selected to perform dangerous missions during World War I. Newbery Medal 1928.

8398 Murphy, Jill. *Dear Hound* (3–5). Illus. by author. 2010, Walker $14.99 (978-0-8027-2190-7). 192pp. Foxes help Alfie, a timid (but large) deerhound puppy, to reunite at last with his beloved family after many adventures. (Rev: BL 8/10; LMC 10/10; SLJ 9/1/10)

8399 Myers, Anna. *Red-Dirt Jessie* (4–7). 1992, Walker $13.95 (978-0-8027-8172-7). In this tale of the Depression era in Oklahoma, 12-year-old Jessie helps keep her family together. (Rev: BCCB 10/92; BL 1/15/93; HB 1–2/93; SLJ 11/92*)

8400 Napoli, Donna Jo. *Mogo, The Third Warthog* (3–5). Illus. by Lita Judge. 2008, Hyperion $15.99 (978-1-4231-0816-0). 208pp. Mogo the warthog is the runt of his litter but is determined to survive on the scary and dangerous savanna, and with the help of a young baboon he manages to do just that. (Rev: BL 6/1–15/08; LMC 3/08; SLJ 8/08)

8401 Naylor, Phyllis Reynolds. *Cuckoo Feathers* (3–5). Illus. by Marcy Ramsey. 2006, Marshall Cavendish $14.95 (978-0-7614-5285-0). 96pp. When the two pigeons Sarah has regarded as her own decamp for a neighboring Chicago apartment, she is reluctant to give them up. (Rev: BL 5/1/06; SLJ 6/06)

8402 Naylor, Phyllis Reynolds. *Saving Shiloh* (4–7). 1997, Simon & Schuster $15.00 (978-0-689-81460-0). In this sequel to the Newbery Medal-winning *Shiloh* and *Shiloh Season*, Marty again encounters the evil Judd Travers, who has been accused of murder. (Rev: BL 9/1/97*; HB 9–10/97; HBG 3/98; SLJ 9/97)

8403 Naylor, Phyllis Reynolds. *Shiloh* (4–8). 1991, Macmillan $16.00 (978-0-689-31614-2). When a beagle follows him home, Marty, from a West Virginia family with a strict code of honor, learns a painful lesson about right and wrong. Newbery Medal 1992. (Rev: BCCB 10/91; BL 12/1/91*; HB 1–2/92; SLJ 9/91)

8404 Naylor, Phyllis Reynolds. *Shiloh Season* (4–8). 1996, Simon & Schuster $15.00 (978-0-689-80647-6). The evil Judd Travers wants his dog back from the Prestons in this sequel to *Shiloh* (1991). (Rev: BCCB 12/96; BL 11/15/96*; HB 11–12/96; SLJ 11/96)

8405 Newman, Lesléa. *Hachiko Waits* (3–5). Illus. by Machiyo Kodaira. 2004, Holt $15.95 (978-0-8050-7336-2). 112pp. This is the fictionalized story of a Japanese Akita who continued — for ten years — to wait at the station for his master's return. (Rev: BL 1/1–15/05; SLJ 11/04)

8406 Nielsen, Virginia. *Batty Hattie* (4–6). 1999, Marshall Cavendish $14.95 (978-0-7614-5047-4). When her mother goes on tour with a jazz band, Harriet is left alone with her uncle and feels extreme loneliness until she rescues a helpless baby bat she finds on the ground. (Rev: BCCB 4/99; BL 3/1/99; HBG 10/99; SLJ 4/99)

8407 Nolan, Lucy. *Home on the Range* (2–4). Illus. by Mike Reed. Series: Down Girl and Sit. 2010, Marshall Cavendish $14.99 (978-0-7614-5649-0). 54pp. City dogs Down Girl and Sit accompany their owners on a trip to a dude ranch and have many adventures. (Rev: SLJ 5/1/10)

8408 Nolan, Lucy. *On the Road* (1–3). Illus. by Mike Reed. 2005, Marshall Cavendish $14.95 (978-0-7614-5234-8). 64pp. The dog who thinks her name is Down Girl relates an exciting car ride to the beach with her friend Sit, fun camping in the woods, and a trip to the vet, all the while commenting on life and owners. (Rev: BL 11/15/05; SLJ 3/06)

8409 Orr, Wendy. *Lost! A Dog Called Bear* (2–4). Illus. by Susan Boase. 2011, Henry Holt $15.99 (978-080508931-8); paper $5.99 (978-08050938-1-0). 112pp. Logan's coping with his parents' divorce and a move to the city when his dog gets lost — at the same time, Hannah's parents won't let her have a dog so she works at an animal shelter; the two meet and become friends. (Rev: BL 9/15/11; LMC 11–12/11)

8410 Paley, Jane. *Hooper Finds a Family: A Hurricane Katrina Dog's Survival Tale* (3–7). Illus. 2011, HarperCollins $15.99 (978-0-06-201103-9). 144pp. A personable yellow Lab orphaned by Hurricane Katrina narrates this inspiring story about adjusting to new surroundings in New York City. e Lexile 540L (Rev: BL 7/11; SLJ 7/11)

8411 Parker, Cam. *A Horse in New York* (4–8). 1989, Avon paper $2.75 (978-0-380-75704-6). To save Blue, the horse she rode at summer camp, from destruction, Tiffin has to convince her parents to board him for the winter. (Rev: BL 12/15/89)

8412 Platt, Chris. *Astra* (3–6). 2010, Peachtree $15.95 (978-156145541-6). 160pp. Lily, 13, is forbidden to ride after her mother's death on the trail, but when she is given ownership of her mother's horse Astra she starts training for the Tevis Cup Endurance Race. Lexile 730L (Rev: BL 9/1/10; LMC 3–4/11; SLJ 3/1/11)

8413 Platt, Chris. *Moon Shadow* (4–7). 2006, Peachtree $14.95 (978-1-56145-382-5). When a wild mustang mare dies giving birth near her Nevada home, 13-year-old Callie vows to raise and train the foal. (Rev: BL 11/1/06; SLJ 1/07)

8414 Platt, Chris. *Storm Chaser* (4–6). 2009, Peachtree $14.95 (978-156145496-9). 178pp. On her family's Nevada dude ranch, 13-year-old Jessie must train her favorite horse, Storm Chaser, for possible sale to the despised Ariel. (Rev: BLO 11/1/09; SLJ 10/09)

8415 Popp, Monika. *Farm Year* (2–4). Illus. by Monika Popp and Regine Frick von Schmuck. 2002, Groundwood $18.95 (978-0-88899-452-3). A young farm boy takes special interest in a Holstein heifer and shepherds her tenderly through her first year of life. (Rev: HBG 10/02; SLJ 6/02)

8416 Pyron, Bobbie. *A Dog's Way Home* (4–7). 2011, HarperCollins $16.99 (978-0-06-198674-1); LB $17.89 (978-0-06-198673-4). 336pp. Told in alternating chapters by Abby, an 11-year-old girl, and Tam, a beloved dog trying to find his way home after the accident in which they both were injured, this tense story ends happily. ⌒ (Rev: BL 2/15/11; SLJ 4/11; VOYA 4/11)

8417 Resnick, Jacqueline. *The Daring Escape of the Misfit Menagerie* (4–6). Illus. by Matthew Cook. 2012, Penguin $16.99 (978-159514588-8). 272pp. A rabbit, a wombat, a dog, and a bear endure harsh treatment at a traveling circus until they manage to escape. e Lexile 730L (Rev: BL 12/15/12; LMC 8–9/13; SLJ 2/13)

8418 Sachar, Louis. *Marvin Redpost: Alone in His Teacher's House* (2–4). 1994, Random LB $11.99 (978-0-679-91949-0); paper $3.99 (978-0-679-81949-3). 83pp. Marvin is upset and confused when the dog he is taking care of dies. (Rev: BL 6/1–15/94)

8419 Salisbury, Graham. *Zoo Breath* (3–5). Illus. by Jacqueline Rogers. Series: Calvin Coconut. 2010, Random House $12.99 (978-0-385-73704-3); LB $18.99 (978-0-385-90642-5). 160pp. In his campaign to be allowed to keep the family dog despite Streak's bad breath, Calvin investigates the problem for his school assignment. e (Rev: SLJ 12/1/10)

8420 Salten, Felix. *Bambi: A Life in the Woods* (5–8). 1926, Pocket paper $4.99 (978-0-671-66607-1). The growing to maturity of an Austrian deer.

8421 Saunders, Susan. *Lucky Lady* (3–7). 2000, HarperCollins $14.95 (978-0-380-97784-0). 144pp. The lives of 12-year-old Jennie and her dispirited grandfather change for the better when the girl buys a wild buckskin filly named Lucky Lady. (Rev: BCCB 5/00; BL 8/00; HBG 10/00; SLJ 7/00)

8422 Schwartz, Virginia Frances. *Nutz!* (3–5). Illus. by Christina Leist. 2012, Orca paper $12.95 (978-18965808-7-6). 144pp. Fat, jealous cat Amos watches disdainfully as his human, Tyler, 10, fawns over their household's newest pet, an injured baby squirrel named Nutz. (Rev: BL 3/1/12; SLJ 4/1/12)

8423 Seuling, Barbara. *Robert and the Great Pepperoni* (2–3). Illus. by Paul Brewer. 2001, Cricket $14.95 (978-0-8126-2825-8). 118pp. Second-grader Robert really wants a dog and he starts a pet-sitting service that eventually but temporarily gives him a chance to look after one. (Rev: HB 1/02; HBG 3/02; SLJ 10/01)

8424 Sherlock, Patti. *Four of a Kind* (5–9). 1991, Holiday $13.95 (978-0-8234-0913-6). Andy's grandfather agrees to lend him money to buy a pair of horses, and he sets his sights on winning the horse-pulling contest at a state fair. (Rev: BL 12/1/91; SLJ 10/91)

8425 Smiley, Jane. *A Good Horse* (4–8). 2010, Knopf $16.99 (978-037586229-8); LB $19.99 (978-037596228-8). 256pp. Thirteen-year-old Abby worries that her colt Jack might be the offspring of a stolen mare at the same time that she is dealing with the sale of her prized Black George. ℮ (Rev: BL 10/15/10; HB 11–12/10; SLJ 12/1/10)

8426 Smiley, Jane. *Pie in the Sky* (4–8). Illus. by Elaine Clayton. 2012, Knopf $16.99 (978-0-375-86968-6); LB $19.99 (978-0-375-96968-3). 176pp. Ninth-grader Abby tackles various horse problems in this story set in 1960s California; the fourth in a series. ℮ (Rev: BLO 10/1/12; HB 9–10/12; SLJ 9/12; VOYA 8/12)

8427 Snelling, Lauraine. *The Winner's Circle* (5–8). Series: Golden Filly. 1995, Bethany House paper $5.99 (978-1-55661-533-7). In this horse story, Trish Evanston, a high school senior who is also a jockey and Triple Crown winner, is being stalked by a mystery man who sends her threatening notes. (Rev: SLJ 10/95; VOYA 4/96)

8428 Springer, Nancy. *A Horse to Love* (4–8). 1987, HarperCollins $11.95 (978-0-06-025824-5). Erin's parents buy her a horse hoping that this will help cure her shyness. (Rev: BL 3/87; SLJ 3/87)

8429 Stauffacher, Sue. *Gator on the Loose!* (4–6). Illus. by Priscilla Lamont. Series: Animal Rescue Team. 2010, Knopf $12.99 (978-0-375-85847-5); LB $15.99 (978-0-375-95847-2). 160pp. Ten-year-old Keisha, daughter of mixed-race parents, helps in her family's animal rescue business, finding suitable homes for animals including an alligator. ⌒ ℮ Lexile 740L (Rev: BL 4/1/10; LMC 8–9/10; SLJ 8/10)

8430 Stauffacher, Sue. *Hide and Seek* (3–5). Illus. by Priscilla Lamont. Series: Animal Rescue Team. 2010, Knopf $12.99 (978-0-375-85849-9); LB $15.99 (978-0-375-95849-6). 160pp. Ten-year-old Keisha Carter and her family come to the rescue when an inquisitive deer gets a plastic pumpkin stuck on its head. ⌒ (Rev: BL 12/1/10; SLJ 12/1/10)

8431 Taylor, Theodore. *Tuck Triumphant* (4–7). 1991, Avon paper $5.99 (978-0-380-71323-3). A 1950s novel about a blind dog in a loving family and the deaf Korean boy they adopt. (Rev: BL 2/1/91)

8432 Townsend, Wendy. *The Sundown Rule* (4–7). 2011, Namelos $18.95 (978-1-60898-099-4). 128pp. Louise's father is on assignment in Brazil and she must live with relatives in a housing development, far from the woods and the animals that Louise so loves. Lexile 750L (Rev: SLJ 4/11)

8433 Van Laan, Nancy. *Busy, Busy Moose* (1–2). Illus. by Amy Rusch. 2003, Houghton $15.00 (978-0-395-96091-2). 48pp. In this sequel to *Moose Tales* (2001), the title character and his friends experience the changing seasons. (Rev: BL 7/03; HB 9/03; HBG 4/04; SLJ 9/03)

8434 Voigt, Cynthia. *Young Fredle* (3–5). Illus. by Louise Yates. 2011, Knopf $16.99 (978-0-375-86457-5); LB $19.99 (978-0-375-96457-2). 224pp. Led astray by his sweet tooth, a young kitchen mouse finds himself cast

out into the dangers of the world at large and has many scary adventures before finding his way home. ⌒ ℮ Lexile 840L (Rev: BL 1/1–15/11; HB 3–4/11; SLJ 2/1/11)

8435 Wallace, Bill. *Coyote Autumn* (4–6). 2000, Holiday House $16.95 (978-0-8234-1628-8). 201pp. During his first autumn in rural Oklahoma, Brad finds an orphan coyote pup that he raises. (Rev: BCCB 11/00; BL 12/15/00; HBG 10/01; SLJ 10/00)

8436 Wallace, Bill. *Goosed!* (2–4). Illus. by Jacqueline Rogers. 2002, Holiday House $16.95 (978-0-8234-1757-5). 128pp. T.P. the dog does not welcome the arrival of a Labrador puppy in his life in this beginning chapter book. (Rev: HBG 3/03; SLJ 12/02)

8437 Wallace, Carol, and Bill Wallace. *The Meanest Hound Around* (2–4). Illus. by John Steven Gurney. 2003, Simon & Schuster $15.95 (978-0-7434-3785-1). In this heartwarming story of canine friendship, Freddie, an abandoned dog, befriends a watchdog named Spike and helps him to escape from his abusive owner. (Rev: HBG 10/03; SLJ 4/03)

8438 Walters, Eric. *Hunter* (4–6). 2012, Orca paper $9.95 (978-14598015-7-8). 208pp. The story of *Catboy* (2011) — about a boy who helps a colony of feral cats — is presented through the eyes of Hunter, one of the cats. ℮ (Rev: BLO 10/15/12; LMC 3–4/13)

8439 Wedekind, Annie. *Wild Blue: The Story of a Mustang Appaloosa* (4–7). 2009, Feiwel & Friends $12.99 (978-0-312-38424-1). Josiah helps a mustang return to her Idaho home. (Rev: BL 6/1–15/09; SLJ 5/09)

8440 Wells, Ken. *Rascal: A Dog and His Boy* (5–8). Illus. by Christian Slade. 2010, Knopf $16.99 (978-037586652-4); LB $19.99 (978-037596652-1). 208pp. A playful beagle puppy named Rascal learns how to be an alert, responsive dog when his young owner, Meely, is in danger, in this novel set in the Louisiana bayou. Lexile 720L (Rev: BL 9/1/10; LMC 1–2/11)

8441 Whelan, Gloria. *Silver* (2–4). Illus. by Stephen Marchesi. 1988, Random paper $3.99 (978-0-394-89611-3). 64pp. Rachel wants to compete in the Alaska Iditarod sled race, and she thinks she can win with her lead dog, Silver. (Rev: BCCB 7–8/88; BL 7/88; SLJ 10/88)

8442 Wilbur, Frances. *The Dog with Golden Eyes* (4–7). 1998, Milkweed paper $6.95 (978-1-57131-615-8). Cassie befriends a white dog that turns out to be an arctic wolf, and she must find his owners before he becomes a target for the police or hunters. (Rev: BCCB 9/98; BL 9/1/98; HBG 3/99; SLJ 7/98; VOYA 8/98)

8443 Woodrow, Allan. *The Pet War* (4–6). 2013, Scholastic $16.99 (978-054551319-7). 272pp. Otto and Lexi, 11 and 12, both want a pet — but should it be a cat or a dog? The two are given a month to raise $500 and whoever turns up the money will get to choose. ℮ (Rev: BL 11/1/13; LMC 3–4/14; SLJ 11/13)

8444 Woods, Shirley. *Jack: The Story of a Beaver* (3–5). Illus. by Celia Godkin. 2002, Fitzhenry & Whiteside $14.95 (978-1-55041-733-3). 96pp. Nature lovers will enjoy the story of the first two years of life for Jack the

Beaver, who evades predators, learns to avoid traps, and finally finds a mate. (Rev: BL 1/1–15/03; SLJ 3/03)

8445 Woods, Shirley. *Tooga: The Story of a Polar Bear* (4–6). Illus. by Muriel Wood. 2004, Fitzhenry & Whiteside $14.95 (978-1-55041-898-9). 96pp. Facts are interwoven into this story of a polar bear cub who makes his long and dangerous way home after floating hundreds of miles on an ice flow. (Rev: SLJ 4/05)

Family Stories

8446 Alcott, Louisa May. *Little Women* (5–9). 1947, Putnam $21.99 (978-0-448-06019-4). One of the many fine editions of this enduring story. Two sequels are *Little Men* and *Jo's Boys*.

8447 Almond, David. *My Dad's a Birdman* (4–6). Illus. by Polly Dunbar. 2008, Candlewick $15.99 (978-0-7636-3667-8). 128pp. Lizzie's father might be crazy but nonetheless she will help him make wings to fly across the River Tyne and win the Great Human Bird Competition. (Rev: BL 3/15/08; HB 5/08; LMC 10/08; SLJ 5/08)

8448 Almond, David. *Slog's Dad* (4–7). Illus. by Dave McKean. 2011, Candlewick $15.99 (978-0-7636-4940-1). 64pp. A young boy grieving after his father's death meets a stranger he believes to be his dad returned with his legs intact. (Rev: BL 3/15/11; SLJ 5/11; VOYA 6/11)

8449 Alvarez, Julia. *How Tía Lola Came to (Visit) Stay* (4–7). 2001, Knopf $15.95 (978-0-375-80215-7). Aunt Lola from the Dominican Republic comes to visit 10-year-old Miguel and his family in Vermont and everywhere she goes she spreads friendliness, enthusiasm, stories, and surprise parties. (Rev: BCCB 4/01; BL 2/15/01; HBG 10/01; SLJ 3/01)

8450 Alvarez, Julia. *How Tía Lola Ended Up Starting Over* (4–7). Series: Tía Lola. 2011, Knopf $15.99 (978-037586914-3); LB $18.99 (978-037596914-0). 160pp. Tía Lola starts a bed-and-breakfast with the help of the children, but it seems that someone wants the business to fail; who can be wishing them ill in this mystery set in Vermont and featuring Latino families? (Rev: BL 11/1/11)

8451 Alvarez, Julia. *How Tía Lola Learned to Teach* (4–7). Series: Tía Lola. 2010, Knopf $15.99 (978-0-375-86460-5); LB $18.99 (978-0-375-96460-2). 144pp. In this sequel to *How Tía Lola Came to (Visit) Stay* (2001), Miguel and Juanita's Dominican aunt is teaching at their school and worrying about her soon-to-expire visa. ⌒ (Rev: BL 12/1/10; HB 1–2/11; LMC 3–4/11; SLJ 11/1/10)

8452 Alvarez, Julia. *How Tía Lola Saved the Summer* (4–7). Series: Tía Lola. 2011, Knopf $15.99 (978-0-375-86727-9); LB $18.99 (978-0-375-96727-6). 160pp. Tía Lola saves the day when three unwelcome girls and their father visit Miguel's Vermont farmhouse, creating a summer camp atmosphere. (Rev: BL 5/1/11; SLJ 7/11)

8453 Baker, Deirdre. *Becca at Sea* (4–6). 2007, Groundwood $16.95 (978-0-88899-737-1). Ten-year-old Becca learns to love her grandmother's rough character as well as the choppy waters that surround her British Columbia island home in this episodic novel. (Rev: HB 1/08; LMC 1/08; SLJ 10/07)

8454 Barshaw, Ruth McNally. *Ellie McDoodle: Have Pen, Will Travel* (3–6). Illus. by author. 2007, Bloomsbury $11.95 (978-1-58234-745-5). 170pp. Ellie survives a summer camping trip with her annoying cousins by playing games and pranks and recording it all in her diary/sketchbook. (Rev: SLJ 6/07)

8455 Bateson, Catherine. *Being Bee* (3–6). 2007, Holiday $16.95 (978-0-8234-2104-6). 144pp. Making a new family is hard for Bee when her father's girlfriend, Jazzi, moves in and begins redecorating; set in Australia. (Rev: BL 10/1/07; HB 11/07; SLJ 10/07)

8456 Bateson, Catherine. *Magenta McPhee* (3–6). 2010, Holiday House $16.95 (978-0-8234-2253-1). 171pp. Magenta goes online to find a dating match for her lonely, divorced father in this funny, realistic story about a teen who writes fantasies. Lexile 640L (Rev: BL 3/1/10; HB 5–6/10; SLJ 3/10)

8457 Bauer, Jutta. *Grandpa's Angel* (1–3). Illus. 2005, Candlewick $12.99 (978-0-7636-2743-0). 48pp. The illustrations — most notably the images of a guardian angel — add another dimension to this captivating tale about an elderly man telling his grandson about the ups and downs of his life; a German import, this includes stories of World War II. (Rev: BL 10/15/05; SLJ 10/05)

8458 Beaty, Andrea. *Cicada Summer* (4–6). 2008, Abrams $15.95 (978-0-8109-9472-0). 176pp. In small-town Illinois, 12-year-old Lilly, who has not spoken since her brother died two years ago, tries to retain her protective silence. (Rev: BL 6/1–15/08; HB 5/08; LMC 10/08; SLJ 6/08)

8459 Bell, Cathleen Davitt. *Little Blog on the Prairie* (5–8). 2010, Bloomsbury $16.99 (978-1-59990-286-9). 288pp. Sentenced to spend a summer at a frontier family history camp in Wyoming, 13-year-old Gen sneaks in a cell phone and reports her experiences back to friends at home even as she becomes more comfortable with the life of 1890. ⌒ ℮ Lexile 820L (Rev: BL 4/1/10; SLJ 5/10)

8460 Bertrand, Diane Gonzales. *Alicia's Treasure* (4–6). 1996, Arte Publico paper $7.95 (978-1-55885-086-6). 125pp. Ten-year-old Alicia spends her first weekend at the beach, thanks to her brother's girlfriend. (Rev: BL 5/1/96; SLJ 7/96)

8461 Birdsall, Jeanne. *The Penderwicks at Point Mouette* (4–7). 2011, Knopf $16.99 (978-0-375-85851-2); LB $19.99 (978-0-375-95851-9). 304pp. Father, his new wife, and young son are away in England and Rosalind is in New Jersey, so Skye finds herself in an unaccustomed role as OAP (oldest available Penderwick) when the three younger sisters go to Maine with Aunt Claire. (Rev: BL 5/1/11; SLJ 7/11)

8462 Birdsall, Jeanne. *The Penderwicks on Gardam Street* (4–7). Series: The Penderwicks. 2008, Knopf $15.99 (978-0-375-84090-6). The loving, close Penderwick sisters, who were introduced in *The Penderwicks*, are loath to see their widower father start dating again and come up with a plan to discourage him. (Rev: BL 5/1/08; SLJ 3/08)

8463 Birdsall, Jeanne. *The Penderwicks: A Summer Tale of Four Sisters, Two Rabbits, and a Very Interesting Boy* (3–6). 2005, Knopf LB $17.99 (978-0-375-93143-7). 192pp. Four sisters, ages 4 to 12, spend a wonderful summer in the Berkshires with their father. (Rev: BL 4/1/05)

8464 Birdseye, Tom. *A Tough Nut to Crack* (3–5). 2006, Holiday $16.95 (978-0-8234-1967-8). 124pp. Cassie, sent from the city to help out at her grandfather's farm after he's injured, is determined to mend a long-standing feud between her father and grandfather. (Rev: BL 1/1–15/07; SLJ 1/07)

8465 Bledsoe, Lucy Jane. *Cougar Canyon* (5–8). 2001, Holiday $16.95 (978-0-8234-1599-1). A family story and environmental tale about a 13-year-old girl named Izzy who fights to save a cougar in the local park. (Rev: BCCB 2/02; BL 2/1/02; HBG 3/02; SLJ 2/02; VOYA 4/02)

8466 Blume, Judy. *Cool Zone with the Pain and the Great One* (3–5). Illus. by James Stevenson. 2008, Delacorte LB $19.99 (978-0-385-90325-7); paper $12.95 (978-0-385-73306-9). 128pp. In alternating chapters, 1st-grader Jake (the Pain) and his 3rd-grader sister Abigail (the Great One) tell stories of sibling rivalry, bullies, stuffed animals, and loose teeth. (Rev: BL 3/1/08; SLJ 6/08) ○

8467 Blume, Judy. *Double Fudge* (4–6). Series: Fudge. 2002, Dutton $15.99 (978-0-525-46926-1). Twelve-year-old Peter Hatcher suffers many trials in this novel, as his younger brother Fudge (Farley) becomes obsessed with money, and a family of long-lost relatives arrives for an extended stay in New York. (Rev: BCCB 11/02; BL 9/15/02; HB 11/02; HBG 3/03; SLJ 9/02)

8468 Blume, Judy. *Friend or Fiend? with the Pain and the Great One* (1–4). Illus. by James Stevenson. 2009, Delacorte $12.99 (978-038573308-3); LB $16.99 (978-038590327-1). 128pp. Third-grader Abigail (the Great One) and her brother Jacob (the Pain) have adventures including a visit to relatives in New York and celebrating their cat Fuzzy's birthday. ○ ℮ Lexile 360L (Rev: BL 4/15/09; SLJ 5/1/09)

8469 Blume, Judy. *Iggie's House* (4–7). 1970, Dell paper $4.99 (978-0-440-44062-8). An African American family moves into Iggie's old house.

8470 Brand, Christianna. *Nurse Matilda* (3–5). Illus. by Edward Ardizzone. 2005, Bloomsbury $16.95 (978-1-58234-670-0). 384pp. Nurse Matilda tries to bring order to a family with innumerable children in this inspiration for the movie "Nanny McPhee." (Rev: BL 3/1/05)

8471 Branford, Anna. *Violet Mackerel's Personal Space* (2–4). Illus. by Elanna Allen. 2013, Atheneum $15.99 (978-144243591-9). 128pp. Violet's mother is planning to marry Vincent, and this means Violet and her brother Dylan face a difficult move; the fourth book in the series. Notable Australian Children's Book. ℮ Lexile 990 (Rev: BLO 9/15/13)

8472 Bredsdorff, Bodil. *Eidi* (4–6). Trans. from Danish by Kathryn Mahaffy. Series: The Children of Crow Cove. 2009, Farrar $16.99 (978-0-374-31267-1). 144pp. This installment in the series tells the story of Eidi, a young girl who leaves her home after the birth of her stepbrother, only to find herself caring for a young orphan who is being abused his stepfather. ALSC Notable Children's Book, 2010. Lexile 810L (Rev: BL 9/1/09*; HB 11–12/09; SLJ 12/09)

8473 Bryant, Ann. *You Can't Fall for Your Stepsister* (4–7). Series: Step-Chain. 2003, Lobster paper $3.95 (978-1-894222-77-8). Ollie, 13, thinks he may be falling in love with his stepsister Frankie, but she ends up becoming his new best friend. (Rev: SLJ 5/04)

8474 Bulion, Leslie. *The Universe of Fair* (3–5). Illus. by Frank W. Dormer. 2012, Peachtree $15.95 (978-1-56145634-5). 264pp. Everything goes wrong when 11-year-old Miller must take his younger sister to the opening day of the annual fair, ruining his elaborate plans for enjoying the event with a degree of independence. Lexile 760L (Rev: BL 10/1/12; SLJ 11/12)

8475 Burch, Robert. *Ida Early Comes over the Mountain* (4–8). 1990, Puffin paper $5.99 (978-0-14-034534-6). The four motherless Sutton children find a new and most unusual housekeeper in Ida.

8476 Burnett, Frances Hodgson. *A Little Princess* (4–6). Illus. by Tasha Tudor. 1987, HarperCollins paper $6.99 (978-0-06-440187-6). 240pp. Sad story of a penniless orphan whose fortune is finally restored.

8477 Butcher, Kristin. *The Gramma War* (4–6). 2001, Orca paper $6.95 (978-1-55143-183-3). 170pp. Annie's life isn't enhanced when her difficult grandmother moves in and takes Annie's room, but an interest in genealogy brings them closer. (Rev: BCCB 1/02; BL 10/1/01; SLJ 9/01)

8478 Byars, Betsy. *Beans on the Roof* (3–5). Illus. 1990, Dell paper $3.99 (978-0-440-40314-2). 80pp. George's sister and the whole family are writing roof poems and George feels awful until he can write one too. (Rev: BCCB 11/88; BL 11/1/88; SLJ 11/88)

8479 Byars, Betsy. *Cracker Jackson* (5–6). 1986, Puffin paper $5.99 (978-0-14-031881-4). 168pp. Eleven-year-old Cracker proves a caring friend to his ex-baby-sitter when he suspects she is a victim of wife beating. (Rev: BL 4/1/85; HB 5/85; SLJ 5/85)

8480 Cameron, Ann. *Spunky Tells All* (2–4). Illus. by Lauren Castillo. Series: Julian and Huey. 2011, Farrar $15.99 (978-0-374-38000-7). 128pp. Spunky the dog narrates this story about the difficulty of communicating with humans and what happens when his family adopts a cat; an illustrated chapter book. (Rev: BL 11/1/11; SLJ 11/1/11*)

8481 Carmichael, Clay. *Wild Things* (5–8). 2009, Front St. $18.95 (978-1-59078-627-7). 248pp. After her mother dies, 11-year-old Zoe goes to live with her sculptor uncle Henry and gradually learns to trust people with the help of a feral cat who alternates narrating with Zoe. ALA Notable Children's Book. (Rev: BL 4/15/09; VOYA 8/09)

8482 Cervantes, Jennifer. *Tortilla Sun* (4–7). 2010, Chronicle $16.99 (978-0-8118-7015-3). 224pp. Izzy, 12, spends a summer in New Mexico with her grandmother and learns about her father and her cultural heritage. (Rev: BLO 5/1/10; LMC 8–9/10; SLJ 6/10)

8483 Cheng, Andrea. *Only One Year* (2–4). Illus. by Nicole Wong. 2010, Lee & Low $16.95 (978-1-60060-252-8). 104pp. Nine-year-old Sharon and her younger sister are devastated when their parents decided to send their 2-year-old brother to spend a year in China with his grandparents. (Rev: BL 2/15/10; LMC 8–9/10; SLJ 4/1/10)

8484 Cheng, Andrea. *Shanghai Messenger* (4–6). Illus. by Ed Young. 2005, Lee & Low $17.95 (978-1-58430-238-4). Xiao Mei, an 11-year-old Chinese American girl, learns about the Chinese half of her heritage on a summer trip to Shanghai. (Rev: BL 8/05; SLJ 9/05)

8485 Cleary, Beverly. *Socks* (4–6). Illus. by Beatrice Darwin. 1973, Avon paper $5.99 (978-0-380-70926-7). 160pp. What happens when the family cat Socks realizes that his position of importance is threatened by the arrival of a baby.

8486 Clifton, Lucille. *The Lucky Stone* (3–5). Illus. by Dale Payson. 1986, Dell paper $3.99 (978-0-440-45110-5). 64pp. Several stories in the life of a girl's great-grandmother linked by the power of a stone.

8487 Cohen, Miriam. *Mimmy and Sophie All Around the Town* (2–3). Illus. by Thomas F. Yezerski. 2004, Farrar $16.00 (978-0-374-34989-9). 80pp. Two girls living in Brooklyn during the Depression experience all the joys and irritations of sisterhood. (Rev: BL 1/1–15/04; SLJ 5/04)

8488 Coman, Carolyn. *Sneaking Suspicions* (4–6). Illus. by Rob Shepperson. 2007, Front St. $16.95 (978-1-59078-491-4). After Ivy's parents are released from prison, she attempts to keep everyone honest as the family sets off to the Florida Everglades to find a long-lost cousin; a sequel to *The Big House* (2004). (Rev: BL 9/15/07; LMC 1/08; SLJ 10/07)

8489 Compestine, Ying Chang. *Crouching Tiger* (K–3). Illus. by Yan Nascimbene. 2011, Candlewick $16.99 (978-0-7636-4642-4). 40pp. Vinson is initially scornful by his Chinese grandfather's tai chi, but comes to recognize that the old man is respected for his prowess. (Rev: BL 12/15/11; HB 1–2/12; SLJ 12/1/11)

8490 Connor, Leslie. *Waiting for Normal* (5–7). 2008, HarperCollins $15.99 (978-0-06-089088-9). Addie lives in a trailer with her mother and looks forward to visits with her stepfather and half sisters, whose life is far more "normal." ALA Notable Children's Book. (Rev: BL 4/1/08; SLJ 2/08)

8491 Corcoran, Barbara. *The Potato Kid* (5–8). 1993, Avon paper $3.50 (978-0-380-71213-7). In spite of her

protests, Ellis must look after an underprivileged girl her mother takes in for the summer. (Rev: BCCB 11/89; BL 11/15/89; HB 1–2/90; SLJ 10/89; VOYA 2/90)

8492 Cotten, Cynthia. *Fair Has Nothing to Do with It* (4–7). 2007, Farrar $16.00 (978-0-374-39935-1). Upset by the death of his grandfather, 12-year-old Michael focuses his energies on an art project to honor his memory. (Rev: BL 4/1/07; SLJ 6/07)

8493 Couloumbis, Audrey. *Jake* (3–6). 2010, Random House $15.99 (978-037585630-3); LB $18.99 (978-037595630-0). 176pp. When his mother breaks her leg, 10-year-old Jake finds himself in the care of his paternal grandfather. **e** (Rev: BL 9/1/10; SLJ 10/10)

8494 Couloumbis, Audrey. *Lexie* (3–5). Illus. by Julia Denos. 2011, Random House $15.99 (978-0-375-85632-7); LB $18.99 (978-0-375-95632-4). 200pp. Lexie, 10, is looking forward to spending time at her family's Jersey beach house with her recently divorced dad until she discovers he is bringing his girlfriend and her sons. **e** Lexile 600L (Rev: HB 7–8/11; SLJ 7/11)

8495 Coville, Bruce, et al. *Amber Brown Is Tickled Pink* (2–5). Illus. by Tony Ross. 2012, Putnam $14.99 (978-0-399-25656-1). 160pp. Coville and Levy bring fans this new book about Paula Danziger's beloved character, in which Amber must negotiate the shallows of her mother's remarriage and her father's discontent. Lexile 530 (Rev: BL 8/12; SLJ 10/12)

8496 Cox, Judy. *Nora and the Texas Terror* (2–4). Illus. by Amanda Haley. 2010, Holiday House $15.95 (978-0-8234-2283-8). 96pp. When 3rd-grader Nora's uncle loses his job, he and his family — including Nora's annoying cousin Ellie — move to live with them in Oregon. Lexile 450L (Rev: BL 12/15/10; SLJ 12/1/10)

8497 Creech, Sharon. *Heartbeat* (3–6). 2004, HarperCollins $15.99 (978-0-06-054022-7). 192pp. Thoughtful 12-year-old Annie, who enjoys running but not competing, faces numerous personal challenges in this story told in free verse. (Rev: BL 2/1/04; HB 5/04; SLJ 2/04)

8498 Creech, Sharon. *Replay* (4–7). 2005, HarperCollins LB $16.89 (978-0-06-054020-3). Twelve-year-old Leo untangles some of the secrets of his boisterous Italian American family when he finds his father's boyhood journal. (Rev: BCCB 11/05; BL 9/1/05*; HBG 4/06; LMC 3–4/06; SLJ 9/05; VOYA 12/05)

8499 Cruz, Maria Colleen. *Border Crossing* (4–8). 2003, Arte Publico paper $9.95 (978-1-55885-405-5). Ceci, 12, can't understand why her Mexican father won't speak Spanish or talk about his home, so she decides to go and investigate. (Rev: BL 11/15/03; SLJ 2/04)

8500 Curtis, Christopher Paul. *The Watsons Go to Birmingham — 1963* (4–8). 1995, Delacorte $16.95 (978-0-385-32175-4); paper $6.50 (978-0-440-41412-4). An African American family returns to Alabama from Michigan to place their troubled son with his grandmother in this novel set in the 1960s. (Rev: BL 8/95; SLJ 10/95*; VOYA 12/95)

8501 Danziger, Paula. *Amber Brown Is Green with Envy* (2–4). Illus. by Tony Ross. 2003, Penguin $15.99 (978-

0-399-23181-0). 160pp. Amber's divorced parents are moving in new directions and the fourth grader finds the tensions difficult to cope with. (Rev: BL 9/1/03; HBG 4/04; SLJ 9/03)

8502 Davies, Jacqueline. *The Bell Bandit* (3–6). Series: Lemonade War. 2012, Houghton Mifflin $15.99 (978-054756737-2). 192pp. Siblings Evan and Jessie investigate the disappearance of the family's bell as they spend Christmas and New Year's at Grandma's house in the aftermath of a devastating fire. ∩ (Rev: BL 4/1/12; LMC 8–9/12)

8503 Delacre, Lulu. *Salsa Stories* (4–7). 2000, Scholastic paper $16.99 (978-0-590-63118-1). After each of her relatives tells a childhood story about a favorite food, Carmen Teresa records them and supplies appropriate recipes. (Rev: BCCB 5/00; BL 5/1/00; HBG 10/00; SLJ 3/00; VOYA 6/00)

8504 Dowell, Frances O'Roark. *Dovey Coe* (4–7). 2000, Simon & Schuster $16.00 (978-0-689-83174-4). The mountain country of North Carolina in 1928 is the setting of this story of a plucky girl who cares for her siblings and who gets involved in a murder trial. (Rev: BL 4/15/00; HBG 10/00; SLJ 5/00; VOYA 6/00)

8505 Draper, Sharon M. *The Birthday Storm* (2–4). 2009, Scholastic $14.99 (978-0-545-07152-9). 112pp. Sassy and her family travel to Florida to celebrate their grandma's birthday, but a hurricane is arriving at the same time — and the local sea turtles are in danger. (Rev: BL 11/15/09; SLJ 11/1/09)

8506 Draper, Sharon M. *Little Sister Is Not My Name* (2–4). 2009, Scholastic $16.99 (978-0-545-07151-2). 112pp. Sassy is the youngest and smallest in her African American family and often feels left out until the day when her size proves useful. (Rev: BL 4/15/09; SLJ 3/09)

8507 Duble, Kathleen Benner. *Bravo Zulu, Samantha!* (5–8). 2007, Peachtree $14.95 (978-1-56145-401-3). Twelve-year-old Samantha unwillingly spends the summer with her grandparents but her retired Air Force grandfather turns out to have an exciting secret. (Rev: BL 6/1–15/07; SLJ 6/07)

8508 Dunmore, Helen. *Brother Brother, Sister Sister* (5–8). 2000, Scholastic paper $4.50 (978-0-439-11322-9). Written in diary format, this is the story of Tanya, once an only child and now surrounded by babies after her mother has quadruplets. (Rev: SLJ 8/00)

8509 Edwards, Nancy. *Mom for Mayor* (3–5). Illus. by Michael Chesworth. 2006, Cricket $15.95 (978-0-8126-2743-5). 144pp. In a last-ditch effort to prevent the sale of a local playground to developers, fifth-grader Eric convinces his mother to run for mayor against the man who engineered the sale plan; an entertaining chapter book with humorous illustrations. (Rev: BL 3/15/06; SLJ 3/06)

8510 Eland, Lindsay. *A Summer of Sundays* (3–6). 2013, Egmont $15.99 (978-160684030-6). 384pp. Sunday Fowler, nearly 12, is in the middle of six siblings and feels totally irrelevant until she makes a discovery in the local library and hopes to gain some attention. **e** Lexile 680 (Rev: BLO 7/13; LMC 1–2/14; SLJ 8/13)

8511 Elliott, Zetta. *Bird* (4–8). Illus. by Shadra Strickland. 2008, Lee & Low $19.95 (978-1-60060-241-2). 48pp. Bird, an African American boy struggling with his brother's death from drugs, finds solace in drawing and the understanding of his uncle in this novel in verse. Coretta Scott King/John Steptoe New Talent Author Award; ALA Notable Children's Book 2009. (Rev: BL 11/1/08; LMC 3–4/09)

8512 Ellis, Sarah. *Odd Man Out* (4–6). 2006, Groundwood $16.95 (978-0-88899-702-9). 160pp. Twelve-year-old Kip spends a summer with his grandmother and five female cousins and learns — from a binder he finds in the attic — about the father he never knew. (Rev: BL 12/1/06; SLJ 12/06)

8513 Ellison, Elizabeth Stow. *Flight* (4–8). 2008, Holiday House $16.95 (978-082342128-2). 245pp. Caught between her unresponsive, oblivious parents and her older brother Evan who's coping with a learning disability, 12-year-old Samantha struggles to advocate for Evan and eventually discovers that her mother is hiding her own disability — that she cannot read. Lexile 710L (Rev: BLO 11/1/08; SLJ 11/1/08)

8514 English, Karen. *Francie* (5–8). 1999, Farrar $17.00 (978-0-374-32456-8). Francie, a black girl growing up in segregated Alabama, places her family in danger when she helps a friend who is escaping a racist employer. (Rev: BCCB 10/99; BL 10/15/99; HB 9–10/99; HBG 3/00; SLJ 9/99; VOYA 2/00)

8515 Fenner, Carol. *Yolonda's Genius* (4–6). 1995, Simon & Schuster paper $17.00 (978-0-689-80001-6). 153pp. African American Yolanda tries to prove that her young brother, who does poorly at school, is really a musical genius. (Rev: BL 6/1–15/95; SLJ 7/95)

8516 Fleischman, Sid. *Bo and Mzzz Mad* (5–7). 2001, Greenwillow LB $15.89 (978-0-06-029398-7). When his father dies, 12-year-old Bo accepts an invitation from relatives despite a longstanding family feud. (Rev: BL 5/15/01*; HB 5–6/01; HBG 10/01; SLJ 5/01)

8517 Fleming, Candace. *Lowji Discovers America* (3–5). 2005, Simon & Schuster $15.95 (978-0-689-86299-1). Lowji, newly arrived in Illinois from his native India, convinces the landlady to keep animals at his apartment building and gets to know his new neighbors. (Rev: BL 3/15/05; SLJ 4/05)

8518 Fletcher, Brian. *Uncle Daddy* (4–6). 2001, Holt $15.95 (978-0-8050-6663-0). 133pp. Nine-year-old Rivers's peaceful life is upset when his long-absent father turns up without warning. (Rev: BCCB 5/01; BL 8/01; HB 7/01; HBG 10/01; SLJ 5/01)

8519 Fletcher, Ralph. *Fig Pudding* (5–7). 1995, Clarion $15.00 (978-0-395-71125-5). A year that brings both tragedy and hilarity in the life of a family of six children. (Rev: BCCB 5/95; BL 5/15/95; SLJ 7/95)

8520 Flood, Pansie Hart. *Secret Holes* (4–6). Illus. by Felicia Marshall. 2003, Carolrhoda LB $15.95 (978-0-87614-923-2). 122pp. After moving with her mother from Florida to a farm in rural South Carolina, 10-year-old Sylvia discovers that her new best friend — 100-year-old Lula Maye — is also her great-grandmother and that the father she'd long believed was dead is very much alive. (Rev: HBG 4/04; SLJ 1/04)

8521 Flood, Pansie Hart. *Sometimey Friend* (3–5). Illus. by Felicia Marshall. 2005, Carolrhoda $15.95 (978-1-57505-866-5). 128pp. While the aunt who raised her travels to Florida, 10-year-old Sylvia Freeman stays in South Carolina with her elderly great-grandmother, an arrangement that suits her fine until her classmates begin poking fun at the old woman. (Rev: BL 11/15/05; SLJ 12/05)

8522 Fogelin, Adrian. *Crossing Jordan* (5–8). Illus. by Suzy Schultz. 2000, Peachtree $14.95 (978-1-56145-215-6). Set in contemporary Florida, this novel tells how 12-year-old Cass must keep her friendship with African American Jemmie a secret from her racist father. (Rev: BCCB 4/00; HBG 10/00; SLJ 6/00)

8523 Fogelin, Adrian. *My Brother's Hero* (5–8). 2002, Peachtree $14.95 (978-1-56145-274-3). When Ben and his family travel to Florida for a vacation, Ben meets a girl named Mica, whose life he finds exciting and mysterious. (Rev: BL 2/1/03; HBG 10/03; SLJ 2/03)

8524 Fosberry, Jennifer. *My Name Is Not Alexander* (1–3). Illus. by Mike Litwin. 2011, Sourcebooks $16.99 (978-1-4022-5433-8). 32pp. A young narrator imagines himself as one historical personality after another — complete with lavish costumes. (Rev: BL 5/1/11; SLJ 6/11)

8525 Fox, Paula. *The Village by the Sea* (5–8). 1988, Orchard $15.95 (978-0-531-05788-9). Emma is staying with an aunt and uncle while her father has heart surgery, and the three interact in complex ways. Also use the re-issued *A Likely Place* (1997). (Rev: BCCB 7–8/88; BL 9/1/88; HB 9–10/88; SLJ 8/88; VOYA 10/88)

8526 Frazier, Sundee T. *Brendan Buckley's Universe and Everything in It* (4–6). 2007, Delacorte $14.99 (978-0-385-73439-4). Brendan's love of rocks leads the mixed-race boy to a relationship with his estranged white grandfather. (Rev: BL 1/1–15/08; LMC 1/08; SLJ 10/07) ∩

8527 Frazier, Sundee T. *The Other Half of My Heart* (4–6). 2010, Delacorte $16.99 (978-0-385-73440-0); LB $19.99 (978-0-385-90446-9). 304pp. Biracial twins Keira and Minna, 11, experience life differently because of their different skin tones and personalities, and entering the Miss Black Pearl Pre-Teen competition underlines this. ∩ ℮ Lexile 750L (Rev: BL 8/10*; LMC 10/10; SLJ 7/10; VOYA 6/10)

8528 Freeman, Martha. *The Trouble with Twins* (3–5). Illus. by Cat B. Smith. 2007, Holiday $16.95 (978-0-8234-2025-4). Two previous books featuring Holly introduced this lively, caring girl who is now coping with her energetic 2-year-old twin brothers. (Rev: BCCB 1/08; BL 12/1/07; SLJ 3/08)

8529 Friedman, Laurie. *Mallory vs. Max* (2–4). Illus. by Tamara Schmitz. 2005, Carolrhoda LB $15.95 (978-1-57505-795-8). 159pp. Eight-year-old Mallory is not

pleased when her brother Max's new puppy gets all the attention. (Rev: SLJ 4/05)

8530 Gantos, Jack. *I Am Not Joey Pigza* (5–8). 2007, Farrar $16.00 (978-0-374-39941-2). Joey's father returns to the Pigza family with lottery winnings, a new name, and promises of a new future based on a diner. ∩ (Rev: BL 8/07; SLJ 9/07)

8531 Gantos, Jack. *Jack Adrift: Fourth Grade Without a Clue* (4–7). 2003, Farrar $16.00 (978-0-374-39987-0). In this prequel to the four previous books, Jack Henry is 9 and has just moved to Cape Hatteras where he has comic experiences and more serious conversations with his dad. (Rev: BL 8/03; HB 11–12/03; HBG 4/04; SLJ 9/03)

8532 Garland, Sherry. *The Lotus Seed* (K–5). Illus. by Tatsuro Kluchi. 1993, Harcourt $16.00 (978-0-15-249465-0). 32pp. A young narrator tells of fleeing her Vietnamese homeland to settle with her family in America. (Rev: BL 3/15/93*; HB 5/93; SLJ 7/93)

8533 Gates, Susan. *Beyond the Billboard* (5–8). 2007, Harcourt $16.00 (978-0-15-205983-5). Ford and Firebird, 13-year-old twins, have grown up secluded from the modern world but their lives are about to change as secrets are revealed. (Rev: BL 6/1–15/07; SLJ 8/07)

8534 Gay, Marie-Louise, and David Homel. *Travels with My Family* (3–5). 2006, Groundwood $15.95 (978-0-88899-688-6). 80pp. Adventures are guaranteed in this family, which takes unusual (and sometimes dangerous) vacations — observed by an older brother with a dry sense of humor. (Rev: BL 5/15/06; SLJ 8/06)

8535 Gewirtz, Adina Rishe. *Zebra Forest* (5–8). 2013, Candlewick $15.99 (978-076366041-3). 208pp. Annie, 11, and her younger brother Rew learn a lot about themselves and their family when they are held hostage — by the father they thought was long dead? ∩ ℮ (Rev: BL 4/1/13; HB 3–4/13; LMC 8–9/13; SLJ 5/13*)

8536 Gifaldi, David. *Listening for Crickets* (3–5). 2008, Holt $16.95 (978-0-8050-7385-0). 192pp. Jake, about to start 5th grade, describes his difficulties at home (feuding parents and a Dad out of work and drinking) and at school and the comfort he gets from telling stories to his younger sister. (Rev: BL 5/15/08; HB 9/08; LMC 3/09)

8537 Glatt, Lisa, and Suzanne Greenberg. *Abigail Iris: The One and Only* (2–4). Illus. by Joy Allen. 2009, Walker $14.99 (978-0-8027-9782-7). 160pp. After spending a vacation with her friend Genevieve, who is an "only," Abigail Iris appreciates her own siblings more. (Rev: BCCB 4/09; BL 3/1/09; SLJ 3/09)

8538 Glatt, Lisa, and Suzanne Greenberg. *Abigail Iris: The Pet Project* (2–4). Illus. by Joy Allen. 2010, Walker $14.99 (978-0-8027-8657-9). 176pp. Abigail Iris is upset that her sister is allergic to her new kitten and feels jealous of her three friends who have no siblings. (Rev: SLJ 4/1/10)

8539 Greene, Stephanie. *Sophie Hartley, on Strike* (3–5). 2006, Clarion $15.00 (978-0-618-71960-0). 152pp. Ten-year-old Sophie and her older sister Nora feel their share of the household chores is too heavy and decide to go on strike. (Rev: BL 1/1–15/07; SLJ 1/07)

8540 Greenfield, Eloise. *Koya DeLaney and the Good Girl Blues* (4–6). 1995, Scholastic paper $2.95 (978-0-590-43299-3). 176pp. Sixth-grader Koya DeLaney, whose talent is a gift of laughter, has some growing up to do when family conflicts arise. (Rev: BCCB 3/92; BL 2/15/92; SLJ 3/92)

8541 Greenfield, Eloise. *Sister* (5–7). Illus. by Moneta Barnett. 1974, HarperCollins $15.99 (978-0-690-00497-7); paper $5.99 (978-0-06-440199-9). Four years in an African American girl's life, as revealed through scattered diary entries, during which she shows maturation, particularly in her attitude toward her sister.

8542 Hamilton, Virginia. *Bluish* (4–6). 1999, Scholastic $16.95 (978-0-590-28879-8). 128pp. Dreenie tries to become friends with a girl nicknamed Bluish, wheelchair-ridden and suffering from cancer, who is in Dreenie's fifth-grade class. (Rev: BCCB 10/99; BL 9/15/99; HBG 3/00; SLJ 11/99)

8543 Hamilton, Virginia. *Second Cousins* (5–8). 1998, Scholastic paper $14.95 (978-0-590-47368-2). In this sequel to *Cousins,* 12-year-old Cammy learns a secret during a family reunion in her small Ohio town. (Rev: BCCB 11/98; BL 8/98; HB 1–2/99; HBG 3/99; SLJ 11/98; VOYA 2/99)

8544 Harrington, Karen. *Sure Signs of Crazy* (5–8). 2013, Little, Brown $16.99 (978-031621058-4). 280pp. Sarah, a rising 7th-grader who survived her mother's attempt to kill her and is now dealing with adolescence and her alcoholic father, finds inventive ways to deal with her difficult situation. ⌒ ℓ Lexile 750 (Rev: BL 8/13*; LMC 11–12/13; SLJ 8/13*)

8545 Harrison, Mette Ivie. *The Monster in Me* (5–8). 2003, Holiday $16.95 (978-0-8234-1713-1). A caring foster family and her growing enjoyment in running make Natalie, 13, more optimistic about life. (Rev: BL 4/1/03; HBG 10/03; SLJ 6/03; VOYA 10/03)

8546 Hausman, Gerald, and Uton Hinds. *The Jacob Ladder* (5–8). 2001, Orchard paper $15.95 (978-0-531-30331-3). This story of a young Jamaican who struggles valiantly to cope with poverty, a charismatic but neglectful father, and the problems of growing up is based on the youth of coauthor Uton Hinds. (Rev: BL 5/1/01; HBG 3/02; SLJ 4/01; VOYA 6/01)

8547 Hermes, Patricia. *Emma Dilemma and the Camping Nanny* (3–6). 2009, Marshall Cavendish $15.99 (978-0-7614-5534-9). 144pp. Nine-year-old Emma is frustrated by her nanny's affection for her boyfriend and by her friend Luisa's defection. What can she do, and will it work? (Rev: BL 3/15/09; SLJ 5/09)

8548 Hermes, Patricia. *Emma Dilemma and the Soccer Nanny* (3–5). 2008, Marshall Cavendish $15.99 (978-0-7614-5301-7). 112pp. Emma, now 9, would like her nanny to chaperone the soccer trip to Washington, not her mother. (Rev: BL 7/08; SLJ 6/08)

8549 Hermes, Patricia. *Emma Dilemma, the Nanny, and the Secret Ferret* (2–4). 2010, Marshall Cavendish $15.99 (978-0-7614-5650-6). 144pp. Young Emma sneaks her pet ferret Marmaduke along on the family vacation, with predictably chaotic results. ℓ Lexile 540L (Rev: SLJ 4/1/10)

8550 Hicks, Betty. *Out of Order* (4–7). 2005, Roaring Brook $15.95 (978-1-59643-061-7). In alternating chapters, four new stepsiblings relate the problems — and the fun — they have had adjusting to life together. (Rev: BL 9/15/05; SLJ 10/05; VOYA 12/05)

8551 Hirsch, Odo. *Darius Bell and the Glitter Pool* (4–7). 2010, Kane/Miller $15.99 (978-193527965-5). 240pp. Broke and desperate, Darius's once wealthy family has nothing to give to the community as its annual thank you, until an earthquake reveals a hidden cave that may provide the answer; set in Australia. Lexile 770L (Rev: BL 9/1/10; LMC 3–4/11)

8552 Hogeweg, Margriet. *The God of Grandma Forever* (4–6). 2001, Front St. $14.95 (978-1-886910-69-0). 112pp. Maria has a difficult relationship with her religious grandmother in this story translated from Dutch. (Rev: BCCB 6/01; BL 9/15/01; HBG 10/01; SLJ 7/01)

8553 Holm, Jenni. *Our Only May Amelia* (4–6). 1999, HarperCollins LB $15.89 (978-0-06-028354-4). Told in diary form, this is the story of 12-year-old May Amelia, who lives with her large family in Washington State in the late 1800s, and of her troubles when her grandmother comes to stay. Newbery Honor Book, 2000. (Rev: BCCB 9/99; BL 9/1/99; HBG 10/99; SLJ 6/99)

8554 Holm, Jennifer L. *The Trouble with May Amelia* (3–6). Illus. by Adam Gustavson. 2011, Simon & Schuster $15.99 (978-1-4169-1373-3). 224pp. May Amelia, a Finnish American 13-year-old, shows her inner strength as she copes with criticism from family and community in this sequel to the Newbery Honor Book; set in 1900 Washington state. ⌒ ℓ Lexile 690L (Rev: BL 3/1/11; HB 5–6/11; SLJ 4/11)

8555 Holt, Kimberly Willis. *Piper Reed, the Great Gypsy* (3–5). Illus. by Christine Davenier. 2008, Holt $14.95 (978-0-8050-8198-5). 160pp. In this sequel to *Piper Reed, Navy Brat* (2007), 9-year-old Piper, a dyslexic, continues her entertaining descriptions of her family life. Her father is away at sea but Piper enjoys various events including a Gypsy Club pet show. (Rev: BL 7/08; HB 9/08) ⌒

8556 Jarrow, Gail. *If Phyllis Were Here* (5–7). 1989, Avon paper $2.75 (978-0-380-70634-1). Libby, age 11, has to learn to adjust to living without her best friend — her grandmother who moves to Florida. (Rev: BL 10/15/87; SLJ 9/87)

8557 Jimenez, Francisco. *The Circuit: Stories from the Life of a Migrant Child* (5–10). 1997, Univ. of New Mexico paper $11.95 (978-0-8263-1797-1). Eleven moving stories about the lives, fears, hopes, and problems of children in Mexican migrant worker families. (Rev: BL 12/1/97)

8558 Johnston, Tony. *Angel City* (2–4). Illus. by Carole Byard. 2006, Philomel $15.99 (978-0-399-23405-7). 40pp. An elderly African American man discovers a Latino baby abandoned in a dumpster and takes the child home to raise as his own. (Rev: BL 6/1–15/06; SLJ 6/06)

8559 Johnston, Tony. *Any Small Goodness: A Novel of the Barrio* (4–7). Illus. by Raul Colon. 2001, Scholastic paper $16.95 (978-0-439-18936-1). Eleven-year-old Arturo Rodriguez, whose Mexican family is new to Los Angeles, describes family life, school, celebrations, and dangers. (Rev: BL 9/15/01; HBG 3/02; SLJ 9/01; VOYA 10/01)

8560 Jones, Kimberly K. *Sand Dollar Summer* (5–8). 2006, Simon & Schuster $15.95 (978-1-4169-0362-8). Annalise's summer in Maine with her mother and younger, often-mute brother Free takes a dramatic turn when a hurricane hits their island. (Rev: BL 5/15/06; HBG 10/06; LMC 1/07; SLJ 6/06*)

8561 Jones, Marcia Thornton. *Ratfink* (3–5). Illus. by C. B. Decker. 2010, Dutton $16.99 (978-0-525-42066-8). 224pp. Fifth-grader Logan slowly learns to accept and even appreciate his aging, forgetful, and embarrassing Grandpa, who actually ends up helping him deal with problems at school and at home. **e** Lexile 630L (Rev: BL 12/15/09*; SLJ 2/10)

8562 Kadohata, Cynthia. *The Thing About Luck* (4–8). Illus. by Julia Kuo. 2013, Atheneum $16.99 (978-141691882-0). 288pp. It seems that 12-year-old Summer's migrant worker Japanese American family has run out of luck — her parents must go to Japan to care for elderly relatives, Summer herself has malaria, her younger brother has his own problems, and her grandparents are not really fit for wheat harvesting; can Summer hold everything together? National Book Award. **e** Lexile 700 (Rev: BL 4/1/13*; HB 7–8/13*; LMC 1–2/14; SLJ 6/13*)

8563 Kehret, Peg. *Runaway Twin* (5–8). 2009, Dutton $16.99 (978-0-525-42177-1). 197pp. Thirteen-year-old Sunny Skyland leaves her Nebraska foster home for Washington state on a quest to find the twin sister from whom she was separated ten years before. Lexile 740L (Rev: BLO 8/09; SLJ 12/09; VOYA 12/09)

8564 Kehret, Peg. *Sisters Long Ago* (5–8). 1992, Pocket paper $3.99 (978-0-671-78433-1). While surviving a near drowning, Willow has a glimpse of herself living another life in ancient Egypt. (Rev: SLJ 3/90)

8565 Kelly, Katy. *Lucy Rose: Big on Plans* (2–4). Illus. by Adam Rex. 2005, Delacorte $12.95 (978-0-385-73204-8). 128pp. Lucy Rose, a precocious 8-year-old, chronicles her busy plans for the summer in her journal. (Rev: BL 8/05; SLJ 6/05)

8566 Kelly, Katy. *Lucy Rose: Busy Like You Can't Believe* (2–4). Illus. by Adam Rex. Series: Lucy Rose. 2006, Delacorte $12.95 (978-0-385-73319-9). 176pp. Now in fourth grade, Lucy Rose reveals in her diary her struggles with her mother's romantic life and learns some important lessons about the perils of eavesdropping. (Rev: BL 10/15/06; SLJ 10/06)

8567 Kennedy, Marlane. *The Dog Days of Charlotte Hayes* (4–7). 2009, Greenwillow $15.99 (978-0-06-145241-3); LB $16.89 (978-0-06-145242-0). 144pp.

Eleven-year-old Charlotte, no dog lover, nonetheless works to find a better home for the St. Bernard her family neglects. **e** Lexile 790L (Rev: BL 2/15/09; SLJ 4/1/09)

8568 Kennedy, Marlane. *Me and the Pumpkin Queen* (4–6). 2007, Greenwillow $15.99 (978-0-06-114022-8). 192pp. In homage to her late mother, 11-year-old Mildred tries for years to grow giant pumpkins to win a contest, and her family and friends provide support along the way. (Rev: BCCB 9/07; BL 7/07; SLJ 8/07)

8569 Kerley, Barbara. *The Extraordinary Mark Twain (According to Susy)* (2–5). Illus. by Edwin Fotheringham. 2010, Scholastic $17.99 (978-0-545-12508-6). 48pp. Thirteen-year-old Susy Clemens decides to set the world straight on her father (Twain) in this unusual book that features pages of Susy's (often misspelled) journal. (Rev: BL 12/1/09; LMC 5–6/10; SLJ 1/1/10*)

8570 Kirby, Susan E. *Ida Lou's Story* (4–6). Series: American Quilts. 2001, Simon & Schuster paper $4.99 (978-0-689-80972-9). 170pp. Lacey likes to hear stories of times past and her great-great-aunt Ida Lou who dreamed of becoming a trapeze artist. (Rev: SLJ 12/01)

8571 Klein, Norma. *Mom, the Wolfman and Me* (5–8). 1972, Avon paper $3.50 (978-0-380-00791-2). Brett's mother is single but the Wolfman is becoming more than a steady boyfriend.

8572 Kline, Lisa Williams. *Season of Change* (5–8). 2013, Zonderkidz $10.99 (978-031074007-0). 208pp. Stepsisters Diana and Stephanie are finally getting along when their parents decide their marriage is in trouble; they head for a retreat leaving the girls to face various difficulties that are described in alternating chapters. The final installment in the series that began with *Summer of the Wolves* (2012). (Rev: BL 7/13; SLJ 8/13)

8573 Klise, Kate. *Far from Normal* (5–8). 2006, Scholastic $16.99 (978-0-439-79447-3). In this sequel to *Deliver Us from Normal* (2005), the Harrisong family makes a deal with the devil when a retailing giant threatens to sue over disparaging remarks made about the chain in a book written by Charles. (Rev: BL 10/15/06; VOYA 4/07)

8574 Krishnaswami, Uma. *Naming Maya* (5–8). 2004, Farrar $16.00 (978-0-374-35485-5). On a trip to India with her mother, 12-year-old Maya learns some important lessons about herself and the real reasons for the breakup of her parents' marriage. (Rev: BL 4/1/04; HB 7–8/04; SLJ 6/04; VOYA 6/04)

8575 Kurtz, Jane. *Anna Was Here* (3–6). 2013, Greenwillow $16.99 (978-006056493-3). 288pp. Anna is prepared for any disaster, except the one that happens — her family has to move suddenly from Colorado to Kansas, where her minister father is needed and everyone is related to her, and Anna must figure out how to prepare for this change. Lexile 610 (Rev: BL 11/1/13; SLJ 9/13)

8576 LaFleur, Suzanne. *Eight Keys* (4–7). 2011, Random House $16.99 (978-0-385-74030-2); LB $19.99 (978-0-385-90833-7). 224pp. Twelve-year-old orphan Elise is having trouble adapting to middle school when she discovers keys to rooms that her late father designed, which help her cope. (Rev: BL 9/1/11; SLJ 8/11)

8577 Leal, Ann Haywood. *A Finders-Keepers Place* (4–6). 2010, Henry Holt $16.99 (978-0-8050-8882-3). 272pp. In this moving family drama set in the 1970s, Esther, 11, realizes in view of her mother's manic depression that it's up to her to find her missing younger sister and then to search for their absent father. (Rev: BL 11/1/10; SLJ 1/1/11)

8578 Levoy, Myron. *The Witch of Fourth Street and Other Stories* (4–7). 1991, Peter Smith $19.75 (978-0-8446-6450-7); paper $5.99 (978-0-06-440059-6). Eight stories about growing up poor on the Lower East Side of New York City.

8579 Lewis, Beverly. *The Chicken Pox Panic* (2–4). Illus. Series: Cul-de-Sac Kids. 1995, Bethany House paper $3.99 (978-1-55661-626-6). 80pp. While recovering from chicken pox, Abby plans a birthday party for her Korean brother; but when he arrives, everyone has chicken pox. Also in the series: *The Double Dabble Surprise* (1995). (Rev: BL 9/1/95)

8580 Lin, Grace. *Dumpling Days* (3–6). 2012, Little, Brown $15.99 (978-031612590-1). 264pp. Pacy and her family travel to their homeland, Taiwan, to celebrate Grandma's birthday, and Pacy finds challenges, a love for dumplings, and a growing understanding of her heritage. ∩ ℯ (Rev: BL 1/1/12; HB 3–4/12; LMC 1–2/12*)

8581 Lindbergh, Anne. *The Worry Week* (5–7). Illus. by Kathryn Hewitt. 1985, Harcourt $12.95 (978-0-15-299675-8); paper $2.95 (978-0-380-70394-4). Left alone with her sisters for a week in Maine, 11-year-old "Legs" spends most of her time tending to and worrying about her siblings. (Rev: BL 6/1/85; HB 9–10/85; SLJ 8/85)

8582 Little, Jean. *Emma's Strange Pet* (1–2). Illus. by Jennifer Plecas. Series: I Can Read. 2003, HarperCollins $15.99 (978-0-06-028350-6). 64pp. In a concession to his sister Emma's allergies, Max gives up his quest for a dog and accepts a lizard in this sweet but challenging book for beginning readers. (Rev: BL 7/03; HBG 4/04; SLJ 10/03)

8583 Little, Kimberley Griffiths. *The Healing Spell* (5–8). 2010, Scholastic $17.99 (978-0-545-16559-4). 368pp. A healer in the Louisiana bayou gives 12-year-old Livie a spell to help coax her mother out of a coma. Lexile 800L (Rev: BL 6/10; LMC 8–9/10; SLJ 11/1/10)

8584 Look, Lenore. *Alvin Ho: Allergic to Camping, Hiking, and Other Natural Disasters* (2–4). Illus. by LeUyen Pham. 2009, Random $15.99 (978-0-375-85705-8). 176pp. Anxious 2nd-grader Alvin Ho is back in another comical, sensitive story centered around his worries over surviving a planned camping trip with his father. (Rev: BCCB 9/09; BLO 6/16/09; HB 8–9/09; SLJ 7/09) ∩

8585 Lupica, Mike. *Miracle on 49th Street* (5–8). 2006, Philomel $17.99 (978-0-399-24488-9). The life of pro basketball star Josh Cameron is turned upside down when 12-year-old Molly Parker turns up claiming to be his daughter. ∩ (Rev: BL 9/1/06; SLJ 11/06)

8586 Lyon, Annabel. *All-Season Edie* (5–7). 2008, Orca paper $8.95 (978-1-55143-713-2). Edie, 11, flirts with witchcraft as a solution to her family's problems and to aid her in her quest for coolness; this is a fast-paced first-person narrative full of humor. (Rev: BL 3/1/08)

8587 Lytton, Deborah. *Jane in Bloom* (5–8). 2009, Dutton $16.99 (978-0-525-42078-1). 182pp. When 12-year-old Jane's "perfect" older sister Lizzie dies of anorexia, Jane's parents separate and the girl is left to cope by herself — which she does with the aid of a babysitter, a puppy, a digital camera, and a new friend. ℯ Lexile HL540L (Rev: BL 2/15/09; SLJ 5/1/09)

8588 McDonough, Alison. *Do the Hokey Pokey* (3–5). Illus. 2001, Front St. $14.95 (978-0-8126-2699-5). 120pp. Shy, friendless Brendan is afraid he will be embarrassed by his boisterous mother when she is chosen to be DJ for the all-school party. (Rev: BCCB 9/01; BL 4/1/01; HBG 10/01; SLJ 5/01)

8589 McDonough, Yona Zeldis. *The Cats in the Doll Shop* (2–5). Illus. by Heather Maione. 2011, Viking $14.99 (978-0-670-01279-4). 128pp. In 1915 Anna, 11, welcomes her cousin Trudie from Russia; Trudie is shy and withdrawn until her love of cats helps her to adjust; a sequel to *The Doll Shop Downstairs* (2009). ℯ (Rev: BL 12/1/11; LMC 3–4/12; SLJ 12/1/11)

8590 Machado, Ana Maria. *Me in the Middle* (4–6). Trans. from Portuguese by David Unger. Illus. by Caroline Merola. 2002, Groundwood $14.95 (978-0-88899-463-9); paper $5.95 (978-0-88899-467-7). 110pp. Young Bel feels close to her late great-grandmother and hears in her mind her accounts of life in Brazil at the turn of the 20th century, but finds her admonitions on behavior difficult to accept. (Rev: BCCB 7–8/02; HBG 10/02; SLJ 8/02)

8591 McKay, Hilary. *Forever Rose* (4–7). 2008, Simon & Schuster $16.99 (978-1-4169-5486-6). Rose, part of the flighty and dramatic Casson family, gets her own book in the series, in which she and her friends cook up a dangerous adventure and her family unveils a series of surprises. (Rev: BL 4/1/08; SLJ 5/08)

8592 McKay, Hilary. *Indigo's Star* (5–8). 2004, Simon & Schuster $15.95 (978-0-689-86563-3). In this sequel to *Saffy's Angel* (2002), Saffy's younger siblings — 12-year-old Indigo and 8-year-old Rose — take a stand against school bullies with the help of a lonely young American called Tom. (Rev: BL 9/15/04; SLJ 9/04*)

8593 McKay, Hilary. *Saffy's Angel* (4–7). 2002, Simon & Schuster $16.00 (978-0-689-84933-6). Saffron learns she was adopted into her artistic family and travels to Italy in search of her roots. (Rev: BCCB 5/02; BL 5/15/02; HB 7–8/02*; HBG 10/02; SLJ 5/02)

8594 McKinnon, Hannah Roberts. *The Properties of Water* (4–7). 2010, Farrar $16.99 (978-0-0374-36145-). 169pp. When her older sister Marni is paralyzed in a diving accident, 12-year-old Lacey's life is turned upside down. (Rev: BL 11/1/10; SLJ 12/1/10)

8595 MacLachlan, Patricia. *All the Places to Love* (5–8). 1994, HarperCollins LB $18.89 (978-0-06-021099-1). This picture book celebrates the love found in an extended rural family and the joy that a new arrival brings. (Rev: BCCB 7–8/94; BL 6/1–15/94*; SLJ 6/94)

8596 MacLachlan, Patricia. *The Boxcar Children Beginning: The Aldens of Fair Meadow Farm* (3–5). Illus. by Tim Jessell. 2012, Whitman $16.99 (978-0-80756-616-9). 144pp. This volume introduces the lives of Henry, Jessie, Violet, and Benny before they became the orphans known as the Boxcar children. **e** Lexile 420 (Rev: BL 8/12; HB 11–12/12; LMC 1–2/13; SLJ 12/12)

8597 MacLachlan, Patricia. *Cassie Binegar* (4–7). 1982, HarperCollins paper $5.99 (978-0-06-440195-1). Cassie is not happy with the disorder in her family situation.

8598 MacLachlan, Patricia. *Kindred Souls* (3–5). 2012, HarperCollins $14.99 (978-0-06-052297-1). 128pp. When Jake's grandfather is hospitalized, the boy makes the old man's dream of rebuilding the sod house where he was born a reality. (Rev: BL 1/12; HB 1–2/12; SLJ 4/1/12)

8599 MacLachlan, Patricia. *The Truth of Me* (2–4). 2013, HarperCollins $14.99 (978-006199859-1). 128pp. A touching and rhythmic chapter book that finds Robbie happily leaving his distant parents and going to spend the summer with his eccentric grandmother, Maddy, whom he loves fiercely and from whom he learns lessons about life and connections. Lexile 420 (Rev: BL 9/1/13; SLJ 7/13)

8600 MacLean, Christine Cole. *Mary Margaret and the Perfect Pet Plan* (3–5). 2004, Dutton $15.99 (978-0-525-47183-7). 168pp. Nearly 9 years old, Mary Margaret wants a pet and makes many efforts to get one, but it's a long time before her allergic father and pregnant mother can see reason. (Rev: BCCB 6/04; SLJ 7/04)

8601 Madison, Alan. *100 Days and 99 Nights* (3–5). Illus. by Julia Denos. 2008, Little, Brown $14.99 (978-0-316-11354-0). 144pp. In this book that combines humor with a stressful situation, 7-year-old Esme tries to remain brave while her military father is away on a tour of duty; she communes with her "bedzoo" of stuffed animals and takes part in a scrap metal drive. (Rev: BL 5/1/08; LMC 1/09; SLJ 6/08)

8602 Mansfield, Creina. *Cherokee* (5–8). 2001, O'Brien paper $7.95 (978-0-86278-368-6). Gene's wonderful life with his jazz musician grandfather, Cherokee, comes to an end when his aunt decides he needs a home and an education. (Rev: SLJ 11/01)

8603 Marsden, Carolyn. *Bird Springs* (3–5). 2007, Viking $14.99 (978-0-670-06193-8). 128pp. Gregory, a 10-year-old Navajo boy, must cope with moving to a new place and missing his estranged father. (Rev: BCCB 9/07; BL 5/15/07; HB 7/07; LMC 11/07; SLJ 5/07)

8604 Marsden, Carolyn. *Silk Umbrellas* (3–6). 2004, Candlewick $14.99 (978-0-7636-2257-2). 144pp. Eleven-year-old Noi hopes to be able to support her family by creating and selling painted silk umbrellas in this story set in a small Thai village. (Rev: BL 2/1/04*; SLJ 3/04)

8605 Martin, Ann M. *Ten Rules for Living with My Sister* (3–6). 2011, Feiwel & Friends $16.99 (978-0-312-

36766-4). 240pp. When their grandfather moves in, 9-year-old Pearl and 13-year-old Lexie have to share a room and find a way to get along. **e** Lexile 790L (Rev: BL 8/11; HB 9–10/11; SLJ 10/1/11; VOYA 10/11)

8606 Martin, Patricia. *Lulu Atlantis and the Quest for True Blue Love* (2–4). Illus. by Marc Boutavant. 2008, Random $15.99 (978-0-375-84016-6). 228pp. With the arrival of a new baby in the house, Lulu — who is seeking True Blue Love — turns more and more to her daddy longlegs friend Harry. (Rev: LMC 3/08; SLJ 3/08)

8607 Martinez, Arturo O. *Pedrito's World* (5–7). 2007, Texas Tech Univ. $16.95 (978-0-89672-600-0). In rural south Texas in 1941, 6-year-old Pedrito describes the important things in his life — his first day of school, the death of a friend, a Christmas celebration, his first words of English. (Rev: BL 5/1/07)

8608 Matas, Carol. *Sparks Fly Upward* (4–8). 2002, Clarion $15.00 (978-0-618-15964-2). Set in Manitoba in the early 20th century, this is the story of 12-year-old Rebecca, a Jewish girl, and her life with a Ukrainian foster family. (Rev: BCCB 7–8/02; BL 4/1/02; HBG 10/02; SLJ 3/02)

8609 Matthews, Kezi. *Flying Lessons* (5–7). 2002, Cricket $16.95 (978-0-8126-2671-1). A girl in a small southern town bonds with an eclectic bunch of adults after the airplane in which her mother was traveling disappears. (Rev: BL 12/15/02; HB 1–2/03; HBG 3/03; SLJ 12/02; VOYA 6/03)

8610 Mead, Alice. *Isabella's Above-Ground Pool* (2–4). Illus. by Maryann Cocca-Leffler. 2006, Farrar $16.00 (978-0-374-33617-2). 112pp. Nine-year-old Isabella learns some important lessons about sharing after a tornado sweeps through her small Texas town. (Rev: BL 4/1/06; SLJ 5/06)

8611 Medearis, Angela Shelf. *What Did I Do to Deserve a Sister Like You?* (3–5). Illus. by Don Tate and Mark Galbreath. 2002, Eakin $13.95 (978-1-57168-471-4); paper $7.95 (978-1-57168-642-8). 123pp. Sharie, 10, juggles her dislike of her older sister, her problems with her piano teacher, and a longing to ride on a roller-coaster. (Rev: HBG 10/02; SLJ 5/02)

8612 Meehl, Brian. *Out of Patience* (4–6). 2006, Delacorte LB $17.95 (978-0-385-90320-2). 304pp. Twelve-year-old Jake's dream of escaping his boring Kansas hometown, where his plumber father hopes to open a toilet museum, is put on the back burner when his dad brings home a cursed toilet plunger. (Rev: BL 4/1/06; SLJ 11/06; VOYA 6/06)

8613 Mills, Claudia. *Trading Places* (4–6). 2006, Farrar $16.00 (978-0-374-31798-0). 138pp. Twins Todd and Amy must relinquish their familiar roles when things get tough at home and at school. (Rev: BL 2/1/06; SLJ 5/06)

8614 Mobin-Uddi, Asma. *My Name Is Bilal* (4–7). Illus. by Barbara Kiawk. 2005, Boyds Mills $15.95 (978-1-59078-175-3). When they start at a new school, Muslim Bilal and his sister Ayesha balance pride in their own heritage and their desire to blend in. (Rev: BL 8/05; SLJ 8/05)

8615 Modiano, Patrick. *Catherine Certitude* (4–7). Trans. by William Rodarmor. Illus. by Jean-Jacques Sempé. 2001, Godine $17.95 (978-0-87923-959-6). An adult Catherine reminisces about her life as a youngster in Paris — living with her father, puzzling over his job, going to ballet classes, eating in restaurants — in this stylishly illustrated chapter book delivered in picture-book format. (Rev: BL 12/15/01; HBG 3/02; SLJ 2/02)

8616 Monninger, Joseph. *Wish* (5–8). 2010, Delacorte $17.99 (978-0-385-73941-2); LB $20.99 (978-0-385-90788-0). 208pp. Fifteen-year-old Bee sets out to give her little brother Tommy, an 11-year-old with cystic fibrosis, the experience of a lifetime — a chance to swim with sharks. ℮ (Rev: BL 12/1/10*; SLJ 1/1/11)

8617 Morris, Jennifer. *Come, Llamas* (4–6). 2005, Delacorte LB $17.99 (978-0-385-90229-8). 208pp. Nine-year-old JT describes the summer he plays a growing role in his family's Alaska llama ranch and must deal with his grandfather's illness. (Rev: BL 2/1/05; SLJ 1/05)

8618 Moss, Marissa. *Amelia's Longest, Biggest, Most-Fights-Ever Family Reunion* (3–5). Illus. Series: Amelia. 2006, Simon & Schuster $9.95 (978-0-689-87447-5). 80pp. Amelia first steels herself for a reunion with her father's extended family and then records her experiences. (Rev: BL 8/06; SLJ 9/06)

8619 Mourlevat, Jean-Claude. *The Pull of the Ocean* (5–8). Trans. by Y. Mauder. 2006, Delacorte $15.95 (978-0-385-73348-9). In this modern version of "Tom Thumb," Yann — the smallest and youngest of seven — leads his six older brothers (three sets of twins) away from their dismal home to the ocean that's far to the west, meeting many characters along the way. Batchelder Award. (Rev: BL 12/1/06; SLJ 1/07*)

8620 Mulford, Philippa Greene. *The Holly Sisters on Their Own* (4–6). 1998, Marshall Cavendish $14.95 (978-0-7614-5022-1). Charmaine, age 11, is not happy at the prospect of her older half sister's arrival to spend the summer in New York City, but time produces a friendship. (Rev: BCCB 7–8/98; BL 5/1/98; HBG 10/98; SLJ 4/98)

8621 Murphy, Sally. *Pearl Verses the World* (2–4). Illus. by Heather Potter. 2011, Candlewick $14.99 (978-0-7636-4821-3). 73pp. Lonely young Pearl doesn't fit in at school and longs to be at home with her mother and grandmother, who unfortunately is dying; Pearl recounts her life in non-rhyming verse. (Rev: HB 9–10/11; SLJ 9/1/11)

8622 Namioka, Lensey. *Yang the Third and Her Impossible Family* (4–7). Illus. by Kees de Kiefte. 1996, Bantam paper $4.50 (978-0-440-41231-1). Mary, part of a Chinese family newly arrived in Seattle, is embarrassed by her parents' old-country ways in this humorous story. (Rev: BCCB 5/95; BL 4/15/95; SLJ 8/95)

8623 Nelson, Rosemary. *Hubcaps and Puppies* (3–6). 2002, Napoleon paper $8.95 (978-0-929141-98-5). 184pp. Thirteen-year-old Nikki faces difficult choices, such as whether to allow herself to love a stray puppy so soon after the death of her dog. (Rev: BL 3/1/03)

8624 Nielsen, Susin. *Dear George Clooney, Please Marry My Mom* (5–8). 2010, Tundra $18.95 (978-0-88776-977-1). 240pp. Fed up with her phony new stepmom, and her mother's out-of-control dating, 12-year-old Violet decides that George Clooney would be the perfect dad replacement. ℮ (Rev: BL 9/1/10; SLJ 9/1/10; VOYA 10/10)

8625 Orr, Wendy. *Mokie and Bik* (2–4). Illus. by Jonathan Bean. 2007, Holt $15.95 (978-0-8050-7979-1). Fraternal twins Mokie and Bik live with their mother on a houseboat, enjoy their own private language, and have many adventures. (Rev: BL 6/1–15/07; SLJ 7/07)

8626 Park, Barbara. *The Graduation of Jake Moon* (5–8). 2000, Simon & Schuster $15.00 (978-0-689-83912-2). Jake Moon finds it impossible to cope with his grandfather's gradual disintegration from Alzheimer's disease. (Rev: BCCB 12/00; BL 6/1–15/00; HB 9–10/00; HBG 3/01; SLJ 9/00)

8627 Paros, Jennifer. *Violet Bing and the Grand House* (2–4). Illus. 2007, Viking $14.99 (978-0-670-06151-8). 112pp. Despite her determination not to, Violet Bing finds some things that pique her interest during a summer stay with her Great-Aunt Astrid. (Rev: BL 3/15/07)

8628 Pearce, Emily Smith. *Isabel and the Miracle Baby* (2–4). 2007, Front St. $15.95 (978-1-932425-44-4). Eight-year-old Isabel has her hands full with a new baby in the house, her mother recovering from cancer and her father gone much of the time. (Rev: BL 10/1/07; SLJ 10/07)

8629 Pearsall, Shelley. *All Shook Up* (5–8). 2008, Knopf $15.99 (978-0-375-83698-5). Josh's divorced dad has a new girlfriend and a new job as an Elvis impersonator, much to Josh's horror. (Rev: BL 5/1/08; SLJ 7/08)

8630 Pennypacker, Sara. *Clementine and the Family Meeting* (2–4). Illus. by Marla Frazee. 2011, Hyperion/Disney $14.99 (978-1-4231-2356-9). 160pp. Third-grader Clementine copes with mixed feelings when her parents announce there's a new baby on the way. (Rev: BL 7/11; SLJ 8/1/11)

8631 Pryor, Bonnie. *Toenails, Tonsils, and Tornadoes* (3–5). Illus. 1997, Morrow $15.00 (978-0-688-14885-0). 160pp. Fourth-grader Martin is not too happy when his Aunt Henrietta visits, principally because he has to give up his room. (Rev: BCCB 6/97; BL 5/15/97; SLJ 5/97)

8632 Ransom, Candice F. *Finding Day's Bottom* (4–6). 2006, Carolrhoda $15.95 (978-1-57505-933-4). In this poignant tale set in the Blue Ridge Mountains of Virginia, 11-year-old Jane-Ery slowly comes to appreciate her Grandpap's love after her father's death in an accident. (Rev: BL 10/15/06; SLJ 9/06)

8633 Ransom, Candice F. *Seeing Sky-Blue Pink* (3–5). 2007, Carolrhoda $16.95 (978-0-8225-7142-1). Eight-year-old Maddie adjusts to her new home on a farm after her mother marries a nice man named Sam. (Rev: BCCB 11/07; BL 10/15/07; LMC 1/08; SLJ 10/07)

8634 Rocklin, Joanne. *The Five Lives of Our Cat Zook* (3–6). 2012, Abrams $16.95 (978-141970192-4). 240pp. When their beloved cat Zook falls ill, 10-year-old Oona explains to her younger brother that Zook has only used five of his nine lives — and then explains them all. (Rev: BL 3/15/12*; SLJ 4/12)

8635 Rodowsky, Colby. *Ben and the Sudden Too-Big Family* (3–5). 2007, Farrar $16.00 (978-0-374-30658-8). 120pp. Ben, 10, likes to divide events in his life into "all right" and "not all right," and although his new step-mother and even the arrival of his new adopted sister from China fell into the former category, he's not at all sure about the prospect of a houseful of his stepmother's relatives. (Rev: SLJ 4/07)

8636 Rodowsky, Colby. *That Fernhill Summer* (5–8). 2006, Farrar $16.00 (978-0-374-37442-6). When her grandmother becomes ill, biracial teen Kiara confronts family problems and develops relationships with two white cousins she didn't know existed. (Rev: BL 4/15/06; SLJ 6/06)

8637 Rosenthal, Betsy R. *Looking for Me* (4–7). 2012, Houghton Mifflin $15.99 (978-054761084-9). 176pp. The fourth of 12 children in a Jewish family in 1936 Baltimore, 11-year-old Edith finds it difficult to establish her own identity. ℮ (Rev: BL 4/15/12; SLJ 4/12)

8638 Ryan, Pam Muñoz. *Paint the Wind* (4–7). 2007, Scholastic $16.99 (978-0-439-87362-8). On the death of her grandmother — who has been a distant and strict guardian — orphaned 11-year-old Maya is sent to relatives in Wyoming, where she learns about the love of horses and family. (Rev: BL 11/15/07; LMC 1/08; SLJ 11/07)

8639 St. Anthony, Jane. *Grace Above All* (5–7). 2007, Farrar $16.00 (978-0-374-39940-5). In this gentle story set in the 1960s, 13-year-old Grace expects to have a boring summer watching over her siblings but a neighboring boy and Great Aunt Hilda provide unexpected interest. (Rev: BL 5/15/07; SLJ 7/07)

8640 Salmansohn, Karen. *One Puppy, Three Tales* (4–6). Illus. by author. Series: Alexandra Rambles On! 2001, Tricycle $12.95 (978-1-58246-044-4). Twelve-year-old Alexandra shares vivid details of her life and her relationships with her mother, father, and friends. (Rev: HBG 10/01; SLJ 6/01)

8641 Salmansohn, Karen. *Wherever I Go, There I Am* (4–7). Illus. by author. Series: Alexandra Rambles On! 2002, Tricycle $12.95 (978-1-58246-079-6). Alexandra's journal reveals her angst about issues such as scary movies and becoming a teenager. (Rev: HBG 3/03; SLJ 2/03)

8642 Schirripa, Steven R., and Charles Fleming. *Nicky Deuce: Welcome to the Family* (4–6). 2005, Delacorte $15.95 (978-0-385-73257-4). When his summer camp is abruptly closed, Nicholas Borelli II is sent to Brooklyn for a two-week stay with his Grandma Tutti and learns about his Italian American roots. (Rev: BL 10/1/05; SLJ 8/05)

8643 Seidler, Tor. *Brothers Below Zero* (5–8). 2002, HarperCollins LB $15.89 (978-0-06-029180-8). Artistic Tim, overwhelmed by his athletic younger brother, eventually runs away to the place he has felt most valued. (Rev: BCCB 3/02; BL 1/1–15/02; HBG 10/02; SLJ 4/02)

8644 Shang, Wendy Wan-Long. *The Great Wall of Lucy Wu* (4–6). 2011, Scholastic $17.99 (978-0-545-16215-9). 320pp. Chinese American Lucy's plans for a terrific year in 6th grade go awry when her great-aunt arrives from China and moves into her bedroom; slowly she comes to appreciate the traditions her aunt brings with her. Lexile 700L (Rev: BL 2/15/11; SLJ 2/1/11)

8645 Shearer, Alex. *The Great Blue Yonder* (5–8). 2002, Clarion $15.00 (978-0-618-21257-6). Twelve-year-old Harry, who has died in an accident, experiences afterlife on the Other Side and has the opportunity to review his relations with other family members. (Rev: BCCB 6/02; HBG 10/02; SLJ 4/02; VOYA 6/02)

8646 Sidney, Margaret. *The Five Little Peppers and How They Grew* (4–6). 1981, Buccaneer LB $27.95 (978-0-89966-340-1). The classic of five children growing up many decades ago.

8647 Singer, Nicky. *Under Shifting Glass* (5–8). 2013, Chronicle $16.99 (978-145210921-3). 320pp. A mysterious glass flask becomes a magical totem for Jess, a sensitive 12-year-old who is dealing with the death of a beloved aunt and the birth of conjoined twin brothers. (Rev: BL 3/1/13; LMC 10/13; SLJ 5/13; VOYA 4/13)

8648 Smith, Emily. *Joe vs. the Fairies* (2–4). Illus. by Georgie Birkett. 2006, Trafalgar paper $7.50 (978-0-552-55174-8). 92pp. Joe isn't pleased when his cousins arrive and monopolize his sisters with girlish games, but then he meets a girl who enjoys climbing trees. (Rev: BL 1/1–15/06)

8649 Smith, Janice Lee. *The Monster in the Third Dresser Drawer and Other Stories About Adam Joshua* (3–5). Illus. by Dick Gackenbach. 1981, HarperCollins LB $15.89 (978-0-06-025739-2). 96pp. Adam Joshua faces many everyday problems, including a new baby sister, in these six stories. A sequel is: *The Kid Next Door and Other Headaches: Stories about Adam Joshua* (1984).

8650 Smith, Sherri L. *Hot, Sour, Salty, Sweet* (5–7). 2008, Delacorte $15.99 (978-0-385-73417-2). As her grandmothers, one Chinese American and one African American, argue over food and family, Ana's junior high graduation party gets more and more complicated. (Rev: BL 2/1/08; SLJ 4/08)

8651 Snyder, Laurel. *Penny Dreadful* (3–6). Illus. by Abigail Halpin. 2010, Random House $16.99 (978-0-375-86199-4); LB $19.99 (978-0-375-96199-1). 320pp. When wealthy Penelope Grey's father quits his job, the family is forced to move to a less-opulent Tennessee farm house, where Penny has the freedom she's always wanted. ⌒ ℮ Lexile 740L (Rev: BL 10/1/10*; LMC 1–2/11; SLJ 1/1/11)

8652 Soetoro-ng, Maya. *Ladder to the Moon* (3–5). Illus. by Yuyi Morales. 2011, Candlewick $16.99 (978-0-

7636-4570-0). 48pp. A golden ladder takes young Su-haila and her deceased Grandma Annie on a journey to the moon, where they meet people in need of help; written by Barack Obama's half-sister, this mystical story is a tribute to their mother. Lexile AD830L (Rev: BL 3/1/11*; LMC 8–9/11; SLJ 4/11)

8653 Spinelli, Eileen. *The Dancing Pancake* (3–6). Illus. by Joanne Lew-Vriethoff. 2010, Knopf $12.99 (978-0-375-85870-3); LB $15.99 (978-0-375-95870-0). 256pp. After her parents separate, Bindi, 11, moves with her mother into an apartment over the cafe that her aunt owns, where Bindi finds new friends and understanding. **e** Lexile 440L (Rev: BL 4/1/10; LMC 8–9/10; SLJ 5/10)

8654 Spinelli, Jerry. *Jake and Lily* (4–6). 2012, Harper-Collins $15.99 (978-006028135-9). 352pp. Twins Jake and Lily, 11, cope with growing up and losing the close-ness they've shared since birth. (Rev: BL 2/15/12; HB 5–6/12; SLJ 6/12)

8655 Springer, Nancy. *Separate Sisters* (5–7). 2001, Holi-day $16.95 (978-0-8234-1544-1). Two teenage girls deal with the divorce of their parents in different ways. (Rev: BCCB 2/02; BL 2/1/02; HB 3–4/02; HBG 10/02; SLJ 2/02; VOYA 4/02)

8656 Springstubb, Tricia. *Mo Wren, Lost and Found* (4–6). Illus. by Heather Ross. 2011, HarperCollins $15.99 (978-0-06-199039-7). 256pp. After their mother's death, 10-year-old Mo and her younger sister Dottie must move to the other side of town, attend a new school, and start a new life in an apartment above their father's new busi-ness. (Rev: BL 9/1/11*; SLJ 11/1/11)

8657 Starke, Ruth. *Noodle Pie* (5–7). 2010, Kane/Miller $15.99 (978-1-935279-25-9). 189pp. Andy, an 11-year-old Australian boy, keeps a diary during his visit to Vietnam, the place of his father's birth, recording all the interesting cultural differences and the fun he has with his cousin Minh as they work to revamp the family's res-taurant. Lexile 770L (Rev: BLO 3/15/10; LMC 8–9/10; SLJ 5/10)

8658 Stevenson, Robin. *Record Breaker* (4–6). 2013, Orca paper $9.95 (978-15546995-9-9). 152pp. In On-tario in 1963, 12-year-old Jack tries to distract his un-happy family — reeling from the crib death of his baby sister — by attempting to beat a world record. Lexile 590 (Rev: BL 3/1/13; LMC 10/13; SLJ 6/13)

8659 Stolz, Mary. *Go Fish* (3–5). Illus. by Pat Cummings. 1991, HarperCollins LB $14.89 (978-0-06-025822-1). Thomas and his grandfather spend warm times together. (Rev: BCCB 5/91; BL 5/15/91; HB 7/91; SLJ 5/91*)

8660 Stout, Shawn K. *Penelope Crumb* (3–5). Illus. by Valeria Docampo. 2012, Philomel $14.99 (978-039925728-5). 128pp. Big-nosed Penelope decides to learn more about her family, including her estranged grandfather with an equally large nose. Lexile 730 (Rev: BL 8/12; HB 7–8/12; LMC 3–4/13)

8661 Sullivan, Mary. *Dear Blue Sky* (5–8). 2012, Penguin $16.99 (978-039925684-4). 256pp. Cassie chooses an Iraqi girl's blog for a school assignment when her older brother is deployed to that country and her family life

begins to unravel. **e** (Rev: BL 9/1/12; HB 7–8/12; LMC 1–2/13)

8662 Summers, Laura. *Desperate Measures* (4–7). 2011, Putnam $16.99 (978-0-399-25616-5). 250pp. Vicky, 13, her mentally disabled twin sister Rhianna, and their younger brother Jamie run away to their aunt's cottage to avoid being split up by the foster care system. (Rev: LMC 11–12/11; SLJ 7/11)

8663 Taylor, Sydney. *All-of-a-Kind Family* (3–6). Illus. by Helen John. 1980, Peter Smith $21.25 (978-0-8446-6253-4); Dell paper $4.99 (978-0-440-40059-2). 192pp. Warm and moving stories of Jewish family life in New York City. Also use: *Ella of All-of-a-Kind Family* (1980, Dell paper).

8664 Tilly, Meg. *Porcupine* (5–8). 2007, Tundra $15.95 (978-0-88776-810-1). Jacqueline and her younger broth-er and sister go to Canada to live with a great-grand-mother after their father dies in Afghanistan. (Rev: BL 11/15/07; SLJ 12/07)

8665 Uhlberg, Myron. *The Printer* (2–4). Trans. and il-lus. by Henri Sorensen. 2003, Peachtree $16.95 (978-1-56145-221-7). 32pp. In 1940 New York City, a young boy describes how his deaf father, a printer, alerted his hearing co-workers to a deadly fire in the pressroom; an endnote supplies historical details. (Rev: BL 9/1/03; HBG 4/04; SLJ 12/03)

8666 Urban, Linda. *The Center of Everything* (4–6). 2013, Harcourt $15.99 (978-054776348-4). 208pp. As 6th-grader Ruby Pepperdine waits to read her winning essay at a parade, she reviews the challenges she has faced since the death of her grandmother. **e** Lexile 830 (Rev: BL 2/15/13*; LMC 10/13*; SLJ 4/13)

8667 Van Steenwyk, Elizabeth. *Three Dog Winter* (5–8). 1987, Walker $13.95 (978-0-8027-6718-9). A story of dog racing, this family tale tells of 12-year-old Scott and his Malamute, Kaylah. (Rev: BL 2/1/88; SLJ 12/87)

8668 Vernick, Shirley Reva. *Remember Dippy* (5–8). 2013, Cinco Puntos $16.95 (978-193595548-1); paper $9.95 (978-19359555-8-0). 162pp. Johnny, 14, is not happy to learn he will be spending the summer looking after his older, autistic cousin but eventually comes to appreciate his different abilities. **e** Lexile 700 (Rev: BL 6/13; LMC 5–6/14; SLJ 9/13)

8669 Voigt, Cynthia. *Dicey's Song* (5–9). 1982, Macmil-lan $17.95 (978-0-689-30944-1). This story of Dicey's life with her "Gram" in Maryland won a Newbery Medal (1983). Preceding it was *Homecoming* (1981) and a se-quel is *A Solitary Blue* (1983). (Rev: BL 12/15/89)

8670 Wallace, Bill. *Beauty* (5–7). 1988, Holiday $16.95 (978-0-8234-0715-6). Luke finds the adjustment diffi-cult when he and his mother go to live on his grandfa-ther's Oklahoma farm. (Rev: BCCB 11/88; BL 2/1/89; SLJ 10/88)

8671 Warner, Sally. *Happily Ever Emma* (2–4). Illus. by Jamie Harper. 2010, Viking $14.99 (978-0-670-01084-4). 144pp. Third-grader Emma is unhappy to learn that her divorced mother is dating, but feels very guilty when she deliberately fails to pass on a message. **e** Lexile 790L (Rev: BL 12/15/10; SLJ 1/1/11)

8672 Weeks, Sarah. *My Guy* (4–7). 2001, HarperCollins LB $14.89 (978-0-06-028370-4). Guy and Lana agree on only one thing — they don't want to become part of a blended family — and they set out to make sure it won't happen. (Rev: BCCB 6/01; BL 8/01; HB 7–8/01; HBG 10/01; SLJ 5/01)

8673 Welch, Sheila K. *The Shadowed Unicorn* (4–6). 2000, Front St. $15.95 (978-0-8126-2895-1). Identical twins Brendan and Nick join their older, bossy sister Arni on a hunt for a black unicorn in this family story that borders on fantasy. (Rev: BCCB 10/00; BL 4/15/00; HBG 10/00; SLJ 7/00)

8674 White, Ruth. *Belle Prater's Boy* (5–9). 1996, Farrar $17.00 (978-0-374-30668-7). Set in Appalachia in the 1950s, this moving, often humorous story tells about Gypsy and her unusual cousin Woodrow, who hides a secret involving his mother's disappearance. (Rev: BL 4/15/96; SLJ 4/96*)

8675 White, Ruth. *Tadpole* (5–8). 2003, Farrar $16.00 (978-0-374-31002-8). In this novel set in 1950s Appalachia, uncertain 10-year-old Carolina finds her own strengths when her 13-year-old cousin Tadpole arrives, running away from an abusive uncle. (Rev: BL 5/1/03; HB 5–6/03; HBG 10/03; SLJ 3/03*)

8676 Whittemore, Jo. *Odd Girl In* (5–7). 2011, Simon & Schuster paper $6.99 (978-1-4424-1284-2). 234pp. Unruly Alex, 12, and her older twin brothers are enrolled in a good behavior program after one prank too many, and, despite the various challenges, the whole experience turns out well in this novel full of humor. **e** (Rev: SLJ 3/1/11)

8677 Wilder, Laura Ingalls. *Little House in the Big Woods* (4–7). Illus. by Garth Williams. 1953, HarperCollins LB $17.89 (978-0-06-026431-4); paper $6.99 (978-0-06-440001-5). Outstanding story of a log-cabin family in Wisconsin in the late 1800s. Also use *By the Shores of Silver Lake; Farmer Boy; Little House on the Prairie; Long Winter; On the Banks of Plum Creek; These Happy Golden Years* (all 1953); *Little Town on the Prairie* (1961); *The First Four Years* (1971).

8678 Wiles, Deborah. *Each Little Bird That Sings* (4–6). 2005, Harcourt $16.00 (978-0-15-205113-6). 264pp. Comfort Snowberger, the daughter of undertakers, faces death in her own family for the first time in this engaging and sometimes funny novel set in rural Mississippi. (Rev: BL 3/1/05; SLJ 3/05)

8679 Wiles, Deborah. *Love, Ruby Lavender* (4–6). 2001, Harcourt $16.00 (978-0-15-202314-0). 128pp. Ruby misses her grandmother terribly when she goes to Hawaii on vacation, but over the course of the summer she finds that life goes on and that diversions arise. (Rev: BCCB 9/01; BL 5/1/01; HBG 10/01; SLJ 4/01*)

8680 Williams-Garcia, Rita. *P.S. Be Eleven* (4–7). 2013, Amistad $16.99 (978-006193862-7). 288pp. Delphine and her younger sisters are back in Brooklyn where they find things changed — Pa has a girlfriend, Uncle Darnell

is back from Vietnam but is not the same, and 6th grade poses new challenges for Delphine, who shares with her mother in California; the sequel to *One Crazy Summer* (2010). ALA Notable Children's Book; Amelia Bloomer List; Coretta Scott King Award. ∩ **e** Lexile 770L (Rev: BL 2/15/13*; HB 5–6/13; LMC 11–12/13; SLJ 6/13*)

8681 Williams, Dar. *Lights, Camera, Amalee* (5–7). 2006, Scholastic $16.99 (978-0-439-80352-6). A modest inheritance from a grandmother she barely knew gives 12-year-old Amalee the funds she needs to make a documentary about endangered species. (Rev: SLJ 9/06)

8682 Willis, Patricia. *The Barn Burner* (5–8). 2000, Clarion $15.00 (978-0-395-98409-3). In 1933, 14-year-old Ross, a runaway, becomes involved with the Warfield family whose father is away looking for work. (Rev: BCCB 5/00; BL 4/15/00; HBG 10/00; SLJ 7/00)

8683 Wilson, Nancy Hope. *Mountain Pose* (5–7). 2001, Farrar $17.00 (978-0-374-35078-9). Ellie is surprised to inherit her grandmother's farm, but when she reads the diaries left for her she begins to understand more about her family. (Rev: BCCB 6/01; BL 8/01; HB 7–8/01; HBG 10/01; SLJ 4/01*; VOYA 6/01)

8684 Winget, Dianna Dorisi. *A Smidgen of Sky* (4–6). 2012, Harcourt $16.99 (978-054780798-0). 208pp. Four years after the disappearance of her father's plane, 10-year-old Piper Lee plots to stop her mother's remarriage to a man who has an annoying 10-year-old of his own. **e** Lexile 660L (Rev: BL 11/15/12; LMC 1–2/13; SLJ 1/13)

8685 Wiseman, Eva. *No One Must Know* (4–7). 2004, Tundra paper $8.95 (978-0-88776-680-0). Thirteen-year-old Alexandra, who's been raised as a Catholic in Canada, learns that her parents are really Jewish Holocaust survivors. (Rev: BL 1/1–15/05; SLJ 6/05)

8686 Wishinsky, Frieda. *Just Call Me Joe* (2–4). 2004, Orca paper $4.99 (978-1-55143-249-6). 101pp. Ten-year-old Joseph and his teenage sister have migrated to New York from Russia in 1910 and face many difficulties as they wait for their parents to join them. (Rev: SLJ 5/04)

8687 Wood, Brenda. *The Blossoming Universe of Violet Diamond* (4–7). 2014, Penguin $16.99 (978-039925714-8). 240pp. Biracial Violet, 11, finally gets a chance to meet a member of her dead father's African American family. Lexile 670 (Rev: BL 12/1/13; LMC 5–6/14*; SLJ 3/14*)

8688 Woodson, Jacqueline. *Peace, Locomotion* (4–7). 2009, Putnam $15.99 (978-0-399-24655-5). 144pp. In letters to his little sister Lili, who is living in a separate foster home, 12-year-old Lonnie describes his life and his fears for his foster brother who is away at war. Odyssey Honor Recording 2010. ∩ (Rev: BCCB 1/09; BL 12/15/08; HB 1/09; LMC 5/09; SLJ 1/09)

8689 Yee, Lisa. *Aloha, Kanani* (3–5). Illus. by Sarah Davis. 2011, American Girl $12.95 (978-1-59369-840-9); paper $6.95 (978-1-59369-839-3). 120pp. Kanani, a 10-year-old Hawaiian girl, finds herself less content with her island life when her cousin Rachel arrives from New York City with suitcases of clothes and a dislike of swimming and surfing. (Rev: BL 5/1/11; SLJ 8/11)

8690 Yee, Lisa. *Bobby the Brave (Sometimes)* (2–4). Illus. by Dan Santat. 2010, Scholastic $15.99 (978-0-545-05594-9). 160pp. Bobby worries that his unathletic nature and asthma disappoint his former-football-star dad; he's reassured when he that sees Dad struggles with things like cooking and sewing. **e** Lexile 690L (Rev: BL 12/1/10; HB 9–10/10; SLJ 8/1/10)

8691 Yee, Paul. *A Song for Ba* (2–5). Illus. by Jan Peng Wang. 2004, Douglas & McIntyre $16.95 (978-0-88899-492-9). 32pp. Singing Chinese opera is the forte of three generations of an immigrant family, and even though his father doesn't want him to follow in these footsteps, young Wei Lim is secretly tutored by his grandfather. (Rev: BL 4/1/04; SLJ 6/04)

8692 Yep, Laurence, and Katherine S. Yep. *The Dragon's Child: A Story of Angel Island* (3–6). Illus. 2008, HarperCollins $15.99 (978-0-06-027692-8). 144pp. Yep and his niece blend fact and fiction in this account of Yep's father's journey to America in 1922. (Rev: BCCB 6/08; BL 4/1/08; SLJ 6/08)

8693 Zalben, Jane Breskin. *Brenda Berman, Wedding Expert* (2–4). Illus. by Victoria Chess. 2009, Clarion $16.00 (978-0-618-31321-1). Brenda is not at all sure about the woman named Florrie, who will marry Brenda's favorite uncle, and as for Florrie's niece Lucy . . . (Rev: BCCB 9/09; SLJ 6/09)

Fantasy, Science Fiction, and the Supernatural

8694 Abbott, Tony. *City of the Dead* (5–8). Series: The Haunting of Derek Stone. 2009, Scholastic paper $4.99 (978-0-545-03429-6). 160pp. Derek Stone's normal life ends when his father and brother Ronny are supposedly killed in a train accident; but Ronny then turns up — a changed person — and Derek learns about a similar accident many years before that has sinister overtones. (Rev: BCCB 1/09; BL 1/1–15/09; LMC 5/09)

8695 Abbott, Tony. *Kringle* (5–8). 2005, Scholastic $14.99 (978-0-439-74942-8). In early Britain a 12-year-old orphan named Kringle battles dark forces and discovers his true destiny. (Rev: BCCB 12/05; BL 10/15/05; HBG 4/06; SLJ 10/05; VOYA 2/06)

8696 Abela, Deborah. *The Ghosts of Gribblesea Pier* (3–6). 2011, Farrar $15.99 (978-0-374-36239-3). 240pp. On her 12th birthday, Aurelie learns a secret about ghosts that may help her stop a greedy villain from demolishing her family's amusement park. **e** (Rev: LMC 1–2/12; SLJ 11/1/11)

8697 Adler, C. S. *Good-bye Pink Pig* (5–7). 1986, Avon paper $2.75 (978-0-380-70175-9). Shy Amanda takes comfort in the make-believe world of her miniature pink pig — away from the elegant world of her mother and

easygoing life of her brother — until trouble enters her real and imaginary worlds and she learns to assert herself. (Rev: BCCB 2/86; BL 12/15/85)

8698 Adler, C. S. *Help, Pink Pig!* (5–7). 1991, Avon paper $2.95 (978-0-380-71156-7). Unsure of herself with her mother, Amanda retreats into the world of her miniature pink pig. (Rev: BL 5/1/90; SLJ 5/90)

8699 Ahlberg, Allan. *The Improbable Cat* (4–6). Illus. by Peter Bailey. 2004, Delacorte $9.95 (978-0-385-73186-7). 128pp. The kitten that they adopt grows ever bigger and more powerful, taking over the household, and David and his dog, Billy, are the only ones that can stop it. (Rev: SLJ 8/04)

8700 Alcock, Vivien. *The Haunting of Cassie Palmer* (5–8). 1997, Houghton Mifflin paper $6.95 (978-0-395-81653-0). Cassie finds she is blessed with second sight.

8701 Alexander, Lloyd. *The Rope Trick* (4–7). 2002, Dutton $16.99 (978-0-525-47020-5). A young magician sets out on a challenging journey to master the difficult rope trick. (Rev: BCCB 1/03; BL 10/15/02; HB 11–12/02; HBG 3/03; SLJ 9/02; VOYA 12/02)

8702 Alexander, Lloyd. *Time Cat: The Remarkable Journeys of Jason and Gareth* (4–6). Illus. by Bill Sokol. 1996, Puffin paper $6.99 (978-0-14-037827-6). Jason's cat takes him to various times and places.

8703 Alexander, R. C. *Unfamiliar Magic* (5–8). 2010, Random House $17.99 (978-0-375-85854-3). 368pp. Desi, a young witch whose mother has left on a mysterious quest, must fend for herself with only a cat in human form for companionship. Lexile 650L (Rev: BL 4/15/10; LMC 8–9/10; SLJ 4/10)

8704 Allen, Will. *Swords for Hire: Two of the Most Unlikely Heroes You'll Ever Meet* (5–8). Illus. by David Michael Beck. 2003, CenterPunch paper $6.95 (978-0-9724882-0-4). A spoof of a fantasy in which inexperienced warrior 16-year-old Sam Hatcher and his eccentric mentor Rigby Skeet set off to rescue King Olive, who has been unseated by his evil brother. (Rev: BCCB 6/03; SLJ 8/03)

8705 Almond, David. *Mouse Bird Snake Wolf* (2–5). Illus. by Dave McKean. 2013, Candlewick $17.99 (978-076365912-7). 80pp. In an alternate, strange world run by lazy gods three children — Harry, Sue, and Little Ben — create creatures made of sticks, leaves, and clay, one of which turns on its creators. Lexile 510 (Rev: BL 6/13*; HB 9–10/13; LMC 1–2/14*; SLJ 5/13)

8706 Almond, David. *Skellig* (5–8). 1999, Delacorte $16.95 (978-0-385-32653-7). Michael discovers a ragged man in his garage existing on dead flies in this novel that is part fantasy, part mystery, and part family story. (Rev: BL 2/1/99*; HB 5–6/99; HBG 10/99; SLJ 2/99)

8707 Alphin, Elaine M. *Ghost Soldier* (5–7). 2001, Henry Holt $16.95 (978-0-8050-6158-1). Alex, who has special powers, meets a Civil War ghost and helps him discover what happened to his family. (Rev: BCCB 7–8/01; BL 8/01; HBG 10/02; SLJ 8/01; VOYA 8/01)

8708 Alter, Stephen. *Ghost Letters* (5–8). 2008, Bloomsbury $16.95 (978-1-58234-739-4). Gil tosses a message in a bottle into the sea off the Massachusetts coast and receives a reply from a boy living 100 years in the past; fantasy and the supernatural combine for a chilling and thrilling story. (Rev: BL 1/1–15/08; SLJ 5/08)

8709 Alter, Stephen. *The Phantom Isles* (4–7). 2007, Bloomsbury $16.95 (978-1-58234-738-7). Sixth-graders Courtney, Orion, and Ming join with the librarian of their Massachusetts town in an effort to free ghosts that have become trapped in books. (Rev: BL 2/1/07; SLJ 3/07)

8710 Alton, Steve. *The Malifex* (5–8). 2002, Carolrhoda LB $14.95 (978-0-8225-0959-2). Sam's vacation in contemporary England is complicated by a Wiccan's daughter, the release of the ghost of Merlin's apprentice, and a battle between good and evil. (Rev: BL 9/1/02; HBG 10/03; SLJ 11/02)

8711 Amato, Mary. *The Word Eater* (4–6). Illus. 2000, Holiday House $15.95 (978-0-8234-1468-0). 146pp. Lerner's pet worm Fip likes eating paper, but when he eats paper with an object's name on it, the object itself disappears in this comic fantasy. (Rev: BCCB 9/00; BL 10/15/00; HBG 3/01; SLJ 10/00)

8712 Amoss, Berthe. *Lost Magic* (5–7). 1993, Hyperion $14.95 (978-1-56282-573-7). Fantasy and history mingle in this story set in the Middle Ages about a young girl who knows how to use both healing herbs and magic. (Rev: BL 11/1/93)

8713 Andersen, Jodi. *May Bird and the Ever After* (4–7). Illus. by Leonid Gore. 2005, Simon & Schuster $15.95 (978-0-689-86923-5). After falling into a lake near her home, 10-year-old May Bird finds herself in Ever After, a fantasy underworld inhabited by the souls of the dead. (Rev: BCCB 12/05; BL 10/15/05; HBG 4/06; SLJ 12/05; VOYA 12/05)

8714 Anderson, Jodi Lynn. *May Bird Among the Stars* (4–7). 2006, Simon & Schuster $16.95 (978-0-689-86924-2). In this sequel to *May Bird and the Ever After*, 10-year-old May Bird and her cat Somber Kitty remain trapped in the Afterlife torn between finding a way home and helping to save Ever After from the villainous Bo Cleevil. (Rev: BL 12/1/06; SLJ 11/06)

8715 Anderson, Jodi Lynn. *May Bird, Warrior Princess* (4–7). Series: May Bird. 2007, Atheneum $16.99 (978-0-689-86925-9). Three years after returning from the land of the dead, May Bird and Somber Kitty return to Ever After after falling from a rooftop in the final installment in this inventive fantasy series. (Rev: BL 11/1/07; SLJ 10/07)

8716 Anderson, Kevin J., and Ralph McQuarrie. *Stars Wars: Jabba's Palace Pop-Up Book* (2–4). Illus. 1996, Little, Brown $19.45 (978-0-316-53513-7). 14pp. A pop-up book using sound and pictures to illustrate parts of the *Star Wars* films. (Rev: BL 12/15/96)

8717 Anderson, M. T. *The Chamber in the Sky* (5–8). Series: Norumbegan Quartet. 2012, Scholastic $17.99 (978-054533493-8). 288pp. Brian and Gregory make a last-ditch effort to save the Norumbegans from their enemies by finding a lost chamber in this final installment in the series. ℮ Lexile 680L (Rev: BLO 6/12)

8718 Anderson, M. T. *The Empire of Gut and Bone* (5–8). Series: Norumbegan Quartet. 2011, Scholastic $17.99 (978-0-545-13884-0). 336pp. In the land of New Norumbega, Brian and Gregory plead with the lazy, snooty inhabitants — who live inside an alien body — to resist the Thusser invasion of Vermont; the third volume in the series. (Rev: BL 5/1/11; SLJ 7/11)

8719 Anderson, M. T. *The Game of Sunken Places* (5–8). 2004, Scholastic $16.95 (978-0-439-41660-3). Brian and Gregory, both 13, find themselves embroiled in a dangerous and suspenseful game during a stay at the spooky mansion of Gregory's eccentric Uncle Max. (Rev: BL 4/15/04*; SLJ 9/04; VOYA 6/04)

8720 Anderson, M. T. *Jasper Dash and the Flame-Pits of Delaware* (4–7). 2009, Simon & Schuster $16.99 (978-1-4169-8639-3). 432pp. Jasper Dash, Boy Technonaut, and his sidekicks Lily and Katie delve into an alternate Delaware, find art thieves, and battle strange enemies; a funny parody. ⌒ (Rev: BL 7/09; HB 9/09; SLJ 9/09)

8721 Anderson, M. T. *The Suburb Beyond the Stars* (5–8). 2010, Scholastic $17.99 (978-0-545-13882-6). 240pp. Brian and Gregory discover that Prudence is missing, a strange suburb has appeared near her Vermont home, time is not working properly, and the Thussers threaten destruction; a sequel to *The Game of Sunken Places* (2004). Lexile 620L (Rev: BL 6/10; LMC 11–12/10; SLJ 7/10)

8722 Angus, Jennifer. *In Search of Goliathus Hercules* (3–6). Illus. 2013, Whitman $17.99 (978-080752990-4). 350pp. In the 1890s a 10-year-old boy named Henri discovers he can communicate with insects — and in fact that he is becoming quite like one himself. Lexile 780 (Rev: BL 4/1/13; LMC 1–2/14; SLJ 2/13; VOYA 4/13)

8723 Appelbaum, Susannah. *The Hollow Bettle* (4–7). 2009, Knopf $16.99 (978-0-375-85173-5). 416pp. Eleven-year-old Ivy sets out to find her missing uncle, a healer, in this first installment in a fantasy involving magic, herbs, and poisons. (Rev: BL 6/1–15/09; 12/09; LMC 10/09)

8724 Appelbaum, Susannah. *The Tasters Guild* (4–7). Illus. by Jennifer Taylor. Series: Poisons of Caux. 2010, Knopf $16.99 (978-0-375-85174-2); LB $19.99 (978-0-375-95174-9). 384pp. In this exciting second installment, Poison Ivy and her friends battle new dangers as they work to save King Verdigris. (Rev: BL 11/15/10; SLJ 8/10)

8725 Applegate, K. A. *Animorphs #1: The Invasion* (5–8). 1996, Scholastic paper $4.99 (978-0-590-62977-5). Jake, an average suburban kid, is confronted one night by a creature from space who teaches him how to morph into the forms of other creatures. (Rev: VOYA 12/96)

8726 Arbuthnott, Gill. *The Keepers' Tattoo* (5–8). 2010, Scholastic $17.99 (978-0-545-17166-3). 432pp. In a land called Archipelago, 15-year-old Nyssa and her twin brother bear tattoos that hold the secret to the ancient cult of the Keepers; but her brother is being held by the cruel Alaric, and Nyssa must rescue him. ℮ Lexile 790L (Rev: BLO 5/15/10; LMC 10/10; SLJ 7/10)

8727 Archer, E. *Geek Fantasy Novel* (5–8). 2011, Scholastic $17.99 (978-0-545-16040-7). 320pp. Geeky Ralph, 14, visits his British cousins for the summer and discovers there exactly why his parents have always forbidden him to make wishes; a quirky, humorous fantasy. ℮ Lexile 940L (Rev: BL 4/1/11; LMC 8–9/11; SLJ 11/1/11; VOYA 4/11)

8728 Arkin, Alan. *The Lemming Condition* (4–7). Illus. by Joan Sandin. 1989, HarperCollins paper $9.95 (978-0-06-250048-9). Bubber opposes the mass suicide of his companions in this interesting fable.

8729 Armstrong, Alan. *Looking for Marco Polo* (4–7). Illus. by Tim Jessell. 2009, Random House $16.99 (978-0-375-83321-2); LB $19.99 (978-0-375-93321-9). 304pp. Eleven-year-old Mark hears many stories about famed explorer Marco Polo when recovering from an asthma attack while searching for his missing father in the Gobi Desert. Lexile 830L (Rev: BL 8/09; SLJ 12/09)

8730 Armstrong, Alan. *Whittington* (5–8). Illus. by S. D. Schindler. 2005, Random House LB $16.99 (978-0-375-92864-2). Happy to have found a place to live, Whittington the cat regales the other barnyard animals with tales of his famous forebears. (Rev: BL 5/15/05; SLJ 8/05*)

8731 Armstrong, K. L., and M. A. Marr. *Loki's Wolves* (4–6). Illus. by Vivienne To. Series: Blackwell Pages. 2013, Little, Brown $16.99 (978-031620496-5). 358pp. The first volume in a trilogy in which descendants of Norse gods — including South Dakota middle-schoolers Matt, Fen, and Laurie — must challenge monsters in a final battle to save humanity. ⌂ (Rev: BL 3/15/13; LMC 10/13; SLJ 7/13)

8732 Arnold, Louise. *Golden and Grey (An Unremarkable Boy and a Rather Remarkable Ghost)* (4–6). 2005, Simon & Schuster $15.95 (978-0-689-87473-4). Two misfits — a ghost and an 11-year-old boy — become friends and help each other in their respective communities. (Rev: BL 6/1–15/05)

8733 Arnold, Louise. *Golden and Grey: The Nightmares That Ghosts Have* (4–6). 2006, Simon & Schuster $15.95 (978-0-689-87586-1). In this sequel to *Golden and Grey: An Unremarkable Boy and a Rather Remarkable Ghost*, 11-year-old Tom Golden and his ghostly friend Grey Arthur try to figure out what's causing ghosts to disappear. (Rev: BL 10/15/06; HBG 4/07; LMC 1/07; SLJ 9/06)

8734 Arntson, Steven. *The Wikkeling* (5–8). Illus. by Daniela Jaglenka Terrazzini. 2011, Running Press $18 (978-0-7624-3903-4). 256pp. In the dystopian city of the Addition, Henrietta and her friends Gary and Rose are being menaced by a yellow creature called the Wikkeling that gives them headaches. (Rev: BL 5/1/11; SLJ 5/11)

8735 Arold, Marliese. *Ghost Park: The Vanishing Gate/ The Imposter. Bks. 1 and 2* (4–6). Trans. from German by Alexis L. Spry. Illus. by Barbara Scholz. 2007, North-South $12.95 (978-0-7358-2099-9). 216pp. Max and

Sophie encounter magic and spirits as caretakers of an odd estate in these stories originally published in German. (Rev: SLJ 8/07)

8736 Asimov, Janet. *Norby and the Terrified Taxi* (4–8). 1997, Walker $15.95 (978-0-8027-8642-5). Norby, the bungling robot, is kidnapped, and while trying to find him, Jeff and his friends stumble on a plot by Garc the Great to take over the Federation. This is one of a large series of Norby books suitable for middle school readers. (Rev: BL 1/1–15/98; SLJ 12/97)

8737 Asimov, Janet. *The Package in Hyperspace* (5–7). 1988, Walker LB $14.85 (978-0-8027-6823-0). Two space-wrecked children must fend for themselves as they try to reach Merkina. (Rev: BL 1/1/89; SLJ 11/88)

8738 Asimov, Janet, and Isaac Asimov. *Norby and the Invaders* (5–8). 1985, Walker LB $10.85 (978-0-8027-6607-6). Jeff and his unusual robot Norby travel to a planet to help one of Norby's ancestors. Part of a series that includes *Norby's Other Secret*. (Rev: BL 3/1/86; SLJ 2/86)

8739 Asimov, Janet, and Isaac Asimov. *Norby and Yobo's Great Adventure* (5–8). 1989, Walker LB $13.85 (978-0-8027-6894-0). Norby the robot time-travels to help Admiral Yobo of Mars to trace his family roots. Part of a series that also includes *Norby Down to Earth*. (Rev: BL 10/15/89)

8740 Asimov, Janet, and Isaac Asimov. *Norby Finds a Villain* (4–8). 1987, Walker LB $13.85 (978-0-8027-6711-0). Norby the robot and his human friends set out to free Pera, who has been robot-napped by the traitor Ing, in this sixth book of the Norby series. Also use *Norby and the Queen's Necklace* (1986). (Rev: BL 1/1/88; SLJ 11/87)

8741 Auch, Mary Jane. *I Was a Third Grade Spy* (2–4). Illus. 2001, Holiday House $15.95 (978-0-8234-1576-2). 96pp. Young Josh and Artful the dog who can now speak take turns narrating their entertaining efforts to win the talent show. (Rev: BCCB 7–8/01; BL 5/1/01; HBG 10/01; SLJ 7/01)

8742 Augarde, Steve. *The Various* (4–8). 2004, Random House LB $17.99 (978-0-385-75037-0). Midge, a 12-year-old girl on vacation in the countryside, discovers a tribe of little people known as the Various, who are not as helpless as they seem. (Rev: BL 12/15/03; SLJ 3/04)

8743 Avi. *Bright Shadow* (5–8). 1994, Simon & Schuster paper $4.99 (978-0-689-71783-3). At the death of the great wizard, Morenna finds she possesses the last five wishes in the world. (Rev: SLJ 12/85)

8744 Avi. *The Mayor of Central Park* (3–6). Illus. by Brian Floca. 2003, HarperCollins LB $16.89 (978-0-06-051556-0). 208pp. In New York City's Central Park in 1900, Oscar the squirrel leads the fight against an invading rat pack led by Big Daddy Duds. (Rev: BL 8/03; HBG 4/04; SLJ 12/03)

8745 Avi. *Poppy* (4–6). Illus. 1995, Orchard LB $16.99 (978-0-531-08783-1). Tragedy occurs when a young deer mouse named Poppy disobeys her father and ventures out into the night with her boyfriend. (Rev: BCCB 1/96; BL 10/15/95*; SLJ 12/95*)

8746 Avi. *Poppy and Rye* (4–6). Illus. 1998, Avon $16.99 (978-0-380-97638-6). 160pp. Fearless deer mouse Poppy travels to visit another mouse family, where she foils the plans of some beavers to build a dam and also falls in love with another mouse named Rye. (Rev: BL 5/15/98; HB 7/98; HBG 10/98; SLJ 6/98)

8747 Avi. *Ragweed* (4–6). Illus. 1999, Avon $17.99 (978-0-380-97690-4). Ragweed, a brave young mouse, becomes friends with members of a hip band and leads the opposition against Silversides, an angry white cat. (Rev: BCCB 10/99; BL 5/15/99; HBG 10/99; SLJ 7/99)

8748 Avi. *The Seer of Shadows* (4–7). 2008, HarperCollins $16.99 (978-0-06-000015-8). Horace, a photographer's apprentice in 1872, is told by his boss to fake photographs of ghosts, but discovers that he has the ability to conjure actual ghosts with his camera. ☊ (Rev: BL 2/15/08; SLJ 2/08)

8749 Avi. *Something Upstairs: A Tale of Ghosts* (5–7). 1988, Orchard LB $16.99 (978-0-531-08382-6); paper $5.99 (978-0-380-70853-6). Kenny moves into a house in Rhode Island that is haunted by the ghost of a slave who was murdered in 1800. (Rev: BCCB 9/88; BL 11/1/88; SLJ 10/88)

8750 Avi. *Strange Happenings: Five Tales of Transformation* (4–7). 2006, Harcourt $15.00 (978-0-15-205790-9). Shape-shifting and invisibility are among the transformations in this collection of five fantasy tales. (Rev: BL 3/15/06; SLJ 5/06)

8751 Babbitt, Natalie. *The Search for Delicious* (4–7). Illus. by author. 1969, Farrar $17.00 (978-0-374-36534-9). The innocent task of polling the kingdom's subjects for personal food preferences provokes civil war in a zestful spoof of taste and society.

8752 Babbitt, Natalie. *Tuck Everlasting* (4–6). 1975, Farrar $16.00 (978-0-374-37848-6). 160pp. Violence erupts when the Tuck family members discover that their secret about a spring that brings immortality has been discovered.

8753 Baccalario, Pierdomenico. *The Long-Lost Map* (4–6). Trans. by Leah Janeczko. Series: Ulysses Moore. 2006, Scholastic $12.99 (978-0-439-77439-0). 272pp. Jason and Rick are investigating in ancient Egypt while Jason's twin Julia, back in Cornwall, deals with Oblivia Newton in this exciting, fast-paced sequel to *Door to Time* (2005). (Rev: BL 7/06; SLJ 8/06)

8754 Bach, Shelby. *Of Giants and Ice* (4–7). Series: Ever Afters. 2012, Simon & Schuster $15.99 (978-1-4424-3146-1). 352pp. Young Rory emerges from the shadow of her celebrity parents when she finds herself playing a role in a real magical tale full of fairy-tale fantasy. Lexile 700 (Rev: BLO 8/12; LMC 1–2/13; SLJ 9/12)

8755 Bachmann, Stefan. *The Peculiar* (4–7). 2012, HarperCollins $16.99 (978-0-06-219518-0). 376pp. After fairies lose the war with humans, half-fairy half-human changeling children Bartholomew and Hettie find themselves embroiled in mystery and intrigue in this steam-

punk fantasy. ☊ **e** Lexile 760L (Rev: BL 9/15/12; HB 11–12/12; LMC 3–4/13; SLJ 10/12)

8756 Bachmann, Stefan. *The Whatnot* (4–7). 2013, Greenwillow $16.99 (978-006219521-0). 432pp. Bartholomew Kettle is on a mission to rescue his sister from the faerie world before war breaks out between the humans and the faeries, and he will need the help of a street urchin named Pikey who has the ability to see into the faery realm from the human world. ☊ **e** Lexile 680 (Rev: BLO 11/1/13; SLJ 10/13; VOYA 2/14)

8757 Baggott, Julianna. *The Ever Breath* (4–6). 2009, Delacorte $16.99 (978-0-385-73761-6); LB $19.99 (978-0-385-90676-0). 240pp. After their father goes missing, twins Truman and Camille follow a secret passageway to the Breath World and encounter unusual creatures as they look for the Ever Breath, a magical stone that maintains balance between worlds. **e** Lexile 680L (Rev: BL 10/1/09; LMC 11–12/09; SLJ 1/10)

8758 Baggott, Julianna. *The Prince of Fenway Park* (5–8). 2009, HarperCollins $16.99 (978-0-06-087242-7). 336pp. Twelve-year-old Oscar Egg holds the power to lift the curse affecting the Boston Red Sox. (Rev: BL 5/15/09; SLJ 5/09)

8759 Bailey, Carolyn Sherwin. *Miss Hickory* (4–6). Illus. by Ruth Gannett. 1946, Puffin paper $5.99 (978-0-14-030956-0). 128pp. The adventures of a doll made from an apple branch with a hickory nut head. Newbery Award winner, 1947.

8760 Bailey, Len. *Clabbernappers* (4–6). 2005, Tor $17.95 (978-0-7653-0981-5). 240pp. An exciting land of pirates and chess characters awaits junior rodeo champ Danny Ray when he ventures through a mysterious door at an amusement park. (Rev: BL 1/1–15/05; SLJ 6/05)

8761 Baker-Smith, Grahame. *FArTHER* (2–4). Illus. by author. 2013, Candlewick $17.99 (978-0-7636-6370-4). 40pp. A father's dreams of flying are realized by his son in this beautifully illustrated, evocative picture book. Kate Greenaway Medal. (Rev: BLO 7/13; SLJ 4/13)

8762 Baker, E. D. *The Dragon Princess* (5–8). Series: Tales of the Frog Princess. 2008, Bloomsbury $16.99 (978-159990194-7). 250pp. In hopes of controlling an unfortunate flaw — she turns into a dragon whenever she's upset — 15-year-old princess Millie appeals to the Blue Witch for help in this lighthearted tale. ☊ **e** Lexile 820L (Rev: BLO 11/15/08; VOYA 12/08)

8763 Baker, E. D. *Dragon's Breath* (5–7). 2003, Bloomsbury $15.95 (978-1-58234-858-2). Esmeralda and Eadric help Aunt Grassina find ingredients needed to break the spell that turned Grassina's true love, Haywood, into an otter in this humorous sequel to *The Frog Princess* (2002). (Rev: BL 4/15/04; SLJ 12/03; VOYA 4/04)

8764 Baker, E. D. *Fairy Lies* (5–8). Series: Wings: A Fairy Tale. 2012, Bloomsbury $16.99 (978-159990550-1). 256pp. Half-fairy Tamisin's half-goblin boyfriend Jak endeavors to rescue her when she's kidnapped by King Oberon in this fast-paced sequel to *Wings: A Fairy Tale* (2008). (Rev: BLO 2/15/12; LMC 3–4/12; SLJ 3/12; VOYA 2/12)

8765 Baker, E. D. *The Frog Princess* (5–8). 2002, Bloomsbury $15.95 (978-1-58234-799-8). When Princess Esmeralda kisses the frog, she turns into one herself in this humorous twist on the traditional saga. (Rev: BCCB 2/03; BL 11/15/02; SLJ 1/03; VOYA 12/02)

8766 Baker, E. D. *The Salamander Spell* (4–7). 2007, Bloomsbury $16.95 (978-1-59990-018-6). In this prequel to *The Frog Princess* (2002), 13-year-old Grassina is tired of being overshadowed by her older sister Chartreuse and, accompanied by her snake friend Pippa, runs away to the swamp where she discovers her powers, meets a young magician, and saves the kingdom from werewolves. (Rev: BL 9/15/07; SLJ 12/07)

8767 Baker, E. D. *Wings: A Fairy Tale* (5–8). 2008, Bloomsbury $16.95 (978-1-59990-193-0). Could Tamisin really be a goblin? When she grows wings, she realizes she must be from another world. (Rev: BL 5/15/08)

8768 Baker, Jeannie. *The Hidden Forest* (2–4). Illus. 2000, Greenwillow LB $16.89 (978-0-688-15761-6). 32pp. In this fantasy, Ben is led by his friend Sophie into the underwater world of a kelp forest where they encounter a whale. (Rev: BL 9/1/00; HB 7/00; HBG 10/00; SLJ 5/00)

8769 Ball, Justin, and Evan Croker. *Space Dogs* (4–7). 2006, Knopf $15.95 (978-0-375-83256-7). When a powerful force threatens to destroy Gersbach, the planet's inhabitants dispatch dog-shaped vehicles to Earth in a desperate attempt to head off disaster; they end up battling in the front yard of Amy and Lucy Buckley in this humorous, action-packed story. (Rev: BL 6/1–15/06; SLJ 8/06)

8770 Banks, Kate. *The Magician's Apprentice* (5–8). Illus. by Peter Sís. 2012, Farrar $16.99 (978-037434716-1). 224pp. A complex tale in which 16-year-old Baz becomes apprentice to a magician and makes a long and mystical trip through the desert learning about various truths. ∩ **e** Lexile 740L (Rev: BL 8/12; HB 9–10/12; LMC 3–4/13; SLJ 8/1/12)

8771 Banks, Lynne Reid. *Angela and Diabola* (5–8). 1997, Avon $15.95 (978-0-380-97562-4). A wicked romp that chronicles the lives of twins, the angelic Angela and the truly horrible and destructive Diabola. (Rev: SLJ 7/97)

8772 Banks, Lynne Reid. *Harry the Poisonous Centipede's Big Adventure* (3–5). Illus. 2001, HarperCollins LB $14.89 (978-0-06-029394-9). 192pp. Young centipede Harry finds himself trapped with many of his friends, and they have great adventures finding their way home after escaping. (Rev: BL 6/1–15/01; HBG 10/01; SLJ 5/01)

8773 Banks, Lynne Reid. *The Key to the Indian* (4–8). Series: Indian in the Cupboard. 1998, Avon $16.00 (978-0-380-97717-8). In the fifth book of the Indian in the Cupboard series, Omri and Dad return to the time of Little Bear to help the Iroquois deal with European meddlers. (Rev: BL 11/15/98; HBG 3/99; SLJ 12/98)

8774 Banks, Lynne Reid. *The Mystery of the Cupboard* (4–8). Series: Indian in the Cupboard. 1993, HarperCollins paper $5.99 (978-0-380-72013-2). In this, the fourth book in the series, the young hero Omri uncovers a diary that reveals secrets about his magical cupboard. (Rev: BCCB 6/93; BL 4/1/93; HB 7–8/93; SLJ 6/93; VOYA 10/93)

8775 Banks, Lynne Reid. *The Return of the Indian* (5–7). Illus. by William Celdart. Series: Indian in the Cupboard. 1986, Doubleday $16.95 (978-0-385-23497-9); paper $5.99 (978-0-380-70284-8). Omri brings his plastic Indian figures to life and discovers that his friend Little Bear has been wounded and needs his help. (Rev: BL 9/15/86; HB 11–12/86; SLJ 11/86)

8776 Barlow, Steve, and Steve Skidmore. *Whizzard!* (4–6). Illus. by Fiona Land. Series: Tales of the Dark Forest. 2003, Collins paper $8.95 (978-0-00-710864-0). 252pp. In this fast-paced comic fantasy, Tym, the bumbling apprentice to the local wizard, cooks up a magical potion that endows him with the power to travel at super-fast speed. (Rev: SLJ 2/04)

8777 Barnhill, Kelly. *Iron Hearted Violet* (4–7). Illus. by Iacopo Bruno. 2012, Little, Brown $16.99 (978-0-316-05673-1). 432pp. Princess Violet, a lover of good stories, and her friend Demetrius take on the legendary Nybbas in this well-crafted story. ∩ **e** (Rev: BL 11/1/12; HB 11–12/12; LMC 3–4/13; SLJ 12/12; VOYA 10/12)

8778 Barnhill, Kelly. *The Mostly True Story of Jack* (5–8). 2011, Little, Brown $16.99 (978-0-316-05670-0). 323pp. Dumped with his aunt and uncle, Jack — who has considered himself virtually invisible up till now — soon realizes that there is something strange going on in Hazelwood, Iowa, and he is suddenly the center of attention. ∩ **e** Lexile 740L (Rev: BL 8/11*; LMC 10/11; SLJ 9/1/11; VOYA 8/11)

8779 Barnholdt, Lauren. *Hailey Twitch and the Campground Itch* (2–4). Illus. by Suzanne Beaky. Series: Hailey Twitch. 2011, Sourcebooks paper $6.99 (978-1-4022-2446-1). 144pp. Hailey enjoys a camping vacation with family and friends, but her sprite friend Maybelle's magic seems to be misfiring. (Rev: SLJ 7/11)

8780 Barnholdt, Lauren. *Hailey Twitch Is Not a Snitch* (2–4). Illus. by Suzanne Beaky. Series: Hailey Twitch. 2010, Sourcebooks paper $9.99 (978-14022244-4-7). 160pp. Second-grader Hailey takes responsibility for the havoc created by Maybelle, a sprite who lives in Hailey's dollhouse and is determined to prove that she is not a total follower of rules. Also use *Hailey Twitch and the Great Teacher Switch* (2010). (Rev: BL 7/10; LMC 8–9/10)

8781 Barrett, Tracy. *Cold in Summer* (4–7). 2003, Henry Holt $16.95 (978-0-8050-7052-1). An enjoyable story about a lonely girl who slowly comes to realize that her new friend is a ghost. (Rev: BL 4/1/03; HB 5–6/03; HBG 10/03; SLJ 7/03; VOYA 6/03)

8782 Barrett, Tracy. *On Etruscan Time* (5–8). 2005, Henry Holt $16.95 (978-0-8050-7569-4). Hector, 11, finds himself struggling to rescue an Etruscan boy from execution, in this time-travel fantasy set on an archaeological dig in Italy. (Rev: BL 6/1–15/05; SLJ 7/05)

8783 Barrie, J. M. *Peter Pan* (5–8). 1995, NAL paper $4.95 (978-0-451-52088-3). The classic tale of the boy who wouldn't grow up and of his adventures with the Darling children. (Rev: BL 12/15/87)

8784 Barrie, J. M. *Peter Pan* (5–7). 2000, Chronicle $19.95 (978-0-8118-2297-8). Using illustrations from 15 different artists, this is an unusual, unabridged edition of Barrie's classic fantasy. (Rev: BL 11/1/00; HBG 3/01; SLJ 12/00)

8785 Barron, T. A. *Atlantis Rising* (4–8). 2013, Philomel $17.99 (978-039925757-5). 384pp. A young thief named Promi and a young girl named Atlanta are involved in a battle of good against evil that is linked to the creation of Atlantis. (Rev: BL 7/13; LMC 3–4/14; SLJ 10/13)

8786 Barron, T. A. *Doomraga's Revenge* (5–8). Series: Merlin's Dragon Trilogy. 2009, Philomel $16.99 (978-0-399-25212-9). 256pp. The powerful dragon Basil tackles threats to Avalon while Merlin is preoccupied with personal woes; the middle volume in the trilogy. (Rev: BL 9/1/09; LMC 11–12/09; SLJ 9/09)

8787 Barron, T. A. *Tree Girl* (4–8). 2001, Putnam $14.99 (978-0-399-23457-6). Rowanna, 9, discovers she is descended from tree spirits after she is lured into the woods by a shape-shifting bear cub in this book for middle-graders. (Rev: BCCB 10/01; BL 11/1/01; HBG 3/02; SLJ 10/01; VOYA 10/01)

8788 Barrowman, John, and Carole E. Barrowman. *Hollow Earth* (5–8). 2012, Aladdin $16.99 (978-144245852-9). 400pp. Twelve-year-old twins Matt and Emily have the power to bring art to life, and this puts them in peril from ancient forces. ℮ Lexile 880L (Rev: BL 12/1/12; LMC 5–6/13; SLJ 1/13)

8789 Barrows, Annie. *Ivy and Bean* (1–3). Illus. by Sophie Blackall. 2006, Chronicle $14.95 (978-0-8118-4903-6). 116pp. Seven-year-old Bean takes an instant dislike to Ivy when she moves in across the street, but when Ivy comes to Bean's rescue the two begin to develop a friendship; excellent artwork adds to the story. (Rev: BCCB 6/06; BL 4/1/06*; HBG 10/06; LMC 1/07; SLJ 7/06)

8790 Barrows, Annie. *Ivy and Bean and the Ghost That Had to Go* (1–3). Illus. by Sophie Blackall. 2006, Chronicle $14.95 (978-0-8118-4910-4). Best friends Ivy and Bean try to run off the ghost that's haunting the girls' bathroom at school. (Rev: BL 10/15/06; SLJ 2/07)

8791 Barry, Dave, and Ridley Pearson. *The Bridge to Never Land* (4–6). Series: Never Land. 2011, Hyperion/Disney $18.99 (978-1-4231-3865-5). 448pp. Sarah and Aidan find themselves in danger when they follow clues to the origins of Peter Pan. ♫ (Rev: BL 7/11; SLJ 9/1/11)

8792 Barry, Dave, and Ridley Pearson. *Peter and the Secret of Rundoon* (4–7). Illus. by Greg Call. Series: Starcatchers. 2007, Hyperion $18.99 (978-0-7868-3788-5). In this action-packed conclusion to the Starcatchers trilogy, Peter (Pan, that is) saves the world long before ever meeting Wendy and her siblings. (Rev: BL 11/15/07; SLJ 10/07)

8793 Barry, Dave, and Ridley Pearson. *Peter and the Shadow Thieves* (5–8). Illus. by Greg Call. 2006, Hyperion $18.99 (978-0-7868-3787-8). In this sequel to *Peter and the Starcatchers* (2005), the forever-young Peter and Tinker Bell race to foil the evil plans of Lord Ombra. (Rev: BL 6/1–15/06; SLJ 8/06; VOYA 8/06)

8794 Barry, Dave, and Ridley Pearson. *Peter and the Sword of Mercy* (4–6). Illus. by Greg Call. Series: Starcatchers. 2009, Hyperion/Disney $18.99 (978-1-4231-2134-3). 516pp. This action-packed adventure set in 1901 involves Peter and Molly's daughter Wendy and a magical sword that once belonged to Charlemagne. ℮ Lexile 710L (Rev: BL 2/1/10; LMC 5–6/10; SLJ 3/10; VOYA 2/10)

8795 Base, Graeme. *TruckDogs* (4–6). Illus. 2004, Abrams $16.95 (978-0-8109-5031-3). 192pp. Creatures that are part animal, part vehicle — such as TruckSheep and TruckDogs — star in this story about an assault on their town by the RottWheeler gang. (Rev: BL 2/15/04; SLJ 3/04)

8796 Bateman, Colin. *Running with the Reservoir Pups* (4–7). 2005, Delacorte LB $17.99 (978-0-440-42048-4). Eddie becomes involved with a gang of tough Belfast kids and ends up rescuing kidnapped babies from a horrible fate in this action-packed fantasy, the first installment in a trilogy. (Rev: BL 3/1/05; SLJ 1/05)

8797 Baucom, Ian. *Through the Skylight* (4–6). Illus. by Justin Gerard. 2013, Atheneum $17.99 (978-141691777-9). 400pp. Jared, Shireen, and Miranda, in Venice for a semester with their parents, find themselves embroiled in a dangerous and magical adventure involving animals with strange powers, an evil monk, and children from the time of the Crusades. Lexile 700 (Rev: BL 3/15/13; SLJ 5/13; VOYA 4/13)

8798 Bauer, A. C. E. *Come Fall* (4–7). 2010, Random House $15.99 (978-0-375-85825-3). 240pp. Misfits Salman, Lu, and Blos become friends in 7th grade and deal with bullies, dysfunctional homes, and other problems with some input from Puck, Oberon, and Titania in this fantasy inspired by *A Midsummer Night's Dream*. ℮ (Rev: BL 7/10; LMC 10/10; SLJ 9/1/10)

8799 Bauer, Marion Dane. *The Blue Ghost* (2–4). Illus. by Suling Wang. 2005, Random $11.95 (978-0-375-83179-9). 96pp. Nine-year-old Liz is summoned into the past to help a family of children and a blue ghost. (Rev: BL 9/1/05; SLJ 8/05)

8800 Bauer, Marion Dane. *The Golden Ghost* (2–3). Illus. by Peter Ferguson. 2011, Random House $12.99 (978-0-375-86649-4); LB $15.99 (978-0-375-96649-1). 96pp. A canine ghost awaits Delsie and her friend Todd as they investigated an abandoned house. ℮ (Rev: BL 3/15/11; SLJ 4/11)

8801 Bauer, Marion Dane. *The Red Ghost* (2–4). Illus. by Peter Ferguson. 2008, Random $11.99 (978-0-375-84081-4). A doll that seemed perfect for Jenna's little sister turns out to have sad associations in this companion to *The Blue Ghost* (2005). (Rev: BL 4/15/08; SLJ 4/08)

8802 Bauer, Marion Dane. *The Secret of the Painted House* (3–5). Illus. by Leonid Gore. 2007, Random $11.99 (978-0-375-84079-1). Nine-year-old Emily discovers an old playhouse in the woods inhabited by a little girl ghost who tries to hold Emily and her brother captive. (Rev: BCCB 10/07; BL 5/1/07; SLJ 8/07)

8803 Bauer, Marion Dane. *Touch the Moon* (5–7). Illus. by Alix Berenzy. 1987, Houghton Mifflin $15.00 (978-0-89919-526-1). Angry when she doesn't get a real horse, Jennifer throws away her toy horse gift and learns a lesson in responsibility. (Rev: BCCB 9/87; BL 9/15/87; HB 9–10/87)

8804 Bauer, Marion Dane. *The Very Little Princess* (2–4). Illus. by Elizabeth Sayles. 2010, Random House $12.99 (978-0-375-85691-4); LB $15.99 (978-0-375-95691-1). 128pp. Visiting her grandmother for the first time, 10-year-old Zoey discovers a tiny china doll that comes to life and starts ordering her around. (Rev: BL 11/15/09; LMC 3–4/10; SLJ 4/1/10)

8805 Baum, L. Frank. *The Marvelous Land of Oz* (4–6). Illus. by John R. Neill. 1985, Morrow $25.99 (978-0-688-05439-7). 288pp. This is a facsimile of the original 1904 edition with the illustrations in both color and black and white. Other titles in this series are published by Peter Smith and Amereon in hard cover and Dover and Puffin in paperback.

8806 Baum, L. Frank. *The Wonderful Wizard of Oz* (4–8). Illus. by W. W. Denslow. 2000, HarperCollins $24.99 (978-0-06-029323-9). A handsome facsimile of the 1900 publication on high-quality paper and featuring 24 original color plates and 130 two-color drawings. (Rev: BL 12/1/00)

8807 Baum, L. Frank. *The Wonderful Wizard of Oz: A Commemorative Pop-Up* (4–8). Illus. by Robert Sabuda. 2001, Simon & Schuster $24.95 (978-0-689-81751-9). An extraordinary pop-up version of the classic fantasy told in a condensed text. (Rev: BL 12/1/00; HB 9–10/00; HBG 3/01; SLJ 11/00)

8808 Baum, Roger S. *Dorothy of Oz* (4–6). Illus. by Elizabeth Miles. 1989, Morrow $26.99 (978-0-688-07848-5). 176pp. A story true to the original in which Dorothy is called back to Oz because the Tin Woodman, the Scarecrow, and the Cowardly Lion need help. (Rev: BL 1/1/90; SLJ 10/89)

8809 Bawden, Nina. *Off the Road* (5–9). 1998, Clarion $16.00 (978-0-395-91321-5). In this science fiction novel set in a time when the elderly are exterminated, 11-year-old Tom follows his grandfather to the "savage jungle" Outside the Wall, where the old man hopes to escape his fate, and discovers a different kind of society. (Rev: BCCB 10/98; BL 9/15/98; HBG 10/99; SLJ 11/98)

8810 Beck, Ian. *The Secret History of Tom Trueheart* (4–7). 2007, HarperCollins $16.99 (978-0-06-115210-8). Twelve-year-old Tom Trueheart must try to track down his six older brothers when they mysteriously disappear, suspected victims of the enemy of storytelling. ∩ (Rev: SLJ 2/07)

8811 Beck, W. H. *Malcolm at Midnight* (4–6). Illus. by Brian Lies. 2012, Houghton Mifflin $16.99 (978-0-547-68100-9). 272pp. Malcolm, a small rat adopted by Mr. Binney's 5th-grade class, must investigate the disappearance of Aggy the iguana, one of the members of the Midnight Academy formed by classroom pets at night. ∩ e Lexile 540L (Rev: BL 9/1/12; LMC 3–4/13*; SLJ 10/12)

8812 Becker, Bonny. *Holbrook: A Lizard's Tale* (4–6). Illus. by Abby Carter. 2006, Clarion $15.00 (978-0-618-71458-2). 148pp. Holbrook the lizard takes his best painting to the city in hopes of artistic recognition; this complex animal adventure features take-offs on art world luminaries, the outwitting of the carnivorous Count Rumolde, and revelations about city life. (Rev: BL 1/1–15/07; SLJ 12/06)

8813 Becker, Tom. *Lifeblood* (5–8). Series: Darkside. 2008, Scholastic $16.99 (978-0-545-03742-6). 279pp. In this second action-packed installment in the series, Jonathan, born of a Darkside mother and Lightside father, travels between these contemporary and fantasy worlds as he tries to solve a series of murders. (Rev: LMC 3/08; SLJ 3/09)

8814 Bell, Hilari. *Crown of Earth* (5–8). Series: The Shield, Sword, and Crown. 2009, Simon & Schuster $16.99 (978-1-4169-0598-1). 272pp. In this fast-paced stand-alone sequel to *Sword of Waters* (2008), Prince Edoran endeavors to save the life of the hostage Weasel by enlisting the help of his friend Arisa. Lexile 880L (Rev: BL 12/1/09; SLJ 10/09)

8815 Bell, Hilari. *The Goblin Gate* (5–8). Series: The Goblin Wood. 2010, HarperTeen $16.99 (978-0-06-165102-1). 384pp. Jeriah goes off in search of the spell that will open the gate to the otherworld and release his brother; the sequel to 2003's *The Goblin Wood*. e Lexile 750L (Rev: HB 9–10/10; SLJ 10/1/10)

8816 Bell, Hilari. *Shield of Stars* (5–8). Series: The Shield, the Sword and the Crown. 2007, Simon & Schuster $16.99 (978-1-4169-0594-3). Weasel, 14 and a reformed pickpocket, sets out to rescue Justice Holis, who has given him a home and a job, from the wicked ruler of Deorthas. (Rev: BL 5/15/07; SLJ 5/07)

8817 Bell, Hilari. *The Wizard Test* (5–8). 2005, HarperCollins LB $16.89 (978-0-06-059941-6). Fourteen-year-old Dayven is not thrilled when he learns he has magical abilities until he undergoes wizard training. (Rev: BL 2/1/05; SLJ 3/05)

8818 Bell, Ted. *Nick of Time* (5–8). 2008, St. Martin's $17.95 (978-0-312-38068-7). Villains from the past and present (that is, 1939) show up when plucky young Nick opens a sea chest washed up near his family's lighthouse. (Rev: BL 4/1/08; SLJ 5/08)

8819 Bellairs, John. *The Ghost in the Mirror* (5–8). 1994, Puffin paper $5.99 (978-0-14-034934-4). Fourteen-year-old Rose and white witch Mrs. Zimmerman are transported in time to 1828 on a secret mission. (Rev: SLJ 3/93)

8820 Benz, Derek, and Jon S. Lewis. *The Brimstone Key* (5–8). Series: Grey Griffins: The Clockwork Chronicles. 2010, Little, Brown $15.99 (978-0-316-04522-3). 384pp. Max, Ernie, Natalia, and Hailey use their unusual powers to fight the clockworks — robots who are forming an army — at the Iron Bridge Academy; the first installment in a steampunk trilogy. (Rev: BLO 4/15/10; LMC 8–9/10; SLJ 8/10; VOYA 10/10)

8821 Berkeley, Jon. *The Hidden Boy* (3–6). Series: Bell Hoot Fables. 2010, HarperCollins $16.99 (978-0-06-168758-7). 272pp. Thinking they've won a vacation, members of the Flint family find themselves instead in a very strange place — suddenly minus son Theo — and Bea must find her little brother. Lexile 800L (Rev: BL 12/1/09; LMC 3–4/10; SLJ 4/10)

8822 Berkeley, Jon. *The Lightning Key* (4–7). Illus. by Brandon Dorman. Series: The Wednesday Tales. 2009, HarperCollins $16.99 (978-0-06-075513-3). 399pp. In this fast-moving conclusion to the trilogy Miles sets off in hot pursuit of the thieves who stole the powerful Tiger's Egg, having many adventures on the way. (Rev: SLJ 7/09; VOYA 2/09)

8823 Berkeley, Jon. *The Palace of Laughter: The Wednesday Tales No. 1* (4–7). Illus. by Brandon Dorman. Series: Julie Andrews Collection. 2006, HarperCollins $16.99 (978-0-06-075507-2). Miles Wednesday, an 11-year-old orphan, joins forces with a talking tiger and a diminutive angel named Little to rescue Little's mentor from the Palace of Laughter. (Rev: SLJ 8/06)

8824 Berry, Julie Gardner. *The Rat Brain Fiasco* (3–6). Illus. by Sally Faye Gardner. Series: Splurch Academy for Disruptive Boys. 2010, Grosset & Dunlap paper $6.99 (978-0-448-45359-0). 199pp. Troublemaker Cody Mack is sent off to a supposed reformatory boarding school but soon discovers it is in fact run by monsters with evil intentions toward the students; part prose narrative and part graphic novel, this book mixes humor and suspense. ℮ Lexile 510L (Rev: SLJ 11/1/10)

8825 Berryhill, Shane. *Chance Fortune and the Outlaws* (5–8). Series: Adventures of Chance Fortune. 2006, Tom Doherty Assoc. $17.95 (978-0-7653-1468-0). Despite his lack of superpowers, 14-year-old Josh Blevins manages to bluff his way into Burlington Academy for the Superhuman, and there discovers that evil is afoot. (Rev: SLJ 1/07)

8826 Betancourt, Jeanne. *Ava Tree and the Wishes Three* (2–4). Illus. by Angela Dominguez. 2009, Feiwel & Friends $14.99 (978-0-312-37760-1). It's 8-year-old Ava's birthday and she suddenly realizes that she has a wishing power, but it only allows three wishes a day. (Rev: BL 3/15/09; HB 5/09; LMC 8/09; SLJ 5/09)

8827 Bial, Raymond. *The Fresh Grave: And Other Ghostly Stories* (5–7). 1997, Midwest Traditions paper $13.95 (978-1-883953-22-5). A series of ten short, humorous ghost stories featuring two teenage heroes and their escapades in a small midwestern town. (Rev: SLJ 12/97)

8828 Bial, Raymond. *The Ghost of Honeymoon Creek* (5–8). 1999, Midwest Traditions paper $13.95 (978-1-883953-27-0). While investigating a strange light in a neighboring farm, 15-year-old Hank encounters a ghost. (Rev: BL 9/1/00; HBG 3/01; SLJ 1/01)

8829 Bildner, Phil, and Loren Long. *The Barnstormers: Tales of Travelin' Nine Game 1* (4–7). Illus. by Loren Long. 2007, Simon & Schuster $9.99 (978-1-4169-1863-9). On the road with their late father's traveling baseball team, siblings Griffith, Ruby, and Graham discover a ragged baseball with magical powers. (Rev: BL 4/1/07; SLJ 4/07)

8830 Billingsley, Franny. *The Folk Keeper* (5–8). 1999, Simon & Schuster $16.00 (978-0-689-82876-8); paper $4.99 (978-0-689-84461-4). Orphaned Corinna disguises herself as a boy to become a Folk Keeper, one who guards the fierce Folk who live underground. (Rev: BCCB 10/99; BL 9/1/99; HB 11–12/99; HBG 3/00; SLJ 10/99; VOYA 12/99)

8831 Binding, Tim. *Sylvie and the Songman* (5–8). Illus. by Angela Barrett. 2009, Random $15.99 (978-0-385-75157-5). 224pp. Sylvie's composer father disappears, the animals lose their voices, and a villain arrives. (Rev: BL 6/1–15/09*; SLJ 10/09)

8832 Birney, Betty G. *The Princess and the Peabodys* (5–8). 2007, HarperCollins $15.99 (978-0-06-084720-3). Casey Peabody, a no-nonsense sports-loving 8th grader, is an unlikely constant companion for Princess Eglantine, who is accidentally released from 700 years of imprisonment, but the two do become good friends while efforts are made to return Egg to her medieval home. (Rev: BCCB 11/07; SLJ 1/08)

8833 Black, Holly. *The Ironwood Tree* (3–6). Illus. by Tony DiTerlizzi. Series: The Spiderwick Chronicles. 2004, Simon & Schuster $9.95 (978-0-689-85939-7). 128pp. In the fourth installment in the series, Jared and Simon must rescue Mallory from evil dwarves. (Rev: SLJ 6/04)

8834 Black, Holly. *Lucinda's Secret* (3–6). Illus. by Tony DiTerlizzi. Series: Spiderwick Chronicles. 2003, Simon & Schuster $9.95 (978-0-689-85938-0). 128pp. The Grace siblings visit their Aunt Lucinda to learn more about Arthur Spiderwick's *Field Guide to the Fantastical World Around You*. (Rev: HBG 4/04; SLJ 11/03)

8835 Blackwood, Sage. *Jinx* (4–7). 2013, HarperCollins $16.99 (978-006212990-1). 368pp. Young orphan Jinx, abandoned by his stepfather, finds magic and danger in the dark forest of the Unwald as he searches for a cure to a spell; the first volume in a trilogy, this is followed by *Jinx's Magic* (2014), in which Jinx must travel to a new land. ℮ Lexile 620 (Rev: BL 2/15/13*; HB 5-6/13; SLJ 1/13*)

8836 Blair, Margaret Whitman. *Brothers at War* (4–7). 1997, White Mane paper $7.95 (978-1-57249-049-9). Two brothers and their friend Sarah find themselves transported back in time to the Battle of Antietam in 1862. (Rev: BL 8/97)

8837 Block, Francesca Lia. *The Waters and the Wild* (5–8). 2009, HarperTeen $16.99 (978-0-06-145244-4). 128pp. Bee, 13 and a lonely misfit, believes she was switched at birth with the real Bee. Lexile 680L (Rev: BL 3/15/09; SLJ 7/09)

8838 Blythe, Daniel. *Shadow Breakers* (5–8). 2013, Scholastic $16.99 (978-054547979-0). 256pp. In this suspenseful story set in England, 12-year-old Miranda moves to a coastal town where strange things are happening and becomes friends with some young paranormal investigators. ∩ **e** Lexile 610L (Rev: BL 3/1/13; LMC 8–9/13; SLJ 1/13)

8839 Bode, N. E. *The Slippery Map* (5–8). 2007, HarperCollins $16.99 (978-0-06-079108-7). Orphan Oyster R. Motel, 10, enters the imaginary world of Boneland and discovers that his parents are in danger and that the slippery map has fallen into the hands of evil Dark Mouth. (Rev: BL 11/1/07; SLJ 12/07)

8840 Bode, N. E. *The Somebodies* (5–8). Illus. by Peter Ferguson. 2006, HarperCollins $16.99 (978-0-06-079111-7). Fern and her best friend Howard are determined to foil the Blue Queen's plan to destroy the home of the Anybodies who live in a city beneath Manhattan; the final book in a fast-paced trilogy. (Rev: SLJ 9/06)

8841 Bondoux, Anne-Laure. *Vasco: Leader of the Tribe* (4–7). 2007, Delacorte $15.99 (978-0-385-73363-2). Vasco, a rat with hopes for the future, escapes extermination by humans and boards an ocean liner, where he encounters more obstacles before tackling a dangerous rainforest. (Rev: BL 12/1/07; LMC 1/08; SLJ 3/08)

8842 Boniface, William. *The Hero Revealed* (3–5). Illus. by Stephen Gilpin. Series: Extraordinary Adventures of Ordinary Boy. 2006, HarperCollins $15.99 (978-0-06-077464-6). 320pp. Ordinary Boy is the only resident with no superpowers, but when Superopolis is threatened by the evil Professor Brain-Drain it looks as if Ordinary Boy may be the only one who can save the day. (Rev: BL 6/1–15/06; SLJ 6/06)

8843 Booraem, Ellen. *Small Persons with Wings* (5–7). 2011, Dial $16.99 (978-0-8037-3471-5). 304pp. When Mellie's family inherits a dilapidated inn, they find it swarming with fairy-like beings who are desperate to regain a magical moonstone. **e** Lexile 660L (Rev: BL 1/1–15/11; HB 3–4/11; LMC 11–12/11; SLJ 1/1/11*)

8844 Booraem, Ellen. *Texting the Underworld* (5–8). 2013, Dial $16.99 (978-080373704-4). 320pp. In this story about confronting death, 12-year-old Conor is visited by a banshee named Ashling who brings the bad news that one of Conor's relations will die in the near future, but after Ashling makes the choice of becoming a mortal, it is up to Conor to decide who should die in Ashling's stead. **e** Lexile 590 (Rev: BL 10/1/13; HB 7–8/13; LMC 1–2/14; SLJ 12/13; VOYA 10/13)

8845 Bouwman, H. M. *The Remarkable and Very True Story of Lucy and Snowcap* (5–7). 2008, Marshall Cavendish $16.99 (978-0-7614-5441-0). 288pp. In 1787 on the fictional island of Tatenland, two 12-year-old girls — Lucy, a native Colay, and Snowcap, daughter of a

British governor — investigate why the men have all been turned to stone. (Rev: BLO 10/7/08; LMC 3/09; SLJ 11/08)

8846 Boyce, Frank Cottrell. *Chitty Chitty Bang Bang and the Race against Time* (3–6). Illus. by Joe Berger. 2013, Candlewick $15.99 (978-076365982-0). 240pp. The rambunctious car careens from the Jurassic Age (and a chase by a T. rex) to 1920s New York City and thence to the mythical city of El Dorado, with the Tooting family along for the chaotic ride. (Rev: BLO 4/1/13; SLJ 6/13)

8847 Boyce, Frank Cottrell. *Chitty Chitty Bang Bang: Over the Moon* (4–7). Illus. by Joe Berger. 2014, Candlewick $15.99 (978-076365983-7). 240pp. In this final authorized sequel, the Tootings head back to 1966 and are watching the World Cup when their magical car is stolen. (Rev: BLO 3/1/14; SLJ 3/14)

8848 Boyce, Frank Cottrell. *Cosmic* (4–7). 2010, HarperCollins $16.99 (978-0-06-183683-1). 320pp. Twelve-year-old Liam is so big that he's often mistaken for an adult, and he decides to capitalize on this and enter the Greatest Dad Ever Contest to win a flight into space. ∩ **e** Lexile 670L (Rev: BL 11/15/09*; HB 3–4/10; LMC 3–4/10; SLJ 2/10)

8849 Bozarth, Jan. *Kerka's Book* (3–5). Illus. by Andrea Burden. Series: Fairy Godmother Academy. 2009, Random House LB $10.99 (978-0-375-95183-1); paper $7.99 (978-0-375-85183-4). 224pp. Kerka, soon to turn 13 and training as a fairy godmother, meets many magical creatures when she ventures into the world of Aventurine. (Rev: BLO 11/15/09; SLJ 1/10)

8850 Bradman, Tony. *Voodoo Child* (4–7). Illus. by Martin Chatterton. Series: Tales of Terror. 2005, Egmont paper $7.50 (978-1-4052-1126-0). Megan hopes a voodoo doll will get rid of her father's girlfriend. Other scary titles in this series are *Deadly Game* and *Final Cut* (both 2005). (Rev: SLJ 6/05)

8851 Breathed, Berkeley. *The Last Basselope: One Ferocious Story* (4–7). 2001, Little, Brown paper $5.95 (978-0-316-12664-9). In this imaginative picture book for older readers, Opus and his reluctant adventurers are after the nearly extinct basselope. (Rev: BCCB 1/93; BL 12/15/92; SLJ 1/93)

8852 Breen, M. E. *Darkwood* (5–8). 2009, Bloomsbury $16.99 (978-1-59990-259-3). 288pp. Twelve-year-old Annie flees the home she has shared with her aunt and uncle and finds herself in an even less inviting world that is full of danger but may offer clues to her heritage. (Rev: BCCB 9/09; BL 5/15/09; SLJ 6/09; VOYA 10/09)

8853 Breitrose, Prudence. *Mousenet* (3–6). Illus. by Stephanie Yue. 2011, Hyperion/Disney $16.99 (978-142312489-4). 400pp. Megan, whose uncle has just invented the world's smallest computer, is befriended by a group of mice eager to use the computer to improve their own society — and even the planet. **e** (Rev: BL 10/15/11; SLJ 1/12)

8854 Brennan, Herbie. *Zartog's Remote* (3–5). Illus. by Neal Layton. 2001, Carolrhoda LB $14.95 (978-1-57505-507-7). 96pp. A fearful 8-year-old alien named

Zartog and a feisty 8-year-old girl named Rachel band together when Zartog loses the remote control for his spaceship. (Rev: HBG 10/01; SLJ 4/01)

8855 Briggs, Andy. *Rise of the Heroes* (5–8). Series: Hero.com. 2009, Walker paper $7.99 (978-0-8027-9503-8). 251pp. Downloading superpowers including flight and laser vision proves irresistible to four teens who find their new abilities challenging at first. Lexile 780L (Rev: BL 8/09; SLJ 9/09)

8856 Brodien-Jones, Christine. *The Glass Puzzle* (4–7). Illus. by Charles Santoso. 2013, Delacorte $16.99 (978-038574297-9); LB $19.99 (978-037599087-8). 336pp. On a vacation in Wales, 11-year-old Zoe and her cousin Ian find themselves passing through a portal to the lost, mystical island of Wythernsea. e (Rev: BL 7/13; LMC 11–12/13; SLJ 10/13)

8857 Brodien-Jones, Christine. *The Owl Keeper* (5–8). Illus. by Maggie Kneen. 2010, Delacorte $17.99 (978-0-385-73814-9); LB $20.99 (978-0-385-90710-1). 304pp. Eleven-year-old Max partners with an unusual girl, Rose, who shares his appreciation of the silver owls that the High Echelon wants to destroy, and together they make a perilous journey seeking to fulfill a prophecy. e Lexile 750L (Rev: BL 4/15/10; LMC 8–9/10; SLJ 5/10; VOYA 10/10)

8858 Brown, Calef. *Polkabats and Octopus Slacks: 14 Stories* (3–5). Illus. 1998, Houghton $16.00 (978-0-395-85403-7). 32pp. Nonsense verses introduce some wacky characters, including Kansas City Octopus, who goes out on the town in four-legged bell bottoms. (Rev: BL 3/15/98; HBG 10/98; SLJ 5/98)

8859 Brown, Jeff. *Stanley, Flat Again!* (2–4). Illus. by Scott Nash. Series: Flat Stanley. 2003, HarperCollins LB $16.89 (978-0-06-029826-5). 87pp. Stanley, first seen in *Flat Stanley* (1964), is flat once more and has a series of adventures in this entertaining early chapter book. (Rev: HBG 10/03; SLJ 3/03)

8860 Brown, Jeff, and Sara Pennypacker. *The Mount Rushmore Calamity* (2–4). Illus. by Macky Pamintuan. Series: Flat Stanley's Worldwide Adventures. 2009, HarperTrophy $15.99 (978-0-06-142991-0); paper $4.99 (978-0-06-142990-3). 96pp. In this first installment in a new series, Flat Stanley goes to Mount Rushmore, saves Lincoln, then goes hunting for gold; historical and geographical information are woven into the entertaining story. (Rev: BL 5/15/09; SLJ 8/09)

8861 Bruchac, Joseph. *Dragon Castle* (5–8). 2011, Dial $16.99 (978-0-8037-3376-3). 352pp. A 15-year-old Slovakian prince, Rashko, must contend with the arrival of a rogue army when his parents are away and finds himself relying on the power of an ancestor who slayed a dragon. e Lexile 850L (Rev: BLO 8/11; HB 9–10/11; LMC 1–2/12*; SLJ 8/11)

8862 Bruchac, Joseph. *Whisper in the Dark* (5–8). 2005, HarperCollins $16.99 (978-0-06-058087-2). A frightening Native American legend seems to be coming true for 13-year-old Maddie, descended from a Narragansett chief. (Rev: BL 9/1/05; SLJ 8/05)

8863 Buckingham, Royce. *The Dead Boys* (5–8). 2010, Putnam $16.99 (978-0-399-25222-8). 203pp. Arriving in a Washington town where his mother will work at a nuclear plant, 12-year-old Teddy finds that his new friends are all dead and there is a menacing sycamore tree next door. e Lexile 850L (Rev: SLJ 11/1/10)

8864 Buckingham, Royce. *Demonkeeper* (4–7). 2007, Putnam $15.99 (978-0-399-24649-4). Nat lives in Seattle and looks after mostly harmless demons in his creaky old house — until the day when the scary Beast gets loose and Nat must try to retrieve this orphan-eating demon; this fast-paced romp will please reluctant readers. (Rev: SLJ 9/07)

8865 Buckingham, Royce. *Goblins! An UnderEarth Adventure* (5–8). 2008, Putnam $16.99 (978-0-399-25002-6). 232pp. Twelve-year-old Sam and his 17-year-old friend PJ, son of the only police officer in their small town, discover a scary underworld where goblins live. (Rev: SLJ 11/08)

8866 Buckley, Michael. *The Fairy-Tale Detectives* (4–6). Illus. by Peter Ferguson. Series: Sisters Grimm. 2005, Abrams $14.95 (978-0-8109-5925-5). 304pp. Sent to live with their grandmother after their parents disappear, sisters Daphne and Sabrina Grimm find themselves in a magical town full of fairy tale characters known as Everafters. (Rev: BL 11/15/05; SLJ 1/06; VOYA 8/06) ∩

8867 Buffie, Margaret. *The Seeker* (5–8). 2002, Kids Can $16.95 (978-1-55337-358-2). Emma is involved in a quest to reunite her family and becomes embroiled in interplanetary intrigue and gaming in this sequel to *The Watcher* (2000). (Rev: BL 10/1/02; HBG 10/03; SLJ 11/02; VOYA 4/03)

8868 Buffie, Margaret. *The Watcher* (5–8). 2000, Kids Can $16.95 (978-1-55074-829-1). Sixteen-year-old Emma discovers that she is really a changeling, a Watcher, whose mission is to protect her younger sister from warring factions. (Rev: BL 11/1/00; HBG 3/01; SLJ 10/00; VOYA 2/01)

8869 Burden, Meg. *Northlander: Tales of the Borderlands* (5–8). Series: Tales of the Borderlands. 2007, Brown Barn paper $8.95 (978-0-9768126-8-5). Ellin, a Southling with healing powers and other mystical abilities, is torn between her homeland and her friends in the Northlands. (Rev: BL 1/1–15/08; SLJ 2/08)

8870 Burleigh, Robert. *Flight of the Last Dragon* (1–3). Illus. by Mary GrandPre. 2012, Philomel $16.99 (978-0-399-25200-6). 32pp. In verse and a contemporary setting, this is the story of Ultimon, the last surviving dragon, as he climbs out of the sewers and takes one last flight into the sky. (Rev: BLO 10/15/12; LMC 1–2/13; SLJ 12/12)

8871 Burt, Marissa. *Storybound* (4–7). 2012, HarperCollins $16.99 (978-006202052-9). 416pp. Una Fairchild, 12, is magically transported to the Land of Story where she finds mystery and danger. (Rev: BL 3/15/12; SLJ 8/12)

8872 Butts, Nancy. *The Door in the Lake* (5–8). 1997, Front St $17.95 (978-1-886910-27-0). Twenty-seven months after being abducted by aliens, Joey returns home to find that everything has changed while he has remained the same. (Rev: BCCB 7–8/98; BL 5/15/98; HBG 10/98; SLJ 6/98; VOYA 10/98)

8873 Buzbee, Lewis. *Bridge of Time* (5–8). 2012, Feiwel & Friends $17.99 (978-031238257-5). 304pp. Best friends Lee Jones and Joan Lee, 8th-graders who discover their respective parents are divorcing, wish they could go back to an earlier, better time — and get more than they bargained for. ❤ (Rev: BL 4/1/12; SLJ 5/1/12)

8874 Buzbee, Lewis. *Steinbeck's Ghost* (5–8). 2008, Feiwel & Friends $17.95 (978-0-312-37328-3). Thirteen-year-old Travis is unhappy when his family moves to a new subdivision and he drifts back to his old neighborhood in Salinas, California, John Steinbeck's hometown; there he works to save the Steinbeck Library from closure and finds that characters from Steinbeck novels are coming to life. ∩ (Rev: BL 8/08; SLJ 9/08)

8875 Byng, Georgia. *Molly Moon Stops the World* (5–8). 2004, HarperCollins LB $18.89 (978-0-06-051413-6). Molly Moon, a girl of unusual hypnotic powers, is dispatched to California to foil a power-mad hypnotist called Primo Cell. (Rev: BL 5/1/04; SLJ 5/04)

8876 Byng, Georgia. *Molly Moon's Hypnotic Time Travel Adventure* (4–6). 2005, HarperCollins $16.99 (978-0-06-075032-9). 392pp. When her beloved dog is kidnapped, Molly Moon travels back in time to late 19th-century India where she matches wits the villainous Maharaja of Waqt and meets former versions of herself. (Rev: SLJ 1/06)

8877 Cameron, Eleanor. *The Court of the Stone Children* (5–7). 1990, Puffin paper $6.99 (978-0-14-034289-5). Nina's move with her family to San Francisco is a disaster until she encounters a young ghost in a small museum.

8878 Carlson, Caroline. *Magic Marks the Spot* (4–7). Illus. by Dave Phillips. Series: Very Nearly Honorable League of Pirates. 2013, HarperCollins $16.99 (978-006219434-3). 368pp. With the help of her magic gargoyle, Hilary Westfield runs away from Miss Pimm's Finishing School and joins a group of freelance pirates; the first installment in a swashbuckling adventure/fantasy. Amelia Bloomer. ❤ Lexile 900 (Rev: BLO 9/15/13; SLJ 9/13)

8879 Carman, Patrick. *Atherton: The House of Power* (5–8). 2007, Little, Brown $16.99 (978-0-316-16670-6). Atherton is a socially divided world under threat and 12-year-old Edgar has a book that contains key secrets. ∩ (Rev: BL 5/15/07; LMC 11/07; SLJ 6/07)

8880 Carman, Patrick. *Beyond the Valley of Thorns* (4–6). Series: The Land of Elyon. 2005, Scholastic $11.99 (978-0-439-70094-8). 221pp. In the second installment of this fantasy series, Alexa and her companions confront a host of new dangers as they battle the ogre Abaddon. (Rev: SLJ 10/05; VOYA 12/05)

8881 Carman, Patrick. *The Dark Hills Divide* (4–6). Series: Land of Elyon. 2005, Scholastic $11.95 (978-0-439-70093-1). Alexa, 12, discovers the secrets of her

walled city and a plan to destroy it in this fantasy, the first volume in a trilogy. (Rev: BL 3/1/05; SLJ 4/05)

8882 Carman, Patrick. *The Dark Planet* (5–8). Illus. by Squire Broel. Series: Atherton. 2009, Little, Brown $16.99 (978-0-316-16674-4). 350pp. In the action-driven conclusion to this trilogy, Edgar seeks answers about himself as he desperately works to save the homeland of his friend, Dr. Harding. ∩ (Rev: SLJ 10/09; VOYA 10/09)

8883 Carman, Patrick. *Rivers of Fire* (5–8). Series: Atherton. 2008, Little, Brown $16.99 (978-0-316-16672-0). The planet of Atherton is still in trouble, and Edgar, Samuel, and Isabel fight to save it in this continuation of the story that began in *The House of Power.* (Rev: BL 5/15/08; SLJ 8/08)

8884 Carman, Patrick. *The Tenth City* (4–6). Series: The Land of Elyon. 2006, Scholastic $11.99 (978-0-439-70095-5). 186pp. In the conclusion of this fantasy series, Alexa and her band of supporters face off against Grindall who has kidnapped Yipes, Alexa's diminutive friend. (Rev: SLJ 8/06)

8885 Carman, Patrick. *Things That Go Bump in the Night* (4–6). Series: 3:15 Season One. 2011, Scholastic $12.99 (978-0-545-38475-9). 162pp. Ten chilling stories — each with an audio introduction and a video conclusion, available online — feature young teens in tense situations; requires Internet access or smart phone app. (Rev: LMC 1–2/12; SLJ 11/1/11)

8886 Carmody, Isobelle. *Little Fur: The Legend Begins* (3–5). 2006, Random $12.95 (978-0-375-83854-5). 208pp. Little Fur (who is half elf, half troll) sets out on a journey through the human world to save the trees that she calls home as well as the earth spirit. (Rev: BL 11/15/06; SLJ 11/06)

8887 Carmody, Isobelle. *A Mystery of Wolves* (3–5). Illus. by author. 2008, Random $12.99 (978-0-375-83858-3). 240pp. Little Fur, a half-elf and half-troll girl, sets out on a classic discovery search during which she must uncover the Mystery of Wolves. (Rev: BL 2/1/08)

8888 Carroll, Lewis. *Alice in Wonderland and Through the Looking Glass* (4–7). Illus. by John Tenniel. 1963, Putnam $18.99 (978-0-448-06004-0). One of many recommended editions of these enduring fantasies.

8889 Carroll, Lewis. *Alice Through the Looking-Glass* (4–7). Illus. by Helen Oxenbury. 2005, Candlewick $24.99 (978-0-7636-2892-5). Faithful to the original text, Oxenbury's inviting artwork will draw young readers; a companion to her award-winning *Alice's Adventures in Wonderland* (1999). (Rev: BL 12/15/05*; HBG 4/06; SLJ 12/05)

8890 Carroll, Lewis. *Alice's Adventures in Wonderland* (5–7). 2000, Chronicle $19.95 (978-0-8118-2274-9). This oversize edition of the complete text of Carroll's classic features illustrations from 29 artists. (Rev: BL 11/1/00; HBG 3/01; SLJ 11/00)

8891 Carroll, Lewis. *Alice's Adventures in Wonderland* (5–12). Illus. by Iassen Ghiuselev. 2003, Simply Read $29.95 (978-1-894965-00-2). Interesting illustrations by

Ghiuselev that interpret incidents and characters in a different way highlight this new edition of an old classic. (Rev: BL 2/1/04; SLJ 6/04)

8892 Carroll, Lewis. *Alice's Adventures in Wonderland* (3–5). Illus. by Alison Jay. 2006, Dial $25.99 (978-0-8037-2940-7). 224pp. A handsomely illustrated, faithful retelling of the classic story, with glowing paintings of diverse sizes. (Rev: BL 11/1/06)

8893 Carroll, Lewis. *Through the Looking Glass, and What Alice Found There* (4–7). Illus. by John Tenniel. 1977, St. Martin's $14.95 (978-0-312-80374-2). The sequel to *Alice's Adventures in Wonderland*. One of many editions.

8894 Carroll, Michael. *The Ascension: A Super Human Clash* (5–8). Series: Super Human. 2011, Philomel $16.99 (978-0-399-25624-0). 378pp. Villain Krodin returns in this second installment in the series and is conquered by the teenage superheroes after plenty of struggle and fast-paced action. Lexile 680L (Rev: SLJ 8/11)

8895 Carroll, Michael. *Super Human* (5–8). 2010, Philomel $16.99 (978-0-399-25297-6). 336pp. Four teens with superpowers challenge the Helotry's plans to resurrect an ancient warrior. YALSA Popular Paperbacks for Young Adults Top Ten 2012. e Lexile 690L (Rev: BL 5/1/10; LMC 10/10; SLJ 7/10; VOYA 8/10)

8896 Carroll, Thomas. *The Colony* (4–7). 2000, Sunstone $18.95 (978-0-86534-295-8). Fifth-grader Tony and his bullying arch-enemy Lawrence are shrunk to the size of ants by a Navajo charm and in their new environment join opposing forces. (Rev: HBG 3/01; SLJ 7/00)

8897 Carter, Scott William. *Wooden Bones* (4–7). 2012, Simon & Schuster $15.99 (978-1-4424-2751-8). 148pp. After Pinocchio becomes a real boy, he realizes he has the power to bring wood to life, which endangers both him and his father, Gepetto. e (Rev: LMC 1–2/13; SLJ 8/1/12)

8898 Carus, Marianne, ed. *That's Ghosts for You: 13 Scary Stories* (4–7). Illus. by YongSheng Xuan. 2000, Front St $15.95 (978-0-8126-2675-9). A fine collection of 13 chilling stories set in locations around the world, each with a supernatural twist. (Rev: BL 12/1/00; HBG 3/01; SLJ 12/00)

8899 Catanese, P. W. *Dragon Games* (5–8). Series: The Books of Umber. 2010, Simon & Schuster $16.99 (978-1-4169-7521-2). 384pp. Lord Umber and his ward Happenstance travel to Sarnica in an attempt to sate an unquenchable thirst for knowledge about dragons and a disregard for looming danger. ∩ e Lexile 740L (Rev: BLO 12/1/09; SLJ 7/10)

8900 Catanese, P. W. *The Mirror's Tale: A Further Tales Adventure* (4–7). 2006, Simon & Schuster paper $4.99 (978-1-4169-1251-4). When their father decides to separate his mischievous 13-year-old twin sons for the summer, they switch places and one is sent to the castle of his aunt and uncle where he discovers and falls under the spell of a bewitching mirror. (Rev: SLJ 8/06)

8901 Catmull, Katherine. *Summer and Bird* (5–8). 2012, Dutton $16.99 (978-0-525-95346-3). 384pp. Set in the world of Down, this complex fantasy features young sisters Summer and Bird who separately search for their missing parents in an alternate world. e Lexile 760L (Rev: BL 9/15/12*; SLJ 11/12; VOYA 10/12)

8902 Chan, Gillian. *The Carved Box* (5–8). 2001, Kids Can $16.95 (978-1-55074-895-6). The acquisition of a dog and a carved box ease the transition for orphaned Callum, 15, who has moved from Scotland to Canada to live with his uncle, in this novel which has an element of fantasy that comes to the fore in the dramatic ending. (Rev: BL 10/01; HBG 3/02; SLJ 10/01; VOYA 4/02)

8903 Chapman, Linda, and Steve Cole. *Be a Genie in Six Easy Steps* (3–5). 2009, HarperCollins $16.99 (978-0-06-125219-8). 326pp. Four new stepsiblings are adjusting to life together in the English countryside when they discover a book that can teach them how to become genies, with predictably unpredictable results. A sequel is *The Last Phoenix* (2010). Lexile 590L (Rev: BL 5/15/09; SLJ 12/09)

8904 Chase, Max. *Alien Attack* (3–5). Illus. Series: Star Fighters. 2012, Bloomsbury paper $5.99 (978-15999085-0-2). 128pp. Peri, a student at the Intergalactic Force Academy, and Diesel, a half-Martian, escape an invasion of aliens and challenge them from their high-tech spaceship; an action-packed story full of sci fi treats. (Rev: BL 5/15/12; LMC 10/12)

8905 Choldenko, Gennifer. *No Passengers Beyond This Point* (5–8). 2011, Dial $16.99 (978-0-8037-3534-7). 288pp. Three children sent to live in Colorado find themselves in a disconcerting alternate reality, and their determination to support each other is what pulls them through. ∩ e (Rev: BL 2/1/11; HB 1–2/11; LMC 5–6/11; SLJ 2/1/11; VOYA 4/11)

8906 Churchyard, Kathleen. *Bye for Now: A Wisher's Story* (4–7). 2011, Egmont $15.99 (978-1-60684-190-7). 272pp. Robin, 11, is not enjoying her birthday and wishes she could be someone else; the next day she wakes up in London in the body of 11-year-old Fiona, who has quite a different life — but is it better? e (Rev: BL 9/1/11; SLJ 12/1/11)

8907 Clarke, Judith. *Starry Nights* (5–9). 2003, Front St $15.95 (978-1-886910-82-9). When Jess's family moves to a new house, a ghost seems to be involved in the family's emotional upheavals. (Rev: BL 6/1–15/03; HB 9–10/03; HBG 4/04)

8908 Clayton, Emma. *The Roar* (5–8). 2009, Scholastic $17.99 (978-0-439-92593-8). 496pp. This fast-paced science fiction novel revolves around twins from a society ruined by plagues and chemicals and under the control of an evil government bent on selecting (through arcade games) and training unsuspecting youth for an army. ∩ (Rev: BCCB 5/09; LMC 5/09; SLJ 5/09)

8909 Clayton, Emma. *The Whisper* (5–8). 2012, Scholastic $17.99 (978-054531772-6). 320pp. Telepathic twins Mika and Ellie endeavor to halt the evil that is dividing the population into the poor on one side of The Wall and the megalomaniacs on the other side in this sequel to *The Roar* (2009). e (Rev: BL 3/1/12; SLJ 3/12)

8910 Cody, Matthew. *The Dead Gentleman* (5–8). 2011, Knopf $15.99 (978-037585596-2); LB $18.99 (978-037595596-9). 288pp. A time-traveling device enables Tommy, a 1901 street urchin, to contact modern-day teen Jezebel; the two unite their strengths to save the world from zombies. **e** (Rev: BL 2/1/12; SLJ 3/12)

8911 Cody, Matthew. *Powerless* (5–8). 2009, Knopf $15.99 (978-0-375-85595-5); LB $18.99 (978-0-375-95595-2). 279pp. When Daniel, 12, arrives in Noble's Green he soon learns that all the other kids have superpowers that they will lose when they turn 13. Can Daniel use his intelligence to prevent this? ⌒ **e** Lexile 800L (Rev: BL 10/15/09; LMC 11–12/09; SLJ 1/10)

8912 Cody, Matthew. *Super* (5–8). 2012, Knopf $16.99 (978-0-375-86894-8); LB $19.99 (978-0-375-96894-5). 304pp. Despite his lack of superpowers, 13-year-old Daniel has proved quite effective in the past; now he seems to be acquiring powers as others are losing them. What is going on? ⌒ **e** (Rev: BLO 12/1/12; LMC 1–2/13*; SLJ 12/12)

8913 Cohagan, Carolyn. *The Lost Children* (4–6). 2010, Aladdin $16.99 (978-1-4169-8616-4). 320pp. In this complex fantasy, lonely 12-year-old Josephine is transported to another realm — a medieval world that draws on the energy of children — where she discovers unknown strengths with her new friends Ida and Fargus. **e** Lexile 740L (Rev: BL 1/1/10; LMC 5–6/10; SLJ 3/10)

8914 Cole, Steve. *Riddle of the Raptors* (3–5). Illus. by Charlie Fowkes. Series: Astrosaurs. 2006, Simon & Schuster paper $4.99 (978-0-689-87841-1). In the opening installment of this humorous science fiction series, Teggs, an Earth-orbiting dinosaur, and his crew of astrosaurs, set out to rescue a couple of their plant-eating athletes who were taken captive by meat-eating velociraptors. (Rev: SLJ 8/06)

8915 Cole, Steve. *Z. Rex* (5–8). Series: The Hunting. 2009, Philomel $16.99 (978-0-399-25253-2). 276pp. Scottish teenager Adam has to rely on himself when his dad leaves for a business trip and all manner of scary thugs — including a man-eating dinosaur — show up at his house. (Rev: BL 8/09; LMC 11–12/09; SLJ 10/09)

8916 Coleman, Alice Scovell. *Engraved in Stone* (4–7). Illus. by Anjal Renée Armand. 2003, Tiara $14.95 (978-0-9729846-0-7). A prince and princess who will do anything to avoid their planned marriage set off on a quest to get their fate changed in this humorous fantasy. (Rev: SLJ 12/03)

8917 Coleman, Janet W. *Fast Eddie* (3–4). Illus. by Alec Gillman. 1993, Macmillan LB $13.95 (978-0-02-722815-1). Eddie the raccoon faces danger when he plays tricks on humans. (Rev: SLJ 6/93)

8918 Colfer, Eoin. *Artemis Fowl: The Last Guardian* (5–8). 2012, Disney/Hyperion $18.99 (978-1-42316161-5). 336pp. In this series conclusion, genius Artemis Fowl finds himself up against his familiar — and deadly — rival Opal for the final time. ⌒ **e** (Rev: BLO 10/15/12; SLJ 11/12; VOYA 10/12)

8919 Colfer, Eoin. *The Atlantis Complex* (5–8). Series: Artemis Fowl. 2010, Hyperion $17.99 (978-142312819-9). 368pp. In this seventh title in the series, Artemis combats global warming while struggling to overcome a serious case of the Atlantis Complex, an affliction that causes OCD, paranoia, and multiple personalities. ⌒ **e** Lexile 900L (Rev: BL 10/1/10; VOYA 12/10)

8920 Colfer, Eoin. *The Time Paradox* (4–8). Series: Artemis Fowl. 2008, Hyperion $17.99 (978-1-4231-0836-8). 391pp. Artemis travels back in time to retrieve a substance that will cure his mother's disease. ⌒ **e** Lexile 780L (Rev: SLJ 10/1/08; VOYA 10/08)

8921 Collins, Suzanne. *Gregor and the Code of Claw* (5–9). Series: The Underland Chronicles. 2007, Scholastic $17.99 (978-0-439-79143-4). A mysterious prophecy makes Gregor question himself in this adventure-filled fifth title in the series. (Rev: SLJ 7/07)

8922 Collins, Suzanne. *Gregor and the Curse of the Warmbloods* (4–6). Series: Underland Chronicles. 2005, Scholastic $16.95 (978-0-439-65623-8). 368pp. In this third volume in the series, Gregor, his sister Boots, and his mother travel to the Underland to deal with the terrible plague spreading there. (Rev: BL 7/05; SLJ 7/05; VOYA 10/05)

8923 Collins, Suzanne. *Gregor and the Marks of Secret* (5–8). Series: The Underland Chronicles. 2006, Scholastic $16.99 (978-0-439-79145-8). Gregor, accompanied by his little sister Boots, joins forces with Queen Luxa to defend Underland from attacks by the rat army. (Rev: SLJ 9/06; VOYA 8/06)

8924 Collins, Suzanne. *Gregor the Overlander* (4–7). 2003, Scholastic $17.99 (978-0-439-43536-9). When his baby sister disappears into an air vent, 11-year-old Gregor doesn't hesitate to follow and finds himself in a whole new world, an Underland where an unexpected role awaits him. (Rev: BCCB 1/04; BL 11/15/03*; HB 9–10/03; HBG 9–10/03; LMC 11–12/03; SLJ 11/03; VOYA 10/03)

8925 Collodi, Carlo. *The Adventures of Pinocchio. Rev. ed.* (4–10). Trans. from Italian by M. A. Murray. Illus. by Roberta Innocenti. 2005, Creative Editions $19.95 (978-1-56846-190-8). Nineteenth-century European landscapes provide the backdrop for this appealing retelling of the classic story about the puppet that longed to become a little boy; a revision of the 1988 edition. (Rev: SLJ 12/05)

8926 Collodi, Carlo. *Pinocchio* (3–5). Trans. by Claude Sartirano. Illus. by Quentin Greban. 2010, NorthSouth $19.95 (978-073582324-2). 88pp. A carefully abridged and nicely illustrated version of the story about a puppet whose nose betrays him. (Rev: BL 1/1–15/11)

8927 Columbus, Chris, and Ned Vizzini. *House of Secrets* (4–8). Illus. by Greg Call. 2013, HarperCollins $17.99 (978-006219246-2). 496pp. Cordelia, 15, and her younger siblings Brendan and Eleanor move to a new house in San Francisco and find themselves facing a witch who has kidnapped their parents. **e** Lexile 690L (Rev: BL 3/1/13; SLJ 7/13)

8928 Coman, Carolyn. *The Memory Bank* (4–6). Illus. by Rob Shepperson. 2010, Scholastic $16.99 (978-0-545-21066-9). 288pp. The full-page pen-and-ink and pencil drawings enhance this complex story about Hope Scroggins, who tries to find her younger sister Honey and ends up at the Memory Bank, where memories and dreams are sorted and stored. Lexile 730L (Rev: BL 11/1/10*; LMC 11–12/10; SLJ 12/1/10)

8929 Conly, Jane L. *R-T, Margaret, and the Rats of NIMH* (4–6). Illus. by Leonard Lubin. 1990, HarperCollins LB $14.89 (978-0-06-021364-0); paper $6.99 (978-0-06-440387-0). 288pp. The third installment of the brilliant rodents, in which two human children star. (Rev: BCCB 6/90; BL 5/15/90; SLJ 6/90)

8930 Conly, Jane Leslie. *Impetuous R., Secret Agent* (4–6). Illus. by Bonnie Leick. 2008, Hyperion $17.99 (978-1-4231-0418-6). 288pp. This deft tale follows three cockroach kids and their friendly people as they work to raise enough cash to keep their jazz club home intact. (Rev: BL 9/1/08)

8931 Conly, Jane Leslie. *Racso and the Rats of NIMH* (5–7). Illus. by Leonard Lubin. 1986, HarperCollins LB $17.89 (978-0-06-021362-6). This sequel to the Newbery Medal winner involves once again the smart rodents who wish to live in peace in Thorn Valley. (Rev: BCCB 6/86; BL 6/1/86; SLJ 4/86)

8932 Cook, Eileen. *Wishes for Beginners* (3–5). Series: Fourth Grade Fairy. 2011, Simon & Schuster paper $6.99 (978-1-4169-9812-9). 146pp. Willow, a 4th-grader honing her secret fairy powers, has high hopes of becoming friends with the popular Miranda until her own magic abilities seem to fail her. **e** Lexile 670L (Rev: SLJ 7/11)

8933 Coombs, Kate. *The Runaway Dragon* (5–8). 2009, Farrar $16.99 (978-0-374-36361-1). 304pp. With powerful friends in tow, 16-year-old Princess Meg courageously pursues her dragon, Laddy, through the far reaches of an enchanted forest while dodging the evil witch Malison in this sequel to *The Runaway Princess* (2006). **e** Lexile 780L (Rev: BL 9/1/09; HB 9–10/09; SLJ 9/09)

8934 Coombs, Kate. *The Runaway Princess* (4–7). 2006, Farrar $17.00 (978-0-374-35546-3). In this entertaining takeoff on traditional fairy tales, 15-year-old Princess Meg, angry over being sequestered while princes from far and wide compete for her hand in marriage, escapes and takes matters into her own hands. (Rev: BL 9/1/06; SLJ 9/06)

8935 Cooper, Clare. *Ashar of Qarius* (5–8). 1990, Harcourt $14.95 (978-0-15-200409-5). A teenage girl, two children, and their pets are left alone in a space dome and must find a way to survive. (Rev: BL 5/15/90; SLJ 7/90)

8936 Cooper, Susan. *The Boggart* (4–6). 1993, Macmillan $15.00 (978-0-689-50576-8). 200pp. An old desk unleashes the Boggart, a mischievous spirit who has lived in a Scottish castle for centuries. (Rev: BCCB 3/93; BL 1/15/93; HB 5/93*; SLJ 1/93)

8937 Cooper, Susan. *The Boggart and the Monster* (4–6). 1997, Simon & Schuster paper $16.00 (978-0-689-81330-6). 192pp. The Boggart, a Scottish spirit-creature, wants to accompany young Jessup and Emily when they go to Loch Ness to find the monster. (Rev: BCCB 5/97; BL 3/1/97; HB 5/97; SLJ 5/97)

8938 Cooper, Susan. *Green Boy* (4–8). 2002, Simon & Schuster $16.00 (978-0-689-84751-6). Two young boys discover a futuristic world in which natural resources are depleted and a war to save the environment is being waged. (Rev: BCCB 5/02; BL 3/1/02; HB 5–6/02; HBG 10/02; SLJ 2/02)

8939 Cooper, Susan. *King of Shadows* (5–8). Illus. by John Clapp. 1999, Simon & Schuster $16.00 (978-0-689-82817-1). Nat Field time-travels to 1599 London and assumes the child-actor role of Puck in *A Midsummer Night's Dream*. (Rev: BL 10/15/99*; HB 11–12/99; HBG 3/00; SLJ 11/99)

8940 Cooper, Susan. *Silver on the Tree* (5–7). Series: The Dark Is Rising. 1980, Macmillan $18.00 (978-0-689-50088-6). In this fifth and last volume of a series, Will Stanton and his friends wage a final battle against the Dark, the powers of evil. The first four volumes are *Over Sea, Under Stone* (1966), *The Dark Is Rising* (1973), *The Grey King* (1975), and *Greenwitch* (1985). *The Grey King* won the 1976 Newbery Medal. Margaret A. Edwards Award 2012.

8941 Cooper, Susan. *Victory* (4–7). 2006, Simon & Schuster $16.95 (978-1-4169-1477-8). Homesick Molly finds her fate is intertwined with that of Sam, a child sailor of the 19th century who fought in the Battle of Trafalgar; chapters alternate between the present and the past. (Rev: BL 5/1/06; LMC 11/12/06; SLJ 7/06)

8942 Corder, Zizou. *Lionboy: The Truth* (5–8). 2005, Dial $16.99 (978-0-8037-2985-8). In the final installment in the trilogy, Charlie Ashanti, reunited with his parents in Morocco, is kidnapped by the Corporacy and put on a boat bound for the Caribbean, but the boy wonder calls on his animal friends for help. (Rev: BL 10/1/05; SLJ 9/05; VOYA 12/05)

8943 Coville, Bruce. *Always October* (3–6). 2012, HarperCollins $16.99 (978-0-06-089095-7). 384pp. Combining humor and horror, this story features 12-year-old Jacob and his friend Lily, who find themselves in a monster-filled parallel universe as they try to help a foundling known as Little Dumpling. ⋂ **e** Lexile 730L (Rev: BL 10/1/12; SLJ 9/12)

8944 Coville, Bruce. *The Dragon of Doom* (2–4). Illus. by Katherine Coville. Series: Moongobble and Me. 2003, Simon & Schuster $14.95 (978-0-689-85754-6). 69pp. Young Edward finds life in his hometown of Pigbone terribly boring until a magician named Moongobble arrives and asks the boy to be his assistant. (Rev: HBG 4/04; SLJ 1/04)

8945 Coville, Bruce. *The Ghost in the Big Brass Bed* (4–6). 1991, Bantam paper $4.50 (978-0-553-15827-4). Two ghosts appeal for help to Chris and Nina, who try to solve the mystery surrounding them. (Rev: SLJ 1/92)

8946 Coville, Bruce. *Goblins in the Castle* (5–7). 1992, Pocket paper $4.99 (978-0-671-72711-6). William, now 11, has grown up in Toad-in-a-Cage Castle and knows many of its secret passages. (Rev: BL 2/1/93)

8947 Coville, Bruce. *Juliet Dove, Queen of Love: A Magic Shop Book* (4–8). 2003, Harcourt $17.00 (978-0-15-204561-6). Life changes for shy Juliet, 12, when she is given an amulet and the boys suddenly come flocking to her side. (Rev: BL 1/1–15/04; HBG 4/04; SLJ 12/03)

8948 Coville, Bruce. *The Prince of Butterflies* (3–5). Illus. by John Clapp. 2002, Harcourt $16.00 (978-0-15-201454-4). Migrating monarchs turn a boy into a butterfly so he can help them on their journey in this socially conscious story. (Rev: BL 3/15/02; HBG 10/02; SLJ 5/02)

8949 Coville, Bruce, ed. *A Glory of Unicorns* (5–8). 1998, Scholastic paper $16.95 (978-0-590-95943-8). A collection of stories by fantasy authors, including the editor and his wife, that deal with unicorns. (Rev: BL 6/1–15/98; HBG 10/98; SLJ 5/98; VOYA 8/98)

8950 Cowell, Cressida. *How to Speak Dragonese: By Hiccup Horrendous Haddock III* (3–5). Illus. by author. 2006, Little, Brown $10.99 (978-0-316-15600-4). Young Viking Hiccup is joined by a friend and his dragon as they fight Roman invaders in this entertaining sequel to *How to Train Your Dragon* (2004) and *How to Be a Pirate* (2005). (Rev: SLJ 6/06)

8951 Cowell, Cressida. *How to Train Your Dragon: By Hiccup Horrendous Haddock III: Translated from an Old Norse Legend by Cressida Cowell* (4–8). 2004, Little, Brown paper $10.95 (978-0-316-73737-1). The hilarious account of the fumbling efforts of nerdy Hiccup to capture and train a dragon and to take his rightful place as the next Warrior Chief. Also use *How to Be a Pirate: By Hiccup Horrendous Haddock III* (2005). (Rev: BL 4/15/04; SLJ 7/04)

8952 Cowing, Sue. *You Will Call Me Drog* (5–8). 2011, Carolrhoda $16.95 (978-076136076-6). 288pp. A possessed puppet that won't come off a boy's hand turns out to be a good thing, helping him to stick up for himself. (Rev: BL 9/15/11; LMC 1–2/12; SLJ 2/12)

8953 Cowley, Joy. *Starbright and the Dream Eater* (5–8). 2000, HarperCollins LB $14.89 (978-0-06-028420-6). A child born to a mentally disabled teenage mother and named Starbright is destined to save the earth from the Dream Eater. (Rev: BCCB 7–8/00; BL 4/15/00; HBG 10/00; SLJ 6/00)

8954 Cox, Judy. *The Mystery of the Burmese Bandicoot: The Tails of Frederick and Ishbu* (4–7). Illus. by Omar Rayyan. Series: The Tails of Frederick and Ishbu. 2007, Marshall Cavendish $16.99 (978-0-7614-5376-5). Rats Frederick and Ishbu escape their schoolroom cage and embark on an adventure that involves a shipwreck and a statue with the power to end the world. (Rev: BL 10/1/07; SLJ 12/07)

8955 Craig, Joe. *Jimmy Coates: Assassin?* (4–7). 2005, HarperCollins LB $16.89 (978-0-06-077264-2). Thirty-five percent human and 65 percent technologically engineered assassin, 11-year-old Jimmy Coates faces external dangers and internal struggles, all with action, suspense, and humor. (Rev: BL 5/1/05; SLJ 6/05)

8956 Craig, Joe. *Jimmy Coates: Target* (5–8). 2007, HarperCollins $16.99 (978-0-06-077266-6). Jimmy Coates, mostly robot but part human, chooses his human side and ends up on the run from the government that wants him assassinated. (Rev: BL 6/1–15/07)

8957 Crane, Jordan. *The Clouds Above* (2–4). Illus. 2005, Fantagraphics $18.95 (978-1-56097-627-1). Simon skips school and with his cat, Jack, climbs a magic staircase into a world of adventure. (Rev: BL 10/1/05) [741.5]

8958 Creech, Sharon. *The Unfinished Angel* (4–6). 2009, HarperCollins $15.99 (978-0-06-143095-4). Zola, a young American girl, moves to a small Swiss village with her father, meets an angel, aids a group of orphans, and helps to restore life to the aging community. (Rev: BL 7/09; SLJ 9/09) ∩

8959 Creedon, Catherine. *Blue Wolf* (4–8). 2003, HarperCollins LB $16.89 (978-0-06-050869-2). Fantasy lurks around each corner of this story of Jamie, a 14-year-old for whom running is a retreat from life and who sometimes feels that wolves are right at his heels. (Rev: BCCB 1/04; BL 11/15/03; SLJ 10/03)

8960 Crew, Gary. *The Viewer* (5–9). Illus. by Shaun Tan. 2003, Lothian $16.95 (978-0-85091-828-1). A well-illustrated dark fantasy linked to world catastrophes caused by mankind, from religious persecution to atomic war. (Rev: SLJ 3/04)

8961 Crilley, Mark. *Akiko: The Training Master* (3–6). Illus. by author. Series: Akiko. 2005, Delacorte $9.95 (978-0-385-73043-3). 207pp. Fifth-grader Akiko is in outer space at the Intergalactic Space Patrollers Training Camp in this latest installment in the humorous, lively series. (Rev: SLJ 7/05)

8962 Crilley, Paul. *Rise of the Darklings* (5–8). Series: The Invisible Order. 2010, Egmont $16.99 (978-160684031-3); LB $19.99 (978-160684064-1). 352pp. A fast-paced, multilayered fantasy in which 12-year-old Emily Snow — used to selling watercress on the streets of Victorian London — finds herself in the middle of an ancient war. ∩ Lexile 650L (Rev: BLO 5/15/10; LMC 1–2/11; SLJ 10/1/10)

8963 Cross, Gillian. *Pictures in the Dark* (5–8). 1996, Holiday $16.95 (978-0-8234-1267-9). A boy whose life is miserable uses supernatural means to escape the pressures. (Rev: BCCB 1/97; BL 1/1–15/97)

8964 Crowley, Bridget. *Step into the Dark* (5–7). 2003, Hodder & Stoughton paper $8.95 (978-0-340-84416-8). This ghost story is set in a theater and conveys the attraction of the stage. (Rev: BL 12/1/03)

8965 Crum, Shutta. *Thomas and the Dragon Queen* (3–5). Illus. by Lee Wildish. 2010, Knopf $15.99 (978-0-375-8570-34); LB $18.99 (978-0-375-95703-1). 272pp. A diminutive 12-year-old named Thomas, who has managed to qualify as a knight, sets out to rescue a princess from a dragon. (Rev: BL 7/10; LMC 10/10; SLJ 8/1/10*)

8966 Curry, Jane Louise. *The Black Canary* (5–8). 2005, Simon & Schuster $16.95 (978-0-689-86478-0). Twelve-year-old James, from a biracial family of musicians, resists pressure to develop his own musical abilities until he travels back in time to Elizabethan London and discovers he is also talented. (Rev: BL 2/15/05*; SLJ 3/05)

8967 D'Lacey, Chris. *The Fire Within* (5–8). 2005, Scholastic $12.95 (978-0-439-67343-3). A multilayered fantasy in which British college student David Rain comes to board at the home of Liz Pennykettle and her daughter, Lucy, and discovers that the clay dragons crafted by Liz have magical properties. (Rev: SLJ 10/05)

8968 D'Lacey, Chris. *Gruffen* (K–2). Illus. by Adam Stower. Series: The Dragons of Wayward Crescent. 2009, Scholastic $9.99 (978-0-545-16815-1). 104pp. Nine-year-old Liz's mom makes her a dragon called Gruffen to protect her from a "monster" in her room; Gruffen gets off to a rocky start but eventually solves the problem. Lexile 700L (Rev: HB 1–2/10; LMC 11–12/09; SLJ 5/1/10)

8969 Dadey, Debbie, and Marcia T. Jones. *Leprechauns Don't Play Basketball* (5–8). Illus. by John S. Gurney. 1992, Scholastic paper $3.99 (978-0-590-44822-2). The Bailey Elementary 3rd grade thinks the gym teacher is a leprechaun. (Rev: BL 9/15/92)

8970 Dadey, Debbie, and Marcia T. Jones. *This Side of Magic* (2–5). Illus. by Adam Stower. 2009, Starscape paper $3.99 (978-0-7653-5982-7). 136pp. Two children discover a magical land hidden right next door. (Rev: BL 6/1–15/09)

8971 Dahl, Michael. *Last Son of Krypton* (2–4). Illus. by John Delaney. Series: DC Super Heroes. 2009, Stone Arch $18.99 (978-1-4342-1155-2). 56pp. This action-packed, illustrated chapter book gives the story of Superman's arrival on Earth. (Rev: BLO 4/9/09; SLJ 6/09)

8972 Dahl, Michael. *The Museum Monsters* (2–5). Illus. by Dan Schoening. Series: DC Super Heroes: Superman. 2009, Stone Arch LB $25.32 (978-1-4342-1157-6); paper $5.95 (978-1-4342-1372-3). 56pp. A highly illustrated chapter book introduction to Clark Kent, Lois Lane, and Jimmy Olsen. (Rev: LMC 10/09*; SLJ 6/09)

8973 Dahl, Roald. *The Witches* (3–6). Illus. by Quentin Blake. 1983, Farrar $16.00 (978-0-374-38457-9). 208pp. A boy and his grandmamma save English children from being turned into mice by witches.

8974 Dakin, Glenn. *The Society of Unrelenting Vigilance* (5–7). Series: Candle Man. 2009, Egmont $15.99 (978-1-60684-015-3); LB $18.99 (978-1-60684-047-4). 304pp. Young Theo discovers he has the ability to melt people into puddles in this contemporary fast-paced adventure story with a Victorian feel. (Rev: BL 10/15/09; HB 1–2/10; LMC 11–12/09; SLJ 10/09)

8975 Dale, Anna. *Magical Mischief* (4–6). 2011, Bloomsbury $16.99 (978-1-59990-629-4); paper $7.99 (978-1-59990-630-0). 304pp. When the magic in his bookstore gets out of hand, Mr. Hardbattle and his friends Miss

Quint and 13-year-old Arthur look for a new home for it. (Rev: BL 5/1/11; SLJ 9/1/11)

8976 Dale, Anna. *Whispering to Witches* (4–6). 2004, Bloomsbury $16.95 (978-1-58234-890-2). 304pp. Twelve-year-old Joe Binks's Christmas-time encounter with a novice witch named Twiggy sweeps him into a mission to retrieve a book of potions and spells before it can be put to evil use. (Rev: BL 11/15/04; SLJ 11/04)

8977 Daley, Michael J. *Rat Trap* (4–6). 2008, Holiday $16.95 (978-0-8234-2093-3). 212pp. In this sequel to *Space Station Rat* (2005), Jeff and his genetically engineered friend Rat face the evil Dr. Vivexian. (Rev: BL 9/1/08)

8978 Daley, Michael J. *Shanghaied to the Moon* (5–8). 2007, Putnam $16.99 (978-0-399-24619-7). In the year 2165, 13-year-old Stewart Hale wants above all to become a space pilot like his mother was before she died in a crash; when his father refuses to help him, he runs away and finds himself on a secret mission to the moon. (Rev: BL 5/1/07; SLJ 5/07)

8979 Daley, Michael J. *Space Station Rat* (4–6). 2005, Holiday $15.95 (978-0-8234-1866-4). An escaped lab rat and a lonely boy, both residents of an orbiting space station, become friends and together face many challenges; the fast-paced texts switches from one character to the other. (Rev: BL 8/05; SLJ 8/05)

8980 Dallimore, Jan. *Captain Cal and the Garbage Planet* (1–4). Illus. by Richard Morden. 2010, Picture Window LB $14.99 (978-1-4048-5509-0). 56pp. Captain Cal and his capable team save a distant galaxy from drowning in garbage in this zany, lighthearted tale. Also use *Captain Cal and the Robot Army* (2010). (Rev: BL 2/15/10; LMC 1–2/10; SLJ 2/1/10)

8981 Dashner, James. *A Mutiny in Time* (4–6). Series: Infinity Ring. 2012, Scholastic $12.99 (978-0-545-38696-8). 192pp. Young Dak and Sera use a time travel device to to right historical wrongs; the first book in a series to be written by several authors and including a link to an online adventure. ⌒ ⓔ Lexile 800 (Rev: BL 8/12; LMC 1–2/13*; SLJ 10/12)

8982 Datlow, Ellen, and Terri Windling, eds. *Swan Sister: Fairy Tales Retold* (5–10). 2003, Simon & Schuster $16.95 (978-0-689-84613-7). Retellings by well-known authors of traditional stories are inventive and entertaining. (Rev: BCCB 11/03; BL 9/15/03; HBG 4/04; SLJ 12/03)

8983 De Fombelle, Timothée. *Toby Alone* (4–8). Trans. by Sarah Ardizzone. Illus. by François Place. 2009, Candlewick $16.99 (978-0-7636-4181-8). 384pp. In this gripping eco-fantasy, tiny Toby Lolness, 13, must struggle alone to beat the big corporation that threatens the survival of his tree world. (Rev: BCCB 5/09; HB 5/09; LMC 8/09; SLJ 5/09)

8984 De Mari, Silvana. *The Last Dragon* (5–8). Trans. by Shaun Whiteside. 2006, Hyperion $16.95 (978-0-7868-3636-9). To fulfill a prophecy in which he will play a key role, a young elf named Yorsh, the last of his kind in a world hostile to elves, sets off in search of the last dragon. (Rev: BL 11/1/06; SLJ 1/07)

8985 De Quidt, Jeremy. *The Toymaker* (5–8). 2010, Random House $16.99 (978-0-385-75180-3). 368pp. Orphaned young Mathias finds a piece of paper that holds a valuable secret and must elude his various pursuers in this eerie adventure. **e** Lexile 710L (Rev: BL 7/10*; HB 9–10/10; LMC 11–12/10; SLJ 10/1/10)

8986 de Saint-Exupéry, Antoine. *The Little Prince* (4–8). Trans. from French by Richard Howard. Illus. by author. 2009, Houghton Mifflin $35 (978-0-547-26069-3). 64pp. This effective pop-up presentation will attract new readers to the classic story. (Rev: BL 12/15/09; SLJ 3/10)

8987 DeFelice, Cynthia. *The Ghost and Mrs. Hobbs* (4–6). 2001, Farrar $16.00 (978-0-374-38046-5). 192pp. A ghost asks 11-year-old Allie for help, but scary and mysterious happenings hamper her efforts. (Rev: BL 9/1/01; HB 11/01; HBG 3/02; SLJ 8/01)

8988 Del Negro, Janice M. *Passion and Poison: Tales of Shape-Shifters, Ghosts, and Spirited Women* (5–8). Illus. by Vince Natale. 2007, Marshall Cavendish $16.99 (978-0-7614-5361-1). A collection of seven creepy supernatural tales, each featuring females who face peril and challenges. (Rev: BL 9/1/07; SLJ 12/07)

8989 Delaney, Joseph. *The Ghost Prison* (4–7). Illus. by Scott M. Fischer. 2013, Sourcebooks/Fire $12.99 (978-140229318-4). 112pp. Orphan Billy Caider, a resident of the Home for Unfortunate Boys, gets a job at a haunted castle, guarding prisoners including ghosts. **e** Lexile 780 (Rev: BL 10/1/13; LMC 5–6/14; SLJ 1/14)

8990 Delaney, Joseph. *Revenge of the Witch* (5–8). Illus. by Patrick Arrasmith. Series: The Last Apprentice. 2005, Greenwillow LB $17.89 (978-0-06-076619-1). A scary story in which young Tom, seventh son of a seventh son, becomes an apprentice spook and must protect the people from ghouls, boggarts, and beasties. (Rev: BCCB 10/05; BL 8/05*; HB 11–12/05; HBG 4/06; LMC 3/06; SLJ 11/05; VOYA 8/06)

8991 Deming, Sarah. *Iris, Messenger* (5–8). 2007, Harcourt $16.00 (978-0-15-205823-4). Iris is a miserable outcast whose life takes a turn for the better when the mythology book she gets for her birthday leads her to an amazing discovery. (Rev: SLJ 7/07)

8992 Desplechin, Marie. *Poor Little Witch Girl* (4–6). 2006, Bloomsbury $15.95 (978-1-58234-898-8). 128pp. Eleven-year-old Verbena is learning to deal with the fact that she's a witch even though she longs for a normal life, but when one of her Grandma's spell lessons involves the cutest boy at school she feels her social life is doomed. (Rev: BL 12/1/06; SLJ 12/06)

8993 Deutsch, Stacia, and Rhody Cohon. *King's Courage* (2–4). Illus. by David Wenzel. Series: Blast to the Past. 2006, Simon & Schuster paper $3.99 (978-1-4169-1269-9). 112pp. Abigail and her friends travel back in time on a mission to convince Dr. Martin Luther King, Jr. to continue his civil rights campaign. (Rev: BL 2/1/06)

8994 Diamand, Emily. *Flood and Fire* (4–7). 2011, Scholastic $17.99 (978-0-545-24268-4). 368pp. In this sequel to *Raiders' Ransom* set in a troubled 23rd-century England, Lilly struggles to protect Lexy and their game-playing computer while grappling with tense problems that arise in their dystopian world. **e** Lexile 700L (Rev: BL 7/11; SLJ 7/11)

8995 Diamand, Emily. *Raiders' Ransom* (4–8). 2009, Scholastic $17.99 (978-0-545-14297-7). 352pp. In the early 23rd century, when global warming has put much of Great Britain underwater and at risk from attack by marauding Raiders, 13-year-olds Lilly and Zeph are from opposing tribes but must join forces to rescue the kidnapped daughter of the prime minister. ⌒ Lexile 720L (Rev: BL 12/1/09; LMC 11–12/09; SLJ 12/09)

8996 DiCamillo, Kate. *Flora and Ulysses: The Illuminated Adventures* (3–6). Illus. by K. G. Campbell. 2013, Candlewick $17.99 (978-076366040-6). 240pp. After an unfortunate encounter with a vacuum cleaner a squirrel develops amazing superpowers and flies into the heart of unhappy young Flora. Newbery Medal; ALA Notable Children's Book. (Rev: BL 6/13*; HB 9–10/13; LMC 3–4/14; SLJ 8/13*)

8997 DiCamillo, Kate. *The Magician's Elephant* (4–7). Illus. by Yoko Tanaka. 2009, Candlewick $16.99 (978-0-7636-4410-9). 208pp. Young orphan Peter Augustus Duchene learns from a fortune-teller that his younger sister Adele is still alive and sets off, with an elephant, to find her, facing many challenges along the way. ALA Notable Children's Book. (Rev: BCCB 11/09; BL 7/09*; HB 9/09; SLJ 8/09*; VOYA 8/09)

8998 DiCamillo, Kate. *The Miraculous Journey of Edward Tulane* (2–4). Illus. by Bagram Ibatoulline. 2006, Candlewick $18.99 (978-0-7636-2589-4). Edward Tulane, a china rabbit, learns the meaning of love on an odyssey that begins when he falls into the sea during an ocean voyage. (Rev: BCCB 4/06; BL 1/1–15/06*; HB 3/06; LMC 5/06; SLJ 2/06*) ⌒

8999 DiCamillo, Kate. *The Tale of Despereaux: Being the Story of a Mouse, a Princess, Some Soup, and a Spool of Thread* (3–7). Illus. 2003, Candlewick $17.99 (978-0-7636-1722-6). 272pp. The diminutive mouse named Despereaux inspires confidence despite his odd appearance in this multilayered story involving Princess Pea, peasant girl Miggery Sow, and a rat named Roscuro. Newbery Medal winner, 2004. (Rev: BL 7/03; HB 5/04; SLJ 8/03)

9000 DiTerlizzi, Tony. *A Hero for WondLa* (5–8). Illus. by author. 2012, Simon & Schuster $17.99 (978-141698312-5). 464pp. Eva Nine, 12, who was raised underground by a robot, finds her way to New Attica, a seeming utopia; but she soon discovers a sinister underbelly. ⌒ **e** (Rev: BL 3/15/12; SLJ 6/12; VOYA 6/12)

9001 DiTerlizzi, Tony. *The Search for Wondla* (5–8). 2010, Simon & Schuster $17.99 (978-1-4169-8310-1). 496pp. Eva Nine, 12, who has been raised by a robot in an underground home, finally gets to see the real world and finds it a dangerous place full of bizarre creatures; features many rich illustrations and, using a Webcam, readers can access additional information on Eva Nine's world. ∩ Lexile 760L (Rev: BL 9/1/10; LMC 11–12/10; SLJ 8/10)

9002 DiTerlizzi, Tony, and Holly Black. *The Nixie's Song* (3–6). Illus. by Tony DiTerlizzi. Series: Beyond the Spiderwick Chronicles. 2007, Simon & Schuster $10.99 (978-0-689-87131-3). Nick think his life has changed dramatically when he gains a new stepsister, Laurie, but there's much more to come in this first installment in a new fantasy series by the creators of The Spiderwick Chronicles. (Rev: BL 10/15/07) ∩

9003 Divakaruni, Chitra Banerjee. *The Mirror of Fire and Dreaming* (5–8). 2005, Roaring Brook $16.95 (978-1-59643-067-9). In this sequel to *The Conch Bearer* (2003), 12-year-old Anand continues his magic studies and travels back to Moghul times, where he encounters powerful sorcerers and evil jinns. (Rev: BL 9/1/05; SLJ 12/05)

9004 Doherty, Berlie. *The Goblin Baby* (1–4). Illus. by Lesley Harker. Series: Stepping Stones Fantasy. 2009, Random LB $11.99 (978-0-375-95841-0); paper $4.99 (978-0-375-85841-3). 128pp. When Tam's baby sister is replaced with a changeling, he must go to the land of faeries to set things straight. (Rev: BCCB 6/09; BL 5/15/09; LMC 8/09; SLJ 5/09)

9005 Donaldson, Julia. *The Giants and the Joneses* (3–5). Illus. by Greg Swearingen. 2005, Holt $14.95 (978-0-8050-7805-3). 215pp. In this twist on the tale of Jack and the Beanstalk, filled with invented words, Jumbeelia, a young giantess who lives in Groil, climbs down a "bimplestonk" to a miniature world below where she kidnaps three "iggly plops." (Rev: SLJ 10/05) ∩

9006 Dowell, Frances O'Roark. *Falling In* (4–7). 2010, Simon & Schuster $16.99 (978-1-4169-5032-5). 256pp. Middle-schooler Isabelle Bean suddenly finds herself in an alternate world in which a frightening witch might be her grandmother Grete. ∩ ℮ Lexile 850L (Rev: BL 1/1/10*; LMC 5–6/10; SLJ 4/10)

9007 Downer, Ann. *The Dragon of Never-Was* (4–7). Illus. by Omar Ryyan. 2006, Simon & Schuster $16.95 (978-0-689-85571-9). In this lively sequel to *Hatching Magic* (2003), 12-year-old Theodora Oglethorpe accompanies her father to Scotland to investigate the origin of a mysterious scale and there learns more about her own magical powers. (Rev: BL 6/1–15/06; SLJ 12/06)

9008 Downer, Ann. *Hatching Magic* (4–7). Illus. by Omar Rayyan. 2003, Simon & Schuster $16.95 (978-0-689-83400-4). A procession of a pet dragon, a wizard, and his archenemy travel through time from the 13th century to the 21st century, where an 11-year-old Bostonian becomes involved in their disputes. (Rev: BL 4/15/03; HB 7–8/03; HBG 10/03; SLJ 8/03)

9009 Doyle, Bill. *Attack of the Shark-Headed Zombie* (3–5). Illus. by Scott Altmann. Series: Stepping Stones. 2011, Random House LB $12.99 (978-037596675-0); paper $4.99 (978-037586675-3). 112pp. Compelled to take jobs in order to afford new bikes, Henry and Keats sign up to clean a disheveled and spooky mansion; all

manner of paranormal adventures ensue in this action-packed beginning chapter book. ℮ Lexile 480L (Rev: BL 4/15/11; LMC 10/11)

9010 Doyle, Debra, and James D. MacDonald. *Groogleman* (5–8). 1996, Harcourt $15.00 (978-0-15-200235-0). In this novel set in the future, 13-year-old Dan is immune to the plague that is devastating the countryside and sets out with friend Leesie to help tend the sick. (Rev: BCCB 12/96; SLJ 12/96; VOYA 6/97)

9011 Drago, Ty. *Queen of the Dead* (4–7). Series: The Undertakers. 2012, Sourcebooks/Jabberwocky paper $7.99 (978-1-4022-7-557-9). 432pp. Will Ritter and his Undertaker friends continue their efforts against the zombies even as a new leader, the Queen of the Dead, enters the picture; a sequel to *Rise of the Corpses* (2011). ℮ Lexile 660L (Rev: BL 11/1/12; LMC 5–6/13; SLJ 12/12)

9012 Drago, Ty. *The Undertakers: Rise of the Corpses* (4–7). 2011, Sourcebooks paper $10.99 (978-1-4022-4-785-9). 480pp. Gifted with the ability to see zombies, 12-year-old Will joins the Undertakers, a group determined to thwart the zombies' evil plans. (Rev: BL 5/1/11; SLJ 7/11)

9013 Drake, Salamanda. *Dragonsdale* (3–6). Illus. by Gilly Marklew. 2007, Scholastic $16.99 (978-0-439-87173-0). 288pp. A teen girl yearns to ride the dragons she cares for. (Rev: BCCB 9/07; BL 6/1–15/07; LMC 11/07; SLJ 6/07)

9014 Drexler, Sam, and Fay Shelby. *Lost in Spillville* (5–9). Series: Erika and Oz Adventures in American History. 2000, Aunt Strawberry paper $6.99 (978-0-9669988-1-8). Two teenagers accidentally are transported to the 1930s and must locate an important clock maker to be returned to the 1990s. (Rev: SLJ 11/00; VOYA 12/00)

9015 Driscoll, Laura. *Vidia and the Fairy Crown* (2–3). Illus. by Judith Clarke, et al. Series: Disney Fairies. 2006, Random paper $5.99 (978-0-7364-2372-4). Vidia, a temperamental fairy who lives in Never Land's Pixie Hollow, struggles to clear her name after she's falsely accused of stealing Queen Clarion's crown. (Rev: SLJ 3/06)

9016 Duane, Diane. *Deep Wizardry* (5–8). Series: Young Wizards. 2001, Magic Carpet Books LB $15.25 (978-0-613-36059-3); paper $6.95 (978-0-15-216257-3). Nita and Kit, the two young wizards of *So You Want to Be a Wizard*, again use their powers to prevent a great catastrophe. (Rev: HB 5–6/85)

9017 Duane, Diane. *So You Want to Be a Wizard* (5–8). Series: Young Wizards. 2003, Harcourt $16.95 (978-0-15-204738-2); paper $6.95 (978-0-15-216250-4). Nita and friends embark on a journey to retrieve the Book of Night with Moon.

9018 Duel, John. *Wide Awake in Dreamland* (5–8). 1992, Stargaze $15.95 (978-0-9630923-0-4). An evil warlock threatens to steal a 9-year-old's imagination unless the young boy can find a friendly wizard first. (Rev: BL 3/1/92; SLJ 5/92)

9019 Duey, Kathleen. *Silence and Stone* (3–5). Illus. by Sandara Tang. Series: The Faeries' Promise. 2010, Simon & Schuster $15.99 (978-1-4169-8456-6); paper $4.99 (978-1-4169-8457-3). 109pp. Fairy Alida tells a lie in order to escape from the castle where she has been confined for decades. (Rev: SLJ 9/1/10)

9020 Dunkle, Clare B. *The Hollow Kingdom* (5–8). 2003, Henry Holt $16.95 (978-0-8050-7390-4). A beauty-and-the-beast story with a twist, in which Kate is persuaded to marry a goblin king and move to his underground world. (Rev: BL 11/15/03; HBG 4/04; SLJ 12/03)

9021 Dunkle, Clare B. *The Sky Inside* (4–8). 2008, Atheneum $16.99 (978-1-4169-2422-7). Martin discovers the terrible truth about his flawless, enclosed suburb when he gathers the courage to venture outside it. (Rev: BL 5/15/08; SLJ 5/08)

9022 Dunkle, Clare B. *The Walls Have Eyes* (5–8). 2009, Atheneum $16.99 (978-1-4169-5379-1). Martin continues his life-threatening adventures as he faces the controlling forces of his society in this sci-fi sequel to *The Sky Inside* (2008). (Rev: BL 7/09)

9023 Dunlop, Eileen. *Websters' Leap* (4–7). 1995, Holiday $15.95 (978-0-8234-1193-1). In this time-slip fantasy, Jill gets involved with people who owned a Scottish castle 400 years before. (Rev: BL 10/1/95; SLJ 10/95)

9024 Dunmore, Helen. *Ingo* (5–8). 2006, HarperCollins $16.99 (978-0-06-081852-4). As they search for their missing father, 11-year-old Sapphire and her brother Conor find themselves torn between their home on England's Cornish coast and the Mer people and magical sea world of Ingo. (Rev: BCCB 10/06; BL 9/1/06; HBG 4/07; SLJ 8/06; VOYA 4/06)

9025 Dunmore, Helen. *The Tide Knot* (5–8). 2008, HarperCollins $16.99 (978-0-06-081855-5). 336pp. Part-mermaid siblings Sapphire and Conor, introduced in *Ingo* (2006), must save humans from a huge tidal wave. (Rev: BL 1/1–15/08; HB 1/08; SLJ 2/08)

9026 Dunn, Mark. *The Age of Altertron* (4–7). Series: The Calamitous Adventures of Rodney and Wayne, Cosmic Repairboys. 2009, McAdam/Cage paper $12.95 (978-0-59692-345-4). 150pp. In an alternate 1956 the town of Pitcherville is facing numerous strange calamities that 13-year-old twins Rodney and Wayne attempt to resolve with the aid of a physics teacher; the first installment in a zany series. (Rev: LMC 3–4/10; SLJ 2/10)

9027 Dunrea, Olivier. *Hanne's Quest* (2–4). Illus. 2006, Philomel $16.99 (978-0-399-24216-8). 112pp. Hanne, a young hen in Mem Pockets's henhouse, sets off on a heroic quest to save her owners' farm; excellent illustrations enhance this chapter book. (Rev: BCCB 4/06; BL 2/1/06*; HB 3/06; HBG 10/06; SLJ 2/06)

9028 DuPrau, Jeanne. *The City of Ember* (5–7). Series: Books of Ember. 2003, Random House LB $17.99 (978-0-375-92274-9). Lina and Doon work to find a way out of their isolated and decaying city, where the population is beginning to panic. (Rev: BL 4/15/03; HB 5–6/03; HBG 10/03; SLJ 5/03; VOYA 6/03)

9029 DuPrau, Jeanne. *The Diamond of Darkhold* (4–9). Series: Ember. 2008, Random $16.99 (978-0-375-85571-9). 285pp. Lima and Doon return to Ember to search for a device that may offer hope, and to find food to support the residents of Sparks through the hard winter; the final installment in the series. ∩ (Rev: HB 9/08; SLJ 11/08)

9030 DuPrau, Jeanne. *The People of Sparks* (5–7). Series: Books of Ember. 2004, Random House $15.95 (978-0-375-82824-9). In this sequel to *The City of Ember*, Doon and Lina, plus the 400 people they have led from Ember to the surface of the Earth, seek aid from the people of Sparks. (Rev: BL 4/15/04; HB 7–8/04; SLJ 5/04)

9031 DuPrau, Jeanne. *The Prophet of Yonwood* (4–7). Series: Books of Ember. 2006, Random House $15.95 (978-0-375-87526-7). About 50 years before the time of the Embers series, 11-year-old Nickie hides out at her great-grandfather's estate in Yonwood, North Carolina, and thinks about good and evil as she watches her neighbors react to predictions of doom. ∩ (Rev: BL 5/15/06; SLJ 6/06; VOYA 4/06)

9032 Dyer, Heather. *The Girl with the Broken Wing* (2–4). Illus. by Peter Bailey. 2005, Scholastic $15.99 (978-0-439-74827-8). 160pp. An angel with a broken wing leads twins James and Amanda on some merry adventures. (Rev: BL 11/1/05; SLJ 1/06)

9033 Easton, Patricia Harrison. *Davey's Blue-Eyed Frog* (2–4). Illus. by Mike Wohnoutka. 2003, Clarion $14.00 (978-0-618-18185-8). 104pp. Davey catches a blue-eyed frog that turns out to be a princess in this illustrated chapter book. (Rev: BL 3/1/03; HBG 10/03; SLJ 7/03)

9034 Eaton, Jason Carter. *The Facttracker* (4–7). Illus. by Pascale Constantin. 2008, HarperCollins $15.99 (978-0-06-056434-6). The library turns into the "liebrary" when the town of Traäkerfaxx decides to deal in lies rather than facts in this imaginative and clever story. (Rev: BL 1/1–15/08; SLJ 3/08)

9035 Ebbitt, Carolyn Q. *The Extra-Ordinary Princess* (5–8). 2009, Bloomsbury $16.99 (978-1-59990-340-8). 320pp. A younger, overlooked princess is thrust into the spotlight when an evil uncle tries to take over Gossling, leaving her to rescue her older siblings and save the kingdom. (Rev: BL 5/15/09; LMC 1–2/10; SLJ 9/09)

9036 Edwards, Julie Andrews, and Emma Walton Hamilton. *The Great American Mousical* (4–6). Illus. by Tony Walton. 2006, HarperCollins $15.99 (978-0-06-057918-0). 160pp. In this spoof by actress Julie Andrews and her daughter, a troupe of mice in a condemned Broadway theater are feverishly rehearsing a musical revue when their star goes missing. (Rev: BL 1/1–15/06; SLJ 2/06)

9037 Elliott, David. *Jeremy Cabbage and the Living Museum of Human Oddballs and Quadruped Delights* (4–6). 2008, Knopf $15.99 (978-0-375-84333-4). A humorous fast-paced fantasy about 11-year-old orphan Jeremy, who becomes embroiled in a dispute between the autocratic Baron von Strompie and the outcast cloons of the Living Museum of Human Oddballs and Quadruped Delights. (Rev: BL 3/15/08; SLJ 6/08)

9038 Ellis, Deborah. *True Blue* (5–8). 2012, Pajama $19.95 (978-098694953-1). 240pp. When her friend Casey is arrested for the murder of an 8-year-old girl, 17-year-old Jess finds it hard to support her in the face of widespread suspicion from the people of their town. Lexile 710L (Rev: BL 5/1/12; LMC 11–12/12; SLJ 5/1/12)

9039 Else, Barbara. *The Traveling Restaurant: Jasper's Voyage in Three Parts* (4–7). 2012, Gecko $17.95 (978-187757903-5). 295pp. When the powerful Lady Gall sets Jasper's family in her sights, the 12-year-old sets off on an epic search involving aspects of fantasy, time travel, mystery, and seafaring. (Rev: BLO 4/1/12; HB 5–6/12; SLJ 3/12)

9040 Enthoven, Sam. *The Black Tattoo* (5–8). 2006, Penguin $19.99 (978-1-59514-114-9). In this action-packed fantasy epic set in London and Hell, three teenage friends — Esme, Charlie, and Jack — work together to defeat a demonic entity that has taken possession of Charlie. ⌒ (Rev: BL 9/1/06; SLJ 1/07)

9041 Enthoven, Sam. *Tim, Defender of the Earth* (5–8). 2008, Penguin $19.99 (978-1-59514-184-2). Tim, a huge, T. rex-type fighting monster, breaks out of his underground lab to save London and the world from a crazy scientist — with the help of 14-year-old Anna and her friend Chris. (Rev: BL 1/1–15/08; SLJ 3/08)

9042 Epstein, Adam Jay, and Andrew Jacobson. *The Familiars* (4–6). Illus. by Bobby Chiu. Series: The Familiars. 2010, HarperCollins $16.99 (978-0-06-196108-3). 368pp. A streetwise cat finds himself posing as an assistant to a boy magician and must persuade other "familiars" that he is the genuine thing. Lexile 920L (Rev: BL 6/1/10; SLJ 8/10)

9043 Epstein, Adam Jay, and Andrew Jacobson. *Secrets of the Crown* (4–6). Illus. by Peter Chan and Kei Acedera. Series: The Familiars. 2011, HarperCollins $16.99 (978-0-06-196111-3). 384pp. With human magic gone, three animals — Aldwyn the cat, Skylar the blue jay, and Gilbert the tree frog — set out to wrest control of the Shifting Fortress from the evil rabbit Paksahara and restore the status quo. ℮ Lexile 930L (Rev: BLO 11/15/11; SLJ 8/11; VOYA 12/11)

9044 Etchemendy, Nancy. *The Power of Un* (4–7). 2000, Front St $14.95 (978-0-8126-2850-0). Gib, a young boy, meets a strange old man who gives him an "unner," which can send him back in time in this thought-provoking fantasy. (Rev: BCCB 7–8/00; BL 5/1/00; HBG 10/00; SLJ 6/00; VOYA 6/00)

9045 Etra, Jonathan, and Stephanie Spinner. *Aliens for Breakfast* (3–5). Illus. 1988, Random paper $3.99 (978-0-394-82093-4). Richard meets an alien who needs help to find a secret weapon. (Rev: BCCB 12/88; BL 1/15/89; SLJ 3/89)

9046 Evans, Lissa. *Horten's Incredible Illusions* (3–6). 2012, Sterling $14.95 (978-1-4027-9870-2). 352pp. Stuart, 10, must solve a series of increasingly challenging puzzles as he searches for his great-uncle Tony's will in

this sequel to *Horten's Miraculous Mechanisms* (2012). (Rev: BLO 12/1/12; SLJ 11/12)

9047 Evans, Nate. *Meet the Beast* (2–4). Illus. by Vince Evans. 2010, Sourcebooks paper $4.99 (978-1-4022-4-050-8). 128pp. Nine-year-old Zeke and his little sister receive a tiny monster named Otto, who causes some problems but is also useful at discouraging bullies; this early chapter book is highly illustrated and occasionally jumps into graphic novel format. (Rev: BL 11/1/10; SLJ 3/1/11)

9048 Fagan, Deva. *Circus Galacticus* (4–7). 2011, Harcourt $16.99 (978-054758136-1). 304pp. Frustrated orphan Trix joins a circus that tours the universe in a spaceship and learns to navigate new relationships and explore her past. (Rev: BL 11/15/11; SLJ 1/12; VOYA 12/11)

9049 Fagan, Deva. *The Magical Misadventures of Prunella Bogthistle* (4–8). 2010, Henry Holt $16.99 (978-0-8050-8743-7). 272pp. Prunella isn't very successful as a witch, but during her quest to find the Mirable Chalice, she finds that she has other talents; plenty of details about life as a witch make this an entertaining read. Lexile 640L (Rev: LMC 8–9/10; SLJ 6/10; VOYA 6/10)

9050 Falcone, L. M. *Walking with the Dead* (5–8). 2005, Kids Can $16.95 (978-1-55337-708-5). Alex finds himself entangled in the world of Greek mythology when a mummy in his father's museum awakens to take care of some unfinished business in the underworld. (Rev: BL 3/15/05; SLJ 6/05)

9051 Farland, David. *Of Mice and Magic* (5–8). Illus. by Howard Lyon. Series: Ravenspell. 2005, Covenant Communications $16.95 (978-1-57734-918-1). Ben's magical mouse Amber turns Ben into a mouse and together the two set out to rescue the animals from the pet store. (Rev: SLJ 1/06)

9052 Farrey, Brian. *The Vengekeep Prophecies* (4–7). Illus. by Brett Helquist. 2012, HarperCollins $16.99 (978-0-06-204928-5). 400pp. The Grimjink, a family of thieves in a medieval world, will prove to be saviors of the city of Vengekeep according to a prophecy woven into a tapestry. ℮ Lexile 780L (Rev: BL 12/1/12; SLJ 3/13)

9053 Favole, Robert J. *Through the Wormhole* (5–8). 2001, Flywheel $17.95 (978-1-930826-00-7). Detailed endnotes add historical weight to this story of Michael and Kate, who travel through time to 1778 to aid the Marquis de Lafayette and rescue one of Michael's ancestors. (Rev: BL 3/1/01; SLJ 4/01; VOYA 4/01)

9054 Fawcett, Melissa Jayne, and Joseph Bruchac. *Makiawisug: The Gift of the Little People* (3–5). Illus. by David Wagner. 1997, Little People $19.95 (978-0-9656933-2-5). 28pp. The story of the antics of the American Indian "little people," the Makiawisug. (Rev: BL 9/15/97)

9055 Feiffer, Kate. *Signed by Zelda* (5–7). 2012, Simon & Schuster $16.99 (978-1-4424-3331-1). 234pp. When Nicky's grandmother Zelda goes missing, the boy sets out to find her with the help of his friend Lucy, who analyzes handwriting, and a talking pigeon. **e** Lexile 750L (Rev: HB 7–8/12; LMC 11–12/12; SLJ 5/1/12)

9056 Fergus, Maureen. *Ortega* (5–8). 2010, Kids Can $16.95 (978-1-55453-474-6). 224pp. A gorilla named Ortega has been raised in a laboratory and given the ability to speak, but when he is asked to attend middle school, things go awry. Lexile 1040L (Rev: LMC 10/10; SLJ 7/10)

9057 Fields, Bryan W. *Lunchbox and the Aliens* (3–6). Illus. by Kevan Atteberry. 2006, Holt $16.95 (978-0-8050-7995-1). Two dimwitted aliens — Frazz and Grunfloz — kidnap Lunchbox the basset hound and program him to convert garbage into food; a funny, complex story. (Rev: SLJ 10/06)

9058 Fienberg, Anna. *The Witch in the Lake* (5–8). 2002, Annick LB $18.95 (978-1-55037-723-1); paper $7.95 (978-1-55037-722-4). This story of magic and suspense in 16th-century Italy interweaves fantasy with facts about the time. (Rev: HBG 3/03; SLJ 8/02; VOYA 8/02)

9059 Findon, Joanne. *When Night Eats the Moon* (4–7). 2000, Red Deer paper $7.95 (978-0-88995-212-6). Her flute music and some magic take Holly, a Canadian girl visiting England, back to prehistoric times at Stonehenge when the locals are being threatened with a Celtic invasion. (Rev: BL 8/00; VOYA 6/00)

9060 Fine, Edith Hope. *Cryptomania! Teleporting into Greek and Latin with the CryptoKids* (4–6). Illus. by Kim Doner. 2004, Tricycle $15.95 (978-1-58246-062-8). 44pp. Zander and his friends teleport to various places and times, amassing information on Greek and Latin words for a vocabulary assignment; with extensive index/glossary. (Rev: SLJ 11/04)

9061 Fischbein, Dina. *Really Raoulino* (4–6). Illus. by Bill Crews. 2006, Handprint $15.95 (978-1-59354-151-4). Neither Raoulino, a newcomer at the Metropolitan Zoo, nor his keepers know what kind of animal he is, but he knows that what really matters is getting out of the zoo and back to his island home. (Rev: BL 4/15/06; SLJ 6/06)

9062 Fisher, Catherine. *The Oracle Betrayed* (5–8). 2004, Greenwillow $16.99 (978-0-06-057157-3). This suspenseful story set in an imaginary country that combines aspects of ancient Greece and ancient Egypt involves a young heroine, Mirany, on a dangerous quest. (Rev: BL 2/15/04; HB 3–4/04; SLJ 3/04; VOYA 4/04)

9063 Fisher, Catherine. *The Sphere of Secrets* (5–8). Series: Oracle Prophecies Trilogy. 2005, Greenwillow LB $18.89 (978-0-06-057162-7). Alexos, introduced in *The Oracle Betrayed* (2004), embarks on a journey to the Well of Songs while his friend Mirany serves the Oracle. (Rev: BL 3/15/05; SLJ 3/05)

9064 Flanagan, John. *The Battle for Skandia* (4–7). Series: Ranger's Apprentice. 2008, Philomel $16.99 (978-0-399-24457-5). In book four of the series, Will is saved from death by Halt and Horace, Evanlyn is captured, and the Temujai army closes in. (Rev: BL 4/1/08)

9065 Flanagan, John. *The Burning Bridge* (5–8). Series: Ranger's Apprentice. 2006, Philomel $16.99 (978-0-399-24455-1). Will and his friend Horace again face war and find the safety of the kingdom depends on them. (Rev: BL 5/15/06; SLJ 8/06)

9066 Flanagan, John. *Halt's Peril* (5–8). Series: Ranger's Apprentice. 2010, Philomel $17.99 (978-039925207-5). 320pp. In this ninth installment in the series, Will and Horace defy danger and save Halt by trusting each other and working together. ∩ **e** Lexile 800L (Rev: BL 9/15/10)

9067 Flanagan, John. *The Icebound Land* (4–7). Series: Ranger's Apprentice. 2007, Philomel $16.99 (978-0-399-24456-8). Will, the ranger's apprentice, and Princess Evanlyn are captives on a ship that takes them to Skandia to work as slaves; while the ranger Halt and knight-in-training Horace journey to rescue them but face many obstacles. (Rev: BL 6/1–15/07; SLJ 8/07)

9068 Flanagan, John. *The Kings of Clonmel* (5–8). Series: Ranger's Apprentice. 2010, Philomel $17.99 (978-039925206-8). 368pp. Halt, Will, and Horace work against a cult religion called the Outsiders and they discover secrets from Halt's past in this eighth installment in the series. ∩ Lexile 830L (Rev: BLO 6/10; VOYA 6/10)

9069 Flanagan, John. *The Lost Stories* (5–8). Series: Ranger's Apprentice. 2011, Philomel $17.99 (978-039925618-9). 352pp. A collection of nine stories that give the back story to the Ranger's Apprentice series. ∩ **e** (Rev: BL 11/15/11; SLJ 4/12)

9070 Flanagan, John. *The Outcasts* (5–9). Series: Brotherband Chronicles. 2011, Philomel $18.99 (978-039925619-6). 432pp. In an alternate Scandinavia called Skandia outcasts Hal, Stig, and other 16-year-olds undertake military training and compete with each other in races at sea. ∩ **e** (Rev: BL 11/15/11*; SLJ 2/12)

9071 Flanagan, John. *The Ruins of Gorlan* (5–8). 2005, Philomel $15.99 (978-0-399-24454-4). Will becomes an apprentice ranger and plays a key role in protecting his kingdom in this memorable first installment in a new fantasy series. (Rev: BL 6/1–15/05*; SLJ 6/05)

9072 Flanagan, John. *The Siege of Macindaw* (4–8). Series: Ranger's Apprentice. 2009, Philomel $17.99 (978-039925033-0). 304pp. Will, Horace, and a healer band together with the Skandians to reclaim Castle Macindaw and rescue Alyss in this sixth installment in the series. Also use *The Emperor of Nihon-Ja* (2011). ∩ **e** Lexile 850L (Rev: BLO 4/15/09)

9073 Flavin, Teresa. *The Blackhope Enigma* (5–7). 2011, Candlewick $15.99 (978-0-7636-5694-2). 304pp. A mysterious 16th-century painting draws Sunni, 14, her stepbrother, and an art classmate into its labyrinthine embrace. **e** Lexile 690L (Rev: BL 9/15/11; LMC 11–12/11; SLJ 11/1/11)

9074 Flavin, Teresa. *The Crimson Shard* (5–7). 2012, Candlewick $15.99 (978-0-7636-6093-2). 288pp. Sunni and Blaise find themselves transported to 18th-century London and must solve a mystery and work to find a way home in this sequel to *The Blackhope Enigma* (2011). **e** Lexile 700L (Rev: BL 10/1/12; SLJ 12/12)

9075 Fleming, Ian. *Chitty Chitty Bang Bang* (4–6). Illus. by John Burningham. 1964, Amereon LB $19.95 (978-0-88411-983-8). 159pp. Chitty Chitty Bang Bang, a magical racing car, flies, floats, and has a real talent for getting the Pott family in and out of trouble.

9076 Fletcher, Charlie. *Ironhand* (5–8). Series: The Stoneheart Trilogy. 2008, Hyperion $16.99 (978-1-4231-0177-2). In this sequel to *Stoneheart,* George races against three gruesome veins that have appeared on his body as he takes the Hard Way and searches for the Stoneheart. (Rev: BL 4/15/08; SLJ 6/08)

9077 Fletcher, Charlie. *Silvertongue* (5–8). Series: Stoneheart Trilogy. 2009, Hyperion $16.99 (978-1-4231-0179-6). 480pp. In this final book in the trilogy, George, 13, and Edie, 12, employ their newfound gifts — and receive help from statues come to life — in the fight against the Walker, the Last Knight, and the Ice Devil. (Rev: SLJ 6/1/09; VOYA 4/09)

9078 Fletcher, Charlie. *Stoneheart* (5–8). 2007, Hyperion $16.99 (978-1-4231-0175-8). At the Natural History Museum in London 12-year-old George stumbles upon a parallel world where good statues (or spits) and evil taints are at war. (Rev: BL 5/15/07; SLJ 8/07)

9079 Follett, Ken. *The Power Twins* (4–8). 1991, Scholastic paper $2.75 (978-0-590-42507-0). Three youngsters travel to a planet where large, gentle worms live. (Rev: SLJ 1/91)

9080 Foon, Dennis. *The Dirt Eaters* (5–10). Series: Longlight Legacy Trilogy. 2003, Annick $19.95 (978-1-55037-807-8); paper $9.95 (978-1-55037-806-1). In this well-written first installment of a trilogy, 15-year-old Roan finds himself torn between the peaceful ways of his upbringing and a desire to avenge a murderous attack on his village. (Rev: SLJ 1/04; VOYA 2/04)

9081 Forester, Victoria. *The Girl Who Could Fly* (4–7). 2008, Feiwel & Friends $16.95 (978-0-312-37462-4). Piper McCloud can fly — an ability that unsettles her community — and she is taken to a school for children with unusual abilities, which she soon senses is not quite what it seems. (Rev: BL 6/1–15/08; SLJ 9/08)

9082 Fox, Helen. *Eager's Nephew* (5–8). 2006, Random House LB $17.99 (978-0-385-90904-4). In this sequel to *Eager* (2004), Eager the robot and his nephew Jonquil pay a forbidden visit to Eager's human friends, the Bells; mystery and adventure ensue. (Rev: BL 10/15/06; SLJ 1/07)

9083 Foxlee, Karen. *Ophelia and the Marvelous Boy* (4–6). 2014, Knopf $16.99 (978-038575354-8); LB $19.99 (978-038575355-5). 240pp. Eleven-year-old Ophelia believes firmly in science until, grieving for her dead mother, she discovers a Marvelous Boy who needs her help to escape a 300-year captivity. **e** Lexile 660 (Rev: BL 12/15/13*; LMC 8–9/14; SLJ 3/14*)

9084 Frederick, Heather. *For Your Paws Only* (4–6). Illus. by Sally Wern Comport. Series: Spy Mice. 2005, Simon & Schuster $9.95 (978-1-4169-0573-8). 258pp. Morn-

ing Glory Goldenleaf, lead operative of the Spy Mice Agency, uncovers a plot by evil rat leader Roquefort Dupont to rid the world of mice. (Rev: SLJ 12/05)

9085 French, Jackie. *My Dad the Dragon* (2–4). Illus. by Stephen Michael King. Series: Funny Families. 2007, Stone Arch LB $22.60 (978-1-59889-343-4); paper $7.95 (978-1-59889-436-3). 107pp. Horace receives an assignment from his teacher at knight school to slay a dragon in this chapter book packed with fantasy elements. (Rev: SLJ 7/07)

9086 French, Jackie. *My Mom the Pirate* (2–4). Illus. by Stephen Michael King. Series: Funny Families. 2007, Stone Arch LB $22.60 (978-1-59889-345-8); paper $7.95 (978-1-59889-438-7). 107pp. Cecil time-warps to school every day from a pirate ship roaming the seas 200 years in the past. (Rev: SLJ 7/07)

9087 French, Vivian. *The Bag of Bones* (3–5). Illus. by Ross Collins. Series: Tales from the Five Kingdoms. 2009, Candlewick $14.99 (978-0-7636-4255-6). 256pp. Will Trueheart Gracie Gillypot be able to stop the witch Truda Hangnail's evil plans? (Rev: BL 5/1/09)

9088 French, Vivian. *Princess Daisy and the Dazzling Dragon* (2–4). Illus. by Sarah Gibb. Series: Tiara Club. 2007, HarperCollins $15.99 (978-0-06-112434-1); paper $3.99 (978-0-06-112433-4). Princess Daisy, who attends a special school to perfect her princess skills, has a stressful day in which she must deal with mean Princess Floreen and a baby dragon on the roof. (Rev: SLJ 7/07)

9089 French, Vivian. *The Robe of Skulls* (3–5). Series: Tales from the Five Kingdoms. 2008, Candlewick $14.99 (978-0-7636-3531-2). 208pp. This funny, multilayered story, the first in a series, features — among others — a sorceress who absolutely must have a new gown, a talking bat, and a girl called Gracie who has been locked in the cellar for being too cheerful. (Rev: BCCB 7–8/08; BL 9/1/08; HB 7/08)

9090 Fromental, Jean-Luc. *Broadway Chicken* (5–8). Trans. by Suzi Baker. 1995, Hyperion LB $15.49 (978-0-7868-2048-1). A tale of success and failure with, yes, a dancing chicken as the protagonist. (Rev: BL 12/15/95; SLJ 2/96)

9091 Funke, Cornelia. *Ghost Knight* (4–6). Trans. by Oliver Latsch. Illus. by Andrea Offermann. 2012, Little, Brown $16.99 (978-0-316-05614-4). 352pp. Boarding school newcomer Jon's homesickness vanishes when he's confronted by fearsome ghosts in this exciting story set in Salisbury, England. ∩ **e** (Rev: BL 3/1/12; HB 5–6/12; LMC 8–9/12; SLJ 7/12)

9092 Funke, Cornelia. *Igraine the Brave* (3–5). Trans. by Anthea Bell. Illus. by author. 2007, Scholastic $16.99 (978-0-439-90379-0). 224pp. A medieval fantasy featuring lots of magic and a brave 12-year-old girl named Igraine who longs to be a knight. (Rev: BCCB 2/08; BL 10/1/07; LMC 1/08; SLJ 11/07)

9093 Gaiman, Neil. *Coraline* (5–8). Illus. by Dave McKean. 2002, HarperCollins LB $17.89 (978-0-06-623744-2). An Alice-in-Wonderland type of tale for older readers in which a girl finds an alternate world in the empty apartment next door. (Rev: BCCB 11/02; BL 8/02; HB 11–12/02; HBG 3/03; SLJ 8/02*)

9094 Gaiman, Neil. *Fortunately, the Milk* (3–6). Illus. by Skottie Young. 2013, HarperCollins $14.99 (978-006222407-1). 128pp. A father on a trip to buy milk for his children finds himself whisked off on a time-traveling adventure involving everything from pirates and aliens to dancing dwarfs, but manages to return home with milk still in hand. Lexile 680 (Rev: BL 7/13; HB 11–12/13; LMC 5–6/14; SLJ 10/13)

9095 Gaiman, Neil. *Odd and the Frost Giants* (3–6). Illus. by Brett Helquist. 2009, Harper $14.99 (978-0-06-167173-9). 128pp. Odd, a young Viking, takes off alone to seek adventure and meets three mythological Norse characters who need help defeating a giant in order to return home. (Rev: BL 7/09; HB 11/09) ⌓

9096 Gaiman, Neil, and Michael Reaves. *InterWorld* (5–8). 2007, Eos $16.99 (978-0-06-123896-3). Joey, 16, discovers that he can walk into alternate dimensions where he finds other versions of himself and is recruited into an army of Joeys that battles Lord Dogknife and Lady Indigo, two evil magicians. ⌓ (Rev: BL 9/1/07; SLJ 11/07)

9097 Galante, Cecilia. *Willa Bean's Cloud Dreams* (2–4). Illus. by Kristi Valiant. Series: Little Wings. 2011, Random House LB $12.99 (978-037596947-8); paper $4.99 (978-037586947-1). 112pp. Willa Bean is a young cupid who looks a bit different from the norm, and is nervous about her ability to fly. ℮ (Rev: BL 12/15/11)

9098 García, Laura Gallego. *The Valley of the Wolves* (5–8). Trans. by Margaret Sayers Peden. 2006, Scholastic $16.99 (978-0-439-58553-8). Dana, 10, learns to use her magical powers at an academy of sorcery and wonders about the origins of her best friend and constant companion Kai, visible only to Dana. (Rev: BL 5/15/06; SLJ 6/06; VOYA 6/06)

9099 Gardner, Lyn. *Into the Woods* (4–7). Illus. by Mini Grey. 2007, Random House $16.99 (978-0-385-75115-5). After their mother's death, Storm and her sisters flee the evil Dr. DeWilde and his pack of wolves and find themselves facing many dangers that will be familiar to readers of fairy tales. (Rev: BL 5/1/07; HB 7–8/07; LMC 10/07; SLJ 6/07)

9100 Gardner, Lyn. *Out of the Woods* (3–7). Illus. by Mini Grey. 2010, Random House $17.99 (978-0-385-75154-4); LB $20.99 (978-0-385-75156-8). 320pp. Poking fun at well-known fairy tale tropes, this story features an evil witch, a magic pipe, and three plucky sisters who are ready to face any challenge; a sequel to 2006's *Into the Woods*. (Rev: BLO 2/1/10; HB 3–4/10; SLJ 6/10)

9101 Gardner, Sally. *Magical Kids: The Smallest Girl Ever / The Boy Who Could Fly* (3–6). Illus. by author. 2008, Dial $16.99 (978-0-8037-3159-2). 224pp. This "flip-over" volume holds two short back-to-back novels about children whose lives are changed for the better by magic. (Rev: BL 12/15/08; SLJ 2/09)

9102 Gear, W. Michael, and Kathleen O'Neal Gear. *Children of the Dawnland* (5–8). 2009, Starscape $17.95

(978-0-7653-2019-3). 304pp. Twig dreams the future and sees danger for her world so she takes off on a daring journey to save her people. (Rev: BL 7/09)

9103 George, Jessica Day. *Tuesdays at the Castle* (4–8). 2011, Bloomsbury $16.99 (978-1-59990-644-7). 232pp. Princess Celie, 11, lives in a magical castle that has the power to change itself at will; it also has its favorite people and it comes to the aid of Celie when her parents are in danger. ℮ Lexile 860L (Rev: LMC 1–2/12; SLJ 11/1/11)

9104 Gibbs, Stuart. *The Last Musketeer* (5–8). 2011, HarperCollins $16.99 (978-0-06-204838-7). 256pp. On a trip to Paris 14-year-old Greg is whisked back to 1615 France, where he meets young Aramis, Porthos, and Athos and has adventures including a struggle against Richelieu. Lexile 700L (Rev: BL 10/15/11; LMC 1–2/12; SLJ 10/1/11)

9105 Gidwitz, Adam. *The Grimm Conclusion* (4–7). Series: Tales Dark and Grimm. 2013, Dutton $16.99 (978-052542615-8). 368pp. Twins Jorinda and Joringel are caught in a series of gruesome situations in this concluding book of the Gidwitz trilogy, where, as they learn to fight back, they take over the narrative of the book from the storyteller. ⌓ Lexile 630 (Rev: BL 11/15/13; HB 1–2/14; SLJ 12/13)

9106 Gilden, Mel. *Outer Space and All That Junk* (5–7). 1989, HarperCollins LB $12.89 (978-0-397-32307-4). Myron's uncle is collecting junk, which he believes will help aliens return to their home in outer space. (Rev: BL 12/1/89; SLJ 12/89)

9107 Gilman, Charles. *Professor Gargoyle* (4–6). Illus. by Eugene Smith. Series: Tales from Lovecraft Middle School. 2012, Quirk $13.99 (978-1-59474-591-1). 176pp. Seventh grade at a new school is always a challenge, but Robert finds himself facing the mean science teacher Professor Goyle, two-headed rats, disappearing students, and other scary but funny horrors; the first volume in the series. ⌓ ℮ Lexile 660L (Rev: BL 9/1/12; SLJ 11/12)

9108 Gilman, Charles. *The Slither Sisters* (4–7). Illus. by Eugene Smith. Series: Tales from Lovecraft Middle School. 2013, Quirk $13.99 (978-159474593-5). 176pp. Strange things are going on at Lovecraft and Robert and his friends must stop the evil intentions of popular 13-year-old twins Sarah and Sylvia, who are in fact snake monsters. ℮ Lexile 690L (Rev: BL 3/1/13; SLJ 5/13)

9109 Gliori, Debi. *Witch Baby and Me* (4–6). Illus. by author. Series: Witch Baby and Me. 2010, IPG/Corgi paper $7.99 (978-05525567-6-7). 247pp. Nine-year-old Lily is aware that her baby sister Daisy has unusual powers and seeks to curb their wayward effects. ℮ (Rev: BLO 12/1/10; SLJ 9/1/10)

9110 Gliori, Debi. *Witch Baby and Me After Dark* (3–5). Illus. by author. 2010, IPG/Corgi paper $7.99 (978-05525567-8-1). 208pp. Nine-year-old Lily struggles to keep her baby sister (who's really a witch) in disguise in this British Halloween story. The fourth installment

473

in the series is *Witch Baby and Me on Stage* (2011). ℮ (Rev: BL 9/1/10; SLJ 9/1/10)

9111 Going, K. L. *The Garden of Eve* (5–8). 2007, Harcourt $17.00 (978-0-15-205986-6). When Evie and her father move to a house with an enchanted apple orchard after Evie's mother dies, a ghost and a magical seed help to ease Evie's grief. ∩ (Rev: BL 10/1/07; HB 11–12/07; LMC 1/08; SLJ 12/07)

9112 Golding, Julia. *The Gorgon's Gaze* (4–7). Series: Companions Quartet. 2007, Marshall Cavendish $16.99 (978-0-7614-5377-2). This sequel to *Secret of the Sirens* finds both Connie and the Society for the Protection of Mythical Creatures in danger. (Rev: BL 1/1–15/08)

9113 Golding, Julia. *Mines of the Minotaur* (5–8). Series: The Companions Quartet. 2008, Marshall Cavendish $16.99 (978-0-7614-5302-4). 269pp. This installment in the series features Connie, a 13-year-old who has a gift for communicating with mythical creatures. (Rev: SLJ 10/1/08; VOYA 6/08)

9114 Gonick, Larry. *Attack of the Smart Pies* (4–7). Illus. by author. 2005, Cricket $15.95 (978-0-8126-2740-4). This complex novel with graphic elements blends fantasy, horror, mystery, and humor in the story of Emma, a 12-year-old orphan who flees from her threatening foster father and finds herself in Kokonino County, land of the New Muses. (Rev: SLJ 6/05)

9115 Gopnik, Adam. *The King in the Window* (5–8). 2005, Hyperion $19.95 (978-0-7868-1862-4). Mistaken by window wraiths as their king, 11-year-old Oliver Parker struggles to resist their efforts to pull him into their world. (Rev: BL 10/1/05; SLJ 11/05; VOYA 2/06)

9116 Gordon, Amy. *The Shadow Collector's Apprentice* (4–7). 2012, Holiday House $16.95 (978-082342359-0). 202pp. In 1963, 12-year-old Cully Pennyacre, whose father has mysteriously disappeared leaving him with three aunts, takes a job with an antiques dealer who collects people's shadows. (Rev: BL 4/1/12; LMC 8–9/12; SLJ 4/12)

9117 Gormley, Beatrice. *Best Friend Insurance* (5–7). Illus. by Emily Arnold McCully. 1988, Avon paper $2.50 (978-0-380-69854-7). Maureen finds that her mother has been transformed into a new friend named Kitty. (Rev: SLJ 8/04)

9118 Goto, Hiromi. *The Water of Possibility* (5–7). Illus. by Aries Cheung. Series: In the Same Boat. 2002, Coteau paper $8.95 (978-1-55050-183-4). Sayuri, 12, and her younger brother discover a magical world full of danger in this fantasy that includes many elements of Japanese folklore. (Rev: SLJ 8/02)

9119 Grabenstein, Chris. *The Black Heart Crypt* (5–8). Series: Haunted Mystery. 2011, Random House $16.99 (978-037586900-6); LB $19.99 (978-037596900-3). 336pp. Thirteen-year-old Zack and his friends face vengeful ghosts on Halloween in this scary fourth book in the series. ℮ (Rev: BL 8/11; SLJ 2/12)

9120 Grabenstein, Chris. *The Crossroads* (5–8). 2008, Random House $16.99 (978-0-375-84697-7). Zack sees creepy faces in trees in this ghost story full of action, suspense, and likable characters. (Rev: BL 5/1/08)

9121 Graff, Lisa. *A Tangle of Knots* (3–6). 2013, Penguin $16.99 (978-0-399-25517-5). 240pp. Eleven-year-old orphan Cady has an amazing ability to bake just the right cake for everybody she meets in this multilayered story. Booklist Editors' Choice: Books for Youth. ℮ (Rev: BL 4/1/13*; HB 7–8/13; LMC 10/13; SLJ 3/13)

9122 Grahame, Kenneth. *The Reluctant Dragon* (2–4). Illus. by E. H. Shepard. 1938, Holiday House $15.95 (978-0-8234-0093-5); paper $6.95 (978-0-8234-0755-2). 58pp. Tongue-in-cheek story of a boy who makes friends with a peace-loving dragon. Another fine edition is illustrated by Michael Hague (1983, Holt), and a well-received picture-book version abridged and illustrated by Inga Moore was published in 2004 (Candlewick).

9123 Grahame, Kenneth. *The Wind in the Willows: The Gates of Dawn, Vol. 3* (2–5). Trans. from French by Joe Johnson. Adapted by Michel Plessix. Illus. by author. 2000, NBM $15.95 (978-1-56163-245-9). 31pp. A graphic novel that retells key episodes from Chapters 7, 8, and 9 of *The Wind in the Willows*. (Rev: HBG 3/01; SLJ 7/00)

9124 Gray, Kes. *Nelly the Monster Sitter: Grerks, Squurms, and Water Greeps* (3–6). Illus. by Stephen Hanson. 2009, Penguin paper $7.99 (978-1-59514-259-7). 272pp. Nelly Morton likes the thrill and variety of monster sitting. (Rev: BLO 5/27/09)

9125 Gray, Luli. *Falcon and the Carousel of Time* (4–7). 2005, Houghton Mifflin $15.00 (978-0-618-44895-1). Falcon, 13, and her Aunt Emily travel back to 1903 New York City in this novel that blends elements of *Timespinners* (2003) and the two previous Falcon novels. (Rev: BL 6/1–15/05; SLJ 7/05)

9126 Gray, Luli. *Falcon and the Charles Street Witch* (4–7). 2002, Houghton Mifflin $16.00 (978-0-618-16410-3). In this fantasy follow-up to 1995's *Falcon's Egg*, a 12-year-old girl becomes reacquainted with a dragon she released over New York City and befriends a witch who lives in Greenwich Village. (Rev: BL 3/15/02*; HBG 10/02; SLJ 4/02; VOYA 4/02)

9127 Gray, Luli. *Timespinners* (4–6). 2003, Houghton $15.00 (978-0-618-16412-7). 160pp. While visiting the dioramas in the American Museum of Natural History, twins Allie and Fig Newton are transported backward in time to 1913 France and then to 35,000 B.C. (Rev: BL 3/1/03; HBG 10/03; SLJ 4/03)

9128 Greenburg, Dan. *Secrets of Dripping Fang: The Onts* (3–5). Illus. by Scott M. Fischer. Series: The Onts. 2005, Harcourt $11.95 (978-0-15-205457-1). Despite significant hygiene issues, the orphaned Shluffmuffin twins are adopted by the elderly Mandible sisters and welcomed to the old ladies' mansion in Dripping Fang Forest, where they discover that all is not as it seems. (Rev: SLJ 12/05)

9129 Greer, Gery, and Bob Ruddick. *Max and Me and the Time Machine* (5–8). 1983, HarperCollins paper $4.99

(978-0-06-440222-4). Steve and Max travel back in time to England during the Middle Ages.

9130 Griffin, Adele. *Vampire Island* (4–7). 2007, Putnam $14.99 (978-0-399-23785-0). Three Manhattan youngsters — vegetarian vampire siblings Lexington, Madison, and Hudson — try to behave like normal people but their respective vampire traits keep getting in the way in this lighthearted, action-packed story. (Rev: BL 8/07; LMC 11–12/08; SLJ 8/07)

9131 Griffin, Adele. *Witch Twins* (3–5). 2001, Hyperion $14.99 (978-0-7868-0739-0). 144pp. Fifth-grade twins Claire and Luna are given many opportunities both at home and at school to use their hidden powers as witches. (Rev: BL 4/15/01; HB 9/01; HBG 3/02; SLJ 7/01)

9132 Griffin, Peni R. *The Ghost Sitter* (4–6). 2001, Dutton $14.99 (978-0-525-46676-5). 128pp. A gentle ghost story in which Charlotte tries to help a girl who died 50 years ago to find peace. (Rev: BL 8/01; HB 5/01; HBG 10/01; SLJ 6/01)

9133 Griffin, Peni R. *Switching Well* (5–9). 1993, Penguin paper $5.99 (978-0-14-036910-6). Two girls from different centuries trade places but soon regret their decisions. (Rev: BCCB 7–8/93; BL 6/1–15/93*; SLJ 6/93*; VOYA 8/93)

9134 Guiberson, Brenda Z. *Tales of the Haunted Deep* (3–6). Illus. 2000, Holt $15.95 (978-0-8050-6057-7). 70pp. This collection of ghost stories of the sea contains tales of monsters, pirates, lighthouses, and ships, many of them from folklore. (Rev: BCCB 9/00; BL 6/1–15/00; HBG 10/00; SLJ 11/00)

9135 Guibert, Emmanuel, and Joann Sfar. *Sardine in Outer Space 3* (5–8). Trans. by Elisabeth Brizzi. 2007, Roaring Brook paper $12.95 (978-1-59643-128-7). Sardine and her space-pirate friends tackle Supermuscleman among others in this series of zany adventures. (Rev: BL 3/15/07; SLJ 7/07)

9136 Gutman, Dan. *Abner and Me* (5–8). Series: Baseball Card Adventure. 2005, HarperCollins LB $17.89 (978-0-06-053444-8). Stosh and his mother travel back to visit the Battle of Gettysburg in an effort to learn more about baseball's origins. (Rev: BL 1/1–15/05)

9137 Gutman, Dan. *Babe and Me* (4–7). 2000, Avon $16.99 (978-0-380-97739-0). Joe and his dad time-travel to the 1932 World Series to witness a historic moment with hitter Babe Ruth. (Rev: BL 2/1/00; HBG 10/00; SLJ 2/00; VOYA 4/00)

9138 Gutman, Dan. *Cyberkid* (4–8). 1998, Hyperion LB $14.49 (978-0-7868-2344-4). Yip, a computer-savvy 12-year-old, and his sister, Paige, create a "virtual actor," or "vactor," who breaks out of cyberspace and reveals a serious flaw: his database does not include a conscience. (Rev: BL 6/1–15/98; SLJ 8/98)

9139 Gutman, Dan. *Honus and Me: A Baseball Card Adventure* (4–7). 1997, Avon paper $5.99 (978-0-380-78878-1). Young Joe Stoshack finds a magical baseball card that allows him to travel through time and participate in the 1909 World Series. (Rev: BL 4/15/97; SLJ 6/97)

9140 Gutman, Dan. *Jackie and Me: A Baseball Card Adventure* (4–7). 1999, Avon $16.99 (978-0-380-97685-0). While time-traveling to research a paper on Jackie Robinson, Joe Stoshack becomes an African American and experiences prejudice first hand. (Rev: BL 2/1/99; HBG 10/99; SLJ 3/99)

9141 Gutman, Dan. *Satch and Me* (4–7). Series: Baseball Card Adventure. 2005, HarperCollins LB $16.89 (978-0-06-059492-3). Stosh travels back to 1942 to establish whether Satchel Paige was the fastest pitcher in history and learns about racial discrimination in the process. (Rev: SLJ 2/06; VOYA 4/06)

9142 Haarsma, P. J. *Betrayal on Orbis 2* (5–8). Series: The Softwire. 2008, Candlewick $16.99 (978-0-7636-2710-2). This sequel to *Virus on Orbis I* finds JT and his friends enslaved to aquatic aliens called Samirans on a wormhole ring. (Rev: BL 5/15/08; SLJ 7/08)

9143 Haberdasher, Violet. *Knightley Academy* (4–8). 2010, Simon & Schuster $15.99 (978-1-4169-9143-4). 469pp. Orphan Henry Grim becomes the first commoner to attend the prestigious Knightley Academy, which trains police and other public authorities in the Britonian Isles, and soon uncovers a plot to start war. ℮ Lexile 860L (Rev: BL 2/15/10; SLJ 4/10)

9144 Haberdasher, Violet. *The Secret Prince* (5–8). Series: Knightley Academy. 2011, Aladdin $16.99 (978-1-4169-9145-8). 256pp. Back at Knightley Academy and studying for their knighthood, Henry and his friends start a secret battle society and Henry learns about his parents and his destiny. Lexile 830L (Rev: BL 7/11; LMC 10/11; SLJ 8/11)

9145 Haddix, Margaret Peterson. *Among the Barons* (5–8). 2003, Simon & Schuster $16.95 (978-0-689-83906-1). Luke, a third child who has been living underground in this two-child society, comes close to exposure in this exciting installment in the series that began with *Among the Hidden* (1998). (Rev: BL 5/15/03; HBG 10/03; SLJ 6/03; VOYA 8/03)

9146 Haddix, Margaret Peterson. *Among the Betrayed* (5–9). 2002, Simon & Schuster $16.95 (978-0-689-83905-4). In this third novel in the series that started with *Among the Hidden* (1998), illegal third child Nina faces danger and difficult decisions. (Rev: BCCB 10/02; HBG 10/02; SLJ 6/02; VOYA 6/02)

9147 Haddix, Margaret Peterson. *Among the Brave* (4–7). Series: Shadow Children. 2004, Simon & Schuster $15.95 (978-0-689-85794-2). This sequel to *Among the Barons* (2003) features Trey's efforts to rescue Luke and other third-born children. (Rev: BL 5/15/04; SLJ 6/04)

9148 Haddix, Margaret Peterson. *Among the Enemy* (5–8). Series: Shadow Children. 2005, Simon & Schuster $15.95 (978-0-689-85796-6). Matthias, one of the third children illegal in his society, is mistakenly welcomed into the Population Police; there he is confused by divided loyalties. (Rev: BL 6/1–15/05; SLJ 6/05)

9149 Haddix, Margaret Peterson. *Among the Free* (5–8). Series: Shadow Children. 2006, Simon & Schuster $16.95 (978-0-689-85798-0). Illegal third child Luke inadvertently sets off an uprising that leads to the over-throw of his country's oppressive government. (Rev: BL 6/1–15/06; SLJ 8/06)

9150 Haddix, Margaret Peterson. *Among the Hidden* (5–8). 1998, Simon & Schuster $16.95 (978-0-689-81700-7). In a society where only two children are allowed per family, Luke, the third, endures a secret life hidden from authorities. (Rev: HBG 3/99; SLJ 9/98; VOYA 10/98)

9151 Haddix, Margaret Peterson. *Among the Impostors* (5–7). 2001, Simon & Schuster $16.00 (978-0-689-83904-7). As a third child in a society that allows only two per family, Luke has assumed a new identity and at age 12 enrolls in a nightmarish boarding school. (Rev: BCCB 9/01; BL 4/15/01; HBG 10/01; SLJ 7/01; VOYA 8/01)

9152 Haddix, Margaret Peterson. *Caught* (5–8). Series: Missing. 2012, Simon & Schuster $16.99 (978-141698982-0). 352pp. Jonah and Katherine travel to 1903 Switzerland and Serbia to return Albert Einstein's daughter Lieserl to history, but his wife Mileva, who seems to understand a lot about time travel, is unwilling to let her daughter go. ∩ **e** Lexile 730L (Rev: BL 8/12; SLJ 3/13)

9153 Haddix, Margaret Peterson. *Double Identity* (5–8). 2005, Simon & Schuster $15.95 (978-0-689-87374-4). In this science fiction page-turner, 12-year-old Bethany Cole, left with her aunt after her mother suffers a nervous breakdown, uncovers some shocking family secrets. (Rev: BL 10/1/05; SLJ 11/05; VOYA 10/05)

9154 Haddix, Margaret Peterson. *Risked* (5–8). Series: The Missing. 2013, Simon & Schuster $16.99 (978-141698984-4). 320pp. Jonah, Katherine, and Chip are kidnapped and whisked back through time to 1918, where they might just be able to save someone in one of the most famous families in Russia, the Romanovs; the 6th book in the series. **e** Lexile 770 (Rev: BLO 9/15/13; LMC 1–2/14)

9155 Haddix, Margaret Peterson. *Running Out of Time* (4–7). 1995, Simon & Schuster $16.95 (978-0-689-80084-9). Living in a historical site where the time is the 1840s, Jessie escapes into the present in this fantasy. (Rev: BCCB 11/95; BL 10/1/95; SLJ 10/95*)

9156 Haddix, Margaret Peterson. *Sabotaged* (5–8). Series: The Missing. 2010, Simon & Schuster $16.99 (978-141695424-8). 384pp. Siblings Jonah and Katherine are sent back in time to help a missing child in the mysterious Roanoke Colony, but things do not go as planned. ∩ **e** (Rev: BL 10/1/10; SLJ 7/10)

9157 Haddix, Margaret Peterson. *Sent* (5–8). Series: The Missing. 2009, Simon & Schuster $15.99 (978-1-4169-5422-4). 313pp. In this suspenseful sequel to 2008's *Found,* Chip, Jonah, Katherine, and Alex arrive in 15th-century England through the magic of time travel, and struggle to save Princes Edward and Richard from their fates while watching history unfold. (Rev: BL 8/09; SLJ 10/09)

9158 Haddix, Margaret Peterson. *Torn* (4–6). Series: The Missing. 2011, Simon & Schuster $15.99 (978-141698980-6). 352pp. Time travelers Jonah and Katherine are in peril on Henry Hudson's ill-fated 1611 expedition, unsure that they can preserve history and get back home. (Rev: BL 9/1/11)

9159 Hague, Michael, ed. *The Book of Dragons* (4–7). Illus. by author. 1995, Morrow $21.99 (978-0-688-10879-3). Seventeen classic tales about dragons by such authors as Tolkien and Kenneth Grahame are included in this interesting anthology. (Rev: BL 10/1/95; SLJ 10/95)

9160 Hahn, Mary Downing. *All the Lovely Bad Ones* (4–7). 2008, Clarion $16.00 (978-0-618-85467-7). Travis and Corey encounter ghosts at their grandmother's bed-and-breakfast, which was a poor house long ago. (Rev: BL 5/1/08; SLJ 5/08)

9161 Hahn, Mary Downing. *Deep and Dark and Dangerous* (5–8). 2007, Clarion $16.00 (978-0-618-66545-7). While spending the summer at her aunt's cottage in Maine, 13-year-old Ali meets a mysterious girl named Sissie who seems to know a great deal about a tragic accident that occurred three decades earlier. (Rev: BL 3/15/07; SLJ 5/07)

9162 Hahn, Mary Downing. *Wait Till Helen Comes: A Ghost Story* (5–7). 1986, Houghton Mifflin $15.00 (978-0-89919-453-0); paper $5.99 (978-0-380-70442-2). Things go from bad to worse for Molly and Michael and their stepsister Heather when Heather becomes involved in a frightening relationship with the ghost of a dead child. (Rev: BCCB 10/86; BL 9/1/86; SLJ 10/86)

9163 Hahn, Mary Downing. *Witch Catcher* (4–7). 2006, Clarion $16.00 (978-0-618-50457-2). When Jen and her widowed father move into a rambling old mansion, the 12-year-old girl disregards warnings and investigates an old stone tower behind the house. (Rev: BL 6/1–15/06; SLJ 8/06)

9164 Haig, Matt. *To Be a Cat* (4–6). Illus. by Stacy Curtis. 2013, Atheneum $16.99 (978-144245405-7). 304pp. A quirky book about unhappy young Barney's desire to become a cat and the resulting predicaments when he gets his wish. **e** Lexile 690 (Rev: BLO 7/13; LMC 11–12/13; SLJ 7/13)

9165 Hale, Bruce. *The Big Nap* (2–6). Illus. Series: Chet Gecko Mystery. 2001, Harcourt $14.00 (978-0-15-202521-2). 112pp. Lizard detective Chet Gecko investigates why his classmates are turning into mindless model fourth-graders. (Rev: BL 12/1/01; HBG 3/02; SLJ 10/01)

9166 Hale, Bruce. *The Chameleon Wore Chartreuse* (3–6). Illus. Series: Chet Gecko Mystery. 2000, Harcourt $14.00 (978-0-15-202281-5). 112pp. Using a private-eye style of writing, this humorous mystery involves Chet Gecko, a fourth-grade lizard/investigator, who uncovers a plot to steal the team mascot. (Rev: BCCB 6/00; BL 5/15/00; HBG 3/01; SLJ 8/00)

9167 Hale, Bruce. *Farewell, My Lunchbag* (2–5). Illus. Series: Chet Gecko Mystery. 2001, Harcourt $14.00 (978-0-15-202275-4). Detective Chet Gecko investigates the problem of the mystery food snatcher who is operating in his elementary school. (Rev: BL 3/15/01; HBG 10/01)

9168 Hale, Bruce. *Give My Regrets to Broadway* (3–5). Illus. Series: Chet Gecko Mystery. 2004, Harcourt $14.00 (978-0-15-216700-4). Chet Gecko and sidekick Natalie look for Scott Freeh, who was supposed to play the lead in the school play, *Omlet: The Prince of Denver*. (Rev: BL 5/1/04)

9169 Hale, Bruce. *The Mystery of Mr. Nice* (4–6). Series: Chet Gecko Mystery. 2000, Harcourt $14.00 (978-0-15-202271-6). 112pp. Chet Gecko, the lizard detective, sets out to discover why his school principal is suddenly acting very nicely toward everyone. (Rev: BL 11/1/00; HBG 3/01; SLJ 12/00)

9170 Hale, Bruce. *This Gum for Hire* (3–5). Illus. Series: Chet Gecko Mystery. 2002, Harcourt $14.00 (978-0-15-202491-8). 132pp. Lizard detective Chet Gecko investigates mysterious goings-on on the school football team. (Rev: BL 10/1/02; HBG 3/03; SLJ 9/02)

9171 Hale, Bruce. *Trouble Is My Beeswax: From the Tattered Casebook of Chet Gecko, Private Eye* (3–6). Illus. by author. Series: Chet Gecko Mystery. 2003, Harcourt $14.00 (978-0-15-216718-9). 111pp. Chet Gecko, junior detective, enlists the help of mockingbird sidekick Natalie Attired to investigate cheating at Emerson Hicky Elementary. (Rev: HBG 4/04; SLJ 11/03)

9172 Hale, Shannon. *The Storybook of Legends* (4–7). 2013, Little, Brown $17 (978-031640122-7). 304pp. The children of fairy tale characters, such as Cinderella and Maleficent, attend Ever After High where they are trained to be the next generation of characters in the classic fairy tales, but Raven Queen, the daughter of Snow White's Evil Queen, does not want to follow in her mother's footsteps, instead becoming friends with Apple White (Snow White's daughter). e Lexile 720 (Rev: BLO 11/15/13; SLJ 12/13)

9173 Hall, Teri. *Away* (5–8). 2011, Dial $16.99 (978-0-8037-3502-6). 240pp. In this sequel to *The Line* (2010), Rachel is struggling to adapt to living among the Others and continues to search for father, who she now learns is still alive. (Rev: BLO 9/15/11; SLJ 12/1/11)

9174 Hall, Teri. *The Line* (5–8). 2010, Dial $16.99 (978-0-803-73466-1). 192pp. Rachel lives with her mother on an estate close to the Line, which separates the Unified States from the territory called Away; when she hears a plaintive recording from Away, Rachel feels compelled to act. e Lexile 760L (Rev: BL 2/1/10; LMC 3–4/10; SLJ 4/10)

9175 Halpern, Jake, and Peter Kujawinski. *Dormia* (5–8). Illus. 2009, Houghton $17.00 (978-0-547-07665-2). 512pp. All the action takes place when 12-year-old Alphonso falls asleep and enters a world called Dormia where he must use his special powers or Dormia will die. (Rev: BL 7/09; SLJ 9/09)

9176 Hamilton, Richard. *Jack Bolt and the Highwaymen's Hideout* (2–4). Illus. by Sam Hearn. 2007, Bloomsbury Children's paper $5.95 (978-1-59990-091-9). 192pp. Jack, 10, connects with highwaymen from the

18th century when he discovers that his attic bedroom is a link to other eras. (Rev: BL 12/1/07)

9177 Hamilton, Virginia. *Jaguarundi* (2–5). Illus. by Floyd Cooper. 1994, Scholastic $14.95 (978-0-590-47366-8). 40pp. A wildcat (jaguarundi) persuades a coati to flee across the river to find a new home. (Rev: BCCB 2/95; BL 12/15/94; SLJ 12/94)

9178 Hanson, Mary. *How to Save Your Tail* (2–4). Illus. by John Hendrix. 2007, Random $15.99 (978-0-375-83755-5). 112pp. Captured by palace cats Brutus and Muffin, Bob the rat uses his baking and storytelling skills to keep himself off the dinner menu. (Rev: BL 4/1/07)

9179 Haptie, Charlotte. *Otto and the Flying Twins* (4–7). 2004, Holiday $17.95 (978-0-8234-1826-8). In the City of Trees, Otto is shocked to discover his father is king of the magical Karmidee. The sequel is *Otto and the Bird Charmers* (2005). (Rev: BL 4/15/04; SLJ 6/04)

9180 Hardinge, Frances. *Fly Trap* (5–8). 2011, HarperCollins $16.99 (978-0-06-088044-6). 592pp. Orphan Mosca, her goose, and con man Eponymous Clent journey to the city of Toll, which is divided into the parallel towns of Toll-by-Day and the scary Toll-by-Night. (Rev: BL 3/15/11; HB 5–6/11; SLJ 6/11; VOYA 6/11)

9181 Hardinge, Frances. *Well Witched* (5–8). 2008, HarperCollins LB $17.89 (978-0-06-088039-2); paper $16.99 (978-0-06-088038-5). Ryan, Josh, and Chelle steal from a wishing well and discover that the act has given them undesirable wish-granting powers in this intriguing story. (Rev: BL 5/15/08; SLJ 8/08)

9182 Hardy, Janice. *The Shifter* (5–8). Series: The Healing Wars. 2009, HarperCollins $16.99 (978-0-06-174704-5); LB $17.89 (978-0-06-176177-5). 370pp. Fifteen-year-old Nya and her younger sister have the ability to remove pain, but Nya's gift is more tenuous and puts her in danger. e Lexile 630L (Rev: BL 10/15/09; HB 11–12/09; SLJ 1/10)

9183 Harper, Suzanne. *A Gaggle of Goblins* (4–6). Series: Unseen World of Poppy Malone. 2011, Greenwillow $16.99 (978-0-06-199607-8). 304pp. Poppy Malone, 9-year-old daughter of paranormal investigators, is skeptical of such shenanigans until her family moves to Texas and Poppy meets a goblin in the attic of their house. (Rev: BL 5/1/11; SLJ 11/1/11)

9184 Harris, Lewis. *A Taste for Red* (4–6). 2009, Clarion $16 (978-054714462-7). 176pp. Sixth-grader Svetlana, unsettled by a move, becomes convinced she's a vampire because she sleeps under the bed, has heightened senses, and eats only red foods; but then she meets teacher Ms. Larch, who has a vile odor and an evil smile. (Rev: BL 9/1/09; LMC 10/09; SLJ 9/09)

9185 Harrison, Michelle. *13 Treasures* (5–8). 2010, Little, Brown $15.99 (978-0-316-04148-5). 368pp. Tanya, a 13-year-old whose sleep has been disrupted by fairies, is sent to stay with her grandmother at Elvesden Manor and there uncovers dark secrets that place her in danger. e Lexile 770L (Rev: BL 4/1/10; SLJ 4/10)

9186 Hartinger, Brent. *Dreamquest: Tales of Slumberia* (4–8). 2007, Tom Doherty Assoc. $16.95 (978-0-7653-

1397-3). Julie, 11, is suffering — her parents fight all day and she has nightmares every night — until she wakes up in Slumberia, where her dreams are created, and must escape while there's still a chance. (Rev: LMC 1/08*; SLJ 2/08)

9187 Hartley, A. J. *Darwen Arkwright and the Peregrine Pact* (5–8). Illus. by Emily Osborne. 2011, Penguin $16.99 (978-1-59514-409-6). 448pp. Darwen, 11, receives a mysterious mirror that acts as a portal to another dimension full of battle and magic; his new friend Alexandra helps him make sense of all the mayhem. **e** Lexile 810L (Rev: BLO 10/15/11; SLJ 12/1/11)

9188 Hashimoto, Meika. *The Magic Cake Shop* (3–5). Illus. by Josée Masse. 2011, Random House $15.99 (978-0-375-86822-1); LB $18.99 (978-0-375-96822-8). 176pp. Sent to stay with her Uncle Simon, young Emma triumphs over this loathsome relative with the help of a baker who has some magical abilities. (Rev: BL 10/15/11; SLJ 12/1/11)

9189 Haskell, Merrie. *Handbook for Dragon Slayers* (4–6). 2013, HarperCollins $16.99 (978-006200816-9). 336pp. In this medieval fantasy 13-year-old Princess Tilda, who has a deformed foot and a literary bent, nonetheless has success finding dragons and other magical animals. Lexile 770 (Rev: BLO 7/13; SLJ 12/13)

9190 Haskell, Merrie. *The Princess Curse* (5–8). 2011, HarperCollins $16.99 (978-0-06-200813-8). 336pp. Based on the fairy tale about the dancing princesses, this story set in 15th-century Romania involves 13-year-old Reveka, apprentice to a herbalist, who tries to break the curse on the princesses of Sylvania. **e** Lexile 790L (Rev: BL 10/15/11; SLJ 12/1/11)

9191 Hawes, Jason, and Grant Wilson. *Ghost Hunt: Chilling Tales of the Unknown* (4–8). 2010, Little, Brown $16.99 (978-0-316-09959-2). 304pp. Stories of ghost investigations by the Atlantic Paranormal Society are paired with discussion of the techniques used. Also use *Ghost Hunt 2: More Chilling Tales of the Unknown* (2011). **e** (Rev: SLJ 11/1/10; VOYA 12/10)

9192 Hawking, Lucy, and Stephen Hawking. *George and the Big Bang* (3–6). Illus. by Garry Parsons. 2012, Simon & Schuster $18.99 (978-1-4424-4005-0). 304pp. George and Annie have adventures in Europe and in space even as they learn the latest theories about the universe in this third book in the series that combines factual essays with readable plots. Lexile 960 (Rev: BLO 8/12; SLJ 11/12)

9193 Haworth, Danette. *The Summer of Moonlight Secrets* (4–7). 2010, Walker $16.99 (978-0-8027-9520-5). 288pp. Allie Jo, who lives at a rundown hotel, befriends resident skateboarder Chase and the two spend a summer helping Tara, a girl who is part sea creature and is in danger. Lexile 610L (Rev: BL 6/10; LMC 8–9/10; SLJ 7/10)

9194 Hayter, Rhonda. *The Witchy Worries of Abbie Adams* (4–6). 2010, Dial $16.99 (978-0-8037-3468-5). 256pp. Fifth-grader Abbie, one of a long line of witches and trying to keep her talents hidden, is surprised when her new kitten turns out to be a young Thomas Edison.

How to reverse the process? **e** Lexile 1170L (Rev: BL 2/15/10; LMC 5–6/10; SLJ 4/10)

9195 Heath, Jack. *The Lab* (5–8). 2008, Scholastic $17.99 (978-0-545-06860-4). 352pp. This action-packed thriller features a teen known as Agent Six of Hearts who was created in a lab using a variety of genes and works for an underground organization called The Deck. (Rev: BCCB 12/08; BL 12/1/08; LMC 1/09; SLJ 2/09)

9196 Heath, Jack. *Remote Control* (5–8). 2010, Scholastic $17.99 (978-0-545-07591-6). 326pp. Genetically engineered teen agent Six of Hearts faces a crime lord and the ChaosSonic corporation as he battles to rescue his kidnapped clone-brother Kyntak; a sequel to *The Lab* (2008). **e** Lexile 840L (Rev: BL 4/15/10; SLJ 4/10)

9197 Heintze, Ty. *Valley of the Eels* (5–8). 1993, Eakin $15.95 (978-0-89015-904-0). A dolphin leads two boys to an underwater station where friendly aliens are cultivating trees to replant on their own planet. (Rev: BL 3/1/94)

9198 Helgerson, Joseph. *Horns and Wrinkles* (4–7). 2006, Houghton Mifflin $16.00 (978-0-618-61679-4). Mysterious events are taking place in Blue Wing, Minnesota — the nose of a bully named Duke turns into a rhino horn, and his parents turn to stone — and 12-year-old Claire is drawn into an adventure involving fairies and trolls. ∩ (Rev: BL 9/1/06; SLJ 9/06)

9199 Hemphill, Michael, and Sam Riddleburger. *Stonewall Hinkleman and the Battle of Bull Run* (5–7). 2009, Dial $16.99 (978-0-8037-3179-0). 192pp. At yet another boring Civil War reenactment, 12-year-old Stonewall Hinkleman finds himself whisked back to the First Battle of Bull Run, where he must stop a companion time traveler from reversing the outcome of the war. (Rev: BL 4/15/09; SLJ 5/09)

9200 Henderson, Jason. *Vampire Rising* (5–8). Series: Alex Van Helsing. 2010, HarperTeen $16.99 (978-006195099-5). 224pp. When he is sent to school in Switzerland, 14-year-old Alex Van Helsing learns that vampires are real and that his family has been participating in a vampire-hunting agency called the Polidorium since 1821. **e** Lexile HL780L (Rev: BL 3/1/10; SLJ 5/10; VOYA 6/10)

9201 Henderson, Jason. *Voice of the Undead* (5–8). Series: Alex Van Helsing. 2011, HarperTeen $16.99 (978-0-06-195101-5). 304pp. Vampire hunter Alex Van Helsing has another exciting adventure, this time involving Ultravox, a vampire with special vocal gifts. (Rev: BL 5/1/11; SLJ 9/1/11)

9202 Hennesy, Carolyn. *Pandora Gets Jealous* (4–7). Series: Mythic Misadventures. 2008, Bloomsbury $12.95 (978-1-59990-196-1). A lighthearted take on the myth of Pandora in which Pandy takes a special box to school for show-and-tell. (Rev: BL 11/15/07; LMC 4–5/08; SLJ 3/08)

9203 Herbauts, Anne. *Monday* (3–5). Illus. by author. 2006, Enchanted Lion $16.95 (978-1-59270-057-8). 36pp. This unusual, almost-wordless book will appeal to thoughtful readers who follow a creature called Monday through a cycle of seasons, some shared with his friends Lester Day and Tom Morrow. (Rev: SLJ 4/07)

9204 Hess, Nina. *A Practical Guide to Monsters* (4–7). 2007, Mirrorstone $12.95 (978-0-7869-4809-3). A tongue-in-cheek field guide to common monsters, this companion to the series Knights of the Silver Dragon is geared toward young wizards and features detailed illustrations. (Rev: BL 1/1–15/08)

9205 Hickman, Janet. *Ravine* (4–6). 2002, HarperCollins LB $15.89 (978-0-06-029367-3). 192pp. Jeremy enters a dangerous world of fantasy and adventure through a "time slip" in a ravine. (Rev: BCCB 9/02; BL 7/02; HB 5/02; HBG 10/02; SLJ 10/02)

9206 Higgins, F. E. *The Eyeball Collector* (5–8). 2009, Feiwel & Friends $14.99 (978-0-312-56681-4). 272pp. Young Hector Fitzbaudly seeks revenge for his father's death, setting out to track down the evil, one-eyed Gulliver Truepin. e Lexile 950L (Rev: BL 9/15/09; HB 9–10/09; LMC 1–2/10; SLJ 11/09)

9207 Higgins, F. E. *The Lunatic's Curse* (5–8). 2011, Feiwel & Friends $15.99 (978-031256682-1). 352pp. Rex's quest to solve his father's death leads him to the insane asylum on Lake Beluarum in this page-turner that includes an evil stepmother, steampunk aspects, and cannibalism. e Lexile 810L (Rev: BL 8/11; LMC 11–12/11; SLJ 3/12)

9208 Higgins, Simon. *The Nightmare Ninja* (5–8). Series: Moonshadow. 2011, Little, Brown $15.99 (978-0-316-05533-8). 369pp. Moonshadow contends with the altered emotional state of his former rival, now comrade, Snowhawk as he continues to dodge the evil advances of Silver Wolf's underlings; the second book in the series. (Rev: SLJ 9/1/11)

9209 Highwater, Jamake. *Rama: A Legend* (5–9). 1997, Replica LB $24.95 (978-0-7351-0001-5). When he's wrongfully banished from his father's kingdom and his wife, Sita, is kidnapped, valiant Prince Rama charges back to avenge the evil that's befallen his world. (Rev: BL 11/15/94; SLJ 12/94; VOYA 2/95)

9210 Hill, William. *The Magic Bicycle* (5–8). 1998, Otter Creek paper $13.95 (978-1-890611-00-2). For helping an alien escape, Danny receives a magical bicycle that is capable of transporting him through time and space. (Rev: BL 1/1–15/98; SLJ 3/98)

9211 Hirsch, Odo. *Bartlett and the City of Flames* (3–6). Illus. by Andrew McLean. 2003, Bloomsbury $15.95 (978-1-58234-831-5). 201pp. In this gripping sequel to *Bartlett and the Ice Voyage,* the title character and Jacques le Grand try to free Darian, the son of the Pasha of the City of the Sun, from his captors in the underground City of Flames. (Rev: HBG 4/04; SLJ 12/03)

9212 Hoban, Russell. *The Mouse and His Child* (4–8). Illus. by David Small. 2001, Scholastic paper $16.99 (978-0-439-09826-7). A toy mouse and his child embark on a quest to become "self-winding" and have sometimes scary, sometimes humorous adventures in this enchanting fantasy first published in 1967 and now updated with new illustrations. (Rev: BL 12/1/01; HBG 3/02)

9213 Hobbs, Will. *Go Big or Go Home* (5–8). 2008, HarperCollins $15.99 (978-0-06-074141-9). A meteorite crashes into Brady's bedroom in South Dakota, and Brady soon finds that something in the space debris has changed him. (Rev: BL 4/1/08; HB 5–6/08; SLJ 4/08)

9214 Hodges, Margaret. *Gulliver in Lilliput: From Gulliver's Travels by Jonathan Swift* (4–7). Illus. by Kimberly B. Root. 1995, Holiday $17.95 (978-0-8234-1147-4). The story of Gulliver in the land of the little people is retold with bright, detailed illustrations. (Rev: BCCB 6/95; BL 4/15/95; HB 7–8/95; SLJ 6/95*)

9215 Hodges, Margaret, ed. *Hauntings: Ghosts and Ghouls from Around the World* (5–8). Illus. by David Wenzel. 1991, Little, Brown $16.95 (978-0-316-36796-7). A diverse collection of 16 familiar and lesser-known tales about the supernatural. (Rev: BL 11/15/91; HB 11–12/91; SLJ 11/91) [398.2]

9216 Hoeye, Michael. *No Time Like Show Time* (5–8). Series: A Hermux Tantamoq Adventure. 2004, Putnam $14.99 (978-0-399-23880-2). Hermux the mouse investigates who is responsible for sending threatening letters to famous director Fluster Varmint. (Rev: SLJ 11/04)

9217 Hoeye, Michael. *The Sands of Time* (5–8). Series: A Hermux Tantamoq Adventure. 2002, Putnam $14.99 (978-0-399-23879-6). In this sequel to *Time Stops for No Mouse* (2002), the mouse watchmaker and a chipmunk friend believe that mice were once the slaves of cats. (Rev: HBG 3/03; SLJ 10/02; VOYA 12/02)

9218 Hoeye, Michael. *Time Stops for No Mouse* (5–9). Series: A Hermux Tantamoq Adventure. 2002, Putnam $14.99 (978-0-399-23878-9). Hermux Tantamoq, a mouse, leads a quiet life as a watchmaker until Linka Perflinger turns up and Hermux becomes entangled in mystery and suspense. (Rev: BL 3/15/02*; HB 7–8/02; HBG 10/02; SLJ 5/02; VOYA 6/02)

9219 Hoffman, Alice. *Aquamarine* (4–7). 2001, Scholastic paper $16.95 (978-0-439-09863-2). 112pp. Twelve-year-old friends Hailey and Claire find a lonely mermaid named Aquamarine, and they try to give her love and adventure. (Rev: BCCB 2/01; BL 3/1/01; HBG 10/01; SLJ 3/01; VOYA 4/01)

9220 Hoffman, Nina Kiriki. *Thresholds* (5–7). 2010, Viking $15.99 (978-0-670-06319-2). 256pp. Maya moves with her family to Oregon after her best friend's death and the 7th-grader becomes fascinated with her mysterious neighbors, eventually discovering the portal into a fantastical realm they are guarding. A sequel is *Meeting* (2011). e Lexile 630L (Rev: BL 8/10; LMC 10/10; SLJ 9/1/10)

9221 Holm, Jennifer, and Jonathan Hamel. *The Stink Files, Dossier 001: The Postman Always Brings Mice* (3–5). Illus. by Brad Weinman. 2004, HarperCollins LB $15.89 (978-0-06-052980-2). 144pp. While trying to find out who murdered his owner, Sir Archibald, feline London-based sleuth James Edward Bristlefur is whisked away to New Jersey and a confusing new life amid middle-class children. (Rev: BL 5/1/04; SLJ 6/04)

9222 Holt, K. A. *Brains for Lunch: A Zombie Novel in Haiku?!* (5–8). Illus. by Gahan Wilson. 2010, Roaring Brook $15.99 (978-1-59643-629-9). 96pp. Irreverent, sometimes gross, haiku tell the humorous story of a middle school populated by zombies, humans, and blood-sucking chupacabras. (Rev: BL 6/10; LMC 11–12/10; SLJ 10/1/10)

9223 Holt, K. A. *Mike Stellar: Nerves of Steel* (4–7). 2009, Random $15.99 (978-0-375-84556-7). 272pp. Mike's world is turned upside down when his parents make him move to Mars, and he discovers that they are part of a secret plot. (Rev: BLO 7/6/09)

9224 Holub, Joan, and Suzanne Williams. *Athena the Brain* (4–6). Series: Goddess Girls. 2010, Simon & Schuster paper $5.99 (978-1-4169-8271-5). 176pp. Young Athena, 12, is taken aback when she is informed that she is a daughter of Zeus and must attend a goddess (and godboy) school on Mount Olympus. e Lexile 710L (Rev: BLO 3/1/10; SLJ 4/10)

9225 Hood, Ann. *Angel of the Battlefield* (3–6). Illus. by Karl Kwasny. Series: Treasure Chest. 2011, Grosset & Dunlap $16.99 (978-044845471-9). 192pp. Reeling from their parents' divorce, twins Maisie and Felix, 12, arrive at a historic Rhode Island mansion, where a room full of artifacts transports them back to 1836 where they meet Clara Barton. e (Rev: BLO 10/15/11; LMC 3–4/12)

9226 Horowitz, Anthony. *Evil Star* (5–8). Series: The Gatekeepers. 2006, Scholastic $17.99 (978-0-439-67996-1). In the second installment of this action-packed fantasy series, 14-year-old Matt Freeman travels to Peru to learn more about the possible opening of another gate to the underworld. (Rev: BL 6/1–15/06; SLJ 7/06)

9227 Horowitz, Anthony. *Raven's Gate* (5–8). Series: The Gatekeepers. 2005, Scholastic $17.95 (978-0-439-67995-4). Faced with a choice between jail and life in a remote Yorkshire village, 14-year-old Matt chooses the latter, unaware that he's about to enter a world of frightening evil. (Rev: BL 7/05*; SLJ 7/05; VOYA 10/05)

9228 Horowitz, Anthony. *Return to Groosham Grange: The Unholy Grail* (5–8). Series: Groosham Grange. 2009, Philomel $16.99 (978-0-399-25063-7). 214pp. In this funny and somewhat spooky tale, David competes with a new student to earn Groosham Grange's top prize, the magical cup known as the Unholy Grail; a sequel to *Groosham Grange* (2008). Lexile 690L (Rev: BL 8/09; SLJ 9/09; VOYA 8/09)

9229 Horowitz, Anthony. *The Switch* (5–8). 2009, Philomel $16.99 (978-0-399-25062-0). 192pp. Rich kid Tad Spencer, 13, is not pleased when he finds himself in the body of Bob Snarby, son of carnival workers, until he starts to learn more about his old life. (Rev: BL 12/15/08; LMC 5/09; SLJ 3/09)

9230 Howe, James. *Invasion of the Mind Swappers from Asteroid 6!* (3–6). Illus. by Brett Helquist. 2002, Simon & Schuster $9.95 (978-0-689-83949-8). 96pp. Lessons about writing are hidden in the tale of a delightful dachshund named Howie, who keeps a journal detailing his writing experiences as he pens a story about an alien invasion. Also use *It Came from Beneath the Bed!* (2002). (Rev: BL 8/02; HBG 3/03; SLJ 11/02)

9231 Howell, Troy. *The Dragon of Cripple Creek* (5–8). 2011, Abrams $19.95 (978-0-8109-9713-4). 304pp. Kat, 12, falls into an abandoned mine chute in Colorado and discovers not only gold but an ancient dragon guarding the hoard; Kat inadvertently starts a 21st-century gold rush even as she seeks to protect the dragon and the environment. (Rev: BL 5/1/11; SLJ 7/11)

9232 Hughes, Carol. *Dirty Magic* (5–8). 2006, Random House $17.95 (978-0-375-83187-4). In a desperate attempt to save his little sister's life, 10-year-old Joe Brooks enters a shadowy world where ill children are held captive. (Rev: BL 10/1/06; SLJ 2/07)

9233 Hughes, Carol. *The Princess and the Unicorn* (3–6). 2009, Random $15.99 (978-0-375-85562-7). 288pp. This fantasy story follows Eleanor, an English princess who lays claim to a unicorn she discovers on a hunt, and Joyce, a courageous little forest fairy who sets out to rescue the unicorn and her forest village. (Rev: BL 1/1–15/09; SLJ 5/09)

9234 Hughes, Monica, sel. *What If? Amazing Stories* (5–10). 1998, Tundra paper $6.95 (978-0-88776-458-5). Fourteen fantasy and science fiction short stories by noted Canadian writers are included in this anthology, plus a few related poems. (Rev: BL 2/15/99; SLJ 6/99; VOYA 6/99)

9235 Hulme, John, and Michael Wexler. *The Glitch in Sleep* (5–8). Series: Seems. 2007, Bloomsbury $16.95 (978-1-59990-129-9). When 12-year-old Becker gets a job at the Institute for Fixing and Repair, he discovers that the world as we know it is under the control of the Seems; a humorous and thought-provoking story with plenty of illustrations and lots of entertaining gadgets. (Rev: BL 11/15/07; LMC 1/08; SLJ 11/07)

9236 Hulme, John, and Michael Wexler. *The Split Second* (5–8). Series: The Seems. 2008, Bloomsbury $16.99 (978-159990130-5). 300pp. In this followup to 2007's *The Glitch in Sleep,* 13-year-old Becker Drane sets about using his talents to save a fantastical world beset by horrifying storms. ∩ e Lexile 1030L (Rev: BL 10/15/08; SLJ 1/1/09; VOYA 2/09)

9237 Hunter, Erin. *The Empty City* (4–6). Series: Survivors. 2012, HarperCollins $16.99 (978-006210256-0). 288pp. A dog named Lucky becomes the leader of a pack in the aftermath of an earthquake that leaves them in a city without humans; the first volume in a new series. Lexile 760 (Rev: BL 8/12; VOYA 10/12)

9238 Hunter, Erin. *A Hidden Enemy* (4–6). Series: Survivors. 2013, HarperCollins $16.99 (978-006210260-7). 288pp. Former city dog Lucky returns to his pack to help his friends and agrees to spend undercover time with the fiercer wild pack led by a semi-wolf to learn about their rules and behavior. Lexile 820 (Rev: BL 5/1/13)

9239 Hunter, Erin. *Island of Shadows* (5–8). Series: Seekers: Return to the Wild. 2012, HarperCollins $16.99 (978-006199634-4). 304pp. Bears Toklo, Lusa, and Kallik, missing their former companion Ujurak, encounter many dangers as they make a difficult journey home in this first volume in a new series that is a companion to the Seeker books. (Rev: BL 1/1/12)

9240 Hunter, Erin. *The Sight* (5–7). Series: Warriors: The Power of Three. 2007, HarperCollins $16.99 (978-0-06-089201-2). Three kits — Hollypaw, Jaypaw, and Lionpaw — whose parents were members of the Thunderclan are endowed with special abilities in this series opener that follows the New Prophecy cycle. (Rev: BL 8/07; LMC 11–12/08)

9241 Hunter, Erin. *Sign of the Moon* (5–8). Series: Warriors, Omen of the Stars. 2011, HarperCollins $16.99 (978-006155518-3). 352pp. Jayfeather prepares for a dangerous journey that will reveal truth about the final battle as clan disputes continue; the fourth installment in this series. (Rev: BL 9/1/11)

9242 Hunter, Mollie. *The Mermaid Summer* (5–8). 1988, HarperCollins $15.89 (978-0-06-022628-2). Eric Anderson refuses to recognize the power of the mermaid and leaves his Scottish fishing village after his boat is dashed to pieces on the rocks. (Rev: BCCB 5/88; BL 6/1/88; SLJ 6–7/88)

9243 Hurd, Thacher. *Bongo Fishing* (3–6). 2011, Henry Holt $16.99 (978-0-8050-9100-7). 240pp. A friendly, pop culture-loving alien takes earthling Jason on an entertaining intergalactic adventure that also includes a mysterious character called Dr. Zimburger. Lexile 740L (Rev: BL 2/15/11; LMC 5–6/11; SLJ 2/1/11)

9244 Hurwitz, Johanna. *PeeWee's Tale* (2–5). Illus. 2000, North-South $13.95 (978-1-58717-027-0). 96pp. PeeWee is a little guinea pig whose intelligence and ability to read help him escape danger when he is left in a park. (Rev: BL 10/1/00; HBG 3/01; SLJ 10/00)

9245 Hussey, Charmain. *The Valley of Secrets* (4–7). Illus. by Christopher Crump. 2005, Simon & Schuster $16.95 (978-0-689-87862-6). A detailed, multifaceted novel about an orphan who inherits his great-uncle's estate and, through his uncle's journal, learns about the plight of the Amazon Indians. (Rev: BL 3/1/05; SLJ 2/05)

9246 Hutchins, Hazel. *The Prince of Tarn* (3–5). Illus. 1997, Annick $14.95 (978-1-55037-439-1). The spoiled prince created by his author mother in one of her fantasies comes to life and takes Fred to his kingdom. (Rev: BL 2/15/98; SLJ 2/98)

9247 Ibbotson, Eva. *The Abominables* (3–6). Illus. by Fiona Robinson. 2013, Abrams/Amulet $16.95 (978-141970789-6). 272pp. When Lady Agatha was kidnapped by a family of yetis, she became their governess, and together they were very happy until 100 years later, when reporters discover the yetis, and the group must make a long and challenging trip to England. ◑ Lexile 1010 (Rev: BL 9/15/13*; HB 11–12/13; LMC 3–4/14; SLJ 10/13)

9248 Ibbotson, Eva. *The Great Ghost Rescue* (3–6). Illus. by Kevin Hawkes. 2002, Dutton $15.99 (978-0-525-46769-4). A homeless ghost family moves into a boys' school and meets young Rick, who tries to establish a "sanctuary" for displaced ghosts in this humorous, scary, and sometimes gruesome book. (Rev: BCCB 11/02; BL 7/02; HB 9/02; HBG 3/03; SLJ 8/02)

9249 Ibbotson, Eva. *The Ogre of Oglefort* (4–6). 2011, Dutton $16.99 (978-0-525-42382-9). 256pp. A quirky story about a depressed ogre, a princess, and would-be rescuers who all find a satisfying but unexpected ending. ◑ Lexile 910L (Rev: BL 7/11; HB 7–8/11; LMC 11–12/11; SLJ 8/11)

9250 Iggulden, Conn. *Tollins: Explosive Tales for Children* (3–6). Illus. by Lizzy Duncan. 2009, HarperCollins $16.99 (978-0-06-173098-6). 176pp. Three interlinked stories feature Tollins — winged creatures bigger than fairies; a young Tollin named Sparkler has several adventures, including one in which he saves his people from being used in fireworks production. (Rev: BL 2/15/10*; SLJ 2/1/10)

9251 Irving, Washington. *The Legend of Sleepy Hollow* (4–6). Illus. by Gris Grimly. 2007, Atheneum $16.99 (978-1-4169-0625-4). A faithful adaptation of Irving's classic story, with atmospheric illustrations. (Rev: BL 9/15/07; HB 11/07; LMC 11/07; SLJ 2/08)

9252 Irving, Washington. *The Legend of Sleepy Hollow: Found Among the Papers of the Late Diedrich Knickerbocker* (4–6). Illus. 1999, Ideals $16.95 (978-0-8249-4160-4). A well-illustrated edition of this perennial favorite about Ichabod Crane, the Headless Horseman, and the heiress Katrina Van Tassel. (Rev: BL 10/1/99)

9253 Irving, Washington. *Rip Van Winkle and the Legend of Sleepy Hollow* (5–7). Illus. by Felix O. Darley. 1980, Sleepy Hollow $19.95 (978-0-912882-42-0). A handsome edition of these two classics.

9254 Iserles, Inbali. *The Tygrine Cat* (5–8). 2008, Candlewick $15.99 (978-0-7636-3798-9). Mati, the son of the slain queen of the Tygrine Cats, is being pursued by a killer sent by Suzerain in this feline fantasy. (Rev: BL 5/15/08)

9255 Ita, Sam. *Frankenstein: A Pop-Up Book* (4–7). Illus. by author. 2010, Sterling $26.95 (978-1-4027-5865-2). 8pp. With pop-up features, this abridged graphic novel version is effectively scary. (Rev: BL 12/15/10; SLJ 9/1/10)

9256 Jacques, Brian. *The Angel's Command: A Tale from the Castaways of the Flying Dutchman* (5–9). 2003, Putnam $23.99 (978-0-399-23999-1). This action-packed fantasy, set in the 17th century, is the sequel to *Castaways of the Flying Dutchman*. (Rev: BL 2/1/03; HB 3–4/03; HBG 10/03; SLJ 3/03; VOYA 4/03)

9257 Jacques, Brian. *The Bellmaker* (5–7). Series: Redwall. 1995, Putnam $24.99 (978-0-399-22805-6). This seventh tale in the series of animal fantasies features Mariel, a courageous, outspoken mouse. (Rev: BCCB 4/95; BL 4/1/95; HB 5–6/95; SLJ 8/95)

9258 Jacques, Brian. *Castaways of the Flying Dutchman* (5–9). 2001, Putnam $23.99 (978-0-399-23601-3). A mute boy stows away on the *Flying Dutchman*, a ship that is condemned to sail the seas forever, and there he meets the ghostly crew and the crazed captain in this story in which the boy has many adventures and eventually gains the power of speech and the gift of staying young forever. (Rev: BCCB 3/01; BL 3/1/01; HB 3–4/01; HBG 10/01; SLJ 3/01; VOYA 4/01)

9259 Jacques, Brian. *Doomwyte* (5–8). Illus. by David Elliot. Series: Redwall. 2008, Philomel $23.99 (978-039924544-2). 400pp. In this latest installment in the series, two contemptible new villains are thwarted in their quest for the jeweled eyes of the Great Doomwyte Idol. ◯ Lexile 860L (Rev: BL 9/1/08)

9260 Jacques, Brian. *Eulalia!* (5–8). Series: Redwall. 2007, Philomel $23.99 (978-0-399-24209-0). Lord Asheye, Badger Lord of Salamandastron, wishes to find his successor in this satisfying installment in the long-running series. ◯ (Rev: BL 8/07; SLJ 5/08)

9261 Jacques, Brian. *High Rhulain* (5–8). Illus. by David Elliot. Series: Redwall. 2005, Philomel $23.99 (978-0-399-24208-3). In this eighteenth installment, ottermaid Tiria bravely journeys to the Green Isle to rescue otter kinsmen from evil wildcats. (Rev: BL 9/1/05; SLJ 9/05)

9262 Jacques, Brian. *The Legend of Luke: A Tale from Redwall* (5–8). Series: Redwall. 2000, Putnam $23.99 (978-0-399-23490-3). This book focuses on the building of the abbey, Martin's search for his father Luke, and Luke's heroic career. (Rev: BL 12/15/99; HBG 10/00; SLJ 2/00; VOYA 4/00)

9263 Jacques, Brian. *Loamhedge* (5–8). Series: Redwall. 2003, Putnam $23.99 (978-0-399-23724-9). As Redwall stalwarts including Bragoon and Sarobando seek a cure for a haremaid's ills at Loamhedge Abbey, Redwall itself comes under attack. (Rev: BL 9/15/03; HB 11–12/03; HBG 4/04; SLJ 10/03)

9264 Jacques, Brian. *The Long Patrol* (5–8). Series: Redwall. 1998, Putnam $23.99 (978-0-399-23165-0). In this tenth adventure, the villainous Rapscallions decide to attack the peaceful Abbey of Redwall. (Rev: BCCB 4/98; BL 12/15/97; HB 3–4/98; HBG 10/98; SLJ 1/98)

9265 Jacques, Brian. *Lord Brocktree* (5–8). Series: Redwall. 2000, Putnam $23.99 (978-0-399-23590-0). The villainous Ungatt Trunn and his Blue Hordes invade and capture the mountain fortress Salamandastron. (Rev: BCCB 9/00; BL 9/1/00; HB 9–10/00; HBG 3/01; SLJ 9/00)

9266 Jacques, Brian. *Mariel of Redwall* (5–7). Illus. by Gary Chalk. Series: Redwall. 1992, Putnam $24.99 (978-0-399-22144-6). Fourth in the saga of the animals of Redwall Abbey, this story tells how the great Joseph Bell is brought to the abbey. (Rev: BCCB 3/92; BL 1/15/92*; HB 9–10/92; SLJ 3/92)

9267 Jacques, Brian. *Marlfox* (5–8). Series: Redwall. 1999, Putnam $22.99 (978-0-399-23307-4). The famous tapestry depicting Martin and Warrior has been stolen from Redwall Abbey, and four young would-be heroes set out to recover it. (Rev: BL 12/15/98; HB 1–2/99; HBG 10/99; SLJ 4/99; VOYA 2/99)

9268 Jacques, Brian. *Martin the Warrior* (5–7). Illus. by Gary Chalk. Series: Redwall. 1994, Putnam $23.99 (978-0-399-22670-0). This volume tells how the mouse

Martin the Warrior became the bold, courageous fighter that he is. (Rev: BCCB 1/94; BL 3/1/94; HB 9–10/94; SLJ 1/94)

9269 Jacques, Brian. *Mattimeo* (5–8). Series: Redwall. 1990, Putnam $23.99 (978-0-399-21741-8). The evil fox kidnaps the animal children of Redwall Abbey in this continuation of *Mossflower* (1988) and *Redwall* (1987). (Rev: BL 4/15/90; SLJ 9/90; VOYA 8/90)

9270 Jacques, Brian. *Mossflower* (5–7). Illus. by Gary Chalk. Series: Redwall. 1988, Putnam $24.99 (978-0-399-21549-0); paper $5.99 (978-0-380-70828-4). How a brave and resourceful mouse took power from the evil wildcat. (Rev: BCCB 12/88; BL 11/1/88; SLJ 11/88)

9271 Jacques, Brian. *Outcast of Redwall* (5–8). Series: Redwall. 1996, Philomel $24.99 (978-0-399-22914-5). This episode in the Redwall saga involves the badger Sunflash, his buddy Skarlath the kestrel, and their enemy the ferret Swartt Sixclaw. (Rev: BCCB 3/96; BL 3/1/96; SLJ 5/96; VOYA 10/96)

9272 Jacques, Brian. *The Pearls of Lutra* (5–8). Series: Redwall. 1997, Putnam $23.99 (978-0-399-22946-6). The evil marten Mad Eyes threatens the peaceful Redwall Abbey in this ninth book in the series. (Rev: BCCB 4/97; BL 2/15/97; SLJ 3/97*; VOYA 6/97)

9273 Jacques, Brian. *Rakkety Tam* (5–8). Illus. by David Elliot. Series: Redwall. 2004, Putnam $23.99 (978-0-399-23725-6). When Redwall is threatened by a murderous wolverine called Gulo the Savage, two warrior squirrels — Rakkety Tam McBurl and Wild Doogy Plumm — take action. (Rev: BL 9/15/04; SLJ 9/04)

9274 Jacques, Brian. *A Redwall Winter's Tale* (2–5). Illus. by Christopher Denise. 2001, Penguin $18.99 (978-0-399-23346-3). 80pp. The animals of Redwall Abbey gather once again to enjoy an end-of-autumn festival in this colorful picture book. (Rev: BL 9/1/01; HBG 3/02; SLJ 9/01)

9275 Jacques, Brian. *The Rogue Crew* (5–8). Illus. by Sean Rubin. Series: Redwall. 2011, Philomel $23.99 (978-039925416-1). 400pp. Wearat returns to exact revenge in this satisfying, action-packed final installment of the Redwall series. (Rev: BL 5/1/11)

9276 Jacques, Brian. *The Sable Quean* (5–8). Illus. by Sean Charles Rubin. Series: Redwall. 2010, Philomel $23.99 (978-039925164-1). 416pp. Buckler and other courageous Redwall creatures prepare to battle the evil Sable Quean when the abbey's young inhabitants start disappearing. ◯ (Rev: BLO 12/1/09; VOYA 12/09)

9277 Jacques, Brian. *Salamandastron* (5–7). Illus. by Gary Chalk. Series: Redwall. 1993, Putnam $23.99 (978-0-399-21992-4). These tales are centered on the badgers and hares of the castle of Salamandastron near the sea. (Rev: BCCB 7–8/93; BL 3/15/93; HB 5–6/93; SLJ 3/93)

9278 Jacques, Brian. *Seven Strange and Ghostly Tales* (4–7). 1991, Avon paper $3.99 (978-0-380-71906-8). Seven genuinely scary stories with touches of humor. (Rev: BCCB 12/91; BL 1/1/91*; HB 5–6/92; SLJ 12/91)

9279 Jacques, Brian. *Taggerung* (5–8). Series: Redwall. 2001, Putnam $23.99 (978-0-399-23720-1). The 14th book in the series features an otter named Taggerung who was kidnapped from the abbey as a baby and raised by an outlaw ferret. (Rev: BL 8/01; HB 11–12/01; HBG 3/02; SLJ 10/01; VOYA 10/01)

9280 Jacques, Brian. *Triss* (5–8). 2002, Putnam $23.99 (978-0-399-23723-2). An action-packed installment in the Redwall series in which squirrel Triss, an escaped slave, meets up with the badger Sagax and his friend Scarum. (Rev: BL 9/1/02; HB 1–2/03; HBG 3/03; SLJ 10/02; VOYA 12/02)

9281 James, Mary. *Frankenlouse* (5–8). 1994, Scholastic paper $13.95 (978-0-590-46528-1). Nick, 14, is enrolled at Blister Military Academy, which is run by his father. He escapes into his own comic book creations featuring an insect named Frankenlouse. (Rev: BCCB 11/94; BL 10/15/94; SLJ 11/94; VOYA 12/94)

9282 James, Mary. *The Shuteyes* (4–7). 1994, Scholastic paper $3.25 (978-0-590-45070-6). Chester has some unusual experiences when he journeys to Alert, a land where no one sleeps. (Rev: SLJ 4/93)

9283 Jarvis, Robin. *Thomas: Book Three of the Deptford Histories* (5–8). 2006, Chronicle $17.95 (978-0-8118-5412-2). This prequel to the Deptford Mice trilogy, written as the memoirs of an old sea mouse, contains plenty of battles, storms and heroic deeds and can be read as a stand-alone novel. (Rev: BL 1/1–15/07)

9284 Jarvis, Robin. *The Whitby Witches* (4–7). Illus. by Jess Petersen. 2006, Chronicle $17.95 (978-0-8118-5413-9). Sent to live with their elderly Aunt Alice in the English seaside village of Whitby, 8-year-old Ben — who can see the invisible — and 12-year-old Jennet find themselves swept up in a struggle between good and evil. (Rev: BL 10/1/06; SLJ 10/06)

9285 Jenkins, Emily. *Invisible Inkling* (2–4). Illus. by Harry Bliss. 2011, HarperCollins $14.99 (978-0-06-180220-1). 160pp. A small creature called an Inkling helps Hank navigate 4th grade and its bullies when his best friend moves away. ⓔ Lexile 570L (Rev: BL 6/1/11; HB 7–8/11; SLJ 7/11)

9286 Jenkins, Emily. *Toy Dance Party: Being the Further Adventures of a Bossyboots Stingray, a Courageous Buffalo, and a Hopeful Round Someone Called Plastic* (1–3). Illus. by Paul Zelinsky. 2008, Random $16.99 (978-0-375-83935-1). When their little girl, Honey, develops an interest in Barbie dolls, three old toys misbehave in six interconnected adventures in an attempt to get her to remember them. (Rev: BL 9/1/08)

9287 Jenkins, Emily. *Toys Go Out: Being the Adventures of a Knowledgeable Stingray, a Toughy Little Buffalo, and Someone Called Plastic* (1–3). Illus. by Paul Zelinsky. 2006, Random $16.95 (978-0-375-83604-6). 128pp. Three toys that belong to Little Girl have adventures, embarrassing situations, and scary moments that will be very familiar to young readers; a beginning chapter book. (Rev: BCCB 11/06; BL 10/1/06; HBG 10/07; SLJ 9/06*) ∩

9288 Jenkins, Emily. *The Whoopie Pie War* (2–4). Illus. by Harry Bliss. Series: Invisible Inkling. 2013, HarperCollins $14.99 (978-006180226-3). 160pp. Hank and his invisible pet bandapat must defend his father's ice cream store from the a food truck lady selling competing products in this third volume in the series. Lexile 580 (Rev: BL 7/13; SLJ 12/13)

9289 Jenkins, Jerry B., and Chris Fabry. *The Book of the King* (5–8). Series: The Wormling. 2007, Tyndale paper $5.99 (978-1-4143-0155-6). Owen discovers that there is another world beneath his family's bookstore and that he must battle with dragons to overcome evil forces. (Rev: BL 10/15/07)

9290 Jenkins, Martin. *Jonathan Swift's Gulliver* (5–8). Illus. by Chris Riddell. 2005, Candlewick $19.99 (978-0-7636-2409-5). A retelling of the classic tale using contemporary language and striking artwork. (Rev: BL 3/15/05; SLJ 3/05)

9291 Jennings, Patrick. *Invasion of the Dognappers* (4–6). 2012, Egmont $15.99 (978-160684287-4). 208pp. Despite the adults' incredulity that aliens are stealing the dogs, young Logan and his friends form the Intergalactic Canine Rescue Unit. (Rev: BL 5/15/12; LMC 8–9/12; SLJ 4/12)

9292 Jennings, Patrick. *Wish Riders* (5–8). 2006, Hyperion $15.99 (978-1-4231-0010-2). Combining historical fiction and fantasy, this tale of transformation focuses on Edith, 15, who slaves with four other foster children, cooking and cleaning in a Depression-era logging camp until a mysterious seed pod grows into five horses that spirit the children away to forest adventures. (Rev: BL 1/1–15/07)

9293 Jennings, Richard W. *Ghost Town* (5–8). 2009, Houghton $16.00 (978-0-547-19471-4). 176pp. A teenager discovers a camera with the ability to photograph the dearly departed. (Rev: BL 6/1–15/09; HB 7/09; SLJ 9/09)

9294 Jinks, Catherine. *How to Catch a Bogle* (4–6). Illus. by Sarah Watts. 2013, Harcourt $16.99 (978-054408708-8). 320pp. The first in an expected trilogy, this suspenseful book is filled with details about Victorian London where plucky 10-year-old Birdie is apprenticed to Alfred, a professional bogle (goblin) catcher. ALA Notable Children's Book; Booklist Editors' Choice: Books for Youth. ∩ ⓔ Lexile 790 (Rev: BL 10/1/13*; LMC 1–2/14; SLJ 8/13)

9295 Jinks, Catherine. *Saving Thanehaven* (5–8). 2013, Egmont $15.99 (978-160684274-4). 384pp. Stuck inside a computer game, Noble — who must fight all sorts of battles on his quest to save a princess — is seduced by the ideas of Rufus. But is Rufus reliable? Could he be a virus? ⓔ Lexile 680 (Rev: BL 7/13; LMC 1–2/14; SLJ 8/13)

9296 Jobling, Curtis. *Shadow of the Hawk* (5–7). Series: Wereworld. 2012, Viking $16.99 (978-067078455-4). 432pp. Young werewolf Drew fights for his life while enslaved on the isle of Scoria; the third volume in the series. ⓔ Lexile 910L (Rev: BL 10/1/12; SLJ 9/12)

9297 Johansen, K. V. *The Cassandra Virus* (5–8). 2006, Orca paper $7.95 (978-1-55143-497-1). Computer geek Jordan designs a powerful computer program that takes on a life of its own, spreading via the Internet to other computers and taking control of their operations. (Rev: SLJ 11/06; VOYA 8/06)

9298 Johansen, K. V. *Nightwalker* (5–8). 2007, Orca paper $8.95 (978-1-55143-481-0). Thrown into the dungeon when it's discovered that he possesses a powerful magical ring, young Maurey escapes with the help of a baroness and travels to Talverdin in an effort to find out if he is a nightwalker. (Rev: BL 4/1/07; SLJ 9/07)

9299 Johnson-Shelton, Nils. *The Invisible Tower* (5–8). Series: Otherworld Chronicles. 2012, HarperCollins $16.99 (978-006207086-9). 352pp. Ordinary kid Artie Kingfisher, 12, learns that he is actually King Arthur brought back to life in the 21st century and that he must save the world from disaster. ⏏ ℮ (Rev: BL 3/1/12; SLJ 3/12; VOYA 2/12)

9300 Johnson, Charles. *Pieces of Eight* (5–7). Illus. by Jennie Anne Nelson. 1989, Discovery $9.95 (978-0-944770-00-9). David and Mitchell rouse a sea captain's ghost and get to meet Blackbeard the pirate. (Rev: BL 3/15/89)

9301 Johnson, Crockett. *Magic Beach* (1–3). Illus. 2005, Front St. $18.95 (978-1-932425-27-7). 64pp. A boy and his sister conjure up a magical kingdom by writing words in the sand of a very special beach; originally published as *Castles in the Sand* in 1965. (Rev: BL 11/1/05; SLJ 6/06)

9302 Johnson, Gillian. *Thora and the Green Sea-Unicorn* (3–5). Illus. by author. 2007, HarperCollins $15.99 (978-0-06-074381-9). 288pp. After her family's houseboat is destroyed, half-mermaid Thora and her fully human friend Louella try to track down Thora's missing sea-unicorn in this sequel to *Thora: A Half-Mermaid Tale* (2007). (Rev: BL 6/1–15/07; SLJ 6/07)

9303 Johnson, Gillian. *Thora: A Half-Mermaid Tale* (4–6). Illus. 2005, HarperCollins $15.99 (978-0-06-074378-9). 256pp. Ten-year-old Thora, half girl and half mermaid, on dry land after spending the first ten years of her life at sea, tries to foil the villainous plans of a fat-cat tycoon named Frooty de Mare. (Rev: BL 8/05)

9304 Johnson, Jane. *The Shadow World: The Eidolon Chronicles* (4–7). Illus. by Adam Stower. Series: Eidolon Chronicles. 2007, Simon & Schuster $15.99 (978-1-4169-1783-0). The second book in the series finds Ben entering Eidolon to bring back his sister Ellie, who is being held by the evil Dodman. (Rev: BL 12/1/07; SLJ 11/07)

9305 Johnston, Tony. *The Spoon in the Bathroom Wall* (3–4). 2005, Harcourt $16.00 (978-0-15-205292-8). 134pp. An Arthurian spoof in which fourth grader Martha Snapdragon discovers a jeweled spoon in the wall of the boys' bathroom. (Rev: SLJ 6/05)

9306 Jonell, Lynne. *Hamster Magic* (1–3). Illus. by Brandon Dorman. 2010, Random House LB $15.99 (978-0-375-96660-6). 112pp. Four siblings adjusting to living

in the country get way more than they bargained for when they come across a hamster prepared to grant their wishes. (Rev: BL 12/1/10; LMC 1–2/11; SLJ 1/1/11)

9307 Jonell, Lynne. *The Secret of Zoom* (4–6). 2009, Holt $16.99 (978-0-8050-8856-4). Christina, 10 years old and herself pitch-perfect, discovers that orphans with singing talent are being exploited to generate a fuel known as zoom. (Rev: BL 6/1–15/09; SLJ 11/09*)

9308 Jones, Allan. *Fair Wind to Widdershins* (4–6). Illus. by Gary Chalk. Series: The Six Crowns. 2011, Greenwillow $15.99 (978-0-06-200626-4). 176pp. Trundle the hedgehog and his friends continue their quest to find the notorious Crowns while keeping themselves safe from Captain Grizzletusk in this second installment in the series. Lexile 830L (Rev: BLO 10/15/11; SLJ 3/1/12)

9309 Jones, Allan. *Fire over Swallowhaven* (4–6). Illus. by Gary Chalk. Series: The Six Crowns. 2012, Greenwillow $15.99 (978-006200629-5). 160pp. Trundle, Esmeralda, and Jack's mission to find the third crown in the nest of the phoenix is interrupted by a call to battle. (Rev: BL 3/15/12)

9310 Jones, Allan. *Trundle's Quest* (4–6). Illus. by Gary Chalk. Series: The Six Crowns. 2011, Greenwillow $15.99 (978-0-06-200623-3). 176pp. Trundle the hedgehog's simple life as a lamplighter ends abruptly when Esmeralda, a Romany hedgehog, appears on the scene convinced that Trundle can help her find the Six Crowns of the Badgers of Power. Lexile 860L (Rev: BL 3/1/11; SLJ 5/1/11)

9311 Jones, Diana Wynne. *The Game* (5–8). 2007, Penguin $11.99 (978-0-14-240718-9). Hayley, an orphan who has been raised by her difficult grandparents, now finds herself amid a large, happy family in Ireland with cousins who love to play in the mythosphere, a land of stories where secrets about her past reside. (Rev: BL 12/1/06; SLJ 3/07)

9312 Jones, Diana Wynne. *The Pinhoe Egg* (5–8). Series: Chrestomanci. 2006, Greenwillow $18.89 (978-0-06-113125-7). In this compelling addition to the Chrestomanci series, Marianne Pinhoe and Cat Chant find a strange egg with magical properties. ⏏ (Rev: BL 9/15/06; SLJ 10/06)

9313 Jones, Diana Wynne. *Unexpected Magic: Collected Stories* (5–10). 2004, Greenwillow $16.99 (978-0-06-055533-7). An exciting anthology of 16 tales of mystery and magic by a master of fantasy. (Rev: BL 4/15/04; SLJ 9/04)

9314 Jones, Gareth P. *Constable and Toop* (5–8). 2013, Abrams/Amulet $16.95 (978-141970782-7). 416pp. Set in London during the 1880s, this humorous and intriguing story centers on 14-year-old Sam Toop, an undertaker's son with the ability to communicate with ghosts, who must decide what role to play when crisis strikes. ℮ Lexile 760 (Rev: BL 10/1/13*; LMC 3–4/2014*; SLJ 12/13*; VOYA 10/13)

9315 Jones, Kimberly K. *The Genie Scheme* (4–7). 2009, Simon & Schuster $15.99 (978-1-4169-5554-2). 192pp. When she acquires her personal genie, Janna, 12, learns that material possessions are not the best things to wish for. (Rev: BCCB 6/09; BL 3/15/09; SLJ 3/09)

9316 Joyce, William, and Laura Geringer. *Nicholas St. North and the Battle of the Nightmare King* (3–5). Illus. by William Joyce. Series: The Guardians. 2011, Atheneum $14.99 (978-144243048-8). 240pp. Nicholas St. North defends the village of Santoff Claussen from the Nightmare King and his evil Fearlings, and then must seek five other Guardians to continue the fight in this first installment in the series. (Rev: BL 11/1/11)

9317 Juster, Norton. *The Phantom Tollbooth* (4–6). Illus. by Jules Feiffer. 1972, Knopf $19.95 (978-0-394-81500-8); paper $5.50 (978-0-394-82037-8). 256pp. When Milo receives a tollbooth as a gift, he finds that it admits him to a land where many adventures take place. A favorite fantasy.

9318 Kalman, Maira. *Swami on Rye: Max in India* (4–8). 1995, Viking $14.99 (978-0-670-84646-7). A sophisticated comic novel about a dog who goes to India to find the meaning of life. (Rev: BL 10/15/95; SLJ 11/95)

9319 Kassem, Lou. *A Summer for Secrets* (5–7). 1989, Avon paper $2.95 (978-0-380-75759-6). Laura's ability to communicate with animals causes complications. (Rev: BL 10/1/89)

9320 Kay, Elizabeth. *The Divide* (5–9). 2003, Scholastic $15.95 (978-0-439-45696-8). Felix, a 13-year-old with a heart problem, passes out while on a trip to Costa Rica and wakes up in a world full of mythical creatures. The sequel is *Back to the Divide* (2004). (Rev: BL 6/1–15/03; HBG 4/04; SLJ 9/03; VOYA 8/03)

9321 Kaye, Marilyn. *Here Today, Gone Tomorrow* (5–8). Series: Gifted. 2009, Kingfisher paper $7.99 (978-0-7534-6310-9). 224pp. When her classmates begin mysteriously disappearing, clairvoyant Emily battles low self-esteem and bullying and uses her talents to save them. Lexile HL610L (Rev: BL 11/1/09; SLJ 10/09)

9322 Kaye, Marilyn. *Out of Sight, Out of Mind* (5–8). Series: Gifted. 2009, Kingfisher paper $7.99 (978-0-7534-6283-6). 240pp. Eighth-grader Amanda, known for her critical aloofness, has a secret — any spark of sympathy causes her to "body snatch" against her will. Then one day she ends up in the body of nerdy Tracey and learns that the "gifted" class is not what it seems. (Rev: BL 5/15/09; LMC 10/09; SLJ 6/09; VOYA 10/09)

9323 Keehn, Sally M. *Gnat Stokes and the Foggy Bottom Swamp Queen* (5–8). 2005, Putnam $16.99 (978-0-399-24287-8). This fantasy, set in the Appalachian mountains, features a 12-year-old girl named Gnat who faces swamp creatures and spells in her quest to rescue Goodlow Pryce. (Rev: BL 3/1/05; SLJ 4/05)

9324 Keehn, Sally M. *Magpie Gabbard and the Quest for the Buried Moon* (5–8). 2007, Philomel $16.99 (978-0-399-24340-0). Thirteen-year-old Magpie Gabbard must fulfill a prophecy and put aside her cussedness in order to save the moon in this exuberant and complex tall tale. (Rev: BL 4/15/07; SLJ 2/07)

9325 Kehret, Peg. *Ghost's Grave* (5–8). 2005, Dutton $16.99 (978-0-525-46162-3). Josh expects to be bored when he stays in his aunt's old house, but the ghost of a coal miner who died in 1903 livens things up. (Rev: BL 5/15/05; SLJ 10/05)

9326 Kehret, Peg. *Spy Cat* (4–6). 2003, Dutton $15.99 (978-0-525-47046-5). 192pp. Clever cat Pete, who understands everything but is frustrated by his inability to speak, plays a lead role in tracking down the neighborhood burglars. (Rev: BL 1/1–15/03; HBG 10/03; SLJ 1/03)

9327 Kelley, Jane. *The Girl Behind the Glass* (3–5). 2011, Random House $16.99 (978-0-375-86220-5); LB $19.99 (978-0-375-96220-2). 192pp. Hannah, 11, is the only member of her family who can sense the spirit of the girl who died in her house 80 years earlier. (Rev: BL 9/1/11; SLJ 9/1/11)

9328 Kelly, Jacqueline. *Return to the Willows* (4–7). Illus. by Clint Young. 2012, Henry Holt $19.99 (978-0-8050-9413-8). 288pp. Toad, Mole, Rat, and Badger are back in this well-illustrated sequel to *The Wind in the Willows*. **e** Lexile 890L (Rev: BL 10/15/12; SLJ 12/12)

9329 Kempton, Kate. *The World Beyond the Waves: An Environmental Adventure* (5–7). 1995, Portunus $14.95 (978-0-9641330-6-8); paper $8.95 (978-0-9641330-1-3). After being washed overboard during a violent storm, Sam visits a land where she meets ocean animals that have been misused by humans. (Rev: BL 4/15/95; SLJ 3/95)

9330 Kendall, Carol. *The Gammage Cup* (4–7). Illus. by Erik Blegvad. 1990, Harcourt paper $6.00 (978-0-15-230575-8). A fantasy of the Minnipins, a small people of the "land between the mountains."

9331 Kennedy, Kim. *Misty Gordon and the Mystery of the Ghost Pirates* (4–7). Illus. by Greg Call. 2010, Abrams $15.95 (978-0-8109-9357-0). 218pp. Eleven-year-old Misty finds an old diary that draws her into secrets of the past in this mystery involving ghosts and pirates. **e** Lexile 780L (Rev: BL 9/1/10; LMC 1–2/11; SLJ 10/1/10)

9332 Kent, Derek Taylor. *Scary School, by Derek the Ghost* (3–6). Illus. by Scott M. Fischer. 2011, HarperCollins $15.99 (978-006196092-5). 256pp. A series of comic and intriguing vignettes from Scary School — a place where monsters and humans learn together. **e** (Rev: BL 7/11; LMC 11–12/11)

9333 Kerr, P. B. *The Blue Djinn of Babylon* (5–8). Series: Children of the Lamp. 2006, Scholastic $16.99 (978-0-439-67021-0). Philippa Gaunt, 12, is wrongly convicted of cheating and her twin John must rescue her in this action-packed sequel to *The Akhenaten Adventure* (2005). (Rev: BL 3/15/06; SLJ 3/06; VOYA 2/06)

9334 Kessler, Liz. *Emily Windsnap and the Castle in the Mist* (3–6). Illus. by Ledwidge Natacha. 2007, Candlewick $15.99 (978-0-7636-3330-1). Emily's problems as a typical elementary school mermaid take a turn for the worse when King Neptune puts a curse on her. (Rev: BL 9/15/07; SLJ 6/07)

9335 Kessler, Liz. *Emily Windsnap and the Monster from the Deep* (4–7). Series: Emily Windsnap. 2006, Candlewick $15.99 (978-0-7636-2504-7). Half-human and half-mermaid, Emily Windsnap enjoys an idyllic life on Allpoints Island until she inadvertently awakens an evil monster named Kraken; a sequel to *The Tail of Emily Windsnap* (2004). (Rev: BL 6/1–15/06; SLJ 7/06)

9336 Kessler, Liz. *Emily Windsnap and the Siren's Secret* (4–7). Illus. by Natacha Ledwidge. 2010, Candlewick $15.99 (978-0-7636-4374-4). 240pp. Emily helps to resolve a dispute between the merpeople of Shiprock and human developers, and in the process finds some lost sirens and solves a mystery. **e** Lexile 590L (Rev: BLO 3/1/10; SLJ 4/10)

9337 Kessler, Liz. *The Tail of Emily Windsnap* (4–7). Illus. by Sarah Gibb. Series: Emily Windsnap. 2004, Candlewick $15.99 (978-0-7636-2483-5). Twelve-year-old Emily Windsnap, who turns into a mermaid when she gets into the water, learns the truth about her parents. (Rev: BL 5/1/04; SLJ 6/04; VOYA 6/04)

9338 Kessler, Liz. *A Year Without Autumn* (4–7). 2011, Candlewick $15.99 (978-0-7636-5595-2). 304pp. A ride in an old elevator transports 12-year-old Jenni into the future and provides unhappy news about her best friend Autumn's little brother; Jenni manages to return to the present and avert the accident that was in store. **e** (Rev: BLO 11/15/11; LMC 1–2/12; SLJ 12/1/11)

9339 Key, Alexander. *The Forgotten Door* (5–7). 1986, Scholastic paper $4.99 (978-0-590-43130-9). When little Jon falls to earth from another planet, he encounters suspicion and hostility as well as sympathy. A reissue.

9340 Kilworth, Garry. *Attica* (4–8). 2009, IPG/Atom paper $11.95 (978-1-904233-56-5). 352pp. At the top of a house, step-siblings Jordy, Chloe, and Alex find themselves in a strange yet familiar — and threatening — new world. (Rev: BL 4/15/09; VOYA 10/09)

9341 Kimmel, Elizabeth Cody. *The Ghost of the Stone Circle* (5–8). 1998, Scholastic paper $15.95 (978-0-590-21308-0). Fourteen-year-old Cristyn, who is spending the summer in Wales with her historian father, discovers a ghost in the house her father has rented. (Rev: BCCB 3/98; BL 4/15/98; HBG 10/98; SLJ 4/98; VOYA 8/98)

9342 Kimmel, Elizabeth Cody. *Suddenly Supernatural: Scaredy Kat* (5–7). 2009, Little, Brown $10.99 (978-0-316-06685-3). 250pp. Can 13-year-old Kat, who can speak to the dead, and her friend Jac help the spirit of a young boy they find in an abandoned house? ∩ (Rev: HB 3/09; SLJ 3/09)

9343 Kimmel, Eric A. *Don Quixote and the Windmills* (2–4). Illus. by Leonard Everett Fisher. 2004, Farrar $16.00 (978-0-374-31825-3). 32pp. Don Quixote is an appealing hero in this boldly illustrated adaptation in which he mistakes the windmills for giants. (Rev: BL 4/15/04; SLJ 4/04)

9344 King-Smith, Dick. *Lady Lollipop* (2–4). 2001, Candlewick $14.99 (978-0-7636-1269-6). 124pp. Spoiled Princess Penelope chooses a pig named Lollipop as her pet, and Lollipop's poor owner moves to the palace as the pig's keeper. (Rev: BCCB 9/01; BL 4/15/01; HB 5/01; HBG 10/01; SLJ 6/01*)

9345 King-Smith, Dick. *The Mouse Family Robinson* (3–5). Illus. by Nick Bruel. 2008, Roaring Brook $15.95 (978-1-59643-326-7). 80pp. After moving to the perfect catless home, house mouse John Robinson encounters class rivalry between the house mice and the fancy pet mice and suffers the loss of his old mouse friend. (Rev: BL 8/08; LMC 1/09)

9346 King-Smith, Dick. *Pigs Might Fly* (3–5). Illus. by Mary Rayner. 1990, Puffin paper $6.99 (978-0-14-034537-7). 168pp. A pig named Daggie Dogfoot saves the day because he can swim.

9347 King-Smith, Dick. *The Roundhill* (5–7). 2000, Random House paper $4.99 (978-0-440-41844-3). In the English countryside in 1936, 14-year-old Evan meets a mysterious girl who seems to be the Alice of *Alice in Wonderland*. (Rev: BL 1/1–15/01; HBG 3/01; SLJ 12/00)

9348 King-Smith, Dick. *The School Mouse* (3–5). Illus. 1995, Hyperion LB $14.49 (978-0-7868-2029-0). 124pp. Flora's ability to read saves her illiterate mouse parents from eating poison that has been placed around the school where they live. (Rev: BCCB 1/96; BL 10/15/95; SLJ 12/95*)

9349 Kipling, Rudyard. *Rikki-Tikki-Tavi* (3–5). Illus. by Jerry Pinkney. 1997, Morrow $15.89 (978-0-688-14321-3). 40pp. In this classic tale, a mongoose repays a debt of kindness after he has been saved from drowning. (Rev: BL 9/1/97*; HBG 3/98; SLJ 8/97*)

9350 Kirby, Matthew J. *Icefall* (5–8). 2011, Scholastic $17.99 (978-0-545-27424-1). 336pp. In Viking times, Princess Solveig and her siblings are sent to a fortress on a fjord for safety during a war but soon realize that there is a traitor in their midst. ∩ **e** (Rev: BL 11/15/11; SLJ 11/1/11; VOYA 10/11)

9351 Kirby, Matthew J. *The Lost Kingdom* (4–7). 2013, Scholastic $17.99 (978-054527426-5). 352pp. In an alternate 1753 the father-son team of John and Billy Bartram joins a flying-ship expedition to search for a mysterious Welsh settlement with which to make an alliance. Lexile 620 (Rev: BL 9/15/13; LMC 1–2/14; SLJ 11/13)

9352 Kirov, Erica. *Magickeepers: The Eternal Hourglass* (5–8). 2009, Sourcebooks $16.99 (978-1-4022-1501-8). 256pp. The son of a magician discovers magic is real in this melange of ancient underworld shadows and Las Vegas glitter. (Rev: LMC 10/09; SLJ 7/09)

9353 Kladstrup, Kristin. *The Book of Story Beginnings* (4–6). 2006, Candlewick $15.99 (978-0-7636-2609-9). 362pp. In this multilayered fantasy, 12-year-old Lucy tries with the help of a mysterious notebook to unravel the mystery surrounding the disappearance of her great-uncle Oscar in 1914. (Rev: BL 3/1/06; SLJ 4/06)

9354 Klimo, Kate. *The Dragon in the Library* (4–6). Illus. by John Shroades. Series: Dragon Keepers. 2010, Random House $15.99 (978-0-375-85591-7); LB $18.99 (978-0-375-95591-4). 224pp. Dragon Keeper cousins Jesse and Daisy discover that their friend Professor Andersson — and their newly grumpy dragon Emmy — are both in danger in this installment that also introduces a magical library. **e** (Rev: BL 5/15/10; SLJ 9/1/10)

9355 Klimo, Kate. *The Dragon in the Sea* (4–6). Illus. by John Shroades. Series: Dragon Keepers. 2012, Random House $15.99 (978-037587065-1); LB $18.99 (978-037597065-8). 224pp. Jesse, Daisy, and their dragon Emmy head underwater to rescue a newly discovered dragon egg from the snatches of a sea monster. (Rev: BL 5/15/12)

9356 Klimo, Kate. *The Dragon in the Sock Drawer* (4–6). Series: Dragon Keepers. 2008, Random $14.99 (978-0-375-85587-0). 176pp. Ten-year-old cousins Jesse and Daisy become the stand-in parents for a baby dragon and must figure out how to feed and take care of. (Rev: BLO 8/28/08; SLJ 7/08)

9357 Klise, Kate. *Dying to Meet You* (3–6). Illus. by M. Sarah Klise. Series: 43 Old Cemetery Road. 2009, Houghton $15.00 (978-0-15-205727-5). 160pp. An author named Ignatius B. Grumply moves into a Victorian mansion in a town called ghastly and finds he must share with a ghost named Olive and an 11-year-old boy named Seymour; the action takes place in the form of letters between these three and there are many graphic elements. (Rev: BCCB 7–8/09; BL 4/1/09; HB 5/09; SLJ 5/09)

9358 Kloepfer, John. *The Zombie Chasers* (4–7). Illus. by Steve Wolfhard. 2010, HarperCollins $15.99 (978-0-06-185304-3). 224pp. This is a gruesomely humorous — and graphically illustrated — story of a zombified neighborhood in which only Zack, Rice, Zoe, and Madison are normal and must defend themselves against the hungry crowd. **e** Lexile 760L (Rev: BL 4/15/10; LMC 11–12/10; SLJ 11/1/10)

9359 Kluger, Jeffrey. *Nacky Patcher and the Curse of the Dry-Land Boats* (4–7). 2007, Philomel $18.99 (978-0-399-24604-3). When thief Nacky Patcher and orphan Teedie find a sailing ship floating in the lake, they try to persuade the hapless inhabitants of Yole to rally together to rebuild the vessel and escape their oppression by the cruel Baloo family. (Rev: BL 6/1–15/07; SLJ 7/07)

9360 Knudsen, Michelle. *The Dragon of Trelian* (4–7). 2009, Candlewick $16.99 (978-0-7636-3455-1). Calen, a lonely magician's apprentice, and Meg, who is secretly caring for a baby dragon, join forces when they find their kingdom is in danger. (Rev: BCCB 9/09; BL 4/1/09; HB 5/09; LMC 8/09; SLJ 6/09)

9361 Knudsen, Michelle. *The Princess of Trelian* (4–7). 2012, Candlewick $16.99 (978-076365062-9). 448pp. Meg struggles to clear her dragon's name after a rash of attacks plague Lourin. (Rev: BL 3/15/12; HB 5–6/12; VOYA 6/12)

9362 Koller, Jackie F. *If I Had One Wish . . .* (5–8). 1991, Little, Brown $14.95 (978-0-316-50150-7). When 8th-grader Alec is granted his wish that his little brother had never been born, he learns a lesson about charity, kindness, and old-fashioned family values. (Rev: BCCB 12/91; BL 11/1/91; SLJ 11/91)

9363 Korman, Gordon. *The Medusa Plot* (5–8). Series: The 39 Clues: Cahills vs. Vespers. 2011, Scholastic $12.99 (978-054529839-1). 224pp. Amy and Dan Cahill combine their talents to rescue captured friends and family from the evil Vespers. ◠ **e** (Rev: BL 11/1/11; SLJ 4/12)

9364 Kortum, Jeanie. *Ghost Vision* (5–8). Illus. by Dugald Stermer. 1983, Scholastic paper $3.50 (978-0-614-19197-4). A Greenland Inuit realizes that his son has special mystical powers.

9365 Kraatz, Jeramey. *The Cloak Society* (4–6). 2012, HarperCollins $16.99 (978-0-06-209547-3). 288pp. In training to join his family's supervillain business, 12-year-old Alex starts questioning his future intentions when he befriends a young superhero. **e** (Rev: BL 10/15/12; SLJ 12/12)

9366 Krulik, Nancy. *Be Careful What You Sniff For* (1–3). Illus. by Sebastien Braun. Series: Magic Bone. 2013, Grosset & Dunlap paper $4.99 (978-0-448-46-399-5). 128pp. When he finds a magical bone in the backyard Sparky the pup suddenly finds himself outside Buckingham Palace, where he has a series of adventures and meets a bossy corgi. Lexile 420 (Rev: BLO 7/13; LMC 1–2/14; SLJ 8/13)

9367 Krumwiede, Lana. *Archon* (5–8). 2013, Candlewick $16.99 (978-076366402-2). 324pp. Twelve-year-old Taemon's city is only finally beginning to rebuild after Taemon's removal of telekenesis from the inhabitants, but he and his friend Amma must leave Deliverance to find Taemon's father, who is being held prisoner in the Republik. ◠ **e** Lexile 670 (Rev: BLO 9/15/13; SLJ 11/13)

9368 Krumwiede, Lana. *Freakling* (5–8). 2012, Candlewick $15.99 (978-076365937-0). 320pp. When Taemon, 12, loses his psychic abilities, he is cast out from Deliverance to find a mysterious new world where people enjoy using their hands. ◠ **e** (Rev: BL 10/15/12; LMC 3–4/13; SLJ 1/13; VOYA 10/12) [HL600L]

9369 LaFleur, Suzanne. *Listening for Lucca* (5–8). 2013, Random House $16.99 (978-038574299-3); LB $19.99 (978-037599088-5). 240pp. Blending realism and the supernatural, this is the story of 13-year-old Sienna and her family's move to Maine in the hope that a new environment will help her mute brother Lucca. ◠ **e** Lexile 580 (Rev: BL 8/13; LMC 1–2/14; SLJ 9/13*)

9370 Lairamore, Dawn. *Ivy and the Meanstalk* (5–8). 2011, Holiday House $16.95 (978-0-8234-2392-7). 240pp. Princess Ivy and her dragon friend Elridge struggle to set things right by returning a magical harp to the giant's widow in this fractured take on Jack and the Beanstalk. (Rev: BL 10/1/11; LMC 1–2/12; SLJ 9/1/11)

9371 Lairamore, Dawn. *Ivy's Ever After* (5–8). 2010, Holiday House $16.95 (978-0-8234-2261-6). 320pp. A well-meaning but somewhat cowardly dragon rescues a young, independent-minded princess from marrying an evil man. Lexile 980L (Rev: BL 5/15/10; SLJ 8/10)

9372 Landy, Derek. *Playing with Fire* (5–8). Series: Skulduggery Pleasant. 2008, HarperCollins $16.99 (978-0-06-124088-1). Skulduggery and 13-year-old Valkyrie (formerly known as Stephanie) must curb the evil Baron

Vengeous, who plans to bring back to life a terrifying monster called the Grotesquery. (Rev: BL 6/1–15/08; SLJ 7/08)

9373 Landy, Derek. *Skulduggery Pleasant* (5–8). Series: Skulduggery Pleasant. 2007, HarperCollins $17.99 (978-0-06-123115-5). When she inherits her Uncle Gordon's property, plucky 12-year-old Stephanie finds herself swept into an adventure combining magic, mystery, and violence in which her companion is a skeleton named Skulduggery Pleasant. Odyssey Honor Recording 2008. ∩ (Rev: BL 5/1/07; HB 7–8/07; SLJ 6/07)

9374 Langrish, Katherine. *Troll Fell* (5–7). 2004, HarperCollins $16.99 (978-0-06-058304-0). Sent to live with his evil twin uncles after his father's death, 12-year-old Peer Ulfsson seeks a way to foil their plan to sell children to the trolls. (Rev: BL 4/15/04*; SLJ 7/04; VOYA 6/04)

9375 Langrish, Katherine. *Troll Mill* (5–8). 2006, HarperCollins LB $17.89 (978-0-06-058308-8). In this sequel to *Troll Fell* (2004), 15-year-old Peer Ulfsson, who still worries about his cruel uncles and is increasingly involved with Hilde, must help protect a half-selkie baby from trolls and other threats. (Rev: BCCB 3/06; BL 2/1/06*; HBG 10/06; LMC 2/07; SLJ 3/06; VOYA 2/06)

9376 Langton, Jane. *The Dragon Tree* (3–5). Series: Hall Family Chronicles. 2008, HarperCollins $15.99 (978-0-06-082341-2). 176pp. Mortimer Moon, the new tree warden in Walden Pond, is fonder of cutting trees down than conserving them, and when he gets ready to fell a fast-growing new sapling the Hall children rally support to save it, little suspecting that it is in fact a magical Dragon Tree. (Rev: BL 4/1/08; SLJ 8/08)

9377 Langton, Jane. *The Fledgling* (5–7). 1980, HarperCollins LB $17.89 (978-0-06-023679-3); paper $6.99 (978-0-06-440121-0). A young girl learns to fly with her Goose Prince. A sequel is *The Fragile Flag* (1984). Also use *The Diamond in the Window* (1962).

9378 Langton, Jane. *The Mysterious Circus* (3–5). 2005, HarperCollins LB $16.89 (978-0-06-009487-4). Near Walden Pond, the Hall children are visited by an Indian relative bringing a seed that produces elephants. (Rev: BL 5/1/05; SLJ 5/05)

9379 Larwood, Kieran. *Freaks* (5–8). 2013, Scholastic $16.99 (978-054547424-5). 256pp. Set in Victorian London, this combination of steampunk, mystery, and adventure features a wolf girl named Sheba, the members of a freak show, and a plot to snatch poor children from the banks of the Thames. ℮ Lexile 850 (Rev: BL 3/15/13; HB 3–4/13; LMC 8–9/13; SLJ 6/13; VOYA 6/13)

9380 Lasky, Kathryn. *The Capture* (5–8). 2003, Scholastic paper $5.99 (978-0-439-40557-7). Soren, a happy, well-adjusted young barn owl, falls from his nest and is stolen away by a group of owlet thieves bent on reeducation. (Rev: BL 9/15/03; SLJ 10/03)

9381 Lasky, Kathryn. *Daughters of the Sea: Hannah* (4–8). 2009, Scholastic $16.99 (978-0-439-78310-1). 320pp. Orphan Hannah, 15, gets a job as a scullery maid

in 19th-century Boston, meets a young artist who seems to have an incredible understanding of her, and on a trip to the coast starts to recognize how she reacts to the presence of water. ℮ Lexile 800L (Rev: BL 9/1/09; SLJ 10/09; VOYA 2/10)

9382 Lasky, Kathryn. *Felix Takes the Stage* (2–4). Illus. by Stephen Gilpin. Series: The Deadlies. 2010, Scholastic $15.99 (978-054511681-7). 160pp. A family of recluse spiders flee their comfortable home in the Los Angeles symphony hall just ahead of the exterminator. The second book in the series is *Spiders on the Case* (2011), in which spiders foil humans who are stealing rare books from the Boston Public Library. ℮ Lexile 660L (Rev: BL 5/1/10)

9383 Lasky, Kathryn. *Lone Wolf* (5–8). Series: Wolves of the Beyond. 2010, Scholastic $15.99 (978-0-545-09310-1). 240pp. A young wolf with a defective paw is adopted by a mother grizzly bear who teaches him various skills in this first installment in the series. ∩ ℮ Lexile 890L (Rev: BL 12/1/09; LMC 3–4/10; SLJ 3/10)

9384 Lasky, Kathryn. *Lucy* (5–8). Series: Daughters of the Sea. 2012, Scholastic $17.99 (978-043978-312-5). 312pp. Seventeen-year-old Lucy, who has been brought up in New York City by a minister and his ambitious wife, spends the summer in Bar Harbor, Maine, in 1899 and finds out about her sisters, her mother, and her affinity for the sea. ℮ (Rev: BLO 4/15/12)

9385 Lasky, Kathryn. *The Rise of a Legend* (4–7). Series: Guardians of Ga'Hoole. 2013, Scholastic $16.99 (978-054550978-7). 304pp. This prequel recounts the youth of Ezylryb the owl, describing how he learned the art of war and came to influence the fate of his kingdom. Lexile 790 (Rev: BL 7/13; SLJ 2/14)

9386 Lasky, Kathryn. *Shadow Wolf* (5–8). Series: Wolves of the Beyond. 2010, Scholastic $16.99 (978-0-545-09312-5). 272pp. Deformed wolf Faolan struggles to accept his lot as a lowly "gnaw wolf" even as a rival challenges him at every turn. ℮ Lexile 870L (Rev: BL 12/1/10; SLJ 1/1/11)

9387 Law, Ingrid. *Savvy* (5–7). 2008, Dial $16.99 (978-0-803-73306-0). 352pp. On her 13th birthday, Mibs is looking forward to following the pattern of the other Beaumont children and developing a supernatural "savvy" just as her father is hurt in an accident; Mibs and her siblings set off on an adventure-filled journey to be at his side. Newbery Honor; ALA Notable Children's Book; Boston Globe–Horn Book Honor. (Rev: BL 5/15/08*; LMC 10/08; SLJ 5/08; VOYA 2/09)

9388 Law, Ingrid. *Scumble* (5–8). 2010, Dial $16.99 (978-0-8037-3307-7). 416pp. It's Ledge's turn to acquire an unusual power on his 13th birthday in this companion to *Savvy* (2008), and his new ability to create havoc has unwelcome results. ∩ (Rev: BL 7/10*; HB 9–10/10; SLJ 9/1/10)

9389 Lawson, Julie. *Ghosts of the Titanic* (5–8). 2012, Holiday House $16.95 (978-082342423-8). 169pp. Parallel plots and a neat time-travel sequence splice the stories of modern-day class clown Kevin with that of young

1912 seamen Angus, who's been given the grim job of recovering the *Titanic* victims' bodies, in this complex story. (Rev: BL 2/15/12; LMC 11–12/12; SLJ 3/12)

9390 Lawson, Robert. *Rabbit Hill* (4–7). Illus. by author. 1944, Puffin paper $5.99 (978-0-14-031010-8). A warm and humorous story about the small creatures of a Connecticut countryside — each with a distinct personality. Newbery Medal 1945.

9391 Laybourne, Emma. *Missing Magic* (4–7). 2007, Dial $16.99 (978-0-8037-3219-3). Ned, 11, is one of the few students at Leodwych who has no magic, but his practical abilities prove useful when he and two of his classmates are kidnapped. (Rev: BL 7/07; SLJ 9/07)

9392 Layefsky, Virginia. *Impossible Things* (5–8). 1998, Marshall Cavendish $14.95 (978-0-7614-5038-2). Twelve-year-old Brady has several personal and family problems to solve along with taking care of the dragonlike creature that he is hiding. (Rev: HBG 3/99; SLJ 11/98)

9393 Le Guin, Ursula K. *Jane on Her Own* (2–4). Illus. Series: Catwings. 1999, Orchard LB $15.99 (978-0-531-33133-0). 48pp. This fourth installment of the Catwings series features Jane, one of the winged cats, and her experiences when she leaves home to find adventure and friends. (Rev: BCCB 7–8/99; BL 2/1/99; HBG 10/99; SLJ 4/99)

9394 Le Guin, Ursula K. *Wonderful Alexander and the Catwings* (2–4). Illus. Series: Catwings. 1994, Orchard LB $15.99 (978-0-531-08701-5). 48pp. Alexander the kitten helps Jane — one of the flying cats called Catwings — regain her power of speech. (Rev: BL 9/15/94; SLJ 9/94)

9395 Lee, Tanith. *Indigara* (4–7). 2007, Penguin $11.99 (978-0-14-240922-0). Jet and her dog Otis encounter mindless celebrities in the underworld of Planet Obelisk in this humorous meeting of science fiction and pop culture. (Rev: BL 12/15/07; SLJ 12/07)

9396 Leeuwen, Joke van. *Eep!* (4–8). Trans. by Bill Nagelkerke. Illus. by author. 2012, Gecko paper $7.95 (978-18775790-7-3). 152pp. A childless couple's discovery and stewardship of an odd bird-girl bonds them to others who've cared for the creature in this touching, quirky tale. (Rev: BL 3/1/12*; HB 5–6/12; SLJ 3/12)

9397 Legrand, Claire. *The Cavendish Home for Boys and Girls* (4–7). Illus. by Sarah Watts. 2012, Simon & Schuster $16.99 (978-1-4424-4291-7). 352pp. Twelve-year-old Victoria, who strives for perfection, investigates the disappearance of her imperfect friend Lawrence and stumbles on some unpleasant secrets. **e** Lexile 750L (Rev: BLO 11/1/12; SLJ 12/12)

9398 Lemke, Donald. *Emperor of the Airwaves* (2–5). Illus. by Erik Doescher and Mike DeCarlo. Series: DC Super Heroes: Batman. 2009, Stone Arch LB $25.32 (978-1-4342-1153-8); paper $5.95 (978-1-4342-1364-8). 56pp. A highly illustrated chapter book pitting Batman against the Penguin. (Rev: LMC 10/09*; SLJ 6/09)

9399 Lennon, Joan. *Questors* (5–8). 2007, Simon & Schuster $16.99 (978-1-4169-3658-9). When an energy leak threatens the existence of three separate worlds, three youthful half siblings — Bryn, Madlen, and Cam — find they bear a heavy responsibility. (Rev: BL 8/07; HB 1–2/08; LMC 1/08; SLJ 12/07)

9400 Lennon, Joan. *There's a Kangaroo in My Soup!* (2–3). Illus. by Wendy Rasmussen. 2000, Front St. $15.95 (978-0-8126-2898-2). 128pp. Gloria, a runaway circus kangaroo, brings young Kevin out of his shell in this beginning chapter book fantasy. (Rev: SLJ 12/00)

9401 Leonard, Elmore. *A Coyote's in the House* (5–8). 2004, HarperEntertainment $22.00 (978-0-06-072882-3). A coyote named Antwan strikes up a friendship with a couple of pampered dogs from Hollywood. (Rev: BL 5/15/04*)

9402 Lerangis, Peter. *The Colossus Rises* (4–8). Series: Seven Wonders. 2013, HarperCollins $17.99 (978-0-06-207040-1); paper $9.99 (978-00620704-2-5). 368pp. Jack and three other young teens who have a rare genetic abnormality set off to find the artifacts from Atlantis that will save them. ∩ **e** Lexile 580L (Rev: BL 12/1/12; SLJ 3/13)

9403 Leszczynski, Diana. *Fern Verdant and the Silver Rose* (4–8). 2008, Knopf $15.99 (978-0-375-85213-8). 263pp. When her botanist mother Lily is kidnapped, Fern uses her newly discovered talent for communicating with plants to search for her. (Rev: LMC 3/09; SLJ 2/09)

9404 Lethcoe, Jason. *Amazing Adventures from Zoom's Academy* (3–6). Illus. by author. 2005, Ballantine paper $12.95 (978-0-345-48355-3). 151pp. Thirteen-year-old Summer Jones is amazed to find out that her father is a professor at Zoom's Academy for the Super-Gifted; while Summer's powers are being assessed, a move is afoot to attack the academy. (Rev: SLJ 1/06)

9405 Lethcoe, Jason. *Wings* (3–5). 2009, Grosset paper $6.99 (978-0-448-44653-0). 224pp. Fourteen-year-old Edward is sent to boarding school after his mother dies, and there finds that he has wings and is a Guardian with a mission to fulfill. (Rev: BLO 2/9/09; SLJ 8/09)

9406 Levine, Gail C. *Fairy Dust and the Quest for the Egg* (3–5). Illus. by David Christiana. Series: Disney Fairies. 2005, Disney $18.99 (978-0-7868-3491-4). Prilla, a new arrival in the fairy community of Never Land, has trouble fitting in until she's assigned to help repair the magic egg that keeps the inhabitants of Never Land forever young. (Rev: BL 8/05*; HBG 10/06; SLJ 10/05)

9407 Levine, Gail Carson. *Fairies and the Quest for Never Land* (3–5). Illus. by David Christiana. Series: Disney Fairies. 2010, Disney $18.99 (978-1-4231-0935-8). 224pp. In this modern day sequel, Peter Pan returns to whisk one of Wendy Darling's descendants away to Never Land, where she finds unexpected adventures. (Rev: BLO 5/15/10; SLJ 8/1/10)

9408 Levine, Gail Carson. *A Tale of Two Castles* (4–6). 2011, HarperCollins $16.99 (978-0-06-122965-7); LB $17.89 (978-0-06-122966-4). 336pp. Twelve-year-old Elodie finds herself working for a curmudgeonly dragon who teaches her to solve mysteries. ⌒ ℮ Lexile 630L (Rev: BL 3/15/11; HB 5–6/11; SLJ 4/11)

9409 Levine, Gail Carson. *The Two Princesses of Bamarre* (4–7). 2001, HarperCollins LB $17.89 (978-0-06-029316-1). Princess Addie sets out on a quest to find a cure for the Grey Death, a sickness that is destroying her older sister. (Rev: BCCB 10/01; BL 4/15/01; HB 5–6/01; HBG 10/01; SLJ 5/01)

9410 Levy, Elizabeth. *The Principal's on the Roof* (2–4). Illus. by Mordicai Gerstein. Series: Fletcher Mysteries. 2002, Simon & Schuster paper $3.99 (978-0-689-84627-4). Fletcher the dog and Jasper the flea tackle the mystery of the sneezing principal. (Rev: HBG 3/03; SLJ 1/03)

9411 Lewis, C. S. *The Lion, the Witch and the Wardrobe* (5–8). Series: Narnia. 1988, Macmillan LB $22.95 (978-0-02-758200-0). Four children enter the kingdom of Narnia through the back of an old wardrobe. A special edition illustrated by Michael Hague. The other six volumes in this series are *Prince Caspian, The Voyage of the Dawn Treader, The Silver Chair, The Horse and His Boy, The Magician's Nephew*, and *The Last Battle*.

9412 Lewis, C. S. *The Lion, the Witch and the Wardrobe: A Story for Children* (4–7). Illus. by Pauline Baynes. 1988, Macmillan paper $7.95 (978-0-02-044490-9). A beautifully written adventure featuring four children who go into the magical land of Narnia.

9413 Lewis, Josh. *Super Chicken Nugget Boy and the Furious Fry* (2–4). Illus. by Douglas Holgate. Series: Super Chicken Nugget Boy. 2010, Hyperion/Disney $16.99 (978-1-4231-1491-8); paper $4.99 (978-1-4231-1492-5). 144pp. When Fern Goldberg falls into a vat of green liquid, his skin starts turning green whenever he comes into condiments such as ketchup. A sequel is *Super Chicken Nugget Boy and the Pizza Planet People* (2011). (Rev: LMC 11–12/10; SLJ 6/1/10)

9414 Lichtenheld, Tom. *Everything I Know About Monsters: A Collection of Made-up Facts, Educated Guesses, and Silly Pictures About Creatures of Creepiness* (1–4). Illus. by author. 2002, Simon & Schuster $16.95 (978-0-689-84381-5). An appealingly silly guide to the kinds of monsters you find in various places (under the bed, in the closet), with practical tips on monster avoidance. (Rev: HBG 3/03; SLJ 9/02)

9415 Lin, Grace. *Starry River of the Sky* (3–6). Illus. by author. 2012, Little, Brown $17.99 (978-0-316-12595-6). 288pp. The moon is missing from the sky and young Rendi, working at an inn in a village called Clear Sky, shares stories with the visiting Madame Chang that bring respite from the associated problems; a companion to the Newbery Honor Book *Where the Mountain Meets the Moon* (2009). ALA Notable Children's Book; Booklist Editors' Choice: Books for Youth. ⌒ ℮ Lexile 810L (Rev: BL 10/1/12*; HB 11–12/12; LMC 3–4/13*; SLJ 9/12*)

9416 Lin, Grace. *Where the Mountain Meets the Moon* (3–6). Illus. by author. 2009, Little, Brown $16.99 (978-0-316-11427-1). On a quest to help her family, Minli

encounters danger and magic in this story that draws on Chinese legend. (Rev: BL 5/1/09; HB 9/09; SLJ 7/09)

9417 Lindbergh, Anne. *The Hunky-Dory Dairy* (5–7). Illus. by Julie Brinckloe. 1986, Harcourt $14.95 (978-0-15-237449-5); paper $2.75 (978-0-380-70320-3). Zannah visits a community magically removed from the 20th century and enjoys introducing the people to bubble gum, tacos, and other "modern" things. (Rev: BCCB 9/86; BL 4/1/86; SLJ 8/86)

9418 Lindbergh, Anne. *The Prisoner of Pineapple Place* (5–7). 1988, Harcourt $13.95 (978-0-15-263559-6); paper $2.95 (978-0-380-70765-2). Pineapple Place is invisible to everyone except the inhabitants, and somehow finds itself landing in Connecticut. (Rev: BL 7/88; SLJ 8/88)

9419 Lindgren, Astrid. *Ronia, the Robber's Daughter* (4–7). 1985, Puffin paper $5.99 (978-0-14-031720-6). Ronia becomes friendly with the son of her father's rival in this fantasy.

9420 Lipsyte, Robert. *The Twinning Project* (5–8). 2012, Clarion $16.99 (978-0-547-64571-1). 272pp. When Tom discovers that his imaginary friend Eddie is not only real but also his twin living on another Earth 50 years apart, the brothers both become involved in a struggle to save both planets. ℮ Lexile HL570L (Rev: LMC 3–4/13; SLJ 10/12)

9421 Lisle, Holly. *The Silver Door* (5–8). Series: Moon and Sun. 2009, Scholastic $17.99 (978-0-545-00014-7). 386pp. Genna is training to become the Sunrider of prophecy and discovers a lost human city in this danger-laden sequel to *The Ruby Key* (2008). (Rev: BLO 5/27/09; HB 7/09)

9422 Lisle, Janet T. *Afternoon of the Elves* (4–6). 1989, Orchard LB $16.99 (978-0-531-08437-3). 128pp. Hilary discovers that the strange girl named Sara-Kate has a garden inhabited by elves. (Rev: BCCB 10/89; BL 8/89*; HB 9/89; SLJ 9/89*)

9423 Lisle, Janet T. *The Gold Dust Letters* (4–6). 1994, Orchard LB $16.99 (978-0-531-08680-3). 128pp. Angela's father fools her into believing that she is receiving messages from a fairy in an effort to effect a reconciliation. (Rev: BCCB 7–8/94; BL 2/1/94; SLJ 4/94)

9424 Lisle, Janet Taylor. *Highway Cats* (4–7). Illus. by David Frankland. 2008, Philomel $14.99 (978-0-399-25070-5). 128pp. Against all odds, three kittens survive abandonment on the edge of a busy highway and meet up with a group of feral cats; the kittens' unusual abilities become apparent when the cats' scruffy piece of land comes under threat of development. ⌒ (Rev: BL 7/08*; HB 9/08; LMC 1/09; SLJ 11/08)

9425 Littlewood, Kathryn. *Bliss* (3–6). 2012, HarperCollins $16.99 (978-006208423-1). 384pp. When their parents go away, the Bliss children are entrusted with keeping the magical recipes safe, but temptation proves too much and the results are unfortunate. ℮ (Rev: BL 2/1/12; SLJ 2/12; VOYA 12/11)

9426 Llewellyn, Sam. *Darksolstice* (5–8). Series: Lyonesse. 2010, Scholastic $17.99 (978-0-439-93471-8).

365pp. Idris Limpet journeys to Aegypt to rescue his sister Morgan and meets up with the future Knights of the Round Table in this second book in the series. Lexile 790L (Rev: BL 3/1/10; HB 5–6/10; SLJ 5/10)

9427 Llewellyn, Sam. *The Well Between the Worlds* (5–8). Series: Lyonesse. 2009, Scholastic $17.99 (978-0-439-93469-5). 352pp. Its policy of fishing for monsters in the Belowground has threatened the survival of the kingdom of Lyonesse, and 11-year-old Idris — a monstergroom — may be the only hope; the first installment in a series. (Rev: BCCB 2/09; BL 12/15/08; HB 3/09; LMC 5/09; SLJ 5/09; VOYA 2/09)

9428 Loizeaux, William. *Clarence Cochran, a Human Boy* (4–6). Illus. by Anne Wilsdorf. 2009, Farrar $16.00 (978-0-374-31323-4). Inverting Kafka's *The Metamorphosis*, Loizeaux brings us the story of a young cockroach who wakes up to find himself a tiny boy and must struggle against extermination. (Rev: BCCB 6/09; SLJ 4/09)

9429 Loux, Lynn Crosbie. *The Day I Could Fly* (2–4). Illus. by Guy Porfirio. 2003, NorthWord $15.95 (978-1-55971-866-0). A young girl is transformed into a crow for a day. (Rev: SLJ 10/03)

9430 Lovric, Michelle. *The Undrowned Child* (5–7). 2011, Delacorte $17.99 (978-0-385-73999-3); LB $20.99 (978-0-385-90814-6). 464pp. Eleven-year-old Teo, an orphan adopted by two scientists, finds herself taking part in a battle to save 1899 Venice from destruction in this fantasy full of historical detail. **e** Lexile 830L (Rev: BL 6/1/11; LMC 11–12/11; SLJ 8/11*)

9431 Lowe, Natasha. *The Power of Poppy Pendle* (4–6). 2012, Simon & Schuster $15.99 (978-1-4424-4679-3). 272pp. Poppy switches over to the dark side when her parents insist on her practicing magic rather than indulging her passion for baking. **e** (Rev: BLO 9/1/12; LMC 3–4/13; SLJ 10/12)

9432 Lowenstein, Sallie. *Evan's Voice* (5–8). 1998, Lion Stone paper $15.00 (978-0-9658486-1-9). Teenager Jake cares for his catatonic younger brother while seeking civilization's last chance for survival in an area known as the Dead Zone. (Rev: BL 3/1/99; VOYA 6/99)

9433 Lowenstein, Sallie. *Focus* (5–9). 2001, Lion Stone paper $15.00 (978-0-9658486-3-3). The Haldrans leave their planet and relocate to Miners World, where humans live, in order to save their son from discrimination because of his creative intelligence. (Rev: BL 4/15/01; SLJ 8/01; VOYA 8/01)

9434 Lowry, Lois. *Gathering Blue* (5–9). 2000, Houghton Mifflin $16.00 (978-0-618-05581-4). In an inhospitable future world, young Kira must use her courage and her artistic talents. (Rev: BL 6/1–15/00*; HB 9–10/00; HBG 3/01; SLJ 8/00*)

9435 Lowry, Lois. *Gossamer* (5–8). 2006, Houghton Mifflin $16.00 (978-0-618-68550-9). A spirit called Littlest One learns to mix memories that will heal people while they sleep. (Rev: BL 2/15/06; SLJ 5/06*; VOYA 8/06)

9436 Lubar, David. *Beware the Ninja Weenies and Other Warped and Creepy Tales* (4–7). 2012, Starscape $15.99

(978-076533213-4). 192pp. Horror and humor are combined in 33 varied short stories. **e** (Rev: BL 8/12; LMC 1–2/13)

9437 Lubar, David. *The Curse of the Campfire Weenies: And Other Warped and Creepy Tales* (5–7). 2007, Tor $15.95 (978-0-7653-1807-7). Thirty-five creepy stories combine scariness and dark humor in a way that will attract reluctant readers. (Rev: SLJ 12/07)

9438 Lubar, David. *My Rotten Life: Nathan Abercrombie, Accidental Zombie* (4–6). 2009, Starscape paper $5.99 (978-07653163-4-9). 160pp. A social outcast's life turns around thanks to "Hurt-Be-Gone," an experimental drug that renders him a half-dead zombie but has some hidden advantages. (Rev: BL 9/15/09)

9439 Lubar, David. *True Talents* (5–8). 2007, Tor $17.95 (978-0-7653-0977-8). In this sequel to *Hidden Talents* (1999), the paranormally gifted student friends from Edgeview Alternative School flex their extraordinary powers in a series of interconnected adventures; memos, e-mails, and illustrations add to the action-packed narrative. (Rev: BL 3/15/07; SLJ 4/07)

9440 Lubar, David. *The Unwilling Witch* (3–5). Illus. by Marcos Calo. Series: Monsterrific. 2013, Starscape $15.99 (978-076533078-9). 160pp. Angie's suddenly a witch, and now she must figure out how to use her powers for good. (Rev: BLO 9/15/13)

9441 Lubar, David. *The Vanishing Vampire* (3–6). Illus. Series: Monsterrific Tales. 2013, Starscape $15.99 (978-076533077-2). 144pp. Sebastian realizes something is different about him. Has he become a vampire or is there hope his new hunger is temporary? Lexile 550 (Rev: BL 7/13; SLJ 5/13)

9442 Lupica, Mike. *The Batboy* (5–8). 2010, Philomel $17.99 (978-0-399-25000-2). 256pp. Fourteen-year-old Brian gets permission to become a bat boy for the Detroit Tigers despite his mother's misgivings. (Rev: BL 1/1/10; SLJ 4/10)

9443 Luzzatto, Caroline. *Interplanetary Avenger* (4–6). 2005, Holiday House $16.95 (978-0-8234-1933-3). 120pp. Transported to a school on another planet after he opens a mysterious package, middle-schooler Sam must chase after a shape-shifting ne'er-do-well who is threatening Earth; full of gross humor and zany situations. (Rev: SLJ 12/05)

9444 Lyga, Barry. *Archvillain* (4–7). 2010, Scholastic $16.99 (978-0-545-19649-9). 192pp. A plasma storm brings 6th-grader Kyle, already confident and smart, additional strength and intellect, plus the ability to fly; however, to Kyle's dismay, the storm also produces an annoying rival — superpower-endowed Mighty Mike. Lexile 740L (Rev: BL 9/15/10; LMC 11–12/10; SLJ 10/1/10)

9445 Lyga, Barry. *The Mad Mask* (4–7). 2012, Scholastic $17.99 (978-054519651-2). 240pp. Determined to prove that his rival Might Mike is an alien with sinister designs on the world, 12-year-old Kyle (aka the Azure Avenger) teams up with Mad Mask in this fast-paced superhero spoof; a sequel to *Archvillain* (2010). Lexile 810L (Rev: BL 1/1/12; SLJ 3/12)

9446 Lynch, Chris. *Prime Evil* (5–8). Series: Cyberia. 2010, Scholastic $16.99 (978-0-545-02795-3). 148pp. Zane's ability to communicate with animals saves the day when he is sent to Primeval Ranch and must deal with strangely hostile animals and the machinations of the evil Dr. Gristle; the final volume in the trilogy, following *Cyberia* (2009) and *Monkey See, Monkey Don't* (2010). (Rev: BL 1/1–15/11; SLJ 2/1/11)

9447 Lyons, Mary E. *Knockabeg: A Famine Tale* (4–7). 2001, Houghton Mifflin $15.00 (978-0-618-09283-3). In order to protect the people of Knockabeg, faeries battle with the creatures who are causing the blight during the great Irish potato famine. (Rev: BL 11/15/01; HBG 3/02; SLJ 9/01; VOYA 10/01)

9448 Lytle, Robert A. *Three Rivers Crossing* (5–8). 2000, River Road $15.95 (978-0-938682-55-4). After he suffers an accident while fishing, 7th-grader Walker wakes to find he is in the 1820s village of his ancestors. (Rev: BL 5/15/00; SLJ 6/00)

9449 McAllister, Angela. *Digory and The Lost King* (3–5). Illus. by Ian Beck. 2007, Bloomsbury $14.95 (978-1-59990-088-9); paper $5.95 (978-1-59990-089-6). 123pp. Digory sets off in search of his father's missing twin and acquires a baby dragon in this sequel to *Digory the Dragon Slayer*. (Rev: SLJ 7/07)

9450 McAllister, Angela. *Digory the Dragon Slayer* (3–5). Illus. by Ian Beck. 2006, Bloomsbury $14.95 (978-1-58234-722-6); paper $5.95 (978-1-58234-912-1). Digory is a gentle poetry-loving lad who is mistakenly considered knight material and sent off to slay dragons and marry princesses. (Rev: SLJ 8/06)

9451 McAllister, M. I. *Urchin of the Riding Stars* (5–8). Series: Mismantle Chronicles. 2005, Hyperion $17.95 (978-0-7868-5486-8). When his mentor, Captain Crispin, is unjustly accused of slaying the infant prince of Mismantle, Urchin the squirrel is determined to find out who is responsible for the crime. (Rev: BL 10/1/05; SLJ 11/05; VOYA 2/06)

9452 McCaffrey, Laura Williams. *Alia Waking* (5–7). 2003, Clarion $16.00 (978-0-618-19461-2). Alia, 12, and her best friend Kay long to be come "keenten," or warrior women. (Rev: BL 3/1/03; HBG 10/03; SLJ 6/03; VOYA 10/03)

9453 McCarthy, Maureen. *When You Wish Upon a Rat* (3–6). 2012, Abrams/Amulet $16.95 (978-1-4197-0161-0). 288pp. Fed up with life and longing to live in a "normal" family, 11-year-old Ruth is optimistic when she gets three chances from her magical stuffed rat, Rodney. **e** Lexile 690L (Rev: BLO 9/15/12; LMC 3–4/13; SLJ 12/12; VOYA 12/12)

9454 McCaughrean, Geraldine. *A Pack of Lies* (5–7). 1990, Macmillan $16.95 (978-0-7451-1154-4). Stories told by mysterious M.C.C. Berkshire, who wanders into an antique store run by adolescent Ailsa and her mother. (Rev: BCCB 5/89)

9455 MacDonald, Betty. *Hello, Mrs. Piggle-Wiggle* (3–5). Illus. by Hilary Knight. 1957, HarperCollins $16.99 (978-0-397-31715-8); paper $5.99 (978-0-06-440149-4). Introducing the lady who loves all children, good or bad. Further adventures are: *Mrs. Piggle-Wiggle's Farm* (1954); *Mrs. Piggle-Wiggle* (1957); *Mrs. Piggle-Wiggle's Magic* (1957).

9456 McGraw, Eloise. *The Moorchild* (4–6). 1996, Simon & Schuster LB $17.00 (978-0-689-80654-4). Set in the Middle Ages, this fantasy tells of Moql, who is born half human and half fairy, and her difficulties fitting into either world. (Rev: BCCB 6/96; BL 3/1/96*; HB 9/96; SLJ 4/96*)

9457 MacHale, D. J. *The Lost City of Faar* (5–8). Series: Pendragon. 2003, Simon & Schuster paper $5.99 (978-0-7434-3732-5). After saving Denduron from Saint Dane in *The Merchant of Death* (2002), 14-year-old Bobby must confront the shape-changer again in Cloral, a world covered by water. (Rev: SLJ 5/03)

9458 MacHale, D. J. *The Rivers of Zadaa* (5–8). Series: Pendragon. 2005, Simon & Schuster $14.95 (978-1-4169-0710-7). Bobby Pendragon teams up with Loor to foil the villainous Saint Dane's plan to cut off the water supply to Loor's people in Zadaa. (Rev: SLJ 7/05)

9459 MacHale, D. J. *SYLO* (5–8). Series: SYLO Chronicles. 2013, Penguin $17.99 (978-159514665-6). 416pp. Tucker, 14, and his friends are confused when a military operation called SYLO quarantines their island off the coast of Maine, claiming the existence of a deadly virus. **e** (Rev: BL 6/13; LMC 1–2/14; SLJ 9/13)

9460 Mackel, Kathy. *Alien in a Bottle* (4–8). 2004, HarperCollins LB $16.89 (978-0-06-029282-9). An entertaining and action-packed novel in which 8th-grader Sean Winger, an aspiring glassblower, mistakes an alien space ship for an ornate glass bottle and becomes swept up in intergalactic intrigue. (Rev: BL 5/1/04; SLJ 4/04)

9461 McKinty, Adrian. *The Lighthouse Land* (5–8). 2006, Abrams $16.95 (978-0-8109-5480-9). In this first installment in an action-packed science fiction series, Jamie (a 13-year-old who is mute after losing his left arm to bone cancer) and his mother move to an Irish island, where he and a new friend discover an artifact that transports them to a far-off planet in time to help a girl named Wishaway. (Rev: BL 11/15/06; SLJ 1/07)

9462 McKissack, Patricia C. *The Dark-Thirty: Southern Tales of the Supernatural* (5–8). 1992, Knopf $17.99 (978-0-679-91863-9). Ten original stories, rooted in African American history and the oral-storytelling tradition, deal with such subjects as slavery, belief in "the sight," and the Montgomery bus boycott. (Rev: BCCB 12/92; BL 12/15/92; HB 3–4/93; SLJ 12/92*)

9463 McKissack, Patricia C, et al. *Clone Codes* (4–7). 2010, Scholastic $16.99 (978-0-439-92983-7). 192pp. In 2170, 13-year-old Leanna learns about slaves in the Civil War and realizes that her own life is similar; she is not a human being but an enslaved clone. Lexile 680L (Rev: BL 1/1/10; LMC 3–4/10; SLJ 2/10)

9464 MacLachlan, Patricia. *Waiting for the Magic* (3–5). Illus. by Amy June Bates. 2011, Atheneum $15.99 (978-1-4169-2745-7). 160pp. A family suffering disruptions finds some healing when they adopt four dogs and a cat and slowly realize that they can understand the animals' speech. ℮ Lexile 420L (Rev: BL 8/11; LMC 11–12/11; SLJ 10/1/11*)

9465 McMann, Lisa. *Island of Silence* (4–7). Series: The Unwanteds. 2012, Aladdin $16.99 (978-1-44240771-8). 416pp. Magician Mr. Today prepares 14-year-old Alex to become Artime's leader even as his twin, Aaron, plots to take over Quill in this second book in the series. ∩ ℮ Lexile HL820L (Rev: BL 9/1/12; SLJ 2/13)

9466 McMann, Lisa. *The Unwanteds* (4–7). 2011, Simon & Schuster $16.99 (978-1-4424-0768-8). 400pp. In a dystopian land named Quill, Unwanted 13-year-olds with artistic abilities are purged from society; Alex, declared an Unwanted, finds himself in the magical land of Artime, where he learns new skills and worries about his twin brother Aaron, one of the Wanted. (Rev: BLO 9/1/11; SLJ 8/11)

9467 McNamara, Margaret. *Clara and the Magical Charms* (2–4). Illus. by Julia Denos. Series: Fairy Bell Sisters. 2014, HarperCollins $15.99 (978-006222811-6). 128pp. Clara's magical powers seem to be on the rise and she is able to help her gnome friend Rowan when he's on Sheepskerry Island for the Valentine Games. ℮ (Rev: BLO 3/1/14)

9468 McNamara, Margaret. *Sylva and the Fairy Ball* (2–4). Illus. by Julia Denos. Series: Fairy Bell Sisters. 2013, HarperCollins $15.99 (978-006222802-4); paper $4.99 (978-00622280-1-7). 128pp. Sylva, Tinker Bell's younger sister, is disappointed when she is too young to attend the Fairy Ball, but saves the day when she spots trolls headed to the palace; the first installment in an illustrated chapter book series. (Rev: BLO 3/15/13)

9469 McNamee, Eoin. *City of Time* (5–8). Series: The Navigator Trilogy. 2008, Random House $16.99 (978-0-375-83912-2). The moon is inching toward Owen's home planet, causing panic and environmental changes, and Owen travels to the City of Time to try to set things right. (Rev: BL 5/15/08; SLJ 8/08)

9470 McNamee, Eoin. *The Frost Child* (5–8). Illus. by Jon Goodell. Series: The Navigator. 2009, Random $15.99 (978-0-385-73563-6). 352pp. In this action-packed concluding volume to the trilogy the Navigator must once again rally the Resistors to battle against the Harsh. (Rev: BLO 4/24/09; SLJ 10/09)

9471 McNamee, Eoin. *The Navigator: Chosen to Save the World* (5–8). 2007, Random House $15.99 (978-0-375-83910-8). Owen finds himself suddenly in a different world where he and a girl named Cati must battle the Harsh, evil beings who freeze all that they touch and have set time running backward. (Rev: BL 12/1/06; SLJ 3/07)

9472 McNamee, Eoin. *The Ring of Five* (5–7). 2010, Random House $16.99 (978-0-385-73731-9). 352pp. Unhappy young Danny Caulfield gets a chance to go to boarding school and is surprised to find himself at Wilson's Academy of the Devious Arts where he is trained to protect the Upper World from the Lower World. ℮ Lexile 740L (Rev: BL 6/10; LMC 10/10; SLJ 6/10)

9473 McNish, Cliff. *Breathe: A Ghost Story* (4–8). 2006, Carolrhoda LB $15.95 (978-0-8225-6443-0). After the death of his father, young Jack moves with his mother to an old farmhouse in the English countryside, a home that they share with the spirits of four children and the Ghost Mother who enslaved them. (Rev: SLJ 11/06)

9474 McNish, Cliff. *Silver City* (5–8). Series: Silver Sequence. 2006, Carolrhoda $15.95 (978-1-57505-926-6). As the fearsome Roar draws closer to the Earth, Milo, Thomas, Helen, and their friends use their magical powers to keep the threat at bay; a sequel to *The Silver Child* (2005). (Rev: BL 6/1–15/06; SLJ 9/06)

9475 McNish, Cliff. *Silver World* (5–8). Series: The Silver Sequence. 2007, Carolrhoda LB $15.95 (978-1-57505-897-9). In this third volume in the series, Milo and the other children of Coldharbour use their extraordinary powers to protect the Earth from being destroyed by the terrifying monster called "The Roar." (Rev: SLJ 6/07)

9476 Maguire, Gregory. *Four Stupid Cupids* (4–6). Series: Hamlet Chronicles. 2000, Clarion $16.00 (978-0-395-83895-2). 184pp. A far-fetched comedy about four cupids who are freed when the magical vase that Fawn Petros brings to her Vermont school breaks. (Rev: BL 12/1/00; HBG 3/01; SLJ 10/00)

9477 Maguire, Gregory. *Seven Spiders Spinning* (4–6). Illus. by Dirk Zimmer. 1994, Clarion $16.00 (978-0-395-68965-3). 144pp. In this farce, seven tarantulas invade a classroom and go on their separate quests. (Rev: BCCB 10/94; BL 9/15/94; SLJ 10/94)

9478 Mahy, Margaret. *Maddigan's Fantasia* (5–8). 2007, Simon & Schuster $17.99 (978-1-4169-1812-7). When 12-year-old Garland's father is killed, messengers from the future arrive to urge her to travel to a far-off town in search of a solar converter that will prevent future catastrophe. (Rev: BL 12/15/07; HB 11–12/07; LMC 2/08; SLJ 11/07)

9479 Malone, Marianne. *The Sixty-Eight Rooms* (4–6). Illus. by Gina Triplett. 2010, Random House $16.99 (978-0-375-85710-2); LB $19.99 (978-0-375-95710-9). 288pp. Ruthie and her friend Jack discover a way to shrink themselves so they can explore the 68 intricate Thorne Rooms at Chicago's Art Institute. A sequel is *Stealing Magic* (2012). ∩ ℮ Lexile 730L (Rev: BL 1/1/10; LMC 3–4/10; SLJ 2/10)

9480 Malone, Marianne. *Stealing Magic* (4–7). Illus. by Greg Call. Series: A Sixty-Eight Rooms Adventures. 2012, Random House $16.99 (978-037586819-1); LB $19.99 (978-037596819-8). 256pp. Sixth-graders Ruthie and Jack travel back in time to help a Jewish girl in 1937 Paris and a slave girl in antebellum Charleston, South Carolina, in this sequel to *The Sixty-Eight Rooms* (2010) involving the Thorne Rooms at the Art Institute of Chicago. ∩ ℮ (Rev: BL 1/1/12; SLJ 2/12)

9481 Marrone, Amanda. *The Multiplying Menace* (4–7). 2010, Aladdin paper $5.99 (978-1-4169-9033-8). 192pp. Twelve-year-old Maggie's somewhat unpredictable magical talents cause her difficulties until she's sent to live with her grandmother and hones her skills. **e** Lexile 760L (Rev: BL 8/10; LMC 10/10; SLJ 8/10)

9482 Marsden, John. *The Rabbits* (3–6). Illus. by Shaun Tan. 2003, Simply Read $16.95 (978-0-9688768-8-6). In this allegory, native creatures welcome the newcomer rabbits, but the rabbits take over, devastate the landscape, and there is no happy ending. (Rev: SLJ 4/04)

9483 Martin, Ann M., and Laura Godwin. *The Doll People* (3–6). Illus. 2000, Hyperion $15.99 (978-0-7868-0361-3). 272pp. In this fantasy about dolls that are alive, Annabelle Doll tries to solve the mystery of the disappearance of Aunt Sarah Doll in 1955. (Rev: BCCB 1/01; BL 8/00; HBG 3/01; SLJ 11/00)

9484 Martin, Ann M., and Laura Godwin. *The Runaway Dolls* (3–6). Illus. by Brian Selznick. Series: Doll People. 2008, Disney $16.99 (978-0-7868-5584-1). Annabelle Doll runs away with her long-lost sister and into a series of increasingly perilous situations. (Rev: BL 10/1/08; SLJ 10/08) ⌒

9485 Martin, George R. R. *The Ice Dragon* (3–5). Illus. by Yvonne Gilbert. 2006, Tom Doherty Assoc. $12.95 (978-0-7653-1631-8). 106pp. Seven-year-old Adara is a child who loves the cold, and her bond with the ice dragon allows her to rescue her home and family from marauding invaders. (Rev: SLJ 2/07)

9486 Martin, Lisa, and Valerie Martin. *Anton and Cecil: Cats at Sea* (3–7). Illus. by Kelly Murphy. 2013, Algonquin $16.99 (978-161620246-0). 256pp. A tale of two cat brothers, Cecil and Anton, who have exciting and scary adventures aboard 18th-century sailing ships. (Rev: BL 11/1/13; LMC 10/13; SLJ 9/13)

9487 Martin, Rafe. *Birdwing* (5–8). 2005, Scholastic $16.99 (978-0-459-21167-7). This appealing fantasy picks up where "The Six Swans" by the Brothers Grimm ends, chronicling the story of Ardwin, the prince who was turned into a swan and then restored to human form apart from his left arm, which remains a swan's wing. (Rev: BCCB 12/05; BL 11/15/05; HB 1–2/06; SLJ 12/05; VOYA 12/05)

9488 Martini, Clem. *The Mob* (5–8). Series: Feather and Bone: The Crow Chronicles. 2004, Kids Can $16.95 (978-1-55337-574-6). As hundreds of crows of the Kinaar clan come together for their annual socialization at the Gathering Tree, internal conflicts threaten to tear the avian family apart in this first volume in a trilogy. (Rev: BL 10/1/04; SLJ 12/04)

9489 Mason, Timothy. *The Last Synapsid* (4–7). 2009, Delacorte $16.99 (978-0-385-73581-0). 288pp. Before there were dinosaurs, there were reptiles called synapsids and two of them — plus a villain named Jenkins — travel through time to a tiny town in Colorado where Rob and Phoebe try to figure out how to send them back before something terrible happens. (Rev: BCCB 1/09; BLO 2/9/09; LMC 5/09; SLJ 6/09)

9490 Mass, Wendy. *The Last Present* (4–7). Series: Willow Falls. 2013, Scholastic $16.99 (978-054531016-1). 352pp. Thirteen-year-olds Amanda and Leo must work together to help 10-year-old Grace by traveling back in time to make changes in her previous birthdays and undo the curse that has rendered her catatonic; the last installment in the series. ⌒ **e** Lexile 690 (Rev: BLO 9/15/13; LMC 3–4/14; SLJ 10/13)

9491 Masson, Sophie. *Serafin* (5–8). 2000, Saint Mary's paper $5.50 (978-0-88489-567-1). After he saves Calou from being lynched as a witch, Frederick is forced to flee his 17th-century French village with Calou and soon afterward realizes that the girl is a matagot, a half-angel half-human creature. (Rev: SLJ 8/00)

9492 Matas, Carol. *The Edge of When* (5–8). 2012, Fitzhenry & Whiteside paper $12.95 (978-15545519-8-9). 230pp. In three separate but linked stories first published 30 years ago and now updated, 12-year-old Rebecca is transported into the future, at one point to 2050 where a postapocalyptic society is kidnapping healthy children from the past. (Rev: BL 3/15/12)

9493 Matas, Carol, and Perry Nodelman. *Out of Their Minds* (5–8). Series: Minds. 1998, Simon & Schuster $16.00 (978-0-689-81946-9). In this fantasy (the third in the series), Princess Lenora and Prince Coren journey to Andilla to marry but find that some force is upsetting The Balance. (Rev: HBG 3/99; SLJ 9/98; VOYA 2/99)

9494 Matthews, L. S. *A Dog for Life* (5–7). 2006, Delacorte $14.95 (978-0-385-73366-3). Tom is sick and Mouse the dog is banished on grounds of possible infection, so John and Mouse, who can communicate psychically, set out to find Mouse a new home. ⌒ (Rev: BL 12/1/06*; SLJ 10/06)

9495 Mayes, Walter M. *Walter the Giant Storyteller's Giant Book of Giant Stories* (3–5). Illus. by Kevin O'Malley. 2005, Walker $18.95 (978-0-8027-8974-7). Captured by the tiny inhabitants of a Lilliputian-like island, Walter the Giant Storyteller tells a series of stories to convince his captors that giants are not bloodthirsty and mean but rather the victims of character assassination; an oversize volume with dramatic illustrations. (Rev: SLJ 11/05)

9496 Mazer, Anne. *Sister Magic: The Trouble with Violet* (2–4). Illus. by Bill Brown. 2007, Scholastic paper $3.99 (978-0-439-87246-1). The magical aura surrounding her younger sister Violet makes the carefully organized Mabel quite uncomfortable. (Rev: BCCB 10/07; BL 9/1/07; SLJ 9/07)

9497 Meacham, Margaret. *Quiet! You're Invisible* (3–5). 2001, Holiday House $15.95 (978-0-8234-1651-6). 80pp. Fifth-grader Hoby is visited by a boy from the future and must outsmart the middle-school bully to retrieve a stolen part from his new friend's space cruiser. (Rev: BL 1/1–15/02; HBG 3/02; SLJ 11/01)

9498 Mebus, Scott. *Gods of Manhattan* (5–8). Series: Gods of Manhattan. 2008, Dutton $17.99 (978-0-525-47955-0). Rory discovers that he has the ability to see figures from New York history (such as Peter Stuyvesant and Babe Ruth) and that he must use this power to save Manhattan. (Rev: BL 5/15/08; SLJ 4/08)

9499 Mebus, Scott. *Spirits in the Park* (5–8). Series: Gods of Manhattan. 2009, Dutton $17.99 (978-0-525-42148-1). In Mannahatta, the spirit city that exists parallel to the real city, Rory — reluctantly — must find his missing father. (Rev: BLO 4/24/09; SLJ 9/09; VOYA 8/09)

9500 Meddaugh, Susan. *Lulu's Hat* (3–5). Illus. 2002, Houghton $15.00 (978-0-618-15277-3). 64pp. Lulu's deep interest in magic leads her to follow a dog that has jumped into a top hat that has unusual powers. (Rev: BCCB 5/02; BL 5/1/02; HBG 10/02; SLJ 5/02)

9501 Medearis, Angela Shelf. *Haunts: Five Hair-Raising Tales* (4–7). Illus. by Trina Schart Hyman. 1996, Holiday $15.95 (978-0-8234-1280-8). Five stories that contain elements of horror and the supernatural. (Rev: BL 2/1/97; SLJ 4/97)

9502 Meehan, Kierin. *Hannah's Winter* (5–8). 2009, Kane $15.95 (978-1-933605-98-2). 212pp. Hannah, an Australian 12-year-old, finds herself enjoying her stay in Japan and, with her new friends Miki and Hiro, she investigates a mysterious riddle. (Rev: HB 5/09*; SLJ 3/09)

9503 Meloy, Colin. *Under Wildwood* (4–8). Illus. by Carson Ellis. 2012, HarperCollins $17.99 (978-0-06-202471-8). 560pp. Prue and Curtis discover a machinated sweatshop beneath Wildwood, where they're mistaken for deities and trusted with rescuing the children working there; the sequel to *Wildwood* (2011). ⌒ e Lexile 800L (Rev: BL 8/12; SLJ 11/12)

9504 Meloy, Colin. *Wildwood* (4–8). Illus. by Carson Ellis. 2011, HarperCollins $16.99 (978-0-06-202468-8). 560pp. Twelve-year-old Prue enters the Wilderness in search of her brother, who's been abducted by crows, in this richly imagined fantasy. (Rev: BL 7/11; SLJ 8/11*)

9505 Messenger, Norman. *The Land of Neverbelieve* (2–5). Illus. by author. 2012, Candlewick $17.99 (978-076366021-5). 32pp. A thought-provoking look at a richly imagined world of make-believe, featuring an island inhabited by fantastic animals living in lush and magical surroundings; the DK Eyewitness style encourages young readers to revel in the surreal nonsense. (Rev: BLO 12/15/12; LMC 5–6/13*; SLJ 1/13)

9506 Messenger, Shannon. *Keeper of the Lost Cities* (4–7). 2012, Aladdin $16.99 (978-144244593-2). 496pp. At the age of 12 Sophie Foster, who has always known that she is different, learns that she is in fact an elf. e (Rev: BL 11/1/12; LMC 3–4/13; SLJ 1/13)

9507 Messer, Stephen. *Windblowne* (4–7). 2010, Random House $16.99 (978-0-375-86195-6). 304pp. Hoping to become a better kite-maker, Oliver seeks help from his Uncle Gilbert and his talking red kite; together they work to save the trees that support their treehouse village. Lexile 760L (Rev: BL 5/15/10; LMC 8–9/10; SLJ 6/10)

9508 Messner, Kate. *Eye of the Storm* (5–8). 2012, Walker $16.99 (978-0-8027-2313-0). 304pp. In a 2050 world under a constant threat of tornadoes, 13-year-old Jaden

starts to suspect that her scientist father has something to do with the ferocious weather. e Lexile 740L (Rev: SLJ 3/12)

9509 Meyer, Kai. *The Stone Light* (5–7). Trans. from German by Elizabeth D. Crawford. Series: The Dark Reflections Trilogy. 2006, Simon & Schuster $16.95 (978-0-689-87789-6). Desperately searching for help in their fight to free Venice from the evil Egyptian pharaoh, Merle travels on Vermithrax, the flying lion, to Hell in hopes of convincing Lucifer to ally himself with their cause; the sequel to *The Water Mirror* (2005). (Rev: BL 3/15/07; SLJ 1/07)

9510 Meyer, Kai. *The Water Mirror* (4–7). Trans. by Elizabeth D. Crawford. Series: Dark Reflections. 2005, Simon & Schuster $15.95 (978-0-689-87787-2). In an alternate Venice in danger of destruction, 14-year-old Merle, a plucky orphan, finds herself playing a central role; the first volume in a series noted for its setting; sequels are *The Stone Light* (2007) and *The Glass Word* (2008). ⌒ (Rev: BL 1/1–15/06; SLJ 11/05*; VOYA 12/05)

9511 Michael, Livi. *City of Dogs* (5–8). 2007, Putnam $16.99 (978-0-399-24356-1). Sam has always wanted a dog and is happy when Jenny comes to live with him, but Jenny's mission becomes overarching and she must take on friends and foes in this fantasy full of mythological references. (Rev: BCCB 11/07; LMC 11–12/07; SLJ 11/07)

9512 Miéville, China. *Un Lun Dun* (5–9). 2007, Del Rey $17.95 (978-0-345-49516-7). In contemporary London, Zanna and her friend Deeba find themselves on the edge of a strange Unlondon that is awaiting a chosen one. (Rev: SLJ 4/07*)

9513 Milford, Kate. *The Boneshaker* (5–8). 2010, Clarion $17 (978-0-547-24187-6). 384pp. In 1913 Arcane, Missouri, 13-year-old Natalie is suspicious of the owner of a traveling medicine show who has many mysterious machines; but everyone else seems to be taken in by him. ⌒ e Lexile 900L (Rev: BL 5/15/10*; LMC 10/10; SLJ 6/10)

9514 Milford, Kate. *The Broken Lands* (5–8). Illus. by Andrea Offermann. 2012, Clarion $16.99 (978-0-547-73966-3). 464pp. In 1877 Coney Island two orphans find themselves leading an effort to defend New York from evil; a prequel to *The Boneshaker* (2010). e (Rev: BLO 9/1/12; LMC 3–4/13; SLJ 12/12)

9515 Miller, Christopher, and Allan Miller. *Hunter Brown and the Secret of the Shadow* (4–7). Series: Codebearers. 2008, Warner $13.99 (978-1-59317-328-9). 366pp. Pranksters Stretch and Hunter are transported to fantastical Solandra, where they must fight amongst the Codebearers, battling evil and following the wisdom contained in a mysterious book. (Rev: BLO 11/1/08; SLJ 3/1/09)

9516 Miller, Wiley. *The Extraordinary Adventures of Ordinary Basil: The Impossible Flight to Helios* (3–5). 2006, Scholastic $14.99 (978-0-439-85665-2). 128pp. When a man appears outside bored Basil's window in a floating balloon, he hops in and goes on an adventure to Helios, a secret city in the sky where he has exciting adventures in this well-illustrated book set in the late 19th century. (Rev: BL 2/15/07; SLJ 2/07)

9517 Millet, Lydia. *The Fires Beneath the Sea* (4–6). Series: The Dissenters. 2011, Big Mouth $17.99 (978-1-931520-71-3). 256pp. Thirteen-year-old Cara's mother has disappeared, and a sea otter has been communicating with Cara; with her brothers Cara sets out on a quest that involves danger, evil, and ecological concerns. **e** Lexile 780L (Rev: SLJ 8/11)

9518 Milne, A. A. *The World of Pooh: The Complete Winnie-the-Pooh; and the House at Pooh Corner* (1–4). Illus. by E. H. Shepard. 1988, Dutton $24.99 (978-0-525-44447-3). 320pp. A collection of stories about an child's stuffed bear and his friends in the 100 Acre Woods.

9519 Mlynowski, Sarah. *Fairest of All* (4–6). Series: Whatever After. 2012, Scholastic $14.99 (978-054540330-6). 192pp. Abby and her brother Jonah enter Snow White's world via a mysterious mirror, and find themselves wrestling with whether to intercede between her and the poison apple. **e** Lexile 400L (Rev: BL 4/1/12; SLJ 5/1/12)

9520 Molloy, Michael. *The House on Falling Star Hill* (4–8). 2004, Scholastic $16.95 (978-0-439-57740-3). While spending a vacation with his grandparents in a peaceful English village, Tim discovers an alternate world called Tallis and becomes involved in the turmoil taking place there. (Rev: BL 4/15/04; SLJ 4/04)

9521 Molloy, Michael. *The Time Witches* (5–8). 2002, Scholastic paper $4.99 (978-0-439-42090-7). The characters from *The Witch Trade* (2002) return in this sequel in which Abby, a Light Witch, and her friends must travel into the past to foil a plot hatched by the nefarious Wolfbane. (Rev: BL 1/1–15/03; SLJ 8/03)

9522 Moloney, James. *The Book of Lies* (4–6). 2007, HarperCollins $16.99 (978-0-06-057842-8). 368pp. Kidnapped and brought to Mrs. Timmons's Home for Orphans and Foundlings, a young boy awakens with no memory of his former life, but a young girl offers him a single clue that sets him on the trail to his past. (Rev: BL 4/15/07)

9523 Moloney, James. *Trapped* (4–8). Illus. by Shaun Tan. 2008, Stone Arch LB $16.95 (978-1-59889-863-7). David, a skateboarder, can't resist exploring a huge drainpipe even though he knows that two boys once died there in this illustrated book that will appeal to reluctant readers. (Rev: BL 12/15/07; SLJ 2/08)

9524 Moonshower, Candie. *The Legend of Zoey* (4–6). 2006, Delacorte $15.95 (978-0-385-73280-2). 224pp. A multilayered story told in part through the diary entries of Zoey, a modern girl of Native American heritage, who travels back in time to 1811 and meets Prudence, the daughter of white settlers; the two endure the New Madrid earthquakes together. (Rev: BL 7/06; SLJ 12/06)

9525 Moredun, P. R. *The Dragon Conspiracy* (5–8). Series: World of Eldaterra. 2005, HarperCollins LB $17.89 (978-0-06-076664-1). A complex first installment in

which a British schoolboy in 1910 must battle female dragons to save both our world and the magical parallel world of Eldaterra. (Rev: BL 6/1–15/05; SLJ 10/05)

9526 Morris, Gerald. *Parsifal's Page* (5–8). 2001, Houghton Mifflin $16.00 (978-0-618-05509-8). Piers becomes a page to Parsifal and accompanies the innocent young man on his quest to become a knight. (Rev: BCCB 4/01; BL 4/15/01; HB 5–6/01; HBG 10/01; SLJ 4/01; VOYA 6/01)

9527 Morris, Gerald. *The Savage Damsel and the Dwarf* (5–8). 2000, Houghton Mifflin $16.00 (978-0-395-97126-0). Sixteen-year-old Lady Lynet travels to Camelot, in the company of a dwarf, to ask King Arthur's aid in defeating her sister's suitor. (Rev: BL 3/1/00; HB 5–6/00; HBG 10/00; SLJ 5/00; VOYA 6/00)

9528 Morris, Jackie. *The Seal Children* (2–5). Illus. by author. 2004, Frances Lincoln $16.95 (978-1-84507-040-3). The son of a Welsh fisherman and a selkie woman travels to his mother's world beneath the sea and returns with a box of pearls that the people in his village can use to finance a trip to the New World. (Rev: SLJ 7/04)

9529 Morrisette, Sharon. *Toads and Tessellations: A Math Adventure* (K–2). Illus. by Philomena O'Neill. 2012, Charlesbridge $16.95 (978-1-58089-354-1); paper $7.95 (978-1-58089-355-8). 32pp. The importance of tessellations is demonstrated in this story of Enzo, a magician's apprentice of dubious ability in medieval Italy, who attempts to help a shoemaker create 12 pairs of shoes from one piece of fine leather. Lexile 580L (Rev: BLO 9/15/12; LMC 3–4/13; SLJ 8/12)

9530 Morrison, P. R. *Wind Tamer* (4–6). 2006, Bloomsbury $16.95 (978-1-58234-781-3). 336pp. A visit from his uncle convinces 10-year-old Archie Stringweed, who lives in a remote Scottish village, to confront the curse that has hung over his family for generations. (Rev: BL 10/15/06; SLJ 11/06)

9531 Morton-Shaw, Christine. *The Hunt for the Seventh* (5–8). 2008, HarperCollins $16.99 (978-0-06-072822-9). 288pp. Recently moved with his family to the stately Minerva Hall, young Jim finds himself haunted by the ghosts of children who have died in strange accidents. (Rev: BL 1/1–15/09; LMC 3/09; SLJ 5/09)

9532 Moskowitz, Hannah. *Zombie Tag* (5–8). 2011, Roaring Brook $15.99 (978-1-59643-720-3). 240pp. Zombie tag is just a game until 12-year-old Will's older brother Graham suddenly comes back to life. (Rev: BL 12/15/11; SLJ 12/1/11)

9533 Moss, Marissa. *Home Sweet Rome* (4–7). Illus. by author. Series: Mira's Diary. 2013, Sourcebooks/Jabberwocky $12.99 (978-140226609-6). 208pp. In search of her mother Mira travels back to Rome in 1600, where she meets famous artists, philosophers, and scientists. Lexile 760 (Rev: BLO 6/13; SLJ 5/13)

9534 Moss, Marissa. *Mira's Diary: Lost in Paris* (4–7). Illus. by author. 2012, Sourcebooks/Jabberwocky $12.99 (978-1-4022-6606-5). 224pp. Traveling with her father to Paris in search of her missing mother, Mira visits Notre Dame and is transported to the 19th century where she meets Degas and learns about the Dreyfus affair. 🎧 Lexile 730L (Rev: BL 12/1/12; LMC 5–6/13; SLJ 10/12)

9535 Mould, Chris. *The Icy Hand* (4–6). Illus. by author. Series: Something Wickedly Weird. 2008, Roaring Brook $9.95 (978-1-59643-385-4). With help from a talking fish and the ghost of his great-uncle Bartholomew, Stanley battles pirates searching to steal a family heirloom; the second installment in the series. (Rev: HB 11/08; LMC 3/09; SLJ 11/08)

9536 Mull, Brandon. *Seeds of Rebellion* (5–8). Series: Beyonders. 2012, Aladdin $19.99 (978-141699794-8). 512pp. Jason succeeds in traveling from Colorado back to Lyrian in this action-packed story and joins with Rachel and Galloran to fight the evil that is lurking. 🎧 🎧 (Rev: BL 2/1/12; SLJ 3/12)

9537 Mull, Brandon. *Wild Born* (4–7). Series: Spirit Animals. 2013, Scholastic $12.99 (978-054552255-7). 208pp. In the world of Erdas four 11-year-old children — Conor, Abeke, Meilin, and Rollan — learn that they each have an animal spirit within them (a wolf, leopard, giant panda, and falcon respectively) and that they must summon these powerful animals to help them protect the Great Beasts from their malevolent enemy, the Devourer. 🎧 (Rev: BL 11/15/13; LMC 3–4/14; SLJ 10/13)

9538 Mull, Brandon. *A World Without Heroes* (4–7). Series: Beyonders. 2011, Simon & Schuster $19.99 (978-1-4169-9792-4). 464pp. Jason, 14, is transported into an alternate world called Lyrian where he meets another young American, Rachel, and the two set out on a quest to overthrow the evil emperor and find their way home. 🎧 🎧 Lexile 710L (Rev: BL 2/15/11; SLJ 3/1/11; VOYA 8/11)

9539 Muller, Rachel Dunstan. *The Solstice Cup* (5–8). 2009, Orca paper $9.95 (978-1-55469-017-6). 144pp. On a visit to Northern Ireland, tween twins Breanne and Mackenzie ignore warnings about the fairies and find themselves transported into a scary Otherworld. (Rev: BL 5/15/09)

9540 Mullin, Caryl Cude. *A Riddle of Roses* (4–7). 2000, Second Story paper $6.95 (978-1-896764-28-3). Meryl, who has been expelled from school for a year, goes on a quest to Avalon to find her own wisdom. (Rev: BL 2/15/01; VOYA 4/01)

9541 Myers, Walter Dean. *Three Swords for Granada* (3–6). Illus. by John Spiers. 2002, Holiday House $15.95 (978-0-8234-1676-9). 80pp. Sword-wielding Spanish cats stand up to the dogs of the Fidorean Guard in this exciting fantasy set in 1420. (Rev: BL 7/02; HBG 10/03; SLJ 9/02)

9542 Myklusch, Matt. *Jack Blank and the Imagine Nation* (4–7). 2010, Aladdin $16.99 (978-1-4169-9561-6). 480pp. Jack Blank fits right in at St. Barnaby's Home for the Hopeless, Abandoned, Forgotten, and Lost until he destroys a zombie robot and is taken to the Imagine Nation to hone his superpowers and save the world. 🎧 Lexile 780L (Rev: BL 7/10; LMC 10/10; SLJ 9/1/10)

9543 Myklusch, Matt. *The Secret War* (5–8). Series: Jack Blank Adventures. 2011, Aladdin $16.99 (978-1-4169-9564-7). 554pp. In this second complex volume in the series, Jack must deal with a dangerous computer virus while battling the spyware parasite in his own body. The final volume in the trilogy is *The End of Infinity* (2012). (Rev: BLO 9/15/11; LMC 11–12/11; SLJ 11/1/11; VOYA 12/11)

9544 Nash, Scott. *The High-Skies Adventures of Blue Jay the Pirate* (3–6). Illus. by author. 2012, Candlewick $17.99 (978-0-7636-3264-9). 368pp. A band of bird pirates aboard the flying ship Grosbeak, captained by Blue Jay, find themselves facing a variety of dangers even as they teach a young gosling called Gabriel the basics of piracy. 🎧 🎧 Lexile 870L (Rev: BL 9/15/12; LMC 1–2/13; SLJ 10/12; VOYA 8/12)

9545 Naylor, Phyllis Reynolds. *Jade Green: A Ghost Story* (5–8). 2000, Simon & Schuster $16.00 (978-0-689-82005-2). Set in South Carolina about 100 years ago, this ghost story involves Judith Sparrow, age 15, and the mystery surrounding the gruesome death of a girl named Jade Green. (Rev: BL 12/15/99; HBG 10/00; SLJ 2/00; VOYA 6/00)

9546 Naylor, Phyllis Reynolds. *Polo's Mother* (4–6). Illus. by Alan Daniel. Series: Cat Pack. 2005, Simon & Schuster $15.95 (978-0-689-86555-8). 176pp. Polo's mother finally turns up at the Club of Mysteries, but she is not what Polo expected. (Rev: BL 6/1–15/05; SLJ 5/05)

9547 Nelson, D. A. *Dark Isle* (4–6). 2008, Delacorte $15.99 (978-0-385-73630-5). 272pp. After being locked in the cellar by her foster parents, Morag, 10, goes off with a talking rat and a dodo bird to save the world. (Rev: BL 11/15/08; SLJ 1/09)

9548 Nelson, Peter. *Herbert's Wormhole* (4–6). Illus. by Rohitash Rao. 2009, HarperCollins paper $12.99 (978-0-06-168868-3). 256pp. Superkids venture into the near future for some supremely silly fun. (Rev: BL 6/1–15/09)

9549 Nesbet, Anne. *The Cabinet of Earths* (4–7). 2012, HarperCollins $16.99 (978-006196313-1). 272pp. Full of mystery and magic, this book tells of 13-year-old Maya's relocation, with her family, to Paris, where she struggles to keep watch over her young brother while finding herself enchanted by the magical Cabinet of Earths. 🎧 Lexile 800L (Rev: BL 1/1/12; HB 1–2/12; SLJ 5/1/12; VOYA 12/11)

9550 Nesbit, E. *Lionel and the Book of Beasts* (2–4). Illus. by Michael Hague. 2006, HarperCollins $16.99 (978-0-688-14006-9). 48pp. This abridged retelling of Nesbit's classic book tells the story of new young king Lionel, who accidentally unleashes a dragon upon the land. (Rev: BL 12/1/06; SLJ 1/07)

9551 Nesbit, Edith. *The Enchanted Castle* (4–6). Illus. by Paul Zelinsky. 1992, Morrow $25.99 (978-0-688-05435-9). 304pp. A handsome volume that showcases Nesbit's fantasy about four English children and their adventures with a magic ring, first published in 1907. (Rev: BL 12/15/92)

9552 Nesbit, Edith. *Five Children and It* (4–6). Illus. by H. R. Miller. 1981, Buccaneer LB $21.95 (978-0-89966-362-3). 188pp. An enchanting story about a group of children who discover a Psammead, a sand fairy, who both enlivens and confuses their lives. Two more stories about the children: *The Phoenix and the Carpet* (1985); *The Story of the Amulet* (1986).

9553 Newbery, Linda. *Lost Boy* (5–8). 2008, Random House $15.99 (978-0-375-84574-1). New to the town of Hay-on-Wye in Wales, Matt feels the presence of a boy who died there several years before. (Rev: BCCB 3/08; BL 4/1/08; LMC 4–5/08; SLJ 3/08)

9554 Newbery, Linda. *Lucy and the Green Man* (4–6). 2010, Random House $16.99 (978-0-385-75204-6); LB $19.99 (978-0-385-75207-7). 224pp. Lucy's grandfather's mysterious and magical friend Lob comes to live with his granddaughter — the only one who believed he existed — after Grandpa passes away. Lexile 650L (Rev: BL 11/15/10; LMC 5–6/11; SLJ 1/1/11)

9555 Newbound, Andrew. *Ghoul Strike!* (5–8). 2010, Scholastic $16.99 (978-054522938-8). 320pp. Twelve-year-old ghost hunter Alannah Malarra is out of her depth when she faces spirits from another dimension and must call in reinforcements. (Rev: BL 10/15/10; SLJ 1/1/11)

9556 Nielsen, Jennifer A. *The False Prince* (4–7). Series: Ascendance Trilogy. 2012, Scholastic $17.99 (978-054528413-4). 352pp. Most of the royal family of Carthya is dead, and nobleman Conner seeks a child to impersonate the missing younger son and inherit the throne; the first volume in a trilogy. ∩ **e** Lexile 710L (Rev: BL 4/1/12; HB 3–4/12; LMC 8–9/12; SLJ 4/12)

9557 Nielsen, Jennifer A. *The Runaway King* (5–8). Series: Ascendance Trilogy. 2013, Scholastic $17.99 (978-0-545-28415-8). 352pp. In this exciting sequel to *The False Prince* (2012), young Jaron, king of Carthya, is surrounded by enemies even as he struggles to save his realm. ∩ **e** Lexile 710 (Rev: BL 4/1/13; HB 3–4/13; SLJ 4/13; VOYA 6/13)

9558 Nigg, Joseph. *How to Raise and Keep a Dragon* (5–10). Illus. by Dan Malone. 2006, Barron's $18.99 (978-0-7641-5920-6). This whimsical guide to the care and feeding of dragons offers tips for selecting just the right type of dragon, finding the correct equipment and supplies, establishing good modes of communication, and training for competitions. (Rev: SLJ 11/06)

9559 Nimmo, Jenny. *Charlie Bone and the Castle of Mirrors* (4–6). Series: Children of the Red King. 2005, Scholastic $9.95 (978-0-439-54528-0). 432pp. Back for another year at Bloor's Academy, Charlie Bone enlists the help of friends to save Billy Raven from his new adoptive parents. (Rev: BL 9/1/05; SLJ 10/05; VOYA 10/05)

9560 Nimmo, Jenny. *Charlie Bone and the Time Twister* (5–7). 2003, Scholastic $10.99 (978-0-439-49687-2). In 1916 Henry Yewbeam finds a strange marble and is transported to the present-day Bloor's Academy, where Charlie Bone tests his magical abilities in an effort to send him home. A sequel to *Midnight for Charlie Bone* (2003). (Rev: BL 9/15/03; HBG 4/04; SLJ 10/03)

9561 Nimmo, Jenny. *The Chestnut Soldier* (4–6). Series: The Magician Trilogy. 2007, Scholastic $9.99 (978-0-439-84677-6). 203pp. Is a soldier visiting Gywn's Welsh town inhabited by the spirit of Efnisien, an evil prince of lore? The last volume in a trilogy that started with *The Snow Spider* (2006). (Rev: BCCB 5/07; BL 2/15/07) ∩

9562 Nimmo, Jenny. *The Dragon's Child* (2–4). Illus. by Alan Marks. 2008, Scholastic paper $6.99 (978-0-545-06468-2). 107pp. With the help of a slave-girl and a bird, a young dragon named Dando is able to fly. (Rev: BL 8/08; LMC 1/09)

9563 Nimmo, Jenny. *Emlyn's Moon* (3–5). Series: Magician Trilogy. 2007, Scholastic $9.99 (978-0-439-84676-9). 152pp. In this second installment in the trilogy, young magician Gwyn and his friend Nia find they hold the fate of Emlyn Llewelyn in their hands. (Rev: BL 12/15/06) ∩

9564 Nimmo, Jenny. *Griffin's Castle* (5–8). 1997, Orchard LB $17.99 (978-0-531-33006-7). When Dinah and her young mother, Rosalie, move into the rundown mansion owned by Rosalie's boyfriend, Dinah brings to life several carved animals for protection. (Rev: SLJ 6/97; VOYA 8/97)

9565 Nimmo, Jenny. *Midnight for Charlie Bone* (4–6). 2003, Scholastic paper $10.99 (978-0-439-47429-0). 416pp. Charlie Bone, who can look at photographs and hear the conversations and thoughts of the subjects, is sent to Bloor's Academy to enhance his skills and is drawn into a magical battle, makes friends, and becomes immersed in a mystery. (Rev: BL 1/1–15/03; HBG 10/03; SLJ 2/03)

9566 Nimmo, Jenny. *The Secret Kingdom* (4–7). 2011, Scholastic $16.99 (978-0-439-84673-8). 224pp. Charlie Bone introduces this tale of his ancestor Timoken the Red King, who, with his sister Zobayda, finds himself in an action-packed fantasy adventure. The second volume in the series is *The Stones of Ravenglass* (2012). (Rev: BL 10/1/11; SLJ 9/1/11)

9567 Nimmo, Jenny. *The Snow Spider* (3–5). Series: Magician Trilogy. 2006, Scholastic $9.99 (978-0-439-84675-2). 128pp. On Gwyn's 9th birthday his grandmother reveals to him that he's a magician, giving him five gifts to help him with his powers; set in Wales, this story incorporates elements of the local folklore. (Rev: BL 11/15/06)

9568 Nitz, Kristin Wolden. *Saving the Griffin* (3–5). Illus. by Yoshiko Jaeggi. 2007, Peachtree $14.95 (978-1-56145-380-1). During a trip to Italy, two American siblings try to keep their discovery of a baby griffin a secret from family members and others. (Rev: BL 5/15/07; LMC 10/07; SLJ 6/07)

9569 Nix, Garth. *Above the Veil* (5–7). Series: The Seventh Tower. 2001, Scholastic paper $5.99 (978-0-439-17685-9). In episode four in this series, Tal and Milla continue their otherworldly adventures full of action, secrets, and surprising twists and turns. (Rev: SLJ 9/01)

9570 Nix, Garth. *Grim Tuesday* (5–8). Series: Keys to the Kingdom. 2004, Scholastic paper $7.99 (978-0-439-43655-7). Arthur Penhaligon returns in this second installment in the series to the house that holds an alternate universe and there must challenge the evil Grim Tuesday, who threatens to destroy everything; the next volume is *Drowned Wednesday* (2005). (Rev: SLJ 8/04)

9571 Nix, Garth. *Lord Sunday* (5–8). Series: Keys to the Kingdom. 2010, Scholastic $17.99 (978-043970090-0). 320pp. Arthur and his allies meet with great hardship and eventually triumph over the diabolical Lord Sunday in this series conclusion. ⌒ e Lexile 980L (Rev: BL 4/15/10)

9572 Nix, Garth. *Mister Monday* (5–8). Series: The Keys to the Kingdom. 2003, Scholastic paper $6.99 (978-0-439-55123-6). When 7th-grader Arthur Penhaligon receives a healing key from a mysterious stranger, the gift turns out to be a mixed blessing that brings illness and strange creatures seeking to reclaim the key. (Rev: BCCB 1/04; SLJ 12/03)

9573 Nix, Garth. *One Beastly Beast: Two Aliens, Three Inventors, Four Fantastic Tales* (5–7). Illus. by Brian Biggs. 2007, Eos $15.99 (978-0-06-084319-9). Four short stories accompanied by cartoonish illustrations for readers who enjoy fantasy that's not too far out or too scary. (Rev: BCCB 10/07; BL 7/07; SLJ 9/07)

9574 Nix, Garth, and Sean Williams. *Troubletwisters* (4–7). 2011, Scholastic $16.99 (978-054525897-5). 304pp. When their house mysteriously explodes, twins Jaide and Jack, 12, are sent to live with their previously unknown Grandma X, where they discover they have unusual talents, and that a power named The Evil is lurking. (Rev: BL 9/15/11)

9575 Noël, Alyson. *Radiance* (5–8). Series: Riley Bloom. 2010, Square Fish paper $7.99 (978-0-312-62917-5). 192pp. When Riley crosses over into the afterlife, she must adapt to her surroundings by relying on Bodhi, her well-intentioned guide. ⌒ e Lexile 1120L (Rev: LMC 3–4/11; SLJ 9/1/10)

9576 Noël, Alyson. *Shimmer* (5–8). Series: Riley Bloom. 2011, Square Fish paper $7.99 (978-0-312-64-825-1). 192pp. Riley, a dead 12-year-old who is now a Soul Catcher, works with her mentor Bodhi to control the antics of vengeful Rebecca, who died during a slave revolt in 1733. (Rev: BL 5/1/11; SLJ 4/11)

9577 Norcliffe, James. *The Boy Who Could Fly* (5–8). 2010, Egmont $16.99 (978-1-60684-084-9). 304pp. Michael accepts an offer that allows him to fly, and to escape the miserable home for unwanted children where he lives, but is he really better off? Lexile 700L (Rev: BL 7/10; HB 9–10/10; SLJ 4/11)

9578 Nykko. *The Shadow Door* (4–7). Trans. by Carol Klio Burrell. Illus. by Bannister. Series: Elsewhere Chronicles. 2009, Lerner LB $27.93 (978-0-7613-4459-9); paper $6.95 (978-0-7613-3963-2). 48pp. Four friends find a door to a dangerous world peopled with shadowy creatures. (Rev: BL 3/1/09)

9579 Nylund, Eric. *The Resisters* (5–8). 2011, Random House $16.99 (978-0-375-86856-6); LB $19.99 (978-0-375-96856-3). 224pp. Twelve-year-old Ethan learns that his understanding of the world has been false and that adults are all subject to mind control; only prepubescent children are safe and can resist. ⌒ e Lexile 720L (Rev: BL 3/15/11; LMC 10/11; SLJ 7/11)

9580 Nyoka, Gail. *Mella and the N'anga: An African Tale* (5–8). 2006, Sumach paper $9.95 (978-1-894549-49-3). Mella, the daughter of a king in ancient Zimbabwe, with the help of the magical powers she learns from the spiritual adviser called N'anga, strives to save her father's life and realm. (Rev: BL 3/1/06; SLJ 7/06)

9581 O'Brien, Robert C. *Mrs. Frisby and the Rats of NIMH* (5–7). Illus. by Zena Bernstein. 1971, Macmillan $18.00 (978-0-689-20651-1); paper $5.50 (978-0-689-71068-1). Saga of a group of rats made literate and given human intelligence by a series of experiments, who escape from their laboratory to found their own community. Newbery Medal 1972.

9582 O'Dell, Kathleen. *The Aviary* (5–8). 2011, Knopf $15.99 (978-0-375-85605-1); LB $18.99 (978-0-375-95605-8). 352pp. At the turn of the 20th century in Maine, solitary 11-year-old Clara discovers that there is a link between the birds in the aviary in the rose garden and the supposed drowning of five children some years before. (Rev: BL 10/1/11; SLJ 11/1/11)

9583 Ogburn, Jacqueline. *The Bake Shop Ghost* (1–3). Illus. by Marjorie Priceman. 2005, Houghton $16.00 (978-0-618-44557-8). 32pp. The ghost of Cora Lee Merriweather, the bad-tempered owner of a bake shop, scares away all of the bakery's new owners until Annie Washington arrives, determined to stand her ground. (Rev: BCCB 9/05; BL 9/1/05*; HBG 4/06; LMC 5/06; SLJ 10/05)

9584 Okorafor-Mbachu, Nnedi. *The Shadow Speaker* (5–8). 2007, Hyperion $16.99 (978-1-4231-0033-1). West Africa is a very different place in 2070 in this futuristic tale in which Muslim Ejii, 15, shadow-speaks with the queen who had her father killed years earlier. (Rev: BL 3/1/08; SLJ 2/08)

9585 Okorafor-Mbachu, Nnedi. *Zahrah the Windseeker* (5–8). 2005, Houghton Mifflin $16.00 (978-0-618-34090-3). In this appealing debut novel, 13-year-old Zahrah, a "dada girl" readily identifiable by her telltale vine-entwined dreadlocks, struggles to come to terms with her magical powers. (Rev: BL 11/15/05; SLJ 12/05)

9586 Oliver, Lauren. *Liesl and Po* (4–7). Illus. by Kei Acedera. 2011, HarperCollins $16.99 (978-0-06-201451-1). 320pp. A young apothecary's apprentice accidentally switches a box of magic with a vessel containing Liesl's father's ashes, leading to an adventure full of ghosts. ⌒ e Lexile 830L (Rev: BL 9/1/11; SLJ 11/1/11*)

9587 Oliver, Lauren. *The Spindlers* (4–7). 2012, HarperCollins $16.99 (978-0-06-197808-1). 256pp. Liza realizes that her little brother Patrick has been infiltrated by the Spindlers and that he will soon disintegrate and produce hundreds of new Spindlers; Liza is determined to save his soul. ⌒ **e** Lexile 840L (Rev: BL 7/12; LMC 3–4/13; SLJ 9/12*)

9588 Oliver, Lin. *Attack of the Growling Eyeballs* (4–6). Illus. by Stephen Gilpin. Series: Who Shrunk Daniel Funk? 2008, Simon & Schuster $14.99 (978-1-4169-6225-0). 112pp. A sneeze causes Daniel Funk to shrink to toe-size and he then learns two things: that this is a family trait and that he has a twin brother Pablo, who is only an inch high but has a character at least twice his size; a funny action-packed novel. (Rev: BL 4/1/08; LMC 8/08)

9589 Olson, Arielle North, and Howard Schwartz, eds. *Ask the Bones: Scary Stories from Around the World* (5–9). 1999, Viking $16.99 (978-0-670-87581-8). A collection of 22 scary stories about subjects ranging from ghosts to witches and voodoo spells, accompanied by spooky illustrations. (Rev: BCCB 4/99; BL 5/1/99; HB 5–6/99; HBG 10/99; SLJ 4/99)

9590 Oram, Hiawyn. *My Unwilling Witch Goes to Ballet School* (2–4). Illus. by Sarah Warburton. 2009, Little, Brown paper $9.99 (978-0-316-03472-2). 112pp. Poor Rumblewick, a witch's familiar, describes in his diary how he must work overtime trying to get Haggy to behave like a witch when all Haggy wants to do is become a ballerina. (Rev: BL 7/09)

9591 Osborne, Mary Pope. *Moonlight on the Magic Flute* (2–4). Illus. by Sal Murdocca. Series: Magic Tree House. 2009, Random $11.99 (978-0-375-85646-4). Transported back to 18th-century Vienna, Jack and Annie meet a young Mozart and help to save his life. (Rev: BLO 4/23/09) ⌒

9592 Osborne, Mary Pope. *Night of the New Magicians* (2–4). Illus. by Sal Murdocca. Series: Magic Tree House. 2006, Random $11.95 (978-0-375-83035-8). 116pp. Jack and Annie are sent on a magician-searching mission at the 1889 World's Fair. (Rev: BL 5/1/06)

9593 Osterweil, Adam. *The Amulet of Komondor* (5–7). 2003, Front St $15.95 (978-1-886910-81-2). Finding themselves in a parallel world of "Japanimations," Joe and Katie face a mighty challenge, worry about how to get home, and continue their real-world romance in this lighthearted fantasy with *anime*-style illustrations. (Rev: BL 11/15/03; HBG 4/04; SLJ 12/03)

9594 Osterweil, Adam. *The Comic Book Kid* (4–6). Illus. 2001, Front St. $15.95 (978-1-886910-62-1). Brian tries to travel back to 1939 and replace his father's prized Superman #1 comic book. (Rev: BL 5/15/01; HBG 10/01; SLJ 8/01)

9595 Oz, Amos. *Suddenly in the Depths of the Forest* (4–7). Trans. from Hebrew by Sondra Silverston. 2011, Houghton Mifflin $15.99 (978-0-547-55153-1). 144pp. A multilayered story about two children — Maya and Matti — who set out despite their fears to find out why their village has been cursed and all the animals have disappeared; an allegorical fable about tolerance and redemption. **e** Lexile NC1260L (Rev: BL 2/15/11; HB 5–6/11; LMC 10/11*; SLJ 5/11; VOYA 4/11)

9596 Park, Linda Sue. *Archer's Quest* (4–7). 2006, Clarion $16.00 (978-0-618-59631-7). An ancient Korean ruler suddenly appears in the New York State bedroom of 12-year-old Kevin and the two must work out how to get him back home before the Year of the Tiger ends. (Rev: BL 3/15/06; SLJ 5/06)

9597 Paterson, Katherine. *The Field of the Dogs* (3–5). Illus. by Emily Arnold McCully. 2001, HarperCollins LB $14.89 (978-0-06-029475-5). 96pp. Josh, beset by bullies in the Vermont town where he has moved with his mother, discovers that he can understand the language of dogs. (Rev: BCCB 2/01; BL 10/15/01; HBG 10/01; SLJ 2/01)

9598 Paterson, Katherine. *The Wide-Awake Princess* (2–5). Illus. 2000, Clarion $15.00 (978-0-395-53777-0). 48pp. The story of a princess who leaves her castle to find out about the common people in her kingdom and how they live. (Rev: BL 3/15/00; HBG 10/00; SLJ 7/00)

9599 Paterson, Katherine, and John Paterson. *The Flint Heart* (3–6). Illus. by John Rocco. 2011, Candlewick $19.99 (978-0-7636-4712-4). 304pp. The Patersons adapt Eden Philpott's 1910 story about two siblings — Charles and Unity — struggling to rescue their father from the domineering grasp of a cursed piece of flint; the action-packed text is enhanced by striking illustrations. (Rev: BL 9/1/11; SLJ 8/1/11*)

9600 Patten, E. J. *Return to Exile* (5–8). Illus. by John Rocco. Series: Hunter Chronicles. 2011, Simon & Schuster $16.99 (978-1-4424-2032-8). 512pp. Twelve-year-old Sky and his family have moved back to the small town of Exile, Sky's Uncle Phineas has disappeared, and Sky appears to be being targeted by monsters. **e** Lexile 800L (Rev: BL 10/15/11; LMC 5–6/12; SLJ 12/1/11)

9601 Paul, Donita K. *Dragonspell* (4–8). 2004, WaterBrook paper $12.99 (978-1-57856-823-9). Fourteen-year-old Kale is the protagonist of this classic quest tale, set in the world of Amara, with Christian overtones reminiscent of C. S. Lewis. (Rev: SLJ 11/04)

9602 Paver, Michelle. *Oath Breaker* (5–9). Series: Chronicles of Ancient Darkness. 2009, HarperCollins $16.99 (978-0-06-072837-3); LB $17.89 (978-0-06-072838-0). 292pp. When Torak's friend is murdered by a soul-eater, he sets out to get revenge in this fifth book in the series. Lexile 660L (Rev: SLJ 8/09; VOYA 2/09)

9603 Pearce, Philippa. *A Finder's Magic* (3–5). Illus. by Helen Craig. 2009, Candlewick $15.99 (978-0-7636-4072-9). 128pp. When Till loses his dog Bess, he is happy to accept the help of a stranger who asks a variety of animals for pertinent information. (Rev: BCCB 5/09; BLO 5/27/09; SLJ 6/09)

9604 Pearce, Philippa. *Tom's Midnight Garden* (4–7). Illus. by Susan Einzig. 1959, Dell paper $6.99 (978-0-06-440445-7). When the clock strikes 13, Tom visits his garden and meets Hatty, a strange mid-Victorian girl.

9605 Peck, Richard. *The Ghost Belonged to Me* (5–8). 1997, Viking paper $5.99 (978-0-14-038671-4). Richard unwillingly receives the aid of his nemesis, Blossom Culp, in trying to solve the mystery behind the ghost of a young girl. Two sequels are *Ghosts I Have Been* (1977); *The Dreadful Future of Blossom Culp* (1983).

9606 Peck, Richard. *The Mouse with the Question Mark Tail* (3–5). Illus. by Kelly Murphy. 2013, Dial $16.99 (978-080373838-6). 240pp. In the time of Queen Victoria a mouse with an unusual tail sets out to discover his origins. **e** Lexile 680 (Rev: BL 5/1/13*; LMC 11–12/13; SLJ 7/13*)

9607 Peck, Richard. *Secrets at Sea* (4–7). Illus. by Kelly Murphy. 2011, Dial $16.99 (978-0-8037-3455-5). 272pp. In the late 19th century Helena and her mouse siblings must conquer their fears as they accompany the Cranston family (whose house they live in) on an ocean voyage to Europe, meeting many new mice and people as they travel. (Rev: BL 9/1/11; SLJ 9/1/11)

9608 Pemberton, Bonnie. *The Cat Master* (5–8). 2007, Marshall Cavendish $16.99 (978-0-7614-5340-6). A dying Cat Master's telepathic message to his successor — indoor cat but formerly feral Buddy — is intercepted by the evil cat Jett, and Buddy and his friends must fight for justice to be fulfilled. (Rev: BL 6/1–15/07; SLJ 6/07)

9609 Pennell, Christopher. *The Mysterious Woods of Whistle Root* (4–7). Illus. by Rebecca Bond. 2013, Houghton Mifflin $16.99 (978-054779263-7). 224pp. Eleven-year-old orphan Carly Bean Bitters can only sleep during the day and is consequently very lonely until one day she is befriended by a musical rat who invites her to join his small band; together they investigate strange events taking place in the woods. **e** Lexile 790 (Rev: BL 10/1/13; LMC 3–4/14; SLJ 10/13)

9610 Pennypacker, Sara. *Stuart Goes to School* (2–4). Illus. by Martin Matje. 2003, Scholastic $15.95 (978-0-439-30182-4). In this humorous sequel to *Stuart's Cape,* the title character enters the third grade at a new school and finds that having a magical cape can sometimes cause embarrassing problems. (Rev: BL 7/03; SLJ 9/03)

9611 Perrin, Randy. *Time Like a River* (5–7). 1997, RDR $14.95 (978-1-57143-061-8). Margie travels back in time to find a cure for her mother's mysterious illness. (Rev: HBG 3/98; SLJ 3/98)

9612 Perro, Bryan. *The Mask Wearer* (4–7). Trans. by Y. Maudet. 2011, Delacorte $16.99 (978-0-385-73903-0); LB $19.99 (978-0-385-90766-8). 176pp. With the help of mythical animal friends, young Amos Daragon sets out on a quest to find four masks representing earth, wind, fire, and water and thereby defeat the evil threatening his land. **e** Lexile 800L (Rev: BL 2/15/11; LMC 8–9/11*; SLJ 4/11)

9613 Peterson, Will. *Triskellion* (5–9). Series: Triskellion. 2008, Candlewick $16.99 (978-0-7636-3971-6). 368pp. Telepathic twins Adam and Rachel, 14, are spending the summer in an ancient English village and find themselves swept into an adventure involving archaeology, folklore, and an ancient artifact; the first volume in a series. (Rev: BCCB 9/08; LMC 10/08; SLJ 11/08; VOYA 8-08)

9614 Philbrick, Rodman. *REM World* (4–6). 2000, Scholastic $16.95 (978-0-439-08362-1). Ten-year-old Arthur gets stuck in the REM world when he tries to use a REM sleep machine to lose weight. (Rev: BCCB 6/00; BL 5/1/00; HBG 10/00; SLJ 5/00)

9615 Pierce, Tamora. *Briar's Book* (5–9). Series: Circle of Magic. 1999, Scholastic paper $15.95 (978-0-590-55359-9). In this fantasy, Briar, a former street urchin and petty thief, and his teacher, Rosethorn, search for the cause of a deadly plague that is sweeping through their land. (Rev: BL 2/15/99; HBG 10/99; SLJ 3/99; VOYA 6/99)

9616 Pierce, Tamora. *Daja's Book* (5–9). Series: Circle of Magic. 1998, Scholastic paper $15.95 (978-0-590-55358-2). Daja, a mage-in-training, uses her magical powers to create a living vine out of metal, and soon members of the nomadic Traders want to possess it. (Rev: BCCB 12/98; BL 12/1/98; HBG 3/99; SLJ 12/98; VOYA 2/99)

9617 Pierce, Tamora. *Magic Steps* (5–9). Series: The Circle Opens. 2000, Scholastic paper $16.95 (978-0-590-39588-5). Fourteen-year-old Sandry and her friend Pasco use their magic to stop the murders of local merchants. (Rev: BCCB 3/00; BL 3/1/00; HB 5–6/00; HBG 10/00; SLJ 4/00)

9618 Pierce, Tamora. *Street Magic* (5–9). Series: The Circle Opens. 2001, Scholastic paper $16.95 (978-0-590-39628-8). Briar, a 14-year-old former gang member, finds he is again caught between warring gangs when he helps a female street urchin in this futuristic novel. (Rev: BL 4/15/01; HB 3–4/01; HBG 10/01; SLJ 7/01; VOYA 4/01)

9619 Pierce, Tamora. *Tris's Book* (5–9). Series: Circle of Magic. 1998, Scholastic paper $15.95 (978-0-590-55357-5). Tris and her three fellow mages combine forces to fight the pirates who are threatening to destroy their home in this sequel to *Sandry's Book*. (Rev: BCCB 4/98; BL 8/98; HBG 10/98; SLJ 4/98; VOYA 8/98)

9620 Pilkey, Dav. *Ricky Ricotta's Giant Robot vs. the Voodoo Vultures from Venus* (2–4). Illus. by Martin Ontiveros. 2001, Scholastic $16.95 (978-0-439-23624-9). 125pp. Ricky the mouse and his giant robot friend tackle villains from Venus with dastardly plans. (Rev: HBG 10/01; SLJ 5/01)

9621 Pilkey, Dav. *Ricky Ricotta's Mighty Robot vs. the Jurassic Jackrabbits from Jupiter* (2–4). Illus. by Martin Ontiveros. 2002, Scholastic paper $3.99 (978-0-439-37643-3). 127pp. Ricky, his Mighty Robot, and cousin Lucy defeat General Jackrabbit, an invader from Jupiter with nefarious intent. (Rev: SLJ 12/02)

9622 Pilkey, Dav. *Ricky Ricotta's Mighty Robot vs. the Mecha-Monkeys from Mars* (2–4). Illus. by Martin Ontiveros. 2002, Scholastic paper $3.99 (978-0-439-25296-6). 143pp. Ricky and his robot friend battle the fiendish forces of an evil Martian monkey. (Rev: HBG 10/02; SLJ 4/02)

9623 Pilkey, Dav. *Ricky Ricotta's Mighty Robot vs. the Uranium Unicorns from Uranus* (1–3). Illus. by Martin Ontiveros. Series: Ricky Ricotta. 2005, Scholastic $16.99 (978-0-439-37646-4); paper $4.99 (978-0-439-37647-1). Ricky the mouse and his Mighty Robot must foil Uncle Unicorn's evil plot to take over the world. (Rev: SLJ 1/06)

9624 Pipe, Jim. *The Werewolf* (4–7). Series: In the Footsteps Of. 1996, Millbrook LB $24.90 (978-0-7613-0450-0). A horror story in which Bernard, a werewolf, commits terrible acts under the influence of a full moon. (Rev: SLJ 7/96)

9625 Poblocki, Dan. *The Ghost of Graylock* (5–8). 2012, Scholastic $16.99 (978-0-545-40268-2). 272pp. A spooky thriller in which Neil and his sister Bree, spending the summer with their aunts near an abandoned psychiatric hospital, team up with two local youngsters to investigate drownings and a ghost. Best Fiction for YA. **e** Lexile 690L (Rev: BLO 9/1/12; LMC 1–2/13; SLJ 10/12; VOYA 10/12)

9626 Poblocki, Dan. *The Stone Child* (4–6). 2009, Random $15.99 (978-0-375-84254-2). 288pp. Strange things happen when 12-year-old Eddie and his family move to Gatesweed, where horror writer Nathaniel Olmstead lived before he went missing 13 years before. (Rev: BLO 5/27/09; SLJ 11/09)

9627 Poe, Edgar Allan. *Edgar Allan Poe's Tales of Death and Dementia* (5–8). Illus. by Gris Grimly. 2009, Simon & Schuster $18.99 (978-1-4169-5025-7). 136pp. A highly illustrated adaptation of four of Poe's thrillingly macabre stories. (Rev: BL 9/1/09; SLJ 9/09)

9628 Pogue, David. *Abby Carnelia's One and Only Magical Power* (3–6). Illus. by Antonio Caparo. 2010, Roaring Brook $15.99 (978-159643384-7). 288pp. Abby's discovery that she has a perplexing — and totally useless — magical power leads her to Camp Cadabra and some surprising discoveries. ⋒ (Rev: BL 5/15/10; LMC 5–6/10; SLJ 5/10)

9629 Porte, Barbara Ann. *Hearsay: Tales from the Middle Kingdom* (5–8). 1998, Greenwillow $15.00 (978-0-688-15381-6). Each of these 15 entertaining fantasies contains elements of Chinese folklore and culture. (Rev: BCCB 5/98; HBG 10/98; SLJ 6/98)

9630 Potter, Ellen. *Olivia Kidney* (4–6). Illus. by Peter Reynolds. 2003, Penguin $15.99 (978-0-399-23850-5). 160pp. When Olivia's father lands a job as superintendent of a New York City apartment block, the 12-year-old finds the building is full of strange and wonderful characters. (Rev: BL 6/1–15/03; HB 9/03; HBG 4/04; SLJ 6/03)

9631 Potter, Ellen. *Olivia Kidney and the Exit Academy* (4–7). Illus. by Peter H. Reynolds. Series: Olivia Kidney. 2005, Putnam $15.99 (978-0-399-24162-8). After her brother's death, Olivia and her father move into a creepy apartment building where, she discovers, people go to rehearse their deaths. (Rev: BL 3/15/05; SLJ 5/05)

9632 Potter, Ellen. *Olivia Kidney and the Secret Beneath the City* (5–7). Series: Olivia Kidney. 2007, Philomel $16.99 (978-0-399-24701-9). Twelve-year-old Olivia is starting 7th grade at a new arts school and also dealing with other problems real and surreal in this third book in the series. (Rev: BL 5/1/07; SLJ 6/07)

9633 Powell, J. *Big Brother at School* (5–8). Illus. by Paul Savage. Series: Keystone Books. 2006, Stone Arch LB $21.26 (978-1-59889-091-4). At a school where cameras watch students' every move, Lee becomes convinced that the principal and a visiting doctor are aliens and takes step to save his fellow students from abduction. (Rev: SLJ 1/07)

9634 Pratchett, Terry. *Johnny and the Dead* (5–8). Series: Johnny Maxwell. 2006, HarperCollins LB $16.89 (978-0-06-054189-7). In the funny second volume of this trilogy, ghosts of the "post-senior citizens" buried in a local cemetery ask the title character to help block plans to bulldoze their final resting place. (Rev: BL 12/15/05; HB 1–2/06; SLJ 12/05; VOYA 2/06)

9635 Pratchett, Terry. *Only You Can Save Mankind* (5–8). 2005, HarperCollins LB $17.89 (978-0-06-054186-6). It's up to Johnny to save the aliens in a new computer game, and the situation forces him to do some thinking about the very nature of war. (Rev: BL 4/15/05*; SLJ 10/05)

9636 Preller, James. *Home Sweet Horror* (3–6). Illus. by Iacopo Bruno. 2013, Feiwel & Friends paper $5.99 (978-1-250-01-887-8). 112pp. After the death of their mother, Liam, 8, and his older sister Kelly move with their father to a new house that turns out to be haunted. **e** (Rev: BLO 7/13; LMC 1–2/14; SLJ 8/13)

9637 Prevost, Guillaume. *The Book of Time* (5–8). Trans. by William Rodarmor. Series: The Book of Time. 2007, Scholastic $16.99 (978-0-439-88375-7). Sam travels through time — to medieval Scotland, World War I France, and ancient Egypt — to find his missing father and finally discovers he's being held captive in Dracula's castle in this first installment in the series. ⋒ (Rev: BCCB 9/07; BL 7/07; HB 9–10/07; SLJ 11/07)

9638 Primavera, Elise. *The Secret Order of the Gumm Street Girls* (4–7). 2006, HarperCollins $16.99 (978-0-06-056946-4). Four girls who live on Gumm Street have little in common until a series of incidents appear to threaten their picturesque town of Sherbet and Franny, Pru, Cat, and Ivy find themselves on a very Oz-like adventure. (Rev: BL 12/15/06; SLJ 12/06)

9639 Prineas, Sarah. *Found* (4–7). Illus. by Antonio Javier Caparo. Series: The Magic Thief. 2010, HarperCollins $16.99 (978-0-06-137593-4). 368pp. In the third book in the series, Conn is on the run after escaping from prison and heads for Dragon Mountain in an effort to save Wellmet from bad magic. Lexile 730L (Rev: LMC 8–9/10)

9640 Prineas, Sarah. *The Magic Thief* (4–6). 2008, HarperCollins $16.99 (978-0-06-137587-3). 426pp. A young thief named Conn picks the pocket of the wizard Nevery and becomes the magician's apprentice; the first volume in a trilogy. (Rev: BCCB 7–8/08; BL 5/15/08; HB 9/08; SLJ 6/08)

9641 Prineas, Sarah. *Winterling* (5–8). 2012, HarperCollins $16.99 (978-006192103-2). 256pp. Fer accidentally travels to a magical but dangerous world full of strange creatures, where she learns a lot about her family and herself. ⌒ ℮ Lexile 720L (Rev: BLO 11/15/11; SLJ 5/1/12)

9642 Prue, Sally. *Cold Tom* (4–8). 2003, Scholastic $15.95 (978-0-439-48268-4). Tom has disabilities that make him an outcast, and he flees from his elfin tribe to the city inhabited by demons (humans), where he is confronted with his human side. (Rev: BL 9/15/03; HB 7–8/03*; HBG 10/03; SLJ 9/03*; VOYA 10/03)

9643 Pullman, Philip. *Lyra's Oxford* (5–8). Illus. by John Lawrence. 2003, Knopf $10.95 (978-0-375-82819-5). This slim volume takes readers back to the world of Pullman's His Dark Materials trilogy, with maps, postcards, and other ephemera. (Rev: BL 2/1/04; SLJ 1/04; VOYA 6/04)

9644 Quimby, Laura. *The Carnival of Lost Souls* (5–8). 2010, Abrams $16.95 (978-081098980-1). 352pp. Orphaned Jack Carr, a Houdini aficionado, is happy to find a home with Professor Hawthorne but unhappy surprises await him. (Rev: BL 10/15/10; LMC 1–2/11; SLJ 12/1/10)

9645 Quinn, Zoe. *The Caped 6th Grader: Happy Birthday, Hero!* (4–6). Illus. by Brie Spangler. 2006, Random LB $11.99 (978-0-385-90304-2); paper $4.99 (978-0-440-42079-8). 135pp. Zoe Richards has just turned 12 when she finds out she has inherited a gene that gives her super powers; she now must work out how to keep this secret and live her normal life. (Rev: SLJ 9/06)

9646 Radunsky, Vladimir. *I Love You Dude* (2–4). Illus. 2005, Harcourt $16.00 (978-0-15-205176-1). Dude, a young girl's doodle of a blue elephant on the wall of a New York City building, escapes cleanup by the anti-graffiti squad and sets off to find acceptance and a home. (Rev: BL 12/1/05; SLJ 10/05)

9647 Ransom, Candice F. *Bones in the Badlands* (2–4). Illus. by Greg Call. Series: Time Spies. 2006, Wizards of the Coast paper $4.99 (978-0-7869-4028-8). (111pp. In the second volume of this time-travel series, Alex, Mattie, and Sophie find themselves in the Badlands at the close of the 19th century and help a paleontologist protect a cache of dinosaur bones from thieves. (Rev: SLJ 2/07)

9648 Ransom, Candice F. *Secret in the Tower* (2–4). Illus. by Greg Call. Series: Time Spies. 2006, Wizards of the Coast paper $4.99 (978-0-7869-4027-1). In the opening book of this time-travel fantasy series, siblings Alex, Mattie, and Sophie find an antique spyglass that transports them back in time to the Revolutionary Battle of Yorktown in 1781. (Rev: SLJ 2/07)

9649 Rees, Celia. *The Soul Taker* (5–8). 2004, Hodder paper $7.95 (978-0-340-87817-0). Lewis, overweight and lacking confidence, finds himself in thrall to a sinister toy maker. (Rev: BL 1/1–15/04)

9650 Reese, Jenn. *Above World* (5–8). 2012, Candlewick $16.99 (978-076365417-7). 368pp. When her undersea-dwelling people's breathing apparatuses begin to fail, Aluna, 13, sets out for dry land with her friend Hoku, and there they find another society. ⌒ ℮ Lexile 710L (Rev: BL 2/15/12; LMC 8–9/12; SLJ 4/12; VOYA 4/12)

9651 Reeve, Philip. *Goblins* (3–5). 2013, Scholastic $17.99 (978-054522220-4). 352pp. Skarper, a goblin, and Henwyn, an aspiring knight and the son of a cheese maker, form an improbable bond, and set about rescuing princesses and kingdoms, and saving Henwyn from his destiny to become the next evil lord. ℮ Lexile 1020 (Rev: BL 10/1/13; LMC 1–2/14; SLJ 12/13)

9652 Reeve, Philip. *Larklight, or, The Revenge of the White Spiders!, or, To Saturn's Rings and Back!* (5–8). Illus. by David Wyatt. 2006, Bloomsbury $16.95 (978-1-59990-020-9). Art and Myrtle Mumby, who live with their father in a Victorian mansion orbiting the earth, become embroiled in a plot to destroy the solar system; a science fiction romp with a touch of romance and a dollop of Victorian manners. (Rev: BCCB 2/07; BL 10/1/06; HB 11–12/06; HBG 4/07; LMC 2/07; SLJ 11/06*; VOYA 12/06)

9653 Reeve, Philip. *Mothstorm* (5–8). Illus. by David Wyatt. 2008, Bloomsbury $16.99 (978-1-59990-303-3). 320pp. All is calm and all is bright as the Mumbys gather to celebrate Christmas but new threats soon arise, involving a cloud of giant moths and an evil Shaper. (Rev: BLO 4/9/09; HB 1/09; SLJ 12/08)

9654 Reeve, Philip. *No Such Thing as Dragons* (4–7). 2010, Scholastic $16.99 (978-0-545-22224-2). 192pp. A mute boy named Ansel apprenticed to a fraudulent dragon hunter is much surprised to discover that dragons do in fact exist — and are simply hungry animals. ℮ (Rev: BL 8/10; LMC 11–12/10; SLJ 9/1/10)

9655 Reeve, Philip. *Starcross* (5–8). Illus. by David Wyatt. 2007, Bloomsbury $16.95 (978-1-59990-121-3). Starcross is the name of the asteroid belt hotel where Art, Myrtle, and their mother go for a holiday that turns into a strange journey through time; the sequel to *Larklight* (2006). (Rev: BL 11/1/07; HB 1–2/08; SLJ 12/07)

9656 Regan, Dian C. *Princess Nevermore* (5–7). 1995, Scholastic $14.95 (978-0-590-47582-2). A princess from another world gets her wish to visit Earth, where she is befriended by two teenagers, Sarah and Adam. (Rev: BCCB 11/95; SLJ 9/95)

9657 Reiche, Dietlof. *Freddy in Peril* (2–5). Trans. by John Brownjohn. Illus. by Joe Cepeda. 2004, Scholastic $16.95 (978-0-439-53155-9). 208pp. When an evil professor threatens to kidnap Freddy, the golden hamster prodigy, an odd assortment of friends and strangers comes to the hamster's aid. (Rev: BL 4/1/04; SLJ 5/04)

9658 Reiche, Dietlof. *Freddy to the Rescue: Book Three in the Golden Hamster Saga* (3–5). Trans. from German by John Brownjohn. Illus. by Joe Cepeda. Series: Golden Hamster Saga. 2005, Scholastic $16.95 (978-0-439-53157-3). 235pp. It's up to talented golden hamster Freddy (and his cat and a few guinea pigs) to save a tribe of field hamsters in the third book in this funny series. (Rev: SLJ 9/05)

9659 Reinhardt, Dana. *Odessa Again* (4–6). 2013, Random House $15.99 (978-0-385-73956-6); LB $18.99 (978-0-385-90793-4). 208pp. Still adjusting to life after her parents' divorce, 9-year-old Odessa Green is astonished to find herself hurtled back 24 hours in time. **e** (Rev: BL 5/1/13; LMC 11–12/13; SLJ 6/13)

9660 Reisman, Michael. *Simon Bloom, the Gravity Keeper* (4–7). 2008, Dutton $15.99 (978-0-525-47922-2). When a book teaches 11-year-old Simon how to control gravity, velocity, friction, and other physical properties; magic, adventure, and suspense ensue. (Rev: BL 3/1/08; SLJ 4/08)

9661 Reisman, Michael. *Simon Bloom, The Octopus Effect* (4–6). 2009, Dutton $16.99 (978-0-525-42082-8). 304pp. Twelve-year-old Simon, fortified by octopus DNA and with the help of friends, fights to squash the evil Sirabetta's plans for world domination in this sequel to *Simon Bloom, the Gravity Keeper*. (Rev: BLO 1/7/09; LMC 5/09) ∩

9662 Reiss, Kathryn. *Sweet Miss Honeywell's Revenge* (4–7). 2004, Harcourt $17.00 (978-0-15-216574-1). A haunted dollhouse, a parallel story about the original owner of the antique, and the problems of blended family life are intertwined in this story about 12-year-old Zibby Thorne. (Rev: BL 5/1/04; SLJ 8/04)

9663 Renner, Ellen. *Castle of Shadows* (4–7). 2012, Houghton Mifflin $15.99 (978-054774446-9). 400pp. In a fantastic kingdom in the 1850s Princess Charlie,11, sets out to find her missing mother and encounters mystery and adventure. (Rev: BL 3/15/12; SLJ 4/12*)

9664 Rex, Adam. *Cold Cereal* (4–7). Illus. by author. 2012, HarperCollins $16.99 (978-006206002-0). 432pp. A funny and complex fantasy involving humor, secret experiments, parallel stories, and engaging characters both fairy and real. ∩ **e** (Rev: BL 2/1/12; SLJ 2/12*)

9665 Rex, Adam. *The True Meaning of Smekday* (5–8). 2007, Hyperion $16.99 (978-0-7868-4900-0). Gratuity (called Tip) resents having to write an essay about the day aliens took over America in this funny and visually engaging story. (Rev: BL 10/1/07; HB 11–12/07; LMC 1/08; SLJ 11/07)

9666 Rich, Susan, ed. *Half-Minute Horrors* (5–8). 2009, HarperCollins $12.99 (978-0-06-183379-3). 141pp. A collection of varied short horror stories by more than 70 authors. Lexile 720L (Rev: BL 9/15/09; HB 1–2/10; SLJ 1/10)

9667 Richardson, Bill. *After Hamelin* (4–8). 2000, Annick $19.95 (978-1-55037-629-6). In this entertaining fantasy that is a follow-up to the Pied Piper of Hamelin story, Penelope gets the gift of Deep Dreaming and is able to enter the Piper's secret world in the hope of rescuing the children. (Rev: BL 2/15/01; SLJ 4/01; VOYA 4/01)

9668 Richter, Jutta. *The Cat: Or, How I Lost Eternity* (5–8). Trans. by Anna Brailovsky. Illus. by Rotraut Susanne Berner. 2007, Milkweed $14 (978-157131676-9). 63pp. Eight-year-old Christine is late for school every day because a talking alley cat waylays her and together

they discuss everything from math to eternity. Batchelder Honor 2008; ALA Notable Children's Book 2008. Lexile 720L (Rev: BL 3/1/08; SLJ 2/08)

9669 Riddell, Chris. *Ottoline and the Yellow Cat* (2–4). Illus. by author. 2008, HarperCollins $10.99 (978-0-06-144879-9). 176pp. With extensive, engaging illustrations, this is the story of Ottoline Brown's investigation — with the help of her hairy sidekick Mr. Monroe — into the mystery of missing dogs. (Rev: BL 5/15/08; SLJ 7/08)

9670 Riley, James. *Half Upon a Time* (5–9). 2010, Simon & Schuster $15.99 (978-1-4169-9593-7). 388pp. Good-hearted but clumsy Jack and a sassy punk princess set off on a memorable quest to locate her mother, Snow White, in this zany fractured fairy tale. **e** (Rev: LMC 1–2/11; SLJ 3/1/11)

9671 Riordan, Rick. *The Last Olympian* (4–8). Series: Percy Jackson and the Olympians. 2009, Hyperion $17.99 (978-1-4231-0147-5). 314pp. In this final installment in the series, demigod Percy is approaching his important 16th birthday as he moves to protect New York City. ∩ (Rev: BL 5/15/09*; HB 7/09; SLJ 6/09; VOYA 6/09)

9672 Riordan, Rick. *The Lost Hero* (4–8). Series: Heroes of Olympus. 2010, Hyperion/Disney $18.99 (978-142311339-3). 560pp. Teen demigods Piper, Leo, and Jason meet up at Camp Half-Blood and are sent on an urgent quest that takes them across the United States in three days. ∩ **e** Lexile 660L (Rev: BLO 10/1/10; HB 1–2/11; LMC 5–6/11; SLJ 2/1/11)

9673 Riordan, Rick. *The Mark of Athena* (5–8). Series: The Heroes of Olympus. 2012, Disney/Hyperion $19.99 (978-1-42314060-3). 600pp. In the third book in the series, the seven Greek and Roman demigod friends work together to combat threats to the known world. ∩ **e** Lexile 690L (Rev: BLO 10/1/12; SLJ 1/13)

9674 Riordan, Rick. *The Red Pyramid* (5–8). Series: The Kane Chronicles. 2010, Hyperion $17.99 (978-1-4231-1338-6). 528pp. Carter, 14, and Sadie, 12, discover they are descended from Egyptian royalty as they hone their newly evident magical talents while searching for their Egyptologist father, who disappeared after releasing an enemy god from the Rosetta Stone. ∩ **e** Lexile 650L (Rev: BL 5/15/10*; HB 7–8/10; LMC 10/10; SLJ 6/10)

9675 Riordan, Rick. *The Serpent's Shadow* (5–8). Series: Kane Chronicles. 2012, Disney/Hyperion $19.99 (978-142314057-3). 406pp. Siblings Carter and Sade work to defy the impending end of the world by using their magic against the chaos snake Apophis. ∩ **e** Lexile 690L (Rev: BLO 5/1/12; HB 9–10/12; SLJ 9/12)

9676 Riordan, Rick. *The Son of Neptune* (5–8). Series: Heroes of Olympus. 2011, Hyperion $19.99 (978-1-4231-4059-7). 544pp. In this sequel to *The Lost Hero* (2010), Percy Jackson finds himself in Camp Jupiter, a modern refuge for demigods, where he makes friends with Hazel and Frank and together they set off to free Thanatos (Death) and then tackle bigger challenges. ∩ **e** (Rev: BLO 10/1/11; SLJ 12/1/11)

9677 Riordan, Rick. *The Throne of Fire* (5–8). Series: The Kane Chronicles. 2011, Hyperion $18.99 (978-1-4231-4056-6). 464pp. Carter and Sadie must revive the sun god Ra in order to stop Apophis, the snake god of Chaos, from wreaking destruction. (Rev: BL 5/1/11; SLJ 6/11*)

9678 Roach, Marilynne K. *Encounters with the Invisible World* (5–9). Illus. by author. 1977, Amereon $18.95 (978-0-89190-874-6). Spooky stories about witches, demons, spells, and ghosts in New England.

9679 Roberts, Katherine. *Crystal Mask* (5–8). Series: The Echorium Sequence. 2002, Scholastic paper $15.95 (978-0-439-33864-6). The Singers, a group of people who maintain peace in the world through their unusual powers, are confronted by evildoers known as the Frazhin. Also use *Dark Quetzal* (2003). (Rev: BL 4/15/02; HBG 10/02; SLJ 3/02)

9680 Roberts, Laura Peyton. *Green* (5–8). 2010, Delacorte $16.99 (978-0-385-73558-2). 272pp. Thirteen-year-old Lily succeeds her grandmother as Keeper of the Green Clan's gold in this clever, leprechaun-filled story. e Lexile 720L (Rev: BL 12/1/09; LMC 1–2/10; SLJ 2/10)

9681 Rodda, Emily. *The Key to Rondo* (4–7). 2008, Scholastic $16.99 (978-0-545-03535-4). A magic music box takes Leo and his cousin Mimi to the land of Rondo, home to fairy-tale characters and an evil queen. (Rev: BL 12/15/07; SLJ 4/08)

9682 Rodda, Emily. *Rowan and the Keeper of the Crystal* (3–6). Series: Rowan of Rin. 2002, HarperCollins LB $16.89 (978-0-06-029777-0). 208pp. Rowan must take on his mother's duties to choose the next Keeper of the Crystal after she is poisoned in this third book in the series. (Rev: BCCB 4/02; BL 1/1–15/02; HB 3/02; HBG 10/02; SLJ 5/02)

9683 Rodda, Emily. *The Wizard of Rondo* (4–7). 2009, Scholastic $16.99 (978-0-545-11516-2). 400pp. Cousins Leo and Mimi return to the land of Rondo to find a missing wizard and in the process have a confrontation with the evil Blue Queen. (Rev: BL 10/1/09; SLJ 12/09)

9684 Rodgers, Mary, and Heather Hach. *Freaky Monday* (4–7). 2009, HarperCollins $15.99 (978-0-06-166478-6). 192pp. Switching bodies presents some challenges and some welcome changes for a 13-year-old-girl and her teacher; a successor to 1972's *Freaky Friday*. (Rev: BLO 4/14/09; SLJ 6/09)

9685 Rollins, James. *Jake Ransom and the Skull King's Shadow* (5–8). 2009, HarperCollins $16.99 (978-0-06-147379-1). Jake Ransom and his older sister receive a package that may be linked to the disappearance of their archaeologist parents and find themselves transported into a strange and dangerous world. ∩ (Rev: BL 3/15/09; SLJ 9/09)

9686 Ross, Gary. *Bartholomew Biddle and the Very Big Wind* (3–5). Illus. by Matthew Myers. 2012, Candlewick $17.99 (978-0-7636-4920-3). 96pp. Ten-year-old Bartholomew Biddle decides to take a flight using his bedsheet and has several adventures, including playing with pirates and making friends with a boy named Densy who flies along with Bart. (Rev: LMC 3–4/13; SLJ 1/13)

9687 Rowling, J. K. *Harry Potter and the Chamber of Secrets* (4–8). 1999, Scholastic $22.99 (978-0-439-06486-6). During his second year at Hogwarts School of Witchcraft and Wizardry, Harry is baffled when he hears noises no one else can. (Rev: BCCB 9/99; BL 5/15/99*; HB 7–8/99; HBG 10/99; SLJ 7/99; VOYA 10/99)

9688 Rowling, J. K. *Harry Potter and the Goblet of Fire* (4–9). 2000, Scholastic $29.99 (978-0-439-13959-5). This, the fourth installment of Harry Potter's adventures, begins when Voldemort tries to regain the power he lost in his failed attempt to kill Harry. (Rev: BL 8/00*; HB 11–12/00; HBG 3/01; SLJ 8/00)

9689 Rowling, J. K. *Harry Potter and the Half-Blood Prince* (5–12). Illus. by Mary GrandPré. 2005, Scholastic LB $34.99 (978-0-439-78677-5). In this sixth and penultimate volume, Harry, now 16, begins mapping a strategy to defeat the evil Lord Voldemort. (Rev: BL 8/05*; SLJ 9/05; VOYA 10/05)

9690 Rowling, J. K. *Harry Potter and the Order of the Phoenix* (4–12). 2003, Scholastic LB $34.99 (978-0-439-56761-9). Adolescence, adult hypocrisy, and the deadly threat of Voldemort and his evil supporters combine to make Harry's fifth year at Hogwarts as eventful as ever. (Rev: BL 7/03; HB 9–10/03; HBG 10/03; SLJ 8/03; VOYA 8/03)

9691 Rowling, J. K. *Harry Potter and the Prisoner of Azkaban* (4–8). Illus. by Mary GrandPré. 1999, Scholastic $22.99 (978-0-439-13635-8). In this third thrilling adventure, a murderer has escaped from prison and is after our young hero. (Rev: BCCB 10/99; BL 9/1/99*; HB 11–12/99; HBG 3/00; SLJ 10/99)

9692 Rowling, J. K. *Harry Potter and the Sorcerer's Stone* (4–8). 1998, Scholastic $22.99 (978-0-590-35340-3). In this humorous and suspenseful story, 11-year-old Harry Potter attends the Hogwarts School for Witchcraft and Wizardry, where he discovers that he is a wizard just as his parents had been and that someone at the school is trying to steal a valuable stone with the power to make people immortal. (Rev: BCCB 11/98; BL 9/15/98; HB 1–2/99; HBG 3/99; SLJ 10/98; VOYA 12/98)

9693 Rowling, J. K. *The Tales of Beedle the Bard* (5–8). Illus. by author. 2008, Scholastic $12.99 (978-0-545-12828-5). 128pp. Professor Dumbledore's collection of five fairy tales, which he bequeathed to Hermione; with Dumbledore's accompanying commentary. (Rev: BCCB 3/09; BL 1/1–15/09; HB 3/09; SLJ 3/09)

9694 Ruby, Laura. *The Chaos King* (5–8). 2007, HarperCollins $16.99 (978-0-06-075258-3). In this sequel to *The Wall and the Wing* (2006), Gurl — called Georgie now that she has been reunited with her parents — and her friend Bug must put aside their temporary differences and cope with myriad challenges. ∩ (Rev: BCCB 9/07; SLJ 11/07)

9695 Rupp, Rebecca. *Journey to the Blue Moon: In Which Time Is Lost and Then Found Again* (5–8). 2006, Candlewick $15.99 (978-0-7636-2544-3). A multilayered story in which Alex loses his grandfather's pocket watch and takes a trip to the blue moon, where all things lost go; there he finds other searchers and a group that threatens his chances of returning home. (Rev: BL 12/1/06; SLJ 10/06)

9696 Rupp, Rebecca. *The Return of the Dragon* (3–6). 2005, Candlewick $15.99 (978-0-7636-2377-7). 160pp. In this engaging sequel to *The Dragon of Lonely Island* (1998), the Davis siblings return to the island and discover that their friend Fafnyr, a three-headed dragon, is being pursued by an unscrupulous billionaire named J. P. King. (Rev: BL 9/1/05; SLJ 12/05)

9697 Russell, Christine, and Christopher Russell. *The Quest of the Warrior Sheep* (4–7). 2011, Sourcebooks paper $6.99 (978-1-4022-5511-3). 224pp. After a silver object falls from the sky, five sheep set off to contact the sheep god Aries and return the object — which they're convinced is an ancient relic — while pursued by their owners, a few reporters, and a couple of crooks. Also in this series is *The Warrior Sheep Go West* (2011). ℮ Lexile 660L (Rev: BLO 2/14/11; SLJ 5/11)

9698 Russell, Christine, and Christopher Russell. *The Warrior Sheep Down Under* (4–7). 2012, Sourcebooks paper $6.99 (978-14022678-0-2). 256pp. The five intrepid sheep head to Australia to rescue a ewe in this funny third adventure in the series. ℮ Lexile 660L (Rev: BLO 6/12; SLJ 6/12)

9699 Russell, David O., and Andrew Auseon. *Alienated* (5–8). 2009, Simon & Schuster $16.99 (978-1-4169-8298-2). 344pp. Best friends Gene and Vince have fun publishing a tabloid focusing on extraterrestrials until things turn serious and they find themselves embroiled in an intergalactic war. ℮ Lexile 780L (Rev: BL 11/15/09; SLJ 1/10)

9700 Rutkoski, Marie. *The Cabinet of Wonders* (5–8). Series: The Kronos Chronicles. 2008, Farrar $16.95 (978-0-374-31026-4). 272pp. Sprinkled with tidbits of Bohemian history, this volume set in an alternate European Renaissance follows 12-year-old Petra as she works with the Roma to retrieve her father's eyes from an evil prince. ∩ ℮ Lexile 720L (Rev: BL 7/08; HB 1–2/09; SLJ 10/1/08)

9701 Rutkoski, Marie. *The Celestial Globe* (5–8). Series: The Kronos Chronicles. 2010, Farrar $16.99 (978-0-374-31027-1). 304pp. British spy John Dee helps Petra escape Prince Rodolfo, and subsequently enrolls her in magic classes instead of returning her home. Lexile 640L (Rev: BLO 4/15/10; SLJ 4/10)

9702 Rutkoski, Marie. *The Jewel of the Kalderash* (5–8). Series: Kronos Chronicles. 2011, Farrar $16.99 (978-037433678-3). 336pp. Petra embarks on a daring quest to find who created the Gray Men, so she can free her father from this curse in this fast-paced series conclusion. ℮ Lexile 680L (Rev: BL 10/15/11)

9703 Rylant, Cynthia. *The Heavenly Village* (4–7). 1999, Scholastic paper $15.95 (978-0-439-04096-9). A special book about the Heavenly Village — a place where some people stay who are not sure about going to heaven —

and about some of the people who live in this in-between world. (Rev: BL 12/1/99*; HBG 3/00; SLJ 3/00; VOYA 2/00)

9704 Sage, Angie. *Book One: Magyk* (5–8). Illus. by Mark Zug. 2005, HarperCollins LB $18.89 (978-0-06-057732-2). A fantasy of magic, spells, and evil forces, focusing on young Jenna, who was raised by Septimus Heap's family and who now must flee the evil Supreme Custodian. (Rev: BL 3/15/05; SLJ 4/05)

9705 Sage, Angie. *Darke* (5–8). Illus. by Mark Zug. Series: Septimus Heap. 2011, HarperCollins $17.99 (978-006124242-7). 656pp. Jenna and Septimus's 14th birthday celebration is interrupted when a new Darke Domaine opens up and the two — along with Beetle — are called to save the day; the 6th installment in the series. (Rev: BL 5/1/11)

9706 Sage, Angie. *Flyte* (5–8). Illus. by Mark Zug. Series: Septimus Heap. 2006, HarperCollins $17.99 (978-0-06-057734-6). In this fast-paced sequel to *Magyk* (2005), wizard Septimus must protect Princess Jenna from numerous dangers; a CD includes games. (Rev: BL 5/15/06; SLJ 6/06; VOYA 2/06)

9707 Sage, Angie. *Fyre* (5–8). Illus. by Mark Zug. Series: Septimus Heap. 2013, HarperCollins $17.99 (978-006124245-8). 720pp. An action-packed conclusion to the multilayered series in which the quest to relight the Alchemie Fyre tests loyalties and skills. ∩ Lexile 850 (Rev: BLO 7/13)

9708 Sage, Angie. *My Haunted House* (2–4). Illus. by Jimmy Pickering. Series: Araminta Spookie. 2006, HarperCollins $8.99 (978-0-06-077481-3). 132pp. Living in a haunted house suits Araminta Spookie just fine, so she's understandably upset when her Aunt Tabby announces she plans to sell the house. (Rev: SLJ 2/07) ∩

9709 Sage, Angie. *Physik* (5–8). Series: Septimus Heap. 2007, HarperCollins $17.99 (978-0-06-057737-7). When Septimus Heap, apprenticed to a wizard, inadvertently releases the spirit of an evil queen who lived centuries earlier, the ill-tempered monarch unleashes chaos in the kingdom; the third book in the series. ∩ (Rev: BL 4/1/07; SLJ 6/07)

9710 Sage, Angie. *Queste* (5–8). Series: Septimus Heap. 2008, HarperCollins $17.99 (978-0-06-088207-5). In the fourth book of the series, Septimus is sent on a dangerous Queste and tries to rescue his brother Nicko. (Rev: BL 5/15/08; SLJ 6/08)

9711 Sage, Angie. *The Sword in the Grotto* (2–4). Illus. by Jimmy Pickering. Series: Araminta Spookie. 2006, HarperCollins $8.99 (978-0-06-077484-4). In the second book in the series, Araminta and her friend Wanda Wizzard run into trouble when they try to retrieve a sword from a grotto to present to the ghostly Sir Horace for his 500th birthday. (Rev: SLJ 2/07)

9712 Sage, Angie. *Syren* (3–6). Illus. by Mark Zug. Series: Septimus Heap. 2009, HarperCollins $17.99 (978-006088210-5); LB $18.89 (978-006088211-2). 640pp. Wolf Boy is away on a mission while Septimus and his dragon fly off to bring Princess Jenna and the others back from the Harbor; all does not go as planned. (Rev: BL 11/15/09; SLJ 11/09)

9713 St. John, Lauren. *The Elephant's Tale* (5–8). Series: Legend of the Animal Healer. 2010, Dial $16.99 (978-0-8037-3291-9). 221pp. Eleven-year-old Martine, who can communicate with and heal animals, faces the possible loss of her grandmother's South African animal sanctuary in this action-filled final volume in the series. ℮ Lexile 880L (Rev: LMC 10/10; SLJ 7/10)

9714 St. John, Lauren. *The Last Leopard* (4–7). 2009, Dial $16.99 (978-0-8037-3342-8). 208pp. In this third volume about a girl with a gift for healing animals, 11-year-old Martine is on a safari with her grandmother, and she and her best friend Ben must search for an elusive white leopard in grave danger from those who hunt it for its mystical powers. ℮ Lexile 920L (Rev: BL 2/15/09; SLJ 5/1/09)

9715 St. John, Lauren. *The White Giraffe* (5–8). Illus. by David Dean. 2007, Dial $16.99 (978-0-8037-3211-7). After the tragic death of her parents, 11-year-old Martine is sent to live with her grandmother on a large game preserve in South Africa, where she discovers her mystical gifts and exposes poachers who are hunting a rare white giraffe. (Rev: BL 6/1–15/07; LMC 11/07; SLJ 6/07)

9716 Salvatore, R. A., and Geno Salvatore. *The Stowaway* (5–8). Series: Stone of Tymora. 2008, Mirrorstone $17.95 (978-078695094-2). 304pp. In this fantastical maritime tale, young orphan Maimum uses a magical stone to fend off pirates, beasts, and demons. ℮ (Rev: BL 11/15/08)

9717 Sampson, Fay. *Pangur Ban: The White Cat* (5–8). Series: Pangur Ban. 2003, Lion paper $7.95 (978-0-7459-4763-1). A Welsh cat and an Irish monk encounter princesses and mermaids in this fantasy set in the Middle Ages. (Rev: BL 5/15/03; SLJ 11/03)

9718 Sampson, Fay. *Shape-Shifter: The Naming of Pangur Ban* (5–8). Series: Pangur Ban. 2003, Lion paper $7.95 (978-0-7459-4762-4). A Welsh cat pursued by witches befriends an Irish monk in this first book in the series. (Rev: BL 5/15/03)

9719 San Souci, Robert D. *Dare to Be Scared: Thirteen Stories to Chill and Thrill* (4–8). Illus. by David Ouimet. 2003, Cricket $15.95 (978-0-8126-2688-9). A baker's dozen of spooky stories suitable for this age group that feature diverse characters. (Rev: BL 10/1/03; HBG 10/03; SLJ 9/03)

9720 San Souci, Robert D. *Haunted Houses* (4–6). Illus. by Kelly Murphy. 2010, Henry Holt $16.99 (978-0-8050-8750-5). 288pp. Ten creepy haunted house stories feature haunted houses, ghosts, spiders, and other scary situations. ℮ Lexile 900L (Rev: BL 9/1/10; LMC 11–12/10; SLJ 9/1/10)

9721 Sanders, Stephanie S. *Hero in Disguise* (4–7). Series: Villain School. 2012, Bloomsbury $15.99 (978-1-59990-907-3); paper $6.99 (978-1-59990-906-6). 240pp. The students at Villain School are suspicious that

two newcomers are in fact spies from the Hero School. (Rev: BL 10/1/12; SLJ 12/12)

9722 Sanders, Stephanie S. *Villain School: Good Curses Evil* (3–6). 2011, Bloomsbury $15.99 (978-1-59990-610-2). 224pp. Young villains threatening to give up their family's legacy and turn benevolent are given a reeducation in this boarding school story with a supernatural twist. ℮ Lexile 710L (Rev: BL 10/15/11; LMC 3–4/12; SLJ 9/1/11)

9723 Sanderson, Brandon. *Alcatraz Versus the Evil Librarians* (5–8). 2007, Scholastic $16.99 (978-0-439-92550-1). Alcatraz is a 13-year-old boy with unusual powers and a tendency to insert his own thoughts into the narrative, and the librarians are insidious censors of information; fast-paced antics ensure. (Rev: BCCB 2/08; HB 1–2/08; SLJ 11/07)

9724 Sanderson, Brandon. *Alcatraz Versus the Scrivener's Bones* (5–9). 2008, Scholastic $16.99 (978-0-439-92553-2). 320pp. Alcatraz Smedry and his companions face many obstacles as they try to rescue his father from the Library of Alexandria; a pun-filled, humorous fantasy. (Rev: HB 11/08; SLJ 12/08; VOYA 10/08)

9725 Saunders, Kate. *Beswitched* (5–8). 2011, Delacorte $16.99 (978-0-385-74075-3); LB $19.99 (978-0-375-98967-4). 256pp. On her way to boarding school in England, 12-year-old Flora finds herself transported back to 1935 and discovers that her new dorm mates have summoned her. (Rev: BL 11/1/11*; SLJ 12/1/11)

9726 Saunders, Kate. *The Little Secret* (3–6). Illus. by William Carman. 2009, Feiwel & Friends $16.99 (978-0-312-36961-3). 240pp. Eleven-year-old Jane's visit to her new friend's home on a Scottish island turns into adventure when she enters another dimension. (Rev: BL 5/15/09; LMC 10/09; SLJ 8/09)

9727 Saunders, Kate. *Magicalamity* (4–6). 2012, Delacorte $16.99 (978-0-385-74077-7); LB $19.99 (978-0-375-98968-1). 288pp. Eleven-year-old Tom is amazed to find out that he is half fairy and that his father and mortal mother are in trouble; Tom's three fairy godmothers come to the rescue. ℮ Lexile 700L (Rev: BL 12/1/12; LMC 5–6/13; SLJ 4/13*)

9728 Saunders, Kate. *The Whizz Pop Chocolate Shop* (4–6). 2013, Delacorte $16.99 (978-0-385-74301-3); LB $19.99 (978-0-375-99090-8). 304pp. Twins Lily and Oz move to a house inherited from a great-uncle and find talking animals eager to reveal information about the twins' chocolatier ancestors and their magic. ∩ ℮ Lexile 700 (Rev: BL 3/1/13; SLJ 4/13)

9729 Sazaklis, John. *Royal Rodent Rescue* (1–4). Illus. by Art Baltazar. Series: DC Super Pets! 2011, Picture Window LB $22.65 (978-1-4048-6307-1); paper $4.95 (978-1-4048-6622-5). 56pp. Streaky the Super-Cat saves the queen's prized hamster from an evil cat in this action-packed story with integral illustrations. (Rev: SLJ 6/11)

9730 Schade, Susan. *Travels of Thelonious* (4–7). Illus. by Jon Buller. 2006, Simon & Schuster $14.95 (978-0-689-87684-4). This is the engaging, imaginative story of Thelonious, a squirrel who discovers the ruins of a city and searches for clues to the mystery of why humans disappeared. (Rev: BL 4/15/06; SLJ 7/06)

9731 Schaeffer, Susan F. *The Dragons of North Chittendon* (5–7). Illus. by Darcy May. 1986, Simon & Schuster paper $2.95 (978-0-685-14462-6). The story of Arthur, an unruly dragon, and his ESP relationship with the boy Patrick in a story of humans and dragons in and above North Chittendon, Vermont. (Rev: BL 8/86; SLJ 9/86)

9732 Schlitz, Laura Amy. *The Night Fairy* (2–5). Illus. by Angela Barrett. 2010, Candlewick $16.99 (978-0-7636-3674-6). 128pp. Injured by a bat, a young night fairy named Flory must learn to live in a scary new daylight world and finds many unexpected friends. ⌒ Lexile 630L (Rev: BL 1/1/10*; HB 3–4/11; LMC 5–6/10; SLJ 4/1/10*)

9733 Schmid, Susan Maupin. *Lost Time* (5–8). 2008, Philomel $16.99 (978-0-399-24460-5). On the sparsely populated planet Lindos, Violynne searches for her lost parents while living with her aunt Madelyn. (Rev: BL 5/15/08; SLJ 9/08)

9734 Schmidt, Gary D. *Pilgrim's Progress* (4–7). Illus. by Barry Moser. 1994, Eerdmans $22.00 (978-0-8028-5080-5). A simple retelling of the classic in which Christian leaves his home to find the Celestial City. (Rev: BL 11/1/94; SLJ 12/94)

9735 Schmidt, Gary D. *Straw into Gold* (5–8). 2001, Clarion $15.00 (978-0-618-05601-9). Two boys set off to find the answer to the king's riddle and thereby save the lives of rebels, only to discover much more than they had expected. (Rev: BCCB 9/01; HBG 10/01; SLJ 8/01; VOYA 2/02)

9736 Schooley, Bob, and Mark McCorkle. *Liar of Kudzu* (4–6). 2007, Simon & Schuster $15.99 (978-1-4169-1488-4). Pete (who is known as Liar), Justine, and Bobby Ray discover a crashed UFO that holds information about the future and must decide what to do. (Rev: SLJ 5/07)

9737 Schwartz, Alvin. *Scary Stories 3: More Tales to Chill Your Bones* (4–7). Illus. by Stephen Gammell. 1991, HarperCollins LB $17.89 (978-0-06-021795-2); paper $5.99 (978-0-06-440418-1). A modernized version of spooky tales handed down through the years. (Rev: BL 8/91; HB 11–12/91; SLJ 11/91)

9738 Scieszka, Jon. *Hey Kid, Want to Buy a Bridge?* (3–6). Illus. by Adam McCauley. 2002, Viking $15.99 (978-0-670-89916-6). 80pp. The Time Warp Trio is transported back to 1877 in their hometown of Brooklyn and gets to meet Thomas Edison and watch the building of the Brooklyn Bridge. (Rev: BL 2/1/02; HBG 10/02; SLJ 3/02)

9739 Scieszka, Jon. *Me Oh Maya* (2–6). Illus. by Adam McCauley. Series: Time Warp Trio. 2003, Penguin $14.99 (978-0-670-03629-5). 80pp. The Time Warp Trio turn up in Chichen Itza and must derail an evil high priest's plans to sacrifice them to please the harvest gods. (Rev: BL 9/15/03; HBG 4/04; SLJ 12/03)

9740 Scieszka, Jon. *Oh Say, I Can't See* (3–5). Illus. by Adam McCauley. Series: Time Warp Trio. 2005, Viking $14.99 (978-0-670-06025-2). 80pp. The three young time travelers play a key role in George Washington's decision to cross the Delaware River on Christmas Day in 1776. (Rev: BL 11/15/05; SLJ 11/05)

9741 Scieszka, Jon. *Sam Samurai* (4–6). Illus. by Adam McCauley. Series: Time Warp Trio. 2001, Viking $14.99 (978-0-670-89915-9). 80pp. While working on an assignment to write a haiku, the Time Warp Trio is accidentally transported back to 17th-century Japan in this wacky time-travel adventure. (Rev: BL 11/1/01; HBG 3/02; SLJ 11/01)

9742 Scieszka, Jon. *SPHDZ 4 Life!* (4–6). Illus. by Shane Prigmore. Series: Spaceheadz. 2013, Simon & Schuster $15.99 (978-141697957-9); paper $5.99 (978-14169795-8-6). 192pp. In this final installment in the fast-paced and humorous Spaceheadz series Michael K. and his friends, about to graduate from 5th grade, must find the missing Brainwave and save the planet. (Rev: BL 7/13; SLJ 2/14)

9743 Scieszka, Jon. *Summer Reading Is Killing Me* (3–6). Illus. by Lane Smith. 1998, Viking $15.99 (978-0-670-88041-6). 80pp. In this hilarious adventure, the Time Warp Trio get mixed up with characters from books on a summer reading list, such as Dracula, Winnie the Pooh, Long John Silver, and Frankenstein. (Rev: BL 6/1–15/98; HBG 3/99; SLJ 8/98)

9744 Scieszka, Jon. *Tut, Tut* (4–6). Illus. by Lane Smith. 1996, Viking $14.99 (978-0-670-84832-4). The Time Warp Trio find themselves in ancient Egypt in the clutches of the pharaoh's evil priest. (Rev: BL 10/1/96; SLJ 9/04)

9745 Scieszka, Jon. *Viking It and Liking It* (2–4). Illus. by Adam McCauley. 2002, Viking $14.99 (978-0-670-89918-0). 80pp. The Time Warp Trio is thrown into the world of the Vikings and meets challenges including a feisty Leif Ericksson and meals of whale blubber. (Rev: BL 12/1/02; HBG 3/03; SLJ 1/03)

9746 Scieszka, Jon, and Francesco Sedita. *Spaceheadz #1* (3–5). Illus. by Shane Prigmore. Series: SPHDZ. 2010, Simon & Schuster $14.99 (978-1-4169-7951-7). 160pp. Michael's first day of 5th grade gets weird when he's partnered with two kids claiming to be from another planet in this zany space adventure story. Books 2 and 3 were published in 2010 and 2011, respectively. Lexile 580L (Rev: BL 4/1/10; LMC 8–9/10; SLJ 9/1/10*)

9747 Scieszka, Jon, ed. *Guys Read: Other Worlds* (4–7). Illus. by Greg Ruth. Series: Guys Read Library of Great Reading. 2013, HarperCollins $16.99 (978-006196380-3). 352pp. The fourth installment in Scieszka's group of anthologies offers 10 original pieces of fantasy and science fiction targeted to tween and other boys and includes short stories, a graphic story, and a novella by Ray Bradbury. ⌒ ⊖ (Rev: BLO 9/1/13; SLJ 12/13)

9748 Scott, Deborah. *The Kid Who Got Zapped Through Time* (4–7). 1997, Avon $14.00 (978-0-380-97356-9). In this humorous time-travel fantasy, Flattop Kincaid is transported to England during the Middle Ages, where he becomes a serf. (Rev: BL 11/1/97; SLJ 9/97)

9749 Scrimger, Richard. *A Nose for Adventure* (3–6). 2001, Tundra paper $6.95 (978-0-88776-499-8). 184pp. After meeting on a plane to New York City, 13-year-old Alan and sassy, wheelchair-bound Frieda get involved in a smuggling plot at the airport and encounter Norbert, a small alien from Jupiter. (Rev: BL 2/15/01)

9750 Scrimger, Richard. *The Nose from Jupiter* (5–8). 2004, Tundra paper $5.95 (978-0-88776-428-8). Alan doesn't mind that Norbert, an alien from Jupiter, is living in his nose, but Norbert's outspoken remarks often get Alan into trouble. Also use *The Boy from Earth* (2004). (Rev: BL 7/98)

9751 Seabrooke, Brenda. *Stonewolf* (5–8). 2005, Holiday $16.95 (978-0-8234-1848-0). Young orphan Nicholas is taken captive by a group called the Synod but manages to escape, taking with him a sought-after secret formula. (Rev: BL 3/15/05; SLJ 3/05)

9752 Seabrooke, Brenda. *The Vampire in My Bathtub* (4–7). 1999, Holiday $16.95 (978-0-8234-1505-2). After 13-year-old Jeff moves to a new home with his mother, he finds a friendly vampire hidden inside an old trunk. (Rev: BL 1/1–15/00; HBG 3/00; SLJ 12/99)

9753 Seidler, Tor. *Gully's Travels* (4–7). Illus. by Brock Cole. 2008, Scholastic $16.95 (978-0-5450-2506-5). 192pp. Spoiled dog Gulliver's life of luxury is turned upside-down when his master falls for an allergic Frenchwoman and hands the dog over to the doorman; Gully takes off for Paris and other points east. (Rev: BL 9/1/08*; HB 9/08; LMC 1/09; SLJ 8/08)

9754 Selden, George. *The Cricket in Times Square* (3–6). Illus. by Garth Williams. 1960, Farrar $16.00 (978-0-374-31650-1). A Connecticut cricket is transported in a picnic basket to New York's Times Square. Two sequels are: *Tucker's Countryside* (1969); *Harry Cat's Pet Puppy* (1974).

9755 Selfors, Suzanne. *Fortune's Magic Farm* (4–7). Illus. by Catia Chien. 2009, Little, Brown $14.99 (978-0-316-01818-0). 264pp. Ten-year-old Isabelle lives in a soggy place called Runny Cove but knows she came from a place called Nowhere; she leaves her home and finds herself on a journey to a magical place called Fortune's Farm. (Rev: BCCB 5/09; BL 3/15/09; SLJ 3/09)

9756 Selfors, Suzanne. *The Sasquatch Escape* (3–6). Illus. by Dan Santat. Series: Imaginary Veterinary. 2013, Little, Brown $15.99 (978-031620934-2). 208pp. Ben and his friend find a baby dragon, and bring it to the vet in town — soon discovering that this vet treats mythical animals. e Lexile 630 (Rev: BLO 5/15/13; LMC 10/13*; SLJ 6/13)

9757 Sellier, Marie. *Legend of the Chinese Dragon* (2–5). Illus. by Catherine Louis. 2008, North-South $15.95 (978-0-7358-2152-1). In this legend, hostile Chinese tribes overcome their differences and create a creature to protect them — the dragon. (Rev: BL 12/15/07; SLJ 12/07)

9758 Sensel, Joni. *The Farwalker's Quest* (5–8). 2009, Bloomsbury $16.99 (978-1-59990-272-2). 400pp. Not long before the Namingfest in which Ariel expects to be selected as an apprentice Healtouch, Ariel and her friend Zeke find a telling dart that alters their futures. Lexile 660L (Rev: BL 2/15/09; SLJ 4/1/09)

9759 Sensel, Joni. *The Timekeeper's Moon* (5–8). 2010, Bloomsbury $16.99 (978-1-59990-457-3). 352pp. In the future without technology or books introduced in *The Farwalker's Quest* (2009), Ariel and her guardian, Scarl, follow a mysterious map, aware that success is vital. Lexile 700L (Rev: BL 2/1/10; LMC 5–6/10; SLJ 3/10)

9760 Sensel, Joni, and Christian Slade. *Reality Leak* (4–6). 2007, Holt $16.95 (978-0-8050-8125-1). Very strange things start happening when Archibald Keen arrives in Bryan's town to repair a "reality leak." (Rev: SLJ 5/07)

9761 Sepulveda, Luis. *The Story of a Seagull and the Cat Who Taught Her to Fly* (3–6). Trans. by Margaret Sayers Peden. Illus. by Chris Sheban. 2003, Scholastic $15.95 (978-0-439-40186-9). 128pp. Zorba the cat finds himself charged with the responsibilities of raising a seagull chick and teaching it to fly. (Rev: BL 9/1/03; HBG 4/04; SLJ 12/03)

9762 Shalant, Phyllis. *Bartleby of the Big Bad Bayou* (4–6). 2005, Dutton $17.99 (978-0-525-47366-4). Bartleby the turtle and his alligator friend Seezer, both former pets, return to bayou country but find there have been some unwelcome changes while they were away; a sequel to *Bartleby of the Mighty Mississippi* (2000). (Rev: BL 7/05; SLJ 8/05)

9763 Shalant, Phyllis. *The Great Cape Rescue* (3–5). Series: The Society of Super Secret Heroes. 2007, Dutton $15.99 (978-0-525-47404-3). 128pp. A scruffy-looking cape gives Finch and his three best friends the power to deal with school bullies and family problems, so when the cape begins talking and suggests they use its powers to help others, the boys heed its message. (Rev: BL 4/1/07)

9764 Shan, Darren. *A Living Nightmare* (5–8). Series: Cirque du Freak. 2001, Little, Brown $15.95 (978-0-316-60340-9). A supernatural story about a young boy who visits the Cirque Du Freak and is turned into a vampire. (Rev: BL 4/15/01; HBG 10/01; SLJ 5/01; VOYA 4/01)

9765 Shan, Darren. *Lord of the Shadows* (5–10). Series: Cirque du Freak. 2006, Little, Brown $15.99 (978-0-316-15628-8). In the 11th book in the series, part-vampire Darren faces off against Steve Leopard, leader of the Vampaneze, in a battle to determine who will be the next Lord of the Shadows. (Rev: SLJ 9/06)

9766 Shan, Darren. *Tunnels of Blood* (5–8). Series: Cirque du Freak. 2002, Little, Brown $15.95 (978-0-316-60763-6). Darren Shan, teenage half-vampire, sets out to investigate a spate of recent killings for which he believes his vampire master might be responsible. (Rev: BL 8/02; HBG 10/02; SLJ 5/02; VOYA 6/02)

9767 Shan, Darren. *Vampire Mountain* (5–8). Series: Cirque du Freak. 2002, Little, Brown $15.95 (978-0-316-60806-0). Darren Shan, teenage half-vampire, and his mentor travel to Vampire Mountain. The fifth, sixth, and seventh installments in the series are *Trials of Death*, *The Vampire Prince* (both 2003), and *Hunters of the Dusk* (2004). (Rev: BL 8/02; HBG 3/03; SLJ 9/02; VOYA 12/02)

9768 Shan, Darren. *The Vampire's Assistant* (5–8). Series: Cirque du Freak. 2001, Little, Brown $15.95 (978-0-316-60610-3). The creepy, suspenseful second installment about a boy who is "half vampire" and his efforts to adjust to the world of a traveling freak show. (Rev: BL 10/15/01; HBG 3/02; SLJ 8/01; VOYA 10/01)

9769 Sherman, Delia. *Changeling* (5–8). 2006, Viking $16.99 (978-0-670-05967-6). Neef, kidnapped as a baby by fairies, faces exile from her home in New York Between — an alternate Manhattan inhabited by elves, pixies, fairies, and other spirits — when she breaks the rules. (Rev: SLJ 10/06)

9770 Shreve, Susan. *Ghost Cats* (4–7). 1999, Scholastic paper $14.95 (978-0-590-37131-5). A boy, who is trying to adjust to a new family home and the loss of his five cats, is helped when the cats return as ghosts. (Rev: BCCB 12/99; BL 9/1/99; HBG 3/00; SLJ 11/99; VOYA 6/00)

9771 Shusterman, Neal. *Darkness Creeping: Twenty Twisted Tales* (5–8). 2007, Penguin paper $6.99 (978-0-14-240721-9). Four of these creepy stories were written for this collection; others have been published before but are not easily found. (Rev: BL 5/15/07; SLJ 7/07)

9772 Sierra, Judy. *The Gruesome Guide to World Monsters* (5–8). Illus. by Henrik Drescher. 2005, Candlewick $17.99 (978-0-7636-1727-1). A wonderfully ghoulish field guide to more than 60 monsters from world folklore, complete with Gruesomeness Ratings and Survival Tips if appropriate. (Rev: BCCB 9/05; BL 9/15/05*; HBG 4/06; LMC 2/06; SLJ 9/05)

9773 Silberberg, Alan. *Pond Scum* (4–7). 2005, Hyperion $15.99 (978-0-7868-5634-3). Ten-year-old Oliver gains a whole new appreciation for his animal neighbors after he finds a magical gem that allows him to assume the shape of various creatures. (Rev: BL 12/1/05; SLJ 11/05)

9774 Simmons, Michael. *Alien Feast* (5–8). Illus. by George O'Connor. Series: Chronicles of the First Invasion. 2009, Roaring Brook $15.95 (978-1-59643-281-9). 240pp. Aliens have invaded Earth in 2017 and 12-year-old William, who has already faced many adversities in his life, joins up with his friend Sophie and Uncle Maynard to try to rescue Sophie's parents; humor, action, and science fiction conventions add to the drama. (Rev: BCCB 7–8/08; BL 5/15/09; HB 5/09; LMC 5/08; SLJ 8/08)

9775 Simons, Jamie, and E. W. Scollon. *Goners: The Hunt Is On* (4–7). 1998, Avon paper $3.99 (978-0-380-79730-1). Four alien teens from the planet Roma time-travel to Monticello to fetch Thomas Jefferson. (Rev: BL 5/15/98)

9776 Sinykin, Sheri. *Giving Up the Ghost* (5–8). 2007, Peachtree $15.95 (978-1-56145-423-5). Davia is only 13, has asthma, is worried about her mother's cancer,

and afraid of various things; now her dying Aunt Mari wants Davi to help Emilie, a young Creole ghost, to find peace. (Rev: LMC 2/08; SLJ 2/08)

9777 Skelton, Matthew. *The Story of Cirrus Flux* (4–7). 2010, Random House $17.99 (978-0-385-73381-6); LB $20.99 (978-0-385-90398-1). 304pp. In this suspenseful fantasy set in 18th-century London and featuring steampunk-style gadgets, orphan Cirrus must protect a magical token left by his father. ∩ ℮ Lexile 840L (Rev: BL 2/1/10; HB 5–6/10; LMC 5–6/10; SLJ 3/10)

9778 Skurzynski, Gloria. *The Choice* (5–8). Series: The Virtual War Chronologs. 2006, Simon & Schuster $16.95 (978-0-689-84267-2). In the fast-paced concluding installment in the series, 16-year-old Corgan has a final confrontation with the murderous Brigand. (Rev: SLJ 10/06)

9779 Sleator, William. *Hell Phone* (5–8). 2006, Abrams $16.95 (978-0-8109-5479-3). In this dark, suspenseful novel, 17-year-old Nick discovers that the cell phone he bought at a bargain price constantly rings with frightening requests. (Rev: BL 10/1/06; SLJ 11/06)

9780 Slepian, Jan. *Back to Before* (5–7). 1994, Scholastic paper $3.25 (978-0-590-48459-6). Cousins Linny and Hilary travel back to a time before Linny's mother's death and Hilary's parents' separation. (Rev: BCCB 9/93; BL 9/1/93*; SLJ 10/93)

9781 Slote, Alfred. *My Robot Buddy* (5–8). 1986, HarperCollins $12.95 (978-0-397-31641-0). An easily read novel about Danny and the robot that is created for him. (Rev: BL 11/1/87)

9782 Smith, Clete Barrett. *Aliens on Vacation* (5–8). Illus. by Christian Slade. Series: The Intergalactic Bed and Breakfast. 2011, Hyperion/Disney $16.99 (978-1-4231-3363-6). 272pp. Scrub is not pleased to find himself spending a summer at his eccentric grandmother's Washington State bed and breakfast, where he soon discovers things are not at all what they seem. Also use *Alien on a Rampage* (2012) and *Aliens in Disguise* (2013). (Rev: BL 5/1/11; SLJ 7/11)

9783 Smith, Dodie. *The Hundred and One Dalmatians* (3–5). 1981, Avon paper $2.95 (978-0-380-00895-7). 208pp. Pongo and Missis must save the Dalmatian puppies captured by Cruella de Vil.

9784 Smith, Jennifer E. *The Storm Makers* (4–7). Illus. by Brett Helquist. 2012, Little, Brown $16.99 (978-031617958-4). 372pp. Twelve-year-olds Ruby and Simon move with their parents to a Wisconsin farm during a terrible drought, and discover that Simon's strange ties to the weather suggest he may be a very powerful Storm Maker. (Rev: BL 4/1/12; LMC 8–9/12; SLJ 6/12)

9785 Smith, Sherwood. *The Spy Princess* (5–8). 2012, Viking $17.99 (978-0-670-06341-3). 448pp. In a medieval land full of magic, Princess Lilah dresses as a peasant boy and discovers that revolution is brewing. ℮ Lexile 700L (Rev: BL 8/12; LMC 1–2/13; SLJ 9/12)

9786 Smith, Sherwood. *Wren's Quest* (5–8). 1993, Harcourt $16.95 (978-0-15-200976-2). Wren takes time out from magician school to search for clues to her parentage. Sequel to *Wren to the Rescue* (1990). (Rev: BL 4/1/93*; SLJ 6/93)

9787 Smith, Sherwood. *Wren's War* (5–8). 1995, Harcourt $17.00 (978-0-15-200977-9). In this sequel to *Wren to the Rescue* and *Wren's Quest*, Princess Teressa struggles to control herself and her destiny when she finds her parents murdered. (Rev: BL 3/1/95*; SLJ 5/95)

9788 Sniegoski, Tom. *Quest for the Spark, Vol. 1* (4–7). Illus. by Jeff Smith. Series: Bone. 2011, Scholastic $22.99 (978-054514101-7); paper $10.99 (978-05451410-2-4). 224pp. Tom Elm, 12, teams up with a motley crew after he receives a vision telling him to use his necklace to defeat the Nacht, a rogue dragon, in this (illustrated) text addition to the Bone graphic novel series. Lexile 790L (Rev: BL 1/1–15/11; SLJ 3/1/11)

9789 Sniegoski, Tom. *Quest for the Spark, Vol. 2* (4–7). Illus. by Jeff Smith. Series: Bone. 2012, Scholastic $22.99 (978-054514103-1); paper $10.99 (978-05451410-4-8). 224pp. Twelve-year-old Tom proves himself a competent quest leader by obtaining a piece of the Spark that will defeat the evil Nacht. (Rev: BL 2/15/12; SLJ 3/1/12)

9790 Snow, Alan. *Here Be Monsters!* (4–6). Illus. by author. 2006, Simon & Schuster $17.95 (978-0-689-87047-7). 512pp. A complex, inventive, and humor-filled fantasy involving an amazing cast of eccentric characters and a resourceful hero called Arthur. (Rev: BL 5/15/06; SLJ 8/06)

9791 Snow, Alan. *Worse Things Happen at Sea! A Tale of Pirates, Poison, and Monsters* (3–6). Illus. by author. Series: Ratbridge Chronicles. 2013, Simon & Schuster $17.99 (978-068987049-1). 352pp. Many zany adventures ensue when Arthur sneaks aboard the good ship *Laundry* in an effort to find a medicine to cure his grandfather; the sequel to *Here Be Monsters* (2006). ℮ Lexile 770 (Rev: BLO 7/13; LMC 11–12/13; SLJ 8/13)

9792 Snyder, Laurel. *Any Which Wall* (4–7). Illus. by LeUyen Pham. 2009, Random $16.99 (978-0-375-85560-3). 256pp. Four children discover a magic wall in a cornfield and have many adventures traveling through time. (Rev: BCCB 7–8/09; BL 5/15/09; HB 5/09; LMC 8/09; SLJ 6/09; VOYA 4/09)

9793 Snyder, Zilpha Keatley. *The Bronze Pen* (4–6). 2008, Atheneum $16.99 (978-1-4169-4201-6). 208pp. Twelve-year-old Audrey comes into the possession of a magic pen that helps her deal with her father's illness and her quirky new friend; set in the 1970s. (Rev: BL 2/15/08; LMC 10/08; SLJ 3/08)

9794 Snyder, Zilpha Keatley. *The Headless Cupid* (4–7). 1971, Dell paper $4.99 (978-0-440-43507-5). Amanda, a student of the occult, upsets her new family. A sequel is *The Famous Stanley Kidnapping Case* (1985).

9795 Soderberg, Erin. *Welcome to Normal* (2–4). Illus. by Kelly Light. Series: The Quirks. 2013, Bloomsbury $13.99 (978-159990789-5). 240pp. Molly is the only member of her family without a magic "quirk"; will she finally be able to fit in when they move to the town of Normal, Michigan. ℮ Lexile 830 (Rev: BLO 7/13; LMC 10/13)

9796 Somary, Wolfgang. *Night and the Candlemaker* (4–8). 2000, Barefoot $16.99 (978-1-84148-137-1). In this allegory, a candle maker continues with his trade in spite of threats he receives from Night. (Rev: BL 9/15/00; HBG 10/01; SLJ 1/01)

9797 Sonnenblick, Jordan. *Dodger and Me* (4–6). 2008, Feiwel & Friends $16.95 (978-0-312-37793-9). 176pp. Willie starts to understand what he really wants after he is granted three wishes by a large and magical blue chimpanzee. (Rev: BL 3/15/08; SLJ 6/08)

9798 Spalding, Andrea. *The Keeper and the Crows* (3–6). Illus. 2000, Orca paper $5.95 (978-1-55143-141-3). 119pp. Misha sets out to retrieve a key to a magic box that contains Hope, in this fantasy that is a spinoff on the Greek myth about Pandora's Box. (Rev: BL 11/15/00)

9799 Spradlin, Michael. *Menace from the Deep* (4–7). Series: Killer Species. 2013, Scholastic paper $5.99 (978-05455067-1-7). 240pp. Emmet and his scientist father investigate a strange creature found dead in the Everglades. Is it really a man-made predator, and are they all in danger? Lexile 770 (Rev: BLO 7/13; LMC 11–12/13; SLJ 12/13)

9800 Spratt, R. A. *The Adventures of Nanny Piggins* (3–6). Illus. by Dan Santat. 2010, Little, Brown $15.99 (978-0-316-06819-2). 256pp. Parsimonious Mr. Green hires a candy-loving, former circus star pig as nanny to his three children, much to their glee. (Rev: BL 8/10*; LMC 10/10; SLJ 8/10)

9801 Springer, Nancy. *Dussie* (5–8). 2007, Walker $16.95 (978-0-8027-9649-3). When she hits puberty, Dussie, a New York City 13-year-old named for her aunt Medusa, discovers she is a gorgon — and that the talkative snakes that have sprouted from her head may be an inconvenience, as is her ability to turn people to stone. (Rev: BL 11/15/07; SLJ 12/07)

9802 Springer, Nancy. *Sky Rider* (5–8). 2000, HarperCollins paper $4.95 (978-0-380-79565-9). In this contemporary supernatural mystery, Dusty's beloved horse Tazz is cured by a visitor who turns out to be the angry ghost of a teenage boy recently killed on her father's property. (Rev: BCCB 10/99; HBG 3/00; SLJ 8/99)

9803 Stahler, David, Jr. *The Seer* (5–7). Series: The Truesight Trilogy. 2007, HarperCollins $16.99 (978-0-06-052288-9). Jacob, 13, leaves the colony of Harmony, where he is the only person who can see, and seeks both a new life and his childhood friend Delaney, who is a talented musician. (Rev: BCCB 5/07; SLJ 8/07)

9804 Stahler, David, Jr. *Truesight* (5–7). Series: The Truesight Trilogy. 2004, HarperCollins LB $16.89 (978-0-06-052286-5). A race of blind people living in a colony on a distant planet includes one teenager who discovers he can see, and he sees all sorts of flaws in the people of his community. (Rev: SLJ 3/04; VOYA 4/04)

9805 Stanley, Diane. *Bella at Midnight* (5–8). Illus. by Bagram Ibatoulline. 2006, HarperCollins LB $17.89 (978-0-06-077574-2). A fine retelling of the Cinderella story featuring a plucky Bella and a storytelling format.

(Rev: BCCB 4/06; BL 2/1/06*; HB 3–4/06; HBG 10/06; LMC 2/07; SLJ 3/06*; VOYA 2/06)

9806 Stanley, Diane. *The Cup and the Crown* (5–8). 2012, HarperCollins $16.99 (978-0-06-196321-6). 352pp. On a quest to find the Loving Cup, Molly — last seen in *The Silver Bowl* (2011) — discovers Harrowsgode, the mysterious city of her magical ancestors. **e** Lexile 790L (Rev: BL 11/1/12; HB 11–12/12; SLJ 10/12)

9807 Stanley, Diane. *The Princess of Cortova* (5–8). Series: Silver Bowl Trilogy. 2013, HarperCollins $16.99 (978-006204730-4). 320pp. Molly and Tobias accompany King Alaric to the kingdom of Cortova, hoping that a marriage between Alaric and Princess Elizabetta will ease tensions in Westria; this fast-paced final volume in the trilogy is full of exciting strategy. **e** Lexile 850 (Rev: BL 7/13*; LMC 3–4/2014*; SLJ 11/13)

9808 Stanley, Diane. *The Silver Bowl* (5–8). 2011, HarperCollins $16.99 (978-0-06-157543-3). 320pp. A young scullery maid chooses to share the visions she's been keeping silent when foretold events seem to threaten the royal family she works for. Lexile 700L (Rev: BL 4/15/11; SLJ 7/11*)

9809 Stanley, Diane. *The Trouble with Wishes* (2–4). Illus. by author. 2007, HarperCollins $16.99 (978-0-06-055451-4). In this humorous variation on the legend of Pygmalion, a sculptor named Pyg falls in love with a statue of a goddess and wishes she were real; his wish is granted and he soon comes to regret this. (Rev: BL 11/1/06; SLJ 2/07)

9810 Starkey, Dinah, ed. *Ghosts and Bogles* (5–10). 1987, David & Charles $17.95 (978-0-434-96440-6). A collection of 16 British ghost stories, each nicely presented with illustrations. (Rev: SLJ 9/87)

9811 Stead, Rebecca. *First Light* (5–8). 2007, Random House $15.99 (978-0-375-84017-3). On a scientific expedition to Greenland with his parents, 12-year-old Peter meets 14-year-old Thea, a member of a secret society that lives beneath the ice. (Rev: BL 4/15/07; SLJ 8/07)

9812 Steele, Mary Q. *Journey Outside* (5–8). Illus. by Rocco Negri. 1984, Peter Smith $21.75 (978-0-8446-6169-8); paper $5.99 (978-0-14-030588-3). Young Dilar, believing that his Raft People have been circling endlessly in their quest for a "Better Place," sets out to discover the origin and fate of his kind.

9813 Steer, Dugald. *Dr. Ernest Drake's Dragonology: The Complete Book of Dragons* (5–12). 2003, Candlewick $18.99 (978-0-7636-2329-6). Presented as the recently discovered research of a 19th-century scientist, this richly illustrated volume presents a very realistic encyclopedia of dragon facts and figures. (Rev: BL 4/15/04; SLJ 4/04)

9814 Steer, Dugald A. *The Dragon's Eye* (5–8). Series: Dragonology Chronicles. 2006, Candlewick $15.99 (978-0-7636-2810-9). In the late 19th century, Daniel Cook, 12, and his sister Beatrice attend a dragon school run by Dr. Ernest Drake and accompany him on search for the important Dragon's Eye. (Rev: BL 1/1–15/07; SLJ 1/07)

9815 Steig, William. *Abel's Island* (4–6). Illus. by author. 1976, Farrar $15.00 (978-0-374-30010-4). A tale of a pampered mouse who must fend for himself after being marooned on an isolated island.

9816 Stephens, John. *The Emerald Atlas* (4–7). Series: The Books of Beginning. 2011, Knopf $17.99 (978-0-375-86870-2); LB $20.99 (978-0-375-96870-9). 432pp. Siblings Kate, Michael, and Emma have lived in a series of orphanages since their parents disappeared, and now they discover they can travel through time and must deal with both good and evil. ∩ **e** (Rev: BL 3/1/11; HB 3–4/11; LMC 5–6/11; SLJ 6/11*)

9817 Stephens, John. *The Fire Chronicle* (4–7). Series: Books of Beginning. 2012, Knopf $17.99 (978-0-375-86871-9); LB $20.99 (978-0-375-96871-6). 400pp. In this suspense-filled sequel to *The Emerald Atlas* (2011), Kate is transported to 1899 New York while Michael and Emma seek the second volume in the Books of Beginning. ∩ **e** Lexile 780L (Rev: BL 9/15/12; HB 11–12/12; SLJ 10/12*)

9818 Stephens, Sarah Hines. *Midway Monkey Madness* (1–4). Illus. by Art Baltazar. Series: DC Super Pets! 2011, Picture Window LB $22.65 (978-1-4048-6305-7); paper $4.95 (978-1-4048-6619-5). 56pp. Beppo the Super-Monkey saves the day from a malevolent giant gorilla in this action-packed story with integral illustrations. (Rev: SLJ 6/11)

9819 Stevermer, Caroline. *Magic Below Stairs* (4–6). 2010, Dial $16.99 (978-0-8037-3467-8). 208pp. Ten-year-old orphan Frederick, who is surreptitiously guarded by an elf, is selected as a servant and later apprentice to a wizard. (Rev: BL 6/10; SLJ 7/10)

9820 Stewart, Paul. *Freeglader* (4–6). Illus. by Chris Riddell. Series: Edge Chronicles. 2006, Random LB $14.99 (978-0-385-75083-7). 416pp. Librarian knight Rook Barkwater and his friends face daunting challenges on their journey to reach a new home in the Free Glades; the final volume in this fast-paced and complex fantasy. (Rev: BL 12/1/05; SLJ 2/06; VOYA 12/05)

9821 Stewart, Paul. *The Immortals* (5–8). Illus. by Chris Riddell. Series: Edge Chronicles. 2010, Random House $19.99 (978-037583743-2); LB $22.99 (978-037593743-9). 688pp. In this concluding volume in the exciting series, Nate Quarter flees for his life from the phraxmines of the Eastern Woods. **e** (Rev: BL 10/1/10)

9822 Stewart, Paul. *Legion of the Dead* (4–6). Illus. by Chris Riddell. Series: Barnaby Grimes. 2010, Random House $16.99 (978-038575131-5); LB $19.99 (978-038575132-2). 240pp. Victorian-era zombies must be overcome by the hero — dogged young Barnaby — in this cheerfully gruesome historical horror romp. The fourth installment is *Phantom of Blood Alley* (2010). (Rev: BL 2/1/10)

9823 Stewart, Paul. *Muddle Earth* (4–6). Illus. by Chris Riddell. 2007, Delacorte $16.99 (978-0-385-73316-8). 432pp. A funny fantasy in which young Joe Jefferson finds himself transported from his homework to become a saving hero in Muddle Earth. (Rev: BCCB 10/07; BL 6/1–15/07; LMC 10/07; SLJ 9/07)

9824 Stewart, Paul. *Return of the Emerald Skull* (4–6). Illus. by Chris Riddell. 2009, Random $15.99 (978-0-385-75128-5). 224pp. Barnaby Grimes, the messenger boy who travels by rooftop in 19th-century England, learns an ancient Chinese art and uses it when he investigates strange goings-on at Grassington Hall School. (Rev: BL 3/1/09; SLJ 4/09)

9825 Stewart, Paul. *Winter Knights* (4–6). Illus. by Chris Riddell. Series: Edge Chronicles. 2007, Random $12.99 (978-0-375-83741-8). 400pp. Quint and the other Knights Academy students encounter violent winter storms during training in this eighth volume in the series. (Rev: BL 7/07)

9826 Stewart, Paul, and Chris Riddell. *Fergus Crane* (3–5). 2006, Random $14.95 (978-0-385-75088-2). 240pp. Nine-year-old Fergus Crane embarks on a series of magical adventures after a flying box and a winged horse enter his life. (Rev: BL 2/15/06; SLJ 6/06)

9827 Stewart, Paul, and Riddell Chris. *Hugo Pepper* (3–5). Illus. Series: Far-Flung Adventures. 2007, Random $14.99 (978-0-385-75092-9). 272pp. Ten-year-old Hugo Pepper, son of explorers who were eaten by polar bears, sets off on his parents' sled to learn more about his roots and finds himself in Firefly Square, where he finds adventure, intrigue, and eccentricity. (Rev: BL 4/1/07; SLJ 2/07)

9828 Stewart, Sharon. *Raven Quest* (5–8). 2005, Carolrhoda LB $15.95 (978-1-57505-894-8). Tok the raven seeks to restore his good name after being falsely accused of murder and sets off to find the legendary Grey Lords. (Rev: SLJ 1/06; VOYA 12/05)

9829 Stewart, Trenton Lee. *The Mysterious Benedict Society* (4–7). Illus. by Carson Ellis. Series: The Mysterious Benedict Society. 2007, Little, Brown $16.99 (978-0-316-05777-6). Orphan Reynie Muldoon is one of a number of gifted children selected to take part in an effort to infiltrate the Learning Institute for the Very Enlightened; a complex story of mystery and adventure. (Rev: BL 1/1–15/07; SLJ 3/07*)

9830 Stine, R. L. *Goosebumps Wanted: The Haunted Mask* (3–6). 2012, Scholastic $15.99 (978-054541793-8). 240pp. When 12-year-old Lu-Ann puts on a mask that she finds at the bottom of a trunk, it sticks to her skin and she seems suddenly filled with rage; at the same time, her friend Devin is struggling with sinister vines in a Halloween pumpkin patch; a 20th-anniversary, suitably spooky issue. ℮ (Rev: BL 4/15/12)

9831 Stine, R. L. *The Haunting Hour: Chill in the Dead of Night* (5–8). 2001, HarperCollins $14.89 (978-0-06-623605-6). Ten chilling short stories, each with an introduction by the author. (Rev: BCCB 11/01; BL 1/1–15/02; HBG 3/02)

9832 Stine, R. L. *Nightmare Hour* (4–7). 1999, HarperCollins $16.99 (978-0-06-028688-0). Ten scary stories by a master of mystery, with characters that include

aliens, sorcerers, werewolves, witches, and ghosts. (Rev: BL 10/15/99; HBG 3/00; SLJ 12/99)

9833 Stone, David Lee. *The Yowler Foul-up* (5–8). 2006, Hyperion $16.99 (978-0-7868-5597-1). A motley group of would-be heroes tries to stop a plot to turn the people of Dullitch into rocks in this sequel to *The Ratastrophe Catastrophe* (2004). (Rev: BL 4/15/06)

9834 Strasser, Todd. *Hey Dad, Get a Life!* (5–8). 1996, Holiday $15.95 (978-0-8234-1278-5). Twelve-year-old Kelly and her younger sister use the ghost of their dead father to accomplish their everyday chores and finally let their mother know about their secret helper. (Rev: BCCB 3/97; BL 2/15/97; SLJ 3/97)

9835 Stratton, Allan. *The Grave Robber's Apprentice* (5–8). 2012, HarperCollins $16.99 (978-006197608-7). 288pp. Grave robber Hans becomes aware of his royal heritage in this complex fantasy. (Rev: BL 5/15/12*; SLJ 3/12)

9836 Strickland, Brad. *The Curse of the Midions* (5–8). Series: Grimoire. 2006, Dial $12.99 (978-0-8037-3060-1). A trip to London with his parents goes terribly awry when Jarvey Midion finds himself transported to an alternate universe where he must confront the villainous wizard Tantalus Mideon. (Rev: BL 6/1–15/06; SLJ 11/06)

9837 Strickland, Brad. *Tracked by Terror* (5–8). Series: Grimoire. 2007, Dial $15.99 (978-0-8037-3061-8). This sequel to *Curse of the Midions* (2006) finds 12-year-old Jarvey and his friend Betsy navigating a haunted theater and being hunted by animals. (Rev: BL 11/15/07; LMC 11/07; SLJ 2/08)

9838 Strickland, Brad. *The Whistle, the Grave, and the Ghost* (5–8). Series: Lewis Barnavelt. 2003, Dial $16.99 (978-0-8037-2622-2). A silver whistle frees a woman vampire, drawing Lewis Barnavelt and his friends into suspenseful adventures battling an ancient threat. (Rev: BL 8/03; HBG 4/04; SLJ 8/03)

9839 Stringer, Helen. *The Midnight Gate* (5–8). 2011, Feiwel & Friends $17.99 (978-0-312-38764-8). 384pp. Paranormally gifted Belladonna and her friend Steve tackle a dangerous assignment involving a trip to the Land of the Dead. (Rev: BL 5/1/11; SLJ 5/11)

9840 Stringer, Helen. *Spellbinder* (5–8). 2009, Feiwel & Friends $17.99 (978-0-312-38763-1). 384pp. The friendly, benevolent ghosts who populate Belladonna Johnson's world begin to disappear, and the 12-year-old enters the Land of the Dead to find out why. ⌒ ℮ Lexile 840L (Rev: BL 10/15/09; SLJ 10/09; VOYA 2/10)

9841 Stroud, Jonathan. *The Screaming Staircase* (4–7). 2013, Disney/Hyperion $16.99 (978-142316491-3). 384pp. Lucy Carlyle, Anthony Lockwood, and George Cubbins take on some of the ghosts that have been haunting Britain in this tense story. ⌒ ℮ Lexile 720 (Rev: BL 6/13; HB 9–10/13; LMC 3–4/14; SLJ 9/13; VOYA 2/14)

9842 Sutherland, Tui T., and Kari Sutherland. *The Menagerie* (5–8). 2013, HarperCollins $16.99 (978-006078064-7). 288pp. Set in seemingly quiet Xanadu, Wyoming, this lively fantasy full of mythical creatures

— unicorns, phoenixes, griffins — features 7th-grade Logan and his classmate Zoe. **e** Lexile 710 (Rev: BLO 4/1/13; SLJ 5/13)

9843 Sweet, J. H. *Dragonfly and the Web of Dreams* (2–4). Illus. by Tara Larsen Chang. Series: The Fairy Chronicles. 2007, Sourcebooks paper $6.99 (978-1-4022-0873-7). 119pp. Jennifer travels with her fairy friends to the home of the Dream Spider to rebuild the Web of Dreams and help everyone get a good night's sleep in the second book in the series. (Rev: SLJ 8/07)

9844 Tan, Shaun. *The Haunted Playground* (4–6). Illus. by author. 2008, Stone Arch LB $16.95 (978-1-59889-860-6). 64pp. For reluctant readers, this is a suspenseful tale in which Gavin, searching for treasure in a playground one night with his metal detector, encounters sylphlike children. (Rev: BCCB 12/07; BL 11/1/07; SLJ 2/08)

9845 Tanner, Lian. *Museum of Thieves* (4–7). 2010, Delacorte $17.99 (978-0-385-73905-4); LB $20.99 (978-0-385-90768-2). 312pp. In a world where children are chained to their parents until a separation ceremony, 12-year-old Goldie manages to escape and finds herself playing an important role. ∩ (Rev: BL 10/1/10; SLJ 10/1/10)

9846 Taylor, Greg. *Killer Pizza* (5–8). 2009, Feiwel & Friends $14.99 (978-0-312-37379-5). 256pp. Fourteen-year-old Toby's first summer job involves making pizza and hunting monsters. (Rev: BL 5/15/09; SLJ 9/09; VOYA 8/09)

9847 Taylor, Laini. *Faeries of Dreamdark: Blackbringer* (5–8). 2007, Putnam $17.99 (978-0-399-24630-2). With the help of her band of crows, a faerie named Magpie must hunt down devils that the humans have released and keep the dark from consuming the world. (Rev: BL 5/15/07; SLJ 8/07)

9848 Teague, Mark. *The Doom Machine* (4–7). 2009, Scholastic $17.99 (978-0-545-15142-9). 384pp. Set in the 1950s, this zany science fiction yarn follows town troublemaker Jack on an intergalactic journey of discovery to save his uncle's invention from the grips of aliens. Lexile 610L (Rev: BL 10/15/09; HB 1–2/10; LMC 11–12/09; SLJ 10/09; VOYA 10/09)

9849 Teitelbaum, Michael. *The Scary States of America* (5–8). 2007, Delacorte LB $12.99 (978-0-385-90348-6); paper $7.99 (978-0-385-73331-1). A collection of short stories about paranormal events that take place in each of the 50 states. (Rev: BL 6/1–15/07; SLJ 8/07)

9850 Thomas, Shelley Moore. *The Seven Tales of Trinket* (3–5). 2012, Farrar $16.99 (978-0-374-36745-9). 384pp. After the death of her mother 11-year-old Trinket, in the company of Thomas the Pig Boy, sets out to become a storyteller like her father and perhaps reunite with him; set in the Middle Ages, this tale features friendship and magic. **e** Lexile 730L (Rev: BL 10/15/12*; LMC 5–6/13; SLJ 12/12)

9851 Thompson, Kate. *Fourth World* (5–8). Series: Missing Link. 2005, Bloomsbury $16.95 (978-1-58234-650-2). Christie and his older stepbrother Danny go from

Ireland to Scotland, where they discover strange developments at Fourth World, the compound where Danny's scientist mother lives and works, in this first volume of a trilogy. (Rev: BL 5/15/05; SLJ 10/05)

9852 Thompson, Paul B. *The Brightworking* (4–7). Series: The Brightstone Saga. 2012, Enslow $17.95 (978-0-7660-3950-6). 160pp. Mikal, 11-year-old son of a blacksmith, is apprenticed to a powerful wizard in this appealing fantasy featuring political intrigue and a talking metal head. **e** Lexile 630L (Rev: LMC 11–12/12; SLJ 8/1/12; VOYA 6/12)

9853 Thomson, Jamie. *Dark Lord: The Early Years* (5–8). Illus. by Freya Hartas. 2012, Walker $16.99 (978-080272849-4). 336pp. The evil Dark Lord of the Iron Tower of Despair wakes up in the body of a 12-year-old boy in a supermarket parking lot and finds himself facing a very different life, deprived of most of his magical powers. **e** Lexile HL780L (Rev: BL 9/1/12*; LMC 1–2/13; SLJ 2/13; VOYA 8/12)

9854 Thomson, Sarah L. *Dragon's Egg* (3–6). 2007, Greenwillow $15.99 (978-0-06-128848-7). 272pp. Mella, a 12-year-old with a talent for looking after domestic dragons, and her friend Roger must deliver a "true dragon" egg to the Dragontooth Mountains. (Rev: BL 10/1/07; SLJ 1/08)

9855 Thornton, Duncan. *Kalifax* (5–9). Illus. by Yves Noblet. 2000, Coteau paper $8.95 (978-1-55050-152-0). In this fantasy novel, young Tom, with the help of Grandfather Frost, saves the crew of his ship after it becomes trapped in ice. (Rev: SLJ 1/01)

9856 Thornton, Duncan. *The Star-Glass* (5–8). Illus. by Yves Noblet. 2004, Coteau paper $10.95 (978-1-55050-269-5). Tom and Jenny face new challenges in this sequel to the fantasies *Kalifax* and *Captain Jenny and the Sea of Wonders*. (Rev: SLJ 4/04; VOYA 6/04)

9857 Toft, Di. *Wolven* (5–8). 2010, Scholastic $16.99 (978-0-545-17109-0). 336pp. Twelve-year-old Nat is devoted to his unconventional-looking dog, and is astonished when it suddenly morphs into a human boy. Lexile 860L (Rev: BLO 6/10; LMC 11–12/10; SLJ 8/10)

9858 Tolan, Stephanie S. *Who's There?* (5–8). 1994, Morrow $15.00 (978-0-688-04611-8); paper $4.95 (978-0-688-15289-5). Fourteen-year-old Drew is convinced that there is a ghost in her crusty grandfather's house, where she and her brother Evan, who has been mute since their parents' deaths, are currently living. (Rev: BCCB 12/94; BL 9/1/94; SLJ 10/94)

9859 Tolkien, J. R. R. *Roverandom* (4–9). 1998, Houghton Mifflin $17.00 (978-0-395-89871-0); paper $12.95 (978-0-395-95799-8). This fantasy deals with a dog named Roverandom who has the misfortune of insulting a wizard and having to pay the consequences. (Rev: BL 7/98; SLJ 6/98; VOYA 10/98)

9860 Torday, Piers. *The Last Wild* (4–6). 2014, Viking $16.99 (978-067001554-2). 336pp. Twelve-year-old Kester has been in a home for troubled youth and can no longer speak; he is surprised to be asked by cockroaches and pigeons to help save the few animals remaining in this post-apocalyptic world. ∩ **e** Lexile 820 (Rev: BL 3/1/14; LMC 5–6/14; SLJ 2/14)

9861 Townley, Roderick. *The Door in the Forest* (5–8). 2011, Knopf $16.99 (978-0-375-85601-3); LB $19.99 (978-0-375-95601-0). 256pp. Fourteen-year-old Daniel, who cannot lie, and Emily, who has magical powers, travel from their town — which is being occupied by soldiers — to a mysterious nearby island. **e** Lexile 600L (Rev: BL 3/1/11; HB 3–4/11; SLJ 3/1/11)

9862 Townley, Roderick. *Into the Labyrinth* (5–7). 2002, Simon & Schuster $16.95 (978-0-689-84615-1). In this sequel to *The Great Good Thing* (2001), Princess Sylvie and the other characters in their novel become exhausted as their popularity grows and they must rush from chapter to chapter; when the book goes digital, things spiral out of control and Sylvie must defeat an evil "bot" that threatens to destroy them. (Rev: BL 11/1/02; HBG 10/03; SLJ 10/02)

9863 Townsend, Tom. *The Trouble with an Elf* (5–8). Series: Fairie Ring. 1999, Fireworks paper $9.99 (978-0-88092-525-9). The adopted daughter of the king of the elves, Elazandra, journeys through a ring of mushrooms to the world of humans to stop the evil that will destroy both worlds. (Rev: SLJ 4/00)

9864 Trafton, Jennifer. *The Rise and Fall of Mount Majestic* (3–6). Illus. by Brett Helquist. 2010, Dial $16.99 (978-0-8037-3375-6). 344pp. Apathetic 10-year-old Persimmony's life gets more exciting when she finds herself embroiled in a quest to ensure her island's continued well-being; satisfying the tempestuous king, who's 12 years old, adds plenty of comedy to the story. **e** Lexile 930L (Rev: BL 1/1–15/11; LMC 3–4/11; SLJ 3/1/11*)

9865 Trewellard, J. M. *Butterfingers* (4–6). Illus. by Ian Beck. 2007, Random $15.99 (978-0-385-75123-0). 224pp. Ned, a stable boy, is accompanied by many animals — including a dog, a pig, a pony and a mouse — as he endeavors to rescue Princess Bella. (Rev: BL 12/1/07; LMC 11/07; SLJ 9/07)

9866 Tripp, Jenny. *Pete and Fremont* (4–6). Illus. by John Manders. 2007, Harcourt $16.00 (978-0-15-205629-2). 192pp. Circus performers Pete the poodle and Fremont the grizzly bear form a mutually beneficial friendship in this story full of circus lore. (Rev: BL 3/15/07)

9867 Trivas, Tracy. *The Wish Stealers* (4–7). 2010, Simon & Schuster $16.99 (978-1-4169-8725-3). 288pp. A girl named Griffin Penshine receives a box of stolen wishes — pennies dredged from a fountain — and attempts to reunite each one with its owner in order to escape misfortune. **e** Lexile 710L (Rev: BLO 11/15/09; LMC 10/10; SLJ 3/10)

9868 Tunnell, Michael O. *School Spirits* (5–8). 1997, Holiday $15.95 (978-0-8234-1310-2). Three students at creepy Craven Hill School, including the son of the new principal, discover a ghost and solve a decades-old murder mystery involving an 8-year-old boy. (Rev: BCCB 3/98; BL 2/15/98; HBG 3/98; SLJ 3/98; VOYA 8/98)

9869 Turner, Ann W. *Rosemary's Witch* (5–8). 1991, HarperCollins paper $3.95 (978-0-06-440494-5). Rose-mary discovers that her new home is haunted by the spirit of a girl named Mathilda, who's become a witch because of her pain and anger. (Rev: BL 4/1/91; SLJ 5/91*)

9870 Turner, Megan W. *The Queen of Attolia* (5–8). 2000, Greenwillow $15.95 (978-0-688-17423-1). In this sequel to *The Thief*, Gen, a slippery rogue, once more gets involved in the rivalry between two city states. (Rev: BL 4/15/00; HB 7–8/00; HBG 10/00; SLJ 5/00)

9871 Turner, Megan W. *The Thief* (5–8). 1996, Greenwillow $17.99 (978-0-688-14627-6). To escape life imprisonment, Gen must steal a legendary jewel in this first-person fantasy set in olden days. (Rev: BCCB 11/96; BL 1/1–15/97; HB 11–12/96; SLJ 10/96; VOYA 6/97)

9872 Ullman, Barb Bentler. *The Fairies of Nutfolk Wood* (3–5). 2006, HarperCollins $16.99 (978-0-06-073614-9). 256pp. After her parents divorce, 10-year-old Willa and her mother move into a trailer in the woods; here Willa recovers from her stress and, with her elderly neighbor Hazel, befriends the local fairies. (Rev: BL 5/15/06; HBG 10/06; SLJ 7/06)

9873 Ullman, Barb Bentler. *Whistle Bright Magic* (3–6). Series: A Nutfolk Tale. 2010, HarperCollins $16.99 (978-0-06-188286-9). 224pp. Zelly and her mother move to Plunkit after Zelly's grandmother dies, and Zelly yearns for her absent father while helping the Nutfolk save their community from developers; a sequel to *The Fairies of Nutfolk Wood* (2006). Lexile 850L (Rev: BLO 2/1/10; SLJ 2/10)

9874 Umansky, Kaye. *Clover Twig and the Magical Cottage* (4–7). Illus. by Johanna Wright. 2009, Roaring Brook $16.99 (978-1-59643-507-0). 304pp. In this funny, clever tale, 11-year-old Clover gets work cleaning a witch's magical cottage and finds herself protecting the cottage from the witch's evil sister. Lexile 550L (Rev: BL 8/09; HB 9–10/09; LMC 11–12/09; SLJ 9/09)

9875 Umansky, Kaye. *Clover Twig and the Perilous Path* (4–7). Illus. by Johanna Wright. 2012, Roaring Brook $16.99 (978-1-59643-754-8). 256pp. When Clover's baby brother disappears, she enlists the aid of her boss, the good witch Mrs. Eckles, in this sequel to *Clover Twig and the Magical Cottage* (2009). **e** Lexile 570L (Rev: BL 8/12; SLJ 7/12)

9876 Ursu, Anne. *Breadcrumbs* (4–6). 2011, HarperCollins $16.99 (978-0-06-201505-1). 336pp. A shard of glass from an enchanted mirror causes 10-year-old Hazel's friend Jack to be imprisoned by an evil Snow Queen and Hazel must enter a magic wood to rescue him in this richly imagined fantasy featuring several fairy tale tropes. ∩ **e** (Rev: BL 11/15/11; HB 1–2/12; SLJ 11/1/11*)

9877 Ursu, Anne. *The Immortal Fire* (5–8). Series: Cronus Chronicles. 2009, Atheneum $16.99 (978-1-4169-0591-2). 528pp. Thirteen-year-olds Charlotte and Zee take on the task of saving mankind in this action-packed final installment in a series that features many classical references. (Rev: BLO 4/24/09; SLJ 9/09)

9878 Ursu, Anne. *The Real Boy* (4–7). Illus. by Erin McGuire. 2013, HarperCollins $16.99 (978-006201507-5).

352pp. In the city of Asteri, Oscar is the young apprentice of a magician called Caleb, a relatively easy job until an evil force threatens their world. ℯ Lexile 730 (Rev: BL 10/1/13; HB 9–10/13; SLJ 11/13*)

9879 Ursu, Anne. *The Shadow Thieves* (5–8). 2006, Simon & Schuster $16.95 (978-1-4169-0587-5). A plot to reanimate the dead using the essence of living children is foiled by cousins Charlotte and Zee in this story of heroism and mythology that ranges from the Midwest to England to Hades. (Rev: BL 3/1/06; SLJ 4/06)

9880 Ursu, Anne. *The Siren Song* (5–8). Series: Cronus Chronicles. 2007, Atheneum $16.99 (978-1-4169-0589-9). Charlotte, just back from the Underworld (in 2007's *The Shadow Thieves*), goes on a cruise with her cousin Zee and finds herself battling Poseidon and the sea monster Ketos; the second installment in the series that uses elements of Greek mythology. (Rev: BL 11/1/07; HB 7–8/07; SLJ 8/07)

9881 Valente, Catherynne. *The Girl Who Circumnavigated Fairyland in a Ship of Her Own Making* (5–8). Illus. by Ana Juan. 2011, Feiwel & Friends $16.99 (978-0-312-64961-6). 256pp. This quirky, imaginative story features 12-year-old September, who is carried off to Fairyland, where she has some wild and wonderful adventures among the unusual and sometimes sinister inhabitants there. ⌒ ℯ Lexile 920 (Rev: BL 4/15/11; HB 5–6/11; LMC 10/11; SLJ 5/11; VOYA 6/11)

9882 Valente, Catherynne. *The Girl Who Fell Beneath Fairyland and Led the Revels There* (5–8). Illus. by Ana Juan. 2012, Feiwel & Friends $16.99 (978-0-312-64962-3). 272pp. September, 13, realizes that her shadow is draining the magic from Fairyland Above and sets out to put things right in this sequel to *The Girl Who Circumnavigated Fairyland in a Ship of Her Own Making* (2011). ⌒ ℯ Lexile 950L (Rev: BL 10/1/12*; HB 11–12/12; SLJ 9/12)

9883 Valente, Catherynne M. *The Girl Who Soared over Fairyland and Cut the Moon in Two* (5–8). Series: Fairyland. 2013, Feiwel & Friends $16.99 (978-125002350-6). 256pp. Fourteen-year-old September has ventured into Fairyland again, and this time must save the moon from being destroyed by an evil yeti; the 3rd book in the series. ℯ Lexile 930 (Rev: BL 9/15/13*; SLJ 11/13)

9884 Van Allsburg, Chris. *The Wreck of the Zephyr* (2–5). Illus. by author. 1983, Houghton $18.95 (978-0-395-33075-3). 32pp. The story behind the wreck of a sailboat.

9885 Van Belkom, Edo. *Lone Wolf* (5–8). 2005, Tundra paper $8.95 (978-0-88776-741-8). The four teen werewolves adopted by Ranger Brock in *Wolf Pack* (2004) defend their beloved woods against a corrupt developer. (Rev: SLJ 1/06; VOYA 4/06)

9886 Van Cleve, Kathleen. *Drizzle* (5–8). 2010, Dial $16.99 (978-0-8037-3362-6). 368pp. Polly, an 11-year-old who can communicate with plants, lives on a rhubarb farm where it rains at the same time every Monday; when the rains stop, Polly must use her powers of logic

and communication to solve the problem. ⌒ Lexile 650L (Rev: BL 3/1/10; SLJ 4/10)

9887 van Eekhout, Greg. *The Boy at the End of the World* (5–8). 2011, Bloomsbury $16.99 (978-1-59990-524-2). 256pp. The only human survivor of a Life Ark in this post-apocalyptic story, Fisher has instinctive knowledge of many things and sets out to explore his environment in the company of a robot he calls Click. (Rev: BL 5/1/11; SLJ 9/1/11)

9888 Van Eekhout, Greg. *Kid vs. Squid* (4–7). 2010, Bloomsbury $16.99 (978-1-59990-489-4). 208pp. When a girl steals a shrunken head from the Museum of the Strange and Curious, Thatcher and Trudy chase the thief and end up saving a cursed civilization; a lighthearted fantasy full of humor. (Rev: BL 5/15/10; LMC 8–9/10; SLJ 7/10)

9889 Van Tol, Alex. *Shallow Grave* (4–7). Series: Orca Soundings. 2012, Orca LB $16.95 (978-1-4598-0203-2); paper $9.95 (978-1-4598-0202-5). 128pp. For reluctant readers, this is a story about Elliot and Shannon, who encounter a restless spirit when they are assigned to clean up an old boat house. ℯ Lexile HL460L (Rev: BL 10/15/12; LMC 5–6/13; SLJ 4/13)

9890 Vande Velde, Vivian. *Now You See It . . .* (5–8). 2005, Harcourt $17.00 (978-0-15-205311-6). Wendy, 15, puts on a pair of sunglasses and a whole new fantasy world is revealed. (Rev: BL 1/1–15/05; SLJ 1/05)

9891 Vande Velde, Vivian. *Three Good Deeds* (3–5). 2005, Harcourt $16.00 (978-0-15-205382-6). 160pp. Transformed into a goose by a witch's curse, Howard must perform three good deeds to return to human form. (Rev: BL 10/15/05; SLJ 10/05)

9892 Vande Velde, Vivian. *Witch Dreams* (5–8). 2005, Marshall Cavendish $15.95 (978-0-7614-5235-5). Nyssa, a 16-year-old witch, seeks justice for her parents, who were murdered six years earlier. (Rev: BL 12/15/05; SLJ 11/05; VOYA 12/05)

9893 Vanderwal, Andrew H. *The Battle for Duncragglin* (5–7). 2009, Tundra $17.95 (978-0-88776-886-6). 336pp. On a visit to Scotland, 12-year-old Alex and three Scottish children are transported back to a chaotic and dangerous time. (Rev: BL 4/15/09; SLJ 7/09; VOYA 8/09)

9894 Vansickle, Lisa. *The Secret Little City* (5–8). 2000, Palmae $15.95 (978-1-930167-11-7). When 11-year-old Mackenzie moves with her family to a small town in Oregon, she discovers a whole civilization of inch-high people living beneath the floorboards of her new room. (Rev: SLJ 8/00)

9895 Vaupel, Robin. *The Rules of the Universe by Austin W. Hale* (5–8). 2007, Holiday $16.95 (978-0-8234-1811-4). When Austin, 13, discovers that he can alter the molecular structures of people and animals, he conducts careful experiments to determine the limits of this power — and to see if he can save his dying grandfather. (Rev: BL 11/1/07)

9896 Velmans, Hester. *Isabel of the Whales* (4–6). 2005, Delacorte $15.95 (978-0-385-73202-4). An informative fantasy in which a girl becomes a whale and learns about diving, feeding, and communication while she teaches the whales about such dangers as nets and ships. (Rev: SLJ 8/05)

9897 Vernon, Ursula. *Attack of the Ninja Frogs* (2–5). Illus. by author. Series: Dragonbreath. 2010, Dial $12.99 (978-0-8037-3365-7). 206pp. Young dragon Danny and his friend Wendell the iguana travel with exchange student Suki to mythical Japan to seek a way to stop ninja frogs from attacking Suki. (Rev: SLJ 7/1/10)

9898 Vernon, Ursula. *Curse of the Were-Wiener* (2–5). Illus. by author. Series: Dragonbreath. 2010, Dial $12.99 (978-080373469-2). 208pp. In this zany horror story for young readers, Danny Dragonbreath must help his friend Wendell the iguana when a hot dog bites him and he starts to turn into a were-wiener. (Rev: BL 10/15/10)

9899 Vernon, Ursula. *Lair of the Bat Monster* (3–5). Illus. by author. Series: Dragonbreath. 2011, Dial $12.99 (978-080373525-5). 208pp. Danny gets kidnapped by a giant bat monster of legend, and his friend Wendell must rescue him in this lively graphic novel. (Rev: BLO 2/14/11)

9900 Vernon, Ursula. *Nurk: The Strange, Surprising Adventures of a (Somewhat) Brave Shrew* (3–5). Illus. by author. 2008, Harcourt $15.00 (978-0-15-206375-7). 144pp. Nurk the shrew finds unsuspected reserves of courage when he receives a cry for help. (Rev: BLO 7/30/08; SLJ 8/08) ⊙

9901 Vernon, Ursula. *When Fairies Go Bad* (3–5). Illus. by author. Series: Dragonbreath. 2012, Dial $12.99 (978-080373678-8). 208pp. Danny and his friends Wendell and Christiana head to the fairy kingdom in an effort to retrieve Danny's missing mother; the 7th in the series. e Lexile 680L (Rev: BLO 11/1/12)

9902 Verrillo, Erica. *Elissa's Odyssey* (5–8). Series: Phoenix Rising. 2008, Random House $16.99 (978-0-375-83948-1). The second book in the trilogy, following *Elissa's Quest*, finds Elissa in Alhamazar, her mysterious power to speak to animals expanding. (Rev: BL 5/15/08)

9903 Verrillo, Erica. *Elissa's Quest* (5–8). Series: Phoenix Rising. 2007, Random House $16.99 (978-0-375-83946-7). Thirteen-year-old Elissa struggles to control her destiny when she finds out that she is the princess of Castlemar and that her father the king plans to trade her to a desert warlord. (Rev: BL 6/1–15/07; LMC 10/07; SLJ 8/07)

9904 Verrillo, Erica. *World's End* (5–8). Series: Phoenix Rising. 2009, Random $16.99 (978-0-375-83950-4). 336pp. Elissa must escape her father's plans for her in this satisfying final installment in the trilogy. (Rev: BLO 4/24/09; SLJ 9/09)

9905 Voake, Steve. *The Dreamwalker's Child* (5–8). 2006, Bloomsbury $16.95 (978-1-58234-661-8). After being hit by a car, Sam Palmer finds himself in the alternate world of Aurobon, where he learns of a deadly plot to wipe out human life on Earth using a virus transmitted by mosquitoes. (Rev: SLJ 8/06; VOYA 6/06)

9906 Voake, Steve. *The Web of Fire* (5–8). Illus. by Mark Watkinson. 2007, Bloomsbury $17.95 (978-1-58234-737-0). Sam and Skipper are back with new adventures and gadgetry in this fast-paced sequel to *The Dreamwalker's Child* (2006). (Rev: SLJ 6/07)

9907 Voelkel, Jon, and Pamela Voelkel. *Middleworld* (5–8). Series: Jaguar Stones Trilogy. 2007, Smith & Kraus $17.95 (978-1-57525-561-3). Fourteen-year-old Max's parents disappear while working in Central America, and he searches for them with the help of local girl Lola and her knowledge of the mystical elements of Mayan culture. (Rev: BL 11/15/07; SLJ 10/07)

9908 Wade, Rebecca. *The Theft and the Miracle* (5–8). 2007, HarperCollins $16.99 (978-0-06-077493-6). Mystery and supernatural are combined in this story of Hannah, a plain, overweight 12-year-old with artistic abilities, who — with her friend Sam — finds herself on a hunt for a missing religious statue. (Rev: BL 11/15/06; SLJ 1/07)

9909 Wagner, Hilary. *Nightshade City* (5–8). Illus. by Omar Rayyan. Series: Nightshade Chronicles. 2010, Holiday House $17.95 (978-0-8234-2285-2). 320pp. A city of intelligent rats prepares to overthrow its oppressive ruler. Lexile 800L (Rev: BL 9/15/10; LMC 3–4/11; SLJ 1/1/11; VOYA 12/10)

9910 Wagner, Hilary. *The White Assassin* (5–8). Illus. by Omar Rayyan. Series: Nightshade Chronicles. 2011, Holiday House $17.95 (978-0-8234-2333-0). 256pp. Nightshade City's residents work to keep themselves safe from Billycan's devious and conniving ways in this fast-paced sequel to *Nightshade City* (2010). (Rev: BLO 10/15/11; SLJ 10/1/11)

9911 Wallace, Bill. *The Legend of Thunderfoot* (3–5). 2006, Simon & Schuster $15.95 (978-1-4169-0691-9). 160pp. In this appealing animal fantasy, a young roadrunner finds ways to make the most of his oversized feet, swollen out of proportion by a snakebite. (Rev: BL 11/1/06; SLJ 10/06)

9912 Wallace, Carey. *The Ghost in the Glass House* (5–8). 2013, Clarion $16.99 (978-054402291-1). 240pp. Unhappy since her father's death, 12-year-old Clare finds comfort in a glass house and the mysterious ghost of a young boy who lives there. e Lexile 870 (Rev: BL 10/1/13; HB 11–12/13; LMC 3–4/14; SLJ 10/13)

9913 Walsh, Jill Paton. *The Green Book* (4–7). Illus. by Lloyd Bloom. 1982, Farrar paper $4.95 (978-0-374-42802-0). The exodus of a group of Britons from dying Earth to another planet.

9914 Walsh, Pat. *The Crowfield Curse* (5–8). 2010, Scholastic $16.99 (978-0-545-22922-7). 336pp. In England in 1347, 14-year-old orphaned William comes across a hobgoblin and discovers he himself has magical powers, which must be put to good use; this suspenseful story is full of medieval details. ⊙ Lexile 840L (Rev: BL 10/15/10; LMC 11–12/10; SLJ 9/1/10*)

9915 Walsh, Pat. *The Crowfield Demon* (5–8). 2012, Scholastic $16.99 (978-054531769-6). 368pp. In this sequel to *The Crowfield Curse* (2010), young William

— who can see into the spirit world — must deal with a fallen angel threatening Crowfield Abbey and all therein. **e** (Rev: BLO 4/1/12; SLJ 5/1/12) [800L]

9916 Ward, David. *Between Two Ends* (4–6). 2011, Abrams $16.95 (978-081099714-1). 304pp. Twelve-year-old Yeats travels into "The Arabian Nights" to stop the source of his family's present malaise before it harms everyone. (Rev: BL 5/1/11)

9917 Ward, David. *Escape the Mask* (5–8). Series: The Grassland Trilogy. 2008, Abrams $15.95 (978-0-8109-9477-5). Coriko and Pippa escape the Spears, who have been keeping them as slaves, when the Spears are attacked by a mysterious group of warriors; but their adventures do not end there. (Rev: BL 4/15/08)

9918 Warfel, Elizabeth Stuart. *The Blue Pearls* (2–4). Illus. by Veronique Giarrusso. 2001, Barefoot Books $16.99 (978-1-902283-78-4). In this fantasy, a group of angels are preparing a beautiful blue gown for a young mother who is about to die and be welcomed in heaven. (Rev: BL 4/15/01; HBG 10/01; SLJ 7/01)

9919 Waugh, Sylvia. *The Mennyms* (4–8). 1994, Greenwillow $16.00 (978-0-688-13070-1). When their owner dies, a family of rag dolls comes to life and takes over her house in this beginning volume of an extensive series. (Rev: BCCB 5/94; HB 7–8/94; SLJ 4/94)

9920 Waugh, Sylvia. *Mennyms Alive* (4–6). 1997, Greenwillow $16.00 (978-0-688-15201-7). 224pp. The last book about the Mennyms, rag dolls who have problems finding a permanent home. (Rev: BL 9/15/97; HB 11/97; HBG 3/98; SLJ 9/97)

9921 Waxman, Sydell, retel. *The Rooster Prince* (2–5). Illus. by Giora Carmi. 2000, Pitspopany $16.95 (978-0-943706-45-0); paper $9.95 (978-0-943706-49-8). 40pp. In 18th-century Russia, a village boy is given the task of curing a prince who is behaving like rooster. (Rev: SLJ 1/01)

9922 Weatherill, Cat. *Barkbelly* (4–7). Illus. by Peter Brown. 2006, Knopf $15.95 (978-0-375-83327-4). A wooden boy being raised by normal parents flees after he accidentally causes a tragedy and searches for his own family. (Rev: BL 5/15/06; SLJ 7/06)

9923 Weatherill, Cat. *Snowbone* (4–7). Illus. by Peter Brown. 2007, Knopf $15.99 (978-0-375-83328-1). Snowbone rallies her fellow Ashenpeakers (a race of wooden beings that are used as slaves) to escape their bondage and end slavery; a companion to *Barkbelly* (2006). (Rev: BL 6/1–15/07; SLJ 12/07)

9924 Weatherill, Cat. *Wild Magic* (4–7). 2008, Walker $16.99 (978-0-8027-9799-5). 288pp. It seems that the Pied Piper (whose real name was Finn) was actually an elf and took the children from Hamelin in hopes of ridding himself of a curse. (Rev: BCCB 1/09; BL 12/1/08; LMC 1/09; SLJ 11/08)

9925 Webb, Holly. *Lily* (4–7). 2013, Trafalgar Square paper $8.99 (978-14083134-9-7). 256pp. In a world where magic is outlawed, Lily learns that her parents have a sinister plan to use her sister Georgie's abilities. **e** (Rev: BLO 4/1/13)

9926 Weinberg, Karen. *Window of Time* (5–7). Illus. by Annelle W. Ratcliffe. 1991, White Mane paper $9.95 (978-0-942597-18-9). Ben climbs through a window and finds himself 125 years back in time. (Rev: SLJ 7/91)

9927 Welch, R. C. *Scary Stories for Stormy Nights* (5–7). 1995, Lowell House paper $5.95 (978-1-56565-262-0). Ten contemporary horror stories that involve such characters as a werewolf and some pirates. (Rev: BL 5/1/95)

9928 Wells, H. G. *The Time Machine* (3–5). Adapted by Les Martin. Illus. by John Edens. 1990, Random paper $3.99 (978-0-679-80371-3). 93pp. A clever adaptation of a classic science fiction story about a time traveler and his friends. (Rev: SLJ 4/91)

9929 Wells, Kitty. *Paw Power* (2–4). Illus. by Joanna Harrison. Series: Pocket Cats. 2011, Random House $13.99 (978-0-385-75201-5); LB $16.99 (978-0-385-75202-2). 208pp. One of Maddy's ceramic cat figurines comes to life to help her deal with the school bully in this sensitive, accessible story. The third volume in the series is *Feline Charm* (2011). **e** (Rev: BLO 1/1–15/11; SLJ 3/1/11)

9930 Wells, Kitty. *Shadow Magic* (2–4). Illus. by Joanna Harrison. Series: Pocket Cats. 2011, Random House $13.99 (978-0-385-75200-8). 202pp. An aloof ceramic cat figurine gives Maddy the ability to be invisible, which enables her to spy on her secretive cousin who's come to live with the family for awhile. (Rev: SLJ 9/1/11)

9931 Wells, Rosemary. *On the Blue Comet* (5–8). Illus. by Bagram Ibatoulline. 2010, Candlewick $16.99 (978-0-7636-3722-4). 336pp. The crash of 1929 hits 11-year-old Oscar's family hard and the young model train devotee, longing for his old set, discovers a magical train that allows him to visit different times and places. ⌒ (Rev: BL 7/10; HB 9–10/10; LMC 11–12/10; SLJ 9/1/10)

9932 Welsh, M. L. *Mistress of the Storm: A Verity Gallant Tale* (4–8). 2011, Random House $16.99 (978-0-385-75244-2); LB $19.99 (978-0-385-75245-9). 320pp. Twelve-year-old Verity's life takes a turn for the eventful when she uncovers family secrets that lead to a confrontation with a powerful witch. The second installment in the series is *Heart of Stone* (2012). **e** Lexile 750L (Rev: LMC 11–12/11; SLJ 10/1/11*; VOYA 6/11)

9933 Welvaert, Scott R. *The Curse of the Wendigo: An Agate and Buck Adventure* (5–9). Illus. by Brann Garvey. 2006, Stone Arch LB $23.93 (978-1-59889-066-2). Searching for their parents in the vast Canadian wilderness in the late 19th century, 16-year-old Buck and his younger sister Agate find themselves being pursued by the mythical Wendigo; suitable for reluctant readers. (Rev: SLJ 1/07)

9934 Wersba, Barbara. *Walter: The Story of a Rat* (4–7). Illus. by Donna Diamond. 2005, Front St $16.95 (978-1-932425-41-3). Miss Pomeroy, a children's author, develops a friendship with a literary rat named Walter who shares her house in this thoughtful and sophisticated book. (Rev: BCCB 2/06; BL 11/15/05; SLJ 12/05)

9935 West, Jacqueline. *The Second Spy* (4–6). Illus. by Poly Bernatene. Series: The Books of Elsewhere. 2012,

Dial $16.99 (978-080373689-4). 256pp. Olive, 11, is used to strange events at her Victorian house, but when she falls through a hole in the backyard she finds herself facing new dangers. ℮ (Rev: BLO 9/1/12)

9936 West, Jacqueline. *The Shadows* (4–6). Illus. by Poly Bernatene. Series: Books of Elsewhere. 2010, Dial $16.99 (978-0-8037-3440-1). 256pp. When the family moves to a big Victorian house, 11-year-old Olive's emotionally absent parents leave her to explore the mysteries of the old paintings, and an odd pair of glasses that allow her to step inside the art. Also use *Spellbound* (2011) and *The Strangers* (2013). ⌒ ℮ (Rev: BL 6/10; LMC 10/10; SLJ 5/10)

9937 Westall, Robert. *Ghost Abbey* (5–9). 1990, Scholastic paper $3.25 (978-0-590-41693-1). Maggi realizes that the abbey her father is restoring seems to have a life of its own. (Rev: BCCB 2/89; BL 2/1/89; SLJ 3/89; VOYA 6/89)

9938 Westwood, Chris. *He Came from the Shadows* (5–8). 1991, HarperCollins LB $14.89 (978-0-06-021659-7). In a cautionary tale about the dangers of wishing for too much, odd things start to happen after a stranger comes to town. (Rev: BL 4/1/91; SLJ 6/91)

9939 Wharton, Thomas. *The Shadow of Malabron* (5–8). 2009, Candlewick $16.99 (978-0-7636-3911-2). 400pp. A motorcycle crash transports a boy to a magical realm where all the world's stories originate in this imaginative, well-conceived novel about the battle between good and evil. ℮ Lexile 830L (Rev: BL 2/15/10; LMC 1–2/10; SLJ 11/09)

9940 Whelan, Gerard. *Dream Invader* (5–7). 2002, O'Brien paper $7.95 (978-0-86278-516-1). Only Simon's grandmother can break the spell behind the bad dreams he's been having in this supernatural tale set in Ireland. (Rev: BL 9/1/02)

9941 White, E. B. *Charlotte's Web* (3–5). Illus. by Garth Williams. 1952, HarperCollins LB $17.89 (978-0-06-026386-7); paper $7.99 (978-0-06-440055-8). 184pp. Classic, whimsical barnyard fable about a spider who saves the life of Wilbur the pig. Read about the ever-engaging mouse in: *Stuart Little* (1945).

9942 White, E. B. *The Trumpet of the Swan* (3–6). Illus. by Edward Frascino. 1970, HarperCollins LB $14.89 (978-0-06-026398-0); paper $4.95 (978-0-06-440048-0). 222pp. Louis, a voiceless trumpeter swan, is befriended by Sam, learns to play a trumpet, and finds fame, fortune, and fatherhood.

9943 Whitman, John. *Star Wars: The Death Star* (2–5). Illus. by Barbara Gibson. 1997, Little, Brown $15.95 (978-0-316-93592-0). 12pp. Action-packed science fiction is featured in this pop-up book. Also use *Millennium Falcon* (1997). (Rev: BL 12/15/97)

9944 Whittemore, Jo. *Escape from Arylon* (5–8). Series: The Silverskin Legacy. 2006, Llewellyn paper $8.95 (978-0-7387-0869-0). Ainsley and Megan, neighbors with an uneasy friendship, find themselves transported through a portal to Arylon, where they meet many magi-

cal characters and must save the Staff of Lexiam from thieves. ℮ (Rev: SLJ 6/06; VOYA 6/06)

9945 Whybrow, Ian. *Little Wolf's Diary of Daring Deeds* (2–4). Illus. by Tony Ross. 2000, Carolrhoda LB $14.95 (978-1-57505-411-7). 127pp. A beginning chapter book told in hilarious letters by Little Wolf, who is trying to found a school called Adventure Academy with his cousin Yeller. (Rev: HBG 10/00; SLJ 6/00)

9946 Whybrow, Ian. *Little Wolf's Haunted Hall for Small Horrors* (2–4). Illus. by Tony Ross. 2000, Carolrhoda $14.95 (978-1-57505-412-4). Little Wolf, his friend Yeller, and younger brother Smellybreff encounter the ghost of Little Wolf's uncle Bigbad Wolf in this amusing animal fantasy told through letters. (Rev: HBG 3/01; SLJ 9/00)

9947 Whybrow, Ian. *The Unvisibles* (4–6). 2006, Holiday $16.95 (978-0-8234-1972-2). 184pp. Oliver Gasper and Nicky Chew are 12-year-old boys with almost nothing in common, but their lives intersect when Oliver desperately needs a friend to help him reverse the magical chant that rendered him invisible. (Rev: BL 4/15/06; SLJ 5/06)

9948 Wiley, Melissa. *The Prairie Thief* (4–6). 2012, Simon & Schuster $15.99 (978-1-4424-4056-2). 224pp. In Colorado in the late 19th century, 12-year-old Louisa seeks to prove her father's innocence with the help of a magical little Scottish pointy-headed brownie. ℮ (Rev: BL 9/1/12; LMC 1–2/13; SLJ 9/12)

9949 Wilkinson, Carole. *Dragon Moon* (4–6). Series: Dragon Keeper. 2008, Hyperion $16.99 (978-1-4231-1143-6). 368pp. In this final volume in the trilogy set in ancient China, Ping must find a way to take her dragon Kai to the Dragon Haven. (Rev: BL 5/15/08; SLJ 6/08)

9950 Wilkinson, Carole. *Garden of the Purple Dragon* (4–6). 2007, Hyperion $16.99 (978-1-4231-0338-7). 354pp. Twelve-year-old Ping and her charge, baby dragon Kai, face trials and betrayals as Ping strives to protect the line of imperial dragons from dying out in this sequel to *Dragon Keeper* (2005). (Rev: BL 11/1/07; SLJ 9/07)

9951 Williams, Alex. *The Deep Freeze of Bartholomew Tullock* (5–8). 2008, Philomel $16.99 (978-0-399-25185-6). 304pp. Never-ending snow has ruined the Breeze family's fan business and they find themselves in debt to the tyrannical Bartholomew Tullock; with their parents, young Madeline and Rufus succeed in finding the machine that has been causing the constant winter. (Rev: BCCB 11/08; BL 10/1/08; LMC 1/09; SLJ 1/09)

9952 Williams, Maiya. *The Golden Hour* (4–8). 2004, Abrams $16.95 (978-0-8109-4823-5). Thirteen-year-old Rowan and his 11-year-old sister Nina are sent to live with two great-aunts after the death of their mother and find themselves — with their new friends Xanthe and Xavier — transported through a time portal to 1789 Paris. (Rev: BL 3/15/04; SLJ 4/04; VOYA 6/04)

9953 Williams, Maiya. *The Hour of the Cobra* (4–7). 2006, Abrams $16.95 (978-0-8109-5970-5). Xanthe, Xavier, Rowan, and Nina time-travel to ancient Egypt and narrowly avoid altering history in this sequel to

The Golden Hour (2004). (Rev: BL 5/15/06; SLJ 7/06; VOYA 6/06)

9954 Williams, Maiya. *The Hour of the Outlaw* (4–7). 2007, Abrams $16.95 (978-0-8109-9355-6). Xavier and Xanthe, Rowan and Nina travel back in time again — this time to the Old West during the California Gold Rush. (Rev: BL 1/1–15/08; SLJ 1/08)

9955 Williams, Margery. *The Velveteen Rabbit: Or, How Toys Become Real* (2–4). Illus. by Michael Hague. 1983, Holt $16.95 (978-0-8050-0209-6). 48pp. Love brings a toy rabbit to life. One of many fine editions.

9956 Williams, Mark London. *Trail of Bones* (5–8). Series: Danger Boy. 2005, Candlewick $9.99 (978-0-7636-2154-4). Eli, Thea, and Clyne — three characters of very different backgrounds — travel back in time from 2019 to early 19th-century America and become involved with Lewis and Clark and the plight of escaping slaves. (Rev: SLJ 7/05)

9957 Williams, Tad, and Deborah Beale. *The Dragons of Ordinary Farm* (4–7). Illus. by Greg Swearingen. 2009, HarperCollins $16.99 (978-0-06-154345-6). 416pp. Tyler and Lucinda are staying with their great-uncle for the summer and discover the farm is full of mythical animals — dragons, unicorns, and more. (Rev: BLO 4/24/09; LMC 10/09)

9958 Willingham, Bill. *Down the Mysterly River* (4–7). Illus. by Mark Buckingham. 2011, Starscape $15.99 (978-0-7653-2792-5). 336pp. Max, Boy Scout and sleuth, finds himself and three talking animals in a forest, being chased by the mysterious and sinister Blue Cutters. (Rev: BLO 9/1/11; SLJ 12/1/11)

9959 Willis, Alette J. *How to Make a Golem and Terrify People* (5–8). 2012, Floris paper $9.95 (978-08631584-0-7). 240pp. After her home in Edinburgh is broken into, 13-year-old Edda accepts a boy named Michael's help with making a golem to protect her — but things go awry. ℮ (Rev: BLO 4/1/12; LMC 11–12/12; SLJ 6/12)

9960 Wilson, N. D. *The Chestnut King* (4–7). Series: 100 Cupboards. 2010, Random House $16.99 (978-0-375-83885-9); LB $19.99 (978-0-375-93885-6). 496pp. In this trilogy conclusion, young Henry finally meets the Chestnut King, who can help him to defeat the evil witch Nimiane. ∩ ℮ Lexile 670L (Rev: BLO 2/1/10; SLJ 6/10)

9961 Wilson, N. D. *Dandelion Fire* (4–7). 2008, Random $16.99 (978-0-375-83883-5). 480pp. In an attempt to learn more about his birth parents, Henry and his cousin Henrietta again explore in the magical cupboards that lead to other worlds and run up against an evil witch and her powerful minion; a multilayered sequel to *100 Cupboards* (2007). ∩ (Rev: BLO 1/13/09; SLJ 1/09)

9962 Wilson, N. D. *The Dragon's Tooth* (5–8). Series: Ashtown Burials. 2011, Random House $16.99 (978-0-375-86439-1); LB $16.99 (978-0-375-96439-8). 496pp. Cyrus and Antigone struggle to rescue their brother Dan from the clutches of Dr. Phoenix, who is performing experiments on him, in this fast-paced fantasy involving an ancient secret society. ∩ Lexile 640L (Rev: BL 10/15/11*; SLJ 11/1/11*)

9963 Wilson, N. D. *100 Cupboards* (4–7). Series: 100 Cupboards. 2007, Random House $16.99 (978-0-375-83881-1). Henry, a timid 12-year-old, and his braver cousin Henrietta discover a wall of cupboards that lead to alternate worlds. (Rev: BL 12/1/07; HB 1–2/08; LMC 4–5/08; SLJ 4/08)

9964 Winkler, Henry, and Lin Oliver. *Zero to Hero* (3–6). Series: Ghost Buddy. 2012, Scholastic $17.99 (978-0-545-29887-2). 176pp. Billy Broccoli, rising 6th-grader, has a lot to cope with: a new home (his mother has remarried), a new school, and a ghost, who in fact turns out to be quite useful. ∩ ℮ Lexile 800L (Rev: BL 12/15/11; LMC 5–6/12; SLJ 4/1/12)

9965 Winterson, Jeanette. *Tanglewreck* (4–7). 2006, Bloomsbury $16.95 (978-1-58234-919-0). After "time tornadoes" upset the delicate balance of time and space in and around London, 11-year-old Silver embarks on a fantastic odyssey in search of the Timekeeper that, hopefully, can set things right again. (Rev: BL 10/1/06; SLJ 10/06; VOYA 8/06)

9966 Winthrop, Elizabeth. *The Battle for the Castle* (4–7). 1993, Holiday $16.95 (978-0-8234-1010-1). William and friend Jason time-travel to the Middle Ages, where they become involved in a struggle to prevent the return of evil as a ruling power. A sequel to *The Castle in the Attic* (1985). (Rev: BL 9/1/93; HB 7–8/93; SLJ 5/93)

9967 Winthrop, Elizabeth. *The Castle in the Attic* (5–7). 1985, Holiday $16.95 (978-0-8234-0579-4). In an effort to keep his sitter from returning to England, William miniaturizes her and then must find a way to undo the deed. (Rev: BCCB 10/85; BL 1/15/86; SLJ 2/86)

9968 Wollman, Jessica. *Tell Me Who* (4–6). 2009, Dutton $15.99 (978-0-525-42087-3). 224pp. Twelve-year-old Molly becomes extremely popular when she finds a magic machine that predicts who people will marry, but that doesn't ease her worries about her father's upcoming marriage to "the Claw." (Rev: BCCB 2/09; BL 1/1–15/09; SLJ 8/09)

9969 Wood, Beverley, and Chris Wood. *Dog Star* (5–8). 1998, Orca paper $6.95 (978-0-89609-537-3). On a cruise to Alaska with his family, 13-year-old Jeff Beacon encounters a magical pet bull terrier who transports him back in time to the Juneau of 1932. (Rev: VOYA 8/98)

9970 Wood, Beverley, and Chris Wood. *Jack's Knife* (5–9). Series: A Sirius Mystery. 2006, Raincoast paper $7.95 (978-1-55192-709-1). This sequel to *Dog Star* (1998) finds Jack time-traveling with bull terrier Patsy Ann to 1930s Alaska to help solve a mystery at sea. (Rev: SLJ 5/06)

9971 Wood, David. *The Phantom Cat of the Opera* (2–5). Illus. by Peters Day. 2001, Watson-Guptill $16.95 (978-0-8230-4018-6). The classic story is retold with cats as characters, with sumptuous illustrations. (Rev: HBG 10/01; SLJ 11/01)

9972 Woodruff, Elvira. *Orphan of Ellis Island* (4–7). 1997, Scholastic paper $15.95 (978-0-590-48245-5). Left alone on Ellis Island, Dominic finds himself transported in time to the village in Italy his family came from. (Rev: BCCB 3/97; BL 6/1–15/97; SLJ 5/97)

9973 Wrede, Patricia C. *Across the Great Barrier* (5–8). Series: Frontier Magic. 2011, Scholastic $16.99 (978-0-545-03343-5). 352pp. In the second volume of this series set in an alternate Wild West, 18-year-old Eff decides against magic school and joins an expedition to the wilderness beyond the Great Barrier. (Rev: BL 9/1/11; SLJ 9/1/11)

9974 Wrede, Patricia C. *Thirteenth Child* (5–8). 2009, Scholastic $16.99 (978-0-545-03342-8). 352pp. Magical beasts appear on the western frontier in this American history fantasy with a global awareness vibe. (Rev: BCCB 9/09; BL 6/1–15/09; HB 7/09)

9975 Wright, Betty R. *Crandalls' Castle* (4–7). 2003, Holiday $16.95 (978-0-8234-1726-1). This gripping suspense story combines supernatural elements with a look at teen girls' yearning to belong. (Rev: BL 4/1/03; HBG 10/03; SLJ 5/03)

9976 Wright, Betty R. *A Ghost in the House* (5–7). 1991, Scholastic paper $13.95 (978-0-590-43606-9). Bizarre happenings take place when Sarah's elderly aunt moves in. (Rev: BCCB 11/91; BL 1/1/91; SLJ 11/91)

9977 Wright, Randall. *The Silver Penny* (4–7). 2005, Henry Holt $16.95 (978-0-8050-7391-1). In this compelling fantasy set in the 19th century, Jacob — after breaking his leg and facing disability — receives from his great-grandfather a lucky silver penny that gives him access to a supernatural world. (Rev: BCCB 7–8/05; SLJ 8/05; VOYA 10/05)

9978 Wynne-Jones, Tim. *Some of the Kinder Planets* (5–8). 1995, Orchard LB $16.99 (978-0-531-08751-0). Nine imaginative stories about ordinary boys and girls in offbeat situations. (Rev: BCCB 5/95; BL 3/1/95*; HB 1–2/95, 5–6/95, 9–10/95; SLJ 4/95*)

9979 Yep, Laurence. *City of Ice* (5–8). Series: City Trilogy. 2011, Tor $16.99 (978-0-7653-1925-8). 384pp. Scirye and her companions travel to the Arctic Circle in their quest to stop the evil Mr. Roland and dragon Badik from acquiring magical power; the sequel to *City of Fire* (2009). ℮ Lexile 890L (Rev: BL 6/1/11; SLJ 6/11)

9980 Yep, Laurence. *Dragon of the Lost Sea* (5–8). 1982, HarperCollins paper $6.99 (978-0-06-440227-9). Shimmer, a dragon, in the company of a boy, Thorn, sets out to destroy the villain Civet. (Rev: BL 4/15/04)

9981 Yolen, Jane. *Curse of the Thirteenth Fey: The True Tale of Sleeping Beauty* (5–8). 2012, Philomel $16.99 (978-0-399-25664-6). 304pp. This retelling of the Sleeping Beauty story features 13-year-old Gorse, the 13th and youngest fey in her family — and a little accident-prone. ℮ Lexile 880L (Rev: BL 11/15/12; HB 11–12/12; LMC 1–2/13; SLJ 10/12; VOYA 4/13)

9982 Yolen, Jane. *Merlin* (5–8). Series: Young Merlin Trilogy. 1997, Harcourt $16.00 (978-0-15-200814-7). In this concluding volume of a trilogy, Hawk-Hobby (Merlin) escapes from his enemies with a young friend who will later become King Arthur. (Rev: BL 4/15/97; SLJ 5/97)

9983 Yolen, Jane. *Passager* (4–7). Series: Young Merlin Trilogy. 1996, Harcourt $16.00 (978-0-15-200391-3). In medieval England, an abandoned 8-year-old boy named Merlin is taken in by a friendly man who becomes his master. Book two of the trilogy is *Hobby* (1996). (Rev: BL 5/1/96; HB 7–8/96; SLJ 5/96*)

9984 Yolen, Jane. *Wizard's Hall* (4–6). 1991, Harcourt $13.95 (978-0-15-298132-7). 144pp. Henry, an 11-year-old novice wizard, can't seem to get anything right. (Rev: BCCB 7–8/91; BL 3/15/91; SLJ 7/91)

9985 Yolen, Jane, and Adam Stemple. *B.U.G. (Big Ugly Guy)* (4–6). 2013, Dutton $16.99 (978-0-525-42238-9). 328pp. Tired of being bullied, 13-year-old Sammy Greenberg creates a clay golem to protect himself and his only friend Skink; Sammy ignores his rabbi's warnings about the golem and must take steps when it comes alive. Lexile 700 (Rev: BL 3/1/13; HB 3–4/13; LMC 8–9/13; SLJ 4/13)

9986 Yolen, Jane, ed. *Spaceships and Spells* (5–9). 1987, HarperCollins $12.95 (978-0-06-026796-4). A collection of 13 original tales, mostly science fiction but also some fantasy. (Rev: BL 1/15/88; SLJ 11/87)

9987 Yoshi. *The Butterfly Hunt* (5–8). 1991, Picture Book paper $14.95 (978-0-88708-137-8). In this fantasy, a young boy releases a butterfly and forevermore it becomes his own. (Rev: SLJ 6/91)

9988 Young, Steve. *15 Minutes* (5–8). 2006, HarperCollins $15.99 (978-0-06-072508-2). Casey, a 7th-grader who's always late for almost everything, discovers that his grandfather's watch gives him the power to go back 15 minutes. (Rev: SLJ 9/06)

9989 Zahler, Diane. *Princess of the Wild Swans* (4–7). Illus. by Yvonne Gilbert. 2012, HarperCollins $16.99 (978-006200492-5). 224pp. When tasked with making shirts from stinging nettles for each of her five brothers to free them from a curse, 12-year-old Princess Meriel rues her distaste for sewing; based on Grimm's "The Six Swans." (Rev: BL 3/1/12; SLJ 3/12)

9990 Zahler, Diane. *Sleeping Beauty's Daughters* (4–7). 2013, HarperCollins $16.99 (978-006200496-3). 224pp. Twelve-year-old Aurora is the daughter of Sleeping Beauty, and has been cursed with the same spell as her mother, leaving it up to Aurora's sister, Luna, and a young fisherman named Symon to try and keep Aurora awake long enough to get her to the good fairy Emmeline, who can hopefully reverse the spell. ℮ (Rev: BL 10/1/13; LMC 3–4/14; SLJ 9/13)

9991 Zahler, Diane. *The Thirteenth Princess* (4–7). 2010, HarperCollins $15.99 (978-0-06-182498-2). 256pp. Zita learns that she is a king's daughter and that her 12 sisters are under a magic spell. ⌒ Lexile 850L (Rev: BL 12/15/09; LMC 8–9/10; SLJ 3/10)

9992 Zahn, Timothy. *Dragon and Herdsman: The Fourth Dragonback Adventure* (5–8). 2006, Tom Doherty Assoc. $17.95 (978-0-7653-1417-8). With the help of a shape-changing dragon and his friend Alison, 14-year-old Jack Morgan escapes from the Malison Ring. (Rev: SLJ 9/06; VOYA 6/06)

9993 Zakour, John. *Baxter Moon: Galactic Scout* (4–7). 2008, Brown Barn paper $8.95 (978-0-9768126-9-2). Baxter and his crew travel through space to rescue an Aquarian ship from robotic aliens in this entertaining romp. (Rev: BL 5/15/08; SLJ 6/08)

9994 Zappa, Ahmet. *The Monstrous Memoirs of a Mighty McFearless* (4–7). Illus. by author. 2006, Random House $12.95 (978-0-375-83287-1). Written and illustrated by the son of Frank Zappa, this rollicking fantasy follows Mini and Max McFearless, monsterminators who must rescue their father from kidnappers. ∩ (Rev: BL 5/15/06; SLJ 7/06)

Friendship Stories

9995 Barden, Stephanie. *Cinderella Smith* (2–4). Illus. by Diane Goode. 2011, HarperCollins $14.99 (978-0-06-196423-7). 160pp. "Cinderella" Smith navigates the ever-changing waters of elementary school friendships and her predisposition for losing shoes at inopportune times. ℮ Lexile 670L (Rev: BL 4/1/11; HB 5–6/11; SLJ 7/11)

9996 Barrows, Annie. *Doomed to Dance* (1–3). Illus. by Sophie Blackall. Series: Ivy and Bean. 2009, Chronicle $14.99 (978-0-8118-6266-0). 136pp. Disappointed at being cast as squids in their first ballet recital, friends Ivy and Bean figure out a way to get out of performing without letting anyone down in this sixth volume in the series. ∩ ℮ Lexile 530L (Rev: BL 11/1/09; HB 1–2/10; SLJ 1/1/10)

9997 Barrows, Annie. *No News Is Good News* (1–3). Illus. by Sophie Blackall. Series: Ivy and Bean. 2011, Chronicle $14.99 (978-081186693-4). 128pp. After starting a neighborhood newspaper, Ivy and Bean find themselves in the midst of controversy. ∩ (Rev: BL 12/15/11; HB 1–2/12)

9998 Baskin, Nora Raleigh. *The Summer Before Boys* (5–8). 2011, Simon & Schuster $15.99 (978-1-4169-8673-7). 208pp. When her mother is deployed to Iraq, Julia, 12, moves in with her friend Eliza's family but the girls' close bond is threatened by Julia's crush on a boy. ℮ Lexile 720L (Rev: BL 3/1/11; HB 5–6/11; SLJ 4/11)

9999 Blume, Lesley M. M. *Cornelia and the Audacious Escapades of the Somerset Sisters* (4–6). 2006, Knopf $15.95 (978-0-375-83523-0). 272pp. Cornelia befriends the elderly woman who moves in next door and finds her loneliness abated by the woman's fascinating stories of her life. (Rev: BL 7/06; SLJ 9/06)

10000 Bowe, Julie. *My Best Frenemy* (3–6). Series: Friends for Keeps. 2010, Dial $16.99 (978-0-8037-3501-9). 240pp. Fourth-grader Ida May describes her confusion as she tries to choose her friends, especially in the face of a challenging game of truth or dare. (Rev: BLO 5/15/10; SLJ 7/1/10)

10001 Bowe, Julie. *My Last Best Friend* (3–4). 2007, Harcourt $16.00 (978-0-15-205777-0). 146pp. Despite the best efforts of a mean girl named Jenna, Ida seeks out a new friend to get her through fourth grade. (Rev: SLJ 5/07)

10002 Bowe, Julie. *My New Best Friend* (2–4). 2008, Harcourt $16.00 (978-0-15-206498-3). 192pp. Fourth-grader Ida May has a new best friend, and together they try to exploit the potential of a mermaid nightlight to make wishes come true; Ida comes to recognize, however, that Stacey may not always be telling the truth. A sequel to *My Last Best Friend* (2007). (Rev: BLO 7/29/08)

10003 Burnett, Frances Hodgson. *The Secret Garden* (5–8). 1999, Scholastic paper $4.99 (978-0-439-09939-4). An easily read classic about a spoiled girl relocated to England and the unusual friendship she finds there.

10004 Burnett, Frances Hodgson. *The Secret Garden* (4–6). Illus. by Tasha Tudor. 1987, HarperCollins paper $6.99 (978-0-06-440188-3). 256pp. Three children find a secret garden and make it bloom again; the garden, in turn, changes the children. One of many fine editions.

10005 Cabot, Meg. *Glitter Girls, and the Great Fake Out* (3–5). Series: Allie Finkle's Rules for Girls. 2010, Scholastic $15.99 (978-054504047-1). 208pp. Allie ditches her friends in favor of a popular birthday party, and — even worse — lies to them in the process. ∩ ℮ Lexile 830L (Rev: BLO 3/1/10; HB 5–6/10)

10006 Campbell, Ellen Langas. *Raising the Roof* (3–6). Illus. by April D'Angelo. Series: Girls Know How. 2005, NouSoma paper $4.95 (978-0-9743604-1-6). 121pp. A group of fifth-grade girls decide to build a clubhouse with the help of a local construction firm's female CEO. (Rev: SLJ 1/06)

10007 Carlson, Natalie Savage. *The Family Under the Bridge* (3–5). Illus. by Garth Williams. 1958, Harper-Collins LB $17.89 (978-0-06-020991-9); paper $5.99 (978-0-06-440250-7). 112pp. Old Armand, a Paris hobo, finds three children huddled in his hideaway under the bridge and befriends them.

10008 Cotler, Steve. *Cheesie Mack Is Not a Genius or Anything* (4–6). Illus. by Adam McCauley. 2011, Random House $15.99 (978-0-375-86437-7); LB $18.99 (978-0-375-96437-4). 240pp. Ronald (aka "Cheesie") Mack tells readers about the summer after fifth grade when he and his friend Georgie solve a mystery and have many interesting experiences. ℮ Lexile 770L (Rev: BL 4/1/11; HB 5–6/7; SLJ 3/1/11)

10009 Cox, Judy. *That Crazy Eddie and the Science Project of Doom* (2–4). Illus. by Blanche Sims. 2005, Holiday House $15.95 (978-0-8234-1931-9). 88pp. Matt and Eddie's friendship is severely strained, threatening the success of their volcano science fair project. (Rev: BL 6/1–15/05)

10010 Crabtree, Julie. *Discovering Pig Magic* (5–8). 2008, Milkweed $16.95 (978-1-57131-683-7); paper $6.95 (978-1-57131-684-4). 184pp. Thirteen-year-old Matilda and her friends Ariel and Nicki try using magic to resolve the problems they face. (Rev: BCCB 1/09; SLJ 6/09)

10011 Dee, Barbara. *This Is Me from Now On* (5–8). 2010, Aladdin paper $5.99 (978-14169941-4-5). 272pp.

Seventh-grader Evie is fascinated by the new girl next door, who lives totally by her own rules. ℮ (Rev: BLO 11/15/10)

10012 DeLaCroix, Alice. *The Best Horse Ever* (3–5). Illus. by Ronald Himler. 2010, Holiday House $15.95 (978-0-8234-2254-8). 80pp. Abby's new horse leads to friendship troubles in this accessible early chapter book. Lexile 510L (Rev: BL 3/15/10; SLJ 6/1/10)

10013 Dowell, Frances O'Roark. *The Kind of Friends We Used to Be* (4–7). 2009, Atheneum $16.99 (978-1-4169-5031-8). 240pp. Kate and Marylin, whose friendship fell apart in *The Secret Language of Girls* (2005), are now in 7th grade and still heading in separate directions. ⌒ (Rev: BCCB 5/09; BL 3/1/09; SLJ 3/09)

10014 English, Karen. *Nikki and Deja: The Newsy News Newsletter* (1–3). Illus. by Laura Freeman. 2010, Clarion $15 (978-0-547-22247-9). 96pp. African American girls Nikki and Deja struggle with the boundaries between news and gossip while deciding what to print in their neighborhood newsletter. ℮ Lexile 680L (Rev: SLJ 2/1/10)

10015 English, Karen. *Wedding Drama* (1–3). Illus. by Laura Freeman. Series: Nikki and Deja. 2012, Clarion $14.99 (978-054761564-6). 112pp. A class lottery for the chance to attend their teacher's upcoming wedding drives a wedge between African American friends Nikki and Deja. ℮ (Rev: BL 2/15/12; LMC 11–12/12)

10016 Ferber, Brenda A. *Jemma Hartman, Camper Extraordinaire* (3–6). 2009, Farrar $16.95 (978-0-374-33672-1). Jemma's hopes of a great summer sailing with her best friend Tammy are dashed when Tammy turns up with her irritating cousin Brooke. (Rev: BL 5/1/09; SLJ 5/09)

10017 Flake, Sharon G. *The Broken Bike Boy and the Queen of 33rd Street* (3–5). Illus. by Colin Bootman. 2007, Hyperion $15.99 (978-1-4231-0032-4). Queen is a spoiled 5th-grader who thinks she is better than all her classmates until she develops a friendship with the new boy, Leroy. (Rev: BCCB 9/07; BL 6/1–15/07; HB 7/07; LMC 11/07; SLJ 6/07)

10018 Freeman, Martha. *The Trouble with Babies* (2–4). Illus. by Cat B. Smith. 2002, Holiday House $15.95 (978-0-8234-1698-1). Holly must learn to adapt — to her new life in San Francisco with her mother and stepfather, to her new friends, and to the fact that she is going to have a new sibling. (Rev: BCCB 11/02; BL 7/02; HBG 3/03; SLJ 8/02)

10019 Friedman, Laurie. *Happy Birthday, Mallory!* (2–4). Illus. by Tamara Schmitz. Series: Mallory. 2005, Carolrhoda LB $15.95 (978-1-57505-823-8). 159pp. As a special treat, Mallory is allowed to have an old friend come to visit for her ninth birthday in this beginning chapter book. (Rev: SLJ 9/05)

10020 Friedman, Laurie. *Happy New Year, Mallory!* (2–5). Illus. by Jennifer Kalis. Series: Mallory. 2009, Carolrhoda $15.95 (978-082258883-2). 176pp. Appendicitis ruins 9-year-old Mallory's planned New Year's reunion

with her friends from summer camp. Lexile 710L (Rev: BL 9/15/09)

10021 Friedman, Laurie. *Mallory and Mary Ann Take New York* (3–5). Illus. by Jennifer Kalis. Series: Mallory McDonald. 2013, Lerner $15.95 (978-076136074-2). 152pp. The friendship between Mallory and Mary Ann is threatened when only one of them may be allowed to appear on a TV fashion show. ℮ Lexile 670L (Rev: BL 3/1/13)

10022 Friedman, Laurie. *Mallory on Board* (2–4). Illus. by Barbara Pollak. Series: Mallory. 2007, Carolrhoda LB $15.95 (978-0-8225-6194-1). Mallory isn't sure that she likes the idea of her two best friends, Joey and Mary Ann, becoming step siblings in this story set on a cruise ship. (Rev: SLJ 6/07)

10023 Friedman, Laurie. *Mallory on the Move* (2–4). Illus. by Tamara Schmitz. 2004, Carolrhoda $15.95 (978-1-57505-538-1). Mallory, 8, is nervous when her best friend Mary Ann comes to visit her new home and will no doubt meet Mallory's new friend Joey; told in the first person, this book will appeal to new chapter-book readers. (Rev: BL 4/15/04; SLJ 4/04)

10024 Friedman, Laurie. *Three's Company, Mallory!* (3–5). Illus. by Jennifer Kalis. 2014, Lerner $15.95 (978-146770921-7). 160pp. Mallory must cope with the difficulties of sharing her best friend with a newcomer in this 21st installment in the series. ℮ Lexile 760 (Rev: BLO 3/1/14)

10025 Green, Julia. *Tilly's Moonlight Garden* (4–6). Illus. by Paul Howard. 2012, Sourcebooks/Jabberwocky $15.99 (978-140227730-6). 208pp. Tilly is having an anxious time — her family has just moved, her mother is having a difficult pregnancy, and her father is distant — until she discovers a secret garden and a mysterious friend. ℮ Lexile 660L (Rev: BL 10/15/12; LMC 5–6/13; SLJ 1/13)

10026 Greene, Stephanie. *Princess Posey and the Perfect Present* (K–2). Illus. by Stephanie Roth Sisson. 2011, Putnam $12.99 (978-0-399-25462-8). 96pp. First-grader Posey is hurt when her friend's teacher gift outshines her own. ⌒ ℮ (Rev: BL 3/1/11; HB 3–4/11; SLJ 8/1/11)

10027 Greenwald, Lisa. *Sweet Treats and Secret Crushes* (5–8). 2010, Abrams $16.95 (978-0-8109-8990-0). 291pp. It's Valentine's Day, and a snowstorm promises to ruin the romantic plans of 13-year-old BFFs Olivia, Kate, and Georgia, but distributing fortune cookies to neighbors in the Brooklyn, New York, apartment building brings unexpected benefits. (Rev: BL 9/15/10; SLJ 12/1/10)

10028 Greenwald, Sheila. *Rosy Cole's Memoir Explosion: A Heartbreaking Story About Losing Friends, Annoying Family, and Ruining Romance* (3–5). Series: Rosy Cole. 2006, Farrar $16.00 (978-0-374-36347-5). 112pp. Rosy sets out to write a memoir and, in an effort to be entertaining, portrays her friends in a less-than-flattering light. (Rev: BL 5/1/06; SLJ 4/06)

10029 Gregory, Kristiana. *Bronte's Book Club* (3–6). 2008, Holiday $16.95 (978-0-8234-2136-7). 160pp.

Lonely in a new town on the California coast, 12-year-old Bronte starts a book club and finds new friends. (Rev: BL 4/1/08)

10030 Grimes, Nikki. *Make Way for Dyamonde Daniel* (2–4). Illus. by R. Gregory Christie. 2009, Putnam $10.99 (978-0-399-25175-7). 96pp. African American 3rd-grader Dyamonde manages to befriend a new student despite his prickly character. (Rev: BL 5/1/09; LMC 10/09; SLJ 7/09)

10031 Grindley, Sally. *Dear Max* (2–4). Illus. by Tony Ross. 2006, Simon & Schuster $14.95 (978-1-4169-0392-5). 144pp. Max, a 9-year-old aspiring writer, sends a letter to his favorite author, D. J. Lucas, and the two develop an unusual friendship, sharing their problems with writing and life in often-humorous exchanges. Also use *Bravo, Max!* (2007). (Rev: BL 8/06; SLJ 8/06*)

10032 Harper, Charise Mericle. *Just Grace and the Double Surprise* (2–4). Illus. by author. Series: Just Grace. 2011, Houghton Mifflin $14.99 (978-0-547-37026-2). 176pp. Grace, 8, navigates two big changes in her life: her best friend Mimi's family adopts a baby boy instead of the expected girl, and her parents say yes to getting a dog. Lexile 720L (Rev: HB 9–10/11; SLJ 8/1/11)

10033 Harper, Charise Mericle. *Just Grace and the Terrible Tutu* (2–4). Illus. by author. Series: Just Grace. 2011, Houghton Mifflin $15 (978-0-547-15224-0). 176pp. Friends Grace and Mimi, 8, put their heads together to entertain Lily, a spirited 4-year-old with an endless supply of tutus; but the experience makes Mimi worry about the forthcoming arrival of a newly adopted little sister. **e** Lexile 820L (Rev: BL 1/1–15/11; HB 1–2/11; SLJ 4/11)

10034 Hoffman, Mary. *Starring Grace* (2–4). Illus. by Caroline Binch. 2000, Penguin $14.99 (978-0-8037-2559-1). A lively chapter book about young Grace and her many summer adventures with friends, culminating in walk-on roles in a theatrical production. (Rev: BCCB 9/00; BL 2/15/00; HB 3/00; HBG 10/00; SLJ 7/00)

10035 House, Silas, and Neela Vaswani. *Same Sun Here* (5–8). 2012, Candlewick $15.99 (978-076365684-3). 228pp. Twelve-year-old Meena, an immigrant from India living in Chinatown, New York, with her struggling parents, and 12-year-old River, an unemployed Kentucky coal miner's son, become pen pals and through letters and e-mails share their problems and aspirations. **e** Lexile 890L (Rev: BL 3/1/12; LMC 8–9/12; SLJ 4/12*)

10036 Impey, Rose. *Best Friends!* (4–6). Series: The Sleepover Club. 2009, HarperCollins paper $6.99 (978-00072649-4-0). 123pp. The four Sleepover Club girls — Frankie, Kenny, Lyndz, and Fliss — are determined to beat the mean girls in the school competition; the first volume in a British series. (Rev: BL 11/1/09)

10037 Kline, Suzy. *Herbie Jones Moves On* (3–5). 2003, Penguin $14.99 (978-0-399-23635-8). 78pp. Herbie Jones, the title character from eight previous children's books, is back, and this time he's lamenting the imminent departure of his best friend, Raymond. (Rev: HBG 10/03; SLJ 6/03)

10038 Leader, Jessica. *Nice and Mean* (5–7). 2010, Aladdin paper $6.99 (978-1-4169-9160-1). 224pp. Middle-schoolers Sachi and Marina are very different and get off to a bad start when they work together on a video project. **e** Lexile 680L (Rev: BL 7/10; LMC 11–12/10)

10039 Lombard, Jenny. *Drita, My Homegirl* (3–5). 2006, Putnam $15.99 (978-0-399-24380-6). 112pp. Drita, a refugee from Kosovo, and Maxie, a motherless African American girl, connect despite their differences in this story set in a Brooklyn neighborhood. (Rev: BL 5/1/06; SLJ 3/06*)

10040 McDonald, Megan. *Judy Moody: Around the World in 8 1/2 Days* (3–4). Illus. by Peter H. Reynolds. 2006, Candlewick $15.99 (978-0-7636-2832-1). In this new easy-chapter-book adventure, third-grader Judy Moody becomes so obsessed with new friend Amy Namey that she neglects some of her longtime pals. (Rev: SLJ 11/06)

10041 McGhee, Alison. *Snap* (4–6). 2004, Candlewick $15.99 (978-0-7636-2002-8). 132pp. Edwina Beckey, 11, who uses rubber bands to remember things, worries about her friend Sally, whose grandmother is dying. (Rev: BL 5/15/04; SLJ 4/04)

10042 McTighe, Carolyn. *How to Ruin Your Life and Other Lessons School Doesn't Teach You* (3–6). 2010, Red Deer paper $9.95 (978-08899540-1-4). 112pp. PJ and Katie's long friendship is jeopardized when Katie beats PJ in a practice run. (Rev: BL 11/15/10; SLJ 12/10)

10043 Magoon, Kekla. *Camo Girl* (5–8). 2011, Simon & Schuster $15.99 (978-1-4169-7804-6). 224pp. Biracial 6th-grader Ella, an outsider unhappy with her skin tone, is pleased when popular Bailey moves to town and befriends her, but anxious to keep her friendship with the troubled Z. **e** Lexile 600L (Rev: BL 2/1/11; LMC 11–12/11; SLJ 1/1/11)

10044 Martin, Ann M. *The Summer Before* (4–6). 2010, Scholastic $16.99 (978-054516093-3). 224pp. This in-depth prequel to the popular Babysitters Club series provides plenty of character development for each of the four main characters. (Rev: BL 4/1/10)

10045 Medearis, Angela Shelf. *The Adventures of Sugar and Junior* (2–3). Illus. by Nancy Poydar. 1995, Holiday House LB $15.95 (978-0-8234-1182-5). 32pp. A simple story of a friendship between a Hispanic American and an African American youngster and their happy times together. (Rev: BL 10/15/95; SLJ 12/95)

10046 Moss, Marissa. *Amelia's BFF* (3–5). Illus. by author. Series: Amelia's Notebooks. 2011, Simon & Schuster $9.99 (978-1-4424-0376-5). Unpaged. Amelia finds herself caught in the middle between two friends vying for the title of her BFF. (Rev: SLJ 6/11)

10047 Moss, Marissa. *Amelia's Boy Survival Guide* (4–7). Illus. by author. Series: Amelia's Notebooks. 2012, Simon & Schuster $9.99 (978-144244084-5). 80pp. After starting off 8th grade with confidence, Amelia finds herself reeling from an unexpected crush. (Rev: BLO 4/1/12)

10048 Murphy, Sally. *Toppling* (3–5). Illus. by Rhian Nest James. 2012, Candlewick $15.99 (978-0-7636-

5921-9). 128pp. Fifth-grader John is obsessed with his hobby of toppling dominoes until his friend Dom is diagnosed with cancer. (Rev: BLO 10/1/12; LMC 3–4/13; SLJ 9/12)

10049 Myracle, Lauren. *Luv Ya Bunches* (4–6). Series: Flower Power. 2009, Abrams $15.95 (978-081094211-0). 240pp. Four 10-year-old girls — each named after a flower and of different ethnicities — navigate the shoals of 5th grade in this story told through straight narrative, instant messages, blog posts, and even a video script. (Rev: BL 9/15/09*; LMC 1–2/11; SLJ 11/09)

10050 Myracle, Lauren. *Oopsy Daisy* (4–6). Series: Flower Power. 2012, Abrams $16.95 (978-141970019-4). 384pp. The four 5th-grade friends return to help each other through life's ups and downs, including Violet coping with her mom's return from the hospital, Yasamin's conflicts with her parents, and Project Teacherly Lurve, a matchmaking scheme. The 4th title in the series is *Awesome Blossom* (2013). (Rev: BL 2/15/12)

10051 Myracle, Lauren. *Violet in Bloom* (4–6). Series: Flower Power. 2010, Abrams $15.95 (978-0-8109-8983-2). 352pp. The three friends from 2009's *Luv Ya Bunches* are back on a quest to replace their cafeteria's snack food with healthier fare while each dealing with her own concerns. Lexile 700L (Rev: BL 10/1/10; SLJ 12/1/10)

10052 Nagda, Ann Whitehead. *Dear Whiskers* (2–4). Illus. 2000, Holiday House $15.95 (978-0-8234-1495-6). 64pp. For a school assignment, Jenny writes to a younger Saudi Arabian girl in her school and gradually forms a friendship with this reclusive girl who knows little English. (Rev: BCCB 2/01; BL 11/15/00; HB 3/01; HBG 10/01; SLJ 1/01)

10053 O'Connor, Barbara. *Fame and Glory in Freedom, Georgia* (4–6). 2003, Farrar $16.00 (978-0-374-32258-8). 112pp. Sixth-grader Bird finds difficulties and rewards in her campaign to befriend new-boy-at-school Harlem. (Rev: BL 7/03*; HB 7/03; HBG 10/03; SLJ 6/03)

10054 O'Dell, Kathleen. *Agnes Parker . . . Happy Camper?* (4–6). 2005, Dial $16.99 (978-0-8037-2962-9). 160pp. When Agnes and her best friend, Prejean, are assigned to different cabins at science camp, Agnes rightly worries that the two will grow apart. (Rev: BL 1/1–15/05; SLJ 3/05)

10055 O'Dell, Kathleen. *Agnes Parker . . . Keeping Cool in Middle School* (3–6). 2007, Dial $16.99 (978-0-8037-3078-6). 160pp. Now in 7th grade friends Agnes and Prejean take different approaches to the social life and try to cope with bullying and other challenges. (Rev: BL 7/07; SLJ 9/07)

10056 Park, Linda Sue. *Project Mulberry* (5–8). 2005, Clarion $16.00 (978-0-618-47786-9). Working on a silkworm project with her friend Patrick, Korean American Julia also learns about prejudices and friendship. (Rev: BL 8/05; SLJ 5/05)

10057 Pennypacker, Sara. *Clementine* (2–4). Illus. by Marla Frazee. 2006, Hyperion $14.99 (978-0-7868-3882-0). 144pp. Eight-year-old Clementine means

well but seems to find herself spending a lot of time in the school principal's office. (Rev: BL 10/15/06; SLJ 10/06*)

10058 Pennypacker, Sara. *Clementine, Friend of the Week* (2–4). Illus. by Marla Frazee. Series: Clementine. 2010, Hyperion $14.99 (978-1-4231-1355-3). 176pp. The pressure is on when 3rd-grader Clementine is chosen to be Friend of the Week. (Rev: BL 10/1/10; SLJ 7/1/10)

10059 Preller, James. *Along Came Spider* (4–6). 2008, Scholastic $15.99 (978-0-545-03299-5). 144pp. Popular 5th-grader Spider finds it difficult to maintain his friendship with Trey, who displays some antisocial behaviors. (Rev: BL 12/1/08; SLJ 12/08)

10060 Robinson, Sharon. *Slam Dunk!* (4–6). 2007, Scholastic $16.99 (978-0-439-67199-6). 151pp. New to his Harlem school, 6th-grade Jumper struggles to discover if he can be a friend and competitor with a girl. (Rev: BL 9/1/07; SLJ 11/07)

10061 Salmansohn, Karen. *Oh, and Another Thing* (4–6). Illus. by author. Series: Alexandra Rambles On! 2001, Tricycle $12.95 (978-1-58246-045-1). Twelve-year-old Alexandra gets advice on how to handle boys. (Rev: SLJ 2/02)

10062 Stauffacher, Sue. *Donutheart* (4–6). 2006, Knopf $15.95 (978-0-375-83275-8). 208pp. In this sequel to *Donuthead* (2003), Franklin is having trouble making the adjustment to middle school but he sets aside his own preoccupations (hygiene and safety, among them) to come to the aid of Sarah, his best friend. (Rev: BL 11/1/06; SLJ 1/07)

10063 Staunton, Ted. *Two False Moves* (3–5). 2000, Red Deer paper $4.95 (978-0-88995-205-8). 64pp. Relations between classmates Nick and Lindsey deteriorate when Lindsey's parents become prospective buyers of the rented home where Nick and his family live. (Rev: BL 2/15/01)

10064 Stout, Shawn K. *Penelope Crumb Never Forgets* (2–4). Illus. by Valeria Docampo. 2013, Philomel $14.99 (978-0-399-25729-2). 196pp. A trip to a museum — and the feeling that her best friend is abandoning her — spurs Penelope to start her own collection of things that will remind her forever of people who are important to her. € Lexile 760L (Rev: BL 12/15/12; HB 1–2/13; SLJ 3/13)

10065 Tarshis, Lauren. *Emma-Jean Lazarus Fell Out of a Tree* (4–6). 2007, Dial $16.99 (978-0-8037-3164-6). 208pp. Emma-Jean Lazarus is persuaded to use her analytical mind to help a classmate cope with a bully and discovers that social relationships are not always logical. (Rev: BL 3/15/07)

10066 Urban, Linda. *Hound Dog True* (3–6). 2011, Harcourt $15.99 (978-0-547-55869-1). 176pp. Scared of starting classes in a new school, shy 5th-grader Mattie takes comfort in the fact that her uncle is a custodian there, but eventually learns that making friends is up to her. (Rev: BL 9/1/11; SLJ 10/1/11*)

10067 Walliams, David. *Mr. Stink* (4–7). Illus. by Quentin Blake. 2010, Penguin $15.99 (978-159514332-7).

272pp. Twelve-year-old Chloe befriends a smelly tramp despite her mother's crusade to clean up the streets in this funny British book. ∩ ℮ Lexile 730L (Rev: BL 11/15/10*; LMC 1–2/11; SLJ 1/1/11)

10068 Warner, Sally. *Not So Weird Emma* (2–4). Illus. by Jamie Harper. 2005, Viking $14.99 (978-0-670-06005-4). The friendship of third graders Emma McGraw and Cynthia Harbison is fractured when the two start calling each other unflattering names; a sequel to *Only Emma* (2005). (Rev: BL 9/1/05; SLJ 11/05)

10069 Warner, Sally. *Only Emma* (2–4). Illus. by Jamie Harper. Series: Emma. 2005, Viking $14.99 (978-0-670-05979-9). 128pp. In this first book of a series, Emma must deal with a new school, a new apartment, and a week-long visit from 4-year-old Anthony Scarpetto. (Rev: BL 3/1/05; SLJ 4/05)

10070 Wong, Janet S. *Minn and Jake's Almost Terrible Summer* (3–6). Illus. by Genevieve Cote. 2008, Farrar $15.00 (978-0-374-34977-6). 112pp. Two friends, Minn and Jake, finally figure out how to get it better if not exactly right after a move separated them. (Rev: BCCB 9/08; BL 11/15/08; SLJ 8/08)

10071 Yee, Lisa. *Millicent Min, Girl Genius* (4–6). 2003, Scholastic $16.95 (978-0-439-42519-3). 256pp. Eleven-year-old Millicent Min, a child prodigy frustrated by her inability to find friends who are her intellectual equal, decides to hide her genius in order to win Emily as a friend. (Rev: BL 9/1/03; HB 9/03; HBG 4/04; SLJ 3/04)

10072 Yee, Paul. *Shu-Li and Tamara* (2–4). Illus. by Shaoli Wang. 2008, Tradewind paper $7.95 (978-1-896580-93-7). 72pp. Fourth-grader Shu-li is happy to find a friend in her new school in Vancouver, but is it possible that Tamara has been stealing? (Rev: BL 4/1/08; SLJ 9/08)

Growing into Maturity

Family Problems

10073 Adler, C. S. *Ghost Brother* (5–8). 1990, Houghton Mifflin $15.00 (978-0-395-52592-0). After his older brother dies in an accident, 11-year-old Wally finds comfort in his ghost. (Rev: BCCB 5/90; BL 5/15/90; SLJ 5/90; VOYA 8/90)

10074 Adler, C. S. *The No Place Cat* (5–8). 2002, Clarion $15.00 (978-0-618-09644-2). Twelve-year-old Tess runs away from home only to find that life with her father and new stepfamily had its good side after all. (Rev: BCCB 4/02; HBG 10/02; SLJ 3/02)

10075 Adler, C. S. *One Sister Too Many* (5–7). 1989, Macmillan paper $3.95 (978-0-689-71521-1). Casey and her reunited family are being driven crazy by the newest addition — a colicky baby. (Rev: BCCB 3/89; BL 3/15/89; SLJ 4/89)

10076 Amato, Mary. *The Naked Mole Rat Letters* (4–7). 2005, Holiday $16.95 (978-0-8234-1927-2). Through

emails and diary entries, readers learn about Frankie's fear that her father is becoming involved in a new romance. (Rev: BL 6/1–15/05; SLJ 8/05)

10077 Angle, Kimberly Greene. *Hummingbird* (4–6). 2008, Farrar $16.95 (978-0-374-33376-8). 256pp. On a Georgia watermelon farm, 12-year-old March Anne must learn new skills and face much sadness when her grandmother becomes seriously ill. (Rev: BL 7/08; SLJ 9/08)

10078 Atkinson, Elizabeth. *I, Emma Freke* (4–7). 2010, Carolrhoda $16.95 (978-0-7613-5604-2). 232pp. Twelve-year-old Emma, tall and uncertain, learns a lot about herself when she is invited to a family reunion of the father she has never met. (Rev: BL 11/1/10; SLJ 2/1/11*)

10079 Auch, Mary Jane. *Guitar Boy* (5–8). 2010, Henry Holt $16.99 (978-0-8050-9112-0). 272pp. When his mother suffers a brain injury and his father throws him out, 13-year-old Travis's love of guitars and music helps him to survive and even contribute to restoring his family. ∩ Lexile 750L (Rev: BL 11/1/10; LMC 11–12/10; SLJ 9/1/10)

10080 Baptiste, Tracey. *Angel's Grace* (5–8). 2005, Simon & Schuster $15.95 (978-0-689-86773-6). Thirteen-year-old Grace, who has always felt different, embarks on a search for the man she believes is her biological father. (Rev: BL 2/1/05; SLJ 3/05)

10081 Bauer, Joan. *Almost Home* (5–8). 2012, Viking $16.99 (978-0-670-01289-3). 240pp. Sixth-grader Sugar and her mother are able to bounce back from homelessness and depression with the help of their community in a narrative that includes her poems and letters. Lexile 590 (Rev: BL 8/12; HB 9–10/12; LMC 3–4/13*; SLJ 10/12)

10082 Bauer, Joan. *Stand Tall* (5–7). 2002, Putnam $16.99 (978-0-399-23473-6). Tree, a tall 7th grader, has a lot of challenges in this nonetheless humorous novel: his height, his lack of athletic ability, shuffling between his divorced parents' homes, and his veteran grandfather's ailments, to name just a few. (Rev: BCCB 10/02; BL 9/15/02; HB 11–12/02; HBG 3/03; SLJ 8/02)

10083 Bauer, Marion Dane. *Shelter from the Wind* (5–9). 2010, Marshall Cavendish $16.99 (978-0-7614-5687-2). 112pp. Originally published in 1975, this is a story of a girl coming to terms with upheaval in her family including alcoholism, divorce, and remarriage. (Rev: LMC 8–9/10)

10084 Bawden, Nina. *Granny the Pag* (5–8). 1996, Clarion $16.00 (978-0-395-77604-9). Catriona is embarrassed by her grandmother's eccentric ways, such as riding motorbikes and wearing leather jackets, but that doesn't mean she wants to live with her parents instead. (Rev: BCCB 3/96; BL 4/1/96; HB 9–10/96; SLJ 4/96*; VOYA 6/96)

10085 Birdseye, Tom. *Tucker* (5–8). 1990, Holiday $16.95 (978-0-8234-0813-9). A story set in rural Kentucky of a young boy reunited with his younger sister after seven years of separation caused by divorce. (Rev: BL 7/90; SLJ 6/90)

10086 Blume, Judy. *It's Not the End of the World* (5–8). 1972, Dell paper $5.50 (978-0-440-44158-8). Twelve-year-old Karen's world seems to end when her parents are divorced and her older brother runs away.

10087 Brokaw, Nancy Steele. *Leaving Emma* (4–7). 1999, Clarion $15.00 (978-0-395-90699-6). When Emma's best friend moves away and her father is sent to work overseas, the young girl is left with a mother who suffers from bouts of depression. (Rev: BCCB 3/99; BL 3/1/99; HBG 10/99; SLJ 5/99)

10088 Brown, Susan Taylor. *Hugging the Rock* (5–8). 2006, Tricycle $15.95 (978-1-58246-180-9). In this poignant novel told in free-verse poetry, Rachel describes the difficulties she and her dad have in coping after her mother's departure. (Rev: SLJ 9/06)

10089 Bryant, Ann. *One Mom Too Many! Book No. 1* (4–7). Series: Step-Chain. 2003, Lobster paper $3.95 (978-1-894222-78-5). Sarah, 12, is not pleased to discover that both her divorced parents have found new romantic interests. (Rev: SLJ 5/04)

10090 Bunting, Eve. *Is Anybody There?* (4–7). 1990, HarperCollins paper $6.99 (978-0-06-440347-4). Marcus is both scared and angry after his latchkey disappears and things are stolen. (Rev: BCCB 10/88; BL 12/15/88; SLJ 12/88)

10091 Bunting, Eve. *The Summer of Riley* (4–6). 2001, HarperCollins LB $16.89 (978-0-06-029142-6). 176pp. The acquisition of a dog helps William to overcome his distress over his parents' separation and grandfather's death, but then the dog gets in trouble with the law. (Rev: BL 7/01; HBG 10/01; SLJ 6/01)

10092 Butler, Dori Hillestad. *Yes, I Know the Monkey Man* (5–7). 2009, Peachtree $16.95 (978-1-56145-479-2). 208pp. This tense sequel to *Do You Know the Monkey Man?* (2005) flips the narrative to T.J., the discovered twin, as she struggles to connect with her recently found mom and sister and deal with her father's deception. (Rev: BLO 6/16/09; LMC 10/09; SLJ 7/09)

10093 Cardenas, Teresa. *Letters to My Mother* (5–8). Trans. by David Unger. 2006, Groundwood paper $6.95 (978-0-88899-721-0). In unhappy letters to her dead mother, a 10-year-old Cuban girl describes cruelty and prejudice at the hands of her relatives. (Rev: BL 5/1/06; SLJ 8/06)

10094 Cassidy, Cathy. *Indigo Blue* (5–8). 2005, Viking $15.99 (978-0-670-05927-0). As her family life slowly disintegrates, 11-year-old Indigo tries her best to conceal the truth from her friends at school in this realistic story set in Britain. (Rev: BL 10/1/05; SLJ 11/05)

10095 Chambers, Veronica. *Marisol and Magdalena: The Sound of Our Sisterhood* (5–9). 1998, Hyperion LB $15.49 (978-0-7868-2385-7). Hispanic American Marisol is sent to live with her grandmother in Panama for a year, and hopes to track down her absent father. (Rev: BL 10/1/98; SLJ 12/98)

10096 Cheaney, J. B. *The Middle of Somewhere* (5–8). 2007, Knopf $15.99 (978-0-375-83790-6). Put in charge of her learning disabled brother while her mother recovers from knee surgery, 12-year-old Ronnie Sparks comes under even greater pressure when she and her brother accompany their grandfather on a trip to Kansas. (Rev: BL 3/15/07; SLJ 7/07)

10097 Clifford, Eth. *The Remembering Box* (4–6). Illus. 1985, Morrow paper $4.99 (978-0-688-11777-1). Joshua enjoys a special relationship with his grandmother, who shortly before her death gives him a "remembering box" in which she places a girlhood picture of herself. (Rev: BCCB 12/85; BL 12/1/85; HB 3/86)

10098 Clifton, Lutricia. *Freaky Fast Frankie Joe* (4–6). 2012, Holiday House $16.95 (978-082342367-5). 248pp. Twelve-year-old Frankie Joe is uprooted from a Texas trailer park when his mother is arrested, and must adjust to life in Illinois with the father he never met, a stepmother, and four half brothers. (Rev: BL 4/15/12; LMC 8–9/12; SLJ 5/1/12)

10099 Cohn, Rachel. *The Steps* (4–7). 2003, Simon & Schuster $16.95 (978-0-689-84549-9). Annabel resents the complexity of her family life as she reluctantly sets out to visit her father and his new wife, baby, and stepchildren in Australia, but she gradually learns to accept the situation in this humorous portrayal. (Rev: BCCB 2/03; BL 1/1–15/03; HB 5–6/03; HBG 10/03; SLJ 2/03*)

10100 Coman, Carolyn. *What Jamie Saw* (5–8). 1995, Front St $15.95 (978-1-886910-02-7). In this novel seen through the eyes of a young boy, a mother and her family flee her physically abusive husband. (Rev: BCCB 12/95; BL 12/15/95*; SLJ 12/95*)

10101 Connor, Leslie. *Crunch* (5–8). 2010, HarperCollins $16.99 (978-0-06-169229-1); LB $17.89 (978-0-06-169233-8). 336pp. When his parents are stranded on vacation, 14-year-old Dewey must help his older sister look after their three younger siblings and at the same time run their dad's bicycle repair shop and solve the mystery of missing parts. Lexile HL490L (Rev: BL 4/1/10; HB 7–8/10; LMC 11–12/10; SLJ 5/10)

10102 Couloumbis, Audrey. *Getting Near to Baby* (5–9). 1999, Putnam $17.99 (978-0-399-23389-0). When their baby sister dies and their mother sinks into a depression, 12-year-old Willa Jo and Little Sister go to live with a bossy aunt in this story set in North Carolina. (Rev: BCCB 11/99; BL 11/1/99; HB 11–12/99; HBG 3/00; SLJ 10/99; VOYA 2/00)

10103 Couloumbis, Audrey. *Love Me Tender* (5–8). 2008, Random House $16.99 (978-0-375-83839-2). Thirteen-year-old Elvira initially questions her future when after a fight, her father leaves for Vegas to compete in an Elvis-impersonation contest and her pregnant mother takes Elvira and her younger sister to Memphis to reunite with her family. (Rev: BL 2/15/08; SLJ 4/08)

10104 Crist-Evans, Craig. *North of Everything* (4–6). 2004, Candlewick $14.99 (978-0-7636-2098-1). Told from the viewpoint of a young boy, this spare — but moving — novel tells of the joys and tragedies that a family experiences after its move from Miami to a farm in Vermont. (Rev: BL 1/1–15/05; SLJ 11/04)

10105 Danziger, Paula. *Forever Amber Brown* (2–4). Illus. 1996, Penguin $15.99 (978-0-399-22932-9). 101pp. Amber's divorced mother is being courted by Max, and the young girl is concerned. (Rev: BL 11/15/96; SLJ 2/97)

10106 Day, Karen. *Tall Tales* (5–8). 2007, Random House $15.99 (978-0-375-83773-9). As she starts school in yet another new town, 12-year-old Meg conceals her father's alcoholism and abuse, afraid it will frighten off potential friends. (Rev: BL 4/1/07; SLJ 6/07)

10107 de Vries, Maggie. *Somebody's Girl* (3–6). Series: Orca Young Readers. 2011, Orca paper $7.95 (978-1-55469-383-2). 164pp. Martha, a difficult 9-year-old, is upset when she learns her adoptive parents are having a baby. e (Rev: LMC 10/11; SLJ 7/11)

10108 DeFelice, Cynthia. *Wild Life* (4–7). 2011, Farrar $16.99 (978-0-374-38001-4). 192pp. When his parents are posted to Iraq, 12-year-old Erik is sent to his grandparents in North Dakota; unhappy there, he strikes out on his own with his newly adopted dog and manages to survive a time in the wilderness. Lexile 860L (Rev: BLO 6/21/11; LMC 10/11; SLJ 6/11)

10109 Derby, Sally. *Kyle's Island* (5–8). 2010, Charlesbridge $16.95 (978-1-58089-316-9). 192pp. Heartbroken that this will be the last summer at his family's lake cottage — his parents have just divorced — 13-year-old Kyle spends much of his time nursing his anger and fishing with an elderly neighbor who helps him deal with his unhappiness. Lexile 670L (Rev: BL 12/15/09; LMC 5–6/10; SLJ 1/10)

10110 Deuker, Carl. *High Heat* (5–8). 2003, Houghton Mifflin $16.00 (978-0-618-31117-0). Even his baseball prowess seems to desert Shane when his father commits suicide and he must move to a tough new neighborhood and school. (Rev: BL 8/03; HBG 10/03; SLJ 7/03; VOYA 8/03)

10111 Doucet, Sharon Arms. *Fiddle Fever* (4–7). 2000, Clarion $15.00 (978-0-618-04324-8). Felix disobeys his mother, who hates fiddle playing, and builds one out of a cigar box and practices in secret. (Rev: BL 9/1/00; HB 9–10/00; HBG 3/01; SLJ 10/00)

10112 Dowell, Frances O'Roark. *Chicken Boy* (4–7). 2005, Simon & Schuster $15.95 (978-0-689-85816-1). A new friend called Henry brings some comfort into Tobin's sad life. (Rev: BL 5/15/05*; SLJ 7/05*)

10113 Doyle, Eugenie. *Stray Voltage* (5–7). 2002, Front St $16.95 (978-1-886910-86-7). The electrical problems in Ian's family barn reflect the flickering, unpredictable relationships at home, but a wise teacher helps Ian to cope with his circumstances. (Rev: BCCB 1/03; BL 1/1–15/03*; HBG 3/03; SLJ 10/02*; VOYA 2/03)

10114 Ellis, Sarah. *Out of the Blue* (5–7). 1995, Simon & Schuster paper $15.00 (978-0-689-80025-2). Twelve-year-old Megan discovers that she has a 24-year-old half-sister whom her mother gave up for adoption years

ago. (Rev: BCCB 4/95; BL 5/1/95; HB 7–8/95; SLJ 5/95)

10115 Enderle, Dotti. *Man in the Moon* (4–6). Illus. by Kristina Swarner. 2008, Delacorte $14.99 (978-0-385-73566-7). 152pp. In 1961, a mysterious man arrives at the Texas farm where Janine is dreading a summer stuck with her sick brother and teaches them a lot about life; a satisfying novel with a tightly woven plot and realistic characters. (Rev: BCCB 10/08; LMC 8/08; SLJ 9/08)

10116 Farrant, Natasha. *After Iris* (5–8). 2013, Dial $16.99 (978-080373982-6). 256pp. Using her video camera and a diary format to great effect, 12-year-old Bluebell Gadsby documents the struggles of her family after the death of her twin three years before. Lexile 920 (Rev: BLO 7/13; HB 9–10/13; LMC 10/13; SLJ 7/13)

10117 Ferber, Brenda A. *Julia's Kitchen* (5–8). 2006, Farrar $16.00 (978-0-374-39932-0). Eleven-year-old Cara Segal's faith is tested when her mother and sister die in a house fire while Cara is sleeping over at a friend's home. Sydney Taylor Book Award. (Rev: BL 2/1/06; SLJ 4/06)

10118 Fogelin, Adrian. *Anna Casey's Place in the World* (4–6). 2001, Peachtree $14.95 (978-1-56145-249-1). Twelve-year-old orphan Anna must adjust to her new foster home and begin to make friends. (Rev: BL 10/15/01; HBG 3/02; SLJ 12/01)

10119 Foggo, Cheryl. *One Thing That's True* (5–8). 1998, Kids Can $16.95 (978-1-55074-411-8). Roxanne is heartbroken when her older brother runs away after learning that he is adopted. (Rev: BCCB 5/98; BL 2/15/98; HBG 10/98; SLJ 4/98)

10120 Galante, Cecilia. *Willowood* (3–6). 2010, Simon & Schuster $16.99 (978-1-4169-8022-3). 272pp. Lily, 11, struggles to adjust to life in a new city, finding friendship in unexpected places as her busy mother works long hours. e Lexile 630L (Rev: BLO 5/15/10; LMC 5–6/10; SLJ 3/10)

10121 Gallagher, Mary Collins. *Ginny Morris and Dad's New Girlfriend* (3–5). Illus. by Whitney Martin. 2006, Magination $14.95 (978-1-59147-386-2); paper $9.95 (978-1-59147-387-9). 64pp. Ginny is distressed to discover that her divorced father has a girlfriend in this story written to help children dealing with divorce. (Rev: SLJ 2/07)

10122 Gates, Doris. *Blue Willow* (5–8). 1940, Penguin paper $6.99 (978-0-14-030924-9). An easily read novel about a poor girl and the china plate that belonged to her mother. (Rev: BCCB 12/99)

10123 Geisert, Bonnie. *Lessons* (4–6). 2005, Houghton $15.00 (978-0-618-47899-6). 192pp. In 1950s South Dakota, 10-year-old Rachel realizes that her new baby brother is making her father sad; eventually she finds out about the baby who died and did not receive a Christian burial. (Rev: BL 5/15/05; SLJ 5/05)

10124 Giff, Patricia Reilly. *Pictures of Hollis Woods* (5–7). 2002, Random House $15.95 (978-0-385-32655-1). Twelve-year-old Hollis Woods has finally found a foster home where she feels safe, but when the artist who takes her in begins to suffer from dementia, Hollis finds herself in the position of caregiver. Newbery Honor 2003. (Rev: BCCB 12/02; BL 10/15/02; HB 1–2/03; HBG 3/03; SLJ 9/02)

10125 Gilliland, Hap, and William Walters. *Flint's Rock* (5–7). 1996, Roberts Rinehart paper $8.95 (978-1-879373-82-2). Flint, a young Cheyenne, faces problems when he moves with his parents from the reservation to Butte, Montana. (Rev: BCCB 5/96; BL 5/1/96)

10126 Gilmore, Rachna. *Mina's Spring of Colors* (4–7). 2000, Fitzhenry & Whiteside $14.95 (978-1-55041-549-0); paper $8.95 (978-1-55041-534-6). Mina is happy when her grandfather comes from India, but with his arrival comes a culture clash that troubles the girl. (Rev: BL 6/1–15/00; SLJ 9/00; VOYA 12/00)

10127 Gingras, Charlotte. *Emily's Piano* (4–6). Illus. by Stephane Jorisch. 2005, Firefly $18.95 (978-1-55037-913-6); paper $7.95 (978-1-55037-912-9). 64pp. Shaken by the breakup of her parents' marriage, Emily remembers the piano as a symbol of happiness and tracks it down. (Rev: BL 1/1–15/06; SLJ 5/06)

10128 Golding, Theresa Martin. *The Secret Within* (5–8). 2002, Boyds Mills $16.95 (978-1-56397-995-8). Eighth-grader Carly's secret is that her father is abusive and a criminal; the neighbors in the family's new town help her and her mother to finally escape his grip. (Rev: BL 9/15/02; HBG 3/03; SLJ 8/02; VOYA 2/03)

10129 Goobie, Beth. *Something Girl* (5–8). 2005, Orca paper $7.95 (978-1-55143-347-9). Fifteen-year-old Sophie tries to hide the fact that her mother is an alcoholic and her father abusive in this book for reluctant readers. (Rev: BL 7/05; SLJ 12/05)

10130 Goodman, Joan Elizabeth. *Songs from Home* (5–7). 1994, Harcourt paper $4.95 (978-0-15-203591-4). Anna discovers the truth about her father, who has become a drifter in Italy singing for tips in restaurants. (Rev: BCCB 12/94; BL 9/1/94; SLJ 10/94)

10131 Greene, Stephanie. *The Lucky Ones* (5–8). 2008, Greenwillow $16.99 (978-0-06-156586-1). Twelve-year-old Cecile wants things the way they were before her parents began fighting and her sister became interested in boys in this coming-of-age novel set during a summer vacation on an island. (Rev: BL 10/1/08; SLJ 11/08)

10132 Gregory, Nan. *I'll Sing You One-O* (5–8). 2006, Clarion $16.00 (978-0-618-60708-2). Twelve-year-old Gemma is overwhelmed when relatives — including a twin brother — turn up to take her from the foster home she's come to love, and she becomes convinced that an angel will save the day. (Rev: BL 8/06; SLJ 10/06*)

10133 Grimes, Nikki. *Dark Sons* (5–8). 2005, Hyperion $15.99 (978-0-7868-1888-4). Alternating between biblical times and contemporary New York, free-verse narratives express the frustrations of Ishmael — son of Abraham, who must wander the desert with his rejected mother — and of Sam, whose father has left his mother for a young white woman. (Rev: BL 8/05*; SLJ 11/05; VOYA 10/05)

10134 Hahn, Mary Downing. *As Ever, Gordy* (5–8). 1998, Houghton Mifflin $15.00 (978-0-395-83627-9). After his grandmother's death, 13-year-old Gordy must move back to his hometown to live with his older brother, and there he finds himself in a downward spiral. A sequel to *Stepping on Cracks* and *Following My Own Footsteps*. (Rev: BCCB 6/98; BL 5/1/98; HBG 10/98; SLJ 7/98; VOYA 4/99)

10135 Hamilton, Virginia. *Plain City* (5–7). 1993, Scholastic paper $13.95 (978-0-590-47364-4). Buhlaire's life changes dramatically when the father she believed to be dead unexpectedly arrives in town. (Rev: BCCB 11/93; BL 9/15/93*; SLJ 11/93*)

10136 Hansen, Joyce. *One True Friend* (4–7). 2001, Clarion $14.00 (978-0-395-84983-5). Amir's correspondence with his friend Doris comforts him as he tries to fulfill a deathbed promise to his mother to keep his family together. (Rev: BCCB 12/01; BL 12/15/01; HBG 3/02; SLJ 12/01; VOYA 10/01)

10137 Harness, Cheryl. *Just for You to Know* (5–8). 2006, HarperCollins $17.99 (978-0-06-078313-6). Life is turned upside down for 13-year-old Carmen Cathcart, an aspiring artist, when her mother dies during childbirth. (Rev: SLJ 9/06)

10138 Heneghan, James, and Norma Charles. *Bank Job* (5–7). 2009, Orca paper $9.95 (978-1-55143-855-9). 165pp. A gripping read about three foster children who will resort to robbery to stay together. (Rev: BL 5/15/09)

10139 Henkes, Kevin. *The Birthday Room* (5–7). 1999, Greenwillow $19.99 (978-0-688-16733-2). Ben travels to Oregon with his mother to visit Uncle Ian who was responsible for Ben's losing his little finger in an accident. (Rev: BCCB 9/99; BL 7/99; HB 9–10/99; HBG 3/00; SLJ 10/99)

10140 Hermes, Patricia. *You Shouldn't Have to Say Good-bye* (5–8). 1982, Scholastic paper $3.25 (978-0-590-43174-3). A moving novel about a girl whose mother is dying of cancer.

10141 Herschler, Mildred Barger. *The Darkest Corner* (5–9). 2000, Front St $17.95 (978-1-886910-54-6). In this novel set in the Deep South of the 1960s, 10-year-old Teddy is shocked to discover that her beloved dad participated in the lynching of her best friend's father. (Rev: BL 1/1–15/01; HBG 3/01; SLJ 2/01; VOYA 2/01)

10142 Hest, Amy. *Remembering Mrs. Rossi* (3–5). Illus. by Heather Maione. 2007, Candlewick $14.99 (978-0-7636-2163-6). 192pp. The sudden death of 8-year-old Annie's mother, a sixth-grade teacher, shocks those left behind, and while Annie and her father move toward healing, they take comfort in a scrapbook created by her mother's class. (Rev: BL 1/1–15/07)

10143 High, Linda O. *Maizie* (4–8). 1995, Holiday $14.95 (978-0-8234-1161-0). Maizie, a survivor, succeeds in spite of being abandoned by her mother and left with an alcoholic father. (Rev: BCCB 4/95; BL 4/15/95; HB 5–6/95; SLJ 4/95)

10144 Hirahara, Naomi. *1001 Cranes* (4–7). 2008, Delacorte $15.99 (978-0-385-73556-8). Twelve-year-old Angela reluctantly spends the summer with her Japanese American grandparents, where she learns to cope with her parents' separation while creating origami for the family business. (Rev: BL 8/08; SLJ 8/08)

10145 Holcomb, Jerry Kimble. *The Chinquapin Tree* (5–9). 1998, Marshall Cavendish $14.95 (978-0-7614-5028-3). Faced with being sent back to their abusive mother, three youngsters head for the wilderness in this survival story set in Oregon. (Rev: BL 5/1/98; HBG 10/98; SLJ 5/98)

10146 Holmes, Elizabeth. *Tracktown Summer* (5–8). 2009, Dutton $16.99 (978-0-525-47946-8). 256pp. Spending summer with his newly separated and remote father, 12-year-old Jake turns to a 14-year-old neighbor called Adrian for company and eventually discovers the reasons for his strange behavior — he is protecting his mentally ill father. (Rev: BCCB 7–8/09; BL 5/15/09; SLJ 7/09; VOYA 8/09)

10147 Honeycutt, Natalie. *Twilight in Grace Falls* (5–9). 1997, Orchard LB $17.99 (978-0-531-33007-4). A moving novel about the closing of a lumber mill that brings unemployment to 11-year-old Dasie Jenson's father. (Rev: BCCB 6/97; BL 3/15/97*; HB 7–8/97; SLJ 5/97; VOYA 8/97)

10148 Hunter, Evan. *Me and Mr. Stenner* (5–8). 1976, HarperCollins $11.95 (978-0-397-31689-2). Abby's attitudes toward her new stepfather gradually change from resentment to love.

10149 Jackson, Alison. *Eggs over Evie* (4–6). Illus. by Tuesday Mourning. 2010, Henry Holt $16.99 (978-0-8050-8294-4). 224pp. Thirteen-year-old Evie starts off the summer reeling from the news that her new stepmother is expecting a baby, but gains confidence and perspective from a cooking class and her handsome class partner. (Rev: BL 12/15/10; LMC 3–4/11; SLJ 1/1/11*)

10150 Johnson, Angela. *Songs of Faith* (5–8). 1998, Orchard LB $16.99 (978-0-531-33023-4). Doreen is a child of divorce who is particularly upset by her younger brother's problems adjusting after their father moves away. (Rev: BCCB 6/98; BL 2/15/98; HBG 10/98; SLJ 3/98; VOYA 6/98)

10151 Johnston, Lindsay Lee. *Soul Moon Soup* (5–7). 2002, Front St $15.95 (978-1-886910-87-4). When homeless Phoebe and her mother hit bottom, Phoebe goes to live with her grandmother and slowly learns to value her own resources in this story told in verse. (Rev: BCCB 2/03; BL 11/15/02; HB 1–2/03; HBG 3/03; SLJ 11/02)

10152 Jones, Traci L. *Silhouetted by the Blue* (5–8). 2011, Farrar $16.99 (978-0-374-36914-9). 208pp. Serena, an African American 7th-grader, must finally ask for help when her father does not recover from his depression after her mother's death. Lexile 720L (Rev: BL 6/1/11; HB 7–8/11; SLJ 8/11*)

10153 Joosse, Barbara M. *Pieces of the Picture* (5–8). 1989, HarperCollins LB $12.89 (978-0-397-32343-2); paper $3.50 (978-0-06-440310-8). Emily is not happy when she and her mother move to Wisconsin after her

father's death to earn a livelihood running an inn. (Rev: BL 6/1/89; SLJ 4/89)

10154 Klise, Kate. *Deliver Us from Normal* (5–8). 2005, Scholastic $16.95 (978-0-439-52322-6). Charles Harrisong, 11, is embarrassed by his abnormal family life in Normal, Illinois, and horrified when his parents decide to move them all to a houseboat off the Alabama coast. (Rev: BL 3/1/05; SLJ 5/05)

10155 LaFleur, Suzanne. *Love, Aubrey* (4–7). 2009, Random House $15.99 (978-038573774-6); LB $18.99 (978-038590686-9). 272pp. When her mother disappears after her father and sister die in a car accident, 11-year-old Aubrey struggles to cope. ☊ (Rev: BL 8/09*; SLJ 9/09)

10156 Leal, Ann Haywood. *Also Known as Harper* (4–6). 2009, Holt $16.95 (978-0-8050-8881-6). 256pp. Harper has problems — her alcoholic father has left the family, her mother is struggling to make ends meet, and they face eviction — but the poems she writes and some new friends help her to cope. (Rev: BL 3/1/09; SLJ 6/09)

10157 Lewis, Beverly. *Whispers Down the Lane* (5–8). Series: Summerhill Secrets. 1995, Bethany House paper $5.99 (978-1-55661-476-7). An Amish girl agrees to hide Lissa, who has run away from her father's abusive treatment. (Rev: BL 9/1/95; SLJ 2/96)

10158 Little, Kimberley Griffiths. *Circle of Secrets* (4–6). 2011, Scholastic $17.99 (978-0-545-16561-7). 336pp. Shelby, 11, goes to live in the Louisiana bayou with her estranged mother and together they try to resolve conflicts in this story with a mysterious ghost angle. (Rev: BL 12/1/11; SLJ 12/1/11*)

10159 Love, D. Anne. *Semiprecious* (4–6). 2006, Simon & Schuster $16.95 (978-0-689-85638-9). 304pp. Garnet and her sister Opal are left at an aunt's house in small-town Oklahoma while their mother goes off in pursuit of stardom in this novel set in the 1960s. (Rev: BL 7/06; SLJ 9/06)

10160 Luger, Harriett. *Bye, Bye, Bali Kai* (5–7). 1996, Harcourt paper $5.00 (978-0-15-200863-5). Suzie's family hits rock bottom when they are evicted and forced to live in an abandoned building. (Rev: BCCB 3/96; BL 6/1–15/96; SLJ 6/96; VOYA 6/96)

10161 Lupica, Mike. *Hot Hand* (4–6). Series: Comeback Kids. 2007, Philomel $9.99 (978-0-399-24714-9). 165pp. Ten-year-old Billy and his younger brother Ben have a lot to cope with: their parents' separation, their mother's frequent absence, Billy's friction with his father — a demanding basketball coach, and Ben's unappreciated passion for the piano. (Rev: SLJ 10/07)

10162 Lurie, April. *Dancing in the Streets of Brooklyn* (5–9). 2002, Delacorte LB $17.99 (978-0-385-90066-9). Judy, from a Norwegian immigrant family, is devastated to learn that the man she knows as "Pa" is not her birth father in this novel set in 1944. (Rev: BCCB 12/02; BL 11/15/02; HBG 3/03; SLJ 9/02)

10163 McKay, Hilary. *Caddy's World* (4–7). 2012, Simon & Schuster $16.99 (978-144244105-7). 272pp. In this prequel to the series about the Casson family, 12-year-old Caddy is thrown for a loop when her newest sibling,

Rose, is born prematurely and her mother decamps for the hospital, leaving her father to look after the family. **e** Lexile 770L (Rev: BL 5/1/12*; HB 3–4/12; SLJ 3/12*; VOYA 2/12)

10164 McKinnon, Hannah Roberts. *Franny Parker* (5–8). 2009, Farrar $16.00 (978-0-374-32469-8). 160pp. Animal-loving Franny, 12, has been expecting another long hot Oklahoma summer with the usual activities, but then a boy and his mother move in next door and she learns about a different kind of life. (Rev: BCCB 9/09; BL 4/1/09; SLJ 7/09*)

10165 MacLachlan, Patricia. *Edward's Eyes* (3–5). 2007, Atheneum $15.99 (978-1-4169-2743-3). 128pp. When Jake's beloved brother, Edward, dies in an accident, their parents donate Edward's eyes and organs to other children. (Rev: BL 9/1/07; SLJ 10/07)

10166 Marino, Jan. *For the Love of Pete* (5–8). 1994, Avon paper $3.50 (978-0-380-72281-5). Three devoted servants take Phoebe on a journey to find the father she has never met. (Rev: BCCB 7–8/93; BL 6/1–15/93; SLJ 5/93*)

10167 Martin, Patricia A. *Travels with Rainie Marie* (5–7). 1997, Hyperion LB $16.49 (978-0-7868-2212-6). When there is no one to care for her and her five brothers and sisters, Rainie Marie is afraid that her bossy aunt will try to split up the family among various relatives. (Rev: BL 5/15/97; SLJ 7/97)

10168 Martine, Carmela A. *Rosa, Sola* (4–6). 2005, Candlewick $15.99 (978-0-7636-2395-1). Rosa is bereft when the baby brother she's dreamed about is stillborn. (Rev: BCCB 1/06; BL 12/1/05*; HBG 4/06; LMC 11/05; SLJ 10/05)

10169 Mason, Simon. *Moon Pie* (5–8). 2011, Random House $16.99 (978-038575235-0); LB $19.99 (978-038575237-4). 336pp. Martha, 11, looks after her little brother Tug after her mother's death as her father struggles with his drinking. **e** (Rev: BL 11/15/11; HB 11–12/11)

10170 Mazer, Norma Fox. *What I Believe* (5–8). 2005, Harcourt $16.00 (978-0-15-201462-9). When Vicki's father loses his job and the family's fortunes go into free fall, Vicki finds the resulting changes hard to accept and reveals in her poems and journal her coping strategies. (Rev: BL 9/15/05; SLJ 10/05)

10171 Mead, Alice. *Junebug in Trouble* (5–8). 2002, Farrar $16.00 (978-0-374-33969-2). Young Junebug and his mother move out of the housing projects, but Junebug continues to get into the trouble his mother was hoping to avoid. (Rev: BCCB 6/02; BL 4/15/02; HB 5–6/02; HBG 10/02; SLJ 3/02)

10172 Mead, Alice. *Madame Squidley and Beanie* (4–7). 2004, Farrar $16.00 (978-0-374-34688-1). Ten-year-old Beanie's mother has chronic fatigue syndrome and her illness is affecting the 5th-grader's life. (Rev: BL 4/15/04; SLJ 6/04)

10173 Monthei, Betty. *Looking for Normal* (5–8). 2005, HarperCollins LB $16.89 (978-0-06-072506-8). Annie, 12, and her younger brother are sent to live with their

grandparents after their father kills their mother and then himself; unfortunately, life does not improve as they must cope with Grandma's drinking and abuse and Grandpa's indifference. (Rev: BL 6/1–15/05; SLJ 4/05)

10174 Nelson, Theresa. *Earthshine* (5–9). 1994, Orchard LB $17.99 (978-0-531-08717-6). "Slim" decides to live with her father and his lover, who is dying of AIDS. At a support group, she meets Isaiah, whose pregnant mother also has AIDS. (Rev: BL 9/1/94; SLJ 9/94*; VOYA 10/94)

10175 Nelson, Theresa. *Ruby Electric* (5–8). 2003, Simon & Schuster $16.95 (978-0-689-83852-1). The movie script she is writing brings 12-year-old Ruby needed relief from the realities of her life. (Rev: BL 7/03; HB 7–8/03; HBG 10/03; SLJ 6/03*; VOYA 10/03)

10176 Newman, John. *Mimi* (4–7). 2011, Candlewick $15.99 (978-0-7636-5415-3). 192pp. Mimi's mother was killed in an accident and everyone in the family — even the dog — is having trouble dealing with this; the fact that Mimi was adopted from China is mentioned in passing. (Rev: BLO 9/1/11; SLJ 9/1/11)

10177 Nicholls, Sally. *Season of Secrets* (5–8). 2011, Scholastic $16.99 (978-0-545-21825-2). 240pp. Sisters Hannah and Molly are sent to live with their grandparents in northern England after their mother's death, and there they cope very differently with their grief, Molly increasingly absorbed in an inner world. **e** Lexile 620L (Rev: BL 12/15/10; HB 1–2/11; LMC 5–6/11; SLJ 2/1/11)

10178 Nielsen, Susin. *The Reluctant Journal of Henry K. Larsen* (5–8). 2012, Tundra $17.95 (978-1-77049372-8). 224pp. Thirteen-year-old Henry is advised by a therapist to keep a journal as he tries to cope with the upheaval in his family after his older brother kills a school bully and then himself. Best Fiction for YA. **e** Lexile 630L (Rev: BLO 9/15/12; SLJ 1/13*; VOYA 12/12)

10179 Nixon, Joan Lowery. *Maggie Forevermore* (5–8). 1987, Harcourt $13.95 (978-0-15-250345-1). In this sequel to *Maggie, Too* and *And Maggie Makes Three* (both o.p.), 13-year-old Maggie resents spending Christmas with her father and his new wife in California. (Rev: BCCB 4/87; BL 3/1/87; SLJ 3/87)

10180 O'Connor, Barbara. *How to Steal a Dog* (4–6). 2007, Farrar $16.00 (978-0-374-33497-0). 176pp. Desperate to restore some sense of order to her life, in tatters since her father left the family, young Georgina decides to steal a dog and collect a reward. (Rev: BL 3/15/07)

10181 O'Connor, Sheila. *Sparrow Road* (5–8). 2011, Putnam $16.99 (978-0-399-25458-1). 247pp. Raine, 12, ends up meeting her estranged father when she accompanies her mother to a remote artists' retreat for the summer. **e** Lexile 530L (Rev: BL 7/11*; LMC 10/11; SLJ 7/11)

10182 Olson, Gretchen. *Call Me Hope* (4–7). 2007, Little, Brown $15.99 (978-0-316-01236-2). Beaten down by her mother's verbal abuse, 11-year-old Hope screws up the courage to confront her mother and tell her how badly she has been hurt by the name calling. (Rev: BL 3/15/07; SLJ 5/07)

10183 Paratore, Coleen Murtagh. *Sunny Holiday* (3–6). 2009, Scholastic $15.99 (978-0-545-07579-4). Fourth-grader Sunny, who misses her imprisoned father and worries about her always-busy mother, is nevertheless a great optimist and invents one holiday a month to brighten her difficult life. (Rev: BL 1/1–15/09; SLJ 2/09)

10184 Parkinson, Siobhan. *Blue like Friday* (4–7). 2008, Roaring Brook $16.95 (978-1-59643-340-3). In Ireland, tweens Olivia and Hal are unlikely friends but Olivia helps Hal to accept his mother's fiancé. (Rev: BL 3/1/08; SLJ 6/08)

10185 Paterson, Katherine. *Park's Quest* (4–7). 1989, Puffin paper $5.99 (978-0-14-034262-8). A boy search-es for the cause of his father's death in Vietnam. (Rev: BCCB 4/88; HB 7–8/88; SLJ 5/88)

10186 Paterson, Katherine. *The Same Stuff as Stars* (5–7). 2002, Clarion $15.00 (978-0-618-24744-8). An unhappy 11-year-old Angel and her younger brother Bernie are sent to live with their father's grandmother, where An-gel finds comfort in a mysterious man who introduces her to astronomy. (Rev: BCCB 10/02; BL 9/15/02; HB 9–10/02; HBG 3/03; SLJ 8/02*)

10187 Pfeffer, Susan Beth. *Devil's Den* (4–7). 1998, Walker $15.95 (978-0-8027-8650-0). Joey faces the pain of rejection when he seeks out his real father, discovers he is not wanted by him, and must accept living perma-nently with his mom and loving stepfather. (Rev: BCCB 5/98; BL 5/15/98; HBG 10/98; SLJ 6/98)

10188 Porter, Pamela. *Sky* (3–5). Illus. by Mary Jane Gerber. 2004, Groundwood $15.95 (978-0-88899-566-7). 83pp. Georgia, an 11-year-old Native American girl, finds comfort in a foal named Sky after a series of trau-mas including the deaths of her parents, a narrow escape from a burst dam, and an uncomfortable stay in a shelter where she and her grandparents experience prejudice. (Rev: BCCB 12/04; HB 1/05; SLJ 4/05)

10189 Rinn, Miriam. *The Saturday Secret* (4–7). 1998, Alef Design Group paper $7.95 (978-1-881283-26-3). Jason's resentment and anger at having to obey the strict rules imposed by his devout Orthodox Jewish stepfather are made more intense because of his grief at the death of his beloved father. (Rev: BL 10/1/98; SLJ 2/99)

10190 Russo, Marisabina. *A Portrait of Pia* (5–8). 2007, Harcourt $17.00 (978-0-15-205577-6). Overwhelmed by her brother's schizophrenia and her mother's new boyfriend, 12-year-old Pia, already a talented artist, trav-els to Italy to meet her long-absent father and learns how to love her family despite its flaws. (Rev: BL 4/1/07; SLJ 8/07)

10191 Seagraves, Donny Bailey. *Gone from These Woods* (4–7). 2009, Delacorte $15.99 (978-0-385-73629-9). 192pp. With help from a school counselor, Daniel — whose father is an abusive alcoholic — tries to come to terms with the hunting accident in which he shot and killed his beloved uncle. (Rev: BCCB 9/09; BLO 5/27/09; SLJ 9/09)

10192 Shafer, Audrey. *The Mailbox* (5–7). 2006, Dela-corte $15.95 (978-0-385-73344-1). Twelve-year-old Gabe, who has been happy with Uncle Vernon after years in foster care, is shocked when he comes home to find Uncle Vernon dead. ⌒ (Rev: SLJ 11/06)

10193 Sheinmel, Courtney. *All the Things You Are* (5–8). Series: Stella Batts. 2011, Simon & Schuster $15.99 (978-1-4169-9717-7). 256pp. Twelve-year-old Carly's mother is arrested for embezzling, and this has an im-pact on the whole family, particularly affecting Carly's school life. Also use the 5th book in the series: *Who's in Charge* (2013). (Rev: BLO 6/21/11; SLJ 7/11)

10194 Sheinmel, Courtney. *My So-Called Family* (5–8). 2008, Simon & Schuster $15.99 (978-1-4169-5785-0). 194pp. Thirteen-year-old Leah sets out to discover her father — an anonymous sperm donor — and her four recently revealed half-siblings, one of whom is about her age. (Rev: BCCB 10/08; BL 11/15/08; SLJ 12/08)

10195 Sherrard, Valerie. *Tumbleweed Skies* (3–6). 2010, Fitzhenry & Whiteside paper $11.95 (978-15545511-3-2). 153pp. In the summer of 1954, 10-year-old Ellie must go to live with her cold and distant grandmother in Saskatchewan while her salesman father hits the road. (Rev: BL 5/15/10*; LMC 11–12/10; SLJ 3/1/11*)

10196 Shyer, Marlene Fanta. *Fleabiscuit Sings!* (3–6). 2005, Marshall Cavendish $15.95 (978-0-7614-5213-3). 150pp. Twelve-year-old Nicky discovers that Fleabis-cuit, the dog he walks for Mr. Muffin, can sing and adds the pooch to his family's subway performances. (Rev: BCCB 5/05; HB 8–9/05; SLJ 5/05)

10197 Slate, Joseph. *Crossing the Trestle* (5–8). 1999, Marshall Cavendish $14.95 (978-0-7614-5053-5). Set in West Virginia in 1944, this novel centers on 11-year-old Petey and the problems he and his family face after their father is killed in an accident. (Rev: BCCB 12/99; BL 1/1–15/00; HBG 3/00; SLJ 10/99)

10198 Snyder, Laurel. *Bigger Than a Bread Box* (5–8). 2011, Random House $16.99 (978-0-375-86916-7); LB $19.99 (978-0-375-96916-4). 240pp. Twelve-year-old Rebecca turns to a magical bread box for help in put-ting her fractured family back together. ⌒ ℮ Lexile 680L (Rev: BL 10/1/11; SLJ 9/1/11)

10199 Stacey, Cherylyn. *How Do You Spell Abducted?* (4–8). 1996, Red Deer paper $7.95 (978-0-88995-148-8). When their divorced father abducts Deb, Paige, and Cory, the three youngsters must escape from his home in the U.S. and make their way back to their mother in Canada. (Rev: SLJ 12/96)

10200 Stauffacher, Sue. *Harry Sue* (5–8). 2005, Knopf LB $17.99 (978-0-375-93274-8). Both her parents are in prison and 11-year-old Harry Sue Clotkin acts as tough as she can in the face of a difficult life with her grand-mother. (Rev: BL 5/1/05; SLJ 8/05)

10201 Strauss, Linda Leopold. *Really, Truly, Every-thing's Fine* (5–8). 2004, Marshall Cavendish $15.95 (978-0-7614-5163-1). Life changes dramatically for 14-year-old Jill Rider when her father is arrested for jewelry theft. (Rev: BL 5/15/04; SLJ 7/04)

10202 Talbert, Marc. *The Purple Heart* (5–8). 1992, HarperCollins $14.95 (978-0-06-020428-0); paper $3.50 (978-0-380-71985-3). Luke's father has returned from Vietnam an anguished, brooding war hero, and Luke loses his father's Purple Heart, leading to confrontation and reconciliation. (Rev: BL 12/15/91*; SLJ 2/92)

10203 Thomson, John. *A Small Boat at the Bottom of the Sea* (5–7). 2005, Milkweed $16.95 (978-1-57131-657-8); paper $6.95 (978-1-57131-656-1). Upset and angry when he's sent to spend the summer with his ex-con uncle and dying aunt on Puget Sound, 12-year-old Donovan begins to develop a closer relationship with his uncle as his vacation progresses. (Rev: SLJ 10/05; VOYA 4/06)

10204 Trueit, Trudi. *Julep O'Toole: Miss Independent* (4–6). Illus. 2006, Dutton $15.99 (978-0-525-47637-5). 160pp. Eleven-year-old Julep and her mother have differing views on Julep's abilities to make her own decisions; a sequel to *Julep O'Toole: Confessions of a Middle Child* (2005). (Rev: BL 4/15/06; SLJ 3/06)

10205 Viglucci, Patricia C. *Sun Dance at Turtle Rock* (5–7). 1996, Patri paper $4.95 (978-0-9645914-9-3). The child of a racially mixed marriage feels uncomfortable when he visits his white grandfather. (Rev: BL 4/15/96)

10206 Villareal, Ray. *My Father, the Angel of Death* (5–8). 2006, Piñata paper $9.95 (978-1-55885-466-6). Newly relocated to Texas and unhappy with his home life, Jesse Baron wonders what life would be like if his dad were not the well-known wrestler called the Angel of Death; suitable for reluctant readers. (Rev: SLJ 10/06)

10207 Walker, Pamela. *Pray Hard* (5–8). 2001, Scholastic paper $15.95 (978-0-439-21586-2). After Amelia Forest's father dies in an airplane accident for which she feels responsible, her life and that of her family fall apart. ⌂ (Rev: BL 3/1/01; HBG 10/01; SLJ 7/01; VOYA 8/01)

10208 Wallace, Bill. *True Friends* (4–7). 1994, Holiday $15.95 (978-0-8234-1141-2). Everything in Courtney's life becomes a shambles and she must rely on her new friend Judy to help her. (Rev: BCCB 11/94; BL 10/15/94; SLJ 10/94)

10209 Watson, Renée. *What Momma Left Me* (5–8). 2010, Bloomsbury $16.99 (978-1-59990-446-7). 240pp. African American Serenity, 13, tells how she and her brother cope when they go to live with their grandparents after their mother dies and their father disappears. (Rev: BL 5/1/10; LMC 10/10; SLJ 8/10; VOYA 8/10)

10210 Weeks, Sarah. *Jumping the Scratch* (4–6). 2006, HarperCollins $15.99 (978-0-06-054109-5). 176pp. Burdened with a dark secret and in shock after some radical changes in his home life, Jamie Reardon focuses his attention on helping his recently injured aunt to recover her short-term memory. (Rev: BL 2/1/06; SLJ 5/06) ⌂

10211 Wenberg, Michael. *Seattle Blues* (5–8). 2009, WestSide $16.95 (978-1-934813-04-1). When unhappy 13-year-old Maya, spending a reluctant summer with her grandmother in Seattle, finds a musical instrument hidden in the attic she also finds the key to growing into a happier person. (Rev: BLO 1/14/09; SLJ 7/09)

10212 Wilson, Jacqueline. *Cookie* (4–7). Illus. by Nick Sharratt. 2009, Roaring Brook $16.99 (978-1-59643-534-6). 336pp. Beauty Cookson and her mother flee the abusive, boorish yet wealthy Mr. Cookson and start a new life of their own in this endearing tale of redemption. ⌂ Lexile 680L (Rev: BL 9/1/09; LMC 11–12/09; SLJ 10/09)

10213 Woodson, Jacqueline. *Hush* (5–9). 2002, Putnam $15.99 (978-0-399-23114-8). A girl and her family are relocated in the witness protection program after her father, a police officer, testifies against fellow cops in a case that involves racial prejudice. (Rev: BCCB 3/02; BL 1/1–15/02; HB 1–2/02; HBG 10/02; SLJ 2/02*; VOYA 2/02)

10214 Woodworth, Chris. *When Ratboy Lived Next Door* (4–8). 2005, Farrar $16.00 (978-0-374-34677-5). Twelve-year-old Lydia takes an instant dislike to her new neighbor Willis and his pet raccoon, but as she gains a better understanding of the family dynamics that make the boy who he is, she also gains valuable insights into her strained relationship with her mother. (Rev: BCCB 2/05; BL 1/1–15/05; SLJ 3/05)

10215 Zimmer, Tracie Vaughn. *42 Miles* (4–6). Illus. by Elaine Clayton. 2008, Clarion $16.00 (978-0-618-61867-5). 80pp. Nearly 13, JoEllen seeks to integrate the two halves of her life — her weekday life in the city with her mother, who calls her Ellen, and her weekends in the country with her father, who calls her Joey. (Rev: BCCB 6/08; BL 4/1/08; SLJ 4/08)

10216 Zimmer, Tracie Vaughn. *Sketches from a Spy Tree* (3–5). Illus. by Andrew Glass. 2005, Clarion $16.00 (978-0-618-23479-0). 64pp. In a series of poems, a young girl with an identical twin who doesn't always share her views recounts her family's attempts to regain its footing after a devastating divorce. (Rev: BL 8/05; SLJ 8/05)

Personal Problems

10217 Adler, C. S. *Willie, the Frog Prince* (4–7). 1994, Clarion $15.00 (978-0-395-65615-0). Willie's inability to accept responsibility almost causes the loss of his dog, Booboo. (Rev: BL 4/15/94; SLJ 6/94)

10218 Airgood, Ellen. *Prairie Evers* (4–7). 2012, Penguin $15.99 (978-0-399-25691-2). 224pp. Plucky Prairie, 10, has a lot to adjust to: a move to farm life in New York state, the departure of her grandmother, attending school for the first time, and trying to share her family with a troubled classmate. ℮ Lexile 790 (Rev: BL 8/12; LMC 1–2/13; SLJ 9/12) [796.522095496]

10219 Allen, Crystal. *How Lamar's Bad Prank Won a Bubba-Sized Trophy* (5–8). 2011, HarperCollins $16.99 (978-0-06-199272-8). 288pp. Bowling is an important anchor in the difficult life of 13-year-old African American Lamar, but it threatens to undercut his best efforts in this humorous novel about young teen love and emotions. 🎧 **e** Lexile 550L (Rev: BL 3/1/11; SLJ 2/1/11; VOYA 4/11)

10220 Amato, Mary. *Invisible Lines* (5–8). Illus. by Antonio Caparo. 2009, Egmont $15.99 (978-1-60684-010-8); LB $18.99 (978-1-60684-043-6). 336pp. Soccer and science are safe havens for 7th-grader Trevor, who lives in a grim housing project but attends a school for the privileged and has trouble fitting in. Lexile 650L (Rev: BL 11/1/09; SLJ 11/09)

10221 Atkinson, Elizabeth. *From Alice to Zen and Everyone in Between* (5–7). 2008, Carolrhoda $16.95 (978-0-8225-7271-8). Alice moves to a new suburb with her dad and quickly becomes friends with Zen, but when school starts she realizes he's part of the wrong crowd. (Rev: BL 5/1/08; SLJ 9/08)

10222 Auch, Mary Jane. *Seven Long Years Until College* (4–7). 1991, Holiday $13.95 (978-0-8234-0901-3). Natalie runs away from home to join her older sister at college. (Rev: BCCB 1/92; SLJ 10/91)

10223 Axelrod, Amy. *Your Friend in Fashion, Abby Shapiro* (5–7). Illus. by author. 2011, Holiday House $17.95 (978-0-8234-2340-8). 256pp. In 1959, 11-year-old Abby has a hard time making the transition from girlhood to womanhood, and leans on her close-knit Jewish extended family for support and guidance while sharing her problems in letters to Jackie Kennedy. Lexile 710L (Rev: BL 4/15/11; SLJ 4/11)

10224 Bagert, Brod. *Hormone Jungle: Coming of Age in Middle School* (5–8). 2006, Maupin House $23.95 (978-0-929895-87-1). The scrapbook of Christina Curtis's middle-school years tells the story of the poetry war that erupted in sixth grade and of the changing relationships between the young people as they learned more about each other. (Rev: SLJ 6/06)

10225 Banks, Kate. *Lenny's Space* (4–6). 2007, Farrar $16.00 (978-0-374-34575-4). Lenny, a very smart but uncontrolled 9-year-old, learns about friendship and managing his emotions when he makes friends with a boy who has leukemia. (Rev: BCCB 11/07; BL 10/1/07; HB 1/08; SLJ 11/07)

10226 Barnholdt, Lauren. *The Secret Identity of Devon Delaney* (4–7). 2007, Aladdin Mix paper $5.99 (978-1-4169-3503-2). The lies that Devon tells while spending the summer at her grandmother's house come back to bite her when her new friend Lexi moves to Devon's town and attends Devon's middle school. (Rev: BL 8/07; SLJ 8/07)

10227 Bartek, Mary. *Funerals and Fly Fishing* (4–7). 2004, Henry Holt $16.95 (978-0-8050-7409-3). A visit to the grandfather he has never met gives Brad Stanislawski new confidence to deal with the classmates at his new school. (Rev: SLJ 8/04)

10228 Baskin, Nora Raleigh. *Anything But Typical* (4–7). 2009, Simon & Schuster $15.99 (978-1-4169-6378-3). 208pp. This deftly told story centers on Jason, an autistic 6th-grader who can create dynamic stories and relationships on paper but is painfully at a loss in social situ-

ations. ALA Notable Children's Book. 🎧 (Rev: BCCB 4/09; BL 2/1/09; HB 5/09; SLJ 3/09)

10229 Baskin, Nora Raleigh. *Runt* (5–7). 2013, Simon & Schuster $15.99 (978-144245807-9). 200pp. Middle-school bullying is the focus of this novel told from various perspectives. (Rev: BL 7/13; SLJ 8/13)

10230 Bauer, A. C. E. *No Castles Here* (4–7). 2007, Random House $15.99 (978-0-375-83921-4). A magical book, a Big Brother, and a school chorus rescue 11-year-old Augie Boretski from feeling completely lost in his life of poverty and loneliness in Camden, New Jersey. (Rev: BL 12/1/07; SLJ 10/07)

10231 Bauer, Joan. *Close to Famous* (5–8). 2011, Viking $16.99 (978-0-670-01282-4). 256pp. Slow learner and talented baker Foster, 12, and her mother flee her mother's abusive boyfriend to start a new life in West Virginia, where she learns to read and gets the chance to market her baked goods. YALSA Best Fiction for Young Adults 2012. **e** Lexile 540L (Rev: BL 1/1–15/11; HB 1–2/11; LMC 5–6/11; SLJ 3/1/11)

10232 Benjamin, Carol Lea. *The Wicked Stepdog* (4–7). Illus. by author. 1982, Avon paper $2.50 (978-0-380-70089-9). Louise is in the midst of puberty problems and her father's remarriage.

10233 Betancourt, Jeanne. *Kate's Turn* (5–8). 1992, Scholastic $13.95 (978-0-590-43103-3). This story of the young ballerina Kate, who decides the price of fame is too high, shows the grueling, often painful life of a dancer. (Rev: BL 1/1/92; SLJ 2/92)

10234 Bial, Raymond. *Chigger* (4–6). 2012, Motes paper $14 (978-19348943-8-5). 220pp. In the late 1950s straight-laced Luke's family learns to open up and trust rebellious girl Chigger when confronted with evidence of the girl's emotional needs. (Rev: BLO 3/15/12; SLJ 8/12)

10235 Block, Francesca Lia. *House of Dolls* (3–6). Illus. by Barbara McClintock. 2010, HarperCollins $15.99 (978-0-06-113094-6); LB $22.47 (978-0-06-113095-3). 80pp. Emotionally neglected Madison takes her frustration out on her dolls, sending the boys off to "war" and depriving the girls of their beautiful dresses until her grandmother comes to the rescue; gorgeous, detailed illustrations enhance the story. (Rev: BL 3/15/10*; HB 7–8/10; SLJ 6/10)

10236 Blume, Judy. *Then Again, Maybe I Won't* (5–8). 1971, Dell paper $4.99 (978-0-440-48659-6). Thirteen-year-old Tony faces many problems when his family relocates to suburban Long Island.

10237 Boelts, Maribeth. *The PS Brothers* (4–6). 2010, Harcourt $15 (978-0-547-34249-8). 144pp. Friends Russell and Shawn long to have a dog to protect them from bullies and their efforts to raise money lead them to discover an illegal dog-fighting ring. **e** Lexile 810L (Rev: BL 12/15/10; SLJ 11/1/10)

10238 Bradley, Kimberly Brubaker. *Leap of Faith* (4–7). 2007, Dial $16.99 (978-0-8037-3127-1). Abigail finds herself attracted to the new ideas she's learning at the Catholic school where she ended up after being expelled from public school. (Rev: BCCB 9/07; BL 7/07; SLJ 8/07)

10239 Bulion, Leslie. *Uncharted Waters* (4–8). 2006, Peachtree $14.95 (978-1-56145-365-8). Jonah's summer of self-discovery following a dismal school year includes a heroic rescue at sea and excelling at his true talent. (Rev: SLJ 6/06)

10240 Bunting, Eve. *Doll Baby* (5–10). Illus. by Catherine Stock. 2000, Clarion $15.00 (978-0-395-93094-6). A simple, direct narrative in which 15-year-old Ellie explains how being pregnant and having a baby radically changed her life. (Rev: BL 11/1/00; HB 9–10/00; HBG 3/01; SLJ 10/00)

10241 Burch, Robert. *Queenie Peavy* (5–7). 1987, Penguin paper $5.99 (978-0-14-032305-4). Queenie, whose father is in prison, is growing up a defiant, disobedient girl in rural Georgia in the 1930s.

10242 Burg, Shana. *Laugh with the Moon* (4–7). 2012, Delacorte $16.99 (978-038573471-4); LB $19.99 (978-038590469-8). 256pp. Clare, 13, is still grieving for her mother when her doctor father takes her to Malawi, where he works in a hospital; there Clare contends with everyday hardships but finds friendship and comfort. **e** Lexile 740 (Rev: BL 6/12; LMC 10/12; SLJ 6/12)

10243 Caldwell, V. M. *The Ocean Within* (5–7). 1999, Milkweed paper $6.95 (978-1-57131-624-0). Elizabeth, who is on her third set of foster parents since she was orphaned five years before, has built walls of silence around herself that are impossible to penetrate. (Rev: BCCB 1/00; BL 9/1/99; HBG 3/00; SLJ 11/99; VOYA 4/00)

10244 Caldwell, V. M. *Runt* (5–7). 2006, Milkweed $16.95 (978-1-57131-662-2); paper $6.95 (978-1-57131-661-5). Runt, a 13-year-old who is trying to cope with his mother's death and his new living arrangements, becomes close to Mitch, who is dying of cancer. (Rev: SLJ 7/06)

10245 Cameron, Ann. *Colibri* (5–8). 2003, Farrar $17.00 (978-0-374-31519-1). Twelve-year-old Rosa, who was kidnapped from her Mayan village when she was four, seeks to escape from the abusive "uncle" who is exploiting her. (Rev: BCCB 10/03; BL 10/1/03*; HB 9–10/03; HBG 4/04; SLJ 10/03*)

10246 Cameron, Ann. *Gloria's Way* (2–4). 2000, Farrar $15.00 (978-0-374-32670-8). 112pp. In this easy chapter book, readers meet African American Gloria and, in six short episodes, learn about her problems with friendships and family. (Rev: BCCB 2/00; BL 2/15/00; HB 3/00; HBG 10/00; SLJ 3/00)

10247 Caseley, Judith. *Praying to A. L.* (5–8). 2000, Greenwillow $15.95 (978-0-688-15934-4). After her father dies, 12-year-old Sierra transfers all her love to a portrait of Abraham Lincoln given to her by her father. (Rev: BL 5/15/00; HBG 10/00; SLJ 6/00)

10248 Cavanaugh, Nancy J. *This Journal Belongs to Ratchet* (4–7). 2013, Sourcebooks/Jabberwocky $12.99 (978-140228106-8). 320pp. The eclectic journal of Rachel "Rachet" — 11 years old and being home-schooled

by her eco-friendly father — reveals her efforts to learn more about her dead mother, to make friends, and to be normal. Lexile 830 (Rev: BLO 4/1/13; LMC 8–9/13)

10249 Cervantes, Angela. *Gaby, Lost and Found* (4–7). 2013, Scholastic $16.99 (978-054548945-4). 224pp. When Gaby's mother is deported to Honduras, the undocumented 6th-grader finds comfort in her work at the local animal shelter. **e** Lexile 640 (Rev: BLO 8/13; LMC 1–2/14*; SLJ 8/13)

10250 Cleary, Beverly. *Dear Mr. Henshaw* (4–7). Illus. by Paul O. Zelinsky. 1983, Morrow LB $16.89 (978-0-688-02406-2). A Newbery Medal winner (1984) about a boy who pours out his problems in letters to a writer he greatly admires.

10251 Clements, Andrew. *The Jacket* (3–6). Illus. by Dan Gonzalez. 2002, Simon & Schuster $12.95 (978-0-689-82595-8). 80pp. This story about a sixth-grade boy examining race relations and facing his own prejudices is sure to prompt discussion. (Rev: BCCB 3/02; BL 3/1/02; HBG 10/02; SLJ 3/02)

10252 Clements, Andrew. *Troublemaker* (5–8). Illus. by Mark Elliott. 2011, Atheneum $16.99 (978-1-4169-4930-5). 160pp. When his older brother Mitchell gets out of jail a changed character, 6th-grader Clay also decides to reform, but finds it harder than expected. ⌒ Lexile 730L (Rev: BL 6/1/11; HB 7–8/11; LMC 1–2/12; SLJ 7/11)

10253 Collard, Sneed B, III. *Dog Sense* (5–8). 2005, Peachtree $14.95 (978-1-56145-351-1). Unhappy after moving from sunny California to a small town in Montana, 13-year-old Guy Martinez finds solace in time spent with his dog, Streak, and a newfound friend named Luke. (Rev: BL 10/15/05; SLJ 11/05)

10254 Comerford, Lynda B. *Rissa Bartholomew's Declaration of Independence* (3–7). 2009, Scholastic $16.99 (978-0-545-05058-6). 320pp. Everything seems to be different as 6th grade starts, and Clarissa copes (with wry humor) with changes at school and at home. (Rev: BCCB 6/09; BL 5/15/09; SLJ 6/09)

10255 Conford, Ellen. *Hail, Hail Camp Timberwood* (5–7). Illus. by Gail Owens. 1978, Little, Brown $14.95 (978-0-316-15291-4). Thirteen-year-old Melanie's first summer at camp.

10256 Conly, Jane Leslie. *Crazy Lady!* (5–8). 1993, HarperCollins LB $18.89 (978-0-06-021360-2). In a city slum, Vernon forms a friendship with an eccentric woman and helps her care for her disabled teenage son. Newbery Honor 1994; ALA Notable Children's Books 1994; ALA Best Books for Young Adults 1994. (Rev: BCCB 7–8/93; BL 5/15/93*; SLJ 4/93*)

10257 Conway, Celeste. *The Goodbye Time* (4–6). 2008, Delacorte $15.99 (978-0-385-73555-1). Fifth-grader Anna struggles to cope with her brother's departure for college, problems with her best friend Katy, and her own insecurities. (Rev: BCCB 1/09; LMC 3/09; SLJ 2/09)

10258 Cooper, Ilene. *Look at Lucy!* (2–4). Illus. by David Merrell. 2009, Random House LB $11.99 (978-0-375-95558-7); paper $4.99 (978-0-375-85558-0). 112pp.

Bobby enters his beagle, Lucy, in a pet shop "spokespet" contest even though he must overcome his fear of public speaking in order to do so. (Rev: SLJ 10/1/09)

10259 Corriveau, Art. *How I, Nicky Flynn, Finally Get a Life (and a Dog)* (4–7). 2010, Abrams $16.95 (978-081098298-7). 272pp. The gift of a former seeing-eye dog coaxes depressed 11-year-old Nicky Flynn to meet people and explore his new Boston neighborhood. Lexile 670L (Rev: BL 3/1/10; LMC 11–12/10; SLJ 5/10)

10260 Cox, Judy. *Mean, Mean Maureen Green* (2–5). Illus. 1999, Holiday House $15.95 (978-0-8234-1502-1). Lilley is a fearful person who dreads going to school because of a mean neighborhood dog, a school bully, and her new bike without training wheels. (Rev: BCCB 2/00; BL 12/1/99; HBG 10/00; SLJ 3/00)

10261 Crossan, Sarah. *The Weight of Water* (5–8). 2013, Bloomsbury $15.99 (978-159990967-7). 240pp. Searching for her father, Kasienka and her mother travel from Poland to the United Kingdom, where the 12-year-old has many adjustments to make and challenges to face; a love of swimming and the promise of romance bring some comfort. (Rev: BL 7/13; HB 7–8/13; LMC 10/13*; SLJ 6/13)

10262 Crowe, Carole. *Groover's Heart* (4–6). 2001, Boyds Mills $15.95 (978-1-56397-953-8). 144pp. Orphan Charlotte, age 11, has trouble adjusting to the ways of her guardian, wealthy Aunt Viola. (Rev: BL 4/15/01; HBG 10/01; SLJ 4/01)

10263 Curtis, Christopher Paul. *Bud, Not Buddy* (4–6). 1999, Delacorte $15.95 (978-0-385-32306-2). 272pp. In this Newbery Medal winner set in Michigan during the Great Depression, 10-year-old Bud, on the run from his orphanage and his latest foster parents, is determined to find his father. (Rev: BCCB 11/99; BL 9/1/99; HB 11/99; HBG 3/00; SLJ 9/99)

10264 Curtis, Sandra R. *Gabriel's Ark* (2–5). Illus. 1998, Alef Design Group paper $16.95 (978-1-881283-22-5). 64pp. Gabe, who was born disabled, celebrates his bar mitzvah in his own way, thanks to a supportive family and an understanding rabbi. (Rev: BL 10/1/98; SLJ 1/99)

10265 Davis, Katie. *The Curse of Addy McMahon* (4–6). Illus. 2008, Greenwillow $16.99 (978-0-06-128711-4). Sixth-grader Addy fears she is living under a family curse — her father has died, her mother's boyfriend is moving in, she has upset her best friend — and she describes these calamities in an accessible comic strip/diary "autobiogra-strip." (Rev: BL 7/08; SLJ 7/08)

10266 Day, Karen. *A Million Miles from Boston* (5–8). 2011, Random House $15.99 (978-0-385-73899-6); LB $18.99 (978-0-385-90763-7). 224pp. Lucy, 12, contends with her dad's new girlfriend, the shifting social landscape, and a pesky boy from back home who's popped up at their summer vacation home in Maine. (Rev: BL 3/15/11; LMC 10/11; SLJ 6/11)

10267 de Guzman, Michael. *Finding Stinko* (5–8). 2007, Farrar $16.00 (978-0-374-32305-9). On the run from his latest and worst set of foster parents, Newboy, an elective mute, finds new voice with a ventriloquist's dummy;

a compelling book of survival on the streets. (Rev: BL 4/15/07; SLJ 6/07)

10268 Dee, Barbara. *Just Another Day in My Insanely Real Life* (4–7). 2006, Simon & Schuster $15.95 (978-1-4169-0861-6). Cassie must deal with the fallout from her parents' divorce, with her irresponsible older sister and demanding little brother, and with her former best friends in this novel about an all-too-real situation. (Rev: BL 5/15/06; SLJ 8/06)

10269 Dee, Barbara. *Solving Zoe* (4–7). 2009, Simon & Schuster $15.99 (978-1-4169-6128-4). 240pp. Zoe drifts in a sea of bright students and fading friends until her talent for codes and puzzles unlocks her new direction. (Rev: BCCB 6/09; BL 6/1–15/09; SLJ 6/09)

10270 DeGross, Monalisa. *Donavan's Double Trouble* (2–4). Illus. by Amy Bates. 2008, HarperCollins $15.99 (978-0-06-077293-2). 192pp. Fourth-grader Donavan, last seen in *Donavan's Word Jar* (1994), adjusts to his amputee uncle's disability and overcomes his difficulties at school with the help of his supportive African American family. (Rev: BL 12/15/07; SLJ 4/08)

10271 DeKeyser, Stacy. *Jump the Cracks* (5–8). 2008, Flux paper $9.95 (978-0-7387-1274-1). Victoria, 15, sees a little boy being mistreated at a train station and ends up taking him to Georgia — an originally compassionate act that she soon finds will have huge complications. (Rev: BL 3/1/08; SLJ 9/08)

10272 Deriso, Christine Hurley. *Do-Over* (5–8). 2006, Delacorte LB $17.99 (978-0-385-90350-9). Between the recent death of her mother and the move to a new school, 7th-grader Elsa is having a hard time of it, but things look up when her mother mysteriously appears one night and grants her do-over power. (Rev: SLJ 8/06)

10273 Deriso, Christine Hurley. *Talia Talk* (4–6). 2008, Delacorte $15.99 (978-0-385-73620-6). 192pp. Eleven-year-old Talia is coping with friendship problems and her mother's new romance, but she's still unhappy that her talk show host mother told stories about her on the air. (Rev: BCCB 2/09; SLJ 12/08)

10274 DiCamillo, Kate. *Because of Winn-Dixie* (4–6). 2000, Candlewick $15.99 (978-0-7636-0776-0). 184pp. In this Newbery Honor book, lonely 10-year-old India Opal Buloni adopts a stray dog, named Winn-Dixie, who changes her life. (Rev: BCCB 6/00; BL 5/1/00; HB 7/00; HBG 10/00; SLJ 6/00)

10275 DiCamillo, Kate. *The Tiger Rising* (4–6). 2001, Candlewick $12.99 (978-0-7636-0911-5). 128pp. This novel of grieving, friendship, and animal love involves Rob whose mother has just died, an outsider named Sistine with whom he becomes friends, and a caged tiger. (Rev: HB 5/01; HBG 10/01; SLJ 3/01)

10276 Donofrio, Beverly. *Thank You, Lucky Stars* (4–6). 2008, Random $16.99 (978-0-375-83964-1). Early in 5th grade, Ally, abandoned by her friend Betsy, develops a surprising alliance with new girl Tina in this novel full of dance situations and awakening recognition of how to cope with social and family situations. (Rev: BCCB 1/08; BL 1/1–15/08; HB 5/08; SLJ 5/08)

10277 Donovan, Gail. *The Waffler* (2–4). 2013, Dial $16.99 (978-0-8037-3920-8). 208pp. Fourth-grader Monty tries to deal with frustrations at home and at school, but he sometimes has problems deciding between options. ℮ (Rev: BLO 7/13; HB 9–10/13; LMC 1–2/14; SLJ 10/13)

10278 Donovan, Gail. *What's Bugging Bailey Blecker?* (4–6). 2011, Dutton $16.99 (978-0-525-42286-0). 208pp. Set adrift in a new school, Bailey gains maturity by dealing with the loss of a pet, a disappointing party, and an outbreak of head lice. ℮ Lexile 670L (Rev: BL 2/15/11; HB 3–4/11; SLJ 2/1/11)

10279 Dowell, Frances O'Roark. *The Second Life of Abigail Walker* (4–7). 2012, Atheneum $16.99 (978-1-4424-0593-6). 240pp. Abigail, 11, is overweight and bullied until an encounter with a fox spurs her to view her life in a different way. ℮ Lexile 740L (Rev: BL 9/15/12*; LMC 1–2/13; SLJ 10/12)

10280 Dreyer, Ellen. *Speechless in New York: Going to New York* (5–8). Series: Going To. 2000, Four Corners paper $7.95 (978-1-893577-01-5). Jessie is beset with personal problems when she flies to New York from Minnesota with the Prairie Youth Chorale. (Rev: SLJ 3/00)

10281 Dunnion, Kristyn. *Missing Matthew* (4–6). 2004, Red Deer paper $7.95 (978-0-88995-278-2). 112pp. The three girls in the Rebel Rescue Squad decide to investigate the disappearance of 10-year-old Matthew, and instead of a kidnapping they find a sad boy who has run away from home. (Rev: BL 3/1/04; SLJ 5/04)

10282 Ellis, Sarah. *Pick-Up Sticks* (5–8). 1992, Macmillan LB $15.00 (978-0-689-50550-8). A disgruntled teen learns a lesson in life after being sent to live with relatives. (Rev: BL 1/15/92; SLJ 3/92*)

10283 Emery, Joanna. *Brothers of the Falls* (4–6). Illus. by Dave Erickson. 2004, Silver Moon LB $14.95 (978-1-893110-37-3). 92pp. Irish orphan James, 13, arrives in America alone and must find shelter and money to help him search for the brother who was left behind. (Rev: SLJ 8/04)

10284 English, Karen. *Birthday Blues* (2–4). Illus. by Laura Freeman. Series: Nikki and Deja. 2009, Clarion $15.00 (978-0-618-97787-1). Deja, an African American girl, wonders whether her father will come to her eighth birthday party — and whether her classmates will go to a competing event. (Rev: BCCB 4/09; BL 2/1/09; SLJ 1/09)

10285 Erlings, Fridrik. *Benjamin Dove* (5–8). 2007, NorthSouth $15.95 (978-0-7358-2150-7); paper $7.95 (978-0-7358-2149-1). Set in Iceland, this story of four boys' friendship ends in violence when some of the friends take tragically wrong turns in their lives. (Rev: BL 2/1/08; SLJ 12/07)

10286 Evangelista, Beth. *Gifted* (5–8). 2005, Walker $16.95 (978-0-8027-8994-5). George R. Clark is gifted and colossally unpopular with most of his classmates, so he is uneasy about going on his 8th-grade science field trip without his principal-father to protect him from the

bullies; funny and real. (Rev: BL 12/15/05*; HBG 4/06; LMC 11–12/05; SLJ 1/06; VOYA 10/05)

10287 Evans, Douglas. *So What Do You Do?* (5–8). 1997, Front St $14.95 (978-1-886910-20-1). Two middle-schoolers help their beloved former teacher who has become a homeless drunk. (Rev: BCCB 3/98; BL 11/1/97; HBG 3/98; SLJ 1/98; VOYA 2/98)

10288 Flake, Sharon G. *A Freak Like Me* (5–9). 1999, Hyperion paper $5.99 (978-0-7868-1307-0). In her inner-city middle school, Maleeka Madison is picked on by classmates because she is poorly dressed, darker than the others, and gets good grades. (Rev: BL 9/1/98; SLJ 11/98)

10289 Fletcher, Ralph. *Spider Boy* (5–8). 1997, Houghton Mifflin $16.00 (978-0-395-77606-3). Bobby — nicknamed Spider Boy because he knows so much about spiders — has trouble adjusting to his new life in the town of New Paltz, New York. (Rev: BCCB 4/97; BL 6/1–15/97; HB 7–8/97; SLJ 7/97)

10290 Flood, Pansie Hart. *It's Test Day, Tiger Turcotte* (2–3). Illus. by Amy Wummer. 2004, Carolrhoda LB $19.93 (978-1-57505-056-0); paper $6.95 (978-1-57505-670-8). 72pp. Tiger—a boy of multiracial heritage—is already nervous about taking a test, but when it comes to filling in his race, he's genuinely puzzled. (Rev: BCCB 4/04; SLJ 7/04)

10291 Fogelin, Adrian. *The Sorta Sisters* (5–8). Illus. by author. 2007, Peachtree $14.95 (978-1-56145-424-2). Anna, a foster child who lives in Tallahassee, Florida, corresponds with Mica, who lives with her alcoholic father on a boat in the Florida Keys, and their friendship brings them both solace. (Rev: BL 1/1–15/08; SLJ 12/07)

10292 Fogelin, Adrian. *Summer on the Moon* (5–8). 2012, Peachtree $15.95 (978-1-56145-626-0). 240pp. Socko, 13, and his mother move from the gritty inner city to the suburbs, where they will look after an elderly relative, but the situation there is not as simple or satisfactory as they hoped. Lexile 630L (Rev: BL 4/15/12*; LMC 11–12/12; SLJ 7/12)

10293 Fox, Paula. *Monkey Island* (5–8). 1991, Watts LB $16.99 (978-0-531-08562-2). A homeless, abandoned 11-year-old boy in New York City contracts pneumonia and is cared for by a homeless African American teenager and retired teacher, who share their place in the park with him. (Rev: BCCB 10/91*; BL 9/1/91*; HB 9–10/91*; SLJ 8/91)

10294 Fox, Paula. *Western Wind* (5–9). 1993, Orchard LB $17.99 (978-0-531-08652-0). At first resentful of being sent to spend a summer with her grandmother on a Maine island, Elizabeth gradually adjusts and learns a great deal about herself. (Rev: BCCB 9/93; BL 10/15/93; SLJ 12/93*; VOYA 12/93)

10295 Freedman, Paula. *My Basmati Bat Mitzvah* (5–7). 2013, Abrams/Amulet $16.95 (978-141970806-0). 256pp. With the pressure of her approaching bat mitzvah, 12-year-old Tara Bernstein questions both her faith in god and the importance of her mother's Indian heritage. **℮** Lexile 690 (Rev: BL 11/15/13; LMC 3–4/14; SLJ 12/13)

10296 Freeman, Martha. *The Trouble with Cats* (2–4). 2000, Holiday House $15.95 (978-0-8234-1479-6). 76pp. A beginning chapter book about Holly, who is adjusting to a new life in San Francisco with a new stepfather and a new school situation. (Rev: BCCB 4/00; BL 3/15/00; HBG 10/00; SLJ 7/00)

10297 French, Simon. *Where in the World* (5–8). 2003, Peachtree $14.95 (978-1-56145-292-7). A move from Germany to Australia is difficult for Ari, a talented young violinist who spends time living in the past while trying to find ways to cope with the present. (Rev: BL 12/1/03; HBG 4/04; SLJ 12/03*)

10298 Friedman, Aileen. *A Cloak for the Dreamer* (3–5). Illus. by Kim Howard. 1995, Scholastic $16.95 (978-0-590-48987-4). Misha sets out to find his fortune in an amazing cloak designed by his father and brothers. (Rev: BL 2/1/95; SLJ 4/95)

10299 Friesen, Gayle. *Men of Stone* (5–8). 2000, Kids Can $16.95 (978-1-55074-781-2). While Ben Conrad traces his own family roots, he confronts a local bully in this story of a boy's journey to maturity. (Rev: HBG 3/01; SLJ 10/00; VOYA 2/01)

10300 Gale, Eric Kahn. *The Bully Book* (3–6). 2013, HarperCollins $16.99 (978-006212511-8). 240pp. Sixth-grader Eric's journal details his efforts to work out why he is being picked on and to understand the rules of bullying. **℮** Lexile HL620L (Rev: BL 12/15/12; SLJ 2/13)

10301 Garcia, Cristina. *I Wanna Be Your Shoebox* (5–8). 2008, Simon & Schuster $16.99 (978-1-4169-6229-8). Thirteen-year-old Yumi is part Cuban, part Japanese, and part Jewish, and it is only when her terminally ill grandfather, a Russian Jew, tells her his life story that she begins to understand her own identity. (Rev: BL 8/08)

10302 Gardner, Graham. *Inventing Elliot* (5–9). 2004, Dial $16.99 (978-0-8037-2964-3). Despite efforts to avoid bullies at his new high school, 14-year-old Elliot Sutton finds himself embroiled with the Guardians, a group that metes out punishment to those it deems "losers." (Rev: BL 5/15/04; SLJ 3/04; VOYA 4/04)

10303 Geithner, Carole. *If Only* (5–8). 2012, Scholastic $16.99 (978-0-545-23499-3). 336pp. This novel about grief features 8th-grader Corinna learning to navigate the first year after her mother's death from cancer. **℮** Lexile 810L (Rev: BL 3/15/11; LMC 5–6/12; SLJ 3/12)

10304 Gephart, Donna. *As If Being 12 3/4 Isn't Bad Enough, My Mother Is Running for President!* (4–6). 2008, Delacorte $15.99 (978-0-385-73481-3). 224pp. Her mom is running for president and now Vanessa must deal with real fears as well as the typical problems of 7th grade. (Rev: BL 2/15/08; SLJ 2/08)

10305 Gephart, Donna. *Olivia Bean, Trivia Queen* (4–7). 2012, Delacorte $16.99 (978-038574052-4); LB $19.99 (978-037598952-0). 288pp. Olivia's desire to see her father, who now lives in California, fuels her determination to compete in "Kids' Week" on *Jeopardy*; then

her father will really appreciate her? (Rev: BL 5/15/12; SLJ 3/12)

10306 Gervay, Susanne. *I Am Jack* (3–6). Illus. by Cathy Wilcox. 2009, Tricycle $14.99 (978-1-58246-286-8). 128pp. Eleven-year-old Jack is being bullied and having dreadful headaches, but his home life is problematic and it is his friend Anna who initiates change in his life. (Rev: BLO 11/15/09; SLJ 2/1/10)

10307 Gilbert, Barbara Snow. *Stone Water* (5–9). 1996, Front St $15.95 (978-1-886910-11-9). Fourteen-year-old Grant must decide if he will honor his ailing grandfather's wish to help him commit suicide. (Rev: BL 12/15/96; SLJ 12/96*; VOYA 4/97)

10308 Glassman, Miriam. *Call Me Oklahoma!* (2–4). Illus. 2013, Holiday $16.95 (978-0-8234-2742-0). 128pp. Will changing her name make Paige Turner more self-confident and able to deal with a bully? Lexile 720 (Rev: BLO 4/1/13; HB 7–8/13; LMC 11–12/13; SLJ 4/13)

10309 Golding, Theresa Martin. *Kat's Surrender* (5–8). 1999, Boyds Mills $16.95 (978-1-56397-755-8). Thirteen-year-old Kat misses her deceased mother terribly, but she tries to hide it in her friendships for an old man and a wacky girl. (Rev: BL 10/15/99; HBG 3/00; SLJ 11/99; VOYA 4/00)

10310 Gordon, Amy. *The Gorillas of Gill Park* (4–7). 2003, Holiday $16.95 (978-0-8234-1751-3). Shy, lonely Willie comes into his own when he spends the summer with his eccentric Aunt Bridget and meets her zany neighbors. (Rev: BL 6/1–15/03; HBG 10/03; SLJ 5/03)

10311 Gordon, Amy. *The Secret Life of a Boarding School Brat* (5–7). 2004, Holiday House $16.95 (978-0-8234-1779-7). Lydia, already unhappy about her parents' divorce and her grandmother's death, becomes even more miserable at her new boarding school and chronicles her woes in her diary. (Rev: HB 7–8/04; SLJ 8/04)

10312 Gorman, Carol. *Games: A Tale of Two Bullies* (4–7). 2007, HarperCollins $16.99 (978-0-06-057027-9). Instead of suspending Mick and Boot for fighting, their principal requires them to play board games together; after a rocky start punctuated with petty crimes, the boys explore a hidden tunnel together, discovering that they both cope with alcoholic, abusive fathers. (Rev: BL 1/1–15/07; SLJ 1/07)

10313 Graff, Keir. *The Other Felix* (4–6). 2011, Roaring Brook $16.99 (978-1-59643-655-8). 176pp. A young boy coping with nightmares and disengaged parents meets another boy who knows how to fight off monsters. (Rev: BLO 9/15/11; SLJ 12/1/11)

10314 Grant, Vicki. *Hold the Pickles* (5–8). Series: Orca Currents. 2012, Orca LB $16.95 (978-155469921-6); paper $9.95 (978-155469920-9). 112pp. A puny 15-year-old eager for a chance to earn some money dresses up as a hot dog at a food fair, making him a prime target for bullies; for reluctant readers, this action-packed story also involves a mystery. **℮** Lexile HL580L (Rev: BL 3/1/12; LMC 8–9/12; SLJ 5/1/12)

10315 Grant, Vicki. *Pigboy* (5–9). Series: Orca Currents. 2006, Orca $14.95 (978-1-55143-666-1); paper $8.95

(978-1-5314-3643-8). Certain that his classmates' teasing will reach a new high, Dan Hogg dreads the field trip to a pig farm, but he deals well with the challenges that await him as he faces off with an escaped convict; suitable for reluctant readers and gripping enough for others. (Rev: SLJ 12/06)

10316 Gray, Dianne E. *Holding Up the Earth* (5–8). 2000, Houghton Mifflin $15.00 (978-0-618-00703-5). Sarah, a foster child now living on a Nebraska farm, does some research and uncovers stories of the many generations of women who preceded her on the farm and their struggles and problems. (Rev: BL 1/1–15/01; HB 9–10/00; HBG 3/01; SLJ 10/00)

10317 Greene, Bette. *I've Already Forgotten Your Name, Philip Hall!* (4–7). Illus. by Leonard Jenkins. 2004, HarperCollins $15.99 (978-0-06-051835-6). A little white lie that strains her relationship with her best friend, Philip Hall, is only one of the dramas Beth Lambert must deal with in this story set in small-town Arkansas. (Rev: BL 5/1/04; HB 3–4/04; SLJ 3/04; VOYA 6/04)

10318 Greene, Stephanie. *Sophie Hartley and the Facts of Life* (4–6). 2013, Clarion $16.99 (978-054797652-5). 144pp. Sophie's mom has taken a business trip, leaving Dad in charge of the whole Hartley clan, but Sophie has other worries: namely, what to believe about the puberty film that she and her friends will all have to watch next year, and whether she is ready to become a teenager. e Lexile 650 (Rev: BL 11/1/13)

10319 Greenwald, Tommy. *Jack Strong Takes a Stand* (3–6). Illus. by Melissa Mendes. 2013, Roaring Brook $15.99 (978-159643836-1). 240pp. Jack's busy — so busy, in fact, one day he decides that he's tired of being busy, and that he's going on a strike of the couch potato variety. e (Rev: BL 9/15/13; LMC 3–4/14; SLJ 10/13)

10320 Grimes, Nikki. *Planet Middle School* (5–8). 2011, Bloomsbury $15.99 (978-1-59990-284-5). 150pp. African American Joylin, 12, copes with changes to her body and social relationships as she goes through puberty. (Rev: BL 9/15/11; SLJ 12/1/11*)

10321 Grimes, Nikki. *Words with Wings* (3–6). 2013, Boyds Mills/Wordsong $15.95 (978-159078985-8). 96pp. Gabby's parents are getting divorced, and her daydreams are the one thing that's getting her through it all — but she has to learn to balance her daydreaming with succeeding in school; a novel in verse. ALA Notable Children's Book. ∩ Lexile 850 (Rev: BL 9/15/13*; LMC 3–4/14; SLJ 11/13)

10322 Grindley, Sally. *Bravo, Max!* (3–5). Illus. by Tony Ross. 2007, Simon & Schuster $15.99 (978-1-4169-0393-2). 160pp. In his continuing correspondence with his favorite author, 11-year-old Max — first seen in *Dear Max* (2006) — writes about his dislike of his mother's boyfriend, the play Max has written that parallels events in his life, and the joys and agonies of growing up. (Rev: BL 3/15/07)

10323 Grove, Vicki. *Reaching Dustin* (5–8). 1998, Putnam paper $6.99 (978-0-698-11839-3). As part of a 6th-grade assignment, Carly must get to know Dustin Groat,

the class outcast, and as she learns more about him and his family, she realizes that her attitudes toward him in the past have helped create his problems. (Rev: BCCB 3/98; BL 5/1/98; SLJ 5/98)

10324 Gugler, Laurel Dee. *A Piece of Forever* (3–6). 2009, Lorimer paper $8.95 (978-1-55277-026-9). 120pp. In the mid-1950s as a Veterans Day ceremony approaches, Rose struggles with her Mennonite family's pacifist stance. (Rev: BLO 4/23/09)

10325 Haas, Jessie. *Will You, Won't You?* (5–8). 2000, Greenwillow LB $15.89 (978-0-06-029197-6). Mad (short for Madison) is a shy middle-schooler who comes out of her shell during a summer she spends with her wise grandmother in the country. (Rev: BCCB 10/00; BL 2/1/01; HBG 3/01; SLJ 10/00)

10326 Hahn, Mary D. *Anna on the Farm* (3–5). Illus. 2001, Clarion $15.00 (978-0-618-03605-9). 152pp. When 9-year-old Anna arrives at her aunt and uncle's farm for a week, she finds they have taken in an orphan named Theodore, and a hearty rivalry begins. (Rev: BL 2/15/01; HB 5/01; HBG 10/01; SLJ 3/01)

10327 Hamilton, Virginia. *Drylongso* (3–5). Illus. by Jerry Pinkney. 1992, Harcourt $18.95 (978-0-15-224241-1). During a great duststorm on the prairie in 1975, a tall boy appears who helps Lindy and her family find water. (Rev: BCCB 10/92*; BL 7/92*; HB 9/92; SLJ 1/93)

10328 Han, Jenny. *Clara Lee and the Apple Pie Dream* (2–4). Illus. by Julia Kuo. 2011, Little, Brown $14.99 (978-0-316-07038-6). 160pp. Korean American Clara Lee conquers her fear of public speaking and shyness about her heritage and runs for Little Miss Apple Pie. Lexile 600L (Rev: BL 12/1/10; HB 3–4/11; LMC 1–2/11*; SLJ 2/1/11)

10329 Harper, Charise Mericle. *Still Just Grace* (2–4). Illus. by author. 2007, Houghton $15.00 (978-0-618-64643-2). 160pp. Still searching for her own identity, 3rd-grader Grace (last seen in *Just Grace*, 2007) deals with a variety of problems in this appealing novel presented in a format that will appeal to beginning chapter-book readers. (Rev: BL 9/15/07; SLJ 10/07) ∩

10330 Hays, Tommy. *What I Came to Tell You* (5–8). 2013, Egmont $15.99 (978-160684433-5). 304pp. His love of art and his friendship with a new family across the street help 12-year-old Grover to recover from the death of his mother; set in North Carolina, this book includes details about author Thomas Wolfe. Lexile 770 (Rev: BL 9/1/13; SLJ 11/13)

10331 Helget, Nicole, and Nate LeBoutillier. *Horse Camp* (5–8). 2012, Egmont $15.99 (978-160684351-2). 304pp. Twins Percy and Penny, 12, grudgingly adjust to farm life with their uncle in Minnesota after their mother is arrested. (Rev: BL 5/15/12*; SLJ 6/12)

10332 Henderson, Aileen K. *Treasure of Panther Peak* (4–7). 1998, Milkweed paper $6.95 (978-1-57131-619-6). Twelve-year-old Ellie Williams gradually adjusts to her new home when her mother, fleeing an abusive husband, moves to Big Bend National Park to teach in a one-room school. (Rev: BL 12/1/98; HBG 3/99; VOYA 8/99)

10333 Henkes, Kevin. *Junonia* (4–6). Illus. by author. 2011, HarperCollins $15.99 (978-0-06-196417-6); LB $16.89 (978-0-06-196418-3). 192pp. Nearly 10 years old, Alice is unsettled when she and her parents go to Sanibel as usual in February but things are not the same as always — as she likes them to be. ⌂ (Rev: BL 3/1/11*; HB 5–6/11; LMC 10/11; SLJ 6/11)

10334 Henson, Heather. *Here's How I See It, Here's How It Is* (5–7). 2009, Atheneum $16.99 (978-1-4169-4901-5). 272pp. Twelve-year-old Junebug is a budding actress working at her parents' summer stock theater but suddenly circumstances change and she faces a number of problems including her parents' separation and a boy with Asperger's syndrome. (Rev: BCCB 6/09; BL 4/1/09; SLJ 6/09)

10335 Herrera, Robin. *Hope Is a Ferris Wheel* (3–6). 2014, Abrams/Amulet $16.95 (978-141971039-1). 208pp. A poetry club helps 5th-grader Star to conquer her loneliness and unhappiness. Lexile 860 (Rev: BL 3/1/14; HB 5–6/14; LMC 10/14; SLJ 4/14*)

10336 Hershey, Mary. *My Big Sister Is So Bossy She Says You Can't Read This Book* (4–6). 2005, Random LB $17.99 (978-0-385-90917-4). A realistic story about the various problems 10-year-old Effie faces at school and at home: her grandfather has died, her father is in prison, her best friend has moved away, and her older sister has stolen the Angel Scout funds. A sequel is *Ten Lucky Things That Have Happened to Me Since I Almost Got Hit by Lightning* (2008). (Rev: BL 6/1–15/05; SLJ 6/05)

10337 High, Linda O. *The Summer of the Great Divide* (5–8). 1996, Holiday $15.95 (978-0-8234-1228-0). With the political events of 1969 as a backdrop, 13-year-old Wheezie sorts herself out at her relatives' farm. (Rev: BCCB 7–8/96; BL 6/1–15/96; SLJ 4/96)

10338 Hiranandani, Veera. *The Whole Story of Half a Girl* (4–6). 2012, Delacorte $16.99 (978-038574128-6); LB $19.99 (978-037598995-7). 224pp. Half Jewish, half Hindi Sonia contends with many challenges when her father loses his job and she must leave her private school and attend the local middle school. ℮ (Rev: BL 1/1/12; LMC 11–12/12; SLJ 2/12)

10339 Hobbs, Valerie. *The Last Best Days of Summer* (4–8). 2010, Farrar $16.99 (978-0-374-34670-6). 192pp. Twelve-year-old Lucy is tugged in two directions — she wants to join the "in" crowd at school and yet she does not want to abandon her neighbor Eddie, who has Down syndrome and will be attending the same school. ℮ Lexile 570L (Rev: BL 4/1/10*; LMC 5–6/10; SLJ 4/10)

10340 Holmes, Elizabeth. *Pretty Is* (4–6). 2007, Dutton $16.99 (978-0-525-47813-3). 216pp. Erin must deal with a mean former friend and an unconventional older sister as she waits for the summer before sixth grade to end. (Rev: BCCB 7–8/07; SLJ 7/07)

10341 Holmes, Sara Lewis. *Letters from Rapunzel* (5–8). 2007, HarperCollins $15.99 (978-0-06-078073-9). In letters to an unknown correspondent, Cadence — who

calls herself Rapunzel — describes her father's depression and her sense of being alone. (Rev: SLJ 2/07)

10342 Horrocks, Anita. *Almost Eden* (5–8). 2006, Tundra paper $9.95 (978-0-88776-742-5). Elsie is a Mennonite girl who must deal with her mother's depression, the onset of puberty, and religious doubts in this story set in Canada in the 1960s. (Rev: BL 5/15/06)

10343 Horvath, Penny. *Everything on a Waffle* (5–7). 2001, Farrar $16.00 (978-0-374-32236-6). Eleven-year-old Primrose Squarp does not believe her parents drowned during a storm. In the meantime she is moved from pillar to post, ending up as a foster child to an elderly couple. (Rev: BCCB 3/01*; BL 2/15/01; HB 5–6/01*; HBG 10/01; SLJ 4/01; VOYA 6/01)

10344 Horvath, Polly. *The Vacation* (5–7). 2005, Farrar $16.00 (978-0-374-30870-4). When his parents go to Africa as missionaries, 12-year-old Henry is taken on an eye-opening, cross-country trip by his eccentric maiden aunts, Magnolia and Pigg; comedy and weirdness ensue. (Rev: BCCB 10/05; BL 6/05; HB 7–8/05; SLJ 8/05*)

10345 Houtman, Jacqueline Jaeger. *The Reinvention of Edison Thomas* (5–8). 2010, Front St $17.95 (978-1-59078-708-3). 192pp. Eddy is bright and loves science and inventing but has great difficulty getting along with the other students and is often the butt of pranks. Lexile 780L (Rev: BL 4/1/10; LMC 10/10; SLJ 6/10)

10346 Howe, James. *Addie on the Inside* (5–8). 2011, Atheneum $16.99 (978-1-4169-1384-9). 224pp. Seventh grade brings a combination of challenges for Addie Carle in this verse companion to *The Misfits* (2001) and *Totally Joe* (2005). ℮ (Rev: BL 6/1/11; SLJ 8/11*)

10347 Hurwitz, Michele Weber. *Calli Be Gold* (4–6). 2011, Random House $15.99 (978-0-385-73970-2); LB $18.99 (978-0-385-90802-3). 208pp. Calli, a quiet and thoughtful 11-year-old, resists her parents' efforts to mold her as another of the family's overachievers. ℮ (Rev: BL 3/15/11; SLJ 6/11)

10348 Johnson, Emily Rhoads. *Write Me If You Dare!* (4–6). 2000, Front St $15.95 (978-0-8126-2944-6). 208pp. While coping with her mother's death and her father's new girlfriend, 11-year-old Maddie decides that her pen pal is really a ghost. (Rev: BCCB 12/00; BL 11/1/00; HB 1/01; HBG 3/01; SLJ 11/00)

10349 Jukes, Mavis. *Smoke* (4–6). 2009, Farrar $16.95 (978-0-374-37085-5). 176pp. Twelve-year-old Colt struggles with his parents' divorce, a move to California, his mother's new boyfriend, and finally the disappearance of his cat Smoke; he sets off to find the missing cat. (Rev: BCCB 4/09; BL 4/1/09; HB 3/09)

10350 Kane, Kim. *Pip: The Story of Olive* (5–8). 2009, Random $15.99 (978-0-385-75171-1). When her friend Mathilda drops her, lonely Olive suddenly finds she has a twin sister called Pip, who is as bright and adventurous as Olive is pale and retiring; with Pip beside her, Olive decides to look for the father she never met. (Rev: BCCB 7–8/09; SLJ 7/09)

10351 Kaye, Marilyn. *Real Heroes* (5–7). 1993, Avon paper $3.50 (978-0-380-72283-9). Kevin finds he is in the middle of a situation involving quarrels between parents and between best friends, and a controversy about a teacher who is HIV positive. (Rev: BCCB 5/93; BL 4/1/93)

10352 Keene, Carolyn. *Love Times Three* (5–8). Series: River Heights. 1991, Pocket paper $3.50 (978-0-671-96703-1). Nikki has a crush on Tim, but Brittany wants him too. (Rev: BL 12/15/89)

10353 Kelley, Jane. *The Desperate Adventures of Zeno and Alya* (4–6). 2013, Feiwel & Friends $15.99 (978-125002348-3). 208pp. In this inspiring story about hope and friendship, young Alya has leukemia and finds comfort in an orphaned gray parrot that appears at her window looking for food. ℮ Lexile 520 (Rev: BL 10/1/13; LMC 3–4/14; SLJ 9/13)

10354 Kerr, Dan. *Candy on the Edge* (5–8). 2002, Coteau paper $8.95 (978-1-55050-189-6). Candy, an 8th grader, finds herself drawn into a world of crime as she makes new friends and falls for Ramon. (Rev: SLJ 5/02)

10355 Kerz, Anna. *The Mealworm Diaries* (3–5). 2009, Orca paper $9.95 (978-1-55143-982-2). 176pp. Jeremy, still upset about his father's death, has trouble adjusting to his new school in Toronto, especially his difficult science-fair partner Aaron. (Rev: BL 4/15/09)

10356 Khan, Rukhsana. *Wanting Mor* (5–8). 2009, Greenwood $17.95 (978-0-88899-858-3). 192pp. This is a harrowing tale about a young Afghani girl, Jameela, who faces abuse, abandonment, and an orphanage after the death of her mother; based on a true story. (Rev: BCCB 9/09; BL 4/1/09; HB 7/09; LMC 10/09)

10357 Killien, Christi. *Artie's Brief: The Whole Truth, and Nothing But* (5–7). 1989, Avon paper $2.95 (978-0-380-71108-6). Sixth-grader Artie deals with the suicide of his older brother. (Rev: BL 5/15/89)

10358 Kimmel, Elizabeth Cody. *Lily B. on the Brink of Love* (5–8). 2005, HarperCollins LB $16.89 (978-0-06-075543-0). In this charming sequel to *Lily B. on the Brink of Cool* (2003), the title character, an aspiring writer and advice columnist for her school paper, needs counsel herself when she falls in love. (Rev: BL 10/1/05; SLJ 7/05)

10359 Kimmel, Elizabeth Cody. *Spin the Bottle* (5–7). 2008, Dial $16.99 (978-0-8037-3191-2). Phoebe gets a small part in a middle-school play and must deal with spin-the-bottle games, the popular crowd, and changing friendships. (Rev: BL 5/1/08; SLJ 6/08)

10360 Kimmel, Haven. *Kaline Klattermaster's Tree House* (3–5). Illus. by Peter Brown. 2007, Atheneum $15.99 (978-1-4169-5207-7). 150pp. Third-grader Kaline is easily distracted and finds that his imaginary world — especially a tree house where he pretends he has two older brothers — helps him deal with everyday problems including his father's disappearance and bullies at school. (Rev: BCCB 4/08; BL 12/15/07)

10361 Kinney, Jeff. *Diary of a Wimpy Kid* (5–8). Series: Diary of a Wimpy Kid. 2007, Abrams $14.95 (978-0-8109-9313-6). Greg Heffley writes in his very funny journal about the highlights — and the frequent low mo-

ments — of his first year in middle school. (Rev: BL 4/1/07; SLJ 4/07; VOYA 4/07)

10362 Korman, Gordon. *Liar, Liar, Pants on Fire* (2–4). Illus. by JoAnn Adinolfi. 1997, Scholastic $14.95 (978-0-590-27142-4). Third-grader Zoe lies so much that no one believes her when she tells the truth. (Rev: HBG 3/98; SLJ 9/97)

10363 Korman, Gordon. *Ungifted* (5–8). 2012, HarperCollins $16.99 (978-0-06-174266-8); LB $17.89 (978-0-06-174268-2). 288pp. Delinquent Donovan finds himself wrongly assigned to the gifted kids' school, where he joins the robotics team and discovers hidden talents. ∩ ℮ Lexile 730L (Rev: BL 7/12; SLJ 10/12; VOYA 6/12)

10364 Kornblatt, Marc. *Izzy's Place* (4–7). 2003, Simon & Schuster $16.95 (978-0-689-84639-7). Summer with his grandmother proves more rewarding than 10-year-old Henry anticipated as he makes friends and gains a new outlook on life. (Rev: BL 6/1–15/03; HBG 10/03; SLJ 7/03)

10365 Koss, Amy Goldman. *The Girls* (5–9). 2000, Dial $17.99 (978-0-8037-2494-5). In chapters narrated by different protagonists, this book tells of Maya who has been dropped for no apparent reason from a clique of five popular girls in the middle school she attends. (Rev: BCCB 6/00; BL 8/00; HB 7–8/00; HBG 10/00; SLJ 6/00)

10366 Krech, R.W. *Love Puppies and Corner Kicks* (5–8). 2010, Dutton $16.99 (978-0-525-42197-9). 192pp. American Andrea DiLorenzo, 13, moves to Scotland and initially has trouble making friends and is distressed when her stutter returns; however, her soccer skills help her overcome her loneliness and adjust to her new life. ℮ Lexile 530L (Rev: LMC 1–2/10; SLJ 4/10)

10367 Krumgold, Joseph. *Onion John* (5–8). Illus. by Symeon Shimin. 1959, HarperCollins LB $17.89 (978-0-690-04698-4); paper $5.99 (978-0-06-440144-9). A Newbery Medal winner (1960) about a boy's friendship with an old man. Also use the Newbery winner . . . *And Now Miguel* (1954).

10368 Lawson, Julie. *Turns on a Dime* (5–8). 1999, Stoddart paper $7.95 (978-0-7737-5942-8). In this sequel to *Goldstone* (1998), set in British Columbia, 11-year-old Jo faces many new situations, including finding a boyfriend, discovering that she is adopted, and learning that her beloved babysitter is pregnant. (Rev: SLJ 6/99)

10369 Lean, Sarah. *A Dog Called Homeless* (4–7). 2012, HarperCollins $16.99 (978-0-06-212220-9). 208pp. A large dog, a disabled boy, and a homeless man help 5th-grader Cally start to communicate again as she recovers from her mother's death a year earlier. ℮ Lexile 660L (Rev: BL 9/1/12*; HB 9–10/12; SLJ 12/12)

10370 Lee, Jenny. *Elvis and the Underdogs* (4–6). Illus. by Kelly Light. 2013, HarperCollins $16.99 (978-006223554-1). 304pp. A giant, talking therapy dog helps diminutive 10-year-old Benji, who has various physical problems, to deal with problems and build self-confidence. Booklist Editors' Choice: Books for Youth, 2013. 🎧 **e** Lexile 760 (Rev: BL 4/1/13*; SLJ 6/13*)

10371 Lemieux, Michele. *Stormy Night* (4–8). Illus. by author. 1999, Kids Can $15.95 (978-1-55074-692-1). A long picture book in which a young girl who can't sleep ponders questions that are common to preteen girls. (Rev: BL 12/1/99; HBG 3/00; SLJ 12/99)

10372 Lester, Alison. *The Quicksand Pony* (5–8). 1998, Houghton Mifflin $15.00 (978-0-395-93749-5). In this novel set in Australia, 17-year-old Joycie fakes a drowning and seeks a new life in the bush with her infant son, but two young girls stumble on the truth nine years later. (Rev: BCCB 10/98; BL 12/15/98; HB 1–2/99; HBG 3/99; SLJ 10/98; VOYA 2/99)

10373 Levy, Elizabeth. *Cheater, Cheater* (5–8). 1994, Scholastic paper $3.50 (978-0-590-45866-5). Lucy Lovello has been labeled a cheater and even her teachers don't trust her. When she finds her best friend cheating, she faces a moral dilemma. (Rev: BL 10/1/93; SLJ 10/93; VOYA 12/93)

10374 Lewis, Beverly. *Catch a Falling Star* (5–8). Series: Summerhill Secrets. 1995, Bethany House paper $5.99 (978-1-55661-478-1). An Amish boy faces excommunication when he begins paying too much attention to a non-Amish girl. (Rev: BL 3/15/96)

10375 Lewis, Beverly. *Night of the Fireflies* (5–8). Series: Summerhill Secrets. 1995, Bethany House paper $5.99 (978-1-55661-479-8). In this sequel to *Catch a Falling Star* (1995), Levi, an Amish boy, tries to save his young sister, who has been struck by a car. (Rev: BL 3/15/96)

10376 Little, Jean. *Birdie for Now* (3–5). Illus. 2002, Orca paper $5.95 (978-1-55143-203-8). 160pp. Troubled, hyperactive Dickon moves to a new home and finds joy and self-knowledge when he gets the opportunity to train an abused dog. (Rev: BL 11/1/02; SLJ 12/02)

10377 Littman, Sarah Darer. *Confessions of a Closet Catholic* (4–7). 2005, Dutton $15.99 (978-0-525-47365-7). Since she made friends with Mac, a Catholic girl, 11-year-old Justine has been questioning her Jewish faith. Sidney Taylor Book Award 2006. (Rev: SLJ 1/05)

10378 Liu, Cynthea. *Paris Pan Takes the Dare* (5–7). 2009, Putnam $16.99 (978-0-399-25043-9). 256pp. New girl Paris Pan, a 12-year-old Chinese American, is pleased to be asked to join a clique but distressed when she hears about The Dare. (Rev: BLO 5/27/09; SLJ 8/09)

10379 Look, Lenore. *Alvin Ho: Allergic to Girls, School, and Other Scary Things* (2–4). Illus. by LeUyen Pham. 2008, Random $15.99 (978-0-375-83914-6). 160pp. Chinese American Alvin Ho, a timid second-grader who becomes mute when he arrives at school, survives a number of challenges at home and at school. (Rev: BL 7/08; SLJ 8/08)

10380 Lopez, Diana. *Confetti Girl* (4–7). 2009, Little, Brown $15.99 (978-0-316-02955-1). Sixth-grader Lina Flores, living in Texas, struggles to cope with her mother's death, her best friend's problems, her schoolwork, and typical middle-school friendship and romantic chal-

lenges; this coming-of-age story is sprinkled with Spanish phrases. (Rev: BL 5/15/09; SLJ 7/09)

10381 Ludwig, Trudy. *Confessions of a Former Bully* (3–5). Illus. by Beth Adams. 2010, Tricycle $15.99 (978-1-58246-309-4). 48pp. Recording her experiences in her notebook, bully Katie slowly learns to correct her bad behavior when she's referred to the school counselor. Lexile 810L (Rev: BL 9/1/10; LMC 3–4/11; SLJ 8/1/10)

10382 Ludwig, Trudy. *Sorry!* (2–5). Illus. by Maurie J. Manning. 2006, Tricycle $15.95 (978-1-58246-173-1). Jack learns about insincere apologies when he makes friends with the popular Charlie; appended are an author's note, discussion questions, and "Apology Dos and Don'ts." (Rev: SLJ 12/06)

10383 McClintock, Norah. *Back* (5–8). 2009, Orca LB $16.95 (978-1-55143-991-4); paper $9.95 (978-1-55143-989-1). The compelling story of Jojo, who returns from prison to an unwelcoming community. (Rev: BL 4/15/09)

10384 McGhee, Alison. *Julia Gillian: (And the Quest for Joy)* (4–5). Illus. by Drazen Kozjan. 2009, Scholastic $16.99 (978-0-525-03350-3). 320pp. Julia is beset with an assortment of problems in this funny and spirited look at a 5th-grader's life at home and at school. (Rev: HB 5/09; SLJ 7/09)

10385 MacLachlan, Patricia. *The Facts and Fictions of Minna Pratt* (5–7). 1988, HarperCollins paper $6.99 (978-0-06-440265-1). A budding young cellist on the verge of adolescence experiences her first boyfriend. (Rev: BCCB 4/88; BL 6/15/88; SLJ 6–7/88)

10386 MacLachlan, Patricia. *Unclaimed Treasures* (5–8). 1984, HarperCollins paper $6.99 (978-0-06-440189-0). A romantic story of a young girl finding herself.

10387 MacLean, Christine Cole. *Mary Margaret, Center Stage* (3–5). Illus. by Vicky Lowe. 2006, Dutton $15.99 (978-0-525-47597-2). 176pp. Longtime teacher's pet Mary Margaret is jealous when a new girl joins her fourth-grade class and begins to steal the spotlight. (Rev: BL 2/1/06; SLJ 6/06)

10388 Margolis, Leslie. *Girls Acting Catty* (4–6). 2009, Bloomsbury $15.99 (978-1-59990-237-1). 208pp. Sixth-grader Annabelle faces many challenges: a group of mean girls at school, her mother's forthcoming marriage, her cute future stepbrother, her first bra . . . The third book in the series is *Everybody Bugs Out* (2011). 🎧 (Rev: SLJ 12/09)

10389 Marino, Nan. *Neil Armstrong Is My Uncle and Other Lies Muscle Man McGinty Told Me* (3–6). 2009, Roaring Brook $16.95 (978-1-59643-499-8). 160pp. In 1969, a scornful 10-year-old Tammy takes out her anger at life on a boastful foster child called Douglas (aka Muscle Man McGinty). (Rev: BCCB 7–8/09; BL 4/15/09; LMC 10/09; SLJ 6/09)

10390 Martinez, Claudia Guadalupe. *The Smell of Old Lady Perfume* (4–6). 2008, Cinco Puntos $15.95 (978-1-933693-18-7). 256pp. Already stressed by problems at school, sixth-grader Chela is overwhelmed when her father suffers a stroke and her grandmother (she of the old lady perfume) comes to stay. (Rev: BL 9/1/08; SLJ 9/08)

10391 May, Eleanor. *Ty's Triple Trouble* (2–4). Illus. by Amy Wummer. Series: Social Studies Connects. 2007, Kane paper $4.99 (978-1-57565-237-5). 32pp. A cheerful yet cautionary tale about what happens when Ty takes on too much at once, this story encourages readers to consider volunteering. (Rev: SLJ 6/07)

10392 Millard, Glenda. *The Naming of Tishkin Silk* (4–6). Illus. by Patrice Barton. 2009, Farrar $15.99 (978-0-374-35481-7). 112pp. Since his baby sister died and his mother has been in hospital, Griffin Silk has had to cope with making the difficult transition from home-schooling to public school. Lexile 930L (Rev: BL 11/1/09; LMC 11–12/09; SLJ 12/1/09)

10393 Mills, Claudia. *Makeovers by Marcia* (4–7). Series: West Creek Middle School. 2005, Farrar $16.00 (978-0-374-34654-6). Marcia learns that beauty is more than skin deep — and that there are more important things than the school dance — when she gives makeovers to the women in a nursing home. (Rev: BL 3/1/05; SLJ 2/05)

10394 Mills, Claudia. *Perfectly Chelsea* (3–5). Illus. by Jacqueline Rogers. 2004, Farrar $16.00 (978-0-374-31244-2). 128pp. Perfectionist fourth-grader Chelsea must question her own behavior in this story in which religion plays a large role. (Rev: BL 2/1/04; HB 5/04; SLJ 5/04)

10395 Morgan, Nicola. *Chicken Friend* (5–7). 2005, Candlewick $15.99 (978-0-7636-2735-5). When her family moves to the country, Becca tries too hard to be cool and winds up in trouble in this story told from a believable pre-teen point of view. (Rev: BL 3/1/05; SLJ 4/05)

10396 Morris, Taylor. *Blowout* (5–8). Illus. by Anne Keenan Higgins. Series: Hello, Gorgeous! 2011, Grosset & Dunlap paper $6.99 (978-04484552-6-6). 224pp. Mickey, 13, is sure her ship has come in when she gets a job working at her mother's salon, but she finds getting in with the popular crowd isn't as easy as she'd hoped. (Rev: BL 4/1/11)

10397 Moulton, Erin E. *Tracing Stars* (4–6). 2012, Philomel $16.99 (978-039925696-7). 224pp. Rising 6th-grader Indie Lee sets out to reclaim her missing pet lobster and become the kind of girl who won't embarrass her popular sister over the course of one short summer. (Rev: BL 5/15/12*; HB 7–8/12; LMC 11–12/12; SLJ 6/12)

10398 Musgrove, Marianne. *Lucy the Good* (3–5). Illus. by Cheryl Orsini. 2010, Henry Holt $16.99 (978-0-8050-9051-2). 177pp. Seven-year-old Lucy attempts to control her bad behavior when her Dutch great-aunt comes to visit them in Australia. *e* Lexile 570L (Rev: BL 10/1/10; HB 11–12/10; SLJ 11/1/10)

10399 Myers, Walter Dean. *A Star Is Born* (5–8). Series: The Cruisers. 2012, Scholastic $17.99 (978-043991628-8). 176pp. LaShonda's costume designs provide her an opportunity to leave the group home behind — but can

she be parted from her younger, autistic brother? ♫ Lexile 810L (Rev: BL 7/12; LMC 3–4/13; SLJ 8/12)

10400 Myracle, Lauren. *Ten* (3–5). Series: Winnie Years. 2011, Dutton $16.99 (978-0-525-42356-0). 272pp. This volume follows Winnie's life from her 10th birthday through her 11th and the various challenges she faces with humor and courage. *e* (Rev: BL 6/1/11; SLJ 9/1/11)

10401 Nagda, Ann Whitehead. *Tarantula Power!* (2–4). Illus. by Stephanie Roth. 2007, Holiday $15.95 (978-0-8234-1991-3). 96pp. With the help of schoolmates and a pet tarantula, a 4th-grader helps a younger student overcome being bullied. (Rev: BL 7/07; LMC 11/07; SLJ 6/07)

10402 Neri, G. *Chess Rumble* (5–8). Illus. by Jesse Joshua Watson. 2007, Lee & Low $18.95 (978-1-58430-279-7). Marcus learns to channel his anger — over his sister's death and his father's absence — into chess, and tells about it in free verse. ALA Notable Children's Book 2008. (Rev: BL 1/1–15/08; SLJ 11/07)

10403 Nielsen, Susin. *Word Nerd* (4–8). 2008, Tundra $18.95 (978-0-88776-875-0). 256 Twelve-year-old Ambrose, tired of moving and suffering bullies, makes friends with a 25-year-old ex-con neighbor who introduces him to Scrabble and broadens his horizons. (Rev: BCCB 9/08; BLO 12/30/08; SLJ 12/08)

10404 Palacio, R. J. *Wonder* (5–8). 2012, Knopf $15.99 (978-037586902-0); LB $18.99 (978-037596902-7). 320pp. Augie Pullman, a 10-year-old with facial abnormalities who has been homeschooled, is sent to a private school in Manhattan with repercussions for himself and others. YALSA Amazing Audiobooks Top Ten 2013; ALA Notable Children's Book 2013. ♫ *e* (Rev: BL 2/1/12*; HB 7–8/12; SLJ 2/12*)

10405 Paratore, Coleen Murtagh. *Mack McGinn's Big Win* (4–7). 2007, Simon & Schuster $15.99 (978-1-4169-1613-0). Mack is unhappy about his family's move to a new neighborhood and jealous of the attention his older brother gets for his athletic abilities, until a heroic act on Mack's part changes perceptions. (Rev: BL 7/07; SLJ 8/07)

10406 Parkinson, Siobhan. *Second Fiddle* (4–7). 2007, Roaring Brook $16.95 (978-1-59643-122-5). Mags and Gillian attempt to track down Gillian's father in the hopes that he will help finance her education at a music school in England. (Rev: BCCB 6/07; BL 2/15/07; HB 3–4/07; SLJ 6/07)

10407 Paterson, Katherine. *The Great Gilly Hopkins* (4–6). 1978, HarperCollins LB $17.89 (978-0-690-03838-5); paper $5.99 (978-0-06-440201-9). 192pp. Precocious Gilly bounces from one foster home to another.

10408 Patron, Susan. *The Higher Power of Lucky* (4–6). Illus. by Matt Phelan. 2006, Simon & Schuster $16.95 (978-1-4169-0194-5). 144pp. In a tiny California hamlet called Hard Pan, 10-year-old Lucky feels constantly uncertain about her life and seeks a "higher power" that will bring her some peace. Newbery Medal, 2007. (Rev: BL 12/1/06; SLJ 12/06) ♫

10409 Patron, Susan. *Lucky for Good* (3–6). Illus. by Erin McGuire. Series: Lucky's Hard Pan Trilogy. 2011, Atheneum $16.99 (978-1-4169-9058-1). 224pp. Lucky, now 11, copes with a challenge to her mother's cafe and her friends' problems with some help from the people of Hard Pan, California; the last volume in the trilogy that began with *The Higher Power of Lucky* (2006). ∩ Lexile 980L (Rev: BL 6/1/11; HB 7–8/11; SLJ 8/11)

10410 Patterson, James, and Chris Tebbetts. *Middle School: Get Me out of Here!* (4–7). Illus. by Laura Park. 2012, Little, Brown $15.99 (978-031620671-6). 288pp. When his mother loses her job, she and Rafe move in with Grandma and the 7th-grader must attend a new school. ∩ (Rev: BL 5/1/12; SLJ 6/12)

10411 Patterson, Nancy Ruth. *Ellie Ever* (3–5). Illus. by Patty Weise. 2010, Farrar $15.99 (978-0-374-32108-6). 128pp. After losing everything in the hurricane that killed her father, Ellie and her mother move to a horse farm, and Ellie attends a school where a false rumor spreads that she is a princess. Lexile 820L (Rev: BL 9/1/10; HB 9–10/10; LMC 11–12/10; SLJ 9/1/10)

10412 Paulsen, Gary. *The Amazing Life of Birds: (The Twenty-Day Puberty Journal of Duane Homer Leech)* (5–7). 2006, Random House $13.95 (978-0-385-74660-1). Having a bad time with the onset of puberty and its accompanying embarrassments — amusingly confided in his journal — 12-year-old Duane identifies with a baby bird developing in a nest outside his window. (Rev: SLJ 10/06)

10413 Paulsen, Gary. *Brian's Return* (5–8). 1999, Delacorte $15.95 (978-0-385-32500-4). Brian, the hero of *Brian's Winter,* becomes so disheartened with life at school away from the wilderness that he decides to leave society behind forever. (Rev: BL 2/1/99; HB 1–2/99; HBG 10/99; SLJ 2/99)

10414 Paulsen, Gary. *The Cookcamp* (5–7). 1991, Orchard paper $15.95 (978-0-531-05927-2). After a 5-year-old boy discovers his mother is having an affair, he is sent off to northern Minnesota in this World War II story. (Rev: BCCB 3/91; BL 3/1/91; HB 3–4/91; SLJ 2/91*)

10415 Paulsen, Gary. *Crush: The Theory, Practice, and Destructive Properties of Love* (5–8). Series: Liar, Liar. 2012, Random House $12.99 (978-038574230-6); LB $15.99 (978-037599054-0). 176pp. Too scared to ask Tina Zabinski for a date, 14-year-old Kevin decides to investigate how relationships work and launches a series of often ill-fated romance projects, including a speed dating night at school; a companion to *Liar, Liar* and *Flat Broke* (both 2011). ∩ ℮ (Rev: BL 4/15/12; HB 5–6/12; LMC 10/12; SLJ 4/12)

10416 Paulsen, Gary. *Flat Broke: The Theory, Practice and Destructive Properties of Greed* (5–8). Series: Liar, Liar. 2011, Random House $12.99 (978-0-385-74002-9); LB $15.99 (978-0-385-90818-4). 128pp. When his allowance is cut off because of his behavior in *Liar Liar* (2011), 14-year-old Kevin schemes up some clever ways to make money that don't always go over so well with his customers. ∩ ℮ Lexile 810L (Rev: BL 6/1/11; HB 9–10/11; SLJ 7/11)

10417 Paulsen, Gary. *Liar, Liar* (5–8). Series: Liar, Liar. 2011, Random House $12.99 (978-0-385-74001-2); LB $15.99 (978-0-385-90817-7). 128pp. Fourteen-year-old Kevin lies to make life easier until he finally gets in too deep and has to work out a way to extricate himself. ∩ (Rev: BL 3/1/11; HB 3–4/11; LMC 8–9/11; SLJ 6/11)

10418 Paulsen, Gary. *Paintings from the Cave: Three Novellas* (5–9). 2011, Random House $15.99 (978-0-385-74684-7); LB $18.99 (978-0-385-90921-1). 162pp. Lonely children trying to overcome abuse or neglect use various strategies in these three stories that reflect the author's own difficult childhood. ℮ Lexile 880L (Rev: LMC 5–6/12; SLJ 12/1/11)

10419 Paulsen, Gary. *Vote* (5–8). Series: Liar, Liar. 2013, Random House $12.99 (978-038574228-3). 144pp. Kevin Spencer, 14, decides to run for president of the student body in an effort to attract the attention of Tina Zabinski. ∩ ℮ Lexile 820 (Rev: BL 5/1/13; SLJ 8/13)

10420 Perkins, Mitali, ed. *Open Mic: Riffs on Life between Cultures in Ten Voices* (5–8). 2013, Candlewick $15.99 (978-076365866-3). 144pp. A collection of stories about young people bridging cultures in various different ways, told with humor and sensitivity. ℮ (Rev: BL 9/1/13; HB 9–10/13; SLJ 9/13)

10421 Peterseil, Tehila. *The Safe Place* (5–8). 1996, Pitspopany $16.95 (978-0-943706-71-9); paper $12.95 (978-0-943706-72-6). A moving story of an Israeli girl and the problems she faces at school because of a learning disability. (Rev: SLJ 12/96)

10422 Philbrick, Rodman. *The Fire Pony* (5–8). 1996, Scholastic paper $14.95 (978-0-590-55251-6). Rescued from a foster home by his half-brother Joe, Roy hopes that life will be better on the ranch where Joe finds work. (Rev: BCCB 7–8/96; BL 5/1/96; HB 7–8/96; SLJ 9/96; VOYA 10/96)

10423 Pitchford, Dean. *Captain Nobody* (4–6). 2009, Putnam $16.99 (978-0-399-25034-7). 192pp. Newt is a quiet 10-year-old boy who struggles while his football-playing older brother enjoys popularity until tragedy strikes and Newt finds a unique way to contribute to society and hopefully help his brother. (Rev: BL 7/09) ∩

10424 Polikoff, Barbara Garland. *Why Does the Coqui Sing?* (5–8). 2004, Holiday $16.95 (978-0-8234-1817-6). Thirteen-year-old Luz and her brother Rome have trouble adjusting when they move from Chicago to Puerto Rico with their mother and stepfather. (Rev: BL 5/15/04; SLJ 6/04)

10425 Porter, Tracey. *A Dance of Sisters* (5–8). 2002, HarperCollins LB $17.89 (978-0-06-029239-3). When a young ballet dancer's dreams are dashed, she is comforted by her sister. (Rev: BCCB 1/03; BL 2/15/03; HBG 3/03; SLJ 1/03)

10426 Preller, James. *Bystander* (5–8). 2009, Feiwel & Friends $16.99 (978-0-312-37906-3). 226pp. Seventh-grader Eric moves to a new town and is quickly befriended by the charismatic school bully, prompting him to question the morality of his own bystander status. **e** Lexile HL600L (Rev: BL 10/1/09; LMC 10/09; SLJ 1/10; VOYA 2/10)

10427 Reinhardt, Dana. *The Summer I Learned to Fly* (5–8). 2011, Random House $15.99 (978-0-385-73954-2); LB $18.99 (978-0-385-90792-7). 224pp. In the summer of 1986, 13-year-old Drew (aka Birdie) finally finds a friend in runaway Emmett, and he helps her cope with the fact that her widowed mother is dating. ⌂ **e** Lexile 750L (Rev: BL 6/1/11; HB 7–8/11; LMC 11–12/11; SLJ 6/11; VOYA 6/11)

10428 Richter, Jutta. *Beyond the Station Lies the Sea* (3–6). Trans. by Anna Brailovsky. 2009, Milkweed $14 (978-157131690-5). 96pp. Hoping to get to the sea, homeless 9-year-old Niner and his older friend Cosmos sell Niner's guardian angel to a rich woman, with predictably grim consequences. **e** Lexile 580L (Rev: BL 9/15/09; HB 9–10/09; LMC 3–4/10; SLJ 11/09; VOYA 2/10)

10429 Roberts, Marion. *Sunny Side Up* (5–8). Illus. 2009, Random $15.99 (978-0-385-73672-5). 224pp. An 11-year-old Australian girl struggles to balance a complex set of relationships that include divorced parents with newly emerging families, a long-lost grandmother and a best friend whose sudden interest in a boy threatens their pizza delivery business. (Rev: BCCB 2/09; BL 1/1–15/09; SLJ 2/09)

10430 Rosen, Michael. *Michael Rosen's Sad Book* (2–4). Illus. by Quentin Blake. 2005, Candlewick $16.99 (978-0-7636-2597-9). 32pp. An honest and very moving look at the author's grief over the death of his son. (Rev: BL 5/15/05; SLJ 3/05)

10431 Rottman, S. L. *Hero* (5–8). 1997, Peachtree $14.95 (978-1-56145-159-3). When his home life becomes unbearable, Sean is sent to Carbondale Ranch, where his sense of self-worth gradually grows. (Rev: BL 12/1/97; HBG 3/98; SLJ 12/97; VOYA 12/97)

10432 Roy, James. *Max Quigley: Technically Not a Bully* (4–7). Illus. by author. 2009, Houghton $12.95 (978-0-547-15263-9). 208pp. Max Quigley is a bully, although he doesn't see himself this way, and he is forced to spend time with smart but nerdy classmate Triffin in hopes that each will learn from the other. (Rev: BCCB 6/09; BL 3/15/09; HB 5/09)

10433 Ryan, Mary C. *The Voice from the Mendelsohns' Maple* (5–7). Illus. by Irena Roman. 1990, Little, Brown $13.95 (978-0-316-76360-8). Penny tries to cope with many problems, including finding out the identity of the woman who is hiding in the neighbor's maple tree. (Rev: SLJ 12/89)

10434 Rylant, Cynthia. *Missing May* (5–8). 1992, Orchard LB $15.99 (978-0-531-08596-7). Caring about each other is the tender message in this story of 12-year-old Summer, who, along with her uncle, must cope with the death of her beloved aunt. Newbery Medal 1993. (Rev: BCCB 3/92*; BL 2/15/92*; HB 3–4/92; SLJ 3/92*)

10435 Sachar, Louis. *Marvin Redpost: Why Pick on Me?* (2–4). Illus. by Barbara Sullivan. 1993, Random LB $11.99 (978-0-679-91947-6); paper $3.99 (978-0-679-81947-9). 40pp. Marvin becomes a social outcast after he is wrongfully accused of picking his nose. (Rev: BCCB 2/93; BL 5/1/93)

10436 Sachar, Louis. *Small Steps* (5–8). 2006, Delacorte LB $18.99 (978-0-385-90333-2). Two years after being released from Camp Green Lake, African American 17-year-old Armpit is home in Texas and trying to find good work, which is hard when you have a record, when X-Ray turns up with an interesting proposal; a sequel to *Holes* (1998). (Rev: BL 1/1–15/06*; SLJ 1/06; VOYA 2/06)

10437 Santucci, Barbara. *Loon Summer* (1–4). Illus. by Andrea Shine. 2001, Eerdmans $16.00 (978-0-8028-5182-6). Rainie has fun at the lake with her newly separated father and, although she wishes her mother were there, she learns to accept that things have changed. (Rev: SLJ 8/01)

10438 Sawyer, Kim Vogel. *Katy's Debate* (5–8). Series: Katy Lambright. 2010, Zondervan paper $9.99 (978-0-310-71923-6). 204pp. Katy, a Mennonite, is adjusting to high school and enjoying the debating team when she learns her father is considering remarriage. Can she dissuade him? In *Katy's Homecoming* (2011), Katy struggles to find a balance between her modest religion and popularity at school. *Katy's Decision* (2011) is the fourth book in the series. (Rev: SLJ 8/11)

10439 Say, Allen. *The Sign Painter* (5–9). 2000, Houghton Mifflin $17.00 (978-0-395-97974-7). An Asian American youth who wants to be a serious artist gets a job painting signboards scattered through the desert. (Rev: BL 10/1/00; HB 9–10/00; HBG 3/01; SLJ 9/00)

10440 Schumacher, Julie. *The Book of One Hundred Truths* (5–8). 2006, Delacorte $15.95 (978-0-385-73290-1). While spending the summer with her grandparents at the Jersey shore, 12-year-old Thea finds herself babysitting her younger cousin Jocelyn and struggling to keep private the truths she is listing in her diary. (Rev: BL 11/1/06)

10441 Shreve, Susan. *Kiss Me Tomorrow* (5–8). 2006, Scholastic $16.99 (978-0-439-68047-9). Alyssa (aka Blister) is not having a good 7th grade; she feels abandoned by best friend Jonah although she's quick to help him when he's in trouble; she is unhappy about her mother's new boyfriend; and she worries about everything else from clothes to sex. (Rev: BL 9/15/06; SLJ 10/06)

10442 Shura, Mary Francis. *The Sunday Doll* (5–7). 1988, Avon paper $2.95 (978-0-380-70618-1). Thirteen-year-old Emmy is miffed when the family won't tell her what has happened to upset her older sister Jayne, until she learns that Jayne's boyfriend has committed suicide. (Rev: BCCB 7–8/88; BL 7/88; SLJ 8/88)

10443 Siebold, Jan. *My Nights at the Improv* (4–8). 2005, Whitman $14.95 (978-0-8075-5630-6). Lizzie, a shy 8th-grader whose father died two years before, learns how to speak out by eavesdropping on an improvisational theater class, in the process also learning about bullying Vanessa. (Rev: BCCB 7–8/05; SLJ 11/05)

10444 Silverman, A. O. *Mirror Mirror: Twisted Tales* (5–8). 2002, Scholastic paper $15.95 (978-0-439-29593-2). Disturbing stories serve as metaphors for the problems of drug use, divorce, homelessness, and other ills. (Rev: BL 9/1/02; HBG 10/02; SLJ 8/02; VOYA 6/02)

10445 Slepian, Jan. *The Broccoli Tapes* (5–8). 1989, Scholastic paper $3.50 (978-0-590-43473-7). Sara uses tapes during her stay in Hawaii to keep up with her class oral history project. (Rev: BCCB 4/89; BL 4/15/89; SLJ 4/89; VOYA 6/89)

10446 Smith, Yeardley. *I, Lorelei* (5–8). 2009, HarperCollins $16.99 (978-0-06-149344-7). 352pp. In diary entries addressed to her dead cat, 11-year old Lorelei talks about her parents' failing marriage, her friends at her private school in Washington, D.C., a cute boy named Bo, and her efforts to land a role in the school play. (Rev: BL 1/1–15/09; SLJ 3/09)

10447 Sonenklar, Carol. *My Own Worst Enemy* (5–8). 1999, Holiday $15.95 (978-0-8234-1456-7). In this first-person narrative, Eve Belkin finds there is a price to pay when she outdoes herself to be popular in her new school. (Rev: BL 5/15/99; HBG 9/99; SLJ 8/99; VOYA 10/99)

10448 Soto, Gary. *Mercy on These Teenage Chimps* (5–8). 2007, Harcourt $16.00 (978-0-15-206022-0). Friends Ronnie Gonzalez and Joey Rios have just turned 13 and are wrestling with physical and emotional changes. (Rev: BL 12/1/06; SLJ 2/07)

10449 Soto, Gary. *The Pool Party* (4–7). Illus. by Robert Casilla. 1992, Delacorte $13.95 (978-0-385-30890-8). Rudy, part of a Mexican American family, has growing-up problems. (Rev: SLJ 6/93)

10450 Spinelli, Jerry. *Eggs* (4–7). 2007, Little, Brown $15.99 (978-0-316-16646-1). Two troubled children — 9-year-old David and 13-year-old Primrose — forge an unlikely friendship. (Rev: BL 4/1/07; SLJ 7/07)

10451 Spinelli, Jerry. *Wringer* (4–7). 1997, HarperCollins LB $17.89 (978-0-06-024914-4). A sensitive boy must participate in the massacre of thousands of pigeons released at an annual fair. (Rev: BL 9/1/97*; HB 9–10/97; HBG 3/98; SLJ 9/97*)

10452 Sternberg, Julie. *Like Bug Juice on a Burger* (2–4). Illus. by Matthew Cordell. 2012, Abrams/Amulet $14.95 (978-1-4197-0190-0). 176pp. Although Eleanor hates summer camp at first, she gradually adapts and finds she quite enjoys it. Lexile 450 (Rev: BLO 4/1/13; SLJ 4/13)

10453 Sternberg, Julie. *Like Pickle Juice on a Cookie* (2–4). Illus. by Matthew Cordell. 2011, Abrams $14.95 (978-0-8109-8424-0). 128pp. Eleanor copes with her long-time babysitter Bibi's departure to Florida and learns to adjust to a new one in this early chapter book. Gryphon Award. **e** Lexile 440L (Rev: BL 2/15/11; HB 5–6/11; LMC 8–9/11; SLJ 4/11)

10454 Stevenson, Robin. *Impossible Things* (5–7). 2008, Orca paper $8.95 (978-1-55143-736-1). Cassidy be-

friends a new girl in town who claims to have magical powers in the hopes that she can become magical too and overpower mean girls and bullies. (Rev: BL 4/15/08; SLJ 8/08)

10455 Stewart, Jennifer J. *The Bean King's Daughter* (5–7). 2002, Holiday $15.95 (978-0-8234-1644-8). Phoebe, a 12-year-old heiress, reluctantly learns about herself and her young stepmother while at an Arizona ranch. (Rev: BL 9/1/02; HBG 10/02; SLJ 7/02)

10456 Stone, Phoebe. *The Boy on Cinnamon Street* (4–7). 2012, Scholastic $16.99 (978-054521512-1). 240pp. Diminutive 7th-grader Louise, who has suffered tragedy in her life and lives with her grandparents, finds herself opening up when her friend Reni helps her with the mystery of a secret admirer. **e** Lexile 720L (Rev: BL 3/1/12*; HB 1–2/12; LMC 3–4/12; SLJ 1/12; VOYA 2/12)

10457 Stone, Phoebe. *Deep Down Popular* (4–6). 2008, Scholastic $16.99 (978-0-439-80245-1). When Conrad hurts his leg and starts wearing a brace, his popularity wanes and tomboy Jessie Lou, who has a major crush on him, finds herself forming a real friendship with him. (Rev: BL 3/15/08*; LMC 3/08; SLJ 3/08)

10458 Stout, Shawn K. *Fiona Finkelstein, Big-Time Ballerina!!* (2–4). Illus. by Angela Martini. 2009, Aladdin $14.99 (978-1-4169-7927-2). 176pp. Missing her absent mother, ballerina wannabe Fiona, 9, bravely overcomes her stage fright with the help of her kind dad. (Rev: BL 9/15/09; SLJ 1/1/10)

10459 Strasser, Todd. *CON-fidence* (5–8). 2002, Holiday $16.95 (978-0-8234-1394-2). Shy Lauren falls under the spell of the dazzling Celeste, failing to perceive Celeste's underlying motives. (Rev: BCCB 2/03; BL 4/15/03; HBG 10/03; SLJ 1/03; VOYA 4/03)

10460 Swallow, Pamela Curtis. *It Only Looks Easy* (4–7). 2003, Millbrook $15.95 (978-0-7613-1790-6). Kat's problems start when her dog is hit by a car and she "borrows" a bicycle to get to the vet only to have it stolen from her. (Rev: BL 4/15/03; HBG 10/03; SLJ 4/03)

10461 Tan, Shaun. *Lost and Found: Three by Shaun Tan* (5–10). Illus. by author. 2011, Scholastic $21.99 (978-0-545-22924-1). 128pp. A beautifully illustrated collection of three stories first published in Australia and dealing with loss. ALA Notable Children's Book 2012. (Rev: BL 4/1/11; HB 5–6/11; SLJ 4/11*)

10462 Tolan, Stephanie S. *Listen!* (4–7). 2006, HarperCollins $15.99 (978-0-06-057925-8). Lonely after the death of her mother and the departure of her best friend for the summer, 12-year-old Charley finds solace in a stray dog. (Rev: BL 4/1/06)

10463 Tolan, Stephanie S. *Wishworks Inc* (3–5). Illus. by Amy June Bates. 2009, Scholastic $15.99 (978-0-545-03154-7). 160pp. A bullied 3rd-grader named Max, struggling to adjust to his parents' divorce and a new school, finally gets a dog but it's not quite the dog he had imagined in his daydreams. (Rev: BL 4/1/09; HB 9/09; SLJ 7/09)

10464 Tolliver, Ruby C. *Sarita, Be Brave* (3–6). 1999, Eakin $14.95 (978-1-57168-184-3). 144pp. After the deaths of her grandmother and mother, 12-year-old Sara leaves Honduras for an eventful truck trip to Texas where she encounters problems and hardships before making a good adjustment. (Rev: HBG 3/00; SLJ 8/99)

10465 Toten, Teresa. *The Onlyhouse* (5–8). 1996, Red Deer paper $7.95 (978-0-88995-137-2). Eleven-year-old Lucija, whose family was originally from Croatia, relocates to a new house in suburban Toronto after several years in a dense downtown neighborhood with a large immigrant population, and must adjust to a new school, peer pressures, and bullies. (Rev: SLJ 7/96)

10466 Tracy, Kristen. *Camille McPhee Fell Under the Bus . . . .* (3–5). 2009, Delacorte $16.99 (978-0-385-73687-9); LB $19.99 (978-0-385-90633-3). 293pp. Camille, a 4th-grader whose best friend has moved away and whose parents' marriage is troubled, reacts by isolating herself. (Rev: BL 8/09; SLJ 11/1/09*)

10467 Tracy, Kristen. *The Reinvention of Bessica Lefter* (4–7). 2011, Delacorte $15.99 (978-0-385-73688-6); LB $18.99 (978-0-385-90634-0). 320pp. Eager to shuck off her elementary school persona, Bessica decides on a series of brash and ill-fated attempts to change her appearance in time for the beginning of 6th grade. **e** Lexile 570L (Rev: BL 1/1–15/11; SLJ 3/1/11)

10468 Vail, Rachel. *Ever After* (5–9). 1994, Orchard LB $16.99 (978-0-531-08688-9). Fourteen-year-old Molly is trying to act maturely but always seems to mess things up. (Rev: BCCB 4/94; BL 3/1/94; HB 5–6/94, 7–8/94; SLJ 5/94*; VOYA 6/94)

10469 Walliams, David. *The Boy in the Dress* (4–7). Illus. by Quentin Blake. 2009, Penguin $15.99 (978-1-59514-299-3). 240pp. British 12-year-old Dennis discovers he's interested in fashion — and enjoys wearing dresses — in this funny story that includes some slapstick moments but also some difficult ones with his father and brother. Stonewall Honor 2011. (Rev: BL 11/1/09; SLJ 12/09)

10470 Walpole, Peter. *The Healer of Harrow Point* (4–7). 2000, Hampton Roads paper $11.95 (978-1-57174-167-7). A novel of love and compassion about a boy who is promised a hunting trip for his twelfth birthday but wonders if he can kill a deer, particularly after seeing one killed by poachers and after meeting Emma, who can heal animals with her touch. (Rev: SLJ 10/00)

10471 Weissman, Elissa Brent. *Nerd Camp* (4–6). 2011, Atheneum $15.99 (978-1-4424-1703-8). 272pp. Nerdy 10-year-old Gabe tries to hide his intellectual abilities from cool Zack, who's about to become his stepbrother. (Rev: BL 5/1/11; SLJ 6/11)

10472 Wetter, Bruce. *The Boy with the Lampshade on His Head* (5–8). 2004, Simon & Schuster $16.95 (978-0-689-85032-5). Painfully shy, 11-year-old Stanley Krakow maintains a low profile but a rich inner life until he makes friends with an abused girl and finds the inner strength to be a real hero. (Rev: BL 5/1/04; SLJ 8/04)

10473 Williams, Laura E. *Slant* (5–8). 2008, Milkweed $16.95 (978-1-57131-681-3); paper $6.95 (978-1-

57131-682-0). 160pp. Lauren, an 8th-grader and Korean American adoptee, wants to have surgery to make her eyes more Western in this compelling story of identity, culture, and belonging. (Rev: BLO 1/13/09; LMC 3–4/09; SLJ 12/08)

10474 Willner-Pardo, Gina. *Prettiest Doll* (4–7). 2012, Clarion $16.99 (978-054768170-2). 240pp. After a childhood of beauty pageant successes, 13-year-old Olivia is feeling overwhelmed when asked to sing; she takes to the road with Danny, a 15-year-old with his own problems. **e** Lexile 680L (Rev: BL 7/12; HB 1–2/13; SLJ 2/13; VOYA 8/12)

10475 Wilson, Johnniece M. *Poor Girl* (5–7). 1992, Scholastic $13.95 (978-0-590-44732-4). A first-person story about Miranda, who spends the summer trying to earn money for contact lenses before the fall. (Rev: BCCB 4/92; BL 8/92; SLJ 4/92)

10476 Wojciechowska, Maia. *Shadow of a Bull* (5–8). Illus. by Alvin Smith. 1964, Macmillan $16.95 (978-0-689-30042-4). Manolo, surviving son of a great bullfighter, has his own "moment of truth" when he faces his first bull. Newbery Medal 1965.

10477 Wolfson, Jill. *Home, and Other Big, Fat Lies* (5–7). 2006, Henry Holt $16.95 (978-0-8050-7670-7). Shuttled through the foster care system for much of her life, 11-year-old Whitney isn't expecting much out of her latest stop with a family in remote northern California, but her interest in nature — and some new friendships — open her eyes to the importance of fighting for what you believe in. (Rev: SLJ 12/06)

10478 Wolfson, Jill. *What I Call Life* (5–8). 2005, Henry Holt $16.95 (978-0-8050-7669-1). Five young girls — all refugees from troubled families — find friendship and strength during their stay in a group home run by a wise Knitting Lady. (Rev: BCCB 9/05; BL 11/1/05; HBG 4/06; LMC 4–5/06; SLJ 9/05; VOYA 12/05)

10479 Wright, Betty R. *The Summer of Mrs. MacGregor* (5–8). 1986, Holiday $15.95 (978-0-8234-0628-9). Meeting an exotic teenager who calls herself Mrs. Lillina MacGregor helps Linda solve her problem of jealousy toward her older sister. (Rev: BCCB 12/86; BL 11/1/86; SLJ 11/86; VOYA 4/87)

10480 Young, Karen Romano. *Doodlebug* (3–5). Illus. by author. 2010, Feiwel & Friends $14.99 (978-0-312-56156-7). 112pp. Twelve-year-old Dodo family's move from Southern California to San Francisco is related to her own ADD-related school problems, and starts a notebook documenting her life and problems. (Rev: BL 9/15/10; SLJ 1/1/11)

10481 Young, Ronder T. *Moving Mama to Town* (5–8). 1997, Orchard LB $18.99 (978-0-531-33025-8). Although his father is a gambler and a failure, Fred never loses faith in him in this story of a boy who must help support his family although he's only 13. (Rev: BL 6/1–15/97; HB 7–8/97; SLJ 6/97)

10482 Zinnen, Linda. *The Truth About Rats, Rules, and Seventh Grade* (5–7). 2001, HarperCollins LB $15.89 (978-0-06-028800-6). Larch, who faces multiple problems at home and at school, tries to live her life by a set of unemotional rules, but a friendly stray dog and the discovery of the truth about her father's death make these rules hard to keep. (Rev: BCCB 6/01; BL 4/1/01*; HBG 10/01; SLJ 2/01)

Physical and Emotional Problems

10483 Abbott, Tony. *Firegirl* (5–8). 2006, Little, Brown $15.99 (978-0-316-01171-6). Tom, already an outsider at his Catholic school, bravely befriends a girl scarred by burns even when his classmates ostracize and ridicule her. (Rev: BL 7/06; SLJ 7/06)

10484 Auch, Mary Jane. *One-Handed Catch* (4–6). 2006, Holt $16.95 (978-0-8050-7900-5). 256pp. In this inspiring novel set just after World War II, 11-year-old Norm strives to live a normal life after he loses a hand in an accident, succeeding not only in music and art but also baseball. (Rev: BL 10/1/06; SLJ 11/06)

10485 Blume, Judy. *Deenie* (5–8). 1982, Dell paper $5.50 (978-0-440-93259-8). Instead of becoming a model, Deenie must cope with scoliosis and wearing a back brace.

10486 Brooks, Bruce. *Vanishing* (5–8). 1999, Harper-Collins LB $14.89 (978-0-06-028237-0). A challenging novel about a hospitalized girl who gives up eating so she can't be sent home to her dysfunctional family, and the boy she meets who is in remission from a fatal disease. (Rev: BL 5/15/99; HB 5–6/99; HBG 10/99; SLJ 6/99; VOYA 10/99)

10487 Buckley, James. *The Very Ordered Existence of Merilee Marvelous* (5–8). 2007, Greenwillow $16.99 (978-0-06-123197-1). Marilee, a bright young girl with Asperger's syndrome, enjoys order in her life until a new boy in town — Biswick, who has fetal alcohol syndrome — decides to attach himself to her. (Rev: BL 9/1/07; SLJ 10/07)

10488 Butts, Nancy. *Cheshire Moon* (5–7). 1996, Front St $14.95 (978-1-886910-08-9). A friendless deaf girl grieves for a cousin who has drowned at sea in this novel in an island setting. (Rev: BL 10/15/96; SLJ 11/96; VOYA 4/97)

10489 Byars, Betsy. *The Summer of the Swans* (5–7). Illus. by Ted Coconis. 1970, Puffin paper $5.99 (978-0-14-031420-5). The story of a 14-year-old named Sara — moody, unpredictable, and on the brink of womanhood — and how her life changes when her younger, mentally retarded brother disappears. Newbery Medal 1971.

10490 Carter, Anne Laurel. *In the Clear* (4–7). 2001, Orca paper $6.95 (978-1-55143-192-5). A 12-year-old Canadian polio survivor in the 1950s works through her fears and struggles to recapture her lost childhood. (Rev: BL 11/15/01; SLJ 1/02)

10491 Deans, Sis. *Rainy* (4–6). 2005, Holt $16.95 (978-0-8050-7831-2). 208pp. Rainy, an energetic 10-year-old girl with attention deficit hyperactivity disorder whose parents reject medication, has trouble at summer camp. (Rev: BL 8/05; SLJ 10/05; VOYA 10/05)

10492 Denenberg, Barry. *Mirror, Mirror on the Wall: The Diary of Bess Brennan* (4–8). Series: Dear America. 2002, Scholastic paper $10.95 (978-0-439-19446-4). When she comes home at weekends, 12-year-old Bess, who has lost her sight, shares her new life and school experiences with her twin sister, in this novel set in the Depression that includes many details of how the blind cope. (Rev: BL 10/1/02; HBG 3/03; SLJ 10/02)

10493 Draper, Sharon M. *Out of My Mind* (5–8). 2010, Simon & Schuster $16.99 (978-1-4169-7170-2). 304pp. Intelligent 10-year-old Melody, who has cerebral palsy, describes the frustrations of her life, which are somewhat alleviated when she gets a specially adapted computer and can interact with students in a regular classroom. ∩ ℮ Lexile 700L (Rev: BL 1/1/10*; HB 3–4/10; LMC 5–6/10; SLJ 3/10)

10494 Erskine, Kathryn. *Mockingbird* (4–7). 2010, Philomel $15.99 (978-0-399-25264-8). 240pp. Ten-year-old Caitlin, who has Asperger's syndrome and recently lost her older brother in a school shooting, struggles to find closure. National Book Award 2010; ALA Notable Children's Books 2011. ∩ ℮ Lexile 630L (Rev: BL 2/15/10; HB 3–4/10; LMC 5–6/10; SLJ 4/10)

10495 Farnes, Catherine. *Snow* (5–9). 1999, Bob Jones Univ $6.49 (978-1-57924-199-5). A thoughtful novel about an albino girl's problems being accepted, even among students who profess to have Christian charity. (Rev: BL 7/99)

10496 Galante, Cecilia. *Hershey Herself* (5–8). 2008, Aladdin paper $5.99 (978-1-4169-5463-7). While living at a shelter for battered women with her mother and younger sister, Hershey discovers real friends and a real talent. (Rev: BL 5/15/08)

10497 Gantos, Jack. *Joey Pigza Loses Control* (4–7). 2000, Farrar $16.00 (978-0-374-39989-4). Joey, a hyperactive kid, tries to please his father but goes haywire when his father destroys his medication in this Newbery Honor Book. (Rev: BCCB 9/00*; BL 9/1/00*; HB 9–10/00; HBG 3/01; SLJ 9/00; VOYA 2/01)

10498 Gantos, Jack. *Joey Pigza Swallowed the Key* (4–8). 1998, Farrar $16.00 (978-0-374-33664-6). Joey, who suffers from attention deficit disorder, causes so much trouble that he is sent to a special education center, where he learns to cope with his problem. (Rev: BCCB 11/98; BL 12/15/98; HB 11–12/98; HBG 3/99; SLJ 12/98*; VOYA 2/99)

10499 Gantos, Jack. *What Would Joey Do?* (5–8). 2002, Farrar $16.00 (978-0-374-39986-3). Hyperactive Joey is nearly overwhelmed by the antics of his parents, his dying grandmother, and the needs of his blind homeschool partner, but manages to cope in his own unusual way in this final installment in the Joey Pigza trilogy. (Rev: BCCB 11/02; BL 10/1/02*; HB 11–12/02; HBG 3/03; SLJ 9/02*; VOYA 12/02)

10500 Gould, Marilyn. *Golden Daffodils* (5–7). 1991, Allied Crafts paper $10.95 (978-0-9632305-1-5). Janis adjusts to her impairment resulting from cerebral palsy.

10501 Gould, Marilyn. *The Twelfth of June* (5–8). 1994, Allied Crafts LB $12.95 (978-0-9632305-4-6). Janis, who has cerebral palsy, is suffering the first pangs of adolescence and is still fighting the battle to be treated like other girls her age, in this sequel to *Golden Daffodils* (1982). (Rev: SLJ 11/86; VOYA 12/86)

10502 Graff, Lisa. *The Thing About Georgie* (3–5). 2007, HarperCollins $15.99 (978-0-06-087589-3). 224pp. Nine-year-old Georgie's school and family problems, compounded by his dwarfism, are sensitively explored in this upbeat, often funny novel. (Rev: BL 1/1–15/07; SLJ 2/07)

10503 Graff, Lisa. *Umbrella Summer* (4–6). 2009, HarperCollins $15.99 (978-0-06-143187-6). 240pp. It takes time and friends to help 9-year-old Annie get over her brother's death and stop seeing danger around every corner. (Rev: BCCB 7–8/09; BL 8/09; HB 7/09; SLJ 6/09)

10504 Haddix, Margaret P. *Because of Anya* (3–6). 2002, Simon & Schuster $15.95 (978-0-689-38298-7). 128pp. Anya's friend Keely rallies round when Anya must wear a wig because of her alopecia. (Rev: SLJ 11/02)

10505 Hartry, Nancy. *Watching Jimmy* (5–8). 2009, Tundra $16.95 (978-0-88776-871-2). 144pp. Carolyn saw the "accident" that left her friend Jimmy brain-damaged and she keeps her mouth shut until she just can't keep quiet anymore. (Rev: BL 6/1–15/09; SLJ 6/09)

10506 Howe, James. *A Night Without Stars* (5–7). 1983, Avon paper $2.95 (978-0-380-69877-6). A novel about a young girl's hospitalization and serious operation.

10507 Jung, Reinhardt. *Dreaming in Black and White* (5–8). Trans. from German by Anthea Bell. 2003, Penguin $15.99 (978-0-8037-2811-0). A boy with disabilities has waking dreams in which he travels back to Nazi Germany and suffers at the hands of his classmates, teachers, and eventually his father, in this compelling novel translated from German. (Rev: BCCB 9/03; BL 5/15/03; HB 9–10/03*; HBG 4/04; SLJ 8/03)

10508 Kachur, Wanda G. *The Nautilus* (5–7). 1997, Peytral paper $7.95 (978-0-9644271-5-0). A compassionate novel about a girl's rehabilitation after receiving spinal cord injuries in an automobile accident. (Rev: SLJ 9/97)

10509 Kelley, Ann. *Inchworm* (5–8). 2009, Luath paper $12.95 (978-1-906307-62-2). 203pp. Recovering from a heart and lung transplant, 12-year-old Gussie is living in London and missing Cornwall, worrying about her parents' divorce, and hoping to live to the age of 22. (Rev: SLJ 4/09; VOYA 4/09)

10510 Kerz, Anna. *Better Than Weird* (4–7). 2011, Orca paper $9.95 (978-1-55469-362-7). 224pp. Sixth-grader Aaron struggles to calm his excitable behavior, deal with a bully, and to make some friends in advance of the arrival of the father he has not seen in eight years. **e** Lexile 560L (Rev: BL 4/1/11; SLJ 5/11; VOYA 4/11)

10511 Kwasney, Michelle D. *Itch* (5–8). 2008, Henry Holt $16.95 (978-0-8050-8083-4). When Itch and her grandmother move from Florida to Ohio, Itch makes friends with a popular girl who has a sad secret. (Rev: BL 4/15/08; SLJ 9/08)

10512 Lachtman, Ofelia Dumas. *Leticia's Secret* (5–8). 1997, Arte Publico $14.95 (978-1-55885-205-1); paper $7.95 (978-1-55885-209-9). Rosario, from a Mexican American family, shares many adventures with her cousin, the pretty Leticia, and is devastated to learn that she has a fatal disease. (Rev: SLJ 1/98)

10513 Lafaye, A. *Water Steps* (4–7). 2009, Milkweed $16.95 (978-1-57131-687-5); paper $6.95 (978-1-57131-686-8). 188pp. Terrified of water since seeing her family drown as a little girl, 11-year-old Kyna finds she must spend the summer at Lake Champlain with her adoptive parents, who are trying to help her overcome her fears. ⌒ Lexile 790L (Rev: BL 3/15/09; SLJ 9/09)

10514 McDaniel, Lurlene. *To Live Again* (5–9). 2001, Bantam paper $4.99 (978-0-553-57151-6). After three years of remission from leukemia, 16-year-old Dawn has a stroke that produces a terrible bout of depression. (Rev: BL 3/1/01)

10515 McDonald, Megan. *Judy Moody Gets Famous* (2–4). Illus. by Peter Reynolds. 2001, Candlewick $15.99 (978-0-7636-0849-1). In this beginning chapter book, Judy Moody is plagued by jealousy until she manages to become famous anonymously and finds she enjoys it. (Rev: HB 9/01; HBG 3/02; SLJ 10/01)

10516 MacKall, Dandi Daley. *Larger-Than-Life Lara* (4–6). 2006, Dutton $16.99 (978-0-525-47726-6). 192pp. Ten-year-old Laney uses the writing skills she has learned to recount fat Lara's arrival at school and her amazing ability to shrug off slights. (Rev: BL 8/06; SLJ 9/06)

10517 Marino, Jan. *Eighty-Eight Steps to September* (5–7). 1989, Avon paper $2.95 (978-0-380-71001-0). Amy and Robbie have the usual sibling rivalry, until Robbie develops leukemia. (Rev: BCCB 5/89; BL 8/89)

10518 Matlin, Marlee, and Doug Cooney. *Nobody's Perfect* (4–6). 2006, Simon & Schuster $15.95 (978-0-689-86986-0). 240pp. Fourth-grader Megan, who is deaf, has a hard time understanding why the new girl at school seems unfriendly in this sequel to *Deaf Child Crossing* (2002). (Rev: BL 7/06; SLJ 8/06)

10519 Nails, Jennifer. *Next to Mexico* (4–6). 2008, Houghton $16.00 (978-0-618-96635-6). 235pp. Both new to Tucson's Susan B. Anthony Middle School, Lylice and Mexico (newly arrived from Nogales, a talented artist, and a diabetic) form a fragile friendship. (Rev: BCCB 12/08; SLJ 12/08; VOYA 10/08)

10520 Nicholls, Sally. *Ways to Live Forever* (3–7). 2008, Scholastic $16.99 (978-0-545-06948-9). 224pp. Eleven-year-old Sam tells a poignant first-person story of his losing struggle with leukemia. ALA Notable Children's Book. (Rev: BCCB 11/08; BL 11/15/08; HB 9/09;1/09; SLJ 11/08)

10521 Polacco, Patricia. *The Lemonade Club* (2–4). Illus. by author. 2007, Philomel $16.99 (978-0-399-24540-4). In 5th grade, Traci discovers that both her best friend and her teacher have cancer; based on a true story. (Rev: BL 10/1/07; LMC 11/07; SLJ 10/07)

10522 Riskind, Mary. *Apple Is My Sign* (5–6). 1995, Houghton paper $6.95 (978-0-395-65747-8). 160pp. A deaf and mute boy is sent to a special school in the early 1900s.

10523 Seidler, Tor. *The Silent Spillbills* (5–8). 1998, HarperCollins LB $14.89 (978-0-06-205181-3). Katrina faces problems trying to overcome her stuttering but stands up to her tyrannical grandfather to help save from extinction a rare bird known as the silent spillbill. (Rev: BCCB 1/99; BL 12/15/98; HBG 3/99; SLJ 4/99)

10524 Selznick, Brian. *Wonderstruck* (4–8). Illus. by author. 2011, Scholastic $29.99 (978-0-545-02789-2). 640pp. Two parallel stories set 50 years apart involve lonely children who've lost their hearing and run off to New York City to discover themselves; Ben's story unfolds in text, Rose's in pictures. ALA Notable Children's Book 2012. Lexile 830L (Rev: BL 8/11*; HB 9–10/11; SLJ 8/11*; VOYA 10/11)

10525 Shreve, Susan. *The Lovely Shoes* (5–8). 2011, Scholastic $16.99 (978-0-439-68049-3). 256pp. In 1950s Ohio 14-year-old Franny, a girl with a curled-in foot and clunky orthopedic shoes — and a beautiful, fashion-obsessed mother, goes to Italy to see shoe designer Salvatore Ferragamo and finds the attention she deserves. Lexile 1030L (Rev: HB 9–10/11; SLJ 10/1/11)

10526 Shyer, Marlene Fanta. *Welcome Home, Jellybean* (5–8). 1978, Macmillan paper $4.99 (978-0-689-71213-5). Twelve-year-old Neil encounters a near-tragic situation when his older retarded sister comes home to stay.

10527 Snyder, Zilpha Keatley. *The Witches of Worm* (5–8). Illus. by Alton Raible. 1972, Dell paper $5.50 (978-0-440-49727-1). A deeply disturbed girl believes that her selfish and destructive acts are caused by bewitchment.

10528 Strachan, Ian. *The Flawed Glass* (5–8). 1990, Little, Brown $14.95 (978-0-316-81813-1). Physically disabled Shona makes friends with an American boy on an island off the Scottish coast. (Rev: BCCB 11/90; BL 12/1/90; SLJ 1/91)

10529 Striegel, Jana. *Homeroom Exercise* (4–7). 2002, Holiday $16.95 (978-0-8234-1579-3). A 12-year-old who dreams of becoming a professional dancer is diagnosed with juvenile rheumatoid arthritis. (Rev: BL 3/1/02; HBG 10/02; SLJ 6/02; VOYA 8/02)

10530 Warner, Sally. *This Isn't About the Money* (4–6). 2002, Viking $15.99 (978-0-670-03574-8). 224pp. Twelve-year-old Janey, disfigured in the car crash that killed her parents, tries to adjust to her new life in Arizona with her grandfather and great-aunt. (Rev: BCCB 12/02; BL 9/1/02; HBG 3/03; SLJ 9/02)

10531 White, Andrea. *Window Boy* (5–8). 2008, Bright Sky $17.95 (978-193397914-4). 256pp. Twelve-year-old Sam invents a relationship with his hero Winston Churchill to help him cope with cerebral palsy and a difficult family life in 1968 England. Lexile 700L (Rev: BLO 8/08; SLJ 10/1/08)

10532 Zimmer, Tracie Vaughn. *Reaching for the Sun* (5–8). 2007, Bloomsbury $14.95 (978-1-59990-037-7). Seventh-grader Josie faces daunting troubles: school, loneliness, cerebral palsy, and her rural area's development; a new, science-loving neighbor becomes a friend and Josie redefines her relationship with her mother in this appealing verse novel. (Rev: BL 1/1–15/07; SLJ 3/07)

Historical Fiction and Foreign Lands

General and Miscellaneous

10533 Abdul-Jabbar, Kareem, and Raymond Obstfeld. *What Color Is My World? The Lost History of African-American Inventors* (3–6). Illus. by Ben Boos. 2012, Candlewick $17.99 (978-076364564-9). 44pp. Using the framework of a fictional story about young twins helping a handyman work on their home, this book presents information on 16 often-unknown African American inventors. (Rev: BL 2/1/12; SLJ 2/12)

10534 Akbarpour, Ahmad. *Good Night, Commander* (5–8). Illus. by Morteza Zahedi. 2010, Groundwood $17.95 (978-0-88899-989-4). 24pp. Childlike illustrations accompany this account of a young Iranian boy's devastating wartime experiences. (Rev: BL 5/1/10; LMC 8–9/10; SLJ 5/1/10)

10535 Angus, Sam. *Soldier Dog* (5–8). 2013, Feiwel & Friends $16.99 (978-125001864-9). 224pp. A dramatic tale of a 14-year-old boy's miserable family life and decision to head for the battlefields of World War I, where he works with brave dogs. ALA Notable Children's Book. e Lexile 870 (Rev: BL 4/15/13; LMC 10/13; SLJ 5/13*)

10536 Bell, Helen. *Idjhil: And the Land Cried for Its Lost Soul* (3–6). Illus. by author. 2003, Cygnet paper $11.95 (978-1-876268-90-9). 40pp. The life of Idjhil, a happy aboriginal boy in Western Australia, is turned upside down when he is forcibly removed from his family and relocated by the government. (Rev: SLJ 10/03)

10537 Bourke, Pat. *Yesterday's Dead* (5–8). 2012, Second Story paper $11.95 (978-19269203-2-0). 232pp. In the face of the 1918 flu epidemic, doctor's aide Meredith, 13, must find a way to stay healthy as one adult after another contracts the flu. (Rev: BLO 3/15/12; SLJ 4/12; VOYA 6/12)

10538 Broome, Errol. *Gracie and the Emperor* (4–6). 2005, Annick $18.95 (978-1-55037-891-7); paper $7.95 (978-1-55037-890-0). 123pp. Life changes dramatically for 11-year-old Gracie when Napoleon Bonaparte is exiled to the island of St. Helena, where the girl lives with her widowed father. (Rev: SLJ 12/05)

10539 Campbell, Nicola I. *Shi-shi-etko* (2–4). Illus. by Kim LaFave. 2005, Groundwood $16.95 (978-0-88899-659-6). 32pp. A young Canadian Indian girl savors the final few days before she is to be sent away to residential school, far from her family. (Rev: BL 11/1/05; SLJ 11/05)

10540 Carbone, Elisa. *Blood on the River: James Town, 1607* (5–8). 2006, Viking $16.99 (978-0-670-06060-3). As a page for Captain John Smith in the Jamestown Colony, 11-year-old Samuel Collier experiences firsthand the hardships and adventures that confront the settlers; a powerful, historically detailed novel. (Rev: BL 4/15/06; LMC 1/07; SLJ 7/06*)

10541 Crew, Gary. *Troy Thompson's Excellent Poetry Book* (4–7). Illus. by Craig Smith. 2003, Kane/Miller $14.95 (978-1-929132-52-2). Troy Thompson, an 11-year-old Australian boy, uses different forms of poetry to express his feelings about various elements of his life, participating in a yearlong literature assignment and, we learn at the end, winning the grand prize. (Rev: SLJ 1/04)

10542 Cushman, Karen. *Matilda Bone* (4–8). 2000, Clarion $15.00 (978-0-395-88156-9). Set in the 14th century, this novel describes the development of Matilda, 13, who serves as an assistant to the local bone setter in exchange for food and shelter. (Rev: BCCB 12/00; BL 8/00; HB 11–12/00; HBG 3/01; SLJ 9/00*; VOYA 12/00)

10543 Duble, Kathleen Benner. *Quest* (5–8). 2008, Simon & Schuster $16.99 (978-1-4169-3386-1). Through the thoughts of four characters, two of them on Henry Hudson's ship *Discovery*, readers will learn of the significance of the voyage to find the Northwest Passage and why it failed. (Rev: BL 4/15/08; SLJ 8/08)

10544 Edinger, Monica. *Africa Is My Home: A Child of the Amistad* (3–6). Illus. by Robert Byrd. 2013, Candlewick $17.99 (978-076365038-4). 64pp. Magulu is brought to America on the *Amistad,* the slave ship famous for the rebellion by its passengers; after the long court battle that resulted, Magulu finally gets permission to return home to Africa. Lexile 890 (Rev: BL 11/1/13; LMC 3–4/14; SLJ 8/13*)

10545 Fitz-Gibbon, Sally. *Lizzie's Storm* (3–5). Illus. by Muriel Wood. Series: New Beginnings. 2004, Fitzhenry & Whiteside $14.95 (978-1-55041-793-7); paper $7.95 (978-1-55041-795-1). Orphaned in 1931 at the age of 10, Lizzie leaves London to live with relatives on the challenging Canadian prairie and shows her mettle when a dangerous dust storm hits the farm. (Rev: BL 9/1/04; SLJ 10/04)

10546 Goldring, Ann. *Spitfire* (4–6). 2002, Raincoast paper $6.95 (978-1-55192-490-8). 160pp. A Canadian girl is determined to compete in a boys-only soapbox derby in this novel set in 1943. (Rev: BL 5/15/02; SLJ 4/02)

10547 Grant, K. M. *Green Jasper* (5–9). Series: The de Granville Trilogy. 2006, Walker $16.95 (978-0-8027-8073-7). Will and Gavin, introduced in *Blood Red Horse* (2005), come home from the crusade to find England in chaos and Gavin's beloved Ellie abducted by Constable de Scabious; a multilayered medieval adventure story. (Rev: SLJ 6/06; VOYA 8/06)

10548 Gray, Elizabeth Janet. *Adam of the Road* (5–8). Illus. by Robert Lawson. 1942, Puffin paper $7.99 (978-

0-14-032464-8). Adventures of a 13th-century minstrel boy. Newbery Medal 1943.

10549 Harlow, Joan Hiatt. *Secret of the Night Ponies* (4–6). 2009, Simon & Schuster $16.99 (978-141690783-1). 336pp. In 1965 Newfoundland 13-year-old Jessie participates in three daring rescues — of shipwreck victims, an abused orphan, and a herd of wild ponies. e Lexile 670L (Rev: BL 11/1/09; SLJ 11/09)

10550 Hollyer, Belinda. *River Song* (5–8). 2008, Holiday $16.95 (978-0-8234-2149-7). Set in New Zealand, this story of a half-Maori girl torn between two cultures is infused with magical elements from Maori legend. (Rev: BL 5/1/08; SLJ 6/08)

10551 Hughes, Susan. *The Island Horse* (3–5). Illus. by Alicia Quist. 2012, Kids Can $16.95 (978-1-55453-592-7). 160pp. Reeling from the death of her mother, Ellie, 9, channels her grief into a crusade to protect her island's wild ponies in this moving story set in the 1800s. (Rev: BL 3/15/12; SLJ 4/1/12)

10552 James, Helen Foster, and Virginia Shin-Mui Loh. *Paper Son: Lee's Journey to America* (3–6). Illus. by Wilson Ong. 2013, Sleeping Bear $16.99 (978-1-58536-833-4). 40pp. Twelve-year-old Lee reluctantly leaves China and travels to California in 1926, where he faces a grueling interrogation by the immigration officials at Angel Island. Lexile AD490 (Rev: BL 6/13*; SLJ 5/13)

10553 Kerz, Anna. *The Gnome's Eye* (4–7). 2010, Orca paper $9.95 (978-1-55469-195-1). 224pp. Theresa, 10, describes her Yugoslav family's journey from an Austrian refugee camp to Toronto, Canada, where Theresa struggles to make the transition to a new language, a new school, and a new culture in the early 1950s. e Lexile 650L (Rev: BL 5/15/10; LMC 11–12/10; SLJ 8/10)

10554 Kirkpatrick, Katherine. *Escape Across the Wide Sea* (4–6). 2004, Holiday House $17.95 (978-0-8234-1854-1). This gripping novel follows 9-year-old Daniel and his Huguenot family as they flee religious persecution in their native France and find themselves on a slave ship to the New World. (Rev: BL 1/1–15/05; SLJ 11/04)

10555 Lawson, Sue. *Ferret Boy* (4–6). Illus. by Annie Mertzlin. Series: Takeaways. 2003, Lothian paper $8.95 (978-0-7344-0465-7). 256pp. Josh Trimble faces unexpected challenges when, in a hasty moment, he agrees to race his beloved pet ferret in a derby. (Rev: SLJ 8/03)

10556 Lester, Alison. *Sophie Scott Goes South* (2–4). Illus. by author. 2013, Houghton Mifflin $17.99 (978-054408895-5). 40pp. Nine-year-old Sophie travels with her father to Antarctica aboard his icebreaker, the *Aurora Australis,* and shares in her illustrated diary details of her journey and all she has learned. USBBY Outstanding International Book. Lexile 840 (Rev: BL 11/1/13*; HB 11–12/13; LMC 11–12/13; SLJ 12/13)

10557 Logan, Claudia. *The 5,000-Year-Old Puzzle: Solving a Mystery of Ancient Egypt* (3–5). Illus. by Melissa Sweet. 2002, Farrar $17.00 (978-0-374-32335-6). 48pp. Part fact and part fiction, this picture book for older children takes readers along on an actual 1924 expedition to uncover tombs from the days of ancient Egypt. (Rev: BL 4/15/02; HBG 10/02; SLJ 6/02)

10558 Mallam, Sally. *Dende Maro: The Golden Prince* (2–4). Illus. by author. 2009, Hoopoe $17.99 (978-1-933779-48-5). 40pp. This title offers an original creation myth in which a golden prince teaches the ancients how to live. (Rev: BL 6/1–15/09; LMC 8/09; SLJ 6/09)

10559 Martin, Ann M. *Better to Wish* (5–7). Series: Family Tree. 2013, Scholastic $16.99 (978-054535942-9). 240pp. In 1930s Maine 8-year-old Abby has a lot to cope with — a difficult father, a troubled mother, a younger brother with developmental disabilities — but also a lot to hope for; the novel follows her life over a period of 23 years and is the first in a series that will feature succeeding generations. ⌒ Lexile 790 (Rev: BL 6/13; HB 7–8/13; LMC 11–12/13; SLJ 6/13)

10560 Miles, Victoria. *Magnifico* (4–6). 2006, Fitzhenry & Whiteside $15.95 (978-1-55041-960-3). 262pp. Mariangela Benitti must endure teasing and torturous practice to master the accordion, an instrument foisted upon her by her immigrant Italian family, in this story set in Canada in 1939. (Rev: BL 7/06; SLJ 7/06)

10561 Parker, Toni Trent. *Sienna's Scrapbook: Our African American Heritage Trip* (3–6). Illus. by Janell Genovese. 2005, Chronicle $15.95 (978-0-8118-4300-3). 61pp. Sienna, a young African American girl, keeps a scrapbook of her family's summer trip to important sites in the history of black Americans; Sienna's humorous comments, varied ephemera, and appealing illustrations add to the appeal. (Rev: SLJ 1/06)

10562 Pernoud, Regine. *A Day with a Miller* (4–7). Trans. by Dominique Clift. Illus. by Giorgio Bacchin. 1997, Runestone LB $22.60 (978-0-8225-1914-0). A description of the life of a miller and his family in the 12th century and how hydraulic energy was being introduced at that time. (Rev: HBG 3/98; SLJ 3/98)

10563 Platt, Richard. *Roman Diary: The Journal of Iliona of Mytilini, Who Was Captured and Sold As a Slave in Rome, AD 107* (3–6). Illus. by David Parkins. 2009, Candlewick $18.99 (978-0-7636-3480-3). 64pp. In A.D. 107, Iliona and her brother Apollo are captured by pirates and become Roman slaves; Iliona leads a relatively easy life that she documents carefully in her diary. This oversized picture book includes useful back matter. (Rev: BLO 5/27/09; SLJ 6/09)

10564 Polisar, Barry Louis. *Stolen Man: The Story of the Amistad Rebellion* (3–5). 2006, Rainbow Morning Music paper $7.95 (978-0-938663-50-8). 7.95pp. An account of the *Amistad* slave rebellion of 1839 from the perspective of a slave named Sengbe Pieh (later known at Joseph Cinque). (Rev: BL 2/1/07)

10565 Reynolds, Susan. *The First Marathon: The Legend of Pheidippides* (2–4). Illus. by Daniel Minter. 2006, Albert Whitman $16.95 (978-0-8075-0867-1). The role of long-distance runner Pheidippides in the important Battle of Marathon is told in a dramatic, fictionalized text with large illustrations and an informative afterword. (Rev: BL 2/15/06; SLJ 3/06)

10566 Rosen, Michael J. *Sailing the Unknown: Around the World with Captain Cook* (1–4). Illus. by Maria Cristina Pritelli. 2012, Creative Editions $17.99 (978-156846216-5). 40pp. This fictionalized diary chronicles the adventures of 11-year-old Nicholas as he sails the world aboard Captain Cook's *Endeavour* starting in 1768. Lexile 800 (Rev: BLO 1/13; SLJ 1/13*)

10567 Rosen, Sidney, and Dorothy S. Rosen. *The Magician's Apprentice* (5–8). 1994, Carolrhoda LB $19.95 (978-0-87614-809-9). An orphan in a French abbey in the Middle Ages is accused of having a heretical document in his possession and is sent to spy on Roger Bacon, the English scientist. (Rev: BL 5/1/94; SLJ 6/94)

10568 Russell, Christopher. *Dogboy* (4–6). 2006, Greenwillow $15.99 (978-0-06-084116-4). Twelve-year-old Brind, who was raised with dogs and now is renowned for his talent as a kennel boy, faces many challenges and finds a new friend, Aurelie, in this novel set amid the Hundred Years War between France and England. (Rev: BL 4/15/06; SLJ 8/06; VOYA 8/06)

10569 Russell, Christopher. *Hunted* (5–8). 2007, HarperCollins $15.99 (978-0-06-084119-5). Set in the Middle Ages, this is the exciting tale of two teens who run away after being falsely accused of bringing the Black Death to the manor in which they work. (Rev: SLJ 6/07)

10570 Shulevitz, Uri. *The Travels of Benjamin of Tudela: Through Three Continents in the Twelfth Century* (4–7). 2005, Farrar $17.00 (978-0-374-37754-0). Based on Benjamin's diaries, this picture book, which is incredibly detailed in both illustrations and text, tells of his perilous journey through parts of Europe, the Mediterranean, and the Middle East. Sidney Taylor Book Honor 2006. (Rev: BL 3/15/05*; SLJ 4/05)

10571 Skrypuch, Marsha Forchuk. *Aram's Choice* (3–5). Illus. by Muriel Wood. 2006, Fitzhenry & Whiteside $14.95 (978-1-55041-352-6); paper $8.95 (978-1-55041-354-0). 72pp. Aram, a 12-year-old refugee from the Armenian genocide in Turkey in the early 1900s, travels with other orphans to a new home in Canada; based on truth, this compelling story contains many interesting facts and a historical note follows the text. (Rev: BL 8/06; SLJ 9/06)

10572 Skrypuch, Marsha Forchuk. *Call Me Aram* (3–5). Illus. by Muriel Wood. Series: New Beginnings. 2009, Fitzhenry & Whiteside $16.95 (978-1-55455-000-5); paper $10.95 (978-1-55455-001-2). This short novel about an Armenian orphan in Canada who grapples with losing his identity in a new country is a sequel to *Aram's Choice* (2006). (Rev: BLO 6/16/09)

10573 Skrypuch, Marsha Forchuk. *Silver Threads* (2–4). Illus. by Michael Martchenko. 2004, Fitzhenry & Whiteside $16.95 (978-1-55041-901-6). 32pp. This picture-book story of Ukrainian immigrants' bittersweet experiences in early-20th-century Canada is based on the lives of the author's grandparents. (Rev: BL 12/1/04; SLJ 1/05)

10574 Spradlin, Michael P. *Keeper of the Grail* (5–8). Series: The Youngest Templar. 2008, Putnam $17.99 (978-

0-399-24763-7). 248pp. Fourteen-year-old Tristan, who has been raised by monks, becomes a squire to a Templar knight and finds himself journeying to the Holy Land and returning with the Holy Grail; an action-packed, first-person narrative. The second and third books in the series are *Trail of Fate* (2009) and *Orphan of Destiny* (2010). ⋒ Lexile 830L (Rev: BL 9/15/08; LMC 1–2/09; SLJ 2/1/09)

10575 Valgardson, W. D. *Sarah and the People of Sand River* (3–5). Illus. by Ian Wallace. 1996, Douglas & McIntyre $16.95 (978-0-88899-255-0). 56pp. An Icelandic family, now relocated in Manitoba, Canada, is helped by Cree Indians. (Rev: BCCB 12/96; BL 11/1/96*; SLJ 12/96) [398.2]

10576 Williams, Karen Lynn, and Khadra Mohammed. *Four Feet, Two Sandals* (1–3). Illus. by Doug Chayka. 2007, Eerdmans $17.00 (978-0-8028-5296-0). 32pp. Two 10-year-olds in a refugee camp on the Afghanistan-Pakistan border become friends when they discover that between them they own a beautiful pair of sandals. (Rev: BL 9/15/07; LMC 1/08; SLJ 10/07)

10577 Williams, Marcia. *Chaucer's Canterbury Tales* (4–8). 2007, Candlewick $16.99 (978-0-7636-3197-0). The exploits of Chaucer's pilgrims are recounted in age-appropriate double-page spreads that are alive with action and humor; the illustrations help to define the more difficult words. ALA Notable Children's Book 2008. (Rev: BL 2/15/07; HB 3–4/07; LMC 8–9/07; SLJ 3/07*)

Prehistory

10578 Denzel, Justin. *Boy of the Painted Cave* (5–7). 1988, Putnam $17.99 (978-0-399-21559-9). The story of a boy who longs to be a cave artist, set in Cro Magnon times. (Rev: BL 11/1/88; SLJ 11/88)

10579 Ross, Stewart. *Curse of the Crocodile God* (3–6). Illus. by Inklink. 2007, DK $14.99 (978-0-7566-2564-1); paper $3.99 (978-0-7566-2563-4). Two thirteen-year-olds in ancient Egypt solve a murder mystery in this story that will get children interested in studying this time period. (Rev: SLJ 5/07)

Africa

10580 Atinuke. *Anna Hibiscus* (1–3). Illus. by Lauren Tobia. 2010, Kane/Miller paper $5.99 (978-19352797-3-0). 112pp. A beginning chapter book set in modern Africa, this tells stories about Anna and her twin younger brothers Double and Trouble. Also in this series is *Anna Hibiscus' Song* (2011). Boston Globe–Horn Book Honor Award. ⋒ Lexile 670L (Rev: BLO 12/1/10; LMC 1–2/11)

10581 Atinuke. *Good Luck, Anna Hibiscus!* (1–3). Illus. by Lauren Tobia. 2011, Kane/Miller paper $5.99 (978-1-61067-007-4). 112pp. African child Anna Hibiscus prepares for her first trip to Canada to visit her grandmother. Also use *Have Fun, Anna Hibiscus!* (2011), which tells the story of her snowy time in Canada. (Rev: HB 5–6/11; SLJ 8/1/11)

10582 Atinuke. *The No. 1 Car Spotter* (2–5). Illus. by Warwick Johnson Cadwell. 2011, Kane/Miller paper $5.99 (978-16106705-1-7). 112pp. When a Corolla is abandoned near his isolated African village, Oluwalase figures out a way to make it run, and the village is able to bring its goods to market for the first time. (Rev: BL 10/1/11; LMC 3–4/12)

10583 Burns, Khephra. *Mansa Musa: The Lion of Mali* (4–7). Illus. by Diane Dillon and Leo Dillon. 2001, Harcourt $18.00 (978-0-15-200375-3). Lavish illustrations complement this handsome, challenging book about Mansa Musa's journey from a rural village boyhood to becoming the king of Mali. (Rev: BL 12/1/01; HB 11–12/01; HBG 3/02; SLJ 10/01)

10584 Ellis, Deborah. *The Heaven Shop* (5–8). 2004, Fitzhenry & Whiteside $16.95 (978-1-55041-908-5). The AIDS epidemic has a devastating impact on the family of Binti, a 13-year-old Malawi girl. (Rev: BL 9/1/04; SLJ 10/04)

10585 Farmer, Nancy. *Clever Ali* (2–4). Illus. by Gail de Marcken. 2006, Scholastic $17.99 (978-0-439-37014-1). This beautifully written and illustrated picture book for older children, based on a true story of medieval Egypt, features 7-year-old Ali, who must find a way to outwit an evil sultan. (Rev: BL 10/1/06; SLJ 10/06)

10586 Farmer, Nancy. *Do You Know Me?* (4–6). Illus. by Shelley Jackson. 1993, Orchard LB $16.99 (978-0-531-08624-7). 112pp. There are culture clashes (many amusing) when 9-year-old Tapiwa's uncle comes from rural Mozambique to live with her family in the city. (Rev: BL 4/1/93; SLJ 4/93)

10587 Gregory, Kristiana. *Cleopatra VII: Daughter of the Nile* (5–8). Series: Royal Diaries. 1999, Scholastic paper $10.95 (978-0-590-81975-6). This mock-diary recounts various events in the life of 12-year-old Cleopatra who, even at that age, was involved in palace intrigue. (Rev: BL 1/1–15/00; HBG 3/00; SLJ 10/99)

10588 Grifalconi, Ann. *The Village That Vanished* (2–5). Illus. by Kadir Nelson. 2002, Dial $16.99 (978-0-8037-2623-9). 40pp. African villagers escape slavers by dismantling their village piece by piece. (Rev: BCCB 11/02; BL 9/15/02; HB 9/02; HBG 3/03; SLJ 12/02)

10589 Kurtz, Jane. *The Storyteller's Beads* (5–8). 1998, Harcourt $15.00 (978-0-15-201074-4). Two Ethiopian refugees, one a girl from a traditional Ethiopian culture and the other a blind Jewish girl, overcome generations of prejudice against Jews when they face common danger as they flee war and famine during the 1980s. (Rev: BCCB 9/98; BL 5/1/98; HBG 10/98; SLJ 7/98; VOYA 10/98)

10590 Levitin, Sonia. *Dream Freedom* (5–9). 2000, Harcourt $17.00 (978-0-15-202404-8). A novel that graphically portrays the plight of Sudanese slaves, juxtaposed with the story of an American 5th-grade class that joins the fight to free them. (Rev: BL 11/1/00; HBG 3/01; SLJ 10/00; VOYA 12/00)

10591 McCall Smith, Alexander. *Akimbo and the Elephants* (3–5). Illus. by LeUyen Pham. 2005, Bloomsbury $9.95 (978-1-58234-686-1). Ten-year-old Akimbo, who lives with his ranger father on an African game preserve, helps to track down poachers who are killing full-grown elephants for their ivory tusks. Also use *Akimbo and the Lions* (2005), in which he adopts a lion cub. (Rev: BL 9/1/05; SLJ 11/05)

10592 McCaughrean, Geraldine. *Casting the Gods Adrift: A Tale of Ancient Egypt* (5–8). Illus. by Patricia D. Ludlow. 2003, Cricket $15.95 (978-0-8126-2684-1). History and fiction are intertwined in this well-illustrated, suspenseful novel about two boys who are content to be taken in by the Pharoah Akhenaten, and a father enraged by the Pharaoh's refusal to worship the traditional Egyptian gods. (Rev: BCCB 10/03; BL 10/15/03; HBG 4/04; SLJ 8/03)

10593 McKissack, Patricia C. *Never Forgotten* (4–8). Illus. by Leo Dillon. 2011, Random House $18.99 (978-0-375-84384-6); LB $21.99 (978-0-375-94453-6). 48pp. Full of magical realism, this is the wrenching story, told in free verse, of a father left behind in West Africa after his son is taken to America in a slave ship. Coretta Scott King Author Honor 2012; ALA Notable Children's Book 2012. ℮ (Rev: BL 9/1/11*; SLJ 9/1/11*)

10594 McKissack, Patricia C. *Nzingha: Warrior Queen of Matamba* (5–8). Series: Royal Diaries. 2000, Scholastic paper $10.95 (978-0-439-11210-9). Based on fact, this is the story of 17th-century African queen Nzingha who, in present-day Angola, resisted the Portuguese colonizers and slave traders. (Rev: BL 11/1/00; HBG 3/01; SLJ 12/00)

10595 Mankell, Henning. *Secrets in the Fire* (4–8). 2003, Annick $14.95 (978-1-55037-801-6); paper $7.95 (978-1-55037-800-9). This is the true story of Sofia, a courageous Mozambican girl who lost both legs — and her sister — when a landmine exploded. (Rev: BL 12/15/03*; SLJ 5/04)

10596 Marsden, Carolyn, and Philip Matzigkeit. *Sahwira: An African Friendship* (5–8). 2009, Candlewick $15.99 (978-0-7636-3575-6). 208pp. In Rhodesia in the late 1960s, Evan, son of a white American teacher, and Blessing, son of a Shona pastor, find their friendship is challenged by the political and racial tensions that surround them. (Rev: BCCB 7–8/09; BL 4/15/09; SLJ 5/09; VOYA 6/09)

10597 Marston, Elsa. *The Ugly Goddess* (5–8). 2002, Cricket $16.95 (978-0-8126-2667-4). In 523 B.C. Egypt, a 14-year-old Egyptian princess, a young Greek soldier who is in love with her, and an Egyptian boy become embroiled in a mystery adventure that blends fact, fiction, and fantasy. (Rev: BL 1/1–15/03; HBG 3/03; SLJ 12/02)

10598 Michael, Jan. *City Boy* (5–8). 2009, Clarion $16.00 (978-0-547-22310-0). 192pp. In Malawi, after his parents' deaths from AIDS, Sam must swap his urban environment for his aunt's one-room hut. (Rev: BL 5/1/09; HB 9/09)

10599 Milway, Katie Smith. *Mimi's Village: And How Basic Health Care Transformed It* (2–5). Illus. by Eugenie Fernandes. Series: CitizenKid. 2012, Kids Can $18.95 (978-1-55453-722-8). 32pp. Young Mimi's family helps to bring better health care to a rural Kenyan village through some simple and some ambitious measures. Lexile 980L (Rev: BL 9/15/12; LMC 5–6/13; SLJ 10/12)

10600 Milway, Katie Smith. *One Hen: How One Small Loan Made a Big Difference* (2–5). Illus. by Eugenie Fernandes. 2008, Kids Can $18.95 (978-1-55453-028-1). In a village in rural Ghana where microlending is being introduced, young Kojo gets enough money to buy a hen; the eggs from the hen give him enough money to buy another and he eventually creates a large enterprise and is able in turn to help others. (Rev: BCCB 3/08; BL 6/1–15/08; LMC 5/08; SLJ 5/08)

10601 Mwangi, Meja. *The Mzungu Boy* (5–8). 2005, Groundwood $15.95 (978-0-88899-653-4). In 1950s Kenya, a 12-year-old Kenyan boy becomes friendly with the white landowner's son despite both families' disapproval. (Rev: BL 8/05; SLJ 11/05)

10602 Naidoo, Beverley. *Journey to Jo'burg: A South African Story* (4–6). Illus. by Eric Velasquez. 1986, HarperCollins paper $4.99 (978-0-06-440237-8). 96pp. The story of Naledi, from a South African village, who travels to the city with her brother to seek their mother, who works in the home of whites, because their baby sister is dying. (Rev: BCCB 5/86; BL 3/25/86; SLJ 8/86)

10603 Naidoo, Beverley. *No Turning Back* (5–9). 1997, HarperCollins $15.89 (978-0-06-027506-8). Jaabu, a homeless African boy, looks for shelter in contemporary Johannesburg. (Rev: BCCB 2/97; BL 12/15/96*; HB 3–4/97; SLJ 2/97; VOYA 10/97)

10604 Platt, Richard. *Egyptian Diary: The Journal of Nakht* (4–6). Illus. by David Parkins. 2005, Candlewick $17.99 (978-0-7636-2756-0). 64pp. Nakht, a 9-year-old Egyptian boy training to become a scribe like his father, records in his journal observations about life in ancient Memphis, giving readers a good idea of Egyptian culture that is bolstered by the back matter. (Rev: BL 11/15/05; SLJ 2/06)

10605 Turner, Ann. *Maïa of Thebes: 1463 B.C.* (4–6). Series: Life and Times. 2005, Scholastic $10.95 (978-0-439-65223-0). 160pp. In the time of Queen Hatshepsut, 13-year-old Maïa finds her life in danger. (Rev: BL 6/1–15/05)

10606 Williams, Mary. *Brothers in Hope: The Story of the Lost Boys of Sudan* (3–5). Illus. by R. Gregory Christie. 2005, Lee & Low $17.95 (978-1-58430-232-2). 40pp. Garang, a Sudanese boy, flees to Ethiopia and then Kenya, where he finds a home in a refugee camp and hopes to find a way to get to America; this first-person account includes evocative paintings. (Rev: BL 5/1/05; SLJ 6/05)

10607 Yohalem, Eve. *Escape Under the Forever Sky* (5–8). 2009, Chronicle $16.99 (978-0-8118-6653-8). 228pp. Lucy, 13-year-old daughter of the U.S. ambassador to Ethiopia, sneaks out of the house and is kidnapped; her survival skills help her when she manages to escape. (Rev: BL 5/1/09; SLJ 5/09)

Asia

10608 Alexander, Lloyd. *Dream-of-Jade: The Emperor's Cat* (3–5). Illus. by D. Brent Burkett. 2005, Cricket $16.95 (978-0-8126-2736-7). 48pp. Dream-of-Jade, a talking cat, develops a close friendship with a lonely Chinese emperor. (Rev: BL 9/15/05; HBG 4/06; SLJ 11/05)

10609 Coatsworth, Elizabeth. *The Cat Who Went to Heaven* (4–6). Illus. by Lynd Ward. 1990, Simon & Schuster LB $17.00 (978-0-02-719710-5). 72pp. A charming legend of a Japanese artist, his cat, and a Buddhist miracle. Newbery Medal winner, 1931.

10610 Conlogue, Ray. *Shen and the Treasure Fleet* (5–8). 2007, Annick $21.95 (978-1-55451-104-4); paper $11.95 (978-1-55451-103-7). Shen and his sister Chang try to free their mother and learn their father's fate while at sea with Zheng He's "treasure fleet" in early 15th-century China. (Rev: BL 11/15/07)

10611 D'Adamo, Francesco. *Iqbal: A Novel* (4–7). 2003, Simon & Schuster $15.95 (978-0-689-85445-3). The sad story of the death of Iqbal, the young child labor activist, is brought to life through the fictional narrative of a young Pakistani girl who worked with him in the carpet factories. (Rev: BL 11/1/03; HB 11–12/03; HBG 4/04; SLJ 11/03)

10612 Ellis, Deborah. *The Breadwinner* (5–7). 2001, Groundwood $15.95 (978-0-88899-419-6). In Kabul under the strict rule of the Taliban, Parvana dresses as a boy so she can work to feed the remaining women in her family. (Rev: BL 3/1/01; HBG 10/01; SLJ 7/01; VOYA 6/01)

10613 Ellis, Deborah. *Mud City* (4–7). Series: Breadwinner Trilogy. 2003, Douglas & McIntyre $15.95 (978-0-88899-518-6). Feisty Afghan refugee Shauzia sets off on her own, dreaming of a life of freedom in France and prepared to dress as a boy and beg, but circumstances force her back to the camp on the Pakistan border in this final novel in the trilogy. (Rev: BL 11/15/03; HBG 4/04; SLJ 11/03)

10614 Ellis, Deborah. *My Name Is Parvana* (5–8). Series: Breadwinner. 2012, Groundwood $16.95 (978-1-55498-297-4). 204pp. Parvana is now 15 and uncooperative with her American captors in this sequel to the moving books about life in turbulent Afghanistan. e Lexile 670L (Rev: BL 10/15/12; SLJ 10/12*)

10615 Ellis, Deborah. *No Ordinary Day* (4–7). 2011, Groundwood $16.95 (978-1-55498-134-2). 144pp. Valli, a poor Indian orphan who has a fear of lepers, is horrified to hear that she herself has the disease. ALA Notable Children's Book 2012. (Rev: BL 11/1/11*; SLJ 9/1/11*)

10616 Fleischman, Sid. *The White Elephant* (3–5). Illus. by Robert McGuire. 2006, Greenwillow $15.99 (978-0-06-113136-3). 112pp. Run Run, a young elephant

trainer, angers Prince Noi and as a punishment is given a white elephant that he must care for but cannot put to work because of its rarity. (Rev: BL 9/1/06; SLJ 10/06)

10617 Harrison, Troon. *The Horse Road* (4–7). 2012, Bloomsbury $16.99 (978-1-59990-846-5). 304pp. In ancient central Asia horse-crazy Kalli, a young teen, must act to save her beloved horses from invaders; a history-rich novel with lots of detail. e Lexile 1050L (Rev: BL 8/12; LMC 10/12; SLJ 9/12)

10618 Ho, Minfong. *The Clay Marble* (5–9). 1991, Houghton Mifflin $12.00 (978-0-395-77155-6). After fleeing from her Cambodian home in the early 1980s, 12-year-old Dara is separated from her family during an attack on a refugee camp on the Thailand border. (Rev: BL 11/15/91; SLJ 10/91)

10619 Hoobler, Dorothy, and Thomas Hoobler. *The Sword That Cut the Burning Grass* (5–8). Series: The Samurai Mysteries. 2005, Philomel $10.99 (978-0-399-24272-4). In this fourth book about the aspiring young samurai, Seikei tackles a challenging task involving the teenage emperor. (Rev: BL 5/1/05; SLJ 10/05)

10620 Huynh, Quang Nhuong. *The Land I Lost: Adventures of a Boy in Vietnam* (5–8). Illus. by Mai Vo Dinh. 1990, HarperCollins $15.89 (978-0-397-32448-4); paper $5.99 (978-0-06-440183-8). The story of a boy's growing up in rural Vietnam before the war.

10621 Jiang, Ji-Li. *Red Kite, Blue Kite* (1–3). Illus. by Greg Ruth. 2013, Disney/Hyperion $17.99 (978-142312753-6). 32pp. When his father is taken to a labor camp during the Cultural Revolution, he and Tai Shan communicate through flying the kites they both love. Asian Pacific American Award for Literature: Picture Book. Lexile 630 (Rev: BL 1/13; LMC 5–6/13*; SLJ 1/13)

10622 Kang, Hildi. *Chengli and the Silk Road Caravan* (4–6). 2011, Tanglewood $14.95 (978-1-933718-54-5). 200pp. In 7th-century China, 13-year-old Chengli sets out on an adventure along China's Silk Road in a quest to learn more about the father he never knew. (Rev: BLO 10/1/11; LMC 1–2/12; SLJ 10/1/11)

10623 Kelly, Lynne. *Chained* (4–7). 2012, Farrar $16.99 (978-037431237-4). 256pp. Hastin, 10, takes a job looking after a young elephant who is mistreated by a cruel circus owner in this moving story set in northern India. e Lexile 770L (Rev: BL 6/12; HB 7–8/12; LMC 8/12*; SLJ 6/12)

10624 La Valley, Josanne. *The Vine Basket* (5–8). 2013, Clarion $16.99 (978-054784801-3). 256pp. Mehrigul, a Uyghur girl living in China and yearning to go to school, is skilled at making beautiful baskets; can she translate this into a brighter future for herself and her family? Amelia Bloomer List. ⌾ e Lexile 740 (Rev: BL 4/15/13; LMC 10/13; SLJ 5/13*)

10625 Lasky, Kathryn. *Jahanara: Princess of Princesses* (4–8). Series: Royal Diaries. 2002, Scholastic paper $10.95 (978-0-439-22350-8). Princess Jaharana, the daughter of Shah Jahan (who built the Taj Mahal) writes detailed diary accounts of her 17th-century life, with rich descriptions of her surroundings, palace intrigues, and dealing with her family. (Rev: BL 1/1–15/03; HBG 3/03; SLJ 1/03)

10626 Lloyd, Alison. *Year of the Tiger* (5–8). 2010, Holiday House $16.95 (978-0-8234-2277-7). 208pp. In ancient China two 12-year-old boys from different backgrounds become friends amid turbulent times. Lexile 600L (Rev: BL 4/15/10; LMC 10/10; SLJ 6/10)

10627 Louis, Catherine. *Liu and the Bird: A Journey in Chinese Calligraphy* (2–4). Trans. by Sibylle Kazeroid. Illus. by Feng Xiao Min. 2006, North-South $16.95 (978-0-7358-2050-0). 40pp. A young Chinese girl draws for her grandfather the things she saw on her journey to visit him in this introduction to calligraphic symbols. (Rev: BL 4/15/06; SLJ 4/06)

10628 Malaspina, Ann. *Yasmin's Hammer* (2–5). Illus. by Doug Chayka. 2010, Lee & Low $18.95 (978-1-60060-359-4). 40pp. Yasmin struggles to raise money so she and her sister can attend school in Dhaka, Bangladesh. (Rev: BL 5/15/10; LMC 10/10; SLJ 7/1/10)

10629 Marsden, Carolyn, and Thay Phap Niem. *The Buddha's Diamonds* (3–5). 2008, Candlewick $14.99 (978-0-7636-3380-6). 112pp. Ten-year-old Vietnamese Tinh struggles to help his family after a cyclone devastates his small fishing village; includes Buddhist concepts, a glossary, and endnotes. (Rev: BL 3/15/08; LMC 3/08; SLJ 6/08)

10630 Myers, Walter Dean. *Patrol: An American Soldier in Vietnam* (4–8). Illus. by Ann Grifalconi. 2002, HarperCollins LB $17.89 (978-0-06-028364-3). A penetrating picture book for older readers told in narrative verse from the perspective of a teenage soldier in Vietnam. (Rev: BL 3/15/02; HB 7–8/02; HBG 10/02; SLJ 5/02)

10631 Neuberger, Anne E. *The Girl-Son* (3–6). Illus. 1994, Carolrhoda LB $21.27 (978-0-87614-846-4). Based on fact, this is the story of a Korean girl born in 1896 and her fight for women's rights. (Rev: BCCB 2/95; BL 1/1/95; SLJ 2/95)

10632 Neville, Emily C. *The China Year* (5–8). 1991, HarperCollins $15.95 (978-0-06-024383-8). Henri, 14, has left her New York City home, school, and friends to go to Peking University for a year with her father. (Rev: BL 5/1/91; SLJ 5/91)

10633 Noyes, Deborah. *When I Met the Wolf Girls* (3–5). Illus. by August Hall. 2007, Houghton $17.00 (978-0-618-60567-5). 40pp. An orphan girl named Bulu narrates this story, based on truth, about two young girls raised by wolves and their difficulties adapting to life at an Indian orphanage. (Rev: BL 3/15/07)

10634 Park, Linda Sue. *The Kite Fighters* (4–6). 2000, Clarion $15.00 (978-0-395-94041-9). 144pp. Contests involving kite flying are the subject of this exciting novel set in 15th-century Korea. (Rev: BCCB 6/00; BL 4/1/00; HB 5/00; HBG 10/00; SLJ 6/00)

10635 Park, Linda Sue. *Seesaw Girl* (4–7). 1999, Clarion $14.00 (978-0-395-91514-1). In 17th-century Korea, 12-year-old Jade Blossom wanders away from her aristocratic palace and discovers the reality and poverty of

the world outside. (Rev: BCCB 12/99; BL 9/1/99; HBG 3/00; SLJ 9/99)

10636 Park, Linda Sue. *A Single Shard* (4–8). 2001, Clarion $15.00 (978-0-395-97827-6). This Newbery Medal winner describes a Korean boy's journey through unknown territory to deliver two valuable pots. (Rev: BCCB 3/01; BL 4/1/01*; HBG 10/01; SLJ 5/01*)

10637 Park, Linda Sue. *When My Name Was Keoko* (5–9). 2002, Clarion $16.00 (978-0-618-13335-2). A young brother and sister tell, in first-person accounts, what life was like during the Japanese occupation of Korea. (Rev: BCCB 5/02; BL 3/1/02; HB 5–6/02; HBG 10/02; SLJ 4/02)

10638 Paterson, Katherine. *The Master Puppeteer* (4–7). Illus. by Haru Wells. 1989, HarperCollins paper $5.99 (978-0-06-440281-1). Feudal Japan is the setting for this story about a young apprentice puppeteer and his search for a mysterious bandit.

10639 Paterson, Katherine. *Of Nightingales That Weep* (4–7). Illus. by Haru Wells. 1974, HarperCollins paper $6.99 (978-0-06-440282-8). A story set in feudal Japan tells of Takiko, a samurai's daughter, who is sent to the royal court when her mother remarries.

10640 Paterson, Katherine. *The Sign of the Chrysanthemum* (5–7). Illus. by Peter Landa. 1973, HarperCollins LB $14.89 (978-0-690-04913-8); paper $5.99 (978-0-06-440232-3). At the death of his mother, a young boy sets out to find his samurai father in 12th-century Japan.

10641 Peet, Mal, and Elspeth Graham. *Cloud Tea Monkeys* (2–4). Illus. by Juan Wijngaard. 2010, Candlewick $15.99 (978-0-7636-4453-6). 56pp. Friendly monkeys come to young Tashi's aid when her mother is too ill to work in the tea plantation in the Himalayas. (Rev: BL 2/15/10; LMC 8–9/10; SLJ 4/1/10)

10642 Perkins, Mitali. *Bamboo People* (5–8). 2010, Charlesbridge $16.95 (978-1-58089-328-2). 272pp. Contemporary Burma is seen through the perspectives of two protagonists — 15-year-old Chiko, reluctant soldier and son of an imprisoned doctor, and Tu Reh, a Karenni refugee. YALSA Top Ten Best Fiction for Young Adults 2011. ♫ Lexile 680L (Rev: BL 5/15/10; HB 7–8/10; LMC 11–12/10; SLJ 11/1/10*)

10643 Perkins, Mitali. *Rickshaw Girl* (2–5). Illus. by Jamie Hogan. 2007, Charlesbridge $13.95 (978-1-58089-308-4). Naima is a talented painter of the traditional alpana patterns but she longs to do more to help her poor Bangladeshi family, even driving her father's rickshaw, an occupation forbidden to girls. (Rev: BCCB 5/07; BL 11/1/06; HB 5/6–07; LMC 5/07; SLJ 4/07)

10644 Place, Francois. *The Old Man Mad About Drawing* (5–8). Trans. by William Rodarmor. 2003, Godine $19.95 (978-1-56792-260-8). In 19th-century Edo (now Tokyo), Tojiro, a 9-year-old orphan who sells rice cakes, becomes the assistant to a famous old artist. (Rev: BL 3/15/04*; HB 3–4/04; SLJ 5/04)

10645 Reedy, Trent. *Words in the Dust* (5–8). 2011, Scholastic $17.99 (978-0-545-26125-8). 266pp. Learning to read and the unexpected opportunity to have her cleft palate repaired give 13-year-old Afghani Zulaikha a new outlook on life. ♫ Lexile 670L (Rev: BL 1/1–15/11; LMC 5–6/11; SLJ 2/1/11)

10646 Rocco, John. *Fu Finds the Way* (3–5). Illus. by author. 2009, Hyperion $16.99 (978-1-4231-0965-5). 40pp. Young Fu averts a deadly duel by impressing a great warrior with his mastery of the tea ceremony in this handsome picture book. (Rev: BLO 1/1/10; LMC 3–4/10; SLJ 10/1/09)

10647 Russell, Ching Yeung. *Child Bride* (4–7). 1999, Boyds Mills $15.95 (978-1-56397-748-0). Set in China in the early 1940s, this is the story of 11-year-old Ying, her arranged marriage, and an understanding bridegroom who allows her to go home to her ailing grandmother. (Rev: BL 3/1/99; HBG 10/99; SLJ 4/99)

10648 Russell, Ching Yeung. *Lichee Tree* (4–7). 1997, Boyds Mills $15.95 (978-1-56397-629-2). Growing up in China during the 1940s, Ying dreams of selling lichee nuts and visiting Canton. (Rev: BCCB 4/97; BL 3/15/97; SLJ 6/97)

10649 Russell, Ching Yeung. *Tofu Quilt* (3–6). 2009, Lee & Low $16.95 (978-160060423-2). 136pp. A novel in free verse about a young girl determined to be a writer, who struggles with societal restrictions in 1960s Hong Kong. ℮ (Rev: BL 11/1/09; SLJ 10/09)

10650 Say, Allen. *The Boy in the Garden* (K–2). Illus. by author. 2010, Houghton Mifflin $17.99 (978-0-547-21410-8). 32pp. The ancient Japanese folk tale about a crane that turns into a woman is revisited in this quiet, evocative story about young Jori. ℮ (Rev: BL 9/1/10; HB 9–10/10; LMC 5–6–11*; SLJ 10/1/10)

10651 Say, Allen. *Tea with Milk* (4–8). 1999, Houghton Mifflin LB $17.00 (978-0-395-90495-4). A picture book about the author's mother, who was forced by her father to leave her California residence and return to the family's original home in Japan. (Rev: BCCB 6/99; BL 3/15/99*; HB 7–8/99; HBG 10/99; SLJ 5/99) [952]

10652 Sheth, Kashmira. *Boys Without Names* (4–7). 2010, HarperCollins $15.99 (978-0-06-185760-7). 320pp. Eleven-year-old Gopal's rural family cannot make ends meet and heads for Mumbai where the boy looks for work only to find himself a captive in a soul-crushing sweatshop. ℮ Lexile 670L (Rev: BL 11/15/09; SLJ 1/10)

10653 Smith, Icy. *Half Spoon of Rice: A Survival Story of the Cambodian Genocide* (4–7). Illus. by Sopaul Nhem. 2010, East West Discovery Press $19.95 (978-0-9821675-8-8). 44pp. Nine-year-old Nat relates his shocking experiences after the Khmer Rouge force millions to leave Phnom Penh and work in the fields; a moving picture book for older readers. (Rev: BL 12/15/09; LMC 5–6/10; SLJ 12/09)

10654 Sreenivasan, Jyotsna. *Aruna's Journeys* (4–7). 1997, Smooth Stone paper $6.95 (978-0-9619401-7-1). Aruna denies her Indian heritage until she spends a summer in Bangalore, India. (Rev: BL 7/97)

10655 Suneby, Elizabeth. *Razia's Ray of Hope: One Girl's Dream of an Education* (3–5). Illus. by Suana Ver-

elst. 2013, Kids Can $19.95 (978-155453816-4). 36pp. Young Razia wants to go to the new girl's school that is being opened in her rural Afghani village, but her father and brother are against girls being educated; inspired by a true story. USBBY Outstanding International Picture Book. Lexile 680 (Rev: BL 9/15/13; SLJ 9/13)

10656 Tenzing, Norbu. *Himalaya* (3–5). Trans. from French by Shelley Tanaka. Illus. by author. 2002, Groundwood $16.95 (978-0-88899-480-6). A gripping saga, beautifully illustrated, about the Dolpo people of Nepal, their grueling treks through the mountains, and the transfer of leadership. (Rev: HBG 3/03; SLJ 1/03)

10657 Tenzing, Norbu, and Stephane Frattini. *Secret of the Snow Leopard* (3–5). Trans. from French by Shelley Tanaka. Illus. by Tenzing Norbu. 2004, Groundwood $16.95 (978-0-88899-544-5). In beautifully illustrated Nepal, young Tsering defies his stepfather and travels through a dangerous pass where his father lost his life; there he encounters a snow leopard and must draw on his inner strength. (Rev: SLJ 8/04)

10658 Thomason, Mark. *Moonrunner* (4–8). 2009, Kane/Miller $15.95 (978-1-935279-03-7). 217pp. In 1890s Australia, Casey, 12, copes with a difficult transition to a new home by befriending a spirited wild stallion that he decides to save from captivity at all costs. Lexile 620L (Rev: BL 4/15/09; SLJ 6/1/09)

10659 Vejjajiva, Jane. *The Happiness of Kati* (4–7). Trans. by Prudence Borthwick. 2006, Simon & Schuster $15.95 (978-1-4169-1788-5). Nine-year-old Kati's mother is dying and the identity of her father is a mystery in this story set in Thailand. (Rev: BL 5/15/06; SLJ 6/06)

10660 Whelan, Gloria. *Goodbye, Vietnam* (5–8). 1992, Turtleback paper $11.65 (978-0-606-05848-3). Young Mai and her family escape from Vietnam to Hong Kong, suffering through a difficult boat journey; originally published in 1992. (Rev: BL 4/15/06; HB 1/93; SLJ 9/92)

10661 Whitesel, Cheryl Aylward. *Blue Fingers: A Ninja's Tale* (5–8). 2004, Clarion $15.00 (978-0-618-38139-5). In 16th-century Japan, 12-year-old Koji is trained to become a ninja warrior. (Rev: BL 3/15/04; SLJ 3/04)

10662 Whitesel, Cheryl Aylward. *Rebel: A Tibetan Odyssey* (5–8). 2000, HarperCollins $16.99 (978-0-688-16735-6). In Tibet about a century ago, a young boy named Thunder is sent to live with his uncle, an important lama in a Buddhist monastery. (Rev: BCCB 5/00; BL 4/15/00; HBG 3/01; SLJ 7/00)

10663 Wu, Priscilla. *The Abacus Contest: Stories from Taiwan and China* (5–8). 1996, Fulcrum $15.95 (978-1-55591-243-7). Six simple short stories explore life in a Taiwanese city. (Rev: BL 7/96; SLJ 6/96)

10664 Yep, Laurence. *Lady of Ch'iao Kuo: Warrior of the South* (5–8). Series: Royal Diaries. 2001, Scholastic $10.95 (978-0-439-16483-2). In this volume of the Royal Diaries series, the teenage Princess Redbird of the Hsien tribe must use her diplomatic skills to save the lives of both her own people and Chinese colonists in the 6th century A.D. Historical notes add background information. (Rev: BL 11/1/01)

10665 Yue, Guo, and Clare Farrow. *Little Leap Forward: A Boy in Beijing* (3–6). Illus. by Helen Cann. 2008, Barefoot Books $16.99 (978-1-84686-114-7). 126pp. A caged bird teaches 8-year-old Leap Forward about freedom in this moving story set during the 1960s Cultural Revolution in China; based on the author's childhood. (Rev: BL 8/08; HB 9/08)

Europe

10666 Anholt, Laurence. *Leonardo and the Flying Boy* (2–4). Illus. 2000, Barron's $15.99 (978-0-7641-5225-2). 32pp. A fictionalized account of da Vinci's life and accomplishments as reflected in anecdotes about his young apprentices. (Rev: BL 1/1–15/01; SLJ 2/01)

10667 Attema, Martha. *Daughter of Light* (3–5). Illus. 2001, Orca paper $4.99 (978-1-55143-179-6). 138pp. In this affecting novel, which takes place in the Nazi-occupied Netherlands during World War II, a 9-year-old girl braves German soldiers and risks her freedom to help her pregnant mother. (Rev: BL 2/1/02; SLJ 12/01)

10668 Banks, Lynne Reid. *Tiger, Tiger* (5–8). 2005, Delacorte LB $17.99 (978-0-385-90264-9). Two tiger cubs arrive in Rome destined for different fates; Brute is trained to be a killer of men in the Colosseum while Boots becomes a pet for the caesar's daughter, a decision with dangerous consequences. (Rev: BL 5/15/05; SLJ 6/05)

10669 Barrow, Randi. *Saving Zasha* (4–7). 2011, Scholastic $16.99 (978-0-545-20632-7). 240pp. In Russia at the end of World War II, a young boy finds a beautiful German shepherd in the woods, and becomes determined to shield the dog from the anti-German sentiment that is running rampant. ◑ (Rev: BL 2/1/11; SLJ 4/11)

10670 Bawden, Nina. *The Real Plato Jones* (5–8). 1993, Clarion $15.00 (978-0-395-66972-3). British teen Plato Jones and his mother return to Greece for his grandfather's funeral, where Plato discovers that his grandfather may have been a coward and traitor while serving in the Greek Resistance. (Rev: BCCB 11/93; BL 10/15/93; SLJ 11/93*)

10671 Bradley, Kimberly Brubaker. *The Lacemaker and the Princess* (4–8). 2007, Simon & Schuster $16.99 (978-1-4169-1920-9). As the French Revolution gathers strength, a young lace maker becomes the companion of Princess Marie-Thérèse, daughter of Marie Antoinette and King Louis XVI, and witness the growing social unrest. (Rev: BL 4/15/07; SLJ 7/07)

10672 Calkhoven, Laurie. *Michael at the Invasion of France, 1943* (4–7). 2012, Dial $16.99 (978-080373724-2). 144pp. Michael, 13, finds ways to contribute to the Resistance in Nazi-occupied France. ℮ Lexile 660L (Rev: BL 2/1/12; SLJ 3/12)

10673 Clark, Kathy. *Guardian Angel House* (5–8). Series: Holocaust Remembrance. 2009, Second Story paper $14.95 (978-1-897187-58-6). 200pp. Two Jewish sisters

— 12-year-old Susan and 6-year-old Vera — find a safe haven from the Nazis in the Guardian Angel House, a Catholic convent in Budapest; based on the experiences of the author's aunt. (Rev: SLJ 2/10; VOYA 2/10)

10674 *Clay Man: The Golem of Prague* (5–8). Retold by Irene N. Watts. Illus. by Kathryn E. Shoemaker. 2009, Tundra $19.95 (978-0-88776-880-4). 84pp. Told from the perspective of pensive 13-year-old Jacob, the story of the magical golem who protected the Jews of 16th-century Prague is illustrated in striking black-and-white drawings. ℮ Lexile 780L (Rev: BLO 12/1/09; SLJ 3/10)

10675 Clements, Bruce. *A Chapel of Thieves* (4–6). 2002, Farrar $16.00 (978-0-374-37701-4). In this sequel to *I Tell a Lie Every So Often* (1974), Henry, an adventurous 15-year-old, journeys across the Atlantic to Paris in 1849 to rescue his older brother from a gang of thieves. (Rev: BCCB 4/02; BL 3/15/02; HBG 10/02; SLJ 5/02)

10676 Creech, Sharon. *The Castle Corona* (4–7). Illus. by David Diaz. 2007, HarperCollins $18.99 (978-0-06-084621-3). This lively and entertaining fairy tale set in medieval Italy follows a pair of orphaned peasant children named Pia and Enzio who become tasters for the royal family of Castle Corona. ◑ (Rev: BL 9/1/07; SLJ 10/07)

10677 Curtis, Chara M. *No One Walks on My Father's Moon* (4–8). 1996, Voyage LB $16.95 (978-0-9649454-1-8). A Turkish boy is accused of blasphemy when he states that a man has walked on the moon. (Rev: BL 11/15/96)

10678 Davis, Tony. *Future Knight* (2–4). Illus. by Gregory Rogers. 2009, Delacorte $12.99 (978-038573800-2); LB $15.99 (978-038590706-4). 160pp. In 1409 Roland Wright, 10-year-old son of a blacksmith, aspires to become a knight; this story is full of details of the time. (Rev: BL 11/15/09; SLJ 8/09)

10679 de Cervantes, Miguel, and Martin Jenkins. *Don Quixote* (5–8). Illus. by Chris Riddell. 2009, Candlewick $27.99 (978-0-7636-4081-1). Suitably lighthearted, this is a faithful and nicely illustrated retelling of the story of Don Quixote and his exploits. (Rev: BL 4/15/09)

10680 DeJong, Meindert. *Wheel on the School* (4–7). Illus. by Maurice Sendak. 1954, HarperCollins LB $18.89 (978-0-06-021586-6); paper $6.95 (978-0-06-440021-3). The storks are brought back to their island by the schoolchildren in a Dutch village. Newbery Medal 1955.

10681 Deverell, Catherine. *Stradivari's Singing Violin* (3–5). Illus. by Andrea Shine. 1992, Carolrhoda LB $13.95 (978-0-87614-732-0). 48pp. A fictional account of the historical figure behind what is perhaps the world's best-known musical instrument. (Rev: BL 2/15/93)

10682 Dowswell, Paul. *Prison Ship: Adventures of a Young Sailor* (5–9). 2006, Bloomsbury $16.95 (978-1-58234-676-2). In this action-packed sequel to *Powder Monkey* set at the beginning of the 19th century, 13-year-old English sailor Sam Witchall is falsely convicted of theft and sent off to prison in Australia, where he escapes into the Outback. (Rev: SLJ 12/06)

10683 Eisner, Will. *The Last Knight: An Introduction to Don Quixote by Miguel de Cervantes* (4–8). 2000, NBM $15.95 (978-1-56163-251-0). Using an engaging text and a comic book format, this is a fine retelling of Cervantes' classic. (Rev: BL 6/1–15/00; HBG 10/00; SLJ 7/00)

10684 Ellis, Deborah. *A Company of Fools* (5–8). 2002, Fitzhenry & Whiteside $15.95 (978-1-55041-719-7). Quiet Henri and free-spirited Micah try to cheer the people of a France devastated by the Black Death of 1348 by singing. (Rev: BCCB 1/03; BL 1/1–15/03; HB 1–2/03; HBG 3/03; VOYA 2/03)

10685 Fagan, Cary. *Daughter of the Great Zandini* (3–5). Illus. by Cybele Young. 2001, Tundra LB $16.95 (978-0-88776-534-6). 57pp. The Great Zandini's son has been groomed to follow in his father's magician footsteps, but it is Fanny, the neglected daughter, who is the success in this story set in 19th-century Paris. (Rev: HBG 3/02; SLJ 4/02)

10686 Fletcher, Susan. *Falcon in the Glass* (5–8). 2013, Simon & Schuster $16.99 (978-144242990-1). 320pp. In Italy in the late 1400s young Renzo struggles to learn glassmaking with the help of a girl named Letta, who has a strange connection to birds. e Lexile 660 (Rev: BL 7/13; HB 9–10/13; LMC 11–12/13; SLJ 8/13)

10687 Ford, Michael. *Birth of a Warrior* (5–8). 2008, Bloomsbury $16.99 (978-0-8027-9794-0). 256pp. Lysander's Spartan heritage is in conflict with his fondness for the Helot villages with whom he grew up in this exciting, sometimes violent, sequel to *The Fire of Ares* (2008). (Rev: BLO 12/18/08; SLJ 2/09)

10688 Ford, Michael. *The Fire of Ares* (4–6). Series: Spartan Quest. 2008, Walker $16.95 (978-0-8027-9744-5). 250pp. In ancient Sparta, a young slave called Lysander is rescued by a man who recognizes Lysander's amulet as once belonging to his son. (Rev: BL 4/1/08; LMC 8/08; SLJ 4/08)

10689 French, Jackie. *Rover* (5–8). 2007, HarperCollins $17.99 (978-0-06-085078-4). When Vikings raid Hekja's Scottish village, she and her puppy are taken to Greenland, where she's enslaved to Freydis, Leif Erikson's sister; Hekja's dog can spot icebergs, and the two accompany Freydis on her voyage to North America in this compelling, historically accurate story. (Rev: BL 1/1–15/07; SLJ 6/07)

10690 Gilson, Jamie. *Stink Alley* (4–7). 2002, HarperCollins LB $15.89 (978-0-06-029217-1). Twelve-year-old orphan Lizzy Tinker, a Separatist who fled England with her family for Holland in 1608, is befriended by the boy who would one day be known as Rembrandt. (Rev: BCCB 9/02; BL 4/15/02; HB 9–10/02; HBG 3/03; SLJ 7/02)

10691 Glaser, Linda. *Bridge to America* (3–5). 2005, Houghton $16.00 (978-0-618-56301-2). 208pp. Fivel, a young Jew from Poland, describes his life in the shtetl, the agonizing wait for money to fund his family's journey to join his father in the United States, and the diffi-

culties in adjusting when he arrives. (Rev: BL 8/05; SLJ 11/05)

10692 Gonzalez, Christina Diaz. *A Thunderous Whisper* (5–8). 2012, Knopf $16.99 (978-037586929-7); LB $19.99 (978-037596929-4). 304pp. During the Spanish Civil War 12-year-old Ani and Mathias, a 14-year-old German Jew, become friends and work for the rebels resisting Franco in the weeks before the bombing of Guernica. e Lexile 660L (Rev: BL 12/15/12; LMC 1–2/13; SLJ 1/13)

10693 Gordon, Sharon. *Greece* (2–4). Illus. Series: Discovering Cultures. 2003, Benchmark LB $25.64 (978-0-7614-1718-7). 48pp. This well-illustrated overview of Greece and its people includes the usual information offered for this age group, plus some less well-known details. (Rev: SLJ 4/04) [949.5]

10694 Greene, Jacqueline Dembar. *The Secret Shofar of Barcelona* (1–3). Illus. by Doug Chayka. 2009, Lerner LB $17.95 (978-0-8225-9915-9); paper $7.95 (978-0-8225-9944-9). 32pp. A brave Jew who stays loyal to his faith in post-Inquisition Spain contrives clever ways to continue celebrating his religious traditions in this inspiring story. (Rev: BL 11/15/09; LMC 11–12/09; SLJ 10/1/09)

10695 Gregory, Kristiana. *Catherine: The Great Journey* (4–7). Series: Royal Diaries. 2005, Scholastic $10.99 (978-0-439-25385-7). The imagined diary of Catherine the Great's teenage years and her engagement to the Grand Duke of Russia; plenty of historical background gives readers a sense of Catherine's times. (Rev: SLJ 5/06)

10696 Gregory, Kristiana. *Eleanor: Crown Jewel of Aquitaine* (3–6). Series: Royal Diaries. 2002, Scholastic $10.95 (978-0-439-16484-9). 192pp. Eleanor's fictional diary details her daily life in the 12th century — as a child and later as a queen — giving readers a good sense of her times. (Rev: BL 2/1/03; HBG 3/03; SLJ 1/03)

10697 Hartnett, Sonya. *The Midnight Zoo* (5–8). Illus. by Andrea Offermann. 2011, Candlewick $16.99 (978-0-7636-5339-2). 208pp. Caged animals share their horrors with Romany brothers Andrej, 12, and Tomas, 9, who are fleeing a German attack in World War II. ⌒ e Lexile 940L (Rev: BL 8/11; HB 9–10/11; LMC 11–12/11; SLJ 9/1/11; VOYA 10/11)

10698 Hartnett, Sonya. *The Silver Donkey* (5–8). Illus. by Don Powers. 2006, Candlewick $15.99 (978-0-7636-2937-3). Two young French children find and help a wounded World War I soldier in the woods near their home, and as he heals he tells them stories about the tiny silver donkey he carries with him. (Rev: BL 11/15/06; SLJ 12/06)

10699 Holub, Josef. *The Robber and Me* (5–8). Trans. from German by Elizabeth D. Crawford. 1997, Henry Holt $16.95 (978-0-8050-5591-7). On his way to live with his uncle, an orphan is helped by a mysterious stranger and he must later make a decision about whether to stand up to his uncle and the town authorities to clear the name of this man in this novel set in 19th-century Germany. (Rev: SLJ 12/97*)

10700 Ibbotson, Eva. *The Star of Kazan* (4–8). Illus. by Kevin Hawkes. 2004, Dutton $16.99 (978-0-525-47347-3). Set in the Austro-Hungarian empire, this richly detailed and very readable novel tells the story of 12-year-old Annika, who gets a rude awakening when her aristocratic mother whisks her away from her adoptive family. (Rev: BL 10/15/04*; SLJ 10/04*)

10701 Jones, Terry. *The Lady and the Squire* (5–7). 2001, Pavilion $22.95 (978-1-86205-417-2). A beautiful aristocrat joins Tom and Ann as they make their way through a war-torn countryside to the papal court at Avignon. (Rev: BL 2/15/01; SLJ 3/01)

10702 Jorgensen, Norman. *In Flanders Fields* (4–7). Illus. by Brian Harrison-Lever. 2002, Fremantle Arts Centre $22.95 (978-1-86368-369-2). During a Christmas Day ceasefire in the World War I trenches, a soldier rescues a trapped robin. (Rev: SLJ 2/03)

10703 Juster, Norton. *Alberic the Wise* (4–8). Illus. by Leonard Baskin. 1992, Picture Book $16.95 (978-0-88708-243-6). In this picture book set in the Renaissance, Alberic becomes an apprentice to a stained-glass maker. (Rev: BCCB 2/93; BL 1/15/93; SLJ 3/93)

10704 Kanefield, Teri. *Rivka's Way* (4–8). 2001, Front St $15.95 (978-0-8126-2870-8). Daily life inside and outside the Prague ghetto in 1778 is explored in this novel about an unconventional Jewish girl, 15-year-old Rivka Liebermann. (Rev: BCCB 3/02; BL 4/1/01; HBG 10/01; SLJ 3/01; VOYA 10/01)

10705 Kelly, Eric P. *The Trumpeter of Krakow* (5–9). Illus. by Janina Domanska. 1966, Macmillan $17.95 (978-0-02-750140-7); paper $4.99 (978-0-689-71571-6). Mystery surrounds a precious jewel and the youthful patriot who stands watch over it in a church tower in this novel of 15th-century Poland. Newbery Medal 1929.

10706 Kimmel, Elizabeth C. *Before Columbus: The Leif Eriksson Expedition: A True Adventure* (3–6). Series: Landmark Books. 2003, Random $14.95 (978-0-375-81347-4). Kimmel extrapolates from the little that is known about Eriksson's life and adventures to create a portrait of a bold Viking explorer. (Rev: BL 7/03; HBG 4/04; SLJ 10/03) [970.01]

10707 Kingfisher, Rupert. *Madame Pamplemousse and Her Incredible Edibles* (4–6). Illus. by Sue Hellard. 2008, Bloomsbury $15.99 (978-1-59990-306-4). In this foodfest of a novel, a young Parisian girl named Madeleine is sent by her restaurateur Uncle Lard to spy on Madame Pamplemousse and discover her culinary secrets. (Rev: BLO 8/28/08; LMC 1/09)

10708 Knight, Joan MacPhail. *Charlotte in Giverny* (4–6). Illus. 2000, Chronicle $15.95 (978-0-8118-2383-8). 64pp. In this novel set in France in the 1890s a young American girl gets to know many of the American artists who are studying with Monet at Giverny and even meets the reclusive painter himself. (Rev: BL 7/00; HBG 10/00; SLJ 6/00)

10709 Knight, Joan MacPhail. *Charlotte in Paris* (3–6). Illus. by Melissa Sweet. 2003, Chronicle $16.95 (978-0-8118-3766-8). It's 1893, and Charlotte — of *Charlotte in Giverny* (2000) — is now living in Paris and details in her journal all the places she goes and the people she meets. (Rev: HBG 4/04; SLJ 1/04)

10710 Lasky, Kathryn. *Broken Song* (5–8). 2005, Viking $15.99 (978-0-670-05931-7). Reuven Bloom, a 15-year-old Jew and promising violinist, escapes from late 19th-century Russia with his baby sister, the only surviving member of his family. (Rev: BL 1/1–15/05; SLJ 3/05)

10711 Lasky, Kathryn. *Dancing Through Fire* (4–7). Series: Portraits. 2005, Scholastic paper $9.99 (978-0-439-71009-1). The Franco-Prussian War interrupts the dreams of 13-year-old Sylvie, a student at the Paris Opera Ballet in the 1870s. (Rev: BCCB 1/06; BL 12/1/05; SLJ 11/05)

10712 Lasky, Kathryn. *Marie Antoinette: Princess of Versailles* (5–8). Series: Royal Diaries. 2000, Scholastic paper $10.95 (978-0-439-07666-1). This fictional diary covers two years in the life of Marie Antoinette, beginning in 1769 when the 13-year-old was preparing for her fateful marriage. (Rev: BL 4/15/00; HBG 10/00; SLJ 5/00; VOYA 6/00)

10713 Lasky, Kathryn. *Mary, Queen of Scots: Queen Without a Country* (5–8). Series: Royal Diaries. 2002, Scholastic paper $10.95 (978-0-439-19404-4). Part of the Royal Diary series, this is a fictional diary of the year 1553, when Mary was betrothed to the son of King Henry II of France. (Rev: BL 5/15/02; HBG 10/02; SLJ 6/02)

10714 Lawrence, Caroline. *The Charioteer of Delphi* (5–8). Series: Roman Mysteries. 2007, Roaring Brook $16.95 (978-1-59643-085-3). Flavia, Jonathan, Nubia, and Lupus find themselves involved in chariot racing in Rome. (Rev: BL 8/07)

10715 Lawrence, Caroline. *Gladiators from Capua* (5–8). Series: Roman Mysteries. 2005, Roaring Brook $16.95 (978-1-59643-074-7). In their search for Jonathan, who may be alive after all, Flavia, Lupus, and Nubia venture into the coliseum and witness gladiator fights. (Rev: BL 12/1/05; SLJ 2/06)

10716 Lawrence, Iain. *The Smugglers* (5–8). 1999, Delacorte $15.95 (978-0-385-32663-6). In this continuation of *The Wreckers,* 16-year-old John Spencer faces more adventures aboard the *Dragon,* where he faces powerful enemies and must bring the ship safely to port. (Rev: BCCB 7–8/99; BL 4/1/99*; HB 5–6/99; HBG 10/99; SLJ 6/99)

10717 Leeds, Constance. *The Unfortunate Son* (5–8). 2012, Viking $16.99 (978-0-670-01398-2). 256pp. Born in 15th-century France, Luc, who is highly intelligent but has only one ear, is captured and sold into slavery but manages still to lead a lucky — and perhaps romantically successful — life. ⊖ Lexile 690L (Rev: BL 7/12; SLJ 9/12*)

10718 Lewis, J. Patrick. *The Stolen Smile* (3–6). Illus. by Gary Kelley. 2004, Creative Editions $17.95 (978-1-

56846-192-2). 40pp. Vincenzo Peruggia tells the story, based on real events, of his theft of the Mona Lisa from the Louvre in 1911. (Rev: SLJ 1/05)

10719 Littlesugar, Amy. *Willy and Max: A Holocaust Story* (2–4). Illus. by William Low. 2006, Philomel $15.99 (978-0-399-23483-5). 40pp. When the Nazis invade Belgium, Jewish boy Max and his family must flee, leaving a precious painting with the gentile family of Max's friend Willy; many years later, the painting — which was taken by the Nazis — is returned to Max's son in America; an author's note discusses the wholesale theft of artworks by the Germans. (Rev: BL 1/1–15/06; SLJ 3/06)

10720 McDonough, Yona Zeldis. *The Doll with the Yellow Star* (3–5). Illus. by Kimberly B. Root. 2005, Holt $16.95 (978-0-8050-6337-0). 64pp. Claudine, an 8-year-old Jewish girl living in France during the Nazi occupation, is sent to safety in America. (Rev: BL 9/1/05; SLJ 10/05)

10721 McKay, Sharon E. *Charlie Wilcox* (5–8). 2000, Stoddart paper $7.95 (978-0-7737-6093-6). This is the story of a 14-year-old Canadian boy who becomes involved in the trench warfare in France during World War I. (Rev: SLJ 11/00)

10722 Marsden, Carolyn. *My Own Revolution* (5–8). 2012, Candlewick $16.99 (978-0-7636-5395-8). 192pp. In 1960s Czechoslovakia, 14-year-old Patrik rebels against the regime and his family decides to flee to Italy. (Rev: BL 10/15/12; SLJ 10/12)

10723 Marsden, Carolyn. *Take Me with You* (4–7). 2010, Candlewick $14.99 (978-0-7636-3739-2). 176pp. In Italy after World War II best friends Pina and Susanna, both 11, are still at the orphanage and hoping for eventual adoption even if it means separation. (Rev: BL 1/1/10*; LMC 5–6/10; SLJ 3/10)

10724 Meyer, Carolyn. *Anastasia: The Last Grand Duchess, Russia, 1914* (4–8). Series: Royal Diaries. 2000, Scholastic paper $10.95 (978-0-439-12908-4). Anastasia's fictional diary begins when she is 12 in 1914 and ends with her captivity in 1918. (Rev: HBG 10/01; SLJ 10/00; VOYA 4/01)

10725 Meyer, Susan Lynn. *Black Radishes* (4–7). 2010, Delacorte $16.99 (978-0-385-73881-1); LB $19.99 (978-0-385-90748-4). 240pp. In World War II France, young Gustave, a Jew, takes personal risks to help the Resistance. Sydney Taylor Book Honor 2011. (Rev: BL 12/15/10; SLJ 1/1/11)

10726 Mitchell, Jack. *The Ancient Ocean Blues* (5–8). 2008, Tundra paper $9.95 (978-08877683-2-3). 128pp. In 63 B.C. Greece, teenager Marcus Oppius arrives in Athens on an espionage mission for Julius Caesar. ℮ Lexile 800L (Rev: BLO 11/15/08; SLJ 5/1/09)

10727 Mitchell, Jack. *The Roman Conspiracy* (5–9). 2005, Tundra paper $8.95 (978-0-88776-713-5). In this compelling historical thriller set in the Roman Empire, young Aulus Spurinna travels to Rome in a desperate attempt to protect his homeland of Etruria from military pillagers. (Rev: SLJ 11/05)

10728 Morpurgo, Michael. *An Elephant in the Garden* (4–8). 2011, Feiwel & Friends $16.99 (978-0-312-59369-8). 208pp. On the eve of the Allied bombing of Dresden in 1945, Lizzie and her family rescue a zoo elephant named Marlene and together they flee toward the west. (Rev: BL 10/1/11; SLJ 9/1/11)

10729 Morpurgo, Michael. *Meeting Cezanne* (2–5). Illus. by Francois Place. 2013, Candlewick $15.99 (978-076364896-1). 80pp. Ten-year-old Yannick is reluctant to spend the summer in Provence until he learns that Cézanne loved the area — and there he meets another special artist. ℮ Lexile 800 (Rev: BL 11/1/13; LMC 3–4/14)

10730 Morpurgo, Michael. *Toro! Toro!* (4–6). Illus. by Michael Foreman. 2004, Collins paper $7.95 (978-0-00-710718-6). 128pp. During the Spanish Civil War, young Antonio bonds with a bull calf born on the family farm but must let it go when the Nationalists attack their village. (Rev: BL 2/15/04; SLJ 5/04)

10731 Moss, Marissa. *Galen: My Life in Imperial Rome* (3–6). Illus. 2002, Harcourt $15.00 (978-0-15-216535-2). 48pp. Historically accurate details about life in the house of Roman Emperor Augustus are revealed through the eyes of a fictitious Greek slave in a gripping text accompanied by maps, glossary, and captioned illustrations. (Rev: BL 12/15/02; HBG 3/03; SLJ 10/02)

10732 O'Brien, Annemarie. *Lara's Gift* (5–8). 2013, Knopf $16.99 (978-030793174-0); LB $19.99 (978-037597105-1). 208pp. In imperial Russia Lara loves the borzoi hunting dogs her father breeds and hopes to succeed him as a kennel steward, but her hopes are dashed when her baby brother is born. ℮ Lexile 780 (Rev: BL 8/13; LMC 1–2/14; SLJ 9/13*)

10733 Parry, Rosanne. *Second Fiddle* (5–8). 2011, Random House $16.99 (978-0-375-86196-3); LB $19.99 (978-0-375-96196-0). 240pp. In 1990 Berlin, three 8th-grade American girls rescue a soldier beaten by Soviet officers and plot to get him safely to Paris. ♫ ℮ Lexile 810L (Rev: BL 4/15/11; SLJ 3/1/11)

10734 Pyron, Bobbie. *The Dogs of Winter* (5–9). 2012, Scholastic $16.99 (978-0-545-39930-2). 320pp. In 1990s Russia a 5-year-old boy living on the streets joins a pack of street dogs and scavenges with them. ℮ Lexile HL610L (Rev: BL 12/15/12*; HB 1–2/13; SLJ 12/12)

10735 Rappaport, Doreen. *The Secret Seder* (2–4). Illus. by Emily Arnold McCully. 2005, Hyperion $16.99 (978-0-7868-0777-2). 40pp. Young Jacques attends a secret seder in Nazi-occupied France. (Rev: BL 1/1–15/05; SLJ 2/05)

10736 Richardson, Nan. *The Pearl* (3–5). Illus. by Alexandra Young. 2011, Umbrage $17.95 (978-1-884167-24-9). Unpaged. This Russian Cinderella story set in the 18th century involves a wealthy, music-loving man and a peasant girl with a lovely voice and features beautiful illustrations and lyrical text. (Rev: SLJ 8/1/11)

10737 Richter, Jutta. *The Summer of the Pike* (4–7). Trans. by Anna Brailovsky. Illus. by Quint Buchholz. 2006, Milkweed $16.95 (978-1-57131-671-4); paper $6.95 (978-1-57131-672-1). Anna, Daniel, and Lucas, who live on the grounds of a German manor, spend a difficult summer as Anna wishes for a closer relationship with her mother and the boys' mother is slowly dying of cancer; translated from German. (Rev: BL 1/1–15/07; SLJ 12/06)

10738 Riordan, James. *Escape from War* (4–6). 2005, Kingfisher paper $6.95 (978-0-7534-5794-8). 192pp. Parallel, intersecting stories present an English boy called Frank and a German Jewish refugee called Hannah and their experiences in the English countryside during World War II. (Rev: BL 5/15/05)

10739 Robertson, Bruce. *Marguerite Makes a Book* (3–6). 1999, Getty Museum $19.95 (978-0-89236-372-8). 48pp. A stunning picture book for older readers, set in 15th-century Paris, in which young Marguerite takes over her father's book-painting craft when the old man become too infirm to work. (Rev: BL 11/15/99; HBG 3/00; SLJ 1/00)

10740 Roy, Jennifer. *Yellow Star* (5–8). 2006, Marshall Cavendish $16.95 (978-0-7614-5277-5). The fictionalized story, told in first-person free-verse chapters introduced by historical notes, of the author's aunt Syvia, a Holocaust survivor who spent much of her childhood in the grim Lodz ghetto. ∩ (Rev: BL 4/15/06; SLJ 7/06*; VOYA 6/06)

10741 Rubalcaba, Jill. *The Wadjet Eye* (5–8). 2000, Clarion $15.00 (978-0-395-68942-4). After mummifying his dead mother, Damon sets off to find his father and is later hired by Cleopatra as a spy in this action-filled novel set in the Roman Empire of 45 B.C. (Rev: BL 5/15/00; HBG 10/00; SLJ 6/00; VOYA 6/00)

10742 Rundell, Katherine. *Rooftoppers* (4–6). 2013, Simon & Schuster $16.99 (978-144249058-1). 288pp. Twelve-year-old Sophie and her guardian Charles Maxim, who came together after a shipwreck, go in search of the girl's mother in this novel set in Paris and Victorian England. ALA Notable Children's Book. ∩ ℮ Lexile 490 (Rev: BL 9/1/13*; SLJ 12/13*)

10743 Scarrow, Simon. *Fight for Freedom* (5–8). 2012, Hyperion $16.99 (978-142315101-2). 272pp. An exciting story set in ancient Rome about 10-year-old Marcus who is forced to become a gladiator but is determined to gain freedom and save his mother. ℮ (Rev: BL 4/15/12; LMC 5–6/12; SLJ 3/12)

10744 Schwartz, Ellen. *Jesse's Star* (2–5). Illus. 2000, Orca paper $4.99 (978-1-55143-143-7). 108pp. Jesse travels back in time and becomes his great-great-grandfather, a Jewish boy growing up in Russia, reliving his part in helping villagers and himself escape the pogroms and make their way to Canada. (Rev: BL 7/00; SLJ 11/00)

10745 Scott, Elaine. *Secrets of the Cirque Medrano* (5–8). 2008, Charlesbridge $15.95 (978-1-57091-712-7). In Montmartre, Paris, in 1904, 14-year-old Brigitte works in her aunt's cafe and meets the young artist Pablo Picasso and the circus performers who posed for his painting *Family of Saltambiques*. (Rev: BL 1/1–15/08; LMC 10/08; SLJ 3/08)

10746 Shefelman, Janice Jordan. *Anna Maria's Gift* (3–5). Illus. by Robert Papp. 2010, Random House $12.99 (978-0-375-85881-9); LB $15.99 (978-0-375-95881-6). 112pp. Three girls contend with love, loss, and jealousy at an orphanage in 1715 Venice, where they receive violin instruction from Antonio Vivaldi. ℮ Lexile 470L (Rev: BL 4/15/10; LMC 8–9/10; SLJ 4/1/10)

10747 Spring, Debbie. *The Righteous Smuggler* (4–6). Series: Holocaust Remembrance. 2006, Second Story paper $5.95 (978-1-896764-97-9). 160pp. Hendrik, the 12-year-old son of a Dutch fisherman, helps his father to smuggle Jews out of the country after Germany invades the Netherlands. (Rev: BL 1/1–15/06; SLJ 4/06)

10748 Stuchner, Joan Betty. *Honey Cake* (3–5). Illus. by Cynthia Nugent. 2008, Random $11.99 (978-0-375-85189-6). 112pp. David, a 10-year-old Jewish boy living in Copenhagen, Denmark, becomes involved in the Resistance during World War II. (Rev: BL 7/08)

10749 Tak, Bibi Dumon. *Soldier Bear* (4–8). Trans. by Laura Watkinson. Illus. by Philip Hopman. 2011, Eerdmans $13 (978-0-8028-5375-2). 144pp. Based on a true story, this engaging novel is about a bear called Voytek that served in the Polish army in World War II and boosts morale while also carrying live ammunition. Batchelder Award 2012; ALA Notable Children's Book 2012. ℮ Lexile 780L (Rev: BL 10/15/11; HB 11–12/11; LMC 1–2/12; SLJ 11/1/11)

10750 Thompson, Kate. *Most Wanted* (3–5). Illus. by Jonny Duddle. 2010, HarperCollins $15.99 (978-0-06-173037-5). 128pp. A baker's son finds himself in charge of the mad ruler's horse in this action-packed story based on the emperor Caligula. (Rev: BL 10/15/10; HB 1–2/11; LMC 1–2/11; SLJ 11/1/10)

10751 Thor, Annika. *The Lily Pond* (4–6). Trans. by Linda Schenck. 2011, Delacorte $16.99 (978-038574039-5); LB $19.99 (978-038590838-2). 224pp. Thirteen-year-old Stephie, an Austrian Jewish refugee, adjusts to life in the Swedish city of Gothenburg and makes friends while worrying about her parents in Vienna. ∩ (Rev: BL 12/1/11; HB 1–2/12; SLJ 1/12)

10752 Trottier, Maxine. *The Paint Box* (2–4). Illus. by Stella East. 2003, Fitzhenry & Whiteside $16.95 (978-1-55041-804-0). A compelling fictional story about Marietta, daughter of Tintoretto and talented artist herself, with beautiful illustrations and background information on the era. (Rev: BL 5/15/2003; SLJ 5/03)

10753 Visconti, Guido. *The Genius of Leonardo* (3–6). Trans. by Mark Roberts. Illus. 2000, Barefoot Books $16.99 (978-1-84148-301-6). 40pp. Using many quotes from the writings of Leonardo da Vinci, this novel tries to re-create this great man's in the eyes of his servant, Giacomo. (Rev: BCCB 10/00; BL 9/15/00; HBG 10/01; SLJ 9/00)

10754 Wild, Margaret. *Let the Celebrations Begin!* (3–6). Illus. by Julie Vivas. 1991, Watts LB $16.99 (978-0-531-08537-0). 32pp. A picture book for older children about a group of Polish women in the Belsen death camp who organized a party for the surviving children after liberation. (Rev: BCCB 9/91; BL 8/91; SLJ 7/91)

10755 Williams, Laura E. *The Spider's Web* (5–7). 1999, Milkweed paper $6.95 (978-1-57131-622-6). Lexi, a modern German girl, joins a racist skinhead organization and discovers the consequences of irrational hatred — from her own actions and from speaking with an older woman who was once a member of Hitler's Youth. (Rev: BL 6/1–15/99; HBG 10/99)

10756 Winter, Jonah. *The 39 Apartments of Ludwig van Beethoven* (3–5). Illus. by Barry Blitt. 2006, Random $15.95 (978-0-375-83602-2). 40pp. A funny "mockumentary" about Beethoven's constant moving from one apartment to another — along with his five legless pianos — and the putative reasons for these moves. (Rev: BL 8/06; SLJ 10/06)

Great Britain and Ireland

10757 Armstrong, Alan. *Raleigh's Page* (5–7). Illus. by Tim Jessell. 2007, Random House $16.99 (978-0-375-83319-9). As page to Walter Raleigh, 11-year-old Andrew learns about court life, becomes embroiled in intrigues, and has adventures that include visiting the New World. (Rev: BL 8/07; HB 11–12/07; LMC 11/07; SLJ 11/07)

10758 Avi. *Crispin: At the Edge of the World* (5–8). 2006, Hyperion $16.99 (978-0-7868-5152-2). In this compelling sequel to *Crispin: The Cross of Lead*, Bear, who Crispin now regards as a father, is seriously wounded and they make friends with a disfigured girl named Troth; Crispin now finds himself making decisions for the three. ∩ (Rev: BCCB 1/07; BL 9/15/06; HB 9–10/06; HBG 4/07; LMC 2/07; SLJ 10/06*; VOYA 10/06)

10759 Avi. *Crispin: The Cross of Lead* (5–8). 2002, Hyperion paper $6.99 (978-0-7868-1658-3). 320pp. Thirteen-year-old orphan Crispin seeks protection from a juggler named Bear in this complex novel set in medieval England. Newbery Medal. (Rev: BL 5/15/02; HB 9/02; HBG 3/03; SLJ 6/02*)

10760 Avi. *Crispin: The End of Time* (5–8). 2010, HarperCollins $16.99 (978-0-06-174080-0); LB $17.89 (978-0-06-174082-4). 240pp. Still heading for Iceland, Crispin leaves Troth at a convent that needs a healer and continues on alone, soon finding himself in danger from a group of traveling musicians. ∩ e Lexile 690L (Rev: BL 4/15/10; HB 7–8/10; SLJ 6/10)

10761 Blackwood, Gary. *Shakespeare Stealer* (5–8). 1998, NAL $16.95 (978-0-525-45863-0). A 14-year-old apprentice at the Globe Theater is sent by a rival theater company to steal Shakespeare's plays. (Rev: BL 6/1–15/98; HB 7–8/98; HBG 10/98; SLJ 6/98; VOYA 8/98)

10762 Blackwood, Gary. *Shakespeare's Spy* (5–8). 2003, Dutton $16.99 (978-0-525-47145-5). Romance and intrigue are at hand as Widge continues his career at the Globe Theatre in this sequel to *The Shakespeare Stealer* (1998) and *Shakespeare's Scribe* (2000). (Rev: BL 9/1/03; HB 11–12/03; HBG 4/04; SLJ 10/03)

10763 Bowler, Tim. *Playing Dead* (5–8). Series: Blade. 2009, Philomel $16.99 (978-0-399-25186-3). 240pp. Full of British slang and violence, this speedily paced thriller features 14-year-old Blade, a street kid with an instinct for survival amid a culture of gangs. (Rev: BL 5/1/09; HB 5/09; LMC 10/09; SLJ 8/09; VOYA 6/09)

10764 Boyne, John. *Stay Where You Are and Then Leave* (5–7). Illus. by Oliver Jeffers. 2014, Henry Holt $16.99 (978-162779031-4). 256pp. After World War I has ended, 9-year-old Alfie is shining shoes at a London station when he finds out that his father is alive but suffering from shell-shock and mental problems. Lexile 880 (Rev: BL 3/1/14; HB 5–6/14; LMC 10/14; SLJ 3/14)

10765 Bunting, Eve. *Walking to School* (2–4). Illus. by Michael Dooling. 2008, Clarion $16.00 (978-0-618-26144-4). A Catholic girl passing through a Protestant neighborhood in Northern Ireland experiences both heckling and an enriching moment with a Protestant girl; an author's note provides context. (Rev: BL 9/1/08; SLJ 9/08)

10766 Buzbee, Lewis. *The Haunting of Charles Dickens* (5–8). Illus. by Greg Ruth. 2010, Feiwel & Friends $17.99 (978-0-312-38256-8). 368pp. Twelve-year-old Meg searches the streets of 1862 London for her missing brother Orion, accompanied by a family friend, the famed author Charles Dickens. e Lexile 910L (Rev: BL 11/1/10; LMC 1–2/11; SLJ 11/10; VOYA 2/11)

10767 Cassidy, Cathy. *Scarlett* (5–8). 2006, Viking $16.99 (978-0-670-06068-9). Much to her surprise (and with some help from a mysterious boy), 12-year-old Scarlett actually enjoys living in Ireland with her father and his new family. (Rev: BL 12/1/06)

10768 Chaucer, Geoffrey. *Canterbury Tales* (4–8). Adapted by Barbara Cohen. Illus. by Trina Schart Hyman. 1988, Lothrop $26.99 (978-0-688-06201-9). Several of the popular stories are retold with handsome illustrations by Trina Schart Hyman. (Rev: BL 9/1/88; SLJ 8/88)

10769 Cottrell Boyce, Frank. *Framed* (4–7). 2006, HarperCollins $16.99 (978-0-06-073402-2). Life changes dramatically for 9-year-old Dylan Hughes and his quiet Welsh village when priceless art from London's National Gallery is temporarily stored in a nearby quarry. ∩ (Rev: BL 9/1/06; SLJ 8/06*)

10770 Cushman, Karen. *Alchemy and Meggy Swann* (4–8). 2010, Clarion $16 (978-0-547-23184-6). 176pp. In Elizabethan England, 13-year-old Meggy, who needs sticks to walk, arrives in London to work with the father who abandoned her years before; as she adapts to city life she also comes to believe that her father is in serious trouble and determines to save him. Odyssey Honor Recording 2011. ∩ (Rev: BL 3/1/10*; LMC 10/10; SLJ 4/10)

10771 Cushman, Karen. *Will Sparrow's Road* (5–7). 2012, Clarion $16.99 (978-0-547-73962-5). 224pp. In Elizabethan England young Will Sparrow has many adventures on the road and learns a lot about character. ∩ e (Rev: BL 10/1/12; HB 11–12/12; LMC 11–12/12; SLJ 11/12)

10772 De Angeli, Marguerite. *The Door in the Wall* (5–7). Illus. by Marguerite De Angeli. 1990, Dell paper $5.50 (978-0-440-40283-1). Crippled Robin proves his courage in plague-ridden 19th-century London. Newbery Medal 1950.

10773 Deedy, Carmen Agra, and Randall Wright. *The Cheshire Cheese Cat: A Dickens of a Tale* (4–6). Illus. by Barry Moser. 2011, Peachtree $16.95 (978-1-56145-595-9). 228pp. In Ye Old Cheshire Cheese Inn in 19th-century London, a cat named Skilley befriends a mouse named Pip and protects the mice and a raven from a hungry alley cat, all under the amused eyes of customer Charles Dickens. ∩ Lexile 740L (Rev: BLO 3/1/12; SLJ 9/1/11*)

10774 Dhami, Narinder. *Bhangra Babes* (5–8). Series: Babes. 2006, Delacorte $14.95 (978-0-385-73318-2). Their troublesome auntie's marriage plans go awry in this funny, engaging final volume of the trilogy about the Bindi sisters who are adapting their Indian heritage to life in England. (Rev: BL 4/15/06; SLJ 6/06)

10775 Doherty, Berlie. *Street Child* (5–7). 1994, Orchard LB $18.99 (978-0-531-08714-5). The story of a street urchin in Victorian London who is forced to work on a river barge until he escapes. (Rev: BCCB 11/94; BL 9/1/94; SLJ 10/94)

10776 Dowswell, Paul. *Battle Fleet* (5–8). 2008, Bloomsbury $16.95 (978-1-59990-080-3). Young Sam is again on the high seas, this time on Lord Nelson's ship for the battle of Trafalgar. A follow-up to *Powder Monkey* and *Prison Ship*. (Rev: BL 4/15/08; SLJ 9/08)

10777 Dowswell, Paul. *Powder Monkey: Adventures of a Young Sailor* (5–9). 2005, Bloomsbury $16.95 (978-1-58234-675-5). In this stirring historical novel set in the opening years of the 19th century, 13-year-old Sam Witchall begins his career at sea as a "powder monkey," assisting the gun crews on a warship. (Rev: SLJ 11/05; VOYA 10/05)

10778 Duey, Kathleen. *Lara and the Gray Mare* (4–6). Series: Hoofbeats. 2005, Dutton paper $4.99 (978-0-14-240230-6). 128pp. In medieval Ireland, 9-year-old Lara cares for her beloved gray mare as the animal suffers through a difficult pregnancy. (Rev: BL 2/1/05)

10779 Flegg, Aubrey. *Katie's War* (5–8). 2000, O'Brien paper $7.95 (978-0-86278-525-3). Set during Ireland's fight for independence from England, this story shows a girl torn between two sides when her father wants peace and her brother is preparing to use force. (Rev: BL 12/1/00)

10780 Giff, Patricia Reilly. *Maggie's Door* (3–6). 2003, Random LB $17.99 (978-0-385-90095-9). 160pp. In this poignant sequel to *Nory Ryan's Song*, Nory and her friend Sean describe in alternating chapters the horrors of their voyages — and their enduring spirit and optimism — from their native Ireland to join relatives in America. (Rev: BL 9/15/03; HB 9/03; HBG 4/04; SLJ 9/03)

10781 Gilman, Laura Anne. *Grail Quest: The Camelot Spell* (5–8). Series: Grail Quest. 2006, HarperCollins LB $14.89 (978-0-06-077280-2). On the eve of King Arthur's quest for the Holy Grail, three young teens of different backgrounds — Gerard, Newt, and Ailias — must reverse a spell crippling all adults. (Rev: BL 2/1/06; SLJ 6/06)

10782 Graber, Janet. *The White Witch* (5–8). 2009, Roaring Brook $16.95 (978-1-59643-337-3). 160pp. Set in 17th-century England, and with period prose that some may find challenging, this is a suspenseful story about 14-year-old Gwendoline's trials when the Great Plague breaks out. (Rev: BL 4/15/09; LMC 10/09; SLJ 7/09; VOYA 6/09)

10783 Grahame, Kenneth. *The Wind in the Willows* (4–7). Illus. by E. H. Shepard. 1983, Macmillan $19.95 (978-0-684-17957-5). The classic that introduced Mole, Ratty, and Mr. Toad. Two of many other editions are: illus. by Michael Hague (1980, Henry Holt); illus. by John Burningham (1983, Viking).

10784 Grant, Alan. *The Strange Case of Dr. Jekyll and Mr. Hyde* (5–8). Illus. by Cam Kennedy. 2008, Tundra paper $11.95 (978-08877688-2-8). 40pp. In this condensed adaptation of Robert Louis Stevenson's classic tale, Grant and Kennedy bring their comic sensibilities to bear with concise, fast-paced text and brilliant, atmospheric illustrations. (Rev: BL 9/1/08; SLJ 11/08; VOYA 8/08)

10785 Griffin, Margot. *Dancing for Danger: A Meggy Tale* (4–6). Illus. 2001, Stoddart $6.95 (978-0-7737-6136-0). 112pp. Meggy shows real bravery when her forbidden "hedge school" is under threat in 19th-century Ireland. (Rev: BL 6/1–15/01; SLJ 2/02)

10786 Harrison, Cora. *The Famine Secret* (5–7). Illus. by Orla Roche. Series: Drumshee Timeline. 1998, Irish American paper $6.95 (978-0-86327-649-1). In 1847 the four McMahon children are orphaned and sent to an Irish workhouse, but their determination prevails and they are soon plotting to regain their home. (Rev: SLJ 12/98)

10787 Harrison, Cora. *The Secret of Drumshee Castle* (5–7). Illus. by Orla Roche. Series: Drumshee Timeline. 1998, Irish American paper $6.95 (978-0-86327-632-3). Grace Barry, the orphaned heiress to a castle in Ireland during Elizabethan times, flees to England to escape threats by her acquisitive guardians. (Rev: SLJ 12/98)

10788 Harrison, Cora. *The Secret of the Seven Crosses* (4–7). 1998, Wolfhound paper $6.95 (978-0-86327-616-3). In medieval Ireland, three youngsters hope to find hidden treasure by examining sources in their monastery library. Preceded by *Nauala and Her Secret Wolf* and followed by *The Secret of Drumshee Castle*. (Rev: BL 12/15/98)

10789 Heneghan, James. *Safe House* (5–8). 2006, Orca paper $7.95 (978-1-55143-640-1). Twelve-year-old Liam Fogarty is forced to go on the run after he sees the face of one of the gunmen who killed his mother and father in their Belfast home. (Rev: BL 11/1/06; SLJ 1/07)

10790 Holmes, Victoria. *The Horse from the Sea* (5–8). 2005, HarperCollins LB $16.89 (978-0-06-052029-8).

In 1588, Nora, an Irish girl, defies the English and helps a young Spanish sailor and a beautiful stallion, survivors of a shipwreck. (Rev: BL 5/15/05; SLJ 8/05)

10791 Hooper, Mary. *At the Sign of the Sugared Plum* (5–8). 2003, Bloomsbury $16.95 (978-1-58234-849-0). The horrors of the bubonic plague and the squalor of 17th-century London are brought to life in this story of Hannah and her sister Sarah, owner of a sweetmeats shop. (Rev: BL 9/15/03; HBG 4/04; SLJ 8/03; VOYA 10/03)

10792 Kirwan, Anna. *Victoria: May Blossom of Britannia* (5–8). Series: Royal Diaries. 2001, Scholastic paper $10.95 (978-0-439-21598-5). Young Victoria's fictional diary describes her over-regimented life at the ages of 10 and 11; background material adds some historical context to this account of the girl who grew up to rule England. (Rev: BL 12/1/01; HBG 10/02; SLJ 1/02; VOYA 2/02)

10793 Knight, Joan MacPhail. *Charlotte in London* (2–5). Illus. by Melissa Sweet. 2008, Chronicle $16.99 (978-0-8118-5635-5). 52pp. Charlotte is in London in this installment in the series that began with *Charlotte in Giverny* (2000) and with her friend Lizzy visits many landmarks and meets interesting artists and writers, all recorded in her diary. (Rev: BL 3/15/09; SLJ 3/09)

10794 Lasky, Kathryn. *Elizabeth I: Red Rose of the House of Tudor* (4–7). Series: Royal Diaries. 1999, Scholastic paper $10.95 (978-0-590-68484-2). Told in diary form, this is a fictionalized account of Elizabeth I's childhood after her mother was killed and she lived with her father, Henry VIII, and Catherine Parr. (Rev: BCCB 12/99; BL 9/15/99; HBG 3/00; SLJ 10/99)

10795 Lasky, Kathryn. *Hawksmaid: The Untold Story of Robin Hood and Maid Marian* (5–8). 2010, HarperCollins $16.99 (978-0-06-000071-4). 304pp. The back story for Robin Hood's Maid Marian is explored in this inspiring story of a young girl who uses her falconry skills to steal from the rich. e Lexile 780L (Rev: BL 5/15/10; LMC 5–6/10; SLJ 7/10)

10796 Lawrence, Iain. *The Wreckers* (5–8). 1998, Bantam paper $5.50 (978-0-440-41545-9). In this historical novel, young John Spencer narrowly escapes with his life after the ship on which he is traveling is wrecked off the Cornish coast, lured to its destruction by a gang seeking to plunder its cargo. (Rev: BCCB 6/98; BL 6/1–15/98; HB 7–8/98*; HBG 10/98; SLJ 6/98; VOYA 2/99)

10797 Love, D. Anne. *The Puppeteer's Apprentice* (3–6). 2003, Simon & Schuster $16.95 (978-0-689-84424-9). 192pp. In medieval England, an orphan girl called Mouse runs away to become a puppeteer's apprentice. (Rev: BL 3/15/03; HBG 10/03; SLJ 5/03)

10798 McKay, Hilary. *Wishing for Tomorrow* (3–6). Illus. by Nick Maland. 2010, Simon & Schuster $16.99 (978-1-4424-0169-3). 273pp. More than a hundred years after publication of Frances Hodgson Burnett's *A Little Princess,* this sequel tells the story of what happens after Sara Crewe leaves the Select Seminary for Young Ladies. ∩ Lexile 800L (Rev: HB 1–2/10; LMC 8–9/10; SLJ 3/10)

10799 McKenzie, Nancy. *Guinevere's Gift* (5–8). 2008, Knopf $15.99 (978-0-375-84345-7). As a young orphan, the plucky Guinevere lives with her aunt, Queen Alyse, and involves herself in castle intrigue, coming to realize that her destiny may be closer to prophecy than she thought. (Rev: BL 6/1–15/08; SLJ 4/08)

10800 McRobbie, David. *Vinnie's War* (5–8). Illus. 2012, IPG/Allen & Unwin paper $14.99 (978-17423757-6-2). 210pp. Vinnie, 13, has trouble adjusting when he is evacuated from London to the country in World War II, but his music and some new friends bring him comfort. e (Rev: BLO 8/12; SLJ 1/13)

10801 Mayer, Marianna. *Sir Walter Scott's Ivanhoe* (4–6). Illus. by John Rush. 2004, Chronicle $17.95 (978-1-58717-248-9). 56pp. An attractive, large-format adaptation of the classic romantic adventure, with rich illustrations. (Rev: BL 2/1/05; SLJ 1/05)

10802 Morpurgo, Michael. *Sir Gawain and the Green Knight* (4–7). Illus. by Michael Foreman. 2005, Candlewick $18.99 (978-0-7636-2519-1). Morpurgo retells in contemporary prose the story of the Green Knight's challenge to the court of King Arthur. (Rev: BL 11/1/04*; SLJ 10/04)

10803 Morpurgo, Michael. *War Horse* (5–8). 2007, Scholastic $16.99 (978-0-439-79663-7). This gripping tale of World War I and all its horrors is told from the point of view of Joey, an English farm horse that's been drafted for service on the battlefront. (Rev: BL 4/1/07)

10804 Morris, Gerald. *The Adventures of Sir Gawain the True* (3–5). Illus. by Aaron Renier. Series: Knights' Tales. 2011, Houghton Mifflin $14.99 (978-054741855-1). 128pp. Sir Gawain eventually learns the essence of courtliness and courtesy in this irreverent fractured tale. e Lexile 770L (Rev: BL 4/1/11)

10805 Morris, Gerald. *The Adventures of Sir Givret the Short* (3–5). Illus. by Aaron Reneir. Series: Knights' Tales. 2008, Houghton $15.00 (978-0-618-77715-0). 112pp. This entertaining medieval tale follows Sir Givret who is short on height but long on wily ways as he helps a brother knight rescue his fair maiden. (Rev: BL 2/1/09; SLJ 1/09)

10806 Morris, Gerald. *The Ballad of Sir Dinadan* (5–9). 2003, Houghton Mifflin $16.00 (978-0-618-19099-7). An amusing retelling from Arthurian legend that features the younger brother of Sir Tristram as a music lover and reluctant knight. (Rev: BL 5/1/03; HB 5–6/03; HBG 10/03; SLJ 4/03*; VOYA 6/03)

10807 Morris, Gerald. *The Quest of the Fair Unknown* (5–8). 2006, Houghton Mifflin $16.00 (978-0-618-63152-0). To fulfill the deathbed plea of his mother, Beaufils sets off to find his long-absent father, a knight in the court of King Arthur. (Rev: BL 10/15/06; SLJ 11/06)

10808 Morris, Gerald. *The Squire, His Knight, and His Lady* (5–9). 1999, Houghton Mifflin $16.00 (978-0-395-91211-9). This is a retelling, from the perspective of a knight's squire, of the classic story of Sir Gawain and the Green Knight. (Rev: BL 5/1/99; HBG 10/99; SLJ 5/99; VOYA 8/99)

10809 Morris, Gerald. *The Squire's Tale* (5–9). 1998, Houghton Mifflin $16.00 (978-0-395-86959-8). The peaceful existence of 14-year-old Terence is shattered when he becomes the squire of Sir Gawain and becomes involved in a series of quests. (Rev: BL 4/15/98; HB 7–8/98; SLJ 7/98; VOYA 8/98)

10810 Nelson, Mary Elizabeth. *Catla and the Vikings* (5–8). 2012, Orca paper $9.95 (978-14598005-7-1). 192pp. In northern England in 1066, 13-year-old Catla survives a Viking attack and journeys to a neighboring town to warn the citizens, facing her fears as she goes. **e** Lexile 640L (Rev: BL 4/15/12; LMC 10/12; SLJ 6/12)

10811 Priestley, Chris. *The White Rider* (5–8). 2005, Corgi paper $8.99 (978-0-440-86608-4). In this riveting sequel to *Death and the Arrow*, 16-year-old Tom Marlowe is swept up in a series of intrigues in early 18th-century London. (Rev: BL 10/15/05)

10812 Rogers, Gregory. *The Boy, the Bear, the Baron, the Bard* (K–2). Illus. by author. 2004, Roaring Brook $15.95 (978-1-59643-009-9). 32pp. A young boy finds himself transported to Elizabethan England and has many adventures, including encounters with Shakespeare and the Queen, in this wordless picture book. (Rev: BL 10/1/04; LMC 3/05; SLJ 12/04*)

10813 Schlitz, Laura Amy. *Splendors and Glooms* (4–8). 2012, Candlewick $17.99 (978-076365380-4). 400pp. When Clara vanishes on her 12th birthday, suspicion falls on the puppeteer who entertained her and his two young orphan assistants in this novel set in 1860 Britain with elements of fantasy, a witch, and three children facing danger. Newbery Honor Book 2013. ∩ **e** Lexile 670L (Rev: BL 6/12*; HB 9–10/12; LMC 3–4/13; SLJ 8/1/12*; VOYA 10/12)

10814 Schmidt, Gary D. *Anson's Way* (5–9). 1999, Houghton Mifflin $16.00 (978-0-395-91529-5). During the reign of George II, Anson begins his proud career in the British army as part of the forces occupying Ireland, then becomes disillusioned as he develops a growing respect and concern for the Irish. (Rev: BL 4/1/99*; HBG 10/99; SLJ 4/99; VOYA 8/99)

10815 Smith, Jenny. *Diary of a Parent Trainer* (5–8). 2012, Random House $12.99 (978-0-385-74198-9); LB $15.99 (978-0-375-99035-9). 312pp. In her journal, 13-year-old Katie explains how to deal with adult relatives, but her mother's relationship with boyfriend Stuart poses particular problems; a humorous novel set in Great Britain. **e** Lexile 860L (Rev: LMC 10/12; SLJ 7/12)

10816 Snicket, Lemony. *The Austere Academy* (4–6). Illus. Series: Unfortunate Events. 2000, HarperCollins LB $14.89 (978-0-06-028884-6). 240pp. The Baudelaire orphans endure horrible hardships when they enroll as students at Prufrock Academy, where their only friends — the Quagmire orphans — are kidnapped by wicked Count Olaf. (Rev: BL 10/15/00)

10817 Stevenson, Robert Louis. *The Strange Case of Dr. Jekyll and Mr. Hyde* (5–8). Series: Whole Story. 2003, Barnes & Noble paper $3.95 (978-1-59308-054-9). Using lively ink-and-watercolor illustrations, this book offers the complete text of the classic in an attractive format. (Rev: BL 5/1/00; HBG 10/00)

10818 Thomas, Jane Resh. *The Counterfeit Princess* (5–8). 2005, Clarion $15.00 (978-0-395-93870-6). Iris, a young English girl with an uncanny resemblance to Princess Elizabeth (soon to be Elizabeth I), finds herself embroiled in intrigue in this novel set in the 16th century. (Rev: BL 11/15/05; SLJ 10/05)

10819 Updale, Eleanor. *Johnny Swanson* (4–6). 2011, Random House $16.99 (978-0-385-75198-8); LB $19.99 (978-0-385-75199-5). 384pp. Eleven-year-old Johnny ends up solving a murder and acquitting his mother of the crime in this inspiring hard-luck mystery set in 1929 England. **e** Lexile 740L (Rev: BL 5/1/11; HB 3–4/11; SLJ 3/1/11)

10820 Vogiel, Eva. *Friend or Foe?* (5–8). 2001, Judaica $19.95 (978-1-880582-66-4). In this novel set in London during 1948, the girls of the Migdal Binoh School for Orthodox Jewish girls notice strange happenings when the Campbell family moves next door. (Rev: BL 4/1/01)

10821 Whitehouse, Howard. *The Strictest School in the World: Being the Tale of a Clever Girl, a Rubber Boy and a Collection of Flying Machines, Mostly Broken* (5–8). Illus. by Bill Slavin. 2006, Kids Can $16.95 (978-1-55337-882-2); paper $6.95 (978-1-55337-883-9). Raised in India where her father is a British colonial official, Emmaline Cayley is upset when her parents send her to a strict school in England, so she hatches a plan to escape; an appealing blend of humor, fantasy, and Gothic atmosphere. (Rev: SLJ 11/06)

10822 Wiley, Melissa. *Beyond the Heather Hills* (3–5). Illus. by Renee Graef. Series: Martha Years. 2003, HarperCollins paper $6.99 (978-0-06-440715-1). Set in 18th-century Scotland, this fourth volume continues the series on Laura Ingalls Wilder's great-grandmother. Here, she leaves home at age 10 to live with her married older sister. (Rev: BL 5/15/03; HBG 10/03)

10823 Williams, Marcia. *Archie's War* (3–6). Illus. by author. 2007, Candlewick $17.99 (978-0-7636-3532-9). 48pp. World War I comes to dramatic life in a British boy's scrapbook of cartoon drawings, news items, letters, and so forth spanning the years from 1914 to the end of the war. (Rev: BCCB 2/08; LMC 5/08*; SLJ 3/08; VOYA 2/08)

10824 Woelfle, Gretchen. *All the World's a Stage: A Novel in Five Acts* (4–7). Illus. by Thomas Cox. 2011, Holiday House $16.95 (978-0-8234-2281-4). 176pp. When he is caught picking pockets, 12-year-old Kit is offered a chance to redeem himself by working as a stage hand, and participates in the construction of the Globe Theatre in this atmospheric story set in Elizabethan England. (Rev: BL 4/15/11; HB 5–6/11; LMC 10/11; SLJ 5/11)

10825 Wood, Maryrose. *The Hidden Gallery* (4–6). Illus. by Jon Klassen. Series: The Incorrigible Children of Ashton Place. 2011, HarperCollins $15.99 (978-0-06-179112-3). 320pp. Governess Penelope contends with the challenges of taking care of her wolf-like young charges in London, where they attract mischief and spread mayhem wherever they go. ∩ ℮ Lexile 960L (Rev: BL 2/1/11*; SLJ 3/1/11)

10826 Wood, Maryrose. *The Mysterious Howling* (4–6). Illus. by Jon Klassen. Series: The Incorrigible Children of Ashton Place. 2010, HarperCollins $15.99 (978-0-06-179105-5). 288pp. Penelope, 15, is hired as governess for three feral children that Lord Frederick has determined must become civilized in time for the estate's Christmas party; set in 19th-century England. ∩ ℮ Lexile 1000L (Rev: BL 12/15/09*; HB 5–6/10; SLJ 5/10)

10827 Wood, Maryrose. *The Unseen Guest* (4–7). Series: The Incorrigible Children of Ashton Place. 2012, HarperCollins $15.99 (978-006179118-5). 240pp. The three children raised by wolves threaten to undo their years of training by nanny Penelope and return to the wild. ∩ ℮ (Rev: BL 3/15/12*; SLJ 4/12; VOYA 4/12)

10828 Woodruff, Elvira. *Fearless* (5–8). 2008, Scholastic $16.99 (978-0-439-67703-5). Young brothers Digory and Cubby are befriended by Henry Winstanley, the builder of a unusual lighthouse on the Cornish coast, in this intriguing and action-packed story, set in 1703, about bravery and sacrifice. (Rev: BL 5/1/08; LMC 4–5/08; SLJ 4/08)

10829 Woodruff, Elvira. *The Ravenmaster's Secret* (4–7). 2003, Scholastic $15.95 (978-0-439-28133-1). Eleven-year-old Forrest becomes embroiled in dangerous intrigue in this story set inside the Tower of London in the early 18th century, with a glossary and historical notes appended. (Rev: BL 1/1–15/04; SLJ 1/04; VOYA 4/04)

Canada, Latin America, and the Caribbean

10830 Agosin, Marjorie. *I Lived on Butterfly Hill* (5–8). Illus. by Lee White. 2014, Atheneum $16.99 (978-141695344-9). 464pp. When Chile is taken over by a ruthless regime, 11-year-old Celeste must leave her beloved Valparaiso and go to live with her aunt in Maine, where she struggles to adjust. ℮ Lexile 770 (Rev: BL 3/1/14*; LMC 8–9/14; SLJ 5/14)

10831 Belpre, Pura. *Firefly Summer* (5–8). 1996, Piñata paper $9.95 (978-1-55885-180-1). This gentle novel depicts family and community life in rural Puerto Rico at the turn of the 20th century as experienced by young Teresa Rodrigo, who has just completed 7th grade. (Rev: SLJ 2/97; VOYA 4/97)

10832 Burg, Ann E. *Serafina's Promise* (5–8). 2013, Scholastic $16.99 (978-0-54553564-9). 304pp. In a poor village in Haiti, Serafina dreams of going to school and becoming a doctor, but an earthquake means she must first help her stricken family. ALA Notable Children's Book. ℮ (Rev: BL 10/15/13; LMC 3–4/14; SLJ 11/13*)

10833 Caswell, Maryanne. *Pioneer Girl* (5–8). Illus. by Lindsay Grater. 2001, Tundra $16.95 (978-0-88776-550-6). In letters to her grandmother, a 14-year-old girl describes the hardships and interesting experiences of her journey from Ontario to the prairies in the late 1880s. (Rev: HBG 10/01; SLJ 10/01)

10834 Crook, Connie Brummel. *The Hungry Year* (5–8). 2001, Stoddart paper $7.95 (978-0-7737-6206-0). Twelve-year-old Kate must care for her brothers and handle the household chores during a severe Canadian winter in the late 1700s. (Rev: BL 1/1–15/02; SLJ 11/01)

10835 Crook, Connie Brummel. *The Perilous Year* (5–7). 2003, Fitzhenry & Whiteside paper $8.95 (978-1-55041-818-7). In this fast-paced sequel to *The Hungry Year* (2001), 11-year-old twins Alex and Ryan face constant challenges and adventures — including more encounters with pirates — in 18th-century Canada. (Rev: SLJ 3/04)

10836 Danticat, Edwidge. *Anacaona, Golden Flower: Haiti, 1490* (5–8). Series: Royal Diaries. 2005, Scholastic $10.95 (978-0-439-49906-4). In 15th-century Haiti, Anacaona, a girl of royal heritage, records her people's struggles against the Spanish explorers. (Rev: BL 5/15/05)

10837 Downie, Mary Alice, and John Downie. *Danger in Disguise* (5–8). Series: On Time's Wing. 2001, Roussan paper $6.95 (978-1-896184-72-2). Young Jamie, a Scot raised in Normandy in secrecy, is scooped up to serve in the British navy and sent to Quebec to fight the French in this complex tale of adventure and intrigue set in the mid-18th century. (Rev: SLJ 5/01)

10838 Eboch, Chris. *The Well of Sacrifice* (5–8). 1999, Houghton Mifflin $16.00 (978-0-395-90374-2). In this novel set during Mayan times, Eveningstar Macaw sets out to avenge the death of her older brother, Smoke Shell. (Rev: BL 4/1/99; HBG 10/99; SLJ 5/99; VOYA 2/00)

10839 Ellis, Deborah. *Sacred Leaf: The Cocalero Novels* (5–8). Series: The Cocalera Novels. 2007, Groundwood $16.95 (978-0-88899-751-7). Twelve-year-old Diego is living with a family of poor Bolivian coca farmers when their crop is destroyed by soldiers and they join a national protest. (Rev: BL 1/1–15/08; SLJ 12/07)

10840 Ellis, Leanne Statland. *The Ugly One* (4–8). 2013, Clarion $16.99 (978-054764023-5). 240pp. Despite the horrible scar that disfigures her face, 12-year-old Inca girl Micay finds success as a shaman. Lexile 810 (Rev: BLO 7/13; LMC 10/13)

10841 Engle, Margarita. *Wild Book* (5–8). Illus. 2012, Harcourt $16.99 (978-054758131-6). 144pp. Dyslexic Josefa comes to understand the freeing power of words in this story set in 1912 Cuba; based on the life of the author's grandmother. ℮ (Rev: BL 3/1/12; LMC 11–12/12; SLJ 3/12)

10842 Gantos, Jack. *Jack's New Power: Stories from a Caribbean Year* (5–8). 1995, Farrar $16.00 (978-0-374-33657-8); paper $5.95 (978-0-374-43715-2). Eight stories about the interesting people Jack meets when his family moves to the Caribbean. A sequel to *Heads or Tails* (1994). (Rev: BCCB 12/95; BL 12/1/95; SLJ 11/95*)

10843 Harrison, Troon. *A Bushel of Light* (5–8). 2001, Stoddart paper $7.95 (978-0-7737-6140-7). Fourteen-year-old orphan Maggie juggles her need to search for her twin sister and her responsibilities for 4-year-old

Lizzy, in this novel set in Canada in the early 1900s. (Rev: SLJ 10/01)

10844 Haworth-Attard, Barbara. *Home Child* (5–8). 1996, Roussan paper $6.95 (978-1-896184-18-0). Set in Canada during the early 1900s, this is the story of 13-year-old Arthur Fellowes, a London orphan who is treated like an outcast when he joins the Wilson family as a home child (that is, a cheap farm laborer). (Rev: VOYA 8/97)

10845 Hobbs, Will. *Crossing the Wire* (5–8). 2006, HarperCollins $15.99 (978-0-06-074138-9). Victor, a teenage Mexican boy who is the sole support for his family, decides to risk the dangerous crossing into the United States in search of work. ⌒ (Rev: BL 5/1/06; SLJ 5/06; VOYA 4/06)

10846 Holeman, Linda. *Promise Song* (5–8). 1997, Tundra paper $6.95 (978-0-88776-387-8). In 1900, Rosetta, an English orphan who has been sent to Canada, becomes an indentured servant. (Rev: BL 6/1–15/97; SLJ 10/97)

10847 Ibbotson, Eva. *Journey to the River Sea* (5–8). 2002, Dutton $17.99 (978-0-525-46739-7). Orphaned Maia journeys from 1910 London to live with relatives in Brazil in this complex story that involves an unwelcoming family, a beloved governess, a child actor, a runaway, and the wonders of Brazil, all presented with a mix of drama and humor. (Rev: BCCB 4/02; BL 12/15/01; HB 1–2/02; HBG 10/02; SLJ 1/02*; VOYA 12/01)

10848 Jocelyn, Marthe. *Mable Riley: A Reliable Record of Humdrum, Peril, and Romance* (5–10). 2004, Candlewick $15.99 (978-0-7636-2120-9). This is a charming, humorous diary set in 1901 by a 14-year-old girl who accompanies her sister when she becomes a teacher in Stratford, Ontario. (Rev: BL 3/1/04; HB 5–6/04; SLJ 3/04; VOYA 6/04)

10849 Lawson, Julie. *Goldstone* (5–8). 1998, Stoddart paper $7.95 (978-0-7737-5891-9). Karin, a 13-year-old Swedish Canadian girl, lives with her family in a mountainous town in British Columbia in 1910 when heavy winter snows bring avalanches that cause death and destruction. (Rev: BL 7/97; SLJ 5/98)

10850 Lowery, Linda. *Truth and Salsa* (4–7). 2006, Peachtree $14.95 (978-1-59145-366-6). Staying with her grandmother in Mexico after her parents separate, Haley makes a new friend and learns about people living on the edge of poverty. (Rev: SLJ 7/06)

10851 Major, Kevin. *Ann and Seamus* (5–9). Illus. by David Blackwood. 2003, Groundwood $16.95 (978-0-88899-561-2). Based on an early 19th-century shipwreck off the coast of Newfoundland, this historical novel in verse chronicles the romance that develops between 17-year-old Ann Harvey and the Irish teenager she rescues from the ship. (Rev: BL 3/1/04; HB 3–4/04; SLJ 2/04; VOYA 4/04)

10852 Mordecai, Martin. *Blue Mountain Trouble* (5–8). 2009, Scholastic $16.99 (978-0-545-04156-0). 336pp. A strange goat appears to 11-year-old twins Pollyread and Jackson, who live high in the Blue Mountains of

Jamaica, and coincidentally there is a series of strange events. (Rev: BL 4/15/09; HB 5/09; SLJ 7/09)

10853 Ryan, Pam Muñoz. *The Dreamer* (4–8). Illus. by Peter Sís. 2010, Scholastic $17.99 (978-0-439-26970-4). 384pp. Ryan imagines the young life of the poet Pablo Neruda, who was shy, afraid of his demanding father, and interested in nature and the lives of the indigenous Indians of Chile. Belpré Medal 2011; ALA Notable Children's Book 2011; Boston Globe–Horn Book Honor 2010. ⌒ Lexile 650L (Rev: BL 2/1/10*; HB 3–4/10; LMC 3–4/10; SLJ 4/10)

10854 Schwartz, Virginia Frances. *Messenger* (5–9). 2002, Holiday $17.95 (978-0-8234-1716-2). This story of the hardships and joys of a Croatian family living in Ontario's mining towns in the 1920s and 1930s is based on the lives of the author's mother and grandmother. (Rev: HBG 3/03; SLJ 11/02; VOYA 12/02)

10855 Taylor, Joanne. *There You Are: A Novel* (4–7). 2004, Tundra paper $8.95 (978-0-88776-658-9). On post-World War II Cape Breton Island, 12-year-old Jeannie lives in a remote community and longs for a friend. (Rev: SLJ 11/04)

10856 Trottier, Maxine. *A Circle of Silver* (5–8). 2000, Stoddart paper $7.95 (978-0-7737-6055-4). Set in the 1760s, this is the story of 13-year-old John MacNeil who is sent to Canada by his father to toughen him up. (Rev: SLJ 9/00)

Middle East

10857 Abdel-Fattah, Randa. *Where the Streets Had a Name* (5–8). 2010, Scholastic $17.99 (978-0-545-17292-9). 304pp. Thirteen-year-old Palestinian Hayaat faces checkpoints and curfews when she travels from Bethlehem to Jerusalem in search of some soil she hopes will bring relief to her sick grandmother. ⌒ Lexile 740L (Rev: BL 10/1/10; HB 1–2/11; LMC 1–2/11; SLJ 11/1/10; VOYA 4/10)

10858 Carmi, Daniella. *Samir and Yonatan* (4–8). Trans. from Hebrew by Yael Lotan. 2000, Scholastic paper $15.95 (978-0-439-13504-7). Samir, a young Palestinian, is sent to a Jewish hospital for surgery and there he meets some Jewish contemporaries. (Rev: BCCB 4/00; BL 2/1/00; HBG 10/00; SLJ 3/00; VOYA 6/00)

10859 Levine, Anna. *Running on Eggs* (5–9). 1999, Front St $15.95 (978-0-8126-2875-3). The story of two girls — one Jewish and the other Palestinian — and a friendship that withstands cultural and political differences. (Rev: BCCB 11/99; BL 1/1–15/00; HBG 3/00; SLJ 12/99; VOYA 2/00)

10860 Pal, Erika. *Azad's Camel* (1–3). Illus. by author. 2010, Frances Lincoln $17.95 (978-1-84507-982-6). 40pp. A reluctant young camel jockey discovers his camel can talk and together the two plan their escape from the grueling, dangerous sport. Lexile AD450L (Rev: BL 9/1/10; SLJ 9/1/10)

United States

NATIVE AMERICANS

10861 Armstrong, Nancy M. *Navajo Long Walk* (4–7). 1994, Roberts Rinehart $8.95 (978-1-879373-56-3). The story of the Long Walk of the Navajo in 1864 and their confinement in an internment camp are vividly told. (Rev: BL 10/1/94; SLJ 1/95)

10862 Bruchac, Joseph. *A Boy Called Slow: The True Story of Sitting Bull* (5–8). Illus. by Rocco Baviera. 1995, Putnam $17.99 (978-0-399-22692-2). The story of the boyhood of Sitting Bull, who, because of his sluggishness, had been called Slow. (Rev: BCCB 4/95; BL 3/15/95; HB 9–10/95; SLJ 10/95)

10863 Bruchac, Joseph. *Crazy Horse's Vision* (2–4). Illus. by S. D. Nelson. 2000, Lee & Low $16.95 (978-1-880000-94-6). 40pp. This is the story of how a young Native American boy, nicknamed Curly, gained the name Crazy Horse and became a leader of the Lakota. (Rev: BCCB 9/00; BL 5/15/00; HB 7/00; HBG 10/00; SLJ 7/00)

10864 Bruchac, Joseph. *The Journal of Jesse Smoke: The Trail of Tears, 1838* (5–8). Series: My Name Is America. 2001, Scholastic paper $10.95 (978-0-439-12197-2). Jesse, a 16-year-old Cherokee, chronicles in his diary the tribe's forced journey to Oklahoma and tries to understand the reasons behind this cruel action. (Rev: BL 7/01; HBG 10/01; SLJ 7/01; VOYA 8/01)

10865 Bruchac, Marge. *Malian's Song* (2–4). Illus. by William Maughan. 2006, Vermont Folklife Center $16.95 (978-0-916718-26-8). 32pp. Malian, a young Abenaki girl, tells how she fled to safety while her father died defending the family's home in 1759; the story of this British raid was passed from generation to generation. This text includes Abenaki words as well as details of Abenaki life. (Rev: BL 8/06; SLJ 1/07)

10866 Burks, Brian. *Runs with Horses* (5–9). 1995, Harcourt paper $6.00 (978-0-15-200994-6). An adventure story set in 1886 in which 16-year-old Runs with Horses completes his Apache warrior training by performing feats of endurance, survival, and daring, and partly as a result of information he gathers during raids, his tribe realizes that they can no longer continue to resist the white man. (Rev: BL 11/1/95; SLJ 11/95; VOYA 2/96)

10867 Edwardson, Debby Dahl. *Blessing's Bead* (5–8). 2009, Farrar $16.99 (978-0-374-30805-6). 192pp. Two narratives — the first set in 1917 and the second in 1989 — tell the stories of Inupiaq Eskimo teenagers and the quite different challenges they face. (Rev: BL 10/15/09*; LMC 11–12/09; SLJ 11/09)

10868 Erdrich, Louise. *Chickadee* (4–7). Series: Birchbark House. 2012, HarperCollins $15.99 (978-0-06-057790-2). 208pp. In 1866 the Omakayas set off on a dangerous, wintertime expedition on the Great Plains to find their son Chickadee, 8, who's been kidnapped; the fourth book in the series. Scott O'Dell Historical Fiction Award. Lexile 800 (Rev: BL 8/12; HB 9–10/12; SLJ 9/12*)

10869 Erdrich, Louise. *The Game of Silence* (5–8). 2005, HarperCollins LB $16.89 (978-0-06-029790-9). As 9-year-old Omakayas is coming of age, the intrusion of the European settlers increasingly impacts the Ojibwe lifestyle in this sequel to *The Birchbark House* (1999). (Rev: BL 5/15/05*; SLJ 7/05)

10870 Erdrich, Louise. *The Porcupine Year* (4–7). Illus. by author. 2008, HarperCollins $15.99 (978-0-06-029787-9). In this sequel to *The Birchbark House* (1999) and *The Game of Silence* (2005), Omakayas is now 12 and the family is traveling north, looking for a new home far from the intruding white settlers. (Rev: BL 6/1–15/08; SLJ 9/08)

10871 Grutman, Jewel, and Gay Matthaei. *The Ledgerbook of Thomas Blue Eagle* (4–8). Illus. by Adam Cvijanovic. 1994, Thomasson-Grant $17.95 (978-1-56566-063-2). A young Native American boy attends a white man's school but tries to retain his own identity and culture in this story that takes place in the West 100 years ago. (Rev: SLJ 12/94)

10872 Howard, Ellen. *The Crimson Cap* (5–8). 2009, Holiday House $16.95 (978-0-8234-2152-7). 208pp. Eleven-year-old Pierre Talon finds himself living with the Hasinai Indians after setting out on an ill-fated mission with explorer La Salle. Lexile 720L (Rev: BLO 12/1/09; LMC 1–2/10; SLJ 11/09)

10873 Hudson, Jan. *Sweetgrass* (5–8). 1989, Scholastic paper $3.99 (978-0-590-43486-7). A description of the culture of the Dakota Indians in the 1830s. (Rev: BCCB 4/89; BL 4/1/89; SLJ 4/89)

10874 Kittredge, Frances. *Neeluk: An Eskimo Boy in the Days of the Whaling Ships* (3–5). Illus. by Howard Rock. 2001, Alaska Northwest paper $18.95 (978-0-88240-545-2). 88pp. Illustrations by an Inupiat artist combine with simple stories to present the Inupiat way of life in the late 1800s. (Rev: BL 8/01; HBG 3/02; SLJ 1/02)

10875 Maher, Ramona. *Alice Yazzie's Year* (3–6). Illus. by Shonto Begay. 2004, Tricycle $15.95 (978-1-58246-080-2). 40pp. Reissued with new illustrations, this picture book written in verse chronicles a year in the life of an 11-year-old Navajo girl. (Rev: BL 8/03; HBG 4/04; SLJ 11/03)

10876 Marchand, Peter. *What Good Is a Cactus?* (3–5). Illus. by Craig Brown. 1994, Roberts Rinehart paper $7.95 (978-1-879373-83-9). Through talking to a wise Native American and observing nature, a scientist realizes the importance of all living things and the role each plays. (Rev: SLJ 11/94)

10877 Matthaei, Gay, and Jewel Grutman. *The Sketchbook of Thomas Blue Eagle* (4–7). 2001, Chronicle $16.95 (978-0-88182-908-2). Through drawings and narration, the Lakota artist Thomas Blue Eagle tells how he joined Buffalo Bill's show, traveled to Europe, and made enough money to marry. (Rev: BCCB 5/01; BL 4/1/01)

10878 O'Dell, Scott, and Elizabeth Hall. *Thunder Rolling in the Mountains* (5–9). 1992, Dell paper $5.50 (978-0-440-40879-6). From the viewpoint of Chief Joseph's daughter, this historical novel concerns the forced removal of the Nez Perce from their homeland in 1877. (Rev: BL 6/15/92*; SLJ 8/92)

10879 Osborne, Mary Pope. *Standing in the Light: The Captive Diary of Catharine Carey Logan* (3–6). Illus. Series: Dear America. 1998, Scholastic $10.95 (978-0-590-13462-0). 192pp. After 13-year-old Caty and her younger brother are captured by Lenape Indians in rural Pennsylvania in 1763, they gradually learn to appreciate the values in this foreign culture. (Rev: BL 10/15/98; HBG 3/99; SLJ 1/99)

10880 Parry, Rosanne. *Written in Stone* (4–7). 2013, Random House $16.99 (978-037586971-6); LB $19.99 (978-037596971-3). 208pp. In the Pacific Northwest in the 1920s a Native American girl strives to recover from the deaths of her mother and baby sister during the flu pandemic, followed by that of her father on a whale hunt. e Lexile 810 (Rev: BL 6/13; LMC 11–12/13; SLJ 6/13)

10881 Patent, Dorothy Hinshaw. *The Buffalo and the Indians: A Shared Destiny* (4–8). Illus. by William Muñoz. 2006, Clarion $18.00 (978-0-618-48570-3). This beautifully illustrated title explores the unique bonds — both spiritual and economic — between Native Americans and the American bison. (Rev: BL 6/1/06*; HBG 4/07; LMC 2/07; SLJ 8/06*) [978.004]

10882 Pitts, Paul. *Racing the Sun* (5–7). 1988, Avon paper $6.99 (978-0-380-75496-0). Brandon begins to understand his Navajo heritage after his grandfather comes to live with him. (Rev: BL 9/15/88; SLJ 2/89)

10883 Raczek, Linda. *Rainy's Powwow* (3–5). Illus. by Gary Bennett. 1999, Northland $15.95 (978-0-87358-686-3). 32pp. Lorraine is seeking to develop her own special dance at the powwow, when an eagle feather changes her hopes. (Rev: BL 4/1/99; HBG 10/99; SLJ 6/99)

10884 Roop, Peter. *The Buffalo Jump* (2–4). Illus. by Bill Farnsworth. 1996, Northland LB $14.95 (978-0-87358-616-0). Little Blaze, a Native American boy, saves his older brother's life during a buffalo hunt. (Rev: SLJ 2/97)

10885 Schwartz, Virginia Frances. *Initiation* (5–8). 2003, Fitzhenry & Whiteside $15.95 (978-1-55005-053-0). Kwakiuti Indian twins Nana and Nanolatch prepare to face the responsibilities of adulthood in this story set on the West Coast of North America in the 15th century. (Rev: SLJ 3/04) [813]

10886 Smith, Patricia Clark. *Weetamoo: Heart of the Pocassets, Massachusetts — Rhode Island, 1653* (5–8). Series: Royal Diaries. 2003, Scholastic $10.95 (978-0-439-12910-7). Weetamoo prepares to succeed her father as leader of the tribe and describes relationships with the European settlers and how daily life changes with the seasons. (Rev: BL 12/15/03; HBG 4/04; SLJ 1/04)

10887 Sneve, Virginia Driving Hawk. *Bad River Boys: A Meeting of the Lakota Sioux with Lewis and Clark* (2–4). Illus. by Bill Farnsworth. 2005, Holiday $16.95 (978-0-8234-1856-5). 32pp. Based on an entry from William Clark's journal, this fictional story tells of an encounter between three Lakota boys and members of Lewis and Clark's Corps of Discovery expedition. (Rev: BL 11/15/05; SLJ 11/05)

10888 Tapahonso, Luci. *Songs of Shiprock Fair* (2–4). Illus. by Anthony Chee Emerson. 1999, Kiva $15.95 (978-1-885772-11-4). This is the story of the oldest fair in the Navajo Nation at Shiprock, New Mexico, as seen through the eyes of a little girl who experiences it from the early preparations to the ceremonial dances on the last night. (Rev: HBG 3/00; SLJ 4/00)

10889 Tingle, Tim. *Crossing Bok Chitto* (2–4). Illus. by Jeanne Rorex Bridges. 2006, Cinco Puntos $17.95 (978-0-938317-77-7). 40pp. Martha Tom, a young Choctaw girl in 1800s Mississippi, befriends a slave boy and his family and leads them to freedom when they face a crisis. (Rev: BCCB 7–8/06; BL 4/15/06*; LMC 11/06)

10890 Vick, Helen H. *Shadow* (5–7). Series: Courage of the Stone. 1998, Roberts Rinehart $15.95 (978-1-57098-218-7); paper $9.95 (978-1-57098-195-1). Shadow, an independent Pueblo Indian girl in pre-Columbian Arizona, leaves her home to rescue her father. (Rev: SLJ 10/98)

10891 Virginia Driving Hawk, Sneve. *Lana's Lakota Moons* (5–8). 2008, Univ. of Nebraska paper $12.95 (978-0-8032-6028-3). Lori and Lana, Lakotas whose lives are a combination of Native American tradition and modern American culture, have disturbing premonitions about the future that sadly come true in this thoughtful, moving story. (Rev: BL 5/1/08)

10892 Von Ahnen, Katherine. *Heart of Naosaqua* (4–6). Illus. 1996, Roberts Rinehart paper $9.95 (978-1-57098-010-7). 160pp. In 1823, Naosaqua and her people, the Mesquakie Indians, must find a new home. (Rev: BL 7/96)

10893 Wyss, Thelma Hatch. *Bear Dancer: The Story of a Ute Girl* (4–7). 2005, Simon & Schuster $15.95 (978-1-4169-0285-0). In this fact-based historical novel, life is turned upside down for Elk Girl, a member of the Tabaguache Ute, when she is kidnapped by a rival tribe. (Rev: BL 10/15/05; SLJ 10/05)

COLONIAL PERIOD

10894 Atkins, Jeannine. *Anne Hutchinson's Way* (2–4). Illus. by Michael Dooling. 2007, Farrar $17.00 (978-0-374-30365-5). 32pp. Through the eyes of young Susanna, who has 10 older siblings, readers learn about Massachusetts in 1634 and the issue of religious freedom; based on the story of Anne Hutchinson, Susanna's mother, who was banished for her renegade beliefs. (Rev: BL 7/07; SLJ 8/07)

10895 Butler, Amy. *Virginia Bound* (4–7). 2003, Clarion $15.00 (978-0-618-24752-3). Thirteen-year-old Rob is kidnapped in London and shipped to Virginia as an indentured servant to work on a tobacco farm in 1627. (Rev: BL 3/1/03; HBG 10/03; SLJ 6/03)

10896 Cocca-Leffler, Maryann. *Spotlight on Stacey* (2–4). Illus. by author. Series: Social Studies Connects. 2007, Kane paper $4.99 (978-1-57565-236-8). 32pp. A thoughtful aunt and a trip to a colonial village help Stacey prepare for a role in a play. Readers will learn facts about colonial times from Stacey's research. (Rev: SLJ 6/07)

10897 Collier, James Lincoln. *The Corn Raid: A Story of the Jamestown Settlement* (5–9). 2000, Jamestown paper $5.95 (978-0-8092-0619-3). History and fiction mix in this adventure tale set in the Jamestown settlement and featuring a 12-year-old indentured servant and his cruel master. (Rev: SLJ 4/00)

10898 Durrant, Lynda. *The Beaded Moccasins: The Story of Mary Campbell* (5–9). 1998, Clarion $15.00 (978-0-395-85398-6). Told in the first person, this is a fictionalized account of the true story of 12-year-old Mary Campbell who was captured by the Delaware Indians in 1759. (Rev: BCCB 5/98; BL 3/15/98; HBG 10/98; SLJ 6/98; VOYA 12/98)

10899 Edmonds, Walter D. *The Matchlock Gun* (5–7). Illus. by Paul Lantz. 1941, Putnam $16.99 (978-0-399-21911-5). Exciting, true story of a courageous boy who protected his mother and sister from the Indians of the Hudson Valley. Newbery Medal 1942.

10900 Field, Rachel. *Calico Bush* (5–7). Illus. by Allen Louis. 1987, Macmillan $17.95 (978-0-02-734610-7). This 1932 Newbery Honor Book is an adventure story of a French girl "loaned" to a family of American pioneers in Maine in the 1740s.

10901 Grote, JoAnn A. *Queen Anne's War* (5–8). Series: The American Adventure. 1998, Chelsea LB $15.95 (978-0-7910-5045-3). During Queen Anne's War in 1710, Will Smith's family becomes involved in the attempt to drive the French out of New England, but 11-year-old Will is preoccupied with a jealous classmate. (Rev: HBG 3/99; SLJ 1/99)

10902 Hermes, Patricia. *Salem Witch* (5–8). Series: My Side of the Story. 2006, Kingfisher paper $7.95 (978-0-7534-5991-1). Two teenage friends develop different views during the witch trials in 17th-century Salem, and readers can flip the book to read each person's opinion. (Rev: SLJ 2/07)

10903 Hermes, Patricia. *Season of Promise* (3–6). Series: My America, Elizabeth's Jamestown Colony Diary. 2002, Scholastic $10.95 (978-0-439-38898-6). 108pp. In 1611, ten-year-old Elizabeth continues to describe life in Jamestown as her twin brother Caleb returns, her father plans to remarry, and there is food to eat, although the colonial leaders are strict. (Rev: HBG 3/03; SLJ 2/03)

10904 Howard, Ginger. *William's House* (K–3). Illus. by Larry Day. 2001, Millbrook LB $22.90 (978-0-7613-1674-9). 32pp. An informative story that describes how a colonist built a house like the one he left behind in England and gradually had to change and modify it to adjust to a new climate and environment. (Rev: BL 3/15/01*; HBG 10/01; SLJ 3/01)

10905 Hurst, Carol Otis, and Rebecca Otis. *A Killing in Plymouth Colony* (5–7). 2003, Houghton Mifflin $15.00 (978-0-618-27597-7). John Bradford, the son of the governor of Plymouth Colony, has always struggled to gain

his father's approval and feels an affinity toward an outcast who is accused of murder. (Rev: BL 12/1/03; HBG 4/04; SLJ 10/03)

10906 Karr, Kathleen. *Worlds Apart* (4–7). 2005, Marshall Cavendish $15.95 (978-0-7614-5195-2). In 1670 South Carolina, Christopher — a teenage settler — and Sewee Indian Asha-po become friends. (Rev: BCCB 5/05; SLJ 5/05)

10907 Karwoski, Gail. *Surviving Jamestown: The Adventures of Young Sam Collier* (5–7). Illus. by Paul Casale. 2001, Peachtree $14.95 (978-1-56145-239-2); paper $8.95 (978-1-56145-245-3). Full of facts, this novel tells the story of a 12-year-old English boy who sails in 1606 for the colony of Virginia, with details of the struggles the colonists faced. (Rev: HBG 10/01; SLJ 8/01; VOYA 8/01)

10908 Ketchum, Liza. *Where the Great Hawk Flies* (4–7). 2005, Clarion $16.00 (978-0-618-40085-0). The Coombs family and the Tuckers have trouble getting along — even the young boys — because Mrs. Tucker is a Pequot Indian and the Coombs suffered mightily during an Indian raid seven years before. (Rev: BCCB 12/05; BL 9/15/05*; HB 1–2/06; LMC 1/06; SLJ 1/06; VOYA 4/06)

10909 Kimmel, Eric A. *Blackbeard's Last Fight* (2–4). Illus. by Leonard Everett Fisher. 2006, Farrar $17.00 (978-0-374-30780-6). 32pp. In the early 18th century, cabin boy Jeremy Hobbs hears conflicting reports about Blackbeard the pirate and witnesses his capture and execution; vivid paintings (avoiding the final scene) add to the exciting story. (Rev: BL 3/1/06; SLJ 5/06)

10910 Lasky, Kathryn. *A Journey to the New World: The Diary of Remember Patience Whipple* (4–7). Series: Dear America. 1996, Scholastic paper $10.95 (978-0-590-50214-6). Using diary entries as a format, this is the story of 12-year-old Mem Whipple, her journey on the *Mayflower*, and her first year in the New World. (Rev: BCCB 10/96; HB 9–10/96; SLJ 8/96; VOYA 10/96)

10911 Ovecka, Janice. *Cave of Falling Water* (4–8). Illus. by David K. Fadden. 1992, New England paper $10.95 (978-0-933050-98-3). A cave in the hills of Vermont plays a part in the lives of three girls, one an Indian and one white, both from colonial times, and the last, a contemporary adolescent. (Rev: BL 5/1/93)

10912 Rinaldi, Ann. *The Journal of Jasper Jonathan Pierce: A Pilgrim Boy, Plymouth, 1620* (4–8). 2000, Scholastic paper $10.95 (978-0-590-51078-3). This fictionalized account of the Pilgrims in journal format follows the adventures of a 14-year-old indentured servant aboard the *Mayflower* and during his first year in the New World. (Rev: BL 2/15/00; HBG 10/00; SLJ 7/00)

10913 Russell, Krista. *The Other Side of Free* (5–8). 2013, Peachtree $16.95 (978-156145710-6). 256pp. In 1739, 13-year-old Jem joins escaped slaves in Spanish Florida but he finds he is uncertain of his current situation and where his loyalties should lie. Lexile 650 (Rev: BL 11/1/13; LMC 5–6/14; SLJ 1/14)

10914 Schwabach, Karen. *A Pickpocket's Tale* (5–8). 2006, Random House LB $17.99 (978-0-375-93379-0). After being caught picking pockets on the streets of London in 1730, 10-year-old orphan Molly is exiled to America where she learns many new things from the Jewish family to which she is indentured. (Rev: BL 11/15/06; SLJ 11/06)

10915 Stainer, M. L. *The Lyon's Cub* (5–9). 1998, Chicken Soup LB $9.95 (978-0-9646904-5-5); paper $6.95 (978-0-9646904-6-2). This novel, a continuation of *The Lyon's Roar* (1997), tells what happened to the settlers of the lost colony of Roanoke and their life with peaceful Indian tribes. Continued in *The Lyon's Pride* (1998). (Rev: SLJ 8/98)

10916 Strickland, Brad. *The Guns of Tortuga* (5–8). 2003, Simon & Schuster paper $4.99 (978-0-689-85297-8). Young Davy helps the crew of the *Aurora* defeat a band of pirates in this sequel to *Mutiny!* (Rev: BL 2/1/03; SLJ 3/03)

10917 Tripp, Valerie. *Changes for Felicity: A Winter Story* (2–5). Illus. by Dan Andreasen. Series: American Girl. 1992, Pleasant $12.95 (978-1-56247-038-8); paper $6.95 (978-1-56247-037-1). In this story of a girl who lives in colonial Williamsburg, the father of her best friend is jailed as a Loyalist. Also use: *Felicity Saves the Day: A Summer Story;* and *Happy Birthday, Felicity* (both 1992). (Rev: BL 5/1/92)

10918 Tripp, Valerie. *Felicity Learns a Lesson: A School Story* (3–5). Illus. by Dan Andreasen. Series: American Girl. 1991, Pleasant paper $6.95 (978-1-56247-007-4). Felicity learns to control her temper in this story set in colonial Williamsburg. (Rev: BL 1/1/91; SLJ 1/92)

10919 Tripp, Valerie. *Felicity's Surprise: A Christmas Story* (3–5). Illus. by Dan Andreasen. Series: American Girl. 1991, Pleasant paper $6.95 (978-1-56247-010-4). The family must depend more on Felicity when her mother is ill, in this story of colonial Williamsburg. (Rev: BL 1/1/91; SLJ 1/92)

10920 Troeger, Virginia B. *Secret Along the St. Mary's* (3–5). Illus. by Michael-Che Swisher. Series: Mysteries in Time. 2003, Silver Moon LB $14.95 (978-1-893110-35-9). 92pp. Motherless 12-year-old Susannah, who must keep house for her father and brother in 17th-century Maryland, faces tough choices — some involving indentured servitude — in this story that interweaves historical fact. (Rev: SLJ 3/04)

10921 Wisler, G. Clifton. *This New Land* (5–9). 1987, Walker LB $14.85 (978-0-8027-6727-1). Twelve-year-old Richard and his family begin a new life in Plymouth, Massachusetts, in 1620. (Rev: BL 3/15/88; SLJ 11/87)

THE REVOLUTION

10922 Alsheimer, Jeanette E., and Patricia J. Friedle. *The Trouble with Tea* (5–8). 2002, Pentland $15.95 (978-1-57197-299-6). When Patience visits her friend Anne in Boston in 1773, she witnesses many of the events that led to the American Revolution. (Rev: BL 6/1–15/02)

10923 Anderson, Laurie Halse. *Forge* (5–8). 2010, Simon & Schuster $16.99 (978-1-4169-6144-4). 2pp. In this sequel to 2008's *Chains,* recently freed slave Curzon, 15, is on the run during the time of the American Revolution, eventually joining the army to battle the British at Saratoga. ⌒ ℮ Lexile 820L (Rev: BL 9/15/10; HB 11–12/10; LMC 1–2/11; SLJ 10/1/10)

10924 Armstrong, Jennifer. *Thomas Jefferson: Letters from a Philadelphia Bookworm* (5–8). Series: Dear Mr. President. 2001, Winslow $8.95 (978-1-890817-30-5). Twelve-year-old Amelia and President Jefferson discuss the events of the times in a continuing exchange of letters. (Rev: BL 5/15/01; HBG 10/01; SLJ 6/01; VOYA 8/01)

10925 Avi. *The Fighting Ground* (5–9). Illus. by Ellen Thompson. 1984, HarperCollins LB $16.89 (978-0-397-32074-5); paper $5.99 (978-0-06-440185-2). Thirteen-year-old Jonathan marches off to fight the British. (Rev: BL 4/87)

10926 Bartoletti, Susan C. *The Flag Maker* (1–4). Illus. by Claire A. Nivola. 2004, Houghton $16.00 (978-0-618-26757-6). 32pp. In this story of the British attack on Fort McHenry, Bartoletti focuses on the 13-year-old girl who helped her mother sew the garrison's huge American flag. (Rev: BL 3/1/04*; HB 5/04; SLJ 4/04)

10927 Brown, Don. *Henry and the Cannons: An Extraordinary True Story of the American Revolution* (K–3). Illus. by author. 2013, Roaring Brook $16.99 (978-1-59643-266-6). 32pp. The well-illustrated, fascinating story of a bookseller named Henry Knox who succeeded in hauling 59 cannons a distance of about 300 miles to Fort Ticonderoga in the winter of 1775. ℮ Lexile AD820L (Rev: BL 12/15/12*; HB 1–2/13; SLJ 1/13*)

10928 Bruchac, Joseph. *The Arrow over the Door* (4–7). 1998, Dial $15.99 (978-0-8037-2078-7). Two boys, one a Quaker and the other a Native American, share the narration of this story that takes place immediately before the Battle of Saratoga in 1777. (Rev: BCCB 4/98; BL 2/15/98; HBG 10/98; SLJ 4/98)

10929 Calkhoven, Laurie. *Daniel at the Siege of Boston, 1776* (4–7). Series: Boys of Wartime. 2010, Dutton $16.99 (978-052542144-3). 176pp. Twelve-year-old Daniel finds the courage to reveal a traitor to General Washington in this coming-of-age story set in Revolutionary War-era America. Lexile 710L (Rev: BL 2/1/10; LMC 5–6/10)

10930 Cooper, Afua. *My Name Is Phillis Wheatley: A Story of Slavery and Freedom* (5–8). 2009, Kids Can $16.95 (978-1-55337-812-9). 152pp. Set in Senegal, Boston, and London, this first-person account tells the fictionalized true story of Phillis Wheatley, the 18th-century slave who became a renowned poet. Lexile 790L (Rev: BL 9/1/09; SLJ 10/09)

10931 DeFelice, Cynthia. *The Ghost of Poplar Point* (4–6). 2007, Farrar $16.00 (978-0-374-32540-4). Allie, 12, and her friend Dub learn about a 1770s massacre in this fourth ghost story in the series. (Rev: BL 9/15/07; SLJ 10/07)

10932 Dell, Pamela. *Freedom's Light: A Story About Paul Revere's Midnight Ride* (4–6). Series: Scrapbooks of America. 2002, Tradition LB $28.50 (978-1-59187-016-6). 47pp. Fact and fiction are interwoven in this story of 12-year-old Mary Cates, a polisher in Revere's silver shop who becomes a spy when she discovers that a co-worker is plotting against Revere. (Rev: SLJ 5/03)

10933 Demas, Corinne. *If Ever I Return Again* (5–8). 2000, HarperCollins LB $15.89 (978-0-06-028718-4). Twelve-year-old Celia describes life aboard a whaling ship in letters home to her cousin. (Rev: BCCB 6/00; BL 4/1/00; HBG 10/00; SLJ 8/00)

10934 Duey, Kathleen. *Silence and Lily: 1773* (3–6). Series: Hoofbeats. 2007, Dutton $15.99 (978-0-525-47852-2). 160pp. With war on the horizon and constant chores at home, Silence longs to spend time with her beloved horse Lily. (Rev: BL 10/1/07)

10935 Durrant, Lynda. *Betsy Zane, the Rose of Fort Henry* (5–8). 2000, Clarion $15.00 (978-0-395-97899-3). Toward the end of the Revolutionary War, Betsy sets out alone from Philadelphia to rejoin her five brothers in western Virginia. (Rev: BCCB 10/00; BL 9/15/00; HBG 3/01; SLJ 4/01)

10936 Elliott, L. M. *Give Me Liberty* (5–8). 2006, HarperCollins $16.99 (978-0-06-074421-2). Nathaniel Dunn, a 13-year-old indentured servant in colonial Virginia, is taken under the wing of an elderly schoolmaster and watches as the revolutionary movement grows and affects his own behavior. (Rev: BL 10/1/06; SLJ 9/06)

10937 Fritz, Jean. *George Washington's Breakfast* (3–5). Illus. by Paul Galdone. 1998, Penguin paper $6.99 (978-0-698-11611-5). 43pp. George W. Allen knows all there is to know about our first president — except what he had for breakfast.

10938 Giff, Patricia Reilly. *Storyteller* (4–7). 2010, Random House $15.99 (978-0-375-83888-0); LB $18.99 (978-0-375-93888-7). 176pp. While staying with an aunt, Elizabeth uncovers the story of an 18th-century ancestor whose dramatic Revolutionary War experiences culminated in the Battle of Oriskany. e Lexile HL610L (Rev: BL 9/15/10; LMC 1–2/11; SLJ 11/1/10)

10939 Goodman, Joan Elizabeth. *Hope's Crossing* (5–8). 1998, Houghton Mifflin $16.00 (978-0-395-86195-0). Kidnapped by British loyalists during the Revolution, Hope must try to escape and find her way home. (Rev: BCCB 7–8/98; BL 6/1–15/98; HBG 10/98; SLJ 5/98; VOYA 8/98)

10940 Gregory, Kristiana. *Cannons at Dawn: The Second Diary of Abigail Jane Stewart* (4–8). Series: Dear America. 2011, Scholastic $12.99 (978-0-545-21319-6); LB $16.99 (978-0-545-28088-4). 256pp. Abigail and her family follow the Continental Army after their Valley Forge home burns down and the 13-year-old matures as the war progresses. e (Rev: SLJ 7/11)

10941 Gregory, Kristiana. *Five Smooth Stones: Hope's Diary* (3–5). Series: My America. 2001, Scholastic $10.95 (978-0-439-14827-6). 112pp. Set in 1776 Philadelphia and told in diary format, this novel tells of a 9-year-old girl and her family's problems at the beginning of the Revolutionary War. (Rev: BL 1/1–15/01; HBG 10/01)

10942 Gregory, Kristiana. *We Are Patriots: Hope's Revolutionary War Diary, Book Two* (2–4). Series: My America. 2002, Scholastic $10.95 (978-0-439-21039-3); paper $4.99 (978-0-439-36906-0). 108pp. Ten-year-old Hope tells her diary the details of the war raging around Philadelphia in 1777. (Rev: HBG 10/02; SLJ 8/02)

10943 Jones, Elizabeth McDonald. *Peril at King's Creek: A Felicity Mystery* (3–5). Series: American Girl Mysteries. 2006, Pleasant paper $6.95 (978-1-59369-101-1). Spending the summer of 1776 at her family's Virginia plantation, Felicity hears reports that British troops are raiding the farms of patriots and becomes suspicious of a visitor who shows a lot of interest in her horse. (Rev: BL 6/1–15/06; SLJ 4/06)

10944 Kirkpatrick, Katherine. *Redcoats and Petticoats* (3–5). Illus. by Ronald Himler. 1999, Holiday House $16.95 (978-0-8234-1416-1). When 13-year-old Thomas Strong is out on some unusual errands, he is unaware at first that he is part of a spy network conveying messages to the forces of George Washington during the Revolutionary War. (Rev: BL 3/1/99; HBG 10/99; SLJ 4/99)

10945 Moore, Ruth Nulton. *Distant Thunder* (5–8). Illus. by Allan Eitzen. 1991, Herald paper $6.99 (978-0-8361-3557-2). During the Revolution, when wounded Americans are sent to Pennsylvania to recover, young Kate experiences the horrors of war. (Rev: BCCB 1/92; SLJ 1/92)

10946 Noble, Trinka Hakes. *The Scarlet Stockings Spy* (2–4). Illus. by Robert Papp. 2004, Sleeping Bear $16.95 (978-1-58536-230-1). Maddy Rose, a young seamstress in revolutionary-era Philadelphia, devises a clever signaling system to keep patriot forces informed about what ships are docked in the city's harbor. (Rev: BL 2/1/05)

10947 Pryor, Bonnie. *Captain Hannah Pritchard: The Hunt for Pirate Gold* (5–8). Series: Historical Fiction Adventures. 2011, Enslow LB $27.93 (978-0-7660-3817-2). 160pp. Still disguised as Jack, Hannah Pritchard leads her crew on missions for the Continental navy while searching for lost pirate treasure in this final installment in the trilogy set during the American Revolution. (Rev: BLO 10/15/11; SLJ 2/12; VOYA 12/11)

10948 Roop, Peter, and Connie Roop. *An Eye for an Eye: A Story of the Revolutionary War* (5–9). 2000, Jamestown paper $5.95 (978-0-8092-0628-5). During the Revolutionary War, Samantha, disguised as boy, sets out to save her brother who is being held prisoner on a British ship. (Rev: BCCB 7–8/00; SLJ 4/00)

10949 Thomas, Velma M. *Lest We Forget: The Passage from Africa to Slavery and Emancipation* (5–8). 1997, Crown $29.95 (978-0-609-60030-6). An interactive book about slavery based on material from the Black Holocaust Museum. (Rev: BL 12/15/97) [973.6]

10950 Tripp, Valerie. *Very Funny, Elizabeth!* (3–5). Illus. by Dan Andreasen. Series: American Girl. 2005, American Girl paper $6.95 (978-1-59369-061-8). 81pp. Ten-year-old Elizabeth Cole and her friend Felicity, who are growing up in Revolutionary-era Williamsburg, enjoy teasing Elizabeth's older sister Annabelle in this volume that provides historical detail. (Rev: SLJ 3/06)

10951 Woodruff, Elvira. *George Washington's Spy* (4–6). 2010, Scholastic $16.99 (978-0-545-10487-6). 230pp. Ten-year-old Matt and his younger sister travel back in time with some friends and become embroiled in the American Revolution as they learn about both sides in the conflict. (Rev: LMC 3–4/11; SLJ 12/1/10)

THE YOUNG NATION, 1789–1861

10952 Arbuckle, Scott. *Zeb, the Cow's on the Roof Again! And Other Tales of Early Texas Dwellings* (3–7). Illus. by author. 1996, Eakin $15.95 (978-1-57168-102-7). 128pp. Four youngsters tell about their dwellings in stories that take place at various times in Texas history. (Rev: SLJ 4/97)

10953 Barker, M. P. *A Difficult Boy* (5–9). 2008, Holiday $16.95 (978-0-8234-2086-5). Indentured to a shopkeeper against his will, Ethan befriends young Daniel, a young Irishman, and the two find friendship and a joint love of horses in this story set in 1839 Massachusetts. (Rev: BL 4/15/08; SLJ 5/08)

10954 Blos, Joan W. *Letters from the Corrugated Castle: A Novel of Gold Rush California, 1850–1852* (4–8). 2007, Simon & Schuster $17.99 (978-0-689-87077-4). Reunited with a mother long believed to be dead, 13-year-old Eldora must learn to adjust to living a life of comfort in San Francisco; newspaper articles and her correspondence with Luke, who hopes to find a fortune, reveal much about life during the Gold Rush. (Rev: BL 4/15/07; SLJ 6/07)

10955 Broyles, Anne. *Priscilla and the Hollyhocks* (2–4). Illus. by Anna Alter. 2008, Charlesbridge $15.95 (978-1-57091-675-5). 32pp. A hollyhock patch is a source of comfort for a young slave girl separated from her mother; she has hollyhock seeds in her pocket when she is later purchased by a Cherokee family, and it is on the Trail of Tears that she finds her freedom and can eventually plant her own patch. (Rev: BL 2/1/08; LMC 10/08; SLJ 3/08)

10956 Buckey, Sarah Masters. *Meet Marie-Grace* (4–6). Illus. by Christine Kornacki. 2011, American Girl $12.95 (978-1-59369-651-1); paper $6.95 (978-15936965-2-8). 120pp. Reserved Massachusetts girl Marie-Grace is able to handle the boisterous nature of 1853 New Orleans with the help of a new friend, Cécile, who is black. **e** Lexile 750L (Rev: BL 10/15/11; SLJ 4/1/12)

10957 Cooper, Afua. *My Name Is Henry Bibb: A Story of Slavery and Freedom* (5–8). 2009, Kids Can $16.95 (978-1-55337-813-6). 160pp. Based on a true story, this gritty first-person account of Henry Bibb, the son of a black woman and a white plantation owner in 19th-century Kentucky, depicts the cruelty, humiliation, and yearning for freedom that was part of a slave's daily ex-perience. Lexile 800L (Rev: BL 8/09; LMC 11–12/09; SLJ 10/09)

10958 Crook, Connie Brummel. *Laura Secord's Brave Walk* (2–5). Illus. by June Lawrason. 2001, Second Story $14.95 (978-1-896764-34-4). During the War of 1812, Laura Secord hears American soldiers' plans to attack at Beavers Dam, and sets off on a dangerous journey to warn the British in this novel with realistic battlefield illustrations. (Rev: SLJ 7/01)

10959 Dahlberg, Maurine F. *The Story of Jonas* (4–7). 2007, Farrar $16.00 (978-0-374-37264-4). In the mid-1800s, Jonas, a 13-year-old slave, is sent on an expedition to find gold in the Kansas Territory and realizes that freedom is not beyond his grasp. (Rev: BL 4/07; SLJ 4/07)

10960 DeFelice, Cynthia. *Bringing Ezra Back* (4–6). 2006, Farrar $16.00 (978-0-374-39939-9). 160pp. In this sequel to *Weasel* (1990), 12-year-old Nathan travels from Ohio to Pennsylvania in 1840 in an attempt to locate and help Ezra, the man grievously injured by Weasel. (Rev: BL 8/06; SLJ 9/06)

10961 Donaldson, Joan. *A Pebble and a Pen* (5–8). 2000, Holiday $15.95 (978-0-8234-1500-7). In 1853, to avoid an arranged marriage, 14-year-old Matty runs away to study penmanship at Mr. Spencer's famous Ohio school. (Rev: BCCB 12/00; BL 1/1–15/01; HBG 10/01; SLJ 12/00; VOYA 2/01)

10962 Duble, Kathleen Benner. *Hearts of Iron* (5–8). 2006, Simon & Schuster $15.95 (978-1-4169-0850-0). In a Connecticut iron-working community in the early 19th century, two young lovers rebel against their families' plans for their future. (Rev: BL 9/15/06; SLJ 11/06)

10963 Duey, Kathleen, and Karen A. Bale. *Hurricane: Open Seas, 1844* (5–7). Series: Survival! 1999, Simon & Schuster paper $4.50 (978-0-689-82544-6). This exciting sea story, set in 1844, tells of two youngsters who are on a whaler when a killer hurricane strikes. (Rev: SLJ 8/99)

10964 Frost, Helen. *Salt: A Story of Friendship in a Time of War* (5–8). 2013, Farrar $17.99 (978-037436387-1). 176pp. During the War of 1812, 12-year-olds Anikwa of the Miami tribe and James, from a fort trading post, try to maintain their friendship amid the strife that surrounds them. (Rev: BL 6/13*; HB 7–8/13; LMC 1–2/14; SLJ 7/13; VOYA 6/13)

10965 Garland, Sherry. *In the Shadow of the Alamo* (5–8). Series: Great Episodes. 2001, Harcourt $17.00 (978-0-15-201744-6). Fifteen-year-old Lorenzo Bonifacio, a conscript in the Mexican army of Santa Ana, describes the harsh life of the soldiers and the family members who follow them on the trek to Texas and the battle of the Alamo. (Rev: BCCB 1/02; BL 10/15/01; HB 11–12/01; HBG 3/02; SLJ 12/01; VOYA 10/01)

10966 Giblin, James Cross. *The Boy Who Saved Cleveland* (3–6). Illus. by Michael Dooling. 2006, Holt $15.95 (978-0-8050-7355-3). 64pp. This fact-based story recounts the trials of 10-year-old Seth Doan who helped to nurse early settlers of Cleveland, Ohio, through a malaria outbreak in the late 18th century. (Rev: BL 4/15/06; SLJ 5/06)

10967 Greenwood, Barbara. *The Last Safe House: A Story of the Underground Railroad* (3–6). Illus. by Heather Collins. 1998, Kids Can $16.95 (978-1-55074-507-8); paper $10.95 (978-1-55074-509-2). 119pp. Using a Canadian family's participation in the Underground Railroad in 1856 as a framework, this book supplies good background on the railroad's organization, accomplishments, and the fight against slavery. (Rev: HBG 3/99; SLJ 1/99)

10968 Guccione, Leslie D. *Come Morning* (4–7). 1995, Carolrhoda LB $19.15 (978-0-87614-892-1). A young boy takes over his father's duties as a conductor on the Underground Railroad. (Rev: BCCB 1/96; HB 11–12/95; SLJ 11/95)

10969 Helgerson, Joseph. *Crows and Cards* (4–7). Illus. by Peter De Seve. 2009, Houghton $16.00 (978-0-618-88395-0). 352pp. In the mid-19th century, 12-year-old Zeb is sent off to become a tanner but on the riverboat to St. Louis meets a gambler who offers a more enticing life. (Rev: BL 4/15/09; HB 5/09; LMC 10/09; SLJ 8/09)

10970 Higgins, Joanna. *Waiting for the Queen* (5–8). 2013, Milkweed $16.95 (978-157131700-1). 256pp. Eugenie and her family have fled France to escape the French Revolution, but they find that life in America is very different, and that the families they have hired to help them do not want to be servants, particularly not Hannah, a maid for Eugenie; the girls bond over the mistreatment of a slave and form an unlikely friendship. (Rev: BL 11/1/13; LMC 3–4/14; SLJ 8/13; VOYA 8/13)

10971 Hill, Donna. *Shipwreck Season* (5–8). 1998, Clarion $16.00 (978-0-395-86614-6). In the 1800s, 16-year-old Daniel joins a crew of seamen who patrol America's eastern coastline, rescuing people and cargo from shipwrecks. (Rev: BCCB 7–8/98; BL 6/1–15/98; HBG 3/99; SLJ 6/98)

10972 Hilts, Len. *Timmy O'Dowd and the Big Ditch: A Story of the Glory Days on the Old Erie Canal* (5–7). 1988, Harcourt $13.95 (978-0-15-200606-8). Timmy and his cousin Dennis don't get along, but when the canals threaten to flood, they realize each other's strengths and stamina. (Rev: BCCB 12/88; BL 10/1/88; SLJ 12/88)

10973 Houston, Gloria. *Bright Freedom's Song: A Story of the Underground Railroad* (4–7). 1998, Harcourt $17.00 (978-0-15-201812-2). A tense, dramatic story about a girl who helps her parents operate a North Carolina station on the Underground Railroad. (Rev: BCCB 1/99; BL 11/1/98; HBG 3/99; SLJ 12/98; VOYA 2/99)

10974 Howard, Ellen. *The Log Cabin Wedding* (2–4). Illus. by Ronald Himler. 2006, Holiday $15.95 (978-0-8234-1989-0). 48pp. Elvirey is upset when her widowed father falls in love with the Widow Aiken in this chapter-book sequel to the picture books *Log Cabin Quilt* (1996), *The Log Cabin Christmas* (2000), and *The Log Cabin Church* (2002). (Rev: BL 9/15/06; SLJ 12/06)

10975 Hurst, Carol Otis. *Through the Lock* (5–8). 2001, Houghton Mifflin $15.00 (978-0-618-03036-1). In this novel set in Connecticut in the first half of the 19th century, a young orphan named Etta shares many adventures with a boy who lives in an abandoned cabin by a canal. (Rev: BCCB 3/01; BL 4/1/01; HB 3–4/01; HBG 10/01; SLJ 3/01; VOYA 4/01)

10976 Hyatt, Patricia Rusch. *The Quite Contrary Man: A True American Tale* (K–3). Illus. by Kathryn Brown. 2011, Abrams $16.95 (978-0-8109-4065-9). 32pp. In early 19th-century New England, Joseph Palmer refuses to shave his beard as the law requires and is eventually sent to jail in this story of an independent spirit. Lexile AD840L (Rev: BL 4/1/11; LMC 8–9/11; SLJ 3/1/11)

10977 Ketchum, Liza. *Orphan Journey Home* (5–7). 2000, Avon $15.99 (978-0-380-97811-3). When their parents die in southern Illinois in 1828, Jesse and her three siblings must find their way to their grandmother in eastern Kentucky. (Rev: BCCB 6/00; BL 6/1–15/00; HBG 10/00; SLJ 8/00)

10978 Kroll, Steven. *John Quincy Adams: Letters from a Southern Planter's Son* (4–6). Illus. Series: Dear Mr. President. 2001, Winslow $9.95 (978-1-890817-93-0). 122pp. A fictional correspondence between a young boy and President John Quincy Adams details historical events and gives insight into Adams's character and concerns. (Rev: BL 1/1–15/02; HBG 3/02; SLJ 12/01)

10979 Lester, Julius. *The Old African* (4–7). Illus. by Jerry Pinkney. 2005, Dial $19.99 (978-0-8037-2564-5). An elderly slave who never speaks uses his acute mental powers to relieve the pain of his people on a Georgia plantation. (Rev: BL 7/05*; SLJ 9/05; VOYA 12/05)

10980 McKissack, Patricia C. *A Picture of Freedom: The Diary of Clotee, a Slave Girl* (4–6). 1997, Scholastic $9.95 (978-0-614-25386-3). 208pp. Using a diary format, this novel describes the life of slaves on a Southern plantation as seen through the eyes of a young slave girl. (Rev: BL 4/15/97; SLJ 9/97)

10981 McKissack, Patricia C., and Fredrick McKissack. *Let My People Go* (5–8). 1998, Simon & Schuster $20.00 (978-0-689-80856-2). This novel set in the early 19th century combines Bible stories and the hardships endured by slaves as told by Price Jefferson, a former slave who is now an abolitionist living in South Carolina. (Rev: BCCB 12/98; BL 10/1/98; HBG 3/99; SLJ 11/98)

10982 Mazer, Harry. *My Brother Abe: Sally Lincoln's Story* (4–6). 2009, Simon & Schuster $15.99 (978-1-4169-3884-2). 208pp. Mazer expands the facts we know about Lincoln's sister Sally into a story about the family's hard-scrabble life in the early 19th-century Midwest. (Rev: BCCB 2/09; BL 1/1–15/09; LMC 5/09; SLJ 2/09)

10983 Minahan, John A. *Abigail's Drum* (2–5). Illus. 1995, Pippin $15.95 (978-0-945912-25-5). 64pp. During the War of 1812, Rebecca and Abigail try to save their father, who has been captured by the British. (Rev: BCCB 2/96; BL 2/15/96; SLJ 2/96)

10984 Monjo, F. N. *The Drinking Gourd* (2–4). Illus. by Fred Brenner. 1970, HarperCollins LB $16.89 (978-0-06-024330-2); paper $3.99 (978-0-06-444042-4). A New England white boy helps a black family escape on the Underground Railroad.

10985 Myers, Anna. *The Grave Robber's Secret* (4–7). 2011, Walker $16.99 (978-0-8027-2183-9). 224pp. In 19th-century Philadelphia, 12-year-old Robby Hare has helped his father to rob graves, but he suspects that actual murder may be afoot when a boarder called Mr. Burke moves in; loosely based on the murders that took place in Edinburgh, Scotland, in the early 1800s. **e** Lexile 650L (Rev: BL 4/15/11; LMC 3–4/11; SLJ 3/1/11)

10986 Nolen, Jerdine. *Eliza's Freedom Road: An Underground Railroad Diary* (4–7). 2011, Simon & Schuster $14.99 (978-1-4169-5814-7). 160pp. House slave Eliza, 12, describes in her diary her escape from a cruel master with the help of the Underground Railroad, and records some of the stories she has heard and read; set in 1855. **e** Lexile 670L (Rev: BLO 1/1–15/11; SLJ 2/1/11)

10987 Nordan, Robert. *The Secret Road* (5–9). 2001, Holiday $16.95 (978-0-8234-1543-4). Young Laura helps an escaped slave on a long and suspenseful journey to freedom by posing as her sister. (Rev: BL 9/15/01; HBG 3/02; SLJ 10/01; VOYA 12/01)

10988 Olson, Tod. *How to Get Rich in the California Gold Rush: An Adventurer's Guide to the Fabulous Riches Discovered in 1848* (4–8). Illus. by Scott Allred. 2008, National Geographic $16.95 (978-142630315-9); LB $25.90 (978-142630316-6). 48pp. In this fictional story set in factual historical context, three young men head west to become gold barons and reach the conclusion that they're better off seeking their fortune in other ways. Lexile NC990L (Rev: BL 10/15/08; SLJ 12/08*; VOYA 2/09)

10989 Paterson, Katherine. *Jip: His Story* (5–9). 1998, Puffin paper $6.99 (978-0-14-038674-5). Jip, a foundling boy in Vermont of the 1850s, wonders about his origins, particularly after he finds he is being watched by a mysterious stranger. (Rev: BCCB 12/96; BL 9/1/96*; HB 11–12/96; SLJ 10/96*; VOYA 4/97)

10990 Platt, Kin. *A Mystery for Thoreau* (5–8). 2008, Farrar $16 (978-037435337-7). 176pp. In mid-19th-century Concord, Massachusetts, teen journalist Oliver Puckle investigates a murder near Thoreau's cabin at Walden Pond; both humorous and melodramatic, this novel conveys much about the time and place. (Rev: BL 11/1/08; SLJ 12/08; VOYA 12/08)

10991 Rappaport, Doreen. *Freedom River* (3–5). Illus. 2000, Hyperion $14.99 (978-0-7868-0350-7). 32pp. Based on fact, this is a picture book for older readers that tells how John Parker, an ex-slave, helped a family to escape from Kentucky via the Underground Railroad. (Rev: BL 10/1/00; HBG 3/01; SLJ 10/00)

10992 Raven, Margot Theis. *Night Boat to Freedom* (1–3). Illus. by E. B. Lewis. 2006, Farrar $16.00 (978-0-374-31266-4). Twelve-year-old Christmas John, urged on by Granny Judith, helps dozens of slaves escape to freedom, but when she tells the boy that he, too, must flee, he refuses to go without her; text and illustrations blend to make this a touching story. (Rev: BCCB 12/06; BL 10/15/06; SLJ 11/06)

10993 Rinaldi, Ann. *The Blue Door* (5–8). Series: Quilt. 1996, Scholastic paper $15.95 (978-0-590-46051-4). In this final volume of the Quilt trilogy — following *A Stitch in Time* (1994) and *Broken Days* — Amanda is forced to take a mill job in Lowell, Massachusetts, after an adventurous trip north from her South Carolina home. (Rev: BL 11/1/96; VOYA 2/97)

10994 Rinaldi, Ann. *The Ever-After Bird* (5–8). 2007, Harcourt $17.00 (978-0-15-202620-2). CeCe travels with her uncle, an abolitionist and ornithologist, to Georgia to search for a rare bird and help slaves get to the Underground Railroad. (Rev: BL 11/1/07; LMC 1/08; SLJ 12/07)

10995 Roseman, Kenneth. *The Other Side of the Hudson: A Jewish Immigrant Adventure* (5–8). Series: Do-It-Yourself Adventure. 1993, UAHC paper $11.95 (978-0-8074-0506-2). Using an interactive format, readers can choose various destinations for a young male Jewish immigrant after he arrives in New York City from Germany in 1851. (Rev: SLJ 6/94)

10996 Sanchez, Anita. *The Invasion of Sandy Bay* (5–8). 2008, Boyds Mills $16.95 (978-1-59078-560-7). 152pp. Twelve-year-old Lemuel attempts to save his little fishing village during the War of 1812 when he spots a British warship in the harbor; with extensive historical endnotes. (Rev: BL 10/1/08; LMC 1/02; VOYA 10/08)

10997 Schneider, Mical. *Annie Quinn in America* (5–9). 2001, Carolrhoda LB $15.95 (978-1-57505-510-7). In 1847, young Annie and her brother travel from Ireland, a land ravaged by the potato famine, to America, a land fraught with dangers of its own. (Rev: BL 11/15/01; HBG 3/02; SLJ 9/01)

10998 Schwartz, Virginia Frances. *Send One Angel Down* (5–8). 2000, Holiday $16.95 (978-0-8234-1484-0). This is the story of a young slave girl, Eliza, the skills she learns on the plantation, and how this knowledge helps her when she gains freedom. (Rev: BL 6/1–15/00; HB 7–8/00; HBG 10/00; SLJ 8/00)

10999 Siegelson, Kim L. *Escape South* (2–4). Illus. by Shelley Jackson. Series: Road to Reading. 2000, Golden $10.99 (978-0-307-46504-7). This easy chapter book tells, in fictionalized form, how some runaway slaves were given shelter and land by the Seminole Indians in Florida and later left for land out west. (Rev: BL 2/15/01; HBG 3/01)

11000 Siegelson, Kim L. *In the Time of the Drums* (2–5). Illus. by Brian Pinkney. 1999, Hyperion LB $16.49 (978-0-7686-2386-4). Told from the standpoint of a young African American, this is the legend of the slave rebellion at Ibo's Landing in South Carolina's Sea Islands. (Rev: BL 4/1/99)

11001 Stiles, Martha Bennett. *Sailing to Freedom* (4–8). 2012, Henry Holt $16.99 (978-0-8050-9238-7). 246pp. Ray, 12, joins his uncle's ship as a cook's helper in the mid-19th century and discovers that they are transporting an escaping slave to safety in the north. **e** Lexile 890L (Rev: LMC 1–2/13; SLJ 8/1/12)

11002 Stowe, Cynthia M. *The Second Escape of Arthur Cooper* (5–7). 2000, Marshall Cavendish LB $14.95 (978-0-7614-5069-6). Based on a true story, this novel tells of Arthur Cooper, an escaped slave, and the Quakers on Nantucket Island who saved him from slave catchers in 1822. (Rev: BL 8/00; HBG 3/01; SLJ 10/00)

11003 Trottier, Maxine. *Under a Shooting Star* (5–8). Series: The Circle of Silver Chronicles. 2002, Stoddart paper $7.95 (978-0-7737-6228-2). During the War of 1812, a 15-year-old boy who is half English and half Oneida Indian struggles with conflicting loyalties as he tries to protect the two American girls he is escorting. (Rev: SLJ 5/02)

11004 Turner, Glennette Tilley. *Running for Our Lives* (5–7). 1994, Holiday $16.95 (978-0-8234-1121-4). A thoroughly researched novel about a boy and his family who escape slavery in the 1850s and traveled on the Underground Railroad to Canada. (Rev: BCCB 6/94; BL 6/1–15/94; SLJ 4/94)

11005 Wait, Lea. *Finest Kind* (4–7). 2006, Simon & Schuster $16.95 (978-1-4169-0952-1). When his family falls on hard times and is forced to move from Boston to Maine in the 1830s, 12-year-old Jake Webber finds himself shouldering new responsibilities, including looking after his disabled younger brother. (Rev: BL 10/15/06; SLJ 11/06)

11006 Wait, Lea. *Seaward Born* (4–7). 2003, Simon & Schuster $16.95 (978-0-689-84719-6). Michael, a young slave, makes a dangerous journey to Canada and freedom in this dramatic historical novel. (Rev: BL 2/15/03; HBG 10/03; SLJ 1/03)

11007 Wall, Bill. *The Cove of Cork* (5–9). 1999, Irish American paper $7.95 (978-0-85635-225-6). In this novel, the third in a trilogy revolving around the War of 1812, an Irish lad, the first mate of the American schooner *Shenandoah*, sees action in a battle against a British vessel and eventually wins the hand of the granddaughter of a shipbuilding magnate. (Rev: SLJ 7/99)

11008 Wanttaja, Ronald. *The Key to Honor* (5–9). 1996, Fireworks paper $9.99 (978-0-88092-270-8). During the War of 1812, midshipman Nate Lawton has doubts about his courage in battle and worries about his father, who has been taken prisoner by the British. (Rev: VOYA 8/96)

11009 Whelan, Gloria. *Farewell to the Island* (5–8). 1998, HarperCollins $16.95 (978-0-06-027751-2). In this sequel to *Once on This Island,* Mary leaves her Michigan home after the War of 1812 and travels to England where she falls in love with Lord Lindsay. (Rev: BL 12/1/98; HBG 3/99; SLJ 1/99)

11010 Whelan, Gloria. *Friend on Freedom River* (3–5). Illus. by Gijsbert van Frankenhuyzen. 2005, Sleeping Bear $16.95 (978-1-58536-222-6). In 1850, on a cold December night on the Detroit River, young Louis is asked to ferry runaway slaves to Canada. (Rev: BL 5/15/04; SLJ 6/05)

11011 Whelan, Gloria. *Once on This Island* (4–7). 1995, HarperCollins LB $14.89 (978-0-06-026249-5). In 1812, Mary and her older brother and sister must tend the family farm on Mackinac Island when their father goes off to war. (Rev: BCCB 11/95; BL 10/1/95; SLJ 11/95; VOYA 2/96)

11012 Wiley, Melissa. *On Tide Mill Lane* (4–8). 2001, HarperCollins $16.95 (978-0-06-027013-1). Charlotte experiences a number of household crises in Roxbury, Massachusetts, where she lives with her blacksmith father at the time of the War of 1812. (Rev: BL 2/15/01; HBG 10/01)

11013 Woods, Brenda. *My Name Is Sally Little Song* (4–7). 2006, Putnam $15.99 (978-0-399-24312-7). Eleven-year-old Sally, a slave on a Georgia plantation at the beginning of the 19th century, escapes with her family and heads south to seek refuge with the Seminole Indians. (Rev: BCCB 11/06; BL 8/06; HBG 4/07; SLJ 9/06)

11014 Wright, Courtni C. *Journey to Freedom: A Story of the Underground Railroad* (3–5). Illus. by Griffith Gershom. 1994, Holiday House LB $17.95 (978-0-8234-1096-5). 28pp. A picture book that tells of 8-year-old Joshua and his flight to freedom on the Underground Railroad. (Rev: BL 11/15/94; SLJ 1/95)

11015 Wyeth, Sharon Dennis. *Flying Free: Corey's Underground Railroad Diary* (2–4). Illus. Series: My America. 2002, Scholastic $10.95 (978-0-439-24443-5). 112pp. In diary form, this novel traces the travels of Corey, a black boy, and his family to freedom in Canada via the Underground Railroad. (Rev: BL 6/1–15/02; HBG 10/02; SLJ 8/02)

PIONEERS AND WESTWARD EXPANSION

11016 Altman, Linda J. *The Legend of Freedom Hill* (2–4). Illus. by Cornelius Van Wright and Ying-Hwa Hu. 2000, Lee & Low $15.95 (978-1-58430-003-8). 32pp. Set in Gold Rush California, this novel tells how Rosabel, the daughter of a runaway slave, and her Jewish friend Sophia pan enough gold to buy the freedom of Rosabel's mother. (Rev: BL 11/1/00; HBG 3/01; SLJ 8/00)

11017 Applegate, Stan. *The Devil's Highway* (5–8). Illus. by James Watling. 1998, Peachtree paper $8.95 (978-1-56145-184-5). In this adventure novel set in the early 1800s, 14-year-old Zeb and his horse, Christmas, set out on the bandit-infested Natchez Trail to search for the boy's grandfather. (Rev: SLJ 2/99)

11018 Bauer, Marion Dane. *Land of the Buffalo Bones: The Diary of Mary Elizabeth Rodgers, an English Girl in Minnesota* (4–8). Series: Dear America. 2003, Scholastic $12.95 (978-0-439-22027-9). Based on real-life events, Polly Rodgers's diary reveals the hardships endured by a group of English settlers who arrived in Minnesota in 1873. (Rev: BL 5/15/03; HBG 10/03; SLJ 9/01)

11019 Benner, J. A. *Uncle Comanche* (5–8). 1996, Texas Christian Univ. paper $12.95 (978-0-87565-152-1). Based on fact, this is the story of the adventures of 12-year-old Sul Ross, who runs away from home in pre-Civil War Texas and is pursued by a family friend nicknamed Uncle Comanche. (Rev: VOYA 10/96)

11020 Blakeslee, Ann R. *A Different Kind of Hero* (5–7). 1997, Marshall Cavendish $14.95 (978-0-7614-5000-9). In 1881 Colorado, Renny is criticized for befriending and helping a Chinese boy new to town. (Rev: BL 9/1/97; HBG 3/98; SLJ 1/98)

11021 Chrismer, Melanie. *Phoebe Clappsaddle for Sheriff* (1–3). Illus. by Virginia M. Roeder. 2003, Pelican $15.95 (978-1-58980-127-1). In this rollicking tale set in the early years of Texas's statehood, diminutive Phoebe Clappsaddle fills in as sheriff when she's selected by the governor to meet the stagecoach carrying the town's new schoolteacher. (Rev: HBG 4/04; SLJ 1/04)

11022 Collier, James Lincoln. *Wild Boy* (5–8). 2002, Marshall Cavendish $15.95 (978-0-7614-5126-6). After knocking his father out during an argument, 12-year-old Jesse runs away from his frontier home to live in the mountains, where he has many adventures, learns many skills, and reflects on his own characteristics before finally deciding to return home in this story that appears to be set in the 19th century. (Rev: BL 11/1/02; HBG 10/03; SLJ 11/02)

11023 Couloumbis, Audrey. *The Misadventures of Maude March, or, Trouble Rides a Fast Horse* (5–8). 2005, Random House LB $17.99 (978-0-375-93245-8). When their aunt and sole guardian is killed, Maude and Sallie March rebel against their new foster family and set off on their own in this rollicking tale of the Old West. (Rev: SLJ 9/05)

11024 Cullen, Lynn. *Nelly in the Wilderness* (5–8). 2002, HarperCollins LB $15.89 (978-0-06-029134-1). Set in the Indiana frontier of 1821, 12-year-old Nelly and her brother, Cornelius, must adjust to a new stepmother after their beloved Ma dies. (Rev: BCCB 5/02; BL 4/1/02; HB 7–8/02; HBG 10/02; SLJ 2/02)

11025 Cushman, Karen. *The Ballad of Lucy Whipple* (5–8). 1996, Clarion $16.00 (978-0-395-72806-2). Lucy hates being stuck in the California wilderness with an overbearing mother who runs a boarding house. (Rev: BCCB 9/96; BL 8/96*; HB 9–10/96; SLJ 8/96*; VOYA 12/96)

11026 Dallas, Sandra. *The Quilt Walk* (4–7). 2012, Sleeping Bear $18.95 (978-1-58536800-6). 215pp. Traveling west to Colorado in 1864, 10-year-old Emmy learns to make quilts — and friends — while facing many challenges. (Rev: BLO 10/15/12; SLJ 1/13)

11027 Durrant, Lynda. *The Sun, the Rain, and the Apple Seed: A Novel of Johnny Appleseed's Life* (5–8). 2003, Clarion $15.00 (978-0-618-23487-5). This fictionalized biography of John Chapman's life focuses on his eccentricities. (Rev: BL 5/15/03; HBG 10/03; SLJ 5/03)

11028 Ferris, Jean. *Much Ado About Grubstake* (5–8). 2006, Harcourt $17.00 (978-0-15-205706-0). Sixteen-year-old Arley, owner of her family's mine and boarding house in 1888 Grubstake, Colorado, becomes suspicious when a stranger takes an unusual interest in the rundown mining town; adventure, romance, and humor are combined in this mystery. (Rev: BL 8/06; SLJ 11/06)

11029 Finley, Mary Peace. *Meadow Lark* (5–8). Series: Santa Fe Trail trilogy. 2003, Filter $15.95 (978-0-86541-070-1). In this sequel to *Soaring Eagle* (1993) and *White Grizzly* (2000) set in 1845, Teresita Montoya, 13, has various adventures on the Santa Fe Trail as she searches for her older brother and for a new life for herself. (Rev: BL 12/1/03; HBG 4/04; SLJ 2/04)

11030 Finley, Mary Peace. *White Grizzly* (5–9). 2000, Filter $15.95 (978-0-86541-053-4); paper $8.95 (978-0-86541-058-9). Fifteen-year-old Julio sets out on an arduous journey along the Santa Fe Trail to discover his true identity. (Rev: BL 12/1/00; HBG 10/01; SLJ 1/01; VOYA 2/01)

11031 Fleischman, Paul. *The Borning Room* (5–8). 1991, HarperCollins paper $4.99 (978-0-06-447099-5). Georgina remembers important turning points in her life and the role played by the room set aside for giving birth and dying in her grandfather's house in 19th-century rural Ohio. (Rev: BCCB 9/91; BL 10/1/91*; HB 11–12/91*; SLJ 9/91*)

11032 Fleischman, Sid. *Bandit's Moon* (3–6). Illus. 1998, Greenwillow $17.99 (978-0-688-15830-9). 144pp. Based partly on fact, this is a humorous adventure story about Annyrose, a young girl who, disguised as a boy, joins a band of Mexican bandits led by Wakeen, the notorious robber. (Rev: BCCB 11/98; BL 10/1/98*; HB 11/98; HBG 3/99; SLJ 9/98)

11033 Fleischman, Sid. *Jim Ugly* (4–6). Illus. by Joseph A. Smith. 1992, Greenwillow $17.99 (978-0-688-10886-1). In the time of the Old West, Jake — accompanied by his dad's mongrel dog — sets off in search of his missing father. (Rev: BCCB 3/92*; BL 5/15/92; SLJ 4/92)

11034 Galbraith, Kathryn O. *Arbor Day Square* (PS–3). Illus. by Cyd Moore. 2010, Peachtree $16.95 (978-1-56145-517-1). 32pp. A girl and her father decide to plant trees in their frontier prairie town, kicking off an annual Arbor Day tradition in this charming story. (Rev: BL 4/15/10; SLJ 4/1/10)

11035 Garland, Sherry. *Valley of the Moon: The Diary of Rosalia de Milagros* (5–8). 2001, Scholastic paper $10.95 (978-0-439-08820-6). Rosalia, a 13-year-old orphan, keeps a diary about working on a California ranch in 1846. (Rev: BL 4/1/01; HBG 3/02; SLJ 4/01; VOYA 8/01)

11036 Glaze, Lynn. *Seasons of the Trail* (4–6). Illus. by Matthew Archambault. 2000, Silver Moon LB $14.95 (978-1-893110-20-5). 92pp. To avoid the oncoming Civil War, 14-year-old Lucy Scott and her family leave their home in Missouri and journey to California by covered wagon. (Rev: HBG 3/01; SLJ 1/01)

11037 Gregory, Kristiana. *Across the Wide and Lonesome Prairie: The Oregon Trail Diary of Hattie Campbell* (4–7). Series: Dear America. 1997, Scholastic paper $10.95

(978-0-590-22651-6). In a diary format, this novel chronicles the hardships that pioneers endured during a trip west on the Oregon Trail. (Rev: SLJ 3/97)

11038 Gregory, Kristiana. *My Darlin' Clementine* (4–7). 2009, Holiday $16.95 (978-0-8234-2198-5). 208pp. Based on the traditional folk song, this is the story of 16-year-old Clementine, who in Idaho Territory in the late 1860s has to deal with family problems including her father's gambling and drinking while still hoping to become a doctor. (Rev: BL 4/15/09; SLJ 5/09; VOYA 6/09)

11039 Gregory, Kristiana. *Seeds of Hope: The Gold Rush Diary of Susanna Fairchild* (4–8). 2001, Scholastic paper $10.95 (978-0-590-51157-5). After Susanna's mother dies in 1849, the 14-year-old takes over her journal and describes the hardships she and her sisters face when their father decides to move the family to California in search of gold. (Rev: BL 9/1/01; HBG 10/01; SLJ 7/01; VOYA 10/01)

11040 Hahn, Mary Downing. *The Gentleman Outlaw and Me — Eli: A Story of the Old West* (5–8). 1996, Clarion $16.00 (978-0-395-73083-6). In frontier days, Eliza, masquerading as a boy, travels west in search of her father. (Rev: BCCB 4/96; BL 4/1/96; HB 9–10/96; SLJ 5/96; VOYA 6/96)

11041 Hart, Alison. *Anna's Blizzard* (3–5). Illus. by Paul Bachem. 2005, Peachtree $12.95 (978-1-56145-349-8). 141pp. Twelve-year-old Anna Vail loves life on the prairie although she lacks confidence at school, but when a blizzard traps children in the schoolhouse, it's Anna and her faithful pony who guide them all to safety. (Rev: SLJ 10/05)

11042 Heisel, Sharon E. *Precious Gold, Precious Jade* (5–8). 2000, Holiday $16.95 (978-0-8234-1432-1). At the end of the Gold Rush in southern Oregon, two sisters create hostilities when they befriend a Chinese family that has moved to town. (Rev: BCCB 4/00; HBG 10/00; SLJ 4/00)

11043 Helldorfer, M. C. *Hog Music* (K–4). Illus. by S. D. Schindler. 2000, Viking $15.99 (978-0-670-87182-7). Set in the first half of the 19th century, this book chronicles the routes and vehicles involved in transporting a hat from the east to Illinois. (Rev: BCCB 9/00; HBG 10/00; SLJ 5/00)

11044 Hermes, Patricia. *A Perfect Place: Joshua's Oregon Trail Diary* (3–5). Series: My America. 2002, Scholastic $10.95 (978-0-439-19999-5). 112pp. In this sequel to *Westward to Home* (2000), 9-year-old Joshua records the difficult conditions in the Willamette Valley as winter closes in. (Rev: BL 1/1–15/03; HBG 3/03; SLJ 11/02)

11045 Holland, Isabelle. *The Promised Land* (5–8). 1996, Scholastic paper $15.95 (978-0-590-47176-3). Orphaned Maggie and Annie, who have been happily living with the Russell family on the Kansas frontier for three years, are visited by an uncle who wants them to come home with him to Catholicism and their Irish heritage in New York City. A sequel to *The Journey Home*. (Rev: BL 4/15/96; SLJ 8/96; VOYA 6/96)

11046 Holling, Holling C. *Tree in the Trail* (4–7). Illus. by author. 1942, Houghton Mifflin $20.00 (978-0-395-18228-4); paper $11.95 (978-0-395-54534-8). The history of the Santa Fe Trail, described through the life of a cottonwood tree, a 200-year-old landmark to travelers and a symbol of peace to the Indians.

11047 Holm, Jennifer L. *Boston Jane: An Adventure* (5–8). 2001, HarperCollins LB $17.89 (978-0-06-028739-9). A well-bred young woman faces hardships as she searches the 19th-century Washington Territory for her lost fiancé. (Rev: BL 9/1/01; HB 9–10/01; HBG 3/02; SLJ 8/01)

11048 Holm, Jennifer L. *Boston Jane: The Claim* (5–8). 2004, HarperCollins $15.99 (978-0-06-029045-0). In the third installment in Jane's story, an old rival named Sally and a former suitor cause difficulties for Jane. (Rev: BL 3/1/04; SLJ 5/04; VOYA 4/04)

11049 Holm, Jennifer L. *Boston Jane: Wilderness Days* (5–8). 2002, HarperCollins LB $18.89 (978-0-06-029044-3). Jane's continued adventures in 1854 Washington Territory include helping to stop a murderer and adjusting to the hardships of pioneer life. (Rev: BL 9/1/02; HB 9–10/02; HBG 3/03; SLJ 10/02)

11050 Hooks, William H. *Pioneer Cat* (2–4). Illus. by Charles Robinson. 1988, Random paper $3.99 (978-0-394-82038-5). 64pp. Kate smuggles a cat aboard the prairie schooner as the family heads west on the Oregon Trail. (Rev: BCCB 12/88; BL 1/15/89; SLJ 3/89)

11051 Hopkinson, Deborah. *Cabin in the Snow* (2–4). Series: Prairie Skies. 2002, Simon & Schuster paper $3.99 (978-0-689-84351-8). 80pp. Charlie must care for his pregnant mother while his father is away in this story set in Kansas during the free-state movement. (Rev: BL 12/15/02; HBG 3/03; SLJ 1/03)

11052 Hopkinson, Deborah. *Our Kansas Home* (3–5). Illus. by Patrick Faricy. Series: Prairie Skies. 2003, Simon & Schuster paper $3.99 (978-0-689-84353-2). 80pp. In this final volume in the trilogy, Charlie and his father tangle with pro-slavery ruffians and Charlie helps a runaway slave. (Rev: BL 3/1/03; HBG 10/03; SLJ 3/03)

11053 Hopkinson, Deborah. *Sailing for Gold* (2–4). Illus. by Bill Farnsworth. Series: Ready-for-Chapters. 2004, Simon & Schuster paper $3.99 (978-0-689-86031-7). 64pp. The first installment in an exciting and information-packed trilogy about orphan David Hill, 11, who sets off from Seattle for the Klondike in search of his uncle. (Rev: BL 1/1–15/04; SLJ 7/04)

11054 Karr, Kathleen. *Exiled: Memoirs of a Camel* (4–8). 2004, Marshall Cavendish $15.95 (978-0-7614-5164-8). This fascinating story of the U.S. Camel Corps is told from the viewpoint of Ali, an Egyptian camel drafted for service in this shortlived branch of the United States Army. (Rev: BL 5/1/04; SLJ 5/04)

11055 Karr, Kathleen. *Oregon Sweet Oregon* (5–8). Series: Petticoat Party. 1997, HarperCollins LB $14.89 (978-0-06-027234-0). This novel, set in Oregon City, Oregon, from 1846 through 1848, recounts the adventures of 13-year-old Phoebe Brown and her family when they stake a land claim along the Willamette River. (Rev: BL 7/97; SLJ 7/98)

11056 Karwoski, Gail. *Seaman: The Dog Who Explored the West with Lewis and Clark* (4–8). 1999, Peachtree paper $8.95 (978-1-56145-190-6). This historical novel dramatizes the story of Seaman, the Newfoundland dog that accompanied Lewis and Clark on their expedition. (Rev: BL 8/99; HBG 10/03; SLJ 10/99)

11057 Kent, Deborah. *Blackwater Creek* (4–6). Series: Saddles, Stars, and Stripes. 2005, Kingfisher $8.95 (978-0-7534-5885-3). 152pp. In 1849 California, Hungarian immigrant Erika looks after horses for a local rancher while her brother and father search for gold. (Rev: SLJ 3/06)

11058 Kent, Deborah. *Riding the Pony Express* (3–7). Series: Saddles, Stars, and Stripes. 2006, Kingfisher $8.95 (978-0-7534-6001-6). 149pp. Despite the fact that her father has died and her brother is accused of robbery, 15-year-old Lexie has no intention of being shipped back East and, disguising herself as a boy, sets off on her own along the Pony Express trail to prove her brother innocent. (Rev: SLJ 8/06)

11059 Kent, Peter. *Quest for the West: In Search of Gold* (3–6). Illus. 1997, Millbrook LB $21.40 (978-0-7613-0302-2). 32pp. The Hornik family leave their Czech homeland in 1849 to find a new life in the United States in this novel with excellent pen-and-ink and watercolor illustrations. (Rev: BL 12/1/97; SLJ 6/98)

11060 Kerr, Rita. *Texas Footprints* (4–7). 1988, Eakin $13.95 (978-0-89015-676-6). A tale of the author's great-great-grandparents who went to Texas in 1823. (Rev: BL 3/1/89)

11061 Ketchum, Liza. *Newsgirl* (4–7). 2009, Viking $16.99 (978-0-670-01119-3). 336pp. Set in 1851 San Francisco, this is the story of 12-year-old Amelia, who dresses as a boy to sell newspapers and eventually becomes a news item herself. Lexile 640L (Rev: BL 9/15/09; SLJ 9/09)

11062 Kimmel, Elizabeth C. *The Adventures of Young Buffalo Bill: In the Eye of the Storm* (3–7). Series: Adventures of Young Buffalo Bill. 2003, HarperCollins LB $16.89 (978-0-06-029116-7). 144pp. At the age of nine, young Bill must look after the Kansas homestead in his father's absence and feels resentment against these heavy duties. (Rev: BL 1/1–15/03; HBG 10/03; SLJ 2/03)

11063 Lasky, Kathryn. *The Journal of Augustus Pelletier: The Lewis and Clark Expedition* (4–6). Series: My Name Is America. 2000, Scholastic $10.95 (978-0-590-68489-7). 172pp. Fourteen-year-old Augustus Pelletier, half French and half Omaha Indian, relates his adventures into unknown territory. (Rev: HBG 10/01)

11064 Laurgaard, Rachel K. *Patty Reed's Doll: The Story of the Donner Party* (3–6). Illus. by Elizabeth Michaels. 1989, Tomato Enterprises paper $9.95 (978-0-9617357-2-2). 144pp. A fantasy seen through the eyes of a doll about a survivor of the Donner Party. A reissue. (Rev: SLJ 11/89)

11065 Levine, Ellen. *The Journal of Jedediah Barstow: An Emigrant on the Oregon Trail* (4–7). Series: My Name Is America. 2002, Scholastic $10.95 (978-0-439-06310-4). Jedediah continues his mother's journal about their experiences on the Oregon Trail after she and the rest of his family are drowned while crossing a river. (Rev: BL 2/15/03; HBG 10/03; SLJ 11/02)

11066 Levitin, Sonia. *Clem's Chances* (4–7). 2001, Scholastic paper $17.95 (978-0-439-29314-3). Fourteen-year-old Clem becomes acquainted with the hardships and rewards of frontier life when he travels to California to find his father in 1860. (Rev: BL 9/15/01; HB 11–12/01; HBG 3/02; SLJ 10/01)

11067 Love, D. Anne. *Bess's Log Cabin Quilt* (2–5). Illus. by Ronald Himler. 1995, Holiday House $15.95 (978-0-8234-1178-8). 72pp. In frontier Oregon, Bess hopes that by winning a quilt contest she can help ease her family's financial problems. (Rev: BCCB 6/95; BL 2/15/95; SLJ 6/95)

11068 Luger, Harriett. *The Last Stronghold: A Story of the Modoc Indian War, 1872-1873* (5–8). 1995, Linnet paper $17.50 (978-0-208-02403-9). The Modoc Indian War of 1872-1873 is re-created in this story involving three young people: Charka, a Modoc youth; Ned, a frontier boy; and Yankel, a Russian Jew who has been tricked into joining the army. (Rev: VOYA 6/96)

11069 MacBride, Roger L. *In the Land of the Big Red Apple* (3–7). Illus. by David Gilleece. 1995, HarperCollins LB $15.89 (978-0-06-024964-9). 352pp. In the mid-1890s, the farm at Rocky Ridge, where Rose Wilder Lane is growing up, gradually prospers. (Rev: BL 5/15/95; SLJ 9/95)

11070 MacBride, Roger L. *Little Farm in the Ozarks* (3–6). Illus. 1994, HarperCollins paper $7.99 (978-0-06-440510-2). 304pp. Based on the journals of Rose Wilder Lane, this novel tells about the Wilder family's first spring and summer in Mansfield, Missouri. (Rev: BL 5/1/94)

11071 MacBride, Roger L. *Little House on Rocky Edge* (3–7). Illus. by David Gilleece. 1993, HarperCollins paper $7.99 (978-0-06-440478-5). 304pp. This reworking of Laura Ingalls Wilder's material tells the story from Rose's perspective of the Wilder family's move from South Dakota to Missouri. This is the first part of a projected five-part series. (Rev: BL 6/1–15/93)

11072 MacBride, Roger L. *New Dawn on Rocky Ridge* (4–7). Series: Rocky Ridge. 1997, HarperCollins paper $7.99 (978-0-06-440581-2). This part of the Wilder family story covers 1900-1903 and focuses on Rose's difficult early teen years. (Rev: BL 11/1/97; HBG 3/98; SLJ 2/98)

11073 McDonald, Brix. *Riding on the Wind* (5–10). 1998, Avenue paper $5.95 (978-0-9661306-0-7). In frontier Wyoming during the early 1860s, 15-year-old Carrie Sutton is determined to become a rider in the Pony Express after her family's ranch has been chosen as a relay station. (Rev: SLJ 1/99)

11074 McKissack, Patricia C. *Run Away Home* (4–7). 1997, Scholastic paper $14.95 (978-0-590-46751-3). In 1888 rural Alabama, a young African American girl helps shelter a fugitive Apache boy. (Rev: BL 10/1/97; HB 11–12/97; HBG 3/98; SLJ 11/97)

11075 MacLachlan, Patricia. *Grandfather's Dance* (4–6). Series: Sarah Plain and Tall. 2006, HarperCollins $14.99 (978-0-06-027560-0). 96pp. At Anna's wedding, Cassie, the fourth-grade daughter of Sarah (of *Sarah Plain and Tall*), mulls over her bonds with the rest of the family in this closing installment in the series. (Rev: BL 7/06; SLJ 11/06)

11076 MacLachlan, Patricia. *Sarah, Plain and Tall* (3–5). Illus. by Marcia Sewall. 1985, HarperCollins LB $16.89 (978-0-06-024102-5); paper $5.99 (978-0-06-440205-7). 64pp. Two children wait on the prairie for the arrival of their new stepmother, who has answered their father's ad for a wife. Newbery Medal winner, 1986. (Rev: BCCB 5/85; BL 5/1/89; SLJ 5/85)

11077 McMullan, Kate. *As Far as I Can See: Meg's Prairie Diary* (2–4). Series: My America. 2002, Scholastic $10.95 (978-0-439-42517-9). 112pp. City girl Meg describes her new life in Kansas, where she and her brother have been sent to avoid a cholera epidemic in 1856, and writes about the help she gives to a runaway slave. (Rev: BL 10/1/02; HBG 3/03; SLJ 8/02)

11078 McMullan, Kate. *A Fine Start: Meg's Prairie Diary* (4–6). Series: My America. 2003, Scholastic LB $12.95 (978-0-439-37061-5). 106pp. In this fictional diary, 9-year-old Meg recounts the hardships her family endures on the prairies of the Kansas Territory. (Rev: HBG 4/04; SLJ 1/04)

11079 Milligan, Bryce. *With the Wind, Kevin Dolan: A Novel of Ireland and Texas* (5–7). 1987, Corona paper $7.95 (978-0-931722-45-5). The story of Kevin and Tom, brothers who leave the famine in Ireland in the 1830s and head for America. (Rev: BL 8/87; SLJ 9/87)

11080 Moeri, Louise. *Save Queen of Sheba* (5–7). 1990, Avon paper $3.50 (978-0-380-71154-3). Young David survives a wagon train massacre and must take care of his young sister.

11081 Myers, Laurie. *Lewis and Clark and Me: A Dog's Tale* (3–6). Illus. by Michael Dooling. 2002, Holt $16.95 (978-0-8050-6368-4). The Lewis and Clark expedition told from the point of view of Seaman, Lewis's Newfoundland dog, with excerpts from Lewis's journal, illustrations and a map of the route. (Rev: BL 9/1/02; HB 9/02; HBG 3/03; SLJ 9/02)

11082 Naylor, Phyllis Reynolds. *Emily and Jackson Hiding Out* (3–5). Illus. by Ross Collins. 2012, Delacorte $14.99 (978-0-385-74097-5); LB $17.99 (978-0-375-98978-0). 176pp. In this western adventure companion to *Emily's Fortune* (2010), the evil Uncle Victor reappears in time to endanger orphans' Emily and Jackson's newfound security. Lexile 870 (Rev: BL 8/12; LMC 1–2/13; SLJ 8/12)

11083 Naylor, Phyllis Reynolds. *Emily's Fortune* (3–5). Illus. by Ross Collins. 2010, Delacorte $14.99 (978-0-385-73616-9); LB $17.99 (978-0-385-90589-3). 160pp. A lively story in which newly orphaned Emily, now an heiress, travels (with her turtle Rufus and new friend Jackson) west by stagecoach to her aunt's home and must outsmart the evil Victor en route. (Rev: BL 4/15/10; LMC 10/10; SLJ 6/1/10*)

11084 Nixon, Joan Lowery. *In the Face of Danger* (5–8). 1996, Bantam paper $4.99 (978-0-440-22705-2). Megan fears she will bring bad luck to her adoptive family in this story set in the prairies of Kansas. This is the third part of the Orphan Train Quartet. (Rev: SLJ 12/88; VOYA 12/88)

11085 Oatman, Eric. *Cowboys on the Western Trail: The Cattle Drive Adventures of Josh McNabb and Davy Bartlett* (4–7). Series: I Am America. 2004, National Geographic paper $6.99 (978-0-7922-6553-5). The excitement of a cattle drive is shown in the journals and letters of two young teen boys in this blend of fact and fiction set in 1887 and presented in an appealing magazine format. (Rev: BL 5/15/04)

11086 O'Dell, Scott. *Streams to the River, River to the Sea: A Novel of Sacagawea* (5–9). 1986, Houghton Mifflin $16.00 (978-0-395-40430-0). A fictionalized portrait of the real-life Indian woman who traveled west with Lewis and Clark on their famous journey. (Rev: BL 3/15/86; HB 9–10/86; SLJ 5/86; VOYA 6/86)

11087 Olson, Tod. *How to Get Rich on the Oregon Trail: My Adventures Among Cows, Crooks, and Heroes on the Road to Fame and Fortune* (4–8). Illus. by Scott Allred. 2009, National Geographic $16.95 (978-1-4263-0412-5). 48pp. In his journal, 15-year-old Will Reed records the events of his family's 1852 journey to Oregon. (Rev: BCCB 5/09; BL 3/1/09; LMC 10/09; SLJ 5/09)

11088 Patron, Susan. *Behind the Masks: The Diary of Angeline Reddy* (4–8). Series: Dear America. 2012, Scholastic $12.99 (978-054530437-5). 304pp. In California in 1880, 14-year-old Angeline investigates her father's disappearance and meets a variety of obstacles, including a ghost and a gang of vigilantes. (Rev: BL 12/15/11; SLJ 1/12; VOYA 12/11)

11089 Paulsen, Gary. *The Legend of Bass Reeves* (5–8). 2006, Random House $15.95 (978-0-385-74661-8). This fictionalized biography profiles the little-known life and career of Bass Reeves, the former slave who became one of the West's most effective lawmen. (Rev: BCCB 10/06; BL 6/1–15/06; HBG 10/07; SLJ 8/06)

11090 Pearsall, Shelley. *Crooked River* (4–6). 2005, Knopf LB $17.99 (978-0-375-92389-0). 256pp. In early-19th-century Ohio, 13-year-old Rebecca learns about truth and justice as she watches the plight of a Native American accused of killing a trapper. (Rev: BL 5/15/05)

11091 Philbrick, Rodman. *The Journal of Douglas Allen Deeds: The Donner Party Expedition* (5–7). Series: My Name Is America. 2001, Scholastic paper $10.95 (978-0-439-21600-5). A fictional account of the Donner Party's hardships as written in a 15-year-old orphaned boy's journal. (Rev: BL 1/1–15/02; HBG 3/02; SLJ 12/01)

11092 Rinaldi, Ann. *The Second Bend in the River* (5–9). 1997, Scholastic paper $15.95 (978-0-590-74258-0). In Ohio in 1798, 7-year-old Rebecca begins a long-lasting friendship with the Shawnee chief Tecumseh that eventually leads to a marriage proposal. (Rev: BCCB 3/97; BL 2/15/97; HBG 3/98; SLJ 6/97)

11093 Rose, Caroline. *May B* (3–7). 2012, Random House $15.99 (978-158246393-3); LB $18.99 (978-158246412-1). 240pp. May, 11, a housemaid to a young family in a Kansas sod house in the late 1870s, struggles to survive when the husband and wife leave her alone to care for the house. ALA Notable Children's Book 2013. **e** Lexile 680L (Rev: BL 1/1/12; HB 1–2/12; LMC 3–4/12)

11094 Schultz, Jan Neubert. *Battle Cry* (5–9). 2006, Carolrhoda LB $15.95 (978-1-57505-928-0). Native American Chaska and white settler Johnny are drawn into the bloody 1862 Dakota Conflict in this dramatic tale. (Rev: SLJ 7/06)

11095 Schultz, Jan Neubert. *Horse Sense* (5–7). 2001, Carolrhoda LB $15.95 (978-1-57505-998-3); paper $6.95 (978-1-57505-999-0). Fourteen-year-old Will and his father do not get along, but they join a posse tracking dangerous outlaws in this adventure based on a true story. (Rev: BL 8/01; HBG 3/02; VOYA 12/01)

11096 Scillian, Devin. *Pappy's Handkerchief* (2–4). Illus. by Chris Ellison. Series: Tales of Young Americans. 2007, Sleeping Bear $17.95 (978-1-58536-316-2). 32pp. Moses, a young African American boy from Baltimore, must take on a lot of responsibility after a series of accidents befall his family during the Oklahoma Land Run. (Rev: BL 10/1/07; SLJ 1/08)

11097 Seeley, Debra. *Grasslands* (5–8). 2002, Holiday $16.95 (978-0-8234-1731-5). The hard life on the prairie disappoints a 13-year-old newcomer from Virginia until he has the chance to ride as a cowboy in this novel set in the late 19th century. (Rev: BL 11/1/02; HBG 3/03; SLJ 1/03*; VOYA 12/02)

11098 Shaw, Janet. *Happy Birthday Kirsten!* (3–5). Illus. 1987, Pleasant $12.95 (978-0-937295-88-5); paper $6.95 (978-0-937295-33-5). 72pp. It is 1854 in Minnesota and Kirsten looks forward to the gift of a day off from household chores. Also use: *Changes for Kirsten; Kirsten Saves the Day* (both 1988). (Rev: BL 4/1/88)

11099 Shaw, Janet. *Kirsten Learns a Lesson: A School Story* (3–5). Illus. 1986, Pleasant LB $12.95 (978-0-937295-82-3); paper $6.95 (978-0-937295-10-6). 72pp. Kirsten, a young immigrant girl, lives with her Swedish family in 1854 Minnesota. Others in this series are: *Kirsten's Surprise: A Christmas Story; Meet Kirsten: An American Girl* (both 1986). (Rev: BL 12/1/86)

11100 Sommerdorf, Norma. *Red River Girl* (4–7). 2006, Holiday $16.95 (978-0-8234-1903-6). In 1846 after her Ojibwa mother dies, 12-year-old Metis girl Josette starts a journal that documents her family's journey by wagon train from Canada to St. Paul, Minnesota, where they settle and she becomes a teacher. (Rev: BL 11/15/06; SLJ 12/06)

11101 Thomas, Joyce C. *I Have Heard of a Land* (3–6). Illus. by Floyd Cooper. 1998, HarperCollins LB $14.89 (978-0-06-023478-2). 32pp. This tribute to the pioneer spirit tells, through the eyes of a black woman, what it was like to come to the untamed frontier, build a home, and put down roots. (Rev: BCCB 6/98; BL 2/15/98*; HBG 10/98; SLJ 7/98)

11102 Tripp, Valerie. *Happy Birthday, Josefina! A Springtime Story* (3–5). Series: American Girls. 1998, Pleasant $12.95 (978-1-56247-588-8); paper $6.95 (978-1-56247-587-1). In the New Mexico of 1824, Josefina discovers she can become a healer after she cures a friend bitten by a rattlesnake. (Rev: BL 8/98; HBG 3/99)

11103 Tripp, Valerie. *Josefina Saves the Day: A Summer Story* (3–5). Illus. Series: American Girls. 1998, Pleasant $12.95 (978-1-56247-590-1); paper $6.95 (978-1-56247-589-5). 68pp. A heavily illustrated novel, set in the New Mexico of 1824, in which young Josefina's father must decide whether or not to trust an American trader. (Rev: BL 8/98; HBG 3/99)

11104 Tripp, Valerie. *Meet Josefina: An American Girl* (3–5). Illus. Series: American Girls. 1997, Pleasant paper $6.95 (978-1-56247-515-4). In this story set in 1824 on a Mexican ranch in what is now New Mexico, the young heroine helps manage the ranch after her mother's death. Also use *Josefina Learns a Lesson: A School Story* (1997). (Rev: BL 10/1/97; HBG 3/98; SLJ 12/97)

11105 Whelan, Gloria. *Miranda's Last Stand* (4–7). 1999, HarperCollins LB $14.89 (978-0-06-028252-3). After her husband was killed at Little Big Horn, Miranda's mother can't bear to be around Indians, including Sitting Bull, who works with her at Buffalo Bill's Wild West Show. (Rev: BL 11/1/99; HBG 3/00; SLJ 11/99)

11106 Whelan, Gloria. *Return to the Island* (4–7). 2000, HarperCollins LB $15.89 (978-0-06-028254-7). In the early 19th century on Mackinac Island, Mary must decide between two men who love her: White Hawk, an orphan raised by a white family, and James, an English painter. (Rev: BL 1/1–15/01; HBG 3/01; SLJ 12/00)

11107 Wilder, Laura Ingalls. *The Long Winter* (5–8). 1953, HarperCollins LB $17.89 (978-0-06-026461-1). Number six in the Little House books. In this one, the Ingalls face a terrible winter with only seed grain for food.

11108 Wilkes, Maria D. *Little Clearing in the Woods* (3–6). Illus. by Dan Andreasen. Series: The Caroline Years. 1998, HarperCollins LB $15.89 (978-0-06-026998-2). 315pp. Caroline Quiner (the mother of Laura Ingalls Wilder) and her family move to a small cabin in the woods, where her widowed mother takes a job cooking for neighborhood laborers. (Rev: HBG 10/98; SLJ 10/98)

11109 Wilkes, Maria D. *Little House in Brookfield* (3–6). Illus. by Dan Andreasen. Series: The Brookfield Years. 1996, HarperCollins paper $6.99 (978-0-06-440610-9). 298pp. This spinoff from the *Little House* books tells of the childhood in Brookfield, Wisconsin, of Caroline Quiner, who much later would become the mother of Laura Ingalls Wilder. (Rev: SLJ 8/96)

11110 Wisler, G. Clifton. *All for Texas: A Story of Texas Liberation* (4–8). 2000, Jamestown paper $5.95 (978-0-8092-0629-2). A thirteen-year-old boy tells about moving west with his family in 1838 to Texas, where his father has been promised land if he will fight against Mexico. (Rev: BCCB 7–8/00; SLJ 8/00)

11111 Yep, Laurence. *The Journal of Wong Ming-Chung* (4–7). 2000, Scholastic paper $10.95 (978-0-590-38607-4). Told in diary format beginning in October 1851, this is the story of a Chinese boy nicknamed Runt who travels from his native country to join an uncle in the gold mining fields of America. (Rev: BL 4/1/00; HBG 10/00; SLJ 4/00; VOYA 6/00)

11112 Yolen, Jane. *Elsie's Bird* (K–3). Illus. by David Small. 2010, Philomel $17.99 (978-0-399-25292-1). 40pp. Elsie and her father leave Boston after Elsie's mother dies and head for Nebraska, where the city-loving girl feels alone and scared until her pet canary escapes and Elsie must brave the prairie to retrieve him. Lexile AD890L (Rev: BL 8/10; HB 9–10/10; LMC 1–2/11*; SLJ 9/1/10*)

11113 Young, Judy. *Minnow and Rose* (3–5). Illus. by Bill Farnsworth. Series: Tales of Young Americans. 2009, Sleeping Bear $17.95 (978-1-58536-421-3). 40pp. In the mid-1800s, Rose, who is traveling west with her family, meets a Native American girl named Minnow and the two learn about each other's lives. (Rev: BL 3/1/09)

THE CIVIL WAR

11114 Avi. *Iron Thunder* (5–8). 2007, Hyperion $14.99 (978-1-4231-0446-9). Tom, a 13-year-old naval yard worker and later crew member, describes the construction of the *Monitor,* the perilous voyage to the Union blockade, and the ensuing battle with the *Merrimac*; period photographs and newspaper headlines add historic context. (Rev: BL 8/07; LMC 11/07; SLJ 9/07)

11115 Brill, Marlene Targ. *Diary of a Drummer Boy* (4–7). 1998, Millbrook LB $23.90 (978-0-7613-0118-9). Using a diary format, this novel tells of a 12-year-old's experiences as a drummer in the Union Army during the Civil War. (Rev: BL 3/1/98; HBG 10/98; SLJ 5/98)

11116 Calkhoven, Laurie. *Will at the Battle of Gettysburg, 1863* (4–7). Series: Boys of Wartime. 2011, Dutton $16.99 (978-0-525-42145-0). 227pp. Twelve-year-old Will lives in Gettysburg and dreams of being a drummer boy in the Union Army until the war comes right to his doorstep. e (Rev: SLJ 3/1/11)

11117 Crist-Evans, Craig. *Moon over Tennessee: A Boy's Civil War Journal* (4–7). 1999, Houghton Mifflin $15.00 (978-0-395-91208-9). In free-verse diary entries, 13-year-old Crist-Evans reports on the Civil War from his vantage point in a camp behind the front lines. (Rev: BCCB 6/99; BL 5/15/99; HBG 10/99; SLJ 8/99; VOYA 10/99)

11118 Denslow, Sharon Phillips. *All Their Names Were Courage* (4–6). 2003, HarperCollins LB $15.99 (978-0-06-623810-4). Eleven-year-old Sallie Burd writes to her soldier brother about her quest to learn about the horses of Union and Confederate generals. (Rev: BL 8/03; HBG 4/04; SLJ 10/03)

11119 Donahue, John. *An Island Far from Home* (4–7). 1994, Carolrhoda LB $15.95 (978-0-87614-859-4). Joshua, a Union supporter, forms an unusual friendship through corresponding with a young Southern soldier who is a prisoner of war. (Rev: BCCB 2/95; BL 2/15/95; SLJ 2/95)

11120 Durrant, Lynda. *My Last Skirt* (5–8). 2006, Clarion $16.00 (978-0-618-57490-2). After migrating from Ireland to America, Jennie Hodgers, who prefers wearing pants to skirts, adopts the persona of Albert Cashier and joins the Union army in this novel based on a true story. (Rev: BL 2/15/06; SLJ 4/06*)

11121 Ernst, Kathleen. *Hearts of Stone* (5–8). 2006, Dutton $16.99 (978-0-525-47686-3). Fifteen-year-old Hannah and her three younger siblings struggle to survive after they're orphaned in Civil War Tennessee. (Rev: BL 11/1/06; SLJ 12/06)

11122 Ernst, Kathleen. *Retreat from Gettysburg* (5–8). 2000, White Mane LB $17.95 (978-1-57249-187-8). When a doctor orders 14-year-old Chig and his mother to care for a wounded Confederate soldier, the boy finds it hard to be kind to a man who belongs to the side that killed his father and brothers. (Rev: BL 9/15/00; HBG 10/01; SLJ 12/00)

11123 Fleischner, Jennifer. *Nobody's Boy* (5–8). 2006, Missouri Historical Society $12.95 (978-1-883982-58-4). George's mother buys freedom for herself and her son; she goes on to work for Mrs. Lincoln in the White House while George chooses the more dangerous avenue of helping slaves find freedom. (Rev: BL 2/1/07)

11124 Garrity, Jennifer Johnson. *The Bushwhacker: A Civil War Adventure* (5–8). Illus. by Paul Bachem. 1999, Peachtree paper $8.95 (978-1-56145-201-9). The clash of divided loyalties is the main conflict in this story of a boy torn between his Unionist feelings and the friendship he feels towards his protector, a Confederate sympathizer. (Rev: SLJ 4/00)

11125 Hart, Alison. *Fires of Jubilee* (5–7). 2003, Simon & Schuster paper $4.99 (978-0-689-85528-3). Abby, 13, is suddenly a free person when the Civil War ends and finally able to search for her mother, who left long before. (Rev: BL 11/1/03; SLJ 3/04)

11126 Hawk, Fran. *The Story of the H. L. Hunley and Queenie's Coin* (3–5). Illus. by Dan Nance. 2004, Sleeping Bear $16.95 (978-1-58536-218-9). 40pp. This story of the ill-fated Confederate submarine *H. L. Hunley* focuses on the lucky coin given to its developer by his fiancee. (Rev: BL 1/1–15/05; SLJ 5/05)

11127 Hughes, Pat. *Seeing the Elephant: A Story of the Civil War* (2–4). Illus. by Ken Stark. 2007, Farrar $16.00 (978-0-374-38024-3). A 10-year-old boy, who longs to fight for the Union with his older brothers, learns about war when he meets a captured Confederate soldier. (Rev: SLJ 11/07)

11128 Hurst, Carol Otis. *Torchlight* (4–7). 2006, Houghton Mifflin $16.00 (978-0-618-27601-1). As tension mounts between the Yankee and Irish immigrant settlers in a Massachusetts town in 1864, Charlotte and Maggie struggle to maintain their friendship. (Rev: BL 12/1/06; SLJ 1/07)

11129 Keehn, Sally M. *Anna Sunday* (4–8). 2002, Putnam $18.99 (978-0-399-23875-8). In 1863, 12-year-old Anna travels with her younger brother from Pennsylvania to Virginia to find her wounded father. (Rev: BCCB 9/02; BL 6/1–15/02; HBG 10/02; SLJ 6/02; VOYA 8/02)

11130 Kent, Deborah. *Chance of a Lifetime* (4–6). Series: Saddles, Stars, and Stripes. 2005, Kingfisher $8.95 (978-0-7534-5884-6). 173pp. In 1863, 14-year-old Jacquetta May Logan enlists the help of a slave girl to hide her family's Morgan horses from advancing Union forces. (Rev: SLJ 3/06)

11131 Kluger, Jeffrey. *Freedom Stone* (5–7). 2011, Philomel $16.99 (978-0-399-25214-3). 320pp. Young slave Lillie struggles to clear her father's name and gain freedom for herself, her brother, and her mother with the help of a magical stone from Africa. **e** Lexile 1030L (Rev: BL 2/1/11*; LMC 5–6/11; SLJ 6/11)

11132 Love, D. Anne. *Three Against the Tide* (5–8). 1998, Holiday $15.95 (978-0-8234-1400-0). In this Civil War novel, 12-year-old Confederate Susanna Simons must care for her two younger brothers when Yankee troops invade South Carolina. (Rev: BL 12/1/98; HBG 10/99; SLJ 1/99)

11133 Lyons, Mary E., and Muriel M. Branch. *Dear Ellen Bee: A Civil War Scrapbook of Two Union Spies* (5–8). 2000, Atheneum $17.00 (978-0-689-82379-4). Set in Richmond, Virginia, before and during the Civil War, this novel, based on fact, tells how a strong-willed lady and her emancipated slave get involved in a spying adventure. (Rev: BCCB 10/00; BL 11/1/00; HBG 3/01; SLJ 10/00; VOYA 2/01)

11134 McGowen, Tom. *Jesse Bowman: A Union Boy's War Story* (5–8). Series: Historical Fiction Adventure. 2008, Enslow LB $20.95 (978-0-7660-2929-3). The story of a young soldier who is horrified by the brutality of the Civil War. (Rev: BL 4/15/08; SLJ 7/08)

11135 McMullan, Margaret. *How I Found the Strong: A Civil War Story* (5–9). 2004, Houghton Mifflin $15.00 (978-0-618-35008-7). The Civil War changes the way a boy looks at life when it takes away his father and brother and comes close to his Mississippi home. (Rev: BL 2/15/04; SLJ 4/04; VOYA 6/04)

11136 Myers, Laurie. *Escape by Night: A Civil War Adventure* (3–5). Illus. by Amy June Bates. 2011, Henry Holt $14.99 (978-0-8050-8825-0). 128pp. When Tommy, the son of a Presbyterian minister in Georgia during the Civil War, returns a soldier's journal to its rightful owner, he discovers the man is a Yankee in disguise, and he must make a difficult decision. (Rev: BL 4/15/11; LMC 11–12/11; SLJ 6/11)

11137 Noble, Trinka Hakes. *The Last Brother: A Civil War Tale* (2–4). Illus. by Robert Papp. 2006, Sleeping Bear $17.95 (978-1-58536-253-0). 48pp. Eleven-year-old Gabe, who has lost two brothers in battle, joins the

Union Army with older brother Davy and learns to be a bugler. (Rev: BL 9/1/06; SLJ 12/06)

11138 Owens, L. L. *The Code of the Drum* (3–6). Illus. by Margaret Sanfilippo. Series: Cover-to-Cover Books. 2000, Perfection Learning $16.95 (978-0-7807-9654-6); paper $8.95 (978-0-7891-5310-4). When his father is killed in the Civil War, 12-year-old Jacob McCoy joins his dad's Union regiment as a drummer boy. (Rev: SLJ 12/00)

11139 Paulsen, Gary. *Soldier's Heart* (5–8). 1998, Delacorte $15.95 (978-0-385-32498-4). A powerful novel about the agony of the Civil War, based on the real-life experiences of a Union soldier who was only 15 when he went to war. (Rev: BCCB 9/98; BL 6/1–15/98*; HB 11–12/98; HBG 3/99; SLJ 9/98; VOYA 10/98)

11140 Philbrick, Rodman. *The Mostly True Adventures of Homer P. Figg* (4–7). 2009, Scholastic $16.99 (978-0-439-66818-7). 224pp. There's comedy in the midst of war and innocence in the midst of knavery as Homer runs away from from his evil uncle and has many adventures while seeking to save the brother forced to join the Union Army. Newbery Honor 2010; ALA Notable Children's Book. ∩ (Rev: BCCB 1/09; BL 1/1–15/09; HB 1/09; SLJ 1/09)

11141 Pinkney, Andrea Davis. *Abraham Lincoln: Letters from a Slave Girl* (4–7). Series: Dear Mr. President. 2001, Winslow $8.95 (978-1-890817-60-2). Twelve-year-old Lettie Tucker, a slave, exchanges thought-provoking letters with President Abraham Lincoln in this story set in the 1860s packed with interesting illustrations. (Rev: BCCB 2/02; BL 9/1/01; HBG 3/02; SLJ 9/01)

11142 Polacco, Patricia. *Just in Time, Abraham Lincoln* (3–5). Illus. by author. 2011, Putnam $17.99 (978-0-399-25471-0). 48pp. Video gamers Michael and Derek find themselves unexpectedly involved in the battle of Antietam when they dress as Union soldiers. Lexile 570L (Rev: BL 2/1/11; LMC 5–6/11*; SLJ 3/1/11)

11143 Polacco, Patricia. *Pink and Say* (K–5). Illus. 1994, Penguin $16.99 (978-0-399-22671-7). 32pp. Based on a true incident during the Civil War, this book tells of the friendship of two Union soldiers: Say, a white man who is rescued by a black man, Pinkus, known as Pink. (Rev: BCCB 9/94; BL 9/1/94; HB 11/94; SLJ 10/94*)

11144 Porter, Connie. *Addy Learns a Lesson* (3–6). Illus. by Melodye Rosales. Series: American Girls. 1993, Pleasant $12.95 (978-1-56247-078-4); paper $6.95 (978-1-56247-077-7). 70pp. In the year 1864, young Addy and her mother try to escape slavery by fleeing to the North after her father is sold again and they are separated. (Rev: BL 8/93; SLJ 1/94)

11145 Porter, Connie. *Addy Saves the Day: A Summer Story* (2–4). Illus. by Bradford Brown. 1994, Pleasant paper $6.95 (978-1-56247-083-8). 59pp. In this novel set in Philadelphia in 1864, Addy, a former slave, and her family try to make money to search for relatives lost in the Civil War. Also use *Happy Birthday, Addy!* (1994). (Rev: BL 11/1/94; SLJ 11/94)

11146 Rappaport, Doreen. *Freedom Ship* (2–4). Illus. by Curtis James. 2006, Hyperion $15.99 (978-0-7868-0645-4). Slaves seize control of a Confederate steamship and turn it over to Union forces in this fictionalized version of a real event that is followed by a fascinating historical note. (Rev: BL 10/1/06; SLJ 11/06)

11147 Rinaldi, Ann. *Juliet's Moon* (5–8). Series: Great Episodes. 2008, Harcourt paper $17.00 (978-0-15-206170-8). Juliet's home and family are destroyed by the Civil War, and she and her brother, Seth, must fight and even kill to survive in this novel, which is loosely based on actual events. (Rev: BL 4/15/08)

11148 Rinaldi, Ann. *My Vicksburg* (5–8). 2009, Harcourt $16.00 (978-0-15-206624-6). 160pp. In 1863 Vicksburg, Mississippi, families choose to live in caves for safety and 13-year-old Claire Louise worries about the members of her family serving on different sides of the war. (Rev: BL 4/15/09; SLJ 7/09; VOYA 8/09)

11149 Schwabach, Karen. *The Storm Before Atlanta* (5–8). 2010, Random House $16.99 (978-0-375-85866-6); LB $19.99 (978-0-375-95866-3). 320pp. Jeremy dreams of glory when he joins the Union Army, but as the war progresses and he meets an escaped slave, Dulcie, and a Confederate soldier named Charlie, reality sets in. **e** (Rev: BL 1/1–15/11; SLJ 2/1/11)

11150 Spain, Susan Rosson. *The Deep Cut* (5–8). 2006, Marshall Cavendish $16.99 (978-0-7614-5316-1). Thirteen-year-old Lonzo, often considered "slow," finally gains the respect of his father for his actions during the hostilities. (Rev: BL 12/1/06*; SLJ 12/06)

11151 Stolz, Mary. *A Ballad of the Civil War* (4–6). Illus. 1997, HarperCollins LB $13.89 (978-0-06-027363-7). 64pp. Based on a Civil War ballad, this is the story of two Southern brothers who enlist on opposite sides. (Rev: BL 10/1/97; SLJ 2/98)

11152 Thomas, Carroll. *Blue Creek Farm* (4–8). 2001, Smith & Kraus paper $9.95 (978-1-57525-243-8). In Kansas of the 1860s, Matty Trescott and her father manage a farm and feel the effects of the Civil War. (Rev: BL 4/1/01; VOYA 6/01)

11153 Wells, Rosemary. *Lincoln and His Boys* (3–5). Illus. by P. J. Lynch. 2009, Candlewick $16.99 (978-0-7636-3723-1). Inspired by an essay written by Lincoln's son Willie, Wells presents three vignettes about the president and his two younger sons in the White House during the Civil War years. (Rev: BCCB 1/09; BL 1/1–15/09; LMC 5/09; SLJ 1/09)

11154 Winnick, Karen B. *Cassie's Sweet Berry Pie* (1–3). Illus. 2005, Boyds Mills $16.95 (978-1-56397-984-2). 32pp. When Yankee soldiers are approaching, Cassie must think quickly to protect her younger siblings in this story of the Civil War. (Rev: BL 2/15/05; SLJ 3/05)

RECONSTRUCTION TO WORLD WAR II, 1865–1941

11155 Abraham, Susan Gonzales, and Denise Gonzales Abraham. *Cecilia's Year* (4–7). 2004, Cinco Puntos $16.95 (978-0-938317-87-6). Inspired by the real-life story of the authors' mother, this is the story of a 14-year-old Hispanic American girl's determination to defy cultural tradition and continue her schooling in Depression-era New Mexico. (Rev: BL 1/1–15/05; SLJ 4/05)

11156 Adler, Susan S. *Meet Samantha: An American Girl* (3–5). Illus. 1986, Pleasant LB $12.95 (978-0-937295-80-9); paper $6.95 (978-0-937295-04-5). 72pp. Samantha is an orphan living with her wealthy grandmother in the America of 1904. Two others in the series are: *Samantha Learns a Lesson; Samantha's Surprise* (both 1986). (Rev: BL 12/1/86)

11157 Alter, Judith. *Luke and the Van Zandt County War* (5–9). 1984, Texas Christian Univ $14.95 (978-0-912646-88-6). Life in Reconstruction Texas as seen through the eyes of two 14-year-olds. (Rev: SLJ 3/85)

11158 Arato, Rona. *Ice Cream Town* (5–8). 2007, Fitzhenry & Whiteside paper $11.95 (978-1-55041-591-9). Ten-year-old Sammy Levin, a recent Jewish immigrant from Poland, finds it tough to adjust to his new life on the streets of New York City's Lower East Side in the early 1900s. (Rev: BL 4/1/07; SLJ 6/07)

11159 Armstrong, Jennifer. *Theodore Roosevelt: Letters from a Young Coal Miner* (3–6). Illus. Series: Dear Mr. President. 2000, Winslow $8.95 (978-1-890817-27-5). 128pp. Using fictional letters between a 13-year-old Pennsylvania coal miner and Teddy Roosevelt, this book introduces the hardships of a miner's life as well as the character and administration of President Roosevelt. (Rev: BL 3/1/01; HBG 10/01)

11160 Atwell, Debby. *Pearl* (K–3). Illus. 2001, Houghton $16.00 (978-0-395-88416-4). Pearl, a woman in her 90s, covers a substantial part of American history in her reminiscences, which stretch from her grandfather's encounter with George Washington through World Wars I and II and her hope that her great-granddaughter might someday go to the moon. (Rev: BCCB 4/01; BL 5/1/01; HBG 10/01; SLJ 6/01)

11161 Avi. *City of Orphans* (5–8). Illus. by Greg Ruth. 2011, Simon & Schuster $16.99 (978-1-4169-7102-3). 368pp. Newsboy Maks, 13, contends with filthy living conditions, poverty, and the predicament of his sister, who's been falsely accused of stealing a watch from the Waldorf Hotel in this tense story set in 1893 New York City. ⌒ **e** Lexile HL570L (Rev: BL 8/11*; HB 9–10/11; LMC 11–12/11; SLJ 8/11)

11162 Avi. *The Secret School* (3–6). 2001, Harcourt $16.00 (978-0-15-216375-4). Rather than risking her future education, 14-year-old Ida Bidson takes over as teacher and runs a secret school when the one-room schoolhouse in their mountain district is suddenly closed in 1925. (Rev: BCCB 10/01; HB 11/01; HBG 3/02; SLJ 9/01)

11163 Avi. *Silent Movie* (K–3). Illus. by C. B. Mordan. 2003, Simon & Schuster $16.95 (978-0-689-84145-3). 48pp. In black-and-white silent-movie format, this is the story of an immigrant mother and son arriving in America in the early 20th century, the difficulties they have finding Papa, and the near-miraculous reunion. (Rev: BL 3/1/03*; HB 3/03; HBG 10/03; SLJ 3/03)

11164 Bader, Bonnie. *East Side Story* (3–5). Series: Stories of the States. 1993, Silver Moon LB $14.95 (978-1-881889-22-9). 72pp. The story of an 11-year-old Jewish immigrant girl and her sister, both of whom work in the Triangle Shirtwaist Factory in New York City during the early 1900s. (Rev: SLJ 2/94)

11165 Bartoletti, Susan Campbell. *Down the Rabbit Hole: The Diary of Pringle Rose* (4–7). Series: Dear America. 2013, Scholastic $12.99 (978-0-545-29701-1). 256pp. In 1871, 14-year-old Pringle Rose finds herself running away from Scranton to Chicago and facing many challenges in an effort to protect her Down syndrome brother after the deaths of their parents. (Rev: BL 3/1/13; SLJ 3/13)

11166 Beard, Darleen Bailey. *The Babbs Switch Story* (5–8). 2002, Farrar $16.00 (978-0-374-30475-1). A young girl saves her sister from a fire on Christmas Eve in 1924 in this fictional account of a real event. (Rev: BL 3/15/02; HBG 10/02; SLJ 3/02; VOYA 4/02)

11167 Birney, Betty. *The Seven Wonders of Sassafras Springs* (3–6). Illus. by Matt Phelan. 2005, Simon & Schuster $16.95 (978-0-689-87136-8). 224pp. It's 1923 and Eben McAllister longs to travel but first he must meet his father's challenge to find the hidden wonders in his small farming community. (Rev: BL 9/1/05; SLJ 8/05)

11168 Blackwood, Gary. *Moonshine* (5–8). 1999, Marshall Cavendish $14.95 (978-0-7614-5056-6). Thirteen-year-old Thad, growing up with his mother in rural Mississippi during the Depression, makes a little extra money by running an illegal still that produces moonshine for the locals. (Rev: BCCB 11/99; BL 9/1/99; HBG 3/00; SLJ 10/99)

11169 Blakeslee, Ann R. *Summer Battles* (5–8). 2000, Marshall Cavendish $14.95 (978-0-7614-5064-1). The story of Kath, age 11, growing up in a small town in Indiana in 1926 and of her father, a preacher, who is attacked for opposing the Ku Klux Klan. (Rev: BCCB 3/00; BL 4/1/00; HBG 10/00; SLJ 4/00)

11170 Blundell, Judy. *A City Tossed and Broken: The Diary of Minnie Bonner* (4–6). Series: Dear America. 2013, Scholastic $12.99 (978-054531022-2). 224pp. In 1906, after her father is cheated out of their tavern, 14-year-old Minnie goes to San Francisco as a maid to heiress Lily Sump, who then dies in the earthquake. Should Minnie impersonate Lily and avenge her parents? **e** Lexile 770L (Rev: BL 3/1/13; SLJ 5/13; VOYA 4/13)

11171 Bolden, Tonya. *Finding Family* (4–7). 2010, Bloomsbury $15.99 (978-1-59990-318-7). 176pp. In Charleston, West Virginia, at the turn of the 20th century, 12-year-old African American Delana learns that many of the stories she was told about her family were pure fiction. (Rev: BL 9/1/10*; LMC 10/10; SLJ 9/1/10)

11172 Boling, Katharine. *1/1/1905* (4–7). 2004, Harcourt $16.00 (978-0-15-205119-8). In alternating voices, 11-year-old mill worker Pauline and her deformed,

stay-at-home twin sister Arlene describe the harsh circumstances of their early 20th-century life. (Rev: BL 5/15/04; HB 7–8/04; SLJ 7/04)

11173 Bond, Victoria, and T. R. Simon. *Zora and Me* (5–8). 2010, Candlewick $16.99 (978-0-7636-4300-3). 192pp. The fictionalized story of Zora Neale Hurston's childhood is told by her best friend Carrie, 10, as they play together and overhear adult secrets in Eatonville, Florida. ⌒ **e** Lexile 860L (Rev: BL 10/15/10*; LMC 11–12/10; SLJ 11/1/10)

11174 Bornstein, Ruth Lercher. *Butterflies and Lizards, Beryl and Me* (5–7). 2002, Marshall Cavendish LB $14.95 (978-0-7614-5118-1). Eleven-year-old Charley befriends an odd woman named Beryl while her mother works hard to make it through the Great Depression. (Rev: BL 5/15/02; HBG 10/02; SLJ 5/02)

11175 Brown, Irene Bennett. *Before the Lark* (5–9). 2011, Texas Tech Univ. paper $18.95 (978-08967272-7-4). 204pp. Cleft-lip sufferer Jocey, 12, contends with bullying and poverty, eventually discovering the empowerment that comes with self-sufficiency in this story set in 19th-century Missouri; a new edition of an award-winning book first published in 1981. (Rev: BLO 10/15/11)

11176 Burandt, Harriet, and Shelley Dale. *Tales from the Homeplace: Adventures of a Texas Farm Girl* (4–8). 1997, Henry Holt $15.95 (978-0-8050-5075-2). A family story that takes place on a Texas cotton farm during the Depression and features spunky 12-year-old heroine Irene and her six brothers and sisters. (Rev: BCCB 7–8/97; HB 5–6/97; SLJ 4/97*; VOYA 12/97)

11177 Burleigh, Robert. *Into the Air: The Story of the Wright Brothers' First Flight* (5–8). Illus. by Bill Wylie. Series: American Heroes. 2002, Harcourt paper $6.00 (978-0-15-216803-2). A high-interest, comic-book presentation of the first flight with fictionalized dialogue. (Rev: HBG 3/03; SLJ 9/02)

11178 Byars, Betsy. *Keeper of the Doves* (5–8). 2002, Viking $14.99 (978-0-670-03576-2). Young Amie McBee is a thoughtful child who loves to write and — unlike her older twin sisters — has the sensitivity to see the softer side of the mysterious Polish immigrant who lives on their estate and keeps doves in this story set at the turn of the 20th century and presented in 26 short, alphabetical chapters. (Rev: BCCB 1/03; BL 10/1/02*; HB 9–10/02*; HBG 3/03; SLJ 10/02)

11179 Carter, Alden R. *Crescent Moon* (5–8). 1999, Holiday $16.95 (978-0-8234-1521-2). In the early part of the 20th century, Jeremy joins Great-Uncle Mac on a log drive where they become friends with a Native American and his daughter and, through them, experience the shame of racial prejudice. (Rev: BCCB 1/00; BL 2/15/00; HB 3–4/00; HBG 10/00; SLJ 3/00; VOYA 6/00)

11180 Celenza, Anna Harwell. *Gershwin's Rhapsody in Blue* (2–4). Illus. by JoAnn E. Kitchel. 2006, Charlesbridge $19.95 (978-1-57091-556-7). 32pp. The story of Gershwin's struggle to produce a concerto in a few short weeks in 1924 is accompanied by CD of the resulting classic. (Rev: BL 11/1/06; SLJ 7/06)

11181 Choldenko, Gennifer. *Al Capone Shines My Shoes* (5–8). 2009, Dial $17.99 (978-0-8037-3460-9). 288pp. In *Al Capone Does My Shirts* (2004), 12-year-old Moose benefited from his acquaintance with the famous gangster; now Capone is demanding help in return. ⌒ ℮ Lexile 620L (Rev: BL 9/1/09; HB 9–10/09; SLJ 9/09; VOYA 10/09)

11182 Clark, Clara Gillow. *Hattie on Her Way* (4–7). Series: Hattie. 2005, Candlewick $15.99 (978-0-7636-2286-2). The sequel to *Hill Hawk Hattie* (2003) finds Hattie living with her grandmother after her mother's death and seeking to solve a family mystery. (Rev: BL 3/1/05; SLJ 3/05)

11183 Crisp, Marty. *White Star: A Dog on the Titanic* (4–6). 2004, Holiday House $16.95 (978-0-8234-1598-4). Sam Harris, a 12-year-old passenger on the *Titanic*, offers to help care for the dogs in the ship's kennel and develops a strong relationship with an Irish setter named Star; back matter gives historical detail on the disaster. (Rev: BL 5/15/04; SLJ 6/04)

11184 Cross, Gillian. *The Great American Elephant Chase* (5–8). 1993, Holiday $17.95 (978-0-8234-1016-3). In 1881, Tad, 15, and young friend Cissie attempt to get to Nebraska with her showman father's elephant, pursued by two unsavory characters who claim they have bought the animal. (Rev: BCCB 6/93; BL 3/15/93*; SLJ 5/93*; VOYA 10/93)

11185 Crowley, James. *Starfish* (4–8). 2010, Hyperion $16.99 (978-1-4231-2588-4). 336pp. Beatrice and Lionel, young Blackfoot Nation children, run away from their boarding school in the early 1900s and hide in the Montana mountains. ℮ (Rev: BL 6/10; LMC 11–12/10; VOYA 12/10)

11186 Cummings, Priscilla. *Saving Grace* (4–7). 2003, Dutton $17.99 (978-0-525-47123-3). Eleven-year-old Grace faces a tough dilemma when a wealthy family offers to adopt her while her own family is suffering grinding poverty and illness during the Depression. (Rev: BCCB 9/03; BL 5/15/03; HBG 10/03; SLJ 6/03; VOYA 10/03)

11187 Currier, Katrina Saltonstall. *Kai's Journey to Gold Mountain* (4–7). Illus. by Gabhor Utomo. 2005, Angel Island $16.95 (978-0-9667352-7-7); paper $10.95 (978-0-9667352-4-6). Based on the experiences of a Chinese immigrant to the United States in the 1930s, this troubling tale describes the internment of 12-year-old Kai on Angel Island in San Francisco Bay. (Rev: BL 2/15/05*)

11188 Cushman, Karen. *Rodzina* (5–9). 2003, Clarion $16.00 (978-0-618-13351-2). On an orphan train going from Chicago to California in 1881, plucky Rodzina worries about her fate and aims to find a better life than some of the other children on the train. (Rev: BCCB 3/03; BL 3/1/03*; HB 5–6/03; HBG 10/03; SLJ 4/03*)

11189 Danneberg, Julie. *Family Reminders* (4–6). Illus. by John Shelley. 2009, Charlesbridge $14.95 (978-1-58089-320-6). 112pp. In an 1890s gold-mining town in Colorado, 10-year-old Mary's life is turned upside down when her father is injured and the family suddenly faces financial hardship. (Rev: BLO 6/19/09; HB 7/09)

11190 Dell, Pamela. *Liam's Watch: A Strange Story of the Great Chicago Fire* (4–6). Series: Scrapbooks of America. 2002, Tradition LB $28.50 (978-1-59187-014-2). 47pp. Twelve-year-old Liam and his family must flee their home during the Great Chicago Fire of 1871; background historical information is provided in boxed notes and a timeline. (Rev: SLJ 5/03)

11191 Dotty, Kathryn Adams. *Wild Orphan* (5–8). 2006, Edinborough $14.95 (978-1-889020-20-4). In the Midwest in the 1920s, Lizbeth's friendship with an independent-minded orphan named Georgiana gives her courage. (Rev: BL 6/1–15/06)

11192 Dudley, David L. *The Bicycle Man* (5–8). 2005, Clarion $16.00 (978-0-618-54233-8). In this poignant portrait of African American life in the rural South during the late 1920s, 12-year-old Carissa develops a mutually beneficial relationship with Bailey, an elderly jack-of-all-trades to whom she and her mother offer a home. (Rev: BL 11/15/05; SLJ 11/05)

11193 Durbin, William. *El Lector* (4–6). 2006, Random $15.95 (978-0-385-74651-9). 160pp. Thirteen-year-old Bella dreams of one day becoming a *lector* like her grandfather, who reads books and newspapers to workers in a Florida cigar factory. (Rev: BL 2/1/06; SLJ 2/06)

11194 Easton, Richard. *A Real American* (4–7). 2002, Clarion $15.00 (978-0-618-03339-3). Against his father's wishes, 11-year-old Nathan befriends Arturo, the son of Italian immigrants newly arrived in a Pennsylvania coal-mining town. (Rev: BCCB 9/02; BL 5/15/02; SLJ 3/02)

11195 Erickson, John R. *Moonshiner's Gold* (5–9). 2001, Viking $15.99 (978-0-670-03502-1). Fourteen-year-old Riley becomes embroiled in exciting intrigue involving moonshiners and corruption in this novel set in Texas in the 1920s. (Rev: HBG 3/02; SLJ 8/01; VOYA 10/01)

11196 Fisher, Leonard Everett. *The Jetty Chronicles* (5–9). 1997, Marshall Cavendish $15.95 (978-0-7614-5017-7). A series of vignettes based on fact about the unusual people the author met while growing up in Sea Gate, New York, at a time when the United States was drifting into World War II. (Rev: BL 10/15/97; HBG 3/98; SLJ 12/97; VOYA 2/98)

11197 Forrester, Sandra. *Leo and the Lesser Lion* (3–6). 2009, Knopf $16.99 (978-037585616-7); LB $19.99 (978-037595616-4). 304pp. Young Bayliss decides to become a nun after she survives the swimming accident that killed her older brother in 1932 Alabama but her resolve is tested when two homeless girls take over Leo's bedroom. ℮ Lexile 870L (Rev: BL 11/1/09; LMC 10/09; SLJ 11/09)

11198 Franklin, Kristine L. *Grape Thief* (5–9). 2003, Candlewick $16.99 (978-0-7636-1325-9). In 1925 Washington State, a boy of Croatian heritage tries to find a way to stay in school even though his family is in financial difficulty. (Rev: BL 10/1/03; SLJ 9/03)

587

11199 Fuqua, Jonathon. *Darby* (4–7). 2002, Candlewick $15.99 (978-0-7636-1417-1). A 9-year-old white girl, Darby, and her family become the target of KKK violence after she protests the killing of a black sharecropper's son in 1926 South Carolina. (Rev: BCCB 7–8/02; BL 3/15/02; HB 3–4/02; HBG 10/02; SLJ 3/02; VOYA 4/02)

11200 Fusco, Kimberly Newton. *The Wonder of Charlie Anne* (5–8). 2010, Knopf $16.99 (978-0-375-86104-8). 272pp. When Charlie Anne's mother dies in the Depression era, cousin Mirabel comes to live with the family and life becomes even tougher; however, a friendship with an African American neighbor — despite the disapproval of bigoted neighbors — brings her comfort. ∩ Lexile 970L (Rev: BL 9/1/10; LMC 11–12/10; SLJ 10/1/10*)

11201 Giff, Patricia Reilly. *R My Name Is Rachel* (4–7). 2011, Random House $15.99 (978-0-375-83889-7); LB $18.99 (978-0-375-93889-4). 176pp. Three formerly city children are left to fend for themselves on an isolated farm in upstate New York when their father must leave to work near Canada during the Great Depression; Rachel, 12, takes solace in her correspondence with an old neighbor. ∩ e Lexile 550L (Rev: BLO 1/12; HB 11–12/11; LMC 5–6/12; SLJ 11/1/11)

11202 Giff, Patricia Reilly. *Water Street* (5–8). 2006, Random House $15.95 (978-0-385-73068-6). In this poignant sequel to *Nory Ryan's Song* (2000) and *Maggie's Door* (2003), set in late 19th-century Brooklyn and told from alternating points of view, 13-year-old Bird Ryan and her new upstairs neighbor Thomas develop a close friendship. ∩ (Rev: BCCB 1/07; BL 8/06; HB 9–10/06; HBG 4/07; LMC 2/07; SLJ 9/06)

11203 Golden, Laura. *Every Day After* (4–6). 2013, Delacorte $15.99 (978-038574326-6); LB $18.99 (978-037599103-5). 224pp. In Depression-era Alabama when her father has deserted the family, young Lizzie must cope with her mother's overwhelming depression and the fear that she herself will be sent to an orphanage. e Lexile 700 (Rev: BLO 7/13; LMC 10/13*; SLJ 7/13)

11204 Goodman, Susan. *Hazelle Boxberg* (2–4). Illus. by Doris Ettlinger. 2004, Simon & Schuster LB $11.89 (978-0-689-84983-1). The moving story, based on truth, of 11-year-old Hazelle's trip to Texas by orphan train and her escape from the family that chooses her from a lineup at the Masonic Hall. (Rev: BL 3/1/04)

11205 Gray, Dianne E. *Together Apart* (5–9). 2002, Houghton Mifflin $16.00 (978-0-618-18721-8). After surviving the blizzard of 1888, Isaac and Hannah discover their love for each other while working for feminist publisher Eliza Moore. (Rev: BCCB 11/02; BL 9/15/02; HB 11–12/02; HBG 3/03; SLJ 12/02; VOYA 2/03)

11206 Greenwood, Barbara. *Factory Girl* (5–8). 2007, Kids Can $18.95 (978-1-55337-648-4); paper $12.95 (978-1-55337-649-1). A story about 12-year-old Emily, who in the early 20th century must take a job in a sweatshop and suffer intolerable conditions, is accompanied by historic photographs of children at work and details of key events on the road to reform. (Rev: BL 2/15/07; LMC 8–9/07; SLJ 5/07)

11207 Gregory, Kristiana. *Earthquake at Dawn* (5–9). Series: Great Episodes. 2003, Harcourt paper $6.99 (978-0-15-204681-1). Based on actual letters and photographs, this historical novel depicts the devastating 1906 San Francisco earthquake. (Rev: BL 4/15/92; SLJ 8/92)

11208 Gregory, Kristiana. *Orphan Runaways* (5–7). 1998, Scholastic paper $15.95 (978-0-590-60366-9). Two brothers run away from a San Francisco orphanage in 1879 to look for an uncle in the gold fields. (Rev: BCCB 3/98; BL 2/15/98; HBG 10/98; SLJ 3/98)

11209 Gundisch, Karin. *How I Became an American* (4–8). Trans. by James Skofield. 2001, Cricket $15.95 (978-0-8126-4875-1). This is the story of Johann, a young German immigrant, who arrives in an Ohio steel town in the early 20th century. (Rev: BL 11/15/01; HBG 3/02; SLJ 12/01; VOYA 4/02)

11210 Gutman, Dan. *Race for the Sky: The Kitty Hawk Diaries of Johnny Moore* (4–7). 2003, Simon & Schuster $15.95 (978-0-689-84554-3). Fact and fiction are interwoven in this diary by 14-year-old John Moore, recording his firsthand observations of the Wright brothers' progress. (Rev: BL 1/1–15/04; SLJ 1/04)

11211 Haas, Jessie. *Chase* (5–9). 2007, HarperCollins $16.99 (978-0-06-112850-9). In mid-19th-century Pennsylvania, Phin Chase witnesses a murder and flees, pursued by a stranger and a horse that seems to have tracking abilities. (Rev: BL 2/1/07; SLJ 4/07)

11212 Haddix, Margaret Peterson. *Uprising* (5–8). 2007, Simon & Schuster $16.99 (978-1-4169-1171-5). Three very different young girls — 15-year-old Italian immigrant Bella, Russian Jewish immigrant Yetta, and privileged Jane — give their perspective of the strike that occurred 13 months before the Triangle Shirtwaist Fire in 1911, protesting working conditions in the garment industry. (Rev: BL 9/15/07; SLJ 9/07)

11213 Hansen, Joyce. *I Thought My Soul Would Rise and Fly: The Diary of Patsy, a Freed Girl* (4–8). Series: Dear America. 1997, Scholastic paper $10.95 (978-0-590-84913-5). In this novel in the form of a diary, a freed slave girl wonders what to do with her life after leaving the plantation. (Rev: BL 12/15/97; HBG 3/98; SLJ 11/97)

11214 Harlow, Joan Hiatt. *Firestorm!* (4–7). 2010, Simon & Schuster $16.99 (978-141698485-6). 336pp. Poppy, a 12-year-old pickpocket, and Justin, 13-year-old son of a wealthy jeweler, become unlikely friends and manage a daring escape from the Great Chicago Fire of 1871; an Afterword distinguishes between fiction and fact. Lexile 660L (Rev: BL 11/15/10; SLJ 2/1/11)

11215 Harper, Jo, and Josephine Harper. *Finding Daddy: A Story of the Great Depression* (1–3). Illus. by Ron Mazellan. 2005, Turtle Bks. $16.95 (978-1-890515-31-7). 42pp. Young Bonnie is bereft when her father must leave home to find work, and she sets out to find him; a timeline, glossary, and song lyrics provide more information about the Great Depression. (Rev: SLJ 9/05)

11216 Harris, Carol Flynn. *A Place for Joey* (4–8). 2001, Boyds Mills $15.95 (978-1-56397-108-2). Twelve-year-old Joey, an Italian immigrant living in Boston in the early 20th century, learns an important lesson through a heroic act. (Rev: BL 9/1/01; HBG 3/02; SLJ 9/01; VOYA 10/01)

11217 Hayles, Marsha. *Breathing Room* (5–9). Illus. 2012, Henry Holt $16.99 (978-0-8050-8961-5). 256pp. Tuberculosis-stricken Evvy is sent to live at a remote sanatorium in this story set in 1940 against the background of war; there, she gains confidence and makes friends. e Lexile 800L (Rev: BLO 8/12; HB 7–8/12; LMC 11–12/12; SLJ 9/12)

11218 Hesse, Karen. *Letters from Rifka* (4–8). 1992, Henry Holt $16.95 (978-0-8050-1964-3). In letters back to Russia, Rifka, 12, recounts her long journey to the United States in 1919, starting with the dangerous escape over the border. (Rev: BCCB 10/92; BL 7/92; HB 9–10/92*; SLJ 8/92*)

11219 Hesse, Karen. *A Time of Angels* (5–8). 1995, Hyperion LB $16.49 (978-0-7868-2072-6). As influenza sweeps her city in 1918, killing thousands, Hannah tries to escape its ravages by moving to Vermont, where an old farmer helps her. (Rev: BCCB 1/96; BL 12/1/95; SLJ 12/95)

11220 Hill, Kirkpatrick. *Dancing at the Odinochka* (4–7). 2005, Simon & Schuster $15.95 (978-0-689-87388-1). An atmospheric life of Erinia — daughter of a Russian father and Athabascan mother — growing up in the 1860s in what is now Alaska. (Rev: BL 8/05; SLJ 8/05)

11221 Hitchcock, Shannon. *The Ballad of Jessie Pearl* (5–8). 2013, Namelos $18.95 (978-160898141-0). 131pp. Set in North Carolina during the early 1920s, this historical novel tells the story of 14-year-old Jessie Pearl Hennings, who has dreams of going to teaching college but must first overcome the challenges facing her family. e (Rev: BL 2/15/13; LMC 8–9/13; SLJ 4/13)

11222 Hobbs, Valerie. *Maggie and Oliver, or, a Bone of One's Own* (3–6). Illus. by Jennifer Thermes. 2011, Henry Holt $15.99 (978-0-8050-9294-3). 192pp. Oliver, a dog abandoned after the death of its owner, and Maggie, an orphaned street urchin, find each other in this initially bleak but ultimately optimistic story set in early-20th-century Boston. (Rev: BL 11/1/11; SLJ 10/1/11)

11223 Hoberman, Mary Ann. *Strawberry Hill* (3–5). Illus. by Wendy A. Halperin. 2009, Little, Brown $15.99 (978-0-316-04136-2). 240pp. When she moves to Strawberry Hill during the Depression, 10-year-old Allie finds no berries, but she does find friendship. (Rev: BL 6/1–15/09; SLJ 7/09)

11224 Holland, Isabelle. *Paperboy* (4–6). 1999, Holiday House $16.95 (978-0-8234-1422-2). 137pp. Growing up in a New York City slum in 1881, 12-year-old Kevin O'Donnell helps out his family by getting a job as a messenger for the owner of the *New York Chronicle*. (Rev: BCCB 10/99; HBG 3/00; SLJ 9/99)

11225 Holm, Jennifer L. *Turtle in Paradise* (4–6). 2010, Random House $16.99 (978-0-375-83688-6); LB $19.99 (978-0-375-93688-3). 208pp. Turtle, 11, is sent to live with relatives in Key West when her mother's new employer turns out to be anti-children in this Depression-era story based on the experiences of the author's great-grandmother. Newbery Honor Book. ⌒ e Lexile 610L (Rev: BL 4/15/10*; LMC 8–9/10; SLJ 4/10)

11226 Hoobler, Dorothy, and Thomas Hoobler. *The First Decade: Curtain Going Up* (4–6). Illus. Series: Century Kids. 2000, Millbrook LB $22.90 (978-0-7613-1600-8). 160pp. Presents the first decade of the 20th century in the life of the Aldriches, a theatrical family living in Maine. (Rev: BCCB 7–8/00; BL 5/1/00; HBG 10/00; SLJ 7/00)

11227 Hoobler, Dorothy, and Thomas Hoobler. *The Second Decade: Voyages* (4–6). Illus. Series: Century Kids. 2000, Millbrook LB $22.90 (978-0-7613-1601-5). 160pp. In the second decade of the 20th century, Peggy Aldrich and her sister photograph the factory workers in Lowell, Massachusetts, explore issues involving child labor and women's suffrage, and feel the effects of the sinking of the *Titanic*. (Rev: BCCB 7–8/00; BL 5/1/00; HBG 10/00; SLJ 7/00)

11228 Hopkinson, Deborah. *Knit Your Bit: A World War I Story* (K–3). Illus. by Steven Guarnaccia. 2013, Putnam $16.99 (978-0-399-25241-9). 32pp. Despite his initial resistance, Mikey enjoys participating in a knitting contest (boys vs. girls) to create hats, scarves, and socks for soldiers at the front. Lexile 460 (Rev: BL 3/15/13*; HB 1–2/13; LMC 8–9/13; SLJ 3/13)

11229 Hopkinson, Deborah. *Sky Boys: How They Built the Empire State Building* (2–4). Illus. by James Ransome. 2006, Random $16.95 (978-0-375-83610-7). 48pp. A young boy and his unemployed father watch as daring workers defy gravity in the construction of New York City's Empire State Building; dramatic illustrations highlight the heights. (Rev: BL 12/1/05; SLJ 2/06)

11230 Hulme, Joy N. *Climbing the Rainbow* (4–6). 2004, HarperCollins LB $16.89 (978-0-06-054304-4). In 1911, 10-year-old Dora's large family moves to New Mexico; there Dora faces various challenges, including starting school and the death of a friend. (Rev: BL 1/1–15/04; SLJ 2/04)

11231 Hurst, Carol Otis. *You Come to Yokum* (3–5). Illus. by Life Kay. 2005, Houghton $15.00 (978-0-618-55122-4). The Carlyle family's move to rural western Massachusetts does nothing to dampen Mrs. Carlyle's enthusiastic — and sometimes embarrassing — support for the women's suffrage movement. (Rev: BL 9/1/05; SLJ 1/06)

11232 Hurwitz, Johanna. *Faraway Summer* (5–7). Illus. by Mary Azarian. 1998, Morrow $14.95 (978-0-688-15334-2). In 1910, a Jewish orphan who lives in a tenement in New York City is thrilled at the thought of spending two weeks on a farm in Vermont, thanks to the Fresh Air Fund. (Rev: BL 3/1/98; HB 7–8/98; HBG 10/98; SLJ 5/98)

11233 Jackson, Alison. *Rainmaker* (5–8). 2005, Boyds Mills $16.95 (978-1-59078-309-2). The farmers in Pidge Martin's town hire a rainmaker in the hopes that she will save their crops in this story set in 1939 Florida. (Rev: BL 3/15/05; SLJ 4/05)

11234 Jocelyn, Marthe. *Earthly Astonishments* (4–8). 2000, Tundra paper $7.95 (978-0-88776-628-2). The setting is New York City in the 1880s and the novel involves a girl who is only 22 inches tall and her career in a glorified freak show. (Rev: BCCB 2/00; HBG 10/00; SLJ 4/00)

11235 Jocelyn, Marthe. *How It Happened in Peach Hill* (5–9). 2007, Random House $15.99 (978-0-375-83701-2). Fifteen-year-old Annie, who does research for her "clairvoyant" mother mainly by pretending she is stupid, longs for a normal life in this compelling novel set in the 1920s. (Rev: BL 1/1–15/07; SLJ 4/07*)

11236 Kelly, Jacqueline. *The Evolution of Calpurnia Tate* (4–7). 2009, Holt $16.95 (978-0-8050-8841-0). 352pp. In Texas at the turn of the 20th century, 11-year-old Calpurnia, the only daughter among seven children, has an independent streak and an interest in natural science that she shares with her grandfather. Newbery Honor 2010; ALA Notable Children's Book. ⌒ Lexile 830L (Rev: BL 5/1/09*; HB 9/09; LMC 10/09; SLJ 5/09*; VOYA 4/09)

11237 Kirwan, Anna. *Of Flowers and Shadows* (4–6). Series: Portraits. 2005, Scholastic $9.99 (978-0-439-71010-7). 182pp. This appealing fictional tale, inspired by Winslow Homer's "Girl and Laurel" painting, tells how Aurelia, an orphan and servant for a family in Townsend, Massachusetts, came to pose for the artist. (Rev: BL 11/15/05; SLJ 11/05)

11238 Klass, Sheila Solomon. *A Shooting Star: A Novel About Annie Oakley* (4–8). 1996, Holiday $15.95 (978-0-8234-1279-2). A fictionalized biography of the woman who rose from poverty to become a famous show-business sharpshooter. (Rev: BL 12/15/96; SLJ 5/97)

11239 Klise, Kate. *Stand Straight, Ella Kate: The True Story of a Real Giant* (K–3). Illus. by M. Sarah Klise. 2010, Dial $16.99 (978-0-8037-3404-3). 32pp. This first-person account is based on the true story of Ella Kate Ewing, born in 1872, who was more than 7 feet tall at the age of 17 and who chose to appear in museum and circus exhibits as a career. Lexile AD640L (Rev: BL 6/10*; LMC 10/10; SLJ 6/1/10)

11240 Koller, Jackie F. *Nothing to Fear* (5–7). 1991, Harcourt $14.95 (978-0-15-200544-3); paper $8.00 (978-0-15-257582-3). Danny Garvey is a first-generation Catholic Irish American growing up in New York City in the 1930s. (Rev: BCCB 3/91; BL 3/1/91; SLJ 5/91)

11241 Korman, Gordon. *Unsinkable* (5–8). Series: Titanic. 2011, Scholastic paper $5.99 (978-0-545-12-331-0). 176pp. A young Irish pickpocket named Paddy finds himself aboard the *Titanic* in this tense historical adventure, the first installment in a series. The second volume is *Collision Course* (2011). Also use *S.O.S.* (2011). ⌒ ℮ Lexile 820L (Rev: BLO 8/11; SLJ 9/1/11)

11242 LaFaye, A. *Walking Home to Rosie Lee* (2–4). Illus. by Keith D. Shepherd. 2011, Cinco Puntos $16.95 (978-1-933693-97-2). 32pp. At the end of the Civil War,

a young slave boy named Gabe heads north in search of his mother, who was sold and sent away from him. (Rev: BL 11/1/11; SLJ 9/1/11)

11243 Larson, Kirby. *The Friendship Doll* (4–6). 2011, Delacorte $15.99 (978-0-385-73745-6); LB $18.99 (978-0-385-90667-8). 202pp. One of the 58 dolls Japan presented to the United States in 1927, Miss Kanagawa, has an inspiring influence on each of the girls she lives with. ℮ Lexile 760L (Rev: BL 7/11; LMC 1–2/12; SLJ 8/11)

11244 Lasky, Kathryn. *Dreams in the Golden Country: The Diary of Zipporah Feldman, a Jewish Immigrant Girl* (4–8). 1998, Scholastic paper $10.95 (978-0-590-02973-5). Twelve-year-old Zipporah Feldman, a Jewish immigrant from Russia, keeps a diary about her life with her family on New York's Lower East Side around 1910. (Rev: BL 4/1/98; HBG 9/98; SLJ 5/98)

11245 Lasky, Kathryn. *A Time for Courage: The Suffragette Diary of Kathleen Bowen, Washington, DC, 1917* (4–6). Series: Dear America. 2002, Scholastic $10.95 (978-0-590-51141-4). Thirteen-year-old Kat records her increasing interest in politics and her activities supporting the women's suffrage movement. (Rev: HBG 10/02; SLJ 8/02)

11246 Latham, Irene. *Leaving Gee's Bend* (5–8). 2010, Putnam $16.99 (978-0-399-25179-5). 240pp. Ten-year-old African American Ludelphia sets out on a dangerous journey to get help for her ailing mother in 1932. Lexile 700L (Rev: BL 2/1/10; LMC 1–2/10; SLJ 1/10; VOYA 2/10)

11247 Lenski, Lois. *Strawberry Girl* (4–6). Illus. by author. 1945, HarperCollins LB $18.89 (978-0-397-30110-2); paper $5.99 (978-0-06-440585-0). 192pp. Lively adventures of a little girl, full of the flavor of the Florida lake country. Newbery Medal winner, 1946.

11248 Levine, Kristin. *The Best Bad Luck I Ever Had* (5–8). 2009, Putnam $16.99 (978-0-399-25090-3). 272pp. In early-20th-century small-town Alabama, 12-year-old Dit is surprised that the new postmaster is African American and disappointed that his daughter is unskilled in baseball, hunting, and fishing; as Emma and Dit become friends they have to deal with racism and injustice. YALSA Amazing Audiobooks Top Ten 2011. ⌒ (Rev: BCCB 4/09; BL 11/15/08; HB 5/09; LMC 3/09; SLJ 1/09)

11249 Lewis, Zoe. *Keisha Discovers Harlem* (3–5). Illus. by Dan Burr and Rich Grot. Series: Magic Attic Club. 1999, Magic Attic LB $17.40 (978-1-57513-144-3). 74pp. Keisha puts on a flapper costume and finds herself transported to New York City during the Harlem Renaissance. (Rev: SLJ 4/99)

11250 Long, Susan Hill. *Whistle in the Dark* (5–8). 2013, Holiday $16.95 (978-082342839-7). 192pp. In the Ozarks in the 1920s, 13-year-old Clem must give up his dreams of attending school and become the next man in his family to join the dangerous profession of lead mining to help pay for his sister's medical bills. Lexile 740 (Rev: BL 9/15/13; HB 1–2/14; LMC 5–6/14; SLJ 10/13)

11251 Lottridge, Celia Barker. *The Listening Tree* (4–8). 2011, Fitzhenry & Whiteside paper $11.95 (978-1-55455-052-4). 154pp. Nine-year-old Ellen, new to city life, gains the courage to talk to strangers when she overhears plans to evict her neighbors in this Depression story set in Canada. Lexile 1240 (Rev: BL 4/15/11; SLJ 5/11; VOYA 4/11)

11252 Love, D. Anne. *I Remember the Alamo* (4–6). 2000, Holiday House $15.95 (978-0-8234-1426-0). 156pp. The McCann family moves to San Antonio and becomes embroiled in the battle of the Alamo and its aftermath in this historical novel. (Rev: BL 1/1–15/00; HB 3/00; HBG 3/00; SLJ 1/00)

11253 Love, D. Anne. *A Year Without Rain* (4–6). 2000, Holiday House $15.95 (978-0-8234-1488-8). 118pp. Set in the late 19th century, this novel tells how Rachel, who lives on the Dakota prairie, tries to thwart her father's plans to remarry. (Rev: BCCB 7–8/00; BL 4/1/00; HB 7/00; HBG 10/00; SLJ 9/00)

11254 Lowry, Lois. *Like the Willow Tree: The Diary of Lydia Amelia Pierce* (4–7). Illus. Series: Dear America. 2011, Scholastic $12.99 (978-0-545-14469-8); LB $16.99 (978-0-545-26556-0). 224pp. Eleven-year-old Lydia and her brother are sent to live with the Shakers at Sabbathday Lake, Maine, when their parents die in the influenza epidemic of 1918. Lexile 830L (Rev: BL 12/1/10; SLJ 2/1/11)

11255 McCaughrean, Geraldine. *The Glorious Adventures of the Sunshine Queen* (5–8). 2011, HarperCollins $16.99 (978-0-06-200806-0). 336pp. In the 1890s, 12-year-old Cissy and two friends have great adventures on a Missouri River paddle steamer when they are pulled out of school because of a diphtheria outbreak. ☊ Lexile 950L (Rev: BL 4/1/11; HB 5–6/11; SLJ 7/11; VOYA 6/11)

11256 MacKall, Dandi Daley. *Rudy Rides the Rails: A Depression Era Story* (3–5). Illus. by Chris Ellison. 2007, Sleeping Bear $17.95 (978-1-58536-286-8). 40pp. Powerful illustrations bring to life this story of a Depression-era teen who hops freight trains in search of work. (Rev: BL 5/1/07; SLJ 6/07)

11257 McKissack, Patricia C. *Color Me Dark: The Diary of Nellie Lee Love, the Great Migration North* (4–6). Series: Dear America. 2000, Scholastic $10.95 (978-0-590-51159-9). 224pp. Told in diary form, this is the fictional story of African American Nellie Lee Love, whose family moves from Tennessee to Chicago in 1919 and encounters prejudice, corruption, and race riots. (Rev: BL 2/15/00; HBG 10/00; SLJ 7/00)

11258 McMullan, Margaret. *When I Crossed No-Bob* (5–8). 2007, Houghton Mifflin $16.00 (978-0-618-71715-6). Addy O'Donnell, 12, manages to separate herself from her violent and racist family in this novel about post-Civil War Mississippi and the beginnings of the Ku Klux Klan. (Rev: BL 10/1/07; HB 1–2/08; SLJ 11/07)

11259 Matas, Carol. *Rosie in New York City: Gotcha!* (3–6). 2003, Simon & Schuster paper $4.99 (978-0-689-85714-0). 124pp. In early-20th-century New York City, 11-year-old Rosie takes a factory job when her mother falls ill. (Rev: BL 5/15/03; SLJ 8/03)

11260 Mattern, Joanne. *Coming to America: The Story of Immigration* (4–8). Illus. by Margaret Sanfilippo. 2000, Perfection Learning $17.95 (978-0-7807-9715-4); paper $8.95 (978-0-7891-2851-5). A fictional presentation centering on the Martini family and their journey from Italy at the turn of the 20th century to find a new home in America. (Rev: HBG 3/01; SLJ 2/01)

11261 Meltzer, Milton. *Tough Times* (5–8). 2007, Clarion $16.00 (978-0-618-87445-3). With detailed historical background, this novel describes the struggles and despair experienced by high school senior Joey Singer and his family as the Depression deepens. (Rev: BL 9/1/07; SLJ 12/07)

11262 Mobley, Jeannie. *Katerina's Wish* (4–6). 2012, Simon & Schuster $15.99 (978-1-44243343-4). 256pp. Katerina's father brought the family from Bohemia to Colorado to work in the coal mines and earn enough to buy a farm, but in 1901 young Katerina has doubts they will achieve this goal. ☊ Lexile 780L (Rev: BL 9/15/12*; LMC 1–2/13; SLJ 8/1/12)

11263 Moss, Jenny. *Winnie's War* (5–8). 2009, Walker $16.99 (978-0-8027-9819-0). 224pp. In 1918 Texas Winnie, 12, must deal with her difficult grandmother, her troubled mother, her overworked father, her two little sisters, and now an epidemic of flu. (Rev: BCCB 2/09; BLO 12/9/08)

11264 Moss, Marissa. *Rose's Journal: The Story of a Girl in the Great Depression* (3–5). Illus. by author. Series: Young American Voices. 2001, Harcourt $15.00 (978-0-15-202423-9). 56pp. In her pink-lined journal, young Rose records the hardships her family faces during the dust storms of 1935 Kansas and details outside events such as the Hauptmann trial. (Rev: HBG 3/02; SLJ 12/01)

11265 Murphy, Claire Rudolf. *Marching with Aunt Susan: Susan B. Anthony and the Fight for Women's Suffrage* (3–6). Illus. by Stacey Schuett. 2011, Peachtree $16.95 (978-1-56145-593-5). 36pp. In 1896 Bessie is not allowed to go hiking with her father and brothers and decides to go to a women's suffrage meeting instead; there she meets Susan B. Anthony and is drawn into the movement. (Rev: BL 12/1/11; LMC 5–6/12*; SLJ 9/1/11)

11266 Myers, Anna. *Hoggee* (5–7). 2004, Walker $16.95 (978-0-8027-8926-6). Despite all his own problems, 14-year-old mule driver Howard decides to do what he can to help a deaf mute girl in this novel set in 19th-century New York State. (Rev: SLJ 11/04)

11267 Nislick, June Levitt. *Zayda Was a Cowboy* (4–7). 2005, Jewish Publication Soc. paper $9.95 (978-0-8276-0817-7). A Jewish grandfather tells his grandchildren about his exploits as a cowboy when he first arrived in America from Eastern Europe; an epilogue gives background and there is a glossary and a bibliography. (Rev: BL 8/05*)

11268 Oneal, Zibby. *A Long Way to Go* (3–5). Illus. by Michael Dooling. 1992, Puffin paper $4.99 (978-0-14-032950-6). 64pp. Lila's life changes when her grandmother is jailed for fighting for women's rights in 1917 America. (Rev: BCCB 9/90; BL 3/1/90; HB 7/90; SLJ 9/90)

11269 Paterson, Katherine. *Bread and Roses, Too* (5–8). 2006, Clarion $16.00 (978-0-618-65479-6). Jake and Rosa, children from different backgrounds, suffer from the effects of the textile workers' strike in early 20th-century Massachusetts. ∩ (Rev: BCCB 3/07; BL 8/06; HB 9–10/06; HBG 4/07; LMC 2/07; SLJ 9/06; VOYA 12/06)

11270 Paterson, Katherine. *Preacher's Boy* (5–8). 1999, Clarion $15.00 (978-0-395-83897-6). In small-town Vermont in 1899, a time of new ideas and technological change, Robbie, the restless, imaginative, questioning son of a preacher, causes unforeseen trouble when he plans his own kidnapping for profit. (Rev: BCCB 10/99; BL 8/99; HB 9–10/99; HBG 3/00; SLJ 8/99)

11271 Peck, Richard. *Fair Weather* (4–6). 2001, Dial $16.99 (978-0-8037-2516-4). A 13-year-old Illinois farm girl and her family take an exciting trip to the 1893 World's Columbian Exposition in Chicago. (Rev: BCCB 10/01; BL 9/1/01; HB 11/01*; HBG 3/02; SLJ 9/01*)

11272 Peck, Richard. *Here Lies the Librarian* (5–8). 2006, Dial $16.99 (978-0-8037-3080-9). Four young female librarians arrive in a small town in Indiana in 1914 and inspire 14-year-old Peewee McGrath to consider her future in different ways. (Rev: BL 3/1/06; SLJ 4/06*; VOYA 2/06)

11273 Peck, Robert Newton. *Arly* (5–8). 1989, Walker $16.95 (978-0-8027-6856-8). A teacher changes the life of a young boy in a migrant camp in Florida in 1927. (Rev: BL 7/89; VOYA 8/89)

11274 Pinkney, Andrea Davis. *Bird in a Box* (4–7). 2011, Little, Brown $16.99 (978-0-316-07403-2). 245pp. Three young boxing fans facing personal challenges come together at the Mercy Home for Negro Orphans and are inspired by the great Joe Louis's victories during the Great Depression. ∩ ℮ (Rev: BL 4/15/11; HB 5–6/11; LMC 10/11; SLJ 3/1/11)

11275 Porter, Tracey. *Billy Creekmore* (5–7). 2007, HarperCollins $16.99 (978-0-06-077570-4). From a grim orphanage to the mines of West Virginia and on to a life in the circus, 10-year-old Billy describes in picaresque style the difficult life of the young and poor in the early 20th century. (Rev: BL 4/15/07; SLJ 7/07)

11276 Porter, Tracey. *Treasures in the Dust* (5–7). 1997, HarperCollins LB $14.89 (978-0-06-027564-8). With alternating points of view, two girls from poor families in Oklahoma's Dust Bowl tell their stories. (Rev: BL 8/97; HB 9–10/97; HBG 3/98; SLJ 12/97*; VOYA 10/98)

11277 Rabe, Berniece. *Hiding Mr. McMulty* (5–8). 1997, Harcourt $18.00 (978-0-15-201330-1). This novel, set in southeast Missouri in 1937, tells a story of race and class conflicts as experienced by 11-year-old Rass. (Rev: BL 10/15/97; HBG 3/98; SLJ 12/97; VOYA 2/98)

11278 Ransom, Candice F. *Fire in the Sky* (3–5). Illus. 1997, Carolrhoda LB $19.93 (978-0-87614-867-9). 72pp. In the late 1930s in New Jersey, Stenny becomes involved in the flight of the dirigible *Hindenburg* and the rescue operation after it burns. (Rev: BL 5/1/97; SLJ 8/97)

11279 Ransom, Candice F. *Jimmy Crack Corn* (3–5). Illus. 1994, Carolrhoda LB $19.95 (978-0-87614-786-3). 56pp. The beginning of the Great Depression as seen through the experiences of a farm family sinking into poverty with no hope for the future. (Rev: BCCB 6/94; BL 7/94; SLJ 6/94)

11280 Ray, Delia. *Ghost Girl: A Blue Ridge Mountain Story* (5–8). 2003, Clarion $16.00 (978-0-618-33377-6). In rural Virginia during the Depression, young April longs to go to the new school built by President Hoover and learn to read, but her family circumstances do not make this easy. (Rev: BCCB 11/03; BL 11/15/03; HB 1–2/04*; HBG 4/04; SLJ 11/03*)

11281 Reich, Susanna. *Penelope Bailey Takes the Stage* (4–7). 2006, Marshall Cavendish $16.95 (978-0-7614-5287-4). A frustrated Penny takes a role in the school play against the wishes of her aunt in this novel set in Victorian San Francisco. (Rev: BL 5/15/06; SLJ 5/06)

11282 Rhodes, Jewell Parker. *Sugar* (3–5). 2013, Little, Brown $16.99 (978-0-31604305-2). 288pp. Plantation hand Sugar resents her life of limited options in this strong Reconstruction-era story. ALA Notable Children's Book. ℮ (Rev: BL 5/15/13; LMC 10/13; SLJ 6/13)

11283 Robinet, Harriette G. *Forty Acres and Maybe a Mule* (4–7). 1998, Simon & Schuster $16.00 (978-0-689-82078-6). After the Civil War, Gideon and other freed slaves begin working the 40 acres of land each has been promised in spite of the opposition of white settlers. (Rev: BL 1/1–15/99; HBG 3/99; SLJ 11/98)

11284 Rockwell, Anne. *Hey, Charleston! The True Story of the Jenkins Orphanage Band* (1–4). Illus. by Colin Bootman. 2013, Carolrhoda LB $16.95 (978-076135565-6). 32pp. Tells the moving story of a minister in South Carolina, a former slave himself, who helps a group of orphans and finds a way for them to form a successful jazz band at the turn of the 20th century. (Rev: BL 11/1/13; LMC 3–4/13; SLJ 9/13) [784.4]

11285 Rogers, Lisa Waller. *Get Along, Little Dogies: The Chisholm Trail Diary of Hallie Lou Wells: South Texas, 1878* (4–7). 2001, Texas Tech Univ. $14.50 (978-0-89672-446-4); paper $8.95 (978-0-89672-448-8). Feisty 14-year-old Hallie Lou records in her diary the details and dangers of a cattle drive from Texas to Kansas. (Rev: HBG 10/01; SLJ 7/01)

11286 Rubright, Lynn. *Mama's Window* (4–6). Illus. by Patricia C. McKissack. 2005, Lee & Low $16.95 (978-1-57480-160-6). 96pp. Sugar, an 11-year-old African American orphan living with his uncle on the Mississippi Delta, fights to ensure that his late mother's dream of a stained-glass window for the local church becomes a reality. (Rev: BL 7/05; SLJ 8/05)

11287 Ryan, Pam Muñoz. *Esperanza Rising* (5–8). 2000, Scholastic paper $17.99 (978-0-439-12041-8). During the Great Depression, poverty forces Esperanza and her mother to leave Mexico and seek work in an agricultural labor camp in California. (Rev: BCCB 12/00; BL 12/1/00; HB 1–2/01; HBG 3/01; SLJ 10/00; VOYA 12/00)

11288 Schwabach, Karen. *The Hope Chest* (4–6). 2008, Random $16.99 (978-0-375-84095-1). Eleven-year-old Violet runs away from home and joins the fight for the women's rights in the 1920s. (Rev: HB 3/08; LMC 3/08; SLJ 3/08)

11289 Sebestyen, Ouida. *Words by Heart* (5–7). 1979, Little, Brown $15.95 (978-0-316-77931-9). Race relations are explored when an African American family moves to an all-white community during the Reconstruction era. (Rev: BL 6/1/88)

11290 Sherman, Eileen B. *Independence Avenue* (5–9). 1990, Jewish Publication Society $14.95 (978-0-8276-0367-7). This story of Russian Jews who immigrate to Texas in 1907 has a resourceful, engaging hero, an unusual setting, and plenty of action. (Rev: BL 2/15/91; SLJ 1/91)

11291 Snyder, Zilpha Keatley. *William S. and the Great Escape* (5–7). 2009, Simon & Schuster $16.99 (978-1-4169-6763-7). 224pp. In a small California town during the Great Depression, the four youngest Baggett siblings flee their coarse, abusive family for their aunt's house after sister Janey's guinea pig is flushed down the toilet. A sequel is *William's Midsummer Dreams* (2011), in which William is living with his Aunt Fiona and playing the role of Puck. ∩ ℮ Lexile 980L (Rev: BL 7/09; LMC 11–12/09; SLJ 10/09)

11292 Stroud, Bettye. *Dance Y'All* (2–4). Illus. by Cornelius Van Wright and Ying-Hwa Hu. 2001, Marshall Cavendish $15.95 (978-0-7614-5065-8). With some help, Jack Henry overcomes his fear of the snake in the barn in this novel set at the beginning of the 20th century. (Rev: HBG 3/02; SLJ 11/01)

11293 Swain, Gwenyth. *Hope and Tears: Ellis Island Voices* (5–8). Illus. 2012, Boyds Mills $17.95 (978-159078765-6). 96pp. Fictionalized personal histories in the form of letters, diary entries, poems, and monologues and dialogues — accompanied by a factual commentary — provide lots of information about the experiences of immigrants arriving at Ellis Island. (Rev: BL 4/15/12; HB 5–6/12; SLJ 5/1/12)

11294 Tarshis, Lauren. *I Survived the Shark Attacks of 1916* (3–7). Illus. by Scott Dawson. Series: I Survived. 2010, Scholastic $16.99 (978-0-545-20688-4). 87pp. Based on the New Jersey shark attacks of 1916, this story follows of group of boys who play pranks on each other, doubting the existence of the shark — until they see it for themselves. Lexile 610L (Rev: SLJ 12/1/10)

11295 Tate, Eleanora E. *Celeste's Harlem Renaissance* (4–7). 2007, Little, Brown $15.99 (978-0-316-52394-3). In the early 1920s Celeste arrives in New York from North Carolina and discovers that her aunt is not the fa-

mous singer and dancer she was told but that the lively spirit of the Harlem Renaissance brings her rewards. (Rev: BL 2/1/07; SLJ 5/07)

11296 Taylor, Sarah Stewart. *Amelia Earhart: This Broad Ocean* (4–7). Illus. by Ben Towle. 2010, Hyperion $17.99 (978-1-4231-1337-9). 96pp. Young Grace, who wants to be a reporter one day, is entranced by Earhart and her bravery in this graphic novel presentation of a portion of Earhart's life. (Rev: BL 3/15/10*; LMC 8–9/10; SLJ 5/10)

11297 Tripp, Valerie. *Changes for Kit: A Winter Story* (3–5). Illus. by Walter Rane. Series: American Girl. 2001, Pleasant $12.95 (978-1-58485-027-4); paper $6.95 (978-1-58485-026-7). 70pp. A section of historical facts and photographs follows the story of Kit seeking clothing donations for children at the local soup kitchen and learning to cope with her grumpy uncle during the Depression. (Rev: BL 12/1/01; HBG 3/02)

11298 Tripp, Valerie. *Changes for Samantha: A Winter Story* (3–5). Illus. by Robert Grace and Nancy Niles. 1988, Pleasant LB $12.95 (978-0-937295-95-3); paper $6.95 (978-0-937295-47-2). 72pp. Wealthy New Yorker Samantha now lives with her aunt and uncle in a series that takes place in 1904 and includes: *Happy Birthday Samantha* (1987); *Samantha Saves the Day* (1988). (Rev: BL 1/1/89; SLJ 2/89)

11299 Tripp, Valerie. *Happy Birthday, Kit! A Springtime Story, 1934* (3–5). Illus. Series: American Girl. 2001, Pleasant $12.95 (978-1-58485-023-6); paper $6.95 (978-1-58485-022-9). 70pp. Kit greets her Aunt Millie's arrival with mixed emotions. (Rev: BL 8/01; HBG 3/02)

11300 Tripp, Valerie. *Kit Learns a Lesson: A School Story* (3–5). Illus. 2000, Pleasant $12.95 (978-1-58485-121-9). 67pp. As the Great Depression grows more serious, it affects all facets of Kit Kittredge's life including her family and school. (Rev: BL 9/1/00; HBG 3/01; SLJ 12/00)

11301 Tripp, Valerie. *Kit Saves the Day: A Summer Story, 1934* (3–5). Illus. Series: American Girl. 2001, Pleasant $12.95 (978-1-58485-025-0); paper $6.95 (978-1-58485-024-3). 68pp. Kit discovers that a hobo's life isn't as much fun as she first thought. (Rev: BL 8/01; HBG 3/02)

11302 Tripp, Valerie. *Meet Kit: An American Girl* (3–5). Illus. by Walter Rane. Series: American Girls. 2000, Pleasant $12.95 (978-1-58485-017-5). 70pp. In 1934, Kit Kittredge and her family feel the effects of the Great Depression when her father loses his job and her mother takes in boarders. (Rev: BL 9/1/00; HBG 3/01; SLJ 12/00)

11303 Tubb, Kristin O'Donnell. *Autumn Winifred Oliver Does Things Different* (4–6). 2008, Delacorte $15.99 (978-0-385-73569-8). 224pp. In the Great Smoky Mountains during the Depression, 11-year-old Autumn and her grandfather try to stop the government from destroying their mountain home. (Rev: BL 11/15/08; LMC 3/09; SLJ 1/09)

11304 Tubb, Kristin O'Donnell. *Selling Hope* (5–8). 2010, Feiwel & Friends $16.99 (978-031261122-4). 224pp. As Halley's Comet approaches in 1910, imaginative 13-year-old Hope sells "anti-comet" pills with the help of a young Buster Keaton. (Rev: BL 11/15/10*; SLJ 12/1/10)

11305 Tucker, Terry Ward. *Moonlight and Mill Whistles* (5–7). 1998, Summerhouse $15.00 (978-1-887714-32-7). Thirteen-year-old Tommy is unaware how his life will change after he meets a gypsy girl named Rhona in this novel set in an early 1900s South Carolina cotton mill town. (Rev: BL 3/1/99; SLJ 5/99)

11306 Vander Zee, Ruth. *Mississippi Morning* (3–6). Illus. by Floyd Cooper. 2004, Eerdmans $16.00 (978-0-8028-5211-3). A picture-book story of a 12-year-old boy in 1933 Mississippi who must come to terms with the racism that is all around him, even in his father. (Rev: BL 10/15/04*; SLJ 9/04)

11307 Vanderpool, Clare. *Moon Over Manifest* (5–8). 2010, Delacorte $16.99 (978-0-385-73883-5); LB $19.99 (978-0-385-90750-7). 351pp. Twelve-year-old Abilene arrives in Manifest in 1936 hoping to learn more about her father, and a box of mementos sets her and her new friends on a journey of discovery. Newbery Medal 2011; ALA Notable Children's Book 2011. ⊙ ℮ (Rev: BL 10/15/10*; LMC 5–6/11; SLJ 11/1/10)

11308 Waldman, Neil. *Say-Hey and the Babe: Two Mostly True Baseball Stories* (4–6). Illus. by author. 2006, Holiday $16.95 (978-0-8234-1857-2). 40pp. Two stories based on fact link a baseball autographed by Babe Ruth and subsequently lost with a stickball player's discovery in a sewer grate 14 years later; sidebars add lots of baseball lore and separate fact from fiction. (Rev: BL 5/15/06; SLJ 7/06)

11309 Waldman, Neil. *They Came from the Bronx: How the Buffalo Were Saved from Extinction* (2–5). Illus. by author. 2001, Boyds Mills $16.95 (978-1-56397-891-3). A Comanche grandmother and grandson await a small herd of buffalo in a story based on efforts to return bison to the plains in 1907. (Rev: HBG 10/02; SLJ 9/01)

11310 Warner, Sally. *Finding Hattie* (5–8). 2001, HarperCollins $15.95 (978-0-06-028464-0). Hattie Knowlton's 1882 journal describes Miss Bulkey's school in Tarrytown, New York, and the people she meets there, including her sophisticated, shallow but popular cousin Sophie. (Rev: BCCB 6/01; BL 2/1/01; HB 5–6/01; HBG 10/01; SLJ 2/01; VOYA 8/01)

11311 Weatherford, Carole Boston. *Dear Mr. Rosenwald* (2–4). Illus. by R. Gregory Christie. 2006, Scholastic $16.99 (978-0-439-49522-6). 32pp. In this fact-based tale from the rural South of the 1920s, 10-year-old Ovella describes her community's efforts to build a new school with seed money from Julius Rosenwald, president of Sears, Roebuck. (Rev: BL 10/1/06; SLJ 10/06*)

11312 Wells, Rosemary, and Tom Wells. *The House in the Mail* (2–5). Illus. by Dan Andreasen. 2002, Viking $16.99 (978-0-670-03545-8). 32pp. A scrapbook-style accounting by a 12-year-old girl of her family's mail-order home in 1927 Kentucky. (Rev: BCCB 2/02; BL 3/1/02; HBG 10/02; SLJ 3/02)

11313 Whelan, Gloria. *The Locked Garden* (3–6). 2009, HarperCollins $15.99 (978-0-06-079094-3). 176pp. At the turn of the 20th century, after their mother's death, Verna and her sister Carlie move with their doctor father to a mental asylum in northern Michigan, where prejudices persist. (Rev: BL 4/15/09; SLJ 7/09)

11314 Winthrop, Elizabeth. *Franklin Delano Roosevelt: Letters from a Mill Town Girl* (5–7). Series: Dear Mr. President. 2001, Winslow $9.95 (978-1-890817-61-9). Fictional letters between Franklin Delano Roosevelt and a 12-year-old girl illustrate living conditions and government policy during the Depression. (Rev: BL 2/1/02; HBG 3/02; SLJ 12/01)

11315 Wolfert, Adrienne. *Making Tracks* (5–7). Series: Adventures in America. 2000, Silver Moon LB $14.95 (978-1-893110-16-8). In this novel set in the Depression, young Henry leaves his foster home to ride the rails to Chicago to find his father. (Rev: BL 7/00; HBG 3/01; SLJ 11/00)

11316 Wyatt, Leslie J. *Poor Is Just a Starting Place* (5–8). 2005, Holiday $16.95 (978-0-8234-1884-8). In rural Kentucky during the Great Depression, 12-year-old Artie longs for a different life. (Rev: BL 6/1–15/05; SLJ 7/05)

11317 Wyss, Thelma Hatch. *A Tale of Gold* (4–6). 2007, Simon & Schuster $15.99 (978-1-4169-4212-2). 160pp. In the late 1890s, a 14-year-old orphan named James sets out from San Francisco heading for the gold fields of Alaska, meeting many interesting characters on the exciting journey. (Rev: BL 10/15/07; SLJ 10/07)

11318 Yep, Laurence. *Dream Soul* (5–8). 2000, HarperCollins LB $14.89 (978-0-06-028309-4). In this sequel to *Star Fisher* (1991), the Lees, a family of Chinese immigrants who live in Clarksburg, West Virginia, in 1927, face conflicts when the children want to celebrate Christmas. (Rev: BCCB 12/00; BL 12/1/00)

11319 Yep, Laurence. *The Earth Dragon Awakes: The San Francisco Earthquake of 1906* (3–5). 2006, HarperCollins $14.99 (978-0-06-027524-2). 128pp. Best friends Henry and Ching, both fans of "penny dreadful" adventure novels, live through the earthquake and realize that their fathers are heroes. (Rev: BL 3/1/06; SLJ 5/06)

11320 Ylvisaker, Anne. *The Luck of the Buttons* (4–6). 2011, Candlewick $15.99 (978-0-7636-5066-7). 240pp. Twelve-year-old Tugs Button's fortunes begin to change when she wins a three-legged race and a Brownie camera in this small-town Iowa story set during the Great Depression. Lexile 730L (Rev: BL 4/15/11; HB 3–4/11; SLJ 4/11)

11321 Yolen, Jane. *Tea with an Old Dragon: A Story of Sophia Smith, Founder of Smith College* (2–4). Illus. by Monica Vachula. 1998, Boyds Mills $15.95 (978-1-56397-657-5). In this historical story set in a 19th-century New England town, a little girl becomes friends with

Miss Sophy Smith, the founder of Smith College. (Rev: HBG 3/99; SLJ 10/98)

WORLD WAR II AND AFTER

11322 Abbott, Tony. *Lunch-Box Dream* (5–8). 2011, Farrar $16.99 (978-0-374-34673-7). 192pp. Two families — one white and one black — traveling through the South in 1959 are brought together by unlikely circumstances in this tense story. (Rev: BL 7/11; SLJ 9/1/11)

11323 Adler, David A. *Don't Talk to Me About the War* (4–7). 2008, Viking $15.99 (978-0-670-06307-9). Tommy tries hard to ignore the problems overseas and at home in this novel set in the Bronx in 1940. (Rev: BL 4/15/08; SLJ 3/08)

11324 Armstrong, Alan. *Racing the Moon* (5–8). Illus. by Tim Jessell. 2012, Random House $16.99 (978-0-375-85889-5); LB $19.99 (978-0-375-95889-2). 212pp. In 1947 Alex, 11, and her older brother are excited when they meet a real scientist who shares their passion for space. e Lexile 780L (Rev: BL 6/12; LMC 10/12; SLJ 8/1/12)

11325 Avi. *Who Was That Masked Man, Anyway?* (5–7). 1992, Orchard LB $17.99 (978-0-531-08607-0). In a story told through dialogue, 6th-grader Frankie lives through World War II by immersing himself in his beloved radio serials. (Rev: BCCB 10/92*; BL 8/92*; HB 3–4/93; SLJ 10/92*)

11326 Bernier-Grand, Carmen T. *In the Shade of the Nispero Tree* (4–7). 1999, Orchard LB $16.99 (978-0-531-33154-5). Prejudice and racism separate two friends in this story set in Ponce, Puerto Rico, during 1961. (Rev: BCCB 3/99; BL 4/1/99; HBG 10/99; SLJ 3/99)

11327 Bishop, Claire Huchet. *Twenty and Ten* (4–6). Illus. by William Pene du Bois. 1984, Peter Smith $21.25 (978-0-8446-6168-1); Puffin paper $5.99 (978-0-14-031076-4). A nun and 20 French children hide ten young refugees from the Nazis.

11328 Blake, Stephanie J. *The Marble Queen* (4–6). 2013, Amazon Children's $16.99 (978-076146227-9). 192pp. In 1959 Freedom Jane McKenzie bucks tradition and is determined to beat the boys to become Marble Queen. (Rev: BL 10/15/12; LMC 5–6/13; SLJ 1/13)

11329 Blume, Lesley M. M. *The Rising Star of Rusty Nail* (4–6). 2007, Knopf $15.99 (978-0-375-83524-7). 288pp. Set in a small Minnesota town in 1953, this is the story of Franny, a musically talented 10-year-old who tries to get a Russian immigrant (suspected of being a Communist spy) to become her piano teacher. (Rev: BL 6/1–15/07*; LMC 10/07; SLJ 7/07)

11330 Borden, Louise. *Across the Blue Pacific* (3–5). Illus. by Robert Andrew Parker. 2006, Houghton $17.00 (978-0-618-33922-8). 48pp. In this poignant fictional memoir, a woman recalls her concern as a fourth grader for the welfare of a neighbor who served on a submarine in the Pacific during World War II; watercolor paintings evoke the mood and time period. (Rev: BCCB 6/06; BL 4/1/06*; HB 5/06; HBG 10/06; LMC 1/07; SLJ 5/06)

11331 Brandeis, Gayle. *My Life with the Lincolns* (5–7). 2010, Henry Holt $16.99 (978-0-8050-9013-0). 256pp. In the summer of 1966, intelligent 12-year-old Mina Edelmann believes that she is the reincarnation of one of Abraham Lincoln's sons as she learns about racism and watches the civil rights movement. ∩ e Lexile 840L (Rev: BL 2/15/10; LMC 5–6/10; SLJ 3/10)

11332 Bryant, Jen. *Kaleidoscope Eyes* (5–7). 2009, Knopf $15.99 (978-0-375-84048-7). 272pp. In 1968 New Jersey, 13-year-old Lyza and her friends search for buried treasure; a compelling free-verse novel that conveys the tensions of the time. (Rev: BL 4/15/09; LMC 8/09; SLJ 6/09; VOYA 6/09)

11333 Buckey, Sarah Masters. *The Light in the Cellar* (3–6). 2007, Pleasant $10.95 (978-1-59369-159-2); paper $6.95 (978-1-59369-158-5). 158pp. Set in the United States during World War II, this story follows Molly and her friend, Emily, as they try to solve the mystery of the disappearance of the town's sugar, which is prized because of rationing (includes historical background information and photographs at the end). (Rev: BL 5/1/07; SLJ 5/07)

11334 Casanova, Mary. *The Klipfish Code* (4–7). 2007, Houghton Mifflin $16.00 (978-0-618-88393-6). Marit and her brother Lars struggle under the restrictions of Nazi-occupied Norway in this action- and suspense-filled novel. (Rev: BL 10/15/07; SLJ 10/07)

11335 Celenza, Harwell. *Duke Ellington's Nutcracker Suite* (2–5). Illus. by Don Tate. 2011, Charlesbridge $19.95 (978-1-57091-700-4). 32pp. A fascinating, fictionalized account of Duke Ellington's re-creation of Tchaikovsky's Nutcracker Suite with Billy Strayhorn; includes CD. (Rev: BL 11/1/11; SLJ 11/1/11)

11336 Cheng, Andrea. *Eclipse* (5–8). 2006, Front St $16.95 (978-1-932425-21-5). In 1952 Cincinnati, 8-year-old immigrant Peti is disappointed when his relatives arrive to live with them; his cousin is a bully and his mother still worries about her father, who cannot get out of Hungary. (Rev: BL 11/1/06)

11337 Coerr, Eleanor. *Mieko and the Fifth Treasure* (4–7). 2003, Puffin paper $5.99 (978-0-698-11990-1). A Japanese girl believes that she will never draw again after she is injured during the atomic bomb attack on Nagasaki. (Rev: BCCB 4/93; BL 4/1/93*; SLJ 7/93)

11338 Coleman, Evelyn. *Freedom Train* (5–8). 2008, Simon & Schuster $15.99 (978-1-4169-5211-4). Clyde, who comes from a poor white family, stands up for himself by refusing to join his father in harassing a black family in this story set in 1947 Atlanta. (Rev: BL 2/1/08)

11339 Conkling, Winifred. *Sylvia and Aki* (4–6). 2011, Tricycle $16.99 (978-1-58246-337-7); LB $19.99 (978-1-58246-438-1). 160pp. Two parallel narratives set in the 1940s follow the lives of Sylvia Mendez, a Mexican American girl whose father sues Orange County, California, in hopes of getting his daughter into school there, and of Aki, a Japanese American girl who misses her home when her family is moved to an internment camp in Arizona. e (Rev: BLO 11/15/11; SLJ 6/11)

11340 Copeland, Cynthia. *Elin's Island* (5–7). 2003, Millbrook LB $22.90 (978-0-7613-2522-2). Raised since infancy by lighthouse keepers, 13-year-old Elin is left on her own to tend the house and light on an eventful night in 1941. (Rev: BL 3/15/03; HBG 10/03; SLJ 7/03)

11341 Couloumbis, Audrey, and Akila Couloumbis. *War Games: A Novel Based on a True Story* (4–7). 2009, Random House $16.99 (978-0-375-85628-0); LB $19.99 (978-0-375-95628-7). 240pp. In Greece in 1941, adventuresome Petros and his family must hide their ties to America when a Nazi commandant comes to live at their house. e Lexile 710L (Rev: BL 10/1/09; HB 11–12/09; LMC 11–12/09; SLJ 10/09)

11342 Crum, Shutta. *Spitting Image* (5–8). 2003, Clarion $15.00 (978-0-618-23477-6). Jessie has a busy summer in 1967 in her Kentucky hometown, tackling family problems and dealing with well-meaning volunteers and reporters who view them as "rural poor." (Rev: BL 3/1/03; HBG 10/03; SLJ 4/03*)

11343 Deedy, Carmen A. *The Yellow Star: The Legend of King Christian X of Denmark* (3–5). 2000, Peachtree $16.95 (978-1-56145-208-8). Although in real life it did not happen, this picture book tells how the King of Denmark wore a Jewish star in World War II to show Hitler that in his country there are only Danes. (Rev: BCCB 11/00; BL 7/00; HBG 3/01; SLJ 9/00)

11344 Dowell, Frances O'Roark. *Shooting the Moon* (4–8). 2008, Atheneum $16.99 (978-1-4169-2690-0). Jamie is surprised when her military father is not pleased about her big brother volunteering to go to Vietnam, until TJ sends home increasingly disturbing photographs of the war. Boston Globe–Horn Book Honor. (Rev: BL 3/15/08; SLJ 5/08)

11345 Elmer, Robert. *Into the Flames* (5–7). Series: Young Underground. 1995, Bethany House paper $5.99 (978-1-55661-376-0). Danish twins are captured by the Gestapo while trying to rescue their uncle during World War II. (Rev: BL 5/15/95; SLJ 8/95)

11346 Erskine, Kathryn. *Seeing Red* (5–8). 2013, Scholastic $16.99 (978-054546440-6). 352pp. It's 1972 and 12-year-old Red Porter's life is changing, and fast: his father has died, his mother wants to move away from Virginia and the only town Red's ever known; in his efforts to stop this move Red learns about his family's history and about racism and injustice. ∩ e Lexile 750 (Rev: BL 9/15/13*; HB 9–10/13; LMC 3–4/14; SLJ 10/13; VOYA 8/13)

11347 Fawcett, Katie Pickard. *To Come and Go Like Magic* (5–8). 2010, Knopf $15.99 (978-0-375-85846-8); LB $18.99 (978-0-375-95846-5). 256pp. A new teacher nurtures 12-year-old Chili Sue Mahoney's desire to leave the depressed town of Mercy Hill, in the Appalachian hills of Kentucky; set in the 1970s. e (Rev: BL 3/1/10; SLJ 2/10; VOYA 4/10)

11348 Ferrari, Michael. *Born to Fly* (4–6). 2009, Delacorte $15.99 (978-0-385-73715-9). 224pp. On Bird's 11th birthday the Japanese attack Pearl Harbor and her whole life changes; her pilot father joins the Air Force

and her friendship with a Japanese American boy named Kenji brings new complications in this action-packed novel. (Rev: BL 5/15/09; SLJ 9/09)

11349 Fitzmaurice, Kathryn. *A Diamond in the Desert* (5–8). 2012, Viking $16.99 (978-067001292-3). 256pp. A young boy at a Japanese internment camp in 1942 gets so caught up in building a baseball diamond that he abandons his younger sister, which has serious consequences. (Rev: BL 3/15/12; LMC 8–9/12; SLJ 2/12)

11350 Fixmer, Elizabeth. *Saint Training* (5–7). 2010, Zondervan $14.99 (978-0-310-72018-8). 256pp. In the turbulent 1960s, 6th-grader Mary Clare is the oldest in a large Catholic family and decides that sainthood will be her — and her family's — salvation. e (Rev: BL 11/15/10; SLJ 11/1/10)

11351 Flood, Pansie Hart. *Sylvia and Miz Lula Maye* (3–5). Illus. by Felicia Marshall. 2002, Carolrhoda $15.95 (978-0-87614-204-2). 120pp. A 10-year-old African American girl and her 100-year-old neighbor form an unlikely friendship in this novel set in 1970s South Carolina. (Rev: BL 2/15/02; HBG 10/02; SLJ 4/02)

11352 Flores-Galbis, Enrique. *90 Miles to Havana* (5–8). 2010, Roaring Brook $16.99 (978-1-59643-168-3). 304pp. A fictionalized account of the author's experience of coming to America from Cuba in the 1960s, when he was separated from his parents and placed in a camp in Miami. Belpré Honor 2011; ALA Notable Children's Book 2011. Lexile 790L (Rev: BL 5/1/10; LMC 8–9/10; SLJ 8/10; VOYA 12/10)

11353 Gantos, Jack. *Dead End in Norvelt* (5–8). 2011, Farrar $15.99 (978-0-374-37993-3). 352pp. Grounded for the entire summer, spirited Jack, 11, finds himself helping to write obituaries and coping with small-town life full of eccentric people in this funny and thoughtful story set in 1962. Newbery Medal 2012; ALA Notable Children's Book 2012. ∩ e Lexile 920L (Rev: BL 8/11; HB 9–10/11; LMC 11–12/11; SLJ 9/1/11)

11354 Geisert, Bonnie. *Prairie Winter* (3–6). 2009, Houghton Mifflin $16 (978-0-618-68588-2). 224pp. A fierce winter on the Great Plains in the 1950s means that 6th-grader Rachel and her sisters can move into town and attend school without interruption, a change that is both thrilling and worrying. e Lexile 720L (Rev: BL 11/1/09; SLJ 1/10; VOYA 12/09)

11355 Giff, Patricia Reilly. *Gingersnap* (4–6). 2013, Random House $15.99 (978-037583891-0); LB $18.99 (978-037593891-7). 160pp. When her brother Rob is reported as missing in action in World War II, 11-year-old Jayna sets out for Brooklyn with her pet turtle in hope of finding her grandmother; a ghost appears to guide her. ∩ e Lexile 540L (Rev: BL 12/15/12; HB 1–2/13; LMC 8–9/13*; SLJ 2/13)

11356 Giff, Patricia Reilly. *Lily's Crossing* (5–8). 1997, Delacorte $15.95 (978-0-385-32142-6). During World War II, motherless Lily loses her father when he is sent to fight in France but becomes friendly with Albert, an orphaned Hungarian refugee. (Rev: BCCB 4/97; BL 2/1/97; HB 3–4/97; SLJ 2/97)

11357 Giff, Patricia Reilly. *Willow Run* (4–6). 2005, Random $15.95 (978-0-385-73067-9). 176pp. Life changes dramatically for 11-year-old Meggie Dillon when her immediate family moves to Michigan so that her father can work in a airplane factory in World War II. (Rev: BCCB 12/05; BL 7/05*; HB 9/05; HBG 4/06; LMC 1/06; SLJ 9/05; VOYA 2/06) ∩

11358 Glatshteyn, Yankev. *Emil and Karl* (5–8). Ed. by Jeffrey Shandler. 2006, Roaring Brook $16.95 (978-1-59643-119-5). Two 9-year-old friends — one Jewish, one Aryan — try to elude the Nazis on the streets of Vienna shortly after Germany's invasion; a fast-paced, moving story initially published in 1940. (Rev: BL 4/15/06; SLJ 6/06*; VOYA 4/06)

11359 Going, K. L. *The Liberation of Gabriel King* (4–6). 2005, Penguin $15.99 (978-0-399-23991-5). 160pp. Ten-year-old Gabriel, a small and fearful white boy in 1976 Georgia, and his assertive African American friend Frita agree to tackle Gabe's (and her) fears and find themselves strong enough to withstand racist attacks. (Rev: BL 5/15/05; SLJ 6/05)

11360 Graff, Nancy Price. *Taking Wing* (5–8). 2005, Clarion $15.00 (978-0-618-53591-0). A multilayered story set in 1942 Vermont and featuring 13-year-old Gus, who, over the course of the book, learns about prejudice, and about killing and death. (Rev: BL 5/15/05*; SLJ 5/05)

11361 Griffis, Molly Levite. *The Feester Filibuster* (4–8). 2002, Eakin $17.95 (978-1-57168-541-4); paper $8.95 (978-1-57168-694-7). John Allen Feester is determined to show he's not a spy in this sequel to *The Rachel Resistance* (2001). (Rev: BL 11/1/02; HBG 10/01)

11362 Gwaltney, Doris. *Homefront* (5–8). 2006, Simon & Schuster $15.95 (978-0-689-86842-9). A young girl must cope with the diverse effects of World War II on her Virginia farming family. (Rev: BCCB 10/06; BL 7/06; SLJ 7/06*)

11363 Hahn, Mary Downing. *Stepping on the Cracks* (5–8). 1991, Houghton Mifflin $16.00 (978-0-395-58507-8); paper $5.99 (978-0-380-71900-6). The compelling story of a 6th-grade girl during World War II and her difficult decision whether to help a pacifist deserter. (Rev: BCCB 12/91*; BL 10/15/91*; HB 11–12/91; SLJ 12/91*)

11364 Harrar, George. *The Wonder Kid* (4–7). Illus. by Anthony Winiarski. 2006, Houghton Mifflin $16.00 (978-0-618-56317-3). As a kid growing up in the 1950s, Jesse contracts polio and with the encouragement of a friend passes the time creating a comic strip hero called the Wonder Kid. (Rev: SLJ 3/07)

11365 Haworth, Danette. *Me and Jack* (3–6). 2011, Walker $16.99 (978-0-8027-9453-6). 240pp. When 6th-grader Josh and his Air Force recruiter father move to the Pennsylvania mountains, the boy must defend his newly acquired and much loved dog from accusations by the hostile local residents; set during the Vietnam War. (Rev: BL 4/1/5/11; SLJ 5/11)

11366 Hemphill, Helen. *Runaround* (5–8). 2007, Front St $16.95 (978-1-932425-83-3). In 1960s Kentucky, motherless 11-year-old Sassy needs more information about love but has trouble finding a source as her Dad is busy with other things, her housekeeper wants her just to act like a young lady, and her sister may be involved with the same handsome neighbor. (Rev: BL 3/1/07*; SLJ 4/07)

11367 Herman, Charlotte. *My Chocolate Year: A Novel with 12 Recipes to Make Your World a Little Sweeter* (3–5). Illus. by LeUyen Pham. 2008, Simon & Schuster $15.99 (978-1-4169-3341-0). 176pp. This portrait of a Jewish family in post-World War II Chicago features Dorrie, a 5th-grader with culinary ambitions and worries about relatives abroad; recipes are sprinkled throughout. (Rev: BLO 7/29/08; SLJ 2/08)

11368 Herrera, Juan Felipe. *Downtown Boy* (5–8). 2005, Scholastic $16.99 (978-0-439-64489-1). This poignant free-verse novel, narrated by 10-year-old Juanito, offers an unflinching look at what life was like for Chicano migrant workers and their families in 1950s California. (Rev: BL 12/15/05; SLJ 1/06; VOYA 4/06)

11369 Hinton, Nigel. *Time Bomb* (5–8). 2006, Tricycle $15.95 (978-1-58246-186-1). Coming of age in post-World War II London, four 12-year-old friends who have lost their trust in adults discover an unexploded German bomb and set in motion a chain of events. (Rev: SLJ 12/06)

11370 Hoestlandt, Jo. *Star of Fear, Star of Hope* (2–4). Trans. by Mark Polizzotti. Illus. by Johanna Kang. 1995, Walker LB $16.85 (978-0-8027-8374-5). 32pp. In World War II–occupied France, Helen witnesses the growing persecution of her Jewish friend Lydia. (Rev: BCCB 6/95; BL 5/1/95; HB 9/95; SLJ 8/95)

11371 Holm, Jennifer L. *Penny from Heaven* (5–8). 2006, Random House $15.95 (978-0-375-83687-9). Set in 1953, this is the story of how 12-year-old Penny gets to know her late father's lively Italian American family and comes to understand the circumstances surrounding her father's death. Newbery Honor 2007. (Rev: BL 4/15/06; HB 3–4/07; SLJ 7/06)

11372 Hoobler, Dorothy, and Thomas Hoobler. *The 1940s: Secrets* (3–6). Illus. Series: Century Kids. 2001, Millbrook LB $22.90 (978-0-7613-1604-6). 176pp. The story of various branches of the Aldrich family and their contributions to the home front during World War II. (Rev: BL 4/1/01; HBG 10/01; SLJ 5/01)

11373 Hostetter, Joyce Moyer. *Blue* (4–7). 2006, Boyds Mills $16.95 (978-1-59078-389-4). When her father leaves for World War II, Ann Fay, the oldest of four children, struggles to keep up with the chores in their North Carolina home until polio strikes the community. (Rev: BL 2/15/06; SLJ 6/06)

11374 Jones, Traci L. *Finding My Place* (5–8). 2010, Farrar $16.99 (978-0-374-33573-1). 208pp. In mid-1970s Denver, Tiphanie starts her freshman year as the only black girl in her school and discovers that there are other outsiders. **e** Lexile 750L (Rev: BL 4/15/10; LMC 8–9/10; SLJ 6/10)

11375 Judge, Lita. *One Thousand Tracings: Healing the Wounds of World War II* (3–6). Illus. by author. 2007, Hyperion $15.99 (978-1-4231-0008-9). 40pp. Set in postwar America, this is a beautifully illustrated story of a little girl in the Midwest who helps her mother prepare care packages to be sent to Europeans who lack many basic necessities, including clothing and shoes. (Rev: BL 5/15/07; SLJ 7/07)

11376 Kacer, Kathy. *The Night Spies* (4–7). 2003, Second Story paper $5.95 (978-1-896764-70-2). Hiding from the Nazis, Gabi and her family can leave their cramped quarters only at night, but Gabi and her cousin Max manage to help the partisans. (Rev: BL 1/1–15/04; SLJ 3/04)

11377 Kadohata, Cynthia. *Weedflower* (5–8). 2006, Simon & Schuster $16.95 (978-0-689-86574-9). Sumiko and her Japanese American family are moved from their California flower farm to an internment camp in Arizona after the attack on Pearl Harbor; there she grows a garden and befriends a local Mojave boy. ∩ (Rev: BL 4/15/06*; HB 7–8/06; SLJ 7/06*)

11378 Kerley, Barbara. *Greetings from Planet Earth* (4–6). 2007, Scholastic $16.99 (978-0-439-80203-1). In 1977, as he considers a class project on space exploration, 12-year-old Theo is more preoccupied with family questions — why can he never discuss his father, who never returned from Vietnam? (Rev: BL 4/15/07)

11379 Kinsey-Warnock, Natalie. *True Colors* (4–6). 2012, Knopf $15.99 (978-0-375-86099-7). 256pp. In early 1950s Vermont during a community celebration, 10-year-old Blue sets out to find the mother who abandoned her as a baby. **e** Lexile 890L (Rev: BL 12/1/12; LMC 3–4/13*; SLJ 11/12)

11380 Klages, Ellen. *The Green Glass Sea* (4–7). 2006, Viking $16.99 (978-0-670-06134-1). In 1943, talented 10-year-old Dewey goes to live with her father at the Los Alamos compound, a tense place where she initially has trouble making friends. ∩ (Rev: BL 11/15/06; SLJ 11/06)

11381 Klages, Ellen. *White Sands, Red Menace* (5–8). 2008, Viking $16.99 (978-0-670-06235-5). In this riveting sequel to *The Green Glass Sea* (2006), Dewey's father has died and she is living near Los Alamos with her friend Suze, whose father is working on a new rocket for the space race. (Rev: BL 8/08)

11382 Kochenderfer, Lee. *The Victory Garden* (4–6). 2002, Delacorte $14.95 (978-0-385-32788-6). 166pp. Eleven-year-old Teresa writes to her pilot brother and helps her father tend a victory garden in this tale set in Kansas in 1943. (Rev: BCCB 3/02; BL 3/1/02; HBG 10/02; SLJ 1/02)

11383 Kogawa, Joy. *Naomi's Tree* (3–5). Illus. by Ruth Ohi. 2009, Fitzhenry & Whiteside $19.95 (978-1-55455-055-5). 32pp. Interned in Canada during World War II, Naomi clings to memories of the cherry tree planted by her Japanese grandparents, and of her mother who cannot return from Japan. (Rev: BL 5/1/09)

11384 Lai, Thanhha. *Inside Out and Back Again* (4–7). 2011, HarperCollins $15.99 (978-0-06-196278-3). Based on the author's own childhood experiences, this novel in verse tells the story of 10-year-old Hà and her journey with her mother and brothers from Vietnam to rural Alabama, where she faces many challenges. ALSC Notable Children's Book; National Book Award for Young People's Literature; Newbery Honor Book. **e** Lexile 800L (Rev: BL 1/1–15/11*; HB 3–4/11; SLJ 3/1/11*)

11385 Larson, Kirby. *Duke* (3–6). 2013, Scholastic $16.99 (978-054541637-5). 240pp. In 1944 everyone in Hobie Hanson's family is working for the war effort — except 11-year-old Hobie, who feels like he has more to give and decides to lend his German shepherd, Duke, to Dogs for Defense, a decision he soon regrets. **e** (Rev: BL 11/1/13; HB 9–10/13; LMC 1–2/14*; SLJ 10/13) [540]

11386 Larson, Kirby. *The Fences Between Us: The Diary of Piper Davis* (4–7). Series: Dear America. 2010, Scholastic $12.99 (978-0-545-22418-5); LB $16.99 (978-0-545-26232-3). 317pp. Thirteen-year-old Piper describes in her diary the many changes that take place in her life starting in December 1941. (Rev: BL 7/10; SLJ 12/1/10; VOYA 10/10)

11387 Lawrence, Iain. *Gemini Summer* (4–7). 2006, Delacorte $15.95 (978-0-385-73089-1). In the mid-1960s, soon after Danny's brother Beau dies in an accident, a stray dog appears and adopts Danny; Danny becomes devoted to the dog and, because he sees much of Beau in Rocket, he and Rocket set off for Cape Canaveral to realize Beau's dream of seeing the Gemini mission. (Rev: BL 12/15/06; SLJ 11/06)

11388 Lemna, Don. *Out in Left Field* (4–7). Illus. by Matt Collins. 2012, Holiday House $16.95 (978-082342313-2). 224pp. Eleven-year-old Donald has a miserable time in 1947 and into 1948, starting with a humiliating flop in baseball and continuing through other misadventures in this funny sequel to *When the Sergeant Came Marching Home* (2008). (Rev: BL 4/1/12; SLJ 6/12)

11389 Lemna, Don. *When the Sergeant Came Marching Home* (4–7). Illus. by Matt Colins. 2008, Holiday $16.95 (978-0-8234-2083-4). Set in the 1940s, this novel of a family that moves to a farm in Montana paints a realistic picture of the hardships and joys of rural life at that time. (Rev: BL 4/15/08; SLJ 7/08)

11390 Levine, Ellen. *Catch a Tiger by the Toe* (5–8). 2005, Viking $15.99 (978-0-670-88461-2). Jamie's world is turned upside down when her father is put in jail for refusing to reveal the names of other Communists to the House Un-American Activities Committee. (Rev: BL 3/15/05*; SLJ 6/05)

11391 Levine, Kristin. *The Lions of Little Rock* (5–8). 2012, Putnam $16.99 (978-039925644-8). 304pp. In 1958 Little Rock, Arkansas, 12-year-old Marlee, who is already struggling with acute shyness, must deal with the fact that her best friend is thrown out of school because she is a light-skinned black. ∩ (Rev: BL 1/1/12; SLJ 1/12)

11392 Levitin, Sonia. *Journey to America* (5–8). Illus. by Charles Robinson. 1970, Macmillan paper $4.99 (978-0-689-71130-5). A Jewish mother and her three daughters flee Nazi Germany in 1938 and undertake a long and difficult journey to join their father in America. (Rev: BL 9/1/93)

11393 Lieurance, Suzanne. *The Lucky Baseball: My Story in a Japanese-American Internment Camp* (3–6). Series: Historical Fiction Adventures. 2009, Enslow LB $27.93 (978-0-7660-3311-5). 160pp. Twelve-year-old Harry Yakamoto relies on baseball to sustain him through the hardship of his family's internment camp experience in the early 1940s. (Rev: BL 9/1/09; SLJ 1/10)

11394 Lord, Bette Bao. *In the Year of the Boar and Jackie Robinson* (4–6). Illus. by Marc Simont. 1984, Harper-Collins paper $5.99 (978-0-06-440175-3). 176pp. The story of a Chinese girl who leaves China to join her father in New York in 1947.

11395 Lowry, Lois. *Number the Stars* (5–7). 1989, Houghton Mifflin $16.00 (978-0-395-51060-5); paper $5.99 (978-0-440-40327-2). The story of war-torn Denmark and best friends Annemarie Johansen and Ellen Rosen. Newbery Medal 1990. (Rev: BCCB 3/89; BL 3/1/89; SLJ 3/89)

11396 McDowell, Marilyn Taylor. *Carolina Harmony* (4–7). 2009, Delacorte $16.99 (978-0-385-73590-2). 336pp. In 1964 in the Blue Ridge Mountains 10-year-old runaway orphan Carolina begins to recover from the traumas she has experienced. (Rev: BL 2/1/09; SLJ 8/09)

11397 McKissack, Patricia C. *Abby Takes a Stand* (2–4). Illus. by Gordon C. James. Series: Scraps of Time. 2005, Viking $14.99 (978-0-670-06011-5). 112pp. Grandma Gee, an African American, tells her granddaughters about her humiliation when refused entry to a department store restaurant in 1960 and about her efforts to support the civil rights movement. (Rev: BL 5/15/05)

11398 McKissack, Patricia C. *Away West* (3–6). Illus. by Gordon C. James. Series: Scraps of Time. 2006, Viking $14.99 (978-0-670-06012-2). 112pp. In this second volume in the series, the Webster children learn the story of Everett Turner, who works in a livery stable after the Civil War and dreams of living in the African American town of Nicodemus, Kansas. (Rev: BL 4/15/06; SLJ 5/06)

11399 McMullan, Margaret. *Sources of Light* (5–8). 2010, Houghton Mifflin $16 (978-054707659-1). 240pp. A young African American girl copes with racial tensions when her mother moves the family from Pennsylvania to Jackson, Mississippi, after her father's death in Vietnam in 1962. **e** Lexile 840L (Rev: BL 4/15/10; HB 5–6/10; SLJ 5/10; VOYA 8/10)

11400 McSwigan, Marie. *Snow Treasure* (4–7). Illus. by Andre Le Blanc. 1986, Scholastic paper $4.99 (978-0-590-42537-7). Children smuggle gold out of occupied Norway on their sleds.

11401 Madden, Kerry. *Gentle's Holler* (5–8). Series: Maggie Valley. 2005, Viking $16.99 (978-0-670-05998-0). Livy Two, part of a large, poor family living in the North Carolina mountains, learns a lesson when her father is injured. (Rev: BL 3/1/05; SLJ 6/05)

11402 Madden, Kerry. *Jessie's Mountain* (5–8). Series: Maggie Valley. 2008, Viking $16.99 (978-0-670-06154-9). Livy Two and her family are still struggling to make it in this final installment in the series, but they start to turn things around using their love of music. (Rev: BL 2/8/08; SLJ 3/08)

11403 Madden, Kerry. *Louisiana's Song* (5–8). Series: Maggie Valley. 2007, Viking $16.99 (978-0-670-06153-2). Their father is home from the hospital but cannot work, so Livy Two and her nine siblings do everything they can to support their family in this sequel to *Gentle's Holler* (2005) set in North Carolina in 1963. (Rev: BL 6/1–15/07; SLJ 8/07)

11404 Maguire, Gregory. *The Good Liar* (4–6). 1999, Clarion $15.00 (978-0-395-90697-2). 129pp. A first-person novel about a boy growing up in occupied France during World War II and the deception involved when his parents hide a Jewish woman and her daughter. (Rev: BCCB 3/99; BL 4/15/99*; HB 7/99; HBG 10/99; SLJ 5/99)

11405 Martin, Ann M. *The Long Way Home* (5–7). Series: Family Tree. 2013, Scholastic $16.99 (978-054535943-6). 224pp. This second volume in the family epic spans the years from 1955 to 1971 and focuses on identical twins Dana and Julia and the effect on their lives when their father dies. ∩ **e** Lexile 780 (Rev: BL 10/1/13; HB 11–12/13; SLJ 12/13)

11406 Mathews, Ellie. *The Linden Tree* (4–6). 2007, Milkweed $16.95 (978-1-57131-673-8); paper $6.95 (978-1-57131-674-5). 170pp. After her mother's sudden death, 9-year-old Katy Sue must cope with her grief, added responsibilities on the family farm, and the arrival of her mother's sister, Aunt Katherine. (Rev: BCCB 9/07; BL 5/1/07; LMC 10/07; SLJ 9/07)

11407 Matti, Truus. *Mister Orange* (4–6). Trans. by Laura Watkinson. Illus. by Jenni Desmond. 2013, Enchanted Lion $16.95 (978-159270123-0). 164pp. In 1943, when his brother Albie goes off to war, Linus takes over his job as a delivery boy and finds himself befriending a man he calls Mr. Orange — a character based on the painter Mondrian. ALA Notable Children's Book; Mildred L. Batchelder Award; USBBY Outstanding International Book. (Rev: BL 1/13*; SLJ 1/13)

11408 Mercer, Peggy. *There Come a Soldier* (2–4). Illus. by Ron Mazellan. 2007, Handprint $17.95 (978-1-59354-192-7). 40pp. Memories of his youth on a Georgia farm sustain a World War II paratrooper in this picture-book story based on her father's experiences. (Rev: BL 11/15/07; SLJ 11/07)

11409 Morpurgo, Michael. *The Amazing Story of Adolphus Tips* (4–7). 2006, Scholastic $16.99 (978-0-439-79661-3). This is the story of Lily, a 12-year-old British girl who struggles with anger as her father is sent to war in 1943 and her family is relocated to make room for

Allied rehearsals of the Normandy invasion. (Rev: BL 4/15/06; SLJ 8/06)

11410 Moses, Shelia P. *Sallie Gal and the Wall-a-kee Man* (2–4). Illus. by Niki Daly. 2007, Scholastic $15.99 (978-0-439-90890-0). 152pp. African American Sallie Mae, almost 9, lives in a hardscrabble sharecropping community in North Carolina in the 1970s and longs to have new hair ribbons. (Rev: BCCB 2/08; BL 10/1/07; HB 9/07; LMC 1/08; SLJ 9/07)

11411 Myers, Walter Dean. *The Journal of Scott Pendleton Collins: A World War II Soldier* (5–9). Series: My Name Is America. 1999, Scholastic paper $10.95 (978-0-439-05013-5). Through a series of letters, readers get to know 17-year-old Collins, an American soldier who participates in the D-Day invasion of Europe. (Rev: BL 6/1–15/99; HBG 10/99; SLJ 7/99)

11412 Napoli, Donna Jo. *Fire in the Hills* (5–8). 2006, Dutton $16.99 (978-0-525-47751-8). In this fact-based sequel to *Stones in Water* (1997), 14-year-old Roberto returns to Italy after escaping from a Nazi prison camp and joins the resistance movement. (Rev: BL 9/1/06; SLJ 9/06)

11413 Nemeth, Sally. *The Heights, the Depths, and Everything in Between* (5–8). 2006, Knopf LB $17.99 (978-0-375-93458-2). Jake Little, a dwarf, and Lucy Small, who despite her name is unusually tall, become friends and navigate the rough waters of middle school and dealing with parents in this story set in the 1970s. (Rev: BL 7/06)

11414 Newbery, Linda. *At the Firefly Gate* (5–8). 2007, Random House $15.99 (978-0-385-75113-1). Henry befriends a neighbor who was once engaged to another Henry, a Royal Air Force pilot who failed to return from a mission in World War II. When Henry begins to see a mysterious figure at his gate and reenacts the pilot's final flight on a simulator, the war seems not so long ago. (Rev: BCCB 4/07; BL 2/15/07; HB 3–4/07; SLJ 3/07)

11415 Noe, Katherine Schlick. *Something to Hold* (4–7). 2011, Clarion $16.99 (978-0-547-55813-4). 256pp. In the early 1960s Kitty, 11, contends with being one of few white children on an Indian reservation, struggling to make friends while learning about discrimination; includes a map, author's note, glossary, and pronunciation guide. (Rev: BL 10/1/11; SLJ 11/1/11)

11416 O'Connor, Sheila. *Keeping Safe the Stars* (5–7). 2012, Putnam $16.99 (978-0-399-25459-8). 304pp. In rural Minnesota in 1974, 13-year-old Pride must look after her younger sister and brother when their grandfather is hospitalized. ℮ Lexile HL650L (Rev: BL 10/15/12; LMC 3–4/13; SLJ 12/12)

11417 Parker, Marjorie Hodgson. *David and the Mighty Eighth* (4–7). Illus. by Mark Postlethwaite. 2007, Bright Sky $17.95 (978-1-931721-93-6). David is sent to stay on his grandparents' farm in rural England and there befriends an American soldier stationed with the U.S. Eighth Air Force in this novel set in 1944. (Rev: BL 12/15/07)

11418 Parkhurst, Liz. *Under One Flag: A Year at Rohwer* (3–5). Illus. by Tom Clifton. 2005, August House $16.95 (978-0-87483-759-9). 32pp. A young Japanese American intern and the son of the camp administrator become friends during World War II. (Rev: BL 5/15/05; SLJ 4/05)

11419 Pausewang, Gudrun. *Dark Hours* (5–8). Trans. from German by John Brownjohn. 2006, Annick $21.95 (978-1-55451-042-9). In Germany during the closing days of World War II, Gisela and her younger siblings become trapped in an air raid shelter after being separated from their mother and grandmother. (Rev: BL 11/1/06; SLJ 2/07)

11420 Pearsall, Shelley. *Jump into the Sky* (5–8). 2012, Knopf $16.99 (978-0-375-83699-2); LB $19.99 (978-0-375-93699-9). 352pp. Levi, a 13-year-old African American, leaves Chicago to join his father in North Carolina in 1945, only to find that his paratrooper father has just shipped out and Levi must face southern bigotry alone. Booklist Editors' Choice: Books for Youth. ∩ ℮ Lexile 940L (Rev: BL 9/15/12*; LMC 1–2/13*; SLJ 9/12; VOYA 10/12)

11421 Peck, Richard. *On the Wings of Heroes* (4–6). 2007, Dial $16.99 (978-0-8037-3081-6). 148pp. Life before and during World War II is presented from the perspective of Davy Bowman, who lives in small-town America and has an older brother in the Air Force. (Rev: BL 12/1/06; SLJ 4/07*; VOYA 4/07)

11422 Peck, Richard. *A Season of Gifts* (5–8). 2009, Dial $16.99 (978-0-8037-3082-3). 176pp. Spunky, rifle-toting Grandma Dowdel, last seen in *A Long Way from Chicago* (1998) and *A Year Down Yonder* (2000), intervenes in the life of a weak-kneed preacher's son in this tale of neighborly kindness set in 1958 small-town Illinois. ∩ Lexile 690L (Rev: BL 8/09*; HB 9–10/09; SLJ 10/09; VOYA 12/09)

11423 Pérez, L. King. *Remember as You Pass Me By* (5–8). 2007, Milkweed $16.95 (978-1-57131-677-6); paper $6.95 (978-1-57131-678-3). In 1950s Texas racial tensions come between 12-year-old Silvy Lane and her black friend Mabelee. (Rev: LMC 2/08; SLJ 11/07)

11424 Pinkney, Andrea Davis. *With the Might of Angels: The Diary of Dawnie Rae Johnson, Hadley, Virginia, 1954* (5–8). Illus. Series: Dear America. 2011, Scholastic $12.99 (978-0-545-29705-9). 336pp. Dawnie Rae chronicles her life in her diary: she's 12 and has been chosen to integrate an all-white school in her town in 1954 while also facing difficulties at home. ∩ ℮ (Rev: BL 9/1/11; SLJ 9/1/11)

11425 Radin, Ruth Yaffe. *Escape to the Forest: Based on a True Story of the Holocaust* (4–6). Illus. by Janet Hamlin. 2000, HarperCollins LB $13.89 (978-0-06-028521-0). 80pp. A realistic story of a Jewish girl named Sarah and her part in resistance against the Nazis during World War II. (Rev: BCCB 3/00; HBG 10/00; SLJ 3/00)

11426 Ray, Delia. *Singing Hands* (4–7). 2006, Clarion $16.00 (978-0-618-65762-9). Gussie's parents are deaf, which means she can be even more mischievous than the average child in this book set in the 1940s American South. (Rev: BL 5/1/06; SLJ 7/06)

11427 Rodman, Mary Ann. *Jimmy's Stars* (5–8). 2008, Farrar $16.95 (978-0-374-33703-2). Ellie's beloved brother Jimmy's deferments run out and he is sent off to fight in World War II; when news arrives that he has been killed, Ellie finds it almost impossible to believe. (Rev: BL 4/1/08; SLJ 6/08)

11428 Rodman, Mary Ann. *Yankee Girl* (4–8). 2004, Farrar $17.00 (978-0-374-38661-0). In 1964, Alice's family moves from Chicago to Mississippi and 6th-grader Alice must cope not only with the stress of a new school but also with her ambivalence about the only black girl in her class; newspaper headlines introducing each chapter keep the racial violence of the time in the reader's mind. (Rev: BL 3/1/04; SLJ 4/04)

11429 Rogers, Kenny, and Donald Davenport. *Christmas in Canaan* (5–8). 2002, HarperCollins $15.99 (978-0-06-000746-1). In 1960s Texas, after a black boy and a white boy fight on the school bus, the adults decree that the two boys must spend time together, and a difficult start ends in the boys becoming fast friends when they help a wounded dog. (Rev: BL 11/1/02; HBG 3/03; SLJ 10/02; VOYA 4/03)

11430 Salisbury, Graham. *House of the Red Fish* (5–8). 2006, Random House $16.95 (978-0-385-73121-8). After his father is sent to an internment camp, Japanese American teen Tomi rallies the community to help raise his father's sunken fishing boat in this inspiring sequel to *Under the Blood-Red Sun* (2005). (Rev: BL 4/15/06; LMC 10/06; SLJ 8/06)

11431 Say, Allen. *Music for Alice* (4–7). 2004, Houghton Mifflin $17.00 (978-0-618-31118-7). Based on a real story, this is the moving portrait of a Japanese American couple who make the best of the challenges forced upon them during World War II. (Rev: BL 2/1/04; HB 5–6/04; SLJ 4/04)

11432 Scattergood, Augusta. *Glory Be* (3–6). 2012, Scholastic $16.99 (978-054533180-7). 208pp. In 1964, 11-year-old Gloriana faces an obstacle to her usual birthday pool party — desegregation, which has the led the town to close the pool indefinitely. **e** (Rev: BL 1/12; LMC 3–4/12; SLJ 2/12)

11433 Shank, Marilyn Sue. *Child of the Mountains* (4–7). 2012, Delacorte $16.99 (978-038574079-1); LB $19.99 (978-037598969-8). 272pp. In rural Appalachia in 1953, Lydia, 11, confides in her diary as she struggles to come to terms with her brother's death from cystic fibrosis and her mother's stint in jail. **e** (Rev: BL 4/15/12; LMC 8–9/12; SLJ 5/1/12)

11434 Sherman, M. Zachary. *A Time for War* (4–6). Illus. by Fritz Casas. Series: Bloodlines. 2011, Stone Arch LB $23.32 (978-1-4342-2558-0); paper $6.95 (978-1-4342-3097-3). 88pp. In World War II, paratrooper Michael Donovan escapes death and finds he is braver than he thought; nonfiction sections and illustrations add information to the dramatically presented text. (Rev: BL 6/1/11; SLJ 8/11)

11435 Shimko, Bonnie. *The Private Thoughts of Amelia E. Rye* (5–8). 2010, Farrar $16.99 (978-0-374-36131-0). 240pp. Abandoned by her father before birth and feeling unloved by her mother, Amelia finds a friend in Fancy Nelson, a feisty girl who is the first African American in Amelia's class; set in upstate New York in the 1960s. **e** Lexile 790L (Rev: BL 4/15/10*; LMC 5–6/10; SLJ 4/10)

11436 Smiley, Jane. *Gee Whiz* (4–8). Series: Horses of Oak Valley Ranch. 2013, Knopf $16.99 (978-037586969-3); LB $19.99 (978-037596969-0). 272pp. Abby has a lot on her plate: not only is her family housing a champion horse in their stables, but a religious leader's death is bringing changes to her church and her brother is shipping out to Vietnam; the 5th book in the series. **e** Lexile 980 (Rev: BLO 9/15/13; HB 11–12/13; SLJ 12/13; VOYA 2/14)

11437 Smiley, Jane. *The Georges and the Jewels* (4–8). Illus. by Elaine Clayton. 2009, Knopf $16.99 (978-0-375-86227-4); LB $19.99 (978-0-375-96227-1). 256pp. Twelve-year-old Abby cares for her family's horses as a way of escaping isolation, family drama, and her father's strict religious views in 1960s California. **e** Lexile 970L (Rev: BL 9/15/09; HB 11–12/09; SLJ 10/09)

11438 Smith, D. James. *The Boys of San Joaquin* (5–8). 2005, Simon & Schuster $15.95 (978-0-689-87606-6). An episodic tale set in the 1950s, in which 12-year-old Paolo describes events of his life and a mystery involving a half-eaten $20 bill. (Rev: BL 3/1/05; SLJ 1/05)

11439 Smith, D. James. *Probably the World's Best Story About a Dog and the Girl Who Loved Me* (5–8). 2006, Simon & Schuster $15.95 (978-1-4169-0542-4). In 1951 California, 12-year-old Paolo's beloved dog Rufus is dognapped and he enlists the help of his younger brother and a deaf cousin to unravel the mystery while also coping with a new paper route and a budding romance; this sequel to *The Boys of San Joaquin* (2004) introduces a sign language word with each chapter. (Rev: BL 9/1/06; SLJ 8/06)

11440 Smith, Icy. *Mei Ling in China City* (3–5). Illus. by Gayle Garner Roski. 2008, East West Discovery $18.95 (978-0-9701654-8-0). In 1942 Los Angeles, Mei Ling describes life in China City and the family's efforts to raise funds for people back home, and details her efforts to stay in touch with her friend Yayeko, a Japanese friend who has been interned. (Rev: LMC 11/08; SLJ 5/08)

11441 Smith, Roland. *Elephant Run* (5–8). 2007, Hyperion $15.99 (978-1-4231-0402-5). During World War II, 14-year-old Nick is sent to his father's plantation in Burma to escape the London Blitz but ends up running from cruel Japanese occupiers in this suspenseful historical novel. (Rev: BL 2/15/08; SLJ 1/08)

11442 Son, John. *Finding My Hat* (4–8). Series: First Person Fiction. 2003, Scholastic $16.95 (978-0-439-43538-3). Autobiography plays a large part in this frank, often funny novel about the son of Korean immigrants growing up in America in the 1970s and 1980s. (Rev: BL 11/15/03; HBG 4/04; LMC 11–12/03; SLJ 10/03)

11443 Stanley, Diane. *Saving Sky* (5–8). 2010, Harper-Collins $15.99 (978-0-06-123905-2). 199pp. Living on a New Mexico ranch, 7th-grader Sky is isolated from the terrorism affecting the nation until her friend Kareem finds himself under suspicion. (Rev: BL 6/10*; SLJ 9/1/10)

11444 Stone, Phoebe. *The Romeo and Juliet Code* (5–8). 2011, Scholastic $16.99 (978-0-545-21511-4). 300pp. Eleven-year-old Felicity is sent from London to relatives in Maine to protect her from bombardment by the Germans; she becomes friends with adoptee Derek and together they solve a family mystery. (Rev: BL 1/1–15/11; HB 3–4/11; LMC 5–6/11; SLJ 2/1/11)

11445 Stone, Phoebe. *Romeo Blue* (5–8). 2013, Scholastic $16.99 (978-054544360-9). 352pp. Still in Maine, 12-year-old Felicity is suspicious when a man turns up who claims to be the father of her close friend Derek; a sequel to *The Romeo and Juliet Code* (2011). Lexile 790 (Rev: BL 5/1/13*; LMC 11–12/13; SLJ 6/13)

11446 Strasser, Todd. *Fallout* (5–8). 2013, Candlewick $16.99 (978-076365534-1). 272pp. Set against the Cuban missile crisis of the early 1960s, this alternate history switches perspectives between Scott's father's plans for a bomb shelter and the period after an attack as his family and neighbors are trapped in the shelter and running out of patience and options. ⌒ ℮ Lexile 740 (Rev: BL 9/1/13; LMC 5–6/14; SLJ 9/13)

11447 Sullivan, Jacqueline Levering. *Annie's War* (4–7). 2007, Eerdmans $15.00 (978-0-8028-5325-7). In 1946, 10-year-old Annie is having a hard time coping with her father's MIA status and her 19-year-old uncle's emotional problems, and she finds some comfort in imagined conversations with President Truman. (Rev: BL 8/07; SLJ 9/07)

11448 Tarshis, Lauren. *I Survived Hurricane Katrina, 2005* (3–6). Illus. by Scott Dawson. Series: I Survived. 2011, Scholastic $16.99 (978-054520689-1); paper $4.99 (978-05452069-6-9). 112pp. Eleven-year-old Barry Tucker's family is trapped during the storm in this story of heroic behavior. (Rev: BL 2/1/11)

11449 Taylor, Marilyn. *Faraway Home* (5–8). 2000, O'Brien paper $7.95 (978-0-86278-643-4). Taken from his Austrian homeland by the Kindertransport, 13-year-old Karl is sent to County Down in Ireland where he endures the hardship of country life and the hostility of the locals. (Rev: BL 3/1/01)

11450 Testa, Maria. *Almost Forever* (2–5). 2003, Candlewick $14.99 (978-0-7636-1996-1). In free verse, a first grader describes her feelings during the year her father spends as a doctor in the Vietnam War. (Rev: BL 9/1/03; SLJ 10/03)

11451 Toksvig, Sandi. *Hitler's Canary* (5–8). 2007, Roaring Brook $16.95 (978-1-59643-247-5). A Danish family decides to risk everything in order to help Jews escape the Nazis. (Rev: BL 1/1–15/07; SLJ 4/07)

11452 Tooke, Wes. *King of the Mound: My Summer with Satchel Paige* (5–7). 2012, Simon & Schuster $15.99 (978-144243346-5). 160pp. Recovering from a bout

with polio that has left him with a leg brace, 12-year-old Nick is happy to help with odd jobs at the North Dakota stadium where his father is catcher, and to meet the great Satchel Paige. (Rev: BL 2/15/12; SLJ 2/12)

11453 Tripp, Valerie. *Brave Emily* (2–4). Illus. by Nick Backes. 2006, Pleasant $12.95 (978-1-59369-211-7); paper $6.95 (978-1-59369-210-0). 78pp. Sent to live with an American family to escape the bombing of London in World War II, shy third grader Emily has trouble adjusting to the dramatic changes in her life. (Rev: BL 11/1/06; SLJ 2/07)

11454 Tripp, Valerie. *Meet Molly: An American Girl* (3–5). Illus. by C. F. Payne. 1986, Pleasant LB $12.95 (978-0-937295-81-6); paper $6.95 (978-0-937295-07-6). 72pp. Molly is growing up without a father during World War II in America. Others in the series are: *Molly Learns a Lesson* (1986); *Molly's Surprise* (1986); *Molly Saves the Day* (1988); *Happy Birthday, Molly!* (1987); *Changes for Molly* (1988). (Rev: BL 12/1/86)

11455 Tuck, Pamela T. *As Fast as Words Could Fly* (3–8). Illus. by Eric Velasquez. 2013, Lee & Low $18.95 (978-1-60060-348-8). 40pp. This story about school integration in 1960s North Carolina — focusing on 14-year-old Mason Steele and his typing skills — draws on the experiences of the author's father. (Rev: BL 6/13; LMC 11–12/13; SLJ 6/13)

11456 Uchida, Yoshiko. *The Bracelet* (1–5). Illus. by Joanna Yardley. 1993, Penguin $16.99 (978-0-399-22503-1). Emi, a Japanese American girl, is confused and frightened when she is interned in a prison camp during World War II. (Rev: BCCB 9/93; BL 9/15/93; HB 11/93; SLJ 12/93)

11457 Vander Els, Betty. *The Bombers' Moon* (5–7). 1992, Farrar paper $4.50 (978-0-374-30877-3). Missionary children Ruth and Simeon are evacuated to escape the Japanese invasion of China; they will not see their parents for four years. A sequel is *Leaving Point* (1987). (Rev: BCCB 9/85; BL 11/1/85; HB 9–10/85)

11458 Vanderpool, Clare. *Navigating Early* (5–8). 2013, Delacorte $16.99 (978-0-385-74209-2); LB $19.99 (978-0-375-99040-3). 320pp. Sent from Kansas to a boarding school in Maine after his mother's death, Jack has trouble adjusting and joins a strange boy named Early in an eventful trek along the Appalachian Trail tracking a bear. Printz Honor Book; Booklist Editors' Choice: Books for Youth; Best Fiction for YA; ALA Notable Children's Book. ⌒ ℮ Lexile 790L (Rev: BL 12/15/12*; HB 3–4/13; LMC 8–9/13; SLJ 3/13*)

11459 Vogiel, Eva. *Invisible Chains* (5–8). 2000, Judaica $19.95 (978-1-880582-57-2). In 1948, 14-year-old Frumie is sent with her crippled younger sister, Judy, to a boarding school for religiously observant Jewish girls. (Rev: BL 7/00; HBG 10/00)

11460 Wallace, Rich. *War and Watermelon* (5–8). 2011, Viking $15.99 (978-0-670-01152-0). 192pp. In 1969, 12-year-old Brody longs to make the football team, goes to Woodstock, and mediates between his older brother and his father on the subject of Vietnam; presented in a first-person, diary format. **e** Lexile 630L (Rev: BL 7/11; LMC 11–12/11; SLJ 7/11)

11461 Walters, Eric. *War of the Eagles* (5–7). 1998, Orca $14.00 (978-1-55143-118-5); paper $7.95 (978-1-55143-099-7). During the opening months of the war against Japan, a West Coast Canadian boy witnesses the growing prejudice against Japanese Canadians and also becomes aware of his own Indian heritage. (Rev: BL 12/15/98; HBG 3/99; SLJ 12/98)

11462 Waters, Zack C. *Blood Moon Rider* (5–8). 2006, Pineapple $13.95 (978-1-56164-350-9). Abandoned by his stepmother after his father is killed in World War II, 14-year-old Harley Wallace survives an eventful journey to the home of a grandfather he's never met and there finds more excitement waiting. (Rev: SLJ 8/06)

11463 Watson, Renee. *A Place Where Hurricanes Happen* (2–5). Illus. by Shadra Strickland. 2010, Random House $17.99 (978-0-375-85609-9). 40pp. In alternating free-verse voices, four young friends from the same New Orleans neighborhood describe their experiences during and after Hurricane Katrina. (Rev: BL 5/15/10; LMC 11–12/10; SLJ 6/1/10)

11464 Watts, Irene N. *Finding Sophie: A Search for Belonging in Postwar Britain* (5–8). 2002, Tundra paper $6.95 (978-0-88776-613-8). In this sequel to *Remember Me* (2000), World War II has ended and 13-year-old Sophie waits anxiously to hear news of her Jewish family in Germany, at the same time hoping she will not have to leave her happy life in London. (Rev: BL 1/1–15/03; SLJ 3/03; VOYA 8/03)

11465 Watts, Irene N. *Remember Me: A Search for Refuge in Wartime Britain* (5–8). 2000, Tundra paper $7.95 (978-0-88776-519-3). A heart-tugging story of an 11-year-old Jewish girl who, at the beginning of World War II, is transported from her home in Berlin to live in a Welsh mining town where she knows no one and speaks no English. (Rev: BL 12/1/00; SLJ 1/01; VOYA 2/01)

11466 Weston, Elise. *The Coastwatcher* (5–8). 2005, Peachtree $14.95 (978-1-56145-350-4). Vacationing on the South Carolina coast with his family in 1943, 11-year-old Hugh sees some signs that Germans are nearby and is determined to convince the doubting adults that he is right. (Rev: BL 11/1/05; SLJ 3/06)

11467 White, Ruth. *Little Audrey* (5–8). 2008, Farrar $16.00 (978-0-374-34580-8). 160pp. Using the voice of her older sister, the author describes their family life in the late 1940s; 11-year-old Audrey must cope with her own physical problems, her father's drinking, her mother's emotional absence, and her three needy little sisters. (Rev: BL 9/1/08*; SLJ 9/08*; VOYA 8/08)

11468 White, Ruth. *Way Down Deep* (4–7). 2007, Farrar $16.00 (978-0-374-38251-3). In 1944 West Virginia, the arrival of a new family in a town called Way Down Deep suddenly raises questions about the origins of Ruby June, a foundling who has lived there for 10 years. (Rev: BL 3/1/07; SLJ 4/07)

11469 Whittenberg, Allison. *Hollywood and Maine* (5–8). 2009, Delacorte $15.99 (978-0-385-73671-8).

176pp. When her jailbird uncle shows up to displace her from her attic bedroom, 14-year-old Maine Upshaw puts her energy into winning a beauty contest and steps on a lot of toes in this sequel to *Sweet Thang* (2006) set in the 1970s. (Rev: BCCB 3/09; BL 2/1/09; SLJ 2/09)

11470 Wiles, Deborah. *Countdown* (5–7). Series: Sixties Trilogy. 2010, Scholastic $17.99 (978-0-545-10605-4). 400pp. In October 1962 life is tense for 11-year-old Franny, whose father is a fighter pilot, as relations between the United States and the Soviet Union become increasingly strained; extracts from songs and speeches, plus black-and-white photographs, add to readers' understanding. ALA Notable Children's Book. ∩ Lexile 800L (Rev: BL 5/1/10*; HB 5–6/10; LMC 10/10; SLJ 7/10)

11471 Williams-Garcia, Rita. *One Crazy Summer* (4–7). 2010, Amistad $15.99 (978-0-06-076088-5); LB $16.89 (978-0-06-076089-2). 224pp. African American Delphine, 11, and her younger sisters are sent from Brooklyn to visit the mother who abandoned them and moved to California; there they find little welcome and spend time at a community center run by the Black Panthers. Newbery Honor 2011; Scott O'Dell Award for Historical Fiction; Coretta Scott King Award; ALA Notable Children's Book 2011; YALSA Amazing Audiobooks Top Ten 2011. ∩ **e** Lexile 750L (Rev: BL 2/1/10*; HB 3–4/10; LMC 3–4/10; SLJ 3/10)

11472 Williams, Laura E. *Behind the Bedroom Wall* (5–8). 1996, Milkweed paper $6.95 (978-1-57131-606-6). Korinna, a young Nazi, discovers that her parents are hiding a Jewish couple in wartime Germany. (Rev: BL 8/96; SLJ 9/96)

11473 Wilson, John. *Flames of the Tiger* (5–8). 2003, Kids Can $16.95 (978-1-55337-618-7). The horrors of World War II are seen through the eyes of 17-year-old Dieter, who with his younger sister is fleeing his native Germany as the war nears an end. (Rev: SLJ 1/04; VOYA 6/04) [813]

11474 Winkler, Allan M. *Cassie's War* (4–6). 1994, Royal Fireworks paper $9.99 (978-0-88092-106-0). 94pp. Cassie is growing up in California during World War II, which brings internment to her Japanese American friend and death to her soldier father. (Rev: BL 2/1/95)

11475 Wittlinger, Ellen. *This Means War!* (5–8). 2010, Simon & Schuster $16.99 (978-1-4169-7101-6). 224pp. After her best friend Lowell abandons her for the company of boys, 10-year-old Juliet befriends Polly, and the girls become intent on challenging the boys to increasingly risky and dangerous tests of will in this story set during the Cold War. Lexile 740L (Rev: BL 2/1/10; HB 5–6/10; SLJ 4/10)

11476 Woods, Brenda. *The Red Rose Box* (5–8). 2002, Putnam $16.99 (978-0-399-23702-7). In 1953, Leah, a southern black girl, and her family travel to Los Angeles where they find a different culture and more progressive attitudes. (Rev: BCCB 7–8/02; BL 6/1–15/02; HBG 10/02; SLJ 6/02; VOYA 6/02)

11477 Woodworth, Chris. *Georgie's Moon* (5–8). 2006, Farrar $16.00 (978-0-374-33306-5). Seventh-grader Georgie Collins lives her life waiting for her father to return from Vietnam, and is unable to accept his death at first. (Rev: BL 3/1/06; SLJ 4/06)

11478 Yep, Laurence. *Hiroshima* (4–7). 1995, Scholastic paper $9.95 (978-0-590-20832-1). A powerful work of fiction that explores the bombing of Hiroshima in 1945 and its aftermath. (Rev: BCCB 6/95; BL 3/15/95*; HB 9–10/95; SLJ 5/95)

11479 Yep, Laurence. *The Star Maker* (3–5). 2011, HarperCollins $15.99 (978-0-06-025315-8); LB $16.89 (978-0-06-025316-5). 112pp. In 1950s San Francisco 8-year-old Chinese American Artie succeeds in meeting a foolish fireworks promise with the help of his Uncle Chester. Lexile 530L (Rev: BL 11/15/10; SLJ 2/1/11)

11480 Ylvisaker, Anne. *Little Klein* (3–6). 2007, Candlewick $15.99 (978-0-7636-3359-2). 186pp. In the Midwest in the mid-20th century, 9-year-old Harold Klein is younger, smaller, and frailer than his rambunctious brothers but he's tough underneath and with his adopted dog he can be very effective. (Rev: BCCB 3/08; SLJ 1/08; VOYA 2/08)

11481 Zeinert, Karen. *To Touch the Stars: A Story of World War II* (5–8). Series: Jamestown's American Portraits. 2000, Jamestown paper $5.95 (978-0-8092-0630-8). Eighteen-year-old Liz Erickson, who loves to fly airplanes, longs for independence while she investigates possible sabotage in the Women's Airforce Service pilots program. (Rev: SLJ 9/00)

11482 Zucker, Jonny. *The Bombed House* (5–8). Illus. by Paul Savage. Series: Keystone Books. 2006, Stone Arch LB $21.26 (978-1-59889-092-1). This fast-paced story, which will attract reluctant readers, features brothers Ned and Harry Jennings, who find a German soldier hiding in London during World War II. (Rev: SLJ 1/07)

Holidays and Holy Days

11483 Bauer, Caroline Feller, ed. *Halloween: Stories and Poems* (3–6). Illus. by Peter Sís. 1989, HarperCollins LB $14.89 (978-0-397-32301-2). 96pp. An anthology with spooky happenings for reading on Halloween, although not directly related to the holiday. (Rev: BL 9/1/89; SLJ 10/89)

11484 Chaikin, Miriam. *Alexandra's Scroll: The Story of the First Hanukkah* (4–6). Illus. by Stephen Fieser. 2002, Holt $18.95 (978-0-8050-6384-4). Alexandra and her family are caught up in the tumultuous events that lead to the first Hanukkah in this brightly illustrated historical novel. (Rev: BL 9/1/02; HB 9/02; HBG 3/03; SLJ 10/02)

11485 Chaikin, Miriam. *Angel Secrets: Stories Based on Jewish Legend* (4–6). Illus. by Leonid Gore. 2005, Holt $18.95 (978-0-8050-7150-4). In this collection of six short stories based on Jewish folklore, angels do God's

work on Earth as well as in Heaven. (Rev: BL 10/1/05; SLJ 9/05) [296.3]

11486 Codell, Esmé Raji. *Hanukkah, Shmanukkah!* (3–5). Illus. by LeUyen Pham. 2005, Hyperion $16.99 (978-0-7868-5197-3). 48pp. Dickens's *A Christmas Carol* is retold as a Hanukkah tale full of humor and Yiddish phrases; a glossary is provided. (Rev: BL 9/1/05)

11487 Funke, Cornelia. *When Santa Fell to Earth* (3–5). 2006, Scholastic $15.99 (978-0-439-78204-3). 176pp. With the help of his new friends Charlotte and Ben, a good Santa must try to save Christmas from the evil schemes of Gerold Geronimus Goblynch. (Rev: BL 11/15/06; SLJ 10/06)

11488 Henry, O. *The Gift of the Magi* (5–8). Illus. by Carol Heyer. 1994, Ideals $14.95 (978-1-57102-003-1). The classic story of unselfish love at Christmas gets some handsome illustrations. Another fine edition is illustrated by Kevin King (1988, Simon & Schuster). (Rev: BL 8/94)

11489 Jenkins, Emily. *Dangerous Pumpkins* (2–4). Illus. by Harry Bliss. 2012, HarperCollins $14.99 (978-0-06-180223-2). 160pp. In this sequel to *Invisible Inkling* (2011), 9-year-old Hank's invisible bandapat companion causes trouble on Halloween. e Lexile 520L (Rev: BL 10/1/12; HB 9–10/12; SLJ 10/12)

11490 Kimmel, Eric A. *The Spotted Pony: A Collection of Hanukkah Stories* (3–6). Illus. by Leonard Everett Fisher. 1992, Holiday House $15.95 (978-0-8234-0936-5). 70pp. A collection of wonderfully earthy and joyous Jewish folktales. (Rev: BL 11/15/92)

11491 Kline, Suzy. *Horrible Harry and the Holidaze* (2–3). Illus. by Frank Remkiewicz. 2003, Penguin $13.99 (978-0-670-03642-4). Horrible Harry's 3rd-grade class learns about five winter holidays — Three Kings' Day, Korean New Year, Kwanzaa, Hanukkah, and Christmas — while Harry worries about his grandfather's move to a nursing home. (Rev: BL 9/1/03; HBG 4/04; SLJ 10/03)

11492 McDonald, Megan. *Judy Moody and Stink: The Holly Joliday* (2–4). Illus. by Peter H. Reynolds. 2007, Candlewick $14.99 (978-0-7636-3237-3). 96pp. Judy Moody uses toilet paper for her lengthy Christmas list but Stink's request is simple — snow. (Rev: BL 11/15/07; HB 11/07)

11493 Maguire, Gregory. *Five Alien Elves* (3–5). Illus. by Elaine Clayton. 1998, Clarion $15.00 (978-0-395-83894-5). 176pp. On Christmas Eve, five space aliens kidnap the town mayor, and two rival clubs — the Copycats and the Tattletales — join forces to rescue him. (Rev: HBG 3/99; SLJ 10/98)

11494 Mass, Wendy. *11 Birthdays* (4–6). 2009, Scholastic $16.99 (978-0-545-05239-9). 272pp. Born on the same day and friends for their first nine years, Amanda and Leo fell out on their 10th birthday, but their 11th birthday brings a strange time loop, making them relive the day over and over. (Rev: BCCB 2/09; BL 12/15/08)

11495 Matthews, Caitlin. *While the Bear Sleeps: Winter Tales and Traditions* (4–6). Illus. 1999, Barefoot Books $19.95 (978-1-902283-81-4). A satisfying anthology of tales about winter holidays and customs, including Hanukkah, Kwanzaa, Christmas, and Twelfth Night, tied together by a story involving a little girl and her guide, a bear. (Rev: BL 11/15/99; SLJ 10/99)

11496 Montgomery, L. M. *Christmas with Anne and Other Holiday Stories* (4–7). 1996, McClelland & Stewart $12.95 (978-0-7710-6204-9). A collection of 16 short pieces and stories (two from the Anne of Green Gables books) that deal with Christmas. (Rev: BL 9/1/96)

11497 O'Connell, Rebecca. *Penina Levine Is a Potato Pancake* (3–5). Illus. by Majella Lue Sue. 2008, Roaring Brook $16.95 (978-1-59643-213-0). 144pp. Penina is not looking forward to Hanukkah — her best friend will be in Aruba, her favorite teacher is moving away, and Penina will have to deal with her pesky younger sister Mimsy. (Rev: BLO 10/7/08; SLJ 12/08)

11498 Osborne, Mary Pope. *Christmas in Camelot* (2–5). Series: Magic Tree House. 2001, Random LB $13.99 (978-0-375-91373-0). 116pp. Stalwart Jack and Annie time-travel to Camelot and must solve riddles to break the spell of the evil Mordred and save the knights of the Round Table. (Rev: BL 12/15/01; HBG 3/02; SLJ 10/01)

11499 Polacco, Patricia. *Christmas Tapestry* (3–6). Illus. 2002, Penguin $16.99 (978-0-399-23955-7). 160pp. In this heartwarming Christmas story, a boy and his father use a tapestry to cover a hole in a church wall, only to find that the fabric has special meaning to a Jewish couple. (Rev: BCCB 10/02; BL 9/1/02; HBG 3/03; SLJ 10/02)

11500 Pollock, Beth. *Harley's Gift* (3–5). Series: Streetlights. 2008, James Lorimer paper $7.95 (978-1-55028-992-3). 123pp. In Toronto, 11-year-old Harley anticipates Christmas and her father's once-a-year visit with some trepidation. (Rev: BL 5/15/08)

11501 Robinson, Barbara. *The Best Christmas Pageant Ever* (4–6). Illus. by Judith G. Brown. 1972, HarperCollins LB $16.89 (978-0-06-025044-7); paper $5.99 (978-0-06-440275-0). 96pp. When a family of unrestrained children takes over the church Christmas pageant, the results are hilarious.

11502 Ross, Richard. *Arctic Airlift* (1–3). Illus. 2005, Blue Fox $17.00 (978-0-9763119-0-4). Santa's workshop is threatened by a flood, and young ham radio operator Robert picks up the distress call. (Rev: BL 10/15/05; SLJ 10/05)

11503 Russell, Ching Yeung. *Moon Festival* (3–5). Illus. by Christopher Zhong-Yuan. 1997, Boyds Mills $15.95 (978-1-56397-596-7). 32pp. Ying and her friends celebrate the summer Moon Festival in many ways, including making paper lanterns. (Rev: BL 9/15/97; HBG 3/98)

11504 *A Simply Wonderful Christmas: A Literary Advent Calendar* (3–6). Illus. by Silke Leffler. 2006, North-South $25.00 (978-0-7358-2100-2). 133pp. Arranged like an advent calendar, this collection of stories and poems contains a special literary treat for each night in December leading up to Christmas. (Rev: SLJ 10/06)

11505 Steinhöfel, Andreas. *An Elk Dropped In* (2–4). Illus. by Kerstin Meyer. 2006, Boyds Mills $16.95 (978-1-932425-80-2). 79pp. In a German village, an elk named Mr. Moose takes Santa's sleigh out for a practice run and ends up crashing into Billy Wagner's house, where they happily care for him until he recuperates. (Rev: BL 11/15/06; SLJ 10/06)

11506 Thompson, Lauren. *A Christmas Gift for Mama* (3–5). Illus. by Jim Burke. 2003, Scholastic $16.95 (978-0-590-30725-3). 48pp. Inspired by O. Henry's "The Gift of the Magi," this holiday tale tells how Grace trades a treasured belonging to buy a matching figurine for her mother's collection, only to find that her mother disposed of the figurine to buy Grace a gift. (Rev: BL 9/1/03; HBG 4/04; SLJ 10/03)

11507 Van Leeuwen, Jean. *The Great Christmas Kidnapping Caper* (3–5). Illus. by Steven Kellogg. 1975, Dial $12.95 (978-0-685-01454-7). 144pp. A group of mice who live in a dollhouse at Macy's solve the mystery of the disappearance of Santa Claus.

11508 Wiggin, Kate Douglas. *The Birds' Christmas Carol* (3–5). Illus. by Jessie Gillespie. 1941, Houghton $9.95 (978-0-395-07205-9). A beautiful edition of a story first published in 1888. (Rev: HBG 3/98)

11509 Zalben, Jane Breskin. *The Magic Menorah: A Modern Chanukah Tale* (3–5). Illus. by Donna Diamond. 2001, Simon & Schuster $15.00 (978-0-689-82606-1). Twelve-year-old Stanley dreads Hanukkah — lots of annoying relatives arrive and his grandfather always looks sad — but this year a strange man appears from a menorah Stanley finds in the attic and grants him three wishes. (Rev: HBG 3/02; SLJ 10/01)

Humorous Stories

11510 Adderson, Caroline. *Jasper John Dooley: Left Behind* (2–4). Illus. by Ben Clanton. 2013, Kids Can $16.95 (978-1-55453-579-8). 132pp. Despite his trepidation, Jasper manages — with some mishaps — to get through the week that his beloved grandmother is away on a cruise. Lexile 590 (Rev: BLO 6/13; SLJ 4/13)

11511 Ahlberg, Allan. *The Children Who Smelled a Rat* (2–4). Illus. by Katharine McEwen. 2005, Candlewick $15.99 (978-0-7636-2870-3). 80pp. In this action-packed tale about the Gaskitt family, twins Gus and Gloria try to figure out what caused their teacher's weird behavior, taxi driver Mom finds strange packages, and Dad chases after the baby's runaway shopping cart. (Rev: BCCB 11/05; BL 11/1/05; HBG 4/06; LMC 1/06; SLJ 10/05*)

11512 Amato, Mary. *Drooling and Dangerous: The Riot Brothers Return!* (3–5). Illus. by Ethan Long. Series: The Riot Brothers. 2006, Holiday $16.95 (978-0-8234-1986-9). 177pp. Wilbur and Orville Riot return for more zany adventures — as spies, as movie stars, and as school principals. (Rev: BL 5/15/06; HBG 10/06; SLJ 10/06)

11513 Amato, Mary. *Stinky and Successful: The Riot Brothers Never Stop* (2–5). Illus. by Ethan Long. 2007, Holiday House $16.95 (978-0-8234-2100-8). 150pp. Wilbur and Orville turn into helpful knights, tease their mother, and take up science in this imaginative, humorous, and fast-paced book. (Rev: SLJ 10/07)

11514 Anderson, M. T. *Agent Q, or the Smell of Danger!* (4–7). Illus. by Kurt Cyrus. Series: Pals in Peril. 2010, Simon & Schuster $16.99 (978-1-4169-8640-9). 294pp. Crime-fighting teens Lily, Jasper, and Katie are trying to get home to New Jersey after their adventures in Delaware, but the evil Autarch has other things in mind. (Rev: BL 9/15/10*; SLJ 11/1/10)

11515 Anderson, M. T. *Zombie Mommy* (5–8). Illus. by Kurt Cyrus. Series: Pals in Peril. 2011, Simon & Schuster $16.99 (978-144243068-6). 240pp. Lily, Katie, Drgnan, and Jasper Dash, Boy Technonaut must save Lily's mother, who has been possessed by a zombie with ambitions. Lexile 710L (Rev: BL 10/15/11; HB 11–12/11)

11516 Angleberger, Tom. *Fake Mustache: How Jodie O'Rodeo and Her Wonder Horse (and Some Nerdy Kid) Saved the U.S. Presidential Election from a Mad Genius Criminal Mastermind* (4–7). Illus. by Jen Wang. 2012, Abrams Amulet $13.95 (978-1-4197-0194-8). 208pp. In the small town of Hairsprinkle a fake mustache sparks hilarious chaos as 7th-grader Casper takes to robbing banks, hypnotizing residents, becoming mayor . . . and then governor . . . and then president? ∩ e Lexile 710L (Rev: BL 5/15/12; HB 5–6/12; LMC 11–12/12; SLJ 6/12)

11517 Applegate, Katherine. *Don't Swap Your Sweater for a Dog* (1–2). Illus. by Brian Biggs. Series: Roscoe Riley Rules. 2008, HarperCollins $14.99 (978-0-06-114886-6). 79pp. First-grader Roscoe figures a way to enter a pet contest even though he doesn't have a pet in this humorous early chapter book, the third in a series that also includes *Never Glue Your Friends to Chairs* (2008) and *Don't Tap-Dance on Your Teacher* (2009). (Rev: LMC 3/09; SLJ 9/08)

11518 Ardagh, Philip. *Dreadful Acts* (4–7). Illus. by David Roberts. Series: Eddie Dickens. 2003, Henry Holt $14.95 (978-0-8050-7155-9). This zany sequel to *A House Called Awful End* (2002) throws more wild adventures at 12-year-old Eddie Dickens. (Rev: BL 4/15/03; HBG 10/03; SLJ 5/03)

11519 Ardagh, Philip. *Terrible Times* (4–7). Illus. by David Roberts. 2003, Henry Holt $12.95 (978-0-8050-7156-6). Young Eddie Dickens sails for America and encounters all sorts of zany situations in this last installment in the trilogy set in Victorian England. (Rev: BL 2/1/04; SLJ 12/03)

11520 Asch, Frank. *Gravity Buster: Journal #2 of a Cardboard Genius* (3–5). Illus. by author. Series: Cardboard Genius. 2007, Kids Can $14.95 (978-1-55453-068-7); paper $5.95 (978-1-55453-069-4). Alex describes the inventive contraptions that he and his little brother, Jonathan, build to aid in their imaginative play in this sequel to *Star Jumper*. (Rev: SLJ 5/07)

11521 Asch, Frank. *Star Jumper: Journal of a Cardboard Genius* (3–5). 2006, Kids Can $14.95 (978-1-55337-886-0); paper $5.95 (978-1-55337-887-7). 128pp. Intending to escape his little brother, Alex goes about building a spaceship and a duplicator, with some unintended consequences. (Rev: BL 7/06; HBG 10/06; LMC 1/07; SLJ 6/06)

11522 Atwater, Richard, and Florence Atwater. *Mr. Popper's Penguins* (4–6). Illus. by Robert Lawson. 1938, Little, Brown $16.95 (978-0-316-05842-1). Mr. Popper has to get a penguin from the zoo to keep his homesick penguin company; soon there are 12.

11523 Auch, Mary Jane. *I Was a Third Grade Bodyguard* (1–3). Illus. by Herm Auch. 2003, Holiday House $15.95 (978-0-8234-1775-9). 73pp. When third grader Brian volunteers to look after the class chicken during Christmas vacation, the responsibility for watching the bird falls mainly on Arful, Brian's dog. (Rev: HBG 4/04; SLJ 12/03)

11524 Auch, Mary Jane. *I Was a Third Grade Science Project* (2–4). Illus. by Herm Auch. 1998, Holiday House $15.95 (978-0-8234-1357-7). 94pp. Brian tries to hypnotize his dog into believing he's a cat, but the spell works on one of Brian's classmates instead. (Rev: BL 3/15/98; HBG 10/98; SLJ 5/98)

11525 Babbitt, Natalie. *Jack Plank Tells Tales* (2–6). 2007, Scholastic $15.95 (978-0-545-00496-1). Jack, an unsuccessful pirate, searches for a more suitable profession and describes his quest using entertaining, fantastic tales. By the author of *Tuck Everlasting*. (Rev: SLJ 5/07)

11526 Baker, Kim. *Pickle: The (Formerly) Anonymous Prank Club of Fountain Point Middle School* (4–7). Illus. by Tim Probert. 2012, Roaring Brook $15.99 (978-1-59643-765-4). 240pp. Calling themselves the League of Picklemakers, 6th-graders Ben Diaz and friends engage in a series of escalating pranks. e (Rev: BL 11/1/12; HB 11–12/12; LMC 3–4/13; SLJ 11/12)

11527 Banscherus, J. *Detective's Duel* (3–6). Trans. from German by Daniel C. Baron. Illus. by Ralf Butschkow. Series: Klooz. 2007, Stone Arch LB $22.60 (978-1-59889-339-7). 65pp. Klooz's monopoly on detective work is threatened when another boy, King, begins solving mysteries the high-tech way. (Rev: LMC 10/07; SLJ 7/07)

11528 Banscherus, J. *The Great Snake Swindle. Bk. 1* (3–6). Trans. from German by Daniel C. Baron. Illus. by Ralf Butschkow. Series: Klooz. 2007, Stone Arch LB $22.60 (978-1-59889-340-3). 67pp. Sean is scamming his classmates by selling them "magic" balls, but Klooz uncovers his trickery and gets his friends their money back. (Rev: SLJ 7/07)

11529 Baron, Jeff. *I Represent Sean Rosen* (5–8). 2013, Greenwillow $16.99 (978-0-06-218747-5). 336pp. Determined to sell his movie idea to Hollywood, 13-year-old Sean Rosen invents an agent to represent him. e Lexile 660 (Rev: BL 3/15/13; LMC 10/13; SLJ 4/13*)

11530 Barrows, Anne. *Ivy + Bean Break the Fossil Record* (1–3). Illus. by Sophie Blackall. 2007, Chronicle

$14.95 (978-0-8118-5683-6). 132pp. In this hilarious book, all the 2nd-graders are trying to set different new world records, and Ivy and Bean decide to dig in Bean's backyard in hopes of becoming the youngest people ever to find dinosaur bones. (Rev: BL 7/07; SLJ 7/07)

11531 Barry, Dave, and Ridley Pearson. *Science Fair: A Story of Mystery, Danger, International Suspense, and a Very Nervous Frog* (5–8). 2008, Hyperion $18.99 (978-1-4231-1324-9). 400pp. Inept secret agents from Krpshtskan plan to use American middle-school students to build secret weapons in their science fair projects. ◯ (Rev: BL 12/15/08; SLJ 3/09; VOYA 12/08)

11532 Basye, Dale E. *Blimpo: The Third Circle of Heck* (4–7). Illus. by Bob Dob. Series: Heck. 2010, Random House $16.99 (978-037585676-1); LB $19.99 (978-037595676-8). 464pp. Milton Fauster, 11, must help his sister Marlo, who is training as Satan's secretary, and his friend Virgil, who is consigned to the circle for overweight children, in this third installment in the humorous series. In *Fibble: The Fourth Circle of Heck,* set in the city of liars, Marlo wakes up in her younger brother Milton's body. (Rev: BLO 2/15/10)

11533 Basye, Dale E. *Heck: Where the Bad Kids Go* (3–6). 2008, Random $16.99 (978-0-375-84075-3). 304pp. When they die in a freak accident, outgoing 13-year-old Marlo and her timid younger brother Milton find themselves in Heck, a kind of reform school in limbo from which they long to escape; this humorous tale has its dark side but is full of worldplay and classical allusions. (Rev: BL 6/1–15/08; SLJ 9/08)

11534 Basye, Dale E. *Rapacia: The Second Circle of Heck* (4–7). Illus. by Bob Dob. Series: Heck. 2009, Random House $16.99 (978-0-375-84077-7); LB $19.99 (978-0-375-94077-4). 362pp. Marlo joins other young shoplifters in the second circle of Heck, where he is taunted by cool stuff he can never have. ◯ (Rev: BL 5/15/11; SLJ 8/09)

11535 Basye, Dale E. *Snivel: The Fifth Circle of Heck* (4–7). Illus. by Bob Dob. Series: Heck. 2012, Random House $16.99 (978-037586834-4); LB $19.99 (978-037596834-1). 448pp. Deceased Milton and Marlo Fauster save the world from Nikola Tesla's nefarious plot to come back to life. ✎ (Rev: BL 3/15/12; VOYA 10/12)

11536 Bean, Raymond. *Rippin' It Old School* (3–5). 2010, AmazonEncore paper $9.95 (978-1-935597-08-7). 140pp. After the wild success of his first invention (in 2008's *Sweet Farts,* 10-year-old millionaire Keith is struggling to come up with his next big thing, and coping with the jealousy of family and friends. (Rev: BL 9/15/10; SLJ 5/11)

11537 Beaty, Andrea. *Attack of the Fluffy Bunnies* (3–6). Illus. by Dan Santat. 2010, Abrams $12.95 (978-0-8109-8416-5). 192pp. Two twins use their knowledge of horror movies to predict the sequence of events when their summer camp is taken over by giant warrior rabbits. ✎ Lexile 790L (Rev: BL 5/1/10; LMC 11–12/10; SLJ 7/1/10)

11538 Benton, Jim. *Attack of the 50-Foot Cupid* (2–4). Illus. Series: Franny K. Stein, Mad Scientist. 2004, Simon & Schuster $14.95 (978-0-689-86292-2). 112pp. Franny's new lab assistant turns out to be a fairly inept mongrel who succeeds in unleashing a giant, arrow-shooting Cupid in this humorous beginning chapter book. Also use *The Invisible Fran* (2004). (Rev: BL 3/1/04; SLJ 5/04)

11539 Benton, Jim. *The Fran That Time Forgot* (2–4). Illus. by author. Series: Franny K. Stein, Mad Scientist. 2005, Simon & Schuster $14.95 (978-0-689-86294-6). 102pp. Franny travels back in time in an attempt to change her middle name (Kissypie) in this half-funny, half-scary story. (Rev: SLJ 8/05)

11540 Benton, Jim. *Frantastic Voyage* (2–4). Illus. Series: Franny K. Stein, Mad Scientist. 2005, Simon & Schuster $14.95 (978-1-4169-0229-4). When her canine assistant swallows a tiny doomsday device, girl scientist Franny shrinks herself so she can go and retrieve it; gross scenes will attract reluctant readers to this beginning chapter book with black-and-white cartoons. (Rev: BL 1/1–15/06; SLJ 4/06)

11541 Birney, Betty. *Trouble According to Humphrey* (2–4). 2007, Putnam $14.99 (978-0-399-24505-3). 176pp. Humphrey the class hamster describes his concerns about Paul's grades, Mandy's family's financial problems, and other woes in this third, funny installment in the series. (Rev: BL 1/1–15/07; SLJ 2/07)

11542 Birney, Betty. *The World According to Humphrey* (2–5). 2004, Penguin $14.99 (978-0-399-24198-7). 144pp. Humphrey the hamster has a very varied and mostly enjoyable life as the class pet, but he worries about his future at the hands of Mrs. Brisbane. (Rev: BL 3/1/04; SLJ 4/04)

11543 Blume, Judy. *Freckle Juice* (2–5). Illus. by Sonia O. Lisker. 1971, Macmillan $15.00 (978-0-02-711690-8); Dell paper $4.50 (978-0-440-42813-8). 40pp. A gullible second-grader pays 50 cents for a recipe to grow freckles.

11544 Blume, Judy. *Starring Sally J. Freedman as Herself* (4–7). 1977, Dell paper $5.99 (978-0-440-48253-6). A story of a 5th-grader's adventures in New Jersey and Florida in the late 1940s.

11545 Bolger, Kevin. *Zombiekins* (4–6). Illus. by Aaron Blecha. 2010, Penguin paper $10.99 (978-15951417-7-4). 208pp. Chaos and hilarity ensue when 4th-grader Stanley returns from a trip to Dementedyville with a possessed stuffed animal whose bite turns schoolmates into zombies. ✎ Lexile 880L (Rev: BL 6/10; SLJ 10/10)

11546 Bond, Michael. *Paddington Takes the Test* (3–5). Illus. 2002, Houghton $15.00 (978-0-618-18384-5). 144pp. This new edition of a 1980 release about the ever-popular bear sports a new jacket illustration and a larger typeface. (Rev: BL 3/15/02; HBG 10/02)

11547 Boniface, William. *The Return of Meteor Boy?* (4–6). Illus. by Stephen Gilpin. Series: The Extraordinary Adventures of Ordinary Boy. 2007, HarperCollins $16.99 (978-0-06-077467-7). 344pp. Ordinary Boy, the only person in Superopolis without superpowers, suspects that the Amazing Indestructo may have had something to do with Meteor Boy's disappearance in this second book in the series. (Rev: SLJ 8/07)

11548 Bragg, Georgia. *Matisse on the Loose* (4–6). 2009, Delacorte $16.99 (978-0-385-73570-4). A boy who makes copies of famous masterpieces replaces one of the masterworks in a museum with one of his own. (Rev: BL 6/1–15/09; SLJ 7/09)

11549 Brockmeier, Kevin. *Grooves: A Kind of Mystery* (4–7). 2006, HarperCollins LB $17.89 (978-0-06-073692-7). In this funny mystery with science fiction overtones, unprepossessing 7th-grader Dwayne Ruggles finds out that the sounds coming from his blue jeans are really cries for help from imprisoned factory workers. (Rev: BL 2/1/06; SLJ 3/06)

11550 Brooke, William J. *A Is for AARRGH!* (5–8). 1999, HarperCollins LB $14.89 (978-0-06-023394-5). A humorous story about a prehistoric boy, Mog, and his amazing discoveries about language and communication. (Rev: BCCB 11/99; BL 10/15/99; HB 9–10/99; HBG 3/00; SLJ 9/99)

11551 Bruel, Nick. *Bad Kitty for President* (3–5). Illus. by author. 2012, Roaring Brook $13.99 (978-1-59643-669-5). 144pp. Annoyed with all the strays in town, Bad Kitty decides to run for president of the Neighborhood Cat Coalition in this book full of details of voter registration, debate coaching, and media interviews. (Rev: BL 3/15/12; SLJ 4/1/12)

11552 Bruel, Nick. *Bad Kitty School Daze* (2–4). Illus. by author. 2013, Roaring Brook $13.99 (978-159643670-1). 160pp. Kitty's bad behavior results in her being sent to Diabla Von Gloom's School for Wayward Pets along with Puppy, who has drooling problems. **e** Lexile GN630L (Rev: BL 12/15/12)

11553 Bruel, Nick. *Bad Kitty vs. Uncle Murray: The Uproar at the Front Door* (2–4). Illus. by author. 2010, Roaring Brook $13.99 (978-1-59643-596-4). 160pp. Poor Uncle Murray has been left in charge of Bad Kitty and Poor Puppy and his good nature is sorely tried. (Rev: SLJ 8/1/10)

11554 Buckley, Michael. *The Cheerleaders of Doom* (4–7). Illus. by Ethen Beavers. Series: NERDS. 2011, Abrams $14.95 (978-141970024-8). 288pp. When Gertie, a former member of the National Espionage, Rescue, and Defense Society, disrupts the multi-verse with her cheerleading aspirations, Wheezer and the other NERDS swing into action; the third volume in the series. ∩ (Rev: BL 12/1/11; SLJ 2/12)

11555 Byars, Betsy. *Bingo Brown's Guide to Romance* (5–8). 2000, Puffin paper $5.99 (978-0-14-036080-6). Romance, confusion, and comedy occur when Bingo Brown meets his true love in the produce section of the grocery store. (Rev: BL 4/1/92; SLJ 4/92)

11556 Byars, Betsy. *Me Tarzan* (3–5). 2000, HarperCollins LB $15.89 (978-0-06-028707-8). 96pp. Dorothy's Tarzan yell is so effective that she wins the part of Tarzan in the school play, and also finds that animals respond to

her call. (Rev: BCCB 6/00; BL 3/15/00; HB 5/00; HBG 10/00; SLJ 7/00)

11557 Cabot, Meg. *Princess in Waiting* (5–7). Series: Princess Diaries. 2003, HarperCollins $16.99 (978-0-06-009607-6). Princess Mia gets in a royal mess when her duties interfere with her love life. (Rev: BL 5/15/03; HBG 10/03; SLJ 5/03; VOYA 6/03)

11558 Calmenson, Stephanie, and Joanna Cole. *Gator Halloween* (2–4). Illus. 1999, Morrow LB $14.89 (978-0-688-14785-3). 64pp. Amy and Allie's plan to win the best Halloween costume prize gets sidetracked when they try to find a lost pet. (Rev: BL 9/1/99; HBG 3/00; SLJ 9/99)

11559 Calmenson, Stephanie, and Joanna Cole. *Get Well, Gators!* (2–4). Illus. Series: Gator Girls. 1998, Morrow LB $15.89 (978-0-688-14787-7). 64pp. When Allie, who was to sing a duet with Amy at the Swamp Town fair, comes down with swamp flu, Amy is afraid to sing solo in this simple, humorous story. (Rev: BL 11/15/98; HBG 3/99; SLJ 10/98)

11560 Carvell, Tim. *Planet Tad* (5–8). Illus. by Doug Holgate. 2012, HarperCollins $12.99 (978-006193436-0). 256pp. Twelve-year-old Tad's blog recounts everything he goes through — girl problems, school problems, awful summer job — in the year he's in 7th and 8th grades. Lexile 940L (Rev: BL 4/15/12; SLJ 6/12)

11561 Castle, M. E. *Popular Clone* (4–7). 2012, Egmont $15.99 (978-160684232-4). 320pp. Socially inept and bullied scientific genius Fisher is frustrated when he clones himself so he can stay home and play video games while his clone attends school, and it turns out that Fisher Two becomes popular. ∩ **e** (Rev: BL 1/1/12)

11562 Child, Lauren. *Clarice Bean Spells Trouble* (3–5). 2005, Candlewick $15.99 (978-0-7636-2813-0). 192pp. Vowing to be more like Ruby Redfort, a character in books and a TV series, Clarice Bean tries to prepare for an upcoming spelling bee while also vying for a leading part in a school production of *The Sound of Music*. (Rev: BL 9/1/05; SLJ 8/05)

11563 Child, Lauren. *Clarice Bean, Don't Look Now* (2–5). 2007, Candlewick $15.99 (978-0-7636-3536-7). 252pp. Clarice Bean's problems justify her constant worrying: the ceiling falls, her best friend is moving, and a new student arrives arrives from Sweden. (Rev: SLJ 10/07)

11564 Cleary, Beverly. *Ellen Tebbits* (3–5). Illus. by Louis Darling. 1951, Morrow $15.89 (978-0-688-31264-0); Avon paper $5.99 (978-0-380-70913-7). 160pp. Eight-year-old Ellen has braces on her teeth, takes ballet lessons, and, worst of all, wears long woolen underwear.

11565 Cleary, Beverly. *Emily's Runaway Imagination* (3–6). Illus. by Beth Krush and Joe Krush. 1961, Avon paper $5.99 (978-0-380-70923-6). 224pp. Emily's imagination helps get a library for Pitchfork, Oregon, in the 1920s.

11566 Cleary, Beverly. *Henry Huggins* (3–5). Illus. by Louis Darling. 1950, Avon paper $5.99 (978-0-380-70912-0). 160pp. Henry is a small boy with a knack for creating hilarious situations. Others in the series: *Henry and Beezus* (1952); *Henry and Ribsy* (1954); *Henry and the Paper Route* (1957); *Henry and the Clubhouse* (1962). (Rev: HBG 10/01)

11567 Cleary, Beverly. *Otis Spofford* (3–6). Illus. by Louis Darling. 1953, Avon paper $5.99 (978-0-380-70919-9). 192pp. This story of Otis stirring up a little excitement at school is full of humor.

11568 Clifford, Eth. *Harvey's Horrible Snake Disaster* (3–5). 1984, Houghton $15.00 (978-0-395-35378-3). 128pp. Harvey tries to disguise the fact that he is petrified of snakes.

11569 Collins, Ross. *Medusa Jones* (4–7). Illus. by author. 2008, Scholastic $16.99 (978-0-439-90100-0). Yes, Medusa does have snakes for hair, and her friend Mino is half bull; they are part of the outcast group at school, where Theseus and his friends push them around. A trip to Mount Olympus changes all that, since the students must pull together. (Rev: BL 12/1/07; LMC 3/08; SLJ 1/08)

11570 Cooney, Doug. *The Beloved Dearly* (4–6). Illus. by Tony DiTerlizzi. 2002, Simon & Schuster LB $16.00 (978-0-689-83127-0). 192pp. A 12-year-old goes into the pet funeral business in this humorous and inventive novel aimed at a middle-grade audience. (Rev: BCCB 5/02; BL 1/1–15/02; HBG 10/02; SLJ 1/02)

11571 Cooper, Rose. *Secrets from the Sleeping Bag* (5–8). Illus. by author. Series: Blogtastic! 2012, Delacorte $12.99 (978-038574246-7); LB $15.99 (978-037599059-5). 208pp. She has no access to her blog while spending four weeks at summer camp, but Sofia records all the highs and lows in her Pre-Blogging spiral-bound notebook. **e** (Rev: BL 9/1/12; SLJ 8/1/12; VOYA 10/12)

11572 Coven, Wanda. *Heidi Heckelbeck and the Tie-Dyed Bunny* (1–3). Illus. by Priscilla Burris. 2014, 128pp. Heidi gets to take the principal's pet rabbit home for Easter, but the bunny gets into the dyes for the eggs and even Heidi's magic won't help; this early chapter book is 10th in the series. (Rev: BLO 3/1/14)

11573 Cowell, Cressida. *How to Cheat a Dragon's Curse: The Heroic Misadventures of Hiccup the Viking* (3–5). Illus. by author. Series: Hiccup. 2007, Little, Brown $10.99 (978-0-316-11425-7). 244pp. Another zany Hiccup adventure finds our hero on a quest to find the Vegetable That No One Dares Name, a task that involves evading Norbert the Nutjob and training a dragon. Entertaining illustrations add to the fun. (Rev: SLJ 5/07)

11574 Cowley, Joy. *Stories of the Wild West Gang* (3–6). Illus. by Trevor Pye. 2012, Gecko $16.95 (978-1-877579-21-9). 368pp. A compilation of 10 short chapter books set in New Zealand and featuring only child Michael and his fascination with his five rambunctious West cousins and their rowdy exploits. **e** (Rev: BLO 9/15/12; SLJ 10/12)

11575 Cox, Judy. *Third Grade Pet* (2–3). Illus. 1998, Holiday House $15.95 (978-0-8234-1379-9). 93pp. In this easy chapter book, Rosemary takes her class's pet

rat home to save him from the class bully and has problems keeping him hidden and safe. (Rev: BCCB 2/99; BL 12/15/98; HBG 3/99; SLJ 2/99)

11576 Cox, Judy. *Weird Stories from the Lonesome Cafe* (2–5). Illus. 2000, Harcourt $15.00 (978-0-15-202134-4). An easy chapter book in which Sam and his uncle open a roadside cafe to which celebrities come incognito. (Rev: BCCB 4/00; BL 4/15/00; HBG 10/00; SLJ 6/00)

11577 Danziger, Paula. *Amber Brown Goes Fourth* (2–4). Illus. 1995, Penguin $16.99 (978-0-399-22849-0). 112pp. Amber Brown, a fourth-grader unsure of herself, doesn't know how to react to her divorced mother's new boyfriend. (Rev: BCCB 11/95; BL 10/15/95; HB 11/95; SLJ 10/95*)

11578 Danziger, Paula. *Amber Brown Is Feeling Blue* (3–5). Illus. 1998, Penguin $16.99 (978-0-399-23179-7). 32pp. Amber's humorous adventures continue when her divorced mother takes a new boyfriend, her father returns from Paris, and a new girl in her class also has a color-name, Kelly Green. (Rev: BL 12/1/98; SLJ 11/98)

11579 Danziger, Paula. *Amber Brown Is Not a Crayon* (2–4). Illus. by Tony Ross. 1994, Penguin $16.99 (978-0-399-22509-3). 80pp. Amber Brown's close friendship with Justin Daniels will end soon because Justin's family is moving. (Rev: BCCB 6/94; BL 4/15/94; HB 7/94; SLJ 5/94*)

11580 Danziger, Paula. *Amber Brown Sees Red* (2–4). Illus. 1997, Penguin $15.99 (978-0-399-22901-5). 120pp. Amber Brown is now in the fourth grade and is increasingly upset with her parents' custody battles involving her. (Rev: BL 5/15/97; SLJ 7/97)

11581 Danziger, Paula. *I, Amber Brown* (3–6). Illus. by Tony Ross. 1999, Penguin $14.99 (978-0-399-23180-3). 140pp. Amber Brown, daughter of divorced parents, gets her ears pierced when she is with her father, in spite of her mother's objections. (Rev: BL 10/15/99; HBG 3/00; SLJ 11/99)

11582 Danziger, Paula. *You Can't Eat Your Chicken Pox, Amber Brown* (2–4). Illus. by Tony Ross. 1995, Penguin $15.99 (978-0-399-22702-8). 112pp. Amber visits London with her aunt while her parents are getting a divorce. A sequel to *Amber Brown Is Not a Crayon* (1994). (Rev: BCCB 4/95; BL 3/15/95; SLJ 6/95*)

11583 Derby, Kenneth. *The Top 10 Ways to Ruin the First Day of 5th Grade* (4–6). 2004, Holiday House $16.95 (978-0-8234-1851-0). 164pp. Fifth-grader Tony Madison, a big fan of David Letterman's late-night TV show, indulges in increasingly outrageous stunts in an effort to appear on the show. (Rev: BL 2/1/05; SLJ 1/05)

11584 Devillers, Julia, and Jennifer Roy. *Trading Faces* (4–7). 2008, Simon & Schuster $16.99 (978-1-4169-7531-1). 300pp. Middle school twins Emma and Payton have very different social lives — one is popular while the other is brainy — and switch places with interesting results. **e** Lexile HL460L (Rev: SLJ 5/1/09)

11585 Draper, Sharon M. *The Dazzle Disaster Dinner Party* (2–4). 2010, Scholastic $15.99 (978-0-545-07154-

3). 144pp. Ambitious 4th-grader Sassy decides to hold a dinner party for her class, but things do not go quite as planned. Lexile 530L (Rev: BL 12/15/10; SLJ 1/1/11)

11586 du Bois, William Pene. *Twenty-One Balloons* (4–6). Illus. by author. 1947, Puffin paper $6.99 (978-0-14-032097-8). 184pp. Truth and fiction are combined in the adventures of a professor who sails around the world in a balloon. Newbery Medal winner, 1948.

11587 Durand, Hallie. *Dessert First* (2–4). Illus. by Christine Davenier. 2009, Atheneum $14.99 (978-1-4169-6385-1). Eight-year-old Dessert, whose teacher urges students to march to their own drummers, tries to persuade her parents to start dinner with dessert. (Rev: BCCB 9/09; BLO 5/28/09; LMC 8/09; SLJ 7/09)

11588 Elliott, David. *Evangeline Mudd and the Great Mink Escapade* (3–5). 2006, Candlewick $15.99 (978-0-7636-2295-4). Evangeline Mudd, enthusiastic warrior for animal rights, sets out to free a number of minks before they are turned into ballet costumes. (Rev: BL 2/15/06; SLJ 3/06)

11589 Feiffer, Jules. *The Man in the Ceiling* (5–7). 1993, HarperCollins paper $9.99 (978-0-06-205907-9). Jimmy turns to cartooning in an effort to gain some recognition in a family that is intent on ignoring him. (Rev: BCCB 12/93; BL 11/15/93; SLJ 2/94*)

11590 Fleischman, Paul. *The Dunderheads* (3–5). Illus. by David Roberts. 2009, Candlewick $16.99 (978-0-7636-2498-9). 56pp. Miss Breakbone keeps an electric chair in the classroom and the students plan to overthrow the throne. (Rev: BCCB 7–8/09; BL 6/1–15/09; HB 7/09; SLJ 6/09)

11591 Fleischman, Sid. *Chancy and the Grand Rascal* (5–7). Illus. by Eric Von Schmidt. 1966, Little, Brown $14.95 (978-0-316-28575-9); paper $4.95 (978-0-316-26012-1). The boy and his uncle, the grand rascal, combine hard work and quick wits to outsmart a scoundrel, hoodwink a miser, and capture a band of outlaws.

11592 Fleischman, Sid. *The Ghost on Saturday Night* (3–5). Illus. by Eric Von Schmidt. 1974, Little, Brown $14.95 (978-0-316-28583-4). Ten-year-old Opie's efforts to raise money for a saddle involve him in a ghost-raising session and the recovery of money stolen from a bank.

11593 Fleischman, Sid. *McBroom Tells the Truth* (3–5). Illus. by Walter Lorraine. 1981, Little, Brown $12.45 (978-0-316-28550-6). 48pp. A tall tale about a New England farmer named McBroom. Also use: *McBroom and the Great Race* (1980). (Rev: SLJ 1/05)

11594 Fleischman, Sid. *Mr. Mysterious and Company* (3–5). Illus. by Eric Von Schmidt. 1997, Greenwillow $15.00 (978-0-688-14921-5). A traveling magic show during the 1880s makes for an entertaining family story that is also an excellent historical novel.

11595 Fleming, Candace. *The Fabled Fifth Graders of Aesop Elementary School* (3–5). 2010, Random House $15.99 (978-0-375-86334-9); LB $18.99 (978-0-375-96334-6). 176pp. The intrepid Mr. Jupiter steps up to educate the gang of rowdy 5th-graders in this zany story

packed with fable-related hyperbole, a sequel to *The Fabled Fourth Graders of Aesop Elementary School* (2007). ℮ Lexile 660L (Rev: BL 9/1/10; HB 9–10/10; SLJ 9/1/10)

11596 Foley, June. *Susanna Siegelbaum Gives Up Guys* (5–8). 1992, Scholastic paper $3.25 (978-0-590-43700-4). Susanna, a flirt, makes a bet that she can give up guys for three months. (Rev: SLJ 8/91)

11597 Foley, Lizzie K. *Remarkable* (3–7). 2012, Dial $16.99 (978-080373706-8). 304pp. Ordinary enough to be unsuitable for the town of Remarkable's School for the Remarkably Gifted, 10-year-old Jane Doe is the only student in the public school until the trouble-making Grimlet twins and a pirate captain arrive and lead her in a series of adventures. (Rev: BL 3/15/12*; HB 3–4/12; LMC 10/12; SLJ 4/12)

11598 Freeman, Martha. *The Polyester Grandpa* (4–5). 1998, Holiday House $15.95 (978-0-8234-1398-0). 145pp. Grandma turns up with a new husband — brash, uncouth Jimmy Barkenfalt — and 10-year-old Morgan Knight's family has a fit. (Rev: BCCB 1/99; BL 12/1/98; HBG 3/99; SLJ 12/98)

11599 Gannett, Ruth. *My Father's Dragon* (4–6). Illus. by author. 1986, Knopf paper $4.99 (978-0-394-89048-7). 88pp. Hilarious adventures of Elmer Elevator. Also use: *The Dragons of Blueland* (1963); *Elmer and the Dragon* (1987).

11600 Gauthier, Gail. *A Girl, a Boy, and a Monster Cat* (3–4). Illus. by Joe Cepeda. 2007, Putnam $14.99 (978-0-399-24689-0). 83pp. Despite their differences, Brandon and Hannah enjoy playing together after school, spying on Hannah's cat, and avoiding the crazy chihuahua next door. (Rev: BCCB 10/07; HB 7/07; SLJ 8/07)

11601 Gidwitz, Adam. *In a Glass Grimmly* (5–12). 2012, Dutton $16.99 (978-0-525-42581-6). 320pp. Jack and Jill — and a lonely frog — brave many scary situations in this gory yet humorous fairy-tale companion to *A Tale Dark and Grimm* (2010). ALA Notable Children's Book 2013. ☊ ℮ Lexile 630L (Rev: HB 11–12/12; LMC 5–6/13*; SLJ 10/12*; VOYA 12/12)

11602 Giff, Patricia Reilly. *Hunter Moran Saves the Universe* (4–7). 2012, Holiday $16.95 (978-0-8234-1949-4). 128pp. Imaginative 5th-grade twins Hunter and Zack investigate a dentist they believe is planning mayhem. ℮ Lexile 550L (Rev: BL 11/1/12; SLJ 11/12)

11603 Gifford, Peggy. *Moxy Maxwell Does Not Love Practicing the Piano (But She Does Love Being in Recitals)* (3–5). Photos by Valorie Fisher. 2009, Random House $12.99 (978-0-375-84488-1); LB $15.99 (978-0-375-96688-0). 177pp. Ten-year-old Moxy prepares for her recital — planning and constructing her clothes to the extent that she has no time for actual rehearsal. (Rev: BL 12/15/09; SLJ 11/1/09)

11604 Gifford, Peggy. *Moxy Maxwell Does Not Love Writing Thank-you Notes* (2–4). Illus. by Valorie Fisher. 2008, Random $12.99 (978-0-375-84270-2). 176pp. Ten-year-old Moxy knows she has to write these 12 thank-you notes but will she ever actually get around to it? (Rev: BL 9/1/08; HB 9/08; SLJ 8/08)

11605 Gleitzman, Morris. *Toad Away* (4–6). 2006, Random $14.95 (978-0-375-82766-2). 208pp. Limpy, the Australian cane toad, journeys to the Amazon in his quest to find a way to peacefully coexist with humans. (Rev: BL 2/15/06; SLJ 4/06)

11606 Gleitzman, Morris. *Toad Rage* (3–6). 2004, Random $14.95 (978-0-375-82762-4). A plucky Australian cane toad sets out to stop the carnage of his fellow amphibians on the roads. (Rev: BL 3/1/04; SLJ 4/04)

11607 Gorman, Carol. *Lizard Flanagan, Supermodel??* (4–7). 1998, HarperCollins $14.95 (978-0-06-024868-0). Sixth-grader Lizard Flanagan will do anything to make enough money to go by bus from her home in Iowa to a game in Wrigley Field, but is entering a local fashion show for teens going too far? (Rev: BL 11/15/98; HBG 3/99; SLJ 10/98)

11608 Goscinny, René. *Nicholas* (4–6). Trans. from French by Anthea Bell. Illus. by Jean-Jacques Sempé. 2005, Phaidon $19.95 (978-0-7148-4529-6). 128pp. Nicholas, a mischievous schoolboy, and his friends get into one scrape after another in this collection of tales by the author of the *Asterix* comics. (Rev: SLJ 10/05)

11609 Goscinny, René. *Nicholas on Vacation* (2–5). Trans. from French by Anthea Bell. Illus. by Jean-Jacques Sempé. 2006, Phaidon $19.95 (978-0-7148-4678-1). Follow Nicholas on his summer vacation as he travels to the beach with his parents and goes to a camp to stay overnight for the first time. *Nicholas and the Gang* (2007) is the fourth book about the boy who attracts trouble wherever he goes. (Rev: SLJ 3/07)

11610 Gosselink, John. *The Defense of Thaddeus A. Ledbetter* (4–7). 2010, Abrams $14.95 (978-0-8109-8977-1). 240pp. Mastermind and social misfit Thaddeus, 12, spends his time writing a "Prison Diary" and campaigning for his release from unfair In-school Suspension. Lexile 970L (Rev: BL 11/1/10; LMC 1–2/11; SLJ 11/1/10; VOYA 12/10)

11611 Grant, Michael. *The Call* (5–8). Series: The Magnificent 12. 2010, HarperCollins $16.99 (978-006183366-3). 224pp. An ordinary, fearful 12-year-old finds himself pitted against the Pale Queen in this tongue-in-cheek story about overcoming phobias; the first installment in a series. Also use *The Trap*. e Lexile 710L (Rev: BL 11/15/10*)

11612 Green, D. L. *Zeke Meeks vs. the Putrid Puppet Pals* (2–4). Illus. by Josh Alves. 2012, Capstone $21.32 (978-140486803-8); paper $5.95 (978-14048722-3-3). 128pp. Lighthearted gross-out humor adds appeal to this story of 3rd-grader Zeke, who deals with minor annoyances at home — an embarrassing dog, an annoying sister — and a felt finger puppet fad gripping his elementary school. (Rev: BL 3/15/12; LMC 5–6/12)

11613 Greenburg, Dan. *Tell a Lie and Your Butt Will Grow* (2–4). Illus. by Jack E. Davis. Series: Zack Files. 2002, Grosset paper $4.99 (978-0-448-42682-2). 58pp. Andrew, Zack's less-than-truthful partner on a science

fair project, discovers to his dismay that his backside is getting bigger with every fib he tells. (Rev: SLJ 4/03)

11614 Greenwald, Tommy. *Charlie Joe Jackson's Guide to Extra Credit* (4–7). Illus. by J. P. Coovert. 2012, Roaring Brook $14.99 (978-1-59643-692-3). 272pp. Desperate to boost his grades and avoid the dreaded Camp Rituhbukkee (Reading Camp), Charlie Joe signs up for the school play and agrees to be a model in art class; a sequel to 2011's *Charlie Joe Jackson's Guide to Not Reading*. ⌒ (Rev: BL 10/1/12; SLJ 11/12)

11615 Greenwald, Tommy. *Charlie Joe Jackson's Guide to Summer Vacation* (4–7). Illus. by J. P. Coovert. Series: Charlie Joe Jackson's Guide. 2013, Roaring Brook $14.99 (978-159643757-9). 224pp. Sentenced by his parents to a three-week academic camp, Charlie Joe sets out to convert the other residents into "normal" kids like him. Lexile 800 (Rev: BL 5/1/13; SLJ 12/13)

11616 Griffiths, Andy. *Killer Koalas from Outer Space: And Lots of Other Very Bad Stuff That Will Make Your Brain Explode* (4–7). Illus. by Terry Denton. 2011, Feiwel & Friends $12.99 (978-0-312-36789-3). 176pp. Often gross and silly, this collection of short stories, verse, and cartoons featuring "Very Bad" characters — everything from zombie kittens, killer koalas, and inadequate adults — will captivate its intended audience. (Rev: BL 11/1/11; SLJ 10/1/11)

11617 Griffiths, Andy. *The 13-Story Treehouse* (3–5). Illus. by Terry Denton. 2013, Feiwel & Friends $13.99 (978-125002690-3). 256pp. Book creators Andy and Terry, who live in a giant well-equipped treehouse, find plenty of material for their overdue manuscript as they deal with adventures involving giant bananas, flying cats, sea monkeys, and a sea monster pretending to be a mermaid. ⌒ e Lexile 560 (Rev: BL 4/1/13; LMC 10/13; SLJ 5/13)

11618 Gutman, Dan. *Ms. Beard Is Weird!* (1–3). Illus. by Jim Paillot. Series: My Weirder School. 2012, HarperCollins paper $3.99 (978-00620420-9-5). 112pp. Ella Mentry School is the site of a TV reality show in this funny series entry featuring A. J. and her teachers. e Lexile 650L (Rev: BL 9/1/12)

11619 Hamilton, Richard. *Cal and the Amazing Anti-Gravity Machine* (3–5). 2006, Bloomsbury paper $5.95 (978-1-58234-714-1). In this funny chapter book for new readers, 10-year-old Cal — accompanied by his talking dog Frankie — investigates his neighbor's newly developed antigravity machine with unsettling results. (Rev: BL 4/15/06; SLJ 7/06)

11620 Hannan, Peter. *Goofballs in Paradise*. Bk. #2 (2–4). Illus. by author. Series: Super Goofballs. 2007, HarperCollins $15.99 (978-0-06-085214-6); paper $4.99 (978-0-06-085213-9). 162pp. The Goofballs defend everyone's right to be goofy by defeating Mondo Grumpo while at a tropical resort. (Rev: SLJ 6/07)

11621 Hannan, Peter. *That Stinking Feeling*. Bk. #1 (2–4). Illus. by author. Series: Super Goofballs. 2007, HarperCollins $15.99 (978-0-06-085212-2); paper $4.99 (978-0-06-085211-5). 145pp. Amazing Techno Dude and his grandmother, Bodacious Backwoods Woman, round up a group of goofball superhero friends to fight the evil Queen Smellina and Fabian the Flatulent Fiend. (Rev: SLJ 6/07)

11622 Harper, Charise Mericle. *Just Grace* (2–4). Illus. 2007, Houghton $15.00 (978-0-618-64642-5). 144pp. Just Grace (misnamed by her teacher to set her apart from the other three Graces in her class) deals successfully with the usual third-grade problems in this funny chapter book, but her well-intentioned efforts to find a neighbor's cat go awry. (Rev: BL 3/1/07*)

11623 Harper, Charise Mericle. *Just Grace and the Snack Attack* (2–4). Illus. by author. Series: Just Grace. 2009, Houghton Mifflin $15 (978-0-547-15223-3). 176pp. Grace's research into flavored potato chips prompts speculation about various apparently unrelated aspects of her life. Lexile 940L (Rev: BL 3/15/10; HB 11–12/09; SLJ 12/1/09)

11624 Hayes, Daniel. *Eye of the Beholder* (5–8). 1992, Fawcett paper $6.99 (978-0-449-00235-3). Tyler and Lymie are in trouble again when they fake some works of a famous sculptor. (Rev: BL 2/1/93; SLJ 12/92)

11625 Hite, Sid. *Those Darn Dithers* (5–8). 1996, Henry Holt $15.95 (978-0-8050-3838-5). A humorous novel about the dithering Dithers with adventures involving Porcellina the dancing pig and an eccentric who drifts out to sea on a rubber raft. (Rev: BL 12/15/96; SLJ 12/96; VOYA 10/97)

11626 Horvath, Polly. *The Trolls* (3–6). Illus. by Wendy A. Halperin. 1999, Farrar $16.00 (978-0-364-37787-1). Aunt Sally spins some fanciful tales when she entertains two nieces and a nephew left in her care. (Rev: BL 3/1/99*; SLJ 4/99)

11627 Horvath, Polly. *When the Circus Came to Town* (5–8). 1996, Farrar paper $5.95 (978-0-374-48367-8). Opinion is sharply divided in Ivy's town when a circus troupe decides to relocate there. (Rev: BCCB 12/96; BL 11/15/96; SLJ 12/96*)

11628 Howe, Deborah, and James Howe. *Bunnicula: A Rabbit Tale of Mystery* (4–6). Illus. by Alan Daniel. 1979, Macmillan LB $16.00 (978-0-689-30700-3); Avon paper $3.99 (978-0-380-51094-8). 112pp. A dog named Harold tells the story of a rabbit many believe to be a vampire. Two sequels by James Howe are: *Howliday Inn* (1982); *The Celery Stalks at Midnight* (1983).

11629 Howe, James. *Bunnicula Meets Edgar Allan Crow* (4–7). Illus. by Eric Fortune. 2006, Simon & Schuster $15.95 (978-1-4169-1458-7). When world-famous author M. T. Graves and his pet, Edgar Allan Crow, come to stay with the Monroe family, Bunnicula the vampire bunny suspects that the household guests are up to no good. (Rev: BL 1/1–15/07; SLJ 2/07)

11630 Howe, James. *Bunnicula Strikes Again!* (3–6). 1999, Simon & Schuster $15.00 (978-0-689-81463-1). In this sequel to *Bunnicula*, the fanged rabbit, who needs a diet of carrot juice, is again pursued by Chester, who is afraid other vegetables might be endangered. (Rev: BL 10/1/99; HBG 3/00; SLJ 12/99)

11631 Howe, James. *Howie Monroe and the Doghouse of Doom* (3–5). Illus. by Brett Helquist. 2002, Simon & Schuster $9.95 (978-0-689-83951-1). Puppy Howie is self-congratulatory about his literary creation, a funny parody of Harry Potter. (Rev: BL 10/1/02; HBG 3/03)

11632 Howe, James. *The New Nick Kramer or My Life as a Baby-Sitter* (5–9). 1995, Hyperion LB $14.49 (978-0-7868-2053-5). Nick and rival Mitch make an unusual bet on who will win the affections of newcomer Jennifer. (Rev: BL 12/15/95; SLJ 1/96)

11633 Ives, David. *Monsieur Eek* (4–7). 2001, HarperCollins LB $15.89 (978-0-06-029530-1). Thirteen-year-old Emmaline defends a monkey against criminal charges in the not-quite-right town of MacOongafoondsen, population 21. (Rev: BL 6/1–15/01; HBG 3/02; SLJ 6/01)

11634 Jennings, Patrick. *My Homework Ate My Homework* (4–7). 2013, Egmont $15.99 (978-160684286-7). 224pp. Zaritza, a melodramatic 11-year-old seeking a starring role in an upcoming play, is prepared to use any excuse — including the class ferret — to account for her homework shortcomings. Lexile 590 (Rev: BL 4/1/13; LMC 5–6/13; SLJ 6/13)

11635 Jennings, Richard W. *Ferret Island* (5–7). 2007, Houghton Mifflin $16.00 (978-0-618-80632-4). Will and a huge, friendly ferret named Jim are on the run from a ferret gang that has been trained to attack McDonald's restaurants. (Rev: BCCB 5/07; BL 7/07; HB 5–6/07; SLJ 5/07)

11636 Jennings, Richard W. *My Life of Crime* (4–8). 2002, Houghton Mifflin $15.00 (978-0-618-21433-4). Nothing goes right when 6th-grader Fowler decides to "rescue" a caged parrot. (Rev: BL 1/1–15/03; HBG 3/03; VOYA 2/03)

11637 Keller, Laurie. *Bowling Alley Bandit* (2–4). Illus. by author. 2013, Henry Holt $12.99 (978-0-8050-9076-5). 112pp. Arnie the doughnut joins his best friend, Mr. Bing, in his bowling league and solves a mystery in this boisterous blend of text and graphic elements. (Rev: BLO 7/13; LMC 1–2/14*; SLJ 7/13*)

11638 Kelly, Katy. *Melonhead and the Big Stink* (3–5). Illus. by Gillian Johnson. 2010, Delacorte $14.99 (978-0-385-73658-9); LB $17.99 (978-0-385-90617-3). 224pp. Adam "Melonhead" and his friend Sam, rising 5th-graders, do their very best to behave in order to travel to New York to see the smelly "titan arum" that only blooms every seven years. (Rev: BLO 4/15/10; SLJ 7/1/10)

11639 Kelly, Katy. *Melonhead and the Vegalicious Disaster* (3–5). Illus. by Gillian Johnson. 2012, Delacorte $14.99 (978-038574164-4); LB $17.99 (978-037599015-1). 224pp. Adam "Melonhead" is back, suffering from his mother's enthusiasm for vegetables and dealing with school and friendship predicaments. **e** Lexile 470L (Rev: BLO 10/1/12)

11640 Kerrin, Jessica Scott. *Martin Bridge Sound the Alarm!* (2–4). Illus. by Joseph Kelly. Series: Martin Bridge. 2007, Kids Can $14.95 (978-1-55337-976-8); paper $4.95 (978-1-55337-977-5). 110pp. What kid wouldn't like to be locked in a toy store? When this really happens to Martin and his friend, Martin comes up with an ingenious plan to call for help. (Rev: SLJ 5/07)

11641 Kidd, Ronald. *Sammy Carducci's Guide to Women* (5–7). 1995, Dramatic Publg $6.25 (978-0-87129-522-4). A somewhat sexist 6th grader discovers that, where women are concerned, perhaps he is not as irresistible as he thinks he is. (Rev: BCCB 1/92; BL 1/1/92; SLJ 1/92)

11642 Kimmel, Elizabeth Cody. *The Reinvention of Moxie Roosevelt* (5–7). 2010, Dial $16.99 (978-0-8037-3303-9). 256pp. Thirteen-year-old Moxie decides to reinvent herself when she heads off to boarding school, eventually realizing that it's easiest to just be herself. Lexile 780L (Rev: BL 6/10; LMC 1–2/11; SLJ 7/10)

11643 Kinard, Kami. *The Boy Project (Notes and Observations of Kara McAllister)* (5–8). Illus. by author. 2012, Scholastic $12.99 (978-054534515-6). 272pp. Kara employs scientific method to help figure out the best way to land a date, documenting her progress on note cards. e (Rev: BL 3/1/12; SLJ 2/12)

11644 Kinney, Jeff. *Cabin Fever* (5–8). Illus. by author. Series: Diary of a Wimpy Kid. 2011, Abrams $12.95 (978-141970223-5). 224pp. It's the month between Thanksgiving and Christmas, and Greg is tired of having to behave for Santa, especially when the adults in his life are so unreasonable. YALSA Amazing Audiobooks Top Ten 2013. (Rev: BLO 11/1/11)

11645 Kinney, Jeff. *Hard Luck* (5–8). Illus. by author. Series: Diary of a Wimpy Kid. 2013, Abrams/Amulet $13.95 (978-141971132-9). 224pp. Greg finds himself abandoned when his best friend Rowley gets a girlfriend, and unfortunately this means spending even more time with his eccentric extended family — but the real question is, will Greg and Rowley be friends again? e Lexile 1020 (Rev: BLO 11/1/13)

11646 Kinney, Jeff. *The Last Straw* (5–8). Illus. by author. Series: Diary of a Wimpy Kid. 2009, Abrams $12.95 (978-0-8109-7068-7). 224pp. Middle school non-jock Greg Heffley keeps a diary in which he details his angst about his troublesome brothers, his demanding father, and other aspects of life. ⌂ (Rev: BL 2/1/09; SLJ 4/09)

11647 Kinney, Jeff. *Rodrick Rules* (5–8). Illus. by author. Series: Diary of a Wimpy Kid. 2008, Abrams $12.95 (978-0-8109-9473-7). Twelve-year-old Greg Heffley of *Diary of a Wimpy Kid* (2007) will make readers laugh again with this diary that recounts his struggles at home and at school, particularly those involving his annoying older brother Rodrick. (Rev: BL 2/1/08; SLJ 3/08)

11648 Kinney, Jeff. *The Third Wheel* (5–8). Illus. by author. Series: Diary of a Wimpy Kid. 2012, Abrams/Amulet $13.95 (978-141970584-7). 224pp. To his surprise, Greg has a date for the Valentine's Day dance and must leave best friend Rowley to fend for himself; the 7th volume in the series. e Lexile 1060L (Rev: BLO 11/15/12)

11649 Kinney, Jeff. *The Ugly Truth* (5–8). Illus. by author. Series: Diary of a Wimpy Kid. 2010, Abrams $13.95 (978-081098491-2). 224pp. Charging headlong toward puberty, Greg Heffley suffers a series of mor-

tifying tween social gaffes. Lexile 1000L (Rev: BLO 11/1/10; SLJ 5/11)

11650 Kline, Suzy. *Orp Goes to the Hoop* (5–7). 1993, Avon paper $3.50 (978-0-380-71829-0). Seventh-grader Orp gets a chance to play a big part in the basketball team's big game. (Rev: BCCB 7–8/91; BL 7/91; SLJ 7/91)

11651 Klise, Kate. *Regarding the Bathrooms: A Privy to the Past* (4–6). Illus. by M. Sarah Klise. Series: Regarding the . . . 2006, Harcourt $15.00 (978-0-15-205164-8). 160pp. The principal of Geyser Creek Middle School grows increasingly frustrated as unexpected events delay progress on the school's bathroom remodeling project in this multilayered, funny story involving a dollop of Roman/bathroom history and told through letters, memos, newspaper articles, and police reports. (Rev: BL 9/1/06; SLJ 8/06)

11652 Klise, Kate. *Regarding the Bees: A Lesson in Letters, on Honey, Dating and Other Sticky Subjects* (4–6). Illus. by M. Sarah Klise. 2007, Harcourt $15.00 (978-0-15-205711-4). Now in 7th grade, the students at Geyser Creek Middle School must prepare for the Basic Education Evaluation (BEE) standardized test through corresponding via fax and letter with fountain designer Florence Waters. (Rev: BL 11/1/07; SLJ 9/07)

11653 Klise, Kate. *Regarding the Fountain: A Tale, in Letters, of Liars and Leaks* (4–6). Illus. 1998, Avon $16.99 (978-0-380-97538-9). 144pp. Dry Creek's school needs a new water fountain, causing a flurry of letters, memos, and other communications involving the school and fountain designer, Florence Waters. (Rev: BL 8/98; HB 5/98; HBG 10/98; SLJ 6/98)

11654 Klise, Kate. *Regarding the Trees: A Splintered Saga Rooted in Secrets* (4–6). Illus. by M. Sarah Klise. 2005, Harcourt $15.00 (978-0-15-205163-1). In a scrapbook format using letters, news articles, and illustrations, this is the funny, pun-filled, and complex story of a dispute over trimming the trees at the middle school and a community's various interests. (Rev: BL 11/1/05; SLJ 11/05)

11655 Korman, Gordon. *Maxx Comedy: The Funniest Kid in America* (4–6). 2003, Hyperion $15.99 (978-0-7868-0746-8). 160pp. The joke-filled story of Max Carmody's quest to be the funniest kid in America also resonates with themes of friendship and loyalty. (Rev: BL 6/1–15/03; HBG 10/03; SLJ 9/03)

11656 Krishnaswami, Uma. *The Grand Plan to Fix Everything* (4–6). Illus. by Abigail Halpin. 2011, Atheneum $16.99 (978-1-4169-9589-0). 272pp. Eleven-year-old Dini is initially sad when she hears her family is moving to India for two years, but also hopeful that she will get to meet her favorite Bollywood star. (Rev: BL 9/1/11; SLJ 5/11)

11657 Krulik, Nancy. *Trouble Magnet* (2–4). Illus. by Aaron Blecha. Series: George Brown, Class Clown. 2010, Grosset & Dunlap paper $4.99 (978-0-448-45368-2). 128pp. A 4th-grader suffering from a case of enormous belches struggles to control the behavior when he arrives at his new school. (Rev: SLJ 7/1/10)

11658 Kurzweil, Allen. *Leon and the Champion Chip* (3–6). Illus. by Bret Bertholf. 2005, Greenwillow $15.99 (978-0-06-053933-7). 336pp. Leon Zeisel starts fifth grade, plans revenge on bully Henry Lumpkin, and discovers to his amazement that his science class will spend a semester researching the potato chip, his favorite snack food; a funny sequel to *Leon and the Spitting Image* (2003). (Rev: BL 11/1/05; SLJ 3/06)

11659 Laden, Nina. *Romeow and Drooliet* (2–6). Illus. by author. 2005, Chronicle $16.95 (978-0-8118-3973-0). Romance is surely doomed when cat Romeow and dog Drooliet fall for each other. (Rev: SLJ 6/05)

11660 Lawson, Robert. *Ben and Me* (5–8). Illus. by author. 1939, Little, Brown $16.95 (978-0-316-51732-4); paper $5.99 (978-0-316-51730-0). The events of Benjamin Franklin's life, as told by his good mouse Amos, who lived in his old fur cap.

11661 Lawson, Robert. *Captain Kidd's Cat* (3–5). Illus. by author. 1984, Little, Brown paper $7.95 (978-0-316-51735-5). A narrative recount by McDermot, faithful cat of Captain William Kidd.

11662 Lawson, Robert. *Mr. Revere and I* (5–8). Illus. by author. 1953, Little, Brown paper $6.99 (978-0-316-51729-4). A delightful account of certain episodes in Revere's life, as revealed by his horse Scheherazade. (Rev: SLJ 1/05)

11663 Lindgren, Astrid. *Pippi Longstocking* (4–6). Trans. by Florence Lamborn. Illus. by Louis Glanzman. 1950, Puffin paper $5.99 (978-0-14-030957-7). 158pp. A little Swedish tomboy who has a monkey and a horse for companions. Also use: *Pippi Goes on Board* (1957); *Pippi in the South Seas* (1959).

11664 Lowry, Lois. *Anastasia at This Address* (5–9). 1991, Houghton Mifflin $16.00 (978-0-395-56263-5); paper $4.50 (978-0-440-40652-5). The irrepressible Anastasia answers a personal ad, using her mother's picture instead of her own, with typically hilarious results. (Rev: BCCB 3/91; BL 4/1/91; SLJ 8/91)

11665 Lowry, Lois. *Anastasia on Her Own* (5–7). 1985, Houghton Mifflin $16.00 (978-0-395-38133-5); paper $4.50 (978-0-440-40291-6). Seventh-grader Anastasia Krupnik must face both domestic crisis and romance. Another chapter in Anastasia's busy life is recounted in *Anastasia Has the Answers* (1986). (Rev: BL 5/15/85; HB 9–10/85; SLJ 8/85)

11666 Lowry, Lois. *Anastasia's Chosen Career* (5–7). 1987, Houghton Mifflin $16.00 (978-0-395-42506-0); paper $4.50 (978-0-440-40100-1). Thirteen-year-old Anastasia gets some surprises when she begs to go to charm school to change her freaky looks. Anastasia's baby brother is featured in *All About Sam* (1988). (Rev: BCCB 9/87; BL 9/1/87; SLJ 9/87)

11667 Lowry, Lois. *Attaboy, Sam!* (2–5). Illus. by Diane deGroat. 1992, Houghton $16.00 (978-0-395-61588-1). Anastasia Krupnik's little brother, Sam, decides to make

perfume for his mother's birthday. (Rev: BCCB 4/92; BL 2/15/92*; HB 7/92*; SLJ 5/92*)

11668 Lowry, Lois. *The Birthday Ball* (3–5). Illus. by Jules Feiffer. 2010, Houghton Mifflin $16 (978-0-547-23869-2). 192pp. Princess Patricia's 16th birthday — and the time to choose between unappealing suitors — is looming and she takes refuge in disguising herself as a peasant girl and attending the village school. 🎧 **e** Lexile 870L (Rev: BL 3/1/10*; HB 3–4/10; SLJ 3/10)

11669 Lowry, Lois. *See You Around, Sam!* (3–6). Illus. by Diane deGroat. 1996, Houghton $15.00 (978-0-395-81664-6). 144pp. Sam decides to run away to Alaska because his mother won't let him wear his plastic fangs. (Rev: BCCB 11/96; BL 10/1/96*; HB 9/96; SLJ 10/96*)

11670 Lowry, Lois. *Switcharound* (5–7). 1985, Houghton Mifflin $16.00 (978-0-395-39536-3). Caroline and her nemesis brother J.P. must spend the summer with their divorced father's new family in Des Moines. A sequel to *The One Hundredth Thing About Caroline* (1983). (Rev: BCCB 1/86; BL 10/1/85; HB 1–2/86)

11671 Lowry, Lois. *The Willoughbys* (4–6). Illus. by author. 2008, Houghton $16.00 (978-0-618-97974-5). 176pp. The dreadful Willoughby parents take off on vacation and try to sell the house in their absence, leaving their four children — who are in the care of a much-despised nanny — plotting to become "deserving orphans." (Rev: BL 2/15/08; HB 3/08; SLJ 4/08; VOYA 8/08) 🎧

11672 Lowry, Lois. *Zooman Sam* (3–5). Illus. 1999, Houghton $16.00 (978-0-395-97393-6). 160pp. Sam Krupnick is in seventh heaven when he learns to read in his nursery school. (Rev: BCCB 9/99; BL 7/99; HB 9/99; HBG 3/00; SLJ 9/99)

11673 Lubar, David. *Numbed!* (3–5). 2013, Millbrook $15.95 (978-146770594-3). 144pp. Logan and Benedict think math is boring, but when their math skills are numbed by a robot at the Mobius Mathematics Museum, they discover that they use math more than they could have imagined. **e** Lexile 550 (Rev: BLO 9/15/13; LMC 5–6/14; SLJ 8/13)

11674 Lubar, David. *Punished!* (4–7). 2006, Darby Creek $15.95 (978-1-58196-042-6). Thanks to a curse, Logan becomes a non-stop punster and must uncover oxymorons, anagrams, and palindromes to break the spell. (Rev: BL 5/1/06; SLJ 5/06*)

11675 Luper, Eric. *Jeremy Bender vs. the Cupcake Cadets* (3–6). 2011, HarperCollins $15.99 (978-0-06-201512-9). 240pp. After 6th-grader Jeremy damages his father's beloved antique motorboat, he and his friend Slater dress up as girls and hope to win the prize money in a model-sailboat race organized by the Cupcake Cadet club. (Rev: BL 5/1/11; SLJ 6/11)

11676 McCloskey, Robert. *Homer Price* (3–6). Illus. by author. 1943, Puffin paper $6.99 (978-0-14-030927-0). 160pp. Popular and preposterous adventures of a Midwestern boy. Continued in: *Centerburg Tales* (1951).

11677 MacDonald, Amy. *No More Nice* (4–7). 1996, Orchard LB $15.99 (978-0-531-08892-0). A humorous story about a spring vacation spent by a boy with his eccentric great-aunt and -uncle. (Rev: BCCB 10/96; BL 9/1/96; SLJ 9/96)

11678 McDonald, Megan. *Cloudy with a Chance of Boys* (4–6). Series: Sisters Club. 2011, Candlewick $15.99 (978-0-7636-4615-8). 272pp. Is 12-year-old Stevie ready for a boyfriend? She struggles with this idea even as her older sister Alex admires a student named Scott and her younger sister Joey prefers frogs; the third book in the series. ⌒ ℮ Lexile 500L (Rev: BL 3/15/11; SLJ 3/1/11)

11679 McDonald, Megan. *Judy Moody Predicts the Future* (2–4). Illus. by Peter H. Reynolds. Series: Judy Moody. 2003, Candlewick $15.99 (978-0-7636-1792-9). 160pp. Eight-year-old Judy Moody is convinced that she has newfound psychic abilities when she slips on the mood ring from the cereal box. (Rev: BL 9/15/03; HBG 4/04; SLJ 11/03)

11680 McDonald, Megan. *Stink and the Incredible Super-Galactic Jawbreaker* (2–4). Illus. by Peter H. Reynolds. Series: Stink. 2006, Candlewick $12.99 (978-0-7636-2158-2). 128pp. When he discovers that a letter of complaint can yield free candy, Stink — Judy Moody's younger brother — embarks on a letter-writing campaign. (Rev: BL 4/15/06; SLJ 7/06)

11681 McDonald, Megan. *Stink and the Midnight Zombie Walk* (K–3). Illus. by Peter H. Reynolds. Series: Stink. 2012, Candlewick $12.99 (978-076365692-8). 160pp. The book release party for a zombie thriller attracts a lot of attention in this early chapter book. ⌒ (Rev: BL 2/1/12)

11682 McDonald, Megan. *Stink and the Ultimate Thumb-Wrestling Smackdown* (2–4). Illus. by Peter H. Reynolds. Series: Stink. 2011, Candlewick $12.99 (978-076364346-1). 144pp. After flunking gym class, Stink tries thumb-wrestling before deciding to take up karate; lively graphics and wordplay add to the fun. (Rev: BL 1/1–15/11)

11683 McDonald, Megan. *Stink: Solar System Superhero* (2–4). Illus. by Peter H. Reynolds. Series: Stink. 2010, Candlewick $12.99 (978-0-7636-4321-8). 118pp. When 2nd-grader Stink learns that Pluto has been demoted to a dwarf planet, he sets out to restore its status in this entertaining and informative story. ⌒ Lexile 930 (Rev: BL 1/1/10; SLJ 2/1/10)

11684 Mackay, Claire, sel. *Laughs* (5–8). 1997, Tundra paper $6.95 (978-0-88776-393-9). An anthology of humorous stories (and some poems) by several well-known Canadian writers. (Rev: SLJ 9/97)

11685 McKenna, Colleen O'Shaughnessy. *Mother Murphy* (5–7). 1993, Scholastic paper $2.95 (978-0-590-44856-7). With her mother confined to bed, 12-year-old Collette volunteers as mother-for-a-day with disasterous and funny results. (Rev: BCCB 2/92; BL 2/1/92; SLJ 2/92)

11686 MacLachlan, Patricia. *Arthur, for the Very First Time* (4–6). Illus. by Lloyd Bloom. 1980, HarperCollins

paper $4.99 (978-0-06-440288-0). 128pp. Arthur spends a summer on the farm of his aunt and uncle.

11687 McMahen, Chris. *Tabloidology* (4–6). 2009, Orca paper $9.95 (978-1-55469-009-1). It's either close the school newspaper or hire loose cannon Trixie Wilder as a writer. What's a boy to do? (Rev: BL 6/1–15/09)

11688 Maguire, Gregory. *One Final Firecracker* (4–7). Illus. by Elaine Clayton. Series: The Hamlet Chronicles. 2005, Clarion $17.00 (978-0-618-27480-2). In the final pun-filled installment in the series, the rival Tattletales and Copycats must cooperate to defend the class and the soon-to-be-wed Miss Earth from myriad threats. (Rev: SLJ 5/05)

11689 Mason, Simon. *The Quigleys in a Spin* (3–5). Illus. by Helen Stephens. 2006, Random $14.95 (978-0-385-75098-1). Lucy painting her sleeping dad's toenails and having a dreadful birthday party are only two of the funny episodes in this British chapter book. (Rev: BL 1/1–15/06; SLJ 4/06)

11690 Meacham, Margaret. *A Fairy's Guide to Understanding Humans* (5–8). 2007, Holiday $16.95 (978-0-8234-2078-0). Morgan's unreliable fairy godmother tries to improve 14-year-old Morgan's life after her move to a new house and new school in this sequel to *A Mid-Semester Night's Dream* (2004). (Rev: BL 2/1/08; SLJ 2/08)

11691 Mills, Claudia. *Alex Ryan, Stop That!* (4–7). Series: West Creek Middle School. 2003, Farrar $16.00 (978-0-374-34655-3). All Alex's efforts to attract classmate Marcia go awry in this humorous account of 7th-grade and son-father relations. (Rev: BL 4/1/03; HBG 10/03; SLJ 4/03)

11692 Montgomery, Claire, and Monte Montgomery. *Hubert Invents the Wheel* (4–7). Illus. by Jeff Shelly. 2005, Walker $16.95 (978-0-8027-8990-7). Hubert, a struggling 15-year-old inventor in ancient Sumeria, finally finds success when he invents the wheel, but things quickly spin out of control. (Rev: SLJ 11/05)

11693 Morgan, Christopher. *Pirates Drive Buses* (2–4). 2008, Roaring Brook $14.95 (978-1-59643-313-7). 80pp. This zany seagoing adventure opens with brother Bill and sister Heidi on their way to school when they meet their pirate friend and are persuaded to join him on a search for his ship. (Rev: BL 3/1/08; LMC 3/08; SLJ 5/08)

11694 Mulford, Philippa Greene. *Making Room for Katherine* (5–9). 1994, Macmillan $14.95 (978-0-02-767652-5). A 16-year-old is recovering from her father's death when a 13-year-old cousin arrives from Paris to visit for the summer. (Rev: BL 4/15/94; SLJ 5/94; VOYA 8/94)

11695 Naylor, Phyllis Reynolds. *Alice in April* (5–8). 1993, Dell paper $4.50 (978-0-440-91032-9). Alice is back, this time caught between her desire to be a perfect housekeeper and her fascination with her developing body. (Rev: BL 3/1/93; SLJ 6/93)

11696 Naylor, Phyllis Reynolds. *Alice the Brave* (5–7). 1995, Simon & Schuster paper $4.99 (978-0-689-80598-

1). Alice conquers her fear of deep water and also feels the pangs of growing up in this amusing continuation of a popular series. (Rev: BCCB 4/95; BL 5/1/95; HB 7–8/95; SLJ 5/95)

11697 Naylor, Phyllis Reynolds. *Boys Against Girls* (4–6). 1994, Delacorte $14.95 (978-0-385-32081-8). 147pp. Boys and girls try to trick each other into believing that a strange monster exists, and maybe they are right. (Rev: BCCB 11/94; BL 9/1/94; SLJ 11/94)

11698 Naylor, Phyllis Reynolds. *Boys Rock!* (4–6). 2005, Delacorte $15.95 (978-0-385-73140-9). 144pp. To earn extra reading credits over the summer, the Hatford brothers decide to publish a newspaper, an undertaking that becomes even more complicated when they reluctantly ask the Malloy sisters to join them. (Rev: BL 10/1/05; SLJ 1/06)

11699 Naylor, Phyllis Reynolds. *Reluctantly Alice* (5–8). 1991, Macmillan $16.00 (978-0-689-31681-4). Alice's life in the 7th grade seems full of embarrassment. (Rev: BCCB 4/91*; BL 2/1/91; HB 7–8/91; SLJ 3/91*)

11700 Naylor, Phyllis Reynolds. *Who Won the War?* (4–7). 2006, Delacorte LB $17.99 (978-0-385-90172-7). In the last weeks before they return to Ohio (and the last volume in the series), the Malloy sisters mount a last-ditch campaign to prove their superiority over the Hatford boys. (Rev: BL 11/1/06; SLJ 9/06)

11701 Nesbo, Jo. *Doctor Proctor's Fart Powder* (4–7). Illus. by Mike Lowery. 2010, Simon & Schuster $14.99 (978-1-4169-7972-2). 160pp. Dr. Proctor's loud but non-smelly invention launches Nilly into outer space at the beginning of this humorous, action-packed story in which bad people try to steal this wondrous product; set in Norway. ∩ Lexile 830L (Rev: BL 1/1/10; SLJ 2/10)

11702 Nesbo, Jo. *Who Cut the Cheese?* (4–7). Trans. by Tara F. Chance. Illus. by Mike Lowery. Series: Doctor Proctor's Fart Powder. 2012, Aladdin $15.99 (978-144243307-6). 464pp. In this sequel to *Doctor Proctor's Fart Powder* (2010), Nilly, Lisa, and Dr. Procter apply their zany inventions to the burgeoning crises threatening Norway. e Lexile 770L (Rev: BL 1/1/12; LMC 5–6/12; SLJ 6/12)

11703 Norriss, Andrew. *I Don't Believe It, Archie!* (2–5). Illus. by Hannah Shaw. 2012, Random House $12.99 (978-038575250-3); LB $15.99 (978-038575251-0). 128pp. Prone to misadventure, young Archie's stories are never believed in this funny British import. e (Rev: BL 3/1/12*; HB 3–4/12; LMC 3–4/12; SLJ 3/12)

11704 O'Brien, John. *Look . . . Look Again!* (3–6). Illus. by author. 2012, Boyds Mills paper $18.95 (978-15907889-4-3). 64pp. Whimsical cartoon illustrations portray quirky scenarios that will amuse and tease the brain. (Rev: BL 11/15/12; SLJ 1/13)

11705 O'Malley, Kevin. *Captain Raptor and the Moon Mystery* (K–4). Illus. by Patrick O'Brien. 2005, Walker $16.95 (978-0-8027-8935-8). Captain Raptor and his dinosaur crew blast into space to investigate the landing of a UFO — carrying alien humans — on one of Jurassica's moons. (Rev: BCCB 4/05; SLJ 4/05)

11706 O'Malley, Kevin. *Once Upon a Royal Super Baby* (3–5). Illus. by Scott Goto. 2010, Walker $16.99 (978-0-8027-2164-8). 32pp. A boy and girl bicker over their creative writing assignment, the girl imagining a sweet royal baby who can talk to birds while the boy gives him superpowers, a motorcycle, and sunglasses. (Rev: BL 11/1/10; LMC 11–12/10; SLJ 9/1/10)

11707 Parish, Herman. *Amelia Bedelia Means Business* (2–4). Illus. by Lynne Avril. 2013, Greenwillow paper $4.99 (978-0-06-209-496-4). 146pp. Amelia Bedelia comes to the chapter-book reader with this first story about her hapless efforts to earn her share of a coveted bicycle. Lexile 640 (Rev: BL 3/15/13; LMC 8–9/13; SLJ 4/13)

11708 Park, Barbara. *Buddies* (5–8). 1986, Avon paper $2.95 (978-0-380-69992-6). Dinah's dreams of being popular at camp are dashed in this humorous novel because she is forever being accompanied by Fern, the camp nerd. (Rev: BCCB 5/85; BL 4/15/85; SLJ 5/85)

11709 Park, Barbara. *Junie B. Jones and a Little Monkey Business* (2–3). Illus. by Denise Brunkus. 1993, Random paper $3.99 (978-0-679-83886-9). 46pp. Junie is amazed to learn that her new brother is a monkey after grandmother declares, "He's the cutest monkey I've ever seen!" (Rev: BL 3/1/93)

11710 Park, Barbara. *Junie B. Jones and the Stupid Smelly Bus* (2–3). Illus. by Denise Brunkus. 1992, Random $11.99 (978-0-679-92642-9); paper $3.99 (978-0-679-82642-2). 70pp. Junie B. is a cross between Lily Tomlin's Edith Ann and Eloise in this funny story of a youngster on her way to kindergarten. (Rev: BL 12/1/92; SLJ 11/92)

11711 Park, Barbara. *Junie B. Jones Is a Beauty Shop Guy* (2–3). 1998, Random LB $11.99 (978-0-679-98939-4); paper $3.99 (978-0-679-88931-1). Junie B. Jones believes she has a calling to become a barber and, after practicing on various stuffed animals, decides to move on to a human subject — herself. (Rev: BL 11/15/98; SLJ 12/98)

11712 Park, Barbara. *Junie B. Jones Smells Something Fishy* (2–4). Illus. 1998, Random paper $3.99 (978-0-679-89130-7). 67pp. When all her plans to take a pet to school fail, a disappointed Junie brings a fish stick instead and wins a prize for the most well-behaved pet. (Rev: BL 3/15/99)

11713 Park, Barbara. *The Kid in the Red Jacket* (4–6). 1988, Knopf paper $3.99 (978-0-394-80571-9). 128pp. Ten-year-old Howard is having some trouble adjusting to life in Massachusetts when his family moves from Arizona. (Rev: BCCB 3/87; BL 2/15/87; SLJ 3/87)

11714 Park, Barbara. *Operation: Dump the Chump* (3–6). Illus. by Robert Sauber. 1989, Knopf paper $4.99 (978-0-394-82592-2). 128pp. Oscar Winkle devises a plan to get rid of his young brother.

11715 Pastis, Stephan. *Timmy Failure: Mistakes Were Made* (4–7). Illus. by author. 2013, Candlewick $14.99 (978-076366050-5). 304pp. This illustrated comic novel presents 11-year-old Timmy Failure, detective par excellence, and his sidekick, a giant polar bear named Total. **e** Lexile 520L (Rev: BL 12/1/12; LMC 8–9/13; SLJ 5/13)

11716 Patterson, James, and Chris Grabenstein. *I Funny* (4–7). Illus. by Laura Park. 2012, Little, Brown $15.99 (978-0-316-20693-8). 255pp. Aspiring middle school comedian Jamie Grimm uses humor to cope with the fact that he's confined to a wheelchair. ⌒ **e** Lexile 610L (Rev: BL 10/15/12; LMC 3–4/13; SLJ 12/12; VOYA 12/12)

11717 Paulsen, Gary. *Lawn Boy* (5–8). 2007, Random House $12.99 (978-0-385-74686-1). Given his late grandfather's somewhat battered riding mower as a gift, a 12-year-old entrepreneur launches a phenomenally successful lawn care business in this zany, tongue-in-cheek story. (Rev: BL 4/15/07; HB 7–8/07; SLJ 6/07)

11718 Paulsen, Gary. *Lawn Boy Returns* (5–8). Series: Lawn Boy. 2010, Random House $12.99 (978-0-385-74662-5); LB $15.99 (978-0-385-90899-3). 101pp. The enterprising 12-year-old's lawn business grows into a monster and his hippie stockbroker gets him involved in risky high finance — and then there's the sponsorship of a boxer — when all he really wants is to play with the other kids. ⌒ **e** Lexile 920L (Rev: BLO 6/16/10; HB 7–8/10; SLJ 6/10)

11719 Paulsen, Gary. *Masters of Disaster* (4–6). 2010, Random House $12.99 (978-0-385-73997-9); LB $15.99 (978-0-385-90816-0). 112pp. Three boys set out to prove their mettle by undertaking progressively more dangerous dares in this zany and often gross chapter book. ⌒ **e** (Rev: BL 10/1/10; LMC 1–2/11; SLJ 11/1/10)

11720 Peck, Robert Newton. *Higbee's Halloween* (5–7). 1990, Walker LB $14.85 (978-0-8027-6969-5). Higbee decides something must be done about the unruly Striker children. (Rev: SLJ 10/90)

11721 Peirce, Lincoln. *Big Nate: In a Class by Himself* (3–6). Illus. by author. Series: Big Nate. 2010, HarperCollins $12.99 (978-0-06-194434-5); LB $14.89 (978-0-06-194435-2). 224pp. Reacting to a fortune cooking message, 6th-grader Nate sets out to excel all day and instead merely succeeds in racking up a series of detentions. (Rev: BL 3/1/10; SLJ 4/10)

11722 Pennypacker, Sara. *The Talented Clementine* (2–4). Illus. by Marla Frazee. 2007, Hyperion $14.99 (978-0-7868-3870-7). 144pp. Third-grader Clementine views the forthcoming talent show with nothing but dread in this funny chapter book. (Rev: BL 3/15/07) ⌒

11723 Perl, Erica S. *Aces Wild* (4–7). 2013, Random House $15.99 (978-030793172-6); LB $18.99 (978-037597104-4). 224pp. Zelly must tame her rambunctious new puppy Ace before she will be allowed to have a sleepover, but she must do so with the help of her equally uncontrollable Grandpa Ace. ⌒ Lexile 650 (Rev: BLO 7/13; LMC 11–12/13; SLJ 7/13)

11724 Petty, J. T. *Clemency Pogue: Fairy Killer* (3–6). Illus. by Will Davis. 2005, Simon & Schuster $9.95 (978-0-689-87236-5). 125pp. A satirical tale in which Clem-

ency is inadvertently responsible for killing six innocent fairies and must set things right. (Rev: SLJ 4/05)

11725 Petty, J. T. *The Squampkin Patch: A Nasselrogt Adventure* (4–7). Illus. by David Michael Friend. 2006, Simon & Schuster $15.95 (978-1-4169-0274-4). A funny, far-fetched fantasy about two children who escape hard labor at the zipper factory/orphanage (their parents are tied up in tanning beds) and find themselves pursued by squampkins — pumpkin-like creatures — that are out for blood. (Rev: SLJ 7/06)

11726 Pilkey, Dav. *The Adventures of Captain Underpants* (2–4). Illus. 1997, Scholastic $16.99 (978-0-590-84627-1). A superhero spoof in which two boys capture their principal and turn him into Captain Underpants. (Rev: BL 7/97; HBG 3/98; SLJ 12/97)

11727 Pilkey, Dav. *The Adventures of Super Diaper Baby* (2–5). Illus. by author. 2002, Scholastic paper $5.99 (978-0-439-37606-8). 125pp. As a penance for bad behavior, Harold and George are ordered to tackle the topic of good citizenship and instead invent a diaper-clad superhero. (Rev: HBG 10/02; SLJ 6/02)

11728 Pilkey, Dav. *Captain Underpants and the Attack of the Talking Toilets* (3–5). Illus. 1999, Scholastic $16.99 (978-0-590-63136-5). 144pp. George, Harold, and their school principal, who is also Captain Underpants, get involved in an army of teacher-eating toilets led by supercommode Turbo Toilet 2000. (Rev: BCCB 5/99; BL 5/1/99; HBG 10/99; SLJ 6/99)

11729 Pilkey, Dav. *Captain Underpants and the Big, Bad Battle of the Bionic Booger Boy: Part 1: The Night of the Nasty Nostril Nuggets* (2–4). Illus. by author. 2003, Scholastic $16.95 (978-0-439-37609-9); paper $5.99 (978-0-439-37610-5). 173pp. The superhero and sidekicks George and Harold face off against Melvin Sneedley, who's transformed himself into the Bionic Booger Boy. A sequel is *Captain Underpants and the Big, Bad Battle of the Bionic Booger Boy, Part 2: The Revenge of the Ridiculous Robo-Boogers* (2003). (Rev: HBG 4/04; SLJ 1/04)

11730 Pilkey, Dav. *Captain Underpants and the Invasion of the Incredibly Naughty Cafeteria Ladies from Outer Space (and the Subsequent Assault of the Equally Evil Lunchroom Zombie Nerds)* (4–6). Illus. 1999, Scholastic $16.99 (978-0-439-04995-5). 144pp. Another wacky adventure featuring fourth-graders George and Harold, their principal who becomes Captain Underpants, and a threat from outer space. (Rev: BL 9/15/99; HBG 3/00; SLJ 11/99)

11731 Pilkey, Dav. *Captain Underpants and the Perilous Plot of Professor Poopypants* (3–5). Illus. 2000, Scholastic $16.95 (978-0-439-04997-9). 160pp. Captain Underpants, aka Mr. Krupp, an elementary school principal, and students George and Harold combat a mad scientific genius, Pippy Pee-pee Poopypants. (Rev: BL 2/15/00; HBG 10/00; SLJ 5/00)

11732 Pilkey, Dav. *Captain Underpants and the Preposterous Plight of the Purple Potty People* (2–5). Illus. by author. 2006, Scholastic $16.99 (978-0-439-37613-6);

paper $4.99 (978-0-439-37614-3). 175pp. George and Harold find themselves in an alternate universe inhabited by evil versions of themselves. (Rev: SLJ 12/06)

11733 Pilkey, Dav. *Captain Underpants and the Terrifying Return of Tippy Tinkletrousers* (3–5). Illus. by author. 2012, Scholastic paper $9.99 (978-05451753-4-0). 304pp. The trouble-making Tippy Tinkletrousers sends George and Harold back to kindergarten, where they face 6th-grade bully Kipper Krupp without the help of Captain Underpants; the 9th volume in the series. **e** (Rev: BL 9/1/12; SLJ 10/12)

11734 Pilkey, Dav. *Captain Underpants and the Wrath of the Wicked Wedgie Woman* (3–6). Illus. 2001, Scholastic $16.99 (978-0-439-04999-3); paper $5.99 (978-0-439-05000-5). 176pp. George and Harold of Captain Underpants fame create a comic book about their teacher, Mrs. Ribble, whom they dub Wicked Wedgie Woman. (Rev: BL 1/1–15/02; HBG 3/02)

11735 Pinkwater, Daniel. *Adventures of a Cat-Whiskered Girl* (5–8). 2010, Houghton Mifflin $16 (978-0-547-22324-7). 282pp. Fourteen-year-old Audrey, who resembles a cat, has a series of chaotic and wacky adventures around the Hudson river town of Poughkeepsie, encountering characters from other realms, dimensions, and places. (Rev: BL 5/15/10; HB 5–6/10; SLJ 8/10)

11736 Pinkwater, Daniel. *The Artsy Smartsy Club* (4–6). Illus. by Jill Pinkwater. 2005, HarperCollins LB $16.89 (978-0-06-053558-2). 176pp. Chalk sidewalk portraits of Henrietta (the giant chicken of *The Hoboken Chicken Emergency* [1977]) prompt a group of friends to investigate, leading to an exploration of art in general and entertaining efforts to start up a new art festival. (Rev: BL 5/1/05; SLJ 5/05)

11737 Potter, Ellen. *Otis Dooda: Strange but True* (3–6). Illus. by David Heatley. 2013, Feiwel & Friends $13.99 (978-1-250-01176-3). 128pp. A funny story about Otis's misadventures when his family moves from the country into a New York apartment building peopled by zany characters. **e** (Rev: BL 6/13; LMC 10/13; SLJ 9/13)

11738 Raschka, Chris. *Seriously, Norman!* (5–8). Illus. by author. 2011, Scholastic $17.95 (978-0-545-29877-3). 352pp. Twelve-year-old Norman's tutor Balthazar Birdsong assigns him, along with kite flying, to read the dictionary, inspiring some interesting vocabulary in this quirkily amusing book. (Rev: BL 9/15/11; SLJ 11/1/11)

11739 Rees, Douglas. *Uncle Pirate* (2–4). Illus. by Tony Auth. 2008, Simon & Schuster $15.99 (978-1-4169-4762-2). 100pp. Fourth-grader Wilson's life changes for the better when his wicked pirate uncle comes to live with him and reorganizes his poorly run, dangerous school in shocking, amusing ways. (Rev: BCCB 9/08; SLJ 2/09)

11740 Rees, Douglas. *Uncle Pirate to the Rescue* (3–6). Illus. by Tony Auth. 2010, Simon & Schuster paper $5.99 (978-1-4169-7505-2). 112pp. Wilson's elementary school class comes to the rescue when his swashbuckling uncle goes missing at sea in this funny sequel to *Uncle Pirate* (2008). Lexile 570L (Rev: SLJ 3/10)

11741 Rex, Michael. *Icky Ricky: Toilet Paper Mummy* (2–4). Illus. by author. 2013, Random House paper $4.99 (978-0-307-93-167-2). 128pp. For the gross-out crowd this early chapter book features Ricky, an energetic and inventive child with an offbeat view of the world; will appeal to reluctant readers. Lexile 710 (Rev: BLO 7/13; LMC 11–12/13; SLJ 5/13)

11742 Riddell, Chris. *Ottoline Goes to School* (3–6). Illus. by author. 2009, HarperCollins $10.99 (978-0-06-144900-0). 176pp. Ottoline and her doggy best friend Mr. Monroe attend the Alice B. Smith School for the Differently Gifted, where Ottoline does not initially excel; the combination of chapter-book text and graphic novel illustrations is effective. (Rev: SLJ 7/09)

11743 Riddleburger, Sam. *The Qwikpick Adventure Society* (3–6). 2007, Dial $16.99 (978-0-8037-3178-3). 127pp. Lyle, Marilla, and Dave are fascinated by the "poop fountain" at the nearby water treatment plant and record their visit there in a scrapbook. (Rev: BCCB 7–8/07; SLJ 7/07)

11744 Robertson, Keith. *Henry Reed, Inc.* (5–7). Illus. by Robert McCloskey. 1989, Puffin paper $6.99 (978-0-14-034144-7). Told deadpan in diary form, this story of Henry's enterprising summer in New Jersey presents one of the most amusing boys since Tom and Huck. Others in the series *Henry Reed's Journey* (1963); *Henry Reed's Baby-Sitting Service* (1966); *Henry Reed's Big Show* (1970).

11745 Robinson, Barbara. *The Best School Year Ever* (3–5). 1994, HarperCollins LB $16.89 (978-0-06-023043-2). 128pp. Beth has to write a complimentary composition about a classmate who appears to have no redeeming qualities. (Rev: BL 10/15/94; HB 11/94; SLJ 10/94)

11746 Robinson, Barbara. *My Brother Louis Measures Worms and Other Louis Stories* (3–6). 1988, HarperCollins LB $15.89 (978-0-06-025083-6); paper $4.95 (978-0-06-440362-7). 160pp. Events in ten stories of the wild Lawson family. (Rev: BCCB 12/88; BL 11/1/88; SLJ 12/88)

11747 Rockwell, Thomas. *How to Eat Fried Worms* (4–6). Illus. by Emily Arnold McCully. 1973, Watts LB $29.00 (978-0-531-02631-1); Dell paper $4.99 (978-0-440-44545-6). 128pp. In this very humorous story, Billy takes on a bet — he will eat 15 worms in 15 days. His family and friends help devise ways to cook them.

11748 Rodgers, Mary. *Freaky Friday* (4–7). 1972, HarperCollins LB $16.89 (978-0-06-025049-2); paper $5.99 (978-0-06-440046-6). Thirteen-year-old Annabel learns some valuable lessons during the day she becomes her mother. Two sequels are *A Billion for Boris* (1974) and *Summer Switch* (1982). (Rev: BL 4/15/89)

11749 Root, Phyllis. *Aunt Nancy and the Bothersome Visitors* (1–4). Illus. by David Parkins. Series: Aunt Nancy. 2007, Candlewick $16.99 (978-0-7636-3074-4). Old Man Trouble, Cousin Lazybones, Old Woeful, and Mister Death visit Aunt Nancy, but she doesn't let any of them get the better of her in this collection of tall tales. (Rev: BCCB 10/07; HB 9/07; LMC 11/07; SLJ 8/07)

11750 Sachar, Louis. *Sideways Arithmetic from Wayside School* (4–8). Series: Wayside School. 1992, Scholastic paper $4.99 (978-0-590-45726-2). Sue learns a new kind of math and encounters some humorous brainteasers when she transfers to Wayside School. (Rev: BL 12/15/89)

11751 Sandburg, Carl. *Never Kick a Slipper at the Moon* (1–3). Illus. by Rosanne Litzinger. 2008, Holiday $16.95 (978-0-8234-2160-2). 32pp. This humorous Rootabaga story explains exactly why you should not kick slippers at the moon. (Rev: BLO 7/30/08)

11752 Scieszka, Jon. *Squids Will Be Squids: Fresh Morals, Beastly Fables* (2–6). Illus. by Lane Smith. 1998, Viking $17.99 (978-0-670-88135-2). 48pp. This book by the author of the *Stinky Cheese Man* presents 18 contemporary, goofy fables, each with a silly moral attached. (Rev: BCCB 11/98; BL 9/15/98; HB 11/98; HBG 3/99; SLJ 10/98)

11753 Scieszka, Jon, ed. *Guys Read: Funny Business* (4–7). Illus. by Adam Rex. 2010, HarperCollins $16.99 (978-0-06-196374-2); paper $5.99 (978-0-06-196373-5). 256pp. A collection of humorous stories by well-known writers that will appeal to boys. e (Rev: BL 10/1/10*; SLJ 10/1/10; VOYA 2/11)

11754 Scrimger, Richard. *Noses Are Red* (4–7). 2002, Tundra paper $7.95 (978-0-88776-590-2). Norbert, the alien who likes to live in Alan's nose, works to Alan's benefit once again when Alan and a friend meet a variety of perils on a camping trip. (Rev: BL 1/1–15/03; HBG 3/03; SLJ 12/02; VOYA 2/03)

11755 Scroggs, Kirk. *Dracula vs. Grampa at the Monster Truck Spectacular* (2–5). Illus. by author. Series: Wiley and Grampa's Creature Features. 2006, Little, Brown paper $2.99 (978-0-316-05941-1). Grampa provokes Gramma's ire when he takes grandson Wiley to Colonel Dracula's Monster Truck Spectacular on Halloween night; an exciting evening that includes a strong tornado. Also use *Grampa's Zombie BBQ* (2006). (Rev: SLJ 10/06)

11756 Seegert, Scott. *How to Grow Up and Rule the World* (5–8). Illus. by John Martin. Series: Vordak the Incomprehensible. 2010, Egmont $13.99 (978-1-60684-013-9). 200pp. The comically sinister Vordak provides dazzling insights into the mind of an evil genius in this giggle-worthy personal development book, featuring tips on wardrobe, social behavior, housing, and death traps. Lexile NC1140L (Rev: BL 9/1/10; SLJ 12/1/10)

11757 Sherman, Deborah. *The BEDMAS Conspiracy* (5–7). 2011, Fitzhenry & Whiteside paper $9.95 (978-1-55455-181-1). 172pp. Cousins Adam and Daniela are determined to win the middle school talent show with their rock band despite their respective deficiencies. Lexile 660L (Rev: LMC 3–4/12; SLJ 12/1/11)

11758 Sherman, Deborah. *The Triple Chocolate Brownie Genius* (4–6). 2007, Fitzhenry & Whiteside $10.95 (978-1-55455-035-7). 151pp. When Michael, 13, goes

from being a popular class clown to a super smart student, he and his friends discover that a computer chip in the homemade brownies Michael ate has caused the change, which they humorously struggle to reverse. (Rev: BL 12/1/07; SLJ 1/08)

11759 Shipton, Paul. *The Pig Who Saved the World: By Gryllus the Pig* (5–8). 2007, Candlewick $15.99 (978-0-7636-3446-9). In this sequel to *The Pig Scrolls* (2005), Gryllus the pig and his mythological friends — including the young poet Homer — are searching for Circe, the sorceress who can make Gryllus human again. (Rev: BL 10/1/07; SLJ 11/07)

11760 Silberberg, Alan. *The Awesome, Almost 100% True Adventures of Matt and Craz* (5–8). Illus. by author. 2013, Aladdin $16.99 (978-141699432-9). 336pp. Middle-schoolers Matt and Craz, aspiring cartoonists, receive a magic pen and ink that send them off on some riotous adventures. Lexile 830 (Rev: BLO 7/13; LMC 10/13*; SLJ 5/13)

11761 Sitomer, Alan Lawrence. *A Catastrophe of Nerdish Proportions* (5–8). Series: Nerd Girls. 2012, Hyperion/Disney $16.99 (978-1-4231-3997-3). 266pp. Warring groups the Nerd Girls and the ThreePees (Pretty, Popular, Perfect) are sentenced to compete together in the Academic Septathlon. ∩ e Lexile HL720L (Rev: BLO 9/15/12; SLJ 8/1/12)

11762 Skye, Obert. *Potterwookiee: The Creature from My Closet* (4–7). Illus. by author. 2012, Henry Holt $12.99 (978-8050-9451-0). 256pp. From Robert Burnside's closet emerges a creature that is part Chewbacca and part Harry Potter in this funny followup to *Wonkenstein* (2011). e Lexile 820L (Rev: BLO 9/1/12; SLJ 11/12)

11763 Skye, Obert. *Wonkenstein: The Creature from My Closet* (4–7). Illus. by author. 2011, Henry Holt $12.99 (978-0-8050-9268-4). 240pp. Twelve-year-old Rob is uninterested in books and they pile up in his closet — until the day a strange being emerges from the heap, appearing to be a combination of Willy Wonka and Frankenstein, complicating Rob's all-too-average life. Lexile 860L (Rev: BL 10/15/11; SLJ 9/1/11)

11764 Smallcomb, Pam. *The Last Burp of Mac McGerp* (3–5). Illus. by Lizzy Bromley. 2003, Bloomsbury $15.95 (978-1-58234-856-8). 120pp. No one can belch quite like fifth-grader Mac, but his hopes of entering the National Burping Competition are threatened by a strict new school principal. (Rev: BL 2/15/04; HBG 4/04; SLJ 9/03)

11765 Snicket, Lemony. *The Bad Beginning* (4–7). Series: A Series of Unfortunate Events. 1999, HarperCollins $12.99 (978-0-06-440766-3). A humorous story about the ill-fated Beaudelaire orphans and the creepy, wicked villains they never seem to avoid. (Rev: BL 12/1/99; HBG 3/00; SLJ 11/99)

11766 Snicket, Lemony. *The Carnivorous Carnival* (4–8). Illus. by Brett Helquist. Series: A Series of Unfortunate Events. 2002, HarperCollins LB $15.89 (978-0-06-029640-7). The Baudelaire orphans pose as carnival freaks in the ninth volume of this unhappily-ever-after series. (Rev: BL 12/15/02; HBG 3/03; SLJ 1/03)

11767 Snicket, Lemony. *The End* (5–8). Illus. by Brett Helquist. Series: A Series of Unfortunate Events. 2006, HarperCollins $12.99 (978-0-06-441016-8). The Baudelaire orphans find themselves stranded on an island with none other than the villainous Count Olaf; will this be the last installment in the series? (Rev: BL 10/15/06)

11768 Snicket, Lemony. *The Wide Window* (4–7). Series: A Series of Unfortunate Events. 2000, HarperCollins LB $15.89 (978-0-06-028314-8). The three Baudelaire children have a new guardian, timid cousin Josephine, but they are pursued by former keeper Count Olaf. (Rev: BL 2/1/00; HBG 10/00; SLJ 1/00)

11769 Sonnenblick, Jordan. *Dodger for President* (4–6). 2009, Feiwel & Friends $16.99 (978-0-312-37794-6). 176pp. Dodger, the zany blue chimp only visible to Willie and Lizzie, does what he can to support Willie's run for class president with Lizzie as his running mate. (Rev: BL 4/15/09; VOYA 10/09)

11770 Soto, Gary. *Summer on Wheels* (5–8). 1995, Scholastic paper $13.95 (978-0-590-48365-0). In this sequel to *Crazy Weekend* (1994), Hector and Mando take a bike ride from their barrio home in Los Angeles to Santa Monica. (Rev: BL 1/15/95; SLJ 4/95; VOYA 4/95)

11771 Spinelli, Jerry. *The Library Card* (4–8). 1997, Scholastic paper $15.95 (978-0-590-46731-5). Four humorous, poignant stories about how books changed the lives of several youngsters. (Rev: BCCB 3/97; BL 2/1/97; HB 3–4/97; SLJ 3/97; VOYA 10/97)

11772 Stadler, Alexander. *Invasion of the Relatives* (2–4). Illus. by author. Series: Julian Rodriguez. 2009, Scholastic $15.99 (978-0-439-91967-8). 144pp. The fuss and bother surrounding Thanksgiving nearly drives Julian (er, First Officer Julian Rodriguez, space traveler) over the edge, and he expresses his discontent through his computer. (Rev: BL 11/15/09; SLJ 3/1/10)

11773 Standiford, Natalie. *Blonde at Heart* (5–8). Series: Elle Woods. 2006, Hyperion $4.99 (978-0-7868-3843-1). How Elle Woods, the central character of the 2001 movie *Legally Blonde*, became a blond bombshell in her effort to attract the attention of her crush. (Rev: BL 7/06; SLJ 5/06)

11774 Stanley, George E. *Hershell Cobwell and the Miraculous Tattoo* (4–8). 1991, Avon paper $2.95 (978-0-380-75897-5). A junior high boy decides to gain popularity by getting a tattoo. (Rev: BL 3/15/91)

11775 Tayleur, Karen. *Excuses! Survive and Succeed with David Mortimore Baxter* (3–6). Illus. by Brann Garvey. 2006, Stone Arch LB $23.93 (978-1-59889-073-0). 71pp. David is good avoiding work and shares all his excuses for getting out of homework, chores, eating veggies, and more in this hilarious story. (Rev: SLJ 3/07)

11776 Tayleur, Karen. *Secrets! The Secret Life of David Mortimore Baxter* (3–6). Illus. by Brann Garvey. 2006, Stone Arch LB $23.93 (978-1-59889-077-8). 82pp. When a well-known wrestler acknowledges Davey as a trustworthy friend on national TV, Davey gets lots more attention and confidences than he needs. (Rev: SLJ 3/07)

11777 Thompson, Colin. *The Floods: Good Neighbors* (3–6). Illus. by Crab Scrambly. 2008, HarperCollins $15.99 (978-0-06-113196-7). 224pp. The Floods, a family of weird-looking witches and wizards — except for the very normal Betty, are usually easy-going but the behavior of their neighbors, the Dents, pushes them over the edge. (Rev: BL 5/15/08)

11778 Trahey, Jane. *The Clovis Caper* (5–8). 1990, Avon paper $2.95 (978-0-380-75914-9). Martin is so upset at leaving his dog, Clovis, when going to England that Aunt Hortense plots to smuggle the dog out of the country. (Rev: BL 7/90)

11779 Trine, Greg. *The Fake Cape Caper* (2–5). Illus. by Rhode Montijo. Series: Melvin Beederman, Superhero Series. 2007, Holt $16.95 (978-0-8050-8158-9); paper $5.99 (978-0-8050-8159-6). 144pp. Melvin Breederman, superhero in charge of Los Angeles, attends the Superhero's Convention in Las Vegas, leaving his young sidekick to keep Los Angeles safe from evil bad guys and bullies. (Rev: SLJ 11/07)

11780 Trine, Greg. *Melvin Beederman, Superhero: The Curse of the Bologna Sandwich* (2–4). Illus. by Rhode Montijo. Series: Melvin Beederman, Superhero. 2006, Holt $15.95 (978-0-8050-7928-9); paper $5.99 (978-0-8050-7836-7). 138pp. Hapless superhero Melvin is almost defeated by his love for bologna in this installment in the laugh-out-loud series. The adventures continue in *Melvin Beederman, Superhero: The Revenge of the McNasty Brothers* (2005). (Rev: SLJ 5/06)

11781 Trueit, Trudi. *Mom, There's a Dinosaur in Beeson's Lake* (3–5). Illus. by Jim Paillot. Series: Secrets of a Lab Rat. 2010, Simon & Schuster $14.99 (978-1-4169-7593-9). 145pp. Ten-year-old Scab McNally faces many difficult situations in this funny book, including swimming lessons that may reveal his fear of the water. (Rev: SLJ 5/1/10)

11782 Trueit, Trudi. *No Girls Allowed (Dogs Okay)* (2–5). Illus. by Jim Paillot. Series: Secrets of a Lab Rat. 2009, Aladdin $14.99 (978-1-4169-7592-2). 128pp. Nine-year-old bad boy Scab McNally wants a puppy and decides to sell his "sister-repellent" to raise the necessary funds. (Rev: BCCB 3/09; BL 4/1/09; SLJ 3/09) ∩

11783 Tulloch, Richard. *Weird Stuff* (5–8). Illus. by Shane Nagle. 2006, Walker $16.95 (978-0-8027-8058-4). A borrowed pen gives school soccer star Brian Hobble amazing new writing abilities, but they're limited to a single genre — romantic fiction. (Rev: SLJ 8/06)

11784 Uderzo, Albert. *Asterix and Son* (4–8). Trans. by Anthea Bell and Derek Hockridge. 2002, Orion paper $9.95 (978-0-7528-4775-7). In comic-book format, this is the entertaining story of French heroes Asterix and Obelix and how they became guardians of a kidnapped baby. Also use *Asterix and the Black Gold* (2002) and *Asterix and the Great Divide* (2002). (Rev: BL 4/15/02)

11785 Van Draanen, Wendelin. *The Power Potion* (3–6). Illus. by Stephen Gilpin. Series: The Gecko and Sticky.

2010, Knopf $12.99 (978-037584379-2); LB $15.99 (978-037594573-1). 240pp. Dave and his sidekick gecko swap a villain's mysterious potion for a presumably inert substitute, which turns out to cause incapacitating diarrhea; the fourth book in the series. (Rev: BLO 4/15/10)

11786 Van Draanen, Wendelin. *Shredderman: Secret Identity* (3–5). Illus. by Brian Biggs. 2004, Knopf $12.95 (978-0-375-82351-0). 144pp. To get the best of a school bully called Bubba, brainy but somewhat nerdy fifth-grader Nolan makes Bubba the "star" of a Web site. (Rev: BL 2/1/04*; SLJ 5/04)

11787 Vance, Alexander. *The Heartbreak Messenger* (5–8). 2013, Feiwel & Friends $16.99 (978-125002969-0). 288pp. After building a successful business as a "heartbreak messenger," 13-year-old Quentin begins to question the task when various breakups go wrong and when his best friend Abby is affected. e Lexile 670 (Rev: BL 7/13; LMC 1–2/14; SLJ 8/13*)

11788 Vande Velde, Vivian. *8 Class Pets + 1 Squirrel ÷ 1 Dog = Chaos* (2–4). Illus. by Steve Björkman. 2011, Holiday House $15.95 (978-0-8234-236-4-). 67pp. This zany story captures the mounting chaos that is unleashed when a squirrel wakes up a sleeping dog, which leads to an all-out pursuit into and through the halls of an elementary school, adding new animals as they go; the animals all speak, using very different styles that add to the fun. Lexile 740L (Rev: BL 10/15/11; SLJ 12/1/11)

11789 Venuti, Kristin Clark. *The Butler Gets a Break* (4–7). Series: Bellweather Tales. 2010, Egmont $15.99 (978-1-60684-087-0). 240pp. Hospitalized with a broken leg, Benway the butler hears about the escapades of the Bellweathers and worries that he may lose his job; a sequel to *Leaving the Bellweathers* (2009). (Rev: BL 11/1/10; SLJ 11/1/10)

11790 Venuti, Kristin Clark. *Leaving the Bellweathers* (4–7). Series: Bellweather Tales. 2009, Egmont $15.99 (978-160684006-1). 256pp. Butler Tristan Benway is looking forward to ending his tenure with the eccentric Bellweathers and starts a memoir about their outrageous behaviors. ∩ (Rev: BL 9/15/09; HB 11–12/09; SLJ 9/09)

11791 Wallace, Bill. *Ferret in the Bedroom, Lizards in the Fridge* (4–6). 1986, Holiday House $16.95 (978-0-8234-0600-5). 144pp. Liz would certainly win the sixth-grade presidency if it weren't that her zoology teacher-father keeps so many unusual animals around the house and scares away her friends. (Rev: BCCB 7–8/86; BL 6/15/86)

11792 Ware, Cheryl. *Venola in Love* (4–7). Illus. by Kristin Sorra. 2000, Orchard LB $16.99 (978-0-531-33306-8). Told through diary entries, e-mail messages, and class notes, this humorous novel tells how 7th-grader Venola discovers the problems of falling in love. (Rev: BCCB 10/00; HBG 10/01; SLJ 10/00)

11793 Weeks, Sarah. *Oggie Cooder* (3–5). 2008, Scholastic $16.99 (978-0-439-92791-8). 168pp. Fourth-grader Oggie Cooder's talent for nibbling on slices of cheese until they form the outlines of the states wins the

formerly unpopular boy celebrity and some new friends. (Rev: BCCB 2/08; BL 1/1–15/08; SLJ 3/08) ∩

11794 Weiner, Ellis. *The Templeton Twins Have an Idea, Bk. 1* (4–7). Illus. by Jeremy Holmes. Series: The Templeton Twins. 2012, Chronicle $16.99 (978-0-8118-6679-8). 228pp. Resourceful twins Abigail and John, 12, along with their dog, are kidnapped by one of their father's former students and his twin brother. e Lexile 850L (Rev: BL 9/1/12; HB 9–10/12; LMC 8–9/12; SLJ 7/12; VOYA 10/12)

11795 Weiner, Ellis. *The Templeton Twins Make a Scene* (4–6). Illus. by Jeremy Holmes. 2013, Chronicle $16.99 (978-145211184-1). 272pp. Abigail and John Templeton again must save a brilliant invention created by their father from the clutches of the evil Dean D. and Dan D. Dean. e Lexile 830 (Rev: BLO 9/15/13; SLJ 8/13)

11796 Whitehouse, Howard. *The Island of Mad Scientists: Being an Excursion to the Wilds of Scotland, Involving Many Marvels of Experimental Invention, Pirates, a Heroic Cat, a Mechanical Man and a Monkey* (4–7). Illus. by Bill Slavin. Series: The Mad Misadventures of Emmaline and Rubberbones. 2008, Kids Can $17.95 (978-1-55453-236-0); paper $7.95 (978-1-55453-237-7). 262pp. The third and final installment in this fast-paced series involves more running from villains, crazy characters, and many comic moments as the group tries to reach Urrgghh. (Rev: SLJ 2/09)

11797 Wight, Eric. *Frankie Pickle and the Closet of Doom* (2–4). Illus. by author. 2009, Simon & Schuster $12.99 (978-1-4169-6484-1). Frankie Pickle is blessed with a vivid imagination and an outstandingly messy room in this combination chapter book/graphic novel. (Rev: LMC 10/09; SLJ 7/09)

11798 Wisniewski, David. *The Secret Knowledge of Grown-ups* (3–5). Illus. 1998, Lothrop LB $17.89 (978-0-688-15340-3). 48pp. A zany book that explores the truth behind such parental directives as "Drink your milk" and "Don't bite your fingernails." (Rev: BCCB 7–8/98; BL 3/1/98; HBG 10/98; SLJ 3/98)

11799 Wynne-Jones, Tim. *Ned Mouse Breaks Away* (2–4). Illus. by Dusan Petricic. 2003, Groundwood $14.95 (978-0-88899-474-5). 68pp. Ned Mouse attempts an ingenious escape from prison in this surreally funny story. (Rev: SLJ 4/03)

11800 Yee, Lisa. *So Totally Emily Ebers* (5–8). 2007, Scholastic $16.99 (978-0-439-83847-4). In this companion to *Millicent Min, Girl Genius* (2003) and *Stanford Wong Flunks Big-Time* (2005), Emily writes a series of letters to her absent father, telling him about her friends Millicent and Stanford and their tutoring arrangement. (Rev: BL 3/15/07; SLJ 4/07)

11801 Yee, Lisa. *Stanford Wong Flunks Big-Time* (4–7). 2005, Scholastic $16.99 (978-0-439-62247-9). In this rollicking sequel to *Millicent Minn, Girl Genius*, Stanford Wong is upset when his parents hire Millicent, his arch-nemesis, to tutor him in English. (Rev: BL 11/15/05; SLJ 12/05)

11802 Young, Steve. *Winchell Mink: The Misadventure Begins* (4–6). 2004, HarperCollins LB $16.89 (978-0-06-053500-1). Changes in font, musical notes, and asides and commentary add to the humor and liveliness of this fast-paced story involving bullies, time travel, and an 11-year-old boy exchanging bodies with his pet turtle, Hannibal. (Rev: BCCB 9/04; SLJ 6/04)

School Stories

11803 Ada, Alma Flor, and Gabriel Zubizarreta. *Dancing Home* (4–6). 2011, Atheneum $14.99 (978-1-4169-0088-7). 160pp. Margie, 10, tries to hide her Mexican background until her cousin Lupe arrives in California and Margie slowly learns to appreciate her heritage. **e** Lexile 960L (Rev: BL 7/11; SLJ 7/11)

11804 Adderson, Caroline. *Star of the Week* (2–4). Illus. by Ben Clanton. 2012, Kids Can $15.95 (978-1-55453-578-1). 128pp. It's Jasper's turn to be Star of the Week but he finds himself upstaged left and right in this appealing chapter book. (Rev: BL 3/1/12; LMC 10/12; SLJ 3/1/12)

11805 Amato, Mary. *Please Write in This Book* (2–5). Illus. by Eric Brace. 2006, Holiday House $16.95 (978-0-8234-1932-6). 97pp. A teacher's effort to get children writing is only successful after hurtful slurs and rivalries run their course. (Rev: BCCB 3/07; BL 12/15/06; HBG 4/07; SLJ 4/07)

11806 Angleberger, Tom. *The Strange Case of Origami Yoda* (4–6). Illus. by author. 2010, Abrams $12.95 (978-0-8109-8425-7). 160pp. Sixth-grader Tommy vacillates between belief and disbelief when a classmate comes to school with a origami finger puppet that seems to dispense sage advice. ⌒ **e** Lexile 760L (Rev: BL 5/1/10; SLJ 5/10)

11807 Bancks, Tristan. *Mac Slater Hunts the Cool* (5–8). 2010, Simon & Schuster $15.99 (978-1-4169-8574-7). 224pp. Is Mac truly cool? He feels like an outsider at his Australian school, but when he enters a contest to come up with the next cool trend, he gets a chance to prove that outsiders can be cool too. Lexile 690L (Rev: BL 4/1/10; LMC 8–9/10; SLJ 3/10)

11808 Barnes, Derrick. *We Could Be Brothers* (5–8). 2010, Scholastic $17.99 (978-054513573-3). 176pp. African American 8th-graders Robeson and Pacino come from different backgrounds but recognize their common aims as they confront Tariq, a threatening classmate. Lexile HL600L (Rev: BL 11/15/10; VOYA 4/11)

11809 Barshaw, Ruth McNally. *Ellie McDoodle: New Kid in School* (4–7). Illus. by author. 2008, Bloomsbury $12.99 (978-159990238-8). 176pp. In 6th grade at a new school Ellie McDoodle tackles finding friends, horrible school lunches, and various other trials and tribulations recounted through sketches, cartoons, and engaging text. Lexile 510L (Rev: BLO 8/08)

11810 Beam, Matt. *Can You Spell Revolution?* (5–8). 2008, Dutton $17.99 (978-0-525-47998-7). 208pp. New student Clouds McFadden brings together four unlikely classmates to overthrow the lousy administration at Laverton Middle School, using strategies gleaned from history. (Rev: BL 12/1/08; SLJ 1/09)

11811 Becker, Bonny. *The Magical Ms. Plum* (2–4). Illus. by Amy Portnoy. 2009, Knopf $12.99 (978-0-375-85637-2); LB $15.99 (978-0-375-95637-9). 112pp. A talented teacher and her magical closet supply the children in her class with exactly what they need. **e** Lexile 670L (Rev: BL 11/1/09; LMC 11/09; SLJ 11/1/09)

11812 Bertrand, Diane Gonzales. *The Ruiz Street Kids / Los muchachos de la calle Ruiz* (3–6). 2006, Piñata paper $9.95 (978-1-55885-321-8). 240pp. Joe Silva and his friends shun David until they realize he's just insecure; Spanish text follows the English. (Rev: SLJ 10/06)

11813 Birdseye, Tom. *Attack of the Mutant Underwear* (3–6). 2003, Holiday House $16.95 (978-0-8234-1689-9). 199pp. Dreams of past underwear-related humiliation haunt Cody Lee Carson as he prepares to begin fifth grade in a new town; his entertaining diary recounts his progress. (Rev: BL 1/1–15/04; HBG 4/04; SLJ 1/04)

11814 Bulion, Leslie. *The Trouble with Rules* (3–5). 2008, Peachtree $14.95 (978-1-56145-440-2). 137pp. Fourth grade brings new rules — boys and girls can't be friends anymore — but Nadie's got a few ideas of her own. (Rev: LMC 8/08; SLJ 9/08)

11815 Butcher, Kristin. *Cheat* (5–8). 2010, Orca LB $16.95 (978-1-55469-275-0); paper $9.95 (978-1-55469-274-3). 112pp. Eager for acclaim, school newspaper reporter Laurel is disappointed when her story about school cheating is poorly received. (Rev: BL 12/15/10; SLJ 2/1/11)

11816 Buyea, Rob. *Because of Mr. Terupt* (4–6). 2010, Delacorte $16.99 (978-038573882-8); LB $19.99 (978-038590749-1). 208pp. A group of 5th-graders with diverse problems learn a lot from a new teacher in this novel told from several perspectives. (Rev: BL 10/15/10; LMC 5–6/11*; SLJ 12/1/10*)

11817 Buyea, Rob. *Mr. Terupt Falls Again* (4–7). 2012, Delacorte $16.99 (978-0-385-74205-4); LB $19.99 (978-037599038-0). 288pp. Mr. Terupt's students are now in 6th grade and are dealing with coming-of-age problems even as they help their teacher plan his wedding. **e** Lexile 680L (Rev: BLO 12/15/12; SLJ 11/12; VOYA 12/12)

11818 Byars, Betsy. *The 18th Emergency* (4–6). Illus. by Robert Grossman. 1981, Puffin paper $4.99 (978-0-14-031451-9). 128pp. A young boy, nicknamed Mousi, incurs the wrath of the school bully and awaits his inevitable punishment with fear.

11819 Cameron, Ann. *Gloria Rising* (2–4). Illus. by Lis Toft. 2002, Farrar $15.00 (978-0-374-32675-3). 112pp. A young African American girl named Gloria stars in this easy chapter book involving an inspiring woman astronaut and an intimidating fourth-grade teacher. (Rev: BCCB 4/02; BL 2/15/02; HBG 10/02; SLJ 3/02)

11820 Catalanotto, Peter, and Pamela Schembri. *The Secret Lunch Special* (1–3). Illus. by Peter Catalanotto. Series: Second Grade Friends. 2006, Holt $15.95 (978-0-8050-7838-1). Misunderstanding a classmate's remarks, young Emily — new to coping with second grade — worries about the consequences of leaving her lunch bag on the school bus. (Rev: BL 9/1/06; SLJ 9/06)

11821 Cheng, Andrea. *Where the Steps Were* (2–5). Illus. by author. 2008, Boyds Mills $16.95 (978-1-932425-88-8). 144pp. Five multicultural students in Miss D.'s 3rd-grade class speak of their dreams and their sadness that their inner-city Cincinnati school is being demolished. (Rev: BL 3/1/08; HB 5/08; SLJ 5/08)

11822 Clements, Andrew. *Extra Credit* (4–7). Illus. by Mark Elliot. 2009, Atheneum $16.99 (978-1-4169-4929-9). 192pp. Abby, 11, becomes pen pals with a student in Afghanistan. (Rev: BCCB 9/09; BL 6/1–15/09; HB 7/09)

11823 Clements, Andrew. *Frindle* (3–6). Illus. 1996, Simon & Schuster $15.00 (978-0-689-80669-8). 105pp. Nick's desire to get even with a teacher gets out of hand. (Rev: BL 9/1/96; HB 11/96; SLJ 9/96)

11824 Clements, Andrew. *Jake Drake, Class Clown* (2–5). Illus. by Dolores Avendano. 2002, Simon & Schuster $15.00 (978-0-689-83921-4). Jake is determined to make the new student teacher crack a smile. (Rev: HBG 10/02; SLJ 7/02)

11825 Clements, Andrew. *Jake Drake, Teacher's Pet* (3–5). Illus. by Dolores Avendano. 2001, Simon & Schuster $15.00 (978-0-689-83919-1). In this beginning chapter book, Jake Drake faces the worst day of his life — the day he becomes the teacher's pet. (Rev: BL 1/1–15/02; HBG 10/02; SLJ 4/02)

11826 Clements, Andrew. *The Landry News* (3–7). Illus. 1999, Simon & Schuster $15.00 (978-0-689-81817-2). 128pp. When Cara's editorial about a lazy teacher causes him to lose his job, issues of responsibility and freedom of the press emerge. (Rev: BCCB 6/99; BL 6/1–15/99; HB 7/99; HBG 10/99; SLJ 7/99)

11827 Clements, Andrew. *Lost and Found* (3–6). Illus. by Mark Elliot. 2008, Atheneum $16.99 (978-1-4169-0985-9). 176pp. Jay and Ray, 12-year-old twins who would prefer to be seen as individuals, move to a new school and grasp a chance to experiment with taking turns to attend as a single student. (Rev: BL 8/08; HB 9/08) ∩

11828 Clements, Andrew. *Lunch Money* (4–6). Illus. by Brian Selznick. 2005, Simon & Schuster $15.95 (978-0-689-86683-8). 222pp. Greg comes up with a great idea to make money but runs into setbacks when the school bans his product and another student develops a competing one. (Rev: SLJ 8/05)

11829 Clements, Andrew. *No Talking* (3–6). Illus. by Mark Elliott. 2007, Simon & Schuster $15.99 (978-1-4169-0983-5). 160pp. The teachers find it quite unsettling when a boisterous 5th-grade decides to practice silence. (Rev: BCCB 10/07; BL 9/15/07; SLJ 9/07) ∩

11830 Cooper, Rose. *Gossip from the Girls' Room* (5–8). Illus. by author. 2011, Delacorte $12.99 (978-0-385-73947-4); LB $15.99 (978-0-385-90791-0). 200pp. Sixth-grader Sophia's attempts to bring down a popular girl at school by posting gossipy blogs go awry. ℮ (Rev: BL 1/1–15/11; SLJ 3/1/11)

11831 Copeland, Cynthia L. *Dilly for President* (3–5). Illus. by author. 2006, Millbrook paper $6.95 (978-0-7613-2442-3). 64pp. In her diary, Dilly describes her classmates and teachers as she enters fourth grade and decides to run for class president. (Rev: SLJ 4/06)

11832 Cox, Judy. *Ukulele Hayley* (2–4). Illus. by Amanda Haley. 2013, Holiday $16.95 (978-082342863-2). 96pp. Hayley wants to find a talent of her own, and when she discovers that she can play the ukulele, Hayley's not in the background anymore, but helping to save the school's music program; includes tips on playing the instrument. ℮ Lexile 450 (Rev: BLO 9/15/13; LMC 5–6/14; SLJ 10/13)

11833 Creech, Sharon. *Hate That Cat* (3–6). 2008, HarperCollins $15.99 (978-0-06-143092-3). 176pp. In this sequel to *Love That Dog* (2001), Jack is in 5th grade, still writing poetry, and resisting the idea of a pet to replace his beloved dog. (Rev: BL 8/08; HB 11/08) ∩

11834 Daly, Niki. *Bettina Valentino and the Picasso Club* (4–6). Illus. by author. 2009, Farrar $16.00 (978-0-374-30753-0). 112pp. Bettina Valentino is in 5th grade and bowled over by the new art teacher, who needs support when Maxine's parents criticize his teaching; readers learn about various artists and movements. (Rev: BL 3/15/09)

11835 Daneshvari, Gitty. *Class Is Not Dismissed!* (4–7). Series: School of Fear. 2010, Little, Brown $16.99 (978-0-316-03328-2). 320pp. In this lighthearted followup to 2009's *School of Fear*, the four phobia-ridden students return to take another stab at curing their unreasonable and paralyzing fears and together investigate who is stealing from their school. (Rev: BL 10/1/10; SLJ 9/1/10)

11836 Danneberg, Julie. *The Big Test* (1–3). Illus. by Judy Love. 2011, Charlesbridge $16.95 (978-1-58089-360-2); paper $6.95 (978-1-58089-361-9). 32pp. Mrs. Hartwell's class gets lots of practice before the day of the dreaded standardized test. (Rev: BL 8/11; SLJ 7/11)

11837 Devillers, Julia. *New Girl in Town* (3–5). Illus. by Paige Pooler. Series: Liberty Porter, First Daughter. 2010, Simon & Schuster $15.99 (978-1-4169-9128-1). 194pp. First daughter Liberty doesn't sacrifice her ideals in order to win friends when she starts at her new school in Washington, D.C. (Rev: SLJ 9/1/10)

11838 DiSalvo, DyAnne. *The Sloppy Copy Slipup* (3–5). Illus. 2006, Holiday $16.95 (978-0-8234-1947-0). 103pp. Brian Higman complains that he can't find anything interesting to write about, but his teacher and classmates show him that the stuff of his everyday life provides plenty of inspiration. (Rev: BL 3/1/06; SLJ 5/06)

11839 Dowell, Frances O'Roark. *Phineas L. MacGuire . . . Blasts Off!* (2–5). Illus. Series: From the Highly Scientific Notebooks of Phineas L. MacGuire. 2008,

Atheneum $16.99 (978-1-4169-2689-4). Phineas gets a job dog-walking to earn money for Space Camp, and decides to investigate the properties of slobber. (Rev: BLO 7/31/08)

11840 Dowell, Frances O'Roark. *Phineas L. MacGuire . . . Erupts! The First Experiment* (3–5). Illus. by Preston McDaniels. Series: From the Highly Selective Notebooks of Phineas L. MacGuire. 2006, Simon & Schuster $15.95 (978-1-4169-0195-2). 176pp. Science fair success seems unlikely when Phineas L. MacGuire is paired with the obnoxious new kid to work on a fourth-grade science project. (Rev: BL 6/1–15/06; SLJ 6/06)

11841 Durand, Hallie. *Just Desserts* (2–4). Illus. by Christine Davenier. 2010, Atheneum $15.99 (978-1-4169-6387-5). 208pp. Third-grader Dessert is inspired by lessons on the American Revolution to start a club to fight back against annoying siblings, but her good efforts backfire. (Rev: BLO 8/10; LMC 10/10; SLJ 6/1/10)

11842 Edwards, Michelle. *Stinky Stern Forever* (1–3). Illus. Series: Jackson Friends. 2005, Harcourt $14.00 (978-0-15-216389-1). Pa Lia Vang and her second-grade classmates have complex reactions when the class bully dies in an accident. (Rev: BL 9/1/05; SLJ 10/05*)

11843 English, Karen. *Substitute Trouble* (2–4). Illus. by Laura Freeman. 2013, Clarion $14.99 (978-054761565-3). 112pp. Nikki and Deja suffer through substitute teachers when Ms. Shelby-Ortiz is injured. Lexile 740 (Rev: BL 7/13)

11844 Feldman, Jody. *The Seventh Level* (5–8). 2010, Greenwillow $16.99 (978-0-06-195105-3). 304pp. Eager for acceptance into his middle school's secret society, the Legend, Travis is thrilled when he begins receiving the clues and puzzles that, if solved, will grant him admittance. **e** Lexile 630L (Rev: BL 5/1/10; SLJ 10/1/10)

11845 Flood, Pansie Hart. *Tiger Turcotte Takes on the Know-It-All* (2–4). Illus. by Amy Wummer. 2005, Carolrhoda LB $19.93 (978-1-57505-814-6); paper $6.95 (978-1-57505-900-6). 71pp. A beginning chapter book about a second-grade boy-girl rivalry. (Rev: SLJ 7/05)

11846 Frank, Lucy. *The Homeschool Liberation League* (5–8). 2009, Dial $16.99 (978-0-8037-3230-8). 288pp. Eighth-grader Katya is disappointed when home schooling does not turn out to give her the freedom she desires, and she sets out — with the help of a cute violin player named Milo — to change this. (Rev: BCCB 9/09; BLO 5/27/09; HB 9/09; SLJ 8/09)

11847 Fredericks, Mariah. *In the Cards: Love* (5–8). 2007, Simon & Schuster $15.99 (978-0-689-87654-7). Three eighth-grade girls in Manhattan use tarot cards to discover whether Anna will succeed in turning her crush on Declan into a romance; likable, believable characters populate this funny novel. (Rev: BL 1/1–15/07; SLJ 4/07)

11848 Friedman, Laurie. *Mallory Goes Green* (2–5). Illus. by Jennifer Kalis. Series: Mallory. 2010, Carolrhoda $15.95 (978-082258885-6). 160pp. Mallory's enthusiasm for the environment tends to alienate classmates and

adults until she realizes she must take another approach. The 14th book in the series is *Mallory in the Spotlight* (2010) in which a starring role calls friendship tension. (Rev: BL 2/15/10)

11849 Gallagher, Diana G. *Vote! The Complicated Life of Claudia Cristina Cortez* (5–7). Illus. by Brann Garvey. Series: Claudia Cristina Cortez. 2008, Stone Arch LB $23.93 (978-1-4342-0770-8); paper $5.95 (978-1-4342-0866-8). 88pp. Claudia and her classmates deal with the ups and downs of a class election in this visually appealing story for reluctant readers that includes a discussion guide and Internet links. (Rev: LMC 5/09; SLJ 2/09)

11850 Gephart, Donna. *How to Survive Middle School* (5–8). 2010, Delacorte $15.99 (978-038573793-7); LB $18.99 (978-038590701-9). 256pp. Used to being bullied and grieving the loss of his best friend Elliott, 13-year-old David Greenberg finds a new ally in Sophie who boosts his popularity by promoting his YouTube videos. **e** (Rev: BL 3/1/10; SLJ 6/10)

11851 Giblin, James Cross. *Did Fleming Rescue Churchill?* (3–5). Illus. by Erik Brooks. 2008, Holt $16.95 (978-0-8050-8183-1). Jason, a 5th-grade report writer, discovers the pleasures of research as he investigates a possible connection between Alexander Fleming and Winston Churchill. (Rev: BL 3/15/08; LMC 3/08; SLJ 4/08)

11852 Giff, Patricia Reilly. *Look Out, Washington, D.C.!* (2–4). Illus. 1995, Dell paper $3.99 (978-0-440-40934-2). 118pp. A series of setbacks dull Emily's enthusiasm for the field trip the Polk Street School class is taking to Washington, D.C. (Rev: BCCB 7–8/95; BL 6/1–15/95; SLJ 10/95)

11853 Gilson, Jamie. *Bug in a Rug* (2–4). Illus. 1998, Clarion $15.00 (978-0-395-86616-0). 69pp. In this easily read chapter book, the reader follows Richard through a day in the second grade, including the embarrassment of having to wear purple pants — a gift from his visiting Aunt Nannie. (Rev: BL 4/15/98; HBG 10/98; SLJ 6/98)

11854 Gilson, Jamie. *Gotcha!* (2–4). Illus. by Amy Wummer. 2006, Clarion $15.00 (978-0-618-54356-4). Information on spiders is interwoven into a story about second-grader Richard and his relationship with a bully named Patrick; an easy, humorous chapter book with line drawings. (Rev: BL 4/1/06; SLJ 4/06)

11855 Gilson, Jamie. *It Goes Eeeeeeeeeeee!* (2–4). Illus. by Diane deGroat. 1994, Clarion $15.00 (978-0-395-67063-7). 68pp. Patrick, a conceited new boy in school, is put in his place when he spreads misinformation about bats in class and is corrected by Dawn Marie. (Rev: BCCB 5/94; BL 4/1/94; SLJ 6/94)

11856 Graff, Lisa. *The Life and Crimes of Bernetta Wallflower* (4–6). 2008, HarperCollins $15.99 (978-0-06-087592-3). 256pp. The curious and very original Bernetta loses her scholarship when she is falsely accused of cheating, and is willing to try almost anything in order to raise $9,000 so she can return to her school. (Rev: BL 3/1/08; SLJ 2/08)

11857 Graff, Lisa. *Sophie Simon Solves Them All* (3–5). Illus. by Jason Beene. 2010, Farrar $14.99 (978-0-374-37125-8). 112pp. In pursuit of an advanced graphing calculator, friendless whiz-kid Sophie begins charging her classmates for solving their problems in this amusing story. **e** Lexile 680L (Rev: BL 9/15/10; HB 11–12/10; LMC 11–12/10; SLJ 9/1/10)

11858 Greene, Stephanie. *Princess Posey and the First Grade Parade* (K–2). Illus. by Stephanie Roth Sisson. 2010, Putnam $12.99 (978-0-399-25167-2). 96pp. Posey has many anxieties about starting 1st grade in this early chapter book. (Rev: BL 7/10; LMC 10/10; SLJ 6/1/10)

11859 Greenwald, Tommy. *Charlie Joe Jackson's Guide to Not Reading* (4–7). Illus. by J. P. Coovert. 2011, Roaring Brook $14.99 (978-1-59643-691-6). 224pp. Middle-schooler Charlie Joe goes to great lengths to avoid reading, although he is partial to some kinds of books — checkbooks, comic books, and Facebook. (Rev: BL 5/1/11; SLJ 8/11)

11860 Grimes, Nikki. *Rich* (2–4). Illus. by R. Gregory Christie. 2009, Putnam $10.99 (978-039925176-4). 112pp. Dyamonde and Free befriend a new classmate, Damaris, who is homeless and living in a shelter. ∩ **e** (Rev: BL 11/1/09)

11861 Gutman, Dan. *The Homework Machine* (4–6). 2006, Simon & Schuster $15.95 (978-0-689-87678-3). 160pp. A magical homework machine creates an unlikely alliance between a fifth-grade computer geek, a teacher's pet, the class clown, and a slacker. (Rev: BCCB 3/06; BL 2/1/06*; HBG 10/06; LMC 10/06; SLJ 4/06*)

11862 Gutman, Dan. *Miss Laney Is Zany!* (3–5). Illus. by Jim Paillot. Series: My Weird School Daze. 2010, HarperCollins LB $15.89 (978-0-06-155417-9); paper $3.99 (978-0-06-155415-5). 104pp. A.J.'s new game-show-loving speech teacher comes up with a way to solve the school's financial woes in this beginning chapter book with lots of wordplay. (Rev: SLJ 9/1/10)

11863 Gutman, Dan. *Return of the Homework Machine* (4–6). Series: Homework Machine. 2009, Simon & Schuster $15.99 (978-1-4169-5416-3). The four characters from *The Homework Machine* (2006) are now in 6th grade and on the track of the computer chip that powered their device. (Rev: BL 4/15/09; SLJ 7/09)

11864 Harper, Charise Mericle. *Just Grace, Star on Stage* (2–4). Illus. by author. 2012, Houghton Mifflin $15.99 (978-054763412-8). 208pp. In this 9th volume in the series, Grace is initially downcast when she is not picked for the role of fairy queen in the class play. **e** Lexile 690L (Rev: BL 10/1/12)

11865 Herrick, Steven. *Naked Bunyip Dancing* (2–5). Illus. by Beth Norling. 2008, Front St. $16.95 (978-1-59078-499-0). In humorous free verse, this novel follows a class of Australian 11- and 12-year-olds as they interreact with their new hippie teacher. (Rev: BCCB 5/08; BL 4/15/08; HB 5/08; LMC 5/08; SLJ 4/08)

11866 Hill, Kirkpatrick. *The Year of Miss Agnes* (4–6). 2000, Simon & Schuster $16.00 (978-0-689-82933-8). 128pp. Set in northern Canada, this is a gentle story about a schoolteacher named Miss Agnes and the changes she makes in her pupils during the year she teaches in a one-room schoolhouse. (Rev: BCCB 11/00; BL 10/15/00; HB 11/00; HBG 3/01; SLJ 9/00)

11867 Hobbs, Valerie. *Minnie McClary Speaks Her Mind* (4–6). 2012, Farrar $16.99 (978-037432496-4). 224pp. A new teacher inspires 6th-grader Minnie, unsure of herself at a new school, to speak up against prejudice at a board meeting. ∩ **e** Lexile 610L (Rev: BLO 10/15/12; SLJ 1/13)

11868 Hoffman, Mary. *Encore, Grace!* (2–5). Illus. by June Allen. 2003, Penguin $14.99 (978-0-8037-2951-3). 112pp. Grace deals with a class play and difficult friends and family in this chapter book with occasional illustrations. (Rev: BL 12/1/03; HBG 4/04; SLJ 12/03)

11869 Holmes, Sara Lewis. *Operation Yes* (5–8). 2009, Scholastic $16.99 (978-054510795-2). 256pp. Miss Loupe uses improv acting in her 6th-grade class at an Air Force base school, and she is rewarded by her students' loyal support when her brother goes missing in Afghanistan. ∩ (Rev: BL 9/15/09*; HB 11–12/09; SLJ 11/09)

11870 Jacobson, Jennifer. *Andy Shane and the Very Bossy Dolores Starbuckle* (1–3). Illus. by Abby Carter. 2005, Candlewick $15.99 (978-0-7636-1940-4). A bully is making life at school miserable for Andy Shane until his Granny Webb pays a visit to the classroom. (Rev: BL 7/05; SLJ 8/05*)

11871 Jacobson, Jennifer. *Winnie at Her Best* (2–4). Illus. by Alissa Imre Geis. 2006, Houghton $16.00 (978-0-618-47277-2). 112pp. Winnie must choose between helping out a young friend in need or pursuing her new-found interest in art. (Rev: BL 8/06; SLJ 9/06)

11872 Kline, Suzy. *Horrible Harry at Halloween* (2–3). Illus. 2000, Viking $14.99 (978-0-670-88864-1). At Halloween, Harry must solve the mystery of a stolen party costume in this story about Class 3B. (Rev: BL 9/15/00; HBG 3/01; SLJ 9/00)

11873 Kline, Suzy. *Horrible Harry Cracks the Code* (2–4). Illus. by Frank Remkiewicz. 2007, Viking $13.99 (978-0-670-06200-3). 66pp. Readers will unwittingly learn a math lesson as they read about how Harry, a 3rd-grader, tries to figure out a number code used to award daily prizes. (Rev: BL 5/1/07)

11874 Knudson, Mike, and Steve Wilkinson. *Raymond and Graham Rule the School* (2–4). Illus. by Stacy Curtis. 2008, Viking $14.99 (978-0-670-01101-8). 136pp. A funny, feel-good ride through 4th grade as two buddies who expected to revel in being the oldest kids in the school find themselves thwarted at every turn. (Rev: SLJ 9/08)

11875 Korman, Gordon. *The 6th Grade Nickname Game* (4–6). 1998, Hyperion LB $15.49 (978-0-7868-2382-6). 160pp. Typical problems encountered in the sixth grade are faced by Wiley and Jeff along with the anxiety of mounting a campaign to save the substitute teacher, Mr. Hughes. (Rev: BL 10/15/98)

11876 Langston, Laura. *The Trouble with Cupid* (4–8). 2008, Fitzhenry & Whiteside paper $11.95 (978-1-

55455-059-3). 251pp. Eighth-grader Erin is asked to train the school's mascot for a dog food contest and finds the job more complicated and educational than she had expected; the gorgeous Zach Cameron is going to help, though. (Rev: SLJ 2/09; VOYA 6/08)

11877 LeBlanc, Louise. *Maddie's Big Test* (2–4). Illus. by Marie-Louise Gay. 2007, Formac paper $4.95 (978-0-8878-0714-5). 64pp. Maddie, who's much more interested in becoming a star than in math, is so nervous about her test that she decides to cheat. (Rev: BL 4/1/07)

11878 Lee, Lauren. *Stella: On the Edge of Popularity* (5–7). 1994, Polychrome $10.95 (978-1-879965-08-9). A Korean American girl has to choose between being popular and being loyal to her Korean culture. (Rev: BCCB 7–8/94; SLJ 9/94)

11879 Lennon, Maria T. *Confessions of a So-Called Middle Child* (5–8). 2013, HarperCollins $16.99 (978-006212690-0). 288pp. After being expelled from her previous school, 12-year-old Charlie C. Cooper starts over at a new school, where her therapist assigns her the task of befriending the girl who is most bullied. e (Rev: BL 10/1/13; SLJ 9/13)

11880 Lin, Grace. *The Year of the Dog* (3–5). Illus. 2006, Little, Brown $14.99 (978-0-316-06000-4). A 12-year-old Taiwanese American girl chronicles the events of a year that includes a new friend, academic achievements, growing awareness of cultural differences, and a touch of romance. (Rev: BCCB 2/06; BL 1/1–15/06*; HB 3/06; HBG 10/06; SLJ 3/06)

11881 Lin, Grace. *The Year of the Rat* (3–5). Illus. by author. 2008, Little, Brown $14.99 (978-0-316-11426-4). Grace's Taiwanese American family celebrates Chinese New Year as Grace tackles such changes as her best friend moving away and a Chinese boy arriving at her school in this sequel to *The Year of the Dog* (2006). (Rev: BL 11/15/07; HB 5/08; SLJ 3/08)

11882 Look, Lenore. *Ruby Lu, Empress of Everything* (2–4). Illus. by Anne Wilsdorf. 2006, Simon & Schuster $15.95 (978-0-689-86460-5). 176pp. Ruby Lu faces new challenges as she helps her deaf cousin Flying Duck, newly arrived from China, to adjust to school and life in America; a sequel to *Ruby Lu, Brave and True* (2004). (Rev: BL 2/15/06; SLJ 7/06*)

11883 Lovelace, Maud H. *Betsy-Tacy* (3–4). Illus. by Lois Lenski. 1940, HarperCollins paper $5.99 (978-0-06-440096-1). Two 5-year-olds are inseparable at school and at play. One of a popular series. Five sequels are: *Betsy-Tacy and Tib* (1941); *Betsy and Tacy Go over the Big Hill* (1942); *Betsy and Tacy Go Downtown* (1943); *Heaven to Betsy* (1945); *Betsy in Spite of Herself* (1946).

11884 Lowry, Lois. *Gooney Bird and All Her Charms* (2–4). Illus. by Middy Thomas. 2014, Houghton Mifflin $16.99 (978-054411354-1). 150pp. Napoleon the skeleton has come to school with Gooney Bird while her 2nd-grade class studies anatomy, but when Napoleon is stolen, Gooney finds herself playing detective. e Lexile 610 (Rev: BL 11/1/13; SLJ 1/1/14)

11885 Lowry, Lois. *Gooney Bird and the Room Mother* (2–4). Illus. by Middy Thomas. Series: Gooney Bird. 2005, Houghton $15.00 (978-0-618-53230-8). 80pp. Gooney Bird brings in a secret room mother and saves the class Thanksgiving pageant in this sequel to *Gooney Bird Greene*. (Rev: BL 3/1/05; SLJ 5/05)

11886 Lowry, Lois. *Gooney Bird Greene* (2–5). Illus. by Middy Thomas. 2002, Houghton $15.00 (978-0-618-23848-4). Gooney Bird is a colorful character: a new second-grader who has a fondness for dressing outrageously and telling fanciful stories. (Rev: BCCB 10/02; BL 9/1/02; HB 9/02; HBG 3/03; SLJ 11/02)

11887 Lowry, Lois. *Gooney Bird on the Map* (2–4). Illus. by Middy Thomas. 2011, Houghton Mifflin $15.99 (978-0-547-55622-2). 128pp. Gooney Bird comes up with a plan to make staying home for spring break more fun than going on vacation. (Rev: BL 11/1/11; SLJ 10/1/11)

11888 Lowry, Lois. *Gooney the Fabulous* (2–4). Illus. by Middy Thomas. 2007, Houghton $15.00 (978-0-618-76691-8). 96pp. In this third outing, second-grader Gooney Bird Green leads her classmates in writing their own fables after Miss Pidgeon reads them an Aesop's tale. (Rev: BL 1/1–15/07)

11889 Lundquist, Jenny. *Seeing Cinderella* (4–7). 2012, Simon & Schuster $15.99 (978-1-4424-4550-5). 240pp. Callie is most unhappy to be starting 6th grade wearing ugly glasses — until she discovers that they have given her amazing abilities to "read" other people. e Lexile 680L (Rev: SLJ 5/1/12; VOYA 6/12)

11890 McCafferty, Megan. *The (Totally Not) Guaranteed Guide to Popularity, Prettiness and Perfection* (4–7). Series: Jessica Darling's It List. 2013, Little, Brown $17 (978-031624499-2). 240pp. Jessica Darling (first seen as in high school in 2001's *Sloppy Firsts*) is entering junior high in this prequel series and receives a list of tips from her college-age sister. Lexile 810 (Rev: BL 7/13; SLJ 9/13)

11891 McDonald, Megan. *Judy Moody* (2–4). Illus. 2000, Candlewick $15.99 (978-0-7636-0685-5). 196pp. A beginning chapter book about Judy Moody, a third-grader, and her everyday trials and tribulations. (Rev: BCCB 5/00; BL 7/00; HBG 10/00; SLJ 7/00)

11892 McDonald, Megan. *Judy Moody Goes to College* (2–4). Illus. by Peter H. Reynolds. 2008, Candlewick $15.99 (978-0-7636-2833-8). 144pp. When third-grader Judy visits a local college to meet her new math tutor she becomes immersed in a new way of thinking. (Rev: BL 9/1/08) ⌒

11893 McDonald, Megan. *Judy Moody Saves the World!* (2–5). Illus. by Peter Reynolds. 2002, Candlewick $15.99 (978-0-7636-1446-1). Third-grader Judy is busy saving the world with a recycling project in this third installment in the series in which she stars. (Rev: BL 9/1/02; HBG 3/03)

11894 McDonald, Megan. *Stink and the World's Worst Super-Stinky Sneakers* (2–4). Illus. by Peter H. Reynolds. 2007, Candlewick $12.99 (978-0-7636-2834-5). 144pp. Stink, who got his name as a baby, had been intent on winning the smelly sneaker contest but is willing to give up this chance to become one of the judges instead. (Rev: BL 4/15/07)

11895 McElligott, Matthew, and Larry Tuxbury. *Benjamin Franklinstein Lives!* (4–7). Illus. by Matthew McElligott. Series: Benjamin Franklinstein. 2010, Putnam $12.99 (978-0-399-25229-7). 128pp. Science whiz Victor's expectations of winning the school science fair are dashed when a lightning strike revives a dormant Ben Franklin, who had been in secret suspended animation. A sequel is *Benjamin Franklinstein Meets the Fright Brothers* (2011). **e** Lexile 590L (Rev: BL 9/1/10; LMC 11–12/10; SLJ 11/1/10)

11896 MacLachlan, Patricia. *Word After Word After Word* (2–5). 2010, HarperCollins $14.99 (978-0-06-027971-4); LB $15.89 (978-0-06-027972-1). 128pp. Fourth-grader Lucy comes to understand the power of poetry when a visiting author spends time in her class. **e** (Rev: BL 3/15/10*; SLJ 7/1/10)

11897 McMullan, Kate. *School! Adventures at the Harvey N. Trouble Elementary School* (1–4). Illus. by George Booth. 2010, Feiwel & Friends $12.99 (978-0-312-37592-8). 160pp. Heading for school each morning Ron Faster — always in a hurry — is ready to deal with music teacher Doremi Fasollatido and Janitor Iquit. (Rev: LMC 8–9/10; SLJ 8/1/10)

11898 Marsden, Carolyn. *The Gold-Threaded Dress* (3–5). 2002, Candlewick $13.99 (978-0-7636-1569-7). 73pp. Fourth-grader Oy is torn between her desire to make friends and her classmates' interest in her precious Thai dress. (Rev: BCCB 6/02; BL 5/1/02*; HBG 3/03; SLJ 4/02)

11899 Marsden, Carolyn. *The Quail Club* (3–5). 2006, Candlewick $15.99 (978-0-7636-2635-8). 144pp. Thai American fifth-grader Oy faces a cultural dilemma when her school schedules a talent show: honor her heritage with a traditional Thai dance or succumb to her classmate's demand that Oy join her in an American dance; a sequel to *The Gold-Threaded Dress* (2002). (Rev: BL 3/1/06; SLJ 4/06)

11900 Martin, Ann M. *Belle Teal* (4–6). 2001, Scholastic $16.95 (978-0-439-09823-6). 224pp. Fifth-grader Belle befriends the only black student in her class in this story about the early days of desegregation. (Rev: BCCB 2/02; BL 10/1/01; HB 1/02; HBG 3/02; SLJ 9/01)

11901 Messner, Kate. *Marty McGuire* (2–4). Illus. by Brian Floca. 2011, Scholastic $15.99 (978-0-545-14244-1); paper $5.99 (978-0-545-14-246-5). 144pp. An active, nature-loving young girl is reluctantly cast as the princess in the school play and learns a little about drama and improvisation. ∩ Lexile 660L (Rev: BL 6/1/11; LMC 10–11/11; SLJ 12/1/11)

11902 Millard, Glenda. *Layla, Queen of Hearts* (4–6). Illus. by Patrice Barton. 2010, Farrar $15.99 (978-0-374-34360-6). 112pp. Third-grader Layla is at a loss for who to bring to school for Senior Citizens' Day, until she meets charming and scatterbrained Miss Amelie. Lexile 900L (Rev: BLO 3/1/10; SLJ 6/1/10)

11903 Mills, Claudia. *Being Teddy Roosevelt* (3–5). Illus. by R. W. Alley. 2007, Farrar $16.00 (978-0-374-30657-1). In this funny school story, fourth-grader Riley, assigned to research and depict Theodore Roosevelt, employs some of T.R.'s enterprising zeal to obtain an unaffordable saxophone to play in the school band. (Rev: BL 1/1–15/07; SLJ 3/07)

11904 Mills, Claudia. *Fractions = Trouble!* (2–3). Illus. by G. Brian Karas. 2011, Farrar $15.99 (978-0-374-36716-9). 116pp. Third-grader Wilson has difficulty with fractions and grudgingly accepts tutoring while fretting about his science fair project. (Rev: SLJ 6/11)

11905 Mills, Claudia. *Kelsey Green, Reading Queen* (2–4). Illus. by Rob Shepperson. Series: Franklin School Friends. 2013, Farrar $15.99 (978-0-374-37485-3). 128pp. Third-grader Kelsey loves to read and aims to win the school's reading contest until she realizes that helping a struggling reader may be equally rewarding. Lexile 750 (Rev: BLO 6/13; HB 5–6/13; SLJ 8/13)

11906 Mills, Claudia. *Zero Tolerance* (4–7). 2013, Farrar $16.99 (978-037433312-6). 224pp. When 7th-grader Sierra accidentally grabs her mother's lunch bag, which contains a paring knife, she finds she has violated her school's zero tolerance and faces expulsion. Lexile 670 (Rev: BLO 7/13; LMC 10/13; SLJ 6/13)

11907 Mongredien, Sue. *Be My Valentine* (4–6). Series: The Sleepover Club. 2010, IPG/Lion paper $6.99 (978-00072770-5-6). 128pp. Two mean girls exploit Fliss's crush on Ryan in a hurtful Valentine's Day prank, and her friends plan revenge. (Rev: BLO 11/15/09)

11908 Montes, Marisa. *Get Ready for Gabi! A Crazy Mixed-Up Spanglish Day* (3–6). Illus. by Joe Cepeda. 2003, Scholastic $12.95 (978-0-439-51710-2); paper $3.99 (978-0-439-47519-8). 124pp. Third-grader Gabi speaks Spanish at home and English at school, but when a classmate starts causing problems, what comes out of her mouth is a mixture of the two. (Rev: BL 9/1/03; HBG 10/03; SLJ 11/03)

11909 Morgenstern, Susie. *A Book of Coupons* (4–6). Illus. 2001, Viking $13.99 (978-0-670-89970-8). 64pp. An elderly teacher rewards his fifth-grade class with books of coupons that are redeemable for such treats as dancing in class, and not going to the blackboard when summoned. (Rev: BL 4/1/01; HB 5/01; HBG 10/01; SLJ 5/01)

11910 Moss, Marissa. *Amelia's Book of Notes and Note Passing* (3–5). Series: Amelia. 2006, Simon & Schuster $9.95 (978-0-689-87446-8). 80pp. Amelia's world is jarred off-orbit when a new girl joins her class at school and Amelia starts receiving hateful anonymous notes. (Rev: BL 5/1/06)

11911 Moss, Marissa. *Amelia's Most Unforgettable Embarrassing Moments* (3–5). Illus. by author. 2005, Simon & Schuster $9.95 (978-0-689-87041-5). Faced with a three-day class field trip, Amelia worries about whether her bedtime apparel will pass muster; her older sister's presence as a teaching aide adds to her angst but ends up helping her realize she's not alone in her fears. (Rev: SLJ 11/05)

11912 Moss, Marissa. *Amelia's Science Fair Disaster* (4–6). Illus. by author. Series: Amelia's Notebook: Life in Middle School. 2008, Simon & Schuster $9.99 (978-1-4169-6494-0). 80pp. Amelia gets stuck with dreadful partners for a 7th-grade science project. (Rev: BLO 1/13/09)

11913 Moss, Marissa. *Amelia's 6th-Grade Notebook* (4–6). Illus. 2005, Simon & Schuster $10.95 (978-0-689-87040-8). 80pp. Entering middle school, Amelia has to deal with the presence of her older sister and a really mean English teacher. (Rev: BL 7/05; SLJ 10/05)

11914 Moss, Marissa. *The Vampire Dare!* (2–4). Illus. by author. 2011, Simon & Schuster paper $5.99 (978-14424173-7-3). 80pp. Fourth-grader Daphne fills her journal with doodles and musings about coming up with the perfect vampire outfit for Costume Day. (Rev: BL 5/1/11)

11915 Myers, Walter Dean. *The Cruisers* (5–8). 2010, Scholastic $15.99 (978-0-439-91626-4). 123pp. The four low-achieving 8th-grade creators of *The Cruiser* alternative newspaper are assigned the roles of peacekeepers during a Civil War unit with interesting results; set in a Harlem school for the gifted and talented. ∩ Lexile 810L (Rev: BL 9/1/10*; LMC 1–2/11; SLJ 10/1/10)

11916 Nagda, Ann Whitehead. *Kevin Keeps Up* (2–4). 2012, Holiday $15.95 (978-082342657-7). 128pp. His substitute teacher is not as understanding about attention deficits and Kevin worries about completing his report on cheetahs. ℮ Lexile 590L (Rev: BL 10/1/12; LMC 3–4/13)

11917 Naylor, Phyllis Reynolds. *Alice in Blunderland* (3–7). 2003, Simon & Schuster $15.95 (978-0-689-84397-6). 200pp. Fourth-grader Alice is well-intentioned but blunder-prone in this second of three prequels to the Alice books. (Rev: HBG 4/04; SLJ 9/03)

11918 Naylor, Phyllis Reynolds. *Starting with Alice* (3–8). 2002, Simon & Schuster $15.95 (978-0-689-84395-2). 192pp. In this prequel, Alice (first seen in *The Agony of Alice* in 1985) is in third grade in a new school in Maryland, initially has trouble finding friends, and still misses her dead mother. (Rev: BCCB 11/02; BL 11/15/02; HB 9/02; HBG 3/03; SLJ 9/02)

11919 O'Connell, Rebecca. *Penina Levine Is a Hard-Boiled Egg* (4–6). Illus. by Majella Lue Sue. 2007, Roaring Brook $16.95 (978-1-59643-140-9). 176pp. Penina, a feisty Jewish sixth grader troubled by a school assignment involving the Easter bunny, worries that confiding in her parents will only cause more trouble. (Rev: BL 3/15/07)

11920 Papademetriou, Lisa. *Sixth-Grade: Glommers, Norks, and Me* (4–6). 2005, Hyperion $14.99 (978-0-7868-5169-0). 224pp. Allie must contend with squabbling friends and likes to invent new words to do so in this enjoyable look at life in middle school. (Rev: BL 3/15/05; SLJ 5/05)

11921 Park, Barbara. *Junie B. Jones and Her Big Fat Mouth* (2–4). Illus. by Denise Brunkus. 1993, Random $11.99 (978-0-679-94407-2); paper $3.99 (978-0-679-84407-5). 72pp. In this hilarious story of kindergartner Junie B. Jones, the little girl has trouble with the Pledge of Allegiance, keeping quiet in class, and deciding what to be on Job Day. (Rev: BL 11/15/93)

11922 Park, Barbara. *Junie B. Jones and the Yucky Blucky Fruitcake* (2–4). Illus. by Denise Brunkus. Series: Junie B. Jones. 1995, Random paper $3.99 (978-0-679-86694-7). 71pp. A young kindergartner tells about her many troubles at school, where she is always a loser. (Rev: BL 12/15/95)

11923 Park, Barbara. *Junie B., First Grader: Cheater Pants* (1–2). 2003, Random LB $13.99 (978-0-375-92301-2). 96pp. Junie B. is back again, and she's learning some tough lessons about cheating at school. (Rev: BL 9/15/03; HBG 4/04; SLJ 9/03)

11924 Park, Barbara. *Junie B., First Grader: Toothless Wonder* (2–4). Illus. by Denise Brunkus. 2002, Random LB $13.99 (978-0-375-90295-6). 96pp. Junie B. is losing her first tooth and decides to look into the existence of the tooth fairy, which she rather doubts. (Rev: BL 11/1/02; HBG 3/03; SLJ 12/02)

11925 Patterson, James, and Chris Tebbetts. *Middle School, the Worst Years of My Life* (3–6). Illus. by Laura Park. 2011, Little, Brown $15.99 (978-0-316-10187-5). 288pp. Middle school misfit Rafe decides to break every rule in the school's code of conduct and spends his time pulling fire alarms, painting graffiti, and so forth until he is finally expelled and the frustrated adults consider an alternative arts school. (Rev: BL 9/15/11; SLJ 11/1/11*)

11926 Patterson, James, and Lisa Papademetriou. *My Brother Is a Big, Fat Liar!* (4–6). Illus. by Neil Swaab. 2013, Little, Brown $15.99 (978-031620754-6). 304pp. Entering middle school, Georgia finds that her brother Rafe's dreadful reputation is coloring her chances of success. ∩ ℮ Lexile 520 (Rev: BLO 3/15/13; SLJ 5/13)

11927 Peirce, Lincoln. *Big Nate Strikes Again* (3–6). Series: Big Nate. 2010, HarperCollins $13.99 (978-0-06-194436-9); LB $14.89 (978-0-06-194437-6). 224pp. Big Nate must cope with the unbearable Gina, an A-plus student who keeps showing up where he doesn't want her in school. Lexile 430L (Rev: BL 2/1/11; HB 11–12/10; SLJ 12/1/10)

11928 Peschke, Marci. *Daisy's Summer Essay* (2–4). Illus. by M. H. Pilz. Series: Growing Up Daisy. 2011, ABDO LB $25.65 (978-161641114-5). 80pp. Mexican American Daisy Martinez gets help from her *abuela* and creates an excellent show-and-tell project for her 4th-grade class in this first installment in a new series that also includes *Daisy's Fall Festival, Daisy's Field Trip Adventure,* and *Daisy for President* (all 2011). (Rev: BL 5/1/11)

11929 Pinkney, Andrea Davis. *Hold Fast to Dreams* (5–8). 1995, Morrow $16.00 (978-0-688-12832-6). A bright, resourceful African American girl faces problems when she finds she is the only black student in her new middle school. (Rev: BCCB 5/95; BL 2/15/95; HB 9–10/95; SLJ 4/95)

11930 Polacco, Patricia. *Bully* (3–7). Illus. by author. 2012, Putnam $17.99 (978-0-399-25704-9). 48pp. New kids in 6th grade Lyla and Jamie give each other support through the online bullying they suffer from other students. ℮ Lexile 630L (Rev: BL 12/1/12; LMC 3–4/13; SLJ 8/12)

11931 Polacco, Patricia. *The Junkyard Wonders* (2–5). Illus. by author. 2010, Philomel $17.99 (978-0-399-25078-1). 48pp. A creative teacher inspires a classroom of slow learners, insisting that her students have as much potential as anyone else. Lexile 660L (Rev: BL 5/1/10; LMC 10/10; SLJ 7/1/10)

11932 Russell, Rachel Renee. *Tales from a Not-So-Smart Miss Know-It-All* (4–6). Illus. by author. Series: Dork Diaries. 2012, Aladdin $13.99 (978-144244961-9). 336pp. In a move to curb the activities of the snobby Mackenzie Hollister, Nikki joins the school newspaper and becomes its secret advice columnist; the 5th book in the series. ∩ ℮ Lexile 750L (Rev: BLO 11/15/12)

11933 Rylander, Chris. *The Fourth Stall* (4–7). 2011, HarperCollins $15.99 (978-0-06-199496-8). 320pp. Sixth-graders Mac and Vince run a successful business helping fellow students with everything from tests to defense against bullies, but find their friendship tested when they confront a real challenge. (Rev: BL 2/15/11; LMC 5–6/11; SLJ 9/1/11; VOYA 12/11)

11934 Rylander, Chris. *The Fourth Stall, Part II* (4–7). 2012, HarperCollins $15.99 (978-006199630-6). 240pp. Expert problem-solvers Mac and Vince continue to build their advice business (conducted from the washroom) even as their classmates' dilemmas get more and more complex. (Rev: BL 3/1/12; VOYA 12/11)

11935 Sachar, Louis. *Marvin Redpost: Class President* (2–4). Illus. 1999, Random LB $11.99 (978-0-679-98999-8); paper $3.99 (978-0-679-88999-1). In this beginning chapter book, Marvin's third-grade class has a surprise visit from the president of the United States. (Rev: BCCB 4/99; BL 4/15/99; HBG 10/99; SLJ 6/99)

11936 Sachar, Louis. *Wayside School Is Falling Down* (3–6). Illus. by Joel Schick. 1989, Lothrop $15.99 (978-0-688-07868-3); Avon paper $5.99 (978-0-380-75484-7). 192pp. Episodes with the children who inhabit the world's wackiest elementary school. (Rev: BL 5/1/89; SLJ 5/89)

11937 Salisbury, Graham. *Kung Fooey* (3–5). Illus. by Jacqueline Rogers. Series: Calvin Coconut. 2011, Random House $12.99 (978-0-385-73963-4); LB $15.99 (978-0-385-90797-2). 144pp. Calvin is curious about his new classmate Benny who makes various claims that seem unlikely, but also worries when class bully Tito picks on Benny; the sixth installment in the series set in Hawaii. Also use *Dog Heaven* (2010). ℮ (Rev: SLJ 8/1/11)

11938 Sand-Eveland, Cyndi. *Dear Toni* (3–6). Illus. by author. 2008, Tundra $12.95 (978-0-88776-876-7). 129pp. At her new school, 6th-grader Gene initially finds it difficult to write a journal that will not be read for 40 years, but she soon enjoys recording her new and sometimes dramatic life. (Rev: SLJ 2/09)

11939 Schoenberg, Jane. *The One and Only Stuey Lewis: Stories from the Second Grade* (2–3). Illus. by Cambria Evans. 2011, Farrar $16.99 (978-0-374-37292-7). 128pp. Second-grader Stuey contends with familiar school troubles and triumphs in these four short stories. (Rev: BLO 8/11; LMC 11–12/11; SLJ 8/1/11)

11940 Schwartz, Virginia Frances. *The 4 Kids in 5E and 1 Crazy Year* (3–5). 2006, Holiday $16.95 (978-0-8234-1946-3). 261pp. A fifth-grade ESL teacher helps each of her four students find themselves through reading and writing; the story is told through the students' journal entries. (Rev: BL 12/1/06; SLJ 11/06)

11941 Selzer, Adam. *I Put a Spell on You: From the Files of Chrissie Woodward, Spelling Bee Detective* (5–7). 2008, Delacorte $15.99 (978-0-385-73504-9). 247pp. Ambitious adults may be planning to fix the spelling bee at the Gordon Liddy Community School, and sleuth Chrissie Woodward is determined to find out what's going on. (Rev: BCCB 9/08; HB 9/08; SLJ 11/08)

11942 Seuling, Barbara. *Robert and the Practical Jokes* (2–4). Illus. by Paul Brewer. 2006, Cricket $15.95 (978-0-8126-2741-1). In addition to getting in trouble at school and being fooled into eating a worm, Robert attends a wedding and learns to dance. (Rev: BL 5/1/06; SLJ 3/06)

11943 Seuling, Barbara. *Robert Takes a Stand* (2–4). Illus. by Paul Brewer. 2004, Cricket $15.95 (978-0-8126-2712-1). Third-grader Robert tackles a variety of topics — class politics, animal rights, and caring for a new puppy — in this appealing book for beginning readers. Also use *Robert Finds a Way* (2005). (Rev: BL 4/1/04; HB 7/04; SLJ 4/04)

11944 Simon, Coco. *The Cupcake Cure* (4–6). Series: Cupcake Diaries. 2011, Simon & Schuster paper $5.99 (978-14424227-5-9). 160pp. Four girls form a bond during the early days of middle school as they navigate prickly social situations together. (Rev: BL 5/1/11)

11945 Spinelli, Jerry. *Loser* (3–6). 2002, HarperCollins LB $16.89 (978-0-06-000483-5). 224pp. Donald Zinkoff, labeled a "loser" by his classmates, is nonetheless happy and secure, unconcerned about what others think of him. (Rev: BCCB 5/02; BL 5/15/02; HB 7/02; HBG 10/02; SLJ 5/02)

11946 Spinelli, Jerry. *Third Grade Angels* (3–4). Illus. by Jennifer A. Bell. 2012, Scholastic $15.99 (978-0-545-38772-9). 160pp. Suds finds it harder than expected to earn the first halo as a new 3rd-grader in this entertaining prequel to *Fourth Grade Rats* (1991). ∩ ℮ Lexile 390L (Rev: BL 9/15/12; HB 9–10/12; LMC 1–2/13*; SLJ 12/12)

11947 Starkey, Scott. *How to Beat the Bully Without Really Trying* (3–6). 2012, Simon & Schuster $15.99 (978-144241685-7). 272pp. New student Rodney is immediately picked on by the resident bully but gains stature when a stray baseball knocks Josh out cold. (Rev: BL 1/1/12; SLJ 4/12)

11948 Stering, Shirley. *My Name Is Seepeetza* (5–10). 1997, Douglas & McIntyre paper $5.95 (978-0-88899-165-2). Told in diary form, this autobiographical novel about a 6th-grade Native American girl tells of her heartbreak at the terrible conditions at her school, where she is persecuted because of her race. (Rev: BL 3/1/97)

11949 Stewart, Kiera. *Fetching* (5–8). 2011, Hyperion/Disney $16.99 (978-1-4231-3845-7). 304pp. Olivia applies dog training principles to the "pack" of mean cliquish kids at her middle school, but finds that the results are not quite what she expected. e Lexile 740L (Rev: BL 10/15/11; SLJ 11/1/11; VOYA 12/11)

11950 Stine, R. L. *It's the First Day of School . . . Forever!* (4–6). 2011, Feiwel & Friends $15.99 (978-0-312-64954-8). 192pp. Artie's first day at middle school does not go well, and the boy relives the same disastrous events over and over — but is it all a bad dream? ∩ e (Rev: BL 8/11; LMC 11–12/11; SLJ 8/1/11*)

11951 Thomson, Melissa. *Keena Ford and the Secret Journal Mix-Up* (1–3). Illus. by Frank Morrison. 2010, Dial $15.99 (978-0-8037-3465-4). 128pp. Second-grader Keena, an African American living in Washington, D.C., faces difficult choices when Tiffany threatens to share Keena's personal diary with the whole school. e Lexile 780L (Rev: BL 11/15/10; SLJ 10/1/10)

11952 Tracy, Kristen. *Bessica Lefter Bites Back* (4–7). 2012, Delacorte $16.99 (978-038574069-2); LB $19.99 (978-037598961-2). 272pp. Bessica's iffy social standing goes from bad to worse when her friend lets fly a rumor about a nasty foot fungus even as she must work out a strategy for sharing mascot duty. e Lexile 550L (Rev: BL 2/15/12; LMC 8–9/12; SLJ 3/12; VOYA 4/12)

11953 Trueit, Trudi. *Scab for Treasurer?* (2–5). Illus. by Jim Paillot. Series: Secrets of a Lab Rat. 2011, Aladdin $14.99 (978-1-4169-7594-6); paper $4.99 (978-14169611-3-0). 160pp. In a bid to become 4th-grade class president, Scab pledges to eat any food his classmates bring him. ∩ e Lexile 490L (Rev: BL 7/11; SLJ 7/11)

11954 Walters, Eric. *Special Edward* (5–8). 2009, Orca $16.95 (978-1-55469-096-1); paper $9.95 (978-1-55469-092-3). 108pp. Eddy, a lazy sophomore, figures that if he can get himself into special ed class, he won't have to work so hard. (Rev: BL 5/15/09; SLJ 9/09)

11955 Wardlaw, Lee. *101 Ways to Bug Your Friends and Enemies* (5–8). 2011, Dial $16.99 (978-0-8037-3262-9). 288pp. Eighth grade proves challenging to "Sneeze" Wyatt as he attends some classes at high school, falls for Hayley who unfortunately is in love with someone else, and a golfer bullies him. e Lexile 600L (Rev: BLO 10/15/11; SLJ 10/1/11)

11956 Warner, Sally. *EllRay Jakes and the Beanstalk* (1–3). Illus. by Brian Biggs. 2013, Viking $14.99 (978-067078499-8); paper $5.99 (978-01424235-9-2). 144pp. When the scrawny 3rd-grader's best friend forsakes him,

EllRay decides to take up skateboarding to regain his attention. ∩ e Lexile 800 (Rev: BLO 9/1/13)

11957 Warner, Sally. *EllRay Jakes Is a Rock Star!* (2–4). Illus. by Jamie Harper. Series: EllRay Jakes. 2011, Viking $14.99 (978-0-670-01158-2). 144pp. EllRay is eager to have something to bring for show and tell and borrows his geologist dad's crystals without permission — only to find himself in a tight spot when the crystals go missing. e (Rev: BL 12/15/11; SLJ 9/1/11)

11958 Warner, Sally. *EllRay Jakes Is Not a Chicken!* (2–4). Illus. by Jamie Harper. 2011, Viking $14.99 (978-0-670-06243-0). 144pp. EllRay struggles to be good at school, even in the face of bullies, lest his father cancel their upcoming trip to Disneyland. (Rev: BL 6/1/11; LMC 10/11; SLJ 8/1/11)

11959 Warner, Sally. *Super Emma* (2–3). Illus. by Jamie Harper. 2006, Viking $14.99 (978-0-670-06140-2). 90pp. When Emma rescues EllRay from the clutches of a school bully, the reactions of her classmates — including EllRay — are not at all what she expected. (Rev: SLJ 10/06)

11960 Weissman, Elissa Brent. *Standing for Socks* (3–6). 2009, Simon & Schuster $15.99 (978-1-4169-4801-8). 220pp. Fara enjoyed wearing mismatched socks to school in 5th grade, but as she enters 6th grade and runs for class president she wants to be recognized for other achievements. (Rev: BCCB 4/09; BL 3/15/09; SLJ 4/09)

11961 Weissman, Elissa Brent. *The Trouble with Mark Hopper* (4–6). 2009, Dutton $16.99 (978-0-525-42067-5). 240pp. Two boys with the same name, in the same middle school, even looking much alike — confusion and competition reign at first. (Rev: BCCB 9/09; BLO 5/28/09; SLJ 8/09)

11962 Wilkowski, Sue. *The Bad Luck Chair* (3–5). Illus. by CB Decker. 2007, Dutton $15.99 (978-0-525-47794-5). 124pp. Can Addy overcome the misfortune that comes from sitting in her fourth-grade classroom's "bad luck" chair? (Rev: BCCB 10/07; SLJ 7/07)

11963 Winerip, Michael. *Adam Canfield: The Last Reporter* (5–8). 2009, Candlewick $16.99 (978-0-7636-2342-5). 376pp. Featuring teen journalist Adam and his coeditor sidekick Jennifer, this third installment in a series builds upon themes of enterprise, journalistic ethics, and budding romance. ∩ Lexile 710L (Rev: BLO 10/15/09; SLJ 10/09; VOYA 12/09)

11964 Winkler, Henry, and Lin Oliver. *Bookmarks Are People Too!* (1–3). Illus. by Scott Garrett. Series: Here's Hank. 2014, Grosset & Dunlap $14.99 (978-044848239-2); paper $4.99 (978-04484799-7-2). 128pp. In this prequel series Hank Zipzer is in 2nd grade and having trouble finding a role in the school play; awarded a part as a bookmark, Hank goes on to surprise everybody. e Lexile 570 (Rev: BL 3/1/14; SLJ 4/14)

11965 Winkler, Henry, and Lin Oliver. *My Secret Life as a Ping-Pong Wizard* (3–5). Illus. Series: Hank Zipzer. 2005, Grosset $13.99 (978-0-448-43877-1); paper $4.99 (978-0-448-43749-1). When his fifth-grade classmates begin to get serious about sports, dedicated underachiever Hank Zipzer takes up ping-pong and discovers, much to his surprise, that sports can be fun. (Rev: BL 1/1–15/06)

11966 Winston, Sherri. *President of the Whole Fifth Grade* (3–6). 2010, Little, Brown $15.99 (978-0-316-11432-5). 288pp. Brianna is so eager to become class president (and later rich and famous) that she jeopardizes her relationship with her friends. ℮ Lexile 730L (Rev: BL 12/1/10; LMC 1–2/11; SLJ 12/1/10)

11967 Wong, Janet S. *Me and Rolly Maloo* (2–4). Illus. by Elizabeth Buttler. 2010, Charlesbridge $15.95 (978-1-58089-158-5). 128pp. Popular 4th-grader Rolly asks the nerdy Jenna, a math whiz, to provide the answers in the upcoming test; which girl is the cheater? Lexile 740L (Rev: BL 6/10; LMC 1–2/11; SLJ 11/1/10)

11968 Yoo, David. *The Detention Club* (5–8). 2011, HarperCollins $16.99 (978-0-06-178378-4). 304pp. Sixth-grader Peter's zany scheme to boost his faltering popularity lands him in detention in this humorous story about the challenges of middle school. ℮ Lexile 880L (Rev: BL 8/11; HB 9–10/11; SLJ 10/1/11)

11969 Zucker, Naomi. *Callie's Rules* (4–7). 2009, Egmont $15.99 (978-160684027-6). 240pp. Callie, 11, is a smart kid who tries to understand what's necessary to fit in in middle school but feels compelled, along with her family, to take a stand when her school decides to ban "satanic" Halloween celebrations. A sequel is *Write On, Callie Jones* (2010). (Rev: BL 9/1/09; SLJ 8/09)

Short Stories and Anthologies

11970 Ada, Alma Flor, and F. Isabel Campoy. *Yes! We Are Latinos* (3–6). Illus. by David Diaz. 2013, Charlesbridge $18.95 (978-158089383-1). 96pp. In 12 narrative poems starting with "My name is . . .," the authors explore the Latino world and individual experiences. (Rev: BL 9/1/13; LMC 3–4/14; SLJ 8/13)

11971 Asher, Sandy, and David L. Harrison, eds. *Dude! Stories and Stuff for Boys* (4–7). 2006, Dutton $17.99 (978-0-525-47684-9). Selections for boys — poems, short stories, and other works — offer diverse experiences; authors include Sneed B. Collard III, Clyde Robert Bulla, Jane Yolen, and Ron Koertge. (Rev: BL 7/06; HBG 4/07; LMC 1/07; SLJ 8/06; VOYA 12/06)

11972 Avi, sel. *Best Shorts: Favorite Short Stories for Sharing* (5–9). Ed. by Carolyn Shute. Illus. by Chris Raschka. 2006, Houghton Mifflin $16.95 (978-0-618-47603-9). The 24 short stories in this anthology provide a sampling of some of the best writing in a wide variety of genres. (Rev: SLJ 10/06)

11973 Benedictus, David. *Return to the Hundred Acre Wood* (2–4). Illus. by Mark Burgess. 2009, Dutton $19.99 (978-0-525-42160-3). 160pp. A collection of new stories about Christopher Robin and his friends. ♫ ℮ Lexile 940L (Rev: BL 11/1/09; SLJ 1/1/10)

11974 *The Big Book of Horror: 21 Tales to Make You Tremble* (5–7). Illus. by Pedro Rodriguez. 2007, Sterling $12.95 (978-1-4027-3860-9). This collection of 21 horror tales includes stories by Edgar Allan Poe, Charles Dickens, Robert Louis Stevenson, and H. P. Lovecraft. (Rev: BL 3/15/07; SLJ 7/07)

11975 Book Wish Foundation. *What You Wish For: A Book for Darfur* (5–8). 2011, Putnam $17.99 (978-0399-25454-3). 272pp. With a foreword by Mia Farrow and contributions by authors including Alexander McCall Smith, Jane Yolen, Naomi Shihab Nye, and Cynthia Voigt, this is a collection of stories and poems that focus on young people's aspirations, created to benefit the refugees of Darfur. ℮ (Rev: BL 10/1/11*; LMC 1–2/12; SLJ 11/1/11; VOYA 2/12)

11976 Bradman, Tony, ed. *Under the Weather: Stories About Climate Change* (4–7). 2010, Frances Lincoln $16.95 (978-1-84507-930-7). 215pp. This multicultural selection of short stories examines how climate change is affecting people in different parts of the world. (Rev: BL 1/1–15/11; SLJ 1/1/11) [808.83936]

11977 Bruchac, Joseph, et al. *Lay-ups and Long Shots* (4–6). 2008, Darby Creek $15.95 (978-1-58196-078-5). 112pp. A collection of nine short stories featuring a wide range of sports and appealing young people who play them. (Rev: BL 9/15/08)

11978 Canfield, Jack, ed. *Chicken Soup for the Kid's Soul: 101 Stories of Courage, Hope and Laughter* (4–7). 1998, Health Communications paper $14.95 (978-1-55874-609-1). A collection of inspiring true stories, some by well-known people, but mostly by children who sent them to the editors. (Rev: BL 9/1/98; HBG 3/99) [158.1]

11979 Canfield, Jack, ed. *Chicken Soup for the Preteen Soul: 101 Stories of Changes, Choices and Growing Up for Kids Ages 9-13* (5–7). 2000, Health Communications $24.00 (978-1-55874-801-9); paper $14.95 (978-1-55874-800-2). The usual mix of verse and prose written by and for preteens, with the aim of offering inspiration, comfort, and practical advice. (Rev: HBG 10/01; SLJ 4/01) [158.1]

11980 Carus, Marianne, ed. *Fire and Wings: Dragon Tales from East and West* (3–6). Illus. by Nilesh Mistry. 2002, Cricket $17.95 (978-0-8126-2664-3). 146pp. A collection of 15 stories, most of which have appeared in *Cricket* magazine, about all kinds of dragons, by authors including Jane Yolen, Patricia MacLachlan, Eric A. Kimmel, Vida Chu, and E. Nesbit. (Rev: HBG 3/03; SLJ 12/02)

11981 Crebbin, June, ed. *Horse Tales* (4–7). Illus. by Inga Moore. 2005, Candlewick $18.99 (978-0-7636-2657-0). Diverse short stories about horses, with color illustrations. (Rev: BL 9/1/05; SLJ 8/05)

11982 Davis, Donald. *Mama Learns to Drive and Other Stories: Stories of Love, Humor, and Wisdom* (4–7). 2005, August House $17.95 (978-0-87483-745-2). Brief, slow-paced short stories based on his mother, who grew up in the Smoky Mountains in the 1930s, are mixed with tales about the author's own youth in the 1950s. (Rev: BL 8/05; SLJ 10/05)

11983 Editors of McSweeney's. *Noisy Outlaws, Unfriendly Blobs, and Some Other Things* (4–7). 2005, McSweeney's $22.00 (978-1-932416-35-0). Kid-friendly stories by well-known authors including Nick Hornby, Neil Gaiman, and Jon Scieskza. (Rev: BL 9/1/05)

11984 Evans, Douglas. *Mouth Moths: More Classroom Tales* (2–4). Illus. by Larry Di Fiori. 2006, Front St. $15.95 (978-1-932425-23-9). 112pp. The short stories in this collection showcase eccentric students in a third grade classroom. (Rev: BL 11/1/06; SLJ 11/06)

11985 Gac-Artigas, Alejandro. *Off to Catch the Sun* (5–8). 2001, Espacio paper $11.95 (978-1-930879-28-7). Thirteen-year-old author Gac-Artigas explores serious issues through poetry, essays, and short stories. (Rev: BL 1/1–15/02)

11986 Gratz, Alan. *Fantasy Baseball* (5–8). 2011, Dial $16.99 (978-0-8037-3463-0). 304pp. Twelve-year-old Alex finds himself joining an odd baseball league populated by characters from classic children's literature and fairy tales in this multilayered fantastical story. **e** Lexile 730L (Rev: BLO 1/1–15/11; SLJ 4/11)

11987 Hart, Sue. *Tales of the Full Moon* (2–4). Illus. by Chris Harvey. 2006, Fulcrum $16.95 (978-1-55591-582-7). 93pp. Facts about African animals are interwoven into folktale-like stories told by Spinosa the spider. (Rev: BL 7/06)

11988 Hearne, Betsy. *Hauntings and Other Tales of Danger, Love, and Sometimes Loss* (5–8). 2007, Greenwillow $15.99 (978-0-06-123910-6). A collection of 15 eerie stories set in the past (mostly in Ireland), in the present (mostly America), and in the hereafter (mostly Heaven and Hell). (Rev: BL 8/07; LMC 9–10/07; SLJ 11/07)

11989 Hollander, John, ed. *O. Henry* (5–8). Illus. by Miles Hyman. 2006, Sterling $14.95 (978-1-4027-0988-3). A collection of seven O. Henry short stories, including "The Gift of the Magi," with helpful introductions before each story. (Rev: BL 4/15/06; SLJ 5/06)

11990 Holt, Kimberly Willis. *Part of Me: Stories of a Louisiana Family* (5–8). 2006, Henry Holt $16.95 (978-0-8050-6360-8). Reading is the thread that links this collection of short stories that spans four generations of a Louisiana family, from 1939 to the early 21st century. (Rev: BL 9/1/06; SLJ 9/06)

11991 Hurwitz, Johanna, ed. *I Fooled You: Ten Stories of Tricks, Jokes, and Switcheroos* (4–6). 2010, Candlewick $16.99 (978-0-7636-3789-7); paper $6.99 (978-0-7636-4877-0). 192pp. David Adler, Michelle Knudsen, and Megan McDonald are among the 10 authors represented in this diverse collection. (Rev: LMC 5–6/10; SLJ 3/10)

11992 Jocelyn, Marthe, sel. *Secrets* (5–8). 2005, Tundra paper $8.95 (978-0-88776-723-4). A collection of 12 short stories that reveal the importance of secrets. (Rev: SLJ 2/06)

11993 Kantor, Susan, ed. *One-Hundred-and-One African-American Read-Aloud Stories* (3–8). 1998, Black Dog & Leventhal $12.98 (978-1-57912-039-9). 416pp. This book includes folktales, excerpts from novels, biographies, and history books, plus a sampling of songs, poetry, and chants all about African Americans and their heritage. (Rev: SLJ 6/99)

11994 Kibuishi, Kazu, ed. *Explorer: The Mystery Boxes* (4–8). Illus. 2012, Abrams $19.95 (978-141970010-1); paper $10.95 (978-14197000-9-5). 128pp. An anthology of short graphic works all centering on the theme of a mysterious box and its contents. (Rev: BL 2/15/12; HB 5–6/12; LMC 8–8/12; SLJ 3/1/12*; VOYA 4/12)

11995 Lubar, David. *The Battle of the Red Hot Pepper Weenies and Other Warped and Creepy Tales* (4–7). 2009, Tor $15.95 (978-0-7653-2099-5). 192pp. A collection of 35 varied short stories with something for everyone — humor, horror, science fiction, suspense. (Rev: BLO 3/5/09; SLJ 5/09)

11996 Lubar, David. *Invasion of the Road Weenies and Other Warped and Creepy Tales* (4–7). 2005, Tor $16.95 (978-0-7653-1447-5). Entertaining stories about how things don't always work out how you hope or expect; suitable for reluctant readers. (Rev: BL 8/05; SLJ 9/05; VOYA 10/05)

11997 McCall Smith, Alexander. *The Perfect Hamburger and Other Delicious Stories* (3–5). Illus. by Laura Rankin. 2007, Bloomsbury $15.95 (978-1-59990-134-3). 288pp. Three entertaining stories revolving around food and children's creative efforts to solve problems were previously published in Britain. (Rev: BL 10/15/07; LMC 1/08; SLJ 10/07)

11998 McKissack, Patricia C. *Porch Lies: Tales of Slicksters, Tricksters, and Other Wily Characters* (3–5). Illus. by Andre Carrilho. 2006, Random $18.95 (978-0-375-83619-0). 160pp. Ten funny and spooky original stories full of bad characters are based on stories McKissack heard on her grandparents' porch. (Rev: BCCB 10/06; BL 5/15/06; HB 9/06; HBG 4/07; LMC 1/07; SLJ 9/06)

11999 Martin, Ann M., and David Levithan, eds. *Friends: Stories About New Friends, Old Friends, and Unexpectedly True Friends* (4–6). 2005, Scholastic $16.95 (978-0-439-72991-8). 208pp. The many faces of friendship are reflected in this collection of short stories by such well-known authors as Meg Cabot, Pam Muñoz Ryan, and Brian Selznick. (Rev: BL 11/15/05; SLJ 1/06)

12000 Mazer, Anne, ed. *America Street: A Multicultural Anthology of Stories* (5–8). 1993, Persea paper $7.95 (978-0-89255-191-0). Fourteen short stories about growing up in America's diverse society by Robert Cormier, Langston Hughes, Grace Paley, Gary Soto, and others. (Rev: BCCB 11/93; BL 9/1/93; SLJ 11/93; VOYA 12/93)

12001 Morpurgo, Michael, comp. *The Kingfisher Book of Great Boy Stories: A Treasury of Classics from Children's Literature* (4–8). 2000, Kingfisher $19.95 (978-0-7534-5320-9). An attractively illustrated collection of stories from authors including Carlo Collodi, Roald Dahl, Ted Hughes, C. S. Lewis, A. A. Milne, Donald Sobol, and Mark Twain. (Rev: HBG 10/01; SLJ 4/01)

12002 Oldfield, Jenny, comp. *The Kingfisher Book of Horse and Pony Stories* (4–7). 2005, Kingfisher $16.95 (978-0-7534-5850-1). The special relationship between horses and humans is celebrated in this collection of 12 contemporary, fantasy, and historical short stories. (Rev: SLJ 12/05)

12003 Olson, Arielle North, and Howard Schwartz. *More Bones: Scary Stories from Around the World* (4–7). Illus. by E. M. Gist. 2008, Viking $15.99 (978-0-670-06339-0). 176pp. This collection of 22 retellings of scary stories from around the world features witches and wizards, corpses and ghosts, and lots of unexpected twists. (Rev: BL 10/1/08; SLJ 9/08)

12004 O'Malley, Kevin. *Backpack Stories* (2–4). Illus. by author. 2009, Whitman $16.99 (978-0-8075-0504-5). 32pp. Ranging in tone from zany to touching, this book of four short stories is centered around backpacks. (Rev: BL 9/15/09; LMC 10/09; SLJ 9/1/09)

12005 Paulsen, Gary, ed. *Shelf Life: Stories by the Book* (4–7). 2003, Simon & Schuster $16.95 (978-0-689-84180-4). Books are the stars of these 10 stories by well-known authors that show that reading can change lives. (Rev: BL 8/03; HBG 4/04; SLJ 8/03; VOYA 8/03)

12006 Peck, Richard. *Past Perfect, Present Tense* (5–12). 2004, Dial $16.99 (978-0-8037-2998-8). This anthology includes 11 previously published stories and two new ones, with comments on each story's inspiration and tips on writing fiction. (Rev: BL 4/1/04; HB 3–4/04; SLJ 4/04; VOYA 6/04)

12007 Schulman, Janet, sel. *You Read to Me and I'll Read to You: 20th-Century Stories to Share* (K–3). 2001, Knopf $34.95 (978-0-375-81083-1). A selection of stories for beginning readers by authors including Judy Blume, Roald Dahl, Astrid Lindgren, Louis Sachar, and Wiliam Steig. (Rev: HBG 3/02; SLJ 12/01)

12008 Spiegelman, Art, and Francoise Mouly, eds. *Little Lit: Strange Stories for Strange Kids* (4–9). 2001, HarperCollins paper $19.95 (978-0-06-028626-2). This collection of offbeat, imaginative, graphic stories includes something for everyone, from humor to fantasy to horror, from Maurice Sendak to David Sedaris. (Rev: BL 12/15/01; HB 1–2/02; HBG 3/02; SLJ 3/02)

12009 *Sports Shorts* (4–7). 2005, Darby Creek $15.99 (978-1-58196-040-2). Eight writers contribute "semi-autobiographical" tales about their sporting achievements at school, many humorously revealing failings rather than triumphs. (Rev: BL 9/1/05; SLJ 11/05)

12010 Tellegen, Toon. *Far Away Across the Sea* (K–4). Trans. by Martin Cleaver. Illus. by Jessica Ahlberg. 2010, Boxer $12.95 (978-1-907152-37-5). 160pp. Bright watercolor illustrations enhance this collection of short and quirky animal stories. (Rev: BL 10/15/10; LMC 11–12/10; SLJ 11/1/10)

12011 Van Allsburg, Chris, ed. *The Chronicles of Harris Burdick: 14 Amazing Authors Tell the Tales* (3–7). Illus. by editor. 2011, Houghton Mifflin $24.99 (978-0-547-54810-4). 208pp. Well-known authors present stories inspired by the illustrations in Van Allsburg's *The Mysteries of Harris Burdick*. YALSA Best Fiction for Young Adults 2012. e Lexile 840L (Rev: BL 9/1/11; HB 9–10/11; SLJ 8/11; VOYA 10/11)

12012 Weiss, M. Jerry, and Helen S. Weiss, eds. *This Family Is Driving Me Crazy: Ten Stories About Surviving Your Family* (5–8). 2009, Putnam $17.99 (978-0-399-25040-8). 240pp. Gordon Korman, Jack Gantos, Walter Dean Myers, and Nancy Springer are among the authors represented in this collection of varied stories with themes including forgiveness, self-discovery, and compassion in the face of adversity. Lexile 830L (Rev: BL 10/1/09; LMC 11/09; SLJ 10/09; VOYA 2/10)

Sports Stories

12013 Abdul-Jabbar, Kareem, and Raymond Obstfeld. *Sasquatch in the Paint* (5–8). Series: Streetball Crew. 2013, Disney/Hyperion $16.99 (978-142317870-5). 224pp. In this multilayered coming-of-age story, 8th-grader Theo, who has suddenly grown 6 inches but is now totally uncoordinated, must juggle demands on the basketball court, from his "Aca-lympic" team, and from family and friends. e Lexile 660 (Rev: BL 9/1/13; LMC 1–2/14; SLJ 9/13)

12014 Adler, David A. *Mama Played Baseball* (K–3). Illus. by Chris O'Leary. 2003, Harcourt $16.00 (978-0-15-202196-2). Amy and her mother grow closer when Mama starts playing in the first women's pro baseball league during the early 1940s. (Rev: HBG 10/03; SLJ 4/03)

12015 Aronson, Sarah. *Beyond Lucky* (4–7). 2011, Dial $16.99 (978-0-8037-3520-0). 256pp. Soccer looms more important on Ari's radar than his forthcoming bar mitzvah, and he is convinced that the trading card he has found will bring him luck. (Rev: BL 9/1/11; SLJ 8/11)

12016 Barber, Tiki, and Paul Mantell. *Goal Line* (4–7). Illus. 2011, Simon & Schuster $15.99 (978-141699095-6). 176pp. Ronde Barber copes with a case of sibling envy after his twin brother's summer growth spurt in this football-fueled family story. e Lexile 760L (Rev: BLO 8/11)

12017 Barber, Tiki, and Ronde Barber. *End Zone* (4–7). 2012, Simon & Schuster $15.99 (978-1-41699097-0). 176pp. Ninth-grade twins Tiki and Ronde lead their football team as it contends with a variety of setbacks on their road to the state finals. Lexile 830 (Rev: BLO 8/12)

12018 Barber, Tiki, and Ronde Barber, et al. *Red Zone* (4–7). 2010, Simon & Schuster $15.99 (978-141696860-3). 176pp. The Eagles junior-high football team manages to make it to the state championship despite an outbreak of chicken pox. e Lexile 790L (Rev: BL 9/1/10)

12019 Barwin, Steven. *Icebreaker* (4–8). Series: Sports Stories. 2007, Lorimer paper $7.95 (978-1-55028-950-3). Hockey fans will love this book featuring Greg, a junior high school hockey player whose year gets complicated when his stepsister tries out for the team. (Rev: SLJ 7/07)

12020 Barwin, Steven, and Gabriel David Tick. *Slam Dunk* (5–7). Series: Sports Stories. 1999, Orca paper $5.50 (978-1-55028-598-7). An easy read about a junior high basketball team in Canada that goes coed and the problems that result. (Rev: SLJ 1/00)

12021 Bates, Cynthia. *Shooting Star* (4–6). Series: Sports Stories. 2001, Lorimer paper $5.50 (978-1-55028-726-4). Eight-grader Quyen Ha, who was a basketball star at her middle school, has some reservations about her decision to join a bantam team in this novel set in Canada that has information on Vietnamese family life. (Rev: SLJ 1/02)

12022 Bildner, Phil. *The Greatest Game Ever Played* (1–3). Illus. by Zachary Pullen. 2006, Putnam $16.99 (978-0-399-24171-0). 40pp. The legendary 1958 NFL championship game between the New York Giants and the Baltimore Colts comes to life in this appealing story about a father and son struggling to adjust to the loss of their hometown baseball team. (Rev: BL 9/1/06; SLJ 8/06)

12023 Bledsoe, Lucy Jane. *Hoop Girlz* (5–7). 2002, Holiday $16.95 (978-0-8234-1691-2). When 11-year-old River is denied a place on the girls' basketball team, she forms her own team, with her brother as the coach. (Rev: BL 9/1/02; HBG 10/03; SLJ 12/02)

12024 Bo, Ben. *The Edge* (5–8). 1999, Lerner LB $14.95 (978-0-8225-3307-8). Conflicted Declan is sent to a rehabilitation program in Canada's Glacier National Park, where he learns to snowboard and is drawn into a duel with the local champion. (Rev: BCCB 1/00; BL 10/15/99; HBG 3/00; SLJ 1/00; VOYA 4/00)

12025 Bowen, Fred. *The Final Cut* (4–7). Illus. by Ann Barrow. Series: AllStar Sport Story. 1999, Peachtree paper $4.95 (978-1-56145-192-0). A fast-paced novel about four friends and their efforts to make the junior high school basketball team. (Rev: SLJ 7/99)

12026 Bowen, Fred. *Full Court Fever* (3–6). Illus. by Ann Barrow. Series: AllStar Sport Story. 1998, Peachtree paper $4.95 (978-1-56145-160-9). 103pp. Michael and the rest of the seventh-grade basketball team are fearful about the coming match against the eighth graders. (Rev: SLJ 12/98)

12027 Bowen, Fred. *Hardcourt Comeback* (4–7). Series: Fred Bowen Sports Story. 2010, Peachtree paper $5.95 (978-15614551-6-4). 144pp. Basketball star Brett's confidence is shaken when he misses an easy shot and his uneasiness spreads to other areas. (Rev: BL 4/15/10; SLJ 5/10)

12028 Bowen, Fred. *On the Line* (4–7). Illus. by Ann Barrow. 1999, Peachtree paper $4.95 (978-1-56145-199-9). A young boy learns about self-image and open-mindedness while trying to improve his foul shots in this novel about an 8th grader and his basketball skills. (Rev: SLJ 4/00)

12029 Bowen, Fred. *Playoff Dreams* (3–5). Illus. 1997, Peachtree paper $4.95 (978-1-56145-155-5). 112pp.

When Brendan begins to feel that he is the only salvation open to his baseball team, Uncle Jack steps in with some good advice. (Rev: BL 11/1/97; SLJ 3/98)

12030 Bowen, Fred. *T.J.'s Secret Pitch* (3–5). Illus. by Jim Thorpe. Series: AllStar Sport Story. 1996, Peachtree paper $4.95 (978-1-56145-119-7). 104pp. A young Little Leaguer copies the famous pitch of the legendary Truett "Rip" Sewell and achieves fame. (Rev: SLJ 7/96)

12031 Bowen, Fred. *Throwing Heat* (3–5). 2010, Peachtree paper $5.95 (978-15614554-0-9). 136pp. Fastballer Jack, an 8th-grader, learns to control his pitching in this book for baseball fans. (Rev: BL 9/1/10; SLJ 10/1/10)

12032 Bowen, Fred. *Touchdown Trouble* (3–5). 2009, Peachtree paper $5.95 (978-1-56145-497-6). 126pp. Sam's football team must make a difficult decision when it is revealed that their winning score was the result of an illegal fifth-down play; includes an account of a similar situation in a famous 1940 Cornell-Dartmouth game. Lexile 660L (Rev: BL 9/1/09; SLJ 1/10)

12033 Bowen, Fred. *Winners Take All* (3–7). Illus. by Paul Casale. 2000, Peachtree paper $4.95 (978-1-56145-229-3). 104pp. Twelve-year-old Kyle eventually confesses to faking a catch in this story that includes discussion of Christy Mathewson, a pro pitcher in the early 1900s who was admired for his sportsmanship. (Rev: SLJ 4/01)

12034 Brooks, Bruce. *Dooby* (5–8). Series: Wolfbay Wings. 1998, HarperCollins LB $14.89 (978-0-06-027898-4); paper $4.50 (978-0-06-440708-3). Dooby sulks when he is not made captain of his Peewee hockey team, but is completely humiliated to learn he has lost out to a girl. Also recommended in this series is *Reed* (1998). (Rev: HBG 3/99; SLJ 2/99)

12035 Brooks, Bruce. *Prince* (5–8). Series: Wolfbay Wings. 1998, HarperCollins paper $4.50 (978-0-06-440600-0). Prince, the only African American boy on the Wolfbay Wings hockey team, is pressured by his middle school coach to switch to basketball. (Rev: HBG 10/98; SLJ 6/98)

12036 Brooks, Bruce. *Reed* (5–8). Series: Wolfbay Wings. 1998, HarperCollins LB $14.89 (978-0-06-028055-0). Reed, a member of the Wolfbay Wings hockey team, is considered a "puck-hog" and must learn to be more of a team player. (Rev: HBG 3/99; SLJ 2/99)

12037 Brooks, Bruce. *Shark* (5–8). Series: Wolfbay Wings. 1998, HarperCollins LB $14.89 (978-0-06-027570-9); paper $4.50 (978-0-06-440681-9). In spite of being fat, slow, and confused, Shark becomes a valuable player on the Wolfbay Wings hockey team. (Rev: HBG 10/98; SLJ 6/98)

12038 Bruchac, Joseph. *The Warriors* (5–8). 2003, Darby Creek $15.95 (978-1-58196-002-0). Jake Forrest, a Native American teenager and lacrosse whiz, leaves the reservation to attend a private school and encounters many new situations, including a different attitude toward sports. (Rev: BL 12/1/03; HBG 10/01; SLJ 10/03)

12039 Bunting, Eve. *Snowboarding on Monster Mountain* (4–6). Illus. by Karen Ritz. 2003, Cricket $15.95

(978-0-8126-2704-6). 80pp. Facing her fear of heights and her worries about new girl Izzy, 11-year-old Callie agrees to go snowboarding with her best friend Jen. (Rev: BL 1/1–15/04; HBG 4/04; SLJ 1/04)

12040 Butcher, Kristin. *Cairo Kelly and the Man* (4–8). 2002, Orca paper $6.95 (978-1-55143-211-3). When Midge discovers that his baseball team's umpire, Hal Mann, is illiterate, Midge and his friend Kelly set out to solve the problem. (Rev: BL 9/1/02; VOYA 4/03)

12041 Butler, Dori Hillestad. *Sliding into Home* (5–8). 2003, Peachtree $14.95 (978-1-56145-222-4). Joelle, 13, refuses to accept a ban on girls playing baseball when she moves to a small town in Iowa. (Rev: BL 5/1/03; HBG 10/03; SLJ 1/04)

12042 Choat, Beth. *Soccerland* (5–8). Series: The International Sports Academy. 2010, Marshall Cavendish $16.99 (978-0-7614-5724-4). 200pp. Soccer phenom Flora struggles to adjust when she goes from her tiny Maine town to a prestigious soccer camp where her talents aren't as exceptional and the culture is cutthroat. (Rev: BLO 8/10; SLJ 11/1/10)

12043 Christopher, Matt. *Baseball Turnaround* (4–6). 1977, Little, Brown paper $4.50 (978-0-316-14264-9). 160pp. After Sandy has had a brush with the law, he tries to keep this part of his past a secret from his teammates. (Rev: BL 6/1–15/97; SLJ 8/97)

12044 Christopher, Matt. *The Comeback Challenge* (4–6). Illus. 1996, Little, Brown paper $4.50 (978-0-316-14152-9). 160pp. Twelve-year-old Mark has problems with Vince, the captain of his soccer team. (Rev: BL 1/1–15/96; SLJ 1/96)

12045 Christopher, Matt. *Dirt Bike Racer* (3–5). Illus. by Barry Bomzer. 1986, Little, Brown paper $4.50 (978-0-316-14053-9). Ron finds a bike at the bottom of a lake and begins dirt bike racing. Another sports story from the same author is: *Dirt Bike Runaway* (1989).

12046 Christopher, Matt. *The Dog That Pitched a No-Hitter* (2–4). Illus. by Daniel Vasconcellos. 1993, Little, Brown paper $3.95 (978-0-316-14103-1). Mike's dog Harry has powers of ESP and helps Mike with his pitching game. (Rev: BL 5/15/88; SLJ 8/88)

12047 Christopher, Matt. *The Hit-Away Kid* (2–5). Illus. 1988, Little, Brown paper $4.50 (978-0-316-14007-2). 55pp. Barry McGee, left fielder for the Peach Street Mudders, learns a lesson in sportsmanship and telling the truth. Two other baseball stories are: *Supercharged Infield* (1985); *The Spy on Third Base* (1988). (Rev: BCCB 5/88; BL 4/1/88; SLJ 5/88)

12048 Christopher, Matt. *Mountain Bike Mania* (5–7). 1998, Little, Brown paper $4.50 (978-0-316-14292-2). Will is at loose ends with no after-school activities until he becomes involved in a mountain bike club. (Rev: BL 2/1/99; HBG 10/99; SLJ 3/99)

12049 Christopher, Matt. *Penalty Shot* (3–5). Illus. 1997, Little, Brown paper $3.95 (978-0-316-14190-1). Kevin is thrown off the hockey team for bad grades but is determined to get back on. (Rev: BL 1/1–15/97; SLJ 2/97)

12050 Christopher, Matt. *Prime-Time Pitcher* (4–7). 1998, Little, Brown paper $4.50 (978-0-316-14213-7). Koby Caplin becomes arrogant about his winning streak on the baseball team and soon loses games because of his lack of teamwork. (Rev: HBG 3/99; SLJ 12/98)

12051 Christopher, Matt. *Red-Hot Hightops* (4–6). Illus. 1992, Little, Brown paper $4.50 (978-0-316-14089-8). 128pp. Shyness prevents Kelly from showing off her basketball skills or speaking to a boy she likes until she finds a pair of red sneakers in her locker. (Rev: BL 1/15/88)

12052 Christopher, Matt. *Return of the Home Run Kid* (4–7). Illus. by Paul Casale. 1994, Little, Brown paper $4.50 (978-0-316-14273-1). In this sequel to *The Kid Who Only Hit Homers* (1972), Sylvester learns to be more aggressive on the field but gets criticism from his friends. (Rev: BL 4/15/92; SLJ 5/92)

12053 Christopher, Matt. *Snowboard Maverick* (4–7). 1997, Little, Brown paper $4.50 (978-0-316-14203-8). Dennis overcomes his fears and begins snowboarding. (Rev: BL 4/1/98; HBG 3/98; SLJ 3/98)

12054 Christopher, Matt. *Soccer Halfback* (4–6). Illus. by Larry Johnson. 1985, Little, Brown paper $4.50 (978-0-316-13981-6). Everyone wants Jabber to play football, but his favorite sport is soccer.

12055 Clare, Cassandra. *Toby Wheeler: Eighth-Grade Bench Warmer* (5–8). 2007, Delacorte $14.99 (978-0-385-73390-8). Toby, an 8th-grader, joins the basketball team to be closer to his best friend but find himself stuck on the bench, the 12th man. (Rev: BL 9/1/07; SLJ 9/07)

12056 Clippinger, Carol. *Open Court* (5–8). 2007, Knopf $15.99 (978-0-375-84049-4). Thirteen-year-old Holloway ("Hall") is only 13 but must deal with the pressures of competitive tennis as well as everyday stresses of being a teenager. (Rev: SLJ 7/07)

12057 Corbett, Sue. *Free Baseball* (4–7). 2006, Dutton $15.99 (978-0-525-47120-2). An endearing 11-year-old called Felix, who loves baseball and is annoyed that his mother won't tell him more about his Cuban outfielder father, is thrilled when he gets the chance to be batboy for a minor league Florida team. (Rev: BCCB 2/06; SLJ 2/06; VOYA 4/06)

12058 Coy, John. *Around the World* (1–4). Illus. by Antonio Reonegro and Tom Lynch. 2005, Lee & Low $17.95 (978-1-58430-244-5). A fast-paced game of basketball moves from one location to another around the world; the art adds to the energy. (Rev: SLJ 1/06)

12059 Coy, John. *Eyes on the Goal* (4–6). Series: 4 for 4. 2010, Feiwel & Friends $16.99 (978-0-312-37330-6). 176pp. The four friends first seen in *Top of the Order* (2009) are now headed for soccer camp where they finally manage to get on the same team. **e** Lexile 530L (Rev: BLO 2/1/10; LMC 5–6/10; SLJ 4/10)

12060 Coy, John. *Strong to the Hoop* (2–5). Illus. 1999, Lee & Low $16.95 (978-1-880000-80-9). 32pp. In this basketball story, 10-year-old James is drafted to play with the older kids when one of their teammates hurts his ankle. (Rev: BL 12/15/99; HBG 10/00; SLJ 10/99)

12061 Coy, John. *Top of the Order* (4–6). 2009, Feiwel & Friends $16.99 (978-0-312-37329-0). 96pp. Four fifth-grade boys, plus one girl, each have problems but share a love of baseball in this action-packed novel. (Rev: BCCB 4/09; BL 3/1/09; SLJ 3/09)

12062 Drumtra, Stacy. *Face-Off* (4–8). 1992, Avon paper $3.50 (978-0-380-76863-9). T.J. and his twin Brad become rivals for friends and for status on the hockey team. (Rev: BL 4/1/93; SLJ 1/05; VOYA 8/93)

12063 Durant, Alan, sel. *Sports Stories* (5–9). Illus. by David Kearney. Series: Story Library. 2000, Kingfisher $14.95 (978-0-7534-5322-3). A collection of 21 previously published short stories by well-known authors dealing with a variety of sports. (Rev: HBG 10/01; SLJ 11/00)

12064 Fitzgerald, Dawn. *Getting in the Game* (4–7). 2005, Roaring Brook $15.95 (978-1-59643-044-0). In first-person narrative, Joanna Giordano describes her difficult experiences as the only girl on a 7th-grade ice hockey team that doesn't want her, plus her problems with peers, parents, and ailing grandfather. (Rev: BCCB 9/05; BL 3/1/05; SLJ 7/05; VOYA 6/05)

12065 Fitzgerald, Dawn. *Soccer Chick Rules* (5–8). 2006, Roaring Brook $16.95 (978-1-59643-137-9). When her school's sports program is threatened, Tess Munro, a talented 13-year-old soccer player, joins the campaign to win approval for the school levy. (Rev: BL 9/1/06; SLJ 10/06)

12066 Forsyth, C. A. *Power Hitter* (4–6). Series: Sports Stories. 2001, Lorimer paper $5.50 (978-1-55028-732-5). 86pp. A 13-year-old boy goes to visit relatives in Winnipeg for a summer full of baseball, unaware that his parents are divorcing and his mother is ill. (Rev: SLJ 1/02)

12067 Freitas, Donna. *Gold Medal Summer* (5–8). 2012, Scholastic $16.99 (978-054532788-6). 240pp. Joey, 14, is torn between her gymnastic ambitions and the desire to live a normal life. e Lexile 790L (Rev: BL 6/12; LMC 8–9/12; SLJ 6/12)

12068 Garza, Xavier. *Lucha Libre: The Man in the Silver Mask: A Bilingual Cuento* (2–5). Trans. by Luis Humberto Crosthwaite. Illus. by author. 2005, Cinco Puntos $17.95 (978-0-938317-92-0). Young Carlitos goes to a professional wrestling match ("lucha libre") in Mexico City and is thrilled by the sight of his favorite masked wrestler; can it be someone Carlitos knows? (Rev: SLJ 10/05)

12069 Garza, Xavier. *Maximilian and the Mystery of the Guardian Angel* (3–6). Illus. by author. 2011, Cinco Puntos paper $12.95 (978-19336939-8-9). 160pp. Aspiring Mexican wrestler Maximilian, 11, finally meets his hero, El Àngel, and comes face-to-face with the scary villains who want to end his winning streak; in both English and Spanish. (Rev: BLO 1/25/12; SLJ 1/12)

12070 Gassman, Julie. *You Can't Spike Your Serves* (2–4). Illus. by Jorge Santillan. Series: Victory School Superstars. 2011, Stone Arch LB $25.32 (978-1-4342-2231-2). 56pp. Super-talented athlete Alicia hatches a plan to help out a friend at a disadvantaged school in this sports story. (Rev: BL 9/1/11; SLJ 6/11)

12071 Gratz, Alan. *The Brooklyn Nine* (5–8). 2009, Dial $16.99 (978-0-8037-3224-7). 320pp. This saga, told in nine stories or "innings," follows nine generations of a German immigrant family with links to both baseball and Brooklyn. (Rev: BCCB 4/09; BL 2/1/09; HB 3/09; LMC 5/09; SLJ 3/09)

12072 Green, Tim. *Football Champ* (4–8). 2009, HarperCollins $16.99 (978-0-06-162689-0). 288pp. Twelve-year-old Troy, who has an amazing ability to predict football plays, is accused of cheating in this exciting sequel to *Football Genius* (2007). (Rev: BL 9/15/09; SLJ 7/09)

12073 Green, Tim. *Football Genius* (5–8). 2007, HarperCollins $16.99 (978-0-06-112270-5). Troy's football skills are ignored until a linebacker for the Atlanta Falcons sees his ability to predict upcoming plays and uses him as the team's secret weapon. (Rev: BL 5/1/07; SLJ 7/07)

12074 Green, Tim. *Force Out* (4–6). 2013, HarperCollins $16.99 (978-0-06-208959-5). 288pp. The friendship between 6th-graders Joey and Zach is jeopardized as they both aspire to be selected for a Little League all-star team. Lexile 760 (Rev: BL 3/15/13; SLJ 3/13)

12075 Green, Tim. *Unstoppable* (5–8). 2012, HarperCollins $16.99 (978-0-06-208956-4). 342pp. Harrison, a 13-year-old who has had a tough life in a series of foster homes, finally gets lucky and is placed with a loving couple and even a football coach! But his stardom on the field comes to a crashing halt. ⌒ e Lexile 730L (Rev: BL 9/1/12; SLJ 8/1/12; VOYA 8/12)

12076 Gunderson, Jessica. *Don't Break the Balance Beam!* (2–4). Illus. by Jorge Santillan. Series: Sports Illustrated Kids: Victory School Superstars. 2011, Capstone LB $25.32 (978-1-4342-2057-8); paper $5.95 (978-1-4342-2807-9). 56pp. At the Victory School for Super Athletes, Kenzie — who excels on the balance beam — triumphs over athletic humiliation; an early chapter book. Lexile 440L (Rev: BL 1/1–15/11; LMC 3–4/11; SLJ 1/1/11)

12077 Gutman, Dan. *Coach Hyatt Is a Riot!* (3–5). Illus. by Jim Paillot. Series: My Weird School Daze. 2009, HarperCollins LB $15.89 (978-0-06-155408-7); paper $3.99 (978-0-06-155406-3). 106pp. This humorous beginning chapter book about A.J. and his less-than-ideal Pee Wee Football team will appeal to reluctant readers. (Rev: SLJ 6/09)

12078 Gutman, Dan. *Roberto and Me* (4–6). Series: Baseball Card Adventure. 2010, HarperCollins $15.99 (978-006123484-2); LB $16.89 (978-006123485-9). 192pp. Young Stosh travels back in time in an attempt to save baseball star Roberto Clemente's life in this adventure and takes a surprising twist halfway through. ⌒ e Lexile 580L (Rev: BL 1/1/10; VOYA 8/10)

12079 Gutman, Dan. *Ted and Me* (5–8). 2012, HarperCollins $15.99 (978-006123487-3). 208pp. Charged with going back in time to warn FDR of the impending attack of Pearl Harbor, Stosh meets Ted Williams and gets some solid baseball advice. ⌒ ℮ Lexile 630L (Rev: BLO 4/1/12)

12080 Hale, Daniel J., and Matthew LaBrot. *Red Card* (4–7). Series: Zeke Armstrong Mystery. 2002, Top paper $8.95 (978-1-929976-15-7). Someone is trying to kill the soccer coach, and young Zeke sets out to discover who and why. (Rev: SLJ 12/02; VOYA 12/02)

12081 Hall, Donald. *When Willard Met Babe Ruth* (4–6). Illus. by Barry Moser. 1996, Harcourt $16.00 (978-0-15-200273-2). 48pp. A young New Hampshire farm boy and his father have a chance meeting with Babe Ruth. (Rev: BCCB 6/96; BL 3/15/96*; HB 9/96; SLJ 5/96)

12082 Harkrader, L. D. *Airball: My Life in Briefs* (4–7). 2005, Roaring Brook $15.95 (978-1-59643-060-0). Kirby's middle school basketball team begins to improve when their coach — whom Kirby secretly believes is his father — insists the boys practice in their underwear. (Rev: BL 9/1/05; SLJ 11/05; VOYA 10/05)

12083 Haven, Paul. *Two Hot Dogs with Everything* (4–7). Illus. by Tim Jessell. 2006, Random House LB $17.99 (978-0-375-93350-9). Danny, 11, follows many superstitious rituals each time the Sluggers play, but his efforts seem to have no effect until he chews some 108-year-old gum that belonged to the team's founder. (Rev: BL 4/1/06)

12084 Hicks, Betty. *Doubles Troubles* (2–4). Illus. by Simon Gane. Series: Gym Shorts. 2010, Roaring Brook $15.99 (978-159643489-9). 64pp. Henry learns the importance of being kind and gracious in this story of competition on the tennis court and cooperation on a history project. ℮ Lexile 540L (Rev: BL 3/15/10)

12085 Hicks, Betty. *Scaredy-Cat Catcher* (2–4). Illus. by Adam McCauley. Series: Gym Shorts. 2009, Roaring Brook $16.95 (978-1-59643-246-8). 64pp. After breaking his arm while playing catcher, and developing an unfortunate retreating reflex, Rocky gets help from his friends and his dog and makes a comeback. (Rev: SLJ 4/09)

12086 Higgins, M. G. *Power Hitter* (4–6). Series: Travel Team. 2012, Lerner LB $27.93 (978-076138324-6); paper $7.95 (978-076138539-4). 128pp. Sammy Perez's prized slugging ability seems to evaporate when the team switches to wooden bats; for reluctant readers. (Rev: BL 4/15/12; SLJ 4/12)

12087 Hirschfeld, Robert. *Goalkeeper in Charge* (5–7). Series: Christopher Sports. 2002, Little, Brown paper $4.50 (978-0-316-07548-0). Seventh-grader Tina works to overcome her shyness on and off the soccer field. (Rev: BL 9/1/02; HBG 3/03)

12088 Holohan, Maureen. *Catch Shorty by Rosie* (4–8). Series: The Broadway Ballplayers. 1999, Broadway Ballplayers paper $6.95 (978-0-9659091-6-7). Sixth-grader Rosie Jones devotes her time to organizing an all-girls football league while coping with a series of minor personal problems at home and school. (Rev: SLJ 3/00)

12089 Hurwitz, Johanna. *Baseball Fever* (3–6). Illus. by Ray Cruz. 1981, Morrow paper $3.95 (978-0-688-

10495-5). 128pp. Mr. Feldman loathes baseball, but his son Ezra loves it.

12090 Jennings, Patrick. *Out Standing in My Field* (3–5). 2005, Scholastic $16.95 (978-0-439-46581-6). 176pp. Ty, a not-so-talented baseball player, has a revealing conversation with his sister while Ty's team loses yet another game. (Rev: BL 3/15/05; SLJ 4/05)

12091 Johnson, Scott. *Safe at Second* (5–8). 2001, Penguin paper $7.99 (978-0-698-11877-5). The story of the friendship between Paulie and Todd, their love of baseball, and what happens after Todd is hit during a game and loses an eye. (Rev: BL 6/1–15/99; SLJ 7/99; VOYA 8/99)

12092 Kew, Trevor. *Sidelined* (5–8). Series: Sports Stories. 2011, Orca $9.95 (978-155277550-9); LB $16.95 (978-155277551-6). 128pp. Marjan copes with competitive jealousy when her talented friend Vicky lands a spot on an elite soccer team in this story set in Vancouver. (Rev: BLO 8/11)

12093 King, Donna. *Double Twist* (5–8). 2007, Kingfisher paper $5.95 (978-0-7534-6023-8). When her ice-dancing partner injures his knee, 12-year-old Laura Lee scrambles to replace him just one month before the Junior Grand Prix. (Rev: BL 1/1–15/07)

12094 King, Donna. *Game, Set, and Match* (4–6). 2007, Kingfisher paper $5.95 (978-0-7534-6022-1). Carrie's summer at a Florida tennis camp is a time for her to prove her independence and her talent at the sport. (Rev: SLJ 5/07)

12095 Knudson, Mike. *Raymond and Graham: Bases Loaded* (3–5). Illus. by Stacy Curtis. Series: Raymond and Graham. 2010, Viking $14.99 (978-0-670-01205-3). 155pp. Baseball pals Raymond and Graham contend with obstacles on the path to their team winning the Little League Championship in this story presented in slightly larger-than-usual font; a sequel to *Raymond and Graham Rule the School* (2008). (Rev: SLJ 2/1/10)

12096 Levy, Elizabeth. *Tackling Dad* (5–8). 2005, HarperCollins LB $16.89 (978-0-06-000050-9). Cassie, 13, has won a place on the football team but her father won't sign the consent form. (Rev: BL 9/1/05; SLJ 8/05)

12097 Lupica, Mike. *The Big Field* (5–8). 2008, Philomel $17.99 (978-0-399-24625-8). Fourteen-year-old Hutch and his team are going to the Florida State finals, but Hutch's happiness is marred by troubled relationships with his father and a new, difficult teammate. (Rev: BL 12/1/07; SLJ 2/08)

12098 Lupica, Mike. *Million-Dollar Throw* (5–8). 2009, Philomel $17.99 (978-0-399-24626-5). 244pp. Thirteen-year-old Nate Brodie, star quarterback of the school football team, gets a chance to solve his family's money problems when he is selected for the million-dollar football toss during halftime at a pro football game. ⌒ ℮ Lexile 960L (Rev: BL 9/1/09; SLJ 12/09; VOYA 12/09)

12099 Lupica, Mike. *Play Makers* (4–7). Series: Game Changers. 2013, Scholastic $16.99 (978-054538183-3). 224pp. After a successful football season, 6th-grader Ben McBain and his friends find themselves facing new challenges on the basketball court. Lexile 920 (Rev: BLO 11/15/13; SLJ 6/13)

12100 Lupica, Mike. *Shoot-Out* (4–6). Series: Comeback Kids. 2010, Philomel $10.99 (978-039924718-7). 165pp. Accustomed to winning, Jack has a difficult time when he moves to a new school and his soccer team loses its first match. ⌒ Lexile 920L (Rev: BL 9/1/10; SLJ 9/10)

12101 Lupica, Mike. *Summer Ball* (5–8). 2007, Philomel $17.99 (978-0-399-24487-2). Even though his coach offers little encouragement, Danny Walker's determination helps him lead his summer basketball team to victory. (Rev: BL 4/15/07; SLJ 6/07)

12102 Lupica, Mike. *Two-Minute Drill* (4–6). Series: Comeback Kids. 2007, Philomel $9.99 (978-0-399-24715-6). 180pp. Scott Parry, the worst player on the 6th-grade football team finds an unusual way to help his team. (Rev: SLJ 10/07)

12103 Lupica, Mike. *The Underdogs* (5–8). 2011, Philomel $17.99 (978-039925001-9). 256pp. When his economically depressed town cuts funding for his football program, 12-year-old Will Tyler swings into action and revives the team. (Rev: BL 9/1/11)

12104 McEwan, Jamie. *Rufus the Scrub Does Not Wear a Tutu* (2–3). Illus. by John Margeson. 2007, Darby Creek $14.95 (978-1-58196-060-0). 64pp. Rufus takes up ballet and must deal with teasing — until his newfound coordination helps him on the football field. A sequel to *Willy the Scrub* and *Whitewater Scrubs*. (Rev: SLJ 6/07)

12105 Mack, W. C. *Athlete vs. Mathlete* (5–7). 2013, Bloomsbury $16.99 (978-159990915-8); paper $6.99 (978-15999085-8-8). 208pp. Seventh-grade twins Owen, a basketball player, and Russell, an academic whiz, find themselves pitted against each other when Russ is asked to try out for the team and shows unexpected abilities. **e** (Rev: BL 3/15/13; LMC 5–6/13; VOYA 12/12)

12106 Mackel, Kathy. *MadCat* (5–8). 2005, HarperCollins LB $16.89 (978-0-06-054870-4). Madelyn Catherine (aka MadCat), catcher on her local girls' fast-pitch softball team, is at the center of this story about sports, team play, and family involvement. (Rev: BL 2/15/05; SLJ 3/05)

12107 McKissack, Patricia C. *The Home-Run King* (3–6). Illus. by Gordon C. James. Series: Scraps of Time. 2008, Viking $14.99 (978-0-670-01085-1). The Webster cousins learn about about baseball's segregated past when Grandma Gee tells them a story set in 1937 about the Nashville "chitlin' circuit," which provided homes for traveling Negro League players. (Rev: BL 2/1/09; HB 1/09)

12108 Maddox, Jake. *Diving Off the Edge* (4–7). Illus. by Sean Tiffany. Series: Jake Maddox Sports Fiction. 2009, Stone Arch $17.99 (978-1-4342-1205-4). 72pp. A fast-paced story about swimming, peer pressure, and friendship. (Rev: BLO 3/19/09)

12109 Maddox, Jake. *Full Court Dreams* (4–7). Illus. by Tuesday Mourning. Series: Impact. 2008, Stone Arch LB $16.95 (978-1-4342-0469-1). Megan is determined to make the basketball team this year and gives the tryouts her all; for reluctant readers. (Rev: BL 4/1/08)

12110 Maddox, Jake. *Paintball Blast* (4–6). Illus. by Sean Tiffany. Series: Impact Books — A Jake Maddox Sports Story. 2007, Stone Arch LB $22.60 (978-1-59889-322-9). 65pp. Paintball experts Max and Tyler are suspicious about the constant wins registered by a new player named Ryan. Could he be cheating? Reluctant readers enjoy this series, which also includes *Speedway Switch* (2007). (Rev: SLJ 11/07)

12111 Maddox, Jake, and Eric Stevens. *Karate Countdown* (4–7). Illus. by Sean Tiffany. Series: Jake Maddox Sports Fiction. 2009, Stone Arch $17.99 (978-1-4342-1200-9). 72pp. Karate helps Kenny to defuse his anger over his mother's death. (Rev: BLO 3/19/09)

12112 Maddox, Jake, and Lisa Trumbauer. *Kart Crash* (4–7). Illus. by Sean Tiffany. Series: Jake Maddox Sports Story. 2008, Stone Arch $16.95 (978-143420777-7). 72pp. Austin learns the value of teamwork and determination in this fast-paced tale set on the go-kart track. Lexile 470L (Rev: BL 11/15/08)

12113 Mantell, Paul. *Stealing Home* (3–6). Series: Matt Christopher. 2004, Little, Brown paper $4.50 (978-0-316-60742-1). Seventh grader Joey Gallagher enjoys being a baseball star and is not pleased at first to discover the exchange student visiting from Nicaragua, Jesus, also has real talent. (Rev: SLJ 11/04)

12114 Mazer, Abby. *The Amazing Days of Abby Hayes* (3–6). 2000, Scholastic paper $4.99 (978-0-439-14977-8). 144pp. Told in prose, journal entries, and drawings, this is the story of Abby Hayes, who tries without much success to shine at soccer. (Rev: BL 8/00)

12115 Messner, Kate. *Sugar and Ice* (5–7). 2010, Walker $16.99 (978-0-8027-2081-8). 288pp. When Russian skating coach Andrei Grosheva offers 12-year-old farm girl Claire a scholarship to train with the elite in Lake Placid, she encounters a world of mean girls on ice, where competition is everything. (Rev: BL 9/1/10; SLJ 12/1/10)

12116 Mills, Claudia. *Basketball Disasters* (3–6). Illus. by Guy Francis. 2012, Knopf $12.99 (978-037586875-7); LB $15.99 (978-037596875-4). 176pp. Persuaded to join the basketball team by his best friend, Mason has a hard time coping with a serious losing streak and his dad's misguided coaching. **e** (Rev: BL 2/1/12; LMC 3–4/12)

12117 Mills, Claudia. *Gus and Grandpa at Basketball* (2–4). Illus. by Catherine Stock. 2001, Farrar $14.00 (978-0-374-32818-4). In this seventh book in the series, Grandpa helps Gus overcome his anxiety about playing basketball in front of a crowd. (Rev: BL 11/15/01; HB 11/01; HBG 3/02; SLJ 9/01)

12118 Myers, Walter Dean. *Me, Mop, and the Moondance Kid* (5–7). 1988, Dell paper $4.99 (978-0-440-40396-8). The efforts of T.J. and Moondance to get their friend Mop adopted. (Rev: BCCB 12/88; BL 2/1/89; SLJ 1/88)

12119 Nicholson, Lorna Schultz. *Roughing* (5–8). 2005, Lorimer paper $5.50 (978-1-55028-858-2). This story set in a hockey camp in Calgary, Alberta, features Josh, a boy with type 1 diabetes; Peter, a native Canadian; and Peter, a bully who plans to teach Peter a lesson. (Rev: BL 5/15/05; SLJ 9/05)

12120 Nicholson, Lorna Schultz. *Too Many Men* (4–8). Series: Sports Stories. 2007, Lorimer paper $7.95 (978-1-55028-948-0). Hockey player Sam juggles his busy home life with hockey practice as starting goalie. (Rev: SLJ 7/07)

12121 Nitz, Kristin Wolden. *Defending Irene* (5–7). 2004, Peachtree $14.95 (978-1-56145-309-2). When her family moves to Italy for a year, 13-year-old Irene is determined to continue playing soccer, even if it's on the boys' team. (Rev: SLJ 9/04)

12122 Northrop, Michael. *Plunked* (5–8). 2012, Scholastic $16.99 (978-054529714-1). 256pp. Formerly bold and brassy 6th-grader Jack struggles to recover his pluck after being struck in the head by a baseball. **e** Lexile 640L (Rev: BL 3/1/12; LMC 8–9/12; SLJ 4/12; VOYA 6/12)

12123 Park, Linda Sue. *Keeping Score* (4–7). 2008, Clarion $16.00 (978-0-618-92799-9). In 1951 fireman Jim teaches Brooklyn Dodgers fan Maggie, 9, how to score a game and the two remain friends even when Jim is sent to Korea; when Jim is horribly injured, Maggie is determined to help. (Rev: BL 2/1/08; SLJ 3/08)

12124 Patneaude, David. *Haunting at Home Plate* (4–7). 2000, Whitman LB $15.99 (978-0-8075-3181-5). Twelve-year-old Nelson is amazed when mysterious instructions are left on the playing field in this baseball novel about a losing team that suddenly seems to be getting help from a ghost. (Rev: BCCB 11/00; BL 9/1/00; HBG 3/01; SLJ 9/00)

12125 Peers, Judi. *Shark Attack* (5–7). Series: Sports Stories. 1999, Orca paper $6.50 (978-1-55028-620-5). An easily read story set in Canada, in which a young baseball player wants to impress his father but doesn't think he can ever reach his older brother's record. (Rev: SLJ 1/00)

12126 Preller, James. *Six Innings* (5–8). 2008, Feiwel & Friends $16.95 (978-0-312-36763-3). Six innings of a Little League game reveal much about the game's young players and about the young announcer, a player sidelined by cancer. ALA Notable Children's Book 2009. (Rev: BL 4/1/08; SLJ 4/08)

12127 Priebe, Val. *Running Rivals* (4–8). Illus. by Tuesday Mourning. Series: Impact Books: A Jake Maddox Sports Story. 2008, Stone Arch LB $17.95 (978-1-4342-0874-3); paper $5.99 (978-1-4342-0778-4). 72pp. Amy, an African American girl who lives for her running, suffers an injury and faces two months without practice. (Rev: SLJ 3/09)

12128 Richardson, Charisse K. *The Real Lucky Charm* (3–5). 2005, Dial $16.99 (978-0-8037-3105-9); paper $4.99 (978-0-14-240431-7). 96pp. Ten-year-old Mia attributes her basketball skill to the new charm for her bracelet, and is happy to play on the team with her twin brother Marcus; but when she loses the charm her confidence evaporates. (Rev: BL 9/1/05; SLJ 10/05)

12129 Ripken, Cal, Jr. *Hothead* (5–8). 2011, Hyperion/Disney $16.99 (978-1-4231-4000-9). 144pp. Gifted — and frustrated by family woes — 7th-grade shortstop Connor finally learns to control his temper when it threatens to derail his sports career. ∩ **e** Lexile 810L (Rev: BL 2/15/11; SLJ 4/11)

12130 Ripken, Cal, Jr., and Kevin Cowherd. *Super-Sized Slugger* (4–7). Series: Cal Ripken, Jr.'s All-Stars. 2012, Hyperion/Disney $16.99 (978-1-4231-4001-6). 182pp. Eighth-grader Cody must deal with teasing about his weight and now a series of mysterious thefts; can his baseball skills compensate? ∩ **e** Lexile 810L (Rev: SLJ 8/1/12)

12131 Ritter, John H. *The Boy Who Saved Baseball* (5–7). 2003, Putnam $17.99 (978-0-399-23622-8). A small town depends on its baseball team to rescue it from big developers. (Rev: BL 5/1/03*; HBG 4/04; SLJ 6/03; VOYA 8/03)

12132 Ritter, John H. *Choosing Up Sides* (5–9). 1998, Putnam $18.99 (978-0-399-23185-8). Jake is a great southpaw in baseball, but his preacher father forbids the boy to use his left hand for pitching as it is the instrument of Satan. (Rev: BCCB 6/98; BL 5/1/98; HBG 10/98; SLJ 6/98; VOYA 12/98)

12133 Ritter, John H. *The Desperado Who Stole Baseball* (5–8). 2009, Philomel $17.99 (978-0-399-24664-7). 272pp. In the 1880s, 12-year-old Jack Dillon — self-proclaimed baseball whiz — and outlaw Billy the Kid play in a key game in which a California mining town competes against the Chicago White Stockings; a rollicking prequel to *The Boy Who Saved Baseball* (2003). ∩ Lexile 750L (Rev: BL 2/15/09; SLJ 4/1/09)

12134 Ritter, John H. *Fenway Fever!* (5–8). 2012, Philomel $16.99 (978-0-399-24665-4). 230pp. Twelve-year-old "Stats" Pagano's devotion to baseball and the Red Sox is at the center of this story about a family's declining hot dog business and a pitcher's theory about the curse on the Fenway Park team. **e** (Rev: BLO 4/15/12; LMC 11–12/12; SLJ 9/12)

12135 Roberts, Ken. *Thumb on a Diamond* (3–5). Illus. by Leanne Franson. 2006, Groundwood $15.95 (978-0-88899-629-9); paper $6.95 (978-0-88899-705-0). 128pp. The children of a remote fishing village on the coast of British Columbia form a baseball team and enter a regional tournament as part of their scheme to visit a big city. (Rev: BL 6/1–15/06; SLJ 8/06)

12136 Roberts, Kristi. *My Thirteenth Season* (5–8). 2005, Henry Holt $15.95 (978-0-8050-7495-6). When Fran, whose mother has recently died, tries to play baseball for the boys' team in her new town, she is in for a world of trouble. (Rev: BL 3/15/05*; SLJ 3/05)

12137 Rodriguez, Alex. *Out of the Ballpark* (2–4). Illus. by Frank Morrison. 2007, HarperCollins $16.99 (978-0-06-115194-1). The Yankees player draws on his childhood experiences in this story of a determined young athlete who succeeds through hard work. (Rev: BL 3/15/07)

12138 Ross, Jeff. *The Drop* (4–7). Series: Orca Sports. 2011, Orca paper $9.95 (978-1-55469-392-4). 168pp. For reluctant readers, this is an exciting snowboarding adventure story set in the mountains of British Columbia. (Rev: BL 7/11; SLJ 8/11)

12139 Rud, Jeff. *In the Paint* (5–8). 2005, Orca paper $7.95 (978-1-55143-337-0). Matt is glad to make the basketball team but soon finds there are pressures he would prefer to avoid. (Rev: BL 7/05)

12140 Scaletta, Kurtis. *Jinxed!* (2–4). Illus. by Eric Wight. Series: Topps League. 2012, Abrams $15.95 (978-141970286-0); paper $5.95 (978-14197026-1-7). 112pp. Hired as a bat boy for the summer, Chad enjoys the hard work and seeks to help a shortstop who think he is jinxed. **e** (Rev: BLO 5/15/12; LMC 11–12/12)

12141 Scaletta, Kurtis. *Mudville* (4–8). 2009, Knopf $15.99 (978-0-375-85579-5). 272pp. It has been raining in Moundville (aka Mudville) for 22 years, but with the arrival of a foster child named Sturgis the sun suddenly reappears and allows baseball and the interrupted game against Sinister Bend to resume. (Rev: BL 3/1/09; SLJ 3/09)

12142 Scieszka, Jon, ed. *The Sports Pages* (5–8). Illus. by Dan Santat. Series: Guys Read. 2012, HarperCollins $16.99 (978-0-06-196378-0). 272pp. Scieszka, Dan Gutman, Jacqueline Woodson, Chris Crutcher, Joseph Bruchac, and Gordon Korman are among the contributors to this collection of 10 short stories about a variety of sports. ⌒ **e** (Rev: BL 9/1/12; SLJ 11/12; VOYA 10/12)

12143 Scudamore, Beverly. *Misconduct* (4–6). Series: Sports Stories. 2005, Lorimer paper $5.50 (978-1-55028-854-4). Matthew is influenced by a new kid on his hockey team and must figure out if the friendship is worth his integrity. (Rev: SLJ 8/05)

12144 Sherman, M. Zachary. *Impulse* (5–8). Illus. by Caio Majado. Series: Tony Hawk's 900 Revolution. 2011, Capstone LB $25.32 (978-1-4342-3203-8); paper $6.95 (978-1-4342-3452-0). 128pp. Fourteen-year-old foster child Dylan, aka Slider, contends with the mysterious disappearance of his admired older brother in this skateboard-fueled thriller with magical elements; this series appeals to reluctant readers. Lexile 660L (Rev: BLO 8/11; LMC 1–2/12; SLJ 12/1/11; VOYA 10/11)

12145 Smith, Charles R. *Winning Words: Sports Stories and Photographs* (5–8). Illus. by author. 2008, Candlewick $17.99 (978-076361445-4). 80pp. This short story collection from sportswriter Smith interprets some of sport's best themes, including confidence, determination, and motivation, and includes photographs that add interest. Lexile 620L (Rev: BL 9/1/08; SLJ 8/08)

12146 Spring, Debbie. *Breathing Soccer* (5–8). 2008, Thistledown $10.95 (978-189723542-3). 140pp. Asthmatic soccer buff Lisa, 12, gains inspiration from stories of athletes overcoming physical struggles in this believable, happy-ending tale. (Rev: BLO 8/08; SLJ 1/1/09)

12147 Stoudemire, Amar'e. *Home Court* (4–7). Illus. by Tim Jessell. Series: STAT "Standing Tall and Talented". 2012, Scholastic $17.99 (978-054543169-9); paper $5.99 (978-05453875-9-0). 144pp. In this semiautobiographical tale 11-year-old Amar'e works hard at school and enjoys skateboarding — and is ready, with his friends, to take on a trio of older bullies trying to invade their basketball court. **e** Lexile 650L (Rev: BL 6/12)

12148 Swan, Bill. *The Enforcer* (5–8). Series: Canadian Sports Stories. 2008, James Lorimer $8.95 (978-1-55028-981-7); paper $8.95 (978-1-55028-979-4). Hockey is the focus in this book about Jake, a boy with three grandfathers who all intrude into his life in different ways. (Rev: BL 6/1–15/08)

12149 Telander, Rick. *String Music* (4–6). 2002, Cricket $15.95 (978-0-8126-2647-6). 144pp. Robbie, a fifth-grader with plenty of problems, runs away to the big city, sneaks into a basketball game, and meets basketball's greatest player. (Rev: BCCB 7–8/02; BL 5/1/02)

12150 Temple, Bob. *Free Climb* (4–8). Illus. by Sean Tiffany. Series: Impact Books: A Jake Maddox Sports Story. 2008, Stone Arch LB $22.60 (978-1-4342-0784-5); paper $5.99 (978-1-4342-0880-4). 72pp. Fourteen-year-old Amir is convinced to abandon climbing buildings and spend his time at the gym instead. (Rev: SLJ 3/09)

12151 Tocher, Timothy. *Bill Pennant, Babe Ruth, and Me* (5–9). 2009, Cricket $16.95 (978-0-8126-2755-8). 184pp. In 1920, 16-year-old Hank Cobb is put in charge of the Giants' mascot, a Mexican wildcat, and then must keep an eye on the Yankees' new player called Babe Ruth. (Rev: LMC 8/09; SLJ 6/09)

12152 Trembath, Don. *Frog Face and the Three Boys* (4–7). Series: Black Belt. 2001, Orca paper $6.95 (978-1-55143-165-9). Three very different 7th-graders are enrolled in a karate class to teach them discipline. (Rev: BL 3/1/01; SLJ 9/01; VOYA 8/02)

12153 Wallace, Bill. *Never Say Quit* (5–7). 1993, Holiday $16.95 (978-0-8234-1013-2). A group of misfits who don't make the soccer team decide to form one of their own. (Rev: BL 4/15/93)

12154 Wallace, Rich. *Ball Hogs* (3–5). Illus. by Jimmy Holder. Series: Kickers. 2010, Knopf $12.99 (978-0-375-85754-6); LB $15.99 (978-0-375-95754-3). 128pp. Fourth-grader Ben copes with an arrogant teammate in this soccer story. Also use *Fake Out* (2010) and *Game-Day Jitters* (2011). (Rev: SLJ 9/1/10)

12155 Wallace, Rich. *Dunk Under Pressure* (4–6). Series: Winning Season. 2006, Viking $14.99 (978-0-670-06095-5). 119pp. Sixth-grader Dunk (Cornell Duncan), free-throw star, learns about being a team player. (Rev: SLJ 6/06)

12156 Wallace, Rich. *Southpaw* (4–6). Series: Winning Season. 2006, Viking $14.99 (978-0-670-06053-5). 128pp. Jimmy Fleming, who has moved to Hudson City with his recently divorced father, joins his school's baseball team and manages to win the acceptance of his teammates after a shaky start. (Rev: BL 2/15/06; SLJ 3/06; VOYA 2/06)

640

12157 Wallace, Rich. *Sports Camp* (4–6). 2010, Knopf $15.99 (978-0-375-84059-3); LB $18.99 (978-0-375-94059-0). 160pp. Riley, 11, struggles to fit in at a summer athletics camp despite being one of the youngest and lackluster at basketball and softball. Lexile 730L (Rev: BL 3/1/10; SLJ 4/10)

12158 Walters, Eric. *Full Court Press* (3–5). 2001, Orca paper $5.95 (978-1-55143-169-7). 152pp. Though only in the third grade, Nick and Kia decide to try out for the fifth-grade basketball team. (Rev: BL 4/1/01)

12159 Walters, Eric. *Long Shot* (2–5). Illus. by John Mantha. 2002, Orca paper $5.95 (978-1-55143-216-8). 140pp. The new coach of Nick and Kia's basketball team is so unpleasant that all the players walk out. (Rev: SLJ 7/02)

12160 Walters, Eric. *Three on Three* (3–5). Illus. 2000, Orca paper $4.99 (978-1-55143-170-3). 122pp. Third-graders Nick and Kia, excellent basketball players, get the best player in school to join them for a 3-on-3 tournament, but unforeseen problems arise. (Rev: BCCB 6/00; BL 6/1–15/00)

12161 Weatherford, Carole Boston. *Champions on the Bench: The Cannon Street YMCA All-Stars* (2–4). Illus. by Leonard Jenkins. 2007, Dial $16.99 (978-0-8037-2987-2). 32pp. In 1955 South Carolina, 61 white Little League teams refuse to play against an African American team. (Rev: BL 2/1/07; SLJ 1/07)

12162 Webster-Doyle, Terrence. *Breaking the Chains of the Ancient Warrior: Tests of Wisdom for Young Martial Artists* (5–8). 1995, Martial Arts for Peace paper $14.95 (978-0-942941-32-6). A collection of inspirational stories, karate parables, and tests that promote ethical behavior, with accompanying follow-up questions and a message for adult readers. (Rev: SLJ 1/96)

12163 Wolff, Virginia Euwer. *Bat 6* (5–9). 1998, Scholastic paper $16.95 (978-0-590-89799-0). In this novel narrated by the members of the opposing teams, a Japanese American girl just out of an internment camp meets a bitter girl whose father was killed at Pearl Harbor, and the two become rivals in baseball. (Rev: BCCB 6/98; BL 5/1/98*; HBG 10/98; SLJ 5/98; VOYA 6/98)

12164 Wooldridge, Frosty. *Strike Three! Take Your Base* (5–9). Illus. by Pietri Freeman. 2001, Brookfield Reader $16.95 (978-1-930093-01-0); paper $6.95 (978-1-930093-07-2). Baseball provides the setting as two brothers deal individually with the sudden death of their umpire father. (Rev: SLJ 3/02)

12165 Zirpoli, Jane. *Roots in the Outfield* (5–7). 1988, Houghton Mifflin $16.00 (978-0-395-45184-7). Josh spends a summer with his newly married father in Wisconsin and discovers some baseball memorabilia that help him overcome his own fears and ineptness in right field. (Rev: BL 4/1/88; SLJ 5/88)

Traditional Literature

Fairy Tales and Folklore

12166 Aardema, Verna. *The Lonely Lioness and the Ostrich Chicks* (PS–2). Illus. by Yumi Heo. 1996, Knopf LB $18.99 (978-0-679-96934-1). In this Masai story, a lonely lioness is determined to raise an ostrich's four chicks. (Rev: BCCB 2/97; BL 11/15/96; SLJ 12/96*) [398.2]

12167 Aardema, Verna. *Rabbit Makes a Monkey of Lion* (K–1). Illus. by Jerry Pinkney. 1989, Puffin paper $6.99 (978-0-14-054593-7). 32pp. A Swahili tale of a wily little rabbit outwitting the big brawny lion. (Rev: BL 3/1/89; HB 5/89; SLJ 6/89) [398.2]

12168 Aardema, Verna. *Sebgugugu the Glutton: A Bantu Tale from Rwanda, Africa* (4–6). Illus. by Nancy L. Clouse. 1993, Africa World $14.95 (978-0-86543-377-9). 32pp. In this Rwandian folktale, a foolish man loses everything because of his greed. (Rev: BL 4/1/93; SLJ 6/93) [398.2]

12169 Aardema, Verna, ed. *Why Mosquitoes Buzz in People's Ears: A West African Tale* (K–3). Illus. by Leo Dillon and Diane Dillon. 1992, Puffin paper $7.99 (978-0-14-054905-8). 32pp. Bold, stylized paintings illustrate this tale of a mosquito who tells a whopping lie, thus setting off a chain of events. Caldecott Medal winner, 1976. [398.2]

12170 Aardema, Verna, retel. *Bringing the Rain to Kapiti Plain: A Nandi Tale* (PS–2). Illus. by Beatriz Vidal. 1981, Puffin paper $7.99 (978-0-14-054616-3). 32pp. A rhyming book on how the rain was brought to an African plain. [398.2]

12171 Abeya, Elisabet. *Hansel and Gretel / Hansel y Gretel* (K–3). Illus. by Cristina Losantos. 2005, Chronicle $14.95 (978-0-8118-4793-3); paper $6.95 (978-0-8118-4794-0). 32pp. An entertaining, bilingual (Spanish and English) retelling of the classic fairy tale with ink-and-watercolor illustrations. (Rev: BL 8/05; HBG 4/06; SLJ 10/05) [398.2]

12172 Ada, Alma Flor. *The Three Golden Oranges* (K–3). Illus. by Reg Cartwright. 1999, Simon & Schuster $16.00 (978-0-689-80775-6). 32pp. A retelling of the Spanish folktale about the three princes who want wives, and to get them must bring three oranges to a wise old woman. (Rev: BCCB 7–8/99; BL 5/15/99; HBG 10/99; SLJ 7/99) [398.2]

12173 Ada, Alma Flor, and F. Isabel Campoy. *Tales Our Abuelitas Told: A Hispanic Folktale Collection* (3–5). Illus. by Felipe Davalos. 2006, Simon & Schuster $19.95 (978-0-689-82583-5). 128pp. The 12 folk tales in this collection have their roots in Hispanic culture but touch on universal themes; interesting notes add relevance. (Rev: BL 9/1/06; SLJ 9/06) [398.2]

12174 Adler, Naomi. *The Barefoot Book of Animal Tales* (2–4). Illus. by Amanda Hall. 2002, Barefoot Books $19.99 (978-1-84148-941-4). Lovely, vivid illustrations brighten retellings of nine animal tales, including a Native American story and the German classic about the Bremen musicians. (Rev: BL 1/1–15/03; HBG 3/03; SLJ 6/03) [398.2]

12175 Adler, Naomi. *Play Me a Story: Nine Tales About Musical Instruments* (3–6). Illus. 1998, Millbrook LB $23.40 (978-0-7613-0401-2). 80pp. Beginning with the tale of the Pied Piper of Hamelin, this book contains nine stories about musical instruments from different countries, including a Native American story and a myth from ancient Greece. (Rev: BL 7/98; HBG 10/98; SLJ 4/98) [398]

12176 Aesop. *The Aesop for Children* (3–5). Illus. by Milo Winter. 1984, Checkerboard $12.95 (978-1-56288-039-2); paper $5.99 (978-0-590-47977-6). This edition, reissued with the original artwork, includes 126 tales. [398.2]

12177 Aesop. *Fables of Aesop* (4–6). Illus. by David Levine. 1984, Harvard Common $13.95 (978-0-87645-074-1); paper $8.95 (978-0-87645-116-8). 108pp. One of many recommended editions of this classic. [398.2]

12178 Aesop. *The Tortoise and the Hare: An Aesop Fable* (PS–K). Illus. by Janet Stevens. 1984, Holiday House LB $16.95 (978-0-8234-0510-7); paper $6.95 (978-0-8234-0564-0). 32pp. An updated, charming retelling of the classic fable. [398.2]

12179 Ahlberg, Allan. *Previously* (PS–2). Illus. by Bruce Ingman. 2007, Candlewick $16.99 (978-0-7636-3542-8). For children who already know their fairy tales, this is an entertaining cumulative story in reverse involving Goldilocks, Cinderella, Jack and the beanstalk, the gingerbread man, and so forth. (Rev: BCCB 11/07; LMC 1/08; SLJ 11/07) [398.2]

12180 Ahmed, Said Salah. *The Lion's Share / Qayb Libaax: A Somali Folktale* (PS–2). Illus. by Kelly Dupre. 2006, Minnesota Humanities Commission $15.95 (978-1-931016-12-4); paper $7.95 (978-1-931016-13-1). After cooperating to kill a camel, the hungry animals must divide the loot, but as always the "lion's share is not fair." (Rev: BL 1/1–15/07; SLJ 1/07) [398.2]

12181 Aldana, Patricia, ed. *Jade and Iron: Latin American Tales from Two Cultures* (5–8). Trans. by Hugh Hazelton. 1996, Douglas & McIntyre $18.95 (978-0-88899-256-7). Fourteen folktales on a variety of subjects and from many regions in Latin America are retold in this large-format picture book. (Rev: BCCB 1/97; BL 12/1/96) [398.2]

12182 Alderson, Brian. *Thumbelina* (K–2). Illus. by Bagram Ibatoulline. 2009, Candlewick $17.99 (978-0-7636-2079-0). 40pp. Detailed realistic paintings enhance this retelling of the familiar story about a diminutive girl and her adventures. (Rev: BLO 11/1/09; LMC 1–2/10; SLJ 12/1/09)

12183 Alley, Zoe B. *There's a Wolf at the Door* (K–3). Illus. by R. W. Alley. 2008, Roaring Brook $19.95 (978-1-59643-275-8). 32pp. A well-dressed Wolf moves from one bad situation to another in this humorous, oversize collection of five traditional tales. (Rev: BL 9/1/08; HB 11/08; SLJ 9/08) [398.2]

12184 Anaya, Rudolfo. *My Land Sings: Stories from the Rio Grande* (5–9). 1999, Morrow $17.00 (978-0-688-15078-5). A magical collection of 10 stories, set mostly in New Mexico, that deal with Mexican and Native American folklore. (Rev: BL 8/99; HBG 10/00; SLJ 9/99) [398.2]

12185 Andersen, Hans Christian. *Andersen's Fairy Tales* (3–5). Trans. by Anthea Bell. Illus. by Silke Leffler. 2007, North-South $19.95 (978-0-7358-2141-5). 96pp. A handsome, large-format collection of 13 Andersen tales. (Rev: BL 10/15/07; SLJ 12/07) [398.2]

12186 Andersen, Hans Christian. *The Little Match Girl* (2–4). Illus. by Kveta Pacovska. 2005, Putnam $18.99 (978-0-698-40027-6). 32pp. Avant-garde illustrations enliven this retelling of Andersen's beloved fairy tale. (Rev: BL 10/1/05; SLJ 11/05) [398.2]

12187 Andersen, Hans Christian. *Little Mermaids and Ugly Ducklings: Favorite Fairy Tales by Hans Christian Andersen* (4–6). Illus. by Gennady Spirin. 2001, Chronicle $15.95 (978-0-8118-3320-2). 59pp. Handsome, imaginative illustrations of differing styles and sizes enhance six well-known tales. (Rev: BL 12/1/01; HBG 3/02) [398.2]

12188 Andersen, Hans Christian. *The Princess and the Pea* (PS). Illus. by Rachel Isadora. 2007, Putnam $16.99 (978-0-399-24611-1). The classic tale is relocated to a beautifully illustrated East Africa. (Rev: BL 4/15/07) [398.2]

12189 Andersen, Hans Christian. *Thumbelina* (PS–2). Retold and illus. by Brian Pinkney. 2003, Greenwillow LB $17.89 (978-0-688-17477-4). Pinkney's picture-book retelling is faithful to the original and features interesting artwork that differs from his usual style. (Rev: HBG 4/04; SLJ 9/03) [398.2]

12190 Andersen, Hans Christian. *The Ugly Duckling* (PS–1). Illus. by Rachel Isadora. 2009, Putnam $16.99 (978-0-399-25029-3). 32pp. Set in Africa, this gentle retelling has the ugly duckling turning into a black swan. (Rev: BL 5/1/09; SLJ 6/09) [398.2]

12191 Andersen, Hans Christian. *The Ugly Duckling* (K–4). Illus. by Steve Johnson and Lou Fancher. 2008, Candlewick $16.99 (978-0-7636-2159-9). Illustrated with elegant paint-and-collage artwork, this is a worthy retelling of the classic story. (Rev: BCCB 3/08; HB 1/08; SLJ 1/08) [398.2]

12192 Andersen, Hans Christian. *The Ugly Duckling* (K–3). Illus. by Pirkko Vainio. 2009, North-South $16.95 (978-0-7358-2226-9). 32pp. This beautifully illustrated, simple retelling was first published in Switzerland. (Rev: BLO 4/24/09; SLJ 6/09) [398.2]

12193 Andersen, Hans Christian, and Cynthia Rylant. *The Steadfast Tin Soldier* (K–3). Illus. by Jen Corace. 2013, Abrams $17.95 (978-141970432-1). 32pp. A simple, nicely illustrated adaptation of Andersen's classic story about the one-legged tin soldier who falls in love with a toy ballerina. Lexile 813.6 (Rev: BL 4/1/13; HB 7–8/13; LMC 11–12/13)

12194 Anderson, David A. *The Origin of Life on Earth: An African Creation Myth* (2–6). Illus. by Kathleen A. Wilson. 1991, Sights LB $18.95 (978-0-9629978-5-3). This African myth tells how earthly creatures were formed and how the world began spinning. (Rev: SLJ 7/92) [398.2]

12195 Andreasen, Dan. *Rose Red and the Bear Prince* (PS–1). Illus. 2000, HarperCollins LB $16.89 (978-0-06-027967-7). 40pp. In this version of the Brothers Grimm tale, Rose Red helps a wandering bear to break the enchantment that has turned him from a prince to this animal. (Rev: BL 1/1–15/00; HBG 10/00; SLJ 2/00) [398.2]

12196 Andrews, Jan. *Out of the Everywhere: Tales for a New World* (2–6). Illus. by Simon Ng. 2001, Groundwood $19.95 (978-0-88899-402-8). 95pp. Andrews retells stories, setting them in the New World and showing their relevance to immigrants or people seeking new situations. (Rev: HB 9/01; HBG 3/02; SLJ 9/01) [813]

12197 Araujo, Frank P. *Nekane, the Lamina and the Bear: A Tale of the Basque Pyrenees* (K–2). Illus. by Xiao Jun

Li. 1993, Rayve $16.95 (978-1-877810-01-5). 32pp. In this Basque version of the standard fairy tale, Red Riding Hood becomes Nekane, who is stopped by a forest spirit on her way to her uncle's home. (Rev: BCCB 3/94; BL 2/1/94; SLJ 5/94) [398.2]

12198 Araujo, Frank P. *The Perfect Orange: A Tale from Ethiopia* (K–3). Illus. by Xiao Jun Li. Series: Toucan Tales. 1994, Rayve $17.95 (978-1-877810-94-7). In this Ethiopian folktale, a simple girl impresses a king with her generosity, and he rewards her with gold and jewels. (Rev: SLJ 3/95) [398.2]

12199 Arenson, Roberta. *Manu and the Talking Fish* (PS–3). Illus. 2000, Barefoot Books $15.95 (978-1-84148-032-9). 32pp. This Indian variation on the Noah story tells of Manu, a prince, who rescues a fish. When the fish grows up, he warns Manu of an impending flood that will destroy the world. (Rev: BL 4/1/00; SLJ 6/00) [398.2]

12200 Arkhurst, Joyce Cooper. *The Adventures of Spider: West African Folktales* (4–7). Illus. by Jerry Pinkney. 1992, Little, Brown paper $8.99 (978-0-316-05107-1). Six humorous stories featuring the crafty spider. [398.2]

12201 Arnold, Katya, retel. *That Apple Is Mine!* (PS–1). Illus. by Katya Arnold. 2000, Holiday House $15.95 (978-0-8234-1629-5). In this Russian folktale, Bear teaches the animals to share when they all want the same apple. (Rev: HB 1/01; HBG 3/01; SLJ 12/00) [398.2]

12202 Aroner, Miriam. *The Kingdom of Singing Birds* (K–5). Illus. by Shelly O. Haas. 1993, Kar-Ben $13.95 (978-0-929371-43-6); paper $5.95 (978-0-929371-44-3). In this Jewish folktale, a rabbi tells a king that the only way to get his birds to sing is to set them free. (Rev: SLJ 9/93) [398.2]

12203 Artell, Mike. *Jacques and de Beanstalk* (PS–2). Illus. by Jim Harris. 2010, Dial $16.99 (978-0-8037-2816-5). 32pp. In this Cajun adaptation of the classic story, Jacques is depicted as a hard-working youngster lured by the smarmy magic bean man; a glossary provides help with the dialect. (Rev: BLO 2/1/10; SLJ 4/1/10) [398.2]

12204 Artell, Mike. *Petite Rouge: A Cajun Red Riding Hood* (PS–2). Illus. by Jim Harris. 2001, Dial $16.99 (978-0-8037-2514-0). 32pp. The wolf becomes an alligator and the little girl a duck in this Louisiana version of the classic tale. (Rev: BL 7/01; HBG 10/01; SLJ 6/01) [398.2]

12205 Artell, Mike. *Three Little Cajun Pigs* (K–3). Illus. by Jim Harris. 2006, Dial $16.99 (978-0-8037-2815-8). The classic tale is given a funny Cajun spin when a hungry gator fills in for the big, bad wolf. (Rev: HBG 4/07; SLJ 12/06) [398.2]

12206 Asbjornsen, Peter C. *The Three Billy Goats Gruff* (PS–2). Retold by Glen Rounds. Illus. 1993, Holiday House LB $15.95 (978-0-8234-1015-6). 32pp. This veteran illustrator noted for animal drawings illustrates and retells this famous Norweigan folktale. (Rev: BL 4/15/93; HB 7/93; SLJ 6/93*) [398.2]

12207 Asbjornsen, Peter C., and Jörgen Moe. *Norwegian Folk Tales* (3–6). Illus. by Erik Werenskiold and Theodor Kittelsen. 1978, Pantheon paper $14.00 (978-0-394-71054-9). This edition retains the original illustrations from the 1845 edition. [398.2]

12208 Asch, Frank. *Ziggy Piggy and the Three Little Pigs* (PS–1). Illus. 1998, Kids Can $14.95 (978-1-55074-515-3). 32pp. A variation on the story of the three little pigs in which a fourth little pig, Ziggy, rescues his brothers from the wolf and takes them to a raft he made from driftwood. (Rev: BL 11/15/98; HB 11/98; HBG 3/99) [398.2]

12209 Ash, Russell, and Bernard A. Higton, eds. *Aesop's Fables* (3–6). Illus. 1991, Chronicle $17.95 (978-0-87701-780-6). 95pp. More than 50 fables reprinted and illustrated with artists from the past. (Rev: SLJ 3/91) [398.2]

12210 Ashabranner, Brent, and Russell Davis. *The Lion's Whiskers and Other Ethiopian Tales* (4–7). 1997, Linnet LB $19.95 (978-0-208-02429-9). A classic collection of 16 Ethiopian folktales originally published in 1995. (Rev: BL 10/1/97; SLJ 5/97*) [398.2]

12211 Ata, Te. *Baby Rattlesnake* (PS–K). Adapted by Lynn Moroney. Illus. by Veg Reisberg. 1990, Children's Book Pr. $14.95 (978-0-89239-049-6). 32pp. A baby rattlesnake doesn't know how to behave when he is given a rattle before reaching maturity. (Rev: BL 3/1/90; SLJ 4/90) [398.2]

12212 Aylesworth, Jim. *The Gingerbread Man* (PS–2). Illus. by Barbara McClintock. 1998, Scholastic $16.95 (978-0-590-97219-2). 32pp. A traditional retelling of the old folktale about the cheerful elderly couple who created a gingerbread man who comes to life and leads them a merry chase. (Rev: BL 4/1/98; HBG 10/98; SLJ 4/98) [398.21]

12213 Aylesworth, Jim. *The Mitten* (PS–2). Illus. by Barbara McClintock. 2009, Scholastic $16.99 (978-0-439-92544-0). 32pp. In this retelling of a beloved Ukrainian tale, a young boy's lost mitten becomes a warm refuge for a variety of woodland animals. (Rev: BL 11/1/09*; LMC 11–12/09; SLJ 12/1/09*) [398.2]

12214 Balcells, Jacqueline. *The Enchanted Raisin* (3–6). Trans. by Elizabeth G. Miller. Illus. 1989, Latin American Literary Review Pr. paper $11.00 (978-0-935480-38-2). 103pp. Ten contemporary fairy stories by a noted Chilean writer for children. (Rev: BL 12/1/89) [398.2]

12215 Bar-El, Dan. *Such a Prince* (K–2). Illus. by John Manders. 2007, Clarion $16.00 (978-0-618-71468-1). A funny fractured version of a French fairy tale, "Three May Peaches," in which an aging fairy called Libby Gaborchik helps a love-starved Princess Vera. (Rev: SLJ 1/08) [398.2]

12216 Barbosa, Rogerio Andrade. *African Animal Tales* (4–6). Trans. by Feliz Guthrie. Illus. by Cica Fittipaldi. 1993, Volcano $17.95 (978-0-912078-96-0). 63pp. Weak, small animals outwit stronger animals in this collection of ten African folktales. (Rev: BL 2/15/94) [398.2]

12217 Barton, Byron. *The Little Red Hen* (PS–2). Illus. 1993, HarperCollins LB $17.89 (978-0-06-021676-4). A new interpretation of this favorite story of the industrious hen, with appealing illustrations. (Rev: BL 5/1/93; SLJ 7/93) [398.2]

12218 Barton, Byron. *The Three Bears* (PS). Illus. 1991, HarperCollins LB $17.89 (978-0-06-020424-2). 32pp. For the very young, this is a retelling of the story of Goldilocks and the Three Bears. (Rev: BL 1/1/91; SLJ 11/91) [398.2]

12219 Bateman, Teresa. *The Princesses Have a Ball* (K–3). Illus. by Lynne W. Cravath. 2002, Whitman $16.95 (978-0-8075-6626-8). 32pp. A suspicious king asks detectives to find out what his girls are up to, but a cobbler finds the answer first and advises the young ladies to reveal their athletic skills in this basketball version of "The Twelve Dancing Princesses." (Rev: BL 11/1/02; HB 1/03; HBG 3/03; SLJ 12/02) [398.2]

12220 Bateson-Hill, Margaret. *Chanda and the Mirror of Moonlight* (3–4). Illus. by Karin Littlewood. 2001, Zero to Ten $17.95 (978-1-84089-217-8). An evil stepmother tries to trick the prince into marrying her daughter instead of Chanda, but the mirror reveals the truth. (Rev: SLJ 5/02) [398.2]

12221 Batt, Tanya. *The Fabrics of Fairytale: Stories Spun from Far and Wide* (4–6). Illus. 2000, Barefoot Books $19.99 (978-1-84148-061-9). 80pp. This book contains seven retold folktales, each related to a different kind of fabric or an article of clothing, like silk brocade, a patchwork coat, or a feather cloak. Patchwork illustrations are reminiscent of a story quilt. (Rev: BL 11/15/00; HBG 10/01; SLJ 11/00) [398.23]

12222 Batt, Tanya. *The Princess and the White Bear King* (1–3). Illus. by Nicoletta Ceccoli. 2004, Barefoot Books $16.99 (978-1-84148-339-9). 40pp. Borrowing from three traditional folktales, Batt has created a charming story about a beautiful young princess who is kidnapped by a white bear and taken to his stately palace. (Rev: BL 11/1/04; SLJ 1/05) [398.2]

12223 Batt, Tanya Robyn. *A Child's Book of Faeries* (3–5). Illus. by Gail Newey. 2002, Barefoot Books $19.99 (978-1-84148-954-4). Four stories, with snippets of poetry and folklore, introduce the magical world of fairies and leprechauns. (Rev: BL 12/15/02; HBG 3/03; SLJ 1/03) [398.21]

12224 Batt, Tanya Robyn. *The Faerie's Gift* (K–3). Illus. by Nicoletta Ceccoli. 2003, Barefoot Books $16.99 (978-1-84148-998-8). 32pp. A fairy offers a woodcutter one wish, and the wish he makes pleases everyone in his family. (Rev: BL 2/15/03; HBG 10/03; SLJ 6/03) [398.2]

12225 Bazilian, Barbara. *The Red Shoes* (K–2). Illus. 1997, Whispering Coyote $10.95 (978-1-879085-56-5). 40pp. This attractive retelling of Andersen's story has been changed to make it less preachy and gory. (Rev: BL 11/1/97; HBG 3/98; SLJ 10/97) [398.2]

12226 Beach, Milo Cleveland. *The Adventures of Rama* (4–6). Illus. 1983, Smithsonian Institution $15.00 (978-0-934686-51-8). 64pp. Tales from the Hindu epic Ramayana. (Rev: SLJ 2/05) [398.2]

12227 Bedard, Michael, ed. *The Painted Wall and Other Strange Tales* (4–7). 2003, Tundra $16.95 (978-0-88776-652-7). Chinese folktales collected centuries ago are full of action and the supernatural. (Rev: BL 1/1–15/04; SLJ 1/04) [398.2]

12228 Beeler, Selby B. *Throw Your Tooth on the Roof: Tooth Traditions from Around the World* (PS–3). Illus. by G. Brian Karas. 1998, Houghton $16.00 (978-0-395-89108-7). 32pp. As well as some basic facts about teeth, this book outlines lost-tooth traditions from around the world, each of which makes placing the tooth under a pillow to get money from the tooth fairy seem very tame. (Rev: BCCB 11/98; BL 7/98; HBG 3/99; SLJ 9/98) [398]

12229 Behan, Brendan. *The King of Ireland's Son* (3–5). Illus. by P. J. Lynch. 1997, Orchard $16.95 (978-0-531-09549-2). 32pp. A rich retelling of the Irish folktale about three princes who set out to find the origin of the heavenly music that is heard in their land. (Rev: BCCB 4/97; BL 4/15/97; SLJ 6/97) [398.2]

12230 Bell, Anthea. *The Porridge Pot* (K–2). Illus. by Claudia Carls. 2007, Penguin $16.99 (978-0-698-40073-3). 32pp. Eye-catching, detailed illustrations combining sculpture and painting illuminate this folktale about a poor little girl who loses her parents and her shoe in the woods but finds a prince. (Rev: BL 9/1/07; SLJ 11/07) [398.2]

12231 Beneduce, Ann Keay. *Jack and the Beanstalk* (1–3). Illus. by Gennady Spirin. 1999, Penguin $17.99 (978-0-399-23118-6). 32pp. An expanded version of the classic tale, based on a Victorian retelling, in which a fairy figures prominently as Jack's helper. (Rev: BCCB 12/99; BL 11/1/99; HBG 3/00; SLJ 11/99) [398.2]

12232 Berger, Barbara Helen. *All the Way to Lhasa: A Tale from Tibet* (PS–2). Illus. 2002, Penguin $17.99 (978-0-399-23387-6). 32pp. Courage and perseverance win over headlong speed in this tale of two young men journeying to the holy city of Lhasa, with illustrations that contain many Tibetan Buddhist touches. (Rev: BL 10/1/02; HBG 3/03; SLJ 9/02) [398.2]

12233 Bierhorst, John. *The Woman Who Fell from the Sky: The Iroquois Story of Creation* (K–4). Illus. by Robert Andrew Parker. 1993, Morrow LB $14.89 (978-0-688-10681-2). 32pp. Sky Woman, with the help of her two sons, creates the earth. (Rev: BCCB 5/93; BL 3/15/93; HB 5/93; SLJ 4/93) [398.2]

12234 Bierhorst, John, ed. *The People with Five Fingers: A Native Californian Creation Tale* (K–3). Illus. by Robert Andrew Parker. 2000, Marshall Cavendish $15.95 (978-0-7614-5058-0). 32pp. A Native American creation tale about how Coyote put the animals to work to prepare for the arrival of humans in the world. (Rev: BCCB 3/00; BL 4/1/00; HBG 10/00; SLJ 6/00) [398.2]

12235 Bini, Renata, retel. *A World Treasury of Myths, Legends, and Folktales: Stories from Six Continents* (3–6). Trans. from Italian by Alexandra Bonfante-Warren.

Illus. by Mikhail Fiodorov. 2000, Abrams $24.95 (978-0-8109-4554-8). 126pp. These brief retellings of tales from around the world cover many cultures and times; about one-quarter are from Native American sources. (Rev: BL 1/1–15/01; HBG 3/01; SLJ 12/00) [398.2]

12236 Birch, David. *The King's Chessboard* (3–5). Illus. by Devis Grebu. 1988, Puffin paper $6.99 (978-0-14-054880-8). 32pp. A wise man outsmarts a vain king when he is offered a reward. (Rev: BL 5/15/88; SLJ 4/88) [398.2]

12237 Birdseye, Tom. *Look Out, Jack! The Giant Is Back!* (K–3). Illus. by Will Hillenbrand. 2001, Holiday House $16.95 (978-0-8234-1450-5). 32pp. The giant of "Jack and the Beanstalk" fame has a big brother who wants revenge — and Jack narrowly escapes him in this colorful picture book. (Rev: BCCB 10/01; BL 9/1/01; HBG 3/02; SLJ 10/01) [398.2]

12238 Birdseye, Tom. *Soap! Soap! Don't Forget the Soap! An Appalachian Folktale* (3–6). Illus. by Andrew Glass. 1993, Holiday House LB $16.95 (978-0-8234-1005-7). 32pp. An adaptation of a familiar story about a forgetful hero sent to the store by his mother. (Rev: BCCB 6/93; BL 3/15/93; HB 5/93) [398.2]

12239 Blackstone, Stella. *Storytime: First Tales for Sharing* (PS–K). Illus. by Anne Wilson. 2005, Barefoot Books $19.99 (978-1-84148-345-0). 96pp. Seven familiar tales — including such classics as "Goldilocks and the Three Bears" and "The Gingerbread Man" — are faithfully retold and accompanied by attractive collage and acrylic illustrations. (Rev: BL 1/1–15/06; SLJ 11/05) [398.2]

12240 Blades, Ann. *Too Small* (K–2). Illus. by author. 2000, Groundwood $15.95 (978-0-88899-400-4). A variation on the traditional Yiddish tale about a house that becomes crowded when a lot of friends and animals are invited in. (Rev: HBG 3/01; SLJ 10/00) [398.2]

12241 Blair, Eric. *Paul Bunyan* (K–1). Illus. by Micah Chambers-Coldberg. Series: Read-It! Readers Tall Tales. 2005, Picture Window LB $19.93 (978-1-4048-0976-5). 32pp. The familiar tall tale is retold for beginning readers, with colorful illustrations. (Rev: SLJ 7/05) [398.2]

12242 Boada, Francesc. *Cinderella / Cenicienta* (PS–1). Illus. by Monse Fransoy. Series: Bilingual Editions. 2001, Chronicle paper $6.95 (978-0-8118-3090-4). A bilingual version full of humor that stays close to the original tale. (Rev: BL 7/01; HBG 10/01) [398.2]

12243 Bofill, Francesc. *Jack and the Beanstalk / Juan y los frijoles magicos* (2–4). 1998, Chronicle $13.95 (978-0-8118-2062-2). 32pp. Using an easy English/Spanish text, this is an attractive retelling of the classic folktale. (Rev: BL 11/15/98; SLJ 8/98) [398.2]

12244 Bofill, Francesc. *Rapunzel* (K–3). Illus. by Joma. 2006, Chronicle $14.95 (978-0-8118-5059-9); paper $6.95 (978-0-8118-5060-5). 32pp. A nicely illustrated bilingual retelling of the classic tale, with enjoyable twists. (Rev: BL 3/1/06; SLJ 6/06) [398.2]

12245 Borlenghi, Patricia. *Chaucer the Cat and the Animal Pilgrims* (3–6). Illus. by Giles Greenfield. 2000,

Bloomsbury $22.95 (978-0-7475-4491-3). 77pp. A group of animal pilgrims from around the world led by Chaucer the Cat from London tell folk tales on their way to honor Saint Francis at Assisi. (Rev: SLJ 1/01) [398.2]

12246 Bouchard, David. *The Great Race* (3–6). Illus. by Zhong-Yang Huang. 1997, Millbrook LB $21.40 (978-0-7613-0305-3). 32pp. This folktale tells that the order of the animals in the Chinese zodiac was determined by a great race. (Rev: BL 2/1/98; HBG 3/98; SLJ 1/98) [398.2]

12247 Bradman, Tony. *Mr. Wolf Bounces Back* (2–4). Illus. by Sarah Warburton. 2009, Stone Arch LB $23.99 (978-1-4342-1306-8). 56pp. Bradman tells the story of Granny and the wolf after the well-known episode; Granny is lonely and the big bad wolf has become a father and needs a different kind of job. (Rev: LMC 10/09; SLJ 6/09) [398.2]

12248 Breinburg, Petronella. *Stories from the Caribbean* (2–4). Illus. by Syrah Arnold and Tina Barber. Series: Multicultural Stories. 2000, Raintree LB $27.12 (978-0-7398-1334-8). 48pp. Ghost stories, creation fables, and animal stories are included in this interesting anthology. (Rev: HBG 10/00; SLJ 11/00) [398.2]

12249 Brett, Jan. *Gingerbread Baby* (PS–3). Illus. 1999, Penguin $16.99 (978-0-399-23444-6). 32pp. In this updated version of the old tale, Gingerbread Baby escapes and wreaks havoc in the Swiss village where he had been baked. (Rev: BL 11/15/99; HBG 3/00; SLJ 11/99)

12250 Brett, Jan. *The Mitten* (PS–2). Illus. 1990, Penguin $16.99 (978-0-399-21920-7). In this Ukrainian folktale, Nicki loses in the snow one of the mittens that his grandmother knit him. (Rev: BCCB 12/89; BL 9/15/89*; HB 11/89; SLJ 11/89) [398.2]

12251 Brett, Jan. *The Three Snow Bears* (1–3). Illus. by author. 2007, Putnam $16.99 (978-0-399-24792-7). 32pp. In the cold north, an Inuit girl called Aloo-ki loses her sled dogs and comes across an empty igloo in this re-imagining of "Goldilocks and the Three Bears." (Rev: BL 9/15/07; LMC 11/07; SLJ 12/07) [398.2] ⌂

12252 Brett, Jan. *Who's That Knocking on Christmas Eve?* (K–2). Illus. 2002, Penguin $16.99 (978-0-399-23873-4). A beautifully illustrated folktale of a Christmas Eve feast nearly ruined by hungry trolls. (Rev: BCCB 10/02; BL 9/1/02; HBG 3/03; SLJ 10/02)

12253 Brett, Jan, retel. *Beauty and the Beast* (PS–3). Illus. 1989, Houghton $16.00 (978-0-89919-497-4). A smooth, brief retelling of the old classic. (Rev: BCCB 12/89; BL 10/1/89; SLJ 11/89) [398.2]

12254 Brill, Marlene T. *Tooth Tales from Around the World* (K–2). Illus. by Katya Krenina. 1998, Charlesbridge LB $15.95 (978-0-88106-398-1); paper $6.95 (978-0-88106-399-8). 32pp. An outline of the many traditions and beliefs from around the world concerning lost teeth. For example, ancient Egyptians threw their teeth to the sun in the belief that the sun made teeth strong. (Rev: BL 7/98; HBG 10/98) [398]

12255 Brimner, Larry Dane, retel. *Captain Stormalong* (PS–2). Illus. by Chi Chung. Series: Imagination Series:

Tall Tales. 2004, Compass Point LB $26.60 (978-0-7565-0601-8). 32pp. Captain Stormalong, a larger-than-life character who first appeared in an old sea chantey, springs to life again in this spirited retelling of some of his most audacious adventures. (Rev: SLJ 7/04) [398.2]

12256 Brown, Marcia. *Backbone of the King: The Story of Paka'a and His Son Ku* (5–7). Illus. by author. 1984, Univ. of Hawaii $19.00 (978-0-8248-0963-8). A reissue of the book based on a Hawaiian legend of a boy who wants to help his exiled father. [398.2]

12257 Brown, Marcia. *Dick Whittington and His Cat* (K–3). Illus. by author. 1988, Macmillan $16.00 (978-0-684-18998-7). 32pp. A reissue of a Caldecott Honor Book published in 1950 about the boy who went to London to seek his fortune. [398.2]

12258 Brown, Marcia. *Stone Soup* (1–4). Illus. by author. 1979, Macmillan $16.00 (978-0-684-92296-6); paper $5.99 (978-0-689-71103-9). 48pp. An old French tale about three soldiers who make soup from stones. [398.2]

12259 Brown, Stephanie Gwyn. *Professor Aesop's the Crow and the Pitcher* (K–4). Illus. by author. 2003, Tricycle $15.95 (978-1-58246-087-1). A clever crow, temporarily foiled in his attempts to drink from a pitcher, comes up with an ingenious solution. (Rev: HBG 10/03; SLJ 9/03) [398.2]

12260 Bruchac, James, and Joseph Bruchac. *Rabbit's Snow Dance* (PS–2). Illus. by Jeff Newman. 2012, Dial $16.99 (978-0-8037-3270-4). 32pp. In this retelling of a traditional Iroquois tale we learn why Rabbit does not have a long tail. Lexile 640L (Rev: BL 12/1/12; HB 11–12/12; LMC 3–4/13; SLJ 11/12) [398.2089]

12261 Bruchac, James, and Joseph Bruchac, retels. *The Girl Who Helped Thunder and Other Native American Folktales* (3–6). Illus. by Stefano Vitale. 2008, Sterling $14.95 (978-1-4027-3263-8). 96pp. Arranged geographically, this anthology includes stories from diverse peoples, with background information that provides historical and cultural context. (Rev: BCCB 1/09; HB 1/09; LMC 5/09; SLJ 12/08) [398.2]

12262 Bruchac, Joseph. *Dog People: Native Dog Stories* (3–6). Illus. by Murv Jacob. 1995, Fulcrum $14.95 (978-1-55591-228-4). This book contains five very readable stories about the Abenaki Indian children and their dogs. (Rev: SLJ 1/96) [398.2]

12263 Bruchac, Joseph. *Native American Animal Stories* (5–8). 1992, Fulcrum paper $12.95 (978-1-55591-127-0). Animal stories from various Native American tribes, for reading aloud and storytelling. (Rev: BL 9/1/92; SLJ 11/92) [398.2]

12264 Bruchac, Joseph. *Native Plant Stories* (4–8). 1995, Fulcrum paper $12.95 (978-1-55591-212-3). A collection of stories about plants that come from various Native American cultures in North and Central America. (Rev: BL 9/1/95) [398.24]

12265 Bruchac, Joseph, and James Bruchac. *How Chipmunk Got His Stripes: A Tale of Bragging and Teasing* (1–3). Illus. by Ariane Dewey and Jose Aruego. 2001, Dial $16.99 (978-0-8037-2404-4). In this Native American story, squirrel is punished for teasing Big Bear by having the now-familiar chipmunk stripe placed on his back. (Rev: BCCB 3/01; BL 2/1/01; HBG 10/01; SLJ 2/01) [398.24]

12266 Bruchac, Joseph, and James Bruchac. *When the Chenoo Howls* (3–6). Illus. 1998, Walker $16.95 (978-0-8027-8638-8). 128pp. This anthology consists of 12 scary stories from the Northeast woodland Native Americans — most of them traditional folktales together with a few original stories that incorporate legendary characters. (Rev: BCCB 9/98; BL 8/98; HBG 3/99; SLJ 12/98) [398.2]

12267 Bryan, Ashley. *Beat the Story-Drum, Pum-Pum* (K–4). Illus. by author. 1987, Macmillan paper $8.95 (978-0-689-71107-7). 80pp. A retelling of five Nigerian folktales. [398.2]

12268 Bryan, Ashley. *Beautiful Blackbird* (K–2). Illus. 2003, Simon & Schuster $16.95 (978-0-689-84731-8). 40pp. Bold collages illustrate the Zambian tale of Blackbird, who is the envy of all the brightly colored birds in Africa and generously agrees to share his blackening potion, so that all the birds can be black and beautiful. (Rev: BCCB 2/03; BL 1/1–15/03; HB 3/03*; HBG 10/03; SLJ 1/03) [398.2]

12269 Bryan, Ashley. *The Night Has Ears: African Proverbs* (K–3). Illus. 1999, Simon & Schuster $16.00 (978-0-689-82427-2). 32pp. Presenting one proverb per page, this is a collection of 26 aphorisms from various African tribes. (Rev: BL 9/15/99; HBG 3/00; SLJ 1/00) [398.9]

12270 Buehner, Caralyn. *Goldilocks and the Three Bears* (PS–1). Illus. by Mark Buehner. 2007, Dial $16.99 (978-0-8037-2939-1). Three well-behaved bears live in a lovely little log cabin in the woods that a boisterous rope-jumping Goldilocks invades in their absence. (Rev: BL 3/1/07; SLJ 4/07) [398.2]

12271 Bunting, Eve. *Finn McCool and the Great Fish* (1–3). Illus. by Zachary Pullen. 2010, Sleeping Bear $16.95 (978-1-58536-366-7). 32pp. In this story, Ireland's mythological giant seeks wisdom from a salmon. (Rev: BL 4/1/10; SLJ 4/1/10) [398.2]

12272 Burns, Batt. *The King with Horse's Ears and Other Irish Folktales* (3–6). Illus. by Igor Oleynikov. Series: Folktales of the World. 2009, Sterling $14.95 (978-1-4027-3772-5). 96pp. Thirteen Irish tales feature warriors, heroes, fairies, and leprechauns; includes Gaelic words and Celtic-style illustrations. (Rev: BL 3/1/09; SLJ 3/09) [398.2]

12273 Bushyhead, Robert H. *Yonder Mountain: A Cherokee Legend* (PS–3). Illus. by Kristina Rodanas. 2002, Marshall Cavendish $16.95 (978-0-7614-5113-6). 32pp. In this Cherokee folktale, an old chief tests three young men to determine who will be his successor. (Rev: BL 2/15/03; HBG 10/03; SLJ 12/02) [398.2]

12274 Carle, Eric. *The Rabbit and the Turtle* (K–3). Illus. by author. 2008, Scholastic $16.99 (978-0-545-00541-8). 32pp. A collection of Aesop fables, many previously published by Carle, are redesigned here, each ending with the moral. (Rev: BL 6/1–15/08; LMC 10/08) [398.2]

12275 Carpenter, F. R. *Tales of a Chinese Grandmother* (5–7). Illus. by Malthe Hasselriis. 1973, Amereon LB $24.95 (978-0-89190-481-6); paper $8.95 (978-0-8048-1042-5). A boy and a girl listen to 30 classic Chinese tales. [398.2]

12276 Carpenter, Stephen. *The Three Billy Goats Gruff* (PS). Illus. Series: Harper Growing Tree. 1998, Harper-Collins $9.99 (978-0-694-01033-2). 24pp. For the very young, this is a simple but accurate retelling of the old English folktale using double-page pictures. (Rev: BL 5/15/98; HBG 10/98; SLJ 7/98) [398.2]

12277 Carrier, Roch, retel. *The Flying Canoe* (3–6). Trans. from French by Sheila Fischman. Illus. by Sheldon Cohen. 2004, Tundra $15.95 (978-0-88776-636-7). On a New Year's Eve in the mid-19th century, 11-year-old Baptiste and his homesick lumberjack friends are transported home by magical canoe; a French Canadian folktale. (Rev: SLJ 4/05) [398.2]

12278 Casanova, Mary. *The Hunter* (PS–3). Illus. by Ed Young. 2000, Simon & Schuster $16.95 (978-0-689-82906-2). 32pp. This is a Chinese tale of a simple hunter who is granted the ability to understand the language of animals. He bravely tells his people that a great flood is coming and that he has learned of it from the animals, but he is turned to stone for divulging his secret ability. (Rev: BCCB 11/00*; BL 5/15/00; HBG 10/01; SLJ 8/00) [398.2]

12279 Cech, John. *Aesop's Fables* (1–4). Illus. by Martin Jarrie. 2009, Sterling $16.95 (978-1-4027-5298-8). 40pp. A collection of 36 of the lesser-known Aesop tales. (Rev: BLO 4/13/09; SLJ 7/09) [398.2]

12280 Cech, John. *Jack and the Beanstalk* (1–3). Illus. by Robert MacKenzie. 2008, Sterling $14.95 (978-1-4027-3064-1). Yet another variation on the Jack-and-the-beanstalk story with a funny ending and endnotes trace the story's themes to tales throughout history. (Rev: BL 3/15/08; SLJ 5/08) [398.2]

12281 Cech, John. *The Twelve Dancing Princesses* (PS–2). Illus. by Lucy Corvino. 2009, Sterling $14.95 (978-1-4027-4435-8). 28pp. A lushly illustrated retelling of the story about the princesses who mysteriously manage to wear out their shoes every night. (Rev: BL 3/15/09; SLJ 7/09) [398]

12282 Cecil, Laura. *Cunning Cat Stories* (K–2). Illus. by Emma Chichester Clark. 2003, Pavilion $19.95 (978-1-86205-376-2); paper $.00 (978-1-84365-023-2). 80pp. Three feline-themed folk tales — "Puss in Boots," "Sir Pussycat," and "The White Cat" — are retold in this attractively illustrated collection. (Rev: BL 6/1–15/04; SLJ 5/04)

12283 Cecil, Laura, retel. *Wicked Wolf Stories* (K–2). Illus. by Emma Chichester Clark. 2003, Pavilion $19.95 (978-1-86205-460-8); paper $10.95 (978-1-84365-018-8). 80pp. Three popular children's stories featuring wolves are featured in this attractive volume. (Rev: BL 6/1–15/04)

12284 Charles, Veronika M., retel. *Maiden of the Mist: A Legend of Niagara Falls* (1–3). Illus. by Veronika M. Charles. 2001, Stoddart $13.95 (978-0-7737-3297-1); paper $6.95 (978-0-7737-6207-7). A beautifully illustrated story of the maiden who sacrifices herself to the Thunder God in order to save her people from illness. (Rev: SLJ 1/02) [398.2]

12285 Chen, Debby. *Monkey King Wreaks Havoc in Heaven* (4–6). Illus. by Wenhai Ma. 2001, Pan Asian $16.95 (978-1-57227-068-8). 36pp. A retelling of a Chinese tale about the sly Monkey King. (Rev: BL 10/15/01) [398.2]

12286 Child, Lauren. *The Princess and the Pea* (K–3). Illus. by Polly Borland. 2006, Hyperion $16.99 (978-0-7868-3886-8). 40pp. The queen puts a potential bride for her son to the pea-under-the-mattress test in this fractured fairy tale. (Rev: BL 2/15/06; SLJ 3/06*) [398.2]

12287 Chin, Yin-lien C., ed. *Traditional Chinese Folktales* (5–8). Illus. by Lu Wang. 1989, East Gate $44.95 (978-0-87332-507-3). This is a collection of 12 Chinese folktales that express a variety of themes and genres from faithful lovers to trickster tales. (Rev: SLJ 8/89) [398.2]

12288 Chodzin, Sherab, and Alexandra Kohn. *The Wisdom of the Crows and Other Buddhist Tales* (3–5). Illus. 1998, Tricycle $17.95 (978-1-883672-68-3). 80pp. This collection of Asian folktales illustrated with clear watercolors represents various facets of Buddhist thought and beliefs. (Rev: BL 6/1–15/98; SLJ 04/98) [294]

12289 Christelow, Eileen. *Where's the Big Bad Wolf?* (PS–1). Illus. 2002, Clarion $16.00 (978-0-618-18194-0). 32pp. This humorous retelling of the classic tale — featuring cartoon illustrations and dialogue balloons — is written as a mystery, featuring Detective Doggedly in search of BBW (Big Bad Wolf). (Rev: BL 10/15/02; HBG 3/03; SLJ 9/02)

12290 Ciddor, Anna. *Night of the Fifth Moon* (5–8). 2008, Allen & Unwin paper $9.95 (978-1-74114-814-5). 243pp. Set in ancient Ireland and filled with beautiful imagery, this engaging novel tells the story of Ket, who must leave his family and struggle for the chance to become a druid. (Rev: SLJ 5/09; VOYA 10/08)

12291 Claflin, Willy. *The Uglified Ducky: A Maynard Moose Tale* (K–3). Illus. by James Stimson. 2008, August House $18.95 (978-0-87483-858-9). 32pp. Andersen's tale about an ugly duckling is moved to northern Maine where a moose grows up as a member of a duck "fambly"; a humorous read with an accompanying CD. (Rev: LMC 3/09; SLJ 9/08) [398.2]

12292 Clement, Gary. *Just Stay Put: A Chelm Story* (K–4). Illus. 1996, Douglas & McIntyre $14.95 (978-0-88899-239-0). 32pp. A resident of Chelm, Poland, mistakes his hometown for Warsaw. (Rev: BL 9/15/96; SLJ 6/96) [398.2]

12293 Climo, Shirley. *King of the Birds* (PS–3). Illus. by Ruth Heller. 1991, HarperCollins paper $5.95 (978-0-06-443273-3). 32pp. The long-ago legend of how the birds chose a king. (Rev: BL 2/15/88; SLJ 8/88) [398.2]

12294 Climo, Shirley. *The Korean Cinderella* (K–3). Illus. by Ruth Heller. 1993, HarperCollins $17.99 (978-0-06-020432-7). 48pp. After Pear Blossom's mother dies and her father remarries, she is mistreated by her stepmother and stepsister. (Rev: BCCB 6/93; BL 5/1/93; SLJ 8/93) [398.2]

12295 Climo, Shirley. *Tuko and the Birds: A Tale from the Philippines* (1–3). Illus. by Francisco Mora. 2008, Holt $16.95 (978-0-8050-6559-6). 40pp. The birds of Mount Pinatubo are fed up with the noise created by a gecko named Tuko and look for ways to get rid of him; lush illustrations and Filipino words add to this lively folktale. (Rev: BL 4/15/08; HB 5/08; LMC 8/08; SLJ 5/08) [398.2]

12296 Climo, Shirley, retel. *The Little Red Ant and the Great Big Crumb* (PS–2). Illus. by Francisco Mora. 1995, Clarion $16.00 (978-0-395-70732-6). 39pp. A tiny ant seeks help in vain from other animals to move a heavy crumb in this Mexican tale. (Rev: SLJ 11/95) [398.2]

12297 Coburn, Jewell Reinhart. *Domitila: A Cinderella Tale from the Mexican Tradition* (3–5). Illus. 2000, Shen's $16.95 (978-1-885008-13-8). 32pp. This variation on the story of Cinderella comes from the folklore of Hidalgo, Mexico. (Rev: BL 5/15/00; HBG 10/00; SLJ 7/00) [398.2]

12298 Coburn, Jewell Reinhart, and Tzexa Cherta Lee, adapt. *Jouanah: A Hmong Cinderella* (K–3). Illus. by Anne S. O'Brien. 1996, Shen's $15.95 (978-1-885008-01-5). This version of the Cinderella story from the Hmong of Southeast Asia takes place in a peasant village. (Rev: BCCB 12/96; SLJ 3/97) [398.2]

12299 Cohen, Caron L. *The Mud Pony: A Traditional Skidi Pawnee Tale* (K–3). Illus. by Shonto Begay. 1988, Scholastic $15.95 (978-0-590-41525-5). 32pp. The moving story of a boy too poor to have a pony of his own who grows up to become chief of his people. (Rev: BCCB 12/88; BL 12/1/88; SLJ 1/89) [398.2]

12300 Cohen, Daniel. *Railway Ghosts and Highway Horrors* (3–5). Illus. by Stephen Marchesi. 1993, Scholastic paper $2.95 (978-0-590-45423-0). 112pp. Phantom hitchhikers and accident victims fill this anthology of American and British travelers' lore. (Rev: BL 11/15/91) [133.1]

12301 Collins, Sheila Hebert. *Jolie Blonde and the Three Heberts: A Cajun Twist to an Old Tale* (K–4). Illus. by Patrick Soper. 1999, Pelican $15.95 (978-1-56554-324-9). In this Cajun version of Goldilocks, the heroine is Jolie Blonde and the bears are three humans named Hebert whose gumbo is eaten while they are away. (Rev: HBG 10/99; SLJ 6/99) [398.2]

12302 Collodi, Carlo. *The Adventures of Pinocchio* (5–7). Illus. by Iassen Ghiuselev. 2002, Simply Read $29.95 (978-0-9688768-0-0). The full text of the original is used here with effective black-and-white illustrations and several full-page watercolors. (Rev: BL 4/1/02)

12303 Collodi, Carlo. *Pinocchio* (3–5). Illus. by Robert Ingpen. 2005, Purple Bear $19.95 (978-1-933327-00-6).

136pp. A handsome, large-format version of the classic tale about the puppet who wants to become a real boy. (Rev: BL 11/15/05; SLJ 12/05) [398.2]

12304 Compestine, Ying Chang. *The Real Story of Stone Soup* (PS–2). Illus. by Stephanie Jorisch. 2007, Dutton $16.99 (978-0-525-47493-7). 32pp. An officious, lazy fisherman gets his comeuppance when his young assistants convince him that the flavor in the soup comes from carefully chosen stones, while the pictures show the truth. (Rev: BL 1/1–15/07; SLJ 1/07) [398.2]

12305 Conger, David, et al., retels. *Asian Children's Favorite Stories: A Treasury of Folktales from China, Japan, Korea, India, the Philippines, Thailand, Indonesia and Malaysia* (K–4). Illus. by Patrick Yee. 2006, Tuttle $24.95 (978-0-8048-3669-2). 112pp. A collection of 13 tales from different Asian countries including "The Lucky Farmer Becomes King" and "The Crane's Gratitude." (Rev: SLJ 3/07) [398.2]

12306 Connolly, James E. *Why the Possum's Tail Is Bare: And Other North American Indian Nature Tales* (4–7). 1992, Stemmer $15.95 (978-0-88045-069-0); paper $7.95 (978-0-88045-107-9). Nature and folklore are combined in 13 Native American animal tales. (Rev: BL 9/1/85; SLJ 10/85) [398.2]

12307 Conover, Sarah, ed. *Kindness: A Treasury of Buddhist Wisdom for Children and Parents* (4–7). 2001, Eastern Washington Univ. paper $19.95 (978-0-910055-67-3). Thirty-one stories related to Buddhism, including Jataka tales about the Buddha's incarnations, have been effectively translated and adapted for this anthology. (Rev: BL 2/15/01; SLJ 3/01) [294.3]

12308 Cooling, Wendy. *Farmyard Tales from Far and Wide* (PS–2). Illus. by Rosslyn Moran. 1998, Barefoot Books $15.95 (978-1-901223-38-5). 48pp. Each of these seven folktales deals with common farmyard animals and comes from the folklore of a different country. (Rev: BL 11/1/98; SLJ 11/98) [398.2]

12309 Coombs, Kate. *Hans My Hedgehog: A Tale from the Brothers Grimm* (K–3). Illus. by John Nickle. 2012, Atheneum $16.99 (978-141691533-1). 40pp. Half hedgehog, half human, Hans seeks understanding and acceptance in an enchanted woodland, where he proves adept at breaking spells and giving guidance. (Rev: BL 1/1/12; LMC 5–6/12; SLJ 1/12) [398.2]

12310 Cooper, Susan, retel. *The Silver Cow: A Welsh Tale* (K–4). Illus. by Warwick Hutton. 1991, Simon & Schuster paper $5.99 (978-0-689-71512-9). 32pp. A greedy farmer inherits a silver cow from his son, who received it for his harp playing. [398.2]

12311 Copper, Melinda. *Snow White* (K–2). Illus. 2005, Dutton $16.99 (978-0-525-47474-6). 40pp. Animals play the leading roles in this beautifully illustrated version of the classic fairy tale from the Brothers Grimm. (Rev: BL 8/05; SLJ 11/05) [398.2]

12312 Corwin, Oliver J. *Hare and Tortoise Race to the Moon* (K–3). Illus. 2002, Abrams $14.95 (978-0-8109-0566-5). 40pp. In this modern twist on Aesop's classic,

Tortoise and Hare race to the moon in rocket ships. (Rev: BL 10/15/02; HBG 3/03; SLJ 11/02) [398.2]

12313 Courlander, Harold, and George Herzog. *The Cow-Tail Switch: And Other West African Stories* (4–6). Illus. by Madye Lee Chastain. 1988, Holt paper $9.95 (978-0-8050-0298-0). 160pp. Originally published in 1947, this is a fine collection of folktales about foolish and wise men and animals. [398.2]

12314 Craft, K. Y. *Cinderella* (2–4). Illus. 2000, North-South LB $15.88 (978-1-58717-005-8). 32pp. An exquisite version of Cinderella based on the Lang and Rackham text and accompanied by wonderful oil-over-watercolor paintings. (Rev: BCCB 11/00; BL 11/1/00*; HBG 3/01; SLJ 11/00) [398.2]

12315 Craft, Mahlon F. *Sleeping Beauty* (2–4). Illus. by Kinuko Craft. 2002, North-South LB $16.50 (978-1-58717-121-5). 32pp. A beautifully illustrated retelling of the traditional fairy tale. (Rev: BCCB 1/03; BL 9/15/02; HBG 3/03; SLJ 10/02) [398.2]

12316 Crook, Connie Brummel. *Maple Moon* (K–4). Illus. by Scott Cameron. 1998, Stoddart $15.95 (978-0-7737-3017-5). 32pp. A crippled young Mississauga boy accidentally discovers tree sap as a source of food for his people in this adaptation of two Native American folktales. (Rev: BL 4/15/98; SLJ 4/98) [398.2]

12317 Cummings, Pat. *Ananse and the Lizard* (PS–3). Illus. 2002, Holt $16.95 (978-0-8050-6476-6). 40pp. The trickster spider meets his match when a cunning lizard wins the competition for the hand of the chief's daughter. (Rev: BL 11/1/02; HBG 3/03; SLJ 10/02) [398.2]

12318 Curry, Jane Louise. *Hold Up the Sky and Other Native American Tales from Texas and the Southern Plains* (3–7). Illus. 2003, Simon & Schuster $17.95 (978-0-689-85287-9). 176pp. These varied folktales offer a mix of adventure, pourquoi stories, and humor and are accompanied by brief supplementary information about the 14 tribes from which they originated. (Rev: BL 4/1/03; HBG 10/03; SLJ 10/03) [398.2]

12319 Czarnota, Lorna MacDonald. *Medieval Tales That Kids Can Read and Tell* (3–6). Series: World Folktale Collections. 2000, August House $21.95 (978-0-87483-589-2); paper $12.95 (978-0-87483-588-5). 96pp. This collection of folk tales suitable for children to tell features such characters as Robin Hood, William Tell, Robert Bruce, Joan of Arc, and Beowulf. (Rev: HBG 10/00; SLJ 2/01) [398.2]

12320 Czernecki, Stefan, and Timothy Rhodes. *The Sleeping Bread* (1–3). Illus. by Stefan Czernecki. 1992, Hyperion $14.95 (978-1-56282-183-8). 40pp. In this Central American folktale, the tears of a beggar who is driven out of town change the village's bread when they are added to the dough. (Rev: BCCB 9/92; BL 4/15/92; SLJ 8/92) [398.2]

12321 Daly, Niki. *Pretty Salma: Little Red Riding Hood Story from Africa* (PS–2). Illus. 2007, Clarion $16.00 (978-0-618-72345-4). In Ghana, pretty Salma disobeys her grandmother and talks to a strange Mr. Dog, who takes her clothes and tricks Granny into thinking he's Salma. (Rev: BL 2/1/07) [398.2]

12322 Datlow, Ellen, and Terri Windling, eds. *Troll's-Eye View: A Book of Villainous Tales* (5–8). 2009, Viking $16.99 (978-0-670-06141-9). 176pp. The villains in fairy tales get a chance to tell their stories in this collection of varied, original tales and poems by authors including Neil Gaiman, Garth Nix, and Jane Yolen. ALA Notable Children's Book. (Rev: BCCB 7–8/09; BL 3/1/09; LMC 8–9/09; SLJ 4/09)

12323 Davis, Aubrey. *Bone Button Borscht* (K–3). Illus. by Dusan Petricic. 1997, Kids Can $15.95 (978-1-55074-224-4). An Eastern European version of *Stone Soup*, in which a beggar persuades the synagogue caretaker to let him make borscht from his coat buttons. (Rev: BL 11/1/97; SLJ 11/97) [398.2]

12324 Davis, Aubrey. *The Enormous Potato* (PS–1). Illus. by Dusan Petricic. 1998, Kids Can $14.95 (978-1-55074-386-9). 32pp. This variation on the Russian tale about a turnip uses a gigantic potato that again requires the help of everyone, including a tiny mouse, to get it out of the ground. (Rev: BCCB 10/98; BL 11/1/98; HBG 3/99; SLJ 11/98) [398.2]

12325 Davis, Aubrey. *Sody Salleratus* (PS–2). Illus. by Alan Daniel and Lea Daniel. 1998, Kids Can $14.95 (978-1-55074-281-7). 32pp. In this American folktale, a wise squirrel solves the problem of having a bear in town that delights in eating everyone. (Rev: BL 3/15/98; HBG 10/98; SLJ 4/98) [398.2]

12326 Davis, David. *Fandango Stew* (PS–4). Illus. by Ben Galbraith. 2011, Sterling $14.95 (978-1-4027-6527-8). 32pp. This frontier version of the familiar "Stone Soup" tale features two hard-up hombres, Slim and his grandson Luis, who make a delicious pot of soup from one lowly fandango bean. Lexile AD820L (Rev: BL 3/15/11; LMC 8–9/10; SLJ 4/11) [398.2]

12327 Davis, David. *Texas Zeke and the Longhorn* (PS–3). Illus. by Alan Fearl Stacy. 2006, Pelican $15.95 (978-1-58980-348-0). Set in Texas, this version of "The Old Woman and Her Pig" features Old Zeke, who buys a longhorn steer that refuses to be corralled and must turn to a parade of others for help. (Rev: SLJ 9/06) [398.2]

12328 Davis, Donald. *Jack and the Animals* (PS–2). Illus. by Kitty Harvill. 1995, August House $15.95 (978-0-87483-413-0). 32pp. Jack and a group of unhappy animals outwit a gang of robbers in this Appalachian tale. (Rev: BL 10/1/95; SLJ 1/96)

12329 Davis, Donald. *The Pig Who Went Home on Sunday: An Appalachian Folktale* (K–4). Illus. by Jennifer Mazzucco. 2004, August House $16.95 (978-0-87483-571-7). In this Appalachian variation of "The Three Little Pigs," only one youngster heeds his mother's advice and survives to come home at the weekend. (Rev: SLJ 8/04) [398.2]

12330 Davison, Katherine. *Moon Magic: Stories from Asia* (3–5). Illus. 1994, Carolrhoda LB $19.95 (978-0-87614-751-1). A retelling of four Asian myths that deal with the moon and its phases. (Rev: BL 5/15/94; SLJ 6/94) [398.2]

12331 Day, Nancy Raines. *Piecing Earth and Sky Together* (2–4). Illus. by Genna Panzarella. 2001, Shen's $17.95 (978-1-885008-19-0). 32pp. In this creation story from Laos with beautiful illustrations, two heavenly brothers set out to create the sky and the earth. (Rev: BL 4/1/02; HBG 10/02; SLJ 7/02) [398.2]

12332 de Hann, Linda, and Stern Nijland. *King and King* (PS–2). Illus. 2002, Tricycle $15.99 (978-1-58246-061-1). When his mother the queen wants him to marry, a prince falls in love with another prince, and they marry and live happily ever after in this alternative fairy tale. (Rev: BL 7/02; HB 7/02; HBG 10/02; SLJ 3/02) [398.2]

12333 de la Mare, Walter. *The Turnip* (1–4). Illus. by Kevin Hawkes. 1992, Godine $18.95 (978-0-87923-934-3). 32pp. Based on a Grimm brothers tale, the story of a good but poor man with an enormous turnip and his greedy, rich half-brother. (Rev: BL 11/15/92; HB 1/93; SLJ 12/92) [398.2]

12334 de la Paz, Myrna J. *Abadeha: The Philippine Cinderella* (K–3). Illus. by Youshan Tang. 2001, Shen's $16.95 (978-1-885008-17-6). 32pp. A Philippine version of the Cinderella story in which Abadeha is helped by kindly spirits and wins the prince by removing a ring that is stuck on his finger. (Rev: BL 7/01; HBG 3/02; SLJ 12/01) [398.2]

12335 De Montano, Marty Kreipe. *Coyote in Love with a Star* (PS–3). Illus. by Tom Coffin. 1998, Abbeville $14.95 (978-0-7892-0162-1). In this updated pourquoi tale that explains why coyotes howl at the moon, Coyote travels to New York City and there falls in love with a star. (Rev: BL 12/1/98; HB 3/99; HBG 3/99; SLJ 2/99) [398.2]

12336 De Regniers, Beatrice S. *Little Sister and the Month Brothers* (K–3). Illus. by Margot Tomes. 1976, Houghton $8.95 (978-0-8164-3147-2). 48pp. A delightful retelling of an old Slavic tale reminiscent of the Cinderella theme. [398.2]

12337 de Sauza, James. *Brother Anansi and the Cattle Ranch / El Hermano Anansi y el Rancho de Ganada* (3–6). Adapted by Harriet Rohmer. Illus. by Stephen Von Mason. 1989, Children's Book Pr. $14.95 (978-0-89239-044-1). A bilingual retelling of the ancient folktale about the trickster spider, now transplanted to Nicaragua. Two others in this dual-language series are: *Mr. Sugar Came to Town/La Visita del Señor Azucar* (1989); *Uncle Nacho's Hat/El Sombrero de Tio Nacho* (1989). (Rev: BL 11/15/89) [398.2]

12338 Dee, Ruby. *Two Ways to Count to Ten: A Liberian Folktale* (PS–1). Illus. by Susan Meddaugh. 1990, Holt paper $6.95 (978-0-8050-1314-6). 32pp. The antelope outsmarts them all when the king advertises for a successor. (Rev: BL 7/88; SLJ 6–7/88) [398.2]

12339 Deedy, Carmen A. *Martina the Beautiful Cockroach* (K–3). Illus. by Michael Austin. 2007, Peachtree $16.95 (978-1-56145-399-3). 32pp. A surprise ends this rollicking story of how Martina, a lovely cockroach,

chooses a husband; an adaptation of a Cuban folktale. (Rev: BL 10/1/07; LMC 1/08; SLJ 10/07) [398.2] ∩

12340 DeFelice, Cynthia. *Nelly May Has Her Say* (PS–3). Illus. by Henry Cole. 2013, Farrar $16.99 (978-0-374-39899-6). 32pp. Eager to please her new master, Nelly May Nimble, the oldest of 13 needy siblings, accedes to his demands to use special names for ordinary objects — until a crisis erupts. **e** (Rev: BL 3/1/13*; HB 3–4/13; LMC 10/13; SLJ 2/13*) [398.20942]

12341 DeFelice, Cynthia, and Mary DeMarsh. *Three Perfect Peaches* (K–2). Illus. by Irene Trivas. 1995, Orchard LB $16.99 (978-0-531-08722-0). 32pp. In this French folktale, a young farmboy claims the hand of a princess he helped save from death. (Rev: BCCB 4/95; BL 1/15/95; SLJ 4/95) [398.2]

12342 Del Negro, Janice M. *Willa and the Wind* (1–3). Illus. by Heather Solomon. 2005, Marshall Cavendish $16.95 (978-0-7614-5232-4). In this adaptation of an old Norwegian folktale adorned with airy, swirling illustrations, courageous Willa confronts the North Wind and a wicked innkeeper. (Rev: BL 9/1/05; SLJ 12/05) [398.2]

12343 Delacre, Lulu, retel. *Golden Tales: Myths, Legends, and Folktales from Latin America* (4–8). Retold by Lulu Delacre. 1996, Scholastic paper $18.95 (978-0-590-48186-1). Twelve important Latin American folktales from before and after the time of Columbus are featured. (Rev: BL 12/15/96; SLJ 9/96) [398.2]

12344 Delessert, Etienne. *The Seven Dwarfs* (3–4). Illus. 2001, Creative Editions LB $17.95 (978-1-56846-139-7). 32pp. One of Snow White's dwarfs, Stephane, recounts the princess's story in this imaginative take on the fairy tale. (Rev: BL 1/1–15/02; HB 1/02; HBG 3/02) [398.2]

12345 Demi. *The Dragon's Tale and Other Animal Fables of the Chinese Zodiac* (3–6). Illus. 1996, Holt $18.95 (978-0-8050-3446-2). 26pp. A collection of 12 fables that involve the animals in the Chinese zodiac. (Rev: BCCB 1/97; BL 9/15/96; SLJ 10/96) [398.2]

12346 Demi. *The Emperor's New Clothes* (PS–3). Illus. 2000, Simon & Schuster $19.95 (978-0-689-83068-6). 42pp. Employing a Chinese motif in the illustrations, this is a new, interesting, multicultural retelling of the Andersen tale. (Rev: BL 6/1–15/00; HB 5/00; HBG 10/00; SLJ 6/00) [398.2]

12347 Demi. *The Empty Pot* (K–2). Illus. by author. 1990, Holt $16.95 (978-0-8050-1217-0). 32pp. Young Ping finds out that honesty pays when the emperor gives seeds to each child in the kingdom to produce the best flower. (Rev: BL 4/1/90; HB 5/90; SLJ 7/90) [398.2]

12348 Demi. *The Greatest Treasure* (PS–3). Illus. 1998, Scholastic $16.95 (978-0-590-31339-1). In this retelling of a traditional Chinese folktale, poor peasant Li receives a gift of money from his rich neighbor and his lifestyle changes as he begins to worry about how to care for his newfound wealth. (Rev: BL 8/98*; HBG 3/99; SLJ 9/98) [398.2]

12349 Demi. *One Grain of Rice* (3–6). Illus. 1997, Scholastic $19.95 (978-0-590-93998-0). 40pp. Rani outwits the rajah to gain food for her people in this Indian folktale. (Rev: BCCB 2/97; BL 3/1/97*; SLJ 3/97*) [398.2]

12350 Dengler, Marianna. *The Worry Stone* (3–5). Illus. by Sibyl G. Gerig. 1996, Northland LB $15.95 (978-0-87358-642-9). 34pp. When her grandfather dies, Amanda finds that she gets comfort from rubbing a stone that the old man had given to her. (Rev: BL 12/15/96; SLJ 1/97) [398.2]

12351 dePaola, Tomie. *Days of the Blackbird: A Tale of Northern Italy* (K–3). Illus. 1997, Penguin $16.99 (978-0-399-22929-9). 32pp. An Italian tale about a faithful bird that stays through the winter to sing for an ailing duke. (Rev: BL 3/15/97; HB 3/97; SLJ 3/97*)

12352 dePaola, Tomie. *Jamie O'Rourke and the Big Potato: An Irish Folktale* (PS–3). Illus. 1992, Penguin $16.99 (978-0-399-22257-3). 32pp. Lazy Jamie gets a seed from a leprechaun and produces an enormous potato. (Rev: BL 2/15/92; SLJ 4/92) [398.2]

12353 dePaola, Tomie. *The Legend of the Persian Carpet* (K–3). Illus. by Claire Ewart. 1993, Penguin $16.99 (978-0-399-22415-7). 32pp. When his prize diamond is stolen and shattered, a Persian king finds solace in a beautiful new carpet woven for him. (Rev: BL 10/1/93; SLJ 1/94) [398.2]

12354 dePaola, Tomie. *The Legend of the Poinsettia* (K–4). Illus. 1994, Penguin LB $16.99 (978-0-399-21692-3). 32pp. Lucinda is unhappy because she has ruined the blanket that was intended for use in a Christmas procession. (Rev: BL 8/94; HB 11/94; SLJ 4/05) [398.2]

12355 dePaola, Tomie. *The Mysterious Giant of Barletta: An Italian Folktale* (K–3). Illus. by author. 1988, Harcourt paper $6.00 (978-0-15-256349-3). 32pp. A statue of an old lady saves the town from marauders. [398.2]

12356 dePaola, Tomie. *Strega Nona* (PS–2). Illus. by author. 1979, Simon & Schuster paper $6.95 (978-0-671-66606-4). The old Italian folktale retold. Also use: *Big Anthony and the Magic Ring* (1979) and *Strega Nona's Magic Lessons* (1982).

12357 dePaola, Tomie. *Strega Nona: Her Story* (PS–3). Illus. 1996, Penguin $16.99 (978-0-399-22818-6). 32pp. This book supplies background information on the birth and youth of Nona and how she became the village strega. (Rev: BL 9/15/96; HB 11/96; SLJ 10/96) [398.2]

12358 dePaola, Tomie. *Tomie dePaola's Front Porch Tales and North Country Whoppers* (2–5). Illus. by author. 2007, Putnam $17.99 (978-0-399-24754-5). 64pp. Arranged by season, this is a humorous collection of original jokes, tall tales, stories, and short quips inspired by 35 years living in New England. (Rev: BCCB 12/07; BL 11/1/07; SLJ 11/07) [398.2]

12359 dePaola, Tomie, ed. *Tomie dePaola's Favorite Nursery Tales* (PS–3). Illus. by Tomie dePaola. 1986, Penguin $25.99 (978-0-399-21319-9). 128pp. The artist's favorite childhood remembrances in an attractive package. (Rev: BCCB 2/87; BL 11/1/86; SLJ 1/87) [398.2]

12360 dePaola, Tomie, retel. *Fin M'Coul: The Giant of Knockmany Hill* (PS–3). Illus. by Tomie dePaola. 1981, Holiday House LB $16.95 (978-0-8234-0384-4); paper $6.95 (978-0-8234-0385-1). Fin's wife saves him from the most feared giant in Ireland. [398.2]

12361 dePaola, Tomie, retel. *The Legend of the Bluebonnet: An Old Tale of Texas* (K–3). Illus. by Tomie dePaola. 1983, Penguin $16.99 (978-0-399-20937-6). 32pp. This book retells the Comanche Indian story of the origin of the Texas bluebonnet flower. [398.2]

12362 DeSpain, Pleasant. *The Dancing Turtle: A Folktale from Brazil* (K–3). Illus. by David Boston. 1998, August House $15.95 (978-0-87483-502-1). Through trickery, wily Turtle escapes from her human captors in this Brazilian folktale set in a tropical rain forest. (Rev: BL 5/1/98; HBG 10/98; SLJ 5/98) [398.2]

12363 DeSpain, Pleasant. *Sweet Land of Story: Thirty-Six American Tales to Tell* (4–6). Illus. 2000, August House $19.95 (978-0-87483-569-4). This anthology of 36 American folktales ranges from tall tales and Native American stories to Jack tales and traditional ghost stories. (Rev: BL 12/15/00; HBG 10/01; SLJ 12/00) [398.2]

12364 DeSpain, Pleasant. *Tales of Cats* (3–5). Illus. by Don Bell. Series: The Books of Nine Lives. 2003, August House $14.95 (978-0-87483-713-1). Nine folktales about cats from diverse cultures may appeal in particular to reluctant readers. (Rev: HBG 4/04; SLJ 1/04) [398.2]

12365 DeSpain, Pleasant. *Tales of Enchantment* (3–5). Illus. by Don Bell. Series: The Books of Nine Lives. 2003, August House $14.95 (978-0-87483-711-7). 80pp. This collection of nine folk tales offers stories of fantasy and the supernatural from cultures around the world. (Rev: HBG 4/04; SLJ 1/04) [398.2]

12366 DeSpain, Pleasant. *Tales of Nonsense and Tomfoolery* (3–5). Illus. Series: Books of Nine Lives. 2001, August House paper $3.99 (978-0-87483-645-5). 80pp. A collection of tales from around the world that specialize in nonsense. (Rev: BL 7/01) [398.2]

12367 DeSpain, Pleasant. *Tales of Tricksters* (3–5). Illus. Series: Books of Nine Lives. 2001, August House paper $3.99 (978-0-87483-644-8). 80pp. A collection of tales from around the world that specialize in tricksters. (Rev: BL 7/01) [398.2]

12368 DeSpain, Pleasant. *Tales of Wisdom and Justice* (3–5). Illus. Series: Books of Nine Lives. 2001, August House paper $3.99 (978-0-87483-646-2). 80pp. A collection of tales from around the world that specialize in wise decisions. (Rev: BL 7/01) [398.2]

12369 DeSpain, Pleasant. *Tales to Frighten and Delight* (3–5). Illus. by Don Bell. Series: The Books of Nine Lives. 2003, August House $14.95 (978-0-87483-712-4). Nine spine-chilling folktales are collected from cultures around the world. (Rev: HBG 4/04; SLJ 1/04) [398.27]

12370 DeSpain, Pleasant, retel. *Thirty-Three Multicultural Tales to Tell* (3–7). Illus. by Joe Shlichta. Series: American Folklore and Storytelling. 1993, August House paper $15.00 (978-0-87483-266-2). 126pp. An interesting international collection of folktales that span a number of subjects and moods. (Rev: SLJ 6/94) [398.2]

12371 Diakité, Baba Wague. *The Hunterman and the Crocodile: A West African Folktale* (K–3). Illus. 1997, Scholastic $16.95 (978-0-590-89828-7). 32pp. A West African folktale about the Hunterman who runs afoul of Bamba the Crocodile and is helped by Rabbit. (Rev: BCCB 2/97; BL 3/15/97; SLJ 3/97) [398.2]

12372 Diakité, Baba Wague. *The Magic Gourd* (2–4). Illus. 2003, Scholastic $16.95 (978-0-439-43960-2). 32pp. A retelling of a folktale from Mali about a rabbit who, when his magic gourd is stolen, receives a magic rock to help recover it. (Rev: BCCB 3/03; BL 2/15/03; HBG 10/03; SLJ 2/03) [398.2]

12373 Diakité, Baba Wague, retel. *The Hatseller and the Monkeys* (K–3). Illus. by Baba Wague Diakité. 1999, Scholastic $17.99 (978-0-590-96069-4). This is an interesting West African version of the traditional tale about a peddler whose hats are stolen by a group of monkeys. (Rev: BCCB 2/99; HB 5/99; HBG 10/99; SLJ 2/99) [398.2]

12374 Dijkstra, Lida. *Little Mouse* (PS–K). Illus. by Lida Grobler. 2004, Front St. $15.95 (978-1-932425-06-2). 32pp. A retelling of a traditional tale in which a little mouse, accompanied by her adoptive hermit father, searches for "the strongest being on earth" to be her mate. (Rev: BL 1/1–15/05; SLJ 2/05) [398.2]

12375 Dominic, Gloria, adapt. *Brave Bear and the Ghosts: A Sioux Legend* (2–4). Illus. by Charles Reasoner. Series: Native American Lore and Legends. 1996, Rourke LB $19.95 (978-0-86593-429-0). 47pp. A charming trickster tale with a surprise ending from the Sioux. Also use *Coyote and the Grasshoppers: A Pomo Legend* and *Song of the Hermit Thrush: An Iroquois Legend* (both 1996). (Rev: SLJ 3/97) [398.2]

12376 Dorson, Mercedes, and Jeanne Wilmot. *Tales from the Rain Forest: Myths and Legends from the Amazonian Indians of Brazil* (5–8). 1997, Ecco $18.00 (978-0-88001-567-7). Ten entertaining folktales from the Amazonian Indians of Brazil. (Rev: BL 2/15/98; HB 3–4/98; HBG 10/98) [398.2]

12377 Doucet, Sharon Arms. *Lapin Plays Possum: Trickster Tales from the Louisiana Bayou* (4–6). Illus. by Scott Cook. 2002, Farrar $18.10 (978-0-374-34328-6). 64pp. This is a well-illustrated collection of three tales about the trickster rabbit from Cajun country told with many humorous bayou phrases. (Rev: BL 4/15/02; HB 5/02; HBG 10/02; SLJ 4/02) [398.2]

12378 Doucet, Sharon Arms. *Why Lapin's Ears Are Long and Other Tales from the Louisiana Bayou* (4–6). Illus. by David Catrow. 1997, Orchard LB $19.99 (978-0-531-33041-8). 64pp. Three entertaining folktales from Cajun country that feature the trickster rabbit. (Rev: BL 8/97; HB 9/97; HBG 3/98; SLJ 9/97) [398.2]

12379 Downard, Barry, retel. *The Race of the Century* (PS–5). Illus. by reteller. 2008, Simon & Schuster $15.99 (978-1-4169-2509-5). A funny retelling of the race between the tortoise and the hare, in which it is a big media event. (Rev: BCCB 1/08; LMC 3/08; SLJ 2/08) [398.24]

12380 Doyle, Malachy. *The Barefoot Book of Fairy Tales* (K–3). Illus. by Nicoletta Ceccoli. 2005, Barefoot Books $19.99 (978-1-84148-798-4). Twelve fairy tales from around the world are collected in this quirky and accessible anthology. (Rev: BL 12/1/05; SLJ 2/06) [398.2]

12381 Doyle, Malachy. *Tales from Old Ireland* (3–6). Illus. 2000, Barefoot Books $19.99 (978-1-902283-97-5). 96pp. A heady collection of traditional Irish tales that includes the familiar "Children of Lir" and "The Soul Cages." (Rev: BL 11/15/00; HB 3/01; HBG 10/01; SLJ 11/00) [398.2]

12382 Duvall, Deborah L. *The Opossum's Tale: A Grandmother Story* (PS–2). Illus. by Murv Jacob. 2005, Univ. of New Mexico $15.95 (978-0-8263-3694-1). Based on Cherokee folklore, this richly illustrated picture book tells how the opossum got its distinctive hairless tail. (Rev: BL 3/15/06; SLJ 2/06) [398.2]

12383 Dwyer, Mindy, retel. *Coyote in Love* (PS–3). Illus. by Mindy Dwyer. 1997, Alaska Northwest $15.95 (978-0-88240-485-1). This Native American tale of how Crater Lake was formed tells of Coyote's unrequited love for a star. (Rev: SLJ 7/97) [398.2]

12384 Echewa, T. Obinkaram. *The Magic Tree: A Folktale from Nigeria* (PS–3). Illus. by E. B. Lewis. 1999, Morrow LB $15.89 (978-0-688-16232-0). 32pp. In this Nigerian folktale, a young outsider gains power and prestige when a magic udara tree gives him fruit and obeys his commands. (Rev: BCCB 4/99; BL 6/1–15/99*; HBG 10/99; SLJ 8/99) [398.2]

12385 Edens, Cooper, ed. *Princess Stories: A Classic Illustrated Edition* (2–4). Series: Classics Illustrated Editions. 2004, Chronicle $19.95 (978-0-8118-4032-3). 136pp. Familiar stories — by Hans Christian Andersen, the Grimm brothers, and Charles Perrault, among others — of princesses pursuing romantic aspirations are paired with vintage images. (Rev: BL 10/15/04; SLJ 1/05) [398.2]

12386 Edmonds, I. G. *Ooka the Wise: Tales of Old Japan* (3–6). Illus. by Sanae Yamazaki. 1994, Linnet LB $16.00 (978-0-208-02379-7). 96pp. A collection of 17 Japanese folktales featuring the legendary judge Ooka Tadasuke, who is devoted to the cause of justice. (Rev: BL 5/15/94) [398.2]

12387 Egielski, Richard. *Saint Francis and the Wolf* (PS–2). Illus. 2005, HarperCollins $15.99 (978-0-06-623870-8). 40pp. St. Francis communicates with a wolf that has been terrorizing an Italian town and strikes a compromise that satisfies all parties. (Rev: BL 10/1/05*; SLJ 10/05) [398.2]

12388 Ehlert, Lois. *Cuckoo / Cucu* (PS–2). Trans. by Gloria de Aragon Andujar. Illus. 1997, Harcourt $16.00 (978-0-15-200274-9). 40pp. In this Mayan tale, Cuckoo saves the annual harvest of seeds on which the other birds live during the winter. (Rev: BCCB 6/97; BL 4/1/97*; HBG 3/98; SLJ 3/97) [398.2]

12389 Ehlert, Lois. *Moon Rope: A Peruvian Folktale* (4–8). 1992, Harcourt $17.00 (978-0-15-255343-2). In both English and Spanish, this is the story of Fox, who wants to go to the moon and persuades his friend Mole to go along. (Rev: BCCB 12/92; BL 10/15/92*; HB 11–12/92; SLJ 10/92*) [398.2]

12390 Eilenberg, Max. *Beauty and the Beast* (2–4). Illus. by Angela Barrett. 2006, Candlewick $17.99 (978-0-7636-3160-4). A wonderful retelling of the classic tale of Beauty and the Beast, set in the nineteenth century and accompanied by lovely, expressive watercolor illustrations. (Rev: BL 12/1/06; SLJ 12/06*) [398.2]

12391 Eisner, Will. *Sundiata: A Legend of Africa* (5–8). 2003, NBM $15.95 (978-1-56163-332-6). A retelling, in comic book style, of an African folktale about a lame prince who conquers an evil king. (Rev: BL 2/1/03; HBG 10/03; SLJ 2/03) [398.2]

12392 Elya, Susan Middleton. *Rubia and the Three Osos* (PS–2). Illus. by Melissa Sweet. 2010, Hyperion/Disney $15.99 (978-1-4231-1252-5). 40pp. With Spanish words sprinkled throughout, this retelling of Goldilocks set in the Southwest includes a glossary. Lexile AD450L (Rev: BLO 8/10; SLJ 10/1/10) [394.2]

12393 Emberley, Rebecca, and Ed Emberley. *Chicken Little* (PS–K). Illus. by Rebecca Emberley. 2009, Roaring Brook $16.95 (978-1-59643-464-6). 32pp. Bright, colorful collage illustrations full of fun enhance this lively retelling. (Rev: BL 5/1/09; HB 5/09; SLJ 5/09) [398.2]

12394 Endredy, James. *The Journey of Tunuri and the Blue Deer: A Huichol Indian Story* (1–4). 2003, Bear & Company $15.95 (978-1-59143-016-2). 32pp. Based on a traditional folk tale, this gentle story highlighted by traditional yarn art tells how an enchanted deer leads a young Huichol boy on a magical journey to meet the spirits of nature. (Rev: BL 12/1/03; SLJ 1/04) [398.2]

12395 Ensor, Barbara. *Cinderella (As If You Didn't Already Know the Story)* (3–6). Illus. 2006, Random $12.95 (978-0-375-83620-6). 109pp. Cinderella and her prince end up living happily ever after in this retelling, each finding a fulfilling career; Cinderella's letters to her deceased mother tell part of the story. (Rev: SLJ 7/06) [398.2]

12396 Ensor, Barbara. *Thumbelina, Tiny Runaway Bride* (2–5). Illus. by author. 2008, Random $12.99 (978-0-375-83960-3). 160pp. The story of Thumbelina is reimagined in this early chapter book. (Rev: BL 7/08; LMC 8/08; SLJ 11/08) [398.2]

12397 Ernst, Judith, retel. *The Golden Goose King: A Tale Told by the Buddha* (3–6). Illus. by Judith Ernst. 1995, Parvardigar $19.95 (978-0-9644362-0-6). A Jataka tale about a queen who captures the Golden Goose King, who is actually Buddha. (Rev: BL 9/1/95; SLJ 9/95) [398.2]

12398 Ernst, Lisa Campbell. *The Gingerbread Girl* (PS–2). 2006, Dutton $16.99 (978-0-525-47667-2). 32pp. In this whimsical twist on the story of the Gingerbread Boy, his sister proves much more resourceful than her ill-fated sibling. (Rev: BL 9/1/06; SLJ 11/06) [398.2]

12399 Esbensen, Barbara J. *Ladder to the Sky: How the Gift of Healing Came to the Ojibway Nation* (K–3). Illus.

by Helen K. Davie. 1989, Little, Brown $15.95 (978-0-316-24952-2). 32pp. Although the Ojibwa (Chippewa) lost their direct connection to the Great Spirit, they were granted healing powers. (Rev: BCCB 2/90; BL 11/1/89; SLJ 10/89) [398.2]

12400 Escardo i Bas, Merce. *The Three Little Pigs / Los tres cerditos* (K–2). Illus. by Pere Joan. 2006, Chronicle $14.95 (978-0-8118-5063-6). 24pp. The familiar story is told in both English and Spanish, with comic-book style illustrations. (Rev: BL 5/1/06; SLJ 6/06) [398.2]

12401 Escott, John, retel. *The Little Red Hen* (PS–K). Illus. by Annie West. 2003, Gingham Dog $15.95 (978-1-57768-492-3). 32pp. A retelling of the story of the Little Red Hen and her unhelpful friends. (Rev: HBG 4/04; SLJ 4/04) [398.2]

12402 Evetts-Secker, Josephine. *The Barefoot Book of Father and Son Tales* (3–6). Illus. 1999, Barefoot Books $19.95 (978-1-902283-32-6). 80pp. Father-son relationships are explored in this collection of folktales that includes the Daedalus-Icarus myth. (Rev: BL 4/1/99; SLJ 6/99) [398.27]

12403 Evetts-Secker, Josephine. *The Barefoot Book of Mother and Son Tales* (3–6). 1999, Barefoot Books $19.95 (978-1-902283-05-0). 80pp. Using colorful illustrations and a choice of tales from the world's folklore, this collection explores mother-son relationships. (Rev: BL 4/1/99; SLJ 6/99) [398.27]

12404 Evetts-Secker, Josephine. *Little Red Riding Hood* (PS–2). Illus. by Nicoletta Ceccoli. 2004, Barefoot Books $16.99 (978-1-84148-621-5). 32pp. Nicoletta Ceccoli's stunning artwork enlivens this child-friendly retelling. (Rev: BL 3/15/04; SLJ 8/04) [389.2]

12405 Ferris, Jean. *Once Upon a Marigold* (5–8). 2002, Harcourt $17.00 (978-0-15-216791-2). Christian falls in love with Princess Marigold and wins her heart through his bravery in this fairy tale full of fun. (Rev: BCCB 2/03; BL 9/15/02; HB 9–10/02; HBG 3/03; SLJ 11/02; VOYA 12/02)

12406 Ferris, Jean. *Twice Upon a Marigold: Part Comedy, Part Tragedy, Part Two* (5–8). 2008, Harcourt $17.00 (978-0-15-206382-5). Queen Marigold and King Christian, introduced in *Once upon a Marigold*, are now married and Queen Olympia, who fell into a river at the end of the first book, is now dried off and back to her wicked ways. (Rev: BL 4/15/08; SLJ 6/08)

12407 Finch, Mary. *The Little Red Hen and the Ear of Wheat* (PS–K). Illus. by Elisabeth Bell. Series: A Barefoot Beginner Book. 1999, Barefoot Books $15.95 (978-1-902283-47-0). A retelling of the famous folktale about the little red hen who can't find helpers to prepare a loaf of bread. (Rev: SLJ 5/99) [398.2]

12408 Finch, Mary, retel. *The Three Billy Goats Gruff* (PS). Illus. by Roberta Arenson. 2001, Barefoot Books LB $15.99 (978-1-84148-349-8). A gentler version of the tale for this young age group, with colorful goats and a singing troll. (Rev: HBG 3/02; SLJ 11/01) [398.2]

12409 Fleischman, Paul. *Glass Slipper, Gold Sandal* (K–2). Illus. by Julie Paschkis. 2007, Holt $16.95 (978-

0-8050-7953-1). Fleischman interweaves elements of a number of cultures in this unusual and beautifully illustrated retelling of Cinderella. (Rev: BCCB 11/07; BL 11/15/07; HB 1/08; LMC 11/07; SLJ 9/07) [398.2]

12410 Foreman, Michael. *Rock-A-Doodle-Do!* (K–2). Illus. 2000, Andersen $16.95 (978-0-86264-951-7). 32pp. This entertaining version of *The Bremen Town Musicians* takes place in the American Southwest in the 1950s. (Rev: BL 3/1/01)

12411 Forest, Heather. *The Contest Between the Sun and the Wind* (K–3). Illus. by Susan Gaber. 2008, August House $16.95 (978-0-87483-832-9). 32pp. This Aesop fable retells the story of how the wind and the sun battle to make a man take off his coat. (Rev: BL 3/15/08; SLJ 4/08) [398.2]

12412 Forest, Heather. *Stone Soup* (PS–3). Illus. by Susan Gaber. 1998, August House $15.95 (978-0-87483-498-7). 32pp. Using a contemporary village as its setting, this is a handsome retelling of the ancient tale that originated in France and, in a different version, Sweden. (Rev: BL 9/1/98; HBG 10/98; SLJ 5/98) [398.2]

12413 Forest, Heather. *Wisdom Tales from Around the World* (4–7). 1996, August House $27.95 (978-0-87483-478-9); paper $19.95 (978-0-87483-479-6). Fifty fables, folktales, and myths from around the world. (Rev: BCCB 2/97; BL 3/1/97; SLJ 4/97) [398.2]

12414 Forest, Heather. *The Woman Who Flummoxed the Fairies: An Old Tale from Scotland* (K–3). Illus. by Susan Gaber. 1990, Harcourt $14.95 (978-0-15-299150-0). In this retelling of a tale from Scotland, the fairies kidnap a baker so she will make cakes only for them. (Rev: BL 4/1/90; SLJ 6/90) [398.2]

12415 Forest, Heather. *Wonder Tales from Around the World* (4–6). Illus. 1995, August House paper $16.95 (978-0-87483-422-2). 160pp. A collection of 27 traditional stories, some familiar and others never anthologized before. (Rev: BL 11/15/95; SLJ 4/96) [398.2]

12416 Forest, Heather, retel. *The Little Red Hen: An Old Fable* (PS–2). Illus. by Susan Gaber. 2006, August House $16.95 (978-0-87483-795-7). A charming, rhyming version of the classic story featuring a black-and-white cat, a Corgi with a blanket, and a literary mouse as the hen's friends. (Rev: SLJ 11/06) [398.2]

12417 Fox, Paula. *Amzat and His Brothers: Three Italian Tales* (3–5). Illus. by Emily Arnold McCully. 1993, Orchard $16.95 (978-0-531-05462-8). 80pp. Tales retold from a grandfather who lived in a small Italian village. (Rev: BCCB 3/93*; BL 3/15/93; HB 7/93; SLJ 7/93) [398.2]

12418 French, Fiona, retel. *Jamil's Clever Cat: A Folk Tale from Bengal* (PS–2). Illus. by Fiona French and Dick Newby. 1999, Star Bright $13.95 (978-1-887734-72-1). In this tale from Bengal, a cat helps his master gain riches and a bride. (Rev: SLJ 3/00) [398.2]

12419 Froese, Deborah. *The Wise Washerman: A Folktale from Burma* (K–3). Illus. by Wang Kui. 1996, Hyperion LB $15.49 (978-0-7868-2232-4). A jealous neighbor tries to get an industrious washerwoman into trouble in this Burmese folktale. (Rev: BCCB 12/96; SLJ 1/97) [398.2]

12420 Fusek-Peters, Andrew. *The Tiger and the Wise Man* (PS–2). Illus. by Diana Mayo. 2005, Child's Play paper $7.99 (978-1-904550-07-5). 32pp. In this brightly illustrated retelling of a traditional Indian folktale, a wise man may have to pay a very high price for foolishly releasing a vicious tiger from its cage. (Rev: BL 8/05; SLJ 6/05) [398.2]

12421 Gal, Laszlo, and Raffaella Gal. *The Parrot* (K–3). Illus. 1997, Douglas & McIntyre $16.95 (978-0-88899-287-1). In this Italian folktale, a prince assumes the identity of a parrot to help a princess. (Rev: BL 9/15/97; SLJ 10/97) [398.2]

12422 Galdone, Joanna. *The Tailypo: A Ghost Story* (1–3). Illus. by Paul Galdone. 1984, Houghton paper $7.95 (978-0-395-30084-8). In this ghostly story, a mysterious creature returns to retrieve his tail, cut off by an old man. [398.2]

12423 Galdone, Paul. *The Gingerbread Boy* (PS–1). Illus. by author. 1983, Houghton $16.00 (978-0-395-28799-6); paper $6.95 (978-0-89919-163-8). 40pp. Humorous and vigorous illustrations enhance this favorite folktale of the adventures of a runaway gingerbread boy. [398.2]

12424 Galdone, Paul. *Henny Penny* (K–2). Illus. by author. 1979, Houghton $16.00 (978-0-395-28800-9); paper $6.95 (978-0-89919-225-3). 32pp. A retelling of the favorite cumulative folktale of the hen who thought the sky was falling. [398.2]

12425 Galdone, Paul. *The Little Red Hen* (K–2). Illus. by author. 1979, Houghton $15.00 (978-0-395-28803-0); paper $5.95 (978-0-89919-349-6). A little hen works for her lazy housemates in this reworking of the old tale. Another fine edition is: *The Little Red Hen: An Old Story*, illus. by Margot Zemach (1983, Farrar).

12426 Galdone, Paul. *The Monkey and the Crocodile: A Jataka Tale from India* (K–3). Illus. by author. 1969, Houghton paper $6.95 (978-0-89919-524-7). 32pp. A crocodile decides he will catch a monkey. [398.2]

12427 Galdone, Paul. *The Three Bears* (K–2). Illus. by author. 1979, Houghton $16.00 (978-0-395-28811-5); paper $6.95 (978-0-89919-401-1). The illustrations for this familiar story are large, colorful, and humorous; excellent to use with a group. [398.2]

12428 Galdone, Paul. *The Three Billy Goats Gruff* (PS–3). Illus. by author. 1973, Houghton $16.00 (978-0-395-28812-2). 32pp. A troll meets his match. (Rev: SLJ 3/05) [398.2]

12429 Galdone, Paul. *The Three Little Pigs* (PS–1). Illus. by author. 1979, Houghton $16.00 (978-0-395-28813-9). The old folktale told in verse. Another recommended edition is: Illus. by Erik Blegvad (1980, Macmillan).

12430 Galdone, Paul. *The Turtle and the Monkey: A Philippine Tale* (K–2). Illus. by author. 1990, Houghton paper $7.95 (978-0-395-54425-9). 32pp. Turtle asks monkey to help him save a banana tree. [398.2]

12431 Ganeri, Anita. *Islamic Stories* (1–6). Illus. by Rebecca Wallis. Series: Traditional Religious Tales. 2006,

Picture Window LB $26.60 (978-1-4048-1313-7). 32pp. Most of the Islamic stories in this collection recount incidents from the life of Muhammad, but they also touch on Abraham, Hagar, Ishmael, and Moses. (Rev: SLJ 4/06) [297.1]

12432 Gardner, Carol. *Princess Zelda and the Frog* (PS–2). Illus. 2011, Feiwel & Friends $16.99 (978-0-312-60325-0). 40pp. Two bulldogs, one dressed as a princess and one as a frog, add considerable humor to this retelling of the traditional story about a frog that turns into a prince. Lexile AD700L (Rev: BLO 8/11; SLJ 6/11) [398.2]

12433 Garland, Sherry. *Children of the Dragon: Selected Tales from Vietnam* (3–5). Illus. 2001, Harcourt $18.00 (978-0-15-224200-8). 64pp. Six tales from Vietnam are introduced by material on the land, its history, and folk traditions. (Rev: BL 7/01; HBG 3/02; SLJ 10/01*) [398.2]

12434 Gelfand, Shoshana Boyd. *The Barefoot Book of Jewish Tales* (3–6). Illus. by Amanda Hall. 2013, Barefoot $19.99 (978-184686884-9). 80pp. This collection of eight traditional Jewish tales, simply written with illustrations in a variety of media, provides children with a good introduction to Jewish moral values and culture. (Rev: BL 11/15/13) [398.2089]

12435 Geras, Adele. *My Grandmother's Stories: A Collection of Jewish Folk Tales* (1–5). Illus. by Anita Lobel. 2003, Knopf LB $21.99 (978-0-375-92285-5). 96pp. In this beautifully illustrated collection, each of 10 stories is introduced by a young girl's question to her grandmother. (Rev: HBG 4/04; SLJ 8/03) [398.2]

12436 Geras, Adele. *Sleeping Beauty* (2–4). Illus. by Christian Birmingham. 2004, Scholastic $18.95 (978-0-439-58180-6). 64pp. Black-and-white illustrations and a number of beautiful pastels enhance this retelling. (Rev: BL 5/1/04; SLJ 8/04) [398.2]

12437 Gershator, David, and Phyllis Gershator. *Kallaloo! A Caribbean Tale* (PS–3). Illus. by Diane Greenseid. 2005, Marshall Cavendish $16.95 (978-0-7614-5110-5). A hungry grandmother decides to make soup from a shell, and the curious neighbors contribute various ingredients in this West Indian version of "Stone Soup." (Rev: SLJ 6/05) [398.2]

12438 Gershator, Phillis. *Only One Cowry* (K–3). Illus. by David Soman. 2000, Orchard LB $17.99 (978-0-531-33288-7). 32pp. This African folktale in picture-book format tells about tricksters, weddings, and dowries and employs collages made of cut and torn paper to illustrate its events. (Rev: BCCB 1/01; BL 10/15/00; HBG 3/01; SLJ 9/00) [398.2]

12439 Gershator, Phillis. *Tukama Tootles the Flute* (PS–3). Illus. by Synthia Saint James. 1994, Orchard LB $16.99 (978-0-531-08661-2). 32pp. A flute-playing youngster uses his music to escape the clutches of a giant in this folktale from the Virgin Islands. (Rev: BCCB 4/94; BL 5/1/94; HB 5/94; SLJ 4/94) [398.2]

12440 Gershator, Phillis. *Zzzng! Zzzng! Zzzng! A Yoruba Tale* (PS–1). Illus. by Theresa Smith. 1998, Orchard

LB $16.99 (978-0-531-08873-9). 32pp. In this Yoruba folktale from Nigeria, Mosquito faces rejection when he tries to marry above his station and takes out his anger by buzzing and biting. (Rev: BCCB 10/98; BL 8/98; HBG 3/99; SLJ 10/98) [398.2]

12441 Gershator, Phillis, and Alexa Ginsburg. *Wise . . . and Not So Wise: Ten Tales from the Rabbis* (3–6). Series: New Children's Titles. 2004, Jewish Publication Soc. $15.95 (978-0-8276-0755-2). 120pp. Ten stories drawn from traditional Jewish sources present interesting situations and are followed by questions that will provoke thoughtful analysis of their meaning and relevance today. (Rev: BL 10/1/04; SLJ 1/05) [296.1]

12442 Gerson, Mary-Joan. *Fiesta Feminina: Celebrating Women in Mexican Folktales* (4–8). 2001, Barefoot $19.99 (978-1-84148-365-8). This volume includes eight tales from Mexican folklore about strong and magical women, presented with bold illustrations, a pronunciation guide, and a glossary. (Rev: BL 9/15/01; HBG 3/02; SLJ 10/01) [398.2]

12443 Gerstein, Mordicai. *The Shadow of a Flying Bird: A Legend from the Kurdistani Jews* (1–5). Illus. 1994, Hyperion LB $16.49 (978-0-7868-2012-2). 32pp. God comes to earth to claim the life of his faithful servant Moses in this Jewish folktale. (Rev: BL 10/1/94; SLJ 9/94) [398.2]

12444 Gibbons, Gail. *Behold . . . the Dragons!* (K–3). Illus. 1999, Morrow LB $17.89 (978-0-688-15527-8). 32pp. Drawing on the world's folklore, this book follows dragons through different cultures and times. (Rev: BL 5/1/99; HBG 10/99; SLJ 4/99) [398]

12445 Gilchrist, Cherry. *A Calendar of Festivals* (3–7). Illus. 1998, Barefoot Books $18.95 (978-1-901223-68-2). 80pp. This anthology includes folktales and stories for many of the major holidays celebrated annually around the world. (Rev: BL 9/15/98; SLJ 12/98) [394.2]

12446 Gilchrist, Cherry. *Stories from the Silk Road* (3–7). Illus. 1999, Barefoot Books $19.95 (978-1-902283-25-8). 80pp. Seven exotic folktales represent the culture and history of the countries along the fabled Silk Road that stretched from China to Persia. (Rev: BL 9/15/99; SLJ 11/99) [398.27]

12447 Gilchrist, Cherry. *Sun-Day, Moon-Day: How the Week Was Made* (3–5). Illus. by Amanda Hall. 1998, Barefoot Books $18.95 (978-1-901223-63-7). 80pp. Each day of the week is highlighted, with background information and a tale from Greek, Norse, Roman, Babylonian, and other folklore traditions. (Rev: SLJ 9/98) [398.2]

12448 Gilman, Phoebe. *Something from Nothing* (PS–3). Illus. 1993, Scholastic $16.95 (978-0-590-47280-7). 32pp. This folktale tells how a frugal grandfather recycles the material from a jacket to ever smaller objects, ending with the covering for a button. (Rev: BCCB 2/94; BL 9/1/93; HB 11/93; SLJ 1/94) [398.2]

12449 Ginsburg, Mirra. *The Chinese Mirror* (1–3). Illus. by Margot Zemach. 1991, Harcourt paper $6.00 (978-0-15-217508-5). 26pp. An old folktale from Korea tells of a man who brings home a mirror — unknown to his fellow villagers — from a trip to China. (Rev: BCCB 5/88; BL 4/15/88; SLJ 4/88) [398.2]

12450 Gittins, Anne. *Tales from the South Pacific Islands* (4–6). Illus. by Frank Rocca. 1977, Stemmer $12.95 (978-0-916144-02-9). 96pp. Twenty-two folktales from such places as Fiji and Samoa in which the sea and its creatures play prominent roles. [398.3]

12451 Goble, Paul. *The Legend of the White Buffalo Woman* (4–8). 1998, National Geographic $16.95 (978-0-7922-7074-4). In this picture book for older readers recounting a Lakata Indian tale, an earth woman and an eagle mate after a great flood to produce a new people. (Rev: BL 3/15/98; HBG 10/98; SLJ 5/98) [398.2]

12452 Goldman, Judy. *Whiskers, Tails and Wings: Animal Folktales from Mexico* (4–6). Illus. by Fabricio VandenBroeck. 2013, Charlesbridge $16.95 (978-158089372-5). 64pp. Five folktales, each from a different indigenous Mexican group and accompanied by acrylic and watercolor images on textured paper, are retold in this engaging and informative book that gives readers a cultural awareness of various Mexican societies. (Rev: BLO 11/15/13; LMC 3–4/14; SLJ 9/13) [398.20972]

12453 Goode, Diane. *The Dinosaur's New Clothes* (PS–1). Illus. 1999, Scholastic $15.95 (978-0-590-38360-8). 40pp. This variation on the Andersen tale is set in the Palace of Versailles and features dinosaurs as characters. (Rev: BCCB 12/99; BL 11/15/99; HBG 3/00; SLJ 9/99) [398.2]

12454 Gorbachev, Valeri. *Fool of the World and the Flying Ship* (1–3). Illus. by author. 1998, Star Bright $15.95 (978-1-887734-19-6). 40pp. A new adaptation of the Ukrainian tale about a tsar who promises his daughter in marriage to the man who brings him a flying ship. (Rev: SLJ 4/99) [398.2]

12455 Gordon, David. *Hansel and Diesel* (PS–K). 2006, HarperCollins $16.99 (978-0-06-058122-0). 32pp. Hansel and Diesel are two little trucks facing the Wicked Winch in this strikingly illustrated twist on the well-known fairy tale. (Rev: BL 5/1/06; SLJ 7/06) [398.2]

12456 Gray, Luli. *Ant and Grasshopper* (PS–2). Illus. by Giuliano Ferri. 2011, Simon & Schuster $16.99 (978-1-4169-5140-7). 32pp. In this retelling, cautious Ant prepares carefully for winter while happy-go-lucky Grasshopper prefers to play the fiddle and sing, and the two eventually find they are in fact in harmony. (Rev: BL 2/15/11; SLJ 2/1/11*) [398.2]

12457 Gray, Margaret. *The Ugly Princess and the Wise Fool* (3–6). Illus. by Randy Cecil. 2002, Holt $15.95 (978-0-8050-6847-4). There's a happy ending to this tale despite the fact that the princess is ugly and wisdom has been banned from the land. (Rev: BCCB 12/02; BL 11/15/02; HBG 3/03; SLJ 10/02) [398.2]

12458 Greaves, Nick. *When Hippo Was Hairy: And Other Tales from Africa* (4–8). 1988, Barron's paper $11.95 (978-0-8120-4548-2). Thirty-one traditional African tales, a combination of folklore and fact. (Rev: BL 2/15/89; SLJ 2/89) [398.2]

12459 Green, Roger L. *Adventures of Robin Hood* (5–9). 1994, Knopf $15.00 (978-0-679-43636-2); paper $4.99 (978-0-14-036700-3). The exploits of this folk hero are retold in this reissue of a classic version. [398]

12460 Green, Roger L. *Tales of Ancient Egypt* (5–9). 1972, Penguin paper $4.99 (978-0-14-036716-4). A collection of folktales from ancient Egypt including one about the source of the Nile. [398]

12461 Greene, Ellin. *The Little Golden Lamb* (PS–2). Illus. by Rosanne Litzinger. 2000, Clarion $15.00 (978-0-395-71526-0). 32pp. Anyone who touches the lamb with a golden fleece becomes stuck to it in this amusing folktale. (Rev: BCCB 5/00; BL 3/15/00; HB 5/00; HBG 10/00; SLJ 6/00) [398.22]

12462 Grifalconi, Ann. *The Village of Round and Square Houses* (PS–2). Illus. by author. 1986, Little, Brown $16.95 (978-0-316-32862-3). 32pp. This blend of fiction, anthropology, and folklore centers around the central African remote village of Tos. (Rev: BCCB 6/86; BL 6/15/86; SLJ 8/86) [398.2]

12463 Grimm Brothers. *The Complete Grimm's Fairy Tales* (4–6). Illus. by Josef Scharl. 1974, Pantheon paper $18.00 (978-0-394-70930-7). Based on Margaret Hunt's translation, this has become the standard edition of these perennial favorites. [398.2]

12464 Grimm Brothers. *The Elves and the Shoemaker* (PS–K). Retold and illus. by Paul Galdone. 1984, Houghton paper $6.95 (978-0-89919-422-6). 32pp. A poor shoemaker is visited by elves at night. [398.2]

12465 Grimm Brothers. *The Frog Prince* (1–2). Adapted by Sindy McKay. Illus. by George Ulrich. Series: We Both Read. 1998, Treasure Bay $7.99 (978-1-891327-02-5). This fairy tale is retold twice — with an adult's and a child's vocabulary. (Rev: SLJ 12/98) [398.2]

12466 Grimm Brothers. *Household Stories of the Brothers Grimm* (4–7). Illus. by Walter Crane. 1963, Dover paper $9.95 (978-0-486-21080-3). First published in the United States in 1883. [398.2]

12467 Grimm Brothers. *Little Red Riding Hood / Caperucita roja: A Bilingual Book* (K–2). Trans. by James Surges. Illus. by Pau Estrada. 1999, Chronicle $12.95 (978-0-8118-2561-0); paper $6.95 (978-0-8118-2562-7). A bilingual version of the favorite folktale with charming yet scary illustrations. (Rev: SLJ 2/00) [398.2]

12468 Grimm Brothers. *Rumpelstiltskin* (PS–1). Illus. by Paul Galdone. 1985, Houghton $16.00 (978-0-89919-266-6); paper $7.95 (978-0-395-52599-9). 32pp. Bold drawings highlight this straightfoward version of the little man who spins straw into gold. Another fine edition is: Illus. by John Wallner (1984, Prentice). (Rev: BL 6/1/ 5; SLJ 8/85) [398.2]

12469 Grimm Brothers. *Rumpelstiltskin* (PS–2). Retold by Paul O. Zelinsky. Illus. by reteller. 1986, Dutton $16.99 (978-0-525-44265-3). 40pp. Closeups and much detail in the illustrations highlight the retelling of this old favorite. (Rev: BCCB 10/86; BL 9/1/86; SLJ 10/86) [398.2]

12470 Grimm Brothers. *The Shoemaker and the Elves* (K–2). Retold and illus. by Ilse Plume. 1991, Harcourt $14.95 (978-0-15-274050-4). This folktale is relocated to Renaissance Italy, but the plot is the same except that the elves now number four. (Rev: SLJ 1/92) [398.2]

12471 Grimm Brothers. *The Three Feathers* (5–8). Illus. by Eleonore Schmid. 1984, Creative Editions LB $13.95 (978-0-87191-941-0). A version for older readers that is faithful to the original. [398.2]

12472 Grimm Brothers. *The Water of Life: A Tale from the Brothers Grimm* (PS–3). Retold by Barbara Rogasky. Illus. by Trina S. Hyman. 1986, Holiday House LB $16.95 (978-0-8234-0552-7). 40pp. Three brothers journey to find the water of life for their ailing father. (Rev: BCCB 11/86; BL 9/15/86; HB 3/87) [398.2]

12473 Grimm, Jacob, and Wilhelm Grimm. *Rapunzel* (K–3). Trans. by Anthea Bell. Illus. by Dorothee Duntze. 2005, North-South $16.95 (978-0-7358-2013-5). 32pp. Sunny artwork gives this large-format retelling a more lighthearted feel than usual. (Rev: BL 12/1/05; SLJ 11/05) [398.2]

12474 Grimm, Jacob, and Wilhelm Grimm. *Sleeping Beauty* (K–3). Illus. by Maja Dusikova. 2012, North-South $17.95 (978-0-7358-4087-4). 32pp. With soft new illustrations, this is a faithful retelling of the classic fairy tale. (Rev: BL 10/1/12; LMC 5–6/13*; SLJ 12/12) [398.2]

12475 Grimm, Jacob, and Wilhelm Grimm. *Snow White* (1–4). Illus. by Quentin Greban. 2009, NorthSouth $16.95 (978-0-7358-2257-3). 32pp. This faithful retelling features effective illustrations. (Rev: BLO 11/1/09; LMC 11–12/09; SLJ 11/1/09) [398.2]

12476 Gross, Gwen, ed. *Knights of the Round Table* (2–5). Illus. by Norman Green. 1992, Random paper $3.99 (978-0-394-87579-8). 112pp. A retelling of many of the most popular Arthurian legends. (Rev: BCCB 9/85; SLJ 2/86) [398.2]

12477 Gustafson, Scott, sel. *Classic Fairy Tales* (PS–6). Illus. by Scott Gustafson. 2003, Greenwich Workshop $19.95 (978-0-86713-089-8). 144pp. Scott Gustafson's breathtaking artwork highlights these retellings of 10 classic fairy tales, including "Snow White," "Puss in Boots," and "Hansel and Gretel." (Rev: BL 1/1–15/04; SLJ 12/03) [398.2]

12478 Ha, Song. *Indebted as Lord Chom / No Nhu Chua Chom: The Legend of the Forbidden Street* (1–4). Trans. from Vietnamese by William Smith. Illus. by Ly Thu Ha. 2006, East West Discovery $16.95 (978-0-9701654-6-6). 32pp. This engaging Vietnamese folk tale, presented in both English and Vietnamese, explains the origins of two Hanoi street names. (Rev: SLJ 1/07) [398.2]

12479 Hale, Bruce. *Snoring Beauty* (PS–2). Illus. by Howard Fine. 2008, Harcourt $16.00 (978-0-15-216314-3). 44pp. Full of wordplay and fun, this retelling of "Sleeping Beauty" features Princess Margarine and her parents King Gluteus and Queen Esophagus. (Rev: BL 5/15/08; LMC 11/08; SLJ 6/08) [398.2]

12480 Haley, Gail E. *A Story, a Story* (1–4). Illus. by author. 1970, Macmillan LB $17.00 (978-0-689-20511-8); paper $5.99 (978-0-689-71201-2). 36pp. How African "spider stories" began is traced back to the time when Ananse, the Spider Man, made a bargain with the Sky God. Caldecott Medal winner, 1971. [398.2]

12481 Hall, Amanda. *Prince of the Birds* (PS–2). Illus. 2005, Frances Lincoln $15.95 (978-1-84507-102-8). 32pp. A classic love story, set in southern Spain, in which a prince and a princess, each imprisoned in a tower, find each other with the aid of birds. (Rev: BL 5/1/05) [398.2]

12482 Hall, Amanda. *The Stolen Sun: A Story of Native Alaska* (PS–3). Illus. 2002, Eerdmans $17.00 (978-0-8028-5225-0). 32pp. A Native Alaskan tale with folkloric flavor about the creation of the world and its inhabitants. (Rev: BL 2/15/02; HBG 10/02; SLJ 9/02) [398.2]

12483 Hallworth, Grace. *Sing Me a Story: Song and Dance Stories from the Caribbean* (K–3). Illus. by John Clementson. 2002, August House $19.95 (978-0-87483-672-1). Caribbean folktales that involve song are accompanied by music and lyrics as well as lively and evocative collage borders. (Rev: BL 11/1/02; HBG 3/03; SLJ 9/02) [398.2]

12484 Hamilton, Martha, and Mitch Weiss. *The Ghost Catcher* (PS–2). Illus. by Kristen Balouch. 2008, August House $16.95 (978-0-87483-835-0). 32pp. A barber's generosity to his poorer clients enrages his wife, and he cleverly tricks a ghost into providing him with riches; a traditional tale from Bengal. (Rev: BCCB 9/08; BL 5/15/08; LMC 8/08; SLJ 6/08) [398.2]

12485 Hamilton, Martha, and Mitch Weiss. *The Hidden Feast: A Folktale from the American South* (PS–2). Illus. by Don Tate. 2006, August House $16.95 (978-0-87483-758-2). 32pp. Rooster learns an important lesson when he rejects what he believes is cornbread at a party. (Rev: BL 3/1/06; SLJ 4/06) [398.2]

12486 Hamilton, Martha, and Mitch Weiss. *How and Why Stories: World Tales Kids Can Read and Tell* (5–10). 1999, August House $21.95 (978-0-87483-562-5); paper $12.95 (978-0-87483-561-8). This excellent collection of 25 pourquoi (how and why) stories from around the world also contains a useful introduction on folklore, plus tips on delivering each of the tales. (Rev: BL 5/15/00; HBG 3/00; SLJ 1/00) [398.2]

12487 Hamilton, Martha, and Mitch Weiss. *Noodlehead Stories: World Tales Kids Can Read and Tell* (3–5). Illus. 2000, August House $21.95 (978-0-87483-584-7); paper $12.95 (978-0-87483-585-4). Includes 23 humorous stories from around the world, with tips on effective delivery and general storytelling advice. (Rev: BL 2/15/01; HBG 10/01; SLJ 1/01) [389.2]

12488 Hamilton, Martha, and Mitch Weiss. *Priceless Gifts* (K–2). Illus. by John Kanzler. 2007, August House $16.95 (978-0-87483-788-9). 32pp. A Genoese merchant sails to the Spice Islands to trade his goods, receiving a rich reward for bringing cats to a rat-infested island; his jealous competitor seeks the same fortune, with less favorable results. (Rev: BL 6/1–15/07) [398.2]

12489 Hamilton, Virginia. *Bruh Rabbit and the Tar Baby Girl* (K–4). Illus. by James Ransome. 2003, Scholastic $16.95 (978-0-590-47376-7). Rich watercolors and the Gullah dialect make this an appealing retelling of the familiar story. (Rev: HBG 4/04; SLJ 11/03) [398.2]

12490 Hamilton, Virginia. *The Girl Who Spun Gold* (PS–3). Illus. by Leo Dillon and Diane Dillon. 2000, Scholastic $17.95 (978-0-590-47378-1). Stunning illustrations and stirring prose mark this outstanding retelling of the Rumpelstiltskin folktale using a West Indian setting. (Rev: BCCB 12/00; BL 8/00*; HB 9/00; HBG 3/01; SLJ 9/00) [398.2]

12491 Hamilton, Virginia. *Her Stories: African American Folktales, Fairy Tales, and True Tales* (5–8). 1995, Scholastic paper $22.95 (978-0-590-47370-5). Nineteen tales about African American females are retold in the wonderful style of Virginia Hamilton. (Rev: BL 11/1/95*; SLJ 11/95*) [398.2]

12492 Hamilton, Virginia. *The People Could Fly: American Black Folk Tales* (4–9). Illus. by Leo Dillon and Diane Dillon. 1985, Knopf LB $18.99 (978-0-394-96925-1); paper $13.00 (978-0-679-84336-8). A retelling of 24 folktales — some little known, others familiar, such as Tar Baby. (Rev: BCCB 7/85; BL 7/85; SLJ 11/85) [398.2]

12493 Hamilton, Virginia. *A Ring of Tricksters: Animal Tales from North America, the West Indies, and Africa* (3–6). Illus. by Barry Moser. 1997, Scholastic $22.95 (978-0-590-47374-3). 112pp. This is a stunning collection of trickster tales, many from Africa and others that were adapted by slaves to reflect conditions in the West Indies and the United States. (Rev: BL 1/1–15/98; HBG 3/98; SLJ 11/97) [398.2]

12494 Han, Carolyn. *Why Snails Have Shells: Minority and Han Folktales from China* (4–6). Trans. by Jay Han. Illus. 1994, Univ. of Hawaii $7.95 (978-0-8248-1505-9). 73pp. Attractive paintings accompany this splendid collection of 20 folktales from China. (Rev: BL 8/94; SLJ 2/05) [398.2]

12495 Han, Suzanne C. *The Rabbit's Tail: A Story from Korea* (K–3). Illus. by Richard Wehrman. 1999, Holt $15.95 (978-0-8050-4580-2). 32pp. A charming folktale in which Tiger, through a series of misunderstandings, becomes involved with a rabbit that loses its tail. (Rev: BCCB 6/99; BL 2/15/99; HBG 10/99; SLJ 3/99) [398.2]

12496 Harper, Jo. *The Legend of Mexicatl* (K–3). Illus. by Robert Casilla. 1998, Turtle $15.95 (978-1-890515-05-8). 32pp. A handsome retelling of the Mexican legend about the teenage boy who is destined to lead his people out of the desert. (Rev: BL 4/15/98) [398.2]

12497 Harper, Wilhelmina, retel. *The Gunniwolf* (PS–1). Illus. by Barbara Upton. 2003, Dutton $15.99 (978-0-525-46785-4). Harper's classic tale of the Little Girl who disregards warnings and encounters the not-so-fearsome Gunniwolf appears with new illustrations and a woodland setting. (Rev: HBG 10/03; SLJ 9/03) [398.2]

12498 Harris, Jim. *Jack and the Giant: A Story Full of Beans* (K–4). Illus. 1997, Northland LB $15.95 (978-0-87358-680-1). This version of "Jack and the Beanstalk" had Jack living on a ranch in Arizona with his mother, Annie Okey-Dokey. (Rev: BL 2/1/98; HBG 3/98; SLJ 2/98) [398.2]

12499 Harris, Jim, retel. *The Three Little Dinosaurs* (K–3). Illus. by Jim Harris. 1999, Pelican $15.95 (978-1-56554-371-3). In this version the three little pigs folktale, three young brachiosaurs build different homes to withstand the big bad Tyrannosaurus rex. (Rev: HBG 3/00; SLJ 2/00) [398.2]

12500 Harris, Joel Chandler. *Jump! The Adventures of Brer Rabbit* (3–5). Adapted by Van Dyke Parks and Malcolm Jones. Illus. by Barry Moser. 1986, Harcourt $15.95 (978-0-15-241350-7); paper $7.00 (978-0-15-201493-3). 40pp. An edition with tracings of the stories' roots in oral tradition. (Rev: BCCB 11/86; BL 1/1/87; SLJ 11/86) [398.2]

12501 Hartman, Bob. *The Lion Storyteller Book of Animal Tales* (K–3). Illus. by Susie Poole. 2004, Lion paper $13.95 (978-0-7459-4838-6). 116pp. A diverse and entertaining collection of more than 30 tales to do with animals. (Rev: SLJ 8/04) [398.2]

12502 Hartman, Bob. *Mr. Aesop's Story Shop* (K–3). Illus. by Jago. 2011, IPG/Lion $14.99 (978-074596915-2). 48pp. Aesop himself relates 10 familiar fables from his spot in the marketplace in this well-illustrated collection. (Rev: BL 8/11; LMC 5–6/13) [398]

12503 Hasler, Eveline. *A Tale of Two Brothers* (K–3). Trans. by Marianne Martens. Illus. by Kathi Bhend. 2006, North-South $16.95 (978-0-7358-2102-6). 40pp. Hunchbacked brothers Morris and Boris have opposite outlooks on life, and Morris is rewarded for his sunny good nature and enjoyment of all around him. (Rev: BL 9/1/06; SLJ 9/06) [398.2]

12504 Hassett, John, and Ann Hassett. *Can't Catch Me* (PS–2). Illus. by John Hassett. 2006, Houghton $16.00 (978-0-618-70490-3). 32pp. In this lively adaptation of "The Gingerbread Man," an ice cube escapes from the freezer and makes a dash for the sea. (Rev: SLJ 10/06) [398.2]

12505 Hassett, John, and Ann Hassett. *The Three Silly Girls Grubb* (PS–1). Illus. 2002, Houghton $15.00 (978-0-618-14183-8). 32pp. The three Grubb girls must get past Ugly-Boy Bobby in this goofy version of "The Three Billy Goats Gruff." (Rev: BCCB 11/02; BL 9/15/02; HB 9/02; HBG 3/03; SLJ 11/02*) [398.2]

12506 Hayes, Joe. *El Cucuy! A Bogeyman Cuento in English and Spanish* (K–4). Illus. by Honorio Robledo. 2001, Cinco Puntos $15.95 (978-0-938317-54-8). 32pp. A southwestern bogeyman comes down from his mountain to carry off bad children. (Rev: BL 7/01; HBG 10/01; SLJ 7/01) [398.2]

12507 Hayes, Joe. *Little Gold Star / Estrellita de oro: A Cinderella Cuento* (PS–3). Illus. by Gloria Osuna Perez and Lucía Angela Pérez. 2000, Cinco Puntos $15.95 (978-0-938317-49-4). Told in English and Spanish, this is an interesting version of the Cinderella story that is popular in the mountain communities of New Mexico. (Rev: BCCB 7–8/00; BL 5/15/00; HBG 10/00; SLJ 6/00) [398.2]

12508 Hayes, Joe. *Pajaro Verde / The Green Bird* (2–4). Illus. by Antonio Castro L. 2002, Cinco Puntos $16.95 (978-0-938317-65-4). A young woman marries a bird to save him from evil in this New Mexican folktale, told in both Spanish and English, filled with magic and monsters. (Rev: BL 10/15/02; HBG 3/03) [398.2]

12509 Hayes, Joe, retel. *Baila, Nana, Baila/Dance, Nana, Dance: Cuban Folktales in English and Spanish* (3–6). Illus. by Mauricio Trenard Sayago. 2008, Cinco Puntos $20.95 (978-1-933693-17-0). 128pp. Thirteen diverse, bilingual folk tales from Cuba have elements of stories from Spain, Africa, and the Caribbean. (Rev: BCCB 1/09; LMC 5/09; SLJ 2/09) [398.2]

12510 Haylesworth, Jim, retel. *Goldilocks and the Three Bears* (PS–2). Illus. by Barbara McClintock. 2003, Scholastic $16.95 (978-0-439-39545-8). A handsome retelling with traditional illustrations and language that will appeal nonetheless to today's readers. (Rev: HB 11/03; HBG 4/04; SLJ 10/03) [398.2]

12511 Hayward, Linda. *All Stuck Up* (1–3). Illus. by Normand Chartier. 1990, Random paper $3.99 (978-0-679-80216-7). 32pp. The tar baby story featuring Brer Rabbit is retold. (Rev: BCCB 7–8/92; BL 6/1/90; SLJ 8/90) [398.2]

12512 Hedlund, Irene. *Mighty Mountain and the Three Strong Women* (PS–3). Trans. by Judith Elkin. Illus. 1990, Volcano $14.95 (978-0-912078-86-1). A sumo wrestler meets three women who surpass him in strength. (Rev: BL 6/1/90; SLJ 10/90) [398.2]

12513 Helmer, Marilyn. *Three Teeny Tiny Tales* (K–2). Illus. by Veselina Tomova. Series: Once-Upon-a-Time. 2001, Kids Can $10.95 (978-1-55074-841-3). 32pp. "The Elves and the Shoemaker," "The Gingerbread Man," and "Thumbelina" are retold in picture-book format. (Rev: BL 7/01; HBG 3/02; SLJ 6/01) [398.2]

12514 Henderson, Kathy. *Lugalbanda: The Boy Who Got Caught Up in a War* (2–4). Illus. by Jane Ray. 2006, Candlewick $16.99 (978-0-7636-2782-9). 80pp. This retelling of an ancient Sumerian legend recounts how a young prince named Lugalbanda receives the strength he needs for war. (Rev: BL 5/1/06; SLJ 4/06*) [398.2]

12515 Hennessy, B. G., reteller. *The Boy Who Cried Wolf* (PS–1). Illus. by Boris Kulikov. 2006, Simon & Schuster $15.95 (978-0-689-87433-8). 40pp. The fable about the shepherd boy who cried wolf is given vivid new life in this beautifully illustrated, funny picture book. (Rev: BL 2/1/06; SLJ 3/06*) [398.2]

12516 Henrichs, Wendy. *I Am Tama, Lucky Cat: A Japanese Legend* (K–3). Illus. by Yoshiko Jaeggi. 2011, Peachtree $16.95 (978-1-56145-589-8). 32pp. Describes the origins of the beckoning cat and how it came to be a symbol of good luck. (Rev: BLO 11/15/11; SLJ 12/1/11) [398.2]

12517 Heo, Yumi. *The Green Frogs* (K–3). Illus. 1996, Houghton $17.00 (978-0-395-68378-1). Two disobedient frogs decide to honor their mother's last wish in this Korean folktale. (Rev: BCCB 10/96; BL 7/96; HB 11/96) [398.2]

12518 Herman, Gail, retel. *The Lion and the Mouse* (1). Illus. by Lisa McCue. Series: Early Step into Reading. 1998, Random paper $3.99 (978-0-679-88674-7). 32pp. The classic Aesop fable is retold dramatically in a simple text suitable for beginning readers. (Rev: BL 11/1/98; SLJ 2/99) [398.2]

12519 Hester, Denia Lewis. *Grandma Lena's Big Ol' Turnip* (K–2). Illus. by Jackie Urbanovic. 2005, Whitman $16.95 (978-0-8075-3027-6). 32pp. It takes a whole family to pull up the giant turnip in Grandma Lena's garden, but the reward afterward is home-cooked soul food in this story based on Alexei Tolstoy's "The Turnip." (Rev: BL 3/15/05; SLJ 5/05)

12520 Hewitt, Kathryn, adapt. *The Three Sillies* (K–3). Illus. by Kathryn Hewitt. 1989, Harcourt paper $3.95 (978-0-15-286856-7). A suitor sets out to find three sillier people than his betrothed's family. (Rev: BCCB 5/86; BL 4/1/86; SLJ 5/86) [398.2]

12521 Heyer, Carol, retel. *Robin Hood* (2–4). Illus. by Carol Heyer. 1993, Ideals LB $15.00 (978-0-8249-8648-3). This handsome book retells the most famous of Robin Hood's exploits, culminating in the King's pardon. (Rev: SLJ 11/93) [398.2]

12522 Heyer, Marilee. *The Weaving of a Dream: A Chinese Folktale* (3–5). Illus. by author. 1989, Puffin paper $7.99 (978-0-14-050528-3). 32pp. The third of an old widow's sons retrieves her precious brocade, from whence steps the Red Fairy, and all three live happily ever after. (Rev: BL 4/15/86; SLJ 4/86) [398.2]

12523 Hickox, Rebecca. *The Golden Sandal: A Middle Eastern Cinderella Story* (K–3). Illus. by Will Hillenbrand. 1998, Holiday House $17.95 (978-0-8234-1331-7). 32pp. A vivid retelling with atmospheric illustrations of an Iraqi folktale that is a variation of the Cinderella story. (Rev: BCCB 6/98; BL 4/1/98; HB 3/98; HBG 10/98; SLJ 4/98) [398.2]

12524 Hicks, Ray, and Lynn Salsi. *The Jack Tales* (3–5). Illus. 2000, Callaway $24.95 (978-0-935112-58-0). 40pp. Two different versions of each of three plucky Jack tales are effectively presented in print and on a CD. (Rev: BL 11/15/00*; HBG 3/01; SLJ 11/00) [398.2]

12525 Highwater, Jamake. *Anpao: An American Indian Odyssey* (5–8). Illus. by Fritz Scholder. 1993, HarperCollins paper $8.99 (978-0-06-440437-2). A young hero encounters great danger on his way to meet his father, the Sun, in this dramatic American Indian folktale. [398.2]

12526 Hillerman, Tony, ed. *The Boy Who Made Dragonfly: A Zuni Myth* (5–7). Illus. by Laszlo Kubinyi. 1986, Univ. of New Mexico paper $11.95 (978-0-8263-0910-5). A Zuni boy and his little sister are left behind by their tribe and survive hunger and deprivation through the intervention of the Cornstalk Being. [398.2]

12527 Hoberman, Mary Ann. *You Read to Me, I'll Read to You: Very Short Fables to Read Together* (1–4). Illus. by Michael Emberley. 2010, Little, Brown $16.99 (978-0-316-04117-1). 32pp. Designed for two voices, this collection features 13 Aesop fables retold in verse and accompanied by lively illustrations. **e** Lexile AD330L (Rev: BL 1/1–15/11; SLJ 4/11) [811]

12528 Hoberman, Mary Ann. *You Read to Me, I'll Read to You: Very Short Fairy Tales to Read Together* (2–4). Illus. by Michael Emberly. 2004, Little, Brown $16.95 (978-0-316-14611-1). Designed for two voices, this picture book features retellings of eight popular fairy tales. (Rev: BL 7/04; HB 5/04; SLJ 5/04) [398.2]

12529 Hodges, Margaret. *Dick Whittington and His Cat* (PS–2). Illus. by Melisande Potter. 2006, Holiday $16.95 (978-0-8234-1987-6). 32pp. Retells the British legend of the orphan who became Lord Mayor of London. (Rev: BL 5/1/06; SLJ 5/06) [398.2]

12530 Hodges, Margaret. *The Hero of Bremen* (3–6). Illus. by Charles Mikolaycak. 1993, Holiday House LB $17.95 (978-0-8234-0934-1). In this German folktale, a disabled cobbler is helped by the ghost of Roland, the legendary knight who saved the city of Bremen centuries before. (Rev: BCCB 10/93; BL 10/15/93; HB 11/93; SLJ 10/93) [398.2]

12531 Hodges, Margaret. *St. George and the Dragon: A Golden Legend* (2–5). Illus. by Trina S. Hyman. 1984, Little, Brown $16.95 (978-0-316-36789-9). A reworking of the English tale as it appeared in Edmund Spenser's Fairie Queen. Caldecott Medal winner, 1985. [398.2]

12532 Hodges, Margaret. *Up the Chimney* (K–2). Illus. by Amanda Harvey. 1998, Holiday House $15.95 (978-0-8234-1354-6). 32pp. When a girl goes out to seek her fortune, she is helped by all the objects and animals she has helped in the past, but when her uncharitable, cruel sister goes out, her fate is different. (Rev: BCCB 12/98; BL 11/15/98; HBG 3/99; SLJ 1/99) [398.2]

12533 Hodges, Margaret, adapt. *The Boy Who Drew Cats* (K–3). Illus. by Aki Sogabe. 2002, Holiday House $16.95 (978-0-8234-1594-6). 32pp. A young boy's obsession with drawing cats everywhere he goes eventually changes his life in this tale of the supernatural. (Rev: BCCB 4/02; BL 6/1–15/02; HB 5/02; HBG 10/02; SLJ 3/02) [398.2]

12534 Hodges, Margaret, retel. *The Kitchen Knight: A Tale of King Arthur* (3–6). Illus. by Trina S. Hyman. 1990, Holiday House LB $17.95 (978-0-8234-0787-3). A lavishly illustrated version of the story of the king who hides his identity to work in the kitchen at King Arthur's court. (Rev: BCCB 11/90*; HB 3/91; SLJ 1/91) [398.2]

12535 Hoffman, Mary. *Clever Katya: A Fairy Tale from Old Russia* (K–3). Illus. by Marie Cameron. 1998, Barefoot Books $15.95 (978-1-901223-64-4). In this Russian folktale, 7-year-old Katya so impresses the czar with her intelligence that he asks her to visit him in his palace. (Rev: BL 10/1/98; SLJ 10/98) [398.2]

12536 Hoffman, Mary. *A Twist in the Tail: Animal Stories from Around the World* (K–3). Illus. by Jan Ormerod. 1998, Holt $18.95 (978-0-8050-5945-8). 68pp. Ten lively folktales about animals from such places as India, China, Malaysia, and Nigeria are included in this anthology. (Rev: BL 11/15/98; SLJ 11/98) [398.245]

12537 Hofmeyr, Dianne. *The Star-Bearer: A Creation Myth from Ancient Egypt* (3–5). Illus. by Judy Daly. 2001, Farrar $16.00 (978-0-374-37481-5). 32pp. In this picture book for older readers, a creation myth from Egypt is retold in which the god of rain and dew and the god of air emerge from a lotus bud. (Rev: BCCB 3/01; BL 2/15/01) [299]

12538 Hogrogian, Nonny. *The Contest* (3–5). Illus. by author. 1976, Greenwillow $18.89 (978-0-688-84042-6). 32pp. Adaptation of the folktale about two robbers who discover that they are engaged to the same girl. [398.2]

12539 Hogrogian, Nonny. *One Fine Day* (K–3). Illus. by author. 1971, Macmillan $16.00 (978-0-02-744000-3); paper $5.99 (978-0-02-043620-1). Based on an Armenian folktale, this cumulative story is ideal for reading aloud. Caldecott Medal winner, 1972. [398.2]

12540 Holt, Daniel D., sel. *Tigers, Frogs, and Rice Cakes: A Book of Korean Proverbs* (2–4). Illus. by Soma Han Stickler. 1999, Shen's $15.95 (978-1-885008-10-7). Each of the 20 Korean proverbs included are given in both English and Korean, with explanations. (Rev: BCCB 5/99; HBG 10/99; SLJ 6/99) [398.2]

12541 Hong, Chen Jiang. *The Magic Horse of Han Gan* (PS–2). Trans. by Claudia Zoe Bedrick. Illus. 2006, Enchanted Lion $16.95 (978-1-59270-063-9). 38pp. This attractive picture book recounts the moving and dramatic legend of a magical horse created by 9th-century Chinese artist Han Gan. (Rev: BL 11/1/06; SLJ 12/06*) [398.2]

12542 Hong, Lily T. *Two of Everything: A Chinese Folktale* (K–3). Illus. 1993, Whitman LB $16.95 (978-0-8075-8157-5). 32pp. Elderly Mr. Haktak finds a magical brass pot in his garden. (Rev: BL 3/15/93*; HB 7/93*; SLJ 6/93*) [398.2]

12543 Hopkins, Jackie Mims. *The Horned Toad Prince* (PS–2). Illus. by Michael Austin. 2000, Peachtree $15.95 (978-1-56145-195-1). This breezy update of the fairy tale is set in the Southwest and features a frog who demands that the heroine feed him chili. (Rev: BCCB 7–8/00; BL 5/15/00; HBG 10/00; SLJ 4/00) [398.2]

12544 Houston, James. *Tikta'liktak: An Eskimo Legend* (4–6). Illus. by author. 1990, Harcourt paper $10.00 (978-0-15-287748-4). Legend of a young Inuit hunter who is carried out to sea on a drifting ice floe with only his bow and arrows and a harpoon. Also use: *The White Archer: An Eskimo Legend* (1990).

12545 Huck, Charlotte. *The Black Bull of Norroway* (2–4). Illus. by Anita Lobel. 2001, Greenwillow LB $15.89 (978-0-688-16901-5). 40pp. A Scottish beauty-and-the-beast tale, richly illustrated and accompanied by a discussion of the story's origins and variants. (Rev: BCCB 5/01; BL 9/15/01; HB 5/01; HBG 10/01; SLJ 6/01) [398.2]

12546 Huck, Charlotte. *Toads and Diamonds* (K–3). Illus. by Anita Lobel. 1996, Greenwillow $15.89 (978-0-688-13681-9). 32pp. A downtrodden girl is rewarded for her kindness in this retelling of a folktale. (Rev: BCCB 1/97; BL 11/1/96*; HB 11/96; SLJ 9/96) [398.2]

12547 Hull, Robert, retel. *Egyptian Stories* (4–6). Illus. by Noel Bateman and Barbara Loftus. Series: Tales from Around the World. 1994, Thomson Learning LB $24.26 (978-1-56847-155-6). 48pp. Introduces seven traditional tales, including a creation story, as well as life in ancient Egypt. (Rev: SLJ 8/94) [398.2]

12548 Hunt, Angela E. *The Tale of Three Trees: A Traditional Folktale* (K–2). Illus. by Tim Jonke. 1989, Lion $14.99 (978-0-7459-1743-6). 32pp. A folktale about three trees — a manger for the Christ child, a fishing boat that carries Jesus, and timbers that become the cross. (Rev: BL 11/1/89) [398.2]

12549 Hurston, Zora Neale. *Lies and Other Tall Tales* (PS–2). Illus. by Christopher Myers. 2005, HarperCollins $15.99 (978-0-06-000655-6). 40pp. Imaginative illustrations enhance the irreverence of these tall tales collected by Hurston in the 1930s. (Rev: BL 9/15/05*; SLJ 11/05) [398.2]

12550 Hurston, Zora Neale. *The Six Fools* (PS–2). Ed. by Joyce Carol Thomas. Illus. by Ann Tanksley. 2006, HarperCollins $15.99 (978-0-06-000646-4). In this story drawn from the collection of folk tales collected by Zora Neale Hurston during the 1930s, a young groom-to-be travels the world in search of fools as big as his fiancee and her parents. (Rev: BL 2/1/06; SLJ 1/06*) [398.2]

12551 Hurston, Zora Neale, and Joyce Carol Thomas. *The Three Witches* (2–4). Illus. by Faith Ringgold. 2006, HarperCollins $15.99 (978-0-06-000649-5). 32pp. In this adaptation of an African American tale first collected by Zora Neale Hurston, two young siblings escape the clutches of three witches with a little help from their grandmother, three hound dogs, and a snake. (Rev: BL 6/1–15/06; SLJ 8/06) [398.2]

12552 Husain, Shahrukh. *The Wise Fool: Fables from the Islamic World* (1–5). Illus. by Micha Archer. 2011, Barefoot $19.99 (978-1-846-86226-7). 64pp. A retelling of 22 folktales about Mulla Nasreddin Hoca, a wise man remembered for his insightful and humorous stories. (Rev: BL 11/15/11; SLJ 9/1/11) [398.2]

12553 Hutchinson, Duane. *The Gunny Wolf and Other Fairy Tales* (4–6). Illus. 1993, Foundation paper $6.95 (978-0-934988-29-2). 88pp. A total of seven folktales, including Tom Thumb and The Six Swans, are included in this collection. (Rev: BL 5/15/93) [398.2]

12554 Icenoggle, Jodi. `Til the Cows Come Home* (K–4). Illus. by Normand Chartier. 2004, Boyds Mills $15.95 (978-1-56397-987-3). The Jewish folktale "The Button Story," newly set in the American West, follows a piece of leather over the years as it becomes a pair of chaps, then a pair of gloves, and finally a button. (Rev: SLJ 3/04)

12555 Isadora, Rachel. *The Fisherman and His Wife* (PS–1). Illus. by author. 2008, Putnam $16.99 (978-0-399-24771-2). 32pp. The traditional Grimm story is set in Africa in this beautifully illustrated volume. (Rev: BL 4/1/08; HB 3/08; LMC 10/08; SLJ 3/08) [398.2]

12556 Isadora, Rachel. *Hansel and Gretel* (PS–2). Illus. by author. 2009, Putnam $16.99 (978-0-399-25028-6). 32pp. The story of the two innocent children and the wicked witch is moved to an African setting and illustrated with traditional Kente patterns. (Rev: BL 1/1–15/09; SLJ 4/09) [398.2]

12557 Izcoa, Carmen Rivera, adapt. *Mediopollito / Half-a-Chick* (K–3). Illus. by Nívea O. Montáñez. 1996, Ediciones Huracan $10.50 (978-0-929157-43-6). A Puerto Rican folktale about a bird that punishes the king for being mean and selfish. (Rev: BL 2/1/04; SLJ 11/97) [398.2]

12558 Jackson, Bobby L., retel. *Little Red Ronnika* (1–4). Illus. by Rhonda Mitchell. 1998, Multicultural Publns. LB $16.95 (978-1-884242-80-9). 32pp. In this version of Little Red Riding Hood, the characters are all African Americans. Granny is a hip senior and the wolf is a rapper. (Rev: SLJ 1/99) [398.2]

12559 Jackson, Ellen. *Cinder Edna* (PS–3). Illus. by Kevin O'Malley. 1994, Lothrop $17.99 (978-0-688-12322-2). 32pp. Whereas Cinderella is a passive wimp, Cinder Edna is a spirited girl who mows lawns to make money so she can attend the ball. In this book, the two stories are told side by side. (Rev: BL 3/15/94; SLJ 4/94) [398.2]

12560 Jackson, Ellen. *The Impossible Riddle* (K–3). Illus. by Alison Winfield. 1995, Whispering Coyote $14.95 (978-1-879085-93-0). 32pp. In this Russian folktale, a czar hopes to prevent his daughter's marriage by demanding that prospective suitors answer an impossible riddle. (Rev: BL 1/1–15/96) [398.2]

12561 Jacobs, Jimmy. *Moonlight Through the Pines: Tales from Georgia Evenings* (5–7). 2000, Franklin-Sarrett paper $11.95 (978-0-9637477-3-0). A collection of humorous reminiscences, family stories, tall tales, and other examples of folklore, all from the South. (Rev: BL 8/00) [398.2]

12562 Jacobs, Joseph. *Celtic Fairy Tales* (3–6). Illus. by John D. Batten. 1968, Peter Smith $24.00 (978-0-8446-2302-3); Dover paper $7.95 (978-0-486-21826-7). 267pp. A classic collection. Followed by: *More Celtic Fairy Tales* (1969, Dover paper

12563 Jacobs, Joseph. *English Fairy Tales* (3–6). Illus. by John D. Batten. 1969, Peter Smith $23.75 (978-0-8446-2303-0); Dover paper $10.95 (978-0-486-21818-2). A standard collection by a master storyteller. [398.2]

12564 Jaffe, Nina. *The Golden Flower: A Taino Myth from Puerto Rico* (K–3). Illus. by Enrique O. Sánchez. 1996, Simon & Schuster $16.95 (978-0-689-80469-4). The creation of the island of Puerto Rico is told in this Taino myth about a magical pumpkin. (Rev: BCCB 6/96; BL 6/1–15/96; SLJ 7/96) [398.2]

12565 Jaffe, Nina. *Tales for the Seventh Day: A Collection of Sabbath Stories* (3–7). Illus. by Kelly Stribling Sutherland. 2000, Scholastic $15.95 (978-0-590-12054-

8). 73pp. A collection of Jewish tales that honor the traditions and the celebration of the Sabbath. (Rev: BL 12/15/00; HBG 3/01; SLJ 11/00) [398.2]

12566 Jaffe, Nina. *The Way Meat Loves Salt: A Cinderella Tale from the Jewish Tradition* (PS–2). Illus. by Louise August. 1998, Holt $15.95 (978-0-8050-4384-6). A Yiddish folktale that combines King Lear with Cinderella and casts Elijah the Prophet in the role of fairy godmother. (Rev: BCCB 11/98; BL 10/1/98; HB 9/98; HBG 3/99; SLJ 9/98) [398.2]

12567 Jaffe, Nina, and Steve Zeitlin. *The Cow of No Color: Riddle Stories and Justice Tales from Around the World* (5–8). 1998, Henry Holt $17.00 (978-0-8050-3736-4). A collection of folktales from around the world that deal with the theme of justice. (Rev: BCCB 12/98; BL 11/1/98; HBG 3/99; SLJ 12/98) [398.2]

12568 Jaffrey, Madhur. *Seasons of Splendor: Tales, Myths, and Legends from India* (5–8). Illus. by Michael Foreman. 1985, Puffin paper $7.95 (978-0-317-62172-3). Folktales and family stories as well as accounts of Rama and Krishna. (Rev: BCCB 1/86; BL 1/15/86) [398.2]

12569 Janisch, Heinz. *The Fire: An Ethiopian Folk Tale* (PS–2). Trans. by Shelley Tanaka. Illus. by Fabricio Vandenbroeck. 2002, Groundwood $15.95 (978-0-88899-450-9). 32pp. A slave must spend the night on a snow-capped mountain peak with no clothes or shelter to win his freedom in this Ethiopian folktale with evocative double-page paintings. (Rev: BL 12/15/02; HBG 3/03; SLJ 2/03) [398.2]

12570 Jendresen, Erik, and Joshua M. Greene, retels. *Hanuman: Based on Valmiki's Ramayana* (3–6). Illus. by Li Ming. 1998, Tricycle $15.95 (978-1-883672-78-2). A retelling of the section of the Ramayana in which the monkey clan under Hanuman helps Rama rescue his wife Sita. (Rev: BCCB 3/99; HBG 10/99; SLJ 11/98) [398.2]

12571 Johnson-Davies, Denys. *Goha the Wise Fool* (2–4). Illus. by Hany El Saed Ahmed and Hag Hamdy Mohamed Fattouh. 2005, Philomel $16.99 (978-0-399-24222-9). 40pp. Traditional tapestries illustrate a collection of memorable tales about a Middle Eastern trickster-fool called Goha. (Rev: BL 6/1–15/05*; HB 9/05) [398.2]

12572 Johnson, Emily Pauline. *The Lost Island* (2–4). Illus. by Atanas Matsoureff. 2005, Simply Read $16.95 (978-1-894965-07-1). In this retelling of an Indian folktale, an elderly man tells of his search for a mysterious lost island said to hold the bravery of a once-powerful leader of the Squamish. (Rev: BL 1/1–15/05) [398.2]

12573 Jolley, Dan. *Pigling: A Cinderella Story* (3–6). Illus. by Anne Timmons. Series: Graphic Myths and Legends. 2008, Lerner LB $27.93 (978-0-8225-7174-2). 48pp. This brightly illustrated graphic novel tells the story of how Pear Blossom, a Korean Cinderella, eases her sorrow and overcomes her cruel stepmother and stepsister for a happy-ever-after ending. (Rev: BL 9/15/08; LMC 1/09) [398.2]

12574 Jones, Carol. *The Gingerbread Man* (PS–K). Illus. 2002, Houghton $16.00 (978-0-618-18822-2). 32pp. In this spirited retelling, it is nursery rhyme characters who chase the gingerbread boy. (Rev: BL 2/15/02; HBG 10/02; SLJ 4/02) [398.2]

12575 Jones, Carol. *The Hare and the Tortoise* (K–3). Illus. 1996, Houghton $13.95 (978-0-395-81368-3). 32pp. Peepholes and detailed illustrations are used in this retelling of the famous Aesop fable. (Rev: BL 9/1/96; SLJ 9/96) [398.24]

12576 Jones, Jennifer B. *Heetunka's Harvest: A Tale of the Plains Indians* (K–3). Illus. by Shannon Keegan. 1995, Roberts Rinehart $15.95 (978-1-879373-17-4). Nature takes revenge on a thieving Dakota Indian woman who steals from Heetunka the bean mouse. (Rev: BL 1/1/95; SLJ 4/95) [398.2]

12577 Jorisch, Stephane, adapt. *As for the Princess? A Folktale from Quebec* (K–3). Illus. by Stephane Jorisch. 2001, Annick LB $19.95 (978-1-55037-695-1); paper $7.95 (978-1-55037-694-4). A not-very-bright young man finally gets his revenge against a beautiful but light-fingered princess. (Rev: HBG 3/02; SLJ 3/02) [398.2]

12578 Joslin, Mary. *The Lion Classic Wisdom Stories* (4–7). Illus. by Christina Balit. 2013, IPG/Lion $19.99 (978-074596369-3). 128pp. A collection of 28 nicely illustrated tales that convey lessons of wisdom. (Rev: BLO 9/15/13; SLJ 7/13) [398.2]

12579 Kampen, Vlasta van, ed. *Bear Tales: Three Treasured Stories* (PS–1). Illus. 2000, Annick LB $18.95 (978-1-55037-619-7); paper $6.95 (978-1-55037-618-0). 40pp. Three bear stories are retold here, one from Czech sources, one from Russian, and one from Native American folklore. (Rev: BL 6/1–15/00; HBG 10/00; SLJ 10/00) [398.2]

12580 Keats, Ezra Jack. *John Henry: An American Legend* (1–3). Illus. by author. 1965, Knopf paper $5.99 (978-0-394-89052-4). Large, bold figures capture the spirit of the hero who died with a hammer in his hand. [398.2]

12581 Keding, Dan. *Stories of Hope and Spirit: Folktales from Eastern Europe* (3–6). Illus. 2004, August House $18.95 (978-0-87483-727-8). 77pp. A collection of stories that show the diversity of Eastern Europe and entertain while providing life lessons. (Rev: SLJ 7/05) [398.2]

12582 Keens-Douglas, Richard. *Mama God, Papa God: A Caribbean Tale* (K–2). Illus. by Stefan Czernecki. 1999, Crocodile LB $15.95 (978-1-56656-307-9). A Caribbean Island folktale attractively illustrated that tells a creation story centering around Mama God and Papa God and how they created diversity in the people that they made. (Rev: HBG 10/99; SLJ 7/99) [398.2]

12583 Kellogg, Steven. *Paul Bunyan* (K–4). Illus. by author. 1984, Morrow $17.89 (978-0-688-03850-2); paper $6.99 (978-0-688-05800-5). 40pp. Several stories about Paul and the blue ox Babe, all wittily illustrated. (Rev: BL 2/1/04) [398.2]

12584 Kellogg, Steven. *The Pied Piper's Magic* (K–1). 2009, Dial $16.99 (978-0-8037-2818-9). 40pp. Based loosely on the well-known Pied Piper story, this version tells the story of Peterkin whose magic pipe allows him to conjure up words and objects and then transform them — so that troublesome "rats" become "stars," for example. (Rev: BCCB 7–8/09; BL 1/1–15/09; SLJ 5/09) [398.2]

12585 Kellogg, Steven. *Sally Ann Thunder Ann Whirlwind Crockett* (PS–3). Illus. 1995, Morrow $16.89 (978-0-688-14043-4). A humorous look at the life of Davy Crockett's wife and her equally amazing exploits. (Rev: BCCB 9/95; BL 8/95; SLJ 10/95) [398.2]

12586 Kellogg, Steven, retel. *Pecos Bill* (K–3). Illus. by Steven Kellogg. 1986, Scholastic paper $6.99 (978-0-688-09924-4). Humor permeates these tall tales of the American folk hero. (Rev: BCCB 11/86; BL 9/1/86; SLJ 9/86) [398.2]

12587 Ketteman, Helen. *Armadilly Chili* (K–3). Trans. and illus. by Will Terry. 2004, Whitman $16.95 (978-0-8075-0457-4). This charming retelling of the Little Red Hen story is transposed to the American Southwest. (Rev: BL 6/1–15/04; SLJ 5/04) [398.2]

12588 Ketteman, Helen. *The Three Little Gators* (PS–2). Illus. by Will Terry. 2009, Albert Whitman $16.99 (978-0-8075-7824-7). 32pp. Three young alligators build their houses with rocks, sticks, and sand, respectively, in this entertaining version of the "Three Little Pigs" set in Texas. (Rev: BLO 4/24/09; LMC 10/09; SLJ 6/09)

12589 Ketteman, Helen. *Waynetta and the Cornstalk: A Texas Fairy Tale* (K–3). Illus. by Diane Greenseid. 2007, Albert Whitman $16.95 (978-0-8075-8687-7). In this fractured version of "Jack and the Beanstalk" set in Texas, life on the ranch changes for the better when cowgirl Waynetta plants some magic corn and scales a huge cornstalk to find a gigantic ranch inhabited by a giant. (Rev: SLJ 4/07) [398.2]

12590 Kherdian, David. *The Golden Bracelet* (K–4). Illus. by Nonny Hogrogian. 1998, Holiday House $16.95 (978-0-8234-1362-1). An Armenian story about a prince who uses his skill as a weaver to send a message to his wife when he is held prisoner by an evil sorcerer. (Rev: BL 6/1–15/98; HBG 10/98; SLJ 8/98) [398.2]

12591 Kidd, Ronald, ed. *On Top of Old Smoky: A Collection of Songs and Stories from Appalachia* (4–6). Illus. by Linda Anderson. 1992, Ideals $13.95 (978-0-8249-8569-1). A handsome collection of songs and stories from Appalachia with distinctive illustrations. (Rev: BL 12/1/92; SLJ 4/05) [782]

12592 Kilgannon, Eily. *Folktales of the Yeats Country* (5–8). 1990, Mercier paper $10.95 (978-0-85342-861-9). Seventeen folktales that originate in County Sligo in Ireland. (Rev: BL 8/90; SLJ 2/91) [398.2]

12593 Kimmel, Eric A. *The Adventures of Hershel of Ostropol* (K–4). Illus. by Trina S. Hyman. 1995, Holiday House $16.95 (978-0-8234-1210-5). 64pp. Ten Jewish folktales that use as a locale a village community in the Ukraine during the 19th century. (Rev: BL 10/15/95; SLJ 11/95) [398.2]

12594 Kimmel, Eric A. *Anansi and the Magic Stick* (PS–2). Illus. by Janet Stevens. 2001, Holiday House $16.95 (978-0-8234-1443-7). 32pp. Things don't go as Anansi the tricky spider plans when he steals a magic stick to do his work for him. (Rev: BCCB 12/01; BL 9/15/01; HBG 3/02; SLJ 9/01) [398.2]

12595 Kimmel, Eric A. *Anansi and the Moss-Covered Rock* (PS–3). Illus. by Janet Stevens. 1988, Holiday House LB $16.95 (978-0-8234-0689-0); paper $6.95 (978-0-8234-0798-9). 32pp. Anansi the trickster discovers a magic rock that knocks animals out, and then he steals their food. (Rev: BCCB 10/88; BL 10/1/88; SLJ 11/88) [398.2]

12596 Kimmel, Eric A. *Anansi and the Talking Melon* (PS–3). Illus. by Janet Stevens. 1994, Holiday House LB $16.95 (978-0-8234-1104-7). 32pp. Hiding inside a melon, Anansi the Spider tricks all the animals into believing that the melon can speak in this African folktale. (Rev: BCCB 6/94; BL 2/15/94; SLJ 3/94*) [398.2]

12597 Kimmel, Eric A. *Anansi Goes Fishing* (K–3). Illus. by Janet Stevens. 1992, Holiday House LB $16.95 (978-0-8234-0918-1). Lazy but lovable trickster Anansi is outwitted by the clever turtle in this contemporary rendition of an old tale. (Rev: BL 3/15/92; SLJ 5/92) [398.2]

12598 Kimmel, Eric A. *Anansi's Party Time* (PS–2). Illus. by Janet Stevens. 2008, Holiday $16.95 (978-0-8234-1922-7). 32pp. Turtle gets his revenge on the trickster spider Anansi in this humorous folktale. (Rev: BL 9/15/08; LMC 5/09; SLJ 9/08) [398.2]

12599 Kimmel, Eric A. *Baba Yaga: A Russian Folktale* (K–3). Illus. by Megan Lloyd. 1991, Holiday House LB $16.95 (978-0-8234-0854-2). 32pp. A traditional Russian folktale about Marina, whose wicked stepmother sends her to the forest witch. (Rev: BL 5/1/91; SLJ 6/91) [398.2]

12600 Kimmel, Eric A. *Bearhead: A Russian Folktale* (K–3). Illus. by Charles Mikolaycak. 1991, Holiday House LB $16.95 (978-0-8234-0902-0). 32pp. A peasant woman finds an odd-looking foundling with the body of a human and the head of a bear. (Rev: BCCB 12/91; BL 9/1/91; SLJ 10/91) [398.2]

12601 Kimmel, Eric A. *Bernal and Florinda: A Spanish Tale* (K–3). Illus. by Robert Rayevsky. 1994, Holiday House LB $15.95 (978-0-8234-1089-7). 32pp. A comic fairy tale about two Spanish lovers who are united in marriage despite the objections of the bride's father. (Rev: BCCB 9/94; BL 9/15/94; SLJ 11/94) [398.2]

12602 Kimmel, Eric A. *The Birds' Gift: A Ukrainian Easter Story* (PS–3). Illus. by Katya Krenina. 1999, Holiday House $16.95 (978-0-8234-1384-3). 34pp. After saving a group of birds, on Easter morning townspeople find beautifully decorated eggs left behind as gifts. (Rev: BL 4/15/99; HBG 10/99; SLJ 6/99) [398.2]

12603 Kimmel, Eric A. *Boots and His Brothers: A Norwegian Tale* (PS–3). Illus. by Kimberly B. Root. 1992, Holiday House LB $14.95 (978-0-8234-0886-3). 32pp.

In this Norwegian folktale, three brothers set out to seek their fortunes, but only the youngest, Boots, succeeds. (Rev: BCCB 3/92; BL 3/1/92) [398.2]

12604 Kimmel, Eric A. *Cactus Soup* (1–3). Trans. and illus. by Phil Huling. 2004, Marshall Cavendish $16.95 (978-0-7614-5155-6). 32pp. "Stone Soup" meets chiles and beans in this Mexico-based variant involving hungry revolutionary forces. (Rev: BL 9/15/04*; SLJ 10/04) [398.2]

12605 Kimmel, Eric A. *The Castle of Cats: A Story from Ukraine* (PS–2). Retold by Eric A. Kimmel. Illus. by Katya Krenina. 2004, Holiday House $16.95 (978-0-8234-1565-6). 32pp. A farmer tests the mettle of his three sons by sending them on a mission in this story based on a Latvian folktale. (Rev: BL 10/15/04; SLJ 11/04)

12606 Kimmel, Eric A. *Easy Work! An Old Tale* (PS–3). Illus. by Andrew Glass. 1998, Holiday House $17.95 (978-0-8234-1349-2). 32pp. In this variation on the classic Norwegian folktale, farmer McTeague and his wife decide to exchange roles for a day, with disastrous results. (Rev: BL 4/15/98; HBG 10/98; SLJ 6/98) [398.2]

12607 Kimmel, Eric A. *The Fisherman and the Turtle* (K–2). Illus. by Martha Aviles. 2008, Marshall Cavendish $16.99 (978-0-7614-5387-1). A fisherman granted a wish by a green sea turtle finds his greedy wife disagreeing with his choice in this adaptation of "The Fisherman and His Wife," a Grimm tale set in ancient Mexico. (Rev: BL 4/1/08; LMC 10/08; SLJ 5/08) [398.2]

12608 Kimmel, Eric A. *The Flying Canoe: A Christmas Story* (1–3). Illus. by Daniel San Souci. 2011, Holiday House $16.95 (978-082341730-8). 32pp. In this French-Canadian tale, a group of fur traders are spirited away to Montreal via a flying canoe on the night before Christmas. (Rev: BL 9/15/11; SLJ 10/1/11) [398.2]

12609 Kimmel, Eric A. *The Frog Princess: A Tlingit Legend from Alaska* (PS–2). Illus. by Rosanne Litzinger. 2006, Holiday $16.95 (978-0-8234-1618-9). 32pp. A beautiful girl falls in love with and marries a frog, much to the dismay of her Tlingit family. (Rev: BL 5/1/06; SLJ 6/06) [398.2]

12610 Kimmel, Eric A. *Gershon's Monster* (2–4). Illus. by Jon J. Muth. 2000, Scholastic $17.99 (978-0-439-10839-3). 32pp. Based on an early Hasidic legend, this is the story of Gershon and how his sins catch up with him. (Rev: BCCB 10/00; BL 10/1/00; HB 9/00; HBG 3/01; SLJ 9/00) [398.2]

12611 Kimmel, Eric A. *The Gingerbread Man* (PS–K). Illus. by Megan Lloyd. 1993, Holiday House LB $16.95 (978-0-8234-0824-5). 32pp. This is a modern version of a classic tale about the cookie that says he can't be caught. (Rev: BL 3/15/93; SLJ 6/93*) [398.2]

12612 Kimmel, Eric A. *The Goose Girl: A Story from the Brothers Grimm* (4–6). Illus. by Robert Sauber. 1995, Holiday House LB $15.95 (978-0-8234-1074-3). 32pp. A retelling of the Brothers Grimm tale of the young princess who is cheated out of her birthright by a greedy serving girl. (Rev: BL 10/15/95; SLJ 10/95) [398.2]

12613 Kimmel, Eric A. *The Greatest of All: A Japanese Folktale* (PS–3). Illus. by Giora Carmi. 1991, Holiday House LB $17.95 (978-0-8234-0885-6). 32pp. The father of Chuko Mouse is not happy when she tells him she wants to marry a humble, but handsome, field mouse. (Rev: BL 10/15/91; SLJ 10/91) [398.2]

12614 Kimmel, Eric A. *I Know Not What, I Know Not Where: A Russian Tale* (4–6). Illus. by Robert Sauber. 1994, Holiday House LB $16.95 (978-0-8234-1020-0). 64pp. In this Russian fairy tale, a hunter is rewarded for saving an enchanted dove's life by getting help to perform tasks demanded by the czar. (Rev: BCCB 7–8/94; BL 3/1/94; SLJ 6/94) [398.2]

12615 Kimmel, Eric A. *Iron John* (K–4). Illus. by Trina S. Hyman. 1994, Holiday House LB $17.95 (978-0-8234-1073-6). 32pp. An adaptation of a Grimm tale about Prince Walter, who meets Iron John in the forest and breaks a spell that has been cast over him. (Rev: BCCB 12/94; BL 11/1/94; SLJ 12/94) [398.2]

12616 Kimmel, Eric A. *The Jar of Fools: Eight Hanukkah Stories from Chelm* (PS–3). Illus. by Mordicai Gerstein. 2000, Holiday House $18.95 (978-0-8234-1463-5). 56pp. This collection of eight stories — some original plus some traditional Fools of Chelm tales — is filled with silliness and slapstick. (Rev: BL 9/1/00; HB 9/00; HBG 3/01)

12617 Kimmel, Eric A. *Little Red Hot* (PS–1). Illus. by Laura Huliska-Beith. 2013, Amazon/Two Lions $17.99 (978-1-4778-1638-7). 32pp. On her way to take her ailing grandmother a hot pepper pie, Little Red Hot meets Señor Lobo in this fractured version of Little Red Riding Hood. (Rev: BL 4/1/13; LMC 11–12/13; SLJ 6/13)

12618 Kimmel, Eric A. *Medio Pollito: A Spanish Tale* (K–2). Illus. by Valeria Docampo. 2010, Marshall Cavendish $17.99 (978-0-7614-5705-3). 32pp. The half-chick of the traditional folk tale (he has one leg, one eye, one wing . . .) sets off for Madrid and has various adventures with help from friends he meets along the way. (Rev: BL 9/1/10; LMC 1–2/11; SLJ 9/1/10) [398.2094]

12619 Kimmel, Eric A. *Montezuma and the Fall of the Aztecs* (2–5). Illus. by Daniel San Souci. 2000, Holiday House $16.95 (978-0-8234-1452-9). 32pp. After introducing the history and culture of the Aztecs, this picture book covers the reign of Montezuma, the coming of Cortes, and the Aztec leader's defeat. (Rev: BL 1/1–15/00; HBG 10/00; SLJ 3/00) [972]

12620 Kimmel, Eric A. *The Old Woman and Her Pig* (PS–3). Illus. by Giora Carmi. 1992, Holiday House LB $17.95 (978-0-8234-0970-9). 32pp. An excellent retelling of the classic British folktale. (Rev: BL 1/1/93; SLJ 10/92) [398.2]

12621 Kimmel, Eric A. *One Eye, Two Eyes, Three Eyes: A Hutzul Tale* (PS–3). Illus. by Dirk Zimmer. 1996, Holiday House LB $15.95 (978-0-8234-1183-2). 32pp. A traveler unwittingly bargains away his daughter in this Ukrainian tale. (Rev: BL 11/1/96; SLJ 1/97) [398.2]

12622 Kimmel, Eric A. *Onions and Garlic* (PS–3). Illus. by Katya Arnold. 1996, Holiday House $15.95 (978-0-

8234-1222-8). 32pp. In this Hebrew folktale, young Getzel is able to use a sackful of onions to obtain a fortune in diamonds. (Rev: BCCB 6/96; BL 4/1/96; SLJ 7/96) [398.2]

12623 Kimmel, Eric A. *Rimonah of the Flashing Sword: A North African Tale* (K–3). Illus. by Omar Rayyan. 1995, Holiday House LB $15.95 (978-0-8234-1093-4). An Egyptian folktale that is a variation on the Snow White story about a princess fleeing the wrath of a wicked stepmother. (Rev: BL 3/1/95; SLJ 3/95) [398.2]

12624 Kimmel, Eric A. *The Rooster's Antlers: A Story of the Chinese Zodiac* (PS–3). Illus. by YongSheng Xuan. 1999, Holiday House $16.95 (978-0-8234-1385-0). This Chinese folktale tells how Rooster gets his revenge when he isn't chosen by the emperor to be part of the Chinese calendar. (Rev: BCCB 10/99; BL 12/15/99; HBG 3/00; SLJ 10/99) [398.2]

12625 Kimmel, Eric A. *The Runaway Tortilla* (K–2). Illus. by Randy Cecil. 2000, Winslow $16.95 (978-1-890817-18-3). A silly tortilla runs away but is finally caught and eaten by Señor Coyote. (Rev: BCCB 12/00; HBG 10/01; SLJ 10/00) [398.2]

12626 Kimmel, Eric A. *Seven at One Blow: A Tale from the Brothers Grimm* (PS–1). Illus. by Megan Lloyd. 1998, Holiday House $16.95 (978-0-8234-1383-6). 32pp. After amazing himself by killing seven flies on his jelly sandwich with one blow, a little tailor sets out to seek his fortune in this tale from the Brothers Grimm. (Rev: BL 11/15/98; HB 1/99; HBG 3/99; SLJ 12/98) [398.2]

12627 Kimmel, Eric A. *Sirko and the Wolf* (K–3). Illus. by Robert Sauber. 1997, Holiday House LB $15.95 (978-0-8234-1257-0). 32pp. When a dog grows too old to be useful, he strikes a bargain with a wolf in this Ukrainian folktale. (Rev: BL 9/15/97; HBG 3/98; SLJ 11/97) [398.2]

12628 Kimmel, Eric A. *Squash It! A True and Ridiculous Tale* (3–5). Illus. by Robert Rayevsky. 1997, Holiday House LB $15.95 (978-0-8234-1299-0). 32pp. The Spanish tale of the king who adopted a louse as his favorite pet. (Rev: BL 6/1–15/97; HB 7/97; SLJ 7/97) [398.2]

12629 Kimmel, Eric A. *The Tale of Aladdin and the Wonderful Lamp: A Story from the Arabian Nights* (PS–3). Illus. by Ju-Hong Chen. 1992, Holiday House LB $14.95 (978-0-8234-0938-9). 32pp. A humorous retelling of the famous story. (Rev: BL 11/1/92; SLJ 12/92) [398.2]

12630 Kimmel, Eric A. *Ten Suns: A Chinese Legend* (K–3). Illus. by YongSheng Xuan. 1998, Holiday House $15.95 (978-0-8234-1317-1). When the ten sons (suns) of Di Jun decide that they will no longer make their solitary journeys across the sky each day but instead walk together, their father is afraid the combined heat will destroy the earth. (Rev: BCCB 6/98; BL 5/1/98; HBG 10/98; SLJ 5/98) [398.2]

12631 Kimmel, Eric A. *The Three Cabritos* (PS–1). Illus. by Stephen Gilpin. 2007, Marshall Cavendish $16.99 (978-0-7614-5343-7). 32pp. Three goats must cross a bridge into Mexico when they encounter a legendary monster in this lighthearted retelling of "The Three Billy Goats Gruff." (Rev: BCCB 5/07; BL 7/07; SLJ 5/07) [398.2]

12632 Kimmel, Eric A. *The Three Little Tamales* (K–3). Illus. by Valeria Docampo. 2009, Marshall Cavendish $17.99 (978-0-7614-5519-6). 32pp. Three little tamales flee for their lives and build houses made of different materials in this fractured "Three Little Pigs" set in the Southwest. (Rev: BL 3/15/09; LMC 8/09; SLJ 6/09) [398.2]

12633 Kimmel, Eric A. *The Three Princes* (K–3). Illus. by Leonard Everett Fisher. 1994, Holiday House LB $16.95 (978-0-8234-1115-3). 30pp. A beautiful princess shows great wisdom in choosing her husband from the three noble cousins who are her suitors in this Middle Eastern folktale. (Rev: BCCB 4/94; BL 3/1/94*; SLJ 3/94) [398.2]

12634 Kimmel, Eric A. *Three Sacks of Truth: A Story from France* (PS–3). Illus. by Robert Rayevsky. 1993, Holiday House LB $15.95 (978-0-8234-0921-1). In this French folktale, a king promises his daughter to the man who can bring him the perfect peach. (Rev: BCCB 7–8/93; BL 4/15/93; SLJ 7/93) [398.2]

12635 Kimmel, Eric A. *Three Samurai Cats: A Story from Japan* (PS–2). Illus. by Mordicai Gerstein. 2003, Holiday House $16.95 (978-0-8234-1742-1). In this colorful adaptation of a Japanese folktale, a feudal lord seeks help from a trio of samurai cats to rid his castle of a bothersome rat. (Rev: BL 4/15/03; HB 7/03; HBG 10/03; SLJ 6/03) [398.2]

12636 Kimmel, Eric A. *The Two Mountains: An Aztec Legend* (3–5). Illus. 2000, Holiday House $16.95 (978-0-8234-1504-5). 32pp. This Aztec legend tells how two young lovers are transformed into the two mountains that overlook the Valley of Mexico. (Rev: BL 5/15/00; HBG 10/00; SLJ 4/00) [398.2]

12637 Kimmelman, Leslie. *The Little Red Hen and the Passover Matzah* (PS–1). Illus. by Paul Meisel. 2010, Holiday House $16.95 (978-0-8234-1952-4). 32pp. In this version of The Little Red Hen, the plucky protagonist exclaims "Oy gevalt!" as Passover approaches and "What chutzpah!" when her lazy friends show up to the seder dinner she's had to make by herself. (Rev: BL 2/1/10; HB 5–6/10; SLJ 3/1/10*) [398.2]

12638 Knutson, Barbara. *How the Guinea Fowl Got Her Spots: A Swahili Tale of Friendship* (PS–2). Illus. 1990, Carolrhoda LB $15.95 (978-0-87614-416-9). 24pp. Cow returns a favor given by Nganga the Guinea Fowl by giving her spots that can help her hide from enemies. (Rev: BCCB 7–8/90*; BL 6/15/90; HB 9/90; SLJ 9/90) [398.2]

12639 Knutson, Barbara. *Love and Roast Chicken: A Trickster Tale from the Andes Mountains* (PS–2). Illus. Series: Carolrhoda Picture Books. 2004, Carolrhoda $16.95 (978-1-57505-657-9). 32pp. A tiny guinea pig outwits both a fox and a farmer in this trickster tale set in the Andes. (Rev: BL 9/15/04; SLJ 11/04) [398.2]

12640 *Kokopelli, Drum in Belly* (3–5). Trans. and illus. by Gail E. Haley. 2003, Filter $12.95 (978-0-86541-069-5). Rich illustrations enhance this telling of the Native American legend of Kokopelli the Cicada. (Rev: BL 10/15/03; HBG 4/04; SLJ 2/04)

12641 Krasno, Rena, and Yeng-Fong Chiang. *Cloud Weavers: Ancient Chinese Legends* (2–6). 2003, Pacific View $22.95 (978-1-881896-26-5). 96pp. Nearly two dozen Chinese stories — legends, tales from Chinese history, and stories from Chinese literature — are introduced with background information and accompanied by Chinese posters from the early 20th century. (Rev: BL 7/03; SLJ 8/03) [398.2]

12642 Krensky, Stephen. *Bokuden and the Bully: A Japanese Folktale* (2–5). Illus. by Cheryl Kirk Noll. Series: On My Own Folklore. 2008, Millbrook LB $25.26 (978-0-8225-7547-4). In 16th-century Japan and nobleman who is talented with the sword unmans a bullying warrior. (Rev: SLJ 3/09) [398.2]

12643 Krensky, Stephen. *John Henry* (2–4). Illus. by Mark Oldroyd. Series: On Your Own Folklore. 2006, Lerner $25.26 (978-1-57505-887-0). 48pp. Tall tales chronicle some of the amazing feats attributed to John Henry in American railroading folklore. (Rev: BL 9/1/06; SLJ 8/06) [398.2]

12644 Krensky, Stephen, adapt. *Paul Bunyan* (1–4). Illus. by Craig Orback. Series: On My Own Folklore. 2006, Millbrook LB $25.26 (978-1-57505-888-7). 48pp. For beginning readers, this is an introduction to lumberjack Paul Bunyan and his amazing feats. Also use *Pecos Bill* (2006). (Rev: SLJ 8/06) [398.2]

12645 Krishnaswami, Uma. *Stories of the Flood* (4–6). Illus. 1994, Roberts Rinehart $15.95 (978-1-57098-007-7). 41pp. In a picture-book format, nine flood myths from such places as ancient Sumeria and Hawaii are retold. (Rev: BL 2/1/95; SLJ 2/95) [291.13]

12646 Kroll, Steven. *Queen of the May* (PS–3). Illus. by Patience Brewster. 1993, Holiday House LB $15.95 (978-0-8234-1004-0). 32pp. Sylvie becomes Queen of the May in spite of her meddling stepmother and stepsister. (Rev: BL 4/1/93; SLJ 7/93) [398.2]

12647 Krull, Kathleen, ed. *A Pot o' Gold: A Treasury of Irish Stories, Poetry, Folklore and (of Course) Blarney* (4–8). Illus. by David McPhail. 2004, Hyperion $16.99 (978-0-7868-0625-6). This is a comprehensive collection — including riddles, blessing, and battle cries — with attractive and appropriate illustrations. (Rev: BL 2/15/04; SLJ 3/04) [820.8]

12648 Kushner, Lawrence, and Gary Schmidt. *In God's Hands* (1–3). Illus. by Matthew J. Baek. 2005, Jewish Lights $16.99 (978-1-58023-224-1). Jacob, a rich man who believes he is following a divine mandate, bakes loaves of bread and takes them to the synagogue where they are gratefully retrieved by David, a man so poor he can't afford to feed his family. (Rev: BL 10/1/05*; SLJ 10/05) [398.2]

12649 L'Homme, Erik. *Tales of a Lost Kingdom: A Journey into Northwest Pakistan* (3–5). Trans. by Claudia

Zoe Bedrick. Illus. by François Place. 2007, Enchanted Lion $17.95 (978-1-59270-072-1). Three folk tales from Pakistan, each ending with a question and a moral. (Rev: BL 1/1–15/08; SLJ 12/07) [398.209549]

12650 Lach, William, ed. *Fairyland: In Art and Poetry* (3–7). Illus. by Richard Doyle. 2002, Holt $17.95 (978-0-8050-7006-4). 40pp. Illustrations from Richard Doyle's classic *In Fairyland* (1870) are paired with selections from writers including Shakespeare, de la Mare, Langston Hughes, and Laura Ingalls Wilder in a handsome volume suited to browsing. (Rev: HBG 10/02; SLJ 7/02) [398.2]

12651 Laird, Elizabeth. *Beautiful Bananas* (PS–2). Illus. by Liz Pichon. 2004, Peachtree $15.95 (978-1-56145-305-4). In this charming circular folktale, young Beatrice sets off for her grandfather's house with a bunch of bananas balanced on her head; various encounters with animals along the way cause substitutions for the bananas. (Rev: BL 5/1/04; SLJ 4/04) [398.2]

12652 Lake, Mary D., retel. *The Royal Drum: An Ashanti Tale* (K–2). Illus. by Carol O'Malia. 1996, Mondo $14.95 (978-1-57255-140-4). Using a rebus approach, this tale from Ghana tells how Anansi the spider gets all of the animals to participate in making a drum for Lion the king. (Rev: SLJ 11/96) [398.2]

12653 Lang, Andrew. *The Arabian Nights Entertainments* (5–9). 1969, Dover paper $12.95 (978-0-486-22289-9). Aladdin and Sinbad are only two of the characters in these 26 tales of Arabia and the East. (Rev: BL 9/1/89) [398.2]

12654 Lang, Andrew, ed. *Blue Fairy Book* (4–6). 1965, Dover paper $10.95 (978-0-486-21437-5). 390pp. A fine edition of this classic collection. There are 11 other "color" Fairy Books. Some are: *Green Fairy Book* (1965); *Yellow Fairy Book* (1966); *Grey Fairy Book; Orange Fairy Book; Red Fairy Book* (all 1968).

12655 Langton, Jane. *The Queen's Necklace: A Swedish Folktale* (3–5). Illus. by Ilse Plume. 1994, Hyperion LB $16.49 (978-0-7868-2007-8). 40pp. When a queen gives away pearls to help the poor, her cruel king demands her life. (Rev: BL 10/1/94; SLJ 10/94) [398.2]

12656 Langton, Jane. *Saint Francis and the Wolf* (PS–1). Illus. by Ilse Plume. 2007, Godine $16.95 (978-1-56792-320-9). 32pp. A brief retelling of the legend of Francis of Assisi and the wolf that was plaguing Gubbio. (Rev: BL 10/1/07; SLJ 12/07) [398.2]

12657 Langton, Jane. *Salt: From a Russian Folktale* (K–3). Trans. by Alice Plume. Illus. by Ilse Plume. 1992, Hyperion $14.95 (978-1-56282-178-4). A Russian folktale about three brothers who go to sea to seek their fortunes. (Rev: BCCB 1/93; BL 10/15/92; SLJ 12/92) [398.2]

12658 Lansky, Bruce, ed. *Girls to the Rescue Book 2: Tales of Clever, Courageous Girls from Around the World* (3–6). 1996, Meadowbrook LB $3.95 (978-0-671-57375-1). In each of the folktales gathered from around the world, young women must rely on their ingenuity to overcome obstacles. (Rev: SLJ 2/97) [398.2]

12659 Lansky, Bruce, sel. *Girls to the Rescue: Tales of Clever, Courageous Girls from Around the World* (3–6). 1995, Meadowbrook paper $3.95 (978-0-88166-215-3). 100pp. A collection of stories about resourceful young women, many of which originated in the world's folklore. (Rev: SLJ 12/95) [398.2]

12660 LaRochelle, David. *The End* (PS–3). Illus. by Richard Egielski. 2007, Scholastic $16.99 (978-0-439-64011-4). From the beginning — "And they all lived happily ever after" — to the final "Once upon a time" this zany fairy tale keeps up its topsy-turvy nature. (Rev: BL 1/1–15/07; HB 5/07; HBG 10/07; LMC 5/07; SLJ 4/07*) [398.2]

12661 Larrabee, Lisa. *Grandmother Five Baskets* (2–4). Illus. by Lori Sawyer. 1993, Harbinger paper $9.95 (978-0-943173-90-0). 60pp. Using five baskets that have been made by a Poarch Creek Indian woman as a metaphor, different stages of life are explained. (Rev: SLJ 3/94)

12662 Larson, Jean Russell. *The Fish Bride and Other Gypsy Tales* (4–6). Illus. 2000, Linnet $22.50 (978-0-208-02474-9). 90pp. Sixteen tales of romance, adventure, and humor from the rich traditions of Rom or Gypsies are attractively retold in this entertaining collection. (Rev: BL 11/1/00; HB 11/00; HBG 3/01; SLJ 9/00) [398.2]

12663 Lavitt, Edward, and Robert E. McDowell. *Nihancan's Feast of Beaver: Animal Tales of the North American Indians* (2–6). Illus. by Bunny P. Huffman. 1990, Museum of New Mexico paper $12.95 (978-0-89013-211-1). This handsome book contains 36 tales from nine different cultural areas in North America. (Rev: BL 3/1/91) [398.2]

12664 Leavy, Una. *Irish Fairy Tales and Legends* (4–8). 1997, Roberts Rinehart $18.95 (978-1-57098-177-7). An attractive book that contains 10 Irish legends, some going back 2,000 years. (Rev: BL 2/1/98; HBG 10/98; SLJ 2/98) [398.2]

12665 Lee, Jeanne. *I Once Was a Monkey: Stories Buddha Told* (2–4). Illus. 1999, Farrar $16.00 (978-0-374-33548-9). 40pp. This handsome volume contains six *Jatakas* or birth stories from the Buddhist faith. (Rev: BCCB 4/99; BL 3/15/99; HBG 10/99; SLJ 3/99) [294.3]

12666 Lee, Jeanne M. *The Song of Mu Lan* (5–8). 1995, Front St $17.95 (978-1-886910-00-3). Mu Lan disguises herself as a boy and joins the emperor's army in this traditional Chinese tale. (Rev: BL 11/15/95; SLJ 12/95) [398.2]

12667 Lee, Jeanne M, retel. *Toad Is the Uncle of Heaven: A Vietnamese Folk Tale* (4–7). Retold by Jeanne M. Lee. Illus. by Jeanne M. Lee. 1985, Henry Holt paper $6.95 (978-0-8050-1147-0). This book tells the story of Toad who collects companions on his way to see the King of Heaven, who makes rain. (Rev: BL 11/1/85; HB 3–4/86) [398.2]

12668 Levine, Gail C. *Cinderellis and the Glass Hill* (4–6). Illus. 2000, HarperCollins LB $14.89 (978-0-06-028337-7). 96pp. This humorous variation on the Cinderella story has as its central character a boy named Ellis who is ignored by his older brothers but eventually wins the princess Marigold. (Rev: BL 1/1–15/00; HBG 10/00) [398.2]

12669 Levine, Gail C. *The Princess Test* (3–6). Illus. 1999, HarperCollins LB $8.89 (978-0-06-028063-5). 80pp. In this variation on *The Princess and the Pea*, a blacksmith's daughter turns out to be more sensitive than a princess. (Rev: BL 4/15/99) [398.2]

12670 Levine, Gail Carson. *Ella Enchanted* (5–8). 1997, HarperCollins LB $17.89 (978-0-06-027511-2). A spirited, cleverly plotted retelling of the Cinderella story in which Ella is finally paired with the Prince Charmant. (Rev: BCCB 5/97; BL 4/15/97*; HB 5–6/97; SLJ 4/97*; VOYA 8/97)

12671 Lewis, Naomi, and Hans Christian Andersen. *The Snow Queen* (2–4). Illus. by Christian Birmingham. 2008, Candlewick $16.99 (978-0-7636-3229-8). 64pp. Word and image work together to retell this Andersen fairy tale that features a surprisingly warm and lovely Snow Queen. (Rev: BCCB 2/09; BLO 1/13/09; HB 1/09; SLJ 2/09) [398.2]

12672 Lewis, Naomi, retel. *Elf Hill: Tales from Hans Christian Andersen* (K–3). Illus. by Emma Chichester Clark. 1999, Star Bright $20.95 (978-1-887734-70-7). 68pp. A straightforward retelling of nine tales from the familiar "The Princess and the Pea" to the unfamiliar "The Money-Box Pig." (Rev: SLJ 1/00) [398.2]

12673 Liddell, Janice. *Imani and the Flying Africans* (2–5). Illus. by Linda Nickens. 1994, Africa World $14.95 (978-0-86543-365-6); paper $6.95 (978-0-86543-366-3). After hearing about the Flying Africans, who could rise into the air and escape slavery, young Imani dreams that he is captured by kidnappers and uses the same method to achieve freedom. (Rev: SLJ 11/94) [398.2]

12674 Light, Steve. *Puss in Boots* (PS–2). Illus. 2002, Abrams $14.95 (978-0-8109-4368-1). Collages illustrate this faithful version of a favorite folktale. (Rev: BCCB 5/02; BL 4/15/02; HBG 10/02; SLJ 4/02) [398.2]

12675 Lilly, Melinda. *Kwian and the Lazy Sun: African Tales and Myths* (K–3). Series: African Tales and Myths. 1998, Rourke LB $26.60 (978-1-57103-243-0). In this South African tale, a young girl figures out how to get the sun and the moon into the sky. Also use from the same series and author *Tamba and the Chief: A Tenne Tale* and *Warrior Son of a Warrior Son: A Masai Tale* (both 1998). (Rev: SLJ 4/99) [398.2]

12676 Lilly, Melinda, retel. *Spider and His Son Find Wisdom: An Akan Tale* (2–4). Illus. by Charles Reasoner. Series: African Tales and Myths. 1998, Rourke LB $19.95 (978-1-57103-244-7). 31pp. The spider, Anansi, tries to retrieve all the good advice he has given to unappreciative villagers in this Akan tale told in a picture-book format. (Rev: SLJ 3/99) [398.2]

12677 Lilly, Melinda, retel. *Wanyana and Matchmaker Frog: A Bagandan Tale* (2–4). Illus. by Charles Reasoner. Series: African Tales and Myths. 1998, Rourke LB $19.95 (978-1-57103-247-8). 31pp. To repay a kindness he received when in distress, a frog gives a young girl good advice in choosing a husband in this African folk tale. (Rev: SLJ 3/99) [398.2]

12678 Lilly, Melinda, retel. *Zimani's Drum: A Malawian Tale* (2–4). Illus. by Charles Reasoner. Series: African Tales and Myths. 1998, Rourke LB $19.95 (978-1-57103-248-5). 31pp. Blind Zimani rescues his brother and two sisters from the clutches of Mkango the Lion. (Rev: SLJ 3/99) [398.2]

12679 Lin, Grace. *The Red Thread: An Adoption Fairy Tale* (K–3). Illus. by author. 2007, Albert Whitman $16.95 (978-0-8075-6922-1). Lin interweaves a fairy tale based on a traditional Chinese belief with a story about a contemporary adopted child. (Rev: BL 10/15/07; SLJ 9/07) [398.2]

12680 Lind, Michael. *Bluebonnet Girl* (K–3). Illus. by Kate Kiesler. 2003, Holt $16.95 (978-0-8050-6573-2). 40pp. A Comanche legend telling why bluebonnets bloom in Texas. (Rev: BL 3/15/03; HBG 4/04; SLJ 4/03) [398.2]

12681 Linn, Dennis, et al. *What Is My Song?* (2–4). Illus. by Francisco Miranda. 2005, Paulist Press $16.95 (978-0-8091-6722-7). 32pp. In this adaptation of an African folktale, a boy strives to live up to what he believes to be his God-given purpose in life. (Rev: BL 12/1/04)

12682 Linzer, Lila. *Once Upon an Island* (2–5). 1999, Front St. $15.95 (978-1-886910-10-2). 76pp. Four tales about animals (including bees, goats, and doves) from the island of St. Croix are retold in a dialect that captures the lilting rhythms of West Indian English. (Rev: HBG 10/99; SLJ 4/99) [398.2]

12683 Ljungkvist, Laura. *Snow White and the Seven Dwarfs* (PS–2). Illus. 2003, Abrams $14.95 (978-0-8109-4241-7). 38pp. Snow White gets a contemporary look in this beautifully illustrated simple retelling. (Rev: BL 4/15/03; HBG 10/03; SLJ 7/03) [398.2]

12684 Long, Laurel, and Jacqueline Ogburn, retels. *The Lady and the Lion: A Brothers Grimm Tale* (2–4). Illus. by Laurel Long. 2003, Dial $16.99 (978-0-8037-2651-2). Lush oil paintings decorate this romantic adaptation of a Grimm story about a lion who turns into a price at night. (Rev: BL 1/1/04; HBG 4/04; SLJ 2/04) [398.2]

12685 Lorenz, Albert. *Jack and the Beanstalk: How a Small Fellow Solved a Big Problem* (PS–3). Illus. 2002, Abrams $16.95 (978-0-8109-1160-4). Realistic, highly detailed illustrations emphasize the importance of size and Jack's inventiveness. (Rev: BL 10/1/02; HBG 3/03; SLJ 10/02) [398.2]

12686 Lottridge, Celia B., retel. *The Name of the Tree* (K–5). Illus. by Ian Wallace. 1990, Macmillan $16.00 (978-0-689-50490-7). This Bantu tale begins with hungry animals finding a tree laden with every fruit imaginable. (Rev: BCCB 4/90; SLJ 3/90) [398.2]

12687 Louie, Ai-Ling, retel. *Yeh-Shen: A Cinderella Story from China* (2–6). Illus. by Ed Young. 1982, Penguin $16.99 (978-0-399-20900-0). 32pp. A Chinese story about a poor girl living with her cruel stepmother and stepsisters. [398.2]

12688 Love, Hallie N., and Bonni Larson, retels. *Watakame's Journey: The Story of the Great Flood and the New World: A Huichol Indian Tale* (2–6). Illus. 1999, Clear Light $14.95 (978-1-56416-029-4). This is a Mexican version of the Noah story featuring a young boy who is selected by the goddess of all growing things to build a boat to withstand the coming flood. (Rev: SLJ 12/99) [398.2]

12689 Lowell, Susan. *Cindy Ellen: A Wild Western Cinderella* (K–3). Illus. by Jane Manning. 2000, HarperCollins LB $17.89 (978-0-06-027447-4). This version of the Cinderella story features a mean stepmother, a godmother with a six-gun, and a cowboy hero named Joe Prince. (Rev: BCCB 9/00; BL 5/15/00; HBG 10/00) [398.2]

12690 Lowell, Susan. *Dusty Locks and the Three Bears* (PS–1). Illus. by Randy Cecil. 2001, Holt $15.95 (978-0-8050-5862-8). 32pp. A western version of Goldilocks starring a bad-tempered, ill-mannered runaway. (Rev: BCCB 7–8/01; BL 7/01; HB 7/01; HBG 10/01; SLJ 7/01) [398.2]

12691 Lowell, Susan. *The Tortoise and the Jackrabbit* (PS–2). Illus. by Jim Harris. 1994, Northland LB $15.95 (978-0-87358-586-6). 32pp. This favorite Aesop fable is retold with the tortoise an aged grandmother and the hare a conceited egocentric. (Rev: BL 1/15/95; HB 3/05; SLJ 2/95)

12692 Lowery, Linda, and Richard Keep. *The Chocolate Tree: A Mayan Folktale* (PS–3). Illus. by Janice L. Porter. 2008, Lerner LB $25.26 (978-0-8225-7545-0). 48pp. This delicious beginning chapter book features lively words and attractive illustrations that tell the Mayan story of how humans got chocolate. (Rev: BL 9/15/08) [398.2]

12693 Lowry, Amy. *Fox Tails: Four Fables from Aesop* (K–2). Illus. by author. 2012, Holiday House $16.95 (978-0-8234-2400-9). 32pp. Four fables featuring foxes are melded into one in this subtly humorous introduction to Aesop's works for young people. (Rev: BL 2/15/12*; LMC 8=912; SLJ 4/1/12) [398.2]

12694 Luenn, Nancy. *The Miser on the Mountain: A Nisqually Legend of Mount Rainier* (3–6). Illus. by Pierr Morgan. 1997, Sasquatch $15.95 (978-1-57061-082-0). 32pp. An Indian legend set on Ta-co-bet, or Mount Rainier, in which greed leads to a man's downfall. (Rev: BL 9/15/97; HBG 3/98; SLJ 1/98) [398.2]

12695 Lunge-Larsen, Lise. *The Hidden Folk: Stories of Fairies, Gnomes, Selkies, and Other Secret Beings* (3–5). Illus. by Beth Krommes. 2004, Houghton $18.00 (978-0-618-17495-9). 80pp. Drawing on the folkloric traditions of northern Europe, Lunge-Larsen offers up eight tales about magical beings. (Rev: BL 9/1/04) [398.2]

12696 Lunge-Larsen, Lise. *The Troll with No Heart in His Body* (2–4). Illus. 1999, Houghton $18.00 (978-0-395-91371-0). 96pp. A collection of nine Norwegian folktales, including "Three Billy Goats Gruff." (Rev: BCCB 1/00; BL 9/1/99; HB 11/99; HBG 3/00; SLJ 11/99) [398.2]

12697 Lupton, Hugh. *Pirican Pic and Pirican Mor* (2–4). Illus. by Yumi Heo. 2003, Barefoot Books $16.99 (978-1-84148-070-1). A humorous cumulative Celtic folktale recounts the conflict between Pirican Pic and Pirican Mor over the latter's theft of the former's hard-won walnuts. (Rev: BL 4/1/03; HB 7/03; HBG 10/03; SLJ 5/03) [398.2]

12698 Lupton, Hugh. *The Story Tree: Tales to Read About* (PS–2). Illus. by Sophie Fatus. 2001, Barefoot Books $18.99 (978-1-84148-312-2). 64pp. This volume includes seven folktales from around the world, including favorites such as "The Three Billy Goats Gruff" and "The Magic Porridge Pot." (Rev: BL 10/1/01; HBG 3/02; SLJ 11/01) [398.2]

12699 Lupton, Hugh, retel. *Tales of Wisdom and Wonder* (2–6). Illus. by Niamh Sharkey. 1998, Barefoot Books $18.95 (978-1-901223-09-5). 64pp. Seven traditional stories from different cultures, such as Haitian, Cree, West African, Russian, and Irish, are retold in this anthology. (Rev: SLJ 10/98) [398.2]

12700 Lynch, Tom, adapt. *Fables from Aesop* (3–5). Illus. by Tom Lynch. 2000, Viking $15.99 (978-0-670-88948-8). A striking presentation of 13 of the most famous fables from Aesop. (Rev: HBG 10/01; SLJ 10/00) [398.2]

12701 Lyons, Mary. *Roy Makes a Car* (PS–2). Illus. by Terry Widener. 2005, Simon & Schuster $16.95 (978-0-689-84640-3). 32pp. A tall tale about auto mechanic Roy's designn for an accident-proof car, based on a folktale collected by Zora Neale Hurston in the 1930s. (Rev: BL 2/1/05; SLJ 2/05) [398.2]

12702 McBratney, Sam. *One Voice, Please: Favorite Read-Aloud Stories* (2–4). Illus. by Russell Ayto. 2008, Candlewick $15.99 (978-0-7636-3479-7). 176pp. A collection of more than 50 short, traditional stories that are suitable for reading aloud. (Rev: BL 4/1/08; HB 5/08; SLJ 8/08) [398.2]

12703 McCarthy, Ralph F. *The Inch-High Samurai* (K–3). Illus. by Shiro Kasamatsu. 1993, Kodansha $19.95 (4-7700-1758-8). 48pp. Pint-sized Inchy Bo performs some mighty deeds, including fighting an ogre, in this Japanese folktale. (Rev: BL 12/15/93; SLJ 2/94) [398.2]

12704 McCarthy, Ralph F. *The Moon Princess* (3–6). Illus. by Kancho Oda. Series: Children's Classics. 1993, Kodansha $19.95 (4-7700-1756-1). Retellings in verse of three Japanese folktales, one about a virtuous old man and his dog, another a Tom Thumb–like character, and another, the title story, about a couple who find a tiny girl inside a bamboo. (Rev: SLJ 2/94) [398.2]

12705 McCaughrean, Geraldine. *Grandma Chickenlegs* (K–3). Illus. by Moira Kemp. 1999, Carolrhoda $15.95 (978-1-57505-415-5). 32pp. In this classic Russian folktale, young Tatia is sent to the witch's house to borrow a needle and is soon a prisoner of the horrible Baba Yaga. (Rev: BL 10/15/99; HBG 3/00; SLJ 1/00) [398.2]

12706 McClintock, Barbara. *Animal Fables from Aesop* (4–6). Illus. 1991, Godine $18.95 (978-0-87923-913-8). 48pp. The text is an expansion of nine fables complete with dialogue and dramatic situations. (Rev: BCCB 1/92; BL 1/1/92; HB 1/92; SLJ 1/92) [398.2]

12707 McClintock, Barbara. *Cinderella* (K–3). Illus. 2005, Scholastic $15.99 (978-0-439-56145-7). 32pp. This beautifully illustrated adaptation of the classic Cinderella fairy tale is set in the Paris of Louis XIV. (Rev: BL 1/1–15/06; SLJ 10/05*) [398.2]

12708 McClure, Gillian. *The Land of the Dragon King and Other Korean Stories* (3–5). Illus. by author. 2008, Frances Lincoln $19.95 (978-1-84507-805-8). 64pp. A collection of nine varied folktales from Korea — fables and pourquoi and trickster tales — with handsome Korean-inspired illustrations. (Rev: BLO 1/13/09; SLJ 12/08) [398.2]

12709 McDermott, Denis. *The Golden Goose* (PS–2). Illus. 2000, HarperCollins LB $15.89 (978-0-688-11403-9). 32pp. In this version of the Grimm Brothers tale, young Hans is rewarded for helping a troll by the gift of a talking golden goose. (Rev: BL 5/15/00; HBG 10/00; SLJ 7/00) [398.2]

12710 McDermott, Gerald. *Anansi, the Spider: A Tale from the Ashanti* (K–3). Illus. by author. 1972, Holt LB $16.95 (978-0-8050-0310-9); paper $6.95 (978-0-8050-0311-6). 48pp. Because Anansi and his sons quarrel, the moon remains in the sky. [398.2]

12711 McDermott, Gerald. *Jabuti the Tortoise: A Trickster Tale from the Amazon* (K–2). Illus. 2001, Harcourt $16.00 (978-0-15-200496-5). 32pp. A brilliantly colorful retelling of the story of Jabuti, a tortoise who is tricked by a jealous vulture, who in turn is punished as the other birds gain colors and songs. (Rev: BL 9/15/01; HBG 3/02; SLJ 9/01) [398.2]

12712 McDermott, Gerald. *Monkey: A Trickster Tale from India* (PS–2). Illus. by author. 2011, Harcourt $16.99 (978-0-15-216596-3). 32pp. This Buddhist trickster tale, in which Crocodile and Monkey vie for superiority, is enhanced by McDermott's signature illustrations. (Rev: BL 4/15/11; HB 5–6/11; SLJ 4/11*) [398.2]

12713 McDermott, Gerald. *Pig-Boy: A Trickster Tale from Hawai'i* (K–1). Illus. by author. 2009, Harcourt $16.00 (978-0-15-216590-1). A naughty Pig-Boy uses his grandmother's magic to shape-shift and evade the annoyed King and Pele, the goddess of fire, in this story based on Hawaiian myth. (Rev: BCCB 5/09; BL 5/15/09; HB 7/09; SLJ 7/09) [398.2]

12714 McDermott, Gerald. *The Stonecutter: A Japanese Folk Tale* (K–3). Illus. by author. 1975, Puffin paper $6.99 (978-0-14-050289-3). 32pp. The familiar tale of the stonecutter who kept demanding greater power is brilliantly illustrated with colorful, stylized collage paintings. [398.2]

12715 McDermott, Gerald. *Zomo the Rabbit: A Trickster Tale from West Africa* (PS–3). Illus. 1992, Harcourt $14.95 (978-0-15-299967-4). An enduring Nigerian tale of a trickster who is cunning but not always wise. (Rev: BCCB 9/92*; BL 9/15/92*; SLJ 11/92*) [398.2]

12716 MacDonald, Amy. *Please, Malese!* (K–3). Illus. by Emily Lisker. 2002, Farrar $16.00 (978-0-374-36000-9).

32pp. This variation of a Haitian folktale tells the story of wily Malese, a trickster who can convince the villagers of anything. (Rev: BL 8/02; HB 9/02; HBG 3/03; SLJ 9/02) [398.2]

12717 MacDonald, George. *The Golden Key* (2–6). Illus. by Maurice Sendak. 1993, Farrar paper $6.95 (978-0-374-42590-6). 96pp. In this classic fairy tale, two young people search for a keyhole where their golden key will fit. [398.2]

12718 MacDonald, George. *The Light Princess* (1–6). Adapted by Robin McKinley. Illus. by Katie T. Treherne. 1988, Harcourt $13.95 (978-0-15-245300-8). 44pp. A prince breaks the spell of a princess who has been deprived of gravity. (Rev: BL 7/88) [398.2] ∩

12719 MacDonald, Margaret Read. *Conejito: A Folktale from Panama* (K–3). Illus. by Geraldo Vaério. 2006, August House $16.95 (978-0-87483-779-7). 32pp. In this rhyming folktale from Panama, Conejito, a little rabbit, sets off to visit his aunt and along the way cleverly manages to escape the clutches of three fearsome predators. Conejito's song is included, tempting young children to sing along. (Rev: BL 3/15/06; SLJ 4/06) [398.2]

12720 MacDonald, Margaret Read. *Fat Cat* (PS–3). Illus. by Julie Paschkis. 2001, August House $15.95 (978-0-87483-616-5). 32pp. Brilliant illustrations and rhythmic prose are featured in this Danish folktale about a cat that gobbles up anyone who calls him fat, and the cunning mouse that saves them all. (Rev: BL 11/15/01; HBG 3/02; SLJ 1/02) [398.2]

12721 MacDonald, Margaret Read. *Go to Sleep, Gecko! A Balinese Folktale* (PS–2). Illus. by Geraldo Valério. 2006, August House $16.95 (978-0-87483-780-3). Gecko complains repeatedly to Elephant, the village chief, that fireflies are keeping him awake at night, but realizes eventually that it's all part of the natural order. (Rev: SLJ 10/06) [398.2]

12722 MacDonald, Margaret Read. *The Great Smelly, Slobbery, Small-Toothed Dog* (PS–2). Illus. by Julie Paschkis. 2007, Random $16.95 (978-0-87483-808-4). A big, slobbery dog saves a rich man from a thief and chooses as his reward the rich man's daughter in this variant of "Beauty and the Beast." (Rev: BL 11/1/07; LMC 1/08; SLJ 12/07) [398.2]

12723 MacDonald, Margaret Read. *The Old Woman Who Lived in a Vinegar Bottle: A British Fairy Tale* (PS–2). Illus. by Nancy D. Fowlkes. 1995, August House $15.95 (978-0-87483-415-4). In this English folktale, a fairy discovers that there is no pleasing some people when she supplies better housing for an old woman who had been living in a vinegar bottle. (Rev: BL 10/1/95; SLJ 1/96) [398.2]

12724 MacDonald, Margaret Read. *Peace Tales: World Folktales to Talk About* (5–7). 1992, Shoe String LB $25.00 (978-0-208-02328-5); paper $17.50 (978-0-208-02329-2). Stories and proverbs directed toward achieving world peace. (Rev: BL 6/15/92; SLJ 10/92) [398.2]

12725 MacDonald, Margaret Read. *Slop! A Welsh Folktale* (K–2). Illus. by Yvonne Davis. 1997, Fulcrum $15.95 (978-1-55591-352-6). 24pp. In this Welsh folktale, fairies become annoyed when their neighbor continually empties his slop bucket on top of their cottage. (Rev: BL 11/1/97; HBG 3/98; SLJ 11/97) [398.2]

12726 MacDonald, Margaret Read. *Teeny Weeny Bop* (K–2). Illus. by Diane Greenseid. 2006, Albert Whitman $16.95 (978-0-8075-7992-3). 32pp. When Teeny Weeny Bop makes a series of bad decisions, she ends up with a slug as a pet in this silly story that incorporates folkloric features. (Rev: BL 5/15/06; SLJ 8/06) [398.2]

12727 MacDonald, Margaret Read. *Too Many Fairies: A Celtic Tale* (K–2). Illus. by Susan Mitchell. 2010, Marshall Cavendish $17.99 (978-0-7614-5604-9). 32pp. In this Scottish-Irish folktale an old woman who hates housework initially welcomes some helpful fairies but soon finds their noise too irritating — at which point the fairies undo all their good work. (Rev: BL 4/15/10; LMC 8–9/10; SLJ 4/1/10) [398.2]

12728 MacDonald, Margaret Read. *Tunjur! Tunjur! Tunjur! A Palestinian Folktale* (PS–2). Illus. by Alik Arzoumanian. 2006, Marshall Cavendish $16.95 (978-0-7614-5225-6). 32pp. A woman's prayers for a child to love are rewarded with the arrival of a little cooking pot with unfortunate larcenous tendencies. (Rev: BL 3/1/06; SLJ 4/06) [398.2]

12729 MacDonald, Margaret Read, comp. *Earth Care: World Folktales to Talk About* (3–7). 1999, Linnet LB $26.50 (978-0-208-02416-9); paper $17.50 (978-0-208-02426-8). 161pp. These 41 folk stories from 30 countries deal with humans and their relationship to nature. (Rev: BL 1/1–15/00; HBG 3/00; SLJ 4/00) [398.2]

12730 MacDonald, Margaret Read, retel. *The Girl Who Wore Too Much: A Folktale from Thailand* (PS–3). Illus. by Yvonne Davis. 1998, August House $15.95 (978-0-87483-503-8). In this updated folktale from Thailand, a young girl learns the value of simplicity when she wears all her beautiful dresses to a dance and is so weighted down she can't keep up with her friends. (Rev: HBG 10/98; SLJ 6/98) [398.2]

12731 MacDonald, Margaret Read, retel. *A Hen, a Chick and a String Guitar* (PS). Illus. by Sophie Fatus. 2005, Barefoot Books $17.99 (978-1-84148-796-0). An entertaining, musical, and instructive cumulative tale with Chilean origins in which a child's collection of animals grows until he has 16, plus a string guitar; a CD is included. (Rev: BCCB 5/05; SLJ 5/05) [398.2]

12732 Macdonald, Margaret Read, reteller. *The Boy from the Dragon Palace: A Folktale from Japan* (PS–3). Illus. by Sachiko Yoshikawa. 2011, Whitman $16.99 (978-0-8075-7513-0). Unpaged. A greedy flower seller realizes his personal fortunes are tied to the kindness he expresses towards others in this richly illustrated folktale. (Rev: HB 11–12/11; LMC 1–2/12; SLJ 8/1/11) [398.2]

12733 McDonald, Megan. *The Hinky-Pink: An Old Tale* (K–3). Illus. by Brian Floca. 2008, Atheneum $16.99 (978-0-689-87588-5). 48pp. In Florence long ago, Anabel must produce a princess gown in a week, which she could do very well thank you were it not for the little sprite who drives her to distraction. (Rev: BCCB 11/08; BL 9/15/08; HB 11/08; LMC 11/08; SLJ 8/08) [398.2]

12734 McGill, Alice. *Sure as Sunrise: Stories of Bruh Rabbit and His Walkin' Talkin' Friends* (PS–3). Illus. by Don Tate. 2004, Houghton $17.00 (978-0-618-21196-8). 48pp. Characterful illustrations accompany these five trickster tales that McGill learned when she was growing up in an African American community in North Carolina. (Rev: BL 4/15/04*; SLJ 6/04) [398.2]

12735 McGovern, Ann. *Too Much Noise* (K–3). Illus. by Simms Taback. 1967, Houghton $16.00 (978-0-395-18110-2); paper $6.95 (978-0-395-62985-7). 48pp. An old man follows the advice of the village wise man when he complains that his house is too noisy. [398.2]

12736 McGovern, Ann, adapt. *Stone Soup* (PS–1). Illus. by Winslow Pels. 1986, Scholastic paper $3.99 (978-0-590-41602-3). 32pp. The old story of the young man who asks for food and is refused by the old woman, then he asks her for a stone. (Rev: BCCB 2/87; BL 10/15/86; SLJ 11/86) [398.2]

12737 McIntosh, Gavin. *Hausaland Tales from the Nigerian Marketplace* (4–9). 2002, Linnet $22.50 (978-0-208-02523-4). This collection of 12 Nigerian folktales skillfully interweaves details of contemporary Hausa society. (Rev: HBG 3/03; SLJ 11/02) [398.2]

12738 McKay, Sindy, adapt. *Jack and the Beanstalk* (1–2). Illus. by Lydia Halverson. Series: We Both Read. 1998, Treasure Bay $7.99 (978-1-891327-00-1). This traditional English folktale is told twice — with an adult's and a child's vocabulary. (Rev: SLJ 12/98) [398.2]

12739 Maddern, Eric. *The Cow on the Roof* (PS). Illus. by Paul Hess. 2006, Frances Lincoln $15.95 (978-1-84507-374-9). Convinced that he does the lion's share of work, a farmer switches jobs for a day with his wife, only to learn that her chores are not nearly as easy as he had imagined; a traditional tale reset in Wales. (Rev: SLJ 10/06) [398.2]

12740 Maddern, Eric. *The King and the Seed* (K–3). Illus. by Paul Hess. 2009, Frances Lincoln $16.95 (978-1-84507-926-0). 28pp. Young Jack's honesty is rewarded with appointment as heir to the throne in this handsome retelling of a Chinese Mandarin story, featuring detailed watercolor and colored pencil illustrations. (Rev: BL 1/1/10; SLJ 1/1/10) [398.20951]

12741 Maddern, Eric. *Nail Soup* (K–3). Illus. by Paul Hess. 2007, Frances Lincoln $15.95 (978-1-84507-479-1). A Swedish variant of the traditional "Stone Soup," in which a Traveller seeking shelter offers to make a housewife a soup. (Rev: BCCB 1/08; SLJ 4/08) [398.2]

12742 Madrigal, Antonio H. *The Eagle and the Rainbow: Timeless Tales from México* (4–7). Illus. by Tomie dePaola. 1997, Fulcrum $15.95 (978-1-55591-317-5). A collection of wise, wonderful, but little-known folktales from Mexico. (Rev: BL 7/97; HBG 4/04) [398.2]

12743 Mahy, Margaret. *The Seven Chinese Brothers* (K–3). Illus. by Jean Tseng. 1992, Scholastic paper $6.99 (978-0-590-42057-0). 40pp. Each of seven Chinese

brothers has an amazing gift, used to help one another. (Rev: BCCB 7–8/90; BL 4/1/90; HB 7/90; SLJ 3/90*) [398.2]

12744 Malory, Thomas. *Merlin and Making of the King* (4–6). Retold by Margaret Hodges. Illus. by Trina S. Hyman. 2004, Holiday House $16.95 (978-0-8234-1647-9). 40pp. The Arthurian tales of the "Sword in the Stone," "Excalibur," and "The Lady of the Lake" are simply told and beautifully illustrated with rich medieval effects. (Rev: BL 9/15/04; SLJ 9/04*) [398.2]

12745 Malotki, Ekkehart, comp. *The Magic Hummingbird: A Hopi Folktale* (2–4). Illus. by Michael Lacapa. 1996, Kiva $15.95 (978-1-885772-04-6). In this Hopi tale, a boy makes a toy hummingbird that comes to life and helps end a drought by taking the boy and his sister to the fertility god. (Rev: SLJ 11/96) [398.2]

12746 Mama, Raouf. *The Barefoot Book of Tropical Tales* (3–5). Illus. 2000, Barefoot Books $19.95 (978-1-902283-21-0). 64pp. Backed up by extensive source notes, this book contains eight folktales that come from either African or Afro-Caribbean traditions. (Rev: BL 4/1/00; SLJ 9/00) [398.2]

12747 Mama, Raouf, retel. *Why Goats Smell Bad and Other Stories from Benin* (4–8). Retold by Raouf Mama. 1998, Linnet LB $21.50 (978-0-208-02469-5). A delightful collection of 20 folktales from the Fon culture of Benin, handsomely illustrated with woodcuts. (Rev: BCCB 5/98; BL 2/15/98; HBG 9/98; SLJ 4/98) [398.2]

12748 Manna, Anthony L., and Soula Mitakidou. *The Orphan: A Cinderella Story from Greece* (1–4). Illus. by Giselle Potter. 2011, Random House $16.99 (978-0-375-86691-3). 40pp. Mother Nature helps a Greek girl to meet the prince (in church) and escape a life of drudgery with her stepmother and stepsisters. **e** (Rev: BL 10/15/11; HB 11–12/11; LMC 11–12/11; SLJ 9/1/11) [398.2]

12749 Marcantonio, Patricia Santos. *Red Ridin' in the Hood, and Other Cuentos* (3–5). Illus. by Renato Alarcão. 2005, Farrar $16.00 (978-0-374-36241-6). 208pp. Traditional fairy tales are turned inside-out and given Latino flair. (Rev: BL 3/15/05; SLJ 4/05) [398.2]

12750 Marcos, Subcomandante. *The Story of Colors / La Historia de los Colores: A Folktale from the Jungles of Chiapas* (K–4). Trans. by Anne Bar Din. Illus. by Domitila Domínguez. 1999, Cinco Puntos $15.95 (978-0-938317-45-6). This folktale told in both Spanish and English explains the origins of the colors in the world and how the macaw got its bright plumage. (Rev: HBG 10/99; SLJ 5/99) [398.2]

12751 Marshall, Bonnie C., retel. *Tales from the Heart of the Balkans* (3–5). Illus. Series: World Folklore. 2001, Libraries Unlimited $29.00 (978-1-56308-870-4). Marshall retells folk and fairy tales from the region, preceded by historical and cultural information. (Rev: SLJ 2/02) [398.2]

12752 Marshall, James, retel. *Hansel and Gretel* (K–3). Illus. 1990, Puffin paper $7.99 (978-0-14-050836-9). A retelling of the famous story with innovative, often humorous, illustrations. (Rev: SLJ 12/90*) [398.2]

12753 Martin, Rafe. *The Brave Little Parrot* (K–3). Illus. by Susan Gaber. 1998, Penguin $16.99 (978-0-399-22825-4). As a reward for trying to put out a forest fire, a little parrot is given colored plumage in this Indian jataka tale. (Rev: BCCB 3/98; BL 2/15/98; SLJ 5/98) [298.2]

12754 Martin, Rafe. *Foolish Rabbit's Big Mistake* (PS–2). Illus. by Ed Young. 1985, Penguin $17.99 (978-0-399-21178-2). 32pp. A tale from India reminiscent of Chicken Little, about a little rabbit who fears the end of the world and tells everyone that the earth is breaking up. A Jataka tale. (Rev: BCCB 12/85; BL 12/15/85; HB 3/86; SLJ 2/05) [398.2]

12755 Martin, Rafe. *The Rough-Face Girl* (1–4). Illus. by David Shannon. 1992, Penguin LB $16.99 (978-0-399-21859-0). 32pp. This variation on the Cinderella tale takes place in an Algonquin village on the shores of Lake Ontario. (Rev: BL 4/15/92; HB 7/92; SLJ 5/92) [398.2]

12756 Martin, Rafe. *The Storytelling Princess* (PS–3). Illus. by Kimberly B. Root. 2001, Penguin $16.99 (978-0-399-22924-4). A prince and princess who have both refused arranged marriages find their respective criteria are met in each other. (Rev: BCCB 7–8/01; BL 7/01; HBG 3/02; SLJ 9/01) [398.2]

12757 Martin, Rafe. *The Twelve Months* (2–4). Illus. by Vladyana Langer Krykorka. 2001, Stoddart $15.95 (978-0-7737-3249-0). 32pp. In this Russian variation on the Cinderella story, 12 men, representing the 12 months, help the poor young heroine supply the exotic gifts that her mean aunt and cousin demand. (Rev: BL 4/15/01; SLJ 11/01) [398.2]

12758 Martin, Rafe. *The World Before This One* (5–8). Illus. by Calvin Nichols. 2002, Scholastic paper $16.95 (978-0-590-37976-2). Crow, a Seneca Indian, comes upon a storytelling stone that tells him about the origins of the earth in this series of stories. (Rev: BL 2/15/03; HBG 3/03; SLJ 12/02; VOYA 2/03) [398.2]

12759 Mason, Victor, and Gillian Beal, retels. *Balinese Children's Favorite Stories* (1–4). Illus. by Trina Bohan-Tyrie. 2001, Tuttle $16.95 (962-593-440-5). 96pp. Eleven tales from Bali, many of which are about animals, are paired with varied illustrations including detailed Balinese costumes. (Rev: SLJ 5/02) [398.2]

12760 Matthews, Andrew. *Marduk the Mighty and Other Stories of Creation* (4–6). Illus. by Sheila Moxley. 1997, Millbrook LB $22.40 (978-0-7613-0204-9). 96pp. A collection of 24 creation stories, beginning with Genesis and ending with a Norse myth about the fall of the gods. (Rev: BCCB 6/97; BL 6/1–15/97; SLJ 7/97) [291.1]

12761 Matthews, Caitlin. *The Barefoot Book of Princesses* (4–6). Illus. 1998, Barefoot Books $19.99 (978-1-901223-74-3). 64pp. In a collection of fairy tales from around the world, the reader meets a number of princesses (some familiar, such as Sleeping Beauty, others

not) and their challenging situations. (Rev: BL 11/15/98; SLJ 11/98) [398.2]

12762 Matthews, Caitlin. *Fireside Stories: Tales for a Winter's Eve* (K–3). Illus. by Helen Cann. 2007, Barefoot Books $19.99 (978-1-84686-065-2). 96pp. Winter-themed folk tales from Austria, Russia, Canada, and the Czech Republic are among those included here. (Rev: BL 12/1/07; LMC 1/08; SLJ 2/08) [398.2]

12763 Matthews, Caitlin, retel. *Celtic Memories* (1–6). Illus. by Olwyn Whelan. 2003, Barefoot Books $19.99 (978-1-84148-097-8). 80pp. The Celts of Ireland, Wales, Scotland, and Brittany are the source of this well-illustrated collection of folklore, songs, blessings, and poems, which includes informative notes and pronunciation guides. (Rev: BL 1/1–15/04; HBG 4/04; SLJ 3/04) [398.2]

12764 Matthews, John. *Arthur of Albion* (4–8). Illus. by Pavel Tatarnikov. 2008, Barefoot $24.99 (978-184686049-2). 96pp. This compendium includes ten Arthurian legends ranging from familiar to obscure and interspersed with background information. (Rev: BLO 10/15/08) [398.2]

12765 Matthews, John. *The Barefoot Book of Knights* (4–7). Illus. by Giovanni Manna. 2002, Barefoot $19.99 (978-1-84148-064-0). This book contains retellings of seven tales of knights and chivalry from countries around the world. (Rev: BCCB 9/02; BL 4/15/02; HBG 10/02; SLJ 6/02) [398.2]

12766 Matthews, John. *Giants, Ghosts and Goblins* (4–6). Illus. 1999, Barefoot Books $19.95 (978-1-902283-27-2). 80pp. Nine stories of ghosts, some of them friendly, from such faraway places as Australia. (Rev: BL 10/15/99; SLJ 10/99) [398.2]

12767 Matthews, John, and Caitlin Matthews. *The Wizard King and Other Spellbinding Tales* (3–6). Illus. 1998, Barefoot Books $18.95 (978-1-901223-84-2). 80pp. An interesting collection of nine folk and fairy stories from around the world that feature dragons, monsters, spells, and wizards. (Rev: BL 10/15/98; SLJ 12/98) [398.2]

12768 Max, Jill, ed. *Spider Spins a Story: Fourteen Legends from Native America* (3–6). Illus. 1997, Northland $16.95 (978-0-87358-611-5). 72pp. Spider plays a prominent role in these folktales, illustrated by six Native American artists. (Rev: BL 12/15/97; HBG 10/98; SLJ 1/98) [398.2]

12769 Mayer, Marianna. *Baba Yaga and Vasilisa the Brave* (PS–3). Illus. by Kinuko Craft. 1994, Morrow $17.99 (978-0-688-08500-1). Vasilisa survives both the schemes of her wicked stepmother and a visit to the witch Baba Yaga and finally marries the czar. (Rev: BL 6/1–15/94; SLJ 7/94*) [398.2]

12770 Mayo, Gretchen Will. *Earthmaker's Tales: North American Indian Stories About Earth Happenings* (4–6). Illus. 1989, Walker LB $13.85 (978-0-8027-6840-7). 96pp. Legends that center on the earth itself. (Rev: BL 3/1/89) [398.2]

12771 Mayo, Gretchen Will. *Here Comes Tricky Rabbit!* (2–4). Illus. Series: Native American Trickster Tales.

1994, Walker LB $13.85 (978-0-8027-8274-8). 48pp. These five folktales reveal Rabbit to be a wily trickster. (Rev: BCCB 6/94; BL 8/94; SLJ 7/94) [398.2]

12772 Mayo, Gretchen Will. *Star Tales: North American Indian Stories About the Stars* (4–7). Illus. by author. 1987, Walker LB $13.85 (978-0-8027-6673-1). Fourteen tales, each introduced by a one-page commentary on a constellation. (Rev: BL 6/15/87; SLJ 5/87) [398.2]

12773 Mayo, Gretchen Will. *That Tricky Coyote!* (PS–3). Illus. 1993, Walker LB $13.85 (978-0-8027-8201-4). Five short stories from different tribes that deal with the escapades of the trickster Coyote. (Rev: BL 9/1/93; SLJ 9/93) [398.2]

12774 Mayo, Gretchen Will, retel. *Big Trouble for Tricky Rabbit!* (2–4). Illus. by Gretchen Will Mayo. Series: Native American Trickster Tales. 1994, Walker LB $13.85 (978-0-8027-8276-2). 38pp. Using simple vocabulary and short sentences, the author retells five trickster tales from Native American folklore, all involving Rabbit. (Rev: BCCB 6/94; SLJ 7/94) [398.2]

12775 Mayo, Gretchen Will, retel. *Meet Tricky Coyote!* (2–5). Illus. by Gretchen Will Mayo. Series: Native American Trickster Tales. 1993, Walker LB $13.85 (978-0-8027-8199-4). A retelling of some short, humorous Native American stories about the clever trickster coyote. Companion volumes are *That Tricky Coyote!* and *Magical Tales from Many Lands* (both 1993). (Rev: SLJ 9/93) [398.2]

12776 Medearis, Angela Shelf. *The Singing Man* (PS–3). Illus. by Terea D. Shaffer. 1994, Holiday House LB $17.95 (978-0-8234-1103-0). 36pp. Banzar is scorned in his Nigerian village because he wants to become a musician, but eventually he returns to his home in triumph. (Rev: BL 7/94; SLJ 9/94) [398.2]

12777 Medearis, Angela Shelf. *Tailypo: A Newfangled Tall Tale* (K–3). Illus. by Sterling Brown. 1996, Holiday House LB $15.95 (978-0-8234-1249-5). 32pp. A variation on the folktale about a monster that leaves its tail behind in the cabin of an African American boy. (Rev: BL 11/1/96; SLJ 1/97) [398.2]

12778 Medicine Crow, Joseph. *Brave Wolf and the Thunderbird* (PS–3). Illus. by Linda R. Martin. 1998, Abbeville $14.95 (978-0-7892-0160-7). 31pp. Written and illustrated by Native Americans, this is the traditional tale of the kidnapping of Brave Wolf by Thunderbird to assist in the rescue of Thunderbird's chicks from a sea monster. (Rev: BL 12/1/98; HBG 3/99; SLJ 4/99) [398.2]

12779 Meeker, Clare Hodgson. *A Tale of Two Rice Birds: A Folktale from Thailand* (4–8). Illus. by Christine Lamb. 1994, Sasquatch $14.95 (978-1-57061-008-0). Two rice birds are reincarnated as a princess and a farmer's son in this Thai folktale. (Rev: BL 1/15/95; SLJ 11/94) [398.2]

12780 Menchú, Rigoberta, and Dante Liano. *The Honey Jar* (4–6). Trans. by David Unger. Illus. by Domi. 2006, Groundwood $18.95 (978-0-88899-670-1). Menchú, winner of the Nobel Peace Prize, recounts Guatemalan folktales she learned as a child; illustrations reflect

the text in folk-art style. (Rev: BL 3/15/06; SLJ 6/06) [398.2]

12781 Merrill, Jean. *The Girl Who Loved Caterpillars: A Twelfth-Century Tale from Japan* (5–8). Illus. by Floyd Cooper. 1992, Putnam $16.99 (978-0-399-21871-2). The story of a young Izumi who has no interest in lute playing or writing poetry but is fascinated with "creepy crawlies" instead. (Rev: BCCB 11/92; BL 9/1/92*; SLJ 9/92) [398.2]

12782 Miller, Bobbi. *One Fine Trade* (PS–2). Illus. by Will Hillenbrand. 2009, Holiday $16.95 (978-0-8234-1836-7). 32pp. Based on a folk song, this is a cumulative tale about a peddler seeking a dress for his daughter's wedding. (Rev: BCCB 5/09; BLO 5/27/09; SLJ 3/09) [398.2]

12783 Milligan, Bryce. *Brigid's Cloak: An Ancient Irish Story* (1–3). Illus. by Helen Cann. 2002, Eerdmans $16.00 (978-0-8028-5224-3). 32pp. This book with Celtic and early Christian undertones tells the story of Saint Brigid, who is transported to Jerusalem in a vision and helps care for the baby Jesus. (Rev: BL 10/15/02; HBG 3/03; SLJ 2/03) [398.2]

12784 Milligan, Bryce. *The Prince of Ireland and the Three Magic Stallions* (1–3). Illus. by Preston McDaniels. 2003, Holiday House $16.95 (978-0-8234-1573-1). An Irish folktale in which a story saves the lives of the storyteller and his friends. (Rev: BL 3/15/03*; HBG 10/03; SLJ 6/03) [398.2]

12785 Milord, Susan. *Bird Tales from Near and Far* (1–5). Illus. 1999, Williamson $12.95 (978-1-885593-18-4). From many cultures, this collection of folktales about a variety of birds also contains factual information, projects, and crafts. (Rev: BL 2/15/99; SLJ 11/98) [398.2]

12786 Milord, Susan. *Tales Alive! Ten Multicultural Folktales with Activities* (4–6). Illus. 1995, Williamson paper $14.25 (978-0-913589-79-3). 128pp. This book contains 19 folktales plus such related material as riddles, puzzles, and craft projects. (Rev: BL 4/15/95; SLJ 3/95) [398.2]

12787 Milord, Susan, retel. *Tales of the Shimmering Sky: Ten Global Folktales with Activities* (3–6). Illus. by JoAnn E. Kitchel. Series: A Williamson Tales Alive! Book. 1996, Williamson paper $14.25 (978-1-885593-01-6). 128pp. Ten folktales from different cultures explore such topics as the sky, wind, seasons, colors, and the weather, with additional background material and many suggested projects. (Rev: SLJ 2/97) [398.2]

12788 Mitchell, Stephen. *Genies, Meanies, and Magic Rings: Three Tales from the Arabian Nights* (3–5). Illus. by Tom Pohrt. 2007, Walker $16.95 (978-0-8027-9639-4). Mitchell retells "Ali Baba and the 40 Thieves," "Abu Keer and Abu Seer," and "Aladdin and the Magic Lamp." (Rev: BCCB 10/07; BL 10/1/07; HB 9/07; SLJ 10/07) [398.2]

12789 Mitchell, Stephen. *Iron Hans: A Grimms' Fairy Tale* (1–3). Illus. by Matt Tavares. 2007, Candlewick $16.99 (978-0-7636-2160-5). 40pp. In this retelling of a Grimm tale, a young prince comes to the aid of a wild giant man (Iron Hans) only to disappoint the giant and be sent out into the world where he saves the kingdom and regains the support of the giant. (Rev: BL 12/15/07; LMC 1/08; SLJ 11/07) [398.2]

12790 Mitchell, Stephen. *The Tinderbox* (2–4). Illus. by Bagram Ibatoulline. 2007, Candlewick $17.99 (978-0-7636-2078-3). 48pp. A soldier, after both gaining and losing riches, uses a magic tinderbox to summon three huge-eyed dogs, secretly court a princess, and, ultimately, escape death; this rich retelling is enhanced by Ibatoulline's ink illustrations that portray the period setting, people, and creatures. (Rev: BL 1/1–15/07) [398.2]

12791 Mollel, Tololwa M. *Ananse's Feast: An Ashanti Tale* (K–3). Illus. by Andrew Glass. 1997, Clarion $16.00 (978-0-395-67402-4). Akye the turtle gets revenge on Ananse the spider in this gentle Ashanti tale. (Rev: BL 4/15/97; SLJ 5/97) [398.2]

12792 Mollel, Tololwa M. *Kitoto the Mighty* (K–3). Illus. by Kristi Frost. 1998, Stoddart $14.95 (978-0-7737-3019-9). An African folktale about Kitoto, a mouse who sets out to find a force strong enough to protect him from a hawk. (Rev: BCCB 11/98; SLJ 2/99) [398.2]

12793 Mollel, Tololwa M. *Subira Subira* (PS–2). Illus. by Linda Saport. 2000, Clarion $15.00 (978-0-395-91809-8). 32pp. A Tanzanian folktale in which a brave young girl named Tatu is given advice by a spirit woman on how to control her difficult younger brother. (Rev: BCCB 5/00; BL 2/15/00; HBG 10/00; SLJ 4/00) [398.22]

12794 Mollel, Tololwa M. *To Dinner, for Dinner* (PS–3). Illus. by Synthia Saint James. 2000, Holiday House $16.95 (978-0-8234-1527-4). Based on a Tanzanian story, this tale tells of a rabbit, Juhudi, and his tricks to keep from becoming Leopard's dinner. (Rev: BL 9/1/00; HBG 10/01; SLJ 8/00) [398.2]

12795 Molnar, Irma. *One-Time Dog Market at Buda and Other Hungarian Folktales* (5–8). Illus. by Georgeta-Elena Enesel. 2001, Linnet $25.00 (978-0-208-02505-0). A collection of 23 clever, thought-provoking Hungarian folktales for older readers. (Rev: BL 1/1–15/02; HBG 3/02; SLJ 2/02) [398.2]

12796 Montejo, Victor. *White Flower: A Maya Princess* (K–3). Illus. by Rafael Yockteng. 2005, Groundwood $16.95 (978-0-88899-599-5). 36pp. In this reinterpretation of a Spanish folk tale, White Flower, daughter of a Mayan king, uses her magical powers to help a young nobleman and win his heart. (Rev: BL 12/1/05; SLJ 1/06) [398.2]

12797 Montejo, Victor, retel. *Popol Vuh: A Sacred Book of the Maya* (5–8). Trans. by David Under. Retold by Victor Montejo. Illus. by Luis Garay. 1999, Groundwood $19.95 (978-0-88899-334-2). A creation story from the Mayans in a beautifully designed book that features gods, giants, mortals, and animals. (Rev: HBG 3/00; SLJ 12/99) [398.2]

12798 Montes, Marisa. *Juan Bobo Goes to Work* (PS–3). Illus. by Joe Cepeda. 2000, HarperCollins LB $17.89 (978-0-688-16234-4). A charming story — set in Puerto Rico and using many Spanish words and phrases —

about Juan Bobo who makes a rich girl laugh and is rewarded with a ham every Sunday. (Rev: BL 2/1/01; HBG 3/01; SLJ 10/00)

12799 Mora, Pat. *The Night the Moon Fell* (PS–K). Illus. by Domi. 2000, Douglas & McIntyre $16.95 (978-0-88899-398-4). A Mayan myth about how Luna, the moon, is shattered when she falls from the sky and how she gathers strength to repair herself and return to her home. (Rev: BL 9/1/00; HBG 3/01; SLJ 11/00) [398.2]

12800 Mora, Pat. *The Race of Toad and Deer* (PS–1). Illus. by Domi. 2001, Groundwood $15.95 (978-0-88899-434-9). 32pp. This is a newly illustrated and rewritten version of the Mayan take on the tortoise and the hare, first published in 1995. (Rev: BCCB 12/01; BL 12/15/01; HBG 3/02) [398.2]

12801 Moreton, Daniel. *La Cucaracha Martina: A Caribbean Folktale* (PS–2). Illus. 1997, Turtle $14.95 (978-1-890515-03-4). A refined cockroach finally finds her mate, a handsome cricket, in this Caribbean folktale. (Rev: BL 1/1–15/98; SLJ 11/97) [398.2]

12802 Morin, Paul. *Animal Dreaming: An Aboriginal Dreamtime Story* (3–6). Illus. by author. 1998, Harcourt $16.00 (978-0-15-200054-7). A folktale from Australia that tells how three animals — a kangaroo, a turtle, and an emu — try to bring peace to a warring world. (Rev: HBG 10/98; SLJ 3/98) [398.2]

12803 Morpurgo, Michael. *Gentle Giant* (K–3). Illus. by Michael Foreman. 2004, Collins $16.95 (978-0-00-711064-3). 32pp. A lonely giant finds acceptance when he saves the village of Ballyloch from ecological disaster. (Rev: BL 4/15/04; SLJ 5/04) [398.2]

12804 Morpurgo, Michael. *The McElderry Book of Aesop's Fables* (PS–2). Illus. by Emma Chichester Clark. 2005, Simon & Schuster $19.95 (978-1-4169-0290-4). Twenty-one classic fables are retold in conversational style with humorous watercolors. (Rev: BL 5/1/05; SLJ 6/05) [398.2]

12805 Morpurgo, Michael. *The Pied Piper of Hamelin* (3–6). Illus. by Emma Chichester Clark. 2011, Candlewick $16.99 (978-0-7636-4824-4). 64pp. In this attractive retelling narrated by an orphan who uses a crutch, Hamelin is a town with a vast divide between the lives of rich and poor, and the rats are shown invading every inch. (Rev: BL 1/1/12; HB 1–2/12; SLJ 11/1/11) [398.2]

12806 Morris, Gerald. *The Adventures of Sir Lancelot the Great* (3–5). Illus. by Aaron Renier. Series: The Knights' Tales. 2008, Houghton $15.00 (978-0-618-77714-3). 96pp. The brave knight's courageous side is emphasized in this collection of episodes full of humor. (Rev: BCCB 5/08; BL 6/1–15/08; LMC 1/09; SLJ 6/08) [398.2]

12807 Morrison, Toni, and Slade Morrison. *The Ant or the Grasshopper?* (K–5). Illus. by Pascal LeMaitre. Series: Who's Got Game? 2003, Scribner $16.95 (978-0-7432-2247-1). Kid A, an ant, and his close grasshopper buddy Foxy G decide the time for summer fun has passed and begin to prepare for the coming of winter. (Rev: BL 5/15/03; HBG 10/03; SLJ 9/03) [741.5]

12808 Morrison, Toni, and Slade Morrison. *The Tortoise or the Hare* (PS–2). Illus. by Joe Cepeda. 2010, Simon & Schuster $16.99 (978-1-4169-8334-7). 32pp. In this Aesop rewrite, a fast hare and a ponderous tortoise announce that it's not about whether you win or lose, it's about being friends and good sports. (Rev: BL 11/1/10; LMC 11–12/10; SLJ 10/1/10) [398.2]

12809 Moseley, James. *The Ninth Jewel of the Mughal Crown: The Birbal Tales from the Oral Traditions of India* (3–6). Illus. 2001, Summerwind $24.95 (978-0-9704447-1-4). A collection of stories from India that involve the 14th-century Emperor Akbar and his clever and amusing adviser Birbal. (Rev: BL 7/01; SLJ 10/01) [398.2]

12810 Moses, Will. *Hansel and Gretel: A Retelling from the Original Tale by the Brothers Grimm* (K–3). Illus. 2006, Philomel $16.99 (978-0-399-24234-2). 40pp. Moses adheres to the darker side of the Grimm story, adding detailed and lush folk-art illustrations. (Rev: BL 2/1/06; SLJ 3/06) [398.2]

12811 Munduruku, Daniel. *Tales of the Amazon: How the Munduruku Indians Live* (5–8). Trans. by Jane Springer. Illus. by Laurabeatriz. 2000, Groundwood $18.95 (978-0-88899-392-2). This is an interesting view of the life of the human inhabitants of the Amazon rain forest with material on lifestyles, houses, languages, myths, and marriage. (Rev: BL 9/1/03; HBG 3/01; SLJ 9/00) [981]

12812 Murphy, Claire R. *Caribou Girl* (K–3). Illus. by Linda Russell. 1998, Roberts Rinehart $16.95 (978-1-57098-145-6). A young Inuit changes into a caribou to bring the herd to her starving people. (Rev: HBG 10/98; SLJ 7/98) [398.2]

12813 Murphy, Jim. *Fergus and the Night-Demon: An Irish Ghost Story* (1–3). Illus. by John Manders. 2006, Clarion $16.00 (978-0-618-33955-6). 32pp. Out for a night of fun, Fergus O'Mara, a lazy young Irishman, encounters the towering Night-Demon and must try to talk himself out of deep trouble. (Rev: BL 9/1/06; SLJ 8/06)

12814 Murphy, Shirley Rousseau. *Wind Child* (K–4). Illus. by Leo and Diane Dillon. 1999, HarperCollins LB $15.89 (978-0-06-024904-5). 40pp. A romantic fairy tale about a lonely girl whose extraordinary weaving skills attract a prince who falls in love with her. (Rev: BL 6/1–15/99; HBG 10/99; SLJ 4/99) [398.2]

12815 Mutén, Burleigh. *Grandfather Mountain: Stories of Gods and Heroes from Many Cultures* (4–7). Retold by Burleigh Muten. Illus. by Siân Bailey. 2004, Barefoot $19.99 (978-1-84148-789-2). Strong male protagonists are featured in folktales from England, Greece, Ireland, Japan, Mexico, New Zealand, Nigeria, and the Seneca Indians. (Rev: BL 11/15/04; SLJ 1/05) [398.2]

12816 Mutén, Burleigh. *Grandmothers' Stories: Wise Woman Tales from Many Cultures* (3–5). Illus. 1999, Barefoot Books $19.99 (978-1-902283-24-1). An anthology of folktales from around the world that portray older women in a favorable light. (Rev: BL 11/15/99; SLJ 3/00) [398.27]

12817 Muth, Jon J. *Stone Soup* (K–2). Illus. 2003, Scholastic $17.99 (978-0-439-33909-4). In this version of the traditional tale, Buddhist monks want Chinese villagers to learn the joy of sharing, and as contributions come into the soup pot and the mix richens, so do the colors of the lush illustrations. (Rev: BCCB 3/03; BL 1/1–15/03; HB 3/03; HBG 10/03; SLJ 3/03) [398.2]

12818 Myers, Tim. *The Outfoxed Fox* (1–3). Illus. by Ariel Ya-Wen Pang. 2007, Marshall Cavendish $16.99 (978-0-7614-5356-7). In this traditional Japanese play or kyogen, an old fox rejects a young fox's idea and lives to regret it. (Rev: LMC 1/08; SLJ 11/07)

12819 Myers, Tim. *Tanuki's Gift: A Japanese Tale* (K–3). Illus. by Robert Roth. 2003, Marshall Cavendish $16.95 (978-0-7614-5101-3). 32pp. A Japanese folktale of a fond relationship between a Buddhist priest and a magical creature called a tanuki. (Rev: BL 3/15/03; HBG 10/03; SLJ 7/03) [398.2]

12820 Myers, Tim, retel. *The Furry-Legged Teapot* (1–4). Illus. by Robert McGuire. 2007, Marshall Cavendish $16.99 (978-0-7614-5295-9). Yoshi the tanuki changes himself into a teapot but cannot change back until he is saved by the emperor's grandson. By the author of *Tanuki's Gift: A Japanese Tale*. (Rev: SLJ 5/07)

12821 Naidoo, Beverley, reteller. *Aesop's Fables* (1–4). Illus. by Piet Grobler. 2011, Frances Lincoln $18.95 (978-1-84780-007-7). 52pp. Sixteen fables are portrayed in an African setting in this vivid collection that includes a few words from varied African languages. (Rev: SLJ 11/1/11*) [398.2]

12822 Nanji, Shenaaz. *Indian Tales: A Barefoot Collection* (4–6). Illus. by Christopher Corr. 2007, Barefoot Books $19.99 (978-1-84686-083-6). 96pp. A colorful introduction to Indian folklore, with a tale from each of eight different states preceded by background information that adds context. (Rev: BCCB 12/07; BL 11/15/07; LMC 1/08; SLJ 1/08) [398.2]

12823 Nelson, S. D. *Gift Horse: A Lakota Story* (PS–3). Illus. 1999, Abrams $14.95 (978-0-8109-4127-4). Flying Cloud earns his status as a Lakota warrior when he joins a raiding party to return horses stolen by Crow enemies. (Rev: BL 12/1/99; HBG 3/00; SLJ 11/99) [978]

12824 Nesbit, E. *Jack and the Beanstalk* (K–3). Illus. by Matt Tavares. 2006, Candlewick $16.99 (978-0-7636-2124-7). 48pp. Large illustrations with eye-catching perspectives illustrate this retelling that features a lazy, clumsy Jack who succeeds in the end. (Rev: BL 9/15/06; SLJ 11/06*) [398.2]

12825 Nesbit, Edith. *Melisande* (K–3). Illus. by P. J. Lynch. 1989, Harcourt $13.95 (978-0-15-253164-5). 48pp. The fairies take their revenge when a royal family excludes them from the daughter's christening party. (Rev: BL 10/1/89*; HB 11/89; SLJ 1/90) [398.2]

12826 Nikly, Michelle. *The Perfume of Memory* (3–7). Illus. by Jean Claverie. 1999, Scholastic $16.95 (978-0-439-08206-8). In this fairy tale, a young child uses various perfumes to restore the memory of the queen. (Rev: HBG 3/00; SLJ 11/99) [398.2]

12827 Nordenstrom, Michael. *Pele and the Rivers of Fire* (2–4). Illus. 2002, Bess $10.95 (978-1-57306-079-0). 32pp. The power of Pele, the Hawaiian volcano goddess, is brought to life by spectacular, vivid paintings accompanied by a simple retelling of Pele's move to Hawaii from Tahiti and her battles with her sister. (Rev: BL 12/1/02; HBG 3/03; SLJ 1/03) [299]

12828 Norling, Beth. *Sister Night and Sister Day* (PS–2). Illus. 2001, Allen & Unwin $14.95 (978-1-86448-863-0). 32pp. There are quite different outcomes when twin sisters Ruby and Rose go to work for Mother Earth, in this retelling of a Grimm tale. (Rev: BL 8/01; SLJ 6/01) [398.2]

12829 Norman, Howard. *Between Heaven and Earth: Bird Tales from Around the World* (3–7). Illus. by Leo Dillon and Diane Dillon. 2004, Harcourt $22.00 (978-0-15-201982-2). 96pp. Five beautifully illustrated bird-themed folktales hail from Africa, Australia, China, Norway, and Sri Lanka. (Rev: BL 11/1/04) [398.2]

12830 Nunes, Shiho S. *Chinese Fables: "The Dragon Slayer" and Other Timeless Tales of Wisdom* (3–6). Illus. by Lak-Khee Tay-Audouard. 2013, Tuttle $16.95 (978-0-8048-4152-8). 64pp. A collection of 19 cautionary tales from China, accompanied by complementary illustrations. e (Rev: BL 7/13; SLJ 7/13) [398.2]

12831 Ober, Hal. *How Music Came to the World: An Ancient Mexican Myth* (1–4). Illus. by Carol Ober. 1994, Houghton $17.00 (978-0-395-67523-6). 32pp. How music came to the world is the subject of this folktale dating to pre-Columbian times. (Rev: BL 3/15/94; SLJ 10/94) [398.2]

12832 Oberman, Sheldon. *Solomon and the Ant* (5–8). 2006, Boyds Mills $19.95 (978-1-59078-307-8). Nearly 50 traditional Jewish stories are arranged chronologically and accompanied by notes and commentary. (Rev: BL 2/1/06; SLJ 3/06) [398.2]

12833 Ogburn, Jacqueline. *The Magic Nesting Doll* (PS–3). Illus. by Laurel Long. 2000, Dial $17.99 (978-0-8037-2414-3). 32pp. An original fairy tale set in Russia about a girl who inherits a set of nesting dolls with magical powers. (Rev: BL 9/15/00; HBG 3/01; SLJ 12/00) [398.2]

12834 Olaleye, Isaac. *In the Rainfield: Who Is the Greatest?* (K–3). Illus. by Ann Grifalconi. 2000, Scholastic $16.95 (978-0-590-48363-6). 32pp. In this folktale from Nigeria, three elements — Wind, Fire, and Rain — compete to see which is greatest. (Rev: BCCB 2/00; BL 2/15/00; HBG 10/00; SLJ 4/00) [398.2]

12835 Olaondo, Susana. *Julieta, ¿Que Plantaste? / Julieta, What Did You Plant?* (K–2). Illus. 2001, Alfaguara paper $9.95 (9974-671-00-0). 32pp. This folktale about industrious Julieta the armadillo and the indolent but clever fox who tries to outwit her is sprinkled with Uruguayan phrases and accompanied by cartoonlike illustrations. (Rev: BL 12/15/01) [398.2]

12836 Oliver, Narelle. *Mermaids Most Amazing* (2–4). Illus. 2005, Penguin $15.99 (978-0-399-24288-5). 32pp. The origins of folklore and mythology about mermaids

are briefly explored in this attractive import from Australia. (Rev: BL 2/1/05; SLJ 2/05) [398.21]

12837 O'Malley, Kevin. *The Great Race* (K–2). Illus. by author. 2011, Walker $16.99 (978-0-8027-2158-7). 32pp. In an entertaining twist on the tortoise vs. hare story, grumpy Nate Tortoise challenges arrogant Lever Lapin to a race and beats him while he's busy signing autographs. (Rev: BL 4/1/11; LMC 10/11; SLJ 5/1/11) [398.2]

12838 O'Neal, Shaquille. *Shaq and the Beanstalk: And Other Very Tall Tales* (K–4). Illus. by Shane W. Evans. 1999, Scholastic $15.95 (978-0-590-91823-7). 80pp. A collection of fractured fairy tales that feature Shaq O'Neal and such characters as the Big Bad Wolf, the three bears, and a hen that lays golden basketballs. (Rev: HBG 10/00; SLJ 2/00) [398.2]

12839 Onyefulu, Ifeoma. *The Girl Who Married a Ghost and Other Tales from Nigeria* (2–5). Illus. by Julia Cairns. 2010, Frances Lincoln $15.95 (978-1-84780-176-0). 112pp. A collection of stories that reflect the concerns and dreams of the peoples of Nigeria. (Rev: BL 12/15/10; SLJ 3/1/11) [398.2]

12840 Oppenheim, Shulamith Levey. *Iblis* (1–4). Illus. by Ed Young. 1994, Harcourt $15.95 (978-0-15-238016-8). 32pp. In this Islamic version of Adam and Eve's expulsion from Eden, the devil is called Iblis. (Rev: BCCB 4/94; BL 3/15/94; SLJ 4/94) [297]

12841 Oram, Hiawyn. *Not-So-Grizzly Bear Stories* (3–4). 1998, Little Tiger $16.95 (978-1-888444-41-4). An exciting retelling of ten folktales about bears from around the world. (Rev: BL 3/1/99; HBG 3/99; SLJ 4/99) [398.24]

12842 Oram, Hiawyn, retel. *Counting Leopard's Spots: Animal Stories from Africa* (K–4). Illus. by Tim Warnes. 1998, Little Tiger $16.95 (978-1-888444-31-5). 96pp. A handsome book that contains a variety of tales from Africa, including cautionary, pourquoi, and trickster stories. (Rev: BL 8/98; HBG 10/98; SLJ 12/98) [398.2]

12843 Orgel, Doris. *The Bremen Town Musicians and Other Animal Tales from Grimm* (PS–2). Illus. by Bert Kitchen. 2004, Roaring Brook $18.95 (978-1-59643-040-2). 48pp. Six animal-themed fairy tales from the brothers Grimm are accompanied by arresting illustrations. (Rev: BL 1/1–15/05) [398.2]

12844 Orgel, Doris. *Doctor All-Knowing* (PS–2). Illus. by Alexandra Boiger. 2008, Atheneum $16.99 (978-1-4169-1246-0). 40pp. A retelling of a tale about a poor man who seeks to make a better life for himself and his daughter, and succeeds more through luck than good judgment. (Rev: BL 9/1/08) [398.2]

12845 Osborne, Mary Pope. *The Brave Little Seamstress* (K–3). Illus. by Giselle Potter. 2002, Atheneum $16.00 (978-0-689-84486-7). 40pp. A clever retelling of "The Brave Little Tailor" folktale using a saucy young girl as its heroine. (Rev: BCCB 5/02; BL 4/1/02; HBG 10/02; SLJ 4/02) [398.2]

12846 Osborne, Mary Pope. *Kate and the Beanstalk* (PS–3). Illus. by Giselle Potter. 2000, Atheneum $16.00

(978-0-689-82550-7). 40pp. Kate, the daughter of a knight killed by the giant, is the heroine of this delightful version of Jack and the Beanstalk. (Rev: BCCB 1/01; BL 11/15/00*; HBG 3/01; SLJ 10/00) [398.2]

12847 Osborne, Mary Pope. *Sleeping Bobby* (PS–2). Illus. by Giselle Potter. 2005, Simon & Schuster $16.95 (978-0-689-87668-4). In this gender-swapping adaptation of "Sleeping Beauty," a handsome prince is awakened from a deep slumber by the spell-breaking kiss of a lovely princess. (Rev: BL 1/1–15/06; SLJ 10/05) [398.2]

12848 Osborne, Mary Pope, ed. *Mermaid Tales from Around the World* (3–6). Illus. by Troy Howell. 1993, Scholastic $16.95 (978-0-590-44377-7). 96pp. Twelve stories about mermaids collected from the world's folklore. (Rev: BCCB 2/94; BL 10/15/93; SLJ 11/93) [398.21]

12849 Otsuka, Yuzo. *Suho's White Horse: A Mongolian Legend* (PS–3). Trans. by Richard McNamara. Illus. by Suekichi Akaba. 2007, R.I.C. $17.95 (978-1-74126-021-2). 48pp. The sad legend of the invention of the Mongolian fiddle, in which a young shepherd boy's champion horse is seized by an evil ruler. (Rev: BL 4/1/07) [398.2]

12850 Park, Janie Jaehyun. *The Love of Two Stars: A Korean Legend* (K–2). Illus. 2005, Groundwood $16.95 (978-0-88899-672-5). 32pp. An accessible retelling of the Korean folktale in which two lovers, punished for neglecting their work, win support from the birds when they cannot reunite. (Rev: BL 10/15/05; SLJ 11/05) [398.2]

12851 Park, Janie Jaehyun. *The Tiger and the Dried Persimmon* (K–3). Illus. 2002, Groundwood $15.95 (978-0-88899-485-1). Vibrant artwork accompanies this version of a comic Korean folktale about a tiger who misinterprets a woman's words to her child and ends up terrified of persimmons. (Rev: BL 12/15/02; HBG 3/03) [398.2]

12852 Patterson, Jose. *Angels, Prophets, Rabbis and Kings: From the Stories of the Jewish People* (3–6). Illus. by Claire Bushe. 1991, Bedrick LB $24.95 (978-0-87226-912-5). 144pp. A treasure chest of stories and parables. (Rev: BL 9/15/91; SLJ 8/91) [398.2]

12853 Paul, Ann Whitford. *Tortuga in Trouble* (PS–1). Illus. by Ethan Long. 2009, Holiday $16.95 (978-0-8234-2180-0). 32pp. Tortuga the turtle's friends Conejo, Culebra, and Iguana save the day in this version of "Little Red Riding Hood" laced with Spanish words. (Rev: BCCB 3/09; BL 5/1/09; HB 3/09; LMC 10/09; SLJ 2/09) [398.2]

12854 Paye, Won-Ldy, and Margaret H. Lippert. *Head, Body, Legs: A Story from Liberia* (PS–2). Illus. by Julie Paschkis. 2002, Holt $16.95 (978-0-8050-6570-1). This amusing tale from Liberia about disjointed body parts teaches the value of cooperation. (Rev: BL 8/02; HB 5/02; HBG 10/02; SLJ 4/02) [398.2]

12855 Paye, Won-Ldy, and Margaret H. Lippert, retels. *Mrs. Chicken and the Hungry Crocodile* (PS–3). Illus. by Julie Paschkis. 2003, Holt $16.95 (978-0-8050-7047-7). Mrs. Chicken manages to survive a difficult encounter with a crocodile in this newly illustrated folktale from

the Dan people of Liberia that appeared in *Why Leopard Has Spots* (Fulcrum, 1998). (Rev: HB 5/03; HBG 10/03; SLJ 7/03) [398.2]

12856 Paye, Won-Ldy, and Margaret H. Lippert, retels. *The Talking Vegetables* (K–4). Illus. by Julie Paschkis. 2006, Holt $16.95 (978-0-8050-7742-1). In this spirited retelling of a Liberian folk tale, Spider is lazy and chooses not to join with his neighbors in planting a field of vegetables, so when he tries to pick some for his own use the vegetables turn him away. (Rev: SLJ 11/06) [398.2]

12857 Pearce, Philippa. *The Squirrel Wife* (K–3). Illus. by Wayne Anderson. 2007, Candlewick $16.99 (978-0-7636-3551-0). 32pp. When Jack rescues a small green man in the forest, he is rewarded with a baby squirrel who transforms into a human female and becomes his wife, much to the disapproval of his jealous older brother who tries to ruin his happiness. (Rev: BL 11/15/07; LMC 5/08; SLJ 1/08) [398.2]

12858 Pearson, Maggie. *The Fox and the Rooster and Other Tales* (K–3). Illus. by Joanne Moss. 1997, Little Tiger $14.95 (978-1-888444-17-9). 77pp. Fourteen countries — e.g., Norway, Japan, and Ireland — are represented in this collection of folktales. (Rev: BCCB 3/98; BL 2/15/98; HBG 10/98) [398.2]

12859 Pearson, Maggie. *The Headless Horseman and Other Ghoulish Tales* (4–7). 2001, Interlink $18.95 (978-1-56656-377-2). From Bluebeard to Baba Yaga and Ichabod Crane, this is a collection of 14 tales about eerie beings. (Rev: BL 3/1/01; HBG 10/01; SLJ 1/01) [398.2]

12860 Peck, Jan, and David Davis. *The Green Mother Goose: Saving the World One Rhyme at a Time* (PS–1). Illus. by Carin Berger. 2011, Sterling $14.95 (978-1-4027-6525-4). 32pp. Thirty familiar fairy tales are given eco-conscious facelifts in this nicely illustrated collection. Lexile 1140 (Rev: BL 4/15/11; LMC 10/11; SLJ 5/1/11) [811]

12861 Percy, Graham, reteller. *The Ant and the Grasshopper* (1–3). Illus. by reteller. Series: Aesop's Fables. 2009, Child's World LB $27.07 (978-1-60253-201-4). 32pp. Aesop's well-loved fable about the busy ant and the lazy grasshopper gets an update for younger readers. Also use *The Lion and the Mouse* (2009). (Rev: LMC 3–4/10; SLJ 1/1/10) [398.2]

12862 Perkins, John. *Perceval: King Arthur's Knight of the Holy Grail* (4–7). Illus. by Gennady Spirin. 2007, Marshall Cavendish $16.99 (978-0-7614-5339-0). 38pp. A traditional tale of the flawed Perceval, whose decision to follow King Arthur causes his mother to die of a broken heart. Beautiful illustrations make this book lovely to read. (Rev: LMC 10/07; SLJ 7/07)

12863 Perrault, Charles. *The Complete Fairy Tales of Charles Perrault* (4–6). Trans. by Neil Philip and Nicoletta Simborowski. Illus. by Sally Holmes. 1993, Clarion $28.00 (978-0-395-57002-9). 156pp. Eleven tales by Perrault, newly translated and illustrated with watercolors and printed with fine historical notes. (Rev: BL 11/1/93; SLJ 9/93) [398]

12864 Perrault, Charles. *Perrault's Fairy Tales* (4–6). Illus. by Gustave Dore. 1969, Dover paper $10.95 (978-0-486-22311-7). 117pp. A classic edition with illustrations by the French master. [398.2]

12865 Perrault, Charles. *Puss in Boots* (K–3). Illus. by Paul Galdone. 1983, Houghton paper $7.95 (978-0-89919-192-8). 32pp. A recommended version of this favorite French tale, now available with an audio version. [398.2]

12866 Perrault, Charles. *Puss in Boots* (K–4). Illus. by Fred Marcellino. 1990, Farrar $16.00 (978-0-374-36160-0). 32pp. A handsomely illustrated version of this classic tale. (Rev: BCCB 12/90; BL 12/1/90*; HB 3/91*; SLJ 1/91) [398.2]

12867 Peters, Andrew F. *Strange and Spooky Stories* (3–6). Illus. 1997, Millbrook LB $23.90 (978-0-7613-0321-3). 80pp. Nine unusual but appealing tales from North America, the British Isles, Central Europe, and the Czech Republic. (Rev: BL 2/1/98; HBG 3/98) [398.2]

12868 Phelps, Ethel Johnston. *Tatterhood and Other Tales* (3–6). Illus. by Pamela Baldwin-Ford. 1978, Feminist paper $9.95 (978-0-912670-50-8). 192pp. Tales in which women play a vital and decisive role. [398.2]

12869 Philip, Neil. *The Arabian Nights* (4–6). Illus. by Sheila Moxley. 1994, Orchard $19.95 (978-0-531-06868-7). 160pp. With lovely paintings and colorful prose, this is an excellent retelling of 16 of the Arabian Nights stories, including Ali Baba, Scheherazade, and Aladdin. (Rev: BL 12/15/94; HB 5/94; SLJ 12/94*) [398.2]

12870 Philip, Neil. *Noah and the Devil* (PS–3). Illus. by Isabelle Brent. 2001, Clarion $16.00 (978-0-618-11754-3). 32pp. The devil makes trouble aboard the ark in this retelling of the Bible story. (Rev: BL 10/1/01; HBG 3/02; SLJ 8/01) [398.2]

12871 Philip, Neil. *The Pirate Princess and Other Fairy Tales* (4–6). Illus. by Mark Weber. 2005, Scholastic $19.99 (978-0-590-10855-3). 96pp. A large, handsome collection of seven compelling fairy tales/parables written by Nahman ben Simha, a 19th-century Hasidic rabbi — tales that cover themes of true love, adventure, fortune, and health and happiness. (Rev: BL 1/1–15/06; SLJ 3/06) [398.2]

12872 Philip, Neil, ed. *Horse Hooves and Chicken Feet: Mexican Folktales* (4–8). Illus. by Jacqueline Main. 2003, Clarion $19.00 (978-0-618-19463-6). Bright folk-art illustrations accompany 14 stories that feature humor and the importance of the Catholic church. (Rev: BL 10/15/03; HBG 4/04; SLJ 9/03) [398.2]

12873 Philip, Neil, ed. *Stockings of Buttermilk: American Folktales* (4–5). Illus. 1999, Clarion $20.00 (978-0-395-84802-4). 124pp. A collection of 18 folktales that had their roots in Europe (e.g., "Jack and the Beanstalk") but were changed when imported into America — often by African American storytellers. (Rev: BL 9/1/99; HB 11/99; HBG 3/00; SLJ 10/99) [398.2]

12874 Pienkowski, Jan. *The Fairy Tales* (K–3). Trans. by David Walser. Illus. by author. 2006, Viking $19.99 (978-0-670-06189-1). This handsome collection includes four of the genre's best-known stories — "Cinderella," "Hansel and Gretel," "Sleeping Beauty," and "Snow White" — translated from German and illustrated with dramatic silhouettes filled with color. (Rev: BL 11/1/06; SLJ 11/06) [398.2]

12875 Pinkney, Jerry. *Aesop's Fables* (2–4). Illus. 2000, North-South $19.95 (978-1-58717-000-3). 96pp. A first-rate collection of 60 of Aesop's tales retold and illustrated by this acclaimed artist. (Rev: BCCB 12/00; BL 12/15/00*; HB 1/01; HBG 3/01; SLJ 10/00) [398.24]

12876 Pinkney, Jerry. *The Little Red Hen* (PS–K). Illus. 2006, Dial $16.99 (978-0-8037-2935-3). 32pp. Pinkney's colorful artwork breathes new life into the classic tale. (Rev: BL 3/1/06; SLJ 5/06*) [398.2]

12877 Pinkney, Jerry. *Little Red Riding Hood* (PS). Illus. by author. 2007, Little, Brown $16.99 (978-0-316-01355-0). 40pp. A retelling of how Red survives her encounter with the wolf, with old-fashioned watercolor renderings. (Rev: BL 9/1/07; HB 11/07; LMC 3/08; SLJ 10/07) [398.2]

12878 Pinkney, Jerry. *The Nightingale* (K–4). Illus. 2002, Penguin $16.99 (978-0-8037-2426-6). 40pp. The familiar fairy tale of a king and a nightingale with a magical voice is transplanted to Morocco and accompanied by beautiful illustrations. (Rev: BCCB 11/02; BL 9/1/02) [398.2]

12879 Pinkney, Jerry. *Puss in Boots* (1–3). Illus. by author. 2012, Dial $17.99 (978-0-8037-1642-1). 40pp. Detailed illustrations grace this adaptation of the classic tale about a clever cat. (Rev: BL 11/15/12; HB 1–2/13; LMC 5–6/13*; SLJ 12/12) [398.2]

12880 Pinkney, Jerry. *The Tortoise and the Hare* (PS–3). Illus. by author. 2013, Little, Brown $18 (978-031618356-7). 40pp. The traditional story is set in the American Southwest with minimal text. ALA Notable Children's Book. (Rev: BL 8/13*; LMC 1–2/14*; SLJ 9/13*) [398.2]

12881 Pinkney, Jerry. *The Ugly Duckling* (PS–3). 1999, Morrow LB $17.89 (978-0-688-15933-7). 40pp. Gorgeous double-page spreads are used in this handsome retelling of Hans Christian Andersen's classic story. Caldecott Honor Book, 2000. (Rev: BCCB 3/99; BL 3/1/99*; HB 5/99; HBG 10/99; SLJ 5/99) [398.2]

12882 Pirotta, Saviour. *The Golden Slipper: An Ancient Egyptian Fairy Tale and Cinderella* (3–5). Illus. by Alan Marks. Series: Once Upon a World. 2008, Black Rabbit LB $22.95 (978-1-59771-077-0). 32pp. An Egyptian Cinderella tale, featuring a Greek slave girl called Rhodopis, is followed by a traditional version. (Rev: BL 4/1/08) [398.2]

12883 Pirotta, Saviour. *The McElderry Book of Grimm's Fairy Tales* (K–3). Illus. by Emma Chichester Clark. 2006, Simon & Schuster $19.95 (978-1-4169-1798-4). Ten classic Grimm tales are retold in appealing text and illustrations. (Rev: BL 11/1/06; SLJ 11/06) [398.2]

12884 Pitcher, Caroline. *Mariana and the Merchild: A Folk Tale from Chile* (PS–3). Illus. by Jackie Morris.

2000, Eerdmans $17.00 (978-0-8028-5204-5). 32pp. In this Chilean folktale, Mariana, who lives alone on the beach, raises an infant mermaid until she is old enough to survive in the sea. (Rev: BL 3/1/00; HBG 10/00; SLJ 5/00) [398.2]

12885 Piumini, Roberto, reteller. *Goldilocks and the Three Bears* (2–4). Illus. by Valentina Salmaso. Series: Storybook Classics. 2009, Picture Window LB $25.32 (978-1-4048-5499-4). 32pp. A simple retelling with friendly looking bears, this will appeal to newly independent readers; includes discussion questions, a glossary, and advice on writing fairy tales. (Rev: LMC 1–2/10; SLJ 1/1/10) [398.22]

12886 Podwal, Mark. *Golem: A Giant Made of Mud* (K–4). Illus. 1995, Greenwillow LB $14.93 (978-0-688-13812-7). 32pp. A collection of stories about the mysterious shape-changing creature that is associated with Prague. (Rev: BL 10/1/95; SLJ 11/95) [398.2]

12887 Pogorelsky, Antony, and Elizabeth James. *The Little Black Hen* (1–3). Retold by Elizabeth James. Illus. by Gennady Spirin. 2003, Simply Read $16.95 (978-1-894965-03-3). 32pp. This fable, written for Alexei Tolstoi by his uncle, recounts the story of Alyosha, a Russian boy who is granted one wish but is almost undone by his greed and arrogance. (Rev: BL 9/15/03; SLJ 12/03) [398.2]

12888 Pollock, Penny. *The Turkey Girl: A Zuni Cinderella Story* (4–6). Illus. by Ed Young. 1996, Little, Brown $16.95 (978-0-316-71314-6). 32pp. In this Zuni folktale, Turkey Girl's magical transformation ends in disaster when she forgets her promise to return to her flock of birds. (Rev: BCCB 4/96; BL 4/15/96; HB 5/96; SLJ 5/96) [398.2]

12889 Poole, Amy Lowry. *The Ant and the Grasshopper* (PS–1). Illus. 2000, Holiday House $17.95 (978-0-8234-1477-2). 32pp. This version of Aesop's fable is transported to China, and the ink and gouache illustrations on rice paper impart a quaint Oriental look. (Rev: BCCB 12/00; BL 8/00; HBG 3/01; SLJ 9/00) [398.24]

12890 Poole, Amy Lowry. *How the Rooster Got His Crown* (K–3). Illus. 1999, Holiday House $15.95 (978-0-8234-1389-8). 32pp. A little rooster persuades a sun to leave its cave and is rewarded with a crown in this Chinese pourquoi tale. (Rev: BL 4/15/99; HB 5/99; HBG 10/99; SLJ 5/99) [398.2]

12891 Poole, Amy Lowry. *The Pea Blossom* (K–2). Illus. 2005, Holiday House $16.95 (978-0-8234-1864-0). 32pp. A watercolor picture book, set in China, retelling the Hans Christian Andersen tale of a pea that helps a sick little girl. (Rev: BL 3/1/05; SLJ 3/05) [398.2]

12892 Powell, Patricia Hruby. *Ch'at Tó Yiníló' / Frog Brings Rain* (K–3). Ed. by Jessie Ruffenach. Trans. from Navajo by Peter A. Thomas. Illus. by Kendrick Benally. 2006, Salina Bookshelf $17.95 (978-1-893354-08-1). A bilingual retelling of a Navajo story about a frog that helps douse a fire and save the First People. (Rev: SLJ 7/06) [398.2]

12893 Powell, Patricia Hruby. *Zinnia: How the Corn Was Saved* (1–5). Trans. by Peter A. Thomas. Illus. by Kendrick Benally. 2004, Salina Bookshelf $17.95 (978-1-893354-38-8). This authentic retelling, in both Navajo and English, of a folktale about a knowledgeable Spider Woman is notable for its illustrations. (Rev: SLJ 6/04) [398.2]

12894 Price, Kathy. *The Bourbon Street Musicians* (4–6). Illus. by Andrew Glass. 2002, Clarion $16.00 (978-0-618-04076-6). 40pp. A retelling of "The Bremen Town Musicians" moved to New Orleans and with a Cajun beat. (Rev: BL 6/1–15/02; HBG 10/02; SLJ 5/02) [398.2]

12895 Pringle, Laurence. *Imagine a Dragon* (2–4). Illus. by Eujin Kim Neilan. 2008, Boyds Mills $16.95 (978-1-56397-328-4). Pringle explores the history of dragons east and west — from those that tangled with St. George and to legends of Norway, Egypt, and the Far East. (Rev: BL 3/1/08; LMC 3/08; SLJ 7/08) [398.24]

12896 Prokofiev, Sergei. *The Love for Three Oranges* (2–4). Illus. by Elzbieta Gaudasinska. Series: Musical Stories. 2006, Pumpkin House $16.95 (978-0-9646010-3-1). The fairy-tale story, based on the libretto for Prokofiev's opera, of a prince who is cursed to fall in love with three oranges and must steal them from a faraway castle, in the process finding his true love. (Rev: BL 11/15/06; SLJ 10/06) [398.2]

12897 Prokofiev, Sergei. *Peter and the Wolf* (4–8). Adapted by Miguelanxo Prado. Illus. by author. 1998, NBM $15.95 (978-1-56163-200-8). A somber version of the Russian folktale filled with menacing situations and scary settings. (Rev: HBG 10/98; SLJ 6/98) [398.2]

12898 Prose, Francine. *The Angel's Mistake: Stories of Chelm* (PS–4). Illus. by Mark Podwal. 1997, Greenwillow $14.89 (978-0-688-14906-2). 24pp. A series of anecdotes about the city of Chelm — where fools reside — its creation and eventual destruction. (Rev: BCCB 7–8/97; BL 3/1/97; HB 7/97; SLJ 4/97) [398.2]

12899 Prose, Francine. *You Never Know: A Legend of the Lamed-vavniks* (K–4). Illus. by Mark Podwal. 1998, Greenwillow LB $14.89 (978-0-688-15807-1). Gradually the town of Plotchnik realizes that poor Schmuel the Shoemaker is one of God's holy Lamed-vavniks — 36 righteous people living in secret throughout the world. (Rev: BCCB 7–8/98; BL 6/1–15/98; HBG 10/98; SLJ 8/98) [398.2]

12900 Pullman, Philip. *Aladdin and the Enchanted Lamp* (3–5). Illus. by Sophy Williams. 2005, Scholastic $16.95 (978-0-439-69255-7). 64pp. An exotic presentation, full of wit and dramatic art. (Rev: BL 5/1/05) [398.22]

12901 Pullman, Philip. *Puss in Boots: The Adventures of That Most Enterprising Feline* (PS–3). Illus. by Ian Beck. 2001, Knopf $16.95 (978-0-375-81354-2). 32pp. Pullman's version adds a few new characters and a couple of mysteries to be solved. (Rev: BCCB 5/02; BL 7/01; HBG 3/02; SLJ 8/01) [398.2]

12902 Puttapipat, Niroot. *Musicians of Bremen* (PS–2). Illus. 2005, Candlewick $15.99 (978-0-7636-2758-4).

The focus is on music in this retelling that features realistic animals who end up not in Bremen but happily ensconced in a comfortable cottage. (Rev: BL 11/15/05; SLJ 12/05) [398.2]

12903 Pyle, Howard. *The Story of the Grail and the Passing of Arthur* (5–8). Illus. by author. 1985, Macmillan paper $12.95 (978-0-486-27361-7). The last title of a four-volume King Arthur series, first published in 1910. (Rev: BL 12/15/85) [398.2]

12904 Pyle, Howard. *The Wonder Clock: Or Four and Twenty Marvelous Tales* (4–6). Illus. by author. 1915, Dover paper $10.95 (978-0-486-21446-7). 319pp. Tales for each hour of the day, told by figures on a clock. [398.2]

12905 Quattlebaum, Mary. *Sparks Fly High: The Legend of Dancing Point* (PS–2). Illus. by Leonid Gore. 2006, Farrar $16.00 (978-0-374-34452-8). 40pp. In this spirited retelling of a Virginia folktale, Colonel Lightfoot competes with the devil in a dance contest. (Rev: BL 10/15/06; SLJ 12/06) [398.2]

12906 Quoc, Minh. *Tam and Cam / Tam Cam: The Ancient Vietnamese Cinderella Story* (1–4). Trans. from Vietnamese by William Smith. Illus. by Mai Long. 2006, East West Discovery $16.95 (978-0-9701654-4-2). 32pp. Reminiscent of the Cinderella story, this Vietnamese folk tale, offered here in both English and Vietnamese, features a young girl who is mistreated by her stepsister and stepmother but eventually wins the heart of the king. (Rev: SLJ 1/07) [398.2]

12907 Quoc, Tran. *The Tet Pole / Su Tich Cay Neu Ngay Tet: The Story of the Tet Festival* (1–4). Trans. from Vietnamese by William Smith. Illus. by Nguyen Bich. 2006, East West Discovery $16.95 (978-0-9701654-5-9). 32pp. In this charming bilingual Vietnamese folk tale that explains the origins of the Tet festival, Buddha helps a group of poor farmers outwit the demons that have seized control of their fields. (Rev: SLJ 1/07) [398.2]

12908 Raczek, Linda. *Stories from Native North America* (2–4). Illus. by Richard Hook. Series: Multicultural Stories. 2000, Raintree LB $27.12 (978-0-7398-1336-2). 48pp. A fine collection of Native American folktales that represents many geographical locations. (Rev: HBG 10/00; SLJ 11/00) [398.2]

12909 Radunsky, Vladimir. *The Mighty Asparagus* (4–7). 2004, Harcourt $16.00 (978-0-15-216743-1). In this entertaining version of the Russian folktale "The Enormous Turnip" with eye-catching illustrations full of artistic allusions, a gigantic stalk of asparagus sprouts in the courtyard of an Italian king. (Rev: BL 5/15/04; SLJ 7/04) [398.2]

12910 Rae, Jennifer. *Dog Tales* (1–3). Illus. by Rose Cowles. 1999, Tricycle $14.95 (978-1-58246-011-6). 28pp. Six fractured fairy tales are told using dogs as characters. One example is "The Doberman's New Clothes." (Rev: HBG 10/00; SLJ 12/99) [398.2]

12911 Ransome, Arthur. *The Fool of the World and the Flying Ship* (1–4). Illus. by Uri Shulevitz. 1968, Farrar $16.00 (978-0-374-32442-1); paper $6.95 (978-0-374-

42438-1). Colorful, panoramic scenes extend this retelling of a popular Russian folktale about a simple peasant boy who acquires a flying ship. Caldecott Medal winner, 1969. [398.2]

12912 Ransome, Arthur. *Little Daughter of the Snow* (K–3). Ed. by Shena Guild. Illus. by Tom Bower. 2005, Frances Lincoln $15.95 (978-1-84507-297-1). An enchanting adaptation of Ransome's telling of a traditional Russian tale about a childless couple who create a snow girl who magically comes to life. (Rev: BL 12/1/05; SLJ 1/06) [398.2]

12913 Rao, Sandhya, retel. *And Land Was Born* (1–4). Illus. by Uma Krishnaswami. Series: Visual Expressions. 1999, Banyan Tree $19.99 (81-86895-13-2). A delightful creation story from central India that tells how a tortoise helps produce land in a world where only water existed. (Rev: SLJ 7/99) [398.2]

12914 *Rapunzel: Based on the Original Story by the Brothers Grimm* (K–3). Illus. by Sarah Gibb. 2011, Whitman $16.99 (978-0-8075-6804-0). 32pp. Beautifully detailed collage illustrations add appeal to this somewhat softened and sentimentalized version of Rapunzel. (Rev: BL 5/1/11; SLJ 4/11) [398.2]

12915 Rascol, Sabina I. *The Impudent Rooster* (PS–2). Illus. by Holly Berry. 2004, Dutton $16.99 (978-0-525-47179-0). 32pp. A rooster foils the attempts of a greedy nobleman to steal a coin-filled purse intended for the rooster's master in this adaptation of a Romanian folktale. (Rev: BL 2/15/04; HB 5/04; SLJ 4/04) [398.2]

12916 Read MacDonald, Margaret. *Give Up, Gecko!* (PS–1). Illus. by Deborah Melmon. 2013, Amazon/Two Lions $16.99 (978-1-4778-1635-6). 32pp. A group of thirsty desert animals collaborates to find water in this folktale from Uganda. (Rev: BL 4/1/13; SLJ 6/13) [398]

12917 Reneaux, J. J. *Haunted Bayou: And Other Cajun Ghost Stories* (4–8). 1994, August House paper $9.95 (978-0-87483-385-0). Thirteen scary, entertaining folktales from Cajun country are retold effectively. (Rev: SLJ 12/94) [398.2]

12918 Reneaux, J. J. *Why Alligator Hates Dog* (1–3). Illus. by Donnie Lee Green. 1995, August House $15.95 (978-0-87483-412-3). 32pp. Dog loves to torment Alligator, but the wily reptile plots his revenge. (Rev: BL 10/15/95; SLJ 1/96) [398.3]

12919 Repchuk, Caroline. *The Race* (K–3). Illus. by Alison Jay. 2002, Chronicle $15.95 (978-0-8118-3500-8). 24pp. This update has the hare and the tortoise racing around the world. (Rev: BL 4/15/02; HBG 10/02; SLJ 7/02) [398.24]

12920 Riggs, Kate. *Wicked Stepmothers* (K–3). Illus. Series: Happily Ever After. 2013, Creative Education $17.95 (978-160818245-9). 24pp. A review of evil stepmothers featured in traditional fairy tales, offering simple summaries of plots and varied related illustrations. **e** (Rev: BL 4/1/13; LMC 10/13; SLJ 4/13) [398]

12921 Riordan, James. *The Seven Voyages of Sinbad the Sailor* (4–6). Illus. by Shelley Fowles. 2008, Frances Lincoln $18.95 (978-1-84507-531-6). 64pp. A lively retelling of Sinbad's voyages using contemporary language and with detailed maps on the endpapers. (Rev: BLO 7/30/08; LMC 1/09; SLJ 8/08) [398.2]

12922 Riordan, James. *The Songs My Paddle Sings* (2–5). Illus. 1998, Pavilion paper $16.95 (978-1-86205-076-1). An anthology of 20 legends from various Native American peoples, including creation stories, hero legends, and cautionary tales. (Rev: BL 3/15/98; SLJ 5/98) [398.2]

12923 Robbins, Ruth. *Baboushka and the Three Kings* (2–4). Illus. by Nicholas Sidjakov. 1960, Houghton $16.00 (978-0-395-27673-0); paper $6.95 (978-0-395-42647-0). 32pp. The Russian legend of the old woman who refused to follow the three kings in search of the Holy Child. Caldecott Medal winner, 1961. [398.2]

12924 Robbins, Sandra. *The Firefly Star: A Hispanic Folk Tale* (PS–3). Illus. by Iku Oseki. 1995, See-More's Workshop paper $6.95 (978-1-882601-23-3). 32pp. In this Spanish folktale, the important holiday Three Kings' Day almost doesn't take place until a mouse and a ladybug intervene. (Rev: BL 12/1/95; SLJ 2/96) [398.2]

12925 Roberts, Lynn. *Little Red: A Fizzingly Good Yarn* (2–4). Illus. by David Roberts. 2005, Abrams $16.95 (978-0-8109-5783-1). In this variation on the story of Little Red Riding Hood, the heroine is replaced by a little boy named Thomas who tricks the wolf into gulping down a ginger ale and belching up the boy's recently devoured grandmother. (Rev: BL 10/15/05; SLJ 11/05) [398.2]

12926 Roberts, Lynn, retel. *Rapunzel: A Groovy Fairy Tale* (PS–2). Illus. by David Roberts. 2003, Abrams $16.95 (978-0-8109-4242-4). In this retelling set in the 1970s, Rapunzel is locked away in an apartment building by her evil aunt, who chops off Rapunzel's long hair when she discovers the girl is sneaking time with a rock singer. (Rev: HBG 4/04; SLJ 11/03) [398.2]

12927 Rodanas, Kristina, adapt. *The Dragonfly's Tale* (PS–3). Illus. 1992, Houghton $17.00 (978-0-395-57003-6). 28pp. The Ashiwi's waste of food causes the Corn Maiden to bring famine to the village, but a boy and his sister find a way to harvest a successful crop. (Rev: BCCB 6/92; BL 4/1/92; SLJ 7/92) [398.2]

12928 Rogasky, Barbara. *Dybbuk: A Version* (4–6). Illus. by Leonard Everett Fisher. 2005, Holiday $16.95 (978-0-8234-1616-5). 64pp. In this dark tale based on Jewish folklore, a girl is possessed by the spirit of the boy she was destined to marry. (Rev: BL 10/15/05; SLJ 12/05) [398.2]

12929 Rogasky, Barbara. *The Golem* (4–6). Illus. by Trina S. Hyman. 1996, Holiday House $18.95 (978-0-8234-0964-8). 96pp. The story of the giant monster of the 16th century and its use to help protect the Jewish people in Prague from persecution. (Rev: BCCB 9/96; BL 10/1/96*; HB 1/96; SLJ 10/96) [398.2]

12930 Romulo, Liana. *Filipino Children's Favorite Stories* (3–6). Illus. 2001, Periplus $16.95 (962-593-765-X). This is an engaging collection of 14 traditional myths and folktales from the Philippines. (Rev: BL 4/1/01; HBG 3/02; SLJ 11/01) [398.2]

12931 Ros, Roser. *Musicians of Bremen / Los musicos de Bremner* (2–4). Illus. by Pep Montserrat. 2005, Chronicle $14.95 (978-0-8118-4795-7); paper $6.95 (978-0-8118-4796-4). This strikingly illustrated bilingual adaptation of the Grimm tale — in which four aging animals, cast out by their owners, travel to Bremen to join the city band — uses European Spanish. (Rev: BL 11/1/05; SLJ 10/05) [398.2]

12932 Rosales, Melodye. *Leola and the Honeybears: An African-American Retelling of Goldilocks and the Three Bears* (PS–1). Illus. 1999, Scholastic $15.95 (978-0-590-38358-5). 38pp. The changes in the text of this classic tale are minor, but the paintings are outstanding in this version of Goldilocks in which the heroine is an African American. (Rev: BCCB 10/99; BL 11/1/99; HBG 3/00; SLJ 11/99) [398.22]

12933 Rose, Naomi. *Tibetan Tales for Little Buddhas* (PS–2). Trans. by Pasang Tenzin. Illus. by author. 2003, Clear Light $16.95 (978-1-57416-081-9). 63pp. Three traditional folktales are retold In this charming bilingual (English and Tibetan) picture book. (Rev: BL 12/15/04; SLJ 3/05) [398.2]

12934 Rosen, Michael J. *How the Animals Got Their Colors* (5–8). Illus. by John Clemenston. 1992, Harcourt $14.95 (978-0-15-236783-1). Tales from around the world that explain such things as a leopard's spots and the green on a frog's back. (Rev: BCCB 7–8/92; BL 6/15/92; SLJ 9/91) [398.2]

12935 Rossel, Seymour. *Sefer Ha-Aggadah: The Book of Legends for Young Readers* (4–7). Illus. by Judy Dick. 1996, UAHC paper $14.00 (978-0-8074-0603-8). A collection of legends based on stories about the Jewish people from the Old Testament. (Rev: SLJ 3/97) [398.2]

12936 Roth, Rita. *The Power of Song and Other Sephardic Tales* (3–5). Illus. by Alexa Ginsburg. 2007, Jewish Publication Soc. $16.00 (978-0-8276-0844-3). 150pp. An anthology of 13 tales of the Sephardic Jews who lived on the Iberian Peninsula; each story concludes with cultural commentary. (Rev: BL 10/1/07) [389.2]

12937 Rothenberg, Joan. *Yettele's Feathers* (PS–3). Illus. 1995, Hyperion LB $15.49 (978-0-7868-2081-8). 40pp. A rabbi makes Yettele realize how harmful her gossiping can be. (Rev: BL 5/1/95; SLJ 4/95) [398.2]

12938 Rounds, Glen. *Ol' Paul, the Mighty Logger* (3–6). Illus. by author. 1976, Holiday House paper $5.95 (978-0-8234-0713-2). 96pp. An account of the incredible exploits of one of our national folk heroes. [398.2]

12939 Rumford, James. *Beowulf: A Hero's Tale Retold* (5–8). Illus. by reteller. 2007, Houghton Mifflin $17.00 (978-0-618-75637-7). Beautifully illustrated, this is a simplified retelling of the ancient tale about the warrior who defeats the monster Grendel. (Rev: BCCB 11/07; BL 8/07; HB 7–8/07; SLJ 8/07) [398.2]

12940 Runningwolf, Michael. *On the Trail of Elder Brother* (3–6). Illus. 2000, Persea $17.95 (978-0-89255-248-1). Sixteen tales including creation myths and pourquoi stories are included in this collection of Micmac folktales about Glous'gap, called Elder Brother, the embodiment of the Great Spirit. (Rev: BCCB 6/00; BL 7/00; HBG 10/00) [398.2]

12941 Ruskin, John. *The King of the Golden River* (3–5). Illus. by Iassen Ghiuselev. 2005, Simply Read $19.95 (978-1-894965-16-3). 64pp. In this brightly illustrated adaptation of Ruskin's fairy tale, Gluck, a kindhearted lad of 12, is badly treated by his older siblings Hans and Schwartz who are eventually undone by their greed and misanthropy. (Rev: BL 12/1/05) [398.2]

12942 Ryan, Patrick. *Shakespeare's Storybook: Folk Tales That Inspired the Bard* (3–5). Illus. by James Mayhew. 2001, Barefoot Books $19.99 (978-1-84148-307-8). 80pp. A retelling of seven folk tales that may have served as the inspiration for works by Shakespeare. (Rev: BL 11/15/01; HBG 3/02; SLJ 1/02) [822.3]

12943 Rylant, Cynthia. *Hansel and Gretel* (K–2). Illus. by Jen Corace. 2008, Hyperion $16.99 (978-1-4231-1186-3). 40pp. With illustrations that extend the text, this retelling of the classic story emphasizes the children's domestic problems. (Rev: BCCB 11/08; BL 8/08; HB 11/08; SLJ 9/08) [398.2]

12944 Sabuda, Robert. *The Little Mermaid* (1–4). Illus. by author. 2013, Simon & Schuster $29.99 (978-141696080-5). 12pp. A beautifully constructed pop-up version of the Hans Christian Andersen classic about merfolk. (Rev: BL 11/15/13; SLJ 12/13*)

12945 Sakade, Florence, ed. *Japanese Children's Favorite Stories* (2–4). Illus. by Yoshio Kurosaki. 1958, Tuttle $16.95 (978-0-8048-0284-0). 120pp. Twenty folktales traditionally told to Japanese children. [398.2]

12946 Salley, Coleen. *Who's That Tripping over My Bridge?* (K–2). Illus. by Amy Jackson Dixon. 2002, Pelican $15.95 (978-1-56554-890-9). In this retelling of the Norwegian tale, the three Gruff goats live north of Baton Rouge and must cross a bridge guarded by a troll in order to reach the green grasses on the other side. (Rev: HBG 10/02; SLJ 5/02) [398.2]

12947 San José, Christine. *The Emperor's New Clothes* (PS–3). Illus. by Anastassija Archipowa. 1998, Boyds Mills $15.95 (978-1-56397-699-5). 32pp. A new version of Andersen's familiar story in a large-format picture book with graceful watercolor pictures. (Rev: BL 4/1/98; HBG 10/98; SLJ 4/98) [398.2]

12948 San José, Christine. *The Little Match Girl* (PS–3). Illus. by Kestutis Kasparavicius. 2002, Boyds Mills $15.95 (978-1-59078-000-8). 32pp. Lovely illustrations accompany this retelling of the sad story in which the little girl dies. (Rev: BL 10/1/02; HBG 3/03; SLJ 10/02) [398.2]

12949 San José, Christine. *Sleeping Beauty* (K–3). Illus. by Dominic Catalano. 1997, Boyds Mills $14.95 (978-1-56397-636-0). 32pp. Dormouse characters are used in this successful retelling of the traditional fairy tale. (Rev: BL 10/15/97; HBG 3/98; SLJ 9/97) [398.2]

12950 San José, Christine, retel. *Six Swans: A Folktale* (1–4). Illus. by Jes Cole. 2006, Boyds Mills $16.95 (978-1-59078-056-5). Full-page illustrations offering changing perspectives add to the appeal of this retelling,

which the princess herself narrates, of the story of the six brothers who have been changed into swans. (Rev: SLJ 12/06) [398.2]

12951 San Souci, Daniel. *In the Moonlight Mist: A Korean Tale* (PS–3). Illus. by Eujin Kim Neilan. 1999, Boyds Mills $16.95 (978-1-56397-754-1). In this Korean tale, a poor woodcutter saves a deer and, as a reward, is granted his wish to have a wife who loves him. (Rev: BCCB 4/99; BL 3/1/99; HBG 10/99; SLJ 4/99) [398.2]

12952 San Souci, Daniel, retel. *The Rabbit and the Dragon King: Based on a Korean Folk Tale* (1–4). Illus. by Eujin Kim Neilan. 2002, Boyds Mills $17.95 (978-1-56397-880-7). San Souci retells with humor and drama the story of the king who rules the ocean, who in this case is convinced that eating a rabbit's heart will cure his ills. (Rev: SLJ 11/02) [398.2]

12953 San Souci, Robert D. *Brave Margaret: An Irish Adventure* (1–4). Illus. by Sally Wern Comport. 1999, Simon & Schuster $17.00 (978-0-689-81072-5). 40pp. An intrepid girl survives a shipwreck, challenges a giant, and saves her boyfriend in this adaptation of an Irish folktale. (Rev: BCCB 5/99; BL 3/1/99; HBG 10/99; SLJ 9/99) [398.2]

12954 San Souci, Robert D. *Cendrillon: A Caribbean Cinderella* (PS–3). Illus. by Brian Pinkney. 1998, Simon & Schuster $16.00 (978-0-689-80668-1). An enchanting new version of the Cinderella story that is based on a French Creole tale and uses Martinique as its setting. (Rev: BCCB 1/99; BL 10/15/98; HB 11/98; HBG 3/99; SLJ 9/98) [398.2]

12955 San Souci, Robert D. *Cinderella Skeleton* (3–5). Illus. by David Catrow. 2000, Harcourt $16.00 (978-0-15-202003-3). 32pp. A macabre variation on the Cinderella story in which the heroine is a stick-figure skeleton who lives in Boneyard Acres and falls in love with Prince Charnel. (Rev: BCCB 10/00; BL 9/1/00; HB 9/00; HBG 3/01; SLJ 9/00) [398.2]

12956 San Souci, Robert D. *The Faithful Friend* (K–4). Illus. by Brian Pinkney. 1995, Simon & Schuster paper $16.00 (978-0-02-786131-0). 40pp. On the island of Martinique, Hippolyte tries to save his friend's wedding from destruction by the bride's evil uncle. (Rev: BCCB 9/95; BL 4/15/95*; HB 9/95; SLJ 6/95) [398.2]

12957 San Souci, Robert D. *Little Pierre: A Cajun Story from Louisiana* (1–4). Illus. by David Catrow. 2003, Harcourt $16.00 (978-0-15-202482-6). Drawn from Cajun folklore, this variation on the Tom Thumb theme tells how Pierre, dwarfed by his four older brothers, saves the day and rescues his fumbling brothers and the comely Marie-Louise from the Swamp Ogre. (Rev: HBG 4/04; SLJ 1/04) [398.2]

12958 San Souci, Robert D. *Robin Hood and the Golden Arrow* (1–3). Illus. by E. B. Lewis. 2010, Scholastic $17.99 (978-0-439-62538-8). 32pp. Robin Hood dons a disguise to trick the sheriff and win a contest designed to trap him. (Rev: BL 10/15/10; LMC 1–2/11; SLJ 10/1/10) [398.2]

12959 San Souci, Robert D. *The Secret of the Stones* (2–4). Illus. by James Ransome. 1999, Penguin $16.99 (978-0-8037-1640-7). 40pp. In this folktale with roots in both Arkansas and Zaire, a childless couple tries to rescue two orphans who have been turned into pebbles. (Rev: BCCB 1/00; BL 1/1–15/00; HBG 3/00; SLJ 2/00) [398.2]

12960 San Souci, Robert D. *Two Bear Cubs* (K–4). Illus. by Daniel San Souci. 1997, Yosemite $14.95 (978-0-939666-87-4). Two bear cubs fall asleep on a rock that grows into a mountain in this Native American folktale that explains the rock formation known as El Capitan in Yosemite National Park. (Rev: BCCB 3/98; BL 1/1–15/98; SLJ 4/98) [398.2]

12961 San Souci, Robert D., retel. *Sister Tricksters: Rollicking Tales of Clever Females* (3–6). Illus. by Daniel San Souci. 2006, August House $19.95 (978-0-87483-791-9). 69pp. Molly Cottontail, Miz Grasshopper, and Miz Goose are among the characters in this collection of retold tales about memorable female tricksters. (Rev: SLJ 9/06*) [398.2]

12962 San Souci, Robert D., retel. *A Weave of Words* (2–5). Illus. by Raúl Colón. 1998, Orchard LB $17.99 (978-0-531-33053-1). In this Armenian tale, an imprisoned king uses his weaving skills to communicate with his wife. (Rev: BCCB 4/98; HBG 10/98; SLJ 3/98) [398.2]

12963 San Souci, Robert D., retel. *The White Cat: An Old French Fairy Tale* (3–4). Illus. by Gennady Spirin. 1990, Orchard LB $17.99 (978-0-531-08409-0). 32pp. The retelling of the story of three princes who vie for their father's kingdom. (Rev: BCCB 11/90; BL 9/1/90; HB 11/90; SLJ 10/90) [398.2]

12964 Sanderson, Ruth. *Cinderella* (PS–3). Illus. 2002, Little, Brown $15.95 (978-0-316-77965-4). An exquisitely produced version of the Cinderella story with detailed illustrations and an elegant text. (Rev: BL 4/15/02*; HBG 10/02; SLJ 6/02) [398.2]

12965 Sanfield, Steve. *Just Rewards, or Who Is That Man in the Moon and What's He Doing Up There Anyway?* (PS–3). Illus. by Emily Lisker. 1996, Orchard LB $15.99 (978-0-531-08885-2). 32pp. The origin of the belief that there is a man in the moon is retold in this Chinese folktale. (Rev: BL 10/1/96; HB 11/96; SLJ 9/96*) [398.2]

12966 Santangelo, Colony Elliot. *Brother Wolf of Gubbio: A Legend of Saint Francis* (K–3). Illus. 2000, Handprint $15.95 (978-1-929766-07-9). 32pp. In this old Italian tale, Saint Francis tames a wolf that has been terrorizing a village. (Rev: BCCB 1/01; BL 1/1–15/01; HBG 3/01; SLJ 2/01) [398.2]

12967 Sauvant, Henriette. *Rapunzel and Other Magic Fairy Tales* (4–7). Trans. by Anthea Bell. Illus. by author. 2008, Egmont $15.95 (978-1-4052-2702-5). Retellings of fourteen fairy tales, many of them by the Grimm brothers, and some of them grim or even grisly, accompanied by lush illustrations. (Rev: BL 5/1/08; SLJ 7/08) [398.2]

12968 Schlitz, Laura Amy. *The Bearskinner: A Tale of the Brothers Grimm* (3–5). Illus. by Max Grafe. 2007, Candlewick $16.99 (978-0-7636-2730-0). 40pp. This retelling features a destitute soldier who makes a deal with the devil — if he can live for seven years without bathing or grooming while wearing a bearskin, he will be rich; if he fails, he forfeits his soul. (Rev: BCCB 12/07; BL 11/15/07; HB 1/08; LMC 1/08; SLJ 12/07) [398.2]

12969 Schram, Peninnah. *Ten Classic Jewish Children's Stories* (3–6). Illus. 1998, Pitspopany $16.95 (978-0-943706-96-2). 48pp. A volume that contains the retelling of ten traditional Jewish tales — many that illustrate situations in the Torah — with questions to reflect on the lessons taught. (Rev: BL 11/15/98; SLJ 3/99) [296.1]

12970 Schram, Peninnah, retel. *The Magic Pomegranate* (K–2). Illus. by Melanie Hall. 2007, Millbrook LB $25.26 (978-0-8225-6742-4). A retelling of a well known story from the Jewish literature involves three brothers who bring healing gifts to a dying princess and ends happily ever after. (Rev: SLJ 10/07) [398.2]

12971 Schroeder, Alan. *The Tale of Willie Monroe* (1–3). Illus. by Andrew Glass. 1999, Clarion $15.00 (978-0-395-69852-5). 32pp. An adaptation of the Japanese folktale that uses a hillbilly hero instead of a Japanese wrestler. (Rev: BCCB 6/99; BL 4/15/99; HB 3/99; HBG 10/99; SLJ 6/99) [398.2]

12972 Schwartz, Alvin. *More Scary Stories to Tell in the Dark* (4–7). Illus. by Stephen Gammell. 1984, HarperCollins LB $16.89 (978-0-397-32082-0); paper $5.99 (978-0-06-440177-7). Brief tales from folk stories and hearsay with a scary bent. [398.2]

12973 Schwartz, Alvin, ed. *Scary Stories to Tell in the Dark* (3–8). Illus. by Stephen Gammell. 1981, HarperCollins LB $16.89 (978-0-397-31927-5); paper $5.99 (978-0-06-440170-8). 128pp. Ghost stories collected from American folklore. [398.2]

12974 Schwartz, Howard. *Before You Were Born* (PS–2). Illus. by Kristina Swarner. 2005, Roaring Brook $16.95 (978-1-59643-028-0). 32pp. From Jewish legend, this is the story of the angel Lailah, who guides the human soul. (Rev: BL 5/15/05; SLJ 4/05) [398.2089]

12975 Schwartz, Howard, ed. *A Journey to Paradise: And Other Jewish Tales* (1–4). Illus. by Giora Carmi. 2000, Pitspopany $16.95 (978-0-943706-21-4); paper $9.95 (978-0-943706-16-0). 48pp. A collection of eight Jewish folktales that revolve around mystery, magic, and life after death. (Rev: BL 4/15/00; HBG 10/00; SLJ 6/00) [296.1]

12976 Scieszka, Jon. *The Frog Prince Continued* (1–4). Illus. by Steve Johnson. 1991, Viking $15.99 (978-0-670-83421-1). After the princess and the former frog are married, he still keeps hopping about and wonders if he should change back into a frog. (Rev: BCCB 5/91; BL 6/1/91; HB 7/91; SLJ 5/91) [398.2]

12977 Scieszka, Jon. *The True Story of the Three Little Pigs: By A. Wolf* (PS–2). Illus. 1989, Viking $16.99 (978-0-670-82759-6). 32pp. A hip and funny version, from the wolf's point of view. (Rev: BCCB 9/89*; BL 9/1/89; HB 1/90; SLJ 10/89) [398.2]

12978 Scott-Mitchell, Clare. *Cinderella* (PS–2). Illus. by Gordon Fitchett. 2001, Penguin $16.99 (978-0-8037-2577-5). 32pp. In this fresh version of Cinderella all the characters are animals, including the heroine, who is a black-and white cat. (Rev: BL 1/1–15/01; SLJ 2/01) [398.2]

12979 Scott, Nathan Kumar. *Mangoes and Bananas* (2–4). Illus. by T. Balaji. 2006, Tara $14.95 (81-86211-06-3). 32pp. In this retelling of an Indonesian folk tale, clever deer Kanchil and a greedy monkey called Monyet plant a fruit garden together on the agreement that they will share equally; an endnote describes the methods used to create the textile-based illustrations. (Rev: BL 4/1/06; SLJ 6/06) [398.2]

12980 Scott, Nathan Kumar. *The Sacred Banana Leaf* (2–4). Illus. by Radhashyam Raut. 2008, Tara $16.95 (978-8-1862-1128-1). A clever mouse deer trickster named Kanchil falls into a pit and must find a way to persuade other animals to help him out; a beautifully illustrated tale from Indonesia. (Rev: BL 5/15/08; SLJ 6/08) [398.2]

12981 Seabrooke, Brenda. *Wolf Pie* (1–3). Illus. by Liz Callen. 2010, Clarion $16 (978-0-547-04403-3). 48pp. In this fractured fairy tale, Wilfong the wolf fails to blow down the Pygg brothers' nice brick house and instead camps outside, eventually becoming their friend and protector. (Rev: LMC 10/10; SLJ 8/1/10) [398.2]

12982 Seeger, Pete, and Paul Dubois Jacobs. *Abiyoyo Returns* (1–3). Illus. by Michael Hays. 2001, Simon & Schuster $17.00 (978-0-689-83271-0). 40pp. The giant Abiyoyo returns to help the villagers build a dam in this sequel to Seeger's 1986 retelling of a South African folktale. (Rev: BCCB 11/01; BL 11/15/01; HB 11/01; HBG 3/02; SLJ 11/01) [398.2]

12983 Seeger, Pete, and Paul Dubois Jacobs. *Some Friends to Feed: The Story of Stone Soup* (K–2). Illus. by Michael Hays. 2005, Putnam $16.99 (978-0-399-24017-1). This nicely illustrated retelling of the classic story of a hungry soldier and the children who come to his aid is packaged with an audio CD and musical notation. (Rev: BL 9/1/05; SLJ 10/05) [398.2]

12984 Seros, Kathleen, adapt. *Sun and Moon: Fairy Tales from Korea* (2–5). Illus. by Norman Sibley and Robert Krause. 1983, Hollym $18.50 (978-0-930878-25-2). 61pp. A collection of seven stories from Korea. [398.2]

12985 Setterington, Ken. *Hans Christian Andersen's The Snow Queen* (3–5). Illus. by Nelly Hofer and Ernst Hofer. 2000, Tundra $16.95 (978-0-88776-497-4). A secular retelling of the Andersen story illustrated with old-fashioned black-and-white silhouettes. (Rev: BL 12/15/00; HBG 10/01; SLJ 3/01) [398.2]

12986 Setterington, Ken, retel. *Clever Katarina: A Tale in Six Parts* (2–6). Illus. by Nelly Hofer and Ernst Hofer. 2006, Tundra $17.95 (978-0-88776-764-7). 40pp. The artwork shines in this retelling of a Grimm fairy tale originally called "The Peasant's Clever Daughter," in which a beautiful peasant girl called Katarina must solve a riddle to win the king's hand and save her father from being cast into prison. (Rev: SLJ 12/06) [398.2]

12987 Shah, Idries. *The Boy Without a Name* (PS–2). Illus. by Mona Caron. 2000, Hoopoe $17.00 (978-1-883536-20-6). 32pp. Based on an Islamic story, this folktale tells of a boy who visits a wise man to get a name. (Rev: BL 12/1/00; SLJ 2/01) [398.22]

12988 Shah, Idries. *The Clever Boy and the Terrible, Dangerous Animal* (1–4). Illus. by Rose Mary Santiago. 2000, Hoopoe $17.00 (978-1-883536-18-3). In this Middle Eastern folktale, a young boy quiets some villagers by explaining that the animal they fear is really just a melon. (Rev: SLJ 12/00) [398.2]

12989 Shah, Idries. *Fatima the Spinner and the Tent* (PS–2). Illus. by Natasha Delmar. 2006, Hoopoe $18.00 (978-1-883536-42-8); paper $7.99 (978-1-883536-61-9). 32pp. Fatima, daughter of a well-to-do spinner, suffers a series of tragedies that turn out to have taught her useful skills in this retelling of an 18th-century Turkish tale. (Rev: BL 9/15/06; SLJ 11/06) [398.2]

12990 Shah, Idries. *The Lion Who Saw Himself in the Water* (PS–2). Illus. by Ingrid Rodriguez. 1998, Hoopoe $17.00 (978-1-883536-12-1). In this Sufi tale from Islam, a lion is so frightened by his reflection in the water that he can't drink from the pool until a friendly butterfly helps him conquer his fear. (Rev: BL 10/1/98; SLJ 12/98) [398.24]

12991 Shah, Idries. *The Magic Horse* (3–5). Illus. by Julie Freeman. 1998, Hoopoe $17.00 (978-1-883536-11-4). This picture-book version of a Muslim Sufi tale involves two brothers and their separate quests. (Rev: SLJ 2/99) [398.2]

12992 Shah, Idries. *The Man and the Fox* (K–3). Illus. by Sally Mallam. 2006, Hoopoe Bks. $18.00 (978-1-883536-43-5); paper $7.99 (978-1-883536-60-2). A clever fox outwits a man's plot to capture him. (Rev: SLJ 12/06) [398.2]

12993 Shah, Idries. *The Man with Bad Manners* (K–3). Illus. by Rose Mary Santiago. 2003, Hoopoe $18.00 (978-1-883536-30-5). Colorful and simple illustrations lighten this retelling of an Afghani folktale about conflict resolution, now set in the present. (Rev: SLJ 4/04) [398.2]

12994 Shah, Idries. *Neem the Half-Boy* (PS–2). Illus. by Midori Mori and Robert Revels. 1998, Hoopoe $17.00 (978-1-883536-10-7). 32pp. In this story based on an ancient Sufi tale from Islam, Neem remains a half-boy until he successfully confronts a dragon in his lair. (Rev: BL 10/1/98; SLJ 1/99) [398.22]

12995 Shannon, George. *Rabbit's Gift* (PS–1). Illus. by Laura Dronzek. 2007, Harcourt $16.00 (978-0-15-206073-2). 32pp. Rabbit, Donkey, Goat, and Deer all show compassion for one another during a winter storm and share the last turnip in this ancient folktale with a theme common to many cultures. (Rev: BCCB 12/07; BL 11/1/07; SLJ 12/07) [398.2]

12996 Shannon, George. *Stories to Solve: Folktales from Around the World* (4–6). Illus. by Peter Sís. 1985, Morrow paper $4.95 (978-0-688-10496-2). 56pp. Fourteen stories combine puzzles and folklore asking readers how the problem was figured out or the mystery solved. (Rev: BL 12/1/85; HB 9/85; SLJ 9/85) [398.2]

12997 Sharpe, Leah Marinsky, reteller. *The Goat-Faced Girl: A Classic Italian Folktale* (2–4). Illus. by Jane Marinsky. 2009, Godine $16.95 (978-1-56792-393-3). 32pp. A beautiful but lazy princess learns her lesson when her adoptive mother, a sorceress, gives her the head of a goat to teach her a lesson about the value of beauty. (Rev: SLJ 1/1/10*) [398.2]

12998 Shenandoah, Joanne, and Douglas M. George-Kanentiio. *Skywoman: Legends of the Iroquois* (4–8). 1998, Clear Light $14.95 (978-0-940666-99-3). Good writing and effective artwork are combined in this retelling of nine traditional Iroquois tales, including a series of creation stories. (Rev: HBG 10/99; SLJ 2/99) [398.2]

12999 Shepard, Aaron. *King o' the Cats* (1–3). Illus. by Kristin Sorra. 2004, Simon & Schuster $16.95 (978-0-689-82082-3). 32pp. Newly hired church sexton Peter Black, burdened by a reputation for telling tall tales, has difficulty getting anyone to believe accounts of his encounters with a strange group of cats. (Rev: BL 10/15/04; SLJ 8/04) [398.2]

13000 Shepard, Aaron. *Lady White Snake: A Tale from Chinese Opera* (4–6). Illus. by Song Nan Zhang. 2001, Pan Asian $16.95 (978-1-57227-072-5). 30pp. A lavishly illustrated story from Chinese opera about a snake that turns into a beautiful woman. (Rev: BL 10/15/01; SLJ 3/02) [398.2]

13001 Shepard, Aaron. *One-Eye! Two-Eyes! Three-Eyes! A Very Grimm Fairy Tale* (K–2). Illus. by Gary Clement. 2006, Atheneum $16.95 (978-0-689-86740-8). 32pp. A girl with two eyes is the butt of much derision from her one-eyed and three-eyed sisters. (Rev: BL 1/1–15/07; SLJ 1/07) [398.2]

13002 Shepard, Aaron, retel. *Savitri: A Tale of Ancient India* (3–6). Illus. by Vera Rosenberry. 1992, Whitman LB $16.95 (978-0-8075-7251-1). In picture-book format, the retelling of India's epic poem, the Mahabharata. (Rev: BCCB 3/92; BL 3/15/92; SLJ 5/92) [398.2]

13003 Sherman, Josepha. *Magic Hoofbeats: Horse Tales from Many Lands* (2–4). Illus. by Linda Wingerter. 2004, Barefoot Books $19.99 (978-1-84148-091-6). 80pp. Horses with magical abilities are the focus of these brief folktales. (Rev: BL 11/1/04; SLJ 2/05) [398.2]

13004 Sherman, Josepha. *Merlin's Kin: World Tales of the Heroic Magician* (5–8). 1998, August House paper $11.95 (978-0-87483-519-9). A splendid international collection of folktales that feature magicians, sorcerers, shamans, healers, and wizards. (Rev: BL 4/15/99; SLJ 3/99; VOYA 12/98) [398.21]

13005 Sherman, Josepha. *Rachel the Clever and Other Jewish Folktales* (4–6). Illus. 1993, August House paper $10.95 (978-0-87483-307-2). 176pp. Jewish tales gathered from many lands. (Rev: BL 3/15/93) [398.2]

13006 Sherman, Josepha. *Told Tales: Nine Folktales from Around the World* (4–6). Illus. 1995, Silver Moon LB

$14.95 (978-1-881889-64-9). 80pp. A general introduction for beginning storytellers that uses a question-and-answer technique and supplies nine folktales from around the world. (Rev: BL 2/1/96; SLJ 1/96) [398.2]

13007 Shollar, Leah. *A Thread of Kindness: A Tzedaka Story* (2–4). Illus. by Shoshana Mekibel. 2000, Hachai $10.95 (978-1-929628-01-8). 32pp. This traditional tale tells of a poor but virtuous farmer who gains wealth through his kindness to others. (Rev: BL 10/1/00; HBG 10/01; SLJ 1/01) [398.2]

13008 Shulman, Janet. *The Nutcracker* (K–5). Illus. by Renee Graef. 1999, HarperCollins $19.99 (978-0-06-027814-4). An adaptation of Hoffman's story *The Nutcracker and the Mouse King,* with a CD consisting of the narration and some excerpts from the Tchaikovsky ballet. (Rev: BL 9/1/99; HBG 3/00; SLJ 10/99)

13009 Shulman, Lisa. *The Matzo Ball Boy* (PS–1). Illus. by Rosanne Litzinger. 2005, Dutton $15.99 (978-0-525-47169-1). A grandmother preparing chicken soup for the Passover Seder creates a matzo ball boy who jumps from the soup and takes off to see the world in this appealing variation of the Gingerbread Boy. (Rev: BL 2/1/05; SLJ 3/05) [398.2]

13010 Sierra, Judy. *The Beautiful Butterfly: A Folktale from Spain* (K–3). Illus. by Victoria Chess. 2000, Clarion $15.00 (978-0-395-90015-4). This popular Spanish folktale ends happily when the fish that had swallowed Butterfly's new husband — a mouse — spits him out, thus reuniting the happy pair. (Rev: BCCB 5/00; BL 3/15/00; HBG 10/00; SLJ 8/00) [398.2]

13011 Sierra, Judy. *Can You Guess My Name? Traditional Tales Around the World* (3–5). Illus. by Stefano Vitale. 2002, Clarion $21.00 (978-0-618-13328-4). In this handsome volume with lengthy endnotes, Sierra has collected 15 folktales from all corners of the world that are variants of five favorite stories. (Rev: BL 11/15/02; HB 1/03*; HBG 3/03; SLJ 11/02*) [398.2]

13012 Sierra, Judy. *The Gift of the Crocodile* (PS–3). Illus. by Reynold Ruffins. 2000, Simon & Schuster $17.00 (978-0-689-82188-2). 40pp. This is an exotic version of Cinderella, set in the Spice Islands, with a river crocodile serving as Grandmother Crocodile, the fairy godmother. (Rev: BCCB 12/00; BL 1/1–15/01; HB 1/01; HBG 3/01; SLJ 11/00) [398.2]

13013 Sierra, Judy. *Silly and Sillier: Read-Aloud Tales from Around the World* (PS–2). Illus. by Valeri Gorbachev. 2002, Knopf $19.95 (978-0-375-80609-4). These 20 folktales from around the world and the wonderful illustrations that accompany them are sure to bring smiles to young readers' faces. (Rev: BL 12/15/02; HBG 3/03; SLJ 11/02) [398.2]

13014 Sierra, Judy, ed. *Nursery Tales Around the World* (4–6). Illus. by Stefano Vitale. 1996, Clarion $20.00 (978-0-395-67894-7). 114pp. This fascinating work retells folktales with similar themes as they exist in different cultures. (Rev: BCCB 2/96; BL 3/1/96; HB 5/96; SLJ 4/96) [398.2]

13015 Singer, Marilyn. *The Maiden on the Moor* (1–3). Illus. by Troy Howell. 1995, Morrow LB $14.93 (978-0-688-08765-4). In this English ballad, two shepherd brothers discover a young woman lying unconscious and must decide if they should care for her. (Rev: BL 4/15/95; SLJ 4/95) [398.2]

13016 Singer, Marilyn. *Mirror Mirror: A Book of Reversible Verse* (2–5). Illus. by Josée Masse. 2010, Dutton $16.99 (978-0-525-47901-7). 32pp. Clever "reverso" wordplay provides a new angle on some well-loved fairy tales as different pairs of perspectives are offered in verse. Lexile 1040 (Rev: BL 1/1/10*; HB 3–4/10; LMC 5–6/10; SLJ 1/1/10*) [811]

13017 Singh, Rina, and Debbie Lush. *Moon Tales: Myths of the Moon from Around the World* (3–6). 2000, Bloomsbury $22.95 (978-0-7475-4112-7). 77pp. A stylish retelling of folk tales from around the world dealing with the moon and its powers. (Rev: SLJ 3/01) [398.2]

13018 Smith, Chris. *One City, Two Brothers* (K–3). Illus. by Aurelia Fronty. 2007, Barefoot Books $16.99 (978-1-84686-042-3). 32pp. Introduced by King Solomon, this story about the founding of Jerusalem features two caring brothers who try to make sure each has enough grain. (Rev: BL 10/1/07; LMC 1/08; SLJ 12/07) [398.20933]

13019 Smith, Scudder, retel. *Jack and the Beanstalk* (PS–2). Illus. by Felipe López Salán. 2006, Purple Bear $15.95 (978-1-933327-11-2). This retelling of the classic fairy tale is fairly faithful to the original but a bit kinder and gentler in tone. (Rev: SLJ 8/06) [398.2]

13020 Sneed, Brad, retel. *Aesop's Fables* (2–5). Illus. by Brad Sneed. 2003, Dial $16.99 (978-0-8037-2751-9). Contemporary language is used in these lighthearted retellings of 15 tales, with eye-catching illustrations. (Rev: HBG 4/04; SLJ 11/03) [398.2]

13021 Snyder, Dianne. *The Boy of the Three-Year Nap* (K–3). Illus. by Allen Say. 1988, Houghton $16.95 (978-0-395-44090-2). 32pp. In this Japanese folktale adaptation, Taro, who does nothing but eat and sleep, schemes to marry his rich neighbor's daughter. (Rev: BCCB 4/88; BL 4/1/88; HB 5/88) [398.2]

13022 Snyder, Laurel. *Up and Down the Scratchy Mountains* (3–5). Illus. 2008, Random $16.99 (978-0-375-84719-6). 256pp. In the land of Bewilderness, a young milkmaid named Lucy and a prince named Wynston go in search of Lucy's missing mother. (Rev: BL 9/15/08; HB 1/09; SLJ 9/08) [398.2]

13023 Sogabe, Aki, retel. *Aesop's Fox* (K–3). Illus. by Aki Sogabe. 1999, Harcourt $16.00 (978-0-15-201671-5). Several of Aesop's fables involving the fox are interwoven into a single narrative with striking pictures. (Rev: BCCB 11/99; HBG 3/00; SLJ 12/99) [398.2]

13024 Souhami, Jessica. *The Little, Little House* (PS–2). Illus. 2006, Frances Lincoln $15.95 (978-1-84507-108-0). 32pp. Collage artwork breathes new life into the classic rabbinical fable about a poor man who looks for a way to make his family's crowded dwelling more comfortable. (Rev: BL 2/1/06; SLJ 3/06) [309.2]

13025 Souhami, Jessica. *Mrs. McCool and the Giant Cuhullin: An Irish Tale* (K–3). Illus. 2002, Holt $16.95 (978-0-8050-6852-8). 32pp. A giant of Irish lore, Cuhullin, goes in search of another, Finn McCool, to see who is strongest, but Finn's wife turns out to be strongest of all. (Rev: BL 2/15/02; HB 5/02*; HBG 10/02; SLJ 3/02) [398.2]

13026 Souhami, Jessica. *No Dinner! The Story of the Old Woman and the Pumpkin* (PS–1). Illus. 2000, Marshall Cavendish $15.95 (978-0-7614-5059-7). 32pp. In this South Asian folktale, Grandma outwits a wolf, a tiger, and a bear on her way to and from visiting her granddaughter in the forest. (Rev: BCCB 3/00; BL 3/1/00; HBG 10/00; SLJ 4/00) [823.914]

13027 Spencer, Ann. *Song of the Sea: Myths, Tales, and Folklore* (4–6). Illus. 2001, Tundra paper $17.95 (978-0-88776-487-5). 208pp. A handsome and varied collection of sea-related lore from around the world. (Rev: BL 8/01; SLJ 7/01) [398.23]

13028 Spirin, Gennady. *Goldilocks and the Three Bears* (PS–2). Illus. by author. 2009, Marshall Cavendish $17.99 (978-0-7614-5596-7). 32pp. A simple retelling with lush, detailed illustrations. (Rev: BLO 3/18/09; SLJ 3/09) [398.2]

13029 Spirin, Gennady. *Little Red Riding Hood* (K–2). Illus. by author. 2010, Marshall Cavendish $17.99 (978-0-7614-5704-6). 32pp. A handsomely illustrated version that is close to the original and features images inspired by 17th-century Holland. (Rev: BL 11/1/10; LMC 11–12/10; SLJ 9/1/10) [398.2]

13030 Spirin, Gennady. *The Tale of the Firebird* (K–3). Trans. by Tatiana Popova. Illus. 2002, Penguin $16.99 (978-0-399-23584-9). 32pp. The tsar's youngest son survives a number of tests before finding the firebird and winning the love of the beautiful Yelena in this lush picture book that melds three traditional Russian tales. (Rev: BCCB 11/02; BL 11/15/02; HBG 3/03; SLJ 9/02) [398.2]

13031 Squires, Janet. *The Gingerbread Cowboy* (PS–K). Illus. by Holly Berry. 2006, HarperCollins $17.99 (978-0-06-077863-7). 32pp. The familiar tale of the runaway gingerbread boy is given a lively, western twist. (Rev: BL 4/15/06; SLJ 8/06) [398.21]

13032 Stampler, Ann R. *Shlemazel and the Remarkable Spoon of Pohost* (PS–2). Illus. by Jacqueline M. Cohen. 2006, Clarion $16.00 (978-0-618-36959-1). In this adaptation of a traditional Yiddish folk tale, the shtetl's miller uses trickery to transform lazy Shlemazel into a hardworking member of the community. (Rev: BL 6/1–15/06; SLJ 7/06) [398.2]

13033 Stampler, Ann R. *Something for Nothing* (1–3). Illus. by Jacqueline M. Cohen. 2003, Clarion $15.00 (978-0-618-15982-6). 32pp. A clever dog devises a scheme to free his life of three pesky cats in this Jewish folktale. (Rev: BL 5/15/03 ; HBG 10/03; SLJ 4/03) [398.2]

13034 Stampler, Ann Redisch, reteller. *The Rooster Prince of Breslov* (1–3). Illus. by Eugene Yelchin. 2010, Clarion $16.99 (978-0-618-98974-4). 32pp. The well-loved Yiddish folktale about an unlikely old man who cures a prince who is behaving like a rooster is presented with bright illustrations. Lexile AD790L (Rev: HB 9–10/10; LMC 1–2/11; SLJ 10/1/10*)

13035 Stanley, Diane. *Goldie and the Three Bears* (PS–1). Illus. by author. 2003, HarperCollins LB $17.89 (978-0-06-000009-7). Goldie has been looking high and low for a friend "to love with all her heart;" her quest ends when she goes snooping around in the home of the Three Bears. (Rev: HB 9/03; HBG 4/04; SLJ 11/03) [398.2]

13036 Steig, Jeanne. *A Handful of Beans* (PS–3). Illus. by William Steig. 1998, HarperCollins $21.99 (978-0-06-205162-2). 144pp. Six favorite fairy tales, including Rumpelstiltskin, Hansel and Gretel, and Jack and the Beanstalk, are informally retold with cartoon-style drawings. (Rev: BL 11/15/98*; HB 1/99; HBG 3/99; SLJ 12/98) [398.2]

13037 Steptoe, John. *Mufaro's Beautiful Daughters: An African Tale* (PS–2). Illus. by author. 1987, Lothrop LB $17.89 (978-0-688-04046-8). 32pp. Two sisters of opposite natures vie for the hand of the king. (Rev: BCCB 4/87; BL 4/15/87; SLJ 6–7/87) [398.2]

13038 Steptoe, John, retel. *The Story of Jumping Mouse: A Native American Legend* (1–4). 1984, Morrow paper $6.99 (978-0-688-08740-1). The legend of the mouse who, because of good acts, is transformed into an eagle. [398.2]

13039 Stevens, Janet. *Coyote Steals the Blanket: A Ute Tale* (4–6). Illus. 1993, Holiday House LB $17.95 (978-0-8234-0996-9). 32pp. In this amusing legend, a rock chases a coyote after the animal steals a blanket that had covered it. (Rev: BCCB 5/93*; BL 4/1/93; SLJ 6/93) [398.2]

13040 Stevens, Janet. *Old Bag of Bones: A Coyote Tale* (K–4). Illus. 1996, Holiday House LB $16.95 (978-0-8234-1215-0). 32pp. Coyote, who resents growing old, persuades Young Buffalo to share his youth with him in this Shoshone tale. (Rev: BCCB 5/96; BL 5/1/96; HB 7/96; SLJ 5/96*) [398.24]

13041 Stevens, Janet. *Tops and Bottoms* (PS–2). Illus. 1995, Harcourt $16.00 (978-0-15-292851-3). 32pp. An African American folktale about how Hare takes unfair advantage of Bear in a garden project. (Rev: BCCB 4/95; BL 3/15/95*; HB 5/95; SLJ 5/95) [398.2]

13042 Stewig, John W. *Whuppity Stoorie* (2–4). Illus. by Preston McDaniels. 2004, Holiday House $16.95 (978-0-8234-1749-0). 32pp. This picture-book story of a young widow who foils a fairy's attempts to steal her son is set in Scotland, with suitable dialect and illustrations. (Rev: BL 2/15/04; SLJ 3/04) [398.2]

13043 Stihler, Chérie B. *The Giant Cabbage: An Alaska Folktale* (PS–2). Illus. by Jeremiah Trammell. 2003, Sasquatch paper $9.95 (978-1-57061-357-9). In this Alaskan variation on a traditional Russian folktale, Moose enlists the help of a band of animals to get his giant cabbage to the fair for judging. (Rev: SLJ 8/03) [398.2]

13044 Stimpson, Colin. *Jack and the Baked Beanstalk* (PS–2). Illus. by author. 2012, Candlewick $15.99 (978-076365563-1). 40pp. A can of magic baked beans leads Jack to a giant who is bored with counting his gold and instead helps Jack and his mother resurrect their diner business; set during the Depression. Lexile AD830 (Rev: BLO 8/12; LMC 10/12; SLJ 7/12)

13045 Storace, Patricia. *Sugar Cane: A Caribbean Rapunzel* (K–3). Illus. by Raúl Colón. 2007, Hyperion $16.99 (978-0-7868-0791-8). 48pp. Filled with striking illustrations and beautifully descriptive language, this Rapunzel is set on a Caribbean island full of magic. (Rev: BCCB 10/07; BL 7/07; LMC 10/07; SLJ 7/07) [398.2]

13046 Sturges, Philemon. *The Little Red Hen (Makes a Pizza)* (PS–2). Illus. by Amy Ward. 1999, Dutton $15.99 (978-0-525-45953-8). 32pp. In this variation on the classic folktale, the industrious Little Red Hen makes pizza instead of bread. (Rev: BCCB 2/00; BL 11/15/99; HBG 3/00; SLJ 12/99*) [398.2]

13047 Sugiura, Kuniko. *Indonesian Tales of Treasures and Brides* (K–6). Trans. by Matthew Galgani. Illus. by Koji Honda. Series: Asian Folktales Retold. 2007, Heian $16.95 (978-0-89346-951-1). Three traditional Indonesian stories, accompanied by illustrations on every page, tell of brides and grooms and their fortunes. (Rev: SLJ 8/07)

13048 Sugiura, Kuniko, ed. *Indonesian Fables of Feats and Fortunes* (K–6). Trans. by Matthew Galgani. Illus. by Koji Honda. 2007, Heian $16.95 (978-0-89346-950-4). Three traditional Indonesian stories, accompanied by illustrations on every page, tell of animals and people overcoming difficulty. (Rev: SLJ 8/07)

13049 Sutcliff, Rosemary, retel. *Beowulf* (5–8). Retold by Rosemary Sutcliff. Illus. by Charles Keeping. 1984, Smith $24.50 (978-0-8446-6165-0). This is a reissue of the Anglo-Saxon tale published originally in 1962. Also use the King Arthur story, *The Sword and the Circle* (1981, Dutton). [398.2]

13050 Swamp, Chief Jake. *Giving Thanks: A Native American Good Morning Message* (PS–1). Illus. by Erwin Printup. 1995, Lee & Low $15.95 (978-1-880000-15-1). A Mohawk chieftain gives thanks for Mother Earth and the universe that surrounds her. (Rev: BL 10/15/95; SLJ 11/95) [299]

13051 Sweet, Melissa. *Carmine: A Little More Red* (PS–2). Illus. by author. 2005, Houghton $16.00 (978-0-618-38794-6). A fresh and amusing take on the tale of Little Red Riding Hood, told in the form of a sophisticated alphabet book that highlights a different word in the alphabet on each page. (Rev: SLJ 8/05*) [398.2]

13052 Szobody, Michelle. *Beowulf, Book 1: Grendel the Ghastly* (3–6). Illus. by Justin Gerard. 2007, Portland Studios $17.95 (978-0-9797183-0-4). This picture-book presentation of one of Beowulf's adventures makes it accessible to younger readers. (Rev: BL 12/1/07; SLJ 7/08) [398.2]

13053 Taback, Simms. *Joseph Had a Little Overcoat* (PS–2). Illus. 1999, Viking $16.99 (978-0-670-87855-0). 40pp. The many uses of a piece of cloth — from an overcoat to only enough material to cover a button — are the subject of this picture book based on an old Yiddish song. The mixed-media and collage illustrations are warm and lively. Caldecott Medal, 2000. (Rev: BCCB 3/00; BL 1/1–15/00; HBG 3/00; SLJ 1/00) [398.2]

13054 Taback, Simms. *Kibitzers and Fools: Tales My Zayda Told Me* (K–3). Illus. by author. 2005, Viking $16.99 (978-0-670-05955-3). 48pp. Set in the shtetls of Eastern Europe during the late 19th and early 20th centuries, these 13 tales, each of which spotlights a word or two in Yiddish, offer valuable life lessons. (Rev: BL 10/15/05; SLJ 10/05) [398.2]

13055 Talbott, Hudson. *Lancelot* (5–7). 1999, Morrow LB $15.89 (978-0-688-14833-1). A retelling of the life of Lancelot, from his rescue as a child by the Lady of the Lake to his love for Guinevere, marriage to Elaine, and fathering of Galahad. (Rev: BL 9/1/99; HBG 3/00; SLJ 10/99) [398.2]

13056 Tarbescu, Edith. *The Boy Who Stuck Out His Tongue: A Yiddish Folktale* (PS–1). Illus. by Judith C. Mills. 2000, Barefoot Books $15.99 (978-1-84148-067-1). A disobedient son sticks out his tongue and it freezes to a cold iron fence. All the villagers try to free him in this Jewish folktale. (Rev: BCCB 11/00; BL 5/15/00; HBG 3/01; SLJ 9/00) [398.2]

13057 Tarnowska, Wafa'. *The Arabian Nights* (4–8). Illus. by Carole Hénaff. 2010, Barefoot $24.99 (978-1-84686-122-2). 128pp. Eight of Scheherazade's tales — including Aladdin but also ones that will not be familiar to most children — are presented with evocative illustrations. (Rev: BL 1/1–15/11; SLJ 2/1/11*) [398.2]

13058 *Tatanka and the Lakota People: A Creation Story* (1–4). Illus. by Donald F. Montileaux. 2006, South Dakota State Historical Soc. $16.95 (978-0-9749195-8-4). This creation story tells how the Lakota people were tricked into leaving their Underworld with promises of easy living; English and Lakota words are side by side and the illustrations draw on traditional art. (Rev: SLJ 2/07) [398.2]

13059 Taylor, C. J. *All the Stars in the Sky: Native Stories from the Heavens* (2–4). Illus. by author. 2006, Tundra $17.95 (978-0-88776-759-3). 40pp. A collection of seven diverse stories about the night sky from various Native American groups. (Rev: BL 12/1/06) [398.2]

13060 Taylor, C. J. *How We Saw the World: Nine Native Stories of the Way Things Began* (4–6). Illus. 1993, Tundra $17.99 (978-0-88776-302-1). These nine stories from various tribes explain the origin of several animals, like horses, and geographical landmarks, like Niagara Falls. (Rev: BL 11/1/93; SLJ 2/94) [398.3]

13061 Taylor, C. J. *The Secret of the White Buffalo* (K–3). Illus. 1993, Tundra paper $13.95 (978-0-88776-321-2). 24pp. Two Native American scouts encounter a beautiful woman when they set out to track buffalo in this Oglala Indian folktale. (Rev: BL 1/1/94) [398.2]

13062 Tchana, Katrin. *Sense Pass King: A Story from Cameroon* (PS–2). Illus. by Trina S. Hyman. 2002, Holiday House $16.95 (978-0-8234-1577-9). 32pp. Sense Pass King is the name that a child prodigy acquires when she succeeds in discrediting the stupid king and becomes leader of her people. (Rev: BL 11/1/02; HB 11/02; HBG 3/03; SLJ 9/02) [398.2]

13063 Tchana, Katrin Hyman. *The Serpent Slayer and Other Stories of Strong Women* (4–7). Illus. by Trina Schart Hyman. 2000, Little, Brown $21.95 (978-0-316-38701-9). A collection of 18 folktales from around the world featuring brave, creative, and strong women and girls. (Rev: BCCB 11/00*; BL 12/15/00; HB 11–12/00; HBG 3/01; SLJ 11/00) [398.2]

13064 Te Loo, Sanne. *Ping-Li's Kite* (PS–1). Illus. 2002, Front St. $15.95 (978-1-886910-75-1). A young Chinese boy angers the Emperor of the Sky when he flies an undecorated kite in this book based on a Chinese folktale. (Rev: BL 8/02; HBG 10/02; SLJ 5/02) [398.2]

13065 Thomas, Joyce Carol. *The Gospel Cinderella* (PS–2). Illus. by David Diaz. 2004, HarperCollins $15.99 (978-0-06-025387-5). 40pp. In this retelling, the daughter of Queen Mother Rhythm falls into the clutches of Cruel Crooked Foster Mother and can only be saved by her talent as a gospel singer. (Rev: BL 2/15/04; SLJ 5/04) [398.2]

13066 Thompson, Stith, ed. *One Hundred Favorite Folktales* (5–8). Illus. by Franz Altschuler. 1968, Indiana Univ $39.95 (978-0-253-15940-3); paper $19.95 (978-0-253-20172-0). A selection from an international store of folktales. [398.2]

13067 Thomson, Sarah L. *Cinderella* (K–3). Illus. by Nicoletta Ceccoli. 2012, Amazon Children's $17.99 (978-0-7614-6170-8). 32pp. The illustrations will draw readers into this new retelling that is faithful to the original. **e** (Rev: BL 11/1/12; SLJ 1/13) [398.2]

13068 Thurber, James. *Many Moons* (2–4). Illus. by Marc Simont. 1990, Harcourt $14.95 (978-0-15-251872-1). A sick princess asks her father for the moon to help her get better. The original edition, illustrated by Louis Slobodkin, was the 1944 Caldecott Medal winner. (Rev: BL 9/15/90; HB 1/90*; SLJ 1/91) [398.2]

13069 Tingle, Tim. *When Turtle Grew Feathers: A Folktale from the Choctaw Nation* (PS–2). Illus. by Stacey Schuett. 2007, August House $16.95 (978-0-87483-777-3). A rhyming version of a Native American take on the tortoise-and-the-hare legend, with lively illustrations. (Rev: SLJ 5/07)

13070 Tolstoy, Aleksei. *The Gigantic Turnip* (PS–2). Illus. by Niamh Sharkey. Series: Barefoot Beginner. 2000, Barefoot Books $15.95 (978-1-902283-12-8). 40pp. A rather complicated retelling of the popular Russian folktale about a husband and wife who need help to uproot a huge turnip. (Rev: BCCB 7–8/99; SLJ 4/99) [398.2]

13071 Tseng, Grace. *White Tiger, Blue Serpent* (K–3). Illus. by Jean Tseng and Mou-Sien Tseng. 1999, Lothrop $16.00 (978-0-688-12515-8). 32pp. A Chinese folktale in which a young peasant, Kai, faces many dangers while journeying to the palace of the goddess Qin to retrieve a silk brocade. (Rev: BL 8/99; HBG 10/99; SLJ 7/99) [398.2]

13072 Tym, Kate. *Princess Stories from Around the World* (3–5). Illus. by Sophy Williams. 2008, Trafalgar paper $13.95 (978-1-84365-100-0). 64pp. An appealing, large-format collection of traditional tales about princesses of all kinds, told in an up-to-date conversational style with vivid illustrations. (Rev: BLO 7/30/08) [398.2]

13073 Uhlberg, Myron. *Lemuel the Fool* (PS–3). Illus. by Sonja Lamut. 2001, Peachtree $15.95 (978-1-56145-220-0). 32pp. In this Yiddish folktale, a dreamer sets out to see the world but, because he is walking in a circle, finds himself back home. (Rev: BL 4/15/01; HBG 10/01; SLJ 8/01) [398.2]

13074 Ungar, Richard. *Even Higher* (PS–2). Illus. by author. 2007, Tundra $18.95 (978-0-88776-758-6). 32pp. An adaptation of a Eastern European Jewish folktale in which young Reuven he discovers that the rabbi has indeed ascended "even higher" than heaven by secretly cutting wood for a poor widow. (Rev: BL 9/1/07; SLJ 9/07) [398.2]

13075 Valeri, Maria Eulalia. *The Hare and the Tortoise / La liebre y la tortuga* (4–6). Illus. by Max. 2006, Chronicle $14.95 (978-0-8118-5057-5); paper $6.95 (978-0-8118-5058-2). 32pp. A bilingual retelling of the classic fable. (Rev: BL 9/1/06; SLJ 10/06) [398.2]

13076 Vallverdu, Josep. *Aladdin and the Magic Lamp / Aldino y la lampara maravillosa* (4–6). Illus. by Pep Montserrat. 2006, Chronicle $14.95 (978-0-8118-5061-2); paper $6.95 (978-0-8118-5062-9). 32pp. An attractive bilingual retelling. (Rev: BL 9/1/06; SLJ 10/06) [398.22]

13077 Van Kampen, Vlasta. *A Drop of Gold* (PS–2). Illus. 2001, Annick LB $18.95 (978-1-55037-677-7); paper $7.95 (978-1-55037-676-0). 32pp. Spirited artwork illustrates this pourquoi tale of how Mother Nature and her helpers colored the world's birds. (Rev: BL 2/1/02; HBG 3/02; SLJ 1/02) [813]

13078 Van Laan, Nancy. *In a Circle Long Ago: A Treasury of Native Lore from North America* (3–5). Illus. 1995, Knopf LB $21.99 (978-0-679-95807-9). 128pp. Nature is explored in 25 geographically arranged tales, with an introduction to their cultural origins. (Rev: BL 11/15/95; SLJ 11/95) [392.2]

13079 Vande Velde, Vivian. *The Rumpelstiltskin Problem* (4–6). 2000, Houghton $15.00 (978-0-618-05523-4). After a criticism of the logic behind this famous fairy tale, the author presents six new versions of the tale that, supposedly, make more sense. (Rev: BCCB 2/01; HBG 3/01; SLJ 11/00) [398.2]

13080 Villaseñor, Victor. *Little Crow to the Rescue / El cuervito al rescate* (PS–3). Trans. by Elizabeth Cummins Munoz. Illus. by Felipe Ugalde Alcántara. 2005, Arte Publico $15.95 (978-1-55885-430-7). 32pp. In Spanish and English, this is a pourquoi tale about the reasons for crows' disdain for humans. (Rev: BL 10/1/05; SLJ 2/06) [398.2]

13081 Vivian, French. *Henny Penny* (PS–2). Illus. by Sophie Windham. 2006, Bloomsbury $16.95 (978-1-58234-706-6). 32pp. On their way to tell the king that the sky is falling, Henny Penny and her feathered friends fall into the clutches of Foxy Loxy. (Rev: BL 8/06; SLJ 7/06) [398.2]

13082 Vogel, Carole G. *Legends of Landforms: Native American Lore and the Geology of the Land* (4–6). Illus. 1999, Millbrook LB $27.90 (978-0-7613-0272-8). 96pp. This book contains 14 legends about such geological formations as the Grand Canyon and Martha's Vineyard, with scientific background material on each. (Rev: BL 11/15/99; HBG 10/00; SLJ 1/00) [398.2]

13083 Vuong, Lynette Dyer. *The Brocaded Slipper and Other Vietnamese Tales* (5–7). Illus. by Vo-Dinh Mai. 1982, HarperCollins paper $4.95 (978-0-06-440440-2). Five Vietnamese fairy tales, some of which are similar to our own. [398.2]

13084 Waboose, Jan B. *SkySisters* (PS–2). Illus. by Brian Deines. 2000, Kids Can $15.95 (978-1-55074-697-6). 32pp. Two Ojibwaa sisters encounter three guardian spirits — a rabbit, a deer, and a coyote — as they venture out one night to see the Northern Lights. (Rev: BL 11/15/00; HBG 3/01; SLJ 1/01) [398.2]

13085 Wada, Stephanie. *Momotaro and the Island of Ogres* (2–4). Illus. by Kano Naganobu. 2005, George Braziller $21.95 (978-0-8076-1552-2). 398pp. Silk handscrolls from the 19th century illustrate this retelling of the Japanese legend about a child, born from a peach, who succeeds in defeating threatening ogres. (Rev: BL 5/15/05) [398.2]

13086 Wade, Mary Dodson. *No Year of the Cat* (K–2). Illus. by Nicole Wong. 2012, Sleeping Bear $16.95 (978-1-58536-785-6). 32pp. Cat misses her spot in the emperor's animal race and therefore does not make it onto the Chinese zodiac. (Rev: BL 12/15/12; SLJ 1/13) [398.2]

13087 Wahl, Jan. *Little Johnny Buttermilk* (PS–1). Illus. by Jennifer Mazzucco. 1999, August House $15.95 (978-0-87483-559-5). 32pp. An English tale about Little Johnny and how he escapes from a witch after being captured on his way to market. (Rev: BL 12/15/99; HBG 3/00; SLJ 2/00) [398.2]

13088 Waldherr, Kris. *Sacred Animals* (3–6). Illus. 2001, HarperCollins LB $16.89 (978-0-688-16380-8). 48pp. Animal folklore and legends from around the world are organized in four sections — earth, water, fire, and air animals — and surrounded with wonderful illustrations and borders. (Rev: BL 10/1/01; HBG 3/02; SLJ 11/01) [398.2]

13089 Waldman, Debby. *A Sack Full of Feathers* (PS–2). Illus. by Cindy Revell. 2006, Orca $17.95 (978-1-55143-332-5). 32pp. In this vividly portrayed retelling of a Jewish folktale, Yankel learns about the dangers of spreading hurtful gossip. (Rev: BL 10/15/06; SLJ 2/07) [398.2]

13090 Walker, Barbara K., ed. *A Treasury of Turkish Folktales for Children* (4–7). 1988, Shoe String LB $25.00

(978-0-208-02206-6). A witty collection interspersed with riddles. (Rev: BL 10/15/88; SLJ 10/88) [398.2]

13091 Walker, Richard. *The Barefoot Book of Pirates* (4–6). Illus. 1998, Barefoot Books $19.99 (978-1-901223-79-8). 64pp. Pirates and robbers from folklore, including Robin Hood and Pirate Grace, are included in this entertaining collection of folktales from around the world. (Rev: BL 11/15/98; SLJ 9/98) [398.2]

13092 Walker, Richard. *The Barefoot Book of Trickster Tales* (3–6). Illus. 1998, Barefoot Books $18.95 (978-1-902283-08-1). A collection of trickster tales from around the world, including an Anansi story, a Jack tale, a Brer Rabbit adventure, and a Red Riding Hood story from Bengal. (Rev: BL 1/1–15/99; SLJ 11/98) [398]

13093 Wallace, Ian. *Hansel and Gretel* (2–4). Illus. 1996, Douglas & McIntyre $14.95 (978-0-88899-212-3). 32pp. A scary retelling in a contemporary setting of the famous Grimms folktale. (Rev: BL 6/1–15/96; SLJ 5/96) [398.2]

13094 Wang, Gabrielle. *The Race for the Chinese Zodiac* (PS–1). Illus. by Sally Rippin. 2013, Candlewick $14.99 (978-076366778-8). 32pp. In this book about teamwork, honesty, friendship, and idleness, the author uses Chinese-like drawings and simple text to tell the story of the Chinese Zodiac, in which the Jade Emperor, the ruler of Heaven and Earth, summons 13 animals to participate in a race that will determine which 12 animals will become a part of the Zodiac and have a year named after them. (Rev: BLO 11/15/13; SLJ 12/13) [398.2]

13095 Wang, Rosalind C. *The Treasure Chest: A Chinese Tale* (PS–3). Illus. by Will Hillenbrand. 1995, Holiday House LB $15.95 (978-0-8234-1114-6). 32pp. In this Chinese tale, a humble peasant gets help from the Ocean King to fight an evil despot. (Rev: BL 6/1–15/95; SLJ 6/95) [398.2]

13096 Ward, Helen. *The Hare and the Tortoise* (PS–3). Illus. 1999, Millbrook LB $23.90 (978-0-7613-1318-2). 40pp. A witty, straightforward retelling of the fable, illustrated with outstanding watercolor paintings. (Rev: BCCB 6/99; BL 5/15/99*; HBG 10/99; SLJ 7/99) [398.24]

13097 Ward, Helen. *Unwitting Wisdom: An Anthology of Aesop's Fables* (2–5). Illus. 2004, Chronicle $18.95 (978-0-8118-4450-5). 64pp. Arresting ink-and-watercolor illustrations accompany well-worded retellings of a dozen Aesop tales. (Rev: BL 9/15/04; SLJ 10/04) [398.2]

13098 Washington, Donna L. *A Pride of African Tales* (2–5). Illus. by James Ransome. 2004, HarperCollins $16.99 (978-0-06-024929-8). 80pp. These effective retellings introduce African trickster, pourquoi, and other tales from varied cultures. (Rev: BL 3/15/04; SLJ 8/04) [398.2]

13099 Waters, Fiona. *The Emperor and the Nightingale* (PS–3). Illus. by Paul Birkbeck. 2000, Bloomsbury $19.95 (978-0-7475-3559-1). A fine retelling of this classic fairy tale with lavish illustrations and sensitive language. (Rev: BL 11/15/00; SLJ 1/01) [398.2]

13100 Watts, Bernadette. *The Rich Man and the Shoemaker: A Fable by La Fontaine* (2–4). Illus. 2002, North-South LB $16.50 (978-0-7358-4676-0). 32pp. A Renaissance setting graces this tale of the shoemaker who returns a bribe when the gold causes him anxiety. (Rev: BL 10/1/02; HBG 3/03) [398.2]

13101 Watts, Bernadette. *Three Little Pigs* (PS–1). Illus. by author. 2012, NorthSouth $16.95 (978-073584058-4). 32pp. With dramatic, warm artwork, this is a retelling of the classic tale about the pigs being tormented by a wolf. (Rev: BL 1/1/12; LMC 8–9/12; SLJ 1/12) [398.2]

13102 Watts, Bernadette. *The Town Mouse and the Country Mouse: An Aesop Fable* (PS–2). Illus. 1998, North-South LB $15.88 (978-1-55858-988-9). 28pp. A delightful version of the old Aesop fable about two mice that visit each other and discover that home is best. (Rev: BL 11/15/98; HBG 3/99; SLJ 3/99) [398.2]

13103 Weber, Ilse. *Mendel Rosenbusch: Tales for Jewish Children* (3–6). Trans. from German by Ruth Fisher and Hans Fisher. 2001, Herodias $14.00 (978-1-928746-19-5). 102pp. A collection of Czech tales about a poor but wise man who lives behind a synagogue and is visited one night by an angel who gives him a gift — the ability to become invisible. (Rev: HBG 3/02; SLJ 11/01) [398.2]

13104 Webster, M. L, retel. *On the Trail Made of Dawn: Native American Creation Stories* (4–9). Retold by M. L. Webster. 2001, Linnet LB $19.50 (978-0-208-02497-8). The author retells 13 creation stories and places them in cultural context. (Rev: HBG 3/02; SLJ 12/01) [398.2]

13105 Wegman, William. *Cinderella* (PS–2). Illus. 1993, Hyperion $16.95 (978-1-56282-348-1). The characters in this reworking of the Cinderella story are all dogs, but the story remains the same. (Rev: BCCB 7–8/93; BL 5/15/93; SLJ 4/93) [398.2]

13106 Weiss, Jacqueline Shachter. *Young Brer Rabbit: And Other Trickster Tales from the Americas* (4–6). Illus. 1985, Stemmer $14.95 (978-0-88045-037-9); paper $9.95 (978-0-88045-138-3). 80pp. Fifteen stories translated from Spanish, French, and Portuguese. (Rev: BCCB 1/86; BL 3/1/86; SLJ 1/86) [398.2]

13107 Weitzman, David. *Rama and Sita: A Tale from Ancient Java* (1–3). Illus. 2002, Godine $19.95 (978-1-56792-151-9). 32pp. A retelling of the story *The Ramayana*, in the style of Javanese shadow puppetry. (Rev: BL 2/15/03; HBG 10/03; SLJ 6/03) [398.2]

13108 Wenzel, David, and Doug Wheeler. *Fairy Tales of the Brothers Grimm* (4–6). Illus. 1995, NBM $15.95 (978-1-56163-130-8). 48pp. Using a comic book format, some of the best-known tales of the Grimm Brothers are retold, with an emphasis on story-telling pictures. (Rev: BL 4/15/96) [398.2]

13109 Whatley, Bruce. *Wait! No Paint!* (K–2). Illus. 2001, HarperCollins LB $16.89 (978-0-06-028271-4). It's the illustrator himself who threatens the fate of the three little pigs and the big bad wolf in this colorful and inventive retelling. (Rev: BL 8/01; HB 9/01; HBG 3/02; SLJ 7/01) [398.2]

13110 Whipple, Laura. *If the Shoe Fits* (5–8). Illus. by Laura Beingessner. 2002, Simon & Schuster $17.95 (978-0-689-84070-8). A handsome retelling of the Cinderella story using blank verse. (Rev: BCCB 3/02; BL 5/1/02; HBG 10/02; SLJ 8/02) [398.2]

13111 Wiesner, David. *The Three Pigs* (K–6). Illus. by author. 2001, Clarion $16.00 (978-0-618-00701-1). This is a fresh twist on the familiar tale, with excellent and inventive illustrations, that has a bewildered wolf searching for pigs that have been blown into a fantasy universe until they return and set the world to rights. Caldecott Medal winner, 2002. (Rev: BCCB 5/01; BL 5/15/01*; HB 5/01*; HBG 10/01; SLJ 4/01*) [398.2]

13112 Wilcox, Leah. *Falling for Rapunzel* (PS–2). Illus. by Lydia Monks. 2003, Penguin $14.99 (978-0-399-23794-2). In this hilarious variation, Rapunzel misinterprets the prince's pleas, throwing down socks instead of lock, her maid instead of her braid. (Rev: BL 12/1/03; HB 11/03; HBG 4/04; SLJ 12/03) [398.2]

13113 *The Wild Swans* (4–6). Retold by Ken Setterington. Illus. by Ernst Hofer and Nelly Hofer. 2003, Tundra $17.95 (978-0-88776-615-2). 40pp. The story of how Elise saves her brothers from being turned into swans is presented in clear, flowing text and intricate cut-paper art. (Rev: BL 11/15/03; HBG 4/04; SLJ 12/03) [398.2]

13114 Wilde, Oscar. *The Happy Prince* (3–5). Illus. by Robin Muller. 2002, Stoddart $15.95. Wilde's unusual fairy tale in which a swallow and a statue make sacrifices for each other is retold with effective illustrations. (Rev: BL 3/15/02) [398.2]

13115 Willard, Nancy. *Cinderella's Dress* (K–2). Illus. by Jane Dyer. 2003, Scholastic $16.95 (978-0-590-56927-9). With the help of two magpies, a ring hammered from fairy gold, and her fairy godmother, Cinderella finally makes it to the ball despite the best efforts of the horrible stepsisters. (Rev: HBG 4/04; SLJ 11/03) [398.2]

13116 Willard, Nancy. *The Flying Bed* (2–4). Illus. by John Thompson. 2007, Scholastic $16.99 (978-0-590-25610-0). A Florentine baker's business booms after he buys a very special bed, but his greed jeopardizes his luck. (Rev: BCCB 5/07; BL 1/1/07; LMC 8/07; SLJ 4/07) [398.2]

13117 Willey, Margaret. *Clever Beatrice* (PS–3). Illus. by Heather Solomon. 2001, Simon & Schuster $16.00 (978-0-689-83254-3). 40pp. A tall tale from the wilds of Michigan in which a little girl named Beatrice outwits a rich giant. (Rev: BL 7/01; HB 11/01*; HBG 3/02; SLJ 10/01) [398.2]

13118 Willey, Margaret. *Clever Beatrice and the Best Little Pony* (K–2). Illus. by Heather Solomon. 2004, Simon & Schuster $16.95 (978-0-689-85339-5). 40pp. Beatrice triumphs over the lutin, a leprechaun-like being, who seems to be riding her pony at night. (Rev: BL 2/1/05; SLJ 11/04) [398.2]

13119 Williams, Brenda. *The Real Princess: A Mathemagical Tale* (K–2). Illus. by Sophie Fatus. 2008, Barefoot Books $16.99 (978-1-905236-88-6). 40pp. The story of the princess who felt the pea through the mattress

is retold with many opportunities for counting. (Rev: BL 5/15/08; LMC 10/08; SLJ 6/08) [398.2]

13120 Williams, Carol Ann. *Tsubu the Little Snail* (K–3). Illus. by Tatsuro Kiuchi. 1995, Simon & Schuster $15.00 (978-0-671-87167-3). 24pp. Love transforms a snail into a handsome young man in this Japanese folktale. (Rev: BL 6/1–15/95) [398.2]

13121 Williams, Marcia. *The Elephant's Friend and Other Tales from Ancient India* (3–7). Illus. by author. 2012, Candlewick $16.99 (978-076365916-5). 40pp. Eight Indian animal folk tales are retold here and accompanied by colorful comic book illustrations. (Rev: BL 10/1/12; HB 11–12/12; LMC 3–4/13; SLJ 7/12) [398.2]

13122 Wisnewski, Andrea, retel. *Little Red Riding Hood* (PS–3). Illus. by Andrea Wisnewski. 2007, Godine $18.95 (978-1-56792-303-2). Detailed painted prints give this retelling of the fairy tale a classic look. (Rev: SLJ 6/07) [398.2]

13123 Wisniewski, David. *Golem* (3–6). Illus. 1996, Clarion $17.00 (978-0-395-72618-1). The terrifying story of the golem, who was created by Rabbi Loew in the 16th century to help protect his people in the Prague ghetto. Caldecott Medal winner, 1997. (Rev: BCCB 9/96; BL 10/1/96*; SLJ 10/96) [398.2]

13124 Wisniewski, David. *Sundiata: Lion King of Mali* (K–5). Illus. 1992, Houghton $17.00 (978-0-395-61302-3). 32pp. The dying king gives his kingdom to a sickly prince who cannot walk or speak, but in time, he becomes a great and brave leader. (Rev: BL 12/1/92*; HB 3/93; SLJ 10/92*) [398.2]

13125 Wolf, Gita. *Gobble You Up* (K–3). Illus. by Sunita. 2013, Tara $34.95 (978-819231714-4). 40pp. Using a combination of rhyming prose and an ancient form of Indian artwork called mandna, Wolf depicts a Rajasthani folktale about a greedy jackal who eats so many animals (including an elephant) that he eventually explodes and all of the animals break free; each of these books is handmade and numbered. (Rev: BLO 11/15/13; HB 1–2/14; LMC 5–6/14; SLJ 1/1/14)

13126 Wolfson, Evelyn. *Inuit Mythology* (5–9). Illus. by William Sauts Bock. Series: Mythology. 2001, Enslow LB $26.60 (978-0-7660-1559-3). Seven tales from Inuit folklore are accompanied by information on the history and culture of the Inuit peoples. (Rev: BL 4/15/02; HBG 3/02; SLJ 3/02) [398.2]

13127 Wolfson, Margaret Olivia. *The Patient Stone: A Persian Love Story* (3–7). Illus. by Juan Caneba Clavero. 2001, Barefoot Books $16.99 (978-1-84148-085-5). 32pp. This retelling of the story of Fatima, who after many trials earns the love of a prince thanks to a magic stone, is accompanied by beautiful watercolors and handsome borders, as well as an author's note that explains some of the symbolism. (Rev: BL 9/15/01; HBG 3/02; SLJ 2/02) [398.2]

13128 Wolkstein, Diane. *Sun Mother Wakes the World: An Australian Creation Story* (PS–2). Illus. by Bronwyn Bancroft. 2004, HarperCollins $17.99 (978-0-688-13915-5). 32pp. This colorfully illustrated retelling of an aboriginal folktale offers an appealing explanation of the Earth's creation. (Rev: BL 4/15/04; SLJ 4/04) [398.2]

13129 Wolkstein, Diane, retel. *The Glass Mountain* (K–4). Illus. by Louisa Bauer. 1999, Morrow LB $15.89 (978-0-688-14848-5). A lesser-known Grimm Brothers tale in which a young girl is held prisoner in an underground cave by an unpleasant old man named Old Rinkrank. (Rev: BCCB 3/99; HBG 10/99; SLJ 7/99) [398.2]

13130 Wood, Audrey. *Heckedy Peg* (PS–2). Illus. by Don Wood. 1987, Harcourt $16.00 (978-0-15-233678-3); paper $7.00 (978-0-15-233679-0). 32pp. Mother promises gifts to her seven children, all named for days of the week, taken from a 16th-century game still played in England. (Rev: BCCB 12/87; BL 9/15/87; SLJ 11/87) [398.2]

13131 Wooldridge, Connie N. *Wicked Jack* (K–3). Illus. by Will Hillenbrand. 1995, Holiday House LB $16.95 (978-0-8234-1101-6). 32pp. A retelling of the Southern tale about a mean blacksmith who outwits the Devil and his young sons. (Rev: BCCB 12/95; BL 11/1/95; SLJ 12/95*) [398.2]

13132 Wormell, Christopher. *Mice, Morals and Monkey Business: Lively Lessons from Aesop's Fables* (K–3). Illus. 2005, Running Pr. $18.95 (978-0-7624-2404-7). 64pp. The moral messages contained in some of Aesop's most memorable fables are highlighted in striking woodcut illustrations; concise versions of the stories are given at the back of the book. (Rev: BL 9/15/05; SLJ 11/05*) [395]

13133 Xiong, Blia. *Nine-in-One, Grr! Grr!* (3–6). Adapted by Cathy Spagnoli. Illus. by Nancy Hom. 1993, Children's Book Pr. $14.95 (978-0-89239-048-9); paper $7.95 (978-0-89239-110-3). 32pp. In this folktale from Laos, Bird comes up with a trick to prevent the earth from being overpopulated with tigers. A reissue. [398.2]

13134 Xuan, YongSheng. *The Dragon Lover and Other Chinese Proverbs* (K–3). 1999, Shen's $16.95 (978-1-885008-11-4). Illustrated with Chinese paper cuts, this lovely book contains the stories behind five well-known Chinese proverbs. (Rev: BCCB 7–8/99; BL 5/15/99; HBG 10/99; SLJ 8/99) [398.2]

13135 Ye, Ting-xing. *Three Monks, No Water* (K–3). Illus. by Harvey Chan. 1997, Annick LB $16.95 (978-1-55037-443-8); paper $6.95 (978-1-55037-442-1). This story supposedly explains the origin of the Chinese expression "Three monks, no water," which is used when children try to avoid chores. (Rev: BL 2/1/98; SLJ 12/97) [398.2]

13136 Yip, Mingmei. *Chinese Children's Favorite Stories* (3–5). Illus. 2004, Tuttle $18.95 (978-0-8048-3589-3). 96pp. Thirteen varied stories introduce readers to traditional Chinese characters — dragons, emperors, scholars, and so forth. (Rev: BL 2/1/05; SLJ 3/05) [398.2]

13137 Yohannes, Gebregeorgis. *Silly Mammo: An Ethiopian Tale* (PS). Illus. by Bogale Belachew. 2002, African Sun paper $10.00 (978-1-883701-04-8). 32pp. A contemporary Ethiopian village is the setting for this

traditional tale in which a hapless lad gets everything wrong until he kisses a fair lady. (Rev: BL 10/1/02; SLJ 2/03) [398.2]

13138 Yolen, Jane. *The Emperor and the Kite* (K–3). Illus. by Ed Young. 1988, Penguin $16.99 (978-0-399-21499-8). 32pp. Oriental-like paper cuts illustrate this Chinese legend about the unshakable loyalty of the emperor's smallest daughter. First published in 1967. [398.2]

13139 Yolen, Jane. *The Firebird* (PS–3). Illus. by Vladimir Vagin. 2002, HarperCollins LB $17.89 (978-0-06-028539-5). 32pp. An effective retelling of the Russian story that combines elements from the original story with the ballet version. (Rev: BCCB 7–8/02; BL 6/1–15/02; HBG 10/02; SLJ 6/02) [398.2]

13140 Yolen, Jane. *Meow: Cat Stories from Around the World* (1–3). Illus. by Hala Wittwer. 2005, HarperCollins $16.99 (978-0-06-029161-7). 40pp. Ten beautifully illustrated cat stories look at cat — and human — behavior around the world. (Rev: BL 8/05; SLJ 8/05) [398.24]

13141 Yolen, Jane. *Once Upon a Bedtime Story* (K–3). Illus. by Ruth T. Councell. 1997, Boyds Mills $17.95 (978-1-57397-484-4). This is a charming collection of 16 folktales, fairy tales, and fables, chiefly from Europe. (Rev: BL 11/15/97; SLJ 9/97) [398.2]

13142 Yolen, Jane. *Sister Bear: A Norse Tale* (K–2). Illus. by Linda Graves. 2011, Marshall Cavendish $17.99 (978-076145958-3). 32pp. On their way to visit the King of Denmark, Halva and her dancing bear succeed in dealing with a pesky band of trolls. (Rev: BLO 11/15/11; SLJ 10/1/11) [398.2]

13143 Yolen, Jane, and Heidi E. Y. Stemple. *The Barefoot Book of Dance Stories* (1–4). Illus. by Helen Cann. 2010, Barefoot $23.99 (978-1-84686-219-9). 96pp. Eight dance-based folktales and fables from around the world are collected in this beautifully illustrated book that includes notes about the style and steps of each dance (waltz, polka, reels, and so forth). (Rev: BL 1/1–15/11; SLJ 12/1/10) [792.8]

13144 Yolen, Jane, ed. *Mightier than the Sword: World Folktales for Strong Boys* (4–8). Illus. by Raul Colon. 2003, Harcourt $20.00 (978-0-15-216391-4). Yolen has collected stories from countries including Afghanistan, Angola, and China that portray intelligence as an invaluable asset. (Rev: BL 4/1/03; HB 5–6/03; HBG 10/03; SLJ 5/03) [398.2]

13145 Yolen, Jane, ed. *Not One Damsel in Distress: World Folktales for Strong Girls* (3–6). Illus. 2000, Harcourt $21.00 (978-0-15-202047-7). 112pp. A collection of folktales from such different locales as Argentina, Romania, and Germany in which girls face obstacles difficult to surmount. (Rev: BCCB 4/00; BL 3/1/00; HBG 10/00; SLJ 7/00) [398.22]

13146 York, M. J. *The Boy at the Dike: A Dutch Folktale* (K–3). Illus. by Laura Freeman. Series: Folktales from Around the World. 2012, Child's World LB $27.07 (978-161473219-8). 24pp. With appealing illustrations, this is the story of the boy who saved a village with his finger. (Rev: BL 9/15/12; LMC 8–9/13) [398]

13147 York, M. J. *How Many Spots Does a Leopard Have? An African Folktale* (K–3). Illus. by Elizabeth Zunon. Series: Folktales from Around the World. 2012, Child's World LB $27.07 (978-161473217-4). 24pp. Fourteen African animals try but fail to count a prideful leopard's spots. ℮ (Rev: BL 9/15/12; LMC 8–9/13) [398]

13148 York, M. J. *The Tiger, the Brahman, and the Jackal: An Indian Folktale* (K–3). Illus. by Jill Dubin. Series: Folktales from Around the World. 2012, Child's World LB $27.07 (978-161473221-1). 24pp. A tale of trickery involving a Brahman who releases a trapped tiger and a wily jackal who saves the Brahman from being eaten. (Rev: BL 9/15/12; LMC 8–9/13) [398]

13149 Young, Ed. *Hook* (PS–1). Illus. by author. 2009, Roaring Brook $17.95 (978-1-59643-363-2). 32pp. This variation of the Ugly Duckling features a fear-of-flying eaglet hatched by a mother hen. (Rev: BCCB 9/09; BL 6/1–15/09; HB 5/09; LMC 8/09; SLJ 6/09) [398.2]

13150 Young, Ed. *Lon Po Po: A Red-Riding-Hood Story from China* (2–4). Illus. 1989, Penguin $16.99 (978-0-399-21619-0). 32pp. In this variation of the Red Riding Hood story, Mother visits Grandmother, leaving her three children in danger from a marauding wolf. Caldecott Medal winner, 1990. (Rev: BCCB 11/89*; BL 11/15/89; HB 1/90*; SLJ 12/89*) [398.2] 🎧

13151 Young, Ed. *Seven Blind Mice* (PS–3). Illus. 1992, Penguin $17.99 (978-0-399-22261-0). 44pp. A stunning picture book illustrating a version of the old Indian folktale about seven blind men and one elephant. (Rev: BCCB 3/92*; BL 4/1/92*; HB 3/92; SLJ 4/92) [398.2]

13152 Young, Ed. *The Sons of the Dragon King: A Chinese Legend* (3–5). Illus. 2004, Simon & Schuster $16.95 (978-0-689-85184-1). This beautifully illustrated Chinese folktale about the Dragon King and his nine sons recounts how the king comes to accept and take advantage of his sons' unique talents and abilities. (Rev: BL 5/15/04; SLJ 6/04) [398.2]

13153 Young, Ed. *What About Me?* (K–3). Illus. 2002, Penguin $16.99 (978-0-399-23624-2). 40pp. A colorful cumulative tale of Sufi origin about a boy who must provide the grand master with a carpet before he will give the youngster the gift of knowledge. (Rev: BCCB 7–8/02; BL 5/1/02*; HB 7/02; HBG 10/02; SLJ 6/02) [398.2]

13154 Young, Richard, and Judy Dockery Young, eds. *Race with Buffalo: And Other Native American Stories for Young Readers* (3–7). Illus. by Wendell E. Hall. 1994, August House $19.95 (978-0-87483-343-0); paper $9.95 (978-0-87483-342-3). 175pp. This collection of 32 American Indian folktales includes such genres as creation and trickster stories. (Rev: SLJ 8/94) [398.2]

13155 Young, Richard, and Judy Dockery Young, eds. *Stories from the Days of Christopher Columbus: A Multicultural Collection for Young Readers* (5–9). 1992, August House paper $8.95 (978-0-87483-198-6). An anthology of stories translated from a variety of languages, including Italian, Spanish, Portuguese, and Aztec. (Rev: BL 9/15/92; SLJ 7/92) [398.2]

13156 Youngquist, Catherine Valente. *The Three Billygoats Gruff and Mean Calypso Joe* (K–3). Illus. by Kristin Sorra. 2002, Simon & Schuster $16.00 (978-0-689-82824-9). 32pp. The classic story of the three billy goats gets a Caribbean twist, complete with a troll named Calypso Joe. (Rev: BL 8/02; HBG 10/02; SLJ 11/02) [398.2]

13157 Zalben, Jane Breskin. *Hey, Mama Goose* (PS–K). Illus. by Emilie Chollat. 2005, Dutton $15.99 (978-0-525-47097-7). 32pp. Mama Goose, real estate agent, brokers deals in which familiar fairy-tale characters exchange dwellings with one another. (Rev: BL 2/15/05; SLJ 2/05) [398.2]

13158 Zalben, Jane Breskin. *Light* (PS–2). Illus. by author. 2007, Dutton $17.99 (978-0-525-47827-0). 40pp. The importance of light is emphasized in this traditional Jewish story about repairing a broken world. (Rev: BL 10/1/07; LMC 11/07; SLJ 9/07) [398.2]

13159 Zelinsky, Paul O. *Rapunzel* (3–5). Illus. 1997, Dutton $17.99 (978-0-525-45607-0). 48pp. Rich oil paintings illustrate this tale of the enduring power of love. Caldecott Medal winner, 1998. (Rev: BL 11/15/97*; HBG 3/98; SLJ 11/97*) [398.2]

13160 Zemach, Harve. *Duffy and the Devil: A Cornish Tale Retold* (1–3). Illus. by Margot Zemach. 1973, Farrar $17.00 (978-0-374-31887-1); paper $6.95 (978-0-374-41897-7). 40pp. A variant of "Rumpelstiltskin," this folktale is told with humor and verve and boldly illustrated. Caldecott Medal winner, 1974. [398.2]

13161 Zemach, Margot. *It Could Always Be Worse: A Yiddish Folktale* (K–3). Illus. by author. 1976, Scholastic paper $4.95 (978-0-374-43636-0). 32pp. A Yiddish version of an old tale with colorful, humorous illustrations. [398.2]

13162 Zeman, Ludmila. *Sindbad in the Land of Giants* (PS–3). Illus. 2001, Tundra $17.95 (978-0-88776-461-5). 32pp. Sindbad's cunning and courage are tested in this beautifully illustrated adventure. (Rev: BL 8/01; HBG 10/01; SLJ 8/01) [398.2]

13163 Zeman, Ludmila. *Sindbad: From the Tales of the Thousand and One Nights* (3–5). Illus. 1999, Tundra $17.95 (978-0-88776-460-8). 32pp. Using extraordinary illustrations, the author-artist tells the stories of two of the famous voyages of Sinbad, one involving a giant whale and the other featuring a huge bird. (Rev: BL 1/1–15/00*; SLJ 1/00) [813.54]

13164 Zeman, Ludmila, retel. *Sindbad's Secret: From The Tales of the Thousand and One Nights* (2–5). Illus. by Ludmila Zeman. 2003, Tundra $17.95 (978-0-88776-462-2). Sindbad recounts two wondrous escapes and his discovery of the ultimate treasure is this last volume of Zeman's trilogy. (Rev: HBG 10/03; SLJ 3/03) [813.54]

13165 Zunshine, Tatiana, retel. *A Little Story About a Big Turnip* (PS–1). Illus. by Evgeny Antonenkov. 2004, Pumpkin House $15.95 (978-0-9646010-0-0). A simple retelling of the Russian folktale, in which it takes the combined strength of grandfather, grandmother, granddaughter, dog, cat, and mouse to pull the turnip out of the ground. (Rev: SLJ 11/04) [398.2]

Mythology

General and Miscellaneous

13166 Baynes, Pauline. *Questionable Creatures: A Bestiary* (4–6). 2006, Eerdmans $18.00 (978-0-8028-5284-7). 48pp. A great introduction to the mythical animals and creatures that were thought to have existed in medieval times such as unicorns, satyrs, and the phoenix. (Rev: BL 11/15/06; SLJ 4/07) [398.24]

13167 Boughn, Michael. *Into the World of the Dead: Astonishing Adventures in the Underworld* (5–8). 2006, Annick LB $24.95 (978-1-55037-959-4); paper $12.95 (978-1-55037-958-7). This illustrated collection of myths and legends from diverse cultures includes a variety of gods, monsters, and heroes who survived travels to the Underworld. (Rev: SLJ 1/07) [398.2]

13168 Coville, Bruce. *Thor's Wedding Day* (4–7). 2005, Harcourt $15.00 (978-0-15-201455-1). A hilarious retelling of an ancient Norse poem, in which Thor's goat boy describes how he helped Thor to retrieve his stolen magic hammer. (Rev: BL 8/05) [398.2]

13169 Dalal, Anita. *Myths of Oceania* (5–8). Series: Mythic World. 2002, Raintree LB $27.12 (978-0-7398-4978-1). Information about Oceania and its people is included as well as 10 myths about the sea, fishing, and other unique aspects of island living. (Rev: BL 7/02; HBG 10/02) [398.3]

13170 Dalal, Anita. *Myths of Russia and the Slavs* (5–8). Series: Mythic World. 2002, Raintree LB $27.12 (978-0-7398-4979-8). This lavishly illustrated, oversize volume contains 10 myths from Eastern Europe as well as material on the society that created them. (Rev: BL 7/02; HBG 10/02; SLJ 5/02) [398.2]

13171 Daning, Tom. *Mesoamerican Mythology: Quetzalcoatl* (3–6). Illus. 2006, Rosen LB $22.50 (978-1-4042-3401-7). 24pp. A graphic-novel version of the myth about the gods Quetzalcoatl and Tezcatlipoca and how they put their differences aside to defeat the demon caiman of the sea, resulting in the creation of the land and sky. (Rev: SLJ 3/07) [398.2]

13172 Demi. *The Girl Who Drew a Phoenix* (1–3). Illus. by author. 2008, Simon & Schuster $21.99 (978-1-4169-5347-0). 40pp. A girl's persistent efforts to evoke the spirit of the mythical phoenix bird in her drawings eventually meet with success; graceful illustrations with foldouts. (Rev: BL 8/08; LMC 1/09; SLJ 9/08)

13173 Edwards, Katie. *Myths and Monsters: Secrets Revealed* (K–5). Illus. by Simon Mendez. 2004, Charlesbridge LB $16.95 (978-1-57091-581-9); paper $6.95 (978-1-57091-582-6). 29pp. Introduces 10 mythical creatures and shows the real animals on which these "monsters" may have been based. (Rev: SLJ 2/05) [398.24]

13174 Fisher, Leonard Everett. *The Gods and Goddesses of Ancient China* (2–5). 2003, Holiday House $16.95 (978-0-8234-1694-3). 36pp. This colorful picture book introduces 17 deities found in the myths of ancient China and includes a pronunciation guide, glossary, and map. (Rev: BL 7/03; HBG 4/04; SLJ 10/03) [299]

13175 Fisher, Leonard Everett. *Gods and Goddesses of the Ancient Maya* (4–7). 1999, Holiday $16.95 (978-0-8234-1427-7). This book provides a fascinating introduction to Mayan mythology by describing 10 gods and two goddesses. (Rev: BL 2/1/00; HBG 3/00; SLJ 12/99) [299]

13176 Fisher, Leonard Everett. *Gods and Goddesses of the Ancient Norse* (K–4). Illus. 2002, Holiday House $16.95 (978-0-8234-1569-4). An introduction to 15 ancient Norse gods and goddesses, with a pronunciation guide and a family tree. (Rev: BCCB 6/02; BL 3/1/02; HBG 10/02; SLJ 3/02) [293]

13177 Gibbons, Gail. *Behold . . . the Unicorns!* (2–4). Illus. 2001, HarperCollins LB $15.89 (978-0-688-17958-8). 32pp. This handsomely designed book introduces the unicorn and all the myths and symbolism that surround one-horned beasts. (Rev: BCCB 12/01; BL 12/1/01; HBG 3/02; SLJ 12/01) [398.24]

13178 Green, Jen. *Myths of China and Japan* (5–8). Series: Mythic World. 2002, Raintree LB $27.12 (978-0-7398-4977-4). This handsome, oversize book explores the ancient mythology of China and Japan and, in addition to the retelling of 10 myths, contains information on the societies that created them. (Rev: BL 7/02; HBG 10/02) [398.2]

13179 Harris, Geraldine. *Gods and Pharaohs from Egyptian Mythology* (5–8). Illus. by David O'Connor and John Sibbick. 1992, Bedrick LB $24.95 (978-0-87226-907-1). A collection of myths and legends from ancient Egypt. [398.2]

13180 Hyde, Natalie. *Understanding Mesoamerican Myths* (5–8). Illus. Series: Myths Understood. 2012, Crabtree LB $30.60 (978-077874525-9). 48pp. A useful overview of these myths and of the importance of legends to the Aztec, Maya, and Olmec peoples, looking also at their environment, culture, and trade. (Rev: BL 3/15/13; LMC 11–12/13; SLJ 5/13) [299.7]

13181 Hynson, Colin. *Understanding Indian Myths* (5–8). Illus. Series: Myths Understood. 2012, Crabtree LB $30.60 (978-077874524-2). 48pp. A useful overview of these myths and of the importance of religion, environment, culture, and trade involved in their creation. (Rev: BL 3/15/13; LMC 11–12/13)

13182 January, Brendan. *The New York Public Library Amazing Mythology: A Book of Answers for Kids* (5–8). 2000, Wiley paper $14.95 (978-0-471-33205-3). This compendium of information covers Middle Eastern, African, Mediterranean, Asian, Pacific, Northern European, and North and Central American mythology. (Rev: BL 11/1/00; SLJ 9/00) [291.1]

13183 Kopp, Megan. *Understanding Native American Myths* (5–8). Illus. Series: Myths Understood. 2013, Crabtree LB $30.60 (978-077874526-6). 48pp. A useful overview of these myths and of the importance of religion, environment, culture, and trade involved in their creation. (Rev: BL 3/15/13; LMC 11–12/13; SLJ 5/13)

13184 Limke, Jeff. *Isis and Osiris: To the Ends of the Earth* (4–6). Illus. Series: Graphic Myths and Legends. 2006, Lerner $26.60 (978-0-8225-3086-2). 48pp. The lives of ancient Egyptian deities Isis and Osiris are chronicled in graphic-novel format. (Rev: BL 10/15/06; SLJ 11/06) [398.2]

13185 Lorenz, Albert, and Joy Schleh. *The Trojan Horse* (3–5). Illus. 2006, Abrams $17.95 (978-0-8109-5986-6). 40pp. Learn all about the Trojan War in this humorous, visual approach to the Trojan War that offers conversational text, cartoon panels, and cross-sections of the Greek ships, the Trojan horse, and the city of Troy. (Rev: BL 11/15/06; SLJ 11/06) [398.2]

13186 Lunge-Larsen, Lise, retel. *The Adventures of Thor the Thunder God* (3–6). Illus. by Jim Madsen. 2007, Houghton $19.95 (978-0-618-47301-4). Stories of Thor ("protector and defender of civilization"), his family members, and his fellow gods fill the pages of this heavily illustrated volume. (Rev: SLJ 7/07)

13187 Lupton, Hugh, and Daniel Morden. *The Adventures of Odysseus* (3–5). Illus. by Christina Balit. 2006, Barefoot Books $19.99 (978-1-84148-800-4). A large-format picture-book retelling of Homer's classic story, with bright, attractive illustrations and fast-paced, sometimes challenging text. (Rev: BL 12/1/06; SLJ 11/06*) [398.20938]

13188 Malam, John. *Dragons* (4–7). Series: Mythologies. 2010, Black Rabbit LB $28.50 (978-1-59566-982-7). 32pp. Malam looks at dragons, with and without wings, in legends around the world; with color illustrations and many sidebars, this book is aimed at reluctant readers. Also use *Fairies, Giants,* and *Monsters*. (Rev: LMC 10/10; SLJ 4/1/10) [398.24]

13189 Marshall, James Vance. *Stories from the Billabong* (3–5). Illus. by Francis Firebrace. 2009, Frances Lincoln $19.95 (978-1-84507-704-4). A collection of 10 aboriginal stories about creation and nature, with distinctive illustrations. (Rev: BLO 3/24/09; SLJ 5/09) [398.2]

13190 Mutén, Burleigh, retel. *The Lady of Ten Thousand Names: Goddess Stories from Many Cultures* (4–7). Retold by Burleigh Mutén. Illus. by Helen Cann. 2001, Barefoot $19.99 (978-1-84148-048-0). Eight myths that feature goddesses from cultures around the world are retold in this appealing volume. (Rev: HBG 3/02; SLJ 11/01) [291.2]

13191 Napoli, Donna Jo. *Treasury of Egyptian Mythology* (5–8). Illus. by Christina Balit. 2013, National Geographic $24.95 (978-142631380-6). 192pp. An engaging compendium of stories from Egyptian creation mythology. ALA Notable Children's Book. (Rev: BL 10/1/13; LMC 5–6/14*; SLJ 12/13) [398.20932]

13192 Ollhoff, Jim. *Indian Mythology* (4–7). Series: The World of Mythology. 2011, ABDO LB $27.07 (978-1-61714-722-7). 32pp. With chapters on Brahma, Vishnu, Shiva, and Kali, this is a clear introduction to Hindu gods and goddesses. (Rev: BL 2/1/12; SLJ 12/1/11) [398.20954]

13193 Ollhoff, Jim. *Japanese Mythology* (4–7). Series: The World of Mythology. 2011, ABDO LB $27.07 (978-1-61714-723-4). 32pp. With chapters on Amaterasu, O-Kuni-Nushi, and Jimmu, this is a clear introduction to Japanese gods and goddesses. (Rev: BL 2/1/12; SLJ 12/1/11) [398.20952]

13194 Ollhoff, Jim. *Mayan and Aztec Mythology* (4–7). Series: The World of Mythology. 2011, ABDO LB $27.07 (978-1-61714-724-1). 32pp. This appealing introduction to the mythology and legends of the Mayan and Aztec cultures features concise text and eye-catching illustrations and reproductions. (Rev: BL 2/1/12; SLJ 12/1/11) [972.81]

13195 Ollhoff, Jim. *Middle Eastern Mythology* (4–7). Series: The World of Mythology. 2011, ABDO LB $27.07 (978-1-61714-725-8). 32pp. This appealing introduction to the mythology and legends of the Middle East provides information on various Mesopotamian and Canaanite gods and goddesses. (Rev: BL 2/1/12; SLJ 12/1/11) [398.20939]

13196 Penner, Lucille R. *Dragons* (3–5). Trans. and illus. by Peter David Scott. 2004, Random LB $11.99 (978-0-307-46417-0); paper $3.99 (978-0-307-26417-6). 48pp. The dragon's role in the mythologies and cultures of many nations and peoples are explored here. (Rev: BL 8/04) [398.24]

13197 Philip, Neil. *The Illustrated Book of Myths: Tales and Legends of the World* (5–8). Illus. by Nilesh Mistry. 1995, DK paper $19.99 (978-0-7894-0202-8). Ancient myths from both the Old World and the New World have been collected under such headings as creation, destruction, and fertility. (Rev: BL 12/1/95; SLJ 12/95; VOYA 4/96) [291.1]

13198 Schomp, Virginia. *The Ancient Egyptians* (5–7). Series: Myths of the World. 2007, Marshall Cavendish LB $22.95 (978-0-7614-2549-6). Schomp provides background information on the myths of ancient Egypt and retells several of the best-known ones; full-color illustrations add to the appeal. (Rev: LMC 3/08; SLJ 1/08)

13199 Schomp, Virginia. *The Native Americans* (5–7). Series: Myths of the World. 2007, Marshall Cavendish LB $22.95 (978-0-7614-2550-2). Schomp provides background information on the myths of the Native Americans and retells several of the best-known ones; full-color illustrations add to the appeal. (Rev: LMC 3/08; SLJ 1/08)

13200 Schomp, Virginia. *The Norsemen* (5–7). Series: Myths of the World. 2007, Marshall Cavendish LB $22.95 (978-0-7614-2548-9). Schomp provides background information on the myths of Scandinavia and retells several of the best-known ones; full-color illustrations add to the appeal. (Rev: LMC 3/08; SLJ 1/08)

13201 Sherman, Pat. *The Sun's Daughter* (2–4). Illus. by R. Gregory Christie. 2005, Clarion $16.00 (978-0-618-32430-9). 32pp. The harvest is explained through a story based on Iroquois myths. (Rev: BL 3/15/05; SLJ 6/05) [398.2]

13202 Storrie, Paul D. *Beowulf: Monster Slayer: A British Legend* (4–7). Illus. by Ron Randall. Series: Graphic Myths and Legends. 2007, Lerner LB $26.60 (978-0-8225-6757-8). 48pp. An introduction to the ancient legend, carefully presented to preserve the tone of the original story. (Rev: BL 9/07; SLJ 11/07)

13203 Tchana, Katrin Hyman. *Changing Woman and Her Sisters* (5–8). Illus. by Trina Schart Hyman. 2006, Holiday $18.95 (978-0-8234-1999-9). An illustrated collection of traditional stories about ten goddesses from a variety of lesser-known cultures, including Celtic, ancient Mayan, Shinto, Buddhist, and Navajo. (Rev: BCCB 9/06; BL 6/1–15/06; HB 7–8/06; HBG 10/06; LMC 1/07; SLJ 8/06) [398.2]

13204 Thomson, Ruth. *Myths* (2–6). Illus. Series: A First Look at Art. 2005, Chelsea Clubhouse $23.00 (978-0-7910-8316-1). A look at the portrayal of mythological beings and stories in artwork from around the world. Also use *Weather* (2005). (Rev: SLJ 11/05) [398.2]

13205 Williams, Brian. *Understanding Norse Myths* (5–8). Illus. Series: Myths Understood. 2012, Crabtree LB $30.60 (978-077874527-3). 48pp. A useful overview of these myths and of the importance of religion, environment, culture, and trade involved in their creation. (Rev: BL 3/15/13; LMC 11–12/13; SLJ 5/13)

13206 Williams, Marcia. *Ancient Egypt: Tales of Gods and Pharaohs* (3–5). Illus. by author. 2011, Candlewick $16.99 (978-0-7636-5308-8). 48pp. This blend of ancient Egyptian history and mythology features several short tales and comic-strip illustrations with period elements. (Rev: BL 10/1/11; SLJ 9/1/11) [398.2]

13207 Wolfson, Evelyn. *Mythology of the Inuit* (5–9). Illus. by William Sauts Bock. Series: Mythology, Myths, and Legends. 2014, Enslow LB $26.60 (978-0-7660-6177-4). 96pp. Seven tales are accompanied by information on the history and culture of the Inuit peoples. [398.2]

Classical

13208 Bateman, Teresa. *Damon, Pythias, and the Test of Friendship* (PS–3). Illus. by Layne Johnson. 2009, Albert Whitman $16.99 (978-0-8075-1445-0). 32pp. A handsome retelling of the legend about Damon's amazing trust in his friend Pythias. (Rev: BL 5/1/09; SLJ 6/09) [398.20938]

13209 Bryant, Megan E. *Oh My Gods! A Look-It-Up Guide to the Gods of Mythology* (4–7). Series: Mythlopedia. 2010, Franklin Watts LB $39 (978-1-6063-1026-7). 128pp. An irreverent, highly graphic volume that succeeds in conveying lots of information in an entertaining manner; with a useful map of ancient Greece, pronunciation guides, and a list of top 10 things to know about

each divine being. Companion volumes are *All in the Family! A Look-It-Up Guide to the In-Laws, Outlaws, and Offspring of Mythology* (2009), *She's All That! A Look-It-Up Guide to the Goddesses of Mythology* and *What a Beast! A Look-It-Up Guide to the Monsters and Mutants of Mythology* (both 2010). (Rev: BL 10/1/09; LMC 3–4/10) [398.2]

13210 Burleigh, Robert. *Pandora* (3–6). Illus. by Raúl Colón. 2002, Harcourt $17.00 (978-0-15-202178-8). 32pp. A handsome retelling of the Greek myth about Pandora, her longings to open the box, and the terror it produced when she did. (Rev: BCCB 5/02; BL 6/1–15/02; HBG 10/02; SLJ 5/02) [398.2]

13211 Byrd, Robert. *The Hero and the Minotaur: The Fantastic Adventures of Theseus* (2–4). 2005, Dutton $17.99 (978-0-525-47391-6). 40pp. Byrd succeeds in retelling the complex adventures of Theseus in child-friendly narrative and compelling, detailed illustrations. (Rev: BL 7/05; SLJ 8/05*) [398.2]

13212 Catran, Ken. *Voyage with Jason* (5–8). 2003, Lothian paper $10.95 (978-0-7344-0151-9). A new twist on the story of Jason and the Argonauts, narrated by a youth who is part of the eventful three-year quest for the Golden Fleece and concentrating on character as well as adventure. (Rev: SLJ 4/04) [398.2]

13213 Clayton, Sally Pomme. *Persephone* (2–4). Illus. by Virginia Lee. 2009, Eerdmans $18.00 (978-0-8028-5349-3). 26pp. This retelling of the story of the girl who is taken to the Underworld by Hades follows the traditional line and is enhanced by graceful artwork with a classical flavor. (Rev: BL 3/15/09; SLJ 5/09) [398.2]

13214 Climo, Shirley. *Atalanta's Race: A Greek Myth* (3–5). Illus. by Alexander Koshkin. 1995, Clarion $16.00 (978-0-395-67322-5). 32pp. A retelling of the Greek myth about Atalanta, who, abandoned at birth, becomes the world's fastest runner. (Rev: BCCB 6/95; BL 4/15/95; SLJ 4/95*) [398.21]

13215 Curlee, Lynn. *Mythological Creatures: A Classical Bestiary* (4–8). Illus. by author. 2008, Atheneum $17.99 (978-1-4169-1453-2). 40pp. A beautiful book with dreamy color illustrations of creatures that roam through classical mythology, such as gryphons, the Minotaur, Cerberus, and centaurs; each illustration is accompanied by comments about the creature's part in mythology. (Rev: BL 4/1/08; SLJ 5/08) [292.2]

13216 Cuyler, Margery. *Roadsigns: A Harey Race with a Tortoise* (PS–1). Illus. by Steve Haskamp. 2000, Winslow $15.95 (978-1-890817-23-7). 40pp. The Aesop fable of the race between the tortoise and the hare is cleverly retold using road signs and bright, cartoonlike illustrations. (Rev: BL 12/1/00; HBG 3/01; SLJ 9/00) [398.2]

13217 D'Aulaire, Ingri, and Edgar D'Aulaire. *D'Aulaire's Book of Greek Myths* (3–6). Illus. by authors. 1962, Dell paper $18.95 (978-0-440-40694-5). Full-color pictures highlight these brief stories, which are excellent for first readers in mythology. [398.2]

13218 Demi. *King Midas* (2–4). Illus. 2002, Simon & Schuster $19.95 (978-0-689-83297-0). 48pp. Rich illustrations accompany this retelling of the King Midas tale for younger readers. (Rev: BL 3/15/02; HB 5/02; HBG 10/02; SLJ 5/02) [398.2]

13219 DiPrimio, Pete. *The Sphinx* (4–7). Illus. Series: Monsters in Myth. 2010, Mitchell Lane LB $21.50 (978-158415931-5). 48pp. This volume explores the role of the Sphinx in Greek and Egyptian mythology. (Rev: BL 6/1/11) [398.2209182]

13220 Fisher, Leonard Everett. *Cyclops* (1–6). Illus. 1991, Holiday House paper $5.95 (978-0-8234-1062-0). 32pp. The retelling of this classical tale inspires pity and terror in the reader. (Rev: BCCB 12/91; BL 1/1/91*; SLJ 1/92) [398.2]

13221 Fisher, Leonard Everett. *Theseus and the Minotaur* (3–6). Illus. by author. 1988, Holiday House paper $5.95 (978-0-8234-0954-9). 32pp. The story of the birth of Theseus, his adventures, and his killing of the Minotaur. (Rev: BCCB 10/88; BL 10/15/88; SLJ 10/88) [398.2]

13222 Fontes, Justine, and Ron Fontes. *Demeter and Persephone: Spring Held Hostage: A Greek Myth* (1–3). Illus. by Steve Kurth and Barbara Schulz. Series: Graphic Myths and Legends. 2007, Lerner LB $26.60 (978-0-8225-5966-5). 48pp. The myth of Persephone retold in graphic-novel format to reach a wider audience, with imaginative illustrations. (Rev: SLJ 5/07)

13223 Green, Jen. *Myths of Ancient Greece* (5–8). Series: Mythic World. 2001, Raintree LB $27.12 (978-0-7398-3191-5). This volume for older readers separates myth from reality about ancient Greece. (Rev: BL 3/1/02; HBG 3/02; SLJ 12/01) [398.2]

13224 Harris, John. *Strong Stuff: Herakles and His Labors* (4–7). Illus. by Gary Baseman. 2005, Getty $16.95 (978-0-89236-784-9). A lively, tongue-in-cheek account of the 12 labors of ancient Greece's mythical strongman, Herakles (known to the ancient Romans as Hercules). (Rev: BL 11/15/05; SLJ 11/05) [398.2]

13225 Hawthorne, Nathaniel. *Wonder Book and Tanglewood Tales* (5–7). 1972, Ohio State Univ. $72.95 (978-0-8142-0158-9). This is a highly original retelling of the Greek myths, originally published in 1853. (Rev: BL 2/15/04; SLJ 4/04) [398.2]

13226 Homer. *The Odyssey* (3–5). Adapted by Adrian Mitchell. Illus. by Stuart Robertson. 2000, DK $14.99 (978-0-7894-5455-3). 64pp. A handsomely illustrated version of the Odyssey that covers all the major plot developments and the journeys of Odysseus. (Rev: BL 9/1/03; HBG 4/04; SLJ 9/00) [398.2]

13227 Karas, G. Brian. *Young Zeus* (1–4). Illus. by author. 2010, Scholastic $17.99 (978-0-439-72806-5). 48pp. An irreverent, lively account of Zeus's early life, telling how he came to rule heaven and earth. Lexile AD570L (Rev: BL 2/1/10; HB 3–4/10; LMC 5–6/10; SLJ 2/1/10*) [398.2]

13228 Kelly, Sophia. *What a Beast: A Look-It-Up Guide to the Monsters and Mutants of Mythology* (4–7). Illus. Series: Mythlopedia. 2009, Scholastic LB $39 (978-160631028-1); paper $13.95 (978-160631060-1). 128pp. Greek and Roman mythology is given a fresh, modern spin in this irreverent guide to the multi-dimensional beasts of legend. (Rev: BL 3/1/10; LMC 3–4/10*) [398.2]

13229 Kimmel, Eric A. *The McElderry Book of Greek Myths* (K–3). Illus. by Pep Montserrat. 2008, Simon & Schuster $21.99 (978-1-4169-1534-8). 112pp. Simple, clear language, classically inspired computer-generated art, and lots of action are features of theses retellings of stories about such characters as Midas, Icarus, Theseus, and Narcissus. (Rev: BL 1/1–15/08; SLJ 3/08) [398.2]

13230 Low, Alice. *The Macmillan Book of Greek Gods and Heroes* (4–6). Illus. by Arvis Stewart. 1985, Macmillan LB $18.00 (978-0-02-761390-2). 192pp. Well-known myths and legends from ancient Greece in a large-format edition. (Rev: BCCB 11/85; BL 11/15/85; SLJ 1/86) [398.2]

13231 Lupton, Hugh, and Daniel Morden. *The Adventures of Achilles* (5–8). Illus. by Carole Henaff. 2012, Barefoot paper $12.99 (978-1-84686-800-9). 128pp. From his birth and childhood through the Trojan War and his death, this handsome volume focuses on Achilles and the important figures in his life, including many gods and goddesses. Lexile 770L (Rev: BLO 9/1/12; HB 11–12/12; SLJ 10/12)

13232 McCarty, Nick, retel. *The Iliad* (4–8). Retold by Nick McCarty. Illus. by Victor G. Ambrus. 2000, Kingfisher paper $15.95 (978-0-7534-5321-6). This account of the Trojan War uses an exciting text and action-packed illustrations. (Rev: SLJ 1/01) [398.2]

13233 Mayer, Marianna. *Pegasus* (3–6). Illus. by Kinuko Craft. 1998, Morrow $16.99 (978-0-688-13382-5). 40pp. A retelling of the Greek myth about the winged horse Pegasus and how it helped Bellerophon kill Chimera the monster. (Rev: BL 3/15/98; HBG 10/98; SLJ 4/98) [398.2]

13234 Morley, Jacqueline, retel. *Greek Myths* (3–6). Illus. by Giovanni Caselli. 1998, Bedrick $22.50 (978-0-87226-560-8). 96pp. Beginning with the rise of the Titans and ending with Odysseus's wanderings, the myths in this book include those involving Prometheus, Arachne, Psyche, the Minotaur, and Apollo. (Rev: HBG 10/98; SLJ 7/98) [398.2]

13235 Myers, Christopher. *Wings* (PS–4). Illus. 2000, Scholastic $16.95 (978-0-590-03377-0). 40pp. In this modern retelling of the Icarus myth, a young boy who can fly nearly crashes, not because he flies too close to the sun but because repressive adults and bullying kids in the schoolyard try to break his spirit. (Rev: BCCB 12/00; BL 5/15/00; HBG 3/01; SLJ 10/00)

13236 Napoli, Donna Jo. *Treasury of Greek Mythology: Classic Stories of Gods, Goddesses, Heroes and Monsters* (4–7). Illus. by Christina Balit. 2011, National Geographic $24.95 (978-1-4263-0844-4); LB $33.90 (978-1-4263-0845-1). 192pp. This large, eye-catching volume introduces 25 major characters in Greek mythology, outlining each one's origins, realm of power, and legendary story lines; the lyrical text is enhanced by humor and helpful back matter. ALA Notable Children's Book 2012. (Rev: BL 12/1/11; SLJ 10/1/11*) [398.2]

13237 O'Connor, George. *Zeus: King of the Gods* (5–9). Series: Olympians. 2010, First Second paper $9.99 (978-1-59643-431-8). 80pp. The first of a series of graphic novels based on mythology, this is a good introduction to Zeus and his circle. (Rev: BL 1/1/10; LMC 8–9/10; SLJ 3/10) [741.5]

13238 *Odysseus* (4–8). Retold by Geraldine McCaughrean. 2004, Cricket $15.95 (978-0-8126-2721-3). Homer's dramatic story is retold in rhythmic prose. (Rev: BL 12/15/04; SLJ 12/04)

13239 *The Odyssey* (4–7). Retold by Gillian Cross. Illus. by Neil Packer. 2012, Candlewick $19.99 (978-076364791-9). 178pp. A handsome retelling with compelling text and rich, varied illustrations. (Rev: BL 12/1/12; LMC 5–6/13; SLJ 1/13) [883.01]

13240 Orr, Tamra. *The Sirens* (4–7). Illus. 2010, Mitchell Lane LB $21.50 (978-158415930-8). 48pp. This volume explores the importance of the sirens in mythologies around the Mediterranean. (Rev: BL 6/1/11) [398.20938]

13241 Osborne, Mary Pope. *Favorite Greek Myths* (3–6). Illus. by Troy Howell. 1989, Scholastic paper $19.95 (978-0-590-41338-1). This large-format book contains 13 of the best-known stories from classical mythology. (Rev: BL 8/89) [398.2]

13242 Oyibo, Papa. *Big Brother, Little Sister* (PS–3). Illus. by John Clementson. 2000, Barefoot Books $15.95 (978-1-84148-117-3). 40pp. The Aesop fable about the lion and the mouse is retold using an elephant instead of a lion. (Rev: BL 4/1/00; SLJ 8/00)

13243 Philip, Neil, retel. *The Adventures of Odysseus* (3–6). Illus. by Peter Malone. 1997, Orchard $17.95 (978-0-531-30000-8). 72pp. A fine retelling of the epic journey home by Odysseus and his encounters with such creatures as Cyclops, Circe, and the Sirens. (Rev: SLJ 5/97*) [292.1]

13244 Pickels, Dwayne E. *Roman Myths, Heroes, and Legends* (5–8). Series: Costume, Tradition, and Culture: Reflecting on the Past. 1998, Chelsea $28.00 (978-0-7910-5164-1). Using double-page spreads and old collectors' cards as illustrations, this work retells the major Roman myths and introduces their important characters. (Rev: BL 3/15/99; HBG 10/99) [398.2]

13245 Richards, Jean. *The First Olympic Games: A Gruesome Greek Myth with a Happy Ending* (2–4). Illus. 2000, Millbrook LB $23.90 (978-0-7613-1311-3). 32pp. The story of Pelops, who was killed and eaten by his father, Tantalus, restored to life by the gods, and later created the first Olympic Games. (Rev: BCCB 11/00; BL 10/15/00; HBG 10/01; SLJ 11/00) [398.2]

13246 Schomp, Virginia. *The Ancient Greeks* (5–7). Series: Myths of the World. 2007, Marshall Cavendish LB $22.95 (978-0-7614-2547-2). Schomp provides background information on the myths of ancient Greece and

retells several of the best-known ones; full-color illustrations add to the appeal. (Rev: LMC 3/08; SLJ 1/08)

13247 Schulte, Mary. *The Minotaur* (4–6). Series: Monsters. 2008, Gale LB $26.20 (978-0-7377-3590-1). Schulte tells the story of the Minotaur and Theseus's decision to venture into the Labyrinth to slay this half-man half-bull, and then discusses the Minotaur's appearances in popular culture. (Rev: SLJ 12/08) [398]

13248 Stewig, John W. *King Midas* (K–3). Illus. by Omar Rayyan. 1999, Holiday House $17.95 (978-0-8234-1423-9). 32pp. Filled with illustrations containing comic details, this is a fine retelling of the tale about the greedy king who turned his daughter into gold. (Rev: BCCB 3/99; BL 2/15/99; HBG 10/99; SLJ 3/99) [398.2]

13249 Townsend, Michael. *Amazing Greek Myths of Wonder and Blunders* (2–4). Illus. by author. 2010, Dial $14.99 (978-080373308-4). 160pp. An engaging graphic-novel version of some well-known myths, offering an accessible glimpse of the ancient world with touches of contemporary humor. (Rev: BL 1/1/10; LMC 11–12/10; SLJ 1/10; VOYA 6/10) [398.2]

13250 Tracy, Kathleen. *Cerberus* (4–7). Illus. Series: Monsters in Myth. 2010, Mitchell Lane LB $21.50 (978-158415924-7). 48pp. This volume explores the mythological importance of the three-headed dog. (Rev: BL 6/1/11) [398.20938]

13251 Wilbur, Helen L. *Z Is for Zeus: A Greek Mythology Alphabet* (3–6). Illus. by Victor Juhasz. 2008, Sleeping Bear $17.95 (978-1-58536-341-4). An appealing alphabetical introduction to classic Greek stories and heroes, with poetic text and detailed illustrations. (Rev: BLO 2/8/08; LMC 10/08; SLJ 10/08) [292.1]

13252 Woff, Richard. *A Pocket Dictionary of Greek and Roman Gods and Goddesses* (4–8). 2003, Getty $9.95 (978-0-89236-706-1). Varied reproductions from the British Museum add visual appeal to this brief who's who. (Rev: SLJ 2/04) [292.2]

Nursery Rhymes

13253 Ada, Alma Flor, and F. Isabel Campoy, sels. *Pio Peep! Traditional Spanish Nursery Rhymes/Rimas Tradicionles en Espanol* (PS–2). 2003, HarperCollins LB $16.89 (978-0-688-16020-3). 64pp. A charming bilingual English/Spanish collection of nursery rhymes from various Spanish-speaking countries. (Rev: HBG 10/03; SLJ 7/03) [398.8]

13254 Ashburn, Boni. *Builder Goose: It's Construction Rhyme Time!* (1–3). Illus. by Sergio De Giorgi. 2012, Sterling $14.95 (978-140277118-7). 32pp. For the mechanically minded, this is a collection of nursery rhymes recast to include heavy equipment. (Rev: BL 3/1/12; SLJ 5/1/12) [398.8]

13255 Beaton, Clare. *Playtime Rhymes for Little People* (PS–K). Illus. 2001, Barefoot Books $18.99 (978-1-84148-425-9). 64pp. Forty familiar children's rhymes are accompanied by embroidered collages. (Rev: BCCB 12/01; BL 10/15/01; HBG 3/02; SLJ 11/01) [398.8]

13256 Beaton, Clare, comp. *Mother Goose Remembers* (PS). Illus. by Clare Beaton. 2000, Barefoot Books $18.99 (978-1-84148-073-2). 64pp. A highly appealing collection of 46 Mother Goose rhymes with pictures made of felt and other fabrics. (Rev: HBG 3/01; SLJ 9/00)

13257 Cabrera, Jane. *Old Mother Hubbard* (PS). Illus. 2001, Holiday House $15.95 (978-0-8234-1659-2). 32pp. Old Mother Hubbard's dog is up to some new tricks in this colorful and imaginative rendition of the familiar nursery rhyme. (Rev: BCCB 11/01; BL 9/1/01; HBG 3/02; SLJ 1/02) [821.7]

13258 Cabrera, Jane. *Twinkle, Twinkle, Little Star* (PS–K). Illus. by author. 2012, Holiday $16.95 (978-0-8234-2519-8). 32pp. With new verses following the well-known first one, this is a bright rendition of the traditional nursery song, featuring parents and children, animal and human. (Rev: BL 10/1/12; SLJ 12/12) [821]

13259 Catalano, Dominic. *Hush! A Fantasy in Verse* (PS). Illus. by author. 2003, Gingham Dog $14.95 (978-1-57768-679-8). In this charming variation on the traditional nursery song/rhyme "Hush Little Baby," a father tries to comfort his young daughter after she wakes up from a bad dream. (Rev: HBG 4/04; SLJ 1/04)

13260 Chapman, Jane. *Sing a Song of Sixpence: A Pocketful of Nursery Rhymes and Tales* (PS). 2004, Candlewick $15.99 (978-0-7636-2545-0). 64pp. Striking acrylic artwork highlights this collection of familiar nursery rhymes and three fairy tales ("Goldilocks," "The Three Little Pigs," and "The Little Red Hen"). (Rev: BL 9/1/04; SLJ 10/04) [398.8]

13261 Conway, David. *The Great Nursery Rhyme Disaster* (PS–2). Illus. by Melanie Williamson. 2009, Tiger Tales $15.95 (978-1-58925-080-2). 32pp. Little Miss Muffet looks for adventure in other nursery rhymes such as "Jack and Jill" and "Hey Diddle, Diddle" only to realize, after many exciting and colorful moments, that her own rhyme is where she belongs. (Rev: LMC 10/09; SLJ 5/09)

13262 Crews, Nina. *The Neighborhood Mother Goose* (PS–2). Photos by author. 2004, Greenwillow LB $18.89 (978-0-06-051574-4). "Mother" in this case is a real goose in a city park, and the illustrations portray urban youngsters and scenery. (Rev: HB 5/04; SLJ 1/04) [398.8]

13263 Duffy, Chris, ed. *Nursery Rhyme Comics: 50 Timeless Rhymes from 50 Celebrated Cartoonists* (PS–3). Illus. 2011, First Second $18.99 (978-159643600-8). 128pp. Talented cartoonists draw richly imagined versions of familiar nursery rhymes in this inspired collection. (Rev: BL 11/15/11*; SLJ 9/1/11) [741.5]

13264 Edwards, Pamela Duncan. *The Neat Line: Scribbling Through Mother Goose* (PS–2). Illus. by Diana Cain Bluthenthal. 2005, HarperCollins LB $17.89 (978-0-06-623971-2). 32pp. A baby scribble grows up to be a Neat Line and works its way into a book of nursery

rhymes to help the familiar characters out of their predicaments. (Rev: BL 3/15/05; SLJ 5/05)

13265 Edwards, Pamela Duncan, retel. *Miss Polly Has a Dolly* (PS–1). Illus. by Elicia Castaldi. 2003, Penguin $15.99 (978-0-399-23857-4). A rhyming rope-jumping chant is expanded and set to music, with finger-play motions provided. (Rev: HBG 4/04; SLJ 11/03)

13266 Engelbreit, Mary. *Mary Engelbreit's Mother Goose: One Hundred Best-Loved Verses* (PS–1). 2005, HarperCollins $19.99 (978-0-06-008171-3). 128pp. Popular illustrator Engelbreit offers her artistic interpretation of 100 well-known and less-familiar nursery rhymes. (Rev: SLJ 3/06) [398.8]

13267 Fitzgerald, Joanne. *Yum! Yum!* (PS–K). Illus. by author. 2008, Fitzhenry & Whiteside $18.95 (978-1-55041-888-0). 32pp. Nursery rhymes featuring food are illustrated with charming watercolor illustrations. (Rev: BL 12/1/07; SLJ 12/07) [398.8]

13268 French, Vivian. *The Daddy Goose Treasury* (PS–K). Illus. by AnnaLaura Cantone, et al. 2006, Scholastic $18.99 (978-0-439-79608-8). 93pp. Daddy Goose, a relative of Mother Goose, provides the back stories for nursery rhymes such as "Little Miss Muffet" and "Old King Cole." (Rev: SLJ 9/06) [398.8]

13269 Fyleman, Rose. *Mary Middling and Other Silly Folk: Nursery Rhymes and Nonsense Poems* (PS). Illus. by Katja Bandlow. 2004, Clarion $16.00 (978-0-618-38141-8). 28pp. Catchy rhymes first published in 1931 are revived in picture-book form with suitably silly illustrations. (Rev: BL 11/15/04; SLJ 9/04) [821]

13270 Green, Alison. *Mother Goose's Storytime Nursery Rhymes* (PS–1). Illus. by Axel Scheffler. 2007, Scholastic $19.99 (978-0-439-90306-6). 128pp. Mother Goose is an actual goose in this collection, telling her little ones rhyming stories that a heron writes down. Young listeners will enjoy the appealing illustrations. (Rev: SLJ 8/07)

13271 Grey, Mini. *The Adventures of the Dish and the Spoon* (K–3). 2006, Knopf $16.95 (978-0-375-83691-6). 32pp. This tale fleshes out the adventures of the Dish that ran away with the Spoon, a romance that goes bad when the two rob a bank to continue financing their high life. (Rev: BL 6/1–15/06; SLJ 4/06)

13272 Hale, Sarah Josepha. *Mary Had a Little Lamb* (PS–1). Illus. by Laura Huliska-Beith. 2011, Marshall Cavendish $12.99 (978-0-7614-5824-1). 24pp. A timeless, lively new version of the nursery classic. (Rev: BL 3/15/11; SLJ 3/1/11) [811]

13273 Hallworth, Grace, ed. *Down by the River: Afro-Caribbean Rhymes, Games, and Songs for Children* (PS–1). Illus. by Caroline Binch. 1996, Scholastic $16.95 (978-0-590-69320-2). 40pp. More than 20 playground rhymes from the Caribbean are included in this joyful book illustrated with watercolors. (Rev: BCCB 1/97; BL 10/15/96; SLJ 12/96) [811]

13274 Harper, Charise Mericle. *There Was a Bold Lady Who Wanted a Star* (PS–2). Illus. 2002, Little, Brown $15.95 (978-0-316-14673-9). 32pp. "The Little Old

Lady Who Swallowed a Fly" is traded in for a modern lady who tries various modes of transport in her efforts to catch a star. (Rev: BCCB 11/02; BL 11/15/02; HBG 3/03; SLJ 9/02) [782]

13275 *Hickory, Dickory, Dock: And Other Favorite Nursery Rhymes* (PS). Illus. by Sanja Rescek. 2006, Tiger Tales $7.95 (978-1-58925-786-3). A gentle board-book collection of classic nursery rhymes illustrated with cartoon art. Also use *Twinkle, Twinkle, Little Star: And Other Favorite Bedtime Rhymes* (2006). (Rev: SLJ 4/06) [398.8]

13276 Hillenbrand, Will. *Mother Goose Picture Puzzles* (PS–1). Illus. by author. 2011, Marshall Cavendish $17.99 (978-0-7614-5808-1). 40pp. Twenty nursery rhymes, some familiar and some more obscure, are presented in rebus format. e (Rev: BL 3/1/11; SLJ 4/11*) [398.2]

13277 Hines, Anna Grossnickle. *1, 2, Buckle My Shoe* (PS–K). Illus. by author. 2008, Harcourt $16.00 (978-0-15-206305-4). Patchwork illustrations adorn this version of the popular counting nursery rhyme. (Rev: BL 5/15/08; SLJ 5/08)

13278 Hoberman, Mary Ann. *Bill Grogan's Goat* (PS–3). Illus. by Nadine Bernard Westcott. 2002, Little, Brown $14.95 (978-0-316-36232-0). 32pp. The classic nonsense rhyme about Bill Grogan and the goat that is always in trouble is retold with clever illustrations. (Rev: BL 4/15/02; HBG 10/02; SLJ 4/02)

13279 Hoberman, Mary Ann. *You Read to Me, I'll Read to You: Very Short Mother Goose Tales to Read Together* (1–4). Illus. by Michael Emberley. 2005, Little, Brown $16.99 (978-0-316-14431-5). 32pp. Variations on familiar Mother Goose rhymes, meant to be read aloud by two readers. (Rev: SLJ 9/05) [398.2]

13280 Horowitz, Dave. *Humpty Dumpty Climbs Again* (PS–K). Illus. by author. 2008, Putnam $16.99 (978-0-399-24773-6). 32pp. Humpty Dumpty is roused from his post-traumatic depression by the news that one of the king's horses is in trouble. (Rev: BL 12/15/08; HB 1/09; LMC 1/09; SLJ 10/08)

13281 *The House That Jack Built* (K–2). Illus. by Diana Mayo. 2001, Barefoot Books $15.99 (978-1-84148-251-4). Double-page illustrations in bold colors bring new life to the classic rhyme. (Rev: BL 10/15/01; HBG 3/02; SLJ 1/02) [398.8]

13282 Hysom, Dennis. *Wooleycat's Musical Theater* (PS–1). Illus. by Christine Walker. Series: Wooleycat's Favorite Nursery Rhymes. 2003, Tortuga $18.95 (978-1-889910-25-3). 32pp. Ten nursery rhymes are retold with new twists (the cow that jumped over the moon becomes an astronaut, for instance) and set to music on an accompanying CD. (Rev: SLJ 4/04) [398.8]

13283 *If You Love a Nursery Rhyme* (PS–K). Illus. by Susanna Lockheart. 2009, Barron's $18.99 (978-0-7641-6186-5). A large-format collection of 12 nursery rhymes, several with gatefold pages that offer a choice of illustrations. (Rev: BL 4/15/09) [398.8]

13284 Kadair, Deborah Ousley. *There Was an Ol' Cajun* (K–3). Illus. by author. 2002, Pelican $15.95 (978-1-56554-917-3). Instead of a fly, the ol' Cajun swallows all manner of swamp life before coming across an alligator. (Rev: HBG 10/02; SLJ 12/02) [398.8]

13285 Linch, Tanya. *Three Little Kittens* (PS–K). Illus. by author. 2001, Gullane $12.95 (978-1-86233-204-1). The kittens' mittens are lost and dirtied, then found and washed, all with mother's forgiveness. (Rev: SLJ 1/02) [398.2]

13286 McMullan, Kate. *Baby Goose* (PS). Illus. by Pascal LeMaitre. 2004, Hyperion $15.99 (978-0-7868-0430-6). 34pp. Traditional nursery rhymes follow the hands around the clock and feature child-friendly adaptations and illustrations. (Rev: BL 11/15/04; SLJ 11/04) [398.8]

13287 Marshall, James. *James Marshall's Mother Goose* (PS–1). Illus. by author. 1979, Farrar paper $6.95 (978-0-374-43723-7). 40pp. An ebullient, breezy treatment of traditional material. [398.8]

13288 Martin, Bill. *"Fire! Fire!" Said Mrs. McGuire* (PS–1). Illus. by Vladimir Radunsky. 2006, Harcourt $16.00 (978-0-15-205725-1). A group of mice sound the alarm when they think they see a fire through a keyhole in this rhyming picture book; a final cutout reveals candles on the cat's birthday cake. (Rev: BL 5/1/06; SLJ 6/06) [811]

13289 Mavor, Salley. *Pocketful of Posies: A Treasury of Nursery Rhymes* (PS–K). Illus. by author. 2010, Houghton Mifflin $21.99 (978-0-618-73740-6). 72pp. Familiar and not-so-familiar nursery rhymes and verses are presented with boldly textured illustrations that may incorporate shells, seeds, beads, and driftwood. ALSC Notable Children's Book, 2011; Boston Globe–Horn Book Award. e (Rev: BLO 8/10; HB 11–12/10; SLJ 9/1/10) [398.8]

13290 Montgomery, Michael G., and Wayne Montgomery. *Over the Candlestick: Classic Nursery Rhymes and the Real Stories Behind Them* (PS). Illus. by Michael G. Montgomery. 2002, Peachtree $16.95 (978-1-56145-259-0). 32pp. A large-format collection of classic nursery rhymes and a bit of the history behind them, with full-page illustrations. (Rev: BL 3/15/02; HBG 10/02; SLJ 6/02) [398.8]

13291 Moses, Will. *Mary and Her Little Lamb: The True Story of the Famous Nursery Rhyme* (1–3). Illus. by author. 2011, Philomel $17.99 (978-0-399-25154-2). 40pp. The true story behind the nursery rhyme — involving a sickly lamb, a kind young girl, and an 1800s Massachusetts schoolhouse — is presented with folk-art illustrations. (Rev: SLJ 9/1/11)

13292 Moses, Will. *Will Moses Mother Goose* (PS–1). Illus. by author. 2003, Philomel $17.99 (978-0-399-23744-7). 61pp. A whimsically illustrated collection of nursery rhymes and riddles, some well known and others less familiar. (Rev: HBG 4/04; SLJ 9/03) [398.8]

13293 Mother Goose. *Mother Goose: A Canadian Sampler* (PS–1). 1996, Groundwood $18.95 (978-0-88899-213-0). 63pp. Using illustrations from 29 of Canada's prominent picture book illustrators, this is a fine edition of Mother Goose rhymes. (Rev: SLJ 5/96)

13294 Mother Goose. *Tomie dePaola's Mother Goose* (PS–1). Illus. by Tomie dePaola. 1985, Penguin $25.99 (978-0-399-21258-1). Large format and lavish illustrations accompany these old favorites. (Rev: BCCB 11/85; BL 9/1/85; HB 1/86) [398.8]

13295 *My First Nursery Rhymes* (PS). Illus. by Bruce Whatley. Series: Growing Tree. 1999, HarperCollins $10.99 (978-0-694-01205-3). 24pp. A joyous collection of ten favorite rhymes, including "Little Bo-Peep" and "Humpty Dumpty." (Rev: BL 2/1/99; HBG 10/99; SLJ 4/99) [398.8]

13296 Opie, Iona, ed. *Here Comes Mother Goose* (PS). Illus. by Rosemary Wells. 1999, Candlewick $21.99 (978-0-7636-0683-1). More than 50 well-known nursery rhymes are given fresh interpretations through clever new illustrations. (Rev: BCCB 12/99; BL 10/1/99*; HB 11/99; HBG 3/00; SLJ 10/99) [398.8]

13297 Opie, Iona, ed. *Mother Goose's Little Treasures* (PS–K). Illus. by Rosemary Wells. 2007, Candlewick $17.99 (978-0-7636-3655-5). 56pp. Twenty-two little-known rhymes are collected here. (Rev: BL 9/1/07; SLJ 9/07) [398.8]

13298 Opie, Iona, ed. *My Very First Mother Goose* (PS). Illus. by Rosemary Wells. 1996, Candlewick $21.99 (978-1-56402-620-0). 108pp. A basic collection of 60 standard rhymes illustrated with imagination and charm. (Rev: BCCB 12/96; BL 9/1/96; HB 11/96; SLJ 10/96*) [398.8]

13299 Oxenbury, Helen. *The Helen Oxenbury Nursery Collection* (PS–1). Illus. 2004, Knopf LB $21.99 (978-0-375-92992-2). 96pp. This charming collection of poems, rhymes, and stories is drawn from previous books that are now out of print. (Rev: BL 12/1/04) [398.8]

13300 Pearson, Tracey Campbell. *Little Miss Muffet* (PS). Illus. by author. 2005, Farrar $5.95 (978-0-374-30862-9). This adaptation of the popular nursery rhyme shows a young girl acting out the story line, spider and all. (Rev: SLJ 10/05) [398.8]

13301 Pierce, Terry, ed. *Counting Your Way: Number Nursery Rhymes* (PS–K). Illus. by Andrea Petrlik Huseinovic. 2007, Picture Window $25.26 (978-1-4048-2346-4). Twenty familiar rhymes featuring numbers are highlighted on attractively illustrated pages. (Rev: BL 4/1/07) [398.8]

13302 Pinkney, Jerry. *Three Little Kittens* (PS–1). Illus. by author. 2010, Dial $16.99 (978-0-8037-3533-0). 32pp. The classic nursery rhyme of three kittens and their mittens is reinterpreted here with chant-along refrains and evocative pencil-and-watercolor art. (Rev: BL 9/1/10; SLJ 9/1/10) [398.8]

13303 Ross, Tony. *Three Little Kittens and Other Favorite Nursery Rhymes* (PS). Illus. by author. 2009, Holt $16.95 (978-0-8050-8885-4). A grandfather reading to his grandaughter is the framing concept that opens and closes this large-format collection of 49 Mother Goose

rhymes, each featuring its own watercolor illustration. (Rev: BCCB 7–8/09; BL 2/1/09; SLJ 4/09) [398.8]

13304 Sabuda, Robert. *Movable Mother Goose* (PS–1). 1999, Simon & Schuster $19.95 (978-0-689-81192-0). Pop-ups and flaps are used to illustrate this collection of favorite Mother Goose rhymes. (Rev: BL 12/15/99; HBG 3/00; SLJ 2/00)

13305 Sayre, April P. *Trout, Trout, Trout! A Fish Chant* (PS–2). Illus. by Trip Park. 2004, NorthWord $15.95 (978-1-55971-889-9). Bright cartoon illustrations complement this bouncy fish-related chant. (Rev: SLJ 7/04) [597.17]

13306 Scanlon, Elizabeth Garton. *A Sock Is a Pocket for Your Toes: A Pocket Book* (PS–2). Illus. by Robin P. Glasser. 2004, HarperCollins $15.99 (978-0-06-029526-4). This delightful rhyme book takes a broad brush to the concept of pockets — picturing a cave as a pocket for bears and ears as pockets for whispers. (Rev: BL 2/15/04; SLJ 2/04) [811]

13307 Sierra, Judy. *Monster Goose* (K–3). Illus. by Jack E. Davis. 2001, Harcourt $16.00 (978-0-15-202034-7). 56pp. Gruesome, gross, and goofy versions of familiar Mother Goose rhymes. (Rev: BCCB 12/01; BL 9/15/01; HBG 3/02; SLJ 9/01) [811]

13308 Sierra, Judy. *Schoolyard Rhymes* (K–3). Illus. by Melissa Sweet. 2005, Knopf $15.95 (978-0-375-82516-3). 40pp. This collection of schoolyard rhymes includes such favorites as "Liar, Liar, Pants on Fire" and "Lady with the Alligator Purse." (Rev: BL 8/05; SLJ 10/05) [398.8]

13309 Siomades, Lorianne. *Three Little Kittens* (PS–1). Illus. 2000, Boyds Mills $12.95 (978-1-56397-845-6). 32pp. The classic nursery rhyme is given a bright, mischievous treatment that involves both the kittens and some thieving mice. (Rev: BL 2/15/00; HBG 10/00; SLJ 4/00)

13310 Spicer, Maggee, and Richard Thompson. *When They Are Up . . .* (PS–3). Illus. by Kirsti Anne Wakelin. 2004, Fitzhenry & Whiteside $14.95 (978-1-55041-707-4). This imaginative twist on the nursery song about the Duke of York's 10,000 men has them involved in such things as capturing armadillos and knitting socks; music and lyrics are appended. (Rev: SLJ 5/04) [811]

13311 Stevens, Janet, and Susan Stevens Crummel. *And the Dish Ran Away with the Spoon* (K–3). Illus. 2001, Harcourt $17.00 (978-0-15-202298-3). 48pp. Familiar nursery rhymes are reworked with droll results. (Rev: BL 4/1/01*; HB 7/01; HBG 10/01; SLJ 5/01)

13312 *Sylvia Long's Mother Goose* (PS–K). Illus. by Sylvia Long. 1999, Chronicle $19.95 (978-0-8118-2088-2). 109pp. Animals, reptiles, and insects replace humans in the delightful illustrations featured in this Mother Goose anthology. (Rev: BCCB 12/99; BL 11/15/99; HBG 3/00; SLJ 12/99*) [398.8]

13313 Taback, Simms. *This Is the House That Jack Built* (PS–2). Illus. 2002, Penguin $15.99 (978-0-399-23488-0). 32pp. An inventive, spirited take on the traditional nursery rhyme that focuses on the house and its contents.

(Rev: BCCB 10/02; BL 10/1/02*; HB 11/02; HBG 3/03; SLJ 9/02*) [398.8]

13314 Taylor, Jane. *Twinkle, Twinkle, Little Star* (PS–1). Illus. by Jerry Pinkney. 2011, Little, Brown $16.99 (978-0-316-05696-0). Unpaged. A little chipmunk gazes into the sky and wonders at the sights he sees in this imaginative and beautifully illustrated picture book. (Rev: SLJ 11/1/11*) [821]

13315 Thompson, Sarah L. *Around the Neighborhood: A Counting Lullaby* (PS–2). Illus. by Jana Christy. 2012, Amazon Children's $16.99 (978-0-7614-6164-7). 32pp. A variety of animals are introduced along with numbers 1 through 10 in this version of "Over in the Meadow." (Rev: BL 11/1/12; SLJ 1/13) [398.8]

13316 Tildes, Phyllis Limbacher. *Will You Be Mine? A Nursery Rhyme Romance* (PS–K). Illus. by author. 2011, Charlesbridge $17.95 (978-1-58089-244-5); paper $7.95 (978-1-58089-245-2). 32pp. Eighteen Mother Goose rhymes are arranged so they tell a larger story about a cat and poodle's nuptials in this attractively illustrated book. e (Rev: BL 1/1–15/11; SLJ 2/1/11) [398.8]

13317 Trapani, Iza. *Here We Go 'Round the Mulberry Bush* (PS–1). Illus. by author. 2006, Charlesbridge paper $6.95 (978-1-58091-699-8). Animals feast on a vegetable garden in this take on the familiar nursery rhyme. (Rev: SLJ 7/06) [398.8]

13318 Trapani, Iza, retel. *Mary Had a Little Lamb* (PS–1). Illus. by Iza Trapani. 1998, Whispering Coyote $16.95 (978-1-58089-009-0). An expanded version of the nursery rhyme in which the little lamb has misadventures in a farmyard. (Rev: HBG 3/99; SLJ 11/98)

13319 Unobagha, Uzo. *Off to the Sweet Shores of Africa* (PS). Illus. by Julia Cairns. 2000, Chronicle $16.99 (978-0-8118-2378-4). Playful verses about African subjects are contained in this collection that seems inspired by Mother Goose. (Rev: BL 11/1/00; HBG 3/01; SLJ 10/00) [811]

13320 Wells, Rosemary. *The Itsy-Bitsy Spider* (PS). Illus. Series: Bunny Reads Back. 1998, Scholastic $5.99 (978-0-590-02911-7). 16pp. The familiar nursery rhyme about a tiny spider climbing a waterspout is presented in a clever format in this board book. (Rev: BL 12/15/98; HBG 3/99; SLJ 2/99)

13321 Yolen, Jane, ed. *The Lap-Time Song and Play Book* (PS). Illus. by Margot Tomes. 1989, Harcourt $15.95 (978-0-15-243588-2). 32pp. A collection of 16 nursery games and songs with a history for each and simple piano arrangements. (Rev: BL 10/1/89; HB 11/89; SLJ 10/89) [782.42]

13322 Yolen, Jane, ed. *This Little Piggy* (PS). Illus. by Will Hillenbrand. 2006, Candlewick $19.99 (978-0-7636-1348-8). 80pp. A large-format anthology of rhymes, songs, lap games, and finger plays of various kinds, with annotations, pig-filled illustrations, musical notations, and an accompanying CD. (Rev: BL 1/1–15/06*; SLJ 2/06*) [398.8]

13323 Zelinsky, Paul O. *Knick-Knack Paddywhack! A Moving Parts Book* (PS–3). Illus. 2002, Dutton $18.99

(978-0-525-46908-7). 8pp. This miracle of pull-tabs and flaps is a delicious combination of familiar, bouncy rhyme and counting song full of comedy and small details. (Rev: BCCB 2/03; BL 11/1/02; HB 1/03; HBG 3/03; SLJ 12/02) [782.42164]

Poetry

General

13324 Adedjouma, Davida, ed. *The Palm of My Heart: Poetry by African American Children* (1–4). Illus. by R. Gregory Christie. 1996, Lee & Low $15.95 (978-1-880000-41-0). 32pp. Twenty poems by African American children about the beauty and joy of being black. (Rev: BCCB 12/96; BL 2/15/97; SLJ 1/97) [811]

13325 Adoff, Arnold. *Roots and Blues: A Celebration* (4–8). Illus. by R. Gregory Christie. 2011, Clarion $17.99 (978-054723554-7). 96pp. In prose and poetry, Adoff explores the history of the blues from the days of slavery to the present. (Rev: BL 2/15/11*; LMC 1–2/11; SLJ 2/1/11*) [811]

13326 Adoff, Arnold. *Touch the Poem* (PS–3). Illus. by Lisa Desimini. 2000, Scholastic $16.95 (978-0-590-47970-7). 32pp. Common childhood experiences like walking on a beach or feeling the fuzz on a peach are explored in this collection of original poems illustrated with photographs. (Rev: BCCB 2/00; BL 3/15/00; HBG 10/00; SLJ 6/00) [811]

13327 Adoff, Jaime. *Small Fry* (1–3). Illus. by Mike Reed. 2008, Dutton $16.99 (978-0-525-46935-3). 32pp. This collection of 19 poems explores the pros and cons of being short. (Rev: BCCB 11/08; BL 11/15/08; LMC 1/09; SLJ 11/08) [811]

13328 Agard, John. *Half-Caste and Other Poems* (4–7). 2005, Hodder $16.99 (978-0-340-89382-1). Guyana-born Agard offers a collection of his saucy, Caribbean-flavored poetry dealing with topics such as tolerance and diversity that young people will recognize. (Rev: BL 10/15/05; HB 1–2/06; HBG 4/06; SLJ 1/06; VOYA 2/06) [811]

13329 Alarcón, Francisco X. *Poems to Dream Together / Poemas para soñar juntos* (3–5). Illus. by Paula Barragán. 2005, Lee & Low $16.95 (978-1-58430-233-9). 32pp. A collection of short, bilingual poems about aspirations. (Rev: BL 7/05; HBG 10/05; LMC 1/06; SLJ 10/05) [811]

13330 Anaya, Rudolfo. *Elegy on the Death of Cesar Chavez* (4–7). 2000, Cinco Puntos $16.95 (978-0-938317-51-7). This is an elegiac poem that celebrates the life, work, and struggle of the respected labor leader. (Rev: BL 12/15/00; HBG 3/01; SLJ 1/01) [811]

13331 Andrews, Julie, and Emma Walton Hamilton. *Julie Andrews' Treasury for All Seasons: Poems and Songs to Celebrate the Year* (2–5). Illus. by Marjorie Priceman. 2012, Little, Brown $19.99 (978-0-316-04051-8).

192pp. Arranged chronologically, this is a wide-ranging collection of poems and verses relating to holidays, the seasons, various rites of passage. ⋒ (Rev: BL 10/15/12; SLJ 11/12) [808.81]

13332 Andrews, Sylvia. *Dancing in My Bones* (PS). Illus. by Ellen Mueller. 2001, HarperCollins $10.99 (978-0-694-01316-6). 24pp. A multicultural cast of kids dance their way through a park, adding lines to a rhyme along the way. (Rev: BL 11/1/01; HBG 3/02; SLJ 12/01) [811]

13333 Appelt, Kathi. *My Father's House* (PS–2). Illus. by Raúl Colón. 2007, Viking $16.99 (978-0-670-03669-1). Through verse and colorfully rendered illustrations, this book expresses thanks to the Creator for the Earth's beauty and diversity. (Rev: BL 5/15/07; SLJ 8/07) [811]

13334 Archer, Peggy. *From Dawn to Dreams: Poems for Busy Babies* (PS). Illus. by Hanako Wakiyama. 2007, Candlewick $15.99 (978-0-7636-2467-5). Beautiful illustrations of adorable babies accompany poems about little ones' daily routines. (Rev: SLJ 7/07)

13335 Argueta, Jorge. *A Movie in My Pillow / Una Pelicula en Mi Almohada* (4–8). Illus. by Elizabeth Gomez. 2001, Children's $15.95 (978-0-89239-165-3). The author remembers in poetry his family's immigration to the United States from El Salvador, with each poem accompanied by the translation and rich illustrations. (Rev: BL 10/1/01; HBG 10/01; SLJ 5/01*) [861]

13336 Argueta, Jorge. *Sopa de frijoles / Bean Soup: Un poema para cocinar / A Cooking Poem* (1–3). Illus. by Rafael Yockteng. 2009, Groundwood $18.95 (978-0-88899-881-1). In Spanish and English this is a free-verse recipe for bean soup. (Rev: BL 3/15/09; SLJ 4/09) [861]

13337 Argueta, Jorge. *Talking with Mother Earth / Hablando con Madre Tierra: Poems / Poemas* (3–8). Illus. by Lucía Angela Pérez. 2006, Groundwood $15.95 (978-0-88899-626-8). Beautiful bilingual poems give voice to a young Central American Indian's feelings of kinship with nature. (Rev: HBG 4/07; LMC 1/07; SLJ 10/06) [811]

13338 Attenborough, Liz, ed. *Poetry by Heart: A Child's Book of Poems to Remember* (3–5). Illus. 2001, Scholastic $17.95 (978-0-439-29657-1). An eclectic, enchanting collection of poetry for younger readers. (Rev: BL 1/1–15/02; HBG 10/02; SLJ 2/02) [811.54]

13339 Bagert, Brod. *Shout! Little Poems That Roar* (K–2). Illus. by Sachiko Yoshikawa. 2007, Dial $16.99 (978-0-8037-2972-8). This appealing collection of 21 energetic rhyming poems celebrates the wonders — and occasional disappointments — of childhood. (Rev: BL 2/1/07; SLJ 2/07) [811]

13340 Barbe, Walter B., sel. *A School Year of Poems: 180 Favorites from Highlights* (K–3). Illus. by Dennis Hockerman. 2005, Boyds Mills paper $11.95 (978-1-59078-395-5). 116pp. The poems in this anthology are divided into nine child-friendly categories, including animals, weather, and holidays. (Rev: SLJ 10/05) [811]

13341 Bauer, Caroline Feller, ed. *Rainy Day: Stories and Poems* (3–5). Illus. by Michele Chessare. 1986, HarperCollins LB $15.89 (978-0-397-32105-6). 96pp. Poems

and stories from mostly well-known children's poets such as John Ciardi and Langston Hughes. Also use: *Snowy Day: Stories and Poems* (1986). (Rev: BCCB 9/86; BL 7/86; SLJ 9/86)

13342 Bauer, Marion Dane. *Love Song for a Baby* (PS–K). Illus. by Dan Andreasen. 2002, Simon & Schuster $15.95 (978-0-689-82268-1). A tender poem about parents' love for their growing baby, with excellent oil paintings and rhyming text. (Rev: BL 9/1/02; HBG 3/03; SLJ 8/02) [811]

13343 Baylor, Byrd. *The Way to Start a Day* (3–5). Illus. by Peter Parnall. 1978, Macmillan $16.00 (978-0-684-15651-4); paper $5.99 (978-0-689-71054-4). A poetic tribute to the many ways people have greeted a new day.

13344 Becker, Helaine. *Mama Likes to Mambo* (K–2). Illus. by John Beder. 2002, Stoddart $15.95 (978-0-7737-3316-9). 32pp. A collection of amusing, attractively illustrated poems of differing lengths on varied subjects. (Rev: BL 9/15/02; HBG 10/02; SLJ 5/02) [811]

13345 Bennett, Jill, ed. *A Cup of Starshine: Poems and Pictures for Young Children* (PS–1). Illus. by Graham Percy. 1991, Harcourt $16.95 (978-0-15-220982-7). 64pp. These include the traditional rhymes with modern verse and full-color drawings. (Rev: BL 10/15/91; SLJ 12/91) [811]

13346 Bernier-Grand, Carmen. *Cesar: ¡Si, Se Puede! Yes, We Can!* (3–6). Illus. by David Diaz. 2004, Marshall Cavendish $16.95 (978-0-7614-5172-3). 48pp. A series of 19 free-verse poems chronicles the life of Cesar Chavez, from his migrant worker childhood to his leadership in the struggle for farm workers' rights. (Rev: BL 10/15/04; SLJ 10/04) [811]

13347 Berry, James, ed. *Around the World in Eighty Poems* (3–5). Illus. by Katherine Lucas. 2002, Chronicle $19.95 (978-0-8118-3506-0). 96pp. A collection of poems from countries around the world, illustrated with paintings. (Rev: BCCB 1/03; BL 7/02; HBG 3/03; SLJ 4/03) [808.81]

13348 Berry, James, ed. *Classic Poems to Read Aloud* (4–8). 1995, Kingfisher $18.95 (978-1-85697-987-0). Jamaican writer Berry has collected old favorites, mostly British, along with new voices usually excluded from the literary canon. (Rev: BL 5/1/95; SLJ 5/95) [811]

13349 Blake, Quentin. *All Join In* (PS–2). Illus. 1991, Little, Brown $14.95 (978-0-316-09934-9). 32pp. The theme of cooperation is explored in six bright poems. (Rev: BCCB 5/91; BL 4/15/91; SLJ 7/91) [821]

13350 Boling, Katharine. *New Year Be Coming! A Gullah Year* (K–3). Illus. by Daniel Minter. 2002, Whitman $16.99 (978-0-8075-5590-3). 32pp. These twelve poems — one for each month of the year — are written in the unique Gullah dialect of a group of African Americans living on the coast of South Carolina and Georgia. (Rev: BCCB 1/03; BL 11/15/02; HB 11/02; HBG 3/03; SLJ 9/02) [811]

13351 Borden, Louise. *America Is . . .* (2–4). Illus. by Stacey Schuett. 2002, Simon & Schuster $16.95 (978-0-689-83900-9). 40pp. This patriotic poem for younger readers examines life in America through many prisms. (Rev: BL 8/02; HBG 10/02; SLJ 6/02) [811]

13352 Brand, Dionne. *Earth Magic* (4–7). Illus. by Eugenie Fernandes. 2006, Kids Can $14.95 (978-1-55337-706-1). In her first collection of poetry for young people, Brand writes about life in Trinidad, the island of her birth. (Rev: BL 4/1/06; SLJ 7/06) [811]

13353 Brooks, Gwendolyn. *Bronzeville Boys and Girls* (K–4). Illus. by Faith Ringgold. 2007, HarperCollins $16.99 (978-0-06-029505-9). 41pp. This newly illustrated collection of poems by Pulitzer Prize-winner Gwendolyn Brooks, originally published in 1956, celebrates the universal joys of childhood. (Rev: BL 2/1/07; SLJ 2/07) [811]

13354 Brown, Calef. *Soup for Breakfast* (PS–2). Illus. by author. 2008, Houghton $16.00 (978-0-618-91641-2). 32pp. A collection of playful poetry about food. (Rev: BL 11/15/08; HB 3/09; SLJ 2/09) [811]

13355 Brown, Margaret Wise. *Give Yourself to the Rain: Poems for the Very Young* (PS–1). Illus. by Teri L. Weidner. 2002, Simon & Schuster $16.95 (978-0-689-83344-1). A collection of 24 previously unpublished poems for young readers, illustrated in beautiful warm pastels. (Rev: BL 2/15/02; HBG 10/02; SLJ 3/02) [811]

13356 Bruchac, Joseph, and Jonathan London. *Thirteen Moons on Turtle's Back: A Native American Year of Moons* (1–5). Illus. by Thomas Locker. 1997, Putnam paper $6.99 (978-0-399-22141-5). 32pp. For each of the 13 moon cycles in a year, this book contains a poem and an oil painting illustrating it. (Rev: BL 3/1/92; SLJ 7/92) [811.54]

13357 Bryan, Ashley. *Sing to the Sun: Poems and Pictures* (2–6). Illus. 1996, HarperCollins paper $7.99 (978-0-06-443437-9). Short poems with a Caribbean lilt. (Rev: BCCB 10/92; BL 10/15/92; HB 3/93; SLJ 10/92) [811.54]

13358 Bunting, Eve. *Sing a Song of Piglets: A Calendar in Verse* (PS–1). Illus. by Emily Arnold McCully. 2002, Clarion $16.00 (978-0-618-01137-7). 32pp. Readers follow a pair of piglets through the year, with lively watercolors that match the bounciness of the simple rhymes. (Rev: BL 11/15/02; HBG 3/03; SLJ 8/02) [811]

13359 Burkholder, Kelly. *Poetry* (2–5). Series: Artistic Adventures. 2001, Rourke LB $23.93 (978-1-57103-354-3). 24pp. This book explains the basic elements of poetry like rhythm, rhyme, and repetition, introduces different types of poems, and gives advice on how to write your own poetry. (Rev: SLJ 2/01) [811]

13360 Burleigh, Robert. *Langston's Train Ride* (3–6). Trans. and illus. by Leonard Jenkins. 2004, Scholastic LB $16.99 (978-0-439-35239-0). 32pp. Langston Hughes's well-known poem "The Negro Speaks of Rivers," written when he was only 18, is beautifully complemented by the collage artwork. (Rev: BL 9/15/04) [811]

13361 Carlson, Lori M. *Sol a Sol* (2–5). Illus. by Emily Lisker. 1998, Holt $17.00 (978-0-8050-4373-0). A bilingual anthology of poems that describe the daily activities of a Hispanic family. (Rev: BCCB 5/98; BL 4/1/98; HB 5/98; HBG 10/98; SLJ 3/98) [808]

13362 Carney, Mary Lou, ed. *Absolutely Angels: Poems for Children and Other Believers* (PS–3). Illus. by Viqui Maggio. 1998, Boyds Mills $14.95 (978-1-56397-708-4). A collection of poems, mostly by contemporary poets, about the role of angels as protectors and helpers. (Rev: BL 11/1/98; HBG 3/99; SLJ 11/98) [808.81]

13363 Chaucer, Geoffrey. *The Canterbury Tales* (5–9). 1985, Checkerboard $14.95 (978-1-56288-259-4). An adaptation for young readers of 13 tales that still keep the flavor and spirit of the originals. (Rev: SLJ 2/86) [826]

13364 Chorao, Kay, ed. *Rhymes Round the World* (PS–2). Illus. by Kay Chorao. 2009, Dutton $16.99 (978-0-525-47875-1). Forty light poems and songs, many of them familiar, take children on a world tour. (Rev: BL 3/1/09; SLJ 2/09) [821]

13365 Cleary, Brian P. *Rainbow Soup: Adventures in Poetry* (3–6). Illus. by Neal Layton. 2004, Carolrhoda $16.95 (978-1-57505-597-8). 96pp. In multiple poetry forms, Cleary celebrates various aspects of children's everyday lives, including school, sports, and food. (Rev: BL 4/1/04; SLJ 6/04) [808.1]

13366 Clifton, Lucille. *Everett Anderson's Goodbye* (K–2). Illus. by Ann Grifalconi. 1983, Holt paper $5.95 (978-0-8050-0800-5). 32pp. Poems about a young African American boy. (Rev: BL 3/1/04)

13367 Cooling, Wendy. *Come to the Great World: Poems from Around the Globe* (PS–3). Illus. by Sheila Moxley. 2004, Holiday House $16.95 (978-0-8234-1822-0). 32pp. Diverse poems about children and the issues that affect them are illustrated with colorful paintings. (Rev: BL 3/15/04; SLJ 4/04) [811]

13368 Cooney, Barbara, retel. *Chanticleer and the Fox* (1–4). Illus. by Barbara Cooney. 1958, HarperCollins LB $17.89 (978-0-690-18562-1); paper $3.95 (978-0-690-04318-1). Chaucer's Nun's Priest Tale retold by the illustrator. Caldecott Medal winner, 1959.

13369 Crawley, Dave. *Reading, Rhyming, and 'Rithmetic* (1–3). Illus. by Liz Callen. 2010, Boyds Mills $17.95 (978-1-59078-565-2). 32pp. A humorous collection of 20 poems about all aspects of school life. (Rev: LMC 8–9/10; SLJ 4/1/10) [811]

13370 Creech, Sharon. *Who's That Baby? New-Baby Songs* (PS–2). Illus. by David Diaz. 2005, HarperCollins $15.99 (978-0-06-052939-0). 32pp. In this collection of short poems and songs, Creech chronicles the early days of a newborn baby and its interaction with the world around it. (Rev: BL 8/05) [811]

13371 Dahl, Roald. *Vile Verses* (5–8). 2005, Viking $25.00 (978-0-670-06042-9). New illustrations adorn the poems in this aptly titled collection. (Rev: BL 11/1/05; SLJ 11/05*) [811]

13372 Dakos, Kalli. *A Funeral in the Bathroom: And Other School Bathroom Poems* (3–5). Illus. by Mark Beech. 2011, Whitman $14.99 (978-0-8075-2675-0). 48pp. A collection of poems on an unusual topic: activities that take place in a school bathroom (including the funeral for a goldfish). (Rev: LMC 1–2/12; SLJ 8/1/11) [811]

13373 Dawes, Kwame Senu Neville. *I Saw Your Face* (3–5). Illus. by Tom Feelings. 2005, Dial $16.99 (978-0-8037-1894-4). Sketches of black faces around the world are paired with evocative poetry celebrating their global reach. (Rev: BL 2/1/05; SLJ 3/05) [811]

13374 De Regniers, Beatrice S., ed. *Sing a Song of Popcorn: Every Child's Book of Poems* (PS–6). Illus. by Marcia Brown. 1988, Scholastic $18.95 (978-0-590-43974-9). 160pp. A treasure from highly regarded poets, with exciting artwork. (Rev: BCCB 10/88; BL 8/88; SLJ 8/88)

13375 Di Pasquale, Emanuel. *Cartwheel to the Moon: My Sicilian Childhood* (3–6). Illus. by K. Dyble Thompson. 2003, Cricket $16.95 (978-0-8126-2679-7). 64pp. Di Pasquale's poems paint a vivid word picture of his chidhood in Sicily during the 1940s and 1950s. (Rev: BL 4/1/03; HBG 10/03; SLJ 7/03) [811]

13376 Dotlich, Rebecca. *Lemonade Sun and Other Summer Poems* (PS–3). Illus. by Jan S. Gilchrist. 1998, Boyds Mills paper $15.95 (978-1-56397-660-5). 32pp. This book of poems shows children in everyday situations and depicts their sense of wonder. (Rev: BL 2/15/98; HBG 10/98; SLJ 3/98) [811]

13377 Dotlich, Rebecca Kai. *In the Spin of Things: Poetry of Motion* (2–5). Illus. by Karen M. Dugan. 2003, Boyds Mills $16.95 (978-1-56397-145-7). 32pp. Everyday items whirl into motion in this collection of freeform poems. (Rev: BL 4/1/03; HBG 10/03; SLJ 3/03) [811]

13378 Dotlich, Rebecca Kai. *Over in the Pink House* (PS–2). Illus. by Melanie Hall. 2004, Boyds Mills $15.95 (978-1-59078-027-5). 32pp. Rhythm and sound trump meaning in this collection of rhyming verses. (Rev: BL 5/1/04; SLJ 4/04) [796.2]

13379 Dotlich, Rebecca Kai. *When Riddles Come Rumbling: Poems to Ponder* (2–5). Illus. 2001, Boyds Mills $16.95 (978-1-56397-846-3). 32pp. Short, rhythmic poems along with picture clues form riddles about everyday objects. (Rev: BL 11/1/01; HBG 3/02; SLJ 10/01) [811]

13380 *Dream Makers: Young People Share Their Hopes and Aspirations* (3–6). Illus. by Neil Waldman. 2003, Boyds Mills $15.95 (978-1-59078-178-4). The dreams and aspirations of 42 American boys and girls are collected in this attractive large-format volume of rhyming and free verse marking the 150th anniversary of the Children's Aid Society. (Rev: BL 9/1/03; HBG 4/04; SLJ 12/03) [811]

13381 *Drift Upon a Dream: Poems for Sleepy Babies* (PS–1). Illus. by Melanie Williamson. 2004, Charlesbridge paper $6.95 (978-1-57091-578-9). 32pp. This anthology of 21 bedtime poems includes selections by Tennyson, Lee Bennett Hopkins, Eve Merriam, Eleanor Farjeon, and by Foster himself. (Rev: BL 9/1/04) [811]

13382 Durango, Julia. *Under the Mambo Moon* (3–5). Illus. by Fabricio VandenBroeck. 2011, Charlesbridge $12.95 (978-1-57091-723-3). 48pp. Poems celebrate the Latin American people, music, and dance that young Marisol sees and hears at her father's record store. Lexile 840L (Rev: BL 6/1/11; SLJ 7/11) [811]

13383 Eastwick, Ivy O. *I Asked a Tiger to Tea* (2–6). Illus. by Melanie Hall. 2002, Boyds Mills $15.95 (978-1-56397-515-8). 32pp. This is a richly illustrated, lyrical collection of poems about nature and childhood. (Rev: BL 12/15/02; HBG 3/03; SLJ 11/02) [811.54]

13384 Eastwick, Ivy O. *Some Folks Like Cats and Other Poems* (1–3). Ed. by Walter B. Barbe. Illus. by Mary Kurnich Maass. 2002, Boyds Mills $15.95 (978-1-56397-450-2). 28pp. A collection of 20 of the author's poems that deal with such subjects as sunflowers, leaves, rain, and small animals. (Rev: BL 4/15/02; HBG 10/02; SLJ 7/02) [811.54]

13385 Eccleshare, Julia, ed. *First Poems* (PS–3). Illus. by Selina Young. 1994, Bedrick $16.95 (978-0-87226-373-4). A collection of happy, often humorous poems, including a number of old favorites and several by contemporary poets. (Rev: BL 7/94; SLJ 8/94) [821]

13386 Esbensen, Barbara J. *Who Shrank My Grandmother's House? Poems of Discovery* (1–3). Illus. by Eric Beddows. 1992, HarperCollins $15.00 (978-0-06-021827-0). 48pp. This book presents a celebration of everything in a collection of 23 poems. (Rev: BCCB 4/92; BL 6/1/92; HB 5/92; SLJ 4/92*) [811]

13387 Evans, Dilys, ed. *Monster Soup and Other Spooky Poems* (PS–1). Illus. by Jacqueline Rogers. 1992, Scholastic $14.95 (978-0-590-45208-3). 40pp. Watercolor paintings illustrate 16 poems that monster fans are sure to love. (Rev: BL 8/92; SLJ 10/92) [811]

13388 Ferris, Helen, ed. *Favorite Poems Old and New* (4–6). Illus. by Leonard Weisgard. 1957, Doubleday $24.95 (978-0-385-07696-8). 598pp. A book brimming with all kinds of poetry — lyrics, rhymes, doggerel, songs. (Rev: HB 5/04)

13389 Field, Eugene. *Wynken, Blynken, and Nod: A Dutch Lullaby* (PS–1). Illus. by Giselle Potter. 2008, Random $16.99 (978-0-375-84196-5). 40pp. A large-format, dreamy interpretation of the classic bedtime poem. (Rev: BL 5/15/08; HB 5/07; SLJ 7/08) [811]

13390 Fisher, Aileen. *I Heard a Bluebird Sing* (2–5). Illus. by Jennifer Emery. 2002, Boyds Mills $18.95 (978-1-56397-191-4). The 41 poems included in this anthology were selected by children around the United States; they are preceded by excerpts from an article by Fisher and by introductions to the thematically organized sections. (Rev: BL 11/15/02; HBG 3/03; SLJ 10/02) [811.54]

13391 Fisher, Aileen. *Sing of the Earth and Sky: Poems About Our Planet and the Wonders Beyond* (2–4). Illus. 2001, Boyds Mills $15.95 (978-1-56397-802-9). 48pp. A collection of short original poems that are divided into four subjects: earth, sun, moon, and stars. (Rev: BL 3/15/01; HBG 10/01) [811]

13392 Fleischman, Paul. *Big Talk: Poems for Four Voices* (4–7). 2000, Candlewick $17.99 (978-0-7636-0636-7). This collection of spirited, evocative poems for four voices to read aloud covers a variety of topics. (Rev: BCCB 4/00; BL 6/1–15/00; HB 5–6/00; HBG 10/00; SLJ 6/00) [811]

13393 Fletcher, Ralph. *Buried Alive: The Elements of Love* (5–8). 1996, Simon & Schuster $14.00 (978-0-689-80593-6). A series of free-verse poems that explore various aspects of love — puppy and otherwise. (Rev: BCCB 6/96; BL 5/1/96; SLJ 5/96; VOYA 10/96) [811]

13394 Fletcher, Ralph. *Have You Been to the Beach Lately? Poems* (4–7). Photos by Andrea Sperling. 2001, Scholastic paper $15.95 (978-0-531-30330-6). More than 30 chatty poems, illustrated with black-and-white photographs, are written from the perspective of a smart and funny 11-year-old. (Rev: HBG 10/01; SLJ 8/01) [811]

13395 Fletcher, Ralph. *Moving Day* (3–6). Illus. by Jennifer Emery. 2006, Boyds Mills $17.95 (978-1-59078-339-9). Free-verse poems give voice to the feelings of a 12-year-old who is leaving behind the only world he's known and moving to a new and unfamiliar place. (Rev: SLJ 12/06*) [811]

13396 Fletcher, Ralph. *Relatively Speaking: Poems About Family* (5–7). 1999, Orchard LB $15.99 (978-0-531-33141-5). From an 11-year-old boy's point of view, these original poems explore relationships as family members go through periods of change. (Rev: BCCB 5/99; BL 7/99; HBG 10/99; SLJ 4/99) [811]

13397 Fletcher, Ralph. *A Writing Kind of Day* (3–5). Illus. by April Ward. 2005, Boyds Mills $17.95 (978-1-59078-276-7); paper $9.95 (978-1-59078-353-5). 32pp. A collection of 27 poems by a young author who isn't afraid to write about the everyday and even the silly. (Rev: BL 3/15/05; SLJ 4/05) [811]

13398 Flood, Nancy Bo. *Cowboy Up! Ride the Navajo Rodeo* (2–4). Illus. 2013, Boyds Mills/Wordsong $17.95 (978-1-59078-893-6). 48pp. Using a combination of prose and verse as well as photographs, this is a dramatic introduction to the activities at a rodeo. (Rev: BLO 7/13; LMC 10/13; SLJ 3/13) [811]

13399 Forman, Ruth. *Young Cornrows Callin Out the Moon* (PS). Illus. by Cbabi Bayoc. 2007, Children's Book Pr. $16.95 (978-0-89239-218-6). 32pp. A happy poem about summer life among the brownstones of South Philadelphia. (Rev: BL 2/1/07) [811]

13400 Franco, Betsy. *Counting Our Way to the 100th Day! 100 Poems and 100 Pictures to Celebrate the 100th Day of School* (K–2). Illus. by Steven Salerno. 2004, Simon & Schuster $15.95 (978-0-689-84793-6). 48pp. Many of the 100 poems in this stylishly illustrated collection focus on the number "100" and will help students count down the first 100 days of school. (Rev: BL 8/04; SLJ 7/04) [811]

13401 Franco, Betsy. *Messing Around on the Monkey Bars and Other School Poems for Two Voices* (2–4). Illus. by Jessie Hartland. 2009, Candlewick $17.99 (978-

0-7636-3174-1). Nineteen lively school-themed poems are suitable for two or more voices. (Rev: BCCB 5/09; BL 5/15/09; HB 7/09; LMC 10/09; SLJ 11/09) [811]

13402 Frank, John. *Keepers: Treasure-Hunt Poems* (2–5). Illus. 2008, Roaring Brook $17.95 (978-1-59643-197-3). 64pp. Short poems focus on treasures of all kinds — sea glass, baseball cards, pottery jars, and so forth. (Rev: BL 3/15/08; SLJ 6/08) [811]

13403 Frost, Helen. *Spinning Through the Universe: A Novel in Poems from Room 214* (5–7). 2004, Farrar $16.00 (978-0-374-37159-3). A variety of poetic forms — including haiku, tercelle, sonnet, pantoun, and tanka — are used in these diverse and compelling poems about the lives of a fifth-grade teacher and her students. (Rev: BL 4/1/04; SLJ 4/04) [811]

13404 Gaiman, Neil. *Instructions* (K–3). Illus. by Charles Vess. 2010, HarperCollins $14.99 (978-006196030-7). 40pp. A poetic guide to navigating fairy tales and returning home again. (Rev: BLO 6/10; VOYA 10/10) [821]

13405 George, Kristine O'Connell. *Emma Dilemma: Big Sister Poems* (PS–3). Illus. by Nancy Carpenter. 2011, Clarion $16.99 (978-0-618-42842-7). 48pp. Big sister Jessica finds her little sister Emma a source of joy and extreme annoyance, as expressed in 34 evocative poems. (Rev: BL 5/1/11; SLJ 2/1/11*) [811]

13406 George, Kristine O'Connell. *Fold Me a Poem* (1–3). Illus. by Lauren Stringer. 2005, Harcourt $16.00 (978-0-15-202501-4). A boy creates origami animals and then uses them for imaginative play in this book of 32 poems. (Rev: BL 3/15/05; SLJ 3/05) [811]

13407 George, Kristine O'Connell. *Swimming Upstream: Middle School Poems* (5–8). Illus. by Debbie Tilley. 2002, Clarion $14.00 (978-0-618-15250-6). Brief poems describe how one girl navigates the rapids of middle school, discussing everything from school lunches and lockers to making friends and relationships with boys. (Rev: BL 1/1–15/03; HB 1–2/03; HBG 3/03; SLJ 9/02) [811]

13408 George, Kristine O'Connell. *Toasting Marshmallows: Camping Poems* (K–4). Illus. by Kate Kiesler. 2001, Clarion $16.00 (978-0-618-04597-6). 48pp. Thirty simple poems clearly depict a family camping trip, from the details of pitching a tent to the wonders of the natural world, with attractive and varied artwork. (Rev: HBG 10/01; SLJ 7/01*) [811]

13409 Gerstein, Mordicai. *Dear Hot Dog: Poems About Everyday Stuff* (K–3). Illus. by author. 2011, Abrams $16.95 (978-0-8109-9732-5). 32pp. Topics from falling asleep to eating spaghetti are captured in this accessible collection. (Rev: BL 12/15/11; LMC 1–2/12*; SLJ 10/1/11) [811]

13410 Gilchrist, Jan Spivey. *My America* (K–2). Illus. by Ashley Bryan. 2007, HarperCollins $16.99 (978-0-06-079104-9). 40pp. Celebrates the diversity of America in its landscape, animal life, and people. (Rev: BL 4/15/07) [813]

13411 Gilooly, Eileen, ed. *Rudyard Kipling* (4–8). Illus. by Jim Sharpe. 2000, Sterling $14.95 (978-0-8069-

4484-5). This book contains complete poems or excerpts from 28 poems by this well-liked writer including "If" and "The Ballad of East and West." (Rev: HBG 3/01; SLJ 5/00) [821]

13412 Giovanni, Nikki. *Knoxville, Tennessee* (PS–3). Illus. by Larry Johnson. 1994, Scholastic $14.95 (978-0-590-47074-2). 32pp. Nikki Giovanni re-creates the summers she spent growing up in Knoxville and the simple pleasures she enjoyed. (Rev: BCCB 7–8/94; BL 2/15/94; HB 9/94; SLJ 4/94) [811]

13413 Giovanni, Nikki. *The Sun Is So Quiet* (K–2). Illus. by Ashley Bryan. 1996, Holt $14.95 (978-0-8050-4119-4). Thirteen poems that depict everyday occurrences, with illustrations that feature African American children in many cultures. (Rev: BL 10/15/96; SLJ 1/97) [811]

13414 Giovanni, Nikki, ed. *Hip Hop Speaks to Children: A Celebration of Poetry with a Beat* (3–5). Illus. by Kristen Balouch. 2008, Sourcebooks $19.99 (978-1-4022-1048-8). 72pp. Fifty-one poems — by authors including Langston Hughes, Gwendolyn Brooks, Eloise Greenfield, Tupac Shakur, and Queen Latifah — provide a historical collage of African American poetry in print and voice; accompanying CD. (Rev: BL 9/15/08) [811]

13415 Grady, Cynthia. *I Lay My Stitches Down* (4–7). Illus. by Michele Wood. 2012, Eerdmans $17 (978-080285386-8). 34pp. Drawing from the structures and discipline of a quilt, these free-verse poems — each consisting of 10 lines of 10 syllables — explore various aspects of the African American experience. (Rev: BL 2/1/12; HB 1–2/12; LMC 5–6/12; SLJ 1/12) [1.3.2.2]

13416 Graham, Joan B. *Flicker Flash* (3–6). Illus. 1999, Houghton $16.00 (978-0-395-90501-2). 32pp. A collection of verses in geometric forms associated with light, among them a camera, a firefly, a lightbulb, and fireworks. (Rev: BL 1/1–15/00; HBG 3/00; SLJ 12/99*) [811]

13417 *Grandad's Tree: Poems About Families* (2–4). Illus. by Julia Cairns. 2003, Barefoot Books $16.99 (978-1-84148-541-6). 32pp. Twenty poems complemented by watercolor illustrations explore various aspects of family life; poets featured include Eloise Greenfield, Judith Viorst, Christina Rossetti, and Carl Sandburg. (Rev: BL 4/1/03; HBG 10/03) [811.008]

13418 Grandits, John. *Blue Lipstick: Concrete Poems* (5–9). Illus. by author. 2007, Clarion $15.00 (978-0-618-56860-4); paper $5.95 (978-0-618-85132-4). A visually entertaining collection of poems about Jessie, a 9th-grader whose main concerns are clothes, friends, and conflicts with her parents. ALA Notable Children's Book 2008. (Rev: SLJ 7/07) [811]

13419 Greenberg, David T. *The Book of Boys (for Girls) and The Book of Girls (for Boys)* (K–3). Illus. by Joy Allen. 2005, Little, Brown $15.99 (978-0-316-36210-8). 32pp. Rhyming text presents opposing points of view from the two genders on a variety of everyday issues. (Rev: BL 5/15/05) [811]

13420 Greenberg, Jan, ed. *Heart to Heart: New Poems Inspired by Twentieth-Century American Art* (5–10).

2001, Abrams $19.95 (978-0-8109-4386-5). This book contains specially commissioned poems from well-known writers to accompany some of the finest artworks of the 20th century. (Rev: BL 3/15/01*; HBG 10/01; SLJ 4/01*; VOYA 8/01) [811]

13421 Greenfield, Eloise. *The Great Migration: Journey to the North* (2–4). Illus. by Jan Spivey Gilchrist. 2010, HarperCollins $16.99 (978-0-06-125921-0). 32pp. Free verse poems tell the story of the migration of a million African Americans from the rural South to the industrial North between 1915 and 1930, and eloquently express their hopes and regrets. **e** Lexile 730L (Rev: BL 2/1/11*; HB 1–2/11; SLJ 4/11*) [811]

13422 Greenfield, Eloise. *Honey, I Love* (PS–2). Illus. by Jan S. Gilchrist. 2003, HarperCollins LB $18.89 (978-0-06-009124-8). 32pp. An illustrated collection of poems about the loves of a young African American girl (such as her mother, car rides, swimming), first published in 1978. (Rev: BL 2/15/03; HBG 10/03; SLJ 2/03) [811.54]

13423 Greenfield, Eloise. *Honey, I Love, and Other Love Poems* (2–4). Illus. by Diane Dillon and Leo Dillon. 1978, HarperCollins $16.99 (978-0-690-01334-4); paper $6.99 (978-0-06-443097-5). 48pp. Sixteen poems on family love and friendship as experienced by an African American girl.

13424 Greenfield, Eloise. *Nathaniel Talking* (2–5). Illus. by Jan S. Gilchrist. 1988, Writers & Readers $12.95 (978-0-86316-200-8). 32pp. Simple poems on an African American's recollection of childhood. (Rev: BL 12/15/89; HB 9/90; SLJ 8/89) [811]

13425 Greenfield, Eloise. *Under the Sunday Tree* (2–5). Illus. by Amos Ferguson. 1988, HarperCollins paper $10.99 (978-0-06-443257-3). 48pp. Poems of life in the Bahamas. (Rev: BCCB 12/88; HB 11/88)

13426 Greenfield, Eloise. *When the Horses Ride By: Children in the Times of War* (2–4). Illus. by Jan Spivey Gilchrist. 2006, Lee & Low $17.95 (978-1-58430-249-0). 40pp. The poems in this collection celebrate the resiliency of children and their ability to rise above the horrors of war and conflict around the world. (Rev: BL 6/1–15/06; SLJ 9/06) [811]

13427 Grimes, Nikki. *Danitra Brown Leaves Town* (PS–3). Illus. by Floyd Cooper. 2002, HarperCollins LB $16.89 (978-0-688-13156-2). 32pp. Best friends Danitra and Zuri describe their very different summer experiences through letters in this book of free-verse poems. (Rev: BCCB 4/02; BL 2/15/02; HBG 10/02; SLJ 2/02) [811]

13428 Grimes, Nikki. *A Dime a Dozen* (5–8). 1998, Dial $17.99 (978-0-8037-2227-9). Through a series of original poems, the writer explores her childhood: its happy moments, its painful memories — including divorce, foster homes, and parents with drinking and gambling problems — and her search for herself as a teenager. (Rev: BL 12/1/98; HBG 3/99; SLJ 11/98; VOYA 4/99) [811]

13429 Grimes, Nikki. *My Man Blue* (2–5). Illus. by Jerome Lagarrigue. 1999, Dial $16.99 (978-0-8037-2326-9). 32pp. In a series of lyrical poems, Damon describes being a child in Harlem and his friendship for an older man, Blue, whose son was killed on the streets. (Rev: BL 10/15/99; HBG 10/99; SLJ 5/99) [811]

13430 Grimes, Nikki. *Oh, Brother!* (2–4). Illus. by Mike Benny. 2008, Greenwillow $16.99 (978-0-688-17294-7). 32pp. In this collection of poems about a multicultural family, Xavier struggles to adjust to his new, younger stepbrother, Chris. (Rev: BL 12/1/07; SLJ 2/08) [811]

13431 Grimes, Nikki. *A Pocketful of Poems* (K–3). Illus. by Javaka Steptoe. 2001, Clarion $15.00 (978-0-618-93868-1). Poems by a young African American girl named Tiana about urban topics — pigeons, baseball, the moon — are presented in double-page spreads, each traditional poem facing a haiku. (Rev: BL 2/15/01*) [811]

13432 Grimes, Nikki. *Shoe Magic* (2–5). Illus. by Terry Widener. 2000, Orchard LB $17.99 (978-0-531-33286-3). 32pp. In this collection of poems about different kinds of shoes, each shoe embodies a young person's pride in accomplishment and hope for the future. (Rev: BL 9/15/00; HBG 3/01; SLJ 10/00) [811]

13433 Grimes, Nikki. *Stepping Out with Grandma Mac* (4–7). 2001, Orchard paper $16.95 (978-0-531-30320-7). A loving 10-year-old girl describes a very independent grandmother. (Rev: BL 5/15/01*; HBG 10/01; SLJ 7/01) [811.54]

13434 Grimes, Nikki. *Tai Chi Morning: Snapshots of China* (4–8). Illus. by Ed Young. 2004, Cricket $15.95 (978-0-8126-2707-7). Grimes's journal in verse describes her impressions on a tour of China. (Rev: BL 3/1/04; SLJ 5/04) [811]

13435 Grimes, Nikki. *Thanks a Million* (1–3). Illus. by Cozbi A. Cabrera. 2006, Greenwillow $16.99 (978-0-688-17292-3). 32pp. Poetry in various forms celebrates the joys of showing gratitude for everyday kindnesses and pleasures. (Rev: BL 3/15/06; SLJ 3/06) [811]

13436 Grimes, Nikki. *What Is Goodbye?* (4–8). Illus. by Raul Colon. 2004, Hyperion $15.99 (978-0-7868-0778-9). A brother and sister mourn the death of their older brother in poems in alternating voices. (Rev: BL 5/1/04; SLJ 6/04) [811]

13437 Grimes, Nikki. *When Daddy Prays* (PS–K). Illus. by Tim Ladwig. 2002, Eerdmans $16.00 (978-0-8028-5152-9). 32pp. An African American child's impressions of his father's reliance on faith during everyday activities such as gardening, attending a baseball game, and celebrating the New Year. (Rev: BL 3/1/02; HBG 10/02; SLJ 4/02) [811.54]

13438 Gunning, Monica. *America, My New Home* (2–5). Illus. by Ken Condon. 2004, Boyds Mills $16.95 (978-1-59078-057-2). In a series of poems, a young Jamaican girl, newly arrived in the United States, tells about her initial reactions to life in America and her homesickness for her native Caribbean island. (Rev: BL 8/05) [811]

13439 Gunning, Monica. *Under the Breadfruit Tree* (3–6). Illus. 1998, Boyds Mills $15.95 (978-1-56397-539-4). These 38 poems describe the Caribbean peoples and their culture from the standpoint of a young Jamaican

girl. (Rev: BL 2/15/98; HB 7/04; HBG 10/98; SLJ 4/98) [811]

13440 Hague, Michael, sel. *The Book of Fairy Poetry* (K–5). Illus. by Michael Hague. 2004, HarperCollins $19.99 (978-0-688-14004-5). 156pp. An oversize collection of varied works by poets including Walter de la Mare, Sir Walter Scott, Annie R. Rentoul, and Shakespeare. (Rev: SLJ 5/05) [811]

13441 Hale, Glorya, ed. *An Illustrated Treasury of Read-Aloud Poems for Young People: More Than 100 of the World's Best-Loved Poems for Parent and Child to Share* (2–6). Illus. 2003, Black Dog & Leventhal $14.95 (978-1-57912-289-8). 192pp. This thematically organized anthology of poetry — perfect for reading aloud — contains more than 100 poems from such well-known American and English poets as Maya Angelou, Robert Frost, Rudyard Kipling, Henry Wadsworth Longfellow, and William Wordsworth. (Rev: HBG 4/04; SLJ 11/03) [821.008]

13442 Hall, Donald. *The Man Who Lived Alone* (4–7). 1998, Godine paper $11.95 (978-1-56792-050-5). A narrative poem concerning a man who ran away from abuse to see the world and returns in later life.

13443 Hall, Donald, ed. *The Oxford Illustrated Book of American Children's Poems* (PS–4). Illus. 1999, Oxford $25.00 (978-0-19-512373-9). 93pp. From classics like *A Visit from St. Nicholas* to works by Robert Frost, Shel Silverstein, Nikki Giovanni, Karla Kuskin, and others, this is an attractive anthology, perfect for reading aloud. (Rev: BL 1/1–15/00; HBG 3/00; SLJ 1/00) [811]

13444 Harley, Avis. *Fly with Poetry: An ABC of Poetry* (3–5). Illus. by author. 2000, Boyds Mills $13.95 (978-1-56397-798-5). 48pp. A collection of 27 original short poems, generally one for each letter of the alphabet (Y leaves space to write one's own poem). (Rev: SLJ 9/00) [811]

13445 Harrison, David L. *The Alligator in the Closet: And Other Poems Around the House* (2–4). Illus. by Jane Kendall. 2003, Boyds Mills $16.95 (978-1-56397-944-6). 48pp. Common childhood experiences in the home are the focus of these short and accessible poems. (Rev: BL 4/1/03) [811]

13446 Harrison, David L. *Pirates* (3–6). Illus. by Dan Burr. 2008, Boyds Mills $17.95 (978-1-59078-455-6). A realistic look, in poetry, at the lives of pirates; lush paintings accompany the 20 poems. (Rev: BCCB 9/08; SLJ 6/09) [811]

13447 Harrison, David L. *The Purchase of Small Secrets* (3–5). Illus. by Meryl Henderson. 1998, Boyds Mills $14.95 (978-1-56397-054-2). 48pp. This introspective collection of poems touches upon some of the landmark occasions in a boy's journey to maturity, such as fistfights, flirting, and shooting a gun. (Rev: HBG 3/99; SLJ 11/98) [811]

13448 Harrison, David L. *Vacation: We're Going to the Ocean* (2–4). Illus. by Rob Shepperson. 2009, Boyds Mills $16.95 (978-1-59078-568-3). 64pp. A boy narrates in verse the ups and downs of a family visit to the beach. (Rev: BL 5/1/09; SLJ 6/09) [811]

13449 Harrison, Michael, and Christopher Stuart-Clark, comps. *The Oxford Treasury of Time Poems* (4–9). 1999, Oxford LB $25.00 (978-0192761750). From John Milton and William Blake to W. H. Auden and Sylvia Plath, this anthology contains poetry and thoughts about time. (Rev: SLJ 7/99) [811]

13450 Hayford, James. *Knee-Deep in Blazing Snow: Growing Up in Vermont* (4–7). Illus. by Michael McCurdy. 2005, Boyds Mills $17.95 (978-1-59078-338-2). Hayford's simple, quiet poems evoke a simpler country life. (Rev: BL 1/1–15/06; SLJ 11/05) [811]

13451 Heard, Georgia, ed. *The Arrow Finds Its Mark: A Book of Found Poems* (3–6). Illus. by Antoine Guilloppe. 2012, Roaring Brook $16.99 (978-159643665-7). 48pp. An interesting anthology of "found" poems — from lists, advertisement, signs, tweets — that show poetry existing wherever you look. (Rev: BL 4/1/12; LMC 5–6/12; SLJ 4/12) [811]

13452 Heard, Georgia, ed. *Falling down the Page: A Book of List Poems* (3–6). 2009, Roaring Brook $16.95 (978-1-59643-220-8). 48pp. This handsomely designed volume presents 45 list poems by contemporary authors including Jane Yolen, Lee Bennett Hopkins, and Eileen Spinelli. (Rev: BCCB 5/09; BL 3/1/09; SLJ 4/09) [811]

13453 Heidbreder, Robert. *Noisy Poems for a Busy Day* (PS–2). Illus. by Lori Joy Smith. 2012, Kids Can $16.95 (978-1-55453-706-8). 40pp. Thirty poems chronicle the events of a child's day, emphasizing the various noises that crop up. ℮ (Rev: BL 10/15/12; SLJ 10/12) [811]

13454 High, Linda Oatman. *A Humble Life: Plain Poems* (2–4). Illus. by Bill Farnsworth. 2001, Eerdmans $17.00 (978-0-8028-5207-6). 40pp. Graceful poems and evocative paintings depict a year in a Mennonite and Amish county in Pennsylvania. (Rev: BL 12/15/01; HBG 3/02; SLJ 10/01) [811]

13455 Hines, Anna Grossnickle. *Peaceful Pieces: Poems and Quilts About Peace* (2–5). Illus. by author. 2011, Henry Holt $16.99 (978-0-8050-8996-7). 32pp. Beautiful quilts provide a backdrop for poems about peace and tolerance. (Rev: BL 1/1–15/11*; LMC 5–6/11; SLJ 2/1/11) [811]

13456 Hittleman, Carol G., and Daniel R. Hittleman, eds. *A Grand Celebration: Grandparents in Poetry* (3–7). Illus. by Kay Life. 2002, Boyds Mills $16.95 (978-1-56397-901-9). 32pp. This anthology of 26 poems about grandparents represents a variety of cultures, levels of activity, and ages. (Rev: BL 4/1/02; HBG 10/02; SLJ 6/02) [808.819]

13457 Hoberman, Mary Ann. *The Tree That Time Built: A Celebration of Nature, Science, and Imagination* (3–7). 2009, Sourcebooks $19.99 (978-1-4022-2517-8). 224pp. A well-chosen selection of classic and contemporary poems that contemplate various aspects of the natural world. (Rev: BL 12/15/09; LMC 1–2/10; SLJ 1/10) [811]

13458 Hoberman, Mary Ann. *You Read to Me, I'll Read to You: Very Short Scary Tales to Read Together* (PS–2). Illus. by Michael Emberley. 2007, Little, Brown $16.99 (978-0-316-01733-6). 32pp. Not-very-scary poems for two voices feature a variety of monsters and ghouls. (Rev: BL 5/1/07; SLJ 9/07) [811.54]

13459 Hoberman, Mary Ann. *You Read to Me, I'll Read to You: Very Short Stories to Read Together* (2–3). Illus. by Michael Emberley. 2001, Little, Brown $15.95 (978-0-316-36350-1). A collection of short poems designed to be spoken aloud by two readers. (Rev: BL 8/01; HB 11/01; HBG 3/02; SLJ 8/01*) [811.54]

13460 Hoberman, Mary Ann, ed. *Forget-Me-Nots: Poems to Learn by Heart* (3–5). Illus. by Michael Emberley. 2012, Little, Brown $19.99 (978-031612947-3). 144pp. One hundred and twenty-three accessible, memorizable poems are collected in this appealing volume that features some of poetry's biggest names. (Rev: BL 4/1/12; HB 5–6/12; LMC 8–9/12; SLJ 6/1/12) [811]

13461 Hollander, John, ed. *American Poetry* (4–10). Illus. by Sally Wern Comport. Series: Poetry for Young People. 2004, Sterling $14.95 (978-1-4027-0517-5). A colorful celebration of American life, containing 26 poems by well-known poets including Robert Frost, Walt Whitman, Maya Angelou, and Langston Hughes. (Rev: SLJ 8/04) [811]

13462 Hollyer, Belinda, ed. *The Kingfisher Book of Family Poems* (3–5). Illus. by Holly Swain. 2003, Kingfisher $18.95 (978-0-7534-5557-9). 224pp. Poems in this large and varied anthology touch on all aspects of family life and emotions. (Rev: BL 5/1/03; HBG 10/03; SLJ 7/03) [821.008]

13463 Hollyer, Belinda, sel. *She's All That! Poems About Girls* (4–7). Illus. by Susan Hellard. 2006, Kingfisher $14.95 (978-0-7534-5852-5). Poems celebrate today's diverse girls and their interests and concerns, with breezy, hip illustrations. (Rev: SLJ 7/06) [811]

13464 Hooper, Patricia. *Where Do You Sleep, Little One?* (PS–K). Illus. by John Winch. 2001, Holiday House $16.95 (978-0-8234-1668-4). Animals answer the title's question in verse, and gather around a manger to see a sleeping child in this book that features beautiful collage illustrations. (Rev: BL 9/1/01; HBG 3/02; SLJ 9/01) [811]

13465 Hopkins, Lee Bennett. *City I Love* (2–4). Illus. by Marcellus Hall. 2009, Abrams $16.95 (978-0-8109-8327-4). Eighteen poems celebrate the urban wonders of cities around the world. (Rev: BL 3/15/09; SLJ 3/09) [811]

13466 Hopkins, Lee Bennett, ed. *America at War: Poems Selected by Lee Bennett Hopkins* (5–8). Illus. by Stephen Alcorn. 2008, Simon & Schuster $21.99 (978-1-4169-1832-5). A collection of 50-plus poems about American wars from the Revolutionary War to the conflict in Iraq, many centered on the pain felt by soldiers and their families. (Rev: BL 3/1/08; SLJ 3/08) [811]

13467 Hopkins, Lee Bennett, ed. *Behind the Museum Door* (K–3). Illus. by Stacey Dressen-McQueen. 2007,

Abrams $16.95 (978-0-8109-1204-5). 32pp. The poems in this anthology celebrate the sights and sensations found within the walls of a museum. (Rev: BL 4/1/07) [811]

13468 Hopkins, Lee Bennett, ed. *Days to Celebrate: A Full Year of Poetry, People, Holidays, History, Fascinating Facts, and More* (4–7). Illus. by Stephen Alcorn. 2005, Greenwillow LB $19.89 (978-0-06-000766-9). A wide-ranging collection organized by month, each introduced by a calendar page that highlights important dates. (Rev: BL 1/1–15/05; SLJ 1/05) [811]

13469 Hopkins, Lee Bennett, ed. *Good Books, Good Times* (K–3). Illus. by Harvey Stevenson. 1990, HarperCollins LB $16.89 (978-0-06-022528-5). 32pp. Fourteen short poems celebrate book reading. (Rev: BL 11/15/90; HB 1/91; SLJ 10/90*) [811]

13470 Hopkins, Lee Bennett, ed. *Got Geography!* (4–7). Illus. by Philip Stanton. 2006, Greenwillow LB $17.89 (978-0-06-055602-0). Poems celebrate the joys of travel and the maps that guide the way. (Rev: BL 2/1/06; SLJ 5/06) [811]

13471 Hopkins, Lee Bennett, ed. *Hamsters, Shells, and Spelling Bees: School Poems* (PS–3). Illus. by Sachiko Yoshikawa. Series: I Can Read! 2008, HarperCollins $16.99 (978-0-06-074112-9). 48pp. Suitable for beginning readers, these poems about school life were written by well-known poets such as Jane Yolen and Alice Schertle and feature a variety of formats. (Rev: BL 6/1–15/08; SLJ 8/08) [811]

13472 Hopkins, Lee Bennett, ed. *Hand in Hand* (5–8). 1994, Simon & Schuster $21.95 (978-0-671-73315-5). An overview of the history of American poetry, with an interesting selection of poems arranged chronologically. (Rev: BCCB 1/95; BL 1/1/95; SLJ 12/94; VOYA 4/95) [811]

13473 Hopkins, Lee Bennett, ed. *Incredible Inventions* (1–4). Illus. by Julia Sarcone-Roach. 2009, Greenwillow $17.99 (978-0-06-087245-8). 32pp. A collection of 16 diverse poems celebrating inventions from blue jeans to Band-Aids, fig newtons to roller coasters. (Rev: BL 12/1/08; SLJ 2/09) [600]

13474 Hopkins, Lee Bennett, ed. *Lives: Poems About Famous Americans* (3–6). Illus. 1999, HarperCollins $17.99 (978-0-06-027767-3). 40pp. Fourteen poems — 12 new to this collection — celebrate the lives of such famous Americans as Sacagawea, Thomas Edison, Eleanor Roosevelt, and Rosa Parks. (Rev: BL 3/15/99; HBG 10/99; SLJ 6/99) [811.008]

13475 Hopkins, Lee Bennett, ed. *Oh, No! Where Are My Pants?* (PS–2). Illus. by Wolf Erlbruch. 2005, HarperCollins LB $17.89 (978-0-688-17861-1). Simple works by well-known poets about the impact of everyday disasters are paired with lovely illustrations. (Rev: BL 2/15/05; SLJ 2/05) [811]

13476 Hopkins, Lee Bennett, ed. *Surprises* (K–4). Illus. by Megan Lloyd. 1984, HarperCollins paper $3.99 (978-0-06-444105-6). 64pp. A collection of simple poems for beginning readers.

13477 Hopkins, Lee Bennett, ed. *Wonderful Words: Poems About Reading, Writing, Speaking, and Listening* (3–6). Illus. by Karen Barbour. 2004, Simon & Schuster $16.95 (978-0-689-83588-9). 32pp. This colorfully illustrated collection of poems celebrates the wonders of language. (Rev: BL 2/1/04; SLJ 3/04) [811]

13478 Hopkins, Lee Bennett, sel. *My America: A Poetry Atlas of the United States* (3–8). Illus. by Stephen Alcorn. 2000, Simon & Schuster $19.95 (978-0-689-81247-7). 83pp. Seven regions of the United states including Washington, D.C., are explored in this anthology of 51 poems by 40 different poets. (Rev: BCCB 10/00; BL 9/1/03; HBG 3/01; SLJ 9/00) [811]

13479 Hopkins, Lee Bennett, selector. *Amazing Faces* (2–5). Illus. by Chris Soentpiet. 2010, Lee & Low $18.95 (978-1-60060-334-1). 40pp. A collection of multicultural poems celebrating human emotions, with contributions from authors including Joseph Bruchac, Pat Mora, Jane Yolen, and Langston Hughes, and illustrated with rich watercolors. (Rev: BL 4/15/10; LMC 10/10; SLJ 5/10) [811]

13480 Hopkins, Lee Bennett, selector. *I Am the Book* (2–5). Illus. by Yayo. 2011, Holiday House $16.95 (978-0-8234-2119-0). 32pp. Thirteen poems by writers including Naomi Shihab Nye, Jane Yolen, and Karla Kuskin celebrate the pleasures of books and reading. (Rev: BL 3/1/11; SLJ 4/11) [811]

13481 Hubbell, Patricia. *City Kids* (PS–1). Illus. by Teresa Flavin. 2001, Marshall Cavendish $15.95 (978-0-7614-5079-5). 32pp. Simple poems and cheery pictures show kids engaged in such big-city activities as playing stickball, skipping rope, and stretching up like a skyscraper. (Rev: BL 3/1/01; HBG 10/01) [811]

13482 Hudson, Wade, ed. *Pass It On: African-American Poetry for Children* (PS–3). Illus. by Floyd Cooper. 1993, Scholastic $15.95 (978-0-590-45770-5). 32pp. A fine anthology with contributions by such writers as Langston Hughes and Gwendolyn Brooks. (Rev: BL 1/15/93*) [811]

13483 Hughes, Langston. *I, Too, Am America* (K–4). Illus. by Bryan Collier. 2012, Simon & Schuster $16.99 (978-144242008-3). 40pp. Hughes's famous poem is accompanied by inspiring, evocative illustrations; with an illustrator's note about the role of Pullman porters. (Rev: BL 4/1/12; LMC 10/12*; SLJ 6/1/12) [811]

13484 Hughes, Langston. *My People* (PS–3). Illus. by Charles R. Smith Jr. 2009, Atheneum $17.99 (978-1-4169-3540-7). 40pp. With striking sepia portraits of African Americans of all ages, Smith brings new life to Hughes's brief poem. (Rev: BL 2/1/09; LMC 5/09; SLJ 2/09) [811]

13485 Hughes, Langston. *The Negro Speaks of Rivers* (K–3). Illus. by E. B. Lewis. 2009, Disney $16.99 (978-0-7868-1867-9). 32pp. The classic poem about the link between waterways and African American experience is beautifully illustrated. (Rev: BL 11/15/08; LMC 5/09; SLJ 2/09) [811]

13486 Hughes, Ted. *Collected Poems for Children* (4–8). Illus. by Raymond Briggs. 2007, Farrar $18.00 (978-0-374-31429-3). A nicely illustrated collection of 250 British-flavored children's poems by the late Hughes, some funny, some serious, some even scary. (Rev: BL 2/15/07; HB 7–8/07; LMC 11–12/07; SLJ 3/07) [811]

13487 *In Daddy's Arms I Am Tall: African Americans Celebrating Fathers* (3–5). Illus. by Javaka Steptoe. 1997, Lee & Low $15.95 (978-1-880000-31-1). An impressively illustrated book of poems about African American fathers and their many roles. (Rev: BL 2/15/98*; HB 5/05; HBG 3/98; SLJ 2/98) [811]

13488 Iyengar, Malathi Michelle. *Tan to Tamarind: Poems About the Color Brown* (K–3). Illus. by Jamel Akib. 2009, Children's Book Pr. $16.95 (978-0-89239-227-8). 32pp. A poetic celebration of the color brown — in skin tones, foods, nature — with an emphasis on the beauty of diversity. (Rev: BL 3/15/09; SLJ 5/09) [811]

13489 Jackson, Rob. *Weekend Mischief* (2–5). Illus. by Mark Beech. 2010, Boyds Mills $17.95 (978-1-59078-494-5). 32pp. A young boy's weekend is captured in this collection of 20 lively poems full of humor. (Rev: LMC 5–6/10; SLJ 4/1/10) [811]

13490 Janeczko, Paul B. *The Place My Words Are Looking For: What Poets Say About and Through Their Work* (4–9). 1990, Macmillan $17.95 (978-0-02-747671-2). A collection of works by some of the best contemporary poets. (Rev: BCCB 7–8/90; BL 5/1/90; HB 5–6/90*; SLJ 5/90; VOYA 6/90) [811]

13491 Janeczko, Paul B, sel. *A Foot in the Mouth: Poems to Speak, Sing, and Shout* (4–7). Illus. by Chris Raschka. 2009, Candlewick $17.99 (978-0-7636-0663-3). 64pp. Appealing poems ranging from evocative to nonsensical are chosen for their suitability to be read aloud and organized into useful categories. (Rev: BL 2/15/09*; HB 3–4/09; SLJ 3/1/09*; VOYA 2/10) [811]

13492 Janeczko, Paul B., ed. *Dirty Laundry Pile* (3–6). 2001, HarperCollins LB $16.89 (978-0-688-16252-8). 40pp. An anthology of 27 poems told from the standpoint of an object or an animal such as a seashell, a cat, and a tree. (Rev: BL 4/15/01*; HB 7/01*; HBG 10/01; SLJ 8/01) [811]

13493 Janeczko, Paul B., ed. *A Kick in the Head: An Everyday Guide to Poetic Forms* (4–6). Illus. by Chris Raschka. 2005, Candlewick $17.99 (978-0-7636-0662-6). 64pp. Twenty-nine different types of poems (sonnets, ballads, haiku, etc.) are introduced; some funny, some sad, some silly, but all engaging and accompanied by beautiful collages. (Rev: BL 3/15/05; SLJ 3/05) [811.008]

13494 Janeczko, Paul B., sel. *Hey, You! Poems to Skyscrapers, Mosquitoes, and Other Fun Things* (1–4). 2007, HarperCollins $15.99 (978-0-06-052347-3). 40pp. These short poems — which include works by Ogden Nash, Nikki Grimes, Douglas Florian — directly address a diverse range of animals, inanimate objects, and concepts, from the lowly dust mite to black holes. (Rev: BL 4/15/07) [811]

13495 Johnson, Dave, ed. *Movin': Teen Poets Take Voice* (5–10). Illus. by Chris Raschka. 2000, Orchard $15.95 (978-0-531-30258-3); paper $6.95 (978-0-531-07171-7). An anthology of poems by teens who participated in New York Public Library workshops or submitted their work via the Web. (Rev: BL 3/15/00; HBG 10/00; SLJ 5/00; VOYA 6/00) [811]

13496 Johnson, Dinah. *Black Magic* (PS–2). Illus. by R. Gregory Christie. 2010, Henry Holt $15.99 (978-0-8050-7833-6). 32pp. A young African American girl considers all the best things about the color black. (Rev: BL 2/1/10*; LMC 1–2/10; SLJ 2/1/10) [811]

13497 Johnson, Dinah. *Hair Dance!* (K–3). Illus. 2007, Holt $16.95 (978-0-8050-6523-7). 32pp. Color photographs and rhythmic verses celebrate African American hair in diverse styles. (Rev: BCCB 12/07; BL 12/15/07; SLJ 11/07) [811]

13498 Johnston, Tony. *The Ancestors Are Singing* (4–8). Illus. by Karen Barbour. 2003, Farrar $16.00 (978-0-374-30347-1). Mexico's geography, history, and culture are portrayed in poems full of vivid images. (Rev: BL 4/1/03; HBG 10/03; SLJ 4/03; VOYA 10/03) [811]

13499 Johnston, Tony. *My Mexico / México Mío* (K–3). Illus. by F. John Sierra. 1996, Penguin $16.99 (978-0-399-22275-7). 36pp. Mexican scenes are presented in double-page spreads with 18 poems in both English and Spanish. (Rev: BCCB 7–8/96; HB 5/96; SLJ 4/96) [811]

13500 Johnston, Tony. *Voice from Afar: Poems of Peace* (3–6). Illus. by Susan Guevara. 2008, Holiday House $16.95 (978-0-8234-2012-4). Using diverse poetic forms, Johnston reflects on war and peace. (Rev: BL 12/15/08; SLJ 12/08) [811]

13501 Judd, Jennifer Cole, and Laura Wynkoop, eds. *An Eyeball in My Garden: And Other Spine-Tingling Poems* (4–6). Illus. by Johan Olander. 2010, Marshall Cavendish $15.99 (978-0-7614-5655-1). 64pp. Forty-four creepy poems run the gamut from comic to downright eerie in this illustrated collection. ℮ (Rev: LMC 1–2/11; SLJ 11/1/10) [811]

13502 Katz, Bobbi. *Once Around the Sun* (K–2). Illus. by LeUyen Pham. 2006, Harcourt $16.00 (978-0-15-216397-6). 40pp. Simple, happy poems celebrate the highlights of each month in an urban neighborhood. (Rev: BL 4/15/06; SLJ 5/06) [811]

13503 Katz, Bobbi. *Trailblazers: Poems of Exploration* (3–8). Illus. by Carin Berger. 2007, HarperCollins $18.99 (978-0-688-16533-8). 208pp. Poems about 120 explorers throughout the world and across the ages will arouse new interest in these figures. (Rev: SLJ 7/07)

13504 Katz, Bobbi, ed. *Pocket Poems* (PS–1). Illus. by Marylin Hafner. 2004, Dutton $15.99 (978-0-525-47172-1). This collection of playful short poems is organized into chronological periods throughout the day. Also use *More Pocket Poems* (2009). (Rev: BL 2/1/04; SLJ 2/04) [811]

13505 Katz, Susan. *Mrs. Brown on Exhibit and Other Museum Poems* (2–4). Illus. by R. W. Alley. 2002, Simon & Schuster $16.95 (978-0-689-82970-3). 40pp. A collection of poems about Mrs. Brown's class field trips to museums and the many discoveries they find there. (Rev: BL 6/1–15/02; HBG 3/03; SLJ 8/02) [811]

13506 Katz, Susan. *The President's Stuck in the Bathtub: Poems About the Presidents* (2–5). Illus. by Robert Neubecker. 2012, Clarion $17.99 (978-054718221-6). 64pp. Interesting and often comic bits of presidential trivia are collected in this appealing collection of poems with cartoon illustrations. **e** (Rev: BL 1/1/12; LMC 10/12; SLJ 2/12) [811]

13507 Kennedy, Caroline. *Poems to Learn by Heart* (4–8). Illus. by Jon J Muth. 2013, Disney/Hyperion $19.99 (978-142310805-4). 192pp. A wide-ranging collection of more than 100 poems organized into chapters such as "poems about the self," "poems about family," and "poems about friendship and love." ALA Notable Children's Book. (Rev: BLO 4/1/13*; SLJ 6/13*; VOYA 10/13) [811]

13508 Kennedy, Caroline, ed. *A Family of Poems: My Favorite Poetry for Children* (4–7). Illus. by Jon J Muth. 2005, Hyperion $19.95 (978-0-7868-5111-9). This collection of poems for children includes a number of Kennedy family favorites. (Rev: BL 10/15/05; SLJ 12/05*) [811]

13509 Kennedy, X. J., and Dorothy M. Kennedy, eds. *Talking Like the Rain: A First Book of Poems* (PS–3). Illus. by Jane Dyer. 1992, Little, Brown $19.95 (978-0-316-48889-1). This is a cheerful collection of 100 well-illustrated poems in a variety of subjects and moods. (Rev: BCCB 7–8/92; BL 3/15/92; HB 7/92; SLJ 6/92) [821]

13510 Kipling, Rudyard. *If: A Father's Advice to His Son* (4–6). Photos by Charles R. Smith Jr. 2007, Simon & Schuster $14.99 (978-0-689-87799-5). Kipling's classic poem is given new life in this attractive volume full of photographs of boys and young men competing in a wide array of athletic events. (Rev: SLJ 2/07) [811]

13511 Lansky, Bruce, ed. *No More Homework! No More Tests! Kids' Favorite Funny School Poems* (2–6). Illus. 1997, Meadowbrook LB $8.00 (978-0-671-57702-5). 80pp. Humorous, often outrageous, poems that deal with real and fantastic school situations. (Rev: BL 9/15/97) [811]

13512 Larios, Julie. *Imaginary Menagerie: A Book of Curious Creatures* (K–3). Illus. by Julie Paschkis. 2008, Harcourt $16.00 (978-0-15-206325-2). 32pp. Gargoyles, trolls, dragons, and centaurs are among the creatures in these short, rhythmic poems accompanied by folk paintings that extend the words. (Rev: BL 3/15/08; SLJ 6/08) [811]

13513 Lawson, JonArno. *Black Stars in a White Night Sky* (4–7). Illus. by Sherwin Tjia. 2008, Boyds Mills $16.95 (978-1-59078-521-8). An eclectic collection of poems — some silly, some serious, and all full of unusual turns of phrase and wordplay. (Rev: BL 2/15/08; SLJ 4/08) [811]

13514 Lawson, JonArno. *Think Again* (5–8). Illus. by Julie Morstad. 2010, Kids Can $16.95 (978-1-55453-423-

4). 64pp. Forty-eight poems look at the uncertainty and poignancy of first love. (Rev: BL 3/15/10; LMC 8–9/10) [811]

13515 Lear, Edward. *The Owl and the Pussycat* (5–10). Illus. by Stephane Jorisch. Series: Visions in Poetry. 2007, Kids Can $16.95 (978-1-55337-828-0); paper $9.95 (978-1-55453-232-2). A charmingly illustrated version of Lear's classic poem using watercolor and ink. (Rev: SLJ 1/08)

13516 Lee, Claudia M., ed. *Messengers of Rain and Other Poems from Latin America* (2–6). Illus. by Rafael Yockteng. 2002, Groundwood $18.95 (978-0-88899-470-7). 80pp. An anthology of more than 60 poems on a wide range of topics, translated from Spanish, by well-known and less-familiar writers. (Rev: SLJ 1/03) [811]

13517 Lesynski, Loris. *Dirty Dog Boogie* (2–5). Illus. by author. 1999, Annick LB $16.95 (978-1-55037-572-5); paper $6.95 (978-1-55037-573-2). 32pp. A joyous collection of poems that are filled with musical rhythms and quirky language. (Rev: HBG 10/99; SLJ 7/99) [811]

13518 Lesynski, Loris. *Zigzag: Zoems for Zindergarten* (PS–K). Illus. by author. 2004, Annick LB $19.95 (978-1-55037-875-7); paper $8.95 (978-1-55037-882-5). 32pp. Great for reading aloud, thse poems feature nonsense verse and bouncy rhythms. (Rev: BL 12/1/04; SLJ 1/05) [811]

13519 Levin, Jonathan, ed. *Walt Whitman: Poetry for Young People* (5–9). 1997, Sterling $14.95 (978-0-8069-9530-4). After a brief biographical sketch, this volume contains 26 poems and excerpts from longer poems, each introduced with an analysis. (Rev: HBG 3/98; SLJ 11/97) [811]

13520 Lewis, Claudia. *Long Ago in Oregon* (3–7). Illus. by Joel Fontaine. 1987, HarperCollins $11.95 (978-0-06-023839-1). Short poems that recall the nostalgia of childhood in Oregon in the early 1900s. (Rev: BCCB 5/87; BL 7/87; SLJ 9/87)

13521 Lewis, J. Patrick. *Blackbeard: The Pirate King* (3–5). 2006, National Geographic $16.95 (978-0-7922-5585-7). 26pp. Poems about the infamous pirate are accompanied by diverse artwork. (Rev: BL 5/1/06; SLJ 12/06) [811]

13522 Lewis, J. Patrick. *Freedom Like Sunlight: Praisesongs for Black Americans* (5–12). 2000, Creative $17.95 (978-1-56846-163-2). This collection of original poems pays tribute to such important African Americans as Sojourner Truth, Arthur Ashe, Rosa Parks, Marian Anderson, Malcolm X, and Langston Hughes. (Rev: BL 9/15/00*; HBG 3/01; SLJ 12/00) [811]

13523 Lewis, J. Patrick. *Heroes and She-roes: Poems of Amazing and Everyday Heroes* (4–7). Illus. by Jim Cooke. 2005, Dial $16.99 (978-0-8037-2925-4). Helen Keller, Rosa Parks, and Gandhi are among the courageous individuals featured in this collection of poems. (Rev: BL 1/1–15/05; SLJ 3/05) [811]

13524 Lewis, J. Patrick. *The House* (4–7). Illus. by Roberto Innocenti. 2009, Creative Education $19.95 (978-1-56846-201-1). 64pp. This unusual picture book for older children uses poetry and arresting images to present the passing of time from the perspective of a house. (Rev: BL 12/15/09; LMC 3–4/10; SLJ 1/10) [811]

13525 Lewis, J. Patrick. *Please Bury Me in the Library* (2–4). Illus. by Kyle M. Stone. 2005, Harcourt $16.00 (978-0-15-216387-7). 32pp. Sixteen original poems celebrate the joys of reading. (Rev: BL 2/15/05; SLJ 6/05) [811]

13526 Lewis, J. Patrick. *Skywriting: Poems to Fly* (4–7). Illus. by Laszlo Kubinyi. 2010, Creative Editions $17.95 (978-156846203-5). 32pp. This anthology of poems celebrates the adventure of flight, examining scenes in history from the myth of Icarus to the modern day. (Rev: BL 11/15/10; LMC 1–2/11; SLJ 11/1/10) [811.54]

13527 Lewis, J. Patrick. *The Underwear Salesman: And Other Jobs for Better or Verse* (2–5). Illus. by Serge Bloch. 2009, Atheneum $16.99 (978-0-689-85325-8). 64pp. Nearly 50 poems full of wordplay look at a variety of occupations. (Rev: BL 3/1/09; SLJ 4/09) [811]

13528 Lewis, J. Patrick. *Vherses: A Celebration of Outstanding Women* (4–7). Illus. by Mark Summers. 2005, Creative $18.95 (978-1-56846-185-4). The accomplishments of 14 notable and diverse women — including Emily Dickinson, Georgia O'Keeffe, and Venus and Serena Williams — are celebrated in an appealing blend of poetry and art. (Rev: BL 12/15/05) [811]

13529 Lewis, J. Patrick. *When Thunder Comes: Poems for Civil Rights Leaders* (4–7). Illus. by Jim Burke. 2013, Chronicle $16.99 (978-1-4521-0119-4). 44pp. With rich and diverse images this collection of poems introduces 17 civil rights leaders from countries around the world. (Rev: BL 2/15/13*; SLJ 4/13) [811]

13530 Lewis, J. Patrick. *A World of Wonders: Geographic Travels in Verse and Rhyme* (3–5). Illus. by Alison Jay. 2002, Dial $16.99 (978-0-8037-2579-9). 40pp. Geographic terminology and facts are skillfully woven into verse in this attractive volume that touches on topics including seas, deserts, the poles, and the equator. (Rev: BL 3/15/02; HB 3/02; HBG 10/02; SLJ 4/02) [811]

13531 Lewis, J. Patrick. *The World's Greatest Poems* (1–4). Illus. by Keith Graves. 2008, Chronicle $16.99 (978-0-8118-5130-5). 33pp. Twenty-five nicely illustrated, diverse poems celebrate achievements documented in the *Guinness Book of Record,* chosen for their quirky content. (Rev: HB 7/08; SLJ 4/08)

13532 Lewis, J. Patrick, and Douglas Florian. *Poem-Mobiles: Crazy Car Poems* (K–3). Illus. by Jeremy Holmes. 2014, Random House $17.99 (978-037586690-6). 40pp. A collection of quirky poems about cars that provide humor and inventive language. (Rev: BL 12/15/13; LMC 10/14*; SLJ 2/14) [811]

13533 Lewis, J. Patrick, and Paul B. Janeczko. *Birds on a Wire* (2–4). Illus. by Gary Lippincott. 2008, Boyds Mills $17.95 (978-1-59078-383-2). 32pp. Realistic illustrations accompany this renga, a Japanese form of poetry in which one author writes a three-line verse and a second author writes the two lines following. (Rev: BCCB 9/08; BL 8/08; LMC 1/09) [811]

13534 Lewis, J. Patrick, and Rebecca Kai Dotlich. *Castles: Old Stone Poems* (4–7). Illus. by Dan Burr. 2006, Boyds Mills $18.95 (978-1-59078-380-1). The poems in this attractive collection celebrate castles of past and present. (Rev: BL 10/1/06; SLJ 10/06) [811]

13535 Lillegard, Dee. *Go!* (PS). Illus. 2006, Knopf $14.95 (978-0-375-82387-9). 32pp. The short rhyming poems in this collection celebrate motion and things that move, ranging from skateboards and lawnmowers to garbage trucks and school buses. (Rev: BL 11/1/06; SLJ 12/06) [811]

13536 Lindbergh, Reeve. *On Morning Wings* (PS–1). Illus. by Holly Meade. 2002, Candlewick $15.99 (978-0-7636-1106-4). A poem, based on Psalm 139 and illustrated in watercolors, thanking God for His loving care. (Rev: BL 9/15/02; HBG 3/03; SLJ 12/02)

13537 Little, Jean. *I Gave My Mom a Castle* (4–7). Illus. by Kady MacDonald Denton. 2004, Orca paper $7.95 (978-1-55143-253-3). Gifts — expected and unexpected, rewarding and trying — are the theme of this diverse collection of prose poems. (Rev: BL 3/1/04; SLJ 4/04) [811]

13538 Longfellow, Henry Wadsworth. *The Children's Hour* (K–2). Illus. by Glenna Lang. 1993, Godine $17.95 (978-0-87923-971-8). 32pp. The classic poem is illustrated with paintings depicting Longfellow spending time with his children. (Rev: BL 11/15/93) [811]

13539 Longfellow, Henry Wadsworth. *The Children's Own Longfellow* (5–8). 1908, Houghton Mifflin $20.00 (978-0-395-06889-2). Eight selections from the best-known and best-loved of Longfellow's poems. (Rev: BL 2/15/04*; SLJ 3/04)

13540 Longfellow, Henry Wadsworth. *Hiawatha and Megissogwon* (4–7). Illus. by Jeffrey Thompson. 2001, National Geographic $16.95 (978-0-7922-6676-1). Artwork with an authentic Native American feel illustrates Hiawatha's exciting adventures in the "Pearl-Feather" section of Longfellow's epic poem. (Rev: BCCB 3/02; BL 11/15/01; HBG 3/02; SLJ 9/01) [811]

13541 Longfellow, Henry Wadsworth. *The Midnight Ride of Paul Revere* (2–4). Illus. by Christopher Bing. 2001, Handprint $17.95 (978-1-929766-13-0). 40pp. Bing's design juxtaposes historical objects, watercolors, and scratchboard work to great effect in this rendering of Longfellow's famous poem that also includes maps and notes. (Rev: BCCB 2/02; BL 12/15/01; HB 3/02; HBG 10/02; SLJ 12/01*) [811]

13542 Longfellow, Henry Wadsworth. *Paul Revere's Ride* (2–5). Illus. by Monica Vachula. 2003, Boyds Mills $16.95 (978-1-56397-799-2). 32pp. Longfellow's famous poem, with attractive illustrations that show background scenery. (Rev: BL 2/1/03; HBG 10/03; SLJ 5/03) [811]

13543 Longfellow, Henry Wadsworth. *Paul Revere's Ride: The Landlord's Tale* (2–5). Illus. by Charles Santore. 2003, HarperCollins LB $17.89 (978-0-06-623747-3). 40pp. The poem about Revere's famous ride is accompanied here by dramatic illustrations that convey a sense of urgency. (Rev: BL 2/1/03; HBG 10/03; SLJ 3/03) [811]

13544 Longfellow, Henry Wadsworth. *The Song of Hiawatha* (3–10). Illus. by Margaret Early. 2003, Handprint $16.95 (978-1-59354-002-9). A beautifully illustrated edition of the epic poem that traces the eventful life of the Native American leader. (Rev: HBG 4/04; SLJ 1/04) [811]

13545 Lupton, Hugh, ed. *The Songs of Birds: Stories and Poems from Many Cultures* (4–7). 2000, Barefoot $19.95 (978-1-84148-045-9). A beautifully illustrated collection of stories (mostly creation myths) and poems about birds culled from a wide range of cultures. (Rev: BL 3/15/00; SLJ 9/00) [808.819]

13546 McCord, David. *All Day Long: Fifty Rhymes of the Never Was and Always Is* (4–7). Illus. by Henry B. Kane. 1975, Little, Brown paper $6.95 (978-0-316-55532-6). A collection of poems on a variety of subjects, chiefly times that are important in childhood.

13547 McCord, David. *One at a Time: His Collected Poems for the Young* (3–8). Illus. by Henry B. Kane. 1986, Little, Brown $18.95 (978-0-316-55516-6). All seven of the poet's anthologies in one handsome volume.

13548 McGough, Roger, sel. *The Kingfisher Book of Funny Poems* (4–7). Illus. by Caroline Holden. 2002, Kingfisher $19.00 (978-0-7534-5480-0). An anthology of poems arranged by theme that includes many by familiar names such as Ogden Nash, Lewis Carroll, and Shel Silverstein. (Rev: SLJ 6/02) [811]

13549 Martin, Bill, Jr., and Michael Sampson, eds. *The Bill Martin Jr. Big Book of Poetry* (PS–3). Illus. 2008, Simon & Schuster $21.00 (978-1-4169-3971-9). 176pp. This good-looking collection contains nearly 200 illustrated poems from mainly well-known poets. (Rev: BL 11/15/08; HB 1/09; LMC 3/09; SLJ 12/08) [811]

13550 Marzollo, Jean. *I Love You: A Rebus Poem* (PS). Illus. by Suse MacDonald. 2000, Scholastic paper $7.95 (978-0-590-37656-3). 40pp. A rebus puzzle book is used to present a series of simple poems about loving one another. (Rev: BL 12/15/99; HBG 10/00; SLJ 2/00) [811.54]

13551 Mavor, Salley, ed. *You and Me: Poems of Friendship* (PS–3). Illus. 1997, Orchard LB $17.99 (978-0-531-33045-6). 32pp. An anthology of 19 enjoyable poems that celebrate the joys and problems that come with friendships. (Rev: BL 7/97; HBG 3/98; SLJ 9/97) [811]

13552 Maynard, John, ed. *Alfred, Lord Tennyson* (5–8). Illus. by Allen Garns. Series: Poetry for Young People. 2004, Sterling $14.95 (978-0-8069-6612-0). This large-format introduction to Tennyson's works includes an informative profile of the poet, selections accompanied by notes, and rich illustrations. (Rev: BL 2/15/04) [821]

13553 Maynard, John, ed. *Poetry for Young People: William Blake* (4–6). Illus. by Alessandra Cimatoribus. 2007, Sterling $14.95 (978-0-8069-3647-5). 48pp. A selection of Blake's poems follow a brief biography and a review of his literary importance. (Rev: BL 4/1/07) [811]

13554 Medina, Jane. *The Dream on Blanca's Wall / El sueño pegado en la pared de Blanca: Poems in English and Spanish / Poemas en ingles y espanol* (4–6). Illus. by Robert Casilla. 2004, Boyds Mills $16.95 (978-1-56397-740-4); paper $9.95 (978-1-59078-264-4). Sixth-grader Blanca has wanted to be a teacher since the second grade; poems in English and Spanish describe her dreams and the looming personal and economic challenges. (Rev: SLJ 4/04) [811]

13555 Medina, Jane. *My Name Is Jorge: On Both Sides of the River* (3–7). Illus. by Fabricio Vandenbroeck. 1999, Boyds Mills $15.95 (978-1-56397-811-1). An immigrant boy from Mexico describes his experiences in a series of 27 poems in English and Spanish. (Rev: HBG 3/00; SLJ 2/00) [811]

13556 Medina, Tony. *DeShawn Days* (2–5). Illus. by R. Gregory Christie. 2001, Lee & Low $16.95 (978-1-58430-022-9). DeShawn is a young African American boy who describes in verse his home in the projects, the constant sound of sirens, the grim news on TV, his friends, and the music they enjoy. (Rev: HBG 10/01; SLJ 7/01*) [811]

13557 Medina, Tony. *Love to Langston* (3–6). Illus. by R. Gregory Christie. 2002, Lee & Low $16.95 (978-1-58430-041-0). A celebration in poetry of the life and work of poet Langston Hughes, with biographical notes appended. (Rev: BCCB 3/02; BL 2/15/02; HBG 10/02; SLJ 3/02) [811]

13558 Merchant, Natalie. *Leave Your Sleep: A Collection of Classic Children's Poetry* (PS–3). Illus. by Barbara McClintock. 2012, Farrar $24.99 (978-0-374-34368-2). 48pp. Nineteen classic poems are brought to life in detailed paintings and music (a CD is included). (Rev: BL 10/15/12; HB 1–2/13; SLJ 1/13*) [808.81]

13559 Micklos, John, comp. *Grandparent Poems* (K–4). Illus. by Layne Johnson. 2004, Boyds Mills $15.95 (978-1-56397-900-2). 32pp. A collection of more than 20 poems by contemporary poets about grandparents and the special relationships between generations. (Rev: SLJ 3/04) [811]

13560 Micklos, John, ed. *Daddy Poems* (3–5). Illus. 2000, Boyds Mills $15.95 (978-1-56397-735-0). 32pp. This anthology of poems about dads and how they interact with their children contains the work of both well-known and less-well-known poets. (Rev: BL 8/00; HBG 10/00; SLJ 10/00) [811]

13561 Micklos, John, ed. *Mommy Poems* (K–3). Illus. by Lori McElrath-Eslick. 2001, Boyds Mills $16.95 (978-1-56397-849-4); paper $9.95 (978-1-56397-908-8). 32pp. An anthology of 18 poems about mothers by such writers as Gary Soto and Nikki Giovanni. (Rev: BL 3/15/01; HBG 10/01) [811]

13562 Micklos, John, Jr. *No Boys Allowed: Poems About Brothers and Sisters* (PS–3). Illus. by Kathleen O'Malley. 2006, Boyds Mills $15.95 (978-1-59078-051-0). 31pp. A collection of poems that address with love and humor the sometimes-tricky relationship between brothers and sisters. (Rev: SLJ 5/06) [811]

13563 Miller, Kate. *Poems in Black and White* (4–7). 2007, Boyds Mills $17.95 (978-1-59078-412-9). The poems and striking artwork in this slim volume explore images in black and white. (Rev: BL 4/1/07; SLJ 5/07) [811]

13564 Mitchell, Stephen. *The Wishing Bone and Other Poems* (3–6). Illus. by Tom Pohrt. 2003, Candlewick $16.99 (978-0-7636-1118-7). 56pp. Whimsical illustrations accompany these humorous and thought-provoking poems. (Rev: BL 4/1/03; HB 7/03; HBG 10/03; SLJ 5/03) [811]

13565 Mitton, Tony. *Rumble, Roar, Dinosaur! More Prehistoric Poems with Lift-the-Flap Surprises!* (PS–2). Illus. by Lynne Chapman. 2010, Kingfisher $12.99 (978-0-7534-1932-8). Unpaged. This interactive book of poems combines playful poems with appealing illustrations. (Rev: SLJ 5/1/10) [811]

13566 Moore, Lilian. *Beware, Take Care: Fun and Spooky Poems* (PS–1). Illus. by Howard Fine. 2006, Holt $16.95 (978-0-8050-6917-4). Fifteen creepy poems about ghosts and monsters were first published more than 30 years ago. (Rev: BL 9/1/06; SLJ 10/06) [811]

13567 Mora, Pat. *Confetti* (1–4). Illus. by Enrique O. Sánchez. 1996, Lee & Low $15.95 (978-1-880000-25-0). 32pp. A series of poems that mingle Spanish expressions with basic English. (Rev: BL 11/15/96; SLJ 11/96) [811]

13568 Mora, Pat. *Join Hands* (K–3). Illus. by George Ancona. 2008, Charlesbridge $15.95 (978-1-58089-202-5); paper $6.95 (978-1-58089-203-2). 32pp. Celebrating creativity, this imaginative poem uses the Malaysian *pantoum* format and is illustrated with photographs of children in action. (Rev: BLO 7/30/08) [811]

13569 Mora, Pat. *Yum! Mmmm! Que rico!* (1–4). Illus. by Rafael Lopez. 2007, Lee & Low $16.95 (978-1-58430-271-1). Haiku poems introduce readers to foods native to the Americas including blueberry, papaya, vanilla, and corn. (Rev: BCCB 12/07; BL 12/1/07; LMC 1/08; SLJ 9/07) [811]

13570 Mora, Pat, ed. *Love to Mama: A Tribute to Mothers* (PS–4). Illus. by Paula Barragán. 2001, Lee & Low $16.95 (978-1-58430-019-9). 32pp. A celebration of Latina mothers and grandmothers that ends with a glossary and notes about the poets. (Rev: BL 5/1/01; HB 7/01; HBG 10/01; SLJ 4/01*) [811]

13571 Mordhorst, Heidi. *Squeeze: Poems from a Juicy Universe* (2–4). Illus. by Jesse Torrey. 2005, Boyds Mills $16.95 (978-1-59078-292-7). 32pp. Twenty-four free-form poems and color photographs celebrates the experiences that are the essence of childhood. (Rev: BL 10/15/05; SLJ 3/06) [811]

13572 Morgenstern, Constance. *Waking Day* (4–7). 2006, North Word $17.95 (978-1-55971-919-3). In a picture book for older readers, Morgenstern melds Impressionist works with lines from her own poetry. (Rev: BL 2/15/06) [811]

13573 Morninghouse, Sundaira. *Nightfeathers* (PS–K). Illus. by Jody Kim. 1990, Open Hand $9.95 (978-0-940880-27-6); paper $4.95 (978-0-940880-28-3). 32pp. In 24 short poems, a typical day in the life of an African American child is portrayed. (Rev: BL 6/1/90) [811]

13574 Morris, Jackie, comp. *The Barefoot Book of Classic Poems* (3–9). Illus. by Jackie Morris. 2006, Barefoot Books $19.99 (978-1-905236-56-5). 128pp. A handsomely illustrated anthology of nearly 75 classic poems, with works by such well-known writers as Robert Frost, John Donne, Robert Louis Stevenson, and William Wordsworth. (Rev: SLJ 1/07) [811]

13575 Moss, Jeff. *Bone Poems* (3–5). Illus. by Tom Leigh. 1997, Workman $14.95 (978-0-7611-0884-9). 78pp. A group of rhymes that explore facts about dinosaurs and make paleontology fun. (Rev: HBG 3/98; SLJ 12/97*) [811]

13576 Moss, Jeff. *The Butterfly Jar* (2–5). Illus. by Chris L. Demarest. 1989, Bantam $17.95 (978-0-553-05704-1). Upbeat poetry, including the silly and the serious. (Rev: BL 2/1/90; SLJ 7/90) [811]

13577 Mozelle, Shirley. *The Kitchen Talks* (PS–2). Illus. by Petra Mathers. 2006, Holt $15.95 (978-0-8050-7143-6). 32pp. This collection of short poems — often involving riddles — reveals the innermost thoughts of inanimate objects from the kitchen. (Rev: BL 3/15/06; SLJ 4/06) [811]

13578 Mullins, Tom, ed. *Running Lightly . . . : Poems for Young People* (4–9). 1998, Mercier paper $12.95 (978-1-85342-193-8). A charming collection of old songs and ballads, nonsense rhymes, and lyrics. (Rev: BL 5/15/98; SLJ 7/98) [811]

13579 Muse, Daphne, ed. *The Entrance Place of Wonders: Poems of the Harlem Renaissance* (3–5). Illus. by Charlotte Riley-Webb. 2006, Abrams $16.95 (978-0-8109-5997-2). 32pp. Lively oil paintings illustrate this collection of 20 child-friendly poems from the Harlem Renaissance. (Rev: BL 2/1/06; SLJ 3/06) [811]

13580 Myers, Walter Dean. *Angel to Angel: A Mother's Gift of Love* (4–8). 1998, HarperCollins LB $15.89 (978-0-06-027722-2). A photo/poetry montage with 10 distinctly styled poems and photographs focusing on African American mothers and children, and reflecting the relationship between words and pictures. (Rev: BL 2/15/98; HBG 10/98; SLJ 6/98) [811]

13581 Myers, Walter Dean. *Blues Journey* (5–8). Illus. by Christopher Myers. 2003, Holiday $18.95 (978-0-8234-1613-4). Poems reflecting the soulfulness of blues music, accompanied by illustrations. (Rev: BL 2/15/03; HB 5–6/03; HBG 10/03; SLJ 4/03*; VOYA 4/03) [811]

13582 Myers, Walter Dean. *Jazz* (3–5). Illus. by Christopher Myers. 2006, Holiday $18.95 (978-0-8234-1545-8). 48pp. This vibrant blend of poetry and artwork celebrates jazz and the musicians who helped to shape this uniquely American brand of music. (Rev: BCCB 2/07; BL 9/1/06; HBG 4/07; SLJ 9/06) [811]

13583 Myers, Walter Dean, and Christopher Myers. *We Are America: A Tribute from the Heart* (4–8). 2011, HarperCollins $16.99 (978-0-06-052308-4). 40pp. Fourteen short, free-verse poems explore key events and figures in American history ranging from Tecumseh and Abraham Lincoln to Jimi Hendrix and Barbara Jordan. (Rev: BL 5/1/11; SLJ 5/11) [811]

13584 Nelson, Marilyn. *Sweethearts of Rhythm: The Story of the Greatest All-Girl Swing Band in the World* (5–8). Illus. by Jerry Pinkney. 2009, Dial $21.99 (978-0-8037-3187-5). Unpaged. Nelson offers up accessible, rhythmic poems that pay homage to an all-female New Orleans jazz band — the Sweethearts of Rhythm — from the 1940s in this lively, beautifully illustrated book. (Rev: BL 10/15/09; HB 11–12/09; LMC 11–12/09; SLJ 10/09; VOYA 12/09) [811]

13585 New, William. *The Year I Was Grounded* (4–7). Illus. by Robert Kakegamic. 2009, Tradewind paper $12.95 (978-1-896580-35-7). 104pp. Stuck at home, Geordie finds plenty of time to write in his journal, recording events and thoughts in a variety of poetic forms. (Rev: BL 5/1/09; SLJ 7/09) [811]

13586 Nicholls, Judith, ed. *Someone I Like: Poems About People* (3–5). Illus. 2000, Barefoot Books $16.95 (978-1-84148-004-6). 40pp. This anthology of 26 poems explores children's feelings for family members and friends. (Rev: BL 4/1/00; SLJ 7/00) [808.819]

13587 Nikola-Lisa, W. *Bein' with You This Way* (PS–2). Illus. by Michael Bryant. 1994, Lee & Low $15.95 (978-1-880000-05-2). 32pp. A rap poem led by an African American girl talks about racial tolerance. (Rev: BL 7/94; SLJ 7/94) [811]

13588 Norman, Lissette. *My Feet Are Laughing* (K–3). Illus. by Frank Morrison. 2006, Farrar $16.00 (978-0-374-35096-3). 32pp. In this collection of 16 energetic free-verse poems with evocative illustrations, a young Dominican American girl describes her family and life in New York City's Harlem. (Rev: BL 4/1/06; SLJ 5/06) [811]

13589 Oliver, Lin. *Little Poems for Tiny Ears* (PS). Illus. by Tomie dePaola. 2014, Penguin $16.99 (978-039916605-1). 32pp. Using cheerful pastel images and highly readable poems, Oliver and dePaola create an engaging world of childhood experiences. (Rev: BL 11/15/13*; SLJ 2/14) [811]

13590 *Once Upon a Poem: Favorite Poems That Tell Stories* (4–7). 2004, Scholastic $18.95 (978-0-439-65108-0). This appealing collection of 15 narrative poems includes offerings from Lewis Carroll, Longfellow, C. S. Lewis, Roald Dahl, Edward Lear, and Robert Service. (Rev: BL 1/1–15/05; SLJ 1/05) [811]

13591 O'Neill, Mary. *Hailstones and Halibut Bones* (PS–3). Illus. by Leonard Weisgard. 1973, Doubleday paper $8.95 (978-0-385-41078-6). Imaginative poems about color. (Rev: BL 3/1/04)

13592 Paraskevas, Betty. *Junior Kroll* (2–4). Illus. by Michael Paraskevas. 1993, Harcourt $13.95 (978-0-15-241497-9). Fifteen poems about a mischievous boy and his adventures. (Rev: BCCB 5/93; BL 3/1/04; SLJ 6/93) [822]

13593 Park, Linda Sue. *Tap Dancing on the Roof: Sijo (Poems)* (3–6). Illus. by Istvan Banyai. 2007, Clarion $16.00 (978-0-618-23483-7). 48pp. Using a traditional form of poetry from Korea, *sijo*, Park presents images of everyday experiences such as lunchtime and school while also encouraging readers to experiment with their own *sijo*. (Rev: BCCB 11/07; BL 12/1/07; HB 1/08; SLJ 11/07) [811]

13594 Paschen, Elise, ed. *Poetry Speaks to Children* (3–5). Illus. 2005, Sourcebooks $19.95 (978-1-4022-0329-9). 112pp. A broad selection of poems (nearly 100) representing many genres and poets, with an accompanying CD. (Rev: BL 12/15/05; SLJ 1/06) [811]

13595 Pearson, Susan, ed. *The Drowsy Hours: Poems for Bedtime* (PS–1). Illus. by Peter Malone. 2002, HarperCollins LB $16.89 (978-0-06-029421-2). 40pp. This thoughtful anthology captures the bedtime mood perfectly, but will be appreciated any time of the day. (Rev: BL 10/15/02; HBG 10/02; SLJ 6/02) [811.008]

13596 Perdomo, Willie. *Visiting Langston* (2–4). Illus. by Bryan Collier. 2002, Holt $15.95 (978-0-8050-6744-6). A young girl anticipates in poetry a visit to poet Langston Hughes's house in Harlem. (Rev: BCCB 3/02; BL 2/15/02; HBG 10/02; SLJ 4/02) [811]

13597 Philip, Neil, ed. *The Fish Is Me: Bathtime Rhymes* (PS). Illus. by Claire Henley. 2002, Clarion $16.00 (978-0-618-15939-0). 28pp. These 18 rhymes are drawn from poets from several countries, and will immediately appeal to children, whether they enjoy baths or not. (Rev: BL 11/1/02; HBG 3/03; SLJ 8/02) [811.008]

13598 Philip, Neil, ed. *Hot Potato: Mealtime Rhymes* (PS–1). Illus. by Claire Henley. 2004, Clarion $16.00 (978-0-618-31554-3). 32pp. The bouncy rhyming poems in this vividly illustrated picture-book collection focus on the sounds and rhythms of eating. (Rev: BL 4/15/04; SLJ 5/04) [811]

13599 Philip, Neil, ed. *Songs Are Thoughts: Poems of the Inuit* (K–4). Illus. by Maryclare Foa. 1995, Orchard $15.95 (978-0-531-06893-9). 32pp. Short Inuit poems are featured in double-page spreads, each containing a poem and an illustration. (Rev: BCCB 5/95; BL 4/15/95; SLJ 4/95) [897]

13600 Podwal, Mark. *Jerusalem Sky: Stars, Crosses, and Crescents* (3–5). Illus. 2005, Doubleday $15.95 (978-0-385-74689-2). 32pp. In poems and paintings, Podwal celebrates the power and majesty of Jerusalem, a city sacred to three religions: Christianity, Islam, and Judaism. (Rev: BL 10/1/05*; SLJ 9/05) [811]

13601 Pomerantz, Charlotte. *Thunderboom! Poems for Everyone* (PS–2). Illus. by Rob Shepperson. 2006, Front St. $17.95 (978-1-932425-40-6). 48pp. There's something for everyone in this diverse collection of poems ranging from boisterous to playful to quiet. (Rev: BL 4/1/06; SLJ 5/06) [811]

13602 Prelutsky, Jack. *Be Glad Your Nose Is on Your Face and Other Poems* (K–5). Illus. by Brandon Dorman. 2008, Greenwillow $22.99 (978-0-06-157653-9). 208pp. More than 100 poems by the first Children's Poet Laureate are collected in this brightly illustrated volume. (Rev: BLO 3/5/09; SLJ 3/09) [811]

13603 Prelutsky, Jack. *The Frogs Wore Red Suspenders* (PS–3). Illus. by Petra Mathers. 2002, Greenwillow LB $17.89 (978-0-688-16720-2). 64pp. Splendid illustrations accompany whimsical rhymes in this charming book for preschoolers and young readers. (Rev: BCCB 3/02; BL 3/15/02; HB 3/02; HBG 10/02; SLJ 2/02*) [811]

13604 Prelutsky, Jack. *Me I Am!* (PS–2). Illus. by Christine Davenier. 2007, Farrar $16.00 (978-0-374-34902-8). 32pp. Prelutsky's previously published poem about individuality and diversity is shown in dynamic illustrations of three different children. (Rev: BL 4/1/07) [811]

13605 Prelutsky, Jack. *Monday's Troll* (4–6). Illus. by Peter Sís. 1996, Greenwillow $15.89 (978-0-688-14373-2). 40pp. Seventeen original poems that deal with supernatural beings like witches, trolls, wizards, and ogres. (Rev: BCCB 3/96; BL 4/15/96; HB 5/96; SLJ 4/96*) [811]

13606 Prelutsky, Jack. *Nightmares: Poems to Trouble Your Sleep* (5–8). Illus. by Arnold Lobel. 1976, Greenwillow LB $17.89 (978-0-688-84053-2). Shuddery, macabre poems that will frighten but amuse a young audience. A sequel is *The Headless Horseman Rides Tonight: More Poems to Trouble Your Sleep* (1980).

13607 Prelutsky, Jack. *A Pizza the Size of the Sun* (3–6). Illus. by James Stevenson. 1996, Greenwillow $19.89 (978-0-688-13236-1). Humorous, imaginative light verses explore a variety of subjects. (Rev: BCCB 9/96; BL 9/15/96*; HB 9/96; SLJ 9/96*) [811]

13608 Prelutsky, Jack. *Scranimals* (2–4). Illus. by Peter Sís. 2002, HarperCollins LB $18.89 (978-0-688-17820-8). 48pp. The imaginary animals that inhabit Scranimal Island (the "Bananconda" and the "Orangutangerine," for example) are described in fanciful verse and art. (Rev: BCCB 10/02; BL 9/15/02; HB 1/03; HBG 3/03; SLJ 9/02*) [811]

13609 Prelutsky, Jack. *The Silver Moon: Lullabies and Cradle Songs* (PS–1). Illus. by Jui Ishida. 2013, Greenwillow $17.99 (978-0-06-201467-2). 48pp. Twenty short and effective lullabies are illustrated with dreamlike paintings; with musical notations for four of the poems. (Rev: BL 7/13; SLJ 9/13) [811]

13610 Prelutsky, Jack. *The Swamps of Sleethe: Poems from Beyond the Solar System* (3–5). Illus. by Jimmy Pickering. 2009, Knopf $16.99 (978-0-375-84674-8). 40pp. An entertaining collection of poems full of wordplay and grisly, fascinating horror, with suitably macabre illustrations. (Rev: BL 3/1/09; HB 5/09; SLJ 3/09) [811]

13611 Prelutsky, Jack, ed. *The Random House Book of Poetry for Children* (2–6). Illus. by Arnold Lobel. 1983, Random LB $21.99 (978-0-394-95010-5). 248pp. Old standbys and new gems are included in this fine anthology of 572 poems.

13612 Prelutsky, Jack, ed. *Read a Rhyme, Write a Rhyme* (3–5). Illus. by Meilo So. 2005, Knopf $16.95 (978-0-375-82286-5). 32pp. Organized in themes — dogs, bugs, birthdays, and so forth — this anthology groups poems on spreads and on each encourages readers to finish an uncompleted "poemstart." (Rev: BL 11/15/05; SLJ 11/05) [811]

13613 Prelutsky, Jack, ed. *The 20th Century Children's Poetry Treasury* (3–5). Illus. 1999, Random $19.95 (978-0-679-89314-1). On each of the illustrated two-page spreads, there are four to six poems on a single theme, for a total of more than 200 poems by 137 poets. (Rev: BL 12/15/99; HBG 3/00; SLJ 12/99*) [811]

13614 Quattlebaum, Mary. *Family Reunion* (2–3). Illus. by Andrea Shine. 2004, Eerdmans $16.00 (978-0-8028-5237-3). 32pp. Ten-year-old Jodie's summer trip to a family reunion is engagingly portrayed in this collection of varied short poems. (Rev: BL 4/1/04; SLJ 6/04) [811]

13615 Raczka, Bob. *Lemonade: And Other Poems Squeezed from a Single Word* (2–5). Illus. by Nancy Doniger. 2011, Roaring Brook $16.99 (978-1-59643-541-4). 48pp. Word puzzles combine with short pitty verses in this fascinating collection of 22 poems. (Rev: BL 12/15/10*; HB 3–4/11; LMC 5–6/11; SLJ 5/11) [811]

13616 Richards, Beah E. *Keep Climbing, Girls* (K–3). Illus. by R. Gregory Christie. 2006, Simon & Schuster $15.95 (978-1-4169-0264-5). 32pp. "Keep climbing" is the recommendation for girls in this beautifully illustrated poem written by the late African American actress. (Rev: BL 2/1/06; SLJ 2/06*) [811]

13617 Rogasky, Barbara, ed. *Leaf by Leaf: Autumn Poems* (5–8). Illus. by Marc Tauss. 2001, Scholastic paper $16.95 (978-0-590-25347-5). Verses by poets including Shelley, Yeats, and Whitman accompany stunning autumnal photographs. (Rev: BL 7/01; HBG 3/02; SLJ 9/01*) [811.008]

13618 Rosen, Michael. *The Best of Michael Rosen* (3–5). Illus. by Quentin Blake. 1995, Wetlands paper $16.95 (978-1-57143-046-5). 136pp. Sixty-five insightful, often lighthearted poems by the popular English poet. (Rev: BL 2/1/96; SLJ 5/05) [808.81]

13619 Rosen, Michael, ed. *Poems for the Very Young* (PS–2). Illus. by Bob Graham. 1993, Kingfisher $17.95 (978-1-85697-908-5). 80pp. A delightful collection of rhymes for young children, chiefly from American and British sources and illustrated with charming cartoonlike drawings. (Rev: BL 1/1/94*; SLJ 1/94) [821]

13620 Rossetti, Christina. *Sing Song: A Nursery Rhyme Book* (K–3). Illus. by Arthur Hughes. 1969, Dover paper $7.95 (978-0-486-22107-6). 130pp. Many of the poems are about small creatures and familiar objects and have a singing quality that young children enjoy.

13621 Rosten, Norman. *A City Is* (PS–2). Illus. by Melanie Hope Greenberg. 2004, Holt $16.95 (978-0-8050-6793-4). Varied short poems in free verse evoke both the hustle and bustle and the quiet moments of life in a city, many of them specifically about New York. (Rev: BL 3/1/04; SLJ 4/04) [811]

13622 Rowden, Justine. *Paint Me a Poem: Poems Inspired by Masterpieces of Art* (4–7). 2005, Boyds Mills $16.95 (978-1-59078-289-7). Each of the 14 poems in this collection is inspired by a famous painting from the

National Gallery of Art. (Rev: BL 11/1/05; SLJ 10/05) [811.54]

13623 Ruddell, Deborah. *A Whiff of Pine, a Hint of Skunk: A Forest of Poems* (1–3). Illus. by Joan Rankin. 2009, Simon & Schuster $16.99 (978-1-4169-4211-5). 40pp. Poetry and facts are interwoven in this whimsical look at the lives of plants and animals in a forest. (Rev: BCCB 3/09; BL 3/15/09; LMC 8/09; SLJ 4/09*) [811]

13624 Rylant, Cynthia. *Baby Face: A Book of Love for Baby* (PS). Illus. by Diane Goode. 2008, Simon & Schuster $16.99 (978-1-4169-4909-1). Six little poems highlight various activities of a multicultural group of babies. (Rev: BL 3/1/08; SLJ 8/08) [811]

13625 Rylant, Cynthia. *The Stars Will Still Shine* (PS–1). Illus. by Tiphanie Beeke. 2005, HarperCollins $16.99 (978-0-06-054639-7). 40pp. In rhyming text, the author celebrates the continuity of life and such constants as the sky, stars, birds, and church bells. (Rev: BL 10/15/05; SLJ 10/05) [811]

13626 Salas, Laura Purdie. *BookSpeak! Poems About Books* (2–5). Illus. by Josee Bisaillon. 2011, Clarion $16.99 (978-0-547-22300-1). 32pp. This quirky collection of diverse poems looks at all the aspects of books, from plot to cover and index. (Rev: BLO 11/15/11; SLJ 12/1/11) [811]

13627 Schertle, Alice. *Button Up!* (PS–2). Illus. by Petra Mathers. 2009, Harcourt $16.00 (978-0-15-205050-4). Articles of clothing describe their roles and characteristics in verse accompanied by humorous illustrations. (Rev: BCCB 6/09; BL 5/15/09; HB 5/09; SLJ 5/09) [811]

13628 Schertle, Alice. *Keepers* (1–4). Illus. by Ted Rand. 1996, Lothrop LB $15.89 (978-0-688-11635-4). A collection of original poems in which everyday objects become transformed through one's imagination. (Rev: BL 10/15/96; SLJ 12/96) [811]

13629 Schertle, Alice. *Teddy Bear, Teddy Bear* (PS–2). Illus. by Linda Hill Griffith. 2003, HarperCollins LB $16.99 (978-0-688-16871-1). Subjects dear to children are presented in bouncy poems. (Rev: HBG 10/03; SLJ 7/03) [811]

13630 Schertle, Alice. *When the Moon Is High* (PS). Illus. by Julia Noonan. 2003, HarperCollins LB $16.89 (978-0-688-15144-7). When baby can't fall asleep, Daddy decides to take a moonlight stroll with the child in his arms and on their way they encounter a number of nighttime creatures. (Rev: HBG 10/03; SLJ 7/03) [811]

13631 Schmidt, Gary D., ed. *Robert Frost* (5–7). Illus. by Henri Sorensen. Series: Poetry for Young People. 1994, Sterling $14.95 (978-0-8069-0633-1). An anthology of 25 poems suitable for young people, with watercolor illustrations that picture the New England landscape that Frost loved. (Rev: BL 12/1/94; SLJ 2/95) [811]

13632 Schoonmaker, Frances, ed. *Edna St. Vincent Millay* (3–7). Illus. Series: Poetry for Young People. 2000, Sterling $14.95 (978-0-8069-5928-3). 48pp. A representative collection of Millay's poetry illustrated with

evocative watercolors. (Rev: BL 3/15/00; HBG 10/00; SLJ 2/00) [811]

13633 Schoonmaker, Frances, ed. *Henry Wadsworth Longfellow* (4–8). Series: Poetry for Young People. 1999, Sterling $14.95 (978-0-8069-9417-8). A generous, carefully selected presentation of Longfellow's poetry illustrated by full-color paintings and accompanied by biographical notes. (Rev: BL 3/15/99; HBG 9/99; SLJ 3/99) [811]

13634 Shange, Ntozake. *Ellington Was Not a Street* (3–5). Illus. by Kadir Nelson. 2004, Simon & Schuster $15.95 (978-0-689-82884-3). 40pp. Adapted from Shange's poem "Mood Indigo," this richly illustrated picture book for older readers celebrates his childhoold home and the many African American intellectuals and artists who visited. (Rev: BL 2/15/04; SLJ 1/04) [811]

13635 Shange, Ntozake. *Freedom's a-Callin Me* (4–7). Illus. by Rod Brown. 2012, HarperCollins $16.99 (978-0-06-133741-3). 32pp. Poems and paintings capture the danger, strife, and hope experienced by those who strove to escape from slavery via the Underground Railroad. (Rev: BL 2/1/12; HB 1–2/12; SLJ 12/1/11) [811]

13636 Shange, Ntozake. *We Troubled the Waters* (4–8). Illus. by Rod Brown. 2009, Amistad $16.99 (978-0-06-133735-2); LB $17.89 (978-0-06-133737-6). Unpaged. This is a moving collection of unflinching poems portraying the brutality of racism, with stark artwork. (Rev: BL 10/1/09*; SLJ 12/09) [811]

13637 Shapiro, Sheryl, and Simon Shapiro. *Better Together* (PS–1). Illus. by Dusan Petricic. 2011, Annick $19.95 (978-1-55451-279-9); paper $8.95 (978-1-55451-278-2). 32pp. Combinations of different everyday substances, foods, people, and even activities are explored in 13 funny poems. (Rev: BL 6/1/11; SLJ 7/11) [811]

13638 Shields, Carol Diggory. *BrainJuice: American History Fresh Squeezed!* (4–8). Illus. by Richard Thompson. 2002, Handprint $14.95 (978-1-929766-62-8). A timeline runs across the tops of these pages of poems about events in American history. (Rev: HBG 3/03; SLJ 1/03) [811]

13639 Shields, Carol Diggory. *Someone Used My Toothbrush! And Other Bathroom Poems* (PS–3). Illus. by Paul Meisel. 2010, Dutton $16.99 (978-0-525-47937-6). 40pp. Everything from brushing teeth to doing icky chores is presented in this playful collection of bathroom poems. (Rev: BL 4/1/10; LMC 8–9/10; SLJ 5/1/10) [811]

13640 Sidman, Joyce. *Eureka! Poems About Inventors* (4–6). Illus. by K. Bennett Chavez. 2002, Millbrook LB $24.90 (978-0-7613-1665-7). 48pp. Sidman celebrates the lives and inventions of people throughout history in a chronological collection of free-verse poetry. (Rev: BL 10/15/02; HBG 3/03; SLJ 1/03) [811.54]

13641 Sidman, Joyce. *This Is Just to Say: Poems of Apology and Forgiveness* (4–7). Illus. by Pamela Zagarenski. 2007, Houghton Mifflin $16.00 (978-0-618-61680-0). Poems of all kinds written by a fictional 6th-grade class to say "sorry" are paired with responses from the recipients. (Rev: BL 5/15/07; SLJ 5/07) [811]

13642 Siebert, Diane. *Heartland* (K–4). Illus. by Wendell Minor. 1989, HarperCollins paper $6.99 (978-0-06-443287-0). 32pp. A lyrical celebration of the Midwest. (Rev: BL 3/1/89; SLJ 5/89)

13643 Siebert, Diane. *Motorcycle Song* (K–4). Illus. 2002, HarperCollins LB $16.89 (978-0-06-028733-7). 32pp. Invigorating poetry and energetic artwork capture the thrill of a motorcycle ride. (Rev: BL 2/1/02; HBG 10/02; SLJ 4/02) [793.73]

13644 Siebert, Diane. *Tour America: A Journey Through Poems and Art* (4–7). 2006, Chronicle $17.95 (978-0-8118-5056-8). Natural and manmade sights across America are celebrated in this appealing collection of poetry and art. (Rev: BL 6/1–15/06; SLJ 6/06*) [811]

13645 Silverstein, Shel. *Falling Up* (3–6). Illus. 1996, HarperCollins LB $19.89 (978-0-06-024803-1). More than 150 delightful original poems that amuse and amaze. (Rev: BCCB 6/96; BL 7/96*; HB 9/96; SLJ 7/96) [811]

13646 Simon, Seymour, ed. *Star Walk* (4–8). 1995, Morrow LB $14.93 (978-0-688-11887-7). Simple poems and outstanding photographs create an impressive introduction to stars and outer space. (Rev: BL 3/1/95; SLJ 4/95) [811]

13647 Singer, Marilyn. *All We Needed to Say: Poems About School from Tanya and Sophie* (PS–3). Illus. by Lorna Clark. 1996, Simon & Schuster $15.00 (978-0-689-80667-4). Two girls compare their school experiences in a series of short monologues. (Rev: BCCB 9/96; BL 8/96; SLJ 9/96) [811]

13648 Singer, Marilyn. *Central Heating: Poems About Fire and Warmth* (3–5). Illus. by Meilo So. 2005, Knopf LB $17.99 (978-0-375-82912-3). 48pp. From the warmth of chili peppers and roasted marshmallows to the heat of electricity and bombs, Singer explores the properties of fire. (Rev: BL 12/1/04; SLJ 1/05*) [811]

13649 Singer, Marilyn. *Follow Follow: A Book of Reverso Poems* (2–5). Illus. by Josee Masse. 2013, Dial $16.99 (978-080373769-3). 32pp. A collection of reverso poems (which can be read in two directions, with some changes in punctuation) based on classic fairy tales. (Rev: BL 1/13; LMC 8–9/13*; SLJ 4/13) [811]

13650 Singer, Marilyn. *A Stick Is an Excellent Thing: Poems Celebrating Outdoor Play* (PS–1). Illus. by LeUyen Pham. 2012, Clarion $16.99 (978-054712493-3). 40pp. This collection of infectious poems celebrating outdoor play is enhanced by bright, colorful illustrations and an engaging layout. (Rev: BL 1/1/12; HB 1–2/12; SLJ 1/12) [811]

13651 Sklansky, Amy E. *Out of This World: Poems and Facts About Space* (3–5). Illus. by Stacey Schuett. 2012, Knopf $17.99 (978-0-375-86459-9); LB $20.99 (978-037596459-6). 40pp. Twenty diverse poems accompanied by attractive digital illustrations treat the subjects of space travel and astronomy. (Rev: BL 4/1/12; LMC 8–9/12; SLJ 4/1/12) [811]

13652 Smith, Hope Anita. *Keeping the Night Watch* (5–8). Illus. by E. B. Lewis. 2008, Henry Holt $18.95 (978-0-8050-7202-0). In this equally poetic and well-illustrated sequel to *The Way a Door Closes* (2003), 13-year-old C.J.'s father is back home but the family's foundation remains shaky at first. Coretta Scott King Author Honor Book. (Rev: BL 3/15/08; SLJ 6/08) [811]

13653 Smith, Hope Anita. *Mother Poems* (4–7). Illus. by author. 2009, Henry Holt $16.95 (978-0-8050-8231-9). 80pp. In simple free-verse poems, a young African American girl expresses her love for her mother, and the loss she feels upon her death. ALA Notable Children's Book 2010. (Rev: BL 2/15/09; SLJ 4/1/09) [811]

13654 Smith, Hope Anita. *The Way a Door Closes* (5–8). Illus. by Shane W. Evans. 2003, Henry Holt $18.95 (978-0-8050-6477-3). A series of poems convey the feelings of a 13-year-old African American boy whose warm, loving home is destroyed when his father loses his job. (Rev: BL 5/1/03; HBG 10/03; SLJ 5/03*) [811]

13655 Smith, William Jay, comp. *Up the Hill and Down: Poems for the Very Young* (PS–2). Illus. by Allan Eitzen. 2003, Boyds Mills $16.95 (978-1-56397-028-3). 32pp. Robert Louis Stevenson, Aileen Fisher, and Marchette Chute are among the writers represented in this collection of nearly 30 poems. (Rev: HBG 4/04; SLJ 11/03) [811]

13656 Sneve, Virginia Driving Hawk, ed. *Dancing Teepees: Poems of American Indian Youth* (3–8). Illus. by Stephen Gammell. 1989, Holiday House LB $17.95 (978-0-8234-0724-8); paper $8.95 (978-0-8234-0879-5). 32pp. A collection of traditional tribal prayers, songs, and short poems. (Rev: BCCB 5/89; BL 5/15/89; SLJ 6/89)

13657 *Songs, Seas, and Green Peas: Poems for Anywhere* (K–4). Series: Poetry Parade. 2000, Heinemann LB $21.36 (978-1-57572-400-3). 32pp. A collection of poems by both well-known and obscure poets that contains no particular theme or subjects. Also use *Wishes, Wings, and Other Things: Poems for Anytime* (2000). (Rev: HBG 3/01; SLJ 2/01) [811]

13658 Soto, Gary. *Canto Familiar* (4–6). Illus. 1995, Harcourt $18.00 (978-0-15-200067-7). 88pp. Simple poems, many involving Mexican Americans, celebrate experiences at school, home, and in the street. A companion to *Neighborhood Odes* (1992). (Rev: BL 10/1/95; SLJ 12/95*) [811]

13659 Soto, Gary. *Fearless Fernie: Hanging Out with Fernie and Me* (4–6). Illus. by Regan Dunnick. 2002, Penguin $14.99 (978-0-399-23615-0). 64pp. Older readers are invited into the mind and life of an unnamed middle-school boy in this exceptional collection of poems. (Rev: BL 3/15/02; HB 7/02; HBG 10/02; SLJ 3/02*) [811]

13660 Soto, Gary. *Neighborhood Odes* (4–6). Illus. by David Diaz. 1992, Harcourt $15.95 (978-0-15-256879-5). 80pp. Unrhymed verses celebrate such items in a Mexican-American neighborhood as pinatas, weddings, libraries, and tennis shoes. (Rev: BL 6/15/92; HB 5/92*; SLJ 5/92) [811]

13661 Spinelli, Eileen. *Tea Party Today: Poems to Sip and Savor* (1–3). Illus. by Karen M. Dugan. 1999, Boyds Mills $15.95 (978-1-56397-662-9). 32pp. Tea and teatime inspired this group of poems about the ceremony and the emotions it evokes. (Rev: BL 4/1/99; HBG 10/99; SLJ 4/99) [811.54]

13662 Stavans, Ilan, ed. *Wachale! Poetry and Prose About Growing Up Latino in America* (5–8). 2001, Cricket $16.95 (978-0-8126-4750-1). A bilingual anthology about Latino experiences, both in the past and in the present. (Rev: BCCB 2/02; BL 2/1/02; HBG 10/02; SLJ 2/02; VOYA 6/02) [810.8]

13663 Stevenson, James. *Candy Corn* (2–5). Illus. 1999, Greenwillow $16.99 (978-0-688-15837-8). 56pp. Humorous recollections and details of ordinary life are the subjects of this delightful book of poems illustrated with ink-and-watercolor pictures. (Rev: BCCB 5/99; BL 3/15/99*; HB 7/99; HBG 10/99; SLJ 5/99) [811]

13664 Stevenson, James. *Cornflakes: Poems* (3–5). Illus. 2000, Greenwillow $16.99 (978-0-688-16718-9). 48pp. An eclectic collection of short verses on many subjects, illustrated with bright, clear, ink-and-watercolor pictures. (Rev: BL 3/15/00; HB 7/00; HBG 10/00; SLJ 6/00) [811]

13665 Stevenson, Robert Louis. *Block City* (PS). Illus. by Daniel Kirk. 2005, Simon & Schuster $14.95 (978-0-689-86964-8). 32pp. Stevenson's 1883 poem gets new life in a picture book that shows the joys of building — and then destroying — towers of building blocks. (Rev: BL 6/1–15/05) [811]

13666 Stevenson, Robert Louis. *A Child's Garden of Verses* (K–4). Illus. 1989, Chronicle $17.95 (978-0-87701-608-3). 121pp. A handsome edition of the old favorite, using some 100 19th-century illustrations. (Rev: BL 11/1/89*; SLJ 2/90) [821]

13667 Stevenson, Robert Louis. *A Child's Garden of Verses* (PS–5). Illus. by Barbara McClintock. 2011, HarperCollins $17.99 (978-0-06-028228-8). 80pp. McClintock's blend of charming spot art and full-page illustrations will attract new readers to the poems originally published in 1885. (Rev: HB 7–8/11; SLJ 8/1/11) [811]

13668 Stevenson, Robert Louis. *Poetry for Young People: Robert Louis Stevenson* (3–5). Illus. Series: Poetry for Young People. 2000, Sterling $14.95 (978-0-8069-4956-7). 48pp. Chosen mainly from *A Child's Garden of Verses,* this is a representative collection of Stevenson's work for children preceded by a biographical note. (Rev: BL 3/15/00; HBG 10/00; SLJ 7/00) [821]

13669 Stockland, Patricia M., comp. *Cobwebs, Chatters, and Chills: A Collection of Scary Poems* (3–6). Illus. by Sara Rojo Perez. Series: The Poet's Toolbox. 2004, Compass Point LB $23.93 (978-0-7565-0565-3). 32pp. An illustrated anthology of poems by well-known writers that demonstrate poetic forms and concepts. (Rev: SLJ 6/04) [811]

13670 Stockland, Patricia M., comp. *The Free and the Brave: A Collection of Poems About the United States* (3–6). Illus. by Sara Rojo Perez. Series: The Poet's Toolbox. 2004, Compass Point LB $23.93 (978-0-7565-0563-9). 32pp. Patriotic poetry by authors ranging from Carl Sandburg to Ogden Nash is illustrated with cartoon art and used to demonstrate poetic concepts. (Rev: SLJ 6/04) [811]

13671 Sturges, Philemon. *Down to the Sea in Ships* (3–5). Illus. by Giles Laroche. 2005, Penguin $16.99 (978-0-399-23464-4). Birch canoes, Viking ships, cod schooners, and modern ferries are among the vessels depicted in stunning illustrations and varied verses. (Rev: BL 5/15/05; SLJ 6/05) [811]

13672 Swados, Elizabeth. *Hey You! C'mere: A Poetry Slam* (2–5). Illus. by Joe Cepeda. 2002, Scholastic $16.95 (978-0-439-09257-9). 47pp. A collection of poems, presented by a group of urban children, that reflect their everyday concerns. (Rev: BL 4/15/02; HBG 10/02; SLJ 4/02) [811]

13673 Swaim, Jessica. *Scarum Fair* (2–4). Illus. by Carol Ashley. 2010, Boyds Mills $17.95 (978-1-59078-590-4). 32pp. A collection of spookily humorous poems about the weird offerings at the tents and booths of Scarum Fair. (Rev: BLO 10/15/10; LMC 1–2/11; SLJ 11/1/10) [811]

13674 Swenson, May. *The Complete Poems to Solve* (5–8). Illus. by Christy Hale. 1993, Macmillan $13.95 (978-0-02-788725-9). From simple riddles to more complex questions, each of these poems contains a puzzle. (Rev: HB 3–4/93; SLJ 5/93) [811]

13675 Szekeres, Cyndy, ed. *A Small Child's Book of Cozy Poems* (PS). Illus. 1999, Scholastic $6.95 (978-0-590-38364-6). 32pp. From Mother Goose to nonsense verse, this is a sweet collection of rhymes for the very young. (Rev: BL 2/1/99; HBG 10/99; SLJ 4/99) [811.008]

13676 Taberski, Sharon, ed. *Morning, Noon, and Night: Poems to Fill Your Day* (PS–3). Illus. by Nancy Doniger. 1996, Mondo $14.95 (978-1-57255-128-2). 32pp. The day's activities are traced in 29 poems by well-known writers. (Rev: BL 12/15/96; SLJ 5/96) [811]

13677 Tadjo, Veronique. *Talking Drums: A Selection of Poems from Africa South of the Sahara* (4–8). Illus. by author. 2004, Bloomsbury $15.95 (978-1-58234-813-1). Arranged by theme, these 75 poems — traditional and contemporary — cover a broad range of topics. (Rev: BL 3/1/04; SLJ 4/04; VOYA 4/04) [811]

13678 Temperley, Howard. *In the Days of Dinosaurs: A Rhyming Romp Through Dino History* (3–5). Illus. by Michael Kline. 2004, Williamson paper $12.95 (978-0-8249-8662-9). 61pp. Nearly 40 humorous and fact-filled poems describe specific dinosaurs and reflect on dinosaur-related issues. (Rev: SLJ 3/05) [811]

13679 Tennyson, Alfred Lord. *The Lady of Shalott* (5–7). Illus. by Genevieve Cote. 2005, Kids Can $16.95 (978-1-55337-874-7). The setting of Tennyson's "The Lady of Shalott" is moved from the England of King Arthur to the streets of an early 20th-century city in this beautifully illustrated adaptation. (Rev: BL 10/1/05; SLJ 12/05) [821]

13680 Thaler, Mike. *Pig Little* (PS–1). Illus. by Paige Miglio. 2006, Holt $16.95 (978-0-8050-6977-8). A little pig describes all the fun of a day at the beach with his mommy. (Rev: SLJ 7/06) [811]

13681 Thomas, Dylan. *A Child's Christmas in Wales* (5–8). Illus. by Trina Schart Hyman. 1985, Holiday $16.95 (978-0-8234-0565-7). A prose poem about the poet's childhood in a small Welsh village. [821.912]

13682 Thomas, Joyce Carol. *The Blacker the Berry* (PS–2). Illus. by Floyd Cooper. 2008, HarperCollins $16.99 (978-0-06-025375-2). 32pp. The many skin shades of an African heritage are celebrated in this collection of poems. (Rev: BCCB 7–8/08; BL 5/15/08; HB 8–9/08; SLJ 8/08) [811]

13683 Troupe, Quincy. *Little Stevie Wonder* (2–4). Illus. by Lisa Cohen. 2005, Houghton $18.00 (978-0-618-34060-6). 32pp. Vibrant illustrations highlight this free-verse account of Stevie Wonder's childhood and early success. (Rev: BL 2/1/05; SLJ 6/05) [811]

13684 VanDerwater, Amy Ludwig. *Forest Has a Song* (K–3). Illus. by Robbin Gourley. 2013, Clarion $16.99 (978-0-618-84349-7). 40pp. Twenty-six rich poems accompanied by watercolor illustrations celebrate the joys of nature. (Rev: BLO 4/1/13; LMC 8–9/13; SLJ 6/13) [811]

13685 Vecchione, Patrice, ed. *Whisper and Shout: Poems to Memorize* (4–6). 2002, Cricket $16.95 (978-0-8126-2656-8). 144pp. An anthology of 55 accessible poems (many by contemporaries) with a lengthy introduction on poetry and a closing section on resources and biographies. (Rev: BL 4/15/02; HBG 10/02; SLJ 5/02) [811]

13686 Vestergaard, Hope. *Digger, Dozer, Dumper* (PS–1). Illus. by David Slonim. 2013, Candlewick $15.99 (978-0-7636-5078-0). 32pp. Sixteen poems celebrate the capabilities of vehicles ranging from cherry pickers and street sweepers to bulldozers and semis. (Rev: BL 7/13; SLJ 7/13*) [811]

13687 Vestergaard, Hope. *I Don't Want to Clean My Room: A Mess of Poems About Chores* (PS–2). Illus. by Carol Koeller. 2007, Dutton $16.99 (978-0-525-47776-1). Simple, upbeat poems feature children helping out around the house and finding satisfaction in doing a good job. (Rev: SLJ 7/07)

13688 Viorst, Judith. *If I Were in Charge of the World and Other Worries: Poems for Children and Their Parents* (5–8). 1984, Macmillan paper $5.99 (978-0-689-70770-4). Easily read poems focus on topics familiar to young people. [811]

13689 Walker, Rob D. *Mama Says: A Book of Love for Mothers and Sons* (PS–3). Illus. by Leo and Diane Dillon. 2009, Scholastic $16.99 (978-0-439-93208-0). 32pp. In 12 languages — including Hebrew, Arabic, Cherokee, Russian, and English — this is a celebration of the ways in which mothers guide their children. (Rev: BL 4/15/09; SLJ 5/09) [811]

13690 Wallace, Daisy, ed. *Ghost Poems* (4–7). Illus. by Tomie dePaola. 1979, Holiday paper $4.95 (978-0-8234-0849-8). New and old poems to delight and frighten young readers.

13691 Wallace, Daisy, ed. *Witch Poems* (3–6). Illus. by Trina S. Hyman. 1976, Holiday House LB $14.95 (978-0-8234-0281-6); paper $4.95 (978-0-8234-0850-4). Eighteen poems chosen from several different sources on a wide variety of witches.

13692 Waters, Fiona, comp. *Dark as a Midnight Dream: Poetry Collection 2* (5–8). Illus. by Zara Slattery. 1999, Evans Brothers $24.95 (978-0-237-51845-5). An extensive anthology of poetry arranged by subjects such as "Mythical Creatures" and "City Life" that features such writers as Robert Browning, William Shakespeare, William Butler Yeats, William Wordsworth, Langston Hughes, and Carl Sandburg. (Rev: SLJ 11/99) [811]

13693 Weatherford, Carole Boston. *Birmingham, 1963* (3–6). Illus. 2007, Boyds Mills $17.95 (978-1-59078-440-2). 32pp. An anonymous fictional 10-year-old tells, in free verse, the story of the Ku Klux Klan church bombing in 1963 that killed four young girls. (Rev: BL 9/15/07; LMC 10/07; SLJ 12/07) [811]

13694 Weatherford, Carole Boston. *Sidewalk Chalk: Poems of the City* (3–6). Illus. by Dimitrea Tokunbo. 2001, Boyds Mills $15.95 (978-1-56397-084-9). 32pp. Poems about the pleasures of urban life are accompanied by colorful full-page illustrations. (Rev: BL 9/15/01; HBG 3/02; SLJ 1/02) [811]

13695 Weisburd, Stefi. *Barefoot: Poems for Naked Feet* (K–3). Illus. by Lori McElrath-Eslick. 2008, Boyds Mills $16.95 (978-1-59078-306-1). The pleasures and perils of bare feet are explored in 27 poems and watercolor illustrations. (Rev: BL 2/15/08; LMC 3/08; SLJ 8/08) [811]

13696 Whipple, Laura. *Eric Carle's Dragons Dragons and Other Creatures That Never Were* (2–6). Illus. by Eric Carle. 1991, Penguin $21.99 (978-0-399-22105-7). 69pp. This is a collection of poems about dragons and other mythological creatures illustrated by Eric Carle. (Rev: BCCB 12/91; BL 11/1/91; HB 11/91; SLJ 10/91) [811]

13697 Whitman, Walt. *Nothing but Miracles* (K–2). Illus. by Susan L. Roth. 2003, National Geographic $15.95 (978-0-7922-6143-8). A joyful cat family, shown in naive collages, illustrates the words to Whitman's poem from *Leaves of Grass*. (Rev: HBG 4/04; SLJ 1/04) [811.3]

13698 Whitman, Walt. *When I Heard the Learn'd Astronomer* (K–3). Illus. by Loren Long. 2004, Simon & Schuster $16.95 (978-0-689-86397-4). A young boy's growing appreciation of the universe around him is shown in vivid acrylic artwork and the Whitman verse. (Rev: BL 11/15/04*) [811]

13699 Wilbur, Richard. *Runaway Opposites* (4–6). Illus. by Henrik Drescher. 1995, Harcourt $15.00 (978-0-15-258722-2). 32pp. An intriguing, involved book of poems that deal with synonyms and antonyms. (Rev: BCCB 4/95; BL 4/15/95; SLJ 5/95) [811]

13700 Willard, Nancy. *A Visit to William Blake's Inn: Poems for Innocent and Experienced Travelers* (2–5). Illus. by Alice Provensen and Martin Provensen. 1981, Harcourt $16.00 (978-0-15-293822-2); paper $7.00 (978-0-15-293823-9). 44pp. A collection of poems that won the Newbery Award, 1982.

13701 Wilson, Edwin Graves, ed. *Maya Angelou* (4–10). Illus. by Jerome Lagarrigue. Series: Poetry for Young People. 2007, Sterling $14.95 (978-1-4027-2023-9). 48pp. Twenty-five carefully selected poems — with commentary, footnotes, and illustrations — are introduced by information on Angelou's life and influences. (Rev: SLJ 10/07*) [811]

13702 Winnick, Karen B. *A Year Goes Round: Poems for the Months* (K–2). Illus. by author. 2001, Boyds Mills $15.95 (978-1-56397-898-2). A look at the months of the year in short, simple poems about children's activities. (Rev: HBG 3/02; SLJ 11/01) [811]

13703 Winters, Kay. *Voices of Ancient Egypt* (3–6). Illus. by Barry Moser. 2003, National Geographic $16.95 (978-0-7922-7560-2). 32pp. Two-page spreads introduce ancient Egyptian workers — among them a scribe, a pyramid builder, and a herdsman — who describe their lives in first-person free verse. (Rev: BL 9/15/03; HBG 4/04; SLJ 9/03) [932]

13704 Wong, Janet S. *Knock on Wood: Poems About Superstitions* (2–5). Illus. by Julie Paschkis. 2003, Simon & Schuster $17.95 (978-0-689-85512-2). 40pp. Vampires, ghosts, broken mirrors, and black cats are just some of the topics of these aptly illustrated poems about potential bad luck. (Rev: BL 11/15/03; HB 9/03; HBG 4/04; SLJ 12/03)

13705 Wong, Janet S. *Twist: Yoga Poems* (3–5). Illus. by Julie Paschkis. 2007, Simon & Schuster $17.99 (978-0-689-87394-2). 32pp. Short, accessible poems, each focusing on a familiar pose, consider both physical and philosophical aspects of yoga, while illustrations feature multiethnic practitioners and colorful borders of animals and plants. (Rev: BL 1/1–15/07) [811]

13706 Woodson, Jacqueline. *Locomotion* (3–6). 2003, Penguin $15.99 (978-0-399-23115-5). 128pp. A young boy whose parents have died and whose sister is in a different foster home expresses his grief through poetry. (Rev: BCCB 3/03; BL 2/15/03; HB 3/03*; HBG 10/03; SLJ 1/03) [811]

13707 Worth, Valerie. *Peacock and Other Poems* (3–6). Illus. by Natalie Babbitt. 2002, Farrar $15.00 (978-0-374-35766-5). 48pp. A posthumously published collection of 26 poems in the author's signature style, beautifully illustrated with detailed pencil drawings. (Rev: BCCB 6/02; BL 8/02; HB 7/02*; HBG 10/02; SLJ 5/02) [811]

13708 Worthen, Tom, ed. *Broken Hearts . . . Healing: Young Poets Speak Out on Divorce* (5–9). Illus. by Kyle Hernandez. Series: Young Poets Speak Out. 2001, Poet Tree $26.95 (978-1-58876-150-7); paper $14.95 (978-1-58876-151-4). This large selection of poems written by

their peers about divorce, family breakups, and blended families will resonate with young readers. (Rev: SLJ 9/01; VOYA 10/01) [811]

13709 Xinran Xue. *Motherbridge of Love* (PS–2). Illus. by Josee Masse. 2007, Barefoot Books $16.99 (978-1-84686-047-8). 32pp. The illustrations for this lyrical poem directed at an adopted girl show a happy girl with Chinese features and her birth mother and adoptive mother. (Rev: BL 10/15/07; LMC 3/08; SLJ 1/08) [895.1]

13710 Yolen, Jane. *O Jerusalem* (4–6). Illus. by John Thompson. 1996, Scholastic $15.95 (978-0-590-48426-8). A group of original poems that explore the importance of Jerusalem in Judaism, Christianity, and Islam. (Rev: BL 2/1/96*; SLJ 3/96*) [811]

13711 Yolen, Jane. *Sacred Places* (5–9). 1996, Harcourt $16.00 (978-0-15-269953-6). An international collection of informational poems about the places sacred to various faiths. (Rev: BCCB 12/00; BL 10/1/96; SLJ 3/96) [811]

13712 Yolen, Jane, and Andrew F. Peters, eds. *Here's a Little Poem* (PS). Illus. by Polly Dunbar. 2007, Candlewick $21.99 (978-0-7636-3141-3). 112pp. This appealing anthology of more than 60 diverse poems includes works by Jack Prelutsky, Langston Hughes, Rosemary Wells, Gertrude Stein, A. A. Milne, Robert Louis Stevenson. (Rev: BL 4/1/07) [811]

13713 Yolen, Jane, and Andrew Fusek Peters, eds. *Switching on the Moon* (PS–1). Illus. by G. Brian Karas. 2010, Candlewick $21.99 (978-0-7636-4249-5). 95pp. An elegant anthology of 60 bedtime poems by writers including Tennyson, Plath, Langston Hughes, and Lee Bennett Hopkins. (Rev: BL 10/1/10; HB 11–12/10; SLJ 10/1/10*) [398.6]

13714 Yolen, Jane, and Heidi Stemple. *Dear Mother, Dear Daughter* (3–5). Illus. 2001, Boyds Mills $15.95 (978-1-56397-886-9). 32pp. Using simple verses this book consists of double-page spreads; on one side is a letter from a daughter to her mother, on the other the reply. (Rev: BL 3/15/01; HBG 10/01) [811]

13715 Yolen, Jane, and Rebecca Kai Dotlich. *Grumbles from the Forest* (4–6). Illus. by Matt Mahurin. 2013, Boyds Mills/Wordsong $16.95 (978-1-59078-867-7). 48pp. Fairy tales are told from a variety of perspectives in 15 pairs of poems — the pea that got crushed by a princess, the giant's wife who helps Jack escape, and so forth. (Rev: BLO 4/1/13; HB 3–4/13; LMC 10/13; SLJ 4/13)

13716 Zimmer, Tracie Vaughn. *Steady Hands: Poems About Work* (4–7). Illus. by Megan Halsey. 2009, Clarion $16.00 (978-0-618-90351-1). Short poems celebrate a variety of contemporary occupations from bakers to surgeons to dog walkers. (Rev: BL 1/1–15/09; SLJ 4/09) [811]

Animals

13717 Alonzo, Sandra. *Gallop-o-Gallop* (1–4). Illus. by Kelly Murphy. 2007, Dial $16.99 (978-0-8037-2967-4). All sorts of horses — tame and wild, working in rodeos, farms, and ranches —are represented in this collection of poems accompanied by beautiful artwork. (Rev: SLJ 6/07)

13718 Andreae, Giles. *Rumble in the Jungle* (PS). Illus. by David Wojtowycz. 1997, Little Tiger $14.95 (978-1-888444-08-7). A collection of poems about the animals that a small group of ants encounter as they march through the jungle. (Rev: HBG 3/98; SLJ 11/97) [811]

13719 Blackaby, Susan. *Nest, Nook and Cranny* (3–6). Illus. by Jamie Hogan. 2010, Charlesbridge $15.95 (978-1-58089-350-3). 60pp. A collection of diverse poems about animals and their habitats. (Rev: BL 2/1/10; LMC 11–12/10; SLJ 3/10) [811]

13720 Bulion, Leslie. *At the Sea Floor Café: Odd Ocean Critter Poems* (5–8). Illus. by Leslie Evans. 2011, Peachtree $14.95 (978-1-56145-565-2). 45pp. Eighteen poems provide compelling glimpses into the lives of some of the more interesting and bizarre marine creatures. (Rev: LMC 11–12/11; SLJ 4/11) [811]

13721 Carryl, Charles Edward. *The Camel's Lament* (K–3). Illus. by Charles Santore. 2004, Random LB $18.99 (978-0-375-91426-3). 32pp. Stunning watercolors breathe new life into Edward Carryl Charles's poem about the lowly camel. (Rev: BL 7/04; SLJ 10/04*) [811]

13722 Chernaik, Judith, ed. *Carnival of the Animals: Poems Inspired by Saint-Saëns' Music* (K–3). Illus. by Satoshi Kitamura. 2006, Candlewick $16.99 (978-0-7636-2960-1). In this brightly illustrated title, which is bundled with an audio CD, poets offer their profiles of animal characters portrayed musically in the Saint-Saëns classic. (Rev: BCCB 5/06; BL 3/15/06*; HBG 10/06; LMC 10/06; SLJ 4/06) [811]

13723 Crawley, Dave. *Dog Poems* (PS–2). Illus. by Tamara Petrosino. 2007, Boyds Mills $16.95 (978-1-59078-454-9). 32pp. Lighthearted rhyming poems look at dogs and their relations with humans. (Rev: BCCB 10/07; BL 9/1/07; SLJ 8/07) [811]

13724 De Vos, Philip. *Carnival of the Animals* (1–4). Illus. by Piet Grobler. 2000, Front St. $16.95 (978-1-886910-47-8). 38pp. Surreal paintings accompany clever verses to bring to life the Saint-Saens musical fantasy. (Rev: BL 8/00; HBG 10/00; SLJ 7/00) [821]

13725 Ehlert, Lois. *Lots of Spots* (PS–1). Illus. by author. 2010, Simon & Schuster $17.99 (978-1-4424-0289-8). 40pp. Collages and brief poems accompany illustrations of animals that sport spots. (Rev: BL 4/15/10; LMC 5–6/10; SLJ 8/1/10)

13726 Elliott, David. *In the Sea* (PS–2). Illus. by Holly Meade. 2012, Candlewick $16.99 (978-0-7636-4498-7). 32pp. Twenty different marine creatures are presented alongside simple odes to their habits and habitats. (Rev: BL 2/1/12*; SLJ 4/1/12) [811]

13727 Elliott, David. *In the Wild* (PS–2). Illus. by Holly Meade. 2010, Candlewick $16.99 (978-0-7636-4497-0). 32pp. With woodcut illustrations, this is a collection of short poems celebrating wild animals. (Rev: BL 7/10; LMC 11–12/10; SLJ 7/1/10*) [811]

13728 Elliott, David. *On the Farm* (PS–2). Illus. by Holly Meade. 2008, Candlewick $16.99 (978-0-7636-3322-6). 32pp. The animals of an appealing farmyard are celebrated in verse and woodblock and watercolor illustrations. (Rev: BCCB 3/08; BL 5/15/08; HB 3/08; SLJ 2/08) [636]

13729 Fleischman, Paul. *I Am Phoenix: Poems for Two Voices* (4–9). 1985, HarperCollins paper $5.99 (978-0-06-446092-7). A group of love poems about birds that are designed to be read by two voices or groups of voices. (Rev: BL 12/1/85) [811]

13730 Fleischman, Paul. *Joyful Noise: Poems for Two Voices* (3–6). Illus. by Eric Beddows. 1988, HarperCollins LB $16.89 (978-0-06-021853-9); paper $5.99 (978-0-06-446093-4). Poems for reading aloud that explore the lives of insects. Newbery Medal winner, 1989. (Rev: BL 2/15/88; HB 5/88; SLJ 2/88)

13731 Florian, Douglas. *Bow Wow Meow Meow* (PS–2). Illus. 2003, Harcourt $17.00 (978-0-15-216395-2). 56pp. A collection of offbeat poems about cats and dogs, accompanied by watercolor illustrations. (Rev: BL 2/1/03*; HB 5/03; HBG 10/03; SLJ 5/03) [811]

13732 Florian, Douglas. *Dinothesaurus: Prehistoric Poems and Paintings* (K–3). Illus. by author. 2009, Atheneum $17.99 (978-1-4169-7978-4). Twenty humorous poems provide puns and facts about dinosaurs in this accessible book with collage art and a pronunciation guide. (Rev: BCCB 2/09; BL 3/1/09; HB 3/09; SLJ 5/09) [811]

13733 Florian, Douglas. *Insectlopedia* (3–5). Illus. 1998, Harcourt $16.00 (978-0-15-201306-6). 56pp. A well-designed book of poems about insects and spiders. (Rev: BCCB 7–8/98; BL 3/15/98; SLJ 4/98) [811]

13734 Florian, Douglas. *Lizards, Frogs, and Polliwogs* (3–5). Illus. 2001, Harcourt $16.00 (978-0-15-202591-5). 48pp. Playful poetry and imaginative artwork are combined in this book of short original poems about a variety of reptiles and amphibians. (Rev: BL 3/15/01*; HB 5/01; HBG 10/01) [811]

13735 Florian, Douglas. *Mammalabilia* (2–4). Illus. 2000, Harcourt $16.00 (978-0-15-202167-2). 48pp. Twenty-one short, clever rhymes and inventive illustrations examine various members of the animal kingdom. (Rev: BCCB 3/00; BL 3/15/00; HB 3/00; HBG 10/00; SLJ 4/00) [811]

13736 Florian, Douglas. *Omnibeasts: Animal Poems and Paintings* (1–4). 2004, Harcourt $18.00 (978-0-15-205038-2). 96pp. Entertaining wordplay and inventive shapes add to this inviting collection of poems and art about animals. (Rev: BL 10/15/04; SLJ 10/04) [811]

13737 Florian, Douglas. *Zoo's Who: Poems and Paintings* (K–3). Illus. 2005, Harcourt $17.00 (978-0-15-204639-2). 56pp. Clever, brief verses about all sorts of animals (not just the ones found in zoos) are accompanied by unusual art. (Rev: BL 3/15/05; SLJ 4/05) [811]

13738 Franco, Betsy. *A Curious Collection of Cats* (PS–3). Illus. by Michael Wertz. 2009, Tricycle $16.99 (978-1-58246-248-6). 32pp. Thirty-four concrete poems celebrate cats' essential catness. (Rev: BCCB 7–8/09; BL 3/15/09; HB 5/09; SLJ 4/09) [811]

13739 Franco, Betsy. *A Dazzling Display of Dogs* (K–3). Illus. by Michael Wertz. 2011, Tricycle $16.99 (978-1-58246-343-8). 40pp. All aspects of dogs are explored in these 34 funny, energetic, concrete poems. (Rev: BL 12/15/10; HB 1–2/11; SLJ 1/1/11*) [811]

13740 Frost, Robert. *The Runaway* (PS–2). Illus. by Glenna Lang. 1998, Godine $17.95 (978-1-56792-006-2). 32pp. Lovely illustrations accompany this poem about a colt's reaction to the first snowfall. (Rev: BL 3/1/99; HBG 3/99; SLJ 3/99) [811]

13741 George, Kristine O'Connell. *Little Dog and Duncan* (PS–2). Illus. by June Otani. 2002, Clarion $14.00 (978-0-618-11758-1). Preschoolers and beginning readers alike will enjoy the gentle poetry and charming watercolors in this story of two dogs having a sleepover. (Rev: BL 3/1/02; HB 7/02*; HBG 10/02; SLJ 3/02*) [811]

13742 George, Kristine O'Connell. *Little Dog Poems* (PS–K). Illus. by June Otani. 1999, Clarion $13.00 (978-0-395-82266-1). Charming watercolors illustrate these simple, original poems about a little girl and her beloved dog. (Rev: BL 3/15/99; HB 3/99; HBG 10/99; SLJ 5/99) [811]

13743 Ghigna, Charles. *Animal Tracks: Wild Poems to Read Aloud* (K–3). Illus. by John Speirs. 2004, Abrams $14.95 (978-0-8109-4841-9). 38pp. Animals occupy center stage in this collection of 32 brief, illustrated poems, many of which will generate a laugh. (Rev: BL 5/1/04; SLJ 4/04) [811]

13744 Gibson, Amy. *Around the World on Eighty Legs* (PS–3). Illus. by Daniel Salmieri. 2011, Scholastic $18.99 (978-0-439-58755-6). 56pp. Poems full of humor and wordplay introduce animals around the world, organized by continent. (Rev: BL 2/1/11; HB 3–4/11; SLJ 2/1/11) [811]

13745 Gottfried, Maya. *Good Dog* (K–3). Illus. by Robert Rahway Zakanitch. 2005, Knopf LB $17.99 (978-0-375-93049-2). Free-verse poems express the thoughts of a variety of canine personalities and their views of their human companions. (Rev: SLJ 4/05) [811]

13746 Gottfried, Maya. *Our Farm: By the Animals of Farm Sanctuary* (K–3). Illus. by Robert Rahway Zakanitch. 2010, Knopf $17.99 (978-0-375-86118-5). 40pp. Abused farm animals at a shelter describe their happy lives in this handsome collection of poems. ℮ (Rev: BL 3/1/10; LMC 3–4/10; SLJ 1/1/10) [811]

13747 Harley, Avis. *African Acrostics: A Word in Edgewise* (4–7). Illus. by Deborah Noyes. 2009, Candlewick $17.99 (978-0-7636-3621-0). 40pp. Poems featuring acrostic puzzles are paired with photographs of animals in Africa. (Rev: BL 7/09; SLJ 6/09*) [811.6]

13748 Harley, Avis. *The Monarch's Progress: Poems with Wings* (3–5). Illus. by author. 2008, Boyds Mills $16.95 (978-1-59078-558-4). Eighteen diverse poems celebrating butterflies — monarchs in particular —are accompanied by detailed drawings and factual notes. (Rev: BL 2/15/08; SLJ 8/08) [811]

13749 Harley, Avis. *Sea Stars* (1–5). Photos by Margaret Butschler. 2006, Boyds Mills $16.95 (978-1-59078-429-7). 35pp. Short poems of varied constructions and close-up color photographs introduce a number of sea creatures. (Rev: SLJ 10/06) [811]

13750 Hauth, Katherine B. *What's for Dinner? Quirky, Squirmy Poems from the Animal World* (2–5). Illus. by David Clark. 2011, Charlesbridge $16.95 (978-1-57091-471-3); paper $7.95 (978-1-57091-472-0). 48pp. Twenty-nine fun poems focus on the different ways the world's animals get their dinner. ℮ (Rev: BL 2/15/11; LMC LMC 10/11; SLJ 3/1/11) [811]

13751 Hoberman, Mary Ann. *A Fine Fat Pig* (K–5). Illus. by Malcah Zeldis. 1991, HarperCollins $14.95 (978-0-06-022425-7). These 14 poems deal with animals, their characteristics, and habits. (Rev: HB 5/91; SLJ 4/91) [811]

13752 Hollander, John, ed. *Animal Poems* (5–7). Illus. by Simona Mulazzani. Series: Poetry for Young People. 2005, Sterling $14.95 (978-1-4027-0926-5). A collection of classic poems (by such poets as Blake, Frost, Melville, and Yeats) accompanied by artwork and explanatory notes. (Rev: BL 4/1/05; SLJ 3/05) [808.81]

13753 Howitt, Mary. *The Spider and the Fly* (2–5). Illus. by Tony DiTerlizzi. 2002, Simon & Schuster $16.95 (978-0-689-85289-3). 40pp. Outstanding monochrome artwork brings new life to the classic poem. Caldecott Honor Book, 2003. (Rev: BCCB 11/02; BL 10/1/02; HBG 3/03; SLJ 9/02*) [811]

13754 Hubbell, Patricia. *Earthmates* (K–4). Illus. by Jean Cassels. 2000, Marshall Cavendish $15.95 (978-0-7614-5062-7). 32pp. A collection of impressive poems about such animals as a lion, rat, frog, bat, and deer. (Rev: BL 3/15/00; HBG 10/00; SLJ 3/00) [811]

13755 Jackson, Rob. *Animal Mischief* (2–4). Illus. by Laura Jacobsen. 2006, Boyds Mills $15.95 (978-1-59078-254-5). 32pp. The oddities of animal behavior and appearance are celebrated from a biologist's point of view in this collection of 18 amusing poems. (Rev: BL 4/1/06; SLJ 5/06) [811]

13756 Johnston, Tony. *Cat, What Is That?* (1–4). Illus. by Wendell Minor. 2001, HarperCollins LB $16.89 (978-0-06-027743-7). 32pp. Abstract verses and detailed, realistic illustrations bring to life cats of all kinds in a variety of typical feline activities. (Rev: BL 10/1/01; HBG 3/02; SLJ 9/01)

13757 Johnston, Tony. *Gopher Up Your Sleeve* (PS–3). Illus. by Trip Park. 2002, Rising Moon $15.95 (978-0-87358-794-5). Humorous poems about animals are accompanied by fanciful illustrations. (Rev: HBG 10/02; SLJ 11/02) [811]

13758 Kiesler, Kate. *Wings on the Wind: Bird Poems* (PS–2). Illus. 2002, Clarion $14.00 (978-0-618-13333-8). 32pp. Vivid oil paintings are used to illustrate this collection of poems about birds by such writers as Edward Lear, Carl Sandburg, and Margaret Wise Brown. (Rev: BL 4/15/02; HBG 10/02; SLJ 4/02) [811.008]

13759 Kirk, Daniel. *Cat Power!* (1–4). Illus. by author. 2007, Hyperion $18.99 (978-1-4231-0081-2). 48pp. Eighteen poems celebrate all things feline — even the litter box; a CD of songs is included in this companion to *Dogs Rule!* (2003). (Rev: SLJ 11/07) [811]

13760 Kumin, Maxine. *Mites to Mastodons: A Book of Animal Poems* (2–4). Illus. by Pamela Zagarenski. 2006, Houghton $16.00 (978-0-618-50753-5). 32pp. Animals large and small are celebrated in poems that both appeal and convey information; the whimsical collage illustrations add another dimension. (Rev: BL 10/1/06; SLJ 10/06) [811]

13761 Kuskin, Karla. *Toots the Cat* (PS–2). Illus. by Lisze Bechtold. 2005, Holt $16.95 (978-0-8050-6841-2). 32pp. Poems celebrate the life and adventures of Toots, an independent-minded cat. (Rev: BL 9/1/05; SLJ 1/06) [811.54]

13762 Larios, Julie. *Yellow Elephant: A Bright Bestiary* (K–3). Illus. by Julie Paschkis. 2006, Harcourt $16.00 (978-0-15-205422-9). 32pp. Using vivid, folk-art illustrations of animals and nature, this collection of poems looks at colors and animals. (Rev: BCCB 5/06; BL 3/15/06*; HBG 10/06; LMC 11/06; SLJ 4/06) [811]

13763 Levy, Constance. *I'm Going to Pet a Worm Today and Other Poems* (3–5). Illus. by Ronald Himler. 1991, Macmillan $14.00 (978-0-689-50535-5). 48pp. This book of original poems celebrates such creatures of nature as spiders, worms, and beetles. (Rev: BCCB 2/92*; BL 11/15/92; SLJ 10/91) [811]

13764 Lewis, J. Patrick. *What's Looking at You, Kid?* (PS–1). Illus. by Renee Graef. 2012, Sleeping Bear $14.95 (978-158536793-1). 32pp. Bright illustrations provide clues to lively rhymed riddles about animals and insects. (Rev: BLO 4/15/12; SLJ 5/1/12) [818]

13765 Livingston, Myra Cohn, ed. *If You Ever Meet a Whale* (1–4). Illus. by Leonard Everett Fisher. 1992, Holiday House LB $14.95 (978-0-8234-0940-2). 32pp. Seventeen whale poems with full-color paintings. (Rev: BL 11/15/92) [811]

13766 Luján, Jorge. *Rooster / Gallo* (PS–1). Illus. by Manuel Monroy. 2004, Groundwood $14.95 (978-0-88899-558-2). 24pp. Brief poetic text celebrates the rooster and its relationship to the cycle of day and night. (Rev: BL 5/15/04; HB 3/04; SLJ 9/04) [811]

13767 MacLachlan, Patricia, and Emily MacLachlan Charest. *Cat Talk* (PS–2). Illus. by Barry Moser. 2013, Amistad/Katherine Tegen $17.99 (978-0-06-027978-3). 32pp. An attractive collection of 13 poems told from the perspectives of thoughtful cats. (Rev: BL 3/1/13; SLJ 3/13) [811]

13768 MacLachlan, Patricia, and Emily MacLachlan Charest. *I Didn't Do It* (PS–3). Illus. by Katy Schneider.

2010, HarperCollins $16.99 (978-0-06-135833-3); LB $17.89 (978-0-06-135834-0). Unpaged. Fourteen free poems are told from the dogs' perspective and convey doggy complaints and joys. (Rev: SLJ 10/1/10) [811]

13769 MacLachlan, Patricia, and Emily MacLachlan Charest. *Once I Ate a Pie* (2–4). Illus. by Katy Schneider. 2006, HarperCollins $17.99 (978-0-06-073531-9). 40pp. An appealing bunch of dogs reveal in poems things they love and various doggy characteristics. (Rev: BL 5/1/06; SLJ 5/06) [811.54]

13770 Maddox, Marjorie. *A Crossing of Zebras: Animal Packs in Poetry* (2–5). Illus. by Philip Huber. 2008, Boyds Mills (978-1-59078-510-2). 32pp. Fourteen brief poems about animals use alliteration and inventive collective nouns, such as "a rumba of rattlesnakes." (Rev: LMC 3/08; SLJ 7/08) [811]

13771 Mitton, Tony. *Gnash, Gnaw, Dinosaur! Prehistoric Poems with Lift-the-Flap Surprises!* (PS–3). Illus. by Lynne Chapman. 2009, Kingfisher $12.99 (978-0-7534-6226-3). Unpaged. A variety of different dinosaurs are accompanied by short, well-executed rhymes describing their habits in this brightly illustrated volume for budding dino buffs. (Rev: SLJ 11/1/09) [811]

13772 Nichol, Barbara. *Biscuits in the Cupboard* (K–4). Illus. by Philippe Beha. 1998, Stoddart $12.95 (978-0-7737-3025-0). 32pp. A delightful collection of poems about dogs, written entirely from their point of view. (Rev: BL 3/1/04; SLJ 3/98) [808]

13773 Pearson, Susan. *Squeal and Squawk: Barnyard Talk* (K–3). Illus. by David Slonim. 2004, Marshall Cavendish $16.95 (978-0-7614-5160-0). 31pp. Humorous illustrations enhance poems about barnyard animals, from a lovelorn rooster to flying pigs. (Rev: SLJ 6/04) [811]

13774 Pearson, Susan. *Who Swallowed Harold?* (K–4). Illus. by David Slonim. 2005, Marshall Cavendish $16.95 (978-0-7614-5193-8). 31pp. Eighteen humorous poems look at children's relationships with their pets. (Rev: BL 2/1/04*; SLJ 4/05) [811]

13775 Polisar, Barry L. *Insect Soup: Bug Poems* (K–4). Illus. by David Clark. 1999, Rainbow $14.95 (978-0-938663-22-5). Fifteen original poems about insects that are sometimes humorous, sometimes gross, and sometimes amazing. (Rev: SLJ 8/99) [811]

13776 Prelutsky, Jack. *The Carnival of the Animals by Camille Saint-Saëns* (1–4). Illus. by Mary GrandPré. 2010, Knopf $19.99 (978-0-375-86458-2); LB $22.99 (978-0-375-96458-9). Unpaged. Poems composed to accompany Saint-Saëns' beloved orchestral work are collected here; a CD of the music and Prelutsky's readings is included. (Rev: LMC 11–12/10; SLJ 12/1/10*) [811]

13777 Prelutsky, Jack. *If Not for the Cat* (PS–3). Illus. by Ted Rand. 2004, Greenwillow LB $17.89 (978-0-06-059678-1). Seventeen haiku poems explore life from the vantage point of various animals. (Rev: BL 10/1/04; SLJ 10/04) [811]

13778 Prelutsky, Jack. *Tyrannosaurus Was a Beast* (2–5). Illus. by Arnold Lobel. 1988, Morrow paper $6.99 (978-

0-688-11569-2). 32pp. Poems and watercolor portraits bring dinosaurs to life. (Rev: BCCB 9/88; BL 8/88; HB 9/88)

13779 Prelutsky, Jack, ed. *The Beauty of the Beast: Poems from the Animal Kingdom* (3–7). Illus. by Meilo So. 1997, Knopf $25.00 (978-0-679-87058-6). 101pp. A wonderful, beautifully illustrated collection of more than 200 animal poems by 20th-century writers whose works are arranged by animal genus. (Rev: BL 9/15/97; HBG 3/98; SLJ 1/98*) [811]

13780 Prevert, Jacques. *How to Paint the Portrait of a Bird* (K–3). Trans. and illus. by Mordicai Gerstein. 2007, Roaring Brook $14.95 (978-1-59643-215-4). A beautifully illustrated and translated version of French surrealist Prévert's poem, featuring a boy who follows directions that start with painting a cage with an open door for the bird to fly in, then erasing the cage and replacing it with a forest. (Rev: BCCB 2/08; BL 11/15/07; HB 1/08; LMC 11/07; SLJ 1/08) [841]

13781 Rosen, Michael J. *The Cuckoo's Haiku: And Other Birding Poems* (3–6). Illus. by Stan Fellows. 2009, Candlewick $17.99 (978-0-7636-3049-2). Haiku poems and lovely watercolors introduce 24 familiar North American birds. (Rev: BCCB 3/09; SLJ 4/09; VOYA 8/09) [811]

13782 Rosen, Michael J. *The Hound Dog's Haiku and Other Poems for Dog Lovers* (2–4). Illus. by Mary Azarian. 2011, Candlewick $17.99 (978-0-7636-4499-4). 56pp. Beautiful woodcut illustrations enhance this collection of dog-related poetry. (Rev: BL 8/11; HB 9–10/11; LMC 11–12/11; SLJ 8/11) [811]

13783 Ruddell, Deborah. *Today at the Bluebird Cafe: A Branchful of Birds* (1–3). Illus. by Joan Rankin. 2007, Simon & Schuster $15.99 (978-0-689-87153-5). 40pp. Paired with light-filled watercolors, these playful poems combine imaginative anthropomorphizing with facts about birds. (Rev: BL 1/1–15/07; SLJ 2/07*) [811]

13784 Ryder, Joanne. *Toad by the Road: A Year in the Life of These Amazing Amphibians* (2–4). Illus. by Maggie Kneen. 2007, Holt $16.95 (978-0-8050-7354-6). 32pp. This collection of poems chronicles a year in the life of a toad. (Rev: BL 4/1/07; SLJ 4/07) [811]

13785 Schmidt, Amy. *Loose Leashes* (K–2). Illus. by Ron Schmidt. 2009, Random $16.99 (978-0-375-85641-9). 40pp. A variety of dogs — portrayed in poses that complement the poems — express their individual aspirations, complaints, and opinions in verse. (Rev: BL 1/1–15/09; SLJ 2/09) [811]

13786 Sidman, Joyce. *Meow Ruff: A Story in Concrete Poetry* (1–3). Illus. by Michelle Berg. 2006, Houghton $16.00 (978-0-618-44894-4). Recounted in concrete — or visual — poetry, this simple tale with creative graphics tells how a friendship develops between a cat and dog seeking shelter from a storm. (Rev: BCCB 5/06; BL 3/15/06*; HB 5/06; HBG 10/06; SLJ 7/06) [811]

13787 Sierra, Judy. *Antarctic Antics: A Book of Penguin Poems* (PS–2). Illus. by Jose Aruego and Ariane Dewey. 1998, Harcourt $16.00 (978-0-15-201006-5). 32pp.

Thirteen poems of varying length and accompanying pictures describe the behavior and play of baby penguins in their Antarctic home. (Rev: BL 5/1/98; HBG 10/98; SLJ 5/98) [811]

13788 Singer, Marilyn. *The Company of Crows: A Book of Poems* (2–4). Illus. by Linda Saport. 2002, Clarion $16.00 (978-0-618-08340-4). The intelligent crow is presented in poems written from the viewpoint of onlookers, including children, a farmer, and other animals. (Rev: BL 11/15/02; HBG 3/03; SLJ 11/02) [811]

13789 Singer, Marilyn. *Fireflies at Midnight* (2–4). Illus. by Ken Robbins. 2003, Simon & Schuster $16.95 (978-0-689-82492-0). 32pp. Computer-enhanced photograph collages illustrate verses about animals and their behavior on a summer day. (Rev: BL 4/1/03; HBG 10/03; SLJ 5/03) [811]

13790 Sklansky, Amy E. *From the Doghouse: Poems to Chew On* (1–4). Illus. 2002, Holt $17.95 (978-0-8050-6673-9). 44pp. A delightful collection of poems from the canine perspective about things dogs like — walks in the park and car rides, for example — and things dogs don't like — such as fleas and baths. (Rev: HBG 3/03; SLJ 8/02) [811]

13791 Spinelli, Eileen. *Song for the Whooping Crane* (PS–3). Illus. by Elsa Warnick. 2000, Eerdmans $16.00 (978-0-8028-5172-7). 32pp. A poem that celebrates the endangered whooping crane, its beauty, and its life cycle. (Rev: BL 10/1/00; HBG 3/01; SLJ 3/01) [811]

13792 Stockland, Patricia M., ed. *Fur, Fangs, and Footprints: A Collection of Animal Poems* (3–6). Illus. by Sara Rojo Perez. Series: Poet's Toolbox. 2004, Compass Point LB $23.93 (978-0-7565-0562-2). 32pp. Poems about animals by a selection of writers introduce various poetry concepts. (Rev: BL 4/1/04) [808.81]

13793 Swinburne, Stephen R. *Ocean Soup: Tide-Pool Poems* (1–3). Illus. by Mary Peterson. 2010, Charlesbridge $16.95 (978-1-58089-200-1); paper $7.95 (978-1-58089-201-8). 32pp. Tide-pool animals are introduced in first-person verse accompanied by factual information and illustrations in this large-format book. (Rev: BL 1/1/10; SLJ 4/1/10) [811]

13794 Tiller, Ruth. *Cats Vanish Slowly* (K–3). Illus. by Laura L. Seeley. 1995, Peachtree $16.95 (978-1-56145-106-7). 32pp. Twelve poems about the cats (including B.P., for "bad penny") that are found on the farm of the author's grandmother. (Rev: BL 1/1–15/96; SLJ 1/96) [811]

13795 Whipple, Laura, ed. *Eric Carle's Animals Animals* (PS–3). Illus. by Eric Carle. 1989, Penguin $22.99 (978-0-399-21744-9). Eric Carle's collages illustrate various writers' poems, each dealing with an animal. (Rev: BCCB 10/89*; BL 9/1/89*; HB 11/89; SLJ 11/89) [811]

13796 Worth, Valerie. *Animal Poems* (4–7). 2007, Farrar $17.00 (978-0-374-38057-1). A diverse, sometimes challenging collection of poems highlighting animals' individual characteristics. (Rev: BL 4/1/07; SLJ 4/07*) [811]

13797 Yang-Huan. *Homes* (PS–K). Illus. by Hsiao-yen Huang. 2005, Heryin $13.99 (978-0-9762056-3-0). 32pp. A brief, gentle poem about nature and the homes of diverse animals ends with a final spread of parents and children in a comfortable, sunlit home. (Rev: BL 12/1/05) [895.1]

13798 Yolen, Jane. *Count Me a Rhyme: Animal Poems by the Numbers* (3–5). Illus. by Jason Stemple. 2006, Boyds Mills $17.95 (978-1-59078-345-0). 32pp. Poet mother and photographer son team up to create this attractive combination of counting book (nonet, novena, IX, and so forth) and nature study. (Rev: BL 4/1/06; SLJ 4/06) [811]

13799 Yolen, Jane. *An Egret's Day* (3–6). Illus. 2010, Boyds Mills $17.95 (978-1-59078-650-5). 32pp. This collection of photographs and short poems presents a look at the great egret's habitat, habits, and unique life. (Rev: BL 1/1/10; LMC 5–6/10; SLJ 3/1/10) [811]

13800 Yolen, Jane. *Fine Feathered Friends: Poems for Young People to Perform* (3–6). Illus. by Jason Stemple. 2004, Boyds Mills $17.95 (978-1-59078-193-7). 32pp. Poetry and photographs combine to convey striking images of individual species of birds. (Rev: BL 11/1/04; SLJ 12/04) [811]

13801 Yolen, Jane. *A Mirror to Nature: Poems About Reflection* (2–5). Illus. by Jason Stemple. 2009, Boyds Mills $17.95 (978-1-59078-624-6). 32pp. Eye-catching photographs of animals and their reflections are accompanied by short verses. (Rev: BL 3/15/09; SLJ 6/09) [811]

13802 Yolen, Jane. *Wild Wings: Poems for Young People* (3–6). Illus. by Jason Stemple. 2002, Boyds Mills $19.95 (978-1-56397-904-0). 32pp. Unusual photographs accompany beautiful poems about birds. (Rev: BL 5/15/02; HBG 10/02; SLJ 6/02) [811.54]

13803 Ziefert, Harriet, and Fred Ehrlich. *A Bunny Is Funny: And So Is This Book!* (PS–3). Illus. by Todd McKie. 2008, Blue Apple $16.95 (978-1-934706-03-9). Short poems celebrate key characteristics of 19 different animals. (Rev: LMC 10/08; SLJ 7/08) [811]

Haiku

13804 Clements, Andrew. *Dogku* (2–4). Illus. by Tim Bowers. 2007, Simon & Schuster $16.99 (978-0-689-85823-9). 32pp. Told in haiku form, this is an entertaining story about a stray dog adapting to family life. (Rev: BL 5/1/07; LMC 10/07; SLJ 7/07) [811]

13805 Donegan, Patricia. *Haiku: Asian Arts and Crafts for Creative Kids* (4–8). 2004, Tuttle $14.95 (978-0-8048-3501-5). Haiku advice and exercises follow an introduction to the verse form. (Rev: BL 3/15/04; SLJ 8/04) [372.6]

13806 *In the Eyes of the Cat: Japanese Poetry for All Seasons* (PS–3). Trans. by Tze-si Huang. Illus. by Demi. 1994, Holt paper $6.95 (978-0-8050-3383-0). 80pp. These short Japanese poems, known as haiku, use words

and images appreciated by young readers. (Rev: BCCB 5/92; BL 4/15/92; SLJ 5/92) [895.6]

13807 Issa, Kobayashi. *Today and Today* (K–3). Illus. by G. Brian Karas. 2007, Scholastic $16.99 (978-0-439-59078-5). 40pp. Issa's haiku are woven together to create a poetic tapestry chronicling a year in the life of a family. (Rev: BL 4/1/07) [895.6]

13808 Janeczko, Paul B., and J. Patrick Lewis. *Wing Nuts: Screwy Haiku* (2–4). Illus. by Tricia Tusa. 2006, Little, Brown $14.99 (978-0-316-60731-5). 32pp. This picture book introduces readers to *senryu*, a poetic form similar to haiku but generally humorous and focused more on people than nature. (Rev: BL 3/15/06; SLJ 5/06) [811]

13809 Janeczko, Paul B., ed. *Stone Bench in an Empty Park* (5–12). 2000, Orchard LB $16.99 (978-0-531-33259-7). An inspired collection of haiku from a variety of poets, illustrated with stunning black-and-white photographs. (Rev: BCCB 6/00; BL 3/15/00*; HB 3–4/00; HBG 10/00; SLJ 3/00) [811]

13810 Raczka, Bob. *Guyku: A Year of Haiku for Boys* (1–3). Illus. by Peter H. Reynolds. 2010, Houghton Harcourt $16.99 (978-0-547-24003-9). Unpaged. Addressing the seasons in order, this collection of haiku poetry celebrates the activities typical of boys in the outdoors. (Rev: BL 6/1/10; HB 11–12/10; LMC 5–6/11*; SLJ 9/1/10*) [811]

13811 Yolen, Jane. *Least Things: Poems About Small Natures* (K–5). Photos by Jason Stemple. 2003, Boyds Mills $17.95 (978-1-59078-098-5). 32pp. The wonders of nature are celebrated in this appealing blend of haikus by Jane Yolen and vibrant color photographs by her son, Jason Stemple. (Rev: HBG 4/04; SLJ 10/03) [811]

Holidays

13812 Brown, Calef. *Hallowilloween: Nefarious Silliness from Calef Brown* (2–5). Illus. by author. 2010, Houghton Harcourt $16.99 (978-0-547-21540-2). Unpaged. A collection of nonsense verse about zombies, werewolves, and other things Halloween, with suitably wacky illustrations. (Rev: SLJ 8/1/10*) [811]

13813 Cunningham, Julia. *The Stable Rat and Other Christmas Poems* (3–6). Illus. by Anita Lobel. 2001, Greenwillow LB $15.89 (978-0-688-17800-0). 24pp. These interconnected poems portray Christmas from the viewpoint of the animal and other observers, with vivid artwork. (Rev: BCCB 11/01; BL 9/15/01; HB 11/01; HBG 3/02; SLJ 10/01) [811]

13814 Fisher, Aileen. *Do Rabbits Have Christmas?* (PS–2). Illus. by Sarah Fox-Davies. 2007, Holt $16.95 (978-0-8050-7491-8). 32pp. Fifteen short poems accompanied by appealing illustrations describe the joys of the season. (Rev: BL 10/15/07; HB 11/07) [811]

13815 Ghigna, Charles, and Debra Ghigna. *Christmas Is Coming* (PS–3). Illus. by Mary O'Keefe. 2000, Charlesbridge $15.95 (978-0-88106-113-0). 32pp. A number of Christmas preparations, like selecting a tree and baking cookies, are depicted in these 27 original poems with expressive illustrations. (Rev: BL 9/1/00; HBG 3/01) [811]

13816 Grimes, Nikki. *At Jerusalem's Gate: Poems of Easter* (5–8). Illus. by David Frampton. 2005, Eerdmans $20.00 (978-0-8028-5183-3). More than 20 poems are introduced by thoughtful paragraphs and enhanced by handsome illustrations. (Rev: BL 2/15/05; SLJ 3/05) [232.96]

13817 Harrison, Michael, and Christopher Stuart-Clark, eds. *Bright Star Shining: Poems for Christmas* (3–8). Illus. 1998, Eerdmans $15.00 (978-0-8028-5177-2). 48pp. Illustrated by three different artists, this is a fine collection of 32 Christmas poems. (Rev: BL 9/1/98; HBG 3/99) [808.81]

13818 Hopkins, Lee Bennett, ed. *Christmas Presents: Holiday Poetry* (K–3). Illus. by Melanie W. Hall. Series: An I Can Read Book. 2004, HarperCollins LB $16.89 (978-0-06-008055-6). 32pp. Twelve Christmas poems explore all aspects of the holiday and demonstrate different styles and devices. (Rev: BL 8/04; SLJ 10/04) [811]

13819 Hopkins, Lee Bennett, sel. *Halloween Howls: Holiday Poetry* (K–3). Illus. by Stacey Schuett. 2005, HarperCollins $15.99 (978-0-06-008060-0). 32pp. A dozen previously published poems celebrate the sights, sounds, and smells of Halloween; suitable for beginning readers. (Rev: SLJ 10/05) [811]

13820 Horton, Joan. *Halloween Hoots and Howls* (2–5). Illus. 1999, Holt $15.95 (978-0-8050-5805-5). 32pp. A collection of amusing — sometimes wacky — poems about Halloween. (Rev: BCCB 9/99; BL 9/1/99; HBG 3/00; SLJ 10/99) [811]

13821 Johnston, Tony. *Noel* (K–4). Illus. by Cheng-Khee Chee. 2005, Carolrhoda LB $15.95 (978-1-57505-752-1). A church bell's chimes summon humans and animals to worship on Christmas Eve in this lyrical poem accompanied by beautiful impressionistic watercolors. (Rev: SLJ 10/05) [811]

13822 Koontz, Dean. *Every Day's a Holiday: Amusing Rhymes for Happy Times* (3–6). Illus. by Phil Parks. 2003, HarperCollins LB $18.89 (978-0-06-008585-8). 144pp. Each of the 64 poems in this collection celebrates a special day on the calendar — holidays and other landmark days, such as the beginning of autumn and the shortest day of the year. (Rev: HBG 4/04; SLJ 10/03) [811]

13823 Lansky, Bruce, et al. *Happy Birthday to Me! Kids Pick the Funniest Birthday Poems* (2–5). Illus. by Jack Lindstrom. 1998, Meadowbrook $8.95 (978-0-671-57703-2). 27pp. Nine poets are represented in this joyous collection of 21 poems that celebrate birthdays. (Rev: SLJ 5/98) [811]

13824 Livingston, Myra Cohn, ed. *Celebrations* (1–4). Illus. by Leonard Everett Fisher. 1985, Holiday House LB $16.95 (978-0-8234-0550-3); paper $6.95 (978-0-8234-0654-8). 32pp. A handsome book of verse illustrating 16 celebrations, such as Valentine's Day, birthdays, and Easter. (Rev: BCCB 4/85; BL 4/1/85; HB 5/85)

13825 Livingston, Myra Cohn, ed. *Christmas Poems* (PS–3). Illus. by Trina S. Hyman. 1984, Holiday House LB $16.95 (978-0-8234-0508-4). A collection of 18 poems, half of which were commissioned for the volume.

13826 Livingston, Myra Cohn, ed. *Poems for Jewish Holidays* (K–6). Illus. by Lloyd Bloom. 1986, Holiday House LB $15.95 (978-0-8234-0606-7). 32pp. Poems that contain the essence of major Jewish holidays. (Rev: BCCB 2/87; BL 11/1/86; HB 1/87)

13827 Livingston, Myra Cohn, ed. *Valentine Poems* (3–6). Illus. 1987, Holiday House LB $16.95 (978-0-8234-0587-9). 32pp. Sprightly poems from established names and modern ones, too. (Rev: BL 1/15/87; SLJ 12/86)

13828 Moore, Clement C. *The Night Before Christmas* (PS–1). Ed. by Cooper Edens and Harold Darling. Illus. 1998, Chronicle $16.95 (978-0-8118-1712-7). 44pp. This new edition of the classic poem uses illustrations that originally appeared between 1890 and 1928. (Rev: BL 10/1/98; HBG 3/99; SLJ 10/98) [811]

13829 Moore, Clement C. *The Night Before Christmas* (PS–2). Illus. by Jan Brett. 1998, Penguin LB $16.99 (978-0-399-23190-2). This version of the classic Christmas poem contains illustrations of a Victorian house, an old-world Santa, and two stowaway elves. (Rev: HBG 3/99; SLJ 10/98) [811]

13830 Moore, Clement C. *The Night Before Christmas* (PS–3). Illus. by Tomie dePaola. 1980, Holiday House LB $16.95 (978-0-8234-0414-8); paper $6.95 (978-0-8234-0417-9). 32pp. A lovely edition of this popular and loved Christmas poem. Another edition is: Illus. by Anita Lobel (Knopf 1996).

13831 Moore, Clement C. *The Night Before Christmas* (PS–1). Illus. by Cheryl Harness. 1990, Random $8.99 (978-0-394-82698-1). A traditional treatment of the classic holiday poem. (Rev: BL 11/1/90; HB 11/90) [811]

13832 Moore, Clement C. *The Night Before Christmas* (PS–2). Illus. by Holly Hobbie. 2013, Little, Brown $18 (978-031607018-8). 40pp. The star of this work is not the well-known poem, but the illustrations, which are shown from the perspective of a toddler and done in a mixture of watercolor, gouache, and ink. (Rev: BLO 9/15/13; HB 11–12/13; SLJ 10/13) [811]

13833 Moore, Clement C. *The Night Before Christmas* (PS–2). Illus. by Will Moses. 2006, Philomel $16.99 (978-0-399-23745-4). Folk artist Will Moses portrays the traditional poem in nostalgic paintings full of welcoming houses lit by candles. (Rev: BL 9/15/06; SLJ 10/06) [811]

13834 Moore, Clement C. *The Night Before Christmas* (PS–2). Illus. by Gennady Spirin. 2006, Marshall Cavendish $16.99 (978-0-7614-5298-0). 32pp. Spirin's interpretation of the poem is set in a quaint European village of days gone by, with illustrations full of contrasting light. (Rev: BL 9/15/06; SLJ 10/06) [811]

13835 Moore, Clement C. *The Night Before Christmas* (PS–2). Illus. by Tasha Tudor. 1999, Little, Brown $14.95 (978-0-316-85579-2). Wild and domestic animals on a Vermont farm form an important part of the illustrations in this version of the classic poem. (Rev: HBG 3/00; SLJ 10/99) [811]

13836 Moore, Clement C. *The Night Before Christmas* (PS–2). Illus. by Richard Jesse Watson. 2006, Harper-Collins $16.99 (978-0-06-075741-0). 40pp. Moore's classic poem features a high-tech sleigh complete with a fully equipped cockpit, multicultural elves, and dynamic, realistic art. (Rev: BL 9/15/06; SLJ 10/06) [811]

13837 Moore, Clement C. *The Night Before Christmas* (PS–3). Illus. by Bruce Whatley. 1999, HarperCollins LB $16.89 (978-0-06-028380-3). 40pp. The pictures in this attractive edition of the favorite poem depict events from the father's point of view. (Rev: BL 9/1/99*; HBG 3/00; SLJ 10/99) [811]

13838 Moore, Clement C. *The Night Before Christmas* (K–3). Illus. by Lisbeth Zwerger. 2005, Penguin $15.99 (978-0-698-40030-6). 32pp. The immortal Christmas poem is given new life in the dream-like blue and green artwork accented by the red suit. (Rev: BL 10/15/05; SLJ 10/05) [811]

13839 Moore, Clement C. *The Night Before Christmas: Or, a Visit of St. Nicholas* (PS–3). Illus. 1989, Penguin $19.99 (978-0-399-21614-5). 32pp. This handsomely produced edition of the famous poem was illustrated years ago by a now-forgotten artist. (Rev: BL 9/15/89) [811]

13840 Moore, Clement C. *The Teddy Bears' Night Before Christmas* (PS–K). Illus. by Monica Stevenson. 1999, Scholastic $12.95 (978-0-590-03243-8). 40pp. Photographs of stuffed animals in snowy scenes illustrate this version of the classic rhyme. (Rev: BL 9/1/99; HBG 3/00; SLJ 10/99) [811]

13841 Moore, Clement C. *'Twas the Night Before Christmas; or, Account of a Visit from St. Nicholas* (PS–2). Illus. by Matt Tavares. 2002, Candlewick $16.00 (978-0-7636-1585-7). 32pp. The classic, original version of the poem, accompanied by old-fashioned artwork. (Rev: BL 9/1/02; HBG 3/03) [811]

13842 Prelutsky, Jack. *It's Christmas!* (PS–1). Illus. by Marylin Hafner. Series: I Can Read. 2008, Greenwillow $16.99 (978-0-06-053706-7). 48pp. For beginning readers, this is a collection of happy verses about various aspects of Christmas. (Rev: BL 12/1/08; HB 11/08) [811]

13843 Prelutsky, Jack. *It's Valentine's Day* (1–4). Illus. by Yossi Abolafia. 1985, Scholastic paper $2.50 (978-0-590-40979-7). 48pp. Bright, humorous poems in celebration of love and Valentine's Day.

13844 *A Small Treasury of Easter: Poems and Prayers* (K–4). Illus. by Susan Spellman. 1997, Boyds Mills $8.95 (978-1-56397-647-6). 32pp. An illustrated collection of secular and religious Easter poems, divided into two parts: "A Time to Play" and "A Time to Pray." (Rev: SLJ 7/97) [811]

13845 Snell, Gordon. *'Twas the Day After Christmas* (PS–2). Illus. by Sean Delonas. 2003, HarperCollins LB $16.89 (978-0-06-028953-9). This amusing variation on Clement C. Moore's holiday poem paints a portrait of

the somewhat messy day after Christmas from the viewpoint of a tiny mouse. (Rev: HBG 4/04; SLJ 10/03) [811]

13846 Whitehead, Jenny. *Holiday Stew: A Kid's Portion of Holiday and Seasonal Poems* (K–3). Illus. by author. 2007, Holt $17.95 (978-0-8050-7715-5). 64pp. Holidays big and small are celebrated in these 78 child-centered poems. (Rev: BL 5/15/07; SLJ 5/07) [811]

Humorous Poetry

13847 Agee, Jon. *Orangutan Tongs* (1–4). Illus. by author. 2009, Hyperion $16.99 (978-1-4231-0315-8). 32pp. Full of elaborate tongue twisters, this is a collection of funny verses. (Rev: BCCB 4/09; BL 3/1/09; HB 3/09; LMC 5/09; SLJ 3/09) [818]

13848 Aylesworth, Jim. *The Burger and the Hot Dog* (K–3). Illus. by Stephen Gammell. 2001, Simon & Schuster $16.95 (978-0-689-83897-2). 32pp. A collection of funny poems about anthropomorphic foods with effective, messy illustrations. (Rev: BCCB 12/01; BL 10/1/01; HBG 3/02; SLJ 1/02) [811]

13849 Bagert, Brod. *Giant Children* (K–3). Illus. by Tedd Arnold. 2002, Dial $16.99 (978-0-8037-2556-0). 32pp. Side-splitting artwork is the perfect accompaniment to this eclectic collection of poems for young readers. (Rev: BL 8/02; HBG 3/03; SLJ 8/02) [811]

13850 Bagert, Brod. *School Fever* (1–3). Illus. by Robert Neubecker. 2008, Dial $16.99 (978-0-8037-3201-8). 40pp. Quirky first-person poems chronicle a boy's school day, from morning "fever" to bullies to his crush on his teacher. (Rev: BL 8/08; LMC 11/08; SLJ 7/08) [811]

13851 Billings, John. *My Pet Crocodile and Other Slightly Outrageous Verse* (PS–3). Illus. by Janette Todd. 1993, Chokecherry $16.95 (978-1-884035-55-5). 128pp. Humorous poems on such subjects as bungee jumping, nose picking, and bubble gum. (Rev: BL 1/1/94) [811]

13852 Brewton, Sara, ed. *Of Quarks, Quasars and Other Quirks: Quizzical Poems for the Supersonic Age* (5–8). Illus. by Quentin Blake. 1977, HarperCollins LB $13.89 (978-0-690-04885-8). Contemporary poems that poke fun at such modern innovations as transplants and water beds.

13853 Brown, Calef. *Dutch Sneakers and Flea Keepers: 14 More Stories* (3–5). Illus. 2000, Houghton $16.00 (978-0-618-05183-0). 32pp. A collection of original poems that introduce the reader to several odd and eccentric characters, such as the Flea Keepers, who train fleas for cash. (Rev: BCCB 7–8/00; BL 4/1/00; HBG 10/00; SLJ 4/00) [811.54]

13854 Brown, Calef. *Flamingos on the Roof* (3–5). Illus. 2006, Houghton $16.00 (978-0-618-56298-5). 64pp. A delightful collection of nonsense poems accompanied by funky illustrations. (Rev: BL 4/15/06; SLJ 7/06) [811]

13855 Bush, Timothy. *Ferocious Girls, Steamroller Boys, and Other Poems in Between* (1–4). Illus. by author. 2000, Orchard LB $17.99 (978-0-531-33250-4). A funny book that uses seven poems to explore unusual boys and girls and their strange behavior. (Rev: HBG 10/00; SLJ 7/00) [811]

13856 Carroll, Lewis. *Jabberwocky* (3–5). Illus. by Christopher Myers. 2007, Hyperion $15.99 (978-1-4231-0372-1). Vibrant artwork supports a reinterpretation of the classic nonsense poem set on a contemporary basketball court. (Rev: BL 9/1/07; LMC 11/07; SLJ 8/07) [821]

13857 Ciardi, John. *You Read to Me, I'll Read to You* (4–6). Illus. by Edward Gorey. 1987, HarperCollins paper $7.99 (978-0-06-446060-6). 64pp. A collection of original verse for both adults and children.

13858 Cole, William, ed. *Poem Stew* (2–6). Illus. by Karen Ann Weinhaus. 1981, HarperCollins $7.66 (978-0-397-31963-3). 96pp. A collection of 57 witty poems about food.

13859 Cox, Kenyon. *Mixed Beasts* (3–5). Illus. by Wallace Edwards. 2005, Kids Can $17.95 (978-1-55337-796-2). Nonsense poems about beasts such as the kangarooster and bumblebeaver are accompanied by full-page, detailed illustrations. (Rev: SLJ 1/06) [811]

13860 Dakos, Kalli. *The Bug in Teacher's Coffee: And Other School Poems* (K–2). Illus. by Mike Reed. Series: An I Can Read Book. 1999, HarperCollins LB $16.89 (978-0-06-027940-0). 38pp. For beginning readers, a book of humorous poetry with zany illustrations that use everyday objects found in a school. (Rev: HBG 3/00; SLJ 12/99) [811]

13861 Florian, Douglas. *Bing Bang Boing* (4–6). Illus. 1994, Harcourt $16.00 (978-0-15-233770-4). A lighthearted, imaginative collection of short, humorous verses. (Rev: BCCB 11/94; BL 12/1/94; SLJ 11/94) [811]

13862 Florian, Douglas. *Laugh-Eteria* (3–5). Illus. 1999, Harcourt $17.00 (978-0-15-202084-2). 158pp. A collection of 150 original, humorous poems that will appeal to a child's sometimes gross sense of humor. (Rev: BCCB 4/99; BL 3/15/99; HBG 10/99; SLJ 6/99) [811]

13863 Florian, Douglas. *Shiver Me Timbers! Pirate Poems and Paintings* (K–3). Illus. by Robert Neubecker. 2012, Simon & Schuster $16.99 (978-1-4424-1321-4). 32pp. A funny collection of 19 poems featuring wacky pirates and their exploits, enhanced by inventive wordplay and ink and color drawings. **e** (Rev: BL 9/15/12; HB 9–10/12; LMC 1–2/13; SLJ 8/12*) [811]

13864 Grandits, John. *Technically, It's Not My Fault: Concrete Poems* (4–6). Illus. by author. 2004, Clarion paper $5.95 (978-0-618-50361-2). Eleven-year-old Robert's unique — and sometimes gross — vision of the world around him is expressed in arresting poetry with an inventive presentation. (Rev: BL 12/15/04; SLJ 4/05) [811]

13865 Greenberg, David. *Don't Forget Your Etiquette! The Essential Guide to Misbehavior* (1–3). Illus. by Nadine Bernard Westcott. 2006, Farrar $16.00 (978-0-374-34990-5). 40pp. In humorous poems, "Miss Information" dispenses advice that turns proper etiquette on its head. (Rev: BL 10/1/06; SLJ 10/06) [811]

13866 Greenfield, Eloise. *Brothers and Sisters: Family Poems* (1–4). Illus. by Jan Spivey Gilchrist. 2009, HarperCollins $17.99 (978-0-06-056284-7). 32pp. This collection of 25 short poems chronicles the pleasures and perils of life with siblings; illustrations feature African American characters in watercolor-and-ink. (Rev: BL 2/1/09; HB 3/09; SLJ 1/09) [811]

13867 Greenfield, Eloise. *I Can Draw a Weeposaur and Other Dinosaurs* (K–3). Illus. by Jan S. Gilchrist. 2001, Greenwillow LB $14.89 (978-0-688-17635-8). 31pp. A group of poems about fanciful, imaginary dinosaurs along with drawings of them by the girl who dreamed them up. (Rev: HBG 10/01; SLJ 3/01) [811]

13868 Grimes, Nikki. *Is It Far to Zanzibar? Poems About Tanzania* (PS–3). Illus. by Betsy Lewin. 2000, Lothrop LB $15.89 (978-0-688-13158-6). 32pp. A series of rhyming, singsong verses that fancifully describe life in Tanzania. (Rev: BL 3/15/00; HBG 10/00; SLJ 5/00) [811]

13869 Grossman, Bill. *Timothy Tunny Swallowed a Bunny* (PS–2). Illus. by Kevin Hawkes. 2001, HarperCollins $14.95 (978-0-06-028010-9). 32pp. Eighteen nonsense poems explore comic situations, such as the boy who grew a new nose every year. (Rev: BCCB 2/01; BL 2/15/01; HB 3/01*; HBG 10/01; SLJ 3/01)

13870 Hopkins, Lee Bennett, ed. *Dizzy Dinosaurs: Silly Dino Poems* (K–2). Illus. by Barry Gott. Series: I Can Read! 2011, HarperCollins $16.99 (978-0-06-135839-5); paper $3.99 (978-0-06-135841-8). 48pp. Humorous poems about dinosaurs by writers including Marilyn Singer, Douglas Florian, and Rebecca Kai Dotlich are targeted at newly independent readers. (Rev: HB 3–4/11; SLJ 5/1/11) [811]

13871 Horton, Joan. *Hippopotamus Stew: And Other Silly Animal Poems* (PS–2). Illus. by JoAnn Adinolfi. 2006, Holt $16.95 (978-0-8050-7350-8). 32pp. A menagerie of wacky animals — and humans — is introduced in this collection of 21 nonsense poems illustrated with lively, funny collages. (Rev: BL 2/1/06; SLJ 3/06) [811]

13872 Horton, Joan. *I Brought My Rat for Show-and-Tell* (1–3). Trans. and illus. by Melanie Siegel. Series: All Aboard Poetry Reader. 2004, Penguin LB $3.99 (978-0-448-43364-6). 48pp. The eye-catching cartoon illustrations and nonsensical rhyming poems in this collection will appeal to beginning readers. (Rev: BL 8/04; SLJ 10/04) [811]

13873 Janeczko, Paul B., ed. *A Poke in the I: A Collection of Concrete Poems* (3–8). Illus. by Chris Raschka. 2001, Candlewick $15.99 (978-0-7636-0661-9). 36pp. A collection of original humorous poems each of which takes a different shape on the page, for example, the poem about a popsicle is on a stick. (Rev: BL 3/15/01*; HB 7/01*; HBG 10/01) [811.008]

13874 Katz, Alan. *Oops!* (2–5). Illus. by Edward Koren. 2008, Simon & Schuster $17.99 (978-1-4169-0204-1). A collection of 100 little rhyming poems that employ wordplay, puns, and pure nonsense. (Rev: BL 3/1/08; SLJ 4/08) [811]

13875 Katz, Alan. *Poems I Wrote When No One Was Looking* (3–5). Illus. by Edward Koren. 2011, Simon & Schuster $17.99 (978-1416935186). 176pp. This book of comically irreverent poems covers such topics as changing a diaper, spelling mistakes, and embarrassing situations. ℮ (Rev: BL 1/1/10; LMC 1–2/12; SLJ 11/1/11) [811]

13876 Kennedy, X. J. *Uncle Switch: Loony Limericks* (1–3). Illus. by John O'Brien. 1997, Simon & Schuster $15.00 (978-0-689-80967-5). 32pp. Twenty-two funny limericks involving the dimwitted Uncle Switch. (Rev: BCCB 4/97; BL 5/1/97; SLJ 4/97) [811]

13877 Kinerk, Robert. *Oh, How Sylvester Can Pester! And Other Poems More or Less About Manners* (PS–2). Illus. by Drazen Kozjan. 2011, Simon & Schuster $16.99 (978-1-4169-3362-5). 32pp. Full of wordplay, these 20 funny poems focus on etiquette. (Rev: BL 2/15/11; HB 3–4/11; SLJ 3/1/11) [811]

13878 Korman, Gordon, and Bernice Korman. *The D- Poems of Jeremy Bloom: A Collection of Poems About School, Homework, and Life (Sort Of)* (4–6). 1992, Scholastic paper $3.50 (978-0-590-44819-2). 98pp. The engaging and funny poems of rambunctious sixth-grader Jeremy Bloom. (Rev: BL 1/15/93; SLJ 2/93) [811]

13879 Lansky, Bruce, ed. *A Bad Case of the Giggles: Kids' Favorite Funny Poems* (2–5). Illus. by Stephen Carpenter. 1994, Meadowbrook $14.00 (978-0-88166-213-9). 132pp. A great collection of humorous poems that includes puns, tongue twisters, and parodies, many by well-known writers. (Rev: BL 11/15/94; SLJ 2/95) [811]

13880 Lansky, Bruce, ed. *Miles of Smiles: Kids Pick the Funniest Poems, Book 3* (2–6). Illus. by Stephen Carpenter. 1998, Meadowbrook $16.00 (978-0-88166-313-6). 115pp. A collection of 72 humorous poems some of them earthy in content and dealing with subjects such as underwear and bathroom humor. (Rev: HBG 3/99; SLJ 11/98) [811]

13881 Lansky, Bruce, ed. *Rolling in the Aisles: A Collection of Laugh-Out-Loud Poems* (3–6). Illus. by Stephen Carpenter. 2004, Meadowbrook $17.00 (978-0-88166-473-7). 115pp. Organized by kid-friendly topics, these poems — many by familiar authors and selected by young readers — are accompanied by large cartoons. (Rev: SLJ 1/05) [811]

13882 Lear, Edward. *Complete Nonsense Book of Edward Lear* (4–6). Illus. by author. 1951, Dover paper $11.95 (978-0-486-20167-2). 287pp. Verse, prose, drawings, alphabets, and other amusing absurdities.

13883 Lear, Edward. *His Shoes Were Far Too Tight* (2–5). Ed. by Daniel Pinkwater. Illus. by Calef Brown. 2011, Chronicle $16.99 (978-0-8118-6792-4). 40pp. Ten poems showcasing Lear's talent for absurdity are collected in this brightly illustrated book. (Rev: BL 6/1/11; LMC 10/11; SLJ 6/11) [821]

13884 Lear, Edward. *The Owl and the Pussycat* (PS–1). Illus. by Jan Brett. 1991, Penguin $16.99 (978-0-399-21925-2). 32pp. Beautiful double-page spreads enhance

the enchantment of this retelling. (Rev: BL 3/1/91*; SLJ 2/91*) [821]

13885 Lear, Edward. *The Owl and the Pussycat* (PS–1). Illus. by James Marshall. 1998, HarperCollins LB $15.89 (978-0-06-205011-3). 32pp. Fresh and funny artwork from James Marshall highlight this edition of the classic nonsense poem. (Rev: BL 2/1/99; HB 3/99; HBG 10/99; SLJ 12/98) [821]

13886 Lear, Edward. *The Owl and the Pussycat* (PS–4). Illus. by Anne Mortimer. 2006, HarperCollins $15.99 (978-0-06-027228-9). The beloved old rhyme, illustrated in a lush, lovely style. (Rev: SLJ 7/06) [811]

13887 Lear, Edward. *Poetry for Young People* (3–5). Ed. by Edward Mendelson. Illus. by Huliska-Beit Laura. 2002, Sterling $14.95 (978-0-8069-3077-0). 48pp. An introduction to the limericks and poetry of Edward Lear. (Rev: BL 3/1/02; HBG 10/02) [821]

13888 Lear, Edward. *The Quangle Wangle's Hat* (PS–2). Illus. by Louise Voce. 2005, Candlewick $15.99 (978-0-7636-1289-4). The Quangle Wangle, all alone in his tree, is glad when his giant hat becomes home to other animals as fanciful as he. (Rev: BL 3/1/05; SLJ 1/05) [811]

13889 Lesynski, Loris. *Nothing Beats a Pizza* (3–6). Illus. by author. 2001, Annick LB $18.95 (978-1-55037-701-9); paper $7.95 (978-1-55037-700-2). 32pp. Lesynski's verses take a humorous approach to the serious topic of pizza. (Rev: HBG 3/02; SLJ 2/02) [811]

13890 Levine, Gail Carson. *Forgive Me, I Meant to Do It: False Apology Poems* (2–5). Illus. by Matthew Cordell. 2012, HarperCollins $15.99 (978-006178725-6). 80pp. Borrowing from William Carlos Williams' poem "This Is Just to Say," Levine creates a collection of lighthearted poems poking fun in various directions including fairy tales. (Rev: BL 3/1/12*; HB 3–4/12; SLJ 2/12) [811]

13891 Lewis, J. Patrick. *If You Were a Chocolate Mustache* (2–5). Illus. by Matthew Cordell. 2012, Boyds Mills/Wordsong $18.95 (978-1-59078-927-8). 160pp. Readers will romp through this collection of humorous yet informative poems full of wordplay written by the U.S. Children's Poet Laureate and featuring a wide variety of styles accompanied by pen-and-ink drawings that add to the fun. (Rev: BL 12/15/12; LMC 5–6/13; SLJ 10/12) [811]

13892 Lewis, J. Patrick. *Once Upon a Tomb: Gravely Humorous Verses* (2–4). Illus. by Simon Bartram. 2006, Candlewick $16.99 (978-0-7636-1837-7). 32pp. This collection of amusing epitaphs marks the passing of such diverse individuals as an underwear salesman, dairy farmer, schoolteacher, food critic, and fortune teller. (Rev: BL 8/06; SLJ 8/06) [811]

13893 Lewis, J. Patrick. *Tulip at the Bat* (K–3). Illus. by Amiko Hirao. 2007, Little, Brown $16.99 (978-0-316-61280-7). 32pp. The Boston Beasts are up against the New York Pets in this silly, pun-filled World Series championship game. (Rev: BL 4/1/07) [811]

13894 Lewis, J. Patrick, and Jane Yolen. *Last Laughs: Animal Epitaphs* (2–4). Illus. by Jeffrey Stewart Timmins. 2012, Charlesbridge $16.95 (978-1-58089-260-5). 32pp.

Dark humor reigns in this collection of epitaphs full of wordplay; this picture book will amuse many readers but may horrify others. (Rev: BL 9/15/12*; LMC 3–4/13; SLJ 7/12) [811]

13895 McGough, Roger, ed. *Wicked Poems* (4–8). Illus. by Neal Layton. 2005, Bloomsbury paper $15.00 (978-0-7475-6195-8). Misbehavior of varying degrees is displayed in this varied collection of poems accompanied by cartoons. (Rev: SLJ 1/05) [811]

13896 Mendelson, Edward, ed. *Poetry for Young People: Lewis Carroll* (3–5). Illus. 2001, Sterling $14.95 (978-0-8069-5541-4). The poetry that is scattered throughout Lewis Carroll's books is collected here, including some of his nonsense creations like *Jabberwocky*. (Rev: BL 3/1/01; HBG 10/01; SLJ 3/01) [821]

13897 Morrison, Lillian. *I Scream, You Scream: A Feast of Food Rhymes* (3–5). Illus. 1997, August House $12.95 (978-0-87483-495-6). 96pp. Food is the subject of this humorous collection of rhymes, autograph-book verses, tongue twisters, and jokes. (Rev: BL 11/15/97; HBG 3/98; SLJ 11/97) [811]

13898 Nash, Ogden. *The Adventures of Isabel* (PS–2). Illus. by Bridget S. Taylor. 2008, Sourcebooks $16.95 (978-1-4022-1027-3). 32pp. With large bright watercolors, Taylor illustrates the Nash poem about a brave girl who takes on all scary challenges; an accompanying CD offers an audio of Nash reading the verses. (Rev: BL 6/1–15/08; SLJ 6/08) [811.54]

13899 Nesbitt, Kenn. *My Hippo Has the Hiccups: And Other Poems I Totally Made Up* (2–5). Illus. by Ethan Long. 2009, Sourcebooks $17.99 (978-1-4022-1809-5). 172pp. This fun and wacky collection of 100 poems (39 read by the author on the included CD) entertains with its unusual subjects such as angry stew vegetable and pink-headed zebras. (Rev: LMC 10/09; SLJ 5/09) [811]

13900 Opie, Iona, and Peter Opie, eds. *I Saw Esau: The Schoolchild's Pocket Book* (2–5). Illus. by Maurice Sendak. 1992, Candlewick $19.99 (978-1-56402-046-8). 160pp. Schoolyard folk rhymes that are absurd, fierce, vulgar, and compelling. (Rev: BCCB 5/92*; BL 4/15/92*; SLJ 6/92*) [811]

13901 Paraskevas, Betty. *Junior Kroll and Company* (K–3). Illus. by Michael Paraskevas. 1994, Harcourt $13.95 (978-0-15-292855-1). A mischievous, shrewd toddler has a series of adventures, like learning to waltz with Cousin Blanche. (Rev: BL 4/15/94; SLJ 5/94) [811]

13902 Perry, Andrea. *Here's What You Do When You Can't Find Your Shoe: Ingenious Inventions for Pesky Problems* (3–5). Illus. by Alan Snow. 2003, Simon & Schuster $16.95 (978-0-689-83067-9). 40pp. Humorous poems imagine the invention of such child-friendly innovations as a spray that will empty the family shopping cart of offensive vegetables and a leaf-eater to help with raking. (Rev: BL 4/1/03; HBG 10/03; SLJ 5/03) [811]

13903 Perry, Andrea. *The Snack Smasher: And Other Reasons Why It's Not My Fault* (2–5). Illus. by Alan Snow. 2007, Simon & Schuster $16.99 (978-0-689-85469-9). 33pp. These humorous poems provide whim-

sical explanations for some of life's most puzzling mysteries. (Rev: SLJ 2/07) [811]

13904 Phinn, Gervase. *What I Like! Poems for the Very Young* (PS–K). Illus. by Jane Eccles. 2005, Child's Play paper $7.99 (978-1-904550-12-9). 32pp. A lively collection of amusing rhymes and illustrations about subjects close to young children's hearts. (Rev: BL 5/1/05) [811]

13905 Prelutsky, Jack. *Awful Ogre Running Wild* (K–3). Illus. by Paul Zelinsky. 2008, Greenwillow $17.99 (978-0-06-623866-1). The Awful Ogre rides again as he sets out on his summer vacation in this new volume of 17 humorous first-person poems illustrated with chaotic good cheer. (Rev: BL 9/1/08) [811]

13906 Prelutsky, Jack. *Awful Ogre's Awful Day* (PS–3). Illus. by Paul Zelinsky. 2001, Greenwillow LB $16.89 (978-0-688-07779-2). 40pp. Humorous poems look at an ogre's daily routine — from breakfast to bedtime — with amusing illustrations. (Rev: BCCB 9/01; BL 10/15/01; HB 9/01; HBG 3/02; SLJ 9/01*) [811.54]

13907 Prelutsky, Jack. *Behold the Bold Umbrellaphant and Other Poems* (3–5). Illus. by Carin Berger. 2006, Greenwillow LB $17.89 (978-0-06-054318-1). Combinations of animals and objects — alarmadillo, spatuloon, panthermometer, tubaboon, to name just a few — star in these 17 silly poems. (Rev: BL 9/1/06; SLJ 10/06*) [811]

13908 Prelutsky, Jack. *In Aunt Giraffe's Green Garden* (PS–3). Illus. by Petra Mathers. 2007, Greenwillow $16.99 (978-0-06-623868-5). 32pp. Silly poetry and clever illustrations highlight this book about animal friends vacationing in various U.S. locations. (Rev: BL 7/07; SLJ 8/07) [811] ∩

13909 Prelutsky, Jack. *It's Raining Pigs and Noodles* (PS–3). Illus. by James Stevenson. 2000, Greenwillow LB $18.89 (978-0-06-029195-2). 160pp. There are more than 100 nonsense rhymes in this delightful collection; scribbly drawings carry on the humor. (Rev: BCCB 10/00; BL 11/1/00; HBG 3/01; SLJ 11/00) [811]

13910 Prelutsky, Jack. *I've Lost My Hippopotamus* (2–4). Illus. by Jackie Urbanovic. 2012, Greenwillow $18.99 (978-0-06-201457-3). 144pp. More than 100 diverse poems full of funny wordplay focus on many topics. (Rev: BL 12/15/11; SLJ 2/1/12*) [811]

13911 Prelutsky, Jack. *My Dog May Be a Genius* (2–5). Illus. by James Stevenson. 2008, Greenwillow $18.99 (978-0-06-623862-3). 160pp. A collection of well-crafted silly poetry accompanied by cartoon illustrations. (Rev: BL 3/1/08; HB 3/08; LMC 11/08; SLJ 2/08) [811] ∩

13912 Prelutsky, Jack. *The New Kid on the Block: Poems* (3–6). Illus. by James Stevenson. 1984, Greenwillow $18.89 (978-0-688-02272-3). 160pp. A collection of over 100 humorous poems by this prolific master.

13913 Prelutsky, Jack. *Ride a Purple Pelican* (PS–2). Illus. by Garth Williams. 1986, Greenwillow $18.99 (978-0-688-04031-4). New verses that sound like old favorites. (Rev: BL 10/1/86; HB 1/87; SLJ 11/86)

13914 Prelutsky, Jack. *Something Big Has Been Here* (4–6). Illus. by James Stevenson. 1990, Greenwillow $17.99 (978-0-688-06434-1). A bountiful collection of witty poems. (Rev: BCCB 12/90; BL 9/1/90*; HB 11/90*; SLJ 10/90*) [811]

13915 Prelutsky, Jack. *Stardines Swim High Across the Sky: And Other Poems* (1–5). Illus. by Carin Berger. 2013, Greenwillow $17.99 (978-0-06-201464-1). 40pp. Stardines, slobsters, braindeer, and panteaters are among the fantastic creatures portrayed in poems and clever illustrations. ∩ (Rev: BL 12/1/12; HB 3–4/13; SLJ 2/13) [811]

13916 Prelutsky, Jack. *What a Day It Was at School!* (K–2). Illus. by Doug Cushman. 2006, Greenwillow $16.99 (978-0-06-082335-1). This collection of poems — some fantastical and some realistic but all humorous — celebrates the school experience. (Rev: BL 8/06; SLJ 7/06) [811]

13917 Prelutsky, Jack, selector. *There's No Place Like School* (K–3). Illus. by Jane Manning. 2010, HarperCollins $16.99 (978-0-06-082338-2); LB $17.89 (978-0-06-082339-9). 32pp. A collection of 18 short, humorous poems by writers including Lee Bennett Hopkins, Carol Diggory Shields, and Prelutsky himself. (Rev: BL 8/10; SLJ 7/1/10) [811]

13918 Proimos, James. *If I Were in Charge the Rules Would Be Different* (3–5). Illus. 2002, Scholastic $16.95 (978-0-439-20864-2). 80pp. Playful poems about childhood, with humorous illustrations. (Rev: BL 5/15/02; HBG 10/02; SLJ 3/02) [811]

13919 Rash, Andy. *The Robots Are Coming* (2–5). Illus. 2000, Scholastic $15.95 (978-0-439-06306-7). 40pp. This collection of 16 original poems includes as subjects an abominable snowman, a werewolf, and the Loch Ness Monster. (Rev: BCCB 12/00; BL 11/15/00; HBG 3/01; SLJ 11/00) [811]

13920 Rasmussen, Halfdan. *A Little Bitty Man: And Other Poems for the Very Young* (PS–K). Trans. from Danish by Marilyn Nelson and Pamela Espeland. Illus. by Kevin Hawkes. 2011, Candlewick $15.99 (978-0-7636-2379-1). 32pp. This illustrated collection contains 13 of the Danish poet Rasmussen's nonsense poems. (Rev: BL 9/15/11; HB 9–10/11; SLJ 8/1/11*) [831]

13921 Rex, Adam. *Frankenstein Makes a Sandwich* (2–5). Illus. by author. 2006, Harcourt $16.00 (978-0-15-205766-4). Laugh-out-loud poems reveal untold episodes in the lives of some favorite monsters. (Rev: SLJ 9/06*) [811]

13922 Rosen, Michael. *Bananas in My Ears: A Collection of Nonsense Stories, Poems, Riddles, and Rhymes* (1–3). Illus. by Quentin Blake. 2012, Candlewick $15.99 (978-0-7636-6248-6). 96pp. A quirky collection full of wordplay and divided into four sections: Breakfast, Seaside, Doctor, and Under the Bed. (Rev: BLO 10/15/12; SLJ 2/13) [811]

13923 Shapiro, Karen Jo. *Because I Could Not Stop My Bike-and Other Poems* (3–6). Illus. by Matt Faulkner. 2003, Charlesbridge LB $15.95 (978-1-58049-035-9).

32pp. With apologies to the authors, Shapiro borrows rhymes and meters from 26 classic poems and transforms them for today's young readers. (Rev: HBG 4/04; SLJ 8/03) [811]

13924 Shields, Carol Diggory. *Almost Late to School and More School Poems* (1–3). Illus. by Paul Meisel. 2003, Penguin $15.99 (978-0-525-45743-5). 32pp. Humorous poems and vivid cartoon illustrations highlight a variety of elementary-school experiences. (Rev: BL 8/03; HBG 4/04; SLJ 8/03) [811]

13925 Silverstein, Shel. *Every Thing On It* (2–7). Illus. by author. 2011, HarperCollins $19.99 (978-0-06-199816-4). 208pp. This posthumous Silverstein collection features drawings and poems taken from the author's personal archive and never previously published. (Rev: BL 9/1/11; SLJ 9/1/11*) [811]

13926 Silverstein, Shel. *Runny Babbit: A Billy Sook* (2–4). Illus. 2005, HarperCollins LB $18.89 (978-0-06-028404-6). 96pp. Runny Babbit and friends including Toe Jurtle and Goctor Doose feature in clever spoonerist poems. (Rev: BL 5/1/05; SLJ 4/05) [811]

13927 Silverstein, Shel. *Where the Sidewalk Ends* (3–6). Illus. by author. 1974, HarperCollins LB $19.89 (978-0-06-025668-5). 176pp. The author explores various facets and interests of children, with appropriate cartoonlike drawings. Also use: *A Light in the Attic* (1981).

13928 Smith, William J. *Laughing Time: Collected Nonsense* (3–5). Illus. by Fernando Krahn. 1990, Farrar paper $3.50 (978-0-374-44315-3). 176pp. New poems have been added to this satisfyingly silly collection. Revision of the 1980 edition. (Rev: BL 2/15/90; SLJ 3/91) [811]

13929 Soto, Gary. *Worlds Apart: Traveling with Fernie and Me* (4–6). Illus. by Greg Clarke. 2005, Penguin $15.99 (978-0-399-24218-2). 64pp. Fernie and his best friend go on a globe-trotting adventure in this book composed of poems illustrated in black and white. (Rev: BL 3/15/05; SLJ 3/05) [811]

13930 Steig, Jeanne. *Alpha Beta Chowder* (5–8). 1992, HarperCollins LB $14.89 (978-0-06-205007-6). A collection of nonsense verses celebrating the joy of words — their sound and meaning — with each verse playing with a letter of the alphabet. (Rev: BL 11/15/92; SLJ 12/92) [811]

13931 Steinberg, David. *Grasshopper Pie and Other Poems* (K–2). Illus. by Adrian C. Sinnott. Series: All Aboard Poetry Reader. 2004, Grosset paper $3.99 (978-0-448-43347-9). 48pp. Nonsense poetry with bouncy illustrations is full of arresting rhymes. (Rev: BL 7/04; SLJ 10/04) [811]

13932 Stockland, Patricia M., ed. *Recess, Rhyme, and Reason: A Collection of Poems About School* (3–6). Illus. by Sara Rojo Perez. 2004, Compass Point LB $23.93 (978-0-7565-0564-6). 32pp. This lighthearted anthology of poems about school is designed to entertain and to educate young readers about different poetry concepts. (Rev: BL 4/1/04; SLJ 6/04) [808.81]

13933 Tripp, Wallace, ed. *A Great Big Ugly Man Came Up and Tied His Horse to Me: A Book of Nonsense Verse* (K–3). Illus. by Wallace Tripp. 1974, Little, Brown LB $14.95 (978-0-316-85280-7). 48pp. The hilarious drawings that accompany this selection of nonsense verses make this an especially entertaining book.

13934 Turner, Steve. *Dad, You're Not Funny and Other Poems* (3–5). Illus. by David Mostyn. 2000, Lion $16.95 (978-0-7459-4024-3). 96pp. A collection of humorous light verse from this well-known English writer. (Rev: BL 9/15/03; HBG 4/04; SLJ 11/00) [821]

13935 Weinstock, Robert. *Food Hates You, Too* (1–3). Illus. by author. 2009, Hyperion $15.99 (978-1-4231-1391-1). Nineteen funny poems present a different perspective on the topic of food. (Rev: BCCB 1/09; BL 1/1–15/09; LMC 5/09; SLJ 1/09) [808.1]

13936 Westcott, Nadine Bernard. *The Lady with the Alligator Purse* (PS–1). Illus. by author. 1988, Little, Brown paper $4.95 (978-0-316-93136-6). The lady with the alligator purse chooses pizza instead of penicillin in this jump-rope rhyme. (Rev: BL 3/15/88; HB 5/88; HBG 4/04)

13937 Wheeler, Lisa. *Spinster Goose: Twisted Rhymes for Naughty Children* (K–3). Illus. by Sophie Blackall. 2011, Simon & Schuster $16.99 (978-1-4169-2541-5). 48pp. Naughty characters from various nursery rhymes and children's stories are sent to live with the crooked Spinster Goose (sister of Mother Goose) in these darkly funny rhymes. (Rev: BL 2/15/11; HB 5–6/11; SLJ 3/1/11) [811]

13938 Whitehead, Jenny. *Lunch Box Mail and Other Poems* (2–4). Illus. 2001, Holt $16.95 (978-0-8050-6259-5). 48pp. Everyday life and experiences are captured in this collection of poems that emphasizes the humorous side of life. (Rev: BL 4/1/01; HBG 3/02; SLJ 10/01) [811]

13939 Wilson, Karma. *What's the Weather Inside?* (2–5). Illus. by Barry Blitt. 2009, Simon & Schuster $17.99 (978-1-4169-0092-4). A humorous collection of more than 100 poems full of wordplay that focus mainly on a child's world. (Rev: BCCB 5/09; SLJ 7/09) [811]

Nature and the Seasons

13940 Alarcón, Francisco X. *Angels Ride Bikes and Other Fall Poems: Los Angeles Andan en Bicicleta y Otros Poems de Otoño* (K–3). Illus. by Maya Christina Gonzalez. 1999, Children's Book Pr. $15.95 (978-0-89239-160-8). 32pp. Twenty poems written in English and Spanish tell about the fall season in Los Angeles. (Rev: BL 12/1/99; HBG 3/00; SLJ 10/99) [811.54]

13941 Alarcón, Francisco X. *Iguanas in the Snow and Other Winter Poems / Iguanas en la Nieve y Otros Poemas de Invierno* (1–3). Illus. by Maya Christina Gonzalez. 2001, Children's Book Pr. $15.95 (978-0-89239-168-4). A collection of poems about the beauty of winter in northern California, in Spanish and English. (Rev: BL 10/1/01; HBG 3/02; SLJ 8/01) [811]

13942 Baird, Audrey B. *A Cold Snap! Frosty Poems* (2–5). Illus. by Patrick O'Brien. 2002, Boyds Mills $15.95 (978-1-56397-633-9). 32pp. Effective poems and illustrations capture winter's chill. (Rev: BL 9/15/02; HBG 3/03; SLJ 12/02) [811.54]

13943 Baird, Audrey B. *Storm Coming!* (2–4). Illus. by Patrick O'Brien. 2001, Boyds Mills $15.95 (978-1-56397-887-6). 32pp. Twenty-two original poems explore the nature and effects of storms from many points of view. (Rev: BL 3/15/01; HBG 10/01) [811]

13944 Bishop, Rudine Sims, comp. *Wonders: The Best Children's Poems of Effie Lee Newsome* (K–3). Illus. by Lois Mailou Jones. 1999, Boyds Mills paper $8.95 (978-1-56397-825-8). 40pp. A collection of original nature poems by Effie Lee Newsome that were published 60 years ago and were long out of print. (Rev: BCCB 2/00; HBG 3/00; SLJ 4/00) [811]

13945 Buchanan, Ken, and Debby Buchanan. *It Rained on the Desert Today* (2–4). Illus. by Libba Tracy. 1994, Northland LB $14.95 (978-0-87358-575-0). 32pp. A rainstorm in the desert is evoked in free verse and evocative watercolors. (Rev: BL 10/15/94; SLJ 8/94) [811]

13946 Caduto, Michael J. *Earth Tales from Around the World* (5–8). 1997, Fulcrum paper $17.95 (978-1-55591-968-9). This collection of 48 folktales from around the world emphasizes respect for the natural world. (Rev: BL 4/1/98; SLJ 5/98; VOYA 4/98) [398.27]

13947 Cameron, Eileen. *Canyon* (3–5). Illus. by Michael Collier. 2002, Mikaya $16.95 (978-1-931414-03-6). 32pp. Water flows from mountains to rivers to a canyon in this poetic book illustrated with striking photographs of nature. (Rev: BL 5/15/02; HBG 10/02; SLJ 5/02) [811]

13948 Cooling, Wendy. *All the Wild Wonders: Poems of Our Earth* (2–5). Illus. by Piet Grobler. 2010, Frances Lincoln $19.95 (978-1-84780-073-2). 48pp. John Milton, William Blake, and Ogden Nash are among the more than 30 poets represented in this anthology of poems about nature and the environment. (Rev: BL 11/1/10; SLJ 1/1/11) [811]

13949 Coombs, Kate. *Water Sings Blue* (1–4). Illus. by Meilo So. 2012, Chronicle $16.99 (978-081187284-3). 32pp. Beautiful watercolor illustrations accompany a range of poems celebrating underwater and seashore life. (Rev: BL 4/15/12*; HB 7–8/12; LMC 8–9/12*; SLJ 5/1/12*) [811]

13950 Cyrus, Kurt. *Oddhopper Opera: A Bug's Garden of Verses* (3–5). Illus. 2001, Harcourt $16.00 (978-0-15-202205-1). A variety of garden creatures are featured in both the art and the poems in this original collection. (Rev: BL 3/15/01; HBG 10/01) [811]

13951 Davies, Nicola. *Outside Your Window: A First Book of Nature* (PS–2). Illus. by Mark Hearld. 2012, Candlewick $19.99 (978-0-7636-5549-5). 108pp. A large-format, poetic introduction to the seasons and the related changes in nature. (Rev: BL 4/1/12; SLJ 4/1/12) [808.81]

13952 Esbensen, Barbara J. *Swing Around the Sun* (K–3). Illus. 2003, Carolrhoda LB $16.95 (978-0-87614-143-4). The seasons are the focus of this collection that is illustrated by four well-known artists. (Rev: HBG 10/03; SLJ 3/03) [811]

13953 Farrar, Sid. *The Year Comes Round: Haiku through the Seasons* (PS–3). Illus. by Ilse Plume. 2012, Whitman $16.99 (978-0-8075-8129-2). 32pp. Haiku poems describe the changing seasons in this nicely illustrated volume that also includes basic scientific information. ALA Notable Children's Book. (Rev: BL 11/15/12; LMC 1–2/13; SLJ 8/12) [811]

13954 Florian, Douglas. *Autumnblings: Poems and Paintings* (2–5). Illus. by author. 2003, Greenwillow LB $17.89 (978-0-06-009279-5). 48pp. Rhyming verse, creative word play, and lovely illustrations bring autumn to life. (Rev: HB 11/03; HBG 4/04; SLJ 10/03) [811]

13955 Florian, Douglas. *Comets, Stars, the Moon and Mars* (3–5). Illus. 2007, Harcourt $16.00 (978-0-15-205372-7). 56pp. Large-format, double-page spreads combine mixed-media illustrations with lyrical poems about celestial bodies. (Rev: BL 4/1/07) [811]

13956 Florian, Douglas. *Handsprings* (K–3). Illus. 2006, Greenwillow $15.99 (978-0-06-009280-1). Florian follows *Winter Eyes* (1999), *Summersaults* (2002), and *Autumnblings* (2003) with a volume of breezy poems about the joys of spring. (Rev: BL 3/15/06; SLJ 4/06) [811]

13957 Florian, Douglas. *Poetrees* (3–6). Illus. by author. 2010, Simon & Schuster $16.99 (978-1-4169-8672-0). 48pp. Striking, atmospheric illustrations enhance this poetic celebration of trees that is full of wordplay. (Rev: BL 3/1/10; HB 3–4/10; LMC 5–6/10; SLJ 2/1/10) [811]

13958 Florian, Douglas. *Summersaults* (K–4). Illus. 2002, HarperCollins LB $17.89 (978-0-06-029268-3). 48pp. The freedom and beauty of summer are evoked in this collection of short, rhymed poems with playful pictures. (Rev: BCCB 5/02; BL 4/1/02; HB 7/02; HBG 10/02; SLJ 5/02*)

13959 Florian, Douglas. *UnBEElievables: Honeybee Poems and Paintings* (2–5). Illus. by author. 2012, Simon & Schuster $16.99 (978-1-4424-2652-8). 32pp. This collection of informative poems explores the world of honeybees — their social order, hive structure, pollination, and threats facing them. (Rev: BL 4/1/12; HB 3–4/12; LMC 8–9/12*; SLJ 2/1/12) [811]

13960 Florian, Douglas. *Winter Eyes* (K–4). Illus. 1999, Greenwillow $16.99 (978-0-688-16458-4). A series of short, quiet poems that show the effects of winter on a small child. (Rev: BCCB 11/99; BL 11/1/99; HB 11/99; HBG 3/00; SLJ 9/99) [811.54]

13961 Geis, Jacqueline. *Where the Buffalo Roam* (PS–3). Illus. 1992, Ideals LB $14.00 (978-0-8249-8584-4). With illustrations and verses to the familiar cowboy tune, the American Southwest is celebrated. (Rev: BL 11/15/92; SLJ 1/93) [811]

13962 George, Kristine O'Connell. *The Great Frog Race and Other Poems* (4–6). Illus. by Kate Kiesler. 1997, Clarion $16.00 (978-0-395-77607-0). 40pp. A richly

atmospheric picture book that captures some of the outdoor activities of children, including watching captured frogs race. (Rev: BCCB 6/97; BL 3/15/97*; SLJ 4/97*) [811]

13963 George, Kristine O'Connell. *Old Elm Speaks: Tree Poems* (2–6). Illus. by Kate Kiesler. 1998, Clarion $16.00 (978-0-395-87611-4). A collection of original poems that celebrates every wonderful aspect of trees. (Rev: BL 9/1/98*; HBG 3/99; SLJ 9/98) [811]

13964 Gerber, Carole. *Seeds, Bees, Butterflies, and More!: Poems for Two Voices* (2–5). Illus. by Eugene Yelchin. 2013, Henry Holt $17.99 (978-0-8050-9211-0). 32pp. Multiple poems about nature fill this book designed to be read by two people in alternating voices; also included are sections of prose that further explain the ecological concepts described. (Rev: BL 1/13; LMC 8–9/13; SLJ 1/13) [811]

13965 Harrison, David L. *Wild Country* (4–6). Illus. 1999, Boyds Mills $14.95 (978-1-56397-784-8). 48pp. A collection of original nature poems that celebrates such natural wonders as butterflies, mountains, and forests. (Rev: BL 11/15/99; HBG 3/00; SLJ 12/99) [811]

13966 Havill, Juanita. *I Heard It from Alice Zucchini: Poems About the Garden* (K–3). Illus. by Christine Davenier. 2006, Chronicle $15.95 (978-0-8118-3962-4). The science and magic of gardening are celebrated in this collection of poems illustrated with pen-and-ink and watercolor sketches. (Rev: BL 4/1/06; SLJ 4/06*) [811]

13967 Hazeltine, Alice I., and Elva Smith, eds. *The Year Around: Poems for Children* (4–6). Illus. by Paula Hutchison. 1973, Ayer $15.00 (978-0-8369-6403-5). A collection of seasonal poems.

13968 Highwater, Jamake. *Songs for the Seasons* (PS–4). Illus. by Sandra Speidel. 1995, Lothrop LB $14.93 (978-0-688-10659-1). A gentle look at the changes that occur with plants and animals during the cycle of the four seasons. (Rev: BL 4/15/95; SLJ 4/95) [811]

13969 Hines, Anna Grossnickle. *Winter Lights: A Season in Poems and Quilts* (1–3). Illus. 2005, Greenwillow $16.99 (978-0-06-000817-8). 32pp. The lights and warmth of various winter holidays are celebrated in a collection of poems and quilts. (Rev: BL 9/1/05*; SLJ 10/05*) [811]

13970 Hopkins, Lee Bennett. *Sky Magic* (1–3). Illus. by Mariusz Stawarski. 2009, Dutton $17.99 (978-0-525-47862-1). Fourteen poems — from writers including Carl Sandburg, Alice Schertle, and Ashley Bryan — celebrate various features of the sky and are accompanied by dreamy illustrations. (Rev: HB 7/09; SLJ 6/09) [811]

13971 Hopkins, Lee Bennett, ed. *Sharing the Seasons: A Book of Poems* (2–5). Illus. by David Diaz. 2010, Simon & Schuster $21.99 (978-1-4169-0210-2). 88pp. With 48 poems — 12 for each season — this well-illustrated collection represents the works of well-known writers including Carl Sandburg, Joseph Bruchac, and Hopkins himself. (Rev: BL 3/1/10*; LMC 3–4/10; SLJ 6/1/10) [811]

13972 Hopkins, Lee Bennett, ed. *Small Talk: A Book of Short Poems* (2–4). Illus. by Susan Gaber. 1995, Harcourt $14.00 (978-0-15-276577-4). Short poems by distinguished authors are arranged according to seasonal changes. (Rev: BCCB 5/95; BL 8/95; HB 5/95; SLJ 5/95*) [811]

13973 Hubbell, Patricia. *Black Earth, Gold Sun* (2–6). 2001, Marshall Cavendish $15.95 (978-0-7614-5090-0). 32pp. Watercolor illustrations echo the sentiments of these poems about the delights of a garden. (Rev: BL 9/15/01; HBG 3/02; SLJ 11/01) [811.54]

13974 Hundal, Nancy. *Prairie Summer* (3–5). Illus. 1999, Fitzhenry & Whiteside $16.95 (978-1-55041-403-5). 32pp. A poem, illustrated with impressionistic paintings, that depicts life on the prairie. (Rev: BL 11/1/99) [813.54]

13975 Katz, Susan. *Looking for Jaguar: And Other Rain Forest Poems* (2–4). Illus. by Lee Christiansen. 2005, Greenwillow LB $16.89 (978-0-06-029793-0). 40pp. Nineteen poems introduce the flora and fauna of the world's rain forests; supplementary features include an essay about the importance of these habitats and a compilation of relevant facts and figures. (Rev: BL 2/15/05; SLJ 3/05) [811]

13976 Lewis, J. Patrick. *Earth and Us — Continuous: Nature's Past and Future* (K–3). Illus. by Christopher Canyon. Series: Sharing Nature with Children. 2001, Dawn $16.95 (978-1-58469-024-5); paper $7.95 (978-1-58469-023-8). 32pp. A book of attractively illustrated poems about the wonders of the earth and our responsibility to care for it. (Rev: BL 9/1/01; HBG 3/02) [550]

13977 Livingston, Myra Cohn. *Calendar* (PS–K). Illus. by Will Hillenbrand. 2007, Holiday $16.95 (978-0-8234-1725-4). This simple poem, colorfully illustrated with mixed-media artwork, highlights the special features of the months of the year. (Rev: BL 4/1/07) [811.54]

13978 Livingston, Myra Cohn. *A Circle of Seasons* (3–5). Illus. by Leonard Everett Fisher. 1982, Holiday House paper $5.95 (978-0-8234-0656-2). 32pp. A group of poems that brings the seasons to life.

13979 Livingston, Myra Cohn. *Up in the Air* (3–5). Illus. by Leonard Everett Fisher. 1989, Holiday House LB $14.95 (978-0-8234-0736-1). A celebration of flight begins as an airliner takes off. (Rev: BCCB 5/89; BL 5/15/89)

13980 Luján, Jorge. *Colors! Colores!* (K–3). Trans. by John Oliver Simon. Illus. by Piet Grobler. 2008, Groundwood $17.95 (978-0-88899-863-7). 24pp. This bilingual book celebrating color offers short free-verse poems in English and Spanish illustrated with playful watercolors. (Rev: BLO 2/9/09; LMC 8/09; SLJ 5/08) [811]

13981 Merriam, Eve. *The Singing Green: New and Selected Poems for All Seasons* (3–7). Illus. by Kathleen C. Howell. 1992, Morrow $14.00 (978-0-688-11025-3). 112pp. The wordplay romps and frolics in this celebration of sun, trees, and the child in us all. (Rev: BCCB 2/93; BL 12/1/92; HB 1/93; SLJ 12/92) [811]

13982 Mora, Pat. *The Desert Is My Mother / El Desierto Es Mi Madre* (PS–3). Illus. by Daniel Lechon. 1994, Arte Publico $14.95 (978-1-55885-121-4). In this bilingual book of poems, everyday life in the desert is seen through the eyes of a child. (Rev: BL 1/15/95) [811]

13983 Mordhorst, Heidi. *Pumpkin Butterfly: Poems from the Other Side of Nature* (2–5). Illus. by Jenny Reynish. 2009, Boyds Mills $16.95 (978-1-59078-620-8). 32pp. Twenty-three poems about nature are varied in both form and subject. (Rev: BL 11/1/09; LMC 1–2/10; SLJ 12/09) [811]

13984 Muth, Jon J. *Hi, Koo! A Year of Seasons* (PS–3). Illus. by author. 2014, Scholastic $17.99 (978-054516668-3). 32pp. Twenty-six haikus about the seasons feature the little panda Koo. (Rev: BL 12/15/13; LMC 10/14*; SLJ 2/14) [811]

13985 Nicholls, Judith, comp. *The Sun in Me: Poems About the Planet* (1–4). Illus. by Beth Krommes. 2003, Barefoot Books $16.99 (978-1-84148-058-9). 40pp. An anthology of poems from different places and times that celebrate nature. (Rev: HBG 10/03; SLJ 3/03) [811]

13986 Paolilli, Paul, and Dan Brewer. *Silver Seeds* (K–2). Illus. by Lou Fancher and Steve Johnson. 2001, Viking $15.99 (978-0-670-88941-9). 32pp. In each of these 15 nature poems the first letters of each line spell out the name of the poem. (Rev: BL 12/15/00; HBG 10/01) [811.6]

13987 Peters, Lisa Westberg. *Earthshake: Poems from the Ground Up* (2–4). Illus. by Cathie Felstead. 2003, HarperCollins LB $17.89 (978-0-06-029266-9). 32pp. Twenty-two poems exploring various aspects of earth science — including fossils, tectonic plates, lava, and strata — are accompanied by relevant collages in this large-format book. (Rev: BL 11/15/03; HBG 4/04; SLJ 9/03) [811]

13988 Powell, Consie. *Amazing Apples* (PS–4). Illus. by author. 2003, Whitman LB $16.99 (978-0-8075-0399-7). Simple acrostic poems follow an apple orchard through the seasons. (Rev: HBG 4/04; SLJ 10/03) [811]

13989 Prelutsky, Jack. *Dog Days: Rhymes Around the Year* (PS–K). Illus. by Dyanna Wolcott. 1999, Knopf LB $16.00 (978-0-375-80104-4). In these 12 original poems, one for each month, a dog reveals his favorite activities in each season. (Rev: BL 11/1/99) [811]

13990 Prelutsky, Jack. *It's Snowing! It's Snowing! Winter Poems* (K–3). Illus. by Yossi Abolafia. Series: I Can Read. 2006, HarperCollins $15.99 (978-0-06-053715-9). 48pp. Sixteen loosely connected, easily read poems celebrate the joys of winter. (Rev: BL 1/1–15/06; SLJ 7/06) [811]

13991 Rickey, Ann Heiskell. *Bugs and Critters I Have Known* (3–6). Illus. by Ardeane Heiskell Smith. 1998, Old Canyon $12.95 (978-0-9667834-1-4). Illustrated with pen-and-ink drawings, this humorous collection of original poems deals mainly with insects. (Rev: SLJ 6/99) [811]

13992 Roemer, Heidi. *Come to My Party: And Other Shape Poems* (PS–3). Trans. and illus. by Hideko Takahashi. 2004, Holt $17.95 (978-0-8050-6620-3). 32pp. Organized by season, this collection of brief poems explores common experiences and introduces interesting sounds and shapes. (Rev: BL 6/1–15/04; HB 5/04; SLJ 5/04) [811]

13993 Rogasky, Barbara. *Winter Poems* (3–6). Illus. by Trina S. Hyman. 1994, Scholastic $15.95 (978-0-590-42872-9). 40pp. An anthology of poems that deal with winter around the world and activities associated with it. (Rev: BCCB 1/95; BL 9/15/94; HB 11/94; SLJ 10/94*) [811]

13994 Shakespeare, William. *Winter Song: A Poem by William Shakespeare* (K–4). Illus. by Melanie Hall. 2006, Boyds Mills $15.95 (978-1-59078-275-0). Wintry illustrations depict an Elizabethan scene as the backdrop for the poem that appears at the conclusion of his play, *Love's Labor's Lost*. (Rev: SLJ 11/06) [821.3]

13995 Shannon, George. *Busy in the Garden* (PS–2). Illus. by Sam Williams. 2006, Greenwillow $15.99 (978-0-06-000464-4). This collection of 24 lively poems celebrates the joys — and headaches — of a backyard garden. (Rev: BL 1/1–15/06; SLJ 2/06) [811]

13996 Sidman, Joyce. *Butterfly Eyes and Other Secrets of the Meadow* (3–5). Illus. by Beth Krommes. 2006, Houghton $16.00 (978-0-618-56313-5). 48pp. The diversity of life in and around a country meadow is celebrated in poems that include both scientific facts and riddles. (Rev: BL 10/1/06; SLJ 10/06*) [811]

13997 Sidman, Joyce. *Dark Emperor and Other Poems of the Night* (3–6). Illus. by Rick Allen. 2010, Houghton Mifflin $16.99 (978-0-547-15228-8). 32pp. Poetry and science are combined with rich illustrations in this collection of diverse poems about life in the woods at night. Newbery Honor Book. e (Rev: BL 6/1/10*; HB 9–10/10; LMC 1–2/11; SLJ 8/10) [811]

13998 Sidman, Joyce. *Just Us Two: Poems About Animal Dads* (1–4). Illus. by Susan Swan. 2000, Millbrook LB $22.90 (978-0-7613-1563-6). Using double-page illustrations, this book of 11 original poems is about different fathers in the animal world. (Rev: HBG 3/01; SLJ 12/00) [811]

13999 Sidman, Joyce. *Red Sings from Treetops: A Year in Colors* (PS–1). Illus. by Pamela Zagarenski. 2009, Houghton $16.00 (978-0-547-01494-4). The seasons are defined by their colors in evocative text and illustrations. (Rev: BCCB 3/09; BL 5/1/09; HB 3/09; SLJ 4/09) [811]

14000 Sidman, Joyce. *Song of the Waterboatman and Other Pond Poems* (3–5). Illus. by Becky Prange. 2005, Houghton $16.00 (978-0-618-13547-9). 32pp. Poems that teach about the ecology of a pond are accompanied by woodcut illustrations. Caldecott Honor Book, 2006. (Rev: BL 3/15/05) [811]

14001 Sidman, Joyce. *Swirl by Swirl: Spirals in Nature* (PS–3). Illus. by Beth Krommes. 2011, Houghton Mifflin $16.99 (978-0-547-31583-6). 40pp. A fascinating look at spirals in nature, with informative and lyrical free-verse text and eye-catching scratchboard illustrations. (Rev: BL 9/1/11*; SLJ 9/1/11*) [811]

14002 Sidman, Joyce. *Ubiquitous: Celebrating Nature's Survivors* (2–5). Illus. by Beckie Prange. 2010, Houghton Mifflin $17 (978-0-618-71719-4). 40pp. Beautifully illustrated, this collection of poetry and prose conveys factual information and playful imagery about organisms ranging from bacteria to coyotes to humans. e (Rev: BL 1/1/10*; SLJ 3/1/10*) [811]

14003 Siegen-Smith, Nikki, ed. *Sea Dream: Poems from Under the Waves* (2–5). Illus. by Joel Stewart. 2002, Barefoot Books $16.99 (978-1-84148-905-6). 40pp. An absorbing anthology of 26 poems about sea creatures both real and imagined. (Rev: BL 10/15/02; HBG 3/03; SLJ 12/02) [808.81]

14004 Singer, Marilyn. *A Full Moon Is Rising* (2–4). Illus. by Julia Cairns. 2011, Lee & Low $19.95 (978-1-60060-364-8). 48pp. Seventeen poems follow a full moon as it rises around the globe. (Rev: BL 5/1/11; SLJ 6/11) [811]

14005 Spinelli, Eileen. *Polar Bear, Arctic Hare: Poems of the Frozen North* (PS–2). Illus. by Eugenie Fernandes. 2007, Boyds Mills $16.95 (978-1-59078-344-3). 48pp. Twenty-four poems about the animals of the Arctic are paired with large acrylic paintings. (Rev: BL 4/15/07) [811]

14006 Stevenson, Robert Louis. *The Moon* (PS–1). Illus. by Tracey Campbell Pearson. 2006, Farrar $16.00 (978-0-374-35046-8). 40pp. Stevenson's poem "The Moon" becomes a story of a boy and his father viewing the moon and nocturnal animals on a private nighttime boat trip. (Rev: BL 7/06; HBG 4/07; SLJ 9/06*) [821]

14007 Thomas, Patricia. *Nature's Paintbox: A Seasonal Gallery of Art and Verse* (2–4). Illus. by Craig Orback. 2007, Lerner $16.95 (978-0-8225-6807-0). 32pp. Verses about the seasons are paired with illustrations in different media — pen and ink for winter, pastel chalk for spring, watercolors for summer, and oils for fall. (Rev: BL 10/15/07; LMC 1/08; SLJ 11/07) [811]

14008 Updike, John. *A Child's Calendar* (3–5). Illus. by Trina S. Hyman. 1999, Holiday House $16.95 (978-0-8234-1445-1). Updike has written a poem for each month, depicting seasonal activities of a multiracial family in rural New Hampshire. Caldecott Honor Book, 2000. (Rev: BCCB 3/00; BL 9/1/99; HBG 3/00; SLJ 9/99) [811]

14009 Van Wassenhove, Sue. *The Seldom-Ever-Shady Glades* (3–5). Illus. by author. 2008, Boyds Mills $17.95 (978-1-59078-352-8). 32pp. Poems and quilted illustrations express delight in the natural world in this tour of the diversity of the Everglades. (Rev: BL 2/15/08; LMC 3/08*; SLJ 5/08) [811]

14010 Walker, Alice. *There Is a Flower at the Tip of My Nose Smelling Me* (K–3). Illus. by Stefano Vitale. 2006, HarperCollins $16.99 (978-0-06-057080-4). Brief poems celebrate the interconnectedness between nature and humanity. (Rev: BL 4/1/06; SLJ 5/06) [811]

14011 Whipple, Laura, comp. *A Snowflake Fell: Poems About Winter* (PS–3). Illus. by Hatsuki Hori. 2003, Barefoot Books $16.99 (978-1-84148-033-6). 40pp. Beautifully illustrated, this anthology includes diverse poems about winter by poets including Douglas Florian, Nancy Wood, James Whitcomb Riley, and Marilyn Singer. (Rev: HBG 4/04; SLJ 11/03) [811]

14012 Windham, Sophie. *The Mermaid and Other Sea Poems* (3–5). Illus. 1996, Scholastic $16.95 (978-0-590-20898-7). 32pp. Sea creatures from mermaids to fish are featured in 18 poems by well-known writers. (Rev: BL 2/1/96; SLJ 5/96) [821]

14013 Yang-Huan. *Where Is Spring?* (PS–K). Illus. by H. Y. Huang and A. Yang. 2007, Heryin $15.95 (978-0-9762-0568-5). Sweet illustrations accompany a Chinese poet's interpretation of the joys of the season. (Rev: SLJ 8/07)

14014 Yolen, Jane. *Color Me a Rhyme: Nature Poems for Young People* (4–6). Illus. 2000, Boyds Mills $19.95 (978-1-56397-892-0). 32pp. Using related photos as illustrations, these poems each evoke a particular color in nature. (Rev: BL 10/15/00*; HBG 3/01; SLJ 12/00) [811.54]

14015 Yolen, Jane. *Shape Me a Rhyme: Nature's Forms in Poetry* (3–6). Photos by Jason Stemple. 2007, Boyds Mills $17.95 (978-1-59078-450-1). Words and photographs work together in this collection of verses about shapes in nature. (Rev: SLJ 11/07) [811]

14016 Yolen, Jane. *Snow, Snow: Winter Poems for Children* (2–5). Illus. by Jason Stemple. 1998, Boyds Mills $16.95 (978-1-56397-721-3). 32pp. Inspired by photographs of snow scenes, these original poems depict occurrences and express various moods involving winter landscapes and activities. (Rev: BCCB 10/98; BL 11/15/98; HBG 3/99; SLJ 12/98) [811.5]

14017 Yolen, Jane, sel. *Once Upon Ice: And Other Frozen Poems* (4–8). 1997, Boyds Mills $19.95 (978-1-56397-408-3). A collection of 17 poems inspired by photographs of ice formations, which are also included. (Rev: BL 2/1/97; SLJ 3/97) [811]

Sports

14018 Fehler, Gene. *Change-Up: Baseball Poems* (3–5). Illus. by Donald Wu. 2009, Clarion $16.00 (978-0-618-71962-4). Poems about baseball chronicle anticipation of the oncoming season and the following dreams and successes. (Rev: BCCB 3/09; BL 3/15/09) [811]

14019 Gutman, Dan. *Casey Back at Bat* (2–4). Illus. by Steve Johnson. 2007, HarperCollins $16.99 (978-0-06-056025-6). 32pp. Gutman playfully extends Thayer's classic poem as Casey wallops the baseball around the world and back in time, bumping against the poor Leaning Tower of Pisa and knocking the nose off the Sphinx; glowing, textured illustrations borrowed from 19th-century art extend the fun. (Rev: BL 1/1–15/07; SLJ 1/07*) [811]

14020 Hopkins, Lee Bennett, ed. *Extra Innings: Baseball Poems* (4–6). Illus. by Scott Medlock. 1993, Harcourt $16.00 (978-0-15-226833-6). 48pp. Nineteen poems about baseball. (Rev: BL 3/15/93; SLJ 4/93) [811]

14021 Hopkins, Lee Bennett, ed. *Opening Days: Sports Poems* (3–6). Illus. by Scott Medlock. 1996, Harcourt $16.00 (978-0-15-200270-1). There are 18 poems in this collection dealing with a variety of sports, each accompanied by a full-page painting. (Rev: BL 2/15/96; HB 5/96; SLJ 5/96) [811]

14022 Hopkins, Lee Bennett, ed. *Sports! Sports! Sports! A Poetry Collection* (1–3). Illus. by Brian Floca. 1999, HarperCollins LB $15.89 (978-0-06-027801-4). The thrills and excitement of sports activities are captured in this collection of poems by several authors, including the editor. (Rev: BCCB 2/99; BL 4/1/99; HB 1/99; HBG 10/99; SLJ 3/99) [811]

14023 Korman, Gordon, and Bernice Korman. *The Last-Place Sports Poems of Jeremy Bloom: A Collection of Poems About Winning, Losing, and Being a Good Sport (Sometimes)* (3–6). 1996, Scholastic paper $3.99 (978-0-590-25516-5). 92pp. A book that explores the world of sports by using different kinds of poetry, from haiku to narrative verse. (Rev: SLJ 4/97) [811]

14024 Maddox, Marjorie. *Rules of the Game: Baseball Poems* (5–8). Illus. by John Sandford. 2009, Boyds Mills $16.95 (978-1-59078-603-1). Maddox celebrates the game of baseball in this collection of more than 40 brief poems with titles such as "View from the Dugout" and "Sacrifice Bunt." (Rev: BL 4/15/09; SLJ 5/09) [811]

14025 Morrison, Lillian. *Way to Go! Sports Poems* (4–8). Illus. by Susan Spellman. 2001, Boyds Mills $16.95 (978-1-56397-961-3). Sport lovers will appreciate this collection of poems full of rhythm and life, with vibrant illustrations. (Rev: HBG 3/02; SLJ 10/01) [811]

14026 Morrison, Lillian, ed. *At the Crack of the Bat* (4–6). Illus. by Steve Cieslawski. 1992, Little, Brown LB $15.49 (978-1-56282-177-7). 64pp. Full-color paintings add to the hero-loving glory of this all-American sport. (Rev: BCCB 5/92; BL 8/92; SLJ 6/92) [811]

14027 Prelutsky, Jack. *Good Sports: Rhymes About Running, Jumping, Throwing, and More* (K–5). Illus. by Chris Raschka. 2007, Knopf $16.99 (978-0-375-83700-5). The rhyming poems in this collection celebrate the excitement of participating in a wide variety of sports and other physical activities. (Rev: BL 3/1/07*; SLJ 2/07) [811]

14028 Smith, Charles R. *Diamond Life: Baseball Sights, Sounds, and Swings* (1–4). Illus. 2004, Scholastic $15.95 (978-0-439-43180-4). Brightly illustrated, the poems — some of them cleverly shaped — in this collection celebrate baseball and its players. (Rev: BL 3/1/04; SLJ 3/04) [796.357]

14029 Smith, Charles R. *Hoop Kings* (4–7). 2004, Candlewick $14.99 (978-0-7636-1423-2). This celebration of basketball, presented in a blend of rap-style poetry with eye-catching photographs, focuses on 12 of the biggest stars. (Rev: BL 2/15/04; SLJ 3/04) [811]

14030 Thayer, Ernest L. *Casey at the Bat* (5–10). Illus. by Joe Morse. Series: Visions in Poetry. 2006, Kids Can $16.95 (978-1-55337-827-3). The famous poem is reimagined in a contemporary setting, with a multicultural crowd and modern technology grounding the poem in the here-and-now. (Rev: SLJ 6/06) [811]

14031 Thayer, Ernest L. *Casey at the Bat* (2–6). Illus. by LeRoy Neiman. 2002, HarperCollins $19.95 (978-0-06-009068-5). 96pp. The famous baseball poem, illustrated in a bold, striking manner; with an introduction by Jose Torre. (Rev: BCCB 1/01*; BL 9/1/02) [811]

14032 Thayer, Ernest L. *Casey at the Bat: A Ballad of the Republic Sung in the Year 1888* (K–3). Illus. by Christopher Bing. 2000, Handprint $17.95 (978-1-929766-

00-0). 32pp. Fictional clippings and scratchboard engravings are used as illustrations to give an actual-event atmosphere to this poem about Casey's terrible defeat at bat. Caldecott Honor Book, 2001. (Rev: BCCB 1/01*; BL 2/15/01; HB 3/01; HBG 10/01; SLJ 1/01) [811.5]

14033 Thayer, Ernest L. *Casey at the Bat: A Ballad of the Republic Sung in the Year 1888* (4–8). Illus. by C. F. Payne. 2003, Simon & Schuster $16.95 (978-0-689-85494-1). An impossibly muscular Casey is the star of this version of the classic baseball poem. (Rev: BCCB 1/01*; BL 2/1/03; HBG 10/03; SLJ 3/03*) [811]

Biography

Adventurers and Explorers

Collective

14034 Clements, Gillian. *The Picture History of Great Explorers* (2–4). Illus. 2005, Frances Lincoln $19.95 (978-1-84507-075-5). 96pp. A comprehensive and very visual guide, suitable for browsers, to explorers from prehistory through space travel. (Rev: BL 1/1–15/06)

14035 Cummins, Julie. *Women Explorers: Perils, Pistols, and Petticoats* (4–7). Illus. by Cheryl Harness. 2012, Dial $17.99 (978-080373713-6). 48pp. This tribute to female explorers focuses on 10 fearless and brilliant adventurers virtually unheard of in the history books. (Rev: BL 3/1/12; SLJ 3/12) [920]

14036 Gifford, Clive. *10 Explorers Who Changed the World* (5–8). Illus. by David Cousens. 2008, Kingfisher $14.95 (978-0-7534-6103-7). 64pp. Marco Polo, Magellan, and Roald Amundsen are among the explorers briefly profiled in this bright volume with cartoon illustrations and a strong sense of adventure. (Rev: BL 12/1/08; SLJ 2/09) [920]

14037 Gogerly, Liz. *Amundsen and Scott's Race to the South Pole* (4–6). Series: Great Journeys Across Earth. 2007, Heinemann LB $31.43 (978-1-4034-9753-6); paper $8.99 (978-1-4034-9761-1). Useful for reports, this volume is a colorful introduction to the men who raced to the South Pole. (Rev: LMC 1/08; SLJ 4/08)

14038 Gueldenpfennig, Sonia. *Spectacular Women in Space* (4–6). Series: The Women's Hall of Fame. 2005, Second Story paper $7.95 (978-1-896764-88-7). 111pp. After a history of women's achievements in the field of space exploration, this volume profiles 10 women who made significant contributions. (Rev: SLJ 4/05)

14039 Hagglund, Betty. *Epic Treks* (5–9). Illus. by Peter Bull. Series: Epic Adventure. 2011, Kingfisher $19.99 (978-0-7534-6668-1). 64pp. An exciting account of explorers' expeditions — including those of Lewis and Clark, Stanley and Livingston, and Amundsen and Scott, and the less-known Burke and Wills — with many

graphics and technical details. (Rev: BL 11/1/11; SLJ 11/1/11) [920]

14040 Jones, Charlotte Foltz. *Westward Ho! Explorers of the American West* (5–8). 2005, Holiday $22.95 (978-0-8234-1586-1). Intriguing narrative describes the lives and adventures of 11 explorers, including Zebulon Pike and John Wesley Powell. (Rev: BL 5/1/05; SLJ 8/05) [920]

14041 Kerr, Jim. *Hillary and Norgay's Mount Everest Adventure* (4–6). Series: Great Journeys Across Earth. 2007, Heinemann LB $31.43 (978-1-4034-9755-0); paper $8.99 (978-1-4034-9763-5). 48pp. Useful for reports, this volume is a colorful introduction to expedition, the men who conquered the mountain, and the science used. (Rev: LMC 1/08; SLJ 4/08)

14042 Kimmel, Elizabeth Cody. *The Look-It-Up Book of Explorers* (5–9). 2004, Random House LB $17.99 (978-0-375-92478-1); paper $10.99 (978-0-375-82478-4). Chronologically arranged spreads introduce explorers from Leif Eriksson to Robert Ballard, with maps, illustrations, and historical context. (Rev: SLJ 1/05) [920]

14043 McLean, Jacqueline. *Women of Adventure* (5–9). Series: Profiles. 2003, Oliver LB $19.95 (978-1-881508-73-1). Seven 19th- and 20th-century women with diverse interests who broke social barriers by exploring far from home are profiled here, with biographical information, photographs, and maps. (Rev: BCCB 5/03; HBG 10/03; SLJ 7/03; VOYA 8/03) [910]

14044 Mooney, Carla. *Explorers of the New World: Discover the Golden Age of Exploration* (3–7). Illus. by Tom Casteel. Series: Build It Yourself. 2011, Nomad paper $15.95 (978-1-936313-44-0). 120pp. With chapters focusing on Columbus, Cabot, Magellan, and the Spanish conquistadors, this volume gives an overview of the men who discovered and later explored the New World. (Rev: SLJ 9/1/11) [910.9]

14045 Mundy, Robyn, and Nigel Rigby. *Epic Voyages* (5–9). Illus. Series: Epic Adventure. 2011, Kingfisher $19.99 (978-0-7534-6574-5). 64pp. Magellan, Cook,

Shackleton, Heyerdahl, and the more recent Chichester are the focus of this large-format volume full of gripping accounts and color photographs. (Rev: BL 11/1/11; SLJ 5/11) [910.4]

14046 Phelan, Matt. *Around the World* (4–7). Illus. by author. 2011, Candlewick $24.99 (978-076363619-7). 240pp. In graphic novel form, Phelan tells the story of three 19th-century adventurers inspired by Verne's *Around the World in Eighty Days*: Thomas Stevens, a bicyclist; reporter Nellie Bly; and retired sea captain Joshua Slocum. (Rev: BL 9/15/11*; HB 11–12/11; LMC 1–2/12; SLJ 9/1/11) [920]

14047 Rooney, Frances. *Extraordinary Women Explorers* (5–8). Series: Women's Hall of Fame. 2005, Second Story paper $7.95 (978-1-896764-98-6). Women endowed with curiosity and courage are celebrated in this text-dense volume. (Rev: BL 3/1/06; SLJ 12/05) [910]

14048 St. George, Judith. *So You Want to Be an Explorer?* (2–4). Illus. by David Small. 2005, Philomel $16.99 (978-0-399-23868-0). 56pp. This lighthearted overview of explorers celebrates the accomplishments of diverse figures and distinguishes between "good" and "bad" explorers according to their treatment of native peoples. (Rev: BL 9/15/05; SLJ 9/05)

14049 Sharp, Anne Wallace. *Daring Pirate Women* (5–8). Series: Biography. 2002, Lerner LB $27.93 (978-0-8225-0031-5). 112pp. Profiles are given of notorious and ruthless female pirates such as Anne Bonny, Mary Read, and Grace O'Malley. (Rev: BL 6/1–15/02; HBG 10/02; SLJ 8/02)

14050 Stone, Tanya Lee. *Almost Astronauts: 13 Women Who Dared to Dream* (5–8). 2009, Candlewick $24.99 (978-0-7636-3611-1). 144pp. The story of the 13 women who fought to prove they were just as qualified, intelligent, and brave as the men who were training as astronauts in the early 1960s. Sibert Medal 2010; Boston Globe–Horn Book nonfiction Honor 2009; ALA Notable Children's Book 2010. ∩ (Rev: BL 2/15/09; HB 3–4/09; LMC 8–9/09; SLJ 3/1/09*; VOYA 2/09) [920]

14051 Thompson, Gare. *Roald Amundsen and Robert Scott Race to the South Pole* (2–4). Illus. Series: National Geographic History Chapters. 2007, National Geographic LB $17.90 (978-1-4263-0187-2). 48pp. Featuring simple text and many illustrations, this volume tells the compelling story of the competition between the two explorers. (Rev: BL 10/15/07; SLJ 1/08)

14052 Weatherly, Myra. *Women Pirates: Eight Stories of Adventure* (4–7). 1998, Morgan Reynolds LB $21.95 (978-1-883846-24-4). These stories of eight women pirates from the 17th and 18th centuries — including Grace O'Malley, Maria Cobham, and Rachel Wall — are enlivened by period prints and portraits and good maps. (Rev: BCCB 4/98; BL 4/15/98; HBG 3/99; SLJ 7/98; VOYA 10/98) [920]

14053 Yolen, Jane. *Sea Queens: Women Pirates around the World* (4–7). Illus. by Christine Joy Pratt. 2008, Charlesbridge $18.95 (978-1-58089-131-8). Yolen introduces 12 women pirates — from Artemisia in the 5th

century B.C. to Madame Ching in the 19th century and including the well-known Anne Bonny. (Rev: BL 6/1–15/08; SLJ 7/08) [920]

Individual

ACABA, JOE

14054 Hord, Colleen. *Joe Acaba* (1–4). Illus. Series: Little World Biographies. 2013, Rourke LB $16.50 (978-161810151-8); paper $7.95 (9781618102843). 24pp. An inspiring photo-filled profile of the first Puerto Rican astronaut. (Rev: BL 4/1/13) [921]

ANZA, JUAN BAUTISTA DE

14055 Bankston, John. *Juan Bautista de Anza* (5–7). Series: Latinos in American History. 2003, Mitchell Lane LB $29.95 (978-1-58415-196-8). The biography of the Spanish explorer of the American Southwest who was a governor of New Mexico in the late 18th century. (Rev: BL 1/1–15/04) [921]

ARMSTRONG, NEIL

14056 Byers, Ann. *Neil Armstrong: The First Man on the Moon* (4–7). Illus. Series: The Library of Astronaut Biographies. 2004, Rosen LB $29.25 (978-0-8239-4461-3). 112pp. A lively overview focusing mainly on Armstrong's education and training. (Rev: SLJ 1/05)

14057 Zemlicka, Shannon. *Neil Armstrong* (2–5). Illus. Series: History Maker Bios. 2002, Lerner LB $26.60 (978-0-8225-0395-8). 48pp. A simple, absorbing account of the life of the first man to reach the moon, with helpful sidebars that amplify material in the text. (Rev: HBG 3/03; SLJ 12/02)

BALBOA, VASCO NUNEZ DE

14058 Otfinoski, Steven. *Vasco Nunez de Balboa: Explorer of the Pacific* (5–8). Series: Great Explorations. 2004, Benchmark LB $29.93 (978-0-7614-1609-8). 79pp. After material on Balboa's early life, Otfinoski looks at the Spanish explorer's trip to the Pacific. (Rev: SLJ 3/05)

BECKWOURTH, JAMES

14059 Gregson, Susan R. *James Beckwourth: Mountaineer, Scout, and Pioneer* (5–8). Series: Signature Lives. 2005, Compass Point LB $34.60 (978-0-7565-1000-8). Beckwourth was one of the first African Americans to play a role in the exploration of the West. (Rev: SLJ 2/06) [921]

BOONE, DANIEL

14060 Armentrout, David, and Patricia Armentrout. *Daniel Boone* (2–4). Series: Discover Someone Who Made a Difference. 2001, Rourke LB $14.95 (978-1-58952-052-3). 24pp. As well as a life of this famous outdoorsman, this biography explains how he has influenced our lives today. (Rev: BCCB 3/02; BL 1/1–15/02; SLJ 3/02)

14061 Calvert, Patricia. *Daniel Boone: Beyond the Mountains* (5–8). Series: Great Explorations. 2001, Marshall Cavendish LB $29.93 (978-0-7614-1243-4). 79pp. An attractive biography of the American pioneer who explored the Cumberland Gap region and helped settlers in the Kentucky region. (Rev: BCCB 3/02; BL 4/1/02; HBG 3/02; SLJ 3/02)

14062 Kozar, Richard. *Daniel Boone and the Exploration of the Frontier* (4–6). Series: Explorers of New Worlds. 2000, Chelsea LB $25.00 (978-0-7910-5510-6). 63pp. Using a variety of illustrations and a crisp text, this book gives good information about Daniel Boone and the forces that inspired him to explore the frontier. (Rev: HBG 10/00; SLJ 7/00)

14063 McCarthy, Pat. *Daniel Boone* (5–8). Series: Historical American Biographies. 2000, Enslow LB $26.60 (978-0-7660-1256-1). A well-organized and thoroughly documented biography of the legendary pioneer and hero of the American Revolution who died in 1820. (Rev: BL 1/1–15/00; HBG 10/00; SLJ 5/00)

14064 Riehecky, Janet. *Daniel Boone* (3–6). Series: Raintree Biographies. 2003, Raintree LB $25.69 (978-0-7398-5672-7). 32pp. A simple biography of the pioneer's life and achievements, with sidebar features containing primary and background material. (Rev: BCCB 3/02; HBG 3/03; SLJ 3/03)

14065 Spradlin, Michael P. *Daniel Boone's Great Escape* (K–2). Illus. by Ard Hoyt. 2008, Walker $16.95 (978-0-8027-9581-6). 32pp. Spradin focuses on a time when Boone was captured by Shawnee warriors. (Rev: BL 7/08; LMC 8/08; SLJ 7/08)

BROADWICK, GEORGIA "TINY"

14066 Roberson, Elizabeth Whitley. *Tiny Broadwick: The First Lady of Parachuting* (4–8). 2001, Pelican paper $9.95 (978-1-56554-780-3). Less than 5 feet tall, "Tiny" Broadwick joined a hot-air balloon act as a teenager and became the first woman to jump with a parachute. (Rev: BL 7/01) [797.5]

BURTON, RICHARD FRANCIS

14067 Young, Serinity. *Richard Francis Burton: Explorer, Scholar, Spy* (5–9). Series: Great Explorations. 2006, Benchmark LB $32.79 (978-0-7614-2222-8). 80pp. This biography chronicles the English adventurer's explorations in Africa, the Middle East, South Asia, and South America and looks at his interest in the cultures of the people he encountered there. (Rev: SLJ 1/07) [921]

BYRD, ADMIRAL RICHARD EVELYN

14068 Burleigh, Robert. *Black Whiteness: Admiral Byrd Alone in the Antarctic* (4–8). Illus. by Walter L. Krudop. 1998, Simon & Schuster $16.95 (978-0-689-81299-6). An outstanding picture biography, with generous quotations from Byrd's diary that describe his great endurance and his lonely vigil in a small underground structure in

the Antarctic. (Rev: BL 1/1–15/98*; HB 3–4/98; HBG 10/98; SLJ 3/98) [921]

14069 Seiple, Samantha. *Byrd and Igloo: A Polar Adventure* (4–7). Illus. 2013, Scholastic $16.99 (978-054556276-8). 192pp. A terrier named Igloo recounts his adventures in the Arctic and Antarctic with Richard E. Byrd; classified as nonfiction, this draws on primary sources and includes archival photographs. e (Rev: BL 12/1/13; LMC 1–2/14*; SLJ 10/13)

CABEZA DE VACA, ALVAR NUNEZ

14070 Menard, Valerie. *Alvar Nunez Cabeza de Vaca* (5–7). Series: Latinos in American History. 2002, Mitchell Lane LB $29.95 (978-1-58415-153-1). A biography of the 16th-century Spanish nobleman who lived with Native Americans for eight years and who claimed Florida, Louisiana, and Texas for Spain. (Rev: BL 2/15/03; HBG 10/03) [921]

14071 Waldman, Stuart. *We Asked for Nothing: The Remarkable Journey of Cabeza de Vaca* (5–8). Illus. by Tom McNeely. Series: A Great Explorers Book. 2003, Mikaya $19.95 (978-1-931414-07-4). 46pp. Drawing on the writings of Cabeza de Vaca, Waldman tells the riveting story of the Spaniard's eight years in 16th-century Texas and Mexico. (Rev: SLJ 2/04)

CABOT, JOHN

14072 Doak, Robin. *Cabot: John Cabot and the Journey to North America* (4–6). Series: Exploring the World. 2003, Compass Point LB $23.93 (978-0-7565-0420-5). 48pp. Chronicles his 1497 voyage, with material on his early life and with rich historical context, including the impact of these foreigners' arrival on the native inhabitants. (Rev: SLJ 12/03)

14073 Shields, Charles J. *John Cabot and the Rediscovery of North America* (4–8). Series: Explorers of New Worlds. 2001, Chelsea $25.00 (978-0-7910-6438-2); paper $25.00 (978-0-7910-6439-9). 63pp. An absorbing biography that focuses on Cabot's expeditions at the end of the 15th century in search of a passage to Asia. (Rev: SLJ 3/02)

CARSON, KIT

14074 Boraas, Tracey. *Kit Carson: Mountain Man* (4–6). Series: Let Freedom Ring. 2002, Capstone LB $23.93 (978-0-7368-1349-5). 48pp. An absorbing account of the life and exploits of the legendary trapper and scout. (Rev: HBG 3/03; SLJ 2/03)

CARTIER, JACQUES

14075 Blashfield, Jean F. *Cartier: Jacques Cartier in Search of the Northwest Passage* (4–6). Series: Exploring the World. 2001, Compass Point LB $23.93 (978-0-7565-0122-8). 48pp. The story of Cartier's efforts to find a route to China, with color reproductions of maps, paintings, and prints, and information on his contemporaries. (Rev: SLJ 1/02)

CHAMPLAIN, SAMUEL DE

14076 Faber, Harold. *Samuel de Champlain: Explorer of Canada* (5–8). Series: Great Explorations. 2004, Benchmark LB $29.93 (978-0-7614-1608-1). Drawing on Champlain's own accounts, this well-illustrated volume examines his voyages to Canada and achievements as governor of New France. (Rev: SLJ 3/05) [921]

14077 Moore, Christopher. *Champlain* (4–6). Illus. by Francis Back. 2004, Tundra $18.95 (978-0-88776-657-2). 56pp. This attractive, revised edition chronicles the French explorer's early-17th-century journeys in eastern Canada and places his importance in historical context. (Rev: BL 10/15/04; SLJ 11/04)

14078 Sherman, Josepha. *Samuel de Champlain: Explorer of the Great Lakes Region and Founder of Quebec* (4–7). Series: The Library of Explorers and Exploration. 2003, Rosen LB $33.25 (978-0-8239-3629-8). In addition to covering Champlain's life, this volume places his explorations in historical context and gives interesting information on the fur trade and relations with Native Americans. (Rev: SLJ 9/03) [971.01]

COCHRAN, JACQUELINE

14079 Smith, Elizabeth Simpson. *Coming Out Right: The Story of Jacqueline Cochran, the First Woman Aviator to Break the Sound Barrier* (5–8). 1991, Walker LB $15.85 (978-0-8027-6989-3). From her impoverished childhood to her triumphs in the air and later, this is the story of a female aviation pioneer. (Rev: BL 4/15/91; SLJ 5/91) [921]

COLEMAN, BESSIE

14080 Borden, Louise, and Mary Kay Kroeger. *Fly High! The Story of Bessie Coleman* (1–4). Illus. by Teresa Flavin. 2001, Simon & Schuster $16.00 (978-0-689-82457-9). 40pp. A highly illustrated, short biography of airplane pilot Bessie Coleman, who in 1921 became the first African American to get a pilot's license. (Rev: BCCB 2/01; BL 2/15/01; HBG 10/01; SLJ 1/01)

14081 Braun, Eric. *Bessie Coleman* (K–2). Series: First Biographies. 2005, Capstone LB $17.26 (978-0-7368-4229-7). 24pp. With its simple sentences and clear black-and-white photographs, this profile of the first African American woman to earn a pilot's license gives basic, introductory information. (Rev: SLJ 2/06)

14082 Fisher, Lillian M. *Brave Bessie: Flying Free* (4–7). 1995, Hendrick-Long $16.95 (978-0-937460-94-8). This biography tells of the struggles of Bessie Coleman, who became the first African American aviatrix in the United States. (Rev: BL 2/15/96; SLJ 2/96) [921]

14083 Grimes, Nikki. *Talkin' About Bessie: The Story of Aviator Elizabeth Coleman* (2–5). Illus. by E. B. Lewis. 2002, Scholastic $16.95 (978-0-439-35243-7). 48pp. In this unusual biography, Grimes uses the voices of friends and relatives at Coleman's funeral to tell the story of her love of flying and her achievements as the first African American woman flyer. (Rev: BL 11/15/02; HB 1/03*; HBG 3/03; SLJ 10/02)

14084 Plantz, Connie. *Bessie Coleman: First Black Woman Pilot* (4–8). 2001, Enslow LB $26.60 (978-0-7660-1545-6). 128pp. This is a readable biography that breathes life into Coleman's childhood, training as a pilot, and tragic death. (Rev: HBG 3/02; SLJ 1/02)

COLUMBUS, CHRISTOPHER

14085 Adler, David A. *A Picture Book of Christopher Columbus* (K–3). Illus. by John Wallner. Series: Picture Book Biographies. 1991, Holiday House LB $16.95 (978-0-8234-0857-3); paper $6.95 (978-0-8234-0949-5). 32pp. The life of this famous explorer is described in simple text and many illustrations. (Rev: BL 6/1/91; SLJ 5/91)

14086 Bailey, Gerry, and Karen Foster. *Columbus's Chart* (3–5). Illus. by Leighton Noyes and Karen Radford. Series: Stories of Great People. 2008, Crabtree LB $29.27 (978-0-7787-3686-8); paper $9.95 (978-0-7787-3708-7). 40pp. At an antique market, fictitious characters Digby Platt and his older sister Hannah find a chart belonging to Columbus and learn lots of facts about the man and his explorations. (Rev: LMC 11/08; SLJ 7/08)

14087 Clare, John D., ed. *The Voyages of Christopher Columbus* (5–8). Series: Living History. 1992, Harcourt $16.95 (978-0-15-200507-8). Using actors and backdrops of the period, this account reconstructs each of Columbus's New World voyages. (Rev: SLJ 11/92) [921]

14088 Demi. *Columbus* (3–5). Illus. by author. 2012, Amazon Children's $19.99 (978-0-76146167-8). 64pp. An attractive and balanced profile of the explorer that covers both faults and accomplishments. (Rev: BL 11/1/12; SLJ 1/13) [921]

14089 Molzahn, Arlene Bourgeois. *Christopher Columbus: Famous Explorer* (3–5). Illus. Series: Explorers! 2003, Enslow LB $23.93 (978-0-7660-2066-5). 48pp. Arresting illustrations and well-written text make this an appealing volume. (Rev: HBG 10/03; SLJ 8/03)

14090 Reis, Ronald A. *Christopher Columbus and the Age of Exploration for Kids: With 21 Activities* (5–8). Illus. 2013, Chicago Review paper $16.95 (978-16137467-4-5). 160pp. This balanced profile of Columbus, his voyages, his discoveries, and his treatment of indigenous peoples is enhanced by details of his personal life and by activities that extend the text. (Rev: BL 11/1/13; SLJ 12/13) [921]

COOK, CAPTAIN JAMES

14091 Bingham, Jane. *Captain Cook's Pacific Explorations* (4–6). Series: Great Journeys Across Earth. 2007, Heinemann LB $31.43 (978-1-4034-9756-7); paper $8.99 (978-1-4034-9764-2). 48pp. Useful for reports, this volume is a colorful introduction to the 18th-century expeditions of Captain Cook and explains the science involved. (Rev: LMC 1/08; SLJ 4/08)

14092 Meltzer, Milton. *Captain James Cook: Three Times Around the World* (5–8). Series: Great Explorations. 2001, Marshall Cavendish LB $28.50 (978-0-

7614-1240-3). 80pp. Using both text and illustrations, this is a fine biography of the English mariner and explorer who, among other feats, explored the west coast of North America. (Rev: BL 4/1/02; HBG 3/02)

CORONADO, FRANCISCO VASQUEZ DE

14093 Doak, Robin. *Coronado: Francisco Vásquez de Coronado Explores the Southwest* (4–6). Series: Exploring the World. 2001, Compass Point LB $23.93 (978-0-7565-0123-5). 48pp. The story of Coronado's quest for gold in the Southwest, with color reproductions of maps, paintings, and prints, and information on his contemporaries. (Rev: SLJ 1/02)

CORTES, HERNAN

14094 West, David, and Jackie Gaff. *Hernan Cortes: The Life of a Spanish Conquistador* (4–6). Illus. by Jim Eldridge. Series: Rosen's Graphic Nonfiction. 2005, Rosen LB $29.25 (978-1-4042-0244-3). 48pp. The story of the explorer's life in a comic-book format. (Rev: BL 3/15/05)

CREESY, ELEANOR

14095 Fern, Tracey. *Dare the Wind: The Record-Breaking Voyage of Eleanor Prentiss and the Flying Cloud* (1–3). Illus. by Emily Arnold McCully. 2014, Farrar $17.99 (978-037431699-0). 40pp. This compelling account introduces Ellen Prentiss, a fearless ship's navigator who in 1851 piloted a clipper from New York to San Francisco around Cape Horn, setting a new record. (Rev: BL 12/15/13; LMC 10/14*; SLJ 4/14) [921]

CROCKETT, DAVY

14096 Alphin, Elaine M. *Davy Crockett* (2–4). Illus. Series: History Maker Bios. 2002, Lerner LB $26.60 (978-0-8225-0393-4). Legend and fact are clearly separated in this biography that looks mainly at Crockett's career. (Rev: HBG 3/03; SLJ 12/02)

14097 Feeney, Kathy. *Davy Crockett* (2–4). Series: Photo-Illustrated Biographies. 2002, Capstone LB $22.60 (978-0-7368-1110-1). Crockett's life and contributions to the exploration of the West are presented, with care to distinguish between fact and legend. (Rev: SLJ 7/02)

14098 Krensky, Stephen. *Davy Crockett: A Life on the Frontier* (1–3). Illus. by Debra Bandelin and Bob Dacey. Series: Ready-to-Read Stories of Famous Americans. 2004, Simon & Schuster paper $3.99 (978-0-689-85944-1). Krensky provides both legend and fact in this engaging biography of the frontiersman. (Rev: BL 12/1/04; SLJ 3/05)

DA GAMA, VASCO

14099 Calvert, Patricia. *Vasco da Gama: So Strong a Spirit* (5–8). Series: Great Explorations. 2004, Benchmark LB $29.93 (978-0-7614-1611-1). After material on da Gama's early life, Calvert looks at the 15th-century Portuguese explorer's voyages. (Rev: SLJ 3/05) [921]

14100 Draper, Allison Stark. *Vasco da Gama: The Portuguese Quest for a Sea Route from Europe to India* (5–8). Illus. Series: Library of Explorers and Exploration. 2003, Rosen LB $33.25 (978-0-8239-3632-8). 112pp. Da Gama's achievements and brutal behavior are given equal exposure in this well-illustrated volume. (Rev: BL 6/1–15/03)

14101 Kratoville, Betty Lou. *Vasco da Gama* (4–7). Series: Trade Route Explorers. 2000, High Noon paper $17.00 (978-1-57128-168-5). The story of the famous explorer who rounded the Cape of Good Hope and visited India, told in a simple, interesting account. (Rev: SLJ 3/01) [921]

DE SOTO, HERNANDO

14102 Stein, R. Conrad. *Hernando De Soto: A Life of Adventure* (4–6). Illus. Series: A Proud Heritage: The Hispanic Library. 2005, Child's World LB $28.50 (978-1-59296-385-0). 40pp. The story of the Spaniard's life and explorations in the New World. [921]

14103 Whiting, Jim. *Hernando de Soto* (5–7). Series: Latinos in American History. 2002, Mitchell Lane LB $29.95 (978-1-58415-147-0). A simple biography of the Spanish explorer who discovered the Mississippi River in the 16th century while traveling through what is now the southern United States. (Rev: BL 2/15/03; HBG 10/03; SLJ 6/03) [921]

DRAKE, SIR FRANCIS

14104 Gallagher, Jim. *Sir Francis Drake and the Foundation of a World Empire* (4–8). Series: Explorers of New Worlds. 2000, Chelsea $31.00 (978-0-7910-5950-0); paper $25.00 (978-0-7910-6160-2). 63pp. This appealing and readable biography of Sir Francis Drake presents his life from childhood and details his major accomplishments, with photographs, sidebar features, documents, and maps. (Rev: HBG 10/01; SLJ 4/01)

14105 Rice, Earle, Jr. *Sir Francis Drake: Navigator and Pirate* (5–8). Series: Great Explorations. 2002, Benchmark LB $29.93 (978-0-7614-1483-4). 76pp. A profile of the 16th-century British explorer who circumnavigated the globe and fought the Spanish Armada, with maps, timeline, and reproductions. (Rev: HBG 10/03; SLJ 6/03)

EARHART, AMELIA

14106 Brown, Jonatha A. *Amelia Earhart* (2–4). Illus. Series: People We Should Know. 2005, Gareth Stevens LB $21.00 (978-0-8368-4465-8). 24pp. An easy-to-read basic biography of the famous pilot, with photographs. (Rev: BL 3/1/05)

14107 Bull, Angela. *Flying Ace: The Story of Amelia Earhart* (2–4). Illus. by Chris Forsey. Series: Eyewitness Reader. 2000, DK $14.99 (978-0-7894-5436-2); paper $3.99 (978-0-7894-5435-5). 48pp. An interesting biography for beginning readers that reveals many details of Earhart's life and speculates on the cause of her disappearance. (Rev: HBG 10/00; SLJ 7/00)

14108 Burleigh, Robert. *Night Flight: Amelia Earhart Crosses the Atlantic* (1–4). Illus. by Wendell Minor. 2011, Simon & Schuster $16.99 (978-1-4169-6733-0). 40pp. Amelia Earhart's white-knuckle flight across the Atlantic in 1932 is described in spare, lyrical free verse text and gouache and watercolor illustrations. Lexile AD500L (Rev: BL 2/1/11*; HB 3–4/11; LMC 5–6/11; SLJ 2/1/11) [921]

14109 Feinstein, Stephen. *Read About Amelia Earhart* (2–4). Series: I Like Biographies! 2006, Enslow LB $21.26 (978-0-7660-2582-0). 24pp. For early researchers, this is an introductory biography that includes information on Earhart's youth and her work during World War I. (Rev: SLJ 4/06)

14110 Fleming, Candace. *Amelia Lost: The Life and Disappearance of Amelia Earhart* (4–7). Illus. 2011, Random House $18.99 (978-0-375-84198-9); LB $21.99 (978-0-375-94598-4). 128pp. Fleming uses twin narratives — one a biographical overview of Earhart's life and the other the drama of her final flight — to create a compelling and suspenseful account. ALA Notable Children's Book 2012. Lexile 930L (Rev: BL 12/1/10; HB 3–4/11; LMC 8–9/11*; SLJ 3/1/11*) [921]

14111 Lakin, Patricia. *Amelia Earhart: More Than a Flier* (2–3). Illus. by Alan Daniel and Lea Daniel. Series: Childhood of Famous Americans. 2003, Simon & Schuster paper $3.99 (978-0-689-85575-7). 46pp. A simple, colorful account of Earhart's childhood, love for adventure, and achievements as a woman aviator. (Rev: HBG 10/03; SLJ 10/03)

14112 Lauber, Patricia. *Lost Star: The Story of Amelia Earhart* (5–7). 1988, Scholastic paper $4.50 (978-0-590-41159-2). A candid biography of the famed lost aviator. (Rev: BL 10/1/88; SLJ 12/88) [921]

14113 Mara, Wil. *Amelia Earhart* (K–2). Series: Rookie Biographies. 2002, Children's Book Pr. LB $20.50 (978-0-516-22522-7); paper $4.95 (978-0-516-27338-9). 32pp. For beginning readers, this is a simple introduction to the famed aviatrix. (Rev: SLJ 12/02)

14114 Micklos, John, Jr. *Unsolved: What Really Happened to Amelia Earhart?* (4–8). 2006, Enslow LB $31.93 (978-0-7660-2365-9). 144pp. The mystery of Earhart's last flight makes this a compelling read, even for researchers, and it provides what they need in terms of information about her childhood and motivations, photographs, maps, and so forth. (Rev: SLJ 7/07)

14115 Sloate, Susan. *Amelia Earhart: Challenging the Skies* (5–8). 1990, Fawcett paper $6.99 (978-0-449-90396-4). The aviator's life story is told along with an examination of all the theories concerning her disappearance. (Rev: SLJ 6/90) [921]

14116 Tanaka, Shelley. *Amelia Earhart: The Legend of the Lost Aviator* (2–4). Illus. by David Craig. 2008, Abrams $18.95 (978-0-8109-7095-3). 48pp. With archival photographs and original art, this picture-book biography for older readers tells the story of Amelia's life and love of planes. (Rev: BCCB 9/08; BL 6/1–15/08; SLJ 11/08)

ELDER, RUTH

14117 Cummins, Julie. *Flying Solo: How Ruth Elder Soared into America's Heart* (1–3). Illus. by Malene R. Laugesen. 2013, Roaring Brook $17.99 (978-1-59643-509-4). 32pp. Tells the story of a contemporary of Amelia Earhart who was unsuccessful in an attempt to fly solo across the Atlantic but carried on flying nonetheless. (Rev: BL 6/13; HB 9–10/13; SLJ 7/13) [921]

ERIKSON, LEIF

14118 Bankston, John. *Leif Erikson* (5–8). Illus. Series: Junior Biographies from Ancient Civilizations. 2013, Mitchell Lane LB $29.95 (978-161228430-9). 48pp. Leif Erikson's journey to North America, making him one of the first to venture to the continent, is covered in depth in this book, complete with sidebars discussing the society and times in which Erikson lived. e (Rev: BL 11/1/13; LMC 3–4/14)

14119 Klingel, Cynthia, and Robert B. Noyed. *Leif Eriksson: Norwegian Explorer* (3–5). Series: Spirit of America: Our People. 2002, Child's World LB $27.07 (978-1-56766-163-7). 32pp. Eriksson's story is placed in the context of Viking exploration, settlement, society, and family life. (Rev: SLJ 12/02)

FREMONT, JOHN C.

14120 Faber, Harold. *John Charles Fremont: Pathfinder to the West* (5–8). Series: Great Explorations. 2002, Benchmark LB $29.93 (978-0-7614-1481-0). 79pp. A profile of the 19th-century explorer who helped open the American West to settlers, with maps, timeline, and reproductions. (Rev: HBG 10/03; SLJ 6/03)

GAGARIN, YURI

14121 Feldman, Heather. *Yuri Gagarin: The First Man in Space* (2–3). Series: Space Firsts. 2003, Rosen LB $21.25 (978-0-8239-6245-7). 24pp. This brief biography includes information on the cosmonaut's early life, training, and first, pioneering flight into space. (Rev: SLJ 11/03)

HENRY THE NAVIGATOR

14122 Gallagher, Aileen. *Prince Henry the Navigator: Pioneer of Modern Exploration* (5–8). Illus. Series: Library of Explorers and Exploration. 2003, Rosen LB $33.25 (978-0-8239-3621-2). 112pp. During the 15th century, Prince Henry of Portugal spurred others to seek a route to India, claim new territory, and spread Christianity. (Rev: BL 6/1–15/03)

HENSON, MATTHEW

14123 Armentrout, David, and Patricia Armentrout. *Matthew Henson* (1–3). Illus. Series: Discover a Life of an American Legend. 2003, Rourke LB $20.64 (978-1-58952-658-7). 24pp. An introduction to the life and achievements of the African American polar explorer. (Rev: BL 2/1/04; SLJ 3/04)

14124 Hoena, B. A. *Matthew Henson: Arctic Adventurer* (4–7). Illus. by Phil Miller. Series: Graphic Biographies. 2005, Capstone LB $26.60 (978-0-7368-4634-9). The life of the African American explorer is presented in speedy, user-friendly, classic comic book format. (Rev: BL 11/1/05) [910]

14125 Johnson, Dolores. *Onward: A Photobiography of African-American Polar Explorer Matthew Henson* (5–8). Series: National Geographic Photobiography. 2005, National Geographic LB $27.90 (978-0-7922-7915-0). The extraordinary life and achievements of African American explorer Matthew Henson are beautifully documented in this volume that also discusses the racism that Henson faced. (Rev: BCCB 5/06; BL 12/15/05*; HB 5–6/06; HBG 10/06; LMC 8–9/06; SLJ 3/06*; VOYA 6/06) [910]

14126 Weatherford, Carole Boston. *I, Matthew Henson: Polar Explorer* (2–5). Illus. by Eric Velasquez. 2007, Walker $16.95 (978-0-8027-9688-3). 32pp. This first-person poetic narrative traces the explorer's life from the age of 13 and reveals his many talents and his determination in the face of considerable challenges. (Rev: BL 2/1/08; HB 3/08; LMC 5/08; SLJ 1/08*)

14127 Weidt, Maryann N. *Matthew Henson* (2–4). Illus. Series: History Maker Bios. 2002, Lerner LB $26.60 (978-0-8225-0397-2). 48pp. Henson's explorations are the main focus of this biography that touches on his youth. (Rev: SLJ 12/02)

HILLARY, SIR EDMUND

14128 Brennan, Kristine. *Sir Edmund Hillary: Modern-Day Explorer* (4–8). Series: Explorers of New Worlds. 2000, Chelsea $25.00 (978-0-7910-5953-1); paper $25.00 (978-0-7910-6163-3). 63pp. An appealing overview of the life and accomplishments of the mountaineer and explorer, with photographs and maps. (Rev: SLJ 4/01)

14129 Coburn, Broughton. *Triumph on Everest: A Photobiography of Sir Edmund Hillary* (5–8). 2000, National Geographic $17.95 (978-0-7922-7114-7). Using many quotations and excellent photographs, this work records the lifetime accomplishments of one of the first men to reach the top of Mount Everest. (Rev: BCCB 9/00; HBG 3/01; SLJ 10/00) [921]

14130 Elish, Dan. *Edmund Hillary: First to the Top* (5–9). Series: Great Explorations. 2006, Benchmark LB $32.79 (978-0-7614-2224-2). This biography focuses on the New Zealand mountain climber's 1953 conquest of Mount Everest and includes coverage of Sherpa Tenzing Norgay. (Rev: SLJ 1/07) [921]

14131 Stewart, Whitney. *Sir Edmund Hillary: To Everest and Beyond* (5–8). Photos by Anne B. Keiser. Series: Newsmakers. 1996, Lerner LB $30.35 (978-0-8225-4927-7). The life of this famous mountain climber is presented with interesting details about his other interests, including bee keeping, conservation, and helping the Sherpa people. (Rev: SLJ 9/96) [921]

HUDSON, HENRY

14132 Doak, Robin. *Hudson: Henry Hudson Searches for a Passage to Asia* (4–6). Series: Exploring the World. 2003, Compass Point LB $23.93 (978-0-7565-0422-9). 48pp. Traces the four voyages of English-born explorer Henry Hudson in search of a short navigable route from Europe to the Far East. (Rev: LMC 11/03; SLJ 12/03)

14133 Saffer, Barbara. *Henry Hudson: Ill-Fated Explorer of North America's Coast* (4–8). Series: Explorers of New Worlds. 2001, Chelsea $25.00 (978-0-7910-6436-8); paper $25.00 (978-0-7910-6437-5). 63pp. This absorbing biography focuses on Hudson's early 17th-century expeditions from England in search of a sea route to the Far East. (Rev: HBG 10/02; SLJ 3/02)

14134 Weaver, Janice. *Hudson* (3–6). Illus. by David Craig. 2010, Tundra $22.95 (978-0-88776-814-9). 48pp. A dramatic account of Henry Hudson's often unsuccessful explorations and his abandonment by a mutinous crew. (Rev: BL 6/1/10*; LMC 3–4/11; SLJ 9/1/10) [921]

JEMISON, MAE

14135 Braun, Eric. *Mae Jemison* (K–2). Series: First Biographies. 2005, Capstone LB $17.26 (978-0-7368-4231-0). 24pp. With its simple sentences and clear black-and-white photographs, this profile of the first African American woman to become an astronaut gives basic, introductory information. (Rev: SLJ 2/06)

14136 Feinstein, Stephen. *Mae Jemison* (1–4). Series: African-American Heroes. 2007, Enslow LB $21.26 (978-0-7660-2762-6). 24pp. A basic and straightforward look at the life of the African-American astronaut, with photographs. (Rev: SLJ 8/07)

14137 Kraske, Robert. *Mae Jemison: Space Pioneer* (1–3). Series: Fact Finders Biographies. 2006, Capstone LB $22.60 (978-0-7368-6420-6). 32pp. Large, easy-to-read print recounts the life of the first African American astronaut from her childhood through her resignation from NASA in 1994. (Rev: SLJ 1/07)

14138 Naden, Corinne J., and Rose Blue. *Mae Jemison: Out of This World* (2–5). Illus. Series: Gateway. 2003, Millbrook LB $23.90 (978-0-7613-2570-3). 48pp. The life story of the first African American woman in space. (Rev: BL 2/15/03; HBG 10/03)

14139 Raum, Elizabeth. *Mae Jemison* (3–5). Illus. Series: American Lives. 2005, Heinemann LB $18.75 (978-1-4034-6942-7). 32pp. This is a brief but thorough and easily understood account of the first African American woman to become an astronaut. (Rev: BL 2/15/06)

14140 Streissguth, Thomas. *Mae Jemison* (2–4). Illus. Series: Explore Space! 2003, Capstone LB $22.60 (978-0-7368-1626-7). 24pp. A slim, basic biography of the first African American woman to travel in space. (Rev: HBG 10/03; SLJ 3/04)

LA SALLE, CAVELIER DE

14141 Faber, Harold. *La Salle: Down the Mississippi* (5–8). Series: Great Explorations. 2001, Marshall Cavendish LB $29.93 (978-0-7614-1239-7). 80pp. The exciting story of the French explorer who traveled down the Mississippi River to the Gulf of Mexico and named the region Louisiana. (Rev: BL 4/1/02; HBG 3/02; SLJ 3/02)

14142 Goodman, Joan Elizabeth. *Despite All Obstacles: La Salle and the Conquest of the Mississippi* (3–6). Illus. by Tom McNeely. Series: Great Explorers. 2001, Mikaya $19.95 (978-1-931414-01-2). 48pp. Journal entries, excerpts from letters, a map, and attractive illustrations enhance this life of explorer Rene-Robert Cavalier, Sieur de La Salle. (Rev: BL 1/1–15/02; HBG 10/02; SLJ 4/02)

LEWIS AND CLARK

14143 Adler, David A. *A Picture Book of Lewis and Clark* (2–4). Illus. by Ronald Himler. Series: Picture Book Biographies. 2003, Holiday House $16.95 (978-0-8234-1735-3). 32pp. Biographical information about the two explorers and information on the expedition itself are found in this accessible book. (Rev: BL 2/15/03; HBG 10/03; SLJ 3/03)

LIVINGSTONE, DAVID

14144 Otfinoski, Steven. *David Livingstone: Deep in the Heart of Africa* (5–9). Series: Great Explorations. 2006, Benchmark LB $32.79 (978-0-7614-2226-6). 79pp. This biography focuses on the three decades during which the Scottish-born adventurer explored central Africa. (Rev: SLJ 1/07) [921]

MAGELLAN, FERDINAND

14145 Burgan, Michael. *Magellan: Ferdinand Magellan and the First Trip Around the World* (4–6). Series: Exploring the World. 2001, Compass Point LB $23.93 (978-0-7565-0125-9). 48pp. An encompassing look at Magellan's achievements with excellent illustrations, a timeline, and Web site information. (Rev: SLJ 1/02)

14146 Burnett, Betty. *Ferdinand Magellan: The First Voyage Around the World* (4–7). Series: The Library of Explorers and Exploration. 2003, Rosen LB $33.25 (978-0-8239-3617-5). In addition to covering Magellan's life, this volume places his 16th-century voyage in historical context and gives interesting information on the funding of such expeditions and life at sea. (Rev: SLJ 9/03) [910]

14147 Gallagher, Jim. *Ferdinand Magellan and the First Voyage Around the World* (4–6). Series: Explorers of New Worlds. 2000, Chelsea LB $31.00 (978-0-7910-5508-3). 63pp. With well-chosen illustrations and a lively text, this book re-creates the historic voyages of Magellan, the first man to circle the globe. (Rev: HBG 10/00; SLJ 7/00)

14148 Levinson, Nancy Smiler. *Magellan and the First Voyage Around the World* (5–8). 2001, Clarion $19.00 (978-0-395-98773-5). A straightforward biography of Magellan, with information on his times and insightful analysis of his character. (Rev: BCCB 2/02; BL 2/1/02; HB 1–2/02; HBG 3/02; SLJ 1/02) [910.92]

14149 Meltzer, Milton. *Ferdinand Magellan: First to Sail Around the World* (5–8). Illus. Series: Great Explorations. 2001, Benchmark LB $29.93 (978-0-7614-1238-0). 80pp. An encompassing look at Magellan's achievements is complemented by excellent illustrations, a timeline, and Web site information. (Rev: BL 1/1–15/02; HBG 3/02; SLJ 3/02)

14150 Molzahn, Arlene Bourgeois. *Ferdinand Magellan: First Explorer Around the World* (3–5). Series: Explorers! 2003, Enslow LB $23.93 (978-0-7660-2068-9). 48pp. Illustrations and maps enhance this account of Magellan's life and travels. (Rev: HBG 10/03; SLJ 9/03)

14151 Waldman, Stuart. *Magellan's World* (4–7). Illus. by Gregory Manchess. Series: Great Explorers. 2007, Mikaya $22.95 (978-1-931414-19-7). 48pp. "Magellan was driven to ever-greater extremes of brilliance, courage, brutality and madness as he sailed around the world," states this book, which offers an unvarnished portrait of the explorer as well as beautiful illustrations and maps. (Rev: BL 11/1/07)

MALLORY, GEORGE

14152 Salkeld, Audrey. *Mystery on Everest: A Photobiography of George Mallory* (5–8). Series: Photobiography. 2000, National Geographic $17.95 (978-0-7922-7222-9). The life of the famous English mountain climber George Mallory, who died in 1924 in a climbing accident on Mount Everest, written by a member of the team that discovered his body in 1999. (Rev: BCCB 9/00; BL 11/1/00; HBG 3/01; SLJ 11/00) [921]

MARKHAM, BERYL

14153 Markham, Beryl. *The Good Lion* (K–3). Illus. by Don Brown. 2005, Houghton $16.00 (978-0-618-56306-7). 32pp. In this excerpt from her autobiography, author/pilot/adventurer Markham recalls how as a girl she was attacked by a supposedly tame lion on an East African farm. (Rev: BL 9/15/05; SLJ 10/05)

OCHOA, ELLEN

14154 Iverson, Teresa. *Ellen Ochoa* (4–8). Series: Hispanic-American Biographies. 2005, Raintree LB $32.86 (978-1-4109-1299-2). The personal and professional life of the first Hispanic American woman astronaut. (Rev: SLJ 1/06) [921]

14155 Johnston, Lissa. *Ellen Ochoa: Pioneering Astronaut* (2–4). Illus. Series: Fact Finders Biographies: Great Hispanics. 2006, Capstone LB $23.93 (978-0-7368-5438-2). 32pp. A brief profile of the life and career of America's first Hispanic woman to travel into space; NASA and personal photographs are included, along with timelines and research resources. (Rev: BL 4/1/06)

14156 Latham, Donna. *Ellen Ochoa: Reach for the Stars!* (2–4). Series: Defining Moments. 2005, Bearport LB $25.27 (978-1-59716-076-6). 32pp. A clearly written account of Ochoa's life, with information on her childhood and education. (Rev: SLJ 2/06)

14157 Paige, Joy. *Ellen Ochoa: The First Hispanic Woman in Space* (4–7). Illus. Series: The Library of Astronaut Biographies. 2004, Rosen LB $29.25 (978-0-8239-4457-6). 112pp. A lively overview focusing mainly on Ochoa's education and training. (Rev: SLJ 1/05)

OTERO, KATHERINE STINSON

14158 Petrick, Neila Skinner. *Katherine Stinson Otero: High Flyer* (K–3). Illus. by Daggi Wallace. 2006, Pelican $15.95 (978-1-58980-368-8). 32pp. The story of one of the first American women pilots, with information about her world travels and plenty of illustrations. (Rev: SLJ 6/06)

PATCH, SAM

14159 Cummins, Julie. *Sam Patch: Daredevil Jumper* (2–4). Illus. by Michael Allen Austin. 2009, Holiday $16.95 (978-0-8234-1741-4). Sam Patch, who was born in the early 19th century, is remembered for his amazing jumping stunts; a leap into Genesee Falls in 1929 proved his undoing. (Rev: BLO 4/29/09; SLJ 3/09)

PEARY, ROBERT E.

14160 Calvert, Patricia. *Robert E. Peary: To the Top of the World* (5–8). Series: Great Explorations. 2001, Marshall Cavendish LB $29.93 (978-0-7614-1242-7). 80pp. The exciting story of the Arctic explorer who, after several attempts, reached the North Pole in 1909. (Rev: BL 4/1/02; HBG 3/02; SLJ 3/02)

PIKE, ZEBULON

14161 Calvert, Patricia. *Zebulon Pike: Lost in the Rockies* (5–8). Series: Great Explorations. 2004, Benchmark LB $29.93 (978-0-7614-1612-8). 96pp. Presents the life and career of the army officer who explored the West and Southwest. (Rev: SLJ 3/05)

14162 Witteman, Barbara. *Zebulon Pike: Soldier and Explorer* (4–6). Series: Let Freedom Ring. 2002, Capstone LB $23.93 (978-0-7368-1351-8). 48pp. An absorbing account of the life and exploits of the explorer who discovered Pikes Peak. (Rev: HBG 3/03; SLJ 2/03)

POLO, MARCO

14163 Demi. *Marco Polo* (4–7). Illus. by author. 2008, Marshall Cavendish $19.99 (978-0-7614-5433-5). 64pp. A visually impressive picture-book biography of the explorer who made an incredible journey from Europe to China taking nearly a quarter of a century; with a double-page map. (Rev: BL 10/1/08; LMC 3/09*; SLJ 9/08*) [910.4]

14164 Otfinoski, Steven. *Marco Polo: To China and Back* (4–8). Series: Great Explorations. 2002, Benchmark LB $29.93 (978-0-7614-1480-3). 77pp. Readable text accompanied by many illustrations and sidebar features traces Polo's life and adventures. (Rev: HBG 10/03; SLJ 5/03)

14165 Senker, Cath. *Marco Polo's Travels on Asia's Silk Road* (4–6). Series: Great Journeys Across Earth. 2007, Heinemann LB $31.43 (978-1-4034-9751-2); paper $8.99 (978-1-4034-9759-8). 48pp. Useful for reports, this volume is a colorful introduction to Marco Polo's amazing adventures. (Rev: LMC 1/08; SLJ 4/08)

14166 Smalley, Roger. *The Adventures of Marco Polo* (4–6). Illus. by Brian Bascle. Series: Graphic Library. 2005, Capstone LB $26.60 (978-0-7368-3830-6). 32pp. This story of the explorer's life is presented in comic-book format. (Rev: BL 3/15/05)

PONCE DE LEON, JUAN

14167 Harmon, Dan. *Juan Ponce de León and the Search for the Fountain of Youth* (4–6). Series: Explorers of New Worlds. 2000, Chelsea LB $31.00 (978-0-7910-5517-5). 63pp. As well as the life of Ponce de Leon and his exploits, this book gives good background information on the social and political forces that inspired him. (Rev: HBG 10/00; SLJ 7/00)

14168 Otfinoski, Steven. *Juan Ponce de Leon: Discoverer of Florida* (5–8). Series: Great Explorations. 2004, Benchmark LB $29.93 (978-0-7614-1610-4). 76pp. A well-illustrated account of the explorer's life and discoveries, dismissing the idea that he was really searching for the fountain of youth. (Rev: SLJ 3/05)

14169 Whiting, Jim. *Juan Ponce de Leon* (5–7). Series: Latinos in American History. 2002, Mitchell Lane LB $29.95 (978-1-58415-149-4). This is the story of the man who is credited with discovering Florida in 1513 while searching for the fountain of youth. (Rev: BL 2/15/03; HBG 10/03; SLJ 6/03) [921]

14170 Worth, Richard. *Ponce de Leon and the Age of Spanish Exploration in World History* (5–9). Series: In World History. 2003, Enslow LB $26.60 (978-0-7660-1940-9). 112pp. As well as a biography of this great adventurer from Spain, this book describes the work of other Spanish explorers in the Americas. (Rev: BL 11/15/03; HBG 4/04)

POWELL, JOHN WESLEY

14171 Ray, Deborah Kogan. *Down the Colorado: John Wesley Powell, the One-Armed Explorer* (3–5). Illus. by author. 2007, Farrar $17.00 (978-0-374-31838-3). 48pp. Primary source material as well as beautiful color illustrations help make this biography of the famous naturalist worth reading. (Rev: BL 6/1–15/07; HB 1/08; SLJ 12/07)

14172 Ross, Michael E. *Exploring the Earth with John Wesley Powell* (3–5). Series: Naturalist's Apprentice. 2000, Carolrhoda $19.93 (978-1-57505-254-0). 48pp. This biography of the noted explorer, geologist, and naturalist covers his important expeditions into the Grand Canyon and the Colorado plateau region. (Rev: BL 4/15/00; SLJ 8/00)

QUIMBY, HARRIET

14173 Moss, Marissa. *Brave Harriet* (2–4). Illus. by C. F. Payne. 2001, Harcourt $17.00 (978-0-15-202380-5). 32pp. A picture book for older readers telling in first person the story of Harriet Quimby, the first woman to fly solo across the English Channel. (Rev: BL 7/01; HBG 3/02; SLJ 9/01)

14174 Whitaker, Suzanne George. *The Daring Miss Quimby* (1–3). Illus. by Catherine Stock. 2009, Holiday House $16.95 (978-082341996-8). 32pp. The story of Harriet Quimby, the first American woman to earn a pilot's license. (Rev: BL 8/09; LMC 3–4/10; SLJ 8/1/09) [921]

RALEIGH, SIR WALTER

14175 Korman, Susan. *Sir Walter Raleigh: English Explorer and Author* (4–6). Series: Colonial Leaders. 2001, Chelsea LB $27.50 (978-0-7910-5969-2); paper $27.50 (978-0-7910-6126-8). 80pp. Korman gives readers a good overview of the many sides of Raleigh, covering his roles as soldier, scientist, and courtier as well as his efforts to colonize Virginia. (Rev: SLJ 7/01)

RAMON, ILAN

14176 Sofer, Barbara. *Ilan Ramon: Israel's Space Hero* (4–8). 2004, Lerner LB $16.95 (978-1-58013-115-5); paper $6.95 (978-1-58013-116-2). The story of the first Israeli astronaut, from his early life and schooling to his selection for the crew of the ill-fated Columbia space shuttle that broke apart on re-entry in 2003. (Rev: SLJ 6/04) [921]

RIDE, SALLY

14177 Hurwitz, Jane, and Sue Hurwitz. *Sally Ride: Shooting for the Stars* (5–8). 1989, Ballantine paper $6.99 (978-0-449-90394-0). An interestingly written account in paperback format of the female space pioneer. (Rev: BL 12/15/89; SLJ 2/90; VOYA 2/90) [921]

14178 Riddolls, Tom. *Sally Ride: The First American Woman in Space* (5–8). Illus. 2010, Crabtree LB $31.93 (978-077872541-1). 112pp. Chronicling her life from youth to adulthood, this biography presents a straightforward and clearly written portrait of astronaut Sally Ride. (Rev: BL 1/1–15/11) [911]

14179 Wade, Linda R. *Sally Ride: The Story of the First American Female in Space* (4–5). Series: Unlocking the Secrets of Science. 2002, Mitchell Lane LB $25.70 (978-1-58415-139-5). 56pp. Profiles the first American woman to travel in space. (Rev: HBG 10/03)

SCOTT, BLANCHE STUART

14180 Cummins, Julie. *Tomboy of the Air: Daredevil Pilot Blanche Stuart Scott* (3–6). Illus. 2001, HarperCollins LB $17.89 (978-0-06-029243-0). 80pp. Scott was a daredevil from childhood, graduating from driving cars to stunt-flying, and was the first American woman flyer. (Rev: BL 5/15/01; HB 5/01; HBG 3/02; SLJ 6/01*)

SELKIRK, ALEXANDER

14181 Kraske, Robert. *Marooned: The Strange but True Adventures of Alexander Selkirk, the Real Robinson Crusoe* (5–8). Illus. by Robert Andrew Parker. 2005,

Clarion $15.00 (978-0-618-56843-7). The adventurous life of Alexander Selkirk, the Scottish navigator who served as the model for Daniel Defoe's *Robinson Crusoe*. (Rev: BL 11/15/05; SLJ 12/05) [996.1]

SERRA, JUNÍPERO

14182 Whiting, Jim. *Junípero José Serra* (5–7). Series: Latinos in American History. 2003, Mitchell Lane LB $29.95 (978-1-58415-187-6). Profiles the monk who was responsible for founding nine California missions and converting thousands of Native Americans to Christianity. (Rev: BL 1/1–15/04; SLJ 3/00) [921]

SHACKLETON, SIR ERNEST

14183 Calvert, Patricia. *Sir Ernest Shackleton: By Endurance We Conquer* (4–8). Series: Great Explorations. 2002, Benchmark LB $29.93 (978-0-7614-1485-8). 80pp. Readable text accompanied by many illustrations and sidebar features traces Shackleton's life and adventures. (Rev: HBG 10/03; SLJ 5/03)

14184 Kostyal, K. M. *Trial by Ice: A Photobiography of Sir Ernest Shackleton* (4–8). 1999, National Geographic $17.95 (978-0-7922-7393-6). A biography that details the life of Sir Ernest Shackleton, his 1915 Antarctic expedition, and the survival of the explorers aboard the *Endurance*. (Rev: BCCB 12/99; BL 12/1/99; HBG 3/00; SLJ 3/00) [921]

14185 Marcovitz, Hal. *Sir Ernest Shackleton and the Struggle Against Antarctica* (4–6). Illus. Series: Explorers of New Worlds. 2001, Chelsea LB $25.00 (978-0-7910-6424-5). 63pp. Photographs from Shackleton's last expedition and quotations from his own writings add interest to this exploration of his motivations and his voyages. (Rev: HBG 10/02; SLJ 4/02)

SHEPARD, ALAN

14186 Orr, Tamra. *Alan Shepard: The First American in Space* (4–7). Illus. Series: The Library of Astronaut Biographies. 2004, Rosen LB $29.25 (978-0-8239-4455-2). 112pp. A lively overview focusing mainly on Shepard's education and training. (Rev: SLJ 1/05)

SMITH, ELINOR

14187 Brown, Tami Lewis. *Soar, Elinor!* (2–4). Illus. by Francois Roca. 2010, Farrar $16.99 (978-0-374-37115-9). 40pp. Introduces the life of Elinor Smith, who became a licensed pilot at the age of 16 in 1928 and went on to become a test pilot. Lexile AD780L (Rev: BL 12/15/10; LMC 1–2/11; SLJ 11/1/10) [921]

SMITH, JEDEDIAH

14188 Nelson, Sharlene, and Ted Nelson. *Jedediah Smith* (3–6). Series: Watts Library. 2004, Scholastic LB $25.50 (978-0-531-12287-7). 64pp. Jedediah Smith's explorations of the American West are covered here with many illustrations, maps, a timeline, and other helpful features. (Rev: BL 6/1–15/04)

SMITH, JOHN

14189 Doak, Robin. *Smith: John Smith and the Settlement of Jamestown* (4–6). Series: Exploring the World. 2003, Compass Point LB $23.93 (978-0-7565-0423-6). 48pp. Examines the important role played by John Smith in opening North America to European settlement. (Rev: SLJ 12/03)

14190 Schanzer, Rosalyn. *John Smith Escapes Again!* (4–6). 2006, National Geographic $16.95 (978-0-7922-5930-5). 64pp. While the accuracy of Smith's writings, used as the basis for Schanzer's account, is controversial (and examined in an author's note), this volume's stellar design and compelling writing combine to illuminate a poorly understood figure in the history of colonial America. (Rev: BL 1/1–15/07; SLJ 11/06)

WHITMAN, NARCISSA

14191 Harness, Cheryl. *The Tragic Tale of Narcissa Whitman and a Faithful History of the Oregon Trail* (4–7). Illus. 2006, National Geographic $16.95 (978-0-7922-5920-6). 144pp. A biography of Narcissa Whitman, the first woman to cross the Rockies on the perilous Oregon Trail in order to bring her Christian beliefs to the Indians of that area. (Rev: BL 12/1/06)

Artists, Composers, Entertainers, and Writers

Collective

14192 Ball, Heather. *Magnificent Women in Music* (4–7). Series: The Women's Hall of Fame. 2006, Second Story paper $7.95 (978-1-897187-02-9). 108pp. Ten women from different times and with different musical gifts are profiled here, including Clara Schumann, Marian Anderson, and k.d. lang. (Rev: SLJ 7/06)

14193 Benedict, Kitty, and Karen Covington. *The Literary Crowd: Writers, Critics, Scholars, Wits* (5–9). Series: Remarkable Women. 2000, Raintree LB $32.82 (978-0-8172-5732-3). 80pp. Profiles of 150 women writers and others associated with the literary world, including Virginia Woolf, Jane Austen, and Maya Angelou. (Rev: SLJ 8/00)

14194 Bostrom, Kathleen Long. *Winning Authors: Profiles of the Newbery Medalists* (5–10). Series: Popular Authors. 2003, Libraries Unlimited $52.00 (978-1-56308-877-3). Report writers will find useful information on the authors who won this prestigious award, including quotations and material on experiences that relate to the winning books. (Rev: SLJ 6/04; VOYA 6/04) [920]

14195 Bredeson, Carmen. *American Writers of the 20th Century* (5–8). 1996, Enslow LB $20.95 (978-0-89490-704-3). Ten writers for adults, including Toni Morrison and F. Scott Fitzgerald, are introduced in brief profiles. (Rev: BL 6/1–15/96; SLJ 9/96) [920]

14196 Cotter, Charis. *Born to Write: The Remarkable Lives of Six Famous Authors* (4–8). 2009, Annick $24.95 (978-1-55451-192-1); paper $14.95 (978-1-55451-191-4). 168pp. E. B. White, C. S. Lewis, and Madeleine L'Engle are among the authors featured in this interesting volume that discusses the writers that inspired them. (Rev: BL 12/15/09; SLJ 12/09) [920]

14197 Covington, Karen. *Creators: Artists, Designers, Craftswomen* (5–9). Series: Remarkable Women. 2000, Raintree LB $32.85 (978-0-8172-5725-5). 80pp. Mary Cassatt, Georgia O'Keefe, Frido Kahlo, and Beatrix Potter are four of the 150 female artists celebrated in this collective biography. (Rev: BL 6/1–15/00; SLJ 8/00)

14198 Cummins, Julie. *Women Daredevils: Thrills, Chills, and Frills* (3–6). Illus. by Cheryl Harness. 2008, Dutton $17.99 (978-0-525-47948-2). 48pp. Cummins chronicles the daring feats of 14 women in the late 18th and early 19th centuries — a human cannonball, a bareback rider, wing walkers, and so forth — providing historical context and a full-page portrait of each fearless performer. (Rev: BCCB 2/08; BL 11/15/07; SLJ 1/08)

14199 Datnow, Claire. *American Science Fiction and Fantasy Writers* (5–8). Series: Collective Biographies. 1999, Enslow LB $26.60 (978-0-7660-1090-1). Science fiction and fantasy writers profiled in this book include Asimov, Heinlein, Bradbury, Anderson, Norton, L'Engle, and Le Guin. (Rev: BL 4/15/99; VOYA 6/99) [920]

14200 Dillon, Leo, and Diane Dillon. *Jazz on a Saturday Night* (1–3). Illus. by Leo Dillon. 2007, Scholastic $16.99 (978-0-590-47893-9). 40pp. This engaging picture-book collective biography sets up a clever mythical jam session that brings together jazz greats; with accompanying CD. (Rev: BL 9/15/07; LMC 10/07; SLJ 9/07)

14201 Ford, Carin T. *Legends of American Dance and Choreography* (5–7). Series: Collective Biographies. 2000, Enslow LB $26.60 (978-0-7660-1378-0). 128pp. This collective work presents 10 short biographies of such dance luminaries as George Balanchine and Martha Graham. (Rev: BL 6/1–15/00; HBG 10/00; SLJ 7/00)

14202 Gaines, Ann Graham. *American Photographers: Capturing the Image* (4–7). Series: Collective Biographies. 2002, Enslow LB $26.60 (978-0-7660-1833-4). 112pp. The lives and contributions of 10 well-known photographers are presented with photographs and a brief history of photography. (Rev: HBG 10/02; SLJ 10/02)

14203 George-Warren, Holly. *Honky-Tonk Heroes and Hillbilly Angels: The Pioneers of Country and Western*

Music (4–6). Illus. by Laura Levine. 2006, Houghton $16.00 (978-0-618-19100-0). 32pp. Loretta Lynn, Gene Autry, Patsy Cline, and the Carter family are just some of the artists covered in short biographies. (Rev: BL 6/1–15/06; SLJ 6/06)

14204 Gourse, Leslie. *Sophisticated Ladies: The Great Women of Jazz* (5–8). Illus. by Martin French. 2007, Dutton $19.99 (978-0-525-47198-1). Profiles 14 female jazz singers, with full-color portraits, biographical details, and comments on vocal style and importance. (Rev: BL 12/15/06; SLJ 5/07)

14205 Govenar, Alan. *Extraordinary Ordinary People: Five American Masters of Traditional Arts* (5–8). 2006, Candlewick $19.99 (978-0-7636-2047-9). 96pp. Five American artists, recipients of National Endowment for the Arts fellowships, who practice unique — but traditional — art forms are profiled here. (Rev: BL 9/1/06; SLJ 8/06*)

14206 Hasday, Judy. *Extraordinary People in the Movies* (5–9). Series: Extraordinary People. 2003, Children's LB $40.00 (978-0-516-22348-3); paper $16.95 (978-0-516-27857-5). 288pp. Brief biographies of individuals associated with the movie business are arranged chronologically by date of birth and interspersed with short essays on related topics. (Rev: SLJ 7/03)

14207 Hill, Christine M. *Ten Terrific Authors for Teens* (5–7). Series: Collective Biographies. 2000, Enslow LB $26.60 (978-0-7660-1380-3). Among the authors profiled are Judy Blume, Virginia Hamilton, Julius Lester, Lois Lowry, Katherine Paterson, Gary Soto, and Lawrence Yep. (Rev: BL 9/15/00; HBG 10/01; SLJ 12/00; VOYA 8/01) [920]

14208 Holme, Merilyn, and Bridget McKenzie. *Expressionists* (5–9). Series: Artists in Profile. 2002, Heinemann LB $28.50 (978-1-58810-647-6). Introduces the movement and gives biographical information on the major artists and their key works, with reproductions and photographs. Also use *Impressionists* and *Pop Artists* (both 2002). (Rev: HBG 3/03; SLJ 3/03) [759.06]

14209 Ishizuka, Kathy. *Asian American Authors* (5–9). Series: Collective Biographies. 2000, Enslow LB $26.60 (978-0-7660-1376-6). 128pp. Writers for children (including Laurence Yep) and for adults (such as Amy Tan) are included in this collective biography of 10 Asian American writers. (Rev: HBG 10/01; SLJ 3/01)

14210 Krull, Kathleen. *Lives of the Musicians: Good Times, Bad Times (And What the Neighbors Thought)* (5–8). 1993, Harcourt $20.00 (978-0-15-248010-3). Biographies of 16 musical giants, from Vivaldi, Mozart, and Beethoven to Gershwin, Joplin, and Woody Guthrie. (Rev: BL 4/1/93*; SLJ 5/93*) [920]

14211 Marcus, Leonard S. *A Caldecott Celebration: Seven Artists and Their Paths to the Caldecott Medal* (3–8). Illus. 2008, Walker $19.95 (978-0-8027-9703-2). 56pp. An updated version of the 1998 edition, this volume features seven Caldecott-winning artists (one for each decade of the award), introducing their prize-winning books and supplying background information on each.

The artists are Sendak, McCloskey, Marcia Brown, Steig, Van Allsburg, Wiesner, and now Gerstein. (Rev: HB 11/08; LMC 5/08; SLJ 4/08) [920]

14212 Marcus, Leonard S. *Pass It Down: Five Picture-Book Families Make Their Mark* (5–8). 2007, Walker $19.95 (978-0-8027-9600-4). 56pp. Multigenerational families of picture book authors/illustrators are featured here: Donald Crews, Ann Jonas, and Nina Crews; Clement, Edith, and Thacher Hurd; Walter Dean and Christopher Myers; Jerry and Brian Pinkney; and Harlow, Anne, and Lizzy Rockwell. (Rev: BL 12/15/06; SLJ 1/07)

14213 Marquez, Heron. *Latin Sensations* (5–9). 2001, Lerner LB $27.93 (978-0-8225-4993-2); paper $7.95 (978-0-8225-9695-0). 112pp. A collective biography that features profiles of Selena, Ricky Martin, Jennifer Lopez, Marc Anthony, and Enrique Iglesias. (Rev: HBG 10/01; SLJ 3/01)

14214 Nobleman, Marc Tyler. *Boys of Steel: The Creators of Superman* (1–3). Illus. by Ross MacDonald. 2008, Knopf $16.99 (978-0-375-83802-6). 40pp. With evocative illustrations by MacDonald, Nobleman introduces Joe Shuster and Jerry Siegel, the creators of Superman, and describes their long-running dispute with DC Comics. (Rev: BCCB 10/08; BL 6/1–15/08; HB 7/08; LMC 11/08)

14215 Raczka, Bob. *Before They Were Famous: How Seven Artists Got Their Start* (4–7). Illus. 2010, Millbrook LB $25.26 (978-0-7613-6077-3). 32pp. Durer, Michelangelo, Gentileschi, Sargent, Paul Klee, Picasso, and Salvador Dali are the artists featured here, each with a page devoted to their childhood plus early artwork and several other works including a self-portrait. (Rev: BL 11/1/10; LMC 3–4/11; SLJ 1/1/11) [920]

14216 Rubin, Susan G. *The Yellow House: Vincent van Gogh and Paul Gauguin Side by Side* (K–3). Illus. by Joseph A. Smith. 2001, Abrams $17.95 (978-0-8109-4588-3). 40pp. Juxtaposed illustrations introduce the works of Vincent van Gogh and Paul Gauguin who, for a short time in 1888, lived and worked together in a studio in the south of France. (Rev: BL 11/15/01; HBG 3/02; SLJ 1/02)

14217 Shone, Rob. *War Correspondents* (4–6). Illus. by Chris Forsey. Series: Graphic Careers. 2009, Rosen LB $21.95 (978-1-4042-1449-1). Ernie Pyle and Sydney Schanberg are two of the correspondents profiled in this volume that combines a text section with comic-book-style pages. (Rev: BL 1/1–15/09)

14218 Tate, Eleanora E. *African American Musicians* (4–7). Series: Black Stars. 2000, Wiley $24.95 (978-0-471-25356-3). This collective biography highlights both past and present contributions to different kinds of music by several African Americans. (Rev: BL 7/00; HBG 3/01; SLJ 7/00) [920]

Artists

ALBERS, JOSEF

14219 Wing, Natasha. *An Eye for Color: The Story of Josef Albers* (3–6). Illus. by Julia Breckenreid. 2009, Holt $16.99 (978-0-8050-8072-8). 40pp. Artist Josef Alber's early life is mentioned, but this book concentrates on his well-known color theory and includes pages dedicated to his color experiments, a glossary, a color wheel, and several projects. (Rev: BL 7/09; SLJ 9/09)

AUDUBON, JOHN JAMES

14220 Armstrong, Jennifer. *Audubon: Painter of Birds in the Wild Frontier* (2–4). Illus. by Jos. A. Smith. 2003, Abrams $17.95 (978-0-8109-4238-7). 38pp. An excellent introduction to the early life of naturalist-painter John James Audubon, this large-format picture book recounts many of the artist's experiences on the American frontier, including his meeting with the legendary Daniel Boone. (Rev: BL 4/1/03; HBG 10/03; SLJ 5/03)

14221 Burleigh, Robert. *Into the Woods: John James Audubon Lives His Dream* (2–5). Illus. by Wendell Minor. 2003, Simon & Schuster $16.95 (978-0-689-83040-2). 40pp. Charming watercolors and selections of Audubon's own detailed drawings combine with simple, poetic text and quotes from Audubon's journals to give a good picture of the bird-lover who rejected urban life. (Rev: BL 1/1–15/03; HBG 10/03; SLJ 2/03)

14222 Davies, Jacqueline. *The Boy Who Drew Birds: A Story of John James Audubon* (2–4). Illus. by Melissa Sweet. 2004, Houghton $16.00 (978-0-618-24343-3). 32pp. This engaging biography focuses on Audubon's early enthusiasm for birds and his decision to band them to trace their movements. (Rev: BL 11/1/04)

14223 Roop, Peter, and Connie Roop, eds. *Capturing Nature* (5–7). Illus. by Rick Farley. 1993, Walker LB $17.85 (978-0-8027-8205-2). Audubon's prints and original paintings and excerpts from his journals are combined to produce a stunning biography. (Rev: BCCB 12/93; BL 12/15/93; SLJ 1/94) [921]

BOTTICELLI, SANDRO

14224 Connolly, Sean. *Botticelli* (4–8). Series: Lives of the Artists. 2005, World Almanac LB $31.00 (978-0-8368-5648-4). A tall, slender volume full of facts about Botticelli's life and times, with many color reproductions. (Rev: BL 6/1–15/04; SLJ 3/05) [921]

BRADY, MATHEW

14225 Pflueger, Lynda. *Mathew Brady* (5–8). Series: Historical American Biographies. 2001, Enslow LB $26.60 (978-0-7660-1444-2). 128pp. A biography of the photographer known primarily for his coverage of the Civil War, illustrated with many of his works. (Rev: BL 1/1–15/02; HBG 10/01; SLJ 9/01; VOYA 2/02)

BRUEGEL, PIETER

14226 Woodhouse, Jane. *Pieter Bruegel* (3–4). Series: The Life and Work Of. 2000, Heinemann LB $21.36 (978-1-57572-344-0). 32pp. This biography of the Flemish painter includes many examples of his paintings of earthy peasants and their surroundings. (Rev: BL 10/15/00; HBG 10/01; SLJ 2/01)

BRYAN, ASHLEY

14227 Bryan, Ashley. *Words to My Life's Song* (3–7). Illus. by author. 2009, Atheneum $18.99 (978-1-4169-0541-7). 64pp. Full of art, this autobiography chronicles Bryan's rich life and the ever-present importance of drawing and painting, even during war. ALA Notable Children's Book. (Rev: BCCB 1/09; BL 12/15/08*; HB 1–2/09; LMC 8–9/09; SLJ 2/09*) [921]

CALDECOTT, RANDOLPH

14228 Hegel, Claudette. *Randolph Caldecott: An Illustrated Life* (5–9). Series: Avisson Young Adult. 2004, Avisson $27.50 (978-1-888105-60-5). Many of Caldecott's drawings are included in this account of the artist's life and work, with coverage of the children's award named in his honor. (Rev: BL 10/1/04; SLJ 11/04) [741.6]

CALDER, ALEXANDER

14229 Stone, Tanya L. *Sandy's Circus: A Story About Alexander Calder* (1–3). Illus. by Boris Kulikov. 2008, Viking $16.99 (978-0-670-06268-3). 40pp. In this picture-book biography, Stone tells the story of the young Calder's interest in wire sculptures and circus structures that preceded his famous mobiles. (Rev: BCCB 9/08; BL 6/1–15/08; HB 9/08; SLJ 9/08)

CARLE, ERIC

14230 Carle, Eric. *Flora and Tiger: 19 Very Short Stories from My Life* (4–8). 1997, Putnam $17.99 (978-0-399-23203-9). An autobiography of the famous picture-book artist who was born in Germany but who has lived in the United States since 1952. (Rev: BL 12/15/97; HBG 3/98; SLJ 2/98) [921]

CARR, EMILY

14231 Bogart, Jo Ellen. *Emily Carr: At the Edge of the World* (4–8). Illus. by Maxwell Newhouse. 2003, Tundra $18.95 (978-0-88776-640-4). This picture book for older readers presents the life and work of the Canadian artist and writer who became famous for her depictions of the native peoples of the Pacific Coast. (Rev: BL 11/1/03; HBG 4/04; SLJ 12/03) [759.11]

14232 Debon, Nicolas. *Four Pictures by Emily Carr* (5–9). 2003, Douglas & McIntyre $15.95 (978-0-88899-532-2). This small comic-book biography uses four of Carr's paintings to introduce chapters that trace the Canadian artist's life and interest in Native Americans. (Rev: BL 12/1/03; HB 1–2/04; HBG 3/02; SLJ 11/03) [759.11]

14233 Griek, Susan Vande. *The Art Room* (PS–3). Illus. by Pascal Milelli. 2002, Groundwood $15.95 (978-0-88899-449-3). 24pp. This biography of the West Coast Canadian artist concentrates on her teaching of young students and the inspiration she gave them. (Rev: BL 4/1/02; HBG 10/02; SLJ 6/02)

CASSATT, MARY

14234 Ferrara, Cos. *Mary Cassatt: The Life and Art of a Genteel Rebel* (5–8). Series: Girls Explore, Reach for the Stars. 2005, Girls Explore $20.00 (978-0-9749456-3-7). Cassatt's art, shown in small full-color reproductions, is introduced in this biography that also discusses her independence and feminist views. (Rev: BL 2/15/05) [921]

14235 Harris, Lois V. *Mary Cassatt: Impressionist Painter* (2–4). Illus. 2007, Pelican $15.95 (978-1-58980-452-4). American Impressionist Cassatt is the subject of this simple biography containing basic and personal facts about her life and work along with a generous number of reproductions. (Rev: BL 11/1/07; SLJ 12/07)

14236 Hoena, Blake A. *Mary Cassatt* (2–4). Series: Masterpieces: Artists and Their Works. 2003, Capstone LB $22.60 (978-0-7368-2229-9). 24pp. A small-format introductory biography of the artist featuring simple text and color reproductions, with emphasis on Cassatt's association with the Impressionists and how she faced prejudice because of her gender. (Rev: SLJ 3/04)

14237 O'Connor, Jane. *Mary Cassatt: Family Pictures* (3–4). Illus. by Jennifer Kalis. Series: Smart and Art. 2003, Grosset paper $5.99 (978-0-448-43152-9). 32pp. Presented as a school report, this is a simple but appealing overview of the artist's life. (Rev: HBG 10/03; SLJ 7/03)

14238 Streissguth, Thomas. *Mary Cassatt* (4–8). Series: Trailblazers. 1999, Lerner LB $27.93 (978-1-57505-291-5). Full-color illustrations enhance this biography of the American painter who was associated with the Impressionists and spent most of her adult life in France. (Rev: BL 5/1/99; HBG 10/99; SLJ 9/99) [921]

CÉZANNE, PAUL

14239 Burleigh, Robert. *Paul Cézanne: A Painter's Journey* (4–7). Illus. 2006, Abrams $17.95 (978-0-8109-5784-8). 32pp. A lavishly illustrated and thoughtfully written profile of Cézanne's life and art. (Rev: BL 2/15/06; SLJ 3/06)

14240 Tracy, Kathleen. *Paul Cézanne* (4–7). Series: Art Profiles for Kids. 2007, Mitchell Lane LB $29.95 (978-1-58415-565-2). Suitable for both research and browsing, this examination of the artist's life and times includes many reproductions and interesting sidebars. (Rev: LMC 2/08; SLJ 12/07) [921]

CHAGALL, MARC

14241 Landmann, Bimba. *I Am Marc Chagall* (2–4). Illus. 2006, Eerdmans $18.00 (978-0-8028-5305-9). 40pp. Loosely inspired by Chagall's *My Life*, this first-

person narrative describes Chagall's life from childhood through emigration to the United States and features painterly illustrations. (Rev: BL 1/1–15/06; SLJ 4/06)

14242 Lemke, Elisabeth, and Thomas David. *Marc Chagall: What Colour Is Paradise?* (4–8). Illus. Series: Adventures in Art. 2001, Prestel $14.95 (978-3-7913-2393-0). 28pp. Using Chagall's biographical paintings as a focus, this innovative biography tells of his life, career, and work. (Rev: BL 1/1–15/01; SLJ 4/01)

14243 Lewis, J. Patrick, and Jane Yolen. *Self-Portrait with Seven Fingers: The Life of Marc Chagall in Verse* (5–8). Illus. by Marc Chagall. 2011, Creative Editions $18.99 (978-156846211-0). 32pp. Poems by writers including Yolen and Lewis accompany reproductions of Chagall's works in this elegant large-format book. (Rev: BL 12/15/11; SLJ 1/12) [921]

14244 Markel, Michelle. *Dreamer from the Village: The Story of Marc Chagall* (K–3). Illus. by Emily Lisker. 2005, Holt $16.95 (978-0-8050-6373-8). 40pp. This excellent profile traces the artist's life and career and introduces the importance of his work; browsers may find this more useful than report writers. (Rev: BL 8/05; SLJ 9/05)

14245 Mason, Antony. *Marc Chagall* (4–8). Series: Lives of the Artists. 2005, World Almanac LB $31.00 (978-0-8368-5649-1). A tall, slender volume full of facts about Chagall's life and times, with many color reproductions. (Rev: BL 6/1–15/04; SLJ 3/05) [921]

14246 Venezia, Mike. *Marc Chagall* (2–4). Series: Getting to Know. 2000, Children's Book Pr. LB $28.00 (978-0-516-21055-1). A biography of the innovative 20th-century painter told with an easy-to-read text, full-color reproductions, and amusing cartoons. (Rev: BL 5/15/00)

CLOSE, CHUCK

14247 Close, Chuck. *Face Book* (5–8). Illus. 2012, Abrams $18.95 (978-141970163-4). 64pp. Portrait artist Chuck Close offers insight into his creative process and how he has dealt with disability; with 14 beautifully reproduced works that can be mixed and matched. (Rev: BL 3/15/12; HB 5–6/12; SLJ 6/12) [921]

DA VINCI, LEONARDO

14248 Augarde, Steve. *Leonardo da Vinci* (4–8). Illus. by Leo Brown. Series: Lifelines. 2009, Kingfisher $16.99 (978-0-7534-6174-7). 64pp. This book opens with an illustrated, diary-style narrative in which a fictional 10-year-old apprentice to Leonardo da Vinci reveals glimpses into the artist's personality, process, and intellect; the second half of the book looks at everyday life in the Renaissance and details of da Vinci's work. (Rev: BL 11/1/09; SLJ 1/10) [921]

14249 Barretta, Gene. *Neo Leo: The Ageless Ideas of Leonardo da Vinci* (1–3). Illus. by author. 2009, Holt $16.99 (978-0-8050-8703-1). A visually appealing book that juxtaposes Leonardo da Vinci's original plans for several inventions with the modern end-result. (Rev: BL 7/09; SLJ 8/09)

14250 Byrd, Robert. *Leonardo, Beautiful Dreamer* (4–6). Illus. by author. 2003, Penguin $17.99 (978-0-525-47033-5). 40pp. This large-format overview of da Vinci's life and work is beautifully illustrated and packed with information that is presented in varied and appropriate styles. (Rev: BL 8/03; HB 9/03; HBG 4/04; SLJ 9/03)

14251 Herbert, Janis. *Leonardo da Vinci for Kids: His Life and Ideas* (4–8). 1998, Chicago Review paper $16.95 (978-1-55652-298-7). This biography of Leonardo da Vinci contains background information on history, art techniques, science, and philosophy. (Rev: BL 3/1/99; SLJ 4/99) [921]

14252 Krull, Kathleen. *Leonardo da Vinci* (5–8). Illus. by Boris Kulikov. Series: Giants of Science. 2005, Viking $15.99 (978-0-670-05920-1). The less attractive features of da Vinci's times are covered here, along with the artist's childhood and adolescence and his development into both an artist and a scientist, drawing connections between the two disciplines and incorporating much from da Vinci's notebooks. (Rev: BL 9/1/05; SLJ 10/05*) [921]

14253 Kuhne, Heinz. *Leonardo da Vinci: Dreams, Schemes, and Flying Machines* (4–8). Series: Adventures in Art. 2000, Prestel $14.95 (978-3-7913-2166-0). This well-illustrated biography covers da Vinci's accomplishments as a scientist, engineer, inventor, and artist. (Rev: BL 7/00) [921]

14254 Mason, Antony. *Leonardo da Vinci* (4–8). 1994, Barron's paper $8.99 (978-0-8120-1997-1). A brief biography that chronicles the achievements of this multifaceted genius and supplies pictures of some of his great triumphs. (Rev: BL 12/1/94) [921]

14255 O'Connor, Barbara. *Leonardo da Vinci: Renaissance Genius* (5–8). Series: Trailblazer Biographies. 2002, Carolrhoda LB $27.93 (978-0-87614-467-1). An excellent biography that details Leonardo's life from childhood, discusses some of his famous paintings, and looks at his inventions and experiments. (Rev: BL 3/15/03; HBG 3/03; SLJ 11/02; VOYA 8/03) [921]

14256 Reed, Jennifer. *Leonardo da Vinci: Genius of Art and Science* (4–7). Series: Great Minds of Science. 2005, Enslow LB $26.60 (978-0-7660-2500-4). Reed describes da Vinci's wide-ranging achievements — showing, for example, his urban planning ideas, his design for a flying machine, and his anatomical drawings — and emphasizes his originality and creativity. (Rev: SLJ 6/05) [921]

DALI, SALVADOR

14257 Anderson, Robert. *Salvador Dali* (5–8). Illus. Series: Artists in Their Time. 2002, Watts LB $24.00 (978-0-531-12231-0). 48pp. This volume presents Dali's life and influence with many illustrations, news clippings, and useful information. (Rev: BL 10/15/02)

DAVE THE POTTER

14258 Cheng, Andrea. *Etched in Clay: The Life of Dave, Enslaved Potter and Poet* (5–8). Illus. by author. 2013, Lee & Low $17.95 (978-160060451-5). 160pp. This portrait in verse focuses on the life of a slave who took many risks as he created his pots, jugs, and jars and not only signed them but added simple verses. Lexile 790L (Rev: BL 2/1/13; HB 1–2/13; LMC 8–9/13*; SLJ 2/13*) [738.092]

14259 Hill, Laban Carrick. *Dave the Potter: Artist, Poet, Slave* (K–3). Illus. by Bryan Collier. 2010, Little, Brown $16.99 (978-0-316-10731-0). 40pp. This picture book chronicles the life of Dave, an unusual 19th-century slave who was a skilled and prolific potter. (Rev: BL 11/1/10; LMC 11–12/10; SLJ 8/1/10*) [921]

DE KOONING, WILLEM

14260 Hawes, Louise. *Willem de Kooning: The Life of an Artist* (4–6). Series: Artist Biographies. 2002, Enslow LB $23.93 (978-0-7660-1884-6). 48pp. Covers de Kooning's life from youth, his artistic techniques and work habits, and the impact of his lifestyle. (Rev: HBG 10/03; SLJ 3/03)

DEGAS, EDGAR

14261 Venezia, Mike. *Edgar Degas* (2–4). Illus. Series: Getting to Know. 2000, Children's Book Pr. LB $28.00 (978-0-516-21593-8); paper $6.95 (978-0-516-27172-9). 32pp. An easy-to-read text, several reproductions, and humorous cartoons are used to introduce the life and works of this French master. (Rev: BL 9/15/00)

DELACROIX, EUGENE

14262 Venezia, Mike. *Eugene Delacroix* (1–3). Illus. Series: Getting to Know the World's Greatest Artists. 2003, Children's Pr. LB $28.00 (978-0-516-22576-0); paper $6.95 (978-0-516-26976-4). An easy-to-read text and humorous cartoons are used to introduce this famous French artist and his work. [921]

DESJARLAIT, PATRICK

14263 Williams, Neva. *Patrick DesJarlait: Conversations with a Native American Artist* (5–7). 1994, Lerner LB $22.60 (978-0-8225-3151-7). A beautifully illustrated biography of the Native American artist who worked at the Red Lake Indian Reservation in Minnesota. (Rev: BL 1/1/95; SLJ 1/95) [921]

DISNEY, WALT

14264 Ford, Barbara. *Walt Disney* (4–8). 1989, Walker LB $17.00 (978-0-8027-6865-0). The story of Disney's youth and his struggle to fulfill his dreams. (Rev: BL 5/15/89) [791.430924]

ELLABBAD, MOHIEDDIN

14265 Ellabbad, Mohieddin. *The Illustrator's Notebook* (5–10). Trans. from French by Sarah Quinn. Illus. by author. 2006, Groundwood $16.95 (978-0-88899-700-

5). 30pp. In this fascinating journal printed from right to left, Egyptian-born illustrator Ellabbad reflects on the influences that led him to a life in art and offers valuable insights into Arabic cultural sensibilities. (Rev: SLJ 8/06)

FRAZEE, MARLA

14266 Llanas, Sheila Griffin. *Marla Frazee* (3–5). Illus. Series: Children's Illustrators. 2012, ABDO LB $16.95 (978-161783246-8). 24pp. This volume explores the life from childhood of the illustrator who has earned two Caldecott Honors. (Rev: BL 5/1/12; SLJ 5/1/12) [921]

GÁG, WANDA

14267 Ray, Deborah Kogan. *Wanda Gág: The Girl Who Lived to Draw* (2–4). Illus. by author. 2008, Viking $16.99 (978-0-670-06292-8). 40pp. Covering the life of the creator of *Millions of Cats* from her childhood in Bohemia, Ray emphasizes Gág's lifelong interest in art and includes many quotations. (Rev: BCCB 12/08; BL 12/15/08; LMC 11/08; SLJ 10/08)

GAUDI, ANTONI

14268 Rodriguez, Rachel. *Building on Nature: The Life of Antoni Gaudi* (1–3). Illus. by Julie Paschkis. 2009, Holt $16.99 (978-0-8050-8745-1). Full of poetic language and rich images, this is an appealing profile of the innovative Catalonian architect. (Rev: BL 6/1–15/09; LMC 10/09)

GAUGUIN, PAUL

14269 Anderson, Robert. *Paul Gauguin* (4–8). Series: Artists in Their Time. 2003, Watts LB $24.00 (978-0-531-12239-6); paper $6.95 (978-0-531-16647-5). 46pp. An interesting life of Gauguin, with reproductions of his works and of those of fellow painters, with a timeline that adds historical context. (Rev: SLJ 6/03)

GEHRY, FRANK

14270 Bodden, Valerie. *Frank Gehry* (4–7). Series: Xtraordinary Artists. 2008, Creative Education LB $32.80 (978-1-58341-662-4). 48pp. Bodden provides an interesting overview of the architect's life with well-chosen illustrations. (Rev: LMC 8/09; SLJ 4/09)

GIACOMETTI, ALBERTO

14271 Gaff, Jackie. *Alberto Giacometti* (5–8). Series: Artists in Their Time. 2002, Watts LB $24.00 (978-0-531-12224-2); paper $6.95 (978-0-531-16617-8). 48pp. The life of this Italian artist noted for his elongated sculptures is re-created with comments on his social period and reproductions of his work. (Rev: BL 10/15/02)

GIOTTO

14272 Venezia, Mike. *Giotto* (2–4). Series: Getting to Know. 2000, Children's Book Pr. LB $22.00 (978-0-516-21592-1). The story of the Florentine Renaissance artist and architect who influenced all of European paint-ing is told in text, reproductions, and witty cartoons. (Rev: BL 5/15/00)

GORMAN, R. C.

14273 Hermann, Spring. *R. C. Gorman: Navajo Artist* (4–8). Series: Multicultural Junior Biographies. 1995, Enslow LB $20.95 (978-0-89490-638-1). The story of this contemporary Native American artist, who reflects his heritage in his work. (Rev: BL 2/15/96; SLJ 3/96) [921]

GOWNLEY, JIMMY

14274 Gownley, Jimmy. *The Dumbest Idea Ever!* (5–9). Illus. by author. 2014, Scholastic $24.99 (978-054545346-2); paper $11.99 (978-054545347-9). 240pp. The creator of the Amelia Rules series explains, with humor, what inspired him to turn to the drawing board and find success there. ℮ (Rev: BL 12/15/13; LMC 8–9/14*; SLJ 5/14)

GOYA, FRANCISCO

14275 Wood, Alix. *Francisco Goya* (3–6). Illus. Series: Artists Through the Ages. 2013, Windmill LB $25.25 (978-161533624-1). 32pp. An easy-to-read and relatively detailed profile of Goya and his work, covering tapestries, altarpiece paintings, portraits, war images, and frescoes. ℮ (Rev: BL 4/1/13; LMC 11–12/13; SLJ 4/13) [921]

GUYTON, TYREE

14276 Shapiro, J. H. *Magic Trash: A Story of Tyree Guyton and His Art* (2–4). Illus. by Vanessa Brantley-Newton. 2011, Charlesbridge $15.95 (978-1-58089-385-5). 32pp. A picture-book biography of the artist who sees art in all kinds of everyday environments. (Rev: BL 11/1/11; SLJ 11/1/11) [921]

HOKUSAI, KATSUSHIKA

14277 Ray, Deborah Kogan. *Hokusai* (2–4). Illus. 2001, Farrar $18.00 (978-0-374-33263-1). Covers the life of Japanese artist Hokusai from birth, with excellent descriptions of life in late 18th- and 19th-century Japan. (Rev: BL 11/1/01; HBG 3/02; SLJ 12/01*)

HOMER, WINSLOW

14278 *Winslow Homer* (1–3). Illus. by Mike Venezia. Series: Getting to Know the World's Greatest Artists. 2004, Scholastic LB $6.95 (978-0-516-26979-5). 32pp. This beautifully illustrated biography chronicles the life and work of the late-19th-century American artist. (Rev: BL 6/1–15/04)

HOPPER, EDWARD

14279 Foa, Emma. *Edward Hopper* (4–8). Series: Artists in Their Time. 2003, Watts LB $24.00 (978-0-531-12240-2); paper $6.95 (978-0-531-16641-3). 46pp. An interesting life of Hopper, with reproductions of his works and of those of fellow painters, and a timeline that adds historical context. (Rev: SLJ 6/03)

14280 Lyons, Deborah. *Edward Hopper: Summer at the Seaside* (4–8). Series: Adventures in Art. 2003, Prestel $14.95 (978-3-7913-2737-2). The story of the American painter who died in 1967, with a good analysis of many of his important works. (Rev: BL 11/15/03; SLJ 9/03) [921]

14281 Rubin, Susan Goldman. *Edward Hopper: Painter of Light and Shadow* (5–8). Illus. 2007, Abrams $18.95 (978-0-8109-9347-1). Along with a life of the painter, Rubin provides good reproductions of his work plus discussion of his themes, images, and technique. (Rev: BL 9/1/07; SLJ 10/07)

14282 Spangenburg, Ray, and Kit Moser. *Edward Hopper: The Life of an Artist* (3–5). Series: Artist Biographies. 2002, Enslow LB $23.93 (978-0-7660-1881-5). 48pp. A look at the life and work of the artist and his realistic paintings. (Rev: HBG 10/03; SLJ 4/03)

KAHLO, FRIDA

14283 Frith, Margaret. *Frida Kahlo: The Artist Who Painted Herself* (3–5). Illus. by Tomie dePaola. Series: Smart About Art. 2003, Grosset paper $5.99 (978-0-448-42677-8). 32pp. This picture-book biography presents the life of the Mexican artist as seen through the eyes of a young girl who is researching her for a school report. (Rev: HB 11/03; HBG 4/04; SLJ 11/03)

14284 Garza, Hedda. *Frida Kahlo* (5–9). Series: Hispanics of Achievement. 1994, Chelsea LB $21.95 (978-0-7910-1698-5); paper $9.95 (978-0-7910-1699-2). 119pp. Known once only as the wife of Diego Rivera, this painter, who lived most of her life in Mexico, is now considered a great artist. (Rev: BL 3/1/94)

14285 Guzmán, Lila, and Rick Guzmán. *Frida Kahlo: Painting Her Life* (3–5). Series: Famous Latinos. 2006, Enslow LB $22.60 (978-0-7660-2643-8). 32pp. A brief, accessible portrait of the Mexican artist, chronicling her personal life and artistic accomplishments in text for young readers that will also suit older reluctant readers. (Rev: BL 10/15/06; SLJ 2/07)

14286 Holzhey, Magdalena. *Frida Kahlo: The Artist in the Blue House* (4–8). Series: Adventures in Art. 2003, Prestel $14.95 (978-3-7913-2863-8). A colorful introduction to this Mexican painter with an interesting analysis of individual paintings. (Rev: BL 11/15/03; SLJ 9/03) [921]

14287 Laidlaw, Jill A. *Frida Kahlo* (5–8). Series: Artists in Their Time. 2003, Watts LB $24.00 (978-0-531-12236-5); paper $6.95 (978-0-531-16642-0). 46pp. An interesting life of Kahlo, with reproductions of her works and a timeline and informative sidebars that add historical context. (Rev: SLJ 6/03)

14288 Novesky, Amy. *Me, Frida* (1–3). Illus. by David Diaz. 2010, Abrams $16.95 (978-0-8109-8969-6). 32pp. Imaginative illustrations enliven this picture-book biography of Frida Kahlo, emphasizing how she came into her own as an artist after moving to San Francisco with her husband Diego Rivera. (Rev: BL 11/1/10; LMC 11–12/10; SLJ 12/1/10) [921]

14289 Winter, Jonah. *Frida* (PS–3). Illus. by Ana Juan. 2002, Scholastic $16.95 (978-0-590-20320-3). 32pp. An inspirational biography of Mexican artist Frida Kahlo. (Rev: BCCB 2/02; BL 3/1/02; HB 3/02; HBG 10/02; SLJ 3/02)

14290 Woronoff, Kristen. *Frida Kahlo: Mexican Painter* (3–5). Series: Famous Women Juniors. 2002, Gale LB $23.70 (978-1-56711-594-9). 32pp. This account focuses on Kahlo's youth and the events that led to her life as an artist. (Rev: SLJ 9/02)

KIRBY, JACK

14291 Hamilton, Sue. *Jack Kirby* (4–8). Series: Comic Book Creators. 2007, ABDO LB $16.95 (978-1-59928-298-5). A biography of comic book legend Kirby, with information on his childhood, early career, and work on comics such as the *Incredible Hulk* and *Captain America*. (Rev: BL 5/1/07) [921]

KLEE, PAUL

14292 Laidlaw, Jill A. *Paul Klee* (5–8). Series: Artists in Their Time. 2002, Watts LB $24.00 (978-0-531-12230-3). 46pp. Photographs, reproductions, maps, and a timeline that links world events with events in the artist's life make this suitable both for browsing and report writing. (Rev: BL 10/15/02; SLJ 1/03)

LANGE, DOROTHEA

14293 Venezia, Mike. *Dorothea Lange* (2–4). Illus. Series: Getting to Know. 2000, Children's Book Pr. LB $28.00 (978-0-516-22026-0); paper $6.95 (978-0-516-27171-2). 32pp. A biography — enriched with amusing cartoons — of the famous American photographer noted mainly for her haunting pictures of migrant workers and victims of the Great Depression. (Rev: BL 9/15/00)

LAWRENCE, JACOB

14294 Duggleby, John. *Story Painter: The Life of Jacob Lawrence* (5–8). 1998, Chronicle $16.95 (978-0-8118-2082-0). Using 50 color reproductions, this biography of the great African American illustrator and painter tells how he moved to Harlem in the 1930s and developed his own techniques and style. (Rev: BCCB 1/99; BL 10/15/98; HB 3–4/99; HBG 3/99; SLJ 12/98) [921]

14295 Leach, Deba Foxley. *I See You I See Myself: The Young Life of Jacob Lawrence* (5–9). Illus. by Jacob Lawrence. 2002, Phillips Collection $20.00 (978-0-943044-26-2). 64pp. A look at the early life and work of the African American artist, with information on his paintings as a teen. (Rev: SLJ 12/02)

LEE, STAN

14296 Hamilton, Sue. *Stan Lee* (3–5). Illus. Series: Comic Book Creators. 2007, ABDO LB $16.95 (978-1-59928-301-2). 32pp. Comics fans will enjoy this introduction to part of the team behind Spider-Man, the X-Men, the Hulk, and other superheroes. Vintage strips are included. (Rev: SLJ 8/07)

14297 Miller, Raymond H. *Stan Lee: Creator of Spider-Man* (4–8). Series: Inventors and Creators. 2006, Gale LB $26.20 (978-0-7377-3447-8). Superhero fans will enjoy this biography of the man behind Spider-Man and other comic-book characters. (Rev: SLJ 6/06) [921]

LEWIS, MAUD

14298 Bogart, Jo Ellen. *Capturing Joy: The Story of Maud Lewis* (3–6). Illus. by Mark Lang. 2002, Tundra $16.95 (978-0-88776-568-1). The story of the life and work of the Canadian artist who used a folk-art style. (Rev: BL 6/1–15/02; HBG 10/02; SLJ 7/02)

LICHTENSTEIN, ROY

14299 Rubin, Susan Goldman. *Whaam! The Art and Life of Roy Lichtenstein* (4–7). Illus. 2008, Abrams $18.95 (978-081099492-8). 48pp. With many reproductions of his works and thoughtful, engaging text, this eye-catching book offers a portrait of Roy Lichtenstein and his diverse artistic achievements. Lexile 1030L (Rev: BL 11/1/08; HB 1–2/09; SLJ 10/1/08) [921]

MATISSE, HENRI

14300 Anholt, Laurence. *Matisse: The King of Color* (1–3). Illus. by author. Series: Anholt's Artists. 2007, Barron's $14.99 (978-0-7641-6047-9). 32pp. This colorful picture book tells the story behind Matisse's creation — when he is in his 80s — of stained glass windows for a nunnery chapel. (Rev: BL 11/15/07; SLJ 2/08)

14301 Hollein, Max, and Nina Hollein. *Matisse: Cut-Out Fun with Matisse* (4–8). Series: Adventures in Art. 2003, Prestel $14.95 (978-3-7913-2858-4). This large-formatted book that originated in Germany, successfully introduces the life and work of the great French master. (Rev: BL 11/15/03; HBG 3/02; SLJ 8/01) [921]

14302 Parker, Marjorie Blain. *Colorful Dreamer: The Story of Artist Henri Matisse* (K–3). Illus. by Holly Berry. 2012, Dial $16.99 (978-0-8037-3758-7). 32pp. A nicely illustrated picture-book biography that emphasizes the artist's frustrating early life and his discovery of the world of color. Lexile 600L (Rev: BL 11/1/12*; HB 3–4/13; LMC 3–4/13; SLJ 11/12*) [921]

14303 Sturm, Ellen. *Matisse* (2–4). Series: Masterpieces: Artists and Their Works. 2003, Capstone LB $22.60 (978-0-7368-2227-5). 24pp. A small-format introductory biography of the artist featuring simple text and color reproductions and including material on his early life, training, and influences. (Rev: SLJ 3/04)

14304 Welton, Jude. *Henri Matisse* (5–8). Series: Artists in Their Time. 2002, Watts LB $24.00 (978-0-531-12228-0); paper $6.95 (978-0-531-16621-5). 48pp. The artistic and social periods during which Matisse worked are re-created along with a biography and several color examples of his work. (Rev: BL 10/15/02; SLJ 1/03)

14305 Winter, Jeanette. *Henri's Scissors* (K–3). Illus. by author. 2013, Simon & Schuster $16.99 (978-1-4424-6484-1). 40pp. Celebrating Henri Matisse's cut-paper works, this is a handsome account of the artist's adapta-

tions in later life. Booklist Editors' Choice: Books for Youth. ℮ (Rev: BL 6/13*; HB 8–9/13; LMC 1–2/14; SLJ 6/13) [921]

MICHELANGELO

14306 Connolly, Sean. *Michelangelo* (5–8). Series: The Lives of the Artists. 2004, World Almanac LB $31.00 (978-0-8368-5600-2). A tall, slender volume full of facts about Michelangelo's life and times, with many color reproductions. (Rev: SLJ 8/04) [921]

14307 Tames, Richard. *Michelangelo Buonarroti* (3–4). Series: The Life and Work Of. 2000, Heinemann LB $21.36 (978-1-57572-343-3). 32pp. A brief biography of Michelangelo that gives examples of some of his finest works, including the Sistine Chapel. (Rev: BL 10/15/00; HBG 10/01; SLJ 2/01)

14308 Whiting, Jim. *Michelangelo* (4–7). Series: Art Profiles for Kids. 2007, Mitchell Lane LB $29.95 (978-1-58415-562-1). Suitable for both research and browsing, this examination of the artist's life and times includes many reproductions and interesting sidebars. (Rev: LMC 2/08; SLJ 12/07) [921]

MONET, CLAUDE

14309 Connolly, Sean. *Claude Monet* (4–8). Series: Lives of the Artists. 2005, World Almanac LB $31.00 (978-0-8368-5650-7). A tall, slender volume full of facts about Monet's life and times, with many color reproductions. (Rev: BL 6/1–15/04; SLJ 3/05) [921]

14310 Connolly, Sean. *Claude Monet* (3–4). Series: The Life and Work Of. 1999, Heinemann LB $21.36 (978-1-57572-956-5). 32pp. This is a simple introduction to the life and works of Monet, with photos showing him at different stages in his career. (Rev: BL 2/15/00; SLJ 1/00)

14311 Hodge, Susie. *Claude Monet* (5–8). Illus. Series: Artists in Their Time. 2002, Watts LB $24.00 (978-0-531-12226-6). 46pp. Photographs, reproductions, maps, and a timeline that links world events with events in the artist's life make this suitable both for browsing and report writing. (Rev: SLJ 1/03)

14312 Kelley, True. *Claude Monet: Sunshine and Water-lilies* (2–4). Illus. Series: Smart About Art. 2001, Penguin paper $5.99 (978-0-448-42522-1). An interesting overview of Claude Monet's life and work, presented in the Smart About Art school-report format with cartoon drawings. (Rev: BL 11/1/01; HBG 3/02; SLJ 11/01)

14313 Maltbie, P. I. *Claude Monet: The Painter Who Stopped the Trains* (3–5). Illus. by Jos. A. Smith. 2010, Abrams $18.95 (978-0-8109-8961-0). 32pp. This picture book tells the story of how Monet's son's love for trains inspired his father to create wonderful Impressionist scenes at Paris's first train station. (Rev: BL 11/1/10; LMC 11–12/10; SLJ 10/1/10) [921]

14314 Whiting, Jim. *Claude Monet* (4–7). Series: Art Profiles for Kids. 2007, Mitchell Lane LB $29.95 (978-1-58415-563-8). Suitable for both research and browsing, this examination of the artist's life and times includes many reproductions and interesting sidebars. (Rev: LMC 2/08; SLJ 12/07) [921]

MORAN, THOMAS

14315 Judge, Lita. *Yellowstone Moran: Painting the American West* (1–3). Illus. by author. 2009, Viking $16.99 (978-0-670-01132-2). 32pp. In 1871 artist Thomas Moran joined an expedition to the West, documenting his journey in paint and his journal. (Rev: BL 11/1/09; LMC 11–12/09; SLJ 9/1/09) [921]

MORGAN, JULIA

14316 Mannis, Celeste Davidson. *Julia Morgan Built a Castle* (2–4). Illus. by Miles Hyman. 2006, Viking $17.99 (978-0-670-05964-5). 40pp. This intriguing large-format biography covers the life of Julia Morgan, who grew up in the late 19th century, achieved many "firsts" for women in the field, and designed many impressive buildings — including William Randolph Hearst's huge castle at San Simeon. (Rev: BL 11/15/06; SLJ 11/06)

MOSES, GRANDMA

14317 Wallner, Alexandra. *Grandma Moses* (PS–3). Illus. 2004, Holiday House $16.95 (978-0-8234-1538-0). 32pp. Moses did not become an active artist until late in life; this picture book illustrated in a style reminiscent of the artist's primitives also describes her early years. (Rev: BL 3/1/04; HB 7/04; SLJ 5/04)

MOUNT, WILLIAM SIDNEY

14318 Howard, Nancy S. *William Sidney Mount: Painter of Rural America* (4–7). 1994, Sterling $14.95 (978-1-871922-75-2). An interactive book that explores the work and paintings of the 19th-century American painter William Sidney Mount. (Rev: BL 1/15/95) [921]

NAST, THOMAS

14319 Pflueger, Lynda. *Thomas Nast: Political Cartoonist* (5–8). Series: Historical American Biographies. 2000, Enslow LB $26.60 (978-0-7660-1251-6). 128pp. An informative, entertaining, and well-written biography of this influential political cartoonist and critic. (Rev: BL 9/15/00; HBG 10/01; SLJ 11/00)

NOGUCHI, ISAMU

14320 Hale, Christy. *The East-West House: Noguchi's Childhood in Japan* (3–6). Illus. by author. 2009, Lee & Low $17.95 (978-1-60060-363-1). 32pp. A biography of Isamu Noguchi, Japanese American artist, sculptor, and landscape architect, focusing on his boyhood in Japan and his problems with being biracial. (Rev: BL 11/1/09; LMC 11–12/09; SLJ 9/1/09) [921]

O'KEEFFE, GEORGIA

14321 Bryant, Jen. *Georgia's Bones* (2–4). Illus. by Bethanne Andersen. 2005, Eerdmans $16.00 (978-0-8028-5217-5). 32pp. This beautifully illustrated book introduces readers to Georgia O'Keeffe's life and preoc-

cupation with shapes and structures. (Rev: BL 2/15/05; SLJ 4/05)

14322 Kucharczyk, Emily Rose. *Georgia O'Keeffe: Desert Painter* (3–5). Series: Famous Women Juniors. 2002, Gale LB $23.70 (978-1-56711-592-5). 32pp. This account focuses on the artist's youth and the events that led to her life as an artist. (Rev: SLJ 9/02)

14323 Rodríguez, Rachel Victoria. *Through Georgia's Eyes* (K–3). Illus. by Julie Paschkis. 2006, Holt $16.95 (978-0-8050-7740-7). 32pp. O'Keeffe's life — including her childhood — and work are presented in compelling text and vibrant illustrations. (Rev: BCCB 4/06; BL 2/15/06*; HB 5/06; HBG 10/06; LMC 10/06; SLJ 3/06)

14324 Spangenburg, Ray, and Kit Moser. *Georgia O'Keeffe: The Life of an Artist* (2–4). Illus. Series: Artist Biographies. 2002, Enslow LB $23.93 (978-0-7660-1882-2). 48pp. This informative profile of American painter Georgia O'Keeffe includes a timeline, glossary, list of Web sites, and full-color reproductions of selected O'Keeffe paintings. (Rev: BL 4/1/03; HBG 10/03)

OBATA, CHIURA

14325 Ross, Michael E. *Nature Art with Chiura Obata* (3–6). Series: Naturalist's Apprentice. 2000, Lerner $19.95 (978-1-57505-378-3). 48pp. From his childhood in Japan to his move to the U.S. in 1903 to his death in 1975, this is the story of the great painter who used Japanese painting techniques to depict the American landscape. (Rev: BCCB 3/00; BL 2/1/00; HBG 10/00; SLJ 4/00)

OHR, GEORGE E.

14326 Greenberg, Jan, and Sandra Jordan. *The Mad Potter: George E. Ohr, Eccentric Genius* (3–6). Illus. 2013, Roaring Brook $17.99 (978-1-59643810-1). 56pp. George Ohr's inventive pots brought him little respect from the art community of the late 19th century, but his talents were finally recognized in the late 20th century. ALA Notable Children's Book. e (Rev: BL 11/1/13*; LMC 5–6/14; SLJ 9/13*) [921]

PARKS, GORDON

14327 Parr, Ann. *Gordon Parks: No Excuses* (3–5). Illus. by Kathryn Breidenthal. 2006, Pelican $15.95 (978-1-58980-411-1). African American photographer Parks's camera work takes center stage in this brief, large-format biography. (Rev: BL 7/06; SLJ 6/06)

PEI, I. M.

14328 Englar, Mary. *I. M. Pei* (3–5). Illus. Series: Asian-American Biographies. 2005, Raintree LB $32.86 (978-1-4109-1056-1). Profiles the life and career of the Chinese American architect who designed many notable structures, with sidebars that add historical context. (Rev: BL 10/15/05; SLJ 3/06)

PICASSO, PABLO

14329 Gogerly, Liz. *Pablo Picasso: Master of Modern Art* (3–5). 2004, Raintree LB $29.93 (978-0-7398-6628-3). 48pp. Picasso's youth, education, and artistic evolution are strong features of this biography that includes photographs, quotations, and a timeline. (Rev: SLJ 1/05)

14330 Hodge, Susie, and Pablo Picasso. *Pablo Picasso* (4–8). Series: Lives of the Artists. 2004, Gareth Stevens LB $11.95 (978-0-8368-5606-4). 48pp. Works by the young Picasso are a feature of this well illustrated profile. (Rev: BL 6/1–15/04)

14331 Jacobson, Rick. *Picasso: Soul on Fire* (4–7). Illus. by author and Laura Fernandez. 2004, Tundra $15.95 (978-0-88776-599-5). Oil paintings of the Spanish-born artist, along with reproductions of some of his best-known pieces, introduce his work and brief facts about his life. (Rev: BL 11/1/04) [921]

14332 Penrose, Antony. *The Boy Who Bit Picasso* (2–4). Illus. 2011, Abrams $16.95 (978-0-8109-9728-8). 48pp. The author recalls episodes shared with Picasso — his parents were friends of the artist — in this visually pleasing book that includes photographs taken by Penrose's mother. Lexile 800L (Rev: BL 6/1/11; SLJ 6/11) [709.2]

14333 Pfleger, Susanne. *A Day with Picasso* (4–7). Series: Adventures in Art. 2000, Prestel $14.95 (978-3-7913-2165-3). 30pp. An introduction to the life and work of Picasso, including many full-color reproductions. (Rev: BL 2/15/00; SLJ 2/00)

14334 Scarborough, Kate. *Pablo Picasso* (5–8). Series: Artists in Their Time. 2002, Watts LB $24.00 (978-0-531-12229-7); paper $6.95 (978-0-531-16622-2). 48pp. This biography of the 20th century's most famous artist is accompanied by material on the social conditions of his time. (Rev: BL 10/15/02; SLJ 1/03)

14335 Wallis, Jeremy. *Pablo Picasso* (5–8). Series: Creative Lives. 2001, Heinemann LB $27.07 (978-1-58810-206-5). 64pp. Picasso's eccentricities are highlighted in this volume that covers his life, his family, and his work. (Rev: HBG 10/02; SLJ 3/02)

PINKNEY, JERRY

14336 Llanas, Sheila Griffin. *Jerry Pinkney* (3–5). Illus. Series: Children's Illustrators. 2012, ABDO LB $16.95 (978-161783247-5). 24pp. Portrays Pinkney's life from childhood, including his struggle with dyslexia, and his success as an award-winning illustrator. (Rev: BL 5/1/12; SLJ 5/1/12) [921]

PIPPIN, HORACE

14337 Bryant, Jen. *A Splash of Red: The Life and Art of Horace Pippin* (1–4). Illus. by Melissa Sweet. 2013, Knopf $17.99 (978-0-375-86712-5). 40pp. Introduces Horace Pippin, a self-taught African American folk art painter who succeeded despite a bullet wound to his right arm during World War I. Sibert Honor; ALA Notable Children's Book; Booklist Editors' Choice:

Books for Youth. ℮ Lexile 610L (Rev: BL 11/1/12*; HB 1–2/13; LMC 8–9/13; SLJ 1/13*) [921]

14338 Venezia, Mike. *Horace Pippin* (3–5). Illus. by author. Series: Getting to Know the World's Greatest Artists. 2007, Children's Pr. LB $28.00 (978-0-531-18527-8). 32pp. Simply written but packed with information, this is an attractive profile of the African American artist known for his naive paintings of life during slavery and segregation. (Rev: SLJ 2/08)

POLITI, LEO

14339 Stalcup, Ann. *Leo Politi: Artist of the Angels* (4–9). Illus. by Leo Politi. 2004, Silver Moon $24.95 (978-1-893110-38-0). The life of the American-born man who spent his formative years in Italy and returned as an adult to make his home in Los Angeles and protray the ethnic communities there in his books for children. (Rev: SLJ 4/05) [921]

POLLOCK, JACKSON

14340 Bennett, Leonie. *Jackson Pollock* (1–3). Illus. Series: Life and Work. 2005, Heinemann LB $22.79 (978-1-4034-5073-9). 32pp. The life and work of the artist, with photographs of both. (Rev: BL 3/15/05)

14341 Oliver, Clare. *Jackson Pollock* (5–8). Series: Artists in Their Time. 2003, Watts LB $24.00 (978-0-531-12237-2). 46pp. An interesting life of Pollock, with reproductions of his works and of those of fellow painters, and a timeline that adds historical context. (Rev: SLJ 5/03)

REAM, VINNIE

14342 Fitzgerald, Dawn. *Vinnie and Abraham* (2–4). Illus. by Catherine Stock. 2007, Charlesbridge paper $7.95 (978-1-5709-1644-1). This charmingly illustrated picture-book biography illuminates the life of Vinnie Ream, who was not only one of the U.S. Postal Service's first female workers but was also a talented artist and did a life-size sculpture of President Lincoln. (Rev: BL 1/1–15/07)

REMBERT, WINFRED

14343 Rembert, Winfred. *Don't Hold Me Back: My Life and Art* (4–7). 2003, Cricket $19.95 (978-0-8126-2703-9). Rembert reflects on his life in the South as a sharecropper's son — picking cotton, dealing with racism, the civil rights movement — and displays his evocative works of art with comments on their creation. (Rev: BL 11/1/03*; HBG 4/04; SLJ 12/03*) [759.1]

REMBRANDT VAN RIJN

14344 De Bie, Ceciel, and Martijn Leenen. *Rembrandt: See and Do Children's Book* (3–7). Illus. 2001, Getty $19.95 (978-0-89236-621-7). 64pp. An effectively organized biography is combined with activities that encourage children to look closely at the art. (Rev: HBG 3/02; SLJ 4/02)

14345 Mason, Antony. *Rembrandt* (4–8). Series: Lives of the Artists. 2005, World Almanac LB $31.00 (978-0-8368-5651-4). A tall, slender volume full of facts about Rembrandt's life and times, with many color reproductions. (Rev: BL 6/1–15/04; SLJ 3/05) [921]

14346 Mis, Melody S. *Rembrandt* (3–5). Illus. Series: Meet the Artist. 2007, Rosen LB $15.95 (978-1-4042-3840-4). With at least one captioned reproduction on every spread, this is a basic biography of the artist and his career. (Rev: BL 11/1/07; SLJ 1/08)

14347 Niz, Xavier. *Rembrandt* (2–4). Series: Masterpieces: Artists and Their Works. 2003, Capstone LB $22.60 (978-0-7368-2230-5). 24pp. An introductory biography of the 17th-century artist, including material on his childhood and early training plus discussion of his techniques. (Rev: SLJ 3/04)

RENOIR, PIERRE-AUGUSTE

14348 Somervill, Barbara A. *Pierre-Auguste Renoir* (5–8). Series: Art Profiles for Kids. 2007, Mitchell Lane LB $29.95 (978-1-58415-566-9). A brief introduction to the artist's life and work and the times in which he lived, with reproductions of his art. (Rev: BL 1/1–15/08; LMC 2/08; SLJ 12/07) [921]

RINGGOLD, FAITH

14349 Venezia, Mike. *Faith Ringgold* (3–5). Illus. by author. Series: Getting to Know the World's Greatest Artists. 2007, Children's Pr. LB $28.00 (978-0-531-18526-1). Simply written but packed with information, this is an attractive profile of the African American artist known for her children's books and story quilts. (Rev: SLJ 2/08)

RIVERA, DIEGO

14350 Bankston, John. *Diego Rivera* (5–7). Series: Latinos in American History. 2003, Mitchell Lane LB $29.95 (978-1-58415-208-8). A biography of the famous 20th-century Mexican artist who is best known for his murals with political overtones. (Rev: BL 1/1–15/04; HBG 4/04; SLJ 2/04) [921]

14351 Guzmán, Lila, and Rick Guzmán. *Diego Rivera: Artist of Mexico* (3–4). Series: Famous Latinos. 2006, Enslow LB $22.60 (978-0-7660-2641-4). The Mexican artist's life is described in easy-to-understand language, focusing in particular on his vibrantly colored murals. (Rev: SLJ 2/07)

14352 Kent, Deborah. *Diego Rivera: Painting Mexico* (3–6). Series: A Proud Heritage. 2005, Child's World LB $28.50 (978-1-59296-384-3). 40pp. Covers Rivera's childhood and education, discussing in age-appropriate language his four marriages and how his communist leanings are reflected in his paintings. (Rev: SLJ 6/05)

14353 Marin, Guadalupe Rivera. *My Papa Diego and Me / Mi papa Diego y yo: Memories of My Father and His Art / Recuerdos de mi padre y su arte* (2–4). Illus. by Diego Rivera. 2009, Children's Book Press $17.95 (978-089239228-5). 32pp. This bilingual biography pairs 13 Diego Rivera paintings with his daughter's recollections about these works and their creation. (Rev: BL 11/1/09; HB 11–12/09; LMC 11–12/09) [921]

14354 Tonatiuh, Duncan. *Diego Rivera: His World and Ours* (1–3). Illus. by author. 2011, Abrams $16.95 (978-0-8109-9731-8). 40pp. In addition to introducing the artist and his work, this volume speculates about what Rivera would paint if he were alive today. (Rev: BL 5/1/11; SLJ 4/11) [921]

ROCKWELL, NORMAN

14355 Gherman, Beverly. *Norman Rockwell: Storyteller with a Brush* (4–7). 2000, Simon & Schuster $19.95 (978-0-689-82001-4). An appealing biography of this New England artist who reflected mid-20th-century American life and values in his many paintings. (Rev: BCCB 7–8/00; BL 2/15/00; HB 3–4/00; HBG 10/00; SLJ 2/00) [921]

14356 Roy, Jennifer, and Gregory Roy. *Norman Rockwell: The Life of an Artist* (4–6). Series: Artist Biographies. 2002, Enslow LB $23.93 (978-0-7660-1883-9). 48pp. Rockwell's early interest in art and his popularity are highlighted in this account of his life and work. (Rev: HBG 10/03; SLJ 3/03)

14357 Venezia, Mike. *Norman Rockwell* (2–4). Series: Getting to Know. 2000, Children's Book Pr. LB $28.00 (978-0-516-21594-5). 32pp. The popular American artist is introduced with many full color reproductions, a lively text, and some amusing cartoons. (Rev: BL 1/1–15/01)

RODIN, AUGUSTE

14358 Tames, Richard. *Auguste Rodin* (3–4). Series: The Life and Work Of. 2000, Heinemann LB $21.36 (978-1-57572-342-6). 32pp. This book chronicles the life and work of Rodin and includes material on the events that influenced his growth and development as an artist. (Rev: BL 10/15/00; HBG 10/01)

ROUSSEAU, HENRI

14359 Markel, Michelle. *The Fantastic Jungles of Henri Rousseau* (K–3). Illus. by Amanda Hall. 2012, Eerdmans $17 (978-0-8028-5364-6). 34pp. A lush portrait of the self-taught painter and his long road to fame. (Rev: BL 9/15/12*; HB 11–12/12; LMC 1–2/13; SLJ 9/12*) [921]

14360 Venezia, Mike. *Henri Rousseau* (2–4). Series: Getting to Know the World's Greatest Artists. 2002, Children's Book Pr. LB $28.00 (978-0-516-22495-4); paper $6.95 (978-0-516-26998-6). 32pp. An easy-to-read text and humorous cartoons are used to introduce this famous French artist and his work. (Rev: BL 4/1/02)

SARGENT, JOHN SINGER

14361 Kreiter, Eshel, and Marc Zabludoff. *John Singer Sargent: The Life of an Artist* (2–4). Illus. Series: Artist Biographies. 2002, Enslow LB $23.93 (978-0-7660-1879-2). 48pp. This concise, well-illustrated introduction to the life and work of the American painter includes a glossary, timeline, and list of Web sites. (Rev: BL 4/1/03; HBG 10/03)

SAY, ALLEN

14362 Say, Allen. *Drawing from Memory* (4–7). Illus. by author. 2011, Scholastic $17.99 (978-0-545-17686-6). 64pp. Say tells the story of his creative awakening in words and illustrations, beginning with his childhood in World War II Japan. Sibert Honor 2012; ALA Notable Children's Book 2012. Lexile HL560L (Rev: BL 8/11*; SLJ 9/1/11*) [921]

SCHULZ, CHARLES

14363 Gherman, Beverly. *Sparky: The Life and Art of Charles Schulz* (4–8). Illus. 2010, Chronicle $16.99 (978-0-8118-6790-0). 128pp. A graphic-format biography of the creator of *Peanuts,* with many excerpts from the comic strip. (Rev: BL 6/10; SLJ 8/10; VOYA 6/10) [921]

14364 Marvis, Barbara. *Charles Schulz: The Story of the Peanuts Gang* (4–8). Series: Robbie Reader. 2004, Mitchell Lane LB $25.70 (978-1-58415-289-7). This photo-filled biography traces Schulz's life and his love of cartoons; it is especially suitable for reluctant readers. (Rev: BL 9/1/05)

14365 Whiting, Jim. *Charles Schulz* (3–4). Series: Real-Life Reader Biographies. 2002, Mitchell Lane LB $15.95 (978-1-58415-131-9). 32pp. A simple retelling of the life of the talented storyteller and cartoonist who created the comic strip "Peanuts." (Rev: BL 9/15/02; SLJ 4/03)

14366 Woods, Mae. *Charles Schulz* (2–4). Series: Children's Authors. 2000, ABDO LB $21.35 (978-1-57765-425-4). An attractive, brief biography of the creator of Peanuts and the gang. (Rev: HBG 3/01; SLJ 1/01)

SELZNICK, BRIAN

14367 Llanas, Sheila Griffin. *Brian Selznick* (3–5). Illus. Series: Children's Illustrators. 2012, ABDO LB $16.95 (978-161783248-2). 24pp. Covers Selznick's love of books as a child and his progression to become the acclaimed artist he is today. (Rev: BL 5/1/12; SLJ 5/1/12) [921]

SEURAT, GEORGES

14368 Burleigh, Robert. *Seurat and la Grande Jatte: Connecting the Dots* (3–6). 2004, Abrams $17.95 (978-0-8109-4811-2). 32pp. The well-known painting of "La Grande Jatte" serves as an introduction to Seurat's work and time in this oversized picture book for older readers. (Rev: BL 6/1–15/04; SLJ 6/04)

SIMMONS, PHILIP

14369 Lyons, Mary E. *Catching the Fire: Philip Simmons, Blacksmith* (4–8). 1997, Houghton Mifflin $17.00 (978-0-395-72033-2). A biography of the contemporary African American craftsman and artist from Charleston, South Carolina, with extensive quotations from personal interviews. (Rev: BL 9/1/97; HBG 3/98; SLJ 9/97) [921]

SIMON, JOE

14370 Hamilton, Sue. *Joe Simon* (3–5). Illus. Series: Comic Book Creators. 2007, ABDO LB $16.95 (978-1-59928-300-5). 32pp. Comics fans will enjoy this introduction to part of the team behind Captain America and other superheroes. Vintage strips are included. (Rev: SLJ 8/07)

THIEBAUD, WAYNE

14371 Rubin, Susan Goldman. *Delicious: The Life and Art of Wayne Thiebaud* (5–8). Illus. 2007, Chronicle $15.95 (978-0-8118-5168-8). 108pp. Paintings (by Thiebaud, of course) of gum balls and cupcakes on the cover of this nicely designed volume draw readers in to the story of a man who paints "happy pictures." (Rev: BL 2/15/08; SLJ 3/08)

TITIAN

14372 Venezia, Mike. *Titian* (1–3). Illus. Series: Getting to Know the World's Greatest Artists. 2003, Children's Pr. LB $28.00 (978-0-516-22575-3); paper $6.95 (978-0-516-26975-7). 32pp. An easy-to-read text and humorous cartoons are used to introduce this famous Italian artist and his work. [921]

TOULOUSE-LAUTREC, HENRI

14373 Burleigh, Robert. *Toulouse-Lautrec: The Moulin Rouge and the City of Light* (3–5). Illus. 2005, Abrams $17.95 (978-0-8109-5867-8). 32pp. A biography of the French artist, with plenty of colorful reproductions of his work and information about the Paris of his day. (Rev: BL 3/1/05; SLJ 5/05)

TRAYLOR, BILL

14374 Tate, Don. *It Jes' Happened: When Bill Traylor Started to Draw* (2–4). Illus. by R. Gregory Christie. 2012, Lee & Low $17.95 (978-160060260-3). 32pp. Born into slavery and freed at the end of the Civil War, Bill Traylor started to draw at the age of 85 in 1939, producing moving works until his death in 1949. (Rev: BL 5/15/12*; HB 5–6/12; LMC 11–12/12; SLJ 6/1/12*) [921]

TURNER, JOSEPH

14375 Woodhouse, Jane. *Joseph Turner* (3–4). Series: The Life and Work Of. 2000, Heinemann LB $21.36 (978-1-57572-345-7). 32pp. The life and works of this English painter noted chiefly for his luminous seascapes are covered in this brief, well-illustrated biography. (Rev: BL 10/15/00; HBG 10/01)

VAN GOGH, VINCENT

14376 Bodden, Valerie. *Vincent van Gogh* (4–7). Series: Xtraordinary Artists. 2008, Creative Education LB $32.80 (978-1-58341-663-1). Bodden provides an interesting overview of the artist's life with well-chosen illustrations and excerpts from his own writing. (Rev: LMC 8/09; SLJ 4/09)

14377 Bucks, Brad, and Joan Holub. *Vincent van Gogh: Sunflowers and Swirly Stars* (2–4). Series: Smart About Art. 2001, Grosset $5.99 (978-0-448-42521-4). Using lively cartoon drawings and reproductions of the artist's works, the life and output of van Gogh are introduced through the eyes of a young student. (Rev: BL 1/1–15/02; HBG 3/02)

14378 Green, Jen. *Vincent van Gogh* (5–8). Series: Artists in Their Time. 2002, Watts LB $24.00 (978-0-531-12238-9). 48pp. The life and times of this 20th-century artistic genius are covered, with a number of reproductions of his paintings. (Rev: BL 10/15/02)

VELAZQUEZ, DIEGO

14379 *Diego Velazquez* (1–3). Illus. by Mike Venezia. Series: Getting to Know the World's Greatest Artists. 2004, Scholastic LB $6.95 (978-0-516-26980-1). Full-color reproductions and cartoons add to the basic information about the life of the 17th-century Spanish painter. (Rev: BL 6/1–15/04)

VERMEER, JOHANNES

14380 Mis, Melody S. *Vermeer* (2–4). Series: Meet the Artist. 2007, Rosen LB $15.95 (978-1-4042-3843-5). 24pp. Vermeer's life and work are covered in this clear, well-designed volume. (Rev: BL 10/15/07)

14381 Venezia, Mike. *Johannes Vermeer* (2–4). Series: Getting to Know the World's Greatest Artists. 2002, Children's Book Pr. LB $28.00 (978-0-516-22282-0); paper $6.95 (978-0-516-26999-3). 32pp. The life and work of this Dutch master are presented with a simple text and many cartoons. (Rev: BL 4/1/02)

WALDMAN, NEIL

14382 Waldman, Neil. *Out of the Shadows: An Artist's Journey* (5–8). Illus. 2006, Boyds Mills $21.95 (978-1-59078-411-2). 144pp. In this candid memoir, Waldman describes how his challenging childhood experiences influenced him as an artist. (Rev: BL 4/15/06; SLJ 5/06)

WANG YANI

14383 Zhensun, Zheng, and Alice Low. *A Young Painter: The Life and Paintings of Wang Yani — China's Extraordinary Young Artist* (5–8). 1991, Scholastic paper $17.95 (978-0-590-44906-9). The story of a self-taught prodigy whose paintings are highly regarded in China. Includes many examples of her unique work, based on the traditional Chinese style. (Rev: BCCB 9/91; BL 10/1/91*; SLJ 8/91) [921]

WARHOL, ANDY

14384 Bolton, Linda. *Andy Warhol* (5–8). Series: Artists in Their Time. 2002, Watts LB $24.00 (978-0-531-12225-9); paper $6.95 (978-0-531-16618-5). 48pp. This biography includes material on the social period in which Warhol worked. (Rev: BL 10/15/02)

14385 Christensen, Bonnie. *Fabulous! A Portrait of Andy Warhol* (3–6). Illus. by author. 2011, Henry Holt $16.99 (978-0-8050-8753-6). 40pp. An inspiring profile of Warhol as a boy facing many challenges who nonetheless went on to become a success. (Rev: BL 6/1/11; HB 7–8/11; LMC 10/11; SLJ 5/1/11*) [921]

14386 Ford, Carin T. *Andy Warhol: The Life of an Artist* (3–5). Series: Artist Biographies. 2002, Enslow LB $23.93 (978-0-7660-1880-8). 48pp. Warhol's personal life is covered in this brief biography that also introduces his famous works. (Rev: HBG 10/03; SLJ 4/03)

14387 Rubin, Susan G. *Andy Warhol: Pop Art Painter* (4–7). Illus. 2006, Abrams $18.95 (978-0-8109-5477-9). 48pp. This picture-book biography chronicles Warhol's life and career, focusing in particular on his art and his childhood in Pittsburgh; there are many reproductions plus a timeline and a glossary. (Rev: BL 11/1/06; SLJ 11/06)

14388 Warhola, James. *Uncle Andy's: A Faabbbulous Visit with Andy Warhol* (K–3). Illus. 2003, Penguin $16.99 (978-0-399-23869-7). 32pp. A young boy (the author as a child) enjoys visiting his eccentric artist uncle, Andy Warhol, and is inspired by his work. (Rev: BL 2/15/03; HB 3/03; HBG 10/03; SLJ 4/03)

WILHEIM, LILY RENEE

14389 Robbins, Trina. *Lily Renee, Escape Artist: From Holocaust Survivor to Comic Book Pioneer* (4–7). Illus. by Anne Timmons. 2011, Lerner LB $29.27 (978-076136010-0); paper $7.95 (978-076138114-3). 96pp. With helpful back matter that provides historical context, this is the story of a Jewish girl who escapes from Germany in 1939 and goes on to become a cartoonist in America. Sydney Taylor Book Honor 2012. e Lexile GN510L (Rev: BL 10/15/11; LMC 3–4/12; SLJ 11/1/11; VOYA 12/11) [921]

WOOD, GRANT

14390 Duggleby, John. *Artist in Overalls: The Life of Grant Wood* (4–8). 1996, Chronicle $15.95 (978-0-8118-1242-9). The life of this American artist tells of his difficult struggle with poverty and his great attachment to the Midwest. (Rev: BCCB 6/96; BL 4/15/96; HB 7–8/96; SLJ 5/96) [921]

WOOD, MICHELE

14391 Igus, Toyomi. *Going Back Home: An Artist Returns to the South* (4–8). 1996, Children's $16.95 (978-0-89239-137-0). The author re-creates the family history and life of the African American illustrator Michele Wood. (Rev: BCCB 12/96; BL 9/15/96; SLJ 7/97) [921]

WRIGHT, FRANK LLOYD

14392 Mayo, Gretchen Will. *Frank Lloyd Wright* (5–8). Series: Trailblazers of the Modern World. 2004, World Almanac LB $31.00 (978-0-8368-5101-4). Report writers will find useful information on Wright's life, achievements, and lasting contributions. (Rev: SLJ 7/04) [921]

14393 Middleton, Haydn. *Frank Lloyd Wright* (5–8). Series: Creative Lives. 2001, Heinemann LB $27.07 (978-1-58810-203-4). 64pp. An attractive look at the architect's life and career with illustrations and a useful timeline. (Rev: HBG 10/02; SLJ 3/02)

WU DAOZI

14394 Look, Lenore. *Brush of the Gods* (K–3). Illus. by Meilo So. 2013, Random House $17.99 (978-037587001-9). 40pp. A beautifully illustrated picture book blending fiction and biography to tell the story of the Tang dynasty painter Wu Daozi, who created a wonderful mural for the emperor. e Lexile 580 (Rev: BL 5/15/13*; LMC 11–12/13; SLJ 5/13*)

YOUNG, ED

14395 Young, Ed, and Libby Koponen. *The House Baba Built: An Artist's Childhood in China* (3–5). Illus. by Ed Young. 2011, Little, Brown $17.99 (978-0-316-07628-9). 48pp. Young's illustrations and Koponen's text tell the story of the artist's childhood in Shanghai as World War II grew closer. (Rev: BL 9/1/11*; SLJ 9/1/11*) [921]

ZHANG, ANGE

14396 Zhang, Ange. *Red Land, Yellow River: A Story from the Cultural Revolution* (5–8). 2004, Groundwood $16.95 (978-0-88899-489-9). In this compelling autobiography, artist Ange Zhang tells how he came of age during one of the most turbulent periods in modern Chinese history — the Cultural Revolution of the late 1960s. (Rev: BL 12/1/04*; SLJ 12/04) [921]

Composers

BACH, JOHANN SEBASTIAN

14397 Lynch, Wendy. *Bach* (K–3). Series: Lives and Times. 2000, Heinemann LB $19.92 (978-1-57572-214-6). 24pp. A brief account of the highlights of Bach's life illustrated with drawings and photographs. (Rev: SLJ 9/00)

BEETHOVEN, LUDWIG VAN

14398 Viegas, Jennifer. *Beethoven's World* (5–8). Series: Music Throughout History. 2007, Rosen LB $29.25 (978-1-4042-0724-0). 64pp. Six biographical chapters cover the composer's early life, family, personal life, musical training, compositions, and influences, with photographs of key people and places. (Rev: SLJ 1/08)

BERLIN, IRVING

14399 Furstinger, Nancy. *Say It with Music: The Story of Irving Berlin* (5–9). Series: Masters of Music. 2003, Morgan Reynolds LB $23.95 (978-1-931798-12-9). Well-researched and very readable, this account traces Berlin's life from Russia to the United States and his

popular and lasting success as a songwriter. (Rev: BL 6/1–15/03; HBG 4/04; SLJ 10/03) [780.92]

BERLIOZ, HECTOR

14400 Whiting, Jim. *The Life and Times of Hector Berlioz* (5–7). Series: Masters of Music: The World's Greatest Composers. 2004, Mitchell Lane LB $20.95 (978-1-58415-259-0). A brief biography of the talented and troubled creator of the *Symphonie fantastique*. (Rev: SLJ 2/05) [921]

BERNSTEIN, LEONARD

14401 Blashfield, Jean F. *Leonard Bernstein: Composer and Conductor* (4–7). Series: Ferguson Career Biographies. 2001, Ferguson LB $25.00 (978-0-89434-337-7). Numerous black-and-white photographs accompany the easily read text in this interesting account of Bernstein's life and career. (Rev: SLJ 7/01) [780]

14402 Rubin, Susan Goldman. *Music Was It: Young Leonard Bernstein* (5–10). Illus. 2011, Charlesbridge $19.95 (978-1-58089-344-2). A compelling account of the composer/conductor's youth through the age of 25 and his determination to succeed in music despite his father's resistance to the idea. ALA Notable Children's Book; Sydney Taylor Award. (Rev: BL 2/15/11*; HB 5–6/11; LMC 8–9/11; SLJ 3/1/11)

CHOPIN, FREDERIC

14403 Malaspina, Ann. *Chopin's World* (5–8). Series: Music Throughout History. 2007, Rosen LB $29.25 (978-1-4042-0723-3). 64pp. Six biographical chapters cover the composer's early life, family, personal life, musical training, compositions, and influences, with photographs of key people and places. (Rev: SLJ 1/08)

D'AREZZO, GUIDO

14404 Roth, Susan L. *Do Re Mi: If You Can Read Music, Thank Guido d'Arezzo* (K–5). Illus. by author. 2007, Houghton $17.00 (978-0-618-46572-9). 40pp. This colorful fictionalized biography of Guido d'Arezzo focuses on the 11th-century Italian monk's development of a musical notation system. (Rev: BL 12/1/06; SLJ 2/07)

FOSTER, STEPHEN

14405 Pancella, Peggy. *Stephen Foster: The Man Behind Our Best-Loved Songs* (1–3). Series: Lives and Times. 2005, Heinemann LB $24.21 (978-1-4034-6748-5). 32pp. Profiles the composer's life and examines the qualities that made his songs so popular with Americans. (Rev: SLJ 2/06)

GERSHWIN, GEORGE

14406 Reef, Catherine. *George Gershwin: American Composer* (5–8). Series: Masters of Music. 2000, Morgan Reynolds LB $23.95 (978-1-883846-58-9). This biography traces the life one of America's great composers, giving insight into his personality, family, and times. (Rev: BL 2/15/00; HBG 10/00; SLJ 3/00) [921]

14407 Whiting, Jim. *The Life and Times of George Gershwin* (4–6). Series: Masters of Music: The World's Greatest Composers. 2004, Mitchell Lane LB $20.95 (978-1-58415-279-8). 48pp. The challenges that Gershwin faced in both his personal and professional lives are discussed and placed in historical perspective. (Rev: SLJ 5/05)

GUTHRIE, WOODY

14408 Coombs, Karen Mueller. *Woody Guthrie: America's Folksinger* (4–6). Series: Trailblazer Biographies. 2002, Carolrhoda LB $27.93 (978-1-57505-464-3). 120pp. A balanced look at the life of the singer/songwriter who died in 1967. (Rev: HBG 10/02; SLJ 7/02)

HANDEL, GEORGE FRIDERIC

14409 Anderson, M. T. *Handel, Who Knew What He Liked* (3–6). Illus. by Kevin Hawkes. 2001, Candlewick $16.99 (978-0-7636-1046-3). 48pp. Here's an irreverent large-format account of the interesting life of composer Handel, including lively anecdotes and detailed, dramatic illustrations that give a flavor of the time with a dollop of humor. (Rev: BCCB 1/02; BL 12/15/01; HB 11/01*; HBG 3/02; SLJ 12/01*)

14410 Lee, Lavina. *Handel's World* (5–8). Series: Music Throughout History. 2007, Rosen LB $29.25 (978-1-4042-0726-4). 64pp. Six biographical chapters cover the composer's early life, family, personal life, musical training, compositions, and influences, with photographs of key people and places. (Rev: LMC 1/08; SLJ 1/08)

HAYDN, FRANZ JOSEPH

14411 Norton, James R. *Haydn's World* (5–8). Series: Music Throughout History. 2007, Rosen LB $29.25 (978-1-4042-0727-1). Six biographical chapters cover the composer's early life, family, personal life, musical training, compositions, and influences, with photographs of key people and places. (Rev: SLJ 1/08)

IVES, CHARLES

14412 Gerstein, Mordicai. *What Charlie Heard* (3–5). Illus. 2002, Farrar $17.00 (978-0-374-38292-6). 40pp. This picture-book biography focuses on the American composer Charles Ives and his childhood influences. (Rev: BCCB 4/02; BL 4/1/02; HB 5/02*; HBG 10/02; SLJ 3/02)

14413 Stanbridge, Joanne. *The Extraordinary Music of Mr. Ives: The True Story of a Famous American Composer* (1–3). Illus. by author. Series: Ives, Charles. 2012, Houghton Mifflin $16.99 (978-054723866-1). 32pp. Tells the story of Charles Ives, an experimental composer known for the piece he created after the sinking of the *Lusitania* in 1915. Lexile AD830L (Rev: BL 11/1/12; LMC 10/12) [921]

JOPLIN, SCOTT

14414 Bankston, John. *The Life and Times of Scott Joplin* (5–7). Series: Masters of Music: The World's Greatest Composers. 2004, Mitchell Lane LB $20.95 (978-1-58415-270-5). Joplin's career as a ragtime piano player and composer is documented, with coverage of his African American heritage. (Rev: SLJ 2/05) [921]

14415 Gillis, Jennifer Blizin. *Scott Joplin: The King of Ragtime* (2–4). Illus. Series: Lives and Times. 2005, Heinemann LB $16.95 (978-1-4034-6789-8). 32pp. Brief, large text and illustrations cover Joplin's childhood, musical career, death, and later popularity. (Rev: BL 11/1/05)

JOSEPH BOULOGNE, CHEVALIER DE SAINT-GEORGE

14416 Brewster, Hugh. *The Other Mozart: The Life of the Famous Chevalier de Saint-George* (4–6). Illus. by Eric Velasquez. 2006, Abrams $18.95 (978-0-8109-5720-6). 32pp. A captivating picture-book biography of Joseph Bologne Saint-George, a famous 18th-century composer who was the son of a white plantation owner in Guadeloupe and a black slave. (Rev: BL 2/1/07)

14417 Cline-Ransome, Lesa. *Before There Was Mozart: The Story of Joseph Boulogne, Chevalier de Saint-George* (1–3). Illus. by James E. Ransome. 2011, Random House $17.99 (978-0-375-83600-8); LB $20.99 (978-0-375-93621-0). 40pp. Mozart contemporary Joseph Boulogne rose from his obscure West Indian half-French, half-slave background to become a noted musical protégé. Lexile 1110L (Rev: BL 2/15/11; HB 3–4/11; LMC 5–6/11; SLJ 2/1/11) [921]

MESSIAEN, OLIVIER

14418 Bryant, Jen. *Music for the End of Time* (4–7). Illus. by Beth Peck. 2005, Eerdmans $17.00 (978-0-8028-5229-8). This fictionalized picture-book biography tells how French soldier Olivier Messiaen composed and performed music while in a German prison camp during World War II. (Rev: BL 9/1/05; SLJ 12/05) [921]

MOZART, WOLFGANG AMADEUS

14419 Allman, Barbara. *Musical Genius: A Story About Wolfgang Amadeus Mozart* (3–5). Illus. by Janet Hamlin. Series: Creative Minds Biographies. 2004, Carolrhoda LB $22.60 (978-1-57505-604-3); paper $6.95 (978-1-57505-637-1). An accessible introduction to Mozart that starts with his childhood. (Rev: SLJ 8/04)

14420 Ekker, Ernst A. *Wolfgang Amadeus Mozart: A Musical Picture Book* (3–6). Illus. by Doris Eisenburger. 2006, North-South $20.00 (978-0-7358-2056-2). 32pp. A musical CD accompanies this biography that covers the composer's life and career and adds personal details. (Rev: SLJ 5/06)

14421 Lynch, Wendy. *Mozart* (K–3). Series: Lives and Times. 2000, Heinemann LB $19.92 (978-1-57572-219-1). After a brief biography of Mozart, there is a section on how young readers can learn more about him. (Rev: SLJ 9/00)

14422 Riggs, Kate. *Wolfgang Amadeus Mozart* (4–7). Series: Xtraordinary Artists. 2008, Creative Education LB $32.80 (978-1-58341-664-8). 48pp. Bodden provides an interesting overview of the composer's life with well-chosen illustrations and excerpts from his own writing. (Rev: LMC 8/09; SLJ 4/09)

14423 Ross, Stewart. *Wolfgang Amadeus Mozart: Musical Genius* (3–5). Series: Famous Lives. 2004, Raintree LB $29.93 (978-0-7398-6627-6). 48pp. A simple, lively, and well-illustrated biography that chronicles Mozart's major works. (Rev: SLJ 1/05)

14424 Sís, Peter. *Play, Mozart, Play!* (K–3). Illus. 2006, Greenwillow $16.99 (978-0-06-112181-4). This beautifully illustrated picture-book biography with a simple text focuses on the musical prodigy's childhood. (Rev: BL 3/15/06; SLJ 5/06*)

14425 Stanley, Diane. *Mozart: The Wonder Child* (3–5). Illus. by author. 2009, Collins $17.99 (978-0-06-072674-4). A puppet play forms the framework for this account of Mozart's often difficult life and early acceptance as an accomplished composer. (Rev: BCCB 2/09; BL 12/15/08; SLJ 2/09)

14426 Weeks, Marcus. *Mozart: The Boy Who Changed the World with His Music* (5–8). Series: World History Biographies. 2007, National Geographic $17.95 (978-1-4263-0002-8). 64pp. An attractive, well-organized life of the young composer, with details of his music lessons and instruments, his first job, and his later financial worries. (Rev: SLJ 6/07)

NEWTON, JOHN

14427 Granfield, Linda. *Amazing Grace: The Story of the Hymn* (4–8). 1997, Tundra $15.95 (978-0-88776-389-2). The life story of John Newton, a sea captain in the slave trade who later rejected slavery, became a minister, and wrote several hymns, including "Amazing Grace." (Rev: SLJ 8/97) [921]

SATIE, ERIK

14428 Anderson, M. T. *Strange Mr. Satie* (1–3). Illus. by Petra Mathers. 2003, Penguin $16.99 (978-0-670-03637-0). 32pp. The offbeat life and unusual music of French composer Erik Satie are explored in this engaging picture-book biography. (Rev: BL 11/1/03; HB 9/03; HBG 4/04; SLJ 10/03)

SCHUBERT, FRANZ PETER

14429 Bankston, John. *The Life and Times of Franz Peter Schubert* (4–6). Series: Masters of Music. 2003, Mitchell Lane LB $29.95 (978-1-58415-177-7). 48pp. Bankston examines the short but prolific life and career of the 19th-century Austrian composer and includes interesting sidebars that add context. (Rev: SLJ 2/04)

SOUSA, JOHN PHILIP

14430 Gillis, Jennifer Blizin. *John Philip Sousa: The King of March Music* (1–3). Series: Lives and Times. 2005, Heinemann LB $24.21 (978-1-4034-6751-5). 32pp. The youth and adult accomplishments of the composer of marches are covered in this interesting volume. (Rev: SLJ 2/06)

VERDI, GIUSEPPE

14431 Bauer, Helen. *Verdi for Kids: His Life and Music with 21 Activities* (5–8). Illus. 2013, Chicago Review paper $16.95 (978-1-61374-500-7). 144pp. Activities extend this profile of the 19th-century Italian composer and his work and times. (Rev: BL 6/13; SLJ 4/13) [921]

14432 Whiting, Jim. *The Life and Times of Giuseppe Verdi* (4–6). Series: Masters of Music: The World's Greatest Composers. 2004, Mitchell Lane LB $20.95 (978-1-58415-281-1). The challenges that Verdi faced in both his personal and professional lives are discussed and placed in historical perspective. (Rev: SLJ 5/05)

VIVALDI, ANTONIO

14433 Shefelman, Janice. *I, Vivaldi* (2–5). Illus. by Tom Shefelman. 2008, Eerdmans $18.00 (978-0-8028-5318-9). 32pp. A charming, first-person account of Vivaldi's childhood and the tensions between his love of music and his mother's determination that he become a priest. (Rev: HB 1/08; LMC 10/08; SLJ 3/08)

Entertainers

ABDUL, PAULA

14434 Zannos, Susan. *Paula Abdul* (4–8). Series: Real-Life Reader Biographies. 1999, Mitchell Lane LB $15.95 (978-1-883845-74-2). A brief biography of this choreographer and recording artist that recounts her many problems, including a struggle with bulimia and a series of failed marriages. (Rev: BL 6/1–15/99) [921]

AGUILERA, CHRISTINA

14435 Granados, Christine. *Christina Aguilera* (3–4). Series: Real-Life Reader Biographies. 2000, Mitchell Lane LB $15.95 (978-1-58415-044-2). 32pp. The story of the little girl with the big voice who started out as a member of the *New Mickey Mouse Club*. (Rev: BL 11/15/00)

AILEY, ALVIN

14436 Cruz, Barbara C. *Alvin Ailey: Celebrating African-American Culture in Dance* (5–9). Series: African-American Biographies. 2004, Enslow LB $26.60 (978-0-7660-2293-5). 112pp. Ailey's life and contributions to dance are detailed, including a chapter on the classic "Revelations" and information on his contemporaries. (Rev: SLJ 1/05)

ALONSO, ALICIA

14437 Bernier-Grand, Carmen T. *Alicia Alonso: Prima Ballerina* (5–8). Illus. by Raúl Colón. 2011, Marshall Cavendish $19.99 (978-0-7614-5562-2). 64pp. Cuban ballerina Alicia Alonso's success in overcoming personal disability is chronicled in this free-verse biography. (Rev: BL 9/1/11*; SLJ 9/1/11) [921]

ANDERSON, MARIAN

14438 Freedman, Russell. *The Voice That Challenged a Nation: Marian Anderson and the Struggle for Equal Rights* (4–8). 2004, Houghton Mifflin $18.00 (978-0-618-15976-5). Beautifully illustrated with period photographs, this picture-book biography of the African American vocalist describes her life and the events leading up to her historic concert at the Lincoln Memorial. (Rev: BL 6/1–15/04; HB 5–6/04; SLJ 7/04) [921]

14439 Hopkinson, Deborah. *Sweet Land of Liberty* (3–7). Illus. by Leonard Jenkins. 2007, Peachtree $16.95 (978-1-56145-395-5). 32pp. With bold illustrations, this volume traces the life of Oscar Chapman, a white government official who spent much of his life fighting injustice, most notably finding a public venue for singer Marian Anderson after she was denied the right to perform in Constitution Hall. (Rev: BL 4/15/07)

14440 McKissack, Patricia C., and Fredrick McKissack. *Marian Anderson: A Great Singer. Rev. ed.* (2–4). Illus. Series: Great African Americans. 2001, Enslow LB $18.60 (978-0-89490-303-8). 32pp. A biography of the great American concert singer, the first African American to sing with the Metropolitan Opera in New York City. (Rev: SLJ 11/91)

14441 Ryan, Pam Muñoz. *When Marian Sang: The True Recital of Marian Anderson* (K–3). Illus. by Brian Selznick. 2002, Scholastic $17.99 (978-0-439-26967-4). This large-format picture-book biography presents Anderson's life in glowing words and pictures and interweaves the spirituals that Anderson sang. (Rev: BL 11/15/02; HB 11/02; HBG 3/03; SLJ 11/02*)

ARMSTRONG, LOUIS

14442 Kimmel, Eric A. *A Horn for Louis* (2–4). Illus. by James Bernardin. Series: Stepping Stones. 2005, Random $11.95 (978-0-375-83252-9). 96pp. This beginning chapter book tells the story of how jazz musician Louis Armstrong got his first cornet and evokes New Orleans in the early 1900s. (Rev: BL 2/1/06; SLJ 2/06)

14443 McKissack, Patricia C., and Fredrick McKissack. *Louis Armstrong: Jazz Musician. Rev. ed.* (2–4). Illus. Series: Great African Americans. 2001, Enslow LB $18.60 (978-0-89490-307-6). 32pp. A simple biography of this well-loved American musician. (Rev: BL 1/1/92; SLJ 2/92)

14444 Weinstein, Muriel Harris. *Play, Louis, Play! The True Story of a Boy and His Horn* (3–5). Illus. by Frank Morrison. 2010, Bloomsbury $15.99 (978-159990375-0). 128pp. Explores Louis Armstrong's childhood from the point of view of his first cornet, bought from a pawn shop. (Rev: BL 2/1/11; LMC 3–4/11; SLJ 4/11) [921]

ASTAIRE, FRED AND ADELE

14445 Orgill, Roxane. *Footwork: The Story of Fred and Adele Astaire* (3–5). Illus. by Stephane Jorisch. 2007, Candlewick $17.99 (978-0-7636-2121-6). 48pp. This account follows Fred and his older sister Adele as they leave Nebraska at a young age to attend school in New York and go on to become a successful vaudeville act and find success on Broadway. (Rev: BCCB 1/08; BL 11/1/07; LMC 1/08; SLJ 12/07)

BAKER, JOSEPHINE

14446 Winter, Jonah. *Jazz Age Josephine* (K–3). Illus. by Marjorie Priceman. 2012, Atheneum $16.99 (978-141696123-9). 40pp. This picture-book biography introduces the dancer and describes her accomplishments and the considerable obstacles she faced. (Rev: BL 11/1/11*) [921]

BARNUM, P. T.

14447 Fleming, Alice. *P. T. Barnum: The World's Greatest Showman* (5–8). 1993, Walker LB $15.85 (978-0-8027-8235-9). A look at the circus owner's childhood and various successful entrepreneurial ventures. (Rev: BL 1/15/94; SLJ 12/93; VOYA 2/94) [921]

14448 Fleming, Candace. *The Great and Only Barnum: The Tremendous, Stupendous Life of Showman P. T. Barnum* (4–8). Illus. by Ray Fenwick. 2009, Random $18.99 (978-0-375-84197-2). 160pp. The story of Barnum's rags-to-success life providing entertainment to the public, with frank discussion of some of his methods and personality defects. ALA Notable Children's Book. (Rev: BL 6/1–15/09*; HB 9/09; LMC 10/09; SLJ 9/09*) [921]

14449 Warrick, Karen Clemens. *P. T. Barnum: Genius of the Three-Ring Circus* (5–8). Series: Historical American Biographies. 2001, Enslow LB $26.60 (978-0-7660-1447-3). 112pp. The story of the showman and creator of "The Greatest Show on Earth" who presented such attractions as General Tom Thumb and Jenny Lind. (Rev: BL 4/15/01; HBG 10/01; SLJ 7/01)

BARRYMORE, DREW

14450 Zannos, Susan. *Drew Barrymore* (3–4). Series: Real-Life Reader Biographies. 2000, Mitchell Lane LB $15.95 (978-1-58415-035-0). 32pp. The ups and downs in the career and life of the actress who starred in such films as *E. T.* as a child are touched on in this brief biography. (Rev: BL 11/15/00)

BATES, PEG LEG

14451 Barasch, Lynne. *Knockin' on Wood: Starring Peg Leg Bates* (2–3). 2004, Lee & Low $16.95 (978-1-58430-170-7). 32pp. In the early 20th century, African American Clayton "Peg Leg" Bates found fame as a dancer despite losing a leg in a childhood accident and despite his race. (Rev: BL 6/1–15/04; SLJ 6/04)

BEATLES (MUSICAL GROUP)

14452 Krull, Kathleen, and Paul Brewer. *The Beatles Were Fab (and They Were Funny)* (2–4). Illus. by Stacy Innerst. 2013, Harcourt $16.99 (978-0-547-50991-4). 40pp. Focusing on their sense of humor, this is a good picture-book introduction to the Beatles and their impact on the world. (Rev: BL 3/1/13; HB 5–6/13; LMC 8–9/13; SLJ 5/13) [921]

14453 Roberts, Jeremy. *The Beatles* (5–8). Series: Biography. 2001, Lerner LB $27.93 (978-0-8225-4998-7). This is the story of the Beatles, from Liverpool to international stardom and eventual separation. (Rev: BL 4/1/02; HBG 10/02)

BEYONCÉ

14454 Bednar, Chuck. *Beyoncé* (5–8). Series: Transcending Race in America. 2010, Mason Crest $22.95 (978-1-4222-1607-1). 64pp. Beyoncé Knowles is of African American and Creole descent, and this biography explains how she feels her background has influenced her life. Lexile 1180L (Rev: LMC 3–4/10; SLJ 1/10) [921]

BIEBER, JUSTIN

14455 Bieber, Justin. *Justin Bieber: First Step 2 Forever: My Story* (4–8). 2010, HarperCollins $21.99 (978-0-06-203974-3). 240pp. Bieber tells the story of his rise to stardom and includes many photographs of himself. **e** (Rev: SLJ 1/1/11; VOYA 2/11) [921]

14456 Tieck, Sarah. *Justin Bieber: Pop Music Superstar* (3–5). Illus. Series: Big Buddy Biographies. 2012, ABDO LB $19.95 (978-1-61783224-6). 32pp. An attractive profile of the singer, covering his childhood and family, his concert tours, and the awards he has won. (Rev: BL 10/15/12) [921]

BLACK, JACK

14457 Mitchell, Susan K. *Jack Black* (3–6). Series: Today's Superstars. Entertainment. 2008, Gareth Stevens LB $24.00 (978-0-8368-9237-6). 32pp. This brief profile is mostly about Black's professional life with a few personal details, plus Web sites and DVDs for more information. (Rev: SLJ 2/09)

BLACK, SHIRLEY TEMPLE

14458 Bankston, John. *Shirley Temple: Child Star* (4–6). Series: A Blue Banner Biography. 2003, Mitchell Lane LB $25.70 (978-1-58415-172-2). 32pp. This brief biography of Shirley Temple Black focuses primarily on her years as one of America's most popular child stars but also touches on key events in her adult life, including her involvement in Republican politics and her appointment as U.S. ambassador to Ghana. (Rev: SLJ 11/03)

BOONE, JOHN WILLIAM

14459 Harrah, Madge. *Blind Boone* (5–8). 2003, Carolrhoda LB $30.60 (978-1-57505-057-7). The son of a runaway slave, Boone became blind as an infant but soon revealed a musical talent and went on to become a composer and concert pianist. (Rev: BL 12/1/03; HBG 3/02; SLJ 10/01) [781.64]

BRANDY

14460 Newman, Michael. *Brandy* (5–8). Series: Galaxy of Superstars. 2000, Chelsea $25.00 (978-0-7910-5781-0). 64pp. A biography of the famous singer and star of *Moesha*. (Rev: BL 12/15/00; HBG 10/01)

BULLOCK, SANDRA

14461 Hill, Anne E. *Sandra Bullock* (5–8). Series: People in the News. 2000, Lucent LB $27.45 (978-1-56006-711-5). 96pp. Quotations from Bullock and others expand this biography and explain how and why she has gained prominence as a Hollywood actress. (Rev: BL 9/15/00)

14462 Zannos, Susan. *Sandra Bullock* (3–4). Series: Real-Life Reader Biographies. 2000, Mitchell Lane LB $24.95 (978-1-58415-027-5). 32pp. A simple biography of the movie actress that stresses her hard work and determination. (Rev: BL 11/15/00; SLJ 1/01)

CAMERON, JAMES

14463 Etingoff, Kim. *James Cameron: From Truck Driver to Director* (5–8). Illus. Series: Extraordinary Success with a High School Diploma or Less. 2012, Mason Crest LB $22.95 (978-1-42222481-6). 64pp. The focus here is on achievement without a college education, and this profile looks at the career of the *Terminator* director. (Rev: BLO 9/1/12; LMC 5–6/13) [921]

CHAPLIN, CHARLIE

14464 Turk, Ruth. *Charlie Chaplin: Genius of the Silent Screen* (5–9). 2000, Lerner LB $30.35 (978-0-8225-4957-4). 112pp. A competent overview of this great movie maker's life from his childhood in England to his exile in Switzerland. (Rev: BL 2/15/00; HBG 10/00; SLJ 4/00)

CISNEROS, EVELYN

14465 Krohn, Katherine. *Evelyn Cisneros: Prima Ballerina* (1–3). Series: Fact Finders, Biographies, Great Hispanics. 2006, Capstone LB $23.93 (978-0-7368-6416-9). 32pp. Large, easy-to-read print recounts the life of the Mexican American ballerina from childhood until her retirement from the San Francisco Ballet. (Rev: SLJ 1/07)

COLTRANE, JOHN

14466 Golio, Gary. *Spirit Seeker: John Coltrane's Musical Journey* (4–7). Illus. by Rudy Gutierrez. 2012, Clarion $17.99 (978-0-547-23994-1). 48pp. With vibrant illustrations, this is a compelling biography of the jazz musician and his challenges. (Rev: BL 11/1/12; HB 11–12/12; LMC 11–12/12; SLJ 12/12*) [921]

14467 Weatherford, Carole Boston. *Before John Was a Jazz Giant: A Song of John Coltrane* (K–3). Illus. by Sean Qualls. 2008, Holt $16.95 (978-0-8050-7994-4). Coltrane's intense interest in sound and music as a young boy is the focus of this biography. (Rev: BCCB 4/08; BL 2/1/08; HB 5/08; LMC 8/08; SLJ 4/08)

COSBY, BILL

14468 Haskins, Jim. *Bill Cosby: America's Most Famous Father* (5–7). 1988, Walker LB $17.00 (978-0-8027-6786-8). The childhood and career of this famous entertainer. (Rev: BL 6/1/88) [921]

CRUZ, CELIA

14469 Chambers, Veronica. *Celia Cruz, Queen of Salsa* (2–4). Illus. by Julie Maren. 2005, Dial $16.99 (978-0-8037-2970-4). From her childhood in Cuba to her status as a global superstar, this is the story of the salsa singer, with a discography and glossary of Spanish words. (Rev: BL 5/15/05)

CYRUS, MILEY

14470 Magid, Jennifer. *Miley Cyrus/Hannah Montana* (3–6). Series: Today's Superstars. Entertainment. 2008, Gareth Stevens LB $24.00 (978-0-8368-9236-9). 32pp. Miley Cyrus's biography is mostly about her professional life with a few personal details such as her education and friend issues. (Rev: SLJ 2/09)

DAMON, MATT

14471 Greene, Meg. *Matt Damon* (5–8). Series: Galaxy of Superstars. 2000, Chelsea $25.00 (978-0-7910-5779-7). An entertaining biography of the actor who gained star status as the cowriter and lead actor in *Good Will Hunting*. (Rev: BL 12/15/00; HBG 10/01) [921]

DAVIS, MILES

14472 Dell, Pamela. *Miles Davis: Jazz Master* (5–8). Series: Journey to Freedom. 2005, Child's World LB $28.50 (978-1-59296-232-7). An easy-to-read biography that deals frankly with the trumpeter's addiction to heroin and his difficult personality. (Rev: SLJ 8/05) [921]

DICAPRIO, LEONARDO

14473 Stauffer, Stacey. *Leonardo DiCaprio* (5–8). Series: Galaxy of Superstars. 1999, Chelsea $25.00 (978-0-7910-5151-1); paper $25.00 (978-0-7910-5326-3). The story of this young actor's life, with special attention to his role in *Titanic*. (Rev: BL 4/15/99; HBG 10/99; SLJ 5/99) [921]

DION, CELINE

14474 Lutz, Norma Jean. *Celine Dion* (5–8). Series: Galaxy of Superstars. 2000, Chelsea $25.00 (978-0-7910-5777-3). 64pp. The story of the amazing career of this French Canadian singer and how she gained worldwide popularity. (Rev: BL 10/15/00; HBG 10/01)

DJ KOOL HERC

14475 Hill, Laban Carrick. *When the Beat Was Born: DJ Kool Herc and the Creation of Hip Hop* (2–4). Illus. by Theodore Taylor. 2013, Roaring Brook $17.99 (978-1-59643-540-7). 32pp. A picture-book profile of the hip-hop DJ who was born in Jamaica and moved to the United States, where he was known for innovations. ALA Notable Children's Book. ☻ (Rev: BL 7/13; LMC 1–2/14; SLJ 8/13) [921]

DUFF, HULARY

14476 Kjelle, Marylou Morano. *Hilary Duff: Actress and Singer* (2–4). Illus. Series: Robbie Reader. 2004, Mitchell Lane LB $25.70 (978-1-58415-295-8). 32pp. This photo-filled biography traces the life of Hilary Duff and is especially suitable for reluctant readers. [921]

DUNHAM, KATHERINE

14477 O'Connor, Barbara. *Katherine Dunham: Pioneer of Black Dance* (5–8). Illus. 2000, Carolrhoda LB $30.35 (978-1-57505-353-0). 104pp. A fine biography of the African American choreographer who used her study of anthropology to create works for her own dance company and for stage and screen productions. (Rev: BL 5/15/00; HBG 10/00; SLJ 7/00; VOYA 2/01)

DYLAN, BOB

14478 Golio, Gary. *When Bob Met Woody: The Story of the Young Bob Dylan* (3–5). Illus. by Marc Burckhardt. 2011, Little, Brown $17.99 (978-031611299-4). 40pp. The young Bob Zimmerman's fortune-changing trip from Minnesota to New York City to visit his idol Woody Guthrie is encapsulated in this biography that includes useful back matter. (Rev: BL 3/1/11; LMC 10/11) [921]

EFRON, ZAC

14479 Keedle, Jayne. *Zac Efron* (3–6). Series: Today's Superstars. Entertainment. 2008, Gareth Stevens LB $24.00 (978-0-8368-9239-0). 32pp. This brief profile is mostly about Efron's professional life with a few personal details, plus Web sites and DVDs for more information. (Rev: SLJ 2/09)

ESTEFAN, GLORIA

14480 Benson, Michael. *Gloria Estefan* (4–6). Series: A&E Biography. 2000, Lerner LB $27.93 (978-0-8225-4982-6). 112pp. A candid look at a singer who is also a devoted wife and mother, a humanitarian, and an outstanding performer. (Rev: BL 6/1–15/00; HBG 10/00)

FERRERA, AMERICA

14481 Anderson, Sheila. *America Ferrera: Latina Superstar* (5–8). Illus. Series: Hot Celebrity Biographies. 2009, Enslow LB $23.93 (978-0-7660-3210-1). A celebrity biography of a Latina role model. (Rev: BL 6/1–15/09) [921]

FITZGERALD, ELLA

14482 Orgill, Roxane. *Skit-Scat Raggedy Cat: Ella Fitzgerald* (2–4). Illus. by Sean Qualls. 2010, Candlewick $17.99 (978-0-7636-1733-2). 48pp. Ella Fitzgerald's rise from poverty to fame is chronicled in this compelling story full of jazz-infused language. (Rev: BL 6/10; LMC 11–12/10; SLJ 7/1/10) [921]

14483 Pinkney, Andrea D. *Ella Fitzgerald: The Tale of a Vocal Virtuosa* (3–5). Illus. by Brian Pinkney. 2002, Hyperion $16.99 (978-0-7868-0568-6). 32pp. A picture-book biography told by Scat Cat Monroe with a lengthy text about the singer's life and the thrill of witnessing one of her performances. (Rev: BL 4/1/02; HBG 10/02; SLJ 5/02)

GELLAR, SARAH MICHELLE

14484 Powell, Phelan. *Sarah Michelle Gellar* (3–4). Series: Real-Life Reader Biographies. 2000, Mitchell Lane LB $15.95 (978-1-58415-034-3). 32pp. This short biography tells the story of the popular star of *Buffy the Vampire Slayer,* who began acting at age 4. (Rev: BL 11/15/00)

GILLESPIE, DIZZY

14485 Winter, Jonah. *Dizzy* (2–4). Illus. by Sean Qualls. 2006, Scholastic $16.99 (978-0-439-50737-0). 48pp. This compelling account of trumpeter Dizzy Gillespie's life and career is enhanced by vivid, eye-catching illustrations. (Rev: BL 11/1/06*; SLJ 10/06*)

GOULD, GLENN

14486 Konieczny, Vladimir. *Struggling for Perfection: The Story of Glenn Gould* (3–5). Illus. by Chrissie Wysotski. Series: Stories of Canada. 2004, Napoleon $16.95 (978-0-929141-13-8). 96pp. The Canadian-born pianist's talents and eccentricities are all discussed in this entertaining volume. (Rev: BL 7/04; SLJ 9/04)

GRAHAM, MARTHA

14487 Freedman, Russell. *Martha Graham: A Dancer's Life* (4–8). 1998, Clarion $19.00 (978-0-395-74655-4). Martha Graham's amazing talents, driving force, and complex personality are well depicted in this handsomely illustrated biography. (Rev: BCCB 6/98; BL 4/1/98; SLJ 5/98; VOYA 8/98) [921]

HANSON (MUSICAL GROUP)

14488 Powell, Phelan. *Hanson* (5–8). Series: Galaxy of Superstars. 1999, Chelsea $25.00 (978-0-7910-5148-1); paper $3.94 (978-0-7910-5325-6). An attractive volume with information on the three-brother singing group that hails from Tulsa, Oklahoma. (Rev: BL 4/15/98; HBG 10/99) [921]

HART, MELISSA JOAN

14489 Gaines, Ann Graham. *Melissa Joan Hart* (3–4). Series: Real-Life Reader Biographies. 2000, Mitchell Lane LB $15.95 (978-1-58415-036-7). 32pp. A simple profile of the TV actress best known for her roles as Clarissa and Sabrina. (Rev: BL 11/15/00)

HEMSWORTH, LIAM

14490 Shaffer, Jody Jensen. *Liam Hemsworth: The Hunger Games' Strong Survivor* (3–6). Illus. Series: Pop Culture Bios: Action Movie Stars. 2013, Lerner LB $26.60 (978-1-46770742-8). 32pp. With an appealing design, full-color photographs, and easy-to-read text, this entry in the series introduces the Australian actor's life and work. ❡ (Rev: BL 6/13; SLJ 4/13) [921]

HENDRIX, JIMI

14491 Golio, Gary. *Jimi: Sounds Like a Rainbow: A Story of the Young Jimi Hendrix* (3–5). Illus. by Javaka Steptoe. 2010, Clarion $16.99 (978-0-618-85279-6). 32pp. This picture-book biography focuses on Jimi's childhood and early interest in music. (Rev: BL 11/1/10; LMC 1–2/11*; SLJ 9/1/10*) [921]

HENSON, JIM

14492 Durrett, Deanne. *Jim Henson* (2–5). Illus. Series: Inventors and Creators. 2002, Gale LB $23.70 (978-0-7377-0996-4). This look at the life of the Muppets creator includes lots of details on the popular characters. (Rev: BL 11/1/02)

14493 Krull, Kathleen. *Jim Henson: The Guy Who Played with Puppets* (4–7). Illus. by Steve Johnson. 2011, Random House $16.99 (978-0-375-85721-8); LB $19.99 (978-0-375-95721-5). 40pp. A portrait of the creator of the Muppets, with details of his first job on TV at the age of 16. (Rev: BL 11/1/11; SLJ 10/1/11) [921]

HEPBURN, AUDREY

14494 Cardillo, Margaret. *Just Being Audrey* (1–3). Illus. by Julia Denos. 2011, HarperCollins $16.99 (978-0-06-185283-1). 32pp. This well-organized biography offers a glimpse into the life of the beautiful and famously kind actress. (Rev: BL 12/1/10; SLJ 4/11) [921]

HEWITT, JENNIFER LOVE

14495 Severs, Vesta-Nadine. *Jennifer Love Hewitt* (3–4). Series: Real-Life Reader Biographies. 2000, Mitchell Lane LB $24.95 (978-1-58415-032-9). 32pp. The story of the popular actress who has been a professional since doing Barbie commercials for Mattel as a preteen. (Rev: BL 11/15/00)

HILL, FAITH

14496 Hinman, Bonnie. *Faith Hill* (5–9). 2001, Chelsea $25.00 (978-0-7910-6471-9). 64pp. A look at the life and career of the country music star, with information on Nashville's Grand Ole Opry. (Rev: HBG 10/02; SLJ 4/02)

HOLMES, KATIE

14497 Boulais, Sue. *Katie Holmes* (3–4). Series: Real-Life Reader Biographies. 2000, Mitchell Lane LB $15.95 (978-1-58415-038-1). A brief biography of the young actress who wisely completed high school before accepting the role in *Dawson's Creek* that made her famous. (Rev: BL 11/15/00)

HOUDINI, HARRY

14498 Adler, David A., and Michael S. Adler. *A Picture Book of Harry Houdini* (K–2). Illus. by Matt Collins. Series: Picture Book Biographies. 2009, Holiday $17.95 (978-0-8234-2059-9). 32pp. Paintings of Houdini's performances enliven information about his life and career choice. (Rev: BL 7/09)

14499 Biskup, Agnieszka. *Houdini: The Life of the Great Escape Artist* (2–4). Illus. by Pat Kinsella. Series: American Graphic. 2011, Capstone LB $29.32 (978-142965474-6). 32pp. Presents Houdini's various feats in graphic-novel format and includes an account of his death. (Rev: BL 3/15/11) [921]

14500 Carlson, Laurie. *Harry Houdini for Kids: His Life and Adventures with 21 Magic Tricks and Illusions* (4–8). Illus. 2009, Chicago Review paper $16.95 (978-1-55652-782-1). 144pp. This attractive biography full of illustrations and sidebars also includes 21 simple tricks. e (Rev: BL 2/15/09; SLJ 4/1/09) [921]

14501 Cox, Clinton. *Houdini: Master of Illusion* (5–9). Illus. 2001, Scholastic paper $16.95 (978-0-590-94960-6). 208pp. A fast-paced account of the life of the world-famous magician from childhood on, with eight pages of photographs and reproductions. (Rev: BL 11/15/01; HB 1/02; HBG 3/02; SLJ 12/01; VOYA 2/02)

14502 Fleischman, Sid. *Escape! The Story of the Great Houdini* (4–8). 2006, HarperCollins $18.99 (978-0-06-085694-6). 210pp. A lively and entertaining biography by a great writer and professional magician, who reveals just enough of the magic behind the tricks; includes many photographs. Boston Globe–Horn Book Honor 2007. (Rev: SLJ 8/06*; VOYA 6/06)

14503 Lalicki, Tom. *Spellbinder: The Life of Harry Houdini* (5–8). Illus. 2000, Holiday $18.95 (978-0-8234-1499-4). 88pp. A biography of Elrich Weiss, aka Harry Houdini, and his career as a magician and escape artist. (Rev: BCCB 3/01; BL 9/1/00; HBG 3/01; SLJ 9/00; VOYA 12/00)

14504 MacLeod, Elizabeth. *Harry Houdini* (2–3). Illus. by John Mantha. Series: Kids Can Read. 2009, Kids Can $14.95 (978-1-55453-298-8); paper $3.95 (978-1-55453-299-5). 32pp. This accessible biography concentrates on the renowned magician's most sensational feats. (Rev: SLJ 1/1/10) [921]

14505 MacLeod, Elizabeth. *Harry Houdini: A Magical Life* (4–6). Illus. Series: Snapshots: Images of People & Places in History. 2005, Kids Can $14.95 (978-1-55337-769-6); paper $6.95 (978-1-55337-770-2). 32pp. This concise biography separates fact from fiction in describing Houdini's life and feats. (Rev: BL 10/15/05; SLJ 4/06)

14506 Weaver, Janice. *Harry Houdini: The Legend of the World's Greatest Escape Artist* (4–7). Illus. by Chris Lane. 2011, Abrams $18.95 (978-1-4197-0014-9). 48pp. Covers Houdini's life and career as well as his interest in exposing fake mediums; historical sidebars add interest. (Rev: BL 12/1/11; LMC 3–4/12; SLJ 11/1/11*) [921]

IGLESIAS, ENRIQUE

14507 Granados, Christine. *Enrique Iglesias* (3–4). Series: Real-Life Reader Biographies. 2000, Mitchell Lane LB $15.95 (978-1-58415-045-9). 32pp. A profile of the son of singer Julio Iglesias and how he started out in show business as Enrique Martinez because he wanted

to gain recognition based not his father's name but on his own ability. (Rev: BL 11/15/00)

JACKSON, JANET

14508 Dyson, Cindy. *Janet Jackson* (4–7). Series: Black Americans of Achievement. 2000, Chelsea $32.00 (978-0-7910-5283-9). 109pp. The life story of the popular singer and the ups and downs of her career. (Rev: BL 6/1–15/00; HBG 10/00)

JACKSON, MICHAEL

14509 Collins, Terry. *King of Pop: The Story of Michael Jackson* (4–7). Illus. by Michael Byers. 2012, Capstone LB $29.99 (978-142966015-0); paper $7.95 (978-142967994-7). 32pp. Though it omits the more controversial aspects of Jackson's life, this biography does include information about Jackson's turbulent early life. (Rev: BL 3/15/12) [921]

14510 Graves, Karen Marie. *Michael Jackson* (5–8). Series: People in the News. 2001, Lucent LB $35.15 (978-1-56006-707-8). The unusual life of this show business legend is outlined in text and photographs. (Rev: BL 4/1/02)

14511 Krohn, Katherine. *Michael Jackson: Ultimate Music Legend* (4–6). 2010, Lerner LB $26.60 (978-0-7613-5762-9). 48pp. Covering some of the unhappier aspects, Krohn gives a concise account of the performer's life, with emphasis on his childhood and the Jackson 5 and then on his later career and personal life. (Rev: BL 2/1/11; SLJ 5/10) [921]

14512 Pratt, Mary K. *Michael Jackson: King of Pop* (5–8). Series: Lives Cut Short. 2009, ABDO LB $32.79 (978-1-60453-788-8). 112pp. From his childhood through performing in the Jackson 5, then going solo, and the various controversies of his later life, this is a balanced profile of the performer who died at the age of 50. (Rev: BL 2/1/10; SLJ 3/10) [921]

JACKSON, SAMUEL L.

14513 Dils, Tracey E. *Samuel L. Jackson* (4–7). Series: Black Americans of Achievement. 2000, Chelsea $30.00 (978-0-7910-5281-5). 104pp. The life story of the African American actor who has portrayed diverse characters in films including *Pulp Fiction* and *A Time to Kill*. (Rev: BL 6/1–15/00; HBG 10/00)

JAY-Z

14514 Gunderson, Jessica. *Jay-Z: Hip-Hop Icon* (5–7). Illus. by Pat Kinsella. Series: American Graphic. 2012, Capstone LB $29.99 (978-142966017-4); paper $7.95 (978-142967993-0). 32pp. This evenhanded graphic-novel biography of Jay-Z focuses on the less glamorous aspects of stardom, showing readers the hard work and shrewd decision making it takes to succeed. (Rev: BL 3/15/12) [921]

14515 Heos, Bridget. *Jay-Z* (5–8). Illus. Series: Library of Hip-Hop Biographies. 2009, Rosen LB $26.50 (978-1-4358-5052-1). From his childhood rhymes to his adolescent drug dealing, his first hit single, and his marriage to Beyoncé, this is a frank and arresting profile. (Rev: BL 6/1–15/09) [921]

14516 Spilsbury, Richard. *Jay-Z* (5–7). Illus. Series: Titans of Business. 2012, Capstone $32 (978-143296430-6); paper $8.99 (978-14329643-7-5). 48pp. Spilsbury introduces Jay-Z's role as a music industry entrepreneur, as well as covering his hip-hop career. (Rev: BL 11/1/12) [921]

JONAS BROTHERS

14517 Janic, Susan. *Jonas Brothers Forever: The Unofficial Story of Kevin, Joe and Nick* (5–8). Illus. 2009, ECW paper $14.95 (978-1-55022-851-9). 158pp. A well-designed profile of the popular trio, with plenty of photographs. (Rev: BLO 3/24/09) [782.42166092]

KEATON, BUSTER

14518 Brighton, Catherine. *Keep Your Eye on the Kid: The Early Years of Buster Keaton* (3–5). Illus. by author. 2008, Roaring Brook $16.95 (978-1-59643-158-4). A first-person account of the comedian's youth, covering his role in his parents' vaudeville act and his introduction to silent films. (Rev: BCCB 5/08; BL 4/15/08; HB 5/08; LMC 5/08; SLJ 4/08)

KELLAR, HARRY

14519 Jarrow, Gail. *The Amazing Harry Kellar: Great American Magician* (5–8). Illus. 2012, Boyds Mills $17.95 (978-159078865-3). 128pp. Introduces the magician who performed around the world at the turn of the 20th century. Lexile 910L (Rev: BL 6/12; LMC 1–2/13*; SLJ 6/12) [921]

KELLY, EMMETT, SR.

14520 Wilkerson, J. L. *Sad-Face Clown: Emmett Kelly* (5–8). Series: The Great Heartlanders. 2004, Acorn paper $9.95 (978-0-9664470-9-5). The story of Emmett Kelly, Sr., who — as Weary Willie — became possibly the world's most famous circus clown. (Rev: SLJ 4/04) [791.3]

KISS (ROCK GROUP)

14521 Weintraub, Aileen. *KISS: I Wanna Rock and Roll All Night* (5–8). Illus. Series: Rebels of Rock. 2009, Enslow LB $23.95 (978-0-7660-3027-5). 112pp. An accessible account of the flamboyant rock group's ascent to stardom and subsequent revivals. (Rev: BL 4/1/09) [921]

KO, ALEX

14522 Ko, Alex. *Alex Ko: From Iowa to Broadway, My Billy Elliot Story* (4–6). Illus. 2013, HarperCollins $16.99 (978-006223601-2). 320pp. A moving autobiography of the Asian American from Iowa City who found himself in a starring role on Broadway at the age of 13, focusing also on his father's illness and death and other setbacks. (Rev: BL 6/13; SLJ 6/13) [921]

LADY GAGA

14523 Heos, Bridget. *Lady Gaga* (5–8). Illus. 2011, Rosen LB $26.50 (978-143583574-0). 48pp. This biography chronicles Gaga's fairly conventional childhood growing up in Manhattan and documents her fast rise to fame. (Rev: BL 4/1/11) [921]

LATIFAH, QUEEN

14524 Bloom, Sara R. *Queen Latifah* (4–7). Series: Black Americans of Achievement. 2001, Chelsea $30.00 (978-0-7910-6287-6). Numerous photographs add interest to this biography of the amazing singer-actress and her rise to fame. (Rev: BL 4/1/02; HBG 10/02; SLJ 6/02)

14525 Ruth, Amy. *Queen Latifah* (5–8). Series: A&E Biography. 2000, Lerner LB $27.93 (978-0-8225-4988-8). 112pp. The story of the female rap singer who used her positive attitudes, hard work, and determination to get ahead. (Rev: BL 3/1/01; HBG 10/01)

LAWRENCE, JENNIFER

14526 Krohn, Katherine. *Jennifer Lawrence: Star of The Hunger Games* (4–7). Illus. 2012, Lerner LB $26.60 (978-076138642-1); paper $8.95 (978-076138665-0). 48pp. Hunger Games star Jennifer Lawrence's meteoric rise to fame is captured in this colorful biography that looks at her life chronologically and includes many quotations and photographs. **e** Lexile 900L (Rev: BL 2/1/12; SLJ 1/12) [921]

LEDGER, HEATH

14527 Watson, Stephanie. *Heath Ledger: Talented Actor* (5–8). Series: Lives Cut Short. 2009, ABDO LB $32.79 (978-1-60453-789-5). 112pp. The brief life story of the Australian actor who died at the age of 28. (Rev: SLJ 3/10) [921]

LEE, BRUCE

14528 Mochizuki, Ken. *Be Water, My Friend: The Early Years of Bruce Lee* (2–4). Illus. by Dom Lee. 2006, Lee & Low $16.95 (978-1-58430-265-0). 32pp. This picture-book biography focuses on the actor's childhood in Hong Kong and his early interest in martial arts. (Rev: BL 9/1/06; SLJ 11/06)

14529 Tagliaferro, Linda. *Bruce Lee* (5–10). Series: A&E Biography. 2000, Lerner LB $27.93 (978-0-8225-4948-2); paper $7.95 (978-0-8225-9688-2). 112pp. This colorful biography of the famous action star is filled with information about him, his films, and his family. (Rev: HBG 10/00; SLJ 5/00)

LEE, SPIKE

14530 Shields, Charles J. *Spike Lee* (5–7). Illus. 2002, Chelsea $30.00 (978-0-7910-6715-4). 112pp. This look at Spike Lee's career, working methods, and importance includes both strengths and weaknesses and includes many photographs and quotations. (Rev: BL 11/1/02; HBG 3/03)

LENNON, JOHN

14531 Gogerly, Liz. *John Lennon* (4–6). Series: Famous Lives. 2003, Raintree LB $27.12 (978-0-7398-5522-5). 48pp. The story of the legendary member of the Beatles and how he influenced young people to cherish peace and love. (Rev: BL 2/15/03; HBG 10/03)

LIL WAYNE

14532 Earl, C. F. *Lil Wayne* (5–8). Illus. Series: Superstars of Hip-Hop. 2012, Mason Crest LB $19.95 (978-142222532-5). 48pp. This is an appealing profile of the rapper and his adventures and accomplishments. (Rev: BL 10/1/12) [921]

LIMÓN, JOSÉ

14533 Reich, Susanna. *José! Born to Dance: The Story of José Limón* (2–4). Illus. by Raúl Colón. 2005, Simon & Schuster $16.95 (978-0-689-86576-3). 32pp. This biography of the Mexican-born dancer and choreographer emphasizes how the music and events of his childhood impacted his later career. (Rev: BCCB 9/05; BL 8/05*; HBG 4/06; LMC 1/06; SLJ 10/05)

LOMAX, JOHN A.

14534 Hopkinson, Deborah. *Home on the Range: John A. Lomax and His Cowboy Songs* (1–3). Illus. by S. D. Schindler. 2009, Putnam $16.99 (978-0-399-23996-0). 40pp. A picture-book profile of the man who loved cowboy songs and became a musicologist, collecting, documenting, and recording folk songs. (Rev: BCCB 1/09; BL 1/1–15/09; HB 1/09; LMC 5/09; SLJ 1/09)

LOPEZ, JENNIFER

14535 Hill, Anne E. *Jennifer Lopez* (5–8). Series: Galaxy of Superstars. 2000, Chelsea $25.00 (978-0-7910-5775-9). This book chronicles the career of the young Latina star who is a fine singer and actress. (Rev: BL 10/15/00; HBG 10/01) [921]

14536 Menard, Valerie. *Jennifer Lopez* (3–4). Series: Real-Life Reader Biographies. 2000, Mitchell Lane LB $15.95 (978-1-58415-025-1). This popular singer-actress got her big break when she played another young singer, Selena. (Rev: BL 11/15/00)

14537 Tieck, Sarah. *Jennifer Lopez: Famous Entertainer* (3–5). Illus. Series: Big Buddy Biographies. 2012, ABDO LB $19.95 (978-161783225-3). 32pp. An attractive profile of the superstar, covering her childhood and family, her big break, and her life off stage. (Rev: BL 10/15/12) [921]

LUCAS, GEORGE

14538 Shields, Charles J. *George Lucas* (5–7). Illus. Series: Behind the Camera. 2002, Chelsea $30.00 (978-0-7910-6712-3). 112pp. A profile of the famous filmmaker, with information on his strengths and weaknesses, his working methods, and his importance to the American film industry, backed up by many photographs and quotations. (Rev: BL 11/1/02; HBG 3/03)

M.I.A.

14539 Peppas, Lynn. *M. I. A.* (5–8). Illus. Series: Superstars! 2010, Crabtree LB $26.60 (978-077877249-1). 32pp. An interesting profile of the British rap star who came to prominence with the soundtrack of *Slumdog Millionaire*. (Rev: BL 6/1/11) [921]

MARCEAU, MARCEL

14540 Schubert, Leda. *Monsieur Marceau* (2–4). Illus. by Gerard DuBois. 2012, Roaring Brook $17.99 (978-1-59643-529-2). 40pp. Excellent illustrations and brief text introduce the world-famous mime. ℮ (Rev: BL 10/15/12*; HB 9–10/12; LMC 1–2/13; SLJ 8/12*) [921]

14541 Spielman, Gloria. *Marcel Marceau: Master of Mime* (2–5). Illus. by Manon Gauthier. 2011, Lerner/Kar-Ben $17.95 (978-0-7613-3961-8); paper $7.95 (978-0-7613-3962-5). Unpaged. A life of the French mime who was active in the Resistance in World War II and later studied in Paris. (Rev: LMC 11–12/11; SLJ 10/1/11) [921]

MARLEY, BOB

14542 Medina, Tony. *I and I: Bob Marley* (4–8). Illus. by Jesse Joshua Watson. 2009, Lee & Low $19.95 (978-1-60060-257-3). 48pp. This picture-book biography in verse profiles the musician who put reggae into the spotlight. (Rev: BL 6/1–15/09*; LMC 10/09; SLJ 6/09) [782]

MILANO, ALYSSA

14543 Bankston, John. *Alyssa Milano* (3–4). Series: Real-Life Reader Biographies. 2000, Mitchell Lane LB $15.95 (978-1-58415-040-4). The life story of the young actress who grew up on TV's *Who's the Boss* and went on to star in *Charmed*. (Rev: BL 11/15/00)

MILLER, NORMA

14544 Govenar, Alan, ed. *Stompin' at the Savoy: The Story of Norma Miller* (5–8). Illus. by Martin French. 2006, Candlewick $16.99 (978-0-7636-2244-2). 56pp. The energy of Norma Miller, who was still going strong in her early 80s, infuses the pages of this brief biography, made up largely of excerpts from interviews with the legendary African American swing dancer. (Rev: BL 2/1/06; SLJ 3/06)

MILLS, FLORENCE

14545 Schroeder, Alan. *Baby Flo: Florence Mills Lights Up the Stage* (K–3). Illus. by Cornelius Van Wright. 2012, Lee & Low $18.95 (978-160060410-2). 40pp. African American singer and dancer Florence Mills first appeared on stage at the age of 3; the story of this woman who became famous during the Harlem Renaissance will fascinate young readers. (Rev: BL 5/15/12; LMC 10/12; SLJ 6/1/12) [921]

MOZART, MARIA ANNA

14546 Rusch, Elizabeth. *For the Love of Music: The Remarkable Story of Maria Anna Mozart* (1–3). Illus. by Steve Johnson. 2011, Tricycle $16.99 (978-1-58246-326-1). 32pp. A handsomely illustrated life of Mozart's older sister Maria Anna, also a piano virtuoso. (Rev: BL 11/1/10; HB 1–2/11; LMC 10/11; SLJ 1/1/11) [921]

NUREYEV, RUDOLF

14547 Maybarduk, Linda. *The Dancer Who Flew: A Memoir of Rudolf Nureyev* (5–9). 1999, Tundra $18.95 (978-0-88776-415-8). The author, a friend and colleague of Nureyev, not only gives a straightforward biography of the dancer but also tells many backstage stories and introduces his most important roles. (Rev: BL 1/1–15/00; HBG 3/00; SLJ 2/00; VOYA 4/00) [921]

O'DONNELL, ROSIE

14548 Stone, Tanya L. *Rosie O'Donnell: America's Favorite Grown-Up Kid* (4–7). Illus. 2000, Millbrook LB $23.90 (978-0-7613-1724-1). A well-designed, chatty biography of the popular talk-show host and comedienne. (Rev: BL 12/15/00; HBG 3/01)

OAKLEY, ANNIE

14549 Feinstein, Stephen. *Read About Annie Oakley* (2–4). Series: I Like Biographies. 2006, Enslow $21.26 (978-0-7660-2583-7). 24pp. The fascinating life of the sharpshooter is told in simple text and photographs and illustrations. (Rev: BL 7/06; SLJ 4/06)

14550 Krensky, Stephen. *Shooting for the Moon: The Amazing Life and Times of Annie Oakley* (1–4). Illus. by Bernie Fuchs. 2001, Farrar $17.00 (978-0-374-36843-2). 32pp. A combination of simple, concise text and skillful oil paintings convey the life of Annie Oakley, from her childhood to her fame for her shooting skills. (Rev: BL 9/15/01; HBG 3/02; SLJ 9/01)

14551 Landau, Elaine. *Annie Oakley: Wild West Sharpshooter* (3–6). Series: Best of the West Biographies. 2004, Enslow LB $23.93 (978-0-7660-2205-8). 48pp. Period photographs add to this engaging account of Oakley's personal and professional life that will appeal to reluctant readers. (Rev: SLJ 8/04)

14552 Macy, Sue. *Bull's-Eye: A Photobiography of Annie Oakley* (5–8). 2001, National Geographic $17.95 (978-0-7922-7008-9). This book separates fact from fiction in the life of Phoebe Ann Moses Butler, who came to be known as Annie Oakley. (Rev: BL 11/15/01; HBG 3/02; SLJ 10/01; VOYA 4/02) [799.3]

14553 Whiting, Jim. *Annie Oakley* (2–4). Series: A Robbie Reader: What's So Great About? 2006, Mitchell Lane LB $25.70 (978-1-58415-477-8). 32pp. With large text and lots of white space, this introductory biography chronicles the life of the female sharpshooter who became a star attraction with Buffalo Bill's Wild West show. (Rev: SLJ 1/07)

ODETTA

14554 Alcorn, Stephen, and Samantha Thornhill. *Odetta: The Queen of Folk* (2–4). Illus. by Stephen Alcorn. 2010, Scholastic $17.99 (978-0-439-92818-2). 40pp. A spirited introduction to the life and career of folk singer and civil rights activist Odetta, from her birth in 1930 Alabama. (Rev: BL 11/1/10*; LMC 1–2/11; SLJ 11/1/10) [921]

PAUL, LES

14555 Wyckoff, Edwin Brit. *Electric Guitar Man: The Genius of Les Paul* (3–6). Illus. Series: Genius at Work! Great Inventor Biographies. 2008, Enslow LB $16.95 (978-0-7660-2847-0). 32pp. A lively account of the life and work of the musician who invented an early electric guitar and electronic recording devices. (Rev: BL 9/15/08)

PAVLOVA, ANNA

14556 Allman, Barbara. *Dance of the Swan: A Story About Anna Pavlova* (3–6). Illus. by Shelly O. Haas. Series: Creative Minds Biographies. 2001, Carolrhoda LB $21.27 (978-1-57505-463-6). 64pp. Allman presents Pavlova's life from childhood and discusses her love of nature and of children as well as her commitment to ballet. (Rev: HBG 10/01; SLJ 7/01)

PRINZE, FREDDIE, JR.

14557 Wilson, Wayne. *Freddie Prinze, Jr.* (3–4). Series: Real-Life Reader Biographies. 2000, Mitchell Lane LB $15.95 (978-1-58415-063-3). 32pp. The story of the talented performer and actor whose famous father died before he could get to know him. (Rev: BL 11/15/00)

PUENTE, TITO

14558 Brown, Monica. *Tito Puente: Mambo King/Rey del Mambo* (K–3). Illus. by Rafael Lopez. 2013, Rayo $17.99 (978-006122783-7). 32pp. A vibrant, bilingual profile of the Latino musician, emphasizing his enthusiasm at a young age. Belpré Honor; ALA Notable Children's Book. Lexile AD740L (Rev: BL 3/1/13; HB 3–4/13)

14559 Olmstead, Mary. *Tito Puente* (4–7). Series: Hispanic-American Biographies. 2004, Raintree LB $32.86 (978-1-4109-0713-4). A concise account of the life and career of Tito Puente, the popular American bandleader and percussionist who in the 1950s was nicknamed the Mambo King. (Rev: BL 2/1/05; SLJ 8/05) [784.4]

QUINN, ANTHONY

14560 Amdur, Melissa. *Anthony Quinn* (5–9). Series: Hispanics of Achievement. 1993, Chelsea LB $19.95 (978-0-7910-1251-2). The life of this Mexican American actor is told with many interesting asides concerning his career and black-and-white stills from his movies. (Rev: BL 9/15/93) [921]

REESE, DELLA

14561 Dean, Tanya. *Della Reese* (4–7). Series: Black Americans of Achievement. 2001, Chelsea $30.00 (978-0-7910-6291-3). The life and career of this show business giant are outlined with special coverage on her recent successes in television. (Rev: BL 4/1/02)

REEVE, CHRISTOPHER

14562 Apte, Sunita. *Christopher Reeve: Don't Lose Hope!* (3–4). Series: Defining Moments. 2005, Bearport LB $25.27 (978-1-59716-074-2). 32pp. This easy-to-read biography looks at Reeve's childhood as well as his achievements and the challenges he faced. (Rev: SLJ 1/06)

REINHARDT, DJANGO

14563 Christensen, Bonnie. *Django: World's Greatest Jazz Guitarist* (3–6). Illus. by author. 2009, Roaring Brook $17.99 (978-1-59643-422-6). 32pp. Tells the story of how the famous jazz guitar player triumphed over a horrible hand injury. (Rev: BL 11/1/09*; LMC 11–12/09; SLJ 9/1/09*) [921]

RIHANNA

14564 Schuman, Michael A. *Rihanna: Music Megastar* (5–8). Illus. Series: Hot Celebrity Biographies. 2012, Enslow LB $23.93 (978-076603871-4). 48pp. Five short chapters with full-color photographs make this balanced profile appealing to reluctant readers as well as to report writers seeking basic information. (Rev: BL 6/12; SLJ 1/12) [921]

ROBERTS, JULIA

14565 Wilson, Wayne. *Julia Roberts* (3–4). Series: Real-Life Reader Biographies. 2000, Mitchell Lane LB $15.95 (978-1-58415-028-2). 32pp. A simple biography with plenty of pictures of the actress whose career took off after her performance in *Pretty Woman*. (Rev: BL 11/15/00; SLJ 1/01)

ROBESON, PAUL

14566 Greenfield, Eloise. *Paul Robeson. Rev. ed.* (2–5). Illus. by George Ford. 2009, Lee & Low $18.95 (978-1-60060-256-6); paper $9.95 (978-1-60060-262-7). 40pp. This updated biography chronicles the civil rights work of the activist, actor, and singer during the McCarthy era. (Rev: SLJ 6/09)

14567 McKissack, Patricia C., and Fredrick McKissack. *Paul Robeson: A Voice to Remember. Rev. ed.* (2–5). Series: Great African Americans. 2001, Enslow LB $18.60 (978-0-7660-1674-3). 32pp. Presents Robeson's personal and professional life and the hardships he faced because of his race and beliefs. (Rev: HBG 10/01; SLJ 8/01)

ROBINSON, BILL "BOJANGLES"

14568 Dillon, Leo, and Diane Dillon. *Rap a Tap Tap: Here's Bojangles — Think of That!* (PS–2). Illus. 2002, Scholastic $16.99 (978-0-590-47883-0). 32pp. A brilliantly illustrated picture book about legendary tap artist Bill "Bojangles" Robinson. (Rev: BL 10/15/02; HBG 3/03; SLJ 9/02)

ROCK, CHRIS

14569 Blue, Rose, and Corinne J. Naden. *Chris Rock* (4–7). Series: Black Americans of Achievement. 2000, Chelsea $30.00 (978-0-7910-5277-8). The story of the comedian and actor who began his career on *Saturday Night Live* and is noted for his acerbic wit. (Rev: BL 6/1–15/00; HBG 10/00) [921]

14570 Gorman, Jacqueline Laks. *Chris Rock* (3–6). Series: Today's Superstars. Entertainment. 2008, Gareth Stevens LB $24.00 (978-0-8368-9235-2). 32pp. This brief profile is mostly about Chris Rock's professional life with a few personal details, plus Web sites and DVDs for more information. (Rev: SLJ 2/09)

RODRIGUEZ, ROBERT

14571 Marvis, Barbara. *Robert Rodriguez* (5–10). Series: A Real-Life Reader Biography. 1997, Mitchell Lane LB $15.95 (978-1-883845-48-3). This simple, attractive biography of the successful movie maker focuses on his problems growing up in a large family and clinging to his career dreams. (Rev: BL 6/1–15/98; HBG 3/98; SLJ 2/98) [921]

ROGERS, WILL

14572 Donovan, Sandy. *Will Rogers: Cowboy, Comedian, and Commentator* (4–8). Series: Signature Lives. 2007, Compass Point LB $31.93 (978-0-7565-2542-9). This detailed biography of Will Rogers will be useful for report writers. (Rev: SLJ 6/07) [921]

14573 Keating, Frank. *Will Rogers* (K–3). Illus. by Mike Wimmer. 2002, Harcourt $17.00 (978-0-15-202405-5). 32pp. A beautifully illustrated profile of the humorist and newspaper columnist who lived from 1879 to 1935, written by Oklahoma governor Frank Keating. (Rev: BL 9/15/02; HBG 3/03; SLJ 11/02)

RUSSELL, KERI

14574 Hasday, Judy. *Keri Russell* (3–4). Series: Real-Life Reader Biographies. 2000, Mitchell Lane LB $15.95 (978-1-58415-033-6). 32pp. An easily read biography of the young actress who plays Felicity. (Rev: BL 11/15/00)

RYDER, WINONA

14575 Menard, Valerie. *Winona Ryder* (3–4). Series: Real-Life Reader Biographies. 2000, Mitchell Lane LB $15.95 (978-1-58415-039-8). 32pp. A simple biography of the talented actress who appeared in 23 movies before her 30th birthday. (Rev: BL 11/15/00)

SANDLER, ADAM

14576 Seldman, David. *Adam Sandler* (5–8). Series: Galaxy of Superstars. 2000, Chelsea $25.00 (978-0-7910-5773-5). 64pp. An entertaining biography of the actor and comedian who gained notoriety from his roles in *The Waterboy* and *Big Daddy*. (Rev: BL 12/15/00; HBG 10/01)

SARG, TONY

14577 Sweet, Melissa. *Balloons Over Broadway: The True Story of the Puppeteer of Macy's Parade* (K–2). Illus. by author. 2011, Houghton Mifflin $16.99 (978-0-547-19945-0). 40pp. Chronicles the life of Tony Sarg, a boy fascinated with puppets and gadgetry from a young age, and his role in creating the famous Thanksgiving Day parade. (Rev: BL 9/15/11*; SLJ 9/1/11*) [921]

SCHUMANN, CLARA

14578 Allman, Barbara. *Her Piano Sang: A Story About Clara Schumann* (4–7). 1996, Carolrhoda LB $25.55 (978-1-57505-012-6). The story of this groundbreaking composer and pianist who also championed her husband's music. (Rev: BL 1/1–15/97; SLJ 1/97) [921]

14579 Reich, Susanna. *Clara Schumann: Piano Virtuoso* (5–8). 1999, Houghton Mifflin $18.00 (978-0-395-89119-3). A thorough, well-researched biography of this amazing pianist and composer that describes her life as a child prodigy, her marriage to Robert Schumann, and her life promoting his music after his death. (Rev: BL 8/99; HB 3–4/99; HBG 10/99; SLJ 4/99*; VOYA 4/00) [921]

SHAKUR, TUPAC

14580 Harris, Ashley Rae. *Tupac Shakur: Multi-Platinum Rapper* (5–8). Series: Lives Cut Short. 2009, ABDO LB $32.79 (978-1-60453-791-8). 112pp. Focusing on the achievements of a life tragically cut short, this appealing book reveals that Shakur was a gifted student in high school. (Rev: SLJ 3/10) [921]

SIEGEL, SIENA CHERSON

14581 Siegel, Siena Cherson. *To Dance: A Ballerina's Graphic Novel* (5–8). Illus. by Mark Siegel. 2006, Simon & Schuster $17.95 (978-0-689-86747-7). 64pp. In graphic novel format, Siegel tells the story of her dance career, from her introduction to ballet at the age of 6 to her stage debut with the New York City Ballet. Sibert Honor 2007. (Rev: BCCB 1/07; BL 9/1/06; LMC 1/07; SLJ 11/06*; VOYA 4/07)

SILVERSTONE, ALICIA

14582 Powell, Phelan. *Alicia Silverstone* (3–4). Series: Real-Life Reader Biographies. 2000, Mitchell Lane LB $15.95 (978-1-58415-037-4). The life story of this popular young actress who began modeling at age 6 and had been in several movies by the time she turned 20. (Rev: BL 11/15/00)

SIMON, WINSTON

14583 Greenwood, Mark. *Drummer Boy of John John* (PS–3). Illus. by Frane Lessac. 2012, Lee & Low $18.95 (978-1-60060-652-6). 40pp. Vibrant illustrations and rhythmic text tells the story of Winston "Spree" Simon's childhood in the Trinidad and his pioneering use of the steel drum. (Rev: BL 12/15/12; LMC 5–6/13; SLJ 10/12) [921]

SMITH, BESSIE

14584 Manera, Alexandria. *Bessie Smith* (2–5). Series: African-American Biographies. 2003, Raintree LB $28.56 (978-0-7398-6875-1). A simple profile of the singer, with interesting sidebars and good archival photographs that convey a sense of the time in which she lived. (Rev: HBG 4/04; SLJ 11/03)

SMITH, WILL

14585 Miles, Liz. *Will Smith* (3–6). Series: Culture in Action. 2010, Heinemann-Raintree $28.21 (978-1-4109-3397-3). 32pp. With eye-catching photographs and high-interest information, this is a useful biography of the rap star. Lexile 770L (Rev: LMC 3–4/10) [921]

SPIELBERG, STEVEN

14586 Edge, Laura B. *Steven Spielberg: Director of Blockbuster Films* (5–8). Series: People to Know Today. 2008, Enslow LB $23.95 (978-0-7660-2888-3). With many photographs and lists of print and Web resources, this profile provides up-to-date information on the filmmaker's career, personal life, work ethic, and storytelling skills. (Rev: BL 6/1–15/08) [921]

14587 Schoell, William. *Magic Man: The Life and Films of Steven Spielberg* (4–7). 1998, Tudor $18.95 (978-0-936389-57-8). This biography of Spielberg concentrates on how he produces the astonishing special effects for his movies. (Rev: BL 5/15/98; SLJ 2/99) [921]

STEFANI, GWEN

14588 Raum, Elizabeth. *Gwen Stefani* (3–6). Series: Culture in Action. 2010, Heinemann-Raintree $28.21 (978-1-4109-3395-9). 32pp. Everything a reluctant (or avid) reader needs to know about the singer-songwriter, fashion designer, and actress and her successes. Lexile 750L (Rev: LMC 3–4/10) [921]

SUPREMES (MUSICAL GROUP)

14589 Rivera, Ursula. *The Supremes* (4–8). Series: Rock and Roll Hall of Famers. 2002, Rosen LB $29.25 (978-0-8239-3527-7). The Supremes' rise to stardom — and eventual fall from fame without leader Diana Ross — is chronicled here with photographs, glossary, discography, and bibliography. (Rev: BL 10/1/02; SLJ 5/02) [782.421644]

SWIFT, TAYLOR

14590 Reusser, Kayleen. *Taylor Swift* (3–6). Illus. Series: Day by Day with . . . 2010, Mitchell Lane LB $25.70 (978-158415857-8). 32pp. Plenty of color photographs add appeal to this biography of country star Taylor Swift. (Rev: BL 6/1/11) [921]

TATUM, ART

14591 Parker, Robert Andrew. *Piano Starts Here: The Young Art Tatum* (2–4). Illus. by author. 2008, Random $16.99 (978-0-375-83965-8). 32pp. Tatum's youth is well covered in this profile of the jazz pianist who was nearly blind. (Rev: BL 2/1/08; SLJ 2/08)

TWAIN, SHANIA

14592 Gallagher, Jim. *Shania Twain: Grammy Award-Winning Singer* (4–7). Series: Real-Life Reader Biographies. 1999, Mitchell Lane LB $15.95 (978-1-58415-000-8). The story of the entertainer who was adopted into the Ojibwa tribe, began singing in bars at age eight, and went on to marry producer Mutt Lange. (Rev: SLJ 1/00) [921]

TYLER, LIV

14593 Boulais, Sue. *Liv Tyler* (3–4). Series: Real-Life Reader Biographies. 2000, Mitchell Lane LB $15.95 (978-1-58415-041-1). This is the story of the talented model and actress who didn't learn until her teens that her father was Aerosmith's Steven Tyler. (Rev: BL 11/15/00)

VON TRAPP, MARIA

14594 Ransom, Candice F. *Maria von Trapp: Beyond the Sound of Music* (4–6). Illus. Series: Trailblazer Biographies. 2002, Carolrhoda LB $25.26 (978-1-57505-444-5). 112pp. A portrait of Maria von Trapp, based on her own writings, that describes her life in war-torn Austria and move to a ski lodge in Vermont. (Rev: BL 3/1/02; HBG 10/02; SLJ 5/02)

WILLIAMS, ROBIN

14595 Zannos, Susan. *Robin Williams* (3–4). Series: Real-Life Reader Biographies. 2000, Mitchell Lane LB $15.95 (978-1-58415-029-9). 32pp. From playing Mork the alien on TV to winning an Oscar for his film work, this is a brief biography of the famous comedian and actor. (Rev: BL 11/15/00)

WINFREY, OPRAH

14596 Feinstein, Stephen. *Oprah Winfrey* (1–4). Series: African-American Heroes. 2007, Enslow LB $21.26 (978-0-7660-2764-0). 24pp. A basic and straightforward look at the life of the very successful talk-show host, with photographs. (Rev: SLJ 8/07)

14597 Krohn, Katherine. *Oprah Winfrey* (5–8). Series: Biography. 2001, Lerner LB $27.93 (978-0-8225-4999-4). The media genius and talk-show hostess is profiled in an interesting text with many photographs. (Rev: BL 4/1/02; HBG 10/02)

14598 Stone, Tanya Lee. *Oprah Winfrey: Success with an Open Heart* (4–7). Series: Gateway Biographies. 2001, Millbrook LB $23.90 (978-0-7613-1814-9). Oprah's story, with concise text and excellent photographs, will attract and inspire young readers. (Rev: BL 6/1–15/01; HBG 10/01) [791.45]

14599 Weatherford, Carole Boston. *Oprah: The Little Speaker* (1–3). Illus. by London Ladd. 2010, Marshall Cavendish $17.99 (978-0-7614-5632-2). 32pp. This picture-book biography focuses on the first six years of Oprah's life, with her grandmother on a pig farm in Mississippi. (Rev: BL 3/15/10; SLJ 4/1/10) [921]

14600 Westen, Robin. *Oprah Winfrey: "I Don't Believe in Failure"* (5–8). Series: African-American Biography Library. 2005, Enslow LB $31.93 (978-0-7660-2462-5). Winfrey's phenomenal rise to success in the worlds of business and entertainment is placed in social context. (Rev: SLJ 11/05; VOYA 6/06) [921]

WONG, ANNA MAY

14601 Yoo, Paula. *Shining Star: The Anna May Wong Story* (4–6). Illus. by Lin Wang. 2009, Lee & Low $17.95 (978-1-60060-259-7). 32pp. Profile of a pioneer who broke the Asian barriers in the American film industry. (Rev: BL 6/1–15/09; SLJ 7/09)

Writers

ADA, ALMA FLOR

14602 Parker-Rock, Michelle. *Alma Flor Ada: An Author Kids Love* (3–5). Series: Authors Kids Love. 2008, Enslow LB $23.93 (978-0-7660-2760-2). 48pp. A brief biography of the Cuban author with information on her childhood, direct quotations, photographs, and Ada's advice on how to become a writer. (Rev: SLJ 11/08)

ALCOTT, LOUISA MAY

14603 Aller, Susan Bivin. *Beyond Little Women: A Story About Louisa May Alcott* (3–5). Illus. by Qi Z. Wang. Series: Creative Minds Biographies. 2004, Carolrhoda LB $22.60 (978-1-57505-602-9); paper $6.95 (978-1-57505-636-4). An engaging account of Alcott's life from childhood and of the responsibilities she bore as the principal money earner in the family. (Rev: SLJ 8/04)

14604 McDonough, Yona Zeldis. *Louisa: The Life of Louisa May Alcott* (2–4). Illus. by Bethanne Andersen. 2009, Holt $17.99 (978-0-8050-8192-3). 48pp. The author of *Little Women* felt a strong need to support herself and her family, and worked as a nurse during the Civil War before her writing brought her security. (Rev: BL 6/1–15/09; HB 9/09)

14605 Silverthorne, Elizabeth. *Louisa May Alcott* (4–7). Illus. Series: Who Wrote That? 2002, Chelsea $30.00 (978-0-7910-6721-5). 112pp. A look at the life and works of author Louisa May Alcott, with particular emphasis on how her family influenced her work. (Rev: BL 10/15/02; HBG 3/03; SLJ 10/02)

14606 Warrick, Karen Clemens. *Louisa May Alcott: Author of Little Women* (5–8). Series: Historical American Biographies. 2000, Enslow LB $26.60 (978-0-7660-1254-7). 128pp. Using many direct quotations from

Alcott, along with fact boxes, maps, a chronology, and chapter notes, this is an interesting biography of the prolific writer from Pennsylvania. (Rev: BL 3/15/00; HBG 10/00)

ALEICHEM, SHOLOM

14607 Silverman, Erica. *Sholom's Treasure: How Sholom Aleichem Became a Writer* (K–3). Illus. by Mordicai Gerstein. 2005, Farrar $16.00 (978-0-374-38055-7). 40pp. A child-friendly biography of the Yiddish author, emphasizing his difficult youth in a Russian shtetl and his enduring love of stories and fun. (Rev: BL 2/1/05; SLJ 4/05)

ALLENDE, ISABEL

14608 Benatar, Raquel. *Isabel Allende: Recuerdos para un cento / Memories for a Story* (3–5). Trans. by Patricia Petersen. Illus. by Fernando Molinari. 2004, Piñata $15.95 (978-1-55885-379-9). A bilingual picture-book biography that emphasizes the importance of Allende's unusual childhood. (Rev: SLJ 9/04)

ANDERSEN, HANS CHRISTIAN

14609 Hesse, Karen. *The Young Hans Christian Andersen* (3–5). Illus. by Erik Blegvad. 2005, Scholastic $16.99 (978-0-439-67990-9). 48pp. This biography focuses on the Danish storyteller's troubled childhood and how it is reflected in some of his memorable fairy tales. (Rev: BL 11/1/05; SLJ 10/05*)

14610 Varmer, Hjordis. *Hans Christian Andersen: His Fairy Tale Life* (4–7). Trans. by Tina Nunnally. Illus. by Lilian Bregger. 2005, Groundwood $19.95 (978-088899690-9). This large-format, lively biography presents the Danish storyteller's single-minded struggle to rise above adversity. Lexile 870L (Rev: BL 11/1/05; SLJ 6/06) [839.81]

14611 Yolen, Jane. *The Perfect Wizard: Hans Christian Andersen* (1–3). Illus. by Dennis Nolan. 2005, Dutton $16.99 (978-0-525-46955-1). This biography focuses on Andersen's youth, looking in particular at incidents from his childhood that were later incorporated into his fairy tales. (Rev: BL 2/1/05; SLJ 3/05)

ANGELOU, MAYA

14612 Kirkpatrick, Patricia. *Maya Angelou* (5–9). Illus. by John Thompson. Series: Voices in Poetry. 2003, Creative LB $19.95 (978-1-58341-281-7). 48pp. This picture-book biography introduces readers to Angelou's poetry and life from childhood. (Rev: BL 12/1/03; SLJ 12/03)

14613 Raatma, Lucia. *Maya Angelou: Author and Documentary Filmmaker* (4–8). Series: Ferguson Career Biographies. 2001, Ferguson LB $25.00 (978-0-89434-336-0). 127pp. As well as a life of Maya Angelou, this book includes information on how to become a writer, filmmaker, and director. (Rev: SLJ 2/01)

AUSTEN, JANE

14614 Ruth, Amy. *Jane Austen* (5–8). Series: A&E Biography. 2001, Lerner LB $27.93 (978-0-8225-4992-5). This is the intriguing story of Jane Austen, who lived a quiet, obscure life yet produced some of the world's greatest novels. (Rev: BL 6/1–15/01; HBG 10/01; SLJ 11/01)

AVI

14615 Markham, Lois. *Avi* (5–8). 1996, Learning Works paper $7.99 (978-0-88160-280-7). This profile of the gifted writer recounts his triumph over dysgraphia, a learning disability that makes writing difficult, and explores his creative process and the major themes of his work. (Rev: BL 4/1/96; SLJ 8/96) [921]

14616 Sommers, Michael A. *Avi* (5–8). Series: The Library of Author Biographies. 2004, Rosen LB $27.95 (978-0-8239-4522-1). Covers Avi's life and career as a YA author, with analysis of his work, an interview, and lists of works and awards. (Rev: SLJ 1/05) [921]

BARRIE, JAMES

14617 Yolen, Jane. *Lost Boy: The Story of the Man Who Created Peter Pan* (2–4). Illus. by Steve Adams. 2010, Dutton $17.99 (978-0-525-47886-7). 40pp. A compelling and handsome biography of Scotsman James Barrie, with many quotations. (Rev: BL 6/10; LMC 11–12/10; SLJ 7/1/10*) [921]

BAUER, MARION DANE

14618 Bauer, Marion Dane. *A Writer's Story from Life to Fiction* (5–8). 1995, Clarion $14.95 (978-0-395-72094-3); paper $6.95 (978-0-395-75053-7). Readers and aspiring writers will enjoy this famous author's explanations of how she draws on her own experiences to develop her works. (Rev: BL 9/15/95; SLJ 10/95; VOYA 2/96) [813]

BAUM, L. FRANK

14619 Krull, Kathleen. *The Road to Oz: Twists, Turns, Bumps, and Triumphs in the Life of L. Frank Baum* (2–5). Illus. by Kevin Hawkes. 2008, Knopf $17.99 (978-0-375-83216-1). In this picture-book biography readers learn about Baum's life and career as well as gaining insight into the characters and themes of *The Wizard of Oz*. (Rev: BCCB 10/08; BL 6/1–15/08; HB 9/08; LMC 11/08; SLJ 9/08)

BLUME, JUDY

14620 Nault, Jennifer. *Judy Blume* (2–4). Series: My Favorite Writer. 2004, Weigl LB $18.20 (978-1-59036-025-5). 32pp. This attractively illustrated biography of Judy Blume is particularly suitable for report writers. (Rev: BL 4/1/04; SLJ 10/04)

14621 Wheeler, Jill C. *Judy Blume* (2–4). Series: Children's Authors. 2005, ABDO LB $21.35 (978-1-59197-604-2). 24pp. After introducing some of Blume's works, Wheeler discusses the author's childhood, influences on her work, and her determination to write about topics of real concern to children. (Rev: BL 4/1/04; SLJ 4/05)

BRIDWELL, NORMAN

14622 Wheeler, Jill C. *Norman Bridwell* (2–4). Series: Children's Authors. 2005, ABDO LB $21.35 (978-1-59197-605-9). 24pp. After introducing some of Bridwell's works, Wheeler discusses the author's childhood, influences on his work, and his recognition of the limitations of Clifford the Big Red Dog. (Rev: SLJ 4/05)

BRONTË FAMILY

14623 Kenyon, Karen Smith. *The Brontë Family: Passionate Literary Geniuses* (5–9). Series: Lerner Biographies. 2002, Lerner LB $30.35 (978-0-8225-0071-1). An absorbing introduction to the individual members of this literary family, with many illustrations and quotations from letters. (Rev: HBG 3/03; SLJ 1/03; VOYA 2/03) [921]

14624 Reef, Catherine. *The Brontë Sisters: The Brief Lives of Charlotte, Emily, and Anne* (5–9). Illus. 2012, Clarion $18.99 (978-0-547-57966-5). 240pp. A balanced, well-researched, and very readable biography of the three sisters who wrote poetry and novels under men's names. (Rev: BL 6/12*; LMC 1–2/13; SLJ 9/12) [921]

BRUCHAC, JOSEPH

14625 Parker-Rock, Michelle. *Joseph Bruchac: An Author Kids Love* (3–5). Series: Authors Kids Love. 2009, Enslow LB $23.93 (978-0-7660-3060-9). 48pp. With lengthy quotations, this profile touches on Bruchac's childhood and struggle to come to terms with his Native American heritage. (Rev: SLJ 11/1/09) [921]

BUNTING, EVE

14626 McGinty, Alice B. *Meet Eve Bunting* (2–4). Illus. Series: About the Author. 2003, Rosen LB $21.25 (978-0-8239-6411-6). 24pp. Readers learn about Bunting's youth and later life and how and why she started writing for children, with excerpts from her books, reprints from covers, photographs, and other illustrations. (Rev: BL 6/1–15/03; SLJ 3/03)

BURROUGHS, EDGAR RICE

14627 Boerst, William J. *Edgar Rice Burroughs: Creator of Tarzan* (5–8). Illus. Series: World Writers. 2000, Morgan Reynolds LB $23.95 (978-1-883846-56-5). 112pp. A concise biography of the prolific author who created Tarzan and was a pioneer of the science fiction genre. (Rev: BL 7/00; HBG 3/01; SLJ 1/01)

BYARS, BETSY

14628 Byars, Betsy. *The Moon and I* (4–7). 1996, Morrow paper $5.99 (978-0-688-13704-5). A memoir from this well-known children's author, which gives her the opportunity to tell how she likes both writing and snakes. (Rev: BCCB 3/92*; BL 5/15/92; SLJ 4/92) [921]

14629 Cammarano, Rita. *Betsy Byars* (4–7). Series: Who Wrote That? 2002, Chelsea $30.00 (978-0-7910-6720-8). A profile in text and pictures of one of America's best-loved authors and winner of the Newbery and other prizes. (Rev: BL 10/15/02; HBG 3/03) [921]

CAEDMON

14630 Ashby, Ruth. *Caedmon's Song* (1–3). Illus. by Bill Slavin. 2006, Eerdmans $16.00 (978-0-8028-5241-0). 32pp. This picture-book biography introduces young readers to Caedmon, the 7th-century English cowherd who is said to be that country's first poet. (Rev: HBG 10/06; SLJ 3/06)

CHERRY, LYNNE

14631 Cherry, Lynne. *Making a Difference in the World* (3–5). Series: Meet the Author. 2000, Richard C. Owen $14.95 (978-1-57274-373-1). This noted author and illustrator of children's picture books talks about her life and how, when, and why she works. (Rev: BL 7/00; HBG 3/01; SLJ 12/00)

CHRISTIE, AGATHA

14632 Dommermuth-Costa, Carol. *Agatha Christie: Writer of Mystery* (5–9). Series: Biographies. 1997, Lerner LB $30.35 (978-0-8225-4954-3). A biography of the "First Lady of Crime," with material on her personal life, including her two marriages. (Rev: SLJ 8/97; VOYA 4/98)

CISNEROS, SANDRA

14633 Mirriam-Goldberg, Caryn. *Sandra Cisneros: Latina Writer and Activist* (5–8). Series: Hispanic Biographies. 1998, Enslow LB $19.95 (978-0-7760-1045-8). A biography, enlivened with many quotations, of the woman who received Cs and Ds in school and later became a first-rate author and leading Hispanic American activist. (Rev: BL 1/1–15/99; VOYA 10/99) [921]

14634 Warrick, Karen Clemens. *Sandra Cisneros: Inspiring Latina Author* (5–8). Series: Latino Biography Library. 2009, Enslow $31.93 (978-0-7660-3162-3). 128pp. The story of the Mexican American author, the challenges she faced growing up, and how her books reflect her life. (Rev: SLJ 4/10) [921]

CLEARY, BEVERLY

14635 Ring, Susan. *Beverly Cleary* (2–4). Series: My Favorite Writer. 2003, Weigl LB $16.95 (978-1-59036-030-9). 32pp. This attractively illustrated biography is particularly suitable for report writers. (Rev: HBG 3/03)

COVILLE, BRUCE

14636 Parker-Rock, Michelle. *Bruce Coville: An Author Kids Love* (3–5). Series: Authors Kids Love. 2008, Enslow LB $23.93 (978-0-7600-2755-8). 48pp. An engaging biography of the popular author, focusing on his writing and his childhood experiences. (Rev: SLJ 9/08)

CRANE, STEPHEN

14637 Kepnes, Caroline. *Stephen Crane* (5–8). Series: Classic Storytellers. 2004, Mitchell Lane LB $29.95 (978-1-58415-272-9). An introduction to Crane's life, work, and legacy, with background information on relevant historical, cultural, and economic factors. (Rev: BL 1/05; SLJ 1/05) [921]

CRUTCHER, CHRIS

14638 Summers, Michael A. *Chris Crutcher* (5–8). Series: The Library of Author Biographies. 2005, Rosen LB $27.95 (978-1-4042-0325-9). An interview with Crutcher is an interesting addition to this description of the author's life — including his experiences as a novelist, educator, therapist, and child protection advocate — and his works for children. (Rev: SLJ 9/05) [921]

CURTIS, CHRISTOPHER PAUL

14639 Gaines, Ann. *Christopher Paul Curtis* (3–6). Series: Real-Life Reader Biographies. 2001, Mitchell Lane LB $15.95 (978-1-58415-076-3). 32pp. The fascinating story of the determination that took African American Curtis from writing in a journal during breaks on a car assembly line to winning notable awards. (Rev: SLJ 9/01)

DAHL, ROALD

14640 Cooling, Wendy. *D Is for Dahl: A Gloriumptious A-Z Guide to the World of Roald Dahl* (5–8). Illus. by Quentin Blake. 2005, Viking $15.99 (978-0-670-06023-8). For Dahl fans, this is an alphabetically arranged collection of trivia about his life and writings. (Rev: BL 8/05; SLJ 10/05) [823]

14641 Craats, Rennay. *Roald Dahl* (2–4). Series: My Favorite Writer. 2003, Weigl LB $18.20 (978-1-59036-029-3). 32pp. This attractively illustrated biography of Roald Dahl is particularly suitable for report writers. (Rev: SLJ 10/04)

14642 Shields, Charles J. *Roald Dahl* (4–7). Series: Who Wrote That? 2002, Chelsea $30.00 (978-0-7910-6722-2). 106pp. A brief biography of the master of whimsical stories that involve such strange elements as secretive chocolate factories and giant peaches. (Rev: BL 10/15/02; HBG 3/03)

DANZIGER, PAULA

14643 Reed, Jennifer. *Paula Danziger: Voice of Teen Troubles* (5–8). Series: Authors Teens Love. 2006, Enslow LB $31.93 (978-0-7660-2444-1). This profile of the popular author includes interviews in which she discusses her dysfunctional family and her struggles with depression and bulimia. (Rev: BL 9/15/06) [921]

DEPAOLA, TOMIE

14644 Braun, Eric. *Tomie dePaola* (K–2). Series: First Biographies. 2004, Capstone LB $17.26 (978-0-7368-3641-8). 24pp. Very basic information on the author/illustrator's life and work for beginning readers and re-

port writers, with photographs and a timeline. (Rev: SLJ 7/05)

14645 dePaola, Tomie. *Christmas Remembered* (5–8). 2006, Putnam $19.99 (978-0-399-24622-7). 96pp. Folk artist dePaola recalls some of the most memorable Christmases from his past. (Rev: BL 10/1/06; SLJ 10/06)

14646 dePaola, Tomie. *Here We All Are* (2–5). Illus. Series: 26 Fairmount Avenue. 2000, Penguin $13.99 (978-0-399-23496-5). 80pp. A short chapter book that continues Tomie dePaola's *26 Fairmount Avenue* memoir when, as a 5-year-old, he gets a new baby sister. (Rev: BCCB 9/00; BL 5/1/00; HB 5/00; HBG 10/00; SLJ 6/00)

14647 dePaola, Tomie. *I'm Still Scared: The War Years* (2–4). Illus. Series: 26 Fairmount Avenue. 2006, Putnam $13.99 (978-0-399-24502-2). 80pp. DePaola recalls the fears and uncertainties of children growing up in America during World War II in this installment of his autobiographical series. (Rev: BL 4/15/06; SLJ 11/06)

14648 dePaola, Tomie. *On My Way* (2–4). Illus. Series: 26 Fairmount Avenue. 2001, Penguin $13.99 (978-0-399-23583-2). 32pp. A continuation of dePaola's remembrances of his childhood that includes a visit to the 1940 World's Fair. (Rev: BCCB 3/01; BL 12/15/00; HB 3/01; HBG 10/01; SLJ 2/01)

14649 dePaola, Tomie. *Things Will Never Be the Same* (2–4). Illus. Series: 26 Fairmount Avenue. 2003, Penguin $13.99 (978-0-399-23982-3). 80pp. DePaola's autobiography, with his own drawings, continues through 1941, when he turned 7, and details his everyday life until the morning of December 7, when everything changed. (Rev: BCCB 3/03; BL 3/1/03; HBG 10/03; SLJ 5/03)

14650 dePaola, Tomie. *What a Year!* (2–4). Illus. Series: 26 Fairmount Avenue. 2002, Penguin $13.99 (978-0-399-23797-3). 80pp. DePaola's memoirs continues here, taking readers into the life of 6-year-old Tomie from the beginning of 1st grade to New Year's Eve in 1940. (Rev: BCCB 3/02; BL 3/1/02; HB 3/02; HBG 10/02; SLJ 3/02)

14651 dePaola, Tomie. *Why? The War Years: A 26 Fairmount Avenue Book* (2–4). Illus. Series: 26 Fairmount Avenue. 2007, Putnam $14.99 (978-0-399-24692-0). 80pp. Continuing his autobiographical series, dePaola includes many child-appealing vignettes, but focuses on the impact of World War II, concluding with his much-loved cousin's death. (Rev: BL 1/1–15/07)

DICKENS, CHARLES

14652 Hopkinson, Deborah. *A Boy Called Dickens* (3–5). Illus. by John Hendrix. 2012, Random House $17.99 (978-037586732-3); LB $20.99 (978-037596732-0). 40pp. This fictionalized account of young Charles Dickens's life emphasizes his hard childhood and eventual return to school. (Rev: BL 12/15/11*; HB 1–2/12; LMC 3–4/12; SLJ 1/12) [921]

14653 Manning, Mick, and Brita Granström. *Charles Dickens: Scenes from an Extraordinary Life* (3–5). Illus. by Mick Manning. 2011, Frances Lincoln $18.95 (978-184780187-6). 48pp. Using a graphic-novel approach, this simple picture-book biography features first-person passages as well as third-person factual narrative. (Rev: BL 1/1/12; SLJ 1/12) [921]

14654 Rosen, Michael. *Dickens: His Work and His World* (4–7). Illus. by Robert Ingpen. 2005, Candlewick $19.99 (978-0-7636-2752-2). Before reviewing Dickens's major works, Rosen discusses the author's difficult childhood and the social conditions of his times. (Rev: BCCB 3/06; BL 9/15/05*; HBG 4/06; LMC 3/06; SLJ 11/05*) [921]

14655 Wells-Cole, Catherine. *Charles Dickens: England's Most Captivating Storyteller* (4–7). Illus. Series: Historical Notebook. 2011, Candlewick $19.99 (978-0-7636-5567-9). 32pp. A visually appealing introduction to Dickens and his world, using a scrapbook format with double-page spreads covering various aspects of his life and work. (Rev: BLO 11/15/11; LMC 3–4/12; SLJ 11/1/11; VOYA 4/12) [921]

FINGER, BILL

14656 Nobleman, Marc Tyler. *Bill the Boy Wonder: The Secret Co-Creator of Batman* (4–7). Illus. by Ty Templeton. 2012, Charlesbridge $17.95 (978-1-58089-289-6). 48pp. Bill Finger, the overlooked co-creator of Batman comics, gets his due in this interesting biography. Lexile GN970L (Rev: BL 8/12; LMC 3–4/13; SLJ 8/12) [921]

FITZGERALD, F. SCOTT

14657 Bankston, John. *F. Scott Fitzgerald* (5–8). Series: Classic Storytellers. 2004, Mitchell Lane LB $29.95 (978-1-58415-249-1). An introduction to Fitzgerald's life, work, and legacy, with background information on relevant historical, cultural, and economic factors. (Rev: BL 1/05; SLJ 1/05) [921]

FLEISCHMAN, SID

14658 Freedman, Jeri. *Sid Fleischman* (5–9). Series: The Library of Author Biographies. 2004, Rosen LB $27.95 (978-0-8239-4019-6). 112pp. Traces the popular, Newbery-winning author's life and looks at his works, writing process, and inspirations, concluding with an interview and reference material. (Rev: SLJ 9/04)

14659 Parker-Rock, Michelle. *Sid Fleischman: An Author Kids Love* (3–5). Series: Authors Kids Love. 2008, Enslow LB $23.93 (978-0-7660-2757-2). 48pp. A brief biography of the popular author with information on his youth, direct quotations, photographs, and Fleischman's tips on how to become a writer. (Rev: SLJ 11/08)

FLETCHER, RALPH

14660 Fletcher, Ralph. *Marshfield Dreams: When I Was a Kid* (3–5). 2005, Holt $16.95 (978-0-8050-7242-6). 192pp. Children's author Fletcher recalls growing up in coastal Massachusetts as the oldest of nine siblings. (Rev: BL 10/1/05; SLJ 9/05; VOYA 8/05)

FOX, PAULA

14661 Daniel, Susanna. *Paula Fox* (5–8). Series: The Library of Author Biographies. 2004, Rosen LB $27.95 (978-0-8239-4525-2). Covers Fox's life and career, with analysis of her work and its themes, an interview, and lists of works and awards. (Rev: SLJ 1/05) [921]

FROST, ROBERT

14662 Bober, Natalie S. *Papa Is a Poet: A Story about Robert Frost* (1–3). Illus. by Rebecca Gibbon. 2013, Henry Holt $17.99 (978-0-8050-9407-7). 40pp. Told from the perspective of Robert Frost's eldest daughter, Lesley, and based on her journal, Bober relates how Frost became one of America's most famous writers. **e** (Rev: BL 10/1/13; HB 1–2/14; LMC 3–4/14; SLJ 9/13) [921]

14663 Wooten, Sara McIntosh. *Robert Frost: The Life of America's Poet* (5–8). Series: People to Know Today. 2006, Enslow LB $31.93 (978-0-7660-2627-8). A fine introduction to the New England poet whose poetry is loved by young people and adults, with information on his difficult childhood and continuing struggles with depression and financial woes. (Rev: SLJ 1/07) [921]

GANTOS, JACK

14664 Parker-Rock, Michelle. *Jack Gantos: An Author Kids Love* (3–5). Series: Authors Kids Love. 2008, Enslow LB $23.93 (978-0-7600-2756-5). 48pp. An engaging biography of the creator of Joey Pigza and Rotten Ralph, focusing on his writing (he began keeping a journal in 6th grade) and his childhood experiences. (Rev: BL 4/1/08; LMC 3/08; SLJ 9/08)

GEISEL, THEODOR

14665 Carlson, Cheryl. *Dr. Seuss* (K–2). Series: First Biographies. 2004, Capstone LB $17.26 (978-0-7368-3639-5). 24pp. Very basic information on the author's life and work for beginning readers and report writers, with photographs and a timeline. (Rev: SLJ 7/05)

14666 Dean, Tanya. *Theodor Geisel (Dr. Seuss)* (4–7). Illus. Series: Who Wrote That? 2002, Chelsea $30.00 (978-0-7910-6724-6). 112pp. A look at the life and works of the author and illustrator known as Dr. Seuss. (Rev: BL 10/15/02; HBG 3/03)

14667 Foran, Jill. *Dr. Seuss* (2–4). Series: My Favorite Writer. 2003, Weigl LB $16.95 (978-1-59036-028-6). 32pp. This attractively illustrated biography of Theodor Geisel is particularly suitable for report writers. (Rev: SLJ 10/04)

14668 Guillain, Charlotte. *Dr. Seuss* (K–3). Illus. Series: Read and Learn Author Biographies. 2012, Heinemann LB $22 (978-143295959-3). 24pp. For early elementary readers, this simple biography uses a question-and-answer format to introduce students to the works and life of Dr. Seuss. (Rev: BLO 3/1/12; LMC 10/12) [921]

14669 Krull, Kathleen. *The Boy on Fairfield Street: How Ted Geisel Grew Up to Become Dr. Seuss* (3–5). Illus. by Steve Johnson and Lou Fancher. 2004, Random $16.95

(978-0-375-82298-8). 42pp. Concentrating on Geisel's youth, this picture-book biography includes examples of his work. (Rev: BL 2/1/04; SLJ 1/04)

14670 Lynch, Wendy. *Dr. Seuss* (1–4). Series: Lives and Times. 2000, Heinemann LB $19.92 (978-1-57572-216-0). 24pp. A simple biography of Theodor Geisel's alter ego with original drafts of artwork and many photographs. (Rev: HBG 3/01; SLJ 8/00)

14671 Woods, Mae. *Dr. Seuss* (2–4). Illus. Series: Children's Authors. 2000, ABDO $21.35 (978-1-57765-110-9). This book discusses the life and career on Theodor Geisel, better known as Dr. Seuss. (Rev: HBG 3/01; SLJ 1/01)

GIFF, PATRICIA REILLY

14672 Giff, Patricia Reilly. *Don't Tell the Girls: A Family Memoir* (4–7). 2005, Holiday $16.95 (978-0-8234-1813-8). The author tells of the search for her family's roots that led her to Ireland. (Rev: BL 3/1/05; SLJ 7/05) [813]

GRIMM BROTHERS

14673 Hettinga, Donald R. *The Brothers Grimm: Two Lives, One Legacy* (5–8). 2001, Clarion $22.00 (978-0-618-05599-9). An interesting biography that places the brothers' lives in the context of their time and discusses their skills as lexicographers and scholars. (Rev: BL 7/01; HB 1–2/02; HBG 3/02; SLJ 10/01) [430]

HALE, BRUCE

14674 Parker-Rock, Michelle. *Bruce Hale: An Author Kids Love* (3–5). Series: Authors Kids Love. 2008, Enslow LB $23.93 (978-0-7660-2758-9). 48pp. A brief biography of the popular author with information on his youth, direct quotations, photographs, and Hale's advice on how to become a writer. (Rev: SLJ 11/08)

HANDLER, DANIEL

14675 Haugen, Hayley Mitchell. *Daniel Handler: The Real Lemony Snicket* (3–6). Illus. Series: Inventors and Creators. 2005, Gale LB $26.20 (978-0-7377-3117-0). 48pp. The author of the popular A Series of Unfortunate Events books is profiled (and pictured), with discussion of his books. (Rev: SLJ 8/05)

HINTON, S. E.

14676 Kjelle, Marylou Morano. *S. E. Hinton: Author of The Outsiders* (5–8). Series: Authors Teens Love. 2007, Enslow LB $31.93 (978-0-7660-2720-6). A life of the author of the well-known novel, with an "In Her Own Words" section that researchers will find useful. (Rev: SLJ 11/07) [921]

HOMER

14677 Tracy, Kathleen. *The Life and Times of Homer* (5–8). Series: Biography from Ancient Civilizations: Legends, Folklore, and Stories of Ancient Worlds. 2004, Mitchell Lane LB $29.95 (978-1-58415-260-6). Drawing on ancient legends, this is a profile of ancient Greek poet and storyteller Homer. (Rev: BL 10/15/04; SLJ 12/04)

HOPKINS, LEE BENNETT

14678 Hopkins, Lee Bennett. *The Writing Bug* (2–5). Illus. by Diane Rubinger. Series: Meet the Author. 1993, Richard C. Owen $14.95 (978-1-878450-38-8). 32pp. The acclaimed poet, author, and anthologist tells about his life and the experiences that inspire him to write. (Rev: BL 9/1/93; HB 9/93)

14679 Strong, Amy. *Lee Bennett Hopkins: A Children's Poet* (5–8). Series: Great Life Stories. 2003, Watts LB $30.50 (978-0-531-12315-7). 111pp. An inspiring biography that chronicles Hopkins's early struggles and his love for his work. (Rev: SLJ 2/04)

HUGHES, LANGSTON

14680 Bryant, Philip S. *Langston Hughes* (2–5). Series: African-American Biographies. 2003, Raintree LB $28.56 (978-0-7398-6871-3). 64pp. This basic biography profiles Hughes's life and achievements and places them in historical context. (Rev: SLJ 11/03)

14681 McKissack, Patricia C., and Fredrick McKissack. *Langston Hughes: Great American Poet. Rev. ed.* (2–4). Series: Great African Americans. 2002, Enslow LB $18.60 (978-0-7660-1695-8). 32pp. An interesting biography of the African American author noted for both his poetry and fiction and for his role in the Harlem Renaissance. (Rev: BL 7/02; HBG 10/02)

HURSTON, ZORA NEALE

14682 Bryant, Philip S. *Zora Neale Hurston* (2–5). Series: African-American Biographies. 2003, Raintree LB $28.56 (978-0-7398-6872-0). 64pp. A simple profile of the author, with interesting sidebars and good archival photographs that convey a sense of the time in which she lived. (Rev: HBG 4/04; SLJ 11/03)

14683 Fradin, Dennis B., and Judith Bloom Fradin. *Zora! The Life of Zora Neale Hurston* (4–6). Illus. 2012, Clarion $17.99 (978-0-547-00695-6). 192pp. The tumultuous life of African American writer Zora Neale Hurston is chronicled in this inspiring biography. (Rev: BL 2/1/12; HB 11–12/12; LMC 5–6/13; SLJ 9/12; VOYA 4/12) [921]

IRVING, WASHINGTON

14684 Collins, David R. *Washington Irving: Storyteller for a New Nation* (4–8). Series: World Writers. 2000, Morgan Reynolds LB $23.95 (978-1-883846-50-3). This biography introduces the globetrotting American writer and gives details of his work and personality. (Rev: BL 4/1/00; HBG 3/00; SLJ 5/00; VOYA 6/01) [921]

14685 Harness, Cheryl. *The Literary Adventures of Washington Irving* (2–5). Illus. by author. 2008, National Geographic $17.95 (978-1-4263-0438-5). 48pp. An engaging picture-book account of Irving's life, work, and times with attention-grabbing artwork. (Rev: BL 1/1–15/09; SLJ 3/09)

JUANA INES DE LA CRUZ, SISTER

14686 Mora, Pat. *A Library for Juana: The World of Sor Juana Ines* (1–3). Illus. by Beatriz Vidal. 2002, Knopf $15.95 (978-0-375-80643-8). 40pp. This is an absorbing account of the inspiring life of Sor Juana Ines, a child prodigy born in Mexico in the 17th century who became a nun and internationally known scholar and poet. (Rev: BL 11/15/02; HB 11/02; HBG 3/03; SLJ 11/02)

KEHRET, PEG

14687 Kehret, Peg. *Five Pages a Day: A Writer's Journey* (4–7). 2002, Albert Whitman LB $15.99 (978-0-8075-8650-1). Aspiring young writers will particularly enjoy Kehret's account of her writing life, from starting a newspaper about the neighborhood dogs to entering writing contests to her career as an author of children's books. (Rev: BL 12/15/02; HBG 3/03; SLJ 9/02)

KING, STEPHEN

14688 Wilson, Suzan. *Stephen King* (4–6). Series: People to Know. 2000, Enslow LB $26.60 (978-0-7660-1233-2). 128pp. A well-documented, thorough account of the life of this former high-school teacher who became a best-selling writer of suspense and horror novels. (Rev: BL 1/1–15/00; HBG 10/00; SLJ 5/00)

KORMAN, GORDON

14689 Matthews, Sheelagh. *Gordon Korman* (4–6). Illus. Series: Remarkable Writers. 2012, Weigl LB $28.55 (978-161913055-5). 32pp. An appealing profile of the popular writer, with advice for aspiring young writers. (Rev: BL 10/1/12) [921]

LEVINE, GAIL CARSON

14690 McGinty, Alice B. *Meet Gail Carson Levine* (2–4). Series: About the Author. 2003, Rosen LB $18.75 (978-0-8239-6409-3). 24pp. Sample passages, book covers, childhood photographs, and an interview make this an appealing, easy-to-read profile of Levine and her writing career. (Rev: BL 6/1–15/03; SLJ 5/03)

LEWIS, C. S.

14691 Parker, Vic. *C. S. Lewis* (4–7). Series: Writers Uncovered. 2006, Heinemann LB $23.00 (978-1-4034-7336-3). In addition to providing biographical information on Lewis, Parker looks at his books, especially the Narnia series, giving plot outlines and discussing the stories and themes. (Rev: BL 8/06) [921]

LONDON, JACK

14692 Bankston, John. *Jack London* (4–7). Series: Classic Storytellers. 2005, Mitchell Lane LB $29.95 (978-1-58415-263-7). An introduction to London's life, work, and legacy, with background information on relevant historical, cultural, and economic factors. (Rev: BL 1/05) [921]

14693 Streissguth, Thomas. *Jack London* (4–7). Series: A&E Biography. 2000, Lucent LB $27.93 (978-0-8225-4987-1). The story of an adventurer and author who battled personal hardships and wrote eloquently about nature and survival. (Rev: BL 12/15/00; HBG 3/01; SLJ 3/01)

LOVECRAFT, H. P.

14694 Schoell, William. *H. P. Lovecraft: Master of Weird Fiction* (5–8). 2003, Morgan Reynolds LB $23.95 (978-1-931798-15-0). Lovecraft, known for his stories of horror and the supernatural, was born into privilege that ended with his parents' early deaths; his works only received real acclaim after his death. (Rev: BL 9/15/03; HBG 4/04; SLJ 12/03) [813]

LOWRY, LOIS

14695 Lowry, Lois. *Looking Back: A Book of Memories* (4–8). 1998, Houghton Mifflin $17.00 (978-0-395-89543-6). This autobiographical work centers around a series of photographs and the author's comments on each. (Rev: BL 11/1/98; HB 1–2/99; HBG 3/99; SLJ 9/98; VOYA 4/99) [921]

14696 Markham, Lois. *Lois Lowry* (5–8). Series: Meet the Author. 1995, Learning Works paper $7.99 (978-0-88160-278-4). This biography of the Newbery Medal-winning author tells how she became a writer and looks at the personal experiences that are reflected in her books. (Rev: SLJ 1/96) [921]

MAGEE, JOHN

14697 Granfield, Linda. *High Flight: A Story of World War II* (5–7). 1999, Tundra $15.95 (978-0-88776-469-1). The moving story of John Magee, a young Canadian Air Force pilot who was killed in World War II and who is best known for writing the poem "High Flight." (Rev: BCCB 12/99; BL 1/1–15/00; HBG 3/00; SLJ 2/00) [921]

MÁRQUEZ, GABRIEL GARCÍA

14698 Brown, Monica. *My Name Is Gabito: The Life of Gabriel García Márquez* (2–4). Illus. by Raúl Colón. 2007, Northland/Rising Moon $15.95 (978-0-87358-934-5). 32pp. A picture-book biography of the Colombian author covering his youth and explaining his use of magical realism. (Rev: BL 2/1/08; SLJ 3/08*)

MISTRAL, GABRIELA

14699 Brown, Monica. *My Name Is Gabriela / Me llamo Gabriela: The Life of Gabriela Mistral / La vida de Gabriela Mistral* (K–2). Illus. by John Parra. 2005, Luna Rising $15.95 (978-0-87358-859-1). Lyrical first-person text tells the story of the life and writing career of Nobel Prize–winning Chilean poet Gabriela Mistral. (Rev: SLJ 2/06*)

MONTGOMERY, LUCY MAUD

14700 MacLeod, Elizabeth. *Lucy Maud Montgomery: A Writer's Life* (3–5). Illus. 2001, Kids Can LB $14.95 (978-1-55074-487-3). 32pp. Both black-and-white and color illustrations are used to enhance this biography of one of Canada's most famous writers. (Rev: BL 4/1/01; HBG 10/01; SLJ 4/01)

14701 Wallner, Alexandra. *Lucy Maud Montgomery: The Author of Anne of Green Gables* (1–3). 2006, Holiday $16.95 (978-0-8234-1549-6). 32pp. A picture-book life of the author, from her childhood on Prince Edward Island to her marriage to a minister and her success with *Anne*. (Rev: BL 9/15/06; SLJ 12/06)

MORRISON, TONI

14702 Haskins, James. *Toni Morrison: The Magic of Words* (4–6). Illus. Series: Gateway Biographies. 2001, Millbrook $23.90 (978-0-7613-1806-4). Young readers may not be familiar with Morrison's work, but will still enjoy this clearly presented photo-essay introducing her life from childhood, her work, and her support for other writers. (Rev: BL 6/1–15/01; HBG 10/01; SLJ 5/01)

NAYLOR, PHYLLIS REYNOLDS

14703 Naylor, Phyllis Reynolds. *How I Came to Be a Writer. Rev. ed.* (4–9). 2001, Simon & Schuster paper $4.99 (978-0-689-83887-3). Naylor describes the joys and difficulties of life as a writer and includes excerpts of her work in this autobiographical account. (Rev: SLJ 5/01) [921]

NERUDA, PABLO

14704 Brown, Monica. *Pablo Neruda: Poet of the People* (1–3). Illus. by Julie Paschkis. 2011, Henry Holt $16.99 (978-0-8050-9198-4). 32pp. This handsome picture-book biography portrays the at-times turbulent life of the Chilean poet. Lexile AD970L (Rev: BL 1/1–15/11; HB 3–4/11; LMC 5–6/11; SLJ 2/1/11) [921]

14705 DeLano, Poli. *When I Was a Boy Neruda Called Me Policarpo* (4–6). Trans. by Sean Higgins. Illus. by Manuel Monroy. 2006, Groundwood $15.95 (978-0-88899-726-5). 96pp. The author presents his childhood memories of Chilean poet Pablo Neruda along with a number of Neruda's poems. (Rev: BL 7/06; SLJ 5/06)

14706 Ray, Deborah Kogan. *To Go Singing Through the World: The Childhood of Pablo Neruda* (3–5). Illus. 2006, Farrar $17.00 (978-0-374-37627-7). 40pp. A picture-book biography of poet Pablo Neruda, describing his childhood in a Chilean rain forest town and how it shaped his views and writings. (Rev: BL 11/15/06; SLJ 11/06)

NIXON, JOAN LOWERY

14707 Wade, Mary Dodson. *Joan Lowery Nixon: Masterful Mystery Writer* (5–8). Series: Authors Teens Love. 2004, Enslow LB $26.60 (978-0-7660-2194-5). Examines Nixon's life, writings, and her focus on girls of character and strength. (Rev: SLJ 11/04) [921]

PAREDES, AMERICO

14708 Murcia, Rebecca Thatcher. *Americo Paredes* (5–7). Series: Latinos in American History. 2003, Mitchell Lane LB $29.95 (978-1-58415-207-1). The story of the Mexican American author, folklorist, and professor at the University of Texas in Austin who is also famous for establishing a center for intercultural studies. (Rev: BL 1/1–15/04) [921]

PARK, LINDA SUE

14709 Parker-Rock, Michelle. *Linda Sue Park: An Author Kids Love* (3–5). Series: Authors Kids Love. 2009, Enslow LB $23.93 (978-0-7660-3158-6). 48pp. Park discusses her writing and researching process in this clearly written, interview-based biography. (Rev: SLJ 11/1/09) [921]

PATERSON, KATHERINE

14710 Kjelle, Marylou Morano. *Katherine Paterson* (4–7). Series: Classic Storytellers. 2004, Mitchell Lane LB $29.95 (978-1-58415-268-2). Examines the life and times of the award-winning children's author, including her work as a missionary in Japan and how religious faith informs her writing. (Rev: BL 1/1–15/05; SLJ 3/05) [921]

14711 McGinty, Alice B. *Katherine Paterson* (5–8). Series: The Library of Author Biographies. 2005, Rosen LB $27.95 (978-1-4042-0328-0). An interview with Paterson is an interesting addition to this description of the author's life and works for children. (Rev: SLJ 9/05) [921]

PAULSEN, GARY

14712 Gaines, Ann. *Gary Paulsen* (3–6). Series: Real-Life Reader Biographies. 2001, Mitchell Lane LB $15.95 (978-1-58415-077-0). 32pp. Gaines presents Paulsen's difficult childhood, his love of reading, and his fascination with sled dogs and adventure. (Rev: SLJ 9/01)

14713 Paterra, Elizabeth. *Gary Paulsen* (4–7). Series: Who Wrote That? 2002, Chelsea $30.00 (978-0-7910-6723-9). A profile of the prolific author (of almost 200 books) who is best known for his young adult outdoor survival stories. (Rev: BL 10/15/02; HBG 3/03) [921]

14714 Paulsen, Gary. *Caught by the Sea* (5–8). 2001, Delacorte $15.95 (978-0-385-32645-2). The author describes his ongoing love of the sea and the adventures he's had, some funny, some scary. (Rev: BL 9/15/01; HBG 3/02; SLJ 10/01; VOYA 12/01) [818]

14715 Peters, Stephanie True. *Gary Paulsen* (4–8). 1999, Learning Works paper $7.99 (978-0-88160-324-8). A straightforward biography of the outdoorsman and author that tells about his books, his interests, his alcoholism, and his continuing health problems. (Rev: BL 6/1–15/99; SLJ 6/99) [921]

PINKWATER, DANIEL

14716 McGinty, Alice B. *Meet Daniel Pinkwater* (2–4). Illus. Series: About the Author. 2003, Rosen LB $21.25 (978-0-8239-6406-2). 24pp. Readers learn about Pinkwater's youth and later life, his varied interests, how and why he started writing for children, and how he uses his own childhood experiences in his books. (Rev: SLJ 3/03)

POE, EDGAR ALLAN

14717 Frisch, Aaron. *Edgar Allan Poe* (5–9). Illus. by Gary Kelley. Photos by Tina Mucci. Series: Voices in Poetry. 2005, Creative Education LB $31.35 (978-1-58341-344-9). A brief biography that adds atmospheric paintings and photographs to a chronological narrative and excerpts from Poe's works. (Rev: SLJ 3/06) [921]

14718 Kent, Zachary. *Edgar Allan Poe* (5–8). Series: Historical American Biographies. 2001, Enslow LB $26.60 (978-0-7660-1600-2). An informative, well-presented biography of this writer whose unique stories changed the history of American literature. (Rev: BL 1/1–15/02; HBG 3/02; SLJ 9/01)

14719 Lange, Karen E. *Nevermore: A Photobiography of Edgar Allan Poe* (5–8). Illus. 2009, National Geographic $17.95 (978-1-4263-0398-2). 64pp. This readable photo-biography offers an overview of the writer's work and life starting with his difficult childhood and covering his struggles as an adult. (Rev: BCCB 5/09; BL 4/1/09; LMC 10/09; SLJ 4/09*) [921]

14720 Streissguth, Thomas. *Edgar Allan Poe* (5–8). Series: A&E Biography. 2001, Lerner LB $27.93 (978-0-8225-4991-8). The tortured life of this early master of the short story is brought to life in an interesting text and many black-and-white illustrations. (Rev: BL 6/1–15/01; HBG 10/01; SLJ 8/01)

POTTER, BEATRIX

14721 Winter, Jeanette. *Beatrix: Various Episodes from the Life of Beatrix Potter* (PS–2). Illus. 2003, Farrar $15.00 (978-0-374-30655-7). 64pp. Excerpts from Potter's writings are incorporated in this small-format biography that looks mainly at her life as a child and young woman. (Rev: BL 3/1/03; HB 5/03; HBG 10/03; SLJ 3/03)

QUAN, ELIZABETH

14722 Quan, Elizabeth. *Once Upon a Full Moon* (3–5). Illus. by author. 2007, Tundra $19.95 (978-0-88776-813-2). 48pp. Beautifully written from a child's point of view, this memoir traces the Chinese Canadian author's journey as a young girl in the late 1920s to visit her grandmother in China. (Rev: BL 7/07; SLJ 10/07)

RAWLINGS, MARJORIE KINNAN

14723 Cook, Judy, and Laura Lee Smith. *Natural Writer: A Story About Marjorie Kinnan Rawlings* (4–6). Illus. by Laurie Harden. Series: Creative Minds Biographies. 2001, Carolrhoda LB $22.60 (978-1-57505-468-1). This easily read biography with full-page illustrations tells the life story of the author of *The Yearling*. (Rev: HBG 10/01; SLJ 8/01)

REY, MARGRET AND H. A.

14724 Borden, Louise. *The Journey That Saved Curious George: The True Wartime Escape of Margret and H. A. Rey* (3–6). Illus. by Allan Drummond. 2005, Houghton $17.00 (978-0-618-33924-2). 80pp. This handsome large-format volume chronicles the escape from Nazism of Margret and H. A. Rey, the creators of the Curious George books for children. (Rev: BL 10/15/05; SLJ 10/05)

RIVERA, TOMAS

14725 Medina, Jane. *Tomas Rivera* (1–2). Illus. by Edward Martinez. Series: Green Light Reader, Level 2. 2004, Harcourt LB $12.95 (978-0-15-205145-7). 24pp. Medina recounts a life-changing experience from the childhood of Mexican American writer/educator Tomas Rivera. (Rev: BL 7/04)

ROWLING, J. K.

14726 Gaines, Ann. *J. K. Rowling* (3–6). 2001, Mitchell Lane LB $15.95 (978-1-58415-078-7). 32pp. Gaines chronicles Rowling's struggles as a single mother seeking a publisher before *Harry*'s success. (Rev: BCCB 2/02; SLJ 9/01)

14727 Harmin, Karen Leigh. *J. K. Rowling: Author of Harry Potter* (4–7). Series: People to Know Today. 2006, Enslow LB $31.93 (978-0-7660-1850-1). An attractive and accessible biography of the creator of the wildly popular series, with details of her youth, career, and the impact success has had on her life; plus information on aspects of British life that will interest young readers. (Rev: BL 11/1/06) [921]

14728 Peterson-Hilleque, Victoria. *J. K. Rowling: Extraordinary Author* (5–8). Series: Essential Lives. 2010, ABDO LB $32.79 (978-1-61613-517-1). 112pp. This volume describes Rowling's youth and personal life as well as her career, giving information on her efforts to get Harry Potter published, her success, and some of the key characters. (Rev: SLJ 3/1/11) [921]

RUMI

14729 Demi. *Rumi: Whirling Dervish* (5–8). Illus. by author. 2009, Marshall Cavendish $19.99 (978-0-7614-5527-1). This picture-book profile of the 13th-century Persian mystical poet is enhanced by the rich illustrations. (Rev: BL 4/15/09; LMC 10/09; SLJ 6/09) [921]

SACHAR, LOUIS

14730 Greene, Meg. *Louis Sachar* (5–9). Series: The Library of Author Biographies. 2004, Rosen LB $26.50 (978-0-8239-4017-2). 112pp. Traces the popular, Newbery-winning author's life and looks at his works, writing process, and inspirations, concluding with an interview and reference material. (Rev: SLJ 9/04)

SANDBURG, CARL

14731 Meltzer, Milton. *Carl Sandburg: A Biography* (5–10). 1999, Millbrook LB $31.90 (978-0-7613-1364-9).

The story of a literary giant who, in addition to his poetry, is noted for nonfiction works including a biography of Abraham Lincoln. (Rev: BL 12/15/99; HBG 10/00; VOYA 6/00) [921]

SCIESZKA, JON

14732 Scieszka, Jon. *Knucklehead: Tall Tales and Mostly True Stories of Growing Up Scieszka* (4–7). 2008, Viking $16.99 (978-0-670-01106-3). 96pp. Scieszka's entertaining autobiography tells a story of growing up one of six irreverent brothers in Flint, Michigan. ALA Notable Children's Book 2009. ∩ (Rev: BL 9/1/08; HB 11–12/08; LMC 1–2/09; SLJ 10/1/08*; VOYA 12/08) [921]

SENDAK, MAURICE

14733 Braun, Eric. *Maurice Sendak* (K–2). Series: First Biographies. 2004, Capstone LB $17.26 (978-0-7368-3640-1). Very basic information on the author/illustrator's life and work for beginning readers and report writers, with photographs and a timeline. (Rev: SLJ 7/05)

SHAKESPEARE, WILLIAM

14734 Aliki. *William Shakespeare and the Globe* (4–7). 1999, HarperCollins LB $18.89 (978-0-06-027821-2). Shakespeare and Elizabethan England come to life in this detailed picture book that uses many quotations from his plays and also tells of the recent rebuilding of the Globe theater. (Rev: BCCB 4/99; BL 6/1–15/99*; HB 5–6/99; HBG 10/99; SLJ 5/99) [921]

14735 Bailey, Gerry, and Karen Foster. *Shakespeare's Quill* (3–5). Illus. by Leighton Noyes and Karen Radford. Series: Stories of Great People. 2008, Crabtree LB $29.27 (978-0-7787-3691-2); paper $9.95 (978-0-7787-3713-1). Digby Platt and his older sister Hannah learn lots of facts about the man and his writing. (Rev: SLJ 7/08)

14736 Dommermuth-Costa, Carol. *William Shakespeare* (5–8). Series: Biography. 2001, Lerner LB $27.93 (978-0-8225-4996-3). A readable, well-illustrated biography of the Bard of Avon with material on many of his plays. (Rev: BL 4/1/02; HBG 10/02; SLJ 3/02)

14737 Fandel, Jennifer. *William Shakespeare* (5–9). Photos by Marcel Imsand. Series: Voices in Poetry. 2003, Creative Editions LB $19.95 (978-1-58341-283-1). A brief and appealing introduction to Shakespeare's life and work, with examples of his poems, excerpts from his plays, and illustrations. (Rev: SLJ 12/03)

14738 Hilliam, David. *William Shakespeare: England's Greatest Playwright and Poet* (5–8). Series: Rulers, Scholars, and Artists of the Renaissance. 2005, Rosen LB $33.25 (978-1-4042-0318-1). Information on Shakespeare's life and on the theater scene in 16th-century London is interwoven with quotes from the plays and poems. (Rev: BL 8/05) [822.3]

14739 Nettleton, Pamela Hill. *William Shakespeare: Playwright and Poet* (5–9). Series: Signature Lives. 2005, Compass Point $34.60 (978-0-7565-0816-6). Net-

tleton places facts about Shakespeare's life within the context of everyday life of the time, with details about the theater and publishing. (Rev: SLJ 6/05) [921]

SHARMAT, MARJORIE WEINMAN

14740 Wheeler, Jill C. *Marjorie Weinman Sharmat* (2–4). Series: Children's Authors. 2005, ABDO LB $21.35 (978-1-59197-608-0). 24pp. After introducing some of Sharmat's works, Wheeler discusses the author's childhood and influences on her work. (Rev: SLJ 4/05)

SHELLEY, MARY

14741 Darrow, Sharon. *Through the Tempests Dark and Wild: A Story of Mary Shelley, Creator of Frankenstein* (4–7). Illus. by Angela Barren. 2003, Candlewick $16.99 (978-0-7636-0835-4). 40pp. The dramatic story of Mary Shelley's troubled youth is told in this beautifully illustrated, fictionalized picture-book biography. (Rev: BL 6/1–15/03; HBG 10/03; SLJ 6/03)

SILVERSTEIN, SHEL

14742 Ward, S. *Meet Shel Silverstein* (2–3). Series: About the Author. 2001, Rosen LB $18.75 (978-0-8239-5709-5). 24pp. This introduction to the author of "The Giving Tree" describes his life and work. (Rev: SLJ 6/01)

SIMON, SEYMOUR

14743 Simon, Seymour. *From Paper Airplanes to Outer Space* (3–5). Series: Meet the Author. 2000, Richard C. Owen $14.95 (978-1-57274-374-8). 32pp. A noted writer of science books for young people talks about his life and how he writes. (Rev: BL 7/00; HBG 3/01; SLJ 12/00)

SPINELLI, JERRY

14744 McGinty, Alice B. *Meet Jerry Spinelli* (2–4). Illus. Series: About the Author. 2003, Rosen LB $21.25 (978-0-8239-6408-6). 24pp. Readers learn about Spinelli's youth and later life, his varied interests, how and why he started writing for children, and how he uses his own childhood experiences in his books. (Rev: SLJ 3/03)

14745 Seidman, David. *Jerry Spinelli* (5–9). Series: The Library of Author Biographies. 2004, Rosen LB $27.95 (978-0-8239-4016-5). 112pp. Traces the popular, Newbery-winning author's life and looks at his works, writing process, and inspirations, concluding with an interview and reference material. (Rev: SLJ 9/04)

14746 Spinelli, Jerry. *Knots in My Yo-Yo String: The Autobiography of a Kid* (5–8). 1998, Knopf paper $10.95 (978-0-679-88791-1). A frank, delightful memoir of growing up in Norristown, Pennsylvania, during the 1950s by the renowned Newbery Medal-winning writer of fiction for young people. (Rev: BCCB 7–8/98; BL 5/1/98; HBG 10/98; SLJ 6/98; VOYA 12/98) [921]

STEIN, GERTRUDE

14747 Winter, Jonah. *Gertrude Is Gertrude Is Gertrude Is Gertrude* (2–4). Illus. by Calef Brown. 2009, Atheneum $16.99 (978-1-4169-4088-3). 40pp. An engaging picture-book introduction to the world of writer Gertrude Stein, as she hosts a tea party for Picasso, Matisse, Hemingway, and other artists and writers; the illustrations extend the text and add to the lively atmosphere. (Rev: BCCB 1/09; BL 1/1–15/09; SLJ 2/09)

STEINBECK, JOHN

14748 Tracy, Kathleen. *John Steinbeck* (5–8). Series: Classic Storytellers. 2004, Mitchell Lane LB $29.95 (978-1-58415-271-2). An introduction to Steinbeck's life, work, and legacy, with background information on relevant historical, cultural, and economic factors. (Rev: BL 1/05; SLJ 1/05) [921]

STINE, R. L.

14749 Cohen, Joel H. *R. L. Stine* (5–8). Series: People in the News. 2000, Lucent LB $28.70 (978-1-56006-608-8). 96pp. This well-documented biography, illustrated with several black-and-white photographs, tells the story of an author who enjoys scaring his readers. (Rev: BL 6/1–15/00; HBG 10/00; SLJ 8/00)

14750 Parker-Rock, Michelle. *R. L. Stine: Creator of Creepy and Spooky Stories* (5–8). Series: Authors Teens Love. 2005, Enslow LB $26.60 (978-0-7660-2445-8). Stine's writing career is the main focus of this biography that includes an interview. (Rev: SLJ 1/06) [921]

STOWE, HARRIET BEECHER

14751 Adler, David A. *A Picture Book of Harriet Beecher Stowe* (2–4). Illus. by Colin Bootman. Series: Picture Book Biographies. 2003, Holiday House $16.95 (978-0-8234-1646-2). 32pp. This picture-book biography uses realistic oil paintings to reinforce the information about this inspiring woman and the injustices of slavery. (Rev: BL 6/1–15/03; HBG 10/03; SLJ 5/03)

14752 Gelletly, LeeAnne. *Harriet Beecher Stowe: Author of Uncle Tom's Cabin* (3–6). 2001, Chelsea LB $25.00 (978-0-7910-6009-4). Easy-to-read information on Stowe's life and work is accompanied by illustrations and sidebars that profile some of her contemporaries, including Harriet Tubman and William Lloyd Garrison. (Rev: SLJ 10/01)

14753 Griskey, Michèle. *Harriet Beecher Stowe* (5–7). Series: Classic Storytellers. 2005, Mitchell Lane LB $29.95 (978-1-58415-375-7). Good historical and social context makes clear the importance of Stowe's achievements. (Rev: SLJ 11/05) [921]

14754 Sonneborn, Liz. *Harriet Beecher Stowe* (5–8). Series: Leaders of the Civil War Era. 2009, Chelsea House $30 (978-1-60413-302-8). 112pp. Enhanced by a mix of illustrations, period documents, photographs, and concise sidebars, this book provides a balanced look at the author who inspired many to support abolitionism. (Rev: LMC 10/09) [921]

TAYLOR, MILDRED

14755 Houghton, Gillian. *Mildred Taylor* (5–8). Series: The Library of Author Biographies. 2005, Rosen LB $27.95 (978-1-4042-0330-3). An interview with Taylor is an interesting addition to this description of the African American author's life and writings. (Rev: SLJ 9/05) [921]

THOMAS, DYLAN

14756 Thomas, Dylan. *A Child's Christmas in Wales* (3–6). Illus. by Chris Raschka. 2004, Candlewick $17.99 (978-0-7636-2161-2). 32pp. This new edition of Thomas's memoir, first published in 1985, of childhood Christmases in Wales features striking artwork in ink and gouache. (Rev: BL 10/1/04; SLJ 10/04)

THOREAU, HENRY DAVID

14757 Thoreau, Henry David. *Henry David's House* (2–4). Ed. by Steven Schnur. Illus. by Peter M. Fiore. 2002, Charlesbridge $16.95 (978-0-88106-116-1). Using Thoreau's words, this picture book describes the construction of his cottage in the woods near Walden Pond. (Rev: BL 4/1/02; HBG 10/02; SLJ 5/02)

TOLKIEN, J. R. R.

14758 Lynch, Doris. *J. R. R. Tolkien* (5–8). Illus. 2003, Watts LB $30.50 (978-0-531-12253-2). 128pp. An attractive biography that reveals how much the author of *The Lord of the Rings* was influenced by his surroundings and experiences. (Rev: BL 12/15/03; SLJ 7/04)

TWAIN, MARK

14759 Aller, Susan Bivin. *Mark Twain* (5–8). Series: A&E Biography. 2001, Lerner LB $27.93 (978-0-8225-4994-9). The colorful life of one of America's favorite authors is re-created in accessible text, black-and-white photographs, and such additions as interesting sidebars and extensive reading lists. (Rev: BL 6/1–15/01; HBG 10/01)

14760 Anderson, William. *River Boy: The Story of Mark Twain* (1–4). Illus. by Dan Andreasen. 2003, HarperCollins LB $17.89 (978-0-06-028401-5). The importance of the Mississippi in Twain's youth is highlighted in this account that includes coverage of his leaving school at the age of 12, working on a steamboat, searching for gold, and his career as a writer and humorist. (Rev: BL 4/15/03; HBG 10/03; SLJ 3/03)

14761 Armentrout, David, and Patricia Armentrout. *Mark Twain* (1–3). Series: Discover the Life of an American Legend. 2004, Rourke LB $14.95 (978-1-58952-660-0). 24pp. An introductory biography that includes period photographs and other illustrations plus a glossary and pronunciation guide. (Rev: SLJ 3/04)

14762 Brown, Don. *American Boy: The Adventures of Mark Twain* (2–6). Illus. by author. 2003, Houghton $16.00 (978-0-618-17997-8). Presented with wit and visual appeal, this biography focuses on Samuel Clemens's youth. (Rev: HBG 4/04; SLJ 9/03)

14763 Burleigh, Robert. *The Adventures of Mark Twain by Huckleberry Finn* (2–4). Illus. by Barry Blitt. 2010, Simon & Schuster $17.99 (978-0-689-83041-9). 48pp. With the expected colorful narration, Huck Finn tells the story of his creator Mark Twain's life; the humorous, old-fashioned illustrations enhance this picture-book biography and inform readers. Lexile AD750L (Rev: BL 2/15/11; SLJ 3/1/11*) [921]

14764 Fleischman, Sid. *The Trouble Begins at 8: A Life of Mark Twain in the Wild, Wild West* (5–8). 2008, Greenwillow $18.99 (978-0-06-134431-2). This is a spirited account of Twain's adventurous early years and how they formed the foundation for his writing. (Rev: BL 6/1–15/08; SLJ 7/08) [921]

14765 Goldsmith, Howard. *Mark Twain at Work!* (PS–2). Illus. by Frank Habbas. Series: Childhood of Famous Americans. 2003, Simon & Schuster paper $3.99 (978-0-689-85399-9). 31pp. A blend of fact and fiction, this profile of Mark Twain's childhood focuses on a real-life fence-painting scam from Twain's youth that was later incorporated into *Tom Sawyer,* one of his most popular novels. (Rev: HBG 10/03; SLJ 8/03)

14766 Lasky, Kathryn. *A Brilliant Streak: The Making of Mark Twain* (4–7). Illus. by Barry Moser. 1998, Harcourt $18.00 (978-0-15-252110-3). Using many quotations and anecdotes from the author's work, this nicely illustrated biography of Mark Twain concentrates on his first 30 years when he was a steamboat pilot, prospector, reporter, and budding writer. (Rev: BCCB 7–8/98; BL 4/1/98; HB 5–6/98; HBG 10/98; SLJ 4/98) [921]

14767 MacLeod, Elizabeth. *Mark Twain: An American Star* (3–5). Series: Snapshots: Images of People and Places in History. 2008, Kids Can $14.95 (978-1-55337-908-9); paper $6.95 (978-1-55337-909-6). 32pp. This large-format introduction to Twain's life features spreads with text and a quotation on the left and a collage of images on the right. (Rev: BL 4/15/08; SLJ 5/08)

14768 Rasmussen, R. Kent. *Mark Twain for Kids: His Life and Times, 21 Activities* (4–7). Series: For Kids. 2004, Chicago Review paper $14.95 (978-1-55652-527-8). An engaging biography that reveals interesting details of Twain's life and shows how many of the episodes in his books were based on his own experiences. (Rev: BL 9/15/04; SLJ 9/04) [921]

14769 Sherman, Josepha. *Mark Twain* (4–6). Series: Classic Storytellers. 2005, Mitchell Lane LB $29.95 (978-1-58415-374-0). 48pp. In addition to recounting Twain's life and career as an author, this volume touches on the pressing social issues of the day. (Rev: SLJ 2/06)

VERNE, JULES

14770 Schoell, William. *Remarkable Journeys: The Story of Jules Verne* (4–8). Series: World Writers. 2002, Morgan Reynolds LB $23.95 (978-1-883846-92-3). Writing was not Verne's first love, as Schoell explains in this accessible biography. (Rev: BL 6/1–15/02; HBG 10/02; SLJ 9/02) [843.8]

14771 Streissguth, Thomas. *Science Fiction Pioneer: A Story About Jules Verne* (3–6). Illus. by Ralph L. Ramstad. 2000, Carolrhoda LB $22.60 (978-1-57505-440-7). 64pp. This biography traces the life and career of this novelist and how he used his interest and knowledge of science in his works. (Rev: HBG 3/01; SLJ 10/00)

14772 Teeters, Peggy. *Jules Verne: The Man Who Invented Tomorrow* (5–7). 1993, Walker LB $14.85 (978-0-8027-8191-8). The life of the famous writer of science fiction, including his childhood in France. (Rev: BL 3/15/93; SLJ 5/93) [921]

WARNER, GERTRUDE CHANDLER

14773 Wheeler, Jill C. *Gertrude Chandler Warner* (2–4). Series: Children's Authors. 2005, ABDO LB $21.35 (978-1-59197-609-7). 24pp. After introducing some of Warner's works, Wheeler discusses the author's childhood and influences on her work. (Rev: SLJ 4/05)

WARREN, MERCY OTIS

14774 Woelfle, Gretchen. *Write On, Mercy! The Secret Life of Mercy Otis Warren* (2–5). Illus. by Alexandra Wallner. 2012, Boyds Mills $16.95 (978-159078822-6). 40pp. A profile of the woman who, at the time of the Revolution, wrote patriotic plays and poems as well as a three-volume history. (Rev: BL 4/15/12; LMC 11–12/12; SLJ 5/1/12) [921]

WHEATLEY, PHILLIS

14775 Gregson, Susan R. *Phillis Wheatley* (4–6). Illus. Series: Let Freedom Ring. 2001, Capstone LB $23.93 (978-0-7368-1033-3). 48pp. Wheatley's early life, education, marriage, and writing career are placed in historical context and accompanied by excerpts of her poems. (Rev: HBG 3/02; SLJ 7/02)

14776 Kent, Deborah. *Phillis Wheatley: First Published African-American Poet* (4–7). Series: Our People. 2003, Child's World LB $27.07 (978-1-59296-009-5). The life of the 18th-century poet is outlined in this well-illustrated work that features large type and includes historical background. (Rev: SLJ 4/04) [921]

14777 McLendon, Jacquelyn. *Phillis Wheatley: A Revolutionary Poet* (4–7). Series: Library of American Lives and Times. 2003, Rosen LB $34.60 (978-0-8239-5750-7). Kidnapped into slavery from Senegal, Phillis Wheatley became a major voice in the American literary scene. (Rev: BL 6/1–15/03; SLJ 5/03) [921]

14778 Salisbury, Cynthia. *Phillis Wheatley: Legendary African-American Poet* (5–8). Series: Historical American Biographies. 2001, Enslow LB $26.60 (978-0-7660-1394-0). The life story of the first important African American poet, who was brought to America as a slave and bought by a Quaker family who allowed her to develop her talents. (Rev: BL 3/1/01; HBG 10/01; SLJ 7/01)

WHITE, E. B.

14779 Bernard, Catherine. *E. B. White: Spinner of Webs and Tales* (5–8). Series: Authors Teens Love. 2005, Enslow LB $26.60 (978-0-7660-2350-5). An introductory chapter that gives a good overview of White's life is followed by chapters that delve into more detail plus a timeline and an excerpt from a 1969 interview that adds a more personal dimension. (Rev: BCCB 12/05; SLJ 10/05) [921]

14780 Craats, Rennay. *E. B. White* (2–4). Series: My Favorite Writer. 2004, Weigl LB $16.95 (978-1-59036-026-2). 32pp. This attractively illustrated profile of the life and career of the author of classics including *Stuart Little* is particularly suitable for report writers. (Rev: BL 4/1/04; HBG 3/03)

14781 Murcia, Rebecca Thatcher. *E. B. White* (5–8). Series: Classic Storytellers. 2004, Mitchell Lane LB $29.95 (978-1-58415-273-6). An introduction to White's life, work, and legacy, with background information on relevant historical, cultural, and economic factors. (Rev: BL 1/05; SLJ 1/05) [921]

WHITMAN, WALT

14782 Kerley, Barbara. *Walt Whitman: Words for America* (4–8). Illus. by Brian Selznick. 2004, Scholastic $16.95 (978-0-439-35791-3). Whitman's experiences during the Civil War, including his service as a nurse to injured and dying soldiers, are highlighted in this picture-book biography. (Rev: BL 11/15/04; SLJ 11/04) [811]

WILDER, LAURA INGALLS

14783 Armentrout, David, and Patricia Armentrout. *Laura Ingalls Wilder* (1–3). Illus. Series: Discover a Life of an American Legend. 2003, Rourke LB $14.95 (978-1-58952-663-1). Young fans of Wilder will enjoy this brief, photo-filled profile. (Rev: BL 2/1/04)

14784 Berne, Emma Carlson. *Laura Ingalls Wilder* (5–8). Series: Essential Lives. 2007, ABDO LB $22.95 (978-1-59928-843-7). The life of the author of the beloved Little House books, with an emphasis on the hard realities that she faced both as a pioneer child and as an adult during the Great Depression. (Rev: BL 2/1/08; SLJ 3/08) [813]

14785 Strudwick, Leslie. *Laura Ingalls Wilder* (2–4). Series: My Favorite Writer. 2003, Weigl LB $18.20 (978-1-59036-027-9). 32pp. This attractively illustrated biography is particularly suitable for report writers. (Rev: SLJ 10/04)

14786 Wadsworth, Ginger. *Laura Ingalls Wilder: Storyteller of the Prairie* (5–8). Series: Biography. 1997, Lerner LB $27.93 (978-0-8225-4950-5). A solid, readable biography of this author that clarifies the chronology in the Little House books. (Rev: BL 3/1/97; SLJ 4/97) [921]

14787 Wilder, Laura Ingalls. *A Little House Traveler: Writings from Laura Ingalls Wilder's Journeys Across America* (5–8). 2006, HarperCollins $16.99 (978-0-06-072491-7). 352pp. Three of Wilder's diaries — one never before published — chronicle the Little House author's travels with her husband Almanzo and daughter Rose. (Rev: BL 12/15/05; VOYA 4/06)

14788 Woods, Mae. *Laura Ingalls Wilder* (2–3). Series: Children's Authors. 2000, ABDO LB $21.35 (978-1-57765-113-0). 24pp. Eight double-page chapters cover Wilder's life from her birth in 1867 to her death in 1957. (Rev: HBG 3/01; SLJ 3/01)

WILLIAMS, WILLIAM CARLOS

14789 Berry, S. L. *William Carlos Williams* (5–9). Illus. by Yan Nascimbene. Series: Voices in Poetry. 2003, Creative LB $19.95 (978-1-58341-284-8). 48pp. This picture-book biography introduces readers to Williams's poetry and life from childhood. (Rev: BL 12/1/03; HBG 4/04)

14790 Bryant, Jen. *A River of Words: The Story of William Carlos Williams* (2–5). Illus. by Melissa Sweet. 2008, Eerdmans $17.00 (978-0-8028-5302-8). 34pp. This picture-book biography neatly integrates the life story of the doctor poet with excerpts of his poems and mixed-media artwork. Caldecott Honor Book, 2009. (Rev: BL 8/08; LMC 3/09; SLJ 9/08)

WONG, JANET S.

14791 Wong, Janet S. *Before It Wriggles Away* (3–5). Illus. Series: Meet the Authors. 2007, Richard C. Owen LB $14.95 (978-1-57274-861-3). 32pp. Introduces the life and work of the children's poet, with her advice on writing. (Rev: BL 6/1–15/07)

WOODSON, JACQUELINE

14792 Hinton, KaaVonia. *Jacqueline Woodson* (5–8). Series: Classic Storytellers. 2008, Mitchell Lane LB $20.95 (978-1-58415-533-1). The story of Woodson's life, from her childhood in the 1960s to her adulthood — including her lesbian relationship — with photographs and discussions of her work. (Rev: BL 3/3/08; SLJ 8/08) [921]

YACCARINO, DAN

14793 Yaccarino, Dan. *All the Way to America: The Story of a Big Italian Family and a Little Shovel* (PS–3). Illus. by author. 2011, Knopf $16.99 (978-0-375-86642-5). 40pp. Yaccarino tells the story of four generations of his family, starting with his great-grandfather, who came to the United States from Italy with a little shovel and a devotion to hard work and enjoying life. (Rev: BL 3/1/11; SLJ 3/1/11*) [921]

YEP, LAURENCE

14794 McGinty, Alice B. *Meet Laurence Yep* (2–3). Series: About the Author. 2003, Rosen LB $21.25 (978-0-8239-6410-9). 24pp. Sample passages, book covers, childhood photographs, and an interview make this an appealing, easy-to-read profile of the Asian American writer and his career. (Rev: SLJ 5/03)

YOLEN, JANE

14795 McGinty, Alice B. *Meet Jane Yolen* (2–4). Illus. Series: About the Author. 2003, Rosen LB $21.25 (978-0-8239-6407-9). 24pp. Readers learn about Yolen's youth and later life and how and why she started writing for children, with excerpts from her books and reprints of covers. (Rev: SLJ 3/03)

ZINDEL, PAUL

14796 Daniel, Susanna. *Paul Zindel* (5–8). Series: The Library of Author Biographies. 2004, Rosen LB $27.95 (978-0-8239-4524-5). Covers Zindel's career as a YA author, with analysis of his work, an interview, and lists of works and awards. (Rev: SLJ 1/05) [921]

Contemporary and Historical Americans

Collective

14797 Adams, Simon. *The Presidents of the United States* (3–7). 2001, Two-Can $16.95 (978-1-58728-093-1); paper $9.95 (978-1-58728-092-4). 96pp. Double-page spreads give basic information on each president, with interesting anecdotes, timelines, full-color portraits, reproductions, and a carefully chosen quotation. (Rev: SLJ 7/01)

14798 Adler, David A. *Enemies of Slavery* (3–6). Illus. by Donald A. Smith. 2004, Holiday House $16.95 (978-0-8234-1596-0). 32pp. Fourteen Americans who played important roles in the fight against slavery are briefly introduced, with relevant quotations, in this picture book for older children. (Rev: BL 10/1/04; SLJ 3/05)

14799 Adler, David A. *Heroes for Civil Rights* (3–5). Illus. by Bill Farnsworth. 2008, Holiday $16.95 (978-0-8234-2008-7). 32pp. Ralph Abernathy, Fannie Lou Hamer, Martin Luther King Jr., and Thurgood Marshall are among the activists profiled in this attractive volume. (Rev: BL 2/1/08; LMC 3/08; SLJ 1/08)

14800 Adler, David A. *Heroes of the Revolution* (1–4). Illus. by Donald A. Smith. 2003, Holiday House $16.95 (978-0-8234-1471-0). 32pp. Among the 12 men and women profiled here are Crispus Attucks, Deborah Sampson, Molly Pitcher, Ethan Allen, and Thomas Jefferson; each entry includes an illustration, birth and death dates, and the person's contributions to the Revolutionary War. (Rev: HBG 4/04; SLJ 11/03)

14801 Ashby, Ruth. *Extraordinary People* (5–8). Series: Civil War Chronicles. 2002, Smart Apple LB $28.50 (978-1-58340-182-8). 48pp. Key military and civilian figures from both North and South are profiled. (Rev: HBG 3/03; SLJ 2/03; VOYA 4/03)

14802 Barber, James, and Amy Pastan. *Presidents and First Ladies* (4–8). 2002, DK paper $12.99 (978-0-7894-8453-6). For each president and his First Lady, there are biographies, a list of key events, and a box highlighting

an important event during that administration, plus plenty of color illustrations. (Rev: BL 4/1/02; HBG 10/02; SLJ 5/02) [920]

14803 Bausum, Ann. *Our Country's First Ladies* (4–8). 2007, National Geographic $19.95 (978-1-4263-0006-6). 128pp. These profiles of America's first ladies provide material for report writers and enough interest for browsers. (Rev: SLJ 1/07)

14804 Beiden, Tonya. *Portraits of African-American Heroes* (3–5). Illus. by Ansel Pitcairn. 2004, Dutton $18.99 (978-0-525-47043-4). Profiles of figures including Dizzy Gillespie and Gwendolyn Brooks use personal memoirs to draw the reader in. (Rev: BL 3/15/04; SLJ 1/04)

14805 Bowdish, Lynea. *With Courage: Seven Women Who Changed America* (4–6). Illus. 2004, Mondo paper $6.95 (978-1-59336-280-5). 48pp. Rachel Carson, Condoleezza Rice, and Maya Lin are among the seven women profiled for their achievements in mainly male-dominated fields. (Rev: BL 3/1/04; SLJ 7/04)

14806 Brown, Monica. *Side by Side / Lado a lado: The Story of Dolores Huerta and Cesar Chavez / La historia de Dolores Huerta y César Chávez* (2–4). Illus. by Joe Cepeda. 2010, HarperCollins $16.99 (978-006122781-3). 32pp. The parallel stories of workers' rights advocates César Chávez and Dolores Huerta are presented in this brightly illustrated bilingual book. (Rev: BL 11/1/10; SLJ 11/10) [920]

14807 Bruning, John Robert. *Elusive Glory: African-American Heroes of World War II* (5–8). Series: Avisson Young Adult. 2001, Avisson paper $19.95 (978-1-888105-48-3). The true stories of African American servicemen, including six Tuskegee Airmen, who served the United States during World War II. (Rev: BL 1/1–15/02; SLJ 4/02) [940.54]

14808 Buller, Jon. *Smart About the Presidents* (4–7). Illus. by authors. Series: Smart About History. 2004, Penguin paper $5.99 (978-0-448-43372-1). Pertinent facts about each president are conveyed in an informative, accessible style. (Rev: BL 9/1/04; SLJ 4/05) [920]

14809 Burgan, Michael. *Great Women of the American Revolution* (4–6). Series: We the People. 2005, Compass Point LB $26.60 (978-0-7565-0838-8). 48pp. Women's exploits and achievements during the Revolutionary War are placed in historical context. (Rev: SLJ 6/05)

14810 Caravantes, Peggy. *Petticoat Spies: Six Women Spies of the Civil War* (5–8). Illus. 2002, Morgan Reynolds LB $23.95 (978-1-883846-88-6). 112pp. An exciting volume about six women who spied for the Union and Confederacy during the Civil War, with photographs, source notes, a glossary, and a bibliography. (Rev: BL 3/15/02; HBG 10/02; SLJ 8/02)

14811 Cheney, Lynne. *A Is for Abigail: An Almanac of Amazing American Women* (2–4). Illus. by Robin P. Glasser. 2003, Simon & Schuster $16.95 (978-0-689-85819-2). 48pp. Cheney celebrates the contributions of American women in all walks of life, from athletes and performers to inventors and scientists. (Rev: BL 2/1/04; HBG 4/04; SLJ 9/03)

14812 Clinton, Catherine. *When Harriet Met Sojourner* (K–3). Illus. by Shane W. Evans. 2007, HarperCollins $16.99 (978-0-06-050425-0). 32pp. In alternating double-page spreads, Clinton presents the often-difficult lives of Harriet Tubman and Sojourner Truth, ending with a hypothetical meeting between the two in 1864. (Rev: BCCB 2/08; BL 10/15/07; SLJ 4/08)

14813 Cook, Michelle, ed. *Our Children Can Soar: A Celebration of Rosa, Barack, and the Pioneers of Change* (PS–3). Illus. by Cozbi A. Cabrera. 2009, Bloomsbury $16.99 (978-1-59990-418-4). With art by 13 well-known children's book illustrators, this well-presented book profiles 11 key African Americans and their importance in bringing equality. (Rev: BL 4/15/09; SLJ 5/09)

14814 Cooper, Ilene. *A Woman in the House (and Senate): How Women Came to the United States Congress, Broke Down Barriers, and Changed the Country* (5–8). Illus. by Elizabeth Baddeley. 2014, Abrams/Amulet $24.95 (978-141971036-0). 144pp. A lively and interesting introduction to the women who have been elected to government over the past century or so. e (Rev: BLO 3/1/14; LMC 10/14*; SLJ 3/14) [920]

14815 Cox, Clinton. *African American Teachers* (4–7). Series: Black Stars. 2000, Wiley $22.95 (978-0-471-24649-7). A collection of short profiles of important African American teachers who have inspired their students and championed the cause of education. (Rev: BL 7/00; HBG 3/01; SLJ 7/00) [920]

14816 Delano, Marfé Ferguson. *American Heroes* (5–8). 2005, National Geographic LB $45.90 (978-0-7922-7215-1). Fifty men and women whose heroism has helped to shape America are profiled in this attractive large-format volume. (Rev: BL 12/1/05; SLJ 2/06) [920.073]

14817 Doherty, Kieran. *Explorers, Missionaries, and Trappers: Trailblazers of the West* (5–8). Series: Shaping America. 2000, Oliver LB $22.95 (978-1-881508-52-6). Nine important pioneers of the American West are

profiled including a Spanish conquistador, two Spanish priests, John Sutter, Marcus and Narcissa Whitman, and Brigham Young. (Rev: HBG 10/00; SLJ 5/00) [920]

14818 Doherty, Kieran. *Voyageurs, Lumberjacks, and Farmers: Pioneers of the Midwest* (5–8). Series: Shaping America. 2004, Oliver LB $22.95 (978-1-881508-54-0). The lives and accomplishments of eight individuals — including Antoine Cadillac, Jean du Sable, and Josiah and Abigail Snelling — who played key roles in the settlement of the Midwest are placed in historical context, with discussion of the plight of Native Americans in the region. (Rev: SLJ 9/04) [920]

14819 Drucker, Malka. *Portraits of Jewish American Heroes* (3–6). Illus. by Elizabeth Rosen. 2008, Dutton $21.99 (978-0-525-47771-6). 96pp. Twenty contemporary and historical Jewish Americans from many walks of life — including such figures as Albert Einstein, Ruth Bader Ginsburg, Steven Speilberg, Levi Strauss, and Daniel Pearl — are presented in brief but imaginatively presented profiles. (Rev: BL 7/08; SLJ 9/08)

14820 Fleischman, John. *Black and White Airmen: Their True History* (5–8). Illus. 2007, Houghton $20.00 (978-0-618-56297-8). 160pp. At a reunion decades later, white bomber pilot Herb Heilbrun and Tuskegee Airman John Leahr discover how much of World War II they shared although separated by segregation. (Rev: BL 2/1/07)

14821 Fradin, Dennis B. *The Founders: The 39 Stories Behind the U.S. Constitution* (4–7). Illus. by Michael McCurdy. 2005, Walker $22.95 (978-0-8027-8972-3). The 39 men who signed the Constitution are profiled in brief chapters that include information on their home states. (Rev: BL 10/15/05; SLJ 9/05) [973.3]

14822 Freedman, Russell. *Abraham Lincoln and Frederick Douglass: The Story Behind an American Friendship* (5–9). Illus. 2012, Clarion $18.99 (978-054738562-4). 128pp. This attractive title offers a glimpse into the respectful friendship that grew between Frederick Douglass and Abraham Lincoln after Emancipation. ALA Notable Children's Book 2013. (Rev: BL 2/1/12*; HB 5–6/12; SLJ 5/1/12*; VOYA 4/12) [920]

14823 Furbee, Mary Rodd. *Outrageous Women of Civil War Times* (3–6). Series: Outrageous Women. 2003, Jossey-Bass paper $12.95 (978-0-471-22926-1). This fascinating collective biography profiles a number of women — some outrageous, others not — who played important roles during the Civil War era; sidebars, photographs, prints, and paintings add appeal. (Rev: BL 10/1/03)

14824 Furbee, Mary Rodd. *Outrageous Women of Colonial America* (3–6). Illus. Series: Outrageous Women. 2001, Wiley paper $12.95 (978-0-471-38299-7). 120pp. Fourteen women are profiled here, in sections on New England, the middle colonies, and the South. (Rev: BL 5/15/01)

14825 Gherman, Beverly. *First Mothers* (2–4). Illus. by Julie Downing. 2012, Clarion $17.99 (978-0-547-22301-8). 64pp. In chronological order, and with lively illustrations and pertinent facts, this volume introduces the mothers of the 44 presidents. Lexile 870L (Rev: BL 11/1/12; LMC 10/12; SLJ 10/12) [920]

14826 Hacker, Carlotta. *Great African Americans in History* (5–8). Series: Outstanding African Americans. 1997, Crabtree LB $22.60 (978-0-86505-805-7); paper $8.95 (978-0-86505-819-4). There are profiles of 13 great African Americans in American history, including Frederick Douglass, Harriet Tubman, W. E. B. Du Bois, Mary McLeod Bethune, and George Washington Carver. (Rev: BL 9/15/97; SLJ 1/98) [920]

14827 Hall, Brianna. *Great Women of the American Revolution* (3–5). Illus. Series: Story of the American Revolution. 2012, Capstone $26.65 (978-1-42968451-4); paper $7.95 (978-1-4296928-4-7). 32pp. With chapters on "Writing for the Revolution," "Women on the March," "Spies in Petticoats," and "Heroines at Home," this volume gives brief introductions to the contributions of a variety of women. (Rev: BL 10/1/12) [920]

14828 Harmon, Rod. *American Civil Rights Leaders* (5–7). Series: Collective Biographies. 2000, Enslow LB $26.60 (978-0-7660-1381-0). 104pp. This collective biography profiles 10 individuals who are currently or once were active in the civil rights movement in the United States. (Rev: BL 12/15/00; HBG 10/01)

14829 Harness, Cheryl. *Rabble Rousers: 20 Women Who Made a Difference* (3–6). Illus. 2003, Dutton $17.99 (978-0-525-47035-9). 64pp. Girls especially will be drawn to these inspiring two-page accounts of feminists ranging from the famous, such as Susan B. Anthony, to less-known figures, including Ann Lee, founder of the Shaker movement, all presented with handsome sepia portraits, timelines, and addresses of relevant organizations. (Rev: BL 1/1–15/03; HBG 10/03; SLJ 1/03)

14830 Harness, Cheryl. *Remember the Ladies* (4–7). Illus. 2001, HarperCollins $16.99 (978-0-688-17017-2). 64pp. Brief profiles of 100 important American women are each accompanied by a portrait. (Rev: BL 4/15/01; HBG 10/01; SLJ 2/01)

14831 Hoose, Phillip. *We Were There, Too! Young People in U.S. History* (5–8). 2001, Farrar $28.00 (978-0-374-38252-0). Hoose tells the stories of dozens of young people who contributed to the making of America — some famous but many who will be new to readers. (Rev: BCCB 10/01; BL 8/01; HB 9–10/01*; HBG 3/02; SLJ 8/01*) [973]

14832 Hudson, Wade, and Valerie Wesley Wilson. *Afro-Bets Book of Black Heroes from A to Z: An Introduction to Important Black Achievers* (4–7). 1988, Just Us paper $7.95 (978-0-940975-02-6). Forty-nine African American men and women of outstanding accomplishment. (Rev: BL 1/1/89; SLJ 12/88) [920]

14833 Hughes, Chris. *The Constitutional Convention* (5–9). Series: People at the Center Of. 2005, Gale LB $24.95 (978-1-56711-918-3). After an overview of the convention, this volume provides biographical information on key figures including George Washington, Benjamin Franklin, James Madison, and Alexander Hamilton. (Rev: SLJ 6/05) [920]

14834 Kimmel, Elizabeth Cody. *Ladies First: 40 Daring American Women Who Were Second to None* (4–7). 2006, National Geographic $18.95 (978-0-7922-5393-8). 192pp. From well-known women such as Sacagawea and Helen Keller to racing driver Shirley Muldowney and rabbi Sally Priesand, this is a well-written and informative resource. (Rev: SLJ 10/06; VOYA 8/06)

14835 Kramer, Barbara. *Trailblazing American Women* (5–7). Series: Collective Biographies. 2000, Enslow LB $26.60 (978-0-7660-1377-3). 112pp. This collection of biographies profiles women who dared to branch out into new fields and break new ground. (Rev: BL 9/15/00; HBG 10/01; SLJ 12/00)

14836 Krohn, Katherine. *Women of the Wild West* (4–6). Series: A&E Biography. 2000, Lerner LB $27.93 (978-0-8225-4980-2). 112pp. Among its several profiles, this book examines the lives of some infamous women of the Wild West: Calamity Jane, Belle Starr, Pearl Hart, and Annie Oakley. (Rev: BL 6/1–15/00; HBG 3/01; SLJ 9/00)

14837 Krull, Kathleen. *Lives of the Presidents: Fame, Shame (and What the Neighbors Thought)* (4–8). Illus. by Kathryn Hewitt. 1998, Harcourt $20.00 (978-0-15-200808-6). An entertaining collective biography that stresses the human side of U.S. presidents, with interesting, insightful tidbits and details that bring the presidents to life. (Rev: BL 8/98; HB 11–12/98; HBG 3/99; SLJ 9/98) [920]

14838 Lindop, Edmund. *Dwight D. Eisenhower, John F. Kennedy, Lyndon B. Johnson* (4–7). Series: Presidents Who Dared. 1996, Twenty-First Century LB $23.90 (978-0-8050-3404-2). The highlights of these three administrations are presented, preceded by an introduction to the American presidency. (Rev: BL 4/15/96; SLJ 6/96) [920]

14839 Lindop, Edmund. *George Washington, Thomas Jefferson, Andrew Jackson* (4–7). Series: Presidents Who Dared. 1995, Twenty-First Century LB $23.90 (978-0-8050-3401-1). After a general introduction on the duties of the president, brief biographies of three are given, with emphasis on their accomplishments in office. (Rev: BL 1/1–15/96; SLJ 11/95) [920]

14840 Lindop, Edmund. *James K. Polk, Abraham Lincoln, Theodore Roosevelt* (4–7). Series: Presidents Who Dared. 1995, Twenty-First Century LB $23.90 (978-0-8050-3402-8). Highlights and evaluations of the presidencies of Polk, Lincoln, and Theodore Roosevelt. (Rev: BL 1/1–15/96; SLJ 11/95) [920]

14841 Lindop, Edmund. *Richard M. Nixon, Jimmy Carter, Ronald Reagan* (4–8). Series: Presidents Who Dared. 1996, Twenty-First Century LB $23.90 (978-0-8050-3405-9). This account traces salient events in each of these presidents' terms, for example: Nixon and Watergate and relations with China; Carter and ending the war between Egypt and Israel; and Reagan and his arms agreement with the Soviet Union. (Rev: BL 4/15/96; SLJ 6/96) [920]

14842 Lindop, Edmund. *Woodrow Wilson, Franklin D. Roosevelt, Harry S. Truman* (5–8). Series: Presidents Who Dared. 1995, Twenty-First Century LB $23.90 (978-0-8050-3403-5). After an overview of the presidency and brief profiles of these men, this account looks at daring decisions they made as presidents. (Rev: BL 1/1–15/96; SLJ 11/95; VOYA 6/96) [920]

14843 Lynne, Douglas. *Contemporary United States: 1968 to the Present* (5–8). Illus. Series: Presidents of the United States. 2007, Weigl LB $20.35 (978-1-59036-753-7). The lives and times of recent U.S. presidents — from Nixon to George W. Bush — are covered in this eighth volume in the series. (Rev: BL 10/15/07) [973.92092]

14844 McLean, Jacqueline. *Women with Wings* (4–7). Series: Profiles. 2001, Oliver $19.95 (978-1-881508-70-0). An absorbing account of the achievements of women pilots, including Bessie Coleman, Amelia Earhart, and Anne Morrow Lindbergh. (Rev: BL 5/15/01; HBG 10/01; SLJ 10/01) [629.13]

14845 Marvis, Barbara. *Famous People of Asian Ancestry, Vol. 4* (4–7). Series: Contemporary American Success Stories. 1994, Mitchell Lane paper $10.95 (978-1-883845-09-4). A collective biography of Asian Americans, including actor Dustin Nguyen, novelist Amy Tan, and businessman Rocky Aoki. Also use volumes 1 through 3 (2nd ed., 1997). (Rev: BL 10/1/94; SLJ 11/94) [920]

14846 Marvis, Barbara. *Famous People of Hispanic Heritage, Vol. 4* (5–9). 1996, Mitchell Lane paper $12.95 (978-1-883845-29-2). The lives of two Hispanic men and two women who have succeeded in their careers are presented in an easy-to-read style. Other volumes in this series by the same author are available. (Rev: BL 12/15/96; SLJ 1/97; VOYA 2/97) [920]

14847 Masters, Nancy Robinson. *Extraordinary Patriots of the United States of America: Colonial Times to Pre-Civil War* (5–8). Series: Extraordinary People. 2005, Children's Pr. LB $40.00 (978-0-516-24404-4). Interesting 3- to 5-page profiles are arranged chronologically by year of birth. (Rev: SLJ 2/06) [920]

14848 Morin, Isobel V. *Women Chosen for Public Office* (5–7). 1995, Oliver LB $19.95 (978-1-881508-20-5). Nine biographies of women who are involved in the federal government from the superintendent of army nurses to Supreme Court Justice Ruth Bader Ginsburg. (Rev: BL 5/1/95; SLJ 6/95) [920]

14849 Morris, Juddi. *At Home with the Presidents* (4–8). 1999, Wiley paper $13.95 (978-0-471-25300-6). In three to five pages each, this account profiles the presidents of the United States from Washington through Clinton. (Rev: SLJ 3/00) [920]

14850 Morrison, Jessica. *Military* (4–7). Illus. Series: Great African Americans. 2011, Weigl LB $20.99 (978-161690661-0); paper $14.95 (978-161690665-8). 48pp. African Americans who played pivotal roles in America's wars, from the Revolution to Iraq and Afghanistan

are portrayed in this inspiring title. (Rev: BL 2/1/12) [920]

14851 Munson, Sammye. *Today's Tejano Heroes* (5–8). 2000, Eakin $13.95 (978-1-57168-328-1). In alphabetical order, this volume introduces 16 important 20th-century Mexican Americans who have contributed to the history and culture of Texas, including Vikki Carr, Attorney General Dan Morales, and federal judge Hilda Tagle. (Rev: BL 2/1/01) [920]

14852 Obama, Barack. *Of Thee I Sing: A Letter to My Daughters* (K–3). Illus. by Loren Long. 2010, Knopf $17.99 (978-0-375-83527-8); LB $20.99 (978-0-375-93527-5). 40pp. Obama uses the framework of a letter to his daughters to introduce 13 famous Americans who exemplify various virtues. (Rev: BLO 11/15/10*; SLJ 1/1/11) [920]

14853 O'Connor, Jane. *If the Walls Could Talk: Family Life at the White House* (4–7). Illus. by Gary Hovland. 2004, Simon & Schuster $16.95 (978-0-689-86863-4). This inside view of family life within the White House — with caricatures and interesting trivia — is similar to Judith St. George's *So You Want to Be President* (Putnam, 2000). (Rev: BL 8/04; SLJ 9/04)

14854 Pinkney, Andrea Davis. *Let It Shine: Stories of Black Women Freedom Fighters* (5–8). 2000, Harcourt $20.00 (978-0-15-201005-8). This work contains chatty profiles of 10 important African American women, including Sojourner Truth, Rosa Parks, and Shirley Chisholm. (Rev: BCCB 11/00; BL 11/15/00; HB 11–12/00; HBG 3/01; SLJ 10/00; VOYA 12/00) [921]

14855 *Presidents of the United States* (3–6). Illus. Series: Time for Kids. 2006, HarperCollins $17.99 (978-0-06-081554-7). 70pp. Following a discussion of the three branches of government, this browsable volume covers the presidents in chronological order, giving basic personal information and a portrait, political cartoons, notable quotations, and so forth; several presidents are selected for more in-depth information. (Rev: SLJ 10/06)

14856 Raatma, Lucia. *Great Women of the Civil War* (4–6). Series: We the People. 2005, Compass Point LB $26.60 (978-0-7565-0839-5). 48pp. Women's exploits and achievements during the Civil War are placed in historical context. (Rev: BL 5/15/04; HBG 3/98; SLJ 6/05)

14857 Rappaport, Doreen. *In the Promised Land: Lives of Jewish Americans* (4–7). Illus. by Cornelius Van Wright. 2005, HarperCollins LB $16.89 (978-0-06-059395-7). A look at the lives and diverse accomplishments of 13 notable Jewish Americans, including Asser Levy, Harry Houdini, Jonas Salk, and Steven Spielberg. (Rev: BL 1/1–15/05; SLJ 5/05) [920]

14858 Rappaport, Doreen. *We Are the Many: A Picture Book of American Indians* (K–3). Illus. by Cornelius Van Wright and Ying-Hwa Hu. 2002, HarperCollins LB $17.89 (978-0-06-001139-0). 32pp. A collection of 13 brief biographies of Native Americans from different tribes, including Tisquantum (Squanto), Jim Thorpe, and Maria Tallchief. (Rev: BL 10/15/02; HBG 3/03; SLJ 9/02)

14859 Ringstad, Arnold. *Weird-But-True Facts about U.S. Presidents* (1–3). Illus. by Mernie Gallasher-Cole. 2013, Child's World LB $27.07 (978-1-61473-422-2). 32pp. With cartoon illustrations and brief entries on each spread, this volume presents interesting information in an appealing format. **e** (Rev: BL 4/1/13; LMC 11–12/13; SLJ 4/13)

14860 Roop, Connie, and Peter Roop. *Tales of Famous Americans* (3–5). Illus. by Charlie Powell. 2007, Scholastic $17.99 (978-0-439-64116-6). 112pp. With caricatures and anecdotes from their childhoods, this volume introduces figures ranging from George Washington and Pocahontas to Mia Hamm and Yo-Yo Ma. (Rev: BL 11/15/07; SLJ 2/08)

14861 Rosenberg, Aaron. *The Civil War: One Event, Six People* (4–6). Illus. Series: Profiles. 2011, Scholastic paper $6.99 (978-05452375-6-7). 160pp. This collective biography introduces six key players in the Civil War — Abraham Lincoln, Frederick Douglass, Clara Barton, George McClellan, Robert E. Lee, and Mathew Brady — and looks at their importance and influence. (Rev: BL 6/1/11; SLJ 6/11) [920]

14862 Sullivan, Otha Richard. *African American Millionaires* (5–10). Series: Black Stars. 2004, Wiley $24.95 (978-0-471-46928-5). Tyra Banks and Oprah Winfrey are included here, but so are many names that may be unfamiliar to readers, such as William Alexander Leidesdorff and Annie Turnbo Malone. (Rev: SLJ 5/05) [920]

14863 Thimmesh, Catherine. *Madam President: The Extraordinary, True (and Evolving) Story of Women in Politics. Rev. ed.* (4–7). Illus. by Douglas B. Jones. 2008, Houghton Mifflin $17.00 (978-0-618-39666-5); paper $8.95 (978-0-618-97143-5). This update includes profiles of more than 20 women who have been influential in the political arena, including Margaret Chase Smith, Sirimavo Bandaranaike, Margaret Thatcher, Nancy Pelosi, Hillary Clinton, and Condoleezza Rice. (Rev: BL 10/1/04; SLJ 5/08) [920]

14864 Thomson, Sarah L. *What Presidents Are Made Of* (2–4). Illus. by Hanoch Piven. 2004, Simon & Schuster $15.95 (978-0-689-86880-1). Collage caricatures and brief text give wry and unusual portraits of 17 of America's presidents and their outstanding characteristics or interests. (Rev: BL 8/04; SLJ 8/04)

14865 Waldman, Neil. *A Land of Big Dreamers: Voices of Courage in America* (3–5). Illus. by author. 2011, Millbrook $16.95 (978-0-8225-6810-0). 32pp. Thirteen Americans who have shown courage in the face of adversity are represented here in quotations, brief facts, and portraits. (Rev: BL 2/15/11; SLJ 3/1/11) [973]

14866 Warren, Andrea. *We Rode the Orphan Trains* (4–8). 2001, Houghton Mifflin $18.00 (978-0-618-11712-3). Eight moving biographical accounts of men and women, now in their 80s and 90s, who traveled to the Midwest to find new homes and families. (Rev: BCCB 11/01; BL 11/1/01; HBG 3/02; SLJ 11/01; VOYA 12/01) [362.73]

14867 Wheeler, Jill C. *America's Leaders* (4–7). Series: War on Terrorism. 2002, ABDO LB $25.65 (978-1-

57765-661-6). This book contains brief profiles of important American figures in the war against terrorism such as President Bush, Colin Powell, John Ashcroft, and Rudy Giuliani. (Rev: BL 5/15/02; HBG 10/02) [920]

14868 Winter, Jonah. *Wild Women of the Wild West* (3–5). Illus. by Susan Guevara. 2011, Holiday House $16.95 (978-0-8234-1601-1). 40pp. Calamity Jane, Belle Starr, and Annie Oakley are among the 15 women profiled here for their contributions on the western frontier. (Rev: BL 12/1/11; SLJ 11/1/11) [920]

African Americans

BETHUNE, MARY MCLEOD

14869 McKissack, Patricia C., and Fredrick McKissack. *Mary McLeod Bethune: A Great Teacher. Rev. ed.* (2–4). Series: Great African Americans. 2001, Enslow LB $18.60 (978-0-7660-1680-4). An updated biography of the former slave who dedicated her life to the education of African Americans, with new illustrations. (Rev: HBG 3/02; SLJ 5/02)

14870 McKissack, Patricia C., and Fredrick McKissack. *Mary McLeod Bethune: Woman of Courage* (3–5). Illus. Series: Famous African Americans. 2013, Enslow LB $21.26 (978-0-7660-4103-5). 24pp. An accessible account of Bethune's life in five easy chapters with a selection of images. (Rev: BL 4/1/13; LMC 10/13; SLJ 4/13) [921]

14871 Somervill, Barbara A. *Mary McLeod Bethune: African-American Educator* (4–7). Series: Our People. 2003, Child's World LB $27.07 (978-1-59296-008-8). A profile of the African American educator and leader, with sidebars that add historical context. (Rev: SLJ 4/04) [921]

BRIDGES, RUBY

14872 Donaldson, Madeline. *Ruby Bridges* (3–6). Illus. 2009, Lerner LB $27.93 (978-0-7613-4220-5). 48pp. Tells the story of the first African American student to attend a newly integrated school in New Orleans in 1960, with information on Bridges's recent activism. (Rev: BL 2/1/10; SLJ 9/1/09) [921]

BUNCHE, RALPH J.

14873 McKissack, Patricia C., and Fredrick McKissack. *Ralph J. Bunche: Peacemaker. Rev. ed.* (2–4). Series: Great African Americans. 2002, Enslow LB $18.60 (978-0-7660-1701-6). 32pp. The inspiring story of the African American diplomat who was active in UN affairs and won the Nobel Peace Prize in 1950. (Rev: BL 7/02; HBG 10/02)

CARY, MARY ANN SHADD

14874 Ferris, Jeri Chase. *Demanding Justice: A Story About Mary Ann Shadd Cary* (2–4). Illus. by Kimanne

Smith. Series: Creative Minds Biographies. 2003, Carolrhoda LB $22.60 (978-1-57505-177-2); paper $6.95 (978-0-87614-928-7). 64pp. Cary was a free black woman who worked as a teacher and lawyer during the 18th century and sought to improve the lives of other African Americans. (Rev: HBG 10/03; SLJ 8/03)

CRANDALL, PRUDENCE

14875 Jurmain, Suzanne. *The Forbidden Schoolhouse: The True and Dramatic Story of Prudence Crandall and Her Students* (5–8). 2005, Houghton Mifflin $19.00 (978-0-618-47302-1). The inspiring story of Prudence Crandall, who in the 1830s risked ostracism — and worse — from the townspeople of Canterbury, Connecticut, when she opens her academy to young African American women. (Rev: BCCB 11/05; BL 10/1/05*; HB 11–12/05; HBG 4/06; LMC 8–9/05; SLJ 11/05) [370]

14876 Lucas, Eileen. *Prudence Crandall: Teacher for Equal Rights* (1–3). Illus. by Kimanne Smith. 2001, Carolrhoda LB $21.27 (978-1-57505-480-3). 48pp. A biography for beginning readers of Crandall, a Quaker teacher who struggled to run a school for African American students in the 1830s. (Rev: HBG 3/02; SLJ 1/02)

DESMOND, VIOLA

14877 Warner, Jody Nyasha. *Viola Desmond Won't Be Budged!* (2–4). Illus. by Richard Rudnicki. 2010, Groundwood $18.95 (978-0-88899-779-1). Unpaged. This book tells the story of a Canadian black woman who refused to move her seat in a movie theater in 1946. (Rev: BL 11/15/10; LMC 1–2/11; SLJ 12/1/10) [921]

DOUGLASS, FREDERICK

14878 Cline-Ransome, Lesa. *Words Set Me Free: The Story of Young Frederick Douglass* (2–4). Illus. by James E. Ransome. 2012, Simon & Schuster $16.99 (978-141695903-8). 32pp. This picture-book biography of Frederick Douglass emphasizes how learning to read enhanced his life. (Rev: BL 3/15/12) [921]

14879 Lutz, Norma Jean. *Frederick Douglass: Abolitionist and Author* (3–5). Illus. 2001, Chelsea $25.00 (978-0-7910-6003-2); paper $8.95 (978-0-7910-6141-1). This brief introduction to the life of the abolitionist includes material on his youth and education. (Rev: BL 5/1/01)

14880 McKissack, Patricia C., and Fredrick McKissack. *Frederick Douglass: Leader Against Slavery. Rev. ed.* (2–4). Illus. Series: Great African Americans. 2002, Enslow LB $18.60 (978-0-7660-1696-5). 32pp. An updated version of a previously released biography about the slave-turned-abolitionist, which includes archival photographs and Web site information. (Rev: BL 2/15/02; SLJ 5/02)

14881 Sanders, Nancy I. *Frederick Douglass for Kids: His Life and Times, with 21 Activities* (4–7). Illus. 2012, Chicago Review $16.95 (978-156976717-7). 144pp. Activities ranging from making a hat and a cravat to making a paste to keep flies away extend the scope of this informative profile of the orator and abolitionist. **e** (Rev: BL 6/12; LMC 3–4/13*; SLJ 7/12) [921]

14882 Schuman, Michael A. *Frederick Douglass: "Truth Is of No Color"* (4–8). Illus. 2009, Enslow LB $23.95 (978-0-7660-3025-1). This biography tracks the famous abolitionist's life from his childhood escape from slavery into his adult years. (Rev: BL 6/1/09; LMC 11–12/09; SLJ 9/09) [921]

14883 Slade, Suzanne. *Frederick Douglass: Writer, Speaker, and Opponent of Slavery* (K–3). Illus. by Robert McGuire. Series: Biographies. 2007, Picture Window LB $23.93 (978-1-4048-3102-5). 24pp. Beginning readers will benefit from this simple biography of the outspoken abolitionist, with color illustrations. (Rev: SLJ 8/07)

14884 Sterngass, John. *Frederick Douglass* (5–8). Series: Leaders of the Civil War Era. 2009, Chelsea House $30 (978-1-60413-306-6). 112pp. Enhanced by a mix of illustrations, period documents, photographs, and concise sidebars, this book provides a balanced look at the eloquent man who galvanized many in the fight against slavery. (Rev: LMC 10/09) [921]

EVERS, MEDGAR

14885 St. Lawrence, Genevieve. *Medgar Evers* (3–5). Illus. Series: African-American Biographies. 2003, Raintree LB $28.56 (978-0-7398-7028-0). 64pp. An account of the short life of the civil rights leader who was assassinated at the age of 37. (Rev: BL 1/1–15/04; HBG 4/04)

FORTEN, JAMES

14886 Figley, Marty Rhodes. *Prisoner for Liberty* (2–4). Illus. by Craig Orback. Series: On My Own History. 2008, Lerner LB $25.26 (978-0-8225-7280-0); paper $6.95 (978-0-8225-9022-4). For early readers, this is the story of a 15-year-old African American, James Forten, who in the Revolutionary War rejected the chance to escape imprisonment because he was helping a white friend; Forten's later contributions are covered in an Afterword. (Rev: BL 1/1–15/08; SLJ 8/08)

14887 Krebs, Laurie. *A Day in the Life of a Colonial Sailmaker* (2–3). Series: The Library of Living and Working in Colonial Times. 2004, Rosen LB $19.95 (978-0-8239-6231-0). 24pp. Fact and fiction are interwoven as James Forten, an African American living in Philadelphia who became a wealthy man through his innovative sails, goes about his daily business. (Rev: BL 9/1/04)

HAMER, FANNIE LOU

14888 Donovan, Sandy. *Fannie Lou Hamer* (3–5). Illus. Series: African-American Biographies. 2003, Raintree LB $28.56 (978-0-7398-7030-3). 64pp. The life of the woman, the youngest of 20 children of a Mississippi sharecropper, who become a civil rights activist. (Rev: BL 1/1–15/04)

14889 Fiorelli, June Estep. *Fannie Lou Hamer: A Voice for Freedom* (5–10). Series: Avisson Young Adult. 2005, Avisson paper $19.95 (978-1-888105-62-9). Hamer's life, including her youth, are described and placed in the context of events in the United States at the time. (Rev: SLJ 2/06) [921]

HOLMES, BENJAMIN C.

14890 Sherman, Pat. *Ben and the Emancipation Proclamation* (1–3). Illus. by Floyd Cooper. 2010, Eerdmans $16.99 (978-0-8028-5319-6). 32pp. Tells the story of Benjamin Holmes, who surreptitiously learned to read while a young slave, and displayed this talent when a fellow slave prison inmate acquired a copy of the newspaper containing Lincoln's Emancipation Proclamation. (Rev: BL 2/15/10; LMC 10/10; SLJ 2/1/10) [921]

JACKSON, JESSE

14891 Linde, Barbara. *Jesse Jackson* (2–5). Illus. Series: Civil Rights Crusaders. 2011, Gareth Stevens LB $22.60 (978-143395682-9). 24pp. Covers Jackson's involvement in civil rights, his campaign for president, and his subsequent political work. (Rev: BL 10/1/11) [921]

14892 Mis, Melody S. *Meet Jesse Jackson* (2–4). Illus. Series: Civil Rights Leaders. 2008, Rosen $15.95 (978-1-4042-4212-8). 24pp. Jackson's life and accomplishments are placed in the larger context of the civil rights movement. (Rev: BL 6/1–15/08)

14893 Steffens, Bradley, and Dan Wood. *Jesse Jackson* (5–8). Series: People in the News. 2000, Lucent LB $32.45 (978-1-56006-631-6). 126pp. This well-documented look at the life of the religious and civil rights leader gives interesting information on the events and people who influenced him. (Rev: BL 6/1–15/00; HBG 10/00)

JACOBS, HARRIET A.

14894 Fleischner, Jennifer. *I Was Born a Slave: The Story of Harriet Jacobs* (4–8). 1997, Millbrook LB $26.90 (978-0-7613-0111-0). The turbulent life of Harriet Jacobs, who was born into slavery and lived for many years as a fugitive before winning her freedom and becoming an abolitionist. (Rev: BL 9/15/97; HBG 3/98; SLJ 1/98) [921]

KING, CORETTA SCOTT

14895 Bankston, John. *Coretta Scott King and the Story Behind the Coretta Scott King Award* (4–8). Series: Great Achievement Awards. 2003, Mitchell Lane LB $29.95 (978-1-58415-202-6). The story of the widow of Martin Luther King, Jr., her continuing fight for civil rights, and the children's book prize named after her are covered in this biography. (Rev: BL 10/15/03; SLJ 10/03) [921]

14896 Mattern, Joanne. *Coretta Scott King: Civil Rights Activist* (1–3). Illus. Series: Women Who Shaped History. 2003, Rosen LB $19.95 (978-0-8239-6504-5). 24pp. The life of Coretta Scott King, for new readers. (Rev: BL 2/15/03)

14897 Shange, Ntozake. *Coretta Scott* (K–3). Illus. by Kadir Nelson. 2009, Amistad $17.99 (978-0-06-125364-5). 32pp. This artful biography blends simple elegant verse with glowing illustrations to highlight Coretta Scott's life from her childhood days to her civil rights work with her husband, Martin Luther King, Jr. (Rev: BCCB 2/09; BL 1/1–15/09; LMC 10/09; SLJ 1/09)

KING, MARTIN LUTHER, JR.

14898 Adler, David A. *Dr. Martin Luther King, Jr.* (1–3). Illus. by Colin Bootman. Series: Holiday House Reader. 2001, Holiday House $15.95 (978-0-8234-1572-4). A brief account of King's life, achievements, and legacy that will also appeal to older children who are having difficulties reading. (Rev: BL 7/01; SLJ 6/01)

14899 Brown, Jonatha A. *Martin Luther King, Jr.* (2–4). Illus. Series: People We Should Know. 2005, Gareth Stevens LB $21.00 (978-0-8368-4467-2). 24pp. For beginning readers, a simple explanation of King's importance with attractive layout and historical and contemporary photographs. [921]

14900 Bunting, Eve. *The Cart That Carried Martin* (1–4). Illus. by Don Tate. 2013, Charlesbridge $16.95 (978-158089387-9). 32pp. Martin Luther King, Jr.'s funeral procession is the focus of this book, in particular the wooden cart that was pulled by two mules as onlookers sang hymns. **e** (Rev: BL 11/1/13*; LMC 5–6/14; SLJ 11/13) [921]

14901 Darby, Jean. *Martin Luther King, Jr.* (4–8). Series: Lerner Biographies. 1990, Lerner LB $27.93 (978-0-8225-4902-4). An in-depth look at King's life and the civil rights movement. (Rev: BL 7/90; SLJ 11/90) [921]

14902 Farris, Christine King. *March On!* (2–5). Illus. by London Ladd. 2008, Scholastic $17.99 (978-0-545-03537-8). 32pp. A compelling picture book by Martin Luther King Jr.'s older sister, highlighting their childhood together and the 1963 March on Washington. (Rev: BL 8/08)

14903 Farris, Christine King. *My Brother Martin* (K–3). Illus. by Chris Soentpiet. 2003, Simon & Schuster $17.95 (978-0-689-84387-7). 40pp. A fond biography of Dr. Martin Luther King, Jr., by his older sister. (Rev: BL 2/15/03; HB 3/03; HBG 10/03; SLJ 2/03)

14904 January, Brendan. *Martin Luther King Jr.: Minister and Civil Rights Activist* (4–8). Series: Ferguson Career Biographies. 2001, Ferguson LB $25.00 (978-0-89434-342-1). This concise account focuses on King's career as a minister as well as his work as an advocate of civil rights and includes a section on training for the ministry. (Rev: SLJ 4/01)

14905 Jazynka, Kitson. *Martin Luther King, Jr.* (1–3). Illus. 2013, National Geographic LB $13.90 (978-142631060-7); paper $3.99 (9781426310874). 48pp. This brief biography for beginning readers introduces key facts and King's childhood, studies, and contributions, placing him in historical context. (Rev: BL 2/1/13; LMC 11–12/13) [921]

14906 King, Martin Luther, III. *My Daddy, Dr. Martin Luther King, Jr.* (K–3). Illus. by AG Ford. 2013, Amistad $17.99 (978-0-06-028075-8). 40pp. A picture-book memoir of growing up with a famous and committed father, by the second child of the civil rights leader. (Rev: BL 6/13; SLJ 8/13) [921]

14907 Leslie, Tonya. *Martin Luther King, Jr.: A Life of Fairness* (1–3). Illus. by Tina Walski. Series: Blastoff! Readers: People of Character. 2007, Children's Pr. LB

$20.00 (978-0-531-14712-2). 24pp. For beginning readers, this is a simple account of King's life and importance. (Rev: SLJ 1/08)

14908 Lowery, Linda. *Martin Luther King Day* (2–4). Illus. by Hetty Mitchell. 2003, Turtleback LB $17.15 (978-0-87614-299-8). 56pp. Presents the origins of the holiday and discusses the key points of Dr. King's life. (Rev: BL 4/1/87; SLJ 6–7/87)

14909 McKissack, Patricia C., and Fredrick McKissack. *Martin Luther King, Jr.: Man of Peace Rev. ed.* (2–4). Series: Great African Americans. 2001, Enslow LB $18.60 (978-0-7660-1678-1). A newly illustrated edition of this title that includes information on King's early life. (Rev: HBG 3/02; SLJ 5/02)

14910 McLeese, Don. *Martin Luther King, Jr.* (2–5). Series: Equal Rights Leaders. 2002, Rourke LB $20.64 (978-1-58952-286-2). 24pp. Simple text and well-chosen illustrations tell the story of King's life, with good coverage of his youth and education. (Rev: SLJ 1/03)

14911 Myers, Walter Dean. *I've Seen the Promised Land: The Life of Dr. Martin Luther King, Jr.* (1–4). Illus. by Leonard Jenkins. 2004, HarperCollins LB $17.89 (978-0-06-027704-8). A moving and well-illustrated picture-book biography that covers King's political and private lives. (Rev: SLJ 4/04)

14912 Pastan, Amy. *Martin Luther King, Jr.* (5–10). Illus. Series: DK Biography. 2004, DK LB $14.99 (978-0-7566-0491-2); paper $4.99 (978-0-7566-0342-7). 128pp. A heavily illustrated, attractive biography of King that offers broad historical background. (Rev: BL 6/1–15/04)

14913 Patrick, Denise Lewis. *A Lesson for Martin Luther King Jr.* (K–2). Illus. by Rodney S. Pate. Series: Childhood of Famous Americans. 2003, Simon & Schuster paper $3.99 (978-0-689-85397-5). 32pp. A childhood event that helped Martin Luther King Jr. to define his mission in life is the focus of this slim volume. (Rev: HBG 4/04; SLJ 2/04)

14914 Rappaport, Doreen. *Martin's Big Words* (PS–4). Illus. by Bryan Collier. 2007, Hyperion paper $6.99 (978-1-4231-0635-7). 32pp. This picture-book biography interweaves King's own words and a simple narrative to create an inspiring portrait of the man. A paperback edition of the 2001 book that won the 2002 Caldecott Medal. (Rev: BL 10/1/01*; HB 1/02; SLJ 10/01)

14915 Watkins, Angela Farris. *My Uncle Martin's Big Heart* (PS–2). Illus. by Eric Velasquez. 2010, Abrams $18.95 (978-0-8109-8975-7). 32pp. Dr. Martin Luther King's niece tells the happy, gentle story of her relationship with her famous uncle. Lexile AD820L (Rev: BL 9/1/10; LMC 1–2/11; SLJ 10/1/10) [323.092]

14916 Watkins, Angela Farris. *My Uncle Martin's Words for America* (K–4). Illus. by Eric Velasquez. 2011, Abrams $19.95 (978-1-4197-0022-4). 40pp. Referring to key words used in his speeches, Martin Luther King Jr.'s niece describes her uncle's beliefs and work. (Rev: BLO 1/12; SLJ 10/1/11) [921]

LAW, WESTLEY WALLACE

14917 Haskins, James. *Delivering Justice: W. W. Law and the Fight for Civil Rights* (2–4). Illus. by Benny Andrews. 2005, Candlewick $16.99 (978-0-7636-2592-4). A picture-book biography of Westley Wallace Law that chronicles the mail carrier's campaign to win equal treatment for African Americans in his hometown of Savannah, Georgia. (Rev: BL 9/15/05)

LEWIS, JOHN

14918 Haskins, James, and Kathleen Benson. *John Lewis in the Lead: A Story of the Civil Rights Movement* (3–5). Illus. by Benny Andrews. 2006, Lee & Low $17.95 (978-1-58430-250-6). 40pp. This picture-book biography for older readers covers Lewis's civil rights activism, including his role in "Bloody Sunday" in Selma, Alabama, and his political career. (Rev: BL 10/1/06; SLJ 12/06)

LYON, MARITCHA REYMOND

14919 Bolden, Tonya. *Maritcha: A Nineteenth-Century American Girl* (4–7). 2005, Abrams $17.95 (978-0-8109-5045-0). Drawing on primary sources, Bolden tells the story of Maritcha Remond Lyon, a free black girl who succeeded in her fight to attend an all-white high school in Rhode Island in the mid-19th century. Coretta Scott King Illustrator Award and Author Honor Book 2006. (Rev: BL 2/1/05*; SLJ 2/05) [921]

MALCOLM X

14920 Adoff, Arnold. *Malcolm X. Rev. ed.* (3–6). Illus. 2000, HarperCollins paper $4.99 (978-0-06-442118-8). 64pp. This clearly written biography reflects the intense drama of the African American leader's life and death. (Rev: BL 2/15/00)

14921 Benson, Michael. *Malcolm X* (5–8). Series: Biography. 2001, Lerner LB $27.93 (978-0-8225-5025-9). An accessible text and many photographs are used to enliven this biography of the African American civil rights leader who was assassinated in 1965. (Rev: BL 4/1/02; HBG 3/02; SLJ 3/02)

14922 Graves, Renee. *Malcolm X* (3–5). Series: Cornerstones of Freedom. 2003, Children's Pr. LB $26.00 (978-0-516-24224-8). 48pp. A vivid, well-written life of the African American leader. (Rev: SLJ 2/04)

MARSHALL, THURGOOD

14923 Frost, Helen. *Thurgood Marshall* (K–2). Illus. Series: Famous Americans. 2003, Capstone LB $17.26 (978-0-7368-1643-4). This brief biography of Thurgood Marshall introduces young readers to the life and career of the African American attorney who helped bring an end to school segregation and was later appointed to the U.S. Supreme Court. (Rev: HBG 10/03; SLJ 11/03)

14924 Taylor-Butler, Christine. *Thurgood Marshall* (1–2). Series: Rookie Biographies. 2006, Children's Pr. LB $20.50 (978-0-516-25015-1); paper $4.95 (978-0-516-27099-9). 32pp. For beginning readers, this is a simple introduction to the life of the African American jurist from his childhood in Baltimore to his appointment to the U.S. Supreme Court. (Rev: SLJ 9/06)

MASON, BIDDY

14925 Williams, Jean Kinney. *Bridget "Biddy" Mason: From Slave to Businesswoman* (4–6). Illus. Series: Signature Lives: American Frontier Era. 2005, Compass Point $34.60 (978-0-7565-1001-5). 112pp. A life of Bridget "Biddy" Mason, who was born a slave in 1818, traveled west with her Mormon master, gained her freedom, and died in 1891 as one of the richest women in Los Angeles. (Rev: BL 10/15/05; SLJ 3/06; VOYA 6/06)

NORTHUP, SOLOMON

14926 Fradin, Judith Bloom, and Dennis Brindell Fradin. *Stolen into Slavery: The True Story of Solomon Northup, Free Black Man* (5–8). Illus. 2012, National Geographic $18.95 (978-142630937-3); LB $27.90 (978-142630938-0). 128pp. Drawing on his memoir, this dramatic story tells of free black man Northup's ordeal after he was kidnapped and sold into slavery in 1841. **e** (Rev: BL 2/1/12; SLJ 4/12) [921]

PARKS, ROSA

14927 Collard, Sneed B., III. *Rosa Parks: The Courage to Make a Difference* (3–5). Series: American Heroes. 2006, Benchmark LB $28.50 (978-0-7614-2163-4). Parks's life and contributions are clearly described in large typeface and illustrations. (Rev: SLJ 3/07)

14928 Davis, Kenneth C. *Don't Know Much About Rosa Parks* (4–7). Illus. by Sergio Martinez. Series: Don't Know Much About. 2005, HarperCollins paper $4.99 (978-0-06-442126-3). A question-and-answer format, interesting sidebars, and news photographs enliven this profile of Parks, which emphasizes her long-term commitment to civil rights. (Rev: BL 2/1/05) [323]

14929 Dubois, Muriel L. *Rosa Parks* (2–4). Illus. Series: Photo-Illustrated Biographies. 2003, Capstone LB $22.60 (978-0-7368-1607-6). 24pp. A useful introduction to Rosa Parks and her pivotal role in the American civil rights movement. (Rev: HBG 10/03; SLJ 1/04)

14930 Dubowski, Cathy E. *Rosa Parks: Don't Give In!* (2–4). Series: Defining Moments. 2005, Bearport LB $25.27 (978-1-59716-078-0). 32pp. A clearly written account of Parks's life and contribution to the civil rights movement. (Rev: SLJ 2/06)

14931 Fine, Edith Hope. *Rosa Parks: Meet a Civil Rights Hero* (3–4). Illus. Series: Meeting Famous People. 2004, Enslow LB $22.60 (978-0-7660-2099-3). 32pp. The story of Rosa Parks and her role in the struggle for civil rights is recounted in this brief but effective biography. (Rev: BL 2/15/04)

14932 Giovanni, Nikki. *Rosa* (3–5). Illus. by Bryan Collier. 2005, Holt $16.95 (978-0-8050-7106-1). This compelling picture-book biography brings Rosa and her reluctance to accept the status quo into new focus. Caldecott Honor Book, 2006. (Rev: BL 6/1–15/05)

14933 Kittinger, Jo S. *Rosa's Bus: The Ride to Civil Rights* (2–5). Illus. by Steven Walker. 2010, Boyds Mills $17.95 (978-1-59078-722-9). 40pp. The life of Rosa Parks is framed by the story of the bus on which she famously refused to give up her seat. (Rev: BL 11/15/10; SLJ 12/1/10) [323.1196]

14934 McLeese, Don. *Rosa Parks* (2–5). Series: Equal Rights Leaders. 2002, Rourke LB $20.64 (978-1-58952-287-9). 24pp. Simple text and well-chosen illustrations tell the story of Parks's life, with good coverage of her youth and education. (Rev: SLJ 1/03)

14935 Schraff, Anne. *Rosa Parks: "Tired of Giving In"* (4–8). Series: African-American Biography Library. 2005, Enslow LB $31.93 (978-0-7660-2463-2). An accessible profile of Parks and her importance. (Rev: SLJ 10/05) [921]

QUARLLS, CAROLINE

14936 Pferdehirt, Julia. *Caroline Quarlls and the Underground Railroad* (3–6). Illus. Series: Badger Biographies. 2008, Wisconsin Historical Soc. paper $12.95 (978-0-87020-388-6). 110pp. The exciting story of the 16-year-old slave's escape from Missouri and long, difficult journey to freedom in Canada. (Rev: BLO 6/17/08)

RUSTIN, BAYARD

14937 Brimner, Larry Dane. *We Are One: The Story of Bayard Rustin* (5–8). Illus. 2007, Boyds Mills $17.95 (978-1-59078-498-3). 48pp. With lively text, photographs, quotations, and song lyrics, Brimner explains Bayard Rustin's importance in the struggle for civil rights. (Rev: BL 9/1/07; SLJ 11/07)

SHELTON, PAULA YOUNG

14938 Shelton, Paula Young. *Child of the Civil Rights Movement* (2–4). Illus. by Raúl Colón. 2009, Random House $17.99 (978-0-375-84314-3); LB $20.99 (978-0-375-95414-6). 40pp. The daughter of Andrew Young provides a memoir of her childhood experiences as a witness to the civil rights movement, including the exuberant march from Selma to Montgomery. Lexile AD960L (Rev: BL 2/1/10*; LMC 3–4/10; SLJ 12/1/09*) [323.1196]

SMALLS, ROBERT

14939 Halfmann, Janet. *Seven Miles to Freedom: The Robert Smalls Story* (3–5). Illus. by Duane Smith. 2008, Lee & Low $17.95 (978-1-60060-232-0). 32pp. This biography of the slave who stole a Confederate ship and went on to serve in the U.S. Congress tells the story of his escape to the North. (Rev: BL 6/1–15/08; LMC 1/09; SLJ 7/08)

14940 Kennedy, Robert F., Jr. *Robert Smalls: The Boat Thief* (3–6). Illus. by Patrick Faricy. Series: American Heroes. 2008, Hyperion $16.99 (978-1-4231-0802-3). 48pp. The inspiring life of the slave who at the age of 24 masterminded the theft of a Confederate ship and its delivery to the Federal Navy, an event that was only the beginning of a long and influential political career. (Rev: BL 6/1–15/08)

TERRELL, MARY CHURCH

14941 Fradin, Dennis B., and Judith Bloom Fradin. *Fight On! Mary Church Terrell's Battle for Integration* (5–9). 2003, Clarion $18.00 (978-0-618-13349-9). Terrell's efforts to end discrimination are detailed in a readable, large-format biography that includes primary sources and lots of illustrations. (Rev: BL 6/1–15/03; HB 7–8/03; HBG 10/03; SLJ 5/03*; VOYA 6/03) [323]

14942 Lommel, Cookie. *Mary Church Terrell: Speaking Out for Civil Rights* (4–7). Series: African-American Biographies. 2003, Enslow LB $26.60 (978-0-7660-2116-7). 112pp. This interesting account of Terrell's life and her passion for education and activism contains many black-and-white photographs. (Rev: HBG 4/04; SLJ 10/03)

14943 McKissack, Patricia C., and Fredrick McKissack. *Mary Church Terrell: Leader for Equality. Rev. ed.* (2–4). Illus. Series: Great African Americans. 2002, Enslow LB $18.60 (978-0-7660-1697-2). 32pp. An updated version of a previously released biography about the 19th-century activist, including archival photographs and Web site information. (Rev: BL 2/15/02; HBG 10/02; SLJ 5/02)

THURMAN, HOWARD

14944 Issa, Kai Jackson. *Howard Thurman's Great Hope* (3–5). Illus. by Arthur L. Dawson. 2008, Lee & Low $16.95 (978-1-60060-249-8). 32pp. Issa describes the struggles and triumphs of this influential minister and civil rights leader. (Rev: BL 11/15/08; LMC 3/09; SLJ 9/08)

TILLAGE, LEON

14945 Tillage, Leon W. *Leon's Story* (4–9). 1997, Farrar $15.00 (978-0-374-34379-8). An autobiographical account of growing up African American and poor in the segregated South and of participating in the civil rights movement. (Rev: BL 10/1/97*; HB 11–12/97; HBG 3/98; SLJ 12/97) [975.6]

TRUTH, SOJOURNER

14946 Bernard, Catherine. *Sojourner Truth: Abolitionist and Women's Rights Activist* (5–8). Series: Historical American Biographies. 2001, Enslow LB $26.60 (978-0-7660-1257-8). 112pp. The life story of the freed slave who traveled throughout the North preaching emancipation and women's rights before the Civil War. (Rev: BL 4/15/01; HBG 10/01)

14947 Butler, Mary G. *Sojourner Truth: From Slave to Activist for Freedom* (4–8). Series: Library of American Lives and Times. 2003, Rosen LB $34.60 (978-0-8239-5736-1). A forerunner of the modern civil rights movement, Sojourner Truth rose from slavery to become a crusader for good race relations and women's rights. (Rev: BL 6/1–15/03; SLJ 5/03; VOYA 6/03) [921]

14948 Horn, Geoffrey M. *Sojourner Truth: Speaking Up for Freedom* (4–7). Illus. Series: Voices for Freedom: Abolitionist Views. 2009, Crabtree LB $30.60 (978-077874824-3). 64pp. With many images and clear text, this is an attractive profile of the woman who fought for the rights of her people. (Rev: BL 2/1/10) [921]

14949 McKissack, Patricia C., and Fredrick McKissack. *Sojourner Truth: A Voice for Freedom. Rev. ed.* (2–4). Series: Great African Americans. 2002, Enslow LB $18.60 (978-0-7660-1693-4). A simple biography of the black American evangelist and reformer who gained fame as a preacher and fighter for women's suffrage. (Rev: BL 7/02)

14950 Mattern, Joanne. *Sojourner Truth: Early Abolitionist* (1–3). Illus. Series: Women Who Shaped History. 2003, Rosen LB $19.95 (978-0-8239-6502-1). The life of Sojourner Truth, for new readers. (Rev: BL 2/15/03)

14951 Merchant, Peter. *Sojourner Truth: Path to Glory* (3–5). Illus. by Julia Denos. 2007, Simon & Schuster LB $11.89 (978-0-689-87208-2); paper $3.99 (978-0-689-87207-5). 48pp. A biography of the famous abolitionist, accompanied by striking line drawings. (Rev: SLJ 5/07)

14952 Pinkney, Andrea Davis. *Sojourner Truth's Step-Stomp Stride* (K–3). Illus. by Brian Pinkney. 2009, Hyperion $16.99 (978-0-7868-0767-3). 32pp. A dramatic portrait of the freed slave and her passion for abolition, emphasizing the power of speech and energy. (Rev: BL 11/15/09; LMC 5–6/10; SLJ 12/1/09*) [921]

14953 Rockwell, Anne. *Only Passing Through* (4–8). 2000, Knopf $16.95 (978-0-679-89186-4). A moving picture-book biography of Sojourner Truth, who was a pioneer in the struggle for racial equality and devoted her life to the abolitionist movement. (Rev: BCCB 1/01; BL 11/15/00; HB 11–12/00; HBG 3/01; SLJ 12/00) [921]

14954 Roop, Peter, and Connie Roop. *Sojourner Truth* (3–5). Illus. Series: In Their Own Words. 2003, Scholastic paper $4.99 (978-0-439-26323-8). 128pp. A simply written account of the former slave who became an abolitionist, drawing from Truth's own words. (Rev: BL 2/15/03; SLJ 7/03)

TUBMAN, HARRIET

14955 Adler, David A. *Harriet Tubman and the Underground Railroad* (5–8). Illus. 2013, Holiday $18.95 (978-082342365-1). 144pp. This thorough introduction to Tubman's life and achievements provides clear historical context and details her relationships with key figures of the time. (Rev: BL 2/1/13*; LMC 11–12/13; SLJ 2/13; VOYA 6/13) [921]

14956 Gayle, Sharon. *Harriet Tubman and the Freedom Train* (1–3). Illus. by Felicia Marshall. Series: Ready-to-Read Stories of Famous Americans. 2003, Simon & Schuster paper $3.99 (978-0-689-85480-4). A fictionalized account of the former slave's efforts to free others. (Rev: BL 2/15/03; HBG 10/03; SLJ 3/03)

14957 Klingel, Cynthia. *Harriet Tubman: Abolitionist and Underground Railroad Conductor* (3–6). Series:

Our People. 2003, Child's World LB $27.07 (978-1-59296-004-0). 32pp. An interesting profile of Tubman and her anti-slavery activities. (Rev: BL 1/1–15/04; SLJ 4/04)

14958 Malaspina, Ann. *Harriet Tubman* (5–8). Series: Leaders of the Civil War Era. 2009, Chelsea House $30 (978-1-60413-303-5). 112pp. Enhanced by a mix of illustrations, period documents, photographs, and concise sidebars, this book provides a balanced look at the courageous woman who led so many to freedom. (Rev: LMC 10/09) [921]

14959 Mortensen, Lori. *Harriet Tubman: Hero of the Underground Railroad* (K–3). Illus. by Frances Moore. 2007, Picture Window LB $23.93 (978-1-4048-3103-2). 24pp. A simple biography of the slave rescuer, beginning with her childhood and accompanied by illustrations. (Rev: SLJ 8/07)

14960 Sawyer, Kem Knapp. *Harriet Tubman* (5–9). Series: DK Biography. 2010, DK $14.99 (978-0-7566-5807-6); paper $5.99 (978-0-7566-5806-9). 128pp. A well-written and illustrated biography of the famous abolitionist, with a useful timeline and chapter notes. (Rev: BL 4/1/10; SLJ 5/10) [921]

14961 Schraff, Anne. *Harriet Tubman: Moses of the Underground Railroad* (4–8). Series: African-American Biographies. 2001, Enslow LB $26.60 (978-0-7660-1548-7). 128pp. This is an absorbing account of the life of the Underground Railroad leader that covers her work as a nurse, a scout, and a spy. (Rev: HBG 3/02; SLJ 10/01)

14962 Turner, Glennette Tilley. *An Apple for Harriet Tubman* (K–2). Illus. by Susan Ketter. 2006, Albert Whitman $15.95 (978-0-8075-0395-9). 32pp. This picture book poignantly re-creates unhappy incidents from Harriet Tubman's childhood as a slave. (Rev: BL 8/06; SLJ 10/06)

14963 Weatherford, Carole Boston. *Moses: When Harriet Tubman Led Her People to Freedom* (1–3). Illus. by Kadir Nelson. 2006, Hyperion $15.99 (978-0-7868-5175-1). Harriet Tubman's first trip north and her determination to return south to rescue others are celebrated in this moving blend of free verse and beautiful art. Caldecott Honor Book, 2007. (Rev: BL 8/06; SLJ 10/06*)

WASHINGTON, BOOKER T.

14964 Braun, Eric. *Booker T. Washington: Great American Educator* (2–6). Illus. by Cynthia Martin. Series: Graphic Library, Graphic Biographies. 2005, Capstone LB $26.60 (978-0-7368-4630-1). This graphic-novel biography profiles the life and career of the noted African American educator and author. (Rev: SLJ 3/06)

14965 Brimner, Larry Dane. *Booker T. Washington: Getting into the Schoolhouse* (2–4). Series: American Heroes. 2008, Marshall Cavendish $20.95 (978-0-7614-3063-6). 42pp. With sections on "Important Dates" and "Words to Know," this brief biography traces Washington's life from slavery to his work as an educator. (Rev: SLJ 3/09)

14966 McKissack, Patricia C., and Fredrick McKissack. *Booker T. Washington: Leader and Educator. Rev. ed.* (2–4). Illus. Series: Great African Americans. 2001, Enslow LB $18.60 (978-0-7660-1679-8). 32pp. Updated artwork gives this previously published biography of former slave and educator Booker T. Washington a new look. (Rev: BL 1/1–15/02; HBG 3/02)

WATTS, J. C.

14967 Lutz, Norma Jean. *J. C. Watts* (4–7). Series: Black Americans of Achievement. 2000, Chelsea $30.00 (978-0-7910-5338-6). 110pp. The story of a former Oklahoma University football player who entered politics and was first elected to the House of Representatives in 1994. (Rev: BL 6/1–15/00; HBG 10/00)

WELLS-BARNETT, IDA B.

14968 Dray, Philip. *Yours for Justice, Ida B. Wells: The Daring Life of a Crusading Journalist* (2–4). Illus. by Stephen Alcorn. 2008, Peachtree $18.95 (978-1-56145-417-4). A thorough picture-book biography of the black civil rights crusader and journalist who fought to end lynching. (Rev: BL 2/1/08; LMC 3/08; SLJ 4/08)

14969 Fradin, Dennis B., and Judith Bloom Fradin. *Ida B. Wells: Mother of the Civil Rights Movement* (5–10). 2000, Clarion $19.00 (978-0-395-89898-7). An inspiring biography of the African American who was born a slave and went on to become a school teacher, journalist, and an activist who fought for black women's right to vote and helped found the NAACP. (Rev: BL 2/15/00; HB 5–6/00; HBG 10/00; SLJ 4/00*) [921]

14970 McKissack, Patricia C., and Fredrick McKissack. *Ida B. Wells-Barnett: A Voice Against Violence. Rev. ed.* (2–4). Illus. Series: Great African Americans. 2001, Enslow LB $18.60 (978-0-89490-301-4). A simple biography of the founder of the NAACP. (Rev: SLJ 11/91)

14971 Myers, Walter Dean. *Ida B. Wells: Let the Truth Be Told* (2–4). Illus. by Bonnie Christensen. 2008, Collins $16.99 (978-0-06-027705-5). 40pp. An inspirational picture-book profile of the human rights activist who was born into slavery. (Rev: BCCB 11/08; BL 11/15/08; HB 1/08; SLJ 11/08)

14972 Welch, Catherine A. *Ida B. Wells-Barnett: Powerhouse with a Pen* (5–8). Series: Trailblazer Biographies. 2000, Carolrhoda LB $30.35 (978-1-57505-352-3). This book introduces Wells-Barnett, who was born a slave and became a powerful journalist and activist as well as a spokesperson for all African Americans. (Rev: BL 6/1–15/00; HBG 10/00; SLJ 7/00; VOYA 2/01) [921]

WILLIAMS, J. W.

14973 Barbour, Karen. *Mr. Williams* (K–3). Illus. 2005, Holt $16.95 (978-0-8050-6773-6). 32pp. An African American farmer's matter-of-fact recollections of his childhood in Louisiana in the 1930s and 1940s are enhanced by the compelling illustrations. (Rev: BL 9/1/05; SLJ 8/05*)

WOODSON, CARTER G.

14974 Haskins, James, and Kathleen Benson. *Carter G. Woodson: The Man Who Put "Black" in American History* (4–6). Illus. 2000, Millbrook LB $24.90 (978-0-7613-1264-2). 48pp. This biography examines the obstacles and triumphs experienced by the man who created the Association for the Study of Negro Life and History in 1915 and Negro History Week in 1926. (Rev: BL 4/1/00; HBG 10/00; SLJ 7/00)

14975 McKissack, Patricia C., and Fredrick McKissack. *Carter G. Woodson: The Father of Black History. Rev. ed.* (2–4). Series: Great African Americans. 2002, Enslow LB $18.60 (978-0-7660-1698-9). 32pp. A beginning chapter book that covers the life of the black historian who founded the Association for the Study of Negro Life and History in 1915 and began its *Journal of Negro History*. (Rev: BL 7/02)

YORK (C. 1775–1815)

14976 Pringle, Laurence. *American Slave, American Hero: York of the Lewis and Clark Expedition* (3–5). Illus. by Cornelius Wright. 2006, Boyds Mills $17.95 (978-1-59078-282-8). 32pp. This is a careful, well-illustrated picture-book biography of York, the slave who was part of the famous expedition, drawing largely on historical journals. (Rev: BL 11/1/06; SLJ 1/07)

Hispanic Americans

CHAVEZ, CESAR

14977 Adler, David A., and Michael S. Adler. *A Picture Book of Cesar Chavez* (1–4). Illus. by Marie Olofsdotter. 2010, Holiday House $17.95 (978-0-8234-2202-9). 32pp. A thorough and balanced overview of the life of the activist for migrant farm workers. (Rev: BL 7/10; LMC 3–4/11; SLJ 8/1/10) [921]

14978 Apte, Sunita. *Cesar Chavez: We Can Do It!* (3–4). Series: Defining Moments. 2005, Bearport LB $25.27 (978-1-59716-073-5). 32pp. An easy-to-read biography with plenty of photographs, this covers Chavez's childhood as well as his achievements. (Rev: SLJ 1/06)

14979 Braun, Eric. *Cesar Chavez: Fighting for Farmworkers* (2–6). Illus. by Harry Roland, et al. Series: Graphic Library, Graphic Biographies. 2005, Capstone LB $26.60 (978-0-7368-4631-8). 32pp. A graphic-novel biography that introduces the life of the Mexican American labor leader; includes highlighted quotations from primary sources. (Rev: SLJ 3/06)

14980 Brown, Jonatha A. *Cesar Chavez* (5–8). Series: Trailblazers of the Modern World. 2004, World Almanac LB $31.00 (978-0-8368-5097-0). Report writers will find lots of suitable information in this work that covers Chavez's life and accomplishments. (Rev: SLJ 7/04) [921]

14981 Griswold del Castillo, Richard. *César Chávez: The Struggle for Justice / La lucha por la justicia* (2–4). Illus. by Anthony Accardo. 2002, Arte Publico $15.95 (978-1-55885-324-9). 32pp. Bilingual text and full-page paintings bring Mexican American labor leader César Chávez to life. (Rev: BL 12/15/02)

14982 Guzmán, Lila, and Rick Guzmán. *César Chávez: Fighting for Fairness* (3–4). Series: Famous Latinos. 2006, Enslow LB $22.60 (978-0-7660-2370-3). 32pp. A look at Chavez's early life and his peaceful fight for better conditions for migrant workers, with an attractive layout and many photographs. (Rev: SLJ 3/07)

14983 Krull, Kathleen. *Harvesting Hope: The Story of Cesar Chavez* (2–4). Illus. by Yuri Morales. 2003, Harcourt $17.00 (978-0-15-201437-7). 48pp. This inspiring picture-book biography chronicles Chavez's rise from the ranks of migrant workers to a leadership position in the American labor movement. (Rev: BL 6/1–15/03; HB 7/03; HBG 10/03; SLJ 6/03)

14984 McLeese, Don. *Cesar E. Chavez* (2–5). 2002, Rourke LB $14.95 (978-1-58952-285-5). 24pp. Simple text and well-chosen illustrations tell the story of Chavez's life, with good coverage of his youth, education, and early years working in the fields. (Rev: SLJ 1/03)

14985 Tracy, Kathleen. *Cesar Chavez* (5–7). Series: Latinos in American History. 2003, Mitchell Lane LB $29.95 (978-1-58415-224-8). This biography covers the life and accomplishments of the Mexican American labor leader who founded the United Farm Workers. (Rev: BL 1/1–15/04) [921]

14986 Wadsworth, Ginger. *Cesar Chavez* (2–4). Illus. by Mark Schroder. Series: On My Own Biography. 2005, Lerner LB $25.26 (978-1-57505-652-4); paper $5.95 (978-1-57505-764-4). Chavez's own story and the plight of migrant farm workers are intertwined in this picture-book biography. (Rev: BL 5/1/05)

DE PORTOLA, GASPAR

14987 Whiting, Jim. *Gaspar de Portola* (5–7). Series: Latinos in American History. 2002, Mitchell Lane LB $29.95 (978-1-58415-148-7). The story of the Latino governor of "Las Californias" from 1768 to 1770 who was responsible for expelling Jesuits from the area. (Rev: BL 2/15/03; HBG 10/03) [921]

GAC-ARTIGAS, ALEJANDRO

14988 Gac-Artigas, Alejandro. *Yo, Alejandro* (5–7). 2000, Espacio paper $11.95 (978-1-930879-21-8). This is a collection of personal essays written by the author before his 12th birthday about his life in Puerto Rico, the state of Georgia, and later New York City. (Rev: BL 3/1/01) [921]

HUERTA, DOLORES

14989 Gillis, Jennifer Blizin. *Dolores Huerta* (3–6). Series: American Lives. 2005, Heinemann LB $26.79 (978-1-4034-6980-9). 32pp. Using large type and simple text, this volume describes the Mexican American labor leader's efforts to improve working conditions for farm workers. (Rev: SLJ 4/06)

14990 Murcia, Rebecca Thatcher. *Dolores Huerta* (5–7). Series: Latinos in American History. 2002, Mitchell Lane LB $29.95 (978-1-58415-155-5). The story of the gallant woman who worked along with Cesar Chavez to protect the rights of farm workers. (Rev: BL 2/15/03; HBG 10/03) [921]

14991 Van Tol, Alex. *Dolores Huerta: Voice for the Working Poor* (5–8). Illus. Series: Crabtree Groundbreakers Biographies. 2010, Crabtree LB $31.93 (978-077872536-7). 112pp. Dolores Huerta's lifetime of advocacy for farm safety and environmental conscience is portrayed here in clear language and many black-and-white photographs. (Rev: BL 1/1–15/11; VOYA 12/10) [921]

14992 Warren, Sarah. *Dolores Huerta: A Hero to Migrant Workers* (K–3). Illus. by Robert Casilla. 2012, Marshall Cavendish $17.99 (978-076146107-4). 32pp. Dolores Huerta's fight for the rights of migrant workers begins in the classroom, where her students are too hungry and sick to learn. (Rev: BL 4/15/12; LMC 11–12/12; SLJ 5/1/12) [921]

IDAR, JOVITA

14993 Gibson, Karen Bush. *Jovita Idar* (5–7). Series: Latinos in American History. 2002, Mitchell Lane LB $29.95 (978-1-58415-151-7). The inspiring story of the Latin American woman who started San Antonio's first free kindergarten and who founded the League of Mexican American women in 1911 to educate poor children. (Rev: BL 2/15/03; HBG 10/03) [921]

MORENO, LUISA

14994 Moore, Heidi. *Luisa Moreno* (3–6). Series: American Lives. 2005, Heinemann LB $26.79 (978-1-4034-6978-6). 32pp. Using large type and simple text, this volume describes the Guatemalan American social activist's fight to improve working conditions for factory workers, particularly those from Latin America. (Rev: SLJ 4/06)

TENAYUCA, EMMA

14995 Tafolla, Carmen, and Sharyll Tenayuca. *That's Not Fair! / ¡No es justo!* (2–4). Illus. by Terry Ybanez. 2008, Wings $17.95 (978-0-916727-33-8). 40pp. A bilingual picture-book biography of Mexican American labor activist Emma Tenayuca, who worked to improve the lot of factory and farm workers in Texas in the 1920s and 1930s. (Rev: BL 7/08; SLJ 3/09)

Historical Figures and Important Contemporary Americans

ADAMS, SAMUEL

14996 Adler, David A., and Michael S. Adler. *A Picture Book of Samuel Adams* (1–3). Illus. by Ronald Himler. Series: A Picture Book of. 2005, Holiday House $16.95 (978-0-8234-1846-6). 32pp. Historical details are woven into the succinct information on Adams's youth and achievements as an adult. (Rev: BL 6/1–15/05; SLJ 6/05)

14997 Burgan, Michael. *Samuel Adams: Patriot and Statesman* (4–7). Series: Signature Lives (Revolutionary War Era). 2005, Compass Point LB $34.60 (978-0-7565-0823-4). Profiles the man who played a key role in the tax rebellion and Boston Tea Party. (Rev: BL 4/1/05) [921]

14998 Doeden, Matt. *Samuel Adams: Patriot and Statesman* (4–6). Illus. by Tod Smith, et al. Series: Graphic Biographies. 2006, Capstone LB $25.26 (978-0-7368-6500-5). 32pp. This graphic-novel treatment of the story of Samuel Adams, a key figure in the Revolutionary War, will be useful to report-writers and reluctant readers. (Rev: SLJ 5/07)

14999 Fradin, Dennis B. *Samuel Adams: The Father of American Independence* (5–9). 1998, Houghton Mifflin $20.00 (978-0-395-82510-5). An attractive biography of the amazing Sam Adams, whom Jefferson called "the Man of the Revolution." (Rev: BCCB 7–8/98; BL 7/98; SLJ 7/98; VOYA 2/99) [921]

ALBRIGHT, MADELEINE

15000 Byman, Jeremy. *Madam Secretary: The Story of Madeleine Albright* (5–9). Series: Notable Americans. 1997, Morgan Reynolds LB $21.95 (978-1-883846-23-7). The emphasis in this biography is on Albright's public life, first as adviser to various political figures, then as ambassador to the United Nations, and finally as secretary of state. (Rev: BL 12/15/97; SLJ 4/98; VOYA 6/98) [921]

ALLEN, ETHAN

15001 Aronson, Virginia. *Ethan Allen: Revolutionary Hero* (4–6). 2000, Chelsea LB $27.50 (978-0-7910-5974-6); paper $27.50 (978-0-7910-6132-9). 80pp. This introduction to the life of Ethan Allen presents both his triumphs and his failings. (Rev: SLJ 7/01)

15002 Haugen, Brenda. *Ethan Allen: Green Mountain Rebel* (4–7). Series: Signature Lives (Revolutionary War Era). 2005, Compass Point LB $34.60 (978-0-7565-0824-1). Traces the life of the man who, along with Benedict Arnold, led the Green Mountain Boys in capturing Fort Ticonderoga from the British. (Rev: BL 4/1/05; SLJ 8/05) [921]

15003 Raabe, Emily. *Ethan Allen: The Green Mountain Boys and Vermont's Path to Statehood* (4–7). Series:

Library of American Lives and Times. 2001, Rosen LB $34.60 (978-0-8239-5722-4). 112pp. Extraordinary illustrations and fine text tell the story of the controversial founder of Vermont who led the Green Mountain Boys in the capture of Fort Ticonderoga and Crown Point. (Rev: BL 10/15/01)

ARNOLD, BENEDICT

15004 Dell, Pamela. *Benedict Arnold: From Patriot to Traitor* (4–7). Series: Signature Lives (Revolutionary War Era). 2005, Compass Point LB $34.60 (978-0-7565-0825-8). A well-designed and informative profile of the man who betrayed his country. (Rev: BL 4/1/05) [921]

15005 Gaines, Ann Graham. *Benedict Arnold: Patriot or Traitor?* (5–8). Series: Historical American Biographies. 2001, Enslow LB $26.60 (978-0-7660-1393-3). 112pp. Many facets of the character of this controversial American are examined in this well-illustrated volume. (Rev: BL 4/15/01; HBG 10/01; SLJ 6/01)

15006 Gregson, Susan R. *Benedict Arnold* (5–6). Series: Let Freedom Ring. 2001, Capstone LB $23.93 (978-0-7368-1032-6). 48pp. An introduction to Arnold's life and contributions, with discussion of the reasons why he became a traitor. (Rev: HBG 3/02; SLJ 4/02)

15007 Powell, Walter L. *Benedict Arnold: Revolutionary War Hero and Traitor* (5–8). Series: Library of American Lives and Times. 2004, Rosen LB $34.60 (978-0-8239-6627-1). The life of Benedict Arnold, the American patriot who switched his allegiance to the British cause. (Rev: SLJ 7/04) [921]

15008 Sonneborn, Liz. *Benedict Arnold: Hero and Traitor* (4–8). Series: Leaders of the American Revolution. 2005, Chelsea House LB $30.00 (978-0-7910-8617-9). An even-handed introduction to Arnold's life, presented chronologically with occasional factboxes; suitable for report writers. (Rev: SLJ 1/06) [921]

AUSTIN, STEPHEN F.

15009 Haley, James L. *Stephen F. Austin and the Founding of Texas* (5–8). Series: The Library of American Lives and Times. 2003, Rosen LB $34.60 (978-0-8239-5738-5). A concise biography of the pioneer who became one of the founders of Texas. (Rev: SLJ 5/03) [976.4]

BATES, MARTIN VAN BUREN

15010 Andreasen, Dan. *The Giant of Seville: A "Tall" Tale Based on a True Story* (PS–2). Illus. 2007, Abrams $16.95 (978-0-8109-0988-5). 32pp. As a retired circus performer, Martin Van Buren Bates, nearly 8 feet tall, wanted a quiet place to live, and the residents of Seville, Ohio, were determined to give him just that. (Rev: BL 2/1/07)

BILLY THE KID

15011 Bruns, Roger. *Billy the Kid* (5–8). Series: Historical American Biographies. 2000, Enslow LB $26.60 (978-0-7660-1091-8). A well-researched and thorough-

ly documented biography of America's famous outlaw. (Rev: BL 1/1–15/00; HBG 10/00; SLJ 5/00)

15012 Green, Carl R., and William R. Sanford. *Billy the Kid* (3–5). Illus. 2008, Enslow LB $17.95 (978-0-7660-3173-9). 48pp. A revised edition of the life story of the outlaw William H. Bonney, who lived from 1859 to 1881. (Rev: BL 1/1–15/09)

BLY, NELLIE

15013 Butcher, Nancy. *It Can't Be Done, Nellie Bly! A Reporter's Race Around the World* (2–5). Illus. by Jen L. Singh. 2003, Peachtree $12.95 (978-1-56145-289-7). The story of reporter Nellie Bly's attempt to beat the round-the-world journey of Jules Verne's fictional Phineas Fogg. (Rev: BL 3/1/04; HBG 4/04; SLJ 6/04)

15014 Fredeen, Charles. *Nellie Bly: Daredevil Reporter* (5–9). Series: Lerner Biographies. 2000, Lerner LB $25.26 (978-0-8225-4956-7). The story of the daring reporter who traveled around the world in 72 days and was a champion of the women's suffrage movement. (Rev: HBG 10/00; SLJ 3/00) [921]

15015 Krensky, Stephen. *Nellie Bly: A Name to Be Reckoned With* (3–4). Illus. by Rebecca Guay. Series: Milestone. 2003, Simon & Schuster paper $3.99 (978-0-689-85573-3). 80pp. This is an appealing biography of the pioneering woman journalist who made a 72-day trip around the world, with lots of vivid illustrations. (Rev: BL 6/1–15/03; HBG 4/04)

15016 Macy, Sue. *Bylines: A Photobiography of Nellie Bly* (5–7). 2009, National Geographic $19.95 (978-1-4263-0513-9); LB $28.90 (978-1-4263-0514-6). 64pp. This well-researched photobiography of reporter Nellie Bly weaves together maps, period photographs, artifacts, and illuminating captions to paint a memorable portrait. (Rev: BL 8/09; SLJ 10/09) [921]

BOOTH, EDWIN AND JOHN WILKES

15017 Giblin, James Cross. *Good Brother, Bad Brother: The Story of Edwin Booth and John Wilkes Booth* (5–8). 2005, Clarion $22.00 (978-0-618-09642-8). In a compelling and highly readable narrative, Giblin reveals the alcoholism and depression that plagued the theatrical Booth family, the disagreement between the two brothers over the Civil War, and the effects of the assassination on Edwin's later life. (Rev: BL 5/1/05*; SLJ 5/05) [921]

BOWIE, JIM

15018 Edmondson, J. R. *Jim Bowie: Frontier Legend, Alamo Hero* (4–7). Series: Library of American Lives and Times. 2003, Rosen LB $34.60 (978-0-8239-5734-7). 112pp. As well as being a rogue, slave trader, and murderer, Jim Bowie was also a hero of the famous battle of the Alamo. (Rev: BL 6/1–15/03; SLJ 7/03)

15019 Gaines, Ann Graham. *Jim Bowie* (5–8). Series: Historical American Biographies. 2000, Enslow LB $26.60 (978-0-7660-1253-0). A well-documented biography of Jim Bowie, a hero of the revolution in Texas who was best known for fighting in the battle of the Alamo. (Rev: BL 1/1–15/00; HBG 10/00; SLJ 5/00)

BRADFORD, WILLIAM

15020 Doherty, Kieran. *William Bradford: Rock of Plymouth* (5–9). 1999, Twenty-First Century LB $24.90 (978-0-7613-1304-5). Using Bradford's own writings and other contemporary accounts as sources, this is an objective biography of the man who was the governor of the Plymouth Plantation. (Rev: BL 12/1/99; HBG 3/00; SLJ 1/00) [921]

BRADLEY, BILL

15021 Buckley, James, Jr. *Bill Bradley* (5–8). Series: Basketball Hall of Famers. 2002, Rosen LB $29.25 (978-0-8239-3479-9). An easy-to-read, detailed biography of the former athlete, with plenty of photographs. (Rev: BL 9/1/02) [921]

BROWN, JOHN

15022 Brackett, Virginia. *John Brown: Abolitionist* (3–5). Series: Famous Figures of the Civil War Era. 2001, Chelsea LB $25.00 (978-0-7910-6408-5). Told with many color illustrations and a vivid text, this is the story of the obsessive abolitionist who was hanged for treason in 1859. (Rev: BL 4/1/02; HBG 10/02; SLJ 5/02)

15023 Hendrix, John. *John Brown: His Fight for Freedom* (5–8). 2009, Abrams $18.95 (978-0-8109-3798-7). 40pp. Bold illustrations enhance this picture book for older readers that covers the famed abolitionist's life, ideals, and sometimes questionable actions. (Rev: BL 10/15/09*; LMC 3–4/10; SLJ 11/09) [921]

BURR, AARON

15024 Ingram, Scott. *Aaron Burr and the Young Nation* (5–8). Series: Major World Leaders. 2002, Chelsea $28.70 (978-1-56711-250-4). 112pp. The story of the controversial political leader who killed Alexander Hamilton in a duel and later was tried and found guilty of treason. (Rev: BL 1/1–15/03; SLJ 10/02)

15025 Melton, Buckner F. *Aaron Burr: The Rise and Fall of an American Politician* (5–8). Series: Library of American Lives and Times. 2004, Rosen LB $34.60 (978-0-8239-6626-4). 112pp. This engaging biography chronicles the rise and fall of the Revolutionary War hero who was later branded a traitor. (Rev: SLJ 7/04)

CAMPBELL, BEN NIGHTHORSE

15026 Henry, Christopher. *Ben Nighthorse Campbell: Cheyenne Chief and U.S. Senator* (5–8). Series: North American Indians of Achievement. 1994, Chelsea $19.95 (978-0-7919-2046-6). The story of the Cheyenne leader who gained prominence not only among his own people but also in the U.S. Congress. (Rev: BL 6/1–15/93) [921]

CHAMBERLAIN, JOSHUA LAWRENCE

15027 Kennedy, Robert F., Jr. *Joshua Chamberlain and the American Civil War* (3–5). Illus. by Nikita Andreev. 2007, Hyperion $16.99 (978-1-4231-0771-2). 48pp. Joshua Chamberlain served as a Union general during the Civil War, leading his soldiers to battle at Gettysburg and playing a key role at Appomattox. (Rev: BL 12/15/07; LMC 3/08; SLJ 1/08)

CHAPMAN, JOHN

15028 Moses, Will. *Johnny Appleseed: The Story of a Legend* (4–6). Illus. 2001, Penguin $17.99 (978-0-399-23153-7). 32pp. This account of the life of Johnny Appleseed is enhanced by the author's folk-art paintings. (Rev: BL 9/1/01; HBG 3/02; SLJ 9/01)

15029 Warrick, Karen Clemens. *John Chapman: The Legendary Johnny Appleseed* (5–8). Series: Historical American Biographies. 2001, Enslow LB $26.60 (978-0-7660-1443-5). 112pp. An engrossing, nicely illustrated portrait of the man who wandered the Midwest promoting apple cultivation. (Rev: BL 4/15/01; HBG 10/01; SLJ 4/01)

15030 Yolen, Jane. *Johnny Appleseed: The Legend and the Truth* (K–3). Illus. by Jim Burke. 2008, HarperCollins $16.99 (978-0-06-059135-9). 32pp. Yolen looks at both fact and fiction about Appleseed's life and travels in this appealing picture-book biography. (Rev: BL 6/1–15/08; SLJ 10/08)

CODY, BUFFALO BILL

15031 Shields, Charles J. *Buffalo Bill Cody* (3–6). Series: Famous Figures of the American Frontier. 2001, Chelsea LB $25.00 (978-0-7910-6497-9); paper $8.95 (978-0-7910-6498-6). 64pp. An appealing account of Cody's life with black-and-white and full-color illustrations and handy fact boxes. (Rev: SLJ 3/02)

COFFIN, LEVI

15032 Swain, Gwenyth. *President of the Underground Railroad: A Story About Levi Coffin* (3–6). Illus. by Ralph L. Ramstad. Series: Creative Minds Biographies. 2001, Carolrhoda LB $22.60 (978-1-57505-551-0); paper $6.95 (978-1-57505-552-7). 64pp. This is a readable account of the life of Levi Coffin, a Quaker from North Carolina who devoted time and money to helping slaves escape to freedom. (Rev: HBG 10/01; SLJ 7/01)

COUP, W. C.

15033 Covert, Ralph, and G. Riley Mills. *Sawdust and Spangles: The Amazing Life of W.C. Coup* (K–3). Illus. by Giselle Potter. 2007, Abrams $20.95 (978-0-8109-9351-8). 32pp. Coup ran away from home to join the circus at a young age and went on to be come a colleague of P. T. Barnum and creator of the New York Aquarium. (Rev: BLO 1/15/08; LMC 1/08)

CUSTER, GEORGE ARMSTRONG

15034 Anderson, Paul Christopher. *George Armstrong Custer: The Indian Wars and the Battle of the Little Big Horn* (4–8). Series: The Library of American Lives and Times. 2004, Rosen LB $34.60 (978-0-8239-6631-8). The importance of understanding history is emphasized in this balanced and well-illustrated look at Custer's life and stance at Little Big Horn. (Rev: SLJ 7/04) [920]

15035 Kent, Zachary. *George Armstrong Custer* (5–8). Series: Historical American Biographies. 2000, Enslow LB $26.60 (978-0-7660-1255-4). Using extensive chapter notes, a glossary, bibliography, and index, this is a well-documented and objective assessment of Custer's life and deeds. (Rev: BL 1/1–15/00; HBG 10/00)

DAVIS, JEFFERSON

15036 Aretha, David. *Jefferson Davis* (5–8). Series: Leaders of the Civil War Era. 2009, Chelsea House $30 (978-1-60413-297-7). 112pp. Enhanced by a mix of illustrations, period documents, photographs, and concise sidebars, this book provides a balanced look at the leader of the Confederacy. (Rev: LMC 10/09) [921]

15037 Frazier, Joey. *Jefferson Davis: Confederate President* (3–5). Illus. 2001, Chelsea $25.00 (978-0-7910-6006-3); paper $25.00 (978-0-7910-6144-2). 80pp. A brief biography that covers Davis's life, with information on his education, his rise to become president of the Confederacy, and the problems of his administration. (Rev: BL 5/1/01; SLJ 9/01)

DE ZAVALA, LORENZO

15038 Tracy, Kathleen. *Lorenzo de Zavala* (5–7). Series: Latinos in American History. 2002, Mitchell Lane LB $29.95 (978-1-58415-154-8). The biography of the 19th-century Mexican who became vice president of the Republic of Texas and was one of the signers of its constitution. (Rev: BL 2/15/03; HBG 10/03) [921]

DOUGLAS, STEPHEN

15039 Bonner, Mike. *Stephen Douglas: Champion of the Union* (3–5). Series: Famous Figures of the Civil War Era. 2001, Chelsea LB $25.00 (978-0-7910-6402-3). The story of the American politician named the "Little Giant" who engaged in a famous series of debates with Lincoln but later became his staunch supporter. (Rev: BL 4/1/02; HBG 10/02; SLJ 5/02)

EARP, WYATT

15040 Green, Carl R., and William R. Sanford. *Wyatt Earp. Rev. ed.* (4–8). Illus. Series: Outlaws and Lawmen of the Wild West. 2008, Enslow LB $23.93 (978-0-89490-367-0). 48pp. With maps and authentic illustrations, this biography tells the story of the deputy marshal who tried to clean up Tombstone, Arizona. (Rev: BL 10/1/92; SLJ 11/92)

15041 Staeger, Rob. *Wyatt Earp* (3–6). Series: Famous Figures of the American Frontier. 2001, Chelsea LB $25.00 (978-0-7910-6485-6); paper $8.95 (978-0-7910-

6486-3). 64pp. An appealing biography of the famous gunfighter, with black-and-white and full-color illustrations and handy fact boxes. (Rev: HBG 10/02; SLJ 3/02)

EDWARDS, JONATHAN

15042 Lutz, Norma Jean. *Jonathan Edwards: Colonial Religious Leader* (5–7). Series: Colonial Leaders. 2001, Chelsea $27.50 (978-0-7910-5961-6). 80pp. The life of Edwards, a leader in the Great Awakening spiritual movement and preacher among Native American tribes, is presented here with discussion of his contributions and his failings. (Rev: SLJ 5/01)

FARRAGUT, DAVID

15043 Adelson, Bruce. *David Farragut: Union Admiral* (3–5). Series: Famous Figures of the Civil War Era. 2001, Chelsea LB $25.00 (978-0-7910-6416-0). The story of the American admiral who served in the War of 1812 and the Mexican War, and gained fame as a blockade runner during the Civil War. (Rev: BL 4/1/02)

15044 Stein, R. Conrad. *David Farragut: First Admiral of the U.S. Navy* (3–6). Series: A Proud Heritage. 2005, Child's World LB $28.50 (978-1-59296-383-6). 40pp. Covers Farragut joining the navy at the age of 10 and his rise to become an admiral. (Rev: SLJ 6/05)

FRANKLIN, BENJAMIN

15045 Adler, David A. *B. Franklin, Printer* (4–8). 2001, Holiday $19.95 (978-0-8234-1675-2). Quotations, anecdotes, and wonderful illustrations round out this excellent volume about the life and accomplishments of Benjamin Franklin. (Rev: BCCB 2/02; BL 1/1–15/02; HBG 10/02; SLJ 2/02*; VOYA 4/02) [973.3]

15046 Ashby, Ruth. *The Amazing Mr. Franklin: Or the Boy Who Read Everything* (3–5). Illus. by Michael Montgomery. 2004, Peachtree $12.95 (978-1-56145-306-1). Readers will learn about Franklin's youth as well as his later accomplishments in this attractive, small-format volume. (Rev: BL 7/04; SLJ 11/04)

15047 Barretta, Gene. *Now and Ben: The Modern Inventions of Benjamin Franklin* (2–4). 2006, Holt $16.95 (978-0-8050-7917-3). 40pp. Franklin's many interests and inventions are the focus of this reader-friendly overview with appealing illustrations. (Rev: BL 3/1/06; SLJ 3/06)

15048 Byrd, Robert. *Electric Ben: The Amazing Life and Times of Benjamin Franklin* (2–5). Illus. by author. 2012, Dial $17.99 (978-0-8037-3749-5). 40pp. This attractive and informative picture-book biography covers Franklin's life from childhood, placing his accomplishments in historical context and giving the reader a sense of his personality as well as his varied talents. 2013 Boston Globe–Horn Book Nonfiction Book; Robert F. Sibert Honor. (Rev: BL 10/15/12*; HB 1–2/3; LMC 5–6/13*; SLJ 10/12) [921]

15049 Collard, Sneed B., III. *Benjamin Franklin: The Man Who Could Do Just About Anything* (3–5). Series: American Heroes. 2006, Benchmark LB $28.50 (978-0-

7614-2161-0). 40pp. An excellent introductory biography of Franklin, covering his many talents and including attractive well-chosen illustrations and easy-to-read text. (Rev: SLJ 3/07)

15050 Ford, Carin T. *Benjamin Franklin: Inventor and Patriot* (1–3). Illus. Series: Famous Inventors. 2003, Enslow LB $22.60 (978-0-7660-1859-4). For young report writers, this volume presents the salient facts about Franklin in an attractive and accessible manner. (Rev: HBG 10/03; SLJ 1/04)

15051 Fradin, Dennis B. *Who Was Ben Franklin?* (3–5). Illus. by John O'Brien. 2002, Penguin paper $4.99 (978-0-448-42495-8). 112pp. This book traces the fascinating, eclectic life and varied careers of Benjamin Franklin. (Rev: BL 3/1/02; HBG 10/02; SLJ 3/02)

15052 Harness, Cheryl. *The Remarkable Benjamin Franklin* (2–5). 2005, National Geographic $17.95 (978-0-7922-7882-5). 48pp. An appealing profile that combines interesting text with striking illustrations full of details, quotations, and a timeline. (Rev: BCCB 4/06; BL 3/1/06*; HB 3/06; HBG 10/06; LMC 3/06; SLJ 11/05)

15053 Krensky, Stephen. *Ben Franklin and His First Kite* (1–3). Illus. by Bert Dodson. Series: Childhood of Famous Americans. 2002, Simon & Schuster paper $3.99 (978-0-689-84984-8). 31pp. The story of young Franklin's first experiment with a kite is told for beginning readers. (Rev: HBG 3/03; SLJ 10/02)

15054 McCurdy, Michael. *So Said Ben* (3–5). Illus. by author. 2007, Creative Editions LB $17.95 (978-1-56846-147-2). 32pp. Quotations from Ben Franklin are illustrated with humorous woodcut illustrations. (Rev: BL 12/1/07; LMC 5/08; SLJ 1/08)

15055 Nettleton, Pamela Hill. *Benjamin Franklin: Writer, Inventor, Statesman* (K–3). Illus. by Jeff Yesh. Series: Biographies. 2003, Picture Window LB $25.26 (978-1-4048-0186-8). 24pp. A brightly illustrated profile that is suitable for beginning readers. (Rev: SLJ 4/04)

15056 Riley, John. *Benjamin Franklin: A Photo Biography* (1–3). Series: First Biographies. 2000, Morgan Reynolds LB $16.95 (978-1-883846-64-0). 24pp. A very simple biography of Franklin for beginning readers that has a full-page illustration opposite each page of text. (Rev: HBG 10/00; SLJ 8/00)

15057 Rushby, Pamela. *Ben Franklin: Printer, Author, Inventor, Politician* (2–4). Series: National Geographic History Chapters. 2007, National Geographic LB $17.90 (978-1-4263-0191-9). 40pp. Simple sentences, with photographs and drawings, tell the story of Franklin's youth and later accomplishments; a "How to Write an A+ Report" section gives useful advice. (Rev: LMC 1/08*; SLJ 1/08)

15058 Schanzer, Rosalyn. *How Ben Franklin Stole the Lightning* (2–4). Illus. by author. 2003, HarperCollins LB $17.89 (978-0-688-16994-7). A lively account of Franklin's role as an inventor, with a focus on his flying a kite during a rainstorm. (Rev: BCCB 3/03; HBG 10/03; SLJ 1/03)

15059 Schroeder, Alan. *Ben Franklin: His Wit and Wisdom from A–Z* (1–3). Illus. by John O'Brien. 2011, Holiday House $16.95 (978-0-8234-1950-0). 32pp. An attractive, alphabetical tour of Benjamin Franklin's life providing snippets of information about his inventions, personal life, politics, and public service. (Rev: BL 4/15/11; HB 5–6/11; SLJ 4/11) [921]

15060 Sherrow, Victoria. *Benjamin Franklin* (3–4). Series: History Maker Bios. 2002, Lerner LB $26.60 (978-0-8225-0198-5). 48pp. The life of this multitalented genius of the colonial period is presented in a simple text with many illustrations. (Rev: BL 6/1–15/02; HBG 3/03)

15061 Streissguth, Thomas. *Benjamin Franklin* (5–8). Series: A&E Biography. 2001, Lerner LB $27.93 (978-0-8225-4997-0). A readable biography of the many-faceted genius of the newly formed United States. (Rev: BL 4/1/02; HBG 10/02)

15062 Streissguth, Thomas. *Benjamin Franklin* (4–6). Series: Just the Facts Biographies. 2005, Lerner LB $27.93 (978-0-8225-2210-2). 112pp. This attractive and informative biography covers Franklin's youth and education as well as his later life, with interesting factboxes. (Rev: SLJ 2/05)

15063 Van Vleet, Carmella. *Amazing Ben Franklin Inventions You Can Build Yourself* (4–8). 2007, Nomad paper $14.95 (978-0-9771294-7-8). Activities — making invisible ink, wave bottles, kites, and so forth — and the accompanying narrative bring Franklin's inquisitive nature to light. (Rev: LMC 2/08; SLJ 11/07) [921]

GANCI, PETER J.

15064 Ganci, Chris. *Chief: The Life of Peter J. Ganci, a New York Firefighter* (3–5). Illus. 2003, Scholastic $16.95 (978-0-439-44386-9). 40pp. This loving portrait of a New York City firefighter who lost his life on September 11, 2001, was written by his son and is dedicated to firefighters around the world. (Rev: BL 4/15/03; HBG 10/03; SLJ 4/03)

GEE, MAGGIE

15065 Moss, Marissa. *Sky High: The True Story of Maggie Gee* (3–5). Illus. by Carl Angel. 2009, Tricycle $16.99 (978-1-58246-280-6). 32pp. Born with a love of flying, Maggie Gee becomes one of World War II's WASP corps of female pilots; prejudice (she is Asian American) is a side issue. (Rev: BL 6/1–15/09)

GLENN, JOHN

15066 Hilliard, Richard. *Godspeed, John Glenn* (1–3). 2006, Boyds Mills $16.95 (978-1-59078-384-9). 32pp. This picture-book biography offers a brief overview of the astronaut's life but focuses primarily on his first space voyage in the *Friendship 7* capsule. (Rev: BL 10/1/06; SLJ 10/06)

15067 Holden, Henry M. *Trailblazing Astronaut John Glenn* (4–6). Illus. Series: Space Flight Adventures and Disasters. 2004, Enslow LB $25.26 (978-0-7660-5166-9). 48pp. Supported by Web sites, this is an account of the life of the astronaut who went into space twice, decades apart. [921]

15068 Mitchell, Don. *Liftoff: A Photobiography of John Glenn* (4–6). 2006, National Geographic $17.95 (978-0-7922-5899-5). 64pp. This photo-filled biography offers a brief overview of the former astronaut's life and many accomplishments. (Rev: BL 8/06)

15069 Streissguth, Thomas. *John Glenn* (2–4). Illus. Series: Explore Space! 2003, Capstone LB $22.60 (978-0-7368-1625-0). 24pp. A slim, basic profile of the first American to orbit the earth, who went on to be a United States Senator. (Rev: HBG 10/03; SLJ 3/04)

15070 Vogt, Gregory L. *John Glenn's Return to Space* (4–7). Illus. 2000, Twenty-First Century LB $24.90 (978-0-7613-1614-5). 72pp. As well as describing John Glenn's two space flights on the *Mercury* capsule and later the *Discovery,* this biography gives information on astronauts' training and equipment. (Rev: BL 9/15/00; HBG 10/01; SLJ 1/01)

GREENE, NATHANAEL

15071 Mierka, Gregg A. *Nathanael Greene: The General Who Saved the Revolution* (5–8). Illus. Series: Forgotten Heroes of the American Revolution. 2006, OTTN LB $23.95 (978-1-59556-012-4). Employing primary and previously unpublished sources, Mierka's lively text examines Greene's pivotal role as quartermaster general and southern commander in Washington's Revolutionary army. (Rev: BL 1/1–15/07) [973.3]

HALE, NATHAN

15072 Krizner, L. J., and Lisa Sita. *Nathan Hale: Patriot and Martyr of the American Revolution* (4–7). Series: Library of American Lives and Times. 2001, Rosen $31.95 (978-0-8239-5724-8). 112pp. Nathan Hale, executed by the British in 1776, represented the life-and-death issues fought for in the Revolution and became a symbol of courage and patriotism. (Rev: BL 10/15/01)

15073 Tracy, Kathleen. *The Life and Times of Nathan Hale* (5–8). Series: Profiles in American History. 2007, Mitchell Lane LB $19.95 (978-1-58415-447-1). This is an appealing life of Nathan Hale, from his childhood through his execution by the British. (Rev: SLJ 7/07) [921]

15074 Zemlicka, Shannon. *Nathan Hale: Patriot Spy* (2–4). Illus. by Craig Orback. Series: On My Own Biography. 2002, Carolrhoda LB $23.93 (978-0-87614-597-5); paper $5.95 (978-0-87614-905-8). 48pp. For beginning readers, this is an absorbing life of the Revolutionary War hero who was executed for spying. (Rev: HBG 3/03; SLJ 12/02)

HALVORSEN, GAIL S.

15075 Tunnell, Michael O. *Candy Bomber: The Story of the Berlin Airlift's "Chocolate Pilot"* (4–7). 2010, Charlesbridge $18.95 (978-1-58089-336-7); paper $9.95 (978-1-58089-337-4). 120pp. The inspiring story of Lt. Gail S. Halvorsen, who brought joy to the children of West Berlin in 1948, when the city was isolated and short of all supplies. Lexile 1130L (Rev: BL 6/10*; HB 9–10/10; SLJ 7/10) [943]

HAMILTON, ALEXANDER

15076 DeCarolis, Lisa. *Alexander Hamilton: Federalist and Founding Father* (4–7). Series: Library of American Lives and Times. 2003, Rosen LB $31.95 (978-0-8239-5735-4). The story of the military hero of the American Revolution who was the first secretary of the treasury and helped write the Federalist Papers. (Rev: BL 6/1–15/03; SLJ 4/03) [921]

15077 Haugen, Brenda. *Alexander Hamilton: Founding Father and Statesman* (4–7). Series: Signature Lives (Revolutionary War Era). 2005, Compass Point LB $34.60 (978-0-7565-0827-2). Traces the life of the man who became the first secretary of the treasury. (Rev: BL 4/1/05; SLJ 8/05) [921]

15078 Kallen, Stuart A. *Alexander Hamilton* (4–6). Series: Founding Fathers. 2001, ABDO LB $25.65 (978-1-57765-006-5). 64pp. A lively biography of the first secretary of the U.S. Treasury that covers his underprivileged early life and details his importance in the creation of the United States. (Rev: HBG 3/02; SLJ 1/02)

HANCOCK, JOHN

15079 Adler, David A., and Michael S. Adler. *A Picture Book of John Hancock* (2–4). Illus. by Ronald Himler. 2007, Holiday $16.95 (978-0-8234-2005-6). 32pp. This well-illustrated biography of Hancock focuses on his importance to the American Revolution (includes notes, timeline, bibliography and Web sites). (Rev: BL 5/1/07; SLJ 7/07)

15080 Kjelle, Marylou Morano. *The Life and Times of John Hancock* (5–8). Illus. Series: Profiles in American History. 2007, Mitchell Lane LB $19.95 (978-1-58415-443-3). Little-known facts about John Hancock's life make this well-organized biography an interesting read. (Rev: SLJ 7/07) [921]

15081 Raatma, Lucia. *A Signer for Independence: John Hancock* (5–8). Series: We the People. 2009, Compass Point LB $26.65 (978-0-7565-4122-4). 48pp. Accessible and well-illustrated, with a useful timeline, this book provides a balanced look at John Hancock. (Rev: LMC 10/09) [921]

15082 Ransom, Candice F. *John Hancock* (3–4). Illus. Series: History Maker Bios. 2004, Lerner LB $26.60 (978-0-8225-1547-0). 48pp. A simple biography, useful for report writers, with information about Hancock's youth and good photographs and illustrations. (Rev: SLJ 1/05)

HAYSLIP, LE LY

15083 Englar, Mary. *Le Ly Hayslip* (5–8). Series: Asian-American Biographies. 2005, Raintree LB $23.00 (978-1-4109-1055-4). An interesting profile of the Vietnamese-born woman who started the East Meets West Foundation. (Rev: SLJ 3/06) [921]

HENRY, PATRICK

15084 Kukla, Amy, and Jon Kukla. *Patrick Henry: Voice of the Revolution* (4–7). Illus. Series: Library of American Lives and Times. 2001, Rosen $31.95 (978-0-8239-5725-5). 112pp. Detailed text, a variety of illustrations, and a timeline give readers a good understanding of Henry's importance. (Rev: BL 10/15/01)

HESCHEL, ABRAHAM JOSHUA

15085 Rose, Or. *Abraham Joshua Heschel* (4–8). 2003, Jewish Publication Soc. paper $9.95 (978-0-8276-0758-3). A portrait of the rabbi and teacher who was born in Poland, emigrated to the United States, and became a leader in the civil rights movement. (Rev: BL 6/1–15/03; HBG 10/01) [921]

HICKOK, WILD BILL

15086 Green, Carl R., and William R. Sanford. *Wild Bill Hickok. Rev. ed.* (4–8). Illus. Series: Outlaws and Lawmen of the Wild West. 2008, Enslow LB $23.93 (978-0-89490-366-3). 48pp. The life story of the famous frontier marshal in Kansas is retold in text and pictures. (Rev: BL 7/92; SLJ 8/92)

15087 Rosa, Joseph G. *Wild Bill Hickok: Sharpshooter and U.S. Marshal of the Wild West* (4–8). Series: The Library of American Lives and Times. 2004, Rosen LB $34.60 (978-0-8239-6632-5). 112pp. The importance of understanding history is emphasized in this balanced and well-illustrated look at Hickok's life. (Rev: SLJ 7/04)

HOOVER, J. EDGAR

15088 Cunningham, Kevin. *J. Edgar Hoover: Controversial FBI Director* (5–8). Series: Signature Lives. 2005, Compass Point LB $34.60 (978-0-7565-0997-2). This introduction to Hoover's career provides limited personal details, concentrating instead on his political ambitions and tendency to ignore ethical standards. (Rev: SLJ 1/06) [921]

15089 Streissguth, Thomas. *J. Edgar Hoover: Powerful FBI Director* (5–8). Series: Historical American Biographies. 2002, Enslow LB $26.60 (978-0-7660-1623-1). Streissguth looks at Hoover's life from youth, his personality, and his work as head of the FBI, and explores the areas in which his influence was felt, including civil rights and politics. (Rev: HBG 10/02; SLJ 8/02)

HOUSTON, SAM

15090 Boraas, Tracey. *Sam Houston: Soldier and Statesman* (3–5). Illus. Series: Let Freedom Ring. 2002, Capstone LB $23.93 (978-0-7368-1350-1). A thorough look at the life and multiple careers of Sam Houston, who led the fight to wrest Texas from Mexican control. (Rev: HBG 3/03; SLJ 4/03)

15091 Caravantes, Peggy. *An American in Texas: The Story of Sam Houston* (5–8). Series: Founders of the Republic. 2003, Morgan Reynolds LB $23.95 (978-1-931798-19-8). A portrait of the colorful general who be-

came the first president of the Republic of Texas. (Rev: SLJ 5/04) [921]

15092 Harkins, Susan Sales, and William H. Harkins. *Sam Houston* (2–4). Series: A Robbie Reader: What's So Great About? 2006, Mitchell Lane LB $25.70 (978-1-58415-482-2). 32pp. A life of the Virginia native who led the fight for Texas's independence and was elected its first president after it became a republic. (Rev: SLJ 1/07)

15093 Woodward, Walter M. *Sam Houston: For Texas and the Union* (5–8). Series: The Library of American Lives and Times. 2003, Rosen LB $34.60 (978-0-8239-5739-2). A concise biography of the man credited with gaining Texas's independence. (Rev: SLJ 5/03) [976.4]

JACKSON, STONEWALL

15094 Doak, Robin. *Confederate General: Stonewall Jackson* (4–8). Series: We the People. 2009, Compass Point LB $26.65 (978-0-7565-4110-1). 48pp. Doak provides a balanced overview of the life and career of the enigmatic general, with a timeline and well-chosen illustrations. (Rev: LMC 10/09) [921]

15095 Koestler-Grack, Rachel A. *Stonewall Jackson* (5–8). Series: Leaders of the Civil War Era. 2009, Chelsea House $30 (978-1-60413-299-1). 112pp. Enhanced by a mix of illustrations, period documents, photographs, and concise sidebars, this book provides an even-handed profile of the general responsible for some significant military victories. (Rev: LMC 10/09) [921]

JAMES, JESSE

15096 Green, Carl R., and William R. Sanford. *Jesse James. Rev. ed.* (4–8). Illus. Series: Outlaws and Lawmen of the Wild West. 2008, Enslow LB $23.93 (978-0-89490-365-6). 48pp. This easy-to-read text portrays the legendary gunman as both outlaw and hero. (Rev: BL 3/1/92; SLJ 5/92)

JAY, JOHN

15097 Kallen, Stuart A. *John Jay* (4–6). Series: Founding Fathers. 2001, ABDO LB $25.65 (978-1-57765-013-3). 64pp. A lively biography of the first chief justice of the Supreme Court that covers his life and details his importance in the creation of the United States. (Rev: SLJ 1/02)

JOHNSTON, JOSEPH E.

15098 Ditchfield, Christin. *Joseph E. Johnston: Confederate General* (3–5). Series: Famous Figures of the Civil War Era. 2001, Chelsea LB $25.00 (978-0-7910-6412-2). The story of the Confederate general who commanded forces during the Civil War and later served a term in the U.S. House of Representatives. (Rev: BL 4/1/02)

JONES, JOHN PAUL

15099 Bradford, James C. *John Paul Jones and the American Navy* (4–7). Series: Library of American Lives and Times. 2001, Rosen $34.60 (978-0-8239-5726-2). This attractively designed volume combines the life story of the naval hero of the American Revolution with a history of the birth and growth of the American navy. (Rev: BL 10/15/01) [921]

15100 Cooper, Michael L. *Hero of the High Seas: John Paul Jones* (4–7). 2006, National Geographic $21.95 (978-0-7922-5547-5). 128pp. This biography focuses on the Scottish immigrant's naval heroics during the American Revolution and includes a detailed timeline and a useful listing of "Words and Expressions from the Days of Sailing Ships." (Rev: BL 6/1–15/06; SLJ 9/06)

15101 Lutz, Norma Jean. *John Paul Jones: Father of the U.S. Navy* (3–6). Series: Revolutionary War Leaders. 2000, Chelsea LB $31.00 (978-0-7910-5359-1). From his boyhood in Scotland to his death at age 45, this is the biography of a hero of the Revolutionary War. (Rev: HBG 10/00; SLJ 5/00)

15102 Riley, John. *John Paul Jones: A Photo Biography* (1–3). Series: First Biographies. 2000, Morgan Reynolds LB $16.95 (978-1-883846-63-3). 24pp. A heavily illustrated simple biography for beginning readers of the Revolutionary War hero. (Rev: HBG 10/00; SLJ 8/00)

15103 Tibbitts, Alison Davis. *John Paul Jones: Father of the American Navy* (5–8). Series: Historical American Biographies. 2002, Enslow LB $26.60 (978-0-7660-1448-0). The life of the American naval officer noted for his role in the Revolution and for the statement, "I have not yet begun to fight." (Rev: BL 4/1/02; HBG 10/02; SLJ 5/02)

KENNEDY FAMILY

15104 Krull, Kathleen. *The Brothers Kennedy: John, Robert, Edward* (2–4). Illus. by Amy June Bates. 2010, Simon & Schuster $16.99 (978-1-4169-9158-8). 40pp. Profiles the three brothers who became politicians and their mutual support, legacy, and tragedy. (Rev: BL 3/15/10; LMC 8–9/10; SLJ 3/1/10) [921]

KENNEDY, EDWARD M.

15105 McElroy, Lisa Tucker. *Ted Kennedy: A Remarkable Life in the Senate* (4–7). Series: Gateway Biographies. 2009, Lerner LB $25.26 (978-0-7613-4457-5). 48pp. A useful resource for report writers, this biography has all the facts about the late senator's life and political service. (Rev: SLJ 8/09) [921]

KENNEDY, ROBERT F.

15106 Koestler-Grack, Rachel A. *The Assassination of Robert F. Kennedy* (5–8). Series: American Moments. 2005, ABDO LB $25.65 (978-1-59197-931-9). Kennedy's assassination is placed in historical context, with a brief biography and discussion of the aftermath of this tragedy. (Rev: SLJ 11/05) [921]

KEY, FRANCIS SCOTT

15107 Gregson, Susan R. *Francis Scott Key: Patriotic Poet* (3–5). Illus. Series: Let Freedom Ring. 2003, Capstone LB $23.93 (978-0-7368-1554-3). 48pp. Chroni-

cles the life of the lawyer and poet who wrote the words that were eventually to become the lyrics of America's national anthem. (Rev: HBG 10/03; SLJ 9/03)

15108 Kjelle, Marylou Morano. *Francis Scott Key* (1–4). Series: A Robbie Reader, What's So Great About? 2006, Mitchell Lane LB $25.70 (978-1-58415-474-7). 32pp. This brief biography covers the life of the man who wrote "The Star-Spangled Banner." (Rev: SLJ 11/06)

15109 Kulling, Monica. *Francis Scott Key's Star-Spangled Banner* (1–3). Illus. by Richard Walz. Series: Step into Reading. 2012, Random House paper $3.99 (978-03758672-5-5). 48pp. For beginning readers, this is a simple portrait of Key's life and the War of 1812. e (Rev: BL 12/15/11; SLJ 4/1/12) [921]

KNOX, HENRY

15110 Silvey, Anita. *Henry Knox: Bookseller, Soldier, Patriot* (2–5). Illus. by Wendell Minor. 2010, Clarion $17.99 (978-0-618-27485-7). 40pp. This biography tells the little-known story of Henry Knox's journey to procure heavy artillery to defend Boston in 1776, e (Rev: BL 9/1/10*; SLJ 12/1/10) [921]

LAFFITE, JEAN

15111 Rubin, Susan Goldman. *Jean Laffite: The Pirate Who Saved America* (1–4). Illus. by Jeff Himmelman. 2012, Abrams $18.95 (978-081099733-2). 48pp. Tells the story of the Jewish pirate born in Saint-Domingue, who settled in New Orleans, playing a role in the War of 1812, and became a respected businessman. (Rev: BL 3/15/12; SLJ 5/1/12) [921]

LEE, ROBERT E.

15112 Anderson, Paul Christopher. *Robert E. Lee: Legendary Commander of the Confederacy* (4–7). Series: Library of American Lives and Times. 2003, Rosen LB $34.60 (978-0-8239-5748-4). Extensive original sources are used to re-create the life of this Confederate general and the times in which he lived. (Rev: BL 6/1–15/03) [921]

LIEBERMAN, JOSEPH

15113 Feinberg, Barbara S. *Joseph Lieberman: Keeping the Faith* (4–6). Illus. 2001, Millbrook LB $23.90 (978-0-7613-2303-7). 48pp. This profile of the first Jewish candidate for the vice presidency of the United States includes photographs, a timeline, and a bibliography. (Rev: BL 9/15/01; HBG 3/02)

LINCOLN FAMILY

15114 Rabin, Staton. *Mr. Lincoln's Boys: Being the Mostly True Adventures of Abraham Lincoln's Troublemaking Sons Tad and Willie* (2–4). Illus. by Bagram Ibatoulline. 2008, Viking $16.99 (978-0-670-06169-3). 40pp. With only a little embellishment, Rabin presents the antics of Lincoln's two young sons during their days in the White House; Ibatoulline's detailed illustrations add historical atmosphere. (Rev: BL 7/08; LMC 1/09; SLJ 9/08)

MACARTHUR, DOUGLAS

15115 Gaines, Ann Graham. *Douglas MacArthur: Brilliant General, Controversial Leader* (5–8). Series: Historical American Biographies. 2001, Enslow LB $26.60 (978-0-7660-1445-9). 112pp. Using many black-and-white photographs as illustrations, this account gives a well-rounded, unbiased picture of this controversial general. (Rev: BL 4/15/01; HBG 10/01; SLJ 6/01)

15116 Haugen, Brenda. *Douglas MacArthur: America's General* (5–8). Series: Signature Lives. 2005, Compass Point LB $34.60 (978-0-7565-0994-1). This introduction to MacArthur's career provides limited personal details but concentrates instead on his leadership abilities and military achievements. (Rev: SLJ 1/06) [921]

MARION, FRANCIS

15117 Towles, Louis P. *Francis Marion: The Swamp Fox of the American Revolution* (4–7). Series: Library of American Lives and Times. 2001, Rosen LB $34.60 (978-0-8239-5728-6). The life of the Revolutionary War hero known as the Swamp Fox because of his stealthy retreats into the swamp lands. (Rev: BL 1/1–15/02)

MCCAIN, JOHN

15118 Feinberg, Barbara S. *John McCain: Serving His Country* (4–7). Series: Gateway. 2000, Millbrook LB $23.90 (978-0-7613-1974-0). A biography of the senator that tells about his youth and later political career but concentrates on his stint in the navy and his imprisonment during the Vietnam War. (Rev: BL 3/1/01; HBG 10/01) [921]

15119 Wells, Catherine. *John McCain* (5–8). Series: Political Profiles. 2008, Morgan Reynolds LB $27.95 (978-1-59935-046-2). Beginning with his early years and ending just before his nomination as a presidential candidate, this book examines McCain's life as well as his public and military service. (Rev: BL 5/15/08; SLJ 1/08) [921]

MCCLELLAN, GEORGE

15120 Kelley, Brent. *George McClellan: Union General* (3–5). Series: Famous Figures of the Civil War Era. 2001, Chelsea LB $25.00 (978-0-7910-6404-7). The life of this important Union army leader, who was removed from his command by Lincoln, is re-created in pictures and text. (Rev: BL 4/1/02; SLJ 5/02)

MEADE, GEORGE GORDON

15121 Adelson, Bruce. *George Gordon Meade: Union General* (3–5). Series: Famous Figures of the Civil War Era. 2001, Chelsea LB $25.00 (978-0-7910-6410-8). The story of the Civil War general who fought in battles including Bull Run, Antietam, Chancellorsville, and Gettysburg. (Rev: BL 4/1/02; HBG 10/02)

MORRIS, GOUVERNOR

15122 Crompton, Samuel Willard. *Gouverneur Morris: Creating a Nation* (5–8). Series: America's Founding Fathers. 2004, Enslow LB $26.60 (978-0-7660-2213-3). 128pp. An introduction to the life and legacy of Gouvernor Morris, who helped to edit the final draft of the Declaration of Independence. (Rev: SLJ 7/04)

OGLETHORPE, JAMES

15123 Lommel, Cookie. *James Oglethorpe: Humanitarian and Soldier* (4–6). Series: Colonial Leaders. 2001, Chelsea LB $27.50 (978-0-7910-5963-0); paper $27.50 (978-0-7910-6120-6). 80pp. Oglethorpe, the English founder and first governor of the colony of Georgia, was active in a number of areas including prison reform, the guarantee of religious freedom, and relations with Native Americans. (Rev: HBG 10/01; SLJ 7/01)

PAINE, THOMAS

15124 Burgan, Michael. *Thomas Paine: Great Writer of the Revolution* (4–7). Series: Signature Lives (Revolutionary War Era). 2005, Compass Point LB $34.60 (978-0-7565-0830-2). A well designed profile of the revolutionary thinker. (Rev: BL 4/1/05) [921]

15125 McCarthy, Pat. *Thomas Paine: Revolutionary Patriot and Writer* (5–8). Series: Historical American Biographies. 2001, Enslow LB $26.60 (978-0-7660-1446-6). 112pp. A balanced, well-researched biography of the American political theorist and writer who created controversy throughout his lifetime. (Rev: BL 4/15/01; HBG 10/01)

15126 McCartin, Brian. *Thomas Paine: Common Sense and Revolutionary Pamphleteering* (4–7). Series: Library of American Lives and Times. 2001, Rosen $34.60 (978-0-8239-5729-3). The story of the British-born colonialist who heard the cries for liberty around him and whose writings set the stage for the Declaration of Independence. (Rev: BL 10/15/01) [921]

15127 Waxman, Laura Hamilton. *Uncommon Revolutionary: A Story About Thomas Paine* (3–5). Illus. by Craig Orback. Series: Creative Minds Biographies. 2003, Carolrhoda LB $22.60 (978-1-57505-180-2). 64pp. An illustrated biography of the Revolutionary War pamphleteer who supported the cause of American independence. (Rev: HBG 4/04; SLJ 5/04)

PARKHURST, CHARLEY

15128 Kay, Verla. *Rough, Tough Charley* (K–3). Illus. by Adam Gustavson. 2007, Tricycle $15.95 (978-1-58246-184-7). 32pp. The life of Charley Parkhurst, a female stagecoach driver who dressed as a man and whose sex was only revealed after her death. (Rev: BL 6/1–15/07; SLJ 8/07)

PATTON, GEORGE S., JR.

15129 Sutcliffe, Jane. *George S. Patton Jr.* (2–5). Illus. Series: History Maker Bios. 2005, Lerner LB $26.60 (978-0-8225-2436-6); paper $6.95 (978-0-8225-5461-5). 48pp. The life and times of the general, with plenty of information for report writers; includes photographs, drawings, and Web sites. (Rev: SLJ 8/05)

PEARY, MARIE AHNIGHITO

15130 Kirkpatrick, Katherine. *The Snow Baby: The Arctic Childhood of Robert E. Peary's Daring Daughter* (5–8). Illus. 2007, Holiday $16.95 (978-0-8234-1973-9). 48pp. This engaging account of a child growing up partly among the Inuit and partly in her mother's nice home in the United States is based on the autobiography, published in 1934, of Marie Ahnighito Peary, daughter of explorer Robert E. Peary, who was born north of the Arctic Circle in 1893. (Rev: BL 4/15/07; SLJ 3/07)

PELOSI, NANCY

15131 Shichtman, Sandra H. *Nancy Pelosi* (5–8). Series: Political Profiles. 2007, Morgan Reynolds LB $27.95 (978-1-59935-049-3). An admiring portrait of this important political figure, with photographs. (Rev: BL 11/15/07; SLJ 1/08) [328.7]

PENN, WILLIAM

15132 Kroll, Steven. *William Penn: Founder of Pennsylvania* (3–5). Illus. 2000, Holiday House $16.95 (978-0-8234-1439-0). 29pp. This picture book on the life of William Penn discusses his conversion to the Quaker faith and the land grant that was given him in the New World. (Rev: BL 2/15/00; HBG 10/00; SLJ 4/00)

PITCHER, MOLLY

15133 Rockwell, Anne. *They Called Her Molly Pitcher* (3–5). Illus. by Cynthia von Buhler. 2002, Knopf $15.95 (978-0-679-89187-1). The story of the gallant Revolutionary War heroine who offered water to soldiers during the Battle of Monmouth and fired her husband's canon after he was shot. (Rev: BCCB 6/02; BL 4/15/02; HB 5/02; HBG 10/02; SLJ 6/02)

POWELL, COLIN

15134 Blue, Rose, and Corinne J. Naden. *Colin Powell: Straight to the Top. Rev. ed.* (4–8). Series: Gateway Biographies. 1997, Millbrook LB $23.90 (978-0-7613-0256-8); paper $9.95 (978-0-7613-0242-1). A balanced biography of Colin Powell that focuses on his adult life and his stint as chairman of the Joint Chiefs of Staff. (Rev: BL 9/15/97; SLJ 1/98) [921]

15135 Feinstein, Stephen. *Colin Powell* (1–4). Series: African-American Heroes. 2007, Enslow LB $21.26 (978-0-7660-2761-9). 24pp. An easy-to-read account of the African American's life and career, with photographs. (Rev: SLJ 8/07)

15136 Finlayson, Reggie. *Colin Powell* (5–8). Series: A&E Biography. 2003, Lerner LB $27.93 (978-0-8225-4966-6); paper $7.95 (978-0-8225-9698-1). Documents Powell's rise through the military and transition into the political and diplomatic world. (Rev: BL 1/1–15/04; HBG 4/04)

15137 Senna, Carl. *Colin Powell: A Man of War and Peace* (4–8). 1992, Walker LB $16.85 (978-0-8027-8181-9). The life of the general who became the first African American chairman of the Joint Chiefs of Staff. (Rev: BL 3/15/93) [921]

15138 Shichtman, Sandra H. *Colin Powell: "Have a Vision. Be Demanding."* (5–8). Series: African-American Biography Library. 2005, Enslow LB $31.93 (978-0-7660-2464-9). Sandra H. Shichtman profiles former Secretary of State Colin Powell in this title from the African-American Biography Library series. (Rev: SLJ 11/05) [921]

PRINTZ, MICHAEL

15139 Bankston, John. *Michael L. Printz and the Story of the Michael L. Printz Award* (4–8). Series: Great Achievement Awards. 2003, Mitchell Lane LB $19.95 (978-1-58415-182-1). Printz's career as a high school librarian is highlighted in this account of his establishment of the well-known award for YA literature, which includes a list of prize winners. (Rev: BL 10/15/03; SLJ 10/03) [020]

REVERE, PAUL

15140 Ford, Carin T. *Paul Revere: Patriot* (2–4). Series: Heroes of American History. 2003, Enslow LB $22.60 (978-0-7660-2001-6). 32pp. A concise introduction to Revere and his midnight ride, with full-color reproductions. (Rev: HBG 10/03; SLJ 6/03)

15141 Giblin, James Cross. *The Many Rides of Paul Revere* (4–7). Illus. 2007, Scholastic $17.99 (978-0-439-57290-3). 96pp. This well-illustrated, large-format book provides lots of often overlooked information on Paul Revere, covering his childhood, training, career, and role in the American Revolution. (Rev: BL 9/1/07; SLJ 11/07)

15142 Randolph, Ryan P. *Paul Revere and the Minutemen of the American Revolution* (4–7). Series: Library of American Lives and Times. 2001, Rosen $34.60 (978-0-8239-5727-9). 112pp. Fairly large type and many illustrations bring to life Paul Revere, a businessman and family man but also a soldier and spy, and the group of patriots known as the Minutemen. (Rev: BL 10/15/01)

15143 Sutcliffe, Jane. *Paul Revere* (3–4). Series: History Maker Bios. 2002, Lerner LB $26.60 (978-0-8225-0195-4). This basic biography describes the life of this patriot who fought in the Revolutionary War and also worked as a silversmith, dentist, coppersmith, and printer. (Rev: BL 6/1–15/02; HBG 3/03)

15144 Tieck, Sarah. *Paul Revere* (K–3). Series: First Biographies. 2006, ABDO LB $25.65 (978-1-59679-787-1). A beginner's profile of Paul Revere and his contributions to American history, with lots of illustrations, a large typeface, and highlighted words that appear in the glossary. (Rev: SLJ 3/07)

15145 Winter, Jonah. *Paul Revere and the Bell Ringers* (K–2). Illus. by Bert Dodson. 2003, Simon & Schuster paper $3.99 (978-0-689-85635-8). 32pp. This brief profile focuses on a childhood experience that helped to instill a sense of responsibility. (Rev: HBG 4/04; SLJ 2/04)

RICE, CONDOLEEZZA

15146 Cunningham, Kevin. *Condoleezza Rice* (4–8). Series: Journey to Freedom. 2009, Child's World LB $28.50 (978-1-60253-120-8). 32pp. Providing a compelling, inspiring overview of the achievements of Condoleezza Rice, this book includes a timeline. (Rev: BL 3/15/09; LMC 10/09)

15147 Ditchfield, Christin. *Condoleezza Rice: America's Leading Stateswoman*. Rev. ed. (5–8). Series: Great Life Stories. 2006, Watts LB $30.50 (978-0-531-13874-8). An updated version of the 2003 biography, adding information on Rice's role as secretary of state and the continuing events in Iraq. (Rev: SLJ 2/07) [921]

15148 Ryan, Bernard. *Condoleezza Rice: National Security Advisor and Musician* (5–8). 2003, Ferguson LB $25.00 (978-0-8160-5480-0). 155pp. Rice's life and career are detailed, up to the invasion of Iraq. (Rev: SLJ 5/04)

15149 Wade, Mary Dodson. *Condoleezza Rice: Being the Best* (4–7). Illus. 2003, Millbrook LB $23.90 (978-0-7613-2619-9). 48pp. An interesting profile with a focus on Rice's talented youth and southern upbringing. (Rev: BL 3/1/03; HBG 10/03; SLJ 4/03)

ROGERS, ROBERT

15150 Quasha, Jennifer. *Robert Rogers: Rogers' Rangers and the French and Indian War* (4–7). Series: Library of American Lives and Times. 2001, Rosen $34.60 (978-0-8239-5731-6). A beautifully illustrated biography of Major Robert Rogers, who recruited companies of soldiers known as Rogers' Rangers to fight for the British in the French and Indian War. (Rev: BL 10/15/01) [921]

ROSS, BETSY

15151 Duden, Jane. *Betsy Ross* (4–6). Illus. Series: Let Freedom Ring. 2001, Capstone LB $23.93 (978-0-7368-1036-4). Ross's early life, her work as an upholsterer, and the famous sewing of the flag are placed in historical context. (Rev: HBG 3/02; SLJ 7/02)

15152 Harkins, Susan Sales, and William H. Harkins. *The Life and Times of Betsy Ross* (5–8). 2007, Mitchell Lane LB $19.95 (978-1-58415-446-4). This profile provides a balanced account of what is known about the life of Betsy Ross and her role, if any, in creating the American flag. (Rev: SLJ 7/07) [921]

15153 Miller, Susan Martins. *Betsy Ross: American Patriot* (3–6). Series: Revolutionary War Leaders. 2000, Chelsea LB $31.00 (978-0-7910-5360-7). 80pp. The story of the Quaker seamstress who went on to create the most recognized symbol of the United States. (Rev: HBG 10/00; SLJ 5/00)

15154 Randolph, Ryan P. *Betsy Ross: The American Flag and Life in a Young America* (4–7). Series: Library of American Lives and Times. 2001, Rosen $34.60 (978-0-8239-5730-9). This contemporary of George Washington was supposedly the seamstress of the American flag. (Rev: BL 1/1–15/02) [921]

SCHWARZENEGGER, ARNOLD

15155 Sexton, Colleen. *Arnold Schwarzenegger* (5–8). Series: A&E Biography. 2004, Lerner LB $29.27 (978-0-8225-1634-7). 112pp. This evenhanded profile, with many photographs and quotations, covers Schwarzenegger's life from his childhood in Austria to his election as governor of California and appends a list of his films. (Rev: BL 11/1/04)

SEWARD, WILLIAM HENRY

15156 Burgan, Michael. *William Henry Seward: Senator and Statesman* (3–5). Series: Famous Figures of the Civil War Era. 2001, Chelsea LB $25.00 (978-0-7910-6418-4). A clear and concise biography of the man who was secretary of state during the Civil War and who later negotiated the purchase of Alaska from Russia. (Rev: BL 4/1/02; HBG 10/02)

SHERIDAN, PHILIP

15157 Balcavage, Dynise. *Philip Sheridan: Union General* (3–5). Series: Famous Figures of the Civil War Era. 2001, Chelsea LB $25.00 (978-0-7910-6406-1). About 20 full-color illustrations are used with a simple text to tell the story of the Civil War army commander who forced Lee's surrender at Appomattox. (Rev: BL 4/1/02)

STANTON, EDWIN

15158 Allison, Amy. *Edwin Stanton: Union War Secretary* (3–5). Series: Famous Figures of the Civil War Era. 2001, Chelsea LB $25.00 (978-0-7910-6420-7). The fascinating story of the lawyer and public official who was secretary of war during the Civil War and whose feud with President Johnson was legendary. (Rev: BL 4/1/02)

STUART, JEB

15159 Greene, Meg. *James Ewell Brown Stuart: Confederate General* (3–5). Series: Famous Figures of the Civil War Era. 2001, Chelsea LB $25.00 (978-0-7910-6414-6). Known as Jeb Stuart, this distinguished Confederate army leader was killed in 1864 at Spotsylvania Courthouse. (Rev: BL 4/1/02; HBG 10/02)

STUYVESANT, PETER

15160 Krizner, L. J., and Lisa Sita. *Peter Stuyvesant: New Amsterdam, and the Origins of New York* (4–7). Series: Library of American Lives and Times. 2001, Rosen LB $34.60 (978-0-8239-5732-3). The story of New Amsterdam's best-known leader and how the Dutch presence in America influenced our culture for years to come. (Rev: BL 10/15/01; SLJ 7/01*) [921]

SUTTER, JOHN

15161 Engstrand, Iris, and Ken Owens. *John Sutter: Sutter's Fort and the California Gold Rush* (4–8). Series: The Library of American Lives and Times. 2004, Rosen LB $34.60 (978-0-8239-6630-1). The importance of understanding history is emphasized in this balanced and well-illustrated look at Sutter's life. (Rev: SLJ 7/04)

THOMAS, DAVE

15162 Kramer, Barbara. *Dave Thomas: Honesty Pays* (3–5). Illus. 2005, Enslow LB $23.93 (978-0-7660-2375-8). 48pp. An interesting profile of Thomas, the founder of Wendy's, who was adopted at birth and has worked to improve the lives of others. (Rev: BL 4/1/05)

TWEED, WILLIAM "BOSS"

15163 Johnson, Suzan. *Boss Tweed and Tammany Hall* (5–8). Series: Major World Leaders. 2002, Chelsea LB $27.44 (978-1-56711-224-5). 112pp. The amazing life of the corrupt New York politician who defrauded the city of more than $30 million and whose life ended in prison. (Rev: BL 1/1–15/03)

VALLEJO, MARIANO GUADALUPE

15164 Tracy, Kathleen. *Mariano Guadalupe Vallejo* (5–7). Series: Latinos in American History. 2002, Mitchell Lane LB $29.95 (978-1-58415-152-4). The story of the 19th-century military man who supported the U.S. annexation of California and later served in the state's first Senate. (Rev: BL 2/15/03; HBG 10/03) [921]

WEBSTER, DANIEL

15165 Harvey, Bonnie Carman. *Daniel Webster* (5–8). Series: Historical American Biographies. 2001, Enslow LB $26.60 (978-0-7660-1392-6). An engrossing biography of the American statesman, lawyer, and orator who fought to save the Union. (Rev: BL 1/1–15/02; HBG 3/02; SLJ 12/01)

WEBSTER, NOAH

15166 Shea, Pegi Deitz. *Noah Webster: Weaver of Words* (4–7). Illus. by Monica Vachula. 2009, Boyds Mills $18.95 (978-1-59078-441-9). 40pp. This is a large-format, illustrated biography of Webster (1758–1843), who was a man of many interests but is best known for his dictionary of the American language. Lexile 1000L (Rev: BL 11/15/09; LMC 5–6/10; SLJ 11/09) [921]

WELD, THEODORE

15167 Down, Susan Brophy. *Theodore Weld: Architect of Abolitionism* (5–8). Illus. Series: Voices for Freedom: Abolitionist Heroes. 2013, Crabtree LB $30.60 (978-077871062-2). 64pp. Archival photographs, documents, and quotations help to tell the story of abolitionist, writer, editor, speaker, and organizer Theodore Weld and offer an overview of his work and how he became one of the architects of the abolitionist movement in the 1800s. e (Rev: BL 9/1/13; LMC 3–4/14) [921]

WILSON, BILL

15168 White, Tom. *Bill W., a Different Kind of Hero* (4–7). 2003, Boyds Mills $16.95 (978-1-59078-067-1). The founder of Alcoholics Anonymous is the subject of this

biography that describes his long battle with addiction. (Rev: BL 4/15/03; HBG 10/03; SLJ 2/03) [362.292]

YOUNG, BRIGHAM

15169 Gunderson, Cory. *Brigham Young: Pioneer and Prophet* (3–5). Illus. Series: Let Freedom Ring. 2002, Capstone LB $23.93 (978-0-7368-1346-4). With good illustrations, this profile of Young's controversial life includes solid information and historical context. (Rev: HBG 3/03; SLJ 4/03)

15170 Sanford, William R., and Carl R. Green. *Brigham Young: Courageous Mormon Leader* (5–8). Illus. Series: Courageous Heroes of the American West. 2012, Enslow LB $21.26 (978-076604004-5). 48pp. An interesting profile of the religious leader and his challenge-filled westward trek. (Rev: BL 10/1/12; LMC 5–6/13) [921]

Native Americans

BLACK ELK

15171 Nelson, S. D. *Black Elk's Vision: A Lakota Story* (5–8). 2010, Abrams $19.95 (978-0-8109-8399-1). 48pp. A look at the life of the Lakota medicine man who fought in the Battle of Little Bighorn and later traveled with Buffalo Bill's Wild West show before being injured at the massacre at Wounded Knee. ALA Notable Children's Book. (Rev: BL 3/15/10*; SLJ 4/10) [921]

15172 Shaw, Maura D. *Black Elk: Native American Man of Spirit* (4–6). Series: Spiritual Biographies for Young Readers. 2004, SkyLight Paths $12.99 (978-1-59473-043-6). 32pp. The violent aspects of the life of the thoughtful Lakota Sioux warrior named Black Elk are in contrast to his conviction that humans must learn to love and respect the earth and all living things. (Rev: BL 12/15/04)

CHIPETA

15173 Krudwig, Vickie Leigh. *Searching for Chipeta: The Story of a Ute and Her People* (4–7). 2004, Fulcrum paper $12.95 (978-1-55591-466-0). In the second half of the 19th century, Chipeta and her Ute husband worked tirelessly — but ultimately unsuccessfully — to forge an agreement with the U.S. government that would allow the tribe to remain in its traditional homeland. (Rev: BL 9/1/04) [921]

CRAZY HORSE (SIOUX CHIEF)

15174 Birchfield, D. L. *Crazy Horse* (3–6). Series: Raintree Biographies. 2003, Raintree LB $25.69 (978-0-7398-5673-4). A simple biography of the Sioux chief's life and achievements, with sidebar features containing primary and background material. (Rev: HBG 3/03; SLJ 3/03)

15175 Brennan, Kristine. *Crazy Horse* (4–7). Series: Famous Figures of the American Frontier. 2001, Chelsea $25.00 (978-0-7910-6493-1); paper $25.00 (978-0-7910-6494-8). 64pp. Report writers will find this a useful source of information on this Native American leader's adult life and achievements in battle. (Rev: HBG 10/02; SLJ 4/02)

15176 Brimner, Larry Dane. *Chief Crazy Horse: Following a Vision* (2–4). Series: American Heroes. 2008, Marshall Cavendish $20.95 (978-0-7614-3061-2). 42pp. With sections on "Important Dates" and "Words to Know," this brief biography introduces the warrior chief of the Oglala tribe of the Sioux nation. (Rev: SLJ 3/09)

15177 Cunningham, Chet. *Chief Crazy Horse* (4–6). Series: A&E Biography. 2000, Lerner LB $27.93 (978-0-8225-4978-9). 112pp. This biography relates the life of the military leader of the Lakota Indians and tells how he became known for his bravery and ferocity in battle. (Rev: BL 6/1–15/00; HBG 3/01; SLJ 9/00)

15178 Haugen, Brenda. *Crazy Horse: Sioux Warrior* (5–8). Series: Signature Lives. 2005, Compass Point LB $34.60 (978-0-7565-0999-6). Crazy Horse's life and efforts to save his native lands and way of life are documented here. (Rev: SLJ 2/06) [921]

CROW, JOSEPH MEDICINE

15179 Medicine Crow, Joseph. *Counting Coup: Becoming a Crow Chief on the Reservation and Beyond* (5–8). Illus. 2006, National Geographic LB $23.90 (978-0-7922-8328-7); paper $6.95 (978-0-7922-7297-7). 128pp. The memoirs of a Crow chief who was educated in mission and boarding schools and went on to fight in World War II. (Rev: BCCB 5/06; BL 4/15/06; LMC 11/06; SLJ 7/06)

GERONIMO

15180 Feinstein, Stephen. *Read About Geronimo* (2–4). Series: I Like Biographies! 2006, Enslow LB $21.26 (978-0-7660-2598-1). This brief, introductory biography of Geronimo offers an overview of Apache life and the achievements of one of its greatest chiefs. (Rev: SLJ 4/06)

15181 Haugen, Brenda. *Geronimo: Apache Warrior* (5–8). Series: Signature Lives. 2005, Compass Point LB $34.60 (978-0-7565-1002-2). Geronimo's unsuccessful efforts to secure freedom for his people are documented in this attractive book. (Rev: SLJ 2/06) [921]

15182 Thompson, Bill, and Dorcas Thompson. *Geronimo* (4–7). Series: Famous Figures of the American Frontier. 2001, Chelsea $25.00 (978-0-7910-6491-7); paper $8.95 (978-0-7910-6492-4). 64pp. A balanced biography of the Apache leader that report writers will find a useful resource. (Rev: HBG 10/02; SLJ 4/02)

15183 Welch, Catherine A. *Geronimo* (3–5). Illus. Series: History Maker Bios. 2004, Lerner LB $26.60 (978-0-8225-0698-0). 47pp. A well-illustrated profile of the Apache chief who fought strongly against attempts to confine his people to reservations. (Rev: SLJ 4/04)

HAYES, IRA

15184 Nelson, S. D. *Quiet Hero* (3–5). 2006, Lee & Low $16.95 (978-1-58430-263-6). 32pp. Traces the short life of Ira Hayes, a shy Native American who was one of the marines shown raising the flag at Iwo Jima but, despite his acclaim as a hero, slid into depression on his return home. (Rev: BL 9/15/06; SLJ 9/06)

JOSEPH, CHIEF

15185 Biskup, Agnieszka. *Thunder Rolling Down the Mountain: The Story of Chief Joseph and the Nez Perce* (4–7). Illus. by Rusty Zimmerman. Series: American Graphic. 2011, Capstone LB $29.32 (978-142965472-2). 32pp. A graphic novel account of the life of the Nez Perce leader and his efforts on behalf of his people. (Rev: BL 6/1/11) [921]

15186 Klingel, Cynthia, and Robert B. Noyed. *Chief Joseph: Chief of the Nez Perce* (3–6). Illus. Series: Our People. 2002, Child's World LB $27.07 (978-1-56766-165-1). This is an attractive, brief introduction to the leader of the Nez Perce Indians. (Rev: BL 1/1–15/03; SLJ 2/03)

15187 Sutcliffe, Jane. *Chief Joseph* (3–5). Illus. Series: History Maker Bios. 2004, Lerner LB $26.60 (978-0-8225-0696-6). 48pp. Focuses on the famed Nez Perce chief who fought fiercely against European settlers' encroachment on his people's land. (Rev: SLJ 4/04)

JUMPER, BETTY MAE

15188 Annino, Jan Godown. *She Sang Promise: The Story of Betty Mae Jumper: Seminole Tribal Leader* (2–5). Illus. by Lisa Desimini. 2010, National Geographic $17.95 (978-1-4263-0592-4); LB $26.90 (978-1-4263-0593-1). 48pp. Betty Mae Jumper, daughter of a French trapper and a Seminole woman, conquered many challenges to become a leader of the Seminole tribe. (Rev: LMC 3–4/10; SLJ 4/1/10) [921]

LADUKE, WINONA

15189 Silverstone, Michael. *Winona LaDuke: Restoring Land and Culture in Native America* (5–8). Series: Women Changing the World. 2001, Feminist $19.95 (978-1-55861-260-0). 112pp. A candidate for the vice presidency under Ralph Nader in 2000, this author and environmental and Native American rights activist lives on a reservation in Minnesota, where she is dedicated to restoring the land and the culture. (Rev: BL 12/15/01; HBG 10/02)

LOYIE, LARRY

15190 Loyie, Larry, and Constance Brissenden. *As Long as the Rivers Flow* (3–6). Illus. by Heather D. Holmlund. 2003, Douglas & McIntyre $16.95 (978-0-88899-473-8). 40pp. Loyie describes the summer he was 10, living happily among his extended Cree family in the wilds of Alberta but dreading the impending threat of government-enforced boarding school. (Rev: BL 4/15/03; SLJ 10/03)

MENCHU, RIGOBERTA

15191 Menchú, Rigoberta, and Dante Liano. *The Girl from Chimel* (4–7). Trans. by David Unger. Illus. by Domi. 2005, Groundwood $16.95 (978-0-88899-666-4). Rigoberta Menchu, winner of the 1992 Nobel Peace Prize and Maya activist, tells about growing up in the Guatemalan Indian village of Chimel. (Rev: BL 11/1/05; SLJ 2/06) [868]

MONTEZUMA, CARLOS

15192 Capaldi, Gina. *A Boy Named Beckoning: A True Story of Dr. Carlos Montezuma, Native American Hero* (2–4). Illus. by author. 2008, Carolrhoda $16.95 (978-0-8225-7644-0). 32pp. Capaldi traces the life of the Yavapai Indian who was captured as a child but grew up to become a doctor and activist for his people. (Rev: BL 3/15/08; LMC 10/08; SLJ 3/08)

OSCEOLA (SEMINOLE CHIEF)

15193 Koestler-Grack, Rachel A. *Osceola: 1804–1838* (3–6). Illus. Series: American Indian Biographies. 2003, Capstone LB $23.93 (978-0-7368-1211-5). 32pp. In addition to covering Osceola's leadership against American forces, this concise volume looks at his childhood and the Seminole culture. (Rev: HBG 3/03; SLJ 4/03)

PARKER, CHIEF QUANAH

15194 Zemlicka, Shannon. *Quanah Parker* (3–5). Illus. Series: History Maker Bios. 2004, Lerner LB $26.60 (978-0-8225-0724-6). 48pp. Quanah Parker, the last chief of the Comanche, is profiled in this well-illustrated entry that highlights the losses suffered by the Native Americans. (Rev: SLJ 4/04)

PARKER, ELY

15195 Van Steenwyk, Elizabeth. *Seneca Chief, Army General: A Story About Ely Parker* (4–6). Illus. by Karen Ritz. Series: Creative Minds Biographies. 2000, Carolrhoda LB $22.60 (978-1-57505-431-5). 64pp. The story of the Native American who was appointed by Ulysses Grant as Commissioner of Indian Affairs, the first Native American to hold that post. (Rev: HBG 3/01; SLJ 2/01)

POCAHONTAS

15196 Brimner, Larry Dane. *Pocahontas: Bridging Two Worlds* (2–4). Series: American Heroes. 2008, Marshall Cavendish $20.95 (978-0-7614-3065-0). 42pp. With sections on "Important Dates" and "Words to Know," this brief biography traces the life of the Native American woman who helped the Virginia settlers. (Rev: SLJ 3/09)

15197 Nettleton, Pamela Hill. *Pocahontas: Peacemaker and Friend to the Colonists* (K–3). Illus. by Jeff Yesh. 2003, Picture Window LB $25.26 (978-1-4048-0187-5). 24pp. A brightly illustrated profile that is suitable for beginning readers. (Rev: SLJ 4/04)

15198 Raatma, Lucia. *Pocahontas* (1–5). 2001, Compass Point LB $21.26 (978-0-7565-0115-0). 32pp. An acces-

sible and attractive book that is careful to distinguish facts from legends. (Rev: SLJ 1/02)

15199 Sullivan, George. *Pocahontas* (3–5). Series: In Their Own Words. 2002, Scholastic $12.95 (978-0-439-32668-1); paper $4.99 (978-0-439-16585-3). 128pp. After explaining the difference between primary and secondary sources, the author re-creates the life of Pocahontas by quoting from original documents. (Rev: BL 8/02; HBG 10/02; SLJ 11/02)

15200 Zemlicka, Shannon. *Pocahontas* (2–3). Illus. by Jeni Reeves. Series: On My Own Biography. 2002, Carolrhoda LB $23.93 (978-0-87614-598-2); paper $5.95 (978-0-87614-906-5). 48pp. This biography for beginning readers covers the Powhatan Indian's birth, contacts with English settlers, family life, and death, and points out what information is reliable and where exaggeration may occur. (Rev: SLJ 1/03)

POKIAK-FENTON, MARGARET

15201 Jordan-Fenton, Christy, and Margaret Pokiak-Fenton. *Fatty Legs* (4–8). Illus. by Liz Amini-Holmes. 2010, Annick $21.95 (978-1-55451-247-8); paper $12.95 (978-1-55451-246-1). 106pp. This autobiography tells the moving story of a young Inuvialuit girl whose desire to learn to read led her to spend two years in a church-run school that tried to erase the students' identities; set in the 1940s. (Rev: SLJ 12/1/10) [921]

15202 Jordan-Fenton, Christy, and Margaret Pokiak-Fenton. *A Stranger at Home: A True Story* (3–6). Illus. by Liz Amini-Holmes. 2011, Annick $21.95 (978-1-55451-362-8); paper $12.95 (978-1-55451-361-1). 124pp. In this sequel to *Fatty Legs* (2010), Pokiak-Fenton recalls her return to her Inuit village after two years being educated by priests and nuns, and her realization that she has forgotten her own language and is now regarded as an outsider. (Rev: SLJ 12/1/11) [921]

SACAGAWEA

15203 Adler, David A. *A Picture Book of Sacagawea* (1–4). Illus. by Dan Brown. Series: Picture Book. 2000, Holiday House $16.95 (978-0-8234-1485-7). 32pp. The important known facts about Sacagawea, from her birth to the silver dollar in her image, are recounted in this competent biography. (Rev: BL 6/1–15/00; HBG 10/00; SLJ 6/00)

15204 Collard, Sneed B., III. *Sacagawea: Brave Shoshone Girl* (2–4). Illus. Series: American Heroes. 2006, Marshall Cavendish LB $28.50 (978-0-7614-2166-5). 48pp. Archival images add to this life of the Shoshone Indian, which looks at her early life as well as her experiences on the Lewis and Clark expedition. (Rev: BL 1/1–15/07; SLJ 3/07)

15205 DeKeyser, Stacy. *Sacagawea* (3–6). Series: Watts Library. 2004, Scholastic LB $25.50 (978-0-531-12290-7). 64pp. The story of Sacagawea and her journeys with Lewis and Clark's Corps of Discovery is recounted with many illustrations, maps, a timeline, and other helpful features. (Rev: BL 6/1–15/04)

15206 Erdrich, Lise. *Sacagawea* (2–6). 2003, Carolrhoda $16.95 (978-0-87614-646-0). 40pp. This large-format biography of Sacagawea, which features full-page oil paintings, stays close to historical facts as it traces the story of the Shoshone woman who traveled with Lewis and Clark. (Rev: BL 9/1/03; HBG 4/04; SLJ 10/03)

15207 Marcovitz, Hal. *Sacagawea: Guide for the Lewis and Clark Expedition* (4–6). Illus. Series: Explorers of New Worlds. 2000, Chelsea LB $25.00 (978-0-7910-5959-3); paper $25.00 (978-0-7910-6169-5). 63pp. In addition to the usual information on Sacagawea's life, this biography discusses why she has remained such an inspiration. (Rev: SLJ 4/01)

SEQUOYAH (CHEROKEE CHIEF)

15208 Basel, Roberta. *Sequoyah: Inventor of Written Cherokee* (5–8). Series: Signature Lives. 2007, Compass Point LB $31.93 (978-0-7565-1887-5). A life of the Cherokee leader whose efforts to transcribe spoken Cherokee into a written language were not greatly appreciated; this volume will be useful for report writers. (Rev: SLJ 7/07) [921]

15209 Fitterer, C. Ann. *Sequoyah: Native American Scholar* (2–4). Series: Spirit of America: Our People. 2002, Child's World LB $27.07 (978-1-56766-167-5). 32pp. A concise introduction to the life of the Cherokee Indian who invented an alphabet for their language. (Rev: SLJ 12/02)

15210 Klausner, Janet. *Sequoyah's Gift: A Portrait of the Cherokee Leader* (4–7). 1993, HarperCollins LB $16.89 (978-0-06-021236-0). The life of this Cherokee leader is retold, with material on his invention of a written alphabet and his behavior during the Trail of Tears journey. (Rev: BL 9/1/93; HB 9–10/93; SLJ 11/93) [921]

15211 Rumford, James. *Sequoyah: The Cherokee Man Who Gave His People Writing* (1–3). Trans. by Anna Sixkiller Huckaby. Illus. 2004, Houghton $16.00 (978-0-618-36947-8). 32pp. Cherokee translations appear below the English text in this tall slim volume on Sequoyah. (Rev: BL 10/15/04; SLJ 8/04)

SITTING BULL (SIOUX CHIEF)

15212 Aller, Susan Bivin. *Sitting Bull* (3–5). Illus. Series: History Maker Bios. 2004, Lerner LB $26.60 (978-0-8225-0700-0). 47pp. The valiant Sioux chief's life is detailed in this well-illustrated biography that highlights the losses suffered by the Native Americans. (Rev: SLJ 4/04)

15213 Marcovitz, Hal. *Sitting Bull* (3–6). Series: Famous Figures of the American Frontier. 2001, Chelsea LB $25.00 (978-0-7910-6487-0); paper $8.95 (978-0-7910-6488-7). 64pp. The Sioux chief's efforts to improve relations between the Native Americans and the European newcomers are emphasized in this appealing biography. (Rev: SLJ 3/02)

TECUMSEH (SHAWNEE CHIEF)

15214 Koestler-Grack, Rachel A. *Tecumseh: 1768–1813* (3–6). Illus. Series: American Indian Biographies. 2003, Capstone LB $23.93 (978-0-7368-1212-2). 32pp. In addition to covering Tecumseh's efforts to bring together the Native American tribes, this concise volume looks at his childhood and the Shawnee culture. (Rev: HBG 3/03; SLJ 4/03)

TINGLE, TIM

15215 Tingle, Tim. *Saltypie: A Choctaw Journey from Darkness into Light* (3–5). Illus. by Karen Clarkson. 2010, Cinco Puntos $17.95 (978-1-933693-67-5). 40pp. Choctaw storyteller Tingle reflects on his life, recounting the bravery with which his family faced the racism and discrimination that colored their daily life. (Rev: BL 5/1/10; LMC 11–12/10; SLJ 5/1/10) [921]

WALKING COYOTE

15216 Bruchac, Joseph. *Buffalo Song* (1–3). Illus. by Bill Farnsworth. 2008, Lee & Low $17.95 (978-1-58430-280-3). 40pp. Bruchac tells the story of a Salish Indian, Walking Coyote, who worked to save the buffalo from extinction. (Rev: BL 4/1/08; LMC 11/08; SLJ 6/08)

WEBER, EDNAH NEW RIDER

15217 Weber, EdNah New Rider. *Rattlesnake Mesa: Stories from a Native American Childhood* (4–8). 2004, Lee & Low $18.95 (978-1-58430-231-5). In this poignant memoir, Weber tells of her life as a student at a government-run boarding school for Native Americans during the 1920s. (Rev: BL 12/15/04; SLJ 12/04) [921]

WINNEMUCCA, SARAH

15218 Ray, Deborah Kogan. *Paiute Princess: The Story of Sarah Winnemucca* (4–7). Illus. by author. 2012, Farrar $17.99 (978-037439897-2). 48pp. Ray tells the story of the Native American woman born in 1844, whose talent with languages allowed her to bridge two worlds and defend her people in the face of oppression. ◯ ℮ Lexile 1010L (Rev: BL 6/12; HB 5–6/12; LMC 10/12*; SLJ 7/12*) [921]

ZITKALA-SA

15219 Capaldi, Gina, and Q. L. Pearce. *Red Bird Sings: The Story of Zitkala-Sa, Native American Author, Musician, and Activist* (2–4). Illus. by Gina Capaldi. 2011, Carolrhoda $17.95 (978-076135257-0). 32pp. In the late 1800s, a young Sioux girl opted to head east with missionaries instead of staying on the reservation, and her musical skills helped her in her fight for Native American rights; draws on semi-autobiographical stories. (Rev: BL 11/1/11; SLJ 10/1/11*) [921]

Presidents

ADAMS, JOHN

15220 Behrman, Carol H. *John Adams* (5–8). Illus. Series: Presidential Leaders. 2003, Lerner LB $29.27 (978-0-8225-0820-5). 112pp. This biography provides lots of details and illustrations, covering Adams's life and career. (Rev: BL 1/1–15/04)

15221 Feinberg, Barbara S. *John Adams* (5–8). Illus. Series: Encyclopedia of Presidents. 2003, Children's Pr. LB $34.00 (978-0-516-22680-4). 128pp. An informative and appealing account of Adams's life and achievements, with glossary, timeline, and lists of books and Web sites. (Rev: BL 1/1–15/04)

15222 Feinstein, Stephen. *John Adams* (5–9). 2002, Enslow LB $25.26 (978-0-7660-5001-3). 48pp. A well-written and accessible overview of Adams's life and contributions that is extended by a number of recommended Web sites. (Rev: SLJ 6/02)

15223 Harness, Cheryl. *The Revolutionary John Adams* (3–6). Illus. 2002, National Geographic $17.95 (978-0-7922-6970-0). 48pp. Ample quotes, appealing illustrations, and a timeline enhance this biography of America's somewhat neglected second president. (Rev: BL 12/1/02; HBG 3/03; SLJ 2/03)

ADAMS, JOHN AND ABIGAIL

15224 Adler, David A., and Michael S. Adler. *A Picture Book of John and Abigail Adams* (1–3). Illus. by Ronald Himler. Series: Picture Book Biography. 2010, Holiday House $17.95 (978-082342007-0). 32pp. An introduction to the public and private lives of the second president and his wife. (Rev: BL 2/1/10) [921]

15225 Ashby, Ruth. *John and Abigail Adams* (5–8). Series: Presidents and First Ladies. 2005, Gareth Stevens LB $31.00 (978-0-8368-5755-9). An accessible, balanced, and attractive discussion of the Adamses and the contributions each made to their joint lives. (Rev: BL 3/1/05) [921]

ADAMS, JOHN QUINCY

15226 Feinstein, Stephen. *John Quincy Adams* (5–9). 2002, Enslow LB $25.26 (978-0-7660-5002-0). 48pp. Adams's early and later life are covered in this concise biography that includes several pages of annotated Web site recommendations. (Rev: HBG 10/02; SLJ 10/02)

15227 McCollum, Sean. *John Quincy Adams* (4–6). Illus. Series: Encyclopedia of Presidents. 2003, Children's Pr. LB $34.00 (978-0-516-22867-9). 110pp. An updated profile that looks at Adams's life and contributions, providing many illustrations and sidebars. (Rev: SLJ 1/04)

15228 Venezia, Mike. *John Quincy Adams: Sixth President* (1–3). Illus. by author. Series: Getting to Know the U.S. Presidents. 2004, Children's Pr. LB $28.00 (978-0-516-22611-8); paper $7.95 (978-0-516-27480-5). 32pp. This unusual biography takes a light-hearted approach to the key details of the president's life, adding comic-book-style graphics and dialogue bubbles to the large type. (Rev: BL 4/1/04; HBG 4/04; SLJ 4/05)

15229 Walker, Jane C. *John Quincy Adams* (4–6). Series: United States Presidents. 2000, Enslow LB $26.60 (978-0-7660-1161-8). 128pp. A well-organized profile of the man who was a Revolutionary War leader, vice president, and was elected president in 1824. (Rev: BL 10/15/00; HBG 3/01)

ARTHUR, CHESTER A.

15230 Young, Jeff C. *Chester A. Arthur* (4–7). Series: Presidents. 2002, Enslow LB $25.26 (978-0-7660-5077-8). 48pp. As well as an overview of the life and accomplishments of Chester A. Arthur, this book gives a pre-evaluated listing of Web sites where more material can be found. (Rev: BL 12/15/02)

BUCHANAN, JAMES

15231 Young, Jeff C. *James Buchanan* (4–7). Series: Presidents. 2003, Enslow LB $25.26 (978-0-7660-5101-0). 48pp. The story of the fifteenth president who had an extensive political career before becoming president. (Rev: BL 6/1–15/03; HBG 10/03)

BUSH, GEORGE W.

15232 Burgan, Michael. *George W. Bush* (5–8). Illus. Series: Presidents and Their Times. 2012, Marshall Cavendish LB $34.21 (978-160870184-1). 112pp. An appealing, chronological profile that gives an evenhanded account of Bush's life and administrations. (Rev: BL 6/12) [921]

15233 Burgan, Michael. *George W. Bush: Our Forty-Third President* (3–5). Illus. Series: Our Presidents. 2005, Child's World LB $28.50 (978-1-59296-494-9). 48pp. With much material on the war on terrorism, this volume covers Bush's life from childhood through the 2004 elections. [921]

15234 Cohen, Daniel. *George W. Bush: The Family Business* (4–6). Illus. 2000, Millbrook $23.90 (978-0-7613-1851-4). This slim biography ends before the 2000 election that resulted in Bush winning the presidency, but gives valuable information about his youth and family. (Rev: BL 5/1/00; HBG 10/00)

15235 Jones, Veda Boyd. *George W. Bush* (5–8). Illus. Series: Modern World Leaders. 2006, Chelsea House $30.00 (978-0-7910-9217-0). 128pp. This biography traces Bush's life and political career from his 1946 birth in New Haven, Connecticut, through the first five years of his presidency. (Rev: BL 10/15/06)

15236 Kachurek, Sandra J. *George W. Bush* (4–7). Series: United States Presidents. 2004, Enslow LB $26.60 (978-0-7660-2040-5). 128pp. A balanced and well-documented profile with plenty of photographs plus lists of Web sites and places to visit. (Rev: BL 9/15/04)

15237 Marquez, Heron. *George W. Bush* (5–8). Series: Presidential Leaders. 2006, Lerner LB $29.27 (978-0-8225-1507-4). A balanced profile that examines Bush's childhood and adolescence as well as his accomplishments and the controversies surrounding some of his decisions. (Rev: BL 10/15/06) [921]

15238 Ryan, Patrick. *George W. Bush* (1–3). Illus. Series: United States Presidents. 2001, ABDO LB $22.78 (978-1-57765-302-8). 32pp. Report writers will find the basic information they need on Bush's life, with many clear photographs in both color and black and white. (Rev: HBG 10/01; SLJ 9/01)

15239 Thompson, Bill, and Dorcas Thompson. *George W. Bush* (4–8). Series: Childhoods of the Presidents. 2003, Mason Crest $17.95 (978-1-59084-281-2). Bush's privileged childhood and education, his role as eldest son, and the death of his sister from leukemia are covered in an interesting narrative that highlights his character. (Rev: BL 6/1–15/03; SLJ 2/03) [973.931]

15240 Wheeler, Jill C. *George W. Bush* (4–7). Series: War on Terrorism. 2002, ABDO LB $25.65 (978-1-57765-662-3). A brief profile of President Bush with particular emphasis on his war on terrorism. (Rev: BL 5/15/02; HBG 10/02) [921]

15241 Wukovits, John F. *George W. Bush* (5–8). Series: People in the News. 2000, Lucent LB $32.45 (978-1-56006-693-4). 96pp. Published before the 2000 election, this biography uses extensive quotations from Mr. Bush, his friends, and critics. (Rev: BL 9/15/00; HBG 3/01; SLJ 10/00)

CARTER, JIMMY

15242 Kent, Deborah. *Jimmy Carter* (4–7). Series: Encyclopedia of Presidents — Second Series. 2005, Children's Pr. LB $34.00 (978-0-516-22975-1). Updated from the 1989 volume, this new, redesigned edition covers the former president's life and career and adds information about his recent work. (Rev: BL 6/1–15/05) [973.926]

15243 O'Shei, Tim. *Jimmy Carter* (5–9). 2002, Enslow LB $25.26 (978-0-7660-5051-8). 48pp. This introduction to Carter's life, including his childhood, and his contributions contains a long list of recommended Web sites that extend the printed material. (Rev: HBG 10/02; SLJ 6/02)

15244 Santella, Andrew. *James Earl Carter Jr.* (4–7). Series: Profiles of the Presidents. 2002, Compass Point LB $26.60 (978-0-7565-0283-6). A straightforward profile that touches on Carter's southern roots, his successes and failures as president, and his subsequent work in the fields of human rights and democracy. (Rev: SLJ 1/03) [921]

15245 Smith, Betsy. *Jimmy Carter, President* (5–7). 1986, Walker LB $13.85 (978-0-8027-6652-6). A profile of Jimmy Carter and his one-term presidency. (Rev: BL 2/15/87; SLJ 12/86) [921]

CLINTON, BILL

15246 Cwiklik, Robert. *Bill Clinton: President of the 90's. Rev. ed.* (4–8). Series: Gateway Biographies. 1997, Millbrook $22.90 (978-0-7613-0129-5); paper $8.95

(978-0-7613-0146-2). A readable biography that concentrates on Clinton's career as governor of Arkansas and his early years as president. (Rev: BL 9/15/97; SLJ 7/97) [921]

15247 Heinrichs, Ann. *William Jefferson Clinton* (4–8). Series: Profiles of the Presidents. 2002, Compass Point LB $26.60 (978-0-7565-0207-2). This absorbing account of Clinton's life and career covers both the good and bad sides of his presidency and includes a discussion of Hillary's role. (Rev: SLJ 6/02) [921]

15248 Marcovitz, Hal. *Bill Clinton* (4–8). Series: Childhoods of the Presidents. 2003, Mason Crest LB $17.95 (978-1-59084-273-7). This brief, well-illustrated overview of Clinton's childhood and adolescence looks in particular at his relationships with family members, his support for civil rights, and his popularity. (Rev: BL 6/1–15/03; SLJ 2/03) [973.929]

EISENHOWER, DWIGHT D.

15249 Adler, David A. *A Picture Book of Dwight David Eisenhower* (1–3). Illus. Series: Picture Book Biographies. 2002, Holiday House $16.95 (978-0-8234-1702-5). 32pp. Traces the life of the 34th president, Dwight D. Eisenhower, from his childhood in Kansas to his death in 1969. (Rev: BL 10/15/02; HBG 3/03; SLJ 10/02)

15250 Alphin, Elaine M., and Arthur B. Alphin. *Dwight D. Eisenhower* (3–4). Illus. Series: History Maker Bios. 2004, Lerner LB $26.60 (978-0-8225-1544-9). 48pp. A simple biography, useful for report writers, with information about Eisenhower's youth and good photographs and illustrations. (Rev: SLJ 1/05)

15251 Deitch, Kenneth, and Joanne B. Weisman. *Dwight D. Eisenhower: Man of Many Hats* (5–7). Illus. by Jay Connolly. 1990, Discovery LB $14.95 (978-1-878668-02-8). Each stage of Eisenhower's multifaceted career is represented. (Rev: SLJ 2/91) [921]

15252 Raatma, Lucia. *Dwight D. Eisenhower* (4–7). Series: Profiles of the Presidents. 2002, Compass Point LB $26.60 (978-0-7565-0279-9). A straightforward account that focuses on Eisenhower's military career and successes in World War II. (Rev: SLJ 1/03) [921]

15253 Van Steenwyk, Elizabeth. *Dwight David Eisenhower, President* (5–8). 1987, Walker LB $13.85 (978-0-8027-6671-7). The focus is on the career of this war-hero president. (Rev: BL 5/15/87) [921]

FILLMORE, MILLARD

15254 Gottfried, Ted. *Millard Fillmore* (4–7). Series: Presidents and Their Times. 2007, Marshall Cavendish LB $22.95 (978-0-7614-2431-4). 96pp. A clear and thorough life of the president, describing his early years, presidential career, and later life, with discussion of important events that took place during his life. (Rev: SLJ 1/08)

GARFIELD, JAMES A.

15255 Young, Jeff C. *James A. Garfield* (4–7). Series: Presidents. 2003, Enslow LB $25.26 (978-0-7660-5100-

3). 48pp. The story of the twentieth president of the U.S. who served as a major general during the Civil War and was assassinated while he was still in office. (Rev: BL 6/1–15/03)

GRANT, ULYSSES S.

15256 Alter, Judy. *Ulysses S. Grant* (5–9). 2002, Enslow LB $25.26 (978-0-7660-5014-3). 48pp. Grant's early and later life are covered in this concise and balanced biography that includes several pages of annotated Web site recommendations. (Rev: SLJ 10/02)

15257 Crompton, Samuel Willard. *Ulysses S. Grant* (5–8). Series: Leaders of the Civil War Era. 2009, Chelsea House $30 (978-1-60413-301-1). 112pp. Enhanced by a mix of illustrations, period documents, photographs, and concise sidebars, this book provides a balanced look at the most successful leader of the Union Army and president of the United States. (Rev: LMC 10/09) [921]

15258 Sapp, Richard. *Ulysses S. Grant and the Road to Appomattox* (5–8). Series: In the Footsteps of American Heroes. 2006, World Almanac LB $34.00 (978-0-8368-6431-1). This life of Grant includes information on historical sites in sidebar features. (Rev: SLJ 9/06) [921]

HARRISON, WILLIAM HENRY

15259 Gaines, Ann Graham. *William Henry Harrison: Our Ninth President* (4–6). Series: Spirit of America: Our Presidents. 2001, Child's World LB $28.50 (978-1-56766-848-3). 48pp. A well-illustrated and appealing biography that discusses influences that shaped Harrison's policies and looks at his legacy. (Rev: SLJ 12/01)

15260 Venezia, Mike. *William Henry Harrison* (3–4). Illus. Series: Getting to Know the U.S. Presidents. 2005, Children's Pr. LB $28.00 (978-0-516-22614-9); paper $7.95 (978-0-516-27483-6). 32pp. A light-hearted approach to the key details of Harrison's life, adding comic-book-style graphics and dialogue bubbles to the large-type text. [921]

HOOVER, HERBERT

15261 Ruth, Amy. *Herbert Hoover* (5–8). Series: Presidential Leaders. 2004, Lerner LB $29.27 (978-0-8225-0821-2). 112pp. Quotations, photographs, and informative sidebars add to the engaging text about Hoover's life and times. (Rev: SLJ 1/05)

JACKSON, ANDREW

15262 Behrman, Carol H. *Andrew Jackson* (5–8). Series: Presidential Leaders. 2002, Lerner LB $29.27 (978-0-8225-0093-3). Jackson's life and character are brought to life in this narrative that points out his failings as well as his achievements. (Rev: HBG 3/03; SLJ 1/03) [921]

15263 Feinstein, Stephen. *Andrew Jackson* (5–9). 2002, Enslow LB $25.26 (978-0-7660-5003-7). 48pp. A well-written and accessible overview of Jackson's life and contributions that is extended by a number of recommended Web sites. (Rev: SLJ 6/02; VOYA 8/02)

15264 Venezia, Mike. *Andrew Jackson: Seventh President, 1829–1837* (3–4). Illus. Series: Getting to Know the U.S. Presidents. 2005, Children's Pr. LB $28.00 (978-0-516-22612-5); paper $7.95 (978-0-516-27481-2). 32pp. A light-hearted approach to the key details of Jackson's life, adding comic-book-style graphics and dialogue bubbles to the large-type text. [921]

JEFFERSON, THOMAS

15265 Aldridge, Rebecca. *Thomas Jefferson* (5–6). Series: Let Freedom Ring. 2001, Capstone LB $23.93 (978-0-7368-1035-7). 48pp. An introduction to the life and work of Jefferson that touches on his attachment to Sally Hemmings. (Rev: HBG 3/02; SLJ 4/02)

15266 Chew, Elizabeth V. *Thomas Jefferson: A Day at Monticello* (3–6). Illus. by Mark Elliott. 2014, Abrams $18.95 (978-141970541-0). 56pp. Written by a former curator at Monticello, this handsome volume follows Jefferson through a typical day late in his life, revealing much about his habits, his farm, his entertainment, and his history. (Rev: BL 3/1/14; LMC 10/14; SLJ 4/14) [973.4]

15267 Davis, Kenneth C. *Don't Know Much About Thomas Jefferson* (4–7). Illus. by Rob Shepperson. Series: Don't Know Much About. 2005, HarperTrophy paper $4.99 (978-0-06-442128-7). Jefferson's many accomplishments and contributions are presented in a question-and-answer format amplified by sidebar features, maps, and quotations that add context. (Rev: BL 2/1/05; SLJ 5/05) [921]

15268 Ferris, Jeri. *Thomas Jefferson: Father of Liberty* (5–8). 1998, Lerner LB $30.35 (978-1-57505-009-6). This readable biography covers both the public and the private sides of Jefferson's life, with details on his personality and his family. (Rev: BL 3/1/99; HBG 3/99; SLJ 12/98) [921]

15269 Ford, Carin T. *Thomas Jefferson: The Third President* (2–4). Illus. Series: Heroes of American History. 2003, Enslow LB $22.60 (978-0-7660-1861-7). 32pp. Jefferson's life and achievements are covered here, as are questions about his ownership of slaves. (Rev: HBG 10/03; SLJ 9/03)

15270 Gomez, Rebecca. *Thomas Jefferson* (2–3). Illus. Series: First Biographies. 2003, ABDO LB $22.78 (978-1-57765-947-1). For young report writers, this is a simple account of Jefferson's major accomplishments. (Rev: HBG 4/04; SLJ 9/03)

15271 Harness, Cheryl. *Thomas Jefferson* (4–7). 2004, National Geographic $17.95 (978-0-7922-6496-5). Harness paints a personal portrait of Jefferson and his various roles in this picture book, enhanced by maps and eye-catching illustrations. (Rev: BL 2/1/04; SLJ 2/04) [973.4]

15272 Leslie, Tonya. *Thomas Jefferson: A Life of Patriotism* (1–3). Illus. by Tina Walski. Series: Blastoff! Readers. People of Character. 2007, Children's Pr. LB $20.00 (978-0-531-14715-3). 24pp. For beginning readers, this is a simple account of Jefferson's life and goals. (Rev: SLJ 1/08)

15273 Miller, Brandon Marie. *Thomas Jefferson for Kids: His Life and Times with 21 Activities* (5–8). Illus. 2011, Chicago Review paper $16.95 (978-1-56976-348-3). 144pp. Age-appropriate activities (dancing a reel, making a simple microscope) extend this balanced biography that covers personal and political aspects of Jefferson. (Rev: BLO 9/15/11; SLJ 10/1/11) [921]

15274 Nardo, Don. *Thomas Jefferson* (3–6). Series: Encyclopedia of Presidents. 2003, Children's Pr. LB $34.00 (978-0-516-22768-9). 110pp. A well-designed biography with maps, drawings, facts, a timeline, and other features that will be useful for report writers. (Rev: SLJ 4/04)

15275 Reiter, Chris. *Thomas Jefferson* (4–7). Illus. Series: MyReportLinks.com. 2002, Enslow LB $25.26 (978-0-7660-5071-6). 48pp. A concise biography suitable for students doing reports that provides extensive Web links for further research and uses Web site images among the many illustrations. (Rev: BL 9/1/02; HBG 3/03)

15276 Sherrow, Victoria. *Thomas Jefferson* (3–4). Illus. Series: History Maker Bios. 2002, Lerner LB $26.60 (978-0-8225-0197-8). 48pp. A heavily illustrated story of the multitalented man who was also an important president. (Rev: BL 6/1–15/02)

15277 Venezia, Mike. *Thomas Jefferson* (3–4). Illus. Series: Getting to Know the U.S. Presidents. 2004, Children's Pr. LB $28.00 (978-0-516-22608-8); paper $7.95 (978-0-516-27477-5). 32pp. A light-hearted approach to the key details of Jefferson's life, adding comic-book-style graphics and dialogue bubbles to the large-type text. [921]

JOHNSON, ANDREW

15278 Alter, Judy. *Andrew Johnson* (5–8). 2002, Enslow LB $25.26 (978-0-7660-5007-5). 48pp. This overview of Johnson's life and career contains a listing of about 30 Web sites that will extend the information contained in the book. (Rev: SLJ 6/02)

15279 Stevens, Rita. *Andrew Johnson: 17th President of the United States* (5–7). 1989, Garrett LB $21.27 (978-0-944483-16-9). Story of the man who became president on Lincoln's assassination. (Rev: BL 5/1/89) [973.810924]

JOHNSON, LYNDON B.

15280 Colbert, Nancy A. *Great Society: The Story of Lyndon Baines Johnson* (4–8). Illus. 2002, Morgan Reynolds LB $23.95 (978-1-883846-84-8). 144pp. A solid, readable life of the hardworking president that presents fairly both his virtues and defects. (Rev: BL 4/15/02; HBG 3/03; SLJ 8/02)

15281 Levy, Debbie. *Lyndon B. Johnson* (5–9). Series: Presidential Leaders. 2003, Lerner LB $29.27 (978-0-8225-0097-1). A look at the fascinating personal and political life of the president known for his support for

civil rights and for increasing the U.S. involvement in Vietnam. (Rev: HBG 10/03; SLJ 2/03)

KENNEDY, JOHN F.

15282 Anderson, Catherine Corley. *John F. Kennedy* (5–8). Series: Presidential Leaders. 2004, Lerner LB $29.27 (978-0-8225-0812-0). Quotations, photographs, and informative sidebars add to the engaging text about Kennedy's life and times. (Rev: SLJ 1/05) [921]

15283 Heiligman, Deborah. *High Hopes: A Photobiography of John F. Kennedy* (4–6). Ed. by Nancy Feresten. 2003, National Geographic $17.95 (978-0-7922-6141-4). This lavishly illustrated biography looks at Kennedy's achievements and his assassination. (Rev: BL 11/15/03; HBG 4/04; SLJ 4/04)

15284 Hodge, Marie. *John F. Kennedy: Voice of Hope* (5–8). Series: Sterling Biographies. 2007, Sterling $12.95 (978-1-4027-4749-6); paper $5.95 (978-1-4027-3232-4). 124pp. This generally admiring, well-illustrated profile covers Kennedy's life from childhood. (Rev: SLJ 5/07)

15285 Jones, Veda Boyd. *John F. Kennedy* (1–2). Series: Rookie Biographies. 2006, Children's Pr. LB $20.50 (978-0-516-25038-0); paper $4.95 (978-0-516-29797-2). 32pp. For beginning readers, this is a simple introduction to the life of the president. (Rev: SLJ 9/06)

15286 Kaplan, Howard S. *John F. Kennedy* (5–10). Series: DK Biography. 2004, DK paper $4.99 (978-0-7566-0340-3). A heavily illustrated, attractive biography of Kennedy that offers broad historical background. (Rev: BL 6/1–15/04) [921]

15287 Kelly, Tracey. *A Day That Changed History: The Assassination of John F. Kennedy* (4–6). Illus. Series: Turning Points in History. 2013, Black Rabbit LB $35.65 (978-1-59920971-5). 48pp. Using full-page photographs and quotes, Kelly describes JFK's life and career, focusing on his numerous accomplishments, before delving into his assassination and the effect that the tragedy had on the United States and the rest of the world. (Rev: BL 10/1/13; LMC 5–6/14)

15288 Rappaport, Doreen. *Jack's Path of Courage* (2–5). Illus. by Matt Tavares. 2010, Hyperion/Disney $17.99 (978-1-4231-2272-2). 48pp. This picture-book biography covers JFK's life from childhood and features memorable quotations and striking illustrations. Lexile AD780L (Rev: BL 12/15/10; HB 11–12/10; SLJ 10/1/10) [921]

15289 Schultz, Randy. *John F. Kennedy* (4–7). Illus. Series: MyReportLinks.com. 2002, Enslow LB $25.26 (978-0-7660-5012-9). 48pp. A basic, illustrated account of Kennedy's life and accomplishments that provides extensive Web links for students to do further research. (Rev: BL 9/1/02)

15290 Time For Kids Eds., and Ritu Upadhyay. *John F. Kennedy: The Making of a Leader* (3–5). Series: Time for Kids Biographies. 2005, HarperCollins $15.99 (978-0-06-057603-5); paper $3.99 (978-0-06-057602-8). 44pp. Attractive photo-filled pages describe Kennedy's childhood, education, and later life, with interesting sidebar features on topics including Jackie's redecoration of the White House. (Rev: SLJ 2/05)

15291 Todd, Anne. *John F. Kennedy: A Life of Citizenship* (1–3). Illus. by Tina Walski. Series: Blastoff! Readers: People of Character. 2007, Children's Pr. LB $20.00 (978-0-531-14709-2). 24pp. For beginning readers, this is a simple account of Kennedy's life and goals, mentioning the Peace Corps. (Rev: SLJ 1/08)

LINCOLN, ABRAHAM

15292 *Abraham Lincoln: Defender of the Union* (4–6). Series: The Civil War. 2005, Cobblestone $17.95 (978-0-8126-7902-1). This solid profile with excellent illustrations covers Lincoln's childhood, courtship of Mary Todd, family life, political career, and presidency. (Rev: HBG 10/06; SLJ 3/06)

15293 *The Assassination of Abraham Lincoln* (3–6). Illus. by Otha Zachariah Edward Lohse. Series: Graphic Library/Graphic History. 2005, Capstone LB $26.60 (978-0-7368-3831-3). 32pp. This graphic "novel" — factual, but embellished — about the fateful event will appeal to reluctant readers. (Rev: SLJ 7/05)

15294 Aylesworth, Jim. *Our Abe Lincoln* (PS–2). Illus. by Barbara McClintock. 2009, Scholastic $16.99 (978-0-439-92548-8). 40pp. To the tune of "The Old Gray Mare," 12 verses recount key information about Lincoln. (Rev: BCCB 1/09; BL 12/1/08; HB 5/09; SLJ 12/08)

15295 Bryant, Jen. *Abe's Fish: A Boyhood Tale of Abraham Lincoln* (2–4). Illus. by Amy June Bates. 2009, Sterling $15.95 (978-1-4027-6252-9). 40pp. Inspired by few lines in an 1890 biography, this engaging story follows 6-year-old Abe as he presents a fish he has caught to a tired soldier who leaves him pondering the word "freedom." (Rev: BL 1/1–15/09; SLJ 4/09)

15296 Burgan, Michael. *The Assassination of Abraham Lincoln* (3–6). Illus. Series: We the People. 2004, Compass Point LB $26.60 (978-0-7565-0678-0). 48pp. A well-illustrated, concise introduction to Lincoln's untimely death. [921]

15297 Burke, Rick. *Abraham Lincoln* (1–4). Series: American Lives. 2003, Heinemann LB $24.22 (978-1-4034-0155-7). 32pp. This easy-to-understand biography discusses Lincoln's youth and achievements, and includes plentiful, interesting illustrations. (Rev: HBG 10/03; SLJ 7/03)

15298 Burleigh, Robert. *Abraham Lincoln Comes Home* (2–4). Illus. by Wendell Minor. 2008, Holt $16.95 (978-0-8050-7529-1). This volume beautifully integrates history with the story of a little boy watching and waiting for Lincoln's funeral train. (Rev: BL 9/15/08; LMC 3/09)

15299 Collard, Sneed B., III. *Abraham Lincoln: A Courageous Leader* (3–5). Series: American Heroes. 2006, Benchmark $28.50 (978-0-7614-2162-7). 40pp. A basic biography of the sixteenth president, featuring interesting facts about his life and career presented in large typeface with large illustrations. (Rev: SLJ 3/07)

15300 Davis, Kenneth C. *Don't Know Much About Abraham Lincoln* (4–8). Illus. by Rob Shepperson. Series: Don't Know Much About. 2004, HarperCollins LB $15.89 (978-0-06-028820-4). 142pp. A question-and-answer format gives easy access to key details about Lincoln's life. (Rev: BL 2/1/05; SLJ 2/04)

15301 Fontes, Justine, and Ron Fontes. *Abraham Lincoln: Lawyer, Leader, Legend* (2–4). Illus. Series: Dorling Kindersley Readers. 2001, DK $14.99 (978-0-7894-7376-9); paper $3.99 (978-0-7894-7375-2). 48pp. An accessible introduction to Lincoln's life with many facts, illustrations, and maps. (Rev: BCCB 2/02; HBG 10/01; SLJ 8/01)

15302 Ford, Carin T. *Abraham Lincoln: The 16th President* (2–4). Illus. Series: Heroes of American History. 2003, Enslow LB $22.60 (978-0-7660-2000-9). 32pp. A well-illustrated and well-written biography that covers Lincoln's flaws as well as his great achievements. (Rev: HBG 10/03; SLJ 9/03)

15303 Freedman, Russell. *Lincoln: A Photobiography* (4–8). 1987, Houghton Mifflin $20.00 (978-0-89919-380-9); paper $9.95 (978-0-395-51848-9). A no-nonsense, unromanticized look at this beloved president. Newbery Medal 1988. (Rev: BL 12/15/87; SLJ 12/87) [921]

15304 Gilpin, Caroline Crosson. *Abraham Lincoln* (1–3). Illus. 2013, National Geographic LB $13.90 (978-1-42631086-7); paper $3.99 (978-1-42631085-0). 32pp. For beginning readers, this book with two-page chapters and boxed facts and quotations offers a good introduction to Lincoln's life and importance. (Rev: BL 4/15/13; LMC 8–9/13*) [921]

15305 Herbert, Janis. *Abraham Lincoln for Kids: His Life and Times with 21 Activities* (4–8). Illus. 2007, Chicago Review paper $14.95 (978-1-55652-656-5). With many quotations, illustrations, and sidebars, this volume covers Lincoln's life, beliefs, and contributions and includes activities (such as drawing a cartoon and learning Morse code). (Rev: SLJ 10/07) [921]

15306 Holzer, Harold. *The President Is Shot! The Assassination of Abraham Lincoln* (5–8). 2004, Boyds Mills $17.95 (978-1-56397-985-9). A riveting account of Lincoln's assassination, with archival illustrations and historical context. (Rev: BL 3/1/04*; SLJ 2/04) [973.7]

15307 Jackson, Ellen. *Abe Lincoln Loved Animals* (1–3). Illus. by Doris Ettlinger. 2008, Albert Whitman $16.99 (978-0-8075-0123-8). 32pp. This picture book tells a series of stories about Lincoln the animal lover from the time he was a boy until the time he established the presidential tradition of pardoning a turkey on Thanksgiving. (Rev: BL 9/15/08)

15308 Kalman, Maira. *Looking at Lincoln* (K–3). Illus. by author. 2012, Penguin $17.99 (978-039924039-3). 32pp. A young girl recalls facts about Abraham Lincoln's influence on the country as she wonders aloud about aspects of his personal and family life. (Rev: BL 1/12; HB 1–2/12; LMC 8–9/12; SLJ 9/12) [921]

15309 Krull, Kathleen, and Paul Brewer. *Lincoln Tells a Joke: How Laughter Saved the President (and the Country)* (2–4). Illus. by Stacy Innerst. 2010, Harcourt $16 (978-0-15-206639-0). 40pp. Emphasizes Lincoln's use of humor to cope with tense and difficult situations. (Rev: BL 2/15/10; HB 5–6/10; SLJ 3/1/10*) [921]

15310 Mara, Wil. *Abraham Lincoln* (1–2). Illus. Series: Rookie Biographies. 2002, Children's Book Pr. LB $20.50 (978-0-516-22518-0); paper $4.95 (978-0-516-27334-1). A simple account of Lincoln's life for beginning readers. (Rev: BCCB 2/02; SLJ 1/03)

15311 Metzger, Steve. *Lincoln and Grace: Why Abraham Lincoln Grew a Beard* (K–3). Illus. by Ann Kronheimer. 2013, Scholastic paper $6.99 (978-0-545-48-432-9). 40pp. Tells the fascinating story of an 11-year-old girl who suggested to Lincoln that a beard would enhance his chances of winning election. (Rev: BLO 3/15/13; LMC 8–9/13; SLJ 4/13) [921]

15312 Press, David P. *Abraham Lincoln: The Great Emancipator* (5–8). Illus. Series: Voices for Freedom: Abolitionist Heroes. 2013, Crabtree LB $30.60 (978-077871061-5). 64pp. This text uses archival photographs, documents, and quotations to tell the story of abolitionist, lawyer, speaker, and U.S. President Abraham Lincoln and offers an overview of his evolving viewpoints on slavery. (Rev: BL 9/1/13) [921]

15313 Rappaport, Doreen. *Abe's Honest Words: The Life of Abraham Lincoln* (2–4). Illus. by Kadir Nelson. 2008, Hyperion $16.99 (978-1-4231-0408-7). 40pp. Lincoln's own words are combined with Rappaport's free verse and Nelson's powerful art to form an elegant portrait of the president's life and beliefs. (Rev: BCCB 10/08; BL 6/1–15/08; HB 11/08; LMC 1/09; SLJ 10/08)

15314 Roberts, Jeremy. *Abraham Lincoln* (5–7). Series: Presidential Leaders. 2003, Lerner LB $29.27 (978-0-8225-0817-5). 112pp. From childhood through assassination, this is a thorough, well-illustrated, and well-organized account of Lincoln's life. (Rev: SLJ 2/04)

15315 St. George, Judith. *Stand Tall, Abe Lincoln* (2–4). Illus. by Matt Faulkner. 2007, Philomel $16.99 (978-0-399-24174-1). An appealing look at Lincoln's childhood, showing him working on the family farm and developing a love for reading and learning. (Rev: BL 10/1/07; SLJ 11/07)

15316 Schott, Jane A. *Abraham Lincoln* (3–4). Series: History Maker Bios. 2002, Lerner LB $26.60 (978-0-8225-0196-1). Using many true stories, historical photography, and other artwork, this lively biography describes Lincoln's journey from log cabin to the White House. (Rev: BCCB 2/02; BL 6/1–15/02)

15317 Sloate, Susan. *Abraham Lincoln: The Freedom President* (5–8). 1989, Ballantine paper $15.00 (978-0-449-90375-9). An accessible account of the president who led his country through division back to unity. (Rev: BL 12/15/89) [921]

15318 Stone, Tanya Lee. *Abraham Lincoln* (5–10). Series: DK Biography. 2005, DK $14.99 (978-0-7566-0833-0); paper $4.99 (978-0-7566-0834-7). A heavily illustrated, attractive biography of Lincoln that offers broad historical background. (Rev: BL 6/1–15/04) [921]

15319 Sullivan, George. *Abraham Lincoln* (3–5). Illus. Series: In Their Own Words. 2001, Scholastic $12.95 (978-0-439-14750-7); paper $4.99 (978-0-439-09554-9). 128pp. Using speeches, letters, and other primary sources, this is an entertaining, appealing biography of Lincoln. (Rev: BCCB 2/02; BL 4/1/01; HBG 10/01; SLJ 4/01)

15320 Sullivan, George. *Picturing Lincoln: Famous Photographs That Popularized the President* (5–8). 2000, Clarion $16.00 (978-0-395-91682-7). Using five images of Lincoln taken between 1846 and 1864, this book gives historical and biographical information on each and tells how they have been used for posters, button, ribbons, postage stamps, and currency. (Rev: BL 2/1/01; HB 3–4/01; HBG 10/01; SLJ 3/01) [921]

15321 Thomson, Sarah L. *What Lincoln Said* (K–3). Illus. by James Ransome. 2009, Collins LB $18.89 (978-0-06-084820-0). 32pp. This picture-book biography traces Lincoln's life from childhood through signing the Emancipation Proclamation, providing direct quotations throughout. (Rev: BL 9/15/08)

15322 Van Steenwyk, Elizabeth. *When Abraham Talked to the Trees* (K–3). Illus. by Bill Farnsworth. 2000, Eerdmans $16.00 (978-0-8028-5191-8). 32pp. A picture book that tells of Lincoln's youth, his many outdoor activities, and the books he read. (Rev: BL 10/1/00; HBG 3/01; SLJ 12/00)

15323 Waldman, Neil. *Voyages: Reminiscences of Young Abe Lincoln* (5–8). Illus. by author. 2009, Boyds Mills $16.95 (978-1-59078-471-6). 32pp. Blending fiction and nonfiction, these anecdotes about the life of the young Lincoln include direct quotations in a contrasting color. (Rev: BL 3/15/09; SLJ 4/09) [921]

15324 Winters, Kay. *Abe Lincoln: The Boy Who Loved Books* (K–2). Illus. by Nancy Carpenter. 2003, Simon & Schuster $16.95 (978-0-689-82554-5). 40pp. Simple language and detailed illustrations describe Lincoln's childhood and young adult years, with a focus on his love of reading. (Rev: BL 1/1–15/03; HBG 10/03; SLJ 1/03)

MADISON, JAMES

15325 Elish, Dan. *James Madison* (4–7). Series: Presidents and Their Times. 2007, Marshall Cavendish LB $22.95 (978-0-7614-2432-1). A clear and thorough profile of the president, describing his early years, presidential career, and later life, with discussion of important events that took place during his life. (Rev: LMC 5/08; SLJ 1/08)

15326 Kent, Zachary. *James Madison: Creating a Nation* (5–8). Series: America's Founding Fathers. 2004, Enslow LB $26.60 (978-0-7660-2180-8). 128pp. This profile of Madison focuses largely on his public life from the period leading up to the American Revolution through his presidency. (Rev: BL 6/1–15/04)

15327 Santella, Andrew. *James Madison* (3–5). Series: Profiles of the Presidents. 2002, Compass Point LB $26.60 (978-0-7565-0252-2). 64pp. Madison's adult years are the focus of this volume that includes a brief chapter on his youth. (Rev: SLJ 4/03)

15328 Venezia, Mike. *James Madison* (3–4). Illus. Series: Getting to Know the U.S. Presidents. 2004, Children's Pr. LB $28.00 (978-0-516-22609-5); paper $7.95 (978-0-516-27478-2). 32pp. A light-hearted approach to the key details of Madison's life, adding comic-book-style graphics and dialogue bubbles to the large-type text. [921]

MADISON, JAMES AND DOLLEY

15329 Adler, David A., and Michael S. Adler. *A Picture Book of Dolley and James Madison* (K–3). Illus. by Ronald Himler. 2009, Holiday $17.95 (978-0-8234-2009-4). A thorough picture-book biography of the 4th president and his wife, with illustrations that extend the text. (Rev: BLO 5/15/09; SLJ 3/09)

15330 Ashby, Ruth. *James and Dolley Madison* (5–8). Series: Presidents and First Ladies. 2005, Gareth Stevens LB $31.00 (978-0-8368-5757-3). An accessible, balanced, and attractive discussion of the Madisons and the contributions each made to their joint lives. (Rev: BL 3/1/05; SLJ 8/05) [921]

MONROE, JAMES

15331 Teitelbaum, Michael. *James Monroe* (3–5). Series: Profiles of the Presidents. 2002, Compass Point LB $26.60 (978-0-7565-0253-9). 64pp. Monroe's adult years are the focus of this volume that includes a brief chapter on his youth. (Rev: SLJ 4/03)

15332 Venezia, Mike. *James Monroe* (3–4). Illus. Series: Getting to Know the U.S. Presidents. 2004, Children's Pr. LB $28.00 (978-0-516-22610-1); paper $7.95 (978-0-516-27479-9). 32pp. A light-hearted approach to the key details of Monroe's life, adding comic-book-style graphics and dialogue bubbles to the large-type text. [921]

NIXON, RICHARD M.

15333 Aronson, Billy. *Richard M. Nixon* (5–8). Illus. Series: Presidents and Their Times. 2007, Marshall Cavendish LB $22.95 (978-0-7614-2428-4). This biography of the 37th president covers his childhood, his candidacy, and his accomplishments in office, as well as his downfall and impeachment. (Rev: BL 10/15/07; SLJ 1/08) [921]

15334 Marquez, Heron. *Richard M. Nixon* (5–7). Series: Presidential Leaders. 2003, Lerner LB $29.27 (978-0-8225-0098-8). 112pp. The Vietnam War, relations with China, and Watergate all feature prominently in this look at Nixon's private and public life. (Rev: BL 4/15/03; HBG 10/03; SLJ 2/03)

OBAMA, BARACK

15335 Abramson, Jill. *Obama: The Historic Journey* (4–7). Illus. 2009, The New York Times $24.95 (978-0-670-01208-4). 96pp. Striking photographs, informative text drawing on reports from the *New York Times,* and careful explanation of political terms combine to make this a useful and educational biography of the president. (Rev: SLJ 8/09; VOYA 6/09) [921]

15336 Brill, Marlene Targ. *Barack Obama: Working to Make a Difference* (5–8). Series: Gateway Biography. 2006, Lerner LB $23.93 (978-0-8225-3417-4). Obama, the U.S. senator from Illinois, is profiled with details of his family life, education, and entrance to politics. (Rev: BL 3/15/06; SLJ 8/06) [328.73]

15337 Feinstein, Stephen. *Barack Obama* (1–3). Illus. Series: African-American Heroes. 2008, Enslow LB $15.95 (978-0-7660-2893-7). 24pp. This slender biography for young readers chronicles the president's life from childhood with a timeline, reading list, and photographs. (Rev: BL 3/15/08)

15338 Krensky, Stephen. *Barack Obama* (5–9). Illus. 2009, DK $14.99 (978-0-7566-5804-5); paper $5.99 (978-0-7566-5-805-2). 128pp. With the usual DK visual format, this is an attractive portrait of Obama's life, placing his background and experience in historical context. (Rev: BL 4/1/10; SLJ 4/10) [921]

15339 Obama, Barack. *Change Has Come: An Artist Celebrates Our American Spirit* (1–6). Illus. by Kadir Nelson. 2009, Simon & Schuster $12.99 (978-1-4169-8955-4). With compelling images, Nelson celebrates Obama's election. (Rev: LMC 8/09; SLJ 3/09)

15340 Schuman, Michael A. *Barack Obama: "We Are One People"* (5–8). Series: African-American Biography Library. 2008, Enslow LB $23.95 (978-0-7660-2891-3). Opening with Obama's speech at the 2004 Democratic Convention, this biography goes on to cover his life chronologically from childhood through running for president. (Rev: BL 6/1–15/08) [328.730]

15341 von Zumbusch, Amelie. *Barack Obama's Family Tree: Roots of Achievement* (3–5). Illus. Series: Making History: The Obamas. 2010, Rosen LB $21.25 (978-143589390-0). 24pp. Introduces Obama's family history and discusses the influence of his parents and grandparents. (Rev: BL 6/10; LMC 10/10) [921]

15342 Weatherford, Carole Boston. *Obama: Only in America* (3–5). Illus. by Robert T. Barrett. 2010, Marshall Cavendish $17.99 (978-0-7614-5641-4). 48pp. Illustrated with paintings and featuring lyrical prose and excerpts from speeches, this admiring portrait covers the key events in Obama's life. (Rev: BL 5/1/10; LMC 8–9/10; SLJ 4/10) [921]

15343 Wheeler, Jill C. *Barack Obama* (1–4). Illus. Series: United States Presidents. 2009, ABDO LB $18.95 (978-1-60453-481-8). 40pp. This accessible profile is arranged chronologically and includes a timeline, photographs, a useful "Did You Know?" page of facts, and an overview of the U.S. government and the role of the president. (Rev: BL 3/15/09)

15344 Zeiger, Jennifer. *Barack Obama* (4–6). Illus. Series: Cornerstones of Freedom. 2012, Scholastic LB $30 (978-053123050-3); paper $8.95 (978-053128150-5). 64pp. With a map ("What Happened Where"), a timeline, and a list of influential individuals, this biography covers Obama's life through the beginning of his reelection bid. (Rev: BL 4/15/12) [921]

PIERCE, FRANKLIN

15345 Brown, Fern G. *Franklin Pierce* (5–8). Series: Presidents of the United States. 1989, GEC LB $21.27 (978-0-944483-25-1). The story of Pierce, his political life and presidency, plus material on his personal life. (Rev: SLJ 9/89) [921]

POLK, JAMES K.

15346 Venezia, Mike. *James K. Polk: Eleventh President, 1845–1849* (3–4). Illus. Series: Getting to Know the U.S. Presidents. 2005, Children's Pr. LB $28.00 (978-0-516-22616-3); paper $7.95 (978-0-516-27485-0). 32pp. A light-hearted approach to the key details of Polk's life, adding comic-book-style graphics and dialogue bubbles to the large-type text. [921]

REAGAN, RONALD

15347 Burgan, Michael. *Ronald Reagan: A Photographic Story of a Life* (5–8). Illus. Series: DK Biography. 2011, DK $14.99 (978-0-7566-7075-7); paper $5.99 (978-0-7566-7-074-0). 128pp. A visual introduction to the life of the actor who became president. **e** (Rev: BL 6/1/11; SLJ 11/1/11) [921]

15348 Hinkle, Donald Henry. *Ronald Reagan* (4–7). Series: Presidents. 2003, Enslow LB $25.26 (978-0-7660-5112-6). 48pp. The life story of the fortieth president with material on the successes and failures of his two terms. (Rev: BL 6/1–15/03; HBG 10/03)

ROOSEVELT, FRANKLIN D.

15349 Allport, Alan. *Franklin Delano Roosevelt* (5–7). Series: Great American Presidents. 2003, Chelsea House LB $30.00 (978-0-7910-7598-2). 102pp. A concise life of the longest-serving president in U.S. history, from his childhood through his years in the White House, with a foreword by Walter Cronkite. (Rev: SLJ 4/04)

15350 Bardhan-Quallen, Sudipta. *Franklin Delano Roosevelt: A National Hero* (5–8). Series: Sterling Biographies. 2007, Sterling $12.95 (978-1-4027-4747-2); paper $5.95 (978-1-4027-3545-5). 124pp. The author emphasizes the contrast between Roosevelt's privileged background and his concern about social injustice. (Rev: SLJ 5/07)

15351 Burgan, Michael. *Franklin D. Roosevelt* (4–8). Series: Profiles of the Presidents. 2002, Compass Point LB $26.60 (978-0-7565-0203-4). An absorbing introduction to Roosevelt's life and career, with details of his youth and education and the role that his illness played in shaping his character. (Rev: SLJ 6/02) [973.917092]

15352 Freedman, Russell. *Franklin Delano Roosevelt* (5–8). 1990, Houghton Mifflin $20.00 (978-0-89919-379-3). A carefully researched and well-illustrated account of the man and the times. (Rev: HB 3–4/90; SLJ 12/90*) [921]

15353 Haugen, Brenda. *Franklin Delano Roosevelt: The New Deal President* (4–8). Series: Signature Lives. 2006, Compass Point LB $34.60 (978-0-7565-1586-7). Slim but fact-filled, this is a useful biography for report writers, with excerpts from speeches and writings and full discussion of key events in Roosevelt's life. (Rev: SLJ 9/06) [921]

15354 Knapp, Ron. *Franklin D. Roosevelt* (5–9). 2002, Enslow LB $25.26 (978-0-7660-5009-9). 48pp. A listing of recommended Web sites extends the contents of this introduction to Roosevelt's life and presidency. (Rev: HBG 10/02; SLJ 6/02)

15355 Krull, Kathleen. *A Boy Named FDR: How Franklin D. Roosevelt Grew Up to Change America* (3–5). Illus. by Steven Johnson and Lou Fancher. 2011, Knopf $17.99 (978-0-375-85716-4); LB $20.99 (978-0-375-95716-1). Unpaged. Franklin Roosevelt's childhood and young adulthood are described in this picture-book biography that takes readers up to 1924; an epilogue explains his achievements and legacy. (Rev: BL 1/1–15/11; LMC 5–6/11; SLJ 2/1/11) [921]

15356 St. George, Judith. *Make Your Mark, Franklin Roosevelt* (2–5). Illus. by Britt Spencer. Series: Turning Point. 2007, Philomel $16.99 (978-0-399-24175-8). 48pp. Focuses on the president's childhood and his decision as a teenager to move beyond his life of privilege and devote himself to public service. (Rev: BL 11/15/06; SLJ 2/07*)

15357 Van Steenwyk, Elizabeth. *First Dog Fala* (PS–3). Illus. by Michael G. Montgomery. 2008, Peachtree $16.95 (978-1-56145-411-2). 32pp. Meet Fala, the black Scottish terrier who won the hearts of President Franklin Roosevelt and the American people; illustrated with paintings that give us a terrier's-eye view of the FDR White House. (Rev: BL 10/1/08; LMC 3/08)

ROOSEVELT, FRANKLIN D. AND ELEANOR

15358 Ashby, Ruth. *Franklin and Eleanor Roosevelt* (5–8). Series: Presidents and First Ladies. 2005, Gareth Stevens LB $31.00 (978-0-8368-5758-0). An accessible, balanced, and attractive discussion of the Roosevelts and the contributions each made to their joint lives. (Rev: BL 3/1/05) [921]

ROOSEVELT, THEODORE

15359 Brown, Don. *Teedie: The Story of Young Teddy Roosevelt* (1–3). Illus. by author. 2009, Houghton $16.00 (978-0-618-17999-2). 32pp. The story of the president's sickly childhood and how he overcame them to become a man of many, including athletic, interests. (Rev: BL 4/1/09; HB 5/09; SLJ 4/09)

15360 Elish, Dan. *Theodore Roosevelt* (4–7). Series: Presidents and Their Times. 2007, Marshall Cavendish

LB $22.95 (978-0-7614-2429-1). A clear and thorough profile of the president, describing his early years, presidential career, and later life, with discussion of important events that took place during his life. (Rev: SLJ 1/08)

15361 Keating, Frank. *Theodore* (2–6). Illus. by Mike Wimmer. 2006, Simon & Schuster $16.95 (978-0-689-86532-9). 32pp. This attractive and compelling biography of Theodore Roosevelt examines all aspects of his life and emphasizes his loves of nature, reading, and hard work. (Rev: SLJ 3/06*)

15362 Kelley, Alison Turnbull. *Theodore Roosevelt* (5–7). Series: Great American Presidents. 2003, Chelsea House LB $30.00 (978-0-7910-7606-4). An illustrated profile of the 26th president, from his childhood through his public life and legacy. (Rev: SLJ 4/04) [921]

15363 Kraft, Betsy Harvey. *Theodore Roosevelt: Champion of the American Spirit* (5–9). 2003, Clarion $19.00 (978-0-618-14264-4). The determination that carried Roosevelt through a difficult childhood and drove his successful career is emphasized in this engrossing biography of his life and survey of his diverse accomplishments. (Rev: BL 10/15/03; HB 11–12/03; HBG 4/04; SLJ 12/03*; VOYA 10/03) [973.9]

15364 Rappaport, Doreen. *To Dare Mighty Things: The Life of Theodore Roosevelt* (3–5). Illus. by C. F. Payne. 2013, Disney/Hyperion $17.99 (978-142312488-7). 48pp. A vivid picture-book portrait of this president from his sickly childhood to his rise to greatness. (Rev: BL 12/15/13*; LMC 8–9/14*; SLJ 12/13*) [921]

15365 Roosevelt, Theodore. *My Tour of Europe: By Teddy Roosevelt, Age 10* (1–3). Ed. by Ellen Jackson. Illus. by Catherine Brighton. 2003, Millbrook LB $23.90 (978-0-7613-2516-1). This collection of excerpts from Teddy Roosevelt's boyhood journal describes the 10-year-old future president's experiences on a family trip to Europe. (Rev: BL 4/15/03; HBG 10/03; SLJ 6/03)

15366 St. George, Judith. *You're on Your Way, Teddy Roosevelt!* (2–4). Illus. by Matt Faulkner. Series: Turning Point Book. 2004, Philomel $16.99 (978-0-399-23888-8). 48pp. Teddy Roosevelt's childhood is the focus of this picture-book biography that looks at his love for animals and his victory over asthma, which paved the way for his success as both an athlete and a student. (Rev: BL 11/1/04; SLJ 10/04)

15367 Time For Kids Eds., and Lisa DeMauro. *Theodore Roosevelt: The Adventurous President* (3–5). Series: Time for Kids Biographies. 2005, HarperCollins $15.99 (978-0-06-057606-6); paper $3.99 (978-0-06-057604-2). 44pp. Attractive photo-filled pages describe Roosevelt's childhood, education, love for nature, and later life, with interesting sidebar features on topics ranging from the Teddy bear and Mount Rushmore to his "Big Stick" policy. (Rev: BL 3/15/04; SLJ 2/05)

TAYLOR, ZACHARY

15368 Brunelli, Carol. *Zachary Taylor: Our Twelfth President* (4–6). Series: Spirit of America: Our Presidents. 2001, Child's World $28.50 (978-1-56766-836-0). 48pp.

A well-illustrated and appealing biography that discusses influences that shaped Taylor's policies and looks at his legacy. (Rev: SLJ 12/01)

15369 Collins, David R. *Zachary Taylor: 12th President of the United States* (5–7). 1989, Garrett LB $21.27 (978-0-944483-17-6). Tells the life story of a military man elected president in 1848. (Rev: BL 5/1/89) [921]

15370 Venezia, Mike. *Zachary Taylor: Twelfth President, 1849–1850* (3–4). Illus. Series: Getting to Know the U.S. Presidents. 2005, Children's Pr. LB $28.00 (978-0-516-22617-0); paper $7.95 (978-0-516-27486-7). 32pp. A light-hearted approach to the key details of Taylor's life, adding comic-book-style graphics and dialogue bubbles to the large-type text. [921]

TRUMAN, HARRY S

15371 Cannarella, Deborah. *Harry S. Truman* (3–5). Series: Profiles of the Presidents. 2002, Compass Point LB $26.60 (978-0-7565-0278-2). 64pp. Truman's adult years are the focus of this volume that includes a brief chapter on his youth. (Rev: SLJ 4/03)

15372 Lazo, Caroline. *Harry S Truman* (5–7). Illus. Series: Presidential Leaders. 2003, Lerner LB $29.27 (978-0-8225-0096-4). 112pp. Truman's youth, education, family life, and career are all covered in this concise biography full of photographs. (Rev: BL 4/15/03; HBG 10/03)

TYLER, JOHN

15373 Ochester, Betsy. *John Tyler* (4–6). Illus. Series: Encyclopedia of Presidents. 2003, Children's Pr. LB $34.00 (978-0-516-22850-1). An updated profile that looks at Tyler's life and contributions, providing many illustrations and sidebars. (Rev: SLJ 1/04)

15374 Venezia, Mike. *John Tyler* (3–5). Illus. by author. Series: Getting to Know the U.S. Presidents. 2005, Children's Pr. LB $28.00 (978-0-516-22615-6). 32pp. A lighthearted introduction to the 10th president, with plenty of visual information. (Rev: SLJ 7/05)

VAN BUREN, MARTIN

15375 Doak, Robin. *Martin Van Buren* (4–7). 2003, Compass Point LB $26.60 (978-0-7565-0256-0). Van Buren's strengths and weakness receive equal weight in this balanced and readable biography that covers his life from a young age. (Rev: SLJ 11/03) [973.5]

15376 Ellis, Rafaela. *Martin Van Buren: 8th President of the United States* (5–7). 1989, Garrett LB $21.27 (978-0-944483-12-1). The story of a New York governor who became president. (Rev: BL 5/1/89) [921]

15377 Favor, Lesli J. *Martin Van Buren* (3–6). Series: Encyclopedia of Presidents. 2003, Children's Pr. LB $34.00 (978-0-516-22770-2). 110pp. A concise illustrated biography of the eighth president of the United States, with plenty of illustrations and sidebars. (Rev: SLJ 4/04)

15378 Venezia, Mike. *Martin Van Buren: Eighth President 1837–1841* (3–4). Illus. Series: Getting to Know the U.S. Presidents. 2005, Children's Pr. LB $28.00

(978-0-516-22613-2); paper $7.95 (978-0-516-27482-9). 32pp. A light-hearted approach to the key details of Van Buren's life, adding comic-book-style graphics and dialogue bubbles to the large-type text. [921]

WASHINGTON, GEORGE

15379 Adler, David A. *George Washington: An Illustrated Biography* (5–7). 2004, Holiday House $24.95 (978-0-8234-1838-1). Adler presents a balanced and well-researched biography of Washington, giving details of his character as well as information on key events of his time. (Rev: BL 9/15/04; SLJ 12/04) [973.4]

15380 Adler, David A. *President George Washington* (1–3). Illus. by John Wallner. Series: Holiday House Reader. 2005, Holiday $14.95 (978-0-8234-1604-2). 32pp. For beginning readers, this picture-book biography that gives a brief overview of Washington's youth and adult accomplishments uses short sentences, large typeface, and lots of white space. (Rev: BL 9/15/05; SLJ 11/05)

15381 Armentrout, David, and Patricia Armentrout. *George Washington* (1–3). Series: Discover the Life of an American Legend. 2004, Rourke LB $20.64 (978-1-58952-662-4). An introductory book about the first U.S. president, including a glossary and chronology. (Rev: SLJ 3/04)

15382 Burke, Rick. *George Washington* (1–4). Series: American Lives. 2003, Heinemann LB $24.22 (978-1-4034-0158-8). 32pp. Easy to read, this richly illustrated biography covers Washington's life from childhood. (Rev: HBG 10/03; SLJ 7/03)

15383 Chandra, Deborah, and Madeleine Comora. *George Washington's Teeth* (K–3). Illus. by Brock Cole. 2003, Farrar $16.00 (978-0-374-32534-3). 40pp. George Washington's dental problems are examined in lively, witty verses perfectly paired with sprightly watercolors. (Rev: BCCB 2/03; BL 1/1–15/03; HB 3/03*; HBG 10/03; SLJ 1/03)

15384 Collier, James Lincoln. *The George Washington You Never Knew* (4–6). Illus. by Greg Copeland. Series: You Never Knew. 2003, Children's Pr. LB $25.50 (978-0-516-24343-6). 80pp. In an accessible style, Collier reveals the inner man behind the legend, combining historical facts and debunking myths while providing a solid account of the early days of the United States. (Rev: SLJ 1/04)

15385 Delano, Marfe Ferguson. *Master George's People: George Washington, His Slaves, and His Revolutionary Transformation* (5–8). Illus. 2013, National Geographic $18.95 (978-142630759-1); LB $27.90 (978-142630760-7). 64pp. Using primary sources such as George Washington's letters, along with vivid reproductions of paintings and drawings, Delano documents Washington's perspective on slavery, from his inheritance of 10 slaves at the age of 11, to emancipating his slaves in his will. (Rev: BL 2/1/13*; SLJ 2/13) [921]

15386 Ford, Carin T. *George Washington: The First President* (2–4). Series: Heroes of American History. 2003, Enslow LB $22.60 (978-0-7660-1999-7). 32pp. A

concise introduction to the military and political leader. (Rev: HBG 10/03; SLJ 6/03)

15387 Gilpin, Caroline Crosson. *George Washington* (K–1). Illus. Series: National Geographic Kids. 2014, National Geographic paper $3.99 (978-14263146-8-1). 32pp. For beginning readers, this is an attractive biography with enough information for first reports. (Rev: BLO 3/1/14; SLJ 5/14) [921]

15388 Harness, Cheryl. *George Washington* (3–5). Illus. 2000, National Geographic $17.95 (978-0-7922-7096-6). 48pp. A heavily illustrated, large-format biography that covers the important events in Washington's life and describes his personality. (Rev: BL 3/1/00; HBG 10/00; SLJ 4/00)

15389 Hilton, Suzanne. *The World of Young George Washington* (5–8). 1987, Walker $12.95 (978-0-8027-6657-1). Washington as a youth plus detailed information on life in pre-Revolutionary America. (Rev: SLJ 4/87) [921]

15390 Hort, Lenny. *George Washington* (5–10). Series: DK Biography. 2005, DK $14.99 (978-0-7566-0832-3); paper $4.99 (978-0-7566-0835-4). A heavily illustrated, attractive biography of the man born in Virginia. (Rev: BL 6/1–15/04) [921]

15391 Jurmain, Suzanne Tripp. *George Did It* (2–4). Illus. by Larry Day. 2005, Dutton $16.99 (978-0-525-47560-6). 40pp. George Washington's reluctance to take on the responsibilities of the presidency is depicted in lively text and cartoon drawings. (Rev: BL 12/15/05*; SLJ 12/05*)

15392 Keating, Frank. *George: George Washington, Our Founding Father* (2–4). Illus. by Mike Wimmer. 2012, Simon & Schuster $16.99 (978-141695482-8). 32pp. A picture-book biography with full-page paintings and selections from his "Rules of Civility and Decent Behavior in Company and Conversation." (Rev: BL 12/15/11; SLJ 1/12) [921]

15393 McNeese, Tim. *George Washington: America's Leader in War and Peace* (4–8). Series: Leaders of the American Revolution. 2005, Chelsea House LB $30.00 (978-0-7910-8619-3). An even-handed introduction to Washington's life and contributions, presented chronologically with occasional factboxes; suitable for report writers. (Rev: SLJ 1/06) [921]

15394 Mara, Wil. *George Washington* (K–4). Illus. 2002, Children's Book Pr. LB $20.50 (978-0-516-22519-7); paper $4.95 (978-0-516-27335-8). 32pp. A simple account of Washington's life for beginning readers. (Rev: SLJ 1/03)

15395 Miller, Brandon M. *George Washington for Kids: His Life and Times with 21 Activities* (3–6). Illus. 2007, Chicago Review $14.95 (978-1-55652-655-8). 130pp. This absorbing biography offers an unusual amount of information on Washington's personality plus varied activities. (Rev: BL 7/07; SLJ 10/07)

15396 Nettleton, Pamela Hill. *George Washington: Farmer, Soldier, President* (K–3). Illus. by Jeff Yesh. Series: Biographies. 2003, Picture Window LB $25.26

(978-1-4048-0184-4). A brightly illustrated profile that is suitable for beginning readers. (Rev: SLJ 4/04)

15397 Ransom, Candice F. *George Washington* (3–4). Series: History Maker Bios. 2002, Lerner LB $26.60 (978-0-8225-0374-3). 48pp. An introductory biography of the man who was chosen to lead the army and then the country during and after the American Revolution. (Rev: BL 6/1–15/02)

15398 Roberts, Jeremy. *George Washington* (5–7). Series: Presidential Leaders. 2003, Lerner LB $29.27 (978-0-8225-0818-2). This engaging biography chronicles the life and achievements of America's first president and dispels some widely believed myths. (Rev: SLJ 2/04) [921]

15399 Rockwell, Anne. *Big George: How a Shy Boy Became President Washington* (K–3). Illus. by Matt Phelan. 2009, Houghton $17.00 (978-0-15-216583-3). 48pp. Washington is portrayed as a studious, shy boy with a respect for honor who becomes a soldier because he feels it is his duty; his bravery and leadership led to his role as the first president. (Rev: BCCB 2/09; BL 1/1–15/09; HB 3/09; SLJ 2/09)

15400 St. George, Judith. *Take The Lead George Washington* (2–4). Illus. by Daniel Powers. Series: Turning Points. 2005, Penguin $16.99 (978-0-399-23887-1). Washington's first job — as a surveyor, at the age of 16 — is the turning point in this picture-book profile of his transition from childhood to adult. (Rev: BL 12/1/04; SLJ 1/05)

15401 Thomas, Peggy. *Farmer George Plants a Nation* (3–5). Illus. by Layne Johnson. 2008, Boyds Mills $17.95 (978-1-59078-460-0). 32pp. Thomas looks at George Washington's role as a farmer and how his efforts in this area paralleled his work for the new nation. (Rev: BL 2/15/08; LMC 3/08; SLJ 3/08)

WILSON, WOODROW

15402 Randolph, Sallie. *Woodrow Wilson, President* (5–9). Series: Presidential Biography. 1992, Walker LB $15.85 (978-0-8027-8144-4). Offers a concise overview of Wilson's tragic personal and political struggles, his achievements, and his place in history. (Rev: BL 12/15/91; SLJ 3/92) [921]

WILSON, WOODROW AND EDITH

15403 Ashby, Ruth. *Woodrow and Edith Wilson* (5–8). Series: Presidents and First Ladies. 2005, Gareth Stevens LB $31.00 (978-0-8368-5759-7). An accessible, balanced, and attractive discussion of the Wilsons and the contributions each made to their joint lives. (Rev: BL 3/1/05; SLJ 8/05) [921]

First Ladies and Other Women

ADAMS, ABIGAIL

15404 Ching, Jacqueline. *Abigail Adams: A Revolutionary Woman* (4–7). Series: Library of American Lives and Times. 2001, Rosen $34.60 (978-0-8239-5723-1). This biography of Abigail Adams stresses the fact that her husband, John Adams, relied heavily on her advice and that her vision of equality and justice inspired the early consideration of women's rights. (Rev: BCCB 4/01; BL 10/15/01)

15405 Ferris, Jeri Chase. *Remember the Ladies: A Story About Abigail Adams* (3–5). Illus. by Ellen Beier. Series: Creative Minds Biographies. 2000, Carolrhoda LB $22.60 (978-1-57505-292-2). 64pp. A biography of this early first lady that relies heavily on original sources including the writings of Abigail Adams. (Rev: HBG 3/01; SLJ 1/01)

15406 McCarthy, Pat. *Abigail Adams: First Lady and Patriot* (5–8). Series: Historical American Biographies. 2002, Enslow LB $26.60 (978-0-7660-1618-7). The life story of the prolific letter-writer who was wife of the second president of the United States, John Adams. (Rev: BCCB 4/01; BL 4/1/02; HBG 10/02; SLJ 7/02) [921]

15407 Wallner, Alexandra. *Abigail Adams* (K–3). Illus. 2001, Holiday House $16.95 (978-0-8234-1442-0). 32pp. A picture-book biography that examines the life of Abigail Adams, the wife of a president, the mother of another, and a champion of women's rights. (Rev: BL 3/15/01; HB 7/01; HBG 10/01)

ADDAMS, JANE

15408 Armentrout, David, and Patricia Armentrout. *Jane Addams* (2–4). Series: Discover Someone Who Made a Difference. 2001, Rourke LB $14.95 (978-1-58952-054-7). A beginning biography of the famous American social worker who won a Nobel Peace Prize. (Rev: BL 1/1–15/02; SLJ 3/02)

15409 Caravantes, Peggy. *Waging Peace: The Story of Jane Addams* (5–8). 2004, Morgan Reynolds LB $23.95 (978-1-931798-40-2). Covers Addams's life and achievements, with good material on her youth and the lessons she learned from her Quaker father. (Rev: SLJ 2/05) [921]

ANTHONY, SUSAN B.

15410 Edison, Erin. *Susan B. Anthony* (K–2). Illus. Series: Great Women in History. 2013, Capstone LB $21.32 (978-1-62065075-2); paper $5.95 (978-1-62065865-9). 24pp. A slim introduction to Anthony's life and accomplishments, suitable for beginning or struggling readers. (Rev: BL 6/13; SLJ 4/13) [921]

15411 Hopkinson, Deborah. *Susan B. Anthony: Fighter for Women's Rights* (2–4). Illus. by Amy Bates. Series: Ready to Read: Stories of America. 2005, Simon & Schuster paper $3.99 (978-0-689-86909-9). 32pp. This brief biography focuses on Anthony's lifelong fight for women's rights. (Rev: BL 2/1/06; SLJ 5/06)

15412 Klingel, Cynthia, and Robert B. Noyed. *Susan B. Anthony: Reformer* (3–6). Illus. 2002, Child's World LB $27.07 (978-1-56766-171-2). 32pp. An attractive, brief introduction to the life of Susan B. Anthony. (Rev: BL 1/1–15/03)

15413 McLeese, Don. *Susan B. Anthony* (2–5). Series: Equal Rights Leaders. 2002, Rourke LB $20.64 (978-1-58952-284-8). 24pp. Simple text and well-chosen illustrations tell the story of Anthony's life, with good coverage of her youth and education. (Rev: SLJ 1/03)

15414 Malaspina, Ann. *Heart on Fire: Susan B. Anthony Votes for President* (2–4). Illus. by Steve James. 2012, Whitman $16.99 (978-0-8075-3188-4). 32pp. This picture book tells the story of the day Anthony voted in the 1872 presidential election and her subsequent arrest and trial. Amelia Bloomer List. (Rev: BL 9/15/12; LMC 1–2/13; SLJ 8/12) [921]

15415 Orr, Tamra. *The Life and Times of Susan B. Anthony* (5–8). Series: Profiles in American History. 2007, Mitchell Lane LB $19.95 (978-1-58415-445-7). This biography of Anthony traces her life and work in the women's rights movement and contains supplemental facts that will interest readers. (Rev: SLJ 7/07) [921]

15416 Slade, Suzanne. *Susan B. Anthony: Fighter for Freedom and Equality* (2–4). Illus. by Craig Orback. 2007, Picture Window $17.95 (978-1-4048-3104-9). 24pp. An age-appropriate profile that covers Anthony's life from childhood. (Rev: BL 6/1–15/07; SLJ 8/07)

15417 Weidt, Maryann N. *Fighting for Equal Rights: A Story About Susan B. Anthony* (3–5). Illus. by Amanda Sartor. Series: Creative Minds Biographies. 2003, Carolrhoda LB $22.60 (978-1-57505-181-9). 64pp. A straightforward account of the life of the women's rights campaigner, starting with her childhood and schooling, and of the time in which she lived. (Rev: HBG 4/04; SLJ 3/04)

BARTON, CLARA

15418 Dubowski, Cathy E. *Clara Barton: I Want to Help!* (3–5). Illus. Series: Defining Moments. 2005, Bearport LB $25.27 (978-1-59716-075-9). 32pp. This inspiring biography of Clara Barton tells how she overcame her shyness to nurse the wounded on bloody Civil War battlefields and later established the American Red Cross. (Rev: BL 10/15/05; SLJ 2/06)

15419 Francis, Dorothy. *Clara Barton: Founder of the American Red Cross* (4–6). Series: Gateway Greens. 2002, Millbrook LB $23.90 (978-0-7613-2621-2). 48pp. The story of the Red Cross founder who obtained and distributed supplies for the wounded during the Civil War. (Rev: BL 7/02; HBG 3/03)

15420 Hamilton, Leni. *Clara Barton* (5–10). 1987, Chelsea LB $19.95 (978-1-55546-641-1). The story of the Civil War nurse and how she prepared for the founding of the American Red Cross. (Rev: BL 11/1/87) [921]

15421 Koestler-Grack, Rachel A. *The Story of Clara Barton* (4–7). Illus. Series: Breakthrough Biographies. 2004, Chelsea House LB $23.00 (978-0-7910-7312-4). 32pp. From her childhood and early career to her founding of the American Red Cross, this profile gives personal details and historical context. (Rev: BL 3/1/04; SLJ 9/04)

15422 Krensky, Stephen. *Clara Barton* (5–7). Illus. Series: DK Biography. 2011, DK $14.99 (978-0-7566-7279-9); paper $5.99 (978-0-7566-7278-2). 128pp. A life of the woman who nursed the wounded on the battlefields of the Civil War and founded the American Red Cross. ℮ (Rev: BLO 7/11; SLJ 9/1/11) [921]

15423 Somervill, Barbara A. *Clara Barton: Founder of the American Red Cross* (5–8). Series: Signature Lives: Civil War Era. 2007, Compass Point LB $23.95 (978-0-7565-1888-2). Chronicles the life of Clara Barton and provides information on the time in which she worked. (Rev: BL 6/1–15/07) [921]

BLOOMER, ELIZABETH

15424 Reed, Jennifer. *Elizabeth Bloomer: Child Labor Activist* (4–8). Series: Young Heroes. 2006, Gale LB $23.70 (978-0-7377-3615-1). Bloomer became an activist against child labor when she was in middle school and learned about Iqbal Masih, a Pakistani boy sold into slavery. (Rev: SLJ 5/07) [921]

BRIDGMAN, LAURA DEWEY

15425 Alexander, Sally Hobart, and Robert Alexander. *She Touched the World: Laura Bridgman, Deaf-Blind Pioneer* (5–8). 2008, Clarion $18.00 (978-0-618-85299-4). A little-known pioneer in the education of the deaf-blind, Bridgman (two generations older than Helen Keller) is an important figure, and this book ably introduces her to young readers. (Rev: BL 3/1/08; SLJ 3/08) [921]

BUSH, LAURA WELCH

15426 Gormley, Beatrice. *Laura Bush: America's First Lady* (5–8). 2003, Simon & Schuster paper $4.99 (978-0-689-85366-1). A chronological account of Laura Bush's life, with information on her childhood as well as her later public life. (Rev: BL 3/1/03; HBG 10/03; SLJ 5/03) [973.931]

15427 Stone, Tanya L. *Laura Welch Bush* (4–6). Illus. 2001, Millbrook LB $23.90 (978-0-7613-2304-4). A biography of President George W. Bush's wife, with photographs and "fun facts." (Rev: BL 9/15/01; HBG 3/02; SLJ 9/01)

CATT, CARRIE CHAPMAN

15428 Somervill, Barbara. *Votes for Women! The Story of Carrie Chapman Catt* (5–8). Illus. 2002, Morgan Reynolds LB $23.95 (978-1-883846-96-1). This is the story of Carrie Chapman Catt, who devoted her early life to the quest for women's right to vote and later turned her energies to helping Jewish refugees. (Rev: BL 11/15/02; HBG 3/03; SLJ 1/03; VOYA 2/03)

CHILD, LYDIA MARIA

15429 Stux, Erica. *Writing for Freedom: A Story About Lydia Maria Child* (3–5). Illus. Series: Creative Minds Biographies. 2000, Carolrhoda $22.60 (978-1-57505-439-1). A biography of the poet who was also an abolitionist and courageously fought against slavery. (Rev: HBG 10/01; SLJ 1/01)

CLINTON, HILLARY RODHAM

15430 Doak, Robin S. *Hillary Clinton* (3–6). Illus. Series: A True Book: Biography. 2013, Scholastic/Children's Press LB $29 (978-053121906-5). 48pp. This concise profile includes photographs, interesting sidebar, and facts and statistics. (Rev: BL 4/1/13; LMC 11–12/13) [921]

15431 Guernsey, JoAnn Bren. *Hillary Rodham Clinton* (5–8). 2005, Lerner LB $29.27 (978-0-8225-2372-7); paper $7.95 (978-0-8225-9613-4). Traces Clinton's life from childhood, and covers the trials of her husband's second term in office in some detail. (Rev: BL 6/1–15/05; SLJ 7/05) [921]

15432 Wells, Catherine. *Hillary Clinton* (5–8). Series: Political Profiles. 2007, Morgan Reynolds LB $27.95 (978-1-59935-047-9). Readers will learn of the former First Lady and presidential hopeful's life and achievements from this positive portrait. (Rev: BL 11/15/07) [921]

DAY, DOROTHY

15433 Shaw, Maura D. *Dorothy Day: A Catholic Life of Action* (3–6). Illus. by Stephen Marchesi. Series: Spiritual Biographies for Young Readers. 2004, SkyLight Paths $12.99 (978-1-59473-011-5). 32pp. Roman Catholic journalist/social activist Dorothy Day worked to help the homeless and hungry. (Rev: BL 10/1/04)

DIX, DOROTHEA

15434 Herstek, Amy Paulson. *Dorothea Dix* (5–8). Series: Historical American Biographies. 2001, Enslow LB $26.60 (978-0-7660-1258-5). The life of this militant reformer who fought for more humane treatment of the insane. (Rev: BL 1/1–15/02; HBG 3/02; SLJ 1/02)

EDMONDS, SARAH EMMA

15435 Jones, Carrie. *Sarah Emma Edmonds Was a Great Pretender: The True Story of a Civil War Spy* (2–4). Illus. by Mark Oldroyd. 2011, Carolrhoda $17.95 (978-0-7613-5399-7). 32pp. Sarah Emma Edmonds disguised herself as a boy and ran away from her abusive father in the 1850s; this inspiring picture book tells her courageous story. Lexile 780L (Rev: BL 4/15/11; HB 7–8/11; SLJ 4/11) [921]

15436 Moss, Marissa. *Nurse, Soldier, Spy: The Story of Sarah Edmonds, a Civil War Hero* (2–5). Illus. by John Hendrix. 2011, Abrams $18.95 (978-0-8109-9735-6). 48pp. This interesting biography presents short vignettes in the life of Sarah Emma Edmonds, a Canadian woman who lived most of her life as a man, including a stint in the Union Army during the Civil War. (Rev: BL 5/1/11; SLJ 5/1/11) [921]

15437 Reit, Seymour. *Behind Rebel Lines: The Incredible Story of Emma Edmonds, Civil War Spy* (5–8). 1988, Harcourt $12.95 (978-0-15-200416-3); paper $6.00 (978-0-15-200424-8). The remarkable Canadian-born spy who helped to defend the Union in the Civil War. (Rev: BL 3/1/88; SLJ 3/88) [973.785]

FEINSTEIN, DIANNE

15438 McElroy, Lisa. *Meet My Grandmother: She's a United States Senator* (2–4). Series: Grandmothers at Work. 2000, Millbrook LB $22.90 (978-0-7613-1721-0). 32pp. Dianne Feinstein, once mayor of San Francisco and now a U.S. senator, as seen through the eyes of her 6-year-old granddaughter. (Rev: BL 3/15/00; HBG 10/00; SLJ 1/01)

GRAHAM, KATHARINE

15439 Mattern, Joanne. *Katharine Graham and 20th Century American Journalism* (1–4). Series: Women Who Shaped History. 2003, Rosen LB $19.95 (978-0-8239-6500-7). 24pp. The story of the woman who ran the *Washington Post* after her husband's death and who helped uncover the Watergate scandal. (Rev: BL 2/15/03; SLJ 5/03)

GRANDIN, TEMPLE

15440 Montgomery, Sy. *Temple Grandin: How the Girl Who Loved Cows Embraced Autism and Changed the World* (4–8). Illus. 2012, Houghton Mifflin $17.99 (978-054744315-7). 160pp. A fascinating account of how Temple Grandin's autism has allowed her to design facilities that are substantially less threatening to livestock. ALA Notable Children's Book. (Rev: BL 3/15/12; SLJ 4/12*) [921]

HUTCHINSON, ANNE

15441 Mangal, Melina. *Anne Hutchinson: Religious Reformer* (4–6). Series: Let Freedom Ring. 2004, Capstone LB $23.93 (978-0-7368-2454-5). 48pp. Hutchinson was a religious liberal whose outspoken opinions resulted in her banishment from the Massachusetts Bay Colony; she later helped to found the colony of Rhode Island. (Rev: SLJ 8/04)

INGLES, MARY DRAPER

15442 Furbee, Mary Rodd. *Shawnee Captive: The Story of Mary Draper Ingles* (5–8). Illus. 2001, Morgan Reynolds LB $23.95 (978-1-883846-69-5). 112pp. The tragic and exciting story of a pioneer woman captured by Shawnee Indians, her daring escape, and her long and difficult journey home. (Rev: BL 5/15/01; HBG 10/01; SLJ 6/01)

JOHNS, BARBARA ROSE

15443 Kanefield, Teri. *The Girl from the Tar Paper School: Barbara Rose Johns and the Advent of the Civil Rights Movement* (5–8). Illus. 2014, Abrams $19.95

(978-141970796-4). 56pp. Primary sources including photographs, letters, and newspapers tell the story of 16-year-old Barbara Rose Johns, who in the early 1950s led peaceful strikes against the poor education she and her classmates were receiving and brought attention to the fact their sub-par education and schooling conditions were in violation of the 1896 legal doctrine of "separate but equal"; Johns's efforts led to her complaint becoming part of the class action suit that formed the *Brown v. Board of Education* case. ℮ (Rev: BL 10/1/13; LMC 5–6/14*; SLJ 3/14*) [921]

JOHNSON, LADY BIRD

15444 Appelt, Kathi. *Miss Lady Bird's Wildflowers: How a First Lady Changed America* (1–3). Illus. by Joy Fisher Hein. 2005, HarperCollins LB $17.89 (978-0-06-001108-6). 40pp. Lady Bird Johnson's lifelong passion for flowers and her campaign as First Lady to beautify the nation's highways and cities by planting wildflowers are at the center of this volume. (Rev: BL 2/15/05)

KANDER, LIZZIE

15445 Kann, Bob. *A Recipe for Success: Lizzie Kander and Her Cookbook* (5–8). Illus. Series: Badger Biographies. 2006, Wisconsin Historical Soc. paper $12.95 (978-0-87020-373-2). Lizzie Kander was a social reformer in the mid-19th century, responsible among other things for a successful cookbook that benefited the Milwaukee Settlement House; in addition to a profile of Kander, this volume offers interesting information on the time she lived in. (Rev: BL 2/15/07) [921]

KELLER, HELEN

15446 Adler, David A. *Helen Keller* (1–2). Illus. by John C. Wallner. Series: Holiday House Reader. 2003, Holiday House $14.95 (978-0-8234-1606-6). 32pp. Written in simple language that is well suited for early readers, this biography covers Keller's youth and her work as an adult. (Rev: BL 7/03; HBG 4/04; SLJ 11/03)

15447 Garrett, Leslie. *Helen Keller: Biography* (5–10). Series: DK Biography. 2004, DK paper $5.99 (978-0-7566-0339-7). Keller's struggles to conquer her physical disabilities and her worldwide recognition as a political activist and public speaker are covered in the usual rich DK format. (Rev: BL 6/1–15/04) [921]

15448 Hollingsworth, Tamara Leigh. *Helen Keller: A New Vision* (3–5). Illus. Series: Time for Kids Nonfiction Readers. 2012, Teacher Created Materials paper $9.99 (978-14333486-3-1). 48pp. An appealing account of Keller's life, drawing on her own writings and including many sidebars and visual features. (Rev: BL 9/15/12; LMC 5–6/13) [921]

15449 Kent, Deborah. *Helen Keller: Author and Advocate for the Disabled* (3–6). Series: Our People. 2003, Child's World LB $27.07 (978-1-59296-005-7). 32pp. Report writers will find solid material in this biography that includes "Interesting Facts" sidebars. (Rev: BL 1/1–15/04; SLJ 4/04)

15450 Lakin, Patricia. *Helen Keller and the Big Storm* (1–2). Illus. by Diana Magnuson. Series: Childhood of Famous Americans. 2002, Simon & Schuster paper $3.99 (978-0-689-84104-0). 30pp. An anecdote about her teacher rescuing Helen when she is caught in a tree during a storm serves to introduce beginning readers to Helen's character and problems. (Rev: HBG 10/02; SLJ 7/02)

15451 Lawlor, Laurie. *Helen Keller: Rebellious Spirit* (4–8). 2001, Holiday $22.95 (978-0-8234-1588-5). This account puts Keller's life in the context of her time and looks at the opinions and beliefs that made her a "rebellious spirit," with photographs, quotations, a bibliography, and the manual alphabet. (Rev: BL 9/1/01; HB 9–10/01; HBG 3/02; SLJ 9/01*; VOYA 2/02) [362.4]

15452 MacLeod, Elizabeth. *Helen Keller: A Determined Life* (3–5). Illus. Series: Snapshots: Images of People and Places in History. 2004, Kids Can $14.95 (978-1-55337-508-1). Attractive double-page spreads with well-positioned and interesting text make this profile inviting for browsers. (Rev: BL 3/1/04; SLJ 5/04)

15453 Rappaport, Doreen. *Helen's Big World* (2–4). Illus. by Matt Tavares. 2012, Disney/Hyperion $17.99 (978-0-7868-0890-8). 48pp. A large-format, well-designed picture book that covers all aspects of Keller's life from the age of 6 months (when she could still see and hear) and highlights the importance of her teacher, Annie Sullivan. ALA Notable Children's Book. Lexile AD770L (Rev: BL 9/1/12; HB 9–10/12; LMC 3–4/13; SLJ 9/12*) [921]

15454 Shichtman, Sandra H. *Helen Keller: Out of a Dark and Silent World* (4–6). Series: Gateway Greens. 2002, Millbrook LB $23.90 (978-0-7613-2550-5). 48pp. The inspiring story of the woman who overcame multiple handicaps to become a role model for others. (Rev: BL 7/02; HBG 3/03)

15455 Sullivan, George. *Helen Keller* (3–5). Illus. 2001, Scholastic $12.95 (978-0-439-14751-4); paper $4.50 (978-0-439-59555-1). Using excerpts from her biographical works, the author presents an interesting picture of Keller, her problems, and her life. (Rev: BL 4/1/01; HBG 10/01)

15456 Sullivan, George. *Helen Keller: Her Life in Pictures* (4–6). Illus. 2007, Scholastic $17.99 (978-0-439-91815-2). 80pp. This photo-biography spans the life of Keller from infancy to her 80s with black-and-white photographs, simbraille (a print representation of braille characters), and informative back matter. (Rev: BCCB 12/07; BL 11/15/07; LMC 5/08; SLJ 3/08)

15457 Sutcliffe, Jane. *Helen Keller* (2–4). Illus. by Elaine Verstraete. Series: On My Own Biography. 2002, Carolrhoda LB $23.93 (978-0-87614-600-2); paper $5.95 (978-0-87614-903-4). For beginning readers, this is an appealing introduction to Keller's life. (Rev: HBG 3/03; SLJ 12/02)

LAZARUS, EMMA

15458 Glaser, Linda. *Emma's Poem: The Voice of the Statue of Liberty* (K–3). Illus. by Claire A. Nivola. 2010,

Houghton Mifflin $16 (978-0-547-17184-5). 32pp. Moving free verse and detailed mixed-media paintings illustrate the life of Emma Lazarus, who grew up rich but became a champion for poor immigrants. (Rev: BL 2/1/10; SLJ 3/1/10) [921]

15459 Silverman, Erica. *Liberty's Voice: The Story of Emma Lazarus* (1–3). Illus. by Stacey Schuett. 2011, Dutton $17.99 (978-0-525-47859-1). 32pp. Silverman chronicles the life of the humanitarian who was motivated by her empathy toward Russian Jews to write the poem that appears on the Statue of Liberty. Lexile AD810L (Rev: BL 1/1–15/11; SLJ 2/1/11) [921]

LEMLICH, CLARA

15460 Markel, Michelle. *Brave Girl: Clara and the Shirtwaist Makers' Strike of 1909* (K–3). Illus. by Melissa Sweet. 2013, HarperCollins $17.99 (978-0-06-180442-7). 32pp. In this picture-book biography Markel tells the story of Clara Lemlich, an immigrant from Ukraine who inspired garment workers to rebel against their shocking working conditions in the early 1900s. Amelia Bloomer List: 2014. (Rev: BL 11/15/12*; HB 1–2/13; SLJ 1/13*) [921]

LEWIS, IDA

15461 Moss, Marissa. *The Bravest Woman in America: The Story of Ida Lewis* (K–3). Illus. by Andrea U'Ren. 2011, Tricycle $16.99 (978-1-58246-369-8); LB $19.99 (978-158246400-8). 32pp. Lighthouse keeper's daughter Ida Lewis, born in 1842, grows up to fill her father's shoes and rescues many from the sea in her long career. Lexile AD810L (Rev: BL 7/11; HB 7–8/11; LMC 5–6/11; SLJ 7/11) [921]

LINCOLN, MARY TODD

15462 Hull, Mary. *Mary Todd Lincoln* (5–8). Series: Historical American Biographies. 2000, Enslow LB $26.60 (978-0-7660-1252-3). This biography faithfully records the tragic life of Lincoln's widow, whose emotional health declined after the deaths of her son and her husband. (Rev: BL 1/1–15/00; HBG 10/00; SLJ 5/00)

LOCKWOOD, BELVA

15463 Bardhan-Quallen, Sudipta. *Ballots for Belva: The True Story of a Woman's Race for the Presidency* (1–3). Illus. by Courtney A. Martin. 2008, Abrams $16.95 (978-0-8109-7110-3). 32pp. Belva Lockwood was the first woman lawyer to appear before the Supreme Court, and ran for president in 1884. (Rev: BL 11/15/08; LMC 5/09; SLJ 9/08)

15464 Norgren, Jill. *Belva Lockwood: Equal Rights Pioneer* (5–8). Illus. Series: Trailblazer Biographies. 2008, Twenty-First Century $31.93 (978-0-8225-9068-2). 112pp. Norgren introduces the 19th-century woman who worked for the rights of Native Americans and for equal voting rights for all. (Rev: BL 1/1–15/09; SLJ 11/08) [921]

LONGWORTH, ALICE ROOSEVELT

15465 Kerley, Barbara. *What to Do About Alice? How Alice Roosevelt Broke the Rules, Charmed the World, and Drove Her Father Teddy Crazy!* (K–3). Illus. by Edwin Fotheringham. 2008, Scholastic $16.99 (978-0-439-92231-9). 48pp. An entertaining biography of the very original and lively Alice Roosevelt, daughter of president Theodore, with engaging digital art. (Rev: BL 1/1–15/08; SLJ 3/08)

LOW, JULIETTE GORDON

15466 Corey, Shana. *Here Come the Girl Scouts!* (1–4). Illus. by Hadley Hooper. 2012, Scholastic $17.99 (978-0-545-34278-0). 40pp. Tells the story of the formation of Girl Scouts in the United States through a picture-book profile of founder Juliette Gordon Low. (Rev: BL 1/1/12; LMC 8–9/12; SLJ 2/1/12*) [921]

15467 Wadsworth, Ginger. *First Girl Scout: The Life of Juliette Gordon Low* (4–7). Illus. 2011, Clarion $17.99 (978-0-547-24394-8). 224pp. An appealing account of the life of the woman known as Daisy who came from a privileged background, was partially deaf, and founded the Girl Scout movement in the United States. **℮** (Rev: BL 12/1/11; HB 11–12/11; SLJ 10/1/11) [921]

MADISON, DOLLEY

15468 Brown, Don. *Dolley Madison Saves George Washington* (1–3). Illus. by author. 2007, Houghton $16.00 (978-0-618-41199-3). 32pp. A lively biography of Dolley Madison, farm girl turned first lady, who saved George Washington's portrait in 1814 when the British attacked the White House. (Rev: BCCB 11/07; BL 9/1/07; SLJ 9/07)

15469 Klingel, Cynthia, and Robert B. Noyed. *Dolley Madison: First Lady* (2–4). Illus. Series: Spirit of America: Our People. 2002, Child's World LB $27.07 (978-1-56766-170-5). 32pp. A solid introduction to the life of Dolley Madison and her skill as a hostess. (Rev: SLJ 1/03)

15470 Patrick, Jean L. S. *Dolley Madison* (3–4). Illus. Series: History Maker Bios. 2002, Lerner LB $26.60 (978-0-8225-0194-7). 48pp. Using both cartoons and regular illustrations, this is a biography of the brave and gracious first lady who became a famous hostess. (Rev: BL 6/1–15/02; HBG 3/03)

15471 Weatherly, Myra. *Dolley Madison: America's First Lady* (5–8). Series: Founders of the Republic. 2002, Morgan Reynolds LB $23.95 (978-1-883846-95-4). This portrait of Dolley Madison conveys her popularity and courage, with reproductions of period paintings, prints, and maps. (Rev: BL 11/1/02; HBG 3/03; SLJ 3/03) [973.5]

MICHAEL, MOINA BELLE

15472 Walsh, Barbara Elizabeth. *The Poppy Lady: Moina Belle Michael and Her Tribute to Veterans* (2–5). Illus. by Layne Johnson. 2012, Boyds Mills $16.95 (978-1-59078-754-0). 40pp. Walsh tells the story of Moina

Belle Michael's campaign to honor the contributions of the soldiers who fought and died in World War I. (Rev: BL 10/1/12; LMC 3–4/13; SLJ 10/12) [921]

MORRIS, ESTHER

15473 White, Linda Arms. *I Could Do That! Esther Morris Gets Women the Vote* (2–4). Illus. by Nancy Carpenter. 2005, Farrar $16.00 (978-0-374-33527-4). The story of Esther Morris, the little-known suffragist who led a successful campaign to win the vote for women in the Wyoming Territory. (Rev: BL 9/15/05*; SLJ 9/05)

NATION, CARRY A.

15474 Harvey, Bonnie Carman. *Carry A. Nation: Saloon Smasher and Prohibitionist* (5–8). Series: Historical American Biographies. 2002, Enslow LB $26.60 (978-0-7660-1907-2). 128pp. A lively and balanced biography of the prohibitionist who fought alcohol with violence. (Rev: HBG 3/03; SLJ 1/03)

O'CONNOR, SANDRA DAY

15475 McElroy, Lisa. *Sandra Day O'Connor: Supreme Court Justice* (4–6). Series: Gateway Biographies. 2003, Millbrook LB $23.90 (978-0-7613-2502-4). Published before O'Connor announced her plans to retire, this biography chronicles her life and legal career in concise, lively text with many photographs and quotations. (Rev: HBG 4/04; SLJ 1/04)

15476 O'Connor, Sandra Day. *Chico: A True Story from the Childhood of the First Woman Supreme Court Justice* (1–3). Illus. by Dan Andreasen. 2005, Dutton $16.99 (978-0-525-47452-4). Former Supreme Court justice O'Connor gives a good sense of her youth in Arizona in this story about coming across a rattlesnake when riding on her horse Chico as a 6-year-old. (Rev: BL 10/1/05; SLJ 9/05)

15477 Williams, Jean Kinney. *Sandra Day O'Connor: Lawyer and Supreme Court Justice* (4–6). Series: Ferguson Career Biographies. 2001, Ferguson LB $25.00 (978-0-89434-355-1). The story of O'Connor's life from childhood plus information on the confirmation process for Supreme Court appointees and on how to become a lawyer or judge. (Rev: SLJ 5/01)

OBAMA, MICHELLE

15478 Brophy, David Bergen. *Michelle Obama: Meet the First Lady* (4–8). 2008, Collins $16.99 (978-0-06-177991-6); HarperCollins paper $6.99 (978-0-06-177990-9). 128pp. A chronological look at Obama's life from childhood, incorporating many quotations but few photographs. (Rev: BL 3/1/09) [921]

15479 Colbert, David. *Michelle Obama: An American Story* (5–8). Illus. 2009, Houghton $16.00 (978-0-547-24941-4); paper $6.99 (978-0-547-24770-0). 160pp. This profile looks mainly at Obama's ancestry and her childhood and early married life. (Rev: BL 3/1/09) [921]

15480 Hopkinson, Deborah. *Michelle* (K–3). Illus. by AG Ford. 2009, HarperCollins $17.99 (978-0-06-182739-6);

LB $18.89 (978-0-06-182743-3). 32pp. An admiring account of the life of the woman who was born on Chicago's South Side, worked hard to become a success, and became First Lady in 2009. (Rev: BL 11/1/09; SLJ 12/1/09) [921]

15481 Mattern, Joanne. *Michelle Obama* (2–4). Series: A Robbie Reader. What's So Great About . . . ? 2010, Mitchell Lane LB $18.50 (978-1-58415-833-2). 32pp. For early readers, this book covers Michelle Obama's youth and family and her personal and professional achievements. (Rev: BL 6/10; LMC 8–9/10; SLJ 5/1/10) [921]

15482 Weatherford, Carole Boston. *Michelle Obama: First Mom* (2–4). Illus. by Robert T. Barrett. 2010, Marshall Cavendish $17.99 (978-0-7614-5640-7). 32pp. Michelle Obama's domestic side is highlighted in this profile illustrated with sepia-toned oil paintings. (Rev: BL 10/15/10; LMC 11–12/10; SLJ 11/1/10) [921]

15483 Wheeler, Jill C. *Michelle Obama* (2–4). Illus. 2009, ABDO LB $24.21 (978-1-60453-633-1). This introduction to the first lady highlights her childhood and early adult years. (Rev: BL 6/1–15/09)

OBAMA, SASHA

15484 Snyder, Gail. *Sasha* (3–5). Illus. 2009, Mason Crest LB $19.95 (978-1-4222-1480-0). 64pp. A biography of Sasha Obama, the daughter of the president, laced with political background. (Rev: BL 6/1–15/09; SLJ 7/09)

RANKIN, JEANNETTE

15485 Marx, Trish. *Jeannette Rankin: First Lady of Congress* (3–5). Illus. by Dan Andreasen. 2006, Simon & Schuster $18.95 (978-0-689-86290-8). 48pp. This biography uses clear and simple text to chronicle the life and times of the first woman elected to the U.S. House of Representatives. (Rev: BL 1/1–15/06; SLJ 2/06)

ROOSEVELT, ELEANOR

15486 Brown, Jonatha A. *Eleanor Roosevelt* (2–4). Illus. Series: People We Should Know. 2005, Gareth Stevens LB $21.00 (978-0-8368-4468-9). 24pp. For beginning readers, a simple explanation of Eleanor Roosevelt's importance with an attractive layout and historical and contemporary photographs. [921]

15487 Feinberg, Barbara S. *Eleanor Roosevelt: A Very Special Lady* (3–5). Illus. Series: Gateway. 2003, Millbrook LB $23.90 (978-0-7613-2623-6). 48pp. A biography of the First Lady, with photographs, a timeline, and a list of relevant Web sites. (Rev: BL 2/1/03; HBG 10/03; SLJ 4/03)

15488 Freedman, Russell. *Eleanor Roosevelt: A Life of Discovery* (5–9). 1993, Clarion $17.95 (978-0-89919-862-0). This admiring photobiography captures Roosevelt's public role and personal sadness. (Rev: BL 7/93*; SLJ 8/93*; VOYA 2/94) [921]

15489 Jacobson, Ryan. *Eleanor Roosevelt: First Lady of the World* (2–6). Illus. by Gordon Purcell and Barbara

Schulz. Series: Graphic Library, Graphic Biographies. 2005, Capstone LB $26.60 (978-0-7368-4969-2). 32pp. This graphic-novel biography introduces Roosevelt's life and discusses her active support of her husband's domestic programs and her increased involvement in foreign affairs after her husband's death. (Rev: SLJ 3/06)

15490 Jones, Victoria Garrett. *Eleanor Roosevelt: A Courageous Spirit* (5–8). Series: Sterling Biographies. 2007, Sterling $12.95 (978-1-4027-4746-5); paper $5.95 (978-1-4027-3371-0). 124pp. This well-illustrated profile covers Eleanor Roosevelt's life from childhood and discusses her contributions as First Lady, a position she transformed. (Rev: SLJ 5/07)

15491 Koestler-Grack, Rachel A. *The Story of Eleanor Roosevelt* (4–7). Series: Breakthrough Biographies. 2004, Chelsea House LB $23.00 (978-0-7910-7313-1). This brief biography covers Roosevelt's early years as well as her later contributions to her country and to the world. (Rev: BL 3/1/04) [973917]

15492 Lassieur, Allison. *Eleanor Roosevelt: Activist for Social Change* (5–8). Series: Great Life Stories. 2006, Watts LB $30.50 (978-0-531-13871-7). This biography of Eleanor Roosevelt focuses on the first lady's personal life and on her social activism while in the White House and later as an envoy to the United Nations. (Rev: SLJ 2/07) [921]

15493 MacLeod, Elizabeth. *Eleanor Roosevelt: An Inspiring Life* (4–6). 2006, Kids Can $14.95 (978-1-55337-778-8); paper $6.95 (978-1-55337-811-2). 32pp. Traces the first lady's life from her difficult childhood to the humanitarian work that she pursued after the death of her husband, with many quotations and period photographs. (Rev: SLJ 11/06)

15494 Mattern, Joanne. *Eleanor Roosevelt: More than a First Lady* (1–4). Series: Women Who Shaped History. 2003, Rosen LB $19.95 (978-0-8239-6501-4). Through classic photographs and an accessible text, readers will learn about the amazing woman who changed the role of the first lady and had a great influence on world affairs. (Rev: BL 2/15/03)

15495 Rosenberg, Pam. *Eleanor Roosevelt: First Lady, Humanitarian, and World Citizen* (3–6). Series: Our People. 2003, Child's World LB $27.07 (978-1-59296-001-9). 32pp. An accessible life of Roosevelt, emphasizing her contributions to society. (Rev: BL 1/1–15/04)

15496 Somervill, Barbara A. *Eleanor Roosevelt: First Lady of the World* (5–8). Series: Signature Lives: Modern America. 2005, Compass Point $34.60 (978-0-7565-0992-7). An appealing biography that traces the First Lady's life and focuses on her tireless efforts to make life better for America's disadvantaged minorities. (Rev: BL 10/15/05) [973.917]

15497 Westervelt, Virginia Veeder. *Here Comes Eleanor: A New Biography of Eleanor Roosevelt for Young People* (5–8). Series: Avisson Young Adult. 1999, Avisson paper $16.00 (978-1-888105-33-9). A clear account of the life of Eleanor Roosevelt that gives a fine assessment of her

many contributions to humankind. (Rev: BL 2/15/99; SLJ 7/99; VOYA 10/99) [921]

15498 Winget, Mary. *Eleanor Roosevelt* (5–8). Series: A&E Biography. 2000, Lerner LB $27.93 (978-0-8225-4985-7). 112pp. Growing up in a troubled but loving family, Eleanor Roosevelt showed that an ordinary woman can achieve greatness. (Rev: BL 3/1/01; HBG 10/01)

SCIDMORE, ELIZA

15499 Zimmerman, Andrea. *Eliza's Cherry Trees: Japan's Gift to America* (1–3). Illus. by Ju Hong Chen. 2011, Pelican $16.99 (978-1-58980-954-3). 32pp. The story of Eliza Scidmore, a photographer and author who was the first woman to have an important job at the National Geographic Society, and her efforts to bring beautiful Japanese flowering cherry trees to Washington, D.C. Lexile AD670L (Rev: BL 7/11; SLJ 6/11) [975.3]

SHAW, ANNA HOWARD

15500 Brown, Don. *A Voice from the Wilderness: The Story of Anna Howard Shaw* (1–3). Illus. 2001, Houghton $16.00 (978-0-618-08362-6). 32pp. This is the story of Anna Howard Shaw, who came to America in the mid-19th century and overcame adversity to become a teacher and champion of women's suffrage. (Rev: BL 9/15/01; HB 11/01; HBG 3/02; SLJ 9/01)

SMITH, MARGARET CHASE

15501 Plourde, Lynn. *Margaret Chase Smith: A Woman for President* (3–5). Illus. by David McPhail. 2008, Charlesbridge $16.95 (978-1-58089-234-6); paper $7.95 (978-1-58089-235-3). 32pp. Smith, the first woman candidate for president from a major U.S. political party, lived to be 97; this is a chronological account of her life and career in politics. (Rev: BL 4/15/08; LMC 10/08; SLJ 4/08)

SOTOMAYOR, SONIA

15502 Gitlin, Martin. *Sonia Sotomayor: Supreme Court Justice* (5–8). Series: Essential Lives. 2010, ABDO LB $32.79 (978-1-61613-518-8). 112pp. After covering Sotomayor's youth and education, this volume looks at her legal career and explains some of the legal issues in sidebars. (Rev: SLJ 3/1/11) [921]

15503 McElroy, Lisa Tucker. *Sonia Sotomayor: First Hispanic U.S. Supreme Court Justice* (5–8). Illus. Series: Gateway Biographies. 2010, Lerner LB $26.60 (978-0-7613-5861-9). 48pp. This concise, straightforward biography provides an introduction to the first Hispanic Supreme Court justice. Lexile 940L (Rev: BL 6/10; SLJ 5/10) [921]

15504 Winter, Jonah. *Sonia Sotomayor: A Judge Grows in the Bronx / La juez que crecio en el Bronx* (K–3). Illus. by Edel Rodriguez. 2009, Atheneum $16.99 (978-1-44240303-1). 40pp. This bilingual biography focuses on the triumphs and achievements of Supreme Court justice Sonia Sotomayor. (Rev: BL 12/15/09) [921]

STANTON, ELIZABETH CADY

15505 Loos, Pamela. *Elizabeth Cady Stanton* (5–8). Illus. Series: Women of Achievement. 2000, Chelsea $30.00 (978-0-7910-5293-8). 120pp. Drawing largely on Stanton's autobiography, this is the life story of the well-known suffragist of the 19th century. (Rev: BL 2/15/01; HBG 10/01)

15506 Miller, Connie Colwell. *Elizabeth Cady Stanton: Women's Rights Pioneer* (2–6). Illus. by Cynthia Martin. Series: Graphic Library, Graphic Biographies. 2005, Capstone LB $26.60 (978-0-7368-4971-5). 32pp. This graphic-novel biography covers Stanton's role in the women's rights movement and provides links to related online resources. (Rev: SLJ 3/06)

15507 Salisbury, Cynthia. *Elizabeth Cady Stanton: Leader of the Fight for Women's Rights* (5–8). Series: Historical American Biographies. 2002, Enslow LB $26.60 (978-0-7660-1616-3). The life of the fighter for women's suffrage and the organizer of the first women's rights convention. (Rev: BL 4/1/02; HBG 10/02; SLJ 5/02)

15508 Stone, Tanya L. *Elizabeth Leads the Way: Elizabeth Cady Stanton and the Right to Vote* (1–3). Illus. by Rebecca Gibbon. 2008, Holt $16.95 (978-0-8050-7903-6). 32pp. This brief biography introduces young readers to Stanton's fight for women's rights, focusing more on her beliefs than on historical events. (Rev: BL 4/15/08; HB 5/08; LMC 8/08; SLJ 5/08)

STEINEM, GLORIA

15509 Lazo, Caroline Evensen. *Gloria Steinem: Feminist Extraordinaire* (5–7). Series: Lerner Biographies. 1998, Lerner LB $27.93 (978-0-8225-4934-5). The story of Steinem, who overcame a troubled childhood to become a great humanitarian, writer, and leader of the feminist movement. (Rev: BL 7/98; SLJ 7/98) [921]

STINSON, KATHERINE

15510 Winegarten, Debra L. *Katherine Stinson: The Flying Schoolgirl* (4–7). 2001, Eakin $26.95 (978-1-57168-459-2). 115pp. An absorbing introduction to Stinson's accomplishments, which include a whole series of "firsts," that interweaves fiction and fact. (Rev: HBG 10/01; SLJ 6/01)

SULLIVAN, ANNIE

15511 Delano, Marfé Ferguson. *Helen's Eyes: A Photobiography of Annie Sullivan, Helen Keller's Teacher* (4–7). 2008, National Geographic $17.95 (978-1-4263-0209-1). Full of photographs, this attractive, oversize book tells the story of Sullivan's often-sad life. (Rev: BL 6/1–15/08; SLJ 9/08) [921]

TAYLOR, ANNIE EDSON

15512 Van Allsburg, Chris. *Queen of the Falls* (3–5). Illus. by author. 2011, Houghton Mifflin $18.99 (978-0-547-31581-2). 40pp. The fascinating story of the woman who in 1901, at the age of 62, decided to tackle the Niagara Falls in a barrel, seeking funds to keep herself out of the poorhouse. Lexile 1060L (Rev: BL 1/1–15/11; HB 3–4/11; SLJ 3/1/11*)

VAN LEW, ELIZABETH

15513 Vander Hook, Sue. *Civil War Spy: Elizabeth Van Lew* (5–8). Series: We the People. 2009, Compass Point LB $26.65 (978-0-7565-4104-0). 48pp. Accessible and well-illustrated, with a useful timeline, this book provides a balanced look at the canny female spy who provided the Union with key information during the Civil War. (Rev: LMC 10/09) [921]

WALKER, MARY

15514 Harness, Cheryl. *Mary Walker Wears the Pants: The True Story of the Doctor, Reformer, and Civil War Hero* (2–4). Illus. by Carlo Molinari. 2013, Whitman $16.99 (978-0-8075-4990-2). 48pp. An illustrated account of the life of the doctor who received a Medal of Honor for her work on the battlefields of the Civil War. (Rev: BL 6/13; LMC 8–9/13; SLJ 4/13) [921]

WASHINGTON, MARTHA

15515 Raatma, Lucia. *First of First Ladies: Martha Washington* (2–4). Illus. 2009, Compass Point LB $26.65 (978-0-7565-4125-5). 48pp. This title introduces the first lady as a young widow with two children at the time of her marriage to George Washington. (Rev: BL 6/1–15/09)

WILLIAMS, MOLLY

15516 Ochiltree, Dianne. *Molly, by Golly! The Legend of Molly Williams, America's First Female Firefighter* (K–2). Illus. by Kathleen Kemly. 2012, Boyds Mills/Calkins Creek $16.95 (978-1-59078-721-2). 32pp. Ochiltree tells the story of the African American cook who helped fight a house fire during a blizzard in 1818, (Rev: BL 10/15/12; LMC 3–4/13; SLJ 10/12) [921]

WONG, LI KENG

15517 Wong, Li Keng. *Good Fortune: My Journey to Gold Mountain* (4–7). 2006, Peachtree $14.95 (978-1-56145-367-2). 144pp. Wong, who migrated to the United States from China with her mother and sister in 1933, writes about the challenges of adjusting to a new culture. (Rev: BL 3/1/06; SLJ 7/06)

WOODHULL, VICTORIA

15518 Krull, Kathleen. *A Woman for President: The Story of Victoria Woodhull* (3–5). Illus. by Jane Dyer. 2004, Walker $16.95 (978-0-8027-8908-2). Woodhull's fascinating life included working as a spiritualist and financial adviser, amassing wealth, starting a newspaper, and running for president. (Rev: SLJ 9/04)

Scientists, Inventors, Naturalists, and Business Figures

Collective

15519 Aaseng, Nathan. *Business Builders in Computers* (5–8). Series: Business Builders. 2000, Oliver LB $22.95 (978-1-881508-57-1). Bill Gates, Steve Jobs of Apple, and Steve Case of AOL are among the individuals profiled in this interesting volume on the growth of the computer industry. (Rev: BL 2/1/01; HBG 10/01; SLJ 5/01) [338.4]

15520 Aaseng, Nathan. *Business Builders in Fast Food* (5–8). Series: Business Builders. 2001, Oliver $22.95 (978-1-881508-58-8). An interesting look at the creators of fast food empires such as McDonald's and Wendy's. (Rev: BL 9/15/01; HBG 10/01; SLJ 9/01) [381]

15521 Aaseng, Nathan. *Business Builders in Oil* (5–8). Series: Business Builders. 2000, Oliver LB $22.95 (978-1-881508-56-4). This lively introduction to the oil industry provides profiles of key individuals such as John D. Rockefeller, Andrew Mellon, and J. Paul Getty. (Rev: BL 2/1/01; HBG 10/01; SLJ 5/01) [338.2]

15522 Aaseng, Nathan. *Construction: Building the Impossible* (5–9). 2000, Oliver LB $21.95 (978-1-881508-59-5). This book profiles eight famous builders — from Imhotep, who built the first stone pyramids in Egypt, to Frank Crowe, the visionary behind the Hoover Dam. (Rev: BL 5/1/00; HBG 10/00; SLJ 10/00) [920]

15523 Bankston, John. *Francis Crick and James Watson: Pioneers in DNA Research* (5–7). Series: Unlocking the Secrets of Science. 2002, Mitchell Lane LB $17.95 (978-1-58415-122-7). An accessible account of the discovery of the structure of DNA and the lives of the two scientists involved. (Rev: HBG 10/03; SLJ 1/03) [576.5]

15524 Barton, Chris. *The Day-Glo Brothers: The True Story of Bob and Joe Switzer's Bright Ideas and Brand-New Colors* (2–5). Illus. by Tony Persiani. 2009, Charlesbridge $18.95 (978-1-57091-673-1). The story of the two inventive brothers who created glow-in-the-dark paint colors. (Rev: BL 6/1–15/09)

15525 Camp, Carole Ann. *American Women Inventors* (5–10). Illus. Series: Collective Biographies. 2004, Enslow LB $26.60 (978-0-7660-1913-3). 104pp. A collective biography of 10 important American female inventors, their lives, and their discoveries. (Rev: BL 3/1/04)

15526 Cox, Clinton. *African American Healers* (4–7). Series: Black Stars. 1999, Wiley $24.95 (978-0-471-24650-3). Using entries of two to three pages each, this work profiles more than 20 African Americans who have achieved prominence in medicine and related areas. (Rev: BL 2/15/00; HBG 10/00; SLJ 2/00) [910]

15527 Fortey, Jacqueline. *Great Scientists* (5–8). Illus. Series: Eyewitness. 2007, DK $15.99 (978-0-7566-2974-8). 72pp. From Aristotle to Stephen Hawking, this volume offers brief introductions to 30 great scientists, discussing their accomplishments and providing personal information, a timeline, and a few photographs with captions adding historical details. (Rev: BL 9/1/07)

15528 French, Laura. *Internet Pioneers: The Cyber Elite* (5–9). Series: Collective Biographies. 2001, Enslow LB $26.60 (978-0-7660-1540-1). French tells the stories of 10 Internet innovators — including Andrew Grove, Bill Gates, Larry Ellison, and Jeff Bezos — detailing their successes and revealing their very different backgrounds. (Rev: HBG 3/02; SLJ 9/01)

15529 Hansen, Ole Steen. *The Wright Brothers and Other Pioneers of Flight* (4–7). Series: The Story of Flight. 2003, Crabtree $25.27 (978-0-7787-1200-8). In text and pictures, this book introduces the pioneers of flight, with a concentration on the Wright brothers. (Rev: BL 10/15/03) [921]

15530 Harris, Laurie Lanzen, ed. *Biography Today: Profiles of People of Interest to Young Readers* (4–7). Series: Scientists and Inventors. 1996, Omnigraphics LB $39.00 (978-0-7808-0068-7). Profiles of 14 important contemporaries including Carl Sagan and Jane Goodall are accompanied by those of some lesser-known figures, such as geneticist and AIDS fighter Mathilde Krim. (Rev: SLJ 2/97) [920]

15531 Hudson, Wade. *Book of Black Heroes: Scientists, Healers and Inventors* (5–8). 2002, Just Us $9.95 (978-0-940975-97-2). One historic or present-day African American figure is presented on each page of this collective biography of doctors, engineers, and inventors. (Rev: BL 2/15/03) [925]

15532 Indovino, Shaina. *Women in Engineering* (5–8). Illus. Series: Major Women in Science. 2013, Mason Crest LB $22.95 (978-142222926-2). 64pp. Profiles nine female engineers who made significant contributions to the field of engineering, in addition to providing a list of different occupations relevant to the engineering profession. (Rev: BL 10/1/13; LMC 10/14) [920]

15533 Jones, Lynda. *Great Black Heroes: Five Brilliant Scientists* (2–3). Illus. by Ron Garnett. Series: Hello Reader! 2000, Scholastic paper $3.99 (978-0-590-48031-4). This easy-to-read book profiles five African American scientists, among them Ernest Just, a marine biologist, and Percy Lavon Julian, a chemist. (Rev: BL 7/00; SLJ 8/00)

15534 Kang, Zhu. *Science and Scientists* (3–5). Illus. by Hong Tao and Feng Congying. Series: True Stories from Ancient China. 2005, Long River $9.95 (978-1-59265-038-5). 48pp. Profiles the lives and accomplishments of four ancient Chinese scientists — Zhang Heng, Zu Chongzhi, Yi Xing, and Xu Xiake. (Rev: BL 12/1/05)

15535 Kimmel, Elizabeth Cody. *Dinosaur Bone War: Cope and Marsh's Fossil Feud* (4–7). Illus. 2006, Random $11.99 (978-0-375-91349-5); paper $5.99 (978-0-375-81349-8). 128pp. The story of American fossil hunters Edward Cope and Othniel Charles Marsh and the bitter rivalry that led to many dinosaur fossil discoveries and spurred the development of paleontology as a science. (Rev: BL 12/1/06)

15536 Kirsh, Shannon, and Florence Kirsh. *Fabulous Female Physicians* (4–8). 2002, Second Story paper $7.95 (978-1-896764-43-6). Using short chapters and black-and-white photographs, this account profiles 10 mostly unknown female doctors and their accomplishments. (Rev: BL 6/1–15/02; VOYA 8/02) [921]

15537 Krull, Kathleen, and Kathryn Hewitt. *Lives of the Scientists: Experiments, Explosions (and What the Neighbors Thought)* (4–7). Illus. by Kathryn Hewitt. 2013, Houghton Mifflin $20.99 (978-015205909-5). 96pp. Profiles 20 well-known scientists and their idiosyncracies. (Rev: BL 8/13; LMC 5–6/14*; SLJ 8/13) [920]

15538 Lomask, Milton. *Great Lives: Invention and Technology* (5–8). Series: Invention and Technology. 1991, Scribner $23.00 (978-0-684-19106-5). Profiles of great names in invention and technology around the world. (Rev: BL 11/1/91; SLJ 1/92) [920]

15539 McClafferty, Carla Killough. *Tech Titans: One Frontier, Six Bios* (5–7). Illus. 2012, Scholastic paper $6.99 (978-05453657-2). 144pp. Bill Gates, Steve Jobs, Mark Zuckerberg, Larry Page, Sergey Brin, and Jeff Bezos — the men behind Windows, Apple, Face-

book, Google, and Amazon — are profiled here. Lexile 1010L (Rev: BL 4/15/12; LMC 10/12) [920]

15540 McClure, Judy. *Healers and Researchers: Physicians, Biologists, Social Scientists* (5–9). Series: Remarkable Women. 2000, Raintree LB $32.85 (978-0-8172-5734-7). 80pp. This book profiles 150 women from the scientific community including Barbara McClintock, Anna Freud, Jocelyn Elders, and Sushila Nyir. (Rev: SLJ 8/00)

15541 McCutcheon, Marc. *The Kid Who Named Pluto and the Stories of Other Extraordinary Young People in Science* (3–6). Illus. by Jon Cannell. 2004, Chronicle $15.95 (978-0-8118-3770-5). 85pp. A collection of profiles of nine young people who made significant contributions to science while they still were young. (Rev: BL 4/1/04; SLJ 6/04)

15542 Mayberry, Jodine. *Business Leaders Who Built Financial Empires* (5–8). Series: 20 Events. 1995, Raintree LB $27.12 (978-0-8114-4934-2). The biographies of 19 financial wizards and entrepreneurs, beginning with Levi Strauss and Andrew Carnegie and ending with Steven Jobs and Anita Roddick. (Rev: SLJ 7/95) [920]

15543 Mulcahy, Robert. *Medical Technology: Inventing the Instruments* (5–8). Series: Innovators. 1997, Oliver LB $21.95 (978-1-881508-34-2). Seven short biographies of scientists who were responsible for such inventions as the X-ray, stethoscope, thermometer, and electrocardiograph. (Rev: BCCB 7–8/97; SLJ 7/97) [920]

15544 Polking, Kirk. *Oceanographers and Explorers of the Sea* (5–9). Series: Collective Biographies. 1999, Enslow LB $20.95 (978-0-7660-1113-7). Profiles 10 scientists and adventurers who have devoted their lives to the oceans, marine life, and ocean-related pursuits, including Maurice Ewing, who mapped the ocean floor, and Robert Ballard, discoverer of the *Titanic*. (Rev: BL 8/99; SLJ 9/99) [920]

15545 Richie, Jason. *Space Flight: Crossing the Last Frontier* (5–9). Series: Innovators. 2002, Oliver LB $21.95 (978-1-881508-77-9). Biographies of seven men who were instrumental in the development of space flight — including Robert Goddard, Wernher von Braun, and Sergei Korolev — are arranged in chronological order. (Rev: HBG 3/03; LMC 4–5/03; SLJ 4/03) [629.4]

15546 Sherman, Josepha. *Jerry Yang and David Filo: Chief Yahoos of Yahoo* (5–8). Series: Techies. 2001, Millbrook LB $23.90 (978-0-7613-1961-0). This is the story of the creators of Yahoo!, one of the most successful sites in the early days of the World Wide Web. (Rev: BL 4/1/02; HBG 3/02; SLJ 12/01) [921]

15547 Thimmesh, Catherine. *The Sky's the Limit: Stories of Discovery by Women and Girls* (5–7). Illus. by Melissa Sweet. 2002, Houghton Mifflin $16.00 (978-0-618-07698-7). Details discoveries in the sciences, all made by women and girls. A sequel to *Girls Think of Everything* (2000). (Rev: BL 3/1/02; HB 5–6/02; HBG 10/02; SLJ 5/02; VOYA 6/02) [500]

15548 VanCleave, Janice. *Janice VanCleave's Scientists Through the Ages* (4–7). 2003, Wiley paper $12.95 (978-

0-471-25222-1). A collective biography profiling 25 scientists, with explanations of each one's important work and a relevant experiment for the reader to perform. (Rev: BL 12/1/03) [509]

15549 Venezia, Mike. *Steve Jobs and Steve Wozniak: Geek Heroes Who Put the Personal in Computers* (2–4). Illus. by author. Series: Getting to Know the World's Greatest Inventors and Scientists. 2010, Scholastic LB $28 (978-0-531-23730-4). 32pp. With cartoons, images, and accessible large-font text, this is a good introduction to two computer greats. (Rev: BL 5/1/10; SLJ 7/1/10) [920]

15550 White, Casey. *Sergey Brin and Larry Page: The Founders of Google* (5–9). Series: Internet Career Biographies. 2006, Rosen LB $31.95 (978-1-4042-0716-5). The interesting story of the two Stanford graduates who created a company that added a new word to our vocabulary. (Rev: LMC 8–9/07; SLJ 5/07) [920]

15551 Young, Jeff C. *Inspiring African-American Inventors: Nine Extraordinary Lives* (5–8). Illus. Series: Great Scientists and Famous Inventors. 2009, Enslow LB $33.27 (978-159845080-4). 128pp. Nine African American inventors are profiled here, with details of their inventions and links to relevant Web sites. (Rev: BL 2/1/10; VOYA 4/10) [920]

Individual

ALVAREZ, LUIS

15552 Allison, Amy. *Luis Alvarez and the Development of the Bubble Chamber* (5–8). Series: Unlocking the Secrets of Science. 2002, Mitchell Lane LB $25.70 (978-1-58415-140-1). Alvarez was a scientist of wide-ranging interests who won a Nobel Prize for developing a bubble chamber to track atomic particles. (Rev: HBG 3/03; SLJ 2/03; VOYA 6/03) [921]

ANDREESSEN, MARC

15553 Ehrenhaft, Daniel. *Marc Andreessen: Web Warrior* (5–8). Series: The Techies. 2001, Twenty-First Century LB $23.90 (978-0-7613-1964-1). This biography introduces Marc Andreessen, who coauthored the Web-browsing software Mosaic, cofounded the firm Netscape, and was a multimillionaire at age 24. (Rev: BL 3/15/01; HBG 10/01; SLJ 7/01; VOYA 8/01) [921]

ANDREWS, ROY CHAPMAN

15554 Bausum, Ann. *Dragon Bones and Dinosaur Eggs: A Photobiography of Explorer Roy Chapman Andrews* (5–8). 2000, National Geographic $17.95 (978-0-7922-7123-9). A biography of the famous paleontologist who made several important dinosaur discoveries in central Asia and later became director of the American Museum of Natural History in New York City. (Rev: BCCB 5/00*; BL 3/15/00; HBG 10/00; SLJ 3/00) [921]

ANNING, MARY

15555 Goodhue, Thomas. *Curious Bones: Mary Anning and the Birth of Paleontology* (5–8). Illus. 2002, Morgan Reynolds LB $23.95 (978-1-883846-93-0). 112pp. A readable biography of the groundbreaking female paleontologist (1799–1847) that places her achievements in historical context, with a glossary, bibliography, and timeline. (Rev: BL 7/02; HBG 3/03; SLJ 9/02)

15556 Walker, Sally M. *Mary Anning: Fossil Hunter* (2–3). Series: On My Own. 2000, Carolrhoda LB $23.93 (978-1-57505-425-4). Using many original documents as sources, this simple biography tells the life story of Mary Anning, who hunted for fossils on the cliffs of Lyme Regis in England. (Rev: BL 8/00; HBG 3/01; SLJ 12/00)

ARCHIMEDES

15557 Gow, Mary. *Archimedes: Mathematical Genius of the Ancient World* (5–8). Series: Great Minds of Science. 2005, Enslow LB $26.60 (978-0-7660-2502-8). Archimedes' mathematical discoveries are explained and placed in social, scientific, and cultural context. (Rev: SLJ 12/05) [921]

15558 O'Neal, Claire. *Archimedes* (5–8). Illus. Series: Junior Biographies from Ancient Civilizations. 2013, Mitchell Lane LB $29.95 (978-161228437-8). 48pp. The author pays particular attention to the well-known "Eureka!" moment, but also follows the mathematician and inventor's life story, including his youth, and focuses on how he aided Greek civilization with his extensive work. **e** (Rev: BL 11/1/13; LMC 3–4/14) [921]

AVERY, OSWALD

15559 Severs, Vesta-Nadine, and Jim Whiting. *Oswald Avery and the Story of DNA* (4–7). Series: Unlocking the Secrets of Science. 2002, Mitchell Lane LB $25.70 (978-1-58415-110-4). The importance of Avery's early research is reinforced by a description of DNA evidence being used to free wrongly accused prisoners. (Rev: HBG 10/02; SLJ 6/02) [579.3092]

BAER, RALPH

15560 Wyckoff, Edwin Brit. *The Guy Who Invented Home Videos Games: Ralph Baer and His Awesome Invention* (3–5). Illus. 2010, Enslow $22.60 (978-076603450-1). 32pp. Readers learn about the radio repairman who fled Nazi Germany and went on to develop video games. (Rev: BL 3/1/11) [921]

BAIRD, JOHN LOGIE

15561 Reid, Struan. *John Logie Baird* (4–6). Series: Groundbreakers. 2000, Heinemann LB $25.64 (978-1-57572-372-3). 48pp. The ground-breaking inventor of television is featured in this biography that tells of his poor health and his many setbacks. (Rev: HBG 3/01; SLJ 3/01)

BANNEKER, BENJAMIN

15562 Blue, Rose, and Corinne J. Naden. *Benjamin Banneker: Mathematician and Stargazer* (4–6). Illus. Series: Gateway Biographies. 2001, Millbrook LB $23.90 (978-0-7613-1805-7). 48pp. An informative introduction to Banneker's life and achievements as America's "first major black man of science." (Rev: HBG 3/02; SLJ 9/01)

15563 Maupin, Melissa. *Benjamin Banneker* (4–6). Illus. Series: Journey to Freedom. 2009, Child's World LB $28.50 (978-160253117-8). 32pp. The life and accomplishments of African American inventor, astronomer, and activist Benjamin Banneker are presented with a timeline and a glossary. (Rev: BL 2/1/10; LMC 5–6/10) [921]

BARNARD, CHRISTIAAN

15564 Bankston, John. *Christiaan Barnard and the Story of the First Successful Heart Transplant* (4–5). Series: Unlocking the Secrets of Science. 2002, Mitchell Lane LB $25.70 (978-1-58415-120-3). 48pp. A concise but complete look with interesting anecdotal information at the life of the courageous doctor who performed the first successful heart transplant. (Rev: BL 8/02; SLJ 10/02)

BARTRAM, WILLIAM

15565 Ray, Deborah Kogan. *The Flower Hunter: William Bartram, America's First Naturalist* (3–5). Illus. 2004, Farrar $17.00 (978-0-374-34589-1). This brief but information-packed biography of Bartram tells how a childhood interest in his father's botanical studies grew into a full-time occupation as America's first naturalist. (Rev: BL 4/15/04; SLJ 5/04)

BELL, ALEXANDER GRAHAM

15566 Bankston, John. *Alexander Graham Bell and the Story of the Telephone* (5–8). Series: Uncharted, Unexplored, and Unexplained. 2004, Mitchell Lane LB $29.95 (978-1-58415-243-9). As a teacher of the deaf and son of a deaf mother, Bell had a special interest in finding new and better ways to communicate. (Rev: BL 10/15/04) [921]

15567 Berger, Melvin, and Gilda Berger. *Did You Invent the Phone Alone, Alexander Graham Bell?* (3–4). Illus. by Brandon Dorman. Series: Science SuperGiants. 2007, Scholastic paper $4.99 (978-0-439-83381-3). 48pp. "Who made the first telephone call?" "When did telephone service start in the United States?" Using a question-and-answer format, this profile provides biographical and basic scientific information. (Rev: SLJ 2/08)

15568 Carson, Mary Kay. *Alexander Graham Bell: Giving Voice to the World* (5–8). Series: Sterling Biographies. 2007, Sterling LB $12.95 (978-1-4027-4951-3); paper $5.95 (978-1-4027-3230-0). 124pp. Covers Bell's childhood and his lifelong commitment to improving communication. (Rev: SLJ 10/07)

15569 Gaines, Ann. *Alexander Graham Bell* (2–3). Series: Discover the Life of an Inventor. 2001, Rourke LB

$20.64 (978-1-58952-117-9). 24pp. Besides a life of this great inventor, this book describes the science behind the telephone. (Rev: BL 10/15/01; SLJ 1/02)

15570 Garmon, Anita. *Alexander Graham Bell Invents* (2–4). Series: National Geographic History Chapters. 2007, National Geographic LB $17.90 (978-1-4263-0189-6). 40pp. Simple sentences, with photographs and drawings, tell the story of Bell's younger life and later accomplishments; a "How to Write an A+ Report" section gives useful advice. (Rev: LMC 1/08*; SLJ 1/08)

15571 Pollard, Michael. *Alexander Graham Bell: Father of Modern Communication* (5–7). Series: Giants of Science. 2000, Blackbirch LB $27.44 (978-1-56711-334-1). Known primarily for the invention of the telephone, Bell also invented the first hydrofoil, an air-conditioning system, and an early fax machine. (Rev: BL 1/1–15/01; HBG 3/01)

15572 Reid, Struan. *Alexander Graham Bell* (4–6). Series: Groundbreakers. 2000, Heinemann LB $25.64 (978-1-57572-366-2). 48pp. This biography of Bell covers the invention of the telephone plus other innovations he pioneered and his important work with the deaf. (Rev: SLJ 3/01)

15573 Sherrow, Victoria. *Alexander Graham Bell* (1–3). Illus. by Elaine Verstraete. Series: On My Own Biography. 2001, Carolrhoda LB $21.27 (978-1-57505-460-5); paper $5.95 (978-1-57505-533-6). 48pp. Bell's early working years and growing interest in inventions are the focus of this biography that will suit reluctant and beginning readers, with an afterword that covers his personal life and later career. (Rev: HBG 3/02; SLJ 1/02)

15574 Williams, Brian. *Bell and the Science of the Telephone* (4–6). Illus. by David Antram. Series: The Explosion Zone. 2006, Barron's $12.99 (978-0-7641-5972-5). 32pp. This biography focuses on Bell's invention of the telephone and its impact but also touches on the related topics of Morse code, telephone exchanges, and tuning forks. (Rev: SLJ 11/06)

BENZ, KARL

15575 Bankston, John. *Karl Benz and the Single Cylinder Engine* (5–8). Series: Uncharted, Unexplored, and Unexplained. 2004, Mitchell Lane LB $29.95 (978-1-58415-244-6). The first person to build a three-wheeled automobile, Benz went on to design many more-sophisticated cars. (Rev: BL 10/15/04) [921]

BERNERS-LEE, TIM

15576 Gaines, Ann. *Tim Berners-Lee and the Development of the World Wide Web* (4–7). Series: Unlocking the Secrets of Science. 2001, Mitchell Lane LB $25.70 (978-1-58415-096-1). A profile of the man who created the user-friendly way of accessing much of the information on the Internet. (Rev: HBG 10/02; SLJ 2/02) [921]

15577 Stewart, Melissa. *Tim Berners-Lee: Inventor of the World Wide Web* (4–7). Series: Ferguson Career Biographies. 2001, Ferguson LB $25.00 (978-0-89434-367-4). 127pp. Young readers will be fascinated by the details of Berners-Lee's life and career and the accompanying information on the skills needed to become a computer programmer. (Rev: SLJ 10/01)

BEZOS, JEFF

15578 Garty, Judy. *Jeff Bezos* (5–8). Series: Internet Biographies. 2003, Enslow LB $23.93 (978-0-7660-1972-0). A reader-friendly biography of the creator of Amazon.com, with plenty of information on his youth. (Rev: BL 3/15/03; HBG 10/03) [380.1]

15579 Robinson, Tom. *Jeff Bezos: Amazon.com Architect* (5–8). Illus. Series: Publishing Pioneers. 2009, ABDO LB $22.95 (978-160453759-8). 112pp. This positive, informative biography of Amazon founder Jeff Bezos focuses on business innovation. (Rev: BL 12/1/09) [921]

15580 Sherman, Josepha. *Jeff Bezos: King of Amazon* (5–8). 2001, Twenty-First Century LB $23.90 (978-0-7613-1963-4). Jeff Bezos, the genius behind Amazon.com, is introduced along with information on his struggle to found a book company on the Web. (Rev: BL 3/15/01; HBG 10/01; SLJ 7/01; VOYA 8/01) [921]

BLACKWELL, ELIZABETH

15581 Kent, Deborah. *Elizabeth Blackwell: Physician and Health* (3–6). Series: Our People. 2003, Child's World LB $27.07 (978-1-59296-002-6). 32pp. The life and career of Elizabeth Blackwell, the first woman to graduate from medical school and a pioneer in medical education for women. (Rev: SLJ 4/04)

15582 Kline, Nancy. *Elizabeth Blackwell: A Doctor's Triumph* (5–9). Series: Barnard Biography. 1997, Conari paper $11.95 (978-1-57324-057-4). The story of the first woman doctor in America, with generous excerpts from her journal and letters. (Rev: BL 2/15/97; SLJ 6/97; VOYA 12/97) [921]

15583 Peck, Ira. *Elizabeth Blackwell: The First Woman Doctor* (4–5). Illus. 2000, Millbrook $23.90 (978-0-7613-1854-5). 48pp. This solid biography tells the story of the first woman to graduate from medical school in the United States and of her many accomplishments in her field. (Rev: BL 9/15/00; HBG 10/01)

15584 Stone, Tanya Lee. *Who Says Women Can't Be Doctors? The Story of Elizabeth Blackwell* (K–3). Illus. by Marjorie Priceman. 2013, Henry Holt $16.99 (978-080509048-2). 40pp. A picture-book biography of the first American female doctor, describing the barriers she faced and the legacy she left. ℮ (Rev: BL 1/13*; LMC 10/13; SLJ 2/13) [921]

BOMBARDIER, JOSEPH-ARMAND

15585 Older, Jules. *Snowmobile: Bombardier's Dream Machine* (4–6). Illus. by Michael Lauritano. 2012, Charlesbridge $14.95 (978-158089334-3); paper $6.95 (978-15808933-5-0). 64pp. The inspiring story of the inventor of the snowmobile features line drawings and an accessible yet detailed look at the invention. (Rev: BL 3/15/12; SLJ 4/12) [921]

BRAHE, TYCHO

15586 Nardo, Don. *Tycho Brahe: Pioneer of Astronomy* (5–8). Illus. Series: Signature Lives: Scientific Revolution. 2007, Compass Point LB $23.95 (978-0-7565-3309-0). In addition to this Danish scientist's career and discoveries, this well-designed volume explores the basics of scientific investigation and the nature of his breakthroughs. (Rev: BL 12/1/07; SLJ 1/08) [921]

BRAILLE, LOUIS

15587 Freedman, Russell. *Out of Darkness: The Story of Louis Braille* (4–8). 1997, Clarion $16.00 (978-0-395-77516-5). The story of the blind Frenchman who, more than 170 years ago, invented a system of reading using raised dots. (Rev: BCCB 5/97; BL 3/1/97; HB 5–6/97; SLJ 3/97*) [686.2]

BRANSON, RICHARD

15588 Redmond, Shirley Raye. *Richard Branson: Virgin Megabrand Mogul* (5–8). Illus. Series: Innovators. 2011, Gale LB $28.75 (978-073775536-7). 48pp. Tells the success story of the creator of the Virgin Group, offering records and transportation from trains to planes to spaceships. (Rev: BL 12/15/11) [921]

BROWN, BARNUM

15589 Sheldon, David. *Barnum Brown: Dinosaur Hunter* (2–4). Illus. by author. 2006, Walker $16.95 (978-0-8027-9602-8). 32pp. A compelling picture-book biography of dinosaur hunter Barnum Brown, who was fascinated by fossils from a young age and discovered a Tyrannosaurus rex in the early 20th century. (Rev: BL 12/1/06; SLJ 11/06)

BROWN, HELEN GURLEY

15590 Falkof, Lucille. *Helen Gurley Brown: The Queen of Cosmopolitan* (5–8). Series: Wizards of Business. 1992, Garrett LB $17.26 (978-1-56074-013-1). An interesting, accessible, and inspiring biography of the magazine magnate. (Rev: BL 6/15/92; SLJ 7/92) [921]

BURROUGHS, JOHN

15591 Wadsworth, Ginger. *John Burroughs: The Sage of Slabsides* (5–8). 1997, Clarion $16.95 (978-0-395-77830-2). A biography of the American naturalist and essayist who lived in a cabin in the Catskill Mountains and wrote about his observations. (Rev: BCCB 5/97; BL 3/15/97; HB 7–8/97; SLJ 5/97) [508.73]

CANNON, ANNIE JUMP

15592 Gerber, Carole. *Annie Jump Cannon, Astronomer* (3–5). Illus. by Christina Wald. 2011, Pelican $16.99 (978-1-58980-911-6). 32pp. Groundbreaking female astronomer Annie Jump Cannon developed a spectral classification system and a mnemonic device still used by astronomers today; this picture-book biography accurately depicts the hurdles female scientists faced in the late 1800s. (Rev: BL 10/15/11; SLJ 12/1/11) [921]

CARLSON, CHESTER

15593 Zannos, Susan. *Chester Carlson and the Development of Xerography* (4–5). Series: Unlocking the Secrets of Science. 2002, Mitchell Lane LB $25.70 (978-1-58415-117-3). 56pp. The story of the man whose determination to simplify the process of copying documents led to the invention of xerography. (Rev: BL 9/15/02; HBG 3/03; SLJ 11/02)

CAROTHERS, WALLACE

15594 Gaines, Ann Graham. *Wallace Carothers and the Story of DuPont Nylon* (4–5). Series: Unlocking the Secrets of Science. 2001, Mitchell Lane LB $17.95 (978-1-58415-097-8). 56pp. This biography of the inventor of nylon includes information on his suicide. (Rev: BL 10/15/01; SLJ 11/01)

CARSON, RACHEL

15595 Bruchac, Joseph. *Rachel Carson: Preserving a Sense of Wonder* (3–5). Illus. by Thomas Locker. 2004, Fulcrum $17.95 (978-1-55591-482-0). 32pp. Bruchac captures Carson's intense care for the environment and in particular her love of the sea, and includes details of her youth and of her writings. (Rev: BL 7/04; SLJ 6/04)

15596 Ehrlich, Amy. *Rachel: The Story of Rachel Carson* (2–4). Illus. by Wendell Minor. 2003, Harcourt $17.00 (978-0-15-216227-6). 32pp. Fine illustrations enhance this picture-book biography that concentrates on Carson's environmental concerns. (Rev: BL 6/1–15/03; HBG 10/03; SLJ 5/03)

15597 Landau, Elaine. *Rachel Carson and the Environmental Movement* (4–6). Series: Cornerstones of Freedom. 2004, Children's Pr. LB $26.00 (978-0-516-24232-3). 48pp. Carson's life and accomplishments are laid out in clear prose, with photographs and covers of her books. (Rev: SLJ 7/04)

15598 Lawlor, Laurie. *Rachel Carson and Her Book That Changed the World* (2–4). Illus. by Laura Beingessner. 2012, Holiday House $16.95 (978-0-8234-2370-5). 32pp. A moving picture-book tribute to the scientific and ethical contributions that Rachel Carson made to the world. Lexile 890L (Rev: BL 2/15/12; HB 7–8/12; LMC 8–9/12; SLJ 4/1/12) [921]

15599 Scherer, Glenn, and Marty Fletcher. *Who on Earth Is Rachel Carson? Mother of the Environmental Movement* (4–7). Series: Scientists Saving the Earth. 2009, Enslow LB $31.93 (978-1-59845-116-0). 112pp. Readers gain insight into the environmental climate of the 1970s, and the importance of Carson, who strove to raise awareness and end pesticide-related threats to wildlife. (Rev: SLJ 1/10; VOYA 2/10) [921]

15600 Wadsworth, Ginger. *Rachel Carson: Voice for the Earth* (5–7). Series: Lerner Biographies. 1992, Lerner LB $27.93 (978-0-8225-4907-9). The life and work of the conservationist and author, best known for *Silent Spring*. (Rev: BL 6/1/92; HB 7–8/92; SLJ 7/92) [921]

CARVER, GEORGE WASHINGTON

15601 Bolden, Tonya. *George Washington Carver* (3–6). Illus. 2008, Abrams $18.95 (978-0-8109-9366-2). 48pp. An inviting and well-researched biography of this African American scientist, educator, and conservationist, with historical photographs and prints, reproductions of Carver's drawings, and many quotations. (Rev: BL 2/1/08; SLJ 4/08)

15602 Carter, Andy, and Carol Saller. *George Washington Carver* (2–3). Series: On My Own. 2000, Carolrhoda LB $23.93 (978-1-57505-427-8); paper $5.95 (978-1-57505-458-2). 48pp. Born a slave near the end of the Civil War, Carver became famous for helping farmers grow better crops while sharing with them his love of nature. (Rev: BL 8/00; HBG 3/01)

15603 Harness, Cheryl. *The Groundbreaking, Chance-Taking Life of George Washington Carver and Science and Invention in America* (4–6). Illus. by author. 2008, National Geographic $16.95 (978-1-4263-0196-4). This lively biography, which places Carver's life and achievements in historical context, will appeal to general readers as well as to researchers. (Rev: BL 7/08; LMC 10/08; SLJ 7/08)

15604 Krensky, Stephen. *A Man for All Seasons: The Life of George Washington Carver* (2–4). Illus. by Wil Clay. 2008, Collins $16.99 (978-0-06-027885-4). A picture-book introduction to the life of the African American scientist, full of interesting details and with excellent paintings and a useful timeline. (Rev: BL 7/08; LMC 11/08; SLJ 6/08)

15605 McKissack, Patricia C., and Fredrick McKissack. *George Washington Carver: The Peanut Scientist.* Rev. ed. (2–4). Series: Great African Americans. 2002, Enslow LB $18.60 (978-0-7660-1700-9). 32pp. Black-and-white photographs and a readable style are highlights of this biography about the famous African American botanist who was the son of slave parents. (Rev: BL 7/02)

15606 MacLeod, Elizabeth. *George Washington Carver: An Innovative Life* (4–7). Illus. 2007, Kids Can $14.95 (978-1-55337-906-5); paper $6.95 (978-1-55337-907-2). 32pp. Well-organized with attractive graphics, this biography of Carver provides interesting details about his life as well as his major accomplishments. (Rev: SLJ 6/07)

15607 Marzollo, Jean. *The Little Plant Doctor: A Story About George Washington Carver* (K–3). Illus. by Ken Wilson-Max. 2011, Holiday House $16.95 (978-0-8234-2325-5). 32pp. An old Missouri tree narrates this picture-book biography, explaining the care the young Carver took with plants and the challenges he faced. (Rev: BL 3/15/11; SLJ 6/11) [921]

15608 Riley, John. *George Washington Carver: A Photo Biography* (1–3). Series: First Biographies. 2000, Morgan Reynolds LB $16.95 (978-1-883846-62-6). 24pp. With full-page pictures and a simple text this is a biography of the great African American scientist for beginning readers. (Rev: HBG 10/00; SLJ 8/00)

CASE, STEVE

15609 Ashby, Ruth. *Steve Case: America Online Pioneer* (5–8). Series: Techies. 2002, Millbrook LB $23.90 (978-0-7613-2655-7). The story of the Honolulu native who was a leader of AOL and the driving force behind its merger with Time-Warner. (Rev: BL 4/1/02; HBG 10/02) [921]

CHIEN-SHIUNG WU

15610 Cooperman, Stephanie H. *Chien-Shiung Wu: Pioneering Physicist and Atomic Researcher* (5–8). Series: Women Hall of Famers in Mathematics and Science. 2004, Rosen LB $29.25 (978-0-8239-3875-9). This biography describes Wu's life and achievements, explaining how she found a flaw in a widely held assumption about atoms. (Rev: BL 3/1/04; SLJ 9/04) [921]

CLARK, EUGENIE

15611 Butts, Ellen R., and Joyce R. Schwartz. *Eugenie Clark: Adventures of a Shark Scientist* (5–8). Illus. 2000, Linnet $19.50 (978-0-208-02440-4). 107pp. An interesting biography of a contemporary American scientist — an ichthyologist who has produced some startling research on sharks. (Rev: BCCB 2/00; BL 2/15/00; HBG 10/00; SLJ 7/00)

15612 Ross, Michael. *Fish Watching with Eugenie Clark* (3–5). Series: Naturalist's Apprentice. 2000, Lerner LB $19.93 (978-1-57505-384-4). This American scientist of Japanese ancestry has been fascinated by fish since childhood and has turned her interest into a groundbreaking scientific career. (Rev: BL 8/00; HBG 10/00; SLJ 7/00)

COLT, SAMUEL

15613 Wyckoff, Edwin Brit. *The Man Behind the Gun: Samuel Colt and His Revolver* (3–5). Illus. Series: Genius at Work! Great Inventor Biographies. 2010, Enslow LB $22.60 (978-076603446-4). 32pp. Wyckoff chronicles Colt's lifelong interest in things that go bang, and the way in which mass production contributed to his revolver's success. (Rev: BL 3/1/11) [921]

COPERNICUS, NICOLAUS

15614 Andronik, Catherine M. *Copernicus: Founder of Modern Astronomy* (4–8). Series: Great Minds of Science. 2002, Enslow LB $26.60 (978-0-7660-1755-9). This absorbing biography that covers Copernicus's youth and succeeds in explaining necessary scientific concepts also includes activities that reinforce this understanding. (Rev: HBG 10/02; SLJ 6/02) [520.92]

15615 Fradin, Dennis B. *Nicolaus Copernicus: The Earth Is a Planet* (3–6). Illus. by Cynthia von Buhler. 2004, Mondo $15.95 (978-1-59336-006-1). This succinct, illustrated profile of Polish astronomer Copernicus recounts his life and explores how he developed his theory that the planets revolve around the sun. (Rev: BL 4/1/04; SLJ 6/04)

15616 Ingram, Scott. *Nicolaus Copernicus: Father of Modern Astronomy* (5–9). Series: Giants of Science. 2004, Gale LB $26.20 (978-1-56711-489-8). 64pp. Copernicus's life, the influences of the church, and his important contributions to science are presented in clear prose and historical context. (Rev: SLJ 6/05)

CORWIN, JEFF

15617 Corwin, Jeff. *Jeff Corwin: A Wild Life: The Authorized Biography* (4–8). 2009, Puffin paper $5.99 (978-0-14-241403-3). 112pp. Wildlife biologist Jeff Corwin traces the roots of his love of nature and animals in this lively, adventure-rich autobiography. (Rev: BL 12/1/09; SLJ 12/1/09) [921]

COUSTEAU, JACQUES

15618 Bankston, John. *Jacques-Yves Cousteau: His Story Under the Sea* (4–5). Series: Unlocking the Secrets of Science. 2002, Mitchell Lane LB $17.95 (978-1-58415-112-8). 48pp. A concise look at the pioneering undersea explorer and inventor of the aqualung that opened up exploration of the ocean. (Rev: BL 8/02; HBG 3/03; SLJ 9/02)

15619 Berne, Jennifer. *Manfish: The Story of Jacques Cousteau* (K–3). Illus. by Eric Puybaret. 2008, Chronicle $16.99 (978-0-8118-6063-5). 32pp. A lyrical description of the young Cousteau's love of water and how this translated into careers that involved much time underwater. (Rev: BCCB 7–8/08; BL 6/1–15/08; LMC 11/08)

15620 DuTemple, Lesley A. *Jacques Cousteau* (4–6). Series: A&E Biography. 2000, Lerner LB $27.93 (978-0-8225-4979-6). 112pp. This is the story of the pioneering underwater adventurer and filmmaker who spent most of his life exploring the silent world beneath the sea. (Rev: BL 6/1–15/00; HBG 3/01; SLJ 9/00)

15621 King, Roger. *Jacques Cousteau and the Undersea World* (4–6). Illus. Series: Explorers of New Worlds. 2000, Chelsea LB $25.00 (978-0-7910-5956-2); paper $25.00 (978-0-7910-6166-4). This account of Cousteau's life starts with his childhood, and covers his creativity in designing equipment for underwater exploration as well as his other important contributions. (Rev: SLJ 4/01)

15622 Yaccarino, Dan. *The Fantastic Undersea Life of Jacques Cousteau* (K–3). Illus. by author. 2009, Knopf $16.99 (978-0-375-85573-3). 40pp. Starting with Cousteau's childhood, this effective biography traces the oceanographer's love of the sea. (Rev: BCCB 3/09; BL 1/1–15/09; HB 7/09; SLJ 3/09)

CRUM, GEORGE

15623 Taylor, Gaylia. *George Crum and the Saratoga Chip* (2–4). Illus. by Frank Morrison. 2006, Lee & Low $16.95 (978-1-58430-255-1). This attractive picture book recounts how George Crum, a chef of mixed African American and Native American ancestry, invented the potato chip to please a demanding customer and eventually opened his own restaurant. (Rev: BL 4/1/06; SLJ 5/06)

CURIE, MARIE

15624 Birch, Beverley. *Marie Curie, Spanish and English* (5–8). Series: Giants of Science Bilingual. 2005, Gale LB $28.70 (978-1-4103-0505-3). English and Spanish versions of this life of Curie are presented side by side, and the timeline, glossary, and index are also bilingual. (Rev: SLJ 2/06) [921]

15625 Birch, Beverley. *Marie Curie: Courageous Pioneer in the Study of Radioactivity* (5–7). Illus. Series: Giants of Science. 2000, Blackbirch LB $24.95 (978-1-56711-333-4). 64pp. This biography of Marie Curie covers her youth, her struggles to get an education, her marriage, and her scientific career and accomplishments. A bilingual (English/Spanish) version is also available. (Rev: BL 1/1–15/01; HBG 3/01)

15626 Graham, Ian. *Curie and the Science of Radioactivity* (4–6). Illus. by David Antram. Series: The Explosion Zone. 2006, Barron's $12.99 (978-0-7641-5973-2). 32pp. This biography of Marie Curie covers the Polish-born scientist's life and career and explains concepts related to her work, including half-life, transmutation, and the measurement of radiation; suitable for report writers despite cartoon illustrations. (Rev: SLJ 11/06)

15627 Krull, Kathleen. *Marie Curie* (5–8). Illus. by Boris Kulikov. Series: Giants of Science. 2007, Viking $15.99 (978-0-670-05894-5). 128pp. This biography of the Nobel Prize-winning scientist supplies plenty of information about her family life and personality as well as her discoveries and her legacy. ALA Notable Children's Book. (Rev: BL 12/15/07; HB 11/07; SLJ 12/07)

15628 McCormick, Lisa Wade. *Marie Curie* (1–2). Series: Rookie Biographies. 2006, Children's Pr. LB $20.50 (978-0-516-25040-3); paper $4.95 (978-0-516-21445-0). 32pp. For beginning readers, this is a simple overview of the scientist's life with emphasis on her discoveries. (Rev: SLJ 9/06)

15629 MacLeod, Elizabeth. *Marie Curie* (K–3). Illus. by John Mantha. Series: Kids Can Read Alone. 2009, Kids Can $14.95 (978-1-55453-296-4); paper $3.95 (978-1-55453-297-1). For early readers this is an interesting introduction to the Polish scientist and her importance. (Rev: BL 5/1/09)

15630 Poynter, Margaret. *Marie Curie: Discoverer of Radium. Rev. ed.* (4–7). Illus. Series: Great Minds of Science. 2007, Enslow LB $31.93 (978-0-89490-477-6). 128pp. The life and significance of this discoverer of radium are covered, with a chapter of suggested activities. (Rev: BL 1/1/95; SLJ 10/94)

15631 Wishinsky, Frieda. *Manya's Dream: A Story of Marie Curie* (2–5). 2003, Maple Tree $19.95 (978-1-894379-53-3); paper $6.95 (978-1-894379-54-0). 32pp. This inspiring biography of Polish-born scientist Marie Curie focuses principally on the facts of her life, including her childhood in Poland, studies at the Sorbonne in

Paris, and rescue work during World War I. (Rev: BL 12/15/03)

15632 Yannuzzi, Della A. *New Elements: The Story of Marie Curie* (5–10). Illus. Series: Profiles in Science. 2006, Morgan Reynolds $26.95 (978-1-59935-023-3). 144pp. More about the scientist's life than about the significance of her research, this introduction will be helpful to report writers. (Rev: BL 12/1/06; SLJ 1/07)

CURIE, MARIE AND PIERRE

15633 Lin, Yoming S. *The Curies and Radioactivity* (3–5). Illus. Series: Eureka! 2011, Rosen LB $21.25 (978-144885033-4). 24pp. Traces the lives of Marie and Pierre Curie and their important scientific work. (Rev: BL 12/1/11) [921]

DAMADIAN, RAYMOND

15634 Kjelle, Marylou Morano. *Raymond Damadian and the Development of MRI* (5–7). Series: Unlocking the Secrets of Science. 2002, Mitchell Lane LB $25.70 (978-1-58415-141-8). This account focuses on Damadian's scientific accomplishments. (Rev: HBG 10/03; SLJ 1/03) [921]

DARWIN, CHARLES

15635 Anderson, Margaret J. *Charles Darwin: Naturalist. Rev. ed.* (4–7). Illus. Series: Great Minds of Science. 2008, Enslow LB $31.93 (978-0-89490-476-9). 128pp. In addition to a biography of this controversial naturalist, there is a chapter on activities for the reader. (Rev: BL 1/1/95; SLJ 10/94) [921]

15636 Ashby, Ruth. *Young Charles Darwin and the Voyage of the Beagle* (4–7). Illus. by Suzanne Duranceau. 2009, Peachtree $12.95 (978-1-56145-478-5). 132 Focusing on Darwin's five-year voyage on the *Beagle*, this interesting biography includes many direct quotations. (Rev: BL 3/15/09; SLJ 3/09) [921]

15637 Fullick, Ann. *Charles Darwin* (4–6). Series: Groundbreakers. 2000, Heinemann LB $25.64 (978-1-57572-368-6). 48pp. This biography of the scientist who formulated the theory of evolution concentrates on his five-year voyage on the *H.M.S. Beagle*. (Rev: SLJ 2/01)

15638 Gibbons, Alan. *Charles Darwin* (3–6). Illus. by Leo Brown. 2008, Kingfisher $16.95 (978-0-7534-6251-5). 64pp. A fictional cabin boy keeps a diary of Darwin's voyage aboard the *Beagle*, giving personal details as well as observations of scientific studies; an extensive later section of the book discusses the voyage, life at sea, and other facets of Darwin's life. (Rev: BL 1/1–15/09; LMC 5/09*)

15639 Greenberger, Robert. *Darwin and the Theory of Evolution* (5–8). Series: Primary Sources of Revolutionary Scientific Discoveries and Theories. 2005, Rosen LB $29.25 (978-1-4042-0306-8). Profiles English naturalist Charles Darwin and the events that led up to his groundbreaking theory of evolution; useful for brief reports. (Rev: SLJ 11/05) [921]

15640 Krull, Kathleen. *Charles Darwin* (5–8). Illus. by Boris Kulikov. Series: Giants of Science. 2010, Viking $15.99 (978-0-670-06335-2). 128pp. An engaging profile of the famous scientist, covering his life from childhood and explaining his theories. (Rev: BL 12/1/10*; HB 1–2/11; SLJ 3/1/11) [921]

15641 Lasky, Kathryn. *One Beetle Too Many: The Extraordinary Adventures of Charles Darwin* (3–5). Illus. by Matthew Trueman. 2009, Candlewick $17.99 (978-0-7636-1436-2). 48pp. This large-format biography highlights Darwin's curiosity as it explores his life and work. (Rev: BCCB 2/09; BL 1/1–15/09; SLJ 1/09)

15642 Lawson, Kristan. *Darwin and Evolution for Kids: His Life and Ideas with 21 Activities* (5–9). 2003, Chicago Review paper $16.95 (978-1-55652-502-5). The naturalist's life and work are examined in clear, interesting text, with thorough coverage of his five-year research voyage on *H.M.S. Beagle* and the continuing controversy over his theories. (Rev: SLJ 4/04) [921]

15643 McGinty, Alice B. *Darwin* (1–4). Illus. by Mary Azarian. 2009, Houghton $18.00 (978-0-618-99531-8). 48pp. This appealing picture-book biography juxtaposes narrative about his life with quotations from Darwin's journals and letters. (Rev: BL 1/1–15/09; SLJ 3/09)

15644 Schanzer, Rosalyn. *What Darwin Saw: The Journey that Changed the World* (3–6). Illus. by author. 2009, National Geographic $17.95 (978-1-4263-0396-8). 48pp. This brightly illustrated large-format picture book, which focuses mainly on his voyage aboard the *Beagle* and the opinions he forms then, uses many quotations from Darwin's journals, books, and letters and includes a map of the journey. (Rev: BCCB 3/09; BL 3/15/09; SLJ 3/09)

15645 Sís, Peter. *The Tree of Life: Charles Darwin* (4–7). 2003, Farrar $18.00 (978-0-374-45628-3). Highly illustrated, this imaginative and visual biography traces Darwin's life and development as a naturalist, with a focus on his voyages on the *Beagle*. (Rev: BL 10/15/03; HB 11–12/03*; HBG 4/04; SLJ 10/03*) [576.8]

15646 Sproule, Anna. *Charles Darwin: Visionary Behind the Theory of Evolution* (4–7). Illus. Series: Giants of Science. 2003, Gale $26.20 (978-1-56711-655-7). 64pp. Darwin's life and accomplishments are presented in concise text. (Rev: SLJ 1/03)

15647 Wood, A. J. *Charles Darwin and the Beagle Adventure* (5–8). 2009, Candlewick $19.99 (978-0-7636-4538-0). 30pp. Creatively designed to look like Charles Darwin's journal, this book shares a wealth of information about Darwin's journey on the *HMS Beagle* . (Rev: LMC 1–2/10; SLJ 10/09*) [921]

DEERE, JOHN

15648 Hall, Margaret. *John Deere* (2–4). Series: Lives and Times. 2004, Heinemann LB $22.79 (978-1-4034-5327-3). 32pp. Profiles the life and achievements of John Deere, a blacksmith whose invention of an improved farm plow launched the farm equipment business that still bears his name. (Rev: BL 7/04; SLJ 9/04)

DIEMER, WALTER

15649 McCarthy, Meghan. *Pop! The Invention of Bubble Gum* (1–3). Illus. by author. 2010, Simon & Schuster $15.99 (978-1-4169-7970-8). 40pp. A humorous profile of Walter Diemer, the inventor of bubble gum, who was a young accountant in Philadelphia in the 1920s; includes facts about gum. (Rev: BL 4/15/10; HB 5/1/10; LMC 8–9/10; SLJ 5/1/10*) [921]

DOMAGK, GERHARD

15650 Bankston, John. *Gerhard Domagk and the Discovery of Sulfa* (4–5). Series: Unlocking the Secrets of Science. 2002, Mitchell Lane LB $25.70 (978-1-58415-115-9). 56pp. The story of the man who discovered the antibiotic properties of sulfa but whose accomplishments were overshadowed by other advances in antibiotics. (Rev: BL 9/15/02; SLJ 11/02)

DREW, CHARLES

15651 Whitehurst, Susan. *Dr. Charles Drew: Medical Pioneer* (4–6). Series: Journey to Freedom: The African American Library. 2001, Child's World LB $17.95 (978-1-56766-926-8). 40pp. An attractive biography of this pioneering American black scientist who was noted for his research in blood plasma and his work in developing the concept of the Blood Bank. (Rev: BL 12/15/01; HBG 3/02; SLJ 1/02)

DYSON, ESTHER

15652 Jablonski, Carla. *Esther Dyson: Web Guru* (5–8). Series: Techies. 2002, Millbrook LB $23.90 (978-0-7613-2657-1). A leading light in the computer world, Dyson is the owner of EDventure Holdings, and is an active developer of emerging technologies and companies. (Rev: BL 4/1/02; HBG 10/02) [921]

15653 Morales, Leslie. *Esther Dyson: Internet Visionary* (5–8). Series: Internet Biographies. 2003, Enslow LB $23.93 (978-0-7660-1973-7). 48pp. Dyson, a skillful businesswoman, has played an influential role in the development of the Internet as a tool suitable for everyday use. (Rev: HBG 10/03; SLJ 10/03)

EARLE, SYLVIA

15654 Baker, Beth. *Sylvia Earle: Guardian of the Sea* (4–7). Series: Lerner Biographies. 2000, Lerner LB $27.93 (978-0-8225-4961-1). This is a thrilling biography of the famous underwater explorer and marine scientist who was one of the first humans to swim with whales. (Rev: BL 10/15/00; HBG 3/01; SLJ 11/00) [921]

15655 Reichard, Susan E. *Who on Earth Is Sylvia Earle? Undersea Explorer of the Ocean* (4–7). Series: Scientists Saving the Earth. 2009, Enslow LB $31.93 (978-1-59845-118-4). 112pp. An interesting biography of the scientist devoted to underwater exploration and the protection of this environment from threats including oil pollution. (Rev: SLJ 1/10; VOYA 2/10) [921]

EASTMAN, GEORGE

15656 Gillis, Jennifer Blizin. *George Eastman* (2–4). 2004, Heinemann LB $22.79 (978-1-4034-5326-6). 32pp. This concise biography profiles the life and work of George Eastman, whose late-19th-century introduction of the Kodak camera first made photography widely available to the public. (Rev: BL 7/04)

EDISON, THOMAS ALVA

15657 Brown, Don. *A Wizard from the Start: The Incredible Boyhood and Amazing Inventions of Thomas Edison* (1–3). Illus. by author. 2010, Houghton Mifflin $16 (978-0-547-19487-5). 32pp. Edison's boyhood and adolescence are the focus of this inspiring biography, which chronicles Edison's trials at school and hard work as a "news butch" before becoming an inventor. Lexile AD940L (Rev: BL 6/10; SLJ 4/1/10*) [921]

15658 Carlson, Laurie. *Thomas Edison for Kids: His Life and Ideas: 21 Activities* (4–7). Illus. 2006, Chicago Review paper $14.95 (978-1-55652-584-1). Activities allow readers to try some of the inventor's experiments; the biography section covers Edison's personal life as well as his achievements and introduces some of his contemporaries. (Rev: BL 2/15/06; SLJ 6/06) [621.3]

15659 Dooling, Michael. *Young Thomas Edison* (1–3). Illus. 2005, Holiday $16.95 (978-0-8234-1868-8). 40pp. This engaging biography focuses on the inventor's youth, his hearing loss, his homeschooling, and his early experiments. (Rev: BL 1/1–15/06; SLJ 2/06*)

15660 Gaines, Ann. *Thomas Edison* (2–3). Series: Discover the Life of an Inventor. 2001, Rourke LB $20.64 (978-1-58952-122-3). 24pp. A simple, introductory biography that describes Edison's life, contributions, and struggles. (Rev: BL 10/15/01; SLJ 1/02)

15661 Gomez, Rebecca. *Thomas Edison* (2–3). Illus. Series: First Biographies. 2003, ABDO LB $22.78 (978-1-57765-945-7). 32pp. A brief easy-reader overview of the inventor's life and accomplishments. (Rev: HBG 4/04; SLJ 9/03)

15662 Graham, Amy. *Thomas Edison: Wizard of Light and Sound* (5–8). Illus. Series: Inventors Who Changed the World. 2007, Enslow LB $24.95 (978-1-59845-052-1). The text of this profile of Edison and his achievements is augmented by links to carefully evaluated Web sites. (Rev: SLJ 11/07) [921]

15663 Mason, Paul. *Thomas A. Edison* (4–6). Illus. Series: Scientists Who Made History. 2001, Raintree LB $27.12 (978-0-7398-4414-4). This well-illustrated profile of Edison and his life and work will be useful for report writers. (Rev: HBG 10/02; SLJ 2/02)

15664 Mortensen, Lori. *Thomas Edison: Inventor, Scientist, and Genius* (K–3). Illus. by Jeffrey Thompson. Series: Biographies. 2007, Picture Window LB $23.93 (978-1-4048-3105-6). 24pp. An introduction to the inventor for beginning readers who will enjoy learning of Edison's childhood and his achievements as an adult. (Rev: SLJ 8/07)

15665 Sproule, Anna. *Thomas Edison: The World's Greatest Inventor* (5–7). Series: Giants of Science. 2000, Blackbirch paper $24.95 (978-1-56711-331-0). 64pp. A prolific inventor, Edison not only worked on the electric light bulb but also the phonograph, the movie projector, and an early answering machine. (Rev: BL 1/1–15/01; HBG 3/01; SLJ 1/01)

15666 Woodside, Martin. *Thomas A. Edison: The Man Who Lit Up the World* (5–8). Series: Sterling Biographies. 2007, Sterling LB $12.95 (978-1-4027-4955-1); paper $5.95 (978-1-4027-3229-4). 124pp. A concise account of Edison's life from childhood and his many achievements in varied fields. (Rev: SLJ 10/07)

EHRLICH, PAUL

15667 Zannos, Susan. *Paul Ehrlich and Modern Drug Development* (4–5). Series: Unlocking the Secrets of Science. 2002, Mitchell Lane LB $17.95 (978-1-58415-121-0). 56pp. The story of the man often called the "father of modern drug development" and his discovery of a "magic bullet." (Rev: BL 9/15/02; SLJ 3/03)

EINSTEIN, ALBERT

15668 Bankston, John. *Albert Einstein and the Theory of Relativity* (5–8). Series: Unlocking the Secrets of Science. 2002, Mitchell Lane LB $25.70 (978-1-58415-137-1). Einstein's accomplishments and the many challenges he faced are explored in concise text with many black-and-white photographs. (Rev: SLJ 2/03) [921]

15669 Berger, Melvin, and Gilda Berger. *Did It Take Creativity to Find Relativity, Albert Einstein?* (3–4). Illus. by Brandon Dorman. Series: Science SuperGiants. 2007, Scholastic paper $4.99 (978-0-439-83384-4). "What did Einstein discover about light?" "How could scientists test Einstein's theory?" Using a question-and-answer format, this profile provides biographical and basic scientific information. (Rev: SLJ 2/08)

15670 Berne, Jennifer. *On a Beam of Light: A Story of Albert Einstein* (1–3). Illus. by Vladimir Radunsky. 2013, Chronicle $17.99 (978-0-8118-7235-5). 56pp. A colorful biography that focuses on the power of Einstein's intellect and imagination. ALA Notable Children's Book; Booklist Editors' Choice: Books for Youth. ⌒ (Rev: BL 6/13*; HB 5–6/13; LMC 11–12/13; SLJ 4/13*) [921]

15671 Brown, Don. *Odd Boy Out: Young Albert Einstein* (3–5). Illus. 2004, Houghton $16.00 (978-0-618-49298-5). 32pp. Einstein's awkward and unpromising youth is described in this picture-book biography that also introduces his adult achievements. (Rev: BL 9/1/04; SLJ 10/04)

15672 Delano, Marfé Ferguson. *Genius: A Photobiography of Albert Einstein* (5–8). 2005, National Geographic $17.95 (978-0-7922-9544-0). Photographs of the scientist's life, as well as brief explanations of his work, help to make the man and his theories more accessible to young readers; an oversized and engaging volume. (Rev: BL 4/1/05*; SLJ 5/05) [921]

15673 Lakin, Patricia. *Albert Einstein: Genius of the Twentieth Century* (2–4). Illus. by Alan Daniel. Series: Ready-to-Read: Stories of Famous Americans. 2005, Simon & Schuster paper $3.99 (978-0-689-87034-7). 48pp. This effective easy-to-read biography describes Einstein's intelligence and key accomplishments. (Rev: BL 12/1/05)

15674 Lassieur, Allison. *Albert Einstein: Genius of the Twentieth Century* (5–8). Series: Great Life Stories. 2005, Watts LB $30.50 (978-0-531-12401-7). In addition to placing Einstein's life (including his childhood) and contributions in historical and social context, Lassieur explains his theories and their application. (Rev: SLJ 9/05) [921]

15675 MacDonald, Fiona. *Albert Einstein: The Genius Behind the Theory of Relativity* (5–7). Illus. Series: Giants of Science. 2000, Blackbirch LB $27.44 (978-1-56711-330-3). 64pp. As well as his childhood, education, theories, personal life, and international awards, this biography of Albert Einstein assesses his lasting contributions to physics and mathematics. (Rev: BL 1/1–15/01; HBG 3/01; SLJ 1/01)

15676 MacLeod, Elizabeth. *Albert Einstein: A Life of Genius* (5–7). Illus. 2003, Kids Can $14.95 (978-1-55337-396-4); paper $6.95 (978-1-55337-397-1). Small photographs and illustrations accompany this attractive chronological introduction to the life of Einstein that focuses on the man rather than his theories. (Rev: BL 3/1/03; HBG 10/03; SLJ 5/03)

15677 McPherson, Stephanie Sammartino. *Ordinary Genius: The Story of Albert Einstein* (4–7). 1995, Carolrhoda LB $27.93 (978-0-87614-788-7). Good historical background information is given on the life of Einstein plus a clear explanation of his discoveries. (Rev: BL 6/1–15/95; SLJ 9/95) [921]

15678 Meltzer, Milton. *Albert Einstein: A Biography* (3–5). Illus. 2008, Holiday $16.95 (978-0-8234-1966-1). Although brief, this appealing and accessible biography presents lots of solid information on Einstein's life and achievements, including his interests outside science. (Rev: BL 2/1/08; LMC 3/08; SLJ 3/08)

15679 Wyborny, Sheila. *Albert Einstein* (3–6). Series: Inventors and Creators. 2003, Gale LB $23.70 (978-0-7377-1278-0). 48pp. An interesting biography of the German-born physicist and his lasting contributions to scientific knowledge. (Rev: SLJ 6/03)

ELION, GERTRUDE

15680 MacBain, Jennifer. *Gertrude Elion: Nobel Prize Winner in Physiology and Medicine* (5–8). Series: Women Hall of Famers in Mathematics and Science. 2004, Rosen LB $29.25 (978-0-8239-3876-6). Elion, a biochemist and pharmacologist who never earned a doctorate, won a Nobel Prize for her advances in the field of chemotherapy. (Rev: BL 3/1/04; SLJ 9/04) [615]

ELLISON, LARRY

15681 Ehrenhaft, Daniel. *Larry Ellison: Sheer Nerve* (5–8). Series: Techies. 2001, Millbrook LB $23.90 (978-0-7613-1962-7). The life story of one of the world's richest men and co-founder of Oracle, the world's leading supplier of software for information management. (Rev: BL 4/1/02; HBG 3/02; SLJ 12/01) [921]

15682 Peters, Craig. *Larry Ellison: Database Genius of Oracle* (5–8). Series: Internet Biographies. 2003, Enslow LB $23.93 (978-0-7660-1974-4). 48pp. A look at the life and accomplishments of the cofounder of Oracle Corporation. (Rev: HBG 10/03; SLJ 10/03)

ERDOS, PAUL

15683 Heiligman, Deborah. *The Boy Who Loved Math: The Improbable Life of Paul Erdos* (K–3). Illus. by LeUyen Pham. 2013, Roaring Brook $17.99 (978-1-59643-307-6). 48pp. Tells the interesting story of a mathematician who showed talent from a very young age, when he was a child in World War I Hungary. ALA Notable Children's Book, Booklist Editors' Choice: Books for Youth. **e** (Rev: BL 6/13*; HB 5–6/13; LMC 11–12/13; SLJ 5/13) [921]

ERICSSON, JOHN

15684 Wooldridge, Connie N. *Thank You Very Much, Captain Ericsson* (1–5). Illus. by Andrew Glass. 2005, Holiday House $16.95 (978-0-8234-1626-4). The struggles of the Civil-War era inventor are presented in light-hearted text with funny cartoons. (Rev: SLJ 8/05)

FANNING, SHAWN

15685 Mitten, Christopher. *Shawn Fanning: Napster and the Music Revolution* (5–8). Series: Techies. 2002, Millbrook LB $23.90 (978-0-7613-2656-4). Using many photographs and an interesting text, this is the biography of the creator of Napster, a software package for downloading music from computers. (Rev: BL 4/1/02; HBG 10/02; SLJ 6/02) [921]

FARNSWORTH, PHILO

15686 Krull, Kathleen. *The Boy Who Invented TV: The Story of Philo Farnsworth* (3–5). Illus. by Greg Couch. 2009, Knopf $16.99 (978-0-375-84561-1). Krull recounts how the young Farnsworth conceived of the idea of television, explains the underlying scientific concepts, and in an afterword details his loss of the patent. (Rev: BL 6/1–15/09; LMC 10/09)

15687 McPherson, Stephanie Sammartino. *TV's Forgotten Hero: The Story of Philo Farnsworth* (4–7). 1996, Carolrhoda LB $27.93 (978-1-57505-017-1). The biography of the genius who invented electronic television when he was only 14. (Rev: BL 2/1/97; SLJ 2/97) [921]

15688 Roberts, Russell. *Philo T. Farnsworth; the Life of Television's Forgotten Inventor* (4–5). Series: Unlocking the Secrets of Science. 2003, Mitchell Lane LB $25.70 (978-1-58415-176-0). 48pp. This brief biography recounts the bittersweet story of Philo T. Farnsworth, whose pioneering developments in the field of television were never fully acknowledged during his lifetime. (Rev: BL 11/15/03; SLJ 9/03)

FERRIS, GEORGE

15689 Sneed, Dani. *The Man Who Invented the Ferris Wheel: The Genius of George Ferris* (2–4). Illus. Series: Genius Inventors and Their Great Ideas. 2013, Enslow LB $23.93 (978-076604136-3). 48pp. The story of the engineer who created the much-loved wheel for the 1893 World's Fair is followed by a section called "You Be the Inventor." ℮ (Rev: BL 12/15/13; LMC 10/14*; SLJ 3/14) [921]

FIBONACCI, LEONARDO

15690 D'Agnese, Joseph. *Blockhead: The Life of Fibonacci* (3–5). Illus. by John O'Brien. 2010, Henry Holt $16.99 (978-0-8050-6305-9). 40pp. A beautifully illustrated, lighthearted yet informative introduction to the mathematician's childhood, love of numbers, and famous sequence. ∩ Lexile AD570L (Rev: BL 1/1/10; HB 5–6/10; LMC 8–9/10; SLJ 3/1/10) [921]

FLEMING, ALEXANDER

15691 Bankston, John. *Alexander Fleming and the Story of Penicillin* (5–8). Series: Unlocking the Secrets of Science. 2001, Mitchell Lane LB $25.70 (978-1-58415-106-7). This absorbing biography of the Scottish Nobel Prize winner covers his personal life as well as his scientific career. (Rev: HBG 3/02; SLJ 1/02) [616.014092]

15692 Birch, Beverley. *Alexander Fleming: Pioneer with Antibiotics* (4–7). Illus. Series: Giants of Science. 2003, Gale $26.20 (978-1-56711-656-4). 64pp. Fleming's life, education, research, and discovery of penicillin are presented in concise text. (Rev: SLJ 1/03)

15693 Tocci, Salvatore. *Alexander Fleming: The Man Who Discovered Penicillin* (5–8). Series: Great Minds of Science. 2002, Enslow LB $26.60 (978-0-7660-1998-0). 128pp. An absorbing account of Fleming's childhood and later life, with solid information on his contributions to medical science and his legacy. (Rev: HBG 10/02; SLJ 9/02)

FORD, HENRY

15694 Bankston, John. *Henry Ford and the Assembly Line* (4–5). Series: Unlocking the Secrets of Science. 2003, Mitchell Lane LB $17.95 (978-1-58415-173-9). 48pp. This brief biography chronicles the life of Henry Ford and includes photographs and reproductions. (Rev: BL 11/15/03; SLJ 9/03)

15695 Gaines, Ann. *Henry Ford* (2–3). Illus. Series: Discover the Life of an Inventor. 2001, Rourke LB $20.64 (978-1-58952-120-9). 24pp. This biography of Ford concentrates on his influence on the automobile industry. (Rev: BL 10/15/01)

15696 Kulling, Monica. *Eat My Dust! Henry Ford's First Race* (1–2). Series: Step into Reading. 2004, Random LB $11.99 (978-0-375-91510-9); paper $3.99 (978-0-375-81510-2). 48pp. Beginning readers, especially boys, will enjoy this dramatic account of Henry Ford's auto race victory against Alexander Winton. (Rev: BL 8/04)

15697 McCarthy, Pat. *Henry Ford: Building Cars for Everyone* (5–8). Series: Historical American Biographies. 2002, Enslow LB $26.60 (978-0-7660-1620-0). 128pp. Ford is shown as an eccentric but successful father, engineer, and businessman, who made the automobile widely available but expected his workers to suffer difficult conditions. (Rev: HBG 3/03; SLJ 1/03)

15698 Mitchell, Don. *Driven: A Photobiography of Henry Ford* (4–7). 2010, National Geographic $18.95 (978-1-4263-0155-1); LB $27.90 (978-1-4263-0156-8). 64pp. With many photographs and quotations, this is a fine portrait of the founder of the automobile company, frankly discussing his social views, ideals, and character flaws. (Rev: BL 6/10; HB 5–6/10; SLJ 4/10; VOYA 6/10) [338.7]

15699 Roberts, Steven. *Henry Ford* (4–7). Illus. by Planman Technologies. Series: Junior Graphic American Inventors. 2013, Rosen LB $25.25 (978-147770079-2). 32pp. Reluctant readers will enjoy this graphic-novel biography of the man who loved machines from a young age. ℮ (Rev: BL 6/13; LMC 1–2/14; SLJ 4/13) [921]

15700 Schaefer, Lola M. *Henry Ford* (K–2). Series: Famous People in Transportation. 2000, Capstone LB $17.26 (978-0-7368-0546-9). 24pp. For beginning readers, this is a biography of Henry Ford that uses double-page spreads to present important facts about his life and accomplishments. (Rev: HBG 10/00; SLJ 9/00)

FOSSEY, DIAN

15701 Blue, Rose, and Corinne J. Naden. *Dian Fossey: At Home with the Giant Gorillas* (4–6). Series: Gateway Greens. 2002, Millbrook LB $23.90 (978-0-7613-2569-7). 48pp. A brief, nicely illustrated biography of the U.S.-born zoologist who studied the mountain gorilla in its natural habitat in Africa and was killed because of her efforts. (Rev: BL 7/02; HBG 3/03)

15702 Gogerly, Liz. *Dian Fossey* (5–8). Series: Scientists Who Made History. 2003, Raintree LB $27.12 (978-0-7368-5225-8). A riveting profile of the woman who became an expert on gorillas and the militant stance that may have led to her murder. (Rev: BL 3/1/03) [599.884]

15703 Kushner, Jill Menkes. *Who on Earth Is Dian Fossey?: Defender of the Mountain Gorillas* (4–7). Series: Scientists Saving the Earth. 2009, Enslow LB $31.93 (978-1-59845-117-7). 112pp. Readers gain insight into threats facing gorillas and learn about the committed work of Fossey, who strove to save and understand them. (Rev: BL 2/15/10; SLJ 1/10; VOYA 2/10) [921]

15704 Schott, Jane A. *Dian Fossey and the Mountain Gorillas* (2–3). Series: On My Own Biography. 2000, Carolrhoda LB $19.93 (978-1-57505-082-9). 48pp. The exciting story one of the foremost primate researchers of the 20th century, her groundbreaking work observing mountain gorillas in their native habitat, and her efforts to stop their poaching. (Rev: BL 6/1–15/00; HBG 10/00; SLJ 6/00)

FRANKLIN, ROSALIND

15705 Senker, Cath. *Rosalind Franklin* (5–8). Illus. Series: Scientists Who Made History. 2003, Raintree $27.12 (978-0-7398-5226-2). 48pp. An interesting biography of the woman who never gained credit for her contributions to the discovery of the structure of DNA. (Rev: BL 3/1/03; HBG 10/03; SLJ 4/03)

FULTON, ROBERT

15706 Gillis, Jennifer Blizin. *Robert Fulton* (1–4). Series: Lives and Times. 2004, Heinemann LB $22.79 (978-1-4034-5328-0). 32pp. Report writers will find useful information in this biography that has a timeline and "Fact File" boxes. (Rev: SLJ 9/04)

15707 Pierce, Morris A. *Robert Fulton and the Development of the Steamboat* (4–8). Series: Library of American Lives and Times. 2003, Rosen LB $34.60 (978-0-8239-5737-8). The inventor of the steamboat was a man of determination and wide interests who also worked on naval weapons. (Rev: BL 6/1–15/03; SLJ 4/03) [921]

15708 Whiting, Jim. *Robert Fulton* (2–4). Series: A Robbie Reader: What's So Great About? 2006, Mitchell Lane LB $25.70 (978-1-58415-478-5). 32pp. With large text and lots of white space, this introductory biography looks at the life and career of the man responsible for developing the first commercially successful steampowered vessel. (Rev: SLJ 1/07)

GALILEI, GALILEO

15709 Goldsmith, Mike. *Galileo Galilei* (4–6). Illus. Series: Scientists Who Made History. 2001, Raintree LB $27.12 (978-0-7398-4416-8). 48pp. This well-illustrated profile of Galileo and his life and work will be useful for report writers. (Rev: HBG 10/02; SLJ 2/02)

15710 Hightower, Paul. *Galileo: Astronomer and Physicist* (4–7). Series: Great Minds of Science. 1997, Enslow LB $26.60 (978-0-89490-787-6). This biography not only includes material on the life and accomplishments of this courageous scientist but also contains several activities that give an understanding of his work. (Rev: BL 6/1–15/97) [921]

15711 Hilliam, Rachel. *Galileo Galilei: Father of Modern Science* (5–8). Series: Rulers, Scholars, and Artists of the Renaissance. 2005, Rosen LB $33.25 (978-1-4042-0314-3). Ford places Galileo's life and accomplishments in the context of culture and politics of the time. (Rev: SLJ 10/05) [921]

15712 Lewis, J. Patrick. *Galileo's Universe* (3–5). Illus. by Tom Curry. 2005, Creative Editions $24.95 (978-1-56846-183-0). 18pp. This unusual pop-up biography recounts the life of Galileo in rhyming verse. (Rev: BL 12/1/05)

15713 Panchyk, Richard. *Galileo for Kids: His Life and Ideas* (5–9). 2005, Chicago Review paper $16.95 (978-1-55652-566-7). A clearly written and well-illustrated

overview of Galileo's life and scientific achievements, with excerpts from Galileo's writings and suggested activities. (Rev: SLJ 9/05) [921]

15714 Steele, Philip. *Galileo: The Genius Who Faced the Inquisition* (3–6). Series: National Geographic World History Biographies. 2005, National Geographic $17.95 (978-0-7922-3656-6). 64pp. The scientist's place in history is clearly set out in this well-designed, informative book. (Rev: SLJ 6/06)

GATES, BILL

15715 Barton-Wood, Sara. *Bill Gates: Computer Legend* (4–6). Illus. Series: Famous Lives. 2001, Raintree LB $27.12 (978-0-7398-4432-8). 48pp. An introduction to the life and career of Microsoft founder Bill Gates. (Rev: BL 1/1–15/02; HBG 10/02)

15716 Lesinski, Jeanne. *Bill Gates* (4–6). Series: A&E Biography. 2000, Lerner LB $27.93 (978-0-8225-4949-9). 112pp. The story of the man whose name has become synonymous with computers, software, and wealth. (Rev: BL 6/1–15/00; HBG 3/01; SLJ 9/00)

15717 Lockwood, Brad. *Bill Gates: Profile of a Digital Entrepreneur* (5–8). 2007, Rosen LB $31.95 (978-1-4042-1906-9). 112pp. Well-written and updated, this volume on Gates focuses on his career. (Rev: LMC 1/08; SLJ 3/08)

15718 Peters, Craig. *Bill Gates* (5–8). Illus. Series: Internet Biographies. 2003, Enslow LB $23.93 (978-0-7660-1969-0). 48pp. A reader-friendly biography of the creator of Microsoft, with information on his youth as well as his successful later life. (Rev: BL 3/15/03; HBG 10/03)

15719 Sherman, Josepha. *Bill Gates: Computer King* (4–6). Series: Gateway Biographies. 2000, Millbrook LB $23.90 (978-0-7613-1771-5). 48pp. This book successfully tells the story of Bill Gates's life and gives a history of Microsoft. (Rev: HBG 3/01; SLJ 11/00)

15720 Woog, Adam. *Bill Gates* (4–7). Illus. Series: Famous People. 2003, Gale $26.20 (978-0-7377-1400-5). 48pp. Woog covers Gates's childhood, education, interest in computers, and career, with photographs. (Rev: BL 6/1–15/03)

GATES, BILL AND MELINDA

15721 Schuman, Michael A. *Bill Gates: Computer Mogul and Philanthropist* (5–8). 2007, Enslow LB $31.93 (978-0-7660-2693-3). Gates and his wife Melinda and their far-reaching philanthropic efforts are covered in this clearly written volume. (Rev: SLJ 3/08) [921]

GODDARD, ROBERT

15722 Bankston, John. *Robert Goddard and the Liquid Rocket Engine* (4–7). Series: Unlocking the Secrets of Science. 2001, Mitchell Lane LB $17.95 (978-1-58415-107-4). Bankston combines an introduction to Goddard's commitment to rocketry and his difficulty finding funding with an understandable explanation of the scientific challenges. (Rev: HBG 3/02; SLJ 2/02) [621.43]

GOODALL, JANE

15723 January, Brendan. *Jane Goodall: Animal Behaviorist and Writer* (4–7). Series: Ferguson Career Biographies. 2001, Ferguson LB $25.00 (978-0-89434-370-4). 127pp. This easily read biography will appeal in particular to reluctant readers and students seeking quick information for a report. (Rev: SLJ 9/01)

15724 Kittinger, Jo S. *Jane Goodall* (1–2). Series: Scholastic News Nonfiction Readers. 2005, Children's Pr. LB $20.00 (978-0-516-24940-7). 24pp. This simple, photo-filled biography for beginning readers spotlights Goodall's breakthrough work with chimpanzees. (Rev: SLJ 4/06)

15725 Winter, Jeanette. *The Watcher: Jane Goodall's Life with the Chimps* (2–4). Illus. by author. 2011, Random House $17.99 (978-0-375-86774-3); LB $20.99 (978-0-375-96774-0). 48pp. Winter emphasizes Goodall's early passion for nature in this account of her progress to becoming an internationally recognized expert on chimpanzees and the threats they face. (Rev: BL 3/1/11*; HB 3–4/11; LMC 8–9/11; SLJ 4/11) [921]

GUTENBERG, JOHANNES

15726 Feinstein, Stephen. *Johannes Gutenberg: The Printer Who Gave Words to the World* (5–8). Illus. 2008, Enslow LB $33.27 (978-1-59845-077-4). 128pp. A history of printing from the ancient civilizations to the Renaissance is included in this book about Gutenberg's contribution of a movable metal type and printing press. (Rev: SLJ 2/09) [921]

15727 Pollard, Michael. *Johann Gutenberg: Master of Modern Printing* (5–7). Series: Giants of Science. 2001, Blackbirch LB $27.44 (978-1-56711-335-8). 64pp. Good use of illustrations and an interesting text are highlights of this life of the German printer who first used movable type. (Rev: BL 8/1/01; HBG 3/02)

HARRISON, JOHN

15728 Borden, Louise. *Sea Clocks: The Story of Longitude* (2–4). Illus. by Erik Blegvad. 2004, Simon & Schuster $18.95 (978-0-689-84216-0). 48pp. John Harrison's struggles to promote his chronomoter — and to gain credit for its invention — are recounted in an attractive picture-book biography. (Rev: BL 12/1/03; HB 3/04; SLJ 1/04)

15729 Lasky, Kathryn. *The Man Who Made Time Travel* (3–5). Illus. by Kevin Hawkes. 2003, Farrar $17.00 (978-0-374-37488-4). This oversize book presents the story of John Harrison, who worked for 50 years to perfect a timepiece that would track longitude in shipboard navigation. (Rev: BL 3/1/03*; SLJ 4/03)

HARVEY, WILLIAM

15730 Yount, Lisa. *William Harvey: Discoverer of How Blood Circulates.* Rev. ed. (4–8). Illus. Series: Great Minds of Science. 2008, Enslow LB $31.93 (978-0-89490-481-3). 128pp. A biography of the 17th-century scientist that describes early theories about the blood system and the importance of Harvey's discoveries. (Rev: SLJ 2/95) [921]

HEWLETT, WILLIAM

15731 Tracy, Kathleen. *William Hewlett: Pioneer of the Computer Age* (5–7). Series: Unlocking the Secrets of Science. 2002, Mitchell Lane LB $25.70 (978-1-58415-142-5). This accessible account focuses on Hewlett's scientific accomplishments and career in business. (Rev: SLJ 1/03) [921]

HILL, JULIA BUTTERFLY

15732 Fitzgerald, Dawn. *Julia Butterfly Hill: Saving the Redwoods* (4–6). Series: Gateway Greens. 2002, Millbrook LB $23.90 (978-0-7613-2654-0). 48pp. This is a handsome biography of the environmental activist who lived in a 200-foot-tall redwood named Luna from December 1997 to December 1999. (Rev: BL 7/02; HBG 3/03)

HOOKE, ROBERT

15733 Gow, Mary. *Robert Hooke: Creative Genius, Scientist, Inventor* (5–9). Series: Great Minds of Science. 2006, Enslow LB $31.93 (978-0-7660-2547-9). A biography of the 17th-century man of science and arts who made discoveries in many fields and also helped to redesign London after the fire of 1666. (Rev: SLJ 6/07) [921]

HOPPER, GRACE

15734 Mattern, Joanne. *Grace Hopper: Computer Pioneer* (1–4). Series: Women Who Shaped History. 2003, Rosen LB $19.95 (978-0-8239-6505-2). 24pp. The amazing story of the U.S. Navy rear admiral who was a pioneer software engineer and the inventor of the compiler that translates English to the language of the target computer. (Rev: BL 2/15/03; SLJ 5/03)

15735 Murphy, Patricia J. *Grace Hopper: Computer Whiz* (2–4). Series: Famous Inventors. 2004, Enslow LB $22.60 (978-0-7660-2273-7). 32pp. Describes Hopper's trail-blazing achievements and pioneering work in computers. (Rev: SLJ 2/05)

HOUNSFIELD, GODFREY

15736 Zannos, Susan. *Godfrey Hounsfield and the Invention of CAT Scans* (4–5). Series: Unlocking the Secrets of Science. 2002, Mitchell Lane LB $17.95 (978-1-58415-119-7). 56pp. The story of the man who realized that X-rays could be manipulated by computers and later invented the amazingly accurate diagnostic device known as the computerized axial tomography or CAT scanner. (Rev: BL 9/15/02; SLJ 1/03)

HOWARD, LUKE

15737 Hannah, Julie, and Joan Holub. *The Man Who Named the Clouds* (3–5). Illus. by Paige Billin-Frye. 2006, Albert Whitman $16.99 (978-0-8075-4974-2). 40pp. This fascinating book intertwines a profile of Luke Howard, the man who classified clouds into seven types, with a contemporary boy's weather journal. (Rev: BL 8/06; SLJ 10/06)

HUBBLE, EDWIN

15738 Datnow, Claire. *Edwin Hubble: Discoverer of Galaxies* (4–8). Series: Great Minds of Science. 1997, Enslow LB $26.60 (978-0-89490-934-4). A portrait of the great astronomer, noted for his amazing scientific abilities and quirky pretentions. (Rev: BL 12/1/97; HBG 3/98; SLJ 3/98; VOYA 12/97) [921]

IRWIN, STEVE AND BINDI

15739 Breguet, Amy E. *Steve and Bindi Irwin* (5–8). Illus. Series: Conservation Heroes. 2011, Chelsea House LB $35 (978-160413957-0). 160pp. This book describes the conservation efforts of Steve Irwin, who appeared in the *Crocodile Hunter* TV show until his death — and his daughter Bindi's following in his footsteps. (Rev: BL 4/1/11) [921]

IVE, JONATHAN

15740 Hirschmann, Kris. *Jonathan Ive: Designer of the iPod* (5–8). Illus. Series: Innovators. 2007, Gale LB $27.45 (978-0-7377-3533-8). Introduces the man behind this popular gadget; the inside info on Apple is also fascinating. (Rev: BL 12/15/07) [745.2092]

JACKSON, SHIRLEY ANN

15741 O'Connell, Diane. *Strong Force: The Story of Physicist Shirley Ann Jackson* (5–8). Series: Women's Adventures in Science. 2005, Watts LB $31.50 (978-0-531-16784-7). The life and scientific career of Jackson, physicist and former chairman of the U.S. Nuclear Regulatory Commission. (Rev: SLJ 12/05) [921]

JARVIK, ROBERT

15742 Bankston, John. *Robert Jarvik and the First Artificial Heart* (4–5). Series: Unlocking the Secrets of Science. 2002, Mitchell Lane LB $25.70 (978-1-58415-116-6). 48pp. This readable biography with interesting, unexpected facts covers the life and work of the doctor who invented the first artificial heart. (Rev: BL 8/02; HBG 3/03; SLJ 10/02)

JOBS, STEVE

15743 Brashares, Ann. *Steve Jobs: Thinks Different* (5–8). Series: Techies. 2001, Twenty-First Century LB $23.90 (978-0-7613-1959-7). 80pp. The life story of the amazing creator of Apple computers and his phenomenal success as a businessman and entrepreneur. (Rev: BL 3/15/01; HBG 10/01)

15744 Doeden, Matt. *Steve Jobs: Technology Innovator and Apple Genius* (4–7). Illus. Series: Gateway Biographies. 2012, Lerner LB $26.60 (978-146770215-7). 48pp. Tells the story of the creation of Apple and the factors underlying its success. ℮ (Rev: BL 6/12; SLJ 4/12) [921]

15745 Gaines, Ann Graham. *Steve Jobs* (3–4). Series: Real-Life Reader Biographies. 2000, Mitchell Lane LB $15.95 (978-1-58415-026-8). 32pp. The story of the founder of Apple computers who, after leaving the company he built, was brought back to rescue it from mismanagement. (Rev: BL 11/15/00)

15746 Goldsworthy, Steve. *Steve Jobs* (4–7). Illus. Series: Remarkable People. 2011, Weigl LB $27.13 (978-1-61690670-2); paper $12.95 (978-1-61690675-7). 24pp. A generally admiring life of the Apple CEO. (Rev: BL 9/15/11) [921]

15747 Mattern, Joanne. *Steve Jobs* (1–3). Illus. 2013, Scholastic/Children's Press LB $23 (978-0-53124739-6); paper $5.95 (978-0-53124705-1). 32pp. With brief sentences, color photographs, and fast facts, this is a useful introduction to Jobs's life and work for beginning readers. (Rev: BL 4/1/13; SLJ 4/13) [921]

KELLOGG, W. K.

15748 Wyckoff, Edwin Brit. *The Cornflake King: W. K. Kellogg and His Amazing Cereal* (3–5). Illus. Series: Genius at Work! Great Inventor Biographies. 2010, Enslow LB $22.60 (978-076603448-8). 32pp. Wyckoff chronicles Kellogg's early career and his accidental invention of the popular breakfast food. (Rev: BL 3/1/11) [921]

KNIGHT, MARGARET

15749 Brill, Marlene T. *Margaret Knight: Girl Inventor* (2–5). Illus. by Joanne Friar. 2001, Millbrook $22.90 (978-0-7613-1756-2). 32pp. Margaret Knight was driven to invent life- and labor-saving devices by her early experiences working in a textile mill. (Rev: BL 9/15/01; HBG 3/02; SLJ 12/01)

15750 McCully, Emily Arnold. *Marvelous Mattie: How Margaret E. Knight Became an Inventor* (K–3). Illus. 2006, Farrar $16.00 (978-0-374-34810-6). 32pp. The life of the 19th-century inventor of a machine that made paper grocery bags, among other products, and fought a court battle to get a patent. (Rev: BL 2/15/06; SLJ 2/06)

KOLFF, WILLEM

15751 Tracy, Kathleen. *Willem Kolff and the Invention of the Dialysis Machine* (5–8). Series: Unlocking the Secrets of Science. 2002, Mitchell Lane LB $25.70 (978-1-58415-135-7). Kolff invented the dialysis machine in 1942 in the Nazi-occupied Netherlands. (Rev: HBG 3/03; SLJ 12/02) [617.461059092]

KWOLEK, STEPHANIE

15752 Wyckoff, Edwin Brit. *The Woman Who Invented the Thread That Stops Bullets: The Genius of Stephanie Kwolek* (2–4). Illus. Series: Genius Inventors and Their Great Ideas. 2013, Enslow LB $23.93 (978-076604141-7). 48pp. The story of the chemist who invented Kevlar is followed by a section called "You Be the Inventor." ℮ (Rev: BL 12/15/13; LMC 10/14*)

LAGASSE, EMERIL

15753 Albright, Sawyer. *Emeril Lagasse* (4–8). Series: Top Chefs. 2012, Eldorado Ink LB $29.95 (978-1-61900-016-2); paper $16.95 (978-1-61900-017-9). 112pp. Describes the chef's childhood, culinary achievements, and philanthropic work. (Rev: SLJ 7/12) [921]

LAMARR, HEDY

15754 Gaines, Ann. *Hedy Lamarr* (2–3). Illus. Series: Discover the Life of an Inventor. 2001, Rourke LB $20.64 (978-1-58952-119-3). 24pp. The little-known story of the actress Hedy Lamarr and the communications system she devised during World War II, for beginning readers. (Rev: BL 10/15/01; SLJ 1/02)

LAVOISIER, ANTOINE

15755 Yount, Lisa. *Antoine Lavoisier: Founder of Modern Chemistry. Rev. ed.* (4–7). Illus. Series: Great Minds of Science. 2008, Enslow LB $31.93 (978-0-89490-785-2). 128pp. In addition to providing an assessment of the life and works of Lavoisier, called the Father of Chemistry, this book includes several hands-on activities that depend on an understanding of his work. (Rev: BL 6/1–15/97)

LEEUWENHOEK, ANTONI VAN

15756 Yount, Lisa. *Antoni van Leeuwenhoek: First to See Microscopic Life. Rev. ed.* (4–8). Series: Great Minds of Science. 2008, Enslow LB $31.93 (978-0-89490-680-0). 128pp. A brief biography of the Dutch maker of microscopes, who was also the first to examine closely bacteria and blood cells. (Rev: BL 10/15/96; SLJ 12/96)

LEOPOLD, ALDO

15757 Lorbiecki, Marybeth. *Of Things Natural, Wild, and Free: A Story About Aldo Leopold* (4–7). 1993, Carolrhoda LB $15.95 (978-0-87614-797-9). The story of a man who was a great hunter until he realized the importance of the balance in nature, and then turned a tract of farmland into a nature refuge. (Rev: BL 11/1/93; SLJ 11/93) [921]

15758 Yannuzzi, Della A. *Aldo Leopold: Protector of the Wild* (4–6). Series: Gateway Greens. 2002, Millbrook LB $23.90 (978-0-7613-2465-2). 48pp. An attractive biography of the U.S. environmentalist who helped create the first national wildlife area in 1924 and founded the Wilderness Society in 1935. (Rev: BL 7/02; HBG 3/03)

LINNAEUS, CARL

15759 Anderson, Margaret J. *Carl Linnaeus: Father of Classification. Rev. ed.* (4–8). Series: Great Minds of Science. 2009, Enslow LB $31.93 (978-0-89490-786-9). This biography discusses the personal life of Linnaeus, including his explorations in Lapland, but the focus is on the development of his important biological classification system. (Rev: BL 12/1/97; HBG 3/98; SLJ 9/97) [921]

LORENZ, KONRAD

15760 Greenstein, Elaine. *The Goose Man: The Story of Konrad Lorenz* (K–2). Illus. by author. 2010, Clarion $16 (978-0-547-08459-6). 32pp. Animal behaviorist Konrad Lorenz's childhood love of animals led to his Nobel Prize-winning research on geese. (Rev: BL 12/15/09; LMC 8–9/10; SLJ 2/1/10) [921]

MAIMAN, THEODORE H.

15761 Wyckoff, Edwin Brit. *The Man Who Invented the Laser: The Genius of Theodore H. Maiman* (2–4). Illus. Series: Genius Inventors and Their Great Ideas. 2013, Enslow LB $23.93 (978-076604138-7). 48pp. The story of the scientist who invented this useful instrument is followed by a section called "You Be the Inventor." **e** (Rev: BL 12/15/13; LMC 10/14*; SLJ 3/14)

MALONE, ANNIE TURNBO

15762 Wilkerson, J. L. *Story of Pride, Power and Uplift: Annie T. Malone* (4–8). 2003, Acorn $9.95 (978-0-9664470-8-8). Malone, a child of slaves, created beauty products for African American women at the turn of the 20th century and became a wealthy woman and philanthropist. (Rev: BL 3/1/03; SLJ 7/03) [646.7]

MARTINI, HELEN DELANEY

15763 Lyon, George E. *Mother to Tigers* (K–3). Illus. by Peter Catalanotto. 2003, Simon & Schuster $16.95 (978-0-689-84221-4). A picture-book biography of the woman who looked after tiger cubs in her own home before she established a nursery at the Bronx Zoo. (Rev: BL 3/1/03; HB 5/03; HBG 10/03; SLJ 3/03)

MCCLINTOCK, BARBARA

15764 Tracy, Kathleen. *Barbara McClintock: Pioneering Geneticist* (4–7). Series: Unlocking the Secrets of Science. 2001, Mitchell Lane LB $25.70 (978-1-58415-111-1). An absorbing look at the life and research of this Nobel Prize winner. (Rev: HBG 3/02; SLJ 2/02) [921]

MCCOY, ELIJAH

15765 Kulling, Monica. *All Aboard! Elijah McCoy's Steam Engine* (1–3). Illus. by Bill Slavin. Series: Great Idea. 2010, Tundra $17.95 (978-088776945-0). 32pp. A simple introduction to the life and achievements of McCoy, a black inventor born in 1843 who faced many challenges. (Rev: BL 8/10; SLJ 8/10) [921]

MEAD, MARGARET

15766 Horn, Geoffrey M. *Margaret Mead* (5–8). Series: Trailblazers of the Modern World. 2004, World Almanac LB $31.00 (978-0-8368-5099-4). Report writers will find useful information on Mead's life, achievements, and lasting contributions. (Rev: SLJ 7/04) [921]

MENDEL, GREGOR

15767 Bankston, John. *Gregor Mendel and the Discovery of the Gene* (5–8). Series: Uncharted, Unexplored, and

Unexplained. 2004, Mitchell Lane LB $29.95 (978-1-58415-266-8). Profiles the 19th-century Austrian monk who discovered the laws of genetics. (Rev: BL 10/15/04; SLJ 12/04) [921]

15768 Bardoe, Cheryl. *Gregor Mendel: The Friar Who Grew Peas* (2–4). Illus. by Joe A. Smith. 2006, Abrams $18.95 (978-0-8109-5475-5). 32pp. A biography of the father of genetics, with child-friendly explanations of the science and accompanied by beautiful watercolors. (Rev: BL 7/06)

MENDELEYEV, DMITRI

15769 Zannos, Susan. *Dmitri Mendeleyev and the Periodic Table* (5–8). Series: Uncharted, Unexplored, and Unexplained. 2004, Mitchell Lane LB $29.95 (978-1-58415-267-5). This brief biography looks at the life of the inventor of the periodic table, focusing initially on his childhood and offering political context. (Rev: BL 10/15/04) [540]

MERCATOR, GERARDUS

15770 Heinrichs, Ann. *Gerardus Mercator: Father of Modern Mapmaking* (5–12). Series: Signature Lives. 2007, Compass Point LB $31.93 (978-0-7565-3312-0). 112pp. Scientific concepts are presented clearly in this profile that covers Mercator's life, with excerpts from his writing and a timeline that adds historical context. (Rev: SLJ 1/08)

MERIAN, MARIA

15771 Engle, Margarita. *Summer Birds: The Butterflies of Maria Merian* (K–3). Illus. by Julie Paschkis. 2010, Henry Holt $16.99 (978-0-8050-8937-0). 32pp. Maria Merian disproved the popular belief that butterflies were "beasts of the devil" in the 17th century; this inspiring story shows the young scientist and artist pursuing her passions. (Rev: BL 3/15/10*; LMC 5–6/10; SLJ 7/1/10) [921]

MORGAN, ANN

15772 Ross, Michael E. *Pond Watching with Ann Morgan* (3–5). Series: Naturalist's Apprentice. 2000, Carolrhoda $19.93 (978-1-57505-385-1). A biography about the expert on ponds that also serves as a field guide to pond ecology. (Rev: BL 4/15/00; HBG 10/00; SLJ 7/00)

MORSE, SAMUEL

15773 Hall, M. C. *Samuel Morse* (1–4). Series: Lives and Times. 2004, Heinemann LB $22.79 (978-1-4034-5329-7). 32pp. Report writers will find useful information in this biography that has a timeline and "Fact File" boxes. (Rev: SLJ 9/04)

MUIR, JOHN

15774 Armentrout, David, and Patricia Armentrout. *John Muir* (2–4). Illus. 2002, Rourke LB $14.95 (978-1-58952-055-4). A simple introduction for younger readers to the life of naturalist John Muir. (Rev: BL 1/1–15/02; SLJ 3/02)

15775 Dunlap, Julie, and Marybeth Lorbiecki. *John Muir and the Stickeen: An Icy Adventure with a No Good Dog* (2–4). Illus. by Bill Farnsworth. 2004, T&N Children's Publishing $16.95 (978-1-55971-903-2). 32pp. Beautifully illustrated and drawing heavily on Muir's personal journals, this engaging book tells how a dog named Stickeen helped to guide the famed conservationist through a brush with death in Alaska. (Rev: BL 11/15/04)

15776 Locker, Thomas. *John Muir: America's Naturalist* (2–4). 2004, Fulcrum $17.95 (978-1-55591-393-9). 32pp. This brief picture-book biography of the Scottish-born naturalist is beautifully illustrated with paintings of his beloved Yosemite. (Rev: BL 6/1–15/03; HBG 4/04; SLJ 9/03)

MURRAY, JOSEPH E.

15777 Mattern, Joanne. *Joseph E. Murray and the Story of the First Human Kidney Transplant* (5–8). Series: Unlocking the Secrets of Science. 2002, Mitchell Lane LB $25.70 (978-1-58415-136-4). A look at the work of the surgeon who performed the first successful kidney transplant. (Rev: SLJ 12/02; VOYA 6/03) [617.95092]

NEWTON, SIR ISAAC

15778 Anderson, Margaret J. *Isaac Newton: The Greatest Scientist of All Time*. Rev. ed. (4–7). Illus. Series: Great Minds of Science. 2008, Enslow LB $31.93 (978-0-89490-681-7). 128pp. The life of the great English mathematician and physicist who formulated the laws of motion and gravity. (Rev: BL 10/15/96; SLJ 12/96)

15779 Hollihan, Kerrie Logan. *Isaac Newton and Physics for Kids: His Life and Ideas with 21 Activities* (4–8). Illus. 2009, Chicago Review $16.95 (978-1-55652-778-4). 144pp. This well-balanced story offers a picture of the physicist's work and personal life. (Rev: BL 6/1–15/09; LMC 1–2/10; SLJ 8/09) [530.092]

15780 Krull, Kathleen. *Isaac Newton* (5–8). Illus. by Boris Kulikov. Series: Giants of Science. 2006, Viking $15.99 (978-0-670-05921-8). 128pp. Newton's childhood and adult personality are highlighted in this readable biography that gives good explanations of his scientific theories. (Rev: BL 4/1/06; SLJ 3/06*; VOYA 6/06)

15781 Mason, Paul. *Isaac Newton* (4–8). Illus. Series: Scientists Who Made History. 2002, Raintree LB $27.12 (978-0-7398-4845-6). 48pp. Newton's life and contributions are presented in clear text and ample illustrations, with historical detail that places the information in context. (Rev: HBG 10/02; SLJ 9/02)

15782 Steele, Philip. *Isaac Newton: The Scientist Who Changed Everything* (4–7). Illus. Series: National Geographic World History Biographies. 2007, National Geographic $17.95 (978-1-4263-0114-8). 64pp. A colorful, well-designed survey of Newton's life and legacy. (Rev: BL 12/1/07; SLJ 6/07)

NOBEL, ALFRED

15783 Bankston, John. *Alfred Nobel and the Story of the Nobel Prize* (4–8). Series: Great Achievement Awards. 2003, Mitchell Lane LB $29.95 (978-1-58415-168-5). 48pp. An intriguing biography of the inventor of dynamite and the founder of the famous prizes. (Rev: BL 10/15/03; SLJ 9/03)

OMIDYAR, PIERRE

15784 Viegas, Jennifer. *Pierre Omidyar: The Founder of eBay* (5–8). Illus. Series: Internet Career Biographies. 2006, Rosen LB $31.95 (978-1-4042-0715-8). A look at the successful founder of eBay and his hopes for the future. (Rev: BL 10/15/06; SLJ 5/07) [921]

OPPENHEIMER, J. ROBERT

15785 Allman, Toney. *J. Robert Oppenheimer: Father of the Atomic Bomb* (5–9). Series: Giants of Science. 2005, Gale $26.20 (978-1-56711-889-6). Controversial physicist Oppenheimer, who played a key role in the development of the atomic bomb, is profiled in readable text with lots of details for report writers. (Rev: SLJ 7/05) [921]

OTIS, ELISHA

15786 Kulling, Monica. *Going Up! Elisha Otis's Trip to the Top* (1–3). Illus. by David Parkins. Series: Great Idea. 2012, Tundra $17.95 (978-177049240-0). 32pp. A colorful profile of the man whose inventions persuaded the public that elevators would be safe. (Rev: BL 12/1/12) [921]

PASTEUR, LOUIS

15787 Alphin, Elaine M. *Germ Hunter: A Story About Louis Pasteur* (3–6). Illus. by Elaine Verstraete. 2003, Carolrhoda LB $22.60 (978-1-57505-179-6); paper $6.95 (978-0-87614-929-4). Pasteur's early life is covered well in this simple biography that reads more like a novel and is more suitable for reluctant readers than for report writers. (Rev: HBG 10/03; SLJ 7/03)

15788 Armentrout, David, and Patricia Armentrout. *Louis Pasteur* (2–4). Series: Discover Someone Who Made a Difference. 2001, Rourke LB $14.95 (978-1-58952-056-1). This basic biography describes the life and times of Pasteur and how his accomplishments affect our lives today. (Rev: BL 1/1–15/02; SLJ 3/02)

15789 Birch, Beverley. *Louis Pasteur: Father of Modern Medicine* (5–7). Series: Giants of Science. 2001, Blackbirch LB $27.44 (978-1-56711-336-5). 64pp. A readable, well-organized biography of the French chemist whose varied accomplishments include discovery of the process known now as pasteurization. (Rev: BL 8/1/01; HBG 3/02)

15790 Fullick, Ann. *Louis Pasteur* (4–6). 2000, Heinemann LB $25.64 (978-1-57572-373-0). 48pp. As well as covering Pasteur's life, this book tells of the impact of his discoveries on medicine and science. (Rev: SLJ 2/01)

15791 Smith, Linda W. *Louis Pasteur: Disease Fighter. Rev. ed.* (4–8). Illus. Series: Great Minds of Science. 2007, Enslow LB $31.93 (978-0-89490-790-6). 128pp. The story of the "father of microbiology," who discovered pasteurization while working on a wine problem for Napoleon. (Rev: BL 12/1/97; HBG 3/98; SLJ 12/97)

PAULING, LINUS

15792 Zannos, Susan. *Linus Pauling and the Chemical Bond* (4–5). Series: Unlocking the Secrets of Science. 2003, Mitchell Lane LB $25.70 (978-1-58415-123-4). 48pp. This brief biography recounts the life and scientific achievements of American chemist Linus Pauling. (Rev: BL 11/15/03; SLJ 10/03)

PAVLOV, IVAN

15793 Saunders, Barbara R. *Ivan Pavlov: Exploring the Mysteries of Behavior. Rev. ed.* (5–9). Series: Great Minds of Science. 2006, Enslow LB $31.93 (978-0-7660-2506-6). 112pp. This well-written profile chronicles Pavlov's famous experiments and discoveries and shows how his work influenced other branches of science. (Rev: SLJ 6/07)

PINCHOT, GIFFORD

15794 Hines, Gary. *Midnight Forests* (3–5). Illus. by Robert Casilla. 2005, Boyds Mills $16.95 (978-1-56397-148-8). 32pp. Gifford Pinchot, an American who became secretary of agriculture in 1898 and who was responsible for saving large areas of forest in the West, is introduced in this large-format picture-book biography. (Rev: BL 5/15/05; SLJ 4/05)

PULITZER, JOSEPH

15795 Zannos, Susan. *Joseph Pulitzer and the Story Behind the Pulitzer Prize* (4–8). Series: Great Achievement Awards. 2003, Mitchell Lane LB $29.95 (978-1-58415-179-1). Pulitzer's difficulty personality and passion for journalism are highlighted in this account of his establishment of the well-known awards. (Rev: BL 10/15/03; SLJ 9/03) [070.9]

QUADRINO, JAMES

15796 Pearce, Q. L. *James Quadrino: Wildlife Protector* (4–7). Series: Young Heroes. 2006, Gale LB $23.70 (978-0-7377-3612-0). At age 13, James Quadrino took it upon himself to save a fire-ravaged bird sanctuary by building nesting boxes. (Rev: SLJ 6/07) [921]

RICHTER, CHARLES

15797 Zannos, Susan. *Charles Richter and the Story of the Richter Scale* (4–5). Series: Unlocking the Secrets of Science. 2003, Mitchell Lane LB $17.95 (978-1-58415-175-3). 48pp. This brief biography of Charles Richter chronicles the life and achievements of the American physicist and seismologist who is credited with developing the scale for measuring earthquake intensity. (Rev: BL 11/15/03; SLJ 10/03)

RINGLING BROTHERS

15798 Apps, Jerry. *Tents, Tigers, and the Ringling Brothers* (3–7). Illus. Series: Badger Biographies. 2006, Wisconsin Historical Soc. paper $12.95 (978-0-87020-374-9). 114pp. The true story of how the seven Ringling Brothers followed their dreams and began their own circus, describing their day-to-day struggles to keep the business successful. (Rev: BL 2/15/07)

ROBERTS, EDWARD

15799 Zannos, Susan. *Edward Roberts and the Story of the Personal Computer* (5–7). Series: Unlocking the Secrets of Science. 2002, Mitchell Lane LB $25.70 (978-1-58415-118-0). This accessible account focuses on Roberts's accomplishments as an electronic engineer. (Rev: HBG 10/03; SLJ 1/03) [921]

ROCKEFELLER, JOHN D.

15800 Laughlin, Rosemary. *John D. Rockefeller: Oil Baron and Philanthropist* (5–8). Series: American Business Leaders. 2001, Morgan Reynolds LB $21.95 (978-1-883846-59-6). A biography of the determined and skilled businessman who made Standard Oil the dominant company in the oil industry and who was later noted for his philanthropy. (Rev: BL 3/1/01; HBG 10/01; SLJ 7/01) [921]

ROENTGEN, WILHELM

15801 Garcia, Kimberly. *Wilhelm Roentgen and the Discovery of X Rays* (4–5). Series: Unlocking the Secrets of Science. 2002, Mitchell Lane LB $17.95 (978-1-58415-114-2). 48pp. The story of the German physical scientist who stumbled upon X-rays while working on experiments with electricity. (Rev: BL 8/02; HBG 3/03; SLJ 10/02)

ROTHSCHILD, WALTER

15802 Judge, Lita. *Strange Creatures: The Story of Walter Rothschild and His Museum* (1–3). Illus. by author. 2011, Hyperion/Disney $17.99 (978-1-4231-1389-8). 40pp. Lord Walter Rothschild's lifelong fascination with exotic animals spawned one of the most extensive collections of rare and fascinating animals in the world by the time he was 24 years old. Lexile AD950L (Rev: BL 2/15/11; SLJ 2/1/11) [595]

SAGAN, CARL

15803 Butts, Ellen R., and Joyce R. Schwarts. *Carl Sagan* (5–8). Series: A&E Biography. 2000, Lerner LB $27.93 (978-0-8225-4986-4). 112pp. The story of the great astronomer who interested millions in the study of the stars and the question of whether there is life elsewhere in our universe. (Rev: BL 10/15/00; HBG 3/01; SLJ 10/00)

15804 Byman, Jeremy. *Carl Sagan: In Contact with the Cosmos* (5–8). Illus. Series: Great Scientists. 2000, Morgan Reynolds LB $21.95 (978-1-883846-55-8). 112pp. An informative biography of the scientist who popular-

ized astronomy while maintaining a highly productive scholarly life. (Rev: BL 11/1/00; HBG 10/00; SLJ 8/00)

SALK, JONAS

15805 Bankston, John. *Jonas Salk and the Polio Vaccine* (4–5). Series: Unlocking the Secrets of Science. 2001, Mitchell Lane LB $25.70 (978-1-58415-093-0). 56pp. A biography of the famous scientist, with photographs, a glossary, and a list of additional resources. (Rev: BL 10/15/01; SLJ 11/01)

15806 Durrett, Deanne. *Jonas Salk* (2–5). Illus. Series: Inventors and Creators. 2002, Gale LB $23.70 (978-0-7377-1277-3). 48pp. This brief biography presents Salk's life from childhood and his determination to persevere to find a cure for polio, with many photographs, a glossary, and a bibliography. (Rev: BL 11/1/02; SLJ 10/02)

15807 McPherson, Stephanie Sammartino. *Jonas Salk: Conquering Polio* (5–8). Series: Lerner Biographies. 2001, Lerner LB $27.93 (978-0-8225-4964-2). An absorbing account of Salk's life and contributions to medicine that discusses his confrontation with Sabin and the early failures of Salk's vaccine. (Rev: HBG 3/02; SLJ 4/02) [921]

15808 Tocci, Salvatore. *Jonas Salk: Creator of the Polio Vaccine* (4–7). Illus. Series: Great Minds of Science. 2003, Enslow LB $26.60 (978-0-7660-2097-9). 128pp. This book covers the life of the scientist and the importance and impact of the vaccine he developed. (Rev: BL 5/15/03; HBG 10/03)

SANTOS-DUMONT, ALBERTO

15809 Griffin, Victoria. *The Fabulous Flying Machines of Alberto Santos-Dumont* (1–3). Illus. by Eva Montanari. 2011, Abrams $16.95 (978-1-4197-0011-8). 32pp. First flyer Alberto Santos-Dumont's high-society Paris life and his rivalry with Louis Bleriot are documented in this account that also covers his friend Cartier's invention of the wristwatch. (Rev: BL 10/15/11; LMC 1–2/12*; SLJ 9/1/11) [921]

SCHALLER, GEORGE

15810 Turner, Pamela S. *A Life in the Wild: George Schaller's Struggle to Save the Last Great Beasts* (5–8). Illus. 2008, Farrar $21.95 (978-0-374-34578-5). 112pp. Turner traces the environmentalist's work to save gorillas, tigers, lions, snow leopards, and other large endangered animals. (Rev: BCCB 11/08; BL 12/1/08; SLJ 11/08) [590.92]

SESSIONS, KATHERINE OLIVIA

15811 Hopkins, H. Joseph. *The Tree Lady: The True Story of How One Tree-Loving Woman Changed a City Forever* (1–3). Illus. by Jill McElmurry. 2013, Simon & Schuster $16.99 (978-1-4424-1402-0). 32pp. Katherine Olivia Sessions transformed San Diego at the turn of the 20th century, finding trees that could tolerate the arid desert weather. ❷ (Rev: BL 6/13*; HB 9–10/13; LMC 1–2/14; SLJ 10/13*) [921]

SIKORSKY, IGOR

15812 Wyckoff, Edwin Brit. *Helicopter Man: Igor Sikorsky and His Amazing Invention* (3–5). Illus. Series: Genius at Work! Great Inventor Biographies. 2010, Enslow LB $22.60 (978-076603445-7). 32pp. Wyckoff chronicles Sikorsky's devotion to his dream of building a successful helicopter. (Rev: BL 3/1/11) [921]

STRAUSS, LEVI

15813 Van Steenwyk, Elizabeth. *Levi Strauss: The Blue Jeans Man* (5–9). 1988, Walker LB $14.85 (978-0-8027-6796-7). A biography of the Bavarian immigrant, Levi Strauss, who became the blue jeans king of the western world. (Rev: BL 6/15/88; SLJ 10/88; VOYA 8/88) [921]

SUZUKI, HIROMI

15814 Barasch, Lynne. *Hiromi's Hands* (K–3). Illus. 2007, Lee & Low $17.95 (978-1-58430-275-9). 32pp. This picture-book biography of Japanese American sushi chef Hiromi Suzuki begins with the immigration of her father — also a successful sushi chef — to the United States from Japan. (Rev: BL 3/15/07)

TAJIRI, SATOSHI

15815 Mortensen, Lori. *Satoshi Tajiri: Pokémon Creator* (4–7). Illus. 2009, Gale LB $27.45 (978-0-7377-4269-5). 48pp. A brief biography of the Japanese designer known for creating Pokemon and other Nintendo games, with information on his diagnosis with Asperger's syndrome. (Rev: BLO 5/28/09; SLJ 8/09) [921]

TELLER, EDWARD

15816 Bankston, John. *Edward Teller and the Development of the Hydrogen Bomb* (5–8). Series: Unlocking the Secrets of Science. 2001, Mitchell Lane LB $25.70 (978-1-58415-108-1). The life of the scientist born in Hungary who played a key role in the development of the H-bomb. (Rev: HBG 3/02; SLJ 1/02)

TESLA, NIKOLA

15817 Dommermuth-Costa, Carol. *Nikola Tesla: A Spark of Genius* (5–9). 1994, Le⁻ · LB $27.93 (978-0-8225-4920-8). Traces the life and career of this pioneer in the field of electricity. (Rev: BL 12/15/94; SLJ 2/95) [921]

TIENDA, MARTA

15818 O'Connell, Diane. *People Person: The Story of Sociologist Marta Tienda* (5–8). Series: Women's Adventures in Science. 2005, Watts LB $31.50 (978-0-531-16781-6). An informative and accessible profile of sociologist Marta Tienda and her work to create opportunities for people around the world. (Rev: SLJ 12/05) [921]

TORVALDS, LINUS

15819 Brashares, Ann. *Linus Torvalds: Software Rebel* (5–8). Series: Techies. 2001, Millbrook LB $23.90 (978-0-7613-1960-3). The story of the computer genius who created the Linux operating system. (Rev: BL 4/1/02; HBG 3/02; SLJ 12/01) [921]

VEDDER, AMY

15820 Ebersole, Rene. *Gorilla Mountain: The Story of Wildlife Biologist Amy Vedder* (5–8). Series: Women's Adventures in Science. 2005, Watts LB $31.50 (978-0-531-16779-3). An informative and accessible account of Vedder's efforts to protect the endangered mountain gorillas of Rwanda. (Rev: SLJ 12/05)

WAKSMAN, SELMAN

15821 Gordon, Karen. *Selman Waksman and the Discovery of Streptomycin* (5–7). Series: Unlocking the Secrets of Science. 2002, Mitchell Lane LB $25.70 (978-1-58415-138-8). An accessible account of Waksman's life and scientific research. (Rev: HBG 10/03; SLJ 1/03) [921]

WALKER, MADAM C. J.

15822 McKissack, Patricia C., and Fredrick McKissack. *Madam C. J. Walker: Self-Made Millionaire. Rev. ed.* (2–4). Illus. by Michael Bryant. Series: Great African Americans. 2001, Enslow LB $18.60 (978-0-89490-311-3). 32pp. The story of the woman who built a cosmetics empire and became the first self-made African American woman millionaire. (Rev: BL 10/15/92; SLJ 12/92)

15823 Nichols, Catherine. *Madame C. J. Walker* (K–2). Illus. Series: Scholastic News Nonfiction Readers: Biographies. 2005, Scholastic LB $20.00 (978-0-516-24941-4). This brief biography chronicles the inspiring story of the pioneering African American hair-care entrepreneur; large type, simple text, and ample illustrations make this suitable for beginning readers. (Rev: BL 2/1/06; SLJ 4/06)

WALTON, SAM

15824 Blumenthal, Karen. *Mr. Sam: How Sam Walton Built Wal-Mart and Became America's Richest Man* (5–8). Illus. 2011, Viking $17.99 (978-0-670-01177-3). 160pp. A frank profile of the Oklahoma-born man who had a profound influence on the retail face of America — and beyond. ℯ (Rev: BL 6/1/11; HB 7–8/11; LMC 11–12/11; SLJ 7/11) [381]

WANG, VERA

15825 Dakers, Diane. *Vera Wang: A Passion for Bridal and Lifestyle Design* (5–8). Illus. Series: Crabtree Groundbreakers Biographies. 2010, Crabtree LB $31.93 (978-077872535-0). 112pp. Chronicling life from youth to adulthood, this biography presents a straightforward and clearly written portrait of fashion great Vera Wang. Lexile NC1210L (Rev: BL 1/1–15/11) [921]

WEINBERG, ROBERT A.

15826 Gaines, Ann, and Jim Whiting. *Robert A. Weinberg and the Search for the Cause of Cancer* (4–7). Series: Unlocking the Secrets of Science. 2002, Mitchell Lane LB $25.70 (978-1-58415-095-4). The life and achievements of the scientist who specializes in the genetic causes of disease. (Rev: HBG 10/02; SLJ 6/02) [616.9940092]

WELCH, THOMAS BRAMWELL

15827 Carney, Mary Lou. *Dr. Welch and the Great Grape Story* (1–3). Illus. by Sherry Meidell. 2005, Boyds Mills $16.95 (978-1-59078-039-8). 32pp. This picture-book biography traces Thomas Bramwell Welch's efforts to find a nonalcoholic drink based on grapes. (Rev: BL 5/1/05)

WHITNEY, ELI

15828 Gaines, Ann. *Eli Whitney* (2–3). Series: Discover the Life of an Inventor. 2001, Rourke LB $20.64 (978-1-58952-118-6). 24pp. The life of the inventor of the cotton gin is presented simply with material on how this invention works. (Rev: BL 10/15/01)

15829 Gibson, Karen Bush. *The Life and Times of Eli Whitney* (5–8). Illus. Series: Profiles in American History. 2006, Mitchell Lane LB $20.95 (978-1-58415-434-1). An interesting profile of the cotton gin inventor, with period reproductions and relevant sidebar features. (Rev: BL 10/15/06) [609.2]

WOZNIAK, STEPHEN

15830 Riddle, John, and Jim Whiting. *Stephen Wozniak and the Story of Apple Computer* (4–7). Series: Unlocking the Secrets of Science. 2001, Mitchell Lane LB $17.95 (978-1-58415-109-8). A profile of the life and achievements of the co-founder of Apple, who is known for his philanthropy and teaching in elementary schools. (Rev: HBG 10/02; SLJ 2/02) [921]

WRIGHT, WILBUR AND ORVILLE

15831 Berger, Melvin, and Gilda Berger. *Can You Fly High, Wright Brothers?* (3–4). Illus. by Brandon Dorman. Series: Science SuperGiants. 2007, Scholastic paper $4.99 (978-0-439-83378-3). 48pp. Using a question-and-answer format, Berger tells the story of the brothers' life and fascination with aviation. (Rev: SLJ 2/08)

15832 Borden, Louise, and Trish Marx. *Touching the Sky: The Flying Adventures of Wilbur and Orville Wright* (2–4). Illus. by Peter M. Fiore. 2003, Simon & Schuster $18.95 (978-0-689-84876-6). 64pp. Wilbur and Orville are shown as celebrities in this picture book that recounts unusual appearances they made separately. (Rev: BL 9/15/03; HBG 4/04; SLJ 10/03)

15833 Busby, Peter. *First to Fly* (3–5). Illus. by David Craig. 2003, Crown $19.95 (978-0-375-81287-3). 32pp. The obstacles surmounted by the Wright brothers as they took to the sky are handsomely presented in this large, richly illustrated text. (Rev: BL 1/1–15/03; HBG 10/03; SLJ 3/03)

15834 Collins, Mary. *Airborne: A Photobiography of Wilbur and Orville Wright* (4–8). 2003, National Geographic $18.95 (978-0-7922-6957-1). Sixty photographs are only the beginning of this intriguing book packed with information about the brothers and their famous flight. (Rev: BL 2/1/03*; HB 3–4/03; HBG 10/03; SLJ 3/03) [629.13]

15835 Dixon-Engel, Tara, and Mike Jackson. *The Wright Brothers: First in Flight* (5–8). Series: Sterling Biographies. 2007, Sterling LB $12.95 (978-1-4027-4954-4); paper $5.95 (978-1-4027-3231-7). 124pp. The brothers' early life, inspiration, and eventual success are all covered here. (Rev: SLJ 10/07)

15836 Ford, Carin T. *The Wright Brothers: Heroes of Flight* (2–4). Illus. Series: Famous Inventors. 2003, Enslow LB $22.60 (978-0-7660-2002-3). 32pp. Photographs enhance this well-written account of the Wright brothers' inventive abilities. (Rev: HBG 10/03; SLJ 10/03)

15837 Gaines, Ann. *Orville and Wilbur Wright* (2–3). Series: Discover the Life of an Inventor. 2001, Rourke LB $20.64 (978-1-58952-121-6). 24pp. A very simple biography of the Wright brothers with material on their struggles and an explanation of how the airplane works. (Rev: BL 10/15/01)

15838 MacLeod, Elizabeth. *The Wright Brothers: A Flying Start* (3–5). Illus. 2002, Kids Can $14.95 (978-1-55074-933-5). 32pp. Using double-page spreads, with pictures on one and text on the other, this attractive biography is a fine introduction to the Wright brothers and their work. (Rev: BL 4/1/02; HBG 10/02; SLJ 7/02)

15839 McPherson, Stephanie Sammartino, and Joseph Sammartino Gardner. *Wilbur and Orville Wright: Taking Flight* (4–7). Series: Trailblazer Biographies. 2003, Carolrhoda LB $30.60 (978-1-57505-443-8). A well-written, detailed account of the Wright brothers' landmark experiments, enlivened with period photographs and other illustrations. (Rev: SLJ 4/04) [921]

15840 Old, Wendie. *The Wright Brothers* (5–8). Series: Historical American Biographies. 2000, Enslow LB $26.60 (978-0-7660-1095-6). An accurate and objective biography of the heroes of Kitty Hawk, containing chapter notes, a bibliography, and a glossary. (Rev: BL 1/1–15/00; HBG 10/00; SLJ 7/00)

15841 O'Sullivan, Robyn. *The Wright Brothers Fly* (2–4). Series: National Geographic History Chapters. 2007, National Geographic LB $17.90 (978-1-4263-0188-9). 40pp. Simple sentences, with photographs and drawings, tell the story of the Wright brothers' youth and later accomplishments; a "How to Write an A+ Report" section gives useful advice. (Rev: LMC 1/08*; SLJ 1/08)

15842 Reynolds, Quentin. *The Wright Brothers* (5–8). 1963, Random House paper $5.99 (978-0-394-84700-9). An easily read account of the two young men and their dream of flight. [921]

15843 Tieck, Sarah. *Wright Brothers* (K–3). Series: First Biographies. 2007, ABDO LB $25.65 (978-1-59679-790-1). A beginner's profile of Wilbur and Orville Wright and their contributions to the development of the airplane, with lots of illustrations, a large typeface, and highlighted words that appear in the glossary. (Rev: SLJ 3/07)

15844 Yolen, Jane. *My Brothers' Flying Machine: Wilbur, Orville, and Me* (3–5). Illus. by Jim Burke. 2003, Little, Brown $16.95 (978-0-316-97159-1). The story of the Wright brothers is told in free verse by their sister Katherine, who looked after the brothers while they tended to their dream. (Rev: BL 3/1/03; HBG 10/03; SLJ 3/03)

Sports Figures

Collective

15845 Berman, Len. *The Twenty-five Greatest Baseball Players of All Time* (5–8). Illus. 2010, Sourcebooks $16.99 (978-140223886-4). 138pp. Twenty-five of baseball's greatest are profiled in short chapters emphasizing career statistics and triumphs over challenges. (Rev: BL 9/1/10; SLJ 1/1/11; VOYA 12/10) [920]

15846 Bryant, Jill. *Amazing Women Athletes* (4–8). Series: Women's Hall of Fame. 2002, Second Story paper $7.95 (978-1-896764-44-3). This book contains profiles of 10 distinguished women athletes including mountain climber Annie Smith Peck and tennis stars Venus and Serena Williams. (Rev: BL 6/1–15/02; SLJ 8/02) [920]

15847 Christopher, Andre. *Top 10 Men's Tennis Players* (4–7). Series: Sports Top 10. 1998, Enslow LB $17.95 (978-0-7600-1009-9). Brief biographies of past and present tennis greats, with fact boxes, career statistics, and chapter notes. (Rev: BL 3/15/98) [920]

15848 Deane, Bill. *Top 10 Men's Baseball Hitters* (4–7). Series: Sports Top 10. 1998, Enslow LB $17.95 (978-0-7600-1007-5). Brief biographies of great past and present baseball hitters, with fact boxes, career statistics, and chapter notes. (Rev: BL 3/15/98) [920]

15849 Hall, Kirsten. *Kids in Sports: A Chapter Book* (3–6). Series: True Tales. 2004, Children's Pr. LB $22.50 (978-0-516-23733-6); paper $4.95 (978-0-516-24685-7). 48pp. True stories of young people who have excelled in the area of sports. (Rev: SLJ 1/05)

15850 Hotchkiss, Ron. *The Matchless Six: The Story of Canada's First Women's Olympic Team* (5–8). Illus. 2006, Tundra $16.95 (978-0-88776-738-8). 200pp. Profiles the individual athletes and achievements of Canada's groundbreaking women's Olympic team of 1928. (Rev: BL 3/15/06; SLJ 6/06)

15851 Kaminsky, Marty. *Uncommon Champions: Fifteen Athletes Who Battled Back* (5–8). 2000, Boyds Mills $14.95 (978-1-56397-787-9). Profiles of 15 athletes in several different sports who have conquered such mental and physical problems as blindness and drug addiction to achieve their goals. (Rev: BCCB 1/01; BL 11/1/00; HBG 3/01; SLJ 10/00; VOYA 12/00) [921]

15852 Krull, Kathleen. *Lives of the Athletes* (4–7). Illus. by Kathryn Hewitt. 1997, Harcourt $20.00 (978-0-15-200806-2). A collective biography that describes the public and private lives of 20 famous athletes, including Johnny Weissmuller, Red Grange, Babe Didrikson Zaharias, Sonja Henie, and Bruce Lee. (Rev: BCCB 6/97; BL 3/15/97; HB 5–6/97; SLJ 5/97) [920]

15853 Lipsyte, Robert. *Heroes of Baseball: The Men Who Made It America's Favorite Game* (4–7). Illus. 2006, Simon & Schuster $19.95 (978-0-689-86741-5). 96pp. As well as introducing key players of the game, this volume presents a concise history of the sport itself. (Rev: BL 2/15/06; SLJ 4/06)

15854 McDaniel, Melissa. *Pushing the Limits: A Chapter Book* (3–6). Series: True Tales. 2004, Children's Pr. LB $22.50 (978-0-516-23734-3); paper $4.95 (978-0-516-24688-8). 48pp. A look at athletes in the areas of marathon running, triathlons, weight lifting, and sled dog racing. (Rev: SLJ 1/05)

15855 Nichols, Catherine. *Record Breakers: A Chapter Book* (3–6). Series: True Tales. 2004, Children's Pr. LB $22.50 (978-0-516-23732-9); paper $4.95 (978-0-516-24689-5). 48pp. Gertrude Ederle and Mark McGwire are two of the record-setting individuals featured in this volume. (Rev: SLJ 1/05)

15856 Packard, Mary. *Beating the Odds: A Chapter Book* (3–6). Illus. Series: True Tales. 2004, Children's Pr. LB $22.50 (978-0-516-23731-2); paper $4.95 (978-0-516-24682-6). 48pp. Wilma Rudolph (polio) and Lance Armstrong (cancer) are two of the inspiring individuals featured in this volume of true tales about overcoming physical difficulties. (Rev: SLJ 1/05)

15857 Piven, Hanoch. *What Athletes Are Made Of* (2–4). 2006, Simon & Schuster $16.95 (978-1-4169-1002-2).

40pp. Each of the well-known athletes in this visually interesting, offbeat book has an unusual feature to show what he or she is "made of." (Rev: BL 7/06; SLJ 8/06)

15858 Rappoport, Ken. *Guts and Glory: Making It in the NBA* (4–8). 1997, Walker LB $16.85 (978-0-8027-8431-5). The 10 basketball players profiled in this book had to overcome obstacles to get to the top. (Rev: BL 8/97; SLJ 7/97) [920]

15859 Rappoport, Ken. *Ladies First: Women Athletes Who Made a Difference* (5–8). 2005, Peachtree $14.95 (978-1-56145-338-2). Gymnast Nadia Comaneci and dogsled racer Susan Butcher are only two of the many women in diverse sports featured in this collective biography that also gives a brief history of women's participation in sports. (Rev: BL 5/1/05; SLJ 6/05) [920]

15860 Rappoport, Ken. *Profiles in Sports Courage* (4–7). 2006, Peachtree $15.95 (978-1-56145-368-9). 160pp. Twelve stories of bravery on and off the playing field (or court, ring, or track) by men and women from all types of sport and from all around the world. (Rev: BL 7/06; SLJ 6/06)

15861 Roberts, Angela. *NASCAR's Greatest Drivers* (2–4). Illus. 2009, Random LB $11.99 (978-0-375-94813-8); paper $3.99 (978-0-375-94813-1). A basic introduction to NASCAR opens this collective biography suitable for beginning readers. (Rev: BLO 1/7/09)

15862 Rutledge, Rachel. *The Best of the Best in Figure Skating* (4–7). Series: Women of Sports. 1998, Millbrook LB $24.90 (978-0-7613-1302-1). After a brief history of figure skating and mention of its women pioneers, this book devotes separate chapters to the sport's present-day female leaders. (Rev: BL 2/15/99; HBG 10/99) [920]

15863 Rutledge, Rachel. *The Best of the Best in Gymnastics* (5–8). Series: Women of Sports. 1999, Millbrook LB $24.90 (978-0-7613-1321-2); paper $7.95 (978-0-7613-0784-6). After an overview of the sport and its history, the author profiles eight important contemporary female gymnasts, five of whom are American. (Rev: HBG 10/99; SLJ 7/99; VOYA 2/00) [920]

15864 Schilling, Vincent. *Native Athletes in Action!* (4–6). Illus. Series: Native Trailblazers. 2007, 7th Generation paper $9.95 (978-0-9779183-0-0). 125pp. This well-written collective biography profiles 13 Native American athletes from Canada and the United States — many of whom will be unfamiliar to young readers — and focuses on values that helped them succeed. (Rev: BL 9/1/07; SLJ 9/07)

15865 Shea, Therese. *Soccer Stars* (3–5). Series: Greatest Sports Heroes. 2006, Children's Pr. $24.50 (978-0-531-12588-5). 48pp. Profiles some of today's best-known soccer players, including Freddy Adu, David Beckham, and Kristine Lilly. (Rev: BL 9/1/06)

15866 Stout, Glenn. *Baseball Heroes* (3–6). Illus. 2010, Houghton Mifflin paper $5.99 (978-05474170-8-0). 128pp. Hank Greenburg, Jackie Robinson, Fernando Valenzuela, and Ila Borders are profiled in this inspiring,

well-written book about overcoming obstacles. (Rev: BL 9/1/10) [920]

15867 Stout, Glenn. *Yes, She Can! Women's Sports Pioneers* (4–7). 2011, Houghton Mifflin paper $5.99 (978-0-547-41-725-7). 128pp. Profiles women from different backgrounds and eras who made their name in various sports, from Gertrude Eberle through Julie Krone and Danica Patrick. **e** (Rev: BL 5/1/11; SLJ 7/11) [920]

15868 Winter, Jonah. *Beisbol! Latino Baseball Pioneers and Legends* (3–8). Illus. 2001, Lee & Low $16.95 (978-1-58430-012-0). 32pp. Sports fans will appreciate the format here, with statistics and other facts about 14 Latino baseball players presented in trading-card-style profiles. (Rev: BCCB 10/01; BL 10/1/01; HBG 10/01; SLJ 7/01)

15869 Woods, Bob. *Racer Girls* (2–5). Series: Girls Rock! 2006, The Child's World LB $25.64 (978-1-59296-742-1). Profiles female racing car drivers around the world in large text and full-color photographs; suitable for browsing by beginning readers. (Rev: SLJ 4/07)

Automobile Racing

EARNHARDT, DALE, JR.

15870 Stewart, Mark. *Dale Earnhardt Jr.: Driven by Destiny* (5–8). Series: Auto Racing's New Wave. 2003, Millbrook LB $22.90 (978-0-7613-2908-4). An exciting biography of the NASCAR driver who was voted the most popular driver of 2003. (Rev: BL 6/1–15/03; HBG 10/03; SLJ 10/03) [796.72]

GORDON, JEFF

15871 Doeden, Matt. *Jeff Gordon* (3–6). Series: Stars of NASCAR. 2008, Capstone LB $22.60 (978-1-4296-1976-9). 32pp. Simple sentences, color photographs, fact boxes, and statistics make this an appealing profile of the NASCAR driver. (Rev: SLJ 12/08)

15872 Gitlin, Martin. *Jeff Gordon: Racing's Brightest Star* (5–8). Series: Heroes of Racing. 2008, Enslow LB $23.95 (978-0-7660-2997-2). For NASCAR fans, a biography that concentrates on Gordon's victories and charisma. (Rev: BL 4/1/08) [796.72]

JOHNSON, JIMMIE

15873 Doeden, Matt. *Jimmie Johnson* (3–6). Series: Stars of NASCAR. 2008, Capstone LB $22.60 (978-1-4296-1977-6). 32pp. Simple sentences, color photographs, fact boxes, and statistics make this an appealing profile of the NASCAR driver. (Rev: SLJ 12/08)

KAHNE, KASEY

15874 Doeden, Matt. *Kasey Kahne* (3–6). Series: Stars of NASCAR. 2008, Capstone LB $22.60 (978-1-4296-1980-6). 32pp. Simple sentences, color photographs, fact boxes, and statistics make this an appealing profile of the NASCAR driver. (Rev: SLJ 12/08)

LABONTE, TERRY AND BOBBY

15875 Hubbard-Brown, Janet. *The Labonte Brothers* (4–8). Series: Race Car Legends: Collector's Edition. 2005, Chelsea House LB $25.00 (978-0-7910-8767-1). The famous brothers Terry and Bobby Labonte and their racing rivalry and successes are the focus of this readable, photo-filled volume. (Rev: SLJ 5/06) [921]

PATRICK, DANICA

15876 Mello, Tara Baukus. *Danica Patrick* (5–8). Series: Race Car Legends Collector's Edition. 2008, Chelsea House LB $25.00 (978-0-7910-9126-5). An attractive portrait of this history-making race car driver. (Rev: BL 4/15/08) [921]

PETTY FAMILY

15877 Stewart, Mark. *The Pettys: Triumphs and Tragedies of Auto Racing's First Family* (4–8). Illus. 2001, Millbrook LB $24.90 (978-0-7613-2273-3). 64pp. Photographs, quotations, anecdotes, and informative text introduce readers to the famous Petty family and their sometimes tragic involvement in automobile racing. (Rev: BL 9/1/01; HBG 3/02)

STEWART, TONY

15878 Leebrick, Kristal. *Tony Stewart* (4–7). Series: NASCAR Racing. 2004, Capstone LB $23.93 (978-0-7368-2425-5). This profile of auto racing star Tony Stewart chronicles his meteoric rise from go-karts and midget racers to the top ranks of NASCAR. (Rev: BL 4/1/04) [790.72]

UNSER FAMILY

15879 Bentley, Karen. *The Unsers* (4–8). Series: Race Car Legends: Collector's Edition. 2005, Chelsea House LB $25.00 (978-0-7910-8764-0). The famous Unser automobile racing family is the focus of this book that describes their rivalries with the Andretti family and their victories at important races including the Indianapolis 500. (Rev: SLJ 5/06) [921]

Baseball

AARON, HANK

15880 Golenbock, Peter. *Hank Aaron: Brave in Every Way* (2–4). Illus. by Paul Lee. 2001, Harcourt $16.00 (978-0-15-202093-4). Part of this stirring biography focuses on Hank Aaron's goal of breaking Babe Ruth's batting record and the controversy it caused because he was African American. (Rev: BL 2/15/01; HBG 10/01)

15881 Morrison, Jessica. *Hank Aaron: Home Run Hero* (5–8). Illus. Series: Crabtree Groundbreakers Biographies. 2010, Crabtree LB $31.93 (978-077872538-1). 112pp. Morrison covers Hammerin' Hank's life from childhood and his move from the Negro Leagues to ma-

jor-league baseball. Lexile 1080L (Rev: BL 1/1–15/11) [921]

15882 Spencer, Lauren. *Hank Aaron* (4–7). Series: Baseball Hall of Famers. 2003, Rosen LB $29.25 (978-0-8239-3600-7). In 1974, Hank Aaron, an African American, was crowned home run king, taking the title away from Babe Ruth. This is his story. (Rev: BL 6/1–15/03; SLJ 6/03) [921]

15883 Tavares, Matt. *Henry Aaron's Dream* (2–4). Illus. by author. 2010, Candlewick $16.99 (978-0-7636-3224-3). 40pp. In this effective biography, Tavares describes Aaron's youth and the many challenges he faced in achieving his dream of playing major league baseball. (Rev: BL 2/15/10; LMC 5–6/10; SLJ 1/1/10*) [921]

BELL, COOL PAPA

15884 McCormack, Shaun. *Cool Papa Bell* (4–7). Series: Baseball Hall of Famers of the Negro Leagues. 2002, Rosen LB $29.25 (978-0-8239-3474-4). A biography of James Thomas "Cool Papa" Bell of Negro League baseball, who is said to have stolen 175 bases in one season. (Rev: BL 7/02) [921]

BLACKBURNE, LENA

15885 Kelly, David A. *Miracle Mud: Lena Blackburne and the Secret Mud That Changed Baseball* (2–4). Illus. by Oliver Dominguez. 2013, Millbrook LB $16.95 (978-076138092-4). 32pp. For baseball fans, this is a fascinating story about the player who came up with the idea of using mud to make the balls easier to grasp. (Rev: BL 3/1/13; LMC 8–9/13; SLJ 3/13) [921]

BONILLA, BOBBY

15886 Rappoport, Ken. *Bobby Bonilla* (5–9). 1993, Walker LB $15.85 (978-0-8027-8256-4). A biography of the baseball player who rose from poverty in the South Bronx to superstardom and multimillionaire status. (Rev: BL 5/15/93; SLJ 5/93; VOYA 8/93) [921]

CAMPANELLA, ROY

15887 Adler, David A. *Campy: The Story of Roy Campanella* (2–4). Illus. by Gordon C. James. 2007, Viking $15.99 (978-0-670-06041-2). 40pp. African American baseball player joined the Brooklyn Dodgers only a year after Jackie Robinson and was a major star until a 1958 accident left him paralyzed. (Rev: BL 2/1/07; SLJ 4/07)

CLEMENTE, ROBERTO

15888 Kingsbury, Robert. *Roberto Clemente* (4–7). Series: Baseball Hall of Famers. 2003, Rosen LB $29.25 (978-0-8239-3602-1). The story of the National League battling champion who faced racism and discrimination because of his Hispanic background. (Rev: BL 6/1–15/03; SLJ 6/03)

15889 Marquez, Heron. *Roberto Clemente: Baseball's Humanitarian Hero* (4–7). 2005, Carolrhoda LB $30.60 (978-1-57505-767-5). The story of the ballplayer, from his birth in Puerto Rico to his death in a plane crash, with photographs. (Rev: BL 3/15/05; SLJ 5/05) [796.357]

15890 Perdomo, Willie. *¡Clemente!* (1–3). Illus. by Bryan Collier. 2010, Henry Holt $16.99 (978-0-8050-8774-1). 40pp. Tells the story of Clemente's life from the perspective of a boy named for him. (Rev: BL 2/15/10; LMC 5–6/10; SLJ 4/1/10) [921]

15891 Walker, Paul Robert. *Pride of Puerto Rico: The Life of Roberto Clemente* (4–7). 1988, Harcourt paper $6.00 (978-0-15-263420-9). The life of a baseball star and hero who died trying to help others. (Rev: BL 10/1/88; HB 9–10/88; SLJ 1/89) [921]

15892 Winter, Jonah. *Roberto Clemente: Pride of the Pittsburgh Pirates* (2–4). Illus. by Raúl Colón. 2005, Simon & Schuster $16.95 (978-0-689-85643-3). 40pp. Clemente's character, career success, and tragic death are all covered in this engaging picture-book biography. (Rev: BL 2/15/05; SLJ 5/05)

DIMAGGIO, JOE

15893 Sakany, Lois. *Joe DiMaggio* (4–6). Series: Baseball Hall of Famers. 2004, Rosen LB $29.25 (978-0-8239-3779-0). 112pp. Report writers will find solid information on the life and career of the Yankees star. (Rev: SLJ 6/04)

DOBY, LARRY

15894 Crowe, Chris. *Just as Good: How Larry Doby Changed America's Game* (1–3). Illus. by Mike Benny. 2012, Candlewick $32 (978-076365026-1). 32pp. The first African American to play in the American League, Larry Doby was instrumental in securing a championship for the Cleveland Indians in the 1948 World Series. Lexile AD690L (Rev: BL 2/1/12; LMC 5–6/12; SLJ 1/12) [921]

DOUTY, SHEILA CORNELL

15895 Douty, Sheila Cornell, and Judith Cohen. *You Can Be a Woman Softball Player* (3–6). Illus. 2000, Cascade Pass $13.95 (978-1-880599-47-1); paper $7.00 (978-1-880599-46-4). This is the story of Sheila Douty, from her youth, when she was considered a "problem" child, to the 1996 Olympics, where she helped her team win a gold medal. (Rev: BL 7/00)

GAGNE, ERIC

15896 Gagné, Eric, and Greg Brown. *Eric Gagne: Break Barriers* (3–6). Series: Athletes. 2004, Positively for Kids $15.95 (978-0-9634650-6-1). A lively and attractively designed first-person account of Gagne's life and career in baseball, with lots of personal details about his childhood, family life, and sporting successes. (Rev: BL 9/1/04)

GEHRIG, LOU

15897 Buckley, James, Jr. *Lou Gehrig: Iron Horse of Baseball* (5–8). Series: Sterling Biographies. 2010, Sterling $12.95 (978-1-4027-7151-4). 128pp. Details of

Gehrig's life and personality are placed in historical context and enhanced by an appealing layout, plentiful images, and first-person accounts. (Rev: BL 5/1/10; LMC 8–9/10) [921]

15898 Viola, Kevin. *Lou Gehrig* (4–7). Series: Sports Heroes and Legends. 2004, Lerner LB $8.95 (978-0-8225-5311-3). Starting with Gehrig's sad retirement and his "Luckiest Man" speech, this well-written and informative biography goes back to look at his life and successful career. (Rev: BL 9/1/04) [921]

GIBSON, JOSH

15899 Twemlow, Nick. *Josh Gibson* (4–7). Series: Baseball Hall of Famers of the Negro Leagues. 2002, Rosen LB $29.25 (978-0-8239-3475-1). In addition to racial prejudice in the world of baseball, Josh Gibson suffered many personal misfortunes as this life story recounts. (Rev: BL 7/02) [921]

GREENBERG, HANK

15900 McDonough, Yona Zeldis. *Hammerin' Hank: The Life of Hank Greenberg* (K–2). Illus. by Malcah Zeldis. 2006, Walker $16.95 (978-0-8027-8997-6). 32pp. This profile of the first Jewish American baseball star discusses his parents' disapproval of his choice of career, the prejudice he faced, and the difficult decisions he had to make. (Rev: BL 3/1/06; SLJ 4/06*)

15901 Sommer, Shelley. *Hammerin' Hank Greenberg: Baseball Pioneer* (4–7). 2011, Calkins Creek $17.95 (978-1-59078-452-5). 136pp. Pioneering Jewish baseball player Hank Greenberg overcame considerable prejudice in his time on the diamond during the 1930s and 1940s. Sydney Taylor Book Honor 2012. (Rev: BL 3/1/11; SLJ 4/11; VOYA 8/11) [921]

HERSHISER, OREL

15902 Knapp, Ron. *Orel Hershiser* (5–8). Series: Sports Greats. 1993, Enslow LB $17.95 (978-0-89490-389-2). An easily read sports biography that re-creates the great moments in this baseball star's career up to 1993. (Rev: BL 4/1/93) [921]

IRVIN, MONTE

15903 Haegele, Katie. *Monte Irvin* (4–7). Series: Baseball Hall of Famers of the Negro Leagues. 2002, Rosen LB $29.25 (978-0-8239-3477-5). Though recruited into the Negro leagues when he was 17, Irvin, a very talented player, was past his prime when he finally became a major leaguer. (Rev: BL 7/02) [921]

JETER, DEREK

15904 Robinson, Tom. *Derek Jeter: Captain On and Off the Field* (5–8). Series: Sports Stars with Heart. 2006, Enslow LB $31.93 (978-0-7660-2819-7). This biography focuses primarily on Jeter's career in baseball and his work with the philanthropic Turn 2 Foundation. (Rev: BL 9/1/06) [921]

15905 Thornley, Stew. *Derek Jeter* (3–6). Illus. Series: Sports Leaders. 2004, Enslow LB $26.60 (978-0-7660-2035-1). An accessible profile of the shortstop's life and career. [921]

15906 Torres, John A. *Derek Jeter* (3–4). Series: Real-Life Reader Biographies. 2000, Mitchell Lane LB $15.95 (978-1-58415-031-2). 32pp. A brief, attractive biography of the young star of the New York Yankees. (Rev: BL 11/15/00)

JOHNSON, JUDY

15907 Billus, Kathleen. *Judy Johnson* (4–7). Series: Baseball Hall of Famers of the Negro Leagues. 2002, Rosen LB $29.25 (978-0-8239-3476-8). A biography of Johnson covering his years as player, coach, manager, and scout, with black-and-white photographs, glossary, timeline, and lists of additional resources. (Rev: BL 7/02) [796.357]

JOHNSON, MAMIE "PEANUT"

15908 Green, Michelle Y. *A Strong Right Arm: The Story of Mamie "Peanut" Johnson* (4–7). 2002, Dial $15.99 (978-0-8037-2661-1). The life story of the woman who was one of three to play professional baseball and of her career as pitcher with the Negro Leagues' Indianapolis Clowns. (Rev: BL 6/1–15/02*; HBG 3/03; SLJ 8/02; VOYA 8/02)

KOUFAX, SANDY

15909 Winter, Jonah. *You Never Heard of Sandy Koufax?!* (2–4). Illus. by Andre Carrilho. 2009, Random $17.99 (978-0-375-83738-8). 40pp. A compelling picture-book biography of the Jewish player for the Dodgers. (Rev: BCCB 2/09; BL 12/15/08; HB 3/09; SLJ 2/09)

LEONARD, BUCK

15910 Payment, Simone. *Buck Leonard* (4–7). Series: Baseball Hall of Famers of the Negro Leagues. 2002, Rosen LB $29.25 (978-0-8239-3473-7). The story of one of the greatest baseball players of all time, who missed worldwide fame because of his color. (Rev: BL 7/02) [921]

LINCECUM, TIM

15911 Boone, Mary. *Tim Lincecum* (2–4). Illus. Series: Robbie Reader Contemporary Biographies. 2011, Mitchell Lane LB $25.70 (978-161228058-5). 32pp. A profile of the pitcher who led the San Francisco Giants to a World Series championship in 2010. (Rev: BL 12/1/11) [921]

MANLEY, EFFA

15912 Vernick, Audrey. *She Loved Baseball: The Effa Manley Story* (1–3). Illus. by Don Tate. 2010, HarperCollins $16.99 (978-0-06-134920-1). 32pp. The life of the African American who became the first woman to be inducted into the Baseball Hall of Fame and, with her husband, founded the Negro League team that became the Newark Eagles. (Rev: BL 9/1/10; SLJ 11/1/10*) [921]

MANTLE, MICKEY

15913 Marlin, John. *Mickey Mantle* (4–7). Series: Sports Heroes and Legends. 2004, Lerner LB $27.93 (978-0-8225-1796-2). A concise, well-written biography that focuses on Mantle's illustrious career. (Rev: BL 9/1/04; SLJ 11/04) [921]

15914 Weinstein, Howard. *Mickey Mantle* (4–6). Series: Baseball Hall of Famers. 2004, Rosen LB $29.25 (978-0-8239-3782-0). 112pp. Report writers will find solid information on the life and career of the Yankees star. (Rev: SLJ 6/04)

MAYS, WILLIE

15915 Winter, Jonah. *You Never Heard of Willie Mays?!* (2–4). Illus. by Terry Widener. 2013, Random House $17.99 (978-0-375-86844-3). 40pp. With effective illustrations and exciting text, this is a rousing tribute to Mays' accomplishments on the baseball field. **e** (Rev: BL 9/1/12*; HB 1–2/13; LMC 5–6/13*; SLJ 3/13) [921]

MITCHELL, JACKIE

15916 Moss, Marissa. *Mighty Jackie: The Strike-Out Queen* (K–3). Illus. by C. F. Payne. 2004, Simon & Schuster $16.95 (978-0-689-86329-5). Jackie's story opens with the day in 1931 when — at age 17 — she struck out both Lou Gehrig and Babe Ruth. (Rev: BL 1/1–15/04; SLJ 2/04)

PAIGE, SATCHEL

15917 Adler, David A. *Satchel Paige: Don't Look Back* (K–3). Illus. by Terry Widener. Series: Paige, Satchel. 2007, Harcourt $16.00 (978-0-15-205585-1). This picture-book biography gives a the great pitcher's early life and successful career in both the Negro leagues and the majors. (Rev: BL 1/1–15/07)

15918 Cline-Ransome, Lesa. *Satchel Paige* (2–4). Illus. by James Ransome. 2000, Simon & Schuster $16.00 (978-0-689-81151-7). 40pp. The mythic hero of baseball comes to life, with all his swagger and accomplishments, in this biography. (Rev: BCCB 2/00; BL 12/15/99*; HB 3/00; HBG 10/00; SLJ 3/00)

15919 McKissack, Patricia C., and Fredrick McKissack. *Satchel Paige: The Best Arm in Baseball. Rev. ed.* (2–4). Illus. by Michael D. Blegel. Series: Great African Americans. 2002, Enslow LB $18.60 (978-0-89490-317-5). 32pp. The life story of the Hall of Famer who was the first African American pitcher in the American League. (Rev: BL 10/15/92; SLJ 1/93)

15920 Schmidt, Julie. *Satchel Paige* (4–7). Illus. Series: Baseball Hall of Famers of the Negro Leagues. 2002, Rosen LB $29.25 (978-0-8239-3478-2). 112pp. A biography of the famous pitcher who became the oldest rookie ever, with black-and-white photographs, glossary, timeline, and lists of additional resources. (Rev: BL 7/02; VOYA 6/02)

PIKE, LIPMAN

15921 Michelson, Richard. *Lipman Pike: America's First Home Run King* (2–4). Illus. by Zachary Pullen. 2011, Sleeping Bear $16.95 (978-1-58536-465-7). 32pp. Evoking the spirit of baseball's early years in the 1860s, this picture book tells the story of a young Jewish boy who ran fast and was a strong hitter. (Rev: BL 3/1/11; LMC 11–12/11; SLJ 5/1/11) [921]

PUJOLS, ALBERT

15922 Buckingham, Mark. *Albert Pujols: MVP On and Off the Field* (4–7). Illus. 2007, Enslow LB $23.95 (978-0-7660-2866-1). Presents facts on the life of the baseball legend, including his childhood in the Dominican Republic, his move to the United States, his career and accomplishments with the St. Louis Cardinals, and his family. (Rev: BL 9/1/07) [921]

RIPKEN, CAL, JR.

15923 Ripken, Cal, Jr. *The Longest Season: The Story of the Orioles' 1988 Losing Streak* (2–5). Illus. by Ron Mazellan. 2007, Philomel $16.99 (978-0-399-24492-6). 32pp. The famous ballplayer relates the story of that difficult season, and readers will learn that even top athletes experience difficult times. (Rev: SLJ 5/07)

ROBINSON, JACKIE

15924 DeAngelis, Gina. *Jackie Robinson: Overcoming Adversity* (5–8). Illus. Series: Overcoming Adversity. 2000, Chelsea $30.00 (978-0-7910-5897-8). 104pp. Using a highly readable text and black-and-white photographs, this book gives a real picture of Robinson that touches on the reasons he felt extreme anger and his great determination to make a difference. (Rev: BL 2/15/01; HBG 10/01)

15925 Ford, Carin T. *Jackie Robinson: Hero of Baseball* (2–4). Illus. Series: Heroes of American History. 2006, Enslow LB $22.60 (978-0-7660-2600-1). A brief, readable account of Robinson's life and accomplishments, with information about segregation in general. (Rev: BL 2/1/06; SLJ 8/06)

15926 Mara, Wil. *Jackie Robinson* (K–2). Series: Rookie Biographies. 2002, Children's Book Pr. paper $4.95 (978-0-516-27336-5). 32pp. For beginning readers, this is a simple introduction to the legendary baseball player. (Rev: SLJ 12/02)

15927 O'Sullivan, Robyn. *Jackie Robinson Plays Ball* (2–4). Series: National Geographic History Chapters. 2007, National Geographic LB $17.90 (978-1-4263-0190-2). 40pp. Simple sentences, with photographs and drawings, tell the story of Robinson's younger life and later accomplishments; a "How to Write an A+ Report" section gives useful advice. (Rev: LMC 1/08*; SLJ 1/08)

15928 Robinson, Sharon. *Jackie Robinson: American Hero* (3–5). Illus. 2013, Scholastic $16.99 (978-0-545-56915-6). 48pp. With information on his childhood and teen years as well as his career, this is a frank profile of the player who helped to desegregate major league baseball. (Rev: BL 5/1/13; LMC 11–12/13; SLJ 6/13) [921]

15929 Robinson, Sharon. *Jackie's Gift: A True Story of Christmas, Hanukkah, and Jackie Robinson* (K–3). Illus. by E. B. Lewis. 2010, Viking $16.99 (978-067001162-9). 32pp. When young Steve Satlow, whose family bucked the trend and welcomed the African American Robinsons into their neighborhood, mentions that they do not have a Christmas tree, young Jackie Robinson goes to get one — unaware that the Satlows are Jewish. (Rev: BL 2/1/11; SLJ 10/10) [921]

15930 Robinson, Sharon. *Promises to Keep: How Jackie Robinson Changed America* (3–7). Illus. 2004, Scholastic $16.95 (978-0-439-42592-6). 64pp. The inspiring story of Robinson's life and his struggle to break into major league baseball is told by his daughter. (Rev: BL 2/15/04*; SLJ 3/04)

15931 Teitelbaum, Michael. *Jackie Robinson: Champion for Equality* (5–8). Series: Sterling Biographies. 2010, Sterling $12.95 (978-1-4027-7148-4). 128pp. Details of Robinson's life and personality are placed in historical context and enhanced by an appealing layout, plentiful images, and first-person accounts. (Rev: LMC 8–9/10) [921]

15932 Time for Kids Editorial Staff, and Denise Lewis Patrick, eds. *Jackie Robinson: Strong Inside and Out* (2–4). Illus. Series: Time for Kids Biographies. 2005, HarperCollins $15.99 (978-0-06-057601-1); paper $3.99 (978-0-06-057600-4). A lively overview of Robinson's life drawing on the archives of Time-Life and ending with an interview with his daughter Sharon. (Rev: BL 2/1/05)

15933 Wukovits, John F. *Jackie Robinson and the Integration of Baseball* (5–8). Series: Lucent Library of Black History. 2006, Gale LB $32.45 (978-1-59018-913-9). 104pp. The social background to Robinson's achievements is well laid out in this biography suitable for report writers. (Rev: SLJ 3/07)

RUTH, BABE

15934 Fischer, David. *Babe Ruth: Legendary Slugger* (5–8). Series: Sterling Biographies. 2010, Sterling $12.95 (978-1-4027-7147-7). 128pp. Details of Ruth's life and personality are placed in historical context and enhanced by an appealing layout, plentiful images, and first-person accounts. Lexile 1080L (Rev: LMC 8–9/10) [921]

15935 Kelly, David A. *Babe Ruth and the Baseball Curse* (3–5). Illus. by Tim Jessell. 2009, Random LB $11.99 (978-0-375-95603-4); paper $4.99 (978-0-375-85603-7). 112pp. In addition to covering Ruth's childhood and career, Kelly reviews the spotty achievements of the Boston Red Sox after they traded Babe Ruth to the Yankees in 1918. (Rev: BCCB 2/09; BL 1/1–15/09)

15936 Murphy, Frank. *Babe Ruth Saves Baseball!* (1–3). Illus. by Richard Walz. Series: Step into Reading. 2005, Random LB $11.99 (978-0-375-93048-5); paper $3.99 (978-0-375-83048-8). 48pp. Babe Ruth's character comes to the fore in this lively biography for beginning readers. (Rev: BL 6/1–15/05)

15937 Nicholson, Lois. *Babe Ruth: Sultan of Swat* (5–8). 1995, Goodwood $17.95 (978-0-9625427-1-8). This well-written account of the famous slugger explains his lasting influence on baseball. (Rev: SLJ 7/95) [921]

15938 Tavares, Matt. *Becoming Babe Ruth* (1–4). Illus. by author. 2013, Candlewick $16.99 (978-076365646-1). 40pp. This is a compelling picture-book biography of the baseball star, documenting his triumph over an uninspiring start in life. (Rev: BL 1/13*; LMC 8–9/13; SLJ 3/13) [921]

SOCKALEXIS, LOUIS

15939 Wise, Bill. *Louis Sockalexis: Native American Baseball Pioneer* (3–5). Illus. by Bill Farnsworth. 2007, Lee & Low $16.95 (978-1-58430-269-8). 32pp. Colorful illustrations evoke the turn-of-the-century time period in profile the first Native American to play baseball for a major league team. (Rev: BL 7/07; LMC 11/07; SLJ 5/07)

SUZUKI, ICHIRO

15940 Leigh, David S. *Ichiro Suzuki* (4–6). 2004, Lerner LB $27.93 (978-0-8225-1792-4). Suzuki's youth and career in Japan are covered in addition to his contributions in the U.S. major leagues. (Rev: SLJ 11/04)

15941 Levin, Judith. *Ichiro Suzuki* (5–8). Illus. Series: Baseball Superstars. 2007, Chelsea House LB $30.00 (978-0-7910-9440-2). A biography of the record-setting, award-winning Seattle Mariners player from Japan. (Rev: BL 3/18/08) [921]

15942 Stewart, Mark. *Ichiro Suzuki: Best in the West* (4–7). Series: Sports New Wave. 2002, Millbrook LB $22.90 (978-0-7613-2616-8). A well-constructed biography of the famous Japanese Seattle Mariners player that offers information on the game itself as well as statistics, color photographs, and quotations that illustrate his achievements. (Rev: BL 9/1/02; HBG 3/03) [796.357]

WAGNER, HONUS

15943 Yolen, Jane. *All Star! Honus Wagner and the Most Famous Baseball Card Ever* (1–3). Illus. by Jim Burke. 2010, Philomel $17.99 (978-0-399-24661-6). 32pp. Yolen tells the story of Honus Wagner, who seemed an unlikely candidate to become a baseball star. (Rev: BL 2/15/10; LMC 3–4/10; SLJ 3/1/10*) [921]

WEISS, ALTA

15944 Hopkinson, Deborah. *Girl Wonder: A Baseball Story in Nine Innings* (2–4). Illus. by Terry Widener. 2003, Simon & Schuster $16.95 (978-0-689-83300-7). 40pp. Alta Weiss's inspiring story swings along in lyrical prose, relating her adventures as a teenage baseball phenomenon who pitched for a men's team in 1907 at the age of 17. (Rev: BL 1/1–15/03*; HB 3/03; HBG 10/03; SLJ 3/03)

WILLIAMS, TED

15945 McCormack, Shaun. *Ted Williams* (4–6). Series: Baseball Hall of Famers. 2004, Rosen LB $29.25 (978-0-8239-3783-7). 112pp. Report writers will find solid information on the life and career of the Boston Red Sox star. (Rev: SLJ 6/04)

15946 Tavares, Matt. *There Goes Ted Williams: The Greatest Hitter Who Ever Lived* (2–5). Illus. by author. 2012, Candlewick $16.99 (978-076362789-8). 40pp. An admiring portrait of the baseball star that nonetheless mentions his legendary temper in an author's note. (Rev: BLO 2/15/12; HB 1–2/12; LMC 8–9/12; SLJ 1/12) [921]

ZENIMURA, KENICHI

15947 Moss, Marissa. *Barbed Wire Baseball* (2–4). Illus. by Yuko Shimizu. 2013, Abrams $18.95 (978-1-4197-0521-2). 48pp. This is the story of the diminutive Japanese American baseball player Kenichi Zenimura and his efforts to bring the game to his World War II internment camp. ALA Notable Children's Book. (Rev: BL 3/15/13; HB 7–8/13; LMC 10/13; SLJ 4/13) [921]

Basketball

ABDUL-JABBAR, KAREEM

15948 Kneib, Martha. *Kareem Abdul-Jabbar* (5–8). Series: Basketball Hall of Famers. 2002, Rosen LB $29.25 (978-0-8239-3483-6). 112pp. An in-depth look at this basketball great's life, with highlights from his childhood through his NBA career. (Rev: BL 9/1/02)

ANTHONY, CARMELO

15949 Anthony, Carmelo, and Greg Brown. *Carmelo Anthony: It's Just the Beginning* (3–6). Illus. Series: Athletes. 2004, Positively for Kids $15.95 (978-0-9634650-7-8). 48pp. A lively and attractively designed first-person account of Anthony's life and career in basketball, with lots of personal details about his childhood, family life, and sporting successes. [921]

BIRD, SUE

15950 Bird, Sue, and Greg Brown. *Sue Bird: Be Yourself* (3–6). Illus. Series: Athletes. 2004, Positively for Kids $15.95 (978-0-9634650-5-4). A lively and attractively designed first-person account of Bird's life and career in basketball, with lots of personal details about her childhood, family life, and sporting successes. [921]

15951 Boone, Mary. *Sue Bird* (2–4). Illus. Series: Robbie Reader Contemporary Biographies. 2011, Mitchell Lane LB $25.70 (978-161228062-2). 32pp. This profile begins with a career highlight and then provides details of the early life and determination of the Seattle Storm basketball star. (Rev: BL 12/1/11) [921]

BRYANT, KOBE

15952 Savage, Jeff. *Kobe Bryant: Basketball Big Shot* (4–7). Series: Sports Biography. 2000, Lerner LB $22.60 (978-0-8225-3680-2). A very readable, attractive biography of the new NBA sensation that ends with the 1999–2000 season. (Rev: BL 1/1–15/01; HBG 10/01) [921]

15953 Stewart, Mark. *Kobe Bryant: Hard to the Hoop* (4–8). Series: Basketball's New Wave. 2000, Millbrook LB $20.90 (978-0-7613-1800-2). 48pp. The life story of this basketball star who was the son of an NBA player and who became the youngest player in league history to star in the All-Star Game. (Rev: HBG 10/00; SLJ 8/00)

15954 Thornley, Stew. *Super Sports Star Kobe Bryant* (2–5). Illus. Series: Super Sports Stars. 2001, Enslow LB $23.93 (978-0-7660-1514-2). 48pp. Photographs and statistics accompany text about the famous basketball player, from his childhood to his professional career with the L.A. Lakers. (Rev: BL 10/15/01; HBG 3/02)

15955 Torres, John A. *Kobe Bryant* (3–4). Series: Real-Life Reader Biographies. 2000, Mitchell Lane LB $24.95 (978-1-58415-030-5). 32pp. An easily read biography of the well-known basketball player who was a star before he graduated from high school. (Rev: BL 11/15/00)

CARTER, VINCE

15956 Carter, Vince, and Greg Brown. *Vince Carter: Choose Your Course* (3–6). Series: Athletes. 2004, Positively for Kids $15.95 (978-0-9634650-2-3). 48pp. A first-person account of Carter's life and career in basketball, with lots of details about his childhood, family life, and sporting successes. (Rev: BL 9/1/04)

15957 Thornley, Stew. *Super Sports Star Vince Carter* (2–5). Series: Super Sports Stars. 2002, Enslow LB $23.93 (978-0-7660-1805-1). The life of the Toronto Raptors guard-forward is told in an account that features simple text, large type, and many color photographs. (Rev: BL 9/1/02; HBG 10/02)

15958 Torres, John A. *Vince Carter: Slam Dunk Artist* (3–6). Illus. Series: Sports Leaders. 2004, Enslow LB $26.60 (978-0-7660-2173-0). 104pp. An accessible profile of the talented basketball player's life and career. [921]

COOPER, CYNTHIA

15959 Schnakenberg, Robert E. *Cynthia Cooper* (5–9). Series: Women Who Win. 2000, Chelsea $25.00 (978-0-7910-5796-4). 64pp. A biography of this basketball star that focuses on her career and game-related information. (Rev: HBG 3/01; SLJ 2/01; VOYA 4/01)

DUNCAN, TIM

15960 Adams, Sean. *Tim Duncan* (4–7). Series: Sports Heroes and Legends. 2004, Lerner LB $27.93 (978-0-8225-1793-1). A balanced, well-crafted life of the basketball star. (Rev: BL 9/1/04) [921]

15961 Stewart, Mark. *Tim Duncan: Tower of Power* (4–8). Series: Basketball's New Wave. 1999, Millbrook LB $22.90 (978-0-7613-1513-1). Although this biography of basketball's rising star is brief, the information is ample and important topics are all covered. (Rev: HBG 10/00; SLJ 7/00) [921]

GARNETT, KEVIN

15962 Stewart, Mark. *Kevin Garnett: Shake Up the Game* (4–7). Series: Sports New Wave. 2002, Millbrook LB $22.90 (978-0-7613-2615-1). A short biography that chronicles the career of the new star of the Minnesota Timberwolves. (Rev: BL 9/1/02; HBG 10/02) [921]

15963 Thornley, Stew. *Super Sports Star Kevin Garnett* (2–5). Series: Super Sports Stars. 2001, Enslow LB $23.93 (978-0-7660-1515-9). 48pp. Garnett, a small forward for the Minnesota Timberwolves, gets an interesting profile complete with game details and statistics plus plenty of action photographs. (Rev: BL 10/15/01; HBG 3/02)

HARDAWAY, PENNY

15964 Rappoport, Ken. *Super Sports Star Penny Hardaway* (2–5). Illus. Series: Super Sports Stars. 2001, Enslow LB $23.93 (978-0-7660-1516-6). 48pp. Photographs and statistics accompany text about the famous basketball player, from his childhood to his professional career. (Rev: BL 10/15/01; HBG 3/02)

HILL, GRANT

15965 Lowenstein, Felicia. *Grant Hill* (2–5). Series: Super Sports Stars. 2001, Enslow LB $23.93 (978-0-7660-1517-3). Simple sentences and many color photographs are used in this beginning biography of the Orlando Magic forward. (Rev: BL 4/1/02; HBG 10/02)

JAMES, LEBRON

15966 Gagne, Tammy. *LeBron James* (1–3). Illus. Series: Day by Day With. 2010, Mitchell Lane $25.70 (978-158415858-5). 32pp. The talents and positive qualities of the basketball star are presented here in this approachable, well-designed book. (Rev: BL 9/1/10) [921]

15967 Mattern, Joanne. *LeBron James* (2–5). Series: A Robbie Reader. 2004, Mitchell Lane LB $25.70 (978-1-58415-293-4). This photo-filled biography that presents information on James's childhood and career is especially suitable for reluctant readers. (Rev: BL 11/15/04)

15968 Sandler, Michael. *LeBron James: I Love Challenges!* (3–5). Series: Defining Moments: Super Athletes. 2009, Bearport LB $25.27 (978-1-59716-856-4). A look at key events in the life of the basketball player, with a timeline, facts, and engaging anecdotes. (Rev: SLJ 6/09)

JORDAN, MICHAEL

15969 Aaseng, Nathan. *Michael Jordan* (5–8). Series: Sports Greats. 1992, Enslow LB $17.95 (978-0-89490-370-0). Michael Jordan's life, his successes as guard of the Chicago Bulls, and his commercials for TV are discussed in this easily read book. (Rev: BL 10/15/92) [921]

15970 Berger, Phil, and John Rolfe. *Michael Jordan* (4–7). 1990, Little, Brown paper $4.95 (978-0-316-09229-6). This account covers Jordan's childhood and his career development. (Rev: BL 12/15/90; SLJ 4/91) [921]

15971 Cooper, Floyd. *Jump! From the Life of Michael Jordan* (K–3). 2004, Penguin $15.99 (978-0-399-24230-4). Eye-catching illustrations and conversational text reveal the successes and challenges of Jordan's childhood and adolescence. (Rev: BL 9/1/04)

KIDD, JASON

15972 Gray, Valerie A. *Jason Kidd: Star Guard* (5–8). Series: Sports Reports. 2000, Enslow LB $20.95 (978-0-7660-1333-9). The story of the basketball superstar with behind-the-scenes reporting on his life and career. (Rev: BL 10/15/00; HBG 10/00) [921]

15973 Rappoport, Ken. *Jason Kidd: Leader on the Court* (3–6). Illus. Series: Sports Leaders. 2004, Enslow LB $26.60 (978-0-7660-2214-0). 104pp. An accessible profile of the basketball star's life and career. [921]

15974 Thornley, Stew. *Super Sports Star Jason Kidd* (2–5). Series: Super Sports Stars. 2002, Enslow LB $23.93 (978-0-7660-1806-8). 48pp. Complete with game statistics and sports action, this is a simple, attractive biography of the star guard of the New Jersey Nets. (Rev: BL 9/1/02; HBG 10/02)

LESLIE, LISA

15975 Kelley, Brent. *Lisa Leslie* (5–9). Series: Women Who Win. 2000, Chelsea $25.00 (978-0-7910-5794-0). 64pp. This profile of a pioneer in the Women's National Basketball Association contains much game-related information. (Rev: HBG 3/01; SLJ 2/01)

LIEBERMAN-CLINE, NANCY

15976 Greenberg, Doreen, and Michael Greenberg. *A Drive to Win: The Story of Nancy Lieberman-Cline* (4–8). Illus. by Phil Velikan. Series: Anything You Can Do — New Sports Heroes for Girls. 2000, Wish paper $9.95 (978-1-930546-40-0). Based on personal interviews, this is an informative biography of the basketball star Lieberman-Cline. (Rev: SLJ 3/01; VOYA 2/01) [921]

MARBURY, STEPHON

15977 Plum-Ucci, Carol. *Super Sports Star Stephon Marbury* (2–5). Series: Super Sports Stars. 2002, Enslow LB $23.93 (978-0-7660-1810-5). 48pp. An exciting life story of Marbury, the black basketball player who has established a reputation as point guard for the Phoenix Suns. (Rev: BL 2/15/03; HBG 3/03)

MING, YAO

15978 Clark, Travis. *Yao Ming* (5–8). Series: Modern Role Models. 2008, Mason Crest LB $22.95 (978-1-4222-0484-9). 64pp. Yao Ming's great basketball career, his generous charitable works, and his influences are examined in this book, part of a high-interest biography se-

ries that includes a section with information on awards, events, and organizations. (Rev: SLJ 2/09) [921]

15979 Savage, Jeff. *Yao Ming* (2–4). Illus. Series: Amazing Athletes/LernerSports. 2005, Lerner LB $23.93 (978-0-8225-2432-8). 32pp. A well-illustrated introduction to the Chinese-born basketball player. [921]

15980 Young, Jeff C. *Yao Ming: Basketball's Big Man* (3–6). Illus. Series: Sports Leaders. 2005, Enslow LB $26.60 (978-0-7660-2422-9). 104pp. An accessible profile of the Chinese-born basketball player's life and career. [921]

MULLIN, CHRIS

15981 Morgan, Terri, and Shmuel Thaler. *Chris Mullin: Sure Shot* (4–8). Series: Sports Achievers. 1994, Lerner LB $10.13 (978-0-8225-2887-6). The story of this amazing basketball star who overcame many obstacles, including alcoholism. (Rev: BL 1/1/95; SLJ 1/95) [921]

NAISMITH, JAMES

15982 Wyckoff, Edwin Brit. *The Man Who Invented Basketball: James Naismith and His Amazing Game* (2–4). Illus. Series: Genius at Work! Great Inventor Biographies. 2007, Enslow LB $16.95 (978-0-7660-2846-3). 32pp. A compelling biography of the young Canadian who came up with the game of basketball in the late 19th century. (Rev: BL 9/1/07; LMC 11/07; SLJ 7/08)

O'NEAL, SHAQUILLE

15983 Sullivan, Michael J. *Shaquille O'Neal* (5–8). Series: Sports Greats. 1998, Enslow LB $22.60 (978-0-7660-1003-1). The life and career of this well-known basketball star are covered in this easily read biography containing career statistics and many illustrations. (Rev: BL 2/15/99; HBG 10/99) [921]

15984 Torres, John A. *Shaquille O'Neal: Gentle Giant* (3–6). Illus. Series: Sports Leaders. 2004, Enslow LB $26.60 (978-0-7660-2175-4). Report writers and basketball fans will appreciate this overview of Shaq's life and career. (Rev: BL 4/1/04)

PARKER, TONY

15985 MacRae, Sloan. *Meet Tony Parker: Basketball's Famous Point Guard* (3–5). Illus. 2009, PowerKids LB $23.95 (978-1-4358-2710-3). 32pp. A straightforward sports biography of the point guard for the San Antonio Spurs. (Rev: BL 6/1–15/09)

PAYTON, GARY

15986 Mandell, Judith. *Super Sports Star Gary Payton* (2–5). Series: Super Sports Stars. 2001, Enslow LB $23.93 (978-0-7660-1519-7). 48pp. With large type and colorful photographs, this is an easily read biography of the black point guard of the Los Angeles Lakers. (Rev: BL 10/15/01; HBG 3/02)

RICE, GLEN

15987 Rappoport, Ken. *Super Sports Star Glen Rice* (2–5). Series: Super Sports Stars. 2002, Enslow LB $23.93 (978-0-7660-1808-2). 48pp. Large type, colorful photographs, and an appealing format highlight this simple biography of the Houston Rockets star. (Rev: BL 9/1/02; HBG 10/02)

ROSE, DERRICK

15988 Sandler, Michael. *Derrick Rose* (3–5). Illus. Series: Basketball Heroes Making a Difference. 2012, Bearport LB $23.93 (978-161772439-8). 24pp. This positive biography focuses on the charity work of basketball great Derrick Rose. (Rev: BL 4/1/12) [921]

SPREWELL, LATRELL

15989 Pellowski, Michael J. *Super Sports Star Latrell Sprewell* (2–5). Series: Super Sports Stars. 2002, Enslow LB $23.93 (978-0-7660-1811-2). 48pp. With color photographs on each page plus a simple text, this is an exciting biography of the NBA star who plays guard and forward for the New York Knicks. (Rev: BL 9/1/02; HBG 3/03)

STILES, JACKIE

15990 Stewart, Mark. *Jackie Stiles: Gym Dandy* (4–7). Illus. Series: Sports New Wave. 2002, Millbrook LB $22.90 (978-0-7613-2614-4). 48pp. A biography of the WNBA star, with information on her childhood and family, statistics, color photographs, and general material on the game itself. (Rev: BL 9/1/02; HBG 3/03)

STOUDEMIRE, AMAR'E

15991 Sandler, Michael. *Amar'e Stoudemire* (3–5). Illus. Series: Basketball Heroes Making a Difference. 2012, Bearport LB $23.93 (978-161772442-8). 24pp. This profile of the NBA All-Star focuses on his career on the court and his work off the court, helping the needy in both the United States and Africa. (Rev: BL 9/1/12) [921]

SWOOPES, SHERYL

15992 Schweitzer, Karen. *Sheryl Swoopes* (5–8). Series: Modern Role Models. 2008, Mason Crest LB $22.95 (978-1-4222-0491-7). 64pp. Swoopes's decision to reveal that she is gay and expose her financial problems are discussed impartially in this high-interest biography that also includes a section with information on awards, events, and organizations. (Rev: SLJ 2/09)

WADE, DWYANE

15993 DiPrimio, Pete. *Dwyane Wade* (2–4). Illus. Series: Robbie Reader Contemporary Biographies. 2011, Mitchell Lane LB $25.70 (978-161228063-9). 32pp. With career statistics and a chronology, this is a profile of the Miami Heat player who grew up in a tough neighborhood of Chicago. (Rev: BL 12/1/11) [921]

WEBBER, CHRIS

15994 Thornley, Stew. *Chris Webber* (2–5). Series: Super Sports Stars. 2002, Enslow LB $23.93 (978-0-7660-1807-5). A simple biography with many action photographs of Webber, the NBA power forward of the Sacramento Kings. (Rev: BL 4/1/02; HBG 10/02)

WEST, JERRY

15995 Ramen, Fred. *Jerry West* (5–8). Series: Basketball Hall of Famers. 2002, Rosen LB $29.25 (978-0-8239-3482-9). Facts, stories, and full-color photographs are used to bring alive the story of this basketball great, with material on his NBA career and beyond. (Rev: BL 9/1/02) [921]

Boxing

ALI, MUHAMMAD

15996 Bolden, Tonya. *The Champ: The Story of Muhammad Ali* (2–5). Illus. by R. Gregory Christie. 2004, Knopf LB $19.99 (978-0-375-92401-9). 40pp. This engaging biography shows Ali as child, fighter, activist, and poet. (Rev: BL 11/15/04; SLJ 1/05*)

15997 Feinstein, Stephen. *Muhammad Ali* (1–4). 2007, Enslow LB $21.26 (978-0-7660-2763-3). 24pp. A basic and straightforward look at the life of the famous fighter, with photographs. (Rev: SLJ 8/07)

15998 Garrett, Leslie. *The Story of Muhammad Ali* (2–4). Illus. 2002, DK $12.99 (978-0-7894-8516-8); paper $3.99 (978-0-7894-8517-5). 48pp. A chapter-book biography of Muhammad Ali, from childhood to his battle with Parkinson's disease. (Rev: BL 3/1/02; HBG 10/02; SLJ 4/02)

15999 Myers, Walter Dean. *Muhammad Ali: The People's Champion* (1–3). Illus. by Alix Delinois. 2010, Collins $16.99 (978-0-06-029131-0); LB $17.89 (978-0-06-029132-7). 40pp. With quotations and a brisk pace, this is a simple picture-book biography of the prize fighter. (Rev: BL 11/1/09; SLJ 2/1/10) [921]

16000 Smith, Charles R. *Twelve Rounds to Glory: The Story of Muhammad Ali* (5–8). Illus. by Bryan Collier. 2007, Candlewick $19.99 (978-0-7636-1692-2). 80pp. Twelve poems and dynamic mixed-media pictures illustrate the drama of Ali's victories and his life's struggles. Coretta Scott King Author Honor Book, 2008. (Rev: BL 2/1/08; SLJ 12/07)

16001 Timblin, Stephen. *Muhammad Ali: King of the Ring* (5–8). Series: Sterling Biographies. 2010, Sterling $12.95 (978-1-4027-7152-1). 128pp. Details of Ali's life and personality are placed in historical context and enhanced by an appealing layout, plentiful images, and first-person accounts. (Rev: BL 5/1/10; LMC 8–9/10) [921]

16002 Winter, Jonah. *Muhammad Ali: Champion of the World* (3–6). Illus. by François Roca. 2008, Random

$16.99 (978-0-375-83622-0). 32pp. This picture-book biography emphasizes how Ali brought a new spirit to boxing and to sportsmanship. (Rev: BL 2/1/08; SLJ 1/08)

JOHNSON, JACK

16003 Smith, Charles R. *Black Jack: The Ballad of Jack Johnson* (1–3). Illus. by Shane W. Evans. 2010, Roaring Brook $16.99 (978-1-59643-473-8). 40pp. Tells the story of the first African American heavyweight boxing champion, who faced racial prejudice in the early 20th century. (Rev: BL 4/1/10*; LMC 8–9/10; SLJ 7/1/10) [921]

LOUIS, JOE

16004 Adler, David A. *Joe Louis: America's Fighter* (2–6). Illus. by Terry Widener. 2005, Harcourt $16.00 (978-0-15-216489-8). 32pp. This picture-book biography looks at the obstacles the boxer had to overcome to become a world champion. (Rev: BCCB 12/05; BL 9/1/05; HB 1/06; HBG 4/06; LMC 3/06)

16005 De La Peña, Matt. *A Nation's Hope: The Story of Boxing Legend Joe Louis* (1–3). Illus. by Kadir Nelson. 2011, Dial $17.99 (978-0-8037-3167-7). 40pp. Joe Louis's epic fight against German Max Schmeling at Yankee Stadium in 1938 is portrayed in dramatic text and effective illustrations. (Rev: BL 2/1/11*; HB 1–2/11; LMC 5–6/11; SLJ 2/1/11*)

Figure Skating

BOITANO, BRIAN

16006 Boitano, Brian, and Suzanne Harper. *Boitano's Edge: Inside the Real World of Figure Skating* (4–8). 1997, Simon & Schuster $25.00 (978-0-689-81915-5). In this autobiography, Boitano tells about his life, the 1988 Olympics, his training programs, touring, and preparing for competitions. (Rev: BCCB 3/98; BL 2/15/98; SLJ 4/98; VOYA 4/98) [921]

HUGHES, SARAH

16007 Krawiec, Richard. *Sudden Champion: The Sarah Hughes Story* (4–6). Series: Avisson Young Adult. 2002, Avisson paper $19.95 (978-1-888105-53-7). 100pp. A profile of Sarah Hughes, the figure skater who won the gold medal at the 2002 Winter Olympics in Salt Lake City. (Rev: SLJ 4/03)

KWAN, MICHELLE

16008 Stewart, Mark, and Mike Kennedy. *Michelle Kwan: Quest for Gold* (4–6). Illus. 2002, Millbrook LB $24.90 (978-0-7613-2622-9). 64pp. A chronological biography of Chinese American figure skater Michelle Kwan with color photographs. (Rev: BL 3/1/02; HBG 10/02)

Football

BARBER, RONDE AND TIKI

16009 Barber, Tiki, and Paul Mantell. *Kickoff!* (4–6). 2007, Simon & Schuster $15.99 (978-1-4169-3618-3). 156pp. The Barbers reveal much about their lives in junior high and their efforts to make the football team. (Rev: BL 9/1/07; SLJ 12/07)

16010 Barber, Tiki, and Ronde Barber. *By My Brother's Side* (1–3). Illus. by Barry Root. 2004, Simon & Schuster $16.95 (978-0-689-86559-6). 32pp. The NFL player twins describe their energetic youth. (Rev: BL 9/1/04; SLJ 11/05)

16011 Barber, Tiki, and Ronde Barber. *Game Day* (1–3). Illus. by Barry Root. 2005, Simon & Schuster $16.95 (978-1-4169-0093-1). The NFL's Barber twins tell a simple story about their football-playing youth and the rivalry between them. (Rev: BL 9/1/05; SLJ 1/06)

16012 Barber, Tiki, and Ronde Barber. *Teammates* (1–3). Illus. by Barry Root. 2006, Simon & Schuster $16.95 (978-1-4169-2489-0). 32pp. Downcast after their football team loses a game, twin brothers Tiki and Ronde begin a morning practice routine designed to improve Tiki's ball-handling abilities; a large-format picture book illustrated with watercolor-and-gouache paintings. (Rev: BL 9/1/06; SLJ 11/06)

BETTIS, JEROME

16013 Majewski, Stephen. *Jerome Bettis* (5–8). Series: Sports Greats. 1997, Enslow LB $17.95 (978-0-89490-872-9). The great football hero Jerome Bettis and his amazing career are highlighted in this easily read biography. (Rev: BL 2/15/97; VOYA 6/97) [921]

BRADY, TOM

16014 Gatto, Kimberly. *Tom Brady: Never-Quit Quarterback* (3–6). Illus. Series: Sports Leaders. 2005, Enslow LB $26.60 (978-0-7660-2475-5). 104pp. An accessible profile of the quarterback's life and career. [921]

16015 Stewart, Mark. *Tom Brady: Heart of the Huddle* (4–7). Series: Sports New Wave. 2003, Millbrook LB $22.90 (978-0-7613-2907-7). 48pp. The story of the popular young football player who is quarterback for the New England Patriots. (Rev: BL 6/1–15/03; HBG 10/03)

CULPEPPER, DAUNTE

16016 Stewart, Mark. *Daunte Culpepper: Command and Control* (4–7). Series: Sports New Wave. 2002, Millbrook LB $22.90 (978-0-7613-2613-7). This brief biography celebrates the career of the young African American footballer and his achievements as quarterback of the Minnesota Vikings. (Rev: BL 9/1/02; HBG 10/02) [921]

16017 Thornley, Stew. *Super Sports Star Daunte Culpepper* (2–5). Series: Super Sports Stars. 2002, Enslow LB

$23.93 (978-0-7660-2051-1). The life of Culpepper, the black quarterback of the Minnesota Vikings, is excitingly re-created with colorful photographs and interesting game statistics. (Rev: BL 2/15/03; HBG 10/03)

DAVIS, TERRELL

16018 Stewart, Mark. *Terrell Davis: Toughing It Out* (4–8). Series: Football's New Wave. 1999, Millbrook LB $22.90 (978-0-7613-1514-8). A brief biography of this football hero that uses color photographs and many fact boxes. (Rev: HBG 10/00; SLJ 7/00) [921]

FAVRE, BRETT

16019 Thornley, Stew. *Super Sports Star Brett Favre* (2–5). Series: Super Sports Stars. 2002, Enslow LB $23.93 (978-0-7660-2048-1). Using colorful photographs and exciting game details, this is the story of Brett Favre, quarterback of the Green Bay Packers. (Rev: BL 2/15/03; HBG 10/03)

FITZGERALD, LARRY

16020 Sandler, Michael. *Larry Fitzgerald* (2–4). Illus. Series: Football Heroes Making a Difference. 2010, Bearport $22.61 (978-193608758-7). 24pp. Sandler describes the life and achievements of the Arizona Cardinals star along with his efforts to give back to the community. (Rev: BL 9/1/10) [921]

GONZALEZ, TONY

16021 Gonzales, Tony, and Greg Brown. *Tony Gonzalez: Catch and Connect* (3–6). Illus. Series: Athletes. 2004, Positively for Kids $15.95 (978-0-9634650-8-5). 48pp. A lively and attractively designed first-person account of Gonzalez's life and career in football, with lots of personal details about her childhood, family life, and sporting successes. [921]

16022 Sandler, Michael. *Tony Gonzalez* (2–4). Illus. Series: Football Heroes Making a Difference. 2010, Bearport LB $22.61 (978-193608761-7). 24pp. Sandler describes the life and achievements of the record-setting NFL star along with his foundation's efforts to help sick children. (Rev: BL 9/1/10) [921]

JACKSON, BO

16023 Devaney, John. *Bo Jackson: A Star for All Seasons* (5–7). 1992, Walker LB $15.85 (978-0-8027-8179-6). Biography of the Kansas City Royals baseball star, who also played pro football for the Los Angeles Raiders. (Rev: BL 2/15/89; SLJ 1/89) [921]

JOHNSON, BRAD

16024 Johnson, Brad, and Greg Brown. *Brad Johnson: Play with Passion* (3–6). Illus. Series: Athletes. 2004, Positively for Kids $15.95 (978-0-9634650-4-7). 48pp. A lively and attractively designed first-person account of Johnson's life and career in football, with lots of personal details about her childhood, family life, and sporting successes. [921]

JOHNSON, CHRIS

16025 Orr, Tamra. *Chris Johnson* (2–4). Illus. Series: Robbie Reader Contemporary Biographies. 2011, Mitchell Lane LB $25.70 (978-161228064-6). 32pp. This profile of the running back for the Tennessee Titans starts off with a career highlight that draws readers in. (Rev: BL 12/1/11) [921]

LOMBARDI, VINCE

16026 Roensch, Greg. *Vince Lombardi* (4–7). Series: Football Hall of Famers. 2003, Rosen LB $29.25 (978-0-8239-3610-6). 112pp. A lively, detailed, and inspiring biography of the legendary coach for whom the Super Bowl trophy is named. (Rev: SLJ 4/03)

MANNING, PEYTON

16027 Sandler, Michael. *Peyton Manning* (2–4). Illus. Series: Football Heroes Making a Difference. 2011, Bearport LB $22.61 (978-161772311-7). 24pp. Discusses significant moments in the football career of quarterback Peyton Manning and examines his charity work, including his role in beginning the PeyBack Foundation. (Rev: BL 11/1/11) [921]

16028 Stewart, Mark. *Peyton Manning: Rising Son* (4–8). Series: Football's New Wave. 2000, Millbrook LB $22.90 (978-0-7613-1517-9). 48pp. An easily read account of the professional football player's life and family, including a father who also played in the NFL. (Rev: HBG 10/00; SLJ 1/01)

16029 Wilner, Barry. *Peyton Manning: A Football Star Who Cares* (3–6). Illus. Series: Superstar Athletes. 2011, Enslow $23.93 (978-076603774-8). 48pp. This profile celebrates Manning's humanitarian causes while also providing plenty of football fodder. (Rev: BL 9/1/11) [921]

MCNABB, DONOVAN

16030 Mattern, Joanne. *Donovan McNabb: Football Star* (2–4). Illus. Series: Robbie Reader. 2004, Mitchell Lane LB $25.70 (978-1-58415-294-1). This photo-filled biography traces the life and career of Donovan McNabb and is especially suitable for reluctant readers. [921]

MOSS, RANDY

16031 Stewart, Mark. *Randy Moss: First in Flight* (4–8). Series: Football's New Wave. 2000, Millbrook LB $22.90 (978-0-7613-1518-6). The story of the footballer who came from a poor, segregated West Virginia town, was arrested as a young man, but went on to attend college and play professional football. (Rev: HBG 10/00; SLJ 1/01) [921]

16032 Thornley, Stew. *Super Sports Star Randy Moss* (2–5). Series: Super Sports Stars. 2002, Enslow LB $23.93 (978-0-7660-2049-8). 48pp. An easily read biography of the black wide receiver of the Minnesota Vikings. (Rev: BL 2/15/03; HBG 10/03)

PETERSON, ADRIAN

16033 Sandler, Michael. *Adrian Peterson* (2–4). Illus. Series: Football Heroes Making a Difference. 2010, Bearport LB $22.61 (978-1-936087-59-4). 24pp. Sandler describes the life and achievements of the Minnesota Vikings star along with his efforts to give back to the community. (Rev: BL 9/1/10; SLJ 6/1/10) [921]

POLAMALU, TROY

16034 Sandler, Michael. *Troy Polamalu* (2–4). Illus. Series: Football Heroes Making a Difference. 2011, Bearport LB $22.61 (978-161772312-4). 24pp. Looks at the life and career of the football player and at his work with mentally disabled children. (Rev: BL 11/1/11) [921]

RICE, JERRY

16035 Dickey, Glenn. *Jerry Rice* (5–8). Series: Sports Greats. 1993, Enslow LB $17.95 (978-0-89490-419-6). A brief biography of the star football player who gained fame with the San Francisco 49ers. (Rev: BL 9/15/93) [921]

ROMO, TONY

16036 Sandler, Michael. *Tony Romo* (2–4). Illus. Series: Football Heroes Making a Difference. 2010, Bearport $22.61 (978-1-936087-60-0). 24pp. Sandler describes the life and achievements of the Dallas Cowboys star along with his efforts to give back to the community. (Rev: BL 9/1/10; SLJ 6/1/10) [921]

SANCHEZ, MARK

16037 Sandler, Michael. *Mark Sanchez* (2–4). Illus. Series: Football Heroes Making a Difference. 2011, Bearport LB $22.61 (978-161772310-0). 24pp. Looks at the life and career of the football player and at his work with inner-city and diabetic children. (Rev: BL 11/1/11) [921]

SANDERS, BARRY

16038 Knapp, Ron. *Barry Sanders* (5–8). Series: Sports Greats. 1993, Enslow LB $17.95 (978-0-89490-418-9). This brief biography of the star football player contains many action photographs and a separate section on his career statistics. (Rev: BL 9/15/93) [921]

TARKENTON, FRAN

16039 Hulm, David. *Fran Tarkenton* (4–7). Series: Football Hall of Famers. 2003, Rosen LB $29.25 (978-0-8239-3608-3). 112pp. A lively, detailed, and inspiring biography of the star of the Minnesota Vikings and the New York Giants who went on to become a successful businessman. (Rev: SLJ 4/03; VOYA 4/03)

Tennis

AGASSI, ANDRE

16040 Savage, Jeff. *Andre Agassi: Reaching the Top — Again* (4–8). Series: Sports Achievers. 1997, Lerner paper $9.55 (978-0-8225-9750-6). A short, easily read biography of this volatile tennis star. (Rev: BL 1/1–15/98; HBG 3/98) [921]

ASHE, ARTHUR

16041 Cunningham, Kevin. *Arthur Ashe: Athlete and Activist* (5–8). Series: Journey to Freedom: The African American Library. 2005, Child's World LB $28.50 (978-1-59296-228-0). Chronicles the Virginia-born athlete's rise to tennis stardom and his involvement in the fight against apartheid. (Rev: BL 2/1/05) [921]

16042 Hubbard, Crystal. *Game Set Match Champion Arthur Ashe* (4–7). Illus. by Kevin Belford. 2010, Lee & Low $19.95 (978-1-60060-366-2). 48pp. The African American tennis champion's early challenges, successes on the court, and social activism are documented in this picture-book biography. (Rev: BL 10/15/10; LMC 3–4/11; SLJ 3/1/11) [921]

16043 Lazo, Caroline Evensen. *Arthur Ashe* (4–7). Series: A&E Biography. 1999, Lerner $25.26 (978-0-8225-1932-4). The inspiring story of this great African American tennis star and humanitarian is told in a clear, well-organized text with several black-and-white photographs. (Rev: BL 3/15/00) [921]

16044 Mantell, Paul. *Arthur Ashe: Young Tennis Champion* (3–5). Illus. by Meryl Henderson. Series: Childhood of Famous Americans. 2006, Simon & Schuster paper $5.99 (978-0-689-87346-1). Ashe's childhood encounters with prejudice and his success on the tennis court are recounted in this fictionalized biography that is faithful to real events. (Rev: BL 2/1/06)

GIBSON, ALTHEA

16045 Deans, Karen. *Playing to Win: The Story of Althea Gibson* (1–4). Illus. by Elbrite Brown. 2007, Holiday $16.95 (978-0-8234-1926-5). 32pp. A picture-book biography of the tennis star, emphasizing the barriers she had to overcome. (Rev: BL 9/1/07; SLJ 9/07)

16046 Stauffacher, Sue. *Nothing But Trouble: The Story of Althea Gibson* (K–3). Illus. by Greg Couch. 2007, Knopf $16.99 (978-0-375-83408-0). 40pp. The story of how a "nothing but trouble" Harlem girl went on to become a world tennis star. (Rev: BL 2/1/08; HB 11/07; LMC 11/07; SLJ 9/07)

WILLIAMS, VENUS

16047 Sandler, Michael. *Tennis: Victory for Venus Williams* (3–5). Series: Upsets and Comebacks. 2006, Bearport LB $25.27 (978-1-59716-170-1). Venus Williams's determination to keep winning despite physical and emotional challenges is underlined here. (Rev: SLJ 7/06)

873

WILLIAMS, VENUS AND SERENA

16048 Bailey, Diane. *Venus and Serena Williams: Tennis Champions* (5–8). Illus. Series: Sports Families. 2010, Rosen LB $26.50 (978-143583552-8). 48pp. Bailey tells the story of the sisters' childhood in California and their famous rivalry on the courts. (Rev: BL 9/1/10) [921]

16049 Brown, Jonatha A. *Venus and Serena Williams* (2–4). Illus. Series: People We Should Know. 2005, Gareth Stevens LB $14.50 (978-0-86384-470-6). 24pp. For beginning readers, a simple account of the Williams sisters' triumphs with an attractive layout and many photographs. [921]

16050 Stewart, Mark. *Venus and Serena Williams: Sisters in Arms* (4–7). Series: Tennis's New Wave. 2000, Millbrook LB $22.90 (978-0-7613-1803-3). 48pp. A simple biography of the amazing tennis-playing sisters with good coverage of their early lives. (Rev: HBG 3/01; SLJ 3/01)

16051 Stout, Glenn. *On the Court with . . . Venus and Serena Williams* (4–6). Illus. Series: Matt Christopher Sports Bio Bookshelf. 2002, Little, Brown paper $4.95 (978-0-316-13814-7). 128pp. A biography of the tennis greats, with information on their childhoods and family (and the influential role of their father) and details of important matches. (Rev: BL 9/1/02)

Track and Field

COACHMAN, ALICE

16052 Malaspina, Ann. *Touch the Sky: Alice Coachman, Olympic High Jumper* (2–4). Illus. by Eric Velasquez. 2012, Whitman $16.99 (978-0-8075-8035-6). 32pp. First female African American Olympic gold medalist Alice Coachman's struggle from poverty and hardship to stardom is chronicled in this inspiring biography. (Rev: BL 2/1/12; LMC 8–9/12; SLJ 4/1/12) [921]

JONES, MARION

16053 Rutledge, Rachel. *Marion Jones: Fast and Fearless* (4–7). 2000, Millbrook LB $22.90 (978-0-7613-1870-5). 48pp. A biography of the track-and-field star of the 2000 Sydney Olympics that stresses her drive and tenacity. (Rev: HBG 3/01; SLJ 3/01)

LEWIS, RAY

16054 Cooper, John. *Rapid Ray: The Story of Ray Lewis* (5–9). 2002, Tundra paper $8.95 (978-0-88776-612-1). An absorbing profile of the Canadian-born black athlete (and train porter) who won a bronze medal in the 1932 Olympics and the racial hurdles he had to overcome. (Rev: SLJ 6/03) [796.42]

OWENS, JESSE

16055 Gigliotti, Jim. *Jesse Owens: Gold Medal Hero* (5–8). Series: Sterling Biographies. 2010, Sterling $12.95

(978-1-4027-7149-1). 128pp. Details of Owens's life and personality are placed in historical context and enhanced by an appealing layout, plentiful images, and first-person accounts. Lexile 1040L (Rev: LMC 8–9/10) [921]

16056 Israel, Elaine. *Jesse Owens: Running into History* (2–5). Illus. Series: Time for Kids Biographies. 2008, HarperCollins LB $15.99 (978-0-06-057621-9); paper $3.99 (978-0-06-057620-2). 48pp. Follows this runner's life story from Alabama sharecropper family to Olympic champion and later life. (Rev: BLO 3/3/08)

16057 McKissack, Patricia C., and Fredrick McKissack. *Jesse Owens: Olympic Star. Rev. ed.* (2–5). Series: Great African Americans. 2001, Enslow LB $18.60 (978-0-7660-1681-1). This is an updated version of the 1992 book about the African American athlete whose four medals in the 1936 Olympics displeased Hitler, with factual updates, improved illustrations, and lists of print and Internet resources. (Rev: HBG 10/01; SLJ 8/01)

16058 Sutcliffe, Jane. *Jesse Owens* (2–3). Series: On My Own. 2000, Carolrhoda LB $23.93 (978-1-57505-451-3); paper $5.95 (978-1-57505-487-2). 48pp. A simple biography of the athlete who overcame sickness, poverty, and discrimination to become a gold medal winner in Berlin in 1936. (Rev: BL 8/00; HBG 10/01)

RUDOLPH, WILMA

16059 Braun, Eric. *Wilma Rudolph* (K–2). Series: First Biographies. 2005, Capstone LB $17.26 (978-0-7368-4234-1). With its simple sentences and clear black-and-white photographs, this profile of the first African American woman to win three gold medals at a single Olympic Games gives basic, introductory information. (Rev: SLJ 2/06)

16060 Harper, Jo. *Wilma Rudolph: Olympic Runner* (3–6). Illus. by Meryl Henderson. Series: Childhood of Famous Americans. 2004, Simon & Schuster paper $4.99 (978-0-689-85873-4). A moving, fictionalized account of Rudolph's triumph over polio, prejudice, and poverty. (Rev: BL 5/15/04)

16061 Ruth, Amy. *Wilma Rudolph* (4–6). Series: A&E Biography. 2000, Lerner LB $27.93 (978-0-8225-4976-5). 112pp. The inspiring story of the African American athlete who overcame polio and won three gold medals in Olympic track-and-field events in 1960. (Rev: BL 6/1–15/00; HBG 10/00)

16062 Sherrow, Victoria. *Wilma Rudolph* (2–3). Illus. by Larry Johnson. Series: On My Own Biography. 2000, Lerner LB $23.93 (978-1-57505-246-5); paper $5.95 (978-1-57505-442-1). The story of how a young girl whose legs were thin and crooked from polio grew up to win Olympic gold medals for running is told with simplicity and dignity. (Rev: BL 2/15/00; HBG 10/00; SLJ 2/00)

THORPE, JIM

16063 Brown, Don. *Bright Path: Young Jim Thorpe* (K–3). Illus. by author. 2006, Roaring Brook $17.95

(978-1-59643-041-9). 40pp. The importance of athletics in Thorpe's unhappy childhood is emphasized in this nicely illustrated biography. (Rev: SLJ 11/06)

16064 Bruchac, Joseph. *Jim Thorpe: Original All-American* (5–8). 2006, Dial $16.99 (978-0-8037-3118-9). 208pp. Using the first person, this biography chronicles the Native American's youth, his amazing sporting abilities, and his quiet determination to overcome barriers. (Rev: BL 6/1–15/06; SLJ 8/06)

16065 Bruchac, Joseph. *Jim Thorpe's Bright Path* (2–3). Trans. and illus. by S. D. Nelson. 2004, Lee & Low $17.95 (978-1-58430-166-0). 40pp. This inspiring profile of Jim Thorpe focuses on the future Olympic champion's childhood, tracing his life from birth in a log cabin to the start of his scholastic football career at Carlisle Indian School in Pennsylvania. (Rev: BL 8/04; SLJ 6/04)

16066 Labrecque, Ellen. *Jim Thorpe: An Athlete for the Ages* (5–8). Series: Sterling Biographies. 2010, Sterling $12.95 (978-1-4027-7150-7). 128pp. Details of Thorpe's life and personality are placed in historical context and enhanced by an appealing layout, plentiful images, and first-person accounts. (Rev: BL 5/1/10; LMC 8–9/10) [921]

16067 Schuman, Michael A. *Jim Thorpe: "There's No Such Thing as 'Can't'"* (5–8). Series: Americans — The Spirit of a Nation. 2009, Enslow LB $31.93 (978-0-7660-3021-3). 128pp. A dramatic introduction draws readers into this informative and accessible account of Thorpe's life and achievements. (Rev: LMC 11–12/09; SLJ 9/09) [921]

Miscellaneous Sports

ADU, FREDDY

16068 Murcia, Rebecca Thatcher. *Freddy Adu: Young Soccer Superstar* (3–5). Illus. Series: A Robbie Reader. 2005, Mitchell Lane $25.70 (978-1-58415-385-6). 32pp. A brief, photo-filled biography of the young Ghanaian-born soccer phenomenon. (Rev: BL 10/15/05; SLJ 10/05)

ANDERSON, TILLIE

16069 Stauffacher, Sue. *Tillie the Terrible Swede: How One Woman, a Sewing Needle, and a Bicycle Changed History* (K–3). Illus. by Sarah McMenemy. 2011, Knopf $17.99 (978-0-375-84442-3); LB $20.99 (978-0-375-94442-0). 40pp. Tells the story of a Swedish American woman who defied gender barriers and became a famous bicycle racer, even wearing a scandalous pants outfit. Lexile 760L (Rev: BL 2/1/11; HB 3–4/11; LMC 10/11; SLJ 2/1/11) [921]

ARMSTRONG, LANCE

16070 Armstrong, Kristin. *Lance Armstrong: The Race of His Life* (2–3). Illus. Series: All Aboard Reading. 2000,

Penguin paper $3.99 (978-0-448-42407-1). A book for beginning readers that tells about this famous cyclist, his many triumphs, and his battle with cancer — written by his wife. (Rev: BL 12/1/00; HBG 3/01)

16071 Benson, Michael. *Lance Armstrong: Cyclist* (5–8). Series: Ferguson Career Biographies. 2003, Ferguson LB $25.00 (978-0-8160-5479-4). Traces the inspiring life of the great bicycle-racer through his fifth Tour de France win, with an emphasis on his perseverance and optimism. (Rev: SLJ 5/04) [796.6]

16072 Donovan, Sandy. *Lance Armstrong* (2–4). Illus. Series: Amazing Athletes. 2005, Lerner LB $23.93 (978-0-8225-3691-8). 32pp. Armstrong's cycling career is the focus of this easy-reading biography that also touches on his childhood. (Rev: BL 2/15/05; SLJ 3/05)

16073 Garcia, Kimberly. *Lance Armstrong* (3–4). Series: Real-Life Reader Biographies. 2002, Mitchell Lane LB $15.95 (978-1-58415-125-8). 32pp. Using a conversational style and black-and-white photographs, this is a biography of the Tour de France-winning cyclist who overcame cancer. (Rev: BL 9/15/02; SLJ 12/02)

ATLAS, CHARLES

16074 McCarthy, Meghan. *Strong Man: The Story of Charles Atlas* (1–3). Illus. by author. 2007, Knopf $15.99 (978-0-375-82940-6). 40pp. This biography of the legendary fitness pioneer is entertaining and well-illustrated; the author is careful to stick with known facts about the subject's often-embellished life. (Rev: BCCB 7–8/07; BL 6/1–15/07; HB 9/07; SLJ 7/07)

BASS, TOM

16075 Wilkerson, J. L. *From Slave to World-Class Horseman: Tom Bass* (4–8). 2000, Acorn paper $9.95 (978-0-9664470-3-3). A fast-paced narrative about the man who was born a slave and later became such a renowned horseman that he performed for Queen Victoria. (Rev: SLJ 4/00) [921]

BECKHAM, DAVID

16076 Savage, Jeff. *David Beckham* (3–5). Illus. Series: Amazing Athletes. 2008, Lerner LB $23.93 (978-0-8225-8834-4); paper $6.95 (978-0-8225-8975-4). A brief overview of the life of the British soccer star who came to the United States to play for Los Angeles Galaxy. (Rev: BL 6/1–15/08)

CENA, JOHN

16077 Sandler, Michael. *John Cena* (4–7). Illus. Series: Wrestling's Tough Guys. 2012, Bearport LB $23.93 (978-161772573-9). 24pp. Sandler tells the story of the bullied youngster who grew up to be a wrestling champ. (Rev: BL 10/1/12) [921]

DAWES, DOMINIQUE

16078 Washburn, Kim. *Heart of a Champion: The Dominique Dawes Story* (5–8). Series: Zonderkidz Biography. 2012, Zonderkidz paper $6.99 (978-0-310-72268-7).

128pp. A profile of the African American Olympic gymnast, emphasizing her ability to bounce back from disappointments, her religious faith, and her later career as a spokesperson. (Rev: BL 6/12; SLJ 8/1/12) [921]

EDERLE, GERTRUDE

16079 Adler, David A. *America's Champion Swimmer: Gertrude Ederle* (2–4). Illus. by Terry Widener. 2000, Harcourt $16.00 (978-0-15-201969-3). 32pp. A simple biography of the amazing athlete who was the first woman to swim across the English Channel. (Rev: BCCB 4/00; BL 3/15/00*; HB 5/00; HBG 10/00; SLJ 6/00)

HAMILTON, BETHANY

16080 Sandler, Michael. *Bethany Hamilton: Follow Your Dreams!* (3–6). Series: Defining Moments, Overcoming Challenges. 2006, Bearport LB $25.27 (978-1-59716-270-8). 32pp. Surfer Bethany Hamilton lost her left arm in a shark attack when she was only 13; she was back on her surfboard only weeks after the attack and has since worked to raise funds for victims of disasters. (Rev: SLJ 1/07)

HAMM, MIA

16081 Rutledge, Rachel. *Mia Hamm: Striking Superstar* (3–6). Series: Soccer's New Wave. 2000, Millbrook LB $22.90 (978-0-7613-1802-6). 48pp. A fully rounded biography of the soccer star who was a member of the 1991 and 1999 Gold Medal World Cup Soccer teams. (Rev: HBG 10/00; SLJ 7/00)

16082 Zarzycki, Daryl. *Mia Hamm* (2–5). Series: Robbie Reader. 2004, Mitchell Lane LB $25.70 (978-1-58415-286-6). 32pp. This photo-filled biography that presents information on Hamm's childhood and career is especially suitable for reluctant readers. (Rev: BL 11/15/04)

KAHANAMOKU, DUKE

16083 Crowe, Ellie. *Surfer of the Century: The Life of Duke Kahanamoku* (4–7). Illus. by Richard Waldrep. 2007, Lee & Low $18.95 (978-1-58430-276-6). 48pp. A wonderfully illustrated picture-book biography of Duke Kahanamoku, an Olympic Gold Medal swimmer and well-known surfer from Hawaii who was born in 1890. (Rev: BL 9/1/07; SLJ 10/07)

KELLERMAN, ANNETTE

16084 Corey, Shana. *Mermaid Queen: The Spectacular True Story of Annette Kellerman, Who Swam Her Way to Fame, Fortune, and Swimsuit History* (3–6). Illus. by Edwin Fotheringham. 2009, Scholastic $17.99 (978-0-439-69835-1). The title tells the story of this splashy biography. (Rev: BL 6/1–15/09; SLJ 3/09)

LEE, SAMMY

16085 Yoo, Paula. *Sixteen Years in Sixteen Seconds: The Sammy Lee Story* (2–4). Illus. by Dom Lee. 2005, Lee & Low $16.95 (978-1-58430-247-6). 32pp. All about the Korean American Olympic diver, who in 1948 defied prejudice and family expectations to become the first

Asian American to win a gold medal. (Rev: BL 3/15/05; SLJ 4/05)

LEMIEUX, MARIO

16086 Rossiter, Sean. *Mario Lemieux* (4–8). Illus. Series: Hockey Heroes. 2001, Sterling $12.95 (978-1-55054-870-9). 64pp. A detailed look at the career of Pittsburgh Penguin Mario Lemieux. (Rev: BL 2/15/02)

16087 Stewart, Mark. *Mario Lemieux: Own the Ice* (5–8). 2002, Millbrook LB $24.90 (978-0-7613-2555-0); paper $8.95 (978-0-7613-1687-9). A readable biography of the ice hockey star, with photographs, statistics, and information about the athlete's personal life and work ethic. (Rev: BL 9/15/02; HBG 3/03) [796.962]

MONPLAISIR, SHARON

16088 Greenberg, Doreen, and Michael Greenberg. *Sword of a Champion: The Story of Sharon Monplaisir* (4–8). Illus. by Phil Velikan. Series: Anything You Can Do — New Sports Heroes for Girls. 2000, Wish paper $9.95 (978-1-930546-39-4). The life story of the timid, shy high schooler who found her place in fencing via a coach who encouraged her to develop her natural talents. (Rev: SLJ 3/01; VOYA 2/01) [796.8]

MURPHY, ISAAC

16089 Trollinger, Patsi B. *Perfect Timing: How Issac Murphy Became One of the World's Greatest Jockeys* (1–3). Illus. by Jerome Lagarrigue. 2006, Viking $15.99 (978-0-670-06083-2). 32pp. This attractive picture-book biography describes how Isaac Murphy, the Kentucky-born grandson of slaves, became one of horse racing's most illustrious jockeys, riding to victory in three Kentucky Derbys. (Rev: BL 9/1/06; SLJ 12/06)

NASH, KEVIN

16090 Mudge, Jacqueline. *Kevin Nash* (4–7). Series: Pro Wrestling Legends. 2000, Chelsea paper $25.00 (978-0-7910-5828-2). 64pp. This is the biography of the wrestler known as "Diesel." (Rev: BL 10/15/00; HBG 3/01)

PAK, SE RI

16091 Stewart, Mark. *Se Ri Pak: Driven to Win* (4–8). Series: Golf's New Wave. 2000, Millbrook LB $22.90 (978-0-7613-1519-3). The story of the South Korean who won the Ladies Professional Golf Association Championship in 1998. (Rev: HBG 10/00; SLJ 8/00) [921]

PELE (SOCCER PLAYER)

16092 Brown, Monica. *Pele, King of Soccer / Pele, el rey del futbol* (1–3). Illus. by Rudy Gutierrez. 2009, HarperCollins $17.99 (978-0-06-122779-0). 40pp. A bilingual (English/Spanish) profile of the Brazilian soccer player's life, with energetic illustrations. (Rev: BL 11/15/08; SLJ 4/09)

16093 Cline-Ransome, Lesa. *Young Pele: Soccer's First Star* (K–3). Illus. by James Ransome. 2007, Random

$16.99 (978-0-375-83599-5). 40pp. A picture-book biography of the Brazilian-born soccer star who learned to play barefoot using a ball made from a sock full of rags. (Rev: BCCB 3/08; BL 9/1/07; HB 11/07; LMC 11/07; SLJ 8/07)

PHELPS, MICHAEL

16094 Goldish, Meish. *Michael Phelps: Anything Is Possible* (2–4). Illus. Series: Defining Moments: Super Athletes. 2009, Bearport LB $18.95 (978-1-59716-855-7). 32pp. A basic introduction to the Olympic swimmer's life. (Rev: BL 4/1/09; SLJ 6/09)

16095 Phelps, Michael. *How to Train with a T. Rex and Win 8 Gold Medals* (PS–2). Illus. by Ward Jenkins. 2009, Simon & Schuster $17.99 (978-1-4169-8669-0). 32pp. Olympian Michael Phelps explains his rigorous training routines in an appealing and understandable manner. (Rev: BCCB 9/09; BLO 6/19/09)

16096 Zuehlke, Jeffrey. *Michael Phelps* (2–4). Illus. Series: Amazing Athletes/LernerSports. 2005, Lerner LB $23.93 (978-0-8225-2431-1). A well-illustrated introduction to the Olympic swimmer. [921]

REECE, GABRIELLE

16097 Morgan, Terri. *Gabrielle Reece: Volleyball's Model Athlete* (4–7). Series: Sports Achievers. 1999, Lerner LB $22.60 (978-0-8225-3667-3). An accessible biography of the woman who is not only a volleyball champ but also a fashion model and TV personality. (Rev: BL 10/15/99; HBG 3/00) [921]

RIDDLES, LIBBY

16098 Riddles, Libby. *Storm Run: The Story of the First Woman to Win the Iditarod Sled Dog Race* (2–5). Illus. by Shannon Cartwright. 2002, Sasquatch $16.95 (978-1-57061-298-5). 48pp. Initially published in 1986, this first-person account of training and racing in the Iditarod, written by the first woman ever to win it, is bolstered by fresh illustrations. (Rev: BL 3/1/02; HBG 10/02)

ROSENFELD, FANNY BOBBIE

16099 Dublin, Anne. *Bobbie Rosenfeld: The Olympian Who Could Do Everything* (5–8). 2004, Second Story paper $11.95 (978-1-896764-82-5). Fanny Bobbie Rosenfeld migrated from the Ukraine to Canada in 1905, became an outstanding athlete excelling in many sports, and led the Canadian women's relay team to an Olympic gold in 1928. Sidney Taylor Book Honor. (Rev: BL 9/1/04) [921]

TAYLOR, MARSHALL B.

16100 Brill, Marlene Targ. *Marshall "Major" Taylor: World Champion Bicyclist, 1899–1901* (5–8). Series: Trailblazer Biographies. 2007, Lerner LB $31.93 (978-0-8225-6610-6). An inspiring profile of the first African American world cycling champion and his struggles with racism. (Rev: BL 9/1/07) [921]

16101 Cline-Ransome, Lesa. *Major Taylor, Champion Cyclist* (2–4). Illus. by James Ransome. 2004, Simon & Schuster $16.95 (978-0-689-83159-1). Prejudice is a theme throughout this biography of the African American cyclist who won the world championship in 1899. (Rev: BL 2/15/04; SLJ 2/04)

THE ROCK (WRESTLER)

16102 Kjelle, Marylou Morano. *Dwayne "The Rock" Johnson* (1–3). Illus. Series: Robbie Reader Contemporary Biography. 2009, Mitchell Lane LB $17.95 (978-1-58415-722-9). 32pp. For beginning readers, this is an appealing biography of the wrestler/actor. (Rev: BLO 5/27/09)

16103 Ross, Dan. *The Story of the Wrestler They Call "The Rock"* (4–7). Series: Pro Wrestling Legends. 2000, Chelsea $25.00 (978-0-7910-5831-2). 64pp. This is the story of the third-generation wrestler known as "The Rock." (Rev: BL 10/15/00; HBG 3/01)

THOMPSON, JENNY

16104 Greenberg, Doreen, and Michael Greenberg. *Fast Lane to Victory: The Story of Jenny Thompson* (3–6). Illus. by Phil Velikan. Series: Anything You Can Do — New Sports Heroes for Girls. 2001, Wish paper $9.95 (978-1-930546-38-7). 141pp. Swimmer Jenny Thompson's determination to excel and the highlights of her career are presented here. (Rev: SLJ 8/01)

VENTURA, JESSE

16105 Uschan, Michael V. *Jesse Ventura* (5–8). Series: People in the News. 2001, Lucent LB $35.15 (978-1-56006-777-1). From a career in wrestling to a state governorship, this is the story of the amazing Jesse Ventura. (Rev: BL 4/1/02)

WHITE, SHAUN

16106 Doeden, Matt. *Shaun White* (2–4). Series: Amazing Athletes. 2006, Lerner LB $23.93 (978-0-8225-6840-7). 32pp. At the age of 19, snowboarder White won a gold medal at the 2006 Olympics. (Rev: SLJ 1/07)

16107 Schweitzer, Karen. *Shaun White* (5–8). Series: Modern Role Models. 2008, Mason Crest LB $22.95 (978-1-4222-0493-1). Shaun White's story of how he became the best snowboarder and skateboarder is detailed in this book, a high-interest biography that includes information on awards, events, and organizations. (Rev: SLJ 2/09; VOYA 8/09) [921]

WICKENHEISER, HAYLEY

16108 Etue, Elizabeth. *Hayley Wickenheiser: Born to Play* (4–7). 2005, Kids Can paper $6.95 (978-1-55337-791-7). The story of Canadian-born Wickenheiser, a member of Canada's gold medal-winning women's ice hockey team at the Salt Lake City Olympics, who went on to become the first woman to play professional hockey. (Rev: BL 9/1/05) [921]

WIE, MICHELLE

16109 Wheeler, Jill C. *Michelle Wie* (3–5). Illus. Series: Awesome Athletes. 2007, ABDO LB $15.95 (978-1-59928-309-8). 32pp. This brief profile tells the story of golfer Michelle Wie, who became a pro golfer before her 16th birthday. (Rev: BL 5/15/07)

WINKFIELD, JIMMY

16110 Hubbard, Crystal. *The Last Black King of the Kentucky Derby* (2–4). Illus. by Robert McGuire. 2008, Lee & Low $17.95 (978-1-58430-274-2). 40pp. This picture book profiles the life of Jimmy "Wink" Winkfield, a 19th-century African American jockey who overcame discrimination and won the Derby. (Rev: BL 9/1/08)

WOODS, TIGER

16111 Brown, Jonatha A. *Tiger Woods* (2–4). Illus. Series: People We Should Know. 2005, Gareth Stevens LB $21.00 (978-0-8368-4313-2). 24pp. For beginning readers, a simple account of Woods's life and triumphs, with an attractive layout and many photographs. [921]

16112 Collins, David R. *Tiger Woods, Golfing Champion* (5–8). Illus. by Larry Nolte. 1999, Pelican $14.95 (978-1-56554-322-5). A chronologically arranged book ending in 1999 that reveals Tiger Woods's determination and love of the game. (Rev: SLJ 1/00) [921]

16113 Roberts, Jeremy. *Tiger Woods* (5–8). Series: Biography. 2002, Lerner LB $27.93 (978-0-8225-0030-8). The story of the likable wonder boy of golf is told in text and pictures. (Rev: BL 4/1/02; HBG 10/02)

16114 Roberts, Jeremy. *Tiger Woods: Golf's Master* (5–8). Illus. Series: USA Today Lifeline Biographies. 2008, Lerner LB $33.26 (978-158013569-6). 112pp.

Newsy sidebars, photographs, personal stories, and historical context enrich this well-designed biography that also provides thorough descriptions of golf and its gear. (Rev: BL 9/1/08; LMC 3–4/09; SLJ 11/1/08) [921]

16115 Sirimarco, Elizabeth. *Tiger Woods* (3–6). Series: Sports Heroes. 2000, Capstone LB $23.93 (978-0-7368-0581-0). 48pp. This brief biography focuses on Woods's athletic development from childhood and the key accomplishments in his career, with plenty of photographs and statistics. (Rev: SLJ 5/01)

ZAHARIAS, BABE DIDRIKSON

16116 Sutcliffe, Jane. *Babe Didrikson Zaharias: All-Around Athlete* (2–3). Series: On My Own Biography. 2000, Carolrhoda LB $23.93 (978-1-57505-421-6). 48pp. A simple biography of one of the greatest athletes of the 20th century, winner of three medals in track and field at the 1932 Olympics. (Rev: BL 6/1–15/00; HBG 10/00; SLJ 6/00)

16117 Wakeman, Nancy. *Babe Didrikson Zaharias: Driven to Win* (4–7). Series: Biography. 2000, Lerner LB $27.93 (978-0-8225-4917-8). The account focuses on this sportswoman's professional career and her strong personality plus her accomplishments in track and field, basketball, and baseball. (Rev: BL 6/1–15/00; HBG 10/00; SLJ 7/00; VOYA 12/00) [921]

16118 Wallace, Rich, and Sandra Neil Wallace. *Babe Conquers the World: The Legendary Life of Babe Didrikson Zaharias* (5–8). Illus. 2014, Boyds Mills/Calkins Creek $16.95 (978-159078981-0). 272pp. A compelling biography of the woman of Norwegian heritage who excelled in multiple sports. (Rev: BL 3/1/14; LMC 10/14; SLJ 2/14) [920]

World Figures

Collective

16119 Aaseng, Nathan. *The Peace Seekers: The Nobel Peace Prize* (5–8). 1987, Lerner paper $7.95 (978-0-8225-9604-2). Martin Luther King, Jr., and Lech Walesa are among those whose lives and works are introduced. (Rev: BL 2/1/88) [327.1720922]

16120 Avakian, Monique. *Reformers: Activists, Educators, Religious Leaders* (5–9). Series: Remarkable Women. 2000, Raintree LB $32.85 (978-0-8172-5733-0). 80pp. This book contains 150 profiles of woman who, throughout history and from many cultures, have fought for human rights, including Harriet Tubman, Mother Teresa, and Dolores Huerta. (Rev: SLJ 8/00)

16121 Bardhan-Quallen, Sudipta. *The Mexican-American War* (5–9). Series: People at the Center Of. 2005, Gale LB $24.95 (978-1-56711-927-5). After an overview of the war, this volume provides biographical information on key figures including James K. Polk, Abraham Lincoln, Santa Anna, and Zachary Taylor. (Rev: SLJ 6/05) [920]

16122 Billinghurst, Jane. *Growing Up Royal: Life in the Shadow of the British Throne* (4–7). Illus. 2001, Annick $22.95 (978-1-55037-623-4); paper $12.95 (978-1-55037-622-7). 176pp. A look at what it's like to be young and royal, with a focus on the lives of today's British royalty, with color photographs and interesting anecdotes. (Rev: BL 9/1/01; HBG 3/02; SLJ 11/01; VOYA 4/02)

16123 Blue, Rose, and Corinne J. Naden. *People of Peace* (4–7). 1994, Millbrook LB $26.90 (978-1-56294-409-4). Brief biographies of 10 people in modern history who have made great sacrifices for world peace, including Mohandas Gandhi and Desmond Tutu. (Rev: BL 12/15/94; SLJ 2/95) [920]

16124 Chin-Lee, Cynthia. *Akira to Zoltan: Twenty-Six Men Who Changed the World* (3–5). Illus. by Megan Halsey. 2006, Charlesbridge $15.95 (978-1-57091-579-

6). 32pp. A companion to *Amelia to Zora: Twenty-Six Women Who Changed the World* (2005), this volume spotlights the accomplishments of 26 men who have made significant contributions in diverse walks of life, including the arts, sciences, politics, and sports. (Rev: BL 6/1–15/06; SLJ 7/06)

16125 Chin-Lee, Cynthia. *Amelia to Zora: Twenty-Six Women Who Changed the World* (4–7). 2005, Charlesbridge $15.95 (978-1-57091-522-2). Brief information on 26 remarkable and varied women (scientists, artists, athletes, inventors) along with beautiful artwork and quotations from the subjects. (Rev: BL 4/1/05*; SLJ 4/05) [920.72]

16126 Cotter, Charis. *Kids Who Rule: The Remarkable Lives of Five Child Monarchs* (5–8). Illus. 2007, Annick $24.95 (978-1-55451-062-7); paper $14.95 (978-1-55451-061-0). 120pp. King Tutankhamen, Mary Queen of Scots, Queen Christina of Sweden, Emperor Puyi of China, and the fourteenth Dalai Lama are the young rulers included in this interesting book that provides historical context. (Rev: BL 12/15/07)

16127 Gifford, Clive. *10 Kings and Queens Who Changed the World* (4–8). Illus. by David Cousens. 2009, Kingfisher $14.99 (978-0-7534-6252-2). 64pp. With compelling, graphic-novel style artwork, Gifford presents ten of the most notable and influential royal leaders — from Hatshepsut to Elizabeth I — through clear, concise paragraphs in this snazzy research guide. (Rev: BL 6/1–15/09; SLJ 7/09) [929.7]

16128 Haskins, Jim. *African Heroes* (5–8). Series: Black Stars. 2005, Wiley $24.95 (978-0-471-46672-7). Profiles 27 important Africans, both contemporary and from the past, in entries of varying length. (Rev: SLJ 7/05) [920]

16129 Hazell, Rebecca. *The Barefoot Book of Heroic Children* (4–7). Illus. 2000, Barefoot Books $19.95 (978-1-902283-23-4). 96pp. This book presents the lives of 12 heroic children from different times and places, among them Anne Frank, Fanny Mendelssohn, Annie Sullivan, and Iqbal Masih. (Rev: BL 4/15/00)

16130 Hazell, Rebecca. *Heroes: Great Men Through the Ages* (5–8). 1997, Abbeville $19.95 (978-0-7892-0289-5). A collection of 12 biographies, from Socrates to Martin Luther King, Jr., and including Shakespeare, Mohandas Gandhi, Leonardo da Vinci, and Jorge Louis Borges. (Rev: SLJ 6/97) [920]

16131 Hazell, Rebecca. *Heroines: Great Women Through the Ages* (5–8). 1996, Abbeville $19.95 (978-0-7892-0210-9). This is a collective biography of 12 great women spanning the period from ancient Greece to modern times, including Sacagawea, Madame Sun Yat-Sen, Frido Kahlo, Joan of Arc, Harriet Tubman, and Marie Curie. (Rev: SLJ 12/96) [920]

16132 Hughes, Susan. *No Girls Allowed: Tales of Daring Women Dressed as Men for Love, Freedom and Adventure* (4–6). Illus. by Willow Dawson. 2008, Kids Can $16.95 (978-1-55453-177-6); paper $8.95 (978-1-55453-178-3). 80pp. Seven women — starting with Egypt's Hatshepsut — who adopted male identities for a variety of reasons are introduced in graphic novel format. (Rev: BLO 7/29/08; LMC 11/08; SLJ 9/08)

16133 Humphrey, Sandra McLeod. *Dare to Dream! 25 Extraordinary Lives* (4–7). 2005, Prometheus paper $15.98 (978-1-59102-280-0). Twenty-five individuals — including artists, athletes, politicians, and scientists — who overcame obstacles to achieve greatness are profiled, with information on childhood and adult life. (Rev: BL 3/1/05; SLJ 6/05) [920]

16134 Hunter, Ryan Ann. *In Disguise: Stories of Real Women Spies* (5–8). 2004, Beyond Words paper $9.95 (978-1-58270-095-3). Profiles 26 women who risked their lives to spy for causes in which they believed, from 1640 to the Cold War. (Rev: SLJ 8/04) [920]

16135 Krull, Kathleen. *Lives of Extraordinary Women: Rulers, Rebels (and What the Neighbors Thought)* (5–8). Series: Extraordinary Lives. 2000, Harcourt $20.00 (978-0-15-200807-9). Short biographies of women who affected the course of history, from Cleopatra to contemporary Burma's Aung San Suu Kyi. (Rev: BCCB 9/00; BL 9/1/00; HB 11–12/00; HBG 3/01; SLJ 9/00; VOYA 6/01) [920]

16136 Lace, William W. *Leaders and Generals* (5–10). Series: American War. 2000, Lucent LB $28.70 (978-1-56006-664-4). 112pp. The following World War II leaders are profiled: Erwin Rommel, Georgi Zhukov, Erich von Manstein, Yamamoto Isoroku, Douglas MacArthur, Chester Nimitz, Dwight Eisenhower, and Bernard Law Montgomery. (Rev: BL 4/15/00; HBG 10/00; SLJ 6/00)

16137 Landau, Elaine. *Assassins, Traitors, and Spies* (4–6). Illus. Series: Shock Zone: Villains. 2013, Lerner LB $26.60 (978-146770608-7); paper $19.95 (9781467710305). 32pp. Benedict Arnold, Tokyo Rose, Lee Harvey Oswald, and Anna Chapman are among the individuals profiled in this readable, visually appealing volume. (Rev: BL 4/1/13; LMC 11–12/13) [920]

16138 Leon, Vicki. *Outrageous Women of the Middle Ages* (4–7). 1998, Wiley paper $12.95 (978-0-471-17004-4). Using a witty writing style and modern comparisons, this fascinating book profiles a diverse group of amazing women who lived from the 6th through the 14th centuries in Europe, Asia, and Africa. (Rev: BL 4/15/98; SLJ 8/98) [920]

16139 Meltzer, Milton. *Ten Kings and the Worlds They Ruled* (5–8). Illus. by Bethanne Andersen. 2002, Scholastic paper $21.95 (978-0-439-31293-6). Ten kings from around the world and across the ages are discussed in this attractive book that includes impressive portraits and other illustrations. Also use *Ten Queens* (1998). (Rev: BCCB 9/02; BL 7/02; HBG 10/02; SLJ 10/02*) [920.02]

16140 Norris, Kathleen. *The Holy Twins: Benedict and Scholastica* (K–3). Illus. by Tomie dePaola. 2001, Penguin $18.99 (978-0-399-23424-8). 32pp. The abbot who became Saint Benedict and founded the Benedictine order is much better known than his twin sister Saint Scholastica, but the story of both siblings' lives is told here with illustrations that evoke Italy in the sixth century. (Rev: BCCB 7–8/01; BL 10/1/01; HBG 3/02; SLJ 9/01)

16141 Pinkney, Andrea Davis. *Peace Warriors* (5–8). Illus. Series: Profiles. 2013, Scholastic paper $6.99 (978-05455185-7-4). 144pp. A compact volume, this profiles six activists — Mahatma Gandhi, Dorothy Day, Martin Luther King, Jr., Desmond Tutu, the 14th Dalai Lama, and Ellen Johnson Sirleaf — with enough information to inspire readers to investigate further. **e** (Rev: BL 6/13; LMC 1–2/14)

16142 Polansky, Daniel. *The Vietnam War* (4–8). Illus. 2013, Scholastic paper $6.99 (978-05454885-5-6). 144pp. Biographies of Ngo Dinh Diem, John F. Kennedy, Ho Chi Minh, Lyndon B. Johnson, William Westmoreland, and Henry Kissinger focus on their involvement in this conflict and present an interesting overview of the complex viewpoints. (Rev: BL 9/1/13; LMC 8–9/13) [920]

16143 Reed, Jennifer B. *The Saudi Royal Family* (5–8). Illus. Series: Major World Leaders. 2002, Chelsea $30.00 (978-0-7910-7063-5); paper $30.00 (978-0-7910-7187-8). 112pp. Saudi Arabia's ruling royal family is profiled, detailing its rise to power, its Islamic policies, and the various individual rulers, with a look at the contrast between the family's extravagant lifestyle and its religious beliefs. (Rev: BL 1/1–15/03; SLJ 4/03)

16144 Sanderson, Ruth. *More Saints: Lives and Illuminations* (4–7). Illus. 2007, Eerdmans $20.00 (978-0-8028-5272-4). 40pp. A sequel to *Saints: Lives and Illuminations* (2003), this volume adds profiles of 36 saints, this time of the second millennium. (Rev: BL 2/1/07)

16145 Sanderson, Ruth. *Saints: Lives and Illuminations* (4–6). Illus. 2003, Eerdmans $20.00 (978-0-8028-5220-5). 40pp. The lives and deaths of 40 saints, accompanied by painted portraits. (Rev: BL 2/1/03; HBG 10/03; SLJ 5/03)

16146 Schwartz, Heather E. *Girls Rebel! Amazing Tales of Women Who Broke the Mold* (4–7). Illus. 2013, Capstone $33.99 (978-147650232-8). 64pp. Students starting research will find valuable, appealingly formatted

880

information on women from various walks of life — from Sally Ride and Barbara Walters to Temple Grandin and Malala Yousafzai. (Rev: BL 10/1/13; LMC 8–9/14) [920]

16147 Shaw, Maura D. *Ten Amazing People: And How They Changed the World* (4–7). 2002, SkyLight Paths $17.95 (978-1-893361-47-8). Shaw presents 10 well-illustrated biographies of 20th-century religious figures, each with timelines, a quotation, a glossary, and an emphasis on the individual's beliefs. (Rev: BL 10/1/02; HBG 3/03; SLJ 12/02) [200]

16148 Wales, Dirk. *Twice a Hero: Polish American Heroes of the American Revolution* (3–5). Illus. by Lynn Ihsen Peterson. 2007, Great Plains $18.95 (978-0-963245-94-6). 32pp. Profiles two Polish-born heroes — Thaddeus Kosciuszko and Casimir Pulaski — who helped Americans to defeat the British during the Revolutionary War; an accompanying DVD expands the briefer information on Pulaski. (Rev: BL 4/15/07)

16149 Zalben, Jane Breskin. *Paths to Peace: People Who Changed the World* (4–7). Illus. 2006, Dutton $18.99 (978-0-525-47734-1). Zalben profiles 16 individuals who have devoted much of their lives to the goal of making peace a reality. (Rev: BL 1/1–15/06; SLJ 2/06)

Individual

ALEXANDER THE GREAT

16150 Adams, Simon. *Alexander: The Boy Soldier Who Conquered the World* (5–7). Series: National Geographic World History Biographies. 2005, National Geographic LB $27.90 (978-0-7922-3661-0). An attractive, well-illustrated account of Alexander's life and accomplishments, with references to his less-appealing characteristics. (Rev: HBG 4/06; SLJ 9/05) [921]

16151 Demi. *Alexander the Great* (4–7). Illus. by author. 2010, Marshall Cavendish $19.99 (978-0-7614-5700-8). 59pp. The story of the infamous Macedonian conquerer is presented in this concise, beautifully illustrated book. e (Rev: BL 9/15/10; LMC 1–2/11; SLJ 10/1/10) [921]

16152 Greenblatt, Miriam. *Alexander the Great and Ancient Greece* (5–8). Series: Rulers and Their Times. 1999, Marshall Cavendish LB $29.93 (978-0-7614-0913-7). The first part of this biography introduces Alexander the Great and his accomplishments and the second tells about daily life in ancient Greece. (Rev: BL 1/1–15/00; HBG 10/00; SLJ 2/00) [921]

16153 McGowen, Tom. *Alexander the Great: Conqueror of the Ancient World* (5–8). Series: Rulers of the Ancient World. 2006, Enslow LB $27.93 (978-0-7660-2560-8). Excellent for report writers, this biography covers Alexander the Great's life and distinguishes between fact and legend. (Rev: BL 6/1–15/06; SLJ 6/06) [921]

16154 Saunders, Nicholas. *The Life of Alexander the Great* (5–8). Illus. Series: Stories from History. 2006, School Specialty $9.95 (978-0-7696-4713-5); paper

$6.95 (978-0-7696-4694-7). 48pp. Full-color illustrations and graphic-novel format make this engaging biography — which covers the bond between Alexander and his horse as well as his relationship with Hephaestion — attractive to reluctant readers. (Rev: SLJ 1/07)

16155 Shecter, Vicky Alvear. *Alexander the Great Rocks the World* (5–8). Illus. by Terry Naughton. 2006, Darby Creek $18.95 (978-1-58196-045-7). 128pp. Shecter employs an irreverent, kid-appealing tone to accurately present Alexander's amazing travels; cartoons, historical depictions, detailed notes, and resources round out the volume. (Rev: BL 1/1–15/07; SLJ 12/06)

ALLEN, WILL

16156 Martin, Jacqueline Briggs. *Farmer Will Allen and the Growing Table* (1–4). Illus. by Eric-Shabazz Larkin. 2013, Readers to Eaters $17.95 (978-098366153-5). 32pp. Basketball player Will Allen returned to his farming roots, and his Growing Power organization is stimulating gardening efforts far and wide. ALA Notable Children's Book. (Rev: BL 11/1/13*; LMC 1–2/14; SLJ 12/13*)

ANIELEWICZ, MORDECHAI

16157 Callahan, Kerry P. *Mordechai Anielewicz: Hero of the Warsaw Uprising* (5–8). Series: Holocaust Biographies. 2001, Rosen LB $31.95 (978-0-8239-3377-8). The story of Anielewicz and other members of the Jewish resistance in the Warsaw ghetto is told in gripping text accompanied by black-and-white photographs. (Rev: BL 10/15/01) [921]

ARAFAT, YASIR

16158 Headlam, George. *Yasser Arafat* (5–8). Series: A&E Biography. 2003, Lerner LB $29.27 (978-0-8225-5004-4); paper $7.95 (978-0-8225-9902-9). 112pp. The story of the Palestinian leader, his rise to power, and his current status. (Rev: BL 1/1–15/04; HBG 4/04; SLJ 2/04)

16159 Williams, Colleen Madonna Flood. *Yasir Arafat* (5–8). Illus. 2002, Chelsea $30.00 (978-0-7910-6941-7); paper $30.00 (978-0-7910-7186-1). The controversial PLO leader is shown as a man of conviction who struggles to balance the desires of his people and of the rest of the world. (Rev: BL 1/1–15/03; HBG 3/03; SLJ 2/03)

ARISTOTLE

16160 Anderson, Margaret J., and Karen F. Stephenson. *Aristotle: Philosopher and Scientist* (5–8). Series: Great Minds of Science. 2004, Enslow LB $26.60 (978-0-7660-2096-2). 112pp. Aristotle's life, times, and contributions to philosophy and science are examined in concise text. (Rev: SLJ 7/04)

ATTILA THE HUN

16161 Price, Sean Stewart. *Attila the Hun: Leader of the Barbarian Hordes* (5–8). Illus. Series: Wicked History. 2009, Scholastic LB $30.00 (978-0-531-21801-3); paper $5.95 (978-0-531-20737-6). 128pp. This compelling, well-designed biography provides lots of historical context. (Rev: BL 4/15/09; VOYA 6/09) [936]

AUNG SAN SUU KYI

16162 Rose, Simon. *Aung San Suu Kyi* (4–7). Illus. Series: Remarkable People. 2011, Weigl LB $27.13 (978-161690833-1); paper $12.95 (978-161690834-8). 24pp. An admiring, informative profile of the Myanmar activist who won the Nobel Prize. (Rev: BL 9/15/11) [921]

BEGIN, MENACHEM

16163 Brackett, Virginia. *Menachem Begin* (5–8). Series: Major World Leaders. 2002, Chelsea $30.00 (978-0-7910-6946-2). 104pp. The life of the important Israeli prime minister who was in office when peace was declared between Israel and Egypt. (Rev: BL 1/1–15/03; SLJ 2/03)

BHATT, ELA

16164 Sreenivasan, Jyotsna. *Ela Bhatt: Uniting Women in India* (5–8). Series: Women Changing the World. 2000, Feminist $19.95 (978-1-55861-229-7). Inspired by Gandhi, this Indian lawyer founded an organization to help and protect the lives of her country's poorest women and organized a labor union for them. (Rev: BL 9/15/00; HBG 3/01; SLJ 12/00) [921]

BIN LADEN, OSAMA

16165 Louis, Nancy. *Osama bin Laden* (4–7). Series: War on Terrorism. 2002, ABDO LB $25.65 (978-1-57765-663-0). A brief biography of the terrorist leader told through a matter-of-fact text and many color photographs. (Rev: BL 5/15/02; HBG 10/02) [921]

16166 Woolf, Alex. *Osama Bin Laden* (5–8). Series: A&E Biography. 2003, Lerner LB $29.27 (978-0-8225-5003-7); paper $7.95 (978-0-8225-9900-5). 112pp. The story of the leader of the Al Qaeda terrorist movement and his family background in Saudi Arabia. (Rev: BL 1/1–15/04; HBG 4/04; SLJ 2/04)

BLAIR, TONY

16167 Wilson, Wayne, and Jim Whiting. *Tony Blair* (3–6). 2002, Mitchell Lane LB $15.95 (978-1-58415-143-2). 32pp. Blair's colorful youth — as mild rebel and as aspiring rock singer — will draw readers into the story of his later achievements that puts an emphasis on his support of the United States. (Rev: SLJ 12/02)

BONETTA, SARAH FORBES

16168 Myers, Walter Dean. *At Her Majesty's Request: An African Princess in Victorian England* (5–8). 1999, Scholastic paper $17.95 (978-0-590-48669-9). The intriguing story of the African princess who at age 7 was saved from becoming a sacrifice and sent her to England, where she became the ward of Queen Victoria. (Rev: BCCB 2/99; BL 4/1/99; HBG 10/99; SLJ 1/99; VOYA 4/99) [921]

BUDDHA

16169 Gedney, Mona. *The Life and Times of Buddha* (5–7). Series: Biography from Ancient Civilizations: Legends, Folklore, and Stories of Ancient Worlds. 2005, Mitchell Lane LB $29.95 (978-1-58415-342-9). Gedney recounts what is known of the life of Siddartha Gautama, whose search for a better way of living led to the founding of Buddhism. (Rev: SLJ 9/05) [921]

16170 Stewart, Whitney. *Becoming Buddha: The Story of Siddhartha* (3–5). Illus. by Sally Rippin. 2005, Lothian $16.95 (978-0-89346-946-7). 32pp. A picture-book biography of Buddha that chronicles Prince Siddhartha's lifelong search for enlightenment. (Rev: BL 10/1/05; SLJ 11/05)

CAESAR, JULIUS

16171 Galford, Ellen. *Julius Caesar: The Boy Who Conquered an Empire* (5–8). Series: World History Biographies. 2007, National Geographic $17.95 (978-1-4263-0064-6). 64pp. A brief but well-organized biography of Caesar, covering his childhood, adolescence, marriage, military career, rise to power, and murder, and offering pertinent historical context. (Rev: SLJ 6/07)

16172 Saunders, Nicholas. *The Life of Julius Caesar* (5–8). Illus. Series: Stories from History. 2006, School Specialty $9.95 (978-0-7696-4717-3); paper $6.95 (978-0-7696-4697-8). 48pp. Full-color illustrations and graphic-novel format make this engaging biography attractive to reluctant readers. (Rev: SLJ 1/07)

CASTRO, FIDEL

16173 Platt, Richard. *Fidel Castro: From Guerrilla to World Statesman* (5–7). Series: Twentieth-Century History Makers. 2003, Raintree LB $32.85 (978-0-7398-6141-7). 112pp. Platt traces Castro's life from childhood through today, presenting opposing opinions of his achievements in a chapter called "Hero or Monster?" (Rev: HBG 4/04; SLJ 9/03)

16174 Press, Petra. *Fidel Castro: An Unauthorized Biography* (5–7). Series: Heinemann Profiles. 2000, Heinemann LB $24.22 (978-1-57572-497-3). 56pp. An interesting introduction to the life of Cuba's dictator, with photographs that show urban and rural Cuba. (Rev: SLJ 6/01)

CHAMPOLLION, JEAN-FRANCOIS

16175 Rumford, James. *Seeker of Knowledge: The Man Who Deciphered Egyptian Hieroglyphs* (3–5). Illus. 2000, Houghton $16.00 (978-0-395-97934-1). The story of Jean-Francois Champollion, who studied the Rosetta Stone and found the key to understanding Egyptian hieroglyphs. (Rev: BCCB 4/00; BL 4/15/00; HBG 10/00; SLJ 5/00)

CHORN-POND, ARN

16176 Lord, Michelle. *A Song for Cambodia* (3–5). Illus. by Shino Arihara. 2008, Lee & Low $16.95 (978-1-60060-139-2). 32pp. When the Khmer Rouge took over his village in 1975, Arn Chorn was taken from his family and sent to a work camp; there he learned to play the khim, and his love of music supported him through many challenges he faced before being adopted and brought to the United States. (Rev: BL 4/1/08; LMC 10/08; SLJ 4/08)

CHURCHILL, SIR WINSTON

16177 Ashworth, Leon. *Winston Churchill* (5–8). Series: British History Makers. 2002, Cherrytree $17.95 (978-1-84234-072-1). A balanced look at the life and career of the British statesman, with a useful timeline and excellent illustrations. (Rev: SLJ 8/02) [941.082092]

16178 Binns, Tristan Boyer. *Winston Churchill* (5–8). Series: Great Life Stories. 2004, Watts LB $30.50 (978-0-531-12361-4). 127pp. The complex life of Churchill is well portrayed in this biography that covers his youth and career, triumphs and losses, and many and varied interests. (Rev: SLJ 3/05)

16179 Haugen, Brenda. *Winston Churchill: British Soldier, Writer, Statesman* (4–8). 2006, Compass Point LB $34.60 (978-0-7565-1582-9). Slim but fact-filled, this is a useful biography for report writers, with excerpts from speeches and writings and full discussion of key events in Churchill's life. (Rev: SLJ 9/06) [921]

16180 Ridley, Sarah. *Winston Churchill and World War II* (3–5). Illus. Series: History Makers. 2013, Black Rabbit LB $25.65 (978-159771393-1). 24pp. Covers Churchill's childhood, schooling, and military and political career as well as his considerable role in World War II and final years. (Rev: BL 4/1/13; LMC 10/13; SLJ 4/13) [921]

16181 Severance, John B. *Winston Churchill: Soldier, Statesman, Artist* (5–8). 1996, Clarion $19.00 (978-0-395-69853-2). A well-organized, clearly written account of the life and works of Britain's great statesman. (Rev: BL 4/15/96; HB 7–8/96; SLJ 4/96*; VOYA 6/96) [941.084]

CLEOPATRA

16182 Blackaby, Susan. *Cleopatra: Egypt's Last and Greatest Queen* (5–8). Series: Sterling Biographies. 2009, Sterling $12.95 (978-1-4027-6540-7); paper $5.95 (978-1-4027-5710-5). 124pp. A useful and engaging biography for report writers or anyone interested in the renowned queen and her times. (Rev: SLJ 8/09) [921]

16183 Shecter, Vicky Alvear. *Cleopatra Rules! The Amazing Life of the Original Teen Queen* (4–7). 2010, Boyds Mills $17.95 (978-1-59078-718-2). 176pp. Using irreverent teenspeak that will not appeal to all readers, Schecter presents detailed information in a layout full of sidebars and illustrations. Lexile 880L (Rev: BL 10/1/10; LMC 11–12/10; SLJ 10/1/10; VOYA 12/10) [921]

16184 Streissguth, Thomas. *Queen Cleopatra* (4–7). Series: A&E Biography. 2000, Lerner LB $27.93 (978-0-8225-4946-8). 112pp. The story of Cleopatra and her

impact on world history. (Rev: BL 3/15/00; HBG 10/00; SLJ 5/00)

CONFUCIUS

16185 Freedman, Russell. *Confucius: The Golden Rule* (4–8). Illus. by Frederic Clement. 2002, Scholastic paper $17.99 (978-0-439-13957-1). This absorbing account of the life and philosophy of Confucius gives new insight into the character of the man who had so much influence on China. (Rev: BL 10/1/02*; HB 1/03; HBG 3/03; SLJ 9/02*)

CUNXIN, LI

16186 Cunxin, Li. *Dancing to Freedom: The True Story of Mao's Last Dancer* (2–4). Illus. by Anne Spudvilas. 2008, Walker $16.95 (978-0-8027-9777-3). 40pp. The author recalls his difficult early life in rural China, his rigorous training as a ballet dancer, and his defection to the West. (Rev: BCCB 9/08; BL 6/1–15/08; LMC 5/08; SLJ 6/08)

CYR, LOUIS

16187 Debon, Nicolas. *The Strongest Man in the World: Louis Cyr* (2–4). Illus. 2007, Groundwood $17.95 (978-0-88899-731-9). 36pp. The exploits of circus strongman Cyr, a Canadian who amazed audiences in America and Europe at the end of the 19th century, are shown in this visual biography. (Rev: BL 4/1/07)

DALAI LAMA

16188 Gibb, Chris. *The Dalai Lama* (4–6). Series: Famous Lives. 2003, Raintree LB $27.12 (978-0-7398-5520-1). The story of Tibet's exiled political and spiritual leader and of his teachings of peace and civil disobedience. (Rev: BL 2/15/03; HBG 10/03; SLJ 5/03)

16189 Kimmel, Elizabeth Cody. *Boy on the Lion Throne: The Childhood of the 14th Dalai Lama* (5–8). 2009, Roaring Brook $18.95 (978-1-59643-394-6). 160pp. The compelling and wide-ranging story of the childhood of the current Dalai Lama, who was born Lhamo Thondup in 1935. (Rev: BCCB 6/09; SLJ 6/09) [921]

DIANA, PRINCESS OF WALES

16190 Oleksy, Walter. *Princess Diana* (5–8). Series: People in the News. 2001, Lucent LB $27.45 (978-1-56006-579-1). A well-documented life of this tragic, troubled princess, with many quotations and black-and-white photographs. (Rev: BCCB 10/98; BL 4/1/02; HBG 3/01)

DONGPO, SU

16191 Demi. *Su Dongpo: Chinese Genius* (2–4). Illus. 2006, Lee & Low $24.00 (978-1-58430-256-8). 56pp. This picture-book biography chronicles the life and accomplishments of Su Dongpo (also known as Su Shi), a Chinese poet and statesman in the 11th century. (Rev: BL 11/1/06; SLJ 11/06)

ELIZABETH I, QUEEN OF ENGLAND

16192 Adams, Simon. *Elizabeth I: The Outcast Who Became England's Queen* (3–6). Series: National Geographic World History Biographies. 2005, National Geographic $17.95 (978-0-7922-3649-8). 64pp. The queen's life and accomplishments are placed in historical context in this well-designed, informative book. (Rev: HBG 10/06; SLJ 6/06)

16193 Brassey, Richard. *Elizabeth I* (3–5). Series: Brilliant Brits. 2006, Orion paper $8.99 (978-1-84255-233-9). 24pp. The queen up-close and personal, with lots of illustrations in comic-book style and an emphasis on the quirks and the drama of the royal family and their times. (Rev: BL 7/06)

16194 Havelin, Kate. *Elizabeth I* (5–8). Series: Biography. 2002, Lerner LB $27.93 (978-0-8225-0029-2). 112pp. The story of one of the most powerful queens in history and how she learned, at an early age, the politics of survival. (Rev: BCCB 12/99; BL 6/1–15/02; HBG 10/02; SLJ 7/02)

16195 Hollihan, Kerrie Logan. *Elizabeth I, the People's Queen: Her Life and Times: 21 Activities* (4–8). Illus. 2011, Chicago Review paper $16.95 (978-1-56976-349-0). 144pp. The life and times of England's Queen Elizabeth I are given plenty of historical and political context in this well-organized book that includes 21 activities. (Rev: LMC 10/11; SLJ 5/11) [921]

16196 Thomas, Jane Resh. *Behind the Mask: The Life of Queen Elizabeth I* (5–8). 1998, Clarion $20.00 (978-0-395-69120-5). A behind-the-scenes look at the long-lived queen, discussing her childhood, how she overcame opposition to become queen, and her subsequent manipulation of people, the court, and foreigners to attain greatness. (Rev: BL 12/15/98; HB 1–2/99; HBG 3/99; SLJ 12/98*; VOYA 4/99) [921]

ELIZABETH II, QUEEN OF ENGLAND

16197 Barton-Wood, Sara. *Queen Elizabeth II: Monarch of Our Times* (4–6). Illus. Series: Famous Lives. 2001, Raintree LB $27.12 (978-0-7398-4430-4). An affectionate look at the life of Queen Elizabeth II, from childhood through her Golden Jubilee. (Rev: BL 1/1–15/02; HBG 10/02; SLJ 3/02)

FOX, VICENTE

16198 Paprocki, Sherry Beck. *Vicente Fox* (5–8). Series: Major World Leaders. 2002, Chelsea $30.00 (978-0-7910-6944-8). The story of the man who became president of Mexico in July 2000, the first opposition candidate to gain presidential office in more than 70 years. (Rev: BL 1/1–15/03) [921]

FRANCIS, POPE

16199 Watson, Stephanie. *Pope Francis: First Pope from the Americas* (5–8). Illus. 2013, Lerner LB $26.60 (978-146772176-9). 48pp. An interesting and balanced profile of the new pope, covering his youth as well as his work as a cardinal in South America and his early innovations

at the Vatican. **e** (Rev: BL 11/15/13; LMC 8–9/14; SLJ 12/13) [921]

FRANK, ANNE

16200 Alagna, Magdalena. *Anne Frank: Young Voice of the Holocaust* (5–8). Series: Holocaust Biographies. 2001, Rosen LB $26.50 (978-0-8239-3373-0). 112pp. This book describes Anne's childhood, her time spent in hiding, her diary, and her life in the concentration camps. (Rev: BL 10/15/01)

16201 Colbert, David. *Anne Frank* (5–8). Illus. Series: 10 Days That Shook Your World. 2008, Aladdin paper $6.99 (978-1-4169-6445-2). 160pp. Interweaving fact and fiction, Colbert describes 10 important days in Anne Frank's life — from the Netherlands' surrender to the Nazis to March 1945, when Anne is moved to a new camp full of disease. (Rev: BLO 12/8/08) [921]

16202 Frank, Anne. *Anne Frank: The Diary of a Young Girl* (5–8). 1967, Pocket paper $3.95 (978-0-685-05466-6). The moving diary of a young Jewish girl hiding from the Nazis in World War II Amsterdam. [921]

16203 Gold, Alison L. *Memories of Anne Frank: Reflections of a Childhood Friend* (4–8). 1997, Scholastic paper $16.95 (978-0-590-90722-4). Anne Frank's story as told through recollections of her best friend in Amsterdam, Hannah Goslar, a survivor of the Holocaust. (Rev: BL 9/1/97; HBG 3/98; SLJ 11/97) [921]

16204 Hermann, Spring. *Anne Frank: Hope in the Shadows of the Holocaust* (5–7). Series: Holocaust Heroes and Nazi Criminals. 2005, Enslow LB $27.93 (978-0-7660-2531-8). The story of Anne Frank before, during, and after the two years she and her family hid from the Nazis. (Rev: SLJ 11/05) [921]

16205 Hurwitz, Johanna. *Anne Frank: Life in Hiding* (4–7). Illus. by Vera Rosenberry. 1989, Jewish Publication Society $13.95 (978-0-8276-0311-0). This biography describes Anne's life in hiding. (Rev: BL 4/15/89) [921]

16206 Kohuth, Jane. *Anne Frank's Chestnut Tree* (1–3). Illus. by Elizabeth Sayles. 2013, Random House $12.99 (978-0-449-81255-6). 48pp. Beginning readers learn about Anne Frank's life through the lens of her love of the chestnut tree standing outside the Secret Annex. **e** (Rev: BL 7/13; LMC 1–2/14; SLJ 9/13) [921]

16207 Zapruder, Alexandra. *Anne Frank* (2–4). Illus. 2013, National Geographic paper $3.99 (978-14263135-2-3). 48pp. A simply told biography that focuses on Frank's life and how she was forced to alter it because of the Nazi invasion. (Rev: BL 9/15/13; SLJ 2/14) [921]

GANDHI, MAHATMA

16208 Claybourne, Anna. *Gandhi* (4–6). Series: Famous Lives. 2003, Raintree LB $27.12 (978-0-7398-5521-8). 48pp. A brief biography of the Indian leader, his triumphs and hardships, and the story of the nonviolent movement he led. (Rev: BCCB 12/01; BL 2/15/03; HBG 10/03; SLJ 5/03)

16209 Demi. *Gandhi* (3–6). Illus. 2001, Simon & Schuster $19.95 (978-0-689-84149-1). A moving look at a remarkable man that brings to life his character and the time in which he lived. (Rev: BCCB 12/01; BL 6/1–15/01; HB 9/01; HBG 3/02; SLJ 8/01)

16210 Gandhi, Arun, and Bethany Hegedus. *Grandfather Gandhi* (1–4). Illus. by Evan Turk. 2014, Atheneum $17.99 (978-144242365-7). 48pp. Mahatma Gandhi's grandson describes how his grandfather taught him to control anger and find connections with others. (Rev: BL 12/15/13; LMC 8–9/14*; SLJ 2/14) [921]

16211 McGinty, Alice B. *Gandhi: A March to the Sea* (3–5). Illus. by Thomas Gonzalez. 2013, Amazon/Two Lions $17.99 (978-1-4778-1644-8). 32pp. A picture-book account of the 1930 Salt March, in which Gandhi and a group of followers walked 24 days to the sea to protest a tax imposed by the British. e (Rev: BL 6/13; HB 7–8/13; LMC 11–12/13; SLJ 5/13*)

16212 Martin, Christopher. *Mohandas Gandhi* (4–7). Series: A&E Biography. 2000, Lucent LB $27.93 (978-0-8225-4984-0). 112pp. The story of the man who sought to unite and free his people not through violence but by prayer, civil disobedience, and communication. (Rev: BL 12/15/00; HBG 3/01; SLJ 1/01)

16213 Shaw, Maura D. *Gandhi: India's Great Soul* (3–6). Illus. by Stephen Marchesi. Series: Spiritual Biographies for Young Readers. 2004, SkyLight Paths $12.95 (978-1-893361-91-1). An overview of Gandhi's life and beliefs is followed by discussion of how his ideals remain relevant and achievable. (Rev: BL 2/15/04; SLJ 9/04)

16214 Wilkinson, Philip. *Gandhi: The Young Protestor Who Founded a Nation* (4–7). Series: World History Biographies. 2005, National Geographic LB $27.90 (978-0-7922-3648-1). Gandhi's character shines through the straightforward text and interesting anecdotes in this biography that gives historical context plus maps and photographs. (Rev: BL 6/1–15/05) [954.03]

GENGHIS KHAN

16215 Bankston, John. *Genghis Khan* (5–8). Illus. Series: Junior Biographies from Ancient Civilizations. 2013, Mitchell Lane LB $29.95 (978-161228432-3). 48pp. This biography of Genghis Khan explains not only his life, but the lives of his family, as well as the various tribes that he fought with, complete with sidebars to further explain the culture in which he lived. e (Rev: BL 11/1/13; LMC 3–4/14) [921]

16216 Goldberg, Enid A., and Norman Itzkowitz. *Genghis Khan: 13th-Century Mongolian Tyrant* (5–7). Illus. Series: Wicked History. 2007, Scholastic LB $30.00 (978-0-531-12596-0). The bloody deeds of the tyrant are emphasized (this is the Wicked History series, after all), but readers will also learn about ancient Mongolia and its people as well as the few positive results of Genghis Khan's rule. (Rev: BL 12/15/07; LMC 2/08; SLJ 1/08) [921]

16217 Greenblatt, Miriam. *Genghis Khan and the Mongol Empire* (5–8). Series: Rulers and Their Times. 2001, Marshall Cavendish LB $29.93 (978-0-7614-1027-0). This handsomely illustrated book presents, in three parts, a life of Genghis Khan, a section on society during his reign, and a selection of documents of the time. (Rev: BL 1/1–15/02; HBG 3/02; SLJ 2/02)

16218 Nardo, Don. *Genghis Khan and the Mongol Empire* (5–9). Series: World History. 2011, Gale $33.45 (978-1-4205-0326-5). 96pp. An accessible portrait of Genghis Khan, his military reforms, his conquests in western Asia, and his legacy. e (Rev: SLJ 7/11) [921]

GROSS, ELLY BERKOVITS

16219 Gross, Elly Berkovits. *Elly: My True Story of the Holocaust* (4–7). Illus. 2009, Scholastic $14.99 (978-0-545-07494-0). 128pp. A memoir of a woman recalling her experiences as a teenager in a concentration camp and later as a factory slave laborer. (Rev: BL 6/1–15/09; SLJ 9/09) [940.53]

HALILBEGOVICH, NADJA

16220 Halilbegovich, Nadja. *My Childhood Under Fire: A Sarajevo Diary* (4–7). 2006, Kids Can $14.95 (978-1-55337-797-9). 120pp. As a 12-year-old, Halilbegovich kept a diary that reveals the frightening details of her life during the Balkans war. (Rev: BL 5/15/06; SLJ 6/06)

HANH, THICH NHAT

16221 Shaw, Maura D. *Thich Nhat Hanh: Buddhism in Action* (4–6). Illus. by Stephen Marchesi. Series: Spiritual Biographies for Young Readers. 2004, SkyLight Paths $12.95 (978-1-893361-87-4). This brief biography of the Vietnamese Buddhist monk touches lightly on his anti-war activism; it offers an introduction to the benefits of peace and tranquility. (Rev: BL 2/1/04; SLJ 9/04)

HANNIBAL

16222 Warrick, Karen Clemens. *Hannibal: Great General of the Ancient World* (5–8). Series: Rulers of the Ancient World. 2006, Enslow LB $27.93 (978-0-7660-2564-6). The story of Hannibal's life and successes against the Romans are placed in historical context, with details of important battles as well as insight into his character. (Rev: SLJ 6/06) [921]

HATSHEPSUT, QUEEN OF EGYPT

16223 Galford, Ellen. *Hatshepsut: The Princess Who Grew Up to Be King* (4–6). Illus. Series: World History Biographies. 2005, National Geographic $17.95 (978-0-7922-3645-0). 64pp. A life of Hatshepsut, who ruled Egypt about 3,500 years ago, with well-chosen illustrations, interesting sidebars, and clear distinctions between fact and surmise. (Rev: BL 7/05; SLJ 9/05)

HODGMAN, ANN

16224 Hodgman, Ann. *The House of a Million Pets* (3–6). Illus. by Eugene Yelchin. 2007, Holt $16.95 (978-0-8050-7974-6). 272pp. This memoir chronicles the author's ongoing menagerie of animals ranging from hedgehogs and rabbits to owls and a bulbul, and is frank about the deaths as well as the happier experiences. (Rev: BCCB 11/07; BL 9/1/07; HB 1/08; SLJ 12/07)

HONG, CHEN JIANG

16225 Hong, Chen Jiang. *Mao and Me* (4–8). Trans. by Claudia Zoe Bedrick. Illus. by author. 2008, Enchanted Lion $19.95 (978-1-59270-079-0). 96pp. A picture-book memoir about growing up during the Chinese Cultural Revolution, contrasting the personal with the political in often harrowing detail. (Rev: BL 12/15/08; SLJ 2/09)

HUSSEIN, SADDAM

16226 Anderson, Dale. *Saddam Hussein* (5–8). Series: A&E Biography. 2003, Lerner LB $29.27 (978-0-8225-5005-1); paper $7.95 (978-0-8225-9901-2). 112pp. This biography of the Iraqi despot tells his story up to the decision that led to the American invasion. (Rev: BL 1/1–15/04; HBG 4/04; SLJ 2/04)

16227 Shields, Charles J. *Saddam Hussein* (5–8). Series: Major World Leaders. 2002, Chelsea $30.00 (978-0-7910-6943-1). An account of the Iraqi leader's regime, with information on the Iran-Iraq and Persian Gulf wars and on United Nations sanctions and weapons inspections. (Rev: BL 2/1/03; HBG 3/03; SLJ 4/03) [956.7044]

HYPATIA

16228 Love, D. Anne. *Of Numbers and Stars: The Story of Hypatia* (1–3). Illus. by Pam Paparone. 2006, Holiday $16.95 (978-0-8234-1621-9). 32pp. This picture-book biography of Hypatia profiles the life of the female scholar and philosopher whose father's devotion opened up to her worlds that were forbidden to most women. (Rev: BL 4/15/06; SLJ 5/06)

JESUS CHRIST

16229 Demi. *Jesus* (3–5). Illus. 2005, Simon & Schuster $19.95 (978-0-689-86905-1). Striking illustrations illustrate this life of Jesus, told chronologically in the tone of the King James version of the Bible. (Rev: BL 10/1/05; SLJ 10/05)

JOAN OF ARC

16230 Corey, Shana. *Joan of Arc* (2–3). Illus. by Dan Andreasen. Series: Step into Reading. 2003, Random paper $3.99 (978-0-375-80620-9). 48pp. The dramatic story of Joan of Arc is presented in picture-book form for beginning readers. (Rev: BL 7/03; HBG 4/04)

16231 Demi. *Joan of Arc* (3–5). Illus. by author. 2011, Marshall Cavendish $19.99 (978-0-7614-5953-8). 56pp. An elegant picture-book biography portraying the brief but significant life of Joan of Arc, patron saint of France. (Rev: BL 9/1/11; SLJ 10/1/11) [921]

16232 Lee, William W. *Joan of Arc and the Hundred Years' War in World History* (5–9). Series: In World History. 2003, Enslow LB $26.60 (978-0-7660-1938-6). This combination of biography and history tells the story of Joan of Arc and gives details on the long conflict between France and England. (Rev: BL 6/1–15/03; HBG 10/03; SLJ 9/03) [921]

16233 Roberts, Jeremy. *Saint Joan of Arc* (4–6). Series: A&E Biography. 2000, Lerner LB $25.26 (978-0-8225-

4981-9). 112pp. The story of a young woman whose honesty, devotion, and courage inspired an army, a king, and eventually a country to follow her. (Rev: BL 6/1–15/00; HBG 10/00)

16234 Tompert, Ann. *Joan of Arc: Heroine of France* (1–4). Illus. by Michael Garland. 2003, Boyds Mills $15.95 (978-1-59078-009-1). This solid account puts the events in Joan's life in clear historical context. (Rev: BL 3/1/03; HBG 10/03; SLJ 3/03)

16235 Yeatts, Tabatha. *Joan of Arc: Heavenly Warrior* (4–7). Illus. Series: Sterling Biographies. 2009, Sterling $12.95 (978-1-4027-6542-1); paper $5.95 (978-1-4027-5662-7). 124pp. An accessible biography with many illustrations, maps, a timeline, and useful sources. (Rev: BL 2/1/09; SLJ 8/09) [921]

KAMKWAMBA, WILLIAM

16236 Kamkwamba, William, and Bryan Mealer. *The Boy Who Harnessed the Wind* (1–3). Illus. by Elizabeth Zunon. 2012, Dial $16.99 (978-080373511-8). 32pp. In a remote, impoverished Malawi village, 14-year-old Kamkwamba constructed a windmill out of salvaged materials and brought electricity to his neighbors. ⌒ e (Rev: BL 2/15/12; SLJ 1/12) [921]

KOLLEK, TEDDY

16237 Rabinovich, Abraham. *Teddy Kollek: Builder of Jerusalem* (5–8). 1996, Jewish Publication Society $14.95 (978-0-8276-0559-6); paper $9.95 (978-0-8276-0561-9). The story of the former mayor of Jerusalem, who supervised the city's unification after the Six Days War in 1967. (Rev: BL 5/15/96) [921]

KORCZAK, JANUSZ

16238 Adler, David A. *A Hero and the Holocaust: The Story of Janusz Korczak and His Children* (3–5). Illus. by Bill Farnsworth. 2002, Holiday House $16.95 (978-0-8234-1548-9). 32pp. The story of Janusz Korczak's efforts to care for young Jewish children in the Warsaw ghetto and on the trip to the Treblinka death camp, presented in memorable illustrations and a simple text, accompanied by quotes from his diary. (Rev: BL 12/1/02; HBG 3/03; SLJ 3/03)

16239 Bogacki, Tomek. *The Champion of Children: The Story of Janusz Korczak* (4–7). Illus. by author. 2009, Farrar $17.99 (978-0-374-34136-7). 40pp. A brave doctor who gave up his medical practice to found a Jewish orphanage in Poland during World War II and to accompany the children to Treblinka is profiled in this stark but inspiring story. (Rev: BL 10/1/09; LMC 11–12/09; SLJ 12/09) [921]

16240 Spielman, Gloria. *Janusz Korczak's Children* (1–3). Illus. by Matthew Archambault. 2007, Lerner $17.95 (978-1-58013-255-8); Kar-Ben paper $7.95 (978-0-8225-7050-9). 40pp. Spielman tells the story of the Polish doctor who refused to abandon the Jewish orphans he looked after and accompanied them to the death camp at Treblinka. (Rev: BL 10/15/07; LMC 1/08; SLJ 10/07)

KOSSMAN, NINA

16241 Kossman, Nina. *Behind the Border* (5–7). 1994, Lothrop $14.00 (978-0-688-13494-5). This book contains 12 episodes about the author's childhood in Communist Russia before emigrating to the United States. (Rev: BCCB 10/94; BL 8/94; SLJ 10/94) [921]

KOUANCHAO, MALICHANSOUK

16242 Youme. *Mali Under the Night Sky: A Lao Story of Home* (PS–3). Illus. by author. 2010, Cinco Puntos $17.95 (978-1-933693-68-2). 40pp. This is the story of the childhood of Laotian American artist Malichansouk Kouanchao, whose family flees the civil war in Laos and ends up spending time in jail. (Rev: BL 1/1–15/11; LMC 5–6/11; SLJ 11/1/10) [921]

KUBLAI KHAN

16243 Krull, Kathleen. *Kubla Khan: The Emperor of Everything* (3–5). Illus. by Robert Byrd. 2010, Viking $17.99 (978-0-670-01114-8). 48pp. In this vividly illustrated book, Kubla Khan, the first emperor of the Yuan dynasty, matures to enlightened adulthood and ascends the throne. (Rev: BL 7/10; HB 11–12/10; LMC 1–2/11; SLJ 10/1/10*) [921]

LAFAYETTE, MARQUIS DE

16244 Payan, Gregory. *Marquis de Lafayette: French Hero of the American Revolution* (4–7). Illus. Series: Library of American Lives and Times. 2001, Rosen $34.60 (978-0-8239-5733-0). 112pp. Payan introduces the French general who assisted the American cause, with illustrations, maps, and other aids to understanding his times. (Rev: BL 10/15/01)

LAMBKE, BRYAN

16245 Lambke, Bryan, and Tom Lambke. *I Just Am: A Story of Down Syndrome Awareness and Tolerance* (4–10). 2006, Five Star $14.99 (978-1-58985-020-0). 86pp. In this compelling photoessay, a young adult with Down syndrome — with some help from his father — explains what it's like to live with this disability. (Rev: SLJ 10/06)

LAO TZU

16246 Demi. *The Legend of Lao Tzu and the Tao Te Ching* (4–7). Illus. by author. 2007, Simon & Schuster $21.99 (978-1-4169-1206-4). 48pp. A well-designed introduction to the legendary Chinese religious figure Lao Tzu, with 20 verses from the book of wisdom associated with him. (Rev: BL 5/15/07; HB 7/07; LMC 11/07; SLJ 5/07)

LEKUTON, JOSEPH LEMASOLAI

16247 Lekuton, Joseph Lemasolai. *Facing the Lion: Growing Up Maasai on the African Savanna* (5–12). 2003, National Geographic $15.95 (978-0-7922-5125-5). Lekuton, a member of a nomadic Masai tribe and now a teacher in Virginia, remembers his youth in Kenya. (Rev: BCCB 5/06; BL 9/15/03; HBG 4/04; LMC 11–12/06; SLJ 10/03*) [967.62]

LEYSON, LEON

16248 Leyson, Leon. *The Boy on the Wooden Box* (4–7). 2013, Atheneum $16.99 (978-144249781-8). 240pp. Leon Leyson's remarkable narrative details his childhood in Poland where his father worked for Oskar Schindler, who helped the family escape and seek refugee status in the United States after surviving years in the work camps of Nazi Germany. ALA Notable Children's Book. ∩ ℮ (Rev: BL 9/1/13; HB 11–12/13; LMC 3–4/14; SLJ 11/13; VOYA 10/13) [921]

LIU, NA

16249 Liu, Na. *Little White Duck: A Childhood in China* (4–7). Illus. by Andres Vera Martinez. 2012, Graphic Universe LB $29.27 (978-0-76136587-7); paper $9.95 (978-0-76138115-0). 108pp. Using a graphic-novel format Na Liu tells eight stories about her childhood in China during the 1970s. ℮ Lexile 710L (Rev: BLO 9/1/12; HB 9–10/12; LMC 1–2/13*; SLJ 9/12*) [921]

MAATHAI, WANGARI

16250 Johnson, Jen Cullerton. *Seeds of Change: Planting a Path to Peace* (2–4). Illus. by Sonia Lynn Sadler. 2010, Lee & Low $18.95 (978-1-60060-367-9). 40pp. This inspiring story of Nobel Peace Prize laureate Wangari Maathai's environmental activism discusses her education and love of nature in poetic text with colorful illustrations. Lexile 820L (Rev: BL 6/10; LMC 11–12/10; SLJ 4/1/10) [921]

16251 Napoli, Donna Jo. *Mama Miti: Wangari Maathai and the Trees of Kenya* (K–3). Illus. by Kadir Nelson. 2010, Simon & Schuster $16.99 (978-1-4169-3505-6). 40pp. Vibrant collage artwork enhances this picture-book biography of the simple and successful conservation movement Maathai founded in Kenya. (Rev: BL 2/15/10; LMC 5–6/10; SLJ 2/1/10) [921]

16252 Nivola, Claire A. *Planting the Trees of Kenya* (K–3). Illus. by author. 2008, Farrar $16.95 (978-0-374-39918-4). The founder of the Green Belt Movement and first African woman to receive the Nobel Peace Prize is the focus of this simple, clear biography. (Rev: BL 2/15/08; HB 5/08; SLJ 4/08)

16253 Winter, Jeanette. *Wangari's Trees of Peace: A True Story from Africa* (1–3). Illus. by author. 2008, Harcourt $17.00 (978-0-15-206545-4). Wangari Maathai, winner of the 2004 Nobel Peace Prize, grew up in Kenya, was educated in America, and returned to her country to become the founder of the Green Belt Movement. (Rev: BCCB 10/08; BL 12/15/08; LMC 1/09; SLJ 11/08)

MACHIAVELLI, NICCOLÒ

16254 Ford, Nick. *Niccolò Machiavelli: Florentine Statesman, Playwright, and Poet* (5–8). Series: Rulers, Scholars, and Artists of the Renaissance. 2005, Rosen LB $33.25 (978-1-4042-0316-7). Ford places Machiavelli's life and accomplishments in the context of culture and politics of the time. (Rev: SLJ 10/05) [921]

MANDELA, NELSON

16255 Connolly, Sean. *Nelson Mandela: An Unauthorized Biography* (5–7). 2000, Heinemann LB $24.22 (978-1-57572-225-2). 56pp. An appealing biography that contains good background material on South Africa, past and present. (Rev: SLJ 1/01)

16256 Kramer, Ann. *Mandela: The Rebel Who Led His Nation to Freedom* (4–6). Series: National Geographic World History Biographies. 2005, National Geographic $17.95 (978-0-7922-3658-0). 64pp. Mandela's life and accomplishments are placed in the context of the changing political climate in South Africa. (Rev: SLJ 10/05)

16257 Nelson, Kadir. *Nelson Mandela* (PS–3). Illus. by author. 2013, HarperCollins $17.99 (978-0-06-178374-6). 40pp. With large images and clear text, this is an effective portrait of the South African leader for young readers. Coretta Scott King Honor; ALA Notable Children's Book. Lexile 960L (Rev: BL 9/15/12; SLJ 1/13) [921]

MARSHAL, WILLIAM

16258 Weatherly, Myra. *William Marshal: Medieval England's Greatest Knight* (5–8). Illus. 2001, Morgan Reynolds LB $23.95 (978-1-883846-48-0). 112pp. The story of the brave medieval English knight whose accomplishments numbered fighting in tournaments, traveling to the Holy Land, helping to draw up the Magna Carta, and serving as regent when Henry III was a child. (Rev: BCCB 3/01; BL 1/1–15/01; HBG 10/01; SLJ 3/01)

MEDICI, LORENZO DE

16259 Hancock, Lee. *Lorenzo De' Medici: Florence's Great Leader and Patron of the Arts* (5–8). Series: Rulers, Scholars, and Artists of the Renaissance. 2005, Rosen LB $33.25 (978-1-4042-0315-0). Ford places de Medici's life and accomplishments in the context of culture and politics of the time. (Rev: SLJ 10/05) [921]

MILLMAN, ISAAC

16260 Millman, Isaac. *Hidden Child* (4–7). 2005, Farrar $18.00 (978-0-374-33071-2). The author relates his experiences as a child in World War II, when he was hidden in various homes in France to save him from the Nazis. (Rev: BL 6/1–15/05*; SLJ 9/05) [921]

MOHAPATRA, JYOTIRMAYEE

16261 Woog, Adam. *Jyotirmayee Mohapatra: Advocate for India's Young Women* (4–8). Illus. Series: Young Heroes. 2006, Gale LB $27.45 (978-0-7377-3611-3). 48pp. From a village in rural India, Mohapatra became worried at a young age about the challenges facing girls and young women; she went on to found the network of Meena Clubs for which she received the prestigious Youth Action Network award. (Rev: BL 1/1–15/07; SLJ 4/07)

MOTHER TERESA

16262 Demi. *Mother Teresa* (3–5). Illus. 2005, Simon & Schuster $19.95 (978-0-689-86407-0). 40pp. This informative picture-book biography looks at the nun's life, mission, and religious devotion. (Rev: BL 1/1–15/05; SLJ 2/05)

16263 Dils, Tracey E. *Mother Teresa* (4–8). Series: Women of Achievement. 2001, Chelsea $30.00 (978-0-7910-5887-9). 112pp. An absorbing account of the humanitarian's life from her childhood in Albania through her early years in India and her international work with the Missionaries of Charity. (Rev: HBG 3/02; SLJ 11/01)

16264 Ganeri, Anita. *Mother Teresa's Alms Bowl* (2–4). Illus. by Leighton Noyes. Series: Stories of Great People. 2008, Crabtree LB $29.27 (978-0-7787-3690-5); paper $9.95 (978-0-7787-3712-4). A fictional story is used as the framework for solid information about the nun and her work. (Rev: BL 4/1/08; SLJ 7/08)

16265 Morgan, Nina. *Mother Teresa: Saint of the Poor* (4–7). 1998, Raintree paper $7.95 (978-0-8172-7848-9). A biography of the nun whose work with the poor of India made her an international celebrity and earned her a Nobel Peace Prize. (Rev: BL 7/98; HBG 10/98; SLJ 7/98) [921]

16266 Ransom, Candice F. *Mother Teresa* (1–3). Illus. by Elaine Verstraete. Series: On My Own Biography. 2001, Carolrhoda LB $23.93 (978-1-57505-441-4). Mother Teresa's life from childhood and devotion to charitable work are presented in easy-reading text and full-page, realistic art. (Rev: HBG 10/01; SLJ 7/01)

16267 Tilton, Rafael. *Mother Teresa* (4–8). Series: The Importance Of. 2000, Lucent LB $27.45 (978-1-56006-565-4). This thoroughly researched account describes the life of Mother Teresa and gives an honest appraisal of her importance. (Rev: BL 1/1–15/00; HBG 9/00)

16268 Weiss, Ellen. *Mother Teresa: A Life of Kindness* (1–3). Illus. by Tina Walski. Series: Blastoff! Readers: People of Character. 2007, Children's Pr. LB $20.00 (978-0-531-14714-6). 24pp. For beginning readers, this is a simple account of Mother Teresa's life and work for the poor. (Rev: SLJ 1/08)

MUHAMMAD

16269 Demi. *Muhammad* (4–7). 2003, Simon & Schuster $19.95 (978-0-689-85264-0). This readable account of the life of the founding prophet of Islam is accompanied by quotations from the Koran and intricate illustrations. (Rev: BL 6/1–15/03*; HB 7–8/03; HBG 4/04; SLJ 8/03) [297.6]

NAKAHAMA, MANJIRO

16270 Blumberg, Rhoda. *Shipwrecked! The True Adventures of a Japanese Boy* (5–9). Illus. 2001, HarperCollins $16.95 (978-0-688-17484-2). 80pp. The story of a shipwrecked Japanese boy who was adopted by an American sea captain, brought to Massachusetts for an education, and became the first Japanese person to live in the United States. (Rev: BCCB 3/01; BL 2/1/01*; HB 3/01; HBG 10/01; SLJ 2/01)

16271 McCully, Emily Arnold. *Manjiro: The Boy Who Risked His Life for Two Countries* (2–5). Illus. by author. 2008, Farrar $16.95 (978-0-374-34792-5). 40pp. A large-format picture-book biography of the 14-year-old Japanese castaway who was rescued by an American and was influential in acquainting Japan with the outside world. (Rev: BL 9/1/08; HB 11/08)

NAPOLEON I

16272 Burleigh, Robert. *Napoleon: The Story of the Little Corporal* (5–8). Illus. 2007, Abrams $18.95 (978-0-8109-1378-3). 48pp. This informative and attractive biography of Napoleon from his childhood through his final defeat and exile uses an accessible, conversational style. (Rev: BL 6/1–15/07; SLJ 7/07)

NERO

16273 DiPrimio, Pete. *Nero* (5–8). Illus. Series: Junior Biographies from Ancient Civilizations. 2013, Mitchell Lane LB $29.95 (978-161228439-2). 48pp. The Roman emperor Nero is the subject of this biography that puts the chaos of his life into context. **e** (Rev: BL 11/1/13; LMC 3–4/14) [921]

NEZAHUALCOYOTL

16274 Serrano, Francisco. *The Poet King of Tezcoco: A Great Leader of Ancient Mexico* (5–8). Trans. by Trudy Balch. Illus. by Pablo Serrano. 2007, Groundwood $18.95 (978-0-88899-787-6). 48pp. This picture book for older readers introduces the life of Nezahualcoyotl, a 15th-century Toltec royal and poet who brought much advancement to his kingdom. (Rev: BL 6/1–15/07; SLJ 12/07)

NIGHTINGALE, FLORENCE

16275 Armentrout, David, and Patricia Armentrout. *Florence Nightingale* (2–4). Illus. Series: People Who Made a Difference. 2001, Rourke LB $20.64 (978-1-58952-053-0). 24pp. A simple introduction for younger readers to the life of nursing pioneer Florence Nightingale. (Rev: BL 1/1–15/02; SLJ 3/02)

16276 Barnham, Kay. *Florence Nightingale* (4–6). Series: Famous Lives. 2003, Raintree LB $27.12 (978-0-7398-5523-2). 48pp. The inspirational story of the gallant nurse who treated the wounded soldiers on the front lines during the Crimean War. (Rev: BL 2/15/03; HBG 10/03; SLJ 7/03)

16277 Tieck, Sarah. *Florence Nightingale* (K–3). Series: First Biographies. 2006, ABDO LB $25.65 (978-1-59679-786-4). A brief biography that introduces the life and work of the famous nurse in clear text and many photographs and reproductions. (Rev: SLJ 3/07)

NIVOLA, CLAIRE A.

16278 Nivola, Claire A. *Orani: My Father's Village* (2–5). Illus. by author. 2011, Farrar $16.99 (978-0-

374-35657-6). Unpaged. The author reminisces about her childhood spent in a small Sardinian village in this nostalgic memoir with evocative illustrations. SLJ Best Nonfiction Books of 2011; Horn Book Best Nonfiction Books of 2011. Lexile NC1080L (Rev: HB 9–10/11; SLJ 6/11*) [945]

PAHLAVI, MOHAMMED REZA

16279 Barth, Linda. *Mohammed Reza Pahlavi* (5–8). Series: Major World Leaders. 2002, Chelsea $30.00 (978-0-7910-6948-6). 104pp. An engrossing biography of the last Shah of Iran, who ruled during a tumultuous time in the region. (Rev: BL 1/1–15/03)

PETIT, PHILIPPE

16280 Gerstein, Mordicai. *The Man Who Walked Between the Towers* (PS–3). Illus. by author. 2007, Square Fish paper $6.99 (978-0-312-36878-4). This beautifully illustrated book vividly captures the day in 1974 when French aerialist Philippe Petit performed tricks on a high wire strung between the twin towers of New York City's World Trade Center. A paperback edition of the 2003 publication that won the 2004 Caldecott Medal. (Rev: BL BL 11/1/03; HB 11/03; HBG 4/04; SLJ 11/03)

PRINCE WILLIAM

16281 Dougherty, Terri. *Prince William* (5–8). Series: People in the News. 2001, Lucent LB $32.45 (978-1-56006-982-9). Using many quotes, good photographs, and an interesting text, this is a biography of the royal Prince Charming. (Rev: BL 4/1/02)

16282 Landau, Elaine. *Prince William: W.O.W., William of Wales* (4–6). Illus. Series: Gateway Biographies. 2002, Millbrook LB $23.90 (978-0-7613-2120-0). 48pp. A competent biography that explores the life of the very popular prince and his family through text and many color photographs. (Rev: BL 4/15/02; HBG 10/02)

16283 Wyborny, Sheila. *Prince William* (4–7). Illus. Series: Famous People. 2003, Gale $26.20 (978-0-7377-1401-2). 48pp. An interesting biography of the young prince that covers his mother's death and the difficulties of living in the limelight, with lots of color photographs. (Rev: BL 6/1–15/03)

PULASKI, CASIMIR

16284 Collins, David R. *Casimir Pulaski: Soldier on Horseback* (4–8). 1995, Pelican $14.95 (978-1-56554-082-8). A smoothly written biography of the Polish patriot who, though he could scarcely speak English, became an important figure helping the colonists during the Revolutionary War. (Rev: BL 2/15/96) [921]

PUTIN, VLADIMIR

16285 Shields, Charles J. *Vladimir Putin* (5–8). Illus. Series: Major World Leaders. 2002, Chelsea $30.00 (978-0-7910-6945-5). 112pp. Putin's family life, ambitions to be a spy, and accession to power are all covered in this fine biography. (Rev: BL 2/1/03; HBG 3/03; SLJ 3/03)

RINGELBLUM, EMMANUEL

16286 Beyer, Mark. *Emmanuel Ringelblum: Historian of the Warsaw Ghetto* (5–8). Series: Holocaust Biographies. 2001, Rosen LB $31.95 (978-0-8239-3375-4). This true story of a man who recorded events in the Warsaw Ghetto during the Holocaust includes black-and-white photographs. (Rev: BL 10/15/01) [940.53]

RUBIN, SUSAN GOLDMAN

16287 Rubin, Susan G., and Ela Weissberger. *The Cat with the Yellow Star: Coming of Age in Terezin* (3–6). 2006, Holiday House $16.95 (978-0-8234-1831-2). 40pp. A survivor of the Terezin death camp recalls her time there as a child, especially playing the role of a cat in the opera Brundibar; photographs and other features help young children to understand what happened at the camp. (Rev: SLJ 6/06*)

SADAT, ANWAR

16288 Kras, Sara Louise. *Anwar Sadat* (5–8). Series: Major World Leaders. 2002, Chelsea $30.00 (978-0-7910-6949-3). 112pp. An absorbing account of the life of the famous Egyptian leader who shared the 1978 Nobel Peace Prize with Israeli Prime Minister Menachem Begin. (Rev: BL 1/1–15/03; HBG 3/03)

SANTA ANNA, ANTONIO LOPEZ DE

16289 Bankston, John. *Antonio López de Santa Anna* (5–7). Series: Latinos in American History. 2003, Mitchell Lane LB $29.95 (978-1-58415-209-5). A biography of the Mexican general, president, and statesman who is best known for his part in the Battle of the Alamo. (Rev: BL 1/1–15/04; HBG 4/04; SLJ 2/04) [921]

SCHLIEMANN, HEINRICH

16290 Schlitz, Laura Amy. *The Hero Schliemann: The Dreamer Who Dug for Troy* (4–6). Illus. by Robert Byrd. 2006, Candlewick $17.99 (978-0-7636-2283-1). This frank biography of Heinrich Schliemann reveals the flaws in the man who excavated Troy. (Rev: SLJ 9/06)

SENDLER, IRENA

16291 Rubin, Susan Goldman. *Irena Sendler and the Children of the Warsaw Ghetto* (3–6). Illus. by Bill Farnsworth. 2011, Holiday House $18.95 (978-0-8234-2251-7). 32pp. Rubin tells the inspiring story of a young Catholic social worker who risked her life to protect Warsaw Jews from the Nazis. (Rev: BL 4/15/11; LMC 10/11; SLJ 5/11) [940.53]

16292 Vaughan, Marcia. *Irena's Jars of Secrets* (4–7). Illus. by Ron Mazellan. 2011, Lee & Low $18.95 (978-1-60060-439-3). 40pp. A picture-book profile of Irena Sendler, a Polish Catholic social worker who helped save nearly 2,500 children in the Warsaw Ghetto from deportation to the death camps in the early 1940s. Sydney Taylor Book Honor 2012. Lexile 1040L (Rev: BL 12/1/11; LMC 5–6/12; SLJ 11/1/11) [921]

SIEGAL, ARANKA

16293 Siegal, Aranka. *Memories of Babi* (4–7). 2008, Farrar $16.00 (978-0-374-39978-8). The author recalls her pleasant, simple life as a child in Hungary and her closeness to her Jewish grandmother in the years preceding those covered in *Upon the Head of a Goat* (1981). Sidney Taylor Book Honor 2009. (Rev: BL 12/15/07; HB 9–10/08) [947.7]

SILVA, MARINA

16294 Hildebrant, Ziporah. *Marina Silva: Defending Rainforest Communities in Brazil* (5–8). Series: Women Changing the World. 2001, Feminist $19.95 (978-1-55861-292-1). Though battling a serious illness, this gallant woman, once a leader of the native Amazonians, has become a leading figure in protecting the forests of Brazil. (Rev: BL 12/15/01) [921]

SOCRATES

16295 Dell, Pamela. *Socrates: Ancient Greek in Search of Truth* (5–8). Illus. Series: Signature Lives. 2006, Compass Point LB $34.60 (978-0-7565-1874-5). A solid profile of the Greek philosopher that underlines his importance and provides insight into life in ancient Athens. (Rev: BL 10/15/06) [183]

16296 Usher, M. D. *Wise Guy: The Life and Philosophy of Socrates* (2–4). Illus. by William Bramhall. 2005, Farrar $16.00 (978-0-374-31249-7). 40pp. This is a useful but not altogether successful effort to combine a life of Socrates, including his childhood, and a discussion of his philosophical beliefs. (Rev: BL 1/1–15/06; SLJ 1/06)

SON THI ANH, TUYET

16297 Skrypuch, Marsha Forchuk. *Last Airlift: A Vietnamese Orphan's Rescue from War* (4–8). Illus. 2012, Pajama $17.95 (978-098694954-8). 120pp. Tells the story of 8-year-old Son Thi Anh Tuyet, a Vietnamese orphan whose suffering had included polio, who was on the last Canadian flight out of Saigon in 1975. Lexile 670L (Rev: BL 4/15/12; HB 9–10/12; SLJ 4/12) [921]

16298 Skrypuch, Marsha Forchuk. *One Step at a Time: A Vietnamese Child Finds Her Way* (4–8). Illus. 2012, Pajama $17.95 (978-192748501-9). 93pp. This sequel to *Last Airlift* (2012) continues Tuyet's story as she adjusts to her new Toronto family and undergoes surgery for the deformities caused by polio. (Rev: BL 12/1/12; HB 3–4/13; SLJ 2/13) [921]

SOYER, ALEXIS

16299 Arnold, Ann. *The Adventurous Chef: Alexis Soyer* (3–6). Illus. 2002, Farrar $17.00 (978-0-374-31665-5). 40pp. A fascinating, well-illustrated biography that introduces a famous 19th-century chef and innovator who cooked for the rich but also strove to improve nutrition for the poor, the hungry, and the military. (Rev: BL 12/15/02; HB 11/02; HBG 3/03; SLJ 10/02)

ST. COLUMBA

16300 Brown, Don. *Across a Dark and Wild Sea* (K–4). Illus. 2002, Millbrook LB $22.90 (978-0-7613-2415-7). 32pp. The story of the 6th-century Irish monk and scholar Columcille, or Saint Columba, who founded a monastery on the Scottish island of Iona. (Rev: BCCB 5/02; BL 4/1/02*; HB 5/02; HBG 10/02; SLJ 5/02)

ST. FRANCIS OF ASSISI

16301 Kennedy, Robert F., Jr. *Saint Francis of Assisi: A Life of Joy* (2–4). Illus. by Dennis Nolan. 2005, Hyperion $18.99 (978-0-7868-1875-4). Environmental activist Robert F. Kennedy Jr. chronicles the life of Saint Francis of Assisi, his patron saint. (Rev: BL 2/15/05; SLJ 5/05)

ST. HILDEGARD

16302 Winter, Jonah. *The Secret World of Hildegard* (1–4). Illus. by Jeanette Winter. 2007, Scholastic $16.99 (978-0-439-50739-4). This is an interesting introduction to the life and work of Hildegard of Bingen, the medieval mystic, with a focus on her childhood. (Rev: BCCB 10/07; BL 10/1/07; HB 9/07; SLJ 10/07)

ST. THERESE OF LISIEUX

16303 Driscoll, Chris. *God's Little Flower: The Story of St. Therese of Lisieux* (PS–3). Illus. by Patrick Kelley. 2001, Ambassador $13.95 (978-1-929039-05-0). 32pp. A simple, illustrated story of the little girl who became a saint. (Rev: BL 10/1/01; HBG 10/01)

STEINER, MATTHEW

16304 Warren, Andrea. *Escape from Saigon: How a Vietnam War Orphan Became an American Boy* (5–12). 2004, Farrar $17.00 (978-0-374-32224-3). An inspiring account of a young Amerasian war orphan's long journey from Vietnam to a new and successful life in the United States; Long was part of the 1975 Operation Babylift and took the name of Matt Steiner when he was adopted by an American family. (Rev: BL 6/1–15/04*; SLJ 10/04) [959.704]

SUGIHARA, CHIUNE

16305 Gold, Alison L. *A Special Fate: Chiune Sugihara: Hero of the Holocaust* (5–10). 2000, Scholastic paper $15.95 (978-0-590-39525-0). 176pp. The life story of the Japanese diplomat who saved thousands of Jewish lives during the Holocaust while he was stationed in Lithuania. (Rev: BCCB 5/00; BL 4/1/00; HB 5/00; HBG 10/00; SLJ 5/00; VOYA 6/00)

SUZUKI, SHINICHI

16306 Collins, David R. *Dr. Shinichi Suzuki: Teaching Music from the Heart* (4–8). 2001, Morgan Reynolds LB $23.95 (978-1-883846-49-7). 112pp. This account covers Suzuki's childhood, his interest in music, and his development of a successful method of teaching music, especially the violin, to young children. (Rev: BL 12/15/01; HBG 3/02; SLJ 4/02; VOYA 10/03)

TAMANG, JHALAK MAN

16307 Miller, Raymond H. *Jhalak Man Tamang: Slave Labor Whistleblower* (4–7). Series: Young Heroes. 2006, Gale LB $23.70 (978-0-7377-3616-8). This biography chronicles the life of Tamang, who was able to escape a life as a child weaving carpets in Nepal and bring to light the abuses of the industry. (Rev: SLJ 6/07) [921]

TENZING NORGAY

16308 Burleigh, Robert. *Tiger of the Snows: Tenzing Norgay: The Boy Whose Dream Was Everest* (4–6). Illus. by Ed Young. 2006, Simon & Schuster $16.95 (978-0-689-83042-6). 40pp. This picture-book biography of Tenzing Norgay uses beautiful illustrations and poetry to tell the story of the Sherpa guide who conquered Mount Everest in 1953 with Sir Edmund Hillary. (Rev: BL 6/1–15/06; SLJ 6/06)

TOUSSAINT L'OUVERTURE, FRANÇOIS-DOMINIQUE

16309 Rockwell, Anne. *Open the Door to Liberty: A Biography of Toussaint L'Ouverture* (5–8). Illus. by R. Gregory Christie. 2009, Houghton $18.00 (978-0-618-60570-5). 80pp. A well-written and well-researched biography of the freed slave who led a rebellion against the French in 1793 on what is now known as Haiti. (Rev: BL 2/1/09; LMC 10/09; SLJ 3/09) [921]

TRYSZYNSKA, LUBA

16310 Tryszynska-Frederick, Luba. *Luba: The Angel of Bergen-Belsen* (3–6). Illus. by Ann Marshall. 2004, Tricycle $17.99 (978-1-58246-098-7). 48pp. The true story of Luba Tryszynska, a Polish Jew who sheltered and fed more than 50 Dutch Jewish children she found abandoned near her Bergen-Belsen barracks, is recounted in simple, moving prose and accompanied by factual front and back matter. (Rev: BL 11/1/03; HBG 4/04; SLJ 12/03)

TUTANKHAMEN, KING

16311 Hawass, Zahi. *Tutankhamun: The Mystery of the Boy King* (4–7). 2005, National Geographic $17.95 (978-0-7922-8354-6). The director of excavations at key Egyptian archaeological sites offers a fascinating account of the life, death, and burial of King Tut and of new revelations about his fate. (Rev: BL 11/1/05; SLJ 10/05*) [932]

16312 Stewart, David. *You Wouldn't Want to Be Tutankhamen! A Mummy Who Really Got Meddled With* (3–6). Illus. by David Antram. Series: You Wouldn't Want to . . . 2007, Watts LB $28.50 (978-0-531-18725-8); paper $9.95 (978-0-531-18924-5). 32pp. An entertaining look at the boy king and the problems he faced. Cartoons keep the tone light. (Rev: SLJ 8/07)

WALLENBERG, RAOUL

16313 Linnea, Sharon. *Raoul Wallenberg: The Man Who Stopped Death* (5–7). 1993, Jewish Publication Soc. paper $9.95 (978-0-8276-0448-3). This Swedish architect saved thousands of Jews in Hungary from the Nazi Holocaust. (Rev: BL 6/1–15/93) [940]

16314 McArthur, Debra. *Raoul Wallenberg: Rescuing Thousands from the Nazis' Grasp* (5–7). Series: Holocaust Heroes and Nazi Criminals. 2005, Enslow LB $27.93 (978-0-7660-2530-1). A well-documented profile of the courageous Swedish diplomat who saved thousands of Hungarian Jews and disappeared after the end of the war. (Rev: SLJ 11/05) [921]

WIESENTHAL, SIMON

16315 Rubin, Susan Goldman. *The Anne Frank Case: Simon Wiesenthal's Search for the Truth* (4–7). Illus. by Bill Farnsworth. 2009, Holiday $18.95 (978-0-8234-2109-1). This profile of the Nazi hunter and his career starts with an account of Holocaust deniers prompting Wiesenthal to search for the Gestapo officer who arrested Anne Frank's family. (Rev: BCCB 4/09; BL 3/1/09*; SLJ 3/09) [921]

WILLIAM, PRINCE, AND MIDDLETON, KATE

16316 Doeden, Matt. *Prince William and Kate: A Royal Romance* (5–8). Illus. 2011, Lerner LB $26.60 (978-076138029-0). 48pp. Tells the story of Kate and William's individual lives and their relationship, ending with their wedding day; with many photographs and a timeline. (Rev: BL 11/1/11) [921]

XIAOPING, DENG

16317 Stewart, Whitney. *Deng Xiaoping: Leader in a Changing China* (4–7). Series: Lerner Biographies. 2001, Lerner LB $30.35 (978-0-8225-4962-8). An accessible biography of the most powerful man in China from the 1970s until his death, with details of how his reputation was tarnished by the Tiananmen Square massacre. (Rev: BL 9/15/01; HBG 10/01; SLJ 7/01) [921]

YEBOAH, EMMANUEL OFOSU

16318 Currie-Mcghee, Leanne K. *Emmanuel Ofosu Yeboah: Champion for Ghana's Disabled* (4–7). Series: Young Heroes. 2006, Gale LB $23.70 (978-0-7377-3614-4). 48pp. The inspiring story of a disabled Ghanaian who fought for equal rights in a culture that discriminated against the physically challenged. (Rev: SLJ 6/07)

ZHENG HE

16319 Demi. *The Great Voyages of Zheng He* (3–5). Illus. by author. 2012, Shens $21.95 (978-188500845-9). 64pp. An admiring, nicely illustrated profile of the 15th-century Chinese admiral who made seven important voyages with his large fleet, bringing great wealth back to China. (Rev: BL 2/15/13; SLJ 2/13) [921]

16320 Zhang, Hao Yu, and Song Nan Zhang. *The Great Voyages of Zheng He* (4–6). Illus. by Song Nan Zhang. 2005, Pan Asian $16.95 (978-1-57227-088-6). 32pp. The voyages of discovery of Zheng He, a Chinese explorer in the early 1400s, are described in this large-format, richly illustrated volume. (Rev: BL 10/15/05; SLJ 11/05)

The Arts and Language

Art and Architecture

General and Miscellaneous

16321 Agee, Jon, et al. *Why Did the Chicken Cross the Road?* (1–4). Illus. 2006, Dial $16.99 (978-0-8037-3094-6). Why did the chicken cross the road? Fourteen artists — including Chris Raschka, Mo Willems, and Jerry Pinkney — answer the question. (Rev: BCCB 11/06; BL 10/1/06; HBG 4/07; LMC 3/07; SLJ 10/06*)

16322 Ajmera, Maya, and John D. Ivanko. *To Be an Artist* (K–3). Illus. 2004, Charlesbridge $15.95 (978-1-57091-503-1). This photo-filled excursion shows young people in countries around the world participating in various artistic activities; a map pinpoints their locations. (Rev: BL 3/1/04; SLJ 3/04)

16323 Ancona, George. *Murals: Walls That Sing* (5–8). Illus. 2003, Marshall Cavendish $17.95 (978-0-7614-5131-0). 48pp. A photoessay showing murals stretching back from today's urban frescos to the cave paintings of Lascaux. (Rev: BL 4/15/03; HBG 4/04; SLJ 5/03)

16324 Andrews-Goebel, Nancy. *The Pot That Juan Built* (2–4). Illus. by David Diaz. 2002, Lee & Low $16.95 (978-1-58430-038-0). 32pp. This almost-multimedia introduction to the work of Mexican potter Juan Quezada allows the reader to choose between rhyme, prose, illustration, and photography that all describe facets of the artist's life and work. (Rev: BL 9/15/02; HBG 3/03; SLJ 9/02*)

16325 Apodaca, Blanca, and Michael Serwich. *Behind the Canvas: An Artist's Life* (3–6). Illus. Series: Time for Kids. 2012, Teacher Created Materials paper $9.99 (978-14333482-6-6). 48pp. This interesting volume introduces many aspects of an artist's work, providing pertinent facts and thought-provoking questions about creativity and the choices artists must make. Lexile 660L (Rev: BL 11/1/12; LMC 5–6/13*) [750]

16326 Arbogast, Joan Marie. *Buildings in Disguise: Architecture That Looks Like Animals, Food, and Other Things* (4–7). 2004, Boyds Mills $16.95 (978-1-59078-099-2). Buildings in the shapes of milk bottles, elephants, wigwams, and baskets are among the wonders shown in many period and contemporary photographs. (Rev: BL 11/1/04; SLJ 1/05) [720]

16327 *Artist to Artist: 23 Major Illustrators Talk to Children About Their Art* (5–8). Illus. 2007, Philomel $30.00 (978-0-399-24600-5). 64pp. More than 20 children's book illustrators (including Quentin Blake, Leo Lionni, and Tomie dePaola) contribute creative self-portraits and insightful thoughts to this beautiful gatefolded book. (Rev: BL 11/1/07; SLJ 10/07)

16328 Barber, Nicola. *Islamic Art and Culture* (5–8). Series: World Art and Culture. 2005, Raintree LB $32.86 (978-1-4109-1105-6). High-quality color photographs document the architecture, sculpture, painting, pottery, music, dance, and other art forms found in the Islamic world from early times to the present. (Rev: BL 4/1/04)

16329 Bingham, Jane. *Graffiti* (5–7). Illus. Series: Culture in Action. 2009, Raintree LB $28.21 (978-1-4109-3401-7); paper $7.99 (978-1-4109-3418-5). 32pp. Bingham traces the history of graffiti back to cave walls and describes (with examples) modern forms and the pitfalls of indulging in this activity. (Rev: LMC 3–4/10; SLJ 2/10) [751.7]

16330 Bingham, Jane. *Illusion Art* (3–6). Illus. Series: Art off the Wall. 2006, Heinemann LB $32.86 (978-1-4034-8290-7). 56pp. The optical illusion on the cover of this book will draw in young artists who would like to create similar works. Professional artists and their techniques are featured. (Rev: SLJ 5/07)

16331 Bingham, Jane. *Indian Art and Culture* (5–8). Illus. Series: World Art and Culture. 2004, Raintree LB $29.99 (978-0-7398-6607-8). 56pp. High-quality color photographs document the architecture, sculpture, painting, pottery, music, dance, and other art forms found in India from early times to the present. Also use *Aboriginal Art and Culture* (2004). (Rev: BL 4/1/04; SLJ 2/04)

16332 Bingham, Jane. *Michelangelo* (3–6). Series: Culture in Action. 2010, Heinemann-Raintree $28.21 (978-

1-4109-3402-4). 32pp. A high-interest introduction to Michelangelo's work with activities that reinforce literacy and knowledge of the arts. Lexile 770L (Rev: LMC 3–4/10) [709.2]

16333 Bingham, Jane. *Science and Technology* (4–7). Series: Through Artists' Eyes. 2006, Raintree LB $32.86 (978-1-4109-2241-0). 56pp. A brief but interesting exploration of the ways in which artists have documented the progress of science and technology over the years. Also use *Landscape and the Environment* and *Society and Class* (both 2006). (Rev: SLJ 1/07)

16334 Bingham, Jane. *War and Conflict* (3–5). Illus. Series: Through Artists' Eyes. 2006, Raintree LB $23.00 (978-1-4109-2236-6). 56pp. This title examines works of art — fine art but also cartoons, posters, films, stories, plays, and poems — that explore themes of war and conflict. (Rev: BL 8/06; SLJ 1/07)

16335 Blake, Quentin. *Tell Me a Picture* (K–6). Illus. by author. 2003, Millbrook LB $29.90 (978-0-7613-2748-6). 128pp. Adapted from an exhibit at London's National Gallery, this book contains 26 pictures — some from picture books and others from British art galleries — and guidance for finding the story in each. (Rev: HB 7/03; HBG 10/03; SLJ 10/03)

16336 Bos, Samone. *Super Structures* (5–8). Illus. by Alessandro Rabatti. 2008, DK $19.99 (978-0-7566-4088-0). 80pp. Captivating photographs, illustrations, and diagrams enhance the text in this fascinating survey of buildings and structures across history. (Rev: BL 12/1/08; SLJ 3/09) [720]

16337 Brewster, Hugh. *Carnation, Lily, Lily, Rose: The Story of a Painting* (3–5). Illus. by John Singer Sargent. 2007, Kids Can $17.95 (978-1-55453-137-0). 48pp. Kate, an English girl who hopes to be a model for John Singer Sargent's painting *Carnation, Lily, Lily, Rose,* is disappointed when he chooses other children, then relieved when she realizes the difficulty of being an artist's model in this fictionalized story illustrated with photographs and reproductions of Sargent's work and drawing on primary sources. (Rev: BL 11/1/07; LMC 1/08; SLJ 1/08)

16338 Browne, Anthony. *The Shape Game* (K–4). Illus. by author. 2003, Farrar $16.00 (978-0-374-36764-0). 32pp. Browne's inventive account of a visit to an art museum offers plenty of humor and facts about art. (Rev: HB 9/03; HBG 4/04; SLJ 9/03)

16339 Carter, David A. *600 Black Spots: A Pop-up Book for Children of All Ages* (3–6). Illus. by author. 2007, Simon & Schuster $19.99 (978-1-4169-4092-0). 24pp. More suitable for display than circulation, this marvel of paper engineering stimulates its audience with colorful abstract paper sculptures, each spread containing a challenge to find a given number of black spots. (Rev: BL 11/1/07; SLJ 1/08)

16340 Chaplik, Dorothy. *Latin American Arts and Cultures* (5–8). Illus. 2001, Davis $26.95 (978-0-87192-547-3). 128pp. An encompassing look at Latin American art, architecture, and culture, from pre-Columbian

to present-day, complete with pronunciation guide and captioned reproductions or photographs on each page. (Rev: BL 11/1/01)

16341 Chapman, Caroline. *Battles and Weapons: Exploring History Through Art* (4–9). Series: Picture That! 2007, Two-Can $19.95 (978-1-58728-588-2). 64pp. A look at how weapons and war have been depicted in artwork beginning in ancient times and ending in the 1950s. (Rev: SLJ 8/07)

16342 *Children's Book of Art: An Introduction to the World's Most Amazing Paintings and Sculptures* (5–8). Illus. 2009, DK $24.99 (978-0-7566-5511-2). 144pp. This well-designed, large-format volume includes everything from artist profiles to style analysis to how-to instructions. (Rev: BLO 10/1/09; LMC 11–12/09; SLJ 10/09) [700]

16343 Coyne, Jennifer Tarr. *Come Look with Me: Discovering Women Artists for Children* (4–7). Series: Come Look with Me. 2005, Lickle $15.95 (978-1-890674-08-3). Beautifully reproduced examples of works by women artists are paired with brief biographical information and questions that direct the reader's attention to different aspects of art. (Rev: BL 5/1/05; SLJ 6/05) [709]

16344 Cressy, Judith. *Can You Find It?* (2–5). Illus. 2002, Abrams $15.95 (978-0-8109-3279-1). Readers are challenged to search for details (bows, cats, flowers, and other items) within artwork from New York City's Metropolitan Museum of Art. (Rev: BL 2/15/03; HBG 3/03; SLJ 1/03)

16345 Cressy, Judith. *Can You Find It, Too? Search and Discover More Than 150 Details in 20 Works of Art* (2–5). 2004, Abrams $15.95 (978-0-8109-5046-7). 40pp. This sequel to *Can You Find It?* (2003) invites readers to search for features of 20 pieces of art. (Rev: BL 11/1/04)

16346 Cummings, Pat. *Talking with Artists, Vol. 3* (4–8). Series: Talking with Artists. 1999, Clarion $22.00 (978-0-395-89132-2). This is the third volume of interviews with children's artists and includes Peter Sis, Betsy Lewin, and Paul O. Zelinsky, with examples of their works. (Rev: BCCB 4/99; BL 3/15/99; HB 5–6/99; HBG 10/99; SLJ 4/99) [741.6]

16347 D'Harcourt, Claire. *Art Up Close: From Ancient to Modern* (3–5). 2003, Chronicle $19.95 (2-02-059694-6). 63pp. Readers are challenged to find details in 23 representative works that span the history of art; the second part of this oversize book with flaps provides information on the works and artists. (Rev: HBG 4/04; SLJ 12/03)

16348 D'Harcourt, Claire. *Masterpieces Up Close: Western Painting from the 14th to 20th Centuries* (4–8). Trans. from French by Shoshanna Kirk. Series: Up Close. 2006, Chronicle $22.95 (978-0-8118-5403-0). 63pp. An oversize volume that challenges readers to analyze major works of Western art. (Rev: SLJ 7/06)

16349 Delafosse, Claude. *Landscapes* (4–7). Series: First Discovery Art. 1996, Scholastic $11.95 (978-0-590-50216-0). The art and techniques of landscape painting are introduced, with many examples from the masters in various historical periods. (Rev: BL 6/1–15/96; SLJ 7/96) [750]

16350 Delafosse, Claude. *Paintings* (4–7). Series: First Discovery Art. 1996, Scholastic $11.95 (978-0-590-55201-1). A general introduction to painting, with many reproductions and lessons in art appreciation. (Rev: BL 6/1–15/96; SLJ 7/96) [750]

16351 Desnoëttes, Caroline. *Look Closer: Art Masterpieces Through the Ages* (3–6). 2006, Walker $18.95 (978-0-8027-9614-1). Readers' attention to the diverse masterpieces is focused through the innovative use of flaps that ask questions, offer information, and pinpoint areas of interest. (Rev: SLJ 12/06)

16352 Domeniconi, David. *M Is for Masterpiece: An Art Alphabet* (4–6). Illus. by Will Bullas. 2006, Sleeping Bear $17.95 (978-1-58536-276-9). 32pp. An A-to-Z look at the world of art, covering everything from famous artists and artwork to different art styles and the various tools needed. (Rev: BL 12/1/06; SLJ 11/06)

16353 Fisanick, Christina, ed. *Eco-Architecture* (5–10). Series: Opposing Viewpoints. 2008, Gale $36.20 (978-0-7377-3996-1); paper $24.95 (978-0-7377-3997-8). 234pp. This is a wide-ranging discussion of green building techniques and the benefits to the environment. (Rev: SLJ 11/08)

16354 Flatt, Lizann. *Arts and Culture in the Early Islamic World* (5–7). Illus. Series: Life in the Early Islamic World. 2012, Crabtree LB $30.60 (978-077872167-3). 48pp. With excellent illustrations, this attractive volume provides a solid introduction to Islamic calligraphy, architecture, and decorative arts and their importance to the overall culture of the time. (Rev: BL 8/12*; SLJ 8/12) [700.917]

16355 Fritz, Jean. *Leonardo's Horse* (4–7). Illus. by Hudson Talbott. 2001, Putnam $18.99 (978-0-399-23576-4). The story of a Leonardo da Vinci sculpture that was begun in 1493 and finally completed — thanks to the efforts of Charles Dent — in 1999, along with biographical information about da Vinci and examples of his work. (Rev: BCCB 10/01; BL 10/15/01; HB 9–10/01; HBG 3/02; SLJ 9/01) [730]

16356 Glenn, Patricia Brown. *Under Every Roof: A Kid's Style and Field Guide to the Architecture of American Houses* (5–8). 1993, Preservation $16.95 (978-0-89133-214-5). An introduction to the history and styles of architecture of American homes, with a look at more than 70 houses. (Rev: BL 7/94; SLJ 6/94) [728]

16357 Goldberg, Dana, ed. *On My Block: Stories and Paintings by Fifteen Artists* (1–5). 2007, Children's Book Pr. $16.95 (978-0-89239-220-9). 32pp. A visually engaging array of artwork by diverse artists that offer readers a specific sense of place. (Rev: SLJ 12/07)

16358 Goldin, David. *Meet Me at the Art Museum: A Whimsical Look Behind the Scenes* (1–3). Illus. by author. 2012, Abrams $18.95 (978-1-4197-0187-0). 40pp. A ticket stub and a docent's name tag explore a museum after hours, learning about all the activities that

take place there. (Rev: BL 11/1/12; LMC 5–6/13*; SLJ 10/12) [708]

16359 Gonyea, Mark. *Another Book About Design: Complicated Doesn't Make It Bad* (3–5). Illus. by author. 2007, Holt $19.95 (978-0-8050-7576-2). 64pp. Foreground and background, positive and negative space, and repetitive use of shapes are among the design concepts introduced here, with each principle progressing toward a finished picture. (Rev: BCCB 10/07; BL 7/07; SLJ 9/07)

16360 Gonyea, Mark. *A Book About Design: Complicated Doesn't Make It Good* (3–5). Illus. 2005, Hyperion $18.95 (978-0-7868-7575-7). 144pp. A stylish but challenging introduction to the principles of graphic design, covering topics including shape, color, and contrast and providing plenty of illustrations to help young artists see what good design looks like. (Rev: BL 5/1/05; SLJ 7/05)

16361 Guéry, Anne, and Olivier Dussutour. *Alphab'art* (1–4). 2009, Frances Lincoln $19.95 (978-1-84780-013-8). 60pp. This fascinating artistic tour of the alphabet challenges readers to find the individual letters in diverse works of art — some familiar and some lesser-known; the back matter provides context. (Rev: BLO 11/15/09; SLJ 1/10) [421.1]

16362 Hale, Christy. *Dreaming Up: A Celebration of Building* (PS–3). Illus. by author. 2012, Lee & Low $18.95 (978-160060651-9). 40pp. Two-page spreads pair structures created by children with real-life architecture around the world. (Rev: BL 1/13; LMC 5–6/13*; SLJ 10/12) [720]

16363 Harris, Nathaniel. *Mosaics* (4–6). Illus. 2008, PowerKids LB $18.95 (978-1-4042-4438-2). 32pp. This broad introduction defines mosaics and discusses how they are made, then looks at some individual mosaics and provides four craft ideas. (Rev: BL 12/15/08; SLJ 7/09)

16364 Harris, Nathaniel. *Wall Paintings* (4–8). Series: Stories in Art. 2008, Rosen LB $25.25 (978-1-4042-4440-5). 30pp. What are wall paintings? How are they made? After a discussion of mural history and techniques, the author looks at outstanding examples and presents three visually engaging projects with clear directions and interesting stories. (Rev: LMC 8/09; SLJ 7/09)

16365 Henry, Sandi. *Making Amazing Art: 40 Activities Using the 7 Elements of Art Design* (2–5). Illus. by Sarah Cole. Series: Kids Can. 2007, Williamson $16.99 (978-0-8249-6794-9); paper $12.99 (978-0-8249-6795-6). 128pp. This title takes one artistic concept (shape, texture, color, for example) at at time and teams it with projects that clarify and extend the concept. (Rev: SLJ 12/07)

16366 Hibbert, Clare. *Chinese Art and Culture* (5–8). Series: World Art and Culture. 2005, Raintree LB $29.99 (978-1-4109-1107-0). High-quality color photographs document the architecture, sculpture, painting, pottery, music, dance, and other art forms found in China from early times to the present. (Rev: BL 4/1/04)

16367 Hosack, Karen. *Animals* (2–4). Series: How Artists View. 2004, Heinemann LB $24.22 (978-1-4034-4850-7). 32pp. Animals are the subject of this interesting volume in a series that looks at the ways in which artists view and depict various themes. Also in this series are *Nature, Families, Weather, Food,* and *Homes* (all 2004). (Rev: BL 12/1/04)

16368 Hosack, Karen. *Buildings* (4–8). Illus. Series: What Is Art? 2008, Raintree LB $27.50 (978-1-4109-3165-8). 32pp. Hosack introduces a number of kinds of buildings — public spaces, private residences, memorials, and so forth — and discusses their function and form; a bright layout and well-chosen illustrations add appeal. (Rev: SLJ 3/1/09) [720]

16369 Hosack, Karen. *Drawings and Cartoons* (4–8). Illus. Series: What Is Art? 2008, Raintree LB $27.50 (978-1-4109-3163-4). 32pp. Drawings from Michelangelo to modern-day are on display here, accompanied by a paragraph disclosing their purpose and posing questions about their style. (Rev: SLJ 3/1/09) [741]

16370 Hosack, Karen. *Paintings* (4–8). Series: What Is Art? 2008, Raintree LB $27.50 (978-1-4109-3162-7). 32pp. This is an attractive introduction to paintings of many styles, asking readers to consider composition, audience, symbolism, and so forth. (Rev: SLJ 3/09)

16371 Jakab, Cheryl. *Clay* (3–6). Illus. Series: Artists at Work. 2007, Smart Apple LB $27.10 (978-1-58340-775-2). 32pp. Readers will learn how artists work in clay and view some of the pieces they have made — both historical and contemporary. Also in this series, use *Metals, Stone,* and *Wood* (2007). (Rev: SLJ 5/07)

16372 Johmann, Carol A. *Skyscrapers!* (3–6). Illus. by Michael Kline. Series: Kaleidoscope Kids. 2001, Williamson paper $14.25 (978-1-885593-50-4). Cartoonlike drawings and black-and-white photographs are including in this appealing and informative look at skyscrapers, their history, and the structural and design challenges they pose, which also includes a a number of related activities. (Rev: BL 12/15/01; SLJ 3/02)

16373 Khanduri, Kamini. *Japanese Art and Culture* (5–8). Series: World Art and Culture. 2004, Raintree LB $29.99 (978-0-7398-6609-2). High-quality color photographs document the architecture, sculpture, painting, pottery, music, dance, and other art forms found in Japan from early times to the present. (Rev: BL 4/1/04)

16374 Knapp, Ruthie, and Janice Lehmberg. *Impressionist Art* (5–9). Series: Off the Wall Museum Guides for Kids. 1999, Davis paper $9.95 (978-0-87192-385-1). This pocket-size guide supplies an overview of Impressionism and brief introductions to major artists, including Sisley and Monet. (Rev: BL 1/1–15/99) [709.03]

16375 Knapp, Ruthie, and Janice Lehmberg. *Modern Art* (5–9). Series: Off the Wall Museum Guides for Kids. 2001, Davis paper $9.95 (978-0-87192-458-2). A lively and colorful survey of 20th-century art including examples from expressionists, cubists, surrealists, and pop artists. (Rev: BL 8/1/01) [709]

16376 Lach, William. *Can You Hear It?* (K–3). Illus. 2007, Abrams $18.95 (978-0-8109-5721-3). 32pp. A handsome picture book in which reproductions of artistic masterpieces are paired with classical music selections on the accompanying CD; author Lach suggests connections and focal points and provides information on the artists, composers, and musical instruments. (Rev: BL 3/15/07)

16377 Lane, Kimberly. *Come Look with Me: Asian Art* (3–7). Illus. by author. 2008, Charlesbridge $15.95 (978-1-890674-19-9). 32pp. Lane introduces readers to a wide variety of Asian works of art, prefacing each with pertinent questions. (Rev: BLO 6/17/08; SLJ 8/08) [709.5]

16378 Lane, Kimberly. *Come Look with Me: Latin American Art* (4–8). Illus. Series: Come Look with Me. 2007, Charlesbridge $15.95 (978-1-890674-20-5). 32pp. An oversize introduction to Latin American art over the last two centuries, with color reproductions and information on the artists' lives and techniques. (Rev: BL 8/07; LMC 1/08; SLJ 8/07)

16379 Laroche, Giles. *What's Inside? Fascinating Structures Around the World* (4–8). Illus. by author. 2009, Houghton Mifflin $17 (978-0-618-86247-4). Unpaged. This handsome, fact-filled volume looks at both the exteriors and interiors (with people going about activities) of 14 structures ranging from tombs, temples, and castles to skyscrapers and the Sydney Opera House. (Rev: BL 2/15/09; SLJ 5/1/09) [720]

16380 McCully, Emily Arnold. *The Secret Cave: Discovering Lascaux* (1–3). Illus. by author. 2010, Farrar $16.99 (978-0-374-36694-0). 40pp. The 1940 discovery of the striking cave paintings at Lascaux by French schoolboys is the focus of this dramatically illustrated picture book. (Rev: BL 11/1/10; LMC 11–12/10; SLJ 10/1/10*) [944]

16381 MacDonald, Fiona. *Design* (3–5). Illus. Series: Culture Encyclopedia. 2002, Mason Crest LB $18.95 (978-1-59084-476-2). 40pp. The importance of design in such areas as fashion, food, technology, and architecture is discussed in this introduction to style around the world. (Rev: SLJ 3/03)

16382 Mark, Jan. *The Museum Book: A Guide to Strange and Wonderful Collections* (3–5). Illus. by Richard Holland. 2007, Candlewick $18.99 (978-0-7636-3370-7). 56pp. This wide-ranging volume introduces the history of museums and the various kinds of collections — whether scientific, historical, or art-based — found around the world, with interesting information on holy relics and other artifacts and on fakes and mistakes. (Rev: BCCB 12/07; BL 11/1/07; HB 1/08; SLJ 1/08)

16383 Mason, Antony. *Art* (3–5). Illus. Series: Culture Encyclopedia. 2002, Mason Crest LB $18.95 (978-1-59084-475-5). 40pp. An introduction to art over the centuries that looks at all kinds of drawing, painting, sculpture, photography, commercial art, and so forth. (Rev: SLJ 3/03)

16384 Miles, Liz. *Photography* (3–6). Series: Culture in Action. 2010, Heinemann-Raintree $28.21 (978-1-

4109-3400-0). 32pp. Covering everything from the first cameras to today's photojournalists, this title also offers activities that reinforce literacy skills and understanding of the arts. Lexile 780L (Rev: LMC 3–4/10) [771.3]

16385 Monet, Claude. *Monet's Impressions* (K–3). Illus. by author. 2009, Chronicle $15.99 (978-0-8118-7056-6). 48pp. Reproductions of 16 Monet works are presented alongside quotations and snippets of the artist's letters. (Rev: BLO 11/1/09; LMC 1–2/10; SLJ 11/1/09) [759.4]

16386 *My Art Book: Amazing Art Projects Inspired by Masterpieces* (3–6). 2011, DK $15.99 (978-0-7566-7582-0). 80pp. A visually appealing volume of projects associated with 14 famous works of art; they range from the cave paintings of Lascaux to Warhol's pop art and include a variety of materials and techniques. (Rev: SLJ 8/11) [745.5]

16387 Niepold, Mil, and Jean-Yves Verdu. *Oooh! Matisse* (2–4). Illus. by Mil Niepold. 2007, Tricycle $14.95 (978-1-58246-227-1). Using bold, colorful shapes from portions of Matisse's works, the reader is challenged to a visual guessing game and is prompted to look at art from different perspective before the painting is revealed in its entirety. (Rev: BL 11/1/07; SLJ 11/07)

16388 Nilsen, Anna. *Art Auction Mystery* (5–8). 2005, Kingfisher $16.95 (978-0-7534-5842-6). Wannabe art sleuths are challenged to find forgeries hidden in a selection of world-famous paintings. (Rev: BL 11/1/05; SLJ 1/06; VOYA 12/05) [759]

16389 Nilsen, Anna. *Art Fraud Detective* (4–6). Illus. 2000, Kingfisher $15.95 (978-0-7534-5308-7). 48pp. The reader becomes an art forgery detective in this oversize book that compares originals and forgeries of works by such artists as da Vinci, Picasso, and van Gogh. (Rev: BL 10/15/00; HBG 10/01; SLJ 12/00)

16390 Nilsen, Anna. *The Great Art Scandal: Solve the Crime, Save the Show!* (4–9). 2003, Kingfisher $16.95 (978-0-7534-5587-6). Readers must solve a mystery involving an art exhibition in this comic-book-format work that introduces many famous paintings and artists. (Rev: SLJ 3/04) [759.06]

16391 Ogier, Susan. *Objects and Meanings* (5–8). Series: Step-Up Art and Design. 2010, Cherrytree LB $27.10 (978-1-84234-573-3). 32pp. With plenty of photographs, this volume looks at the artistic techniques involved in everything from still life and trompe l'oeil to folk art and using found objects. Also use *People in Action, A Sense of Place,* and *Talking Textiles* (all 2010). (Rev: LMC 10/10; SLJ 5/10) [700]

16392 Paxmann, Christine. *From Mud Huts to Skyscrapers: Architecture for Children* (4–8). Illus. by Anne Ibelings. 2013, Prestel $19.95 (978-379137113-9). 64pp. A fascinating account of construction over the centuries and into the future, with information on architectural style and on the architects themselves. (Rev: BL 1/13; SLJ 5/13*) [720]

16393 Peel, Yana, ed. *Faces for Baby* (PS). Illus. 2013, Candlewick $21.99 (978-0-7636-6433-6). 12pp. An appealing selection of 12 faces featured in modern art that will especially appeal to young children, presented in an oversized board book. (Rev: BL 3/1/13; HB 7–8/13; SLJ 5/13)

16394 Raczka, Bob. *Action Figures: Paintings of Fun, Daring, and Adventure* (3–5). Illus. 2009, Millbrook LB $25.26 (978-0-7613-4140-6). 32pp. Eighteen action-packed paintings by well-known artists represent different styles and eras (from 1450 to 1962), and are accompanied by informative and interesting captions. (Rev: BL 11/1/09; SLJ 10/1/09) [704.9]

16395 Raczka, Bob. *Art Is . . .* (K–5). 2003, Millbrook LB $22.90 (978-0-7613-2874-2). 32pp. An excellent introductory guide to art and its appreciation, this attractive title exposes readers to images of 26 famous works of art, each of which is accompanied by explanatory text discussing the art's significance and quality. (Rev: HBG 10/03; SLJ 10/03)

16396 Raczka, Bob. *Artful Reading* (1–4). Illus. by author. 2007, Millbrook LB $25.26 (978-0-8225-6754-7). 32pp. These 23 artistic studies of a variety of subjects reading books proves yet again that one picture is worth a thousand words; the artists include Degas, Rossetti, and Picasso. (Rev: SLJ 10/07)

16397 Raczka, Bob. *Here's Looking at Me: How Artists See Themselves* (3–5). 2006, Lerner LB $23.93 (978-0-7613-3404-0). 32pp. Self-portraits of important artists throughout the ages, with an emphasis on form and technique. (Rev: BL 5/1/06; SLJ 6/06)

16398 Raczka, Bob. *No One Saw: Ordinary Things Through the Eyes of an Artist* (PS–3). Illus. 2002, Millbrook LB $23.90 (978-0-7613-2370-9). 32pp. Simple verse introduces young readers to the singular viewpoints of modern artists including Georgia O'Keeffe and Vincent van Gogh. (Rev: BL 1/1–15/02; HBG 10/02; SLJ 1/02)

16399 Raczka, Bob. *Unlikely Pairs: Fun with Famous Works of Art* (4–10). 2005, Millbrook LB $23.93 (978-0-7613-2936-7); paper $9.95 (978-0-7613-2378-5). Raczka pairs famous works from different eras and styles (Rodin's "The Thinker" appears to be considering a move on Klee's chessboard, for example); a closing catalog offers factual information. (Rev: SLJ 12/05) [750]

16400 Raczka, Bob. *Where in the World? Around the Globe in 13 Works of Art* (5–8). Illus. Series: Art Adventures. 2007, Lerner LB $23.93 (978-0-8225-6371-6). 32pp. Full-page reproductions and lively text introduce 13 famous works of art, with information on the artist. (Rev: BL 6/1–15/07; SLJ 8/07)

16401 Raimondo, Joyce. *Express Yourself!* (3–5). Illus. Series: Art Explorers. 2005, Watson-Guptill $12.95 (978-0-8230-2506-0). 48pp. Introduces readers to the work of six expressionist painters — Edvard Munch, Vincent van Gogh, Ernest Ludwig Kirchner, Vasily Kandinsky, Willem de Kooning, and Jackson Pollack — and examines a representative work and outlines projects that further illuminate each artist's style. (Rev: BL 11/1/05; SLJ 2/06)

16402 Raimondo, Joyce. *Imagine That! Activities and Adventures in Surrealism* (4–6). Series: New Children's: Art Explorers. 2004, Watson-Guptill $12.95 (978-0-8230-2502-2). 48pp. This engaging volume encourages readers to try their hands at projects that incorporate elements of surrealism. (Rev: BL 12/1/04; SLJ 9/04)

16403 Raimondo, Joyce. *Picture This! Activities and Adventures in Impressionism* (1–5). Illus. 2004, Watson-Guptill $12.95 (978-0-8230-2503-9). 48pp. Monet, Pissarro, and Degas are among the artists used to demonstrate the techniques of Impressionism in this volume faturing discussion and step-by-step activities. (Rev: SLJ 1/05)

16404 Renshaw, Amanda. *The Art Book for Children: Book Two* (3–6). Illus. 2007, Phaidon $19.95 (978-0-7148-4706-1). This volume contains beautifully reproduced works from a variety of time periods and poses questions that encourage close examination. (Rev: BL 11/1/07; SLJ 2/08)

16405 Richards, Julie. *Stadiums and Domes* (4–6). Illus. Series: Smart Structures. 2003, Smart Apple LB $24.25 (978-1-58340-349-5). 32pp. An overview of the use of the dome in construction, from Roman times to the present, with helpful photographs and diagrams. (Rev: SLJ 3/04)

16406 Rolling, James Haywood, Jr. *Come Look with Me: Discovering African American Art for Children* (K–5). Series: Come Look with Me. 2005, Lickle $15.95 (978-1-890674-07-6). 32pp. Twelve examples of African American art, by artists including Romare Bearden and Jacob Lawrence, are paired with background information and questions that encourage young readers to examine the art. (Rev: SLJ 6/05)

16407 Rubin, Susan G. *Degas and the Dance: The Painter and the Petits Rats, Perfecting Their Art* (3–5). Illus. 2002, Abrams $17.95 (978-0-8109-0567-2). 32pp. This volume, with excellent reproductions of preliminary sketches as well as finished works, will attract budding artists and budding ballet dancers; the "petits rats" are young dancers who posed for the painter. (Rev: BL 12/1/02; HBG 3/03; SLJ 12/02)

16408 Rubin, Susan G. *There Goes the Neighborhood: Ten Buildings People Loved to Hate* (4–7). 2001, Holiday $18.95 (978-0-8234-1435-2). 96pp. Many buildings create an uproar from their earliest design but later become nostalgic favorites, among them the Eiffel Tower and Guggenheim Museum, which are profiled here in an absorbing, colorful account that discusses materials and methods of construction. (Rev: BCCB 9/01; BL 8/01; HBG 3/02; SLJ 9/01; VOYA 10/01)

16409 Ruggi, Gilda Williams. *The Art Book for Children* (2–4). Illus. 2005, Phaidon $19.95 (978-0-7148-4511-1). Art critic Ruggi introduces young readers to classic and contemporary works of art and encourages critical thinking and creating connections to children's own experiences. (Rev: BL 11/1/05)

16410 Salvi, Francesco. *The Impressionists. Rev. ed.* (5–8). Illus. by L. R. Galante. Series: Art Masters. 2008, Oliver LB $24.95 (978-1-934545-03-4). A look at the work of the main artists contributing to this movement: Manet, Monet, Renoir, Degas, Cezanne, Pissaro, Sisley, Morisot, Cassatt, Guillaumin, and Caillebotte; the appealing design will please report writers. (Rev: BL 4/15/08) [759.054]

16411 Sayre, Henry M. *Cave Paintings to Picasso: The Inside Scoop on 50 Famous Masterpieces* (3–7). Illus. 2004, Chronicle Bks. $22.95 (978-0-8118-3767-5). 96pp. This short but impressive historical overview chronicles the evolution of the visual arts from prehistoric cave paintings to the 1960s, presenting 50 major works and including historical context and information on the artist. (Rev: BL 11/1/04; SLJ 10/04)

16412 Schulte, Jessica. *Can You Find It Outside?* (2–4). Illus. 2005, Abrams $10.95 (978-0-8109-5795-4). Rhyming text provides clues to help readers find details in these paintings from the collections of New York's Metropolitan Museum of Art. (Rev: BL 11/1/05; SLJ 12/05)

16413 Serres, Alain. *And Picasso Painted Guernica* (4–8). Trans. by Rosalind Price. 2011, Allen & Unwin $24.99 (978-1-74175-994-5). 52pp. This handsome volume explores Picasso's major mural documenting the destruction of Guernica during the Spanish Civil War, and illustrates the evolution of his art. Lexile 900L (Rev: SLJ 1/1/11*)

16414 Shofner, Shawndra. *Sydney Opera House* (3–6). Series: Modern Wonders of the World. 2006, Creative Editions LB $18.95 (978-1-58341-442-2). 32pp. The story of the construction and current uses of the eye-catching Opera House on Sydney's harbor, completed in 1973. (Rev: BL 10/15/06)

16415 Slaymaker, Melissa Eskridge. *Bottle Houses: The Creative World of Grandma Prisbrey* (1–3). Illus. by Julie Paschkis. 2004, Holt $16.95 (978-0-8050-7131-3). 32pp. Grandma Prisbrey's offbeat creations open young readers' eyes to artistic possibilities. (Rev: BL 3/1/04; HB 7/04; SLJ 9/04)

16416 Sousa, Jean. *Faces, Places, and Inner Spaces* (5–8). Illus. 2006, Abrams $18.95 (978-0-8109-5966-8). 48pp. The director of interpretive exhibitions and family programs at the Art Institute of Chicago introduces a variety of works — portraits, landscapes, and abstract pieces — and asks questions that stimulate analysis. (Rev: BL 5/15/06; SLJ 7/06)

16417 Spilsbury, Richard. *Comics and Graphic Novels* (3–6). Illus. Series: Art off the Wall. 2006, Heinemann LB $32.86 (978-1-4034-8286-0). 56pp. The anime-like cover of this book will draw in young artists who would like to create similar works. Professional artists and their techniques are featured. (Rev: SLJ 5/07)

16418 Swain, Sally. *Once Upon a Picture* (1–5). Illus. by author. 2005, Allen & Unwin $16.95 (978-1-74114-001-9). Four world-famous paintings are used as the departure point for storytelling and additional paintings. (Rev: SLJ 2/06)

16419 Thomson, Ruth. *Creatures* (2–5). Illus. Series: First Look at Art. 2004, Chelsea House LB $23.00 (978-0-7910-7945-4). Readers are introduced to the elements of art through a variety of works depicting animals and imaginary creatures. Also use *Portraits* (2004). (Rev: BL 5/1/04; SLJ 9/04)

16420 Thomson, Ruth. *Places* (3–6). Illus. Series: A First Look at Art. 2004, Chelsea Clubhouse LB $23.00 (978-0-7910-7947-8). 32pp. Using famous works representing various styles as examples, this book looks at the depiction of landscapes and other places and includes creative activities. Also use *Families* (2004) and *Celebrations* (2005). (Rev: SLJ 9/04)

16421 Tomecek, Steve. *Art and Architecture* (4–7). Illus. Series: Experimenting with Everyday Science. 2010, Chelsea House LB $35 (978-1-60413-168-0). 174pp. Twenty-five accessible experiments illustrate important concepts in art or architecture ranging from the practical — testing stress on metal, how an arch supports a load — to the more artistic — mixing pigments, how image depth affects perspective. (Rev: SLJ 11/1/10) [701.03]

16422 Van Gogh, Vincent. *Vincent's Colors: Words and Pictures by Vincent van Gogh* (1–3). Ed. by William Lach. 2005, Chronicle $14.95 (978-0-8118-5099-5). 48pp. An excellent introduction to the Dutch artist's works, this attractive volume couples key paintings with excerpts from letters Vincent wrote to his brother Theo. (Rev: BL 11/1/05*; HBG 4/06; SLJ 11/05)

16423 Vogel, Jennifer. *A Library Story: Building a New Central Library* (4–7). 2006, Lerner $26.60 (978-0-8225-5916-0). 64pp. The construction of the new central library in Minneapolis is the topic of this lively, well-illustrated book that looks at the reasons for the building, architectural and engineering concerns, and artistic choices that were made. (Rev: BL 8/06; SLJ 9/06)

16424 Wenzel, Angela. *Edgar Degas: Dance Like a Butterfly* (4–6). Trans. from German by Rosie Jackson. Series: Adventures in Art. 2002, Prestel $14.95 (3-7913-2736-4). Degas's ballet paintings are presented in a way that encourages readers to appreciate movement, light, and color. (Rev: HBG 3/03; SLJ 11/02)

16425 Wenzel, Angela. *Rene Magritte: Now You See It — Now You Don't* (4–7). Series: Adventures in Art. 1998, Prestel $14.95 (978-3-7913-1873-8). An examination of some of the works of Belgian surrealist Rene Magritte. (Rev: BL 8/98; SLJ 8/98) [759.949]

16426 Wenzel, Angela. *Thirteen Art Mysteries Children Should Know* (5–7). Illus. 2011, Prestel $14.95 (978-3-7913-7044-6). 48pp. In chronological order, this volume presents 13 mysteries of the art world, including questions about the Mona Lisa, a Raphael painting, van Gogh's ear, and the identity of graffiti artist Banksy. (Rev: BL 11/1/11; SLJ 10/1/11) [759]

16427 White, Matt. *Cameras on the Battlefield: Photos of War* (5–7). Series: High Five Reading. 2002, Capstone LB $23.93 (978-0-7368-4004-0). For reluctant readers, this is an appealing look at photographs of war, both those that celebrate war and those that document its horrors. (Rev: SLJ 8/02) [779.9355]

16428 Wolfe, Gillian. *Look! Body Language in Art* (3–5). 2004, Lincoln $16.95 (978-1-84507-034-2). 40pp. In this excellent introduction to art appreciation, Wolfe asks readers — incorporating activity ideas and leading questions — to observe the body language depicted in paintings by artists including Vincent van Gogh and Pablo Picasso. (Rev: BL 11/1/04)

16429 Wolfe, Gillian. *Look! Seeing the Light in Art* (3–5). Illus. 2007, Frances Lincoln $16.95 (978-1-84507-467-8). 48pp. Well-known works of art are presented for readers to observe, focusing on the artist's use of light. (Rev: BL 12/15/07)

16430 Zaunders, Bo. *Gargoyles, Girders, and Glass Houses* (3–6). Illus. by Roxie Munro. 2004, Penguin $17.99 (978-0-525-47284-1). Among the architects profiled in this large-format overview of major design and engineering feats are Gustave Eiffel, Antoni Gaudi, and the Roeblings. (Rev: BL 11/1/04; SLJ 12/04)

The Ancient World

16431 Chrisp, Peter. *Ancient Rome* (4–8). Series: History in Art. 2004, Raintree LB $29.93 (978-1-4109-0520-8). 48pp. A look at what art can reveal about the culture and technology of a society. (Rev: SLJ 4/05)

16432 Curlee, Lynn. *Parthenon* (5–8). Illus. by author. 2004, Simon & Schuster $17.95 (978-0-689-84490-4). A beautifully composed overview of the construction and history of the temple built by the ancient Greeks to honor the goddess Athena. (Rev: BL 9/15/04*; HB 7–8/04; SLJ 6/04) [726]

16433 George, Charles. *Pyramids* (5–9). Series: Mysterious and Unknown. 2007, Reference Point LB $24.95 (978-1-60152-027-2). Pyramids around the world are addressed in this well-written text with color photographs; useful for reports. (Rev: SLJ 2/08)

16434 Hinshaw, Kelly Campbell. *Ancient Egypt* (1–3). Series: Art Across the Ages. 2007, Chronicle $14.95 (978-0-8118-5668-3); paper $4.95 (978-0-8118-5669-0). 32pp. Simple text and clear photographs introduce the art treasures of ancient Egypt to beginning and reluctant readers. (Rev: LMC 5/08; SLJ 11/07)

16435 Hinshaw, Kelly Campbell. *The Art of Ancient Mexico* (2–4). Illus. Series: Art Across the Ages. 2007, Chronicle $14.95 (978-0-8118-5670-6); paper $4.95 (978-0-8118-5671-3). 32pp. This beautifully illustrated introduction to the art of ancient Mexico has simple text that is suitable for beginning readers. (Rev: BL 10/15/07; SLJ 11/07)

16436 Knapp, Ruthie, and Janice Lehmberg. *Greek and Roman Art* (5–9). Series: Off the Wall Museum Guides for Kids. 2001, Davis paper $9.95 (978-0-87192-549-7). 72pp. Using many photographs, this account highlights a number of art objects, explains relevant terms associated with them, describes their uses, and gives details on Greek and Roman culture. (Rev: BL 8/1/01)

16437 Langley, Andrew. *Ancient Greece* (4–8). Series: History in Art. 2004, Raintree LB $29.93 (978-1-4109-0517-8). A look at what art can reveal about the culture and technology of a society. (Rev: SLJ 4/05) [709]

16438 Mann, Elizabeth. *The Parthenon: The Height of Greek Civilization* (4–7). Illus. by Yuan Lee. 2006, Mikaya $22.95 (978-1-931414-15-9). 48pp. The engineering feats involved in the construction of the Parthenon are placed in historical and cultural context; includes a foldout spread, a useful map, and many illustrations. (Rev: BL 12/1/06; SLJ 3/07)

16439 Shuter, Jane. *Ancient Chinese Art* (4–6). Illus. Series: Art in History. 2001, Heinemann LB $24.22 (978-1-58810-090-0). 32pp. Painting, calligraphy, bronzes, terracotta, and lacquer and jade are among the art forms featured. (Rev: HB 5/03; HBG 3/02; SLJ 12/01)

16440 Whiting, Jim. *Threat to Ancient Egyptian Treasures* (3–5). Series: A Robbie Reader. On the Verge of Extinction: Crisis in the Environment. 2007, Mitchell Lane LB $25.70 (978-1-58415-588-1). Whiting discusses the threats to important archaeological sites in Egypt; a "What You Can Do" section will help emerging activists. (Rev: LMC 1/08; SLJ 11/07)

Native American Arts and Crafts

16441 January, Brendan. *Native American Art and Culture* (5–8). Series: World Art and Culture. 2005, Raintree LB $32.86 (978-1-4109-1108-7). Pottery, textiles, carving, painting, textiles, and architecture are all discussed, along with body art, ceremonies, songs, and dances; many color photographs are included and a list of museums is appended. (Rev: BL 4/1/04; SLJ 6/05)

16442 Presilla, Maricel E. *Mola: Cuna Life Stories and Art* (5–7). 1996, Henry Holt $17.95 (978-0-8050-3801-9). An examination of the life and art of the Cuna Indians, who live on islands off the coast of Panama. (Rev: BCCB 1/97; BL 10/1/96; SLJ 10/96) [305.48]

16443 Press, Petra. *Native American Art* (4–6). Illus. Series: Art in History. 2001, Heinemann LB $24.22 (978-1-58810-092-4). Rock art, stone sculpture, sand painting, textiles, and basketry are among the kinds of art featured here. (Rev: HBG 3/02; SLJ 12/01)

Middle Ages and the Renaissance

16444 Barter, James. *A Renaissance Painter's Studio* (5–9). Series: The Working Life. 2003, Gale LB $29.95 (978-1-59018-178-2). 112pp. An exploration of daily life for a painter at a time when art was growing in social importance. (Rev: HBG 10/03; SLJ 5/03)

16445 Forward, Toby. *Shakespeare's Globe: An Interactive Pop-up Theatre* (5–8). Illus. by Juan Wijngaard. 2005, Candlewick $19.99 (978-0-7636-2694-5). A large-format pop-up model of the Globe Theatre, with narrative by a Shakespeare colleague and scenes from Shakespeare's plays. (Rev: BL 5/1/05; SLJ 11/05) [792]

16446 Gunderson, Jessica. *Gothic Art* (5–10). Series: Movements in Art. 2008, Creative Education $32.80 (978-1-58341-610-5). 48pp. With good reproductions and clear historical context, Gunderson looks at the era of Gothic art. Also use *Realism* and *Romanticism* (both 2008). (Rev: SLJ 12/08) [709.02]

16447 Macaulay, David. *Building the Book Cathedral* (5–9). 1999, Houghton Mifflin $29.95 (978-0-395-92147-0). The author retells the fascinating story behind the creation of the original *Cathedral* book 25 years ago and adds numerous changes as he leads a tour of the cathedral, such as alterations in scale and page placement. (Rev: BCCB 12/99; BL 11/15/99; HB 9–10/99; SLJ 9/99) [726]

16448 Macaulay, David. *Castle* (5–8). Illus. by author. 1977, Houghton Mifflin $20.00 (978-0-395-25784-5); paper $9.95 (978-0-395-32920-7). Another of the author's brilliant, detailed works, this one on the planning and building of a Welsh castle. [940.1]

16449 Raczka, Bob. *The Vermeer Interviews: Conversations with Seven Works of Art* (3–7). 2009, Millbrook LB $25.26 (978-0-8225-9402-4). 32pp. Raczka uses an interview format here, talking directly to the subjects of seven important Vermeer works and learning about their lives and times. (Rev: LMC 8/09; SLJ 5/09; VOYA 4/09) [759.9492]

16450 Ross, Stewart. *Art and Architecture* (5–8). Series: Medieval Realms. 2004, Gale LB $29.95 (978-1-59018-534-6). 48pp. Romanesque, Gothic, Moorish, and Islamic art and architecture are covered in this well-organized and well-illustrated volume that includes discussions of houses of the poor as well as castles, manors, monasteries, and cathedrals. (Rev: SLJ 3/05)

United States

16451 Albert, Michael. *An Artist's America* (3–8). 2008, Holt $17.95 (978-0-8050-7857-2). Pop artist Albert uses recycled materials to create collages interpreting a number of historic events and trends. (Rev: SLJ 4/08) [709.2]

16452 Baverstock, Alison. *Joseph Cornell: Secrets in a Box* (3–6). Illus. Series: Prestel Adventures in Art. 2003, Prestel $14.95 (3-7913-2928-6). 30pp. The collage boxes of artist Joseph Cornell are explored in detail in this richly illustrated book, which also shows readers how they can make similar creations of their own. (Rev: BL 11/1/03)

16453 Butler, Jerry. *A Drawing in the Sand: A Story of African American Art* (4–7). 1999, Zino $24.95 (978-1-55933-216-3). This oversize book contains two narratives; the first is a history of African American art and artists, the second, an autobiography of Jerry Butler, the African American artist. (Rev: BL 2/15/99*) [704.03]

16454 Curlee, Lynn. *Skyscraper* (4–7). Illus. 2007, Simon & Schuster $17.99 (978-0-689-84489-8). 48pp. Accompanied by striking acrylic paintings, Curlee's detailed narrative explores the architectural history and engineering of skyscrapers. (Rev: BL 1/1–15/07; SLJ 3/07)

16455 Degezelle, Terri. *The U.S. Capitol* (K–2). Series: American Symbols. 2003, Capstone LB $21.26 (978-0-7368-2294-7). 24pp. A well-illustrated profile of the U.S. Capitol, from the initial design contest to the numerous changes and expansions made to the building over the years. (Rev: SLJ 4/04)

16456 Knapp, Ruthie, and Janice Lehmberg. *American Art* (5–9). Series: Off the Wall Museum Guides for Kids. 1999, Davis paper $9.95 (978-0-87192-386-8). An informal pocket-size art appreciation book that features portraits from several centuries of American art, plus various artifacts and furniture. (Rev: BL 1/1–15/99) [709.73]

16457 Leach, Deba Foxley. *Grant Wood: The Artist in the Hayloft* (2–4). Illus. by Grant Wood. Series: Adventures in Art. 2005, Prestel $14.95 (978-3-7913-3401-1). 30pp. Large, color reproductions of Wood's works are accompanied by brief text that will engage readers' attention plus biographical information. (Rev: BL 11/1/05)

16458 Macaulay, David. *Mill* (5–8). Illus. by author. 1983, Houghton Mifflin $19.00 (978-0-395-34830-7); paper $9.95 (978-0-395-52019-2). Rhode Island textile mills of the 19th century are described in text and excellent drawings. [690]

16459 Morrison, Taylor. *The Buffalo Nickel* (2–4). Illus. 2002, Houghton $16.00 (978-0-618-10855-8). 32pp. The story of the artist who designed the buffalo nick-

el, with information about coin production. (Rev: BL 5/15/02; HBG 10/02; SLJ 4/02)

16460 Murray, Julie. *Gateway Arch* (2–3). Illus. Series: All Aboard America. 2003, ABDO LB $21.35 (978-1-57765-671-5). 24pp. This photo-filled book takes young readers on a tour of St. Louis's Gateway Arch, constructed to memorialize the Missouri city's role as a gateway to the West. (Rev: HBG 10/03; SLJ 11/03)

16461 Murray, Julie. *Mount Rushmore* (2–3). Illus. Series: All Aboard America. 2003, ABDO LB $21.35 (978-1-57765-667-8). 24pp. A brief overview of the creation of the giant presidential profiles carved into the mountain. (Rev: HBG 10/03; SLJ 11/03)

16462 Nikola-Lisa, W. *The Year with Grandma Moses* (2–5). Illus. 2000, Holt $20.00 (978-0-8050-6243-4). The seasons as they are experienced in rural America are chronicled in 13 paintings by Grandma Moses; the narrative, some of it drawn from the artist's memoir, describes seasonal activities. (Rev: BCCB 11/00; BL 10/15/00; HBG 3/01; SLJ 10/00)

16463 Pascoe, Elaine, ed. *The Pentagon* (4–7). Series: Super Structures of the World. 2003, Gale LB $24.95 (978-1-56711-867-4). 48pp. An architectural tour of the Pentagon, headquarters of the U.S. Department of Defense. (Rev: SLJ 4/04)

16464 Spilsbury, Richard. *Pop Art* (5–8). Illus. Series: Art on the Wall. 2008, Heinemann LB $23.00 (978-1-4329-1368-7). 48pp. An introduction to the pop art movement and its key figures. (Rev: BL 1/1–15/09; SLJ 4/09)

16465 Weaver, Janice. *Building America* (5–8). Illus. by Bonnie Shemie. 2002, Tundra $17.95 (978-0-88776-606-0). This brief history of architecture in America, from the 17th century to today, features detailed renderings, an illustrated timeline, and a useful glossary. (Rev: HBG 3/03; SLJ 5/03) [721]

Communication

General and Miscellaneous

16466 Marcovitz, Hal. *Bias in the Media* (5–8). Series: Hot Topics. 2010, Gale LB $32.45 (978-1-4205-0224-4). 112pp. With chapters titled "Why Are the Media Biased?," "The Cable Wars," "Citizens as Journalists: Bias in the Blogosphere," "Pockets of Bias," and "Are There Unbiased Media?," this is a useful introduction to assessing the media. (Rev: SLJ 2/1/11) [302.23097]

16467 Platt, Richard. *Communication from Hieroglyphs to Hyperlinks* (4–6). Illus. Series: Kingfisher Knowledge. 2004, Kingfisher $11.95 (978-0-7534-5769-6). 64pp. Tracing the development of communication from early days to modern high-tech media, this colorful overview will attract browsers and reluctant older readers. (Rev: BL 9/1/04; SLJ 11/04)

Codes and Ciphers

16468 Bell-Rehwoldt, Sheri. *Speaking Secret Codes* (4–7). Series: Edge Books: Making and Breaking Codes. 2010, Capstone LB $26.65 (978-1-4296-4569-0). 32pp. Readers learn about spoken codes and how to work with codes, with activities and photographs. Lexile 770L (Rev: SLJ 1/1/11) [302.2]

16469 Blackwood, Gary. *Mysterious Messages: A History of Codes and Ciphers* (5–8). 2009, Dutton $16.99 (978-0-525-47960-4). 170pp. This well-written history clearly explains the ins and outs of codes and ciphers and includes many interesting examples and stories. (Rev: BL 10/15/09; LMC 11–12/09; SLJ 12/09) [652]

16470 Dickson, Louise. *Lu and Clancy's Secret Languages* (1–4). Illus. by Pat Cupples. 2001, Kids Can $14.95 (978-1-55337-025-3); paper $6.95 (978-1-55074-695-2). 40pp. Dog detectives Lu and Clancy hone their knowledge of language (Pig Latin, pictograms, invisible ink, and so forth). Also use *Lu and Clancy's Spy Stuff* (2001). (Rev: HBG 10/01; SLJ 8/01)

16471 Gilbert, Adrian. *Codes and Ciphers* (3–6). Series: Spy Files. 2009, Firefly paper $6.95 (978-1-55407-573-7). 32pp. The Morse code, Navajo code talkers, cipher machines, and secret writing and microdots are among the codes and ciphers described in this volume that also includes historical information and exercises. (Rev: SLJ 4/10) [652]

16472 Gregory, Jillian. *Breaking Secret Codes* (4–7). Series: Edge Books: Making and Breaking Codes. 2010, Capstone LB $26.65 (978-1-4296-4568-3). 32pp. Gregory looks at various kinds of codes and the methods used to break them. Also use *Making Secret Codes* (2010). Lexile 830L (Rev: SLJ 1/1/11) [652]

Flags

16473 Ferry, Joseph. *The American Flag* (5–7). Series: American Symbols and Their Meanings. 2002, Mason Crest LB $18.95 (978-1-59084-026-9). Designs that preceded the familiar flag accompany material on Betsy Ross and Francis Scott Key, illustrations of important flag raisings, and discussion of proper use and treatment of the flag, all in a package that will appeal to reluctant readers. (Rev: SLJ 4/02) [929.9]

16474 Radlauer, Ruth. *Honor the Flag: A Guide to Its Care and Display* (4–7). Illus. by J. J. Smith Moore. 1992, Forest LB $14.95 (978-1-878363-61-9). Lots of information about the American flag and its care. (Rev: BL 10/15/92) [929.92]

16475 Smith, Whitney. *Flag Lore of All Nations* (4–6). Illus. 2001, Millbrook $29.90 (978-0-7613-1753-1). One hundred and ninety-one flags are represented in this book. (Rev: BL 9/1/01; SLJ 9/01)

16476 Williams, Earl P. *What You Should Know About the American Flag* (4–8). 1989, Thomas paper $5.95 (978-

0-939631-10-0). A comprehensive guide to facts and legends, history and traditions concerning the U.S. flag. (Rev: BL 11/15/87) [929.9]

Language and Languages

16477 Beinstein, Phoebe. *Dora's Book of Words / Libro de Palabras de Dora* (PS–2). Trans. by Argentina Palacios Ziegler. Illus. by Thompson Bros. 2003, Simon & Schuster $10.95 (978-0-689-85626-6). 16pp. Dora the Explorer looks at some everyday words loved by children in a format that allows the reader to switch from English to Spanish by pulling on a tab. (Rev: SLJ 3/03)

16478 Cooper, Kay. *Why Do You Speak as You Do? A Guide to World Languages* (5–8). Illus. by Brandon Kruse. 1992, Children's Press LB $14.85 (978-0-8027-8165-9). A simple yet lively presentation of linguistics. (Rev: BCCB 2/93; BL 1/15/93) [400]

16479 Dubosarsky, Ursula. *The Word Snoop* (5–8). Illus. by Tohby Riddle. 2009, Dial $16.99 (978-0-8037-3406-7). 272pp. The character Word Snoop introduces readers to many aspects, old and new, some amazing, of the English language and includes puzzles, secret codes, and humor. (Rev: BLO 6/23/09; HB 9/09; SLJ 9/09) [400]

16480 Edwards, Wallace. *Monkey Business* (4–8). 2004, Kids Can $16.95 (978-1-55337-462-6). Whimsical artwork introduces such common idioms as "opening a can of worms" and "a bull in a china shop"; readers will also enjoy looking for hidden monkeys. (Rev: BL 11/1/04; SLJ 9/04*) [423]

16481 Evans, Lezlie. *Can You Greet the Whole Wide World? 12 Common Phrases in 12 Different Languages* (K–3). Illus. by Denis Roche. 2006, Houghton $16.00 (978-0-618-56327-2). 32pp. A new school year gives a little kitten a chance to greet others in 12 languages, including Arabic, Hindi, Japanese, and Zulu. (Rev: BL 5/1/06; SLJ 6/06)

16482 Guy, Ginger F. *My School / Mi escuela* (PS–1). Illus. by Vivi Escriva. 2006, HarperCollins $12.99 (978-0-06-079101-8). 24pp. An attractive introduction to school vocabulary in English and Spanish. (Rev: BL 8/06; SLJ 6/06)

16483 Klingel, Cynthia. *You Let the Cat Out of the Bag!* (K–3). Illus. by Mernie Gallagher-Cole. Series: Sayings and Phrases. 2007, Child's World LB $22.79 (978-1-59296-903-6). 32pp. This is an entertaining look at common idioms, playfully pairing a literal illustration of the phrase with its actual meaning and background explanation. (Rev: BL 11/15/07; LMC 3/08; SLJ 4/08)

16484 O'Reilly, Gillian. *Slangalicious: Where We Got That Crazy Lingo* (4–6). Illus. by Krista Johnston. 2004, Annick $24.95 (978-1-55037-765-1); paper $12.95 (978-1-55037-764-4). Two computer characters with their own Slangalicious Web site feature in the fictional story that serves as a framework for this entertaining overview of slang. (Rev: BL 12/15/04; SLJ 1/05)

16485 Park, Linda Sue, and Julia Durango. *Yum! Yuck! A Foldout Book of People Sounds* (PS–3). Illus. by Sue Ramá. 2005, Charlesbridge $9.95 (978-1-57091-659-5). 36pp. The different noises that people of different cultures make to express themselves are paired with illustrations of children from around the world. (Rev: SLJ 8/05)

16486 Prap, Lila. *Animals Speak* (PS–2). Illus. 2006, North-South $15.95 (978-0-7358-2058-6). 40pp. More than 40 languages are included in this multilingual guide to the pronunciation of animal sounds in countries around the world. (Rev: BL 3/1/06; SLJ 5/06)

16487 Stojic, Manya. *Hello World! Greetings in 42 Languages Around the Globe!* (K–2). Illus. 2002, Scholastic $14.95 (978-0-439-36202-3). 40pp. Readers learn how to pronounce 42 words for hello, each introduced by a simple, bold painting of a child from the country and the name of the language concerned. (Rev: BL 12/1/02; HBG 3/03; SLJ 12/02)

16488 Takahashi, Peter X. *Jimi's Book of Japanese: A Motivating Method to Learn Japanese* (3–6). Illus. by Yumie Toka. 2002, PB&J paper $18.95 (978-0-9723247-0-0). 72pp. A book featuring the Japanese characters (*kana*) and how to write them, for beginning speakers and writers of the language. (Rev: BL 2/15/03)

Reading, Speaking, and Writing

Books, Printing, Libraries, and Schools

16489 Alexander, Carol. *How to Tell a Folktale* (3–8). Series: Text Styles. 2012, Crabtree LB $26.60 (978-0-7787-1631-0); paper $8.95 (978-0-7787-1636-5). 32pp. This volume explains how to identify folktales, looking at dialogue, setting, plot, theme, characters, and so forth, and gives tips on creative writing. Lexile IG530L (Rev: SLJ 5/1/12) [398.2]

16490 Anderson, Judith. *Education for All* (4–7). Series: Working for Our Future. 2010, Black Rabbit LB $28.50 (978-1-59771-193-7). 32pp. This volume explains why the United Nations chose education for all as one of its eight Millennium Development goals and looks at the various reasons why children do not go to school. (Rev: BL 6/10; LMC 10/10; SLJ 4/10) [370]

16491 Armstrong, Thomas. *You're Smarter Than You Think: A Kid's Guide to Multiple Intelligences* (5–8). 2003, Free Spirit paper $15.95 (978-1-57542-113-1). Eight different intelligences are defined in understandable terms, with quizzes that help readers investigate their own strengths. (Rev: BL 4/15/03; SLJ 6/03; VOYA 6/03) [153.9]

16492 Asimov, Isaac. *Science Fiction: Vision of Tomorrow?* (3–5). Illus. Series: Isaac Asimov's 21st Century Library of the Universe. 2004, Gareth Stevens LB $26.00 (978-0-8368-3952-4). A revised, well-illustrated edition of a previously published book, this discusses the major themes found in science fiction, looking also at real developments that were predicted in advance. (Rev: SLJ 3/05) [500]

16493 Botzakis, Stergios. *Pretty in Print: Questioning Magazines* (4–7). Series: Fact Finders. Media Literacy. 2006, Capstone LB $22.60 (978-0-7368-6764-1). This book explores how magazines capture readers' attention, why they need to do so, and the influences they may have on society; it includes colorful graphics and interesting sidebars. (Rev: SLJ 6/07) [050]

16494 Brown, Don. *Kid Blink Beats the World* (2–5). Illus. by author. 2004, Roaring Brook $16.95 (978-1-59643-003-7). 32pp. Young newspaper vendors' 1899 rebellion against William Randolph Hearst and Joseph Pulitzer is described in this arresting picture book for older children. (Rev: BL 9/15/04)

16495 Cefrey, Holly. *Researching People, Places and Events* (5–8). Series: Digital and Information Literacy. 2010, Rosen LB $26.50 (978-1-4358-5317-1). 48pp. Providing helpful information and advice for undertaking research projects on the Internet, this guide offers tips on the difference between primary and secondary sources, evaluating sources, and avoiding plagiarism. (Rev: LMC 1–2/10; SLJ 3/10) [001.4]

16496 Cornwall, Phyllis. *Put It All Together* (3–6). Illus. Series: Super Smart Information Strategies. 2010, Cherry Lake LB $27.07 (978-1-60279-643-0). 32pp. Presents advice on presenting the results of research, with emphasis on organization and considering both purpose and audience. (Rev: LMC 8–9/10; SLJ 6/10) [372.1]

16497 Curry, Barbara K., and James Michael Brodie. *Sweet Words So Brave: The Story of African American Literature* (5–8). 1996, Zino $24.95 (978-1-55933-179-1). An outline of African American literature, from slave narratives to the great writers of today, such as Nikki Giovanni and Toni Morrison. (Rev: BL 2/15/97*; SLJ 4/97) [810.9]

16498 Davidson, Tish. *School Conflict* (4–8). Series: Life Balance. 2003, Watts LB $20.50 (978-0-531-12251-8); paper $6.95 (978-0-531-15571-4). 80pp. This book examines the various conflicts, including violence, that exist in public education today and how these affect the lives and mental health of students. (Rev: BL 10/15/03; SLJ 3/04)

16499 *Dear Author: Students Write About the Books That Changed Their Lives* (5–9). 1995, Conari paper $9.95 (978-1-57324-003-1). A collection of young adults' letters to authors, both dead and alive, expressing, with wit and honesty, how the authors' books have affected them. (Rev: BL 1/1–15/96; SLJ 11/95) [028.5]

16500 Donovan, Sandy. *Bob the Alien Discovers the Dewey Decimal System* (2–4). Illus. by Martin Haake. Series: In the Library. 2010, Picture Window LB $25.32 (978-1-4048-5757-5). 24pp. A librarian introduces a well-mannered alien in search of information about spiders to the basics of the Dewey Decimal system. Also use *Bored Bella Learns About Fiction and Nonfiction* and *Karl and Carolina Uncover the Parts of a Book* (both 2010). (Rev: LMC 11–12/10; SLJ 4/1/10) [025.4]

16501 Farrell, Juliana, and Beth Mayall. *Middle School: The Real Deal* (5–7). 2001, HarperCollins paper $7.99 (978-0-380-81313-1). Advice on coping with school work, teachers, and social life is presented in an appealing format. (Rev: BL 6/1–15/01; VOYA 8/01) [373.18]

16502 Fontichiaro, Kristin. *Go Straight to the Source* (3–6). Illus. Series: Super Smart Information Strategies. 2010, Cherry Lake LB $27.07 (978-1-60279-640-9). 32pp. Describes how to use primary sources — images, objects, and documents — effectively and how to tie them in with secondary sources. (Rev: SLJ 6/10) [020]

16503 Fontichiaro, Kristin. *Know What to Ask: Forming Great Research Questions* (3–5). Illus. Series: Information Explorer: Super Smart Information Strategies. 2012, Cherry Lake LB $28.50 (978-161080483-7). 32pp. Activities at the end of each section extend and enhance the discussion of forming effective research questions. (Rev: BL 10/15/12; LMC 11–12/13) [001.4]

16504 Forget, Thomas. *The Creation of Captain America* (4–6). Illus. Series: Action Heroes. 2006, Rosen LB $21.95 (978-1-4042-0766-0). 48pp. A look at Captain America, one of Marvel's most famous superheroes and an American icon, and how he was created. (Rev: SLJ 3/07) [741.5]

16505 Funk, Gary. *A Balancing Act: Sports and Education* (5–8). Series: Sports Issues. 1995, Lerner LB $28.75 (978-0-8225-3301-6). A frank, thorough discussion of the many issues involved in sports and their place in educational institutions. (Rev: BL 1/1–15/96; SLJ 9/95) [796.04]

16506 Gaines, Ann Graham. *Don't Steal Copyrighted Stuff!* (5–10). 2008, Enslow LB $28.95 (978-0-7660-2861-6). Students who don't see the harm in cutting and pasting from the Internet will discover that plagiarism can ruin reputations and careers; the story of a writer who got caught brings this truth home, and there are plenty of practical tips on keeping one's work original. (Rev: BL 4/1/08; LMC 3/08) [808]

16507 Gorman, Jacqueline Laks. *The Library* (K–2). Illus. Series: I Like to Visit. 2005, Weekly Reader LB $21.00 (978-0-8368-4452-8). 24pp. A simple photoessay that shows what to expect on a visit to the library. Others in this series include *The Museum*, *The Aquarium*, and *The Playground* (all 2005). (Rev: BL 4/1/05) [027]

16508 Green, Julie. *Write It Down* (3–6). Illus. Series: Super Smart Information Strategies. 2010, Cherry Lake LB $27.07 (978-1-60279-645-4). 32pp. Describes how to find the key information in your research and the use of highlighting, sticky notes, tables, and so forth in enhancing note-taking. (Rev: SLJ 6/10) [371.3]

16509 Guillain, Charlotte. *My First Day at a New School* (K–2). Illus. Series: Growing Up. 2011, Heinemann LB $22 (978-1-4329-4796-5). 24pp. Using simple vocabulary and large color photographs, this reassuring book gives new students a sense of what to expect from their first day at school. (Rev: BL 7/11; SLJ 6/11) [371.002]

16510 Hauser, Jill F. *Wow! I'm Reading! Fun Activities to Make Reading Happen* (PS–3). Illus. by Stan Jaskiel. Series: A Williamson Little Hands Book. 2000, Williamson paper $12.95 (978-1-885593-41-2). 141pp. A collection of activities designed to smooth the path to reading, with references to recommended picture books and bright black-and-white cartoons. (Rev: SLJ 4/01)

16511 Hayward, Linda. *I Am a Book* (1–3). Illus. by Carol Nicklaus. Series: Silly Millies. 2005, Lerner LB $17.90 (978-0-7613-2905-3); paper $4.99 (978-0-7613-1826-2). 32pp. In easy-to-understand text with whimsical illustrations, a book explains how it was made. (Rev: BL 1/1–15/06; SLJ 10/05)

16512 Hughes, Susan. *Off to Class: Incredible and Unusual Schools Around the World* (3–7). Illus. 2011, Owl-Kids $12.95 (978-1-926818-85-6). 64pp. A fascinating look at schools ranging from tent schools in Haiti to schools in caves in China, boat schools, e-mail schools, and more. (Rev: BL 11/1/11; SLJ 9/1/11) [371]

16513 King, M. G. *Librarian on the Roof! A True Story* (K–3). Illus. by Stephen Gilpin. 2010, Whitman $16.99 (978-080754512-6). 32pp. The inspiring story of a spunky Texas librarian who held a rooftop vigil to raise money for her library. (Rev: BL 8/10; LMC 11–12/10; SLJ 10/10) [027.4764]

16514 Koscielniak, Bruce. *Johann Gutenberg and the Amazing Printing Press* (2–5). 2003, Houghton $16.00 (978-0-618-26351-6). 40pp. This history of early book making traces the evolution of the process from the Chinese development of paper up to Johann Gutenberg's 15th-century invention of the printing press. (Rev: BL 7/03; HBG 4/04; SLJ 9/03)

16515 Krensky, Stephen. *Comic Book Century: The History of American Comic Books* (5–8). Illus. Series: People's History. 2007, Lerner LB $30.60 (978-0-8225-6654-0). 112pp. The history of comics is presented as a part of America's history in this illustration- and photo-filled volume. (Rev: BL 10/1/07; LMC 1/08; SLJ 11/07)

16516 McElroy, Lisa, and Abigail Jane Cobb. *Meet My Grandmother: She's a Children's Book Author* (1–4). Photos by Joel Benjamin. 2001, Millbrook LB $22.90 (978-0-7613-1972-6). 31pp. Nine-year-old Vicki Cobb describes her grandmother's work and how books are created and published. (Rev: HBG 3/02; SLJ 8/01)

16517 Marshall, Pam. *From Idea to Book* (PS–2). Series: Start to Finish. 2004, Lerner LB $18.60 (978-0-8225-1385-8). 24pp. The basics of book development are laid out in simple terms for young readers. (Rev: BL 6/1–15/04; SLJ 9/04)

16518 Myron, Vicki, and Bret Witter. *Dewey the Library Cat: A True Story* (4–8). 2010, Little, Brown $15.99 (978-0-316-06871-0). 224pp. A kindhearted librarian takes pity when she finds a freezing kitten in the library's book return in this children's adaptation that focuses on Dewey's everyday adventures. (Rev: BL 5/15/10; LMC 8–9/10; SLJ 6/10) [636.80092]

16519 Pascaretti, Vicki, and Sara Wilkie. *Team Up Online* (3–6). Illus. Series: Super Smart Information Strategies.

2010, Cherry Lake LB $27.07 (978-1-60279-644-7). 32pp. Discusses the best ways of collaborating online on research projects and provides exercises and checklists. (Rev: SLJ 6/10) [025.04]

16520 Rabbat, Suzy. *Find Your Way Online* (3–6). Illus. Series: Super Smart Information Strategies. 2010, Cherry Lake LB $27.07 (978-1-60279-639-3). 32pp. Provides advice on effective research on the Internet, looking specifically at narrowing searches and using subject directories and subscription databases. (Rev: SLJ 6/10) [004.1]

16521 Radabaugh, Melinda. *Going to the Library* (PS–1). Series: First Time. 2003, Heinemann LB $18.50 (978-1-4034-0230-1). A reassuring, simple introduction to a library and its contents. (Rev: HBG 10/03; SLJ 6/03)

16522 Rosen, Suri. *How to Tell a Fable* (3–8). Series: Text Styles. 2012, Crabtree LB $26.60 (978-0-7787-1630-3); paper $8.95 (978-0-7787-1635-8). 32pp. This volume explains how to identify fables, looking at dialogue, setting, plot, theme, characters, and so forth, and gives tips on creative writing. (Rev: SLJ 5/1/12)

16523 Rosenstock, Barb. *Thomas Jefferson Builds a Library* (3–5). Illus. by John O'Brien. 2013, Boyds Mills $16.95 (978-159078932-2). 32pp. Jefferson's lifelong fascination with books is the focus of this attractive picture book. (Rev: BL 8/13; LMC 1–2/14*; SLJ 8/13) [973]

16524 Ruurs, Margriet. *My Librarian Is a Camel: How Books are Brought to Children Around the World* (3–5). Illus. 2005, Boyds Mills $16.95 (978-1-59078-093-0). 32pp. Boats, camels, bicycles, wheelbarrows — this is a look at the unusual means librarians employ to get books to readers in remote areas of the world. (Rev: BL 7/05; SLJ 8/05)

16525 Sawa, Maureen. *The Library Book: The Story of Libraries from Camels to Computers* (3–5). Illus. by Bill Slavin. 2006, Tundra $18.95 (978-0-88776-698-5). 72pp. This appealing study of libraries and their widespread impact traces their history from the ancient Library of Alexandria to electronic texts available from digital archives. (Rev: SLJ 12/06)

16526 Schneider, Meg. *Help! My Teacher Hates Me* (5–8). 1994, Workman paper $7.95 (978-1-56305-492-1). Helpful hints for developing a positive attitude in school. (Rev: BL 3/15/95) [371.8]

16527 Shea, Kitty. *Out and About at the Public Library* (1–3). Illus. by Zachary Trover. 2005, Picture Window LB $26.60 (978-1-4048-1150-8). 24pp. This attractive title takes readers on a field trip to a public library, where they learn about everything from checking out books to using the computer catalog and consulting the reference department. (Rev: SLJ 2/06)

16528 Somervill, Barbara. *The History of the Library* (3–6). Series: Our Changing World: The Timeline Library. 2006, The Child's World LB $27.07 (978-1-59296-438-3). 32pp. An exploration of how books have been made and stored from ancient times to today, with a peek at future developments. (Rev: SLJ 7/06)

16529 StJohn, Amanda. *How to Treat a Book* (K–3). Illus. by Bob Ostrom. 2012, Child's World LB $28.50 (978-161473252-5). 24pp. An owl and a rabbit teach young readers how to look after books, and what happens when you damage one from the library. (Rev: BL 10/1/12) [027.4]

16530 Teitelbaum, Michael. *Making Comic Books* (2–5). Illus. by Howard Bender and David Tanguay. Series: Boys Rock! 2006, The Child's World LB $25.64 (978-1-59296-733-9). 32pp. Follows a comic book's creation from script through storyboard through illustration and lettering; a good choice for beginning and reluctant readers (girls as well as boys). (Rev: SLJ 2/07)

16531 Truesdell, Ann. *Find the Right Site* (3–6). Illus. Series: Super Smart Information Strategies. 2010, Cherry Lake LB $27.07 (978-1-60279-638-6). 32pp. Provides advice on evaluating the content of Web sites. (Rev: SLJ 6/10) [025.042]

16532 Truesdell, Ann. *Fire Away: Asking Great Interview Questions* (3–5). Illus. Series: Information Explorer: Super Smart Information Strategies. 2012, Cherry Lake LB $28.50 (978-161080481-3). 32pp. Activities at the end of each section extend and enhance the discussion of forming effective interview questions. Also use *Wonderful Wikis* (2012), which encourages students to use and create wikis. (Rev: BL 10/15/12; LMC 11–12/13)

16533 Wu, Dana Y. *Our Libraries* (2–4). Series: I Know America. 2001, Millbrook LB $24.90 (978-0-7613-1856-9). 48pp. The Dewey decimal system, the Library of Congress, Banned Books Week, and even MARC records are among the topics covered in this comprehensive overview of libraries. (Rev: HBG 10/01; SLJ 7/01)

Signs and Symbols

16534 Ault, Kelly. *Let's Sign! Every Baby's Guide to Communicating with Grownups* (PS). Illus. by Leo Landry. 2005, Houghton $17.00 (978-0-618-50774-0). 77pp. Simple stories about mealtime, playtime, and bedtime are accompanied by attractive illustrations and depictions of signs used for key words. (Rev: SLJ 12/05)

16535 Bateman, Teresa. *Red, White, Blue and Uncle Who? The Stories Behind Some of America's Patriotic Symbols* (3–6). Illus. by John O'Brien. 2001, Holiday House $16.95 (978-0-8234-1285-3). 64pp. The meaning of patriotic symbols such as Uncle Sam, war memorials, and Mount Rushmore is explained with surprising detail in simple, appealing, and often humorous terms, enhanced by sprightly line drawings. (Rev: BL 12/15/01; HBG 10/02; SLJ 11/01)

16536 Heller, Lora. *Sign Language ABC* (PS–2). Illus. by author. 2012, Sterling $14.95 (978-1-4027-6392-2). 32pp. A clear and accessible guide to the American Sign Language alphabet. (Rev: BL 12/15/11; SLJ 2/1/12) [419]

16537 Heller, Lora. *Sign Language for Kids: A Fun and Easy Guide to American Sign Language* (4–6). 2004, Sterling $14.95 (978-1-4027-0672-1). Color photo-

graphs and clear directions make this an excellent introduction to sign language. (Rev: BL 9/15/04)

16538 Jango-Cohen, Judith. *The Bald Eagle* (K–2). Series: Pull Ahead Books. 2003, Lerner LB $22.60 (978-0-8225-3645-1); paper $5.95 (978-0-8225-4750-1). For beginning report writers, this is a simple, well-illustrated look at the eagle and its choice as a national symbol. (Rev: SLJ 1/04)

16539 Jeffrey, Laura S. *All About Braille: Reading by Touch* (2–4). Illus. Series: Transportation and Communication. 2004, Enslow LB $23.93 (978-0-7660-2184-6). 48pp. A simple, easy-to-read overview of the invention of the Braille system and how it changed the lives of blind people, with true stories. [411]

16540 Kubler, Annie. *My First Signs* (PS). Illus. 2005, Child's Play $6.99 (978-1-904550-39-6). 12pp. An introduction to American Sign Language, for both hearing and deaf children. (Rev: BL 5/15/05)

16541 Lowenstein, Felicia. *All About Sign Language: Talking With Your Hands* (2–4). Illus. Series: Transportation and Communication. 2004, Enslow LB $23.93 (978-0-7660-2028-3). 48pp. A simple, easy-to-read overview of the history of sign language and how it changed the lives of deaf people, with true stories. (Rev: SLJ 12/04)

16542 Lyons, Shelly. *Signs in My Neighborhood* (PS–K). Illus. Series: My Neighborhood. 2013, Capstone LB $24.65 (978-162065098-1); paper $6.95 (9781620658895). 24pp. With simple text, large and bright photographs, and an oversize format, this entry in the series introduces all the signs found in a typical neighborhood and asks readers to look around for more. (Rev: BL 6/13; SLJ 4/13) [302.2]

16543 Mignon, Philippe. *Labyrinths: Can You Escape from the 26 Letters of the Alphabet?* (2–5). Illus. 2002, Firefly $14.95 (978-1-55297-559-6); paper $9.95 (978-1-55297-579-4). A complex and attractive combination of alphabet book, mazes, poetry, and intriguing tidbits both ancient and modern. (Rev: BL 1/1–15/03; HBG 3/03; SLJ 12/02)

16544 Milich, Zoran. *City Signs* (PS–K). Illus. 2002, Kids Can $15.95 (978-1-55337-003-1). A photographic look at worded signs that will leave preschoolers proud of their "reading" skills. (Rev: BL 10/15/02; HB 1/03; HBG 3/03)

16545 Petelinsek, Kathleen, and E. Russell Primm. *At School / En la escuela* (K–2). Illus. by Kathleen Petelinsek. Series: Talking Hands. 2006, The Child's World LB $21.36 (978-1-59296-450-5). 24pp. Students demonstrate simple school-related words using American Sign Language; the text is in both English and Spanish. (Rev: SLJ 6/06)

16546 Searcy, John. *Signs in Our World: Spot the Signs All Around You!* (PS–2). Illus. 2006, DK $15.99 (978-0-7566-1834-6); paper $5.99 (978-0-7566-1827-8). 32pp. A colorful introduction to a wide variety of signs — some wordless — found across America and in some foreign countries. (Rev: BL 4/15/06)

16547 Votry, Kim, and Curt Waller. *Baby's First Signs* (PS–2). Illus. 2001, Gallaudet Univ. $6.95 (978-1-56368-114-1). Basic words are introduced in sign language, showing a child signing and clear directions for signing the word yourself. Also use *More Baby's First Signs* (2001). (Rev: SLJ 2/02)

16548 Warner, Penny. *Signing Fun: American Sign Language Vocabulary, Phrases, Games and Activities* (4–8). Illus. by Paula Gray. 2006, Gallaudet Univ. paper $19.95 (978-1-56368-292-6). This fun-filled introduction to American Sign Language introduces the basic vocabulary of ASL and offers a wide selection of related games and puzzles. (Rev: SLJ 12/06) [419]

16549 Woods, Mary B., and Michael Woods. *Ancient Communication: From Grunts to Graffiti* (5–8). Series: Ancient Technologies. 2000, Runestone LB $25.26 (978-0-8225-2996-5). Beginning with cave paintings and hieroglyphics and ending with modern alphabets and universal languages, this account of the history of communication emphasizes ancient cultures. (Rev: BL 9/15/00; HBG 3/01; SLJ 1/01) [652]

16550 Yanuck, Debbie L. *Uncle Sam* (K–2). Series: American Symbols. 2003, Capstone LB $21.26 (978-0-7368-2295-4). An introduction to Uncle Sam, the bearded symbol of the United States who grew from a political cartoon to an image known around the world. (Rev: SLJ 4/04)

Words and Grammar

16551 Agee, Jon. *Smart Feller Fart Smeller* (2–4). Illus. 2006, Hyperion $14.95 (978-0-7868-3692-5). 64pp. Black-and-white cartoons illustrate this celebration of spoonerisms, such as the one about the smart student who "burned a lunch." (Rev: BCCB 6/06; BL 3/15/06; HB 5/06; HBG 10/06; LMC 11/06; SLJ 5/06)

16552 Alda, Arlene. *Did You Say Pears?* (K–3). Illus. 2006, Tundra $16.95 (978-0-88776-739-5). 32pp. Fun with homonyms and homophones is provided in minimal text and eye-catching photographs. (Rev: BL 3/1/06; HBG 10/06; LMC 10/06; SLJ 6/06)

16553 Amoroso, Cynthia. *Hold Your Horses! (And Other Peculiar Sayings)* (1–3). Illus. by Mernie Gallagher-Cole. Series: Sayings and Phrases. 2011, Child's World LB $25.64 (978-160253681-4). 24pp. A variety of familiar idioms are presented in context and with humorous illustrations. Also use *I'm All Thumbs! (And Other Odd Things We Say)*, *It's a Long Shot! (And Other Strange Sayings)*, and *That's the Last Straw! (And Other Weird Things We Say)* (all 2011). (Rev: BL 4/15/11) [428.1]

16554 Bailey, LaWanda. *Miss Myrtle Frag, the Grammar Nag* (5–9). Illus. by Brian Strassburg. 2000, Absey paper $13.95 (978-1-888842-19-7). A clever book that explains key grammar rules through a series of witty letters from Miss Myrtle Frag. (Rev: SLJ 2/01) [415]

16555 Baker, Rosalie. *In a Word: 750 Words and Their Fascinating Stories and Origins* (4–8). Illus. by Tom Lopes. 2003, Cobblestone $17.95 (978-0-8126-2710-7).

Useful for reference, this guide to the origins and meanings of words and phrases is drawn from a monthly column in *Cobblestone*. (Rev: BL 2/15/04; SLJ 4/04) [422]

16556 Barretta, Gene. *Dear Deer* (K–3). Illus. by Gene Baretta. 2007, Holt $16.95 (978-0-8050-8104-6). 32pp. An entertaining introduction to homophones, featuring Aunt Ant, a moose who loves mousse, and so forth. (Rev: BL 9/15/07; LMC 1/08)

16557 Brennan-Nelson, Denise. *My Daddy Likes to Say* (2–4). Illus. by Jane Monroe Donovan. 2009, Sleeping Bear $15.95 (978-1-58536-432-9). 32pp. Common figures of speech — "cool as a cucumber," "the buck stops here" — are illustrated with humor. (Rev: BLO 4/14/09; SLJ 6/09)

16558 Brennan-Nelson, Denise. *My Momma Likes to Say* (2–4). Illus. by Jane Monroe Donovan. 2003, Sleeping Bear $15.95 (978-1-58536-106-9). 32pp. Illustrations and rhymes expand on the meanings of such phrases as "money doesn't grow on trees" and "cat got your tongue?" (Rev: BL 7/03; SLJ 9/03)

16559 Cleary, Brian P. *Breezier, Cheesier, Newest, and Bluest: What Are Comparatives and Superlatives?* (2–4). Illus. by Brian Gable. Series: Words Are CATegorical. 2013, Millbrook $16.95 (978-076135362-1). 32pp. In the appealing format typical of the series, this volume gives useful examples of comparatives and superlatives. **e** (Rev: BL 3/15/13) [428.1]

16560 Cleary, Brian P. *But and For, Yet and Nor: What Is a Conjunction?* (2–4). Illus. by Brian Gable. Series: Words Are CATegorical. 2010, Millbrook $15.95 (978-082259153-5). 32pp. An appealing introduction to the use of conjunctions, with entertaining illustrations. (Rev: BL 2/1/10) [425]

16561 Cleary, Brian P. *Cool! Whoa! Ah and Oh! What Is an Interjection?* (2–4). Illus. by Brian Gable. Series: Words Are CATegorical. 2011, Millbrook $16.95 (978-158013594-8). 32pp. Frenetic illustrations support many examples of different kinds of interjections. Also use *Thumbtacks, Earwax, Lipstick, Dipstick: What Is a Compound Word?* (2011). (Rev: BL 2/1/11) [428.2]

16562 Cleary, Brian P. *Dearly, Nearly, Insincerely: What Is an Adverb?* (2–4). Illus. by Brian Gable. Series: Words Are CATegorical. 2003, Carolrhoda LB $14.95 (978-0-87614-924-9). 32pp. Energetic illustrations accompany a bouncy rhyming text that introduces adverbs of all kinds. Also use *Lazily, Crazily, Just a Bit Nasally* (2003). (Rev: HBG 10/03; SLJ 3/03)

16563 Cleary, Brian P. *Hairy, Scary, Ordinary: What Is an Adjective?* (PS–3). Illus. by Jenya Prosmitsky. 2000, Lerner $14.95 (978-1-57505-401-8). 32pp. A playful rhyming text helps to explain what an adjective is and how it functions. (Rev: BL 6/1–15/00; HBG 10/00; SLJ 7/00)

16564 Cleary, Brian P. *How Much Can a Bare Bear Bear? What Are Homonyms and Homophones?* (2–5). Illus. by Brian Gable. Series: Words Are CATegorical. 2005, Millbrook LB $15.95 (978-1-57505-824-5).

Rhyming wordplay introduces readers to homonyms and homophones. (Rev: SLJ 11/05)

16565 Cleary, Brian P. *I and You and Don't Forget Who: What Is a Pronoun?* (2–4). Illus. by Brian Gable. Series: Words Are CATegorical. 2004, Carolrhoda $15.95 (978-1-57505-596-1). This clever blend of rhyming text and cartoon drawings makes its lessons about pronouns easy to digest. (Rev: BL 5/1/04; SLJ 7/04)

16566 Cleary, Brian P. *Pitch and Throw, Grasp and Know: What Is a Synonym?* (2–4). Illus. by Brian Gable. Series: Words Are CATegorical. 2005, Carolrhoda $15.95 (978-1-57505-796-5). 32pp. Bright cartoon illustrations of humorous situations introduce synonyms. Also use *Stroll and Walk, Babble and Talk* (2009). (Rev: BL 2/1/05; SLJ 3/05)

16567 Cleary, Brian P. *Rhyme and PUNishment: Adventures in Wordplay* (2–5). Illus. by J. P. Sandy. 2006, Millbrook LB $15.95 (978-1-57505-849-8). 48pp. Puns — some of them quite sophisticated — are delivered inside brief poems accompanied by cartoonish illustrations. (Rev: SLJ 6/06)

16568 Cleary, Brian P. *Stop and Go, Yes and No: What Is an Antonym?* (K–3). Illus. by Brian Gable. Series: Words Are CATegorical. 2006, Millbrook LB $15.95 (978-1-57505-860-3). Simple and not-so-simple antonyms — from "front and back" to "excite and soothe" — are accompanied by amusing drawings; Cleary also explains the use of prefixes such as "un" and "im." Also use *Straight and Curvy, Meek and Nervy* (2009). (Rev: SLJ 6/06)

16569 Cleary, Brian P. *To Root, to Toot, to Parachute: What Is a Verb?* (K–3). Illus. by Jenya Prosmitsky. 2001, Carolrhoda $14.95 (978-1-57505-403-2). 32pp. A delightful, lively introduction to verbs with action-packed illustrations. (Rev: BL 4/15/01; HBG 10/01; SLJ 7/01)

16570 Cleary, Brian P. *Under, Over, By the Clover: What Is a Preposition?* (2–4). Illus. by Brian Gable. 2002, Carolrhoda $14.95 (978-1-57505-524-4). A pack of crazy-colored cartoonlike animals and rhyming text teach younger readers all about prepositions. (Rev: BL 3/1/02; HBG 10/02; SLJ 6/02)

16571 Coffelt, Nancy. *Big, Bigger, Biggest!* (PS–2). Illus. by author. 2009, Holt $16.95 (978-0-8050-8089-6). 32pp. Synonyms, antonyms, and comparisons are introduced by competitive animals. (Rev: BL 3/1/09; SLJ 3/09)

16572 Dahl, Michael. *If You Were a Noun* (1–3). Illus. by Sara Gray. Series: Word Fun. 2006, Picture Window LB $26.60 (978-1-4048-1355-7). 24pp. An attractive and accessible introduction to nouns and their roles in speech. Also use *If You Were a Verb* and *If You Were an Adverb* (2006). (Rev: SLJ 9/06)

16573 Dahl, Michael. *If You Were an Adjective* (1–3). Illus. by Sara Gray. Series: If You Were. 2006, Picture Window LB $26.60 (978-1-4048-1356-4). A picture-book format is used to introduce young readers to adjectives and the role they play in English grammar and sentence structure. (Rev: BL 4/1/06; SLJ 9/06)

16574 Donovan, Sandy. *Keep Your Eye on the Ball: And Other Expressions about Sports* (3–5). Illus. by Aaron Blecha. Series: It's Just an Expression. 2012, Lerner LB $22.60 (978-076137889-1). 32pp. Donovan introduces a number of sports-related idioms with cartoon scenes and photographs. (Rev: BLO 9/1/12; LMC 5–6/13) [428.1]

16575 Donovan, Sandy. *Until the Cows Come Home: And Other Expressions About Animals* (3–5). Illus. 2012, Lerner LB $26.60 (978-076137890-7). 32pp. "Hold your horses" and "sick as a dog" are among the 13 idioms discussed here. (Rev: BL 10/1/12; LMC 5–6/13) [428.1]

16576 *A Drove of Bullocks: A Compilation of Animal Group Names* (3–6). Illus. by author. 2011, Patrick-George paper $12.99 (978-0-9562558-0-8). Unpaged. An imaginatively presented collection of fascinating collective names for groups of animals and birds. Also use *A Filth of Starlings: A Compilation of Bird and Aquatic Animal Group Names* (2011). (Rev: SLJ 7/11)

16577 Edwards, Wallace. *The Cat's Pajamas* (4–7). Illus. by author. 2010, Kids Can $18.95 (978-1-55453-308-4). Unpaged. Rich illustrations depicting animals acting out idioms make clear that these 26 figures of speech cannot be taken literally. Lexile AD820L (Rev: SLJ 2/1/11) [428]

16578 *Flip-a-Word: Pig Wig* (K–2). Illus. by Yukiko Kido. 2006, Blue Apple $12.95 (978-1-59354-175-0); paper $5.95 (978-1-59354-178-1). Bright, colorful pictures introduce three-letter words containing the letter combinations of "at," "ig," and "ug." Also use *Flip-a-Word: Snake Cake* (2006). (Rev: SLJ 11/06)

16579 Hambleton, Laura, and Sedat Turhan. *Monkey Business: Fun with Idioms* (K–3). Illus. by Herve Tullet. Series: Milet Wordwise. 2007, Milet paper $5.99 (978-1-840594-99-7). 28pp. Illustrations provide literal interpretations of such idioms as "monkey business," "I'll give you a hand," and "barking up the wrong tree." (Rev: BL 4/15/07)

16580 Hambleton, Laura, and Sedat Turhan. *Strawberry Bullfrog: Fun with Compound Words* (K–2). Illus. by Sally Hagin. Series: Milet Wordwise. 2007, Milet paper $8.95 (978-1-84059-500-0). The words "honeymoon," "copycat," "cowboy," and "strawberry," along with others, inspire interesting illustrations in this introduction to compound words. (Rev: SLJ 5/07)

16581 Hambleton, Laura, and Sedat Turhan. *Telling Tails: Fun with Homonyms* (K–2). Illus. by Laura Hambleton. Series: Wordwise. 2007, Milet paper $8.95 (978-1-84059-498-0). Sound-alike words with different meanings inspire interesting illustrations in this introduction that includes explanations of the jokes. (Rev: SLJ 5/07)

16582 Heinrichs, Ann. *Interjections* (2–4). Illus. by Dan McGeehan. Series: Language Rules! 2010, Child's World LB $27.07 (978-1-60253-428-5). 24pp. This lively title offers tips and examples of how to use interjections. (Rev: BL 10/1/10; SLJ 12/1/10) [428.2]

16583 Heinrichs, Ann. *Similes and Metaphors* (3–6). Series: The Magic of Language. 2005, The Child's World LB $27.07 (978-1-59296-434-5). 32pp. Advice on using similes and metaphors to brighten sentences is accompanied by attractive graphics and photographs. Also use *Spelling Rules* and *Synonyms and Antonyms* (both 2005). (Rev: SLJ 12/05)

16584 Higgins, Nadia. *Super Apostrophe Saves the Day!* (1–3). Illus. by Mernie Gallagher-Cole. Series: PunctuationBooks. 2012, Child's World LB $27.07 (978-161473265-5). 24pp. The use of apostrophes is demonstrated through a story involving superheroes corralling wayward punctuation marks at Pencil Elementary in Punctuation Junction. (Rev: BLO 9/15/12; SLJ Fall 2012 Series Guide) [428.23]

16585 Klingel, Cynthia. *Go Fly a Kite! (And Other Sayings We Don't Really Mean)* (2–5). Illus. by Mernie Gallagher-Cole. Series: Sayings and Phrases. 2007, The Child's World LB $22.79 (978-1-59296-904-3). 24pp. Introduces more than 20 common idioms and their meanings, with colorful illustrations. Also use *Ack! There's a Bug in My Ear! (And Other Sayings That Just Aren't True)* and *You're Clean as a Whistle! (And Other Silly Sayings)* (2007). (Rev: LMC 3/08; SLJ 4/08)

16586 Kompelien, Tracy. *The Castle Is Cold, Ancient and Old!* (2–5). Series: Synonyms. 2007, ABDO LB $19.93 (978-1-59928-728-7). 24pp. Using plenty of examples, this book introduces readers to synonyms with text and photographs. Also use *Ella Is Right, Smart and Bright!* and *Why Are You Sad and Blue?* (Rev: SLJ 8/07)

16587 Lederer, Richard. *The Circus of Words: Acrobatic Anagrams, Parading Palindromes, Wonderful Words on a Wire, and More Lively Letter Play* (5–8). Illus. by Dave Morice. 2001, Chicago Review paper $12.95 (978-1-55652-380-9). Lovers of words will find lots of entertainment in this selection of challenging exercises. (Rev: SLJ 8/01) [428.1]

16588 Leedy, Loreen, and Pat Street. *There's a Frog in My Throat: 440 Animal Sayings a Little Bird Told Me* (2–5). Illus. by Loreen Leedy. 2003, Holiday House $16.95 (978-0-8234-1774-2). 32pp. An amusing romp through animal-related expressions such as "social butterfly" and "barrel of monkeys." (Rev: BL 3/15/03*; HB 5/03; HBG 10/03; SLJ 4/03)

16589 Lunge-Larsen, Lise. *Gifts from the Gods: Ancient Words and Wisdom from Greek and Roman Mythology* (4–6). Illus. by Gareth Hinds. 2011, Houghton Mifflin $18.99 (978-0-547-15229-5). 96pp. Seventeen everyday words and phrases (Achilles' heel, Pandora's box, victory) with roots in classical mythology are examined here, with excerpts from children's books and relevant illustrations. (Rev: BL 11/1/11; SLJ 10/1/11) [401]

16590 Marsico, Katie. *Conjunctions* (2–4). Illus. by Kathleen Petelinsek. Series: Language Arts Explorer Junior: Parts of Speech. 2013, Cherry Lake LB $25.64 (978-162431181-9). 24pp. Readers learn about conjunctions and their use as they follow a story of a young girl taking her family to an art show. (Rev: BL 10/1/13) [428.2]

16591 Oelschlager, Vanita. *Birds of a Feather: A Book of Idioms and Silly Pictures* (K–3). Illus. by Robin Hegan. 2009, Vanita $17.95 (978-0-9800162-8-4). Idioms are

explained through humorous illustrations, brief paragraphs, and in-depth explanations at the end of the book for older readers. (Rev: BL 7/09)

16592 Oelschlager, Vanita. *Life Is a Bowl Full of Cherries: A Book of Food Idioms and Silly Pictures* (K–3). Illus. by Robin Hegan. 2011, Vanita $15.95 (978-098263663-3); paper $8.95 (978-09826366-2-6). 40pp. Visual representations of food-related puns and idioms ("food for thought") are presented in bright spreads, with brief explanations. (Rev: BL 5/1/11) [440]

16593 Ogburn, Jacqueline K. *Little Treasures: Endearments from Around the World* (PS–3). Illus. by Chris Raschka. 2012, Houghton Mifflin $16.99 (978-054742862-8). 32pp. Readers learn loving terms in 14 languages, including English, Spanish, Hindi, and Chinese. ℮ (Rev: BL 12/15/11; SLJ 1/12) [808.88]

16594 Preciado, Tony. *Super Grammar* (4–7). Illus. by Rhode Montijo. 2012, Scholastic paper $8.99 (978-0-545-42-515-5). 176pp. In comic book style, superheroes introduce the basics of sentences, parts of speech, punctuation marks and so forth. Lexile 970L (Rev: BL 12/1/12; SLJ 12/12) [428]

16595 Pulver, Robin. *Nouns and Verbs Have a Field Day* (K–3). Illus. by Lynn Rowe Reed. 2006, Holiday $16.95 (978-0-8234-1982-1). A companion to *Punctuation Takes a Vacation* (2003) this zany volume features a field day in which verbs and nouns refuse to cooperate with each other. (Rev: BL 4/1/06; SLJ 3/06)

16596 Rayevsky, Kim. *Antonyms, Synonyms and Homonyms* (1–3). Illus. by Robert Rayevsky. 2006, Holiday $16.95 (978-0-8234-1889-3). 32pp. Learn all about antonyms, synonyms, and homonyms with this funny book about an alien trying to make some sense out of life on Earth. (Rev: BL 12/1/06; SLJ 1/07)

16597 Riggs, Kate. *Nouns* (2–4). Illus. Series: Grammar Basics. 2013, Creative Education $17.95 (978-160818238-1). 24pp. With appealing photographs, this series entry helps young readers understand nouns and their importance. Also use *Verbs, Adverbs,* and *Adjectives* (all 2013). (Rev: BL 6/13) [428.2]

16598 Shields, Carol Diggory. *English, Fresh Squeezed! 40 Thirst-for-Knowledge-Quenching Poems* (4–7). Illus. by Tony Ross. Series: BrainJuice. 2005, Handprint $14.95 (978-1-59354-053-1). A humorous, rhyming look at annoying grammatical and other rules of language, with appealing illustrations and useful mnemonic devices. (Rev: BL 2/15/04; HB 5–6/04; SLJ 5/05)

16599 Swanson, Diane. *A Crash of Rhinos, A Party of Jays* (K–2). Illus. by Mariko Ando Spencer. 2006, Annick $19.95 (978-1-55451-048-1); paper $8.95 (978-1-55451-047-4). Introduces collective nouns for groups of animals, including the well-known (a pride of lions) and the obscure (a bouquet of pheasants), and provides interesting facts and eye-catching illustrations. (Rev: BL 1/1–15/07)

16600 Terban, Marvin. *Building Your Vocabulary* (4–8). Illus. Series: Scholastic Guides. 2002, Scholastic paper $12.95 (978-0-439-28561-2). 188pp. In addition to techniques for increasing vocabulary, Terban discusses etymology and how to use a dictionary and thesaurus, giving clear, often entertaining examples throughout. (Rev: SLJ 8/02)

16601 Terban, Marvin. *The Dove Dove: Funny Homograph Riddles* (4–7). Illus. by Tom Huffman. 1988, Houghton Mifflin paper $7.95 (978-0-89919-810-1). Making homographs less puzzling. Also use *Mad As a Wet Hen! and Other Funny Idioms* (1987). (Rev: BL 1/1/89) [818.5402]

16602 Terban, Marvin. *Punctuation Power: Punctuation and How to Use It* (4–9). Illus. by Eric Brace. 2000, Scholastic paper $12.95 (978-0-590-38673-9). 96pp. After a description of each punctuation mark and its uses, this account covers topics including bibliographies, quotations, play scripts, and sentences, and the kinds of punctuation they require. (Rev: SLJ 7/00)

16603 Thomson, Ruth. *A First Thesaurus* (K–3). Illus. 2003, Thameside LB $28.50 (978-1-931983-08-2). 64pp. Pictures and words are combined to introduce youngsters to the thesaurus; children are encouraged to select alternative words from the illustrated choices provided. Also use *A First Word Bank* (2003). (Rev: BL 12/1/02)

16604 Truss, Lynne. *Eats, Shoots, and Leaves: Why, Commas Really Do Make a Difference* (2–4). Illus. by Bonnie Timmons. 2006, Putnam $15.99 (978-0-399-24491-9). 32pp. The scope of Truss's bestseller for adults is narrowed to the role of the comma in this effective picture book full of funny examples of its misuse — "Eat here and get gas," for example. (Rev: BL 9/1/06; SLJ 8/06)

16605 Truss, Lynne. *The Girl's Like Spaghetti: Why, You Can't Manage Without Apostrophes!* (2–4). Illus. by Bonnie Timmons. 2007, Putnam $16.99 (978-0-399-24706-4). Amusing cartoons help teach important lessons about the use of apostrophes. (Rev: BL 7/07; SLJ 7/07)

16606 Verdick, Elizabeth. *Words Are Not for Hurting* (PS). Illus. by Marieka Heinlen. 2004, Free Spirit $11.95 (978-1-57542-156-8). 24pp. Verdick urges children to consider the power of the words they use and to assess their capacity to reassure or to wound. (Rev: BL 10/15/04; SLJ 11/04)

16607 Wilbur, Richard. *Opposites* (5–7). Illus. by author. 1991, Harcourt $11.95 (978-0-15-258720-8). Through verses and cartoonlike illustrations, antonyms are given for a series of words. [811.52]

Writing and Speaking

16608 Adler, Bill, ed. *Kids' Letters to Harry Potter* (3–6). 2001, Carroll & Graf $18.00 (978-0-7867-0890-1). Fans of the Harry Potter novels share thoughts on the books and characters through letters to the boy wizard. (Rev: BL 11/1/01; SLJ 11/01)

16609 Bauer, Marion Dane. *What's Your Story? A Young Person's Guide to Writing Fiction* (5–10). 1992, Clarion paper $7.95 (978-0-395-57780-6). An award-winning

writer gives advice to young authors, including suggestions for planning, writing, and revising. (Rev: BL 4/15/92; SLJ 6/92*) [808.3]

16610 Betz, Adrienne, comp. *Scholastic Treasury of Quotations for Children* (4–8). 1998, Scholastic paper $16.95 (978-0-590-27146-2). From Socrates to Bill Clinton, this is a useful compendium of quotations arranged under 75 subjects. (Rev: SLJ 2/99) [080]

16611 Bullard, Lisa. *You Can Write a Story! A Story-Writing Recipe for Kids* (2–4). Illus. by Deborah Haley Melmon. 2007, Two-Can $16.95 (978-1-58128-587-5). 48pp. The basic ingredients for a good story can be flavored in any way an author/cook can imagine, counsels this entertaining book that makes composition fun. (Rev: SLJ 5/07)

16612 Burkholder, Kelly. *Pen Pals* (2–5). Series: Artistic Adventures. 2001, Rourke LB $23.93 (978-1-57103-353-6). 24pp. This title tells how and why one wants to communicate with others through regular mail and e-mail, with a section on safety tips involving the computer. (Rev: SLJ 2/01)

16613 Burkholder, Kelly. *Stories* (2–5). Series: Artistic Adventures. 2001, Rourke LB $23.93 (978-1-57103-356-7). 24pp. This book introduces different types of writing — descriptive, persuasive, expository, and narrative — with ideas on expressing oneself through writing plus material on editing and revising. (Rev: SLJ 2/01)

16614 Cibula, Matt. *How to Be the Greatest Writer in the World* (4–8). Illus. by Brian Strassburg. 1999, Zino $11.95 (978-1-55933-276-7). A spiral-bound book that presents 88 interesting and engaging exercises to help youngsters who feel they have nothing to write about. (Rev: SLJ 2/00) [808]

16615 Crewe, Sabrina. *War Correspondents* (4–7). Illus. Series: World's Most Dangerous Jobs. 2012, Crabtree LB $24.83 (978-077875103-8). 32pp. A frank look at the dangers journalists face when they cover wars, with color photographs and quotations from primary sources. (Rev: BL 10/15/12) [070.4]

16616 Donoughue, Carol. *The Story of Writing* (4–7). Illus. 2007, Firefly $19.95 (978-1-55407-306-1). From early alphabets through tablets and scrolls, illuminated manuscripts, and the printing press, this is an appealing introduction to the development of writing. (Rev: BL 1/1–15/08)

16617 Dubrovin, Vivian. *Storytelling Adventures: Stories Kids Can Tell* (4–7). Illus. by Bobbi Shupe. 1997, Storycraft paper $14.95 (978-0-9638339-2-1). This book not only includes a selection of stories to tell but also suggests appropriate props to use, with directions on how to make them. (Rev: SLJ 5/97) [808.5]

16618 Dubrovin, Vivian. *Storytelling for the Fun of It* (4–8). Illus. by Bobbi Shupe. 1994, Storycraft paper $16.95 (978-0-9638339-0-7). This useful guide is divided into three parts that give general information, where and what kinds of stories to tell, and how to learn and perform them. (Rev: SLJ 4/94) [808.5]

16619 Fandel, Jennifer. *You Can Write Cool Poems* (1–3). Illus. Series: You Can Write. 2012, Capstone LB $24.65 (978-142967616-8); paper $6.95 (9781429679619). 24pp. With practical tips and lots of examples, this lively, accessible title encourages the very young to try their hands at poetry. (Rev: BL 8/12) [808.1]

16620 Farrell, Tish. *Write Your Own Fantasy Story* (4–8). Series: Write Your Own. 2006, Compass Point LB $33.26 (978-0-7565-1639-0). 64pp. Covering characters, viewpoint, plot, and speech, this is a helpful guide to writing fantasy literature. Also use *Write Your Own Mystery Story* and *Write Your Own Science Fiction Story* (both 2006). (Rev: SLJ 8/06)

16621 Fields, Jan. *You Can Write Great Letters and E-mails* (1–3). Illus. Series: You Can Write. 2012, Capstone LB $24.65 (978-142967613-7); paper $6.95 (9781429679633). 24pp. This lively, accessible title guides young writers on correct formatting and content for both formal and informal written communications. (Rev: BL 8/12) [808.6]

16622 Fletcher, Ralph. *How to Write Your Life Story* (5–8). 2007, HarperCollins $15.99 (978-0-06-050770-1); paper $5.99 (978-0-06-050769-5). 128pp. Writing exercises and examples will help readers to get started on autobiographies or memoirs. (Rev: BL 10/1/07; SLJ 11/07)

16623 Fletcher, Ralph. *Poetry Matters: Writing a Poem from the Inside Out* (4–7). 2002, HarperTrophy paper $5.99 (978-0-380-79703-5). A how-to book for young poets, with ideas on how to make images and "music" with words. (Rev: BL 5/15/02; HBG 10/02; SLJ 2/02*) [808.1]

16624 Gallion, Sue Lowell. *Rick and Rachel Build a Research Report* (4–6). Illus. by Chi Chung. Series: Writing Builders. 2013, Norwood LB $25.27 (978-159953583-8). 32pp. Rick and Rachel learn how to do research and select the information that is important for their report. (Rev: BL 11/15/13; SLJ 12/13) [808.02]

16625 Gilbert, Sara. *Write Your Own Article: Newspaper, Magazine, Online* (4–8). Series: Write Your Own. 2008, Compass Point LB $33.26 (978-0-7565-3855-2). 64pp. A practical guide to selecting a story, interview techniques, choosing viewpoint, developing a story, remaining objective, and so forth, with excerpts as examples. (Rev: SLJ 3/09)

16626 Gutman, Dan. *My Weird Writing Tips* (3–6). Illus. by Jim Paillot. 2013, HarperCollins $16.99 (978-006209107-9). 160pp. An entertaining guide to writing a good, grammatical story or essay. ℮ (Rev: BL 7/13; SLJ 9/13) [808.042]

16627 Hambleton, Vicki, and Cathleen Greenwood. *So, You Want to Be a Writer? How to Write, Get Published, and Maybe Even Make It Big!* (5–8). 2012, Beyond Words $17.99 (978-158270359-6); paper $9.99 (978-15827035-3-4). 192pp. From "What's It Like to Be a Writer" to "How to Get Published: Creating a Proposal" and "Writing as a Career: You Mean I Can Get Paid for That?," this is a thorough overview of the writing

process, covering all formats and genres and providing many examples. (Rev: BL 4/1/12; LMC 8–9/12) [808]

16628 Hamilton, Fran Santoro. *Hands-On English* (4–8). 1998, Portico paper $9.95 (978-0-9664867-0-4). A user-friendly volume that takes a visual approach to illustrate sentence patterns, such as using icons to represent the eight parts of speech, with clear, interesting explanations. Also included are irregular verbs, using modifiers, spelling rules, punctuation and capitalization, homonyms, and how to make outlines. (Rev: SLJ 2/99; VOYA 4/99) [415]

16629 Hamilton, John. *You Write It! Horror* (4–7). Illus. Series: You Write It! 2009, ABDO LB $17.95 (978-1-60453-506-8). 32pp. Tips for budding horror writers cover inspiration, good work habits, effective plots, and how to get published. (Rev: BL 4/1/09) [808.3]

16630 Hamilton, Martha, and Mitch Weiss. *Stories in My Pocket: Tales Kids Can Tell* (4–7). 1997, Fulcrum paper $15.95 (978-1-55591-957-3). This handbook of storytelling for young storytellers includes 30 tales to begin with. (Rev: BL 1/1–15/97) [372.6]

16631 Hershenhorn, Esther. *S Is for Story: A Writer's Alphabet* (3–6). Illus. by Zachary Pullen. 2009, Sleeping Bear $17.95 (978-1-58536-439-8). 40pp. An alphabetical celebration of books and writing. (Rev: BL 10/1/09; SLJ 3/10) [808.3]

16632 Holbrook, Sara. *Wham! It's a Poetry Jam: Discovering Performance Poetry* (2–5). 2002, Boyds Mills paper $9.95 (978-1-59078-011-4). Holbrook includes some of her poems in this guide to performing poetry — how to move, project your voice, express emotion, and so forth. (Rev: HBG 10/02; SLJ 5/02)

16633 Hudson, Wade. *Powerful Words: More Than 200 Years of Extraordinary Writing by African Americans* (5–9). Illus. by Sean Qualls. 2004, Scholastic $19.95 (978-0-439-40969-8). 192pp. Excerpts from the writings and speeches of both well-known and less-familiar African Americans are accompanied by notes on the context and the writer. (Rev: BL 2/15/04; SLJ 2/04)

16634 Janeczko, Paul B, comp. *Poetry from A to Z: A Guide for Young Writers* (4–8). Series: NetGuide. 1994, Simon & Schuster $16.95 (978-0-02-747672-9). This book of 72 poems, alphabetized by topic, gives examples to get young writers started, and the 23 poets represented give advice on how to become a better poet. (Rev: BCCB 3/95; BL 12/15/94; VOYA 5/95) [808.1]

16635 Leedy, Loreen. *Look at My Book: How Kids Can Write and Illustrate Terrific Books* (K–3). Illus. 2004, Holiday House $16.95 (978-0-8234-1590-8). 32pp. This picture book covers all aspects of publishing a work, from initial concept through writing, revision, and selecting design and binding. (Rev: BL 2/15/04; SLJ 4/04)

16636 Levine, Gail Carson. *Writing Magic: Creating Stories That Fly* (5–10). 2006, HarperCollins $16.99 (978-0-06-051961-2); paper $5.99 (978-0-06-051960-5). 167pp. Well-known author Levine provides upbeat, practical tips on such topics as finding story ideas, character and plot development, and investigating the possibility of publication. (Rev: BL 12/15/06; SLJ 2/07*)

16637 Lewis, Catherine. *Thrice Told Tales: Three Mice Full of Writing Advice* (5–8). Illus. by Joost Swarte. 2013, Atheneum $16.99 (978-141695784-3). 144pp. Writing advice is offered with wit and whimsy in this guide that uses a traditional rhyme to focus on the different elements of writing essays, stories, and other forms of literature. **e** (Rev: BL 9/15/13; LMC 3–4/14; SLJ 9/13*) [803]

16638 Litwin, Laura Baskes. *Write Horror Fiction in 5 Simple Steps* (5–8). 2012, Enslow LB $23.93 (978-076603836-3). 48pp. Basic tips on planning and research, organization, and publication accompany advice on writing, examples of the genre, and creepy ideas. (Rev: BL 10/1/12; LMC 5–6/13*) [808.3]

16639 Loewen, Nancy. *Words, Wit, and Wonder: Writing Your Own Poem* (2–4). Illus. by Christopher Lyles. 2008, Picture Window LB $17.99 (978-1-4048-5344-7). 32pp. This primer provides aspiring poets with 12 useful tools. (Rev: BL 4/1/09; SLJ 6/09)

16640 Lynette, Rachel. *Jesse and Jasmine Build a Journal* (4–6). Illus. by Carlos Aon. Series: Writing Builders. 2013, Norwood LB $25.27 (978-159953585-2). 32pp. Two middle-graders record a trip to Yellowstone in this guide to effective journal writing. (Rev: BL 11/15/13) [372.62]

16641 Mack, Jim. *Journals and Blogging* (3–6). Illus. Series: Culture in Action. 2009, Raintree LB $28.21 (978-1-4109-3406-2); paper $7.99 (978-1-4109-3423-9). 32pp. An appealing introduction to writing journals and blogs, with information on Internet etiquette and safety and on well-known practitioners of these arts. (Rev: LMC 3–4/10; SLJ 2/10) [808]

16642 Minden, Cecilia, and Kate Roth. *How to Write a News Article* (2–4). Illus. Series: Language Arts Explorer Junior: Writing. 2012, Cherry Lake LB $24.21 (978-161080308-3). 24pp. A step-by-step guide to producing a simple news story, with useful examples and checklist. Also use *How to Write a How-To* (2012). (Rev: BL 3/15/12; LMC 8–9/13) [808]

16643 Minden, Cecilia, and Kate Roth. *How to Write a Play* (2–4). Illus. Series: Language Arts Explorer Junior. 2012, Cherry Lake LB $25.64 (978-161080490-5). 24pp. Minden explains how to handle characters, dialogue, scenes, and so forth, and offers examples and a checklist. Also in this series: *How to Write a Thank-You Letter, How to Write a Mystery*, and *How to Write a Business Letter* (all 2012). (Rev: BL 12/1/12) [808.2]

16644 Nobleman, Marc Tyler. *Extraordinary E-Mails, Letters, and Resumes* (5–8). Illus. by Kevin Pope. Series: F. W. Prep. 2005, Watts LB $31.00 (978-0-531-16759-5). Advice for students who want to write effective e-mails, letters, and resumés, with an explanation of the importance of communicating clearly. (Rev: SLJ 1/06) [808]

16645 Otfinoski, Steven. *Extraordinary Short Story Writing* (5–8). Illus. by Kevin Pope. Series: F. W. Prep. 2005,

Watts LB $31.00 (978-0-531-16760-1). Tips and activities reinforce the information on writing different types of stories, choosing ideas, and using available resources effectively; a sample short story offers step-by-step guidance. (Rev: SLJ 2/06) [808]

16646 Otfinoski, Steven. *Speaking Up, Speaking Out: A Kid's Guide to Making Speeches, Oral Reports, and Conversation* (5–8). 1996, Millbrook LB $24.90 (978-1-56294-345-5). All kinds of public-speaking situations are introduced, with suggestions on how to be a success at each. (Rev: BL 1/1–15/97; SLJ 1/97) [808.5]

16647 Pelleschi, Andrea. *Neil and Nan Build Narrative Nonfiction* (4–6). Illus. by Yu-Mei Han. Series: Writing Builders. 2013, Norwood LB $25.27 (978-159953586-9). 32pp. A class assignment brings Neil and Nan together to create a nonfiction piece. Also use *Olivia and Oscar Build an Opinion Piece* (2013). (Rev: BL 11/15/13) [372.62]

16648 Prelutsky, Jack. *Pizza, Pigs, and Poetry: How to Write a Poem* (4–6). 2008, Greenwillow paper $5.99 (978-0-06-143448-8). 208pp. An appealing blend of writing tips, examples of the author's own efforts, anecdotes about his life, and a selection of "poemstarts." (Rev: BCCB 6/08; BL 5/1/08; SLJ 6/08)

16649 Raum, Elizabeth. *Poetry* (3–6). Series: Culture in Action. 2010, Heinemann-Raintree $28.21 (978-1-4109-3404-8). 32pp. A high-interest introduction to poetry and the joys of writing and reading it, with activities designed to build literacy and understanding of the arts. Lexile 800L (Rev: LMC 3–4/10) [808.1]

16650 Rivera, Shelia. *The Media War* (5–8). Series: World in Conflict. 2004, ABDO LB $25.65 (978-1-59197-418-5). A brief overview of American journalism's impact on war from the Civil War to the U.S. invasion of Afghanistan. (Rev: BL 4/1/04) [070.1]

16651 Rosinsky, Natalie M. *Write Your Own Biography* (4–8). Series: Write Your Own. 2007, Compass Point LB $31.93 (978-0-7565-3366-3). A helpful guide to writing a biography with excerpts from published works and writing exercises. (Rev: SLJ 12/07) [808]

16652 Rosinsky, Natalie M. *Write Your Own Graphic Novel* (4–8). 2008, Compass Point LB $24.95 (978-075653856-9). 64pp. Rosinsky introduces such helpful concepts as storyboarding, editing, and peer collaboration while providing photos of young writers at work and referencing familiar graphic novels. Lexile 1010L (Rev: BL 11/1/08; SLJ 3/1/09) [741.5]

16653 Roy, Jennifer Rozines. *You Can Write a Story or Narrative* (4–8). Series: You Can Write! 2003, Enslow LB $22.60 (978-0-7660-2085-6). Sound advice for plotting and writing a wide array of different narratives, including adventure, history, fantasy, and folklore. (Rev: SLJ 1/04; VOYA 4/04) [808]

16654 St. John, Amanda. *Bridget and Bo Build a Blog* (2–4). Illus. by Katie McDee. Series: Writing Builders. 2012, Norwood LB $25.27 (978-159953507-4). 32pp. Nine-year-old Bo teaches his friend Bridget how to build and write a blog in this story full of helpful hints and ideas for topics. (Rev: BL 4/1/12*) [808]

16655 Senn, Joyce. *The Young People's Book of Quotations* (5–10). 1999, Millbrook LB $39.90 (978-0-7613-0267-4). Beginning with "accomplishment" and ending with "zoos," this is a collection of 2,000 quotations of special interest to young people, arranged by topic. (Rev: BL 3/1/99*; SLJ 4/99) [082]

16656 Somervill, Barbara. *Backstage at a Newscast* (5–8). Illus. Series: Backstage Pass. 2003, Children's LB $24.50 (978-0-516-24326-9); paper $6.95 (978-0-516-24388-7). 48pp. Somerville provides information on how a newscast is created, along with guidance on careers in journalism. (Rev: BL 5/1/03)

16657 Trueit, Trudi. *Keeping a Journal* (4–8). Illus. 2004, Watts LB $20.50 (978-0-531-12262-4). 80pp. Trueit encourages readers to keep journals, offering tips on getting started, writing prompts and exercises, a calendar of ideas, and alternatives for those who don't enjoy writing, such as scrapbooks and drawing. (Rev: BL 10/15/03; SLJ 3/05)

16658 Veljkovic, Peggy, and Arthur Schwartz, eds. *Writing from the Heart: Young People Share Their Wisdom* (5–9). 2001, Templeton Foundation paper $12.95 (978-1-890151-48-5). A collection of the best essays by young people that have been submitted to the Laws of Life program since it began in 1987. (Rev: SLJ 6/01) [170]

16659 Vinton, Ken. *Alphabet Antics: Hundreds of Activities to Challenge and Enrich Letter Learners of All Ages* (5–8). Illus. by author. 1996, Free Spirit paper $19.95 (978-0-915793-98-3). For each letter of the alphabet, there is a history, how it appears in different alphabets, important words that begin with that letter, a quotation from someone whose name starts with it, and a number of interesting related projects. (Rev: SLJ 1/97) [411]

16660 Wong, Janet S. *You Have to Write* (2–4). Illus. by Teresa Flavin. 2002, Simon & Schuster $17.00 (978-0-689-83409-7). 40pp. Wong uses poetic text and a photo album approach to spur young people to think about writing assignments in new ways. (Rev: BL 7/02; HBG 3/03; SLJ 7/02)

16661 Young, Sue. *Writing with Style* (5–8). Series: Scholastic Guides. 1997, Scholastic $12.95 (978-0-590-50977-0). A guide for the novice writer, with chapters on planning, presenting, and publishing one's work. (Rev: BL 3/1/97; SLJ 5/97) [372.6]

Music

General

16662 Aliki. *Ah, Music!* (1–3). Illus. 2003, HarperCollins LB $17.89 (978-0-06-028727-6). 48pp. Rhythm, harmony, melody, jazz, instruments, and a brief history are among the many aspects of music that Aliki manages to cover in this slim volume. (Rev: BL 6/1–15/03; HB 5/03; HBG 10/03; SLJ 5/03)

16663 Allen, Patrick. *Europe* (4–6). Series: World of Music. 2007, Heinemann LB $31.43 (978-1-4034-9890-8). 48pp. With photographs and discussion of famous players and current styles, this volume offers a broad overview of the music, instruments, and folk traditions of Europe. (Rev: LMC 5/08; SLJ 3/08)

16664 Ayazi-Hashjin, Sherry. *Rap and Hip Hop: The Voice of a Generation* (4–7). Illus. Series: Library of African American Arts and Culture. 1999, Rosen LB $26.50 (978-0-8239-1855-3). 62pp. This account traces the history of rap and hip hop music from their origins in spirituals, jazz, blues, and storytelling traditions; it also gives some information on musicians. (Rev: BL 2/15/00; SLJ 1/00)

16665 Barnes, Deb. *Inside a Rock Band* (2–4). Series: Girls Rock! 2006, Child's World $25.64 (978-1-59296-745-2). 32pp. An inside look at what it's like to be in a professional band. (Rev: BL 11/15/06; SLJ 4/07)

16666 Bertholf, Bret. *The Long Gone Lonesome History of Country Music* (5–8). Illus. 2007, Little, Brown $18.99 (978-0-316-52393-6). 64pp. A chatty survey of country music, discussing its roots and early instruments, tracing the evolution to today's sounds, and introducing some of its greatest performers. (Rev: BL 4/1/07; SLJ 4/07*)

16667 Bryan, Ashley. *Let It Shine: Three Favorite Spirituals* (PS–5). Illus. by author. 2007, Simon & Schuster $16.99 (978-0-689-84732-5). This large-format, beautifully illustrated volume showcases three familiar spirituals: "This Little Light of Mine," "He's Got the Whole

World in His Hands," and "When the Saints Go Marching In." (Rev: BL 11/15/06; SLJ 1/07*)

16668 Cefrey, Holly. *Backstage at a Music Video* (5–8). Illus. Series: Backstage Pass. 2003, Children's paper $6.95 (978-0-516-24386-3). 48pp. The history of music videos is coupled with information on how they are financed and produced, along with guidance on careers in the music business. (Rev: BL 5/1/03)

16669 Celenza, Anna Harwell. *Pictures at an Exhibition* (K–4). Illus. by JoAnn E. Kitchel. 2003, Charlesbridge LB $19.95 (978-1-57091-492-8). 32pp. Drawing on primary-source documents, Celenza has created an arresting account of the friendship that was the catalyst for Mussorgsky's famous piece. (Rev: HBG 4/04; SLJ 4/03)

16670 *Children's Book of Music: An Introduction to the World's Most Amazing Music and Its Creators* (3–6). 2010, DK $24.99 (978-0-7566-6734-4). 142pp. This broad, chronological survey of music looks at musical history, famous composers and musicians, musical instruments, and so forth, and features a visually appealing layout full of photographs and sidebars. (Rev: LMC 3–4/11*; SLJ 1/1/11) [780.9]

16671 Cornish, Melanie J. *The History of Hip Hop* (4–7). Illus. 2009, Crabtree LB $19.95 (978-0-7787-3820-6); paper $8.95 (978-0-7787-3841-1). A single house party in 1973 started hip-hop and it bopped on from there. (Rev: BL 6/1–15/09) [782.42164909]

16672 Corr, Christopher. *Whole World* (PS). Illus. 2007, Barefoot Books $16.99 (978-1-846860-43-0). 32pp. This illustrated version of the classic spiritual (with a sing-along CD) shows children around the world enjoying nature and makes a clear plea for environmental protection. (Rev: BL 4/15/07)

16673 Crossingham, John. *Learn to Speak Music: A Guide to Creating, Performing, and Promoting Your Songs* (5–8). Illus. by Jeff Kulak. 2009, Owlkids paper $17.95 (978-1-897349-65-6). 96pp. An attractive overview of the basics of music with advice on writing music, forming a band, dealing with stage fright, and so forth. (Rev: BL 11/1/09; LMC 1–2/10; SLJ 11/09) [782.42]

16674 Ench, Rick, and Jay Cravath. *North American Indian Music* (5–7). Illus. Series: Watts Library: Indians of the Americas. 2002, Watts LB $25.50 (978-0-531-11772-9); paper $8.95 (978-0-531-16230-9). 64pp. This title looks at the importance of music in the rituals of North American Indian tribes and describes the forms of beat, rhythm, and melody, with illustrations, a glossary, bibliography, and timeline. (Rev: BL 7/02)

16675 Garty, Judy. *Techniques of Marching Bands* (5–8). Series: Let's Go Team. 2003, Mason Crest LB $19.95 (978-1-59084-538-7). 64pp. The slim volume supplies a look at the functions of a marching band, how they operate, and the joys of playing in one. (Rev: BL 10/15/03; SLJ 11/03)

16676 Gatti, Anne, retel. *The Magic Flute* (4–8). Retold by Anne Gatti. Illus. by Peter Malone. 1997, Chronicle $17.95 (978-0-8118-1003-6). An elegant retelling of the Mozart opera, with each scene given a full-color painting and a page of text. The accompanying CD has 16 selections coded to each page. (Rev: SLJ 1/98*) [782.1]

16677 George-Warren, Holly. *Shake, Rattle and Roll: The Founders of Rock and Roll* (4–7). 2001, Houghton Mifflin $16.00 (978-0-618-05540-1). After an informative introduction on the history of rock and roll, there is a series of one-page biographies of famous personalities. (Rev: BL 3/1/01; HBG 10/01; SLJ 5/01*) [781.66]

16678 Greene, Ellin. *Mother's Song: A Lullaby* (PS). Illus. by Elizabeth Sayles. 2008, Clarion $17.00 (978-0-395-71527-7). 32pp. A celebration of a mother's love for her child, with pastel illustrations featuring fairies and a woodland landscape plus original music. (Rev: BL 7/08; SLJ 4/08)

16679 Handyside, Christopher. *Country* (5–9). Series: A History of American Music. 2006, Heinemann LB $31.43 (978-1-4034-8151-1). This history of country music traces the genre from its hillbilly roots to the present and introduces some of its most influential figures, including the Carter family, Johnny Cash, Loretta Lynn, and John Denver. (Rev: SLJ 9/06) [781.642]

16680 Hannah, Johnny. *Hot Jazz Special* (4–6). Illus. 2005, Candlewick $16.99 (978-0-7636-2308-1). This brightly illustrated volume with a fold-out poster celebrates the contributions of jazz players including Louis Armstrong, Duke Ellington, Billie Holliday, Jelly Roll Morton, and Django Reinhardt. (Rev: BL 7/05; SLJ 3/05)

16681 Hasan, Heather. *How to Produce, Release, and Market Your Music* (5–8). Illus. Series: Garage Bands. 2012, Rosen LB $12.95 (978-144885658-9). 64pp. Everything you need to know about making it in the music world, from initial recording through booking shows, establishing copyright, marketing strategies, and use of social media. (Rev: BL 4/1/12) [780.23]

16682 Igus, Toyomi. *I See the Rhythm* (5–8). 1998, Children's $15.95 (978-0-89239-151-6). Using a timeline to set the social context, this title traces African American contributions to such musical forms as the blues, big band, jazz, bebop, gospel, and rock. (Rev: BCCB 7–8/98; BL 2/15/98; SLJ 6/98) [780]

16683 Joel, Billy. *New York State of Mind* (PS–2). Illus. by Izak. 2005, Scholastic $16.99 (978-0-439-55382-7). 32pp. Using Billy Joel's song as the framework, Izak portrays the essence of New York City through a dog's Christmas visit. (Rev: BL 11/15/05)

16684 Levine, Robert. *The Story of the Orchestra* (5–7). Illus. by Meredith Hamilton. 2001, Black Dog & Leventhal $19.98 (978-1-57912-148-8). Orchestra Bob introduces young readers to orchestra history, famous conductors and their eras, and instruments, in a guided tour that includes amusing cartoons, illustrations, and links to selections on the accompanying CD. (Rev: BL 12/15/01; SLJ 9/01) [784.2]

16685 Mack, Jim. *Hip-Hop* (3–6). Series: Culture in Action. 2010, Heinemann-Raintree $28.21 (978-1-4109-3393-5). 32pp. A high-interest introduction to the various forms of hip-hop music and its history, with activities that reinforce literacy and understanding. Lexile 870L (Rev: LMC 3–4/10) [793.3]

16686 McNeil, Keith, and Rusty McNeil. *Colonial and Revolution Songbook: With Historical Commentary* (4–7). 1996, WEM Records paper $11.95 (978-1-878360-08-3). This songbook contains 39 traditional songs from the 17th century through the War of 1812, with brief historical comments for each. (Rev: SLJ 12/96) [973]

16687 Miles, Liz. *Making a Recording* (3–6). Illus. Series: Culture in Action. 2009, Raintree LB $28.21 (978-1-4109-3392-8); paper $7.99 (978-1-4109-3409-3). 32pp. An appealing introduction to recording music, with information on history, techniques, and well-known practitioners of these arts. (Rev: LMC 3–4/10; SLJ 2/10) [781.49]

16688 Miles, Liz. *The Orchestra* (3–6). Series: Culture in Action. 2010, Heinemann-Raintree $28.21 (978-1-4109-3394-2). 32pp. Introduces the structure of an orchestra, what it's like to play in one, and the kinds of music they play, with activities that are designed to reinforce understanding and literacy. Lexile 840L (Rev: LMC 3–4/10) [784.2]

16689 Nelson, Kadir. *He's Got the Whole World in His Hands* (PS–3). Illus. 2005, Dial $16.99 (978-0-8037-2850-9). 32pp. An African American boy savors life with his family and the wonders of the world around him in this picture-book interpretation of the popular spiritual. (Rev: BL 10/1/05*; HBG 4/06; SLJ 9/05)

16690 Olson-Brown, Ellen. *Hush Little Digger* (PS–K). Illus. by Lee White. 2006, Tricycle $12.95 (978-1-58246-160-1). This twist on the popular lullaby "Hush Little Baby" features a father promising his son increasingly large pieces of equipment. (Rev: BL 4/1/06; SLJ 6/06)

16691 Pinkney, Gloria Jean. *Music from Our Lord's Holy Heaven* (2–4). Illus. by Jerry Pinkney, et al. 2005, HarperCollins LB $18.89 (978-0-06-000769-0). 48pp. Children's author Pinkney pairs the lyrics of African

American spirituals with relevant psalms in this beautifully illustrated picture book that comes bundled with an audio CD. (Rev: BL 10/1/05; SLJ 12/05)

16692 Richer, Linda A., and Anita Stoltzfus Breckbill, eds. *Chatter with the Angels: An Illustrated Songbook for Children* (2–6). Illus. 2000, GIA $29.95 (978-1-57999-082-4). An outstanding songbook containing 90 selections of Christian music from different countries and cultures that are printed with piano and guitar arrangements. (Rev: BL 10/1/00; HBG 3/01)

16693 Schaefer, A. R. *Forming a Band* (5–8). Illus. Series: Rock Music Library. 2003, Capstone LB $23.93 (978-0-7368-2146-9). 32pp. A hip and practical guide suitable for reluctant readers. Also use *Booking a First Gig* (2003). (Rev: BL 12/1/03)

16694 Solway, Andrew. *Africa* (4–6). Series: World of Music. 2007, Heinemann LB $31.43 (978-1-4034-9891-5). 48pp. With photographs and discussion of famous players, this volume offers a broad overview of the music, instruments, and folk traditions of Africa. (Rev: LMC 5/08; SLJ 3/08)

16695 Solway, Andrew. *Latin America and the Caribbean* (4–6). Series: World of Music. 2007, Heinemann LB $31.43 (978-1-4034-9889-2). 48pp. With photographs and discussion of famous players and blending of Amerindian, African, and European influences, this volume offers a broad overview of the music, instruments, and traditions of Latin America and the Caribbean. (Rev: SLJ 3/08)

16696 Stringer, Lauren. *When Stravinsky Met Nijinsky: Two Artists, Their Ballet, and One Extraordinary Riot* (2–4). Illus. by author. 2013, Harcourt $16.99 (978-0-547-90725-3). 32pp. This attractive picture book tells the story of the collaboration between the composer and dancer that resulted in the famous *Rite of Spring* — and the riot that greeted this innovative work. ALA Notable Children's Book. Lexile 760L (Rev: BL 11/1/12*; HB 3–4/13; LMC 8–9/13; SLJ 5/13*) [781.5]

16697 *This Little Light of Mine* (PS–2). Illus. by E. B. Lewis. 2005, Simon & Schuster $16.95 (978-0-689-83179-9). 32pp. The words of this familiar African American spiritual spring to life in the vibrant illustrations as a boy moves through his community, sharing experiences. (Rev: BL 2/1/05; SLJ 3/05)

16698 Underwood, Deborah. *Australia, Hawaii, and the Pacific* (4–6). Series: World of Music. 2007, Heinemann LB $31.43 (978-1-4034-9894-6). 48pp. With photographs and discussion of famous players, this volume offers a broad overview of the music, instruments, and traditions of Australia. (Rev: LMC 5/08; SLJ 3/08)

16699 Yolen, Jane. *Apple for the Teacher: Thirty Songs for Singing While You Work* (4–7). 2005, Abrams $24.95 (978-0-8109-4825-9). This collection of work songs, compiled by Yolen and featuring music arrangements by her son Adam Stemple, celebrates 30 diverse occupations from astronaut to weaver. (Rev: BL 10/1/05; SLJ 10/05) [782.42]

Ballads and Folk Songs

16700 Arnold, Tedd. *Catalina Magdalena Hoopensteiner Wallendiner Hogan Logan Bogan Was Her Name* (PS–2). Illus. by author. 2004, Scholastic $10.95 (978-0-590-10994-9). 40pp. A classic camp song serves as inspiration for an unlikely heroine. (Rev: SLJ 8/04) [782.42]

16701 Boynton, Sandra. *Dog Train* (PS–2). Illus. by author. 2005, Workman $17.95 (978-0-7611-3966-9). 64pp. A collection of songs with a distinct rock 'n' roll feel, this book provides spreads for songs that are included on the accompanying CD. (Rev: SLJ 3/06) [782.42]

16702 Burke, Bobby, and Horace Gerlach. *Daddy's Little Girl* (PS–2). Illus. by Maggie Kneen. 2004, HarperCollins $14.99 (978-0-06-028722-1). The 1950s song "Daddy's Little Girl" becomes a book starring a family of rabbits. (Rev: SLJ 5/04) [782.42]

16703 Cabrera, Jane. *Old MacDonald Had a Farm* (PS). Illus. by author. 2008, Holiday $16.95 (978-0-8234-2141-1). A farmer and his animals have fun in this version of the song that ends with the arrival of a human baby. (Rev: BL 3/15/08; SLJ 3/08) [782.42]

16704 Cabrera, Jane. *Row, Row, Row Your Boat* (PS–K). Illus. by author. 2014, Holiday $16.95 (978-082343050-5). 32pp. The traditional song gets a jungle flair in this story featuring a kitten and puppy in a rain forest full of animals. (Rev: BLO 3/1/14; SLJ 5/14) [782.42083]

16705 Crews, Nina. *The Neighborhood Sing-Along* (PS–1). Illus. by author. 2011, Greenwillow $17.99 (978-0-06-185063-9). 64pp. Urban cityscape photographs of multicultural children add appeal to this collection of songs and rhymes. (Rev: BL 4/15/11; HB 5–6/11; SLJ 4/11) [782.42]

16706 Emberley, Rebecca, and Adrian Emberley. *There Was an Old Monster* (PS–K). Illus. by Rebecca Emberley. 2009, Scholastic $16.99 (978-0-545-10145-5). 32pp. A monster swallows more and bigger creatures until he's ready to explode in this twist on the classic cumulative song. (Rev: BL 6/1–15/09; SLJ 6/09) [782.42]

16707 Emmett, Jonathan. *She'll Be Coming 'Round the Mountain* (PS–K). Illus. 2007, Simon & Schuster $16.99 (978-1-4169-3652-7). 32pp. A lively cowgirl dressed in pink pajamas and a huge green hat stars in this rollicking expanded version of the classic song. (Rev: BL 4/1/07; SLJ 3/07) [782.42]

16708 Goembel, Ponder. *Animal Fair* (PS–K). Illus. by author. 2010, Marshall Cavendish $12.99 (978-0-7614-5642-1). 24pp. With detailed, humorous illustrations, this is a retelling of the children's nonsense folk song. (Rev: BL 3/1/10; SLJ 4/1/10) [782.42]

16709 Handyside, Christopher. *Folk* (5–9). 2006, Heinemann LB $31.43 (978-1-4034-8150-4). 48pp. This attractive volume traces the evolution of American folk music from its post-Civil War roots to its influence on the contemporary music scene and introduces some of its most influential figures, including Leadbelly, Woody

Guthrie, Joan Baez, and Bob Dylan. (Rev: SLJ 9/06) [781.62]

16710 *Here We Go Round the Mulberry Bush* (PS–K). Illus. by Sophie Fatus. 2007, Barefoot Books $16.99 (978-1-84686-035-5). An illustrated version of the familiar nursery song, with a discussion of the song's history, the sheet music, and directions for a dance to go along with it. (Rev: BL 6/1–15/07; SLJ 6/07) [782.42]

16711 Isadora, Rachel. *Old Mikamba Had a Farm* (PS–1). Illus. by author. 2013, Penguin $17.99 (978-0-399-25740-7). 40pp. In a nicely illustrated African rendition of the familiar song, Old Mikamba lives in a game park full of exotic animals. ALA Notable Children's Book. (Rev: BL 10/1/13; LMC 3–4/14; SLJ 8/13) [782.42]

16712 Isadora, Rachel. *There Was a Tree* (PS–1). Illus. by author. 2012, Penguin $16.99 (978-0-399-25741-4). 32pp. Set in Africa, this is a lively rendering of the song "And the Green Grass Grew All Around." (Rev: BL 12/1/12; HB 11–12/12; LMC 1–2/13; SLJ 9/12) [782.42]

16713 Katz, Alan. *Mosquitoes Are Ruining My Summer! And Other Silly Dilly Camp Songs* (3–5). Illus. by David Catrow. Series: Silly Dilly. 2011, Simon & Schuster $16.99 (978-1-4169-5568-9). 32pp. Familiar children's songs are given new lyrics describing the woes and wonders of summer camp. (Rev: BL 4/15/11; SLJ 7/11) [782.42]

16714 Lyon, George Ella. *Which Side Are You On? The Story of a Song* (3–5). Illus. by Christopher Cardinale. 2011, Cinco Puntos $17.95 (978-1-933693-96-5). 40pp. The story of the composition of the famed labor rights song "Which Side Are You On?" is presented here against a backdrop of mining company thugs, striking workers, and violence. ∩ (Rev: BL 11/15/11; HB 1–2/12; LMC 5–6/12; SLJ 11/1/11) [782.42]

16715 McGill, Alice. *In the Hollow of Your Hand: Slave Lullabies* (5–7). 2000, Houghton Mifflin $18.00 (978-0-395-85755-7). Family life in the days of slavery is revealed in this moving collection of 13 folk lullabies; a CD of the songs is also included. (Rev: BCCB 1/01; BL 11/15/00; HBG 3/01; SLJ 12/00) [811.008]

16716 Mitchell, Susan K. *The Rainforest Grew All Around* (PS–3). Illus. by Connie McLennan. 2007, Dell $15.95 (978-0-9768823-6-7). 32pp. Adapting the familiar "The Green Grass Grew All Around," this brightly illustrated book introduces young children to a wide variety of rain forest animals and plants. (Rev: BL 6/1–15/07; SLJ 8/07)

16717 Norworth, Jack. *Take Me Out to the Ball Game* (PS–K). Illus. by Amiko Hirao. Series: Children's Favorite Activity Songs. 2011, Imagine $17.95 (978-1-936140-26-8). 16pp. Text and illustrations present the familiar song; an accompanying CD contains songs by Carly Simon, with modified lyrics and a note about Jackie Robinson. (Rev: BL 3/1/11; SLJ 7/11) [782.42]

16718 O'Neal, Debbie Trafton. *Twinkle, Twinkle, Little Star* (PS). Illus. by Benrei Huang. Series: Sing-It. 2003, Augsburg $8.99 (978-0-8066-4350-2). 32pp. This beautifully illustrated book celebrates the familiar children's

song and even adds a new verse written by the author. (Rev: HBG 10/03; SLJ 9/03)

16719 Penner, Fred. *The Cat Came Back* (PS–2). Illus. by Renee Reichert. 2005, Roaring Brook $15.95 (978-1-59643-030-3). 32pp. Excellent artwork elevates the humor of the traditional song about a man determined to rid himself of a pesky cat. (Rev: BL 11/1/05; SLJ 10/05)

16720 Pinkney, Brian. *Hush, Little Baby* (PS). Illus. 2006, Greenwillow $15.99 (978-0-06-055993-9). 32pp. Mama has gone off for the day and it is up to Papa and older brother to look after the little girl; set in an African American family in the early 1900s. (Rev: BL 2/1/06; SLJ 3/06)

16721 Raffi. *This Little Light of Mine* (PS–3). Illus. by Stacey Schuett. Series: Raffi Songs to Read. 2004, Knopf LB $17.99 (978-0-375-92871-0). 32pp. This book-CD package uses the framework of children preparing for a performance of the song, and uses a variety of lights effectively. (Rev: SLJ 7/04)

16722 Sayre, April P. *Hush, Little Puppy* (PS). Illus. by Susan Winter. 2007, Holt $15.95 (978-0-8050-7102-3). 32pp. This gentle picture book captures the joyful friendship of a boy and his puppy as the boy uses his own version of "Hush Little Baby" at bedtime. (Rev: BL 6/1–15/07; SLJ 8/07)

16723 Shulman, Lisa. *Old MacDonald Had a Woodshop* (PS–2). Illus. by Ashley Wolff. 2002, Penguin $17.99 (978-0-399-23596-2). 32pp. Old MacDonald, a female sheep, shares her woodshop with the other farm animals in this entertaining version of the familiar song. (Rev: BL 9/15/02; HB 9/02; HBG 3/03; SLJ 9/02*)

16724 Stotts, Stuart. *We Shall Overcome: The Song That Changed the World* (5–8). Illus. by Terrance Cummings. 2010, Houghton Mifflin LB $18 (978-0-547-18210-0). 80pp. Stotts reviews the history of the song that inspired, encouraged, and comforted those involved in the U.S. civil rights movement; includes a CD with a Pete Seeger recording. Lexile 1080L (Rev: BL 11/1/09; LMC 1–2/10; SLJ 2/10) [782.42162]

16725 Trapani, Iza. *Froggie Went A-Courtin'* (PS–3). Illus. by author. 2002, Charlesbridge LB $15.95 (978-1-58089-028-1). A new, humorous version of the song about Froggie's constant rejections. (Rev: HBG 3/03; SLJ 7/02)

16726 Tyler, Gillian. *Froggy Went a-Courtin'* (PS–2). Illus. 2005, Candlewick $15.99 (978-0-7636-2306-7). 32pp. Eyecatching watercolor-and-ink artwork highlights this adaptation of the familiar folk song about the unlikely romantic relationship between a frog and a mouse. (Rev: BL 1/1–15/05; SLJ 1/05)

16727 Voake, Charlotte. *Tweedle-Dee-Dee* (PS–2). Illus. by author. 2008, Candlewick $16.99 (978-0-7636-3797-2). 32pp. A picture-book version of the folk song "The Green Grass Grew All Around," with appealing illustrations of nature, simple text, plus the music and lyrics. (Rev: BL 6/1–15/08; SLJ 6/08)

16728 Ward, Jennifer. *There Was an Old Monkey Who Swallowed a Frog* (PS–2). Illus. by Steve Gray. 2010,

Marshall Cavendish $16.99 (978-076145580-6). 32pp. A funny cumulative tale about a monkey's strange diet in the jungle. (Rev: BL 3/15/10; LMC 8–9/10) [782.42]

16729 Yarrow, Peter. *Sleepytime Songs* (PS–2). Illus. by Terry Widener. 2008, Sterling $16.95 (978-1-4027-5962-8). 48pp. A collection of bedtime songs, with a CD, from Peter of Peter, Paul and Mary. (Rev: BL 1/1–15/09; SLJ 2/09)

16730 Yarrow, Peter, and Lenny Lipton. *Puff, the Magic Dragon* (PS–2). Illus. by Eric Puybaret. 2007, Sterling $16.95 (978-1-4027-4782-3). 24pp. The classic 1960s song about a friendly dragon is expanded in this picture book with accompanying four-song CD featuring Yarrow (of Peter, Paul, and Mary) and his daughter. (Rev: BL 9/15/07; SLJ 8/07)

Holidays

16731 Boys Choir of Harlem Staff. *O Holy Night: Christmas with the Boys Choir of Harlem* (PS–3). Illus. by Faith Ringgold. 2004, HarperCollins LB $19.89 (978-0-06-051819-6). 40pp. Rich illustrations of an African American holy family and onlookers of all races accompany the words to five Christmas carols, which are featured on the CD. (Rev: BL 9/1/04; SLJ 10/04)

16732 Brebeuf, Jean de. *The Huron Carol* (PS–2). Trans. by Jesse Edgar Middleton. Illus. by Ian Wallace. 2006, Groundwood $16.95 (978-0-88899-711-1). Wallace illustrates in watercolor the 17th-century Christmas carol that sets the Nativity in Huron culture. (Rev: BL 10/15/06; SLJ 10/06)

16733 Cabrera, Jane. *The 12 Days of Christmas* (PS–1). Illus. by author. 2013, Holiday $16.95 (978-082342870-0). 32pp. An adaptation of the traditional carol featuring animals that will appeal to young children. (Rev: BLO 9/15/13; HB 11–12/13; SLJ 10/13) [782.42]

16734 Conahan, Carolyn. *The Twelve Days of Christmas Dogs* (K–3). Illus. 2005, Dutton $15.99 (978-0-525-47486-9). 32pp. A rambunctious parody involving a lot of dogs and one intrusive cat. (Rev: BL 10/15/05; SLJ 10/05)

16735 Feliciano, Jose. *Feliz Navidad: Two Stories Celebrating Christmas* (PS–K). Illus. by David Diaz. 2003, Scholastic $15.95 (978-0-439-51717-1). The lyrics of Feliciano's popular Christmas song are presented in Spanish and English, with beautiful illustrations of Puerto Rican and traditional American festivities. (Rev: HBG 4/04; SLJ 10/03)

16736 Katz, Alan. *Where Did They Hide My Presents? Silly Dilly Christmas Songs* (2–5). Illus. by David Catrow. 2005, Simon & Schuster $15.95 (978-0-689-86214-4). New lyrics for familiar songs celebrate the silly side of Christmas. (Rev: SLJ 10/05)

16737 Long, Laurel. *The Twelve Days of Christmas* (1–3). Illus. by author. 2011, Dial $16.99 (978-080373357-2). 32pp. Handsome paintings conceal hidden gifts in this new interpretation of the traditional carol. (Rev: BL 10/15/11; SLJ 10/1/11) [782.42]

16738 McGinley, Sharon. *The Friendly Beasts* (PS–K). Illus. 2000, Greenwillow $15.95 (978-0-688-17421-7). 24pp. This joyful picture book illustrates the text of the carol "The Friendly Beasts," which describes the roles played by several different animals during the Nativity. (Rev: BCCB 11/00; BL 9/15/00; HBG 10/01)

16739 Neale, John M. *Good King Wenceslas* (PS–2). Illus. by Tim Ladwig. 2005, Eerdmans $16.00 (978-0-8028-5209-0). 32pp. The words of the familiar Christmas carol and oversize double-spread, expressive artwork combine to celebrate the story of King Wenceslas, a 10th-century Bohemian monarch. (Rev: BL 10/15/05; SLJ 10/05)

16740 Orozco, Jose-Luis. *Fiestas: A Year of Latin American Songs of Celebration* (2–4). Illus. by Elisa Kleven. 2002, Dutton $17.99 (978-0-525-45937-8). 56pp. Orozco presents 21 songs in Spanish and English, with music,. (Rev: BL 9/15/02; HBG 3/03)

16741 Ray, Jane. *The Twelve Days of Christmas* (PS–3). Illus. by author. 2011, Candlewick $16.99 (978-076365735-2). 32pp. In the early 20th century, a young woman's small row house fills up with gifts, starting with a partridge in a pear tree and growing ever more abundant. (Rev: BL 10/1/11; SLJ 10/1/11) [782.42]

16742 Spirin, Gennady. *We Three Kings* (K–3). Illus. by author. 2007, Atheneum $16.99 (978-0-689-82114-1). In a Renaissance-reminiscent style, Spirin richly illustrates verses and choruses to the well-known Christmas carol "We Three Kings." (Rev: BL 11/1/07)

16743 Sturges, Philemon. *The Twelve Days of Christmas: A Pinata for the Pinon Tree* (K–2). Illus. by Ashley Wolff. 2007, Little, Brown $16.99 (978-0-316-82323-4). Southwestern images (coyotes yowling, skinks a-skulking) replace the familiar partridges and lords a leaping in this fractured Christmas song. (Rev: BL 9/15/07)

Musical Instruments

16744 Aylmore, Angela. *Banging* (PS–K). Illus. Series: Making Music. 2005, Raintree LB $20.64 (978-1-4109-1604-4). Children show how to use a variety of instruments including drums and Indonesian gongs in this brightly illustrated volume; companion volumes are *Blowing*, *Plucking*, and *Shaking* (all 2005). (Rev: SLJ 1/06)

16745 Barber, Nicola. *Should I Play the Flute?* (3–5). Illus. Series: Learning Musical Instruments. 2006, Heinemann LB $28.21 (978-1-4034-8187-0). 32pp. Chapters answer such questions as "How does a flute make its sound?", "What types of music can you play on a flute?", and "How would I learn to play the flute?" Also use *Should I Play the Piano?* (2006). (Rev: SLJ 2/07)

16746 Crask, Tom. *Should I Play the Drums?* (3–5). Illus. Series: Learning Musical Instruments. 2006, Heinemann

LB $28.21 (978-1-4034-8186-3). 32pp. Answering the title question, this well-organized and attractive volume gives the history of the drums, discusses how their sound is produced, and names famous drum players and drum recordings. Also use *Should I Play the Guitar?* and *Should I Play the Violin?* (both 2006). (Rev: SLJ 2/07)

16747 Day, Eileen M. *I'm Good at Making Music* (PS–1). Series: I'm Good At. 2003, Heinemann LB $18.50 (978-1-4034-0900-3). 24pp. A beginning look at making music on such simple instruments as the triangle, kazoo, and drum. (Rev: HBG 4/04; SLJ 4/04)

16748 Dunleavy, Deborah. *The Kids Can Press Jumbo Book of Music* (2–6). Illus. by Louise Phillips. Series: A Kids Can Press Jumbo Book. 2001, Kids Can paper $14.95 (978-1-55074-723-2). 208pp. Instructions for making a variety of musical instruments from everyday materials are accompanied by suggestions of appropriate music and groupings of instruments. (Rev: SLJ 4/01)

16749 Ganeri, Anita. *Pianos and Keyboards* (4–6). Illus. Series: How the World Makes Music. 2011, Black Rabbit LB $28.50 (978-159920479-6). 32pp. Introduces keyboard instruments from around the world — from the familiar piano and organ to the less common hurdy-gurdy and celeste — with illustrations and clear text. (Rev: BL 10/1/11) [786]

16750 Helsby, Genevieve. *Those Amazing Musical Instruments!* (4–9). Illus. 2007, Sourcebooks $19.95 (978-1-4022-0825-6). 176pp. A CD-ROM is included with this engaging and comprehensive guide to orchestral instruments. (Rev: SLJ 3/08)

16751 Hooper, Maureen Brett. *Highlights Fun to Play Recorder Book: Learn with Easy Steps and Familiar Songs* (2–6). Illus. by Judith Hunt. 2001, Boyds Mills $14.95 (978-1-56397-965-1). Basic instructions for playing the recorder are accompanied by suitable songs that increase in difficulty as the reader progresses through the book. (Rev: SLJ 6/01)

16752 Koscielniak, Bruce. *The Story of the Incredible Orchestra* (K–4). Illus. 2000, Houghton $16.00 (978-0-395-96052-3). 40pp. This account traces the growth of the orchestra and the development of modern musical instruments and also comments on the work of several composers. (Rev: BCCB 6/00; BL 4/15/00; HBG 10/00; SLJ 6/00)

16753 Lynch, Wendy. *Brass* (2–4). Series: Musical Instruments. 2001, Heinemann LB $21.36 (978-1-58810-233-1). A look at the brass family of instruments in words and pictures, with material on the trumpet, tuba, and trombone. (Rev: BL 1/1–15/02; HBG 3/02)

16754 Lynch, Wendy. *Keyboards* (2–4). Illus. Series: Musical Instruments. 2001, Heinemann LB $21.36 (978-1-58810-234-8). 32pp. Lynch introduces younger readers to keyboard instruments, how they work and how they sound, with back matter that includes a glossary and a bibliography. Also use *Percussion* (2001). (Rev: BL 1/1–15/02; HBG 3/02)

16755 Lynch, Wendy. *Strings* (2–4). Series: Musical Instruments. 2001, Heinemann LB $21.36 (978-1-58810-

236-2). 32pp. All the stringed instruments of an orchestra are described in text and pictures with an activity based on creating the simulated sound of stringed instruments. (Rev: BL 1/1–15/02; HBG 3/02)

16756 Lynch, Wendy. *Woodwind* (2–4). Series: Musical Instruments. 2001, Heinemann LB $21.36 (978-1-58810-237-9). 32pp. All the woodwinds — including the clarinet, bassoon, and saxophone — are pictured and described, and common household objects are used to simulate their sounds. (Rev: BL 1/1–15/02; HBG 3/02)

16757 Salzmann, Mary Elizabeth. *What in the World Is a Clarinet?* (K–3). Illus. Series: Musical Instruments. 2012, ABDO LB $25.65 (978-1-61783-203-1). 24pp. A simple introduction to the clarinet, its structure, how it is played, and its role in music. (Rev: BL 4/1/12; SLJ 9/12) [788.6]

16758 Storey, Rita. *The Violin and Other Stringed Instruments* (3–5). Illus. Series: Let's Make Music. 2009, Smart Apple Media LB $19.95 (978-159920212-9). 32pp. This visually appealing book introduces the violin, the guitar, and other stringed instruments and explains how they make music and how they are used. (Rev: BL 11/1/09) [787]

16759 Wiseman, Ann Sayre, and John Langstaff. *Making Music: How to Create and Play 70 Homemade Musical Instruments* (3–5). Illus. by Ann Sayre Wiseman. 2003, Storey Kids paper $9.95 (978-1-58017-512-8). 96pp. Spoons, forks, and flowerpots are among the household items that become musical instruments in this illustrated "how-to" book. (Rev: SLJ 3/04)

National Anthems and Patriotic Songs

16760 Bates, Katharine Lee. *America the Beautiful* (K–3). Illus. by Wendell Minor. 2003, Penguin $18.99 (978-0-399-23885-7). 32pp. Paintings on double-page spreads illustrate the verses of this poem, spanning events in the history of the country. (Rev: HBG 10/03; SLJ 7/03)

16761 Bates, Katharine Lee. *America the Beautiful: Together We Stand* (PS–3). Illus. by Byran Collier. 2013, Scholastic $17.99 (978-0-545-49207-2). 32pp. A celebration of the well-known song, with quotations from presidents and illustrations by 10 children's book artists. (Rev: BL 12/15/12; HB 1–2/13; LMC 10/13; SLJ 3/13) [973]

16762 Berlin, Irving. *God Bless America* (PS). Illus. by Lynn Munsinger. 2002, HarperCollins $15.99 (978-0-06-009788-2). 32pp. The Irving Berlin classic song set to illustration, depicting a family of bears traveling across America. (Rev: BL 8/02; HBG 3/03)

16763 Bowdish, Lynea. *Francis Scott Key and "The Star Spangled Banner"* (K–3). Illus. by Harry Burman. 2002, Mondo $15.95 (978-1-59034-195-7). 32pp. A large-format book for younger readers about Francis Scott Key's penning of the national anthem in 1814. (Rev: BL 12/15/02; HBG 3/03)

16764 Cohan, George M. *You're a Grand Old Flag* (PS–1). Illus. by Warren Kimble. 2007, Walker $16.95 (978-0-8027-9575-5). Images of flags and scenes from the American countryside by artist Warren Kimble illustrate the lyrics to the classic tune. (Rev: SLJ 6/07)

16765 Johnson, James W. *Lift Every Voice and Sing* (PS–3). Illus. by Bryan Collier. 2007, HarperCollins $16.99 (978-0-06-054147-7). 32pp. The well-known song now recognized as the "African American National Hymn" is personally interpreted through collage and watercolor pictures subtly illustrating African American history. (Rev: BL 11/1/07; SLJ 12/07)

16766 Sonneborn, Liz. *The Star-Spangled Banner: The Story Behind Our National Anthem* (3–5). Illus. Series: America in Words and Song. 2004, Chelsea House LB $23.00 (978-0-7910-7337-7). 32pp. This slim volume covers the history of the national anthem and the changes it has undergone over the years. Also use *America the Beautiful: The Story Behind Our National Hymn* (2004). (Rev: BL 4/1/04; HBG 4/04)

16767 Yanuck, Debbie L. *The Star-Spangled Banner* (K–2). Series: American Symbols. 2003, Capstone LB $21.26 (978-0-7368-2293-0). 24pp. An account of the events that inspired Francis Scott Key to write the poem that — more than 100 years later — became the lyrics to the national anthem of the United States. (Rev: SLJ 4/04)

Singing Games and Songs

16768 Allen, Nancy Kelly. *"Happy Birthday": The Story of the World's Most Popular Song* (1–3). Illus. by Gary Undercuffler. 2010, Pelican $16.99 (978-1-58980-675-7). Unpaged. Tells the story of the sisters who wrote the familiar song in the late 19th century, initially with the title "Good Morning to All." (Rev: SLJ 5/1/10) [782.42]

16769 Barnwell, Ysaye M. *We Are One* (PS–2). Illus. by Brian Pinkney. 2008, Harcourt $17.95 (978-0-15-205735-0). 32pp. A song celebrating community, friendship, and peace is illustrated in exuberant scenes and accompanied by a music CD. (Rev: BL 3/1/08; LMC 11/08; SLJ 3/08)

16770 Boynton, Sandra. *Frog Trouble: And Eleven Other Pretty Serious Songs* (K–3). Illus. by author. 2013, Workman $16.95 (978-076117176-8). 70pp. Country music is the focus of this blend of artwork and music, with the lyrics and melody in the text, plus a CD. (Rev: BL 11/1/13; SLJ 11/13) [782.4216420268]

16771 Boynton, Sandra. *Philadelphia Chickens* (PS–5). Illus. by author. 2002, Workman $16.95 (978-0-7611-2636-2). 64pp. A cast of animal characters bounce through pages of lyrics and musical notations, while the songs are performed on the accompanying CD by celebrities including Meryl Streep and Natasha Richardson. (Rev: SLJ 3/03) [782.1]

16772 Cabrera, Jane. *If You're Happy and You Know It!* (PS). Illus. 2005, Holiday House $16.95 (978-0-8234-1881-7). 32pp. Readers clap their hands and stamp their feet along with a cast of assorted animals. (Rev: BL 2/15/05; SLJ 3/05)

16773 Cabrera, Jane. *The Wheels on the Bus* (PS–1). Illus. by author. 2011, Holiday House $16.95 (978-0-8234-2350-7). 32pp. Hyenas, flamingos, crocodiles, and bush babies are among the animals in this jungle version of the familiar song. (Rev: BL 10/1/11; SLJ 9/1/11) [782.42]

16774 *De Colores: Bright with Colors* (PS–3). Illus. by David Diaz. 2008, Marshall Cavendish $16.99 (978-0-7614-5431-1). A visually pleasing illustration of the first two verses of the Spanish folk song. (Rev: BL 3/1/08; SLJ 5/08)

16775 DiPucchio, Kelly. *Sipping Spiders Through a Straw: Campfire Songs for Monsters* (3–5). Illus. by Gris Grimly. 2008, Scholastic $15.99 (978-0-439-58401-2). 40pp. A collection of 18 classic songs that have been reworded to enhance their gross-out quotient. (Rev: BL 5/1/08; SLJ 6/08)

16776 Dylan, Bob. *Man Gave Names to All the Animals* (PS–2). Illus. by Jim Arnosky. 2010, Sterling $17.95 (978-1-4027-6858-3). 32pp. Realistic pencil and acrylic illustrations enhance this updated version of the 1979 Bob Dylan song. (Rev: BL 10/15/10; SLJ 9/1/10) [782.42]

16777 Emberley, Rebecca, and Ed Emberley. *If You're a Monster and You Know It* (PS–K). Illus. by Rebecca Emberley. 2010, Scholastic $16.99 (978-0-545-21829-0). 32pp. Neon-bright monsters are on parade in this boisterous adaptation of the familiar children's song "If You're Happy and You Know It"; a downloadable CD is available on the publisher's Web site. (Rev: BL 9/15/10; SLJ 9/1/10*) [782.42]

16778 *The Farmer in the Dell* (PS). Illus. by Ilse Plume. 2004, Godine $17.95 (978-1-56792-270-7). 28pp. The familiar song is set in Pennsylvania Dutch countryside. (Rev: BL 9/15/04)

16779 Hinojosa, Tish. *Cada Nino / Every Child: A Bilingual Songbook for Kids* (3–6). Illus. by Lucía Angela Pérez. 2002, Cinco Puntos $18.95 (978-0-938317-60-9). 56pp. This is a charming bilingual songbook, with music, presenting 11 traditional and original songs that celebrate the simple things in life. (Rev: BL 6/1–15/02; HBG 10/02)

16780 Hoberman, Mary Ann, adapt. *Mary Had a Little Lamb* (PS–2). Illus. by Nadine Bernard Westcott. Series: Sing-Along Stories. 2003, Little, Brown $15.95 (978-0-316-60687-5). 32pp. Young readers will enjoy this extended version of the popular children's song about Mary and her little lamb that recounts what happens after the lamb gets to school. (Rev: HBG 4/04; SLJ 12/03)

16781 Hort, Lenny. *The Seals on the Bus* (PS–1). Illus. by G. Brian Karas. 2000, Holt $15.95 (978-0-8050-5952-6). 32pp. This variation on the song "The Wheels on the Bus" tells of a series of wild animals who find their way onto a city bus. (Rev: BCCB 5/00; BL 4/1/00; HB 5/00; HBG 10/00; SLJ 5/00)

16782 Jackson, Jill, and Sy Miller. *Let There Be Peace on Earth: And Let It Begin with Me* (PS–2). Illus. by David Diaz. 2009, Tricycle $18.99 (978-158246285-1). 32pp. The lyrics to the popular children's song are given a picture-book update in this book featuring a history of the song, biographical notes on the husband-wife team that created it, information about peace symbols, and musical notations. (Rev: BL 9/15/09; SLJ 12/09) [782.42164]

16783 Kanzler, John. *The Big Rock Candy Mountain* (PS–2). Illus. by author. 2004, Mondo $15.95 (978-1-59336-062-7). 24pp. The folk song becomes a lively picture book as a family goes camping, boating, square dancing, and meets up with interesting creatures including some musical bears; lyrics and music are appended. (Rev: SLJ 5/04)

16784 Katz, Alan. *Are You Quite Polite?* (K–3). Illus. by David Catrow. 2006, Simon & Schuster $15.95 (978-0-689-86970-9). 32pp. Silly verses set to familiar tunes focus on poor behavior (lateness, bad table manners, nose-picking, and so forth), enhanced by suitably lively cartoon art. (Rev: BL 11/15/06; SLJ 10/06)

16785 Katz, Alan. *Going, Going, Gone!* (K–4). Illus. by David Catrow. 2009, Simon & Schuster $16.99 (978-1-4169-0696-4). A humorous collection of familiar tunes with new, sporty lyrics — "On Top of the Bleachers" for example. (Rev: BL 1/1–15/09; SLJ 2/09)

16786 Katz, Alan. *Take Me out of the Bathtub and Other Silly Dilly Songs* (PS–1). Illus. by David Catrow. 2001, Simon & Schuster $15.00 (978-0-689-82903-1). Amusing adaptations of a number of familiar songs are accompanied by equally silly illustrations. (Rev: BL 7/01; HBG 10/01; SLJ 4/01)

16787 Katz, Karen. *The Babies on the Bus* (PS). Illus. by author. 2011, Henry Holt $14.99 (978-0-8050-9011-6). Unpaged. Boisterous illustrations add appeal to this baby-themed take on "The Wheels on the Bus." (Rev: SLJ 6/11) [782.42]

16788 *Knick Knack Paddy Whack* (PS). Illus. by Christiane Engel. 2008, Barefoot Books $16.99 (978-1-84686-144-4). The classic counting song is presented in a tropical setting with a multicultural, musical cast of characters. (Rev: BL 4/1/08; SLJ 5/08)

16789 Lessac, Frane. *Camp Granada: Sing-Along Camp Songs* (2–5). Illus. 2003, Holt $18.95 (978-0-8050-6683-8). 48pp. Colorful, humorous illustrations and a brief story about camp activities form a backdrop for the lyrics to 34 camp songs. (Rev: BL 3/1/03; HBG 10/03; SLJ 6/03)

16790 Loeb, Lisa. *Lisa Loeb's Songs for Movin' and Shakin'* (PS–1). Illus. by Ryan O'Rourke. 2013, Sterling $14.95 (978-140276916-0). 24pp. A toe-tapping collection of 10 songs — five old favorites and five new originals — and accompanying CD. (Rev: BL 4/1/13; SLJ 6/13) [782.42]

16791 Loesser, Frank. *I Love You! A Bushel and a Peck* (PS). Illus. by Rosemary Wells. 2004, HarperCollins LB $16.89 (978-0-06-028550-0). 32pp. Loesser's song from *Guys and Dolls* forms the framework for this charming story of a budding romance between two flirtatious ducklings. (Rev: BL 11/15/04; SLJ 2/05) [782.42]

16792 Long, Ethan. *The Croaky Pokey!* (PS–1). Illus. by author. 2011, Holiday House $14.95 (978-0-8234-2291-3). Unpaged. A rousing version of "Hokey Pokey" featuring a pond full of lively, dancing frogs and a pesky fly. (Rev: SLJ 3/1/11) [782.42]

16793 Miller, J. Philip, and Sheppard M. Greene. *We All Sing with the Same Voice* (PS–K). Illus. by Paul Meisel. 2001, HarperCollins $16.99 (978-0-06-027475-7). 32pp. This book-and-CD set features the Sesame Street song about understanding one another's cultures and the similarities of children all over the world. (Rev: HBG 10/01; SLJ 2/01)

16794 Moore, Mary-Alice. *The Wheels on the School Bus* (K–2). Illus. by Laura Huliska-Beith. 2006, HarperCollins $15.99 (978-0-06-059427-5). 32pp. In this adaptation of the popular song, the action is focused on a bus full of students — and also commuting teachers — as it makes its way to school. (Rev: BL 8/06; SLJ 8/06)

16795 Newcome, Zita. *Head, Shoulders, Knees, and Toes and Other Action Rhymes* (PS). Illus. 2002, Candlewick $15.99 (978-0-7636-1899-5). 64pp. Familiar songs and rhymes, with illustrations of children performing movements to accompany them. (Rev: BL 9/15/02; HBG 3/03; SLJ 10/02)

16796 O'Brien, John. *The Farmer in the Dell* (PS–1). Illus. 2000, Boyds Mills $14.95 (978-1-56397-775-6). 40pp. Hilarious illustrations give new life to this favorite song. (Rev: BL 11/1/00; HBG 3/01; SLJ 9/00)

16797 Quattlebaum, Mary. *Jo MacDonald Had a Garden* (PS–1). Illus. by Laura J. Bryant. 2012, Dawn $16.95 (978-158469164-8); paper $8.95 (978-15846916-5-5). 32pp. In this follow-up to *Jo MacDonald Saw a Pond* (2011), Jo and her cousin Mike plant and care for a vegetable garden. Lexile AD550L (Rev: BLO 4/15/12; LMC 10/12; SLJ 6/1/12) [782.42]

16798 Quattlebaum, Mary. *Jo MacDonald Saw a Pond* (PS–1). Illus. by Laura J. Bryant. 2011, Dawn paper $16.95 (978-1-58469-151-8). 32pp. This updated take on "Old McDonald's Farm" features the farmer's granddaughter discovering a pond and describing eight of its inhabitants; end notes present facts and activities. (Rev: BL 11/1/11; SLJ 12/1/11) [782.42]

16799 Raven, Margot Theis. *Happy Birthday to You! The Mystery Behind the Most Famous Song in the World* (2–5). Illus. by Chris Soentpiet. 2008, Sleeping Bear $17.95 (978-1-58536-169-4). The real story of how "Happy Birthday to You" became the American birthday song. (Rev: BLO 10/7/08; LMC 5/09; SLJ 12/08)

16800 Rueda, Claudia. *Let's Play in the Forest While the Wolf Is Not Around* (PS). Illus. 2006, Scholastic $16.99 (978-0-439-82323-4). The animals of the forest come out to play unaware that the wolf is in fact getting dressed and is hungry — all shown in facing pages — but it turns out that he's just hungry for pancakes; this song is based on a traditional one and the music is appended. (Rev: BL 11/15/06; SLJ 10/06) [782.42]

16801 Salas, Laura Purdie. *From Beginning to End: A Song About Life Cycles* (PS–K). Illus. by Viviana Garofoli. Series: Science Songs. 2008, Picture Window LB $25.32 (978-1-4048-5293-8). 24pp. This sing-along book pairs scientific facts about living things with familiar tunes such as "Are You Sleeping?" to help children retain information. Also use *Home on the Earth: A Song About Earth's Layers* and *Move It! Work It! A Song About Simple Machines*. (Rev: SLJ 5/09)

16802 Sloat, Teri. *There Was an Old Man Who Painted the Sky* (PS–2). Illus. by Stefano Vitale. 2009, Holt $16.95 (978-0-8050-6751-4). Adapting "The Old Woman Who Swallowed a Fly" Sloat tells the story of a prehistoric man whose cave painting is later discovered by a Spanish girl. (Rev: BL 5/15/09; LMC 10/09; SLJ 9/09) [782.42]

16803 Staines, Bill. *All God's Critters* (PS–1). Illus. by Kadir Nelson. 2009, Simon & Schuster $16.99 (978-0-689-86959-4). A rollicking song performed by an exuberant cast of animals, some singing low, some singing high. (Rev: BCCB 2/09; BL 12/15/08; SLJ 1/09)

Performing Arts

Circuses, Fairs, and Parades

16804 Schubert, Leda. *Ballet of the Elephants* (K–3). Illus. by Robert Andrew Parker. 2006, Roaring Brook $17.95 (978-1-59643-075-4). The fascinating story of the collaboration of circus owner John Ringling North, choreographer George Balanchine, and composer Igor Stravinsky to create a ballet featuring 50 elephants with ballerinas on their backs; vivid illustrations accompany the text and the author's note at the end includes a few black-and-white photographs of the performance. (Rev: BL 4/1/06; SLJ 4/06)

Dance

16805 Ancona, George. *¡Olé! Flamenco* (5–8). Photos by author. 2010, Lee & Low $19.95 (978-1-60060-361-7). Unpaged. A photo-essay about the Spanish art form that incorporates dance, music, and song, explaining its history and traditions and following a group of young people who are studying flamenco in Santa Fe, New Mexico. Belpré Honor 2011; ALA Notable Children's Book 2011. (Rev: BL 12/1/10; HB 1–2/11; LMC 5–6/11; SLJ 1/1/11) [793.3]

16806 Augustyn, Frank, and Shelley Tanaka. *Footnotes: Dancing the World's Best-Loved Ballets* (5–8). Illus. 2001, Millbrook LB $24.90 (978-0-7613-2323-5). 96pp. A readable account that introduces ballet from a backstage perspective, with material on how it feels to be a dancer in a large ballet company. (Rev: BL 4/15/01; HBG 10/01; SLJ 6/01*; VOYA 8/01)

16807 Bingham, Jane. *Ballet* (4–8). Series: Dance. 2009, Heinemann LB $31.43 (978-1-4329-1374-8). 48pp. A colorful overview of the origins and evolution of ballet, with discussion of the various skills required, the rig-

orous training, and the complexities of staging a ballet. (Rev: LMC 3–4/09)

16808 Bray-Moffatt, Naia. *Ballet School* (K–3). Illus. 2003, DK $12.99 (978-0-7894-9228-9). 48pp. Ample illustrations grace this friendly, large-format introduction to ballet and its techniques, methods of instruction, costumes, and performances. (Rev: BL 4/15/03; HBG 10/03; SLJ 9/03)

16809 Castle, Kate. *My First Ballet Book* (K–3). 2006, Kingfisher $9.95 (978-0-7534-6026-9). 48pp. The fundamentals of ballet — from basic positions to arabesques, jumps, and pas de deux — are shown in color photographs of ethnically diverse children, accompanied by concise text. (Rev: SLJ 12/06)

16810 Collins, Pat Lowery. *I Am a Dancer* (PS–2). Illus. by Mark Graham. 2008, Lerner LB $22.60 (978-0-8225-6369-3). 32pp. Illustrations of children in motion accompany free-verse poetry about the many ways one can dance. (Rev: BL 6/1–15/08; SLJ 6/08)

16811 Cooper, Elisha. *Dance!* (2–4). Illus. 2001, Greenwillow $16.99 (978-0-06-029418-2). 32pp. This is a very visual introduction to the world of dance, with feathery watercolor illustrations and minimal text. (Rev: BL 9/15/01; HB 11/01; HBG 3/02; SLJ 9/01)

16812 Dillman, Lisa. *Ballet* (4–7). Series: Get Going! Hobbies. 2005, Heinemann LB $27.79 (978-1-4034-6115-5). A photo-filled introduction to ballet, with historical information plus basic positions and steps and exercises to help would-be dancers get in shape; also use *Tap* (2005). (Rev: BL 11/1/05; SLJ 3/06) [792.8]

16813 Friedman, Lise. *Becoming a Ballerina: A Nutcracker Story* (2–5). Illus. by Mary Dowdle. 2012, Viking $18.99 (978-0-670-01392-0). 48pp. Friedman chronicles the story of young Fiona, who has worked hard to become a ballerina and has now won the role of Clara in *The Nutcracker*. Lexile 900L (Rev: BL 9/1/12; HB 11–12/12; LMC 3–4/13; SLJ 10/12)

16814 Frith, Margaret. *Hooray for Ballet!* (2–4). Illus. by Amanda Haley. Series: Smart About the Arts. 2003,

Grosset paper $5.99 (978-0-448-42884-0). 32pp. With plenty of interesting detail, Elizabeth relates the story of her visit to Lincoln Center to see *Swan Lake*. (Rev: HBG 10/03; SLJ 9/03)

16815 Geras, Adele. *Sleeping Beauty* (3–5). Illus. Series: The Magic of Ballet. 2001, David & Charles $10.95 (978-1-86233-246-1). The story of Sleeping Beauty is told from the perspective of four characters. Also use *Swan Lake* (2001). (Rev: BCCB 1/03; BL 7/01; SLJ 11/01)

16816 Gladstone, Valerie. *A Young Dancer: The Life of an Ailey Student* (1–4). Illus. by Jose Ivey. 2009, Holt $18.95 (978-0-8050-8233-3). 48pp. This photoessay shows the dedication of Iman, a 13-year-old African American dancer, as she attends academic classes, music lessons, and long dance practices. (Rev: BCCB 5/09; BL 2/1/09; SLJ 6/09)

16817 Greenberg, Jan, and Sandra Jordan. *Ballet for Martha: Making Appalachian Spring* (2–4). Illus. by Brian Floca. 2010, Roaring Brook $17.99 (978-159643338-0). 48pp. The process of artistic creation is the focus of this book, which provides a glimpse into the collaboration of composer, choreographer, and artist that gave rise to the ballet *Appalachian Spring* in 1944. Lexile AD710L (Rev: BL 7/10*; HB 7–8/10; LMC 10/10; SLJ 8/10) [792.8]

16818 Hayward, Linda. *A Day in the Life of a Dancer* (PS–K). Series: Dorling Kindersley Readers: Jobs People Do. 2001, DK paper $3.99 (978-0-7894-7369-1). Using a very limited vocabulary and simple sentences, this beginning reader explores the everyday life of a ballet dancer. (Rev: BL 8/1/01; HBG 10/01)

16819 Jeffers, Susan. *The Nutcracker* (K–2). Illus. by author. 2007, HarperCollins $16.99 (978-0-06-074386-4). The traditional ballet story is set in the Victorian era and features rich illustrations. (Rev: BL 9/15/07; HB 11/07)

16820 Keeler, Patricia, and Julio Leitao. *Drumbeat in Our Feet* (3–5). Illus. by Patricia Keeler. 2006, Lee & Low $16.95 (978-1-58430-264-3). 32pp. Information on — and illustrations of — traditional African dances are paired with pictures of young Americans learning these dances at a studio in Harlem. (Rev: BL 11/1/06; SLJ 12/06)

16821 Mellow, Mary Kate, and Stephanie Troeller. *Ballet for Beginners* (1–4). 2010, Imagine $14.95 (978-1-936140-01-5). 80pp. Prima Princessa introduces young readers to the movements seen in ballet and shows them around the School of American Ballet and the classes held there. (Rev: BL 2/1/10; SLJ 4/10) [792.8]

16822 Nelson, Marilyn. *Beautiful Ballerina* (K–3). Illus. by Susan Kuklin. 2009, Scholastic $17.99 (978-0-545-08920-3). 32pp. A poem and photographs put readers on the stage with ballerinas from the Dance Theatre of Harlem. (Rev: BL 11/1/09; SLJ 11/1/09) [792.8]

16823 Pavlova, Anna. *I Dreamed I Was a Ballerina* (3–5). Illus. by Edgar Degas. 2001, Simon & Schuster $16.00 (978-0-689-84676-2). 32pp. Beautiful Degas illustrations accompany the true story, in her own words, of

Pavlova's inspiring first visit to a ballet and her subsequent rise to fame. (Rev: BL 12/1/01; HBG 3/02; SLJ 11/01)

16824 Schorer, Suki, and School of American Ballet. *Put Your Best Foot Forward: A Young Dancer's Guide to Life* (4–8). Illus. by Donna Ingemanson. Photos by Chris Carroll. 2005, Workman $9.95 (978-0-7611-3795-5). Practical tips are combined with artistic advice in this helpful guide for young ballet dancers, written by a former principal dancer. (Rev: SLJ 3/06) [792.8]

16825 Thompson, Lauren. *Ballerina Dreams* (K–2). Illus. 2007, Feiwel & Friends $16.95 (978-0-312-37029-9). 40pp. Five little girls with cerebral palsy and other muscular disorders, through hard work and the help of a dancer/physical therapist, realize their dreams of performing in a ballet recital in this true story documented with photographs. (Rev: BL 11/1/07; SLJ 9/07)

16826 Underwood, Deborah. *Ballroom Dancing* (3–6). Series: Culture in Action. 2010, Heinemann-Raintree $28.21 (978-1-4109-3398-0). 32pp. Is ballroom dancing art or sport? This and other questions are addressed in this well-illustrated title with activities designed to build literacy and understanding of the arts. Lexile 710L (Rev: LMC 3–4/10) [793.3]

16827 Wilkes, Angela. *The Best Book of Ballet* (1–4). Series: The Best Book Of. 2000, Kingfisher $12.95 (978-0-7534-5275-2). 32pp. A fine introduction to ballet that includes material on history, famous ballets, a ballet class, basic positions and steps, and what professional dancers do. (Rev: HBG 3/01; SLJ 7/00)

16828 Williams, Ann-Marie. *Learn to Speak Dance: A Guide to Creating, Performing and Promoting Your Moves* (5–8). Illus. by Jeff Kulak. 2011, OwlKids $22.95 (978-1-926818-88-7); paper $14.95 (978-1-926818-89-4). 96pp. A large-format introduction to styles of dance — ballet, ballroom, flamenco, and so forth — with discussion of choreography, preparing for performances, stage fright, and other aspects. (Rev: BL 11/1/11; SLJ 7/11) [792.8]

16829 Yolen, Jane, and Heidi Stemple. *The Barefoot Book of Ballet Stories* (5–7). Illus. by Rebecca Guay. 2004, Barefoot Books $19.99 (978-1-84148-229-3). 96pp. The stories behind seven of the world's classic ballets — including "Cinderella," "The Nutcracker," "Coppelia," and "Sleeping Beauty" — are introduced by a general discussion of ballet as an art form and accompanied by production notes on each work. (Rev: BL 11/1/04; SLJ 12/04)

Marionettes and Puppets

16830 Bryant, Jill, and Catherine Heard. *Making Shadow Puppets* (4–6). Series: Kids Can Do It! 2002, Kids Can $12.95 (978-1-55337-028-4); paper $5.95 (978-1-55337-029-1). Two-dimensional puppets that can be created with easily found materials are presented with good step-by-step instructions. (Rev: BL 9/15/02; HBG 3/03; SLJ 12/02)

Motion Pictures, Radio, and Television

16831 Baker, Frank W. *Coming Distractions: Questioning Movies* (3–6). Illus. Series: Fact Finders: Media Literacy. 2007, Capstone LB $23.93 (978-0-7368-6766-5). 32pp. Readers are encouraged to analyze the images and messages they see projected on the big screen and to be aware of stereotypes and deliberate product placements; the dynamic format adds interest. (Rev: BL 4/1/07)

16832 Fingeroth, Danny. *Backstage at an Animated Series* (4–8). Series: Backstage Pass. 2003, Children's paper $6.95 (978-0-516-24385-6). 48pp. Fingeroth explores the world of animated films, discussing their history, recent technological advances, and the mechanics of production, and suggesting ways to become involved. Also use *Backstage at a Movie Set* (2003). (Rev: SLJ 10/03)

16833 Franks, Katie. *I Want to Be a Movie Star* (2–4). Series: Dream Jobs. 2007, Rosen LB $21.25 (978-1-4042-3619-6). 24pp. Reluctant readers will be drawn to the subject of this book and will learn about the preparation and training required to break into movie stardom. (Rev: SLJ 7/07)

16834 Horn, Geoffrey M. *Movie Animation* (4–6). Series: Making Movies. 2007, Gareth Stevens LB $24.00 (978-0-8368-6837-1). This book provides a brief overview of the production of animated movies and gives snapshots of key figures including Walt Disney and Jayao Miyazaki. (Rev: SLJ 1/07)

16835 Lund, Kristin. *Star Wars, Episode I: Incredible Locations* (3–6). Illus. 2000, DK $19.99 (978-0-7894-6692-1). A visual treat that uses fold-out pages to present drawings and scenes from the movie *The Phantom Menace*. (Rev: BL 1/1–15/01; HBG 3/01)

16836 McCarthy, Meghan. *Aliens Are Coming! The True Account of the 1938 War of the Worlds Radio Broadcast* (1–3). Illus. 2006, Knopf $16.95 (978-0-375-83518-6). 40pp. With varied artwork, this effective picture book presents the 1938 radio broadcast of *War of the Worlds* and the panic that followed in a way that will keep contemporary readers on the edge of their seats. (Rev: BL 2/1/06; SLJ 4/06*)

16837 Miles, Liz. *Movie Special Effects* (3–6). Series: Culture in Action. 2010, Heinemann-Raintree $28.21 (978-1-4109-3399-7). 32pp. A high-interest introduction to the special effects used in movies, with activities that reinforce literacy and understanding. Lexile 920L (Rev: LMC 3–4/10) [778.5]

16838 Reynolds, David West. *Star Wars: Incredible Cross-Sections* (4–8). 1998, DK $19.95 (978-1-78943-480-4). This large-format book includes cross-sections of the TIE fighter, the X-wing fighter, the AT-AT, the Millennium Falcon, Jabba's sail barge, and the Death Star. (Rev: BL 12/15/98) [791.43]

16839 Reynolds, David West. *Star Wars: The Visual Dictionary* (4–8). 1998, DK $19.99 (978-0-7894-3481-4). Using a large-format dictionary approach, the people, creatures, and droids of the *Star Wars* saga are presented, with large photographs of the characters and many stills from the movies. (Rev: BL 12/15/98; HBG 3/99; SLJ 2/99) [791.43]

16840 Spilsbury, Richard. *On the Film Set* (3–6). Illus. Series: Technology at Work. 2008, Raintree LB $19.25 (978-1-4109-3178-8). 32pp. An introduction to the myriad elements that go into making a film. (Rev: BL 12/1/08)

16841 Wan, Guofang. *TV Takeover: Questioning Television* (4–7). Illus. Series: Fact Finders. Media Literacy. 2006, Capstone LB $22.60 (978-0-7368-6763-4). In alerting readers to the motivations behind those who produce television shows, this book fosters critical thinking about the mass media. (Rev: SLJ 6/07) [384.55]

Theater and Plays

16842 Amendola, Dana. *A Day at the New Amsterdam Theatre* (4–9). Photos by Gino Domenico. 2004, Disney $24.95 (978-0-7868-5438-7). A behind-the-scenes look at a production of a musical in the renovated theater in New York City, introducing the wide variety of individuals involved. (Rev: SLJ 1/05) [792]

16843 Bany-Winters, Lisa. *Funny Bones: Comedy Games and Activities for Kids* (3–6). Illus. 2002, Chicago Review paper $14.95 (978-1-55652-444-8). 155pp. In addition to learning games, skits, and songs, readers will find some history of comedy and will gain insight on how to use props, music, makeup, and other techniques to be funny. (Rev: SLJ 12/02)

16844 Birch, Beverley. *Shakespeare's Stories: Comedies* (5–9). Illus. 1990, Bedrick paper $6.95 (978-0-87226-225-6). This is the first of three volumes that retell in attractive, straightforward prose the most popular of his plays. The others are *Shakespeare's Stories: Histories* and *Shakespeare's Stories: Tragedies* (both 1988). (Rev: BL 2/15/89; SLJ 2/89) [813]

16845 Birch, Beverley. *Shakespeare's Stories: Histories* (5–8). 1988, Bedrick paper $6.95 (978-0-87226-226-3). Retelling the classic stories of Shakespeare. (Rev: BL 2/15/89; SLJ 2/89) [813.54]

16846 Birch, Beverley. *Shakespeare's Stories: Tragedies* (5–8). 1988, Bedrick paper $6.95 (978-0-87226-227-0). Retelling the great tragedies. (Rev: BL 2/15/89; SLJ 2/89) [813.54]

16847 Birch, Beverley. *Shakespeare's Tales* (5–8). Illus. by Stephen Lambert. 2002, Hodder $22.95 (978-0-340-79725-9). This appealing and accessible large-format book introduces modern teens to the plots and language of four Shakespeare plays — *Hamlet, Othello, Antony* *and Cleopatra*, and *The Tempest*. (Rev: BL 1/1–15/03; SLJ 4/03) [823.914]

16848 Bruchac, Joseph. *Pushing Up the Sky: Seven Native American Plays for Children* (2–6). Illus. 2000, Dial $21.99 (978-0-8037-2168-5). 96pp. Several folktales from Native American cultures are adapted into simple plays that are easily produced. (Rev: BCCB 2/00; BL 3/1/00; HBG 10/00; SLJ 3/00) [812]

16849 Burdett, Lois. *Hamlet for Kids* (2–4). Series: Shakespeare Can Be Fun! 2000, Firefly LB $19.95 (978-1-55209-522-5); paper $9.95 (978-1-55209-530-0). 64pp. A retelling of *Hamlet* in rhymed couplets with illustrations by the author's students, ages seven to 12. (Rev: HBG 3/01; SLJ 8/00) [822]

16850 Burkholder, Kelly. *Plays* (2–5). Series: Artistic Adventures. 2001, Rourke LB $23.93 (978-1-57103-357-4). Details on putting on a play are given including material on writing scripts, costumes, props, characters, and using voice and movement. (Rev: SLJ 2/01) [792]

16851 Butterfield, Moira. *Hansel and Gretel* (2–4). Photos by Trever Clifford. Illus. by Frances Cony. Series: Playtales. 1997, Heinemann $19.92 (978-1-57572-648-9). 24pp. Contains the script of a play based on this folktale plus direction on how to stage it, from casting and making props to the actual performance. Also use *Sleeping Beauty* (1997). (Rev: BL 4/1/04; HB 3/04; HBG 3/98; SLJ 2/98) [809]

16852 Butterfield, Moira. *Little Red Riding Hood* (2–4). Photos by Trever Clifford. Illus. by Frances Cony. Series: Playtales. 1997, Heinemann $19.92 (978-1-57572-650-2). 24pp. Provides a script based on this fairy tale, as well as a list of parts, directions for production of the play, and instructions for making costumes and sets. Also use *Puss-in-Boots* (1997). (Rev: HBG 3/98; SLJ 3/98) [809]

16853 Chanda, Justin, ed. *Acting Out* (4–8). 2008, Atheneum $16.99 (978-1-4169-6213-7). Young people challenge authority in these one-act plays written by six Newbery Medal winners. (Rev: BL 6/1–15/08) [812]

16854 Coville, Bruce. *William Shakespeare's Hamlet* (4–8). Illus. by Leonid Gore. 2004, Dial $18.99 (978-0-8037-2708-3). This masterful prose retelling makes the famous play accessible to young people. (Rev: BL 5/15/04; SLJ 2/04) [822.3]

16855 Coville, Bruce. *William Shakespeare's Macbeth* (4–8). 1997, Dial $18.99 (978-0-8037-1899-9). Using a picture-book format, the story of Macbeth is retold with emphasis on the supernatural aspects. (Rev: BL 11/1/97; HBG 3/98; SLJ 12/97) [822.3]

16856 Coville, Bruce. *William Shakespeare's Romeo and Juliet* (4–6). 1999, Dial $17.99 (978-0-8037-2462-4). A successful retelling of the Shakespearean tragedy with lushly romantic illustrations. (Rev: BL 12/1/99; HBG 3/00; SLJ 1/00) [822.3]

16857 Coville, Bruce. *William Shakespeare's The Winter's Tale* (4–7). Illus. by LeUyen Pham. 2007, Dial $16.99 (978-0-8037-2709-0). An illustrated prose retell-

ing of the classic tale of jealousy and renewal. (Rev: BL 11/1/07; SLJ 12/07) [822.3]

16858 Coville, Bruce. *William Shakespeare's Twelfth Night* (3–6). Illus. by Tim Raglin. 2003, Dial $16.99 (978-0-8037-2318-4). Coville provides an easy-reading version of the humorous play, accompanied by appealing ink drawings. (Rev: BL 1/1–15/03; HBG 10/03; SLJ 3/03) [822]

16859 Dabrowski, Kristen. *My Second Monologue Book: Famous and Historical People: 100 Monologues for Young Children* (2–6). Series: My First Acting. 2009, Smith & Kraus paper $11.95 (978-1-57525-601-6). 128pp. Monologues are divided into four sections, about familiar people (the doctor, for example), famous Americans, famous foreigners, and imaginary people and folk heroes. Also use *My Third Monologue Book: Places Near and Far: 102 Monologues for Young Children* (2009). (Rev: SLJ 5/09)

16860 Davidson, Rebecca Piatt. *All the World's a Stage* (K–3). Illus. by Anita Lobel. 2003, Greenwillow LB $16.89 (978-0-06-029627-8). This introduction to Shakespeare and nine of his best-known plays takes the form of an extended rhyming poem and action-packed illustrations. (Rev: HBG 10/03; SLJ 5/03) [822.3]

16861 Dunleavy, Deborah. *The Jumbo Book of Drama* (4–8). Illus. by Jane Kurisu. 2004, Kids Can paper $14.95 (978-1-55337-008-6). 208pp. Divided into Acts, this volume covers all aspects of drama and stagecraft, from body movement to lighting and props. (Rev: BL 5/1/04; SLJ 6/04)

16862 Fredericks, Anthony D. *Tadpole Tales and Other Totally Terrific Treats for Readers Theatre* (4–8). 1997, Libraries Unlimited paper $23.00 (978-1-56308-547-5). A delightful collection of scripts for young performers that are spin-offs from folktales, fables, and nursery rhymes. (Rev: BL 3/1/98) [372.67]

16863 Friedman, Lise. *Break a Leg! The Kid's Guide to Acting and Stagecraft* (4–7). Illus. by Mary Dowdle. 2002, Workman paper $14.95 (978-0-7611-2208-1). Some of the topics covered for young would-be actors include analyzing a script, memorizing lines, stage fright, body language, and monologues. (Rev: BL 5/1/02; HBG 10/02)

16864 Gerke, Pamela. *Multicultural Plays for Children Grades K–3* (K–3). 1996, Smith & Kraus paper $19.95 (978-1-57525-005-2). 159pp. Ten entertaining plays, each of which deals with a different racial group. Also use volume 2 (1996), which contains ten plays for grades four to six. (Rev: BL 12/1/96; SLJ 9/96) [812]

16865 Jacobs, Paul Dubois, and Jennifer Swender. *Putting on a Play: Drama Activities for Kids* (3–4). Illus. by Debra Spina Dixon. 2005, Gibbs Smith paper $9.95 (978-1-58685-767-7). 64pp. An excellent introduction to staging a play — as a writer, designer, actor, or any support person — with ideas for story lines and discussion of improvising scenery from everyday materials. (Rev: SLJ 4/06)

16866 Jennings, Coleman A., and Aurand Harris, eds. *A Treasury of Contemporary and Classic Plays for Children: Plays Children Love, Vol. II* (5–8). Illus. by Susan Swan. 1988, St. Martin's $19.95 (978-0-312-01490-2). A group of 20 plays requiring royalties based on such stories as Charlotte's Web, The Wizard of Oz, and The Wind in the Willows. [812.00809282]

16867 Kahle, Peter V. T. *Shakespeare's The Tempest: A Prose Narrative* (5–8). Illus. by Barbara Nickerson. 1999, Seventy Fourth Street $22.95 (978-0-9655702-2-0). An illustrated retelling of Shakespeare's play that uses much of its dialogue. (Rev: SLJ 1/00) [822.3]

16868 Kamerman, Sylvia E., ed. *The Big Book of Large-Cast Plays: 27 One-Act Plays for Young Actors* (5–10). 1994, Plays $12.95 (978-0-8238-0302-6). Thirty short plays on varied subjects, arranged according to audience appeal. (Rev: BL 3/15/95) [812]

16869 Kamerman, Sylvia E., ed. *Thirty Plays from Favorite Stories: Royalty-Free Dramatizations of Myths, Folktales, and Legends from Around the World* (2–4). 1997, Plays paper $15.95 (978-0-8238-0306-4). Thirty short plays based loosely on folktales from around the world. (Rev: SLJ 12/97) [809]

16870 Kamerman, Sylvia, ed. *Great American Events on Stage: 15 Plays to Celebrate America's Past* (5–8). 1996, Plays paper $15.95 (978-0-8238-0305-7). A collection of short plays, each of which revolves around a single incident or individual important in U.S. history. (Rev: SLJ 5/97) [812]

16871 Kindermann, Barbara. *William Shakespeare's Romeo and Juliet* (4–7). Trans. by J. Alison James. Illus. by Christa Unzner. 2006, NorthSouth $17.95 (978-0-7358-2090-6). This well-phrased prose retelling of the ill-fated romance is enhanced by the Renaissance-style illustrations. (Rev: BL 8/06; SLJ 12/06)

16872 Kohl, MaryAnn F. *Making Make-Believe: Fun Props, Costumes, and Creative Play Ideas* (PS–4). 1999, Gryphon paper $14.95 (978-0-87659-198-7). 191pp. Using simple materials, this book supplies ideas for creating 138 different make-believe situations or plays. (Rev: SLJ 10/99) [809]

16873 Krensky, Stephen. *Lizzie Newton and the San Francisco Earthquake* (3–5). Illus. by Jeremy Tugeau. Series: History Speaks. 2010, Millbrook LB $27.93 (978-0-8225-9031-6). 48pp. Ten-year-old Lizzie sets out to find her parents after the 1906 San Francisco earthquake in this partly fictionalized story that is accompanied by a readers' theater script designed for six or more parts. Lexile 410L (Rev: BL 1/1–15/11; SLJ 12/1/10) [979]

16874 McCullough, L. E. *"Now I Get It!": 12 Ten-Minute Classroom Drama Skits for Science, Math, Language, and Social Studies, Vol. I* (4–6). Series: Now I Get It! 2001, Smith & Kraus $11.95 (978-1-57525-161-5). 136pp. In addition to these 12 curriculum-related skits, there are before and after activities, discussion questions, and staging suggestions. Also use *"Now Get It Right!" Volume II* (2001). (Rev: BL 2/1/01) [812]

16875 McCullough, L. E. *Plays for Learning: Israel Reborn: Legends of the Diaspora and Israel's Modern Rebirth for Grades 4–6* (4–6). Series: Young Actors. 2001, Smith & Kraus paper $15.95 (978-1-57525-253-7). 204pp. A collection of 12 plays drawn from a variety of sources that portray the Jewish experience from the expulsion from Israel to the creation of the modern state. (Rev: SLJ 6/02)

16876 McCullough, L. E. *Plays from Fairy Tales: Grades K–3* (1–3). 1998, Smith & Kraus $14.95 (978-1-57525-109-7). 192pp. Using well-known fairy tales as a basis, this collection of original plays includes recommendations for casting, costumes, sets, and related material. (Rev: BL 9/15/98; SLJ 8/98) [812]

16877 McCullough, L. E. *Plays from Mythology: Grades 4–6* (4–6). 1998, Smith & Kraus $14.95 (978-1-57525-110-3). 192pp. This is a collection of original plays based on important world myths such as the stories of Midas and Gilgamesh, with accompanying detailed notes and production tips. (Rev: BL 9/15/98; SLJ 7/98) [812]

16878 McCullough, L. E. *Plays of America from American Folklore for Children Grades K–6* (3–6). Series: Young Actors. 1996, Smith & Kraus paper $14.95 (978-1-57525-038-0). 161pp. A collection of 15 plays from American folklore and history that represent many cultural backgrounds. (Rev: SLJ 8/96) [808.82]

16879 McCullough, L. E. *Plays of the Wild West* (3–7). 1997, Smith & Kraus paper $14.95 (978-1-57525-105-9). 224pp. Both serious and slapstick views of the Wild West are reflected in these 12 plays, mostly musicals. A companion volume is *Plays of the Wild West: Grades K–3* (1997). (Rev: BL 11/1/97; SLJ 1/98) [812]

16880 MacDonald, Margaret Read. *The Skit Book: 101 Skits from Kids* (3–6). Illus. by Marie-Louise Scull. 1990, Shoe String LB $25.00 (978-0-208-02258-5); paper $18.00 (978-0-208-02283-7). 160pp. Funny, silly skits from kids that kids will like. (Rev: BL 6/1/90; SLJ 6/90) [812]

16881 McKeown, Adam. *Julius Caesar* (5–8). Illus. by Janet Hamlin. Series: Young Reader's Shakespeare. 2008, Sterling $14.95 (978-1-4027-3579-0). An accessible retelling to assist students of the play, with engaging illustrations and a tone that is respectful to the original. (Rev: BL 5/15/08; SLJ 6/08) [813.6]

16882 McKeown, Adam. *Romeo and Juliet: Young Reader's Shakespeare* (5–10). Illus. by Peter Fiore. 2004, Sterling $14.95 (978-1-4027-0004-0). Faithful to the original, this retelling uses finely crafted prose and interweaves many of the best-known poetic stanzas. (Rev: BL 8/04; SLJ 10/04) [822.3]

16883 McKeown, Adam, retel. *Macbeth* (5–10). Retold by Adam McKeown. Illus. by Lynne Cannoy. Series: The Young Reader's Shakespeare. 2005, Sterling $14.95 (978-1-4027-1116-9). This conversational prose retelling includes an introduction to the play and incorporates many of the important poetic passages. (Rev: BL 3/1/05; SLJ 5/05) [822.3]

16884 Miller, Helen L. *First Plays for Children* (3–7). 1985, Plays paper $12.95 (978-0-8238-0268-5). 295pp. A useful collection of nonroyalty plays.

16885 Miller, Kimberly M. *Backstage at a Play* (4–8). Series: Backstage Pass. 2003, Children's LB $24.50 (978-0-516-24327-6). 48pp. Miller explores the world of theater, discussing how they are produced and the degree of commitment necessary, and suggesting ways to become involved. (Rev: SLJ 10/03)

16886 Nolan, Paul T. *Folk Tale Plays Round the World: A Collection of Royalty-Free, One-Act Plays About Lands Far and Near* (4–7). 1982, Plays paper $15.00 (978-0-8238-0253-1). Johnny Appleseed and Robin Hood are heroes featured in two of the 17 plays in this collection.

16887 Schlitz, Laura Amy. *Good Masters! Sweet Ladies!* (5–8). Illus. by Robert Byrd. 2007, Candlewick $19.99 (978-0-7636-1578-9). Providing a glimpse into medieval life, a series of interconnected monologues and dialogues feature 23 young people in medieval England and convey information about society at the time. Newbery Medal; ALA Notable Children's Book. ∩ (Rev: BL 8/07*; HB 11–12/07; LMC 11/07; SLJ 8/07) [812.6]

16888 Shakespeare, William. *William Shakespeare* (5–7). Ed. by David Scott Kastan and Marina Kastan. Series: Poetry for Young People. 2000, Sterling $14.95 (978-0-8069-4344-2). In a large format illustrated by paintings, this volume contains three sonnets and 23 short excerpts from the plays of William Shakespeare. (Rev: BL 1/1–15/01; HBG 3/01; SLJ 1/01) [821]

16889 Shepard, Aaron. *Stories on Stage: Children's Plays for Reader's Theater (or Readers Theatre) with 15 Play Scripts from 15 Authors*. 2nd ed. (1–6). 2005, Shepard paper $15.00 (978-0-938497-22-6). 160pp. The 15 story scripts in this collection represent the work of 15 popular writers including Roald Dahl, Louis Sachar, and Harold Courlander. (Rev: SLJ 2/06) [812.5408]

16890 Siberell, Anne. *Bravo! Brava! A Night at the Opera: Behind the Scenes, with Composers, Cast, and Crew* (3–6). Illus. by author. 2001, Oxford $22.95 (978-0-19-513966-2). 64pp. An excellent introduction to the many facets of opera, from its history to behind-the-scenes tasks such as makeup and set design. (Rev: BL 2/15/02; HBG 3/02; SLJ 1/02*)

16891 Slaight, Craig, and Jack Sharrar, eds. *Great Scenes and Monologues for Children* (5–8). Series: Young Actors. 1993, Smith & Kraus paper $12.95 (978-1-880399-15-6). Includes selections from children's novels and fairy tales, as well as adult drama and short stories. (Rev: BL 10/1/93; SLJ 11/93) [808.82]

16892 Stevens, Chambers. *Magnificent Monologues for Kids* (4–8). Ed. by Renee Rolle Whatley. 1999, Sandcastle paper $13.95 (978-1-883995-08-9). A collection of 51 monologues — some best for girls, others for boys — representing different situations and emotions. (Rev: BL 4/1/99; SLJ 8/99) [808.82]

16893 Trimble, Marcia. *Malinda Martha Meets Mariposa: A Star Is Born* (2–4). Illus. by John Lund. 1999, Images LB $15.95 (978-1-891577-57-4). Malinda Martha conjures an unusual play presenting the four stages in the development of the Monarch butterfly with costumed children as cast members. (Rev: SLJ 9/99) [812]

16894 Underwood, Deborah. *Staging a Play* (3–6). Illus. Series: Culture in Action. 2009, Raintree LB $28.21 (978-1-4109-3396-6); paper $7.99 (978-1-4109-3413-0). 32pp. An appealing introduction to stage production, with information on the roles of the director, actors, set and light and sound technicians, costume and makeup experts, and so forth. (Rev: LMC 3–4/10; SLJ 2/10) [792.02]

16895 Van Steenwyk, Elizabeth. *One Fine Day: A Radio Play* (3–5). Illus. by Bill Farnsworth. 2003, Eerdmans $16.00 (978-0-8028-5234-2). 32pp. A fictional conversation between Orville and Wilbur Wright during their first flight is presented in the form of a radio play. (Rev: BL 1/1–15/03; HBG 10/03; SLJ 4/03)

16896 Vigil, Angel. *¡Teatro! Hispanic Plays for Young People* (4–8). 1996, Teacher Ideas paper $25.00 (978-1-56308-371-6). This collection contains 14 English-language scripts that integrate elements of the Hispanic traditions of the Southwest. (Rev: BL 3/1/97; VOYA 6/97) [812]

16897 *William Shakespeare's A Midsummer Night's Dream* (5–9). Illus. by Rod Espinosa. Series: Graphic Shakespeare. 2008, ABDO LB $19.95 (978-1-60270-191-5). 48pp. An entertaining graphic version of *A Midsummer Night's Dream*, using dialogue from the play and featuring commentary on its plot, characters, themes, and other aspects. (Rev: SLJ 1/09) [822]

16898 *William Shakespeare's Hamlet* (5–9). Illus. by Ben Dunn. Series: Graphic Shakespeare. 2008, ABDO LB $19.95 (978-1-60270-188-5). 48pp. An entertaining graphic version of *Hamlet*, using dialogue from the play and featuring commentary on its plot, characters, themes, and other aspects. (Rev: SLJ 1/09) [822]

16899 *William Shakespeare's King Lear* (5–9). Illus. by Ben Dunn. Series: Graphic Shakespeare. 2008, ABDO LB $19.95 (978-1-60270-189-2). 48pp. An entertaining graphic version of *King Lear*, using dialogue from the play and featuring commentary on its plot, characters, themes, and other aspects. (Rev: SLJ 1/09) [822]

History and Geography

History and Geography in General

Miscellaneous

16900 Ajmera, Maya, and John D. Ivanko. *Back to School* (PS–3). Series: It's a Kid's World. 2001, Charlesbridge LB $15.95 (978-1-57091-383-9); paper $6.95 (978-1-57091-384-6). 32pp. This brief look at schooling around the world, with minimal text and color photographs, shows students studying in different situations, unusual methods of getting to school, and various kinds of clothing. (Rev: HBG 3/02; SLJ 6/02)

16901 Arnold, Caroline. *The Geography Book: Activities for Exploring, Mapping, and Enjoying Your World* (4–7). Illus. by Tina Cash Walsh. 2001, Wiley paper $14.95 (978-0-471-41236-6). An organized introduction to several geography concepts along with step-by-step instructions for projects and experiments. (Rev: BL 2/15/02; SLJ 3/02) [910]

16902 Dewey, Jennifer O. *Finding Your Way* (4–6). Illus. 2001, Millbrook LB $23.90 (978-0-7613-0956-7). 64pp. The author relates several tales that involve travel, using one's sense of direction, and becoming lost, in an absorbing text that conveys some basics of map reading. (Rev: BL 5/1/01; HBG 10/01; SLJ 7/01)

16903 Jackson, Ellen. *It's Back to School We Go! First Day Stories from Around the World* (1–3). Illus. by Jan Davey Ellis. 2003, Millbrook LB $23.90 (978-0-7613-2562-8). 32pp. A look at the first day of school in 11 countries, with facts about food, clothes, subjects studied, and games played. (Rev: BL 8/03; HBG 4/04; SLJ 11/03)

16904 Kerley, Barbara. *The World Is Waiting for You* (K–2). Illus. 2013, National Geographic $17.95 (978-1-4263-1114-7); LB $26.99 (978-1-4263-1115-4). 32pp. Full of attractive photographs and accessible text, this appealing volume encourages children to explore the world around them. (Rev: BL 3/1/13; LMC 8–9/13*; SLJ 3/13) [910]

16905 Levy, Joel. *How to Be a World Explorer: Your All-Terrain Training Manual* (4–6). Illus. by James Gulliver Hancock. Series: Not for Parents. 2012, Lonely Planet $17.99 (978-174321425-1). 160pp. Readers learn strategies to cope with a wide variety of challenges in different biomes around the world, with tips on navigation and an "Explorer Bootcamp." (Rev: BL 12/1/12) [910]

16906 Lewis, J. Patrick. *Earth and You: A Closer View: Nature's Features* (2–4). Illus. by Christopher Canyon. 2001, Dawn $16.95 (978-1-58469-016-0); paper $7.95 (978-1-58469-015-3). The author and illustrator present a vivid and lyrical close-up look at natural features of the earth and its plants and animals, urging children to treat their environment with care. (Rev: HBG 10/01; SLJ 4/01)

16907 Moore, Christopher. *From Then to Now: A Short History of the World* (5–8). Illus. by Andrej Krystoforski. 2011, Tundra $25.95 (978-0-88776-540-7). 176pp. Moore offers a broad and fascinating overview of developments in human history from hunter-gatherers to industrialization and the modern, interconnected world. (Rev: BL 5/1/11; SLJ 5/11) [909]

16908 Reynolds, Jan. *Celebrate! Connections Among Cultures* (3–5). Illus. 2006, Lee & Low $16.95 (978-1-58430-253-7). 32pp. Sharing photographs from her travels, the author introduces readers to diverse cultures around the world and their traditions, including the Tuareg of the Sahara, Tibetans, and the Yanomami of the Amazon rain forest. (Rev: BL 3/15/06; SLJ 8/06)

16909 Sloan, Christopher. *Mummies: Dried, Tanned, Sealed, Drained, Frozen, Embalmed, Stuffed, Wrapped, and Smoked . . . and We're Dead Serious* (4–7). Illus. 2010, National Geographic $17.95 (978-1-4263-0695-2); LB $26.90 (978-1-4263-0696-9). 48pp. Mummies from around the world are profiled in this fascinating book featuring plenty of close-up photographs. (Rev: BLO 10/15/10; LMC 3–4/11; SLJ 12/1/10) [393]

16910 Steele, Philip. *Wonders of the World* (4–6). Illus. 2007, Kingfisher $12.95 (978-0-7534-5979-9). 64pp. A broad overview of wonders old and new, including the seven ancient ones plus the Taj Mahal, the canals of Venice, the Empire State Building, the Sydney Opera House, the World Wide Web, and the Hubble telescope. (Rev: BL 5/1/07; LMC 11/07; SLJ 8/07)

Maps and Globes

16911 Anderson, Scoular. *Space Pirates: A Map-Reading Adventure* (2–5). Illus. by author. 2004, Annick $19.95 (978-1-55037-881-8); paper $8.95 (978-1-55037-880-1). Basic map-reading skills are introduced within the framework of a space adventure. (Rev: SLJ 1/05)

16912 Baber, Maxwell. *Map Basics* (4–6). Illus. Series: Map Readers. 2006, Heinemann LB $27.07 (978-1-4034-6794-2). 32pp. This easy-to-understand introduction to mapping offers a brief history of cartography and examines such topics as projections, scale, keys, specialized maps, and the future of cartography; projects and a glossary round out the volume. (Rev: BL 10/15/06)

16913 Bramwell, Martyn. *Central and South America* (4–6). Illus. Series: World in Maps. 2000, Carolrhoda $23.93 (978-0-8225-2912-5). 48pp. This collection of maps of all the countries in Central and South America also covers population, government, languages, currency, size, and capitals. (Rev: BL 10/15/00; HBG 10/01; SLJ 1/01)

16914 Bramwell, Martyn. *How Maps Are Made* (5–8). Series: Maps and Mapmakers. 1998, Lerner LB $22.60 (978-0-8225-2920-0). The difficulties in representing the globe on a flat surface are explored, plus details on how maps are made. (Rev: BL 3/15/99; HBG 3/99; SLJ 2/99) [526]

16915 Bredeson, Carmen. *Looking at Maps and Globes* (1–2). Illus. Series: Rookie Read-About Geography. 2001, Children's Book Pr. LB $20.50 (978-0-516-22351-3). 32pp. An introduction to maps and globes, along with explanations about features such as legends, scale, and the equator. (Rev: BL 11/1/01)

16916 Chancellor, Deborah. *Maps and Mapping* (K–3). Series: Kingfisher Young Knowledge. 2004, Houghton $8.95 (978-0-7534-5759-7). 48pp. Attractive double-page spreads with many illustrations and diagrams present basic information on maps and mapmaking. (Rev: BL 9/1/04)

16917 Gonzales, Doreen. *Up North and Down South: Using Map Directions* (3–5). Illus. Series: First Facts: Map Mania. 2007, Capstone LB $21.26 (978-1-4296-0055-2). 24pp. With photographs, drawings, breezy text introduced by a cartoon bird, and activities, this is an entertaining overview of how to read directions on maps. Also use *Are We There Yet? Using Map Scales* (2007). (Rev: SLJ 2/08)

16918 Jackson, Kay. *Ways to Find Your Way: Types of Maps* (3–5). Illus. Series: First Facts: Map Mania. 2007, Capstone LB $21.26 (978-1-4296-0058-3). 24pp. With photographs, drawings, breezy text introduced by a cartoon bird, and activities, this is an entertaining overview of the various types of maps. (Rev: SLJ 2/08)

16919 Johnson, Jinny. *Maps and Mapping* (2–4). Illus. Series: Inside Access. 2007, Kingfisher $9.95 (978-0-7534-6062-7). 32pp. Clear illustrations add to the usefulness of this introduction to maps that is narrated by an intrepid cartographer named Suki West. (Rev: BL 10/15/07)

16920 Mahaney, Ian F. *Climate Maps* (3–5). Series: Map It! 2006, Rosen LB $21.25 (978-1-4042-3058-3). 24pp. Readers will learn that maps can show much more than cities and roads in this introduction to climate maps. (Rev: SLJ 8/07)

16921 Mahaney, Ian F. *Road Maps* (3–5). Series: Map It! 2006, Rosen LB $21.25 (978-1-4042-3056-9). 24pp. Readers will learn about the features of road maps and how they are used. (Rev: SLJ 8/07)

16922 Oleksy, Walter. *Mapping the World* (5–7). Series: Watts Library: Geography. 2002, Watts LB $25.50 (978-0-531-12029-3); paper $8.95 (978-0-531-16636-9). 64pp. A history of how maps have been made, from the explorers, merchants, and mapmakers of old to the accurate modern products. Also use *Mapping the Seas* and *Maps in History* (both 2002). (Rev: BL 10/15/02)

16923 Ritchie, Scot. *Follow That Map! A First Book of Mapping Skills* (PS–3). Illus. by author. 2009, Kids Can $16.95 (978-1-55453-274-2). 32pp. Readers learn about maps as they follow this story about a girl and her friends searching for her missing dog and cat. (Rev: BL 3/15/09; LMC 8/09)

16924 Robson, Pam. *Maps and Plans* (2–4). Illus. by Tony Kenyon. Series: Geography for Fun. 2001, Millbrook LB $22.90 (978-0-7613-2165-1). This combination of maps, charts, games, and activities introduces some basic concepts in an entertaining way. (Rev: HBG 10/01; SLJ 9/01)

16925 Shores, Erika L. *If Maps Could Talk: Using Symbols and Keys* (3–5). Illus. Series: First Facts: Map Mania. 2007, Capstone LB $21.26 (978-1-4296-0056-9). 24pp. With photographs, drawings, breezy text introduced by a cartoon bird, and activities, this is an entertaining overview of the symbols and keys that appear on maps. (Rev: LMC 3/08; SLJ 2/08)

16926 Waldron, Melanie. *Types of Maps* (3–5). Illus. Series: Let's Get Mapping! 2013, Raintree LB $29.99 (978-141094904-2); paper $7.99 (9781410949110). 32pp. This attractive and informative volume introduces maps of all types — political, physical, statistical, flat/globe, and historical/modern. Also in this series: *Mapping Information* and *How to Read a Map* (2013). (Rev: BL 6/13) [912]

16927 Wilkinson, Philip. *The Kingfisher Student Atlas* (5–8). 2003, Kingfisher $24.95 (978-0-7534-5589-0). An atlas of the earth, with detail on each area's physical characteristics and political boundaries and material on such problems as pollution and deforestation. An accompanying CD offers printable maps. (Rev: SLJ 4/04)

Paleontology and Dinosaurs

16928 Abramson, Andra Serlin, and Jason Brougham, et al. *Inside Dinosaurs* (4–6). Illus. by Jason Brougham. 2010, Sterling $16.95 (978-1-4027-7074-6); paper $9.95 (978-1-4027-7778-3). 49pp. Gatefold features enhance this boldly colored overview of dinosaurs' internal workings. (Rev: LMC 1–2/11; SLJ 12/1/10*) [567.9]

16929 Agenbroad, Larry D., and Lisa Nelson. *Mammoths: Ice-Age Giants* (5–8). Illus. Series: Discovery! 2002, Lerner LB $31.95 (978-0-8225-2862-3). 120pp. A detailed look at mammoths, theories on mammoth extinction, and mammoth discoveries, with sidebar features on topics such as human hunters in the Ice Age, and geologic timelines. (Rev: BL 6/1–15/02; HBG 10/02; SLJ 7/02)

16930 Andreae, Giles. *Dinosaurs Galore!* (PS–3). Illus. by David Wojtowycz. 2005, Tiger Tales $16.95 (978-1-58925-044-4). A varied group of dinosaurs introduces themselves and their characteristcs in humorous rhyming verse. (Rev: SLJ 5/05)

16931 Armentrout, David, and Patricia Armentrout. *Dinosaurs* (PS–2). 2002, Rourke LB $19.95 (978-1-58952-342-5). 32pp. Simple definitions are given for 50 words about dinosaurs, along with a sentence that includes the word. (Rev: SLJ 3/03)

16932 Arnold, Caroline. *Giant Shark: Megalodon, Prehistoric Super Predator* (4–6). Illus. 2000, Clarion $16.00 (978-0-395-91419-9). 32pp. This book introduces the megalodon, an extinct giant shark, and explains how paleontologists have determined its characteristics and how it behaved. (Rev: BL 11/1/00; HBG 3/01; SLJ 11/00)

16933 Arnold, Caroline. *Pterosaurs: Rulers of the Skies in the Dinosaur Age* (2–4). Illus. by Laurie Caple. 2004, Houghton $16.00 (978-0-618-31354-9). 40pp. The pterosaurs — reptiles with a wing span of nearly 40 feet — are introduced here, with plenty of facts and clear illustrations. (Rev: BL 12/1/04)

16934 Arnold, Caroline. *When Mammoths Walked the Earth* (3–5). Illus. by Laurie Caple. 2002, Clarion $16.00 (978-0-618-09633-6). 40pp. An informative, well-illustrated book about key fossil discoveries and the lives of mammoths. (Rev: BL 8/02; HB 11/02; HBG 3/03; SLJ 10/02)

16935 Ashby, Ruth. *Pteranodon: The Life Story of a Pterosaur* (1–3). Illus. by Phil Wilson. 2005, Abrams $14.95 (978-0-8109-5778-7). With simple text and striking images, the author presents what life might have been like for an ancient flying dinosaur. (Rev: SLJ 7/05)

16936 Asimov, Isaac. *What Killed the Dinosaurs?* (3–5). Illus. Series: Isaac Asimov's 21st Century Library of the Universe. 2004, Gareth Stevens LB $26.00 (978-0-8368-3955-5). 32pp. A revised, well-illustrated edition of a previously published book, this discusses possible reasons for the extinction of the dinosaurs and looks at the gigantic Chicxulub crater. (Rev: SLJ 3/05)

16937 Bailey, Jacqui. *The Day of the Dinosaurs* (3–5). Illus. by Matthew Lilly. Series: Cartoon History of the Earth. 2001, Kids Can $16.95 (978-1-55337-073-4); paper $7.95 (978-1-55337-082-6). 32pp. A comic-book-style presentation of the age of the dinosaurs. (Rev: BL 10/15/01; HBG 3/02; SLJ 1/02)

16938 Bailey, Jacqui. *Monster Bones: The Story of a Dinosaur Fossil* (2–4). Illus. by Matthew Lilly. Series: Science Works. 2004, Picture Window LB $26.60 (978-1-4048-0565-1). After a dramatic story that draws the reader in, Bailey explores the process of fossilization and the discovery, classification, reconstruction, and exhibit of fossils. (Rev: SLJ 8/04)

16939 Bardoe, Cheryl. *Mammoths and Mastodons: Titans of the Ice Age* (4–7). Illus. 2010, Abrams $18.95 (978-0-8109-8413-4). 48pp. Two boys discover a perfectly preserved frozen baby mammoth in this story, which offers a glimpse into the lives of these Ice Age giants as well as an introduction to the science of paleontology. Orbis Pictus Honor Award for Outstanding Nonfiction for Children 2011. (Rev: BL 3/15/10; SLJ 4/10) [569]

16940 Barker, Robert T. *Dactyls! Dragons of the Air* (3–4). Illus. by Luis V. Key. Series: Step into Reading. 2005, Random LB $11.99 (978-0-375-93013-3); paper $3.99 (978-0-375-83013-6). 48pp. In conversational, easy-to-understand language, Barker discusses the pterodactyl and its characteristics and conveys the excitement he finds in paleontology. (Rev: SLJ 2/06)

16941 Barner, Bob. *Dinosaur Bones* (PS–2). Illus. 2001, Chronicle $15.95 (978-0-8118-3158-1). The lively cut-paper collage illustrations are the highlight of this book about dinosaurs and their bones. (Rev: BCCB 9/01; BL 11/1/01; HBG 3/02; SLJ 9/01)

16942 Barry, Frances. *Let's Look at Dinosaurs: A Flip-the-Flap Book* (PS–1). Illus. by author. 2011, Candlewick $12.99 (978-0-7636-5354-5). 32pp. With flaps and fold-outs, this wide-format book answers many questions about dinosaurs, taking care to distinguish between fact and conjecture. Lexile 567.9 (Rev: BL 9/1/11; SLJ 8/1/11) [567.9]

16943 Bilgrami, Shaheen. *Amazing Dinosaur Discovery* (PS–3). Illus. by Mike Phillips and Phil Garner. Series: Magic Skeleton. 2002, Sterling $9.95 (978-0-8069-8591-6). 24pp. A visit to a museum introduces younger readers to dinosaurs and their skeletons in this picture book with an appealing format. (Rev: BL 8/02)

16944 Bishop, Nic. *Digging for Bird-Dinosaurs: An Expedition to Madagascar* (4–6). Illus. Series: Scientists in the Field. 2000, Houghton $16.00 (978-0-395-96056-1). Shifting from Madagascar to a lab in New York, this account traces the work of paleontologist Cathy Forster, who is investigating the link between birds and dinosaurs. (Rev: BCCB 5/00; BL 4/15/00*; HB 5/00; HBG 10/00; SLJ 5/00)

16945 Bonner, Hannah. *When Bugs Were Big, Plants Were Strange, and Terrapods Stalked the Earth: A Cartoon Prehistory of Life Before Dinosaurs* (2–5). Illus. 2004, National Geographic $16.95 (978-0-7922-6326-5). 48pp. This fascinating, cartoon-filled excursion into the end of the Paleozoic period more than 250 million years ago offers a blend of natural history and humor. (Rev: BL 2/15/04*; SLJ 2/04)

16946 Bonner, Hannah. *When Dinos Dawned, Mammals Got Munched, and Pterosaurs Took Flight: A Cartoon Prehistory of Life in the Triassic* (4–7). Illus. by author. 2012, National Geographic $17.95 (978-142630862-8); LB $25.90 (978-142630863-5). 48pp. An appealing tour of the Triassic era, focusing on everything from insects to dinosaurs as well as plants, geography, and geology, with eye-catching illustrations, humor, and informative text. (Rev: BL 7/12; LMC 11–12/12) [567.9]

16947 Bonner, Hannah. *When Fish Got Feet, Sharks Got Teeth, and Bugs Began to Swarm* (3–5). Illus. by author. 2007, National Geographic $16.95 (978-1-4263-0078-3). 48pp. Explores life on Earth long before the dinosaurs arrived. (Rev: BCCB 11/07; BL 7/07; HB 1/08; LMC 1/08; SLJ 10/07)

16948 Bradley, Timothy J. *Paleo Bugs: Survival of the Creepiest* (5–8). Illus. by author. 2008, Chronicle $15.99 (978-0-8118-6022-2). The author provides information about prehistoric bugs alongside his own illustrations imagining what they might have looked like in those long-ago days. A companion to *Paleo Sharks*. (Rev: BL 5/15/08; SLJ 7/08) [565]

16949 Bradley, Timothy J. *Paleo Sharks: Survival of the Strangest* (4–7). Illus. 2007, Chronicle $15.95 (978-0-8118-4878-7). 47pp. Well-arranged double-page spreads introduce sharks of prehistoric times and examine how they compare to their modern descendants. (Rev: BL 4/1/07; SLJ 6/07)

16950 Brewster, Hugh. *Dinosaurs in Your Backyard: The Coolest, Scariest Creatures Ever Found in the USA* (3–5). Illus. by Alan Barnard. 2009, Abrams $15.95 (978-0-8109-7099-1). Tyrannosaurus rex, Stegosaurus, and Triceratops are only three of the prehistoric animals introduced in this attractive and informative volume. (Rev: BL 4/15/09; SLJ 6/09)

16951 Brown, Charlotte Lewis. *After the Dinosaurs: Mammoths and Fossil Mammals* (K–3). Illus. by Phil Wilson. Series: An I Can Read Book. 2006, HarperCollins $15.99 (978-0-06-053053-2). 32pp. Double-page spreads introduces some of the mammals — including woolly mammoths and saber-toothed tigers — that followed the dinosaurs; suitable for beginning readers, this solid volume includes a pronunciation guide. (Rev: SLJ 2/07)

16952 Brown, Charlotte Lewis. *The Day the Dinosaurs Died* (1–3). Illus. by Phil Wilson. Series: I Can Read! 2006, HarperCollins $15.99 (978-0-06-000528-3). The author imagines what it would have been like when an asteroid hit the earth 65 million years ago, triggering the demise of the dinosaurs; suitable for beginning readers. (Rev: SLJ 6/06)

16953 Burnie, David. *Dinosaurs* (4–6). Illus. Series: Navigators. 2010, Kingfisher $12.99 (978-0-7534-6414-4). 48pp. Answers many questions about dinosaurs with detailed, lifelike images and concise text organized in eye-catching spreads. (Rev: BL 9/1/10; SLJ 10/1/10) [567.9]

16954 Camper, Cathy. *Bugs Before Time: Prehistoric Insects and Their Relatives* (3–5). Illus. by Steve Kirk. 2002, Simon & Schuster $16.95 (978-0-689-82092-2). 40pp. An eye-catching introduction to the world of prehistoric insects and arthropods. (Rev: BL 3/15/02; HBG 10/02; SLJ 5/02)

16955 Chin, Karen, and Thorn Holmes. *Dino Dung: The Scoop on Fossil Feces* (2–4). Illus. by Karen Carr. Series: Step into Reading. 2005, Random LB $11.99 (978-0-375-92702-7). 48pp. The topic of dinosaur dung makes a fine introduction to the science of paleontology for beginning readers. (Rev: BL 6/1–15/05)

16956 Chrisp, Peter. *Dinosaur Detectives* (2–4). Illus. Series: Dorling Kindersley Readers. 2001, DK $14.99 (978-0-7894-7384-4); paper $3.99 (978-0-7894-7383-7). 48pp. Chrisp interweaves facts about dinosaurs with fictionalized first-person accounts by fossil hunters in a package that makes good browsing for beginning readers. (Rev: HBG 10/01; SLJ 9/01)

16957 Christian, Spencer, and Antonia Felix. *Is There a Dinosaur in Your Backyard? The World's Most Fascinating Fossils, Rocks, and Minerals* (5–8). Series: Spencer Christian's World of Wonders. 1998, Wiley paper $12.95 (978-0-471-19616-7). In addition to discussing dinosaurs, this fascinating book introduces earth science, with interesting details about rocks, minerals, and fossils. (Rev: BL 9/1/98; SLJ 10/98) [552]

16958 Cohen, Daniel. *Allosaurus* (K–2). Illus. Series: Discovering Dinosaurs. 2003, Capstone LB $22.60 (978-0-7368-1618-2). 24pp. A slim, basic overview of the Allosaurus for the beginning reader, with suggested activities and experiments. Also use *Ankylosaurus* and *Brachiosaurus* (both 2003). (Rev: HBG 10/03; SLJ 3/04)

16959 Cohen, Daniel. *Pteranodon* (3–4). Series: Discovering Dinosaurs. 2000, Bridgestone LB $22.60 (978-0-7368-0617-6). 24pp. A basic title that introduces this prehistoric animal. Also use *Stegosaurus* (2000). (Rev: HBG 3/01; SLJ 1/01)

16960 Cooley, Brian, and Mary Ann Wilson. *Make-a-Saurus: My Life with Raptors and Other Dinosaurs* (4–8). Photos by Gary Campbell. 2000, Annick paper $14.95 (978-1-55037-644-9). A two-part book giving a step-by step description of how museum-quality models of dinosaurs are made using the latest discoveries in paleontology, followed by an exploration of how these techniques can be adapted so the reader can make models at home. (Rev: HBG 3/01; SLJ 9/00) [567.9]

16961 Currie, Philip J., and Colleayn O. Mastin. *The Newest and Coolest Dinosaurs* (4–8). 1998, Grasshopper $18.95 (978-1-895910-41-4). Using double-page spreads, this useful volume introduces 15 of the most recent finds in the world of dinosaurs. (Rev: SLJ 1/99) [560]

16962 Cutchins, Judy, and Ginny Johnston. *Giant Predators of the Ancient Seas* (4–7). Series: Southern Fossil Discoveries. 2001, Pineapple $14.95 (978-1-56164-237-3). A look at the reptiles, fish, whales, sharks, and sea snakes that were found in the seas that once covered much of North America, as well as a discussion of the methods scientists used to reconstruct them. (Rev: HBG 3/02; SLJ 12/01) [566]

16963 Dahl, Michael. *Double Bones: The Adventure of Diplodocus* (K–3). Illus. by Garry Nichols. Series: Dinosaur World. 2005, Picture Window $25.26 (978-1-4048-0940-6). 24pp. Facts about the diplodocus appear alongside a simple story about its life in this review of what we know about the dinosaur. Also use *Long Arm: The Adventure of Brachiosaurus* and *Monster Fish: The Adventure of the Ichthyosaurs* (both 2005). (Rev: SLJ 8/05)

16964 De Magalhaes, Roberto Carvalho. *Prehistory* (4–6). Series: Art and Civilization. 2000, Bedrick $16.95 (978-0-87226-615-5). 36pp. Using illustrations of many artifacts, this book explains daily life and culture during prehistoric times. (Rev: HBG 3/01; SLJ 1/01)

16965 Dixon, Dougal. *Amazing Dinosaurs: More Feathers, More Claws, Big Horns, Wide Jaws! 2nd ed.* (5–7). 2007, Boyds Mills $19.95 (978-1-59078-537-9). This carefully updated edition provides new illustrations and text reflecting recent discoveries about dinosaurs. (Rev: SLJ 3/08) [567.9]

16966 Dixon, Dougal. *Ankylosaurus and Other Mountain Dinosaurs* (K–3). Illus. by Steve Weston and James Field. Series: Dinosaur Find. 2004, Picture Window LB $25.26 (978-1-4048-0670-2). 24pp. Basic facts are presented in brief sentences, and include references to the dinosaur's habitat and comparisons to contemporary animals. Also use *Deltadromeus and Other Shoreline Dinosaurs* and *Triceratops and Other Forest Dinosaurs* (2004). (Rev: SLJ 2/05)

16967 Dixon, Dougal. *Dougal Dixon's Amazing Dinosaurs* (3–6). Illus. 2000, Boyds Mills $17.95 (978-1-56397-773-2). 128pp. An attractive, informative field book that introduces groups of dinosaurs and offers solid information on their physical makeup, habits, and special characteristics. (Rev: BL 3/15/00; HBG 10/00; SLJ 5/00)

16968 Dixon, Dougal. *Herbivores* (4–6). Illus. Series: Dinosaurs. 2001, Gareth Stevens LB $26.00 (978-0-8368-2916-7). 36pp. This account explores the world of the herbivore dinosaurs during the Mesozoic Era and discusses related modern species. Also use *Carnivores* and *In the Sky* (2001). (Rev: HBG 3/02; SLJ 3/02)

16969 Dixon, Dougal. *Triceratops: And Other Forest Dinosaurs* (K–2). Series: Dinosaur Find. 2005, Picture Window $25.26 (978-1-4048-0668-9). 24pp. A profile of Triceratops, a large herbivorous dinosaur, and other giant reptiles that also favored forested habitats. (Rev: BL 10/15/04)

16970 Dixon, Dougal. *Tyrannosaurus and Other Dinosaurs of North America* (2–4). Illus. by Steve Weston. Series: Dinosaur Find. 2007, Picture Window LB $25.26 (978-1-4048-2265-8). 24pp. Double-page spreads introduce the prehistoric reptiles that roamed North America with eye-catching art, brief text, and a box that looks at similar contemporary animals. (Rev: BL 3/15/07)

16971 Dixon, Dougal. *World of Dinosaurs and Other Prehistoric Life* (4–6). 2008, Barron's paper $9.99 (978-0-7641-4082-2). 112pp. An accessible guide to prehistoric life with colorful, useful information about each creature including pronunciation of the name and the geographic location of the fossils. (Rev: LMC 5/09*; SLJ 2/09)

16972 Farlow, James O. *Bringing Dinosaur Bones to Life: How Do We Know What Dinosaurs Were Like?* (4–7). Illus. 2001, Watts LB $26.00 (978-0-531-11403-2). 64pp. An interesting look at the life of dinosaurs and at the methods paleontologists use to learn about the beasts, pointing out that although scientists can reconstruct animals from skeletons and fossil evidence, they must always differentiate between fact and educated guesses. (Rev: BL 12/15/01; SLJ 12/01)

16973 Faulkner, Rebecca. *Fossils* (4–6). Series: Geology Rocks! 2007, Raintree LB $31.43 (978-1-4109-2752-1). Plate tectonics, dinosaurs, and fossil fuels are among the topics covered in this appealing and well-organized, high-interest introduction to fossils with color photographs and a section on becoming a paleontologist. (Rev: SLJ 3/08)

16974 French, Vivian. *T. Rex* (PS–2). Illus. by Alison Bartlett. 2005, Candlewick $15.99 (978-0-7636-2184-1). During a visit to a T. rex exhibition, a boy and his grandfather discuss in engaging rhythmic rhyme what is known — and what science has yet to discover — about the prehistoric creature. (Rev: BL 12/1/04)

16975 Gallant, Jonathan R. *The Tales Fossils Tell* (5–9). Series: The Story of Science. 2000, Benchmark LB $29.93 (978-0-7614-1153-6). 80pp. A fascinating introduction to paleontology that explains how the importance of fossils was only clearly understood after the ideas of evolution and extinction were accepted. (Rev: BL 12/15/00; HBG 10/01; SLJ 2/01)

16976 Gallant, Roy A. *Fossils* (3–5). Illus. Series: Kaleidoscope. 2000, Marshall Cavendish $25.64 (978-0-7614-1041-6). 48pp. Beginning with basic information on fossils that shows, for example, how a dying fish can become a fossil, this book goes on to more complex subjects related to paleontology. (Rev: BL 2/1/01; HBG 3/01; SLJ 3/01)

16977 Gibbons, Gail. *Dinosaur Discoveries* (1–3). Illus. 2005, Holiday $16.95 (978-0-8234-1971-5). 32pp. Gibbons reviews dinosaur history in light of new discoveries and tells about paleontologists' ongoing efforts to learn more about these prehistoric creatures. (Rev: BL 10/1/05; SLJ 2/06)

16978 Gibbons, Gail. *Dinosaurs!* (PS–2). Illus. by author. 2008, Holiday $16.95 (978-0-8234-2143-5). 32pp. An accessible overview of dinosaurs and how we have learned about them. (Rev: BL 8/08)

16979 Goldish, Meish. *The Fossil Feud: Marsh and Cope's Bone Wars* (3–5). Series: Fossil Hunters. 2006, Bearport LB $25.27 (978-1-59716-256-2). 32pp. The story of the dramatic 19th-century clash between American paleontologists Othniel Marsh and Edward Cope. (Rev: BL 10/15/06; SLJ 1/07)

16980 Gray, Samantha, and Sarah Walker, eds. *Dinosaur* (3–5). Illus. Series: Eye Wonder. 2001, DK paper $9.99 (978-0-7894-7851-1). Model dinosaurs show how the massive beasts moved, hunted, and lived; theories about their demise are also included. (Rev: BL 12/1/01; HBG 3/02)

16981 Gray, Susan H. *Apatosaurus* (3–5). Illus. Series: Exploring Dinosaurs. 2004, Child's World LB $27.07 (978-1-59296-043-9). 32pp. Following a dramatic scene, information on physical characteristics, behavior, diet, and so forth is presented along with discussion of paleontology as a science. Also use *Oviraptor* and *Iguanodon* (both 2004). (Rev: SLJ 9/04)

16982 Gray, Susan H. *Coelophysis* (3–6). Illus. Series: Exploring Dinosaurs. 2004, Child's World LB $27.07 (978-1-59296-185-6). 32pp. This volume in the Exploring Dinosaurs series looks at the world of the coelophysis, a small but swift carnivore of the late Triassic Period; dramatic scenes draw the reader in to facts and theories about the animals. Also use *Maiasaura* (2004). (Rev: BL 5/1/04; SLJ 9/04)

16983 Gray, Susan H. *Megalosaurus* (3–5). Illus. Series: Exploring Dinosaurs. 2004, Child's World LB $27.07 (978-1-59296-236-5). 32pp. After a fictional opening chapter, there is information the animal's characteristics and behavior plus material on its discovery. Also use *Psittacosaurus* and *Spinosaurus* (both 2004). (Rev: SLJ 2/05)

16984 Green, Jen. *The Dinosaur Museum* (1–4). Illus. by Sebastian Quigley. 2008, National Geographic $19.95 (978-1-4263-0335-7). 20pp. Dramatic dinosaur pop-ups are paired with interactive flaps, tabs, wheels, and mini-books that convey a surprising amount of information. (Rev: BLO 12/16/08)

16985 Guiberson, Brenda. *The Greatest Dinosaur Ever* (K–3). Illus. by Gennady Spirin. 2013, Henry Holt $17.99 (978-080509625-5). 32pp. Twelve large dinosaurs claim the honor of the title in this richly illustrated volume that provides brief information on key characteristics. ℮ (Rev: BL 11/1/13; LMC 1–2/14; SLJ 9/13*) [567.9]

16986 Halls, Kelly Milner. *Dinosaur Mummies: Beyond Bare-Bone Fossils* (4–6). Illus. by Rick Spears. Series: A Junior Library Guild Selection. 2003, Darby Creek $17.95 (978-1-58196-000-6). 48pp. This fascinating book explains how the discovery of fossilized soft-tissue remains of dinosaurs has expanded scientific knowledge about these prehistoric creatures. (Rev: BL 11/1/03; SLJ 12/03)

16987 Hartland, Jessie. *How the Dinosaur Got to the Museum* (K–3). Illus. by author. 2011, Blue Apple $17.99 (978-1-60905-090-0). 40pp. The journey of a diplodocus skeleton from discovery to the halls of the Smithsonian is recounted in double-page spreads that show the contributions of various experts. (Rev: BL 11/1/11; SLJ 11/1/11*) [567.913]

16988 Helm, Charles. *Daniel's Dinosaurs: A True Story of Discovery* (K–3). Photos by author. Illus. by Joan Zimmer. 2004, Maple Tree $16.95 (978-1-897066-06-5); paper $6.95 (978-1-897066-07-2). 32pp. This photoessay tells the story of 8-year-old Daniel Helm's discovery of dinosaur tracks in British Columbia. (Rev: LMC 3/05; SLJ 1/05)

16989 Henry, Michel. *Raptor: The Life of a Young Deinonychus* (2–4). Illus. by Rich Penney. 2007, Abrams $15.95 (978-0-8109-5775-6). A deinonychus matures, mates, and becomes a father. Realistic drawings give readers a glimpse of what scientists think these dinosaurs might have looked like. (Rev: SLJ 5/07)

16990 Holtz, Thomas R, Jr. *Dinosaurs: The Most Complete, Up-to-Date Encyclopedia for Dinosaur Lovers of All Ages* (5–12). Illus. by Luis V. Rey. 2007, Random $34.99 (978-0-375-82419-7). 428pp. Paleontologist

Holtz offers a well-organized overview of dinosaurs and everything dinosaur-related in a well-illustrated volume that will be appreciated by users of many ages (those not interested in cladistics, for example, may find just the information they need on dinosaur eggs). (Rev: HB 1/08; SLJ 12/07)

16991 Hort, Lenny. *Did Dinosaurs Eat Pizza? Mysteries Science Hasn't Solved* (PS–3). Illus. by John O'Brien. 2006, Holt $15.95 (978-0-8050-6757-6). 32pp. A light-hearted look at science's ongoing quest to learn more about what life was like for the dinosaurs. (Rev: BL 4/1/06; SLJ 3/06)

16992 Hughes, Monica. *Flying Giants* (K–2). Illus. Series: I Love Reading! Dino World! 2007, Bearport LB $14.97 (978-1-59716-541-9). 24pp. Beginning readers learn to recognize and pronounce the names of dinosaurs that flew; this small, square book includes colorful illustrations. (Rev: BL 10/15/07; LMC 1/08)

16993 Jeffrey, Gary. *Elasmosaurus: The Long-Necked Swimmer* (2–4). Illus. by Terry Riley. Series: Graphic Dinosaurs. 2009, Rosen LB $25.25 (978-1-4358-2505-5). 32pp. Arresting illustrations grab the reader's interest in this introduction to this marine dinosaur. (Rev: BL 2/1/09)

16994 Jenkins, Steve. *Prehistoric Actual Size* (1–3). Illus. 2005, Houghton $16.00 (978-0-618-53578-1). Dramatic cut-paper artwork offers actual-size representations of anatomical features from such prehistoric creatures as the eight-foot-tall "terror bird" and the Gigantosaurus. (Rev: BCCB 10/05; BL 10/15/05*; HB 1/06; HBG 4/06; LMC 8/06; SLJ 12/05)

16995 Jewitt, Kathryn, and Fiametta Dogi. *3-D Theater: Dinosaurs* (K–3). Illus. 2012, Kingfisher $14.99 (978-075346890-6). 20pp. Effective pop-ups of dinosaurs and their habitats are paired with lots of factual detail. (Rev: BLO 11/15/12) [567.9]

16996 Johnson, Jinny. *Dino Wars* (3–5). Illus. 2005, Abrams $17.95 (978-0-8109-5798-5). 144pp. Dinosaurs are rated by assets including strength, armor, speed, agility, and scariness in this informative guide with a wrestling TV show feel. (Rev: BL 12/15/05; SLJ 2/06)

16997 Johnston, Marianne. *From the Dinosaurs of the Past to the Birds of the Present* (3–5). Illus. Series: Prehistoric Animals and Their Modern-Day Relatives. 2000, Rosen LB $21.25 (978-0-8239-5204-5). 24pp. This account points out the structural similarities between dinosaurs and birds and tells why scientists think they are related. (Rev: BL 12/1/00)

16998 Judge, Lita. *Born to Be Giants: How Baby Dinosaurs Grew to Rule the World* (2–4). Illus. by author. 2010, Roaring Brook $17.99 (978-159643443-1). 48pp. Profiling eight species of dinosaur, this book looks at the babies and how they matured. (Rev: BL 3/1/10; LMC 5–6/10; SLJ 5/10) [500]

16999 Judge, Lita. *How Big Were Dinosaurs?* (K–2). Illus. by author. 2013, Roaring Brook $17.99 (978-159643719-7). 40pp. With detailed, lively illustrations this book compares dinosaurs with contemporary people

and animals. (Rev: BLO 11/15/13; HB 1–2/14; SLJ 12/13*) [567.9]

17000 Keiran, Monique. *Ornithomimus: Pursuing the Bird-Mimic Dinosaur* (4–6). Illus. 2002, Raincoast $26.95 (978-1-55192-348-2). 64pp. A look at the discovery of a featherless beaked fossil in Canada with discussion of fossils and evolution in general, enhanced by color photographs and paintings. (Rev: BL 12/1/02; SLJ 11/02)

17001 Kelsey, Elin. *Finding Out About Dinosaurs* (3–5). Illus. 2000, Owl $19.95 (978-1-895688-97-9). 40pp. Questions about dinosaurs are asked on each double-page spread, and the answers reveal how paleontologists work and what they have learned about these prehistoric animals. (Rev: BL 12/1/00; HBG 3/01; SLJ 10/00)

17002 Kerley, Barbara. *The Dinosaurs of Waterhouse Hawkins* (3–5). Illus. by Brian Selznick. 2001, Scholastic $16.95 (978-0-439-11494-3). 48pp. The true story of Waterhouse Hawkins, the 19th-century British artist who built life-sized dinosaur models; with detailed, dramatic illustrations. Caldecott Honor Book, 2002. (Rev: BCCB 10/01; BL 9/1/01; HBG 3/02; SLJ 10/01)

17003 Kudlinski, Kathleen V. *Boy, Were We Wrong About Dinosaurs!* (K–3). Illus. by S. D. Schindler. 2005, Dutton $15.99 (978-0-525-46978-0). 32pp. Scientists' misconceptions about dinosaurs and other prehistoric creatures are highlighted in interesting, thought-provoking text and realistic illustrations. (Rev: BCCB 1/06; BL 12/1/05*; HB 11/05; HBG 4/06; SLJ 12/05)

17004 Landau, Elaine. *Pterosaurs* (2–4). Illus. Series: True Book Dinosaurs. 2006, Scholastic LB $25.00 (978-0-531-16829-5). 48pp. Colorful clear illustrations add to the appeal of this fact-packed survey of pterosaurs, fossils, and dinosaur extinction. (Rev: BL 1/1–15/07)

17005 Larson, Peter, and Kristin Donnan. *Bones Rock! Everything You Need to Know to Be a Paleontologist* (5–9). 2004, Invisible Cities paper $19.95 (978-1-931229-35-7). A comprehensive, accessible guide to paleontology, describing how to dig for fossils, clean them, keep records, and develop and test theories, with interesting accounts of the authors' experiences. (Rev: SLJ 11/04) [560]

17006 Leedy, Loreen. *My Teacher Is a Dinosaur: And Other Prehistoric Poems, Jokes, Riddles, and Amazing Facts* (2–5). Illus. by author. 2010, Marshall Cavendish $17.99 (978-0-7614-5708-4). 48pp. A lighthearted tour of prehistoric life with an excellent timeline. (Rev: BL 11/1/10; SLJ 1/1/11) [550]

17007 Lessem, Don. *Armored Dinosaurs* (2–4). Illus. by John Bindon. Series: Meet the Dinosaurs. 2004, Lerner LB $23.93 (978-0-8225-1374-2); paper $6.95 (978-0-8225-2570-7). 32pp. Facts about these dinosaurs are presented in a lively narrative that includes present-tense scenes. Also use *Giant Meat-Eating Dinosaurs* and *Horned Dinosaurs* (both 2004). (Rev: SLJ 2/05)

17008 Lessem, Don. *Dinosaur Worlds: New Dinosaurs, New Discoveries* (5–8). 1996, Boyds Mills $19.95 (978-1-56397-597-4). The reader visits various dinosaur digs worldwide in a review of what we know about these amazing creatures. (Rev: BL 11/15/96; SLJ 12/96*) [567.9]

17009 Lessem, Don. *The Fastest Dinosaurs* (2–4). Illus. by John Bindon. Series: Meet the Dinosaurs. 2005, Lerner LB $23.93 (978-0-8225-1422-0); paper $6.95 (978-0-8225-2620-9). 32pp. Which dinosaurs were fastest? And how did scientists find out? Conversational text tackles these questions. Also use *The Smartest Dinosaurs* and *Flying Giants of Dinosaur Time* (both 2005). (Rev: SLJ 7/05)

17010 Lessem, Don. *Feathered Dinosaurs* (2–4). Illus. by John Bindon. Series: Meet the Dinosaurs. 2005, Lerner LB $23.93 (978-0-8225-1423-7); paper $6.95 (978-0-8225-2621-6). 32pp. Simple text and dramatic illustrations explore the link between dinosaurs and birds. (Rev: BL 6/1–15/05)

17011 Lessem, Don. *Sea Giants of Dinosaur Time* (2–3). Illus. by John Bindon. Series: Meet the Dinosaurs. 2005, Lerner LB $23.93 (978-0-8225-1425-1); paper $6.95 (978-0-8225-2623-0). 32pp. The fascinating creatures that filled the prehistoric seas are the focus of this book, complete with illustrations. (Rev: SLJ 9/05)

17012 Lessem, Don. *The Ultimate Dinopedia: The Most Complete Dinosaur Reference Ever* (3–6). Illus. by Franco Tempesta. 2010, National Geographic $24.95 (978-142630164-3); LB $34.90 (978-142630165-0). 272pp. This comprehensive dinosaur encyclopedia includes phonetic spellings and etymological guides along with striking illustrations. Also available as an iPad app. (Rev: BL 12/15/10; LMC 5–6/11) [567.9]

17013 Lewis, Brenda Ralph. *Meat-Eating Dinosaurs* (3–5). Illus. Series: Nature's Monsters: Dinosaurs. 2006, Gareth Stevens LB $23.93 (978-0-8368-6843-2). 32pp. Scary-looking carnivorous dinosaurs roam the pages of this introduction to the meat-eaters. Simple text and brief facts make this a good choice for young readers. (Rev: SLJ 5/07)

17014 Lewis, Brenda Ralph. *Plant-Eating Dinosaurs* (3–5). Illus. Series: Nature's Monsters: Dinosaurs. 2006, Gareth Stevens LB $23.93 (978-0-8368-6844-9). 32pp. Scary-looking herbivores roam the pages of this introduction to the plant-eaters. Simple text and brief facts make this a good choice for young readers. (Rev: SLJ 5/07)

17015 Lewis, Brenda Ralph. *Prehistoric Creatures in the Sea and Sky* (3–5). Illus. Series: Nature's Monsters: Dinosaurs. 2006, Gareth Stevens LB $23.93 (978-0-8368-6845-6). 32pp. Dinosaurs that swam or flew are featured in this introduction. Simple text and brief facts make this a good choice for young readers. (Rev: SLJ 5/07)

17016 Lewis, Brenda Ralph. *Small and Deadly Dinosaurs* (3–5). Illus. Series: Nature's Monsters: Dinosaurs. 2006, Gareth Stevens LB $23.93 (978-0-8368-6846-3). 32pp. The little guys of the prehistoric world are the focus of this book, part of a series. Simple text and brief facts make this a good choice for young readers. (Rev: SLJ 5/07)

17017 Lunis, Natalie. *A T. Rex Named Sue: Sue Hendrickson's Huge Discovery* (3–6). Illus. Series: Fossil Hunters. 2006, Bearport LB $25.27 (978-1-59716-259-3). 32pp. In 1990 Sue Hendrickson discovered a Tyrannosaurus rex skeleton in South Dakota; this is a simply written account of the discovery and the lengthy legal battle to determine custody of the dinosaur remains. (Rev: SLJ 1/07)

17018 McGowan, Chris. *Dinosaur Discovery: Everything You Need to Be a Paleontologist* (3–6). Illus. by Erica Lyn Schmidt. 2011, Simon & Schuster $17.99 (978-1-4169-4764-6). 48pp. Thirteen dinosaurs are briefly highlighted in this book that presents paleontology-related activities — taking molds of teeth, creating mummified skin, and so forth. **e** Lexile 870L (Rev: BL 6/1/11; LMC 11–12/11; SLJ 7/11) [560]

17019 Macleod, Elizabeth. *Monster Fliers: From the Time of the Dinosaurs* (K–3). Illus. by John Bindon. 2010, Kids Can $16.95 (978-1-55453-199-8). 32pp. Nineteen different dinosaurs are described and illustrated in this engaging book that includes comparative sizes and a timeline. (Rev: BL 3/15/10; LMC 8–9/10; SLJ 4/1/10) [567.918]

17020 McMullan, Kate. *Dinosaur Hunters* (2–4). Illus. by John R. Jones. Series: Step into Reading. 2005, Random LB $11.99 (978-0-375-92450-7); paper $3.99 (978-0-375-82450-0). 48pp. A new edition of the easy reader on how fossils are found and studied, with updated text and illustrations. (Rev: BL 9/1/05)

17021 Malam, John. *Dinosaur* (5–8). Illus. 2006, DK $15.99 (978-0-7566-1412-6). 70pp. Tyrannosaurus rex is the star of this attractive book that covers the dinosaur's anatomy, life cycle, and hunting techniques plus archaeological findings and the science that has allowed us to reconstruct the animal from what we know today. (Rev: SLJ 4/07)

17022 Manning, Mick, and Brita Granström. *Dino-Dinners* (K–2). Illus. by Mick Manning. 2007, Holiday $16.95 (978-0-8234-2089-6). 32pp. What did dinosaurs eat? Ten varieties of dinosaurs describe their eating habits in this lighthearted but informative volume. (Rev: BL 9/1/07; LMC 1/08; SLJ 10/07)

17023 Manning, Mick, and Brita Granström. *Dinomania: Things to Do with Dinosaurs* (3–5). Illus. 2002, Holiday House $16.95 (978-0-8234-1641-7). 48pp. This book consists of a series of projects related to dinosaurs, such as creating a diorama of habitats and a mobile of flying creatures. (Rev: BL 6/1–15/02; HBG 10/02; SLJ 4/02)

17024 Manning, Mick, and Brita Granström. *Woolly Mammoth* (K–3). Illus. by Brita Granström. 2009, Frances Lincoln $16.95 (978-1-84507-860-7). 32pp. Rhyming couplets describe the life of a mammoth while sidebars provide more-detailed information for older readers. (Rev: BL 11/15/09; LMC 3–4/10; SLJ 1/1/10) [569.67]

17025 Manning, Phillip Lars. *Dinomummy: The Life, Death, and Discovery of Dakota, a Dinosaur from Hell Creek* (5–8). Illus. 2007, Kingfisher $18.95 (978-0-

7534-6047-4). 32pp. The 2006 discovery of a hadrosaur fossil — so complete its skin was still intact — is the subject of this dramatically designed book that takes readers into the world of paleontology. (Rev: BL 3/3/08)

17026 Markle, Sandra. *Outside and Inside Woolly Mammoths* (4–6). Illus. Series: Outside and Inside. 2007, Walker $17.95 (978-0-8027-9589-2). 40pp. Photographs and digital images add to this account of what we know about mammoths and how they compare with today's elephants. (Rev: BL 5/1/07; HB 7/07; SLJ 6/07)

17027 Matthews, Rupert. *Dinosaur Families: Unearth the Secrets Behind Dinosaur Fossils* (3–6). Series: Dinosaur Dig. 2009, QEB LB $27.10 (978-1-59566-548-5). 32pp. Reluctant readers will enjoy these highly visual books that focus on various aspects of dinosaurs and dinosaur life, with "Wow!" boxes and information on fossils and digs. Also use *Dinosaur Combat, Dinosaur Food,* and *Dinosaurs in Action* (all 2009). (Rev: SLJ 6/09)

17028 Morrison, Taylor. *The Great Unknown* (3–5). Illus. 2001, Houghton $16.00 (978-0-395-97494-0). 32pp. An account of Peale's discovery of mastodon bones in New York state in 1799 and their assembly into a skeleton. (Rev: BCCB 7–8/01; BL 5/1/01; HBG 10/01; SLJ 5/01)

17029 Munro, Margaret. *The Story of Life on Earth* (3–5). Illus. 2000, Douglas & McIntyre $19.95 (978-0-88899-401-1). This informative introduction to the evolution of life on Earth uses double-page spreads to illustrate the flora and fauna of different geological periods. (Rev: BL 11/1/00; HBG 3/01; SLJ 12/00)

17030 Naish, Darren. *Dinosaurs Life Size* (5–7). Illus. 2010, Barron's $14.99 (978-0-7641-6378-4). 80pp. A large-format eye-catching book full of dinosaur facts and pictures of life-size dinosaur parts — jaws, eyes, and claws and so forth — plus fold-out pages including a timeline. (Rev: LMC 3–4/11; SLJ 12/1/10) [567.9]

17031 O'Brien, Patrick. *Mammoth* (K–3). Illus. 2002, Holt $16.95 (978-0-8050-6596-1). O'Brien interweaves historical information about mammoths with contemporary scenes of scientists excavating and identifying a skeleton, in a well-illustrated, large-format overview of these animals that touches on their modern elephant relatives. (Rev: BL 12/1/02; HBG 3/03; SLJ 11/02)

17032 O'Brien, Patrick. *Megatooth* (PS–3). Illus. by author. 2001, Holt $16.95 (978-0-8050-6214-4). O'Brien presents the theories scientists have made about the giant beast also known as the megalodon. (Rev: HBG 10/01; SLJ 6/01)

17033 O'Hearn, Michael. *Triceratops vs. Stegosaurus: When Horns and Plates Collide* (3–5). Illus. Series: Edge Bks. Dinosaur Wars. 2009, Capstone LB $25.32 (978-1-4296-3938-5). 32pp. A triceratops goes head-to-head with a stegosaurus in this attention-grabbing title focusing on the dinosaurs' defenses, weapons, attack styles, and who would likely win in a face-off. Among other titles in the series are *Spinosaurus vs. Giganotosaurus: Battle of the Giants* and *Allosaurus vs. Brachiosaurus: Might Against Height* (both 2009). (Rev: LMC 11–12/10; SLJ 6/1/10) [567.915]

17034 Olien, Becky. *Fossils* (2–4). Series: The Bridgestone Science Library. 2001, Capstone LB $22.60 (978-0-7368-0951-1). Fossils, famous fossil finds, and fuels made from fossils are covered in this slim volume. (Rev: HBG 3/02; SLJ 2/02)

17035 Osborne, Will, and Mary Pope Osborne. *Dinosaurs: A Nonfiction Companion to Dinosaurs Before Dark* (2–4). Illus. by Sal Murdocca. Series: Magic Tree House Research Guide. 2000, Random LB $11.99 (978-0-375-90296-3); paper $4.99 (978-0-375-80296-6). 119pp. Using a time-travel format involving two children, this book discusses the kinds of dinosaurs, their characteristics, misconceptions about them, and the other creatures that lived at the same time. (Rev: HBG 3/01; SLJ 11/00)

17036 Padma, T. V. *The Albertosaurus Mystery: Philip Currie's Hunt in the Badlands* (3–6). Illus. Series: Fossil Hunters. 2006, Bearport LB $25.27 (978-1-59716-254-8). 32pp. Describes paleontologist Philip Currie's search for a site containing the remains of multiple dinosaurs. (Rev: SLJ 1/07)

17037 Press, Judy. *The Kids' Natural History Book: Making Dinos, Fossils, Mammoths and More* (3–5). Illus. Series: Kids Can! 2000, Williamson $12.95 (978-1-885593-24-5). 144pp. A discussion of the animal classification system and how scientists have discovered and organized information about animals, with many related craft projects. (Rev: BL 12/15/00; SLJ 1/01)

17038 Ray, Deborah Kogan. *Dinosaur Mountain: Digging into the Jurassic Age* (4–6). Illus. by author. 2010, Farrar $16.99 (978-0-374-31789-8). 40pp. With readable text and interesting illustrations, Ray tells the exciting story of the "Bone Wars" of the late 19th century and Earl Douglass's discovery of Utah's Dinosaur Mountain. (Rev: BL 2/1/10; LMC 5–6/10; SLJ 5/10) [567.90973]

17039 Relf, Patricia. *A Dinosaur Named Sue: The Story of the Colossal Fossil* (3–6). Illus. 2000, Scholastic $15.95 (978-0-439-09985-1). This is the story of the largest and most complete Tyrannosaurus rex skeleton ever found, how it was transported from South Dakota to the Field Museum in Chicago, and what life was like when Sue was alive. (Rev: BL 12/1/00; HBG 3/01; SLJ 1/01)

17040 Rey, Luis V. *Extreme Dinosaurs* (3–7). Illus. by author. 2001, Chronicle $16.95 (978-0-8118-3086-7). 62pp. Bright, lively illustrations accompany a friendly text that provides lots of information about dinosaur evolution, dinosaur species grouped by continent, and fossil discoveries. (Rev: HBG 3/02; SLJ 9/01)

17041 Sabuda, Robert, and Matthew Reinhart. *Encyclopedia Prehistorica: Dinosaurs* (K–4). Illus. by authors. 2005, Candlewick $26.99 (978-0-7636-2228-2). Beautifully engineered fold-outs introduce a variety of dinosaurs. (Rev: SLJ 9/05)

17042 Sabuda, Robert, and Matthew Reinhart. *Sharks and Other Sea Monsters* (1–3). Series: Encyclopedia Prehistorica. 2006, Candlewick $27.99 (978-0-7636-2229-9). 12pp. Elaborate pop-ups highlight facts about sharks, megalodons, and other prehistoric sea predators. (Rev: BL 6/1–15/06; SLJ 7/06)

17043 Schomp, Virginia. *Ceratosaurus: And Other Horned Meat-Eaters* (3–4). Illus. Series: Prehistoric World. 2005, Benchmark LB $17.95 (978-0-7614-2009-5). 32pp. Vivid illustrations and conversational text introduce the Ceratosaurus and related prehistoric horned animals. Also use *Therizinosaurus* and *Plateosaurus* (both 2005). (Rev: SLJ 3/06)

17044 Schomp, Virginia. *Iguanodon: And Other Spiky-Thumbed Plant-Eaters* (2–4). Illus. Series: Prehistoric World. 2005, Marshall Cavendish LB $17.95 (978-0-7614-2005-7). 32pp. Accessible text and eye-catching images make this an appealing introduction to this prehistoric animal's appearance, diet, habitat, and behavior. (Rev: BL 3/1/06)

17045 Skrepnick, Michael W. *Sinosauropteryx: Mysterious Feathered Dinosaur* (3–4). Illus. by author. Series: I Like Dinosaurs! 2005, Enslow LB $21.26 (978-0-7660-2623-0). 24pp. Introduces the Sinosauropteryx, a small, feathered, poultry-size dinosaur whose fossilized remains were found in China in the mid-1990s. (Rev: SLJ 2/06)

17046 Sloan, Christopher. *Baby Mammoth Mummy: Frozen in Time: A Prehistoric Animal's Journey into the 21st Century* (5–8). Illus. 2011, National Geographic $17.95 (978-1-4263-0865-9); LB $26.90 (978-1-4263-0866-6). 48pp. Tells the story of the discovery in Siberia of the baby mammoth called Lyuba, and discusses what scientists have learned about her world. (Rev: BL 11/15/11; SLJ 12/1/11) [569]

17047 Sloan, Christopher. *Feathered Dinosaurs* (3–6). Illus. 2000, National Geographic $17.95 (978-0-7922-7219-9). 64pp. Using recent paleontological discoveries as its starting point, this book explores what feathered dinosaurs, the distant ancestors of modern birds, might have looked like. (Rev: BL 11/1/00; HBG 3/01; SLJ 11/00)

17048 Sloan, Christopher. *Supercroc and the Origin of Crocodiles* (5–8). 2002, National Geographic $18.95 (978-0-7922-6691-4). A fascinating account of the discovery in Africa of the fossil *Sarcosuchus*, or Supercroc, with additional information on paleontology and crocodile evolution. (Rev: BCCB 5/02; BL 9/15/02; HBG 10/02; SLJ 7/02*) [567.9]

17049 Sloan, Christopher. *Tracking Tyrannosaurs* (5–8). Illus. by Xing Lida. 2013, National Geographic $18.95 (978-142631374-5). 48pp. This useful book is subtitled *Meet T. Rex's Fascinating Family, From Tiny Terrors to Feathered Giants* and traces the dinosaur's lineage from the Jurassic period through modern-day birds. (Rev: BL 11/15/13; SLJ 12/13) [567.912]

17050 Stewart, David. *Dinosaurs* (K–3). Illus. by Nicholas Hewetson. Series: World of Wonder. 2008, Children's Pr. LB $29.00 (978-0-531-20450-4); paper $9.95 (978-0-531-20541-9). 32pp. An effective question-and-answer format and vibrant layouts provide basic infor-

mation on dinosaurs. (Rev: BL 4/1/08; LMC 10/08; SLJ 7/08)

17051 Thompson, Sharon E. *Death Trap: The Story of the La Brea Tar Pits* (4–8). 1995, Lerner LB $28.75 (978-0-8225-2851-7). A history of the 40,000-year-old tar pits in Los Angeles and of the many species of prehistoric animals that were trapped in them, with color photographs. (Rev: BL 6/1–15/95; SLJ 5/95) [560]

17052 Thomson, Sarah L. *Extreme Dinosaurs!* (K–3). Illus. 2007, HarperCollins LB $16.99 (978-0-06-089971-4); paper $6.99 (978-0-06-089967-7). 48pp. Using a conversational question-and-answer format, this volume conveys solid information. (Rev: BLO 1/15/08; SLJ 3/08)

17053 Turner, Alan. *Prehistoric Mammals* (4–6). Illus. by Mauricio Antón. 2004, National Geographic $29.95 (978-0-7922-7134-5). 192pp. Dramatic illustrations and brief text introduce prehistoric mammals that roamed the earth after the time of the dinosaurs. (Rev: BL 11/1/04; SLJ 1/05*)

17054 VanCleave, Janice. *Dinosaurs for Every Kid: Easy Activities That Make Learning Science Fun* (4–7). Series: Science for Every Kid. 1994, Wiley paper $12.95 (978-0-471-30812-6). With accompanying activities, this book explores the world of dinosaurs and how paleontology has discovered, through fossils, how they lived. (Rev: BL 4/1/94; SLJ 7/94) [567.9]

17055 Walker, Sally M. *Fossils* (2–4). Illus. Series: Early Bird Earth Science. 2006, Lerner LB $25.26 (978-0-8225-5945-0). 48pp. Walker explains how fossils are formed, where they're mostly likely to be found, and what can be learned by studying them. (Rev: SLJ 1/07)

17056 Wenzel, Gregory. *Feathered Dinosaurs of China* (4–6). Illus. by author. 2004, Charlesbridge $16.95 (978-1-57091-561-1); paper $6.95 (978-1-57091-562-8). 32pp. A trip more than 100 million years back in time to study the dinosaurs of prehistoric China and their theoretical relationship to modern-day birds. (Rev: SLJ 4/04)

17057 Wenzel, Gregory. *Giant Dinosaurs of the Jurassic* (2–5). Illus. by author. 2004, Charlesbridge $16.95 (978-1-57091-563-5); paper $6.95 (978-1-57091-564-2). 32pp. The lives of a variety of dinosaurs are shown during a typical day in the prehistoric American West. (Rev: BL 10/1/04; SLJ 7/04)

17058 West, David. *Velociraptors and Other Raptors and Small Carnivores* (3–5). Illus. Series: Dinosaurs! 2010, Gareth Stevens LB $26.60 (978-143394224-2). 32pp. Computer-enhanced illustrations give this guide to the razor-toothed velociraptors plenty of immediate appeal. (Rev: BL 10/1/10) [567.912]

17059 Wheeler, Lisa. *Mammoths on the Move* (K–2). Illus. by Kurt Cyrus. 2006, Harcourt $16.00 (978-0-15-204700-9). 32pp. A woolly mammoth migration is the subject of this rhyming book with large illustrations. (Rev: BL 5/1/06; SLJ 6/06)

17060 Williams, Judith. *The Discovery and Mystery of a Dinosaur Named Jane* (5–7). Illus. 2007, Enslow LB $23.93 (978-0-7660-2730-5); paper $13.26 (978-0-

7660-2709-1). A straightforward account of the discovery, excavation and installation of this important fossil find. (Rev: SLJ 7/07)

17061 Woodward, John. *Everything You Need to Know about Dinosaurs and Other Prehistoric Creatures* (3–6). Illus. 2014, DK $15.99 (978-146541575-2). 80pp. In typical DK style, this volume combines visual elements and text on two-page spreads to convey lots of information on dinosaurs, much of it in inventive ways and with discussion of myths and theories. (Rev: BL 3/1/14; LMC 10/14*) [567.9]

17062 Zimmerman, Howard. *Dinosaurs! The Biggest Baddest Strangest Fastest* (2–5). Illus. 2000, Simon & Schuster $17.95 (978-0-689-83276-5). 64pp. An oversize volume that is particularly noteworthy for its excellent illustrations of all sorts of dinosaurs. (Rev: BL 9/1/00; HBG 10/00; SLJ 5/00)

17063 Zoehfeld, Kathleen W. *Did Dinosaurs Have Feathers?* (K–4). Illus. by Lucia Washburn. Series: Let's-Read-and-Find-Out Science. 2004, HarperCollins LB $16.89 (978-0-06-029027-6); paper $5.99 (978-0-06-445218-2). 33pp. Dinosaur fossils and feathers are discussed, with mention of early discoveries and of the links between dinosaurs and birds. (Rev: BL 1/1–15/04; SLJ 2/04)

17064 Zoehfeld, Kathleen W. *Dinosaur Parents, Dinosaur Young: Uncovering the Mystery of Dinosaur Families* (3–6). Illus. Series: Let's-Read-and-Find-Out Science. 2001, Clarion $17.00 (978-0-395-91338-3). 60pp. This book explains what we know about dinosaur parenting and how paleontologists have arrived at this information. (Rev: BL 4/15/01)

17065 Zoehfeld, Kathleen W. *Dinosaur Tracks* (2–4). Illus. by Lucia Washburn. Series: Let's-Read-and-Find-Out Science. 2007, HarperCollins $16.99 (978-0-06-029024-5). 40pp. A look at how dinosaur tracks are discovered and what they can tell us about the animals that made them. (Rev: BL 12/1/06)

17066 Zoehfeld, Kathleen W. *Dinosaurs Big and Small* (PS–1). Illus. by Lucia Washburn. Series: Let's-Read-and-Find-Out Science. 2002, HarperCollins paper $5.99 (978-0-06-445182-6). 40pp. Dinosaurs are compared with buses, elephants, and other items to help children grasp their size. (Rev: BL 7/02; HBG 10/02; SLJ 7/02)

17067 Zoehfeld, Kathleen W. *Terrible Tyrannosaurs* (PS–2). Illus. by Lucia Washburn. 2001, HarperCollins LB $15.89 (978-0-06-027934-9). 40pp. This book highlights the most familiar and most feared dinosaur and tells what we know about it from science. (Rev: BL 2/1/01; HBG 10/01)

Anthropology, Prehistoric Life, and Evolution

17068 Bailey, Jacqui. *The Dawn of Life* (3–5). Illus. by Matthew Lilly. Series: Cartoon History of the Earth. 2001, Kids Can $16.95 (978-1-55337-072-7); paper $7.95 (978-1-55337-081-9). 32pp. The beginnings of plant and animal life on Earth, presented in a comic-book format. Also use *The Birth of the Earth*, *The Day of the Dinosaurs*, and *The Stick and Stone Age* (all 2001). (Rev: BL 10/15/01; HBG 3/02; SLJ 1/02)

17069 Batten, Mary. *Anthropologist: Scientist of the People* (4–7). Series: Scientists in the Field. 2001, Houghton Mifflin $16.00 (978-0-618-08368-8). Striking photographs of a Paraguayan tribe of huntergatherers serve as a powerful backdrop to this explanation of the work of anthropologists. (Rev: BL 8/01; HB 1–2/02*; HBG 3/02; SLJ 9/01) [627]

17070 Corbishley, Mike. *What Do We Know About Prehistoric People?* (4–7). Series: What Do We Know About. 1996, Bedrick LB $18.95 (978-0-87226-383-3). Using double-page spreads, this book explores the known facts about human prehistoric life around the world. (Rev: BL 6/1–15/96) [930.1]

17071 Goldenberg, Linda. *Little People and a Lost World: An Anthropological Mystery* (5–8). 2006, Twenty-First Century LB $29.27 (978-0-8225-5983-2). In 2003, a team of archaeologists and anthropologists discovered the skeleton of what's believed to be a small human being who lived more than 12,000 years ago on Flores Island in Indonesia; this book looks at the controversy over the discovery and the insights it has given into early human life. (Rev: BL 12/1/06; SLJ 4/07) [569.9]

17072 Jenkins, Steve. *Life on Earth: The Story of Evolution* (3–6). Illus. 2002, Houghton $16.00 (978-0-618-16476-9). 40pp. Superb cut-paper illustrations depict the fundamentals of evolution, touching on Darwin, natural selection, and mutation, and ending with an extraordinary timeline. (Rev: BL 12/15/02; HB 9/02*; HBG 3/03; SLJ 12/02)

17073 Lauber, Patricia. *Who Came First? New Clues to Prehistoric Americans* (5–10). 2003, National Geo-

graphic $18.95 (978-0-7922-8228-0). An attractive, oversized volume that encompasses anthropology, archaeology, genetics, and linguistics in its discussion of the provenance of the peoples of the Americas. (Rev: BL 7/03*; HB 7–8/03; HBG 10/03; SLJ 8/03*) [970.01]

17074 Loxton, Daniel. *Evolution: How We and All Living Things Came to Be* (3–8). Illus. by author and Jim W. W. Smith. 2010, Kids Can $18.95 (978-1-55453-430-2). 56pp. Helpful images and question-and-answer sections enhance this accessible presentation of the theory of evolution and the evidence that supports it. (Rev: BLO 2/15/10; LMC 8–9/10; SLJ 5/10) [576.8]

17075 McGowen, Tom. *Giant Stones and Earth Mounds* (4–8). 2000, Millbrook LB $25.90 (978-0-7613-1372-4). A history of the New Stone Age of about 9,000 years ago and the constructions that still exist in the United States today from that period. (Rev: BL 10/1/00; HBG 10/01; SLJ 10/00) [930.1]

17076 Nicolson, Cynthia Pratt. *Totally Human: Why We Look and Act the Way We Do* (3–6). Illus. by Dianne Eastman. 2011, Kids Can $16.95 (978-1-55453-569-9). 40pp. This quirky history of human behavior goes back to the dawn of life to explain some of humanity's weirdest impulses and traits. (Rev: BL 2/15/11; LMC 10/11; SLJ 10/1/11) [576.8]

17077 Pickering, Robert. *The People* (5–8). Series: Prehistoric North America. 1996, Millbrook LB $22.90 (978-1-56294-550-3). An account of the development of the prehistoric North American tribes that may have crossed the land bridge from Asia to the Americas. (Rev: SLJ 4/96) [973.01]

17078 Prap, Lila. *Dinosaurs?!* (K–3). Illus. by author. 2010, NorthSouth $16.95 (978-0-7358-2284-9). Unpaged. A flock of chickens are astonished to think they might be descended from dinosaurs in this humorous and informative look at evolution. (Rev: LMC 10/10; SLJ 3/1/10) [567.9]

17079 Pringle, Laurence. *Billions of Years, Amazing Changes: The Story of Evolution* (5–8). Illus. by Steve

Jenkins. 2011, Boyds Mills $17.95 (978-1-59078-723-6). 96pp. A fascinating, colorful presentation of man's discoveries over time about evolution, with clear explanation of the four core principles plus examples of natural selection and many images. ALA Notable Children's Book 2012. Lexile 1000L (Rev: BL 12/1/11; HB 1–2/12; LMC 1–2/12*; SLJ 12/1/11*) [596.8]

17080 Schertle, Alice. *We* (1–3). Illus. by Kenneth Addison. 2007, Lee & Low $16.95 (978-1-58430-060-1). Well-illustrated and concisely written in poetic form, this introduction to human evolution and ingenuity covers human history from its beginnings in Africa to the present day. (Rev: BL 5/1/07; LMC 11/07; SLJ 5/07)

17081 Sloan, Christopher. *Bury the Dead: Tombs, Corpses, Mummies, Skeletons, and Rituals* (5–9). 2002, National Geographic $18.95 (978-0-7922-7192-5). Young readers will be fascinated by this serious account of burial practices throughout the ages, with timelines, color photographs, diagrams, and clear descriptions of rites around the world. (Rev: BL 12/1/02; HBG 3/03; SLJ 10/02*) [393]

17082 Thimmesh, Catherine. *Lucy Long Ago: Uncovering the Mystery of Where We Came From* (5–7). Illus. 2009, Houghton $18.00 (978-0-547-05199-4). 64pp. The story behind Lucy, a skeleton found in Ethiopia in 1974, that made science rethink how humans evolved. (Rev: BCCB 7–8/09; BL 6/1–15/09; HB 7/09; SLJ 7/09*) [569.9]

17083 Westrup, Hugh. *The Mammals* (5–8). Series: Prehistoric North America. 1996, Millbrook LB $22.90 (978-1-56294-546-6). The woolly mammoth and saber-toothed tiger are two of the prehistoric mammals described in words and pictures. (Rev: BL 5/15/96; SLJ 4/96) [569]

17084 Winston, Robert. *Evolution Revolution* (5–8). Illus. 2009, DK $16.99 (978-0-7566-4524-3). 96pp. This attractive and accessible large-format picture book looks first at creation stories and Darwin's theories before progressing to modern understanding of genetics, evolutionary biology, and the role of DNA. (Rev: BL 3/15/09; SLJ 2/09) [576.82]

945

Archaeology

17085 Arnold, Caroline. *Stone Age Farmers Beside the Sea: Scotland's Prehistoric Village of Skara Brae.* (5–8). 1997, Clarion $16.00 (978-0-395-77601-8). A stunning volume that tells the story of the Stone Age village of Skara Brae, dating to about 3000 B.C., that was unearthed in the Orkney Islands in 1850. (Rev: BCCB 4/97; BL 4/15/97; SLJ 7/97) [930]

17086 Aronson, Marc, and Mike Parker Pearson, Riverside Project. *If Stones Could Speak: Unlocking the Secrets of Stonehenge* (4–6). 2010, National Geographic $17.95 (978-1-4263-0599-3); LB $26.90 (978-1-4263-0600-6). 64pp. This is a fascinating account of recent archaeological discoveries at Stonehenge, with information on the site and its history and on the science of investigating ancient places. Orbis Pictus Honor Award for Outstanding Nonfiction for Children, 2011. Lexile 1070L (Rev: BL 2/1/10*; HB 5–6/10; LMC 3–4/10; SLJ 3/10) [936.2]

17087 Barnes, Trevor. *Archaeology* (4–6). Series: Kingfisher Knowledge. 2004, Houghton $11.95 (978-0-7534-5768-9). 64pp. This colorful overview of archaeological finds and techniques will attract browsers and reluctant older readers. (Rev: BL 9/1/04; SLJ 11/04)

17088 Buell, Janet. *Greenland Mummies* (5–8). Series: Time Travelers. 1998, Twenty-First Century LB $25.90 (978-0-7613-3004-2). By examining mummified human corpses found in Greenland, archaeologists have been able to reconstruct the life and culture of Inuits who lived 500 years ago. (Rev: SLJ 10/98) [930]

17089 Buell, Janet. *Ice Maiden of the Andes* (5–8). Series: Time Travelers. 1997, Twenty-First Century paper $25.90 (978-0-8050-5185-8). The story of the discovery of the frozen body of a young Inca girl who died 500 years ago and of how forensic methods such as DNA testing have revealed insights into Inca society, its religion, and gender roles. (Rev: BL 2/1/98; SLJ 3/98) [985]

17090 Capek, Michael. *Easter Island* (5–8). Series: Unearthing Ancient Worlds. 2008, Lerner LB $30.60 (978-0-8225-7583-2). 80pp. This volume focuses on the statues of Easter Island, exploring their discovery and significance. (Rev: SLJ 10/1/08)

17091 Compoint, Stephane. *Buried Treasures: Uncovering Secrets of the Past* (5–8). Illus. 2011, Abrams $19.95 (978-0-8109-9781-3). 80pp. Suitable mainly for browsing, this volume features eye-catching photographs of discoveries around the world and shots of scientists at work. (Rev: BL 6/1/11; SLJ 7/11) [930.1]

17092 Dean, Arlan. *Terra-Cotta Soldiers: Army of Stone* (4–7). Series: High Interest Books: Digging Up the Past. 2005, Children's Pr. LB $24.50 (978-0-516-25124-0); paper $6.95 (978-0-516-25093-9). For reluctant readers, this is a useful introduction to one of the world's most extraordinary archaeological finds: the 8,000 terracotta warriors of China. (Rev: BL 10/15/05; SLJ 2/06) [931]

17093 Deem, James M. *Bodies from the Ice: Melting Glaciers and the Recovery of the Past* (4–7). Illus. 2008, Houghton $17.00 (978-0-618-80045-2). 64pp. Deem explores what researchers are learning about history and culture as melting glaciers reveal the remains of previously hidden bodies. Sibert Honor; ALA Notable Children's Book. (Rev: BCCB 12/08; BL 12/1/08; HB 1/09; SLJ 12/08*) [599.9]

17094 Funston, Sylvia. *Mummies* (5–7). Illus. by Joe Weissmann. Series: Strange Science. 2000, Owl $19.95 (978-1-894379-03-8); paper $9.95 (978-1-894379-04-5). All kinds of mummified human remains are discussed, from those in ancient Egypt to the 1999 discovery of George Mallory's body on Mount Everest. (Rev: HBG 3/01; SLJ 11/00) [909]

17095 Greene, Meg. *Buttons, Bones, and the Organ-Grinder's Monkey: Tales of Historical Archaeology* (5–8). 2001, Linnet LB $25.00 (978-0-208-02498-5). This introduction to historical archaeology looks at finds at five different sites in the United States. (Rev: BL 10/1/01; HBG 10/02; SLJ 1/02; VOYA 4/02) [973]

17096 Guiberson, Brenda Z. *Mummy Mysteries: Tales from North America* (4–7). Illus. by author. Series: A Redfeather Chapter Book. 1998, Henry Holt $15.95 (978-0-8050-5369-2). Reading like a mystery story, this book focuses on mummies found in North America, how and where they were found, and the information they reveal. (Rev: BCCB 2/99; HBG 3/99; SLJ 12/98) [937]

17097 Halls, Kelly Milner. *Mysteries of the Mummy Kids* (4–6). Illus. 2007, Darby Creek $18.95 (978-1-58196-059-4). Mummified children from around the world are detailed in this compelling survey of the reasons why their bodies were preserved and the ways in which they were found. (Rev: BCCB 5/07; BL 5/1/07; LMC 10/07; SLJ 7/07)

17098 Harris, Nathaniel. *Ancient Maya: Archaeology Unlocks the Secrets of the Maya's Past* (5–8). Series: National Geographic Investigates. 2008, National Geographic $17.95 (978-1-4263-0227-5). With photographs, illustrations, and maps, this book shows how archaeology has uncovered information about the Maya and their culture. (Rev: BL 3/3/08) [972.8]

17099 Harrison, David L. *Cave Detectives: Unraveling the Mystery of an Ice Age Cave* (4–6). Illus. by Ashley Mims. 2007, Chronicle $15.95 (978-0-8118-5006-3). 47pp. This book describes the 2001 discovery of an Ice Age cave and explains how scientists established what prehistoric species lived there. (Rev: BL 5/1/07; SLJ 8/07)

17100 Hartland, Jessie. *How the Sphinx Got to the Museum* (2–4). Illus. by author. 2010, Blue Apple $17.99 (978-1-60905-032-0). 40pp. The life story of Egypt's seven-ton Sphinx is presented in this visually appealing book, which traces the monument's journey from its construction to its current home in New York City's Metropolitan Museum of Art. Lexile AD1120L (Rev: BL 10/1/10*; LMC 3–4/11; SLJ 1/1/11*) [932]

17101 Huey, Lois Miner. *American Archaeology Uncovers the Dutch Colonies* (5–8). Series: American Archaeology. 2009, Marshall Cavendish LB $21.95 (978-0-7614-4263-9). 64pp. Fascinating artifacts and field research bring the Dutch colonies to life in this visually appealing book that includes dig techniques and glimpses at excavation sites. Other recommended titles in this series include *American Archaeology Uncovers the Vikings, American Archaeology Uncovers the Earliest English Colonies, American Archaeology Uncovers the Westward Movement*, and *American Archaeology Uncovers the Underground Railroad* (all 2009). e (Rev: BL 10/1/09; LMC 3–4/10; SLJ 2/1/10) [974.7]

17102 Jameson, W. C. *Buried Treasures of the Atlantic Coast: Legends of Sunken Pirate Treasures, Mysterious Caches, and Jinxed Ships — From Maine to Florida* (4–8). Series: Buried Treasure. 1997, August House $11.95 (978-0-87483-484-0). An account of how buried treasures were acquired and lost and the modern efforts to locate and retrieve them. Also use *Buried Treasures of New England* (1997). (Rev: SLJ 10/97) [910.4]

17103 Kops, Deborah. *Palenque* (5–8). Series: Unearthing Ancient Worlds. 2008, Twenty-First Century LB $30.60 (978-0-8225-7504-7). With many large photographs and interesting text, this volume traces the discovery of the ruins at Palenque in the mid-19th century and the work that has been done since then on this Mayan site. (Rev: LMC 11–12/08; SLJ 2/08)

17104 Lourie, Peter. *The Mystery of the Maya: Uncovering the Lost City of Palenque* (5–8). 2001, Boyds Mills $19.95 (978-1-56397-839-5). The author relates his interesting and often exciting experiences at a dig in Mexico and describes the work of the archaeologists and the history of the site. (Rev: BL 9/15/01; HBG 3/02; SLJ 11/01) [972.75]

17105 Malam, John. *Mummies* (5–8). Series: Kingfisher Knowledge. 2003, Kingfisher $11.95 (978-0-7534-5623-1). A highly illustrated, readable exploration of preserved bodies of all eras and areas of the world. (Rev: HBG 4/04; SLJ 12/03) [393]

17106 Markle, Sandra. *Outside and Inside Mummies* (4–6). Illus. Series: Outside and Inside. 2005, Walker $17.95 (978-0-8027-8966-2). 40pp. This photo-filled title provides an overview of what cutting-edge medical imaging technology reveals about mummies and mummification practices. (Rev: BL 9/15/05; SLJ 8/05)

17107 Panchyk, Richard. *Archaeology for Kids: Uncovering the Mysteries of Our Past with 25 Activities* (5–8). 2001, Chicago Review paper $14.95 (978-1-55652-395-3). An introduction for older readers to the history and scientific method of archaeology, full of illustrations and with interesting activities. (Rev: BL 1/1–15/02; SLJ 12/01) [930.1]

17108 Shuter, Jane. *Ancient China* (4–6). Illus. Series: Excavating the Past. 2005, Heinemann LB $31.43 (978-1-4034-5995-4). The work of archaeologists is clearly shown in this well-illustrated exploration of the early history of China. (Rev: SLJ 2/06)

17109 Smith, K. C. *Exploring for Shipwrecks* (5–7). Series: Shipwrecks. 2000, Watts LB $25.50 (978-0-531-20377-4). 64pp. This book explains and explores the world of underwater archaeology, the techniques and training involved, and gives many examples from specific shipwreck studies. (Rev: BL 10/15/00)

17110 Smith, K. C. *Shipwrecks of the Explorers* (5–7). Illus. Series: Watts Library: Shipwrecks. 2000, Watts LB $25.50 (978-0-531-20378-1). A look at underwater archaeology tells how scientists locate shipwrecks and what the ships reveal about the explorers who sailed in them. There are also descriptions of famous voyages including those of Columbus and Amundsen. (Rev: BL 10/15/00)

17111 Sonneborn, Liz. *Pompeii* (5–8). Series: Unearthing Ancient Worlds. 2008, Lerner LB $30.60 (978-0-8225-7505-4). Concentrating on the original excavation of Pompeii in the 18th century, this book explains how early archaeological digs were conducted. (Rev: BL 4/1/08; SLJ 2/08) [937]

17112 Tanaka, Shelley. *Mummies: The Newest, Coolest and Creepiest from Around the World* (4–7). 2005, Abrams $16.95 (978-0-8109-5797-8). Mummies from across history and around the world are on display in the colorful — and often graphic — pages of this fascinating book. (Rev: BL 12/1/05*; HBG 4/06; LMC 4–5/06; SLJ 12/05*) [393]

17113 Wilcox, Charlotte. *Mummies, Bones, and Body Parts* (4–7). Illus. 2000, Lerner paper $7.95 (978-1-57505-486-5). 64pp. The study of human remains is covered, including material on how death is treated in various cultures, embalming practices, and the work of archaeologists and anthropologists. (Rev: BCCB 9/00; BL 9/1/00; HBG 10/01; SLJ 10/00)

World History

General

17114 Aaseng, Nathan. *You Are the Explorer* (4–8). Series: Great Decisions. 2000, Oliver LB $19.95 (978-1-881508-55-7). In this interactive book about famous explorers, the reader is asked to make decisions similar to those made by real explorers such as Columbus, Cortes, Champlain, and Robert Scott. (Rev: BL 5/1/00; HBG 10/00; SLJ 9/00) [910]

17115 Albee, Sarah. *Poop Happened! A History of the World from the Bottom Up* (4–6). Illus. by Robert Leighton. 2010, Walker LB $20.89 (978-0-8027-9825-1); paper $15.99 (978-0-8027-2077-1). 176pp. A fascinating review of sanitation across the ages, from ancient Egypt and Greece to the problems astronauts face in space; with information on diseases such as cholera and plague. (Rev: BL 2/15/10; LMC 8–9/10; SLJ 5/10) [363.72]

17116 Andryszewski, Tricia. *Walking the Earth: The History of Human Migration* (5–9). 2006, Twenty-First Century LB $27.93 (978-0-7613-3458-3). A thorough introduction to the movements of human population across more than 150,000 years, with many illustrations, maps, and charts. (Rev: HBG 4/07; LMC 3/07; SLJ 1/07; VOYA 12/06) [304.8]

17117 Aronson, Marc, and John W. Glenn. *The World Made New: Why the Age of Exploration Happened and How It Changed the World* (5–8). 2007, National Geographic $17.95 (978-0-7922-6454-5). 64pp. This is an enlightening and well-illustrated survey of world exploration — in particular of European expeditions to the Western Hemisphere in the 15th and 16th centuries — looking at key figures and at the lasting consequences for the people, plants, and animals. (Rev: BL 9/15/07; SLJ 8/07)

17118 Beccia, Carlyn. *The Raucous Royals: Test Your Royal Wits: Crack Codes, Solve Mysteries, and Deduce Which Royal Rumors Are True* (4–7). Illus. by author. 2008, Houghton Mifflin $17 (978-061889130-6). 64pp. Beccia encourages critical thinking in this book that examines the rumors and mystery surrounding eleven royal figure including Richard II, Catherine the Great, Prince Dracula, and Marie Antoinette. (Rev: BL 10/15/08; SLJ 12/08) [929.7]

17119 Blackwood, Gary. *Enigmatic Events* (5–8). Series: Unsolved History. 2005, Marshall Cavendish LB $20.95 (978-0-7614-1889-4). Explores some of history's most enduring mysteries — the disappearance of the dinosaurs and of the *Mary Celeste*, to name only two. (Rev: BL 3/1/06; SLJ 3/06) [904]

17120 Blackwood, Gary L. *Highwaymen* (5–8). Illus. Series: Bad Guys. 2001, Marshall Cavendish LB $29.93 (978-0-7614-1017-1). Period artwork, photographs, and intriguing tales bring real highway robbers, and the times they lived in, to life. (Rev: BL 1/1–15/02; HBG 3/02; SLJ 1/02)

17121 Blackwood, Gary L. *Swindlers* (5–8). Illus. Series: Bad Guys. 2001, Marshall Cavendish LB $29.93 (978-0-7614-1031-7). 72pp. The author presents famous swindlers and cheats throughout history, providing illustrations, source notes, and recommended Web sites and further reading. (Rev: BL 1/1–15/02; HBG 3/02)

17122 Burgan, Michael. *The Spanish Conquest of America: Prehistory to 1775* (5–8). Series: Latino-American History. 2006, Chelsea House LB $35.00 (978-0-8160-6440-3). A thorough and clear account of Spain's influence on the Americas, with discussion of individual explorers as well as the impact on native peoples and the conflicts with other colonial powers. (Rev: BL 3/15/07) [979]

17123 Butts, Ed. *Bodyguards! From Gladiators to the Secret Service* (3–7). Illus. by Scott Plumbe. 2012, Annick $24.95 (978-155451437-3); paper $14.95 (978-1-55451-436-6). 128pp. From samurai to gladiators to bodyguards of Al Capone and Indira Gandhi, this is an entertaining overview of the profession and the tasks these men (and women) perform. (Rev: BL 11/15/12; LMC 8–9/13; SLJ 12/12) [363.28]

17124 Christie, Peter. *The Curse of Akkad: Climate Upheavals That Rocked Human History* (5–8). 2008, Annick $19.95 (978-1-55451-119-8); paper $11.95 (978-1-55451-118-1). The effects of climate change through history are described in segments of one to three pages, making this a good choice for reluctant readers. (Rev: BL 8/08) [551.609]

17125 Connolly, Sean. *Gender Equality* (5–8). Series: Campaigns for Change. 2005, Smart Apple Media LB $29.95 (978-1-58340-515-4). An exploration of women's status and struggles to improve it throughout history; also use *The Right to Vote* (2005). (Rev: SLJ 5/06) [305.42]

17126 Corrigan, Jim. *The 1900s Decade in Photos: A Decade of Discovery* (4–9). Series: Amazing Decades in Photos. 2010, Enslow LB $27.93 (978-0-7660-3129-6). 64pp. With many color photographs and illustrations and simple text, this volume covers events around the world in the first decade of the 20th century. Other titles in this series include *The 1910s Decade in Photos: A Decade That Shook the World, The 1920s Decade in Photos: The Roaring Twenties,* and *The 1930s Decade in Photos: Depression and Hope.* and continue on through the beginning of the 21st century. (Rev: LMC 3–4/10) [973.911]

17127 Deary, Terry. *The Wicked History of the World: History with the Nasty Bits Left In!* (4–7). Illus. by Martin Brown. 2006, Scholastic $10.99 (978-0-439-87786-2). 93pp. This pun-filled survey of world history, with its emphasis on the shadier side, will attract reluctant readers with sections on "Beastly Barbarians," "Rotten Rules," and "Vicious Villains." (Rev: SLJ 12/06)

17128 Defries, Cheryl L. *Seven Natural Wonders of the United States and Canada* (4–7). Series: Seven Wonders of the World. 2005, Enslow LB $25.26 (978-0-7660-5291-8). This tour of seven of North America's natural wonders, including the Grand Canyon, Everglades, and Niagara Falls, is extended by constantly updated links to Web sites. (Rev: SLJ 11/05) [557]

17129 Everett, J. H., and Marilyn Scott Waters. *Haunted Histories: Creepy Castles, Dark Dungeons, and Powerful Palaces* (4–7). 2012, Henry Holt $14.99 (978-0-8050-8971-4). 160pp. Virgil Dante, Ghostarian, shows readers around places (Krak des Chevaliers and the Tower of London, for example), describes life in various dungeons and jails (Newgate Prison, Castle Neuschwanstein, the Bastille), and moves on to ancient palaces and graveyards; includes stories of ghosts and gruesome tortures. e (Rev: LMC 1–2/13; SLJ 7/12) [133.1]

17130 Gelber, Carol. *Masks Tell Stories* (5–7). Series: Beyond Museum Walls. 1993, Millbrook LB $24.90 (978-1-56294-224-3). Explores the nature, meaning, and uses of masks in different cultures at various times. (Rev: BL 8/93) [391]

17131 Gold, Susan Dudley. *Governments of the Western Hemisphere* (5–8). Series: Comparing Continents. 1997, Twenty-First Century LB $24.90 (978-0-8050-5602-0). This book examines the struggles for independence in the United States, Canada, Mexico, Central America,

and South America and the different directions taken by each once independence was achieved, highlighting the diversity across the nations. (Rev: BL 2/1/98; SLJ 3/98) [320.3]

17132 Graham, Amy. *Seven Wonders of the Natural World* (4–7). Series: Seven Wonders of the World. 2005, Enslow LB $25.26 (978-0-7660-5290-1). A tour of seven of the world's natural wonders, including Mount Everest, the Great Barrier Reef, and the Grand Canyon; the text is extended by constantly updated links to Web sites. (Rev: SLJ 11/05)

17133 Guiberson, Brenda Z. *Disasters: Natural and Man-Made Catastrophes Through the Centuries* (5–8). 2010, Henry Holt $18.99 (978-0-8050-8170-1). 256pp. Guiberson presents compelling accounts of 10 well-known disasters including the sinking of the *Titanic*, the Great Chicago Fire, the 1918 flu pandemic, and Hurricane Katrina. (Rev: BL 5/15/10; HB 7–8/10; LMC 8–9/10; SLJ 6/10) [904]

17134 Hansen, Dianne. *Agriculture* (3–5). Series: Yesterday and Today. 2005, Gale LB $23.70 (978-1-56711-827-8). 32pp. A broad overview of the history of agriculture, from the dawn of man through today, with photographs, illustrations and a timelines; suitable for browsing. (Rev: SLJ 7/05)

17135 Harper, Charise Mericle. *Flush! The Scoop on Poop Throughout the Ages* (2–4). Illus. 2007, Little, Brown $15.99 (978-0-316-01064-1). Combining rhyming verse, sidebar facts, and bright illustrations, this paean to poop disposal will fascinate kids drawn to its mix of gross-out humor and arcane historical information. (Rev: BL 1/1–15/07; SLJ 9/06)

17136 Harward, Barnaby. *The Best Book of Pirates* (3–5). Illus. Series: The Best Book Of. 2002, Kingfisher $12.95 (978-0-7534-5449-7). 31pp. Covers pirates through the ages with pirate flags, information on pirate ships and equipment, and a page on contemporary buccaneers. (Rev: HBG 3/03; SLJ 3/03)

17137 Haslam, Andrew. *Living History: The Hands-On Approach to History* (3–6). Illus. Series: Make It Work! 2001, Two-Can $29.95 (978-1-58728-381-9). 256pp. This assemblage of volumes from the Make It Work! series features activities pertaining to daily life in Old Japan, ancient Egypt, ancient Rome, and Native American cultures, such as making togas. (Rev: BL 3/1/02; HBG 3/02)

17138 Hibbert, Clare. *Real Pirates* (3–6). Illus. by John James. 2003, Enchanted Lion $15.95 (978-1-59270-018-9). 48pp. Seagoing bandits of both sexes, from Blackbeard to Anne Bonny, and details of their ships, weapons, and tactics are presented in four geographical areas. (Rev: SLJ 5/04)

17139 Jedicke, Peter. *Great Inventions of the 20th Century* (5–8). Series: Scientific American. 2007, Chelsea House LB $30.00 (978-0-7910-9048-0). With plenty of photographs and clear text, this volume — produced in association with *Scientific American* — presents inventions of the 20th century including cellophane and the microwave in chapters such as "On the Road," "At Home," and "In the Air." (Rev: SLJ 2/08)

17140 Kurlansky, Mark. *The Story of Salt* (4–6). Illus. by S. D. Schindler. 2006, Putnam $16.99 (978-0-399-23998-4). History, science, politics, and technology come together in this story of the sought-after element, adapted from the adult version. (Rev: BL 7/06; SLJ 10/06*)

17141 Lankford, Mary D. *Mazes Around the World* (3–5). Illus. by Karen Dugan. 2008, HarperCollins $16.99 (978-0-688-16519-2). 32pp. Lankford looks at mazes through history, including the Minotaur's labyrinth, religious labyrinths, traditional hedge mazes, and modern water and maize mazes; paintings show each maze's structure. (Rev: BL 4/1/08; LMC 11/06; SLJ 5/08)

17142 Lassieur, Allison. *The History of Pirates: From Privateers to Outlaws* (2–4). Illus. Series: Edge Books: Real World of Pirates. 2006, Capstone LB $23.93 (978-0-7368-6423-7). 32pp. Ideal for beginning readers, this attractive title offers a brief history of pirates with eye-catching illustrations. (Rev: BL 10/15/06)

17143 Lassieur, Allison. *Trade and Commerce in the Early Islamic World* (5–7). Illus. Series: Life in the Early Islamic World. 2012, Crabtree LB $30.60 (978-077872172-7). 48pp. With excellent illustrations, this attractive volume provides a solid introduction to early Islamic trade and commerce and how these activities affected social and cultural life. (Rev: BL 8/12*; SLJ 8/12) [381.0956]

17144 Lauber, Patricia. *What You Never Knew About Beds, Bedrooms, and Pajamas* (2–5). Illus. by John Manders. Series: Around the House History. 2006, Simon & Schuster $16.95 (978-0-689-85211-4). A light history of sleeping customs from the Stone Age to today, with comical commentary in cartoons; suitable for browsing. (Rev: SLJ 2/07)

17145 Lendroth, Susan. *Why Explore?* (K–3). Illus. by Enrique S. Moreiro. 2005, Tricycle $15.95 (978-1-58246-150-2). An interesting overview of human exploration of all kinds over the centuries. (Rev: SLJ 1/06)

17146 Llewellyn, Claire. *Great Discoveries and Amazing Adventures: The Stories of Hidden Marvels and Lost Treasures* (4–7). 2004, Kingfisher $18.95 (978-0-7534-5783-2). Important discoveries — and hoaxes — are described in inviting text, plus many illustrations, factoids, and a foreword by Robert Ballard. (Rev: SLJ 1/05) [509]

17147 Love, Ann, and Jane Drake. *Sweet!* (3–5). Illus. by Claudia Dávila. 2007, Tundra $19.95 (978-0-88776-752-4). This is an appealing survey of candy from ancient history to today, with a running timeline, cartoon illustrations, and many funny and appropriate anecdotes; more suited to browsing than reports. (Rev: BL 2/1/07)

17148 Macaulay, David, and Sheila Keenan. *Castle: How It Works* (K–3). Illus. by David Macaulay. Series: My Readers. 2012, Square Fish $15.99 (978-1-59643-744-9); paper $3.99 (978-1-59643-766-1). 32pp. Beginning readers get a tour of castle structure and castle life in this appealing volume that combines simple but color-

ful text with detailed illustrations. Lexile 500L (Rev: BL 12/1/12*; HB 1–2/13; LMC 1–2/13; SLJ 10/12) [623]

17149 MacDonald, Fiona. *Top 10 Worst Ruthless Warriors You Wouldn't Want to Know!* (4–7). Illus. by David Antram. 2012, Gareth Stevens LB $26.60 (978-143396685-9). 32pp. The exploits of Genghis Khan, Alexander the Great, and Japanese warrior Yoshitsune, among others, are portrayed in this lively and irreverent history that is not for the faint-hearted. Also use *Top 10 Worst Wicked Rulers You Wouldn't Want to Know!* — which introduces Robespierre, Ivan the Terrible, and others. (Rev: BL 4/15/12; SLJ 6/12) [920]

17150 McGowen, Tom. *Assault from the Sea: Amphibious Invasions in the Twentieth Century* (5–8). Series: Military Might. 2002, Twenty-First Century LB $26.90 (978-0-7613-1811-8). 64pp. Invasions launched from the sea during World Wars I and II and the Korean War are the subject of this introduction that includes black-and-white photographs and maps. Also use *Assault from the Sky: Airborne Infantry of World War II* (2002). (Rev: HBG 10/02; SLJ 6/02)

17151 McLaren, Chesley, and Pamela Jaber. *When Royals Wore Ruffles: A Funny and Fashionable Alphabet!* (1–4). Illus. by Chesley McLaren. 2009, Random $16.99 (978-0-375-85166-7). A pleasing alphabetical stroll through all fashion trends from the days of Cleopatra through modern grunge. (Rev: LMC 5/09; SLJ 3/09)

17152 Mara, Wil. *The Seven Continents* (K–2). Series: Rookie Read-About Geography. 2005, Children's Pr. LB $20.50 (978-0-516-22748-1). A broad geographical overview of the continents, with a picture glossary to aid new readers. (Rev: SLJ 7/05)

17153 Markle, Sandra. *Rescues!* (4–7). Illus. 2006, Lerner LB $25.26 (978-0-8225-3413-6). Markle covers rescue efforts in 11 recent disasters (2004 to 2005), giving details of technology used and providing accounts by victims, rescuers, and eyewitnesses. (Rev: BL 4/1/06*; HBG 10/06; LMC 11–12/06; SLJ 8/06; VOYA 6/06) [363.34]

17154 Marsico, Katie. *Stinky Sanitation Inventions* (3–5). Illus. Series: Awesome Inventions You Use Every Day. 2013, Lerner $26.60 (978-146771090-9). 32pp. In this history of sanitation related inventions, Marisco eloquently provides information about toilet paper, portable toilets, diapers, sewers, and other similar products. **e** (Rev: BL 10/1/13; LMC 3–4/14)

17155 Mason, Antony. *People Around the World* (5–7). 2002, Kingfisher $24.95 (978-0-7534-5497-8). An oversize guide to people of different cultures around the world, organized by continent, featuring hundreds of full-color photographs and illustrations, and detailing such topics as diet, language, employment, and leisure of urban and rural dwellers. (Rev: BL 5/1/03; HBG 10/03; SLJ 4/03; VOYA 6/03) [305.8]

17156 Matthews, John. *Pirates* (3–6). 2006, Simon & Schuster $19.95 (978-1-4169-2734-1). The fold-outs, flaps, treasure maps, and other features of this fact-packed interactive book will keep browsers and researchers happy. (Rev: BL 7/06)

17157 Millard, Anne. *A Street Through Time* (4–8). 1998, DK $17.99 (978-0-7894-3426-5). Western European history is traced in this oversize book that contains 14 views of the same riverside location at various times in history, including the Stone Age, Viking times, the Roman period, the Middle Ages, and modern times. (Rev: BL 1/1–15/99; HB 1–2/99; HBG 3/99; SLJ 12/98) [936]

17158 Mooney, Carla. *The Industrial Revolution: Investigate How Science and Technology Changed the World with 25 Projects* (4–7). Illus. by Jen Vaughn. Series: Build It Yourself. 2011, Nomad $21.95 (978-1-936313-81-5); paper $15.95 (978-1-936313-80-8). 128pp. This illustrated title introduces the great minds that gave rise to the Industrial Revolution and showcases their innovations; includes 25 very varied projects. (Rev: BL 12/1/11; SLJ 1/12) [338.0973]

17159 Morris, Neil. *Pirates* (4–6). Illus. Series: Amazing History. 2008, Black Rabbit LB $18.95 (978-1-59920-104-7). 32pp. Double-page spreads look at various aspects of pirates and piracy, including their vessels and equipment, famous individuals, women pirates, and modern forms of piracy. (Rev: BL 4/1/08)

17160 Murrell, Deborah. *Gladiator* (4–7). Series: Qeb Warriors. 2010, Black Rabbit LB $28.50 (978-1-59566-736-6). 32pp. This volume gives arresting descriptions of the lives, battle tactics, and weapons of Roman centurions and Greek hoplites, with maps and eye-catching illustrations. (Rev: LMC 1–2/10)

17161 O'Brien, Patrick. *Mutiny on the Bounty* (4–7). Illus. 2007, Walker $17.95 (978-0-8027-9587-8). 40pp. Clear, balanced narrative and vivid illustrations tell both sides of the story of the famous mutiny and its aftermath. (Rev: BL 1/1–15/07; SLJ 3/07)

17162 Parks, Peggy J. *Clothing* (3–5). Series: Yesterday and Today. 2005, Gale LB $23.70 (978-1-56711-828-5). 32pp. A broad overview of the history of apparel, from the dawn of man through today, with photographs, illustrations and a timelines; suitable for browsing. Also use *Entertainment* (2005). (Rev: SLJ 7/05)

17163 Phillips, Dee. *People of the World* (4–7). Series: Just the Facts. 2006, School Specialty paper $9.95 (978-0-7696-4257-4). Statistics and fast facts on the countries and peoples of the world are presented on double-page spreads. (Rev: BL 4/1/06) [305.8]

17164 Pirotta, Saviour. *Buried Treasure* (3–5). Series: Mysteries of the Past. 2001, Raintree LB $25.69 (978-0-7398-4336-9). 32pp. Egyptian tombs, burial mounds in England, pirate legends, and Nazi loot are among the topics addressed in this overview of underground lore. (Rev: HBG 3/02; SLJ 2/02)

17165 Platt, Richard. *The Scoop on Poop* (4–7). Illus. by John Kelly. 2012, Kingfisher paper $7.99 (978-07534692-3-1). 48pp. An informative and entertaining survey of waste material and its treatment through the ages. (Rev: BL 12/1/12) [392.3]

17166 Price, Sean Stewart. *The Kids' Guide to Lost Cities* (3–5). Illus. Series: Kids' Guides. 2011, Capstone LB $26.65 (978-142966009-9). 32pp. Machu Picchu and Pompeii are among the lost cities discussed in this historical survey. (Rev: BL 2/15/12) [930.1]

17167 Pringle, Laurence. *Ice! The Amazing History of the Ice Business* (4–6). Illus. 2012, Boyds Mills/Calkins Creek $17.95 (978-159078801-1). 80pp. A fascinating account of how we have used and stored ice over the years. (Rev: BL 10/15/12; LMC 3–4/13) [551]

17168 Romanek, Trudee. *Science, Medicine, and Math in the Early Islamic World* (5–7). Illus. Series: Life in the Early Islamic World. 2012, Crabtree LB $30.60 (978-077872170-3). 48pp. With excellent illustrations, this attractive volume provides a solid introduction to science, medicine, and math in the early Islamic world and emphasizes how advanced these fields were. (Rev: BL 8/12*; SLJ 8/12) [509.56]

17169 Roop, Peter, and Connie Roop. *Tales of Famous Animals* (4–8). Illus. by Zachary Pullen. 2012, Scholastic $17.99 (978-0-545-43029-6). 112pp. Roop recounts the achievements of 17 famous animals ranging from Bucephalus to Balto, Seabiscuit, and Punxsutawney Phil. (Rev: BL 12/1/12; SLJ 12/12) [591]

17170 Ross, Stewart. *Conquerors and Explorers* (5–7). Series: Fact or Fiction? 1996, Millbrook LB $26.90 (978-0-7613-0532-3). The subtitle of this work is "The Greed, Cunning, and Bravery of the Travelers and Plunderers Who Opened Up the World." (Rev: BL 10/15/96; SLJ 4/97) [910]

17171 Ross, Stewart. *Into the Unknown: How Great Explorers Found Their Way by Land, Sea, and Air* (4–8). Illus. by Stephen Biesty. 2011, Candlewick $19.99 (978-0-7636-4948-7). 96pp. A handsome and informative overview of 14 important journeys of exploration, starting in 340 B.C. with Pytheas the Greek's voyage to the Arctic Circle and ending in 1969 with Neil Armstrong and Buzz Aldrin's landing on the moon. Boston Globe–Horn Book Honor 2011; ALA Notable Children's Book 2012. (Rev: BL 7/11; HB 5–6/11; LMC 10/11; SLJ 5/11*) [910.9]

17172 Ruggiero, Adriane. *The Ottoman Empire* (5–8). Series: Cultures of the Past. 2002, Marshall Cavendish $29.93 (978-0-7614-1494-0). 80pp. A handsome account that traces the rise and fall of the great Ottoman Empire from its beginning in the 15th century to its collapse and the formation of modern Turkey after World War I. (Rev: BL 1/1–15/03; HBG 3/03; SLJ 2/03)

17173 Rumford, James. *From the Good Mountain: How Gutenberg Changed the World* (1–3). Illus. by author. 2012, Roaring Brook $17.99 (978-1-59643-542-1). 40pp. A profile of Gutenberg and his invention of the moveable printing press is combined with a clear and engaging explanation, presented in riddles, of how books are made. ☐ (Rev: BL 8/12; HB 11–12/12; LMC 1–2/13; SLJ 9/12*) [686.2092]

17174 Rumford, James. *Traveling Man: The Journey of Ibn Battuta, 1325–1354* (3–6). Illus. by author. 2001,

Houghton $16.00 (978-0-618-08366-4). Rumford retells the story of the epic travels across Asia and Africa of the 14th-century explorer and scholar Ibn Battuta, with lyric text that flows through the beautiful illustrations. (Rev: HB 1/02; HBG 3/02; SLJ 10/01)

17175 Rutsala, David. *The Sea Route to Asia* (4–7). Series: Exploration and Discovery. 2002, Mason Crest LB $19.95 (978-1-59084-046-7). 64pp. Rutsala presents Portuguese explorers' efforts to find a route around Africa to Asia, with information on Prince Henry the Navigator, Bartholomeu Dias, and Vasco da Gama. (Rev: SLJ 12/02)

17176 Scandiffio, Laura. *Escapes!* (5–9). Illus. by Stephen MacEachern. Series: True Stories from the Edge. 2004, Annick $18.95 (978-1-55037-823-8); paper $7.95 (978-1-55037-822-1). Ten stories of great escapes and escape attempts, from the first century B.C. to the late 1970s, with a concentration on resourcefulness and bravery. (Rev: SLJ 6/04) [904]

17177 Seibert, Patricia. *We Were Here: A Short History of Time Capsules* (3–6). Illus. 2002, Millbrook LB $22.90 (978-0-7613-0423-4). A history of time capsules, including the Century Safe that was assembled in 1876 and opened in 1976. (Rev: BL 4/1/02; HBG 10/02; SLJ 3/02)

17178 Shapiro, Stephen. *Battle Stations! Fortifications Through the Ages* (5–8). 2005, Annick LB $19.95 (978-1-55037-889-4); paper $7.95 (978-1-55037-888-7). A tall, slim, and very visual overview of fortifications around the world and throughout history. (Rev: BL 9/15/05) [355.7]

17179 Sharp, S. Pearl, and Virginia Schomp. *The Slave Trade and the Middle Passage* (5–8). Series: Drama of African-American History. 2006, Benchmark LB $23.95 (978-0-7614-2176-4). 70pp. A brief overview of the triangular trade between Africa, the American colonies, and Europe, looking at conditions aboard the slave ships. (Rev: SLJ 5/07)

17180 Swain, Ruth Freeman. *Underwear: What We Wear Under There* (2–4). Illus. by John O'Brien. 2008, Holiday $16.95 (978-0-8234-1920-3). 32pp. Swain takes a humorous look at underwear developments through the ages. (Rev: BL 12/1/08; SLJ 12/08)

17181 Swanson, Diane. *Tunnels!* (5–8). Series: True Stories from the Edge. 2003, Annick $18.95 (978-1-55037-781-1); paper $6.95 (978-1-55037-780-4). Ten thrilling stories of tunnel escapes and escapades are accompanied by maps. (Rev: BL 4/15/03; SLJ 5/03) [624.1]

17182 Wells, Don. *The Spice Trade* (5–8). Illus. Series: Great Journeys. 2004, Weigl $26.00 (978-1-59036-208-2); paper $7.95 (978-1-59036-261-7). 32pp. Colorful illustrations and an attractive format will appeal to browsers seeking information about the spice trade; a useful timeline and links to Web sites are included. (Rev: BL 11/1/04)

17183 Wilson, Janet. *Imagine That!* (4–8). Illus. by author. 2000, Stoddart $14.95 (978-0-7737-3221-6). In the form of a reminiscence by 100-year-old Auntie Violet,

this is a brief history of the past century, with major events highlighted. (Rev: SLJ 11/00) [909]

17184 Wojtanik, Andrew. *Afghanistan to Zimbabwe: Country Facts That Helped Me Win the National Geographic Bee* (5–12). 2005, National Geographic paper $12.95 (978-0-7922-7981-5). Facts and figures about the world's 192 independent countries are organized into three categories: Physical, Political, and Environmental/ Economic. (Rev: SLJ 10/05; VOYA 8/05) [910]

17185 Worth, Richard. *The Great Empire of China and Marco Polo in World History* (5–8). Illus. Series: In World History. 2003, Enslow LB $26.60 (978-0-7660-1939-3). 112pp. Quotations from primary documents and excerpts from Polo's own writings add context to this account of his 13th-century journeys to the Far East. (Rev: SLJ 3/04)

17186 Wyatt, Valerie. *Who Discovered America?* (4–7). Illus. by Howie Woo. 2008, Kids Can $17.95 (978-1-55453-128-8); paper $8.95 (978-1-55453-129-5). 40pp. This large-format book examines who arrived on this continent first, introducing the possible candidates and providing lots of interesting information on archaeological finds and how researchers approach this question. (Rev: BL 10/1/08; SLJ 2/09) [970.01]

Ancient History

General and Miscellaneous

17187 Anderson, Jameson. *History and Activities of Ancient China* (3–6). Illus. Series: Hands-on Ancient History. 2006, Heinemann LB $28.21 (978-1-4034-7922-8). 32pp. Social life, arts and culture, games, and holidays and celebrations are covered in this attractive and accessible volume that includes a recipe and two crafts. (Rev: HBG 4/07; SLJ 4/07)

17188 Apte, Sunita. *The Aztec Empire* (3–5). Series: True Book Ancient Civilizations. 2009, Children's Press LB $26 (978-0-531-25227-7). 48pp. Taking care to distinguish between fact and legend, this attractive volume discusses the Aztec empire's people and culture and the ruins that reveal information about them. (Rev: LMC 1–2/10; SLJ 12/1/09) [972]

17189 Ball, Jacqueline, and Richard H. Levey. *Ancient China: Archaeology Unlocks the Secrets of China's Past* (5–8). Illus. Series: National Geographic Investigates. 2006, National Geographic $17.95 (978-0-7922-7783-5). 64pp. After an introduction to China and its history, this volume looks at individual archaeological finds and at the lives revealed; vivid illustrations and good descriptions of archaeological techniques add to the value. (Rev: BL 10/15/06)

17190 Barter, James. *The Ancient Persians* (5–8). Series: Lost Civilizations. 2005, Gale LB $29.95 (978-1-59018-621-3). The lost civilization of the ancient Persians, with information about the society's people, customs, monetary system, and military, with maps and illustrations. (Rev: SLJ 6/06) [935]

17191 Bingham, Jane. *The Ancient World* (5–8). Series: A History of Fashion and Costume. 2005, Facts on File $35.00 (978-0-8160-5944-7). A broad overview of the clothing and personal adornment worn during ancient times, with many visual aids. (Rev: SLJ 5/06) [391]

17192 Broida, Marian. *Ancient Israelites and Their Neighbors: An Activity Guide* (4–7). 2003, Chicago Review paper $16.95 (978-1-55652-457-8). Readers will find out what life was like for the ancient Israelites, Phoenicians, and Philistines through the information and activities in this attractive book. Sidney Taylor Book Honor 2003. (Rev: BL 5/15/03; SLJ 8/03) [933]

17193 Calvert, Patricia. *The Ancient Celts* (5–8). Series: People of the Ancient World. 2005, Watts LB $30.50 (978-0-531-12359-1); paper $9.95 (978-0-531-16845-5). Introduces readers to the arts, religious beliefs, and society of the ancient Celts, with discussion of individual occupations and of the discoveries by archaeologists and anthropologists. (Rev: SLJ 9/05) [973]

17194 Croy, Anita, ed. *Ancient Aztec and Maya* (5–9). Series: Facts at Your Fingertips. 2010, Black Rabbit LB $35.65 (978-1-933834-58-0). 64pp. After presenting historical facts about the Aztec and Mayan civilizations, this volume goes on to look at specific sites and the cultures of these peoples. (Rev: LMC 3–4/10) [972]

17195 Curlee, Lynn. *Seven Wonders of the Ancient World* (3–6). Illus. 2002, Simon & Schuster $17.00 (978-0-689-83182-9). 40pp. An informative introduction for older readers to the wonders of the ancient world, with precise illustrations and thought-provoking text. (Rev: BCCB 3/02; BL 1/1–15/02; HBG 10/02; SLJ 9/02)

17196 Galloway, Priscilla, and Dawn Hunter. *Adventures on the Ancient Silk Road* (5–8). 2009, Annick $24.95 (978-1-55451-198-3); paper $14.95 (978-1-55451-197-6). 164pp. The ancient trade route is brought to life in accounts of three travelers many years apart: the monk Xuanzang, the conqueror Genghis Khan, and the merchant Marco Polo. (Rev: BL 1/1/10; SLJ 12/09) [950]

17197 Greene, Jacqueline D. *Slavery in Ancient Greece and Rome* (4–7). Series: Watts Library: History of Slavery. 2000, Watts LB $25.50 (978-0-531-11693-7). 64pp. Topics covered include the treatment of slaves in Greece and Rome, how they thrived in Greece's democracy, the slave fire brigades, battles of slave gladiators, and the attitudes toward slavery in the early Christian church. (Rev: BL 3/1/01; SLJ 3/01)

17198 Hook, Jason. *Lost Cities* (3–5). Series: Mysteries of the Past. 2001, Raintree LB $25.69 (978-0-7398-4337-6). 32pp. Ur, Knossos, Babylon, and Troy are among the cities addressed in this introduction to the mysteries surrounding the sites and the efforts to uncover the truth. (Rev: HBG 3/02; SLJ 2/02)

17199 Hunter, Erica C. D., and Mike Corbishley. *First Civilizations. Rev. ed.* (5–8). Illus. Series: Cultural Atlas for Young People. 2003, Facts on File $35.00 (978-0-8160-5149-6). 96pp. Colorful topical spreads introduce

readers to the culture, geography, history, and politics of Mesopotamia, Persia, and Assyria. (Rev: SLJ 1/04)

17200 Jestice, Phyllis G. *Ancient Persian Warfare* (3–6). Series: Ancient Warfare. 2010, Gareth Stevens LB $26 (978-1-4339-1973-2). 32pp. In chapters on foot soldiers, fighting with horses, weapons and armor, and war at sea, this volume looks at the armies of ancient Persia and the famous leaders of the time. (Rev: SLJ 6/10) [355.02]

17201 Jovinelly, Joann, and Jason Netelkos. *The Crafts and Culture of the Ancient Hebrews* (5–8). Illus. Series: Crafts of the Ancient World. 2002, Rosen LB $29.25 (978-0-8239-3511-6). 48pp. The crafts of the ancient Hebrews and projects related to them are used to give basic information on their history and how they lived. (Rev: BL 4/1/02)

17202 Levy, Elizabeth. *Awesome Ancient Ancestors! Mound Builders, Maya, and More* (5–8). Illus. by Daniel McFeely. Series: America's Horrible Histories. 2001, Scholastic $12.95 (978-0-439-30349-1); paper $4.99 (978-0-590-10795-2). 156pp. A humorous and chatty cockroach introduces the early inhabitants of North America and Mesoamerica. (Rev: HBG 10/02; SLJ 5/02)

17203 Linnea, Sharon. *Lost Civilizations* (4–7). Illus. by Josh Cochran. Series: Mysteries Unwrapped. 2009, Sterling paper $5.95 (978-1-4027-3984-2). 96pp. This book discusses five famous lost civilizations: Ur, the Mayan Empire, Atlantis, Pompeii, and Angkor Wat. (Rev: BL 7/09)

17204 Maloy, Jackie. *The Ancient Maya* (3–5). Series: True Book Ancient Civilizations. 2009, Children's Press LB $26 (978-0-531-25229-1). 48pp. Taking care to distinguish between fact and legend, this attractive volume discusses the ancient Maya's culture and the ruins that reveal information about them. (Rev: LMC 1–2/10; SLJ 12/1/09) [972]

17205 Miller, Reagan. *Communication in the Ancient World* (5–7). Illus. Series: Life in the Ancient World. 2011, Crabtree LB $19.95 (978-077871733-1); paper $8.95 (978-077871740-9). 32pp. This accessible book explores the development of writing, counting, and calendars in various cultures — Rome, South America, Egypt, Japan — around the ancient world. (Rev: BL 10/1/11; LMC 9–10/12) [302.2]

17206 Newman, Sandra. *The Inca Empire* (3–5). Series: True Book Ancient Civilizations. 2009, Children's Press LB $26 (978-0-531-25228-4). 48pp. Taking care to distinguish between fact and legend, this attractive volume discusses the Inca people and culture and the ruins that reveal information about them. (Rev: BL 10/1/09; LMC 1–2/10; SLJ 12/1/09) [985]

17207 Perl, Lila. *The Ancient Maya* (5–8). Series: People of the Ancient World. 2005, Watts LB $30.50 (978-0-531-12381-2); paper $9.95 (978-0-531-16848-6). Introduces readers to the arts, religious beliefs, and society of the Maya, with discussion of individual occupations and of the discoveries by archaeologists and anthropologists. (Rev: SLJ 9/05) [973]

17208 Price, Massoume. *Ancient Iran* (4–8). Illus. Series: Culture of Iran Youth Series. 2008, Anahita $19.95 (978-0-9809714-0-8). 72pp. After a brief discussion of Iran today, this well-illustrated volume gives a chronological overview of the peoples and culture of ancient Iran. (Rev: SLJ 3/1/09) [935]

17209 Raum, Elizabeth. *What Did the Vikings Do for Me?* (4–7). Illus. Series: Linking Past to Present. 2010, Heinemann LB $29 (978-143293745-4). 32pp. This intriguing overview of Viking history and culture also explains their legacy in aspects including language, justice, and the role of women. (Rev: BL 10/1/10; LMC 1–2/11) [948]

17210 Richardson, Hazel. *Life in Ancient Africa* (4–7). Series: Peoples of the Ancient World. 2005, Crabtree LB $26.60 (978-0-7787-2043-0); paper $8.95 (978-0-7787-2073-7). Introduces the early civilizations of Africa, examining their arts, spiritual beliefs, government, language, and technology; color photographs, sidebars, and timelines add information and appeal. (Rev: SLJ 11/05) [973]

17211 Richardson, Hazel. *Life in Ancient Japan* (4–7). Series: Peoples of the Ancient World. 2005, Crabtree LB $26.60 (978-0-7787-2041-6); paper $8.95 (978-0-7787-2071-3). Introduces ancient Japan's arts, spiritual beliefs, government, language, and technology; color photographs, sidebars, and timelines add information and appeal. (Rev: SLJ 11/05) [952]

17212 Richardson, Hazel. *Life in the Ancient Indus River Valley* (4–7). Series: Peoples of the Ancient World. 2005, Crabtree LB $26.60 (978-0-7787-2040-9); paper $8.95 (978-0-7787-2070-6). Introduces life in the earliest urban civilization on the Indian subcontinent, examining the arts, spiritual beliefs, government, language, and technology; color photographs, sidebars, and timelines add information and appeal. (Rev: SLJ 11/05) [973]

17213 Richardson, Hazel. *Life of the Ancient Celts* (4–7). Series: Peoples of the Ancient World. 2005, Crabtree LB $26.60 (978-0-7787-2045-4); paper $8.95 (978-0-7787-2075-1). Introduces the early Celtic civilization, examining arts, spiritual beliefs, government, language, and technology; color photographs, sidebars, and timelines add information and appeal. (Rev: SLJ 11/05) [973]

17214 Service, Pamela F. *300 B.C.* (5–8). Series: Around the World In. 2002, Benchmark $29.93 (978-0-7614-1080-5). The author explores what was going on in Europe, Africa, Asia, and the Americas in the year 300 B.C. Also use *1200* (2002). (Rev: HBG 3/03; SLJ 2/03) [930]

17215 Smith, K. C. *Ancient Shipwrecks* (5–7). Series: Shipwrecks. 2000, Watts LB $25.50 (978-0-531-20381-1). From the Bronze Age through the Roman Empire, this volume explores the fascinating stories behind ancient wrecks found in the Mediterranean and explored by archaeologists. (Rev: BL 10/15/00)

17216 Sonneborn, Liz. *The Ancient Kushites* (5–8). Series: People of the Ancient World. 2005, Watts LB $30.50 (978-0-531-12380-5). Explores the arts, religious beliefs, and culture of Africa's ancient Kushites, who were also known as Nubians. (Rev: SLJ 9/05) [973]

17217 Stefoff, Rebecca. *The Ancient Mediterranean* (5–8). Series: World Historical Atlases. 2004, Benchmark LB $27.07 (978-0-7614-1641-8). Maps, text, and illustrations give a broad overview of the cultures found in the ancient Mediterranean. Also use *The Ancient Near East* and *The Asian Empires* (both 2004). (Rev: SLJ 2/05) [930]

17218 Trumble, Kelly. *The Library of Alexandria* (5–7). Illus. by Robina MacIntyre Marshall. 2003, Clarion $17.00 (978-0-395-75832-8). An introduction to the famous library, its collection, its scholars, and its destruction by fire. (Rev: BCCB 1/04; BL 11/15/03; HBG 4/04; SLJ 1/04) [027.032]

17219 Wells, Donald. *The Silk Road* (5–8). Series: Great Journeys. 2004, Weigl LB $26.00 (978-1-59036-207-5). Colorful illustrations and an attractive format will appeal to browsers seeking information on this ancient trade route; a useful timeline and links to Web sites are included. (Rev: BL 11/1/04)

17220 Woods, Michael. *Ancient Agriculture: From Foraging to Farming* (5–8). Series: Ancient Technologies. 2000, Runestone LB $25.26 (978-0-8225-2995-8). 88pp. Beginning with prehistoric food-gathering peoples, this book traces the history of plant cultivation and agriculture through each of the great ancient civilizations. (Rev: BL 8/00; HBG 10/00; SLJ 6/00)

17221 Woods, Michael, and Mary B. Woods. *Ancient Medicine: From Sorcery to Surgery* (5–8). Illus. Series: Ancient Technologies. 2000, Lerner LB $25.26 (978-0-8225-2992-7). 88pp. Medical practices in ancient times and cultures — the Stone Age, ancient Egypt, and early Hindu cultures, for example — are discussed in this volume. (Rev: BL 1/1–15/00; HBG 10/00; SLJ 5/00; VOYA 6/00)

17222 Woods, Michael, and Mary B. Woods. *Ancient Transportation: From Camels to Canals* (5–8). Illus. Series: Ancient Technologies. 2000, Lerner LB $25.26 (978-0-8225-2993-4). 88pp. This book covers such topics related to early transportation as the first bridges and roads, early skis and sleds, primitive wagons, and the beginnings of maps. (Rev: BL 1/1–15/00; HBG 10/00; SLJ 6/00; VOYA 6/00)

Egypt and Mesopotamia

17223 Adams, Simon. *Ancient Egypt* (4–6). Illus. Series: Kingfisher Voyages. 2006, Kingfisher $15.95 (978-0-7534-6027-6). 54pp. Viewed from the perspective of an Egyptologist named Dr. Kent Weeks, this is a tour of important sites of ancient Egypt, with discussion of the embalming and engineering practices of the time and the modern technologies that have uncovered the answers to some mysteries. (Rev: SLJ 2/07)

17224 Adamson, Heather. *Ancient Egypt: An Interactive History Adventure* (3–5). Illus. 2009, Capstone LB $27.98 (978-142963415-1). 112pp. In this engaging history book with a choose-your-own-adventure twist, readers select which role they'd like to play in ancient Egypt, from slave to pharaoh. (Rev: BL 7/10; LMC 1–2/10) [932]

17225 Bailey, Linda. *Adventures in Ancient Egypt* (2–5). Illus. Series: Good Times Travel Agency. 2000, Kids Can $14.95 (978-1-55074-546-7); paper $7.95 (978-1-55074-548-1). Using an old travel guide, three children are transported to Egypt in 2500 B.C. where they become acquainted with the sights and sites as well as becoming involved in a series of adventures. (Rev: BL 1/1–15/01; HBG 3/01; SLJ 12/00)

17226 Berger, Melvin, and Gilda Berger. *Mummies of the Pharaohs: Exploring the Valley of the Kings* (4–7). 2001, National Geographic $17.95 (978-0-7922-7223-6). Beginning with King Tut's tomb and continuing through other sites, this book uses stunning photographs and a clear text to describe workings of archaeological digs that are studying Egypt's past. (Rev: BL 2/1/01) [932]

17227 Briscoe, Diana C. *King Tut: Tales from the Tomb* (3–5). Illus. Series: High Five Reading. 2002, Capstone LB $23.93 (978-0-7368-9553-8). 48pp. For reluctant readers, this is a dramatic account of the discovery of the tomb, the life and death of the young Tut, the process of mummification, and the so-called mummy's curse. (Rev: HBG 10/03; SLJ 8/03)

17228 Broida, Marian. *Ancient Egyptians and Their Neighbors: An Activity Guide* (4–8). 1999, Chicago Review paper $16.95 (978-1-55652-360-1). The lives and times of the ancient Egyptians, Nubians, Hittites, and Mesopotamians are examined using text and a series of 40 fascinating projects. (Rev: BL 3/15/00; SLJ 2/00) [939]

17229 Burgan, Michael. *The Curse of King Tut's Tomb* (3–6). Illus. by Barbara Schulz. Series: Graphic Library/ Graphic History. 2004, Capstone LB $26.60 (978-0-7368-3833-7). 32pp. A graphic "novel" — factual, but embellished — about the discovery of Tut's tomb and the legendary curse associated with it; will appeal to reluctant readers. (Rev: SLJ 7/05)

17230 Chrisp, Peter. *Mesopotamia: Iraq in Ancient Times* (4–7). Series: Picturing the Past. 2004, Enchanted Lion $15.95 (978-1-59270-024-0). History and archaeology are the highlights of this nicely illustrated overview of Mesopotamian civilization. (Rev: BL 10/15/04; SLJ 11/04) [935]

17231 Chrisp, Peter. *Pyramid* (4–8). Illus. Series: DK Experience. 2006, DK $15.99 (978-0-7566-1410-2). 67pp. Full-color illustrations, 3-D diagrams, and CT scans make this survey of the construction and importance of the Great Pyramid of Giza informative and attractive. (Rev: SLJ 11/06)

17232 Cline, Eric H., and Jill Rubalcaba. *The Ancient Egyptian World* (5–10). Series: The World in Ancient Times. 2005, Oxford LB $32.95 (978-0-19-517391-8). An overview of ancient Egyptian history and culture, with chronologically arranged chapters covering religion, medicine, clothing, arts, and so forth and introduc-

ing key figures such as Hatshepsut, Tutankhamen, and Cleopatra. (Rev: SLJ 1/06) [932]

17233 Croy, Anita, ed. *Ancient Egypt* (5–9). Series: Facts at Your Fingertips. 2010, Black Rabbit LB $35.65 (978-1-933834-54-2). 64pp. After presenting historical facts about ancient Egypt before and after the pharaohs, this volume goes on to look at specific sites of importance — Abu Simbel, Thebes, Memphis, and so forth. Also use *Ancient Mesopotamia* (2010). (Rev: LMC 3–4/10) [932.222]

17234 Day, Nancy. *Your Travel Guide to Ancient Egypt* (4–8). Series: Passport to History. 2000, Runestone LB $26.50 (978-0-8225-3075-6). Written in the style of a modern-day travel guide, this book on ancient Egypt covers such subjects as sites to see, food, clothing, religious beliefs, politics, and daily life. (Rev: BL 11/15/00; HBG 3/01; SLJ 5/01; VOYA 8/01) [932]

17235 England, Victoria. *Top 10 Worst Things About Ancient Egypt You Wouldn't Want to Know* (4–7). Illus. by David Antram. 2012, Gareth Stevens LB $26.60 (978-143396688-0). 32pp. Starvation, irascible pharaohs, and drudging stone cutting and hauling work are a few of the things ancient Egyptians had to endure; this lively and irreverent history book will appeal to browsers and reluctant readers. (Rev: BL 4/15/12; SLJ 6/12) [932]

17236 Filer, Joyce. *Pyramids* (3–8). Illus. 2006, Oxford Univ. $19.99 (978-0-19-530521-0). 48pp. A detailed introduction to the pyramids of ancient Egypt and their design, their builders, their construction, and their contents; there is also information on pyramids outside Egypt. (Rev: SLJ 7/06)

17237 Gibbons, Gail. *Mummies, Pyramids, and Pharaohs: A Book About Ancient Egypt* (PS–2). 2004, Little, Brown $16.95 (978-0-316-30928-8). 32pp. The history and mysteries of ancient Egypt — including mummies, pharaohs, and pyramids — are explored in an engaging blend of brief, simple narrative and ink-and-watercolor artwork. (Rev: BL 6/1–15/04; SLJ 6/04)

17238 Greene, Jacqueline D. *Slavery in Ancient Egypt and Mesopotamia* (4–7). Series: Watts Library: History of Slavery. 2000, Watts LB $25.50 (978-0-531-11692-0). 64pp. This unusual book covers the earliest forms of slavery, how the pharaohs used slaves to construct the pyramids, and the place of slavery in Hebrew society. (Rev: BL 3/1/01; SLJ 3/01)

17239 Harris, Geraldine. *Ancient Egypt. Rev. ed.* (5–8). Illus. Series: Cultural Atlas for Young People. 2003, Facts on File $35.00 (978-0-8160-5148-9). 96pp. Colorful topical spreads introduce readers to the culture, history, and politics of ancient Egypt. (Rev: SLJ 1/04; VOYA 2/04)

17240 Hawass, Zahi. *Curse of the Pharaohs: My Adventures with Mummies* (4–6). 2004, National Geographic $19.95 (978-0-7922-6665-5). 160pp. Excellent photographs and detailed endmatter add to the interesting discussion of mysteries associated with the tombs of the pharaohs. (Rev: BL 6/1–15/04; SLJ 11/04)

17241 Hibbert, Clare. *Ancient Egypt* (3–6). Illus. by Adam Hook. Series: Rich and Poor in. 2005, Smart Apple LB $27.10 (978-1-58340-720-2). 32pp. Compares the everyday lives of the rich and the poor in ancient Egypt. (Rev: SLJ 5/06)

17242 Hollar, Sherman. *Ancient Egypt* (5–8). Series: Ancient Civilizations. 2011, Britannica Educational LB $31.70 (978-1-61530-523-0). 88pp. This slim volume offers an accessible introduction to the culture, religion, architecture, and inventions of ancient Egypt. ℮ (Rev: SLJ 12/1/11) [932]

17243 Hynson, Colin. *The Building of the Great Pyramid* (5–8). Illus. Series: Stories from History. 2006, School Specialty $9.95 (978-0-7696-4708-1); paper $6.95 (978-0-7696-4692-3). 48pp. Full-color illustrations and graphic novel format make this survey of the ancient engineering feat attractive to reluctant readers. (Rev: SLJ 1/07)

17244 Jestice, Phyllis G. *Ancient Egyptian Warfare* (3–6). Illus. Series: Ancient Warfare. 2010, Gareth Stevens LB $26 (978-1-4339-1971-8). 32pp. In chapters on foot soldiers, fighting with horses, weapons and armor, and war at sea, this volume looks at the armies of ancient Egypt and the famous leaders of the time. (Rev: SLJ 6/10) [355.0]

17245 Jovinelly, Joann, and Jason Netelkos. *The Crafts and Culture of the Ancient Egyptians* (5–8). Series: Crafts of the Ancient World. 2002, Rosen LB $29.25 (978-0-8239-3509-3). 48pp. As well as learning about the mysteries of ancient Egypt, readers can engage in such craft projects as designing a pharaoh's headdress and necklace and re-creating an ancient marbles game. (Rev: BL 5/15/02; SLJ 6/02)

17246 Kaplan, Sarah Pitt. *The Great Pyramid at Giza: Tomb of Wonders* (5–8). Series: Digging Up the Past. 2005, Children's Pr. LB $24.50 (978-0-516-25131-8); paper $6.95 (978-0-516-25095-3). A richly illustrated survey of the important pyramid and the reasons for its creation; suitable for reluctant readers. (Rev: SLJ 2/06) [932]

17247 Kennett, David. *Pharaoh: Life and Afterlife of a God* (4–7). Illus. by author. 2008, Walker $18.95 (978-0-8027-9567-0). This attractive book introduces readers to the elaborate burial of Seti I and in doing so also explains many aspects of life in ancient Egypt, for royalty as well as common people. (Rev: BL 5/1/08; SLJ 2/08) [932]

17248 Lace, William W. *The Curse of King Tut* (5–8). Illus. Series: Mysterious & Unknown. 2007, Reference Point LB $24.95 (978-1-60152-024-1). Readers will learn factual information about the discovery of King Tutankhamen's tomb while searching for the truth about his "curse." (Rev: BL 10/15/07; LMC 2/08; SLJ 2/08) [932]

17249 McCall, Henrietta. *Egyptian Mummies* (3–5). Illus. by David Antram. Series: Fast Forward. 2000, Watts paper $9.95 (978-0-531-16443-3). 32pp. A concise look at mummies and embalming that uses split spreads that

can be opened to reveal additional information. (Rev: SLJ 6/01)

17250 McNeill, Sarah. *Ancient Egyptian People* (4–8). Series: People and Places. 1997, Millbrook LB $21.90 (978-0-7613-0056-4). This basic introduction to the people of ancient Egypt and how they lived consists of several attractive double-page spreads and a brief text. (Rev: BL 2/15/97; SLJ 3/97) [932]

17251 McNeill, Sarah. *Ancient Egyptian Places* (4–8). Series: People and Places. 1997, Millbrook LB $21.90 (978-0-7613-0057-1). Some of the great constructions of ancient Egypt are pictured in a series of elegant double-page spreads with a simple text. (Rev: BL 2/15/97; SLJ 3/97) [932]

17252 Malam, John. *Ancient Egypt* (5–8). Series: Remains to Be Seen. 1998, Evans Brothers $19.95 (978-0-237-51839-4). This introduction to ancient Egypt's culture and history is organized in double-page spreads and is noteworthy for its many sidebars, charts, and illustrations. (Rev: SLJ 9/98) [932]

17253 Malam, John. *Ancient Egypt* (3–6). Illus. Series: Picturing the Past. 2004, Enchanted Lion $15.95 (978-1-59270-021-9). 32pp. Well-written two-page chapters cover geography, history, government, religion, the arts, and home life, with maps, photos and illustrations, and informative sidebars detailing sources. (Rev: SLJ 11/04)

17254 Malam, John. *Ancient Egyptian Jobs* (5–7). Illus. 2002, Heinemann LB $27.07 (978-1-4034-0311-7). 48pp. The daily activities of workers such as scribes, bakers, dancers, jewelers, pyramid builders, and embalmers are described in this slim volume that also offers a general introduction to ancient Egypt. (Rev: HBG 10/03; SLJ 4/03)

17255 Mann, Elizabeth. *The Great Pyramid* (4–7). Series: Wonders of the World. 1996, Mikaya $19.95 (978-0-9650493-1-3). The building of this architectural marvel is told graphically, with details on the society of ancient Egypt. (Rev: BL 2/1/97; SLJ 6/97*) [932]

17256 Manning, Mick, and Brita Granström. *Fly on the Wall: Pharaoh's Egypt* (2–4). Illus. by authors. 2006, Frances Lincoln $15.95 (978-1-84507-100-4). Ancient Egypt's way of life — its history, culture, and mythology in particular — is shown in an appealing scrapbook format full of facts and following several characters as they go about their business. (Rev: SLJ 4/06)

17257 Manning, Ruth. *Ancient Egyptian Women* (5–8). Illus. Series: People in the Past. 2002, Heinemann LB $27.07 (978-1-4034-0313-1). A look at the life of, and options open to, women in ancient Egypt. (Rev: BL 3/1/03; SLJ 4/03)

17258 Minnis, Ivan. *You Are in Ancient Egypt* (3–6). Illus. Series: You Are There! 2004, Raintree LB $26.36 (978-1-4109-0616-8); paper $7.50 (978-1-4109-1008-0). 32pp. In present-tense narrative, Minnis introduces the sites, sounds, food, and varied living conditions of ancient Egypt. (Rev: SLJ 2/05)

17259 Nardo, Don. *Ancient Egypt* (3–6). Illus. 2002, Gale LB $23.70 (978-0-7377-0955-1). A basic introduction to the people of ancient Egypt, nobility and peasants, and to the importance of their religious beliefs. (Rev: SLJ 9/02)

17260 Nardo, Don. *King Tut's Tomb* (3–6). Series: Wonders of the World. 2004, Gale LB $26.20 (978-0-7377-2352-6). 48pp. Nardo discusses what we know of King Tutankhamen's life and death, and describes the discovery of his tomb. (Rev: SLJ 6/05)

17261 Orr, Tamra. *How'd They Do That in Ancient Egypt?* (5–8). Series: How'd They Do That? 2010, Mitchell Lane LB $24.50 (978-1-58415-821-9). 64pp. Covers aspects of life in ancient Egypt, from slaves to pharaohs, ranging from work and play, to hieroglyphs, architecture, religion, and mummies, providing FYInfo sections and a craft (making a reed boat). (Rev: BL 4/1/10; LMC 5–6/10; SLJ 5/10) [932]

17262 Perl, Lila. *The Ancient Egyptians* (4–7). Series: People of the Ancient World. 2004, Watts LB $30.50 (978-0-531-12345-4). 112pp. Pharaohs, mummy makers, farmers, and brewers are among the people presented in this overview of life in ancient Egypt. (Rev: SLJ 2/05)

17263 Pipe, Jim. *You Wouldn't Want to Be Cleopatra! An Egyptian Ruler You'd Rather Not Be* (3–6). Illus. by David Antram. Series: You Wouldn't Want to . . . 2007, Watts LB $28.50 (978-0-531-18726-8); paper $9.95 (978-0-531-18923-6). 32pp. An entertaining look at the queen of Egypt and the problems she faced. Cartoons keep the tone light. (Rev: SLJ 8/07)

17264 Putnam, James. *The Ancient Egypt Pop-Up Book* (5–8). Illus. 2003, Universe $29.95 (978-0-7893-0985-3). Seven imaginatively designed pop-up spreads introduce ancient Egypt, including its pyramids, pharaohs, and mummies. (Rev: SLJ 3/04)

17265 Rubalcaba, Jill. *Ancient Egypt: Archaeology Unlocks the Secrets of Egypt's Past* (3–7). 2006, National Geographic $17.95 (978-0-7922-7784-2). 64pp. This well-illustrated overview of what archaeologists have uncovered about life in ancient Egypt highlights two related events: the 1922 discovery of King Tutankhamen's tomb and the 2005 CT scan of the boy king's mummy. (Rev: SLJ 2/07)

17266 Schomp, Virginia. *Ancient Mesopotamia: The Sumerians, Babylonians, and Assyrians* (5–8). Series: People of the Ancient World. 2004, Watts LB $30.50 (978-0-531-11818-4). 112pp. This fascinating volume covers the history and culture of the Sumerians, Babylonians, and Assyrians, looking at writing, warfare, and the daily life of people ranging from farmers and traders to warriors and nobles. (Rev: SLJ 3/05)

17267 Shuter, Jane. *The Ancient Egyptians* (3–5). Series: History Starts Here! 2000, Raintree LB $25.69 (978-0-7398-1351-5). 32pp. This overview of ancient Egypt includes material on history, culture, daily life, structures, and religion. (Rev: HBG 10/00; SLJ 7/00)

17268 Stewart, David. *You Wouldn't Want to Be an Egyptian Mummy! Disgusting Things You'd Rather Not Know* (4–6). Illus. by David Antram. 2001, Watts LB $29.00

(978-0-531-14597-5); paper $9.95 (978-0-531-16206-4). The symbolism of elaborate Egyptian burials and the process of mummification are explained with many illustrations and cartoon art. (Rev: SLJ 9/01)

17269 Tyldesley, Joyce. *Egypt* (5–8). Illus. Series: Insiders. 2007, Simon & Schuster $16.99 (978-1-4169-3858-3). 64pp. An introduction to ancient Egypt — the pyramids, mummies, Abu Simbel, transportation, arts and crafts, and so forth — with eye-catching illustrations. (Rev: LMC 10/07; SLJ 12/07)

17270 Walker, Jane. *Ancient Egypt* (3–6). Illus. Series: 100 Things You Should Know about. 2002, Mason Crest LB $18.95 (978-1-59084-445-8). 48pp. Organized topically, this collection of 100 facts covers history, government, religion, daily life, dress, and cuisine, and will appeal to reluctant readers. (Rev: SLJ 6/03)

17271 Weitzman, David. *Pharaoh's Boat* (4–7). Illus. by author. 2009, Houghton $17.00 (978-0-547-05341-7). 48pp. Weitzman recounts the fascinating discovery in 1954 of a boat in the Great Pyramid of Giza, explains its origins (it was built as a vehicle to take the Pharaoh Cheops to the afterlife), and details its restoration. ALA Notable Children's Book. (Rev: BCCB 9/09; BL 5/15/09*; HB 5/09; SLJ 4/09*) [932]

17272 Woods, Geraldine. *Science in Ancient Egypt* (4–8). Series: Science of the Past. 1998, Watts paper $8.95 (978-0-531-15915-6). The many contributions to science by the ancient Egyptians, including architecture, astronomy, and mathematics, are outlined in this richly illustrated volume. (Rev: BL 6/1–15/98; HBG 10/98; SLJ 6/98) [932]

Greece

17273 Bailey, Linda. *Adventures in Ancient Greece* (3–5). Illus. by Bill Slavin. Series: Good Times Travel Agency. 2002, Kids Can $14.95 (978-1-55074-534-4); paper $7.95 (978-1-55074-536-8). 48pp. Readers take a trip to ancient Greece and learn about democracy, the Olympics, everyday life, and other aspects in an appealing layout that includes cartoon panels. (Rev: BL 11/1/02; HBG 3/03)

17274 Benduhn, Tea. *Ancient Greece* (1–3). Series: Life Long Ago. 2006, Weekly Reader LB $19.93 (978-0-8368-7782-3). 24pp. Plenty of facts about ancient Greece and its people's customs, beliefs, and political system. An airy design adds to the appeal. (Rev: SLJ 6/07)

17275 Broida, Marian. *Projects About Ancient Greece* (4–6). Illus. Series: Hands-on Ancient History. 2006, Benchmark LB $29.93 (978-0-7614-2259-4). Ten projects — including Minoan bull-dancer paintings, Mycenaean writing, and black-figure pottery — are accompanied by fictionalized scenarios that add context. (Rev: SLJ 4/07)

17276 Caper, William. *Ancient Greece: An Interactive History Adventure* (3–5). Illus. 2009, Capstone LB $29.32 (978-142963417-5). 112pp. In this engaging history book with a choose-your-own-adventure twist, readers select which role they'd like to play in ancient Greece, from slave to philosopher. (Rev: BL 7/10) [938]

17277 MacDonald, Fiona. *You Wouldn't Want to Be a Slave in Ancient Greece! A Life You'd Rather Not Have* (4–6). Illus. by David Antram. Series: You Wouldn't Want To. 2001, Watts LB $29.00 (978-0-531-14600-2); paper $9.95 (978-0-531-16203-3). 32pp. The story of a woman who is kidnapped and taken to Greece as a slave serves as a good starting point to prove the premise of this book. (Rev: SLJ 9/01)

17278 McGee, Marni. *Ancient Greece: Archaeology Unlocks the Secrets of Greece's Past* (3–7). Series: National Geographic Investigates. 2006, National Geographic $17.95 (978-0-7922-7826-9). 64pp. This well-illustrated title looks at archaeologists' efforts over the years to uncover — on land and under the sea — information about life in ancient Greece. (Rev: SLJ 2/07)

17279 Middleton, Haydn. *Ancient Greek Jobs* (4–6). Series: People in the Past. 2002, Heinemann LB $27.07 (978-1-58810-638-4). The tasks of the doctor, banker, farmer, merchant, and other professions are explained and placed in historical context. Also use *Ancient Greek Women* and *Ancient Greek Children*. (Rev: HBG 3/03; SLJ 12/02)

17280 Minnis, Ivan. *You Are in Ancient Greece* (3–6). Illus. Series: You Are There! 2004, Raintree LB $26.36 (978-1-4109-0617-5); paper $7.50 (978-1-4109-1009-7). 32pp. In present-tense narrative, Minnis introduces the sites, sounds, food, and varied living conditions of ancient Greece. (Rev: SLJ 2/05)

17281 Nardo, Don. *Ancient Athens* (5–8). Illus. Series: A Travel Guide To. 2002, Gale $28.70 (978-1-59018-016-7). 112pp. This fact-filled "guidebook" introduces aspiring travelers to everyday life in ancient Athens, in addition to information on climate, geography, important sights, and so forth. (Rev: BL 1/1–15/03; SLJ 2/03)

17282 Nardo, Don. *Ancient Greece* (4–6). Illus. Series: Life During the Great Civilizations. 2004, Gale LB $24.95 (978-1-56711-741-7). 48pp. Nardo explores day-to-day life in ancient Greece, looking at everything from clothes and jobs to social structures and religion.

17283 Nardo, Don. *Greek Temples* (5–7). Illus. Series: Famous Structures. 2002, Watts LB $25.50 (978-0-531-12035-4). 64pp. Nardo looks at the construction, elements, use, and importance of ancient Greek temples, with illustrations. (Rev: BL 9/1/02; SLJ 8/02)

17284 Powell, Anton. *Ancient Greece. Rev. ed.* (5–8). Illus. Series: Cultural Atlas for Young People. 2003, Facts on File $35.00 (978-0-8160-5146-5). 96pp. Colorful topical spreads introduce readers to the culture, history, and politics of ancient Greece, with information on the Olympics, daily life, and women's role. (Rev: SLJ 1/04)

17285 Rice, Rob S. *Ancient Greek Warfare* (3–6). Series: Ancient Warfare. 2010, Gareth Stevens LB $26 (978-1-4339-1972-5). 32pp. In chapters on fortress cities, war on land, and war at sea, this volume looks at the armies

of ancient Greece and at the life and achievements of Alexander the Great. (Rev: SLJ 6/10) [355.02]

17286 Shuter, Jane. *Life in a Greek Temple* (2–4). Illus. Series: Picture the Past. 2005, Heinemann LB $26.79 (978-1-4034-6442-2). 32pp. A basic, attractive overview of Greek temples and their construction as well as the religious beliefs and practices of the ancient Greeks. (Rev: BL 9/15/05)

17287 Shuter, Jane. *Life in a Greek Trading Port* (2–4). Illus. Series: Picture the Past. 2005, Heinemann LB $25.64 (978-1-4034-6444-6). 32pp. This title explores various aspects of everyday life in an ancient Greek port city, including housing, cuisine, clothing, occupations, and leisure pursuits. (Rev: SLJ 11/05)

17288 Solway, Andrew. *Ancient Greece* (3–6). Illus. by Peter Connolly. Series: Ancient World. 2001, Oxford $24.99 (978-0-19-910810-7). 64pp. Exceptional artwork and detailed descriptions of life and institutions in ancient Greece. (Rev: BL 3/1/02; HBG 3/02; SLJ 2/02)

Rome

17289 Anderson, Michael, ed. *Ancient Rome* (5–8). Series: Ancient Civilizations. 2011, Britannica Educational LB $31.70 (978-1-61530-522-3). 88pp. This slim volume offers an accessible introduction to the culture, religion, architecture, and inventions of ancient Rome. **e** (Rev: SLJ 12/1/11) [937]

17290 Beller, Susan Provost. *Roman Legions on the March: Soldiering in the Ancient Roman Army* (5–8). 2007, Twenty-First Century LB $33.26 (978-0-8225-6781-3). After background information on the Roman army, this volume examines the life of the soldiers and provides interesting sidebar features and photographs. (Rev: SLJ 1/08)

17291 Benduhn, Tea. *Ancient Rome* (1–3). Series: Life Long Ago. 2006, Weekly Reader LB $19.93 (978-0-8368-7783-0). 24pp. Plenty of facts about ancient Rome and its people's customs, beliefs, and political system. An airy design adds to the appeal. (Rev: SLJ 6/07)

17292 Blacklock, Dyan. *The Roman Army* (5–8). Illus. by David Kennett. 2004, Walker $17.95 (978-0-8027-8896-2). 48pp. The soldiers, weaponry, fighting techniques, and ingenuity of the Romans are detailed here in clear text and effective cartoon-style illustrations. (Rev: BL 3/1/04*; SLJ 4/04)

17293 Corbishley, Mike. *Ancient Rome. Rev. ed.* (5–8). Illus. Series: Cultural Atlas for Young People. 2003, Facts on File $35.00 (978-0-8160-5147-2). 96pp. Colorful topical spreads introduce readers to the culture, history, and politics of ancient Rome, with information on architecture and major cities of the provinces. (Rev: SLJ 1/04)

17294 Croy, Anita, ed. *Ancient Rome* (5–9). Series: Facts at Your Fingertips. 2010, Black Rabbit LB $35.65 (978-1-933834-56-6). 64pp. From the birth of Rome through the peak of imperial power to the later empire, this well-illustrated volume provides easy access to facts and looks at different areas of the Roman Empire in some detail. (Rev: LMC 3–4/10) [937]

17295 Curry, Jane Louise. *Brave Cloelia: Retold from the Account in the History of Early Rome by the Roman Historian Titus Livius* (2–4). Illus. by Jeff Crosby. 2004, Getty Publications $16.95 (978-0-89236-763-4). A brave Roman girl earns the respect of the Etruscan invader in this picture book based on the writing of Livy. (Rev: BL 11/15/04; SLJ 2/05)

17296 Dargie, Richard. *Ancient Rome* (3–6). Illus. Series: Picturing the Past. 2004, Enchanted Lion $15.95 (978-1-59270-023-3). 32pp. Well-written two-page chapters cover geography, history, government, religion, the arts, and home life, with maps, photos and illustrations, and informative sidebars detailing sources. (Rev: SLJ 11/04)

17297 Dargie, Richard. *Rich and Poor in Ancient Rome* (3–6). Illus. by Adam Hook. 2005, Smart Apple LB $27.10 (978-1-58340-722-6). 32pp. The everyday lives of the rich and the poor in ancient Rome are compared. (Rev: SLJ 5/06)

17298 Deem, James M. *Bodies from the Ash: Life and Death in Ancient Pompeii* (5–8). 2005, Houghton Mifflin $17.00 (978-0-618-47308-3). This photoessay full of vivid illustrations outlines what archaeologists have uncovered about the destruction of Pompeii when Mount Vesuvius erupted nearly 2,000 years ago. (Rev: BL 11/1/05; SLJ 12/05*) [937]

17299 DuTemple, Lesley A. *The Colosseum* (4–7). Series: Great Building Feats. 2003, Lerner LB $27.93 (978-0-8225-4693-1). Using many colorful diagrams and illustrations, this is the story of the construction of the famous colosseum in Rome. (Rev: BL 11/15/03; HBG 4/04) [937]

17300 Ganeri, Anita. *The Ancient Romans* (3–5). Series: History Starts Here! 2000, Raintree LB $25.69 (978-0-7398-1349-2). 32pp. A brief overview that introduces ancient Rome, its daily life, culture, social structure, history, and fall. (Rev: HBG 10/00; SLJ 7/00)

17301 Hanel, Rachael. *Ancient Rome: An Interactive History Adventure* (3–5). Illus. 2009, Capstone LB $29.32 (978-142963416-8). 112pp. In this engaging history book with a choose-your-own-adventure twist, readers select which role they'd like to play in ancient Rome, from slave to senator. (Rev: BL 7/10) [937]

17302 Hanel, Rachael. *Gladiators* (5–8). Series: Fearsome Fighters. 2007, Creative Education LB $31.35 (978-1-58341-535-1). Weapons, armor, fighting techniques, and motivation are all discussed in this description of gladiators in ancient Rome and the kinds of people who were tempted to this career. (Rev: SLJ 1/08)

17303 Hart, Avery, and Sandra Gallagher. *Ancient Rome! Exploring the Culture, People and Ideas of This Powerful Empire* (4–6). Illus. by Michael Kline. Series: A Kaleidoscope Kids Book. 2002, Williamson paper $14.25 (978-1-885593-60-3). 96pp. A fact-filled overview that introduces readers to all aspects of ancient Rome — history, legends and myths, government, transportation, wars, key individuals, and so forth — and provides

activities such as building a triumphal arch. (Rev: SLJ 3/03)

17304 Jovinelly, Joann, and Jason Netelkos. *The Crafts and Culture of the Romans* (5–8). Series: Crafts of the Ancient World. 2002, Rosen LB $29.25 (978-0-8239-3513-0). The daily life and contributions of the ancient Romans are covered, as well as such craft projects as designing a toga. (Rev: BL 5/15/02; SLJ 6/02) [937]

17305 Landau, Elaine. *Exploring Ancient Rome with Elaine Landau* (3–5). Illus. Series: Exploring Ancient Civilizations. 2005, Enslow LB $23.93 (978-0-7660-2337-6). 48pp. The author and her dog Max give readers a tour of ancient Rome's society, trade, engineering, architecture, religion, and food and clothing. (Rev: BL 9/1/05; SLJ 12/05)

17306 MacDonald, Fiona. *Ancient Rome* (3–6). Illus. Series: 100 Things You Should Know about. 2002, Mason Crest LB $18.95 (978-1-59084-446-5). 48pp. Organized topically, this collection of 100 facts covers history, government, religion, daily life, dress, and cuisine, and will appeal to reluctant readers. (Rev: SLJ 6/03)

17307 MacDonald, Fiona. *How to Be a Roman Soldier* (2–5). Illus. by Nicholas Hewetson. Series: How to Be. 2005, National Geographic $14.95 (978-0-7922-3616-0). 32pp. Soldiers' training, weapons, compensation, recreation, and home and family life are all covered in a reader-friendly, well-illustrated format. (Rev: SLJ 12/05)

17308 Malam, John. *You Wouldn't Want to Be a Roman Gladiator! Gory Things You'd Rather Not Know* (4–6). Illus. by David Antram. Series: You Wouldn't Want To. 2001, Watts LB $29.00 (978-0-531-14598-2); paper $9.95 (978-0-531-16204-0). 32pp. Cartoon art belies the grimness of the content in this book in which readers will find plenty of hard information on how gladiators were acquired and trained, their rules of battle, and details of other savage forms of entertainment. (Rev: SLJ 9/01)

17309 Mann, Elizabeth. *The Roman Colosseum* (4–7). Series: Wonders of the World. 1998, Mikaya $19.95 (978-0-9650493-3-7). An oversize book that is crammed with factual material on the Colosseum in Rome. (Rev: BL 12/15/98; SLJ 2/99) [937]

17310 Markel, Rita J. *Your Travel Guide to Ancient Rome* (4–6). Illus. Series: Passport to History. 2003, Lerner LB $26.60 (978-0-8225-3071-8). 96pp. Information about ancient Rome — everything from historical anecdotes to profiles of key indviduals to details of dress and behavior — is conveyed in the style of a travel guide complete with photographs and prints. (Rev: BL 2/15/04; HBG 4/04; SLJ 4/04)

17311 Martin, Michael. *Gladiators* (3–6). Series: Edge Books: Warriors of History. 2006, Capstone LB $23.93 (978-0-7368-6429-9). 32pp. This colorful introduction to gladiators examines the history of this class of professional warriors in ancient Rome, their weapons, and their way of life. (Rev: SLJ 1/07)

17312 Matthews, Rupert. *100 Things You Should Know About Gladiators* (3–6). Illus. Series: Remarkable Man and Beast: Facing Survival. 2010, Mason Crest LB $19.95 (978-142221970-6). 48pp. With plenty of lively photographs and illustrations woven together with cohesive text, this is a useful introduction to gladiators. (Rev: BL 10/15/10; LMC 3–4/11; SLJ 2/1/11) [796.8]

17313 Minnis. *Ancient Rome* (3–6). Series: Raintree Perspectives. 2004, Raintree LB $25.70 (978-1-4109-0618-2). 32pp. Double-page spreads with plenty of illustrations and a low reading level introduce readers to ancient Rome's culture and lifestyle. (Rev: BL 12/1/04; SLJ 2/05)

17314 Nardo, Don. *Ancient Rome* (4–6). Illus. Series: Life During the Great Civilizations. 2004, Gale LB $24.95 (978-1-56711-742-4). Nardo explores day-to-day life in ancient Rome, looking at everything from clothes and jobs to social structures and religion.

17315 Nardo, Don. *Roman Amphitheaters* (5–7). Illus. Series: Famous Structures. 2002, Watts LB $25.50 (978-0-531-12036-1); paper $8.95 (978-0-531-16224-8). 64pp. A clear overview of the construction, elements, use, and importance of ancient Roman amphitheaters, with illustrations. (Rev: BL 9/1/02; SLJ 8/02)

17316 Osborne, Mary Pope. *Pompeii: Lost and Found* (2–4). Illus. by Bonnie Christensen. 2006, Knopf $16.95 (978-0-375-82889-8). 40pp. In addition to describing the eruption of Vesuvius in A.D. 79, Osborne discusses its excavation and how archaeological discoveries allow us to imagine daily life in the city at that time. (Rev: BL 12/1/05; SLJ 1/06)

17317 Osborne, Mary Pope, and Natalie Pope Boyce. *Ancient Rome and Pompeii: A Nonfiction Companion to Vacation Under the Volcano* (2–4). Illus. by Sal Murdocca. 2006, Random $4.99 (978-0-375-83220-8). 128pp. This nonfiction companion to *Vacation Under the Volcano* provides a fascinating introduction to the history and culture of ancient Rome and Pompeii. (Rev: BL 6/1–15/06)

17318 Rice, Rob S. *Ancient Roman Warfare* (3–6). Series: Ancient Warfare. 2010, Gareth Stevens LB $26 (978-1-4339-1974-9). 32pp. In chapters on building an empire, weapons and equipment, camps, and war at sea, this volume looks at the armies of ancient Rome and the famous leaders of the time. (Rev: SLJ 6/10) [355.0]

17319 Solway, Andrew. *Ancient Rome* (3–6). Illus. by Peter Connolly. Series: Ancient World. 2001, Oxford $24.99 (978-0-19-910809-1). Exceptional artwork and detailed descriptions of daily life, culture, religion, and sports in ancient Rome. (Rev: BL 3/1/02; HBG 3/02; SLJ 1/02)

17320 Solway, Andrew. *Rome: In Spectacular Cross-Section* (4–7). Illus. by Stephen Biesty. 2003, Scholastic paper $18.95 (978-0-439-45546-6). An inside look at life in ancient Rome, with views of a private home, the Colosseum, the docks, and a bustling festival. (Rev: BL 2/15/03; HBG 10/03; SLJ 7/03) [937]

17321 Stewart, David. *You Wouldn't Want to Be a Roman Soldier! Barbarians You'd Rather Not Meet* (3–6). Illus. by David Antram. Series: You Wouldn't Want To. 2006, Watts LB $29.00 (978-0-531-12423-9); paper $9.95 (978-0-531-12448-2). 32pp. This book banishes romantic notions about the lives of Roman soldiers, but the cartoon illustrations lighten the portrayal of harsh conditions and deadly challenges. (Rev: SLJ 9/06)

17322 Stroud, Jonathan. *Ancient Rome: A Guide to the Glory of Imperial Rome* (4–7). Series: Sightseers. 2000, Kingfisher $8.95 (978-0-7534-5235-6). This book on ancient Rome is presented like a handbook for tourists, with material on such topics as accommodations, shopping, key sites, etc. (Rev: HBG 3/01; SLJ 9/00) [937]

17323 Williams, Brian. *Ancient Roman Women* (5–8). Illus. Series: People in the Past. 2002, Heinemann LB $27.07 (978-1-58810-632-2). 48pp. A look at the life of, and options open to, women in ancient Rome. (Rev: BL 3/1/03; HBG 10/03; SLJ 4/03)

17324 Williams, Marcia. *The Romans: Gods, Emperors, and Dormice* (3–6). Illus. by author. 2013, Candlewick $16.99 (978-076366581-4). 40pp. With humor and history, a dormouse named Dormeo guides readers through the rise and fall of the Roman Empire, with detailed cartoons that show everyday life, profile key citizens, explain the roles of the gods, and introduce some Latin words. (Rev: BL 10/1/13; LMC 5–6/14; SLJ 11/13) [937]

Aztecs, Incas, and Maya

17325 Calvert, Patricia. *The Ancient Inca* (5–8). Series: People of the Ancient World. 2004, Watts LB $30.50 (978-0-531-12358-4). 128pp. This fascinating volume covers the history and culture of the Inca people, looking at childhood and the daily life of people ranging from farmers to priests, warriors, and emperors. (Rev: SLJ 3/05)

17326 Clare, John D. *Aztec Life* (5–8). Illus. 2006, Saddleback paper $8.95 (978-1-59905-050-8). 32pp. Covers the lifestyle, culture, and traditions of the Aztecs, with quotations from poems and sayings. (Rev: SLJ 9/06)

17327 Dalal, Anita. *Myths of Pre-Columbian America* (5–8). Illus. Series: Mythic World. 2002, Raintree LB $27.12 (978-0-7398-3193-9). 48pp. This volume for older readers separates myth from reality about cultures present in America in pre-Columbian times. (Rev: BL 3/1/02; HBG 3/02; SLJ 12/01)

17328 Day, Nancy. *Your Travel Guide to Ancient Mayan Civilization* (4–8). Series: Passport to History. 2000, Lerner LB $26.50 (978-0-8225-3077-0). 96pp. Using the format of a modern-day travel guide, this book explores the ancient Mayan cities of Uzmal, Tikal, Copan, and others to discover the lifestyles of the Maya, their food, clothes, religion, discoveries, and behavior. (Rev: BL 3/1/01; HBG 10/01; SLJ 4/01)

17329 Gruber, Beth. *Ancient Inca: Archaeology Unlocks the Secrets of Inca's Past* (3–7). Series: National Geographic Investigates. 2006, National Geographic $17.95 (978-0-7922-7827-6). 64pp. This well-illustrated title examines how archaeologists gain knowledge about the ancient Inca civilization of pre-Columbian America, including information on pottery, textiles, and mummies. (Rev: SLJ 2/07)

17330 Hynson, Colin. *You Wouldn't Want to Be an Inca Mummy! A One-Way Journey You'd Rather Not Make* (4–6). Illus. by David Antram. Series: You Wouldn't Want to . . . Ancient Civilization. 2007, Watts LB $29.00 (978-0-531-18744-9). 32pp. Engaging facts, fast action, cartoons, and a touch of humor make for an appealing package about the culture and religion of the Inca people. (Rev: LMC 5/08; SLJ 3/08)

17331 Lewin, Ted. *Lost City: The Discovery of Machu Picchu* (2–4). 2003, Penguin $17.99 (978-0-399-23302-9). 48pp. Striking watercolor spreads grab attention in this picture-book account of the discovery of the lost Inca city. (Rev: BL 7/03; HB 9/03; HBG 4/04; SLJ 6/03)

17332 Lourie, Peter. *Hidden World of the Aztec* (5–8). Illus. 2006, Boyds Mills $17.95 (978-1-59078-069-5). 45pp. This lavishly illustrated title uses modern archaeological projects to introduce the history and culture of the ancient Aztec civilization. (Rev: BL 10/15/06; SLJ 10/06)

17333 MacDonald, Fiona. *How to Be an Aztec Warrior* (2–5). Illus. by David Antram and Mark Bergin. Series: How to Be. 2005, National Geographic $14.95 (978-0-7922-3617-7). 32pp. This attractive title gives readers a look at what life was like for Aztec warriors, touching on such topics as uniforms, weapons, rank, and traditions. (Rev: SLJ 12/05)

17334 MacDonald, Fiona. *You Wouldn't Want to Be an Aztec Sacrifice! Gruesome Things You'd Rather Not Know* (4–6). Illus. by David Antram. Series: You Wouldn't Want To. 2001, Watts LB $29.00 (978-0-531-14602-6); paper $9.95 (978-0-531-16209-5). 32pp. The circumstances of human sacrifice — and potential ways of avoiding this fate — are discussed with some black humor. (Rev: SLJ 3/02)

17335 Mann, Elizabeth. *Machu Picchu* (3–5). Illus. Series: Wonders of the World. 2000, Mikaya $19.95 (978-0-9650493-9-9). 48pp. Beginning with the discovery of Machu Picchu in 1911, this book goes back to trace its construction and history. (Rev: BL 7/00*; HBG 10/00; SLJ 6/00)

17336 Matthews, Rupert. *You Wouldn't Want to Be a Mayan Soothsayer! Fortunes You'd Rather Not Tell* (4–6). Illus. by David Antram. Series: You Wouldn't Want to . . . Ancient Civilization. 2007, Watts LB $29.00 (978-0-531-18746-3). 32pp. Engaging facts, fast action, cartoons, and a touch of humor make for an appealing package about the culture and religion of the Mayan people. (Rev: LMC 5/08; SLJ 3/08)

17337 Silate, Jennifer. *The Inca Ruins of Machu Picchu* (4–6). Illus. Series: Wonders of the World. 2005, Gale LB $26.20 (978-0-7377-3068-5). 48pp. This is a useful, easy-to-read introduction to the current knowledge

about the Incas and the construction of Machu Picchu, with details of contemporary cable-car access and attempts to preserve the site. (Rev: SLJ 7/06)

17338 Wyborny, Sheila. *The Aztec Empire* (4–6). Illus. Series: Life During the Great Civilizations. 2004, Gale LB $24.95 (978-1-56711-736-3). 48pp. Wyborny explores day-to-day life among the Aztecs, looking at everything from clothes and jobs to social structures, medicine, and religion. (Rev: BL 5/15/04; SLJ 8/04)

Middle Ages

17339 Adkins, Jan. *What If You Met a Knight?* (3–5). Illus. 2006, Roaring Brook $16.95 (978-1-59643-148-5). 32pp. Presents a realistic view of the life of knights in the Middle Ages and of their daily responsibilities and challenges. (Rev: BL 8/06; HBG 4/07; LMC 1/07; SLJ 9/06; VOYA 2/07)

17340 Allen, Kathy. *The Horrible, Miserable Middle Ages: The Disgusting Details About Life During Medieval Times* (4–8). Series: Fact Finders: Disgusting History. 2010, Capstone LB $25.32 (978-1-4296-3958-3). 32pp. Allen concentrates on the grosser side of medieval life, describing poor sanitation, rotten food, bugs, medical horrors, and so forth. Lexile 850L (Rev: LMC 11–12/10) [940.1]

17341 Bruce, Julia. *Siege: Can You Capture a Castle?* (3–6). Illus. by Peter Dennis. 2009, Enslow LB $16.95 (978-0-7660-3475-4). A castle under siege is the dramatic frame for solid information about castle design and life on both sides of the walls. (Rev: BL 4/1/09)

17342 Clements, Gillian. *Medieval Castle* (3–6). Illus. by author. Series: Building History. 2009, Sea-to-Sea LB $18.95 (978-1-59771-145-6). 32pp. Answering questions such as "Who built the castles?" and "How did soldiers defend castles?" this volume provides lots of information in the text and in the detailed drawings. (Rev: BLO 3/11/09)

17343 Currie, Stephen. *Miracles, Saints, and Superstition: The Medieval Mind* (5–9). 2006, Gale LB $32.45 (978-1-59018-861-3). Describes the Middle Ages and the role of Christianity at that time. (Rev: SLJ 3/07*) [940.1]

17344 Dunn, John M. *Life During the Black Death* (5–9). Series: The Way People Live. 2000, Lucent LB $28.70 (978-1-56006-542-5). 96pp. This account traces the spread of the Black Death from Mongolia in 1320 to Western Europe and its lasting effects on history, society, and culture. (Rev: HBG 10/00; SLJ 6/00)

17345 Durman, Laura. *Siege* (4–5). Illus. Series: Knights and Castles. 2013, Black Rabbit LB $28.50 (978-184858562-1). 32pp. Double-page spreads look at medieval life during a siege and the roles of the various participants. Also use *Knights* and *Castle Life* (2013). (Rev: BL 6/13; LMC 11–12/13; SLJ 4/13) [355.4]

17346 Ford, Nick. *Jerusalem Under Muslim Rule in the Eleventh Century: Christian Pilgrims Under Islamic Government* (5–9). Series: The Library of the Middle Ages. 2004, Rosen LB $29.25 (978-0-8239-4216-9). Useful for report writers, this volume looks at life in Jerusalem for people of all religions, providing details from primary sources. (Rev: SLJ 8/04) [956.94]

17347 Galloway, Priscilla. *Archers, Alchemists, and 98 Other Medieval Jobs You Might Have Loved or Loathed* (4–6). Illus. by Martha Newbigging. 2003, Annick LB $24.95 (978-1-55037-811-5); paper $14.95 (978-1-55037-810-8). 96pp. One hundred medieval occupations are described in conversational style, with cartoon illustrations and informative castle-shaped sidebars. (Rev: BL 1/1–15/04; SLJ 1/04)

17348 George, Linda S. *800* (5–8). Illus. Series: Around the World. 2003, Marshall Cavendish LB $29.93 (978-0-7614-1085-0). 96pp. This absorbing look at civilizations around the world in the year 800 includes color reproductions, photographs, a timeline, a glossary, and lists of resources. (Rev: BL 6/1–15/03; HBG 3/03)

17349 Gravett, Christopher. *Real Knights: Over 20 True Stories of Battle and Adventure* (4–6). Illus. by John James. 2005, Enchanted Lion $15.95 (978-1-59270-034-9). 48pp. This collection of tales about real-life knights in action includes the exploits of Richard the Lionheart, El Cid, Braveheart, and some others who are less well known. (Rev: SLJ 8/06)

17350 Hanel, Rachael. *Knights* (5–8). Series: Fearsome Fighters. 2007, Creative Education LB $31.35 (978-1-58341-536-8). 48pp. Weapons, armor, fighting techniques, and motivation are all discussed in this description of the knights of the Middle Ages and the kinds of people who were tempted to this career. (Rev: SLJ 1/08)

17351 Haywood, John. *Medieval Europe* (5–9). Series: Time Travel Guides. 2007, Raintree LB $34.29 (978-1-4109-2909-9); paper $9.99 (978-1-4109-2915-0). 64pp. With chapter headings like "Facts," "Everyday Life," and "Things to See and Do," this volume takes an effective travel-guide approach to the Middle Ages, incorporating many visual elements. (Rev: SLJ 1/08)

17352 Helget, Nicole. *Barbarians* (5–8). Illus. Series: Fearsome Fighters. 2012, Creative Education $24.95 (978-160818182-7). 48pp. With many illustrations, maps, and primary documents, this volume looks at such groups as the Celts, Franks, Goths, and Huns that were regarded by the Greeks and Romans as "barbarians," discussing their social mores, weapons, fighting techniques, key figures, and so forth. (Rev: BL 11/1/12; LMC 5–6/13; SLJ 12/12) [940.1]

17353 Hinds, Kathryn. *The Castle* (5–8). Series: Life in the Middle Ages. 2000, Marshall Cavendish LB $29.93 (978-0-7614-1007-2). 80pp. A book that explores the construction and parts of the medieval castle as well as the lifestyles of those who lived in them, from kings and knights to humble servants. (Rev: BL 3/1/01; HBG 3/01; SLJ 3/01)

17354 Hinds, Kathryn. *The Church* (5–8). Series: Life in the Middle Ages. 2000, Marshall Cavendish LB $29.93 (978-0-7614-1008-9). 80pp. Explains the role of the church and the clergy in medieval life as well as giving examples of church construction. (Rev: BL 3/1/01; HBG 3/01; SLJ 3/01)

17355 Hinds, Kathryn. *The Countryside* (5–8). Illus. Series: Life in the Middle Ages. 2000, Marshall Cavendish LB $29.93 (978-0-7614-1006-5). 80pp. The author explains manorialism — a primary social structure in rural areas during the Middle Ages — and describes a medieval village, its residents, and their work and pastimes. (Rev: BL 2/15/01; HBG 3/01; SLJ 3/01)

17356 Kroll, Steven. *Barbarians!* (3–6). Illus. by Robert Byrd. 2009, Dutton $18.99 (978-0-525-47958-1). Goths, Huns, Vikings, and Mongols are the main groupings of "barbarians" discussed in this informative and attractive volume. (Rev: BL 5/1/09; LMC 10/09; SLJ 8/09)

17357 Lassieur, Allison. *The Middle Ages: An Interactive History Adventure* (3–5). 2009, Capstone $27.98 (978-142963418-2). 112pp. In this engaging history book with a choose-your-own-adventure twist, readers select which role they'd like to play in the Middle Ages, from peasant to medieval knight. (Rev: BL 7/10; LMC 1–2/10) [940.1]

17358 MacDonald, Fiona. *How to Be a Medieval Knight* (2–5). Illus. by Mark Bergin. Series: How to Be. 2005, National Geographic $14.95 (978-0-7922-3619-1). Knights' training, equipment, weapons, compensation, tournaments, and peacetime occupations and family life are all covered in a reader-friendly, well-illustrated format. (Rev: SLJ 12/05)

17359 MacDonald, Fiona. *Knights, Castles, and Warfare in the Middle Ages* (5–8). Series: World Almanac Library of the Middle Ages. 2005, World Almanac LB $31.00 (978-0-8368-5895-2). Describes the role of knights, the equipment they used, and their lives and homes. Also use *The Plague and Medicine in the Middle Ages* (2005). (Rev: SLJ 1/06) [940.1]

17360 Marston, Elsa. *The Byzantine Empire* (5–8). Series: Cultures of the Past. 2002, Marshall Cavendish $29.93 (978-0-7614-1495-7). 80pp. Well-written text and colorful graphics present the history and culture of the surviving eastern part of the Roman Empire. (Rev: BL 1/1–15/03; HBG 3/03; SLJ 2/03)

17361 Martin, Alex. *Knights and Castles: Exploring History Through Art* (5–8). Series: Picture That! 2004, Two-Can $19.95 (978-1-58728-441-0). Paintings serve as the vehicle to draw students into the discussion of life in Europe during the late medieval period. (Rev: BL 11/1/04; SLJ 2/05) [940.1]

17362 Martin, Michael. *Knights* (3–6). 2006, Capstone LB $23.93 (978-0-7368-6431-2). 32pp. This colorful overview of knights examines the history, weapons, and way of life of these medieval warriors. (Rev: SLJ 1/07)

17363 Morgan, Gwyneth. *Life in a Medieval Village* (5–7). Illus. by author. 1991, HarperCollins paper $14.95 (978-0-06-092046-3). A story of activities in a medieval village and of the church's importance in life in the Middle Ages. [306.094265]

17364 Olmon, Kyle. *Sabuda and Reinhart Present Castle: Medieval Days and Knights* (3–5). Illus. by Tracy Sabin. 2006, Scholastic $19.99 (978-0-439-54324-8). 6pp. An intriguing look at medieval times and castles featuring three-dimensional pop-up images of everything from the castle itself to drawbridges and catapults. (Rev: BL 11/15/06; SLJ 12/06)

17365 Padrino, Mercedes. *Cities and Towns in the Middle Ages* (5–8). Series: World Almanac Library of the Middle Ages. 2005, World Almanac LB $31.00 (978-0-8368-5893-8). A look at medieval urban living — social structure, government structure, employment, education, religion, food and clothing, and so forth. Also use *Feudalism and Village Life in the Middle Ages* (2005). (Rev: SLJ 1/06) [940.1]

17366 Ross, Stewart. *Monarchs* (5–8). Series: Medieval Realms. 2004, Gale $29.95 (978-1-59018-535-3). This colorfully illustrated, oversize volume explores the structure of European governments during the Middle Ages and such topics as the birth of new nations, wars, and the Crusades. (Rev: BL 10/15/04) [940.1]

17367 Senker, Cath. *The Black Death 1347–1350: The Plague Spreads Across Europe* (4–7). Series: When Disaster Struck. 2006, Raintree LB $32.86 (978-1-4109-2278-6). 56pp. Documents the widespread devastation caused by the plague that spread across Europe in the mid-14th century causing an estimated 20 million deaths and discusses current medical understanding and practices. (Rev: SLJ 1/07)

17368 Steele, Philip. *Castles* (5–7). 1995, Kingfisher $16.95 (978-1-85697-547-6). In this oversized, well-designed book, castles, jousting, armor, and feast days are described. (Rev: BL 8/95; SLJ 4/95) [940.1]

17369 Steele, Philip. *A Knight's City* (1–4). Illus. 2008, Simon & Schuster $18.99 (978-1-4169-6124-6). 32pp. Pop-ups, pull-tabs, large illustrations, and clear text provide a tour of life in a medieval European castle and town. (Rev: BLO 12/16/08; SLJ 12/08)

17370 Steele, Philip. *The Medieval World* (5–8). Series: A History of Fashion and Costume. 2005, Facts on File $35.00 (978-0-8160-5945-4). A broad overview of the clothing and personal adornment worn during this time period, with many visual aids. (Rev: SLJ 5/06) [391]

17371 Steer, Dugald. *Knight: A Noble Guide for Young Squires* (2–6). Illus. by Milivoj Ceran and Neil Chapman. 2006, Candlewick $17.99 (978-0-7636-3062-1). This fact-filled guide to the ways of knighthood is written as though it were a letter of guidance from an imprisoned knight to his son; the delicate flaps and playing pieces for a game called "Squire Fight" will restrict this book's circulation. (Rev: SLJ 2/07)

17372 Tatlock, Ann. *Medieval England* (3–6). Illus. Series: That's Me in History. 2013, Purple Toad LB $29.95 (978-162469000-6). 48pp. William, a 10-year-old baker's son, guides readers through medieval England, pointing out details about everyday life and providing

larger contextual information about feudalism, the Protestant Reformation, and other relevant topics. **e** (Rev: BL 10/1/13; LMC 5–6/14) [942.03]

17373 Walker, Jane. *Knights and Castles* (3–6). Illus. Series: 100 Things You Should Know about. 2002, Mason Crest LB $18.95 (978-1-59084-450-2). 48pp. Information about daily life in the Middle Ages, tournaments, banquets, and battles will appeal to reluctant readers. (Rev: SLJ 6/03)

17374 Woolf, Alex. *Education* (5–8). Series: Medieval Realms. 2004, Gale LB $29.95 (978-1-59018-532-2). Discusses the forms of education available during the Middle Ages — including apprenticeships, song schools, monastic schools, universities — and who was able to enjoy them and what they learned, ending with material on the rise of humanism. (Rev: SLJ 3/05) [370]

Renaissance

17375 Claybourne, Anna. *The Renaissance* (5–9). Series: Time Travel Guides. 2007, Raintree LB $34.29 (978-1-4109-2910-5); paper $9.99 (978-1-4109-2916-7). 64pp. With chapter headings like "Facts," "Everyday Life," and "Things to See and Do," this volume takes an effective travel-guide approach to the Renaissance, incorporating many visual elements. (Rev: SLJ 1/08)

17376 Day, Nancy. *Your Travel Guide to Renaissance Europe* (4–8). Series: Passport to History. 2000, Lerner LB $26.50 (978-0-8225-3080-0). This book uses a travel guide format to introduce the reader to the life and people of Europe from 1350 to 1550 with coverage of culture, style, inventions, religious beliefs, and scientific discoveries. (Rev: BL 3/1/01; HBG 10/01) [940.2]

17377 Prum, Deborah Mazzotta. *Rats, Bulls, and Flying Machines: A History of Renaissance and Reformation* (4–8). Series: Core Chronicles. 1999, Core Knowledge $21.95 (978-1-890517-19-9); paper $11.95 (978-1-890517-18-2). A handsome volume that gives a basic history of the Renaissance and Reformation and highlights the accomplishments of people such as the Medici family, Machiavelli, Michelangelo, Cervantes, Shakespeare, and Gutenberg. (Rev: BL 12/15/99) [909.08]

17378 Schomp, Virginia. *1500* (5–8). Illus. Series: Around the World. 2003, Marshall Cavendish LB $29.93 (978-0-7614-1082-9). 96pp. This absorbing look at civilizations around the world in the year 1500 includes color reproductions, photographs, a timeline, a glossary, and lists of resources. (Rev: BL 6/1–15/03; HBG 3/03)

17379 Schomp, Virginia. *The Italian Renaissance* (5–8). Series: Cultures of the Past. 2002, Marshall Cavendish $29.93 (978-0-7614-1492-6). 80pp. A handsome volume that gives a balanced, well-organized account of the Italian Renaissance, its history, personalities, art, and artifacts. (Rev: BL 1/1–15/03; HBG 3/03)

17380 Waldman, Nomi J. *The Italian Renaissance* (5–7). Series: Daily Life. 2004, Gale LB $26.20 (978-0-7377-

1398-5). 48pp. In simple language, this slim volume describes Italy's rebirth, the blossoming of commerce and culture, and daily life for people of different backgrounds. (Rev: SLJ 2/05)

World War I

17381 Burleigh, Robert. *Fly, Cher Ami, Fly!* (K–2). Illus. by Robert MacKenzie. 2008, Abrams $16.95 (978-0-8109-7097-7). 32pp. The true story of a U.S. Army Signal Corps carrier pigeon that helped to save a battalion in World War I France. (Rev: BL 9/1/08)

17382 Conway, John Richard. *World War I* (4–6). Illus. Series: U.S. Wars. 2003, Enslow LB $25.26 (978-0-7660-5142-3). 48pp. Supported by verified and updated Web links, this is a useful overview of the main events of World War I. (Rev: HBG 4/04)

17383 George, Linda S. *World War I* (5–8). Series: Letters from the Homefront. 2001, Benchmark LB $29.93 (978-0-7614-1096-6). 96pp. Life at the front and at home during the First World War is depicted through letters and other firsthand accounts. (Rev: BL 10/15/01; HBG 3/02)

17384 Granfield, Linda. *Where Poppies Grow: A World War I Companion* (4–7). 2002, Stoddart $16.95 (978-0-7737-3319-0). The horrors of war in the trenches are portrayed in this scrapbook full of photographs, propaganda, and ephemera that includes accounts of two Canadian soldiers. (Rev: BL 6/1–15/02; HBG 10/02; SLJ 7/02) [940.3]

17385 Grant, Reg. *World War I: Armistice 1918* (5–8). Series: The World Wars. 2001, Raintree LB $27.12 (978-0-7398-2753-6). 64pp. The negotiations that ended World War I are detailed here, with discussion of the failure of the League of Nations and the lead-up to World War II. (Rev: SLJ 6/01)

17386 Hamilton, John. *Aircraft of World War I* (5–8). Series: World War I. 2003, ABDO LB $24.21 (978-1-57765-912-9). How aircraft became a valuable military tool for the first time in World War I, and how some of the pilots became internationally famous. (Rev: SLJ 6/04) [940.4]

17387 Hamilton, John. *Battles of World War I* (5–8). Series: World War I. 2003, ABDO LB $24.21 (978-1-57765-913-6). A review of key battles that took place during the three years before the United States entered the conflict in 1917, with information on key figures. (Rev: SLJ 6/04) [940.4]

17388 Hamilton, John. *Events Leading to World War I* (5–8). Series: World War I. 2003, ABDO LB $24.21 (978-1-57765-914-3). An evenhanded description of events and circumstances during the years leading up to World War I in each of the countries that became involved in the conflict. (Rev: SLJ 6/04) [940.3]

17389 Hansen, Ole Steen. *Military Aircraft of WWI* (4–7). Series: The Story of Flight. 2003, Crabtree $25.27 (978-0-7787-1201-5). This book introduces in text and pic-

tures the aircraft used by the allies and enemies during World War I. (Rev: BL 10/15/03) [940.3]

17390 Hansen, Ole Steen. *World War I: War in the Trenches* (5–8). Series: The World Wars. 2001, Raintree LB $27.12 (978-0-7398-2752-9). 64pp. The causes of World War I are introduced, followed by information on the major battles and descriptions of the misery of life in the trenches, with plenty of photographs, reproductions, maps, sidebars, and excerpts from primary sources. (Rev: SLJ 6/01)

17391 Innes, Stephanie, and Harry Endrulat. *A Bear in War* (2–5). Illus. by Brian Deines. 2009, Key Porter $19.95 (978-1-55470-097-4). In World War I, Aileen sends her teddy bear to her father, who is in the trenches; narrated by the bear, the story ends with archival photographs and objects. (Rev: BL 3/1/09; SLJ 4/09)

17392 Murphy, Jim. *Truce: The Day the Soldiers Stopped Fighting* (5–8). 2009, Scholastic $19.99 (978-0-545-13049-3). 144pp. The famous Christmas Truce on the western front in December 1914 is explained in this well-written book that features sepia illustrations and discussion of changing attitudes throughout this long war. (Rev: BL 10/15/09*; HB 11–12/09; LMC 1–2/10; SLJ 11/09) [940.4]

17393 Myers, Walter Dean, and Bill Miles. *The Harlem Hellfighters: When Pride Met Courage* (5–8). Illus. 2006, HarperCollins LB $18.89 (978-0-06-001137-6). 160pp. A tribute to the World War I heroism of the 369th Infantry Regiment, which was made up entirely of African Americans. (Rev: BL 2/1/06; SLJ 4/06)

17394 Preston, Diana. *Remember the Lusitania!* (5–8). Illus. 2003, Walker LB $21.85 (978-0-8027-8847-4). 112pp. This gripping account of the sinking of the *Lusitania* includes many personal stories that will hold young readers' attention. (Rev: BL 4/15/03; HB 7/03; HBG 10/03; SLJ 7/03)

17395 Ross, Stewart. *Assassination in Sarajevo: The Trigger for World War I* (4–9). Illus. by Stefan Chabluk. Series: Point of Impact. 2001, Heinemann LB $24.22 (978-1-58810-074-0). 32pp. The assassination of the Archduke of Austria, a precipitating factor in World War I, is put into context and the alliances among the world's nations at the time are clearly explained. (Rev: HBG 10/01; SLJ 7/01)

17396 Ross, Stewart. *The Battle of the Somme* (5–8). Series: The World Wars. 2003, Raintree LB $28.56 (978-0-7398-5479-2). 64pp. An examination of the first Battle of the Somme in 1916, an all-out assault on entrenched German forces in northern France by British and French troops, and of the enormous carnage involved. (Rev: SLJ 5/04)

17397 Ross, Stewart. *Leaders of World War I* (4–8). Illus. Series: World Wars. 2003, Raintree LB $28.56 (978-0-7398-5481-5). 64pp. Stewart presents concise details on the large cast of world and military leaders involved in this conflict. (Rev: BL 12/1/03; HBG 10/03)

17398 Ross, Stewart. *The Technology of World War I* (4–8). Illus. Series: World Wars. 2003, Raintree LB $28.56

(978-0-7398-5482-2). 64pp. New technologies used during World War I included torpedoes, mines, submarines, tanks, planes with machine guns, and mustard gas; all are shown here with maps, diagrams, period reproductions, and posters. (Rev: BL 12/1/03; HBG 10/03; SLJ 7/03)

17399 Swain, Gwenyth. *World War I* (4–6). Illus. Series: You Choose. 2012, Capstone $31.32 (978-142966020-4); paper $6.95 (978-14296799-7-8). 112pp. This choose-your-own-adventure story emphasizes the choices that had to be made in World War I — a nurse in Belgium must decide whether to stay at her hospital, a British teen can enlist or wait until he is called up, and so forth. (Rev: BL 5/15/12) [940.3]

World War II

17400 Adams, Simon. *World War II* (4–8). Illus. 2000, DK $15.95 (978-0-7894-3298-8). 64pp. Each double-page spread presents a different aspect of World War II, such as the Battle of Britain, military equipment, women at work, and conditions inside the Soviet Union. (Rev: BL 11/1/00)

17401 Adler, David A. *We Remember the Holocaust* (4–7). 1995, Henry Holt paper $14.95 (978-0-8050-3715-9). Through interview excerpts, the terrible days of the Holocaust are remembered. (Rev: SLJ 12/89) [940.54]

17402 Allen, Thomas B. *Remember Pearl Harbor: American and Japanese Survivors Tell Their Stories* (5–9). 2001, National Geographic $17.95 (978-0-7922-6690-7). First-person accounts by Japanese and American men and women give readers a close-up view of the 1941 Japanese attack on Pearl Harbor, with maps and photographs. (Rev: BL 9/1/01; HBG 3/02; SLJ 9/01*; VOYA 10/01) [940.54]

17403 Altman, Linda J. *Crimes and Criminals of the Holocaust* (5–10). Illus. Series: Holocaust in History. 2004, Enslow LB $26.60 (978-0-7660-1995-9). 104pp. This book focuses on the end of World War II and the war crimes trials in Nuremberg as well as other cases such as that of Adolf Eichmann. (Rev: BL 5/1/04)

17404 Altman, Linda J. *The Forgotten Victims of the Holocaust* (5–10). Illus. Series: Holocaust in History. 2003, Enslow LB $26.60 (978-0-7660-1993-5). 104pp. Altman looks at populations victimized by the Nazis that are often overlooked: Poles, Russians, gypsies, homosexuals, and the disabled. Also use *The Jewish Victims of the Holocaust* (2003), which describes Hitler's genocide of the Jews. (Rev: BL 7/03; HBG 4/04; SLJ 10/03)

17405 Altman, Linda J. *Impact of the Holocaust* (5–10). Illus. Series: Holocaust in History. 2004, Enslow LB $26.60 (978-0-7660-1996-6). 104pp. Dscusses the Holocaust's influence in the creation of a homeland for the Jews and a Universal Declaration of Human Rights. (Rev: BL 5/1/04)

17406 Arato, Rona. *The Last Train: A Holocaust Story* (5–8). Illus. 2013, OwlKids $16.95 (978-1-926973-62-3). 144pp. Arato describes the concentration camp experiences of her husband, Paul Auslander, and his older brother Oscar; the boys, along with their mother, are eventually rescued from a boxcar by American soldiers. (Rev: BL 3/1/13; LMC 8–9/13; SLJ 4/13) [940.53]

17407 Auerbacher, Inge. *I Am a Star: Child of the Holocaust* (5–7). 1993, Puffin paper $5.99 (978-0-14-036401-9). The memoirs of a former child survivor of the Terezin concentration camp in Czechoslovakia. (Rev: BCCB 7–8/87; BL 6/1/87; SLJ 4/87) [940.5]

17408 Beller, Susan P. *Battling in the Pacific: Soldiering in World War II* (5–8). 2007, Twenty-First Century LB $33.26 (978-0-8225-6381-5). 112pp. After background information on the war, this volume examines the life of soldiers in the Pacific and provides interesting sidebar features and photographs. (Rev: SLJ 1/08)

17409 Bodden, Valerie. *The Bombing of Hiroshima and Nagasaki* (5–9). Illus. Series: Days of Change. 2007, Creative Education LB $21.95 (978-1-58341-545-0). Survivors of the bombings in both cities recall the horrors of the attacks; a brief background on World War II will help readers to place the bombings in context. (Rev: BL 12/15/07; SLJ 3/08) [940.54]

17410 Brooks, Philip. *The Tuskegee Airmen* (3–6). Illus. Series: We the People. 2004, Compass Point LB $26.60 (978-0-7565-0683-4). A well-illustrated, concise account of the achievements of the African American pilots who flew during World War II.

17411 Burgan, Michael. *Refusing to Crumble: The Danish Resistance in World War II* (5–8). Series: Taking a Stand. 2010, Compass Point LB $31.99 (978-0-7565-4298-6). 64pp. An introduction to the Danish response to the Nazi invasion in 1940, giving the reasons for surrender and highlighting the actions of the underground resistance, brave Danes who worked to save Jews and sabotage the Germans. Lexile 970L (Rev: LMC 11–12/10; VOYA 8/10)

17412 Callery, Sean. *World War II* (5–8). Illus. Series: Discover More. 2013, Scholastic $15.99 (978-054547975-2). 112pp. With well-chosen photographs and links to relevant sites, this is a rewarding overview of the key events and issues of the war, organized by causes, theaters of war, and aftermath. (Rev: BLO 4/1/13; SLJ 5/13) [940.53]

17413 Cooper, Michael L. *Remembering Manzanar: Life in a Japanese Relocation Camp* (4–8). 2002, Clarion $15.00 (978-0-618-06778-7). This evocative account of life in a Japanese American World War II internment center tells its tale through personal accounts of survivors, quotations from the camp newspaper, and revealing photographs. (Rev: BL 1/1–15/03; HBG 10/03; SLJ 2/03) [940.54]

17414 Cretzmeyer, Stacy. *Your Name Is Renée: Ruth Kapp Hartz's Story as a Hidden Child in Nazi-Occupied France* (5–8). 2003, Bt. Bound $22.20 (978-0-613-56879-1). The story of a German Jewish family living in France during the Holocaust, how they survived, and how young Ruth hid in an orphanage run by Catholic nuns. (Rev: BCCB 7–8/99; SLJ 8/99) [940.54]

17415 Crewe, Sabrina, and Dale Anderson. *The Atom Bomb Project* (3–5). Series: Events That Shaped America. 2005, Gareth Stevens LB $26.00 (978-0-8368-3404-8). 32pp. A simple, straightforward account of the Manhattan Project featuring direct quotations, editorial cartoons, photographs, reproductions, and newspaper clippings. (Rev: SLJ 3/05)

17416 De Capua, Sarah. *The Tuskegee Airmen* (4–6). Series: Journey to Freedom. 2009, The Child's World LB $28.50 (978-1-60253-138-3). 32pp. The inspiring story of the World War II squadron of African American pilots. (Rev: SLJ 7/09)

17417 Devaney, John. *America Goes to War: 1941* (5–8). 1991, Walker LB $17.85 (978-0-8027-6980-0). An illustrated, datelined, day-by-day account that covers personal and public events of America's first year of World War II. (Rev: BL 10/1/91; SLJ 8/91) [940.53]

17418 Drez, Ronald J. *Remember D-Day: The Plan, the Invasion, Survivor Stories* (4–8). 2004, National Geographic $17.95 (978-0-7922-6666-2). Filled with period photographs and personal stories, this large-format survey of the Allied invasion of Normandy focuses on the military operation and on the strategic planning that preceded it. (Rev: BL 7/04; SLJ 7/04) [940.54]

17419 Drucker, Olga L. *Kindertransport* (5–8). 1995, Henry Holt paper $8.95 (978-0-8050-4251-1). A true account of a Jewish girl sent from Germany to live in England until she could join her parents in New York City in 1945. (Rev: BCCB 1/93; SLJ 11/92) [940.54]

17420 Dvorson, Alexa. *The Hitler Youth: Marching Toward Madness* (5–9). Series: Teen Witnesses to the Holocaust. 1999, Rosen LB $27.95 (978-0-8239-2783-8). This volume describes how thousands of German boys and girls joined the Hitler Youth, why they were seduced into obeying the Nazis, and how their dreams were eventually shattered. (Rev: BL 4/15/99) [943.086]

17421 Fitzgerald, Brian. *Under Fire in World War II* (4–6). Series: On the Front Line. 2005, Raintree LB $29.93 (978-1-4109-1468-2). 48pp. This is an accessible overview of the key events of World War II, with first-person accounts, photographs, fact boxes, and a timeline. (Rev: SLJ 12/05)

17422 Fox, Anne L., and Eva Abraham-Podietz. *Ten Thousand Children: True Stories Told by Children Who Escaped the Holocaust on the Kindertransport* (5–8). 1998, Behrman paper $12.95 (978-0-87441-648-0). The moving stories of 21 survivors who were part of the rescue operation known as the Kindertransport that took 10,000 Jewish children from Nazi-occupied Europe to freedom during late 1938 and 1939. (Rev: BL 1/1–15/99) [940.53]

17423 Friedman, Laurie. *Angel Girl* (4–6). Illus. by Ofra Amit. 2008, Carolrhoda $16.95 (978-0-8225-8739-2). 32pp. Based on a true concentration camp story, this compelling book tells how 11-year-old Herman is saved

from starvation when a farm girl risks her life to throw him apples. (Rev: BCCB 1/09; BL 8/08; LMC 1/09; SLJ 8/08)

17424 Gitlin, Martin. *World War II on the Home Front* (4–5). Illus. Series: You Choose. 2012, Capstone $31.32 (978-142966019-8); paper $6.95 (978-14296799-8-5). 112pp. This choose-your-own-adventure story emphasizes the politically loaded decisions that had to be made while living on the home front during World War II. (Rev: BL 5/15/12) [973.91]

17425 Gorman, Jacqueline Laks. *Pearl Harbor: A Primary Source History* (5–8). Illus. Series: In Their Own Words. 2009, Gareth Stevens $27.00 (978-1-4339-0047-1). With excerpts from primary sources, narrative text, and many photographs, this is an overview of events leading up to the attack on Pearl Harbor, the attack itself, the aftermath, and its importance today, with profiles of key figures. (Rev: BL 4/1/09) [940.54]

17426 Graham, Ian. *You Wouldn't Want to Be a World War II Pilot! Air Battles You Might Not Survive* (4–8). Illus. by David Antram. Series: You Wouldn't Want to Be. 2009, Franklin Watts LB $29 (978-0-531-21326-1). 32pp. This appealing volume provides facts and examples of the dangers of flying in World War II. Lexile IG910L (Rev: LMC 1–2/10)

17427 Hama, Larry, and Anthony Williams. *The Battle of Iwo Jima: Guerrilla Warfare in the Pacific* (5–8). Illus. Series: Graphic Battles of World War II. 2007, Rosen LB $29.25 (978-1-4042-0781-3). After background text to provide context, this graphic novel account of the battle of Iwo Jima takes readers behind the lines on both sides of the bloody conflict. (Rev: BL 4/1/07; SLJ 7/07) [940.54]

17428 Hodge, Deborah. *Rescuing the Children: The Story of the Kindertransport* (5–12). Illus. 2012, Tundra $17.95 (978-1-77049-256-1). 64pp. Using first-person accounts, accessible text, and effective illustrations, this book tells the story of the 10,000 Jewish children rescued from the Nazis in 1939. (Rev: BL 12/1/12*; SLJ 11/12) [940.53]

17429 Jones, Steven L. *The Red Tails: World War II's Tuskegee Airmen* (4–8). Series: Cover-to-Cover. 2002, Perfection Learning $17.95 (978-0-7569-0251-3); paper $8.95 (978-0-7891-5487-3). The story of the heroic African American squadron of World War II fighter pilots, their successful missions, and the prejudices they faced. (Rev: BL 5/1/02) [940.5404]

17430 Kacer, Kathy. *Hiding Edith: A Holocaust Remembrance Book for Young Readers* (4–7). Illus. 2006, Second Story paper $10.95 (978-1-897187-06-7). 120pp. Focusing on a young Jewish girl named Edith Schwalb, this is the story of a French couple who hid 100 Jewish refugee children during World War II with the help of their town. (Rev: BL 12/1/06; SLJ 12/06)

17431 Kacer, Kathy. *The Underground Reporters: A True Story* (5–8). 2005, Second Story $11.95 (978-1-896764-85-6). Based on real events, this inspiring story tells how a newspaper, published by a group of Jewish teenagers in Budejovice, Czechoslovakia, helped to lift the spirits of the Jewish community during the years of Nazi occupation. (Rev: BL 2/15/05; SLJ 8/05) [940.53]

17432 King, David C. *World War II Days: Discover the Past with Exciting Projects, Games, Activities, and Recipes* (4–6). Illus. by Cheryl K. Noll. Series: American Kids in History. 2000, Wiley paper $12.95 (978-0-471-37101-4). Interspersed with material on the home front during World War II are easy-to-perform projects such as making a victory garden, a flashlight, a periscope, a crystal radio, and a wind vane. (Rev: SLJ 2/01)

17433 Kodama, Tatsuharu. *Shin's Tricycle* (5–8). Trans. by Kazuko Hokumen Jones. Illus. by Noriyuki Ando. 1995, Walker LB $16.85 (978-0-8027-8376-9). A father recalls the life of his young son, who was killed in the bombing of Hiroshima. (Rev: BCCB 12/95; BL 9/1/95*; SLJ 12/95) [940.54]

17434 Komatsu, Kimberly, and Kaleigh Komatsu. *In America's Shadow* (5–8). 2003, Thomas George $35.00 (978-0-9709829-0-2). This account of the internment of Japanese Americans during World War II draws on the memories and archives of the authors' family. (Rev: BL 4/1/03) [940.531]

17435 Kramer, Ann. *Women and War* (5–8). Illus. Series: World War II. 2009, Sea-to-Sea LB $18.95 (978-1-59771-142-5). 32pp. Double-page spreads look at the situation of women during World War II, whether volunteering, serving in the military, working in factories or on farms, or coping with shortages. (Rev: BL 4/1/09; LMC 10/09) [940.53]

17436 Kuhn, Betsy. *Angels of Mercy* (5–8). 1999, Simon & Schuster $18.00 (978-0-689-82044-1). A series of narratives on courage and bravery gives us a fascinating look at the contributions of nurses in World War II. (Rev: BCCB 12/99; BL 10/15/99; HBG 3/00; SLJ 11/99; VOYA 4/00) [940.54]

17437 Langley, Wanda. *Flying Higher: The Women Airforce Service Pilots of World War II* (5–8). Illus. 2002, Linnet $25.00 (978-0-208-02506-7). 128pp. The women who flew in World War II gained little glory for performing many vital tasks; this arresting volume focuses on the director of the service, Jacqueline Cochran, and one of the pilots. (Rev: BL 11/1/02; HBG 3/03; SLJ 8/02; VOYA 12/02)

17438 Levine, Karen. *Hana's Suitcase* (5–8). 2002, Whitman $15.95 (978-0-8075-3148-8). A Japanese curator of a Holocaust exhibit traces the owner of a suitcase and learns the story of young Hana, who died in Auschwitz. Sidney Taylor Book Award 2002. (Rev: BL 3/15/03; HB 5–6/03; HBG 10/03) [940.53]

17439 Levy, Debbie. *The Year of Goodbyes: A True Story of Friendship, Family, and Farewells* (5–8). Illus. 2010, Hyperion $16.99 (978-142312901-1). 144pp. Based on a poetry album created by the author's mother in 1938 as the Jewish family waited for U.S. visas while their German friends disappeared around them. Lexile 910L (Rev: BL 2/15/10; SLJ 5/10) [811]

17440 Levy, Pat. *Causes* (5–9). Series: The Holocaust. 2001, Raintree LB $28.54 (978-0-7398-3257-8). 64pp. Levy discusses the causes of the Holocaust, looking at historical, religious, political, social, and economic factors. Also use *The Death Camps* (2002). (Rev: HBG 10/02; SLJ 2/02; VOYA 4/02)

17441 Levy, Pat. *The Home Front in World War II* (5–8). Series: The World Wars. 2003, Raintree LB $28.56 (978-0-7398-6065-6). 64pp. A description of life on the home front in World War II, both in the Allied countries and the Axis countries, including the bombing, refugees, and various shortages. (Rev: SLJ 5/04)

17442 McGowen, Tom. *Carrier War: Aircraft Carriers in World War II* (5–7). Series: Military Might. 2001, Twenty-First Century LB $26.90 (978-0-7613-1808-8). 64pp. An introduction to the importance of aircraft carriers in World War II, with coverage of Pearl Harbor and major battles in the Pacific. (Rev: HBG 10/01; SLJ 6/01)

17443 McGowen, Tom. *Germany's Lightning War: Panzer Divisions of World War II* (5–8). Series: Military Might. 1999, Twenty-First Century LB $26.90 (978-0-7613-1511-7). After a general history of tank warfare, this account focuses on the Germans' Panzer tank divisions and the part they played in World War II. (Rev: HBG 3/00; SLJ 9/99) [940.54]

17444 McGowen, Tom. *Sink the Bismarck: Germany's Super-Battleship of World War II* (5–8). Series: Military Might. 1999, Twenty-First Century LB $26.90 (978-0-7613-1510-0). A history of German sea power during World War II and the many (eventually successful) British efforts to sink the *Bismarck*. (Rev: HBG 3/00; SLJ 9/99) [940.54]

17445 McNeese, Tim. *The Attack on Pearl Harbor* (5–8). Illus. Series: First Battles. 2001, Morgan Reynolds LB $23.95 (978-1-883846-78-7). 112pp. This book details the 1941 attack on Pearl Harbor and explains the conditions in Japan that led to the assault. (Rev: BL 10/1/01; HBG 3/02; SLJ 1/02; VOYA 12/01)

17446 Marx, Trish. *Echoes of World War II* (5–8). 1994, Lerner LB $14.95 (978-0-8225-4898-0). The true stories of six children around the world whose lives were changed dramatically by World War II. (Rev: BCCB 5/94; BL 9/15/94; SLJ 5/94) [940.53]

17447 Milman, Barbara. *Light in the Shadows* (5–9). 1997, Jonathan David paper $14.95 (978-0-8246-0401-1). Illustrated with powerful woodcut prints, this book tells the story of five Holocaust survivors. (Rev: BL 11/15/97) [940.53]

17448 Nicholson, Dorinda Makanaonalani. *Pearl Harbor Child: A Child's View of Pearl Harbor — from Attack to Peace* (5–8). 1998, Woodson House paper $9.95 (978-1-892858-00-9). This photoessay describes a child's experience during the bombing of Pearl Harbor, the temporary evacuation, and everyday life growing up in Hawaii during World War II. (Rev: BL 1/1–15/99) [996.9]

17449 Nicholson, Dorinda Makanaonalani. *Remember World War II: Kids Who Survived Tell Their Stories* (5–8). Series: Remember. 2005, National Geographic LB

$27.90 (978-0-7922-7191-8). First-person accounts of World War II are given historical context plus illustrations, maps, and so forth; Madeleine Albright contributes an effective introduction. (Rev: BL 7/05; SLJ 8/05) [940.53]

17450 Nobleman, Marc Tyler. *The Sinking of the USS Indianapolis* (4–7). Series: We the People. 2006, Compass Point LB $26.60 (978-0-7565-2031-1). The story of the sinking of the *USS Indianapolis,* two weeks before the end of World War II, is told in straightforward text, with photographs and useful "Did You Know?" features. (Rev: SLJ 1/07)

17451 Panchyk, Richard. *World War II for Kids: A History with 21 Activities* (5–7). 2002, Chicago Review paper $14.95 (978-1-55652-455-4). Features on such topics as living on rations for a day, growing a victory garden, and tracking a ship's movements depict conditions in America and Europe during the war. (Rev: SLJ 12/02) [940.53]

17452 Perl, Lila, and Marion B. Lazan. *Four Perfect Pebbles: A Holocaust Story* (5–9). 1996, Greenwillow $16.99 (978-0-688-14294-0). A memoir of the horror and incredible tribulations suffered by the author's family in the detention camps and later death camps during the Holocaust. (Rev: BL 4/1/96; SLJ 5/96) [940.53]

17453 Raum, Elizabeth. *World War II: An Interactive History Adventure* (3–5). Illus. 2008, Capstone LB $20.99 (978-1-4296-2344-5). 112pp. Find yourself in the thick of World War II and choose between many available roles — an American soldier and a Dutch resistance worker, to name just two. (Rev: BL 4/1/09)

17454 Rice, Earle, Jr. *Blitzkrieg! Hitler's Lightning War* (5–8). Series: Monumental Milestones: Great Events of Modern Times. 2008, Mitchell Lane LB $20.95 (978-1-58415-542-3). The joint air-and-ground attacks that brought Hitler great success at the outset of World War II are the focus of this book that will interest reluctant readers. (Rev: BL 2/15/08) [940.54]

17455 Rogow, Sally M. *Faces of Courage: Young Heroes of World War II* (5–9). 2003, Granville Island $12.95 (978-1-894694-20-9). Based on true stories, this volume presents 12 fictionalized accounts of heroic actions by teenagers under Nazi rule in Europe. (Rev: BL 10/15/03) [940.53]

17456 Rubin, Susan G. *The Flag with Fifty-Six Stars* (4–6). Illus. by Bill Farnsworth. 2005, Holiday House $16.95 (978-0-8234-1653-0). 40pp. A picture book for older readers about the prisoners at the Mauthausen concentration camp and the American flag they sewed — with six extra stars. (Rev: BL 3/15/05; SLJ 5/05)

17457 Rubin, Susan Goldman. *Fireflies in the Dark: The Story of Friedl Dicker-Brandeis and the Children of Terezin* (5–10). 2000, Holiday $18.95 (978-0-8234-1461-1). A heartbreaking picture book that reproduces some of the artwork and writings of the children imprisoned at the Terezin concentration camp, where only 100 of 15,000 children survived. Sidney Taylor Book Honor 2000. (Rev: BCCB 11/00; BL 7/00*; HB 9–10/00; HBG 10/00; SLJ 8/00) [940.53]

17458 Rubin, Susan Goldman. *Searching for Anne Frank: Letters from Amsterdam to Iowa* (5–12). 2003, Abrams $19.95 (978-0-8109-4514-2). A brief penpal exchange between two sisters in Iowa and Anne Frank and her sister serves as the basis for a comparison between life in America and life for Jews in Europe. (Rev: BL 11/1/03; HB 11–12/03; HBG 4/04; SLJ 11/03; VOYA 10/03) [940.5]

17459 Ruelle, Karen Gray, and Deborah Durland DeSaix. *The Grand Mosque of Paris: A Story of How Muslims Rescued Jews During the Holocaust* (3–6). Illus. by Karen Gray Ruelle. 2009, Holiday House $17.95 (978-082342159-6). 40pp. This inspiring book describes how the Muslims of Paris threw their Grand Mosque open to Jews during the Nazi occupation and saved many lives. (Rev: BL 11/15/09; LMC 1–2/10; SLJ 10/09) [940.53]

17460 Russo, Marisabina. *Always Remember Me: How One Family Survived World War II* (3–5). Illus. 2005, Simon & Schuster $16.95 (978-0-689-86920-4). In this moving picture book for older readers, Oma shows her granddaughter family photographs and tells about her Jewish relatives' experiences in the Second World War. (Rev: BL 3/1/05; HBG 9/98; SLJ 4/05)

17461 Sandler, Martin W. *Why Did the Whole World Go to War? And Other Questions about World War II* (3–5). Illus. by Robert Barrett. Series: Good Question! 2013, Sterling $12.95 (978-140279621-0). 32pp. Using a question-and-answer format, this volume focuses on key events of the war that are likely to be of interest to young readers. (Rev: BL 3/15/13; LMC 10/13; SLJ 5/13) [940.53]

17462 Santella, Andrew. *Navajo Code Talkers* (3–6). Illus. Series: We the People. 2004, Compass Point LB $26.60 (978-0-7565-0611-7). 48pp. This absorbing account of the work of the Navajo Code Talkers during World War II includes a chart of code words for the letters of the alphabet. (Rev: BL 5/1/04; SLJ 8/04)

17463 Santella, Andrew. *Pearl Harbor* (4–6). Series: We the People. 2004, Compass Point LB $26.60 (978-0-7565-0680-3). 48pp. A well-illustrated brief discussion of the attack, the events leading up to it, and the building of the memorial. (Rev: SLJ 2/05)

17464 Schroeder, Peter W., and Dagmar Schroeder-Hildebrand. *Six Million Paper Clips: The Making of a Children's Holocaust Memorial* (5–8). Illus. 2004, Kar-Ben $17.95 (978-1-58013-169-8); paper $7.95 (978-1-58013-176-6). 64pp. This is the story of a Tennessee school project in which students collected 11 million paper clips to help them grasp the magnitude of the Holocaust's human toll. (Rev: BL 1/1–15/05; SLJ 7/05)

17465 Seiple, Samantha. *Ghosts in the Fog: The Untold Story of Alaska's WWII Invasion* (5–8). Illus. 2011, Scholastic $16.99 (978-0-545-29654-0). 224pp. Seiple gives us a fascinating and well-researched account of the Japanese invasion and occupation of Alaska in June 1942, including information about the detention of Native Americans. (Rev: BL 12/1/11; LMC 1–2/12; SLJ 11/1/11; VOYA 10/11) [940.54]

17466 Shapiro, Stephen, and Tina Forrester. *Ultra Hush-Hush: Espionage and Special Missions* (5–8). Illus. by David Craig. Series: Outwitting the Enemy. 2003, Annick LB $29.95 (978-1-55037-779-8); paper $14.95 (978-1-55037-778-1). Undercover activities during World War II are the focus of this volume that covers such groups and missions as the Navajo Code Talkers and Britain's double agents. (Rev: BL 8/03; SLJ 5/04) [940.54]

17467 Sheehan, Sean. *The Technology of World War II* (5–8). 2003, Raintree LB $28.56 (978-0-7398-6064-9). 64pp. New technologies introduced during World War II include radar, microwave transmissions, V-1 and V-2 rockets, the jet, codes, chemical and biological weapons, and the atom bomb. (Rev: HBG 10/03; SLJ 7/03)

17468 Sheinkin, Steve. *Bomb: The Race to Build — and Steal — the World's Most Dangerous Weapon* (5–10). 2012, Roaring Brook $19.99 (978-1-59643-487-5). 272pp. A compelling account of the race to build the atom bomb, full of espionage, heroism, and eccentric but brilliant characters. Robert F. Sibert Informational Book Award; Newbery Honor Book; Notable Children's Book; YALSA Award for Excellence in Nonfiction for Young Adults. ⌂ ℮ Lexile 920L (Rev: BL 9/1/12; HB 11–12/12; SLJ 10/12*; VOYA 10/12) [623.4]

17469 Steele, D. Kelly. *Would You Salute? One Child's Story of the Holocaust* (3–4). Illus. by Becky Hyatt Rickenbaker. 2006, Hidden Path $22.95 (978-0-9711534-2-4). Margot, whose mother is Christian and whose father is Jewish, faces difficult choices in Nazi Germany. (Rev: BL 7/06)

17470 Stein, R. Conrad. *World War II in the Pacific* (4–6). Illus. Series: U.S. Wars. 2002, Enslow LB $25.26 (978-0-7660-5093-8). 48pp. Supported by verified and updated Web links, this is a useful overview of the fighting in the Pacific during World War II. Also use *World War II in Europe* (2002). (Rev: HBG 3/03)

17471 Stone, Tanya Lee. *Courage Has No Color: The True Story of the Triple Nickles, America's First Black Paratroopers* (5–9). Illus. 2013, Candlewick $24.99 (978-076365117-6). 160pp. Readers learn about the 555th Parachute Infantry Battalion and these soldiers' contributions during World War II in the face of rampant racism. ℮ (Rev: BL 2/1/13*; LMC 8–9/13; SLJ 1/13*) [940.5403]

17472 Talbott, Hudson. *Forging Freedom* (4–7). Illus. 2000, Putnam $15.99 (978-0-399-23434-7). 64pp. This is the story of Jaap Penraat, a young architectural student in Amsterdam during the Nazi occupation who saved hundreds of Jews from deportation by forging papers and smuggling them out of the city. (Rev: BCCB 11/00; BL 7/00; HB 1/01; HBG 3/01; SLJ 11/00)

17473 Tanaka, Shelley. *Attack on Pearl Harbor: The True Story of the Day America Entered World War II* (5–8). Illus. Series: I Was There. 2001, Hyperion $19.99 (978-0-7868-0736-9). 64pp. An absorbing account of Pearl Harbor that presents the real-life, and very different, experiences of four young men who were there. (Rev: BL 8/01; HBG 10/01; SLJ 11/01; VOYA 12/01)

17474 Taylor, Theodore. *Air Raid — Pearl Harbor: The Story of December 7, 1941* (5–8). 1991, Harcourt paper $6.00 (978-0-15-201655-5). A fine account of why the attack occurred and the effects that were felt around the world. A revised edition. (Rev: SLJ 12/91) [940.54]

17475 van Maarsen, Jacqueline, and Carol Ann Lee. *A Friend Called Anne: One Girl's Story of War, Peace, and a Unique Friendship with Anne Frank* (5–8). 2005, Viking $15.99 (978-0-670-05958-4). Anne Frank's ordinary life before the war, and how things changed once the Nazis arrived, told by Anne's childhood friend. (Rev: BL 4/1/05; SLJ 4/05) [940.53]

17476 Vander Zee, Ruth. *Erika's Story* (3–6). Illus. by Roberto Innocenti. 2003, Creative $15.95 (978-1-56846-176-2). 24pp. A Jewish woman tells how an infant was thrown by her mother from a train headed for a concentration camp. (Rev: BL 11/1/03; HBG 4/04; SLJ 12/03)

17477 Warren, Andrea. *Surviving Hitler: A Boy in the Nazi Death Camps* (5–10). Illus. 2001, HarperCollins LB $17.89 (978-0-06-029218-8). 160pp. The true story of Jack Mandelbaum, who as a teenager survived three years in Nazi death camps through a combination of luck, courage, and friendship. (Rev: BCCB 3/01; BL 1/1–15/01; HB 3/01; HBG 10/01; SLJ 3/01)

17478 Welch, Catherine A. *Children of the Relocation Camps* (3–6). Series: Picture the American Past. 2000, Carolrhoda $22.60 (978-1-57505-350-9). 48pp. The story of the relocation of thousands of Japanese Americans after Pearl Harbor, how the children reacted, and how they built new lives within the camps. (Rev: BL 6/1–15/00; HBG 10/00; SLJ 10/00)

17479 White, Steve. *The Battle of Midway: The Destruction of the Japanese Fleet* (5–9). Illus. by Richard Elson. Series: Graphic Battles of World War II. 2007, Rosen LB $29.25 (978-1-4042-0783-7). 48pp. Historically accurate and detailed, this graphic account will engage readers in the story of an important World War II battle. (Rev: SLJ 7/07) [940.54265933]

17480 Whiteman, Dorit Bader. *Lonek's Journey: The True Story of a Boy's Escape to Freedom* (5–8). 2005, Star Bright $15.95 (978-1-59572-021-4). In this gripping true story that starts in 1939, a young Jew named Lonek survives the Nazis' arrival in Poland, a slave labor camp in Siberia, and the long, perilous journey to Palestine. (Rev: BL 11/15/05*; HBG 4/06; LMC 4–5/06; SLJ 1/06) [940.53]

17481 Whiting, Jim. *The Story of the Holocaust* (5–7). Series: Monumental Milestones: Great Events of Modern Times. 2006, Mitchell Lane LB $29.95 (978-1-58415-400-6). Although slim, this volume conveys a lot of information about the roots and atrocities of the Holocaust. (Rev: SLJ 5/06) [940.53]

17482 Whitman, Sylvia. *Children of the World War II Home Front* (3–6). Series: Picture the American Past. 2001, Carolrhoda LB $22.60 (978-1-57505-484-1). The lifestyle of children in America during World War II is presented through text and historic photographs. (Rev: BL 6/1–15/01; HBG 10/01; SLJ 7/01)

17483 Whitman, Sylvia. *Uncle Sam Wants You!* (5–7). 1993, Lerner LB $30.35 (978-0-8225-1728-3). This work describes the experiences of the many men and women who served in the various armed forces during World War II. (Rev: BL 5/1/93) [940.54]

17484 Wood, Douglas. *Franklin and Winston: A Christmas That Changed the World* (5–8). Illus. by Barry Moser. 2011, Candlewick $16.99 (978-076363383-7). 40pp. In December 1941, Churchill and FDR met and became friends during a tense time, discussing strategies that would have lasting consequences. (Rev: BL 9/15/11*; SLJ 10/1/11) [940.53]

Modern History

17485 Burgan, Michael. *The Berlin Airlift* (4–7). Series: We the People. 2006, Compass Point LB $26.60 (978-0-7565-2024-3). The story of the Berlin Airlift is told in straightforward text, with photographs and useful "Did You Know?" features. (Rev: SLJ 1/07) [943]

17486 Burgan, Michael. *The My Lai Massacre* (5–8). Series: We the People. 2008, Compass Point LB $26.60 (978-0-7565-3849-1). A simple account of the massacre with large photographs, useful for young researchers and reluctant readers. (Rev: SLJ 12/08) [959.704]

17487 Englar, Mary. *The Tet Offensive* (5–8). Series: We the People. 2008, Compass Point LB $26.60 (978-0-7565-3844-6). 48pp. A simple account of the offensive with discussion of its importance and large photographs, useful for young researchers and reluctant readers. (Rev: SLJ 12/08) [959.704]

17488 Gallagher, Jim. *Causes of the Iraq War* (5–8). Series: Road to War. 2005, OTTN LB $22.95 (978-1-59556-009-4). Explores the case put forward for the recent Iraq War, along with the views of those who oppose the conflict with good illustrations and appended material. (Rev: BL 10/15/05) [956.7044]

17489 Gunderson, Cory. *The Need for Oil* (5–8). Series: World in Conflict. 2004, ABDO LB $25.65 (978-1-59197-417-8). This history of conflicts over oil includes useful statistics and will be helpful to students seeking information for reports or background context before the recent Iraq war. (Rev: BL 4/1/04; SLJ 3/04) [338.2]

17490 Holden, Henry M. *The Persian Gulf War* (4–8). Series: U.S. Wars. 2003, Enslow LB $25.26 (978-0-7660-5109-6). 48pp. This concise, interesting account of the conflict in the early 1990s is enhanced by Internet access

to a set of monitored Web links. (Rev: HBG 10/03; SLJ 8/03)

17491 Murdico, Suzanne J. *The Gulf War* (5–9). Series: War and Conflict in the Middle East. 2004, Rosen LB $27.95 (978-0-8239-4551-1). Examines the 1991 war between Iraq and a coalition of nations. (Rev: BL 11/1/04) [956.7]

17492 Santella, Andrew. *The Korean War* (4–7). Series: We the People. 2006, Compass Point LB $26.60 (978-0-7565-2027-4). 48pp. A brief overview of the roots and progress of the conflict between the two parts of a divided nation. (Rev: SLJ 1/07)

17493 Santella, Andrew. *The Persian Gulf War* (3–6). Illus. Series: We the People. 2004, Compass Point LB $26.60 (978-0-7565-0612-4). Provides a concise description of the fall of Kuwait, the formation of the Desert Storm coalition, and the aftermath. [956.7]

17494 Schaffer, David. *The Iran-Iraq War* (5–8). Illus. Series: World History. 2002, Gale LB $32.45 (978-1-59018-184-3). 128pp. Schaffer traces the causes and progress of this long war, incorporating useful primary and secondary source material plus interesting sidebar features. (Rev: BL 5/1/03)

17495 Smith-Llera, Danielle. *Vietnam War POWs* (5–8). Series: We the People. 2008, Compass Point LB $26.60 (978-0-7565-3846-0). 48pp. A simple discussion of the plight of prisoners of war with large photographs, useful for young researchers and reluctant readers. (Rev: SLJ 12/08) [959.704]

17496 Stanley, George E. *America and the Cold War (1949–1969)* (5–8). Series: A Primary Source History of the United States. 2005, World Almanac LB $31.00 (978-0-8368-5830-3). A simple narrative links well-chosen primary sources documenting the key events of the Cold War. Also use *America in Today's World (1969–2004)* (2005). (Rev: BL 4/1/05)

17497 Taylor, David. *The Cold War* (5–9). Illus. Series: 20th Century Perspectives. 2001, Heinemann LB $25.64 (978-1-57572-434-8). 48pp. An easily understood account of the causes of tension between the Soviet Union and the West and the major crises of the "war." (Rev: HBG 3/02; SLJ 11/01)

17498 Willoughby, Douglas. *The Vietnam War* (5–9). Series: 20th Century Perspectives. 2001, Heinemann LB $25.64 (978-1-57572-439-3). 48pp. An easily understood and attractive account of Vietnam's relations with China, and of French and U.S. involvement in the country's affairs. (Rev: SLJ 11/01)

971

Geographical Regions

Africa

General

17499 Banting, Erinn. *The Nile River: The Longest River in the World* (3–6). Illus. Series: Natural Wonders. 2004, Weigl LB $18.20 (978-1-59036-269-3). 32pp. A look at the history of the Nile, the people who live on its banks, the animals and plants it supports, and the environmental threats it faces. (Rev: BL 4/1/04; HBG 3/03; SLJ 4/05)

17500 Bingham, Jane. *African Art and Culture* (5–8). Illus. Series: World Art and Culture. 2004, Raintree LB $29.99 (978-0-7398-6606-1). The indigenous art and culture of Africa from prehistoric times to the present are beautifully captured in this handsome and comprehensive overview. (Rev: BL 4/1/04; SLJ 2/04)

17501 Bowden, Rob. *Africa* (5–8). Series: Continents of the World. 2006, World Almanac LB $34.00 (978-0-8368-5910-2). 64pp. Factboxes and "In Focus" articles add to this overview of the history, geography, people, culture, and so forth of the continent of Africa. (Rev: SLJ 2/06)

17502 Bowden, Rob. *The Nile* (5–7). Series: A River Journey. 2003, Raintree LB $28.56 (978-0-7398-6072-4). 48pp. A trip down the length of East Africa's Nile, from its source to the sea, and a look at its importance to the people who live along it and the challenge of pollution, with photographs, maps, and charts. (Rev: SLJ 3/04)

17503 Bowden, Rob. *Settlements of the Nile* (3–5). Illus. Series: Rivers Through Time. 2005, Heinemann LB $29.93 (978-1-4034-5720-2). 48pp. Traces the history and contemporary life of major settlements along the Nile, discussing environmental and other important issues.

17504 Croze, Harvey. *Africa for Kids: Exploring a Vibrant Continent* (4–7). Illus. 2006, Chicago Review paper $17.95 (978-1-55652-598-8). 176pp. Africa's diver-

sity is highlighted in this accessible volume that covers history, nature, key individuals, and contemporary problems such as poverty, war, AIDS, and the environment; there are 19 activities. (Rev: BL 8/06) [916.22]

17505 Graf, Mike. *Africa* (K–3). Series: Continents. 2002, Capstone LB $21.26 (978-0-7368-1414-0). 24pp. With maps and full-color graphics, this is a brief introduction to the geography, history, flora, fauna, and peoples of Africa. (Rev: HBG 3/03; SLJ 4/03)

17506 Knight, Margy B., and Mark Melnicove. *Africa Is Not a Country* (1–3). Illus. by Anne S. O'Brien. 2000, Millbrook $24.90 (978-0-7613-1266-6). 40pp. This book celebrates the diversity of the African continent by portraying children from various countries and supplying a vignette about each of them. (Rev: BL 11/15/00; HBG 3/01; SLJ 1/01)

17507 Meister, Cari. *Nile River* (3–4). Series: Rivers and Lakes. 2002, ABDO LB $21.35 (978-1-57765-098-0). 24pp. A solid introduction to the Nile, its tributaries, flora and fauna, and the ways in which it has influenced human development in the area throughout history. (Rev: HBG 10/02; SLJ 7/02)

17508 Opini, Bathseba, and Richard B. Lee. *Africans Thought of It: Amazing Innovations* (3–6). Illus. Series: We Thought of It. 2011, Annick LB $21.95 (978-1-55451-277-5); paper $11.95 (978-1-55451-276-8). 48pp. Looks at inventions by Africans in fields as varied as hunting, agriculture, medicine, sports, and the arts. (Rev: LMC 3–4/12; SLJ 10/1/11) [960]

17509 Weintraub, Aileen. *Discovering Africa's Land, People, and Wildlife* (5–8). Series: Continents of the World. 2004, Enslow LB $25.26 (978-0-7660-5204-8). 48pp. An introduction to the geography, history, economy, plants and animals, culture, and peoples of the continent, with discussion of the continuing need for foreign aid in many countries. (Rev: SLJ 11/04)

17510 Woods, Michael, and Mary B. Woods. *Seven Natural Wonders of Africa* (5–8). Series: Seven Natural Wonders. 2009, Twenty-First Century LB $33.26 (978-

0-8225-9071-2). 80pp. The Nile, Victoria Falls, Sahara Desert, Mount Kilimanjaro, Seychelles Islands, Serengeti Plain, and mountain gorillas are the seven wonders featured in this attractive volume. (Rev: BL 4/1/09; LMC 10/09*; SLJ 5/09) [508.6]

Central and Eastern Africa

17511 Allen, Christina. *Hippos in the Night: Autobiographical Adventures in Africa* (4–8). Illus. by Rob Shepperson. 2003, HarperCollins LB $17.89 (978-0-688-17827-7). 144pp. An appealing account of a camping trip through Kenya and Tanzania, with details of the exciting animals and fascinating people encountered on the way. (Rev: BL 4/15/03; HBG 10/03; SLJ 4/03)

17512 Ayodo, Awuor. *Luo* (4–7). Series: Heritage Library of African Peoples. 1995, Rosen LB $29.25 (978-0-8239-1758-7). A portrait of the culture, history, and society of the Luo people, who lived on the shores of Lake Victoria in Kenya. (Rev: BL 3/1/96) [967.8]

17513 Bangura, Abdul Karim. *Kipsigis* (5–8). Series: Heritage Library of African Peoples. 1994, Rosen LB $29.25 (978-0-8239-1765-5). An attractive title that deals with the history and present status of the Kipsigis people of Kenya. (Rev: SLJ 5/95) [967.62]

17514 Barber, Nicola. *Living in the African Savannah* (3–5). Illus. 2007, Raintree LB $27.50 (978-1-4109-2814-6). 32pp. Barber looks at the Maasai people and their life on the savannah, covering homes, food and clothing, school and language, music and dance, and ceremonies. (Rev: SLJ 2/08)

17515 Bessire, Aimee, and Mark Bessire. *Sukuma* (5–8). Series: Heritage Library of African Peoples. 1997, Rosen LB $29.25 (978-0-8239-1992-5). Describes the history, culture, leaders, customs, and present situation of the Sukuma people of Tanzania. (Rev: BL 9/15/97; VOYA 12/97) [967.6]

17516 Bojang, Ali Brownlie. *Sudan in Our World* (5–8). Series: Countries in Our World. 2010, Smart Apple $28.50 (978-1-59920-434-5). 32pp. Bojang covers Sudan's geography, people, culture, economy, government, and future, with frank discussion of the poverty and fighting that have plagued the country. (Rev: SLJ 12/1/10) [962.4]

17517 Corona, Laurel. *Ethiopia* (5–8). Series: Modern Nations of the World. 2000, Lucent LB $29.95 (978-1-56006-823-5). An attractive, well-organized introduction to Ethiopia that gives its history, geography, and culture plus national statistics, a chronology, and bibliographies. (Rev: BL 3/1/01) [963]

17518 Craats, Rennay. *Maasai* (4–6). Illus. Series: Indigenous Peoples. 2005, Weigl $7.95 (978-1-59036-255-6). 32pp. A fascinating and informative overview of the Maasai people, covering history, culture, language, and family life.

17519 De Capua, Sarah. *Malawi in Pictures* (5–8). Illus. Series: Visual Geography. 2009, Lerner LB $31.93 (978-0-8225-1842-6). 80pp. A revised edition of this overview of Malawi's climate, history, geography, culture, education, and other aspects of life in this African nation. (Rev: BL 2/1/89)

17520 Deady, Kathleen W. *Rwanda* (2–5). Illus. Series: Questions and Answers: Countries. 2005, Capstone LB $23.93 (978-0-7368-3759-0). 32pp. Using a question-and-answer format, simple text, large photos, and many factboxes, this is an introduction to Rwanda today, with material on history and traditional culture.

17521 Delzio, Suzanne. *Ethiopia* (2–3). Illus. Series: Many Cultures, One World. 2004, Capstone LB $23.93 (978-0-7368-2449-1). A brief, accessible introduction to Ethiopia and its people, family life, customs, and legends.

17522 Diouf, Sylviane. *Kings and Queens of Central Africa* (4–7). Series: Watts Library: Africa — Kings and Queens. 2000, Watts LB $25.50 (978-0-531-20372-9). 64pp. This look at the political and social evolution of central Africa describes some of its important royalty including the 15th-century Afonso and Bolongongo, the legendary Bakuba king, with a final chapter on the region today. (Rev: BL 3/1/01)

17523 Diouf, Sylviane. *Kings and Queens of East Africa* (4–7). Illus. Series: Watts Library: Africa — Kings and Queens. 2000, Watts LB $25.50 (978-0-531-20373-6). 64pp. This book gives biographical information about royalty in East Africa and through these sketches re-creates the history of this part of Africa. (Rev: BL 2/15/01)

17524 DiPiazza, Francesca. *Sudan in Pictures* (5–8). Illus. Series: Visual Geography. 2006, Lerner LB $31.93 (978-0-8225-1839-6). 80pp. An updated overview of history, culture, geography, economy, education, and health in this African nation. (Rev: BL 2/1/89)

17525 *Ethiopia in Pictures* (5–8). Series: Visual Geography. 1994, Lerner LB $21.27 (978-0-8225-1836-5). Land, history and government, culture, education, religion, and health are covered. (Rev: BL 2/1/89) [963]

17526 Giles, Bridget. *Kenya* (4–8). Series: Nations of the World. 2001, Raintree LB $34.26 (978-0-7398-1290-7). 128pp. From snow-capped mountains to scorching deserts, this geographically and culturally diverse African nation is attractively introduced in this volume. (Rev: BL 12/15/01; HBG 3/02; SLJ 12/01)

17527 Kairi, Wambui. *Kenya* (2–4). Series: We Come From. 2000, Raintree LB $25.69 (978-0-8172-5512-1). A young native guide gives basic facts about Kenya, explains how to cook some delicious dishes, and makes simple toys. (Rev: BL 4/15/00; HBG 10/00)

17528 McQuail, Lisa. *The Masai of Africa* (4–7). Illus. Series: First Peoples. 2001, Lerner LB $23.93 (978-0-8225-4855-3). 48pp. McQuail provides information about the Masai people, covering their history, customs, and contemporary daily life, with photographs. (Rev: BL 10/15/01; HBG 3/02; SLJ 3/02)

17529 *Malawi in Pictures* (5–8). Series: Visual Geography. 1989, Lerner LB $25.55 (978-0-8225-1842-6). An overview of climate, history, geography, culture, education, and other aspects of life. (Rev: BL 2/1/89) [968.97]

17530 Nicolotti, Muriel. *Kuntai: A Masai Child* (K–3). Series: Children of the World. 2005, Gale LB $22.45 (978-1-4103-0290-8). 24pp. Using many photographs, this volume introduces the lifestyle and customs of the Masai, a nomadic people living in East Africa; suitable for browsers rather than report writers. (Rev: SLJ 10/05)

17531 Nnoromele, Salome. *Somalia* (5–8). Series: Modern Nations of the World. 2000, Lucent LB $27.45 (978-1-56006-396-4). 112pp. An introduction to this East African country with material on its history and geography and a large section on daily life. (Rev: BL 5/15/00; HBG 10/00)

17532 Oghojafor, Kingsley. *Uganda* (5–8). Series: Countries of the World. 2004, Gareth Stevens LB $31.00 (978-0-8368-3112-2). 96pp. Introduces readers to the African country's geography, history, people, culture, and government and also takes a look at its relations with other countries and contemporary challenges. (Rev: SLJ 8/04)

17533 Onyefulu, Ifeoma. *Home* (PS–1). Illus. Series: Look at This! 2013, Frances Lincoln $17.99 (978-184780266-8). 28pp. Two-page spreads show objects in the life of a family in Mali. (Rev: BL 10/1/13*) [640]

17534 Parris, Ronald. *Rendille* (5–8). Series: Heritage Library of African Peoples. 1994, Rosen LB $29.25 (978-0-8239-1763-1). With extensive use of black-and-white and color photographs, introduces the history and customs of the Rendille people of Kenya. (Rev: SLJ 5/95) [967.62]

17535 Pateman, Robert. *Kenya* (4–7). Series: Cultures of the World. 1993, Marshall Cavendish LB $35.64 (978-1-85435-572-0). The background story of Kenya is revealed through color photographs and a text that also covers present concerns. (Rev: BL 8/93) [967.62]

17536 Prentzas, G. Scott. *Democratic Republic of the Congo* (4–6). Illus. Series: Social Studies Explorer. 2012, Cherry Lake LB $31.36 (978-161080443-1). 48pp. An attractive, photo-filled overview of this nation, with maps, information on the economy and government, people and culture, and so forth, plus a recipe and a craft. **e** (Rev: BL 3/1/13; LMC 10/13) [967.51]

17537 Pritchett, Bev. *Tanzania in Pictures* (5–8). Illus. Series: Visual Geography. 2007, Lerner LB $31.93 (978-0-8225-1838-9). 80pp. This revised edition contains information on history, geography, economy, religion, and culture. (Rev: BL 2/1/89)

17538 Reynolds, Jan. *Only the Mountains Do Not Move: A Maasai Story of Culture and Conservation* (2–5). Illus. 2011, Lee & Low $18.95 (978-1-60060-333-4). 40pp. Reynolds offers a glimpse into the daily life of a Maasai village in northern Kenya, showing all the ways it has adapted to political, cultural, and environmental challenges. (Rev: BL 9/1/11; SLJ 10/1/11) [305.896]

17539 Roth, Susan L., and Cindy Trumbore. *The Mangrove Tree: Planting Trees to Feed Families* (3–7). Illus. by author. 2011, Lee & Low $19.95 (978-1-60060-459-1). 40pp. In simple cumulative verse, this picture book tells the story of Japanese American biologist Gordon Sato's project to plant mangrove trees in Eritrea and help the surrounding community. ALA Notable Children's Book 2012. (Rev: BL 5/1/11; SLJ 5/1/11*) [577.69]

17540 Roth, Susan L., and Karen Leggett Abouraya. *Hands around the Library: Protecting Egypt's Treasured Books* (2–4). Illus. by Susan L. Roth. 2012, Dial $16.99 (978-0-8037-3747-1). 40pp. With appealing collage art, this tells the story of young people seeking to protect the famous Alexandria Library during the 2011 Egyptian Revolution. (Rev: BL 9/1/12; LMC 11–12/12*; SLJ 9/12) [962.055]

17541 Schemenauer, Elma. *Somalia* (3–5). Series: Faces and Places. 2001, Child's World LB $22.79 (978-1-56766-911-4). Basic facts about Somalia are given in a simple introduction with large type, many color photographs, and a text that emphasizes the everyday life of the people. (Rev: BL 9/15/01; HBG 3/02; SLJ 12/01)

17542 Schemenauer, Elma. *Uganda* (3–5). Series: Countries: Faces and Places. 2003, Child's World LB $25.64 (978-1-56766-941-1). A brief introduction to the geography, history, people, culture, and flora and fauna of this landlocked country. (Rev: SLJ 7/03)

17543 Schemenauer, Elma. *Welcome to Somalia* (1–4). Series: Wecome to the World. 2008, The Child's World LB $27.07 (978-1-59296-976-0). 32pp. As easy introduction to Somalia and its land, people, plants and animals, and so forth, with color photographs, maps, and recipes. (Rev: LMC 10/08; SLJ 9/08)

17544 Schnapper, LaDena. *Teenage Refugees from Ethiopia Speak Out* (5–10). Series: Teenage Refugees Speak Out. 1997, Rosen LB $27.95 (978-0-8239-2438-7). Ethiopian teens now living in America tell of the violence, famine, and civil war that drove them from their country and of their reception in America. (Rev: SLJ 2/98) [963]

17545 Shoveller, Herb. *Ryan and Jimmy: And the Well in Africa That Brought Them Together* (3–6). Illus. 2006, Kids Can $16.95 (978-1-55337-967-6). 55pp. In this inspiring story of one boy's efforts to make a difference in the world, readers learn about Ryan Hreljac, a Canadian boy who raised money to build a well in Africa and worked to rescue Akana Jimmy, the young Ugandan friend abducted by rebels. (Rev: SLJ 11/06)

17546 *Sudan in Pictures* (5–8). Series: Visual Geography. 1990, Lerner LB $25.55 (978-0-8225-1839-6). An overview of history, culture, geography, economy, education, and health. (Rev: BL 2/1/89) [962.4]

17547 Swinimer, Ciarunji C. *Pokot* (5–8). Series: Heritage Library of African Peoples. 1994, Rosen LB $29.25 (978-0-8239-1756-3). Using a good balance of text and visuals, this account describes the history, culture, and present status of the Pokot people of Kenya. (Rev: SLJ 5/95) [967.62]

17548 Tanguay, Bridget. *Kenya* (4–7). Illus. Series: Countries of the World. 2006, National Geographic $19.95 (978-0-7922-7628-9). 64pp. An overview of Kenya with information on the country's history, land, people, government, economy and present issues; excellent color photographs and maps are included. (Rev: SLJ 3/07)

17549 Twagilimana, Aimable. *Hutu and Tutsi* (5–9). Series: The Heritage Library of African Peoples. 1997, Rosen LB $29.25 (978-0-8239-1999-4). A large section of this book is devoted to the current struggle between the Hutu and Tutsi people of central Africa, along with chapters on art and religion. (Rev: SLJ 3/98) [967]

17550 Twagilimana, Aimable. *Teenage Refugees from Rwanda Speak Out* (5–10). Series: Teenage Refugees Speak Out. 1997, Rosen LB $27.95 (978-0-8239-2443-1). Teenage refugees from Rwanda describe the warfare between Tutsi and Hutu peoples, the terrible living conditions that forced them to leave their country, and the challenges and difficulties they have experienced in the United States. (Rev: SLJ 2/98) [967]

17551 Willis, Terri. *Democratic Republic of the Congo* (4–6). Series: Enchantment of the World. 2004, Scholastic LB $37.00 (978-0-516-24250-7). 144pp. Contemporary life, history, geography, culture are all covered in this well-illustrated and well-written volume suitable for report writers. (Rev: BL 9/1/04)

17552 Zeleza, Tiyambe. *Maasai* (5–8). Series: Heritage Library of African Peoples. 1994, Rosen LB $29.25 (978-0-8239-1757-0). An introduction to these people of Kenya and Tanzania, their culture, customs, and history. (Rev: SLJ 5/95) [967.62]

Northern Africa

17553 Barber, Nicola. *Living in the Sahara* (3–5). Series: World Cultures. 2007, Raintree LB $27.50 (978-1-4109-2816-0). 32pp. Barber looks at the people of the desert and various aspects of life there including homes, food and clothing, school and leisure, music and poetry, and celebrations. (Rev: SLJ 2/08)

17554 Bodden, Valerie. *Suez Canal* (3–6). Series: Modern Wonders of the World. 2006, Creative Education LB $27.10 (978-1-58341-441-5). 32pp. An interesting overview of the canal's history, construction, and impact on both world commerce and politics. (Rev: SLJ 12/06)

17555 Giraud, Hervé. *Leila: A Tuareg Child* (K–3). Photos by Jean-Charles Rey. 2005, Gale LB $22.45 (978-1-4103-0545-9). 24pp. Using many photographs, this volume introduces the rootless, nomadic lifestyle of a young Berber girl. (Rev: SLJ 10/05)

17556 Malcolm, Peter. *Libya* (4–7). 1993, Marshall Cavendish LB $35.64 (978-1-85435-573-7). Well-chosen photographs and readable text give good background information as well as material on present problems. (Rev: BL 8/93) [961.2]

17557 Merrick, Patrick. *Morocco* (3–5). Series: Countries: Faces and Places. 2000, Child's World LB $22.79 (978-1-56766-737-0). 32pp. An oversize book filled with color illustrations that describes the history, geography, and people of Morocco. (Rev: BL 4/15/01; HBG 3/01)

17558 Weintraub, Aileen. *The Sahara Desert: The Biggest Desert* (3–5). Illus. Series: Great Record Breakers in Nature. 2001, Rosen $21.25 (978-0-8239-5640-1). Informative text and dramatic full-page photographs introduce the world's biggest desert and its composition, extraordinary range of temperatures, residents, and fossil history. (Rev: BL 12/15/01; SLJ 7/01)

Southern Africa

17559 Bojang, Ali Brownlie. *South Africa in Our World* (5–8). Series: Countries in Our World. 2010, Smart Apple $28.50 (978-1-59920-444-4). 32pp. Bojang covers South Africa's geography, people, culture, economy, government, and future, with frank discussion of such topics as apartheid and AIDS. (Rev: SLJ 12/1/10) [968.06]

17560 Brownlie, Alison. *South Africa* (2–4). Illus. Series: We Come From. 2000, Raintree $25.69 (978-0-8172-5221-2). 32pp. Readers are introduced to South Africa, the homeland of this book's 7-year-old narrator, including its geography, food, weather, work, schools, and other topics. (Rev: BL 4/15/00; HBG 10/00; SLJ 10/00)

17561 Diouf, Sylviane. *Kings and Queens of Southern Africa* (4–7). Illus. Series: Watts Library: Africa — Kings and Queens. 2000, Watts LB $25.50 (978-0-531-20374-3). 64pp. Through the lives of Shaka the Zulu king, Moshoeshoe of the Sotho kingdom, and others, the reader gets a good history of this region before and during the colonial period. (Rev: BL 2/15/01)

17562 Green, Jen. *South Africa* (4–8). Series: Nations of the World. 2001, Raintree LB $34.26 (978-0-7398-1282-2). 128pp. A profile of the strongest industrial nation in Africa, with material on its geography, resources, environment, government, economy, and future. (Rev: BL 6/1–15/01; HBG 10/01)

17563 Langley, Andrew. *Cape Town* (4–7). Series: Great Cities of the World. 2005, World Almanac LB $31.00 (978-0-8368-5045-1). An informative and appealing overview of this major city, with material on its history, its economy, and what it's like to live there. (Rev: BL 4/15/04)

17564 Oluonye, Mary N. *Madagascar* (1–3). Series: Globe-Trotters Club. 2000, Carolrhoda LB $22.60 (978-1-57505-120-8). 48pp. From the monsoons to the comfortable dry season, this is a simple introduction to the island off the coast of Africa that is known as "a World Apart." (Rev: BL 5/15/00; HBG 10/00)

17565 Parker, Linda J. *The San of Africa* (4–6). Series: First Peoples. 2002, Lerner LB $23.93 (978-0-8225-4177-6). This account describes the history and culture of this nomadic people of the Kalahari Desert. (Rev: BL 5/15/02; HBG 10/02)

17566 Rogers, Barbara Radcliffe, and Stillman D. Rogers. *Zimbabwe* (4–7). Series: Enchantment of the World. 2002, Children's LB $37.00 (978-0-516-21113-8). 144pp. This troubled African land is introduced with material on topics including history, geography, people, government, and resources. (Rev: BL 5/15/02; SLJ 7/02)

17567 Rosemarin, Ike. *South Africa* (4–7). Series: Cultures of the World. 1993, Marshall Cavendish LB $35.64 (978-1-85435-575-1). Historical and modern concerns are covered in this look at South Africa. (Rev: BL 8/93) [968]

17568 Ryan, Patrick. *Welcome to South Africa* (1–4). Series: Welcome to the World. 2008, The Child's World LB $27.07 (978-1-59296-977-7). 32pp. As easy introduction to South Africa and its land, people, plants and animals, and so forth, with color photographs, maps, and recipes. (Rev: LMC 10/08; SLJ 9/08)

17569 *South Africa in Pictures* (5–8). Series: Visual Geography. 1996, Lerner LB $25.55 (978-0-8225-1835-8). Focusing on climate, geography, wildlife, and the history of this troubled country. (Rev: BL 8/88) [968.06]

17570 *To Everything There Is a Season* (2–4). Illus. by Jude Daly. 2006, Eerdmans $16.00 (978-0-8028-5286-1). The familiar words from Ecclesiastes are used as the framework for a portrait of life in rural South Africa. (Rev: BL 4/15/06; SLJ 3/06)

17571 Van Wyk, Gary N. *Basotho* (5–7). Series: Heritage Library of African Peoples. 1996, Rosen LB $29.25 (978-0-8239-2005-1). Describes the Basotho people, who live in Lesotho and South Africa, with simple text on their history, religion, social organization, and customs. (Rev: BL 11/15/96; SLJ 3/97) [968]

17572 Van Wyk, Gary N., and Robert Johnson. *Shona* (5–7). Series: Heritage Library of African Peoples. 1997, Rosen LB $29.25 (978-0-8239-2011-2). The Shona people of Zimbabwe are presented in outstanding photographs, with a text that covers their past, their culture, and their present living conditions and problems. (Rev: BL 1/1–15/98) [968]

17573 Wulfsohn, Gisèle. *A Child's Day in a South African City* (K–3). Illus. Series: A Child's Day. 2003, Marshall Cavendish $25.64 (978-0-7614-1407-0). 32pp. A black South African child's experiences in his integrated school and blended family, with explanations of his country's customs and culture. (Rev: BL 2/15/03; HBG 3/03; SLJ 2/03)

17574 *Zimbabwe in Pictures* (5–8). Series: Visual Geography. 1997, Lerner LB $25.55 (978-0-8225-1825-9). Many photographs highlight this overview of Zimbabwe's history, climate, wildlife, and culture. (Rev: BL 4/15/88) [968]

Western Africa

17575 Adeleke, Tunde. *Songhay* (5–7). Series: Heritage Library of African Peoples. 1996, Rosen LB $29.25 (978-0-8239-1986-4). Both historical information and material on contemporary life are given in this account of the African people who live chiefly in Mali, Niger, and Benin. (Rev: BL 11/15/96) [960]

17576 Barr, Gary E. *History and Activities of the West African Kingdoms* (3–6). Illus. Series: Hands-on Ancient

History. 2006, Heinemann LB $28.21 (978-1-4034-7925-9). 32pp. Social life, arts and culture, games, and holidays and celebrations are covered in this attractive and accessible volume that includes a recipe, two crafts, and an activity (a game of Mancala). (Rev: SLJ 4/07)

17577 Boateng, Faustine Ama. *Asante* (5–7). Series: Heritage Library of African Peoples. 1996, Rosen LB $29.25 (978-0-8239-1975-8). This African people living in present-day Ghana is described, with information on history, traditions, and lifestyle. (Rev: BL 11/15/96; SLJ 3/97) [966.7]

17578 Bowden, Rob, and Roy Maconachie. *Nigeria* (5–7). Series: The Changing Face Of. 2003, Raintree LB $28.56 (978-0-7398-6829-4). 48pp. An examination of modern-day Nigeria, with a look at the nation's past difficulties and how it may benefit from its wealth of natural resources. (Rev: SLJ 4/04)

17579 Brook, Larry. *Daily Life in Ancient and Modern Timbuktu* (5–7). 1999, Lerner LB $25.26 (978-0-8225-3215-6). A fascinating look at this ancient West African city that was once a center of commerce and learning. (Rev: BL 9/1/99; HBG 10/99; SLJ 7/99) [966.23]

17580 Brownlie, Alison. *Nigeria* (2–4). Series: We Come From. 2000, Raintree LB $25.69 (978-0-8172-5513-8). 32pp. Using a native child as a guide, this introduction to Nigeria gives basic information on the country plus such specialized coverage as a trip to local markets, making a fish stew, a game of hide and seek, and several recipes. (Rev: BL 4/15/00; HBG 10/00; SLJ 10/00)

17581 Diouf, Sylviane. *Kings and Queens of West Africa* (4–7). Series: Watts Library: Africa — Kings and Queens. 2000, Watts LB $25.50 (978-0-531-20375-0). 64pp. Some of the royal figures covered in this historical survey of West Africa are Emperor Mansa Musa of Mali and Nsate Yalla Mbodj, queen of the Walo of Senegal. (Rev: BL 3/1/01)

17582 Dubois, Muriel L. *Liberia* (2–5). Illus. Series: Questions and Answers: Countries. 2005, Capstone LB $23.93 (978-0-7368-3755-2). 32pp. Using a question-and-answer format, simple text, large photos, and many factboxes, this is an introduction to Liberia today, with material on history and traditional culture.

17583 Hamilton, Janice. *Ivory Coast in Pictures* (5–8). Illus. Series: Visual Geography. 2004, Lerner LB $31.93 (978-0-8225-1828-0). 80pp. This updated edition looks at the geography, history and government, people, cultural life, and economy of West Africa's second-richest nation. (Rev: BL 4/15/88; SLJ 11/88)

17584 Heinrichs, Ann. *Niger* (4–7). Series: Enchantment of the World. 2001, Children's LB $37.00 (978-0-516-21633-1). Niger, a predominately Muslim country that is one of the hottest places in the world, is described in this attractive volume with material on topics such as resources, history, and culture. (Rev: BL 1/1–15/02)

17585 *Liberia in Pictures* (5–8). Series: Visual Geography. 1996, Lerner LB $25.55 (978-0-8225-1837-2). Covers climate, geography, wildlife, vegetation, and natural resources. (Rev: BL 8/88) [966.62]

17586 Murphy, Patricia J. *Nigeria* (3–5). Illus. Series: Discovering Cultures. 2004, Benchmark LB $25.64 (978-0-7614-1795-8). 48pp. An attractive introduction to Nigeria, covering land, people, daily life, education, food, and celebrations, with discussion of the relationships among the many tribes. (Rev: SLJ 6/05)

17587 Nelson, Julie. *West African Kingdoms* (3–5). Series: Ancient Civilizations. 2001, Raintree LB $22.83 (978-0-7398-3581-4). Readers will gain an understanding of the history and culture of the ancient civilizations of Ghana, Mali, and Songhai. (Rev: SLJ 2/02)

17588 *Nigeria in Pictures* (5–8). Series: Visual Geography. 1995, Lerner LB $25.55 (978-0-8225-1826-6). A visual focus on this African land. (Rev: BL 8/88) [966.9]

17589 Nwanunobi, C. O. *Malinke* (5–7). Series: Heritage Library of African Peoples. 1996, Rosen LB $29.25 (978-0-8239-1979-6). Features the culture, history, and contemporary lifeways of the Malinke people, now living along the western coast of Africa. (Rev: BL 11/15/96) [966.23]

17590 Nwanunobi, C. O. *Soninke* (5–7). Series: Heritage Library of African Peoples. 1996, Rosen LB $29.25 (978-0-8239-1978-9). A discussion of the African people found in such countries as Ghana, Mali, Nigeria, and Senegal, with material on history, customs, and present living conditions. (Rev: BL 11/15/96) [966]

17591 Oluonye, Mary N. *Nigeria* (2–4). Illus. Series: Country Explorers. 2007, Lerner LB $27.93 (978-0-8225-7131-5). 48pp. History, geography, culture, sports, animals, and so forth are covered in conversational text and color photographs. (Rev: BL 10/15/07; LMC 1/08; SLJ 12/07)

17592 Onyefulu, Ifeoma. *Here Comes Our Bride! An African Wedding Story* (K–3). Illus. 2004, Lincoln $15.95 (978-1-84507-047-2). 32pp. A Nigerian wedding comes to life in this attractive photoessay that captures all the local traditions and rituals before, during, and after the marriage ceremony. (Rev: BL 9/1/04)

17593 Onyefulu, Ifeoma. *Saying Good-Bye: A Special Farewell to Mama Nkwelle* (PS–2). Illus. 2001, Millbrook $22.90 (978-0-7613-1965-8). 32pp. A young boy describes the two weeks of mourning and the traditional Nigerian village funeral that take place on his great-grandmother's death. (Rev: BL 5/1/01; HB 7/01; HBG 10/01; SLJ 7/01)

17594 Onyefulu, Ifeoma. *Welcome Dede! An African Naming Ceremony* (K–3). Illus. 2005, Frances Lincoln paper $7.95 (978-1-84507-311-4). A dazzling photoessay of a traditional ceremony in a Ghanaian village. (Rev: BL 2/1/05)

17595 Parris, Ronald. *Hausa* (5–7). Series: Heritage Library of African Peoples. 1996, Rosen LB $29.25 (978-0-8239-1983-3). A look at the Hausa people of Niger and Nigeria, with material on history and contemporary life. (Rev: BL 11/15/96) [966]

17596 Provencal, Francis, and Catherine McNamara. *A Child's Day in a Ghanaian City* (1–3). Series: A Child's Day. 2001, Benchmark LB $25.64 (978-0-7614-1223-

6). 32pp. A 7-year-old escorts readers through a typical day in this book that ends with brief information on history, geography, people, religion, and language. (Rev: BL 11/15/01; SLJ 3/02)

17597 Reece, Katherine. *West African Kingdoms: Empires of Gold and Trade* (3–5). Illus. Series: Ancient Civilizations. 2005, Rourke LB $20.95 (978-1-59515-508-5). 48pp. This striking photoessay introduces the culture, geography, people, language, religion, and wildlife of three ancient West African kingdoms — Ghana, Mali, and Songhai. (Rev: BL 3/15/06; SLJ 4/06)

17598 Shuter, Jane. *Ancient West African Kingdoms* (3–5). Illus. Series: History Opens Windows. 2002, Heinemann LB $22.79 (978-1-4034-0255-4). Readers will learn about government, trade, and everyday life in the kingdoms of Ghana, Mali, and Songhai. (Rev: HBG 3/03; SLJ 3/03)

17599 Streissguth, Thomas. *Senegal in Pictures* (5–8). Illus. Series: Visual Geography. 2009, Lerner LB $31.93 (978-0-8225-1827-3). 80pp. An updated look at the geography, history, culture, and economics of Senegal. (Rev: BL 4/15/89; SLJ 11/88)

17600 Taylor, Dereen. *Nigeria* (4–7). Illus. Series: A World of Food. 2010, Oliver LB $24.95 (978-193454514-0). 32pp. This book presents an overview of Nigeria's cuisine, complete with simple recipes, colorful illustrations, and plenty of cultural context. (Rev: BL 4/1/10; LMC 10/10) [394.1]

Asia

General

17601 Bowden, Rob. *Asia* (5–8). Series: Continents of the World. 2006, World Almanac LB $34.00 (978-0-8368-5911-9). Factboxes and "In Focus" articles add to this overview of the history, geography, people, culture, and so forth of the continent of Asia. (Rev: SLJ 2/06) [915]

17602 Bramwell, Martyn. *Southern and Eastern Asia* (4–8). Illus. Series: The World in Maps. 2001, Lerner LB $23.93 (978-0-8225-2916-3). 48pp. For each country in these geographical areas, readers will find a color map, the flag, a box containing important facts, and brief discussions of geography, industry, and economy. Also use *Northern and Western Asia* (2001). (Rev: HBG 10/01; SLJ 7/01)

17603 Dramer, Kim. *The Mekong River* (4–8). Series: Watts Library. 2001, Watts LB $25.50 (978-0-531-11854-2). 63pp. A fact-filled introduction to the history of the Mekong and to the landscape and industry found along it. (Rev: SLJ 5/01)

17604 Hammond, Paula. *China and Japan* (4–8). Illus. Series: Cultures and Costumes: Symbols of Their Period. 2003, Mason Crest LB $19.95 (978-1-59084-436-6). 64pp. A detailed survey of the history of garments and accessories worn by people of all classes in these two Asian nations prior to the 20th century. (Rev: SLJ 3/04)

17605 Helget, Nicole. *Mongols* (5–8). Illus. Series: Fearsome Fighters. 2012, Creative Education $24.95 (978-160818184-1). 48pp. With many illustrations, maps, and primary documents, this volume looks at the Mongols and their society, weapons, fighting techniques, key figures, and so forth. (Rev: BL 11/1/12; LMC 5–6/13; SLJ 12/12)

17606 Kalz, Jill. *Mount Everest* (4–6). Illus. Series: Natural Wonders of the World. 2004, Creative Education LB $18.95 (978-1-58341-325-8). 32pp. After establishing this important mountain's location, this oversized picture book full of color photographs looks at geology, climate, wildlife, people, and other pertinent facts. (Rev: SLJ 1/05)

17607 Kilgallon, Conor. *India and Sri Lanka* (4–8). Illus. Series: Cultures and Costumes: Symbols of Their Period. 2003, Mason Crest LB $19.95 (978-1-59084-443-4). 64pp. A look at the history of garments and accessories worn by all classes of people in India and Sri Lanka up to the end of the 19th century. (Rev: SLJ 3/04)

17608 Major, John S., and Betty J. Belanus. *Caravan to America: Living Arts of the Silk Road* (5–8). 2002, Cricket $24.95 (978-0-8126-2666-7); paper $15.95 (978-0-8126-2677-3). The traditions and skills emanating from the ancient trade routes are shown as surviving today in the work of a rug restorer in New York, an artist-monk in Los Angeles, a cook from Iran, and other examples in this fascinating approach to an interesting subject. (Rev: BL 11/1/02; HB 1–2/03; HBG 3/03; SLJ 2/03; VOYA 6/03) [745]

China

17609 Andersen, Dale. *Ancient China* (3–5). Illus. Series: History in Art. 2004, Raintree LB $29.93 (978-1-4109-0519-2). 48pp. Examples of the era's art and sculpture accompany brief accounts of successive Chinese dynasties, pointing out what art can reveal about the life of the time. (Rev: BL 2/1/05; SLJ 4/05)

17610 Bailey, Linda. *Adventures in Ancient China* (3–5). Illus. by Bill Slavin. Series: Good Times Travel Agency. 2003, Kids Can $14.95 (978-1-55337-453-4). A fictional story about three children whisked magically to ancient China runs in cartoon fashion across the tops of the pages, while a guidebook below looks at everything from farming and transportation to family life and writing. (Rev: HBG 4/04; SLJ 1/04)

17611 Baldwin, Robert F. *Daily Life in Ancient and Modern Beijing* (4–7). Illus. by Ray Webb. Series: Cities Through Time. 1999, Runestone LB $25.26 (978-0-8225-3214-9). Topics introduced in this contrast between Beijing past and present include the arts, religion, school, history, and daily life. (Rev: HBG 10/99; SLJ 7/99) [951]

17612 Barber, Nicola. *Beijing* (4–7). Series: Great Cities of the World. 2004, World Almanac LB $31.00 (978-0-

8368-5028-4). In addition to the usual information on history and people, this attractive volume describes living conditions and leisure time and provides maps and sidebars about contemporary environmental and political issues. (Rev: BL 4/15/04; SLJ 6/04) [951]

17613 Bowden, Rob. *The Yangtze* (5–7). Series: A River Journey. 2003, Raintree LB $28.56 (978-0-7398-6074-8). 48pp. A well-illustrated trip along China's Yangtze River, concentrating on mankind's influence on the river and vice versa, with photographs, maps, and charts. (Rev: SLJ 3/04)

17614 Chan, Arlene. *Awakening the Dragon: The Dragon Boat Festival* (3–6). Illus. by Song Nan Zhang. 2004, Tundra $15.95 (978-0-88776-656-5). 24pp. Bright illustrations accompany this overview of the history and traditions associated with Chinese dragon boat races. (Rev: BL 8/04; SLJ 6/04)

17615 Cole, Joanna. *Imperial China* (1–3). Illus. by Bruce Degen. Series: Ms. Frizzle's Adventures. 2005, Scholastic $16.95 (978-0-590-10822-5). 48pp. From Chinatown, Frizzle and friends are transported by dragon to 11th-century China in this information-packed yet appealing volume combining fact and fiction. (Rev: BL 6/1–15/05)

17616 Costain, Meredith, and Paul Collins. *Welcome to China* (3–5). Illus. Series: Countries of the World. 2001, Chelsea LB $28.00 (978-0-7910-6548-8). 32pp. A very basic overview of the country with information on plants and animals, culture, sports, and schooling. (Rev: HBG 3/02; SLJ 2/02)

17617 Crane, Carol. *D Is for Dancing Dragon* (1–4). Illus. by Zong-Zhou Wang. 2006, Sleeping Bear $17.95 (978-1-58536-273-8). An A to Z journey through China's history and culture, describing various Chinese inventions, the Great Wall, the Chinese New Year, pandas, and so forth. (Rev: SLJ 3/07)

17618 Deedrick, Tami. *China* (3–6). Series: Ancient Civilizations. 2001, Raintree LB $22.83 (978-0-7398-3580-7). 48pp. Deedrick covers the Song, Yuan, and Ming dynasties of the Imperial period, giving good, clear information on history, daily life, culture, and inventions. (Rev: HBG 3/02; SLJ 9/01)

17619 DuTemple, Lesley A. *The Great Wall of China* (4–7). Illus. Series: Great Building Feats. 2003, Lerner LB $27.93 (978-0-8225-0377-4). 80pp. This absorbing account tells the story of the building and importance of the Great Wall of China, with a good selection of illustrations, sidebar features, and maps. (Rev: BL 1/1–15/03; HBG 10/03; SLJ 4/03*)

17620 Ferroa, Peggy. *China* (4–7). Series: Cultures of the World. 1991, Marshall Cavendish LB $35.64 (978-1-85435-399-3). Unusual facts highlight this look at China, with emphasis on culture. (Rev: BL 2/15/92; SLJ 3/92) [951]

17621 Field, Catherine. *China* (4–8). Illus. Series: Nations of the World. 2000, Raintree LB $34.26 (978-0-8172-5781-1). This is a fine introduction to China's past and present that supplies even more interesting information through the use of sidebars. (Rev: BL 10/15/00; HBG 10/00)

17622 Kagda, Falaq. *Hong Kong* (5–8). Series: Cultures of the World. 1998, Marshall Cavendish LB $37.07 (978-0-7614-0692-1). An attractive book that introduces us to Hong Kong's history and geography, its people, and their culture and lifestyles. (Rev: HBG 3/98; SLJ 6/98) [951]

17623 Malaspina, Ann. *The Chinese Revolution and Mao Zedong in World History* (5–8). Series: World History. 2004, Enslow LB $26.60 (978-0-7660-1935-5). 128pp. After a brief overview of Chinese history, Malaspina provides a well-researched introduction to Chinese communism under Mao Zedong, from the early days of the party in the 1920s to the post-Mao reforms. (Rev: SLJ 3/04)

17624 Mann, Elizabeth. *The Great Wall: The Story of Thousands of Miles of Earth and Stone* (4–8). Series: Wonders of the World. 1997, Mikaya $19.95 (978-0-9650493-2-0). The story behind the building of this massive structure, which began as far back as 200 B.C. and involves historical battles for land and power between the Chinese and the nomadic Mongols. (Rev: BL 1/1–15/98; SLJ 12/97) [951]

17625 March, Michael. *China* (2–5). Series: Country File. 2003, Smart Apple LB $24.25 (978-1-58340-236-8). 32pp. An introductory guide to China and its people, well illustrated with maps, charts, and photographs. (Rev: SLJ 3/04)

17626 Marx, Trish. *Elephants and Golden Thrones: Inside China's Forbidden City* (4–7). Illus. by Ellen B. Senisi. 2008, Abrams $18.95 (978-0-8109-9485-0). Full of photographs, this is an inside look at the sights and history of the huge palace complex. (Rev: BL 6/1–15/08; SLJ 7/08) [951]

17627 Meister, Cari. *Yangtze River* (3–4). Series: Rivers and Lakes. 2002, ABDO LB $21.35 (978-1-57765-103-1). A solid introduction to the Yangtze, its tributaries, flora and fauna, and the ways in which it has influenced human development in the area throughout history. (Rev: HBG 10/02; SLJ 7/02)

17628 Michels, Dia L. *Visiting China* (PS). Photos by Michael J. N. Bowles. Series: Look What I See! Where Can I Be? 2003, Platypus Media $16.95 (978-1-930775-15-2). Through the eyes of an infant, readers visit China in this unusual interactive book. (Rev: SLJ 4/04)

17629 Minnis, Ivan. *You Are in Ancient China* (3–6). Series: You Are There! 2004, Raintree LB $26.36 (978-1-4109-0619-9). 32pp. Double-page spreads with plenty of illustrations and a low readling level introduce readers to the culture and lifestyle of the Han Dynasty. (Rev: BL 12/1/04; SLJ 2/05)

17630 Morley, Jacqueline. *You Wouldn't Want to Work on the Great Wall of China! Defenses You'd Rather Not Build* (3–6). Illus. by David Antram. Series: You Wouldn't Want To. 2006, Watts LB $29.00 (978-0-531-12424-6); paper $9.95 (978-0-531-12449-9). 32pp. An unflinching look at what life was like for the workers who built the Great Wall of China, with cartoon illustrations that lighten the grimness. (Rev: SLJ 9/06)

17631 O'Connor, Jane. *The Emperor's Silent Army: Terracotta Warriors of Ancient China* (4–6). 2002, Viking $17.99 (978-0-670-03512-0). 48pp. The beautifully packaged story of the amazing discovery of an army of life-size terracotta soldiers in a field in China in 1974, with information about the emperor who oversaw their construction. (Rev: BL 4/15/02*; HBG 10/02; SLJ 4/02)

17632 Olson, Kay Melchisedech. *China* (2–3). Illus. Series: Many Cultures, One World. 2003, Capstone LB $23.93 (978-0-7368-1531-4). A brief, accessible introduction to China and its people, family life, customs, and legends. (Rev: BL 10/15/03; HBG 10/03; SLJ 12/03)

17633 Olson, Nathan. *China* (3–4). Illus. Series: Fact Finders: Questions and Answers. 2004, Capstone LB $23.93 (978-0-7368-2687-7). 32pp. Using a question-and-answer format, this title introduces China's history, government, economy, education, culture, sports, and lifestyle. (Rev: SLJ 1/05)

17634 Pellegrini, Nancy. *Beijing* (4–8). Photos by Adrian Cooper. Series: Global Cities. 2007, Chelsea House LB $30.00 (978-0-7910-8848-7). 61pp. With plenty of photographs and maps, this volume introduces the history of Beijing as well as its geography, people, environment, transportation, and so forth. (Rev: SLJ 7/07)

17635 Pilon, Pascal, and Elizabeth Thomas. *We Live in China* (4–7). Illus. Series: Kids Around the World. 2006, Abrams $15.95 (978-0-8109-5735-0). 48pp. Four children from different areas of China introduce their region and everyday life; the lack of an index and photo captions limit the book's usefulness for reports, but it will nevertheless serve as an attractive introduction. (Rev: BL 10/15/06; SLJ 2/07)

17636 Qing, Zheng. *China* (4–7). Illus. by Tim Hutchinson. Series: Find Out About. 2007, Barron's $12.99 (978-0-7641-5952-7). 64pp. This well-organized, attractively illustrated guide looks at China's history and contemporary life, and introduces basic phrases in Mandarin. (Rev: BL 4/1/07; SLJ 2/07)

17637 Riehecky, Janet. *China* (2–4). Illus. Series: Country Explorers. 2007, Lerner LB $27.93 (978-0-8225-7129-2). 48pp. Rich in photographs, maps, and illustrations and full of accessible information, this lively book looks at the geography of the land and at all aspects of life there — family life, school life, clothes, medicine, food, sports, and so forth. (Rev: LMC 1/08*; SLJ 12/07)

17638 Schomp, Virginia. *The Ancient Chinese* (4–7). Series: People of the Ancient World. 2004, Watts LB $30.50 (978-0-531-11817-7). 112pp. Emperors, artisans, inventors, and healers are among the people presented in this overview of life in ancient China. (Rev: SLJ 2/05)

17639 Shuter, Jane. *Ancient China* (5–8). Series: Time Travel Guides. 2007, Raintree LB $34.29 (978-1-4109-2729-3). An attractive trip back in time to ancient China, providing details about daily life there — accommodation, food, shopping, and so forth — and suggesting sights to see. (Rev: SLJ 9/07) [931]

17640 So, Sungwan. *In a Chinese City* (2–4). 2001, Benchmark LB $25.64 (978-0-7614-1224-3). 32pp. A 7-year-old escorts readers through a typical day in this book that ends with brief information on history, geography, people, religion, and language. (Rev: HBG 3/02; SLJ 3/02)

17641 So, Sungwan. *Shanyi Goes to China* (PS–2). Series: Children Return to Their Roots. 2006, Frances Lincoln $15.95 (978-1-84507-470-8). 32pp. A little girl named Shanyi visits China with her family, visiting relatives and learning about everything from food and famous sites to calligraphy and religious customs. (Rev: BL 10/15/06; SLJ 12/06)

17642 Tsiang, Sarah. *Warriors and Wailers: One Hundred Ancient Chinese Jobs You Might Have Relished or Reviled* (4–8). Illus. by Martha Newbigging. Series: Jobs in History. 2012, Annick $25.95 (978-155451391-8); paper $16.95 (978-1-55451-390-1). 96pp. Tsiang surveys the social structure of ancient China and the benefits and disadvantages of ranks ranging from highest to lowest. (Rev: BLO 11/1/12; LMC 3–4/13*; SLJ 7/12) [331.700951]

17643 Walker, Kathryn. *Shanghai* (4–7). Series: Great Cities of the World. 2005, World Almanac LB $31.00 (978-0-8368-5046-8). An informative and appealing overview of this important Chinese city, with material on its history, its economy, and what it's like to live there. (Rev: BL 4/15/04)

17644 Wang, Xiaohong. *One Year in Beijing* (1–4). Illus. by Grace Lin. 2006, China Sprout $16.95 (978-0-9747302-5-7). 32pp. Eight-year-old Ling Ling conducts readers on a tour of popular attractions in Beijing, explaining Chinese customs and traditions as she goes; the end matter adds more facts. (Rev: BL 10/15/06; SLJ 3/07)

India

17645 Apte, Sunita. *India* (3–5). Series: A True Book — Geography: Countries. 2009, Children's Pr. LB $26.00 (978-0-531-16890-5). 48pp. An attractive overview of India, covering the differences between city and rural life, weather, daily life and culture, history, and contemporary issues such as recent terrorist attacks. (Rev: SLJ 7/09)

17646 Arnold, Caroline, and Madeleine Comora. *Taj Mahal* (4–7). Illus. by Rahul Bhushan. 2007, Carolrhoda LB $17.95 (978-0-7613-2609-9). A beautifully designed, oversized picture book, this volume on the Taj Mahal and the story behind its construction includes detailed paintings and a fictionalized narrative about the Mogul prince who built it in memory of his wife. (Rev: BL 6/1–15/07; SLJ 7/07)

17647 Bowden, Rob. *The Ganges* (5–7). Series: A River Journey. 2003, Raintree LB $28.56 (978-0-7398-6070-0). 48pp. A detailed look at India's most famous river, its

importance to the people who live along it, and the challenge of pollution, with photographs, maps, and charts. (Rev: SLJ 3/04)

17648 Castelain, Céline, and Aurélien Liutkus. *Asha: A Child of the Himalayas* (K–3). Series: Children of the World. 2005, Gale LB $22.45 (978-1-4103-0286-1). Full-color photographs introduce young readers to Asha, who lives in India's mountainous state of Himachal Pradesh; suitable for browsers rather than report writers. (Rev: SLJ 10/05)

17649 Dalal, Anita. *India* (4–8). Series: Nations of the World. 2001, Raintree LB $34.26 (978-0-7398-1289-1). A fine introduction to this vast, populous country with chapters on the land and cities, past and present, the economy, arts and living, and the future. (Rev: BL 12/15/01; HBG 3/02)

17650 DuTemple, Lesley A. *The Taj Mahal* (4–7). Series: Great Building Feats. 2003, Lerner LB $27.93 (978-0-8225-4694-8). Using many illustrations, this account traces the building of the magnificent tomb that was inspired by one man's love for his wife. (Rev: BL 11/15/03) [954]

17651 Ejaz, Khadija. *Recipe and Craft Guide to India* (4–7). Illus. 2010, Mitchell Lane LB $24.50 (978-158415938-4). 64pp. Cultural and culinary projects introduce readers to many aspects of India. (Rev: BL 1/1–15/11; LMC 1–2/11*) [641.5954]

17652 Flatt, Lizann. *India* (3–5). Series: Facts About Countries. 2009, Sea-to-Sea LB $27.10 (978-1-59771-117-3). 32pp. A well-designed introduction to India with color photographs and statistics and covering geography, history, economy, education, government, culture, and current status. (Rev: SLJ 7/09)

17653 Godard, Philippe. *We Live in India* (3–6). Illus. by Sophie Duffet. Series: Kids Around the World. 2006, Abrams $15.95 (978-0-8109-5736-7). 47pp. Three Indian children from different backgrounds — one Tamil, one Bengali, and one an "untouchable" Hindi — are featured in an overview suitable for browsers. (Rev: SLJ 2/07)

17654 Goodwin, William. *India* (5–8). Series: Modern Nations of the World. 2000, Lucent $27.45 (978-1-56006-598-2). 112pp. An admirable introduction to India that gives material on the land and its past but concentrates on today's population, living conditions, and problems. (Rev: BL 3/15/00; HBG 10/00)

17655 Green, Jen. *Mumbai* (4–8). Photos by Chris Fairclough. Series: Global Cities. 2007, Chelsea House LB $30.00 (978-0-7910-8851-7). 61pp. With plenty of photographs and maps, this overview of the city of Mumbai (formerly Bombay) provides concise information on its history, geography, people, environment, transportation, and so forth. (Rev: SLJ 7/07)

17656 Guile, Melanie. *Culture in India* (4–7). Series: Culture In. 2005, Raintree LB $25.70 (978-1-4109-1134-6). Customs, holidays, clothing, food, and arts and crafts are well covered in this volume that also provides basic information needed for reports and interesting sidebar features on such topics as ancestor worship and celebrities. (Rev: BL 2/15/04; SLJ 5/05) [954]

17657 Mann, Elizabeth. *Taj Mahal* (3–6). Illus. by Alan Witschonke. Series: Wonders of the World. 2008, Mikaya $22.95 (978-1-931414-20-3). 48pp. An interesting account of the building of the Taj Mahal, the love that prompted its construction, and the care that was taken in its incredible design. (Rev: BL 11/15/08; SLJ 1/09)

17658 Olson, Nathan. *India: A Question And Answer Book* (2–5). Illus. Series: Questions and Answers: Countries. 2005, Capstone LB $23.93 (978-0-7368-3751-4). Using a question-and-answer format, simple text, large photos, and many factboxes, this is an introduction to India today, with material on history and traditional culture. (Rev: SLJ 6/05)

17659 Rowe, Percy, and Patience Coster. *Delhi* (4–7). Series: Great Cities of the World. 2005, World Almanac LB $31.00 (978-0-8368-5037-6). An informative and appealing overview of this major Indian city, with material on its history, its economy, and what it's like to live there. (Rev: BL 4/15/04)

17660 Spilsbury, Louise, and Richard Spilsbury. *Living on the Ganges River* (3–5). Illus. Series: World Cultures. 2007, Raintree LB $27.50 (978-1-4109-2820-7). 32pp. The authors look at aspects of life along the Ganges including homes, daily life, food and clothing, school and leisure, and festivals. (Rev: SLJ 2/08)

17661 Spilsbury, Richard. *Settlements of the Ganges River* (3–5). Illus. Series: Rivers Through Time. 2005, Heinemann LB $31.43 (978-1-4034-6526-9). 48pp. Traces the history and contemporary life of major settlements along the Ganges, discussing environmental and other important issues.

17662 Srinivasan, Radhika, and Leslie Jermyn. *India. 2nd ed.* (4–8). Illus. Series: Cultures of the World. 2001, Benchmark LB $37.07 (978-0-7614-1354-7). 144pp. An updated edition of the 1990 title, covering the history, geography, politics, people, arts, culture, and environmental concerns of India. (Rev: HBG 3/02; SLJ 3/02)

17663 Swan, Erin Pembrey. *India* (4–7). Series: Enchantment of the World. 2002, Children's LB $37.00 (978-0-516-21121-3). 144pp. This visually attractive introduction to the past and present of India includes coverage of languages, culture, the people, economy, and government. (Rev: BL 5/15/02)

Japan

17664 Barber, Nicola. *Tokyo* (4–6). Series: Great Cities of the World. 2004, World Almanac LB $31.00 (978-0-8368-5033-8). 48pp. Report writers will find useful information on the Japanese capital's history, culture, and lifestyle. (Rev: SLJ 7/04)

17665 Blumberg, Rhoda. *Commodore Perry in the Land of the Shogun* (5–8). 1985, Lothrop $21.99 (978-0-688-03723-9). Japan was a mysterious country when Perry arrived in 1853 to open its harbors to American ships. (Rev: BL 11/1/85; SLJ 10/85) [952.025]

17666 Boraas, Tracey. *Japan* (3–6). Illus. Series: Countries and Cultures. 2001, Capstone LB $25.26 (978-0-7368-0770-8). 64pp. An overview of history, geography, government, economy, and culture that will be useful for students preparing reports. (Rev: HBG 3/02; SLJ 4/02)

17667 Burgan, Michael. *Japan* (2–5). Illus. Series: Questions and Answers: Countries. 2004, Capstone LB $23.93 (978-0-7368-2478-1). Using a question-and-answer format, simple text, large photos, and many factboxes, this is an introduction to Japan today, with material on history and traditional culture.

17668 Costain, Meredith, and Paul Collins. *Welcome to Japan* (3–5). Illus. Series: Countries of the World. 2001, Chelsea LB $28.00 (978-0-7910-6541-9). 32pp. A basic overview that covers history, government, culture, transportation, plants and animals, sports, and schooling. (Rev: HBG 3/02; SLJ 2/02)

17669 Glaser, Jason, and Don Roley. *Ninja* (3–6). Series: Edge Books: Warriors of History. 2006, Capstone LB $23.93 (978-0-7368-6432-9). 32pp. A colorfully introduction to Japan's ninja warriors, their history, weapons, and way of life. (Rev: SLJ 1/07)

17670 Green, Jen. *Japan* (4–8). Series: Nations of the World. 2001, Raintree LB $34.26 (978-0-8172-5783-5). 128pp. An attractive, fact-filled introduction to this island nation, its rich culture, advanced technology, and wealthy economy. (Rev: BL 6/1–15/01; HBG 10/01)

17671 Hanel, Rachael. *Samurai* (5–8). Series: Fearsome Fighters. 2007, Creative Education LB $31.35 (978-1-58341-538-2). 48pp. Weapons, armor, fighting techniques, and motivation are all discussed in this description of the Japanese feudal warriors and the kinds of people who were tempted to this career. (Rev: SLJ 1/08)

17672 Leavitt, Caroline. *Samurai* (3–5). Illus. Series: Edge Books: Warriors of History. 2006, Capstone LB $23.93 (978-0-7368-6433-6). 32pp. A solid exploration of the history and traditions associated with Japan's samurai warriors, with a wealth of illustrations. (Rev: BL 10/15/06; SLJ 1/07)

17673 MacDonald, Fiona. *How to Be a Samurai Warrior* (2–5). Illus. by John James. Series: How to Be. 2005, National Geographic $14.95 (978-0-7922-3618-4). A glimpse of what life was like for samurai warriors, touching on such fundamentals as clothing, weapons, job requirements, family life, and pay. (Rev: SLJ 12/05)

17674 Malam, John. *You Wouldn't Want to Be a Ninja Warrior! A Secret Job That's Your Destiny* (3–5). Illus. by David Antram. 2012, Scholastic LB $29 (978-0-531-20873-1); paper $9.95 (978-0-531-20948-6). 32pp. Malam looks at the training and weapons of the average ninja, and the skills they needed to develop. (Rev: BL 2/15/12; SLJ 4/1/12) [355.5]

17675 Mofford, Juliet Haines. *Recipe and Craft Guide to Japan* (4–7). Illus. 2010, Mitchell Lane LB $24.50 (978-158415933-9). 64pp. Cultural and culinary projects introduce readers to many aspects of Japan. (Rev: BL 1/1–15/11; LMC 1–2/11*) [641.5952]

17676 Patchett, Kaye. *The Akashi Kaikyo Bridge* (5–8). Illus. Series: Building World Landmarks. 2004, Gale LB $24.95 (978-1-4103-0140-6). 48pp. A concise account of the amazing construction of the bridge that links Shikoku and Honshu islands. (Rev: BL 4/1/04; SLJ 4/05)

17677 Phillips, Charles. *Japan* (3–6). Illus. Series: Countries of the World. 2007, National Geographic LB $27.90 (978-1-4263-0029-5). 64pp. An attractive layout and up-to-date information combine to make this an effective and interesting introduction to the country and its culture. (Rev: SLJ 8/07)

17678 Poisson, Barbara Aoki. *The Ainu of Japan* (4–6). Series: First Peoples. 2002, Lerner LB $23.93 (978-0-8225-4176-9). The Ainu of Japan have shared their homeland with the Japanese for centuries and continue to retain their independent culture. (Rev: BL 5/15/02; HBG 10/02; SLJ 8/02)

17679 Schomp, Virginia. *Japan in the Days of the Samurai* (5–8). Illus. Series: Cultures of the Past. 2001, Marshall Cavendish LB $29.93 (978-0-7614-0304-3). 80pp. A well-illustrated look at the history of Japan, including information on such cultural topics as the tea ceremony and samurai women. (Rev: BL 2/15/02; HBG 3/02; SLJ 3/02)

17680 Shelley, Rex, and Teo Chuu Yong. *Japan. 2nd ed.* (5–8). Series: Cultures of the World. 2001, Benchmark LB $37.07 (978-0-7614-1356-1). An updated edition of the 1996 title, covering the history, geography, politics, people, arts, culture, and environmental concerns of Japan. (Rev: HBG 3/02; SLJ 3/02) [952]

17681 Takabayashi, Mari. *I Live in Tokyo* (1–3). Illus. 2001, Houghton $16.00 (978-0-618-07702-1). Readers learn about the customs, traditions, and everyday activities that are part of a 7-year-old Japanese girl's life. (Rev: BL 9/15/01; HB 11/01*; HBG 3/02; SLJ 10/01)

17682 Turnbull, Stephen. *Real Samurai* (4–6). Illus. by James Field. 2007, Enchanted Lion $15.95 (978-1-59270-060-8). 48pp. An eye-catching volume of information about the ancient samurai covering weapons, warrior practices, codes of honor, and related subjects. (Rev: BL 6/1–15/07; SLJ 7/07)

Other Asian Lands

17683 *Afghanistan in Pictures* (5–8). Series: Visual Geography. 1997, Lerner LB $25.55 (978-0-8225-1849-5). Includes sections on vegetation and wildlife, minerals, cities, history, and government. (Rev: BL 5/1/89) [958.1]

17684 Alberti, Theresa. *Vietnam ABCs* (2–4). Illus. by Alex Blanks. Series: Country ABCs. 2007, Picture Window LB $26.60 (978-1-4048-2251-1). This alphabet-book introduction to Vietnam offers basic information about the Southeast Asian country and its troubled history. (Rev: BL 3/15/07)

17685 Ali, Sharifah Enayat. *Afghanistan. 2nd ed.* (5–9). Series: Cultures of the World. 2006, Benchmark LB $27.95 (978-0-7614-2064-4). A revised and updated edition of the guide to Afghanistan and its history, geogra-

phy, culture, and government including maps and color photographs. (Rev: SLJ 3/07) [958.1]

17686 Barber, Nicola. *Singapore* (4–7). Series: Great Cities of the World. 2005, World Almanac LB $31.00 (978-0-8368-5047-5). An informative and appealing overview of one of the world's most famous cities, with material on its history, its economy, and what it's like to live there. (Rev: BL 4/15/04)

17687 Behnke, Alison. *Angkor Wat* (5–8). Series: Unearthing Ancient Worlds. 2008, Lerner LB $30.60 (978-0-8225-7585-6). 80pp. This volume focuses on the ruins of Angkor Wat, thoroughly explaining the archaeological science that fueled the discoveries and providing color maps, illustrations, and photos. (Rev: SLJ 10/1/08)

17688 Boraas, Tracey. *Thailand* (4–6). Series: Countries and Cultures. 2002, Capstone LB $25.26 (978-0-7368-0940-5). 64pp. The land and people of Thailand are introduced with material on climate, landforms, history, traditions, people, and even a recipe. (Rev: BL 1/1–15/03; HBG 3/03; SLJ 2/03)

17689 Bowden, Rob. *Settlements of the Indus River* (3–5). Illus. Series: Rivers Through Time. 2005, Heinemann LB $29.93 (978-1-4034-5718-9). 48pp. Traces the history and contemporary life of major settlements along the Indus, discussing environmental and other important issues.

17690 Brown, Don. *Far Beyond the Garden Gate: Alexandra David-Neel's Journey to Lhasa* (PS–2). Illus. 2002, Houghton $16.00 (978-0-618-08364-0). 32pp. This is the dramatic story of the long, intrepid travels of the first Western woman to visit the holy city of Lhasa (in 1924) and of her intense interest in Buddhism. (Rev: BL 10/1/02; HB 9/02; HBG 3/03; SLJ 10/02)

17691 Burbank, Jon. *Nepal* (4–7). Series: Cultures of the World. 1991, Marshall Cavendish LB $35.64 (978-1-85435-401-3). The emphasis is on culture as well as the basics of geography, history, government, and people. (Rev: BL 2/15/92) [954.96]

17692 De Capua, Sarah. *Korea* (3–5). Illus. Series: Discovering Cultures. 2004, Benchmark LB $25.64 (978-0-7614-1794-1). An attractive introduction to the Korean peninsula, covering land, people, daily life, education, food, and celebrations, with discussion of the differences between North and South. (Rev: SLJ 6/05)

17693 Ericson, Alex. *Thailand* (3–5). Series: Faces and Places. 2001, Child's World LB $22.79 (978-1-56766-913-8). 32pp. This oversize volume presents basic facts on Thailand with an emphasis on the people and how they live. (Rev: BL 9/15/01; HBG 3/02)

17694 Fiscus, James W. *America's War in Afghanistan* (5–9). Illus. Series: War and Conflict in the Middle East. 2004, Rosen LB $27.95 (978-0-8239-4552-8). 64pp. A well-organized, balanced account of the war between the United States and Afghanistan in the aftermath of the 2001 terrorist attacks on New York and Washington, D.C. (Rev: BL 11/1/04)

17695 Fordyce, Deborah. *Afghanistan* (3–6). Series: Welcome to My Country. 2010, Marshall Cavendish LB

$19.95 (978-1-60870-149-0). 48pp. An overview of the geography, history, government, economy, people, culture, and diet of Afghanistan. (Rev: SLJ 12/1/10) [958.1]

17696 Fordyce, Deborah. *Welcome to Afghanistan* (3–5). Series: Welcome to My Country. 2004, Gareth Stevens LB $27.00 (978-0-8368-2557-2). 48pp. Introduces readers to Afghanistan's geography, history, people, culture, family life, government, religion, and language. (Rev: SLJ 7/04)

17697 Giraud, Hervé. *Basha: A Hmong Child* (K–3). Photos by Jean-Charles Rey. Series: Children of the World. 2005, Gale LB $22.45 (978-1-4103-0547-3). 24pp. Using many photographs, this volume introduces the lifestyle and customs of the Hmong people who live in northern Vietnam; suitable for browsers rather than report writers. Also use *Kradji: A Child of Cambodia* (2005). (Rev: SLJ 10/05)

17698 Gogol, Sara. *A Mien Family* (4–7). Series: Journey Between Two Worlds. 1996, Lerner LB $22.60 (978-0-8225-3407-5); paper $8.95 (978-0-8225-9745-2). The story of a refugee family from the mountainous area of Laos and their journey to the United States. (Rev: BL 11/15/96; SLJ 1/97) [306.85]

17699 Goodman, Jim. *Thailand* (5–9). Series: Cultures of the World. 1991, Marshall Cavendish LB $35.64 (978-1-85435-402-0). Thailand's history, land, and culture. (Rev: BL 3/15/92) [959.3]

17700 Goodman, Susan. *Chopsticks for My Noodle Soup: Eliza's Life in Malaysia* (1–3). Illus. by Michael Doolittle. 2000, Millbrook LB $21.40 (978-0-7613-1552-0). 32pp. A kindergartner from Connecticut visits a Malaysian village with her parents and comments on its daily life and customs in an account illustrated with her father's photographs. (Rev: BL 3/15/00; HBG 10/00; SLJ 5/00)

17701 Guile, Melanie. *Culture in Malaysia* (4–7). Series: Culture In. 2005, Raintree LB $25.70 (978-1-4109-1133-9). Customs, holidays, clothing, food, and arts and crafts are well covered in this volume that also provides basic information needed for reports and interesting sidebar features. (Rev: SLJ 5/05)

17702 Guile, Melanie. *Culture in Vietnam* (3–5). Illus. Series: Culture In. 2005, Raintree LB $25.70 (978-1-4109-1135-3). 32pp. Vietnam's people, language, celebrations and customs are covered, with photographs and maps adding to the appeal. (Rev: BL 3/1/05; SLJ 5/05)

17703 Haberle, Susan E. *North Korea* (2–5). Illus. Series: Questions and Answers: Countries. 2005, Capstone LB $23.93 (978-0-7368-3756-9). 32pp. Using a question-and-answer format, simple text, large photos, and many factboxes, this is an introduction to North Korea today, with material on history and traditional culture.

17704 Haberle, Susan E. *South Korea* (2–5). Illus. Series: Questions and Answers: Countries. 2005, Capstone LB $23.93 (978-0-7368-3761-3). 32pp. Using a question-and-answer format, simple text, large photos, and many factboxes, this is an introduction to South Korea today, with material on history and traditional culture.

17705 Harris, Nathaniel. *Burma (Myanmar)* (4–6). Series: Global Hotspots. 2010, Marshall Cavendish $12.99 (978-0-7614-4758-0). 32pp. An introduction to the turbulent history of Myanmar, ending with a discussion of contemporary problems. (Rev: SLJ 4/10) [959.1]

17706 Heinrichs, Ann. *Pakistan* (2–3). Series: A True Book. 2004, Children's Pr. LB $25.00 (978-0-516-22813-6). 47pp. Geography, history, and daily life are covered in this attractive introduction to Pakistan. (Rev: SLJ 11/04)

17707 Hill, Valerie. *Korea* (3–6). Illus. Series: Ask About Asia. 2002, Mason Crest LB $18.95 (978-1-59084-206-5). 47pp. Geography, history, culture, government, and daily life are presented in double-page spreads with plenty of photographs, reproductions, and maps. (Rev: SLJ 4/03)

17708 Holmes, Jim, and Tom Morgan. *A Child's Day in a Vietnamese City* (K–3). Series: A Child's Day. 2002, Marshall Cavendish LB $25.64 (978-0-7614-1409-4). Present-day Vietnam is introduced through the everyday experiences of a Vietnamese child. (Rev: BL 2/15/03; HBG 3/03)

17709 Knox, Barbara. *Afghanistan* (2–4). Series: Many Cultures, One World. 2004, Capstone LB $23.93 (978-0-7368-2448-4). An interesting introduction to Afghanistan, covering city and country life, family life, laws and customs, seasons, important sights, and even favorite pets. (Rev: SLJ 8/04)

17710 Kummer, Patricia K. *Tibet* (4–8). Series: Enchantment of the World. 2003, Children's Pr. LB $37.00 (978-0-516-22693-4). 144pp. A visually attractive book that covers such topics as the geography, history, government, culture, and people, with a timeline, fast facts, and a recipe. (Rev: SLJ 1/04)

17711 Kwek, Karen, and Jameel Haque. *Pakistan* (3–6). 2010, Marshall Cavendish LB $19.95 (978-1-60870-158-2). 48pp. An overview of the geography, history, government, economy, people, culture, and diet of Pakistan. (Rev: SLJ 12/1/10) [954.91]

17712 Layton, Lesley. *Singapore* (5–8). Series: Cultures of the World. 1990, Marshall Cavendish LB $35.64 (978-1-85435-295-8). As well as history and economy, this introduction to Singapore includes coverage of lifestyles and current problems. (Rev: BL 3/1/91; SLJ 6/91) [959.57]

17713 Levy, Patricia. *Tibet* (4–7). Series: Cultures of the World. 1996, Marshall Cavendish LB $37.07 (978-0-7614-0277-0). Tibet is introduced with general background information, followed by material on its people and their culture, festivals, and food. (Rev: BL 8/96; SLJ 9/96) [951.1]

17714 Lewin, Ted, and Betsy Lewin. *Horse Song: The Naadam of Mongolia* (2–5). Illus. by Ted Lewin. 2008, Lee & Low $19.95 (978-1-58430-277-3). 56pp. An account of the authors' trip to Mongolia, where they watched the annual horse races that are part of the Naadam celebration; a 9-year-old jockey named Tamir teaches them about the event. (Rev: BL 5/1/08; HB 7/08; LMC 10/08; SLJ 6/08)

17715 March, Michael. *Bangladesh* (3–5). Series: Facts About Countries. 2009, Sea-to-Sea LB $27.10 (978-1-59771-113-5). 32pp. A well-designed introduction to Bangladesh with color photographs and statistics and covering geography, history, economy, education, government, culture, and current status. (Rev: SLJ 7/09)

17716 Millett, Sandra. *The Hmong of Southeast Asia* (4–6). Series: First Peoples. 2001, Lerner LB $23.93 (978-0-8225-4852-2). 48pp. This attractive introduction to the Hmong people and their native region and culture also contrasts traditional and modern lifestyles. (Rev: HBG 3/02; SLJ 3/02)

17717 Mirpuri, Gouri, and Robert Cooper. *Indonesia. 2nd ed.* (5–8). Illus. Series: Cultures of the World. 2001, Marshall Cavendish LB $37.07 (978-0-7614-1355-4). An encompassing look at the history, culture, society, and geography of Indonesia. (Rev: BL 3/1/02; HBG 3/02; SLJ 4/02)

17718 Mortenson, Greg, and David Oliver Relin. *Three Cups of Tea: One Man's Journey to Change the World . . . One Child at a Time* (4–8). Illus. 2009, Dial $16.99 (978-0-8037-3392-3). 192pp. Focusing mainly on the young people, this simplified version of Mortenson's bestseller for adults describes his successes building schools in Pakistan and Afghanistan. (Rev: BL 2/1/09; SLJ 2/09) [371]

17719 Mortenson, Greg, and Susan L. Roth. *Listen to the Wind: The Story of Dr. Greg and Three Cups of Tea* (1–3). Illus. by Susan L. Roth. 2009, Dial $16.99 (978-0-8037-3058-8). 32pp. The story of Greg Mortenson's efforts to build schools in the high mountains of Pakistan is told from the point of view of the children of Korphe, who benefited from his extraordinary determination; with effective collage artwork. (Rev: BCCB 3/09; BL 1/1–15/09; LMC 5/09; SLJ 2/09)

17720 Munan, Heidi. *Malaysia* (5–8). Series: Cultures of the World. 1990, Marshall Cavendish LB $35.64 (978-1-85435-296-5). Cultural diversity and lifestyles of the people are two topics covered in this introduction to Malaysia. (Rev: BL 3/1/91) [959.5]

17721 O'Brien, Tony. *Afghan Dreams: Young Voices of Afghanistan* (4–9). Photos by Tony O'Brien. 2008, Bloomsbury $18.99 (978-1-59990-287-6). 74pp. This photo-essay featuring more than 30 young Afghans illustrates their poignant situation and provides background information. ALA Notable Children's Book. (Rev: BCCB 12/08; SLJ 12/08; VOYA 12/08) [305.235092]

17722 Olson, Gillia M. *Afghanistan: A Question and Answer Book* (2–5). Series: Fact Finders. 2004, Capstone LB $23.93 (978-0-7368-2685-3). 32pp. Double-page spreads use simple text, factboxes, and plenty of color photographs to answer pertinent questions about the country's history, geography, government, and culture. (Rev: BL 11/15/04; SLJ 3/05)

17723 Orr, Tamra. *Bangladesh* (5–9). Series: Enchantment of the World Second Series. 2007, Children's Pr.

LB $36.00 (978-0-516-25012-0). Features information on the Asian nation of Bangladesh, including its culture, religion, family life, arts, and sports and looks in particular at the country's struggles with pollution, poor living and working conditions, and political instability. (Rev: BL 8/07) [954.92]

17724 Pang, Guek-Cheng. *Mongolia* (5–8). Series: Cultures of the World. 1999, Marshall Cavendish LB $37.07 (978-0-7614-0954-0). A clear, well-illustrated introduction to this remote land that includes good background information as well as coverage of modern life. (Rev: HBG 10/99; SLJ 10/99) [957]

17725 Pascoe, Elaine, ed. *Into Wild Borneo* (3–6). Series: The Jeff Corwin Experience. 2004, Gale LB $24.95 (978-1-56711-859-9). 48pp. Jeff Corwin of the Animal Planet television series interacts with elephants, apes, and much smaller creatures in Borneo. (Rev: SLJ 4/04)

17726 Raatma, Lucia. *Thailand* (4–6). Illus. Series: Social Studies Explorer. 2012, Cherry Lake LB $31.36 (978-161080441-7). 48pp. An attractive, photo-filled overview of this nation, with maps, information on the economy and government, people and culture, and so forth, plus a recipe and a craft. **e** (Rev: BL 3/1/13; LMC 10/13) [959.3]

17727 Razzak, Shazia. *P Is for Pakistan* (2–5). Photos by Prodeepta Das. 2007, Frances Lincoln $16.95 (978-1-84507-483-8). 28pp. From A to Z, this book introduces words in English or Urdu that convey information on Pakistan's history, culture, or geography. (Rev: SLJ 3/08)

17728 Romano, Amy. *A Historical Atlas of Afghanistan* (4–6). Illus. Series: Historical Atlases of South Asia, Central Asia and the Middle East. 2003, Rosen LB $30.60 (978-0-8239-3863-6). 64pp. This attractive profile that includes many maps and photographs traces Afghanistan's development from prehistoric times to the present. (Rev: SLJ 8/03)

17729 Ryan, Patrick. *Welcome to South Korea* (1–4). Series: Wecome to the World. 2008, The Child's World LB $27.07 (978-1-59296-978-4). As easy introduction to South Korea and its land, people, plants and animals, and so forth, with color photographs, maps, and recipes. (Rev: LMC 10/08; SLJ 9/08)

17730 Sheehan, Sean. *Cambodia* (4–7). Series: Cultures of the World. 1996, Marshall Cavendish LB $37.07 (978-0-7614-0281-7). The troubled land of Cambodia is introduced, with emphasis on its people, their lifestyles, and culture. (Rev: BL 8/96; SLJ 9/96) [959]

17731 Sheehan, Sean, and Shahrezad Samiuddin. *Pakistan* (5–9). Series: Cultures of the World. 2004, Benchmark LB $37.07 (978-0-7614-1787-3). Pakistan's geography, history, economy, and people are all examined, with discussion of interesting aspects of Pakistani culture. (Rev: SLJ 2/05) [954.9]

17732 Shuter, Jane. *The Indus Valley* (3–5). Illus. Series: History Opens Windows. 2002, Heinemann LB $22.79 (978-1-4034-0253-0). 32pp. An overview of government, trade, and everyday life in ancient times in the

Indus Valley that is now in Pakistan and western India. (Rev: HBG 3/03; SLJ 3/03)

17733 Simpson, Judith. *Indonesia* (3–6). Illus. Series: Ask About Asia. 2002, Mason Crest LB $18.95 (978-1-59084-208-9). 47pp. Geography, history, culture, government, and daily life are presenetd in double-page spreads with plenty of photographs, reproductions, and maps. (Rev: HBG 10/03; SLJ 4/03)

17734 Sobol, Richard. *The Life of Rice: From Seedling to Supper* (3–6). Illus. 2010, Candlewick $17.99 (978-0-7636-3252-6). 40pp. A photographer travels around Thailand, documenting the cultural and agricultural importance of rice. (Rev: BL 10/15/10; LMC 11–12/10; SLJ 9/1/10) [633.1]

17735 Sobol, Richard. *The Mysteries of Angkor Wat: Exploring Cambodia's Ancient Temple* (4–6). Photos by Richard Sobol. Series: Traveling Photographer. 2011, Candlewick $17.99 (978-0-7636-4166-5). 48pp. Full of beautiful photographs, this is a fascinating account of the history and mystery surrounding the ancient Cambodian temple. (Rev: LMC 11–12/11; SLJ 8/11) [959.6]

17736 Sobol, Richard. *The Story of Silk: From Worm Spit to Woven Scarves* (2–4). Illus. by author. Series: Traveling Photographer. 2012, Candlewick $17.99 (978-0-7636-4165-8). 40pp. Using many color photographs Sobol describes how a small village in Thailand produces beautiful silk cloth, providing a fascinating of daily life there. (Rev: BL 9/1/12; HB 11–12/12; SLJ 10/12) [595]

17737 *South Korea in Pictures* (5–7). Series: Visual Geography. 1997, Lerner LB $25.55 (978-0-8225-1868-6). An introduction to South Korea that focuses on its politics and economy. (Rev: SLJ 5/90) [951.9]

17738 Stevens, Kathryn. *Afghanistan* (2–4). Series: Faces and Places. 2003, Child's World LB $22.79 (978-1-56766-181-1). This introduction to Afghanistan covers the central Asian country's geography, history, people, culture, government, and economy. (Rev: SLJ 8/03)

17739 Stickler, John, and Soma Han Stickler. *Land of Morning Calm: Korean Culture Then and Now* (3–5). Illus. by authors. 2003, Shen's $16.95 (978-1-885008-22-0). 32pp. An excellent introduction to Korea for young readers, this attractive book covers the history and geography of the peninsula and also examines various cultural aspects. (Rev: BL 10/15/03; SLJ 12/03)

17740 Taus-Bolstad, Stacy. *Pakistan in Pictures. Rev. ed.* (5–9). Series: Visual Geography. 2003, Lerner LB $27.93 (978-0-8225-4682-5). 80pp. This substantially revised volume covers Pakistan's history, geography, culture, and lifestyle. (Rev: SLJ 7/03) [954.9]

17741 *Vietnam in Pictures* (5–8). Series: Visual Geography. 1994, Lerner LB $25.55 (978-0-8225-1909-6). This well-illustrated account of Vietnam covers its history, geography, people, government, and economy. (Rev: BL 11/1/94) [915.97]

17742 Wanasundera, Nanda P. *Sri Lanka* (4–7). Series: Cultures of the World. 1991, Marshall Cavendish LB $213.86 (978-1-85435-397-9). The history, geography,

and culture of Sri Lanka are introduced with an emphasis on contemporary problems. (Rev: BL 2/15/92) [954.93]

17743 Whyte, Mariam. *Bangladesh* (5–9). Series: Cultures of the World. 1998, Marshall Cavendish LB $37.07 (978-0-7614-0869-7). A sympathetic look at the history and geography of Bangladesh, with details of the country's rich background and current problems. (Rev: HBG 10/99; SLJ 6/99) [954.9]

17744 Winter, Jeanette. *Nasreen's Secret School: A True Story from Afghanistan* (2–4). Illus. by author. 2009, Simon & Schuster $16.99 (978-1-4169-9437-4). 40pp. When her father is abducted by the Taliban and her mother disappears, Nasreen goes to live with her grandmother and attends a secret school. e Lexile AD630L (Rev: BL 9/15/09*; HB 11–12/09; LMC 10/09; SLJ 9/1/09) [371.823]

17745 Withington, William A. *Southeast Asia* (5–8). 1988, Gateway $16.95 (978-0-934291-32-3). Sections on lifestyle, land and climate, history and government, festivals, sports, arts, and crafts. (Rev: BL 12/1/88)

17746 Yin, Saw Myat. *Myanmar. Rev. ed.* (4–8). Series: Cultures of the World. 2001, Benchmark LB $37.07 (978-0-7614-1353-0). An introduction to every aspect of Myanmar with useful information on daily life and phonetic pronunciations of many foreign words. Also use *Indonesia* (2001). (Rev: HBG 3/02; SLJ 4/02) [959.1]

Australia and the Pacific Islands

17747 Alter, Judy. *Discovering Australia's Land, People, and Wildlife* (5–8). Series: Continents of the World. 2004, Enslow LB $25.26 (978-0-7660-5207-9). 48pp. An introduction to the geography, history, economy, plants and animals, culture, and people of the continent, showing the contrast between the urban centers on the coasts and the rugged interior. (Rev: SLJ 11/04)

17748 Arnold, Caroline. *Easter Island: Giant Stone Statues Tell of a Rich and Tragic Past* (4–7). 2000, Clarion LB $15.00 (978-0-395-87609-1). This chronological history of Easter Island tells how the stone statues got there and what they mean. (Rev: BCCB 4/00; BL 3/15/00; HB 5–6/00; HBG 10/00; SLJ 4/00) [996.1]

17749 Arnold, Caroline. *Uluru: Australia's Aboriginal Heart* (4–8). Illus. by Arthur Arnold. 2003, Clarion $16.00 (978-0-618-18181-0). Uluru, formerly known as Ayers Rock, is a giant sandstone monolith that changes color in the setting sun and is a spiritual landmark for the native people of the central Australian desert. (Rev: BCCB 12/03; BL 12/15/03; HB 11–12/03; HBG 11–12/03; SLJ 1/04) [994.01]

17750 Banting, Erinn. *The Great Barrier Reef: The Largest Coral Reef in the World* (3–6). Illus. Series: Natural Wonders. 2004, Weigl LB $18.20 (978-1-59036-272-3). 32pp. A look at this giant reef, the living creatures found there, and the dangers it faces. (Rev: SLJ 4/05)

17751 Bartlett, Anne. *The Aboriginal Peoples of Australia* (4–7). Illus. Series: First Peoples. 2001, Lerner LB $23.93 (978-0-8225-4854-6). 48pp. An introduction to the indigenous people of Australia, including their history, customs, and daily life, with photographs. (Rev: BL 10/15/01; HBG 3/02; SLJ 3/02)

17752 Bingham, Jane. *Living in the Australian Outback* (3–5). Series: World Cultures. 2007, Raintree LB $27.50 (978-1-4109-2813-9). 32pp. Bingham looks at various aspects of life in the Outback — plants and animals, food, aboriginal beliefs and culture, and survival techniques. (Rev: SLJ 2/08)

17753 Coffey, Maria, and Debora Pearson. *Jungle Islands: My South Sea Adventure* (4–6). Illus. 2000, Annick LB $26.95 (978-1-55037-597-8); paper $14.95 (978-1-55037-596-1). The waters, land, people, and history of the Solomon Islands are presented in vibrant photos and an interesting narrative. (Rev: BL 1/1–15/01; HBG 3/01; SLJ 12/00)

17754 Darian-Smith, Kate. *Australia, Antarctica, and the Pacific* (5–8). Series: Continents of the World. 2006, World Almanac LB $34.00 (978-0-8368-5912-6). 64pp. Factboxes and "In Focus" articles add to this overview of the history, geography, people, culture, and so forth of the continents of Australia, Antarctica, and island of the Pacific. (Rev: SLJ 2/06)

17755 Darlington, Robert. *Australia* (4–8). Series: Nations of the World. 2001, Raintree LB $34.26 (978-0-7398-1280-8). 128pp. Australia, the world's largest island, is introduced in this attractive volume that gives material on geography, climate, terrain, history, economy, and lifestyles. (Rev: BL 6/1–15/01; HBG 10/01)

17756 Fox, Mary Virginia. *Australia* (1–3). Series: Continents. 2006, Heinemann LB $21.36 (978-1-57572-449-2). 32pp. For beginning report writers, this is a survey of Australia's geography, flora, fauna, weather, and history. (Rev: SLJ 1/07)

17757 Grabowski, John. *Australia* (5–8). Series: Modern Nations of the World. 2002, Gale LB $27.45 (978-1-56006-566-1). The continent Down Under is introduced with coverage of history, natural resources, landmarks, economy, and people. (Rev: BL 12/15/02)

17758 Grupper, Jonathan. *Destination: Australia* (4–6). Illus. 2000, National Geographic $16.95 (978-0-7922-7165-9). 32pp. This stunningly illustrated introduction to Australia covers many subjects but concentrates on its unusual animals. (Rev: BL 6/1–15/00; HBG 10/00; SLJ 5/00)

17759 Jackson, Barbara. *New Zealand* (4–8). Series: Countries of the World. 2008, National Geographic LB $27.90 (978-1-4263-0301-2). 64pp. With lots of color images, this thorough volume looks at the geography, nature, history, culture, government, and economy of New Zealand, with interesting sidebars on customs, celebrations, and so forth. (Rev: SLJ 3/09) [992]

17760 Lester, Alison. *Are We There Yet?* (2–4). Illus. 2005, Kane $15.95 (978-1-929132-73-7). 32pp. A family of five has a great time touring Australia, seeing its sights and enjoying its unique experiences over the course of six months. (Rev: BL 3/15/05; SLJ 4/05)

17761 Lewin, Ted, and Betsy Lewin. *Top to Bottom Down Under* (2–4). Illus. 2005, HarperCollins LB $16.89 (978-0-688-14114-1). With plenty of Australian-speak, the Lewins offer an eye-catching adventure- and animal-filled tour down under. (Rev: BL 1/1–15/05; SLJ 3/05)

17762 Marshall, Diana. *Aboriginal Australians* (3–5). Series: Indigenous Peoples. 2004, Weigl LB $18.20 (978-1-59036-121-4). A fascinating and informative overview of Australia's aboriginals, covering history, culture, language, and family life. (Rev: SLJ 7/04)

17763 Mason, Paul. *Sydney* (4–8). Photos by Rob Bowden. Series: Global Cities. 2007, Chelsea House LB $30.00 (978-0-7910-8849-4). 61pp. With plenty of photographs and maps, this volume introduces the history of Sydney, Australia, as well as its geography, people, environment, transportation, and so forth. (Rev: SLJ 7/07)

17764 Oleksy, Walter. *The Philippines* (4–7). Series: Enchantment of the World. 2000, Children's LB $37.00 (978-0-516-21010-0). 144pp. These South Pacific islands are presented with coverage of history, geography, economy, the people, current problems, culture, and recreation. (Rev: BL 7/00)

17765 Olson, Nathan. *Australia: A Question And Answer Book* (2–5). Illus. Series: Questions and Answers: Countries. 2005, Capstone LB $23.93 (978-0-7368-3747-7). 32pp. Using a question-and-answer format, simple text, large photos, and many factboxes, this is an introduction to Australia today, with material on history and traditional culture. (Rev: SLJ 7/05)

17766 Pelta, Kathy. *Rediscovering Easter Island* (5–9). Series: How History Is Invented. 2001, Lerner LB $28.75 (978-0-8225-4890-4). An assortment of illustrations, maps, and inserts add to this exploration of the mysteries of Easter Island. (Rev: BCCB 7–8/01; HBG 10/01; SLJ 2/02) [996.18]

17767 Rajendra, Vijeya, and Sundran Rajendra. *Australia* (4–7). Series: Cultures of the World. 1991, Marshall Cavendish LB $35.64 (978-1-85435-400-6). Beyond the basics, this volume highlights contemporary problems and concerns in the Land Down Under. (Rev: BL 2/15/92; SLJ 3/92) [994]

17768 Rau, Dana Meachen. *Australia* (3–5). Series: Facts About Countries. 2009, Sea-to-Sea LB $27.10 (978-1-59771-112-8). 32pp. A well-designed introduction to Australia with color photographs and statistics and covering geography, history, economy, education, government, culture, and current status. (Rev: SLJ 7/09)

17769 Schroeder, Holly. *New Zealand ABCs: A Book About the People and Places of New Zealand* (2–4). Illus. by Claudia Wolf. Series: Country ABCs. 2004, Picture Window LB $26.60 (978-1-4048-0178-3). 32pp. Young researchers will find useful facts in this alphabetically organized volume. (Rev: SLJ 8/04)

17770 Shepherd, Donna Walsh. *New Zealand* (4–7). Series: Enchantment of the World. 2002, Children's LB $37.00 (978-0-516-21099-5). 144pp. Some of the subjects covered in this fine introduction to New Zealand are history, people and languages, economy, government, culture, natural resources, and climate. (Rev: BL 5/15/02; SLJ 10/02)

17771 Steele, Philip. *Sydney* (4–6). Series: Great Cities of the World. 2004, World Almanac LB $31.00 (978-0-8368-5032-1). A profile of Australia's oldest and biggest city, well illustrated with photographs. (Rev: SLJ 6/04)

17772 Theunissen, Steve. *The Maori of New Zealand* (4–6). Illus. Series: First Peoples. 2002, Lerner LB $23.95 (978-0-8225-0665-2). 48pp. Full of photographs, this is a wide-ranging introduction to the history and culture of the Polynesian people who settled in New Zealand centuries before the Europeans arrived. (Rev: HBG 3/03; SLJ 6/03)

17773 Turner, Kate. *Australia* (5–8). Series: Countries of the World. 2007, National Geographic LB $27.90 (978-1-4263-0055-4). Excellent photographs and maps make this an appealing introduction to the country's history, geography, government, economy, people, culture, and nature. (Rev: SLJ 10/07) [994]

17774 Underwood, Deborah. *The Easter Island Statues* (3–6). Illus. Series: Wonders of the World. 2004, Gale LB $26.20 (978-0-7377-3065-4). Underwood discusses the construction and symbolism of these famous statues, and includes material on the island's geography, history, and people. (Rev: SLJ 6/05)

17775 Webster, Christine. *Polynesians* (4–6). Illus. Series: Indigenous Peoples. 2004, Weigl LB $18.20 (978-1-59036-123-8). 32pp. Historical and contemporary issues are both covered in this detailed portrait of life among the Polynesian people and how they've endured and adapted to dramatic changes in their homelands. (Rev: BL 4/1/04; SLJ 7/04)

17776 Wojahn, Rebecca Hogue, and Donald Wojahn. *An Australian Outback Food Chain: A Who-Eats-What Adventure* (3–6). Illus. Series: Follow That Food Chain. 2009, Lerner LB $30.60 (978-0-8225-7499-6). 64pp. Dingos and saltwater crocodiles are among the animals introduced in this attractive "choose your own adventure" introduction to plant and animal life in the Outback. (Rev: SLJ 6/09)

Europe

General and Miscellaneous

17777 Bowden, Rob. *Istanbul* (4–8). Photos by Edward Parker. Series: Global Cities. 2007, Chelsea House LB $30.00 (978-0-7910-8850-0). With plenty of photographs and maps, this volume introduces the history of Istanbul as well as its geography, people, environment, transportation, and so forth. (Rev: SLJ 7/07)

17778 Bramwell, Martyn. *Europe* (4–6). Illus. Series: World in Maps. 2000, Carolrhoda $23.93 (978-0-8225-2913-2). 48pp. Portrays the countries of Europe in a

series of maps and accompanying text that supply information on such topics as population, government, geography, cities, and notable physical features. (Rev: BL 10/15/00; HBG 10/01; SLJ 1/01)

17779 *Cyprus in Pictures* (5–8). Series: Visual Geography. 1992, Lerner LB $25.55 (978-0-8225-1910-2). The divided island of Cyprus is introduced, with good background information and material on the standoff between Greece and Turkey up to 1992. (Rev: BL 2/1/93) [956.45]

17780 Flint, David. *Europe* (5–8). Series: Continents of the World. 2006, World Almanac LB $34.00 (978-0-8368-5913-3). Factboxes and "In Focus" articles add to this overview of the history, geography, people, culture, and so forth of the continent of Europe. (Rev: SLJ 2/06) [940]

17781 Holmes, Mary Tavener. *My Travels with Clara* (1–3). Illus. by Jon Cannell. 2007, Getty $17.95 (978-0-89236-880-8). 33pp. A Dutch sea captain describes his travels around Europe with a rhinoceros named Clara in the mid-18th century. (Rev: BL 10/1/07; SLJ 8/07)

17782 Sheehan, Sean. *Malta* (5–9). Series: Cultures of the World. 2000, Marshall Cavendish LB $37.07 (978-0-7614-0993-9). This work covers the culture, geography, and history of Malta with material on such subjects as government, economy, people, lifestyles, and leisure. (Rev: HBG 10/00; SLJ 11/00) [945]

Central and Eastern Europe

17783 Andryszewski, Tricia. *Kosovo: The Splintering of Yugoslavia* (5–8). Illus. Series: Headliners. 2000, Millbrook LB $25.90 (978-0-7613-1750-0). 64pp. Introduced by refugees' accounts of the horror in Kosovo, this book traces the origins of ethnic conflicts in Yugoslavia, with a concentration on events of the past 10 years. (Rev: BL 6/1–15/00; HBG 10/00; SLJ 6/00)

17784 Barber, Nicola. *Istanbul* (3–6). Series: Great Cities of the World. 2005, World Almanac LB $31.00 (978-0-8368-5050-5). 48pp. With color photographs and informative sidebars, this volume introduces the geography, history, culture, religion, work, and recreation of the Turkish city of Istanbul. (Rev: SLJ 11/05)

17785 Corona, Laurel. *Poland* (5–8). Illus. Series: Modern Nations of the World. 2000, Lucent LB $28.70 (978-1-56006-600-2). 126pp. A good history of Poland that also covers Polish achievements and daily life. (Rev: BL 9/15/00; HBG 3/01)

17786 Eboch, Chris. *Turkey* (5–9). Series: Modern Nations of the World. 2003, Gale LB $29.95 (978-1-59018-122-5). This account presents a broad spectrum of material about Turkey including history, geography, and culture. (Rev: BL 11/15/03; SLJ 6/03) [961]

17787 Englar, Mary. *Turkey* (2–5). Illus. Series: Questions and Answers: Countries. 2005, Capstone LB $23.93 (978-0-7368-3762-0). 32pp. Using a question-and-answer format, simple text, large photos, and many factboxes, this is an introduction to Turkey today, with material on history and traditional culture.

17788 Feinstein, Steve. *Turkey in Pictures* (5–8). 1989, Lerner LB $25.55 (978-0-8225-1831-0). An overview of Turkey and its people that includes lots of images. (Rev: BL 8/88) [956.1]

17789 Franchino, Vicky. *Turkey* (4–6). Illus. Series: Social Studies Explorer. 2012, Cherry Lake LB $31.36 (978-161080442-4). 48pp. An attractive, photo-filled overview of this nation, with maps, information on the economy and government, people and culture, and so forth, plus a recipe and a craft. **e** (Rev: BL 3/1/13; LMC 10/13) [956.1]

17790 Harris, Pamela K., and Brad Clemmons. *Welcome to Switzerland* (1–4). Series: Wecome to the World. 2008, The Child's World LB $27.07 (978-1-59296-980-7). 32pp. As easy introduction to Switzerland and its land, people, plants and animals, and so forth, with color photographs, maps, and recipes. (Rev: SLJ 9/08)

17791 *Hungary in Pictures* (5–8). Series: Visual Geography. 1993, Lerner LB $25.55 (978-0-8225-1883-9). Concise text and extensive photographs introduce the land, history, and people of Hungary. (Rev: BL 12/1/93; SLJ 12/93) [943.9]

17792 Kinkade, Sheila. *Children of Slovakia* (2–5). Photos by Elaine Little. Series: The World's Children. 2001, Carolrhoda LB $23.93 (978-1-57505-446-9). 48pp. The daily lives of children in Slovakia are used to introduce the history, geography, and culture of the country, with appealing full-color illustrations, a pronunciation guide, and map. (Rev: HBG 10/01; SLJ 6/01)

17793 LaRoche, Amelia. *We Visit Turkey* (4–8). Illus. Series: Your Land and My Land: The Middle East. 2011, Mitchell Lane LB $33.95 (978-158415956-8). 64pp. With illustrations, photographs, maps, reproductions, a recipe, a craft project, and a timeline, this is a useful overview of the history and geography of Turkey. (Rev: BL 2/1/12) [956.1]

17794 Milivojevic, JoAnn. *Bosnia and Herzegovina* (4–6). Series: Enchantment of the World. 2004, Scholastic LB $37.00 (978-0-516-24247-7). 144pp. Contemporary life, history, geography, culture are all covered in this well-illustrated and well-written volume suitable for report writers. (Rev: BL 9/1/04; SLJ 7/04)

17795 Netzley, Patricia D. *Switzerland* (5–8). Series: Modern Nations of the World. 2001, Lucent LB $27.45 (978-1-56006-821-1). Interesting sidebars, a chronology, and excellent photographs supplement informative text introducing this small country. (Rev: BL 6/1–15/01)

17796 Orr, Tamra. *Slovenia* (5–8). Series: Enchantment of the World. 2004, Children's Pr. LB $37.00 (978-0-516-24249-1). Introduces the history, geography, people, and culture of Slovenia, with plenty of clear photographs and an emphasis on contemporary life. (Rev: BL 9/1/04; SLJ 7/04)

17797 Orr, Tamra. *Turkey* (5–8). Illus. Series: Enchantment of the World, Second Series. 2003, Children's LB $37.00 (978-0-516-22679-8). 144pp. A visually attrac-

tive book that covers such topics as the geography, history, government, culture, and people, with a timeline, fast facts, and a recipe. (Rev: SLJ 5/03)

17798 Ricchiardi, Sherry. *Bosnia: The Struggle for Peace* (5–8). 1996, Millbrook LB $25.90 (978-0-7613-0031-1). An account that gives background information but concentrates on the recent (through 1995) history of Bosnia. (Rev: BL 7/96; SLJ 7/96) [949.702]

17799 Rogers, Lura. *Switzerland* (4–7). Series: Enchantment of the World. 2001, Children's LB $37.00 (978-0-516-21080-3). A highly visual introduction to Switzerland that covers such topics as people and languages, history, natural resources, and climate. (Rev: BL 1/1–15/02)

17800 Sheehan, Sean. *Austria* (4–7). Series: Cultures of the World. 1992, Marshall Cavendish LB $35.64 (978-1-85435-454-9). This introduction to Austria covers its history, lifestyles of the people, and contemporary problems. (Rev: BL 10/15/92) [943.6]

17801 Sheehan, Sean. *Turkey* (4–7). Series: Cultures of the World. 1993, Marshall Cavendish LB $35.64 (978-1-85435-576-8). This introduction to Turkey covers history, culture, economics, and present-day concerns. (Rev: BL 8/93) [956.1]

17802 Stein, R. Conrad. *Austria* (4–7). Series: Enchantment of the World. 2000, Children's LB $37.00 (978-0-516-21049-0). 144pp. A thorough introduction to Austria with material on such subjects as history, the land, government, people, culture, cities, and daily life. (Rev: BL 1/1–15/01)

17803 *Switzerland in Pictures* (5–8). Series: Visual Geography. 1996, Lerner LB $25.55 (978-0-8225-1895-2). With a generous number of color pictures, this account traces the history and geography of Switzerland, with emphasis on the modern nation and its people. (Rev: BL 9/15/96; SLJ 8/98) [949.4]

17804 Willis, Terri. *Romania* (4–7). Series: Enchantment of the World. 2001, Children's LB $37.00 (978-0-516-21635-5). Packed with photographs, original maps, and browser-friendly sidebars, this is a fine introduction to Romania that explores a number of aspects of the past and present of this country. (Rev: BL 1/1–15/02)

France

17805 Bader, Philip. *France* (3–5). Series: Dropping In On. 2001, Rourke LB $28.50 (978-1-55916-280-7). 32pp. A brief tour of France in a hot-air balloon — with stops at interesting places — that includes material on landmarks, the people, food, and growing up. (Rev: SLJ 1/01)

17806 Bailey, Linda. *Adventures in the Ice Age* (3–6). Illus. by Bill Slavin. Series: Good Times Travel Agency. 2004, Kids Can paper $8.95 (978-1-55337-504-3). 48pp. In this sixth installment of the series that blends fact and fiction, the Binkerton children are whisked off to Ice Age France, where they learn facts about life at that time. (Rev: BL 11/1/04)

17807 Corona, Laurel. *France* (5–8). Series: Modern Nations of the World. 2002, Gale LB $29.95 (978-1-56006-760-3). A comprehensive introduction to the land and people of France with material on history, geography, culture, and lifestyles. (Rev: BL 12/15/02) [944]

17808 Costain, Meredith, and Paul Collins. *Welcome to France* (3–5). Illus. Series: Countries of the World. 2001, Chelsea LB $28.00 (978-0-7910-6551-8). 32pp. Young Gregoire introduces daily life, schooling, sports, transport, important places, and so forth, with interesting color photographs. (Rev: HBG 3/02; SLJ 10/01)

17809 Gofen, Ethel C. *France* (4–7). Series: Cultures of the World. 1992, Marshall Cavendish LB $35.64 (978-1-85435-449-5). This account provides information on the history, culture, and people of France and discusses the current problems and concerns. (Rev: BL 10/15/92) [944]

17810 Hoban, Sarah. *Daily Life in Ancient and Modern Paris* (4–7). 2000, Runestone LB $25.26 (978-0-8225-3222-4). This well-illustrated history of Paris is divided chronologically into seven sections, beginning with early Paris and working through the Middle Ages to World War II and the Paris of today. (Rev: BL 2/1/01; HBG 3/01; SLJ 2/01) [944]

17811 Ingham, Richard. *France* (4–8). Illus. 2000, Raintree LB $34.26 (978-0-8172-5782-8). 128pp. A fine introduction to France — its past, its present, and its people — that is particularly noteworthy for its use of graphics. (Rev: BL 10/15/00; HBG 10/00; SLJ 7/00)

17812 LaRoche, Amelia. *Recipe and Craft Guide to France* (4–7). Illus. Series: World Crafts and Recipes. 2010, Mitchell Lane LB $24.50 (978-158415936-0). 64pp. Cultural and culinary projects introduce readers to many aspects of France. (Rev: BL 1/1–15/11; LMC 1–2/11*) [641.5941]

17813 Pipe, Jim. *You Wouldn't Want to Be an Aristocrat in the French Revolution! A Horrible Time in Paris You'd Rather Avoid* (4–6). Illus. by David Antram. Series: You Wouldn't Want to . . . History of the World. 2007, Watts LB $29.00 (978-0-531-18745-6). 32pp. Engaging facts, fast action, cartoons, and a touch of humor make for an appealing package about the French Revolution. (Rev: LMC 5/08; SLJ 3/08)

17814 Plain, Nancy. *Louis XVI, Marie-Antoinette and the French Revolution* (5–8). Series: Rulers and Their Times. 2001, Marshall Cavendish LB $29.93 (978-0-7614-1029-4). In three well-illustrated parts, this book offers a biography of Marie Antoinette, a history of France and its people during the French Revolution, and a generous selection of original documents of the period. (Rev: BL 1/1–15/02; HBG 3/02; SLJ 3/02) [944]

17815 Spengler, Kremena. *France* (2–5). Illus. Series: Questions and Answers: Countries. 2004, Capstone LB $23.93 (978-0-7368-2689-1). Using a question-and-answer format, simple text, large photos, and many factboxes, this is an introduction to France today, with material on history and traditional culture.

17816 Stacey, Gill. *Paris* (4–7). 2004, World Almanac LB $31.00 (978-0-8368-5030-7). This attractive introduction to Paris covers the French capital's history and examines some of its modern-day problems. (Rev: BL 4/15/04; SLJ 6/04) [944]

17817 Stevens, Kathryn. *France* (3–5). Series: Countries: Faces and Places. 2000, Child's World LB $22.79 (978-1-56766-714-1). This basic introduction to France, its history, people, and culture uses simple text, color photographs on each page, and an oversize format. (Rev: BL 4/15/01; HBG 3/01)

17818 Tidmarsh, Celia. *France* (3–5). Series: Facts About Countries. 2009, Sea-to-Sea LB $27.10 (978-1-59771-115-9). 32pp. A well-designed introduction to France with color photographs and statistics and covering geography, history, economy, education, government, culture, and current status. (Rev: SLJ 7/09)

17819 Yuan, Margaret Speaker. *The Arc de Triomphe* (5–8). Series: Building World Landmarks. 2004, Gale LB $24.95 (978-1-4103-0138-3). 48pp. A concise account of the design and construction of this arch, which met financial, political, and technical difficulties. (Rev: SLJ 4/05)

Germany

17820 Barber, Nicola. *Berlin* (4–7). Series: Great Cities of the World. 2005, World Almanac LB $31.00 (978-0-8368-5043-7). An informative and appealing overview of one of the world's most famous cities, with material on its history, its economy, and what it's like to live there. (Rev: BL 4/15/04)

17821 Fuller, Barbara. *Germany* (4–7). Series: Cultures of the World. 1992, Marshall Cavendish LB $35.64 (978-1-85435-530-0). In addition to the usual information on the history and geography of Germany, this account stresses how the people live and their traditions. (Rev: BL 1/1/93) [943]

17822 *Germany in Pictures* (5–8). Series: Visual Geography. 1994, Lerner LB $21.27 (978-0-8225-1873-0). The new united Germany is introduced with a basic text and copious illustrations, including maps, charts, and attractive photographs. (Rev: BL 1/15/95) [943]

17823 Gray, Susan H. *Germany* (1–3). Series: A True Book. 2003, Children's Pr. LB $25.00 (978-0-516-22673-6). 48pp. A blend of easy-to-understand text and colorful illustrations make this overview suitable for beginning readers. (Rev: SLJ 10/03)

17824 Levy, Debbie. *The Berlin Wall* (5–8). Series: Building World Landmarks. 2004, Gale LB $24.95 (978-1-4103-0137-6). 48pp. A concise account of the wall's history and its importance in the struggle between East and West; with a timeline. (Rev: SLJ 4/05)

17825 Nickles, Greg, and Niki Walker. *Germany* (4–8). Series: Nations of the World. 2001, Raintree LB $34.26 (978-0-7398-1285-3). 128pp. A profile of this now united, highly industrialized, and urbanized country, with material on its past, present, and future. (Rev: BL 6/1–15/01; HBG 10/01)

17826 Russell, Henry. *Germany* (5–8). Series: Countries of the World. 2007, National Geographic LB $27.90 (978-1-4263-0059-2). Excellent photographs and maps make this an appealing introduction to the country's history, geography, government, economy, people, culture, and nature. (Rev: SLJ 10/07) [943]

17827 Spengler, Kremena. *Germany* (2–5). Illus. Series: Questions and Answers: Countries. 2004, Capstone LB $23.93 (978-0-7368-2690-7). 32pp. Using a question-and-answer format, simple text, large photos, and many factboxes, this is an introduction to Germany today, with material on history and traditional culture.

Great Britain and Ireland

17828 Allan, Tony. *The Irish Famine: The Birth of Irish America* (4–9). Illus. by Stefan Chabluk. Series: Point of Impact. 2001, Heinemann LB $24.22 (978-1-58810-077-1). Allan traces the causes of the crisis that started in Ireland in 1845, the subsequent wave of emigration to the United States, and the ill feelings created between Britain and Ireland. (Rev: HBG 10/01; SLJ 7/01)

17829 Ashby, Ruth. *Victorian England* (5–8). Series: Cultures of the Past. 2002, Marshall Cavendish $29.93 (978-0-7614-1493-3). 80pp. The political, historical, and cultural aspects of life in England during the reign of Victoria are covered in this handsome volume. (Rev: BL 1/1–15/03; HBG 3/03)

17830 Bean, Rachel. *United Kingdom* (4–8). Illus. Series: Countries of the World. 2007, National Geographic LB $27.90 (978-1-4263-0126-1). This attractive volume full of photographs covers the United Kingdom's geography, history, economy, people, and so forth. (Rev: SLJ 2/08)

17831 Blashfield, Jean F. *Ireland* (4–7). Series: Enchantment of the World. 2002, Children's LB $37.00 (978-0-516-21127-5). 144pp. Using many visual aids and a lively text, this is an introduction to Ireland — the land, the people, and the culture. (Rev: BL 5/15/02; SLJ 12/02)

17832 Boraas, Tracey. *England* (4–6). Series: Countries and Cultures. 2002, Capstone LB $25.26 (978-0-7368-0937-5). 64pp. Using devices such as timelines, maps, sidebars, and a recipe, English history, geography, and culture are introduced. (Rev: BL 1/1–15/03; HBG 3/03; SLJ 7/03)

17833 Brassey, Richard, and Stewart Ross. *The Story of Ireland* (3–5). Illus. 2002, Trafalgar $19.95 (978-1-85881-848-1). Fast-paced narrative and brief biographies tell the history of Ireland from prehistoric times. (Rev: BL 3/1/02)

17834 Chrisp, Peter. *Welcome to the Globe! The Story of Shakespeare's Theater* (3–5). Illus. 2000, DK $12.99 (978-0-7894-6641-9); paper $3.99 (978-0-7894-6640-2). 48pp. The Globe is presented through the words of a variety of characters, real and fictitious, working there and through detailed illustrations. (Rev: HBG 3/01; SLJ 4/01)

17835 Cole, Joanna. *Ms. Frizzle's Adventures: Medieval Castle* (2–5). Illus. by Bruce Degen. Series: The Magic School Bus. 2003, Scholastic $15.95 (978-0-590-10820-1). Ms. Frizzle is on the move again in this amusing and informative large-format volume, this time traveling back in time to medieval England with her student Arnold. (Rev: BL 7/03; HBG 4/04; SLJ 7/03)

17836 Corona, Laurel. *Scotland* (5–8). Series: Modern Nations of the World. 2000, Lucent LB $29.95 (978-1-56006-703-0). 128pp. The history, geography, and culture of Scotland are discussed along with material on daily life in modern Scotland. (Rev: BL 3/1/01)

17837 Dahl, Michael. *England* (3–4). Illus. Series: Fact Finders: Questions and Answers. 2004, Capstone LB $23.93 (978-0-7368-2477-4). Using a question-and-answer format, this title introduces England's history, government, economy, education, culture, sports, and lifestyle. (Rev: SLJ 1/05)

17838 Davis, Kenneth C. *Don't Know Much About the Kings and Queens of England* (4–7). Illus. by S. D. Schindler. Series: Don't Know Much About. 2002, HarperCollins LB $15.89 (978-0-06-028612-5). 48pp. Humorous questions and answers supply information that browsers will enjoy. (Rev: HBG 10/02; SLJ 7/02)

17839 Elgin, Kathy. *Elizabethan England, Vol. 3* (5–8). Series: A History of Fashion and Costume. 2005, Facts on File $35.00 (978-0-8160-5946-1). A broad overview of the clothing and personal adornment worn during this time period, with many visual aids. (Rev: SLJ 5/06) [391]

17840 Gottfried, Ted. *Northern Ireland: Peace in Our Time?* (5–8). Series: Headliners. 2002, Millbrook LB $25.90 (978-0-7613-2252-8). This attractive book gives current and background information on the struggles within Northern Ireland and the causes and possible solutions. (Rev: BL 4/15/02; HBG 10/02; SLJ 3/02)

17841 Greenblatt, Miriam. *Elizabeth I and Tudor England* (5–8). Series: Rulers and Their Times. 2001, Marshall Cavendish LB $29.93 (978-0-7614-1028-7). After a biography of Elizabeth I, this colorful account traces everyday life in Elizabethan times and supplies a selection of primary documents. (Rev: BL 1/1–15/02; HBG 3/02; SLJ 3/02)

17842 Hestler, Anna. *Wales* (5–9). Illus. Series: Cultures of the World. 2001, Marshall Cavendish LB $37.07 (978-0-7614-1195-6). 128pp. Geography, history, government, arts and culture, and lifestyle are all covered in this interesting and attractive volume. (Rev: HBG 10/01; SLJ 11/01)

17843 Hynson, Colin. *Elizabeth I and the Spanish Armada* (5–8). Illus. Series: Stories from History. 2006, School Specialty $9.95 (978-0-7696-4703-6); paper $6.95 (978-0-7696-4629-9). 48pp. A graphic novel presentation of the confrontation between England's Queen Elizabeth I and the Spanish empire, climaxing in the defeat of the Spanish Armada by the English; full-color depictions of battles, fast facts, and maps aid comprehension. (Rev: BL 10/15/06; SLJ 1/07)

17844 Innes, Brian. *United Kingdom* (4–8). Series: Nations of the World. 2001, Raintree LB $34.26 (978-0-7398-1288-4). 128pp. An in-depth look at the nation's geography, climate. terrain, history, government, and lifestyles. (Rev: BL 12/15/01)

17845 *Ireland in Pictures* (5–8). Series: Visual Geography. 1997, Lerner LB $25.55 (978-0-8225-1878-5). Contemporary Ireland is highlighted in this illustrated account. (Rev: BL 12/1/90) [941.5]

17846 Jones, Becky, and Clare Lewis. *The Bumper Book of London: Fun Facts for All the Family* (5–12). Series: Adventure Walks. 2012, Frances Lincoln paper $19.95 (978-0-7112-3145-0). 279pp. This attractive volume provides facts and trivia about London's development since Roman times, highlighting notable sites and interesting details about everyday life throughout the ages. (Rev: SLJ 5/1/12) [942.1]

17847 Levy, Patricia. *Ireland* (4–7). Series: Cultures of the World. 1993, Marshall Cavendish LB $25.95 (978-1-85435-580-5). An account that traces the role of women in Irish history to the present day. (Rev: SLJ 2/94) [941]

17848 Losure, Mary. *The Fairy Ring; or, Elsie and Frances Fool the World* (5–8). Illus. 2012, Candlewick $16.99 (978-076365670-6). 192pp. Losure tells the story of two cousins who as girls in early-20th-century England posed with paintings of fairies and convinced many, including Arthur Conan Doyle, that they were real. ∩ ℮ Lexile 940L (Rev: BL 3/1/12*; HB 3–4/12*; SLJ 5/1/12*; VOYA 2/12) [398]

17849 Lyons, Mary E., ed. *Feed the Children First: Irish Memories of the Great Hunger* (4–8). 2002, Simon & Schuster $17.00 (978-0-689-84226-9). Text, full-color reproductions, and occasional photographs clearly document the suffering of ordinary people during the Irish potato famine. (Rev: BL 12/15/01; HB 3–4/02; HBG 10/02; SLJ 3/02*) [941.5081]

17850 McQuinn, Anna, and Colm McQuinn. *Ireland* (4–8). Series: Countries of the World. 2008, National Geographic LB $27.90 (978-1-4263-0299-2). 64pp. With lots of color images, this thorough volume looks at the geography, nature, history, culture, government, and economy of Ireland, with interesting sidebars on customs, celebrations, and so forth. (Rev: SLJ 3/09) [941.5]

17851 Malam, John. *You Wouldn't Want to Be a Victorian Mill Worker! A Grueling Job You'd Rather Not Have* (4–6). Illus. by David Antram. Series: You Wouldn't Want to . . . History of the World. 2007, Watts LB $29.00 (978-0-531-18747-0). 32pp. Engaging facts, fast action, cartoons, and a touch of humor make for an appealing package about Victorian mill workers. (Rev: LMC 5/08; SLJ 3/08)

17852 *Northern Ireland in Pictures* (5–8). Series: Visual Geography. 1991, Lerner LB $25.55 (978-0-8225-1898-3). This beautiful but troubled land is introduced in text and pictures. (Rev: BL 2/15/92) [941.6]

17853 Oxlade, Chris, and Anita Ganeri. *England* (1–3). Series: A Visit To. 2003, Heinemann LB $22.79 (978-1-4034-0965-2). 32pp. Full of photographs, this is a use-

ful and interesting overview of the country's geography, history, and culture, suitable for beginning readers. Also use *Scotland* and *Wales* (both 2003). (Rev: HBG 10/03; SLJ 7/03)

17854 Ross, Michael Elsohn. *Children of Ireland* (4–6). Series: The World's Children. 2001, Carolrhoda LB $23.93 (978-1-57505-521-3). Outstanding photographs of children are used to introduce this land and the daily lives of its people. (Rev: BL 1/1–15/02; HBG 3/02)

17855 Ross, Michael Elsohn. *Children of Northern Ireland* (2–5). Photos by Felix Rigau. Series: The World's Children. 2001, Carolrhoda LB $23.93 (978-1-57505-433-9). 48pp. This look at the daily lives of children in Northern Ireland introduces the history, geography, and culture of the country, with appealing full-color illustrations, a pronunciation guide, and map. (Rev: HBG 10/01; SLJ 6/01)

17856 Rubbino, Salvatore. *A Walk in London* (1–3). Illus. by author. 2011, Candlewick $16.99 (978-0-7636-5272-2). 40pp. A young girl describes her tour of London with her mother, with details of all the places they visit; captions to the illustrations in this large-format book provide key information. (Rev: BL 5/1/11; SLJ 6/11) [942.1]

17857 Stacey, Gill. *London* (4–8). Series: Great Cities of the World. 2003, World Almanac LB $31.00 (978-0-8368-5022-2). In an appealing blend of text, photographs, quotations, and sidebar features, this volume introduces readers to some of London's history and attractions. (Rev: SLJ 1/04) [942.1]

17858 Stein, R. Conrad. *Scotland* (4–7). Series: Enchantment of the World. 2001, Children's LB $37.00 (978-0-516-21112-1). Numerous pictures, charts, maps, and drawings contribute to a fascinating portrait of Scotland's past and present. (Rev: BL 1/1–15/02)

Greece and Italy

17859 Anderson, Michael, ed. *Ancient Greece* (5–8). Series: Ancient Civilizations. 2011, Britannica Educational LB $31.70 (978-1-61530-513-1). 88pp. This slim volume offers an accessible introduction to the culture, religion, architecture, and inventions of ancient Greece. ℮ (Rev: SLJ 12/1/11) [938]

17860 Barber, Nicola. *Rome* (4–7). Series: Great Cities of the World. 2005, World Almanac LB $31.00 (978-0-8368-5040-6). An informative and appealing overview of one of the world's most famous cities, with material on its history, its economy, and what it's like to live there. (Rev: BL 4/15/04)

17861 Behnke, Alison. *Italy in Pictures. Rev. ed.* (4–8). Illus. Series: Visual Geography. 2002, Lerner LB $27.93 (978-0-8225-0368-2). 80pp. An excellent introduction to Italy that includes material on geography, history, people, economy, and culture with maps, photographs, and illustrations. (Rev: HBG 3/03; SLJ 3/03)

17862 Britton, Tamara. *Greece* (2–4). Series: Countries. 2000, ABDO LB $22.78 (978-1-57765-385-1). A workable introduction to Greece with a focus on modern times. (Rev: HBG 10/01; SLJ 3/01)

17863 Cassidy, Picot. *Italy* (4–8). Series: Nations of the World. 2001, Raintree LB $34.26 (978-0-7398-1287-7). 128pp. A fine overall picture of Italy, its past, its land, its people, its culture, and present-day problems. (Rev: BL 12/15/01; HBG 3/02)

17864 Costain, Meredith, and Paul Collins. *Welcome to Greece* (1–4). Illus. Series: Countries of the World. 2001, Chelsea LB $28.00 (978-0-7910-6545-7). 32pp. An attractive introduction to the land and people of Greece, with a recipe, a craft, a brief page of facts, and many illustrations. (Rev: HBG 3/02; SLJ 12/01)

17865 Croy, Anita, ed. *Ancient Greece* (5–9). Series: Facts at Your Fingertips. 2010, Black Rabbit LB $35.65 (978-1-933834-55-9). 64pp. Crete, Mycenai, Sparta, Olympia, and Athens are among the sites described in this overview of the history and culture of ancient Greece. (Rev: LMC 3–4/10) [938]

17866 Day, Nancy. *Your Travel Guide to Ancient Greece* (4–8). Series: Passport to History. 2000, Runestone LB $26.50 (978-0-8225-3076-3). An outstanding introduction to ancient Greece arranged in the format of a guided tour and covering topics including geography, history, customs, and places to visit in an exciting, interesting way. (Rev: BL 10/15/00*; HBG 3/01; SLJ 2/01) [938]

17867 De Capua, Sarah. *Italy* (2–4). Illus. Series: First Reports. 2003, Compass Point LB $22.60 (978-0-7565-0425-0). 48pp. In this attractive title from the First Reports series, author Sarah E. De Capua introduces readers to the geography, history, people, and culture of Italy. (Rev: SLJ 10/03)

17868 Dubois, Jill, and Xenia Skoura. *Greece. 2nd ed.* (5–8). Series: Cultures of the World. 2003, Benchmark LB $37.07 (978-0-7614-1499-5). In addition to coverage of the geography, history, and economics of Greece, this volume looks at the people and the culture of this Mediterranean nation and provides recipes. (Rev: HBG 10/03; SLJ 8/03) [949.5]

17869 Heinrichs, Ann. *Greece* (4–7). Series: Enchantment of the World. 2002, Children's LB $37.00 (978-0-516-22271-4). 144pp. With many color illustrations, this book gives a fascinating portrait of Greece's past and present with coverage of topics including natural resources, culture, climate, and religion. (Rev: BL 9/15/02; SLJ 12/02)

17870 Hinds, Kathryn. *Venice and Its Merchant Empire* (5–8). Series: Cultures of the Past. 2001, Marshall Cavendish LB $29.93 (978-0-7614-0305-0). A well-illustrated overview of the history of Venice with a focus on the city's glory during the Renaissance. (Rev: BL 2/15/02; HBG 3/02) [945]

17871 Jovinelly, Joann, and Jason Netelkos. *The Crafts and Culture of the Ancient Greeks* (5–8). Series: Crafts of the Ancient World. 2002, Rosen LB $29.25 (978-0-8239-3510-9). As well as basic information on ancient Greece, this book outlines many craft projects. (Rev: BL 5/15/02) [938]

17872 Kotapish, Dawn. *Daily Life in Ancient and Modern Athens* (5–8). Illus. by Bob Moulder. Series: Cities Through Time. 2000, Runestone LB $25.26 (978-0-8225-3216-3). Kotapish explores everyday life, government, and culture in Athens through the ages. (Rev: HBG 3/01; SLJ 5/01) [949.5]

17873 Lamprell, Klay. *Not-for-Parents Rome: Everything You Ever Wanted to Know* (4–7). Illus. 2011, Lonely Planet paper $14.99 (978-17422081-8-3). 96pp. More a source of trivia and amusement than a guidebook, this is nonetheless informative and directed at young visitors to the city; includes many photographs, maps, and images. (Rev: BL 12/1/11) [914.5632]

17874 Macaulay, David. *Rome Antics* (5–8). 1997, Houghton Mifflin $18.00 (978-0-395-82279-1). The reader gets a pigeon-eye view of vistas and buildings as the bird flies over Rome. (Rev: BL 9/15/97; SLJ 11/97*) [945]

17875 Malam, John. *Ancient Greece* (4–7). Series: Picturing the Past. 2004, Enchanted Lion $15.95 (978-1-59270-022-6). This photo-filled volume uses images of ancient Greek artifacts and structures to introduce the civilization's governmental organization, religion, mythology, recreation, and theater. (Rev: BL 10/15/04; SLJ 11/04) [938]

17876 Malam, John. *Exploring Ancient Greece* (5–8). Series: Remains to Be Seen. 1999, Evans Brothers $19.95 (978-0-237-51994-0). Particularly noteworthy in this basic account of the history of ancient Greece are the stunning photographs of temples, theaters, artifacts, and landscapes. (Rev: SLJ 1/00) [938]

17877 Martell, Hazel Mary, and Cleo Kuhtz. *Ancient Greek Civilization* (5–8). Series: Ancient Civilizations and Their Myths and Legends. 2010, Rosen LB $26.50 (978-1-4042-8033-5). 48pp. This volume introduces daily life in ancient Greece and describes religion, agriculture, government, trade, clothing, entertainment, and so forth, at the same time retelling some of the best-known myths. (Rev: LMC 1–2/10) [292.13]

17878 Nardo, Don. *Greece* (5–8). Series: Modern Nations of the World. 2000, Lucent LB $27.45 (978-1-56006-587-6). 128pp. Although there is coverage of ancient Greece, this account stresses modern history, the people today, and current living conditions and problems. (Rev: BL 2/15/00; HBG 10/00; SLJ 6/00)

17879 Olson, Nathan. *Italy* (2–5). Illus. Series: Questions and Answers: Countries. 2005, Capstone LB $23.93 (978-0-7368-3754-5). 32pp. Using a question-and-answer format, simple text, large photos, and many fact-boxes, this is an introduction to Italy today, with material on history and traditional culture.

17880 Parker, Vic. *Pompeii AD 79: A City Buried by a Volcanic Eruption* (4–7). Series: When Disaster Struck. 2006, Raintree LB $32.86 (978-1-4109-2276-2). Parker looks at Pompeii both before and after its destruction by the eruption of Mount Vesuvius, discussing the nature (and likelihood) of volcanic eruptions and what archaeologists have learned from their excavations. (Rev: SLJ 1/07) [937.7]

17881 Peppas, Lynn. *Cultural Traditions in Greece* (2–5). Illus. Series: Cultural Traditions in My World. 2012, Crabtree LB $26.60 (978-077877518-8). 32pp. An overview of the festivals and celebrations that take place in a typical year in Greece. (Rev: BL 2/15/13; LMC 10/13) [394.269495]

17882 Platt, Richard. *Pompeii* (2–5). Illus. by Manuela Cappon. 2007, Kingfisher $16.95 (978-0-7534-6044-3). 48pp. The history of Pompeii, from 750 B.C. to the eruption of Vesuvius and on to the excavation of the site, is chronicled with a focus on a single house. (Rev: BL 10/15/07; LMC 1/08; SLJ 3/08)

17883 Riehecky, Janet. *Greece* (1–3). Series: Countries of the World. 2000, Bridgestone LB $21.26 (978-0-7368-0628-2). 24pp. Full-page photos and current information are the highlights of this basic introduction to Greece. (Rev: HBG 3/01; SLJ 3/01)

Low Countries

17884 Burgan, Michael. *Belgium* (4–7). Series: Enchantment of the World. 2000, Children's LB $37.00 (978-0-516-21006-3). 144pp. This new edition of a standard title contains up-to-date material on such topics as geography and climate, plants and animals, people and culture, the arts, and sports. (Rev: BL 7/00)

17885 De Capua, Sarah. *Netherlands* (2–4). Illus. Series: First Reports. 2003, Compass Point LB $22.60 (978-0-7565-0426-7). 48pp. Simple text introduces readers to basic information on the Netherlands and its geography, history, people, and culture. (Rev: SLJ 10/03)

17886 Heinrichs, Ann. *The Netherlands* (1–3). Series: A True Book. 2003, Children's Pr. LB $25.00 (978-0-516-22675-0). 48pp. A blend of easy-to-understand text and colorful illustrations make this overview suitable for beginning readers. (Rev: SLJ 10/03)

Russia and the Former Soviet States

17887 Aizpuriete, Amanda. *Latvia* (5–8). Trans. by Katarina Hartgers. Photos by Jan Willem Bultje. Series: Looking at Europe. 2006, Oliver $22.95 (978-1-881508-37-3). 48pp. This colorful volume with excellent photographs introduces readers to Latvia's geography, history, people, culture, economy, and lifestyle. (Rev: LMC 3/07; SLJ 1/07)

17888 Bassis, Volodymyr. *Ukraine* (4–7). Series: Cultures of the World. 1997, Marshall Cavendish LB $37.07 (978-0-7614-0684-6). An introduction to this former Soviet state, with emphasis on current history and culture. (Rev: BL 8/97; SLJ 10/97) [947.7]

17889 Bultje, Jan Willem. *Lithuania* (5–8). Trans. by Wilma Hoving. Photos by author. Series: Looking at Europe. 2006, Oliver $22.95 (978-1-881508-43-4). 48pp. This colorful volume with excellent photographs intro-

duces readers to Lithuania's geography, history, people, culture, economy, and lifestyle. (Rev: SLJ 1/07)

17890 Carrion, Esther. *The Empire of the Czars* (4–7). Series: World Heritage. 1994, Children's Press LB $15.00 (978-0-516-08319-3). An overview of Russian history from early times to the breakup of the Soviet Union, with special material on Russia's famous sights, such as Red Square, the Kremlin, and St. Petersburg. (Rev: SLJ 5/95) [947.07]

17891 Corona, Laurel. *Ukraine* (5–8). Series: Modern Nations of the World. 2001, Lucent LB $29.95 (978-1-56006-737-5). This well-illustrated introduction to the former Soviet republic presents material on the people, culture, economy, history, and physical features. (Rev: BL 6/1–15/01) [947]

17892 Frost, Helen. *A Look at Russia* (K–2). Illus. Series: Our World. 2001, Capstone LB $17.26 (978-0-7368-0986-3). 24pp. Brief text and full-page color photographs give a basic introduction to Russia's land, people, and animals. (Rev: HBG 3/02; SLJ 12/01)

17893 Ilyin, Andrey. *A Child's Day in a Russian City* (1–3). Illus. Series: A Child's Day. 2001, Marshall Cavendish $25.64 (978-0-7614-1222-9). 32pp. The events in a typical day for Polina, a 7-year-old Russian girl living in St. Petersburg, with color photographs, sections on history and culture, and other background material. (Rev: BL 11/15/01; HBG 3/02; SLJ 3/02)

17894 Kagda, Sakina. *Lithuania* (4–7). Series: Cultures of the World. 1997, Marshall Cavendish LB $37.07 (978-0-7614-0681-5). An introduction to Lithuania, with material on geography, history, government, culture, daily life, and festivals. (Rev: BL 8/97; SLJ 10/97) [947.93]

17895 Khan, Aisha. *A Historical Atlas of Kyrgyzstan* (4–6). Illus. Series: Historical Atlases of South Asia, Central Asia and the Middle East. 2004, Rosen LB $30.60 (978-0-8239-4499-6). 64pp. This attractive profile that includes many maps and photographs traces Kyrgyzstan's development from prehistoric times to the present. (Rev: SLJ 11/04)

17896 Kollár, Daniel. *Slovakia* (4–7). Series: Looking at Europe. 2006, Oliver $22.95 (978-1-881508-49-6). 48pp. This photo-filled introduction to Slovakia explores its geography, history, people, culture, cuisine, economy, transportation, tourism, and natural resources. (Rev: SLJ 12/06)

17897 Kummer, Patricia K. *Ukraine* (4–7). Series: Enchantment of the World. 2001, Children's LB $37.00 (978-0-516-21101-5). A fine introduction to the past and present of the Ukraine with well-chosen illustrations and material on such topics as resources, daily life, landmarks, languages, and economy. (Rev: BL 1/1–15/02; SLJ 12/01)

17898 Liberman, Sherri. *Historical Atlas of Azerbaijan* (4–6). Illus. 2004, Rosen LB $30.60 (978-0-8239-4497-2). 64pp. Liberman traces the turbulent history of Azerbaijan in this slim volume, concentrating mainly on politics and the ethnic groups that make up the population. (Rev: BL 12/1/04; SLJ 11/04)

17899 Rogers, Stillman D. *Russia* (4–7). Series: Enchantment of the World. 2002, Children's LB $37.00 (978-0-516-22494-7). 144pp. This portrait of Russia in text and illustrations covers such basic subjects as history, resources, geography, people, problems, economy, and culture. (Rev: BL 9/15/02; SLJ 10/02)

17900 Sheehan, Patricia. *Moldova* (5–9). Series: Cultures of the World. 2000, Marshall Cavendish LB $37.07 (978-0-7614-0997-7). This book on the former Soviet republic that borders on the Ukraine covers such topics as culture, land, people, history, resources, and government. (Rev: HBG 10/00; SLJ 11/00) [947]

17901 Spengler, Kremena. *Russia* (2–5). Illus. Series: Questions and Answers: Countries. 2004, Capstone LB $23.93 (978-0-7368-2692-1). Using a question-and-answer format, simple text, large photos, and many factboxes, this is an introduction to Russia today, with material on history and traditional culture.

17902 Steele, Philip. *Moscow* (3–6). Series: Great Cities of the World. 2003, World Almanac LB $31.00 (978-0-8368-5024-6). 48pp. A visit to the Russian capital, well illustrated with photographs, covering the city's history, economy, and people. (Rev: SLJ 3/04)

17903 Veceric, Danica. *Slovenia* (4–7). Series: Looking at Europe. 2006, Oliver $22.95 (978-1-881508-74-8). 48pp. A tour of Slovenia, examining the country's geography, history, people, culture, cuisine, economy, transportation, tourism, and natural resources. (Rev: SLJ 12/06)

17904 Wilson, Neil. *Russia* (4–8). Series: Nations of the World. 2001, Raintree LB $34.26 (978-0-7398-1281-5). 128pp. Colorful photographs, charts, and maps enrich chapters on Russia's past and present, land and cities, economy, art and culture, and possible future developments. (Rev: BL 6/1–15/01; HBG 10/01)

Scandinavia, Iceland, Greenland, and Finland

17905 Alatalo, Jaakko. *A Child's Day in a Nordic Village* (K–3). Series: A Child's Day. 2002, Marshall Cavendish LB $25.64 (978-0-7614-1411-7). 32pp. This book takes a Scandinavian child through a typical day, showing the reader about family, friends, culture, and language. (Rev: BL 2/15/03; HBG 3/03)

17906 Bailey, Linda. *Adventures with the Vikings* (3–5). Illus. by Bill Slavin. Series: Good Times Travel Agency. 2001, Kids Can $14.95 (978-1-55074-542-9); paper $7.95 (978-1-55074-544-3). 48pp. The Binkerton children travel to the age of the Vikings in this comic-book-style story that interweaves fiction and nonfiction. (Rev: BL 10/15/01; HBG 3/02; SLJ 11/01)

17907 Berger, Melvin, and Gilda Berger. *The Real Vikings: Craftsmen, Traders, and Fearsome Raiders* (4–8). 2003, National Geographic $18.95 (978-0-7922-5132-3). A highly illustrated introduction to the Vikings and

their world, with information on their political and social ideals — including democracy — as well as their more fearsome and acquisitive traits. (Rev: BL 12/1/03; HBG 4/04; SLJ 1/04) [948]

17908 Blashfield, Jean F. *Norway* (4–7). Series: Enchantment of the World. 2000, Children's LB $37.00 (978-0-516-20651-6). 144pp. An introduction to Norway that covers such subjects as geography and climate, history and government, mythology and culture, and people and economy. (Rev: BL 7/00)

17909 Boraas, Tracey. *Sweden* (4–6). Series: Countries and Cultures. 2002, Capstone LB $25.26 (978-0-7368-0939-9). 64pp. This introduction to the land and people of Sweden explores topics including history, landforms, government, economics, and traditions. (Rev: BL 1/1–15/03; HBG 3/03)

17910 Butler, Robbie. *Sweden* (4–8). Series: Nations of the World. 2001, Raintree LB $34.26 (978-0-8172-5784-2). 128pp. Colorful maps, charts and graphs, and photographs supplement the text in this fine profile of Sweden. (Rev: BL 6/1–15/01; HBG 10/01)

17911 Corona, Laurel. *Norway* (5–8). Series: Modern Nations of the World. 2000, Lucent LB $29.95 (978-1-56006-647-7). Norway is introduced with coverage of history, geography, and culture plus material on everyday modern life. (Rev: BL 3/1/01) [948.1]

17912 *Denmark in Pictures* (5–8). Series: Visual Geography. 1997, Lerner LB $25.55 (978-0-8225-1880-8). In photographs, maps, charts, and concise text, the land of Denmark and its people are introduced. (Rev: BL 4/1/91; SLJ 7/91) [948]

17913 Dupre, Kelly. *The Raven's Gift: A True Story from Greenland* (K–3). Illus. 2001, Houghton $15.00 (978-0-618-01171-1). An encounter with a raven inspires two men to continue their journey around Greenland, in this effectively illustrated story of an expedition taken by the author's husband. (Rev: BL 8/01; HBG 3/02; SLJ 9/01)

17914 DuTemple, Lesley A. *Sweden* (5–8). Series: Modern Nations of the World. 2000, Lucent LB $28.70 (978-1-56006-588-3). 112pp. A general introduction to Sweden that includes its history and geography but stresses today's living conditions and the people's lifestyles. (Rev: BL 3/15/00; HBG 10/00)

17915 Gan, Delice. *Sweden* (4–7). Series: Cultures of the World. 1992, Marshall Cavendish LB $35.64 (978-1-85435-452-5). This introduction to Sweden gives special coverage of the people and their lifestyles. (Rev: BL 10/15/92) [948.5]

17916 Gunderson, Jessica. *Vikings* (5–8). Illus. Series: Fearsome Fighters. 2012, Creative Education $24.95 (978-160818185-8). 48pp. With many illustrations, maps, and primary documents, this volume looks at the Vikings and their society, weapons, fighting techniques, key figures, and so forth. (Rev: BL 11/1/12; LMC 5–6/13; SLJ 12/12) [948]

17917 Hopkins, Andrea. *Viking Explorers and Settlers* (3–6). Illus. Series: The Viking Library. 2001, Rosen LB $21.25 (978-0-8239-5816-0). 24pp. Beginning report writers will find basic historical information with illustrations, maps, and documents in this slim volume. Also use *Viking Gods and Legends* and *Vikings: The Norse Discovery of America* (both 2002). (Rev: SLJ 6/02)

17918 *Iceland in Pictures* (5–8). Series: Visual Geography. 1996, Lerner LB $25.55 (978-0-8225-1892-1). The history, government, people, and economy of the northern republic of Iceland are covered in words and pictures. (Rev: BL 8/91) [949.12]

17919 Jovinelly, Joann, and Jason Netelkos. *The Crafts and Culture of the Vikings* (5–8). Series: Crafts of the Ancient World. 2002, Rosen LB $29.25 (978-0-8239-3514-7). 48pp. In addition to giving a tour of ancient Scandinavia, this book outlines such craft projects as designing a battle shield and helmet, minting coins, and playing an ancient board game. (Rev: BL 5/15/02)

17920 Kopka, Deborah. *Norway* (1–3). Series: Globe-Trotters Club. 2000, Carolrhoda LB $22.60 (978-1-57505-123-9). 48pp. Double-page spreads with stunning photographs introduce the land and people of Norway, with material on the Vikings, fjords, and skiing. (Rev: BL 10/15/00; HBG 3/01)

17921 Landau, Elaine. *Exploring the World of the Vikings with Elaine Landau* (3–6). Illus. Series: Exploring Ancient Civilizations with Elaine Landau. 2005, Enslow LB $23.93 (978-0-7660-2340-6). 48pp. Readers explore the time of the Vikings along with the author and her dog Max, learning about many aspects of early Norse life and culture, including housing, food, apparel, religion, occupations, and relations with the outside world. (Rev: SLJ 12/05)

17922 Lee, Tan Chung. *Finland* (4–7). Series: Cultures of the World. 1996, Marshall Cavendish LB $37.07 (978-0-7614-0280-0). The small country of Finland with its thousands of lakes is introduced, with emphasis on the people and how they live. (Rev: BL 8/96; SLJ 7/96) [984.97]

17923 McMillan, Bruce. *Going Fishing* (2–4). Illus. 2005, Houghton $16.00 (978-0-618-47201-7). 32pp. Photographs capture a boy and his grandfathers as they fish for cod and lumpfish in Iceland. (Rev: BL 3/1/05; SLJ 5/05)

17924 Manning, Mick, and Brita Granström. *Viking Longship* (3–5). Illus. by Mick Manning. Series: Fly on the Wall. 2007, Frances Lincoln $15.95 (978-1-84507-465-4). Fact and fiction are interwoven as readers learn about Viking life — shipbuilding, meals, clothing, mythology, battles, and so forth. (Rev: BL 11/15/07)

17925 Robinson, Deborah B. *The Sami of Northern Europe* (4–6). Series: First Peoples. 2002, Lerner LB $23.93 (978-0-8225-4175-2). This book describes the life and culture of the Sami, once known as Lapps, who were once primarily reindeer herders. (Rev: BL 5/15/02; HBG 10/02; SLJ 8/02)

17926 Shuter, Jane. *Life in a Viking Town* (2–4). Illus. Series: Picture the Past. 2005, Heinemann LB $25.64 (978-1-4034-6440-8). 32pp. This colorful title gives young readers a sampling of what life was like in a Vi-

king town, covering such topics as dwellings, jobs, food, apparel, and leisure activities. (Rev: SLJ 11/05)

17927 Shuter, Jane. *Life on a Viking Ship* (2–4). Illus. Series: Picture the Past. 2005, Heinemann LB $25.64 (978-1-4034-6441-5). 32pp. This attractive title gives young readers an overview of what life was like on a Viking ship. (Rev: SLJ 11/05)

17928 *Sweden in Pictures* (5–8). Series: Visual Geography. 1993, Lerner LB $21.27 (978-0-8225-1872-3). Gives the background geography and history of Sweden, along with contemporary material. (Rev: BL 12/1/90) [948.5]

17929 Wilcox, Jonathan. *Iceland* (4–7). Series: Cultures of the World. 1996, Marshall Cavendish LB $37.07 (978-0-7614-0279-4). The history, geography, people, and culture of this remote island republic are introduced, with many color photographs. (Rev: SLJ 7/96) [949.12]

17930 Yanuck, Debbie L. *Sweden* (2–3). Illus. Series: Many Cultures, One World. 2004, Capstone LB $23.93 (978-0-7368-2452-1). A brief, accessible introduction to Sweden and its people, family life, customs, and legends. (Rev: SLJ 10/04)

Spain and Portugal

17931 Anderson, Wayne. *The ETA: Spain's Basque Terrorists* (4–8). Series: Inside the World's Most Infamous Terrorist Organizations. 2003, Rosen LB $27.95 (978-0-8239-3818-6). This is the history and present status of the violent organization committed to creating an ethnic homeland separate from Spain. (Rev: BL 10/15/03; SLJ 9/03) [946]

17932 Berendes, Mary. *Welcome to Spain* (1–4). Series: Wecome to the World. 2008, The Child's World LB $27.07 (978-1-59296-979-1). As easy introduction to Spain and its land, people, plants and animals, and so forth, with color photographs, maps, and recipes. (Rev: SLJ 9/08)

17933 Blauer, Ettagale, and Jason Lauré. *Portugal* (4–7). Series: Enchantment of the World. 2002, Children's LB $37.00 (978-0-516-21109-1). This highly visual introduction to Portugal includes accessible information on topics including history, people and language, customs, and economy. (Rev: BL 9/15/02)

17934 Croy, Anita. *Spain* (4–8). Series: Countries of the World. 2010, National Geographic LB $27.90 (978-1-4263-0633-4). 64pp. In addition to giving an overview of the country's geography, people, culture, history, government, economy, and climate, this volume includes special features such as "The Wild West — in Spain!" and "The Real El Cid." (Rev: BL 4/1/10; SLJ 4/10) [946]

17935 Goodman, Joan Elizabeth. *A Long and Uncertain Journey: The 27,000-Mile Voyage of Vasco da Gama* (4–8). Illus. by Tom McNeely. 2001, Mikaya $19.95 (978-0-9650493-7-5). 48pp. Details of Vasco da Gama's explorations and their historical context are accompanied by biographical information, illustrations, journal entries, a map, and a timeline. (Rev: BL 9/1/01; HBG 10/01; SLJ 6/01*; VOYA 8/01)

17936 Heale, Jay. *Portugal* (5–8). Series: Cultures of the World. 1995, Marshall Cavendish LB $37.07 (978-0-7614-0169-8). Present-day conditions in Portugal are emphasized in this account, which also covers history, geography, and culture. (Rev: SLJ 11/95) [914.9]

17937 Kohen, Elizabeth. *Spain* (4–7). Series: Cultures of the World. 1992, Marshall Cavendish LB $35.64 (978-1-85435-451-8). With text, photographs, maps, and fact sheets, the land and people of Spain are introduced. (Rev: BL 10/15/92) [946]

17938 Mann, Kenny. *Isabel, Ferdinand and Fifteenth-Century Spain* (5–8). Series: Rulers and Their Times. 2001, Marshall Cavendish LB $29.93 (978-0-7614-1030-0). Following biographies of these great Spanish rulers, there is a section on the life and culture of their times plus a generous selection of original documents of the period. (Rev: BL 1/1–15/02; HBG 3/02; SLJ 3/02)

17939 *Portugal in Pictures* (5–8). Series: Visual Geography. 1996, Lerner LB $25.55 (978-0-8225-1886-0). Current conditions and problems in Portugal are introduced along with the standard material on history, geography, and social conditions. (Rev: BL 12/15/91) [946.9]

17940 Rogers, Lura. *Spain* (4–7). Series: Enchantment of the World. 2001, Children's LB $37.00 (978-0-516-21123-7). A well-designed book that uses clear text, numerous charts, maps, drawings, and photographs to introduce a number of topics related to Spain and its people. (Rev: BL 1/1–15/02)

17941 Yanuck, Debbie L. *Spain* (2–3). Illus. Series: Many Cultures, One World. 2004, Capstone LB $23.93 (978-0-7368-2451-4). A brief, accessible introduction to Spain and its people, family life, customs, and legends.

The Middle East

General

17942 Barr, Gary E. *History and Activities of the Islamic Empire* (3–6). Illus. Series: Hands-on Ancient History. 2006, Heinemann LB $28.21 (978-1-4034-7926-6). 32pp. Social life, arts and culture, games, and holidays and celebrations are covered in this attractive and accessible volume that includes a recipe and three crafts. (Rev: SLJ 4/07)

17943 Broyles, Matthew. *The Six-Day War* (5–9). Series: War and Conflict in the Middle East. 2004, Rosen LB $27.95 (978-0-8239-4549-8). A well-organized, balanced account of the 1973 war between Israel and its Arab neighbors Egypt, Jordan, and Syria. (Rev: BL 11/1/04; SLJ 1/05)

17944 Fiscus, James W. *The Suez Crisis* (5–9). Series: War and Conflict in the Middle East. 2004, Rosen LB $27.95 (978-0-8239-4550-4). Examines the 1956 con-

flict over control of the canal, involving Egypt, Israel, Britain, and France. (Rev: BL 11/1/04)

17945 Hancock, Lee. *Saladin and the Kingdom of Jerusalem: The Muslims Recapture the Holy Land in AD 1187* (5–9). Series: The Library of the Middle Ages. 2004, Rosen LB $29.25 (978-0-8239-4217-6). 64pp. Useful for report writers, this volume looks at life in Jerusalem under the Crusaders, providing details from primary sources. (Rev: SLJ 8/04)

17946 Hilliam, Paul. *Islamic Weapons, Warfare, and Armies: Muslim Military Operations Against the Crusaders* (5–9). Series: The Library of the Middle Ages. 2004, Rosen LB $29.25 (978-0-8239-4215-2). 64pp. Useful for report writers, this volume looks at the spread of Islam and the conflicts with the Crusaders. (Rev: SLJ 8/04)

17947 Losleben, Elizabeth. *The Bedouin of the Middle East* (4–6). Series: First Peoples. 2002, Lerner LB $23.95 (978-0-8225-0663-8). 48pp. Traditional and contemporary lifestyles are included in this presentation of the Bedouin people, the territory in which they live, and their history, culture, and economy. (Rev: HBG 3/03; SLJ 2/03)

17948 Marx, Trish. *Sharing Our Homeland: Palestinian and Jewish Children at Summer Peace Camp* (3–6). Illus. by Cindy Karp. 2010, Lee & Low $19.95 (978-1-58430-250-5). 48pp. A Muslim girl and a Jewish boy share and learn to appreciate each other's cultures while at summer peace camp. (Rev: BL 5/15/10; LMC 1–2/11; SLJ 10/1/10) [915.69406]

17949 Rivera, Sheila. *Women of the Middle East* (4–6). Series: World in Conflict. 2004, ABDO LB $25.65 (978-1-59197-415-4). For reluctant readers, this title studies the status of contemporary women in Saudi Arabia, Afghanistan, Iran, Egypt, and Israel, looking at the role of religion, politics, and local custom in their lives. (Rev: SLJ 3/04)

17950 Senker, Cath. *The Arab-Israeli Conflict* (5–8). Series: Questioning History. 2004, Smart Apple Media LB $28.50 (978-1-58340-441-6). A clear and balanced discussion of the history and current status of relations between Arabs and Israelis, with a timeline, glossary, and detailed index. (Rev: SLJ 2/05) [956.04]

17951 Steele, Philip. *Middle East* (4–7). Series: Kingfisher Knowledge. 2006, Kingfisher LB $12.95 (978-0-7534-5984-3). Traces the history of the region — extending from Eastern Mediterranean countries into Iraq, Iran, and Afghanistan — as well as its geography, peoples, cultures, religions, economies, and politics. (Rev: SLJ 12/06) [956]

Egypt

17952 Bowden, Rob, and Roy Maconachie. *Cairo* (4–7). Series: Great Cities of the World. 2005, World Almanac LB $31.00 (978-0-8368-5035-2). An informative and appealing overview of one of the world's most famous cities, with material on its history, its economy, and what it's like to live there. (Rev: BL 4/15/04)

17953 Deady, Kathleen W. *Egypt* (1–3). Series: Countries of the World. 2000, Bridgestone LB $21.26 (978-0-7368-0626-8). 24pp. A very basic introduction to Egypt that contains current facts and full-page photos. (Rev: HBG 3/01; SLJ 3/01)

17954 Draper, Allison Stark. *Historical Atlas of Egypt* (4–6). Illus. Series: Historical Atlases of South Asia, Central Asia and the Middle East. 2004, Rosen LB $30.60 (978-0-8239-4498-9). 64pp. This attractive profile that includes many maps and photographs traces Egypt's development from prehistoric times to the present.

17955 Eldash, Khaled, and Dalia Khattab. *A Child's Day in an Egyptian City* (K–3). Series: A Child's Day. 2002, Marshall Cavendish LB $25.64 (978-0-7614-1410-0). 32pp. An accessible introduction to present-day Egypt through the daily life of its children. (Rev: BL 2/15/03; HBG 3/03)

17956 Gutner, Howard. *Egypt* (3–5). Series: A True Book — Geography: Countries. 2009, Children's Pr. LB $26.00 (978-0-531-16889-9). 48pp. An attractive overview of Egypt, covering geography, history, culture, and pertinent statistics. (Rev: SLJ 7/09)

17957 Krebs, Laurie. *We're Sailing Down the Nile: A Journey Through Egypt* (PS–3). Illus. by Anne Wilson. 2007, Barefoot Books $16.99 (978-1-84686-040-9). Readers will learn facts about Egypt's most famous sites and about the country's ancient history and customs in this voyage down the famous river. (Rev: LMC 11/07; SLJ 7/07)

17958 Orr, Tamra. *Egyptian Islamic Jihad* (4–8). Series: Inside the World's Most Infamous Terrorist Organizations. 2003, Rosen LB $27.95 (978-0-8239-3819-3). Dedicated to the overthrow of the secular Egyptian government, this terrorist organization has links to the Al Qaeda terrorist network. (Rev: BL 10/15/03) [962]

17959 Parks, Peggy J. *The Aswan High Dam* (5–8). Series: Building World Landmarks. 2004, Gale LB $24.95 (978-1-56711-329-7). 48pp. This is the fascinating story of the construction of the huge dam on the Nile and the immense technical and social challenges involved. (Rev: SLJ 6/04)

17960 Webster, Christine. *Egypt* (2–5). Illus. Series: Questions and Answers: Countries. 2004, Capstone LB $23.93 (978-0-7368-2688-4). Using a question-and-answer format, simple text, large photos, and many factboxes, this is an introduction to Egypt today, with material on history and traditional culture.

17961 Wilson, Neil. *Egypt* (4–8). Series: Nations of the World. 2001, Raintree LB $34.26 (978-0-7398-1283-9). 128pp. An excellent introduction to the country that housed one of the world's oldest civilizations and is currently a center of Islamic culture and religion. (Rev: BL 6/1–15/01; HBG 10/01)

17962 Zuehlke, Jeffrey. *Egypt in Pictures. Rev. ed.* (4–8). Series: Visual Geography. 2002, Lerner LB $27.93 (978-0-8225-0367-5). Covers Egypt's geography, history,

people, economy, and culture with maps, photographs, and illustrations. (Rev: SLJ 3/03) [962]

Israel (and Palestine)

17963 Boraas, Tracey. *Israel* (4–6). Series: Countries and Cultures. 2002, Capstone LB $25.26 (978-0-7368-0938-2). 64pp. This introduction to Israel includes basic material on history, wildlife, government, geography, and economics. (Rev: BL 1/1–15/03; HBG 3/03; SLJ 4/03)

17964 Bowden, Rob. *Jerusalem* (3–6). Series: Great Cities of the World. 2005, World Almanac LB $31.00 (978-0-8368-5051-2). 48pp. With color photographs and informative sidebars, this volume introduces the geography, history, culture, religion, work, and recreation of Jerusalem. (Rev: SLJ 11/05)

17965 Feinstein, Steve. *Israel in Pictures* (5–8). 1992, Lerner LB $25.55 (978-0-8225-1833-4). An overview of geography, climate, wildlife, and vegetation with photographs, maps, and charts. (Rev: BL 8/88) [956.9405]

17966 Green, Jen. *Israel* (4–8). Series: Nations of the World. 2001, Raintree LB $34.26 (978-0-7398-1286-0). 128pp. A fine, attractive introduction to the land and people of Israel, the nation that was created as a homeland for the Jewish people after World War II. (Rev: BL 6/1–15/01; HBG 10/01)

17967 Gresko, Marcia S. *Israel* (1–3). Series: Globe-Trotters Club. 2000, Carolrhoda LB $22.60 (978-1-57505-118-5). 48pp. From the rocky Negev Desert to the Sea of Galilee, the state of Israel is brought to life in this account that introduces the country through double-page spreads on a variety of subjects. (Rev: BL 5/15/00; HBG 3/01)

17968 Grossman, Laurie M. *Children of Israel* (2–5). Photos by author. Series: The World's Children. 2001, Carolrhoda LB $23.93 (978-1-57505-448-3). 48pp. This look at the daily lives of children in Israel introduces the history, geography, and culture of the country with appealing full-color illustrations, a pronunciation guide, and map. (Rev: HBG 10/01; SLJ 6/01)

17969 Gunderson, Cory. *The Israeli-Palestinian Conflict* (4–6). Series: World in Conflict. 2004, ABDO LB $25.65 (978-1-59197-416-1). A politically balanced introduction to the ongoing conflict between the Israelis and Palestinians, aimed at reluctant readers, with numerous photographs and maps. (Rev: SLJ 3/04)

17970 Hayhurst, Chris. *Israel's War of Independence* (5–9). Series: War and Conflict in the Middle East. 2004, Rosen LB $27.95 (978-0-8239-4548-1). An even-handed overview of Israel's struggle for independence and the ensuing years of violence, with statistics, maps, photographs, and profiles of leaders. (Rev: BL 11/1/04; SLJ 1/05) [956.04]

17971 Saul, Laya. *We Visit Israel* (4–8). Illus. Series: Your Land and My Land: The Middle East. 2011, Mitchell Lane LB $33.95 (978-158415957-5). 64pp. With illustrations, photographs, maps, reproductions, a recipe, a craft project, and a timeline, this is a useful overview of the history and geography of Israel. (Rev: BL 2/1/12) [956.94]

17972 Scharfstein, Sol. *Understanding Israel* (5–7). 1994, KTAV paper $14.95 (978-0-88125-428-0). A heavily illustrated introduction to Israel that covers history, religion, government, culture, and current concerns. (Rev: SLJ 10/94) [956.94]

17973 Sherman, Josepha. *Your Travel Guide to Ancient Israel* (4–8). Illus. Series: Passport to History. 2003, Lerner LB $26.60 (978-0-8225-3072-5). 80pp. An illustrated visit to Israel in the time of King Solomon, with description of foods, housing, clothing, customs, and notable people of that era. (Rev: SLJ 4/04)

17974 Silverman, Maida. *Israel: The Founding of a Modern Nation* (4–7). 1998, Dial LB $15.00 (978-0-8034-2136-3). This account covers 3,000 years of Jewish history, with emphasis on recent centuries, and includes a timeline showing Israel's history from 1948 to 1998. (Rev: BL 5/1/98) [956.94]

17975 Spengler, Kremena. *Israel* (2–5). Illus. Series: Questions and Answers: Countries. 2005, Capstone LB $23.93 (978-0-7368-3753-8). 32pp. Using a question-and-answer format, simple text, large photos, and many factboxes, this is an introduction to Israel today, with material on history and traditional culture.

17976 *Three Wishes: Palestinian and Israeli Children Speak* (5–12). 2004, Groundwood $16.95 (978-0-88899-554-4). 144pp. In an evenhanded presentation that offers an introductory historical overview, 20 first-person accounts relate the experiences of Christian, Jewish, and Muslim young people during the ongoing conflict between Israelis and Palestinians. (Rev: BL 9/1/04*; SLJ 10/04)

17977 Wingate, Katherine. *The Intifadas* (5–9). Series: War and Conflict in the Middle East. 2004, Rosen LB $27.95 (978-0-8239-4546-7). An even-handed overview of the events leading up to the Palestinian uprisings, with statistics, maps, photographs, and profiles of leaders. (Rev: BL 11/1/04) [956.95]

Other Middle Eastern Lands

17978 Anderson, Laurie Halse. *Saudi Arabia* (1–3). Series: Globe-Trotters Club. 2000, Lerner LB $22.60 (978-1-57505-121-5). 48pp. An introduction to this country on the Arabian Peninsula that tells about its landmarks, ethnic groups, oil riches, ancient traditions, and modern conveniences. (Rev: BL 12/15/00; HBG 3/01; SLJ 1/01)

17979 Augustin, Byron. *United Arab Emirates* (4–7). Series: Enchantment of the World. 2002, Children's LB $36.00 (978-0-516-20473-4). 144pp. This important nation is introduced with material on topics including history, natural resources, climate, and people. (Rev: BL 5/15/02; SLJ 9/02)

17980 Augustin, Byron, and Jake Kubena. *Iraq* (5–8). Illus. Series: Enchantment of the World. 2006, Children's Pr. LB $37.00 (978-0-516-24852-3). 144pp. An updated version of a 1998 book on the country, with additional information on ethnic groups, the environment, and continuing violence. (Rev: SLJ 7/06)

17981 Bader, Philip. *Iran* (3–5). Illus. Series: Dropping In On. 2001, Rourke $28.50 (978-1-55916-285-2). This brief tour of Iran via hot-air balloon includes material on geography, famous sights, and the people. (Rev: SLJ 1/01)

17982 Bauer, Brandy. *Iran: A Question And Answer Book* (2–5). Illus. Series: Questions and Answers: Countries. 2005, Capstone LB $23.93 (978-0-7368-3752-1). Using a question-and-answer format, simple text, large photos, and many factboxes, this is an introduction to Iran today, with material on history and traditional culture.

17983 Boueri, Marijean, and Jill Boutros. *Lebanon A to Z: A Middle Eastern Mosaic* (4–8). Illus. by Tatiana Sabbagh. 2006, Publishing Works $25.00 (978-0-9744803-4-3). 77pp. Eleven-year-old Kareem takes readers on a tour through the country's present and past, with an emphasis on cultural traditions and Lebanon's people. (Rev: SLJ 7/06)

17984 Byers, Ann. *Lebanon's Hezbollah* (4–8). Series: Inside the World's Most Infamous Terrorist Organizations. 2003, Rosen LB $27.95 (978-0-8239-3821-6). This is the story of the Lebanese terrorist organization dedicated to installing a conservative Islamic government in Lebanon and to the destruction of Israel. (Rev: BL 10/15/03; SLJ 9/03) [956.92]

17985 Cartlidge, Cherese. *Iran* (5–8). Series: Modern Nations of the World. 2002, Gale LB $29.95 (978-1-56006-971-3). This colorful account gives a comprehensive overview of Iran, including history, geography, and culture. (Rev: BL 12/15/02; SLJ 1/03) [955]

17986 Deady, Kathleen W. *Saudi Arabia* (2–5). Illus. Series: Questions and Answers: Countries. 2005, Capstone LB $23.93 (978-0-7368-3760-6). 32pp. Using a question-and-answer format, simple text, large photos, and many factboxes, this is an introduction to Saudi Arabia today, with material on history and traditional culture. (Rev: HBG 3/02)

17987 Friedman, Mel. *Iraq* (3–5). Series: A True Book — Geography: Countries. 2009, Children's Pr. LB $26.00 (978-0-531-16891-2). 48pp. An attractive overview of Iraq, covering geography, history, culture, people, and the effects of war. (Rev: SLJ 7/09)

17988 Gibson, Karen Bush. *Ancient Babylon* (5–8). Illus. Series: Explore Ancient Worlds. 2012, Mitchell Lane LB $29.95 (978-161228278-7). 48pp. A description of our knowledge of the ancient city, its hanging gardens, systems of writing and justice, with information on Alexander the Great and two crafts (making a sundial and barley bread). (Rev: BL 10/1/12) [935]

17989 Goodwin, William. *Saudi Arabia* (5–8). Series: Modern Nations of the World. 2001, Lucent LB $29.95 (978-1-56006-763-4). The land ruled by the Saud dynasty is presented with details on history, government, geography, resources, and world importance. (Rev: BL 6/1–15/01) [953.8]

17990 Graham, Amy. *Iran in the News: Past, Present, and Future* (5–8). Illus. Series: Middle East Nations in the News. 2006, Enslow LB $33.27 (978-1-59845-022-4). History, culture, people, and current political issues are all covered in this readable overview of Iran that includes links to Web sites that extend the text. (Rev: BL 4/1/06; SLJ 5/06) [955]

17991 Gray, Leon. *Iran* (4–8). Series: Countries of the World. 2008, National Geographic LB $27.90 (978-1-4263-0200-8). Useful for researchers, this book provides basic information about the country as well as data and additional facts presented in sidebars and other features. (Rev: BL 4/15/08) [955.22]

17992 Haskins, James, and Kathleen Benson. *Count Your Way Through Iran* (2–4). Illus. by Farida Zaman. Series: Count Your Way. 2006, Lerner LB $19.93 (978-1-57505-881-8). 24pp. Aspects of Iranian life from 1 to 10 are accompanied by a map and various other key facts. (Rev: BL 8/06)

17993 Hassig, Susan M. *Iraq* (4–7). Series: Cultures of the World. 1992, Marshall Cavendish LB $35.64 (978-1-85435-533-1). This introduction stresses the lifestyles of the people, their religion, and culture. (Rev: BL 1/1/93) [956.7]

17994 Heinrichs, Ann. *Saudi Arabia* (4–7). Series: Enchantment of the World. 2002, Children's LB $37.00 (978-0-516-22287-5). 144pp. Topics covered in the highly visual introduction to Saudi Arabia include history, religion, language, economy, and government. (Rev: BL 9/15/02)

17995 Hestler, Anna. *Yemen* (5–8). Series: Cultures of the World. 1999, Marshall Cavendish LB $37.07 (978-0-7614-0956-4). A fine introduction to this country on the Gulf of Aden with good background information and an overview of modern life. (Rev: HBG 10/99; SLJ 10/99) [956]

17996 Hinman, Bonnie. *We Visit Pakistan* (4–8). Illus. Series: Your Land and My Land: The Middle East. 2011, Mitchell Lane LB $33.95 (978-158415960-5). 64pp. With illustrations, photographs, maps, reproductions, a recipe, a craft project, and a timeline, this is a useful overview of the history and geography of Pakistan. (Rev: BL 2/1/12) [954.91]

17997 *Iran in Pictures* (5–8). Series: Visual Geography. 1992, Lerner LB $21.27 (978-0-8225-1848-8). Basic coverage on this Middle Eastern land and its people. (Rev: BL 5/1/89) [955]

17998 Isaac, Michael. *Historical Atlas of Oman* (4–6). Illus. Series: Historical Atlases of South Asia, Central Asia and the Middle East. 2004, Rosen LB $30.60 (978-0-8239-4500-9). 64pp. This attractive profile that includes many maps and photographs traces Oman's development from prehistoric times to the present.

17999 Janin, Hunt. *Saudi Arabia* (4–7). Series: Cultures of the World. 1992, Marshall Cavendish LB $35.64 (978-1-85435-532-4). The history, geography, economy, language, and people are discussed in this book about Saudi Arabia. (Rev: BL 1/1/93) [953.8]

18000 *Jordan in Pictures* (5–8). 1992, Lerner LB $25.55 (978-0-8225-1834-1). Young readers learn what life is like in this Middle East land. (Rev: BL 2/1/89; SLJ 2/89) [956.9504]

18001 *Lebanon in Pictures* (5–8). Series: Visual Geography. 1992, Lerner LB $25.55 (978-0-8225-1832-7). A country torn apart by strife is the focus of this edition. (Rev: BL 2/1/89) [956.9204]

18002 Lobaido, Anthony C., and Yumi Ng. *The Kurds of Asia* (4–6). Illus. Series: First Peoples. 2002, Lerner LB $23.95 (978-0-8225-0664-5). 48pp. Traditional and contemporary lifestyles are both included in this presentation of the Kurd people, the territory in which they live, and their history, culture, and economy. (Rev: HBG 3/03; SLJ 2/03)

18003 Malhotra, Sonali. *Welcome to Iraq* (3–5). Series: Welcome to My Country. 2004, Gareth Stevens LB $27.00 (978-0-8368-2559-6). 48pp. Introduces readers to Iraq's geography, history, people, culture, family life, government, religion, and language. (Rev: SLJ 7/04)

18004 Marcovitz, Hal. *Kuwait* (5–8). Illus. Series: Modern Middle East Nations. 2003, Mason Crest LB $24.95 (978-1-59084-510-3). 112pp. A thorough introduction to the geography, history, and people of Kuwait, whose wealth makes it an unusual country. (Rev: BL 6/1–15/03; HBG 4/04; SLJ 10/03)

18005 Rajendra, Vijeya, and Gisela Kaplan. *Iran* (4–7). Series: Cultures of the World. 1992, Marshall Cavendish LB $35.64 (978-1-85435-534-8). As well as standard introductory information about Iran, this book tells about how the people live and what the country's present problems are. (Rev: BL 1/1/93) [955]

18006 Romano, Amy. *A Historical Atlas of the United Arab Emirates* (4–6). Illus. 2004, Rosen LB $30.60 (978-0-8239-4501-6). 64pp. A useful supplement to more detailed books on the United Arab Emirates, this title chronicles the country's history from the time of its earliest known settlements to the present. (Rev: BL 12/1/04)

18007 Romano, Amy. *Historical Atlas of Yemen* (4–6). Illus. Series: Historical Atlases of South Asia, Central Asia and the Middle East. 2004, Rosen LB $30.60 (978-0-8239-4502-3). 64pp. This attractive profile that includes many maps and photographs traces Yemen's development from prehistoric times to the present.

18008 Sheehan, Sean. *Lebanon* (5–10). Series: Cultures of the World. 1996, Marshall Cavendish LB $37.07 (978-0-7614-0283-1). A lively, well-written introduction to this war-ravaged country with details on history, economy, culture, religion and foods, including a recipe for a typical dish. (Rev: SLJ 6/97) [569.2]

18009 South, Coleman. *Jordan* (5–10). Series: Cultures of the World. 1996, Marshall Cavendish LB $37.07 (978-0-7614-0287-9). Everyday life in Jordan is the focus of this book that also covers history, religion, culture, geography, festivals, and foods; a single recipe is included. (Rev: SLJ 6/97) [569.5]

18010 Spengler, Kremena. *Iraq: A Question and Answer Book* (2–5). Illus. Series: Fact Finders. 2004, Capstone LB $23.93 (978-0-7368-2691-4). Double-page spreads use simple text, factboxes, and plenty of color photographs to answer pertinent questions about the country's history, geography, government, and culture. (Rev: BL 11/15/04; SLJ 3/05)

18011 Stevens, Kathryn. *Welcome to Iraq* (1–3). Illus. Series: Welcome to the World. 2007, Child's World LB $18.95 (978-1-59296-916-6). 32pp. This simple book looks at life, culture, and wildlife in Iraq and covers recent events in a matter-of-fact style. (Rev: BL 10/15/07)

18012 Van Der Gaag, Nikki, and Felicity Arbuthnot. *Baghdad* (3–6). Series: Great Cities of the World. 2005, World Almanac LB $31.00 (978-0-8368-5049-9). 48pp. With color photographs and informative sidebars, this volume introduces the geography, history, culture, religion, work, and recreation of Baghdad. (Rev: SLJ 11/05)

18013 Wilkes, Sybella. *Out of Iraq: Refugees' Stories in Words, Paintings and Music* (5–9). Illus. 2010, Evans Brothers $17.99 (978-0-237-53930-6). 70pp. A variety of compelling interviews conducted with artists, journalists, teachers, children, and young adults show a moving picture of the humanitarian implications of the 2003 invasion of Iraq. (Rev: BL 10/15/10; SLJ 11/1/10) [305.9]

18014 Wills, Karen. *Jordan* (5–8). Series: Modern Nations of the World. 2001, Lucent LB $29.95 (978-1-56006-822-8). A good profile of Jordan is presented, with basic background material and information on present conditions and the people today. (Rev: BL 6/1–15/01) [956.95]

18015 Winter, Jeanette. *The Librarian of Basra: A True Story from Iraq* (3–5). Illus. 2005, Harcourt $16.00 (978-0-15-205445-8). 32pp. This is the inspiring, true story of an Iraqi librarian's efforts to save the 30,000 books in Basra's library collection from destruction as invading forces neared the city in 2003. (Rev: BL 12/1/04; SLJ 1/05*)

18016 *Yemen in Pictures* (5–8). Series: Visual Geography. 1993, Lerner LB $25.55 (978-0-8225-1911-9). In introduction to this Muslim republic on the Gulf of Aden, with material on its economic and social conditions. (Rev: BL 12/1/93; SLJ 12/93) [953.3]

North and South America (Excluding the United States)

North and South America

18017 Alter, Judy. *Discovering North America's Land, People, and Wildlife* (5–8). Series: Continents of the World. 2004, Enslow LB $25.26 (978-0-7660-5206-2). 48pp. An introduction to the geography, history, economy, plants and animals, culture, and people of the continent, with brief coverage of the Caribbean and Central America. (Rev: SLJ 11/04)

18018 Banting, Erinn. *Galápagos Islands* (3–4). Illus. Series: Wonders of the World. 2012, Weigl LB $19.99 (978-161913523-9). 32pp. An informative introduction to the islands off the coast of Ecuador and their history and flora and fauna, with images, quizzes, a timeline, a recipe, and an activity. (Rev: BL 10/1/12; LMC 8–9/13) [986.6]

18019 Bramwell, Martyn. *North America and the Caribbean* (4–6). Series: World in Maps. 2000, Lerner LB $23.93 (978-0-8225-2911-8). 48pp. A comprehensive and well-illustrated treatment of all the countries that make up North America, from Canada to Mexico and the Caribbean islands. (Rev: BL 10/15/00; HBG 10/01)

18020 Fox, Mary Virginia. *North America* (1–3). Series: Continents. 2006, Heinemann LB $21.36 (978-1-58810-001-6). 32pp. For beginning report writers, this is a survey of North America's geography, flora, fauna, weather, and history. (Rev: SLJ 1/07)

18021 Gunderson, Jessica. *Conquistadors* (5–8). Illus. Series: Fearsome Fighters. 2012, Creative Education $24.95 (978-160818183-4). 48pp. With many illustrations, maps, and primary documents, this volume looks at the Spanish colonists who invaded the Americas and their society, weapons, fighting techniques, key figures, and so forth. (Rev: BL 11/1/12; LMC 5–6/13; SLJ 12/12) [970.01]

18022 Harrison, David L. *Mammoth Bones and Broken Stones: The Mystery of North America's First People* (4–6). Illus. by Richard Hilliard. 2010, Boyds Mills $18.95 (978-159078561-4). 46pp. Harrison looks at our fragments of knowledge about the earliest inhabitants of North America, asking when they arrived and who arrived first, and documenting the artifacts they left behind. Lexile 1040L (Rev: BLO 11/15/10; LMC 3–4/11; SLJ 12/1/10) [970.01]

18023 Mann, Charles C. *Before Columbus: The Americas of 1491* (5–8). 2009, Simon & Schuster $24.99 (978-1-4169-4900-8). 117pp. This clearly written and designed history of pre-Columbian America includes brightly colored illustrations and sidebars that illuminate what for many is a misunderstood period of history. (Rev: BL 9/1/09*; LMC 11–12/09; SLJ 9/09*) [970.01]

18024 Turck, Mary C. *Mexico and Central America: A Fiesta of Cultures, Crafts, and Activities for Ages 8–12* (3–6). 2004, Chicago Review paper $14.95 (978-1-55652-525-4). Turck provides wide-ranging information on Mexico and the countries of Central America, including items on history, geography, and culture, plus recipes, crafts, and activities. (Rev: BL 8/04; SLJ 8/04)

18025 Woods, Michael, and Mary B. Woods. *Seven Natural Wonders of Central and South America* (5–8). Illus. 2009, Twenty-First Century LB $33.26 (978-0-8225-9070-5). 80pp. Angel Falls, the Amazon River, the Atacama Desert, the Galápagos Islands, the Montecristo Cloud Forest, Poás Volcano, and the Andes Mountains are the seven wonders featured in this attractive volume. (Rev: BL 4/1/09; LMC 10/09*; SLJ 5/09) [508.8]

Canada

18026 Beattie, Owen, and John Geiger. *Buried in Ice: The Mystery of a Lost Arctic Expedition* (4–7). Illus. by Janet Wilson. Series: Time Quest. 1993, Scholastic paper $6.95 (978-0-590-43849-0). The story of Sir John Franklin's unsuccessful 1845 expedition from England to find the Northwest Passage. (Rev: BCCB 3/92; BL 4/1/92; SLJ 4/92*) [919.804]

18027 Bial, Raymond. *The Inuit* (5–8). Series: Lifeways. 2001, Marshall Cavendish LB $34.21 (978-0-7614-1212-0). Using clear language and many intriguing illustrations, this is a fine introduction to the Inuit that begins with a folk story on the origins of the people and continues with material on a variety of basic topics. (Rev: BL 1/1–15/02; HBG 3/02; SLJ 4/02)

18028 Boudreau, Hélène. *Life in a Fishing Community* (2–4). Series: Learn About Rural Life. 2009, Crabtree LB $26.60 (978-0-7787-5072-7); paper $8.95 (978-0-7787-5085-7). 32pp. Life in the rural fishing community of Lunenburg, Nova Scotia, is described along with the work involved in fishing and the kinds of fish caught, with information about fishing around the world. (Rev: SLJ 2/1/10) [639.2]

18029 Bowers, Vivien. *Crazy About Canada! Amazing Things Kids Want to Know* (4–6). Illus. by Dianne Eastman. Series: Canadian Geographic Kids. 2006, Maple Tree $28.95 (978-1-897066-47-8); paper $18.95 (978-1-897066-48-5). 96pp. Cartoon figures Vivien and Morton ask questions about various aspects of Canada (geography, history, wildlife, and so forth) in this attractive fact-filled volume. (Rev: BL 4/1/06; SLJ 8/06)

18030 Bowers, Vivien. *Wow Canada! Exploring This Land from Coast to Coast to Coast* (4–6). Illus. 2000, Firefly paper $19.95 (978-1-895688-94-8). 160pp. A family travels across Canada visiting important sites and gathering material on the land and its people in this relaxed travelogue. (Rev: BL 2/15/00; HBG 10/00; SLJ 4/00)

18031 Braun, Eric. *Canada in Pictures. Rev. ed.* (5–9). Series: Visual Geography. 2003, Lerner LB $27.93 (978-0-8225-4679-5). 80pp. An informative and interesting overview of Canada's history, geography, government, economy, and people suitable for both research and browsing. (Rev: HBG 10/03; SLJ 7/03) [971.064]

18032 Butler, Geoff. *Ode to Newfoundland* (1–6). Illus. by author. 2003, Tundra $19.95 (978-0-88776-631-2). 32pp. A picture-book celebration of Newfoundland, with historical notes, lyrics, and music appended. (Rev: HBG 4/04; SLJ 1/04)

18033 Cooper, Michael L. *Klondike Fever: The Famous Gold Rush of 1898* (5–8). 1990, Houghton Mifflin paper $6.95 (978-0-395-54784-7). The events that turned a remote part of the Yukon into a three-ring circus of gold-hungry prospectors. (Rev: BCCB 1/90; BL 11/15/89; HB 1–2/90) [971.9]

18034 Corriveau, Danielle. *The Inuit of Canada* (4–6). Illus. Series: First Peoples. 2001, Lerner $23.95 (978-0-8225-4850-8). 48pp. This attractive introduction to the Inuit people and their native region and culture also contrasts traditional and modern lifestyles. (Rev: BL 2/1/02; HBG 3/02; SLJ 3/02)

18035 Enzoe, Pete, and Mindy Willett. *The Caribou Feed Our Soul* (3–6). Illus. Series: Land Is Our Storybook. 2011, Fitzhenry & Whiteside $16.95 (978-1-897252-67-3). 26pp. The author, a Chipewyan Dene, describes his efforts to protect the caribou of Canada's Northwest Territories and discusses traditional tales and rituals. (Rev: BL 7/11; LMC 10/11; SLJ 6/11) [639]

18036 Greenwood, Barbara. *Gold Rush Fever: A Story of the Klondike, 1898* (4–7). Illus. by Heather Collins. 2001, Kids Can $18.95 (978-1-55074-852-9); paper $12.95 (978-1-55074-850-5). 160pp. Thirteen-year-old Tim and his older brother trek to the Yukon to try to win their fortune in this account that interweaves fact and fiction, with many details about the hardships the miners faced. (Rev: BL 12/15/01; HBG 10/02; SLJ 10/01)

18037 Haugen, Brenda. *Canada ABCs: A Book About the People and Places of Canada* (2–4). Illus. by David Shaw. Series: Country ABCs. 2004, Picture Window LB $26.60 (978-1-4048-0285-8). 32pp. Young researchers will find useful facts in this alphabetically organized volume. (Rev: SLJ 8/04)

18038 Hughes, Susan. *Let's Call It Canada: Amazing Stories of Canadian Place Names* (3–6). Illus. by Clive Dobson and Jolie Dobson. 2003, Maple Tree $26.95 (978-1-894379-49-6); paper $16.95 (978-1-894379-50-2). 96pp. A topically organized compendium of Canadian place names and the interesting stories behind them. (Rev: SLJ 7/03)

18039 Kalman, Bobbie. *Canada: The Culture. Rev. ed.* (4–6). Series: The Lands, Peoples, and Cultures. 2001, Crabtree LB $25.27 (978-0-7787-9360-1); paper $7.95 (978-0-7787-9728-9). 32pp. This revised and updated edition includes Native, French, and English perspectives as well as discussion of refugees. Also use *Canada: The Land* and *Canada: The People* (both 2002). (Rev: SLJ 6/02)

18040 King, David C. *The Inuit* (1–4). Series: First Americans. 2007, Marshall Cavendish LB $20.95 (978-0-7614-2679-0). 48pp. An introduction to these Native Americans, covering their history, culture, beliefs, current status, and future; with an activity and a recipe. (Rev: SLJ 4/08)

18041 Major, Kevin. *Eh? to Zed* (2–4). Illus. 2001, Red Deer $17.95 (978-0-88995-222-5). 32pp. Canadian history and diverse culture are presented in an alphabet running from "Arctic, apple, aurora, Anik" to "Zamboni, zipper, zinc, zed." (Rev: BL 6/1–15/01; SLJ 7/01)

18042 Marx, David F. *Canada* (1–2). Illus. Series: Rookie Readers. 2000, Children's Book Pr. paper $5.95 (978-0-516-27083-8). 32pp. This book for beginning readers gives a quick introduction to Canada, its history, people, and languages. (Rev: BL 12/1/00)

18043 Newhouse, Maxwell. *The RCMP Musical Ride* (4–6). Illus. by author. 2004, Tundra $15.95 (978-0-

88776-683-1). A lively, behind-the-scenes look at the horseback displays performed by the Royal Canadian Mounted Police. (Rev: SLJ 9/04)

18044 Oberman, Sheldon. *The Shaman's Nephew: A Life in the Far North* (4–8). Illus. 2000, Stoddart $18.95 (978-0-7737-3200-1). This first-person narrative explores Inuit art and culture as experienced by Tookoome, an Inuit artist, who reflects on the daily life, beliefs, and myths of his people as presented in his work. (Rev: BL 6/1–15/00; SLJ 7/00)

18045 Olson, Nathan. *Canada* (3–4). Illus. Series: Fact Finders: Questions and Answers. 2004, Capstone LB $23.93 (978-0-7368-2686-0). 32pp. Using a question-and-answer format, this title introduces Canada's history, government, economy, education, culture, sports, and lifestyle. (Rev: SLJ 1/05)

18046 Pang, Guek-Cheng. *Canada. 2nd ed.* (5–9). Series: Cultures of the World. 2004, Benchmark LB $37.07 (978-0-7614-1788-0). History, geography, and culture are all covered in this useful volume that attempts to impart a comprehensive understanding of life in all parts of Canada. (Rev: SLJ 2/05) [971]

18047 Quigley, Mary. *Canada* (1–3). Illus. Series: A Visit To. 2003, Heinemann LB $22.79 (978-1-4034-0964-5). 32pp. Full of photographs, this is a useful and interesting overview of the country's geography, history, and culture, suitable for beginning readers. (Rev: HBG 10/03; SLJ 7/03)

18048 Renaud, Anne. *Pier 21: Stories from Near and Far* (4–7). Illus. by Aries Cheung. Series: Canadian Immigration. 2008, Lobster $16.95 (978-1-897073-70-4). This book is a collection of documents, memories, photographs, and illustrations relating to the site on Halifax Harbor where thousands of immigrants to Canada (in the years 1928 to 1971) started their new lives. (Rev: BL 4/15/08) [325.71]

18049 Robinson, Deborah B. *The Cree of North America* (4–6). Series: First Peoples. 2002, Lerner LB $23.93 (978-0-8225-4178-3). This book describes the culture and history of the Cree of North America, who are found primarily in subarctic Canada. (Rev: BL 5/15/02; HBG 10/02)

18050 Rogers, Barbara Radcliffe, and Stillman D. Rogers. *Canada* (4–7). Series: Enchantment of the World. 2000, Children's LB $37.00 (978-0-516-21076-6). 144pp. This fine introduction to Canada, its land and its people, also contains coverage of its history, economy, plants and animals, languages, sports, and the arts. (Rev: BL 1/1–15/01)

18051 Rowe, Percy. *Toronto* (3–6). Series: Great Cities of the World. 2003, World Almanac LB $31.00 (978-0-8368-5026-0). 48pp. Color photographs enliven this in-depth look at Canada's most populous city, with detailed information on its history, economy, and the lives of its residents. (Rev: SLJ 3/04)

18052 Rowe, Percy, and Patience Coster. *Montreal* (3–6). Series: Great Cities of the World. 2004, World Almanac LB $31.00 (978-0-8368-5039-0). 48pp. Montreal's

history, geography, and economy are described, as are shopping and leisure attractions and the life of the city. (Rev: SLJ 4/05)

18053 Strudwick, Leslie. *Inuit* (4–6). Illus. Series: Indigenous Peoples. 2004, Weigl LB $18.20 (978-1-59036-149-8). 32pp. Historical and contemporary issues are both covered in this detailed portrait of life among the Inuit. (Rev: BL 4/1/04)

18054 Walker, Sally M. *Blizzard of Glass: The Halifax Explosion of 1917* (5–8). Illus. 2011, Henry Holt $18.99 (978-0-8050-8945-5). 160pp. With many archival photographs and compelling narrative, this book tells the story of the explosion of a munitions ship in Halifax harbor in Canada in 1917 following a collision with another vessel; almost 2,000 people were killed. ALA Notable Children's Book 2012. (Rev: BL 11/1/11; SLJ 10/1/11) [971.6]

18055 Weaver, Janice. *Mirror with a Memory: A Nation's Story in Photographs* (4–6). Illus. 2007, Tundra $29.95 (978-0-88776-747-0). 192pp. Archival photographs of Canada's national history — from the 1864 Confederation Conference to the present day — are the focus of this volume, each captioned with commentary and historical information. (Rev: BL 11/15/07; SLJ 12/07)

18056 Whitcraft, Melissa. *The Niagara River* (4–8). Series: Watts Library. 2001, Watts LB $25.50 (978-0-531-11903-7). 63pp. This absorbing and readable account with maps and historical and contemporary photographs looks at the river's history, industry, and impact on the surrounding region. (Rev: SLJ 5/01)

18057 Williams, Brian. *Canada* (3–6). Illus. Series: Countries of the World. 2007, National Geographic LB $27.90 (978-1-4263-0025-7). 64pp. An attractive layout and up-to-date information combine to make this an effective and interesting introduction to the country and its culture. (Rev: SLJ 8/07)

18058 Williams, Suzanne M. *The Inuit* (4–6). Series: Watts Library. 2003, Watts LB $25.50 (978-0-531-12172-6). 63pp. The author profiles an Inuit family in Canada's far north, showing how they combine aspects of traditional and modern life. (Rev: SLJ 5/04)

Mexico

18059 Ancona, George. *The Fiestas* (3–6). Illus. Series: Viva Mexico! 2001, Marshall Cavendish LB $27.07 (978-0-7614-1327-1). One in a series of visually exciting photoessay books for older readers about Mexican culture and traditions that also includes *The Folk Arts* and *The Foods* (both 2001). (Rev: BL 3/1/02; HBG 3/02; SLJ 2/02)

18060 Bingham, Jane. *The Aztec Empire* (5–8). Series: Time Travel Guides. 2007, Raintree LB $34.29 (978-1-4109-2730-9). An attractive trip back in time to the Aztec Empire, providing details about daily life there — accommodation, food, shopping, and so forth — as well as the calendar and festivals. (Rev: LMC 11–12/07; SLJ 9/07) [972]

18061 Burr, Claudia. *Broken Shields* (4–8). 1997, Douglas & McIntyre paper $6.95 (978-0-88899-304-5). From firsthand eyewitness accounts, this is the story of the betrayal of Montezuma at the hands of the Spanish conqueror Cortez. (Rev: BL 12/1/97; HB 11–12/97; HBG 3/98; SLJ 1/98) [972]

18062 Furlong, Kate A. *Mexico* (2–4). Series: Countries. 2000, ABDO LB $22.78 (978-1-57765-390-5). 40pp. An adequate, brief introduction to Mexico that contains excellent photographs, a timeline, and a recipe. (Rev: HBG 10/01; SLJ 3/01)

18063 Gruber, Beth. *Mexico* (4–8). Series: Countries of the World. 2006, National Geographic $19.95 (978-0-7922-7629-6). 64pp. This book covers the geography, people, language, customs, and natural resources of Mexico, with plenty of graphics to add interest to the presentation. (Rev: BL 2/15/07; LMC 5/07)

18064 Hamilton, Janice. *Mexico in Pictures. Rev. ed.* (4–8). Illus. Series: Visual Geography. 2002, Lerner LB $27.93 (978-0-8225-1960-7). 80pp. An excellent introduction to Mexico that includes material on geography, history, people, economy, and culture with maps, photographs, and illustrations. (Rev: HBG 3/03; SLJ 3/03)

18065 Hodgkins, Fran. *Mexico* (2–5). Illus. Series: Questions and Answers: Countries. 2004, Capstone LB $23.93 (978-0-7368-2479-8). 32pp. Using a question-and-answer format, simple text, large photos, and many factboxes, this is an introduction to Mexico today, with material on history and traditional culture. (Rev: SLJ 3/05)

18066 Jovinelly, Joann, and Jason Netelkos. *The Crafts and Culture of the Aztecs* (5–8). Series: Crafts of the Ancient World. 2002, Rosen LB $29.25 (978-0-8239-3512-3). The culture of the Aztecs is covered through a discussion of their crafts and a variety of easily accomplished projects related to them. (Rev: BL 4/1/02; VOYA 6/02) [972]

18067 Kalman, Bobbie. *Mexico: The Culture. Rev. ed.* (4–6). Series: Lands, Peoples, and Cultures. 2008, Crabtree LB $26.60 (978-0-7787-9295-6); paper $8.95 (978-0-7787-9663-3). 32pp. This updated edition contains new photographs and statistics; it covers art, music, dance, language and literature, holidays, cooking, sports, and folklore. Also use *Mexico: The Land* and *Mexico: The People* (2008). (Rev: SLJ 2/09)

18068 Krebs, Laurie. *Off We Go to Mexico! An Adventure in the Sun* (PS–K). Illus. by Christopher Corr. 2006, Barefoot Books $16.99 (978-1-905236-40-4). Readers journey to Mexico, visit some ancient sites and natural wonders, have typical tourist fun, and learn Spanish vocabulary and about Mexican culture. (Rev: BL 3/1/06; SLJ 4/06)

18069 Landau, Elaine. *Mexico* (3–4). Illus. Series: A True Book. 2008, Children's Pr. LB $26.00 (978-0-531-16853-0); paper $6.95 (978-0-531-20727-7). 48pp. A succinct overview of the history, geography and culture of Mexico. (Rev: LMC 10/08; SLJ 9/08)

18070 Laufer, Peter. *Made in Mexico* (K–4). Illus. by Susan L. Roth. 2000, National Geographic $16.95 (978-0-7922-7118-5). A beautifully illustrated book that describes the guitar-making business that flourishes in the remote village of Paracho in Mexico. (Rev: HBG 10/00; SLJ 4/00)

18071 Lewis, Elizabeth. *Mexican Art and Culture* (5–8). Illus. Series: World Art and Culture. 2004, Raintree LB $29.99 (978-0-7398-6610-8). 56pp. The indigenous art and culture of Mexico from prehistoric times to the present are beautifully captured in this handsome and comprehensive overview. (Rev: BL 4/1/04; SLJ 2/04)

18072 Libura, Krystyna. *What the Aztecs Told Me* (4–8). 1997, Douglas & McIntyre paper $6.95 (978-0-88899-306-9). Based on an original 12-volume work written in the 16th century, this book describes the Aztec people from observation and eyewitness accounts. (Rev: BL 12/1/97; HB 11–12/97; HBG 3/98; SLJ 12/97) [972]

18073 Reilly, Mary J. *Mexico* (5–8). Series: Cultures of the World. 1991, Marshall Cavendish LB $35.64 (978-1-85435-385-6). This account emphasizes the geography, history, economy, and lifestyles of the Mexican people. (Rev: BL 4/1/91) [972]

18074 Rosenblum, Morris. *Heroes of Mexico* (5–8). 1972, Fleet $9.50 (978-0-8303-0082-2). A collected group of profiles of people important in the history of Mexico. (Rev: BL 6/87) [972]

18075 Sanna, Ellyn. *Mexico: Facts and Figures* (5–8). Series: Mexico: Our Southern Neighbor. 2002, Mason Crest LB $19.95 (978-1-59084-088-7). 64pp. An introduction to Mexico and its states, with material on history, people and culture today, and issues of importance such as poverty. Also use *The Geography of Mexico*, *The Economy of Mexico*, and *The Government of Mexico*. (Rev: SLJ 12/02)

18076 Somervill, Barbara A. *It's Cool to Learn About Countries: Mexico* (3–6). Series: Social Studies Explorer. 2010, Cherry Lake LB $29.93 (978-1-60279-833-5). 48pp. Readers learn about the geography, population, government, and culture of Mexico; includes a recipe, an art project, and a few activities. (Rev: SLJ 1/1/11) [972]

18077 Streissguth, Thomas. *Mexico* (2–4). Illus. Series: Country Explorers. 2007, Lerner LB $27.93 (978-0-8225-7130-8). 48pp. Rich in photographs, maps, and illustrations and full of accessible information, this lively book looks at the geography of the land and at all aspects of life there — family life, school life, clothes, medicine, food, sports, and so forth. (Rev: LMC 1/08*; SLJ 12/07)

Other Central American Lands

18078 Crandell, Rachel. *Hands of the Rain Forest: The Emberá People of Panama* (1–3). Illus. 2009, Henry Holt $16.99 (978-0-8050-7990-6). 32pp. A photo-essay introducing the lifestyle and traditions of the Emberá people of Panama, with maps and a timeline. (Rev: BL 11/15/09; LMC 11–12/09; SLJ 11/1/09) [972.87]

18079 Deady, Kathleen W. *El Salvador* (2–5). Illus. Series: Questions and Answers: Countries. 2005, Capstone LB $23.93 (978-0-7368-3750-7). 32pp. Using a question-and-answer format, simple text, large photos, and many factboxes, this is an introduction to El Salvador today, with material on history and traditional culture.

18080 Freedman, Russell. *In the Days of the Vaqueros: America's First True Cowboys* (5–9). 2001, Clarion $18.00 (978-0-395-96788-1). Vivid artwork complements this history of the earliest cowboys, the Central American vaqueros who first rode the range in the late 15th century. (Rev: BL 11/15/01*; HB 1–2/02; HBG 3/02; SLJ 9/01) [636.2]

18081 Grandell, Rachel. *Hands of the Maya: Villagers at Work and Play* (K–3). Illus. 2002, Holt $16.95 (978-0-8050-6687-6). 32pp. This photoessay takes readers through a day in a Mayan town and shows typical activities and recreations. (Rev: BL 5/1/02; HB 9/02; HBG 3/03; SLJ 8/02)

18082 Haverstock, Nathan A. *Nicaragua in Pictures* (5–8). 1993, Lerner LB $25.55 (978-0-8225-1817-4). A visit to this controversial country is highlighted by color photographs and clear text. (Rev: BL 10/15/87) [972.85]

18083 *Honduras in Pictures* (4–7). Series: Visual Geography. 1994, Lerner LB $25.55 (978-0-8225-1804-4). Chapters focus on history, culture, education, people, geography, and lifestyles. (Rev: BL 8/87)

18084 Jermyn, Leslie. *Belize* (5–9). Series: Cultures of the World. 2001, Marshall Cavendish LB $37.07 (978-0-7614-1190-1). Geography, history, government, arts and culture, and lifestyle are all covered in this interesting and attractive volume. (Rev: HBG 10/01; SLJ 11/01)

18085 McGaffey, Leta. *Honduras* (5–9). Series: Cultures of the World. 1999, Marshall Cavendish LB $37.07 (978-0-7614-0955-7). After background material on the history and geography of Honduras, this book focuses on modern times and such topics as the economy, population, religion, holidays, and recreation. (Rev: HBG 10/99; SLJ 11/99) [972.8]

18086 Mann, Elizabeth. *Tikal: The Center of the Maya World* (4–8). Illus. by Tom McNeely. Series: Wonders of the World. 2002, Mikaya $19.95 (978-1-931414-05-0). Mann provides an overview for older readers of the Mayan city of Tikal, covering the location, the people, the architecture, the culture, and their sometimes bloodthirsty customs. (Rev: BL 12/15/02; HBG 3/03; SLJ 1/03) [972.81]

18087 Markun, Patricia M. *It's Panama's Canal!* (5–9). 1999, Linnet LB $22.50 (978-0-208-02499-2). This account gives a good background history of the canal plus current information on Panama's control of the zone and its plans for successful management. (Rev: BL 1/1–15/00; HBG 3/00) [972.87]

18088 Morrison, Marion. *Nicaragua* (4–7). Series: Enchantment of the World. 2002, Children's LB $37.00 (978-0-516-20963-0). 144pp. Such topics as geography, history, people, language, economy, and government are covered in this introduction to Nicaragua. (Rev: BL 5/15/02)

18089 Pascoe, Elaine, ed. *Into Wild Panama* (3–6). Series: The Jeff Corwin Experience. 2004, Gale LB $24.95 (978-1-56711-856-8). 48pp. Jeff Corwin of TV's Animal Planet series explores the jungles of Panama, where he encounters such creatures as a frog-eating bat. (Rev: SLJ 4/04)

18090 Shields, Charles J. *Belize* (5–7). Illus. Series: Discovering Central America. 2002, Mason Crest LB $19.95 (978-1-59084-092-4). 64pp. Students needing facts about Belize will find everything here: geography, history, people, and culture, all backed up by maps, photographs, a timeline, and even recipes. (Rev: BL 1/1–15/03)

18091 Shields, Charles J. *Central America: Facts and Figures* (5–7). Illus. Series: Discovering Central America. 2002, Mason Crest LB $19.95 (978-1-59084-099-3). 64pp. This look at Central America as a whole covers history, geography, inhabitants, and cultures. (Rev: BL 1/1–15/03)

18092 Silverstone, Michael. *Rigoberta Menchu: Defending Human Rights in Guatemala* (5–8). 1999, Feminist paper $9.95 (978-1-55861-199-3). In addition to a biography of Nobel Peace Prize winner Rigoberta Menchu, this account presents Guatemala, its civil war, and the efforts to end it. (Rev: BL 3/15/00) [972.81]

Puerto Rico and Other Caribbean Islands

18093 Ancona, George. *Cuban Kids* (3–5). Illus. 2000, Marshall Cavendish $15.95 (978-0-7614-5077-1). This photoessay gives a fine picture of contemporary Cuba as seen through the eyes and actions of the country's children at work and at play. (Rev: BL 12/15/00; HBG 3/01; SLJ 1/01)

18094 Bernier-Grand, Carmen. *Shake It, Morena?* (3–5). Illus. by Lulu Delacre. 2002, Millbrook LB $24.90 (978-0-7613-1910-8). 48pp. This is a collection of games, songs, riddles, and counting rhymes from Puerto Rico with explanations of origins and cultural backgrounds. (Rev: BL 4/15/02; HBG 10/02)

18095 Dubois, Muriel L. *Cuba* (2–5). Illus. Series: Questions and Answers: Countries. 2005, Capstone LB $23.93 (978-0-7368-3749-1). Using a question-and-answer format, simple text, large photos, and many factboxes, this is an introduction to Cuba today, with material on history and traditional culture.

18096 Englar, Mary. *Dominican Republic* (2–3). Illus. Series: Many Cultures, One World. 2004, Capstone LB $23.93 (978-0-7368-2453-8). 32pp. A brief, accessible introduction to the Dominican Republic and its people, family life, customs, and legends.

18097 Furlong, Kate A. *Haiti* (3–5). Illus. Series: The Countries. 2003, ABDO LB $22.78 (978-1-57765-841-2). 40pp. Full-color photographs add to this well-written introduction to Haiti. (Rev: HBG 10/03; SLJ 10/03)

18098 Graves, Kerry A. *Haiti* (4–6). Illus. Series: Countries and Cultures. 2002, Capstone LB $25.26 (978-0-7368-1078-4). An introduction to Haiti's geography, history, and culture, with maps, timelines, and other aids. (Rev: BL 5/15/02; HBG 3/03)

18099 Green, Jen. *Jamaica* (4–8). Series: Countries of the World. 2008, National Geographic LB $27.90 (978-1-4263-0300-5). 64pp. With lots of color images, this thorough volume looks at the geography, nature, history, culture, government, and economy of Jamaica, with interesting sidebars on customs, celebrations, and so forth. (Rev: SLJ 3/09)

18100 Haverstock, Nathan A. *Cuba in Pictures* (5–8). Series: Visual Geography. 1997, Lerner LB $25.55 (978-0-8225-1811-2). A look at America's island neighbor, with color photographs. Also use *Dominican Republic in Pictures* (1997). (Rev: BL 10/15/87) [972.91064]

18101 Hernandez, Romel. *Caribbean Islands: Facts and Figures* (4–6). Illus. 2009, Mason Crest $21.95 (978-1-4222-0622-5). 64pp. This introductory volume to an 11-title series gives an overview of the islands of the Caribbean and their history, geography, economies, people, and cities. (Rev: BLO 3/11/09)

18102 Hernandez, Romel. *Trinidad and Tobago* (4–6). Series: Discovering the Caribbean. 2003, Mason Crest LB $19.95 (978-1-59084-304-8). 63pp. An appealing look at the geography, history, plants and animals, economy, and people of these Caribbean islands, with lots of photographs plus recipes and report ideas. (Rev: SLJ 10/03)

18103 McCarthy, Pat. *The Dominican Republic* (5–8). Series: Top Ten Countries of Recent Immigrants. 2004, Enslow LB $25.26 (978-0-7660-5179-9). Information on the Dominican Republic — culture, history, climate, and people — accompanies an explanation of the reasons for migration to the United States and discussion of the contributions of this community; supported by Web links. (Rev: SLJ 3/05) [304]

18104 Marx, Trish. *Reaching for the Sun: Kids in Cuba* (3–6). Photos by Cindy Karp. 2003, Millbrook LB $25.90 (978-0-7613-2261-0). 48pp. This attractive photoessay documents a Los Angeles children's arts group's month-long visit to Cuba and the personal interaction between visitors and hosts. (Rev: BL 4/15/03; HBG 10/03; SLJ 7/03)

18105 Milivojevic, JoAnn. *Puerto Rico* (1–3). Series: Globe-Trotters Club. 2000, Carolrhoda LB $22.60 (978-1-57505-119-2). 48pp. A simple look at the land and people of Puerto Rico, including natural wonders and such attractions as the Arecibo Observatory, home of the world's largest telescope. (Rev: BL 5/15/00; HBG 10/00; SLJ 9/00)

18106 Milivojevic, JoAnn. *Puerto Rico* (2–3). Series: A Ticket To. 2000, Lerner LB $22.60 (978-1-57505-144-4). A simple introduction to Puerto Rico that covers basic history, geography, and society. (Rev: HBG 10/00; SLJ 9/00)

18107 Orr, Tamra. *Barbados* (3–5). Series: Discovering the Caribbean. 2003, Mason Crest LB $19.95 (978-1-59084-306-2). 63pp. Introduces readers to the geography, history, people, culture, and attractions of Barbados, with recipes and projects. (Rev: HBG 4/04; SLJ 1/04)

18108 Orr, Tamra. *Windward Islands* (4–6). Illus. Series: Discovering the Caribbean. 2003, Mason Crest LB $19.95 (978-1-59084-305-5). 63pp. An appealing look at the geography, history, plants and animals, economy, and people of these Caribbean islands, with lots of photographs plus recipes and report ideas. (Rev: HBG 4/04; SLJ 10/03)

18109 Petersen, Christine, and David Petersen. *Cuba* (3–5). Illus. Series: True Books — Geography. 2001, Children's Book Pr. paper $6.95 (978-0-516-27358-7). 48pp. A colorful overview of Cuba's history and geography, with a positive slant on Castro's influence. (Rev: BL 2/1/02)

18110 Ross, Michael Elsohn. *Children of Puerto Rico* (4–6). Series: The World's Children. 2001, Carolrhoda LB $23.93 (978-1-57505-522-0). This handsome volume filled with color photographs of Puerto Rican children describes the daily life of their island home. (Rev: BL 1/1–15/02; HBG 3/02; SLJ 2/02)

18111 Schreier, Alta. *Cuba* (2–4). Series: A Visit To. 2000, Heinemann LB $21.36 (978-1-57572-380-8). 32pp. An introductory overview of the island nation today, with information on geography, people and culture, language, schools, and transportation presented in large photographs and simple text. (Rev: HBG 10/01; SLJ 4/01)

18112 Temple, Bob. *Dominican Republic* (3–5). Series: Discovering the Caribbean. 2003, Mason Crest LB $19.95 (978-1-59084-301-7). 63pp. Introduces readers to the geography, history, people, culture, and attractions of the Dominican Republic, with a focus on music, plus recipes and projects. (Rev: SLJ 1/04)

18113 Tuck, Jay, and Norma C. Vergara. *Heroes of Puerto Rico* (5–8). 1969, Fleet $9.50 (978-0-8303-0070-9). A series of profiles of famous Puerto Ricans. (Rev: BL 6/87) [972.9]

18114 Will, Emily Wade. *Haiti* (5–8). Series: Modern Nations of the World. 2001, Lucent LB $29.95 (978-1-56006-761-0). The history, geography, and culture of this island country are presented with colorful prose and pictures plus unusual facts contained in sidebars. (Rev: BL 6/1–15/01) [972.94]

18115 Williams, Colleen Madonna Flood. *The Bahamas* (4–6). Series: Discovering the Caribbean. 2003, Mason Crest LB $19.95 (978-1-59084-296-6). 63pp. An appealing look at the geography, history, plants and animals, economy, and people of the Bahamas, with lots of photographs plus recipes and report ideas. (Rev: HBG 4/04; SLJ 10/03)

South America

18116 Allen, Nancy Kelly. *On the Banks of the Amazon / En las orillas del Amazonas* (K–2). Trans. by Eida de la Vega. Illus. by Elizabeth Driessen. 2003, Raven Tree LB $16.95 (978-0-9720192-7-9). 31pp. A lively bilingual introduction to the animals of the Amazon rain forest, featuring two wildlife photographers. (Rev: HBG 4/04; SLJ 12/03)

18117 *Argentina in Pictures* (5–8). Series: Visual Geography. 1994, Lerner LB $25.55 (978-0-8225-1807-5). An overview of climate, wildlife, cities, vegetation, and mineral resources. (Rev: BL 4/15/88; SLJ 5/88) [982]

18118 Aronson, Marc. *Trapped: How the World Rescued 33 Miners from 2,000 Feet Below the Chilean Desert* (4–8). Illus. 2011, Atheneum $16.99 (978-1-4169-1397-9). 144pp. A gripping story of the mine disaster in 2010 and the massive effort to rescue the survivors, with information on geology and mining techniques. (Rev: BL 9/1/11*; SLJ 8/11*) [363.11]

18119 Augustin, Byron. *Bolivia* (4–7). Series: Enchantment of the World. 2001, Children's LB $37.00 (978-0-516-21050-6). With each page containing a color illustration, this attractive book introduces the land and people, economy, culture, and natural resources of Bolivia. (Rev: BL 1/1–15/02)

18120 Bauer, Brandy. *Brazil* (2–5). Illus. Series: Questions and Answers: Countries. 2004, Capstone LB $23.93 (978-0-7368-2481-1). Using a question-and-answer format, simple text, large photos, and many factboxes, this is an introduction to Brazil today, with material on history and traditional culture.

18121 Bingham, Jane. *The Inca Empire* (5–8). Series: Time Travel Guides. 2007, Raintree LB $34.29 (978-1-4109-2731-6). An attractive trip back in time to the Inca Empire, providing details about daily life there — accommodation, food, shopping, and so forth. (Rev: SLJ 9/07) [985]

18122 Boraas, Tracey. *Colombia* (4–6). Illus. Series: Countries and Cultures. 2002, Capstone LB $25.26 (978-0-7368-1076-0). 64pp. An introduction to Colombia that covers many topics including geography, history, and culture, with maps, timelines, and other aids. (Rev: BL 5/15/02; HBG 3/03)

18123 Chin, Jason. *Island: A Story of the Galapagos* (2–4). Illus. by author. 2012, Roaring Brook $16.99 (978-1-59643-716-6). 40pp. This profile of the Galapagos traces the geological evolution as well as that of the plants and animals there, combining fiction and fact in an effective and handsome presentation. ALA Notable Children's Book; Outstanding Science Trade Books for Students K–12. e (Rev: BL 9/15/12; HB 9–10/12; LMC 1–2/13; SLJ 8/12*) [508.866]

18124 *Colombia in Pictures* (5–8). Series: Visual Geography. 1996, Lerner LB $25.55 (978-0-8225-1810-5). Many photographs highlight this visit to a South American nation. (Rev: BL 10/15/87) [986.1]

18125 Corona, Laurel. *Peru* (5–8). Series: Modern Nations of the World. 2001, Lucent LB $28.70 (978-1-56006-862-4). 112pp. Detailed sidebars, a chronology, and national statistics supplement the general information presented in this colorful introduction to Peru. (Rev: BL 6/1–15/01)

18126 Dalal, Anita. *Argentina* (4–8). Series: Nations of the World. 2001, Raintree LB $34.26 (978-0-7398-1279-2). 128pp. A colorful, interesting introduction to Argentina that covers its land and cities, history, culture, present economic conditions, and possible future developments. (Rev: BL 6/1–15/01; HBG 10/01)

18127 Dalal, Anita. *Brazil* (4–8). Series: Nations of the World. 2001, Raintree LB $34.26 (978-0-7398-1284-6). 128pp. A profile of the home of Carnival, the Amazon, and Pele with material attractively presented on its past and present, its people, and its culture. (Rev: BL 6/1–15/01; HBG 10/01)

18128 Deckker, Zilah. *Brazil* (4–8). Series: Countries of the World. 2008, National Geographic LB $27.90 (978-1-4263-0298-5). 64pp. With lots of color images, this thorough volume looks at the geography, nature, history, culture, government, and economy of Brazil, with interesting sidebars on customs, celebrations, and so forth. (Rev: SLJ 3/09) [981]

18129 Dubois, Jill. *Colombia* (5–8). Series: Cultures of the World. 1991, Marshall Cavendish LB $35.64 (978-1-85435-384-9). Background information on Colombia is given as well as coverage of contemporary concerns. (Rev: BL 4/1/91) [986.1]

18130 Dubois, Muriel L. *Peru* (2–5). Illus. Series: Questions and Answers: Countries. 2005, Capstone LB $23.93 (978-0-7368-3758-3). 32pp. Using a question-and-answer format, simple text, large photos, and many factboxes, this is an introduction to Peru today, with material on history and traditional culture.

18131 Eagen, James. *The Aymara of South America* (4–6). Series: First Peoples. 2002, Lerner LB $23.93 (978-0-8225-4174-5). This volume describes the history and present status of the Aymara, who live in the high plains of Peru and Bolivia, where they are known for domesticating the potato. (Rev: BL 5/15/02; HBG 10/02)

18132 Fajardo, Dara Andrea. *A Child's Day in a Peruvian City* (K–3). Series: A Child's Day. 2002, Marshall Cavendish LB $15.95 (978-0-7614-1408-7). 32pp. The reader meets a Peruvian child and learns about culture, work, and play in modern Peru. (Rev: BL 2/15/03; HBG 3/03; SLJ 12/02)

18133 Falconer, Kieran. *Peru* (4–7). Series: Cultures of the World. 1995, Marshall Cavendish LB $37.07 (978-0-7614-0179-7). The focus of this book is on the people of Peru, their lifestyles, artistic endeavors, religion, and leisure activities. (Rev: BL 1/1–15/96; SLJ 4/96) [985]

18134 Fitzpatrick, Anne. *Amazon River* (4–6). Illus. Series: Natural Wonders of the World. 2004, Creative Education LB $27.10 (978-1-58341-322-7). 32pp. After establishing this important river's location, this oversized picture book full of color photographs looks at geology, climate, wildlife, people, and other pertinent facts. (Rev: SLJ 1/05)

18135 Foley, Erin. *Ecuador* (5–8). Series: Cultures of the World. 1995, Marshall Cavendish LB $37.07 (978-0-7614-0173-5). This book supplies good background material on Ecuador but is strongest in describing contemporary conditions. (Rev: SLJ 11/95) [980]

18136 Franchino, Vicky. *It's Cool to Learn About Countries: Brazil* (3–6). Series: Social Studies Explorer. 2010, Cherry Lake LB $29.93 (978-1-60279-827-4). 48pp. Readers learn about the geography, population, government, and culture of Brazil; includes a recipe, an art project, and a few activities. (Rev: SLJ 1/1/11) [981]

18137 Gofen, Ethel C. *Cultures of the World: Argentina* (5–8). Series: Cultures of the World. 1991, Marshall Cavendish LB $213.86 (978-1-85435-380-1). This book provides standard information on history and geography and tells about the contemporary lifestyles of the people. (Rev: BL 4/1/91) [962]

18138 *Guyana in Pictures* (5–8). Series: Visual Geography. 1997, Lerner LB $25.55 (978-0-8225-1815-0). History, climate, wildlife, and major cities are covered in this overview. (Rev: BL 4/15/88) [988.1]

18139 Haverstock, Nathan A. *Paraguay in Pictures* (5–8). Series: Visual Geography. 1995, Lerner LB $25.55 (978-0-8225-1819-8). This overview of Paraguay includes its history to 1987 and possible future developments. (Rev: BL 4/15/88) [989.2]

18140 Jermyn, Leslie. *Paraguay* (5–8). 1999, Marshall Cavendish LB $37.07 (978-0-7614-0979-3). This book about Paraguay covers history, geography, government, and economy as well as such social and cultural topics as religion, the arts, food, and recreation. (Rev: HBG 10/00; SLJ 4/00) [989]

18141 Jones, Helga. *Venezuela* (1–3). Series: Globe-Trotters Club. 2000, Carolrhoda LB $22.60 (978-1-57505-122-2). 48pp. Some of the topics covered in this simple introduction to Venezuela are the land, people, culture, rain forests, and Angel Falls, the highest waterfall in the world. (Rev: BL 5/15/00; HBG 10/00)

18142 Krebs, Laurie. *Up and Down the Andes: A Peruvian Festival Tale* (K–3). Illus. by Aurelia Fronty. 2008, Barefoot Books $16.99 (978-1-84686-203-8). 32pp. A traditional Peruvian festival is described in simple rhymes and attractive acrylic paintings. (Rev: BL 12/15/08; LMC 5/09)

18143 Lichtenberg, Andre. *Brazil* (2–4). Illus. 2000, Raintree $25.69 (978-0-8172-5514-5). 32pp. A young Brazilian boy introduces the reader to his homeland, its geography, food, customs, schools, and everyday life. (Rev: BL 4/15/00; HBG 10/00)

18144 Lourie, Peter. *Lost Treasure of the Inca* (4–7). 1999, Boyds Mills $18.95 (978-1-56397-743-5). A thrilling narrative of a modern search for the gold supposedly hidden by the Incas in the Ecuadorian mountains. (Rev: BCCB 11/99; BL 10/15/99; HBG 3/00; SLJ 11/99) [986.6]

18145 Lourie, Peter. *Tierra del Fuego: A Journey to the End of the Earth* (2–5). Illus. 2002, Boyds Mills $19.95 (978-1-56397-973-6). 48pp. A fascinating first-person look at Tierra del Fuego, the southernmost island off the coast of South America, including its discovery and the fate of its native peoples. (Rev: BL 10/15/02; HBG 3/03; SLJ 9/02)

18146 McNair, Sylvia. *Chile* (4–7). Series: Enchantment of the World. 2000, Children's LB $37.00 (978-0-516-21007-0). 144pp. This attractive new edition of an old title includes material on Chile's land and people, history and government, economics and landmarks, daily life, and sports. (Rev: BL 7/00)

18147 Morrison, Marion. *Ecuador* (4–7). Series: Enchantment of the World. 2000, Children's LB $37.00 (978-0-516-21544-0). 144pp. This book examines the geography and climate of Ecuador, its history, government, language, economy, and people. (Rev: BL 1/1–15/01)

18148 Morrison, Marion. *Guyana* (5–8). Illus. Series: Enchantment of the World, Second Series. 2003, Children's LB $37.00 (978-0-516-22377-3). 144pp. A visually attractive book that covers such topics as the geography, history, government, culture, and people with a timeline, fast facts, and a recipe. (Rev: SLJ 5/03)

18149 Morrison, Marion. *Rio de Janeiro* (4–6). Series: Great Cities of the World. 2004, World Almanac LB $31.00 (978-0-8368-5031-4). Report writers will find useful information on Rio's history, culture, and lifestyle. Also use *Buenos Aires* (2004). (Rev: SLJ 7/04)

18150 Nesbitt, Kris. *My Amazon River Day* (2–5). Illus. 2000, Shedd Aquarium $23.95 (978-0-9701035-0-5). 48pp. This book chronicles everyday life on the banks of the Amazon River in Peru for Patricia, her family, and her friends. (Rev: BL 10/15/00)

18151 Pateman, Robert. *Bolivia* (4–7). Series: Cultures of the World. 1995, Marshall Cavendish LB $37.07 (978-0-7614-0178-0). The people of Bolivia, how they live, and their traditions are some of the topics covered in this general introduction. (Rev: BL 1/1–15/96; SLJ 4/96) [984]

18152 *Peru in Pictures* (5–8). Series: Visual Geography. 1997, Lerner LB $25.55 (978-0-8225-1820-4). An introduction to this South American land, highlighted by color photographs. (Rev: BL 10/15/87) [985]

18153 Spengler, Kremena. *Chile* (2–5). Illus. Series: Questions and Answers: Countries. 2005, Capstone LB $23.93 (978-0-7368-3748-4). Using a question-and-answer format, simple text, large photos, and many factboxes, this is an introduction to Chile today, with material on history and traditional culture.

18154 Tagliaferro, Linda. *Galapagos Islands: Nature's Delicate Balance at Risk* (4–8). Illus. 2001, Lerner LB $27.93 (978-0-8225-0648-5). 88pp. This is a detailed but accessible introduction to the history, geology, wildlife, and ecology of the Galapagos Islands, with maps and photographs. (Rev: BL 9/15/01; HBG 3/02; SLJ 11/01; VOYA 12/01)

18155 Tahan, Raya. *The Yanomami of South America* (4–6). Illus. Series: First Peoples. 2001, Lerner $23.93 (978-0-8225-4851-5). 48pp. This attractive introduction to the Yanomami people and their native region and culture also contrasts traditional and modern lifestyles. (Rev: BL 2/1/02; HBG 3/02; SLJ 3/02)

18156 *Venezuela in Pictures* (4–7). Series: Visual Geography. 1993, Lerner LB $21.27 (978-0-8225-1824-2). The land, people, and government of this oil-rich country are explored in maps, text, and photographs. (Rev: BL 1/1/88) [987]

18157 Walters, Tara. *Brazil* (3–4). Illus. Series: A True Book. 2008, Children's Pr. LB $26.00 (978-0-531-16851-6); paper $6.95 (978-0-531-20725-3). 48pp. A succinct overview of the history, geography, and culture of Brazil. (Rev: LMC 10/08; SLJ 9/08)

18158 Watson, Galadriel. *The Amazon Rain Forest: The Largest Rain Forest in the World* (3–6). Illus. Series: Natural Wonders. 2004, Weigl LB $18.20 (978-1-59036-270-9). 32pp. A look at the history of the rain forest, the people who live there, the animals and plants it supports, and the environmental threats it faces. (Rev: SLJ 4/05)

18159 Webster, Christine. *Yanomami* (3–5). Series: Indigenous Peoples. 2004, Weigl LB $18.20 (978-1-59036-124-5). 32pp. A fascinating and informative overview of the Yanomami people of the Amazon River basin, covering history, culture, language, and family life. (Rev: SLJ 7/04)

18160 Winter, Jane K. *Chile* (5–8). Series: Cultures of the World. 1991, Marshall Cavendish LB $35.64 (978-1-85435-383-2). The geography, history, government, and economy of Chile are some of the topics covered in this fine introduction. (Rev: BL 4/1/91) [983]

18161 Winter, Jane K. *Venezuela* (5–8). Series: Cultures of the World. 1991, Marshall Cavendish LB $35.64 (978-1-85435-386-3). In detailed text and color photographs, the land, people, and contemporary problems and concerns of Venezuela are introduced. (Rev: BL 4/1/91) [987]

Polar Regions

18162 Alexander, Bryan, and Cherry Alexander. *Journey into the Arctic* (1–5). Photos by authors. 2003, Oxford LB $25.00 (978-0-19-522004-9). 48pp. A fascinating tour of Arctic regions takes readers from a village in Greenland through Arctic Canada and Siberia to the North Pole. (Rev: HBG 4/04; SLJ 1/04)

18163 Bagley, Katie. *Antarctica* (K–3). Series: Continents. 2002, Capstone LB $21.26 (978-0-7368-1415-7). 24pp. A brief introduction to the geography, history, flora (mostly lichens and moss), and fauna of Antarctica. (Rev: HBG 3/03; SLJ 4/03)

18164 Baker, Stuart. *Climate Change in the Antarctic* (3–6). Illus. 2009, Marshall Cavendish LB $19.95 (978-076144438-1). 32pp. With chapters on the effects of climate change on the topography, plants, and animals of the Antarctic, this well-illustrated slim volume will be attractive to reluctant readers. (Rev: BL 2/15/10; LMC 3–4/10) [508.3398]

18165 Benduhn, Tea. *Living in Polar Regions* (3–4). Series: Life on the Edge. 2007, Gareth Stevens LB $19.93 (978-0-8368-8343-5). 24pp. After an introduction to the polar regions and the climate of these areas, Benduhn looks at the people who live there, the life they lead, and the problems they face. (Rev: LMC 1/08; SLJ 12/07)

18166 Bledsoe, Lucy Jane. *How to Survive in Antarctica* (5–8). 2006, Holiday $16.95 (978-0-8234-1890-9). 102pp. An account of the author's trips to Antarctica, filled with interesting facts about the frigid land — from wildlife notes to survival tips — plus photographs by the author. (Rev: BCCB 10/06; BL 7/06; HBG 4/07; SLJ 8/06; VOYA 8/06)

18167 Bocknek, Jonathan. *Antarctica: The Last Wilderness* (5–8). Series: Understanding Global Issues. 2003, Smart Apple $19.95 (978-1-58340-356-3). This nicely illustrated book introduces Antarctica with material on climate, animals, exploration, and possible future developments. (Rev: BL 11/15/03; HB 9–10/01; HBG 3/02; SLJ 12/03) [998.9]

18168 Bredeson, Carmen. *After the Last Dog Died: The True-Life, Hair-Raising Adventures of Douglas Mawson and his 1911-1914 Antarctic Expedition* (5–8). 2003, National Geographic $18.95 (978-0-7922-6140-7). This enthralling story of courage in the face of starvation and harsh conditions draws on primary materials including the writings of expedition leader Mawson himself. (Rev: BL 11/1/03; HBG 4/04; SLJ 1/04*) [919.8]

18169 Byles, Monica. *Life in the Polar Lands* (2–5). Illus. by Francis Mosley. 2000, Two-Can LB $9.95 (978-1-58728-557-8); paper $4.95 (978-1-58728-572-1). This is a basic introduction to how plants, animals, and humans manage to survive in the Arctic and Antarctic. (Rev: SLJ 4/01)

18170 Cerullo, Mary. *Life Under Ice* (3–5). Illus. by Bill Curtsinger. 2004, Tilbury House $16.95 (978-0-88448-246-8). 40pp. Plant and animal life above and below the waters of Antarctica are shown in eye-catching color photographs. (Rev: BL 9/15/03; HBG 4/04; SLJ 10/03)

18171 Conlan, Kathy. *Under the Ice* (4–6). Illus. 2002, Kids Can $16.95 (978-1-55337-001-7). 56pp. This photoessay relates the author's exciting experiences doing underwater marine biology research in Antarctica. (Rev: BL 11/1/02; HBG 3/03; SLJ 12/02)

18172 Cordoba, Yasmine A. *Igloo* (3–5). Illus. by Kimberly L. Dawson Kurnizki. Series: Native American Homes. 2001, Rourke LB $28.50 (978-1-55916-277-7). 32pp. Using well-chosen photos and a good text, this book explains the construction of the igloo, its uses, and its place in the culture of the Inuit. (Rev: SLJ 3/01)

18173 Esbensen, Barbara J. *The Night Rainbow* (1–4). Illus. by Helen K. Davie. 2000, Orchard LB $17.99 (978-0-531-33244-3). 32pp. A poetic picture book that discusses the Northern Lights and the many images from different folk traditions that are associated with this phenomenon. (Rev: BL 3/1/00; HBG 10/00; SLJ 4/00)

18174 Fine, Jil. *The Shackleton Expedition* (5–8). Series: Survivor. 2002, Children's LB $24.50 (978-0-516-23904-0); paper $6.95 (978-0-516-23489-2). 48pp. For reluctant readers, this is an accessible and exciting account of how Shackleton's men survived the perils of shipwreck in the ice. (Rev: SLJ 9/02)

18175 Foran, Jill. *Search for the Northwest Passage* (5–8). Series: Great Journeys. 2004, Weigl LB $26.00 (978-1-59036-205-1). Colorful illustrations and an attractive format will appeal to browsers seeking information about the search for a sea route to the West; a useful timeline and links to Web sites are included. (Rev: BL 11/1/04)

18176 Goodman, Susan E. *Life on the Ice* (3–5). Photos by Michael J. Doolittle. 2006, Millbrook LB $22.60 (978-0-7613-2775-2). 32pp. This brief introduction to the world's polar regions explores their geographical remoteness, weather extremes, and the scientific research projects conducted there. (Rev: BL 3/15/06; SLJ 8/06)

18177 Gray, Susan H. *Tundra* (2–5). Series: First Reports. 2000, Compass Point LB $22.60 (978-0-7565-0024-5). 48pp. An informative introduction to the ecosystem, with material on plants and animals, the conditions there, the importance of the biome to the global environment, and features such as the discovery of a woolly mammoth in the permafrost in Russia. (Rev: SLJ 5/01)

18178 Green, Jen. *On the Tundra* (2–5). Illus. Series: Small World. 2002, Crabtree LB $25.27 (978-0-7787-0139-2); paper $8.95 (978-0-7787-0153-8). 32pp. This book for younger readers takes a close look at the creatures that are found in the tundra, and how plant and animal life coexist there. (Rev: BL 10/15/02; SLJ 8/02)

18179 Hooper, Meredith. *Antarctic Journal: The Hidden Worlds of Antarctica's Animals* (5–7). Illus. by Lucia de-Leiris. 2001, National Geographic $16.95 (978-0-7922-7188-8). An exciting account of a summer the author spent at Palmer Station in the Antarctic and the wildlife there. (Rev: BL 6/1–15/01; HBG 10/01; SLJ 3/01) [988]

18180 Johnson, Rebecca. *A Walk in the Tundra* (2–4). Illus. Series: Biomes of North America. 2000, Carolrhoda LB $23.93 (978-1-57505-157-4). A lively account that uses maps, pictures, and text to describe the climate, flora and fauna, and the people of the tundra regions of North America. (Rev: BL 10/15/00; HBG 3/01; SLJ 12/00)

18181 Kimmel, Elizabeth Cody. *Ice Story: Shackleton's Lost Expedition* (4–7). 1999, Clarion $19.00 (978-0-395-91524-0). A fine, accurate, and engrossing description of Shackleton's Imperial Transatlantic Expedition to the Antarctic — one of the great survival stories of all time. (Rev: BL 4/1/99; HBG 10/99; SLJ 4/99) [910.9]

18182 Levinson, Nancy S. *North Pole South Pole* (1–2). Illus. by Diane D. Hearn. 2002, Holiday House $14.95 (978-0-8234-1737-7). 40pp. Basic facts about the two poles for beginning readers. (Rev: HB 1/03; HBG 3/03; SLJ 12/02)

18183 Levy, Janey. *Discovering the Arctic Tundra* (3–5). Series: World Habitats. 2007, Rosen LB $23.95 (978-1-4042-3787-2). 32pp. With photographs and fast facts, this volume covers location, climate, plants and animals, people, threats and conservation efforts, and so forth. (Rev: LMC 3/08; SLJ 1/08)

18184 Love, Ann, and Jane Drake. *The Kids Book of the Far North* (2–4). Illus. 2000, Kids Can $15.95 (978-1-55074-563-4). Topics covered in this introduction to the Arctic include climate and landscape, natural resources, exploration and settlement, and the life, past and present, of the native people. (Rev: BL 9/15/00; SLJ 1/01)

18185 Lynch, Wayne. *The Arctic* (5–9). Series: Our Wild World Ecosystems. 2007, NorthWord $16.95 (978-1-55971-960-5); paper $8.95 (978-1-55971-961-2). 64pp. Lynch introduces the flora and fauna of the Arctic with interesting anecdotes about his own experiences, color photographs, sidebar features, and eco-fact boxes. (Rev: SLJ 5/07)

18186 Markle, Sandra. *Animals Robert Scott Saw: An Adventure in Antarctica* (4–7). Illus. by Phil. Series: Explorers. 2008, Chronicle LB $16.99 (978-0-8118-4918-0). As the title indicates, this book focuses on the animals that explorer Scott took with him to the South Pole in 1912 and those he observed on the way. (Rev: BL 4/1/08) [919.8]

18187 Martin, Jacqueline B. *The Lamp, the Ice, and the Boat Called Fish* (2–4). Illus. 2000, Houghton $15.00 (978-0-618-00341-9). 48pp. The story of the personnel aboard a research boat named Fish and how they survived with the help of some natives after they were trapped in the ice during an Arctic expedition. (Rev: BCCB 2/01; BL 3/1/01; HB 3/01; HBG 10/01)

18188 Matsen, Brad. *An Extreme Dive Under the Antarctic Ice* (4–6). Series: Incredible Deep-Sea Adventures. 2003, Enslow LB $23.93 (978-0-7660-2190-7). 48pp. Readers follow environmental scientists under the cold ice of the Antarctic and discover pollution and other threats. (Rev: HBG 4/04; SLJ 1/04)

18189 Penner, Lucille R. *Ice Wreck* (2–4). Illus. Series: Road to Reading. 2001, Golden $11.99 (978-0-307-46408-8); paper $3.99 (978-0-307-26408-4). An absorbing narrative about Shackleton's disastrous expedition and exciting rescue. (Rev: BL 7/01; HBG 3/02)

18190 Pipe, Jim. *Polar Region Survival* (4–6). Illus. Series: Extreme Habitats. 2007, Gareth Stevens LB $25.27 (978-0-8368-8248-3). 32pp. This well-designed title combines high visual appeal and accessible facts to make an attractive and informative overview of polar regions, the plants and animals that live there, how people use these regions, and the threats to the environment. (Rev: LMC 1/08; SLJ 12/07)

18191 Sandler, Martin W. *Trapped in Ice! An Amazing True Whaling Adventure* (5–8). Illus. 2006, Scholastic $16.99 (978-0-439-74363-1). A gripping account of 1,219 people forced to abandon ship after their whaling vessels became imprisoned in Arctic ice during the early winter of 1871; includes maps, photographs, and journal accounts. (Rev: BL 4/15/06; SLJ 6/06)

18192 Scott, Elaine. *Poles Apart: Why Penguins and Polar Bears Will Never Be Neighbors* (4–8). Illus. 2004, Viking $17.99 (978-0-670-05925-6). 64pp. This fascinating overview of the two polar regions examines their physical characteristics, seasons, wildlife, magnetism, exploration, and the effects of global warming. (Rev: BL 12/1/04; SLJ 12/04)

18193 Sommers, Michael A. *Antarctic Melting: The Disappearing Antarctic Ice Cap* (4–8). Series: Extreme Environmental Threats. 2006, Rosen LB $27.95 (978-1-4042-0741-7). An examination of the impact that global warming has had on Antarctica since 1995, with discussion of the research that takes place on the continent and the work of glaciologists. (Rev: LMC 8–9/07; SLJ 8/07) [363.738]

18194 Steger, Will, and Jon Bowermaster. *Over the Top of the World: Explorer Will Steger's Trek Across the Arctic* (4–7). 1997, Scholastic paper $17.95 (978-0-590-84860-2). Describes the grueling, dangerous adventures involved in a journey across the Arctic Ocean. (Rev: BCCB 2/97; BL 4/15/97; SLJ 4/97*) [919.804]

18195 Stone, Lynn M. *Tundra* (1–3). Illus. Series: Biomes of North America. 2003, Rourke $20.64 (978-1-58952-687-7). 24pp. For young researchers, this is an excellent introduction to this biome, with clear, simple text, photographs, and maps. (Rev: BL 10/15/03)

18196 Theodorou, Rod. *From the Arctic to Antarctica* (2–4). Series: Amazing Journeys. 2000, Heinemann LB $22.79 (978-1-57572-485-0). 32pp. Both the Arctic and Antarctic regions are described in this brief overview that also introduces plant and animal life. (Rev: HBG 3/01; SLJ 7/00)

18197 Wade, Rosalyn. *Polar Worlds* (4–7). Illus. Series: Insiders. 2011, Simon & Schuster $16.99 (978-144243275-8). 64pp. Three-D illustrations draw readers into this overview of the Arctic and Antarctic regions and their topography and flora and fauna, with discussion of exploration, survival measures, and environmental threats. (Rev: BL 12/1/11) [919]

18198 Winner, Cherie. *Life in the Tundra* (5–8). Series: Ecosystems in Action. 2003, Lerner LB $26.60 (978-0-8225-4686-3). In text and pictures, the Arctic tundra is presented with material on the organisms that live there and how human life has changed this ecosystem. (Rev: BL 9/15/03; HBG 10/03) [551.4]

United States

General History and Geography

18199 Ajmera, Maya, and Yvonne Wakim Dennis. *Children of the U.S.A* (3–6). Illus. 2008, Charlesbridge $23.95 (978-1-57091-615-1). This photo-essay com-

pares and contrasts children enjoying themselves in 51 American communities. (Rev: BL 3/1/08; SLJ 2/08)

18200 Andryszewski, Tricia. *Step by Step Along the Appalachian Trail* (4–8). 1998, Twenty-First Century LB $24.90 (978-0-7613-0273-5). A state-by-state tour of the Appalachian Trail, with material on the terrain, elevations, landmarks, and sites along the way. (Rev: BL 3/1/99; HBG 9/99; SLJ 4/99) [973]

18201 Armstrong, Jennifer. *The American Story: 100 True Tales from American History* (4–7). Illus. by Roger Roth. 2006, Knopf $34.95 (978-0-375-81256-9). 368pp. The 100 stories in this large-format collection bring American history to life and include such diverse events as Paul Revere's midnight ride, the first flight of the Wright brothers, the eruption of Mount St. Helens, and the Supreme Court decision resolving the disputed 2000 presidential election. (Rev: BCCB 10/06; BL 8/06; HBG 4/07; SLJ 8/06*)

18202 Backer, Miles. *Travels with Charlie: Way Out West* (1–3). Illus. by Chuck Nitzberg. 2006, Blue Apple $15.95 (978-1-59354-134-7). Charlie the dog visits interesting and quirky sites in the western United States; maps of the states he visits, as well as a U.S. map, will help readers as they follow Charlie on his travels. (Rev: SLJ 6/06)

18203 Bockenhauer, Mark H., and Stephen F. Cunha. *Our Fifty States* (4–10). 2004, National Geographic LB $45.90 (978-0-7922-6992-2). Maps of the states are accompanied by basic facts, photographs, and archival reproductions of key historical events; also includes the U.S. territories. (Rev: SLJ 1/05) [973]

18204 Bowden, Rob. *Settlements of the Mississippi River* (3–5). Illus. Series: Rivers Through Time. 2005, Heinemann LB $29.93 (978-1-4034-5719-6). 48pp. Traces the history and contemporary life of major settlements along the Mississippi, discussing the development of industry and the importance of environmental factors.

18205 Brent, Lynnette R. *At Home: Long Ago and Today* (2–4). Series: Times Change. 2003, Heinemann LB $24.22 (978-1-4034-4531-5). 32pp. A look at how things were "at home" a century or more ago compared with today. (Rev: SLJ 5/04)

18206 Brent, Lynnette R. *At School: Long Ago and Today* (2–4). Series: Times Change. 2003, Heinemann LB $24.22 (978-1-4034-4533-9). 32pp. This book, illustrated with period and contemporary photographs, contrasts a day in school today and a century or so ago. (Rev: SLJ 5/04)

18207 Brent, Lynnette R. *Going Shopping: Long Ago and Today* (2–4). Series: Times Change. 2003, Heinemann LB $24.22 (978-1-4034-4535-3). 32pp. A comparison of what it was like to go shopping more than 100 years ago with what it's like today, illustrated with contemporary and period photographs. (Rev: SLJ 5/04)

18208 Brexel, Bernadette. *The Knights of Labor and the Haymarket Riot: The Fight for an Eight-Hour Workday* (5–8). Series: America's Industrial Society in the 19th Century. 2004, Rosen LB $22.50 (978-0-8239-4028-

8). For reluctant readers, this overview of the struggle to improve working conditions features large print and short chapters. Also use *The Populist Party: A Voice for the Farmers in an Industrial Society* (2004). (Rev: BL 4/1/04)

18209 Buckley, Susan, and Elspeth Leacock. *Journeys for Freedom: A New Look at America's Story* (4–7). Illus. by Rodica Prato. 2006, Houghton $17.00 (978-0-618-22323-7). 48pp. Twenty stories of personal struggles for freedom — ranging from the early 17th century to the late 20th century — feature quotations from primary sources. (Rev: BL 11/15/06; SLJ 1/07)

18210 Buckley, Susan, and Elspeth Leacock. *Kids Make History: A New Look at America's Story* (4–8). Illus. by Randy Jones. 2006, Houghton $17.00 (978-0-618-22329-9). 48pp. Twenty stories of young people who experienced milestone events in American history — from Pocahontas in 1607 to a high school senior on 9/11 — are told in text, quotations, fictionalized dialogue, and illustrations. (Rev: SLJ 1/07)

18211 Burgan, Michael. *Ellis Island* (3–6). Illus. Series: You Choose: History. 2013, Capstone LB $31.32 (978-147650253-3); paper $6.95 (9781476536064). 112pp. Readers choose the paths that three young people will follow through entry to the United States. Also use *The Oregon Trail, The Harlem Renaissance,* and *The Child Labor Reform Movement* (all 2013), which offer similar approaches to history. (Rev: BL 12/1/13; LMC 8–9/14) [304.8]

18212 Burleigh, Robert. *American Moments: Scenes from American History* (3–6). Trans. and illus. by Bruce Strachan. 2004, Holt $18.95 (978-0-8050-7082-8). 48pp. Eighteen chapters present scenes from American history that may lack detail but will arouse interest. (Rev: BL 7/04; SLJ 6/04)

18213 Cheney, Lynne. *Our 50 States: A Family Adventure Across America* (4–6). Illus. by Robin P. Glasser. 2006, Simon & Schuster $17.95 (978-0-689-86717-0). 74pp. Follow a family as they travel all over the United States, visiting interesting destinations and learning historical, geographical, and cultural facts. (Rev: BL 11/15/06; SLJ 1/07)

18214 Collier, Christopher, and James Lincoln Collier. *The Rise of the Cities: 1820–1920* (5–8). Illus. Series: The Drama of American History. 2001, Marshall Cavendish LB $31.36 (978-0-7614-1051-5). 96pp. In this highly illustrated volume, the Colliers paint a broad picture of the process of urbanization in the United States, tracing the problems involved and the growing prominence of cities in American life. (Rev: BL 3/15/01; HBG 10/01; SLJ 7/01)

18215 Colman, Penny. *Girls: A History of Growing Up Female in America* (5–8). 2000, Scholastic paper $18.95 (978-0-590-37129-2). Using diaries, memoirs, letters, magazine articles, and other sources, the author presents a history of girls in America from the first females to cross the Bering Strait to the present day. (Rev: BCCB 2/00; BL 2/1/00; HBG 10/00; SLJ 3/00) [305.23]

18216 Cooper, Jason. *Árboles / Trees* (4–8). Trans. by Blanca Rey. Series: La Guía de Rourke Para los Símbolos de los Estados/Rourke's Guide to State Symbols. 2002, Rourke LB $20.95 (978-1-58952-399-9). The 50 state trees are introduced in bilingual text and illustrations. Also use *Aves / Birds, Banderas / Flags,* and *Flores / Flowers.* (Rev: SLJ 3/03) [582]

18217 Costain, Meredith, and Paul Collins. *Welcome to the United States of America* (3–5). Illus. Series: Countries of the World. 2001, Chelsea LB $28.00 (978-0-7910-6542-6). 32pp. This basic introduction to the land, people, and culture of the United States will be useful in work with new immigrants and ESL students. (Rev: HBG 3/02; SLJ 2/02)

18218 Croy, Elden. *United States* (4–8). Series: Countries of the World. 2010, National Geographic LB $27.90 (978-1-4263-0632-7). 64pp. In addition to giving an overview of the country's geography, people, culture, history, government, economy, and climate, this volume includes special features such as "Mississippi Flyway" and "Go West, Young Man!" (Rev: BL 4/1/10; SLJ 4/10) [973]

18219 DiPiazza, Francesca. *Friend Me! 600 Years of Social Networking in America* (5–8). Illus. 2012, Lerner $33.26 (978-076135869-5). 112pp. From wampum beads and quilting bees to Facebook and Twitter, this is an interesting survey of modes of communication over the centuries. Lexile 1040L (Rev: BL 4/1/12; LMC 10/12; SLJ 4/12; VOYA 6/12) [302.3]

18220 Dolan, Edward F. *The American Indian Wars* (5–8). Illus. 2003, Millbrook LB $29.90 (978-0-7613-1968-9). 112pp. Four hundred years of conflict are covered in this volume that looks at the causes, details the key battles and events, and provides portraits of the key participants. (Rev: BL 12/1/03)

18221 Firestone, Mary. *The Liberty Bell* (K–4). Illus. by Matthew Skeens. Series: American Symbols. 2006, Picture Window LB $23.93 (978-1-4048-3101-8). 24pp. Contemporary-looking illustrations accompany simple text for an introduction to one of America's best-loved symbols. (Rev: SLJ 5/07)

18222 Fischer, Maureen M. *Nineteenth Century Lumber Camp Cooking* (4–7). Series: Exploring History Through Simple Recipes. 2000, Capstone LB $23.93 (978-0-7368-0604-6). 32pp. After describing life in a lumber camp more than a hundred years ago, this book supplies some authentic recipes. (Rev: BL 3/1/01; HBG 10/01; SLJ 4/01)

18223 Floca, Brian. *Lightship* (PS–2). Illus. 2007, Simon & Schuster $16.99 (978-1-4169-2436-4). This is a detailed and attractive account of the role of lightships — which were used where lighthouses were not suitable; the last one in the United States was retired in 1983. (Rev: BL 2/1/07)

18224 Garland, Michael. *Americana Adventure: A Look Again Book* (1–3). Illus. by author. 2008, Dutton $15.99 (978-0-525-47945-1). On the 4th of July Tommy gets the first in a set of clues from his Aunt Jeanne and finds himself on a tour of the country. (Rev: BL 5/15/08; SLJ 6/08)

18225 Gritzner, Charles F. *The United States of America* (4–6). Illus. Series: Modern World Nations. 2007, Chelsea House LB $30.00 (978-0-7910-9511-9). 142pp. This is a very positive overview of the United States' history, geography, government, economy, and culture. (Rev: BLO 5/5/08)

18226 Haban, Rita D. *How Proudly They Wave: Flags of the Fifty States* (4–9). 1989, Lerner LB $23.93 (978-0-8225-1799-3). Pictures of the state flags are accompanied by background information. (Rev: BL 12/15/89; SLJ 3/90) [929.9]

18227 Haskins, James, and Kathleen Benson. *Africa: A Look Back* (5–8). Series: Drama of African-American History. 2006, Benchmark LB $23.95 (978-0-7614-2148-1). Slave narratives form a substantial portion of this survey of African American culture, tracing its roots back to the western part of Africa. (Rev: SLJ 5/07) [967]

18228 Haskins, Lori. *Spooky America: Four Real Ghost Stories* (2–3). Series: Step into Reading. 2003, Golden paper $3.99 (978-0-375-82500-2). 48pp. Truth and legend are intertwined in these illustrated stories set in Massachusetts, Virginia, Colorado, and California. (Rev: BL 10/1/03; HBG 4/04)

18229 Heinz, Brian J. *Nathan of Yesteryear and Michael of Today* (4–6). Illus. by Joanne Friar. 2006, Lerner LB $22.60 (978-0-7613-2893-3). 32pp. This thought-provoking picture book for older students contrasts the daily life of a 12-year-old boy living today and that of his great-great-grandfather, who lived in the 1880s. (Rev: BL 10/15/06)

18230 Hess, Debra. *The American Flag* (3–5). Series: Symbols of America. 2003, Benchmark LB $25.64 (978-0-7614-1709-5). 39pp. A look back at the many variations of the Stars and Stripes before and since the first one was made (according to legend) by Betsy Ross during the Revolutionary War. (Rev: HBG 4/04; SLJ 3/04)

18231 Hess, Debra. *The Liberty Bell* (3–5). Series: Symbols of America. 2003, Benchmark LB $25.64 (978-0-7614-1713-2). 40pp. A look at the Liberty Bell, its role in the Revolution, and why it is cracked. Also use *Statue of Liberty* (2003). (Rev: HBG 4/04; SLJ 3/04)

18232 Hicks, Terry Allan. *The Bald Eagle* (3–5). Series: Symbols of America. 2006, Benchmark LB $28.50 (978-0-7614-2133-7). 40pp. Information on the bald eagle and its selection as the national bird of the United States are accompanied by archival and contemporary images. Also use *Uncle Sam* (2006). (Rev: SLJ 12/06)

18233 Hopkinson, Deborah. *Up Before Daybreak: Cotton and People in America* (5–8). Illus. 2006, Scholastic $18.99 (978-0-439-63901-9). 128pp. A concise, readable history of the American cotton industry with a focus on laborers, especially children; contains archival photographs, reading list, and bibliography. (Rev: BL 4/15/06*; HB 5/06; LMC 11/06; SLJ 6/06*)

18234 Huey, Lois Miner. *Ick! Yuck! Eew! Our Gross American History* (4–6). Illus. 2013, Millbrook LB $26.60 (978-076139091-6). 48pp. A colorful look at the reality of living in America during the 1700s — and the lack of sanitation, hygiene, and medical and dental care along with the presence of insects, germs, smells, and so forth. **e** (Rev: BL 10/1/13; LMC 5–6/14*; SLJ 9/13) [973]

18235 Johnston, Robert D. *The Making of America* (5–8). 2002, National Geographic $29.95 (978-0-7922-6944-1). An informative and balanced overview of American history, this appealing volume divides American history into eight periods; in addition to the narrative, each period includes profiles of two major figures and examines important issues of the time. (Rev: BL 1/1–15/03; HBG 3/03; SLJ 12/02*) [973]

18236 Jordan, Anne Devereaux, and Virginia Schomp. *Slavery and Resistance* (5–8). Illus. 2006, Marshall Cavendish LB $34.21 (978-0-7614-2178-8). 70pp. A well-illustrated, well-organized history of slavery in America from the first colony in Jamestown up until the Civil War. (Rev: BL 2/1/07; SLJ 5/07)

18237 Keenan, Sheila. *Greetings from the 50 States: How They Got Their Names* (4–6). Illus. by Selina Alko. 2008, Scholastic $18.99 (978-0-439-83439-1). In addition to the states' names and how they got them, this breezy volume looks at mottos, physical features, natural resources, history, and key people; includes the District of Columbia. (Rev: BL 12/15/08; LMC 3/09)

18238 Keenan, Sheila. *O, Say Can You See? America's Symbols, Landmarks, and Important Words* (2–5). Illus. by Ann Boyajian. 2004, Scholastic $16.95 (978-0-439-42450-9). 64pp. The bald eagle, the Pledge of Allegiance, and Veteran's Day are among the holidays, landmarks, symbols, and sayings included in this attractive guide. (Rev: BL 10/15/04)

18239 Leacock, Elspeth, and Susan Buckley. *Journeys in Time: A New Atlas of American History* (4–6). Illus. 2001, Houghton $15.00 (978-0-395-97956-3). 48pp. Twenty dramatic stories of "journeys" drawn from true accounts serve to introduce the history of America in an unusual and effective way. (Rev: BL 6/1–15/01; HB 7/01; HBG 10/01; SLJ 6/01)

18240 Leacock, Elspeth, and Susan Buckley. *Places in Time: A New Atlas of American History* (4–6). Illus. 2001, Houghton $15.00 (978-0-395-97958-7). 48pp. In this companion to *Journeys in Time*, 20 significant sites — towns, battlefields, Ellis Island, even a tract house — are used to convey essential elements of American history. (Rev: BL 6/1–15/01; HB 7/01; HBG 10/01; SLJ 6/01)

18241 Lourie, Peter. *Mississippi River* (3–5). Illus. 2000, Boyds Mills $17.95 (978-1-56397-756-5). 48pp. While describing his trip on the Mississippi from Minnesota to Louisiana, the author gives facts about the waterway and the life that surrounds it. (Rev: BCCB 10/00; BL 10/1/00; HBG 3/01; SLJ 10/00)

18242 Lourie, Peter. *On the Trail of Lewis and Clark: A Journey Up the Missouri River* (3–5). Illus. 2002, Boyds

Mills $19.95 (978-1-56397-936-1). Lourie connects his own trip up the Missouri River to the more famous journey that Lewis and Clark took years before. (Rev: BL 4/1/02; HBG 10/02; SLJ 6/02)

18243 Magaziner, Henry Jonas. *Our Liberty Bell* (2–4). Illus. by John O'Brien. 2007, Holiday $15.95 (978-0-8234-1892-3). 32pp. The Liberty Bell's significance throughout American history is examined in this well-designed volume. (Rev: BL 6/1–15/07; LMC 11/07; SLJ 7/07)

18244 Martin, Bill, Jr., and Michael Sampson. *I Pledge Allegiance* (K–4). Illus. by Chris Raschka. 2002, Candlewick $15.99 (978-0-7636-1648-9). 40pp. The Pledge of Allegiance, which was adopted in 1892, is explained to young readers in simple language. (Rev: BCCB 10/02; BL 9/1/02; HBG 3/03; SLJ 12/02)

18245 Masoff, Joy. *We Are All Americans: Understanding Diversity* (4–7). 2006, Five Ponds $26.50 (978-0-9727156-2-1). This celebration of immigration to America — full of photographs, maps, and diagrams — looks at the reasons for migration, the problems involved, and the contributions made by immigrants in all aspects of American life, including music, sports, games, celebrations, literature, food, and art. (Rev: SLJ 1/07)

18246 Michelson, Richard. *Tuttle's Red Barn: The Story of America's Oldest Family Farm* (1–3). Illus. by Mary Azarian. 2007, Putnam $16.99 (978-0-399-24354-7). 40pp. Michelson chronicles the history of the farm that has been in the Tuttle family for 12 generations. (Rev: BL 10/1/07; HB 1/08; LMC 11/07; SLJ 10/07) [975.1]

18247 Miller, Marilyn. *Words That Built a Nation: A Young Person's Collection of Historic American Documents* (4–8). 1999, Scholastic paper $18.95 (978-0-590-29881-0). A collection of 37 documents important in American history — from the Mayflower Compact and the Declaration of Independence to Hillary Rodham Clinton's address to the United Nations Conference on Women and Malcolm X's "The Ballot or the Bullet" speech. (Rev: BL 10/15/99; HBG 3/00; SLJ 2/00) [973]

18248 Miller, Page Putnam. *Landmarks of American Women's History* (5–8). 2004, Oxford LB $32.95 (978-0-19-514501-4). Landmarks — all on the National Register of Historic Places — highlighted for their importance in women's history include Taos Pueblo, New Mexico, chosen for the strong Native American women who lived there; the Wesleyan Chapel at Seneca Falls, where the first women's rights conference was held; and the Boardinghouse at Boott Cotton Mill in Lowell, Massachusetts, home to many young women who worked in the textile industry. (Rev: SLJ 9/04) [973]

18249 Nelson, Robin. *School* (3–6). Series: First Step Nonfiction. 2003, Lerner LB $18.60 (978-0-8225-4640-5). 24pp. Ideal for new readers, this book looks at how early schools differed from those we know today. Also in this series, use *Toys and Games* (2003). (Rev: BL 11/15/03; HBG 4/04; SLJ 12/03)

18250 Neubecker, Robert. *Wow! America!* (PS–K). Illus. 2006, Hyperion $16.99 (978-0-7868-3816-5). 48pp. In

this rollicking sequel to *Wow! City!* (2004), Izzy and Jo visit some of America's most famous sights. (Rev: BL 4/15/06; SLJ 6/06)

18251 Newman, Shirlee P. *Slavery in the United States* (4–7). Series: Watts Library: History of Slavery. 2000, Watts LB $25.50 (978-0-531-11695-1). This account covers the shameful American record concerning slavery with coverage from the African slave trade through plantation life, the Underground Railroad, and abolitionists to the Civil War and emancipation. (Rev: BL 3/1/01)

18252 Pearl, Norman. *The Bald Eagle* (K–4). Illus. by Matthew Skeens. Series: American Symbols. 2006, Picture Window LB $23.93 (978-1-4048-2642-7). 24pp. Children will enjoy learning about how the bald eagle was selected to serve as a symbol of the United States. Contemporary-looking illustrations accompany simple text in this introduction to one of America's best-loved symbols. (Rev: SLJ 5/07)

18253 Prevost, John. *Mississippi River* (3–4). Series: Rivers and Lakes. 2002, ABDO LB $21.35 (978-1-57765-102-4). A solid introduction to the Mississippi, its tributaries, flora and fauna, and the ways in which it has influenced human development in the area throughout history. (Rev: HBG 10/02; SLJ 7/02)

18254 Rubel, David. *Scholastic Atlas of the United States* (3–5). 2000, Scholastic $19.95 (978-0-590-72562-0). 144pp. Arranged by region and then by state, this atlas also contains a text that gives good background on each state plus maps that indicate principal towns, highways, natural resources, national parks, etc. (Rev: HBG 3/01; SLJ 2/01)

18255 Sabuda, Robert. *America the Beautiful* (2–4). Illus. by author. 2004, Simon & Schuster $26.95 (978-0-689-84744-8). 16pp. Elaborate pop-up spreads salute natural and man-made landmarks, including Mount Rushmore, New York City, Mesa Verde, and the Golden Gate Bridge, and the verses of the well-known song. (Rev: BL 11/15/04; SLJ 11/04)

18256 Siebert, Diane. *Mississippi* (3–5). Illus. 2001, HarperCollins LB $17.89 (978-0-688-16446-1). This volume uses free-verse to describe the history associated with the Mississippi River as well as its course from its beginnings in the north to its mouth on the Gulf of Mexico. (Rev: BL 3/15/01; HBG 10/01)

18257 Sills, Leslie. *From Rags to Riches: A History of Girls' Clothing in America* (4–7). 2005, Holiday $16.95 (978-0-8234-1708-7). Changes in clothing over the centuries are linked to the social mores of the time in this appealing volume. (Rev: BL 5/1/05; SLJ 8/05) [391]

18258 Sís, Peter. *The Train of States* (K–3). 2004, Greenwillow LB $18.89 (978-0-06-057839-8). 64pp. Eye-catching circus wagons representing each of the 50 states (the District of Columbia gets the caboose) are arranged in chronological order and accompanied by pertinent facts. (Rev: BL 10/15/04; SLJ 11/04*)

18259 Sonneborn, Liz. *The Pledge of Allegiance: The Story Behind Our Patriotic Promise* (3–5). Illus. Series: America in Words and Song. 2004, Chelsea House LB

$23.00 (978-0-7910-7336-0). 32pp. This slim volume provides the history of the pledge and the changes it has undergone over the years. (Rev: BL 4/1/04; SLJ 5/04)

18260 Stanley, George E. *The New Republic (1763–1815)* (5–8). Illus. Series: A Primary Source History of the United States. 2005, World Almanac LB $31.00 (978-0-8368-5825-9). 48pp. A simple narrative links well-chosen primary sources documenting the key events of the revolutionary period. (Rev: BL 4/1/05; SLJ 7/05)

18261 Talbott, Hudson. *United Tweets of America* (3–5). Illus. by author. 2008, Putnam $17.99 (978-0-399-24520-6). 64pp. An impish look at the 50 states, introduced through a competition between the state birds. (Rev: BL 4/1/08; SLJ 5/08)

18262 Thro, Ellen, and Andrew K. Frank. *Growing and Dividing* (5–8). Series: The Making of America. 2001, Raintree LB $28.54 (978-0-8172-5704-0). 96pp. The story of the development of the eastern United States from the early days of the Republic through the clashes that led to the Civil War. (Rev: BL 4/15/01; HBG 10/01)

18263 *United States in Pictures* (5–8). Series: Visual Geography. 1995, Lerner LB $25.55 (978-0-8225-1896-9). An attractive basic introduction to the geography, history, and people of the United States. (Rev: BL 8/95) [973]

18264 Uschan, Michael V. *Protests and Riots* (5–8). Series: American History. 2010, Gale LB $33.45 (978-1-4205-0278-7). 112pp. Primary source quotes and period photographs enhance this overview of key protests throughout American history. (Rev: SLJ 4/11) [973]

18265 Wacker, Grant. *Religion in Nineteenth Century America* (5–8). Series: Religion in American Life. 2000, Oxford $32.95 (978-0-19-511021-0). This is the story of how religion in America affected such 19th-century events as the westward movement, the Civil War, and immigration, with additional coverage of the careers of such people as Sojourner Truth and Mary Baker Eddy. (Rev: BL 6/1–15/00; HBG 10/00; SLJ 8/00) [973]

18266 West, Delno C., and Jean M. West. *Uncle Sam and Old Glory: Symbols of America* (2–5). Illus. 2000, Simon & Schuster $17.00 (978-0-689-82043-4). From the bald eagle and the Liberty Bell to Smokey the Bear, this is a history of 15 symbols, their origins, and meanings. (Rev: BCCB 1/00; BL 12/15/99; HBG 10/00; SLJ 1/00)

18267 Woods, Michael, and Mary B. Woods. *Seven Natural Wonders of North America* (5–8). Illus. 2009, Twenty-First Century LB $33.26 (978-0-8225-9069-9). 80pp. Dinosaur Provincial Park, Pacific Rim National Park, the redwood forests, Niagara Falls, the Grand Canyon, Yellowstone National Park, and the Paricutín Volcano are the seven wonders featured in this attractive volume. (Rev: BL 4/1/09; LMC 10/09*; SLJ 5/09) [917]

18268 Yaccarino, Dan. *Go, Go America* (3–5). Illus. by author. 2008, Scholastic $17.99 (978-0-439-70338-3). 80pp. The Farley family takes readers on an entertaining and informative tour of the 50 states, with a combination of key facts and interesting trivia. (Rev: BL 3/1/08; LMC 1/08; SLJ 3/08)

18269 Yeh, Phil. *Dinosaurs Across America* (2–4). Illus. by author. 2007, NBM $12.95 (978-1-56163-509-2). 32pp. Patrick Rabbit gets a lesson on the 50 states from some humorous dinosaurs using an appealing graphic format. (Rev: BL 10/15/07; LMC 1/08; SLJ 3/08)

18270 Yorinks, Adrienne. *Quilt of States: Piecing Together America* (5–8). 2005, National Geographic LB $29.90 (978-0-7922-7286-1). With contributions from librarians from all 50 states, this beautifully illustrated volume offers a brief story of each state's accession to the Union, along with other pertinent facts and figures. (Rev: BL 10/1/05; SLJ 12/05) [973]

Historical Periods

NATIVE AMERICANS

18271 Adams, McCrea. *Tipi* (3–5). Illus. by Kimberly L. Dawson Kurnizki. Series: Native American Homes. 2001, Rourke LB $28.50 (978-1-55916-275-3). 32pp. This volume discusses Native American tipis and how, why, where, and by whom they were built. (Rev: SLJ 3/01)

18272 Aloian, Molly, and Bobbie Kalman. *Nations of the Southeast* (3–5). Illus. Series: Native Nations of North America. 2006, Crabtree LB $26.60 (978-0-7787-0385-3); paper $8.95 (978-0-7787-0477-5). 32pp. An interesting overview of the Native American tribes of the American Southeast, examining their culture, language, customs, and contemporary status. (Rev: SLJ 11/06)

18273 Alter, Judy. *Native Americans* (3–5). Series: Spirit of America: Our Cultural Heritage. 2002, Child's World LB $27.07 (978-1-56766-152-1). This account gives an overview of the history of Native Americans, their problems, and the impact of their cultures on present-day American society. (Rev: BL 10/15/02)

18274 Anderson, Dale. *The Anasazi Culture at Mesa Verde* (5–8). Series: Landmark Events in American History. 2003, World Almanac LB $31.00 (978-0-8368-5371-1). The story of the native people from the region around the Four Corners and of their many cultural accomplishment including basketry, pottery, and urban architecture. (Rev: BL 10/15/03) [973]

18275 Beres, Cynthia Breslin. *Longhouse* (3–5). Illus. by Kimberly L. Dawson Kurnizki. 2001, Rourke LB $28.50 (978-1-55916-247-0). 32pp. This book describes the building and uses of the Native American longhouses and the part they played in the culture. (Rev: SLJ 3/01)

18276 Bial, Raymond. *The Apache* (5–8). Series: Lifeways. 2000, Benchmark LB $34.21 (978-0-7614-0939-7). 128pp. Presents the dramatic, often tragic history of the Apache Indians, with biographies of leaders such as Geronimo and a description of the social and cultural life of these nomadic people. (Rev: BL 11/15/00; HBG 3/01; SLJ 3/01)

18277 Bial, Raymond. *The Cheyenne* (5–8). Series: Lifeways. 2000, Benchmark LB $34.21 (978-0-7614-0938-0). 128pp. Part of the Great Plains Indian group, the Cheyenne's daily life, religious beliefs, social system, and history are introduced in this book. (Rev: BL 11/15/00; HBG 3/01; SLJ 3/01)

18278 Bial, Raymond. *The Delaware* (5–9). Series: Lifeways. 2005, Benchmark LB $23.95 (978-0-7614-1904-4). The history, culture, traditions, and present-day life of the Native American tribe, with photographs and other visuals. (Rev: SLJ 6/06) [974.004]

18279 Bial, Raymond. *The Haida* (5–8). Series: Lifeways. 2000, Benchmark LB $34.21 (978-0-7614-0937-3). 128pp. This book describes these Native Americans of the Northwest and introduces their artistic and carving skills, their social system, beliefs, history, and daily life. (Rev: BL 11/15/00; HBG 3/01; SLJ 3/01)

18280 Bial, Raymond. *The Huron* (5–8). Series: Lifeways. 2000, Benchmark LB $34.21 (978-0-7614-0940-3). 128pp. Color pictures and clear text describe this Indian group's past and present and give details of their daily life, religion, and rituals. (Rev: BL 11/15/00; HBG 3/01; SLJ 3/01)

18281 Bial, Raymond. *Longhouses* (2–5). Series: American Community. 2004, Children's Pr. LB $29.00 (978-0-516-23707-7). 48pp. A look at life in the longhouses of the Iroquois living in the Great Lakes region. (Rev: SLJ 1/05)

18282 Bial, Raymond. *The Mandan* (5–9). Series: Lifeways. 2002, Benchmark LB $34.21 (978-0-7614-1415-5). 126pp. Two traditional stories, a recipe, and a language guide accompany information on the history, culture, beliefs, and key figures of the Mandan people. (Rev: HBG 3/03; LMC 8/03; SLJ 6/03)

18283 Bial, Raymond. *The Menominee* (5–9). Series: Lifeways. 2005, Benchmark LB $23.95 (978-0-7614-1903-7). The history, culture, traditions and present-day life of the Native American tribe, with photographs and other visuals. (Rev: SLJ 6/06) [977.4004]

18284 Bial, Raymond. *The Nez Perce* (5–8). Series: Lifeways. 2001, Marshall Cavendish LB $34.21 (978-0-7614-1210-6). This attractively illustrated account gives basic material on the historical and social aspects of this Native American tribe, including their food, clothing, and culture. (Rev: BL 1/1–15/02; HBG 3/02; SLJ 4/02)

18285 Bial, Raymond. *The Powhatan* (5–8). Series: Lifeways. 2001, Marshall Cavendish LB $34.21 (978-0-7614-1209-0). The story of the Powhatan tribe of Virginia, whose members included Pocahontas, with material on their history and various aspects of their culture. (Rev: BL 1/1–15/02; HBG 3/02)

18286 Bial, Raymond. *The Shoshone* (5–8). Series: Lifeways. 2001, Marshall Cavendish LB $34.21 (978-0-7614-1211-3). The story of the Native American tribe of buffalo hunters who lived in the Northwest, with material on their history, culture, language, food, and clothing. (Rev: BL 1/1–15/02; HBG 3/02)

18287 Birchfield, D. L. *The Trail of Tears* (4–7). Series: Landmark Events in American History. 2003, World Almanac LB $31.00 (978-0-8368-5381-0). 48pp. A brief account of the tragic forced removal of Native American

people from their lands by the U.S. government in the mid-19th century. (Rev: SLJ 6/04)

18288 Bjornlund, Lydia. *The Trail of Tears: The Relocation of the Cherokee Nation* (5–8). Series: American History. 2010, Gale LB $33.45 (978-1-4205-0211-4). 104pp. Primary source quotations and period photographs enhance this account of the tragic journey of the Cherokee away from their homeland. (Rev: SLJ 4/11) [975.004]

18289 Broida, Marian. *Projects About American Indians of the Southwest* (3–5). Illus. Series: Hands-on History. 2003, Marshall Cavendish LB $27.07 (978-0-7614-1602-9). 48pp. The 10 simple projects outlined in this book introduce information about the Navajo, Hopi, Zuni, and Pueblo Indians. (Rev: BL 4/1/04; HBG 4/04; SLJ 4/04)

18290 Bruchac, Joseph. *Navajo Long Walk: The Tragic Story of a Proud People's Forced March from Their Homeland* (4–8). Illus. by Shonto Begay. 2002, National Geographic $18.95 (978-0-7922-7058-4). Using revealing words and pictures, this large picture book for older readers re-creates the shameful story of the deadly marches of the Navajo in the 1860s. (Rev: BL 5/1/02; HBG 10/02; SLJ 7/02) [979.1]

18291 Burgan, Michael. *The Trail of Tears* (3–5). Series: We the People. 2001, Compass Point LB $26.60 (978-0-7565-0101-3). 48pp. A well-illustrated, concise introduction to the Cherokee people and the events leading up to their removal from their lands in 1838. (Rev: SLJ 6/01)

18292 Carew-Miller, Anna. *Native American Cooking* (4–7). Illus. Series: Native American Life. 2002, Mason Crest LB $19.95 (978-1-59084-131-0). 64pp. The role of the environment in Native American food choices is emphasized in this overview that is organized by region. Also use *Native American Tools and Weapons* and *What the Native Americans Wore* (both 2002). (Rev: SLJ 2/03)

18293 Collins, David R., and Kris Bergren. *Ishi: The Last of His People* (5–8). Illus. 2000, Morgan Reynolds LB $23.95 (978-1-883846-54-1). This is the story of Ishi, the ill-clad and half-starved man who emerged from the wilderness in California in 1911 and who was believed to be a survivor of the lost Yahi tribe. (Rev: BL 12/1/00; HBG 10/00)

18294 Cooper, Michael L. *Indian School: Teaching the White Man's Way* (5–10). 1999, Clarion $18.00 (978-0-395-92084-8). A moving photoessay about Native American children and how they were removed from their homes and uprooted from their culture to attend Indian boarding schools in an effort to "civilize" them. (Rev: BL 12/1/99; HBG 3/00; SLJ 2/00; VOYA 4/00) [370]

18295 Cory, Steven. *Pueblo Indian* (5–8). Series: American Pastfinder. 1996, Lerner LB $21.27 (978-0-8225-2976-7). Color illustrations and maps accompany this account of the Pueblo Indians and the incredible cities they built. (Rev: BL 7/96) [973]

18296 Crewe, Sabrina, and Dale Anderson. *The Anasazi Culture at Mesa Verde* (3–5). Series: Events That Shaped America. 2003, Gareth Stevens LB $26.00 (978-0-8368-3390-4). Explores what we know about the ancient Anasazi culture of the American Southwest and why they chose to settle in Mesa Verde. (Rev: HBG 10/03; SLJ 10/03)

18297 Cunningham, Kevin, and Peter Benoit. *The Inuit* (3–5). Illus. Series: A True Book: American Indian. 2011, Scholastic LB $28 (978-053120760-4); paper $6.95 (978-053129302-7). 48pp. Introduces the Inuit people and their history, clothing, diet, survival skills, society, and so forth. Also use *The Comanche, The Navajo,* and *The Zuni* (all 2011). (Rev: BL 9/15/11) [979.8004]

18298 DeAngelis, Therese. *The Cherokee: Native Basket Weavers* (3–5). Illus. Series: America's First Peoples. 2003, Capstone LB $23.93 (978-0-7368-1535-2). 32pp. This fascinating overview of the Cherokee provides a basic introduction to the history and culture of the Native American tribe with particular focus on basket weaving skills. (Rev: SLJ 10/03)

18299 DeAngelis, Therese. *The Ojibwa: Wild Rice Gatherers* (3–5). Illus. Series: America's First Peoples. 2003, Capstone LB $23.93 (978-0-7368-1537-6). 32pp. This title from America's First Families series introduces readers to the history and culture of the Ojibwa, an Algonquian-speaking tribe that traditionally lived in the north central United States and nearby Canada. (Rev: HBG 10/03; SLJ 10/03)

18300 Delgado, James P. *Native American Shipwrecks* (5–7). Illus. Series: Watts Library: Shipwrecks. 2000, Watts LB $25.50 (978-0-531-20379-8). 64pp. This book covers the boats that Native Americans made, their uses and voyages, the culture of these peoples, and how underwater archaeologists have explored their wrecks. (Rev: BL 10/15/00)

18301 Dennis, Yvonne Wakim, and Arlene Hirschfelder. *Children of Native America Today* (3–6). Illus. 2003, Charlesbridge $19.95 (978-1-57091-499-7). 64pp. Photos show contemporary Native American young people wearing traditional as well as modern clothes, with maps, reservation locations, and a resource list. (Rev: BL 3/1/03; HBG 10/03; SLJ 10/03)

18302 Dennis, Yvonne Wakim, and Arlene Hirschfelder. *A Kid's Guide to Native American History: More Than 50 Activities* (4–6). Illus. by Gail Rattray. 2009, Chicago Review paper $16.95 (978-15565280-2-6). 256pp. This collection of activities, crafts, recipes, and games illustrates the regional differences between Native American tribes, and looks at their present lives and customs; includes extensive back matter. (Rev: BL 1/1/10; LMC 11–12/10; SLJ 11/09) [970.004]

18303 Denny, Sidney G., and Ernest L. Schusky. *The Ancient Splendor of Prehistoric Cahokia* (4–8). 1997, Ozark paper $3.95 (978-1-56763-272-9). Using the findings at the Cahokia Mounds in southern Illinois as a beginning, the author re-creates the life and culture of

these prehistoric American Indians. (Rev: BL 5/1/97) [977.3]

18304 Englar, Mary. *The Cherokee and Their History* (3–5). Series: We the People. 2005, Compass Point LB $26.60 (978-0-7565-1273-6). 48pp. Suitable for report writers, this history starts with an account of the Trail of Tears and then covers traditions, achievements, life today, and so forth. Also use *The Sioux and Their History* (2006). (Rev: SLJ 9/06)

18305 Englar, Mary. *The Great Plains Indians: Daily Life in the 1700s* (2–4). Series: Native American Life. 2005, Capstone LB $22.60 (978-0-7368-4315-7). 24pp. A brief, attractive introduction to the tribes of the Great Plains, covering their social structure, homes, food, clothing, and traditions. (Rev: SLJ 12/05)

18306 Englar, Mary. *The Pueblo: Southwestern Potters* (3–5). Illus. Series: America's First Peoples. 2003, Capstone LB $23.93 (978-0-7368-1538-3). 32pp. This appealing introduction to the Pueblo people of America's Southwest focuses on their traditional pottery. (Rev: HBG 10/03; SLJ 10/03)

18307 Feinstein, Stephen. *California Native Peoples* (4–6). Illus. Series: Heinemann State Studies. 2003, Heinemann LB $27.07 (978-1-4034-0341-4). From prehistory to today, this attractively illustrated volume looks at the lives and culture of California's native peoples, with particular focus on "outside influences" that brought upheavals. (Rev: HBG 4/04; SLJ 11/03)

18308 Fischer, Laura. *Life on the Trail of Tears* (2–4). Illus. Series: Picture the Past. 2003, Heinemann LB $22.79 (978-1-4034-3800-3). 32pp. The plight of Cherokee children is highlighted in this attractive introduction to the sad story of forced relocation. (Rev: SLJ 6/04)

18309 Fowler, Verna. *The Menominee* (4–7). Series: Indian Nations. 2000, Raintree LB $25.69 (978-0-8172-5458-2). Opening with a folk tale, this book describes the Menominee Indians, their life and culture, and how they were overrun in the 19th century and pushed onto a reservation in northern Wisconsin. (Rev: BL 3/15/01; HBG 10/01) [973]

18310 Gibson, Karen Bush. *The Great Basin Indians: Daily Life in the 1700s* (2–4). Series: Native American Life. 2005, Capstone LB $22.60 (978-0-7368-4318-8). 24pp. A brief, attractive introduction to the tribes of the Great Basin region, covering their social structure, homes, food, clothing, and traditions. (Rev: SLJ 12/05)

18311 Gold, Susan Dudley. *Indian Treaties* (5–8). Series: Pacts and Treaties. 1997, Twenty-First Century LB $24.90 (978-0-8050-4813-1). A history of the successive treaties under which the Native Americans gradually lost their homes and livelihood. (Rev: BL 5/15/97; SLJ 6/97) [323.1]

18312 Gorsline, Marie, and Douglas Gorsline. *North American Indians* (5–8). Illus. by Douglas Gorsline. 1978, Random House paper $3.25 (978-0-394-83702-4). Major tribes are identified and briefly described. [973]

18313 Gray-Kanatiiosh, Barbara A. *Hopi* (2–4). Illus. by Charles Chimerica. Series: Native Americans. 2002,

ABDO LB $22.78 (978-1-57765-598-5). 32pp. An attractive and accessible introduction to the Hopi people that covers homeland, culture, family life, mythology, crafts, war, early contact with the Europeans, and contemporary lifestyle. Also use *Inuit* (2002). (Rev: HBG 10/02; SLJ 8/02)

18314 Gunderson, Mary. *American Indian Cooking Before 1500* (4–7). Series: Exploring History Through Simple Recipes. 2000, Capstone LB $23.93 (978-0-7368-0605-3). 32pp. This book describes the everyday life of Native Americans before Europeans arrived and gives a few simple recipes. (Rev: BL 3/1/01; HBG 10/01; SLJ 7/01)

18315 Hicks, Terry Allan. *The Chumash* (1–4). Series: First Americans. 2007, Marshall Cavendish LB $20.95 (978-0-7614-2678-3). 48pp. An introduction to these Native Americans from the California region, covering their history, culture, beliefs, current status, and future; with an activity and a recipe. (Rev: SLJ 4/08)

18316 Holm, Tom. *Code Talkers and Warriors: Native Americans and World War II* (5–9). Series: Landmark Events in Native American History. 2007, Chelsea House LB $35.00 (978-0-7910-9340-5). How Native Americans have aided their country in wars (many more than WWII are discussed), with an emphasis on Navajo and Comanche code talk. (Rev: BL 12/15/07) [940.54]

18317 Isaacs, Sally Senzell. *Life in a Hopi Village* (1–3). Series: Picture the Past. 2000, Heinemann $21.36 (978-1-57572-314-3). A well-organized, visually attractive account that describes daily life in a Hopi village and covers such topics as food, clothing, shelter, and care of children. (Rev: HBG 3/01; SLJ 11/00)

18318 Jemison, Mary. *The Diary of Mary Jemison: Captured by the Indians* (3–6). Ed. by Connie Roop and Peter Roop. Illus. Series: My Own Words. 2000, Marshall Cavendish LB $27.07 (978-0-7614-1010-2). 64pp. Based on the account published in 1824, this short, nicely illustrated book tells, in a first-person narrative, how Mary Jemison was captured by Indians at age 12 and describes her life with these Native Americans. (Rev: BL 2/15/01; HBG 3/01; SLJ 3/01)

18319 Kirk, Connie Ann. *The Mohawks of North America* (4–7). Series: First Peoples. 2001, Lerner LB $23.93 (978-0-8225-4853-9). 32pp. This book focuses on the history and cultural practices of the Mohawk people and their present status in America. (Rev: BL 10/15/01; HBG 3/02)

18320 Larson, Timothy. *Anasazi* (4–6). Series: Ancient Civilizations. 2001, Raintree LB $22.83 (978-0-7398-3575-3). 48pp. The history, culture, and daily life of the Anasazi Indians are introduced, with maps and photographs and discussion of archaeological studies and the architecture. (Rev: HBG 3/02; SLJ 6/01)

18321 Lassieur, Allison. *The Apsaalooke (Crow) Nation* (2–5). Series: Native Peoples. 2002, Bridgestone LB $21.26 (978-0-7368-1103-3). 24pp. This account describes the history and lifestyle of this Native American

people who lived on the plains around the Yellowstone River. (Rev: BL 6/1–15/02; HBG 3/03)

18322 Lassieur, Allison. *The Arapaho Tribe* (2–5). Series: Native Peoples. 2001, Bridgestone LB $21.26 (978-0-7368-0945-0). 24pp. Covers the history, culture, and lifestyle of this Native American tribe from the Colorado-Wyoming region. (Rev: BL 3/15/02; HBG 3/02)

18323 Lassieur, Allison. *The Blackfeet Nation* (2–5). Series: Native Peoples. 2001, Bridgestone LB $21.26 (978-0-7368-0946-7). 24pp. A brief, colorful introduction to the past and the present of this midwestern Native American nation whose members dyed their moccasins black. (Rev: BL 3/15/02; HBG 3/02)

18324 Lassieur, Allison. *The Choctaw Nation* (2–5). Illus. Series: Native Peoples. 2001, Capstone $21.26 (978-0-7368-0832-3). 24pp. History and contemporary lifestyle are among the topics covered in this introduction to the Choctaw Indians, the first tribe forced to leave its homeland. Also use *The Shoshone People* (2001). (Rev: BL 5/15/01; HBG 10/01; SLJ 8/01)

18325 Lassieur, Allison. *The Creek Nation* (2–5). Series: Native Peoples. 2001, Bridgestone LB $21.26 (978-0-7368-0947-4). This short history of the Creek people covers present status and conditions as well as offering informative text and full-color historical photographs and illustrations. (Rev: BL 3/15/02; HBG 3/02)

18326 Lassieur, Allison. *The Hopi* (2–5). Series: Native Peoples. 2002, Bridgestone LB $21.26 (978-0-7368-1102-6). 24pp. A brief account with many photographs that describes the past and present of this tribe of Pueblo Indians and gives details on the richness of the culture they developed. (Rev: BL 6/1–15/02)

18327 Lassieur, Allison. *The Navajo: A Proud People* (3–5). Series: American Indians. 2005, Enslow LB $23.93 (978-0-7660-2453-3). 48pp. The history of the Navajo (properly called Diné, the book notes), with information about their accomplishments and their lives today. (Rev: SLJ 5/06)

18328 Lassieur, Allison. *The Pequot Tribe* (2–5). Series: Native Peoples. 2001, Bridgestone LB $21.26 (978-0-7368-0948-1). The story of this Eastern Woodlands group of Native Americans is covered briefly in a simple text with many color illustrations. (Rev: BL 3/15/02; HBG 3/02)

18329 Limberland, Dennis, and Mary Em Parrilli. *The Cheyenne* (4–7). Series: Indian Nations. 2000, Raintree LB $25.69 (978-0-8172-5469-8). 48pp. This history of the Cheyenne Indians begins with a folk tale and goes on to describe their lifestyles before and after being sent to reservations in Oklahoma and Montana. (Rev: BL 3/15/01; HBG 10/01)

18330 Littlefield, Holly. *Children of the Indian Boarding Schools* (3–6). Illus. Series: Picture the American Past. 2001, Carolrhoda LB $22.60 (978-1-57505-467-4). A brief, informative text is accompanied by moving photographs that dramatically tell the sad story of Native American children taken from their homes and sent to boarding schools to learn European customs. (Rev: BL 5/15/01; HBG 10/01; SLJ 7/01)

18331 McCarthy, Cathy. *The Ojibwa* (4–7). Series: Indian Nations. 2000, Raintree LB $25.69 (978-0-8172-5460-5). 48pp. A history of the Ojibwa Indians that includes material on the daily life and traditions of this group that now lives in Minnesota, Wisconsin, and central Canada. (Rev: BL 3/15/01; HBG 10/01)

18332 McLester, L. Gordon, and Elisabeth Towers. *The Oneida* (4–7). Series: Indian Nations. 2000, Raintree LB $25.69 (978-0-8172-5457-5). 48pp. The Oneida left their New York lands for Wisconsin and Canada. Beginning with a folk tale, this account describes their past and present with some indication of what the future holds. (Rev: BL 3/15/01; HBG 10/01)

18333 Margolin, Malcolm, and Yolanda Montijo, eds. *Native Ways: California Indian Stories and Memories* (5–8). 1996, Heyday paper $8.95 (978-0-930588-73-1). Reminiscences and stories reflect California Indian culture, both past and present. (Rev: BL 7/96) [979.4]

18334 Mayfield, Thomas Jefferson. *Adopted by Indians: A True Story* (5–8). Ed. by Malcolm Margolin. 1997, Heyday paper $10.95 (978-0-930588-93-9). This is an adaption of the memoirs of a white man who lived with the Choinumne Indians in California for 10 years, beginning in 1850 when he was 8 years old. (Rev: BL 3/1/98) [979.4]

18335 Meyers, Madeleine, ed. *Cherokee Nation: Life Before the Tears* (4–8). Series: Perspectives on History. 1994, Discovery paper $6.95 (978-1-878668-26-4). A history of the Cherokees that emphasizes the leadership of Sequoyah and the life of the tribe before their forced displacement. (Rev: BL 8/94) [970.3]

18336 Monroe, Judy. *The Northwest Indians: Daily Life in the 1700s* (2–4). Series: Native American Life. 2005, Capstone LB $22.60 (978-0-7368-4316-4). A brief, attractive introduction to the tribes of the Pacific Northwest, covering their social structure, homes, food, clothing, and traditions. (Rev: SLJ 12/05)

18337 Morris, Ann. *Grandma Maxine Remembers: A Native-American Family Story* (1–3). Series: What Was It Like, Grandma? 2002, Millbrook LB $22.90 (978-0-7613-2317-4). Native American culture is explored through the memories of a grandmother who tells about her experiences as young girl. An appropriate activity, recipe, and game are appended. (Rev: BL 9/15/02; HBG 10/02; SLJ 10/02)

18338 Nelson, Sharlene, and Ted Nelson. *The Makah* (4–6). Series: Watts Library. 2003, Watts LB $25.50 (978-0-531-12168-9). 63pp. An accessible introduction to the Makah people of the Northwest Pacific Coast, with material on their history and culture. (Rev: SLJ 5/04)

18339 Noble, Trinka Hakes. *The People of Twelve Thousand Winters* (2–5). Illus. by Jim Madsen. Series: Tales of the World. 2012, Sleeping Bear $16.95 (978-158536529-6). 32pp. Full of details of daily life, this account of Lenni Lenape life in an area now part of New Jersey features 10-year-old Walking Turtle, who worries about the fate of his younger cousin, Little Talk, who is disabled. (Rev: BL 5/1/12; SLJ 5/1/12) [974.004]

18340 Nobleman, Marc Tyler. *The Battle of the Little Bighorn* (4–6). Series: We the People. 2001, Compass Point LB $26.60 (978-0-7565-0150-1). A basic overview of Custer's last stand and the motivations of both sides in the battle. (Rev: SLJ 1/02)

18341 Pasqua, Sandra M. *The Navajo Nation* (2–4). Illus. 2000, Bridgestone LB $21.26 (978-0-7368-0499-8). 24pp. This introduction to the largest group of Native Americans in the U.S. briefly covers their history, culture, government, and daily life. (Rev: BL 10/1/00; HBG 10/00; SLJ 12/00)

18342 Patent, Dorothy Hinshaw. *The Horse and the Plains Indians: A Powerful Partnership* (5–8). Illus. by William Muñoz. 2012, Clarion $17.99 (978-054712551-0). 112pp. The changes horses brought to Plains Indian culture are described in this companion to *The Buffalo and the Indians: A Shared Destiny* (2006). (Rev: BL 8/12; LMC 3–4/13; SLJ 5/1/12*) [978.004]

18343 Peters, Russell. *Clambake: A Wampanoag Tradition* (3–5). Illus. by John Madama. Series: We Are Still Here: Native Americans Today. 1992, Lerner LB $21.27 (978-0-8225-2651-3); paper $6.95 (978-0-8225-9621-9). 48pp. Origins and present-day observations of the traditional ceremony that we know as a clambake. (Rev: BCCB 11/92; SLJ 12/92)

18344 Philip, Neil, ed. *A Braid of Lives: Native American Childhood* (4–8). 2000, Clarion $20.00 (978-0-395-64528-4). Twenty vignettes of one or two pages in length give a many-faceted picture of growing up Native American in different parts of the county. (Rev: BL 10/1/00; HBG 10/01; SLJ 6/01; VOYA 4/01) [973]

18345 Philip, Neil, ed. *In a Sacred Manner I Live: Native American Wisdom* (4–8). 1997, Clarion $20.00 (978-0-395-84981-1). More than 30 Native American leaders — including Geronimo and Cochise — are quoted on topics relating to the conduct of life and their beliefs. (Rev: BL 7/97; HBG 3/98; SLJ 12/97) [973]

18346 Press, Petra. *The Pueblo* (3–6). Series: First Reports. 2001, Compass Point LB $22.60 (978-0-7565-0082-5). 48pp. An absorbing, well-illustrated account of the Pueblo people that covers religion, society, history, culture, and lifestyle today. (Rev: SLJ 7/01)

18347 Quigley, Mary. *Mesa Verde* (4–6). Illus. Series: Excavating the Past. 2005, Heinemann LB $31.43 (978-1-4034-5997-8). 48pp. The work of archaeologists is clearly shown in this well-illustrated exploration of the Mesa Verde site and the people who created it. (Rev: SLJ 2/06)

18348 Rasmussen, R. Kent. *Pueblo* (3–5). Illus. by Kimberly L. Dawson Kurnizki. 2001, Rourke LB $28.50 (978-1-55916-249-4). The amazing clay-based homes and villages of the Pueblo Indians are highlighted in this account that explains how they were built, their parts, and their many uses. (Rev: SLJ 3/01)

18349 Ray, Kurt. *Native Americans and the New American Government: Treaties and Promises* (4–6). Illus. Series: Life in the New American Nation. 2004, Rosen LB $22.50 (978-0-8239-4035-6). 32pp. The often fractious relations between Native Americans and the federal government are explored. (Rev: BL 6/1–15/04)

18350 Riehecky, Janet. *The Cree Tribe* (2–5). Series: Native Peoples. 2002, Capstone LB $21.26 (978-0-7368-1366-2). 24pp. A brief introduction to these Plains Indians with details on their past and present and an emphasis on their place in today's world. (Rev: BL 3/15/03; HBG 3/03)

18351 Riehecky, Janet. *The Osage* (2–5). Series: Native Peoples. 2002, Capstone LB $21.26 (978-0-7368-1367-9). 24pp. This introduction to these Plains Indians tells about their history, culture, and how they live today. (Rev: BL 3/15/03; HBG 3/03)

18352 Rosinsky, Natalie M. *The Wampanoag and Their History* (3–6). Illus. Series: We the People. 2005, Compass Point LB $26.60 (978-0-7565-0847-0). 48pp. A concise introduction to the Wampanoag people, their way of life, and the impact of the arrival of the colonists. [974]

18353 Ryan, Marla Felkins, and Linda Schmittroth, eds. *Abenaki* (3–6). Series: Tribes of Native America. 2004, Gale LB $23.70 (978-1-56711-574-1). A richly illustrated look at the Abenaki people of northern New England and southeastern Canada, their history, and their traditional and contemporary customs. Also use *Chickasaw* and *Chinook* (both 2004). (Rev: SLJ 5/04)

18354 Salas, Laura Purdie. *The Trail of Tears, 1838* (4–6). Illus. Series: Let Freedom Ring. 2003, Capstone LB $23.93 (978-0-7368-1559-8). 48pp. Examines the government's removal of the Cherokee from their homelands, their forced march to reservations in Indian Territory, the challenges they faced their, and their status today. (Rev: HBG 10/03; LMC 11/03; SLJ 12/03)

18355 Santella, Andrew. *The Cherokee* (2–3). Series: True Books: American Indians. 2001, Children's Book Pr. paper $6.95 (978-0-516-27315-0). 48pp. This simple, colorful introduction to the Cherokee Indians covers topics such as their homelands, traditions and customs, history, and present status. (Rev: BL 8/1/01)

18356 Schonberg, Marcia. *Ohio Native Peoples* (4–6). Illus. Series: Heinemann State Studies. 2003, Heinemann LB $27.07 (978-1-4034-0667-5). 48pp. This historical survey of the native peoples who have called Ohio home covers roughly 13,000 years of history. (Rev: HBG 4/04; SLJ 10/03)

18357 Seymour, Tryntje Van Ness. *The Gift of Changing Woman* (5–8). 1993, Henry Holt $16.95 (978-0-8050-2577-4). A description of the Apache initiation rite for young women in picture-book format, illustrated by Apache artists. (Rev: BL 11/15/93; SLJ 3/94) [299]

18358 Siegel, Beatrice. *Indians of the Northeast Woodlands* (4–8). Illus. by William Sauts Bock. 1991, Walker LB $14.85 (978-0-8027-8157-4). In question-and-answer format — following the original 1972 edition — this volume contains much information on Native Americans in New England. (Rev: BL 11/15/92) [973]

18359 Smith, Karla. *Virginia Native Peoples* (4–6). 2003, Heinemann LB $27.07 (978-1-4034-0363-6). 48pp. Introduces readers to the native peoples who resided in the state before and after the arrival of European settlers. (Rev: HBG 4/04; SLJ 12/03)

18360 Smithyman, Kathryn, and Bobbie Kalman. *Native North American Foods and Recipes* (3–5). Illus. Series: Native Nations of North America. 2006, Crabtree LB $26.60 (978-0-7787-0383-9); paper $8.95 (978-0-7787-0475-1). Maple sugar, wild rice, squash, and corn are just a few of the foods mentioned in this survey of the Native American diet and methods of food preparation and conservation. (Rev: SLJ 11/06)

18361 Sneve, Virginia Driving Hawk, ed. *Enduring Wisdom: Sayings from Native Americans* (3–6). Illus. by Synthia Saint James. 2003, Holiday House $16.95 (978-0-8234-1455-0). 32pp. A picture-book collection of sayings from 1647 to the present day that are backed up by helpful endnotes. (Rev: BL 3/15/03; HBG 10/03; SLJ 5/03)

18362 Sonneborn, Liz. *The Apache* (3–5). Illus. 2005, Watts LB $25.50 (978-0-531-12295-2). 64pp. Explores the history and culture of the Apache people, with period and contemporary illustrations and a timeline. (Rev: BL 7/05)

18363 Sonneborn, Liz. *The New York Public Library Amazing Native American History: A Book of Answers for Kids* (5–8). 1999, Wiley paper $16.95 (978-0-471-33204-6). Organized by regions and using a question-and-answer approach, this is a fine overview of the history of Native Americans, ending with a chapter on contemporary conditions. (Rev: BL 5/1/00; SLJ 7/00) [970.004]

18364 Stone, Amy M. *Creek* (4–8). Series: Native American Peoples. 2004, Gareth Stevens LB $26.00 (978-0-8368-4217-3). History, tradition, and contemporary life are described with photographs, timeline, fact boxes, and activities. (Rev: SLJ 1/05) [973]

18365 Stout, Mary. *Blackfoot* (4–8). Series: Native American Peoples. 2004, Gareth Stevens LB $26.00 (978-0-8368-4216-6). History, tradition, and contemporary life are described with photographs, timeline, fact boxes, and activities. (Rev: SLJ 1/05) [973]

18366 Sundling, Charles W. *Native Americans of the Frontier* (4–6). Illus. Series: Frontier Land. 2000, ABDO $24.21 (978-1-57765-042-3). 32pp. A simple text and many illustrations are used in this accessible account of the daily life of the American Plains Indians during the 19th century. (Rev: BL 10/15/00; HBG 10/00; SLJ 6/00)

18367 Thompson, Linda. *The California People* (4–7). Series: Native People, Native Lands. 2003, Rourke LB $29.93 (978-1-58952-753-9). One of a well-illustrated series on individual groups of native Americans, with attention to the negative impact of the arrival of European settlers. Other titles in the series include *People of the Northwest and Subarctic*, *People of the Great Basin*, *People of the Northeast Woodlands*, and *People of the Plains and Prairies* (all 2003). (Rev: SLJ 4/04) [979.4]

18368 Walker, Niki, and Bobbie Kalman. *Native North American Wisdom and Gifts* (3–5). Illus. Series: Native Nations of North America. 2006, Crabtree LB $26.60 (978-0-7787-0384-6); paper $8.95 (978-0-7787-0476-8). 32pp. Culture, hunting traditions, medicine and health, language, sports and games, are all covered in this survey of Native American beliefs and respect for the environment. (Rev: SLJ 11/06)

18369 Williams, Suzanne M. *Tlingit Indians* (2–4). Illus. Series: Native Americans. 2003, Heinemann LB $22.79 (978-1-4034-0868-6). 32pp. A look at the Tlingit native people of the northwest Pacific coast and their lives before and after the arrival of white settlers. (Rev: SLJ 5/04)

18370 Wood, Marion, and Brian Williams. *Ancient America. Rev. ed.* (5–8). Illus. Series: Cultural Atlas for Young People. 2003, Facts on File $35.00 (978-0-8160-5145-8). 96pp. Colorful topical spreads introduce readers to Native American history from the end of the Ice Age to the arrival of European explorers and conquerers. (Rev: SLJ 1/04)

18371 Woods, Geraldine. *The Navajo* (5–7). Illus. Series: Watts Library: Indians of the Americas. 2002, Watts paper $8.95 (978-0-531-16227-9). 64pp. This account includes information on history and contemporary issues and covers the Navajo code talkers, land disputes, traditions, housing, and clothing. (Rev: BL 7/02)

18372 Young, Robert. *A Personal Tour of Mesa Verde* (4–7). Series: How It Was. 1999, Lerner LB $30.35 (978-0-8225-3577-5). This book gives a special glimpse into the lives of the Native Americans known as the Puebloans, how they lived, and the culture they developed. (Rev: BL 6/1–15/99; HBG 10/99; SLJ 7/99) [978.8]

18373 Yue, Charlotte, and David Yue. *The Wigwam and the Longhouse* (4–9). Illus. by authors. 2000, Houghton Mifflin $15.00 (978-0-395-84169-3). A well-balanced account that describes the life and history of several tribes of Native Americans from the eastern woodlands. (Rev: HB 7–8/00; HBG 10/00; SLJ 10/00; VOYA 12/00) [973]

18374 Zimmerman, Dwight Jon. *Saga of the Sioux: An Adaptation of Dee Brown's Bury My Heart at Wounded Knee* (5–8). Illus. 2011, Henry Holt $18.99 (978-0-8050-9364-3). 240pp. This adaptation of Dee Brown's classic work provides a short history of the Sioux tribe and examines the events leading up to the Wounded Knee massacre. (Rev: BL 10/1/11; LMC 11–12/11; SLJ 9/1/11; VOYA 8/11) [978]

DISCOVERY AND EXPLORATION

18375 Arenstam, Peter. *Mayflower 1620: A New Look at a Pilgrim Voyage* (5–9). 2003, National Geographic $17.95 (978-0-7922-6142-1). A large-format photoessay of a voyage of the *Mayflower II* — re-creating the original journey — is the backdrop for detail about the 1620 passengers, supplies, navigation techniques, and the new country they arrived in. (Rev: BL 11/1/03; HBG 4/04; SLJ 11/03) [974.4]

18376 Armentrout, David, and Patricia Armentrout. *The Mayflower Compact* (4–7). 2004, Rourke $20.95 (978-1-59515-229-9). 48pp. The reasons for the creation of this document — a political statement signed by a group of *Mayflower* passengers — are thoroughly explored in concise text, accompanied by an array of maps and illustrations. (Rev: BL 10/15/04)

18377 Aykroyd, Clarissa. *Exploration of the California Coast* (4–7). Series: Exploration and Discovery. 2002, Mason Crest LB $19.95 (978-1-59084-043-6). 64pp. Explorers such as Cortes and Drake are covered in this look at 16th-century California. (Rev: SLJ 12/02)

18378 Cook, Peter. *You Wouldn't Want to Sail on the Mayflower! A Trip That Took Entirely Too Long* (3–6). Illus. by Kevin Whelan. Series: You Wouldn't Want to . . . 2005, Watts LB $29.00 (978-0-531-12411-6); paper $9.95 (978-0-531-12391-1). An engaging account of the grim realities and hardships of the Pilgrims' voyage, with cartoon art, a diagram of the ship's layout, and maps. (Rev: SLJ 3/06)

18379 Dell, Pamela. *The Plymouth Colony* (4–6). Series: Let Freedom Ring. 2004, Capstone LB $23.93 (978-0-7368-2463-7). 48pp. With large type and bright design, this volume explores the hardships and triumphs of the Pilgrims. (Rev: SLJ 8/04)

18380 Eisenberg, Jana. *Lewis and Clark: Path to the Pacific* (4–6). Series: Trailblazers of the West. 2005, Children's Pr. LB $24.50 (978-0-516-25126-4); paper $6.95 (978-0-516-25096-0). 48pp. The hardships on this epic expedition, and the relations with Native Americans, are portrayed in short chapters suitable for reluctant readers. (Rev: SLJ 4/06)

18381 Faber, Harold. *Lewis and Clark: From Ocean to Ocean* (5–8). Illus. Series: Great Explorations. 2001, Benchmark LB $29.93 (978-0-7614-1241-0). 80pp. This concise, artfully illustrated volume about the journey of Lewis and Clark includes journal entries, a timeline, and Web site information. (Rev: BL 1/1–15/02; HBG 3/02; SLJ 3/02)

18382 Gioia, Robyn. *America's Real First Thanksgiving: St. Augustine, Florida, September 8, 1565* (3–6). Illus. 2007, Pineapple LB $14.95 (978-1-56164-389-9). 48pp. The first Thanksgiving might have taken place in Florida, claims this author, when the Spanish explorer Pedro Menéndez de Avilés feasted with the Timucua in 1565. (Rev: SLJ 6/07)

18383 Gunderson, Jessica. *The Lewis and Clark Expedition* (4–6). Illus. by Steven Erwin and Keith Williams,. Series: Graphic Library: Graphic History. 2006, Capstone LB $25.26 (978-0-7368-6493-0). 32pp. The difficulty and significance of the expedition are made clear in this graphic presentation. (Rev: SLJ 5/07)

18384 Gunderson, Mary. *Cooking on the Lewis and Clark Expedition* (3–6). 2000, Capstone LB $23.93 (978-0-7368-0354-0). 32pp. As well as historical material on the Lewis and Clark expedition, this book contains a number of modern recipes for food that might have been eaten on this memorable journey. (Rev: HBG 10/00; SLJ 12/00)

18385 Hart, Avery, and Paul Mantell. *Who Really Discovered America? Unraveling the Mystery and Solving the Puzzle* (5–7). Illus. by Michael Kline. Series: A Kaleidoscope Kids Book. 2001, Williamson paper $12.95 (978-1-885593-46-7). 96pp. Several theories are presented about the discovery of America, and students are urged to examine them with open minds, using activities that help them to question and explore. (Rev: SLJ 10/01)

18386 Johmann, Carol A. *The Lewis and Clark Expedition: Join the Corps of Discovery to Explore Uncharted Territory* (4–6). Illus. by Michael Kline. Series: Kaleidoscope Kids. 2002, Williamson paper $14.25 (978-1-885593-73-3). 112pp. This is a wide-ranging and lively history of the expedition, providing profiles of the explorers, excerpts from journals, lists of resources, and activities. (Rev: BL 1/1–15/03; SLJ 3/03)

18387 King, David C. *Projects About the Spanish West* (3–5). Illus. Series: Hands-on History. 2005, Benchmark LB $18.95 (978-0-7614-1982-2). 47pp. The projects outlined in this book — including a yarn picture, a luminaria, an ojo de Dios (eye of God), and a piñata — are designed to help students understand the early Spanish exploration and colonization of the American West. (Rev: SLJ 4/06)

18388 Lourie, Peter. *On the Trail of Sacagawea* (4–6). Illus. 2001, Boyds Mills $18.95 (978-1-56397-840-1). In this handsome pictorial account of a family trip retracing the steps of Lewis and Clark, the author interweaves their contemporary experiences and historical notes. (Rev: BL 5/1/01; HBG 3/02; SLJ 4/01)

18389 Owens, L. L. *Pilgrims in America* (4–6). 2007, Rourke LB $29.93 (978-1-60044-122-6). 48pp. A well-illustrated overview of the Pilgrims who settled in Plymouth, explaining who they were and covering their trip to the New World, the first Thanksgiving, and relations with the native peoples. (Rev: SLJ 4/07)

18390 Patent, Dorothy Hinshaw. *Animals on the Trail with Lewis and Clark* (4–8). Illus. by William Muñoz. 2002, Clarion $18.00 (978-0-395-91415-1). A handsome account of the Lewis and Clark expedition with emphasis on the animals that were discovered during the journey. (Rev: BCCB 5/02; BL 4/15/02*; HB 5–6/02; HBG 10/02; SLJ 4/02) [917.804]

18391 Perritano, John. *Spanish Missions* (3–7). Series: A True Book. 2010, Children's Press LB $26 (978-0-531-20575-4). 48pp. A look at Spanish mission buildings, with beautiful color photographs and discussion of their history and the impact of the missions on the Native Americans. Lexile 950L (Rev: BL 11/15/10; LMC 8–9/10) [266.27]

18392 Pringle, Laurence. *The Dog of Discovery: A Newfoundland's Adventures with Lewis and Clark* (4–6). Illus. by Meryl Henderson. 2002, Boyds Mills $16.95 (978-1590780282). A Newfoundland dog named Seaman was a valued member of the Lewis and Clark expedition, and his story is told here, based on entries in

the explorers' journals and illustrated with drawings and photographs. (Rev: BL 12/1/02; SLJ 3/03)

18393 Quiri, Patricia R. *The Lewis and Clark Expedition* (3–6). Series: We the People. 2000, Compass Point LB $26.60 (978-0-7565-0044-3). 48pp. A profusely illustrated, readable account of the Lewis and Clark expedition that makes for a good introductory overview. (Rev: SLJ 2/01)

18394 Roberts, Russell. *Pedro Menendez de Aviles* (5–7). Series: Latinos in American History. 2002, Mitchell Lane LB $29.95 (978-1-58415-150-0). This account of explorer Pedro Menendez de Aviles's efforts to procure Florida for Spain uses some fictionalized narrative to illustrate the times. (Rev: BL 10/15/02; HBG 3/03; SLJ 10/02) [975.9]

18395 Roop, Peter, and Connie Roop. *River Roads West* (5–8). Illus. 2007, Boyds Mills $19.95 (978-1-59078-430-3). 60pp. The Hudson, Ohio, and Mississippi rivers and the Erie Canal are among the American waterways introduced in this large-format book that discusses the Native American peoples who lived along them and the impact of European exploration and settlement. (Rev: BL 9/15/07; SLJ 9/07)

18396 Stefoff, Rebecca. *Exploration and Settlement* (5–9). Series: Colonial Life. 2007, Sharpe Focus $37.95 (978-0-7656-8108-9). 96pp. With color illustrations and interesting sidebars, this volume looks at the progress of exploration in the 15th and 16th centuries and includes profiles of key explorers. (Rev: SLJ 1/08)

18397 Stefoff, Rebecca. *Exploring the New World* (4–7). Illus. Series: North American Historical Atlases. 2000, Benchmark LB $27.07 (978-0-7614-1056-0). Using historical maps and reproductions, the important explorers and their accomplishments are covered in this slim, attractive volume. (Rev: HBG 3/01; SLJ 1/01)

18398 Steins, Richard. *Exploration and Settlement* (5–8). Illus. Series: Making of America. 2000, Raintree LB $28.54 (978-0-8172-5700-2). 96pp. This account begins with prehistoric migrations to North America and continues with European explorers, including the Spanish, English, French, and Dutch. (Rev: BL 5/1/00; HBG 10/00; SLJ 9/00)

18399 Whiting, Jim. *Francisco Vasquez de Coronado* (5–7). Series: Latinos in American History. 2002, Mitchell Lane LB $29.95 (978-1-58415-146-3). This account of Francisco Vasquez de Coronado's search for the lost cities of gold, and his subsequent trial for cruelty to Native Americans, uses some fictionalized narrative. (Rev: BL 10/15/02; HBG 3/03; SLJ 10/02; VOYA 6/03) [979]

18400 Wittmann, Kelly. *The European Rediscovery of America* (4–7). Series: Exploration and Discovery. 2002, Mason Crest LB $19.95 (978-1-59084-052-8). 64pp. Wittmann looks at the explorers of the 15th and 16th centuries, including Columbus and Cabot. (Rev: SLJ 12/02)

COLONIAL PERIOD

18401 Allman, Melinda, ed. *Primary Sources* (5–8). Series: Thirteen Colonies. 2002, Gale LB $27.45 (978-1-59018-011-2). 112pp. A fascinating collection of primary source material for the young researcher. (Rev: BL 9/15/02; SLJ 10/02)

18402 Altman, Linda J. *Trade and Commerce* (5–9). Series: Colonial Life. 2007, Sharpe Focus $37.95 (978-0-7656-8111-9). 96pp. With color illustrations and interesting sidebars, this volume looks at trade and commerce in the colonies. (Rev: SLJ 1/08)

18403 Bauer, Brandy. *The Virginia Colony* (2–4). Series: Fact Finders: The American Colonies. 2005, Capstone LB $23.93 (978-0-7368-2684-6). 32pp. A very basic overview of the geography, history, religion, and everyday life of the Virginia colony, with large type and short paragraphs. (Rev: SLJ 12/05)

18404 Boraas, Tracey. *The Salem Witch Trials* (4–6). Series: Let Freedom Ring. 2004, Capstone LB $23.93 (978-0-7368-2464-4). A clear explanation of the trials, with background information that aids understanding plus lots of illustrations and a large-size text that will appeal to reluctant readers. (Rev: SLJ 8/04)

18405 Britton, Tamara. *The Georgia Colony* (3–4). Series: The Colonies. 2001, ABDO LB $22.78 (978-1-57765-583-1). The history of the colony is presented here, with information on both the settlers and the Native Americans of the area and on housing, clothing, and the economy. Also use *Roanoke: The Lost Colony* (2001). (Rev: HBG 3/02; SLJ 4/02)

18406 Broida, Marian. *Projects About Colonial Life* (3–5). Illus. Series: Hands-on History. 2003, Marshall Cavendish LB $27.07 (978-0-7614-1603-6). 48pp. The easy-to-follow projects in this slim volume offer students new insights into life in colonial America. (Rev: BL 4/1/04; HBG 4/04; SLJ 3/04)

18407 Brown, Gene. *Discovery and Settlement: Europe Meets the New World (1490-1700)* (5–7). Series: First Person America. 1993, Twenty-First Century LB $20.90 (978-0-8050-2574-3). Using excerpts from original documents, this book covers the exploration of the United States, the Puritans, and the role of Native Americans, African Americans, and women in early colonial days. (Rev: SLJ 3/94) [973.2]

18408 Burgan, Michael. *The Boston Massacre* (3–6). Illus. Series: We the People. 2005, Compass Point LB $26.60 (978-0-7565-0832-6). 48pp. Describes the 1770 protest against the British that ended in violence. [973]

18409 Burgan, Michael. *The Salem Witch Trials* (4–6). Series: We the People. 2005, Compass Point LB $26.60 (978-0-7565-0845-6). 48pp. Details the 1692 trials and places them in historical context. (Rev: SLJ 6/05)

18410 Burgan, Michael. *The Stamp Act of 1765* (3–6). Illus. Series: We the People. 2005, Compass Point LB $26.60 (978-0-7565-0846-3). 48pp. A concise account of the American colonists' rebellion against a new British tax. [973]

18411 Butler, Jon. *Religion in Colonial America* (5–8). Series: Religion in American Life. 2000, Oxford $32.95 (978-0-19-511998-5). This book describes the mix of Catholics, Jews, Africans, Native Americans, Puritans, and various Protestant faiths that coexisted during colonial times. (Rev: BL 6/1–15/00; HBG 10/00) [973.2]

18412 Carter, E. J. *The Mayflower Compact* (4–6). Series: Historical Documents. 2003, Heinemann LB $27.07 (978-1-4034-0803-7). 48pp. A study of the Mayflower Compact, the agreement signed by Pilgrims aboard the *Mayflower* that would effectively form their government in the New World, with suitable illustrations and maps. (Rev: SLJ 5/04)

18413 Daugherty, James. *The Landing of the Pilgrims* (5–7). Illus. by author. 1981, Random House paper $5.99 (978-0-394-84697-2). Based on his own writings, this is the story of the Pilgrims from the standpoint of William Bradford. [974.4]

18414 Day, Nancy. *Your Travel Guide to Colonial America* (4–8). Series: Passport to History. 2000, Lerner LB $26.50 (978-0-8225-3079-4). 96pp. Using a modern-day guidebook format, this account takes the reader back to colonial times with glimpses of the *Mayflower* and visits to such colonies as Jamestown, Virginia, and Plymouth, Massachusetts. (Rev: BL 3/1/01; HBG 10/01; SLJ 4/01)

18415 De Capua, Sarah. *The Virginia Colony* (3–6). Series: Our Thirteen Colonies. 2003, Child's World LB $28.50 (978-1-56766-711-0). 40pp. A profile of colonial-era Virginia, with a concentration on its role in early steps toward U.S. nationhood. (Rev: SLJ 6/04)

18416 Deady, Kathleen W. *The Massachusetts Bay Colony* (2–4). Illus. Series: Fact Finders: American Colonies. 2005, Capstone LB $23.93 (978-0-7368-2676-1). Researchers will find solid information on the colony, covering education, religion, work, trade, and community life. (Rev: BL 10/15/05)

18417 Deady, Kathleen W. *The New Hampshire Colony* (2–4). Series: Fact Finders: The American Colonies. 2005, Capstone LB $23.93 (978-0-7368-2677-8). 32pp. A very basic overview of the geography, history, religion, and everyday life of the New Hampshire colony, with large type and short paragraphs. (Rev: SLJ 12/05)

18418 Doeden, Matt. *The Boston Tea Party* (4–6). Illus. Series: Graphic History. 2005, Capstone LB $26.60 (978-0-7368-3846-7). 32pp. An eye-catching and dramatically worded graphic presentation of the tax revolt.

18419 Doherty, Kieran. *Puritans, Pilgrims, and Merchants: Founders of the Northeastern Colonies* (4–8). 1999, Oliver LB $22.95 (978-1-881508-50-2). A history of each of the northeastern colonies is supplemented with brief biographies of such people as William Bradford, John Winthrop, Peter Stuyvesant, Anne Hutchinson, and William Penn. (Rev: BL 8/99; HBG 3/00; SLJ 1/00) [974]

18420 Doherty, Kieran. *Soldiers, Cavaliers, and Planters: Settlers of the Southeastern Colonies* (4–8). 1999, Oliver LB $22.95 (978-1-881508-51-9). This book focuses on the early southern colonies and their founders and leaders, among them Captain John Smith, Sir Walter Raleigh, and Pedro Menendez de Aviles. (Rev: BL 8/99; HBG 3/00; SLJ 10/99) [975]

18421 Dosier, Susan. *Colonial Cooking* (4–7). Illus. Series: Exploring History Through Simple Recipes. 2000, Capstone LB $23.93 (978-0-7368-0352-6). 32pp. This work covers the home life of the colonialists in the North, with material on kitchens, celebrations, food, and some recipes. (Rev: BL 8/00; HBG 10/00)

18422 Dubois, Muriel L. *The Delaware Colony* (2–4). Series: Fact Finders: The American Colonies. 2005, Capstone LB $23.93 (978-0-7368-2673-0). 32pp. A very basic overview of the geography, history, religion, and everyday life of the Delaware colony, with large type and short paragraphs. (Rev: SLJ 12/05)

18423 Dubois, Muriel L. *The New Jersey Colony* (2–4). Series: Fact Finders: The American Colonies. 2005, Capstone LB $23.93 (978-0-7368-2678-5). 32pp. A very basic overview of the geography, history, religion, and everyday life of the New Jersey colony, with large type and short paragraphs. (Rev: SLJ 12/05)

18424 Englar, Mary. *Dutch Colonies in America* (4–6). Series: We the People. 2008, Compass Point LB $26.60 (978-0-7565-3837-8). 48pp. An introduction to how the Dutch colonies were claimed and explored; also use *French Colonies in America* (2008). (Rev: SLJ 6/09)

18425 Erickson, Paul. *Daily Life in the Pilgrim Colony 1636* (3–5). Illus. Series: Daily Life. 2001, Clarion $20.00 (978-0-618-05846-4). Text, drawings, photographs, and maps describe how the Pilgrims lived at the Plymouth colony in 1636. (Rev: BL 10/1/01; HBG 3/02; SLJ 10/01)

18426 Fischer, Laura. *Life in New Amsterdam* (2–4). Illus. Series: Picture the Past. 2003, Heinemann LB $24.22 (978-1-4034-3798-3). 32pp. A simple, illustrated account of what daily life was like in what is now New York City. (Rev: SLJ 4/04)

18427 Fisher, Leonard Everett. *The Hatters* (4–6). Illus. Series: Colonial Craftsmen. 2000, Marshall Cavendish LB $21.36 (978-0-7614-1146-8). 48pp. This book supplies a glimpse into the hat trade of the 17th and 18th centuries with material on how different hats were made, worn, and marketed. Also use *The Potters* (2000). (Rev: BL 3/15/01; HBG 10/01)

18428 Fisher, Leonard Everett. *The Papermakers* (4–6). Series: Colonial Craftsmen. 2000, Marshall Cavendish LB $21.36 (978-0-7614-1147-5). 48pp. A reissue of this beautifully illustrated work that describes the process of manufacturing, selling, and using paper during colonial times. Also use from the same series *The Tanners* (2000). (Rev: BL 3/15/01; HBG 10/01)

18429 Fishkin, Rebecca. *English Colonies in America* (4–6). Series: We the People. 2008, Compass Point LB $26.60 (978-0-7565-3838-5). 48pp. An introduction to how England's culture shaped the new colonies. (Rev: SLJ 6/09)

18430 Fradin, Dennis B. *Jamestown, Virginia* (3–5). Illus. Series: Turning Points in U.S. History. 2006, Mar-

shall Cavendish LB $29.93 (978-0-7614-2122-1). This volume discusses Jamestown's founding, the dire conditions of its early settlers, and the critical aid provided by Native Americans as well as new arrivals to the settlement. (Rev: BL 1/1–15/07)

18431 Fritz, Jean. *The Lost Colony of Roanoke* (3–5). Illus. by Hudson Talbott. 2004, Penguin $17.99 (978-0-399-24027-0). 64pp. Fritz interweaves facts and speculation in this captivating and well-illustrated account of the lost colony. (Rev: BL 4/1/04; HB 5/04; SLJ 5/04)

18432 Gillis, Jennifer Blizin. *Life in Colonial Boston* (2–4). Illus. Series: Picture the Past. 2003, Heinemann LB $24.22 (978-1-4034-3795-2). 32pp. An introductory look at Boston in the late pre-Revolutionary War era (1760–1773), with information on what life was like for its residents at home, at school, and at work. (Rev: SLJ 4/04)

18433 Gillis, Jennifer Blizin. *Life in New France* (2–4). Illus. Series: Picture the Past. 2003, Heinemann LB $24.22 (978-1-4034-3799-0). 32pp. A sampling of everyday colonial life in "New France" — the French colonies in eastern Canada and Louisiana — with illustrations, timelines, and maps. (Rev: SLJ 4/04)

18434 Girod, Christina M. *South Carolina* (5–8). Series: Thirteen Colonies. 2002, Gale LB $27.45 (978-1-56006-994-2). 96pp. A history of the colony of South Carolina and its people from the early settlements to admission into the United States, told in concise prose with numerous black-and-white illustrations. (Rev: BL 9/15/02)

18435 Green, Carl R. *The French and Indian War* (4–6). Illus. Series: U.S. Wars. 2002, Enslow LB $25.26 (978-0-7660-5090-7). 48pp. Supported by verified and updated Web links, this is a useful overview of the French and Indian Wars. (Rev: BL 10/15/02; HBG 3/03)

18436 Haberle, Susan E. *The South Carolina Colony* (2–4). Series: Fact Finders: The American Colonies. 2005, Capstone LB $23.93 (978-0-7368-2683-9). 32pp. A very basic overview of the geography, history, religion, and everyday life of the South Carolina colony, with large type and short paragraphs. (Rev: SLJ 12/05)

18437 Harkins, Susan Sales, and William H. Harkins. *Georgia: The Debtors Colony* (4–7). Series: Building America. 2006, Mitchell Lane LB $29.95 (978-1-58415-465-5). 48pp. A look at Georgia's early history — including climate, early industry, and population — with information on James Oglethorpe, a key figure who aimed to provide a haven in America for debtors imprisoned in England. (Rev: SLJ 2/07)

18438 Harkins, Susan, and William H. Harkins. *Jamestown: The First English Colony* (4–6). Series: Building America. 2006, Mitchell Lane LB $29.95 (978-1-58415-458-7). 48pp. A mixture of fact and educated conjecture, this well-organized overview of Jamestown underscores the difficulties faced by the settlers who established the first permanent English colony in America. (Rev: BL 10/15/06; SLJ 11/06)

18439 Harness, Cheryl. *Our Colonial Year* (1–3). Illus. 2005, Simon & Schuster $16.95 (978-0-689-83479-0).

40pp. Double-page spreads with short, free-verse text follow everyday life in the 13 colonies through the 12 months of the year, plus a spread for New Year's Day. (Rev: BL 12/1/05; SLJ 12/05)

18440 Hinds, Kathryn. *Daily Living* (5–9). Series: Colonial Life. 2007, Sharpe Focus $37.95 (978-0-7656-8110-2). 96pp. With color illustrations and interesting sidebars, this volume looks at social life in the colonies, exploring food, family life, and so forth. (Rev: SLJ 1/08)

18441 Hinman, Bonnie. *Pennsylvania: William Penn and the City of Brotherly Love* (4–7). Series: Building America. 2006, Mitchell Lane LB $29.95 (978-1-58415-463-1). This history of colonial Pennsylvania explores the reasons why William Penn established the colony in the late 17th century. (Rev: SLJ 2/07) [974.8]

18442 Hossell, Karen. *Delaware 1638–1776* (5–8). Series: Voices from Colonial America. 2006, National Geographic $21.95 (978-0-7922-6408-8). 109pp. This well-illustrated title traces the history of Delaware from the 17th-century massacre of Dutch settlers by Native Americans to the eve of the American Revolution; maps and a timeline make this useful for research. (Rev: SLJ 1/07)

18443 Howarth, Sarah. *Colonial Places* (4–8). Series: People and Places. 1994, Millbrook LB $22.90 (978-1-56294-513-8). Highlights various places of importance in everyday colonial life, such as the meetinghouse and the church. (Rev: BL 5/15/95; SLJ 3/95) [973]

18444 Isaacs, Sally Senzell. *Life in a Colonial Town* (1–3). Series: Picture the Past. 2000, Heinemann LB $21.36 (978-1-57572-312-9). This well-organized account covers such topics as communication, houses, occupations, education, clothing, and food. Similar coverage for colonial cities is given in *Life in America's First Cities* (2000). (Rev: HBG 3/01; SLJ 11/00)

18445 Italia, Bob. *The New York Colony* (3–5). Illus. Series: The Colonies. 2001, ABDO $22.78 (978-1-57765-589-3). 32pp. An overview for younger readers of the New York colony, including information on early history, settlements, everyday life, and other topics. Also use *Roanoke* (2001). (Rev: BL 1/1–15/02; HBG 3/02; SLJ 2/02)

18446 Jackson, Shirley. *The Witchcraft of Salem Village* (4–7). 1963, Random House paper $5.99 (978-0-394-89176-7). An account of the witch-hunting hysteria that hit Salem Village. [133.43097445]

18447 January, Brendan. *The Jamestown Colony* (3–6). Series: We the People. 2000, Compass Point LB $26.60 (978-0-7565-0043-6). 48pp. A heavily illustrated account of the Jamestown colony that is simple in appearance and format. (Rev: SLJ 2/01)

18448 Kalman, Bobbie. *The Blacksmith* (3–5). Illus. by Barbara Bedell. Series: Colonial People. 2002, Crabtree LB $25.27 (978-0-7787-0747-9); paper $8.95 (978-0-7787-0793-6). 32pp. Photographs of reenactments at Williamsburg and Old Salem, North Carolina, add appeal to this description of the work of a colonial black-

smith and the equipment he used. Also use *The Milliner* and *The Woodworker* (2002). (Rev: SLJ 10/02)

18449 Kalman, Bobbie, and Amanda Bishop. *A Slave Family* (3–5). Illus. Series: Colonial People. 2003, Crabtree LB $25.27 (978-0-7787-0746-2); paper $8.95 (978-0-7787-0792-9). 32pp. Describes the lives of slave families during America's colonial period from the early 17th century until the Revolutionary War. (Rev: SLJ 1/04)

18450 Kelly, Martin, and Melissa Kelly. *Government* (5–9). Series: Colonial Life. 2007, Sharpe Focus $37.95 (978-0-7656-8112-6). 96pp. With color illustrations and interesting sidebars, this volume looks at government in the colonies, exploring the Native American tribal organization as well as the colonial structure. (Rev: SLJ 1/08)

18451 Kent, Deborah. *In Colonial New England* (4–8). Series: How We Lived. 1999, Benchmark LB $28.50 (978-0-7614-0905-2). Topics such as home life, childhood, religion, problems, and amusements are covered for the colonial period in New England. Companion volumes are *In the Middle Colonies* and *In the Southern Colonies* (1999). (Rev: HBG 10/00; SLJ 2/00) [973.2]

18452 Lange, Karen. *1607: A New Look at Jamestown* (4–6). Illus. by Ira Block. 2007, National Geographic $17.95 (978-1-4263-0012-7). 48pp. In the light of new information discovered about Jamestown in the late 20th century, this book describes what we now understand about life in the colony. (Rev: BL 12/1/06; SLJ 1/07*)

18453 Lilly, Alexandra. *Spanish Colonies in America* (4–6). Series: We the People. 2008, Compass Point LB $26.60 (978-0-7565-3840-8). 48pp. An introduction to how Spain's culture shaped the new colonies. (Rev: SLJ 6/09)

18454 McKissack, Patricia C., and Fredrick McKissack, Jr. *Hard Labor: The First African Americans, 1619* (5–8). Illus. by Joseph Fiedler. Series: Milestone Books. 2004, Simon & Schuster paper $3.99 (978-0-689-86149-9). Drawing on the meager evidence available, the authors reconstruct the story of the first Africans brought to America. (Rev: BL 2/15/04; SLJ 3/04) [306.3]

18455 McNeese, Tim. *Colonial America: 1543–1763* (5–8). Illus. Series: Discovering U.S. History. 2010, Chelsea House $35 (978-1-60413-349-3). 136pp. Covering more than 200 years, this is a satisfying survey of social and political developments in colonial America, with illustrations, maps, photographs, and interesting sidebar features. **e** (Rev: LMC 11–12/10; SLJ 8/10) [973.2]

18456 McNeese, Tim. *Jamestown* (5–8). Illus. Series: Colonial Settlements in America. 2007, Chelsea House $30 (978-0-7910-9335-1). This overview of the settlement of the colony will be helpful to report writers and includes maps and other graphics. (Rev: BL 7/07; LMC 11/07; SLJ 7/07)

18457 Marsico, Katie. *The Doctor* (3–5). Illus. Series: Colonial People. 2011, Marshall Cavendish LB $20.95 (978-1-60870-412-5). 48pp. Explores the lives of the doctors of the colonial period and the kinds of techniques they had at their disposal. (Rev: BL 12/1/11; SLJ 12/1/11) [610.69]

18458 Martin, Michael. *The Salem Witch Trials* (3–6). Illus. by Brian Bascle. Series: Graphic Library/Graphic History. 2004, Capstone LB $26.60 (978-0-7368-3847-4). This broad overview in graphic-novel format — factual but embellished — of this chapter of American history will appeal to reluctant readers. (Rev: SLJ 7/05)

18459 Marx, Mandy R. *The Maryland Colony* (2–4). Series: Fact Finders: The American Colonies. 2005, Capstone LB $23.93 (978-0-7368-2675-4). A very basic overview of the geography, history, religion, and everyday life of the Maryland colony, with large type and short paragraphs. (Rev: SLJ 12/05)

18460 Miller, Brandon Marie. *Good Women of a Well-Blessed Land: Women's Lives in Colonial America* (5–8). Series: People's History. 2003, Lerner LB $29.27 (978-0-8225-0032-2). The lives and roles of women from all layers of early American society are presented in this well-written account that includes many quotations, maps, and period reproductions. (Rev: BL 5/15/03; HBG 10/03; SLJ 7/03) [305.4]

18461 Miller, Brandon Marie. *Growing Up in a New World* (5–8). Series: Our America. 2002, Lerner LB $26.60 (978-0-8225-0658-4). The thrill of landing in the New World for the first time is re-created through true-life adventures of young people. (Rev: BL 2/15/03; HBG 3/03; SLJ 7/03) [973.2]

18462 Miller, Lee. *Roanoke: The Mystery of the Lost Colony* (4–7). Illus. 2007, Scholastic $18.99 (978-0-439-71266-8). 112pp. Author Miller presents her theory that the colony at Roanoke was sabotaged. (Rev: BL 6/1–15/07; LMC 10/07)

18463 Niz, Xavier. *The Mystery of the Roanoke Colony* (4–6). Illus. by Shannon Eric Denton. Series: Graphic Library: Graphic History. 2006, Capstone LB $25.26 (978-0-7368-6494-7). 32pp. The mystery of this American colony is presented in a graphic format; information following adds depth. (Rev: SLJ 5/07)

18464 Petersen, Christine. *The Glassblower* (3–5). Illus. Series: Colonial People. 2011, Marshall Cavendish LB $20.95 (978-1-60870-413-2). 48pp. Explores the lives and importance of the glassblowers who made a variety of key products in the colonial period. (Rev: BL 12/1/11; SLJ 12/1/11) [666]

18465 Petersen, Christine. *The Tanner* (3–5). Illus. Series: Colonial People. 2011, Marshall Cavendish LB $20.95 (978-1-60870-418-7). 48pp. Explores the lives of the tanners who made a variety of products from leather in the colonial period. Other volumes in this series include *The Tailor* (2011). (Rev: BL 12/1/11; SLJ 12/1/11) [675]

18466 Pipe, Jim. *You Wouldn't Want to Be a Salem Witch: Bizarre Accusations You'd Rather Not Face* (3–5). Illus. by David Antram. Series: You Wouldn't Want To. 2009, Scholastic LB $29.00 (978-0-531-20821-2); paper $9.95 (978-0-531-21047-5). 32pp. Cartoon illustrations and gruesome details make it clear why you wouldn't

want to be involved in the Salem witch trials. (Rev: BLO 3/17/09)

18467 Roop, Connie, and Peter Roop, eds. *Pilgrim Voices: Our First Year in the New World* (4–7). 1995, Walker LB $17.85 (978-0-8027-8315-8). Using first-person sources, the experiences of the Pilgrims from their sea journey to the first Thanksgiving are re-created. (Rev: BL 2/1/96; SLJ 1/96) [974.4]

18468 Schanzer, Rosalyn. *Witches!: The Absolutely True Tale of Disaster in Salem* (5–8). Illus. by author. 2011, National Geographic $16.95 (978-1-4263-0869-7); LB $27.90 (978-1-4263-0870-3). 144pp. With arresting illustrations this is a compelling account of how the illness afflicting two young girls leads to accusations of witchcraft. Sibert Honor 2012; ALA Notable Children's Book 2012. ♫ ℮ (Rev: BL 11/1/11; SLJ 12/1/11*; VOYA 12/11) [133.4]

18469 Schumacher, Tyler. *The Georgia Colony* (2–4). Series: Fact Finders: The American Colonies. 2005, Capstone LB $23.93 (978-0-7368-2674-7). 32pp. A very basic overview of the geography, history, religion, and everyday life of the Georgia colony, with large type and short paragraphs. (Rev: SLJ 12/05)

18470 Sewall, Marcia. *James Towne: Struggle for Survival* (3–5). Illus. 2001, Simon & Schuster $16.00 (978-0-689-81814-1). An 18-year-old carpenter relates his experiences in the colony of Jamestown, sparing little detail of the hardships the settlers faced. (Rev: BL 6/1–15/01; HB 7/01; HBG 10/01; SLJ 6/01)

18471 Sherrow, Victoria. *Huskings, Quiltings, and Barn Raisings: Work-Play Parties in Early America* (4–7). Illus. by Laura LoTurco. 1992, Walker LB $14.85 (978-0-8027-8188-8). How people in early America helped each other with difficult tasks, such as clearing land and raising barns. (Rev: BL 1/15/93) [973.2]

18472 Smith, Carter, ed. *The Arts and Sciences: A Sourcebook on Colonial America* (5–8). Series: American Albums. 1991, Millbrook $25.90 (978-1-56294-037-9). Through many well-captioned illustrations and brief text, this sourcebook traces cultural and scientific life during the U.S. colonial period. (Rev: BL 1/1/92) [973.2]

18473 Stefoff, Rebecca. *Cities and Towns* (5–9). Series: Colonial Life. 2007, Sharpe Focus $37.95 (978-0-7656-8109-6). 96pp. With color illustrations and interesting sidebars, this volume looks at the development of cities and towns from the earlier forts and fishing camps. (Rev: SLJ 1/08)

18474 Stefoff, Rebecca. *The Colonies* (4–7). Series: North American Historical Atlases. 2000, Benchmark LB $27.07 (978-0-7614-1057-7). 48pp. A slim, clearly written account that gives a history of the American colonies, important places, and outstanding people. (Rev: HBG 3/01; SLJ 1/01)

18475 Steins, Richard. *Colonial America* (5–8). Series: Making of America. 2000, Raintree LB $28.54 (978-0-8172-5701-9). 96pp. A brief history of the colonies from

1607 to 1763 with details of their founding, composition, and history. (Rev: HBG 10/00; SLJ 8/00)

18476 Walker, Niki. *Colonial Women* (3–5). Illus. by Barbara Bedell. Series: Colonial People. 2003, Crabtree LB $25.27 (978-0-7787-0749-3); paper $8.95 (978-0-7787-0795-0). 32pp. Examines what life was like for women during America's colonial era. (Rev: SLJ 1/04)

18477 Waxman, Laura Hamilton. *Who Were the Accused Witches of Salem? And Other Questions About the Witchcraft Trials* (3–6). Illus. Series: Six Questions of American History. 2012, Lerner LB $30.60 (978-076135225-9). 48pp. Six thoughtful questions about the Salem Witch trials are considered with reference to the historical and cultural context; includes informative back matter. (Rev: BL 2/1/12; SLJ 3/12) [133.4]

18478 Whitehurst, Susan. *Plymouth: Surviving the First Winter* (2–4). Series: The Library of the Pilgrims. 2001, Rosen LB $21.25 (978-0-8239-5809-2). 24pp. An accessible account of the pilgrims' hard first winter, with details of housing, food, and illness. Also use *William Bradford and Plymouth: A Colony Grows* (2001). (Rev: SLJ 3/02)

18479 Wiener, Roberta, and James R. Arnold. *Connecticut: The History of Connecticut Colony, 1633–1776* (5–8). Series: 13 Colonies. 2004, Raintree LB $31.36 (978-0-7398-6877-5). 64pp. A fact-filled and balanced discussion of the settlement of this area and the problems — political, social, and religious — that confronted the early European inhabitants. Also use *Delaware* and *Maryland* (both 2004). (Rev: SLJ 4/05)

18480 Williams, Jean Kinney. *The Maryland Colony* (3–6). Series: Our Thirteen Colonies. 2003, Child's World LB $28.50 (978-1-56766-615-1). Maps, prints, and other illustrations add to this presentation of Maryland's early history — from its founding in 1634 to early statehood, with coverage of colonial life, relations with Native Americans, and the roles of women and slaves. (Rev: SLJ 6/04)

18481 Wilmore, Kathy. *A Day in the Life of a Colonial Innkeeper* (3–5). Illus. Series: Library of Living and Working in Colonial Times. 2000, Rosen $18.75 (978-0-8239-5430-8). 24pp. In this picture of life at an inn in colonial times, innkeepers Mr. and Mrs. Watkins go about their daily chores — cooking, minding the horses in the stable, cleaning the rooms, and so forth. (Rev: BL 10/15/00)

18482 Wilmore, Kathy. *A Day in the Life of a Colonial Wigmaker* (3–5). Illus. Series: Library of Living and Working in Colonial Times. 2000, Rosen $19.95 (978-0-8239-5426-1). Set in a colonial American wig shop, this account shows how Mr. Hawkins and his staff of wig makers accomplish such tasks as making scull caps, sewing hair onto them, and powdering the finished wigs. (Rev: BL 10/15/00)

18483 Winters, Kay. *Colonial Voices: Hear Them Speak* (4–7). Illus. by Larry Day. 2008, Dutton $17.99 (978-0-525-47872-0). Fictional residents of colonial Boston offer their opinions on independence and revolution in this illustrated book by the author of *Voices of Egypt*. (Rev: BL 5/15/08; LMC 11–12/08; SLJ 6/08*) [973.3]

18484 Worth, Richard. *Colonial America: Building Toward Independence* (5–8). Series: The American Saga. 2006, Enslow LB $31.93 (978-0-7660-2569-1). Tracing the history of the original 13 colonies from the earliest English settlements through the ratification of the Constitution, this volume will be useful for report writers seeking information on politics, government, economy, and culture. (Rev: SLJ 12/06)

18485 Yero, Judith Lloyd. *The Mayflower Compact* (4–7). Series: American Documents. 2006, National Geographic $15.95 (978-0-7922-5891-9). 40pp. Yero distinguishes fact from myth in this examination of the *Mayflower*'s voyage, the colony the Separatists create, and the document they drafted as their governing compact. (Rev: BL 9/15/06; SLJ 10/06)

18486 Yolen, Jane, and Heidi Elizabeth Yolen-Stemple. *Roanoke the Lost Colony: An Unsolved Mystery from History* (2–5). Illus. by Roger Roth. Series: Unsolved Mystery from History. 2003, Simon & Schuster $16.95 (978-0-689-82321-3). 32pp. Fact and fiction are cleverly woven together in this picture book for older children about the disappearance of the colonists of Roanoke, narrated by a young girl who aspires to be a detective. (Rev: BL 7/03; HBG 4/04; SLJ 10/03)

REVOLUTIONARY PERIOD

18487 Allen, Kathy. *The First American Flag* (1–3). Illus. by Siri Weber Feeney. 2009, Picture Window LB $23.99 (978-140485541-0). 32pp. Allen bursts the legend of Betsy Ross and tells the real story of the creation of the flag. (Rev: BL 3/1/10) [929.9]

18488 Ammon, Richard. *Valley Forge* (3–6). Illus. by Bill Farnsworth. 2004, Holiday House $16.95 (978-0-8234-1746-9). 32pp. Details of the hardships suffered by American forces during the winter of 1777–1778 are placed in historical context in this large-format book. (Rev: BL 9/15/04; SLJ 10/04)

18489 Amstel, Marsha. *Sybil Ludington's Midnight Ride* (2–4). Illus. by Ellen Beier. 2000, Carolrhoda LB $23.93 (978-1-57505-211-3); paper $5.95 (978-1-57505-456-8). 48pp. A readable account of 16-year-old Sybil Ludington's exciting midnight ride to spread the word that the British were attacking Danbury, Connecticut. (Rev: HBG 10/00; SLJ 6/00)

18490 Anderson, Dale. *The American Colonies Declare Independence* (5–8). Series: World Almanac Library of the American Revolution. 2005, World Almanac LB $31.00 (978-0-8368-5926-3). Excerpts from primary sources bolster the informative, clearly written text, which is sprinkled with biographical sidebars. Also use *The Causes of the American Revolution*, *The Patriots Win the American Revolution*, and *Forming a New American Government* (all 2005). (Rev: SLJ 1/06) [973.3]

18491 Beller, Susan P. *The Revolutionary War* (5–8). Series: Letters from the Homefront. 2001, Benchmark LB $29.93 (978-0-7614-1094-2). 96pp. An attractive volume that brings events and living conditions during the Revolution alive through a collection of letters and other personal documents. (Rev: BL 10/15/01; HBG 3/02)

18492 Beller, Susan Provost. *Yankee Doodle and the Redcoats: Soldiering in the Revolutionary War* (5–8). Illus. by Larry Day. 2003, Millbrook LB $26.90 (978-0-7613-2612-0). This attractive book covers the plight of the Revolutionary War soldier, with artwork as well as soldiers' letters and other documents adding to the presentation. (Rev: BL 5/15/03; HBG 10/03; SLJ 9/01) [973.3]

18493 Blair, Margaret Whitman. *Liberty or Death: The Surprising Story of Runaway Slaves Who Sided with the British During the American Revolution* (5–8). 2010, National Geographic $18.95 (978-1-4263-0590-0); LB $27.90 (978-1-4263-0591-7). 64pp. Using personal quotes and anecdotes, Blair tells the unhappy story of the runaway slaves who were promised freedom if they fought for the British during the Revolution. Lexile 1160L (Rev: BL 1/1/10*; LMC 5–6/10; SLJ 3/10) [973.3]

18494 Bobrick, Benson. *Fight for Freedom: The American Revolutionary War* (5–8). 2004, Simon & Schuster $22.95 (978-0-689-86422-3). Full-page illustrations face text and "Quick Facts" about topics ranging from the origins and progress of the war to the Continental Congresses, with profiles of key figures and maps. (Rev: BL 11/15/04; SLJ 11/04) [973.3]

18495 Bohannon, Lisa Frederiksen. *The American Revolution* (5–8). Series: Chronicle of America's Wars. 2003, Lerner LB $27.93 (978-0-8225-4717-4). 88pp. Illustrations and maps enliven this overview of the American colonies' struggle for independence, covering the two decades from the French and Indian War to the Treaty of Paris. (Rev: SLJ 3/04)

18496 Brenner, Barbara. *If You Were There in 1776* (4–8). 1994, Bradbury $17.95 (978-0-02-712322-7). The year 1776 is explored, with particular emphasis on the everyday life of young people in the colonies. (Rev: BCCB 6/94; BL 5/15/94; SLJ 6/94) [973.3]

18497 Brown, Don. *Let It Begin Here! April 19, 1775: The Day the American Revolution Began* (2–4). Illus. by author. 2008, Roaring Brook $17.95 (978-1-59643-221-5). 32pp. After introducing the causes of the rebellion, this picture book gives a more detailed account of the first day of fighting and the key characters involved. (Rev: BL 10/1/08; HB 1/09; SLJ 10/08)

18498 Carson, Mary Kay. *Did It All Start with a Snowball Fight? And Other Questions about the American Revolution* (3–5). Series: Good Question! 2012, Sterling $12.95 (978-1-4027-9626-5); paper $5.95 (978-1-4027-8-734-8). 32pp. A breezy, appealing overview of facts and legends relating to the American Revolution, presented chronologically and drawing on interesting primary source materials. (Rev: BL 9/1/12; LMC 3–4/13; SLJ 11/12) [973.3]

18499 Castrovilla, Selene. *Upon Secrecy* (4–7). Illus. by Jeff Crosby and Shelley Ann Jackson. 2009, Boyds Mills

$17.95 (978-1-59078-573-7). 32pp. This illustrated book provides a well-written, slightly fictionalized history of the Culper Spy Ring, a New York City organization instrumental in Washington's ultimate defeat of the British. (Rev: LMC 11–12/09; SLJ 10/09) [973.3]

18500 Cheney, Lynne. *When Washington Crossed the Delaware: A Wintertime Story for Young Patriots* (2–4). Illus. by Peter M. Fiore. 2004, Simon & Schuster $16.95 (978-0-689-87043-9). 40pp. The battles of Trenton and Princeton are described in vivid prose with brief eyewitness quotations. (Rev: BL 10/1/04; SLJ 11/04)

18501 Cook, Peter. *You Wouldn't Want to Be at the Boston Tea Party! Wharf Water Tea You'd Rather Not Drink* (3–6). Illus. by David Antram. Series: You Wouldn't Want To. 2006, Watts paper $9.95 (978-0-531-12447-5). 32pp. A lively look at life in colonial Boston, with some unvarnished realities balanced by the lighthearted cartoon illustrations. (Rev: SLJ 9/06)

18502 Crawford, Laura. *The American Revolution from A to Z* (3–5). Illus. by Judith Hierstein. 2009, Pelican $15.95 (978-1-58980-515-6). Unpaged. Suitable for browsing, this alphabet book covers many topics relating to the American Revolution, from prominent characters and events to the less familiar (Betty Zane and the Battle of the Kegs, for example). (Rev: LMC 1/1/10*; SLJ 1/1/10) [973.3]

18503 Crewe, Sabrina, and Dale Anderson. *Lexington and Concord* (4–6). Series: Events That Shaped America. 2004, Gareth Stevens LB $26.00 (978-0-8368-3398-0). 32pp. The story of the 1775 battle serves as the opening for a well-illustrated and well-organized discussion of the Revolutionary War. (Rev: SLJ 8/04)

18504 Deem, James M. *Primary Source Accounts of the Revolutionary War* (5–8). Series: America's Wars Through Primary Sources. 2006, Enslow LB $33.27 (978-1-59845-004-0). Soldiers' journal entries, letters from home, personal recollections, songs and poetry, and newspaper articles are among the primary sources included in this general history of the war. (Rev: SLJ 4/07) [973.3]

18505 Draper, Allison Stark. *George Washington Elected: How America's First President Was Chosen* (2–4). Illus. Series: Headlines from History. 2001, Rosen LB $19.95 (978-0-8239-5675-3). 24pp. Newspaper headlines and large type make for easy-reading accounts of significant events leading up to and during Washington's tenure. Also use *The Boston Tea Party: Angry Colonists Dump British Tea* (2001). (Rev: SLJ 8/01)

18506 Edwards, Pamela Duncan. *Boston Tea Party* (1–3). Illus. by Henry Cole. 2001, Penguin $16.99 (978-0-399-23357-9). 32pp. Rhythmic text presents the key events in the lead-up to the Tea Party, enlivened by additional commentary from a crew of mice. (Rev: BCCB 6/01; BL 6/1–15/01; HBG 3/02; SLJ 7/01)

18507 Fleming, Thomas. *Everybody's Revolution* (4–7). Illus. 2006, Scholastic $19.99 (978-0-439-63404-5). 96pp. A fascinating introduction to the diverse heroes and heroines of many nationalities who contributed to the success of the American Revolution. (Rev: BL 10/15/06; SLJ 11/06)

18508 Foster, Genevieve, and Joanna Foster. *George Washington's World. Rev. ed.* (5–8). 1997, Beautiful Feet paper $15.95 (978-0-9643803-4-9). A new edition of this 50-year-old book that re-creates what was happening in the world during Washington's life, now with expanded coverage on minorities. (Rev: SLJ 3/98) [909]

18509 Fradin, Dennis B. *The Declaration of Independence* (3–6). Series: Turning Points in U.S. History. 2006, Benchmark LB $29.93 (978-0-7614-2129-0). 45pp. Describes the events leading up to writing of the Declaration of Independence, its composition, and its impact on history. (Rev: SLJ 3/07)

18510 Fradin, Dennis B. *Let It Begin Here! Lexington and Concord: First Battles of the American Revolution* (2–4). Illus. by Larry Day. 2005, Walker LB $17.85 (978-0-8027-8946-4). The story of the battles that began it all, told in an engaging style to appeal to students; with illustrations and information on key figures of the war. (Rev: BL 4/15/05)

18511 Fradin, Dennis B. *The Signers: The 56 Stories Behind the Declaration of Independence* (4–6). Illus. by Michael McCurdy. 2002, Walker $22.95 (978-0-8027-8849-8). 160pp. Report writers will find plenty of information on the 13 colonies and the important individuals of the time in this lively presentation. (Rev: HB 1/03; HBG 3/03; SLJ 11/02)

18512 Freedman, Russell. *The Boston Tea Party* (2–5). Illus. by Peter Malone. 2012, Holiday $17.95 (978-0-8234-2266-1). 40pp. An appealing account of the events leading up to the rebellion against Britain's tax on tea and of the protest itself. Booklist Editors' Choice: Books for Youth, 2012. (Rev: BL 10/1/12*; HB 11–12/12; LMC 5–6/12; SLJ 10/12) [973.3]

18513 Freedman, Russell. *Give Me Liberty! The Story of the Declaration of Independence* (4–7). 2000, Holiday $24.95 (978-0-8234-1448-2). Beginning with the Boston Tea Party, this stirring account introduces characters including Patrick Henry and Paul Revere, events such as the battles at Lexington and Concord, and ends with the Continental Congress and the drawing up of the Declaration of Independence. (Rev: BCCB 10/00; BL 10/1/00*; HB 1–2/01; HBG 3/01; SLJ 10/00) [973.3]

18514 Furgang, Kathy. *The Declaration of Independence and John Adams of Massachusetts* (3–4). Illus. Series: Framers of the Declaration of Independence. 2001, Rosen LB $21.25 (978-0-8239-5590-9). 24pp. Large print and visual interest make this introductory account suitable for reluctant readers. Also use *The Declaration of Independence and Richard Henry Lee of Virginia* and *The Declaration of Independence and Roger Sherman of Connecticut* (both 2002). (Rev: SLJ 5/02)

18515 Furstinger, Nancy. *The Boston Tea Party* (4–6). Illus. Series: Let Freedom Ring. 2002, Capstone LB $23.93 (978-0-7368-1093-7). 48pp. Furstinger gives a concise account of the event and places it in a simple historical context that will be useful for report writers.

Also use *The Boston Massacre* (2002). (Rev: HBG 3/03; SLJ 6/02)

18516 Graves, Kerry A. *The Declaration of Independence: The Story Behind America's Founding Document* (3–5). Series: America in Words and Song. 2003, Chelsea Clubhouse LB $23.00 (978-0-7910-7334-6). 32pp. Details events leading up to America's political break from Britain and the difficulties in framing the document declaring that independence. (Rev: SLJ 5/04)

18517 Green, Carl R. *The Revolutionary War* (4–6). Illus. Series: U.S. Wars. 2002, Enslow LB $25.26 (978-0-7660-5089-1). Supported by verified and updated Web links, this is a useful account of the Revolutionary War. (Rev: BL 10/15/02; HBG 3/03)

18518 Herbert, Janis. *The American Revolution for Kids* (5–8). 2002, Chicago Review paper $14.95 (978-1-55652-456-1). A comprehensive look at the American Revolution from its causes through the early 18th century, with biographical information and interesting features. (Rev: BL 10/1/02; SLJ 11/02) [973.3]

18519 Hossell, Karen. *The Articles of Confederation* (4–6). Series: Historical Documents. 2003, Heinemann LB $27.07 (978-1-4034-0800-6). 48pp. The story of the Articles of Confederation, which served as the first Constitution of the newly independent United States, with a look at what a primary document is and how original documents are preserved. (Rev: SLJ 5/04)

18520 Ingram, Scott. *The Battle of Valcour Bay* (4–6). Series: Triangle Histories of the American Revolution. 2003, Gale LB $22.45 (978-1-56711-778-3). 32pp. A detailed and well-illustrated account of the Revolutionary War battle of Valcour Bay on Lake Champlain. (Rev: SLJ 3/04)

18521 Isaacs, Sally Senzell. *Colonists and Independence* (4–6). Illus. Series: All About America. 2011, Kingfisher LB $19.89 (978-0-7534-6581-3); paper $9.99 (978-0-7534-6513-4). 32pp. With many photographs, paintings, maps, and primary documents, this overview of the colonial settlers and the struggle for independence will be useful for report writers. (Rev: BL 9/1/11; SLJ 8/11) [973]

18522 Jules, Jacqueline. *Unite or Die: How Thirteen States Became a Nation* (2–4). Illus. by Jef Czekaj. 2009, Charlesbridge $16.95 (978-1-58089-189-9); paper $7.95 (978-1-58089-190-5). 48pp. This picture book uses a school play with children dressed as the thirteen states as a framework for introducing the path to nationhood. (Rev: BL 1/1–15/09; SLJ 4/09)

18523 King, David C. *Saratoga* (5–8). Series: Battlefields Across America. 1998, Twenty-First Century LB $26.90 (978-0-7613-3011-0). The significance of the battle at Saratoga in 1777, in which General Burgoyne's British army was defeated, and where and how the history of this battle is preserved today. (Rev: HBG 9/98; SLJ 8/98) [973.3]

18524 Lilly, Melinda. *The Boston Tea Party* (K–2). Illus. by Patrick O'Brien. Series: Reading American History. 2002, Rourke LB $14.95 (978-1-58952-357-9). 24pp. A simple account for beginning readers that introduces the key characters behind the rebellion. (Rev: SLJ 3/03)

18525 McNeese, Tim. *Revolutionary America 1764–1789* (5–8). Series: Discovering U.S. History. 2010, Chelsea House $35 (978-1-60413-350-9). 136pp. McNeese provides a succinct overview of the key events and issues of this period of turmoil, with a chronology and timeline plus illustrations and primary sources. (Rev: LMC 11–12/10) [973.3]

18526 Maestro, Betsy. *Liberty or Death: The American Revolution: 1763–1783* (3–5). Illus. by Giulio Maestro. Series: American Story. 2005, HarperCollins $16.99 (978-0-688-08802-6). 64pp. This attractive volume provides an easy-to-understand overview of the American Revolution and the events that led up to it. (Rev: BL 11/1/05; SLJ 9/05)

18527 Malaspina, Ann. *Phillis Sings Out Freedom: The Story of George Washington and Phillis Wheatley* (2–4). Illus. by Susan Keeter. 2010, Whitman $16.99 (978-0-8075-6545-2). 32pp. Malaspina interweaves the story of Washington's revolutionary efforts with the life and poetry of Phillis Wheatley, a slave who was eventually freed by her owners. (Rev: BL 9/1/10; LMC 11–12/10; SLJ 10/1/10) [973.4]

18528 Martin, Joseph Plumb. *A Revolutionary War Soldier* (3–6). Series: In My Own Words. 2000, Marshall Cavendish LB $27.07 (978-0-7614-1014-0). 64pp. Sly humor is present in diary excerpts that bring to life stirring moments in America's war for independence. (Rev: BL 3/1/01; HBG 3/01; SLJ 3/01)

18529 Miller, Brandon M. *Growing Up in the Revolution and the New Nation* (4–7). Illus. Series: Our America. 2002, Lerner LB $26.60 (978-0-8225-0078-0). 64pp. An in-depth examination of the lives of children during and immediately after the American Revolution, including biographical information about real youngsters. (Rev: BL 10/15/02; HBG 3/03; SLJ 12/02)

18530 Miller, Brandon Marie. *Declaring Independence: Life During the American Revolution* (5–8). Series: People's History. 2005, Lerner LB $29.27 (978-0-8225-1275-2). A thorough look at what life was like during the American Revolution, using primary sources. (Rev: SLJ 9/05; VOYA 6/05) [973.3]

18531 Minor, Wendell. *Yankee Doodle America: The Spirit of 1776 from A to Z* (2–5). Illus. 2006, Putnam $16.99 (978-0-399-24003-4). An attractive and informative alphabetical tour of colonial America. (Rev: BL 4/15/06; SLJ 4/06)

18532 Mortensen, Lori. *Writing the U.S. Constitution* (1–3). Illus. by Siri Weber Feeney. 2009, Picture Window LB $23.99 (978-140485540-3). 32pp. Mortensen provides clear explanations of the concepts underlying the Constitution and places the process of creating it in historical context. Also use *Paul Revere's Ride* (2009). (Rev: BL 3/1/10) [342.7302]

18533 Murphy, Jim. *The Crossing: How George Washington Saved the American Revolution* (5–8). 2010, Scholastic $21.99 (978-0-439-69186-4). 96pp. With many quotations, illustrations, maps, and reproductions, plus clear text, this is an appealing account of Washington's efforts to whip a ragtag army into shape and his various triumphs and failures. (Rev: BL 11/15/10*; SLJ 12/1/10*) [973.3]

18534 Murphy, Jim. *A Young Patriot: The American Revolution as Experienced by One Boy* (5–8). 1996, Clarion $16.00 (978-0-395-60523-3). The American Revolution as seen through the eyes of a 15-year-old volunteer. Margaret A. Edwards Award 2010. (Rev: BCCB 6/96; BL 6/1–15/96*; HB 9–10/96; SLJ 6/96*) [973.3]

18535 Nash, Gary B. *Landmarks of the American Revolution* (5–8). Series: American Landmarks. 2003, Oxford LB $32.95 (978-0-19-512849-9). 158pp. Landmark sites such as Independence Hall, Valley Forge National Historic Park, Faneuil Hall, and Yorktown Battlefield are introduced with excerpts from primary documents such as letters and broadsides. (Rev: SLJ 8/03)

18536 Raatma, Lucia. *The Minutemen* (4–6). Series: We the People. 2005, Compass Point LB $26.60 (978-0-7565-0842-5). 48pp. Describes the role of the Minutemen and their bravery at the battles of Lexington and Concord. (Rev: SLJ 6/05)

18537 St. George, Judith. *The One and Only Declaration of Independence* (1–3). Illus. by Will Hillenbrand. 2005, Penguin $16.99 (978-0-399-23738-6). 48pp. The story of the document's search for a permanent home, presented using questions and answers with cartoon-style illustrations. (Rev: BL 3/1/05; SLJ 6/05)

18538 Schanzer, Rosalyn. *George vs. George: The Revolutionary War as Seen by Both Sides* (5–7). 2004, National Geographic $16.95 (978-0-7922-7349-3). The two sides' differences — and commonalities — are portrayed in an appealing combination of well-written text, colorful art, and speech balloons; sensationalist aspects detract from the overall value. (Rev: BL 11/15/04; SLJ 10/04*) [973.3]

18539 Sheinkin, Steve. *King George: What Was His Problem? Everything Your Schoolbooks Didn't Tell You About the American Revolution* (4–7). Illus. by Tim Robinson. 2008, Roaring Brook $19.95 (978-1-59643-319-9). First published as *The American Revolution* (2005), this is a breezy and often funny collection of stories that history students will remember. (Rev: BL 8/08) [973.3]

18540 Smith, Carter, ed. *The Revolutionary War: A Sourcebook on Colonial America* (5–8). Series: American Albums. 1991, Millbrook $25.90 (978-1-56294-039-3). This volume illustrates the major events leading up to the Revolution and the battles and personalities involved. (Rev: BL 1/1/92) [973.38]

18541 Sobel, Syl. *The Declaration of Independence: How 13 Colonies Became the United States* (3–5). Illus. by Denise Gilgannon. 2008, Barron's paper $6.99 (978-0-7641-3950-5). 48pp. A succinct introduction to the creation of the Declaration of Independence, with background information on the history and beliefs of the time and a description of the government it created. (Rev: LMC 11/08; SLJ 9/08)

18542 Stanley, George E. *The New Republic (1763–1815)* (5–8). Series: A Primary Source History of the United States. 2005, World Almanac LB $31.00 (978-0-8368-5825-9). A simple narrative links well-chosen primary sources documenting the key events of the revolutionary period. (Rev: BL 4/1/05; SLJ 7/05)

18543 Stefoff, Rebecca. *Revolutionary War* (4–7). Illus. Series: North American Historical Atlases. 2000, Benchmark LB $27.07 (978-0-7614-1058-4). Using historical maps and reproductions plus a clear text, this is a basic account of the American Revolution. (Rev: HBG 3/01; SLJ 1/01)

18544 Waxman, Laura Hamilton. *What Are the Articles of Confederation? And Other Questions About the Birth of the United States* (3–6). Illus. Series: Six Questions of American History. 2012, Lerner LB $30.60 (978-076135330-0). 48pp. Six thoughtful questions about the Articles of Confederation are considered with reference to the historical and cultural context; includes informative back matter. (Rev: BL 2/1/12; SLJ 3/12) [342.7302]

18545 Weber, Michael. *The American Revolution* (5–8). Series: Making of America. 2000, Raintree LB $28.54 (978-0-8172-5702-6). 96pp. A fine overview of the American Revolution from the French and Indian War to the creation of the United States. (Rev: BL 7/00; HBG 10/00; SLJ 8/00)

18546 Weber, Michael. *Yorktown* (4–7). Series: Battlefields Across America. 1997, Twenty-First Century LB $26.90 (978-0-8050-5226-8). Background material on the Revolutionary War is given, along with details of the battle and the present-day condition of its site. (Rev: SLJ 1/98) [973.3]

18547 Weber, Michael. *The Young Republic* (5–8). Illus. Series: Making of America. 2000, Raintree LB $28.54 (978-0-8172-5703-3). 94pp. This well-illustrated account begins in the 1780s with the creation of the federal system, the ratification of the Constitution, and the inauguration of Washington as president in 1789. (Rev: BL 5/1/00; HBG 10/00; SLJ 9/00)

18548 Whitelaw, Nancy. *The Shot Heard Round the World: The Battles of Lexington and Concord* (5–8). Illus. 2001, Morgan Reynolds LB $23.95 (978-1-883846-75-6). 112pp. Whitelaw details events from the Boston Massacre in 1770 to the first battles of the Revolution in 1775, with profiles of some of the key players. (Rev: BL 5/15/01; HBG 10/01; SLJ 7/01; VOYA 6/01)

18549 Wister, Sally. *A Colonial Quaker Girl: The Diary of Sally Wister, 1777–1778* (4–6). Series: Diaries, Letters, and Memoirs. 2000, Capstone LB $23.93 (978-0-7368-0349-6). 32pp. This diary of a young girl, kept during the Revolution, reflects everyday family life during this period. (Rev: BL 10/15/00; SLJ 9/00)

18550 Yero, Judith Lloyd. *The Declaration of Independence* (3–5). Series: American Documents. 2006, National Geographic $15.95 (978-0-7922-5397-6). 40pp. Discusses the events that led to this document and the important figures who signed it, with interesting sidebars. (Rev: SLJ 5/06)

THE YOUNG NATION, 1789–1861

18551 Bial, Raymond. *The Strength of These Arms: Life in the Slave Quarters* (5–8). 1997, Houghton Mifflin $16.00 (978-0-395-77394-9). This photoessay re-creates daily life in the slave quarters on large plantations, contrasts it with the luxurious lifestyles of the slave holders, and documents how slaves tried to preserve their heritage, dignity, and hope. (Rev: BL 9/15/97; HBG 3/98; SLJ 11/97) [975]

18552 Bozonelis, Helen Koutras. *Primary Source Accounts of the War of 1812* (5–8). Illus. Series: America's Wars Through Primary Sources. 2006, Enslow LB $33.27 (978-1-59845-006-4). Soldiers' journal entries, letters from the homefront, personal recollections, songs and poetry, and newspaper articles are among the primary sources included in this general history of the war. (Rev: SLJ 4/07) [973.5]

18553 Britton, Tamara. *The Alamo* (3–5). Series: Symbols, Landmarks, and Monuments. 2004, ABDO LB $22.78 (978-1-59197-518-2). 32pp. Historical and contemporary photographs add interest to this presentation of the Alamo's history and significance. (Rev: SLJ 11/04)

18554 Burgan, Michael. *The Alamo* (3–6). Series: We the People. 2001, Compass Point LB $26.60 (978-0-7565-0097-9). 48pp. The major figures are profiled in this overview of the battle, along with maps, photographs, and paintings that bring the story to life. (Rev: SLJ 8/01)

18555 Burgan, Michael. *The Louisiana Purchase* (5–8). Series: We the People. 2002, Compass Point LB $26.60 (978-0-7565-0210-2). 48pp. An accessible, well-illustrated account of the purchase that doubled the size of the United States. (Rev: SLJ 7/02)

18556 Cantor, Carrie Nicholas. *The Mexican War: How the United States Gained Its Western Lands* (4–6). Illus. Series: A Proud Heritage: The Hispanic Library. 2003, Child's World LB $28.50 (978-1-56766-176-7). 40pp. A balanced account of the reasons why the United States went to war and of the progress of the war itself, with material on the prominent individuals, a timeline, and a glossary. (Rev: BL 10/15/03)

18557 Chase, John Churchill. *Louisiana Purchase: An American Story. Rev. ed.* (5–8). 2002, Pelican paper $12.95 (978-1-58980-084-7). The story of the Louisiana Purchase, engagingly told in comic-strip format. (Rev: BL 2/1/03) [973.4]

18558 Coleman, Wim, and Pat Perrin. *The Amazing Erie Canal and How a Big Ditch Opened Up the West* (4–7). Illus. Series: Wild History of the American West. 2006, Enslow LB $33.27 (978-1-59845-017-0). 128pp. Why was the Erie Canal built? What was its impact on American commerce and history? This richly illustrated profile answers those questions and offers a general overview of canals; 30 Internet links are provided for further research. (Rev: BL 10/15/06)

18559 Cosson, M. J. *Yankee Whalers* (4–6). Series: Events in American History. 2007, Rourke LB $29.93 (978-1-60044-140-0). 48pp. Life aboard whaling ships in the 1800s is a major focus of this volume. (Rev: BL 4/1/07; SLJ 4/07)

18560 Coulter, Laurie. *Cowboys and Coffin Makers: One Hundred 19th-Century Jobs You Might Have Feared or Fancied* (3–6). Illus. by Martha Newbigging. 2007, Annick $25.95 (978-1-55451-068-9); paper $16.95 (978-1-55451-067-2). 96pp. Miller, stagecoach driver, farmer, butcher, laundress, and dentist are just a few of the occupations described here. Readers will learn what life was like for all sorts of people during this time in the United States. (Rev: SLJ 6/07)

18561 Currie, Stephen. *Escapes from Slavery* (5–9). Series: Great Escapes. 2003, Gale LB $29.95 (978-1-59018-276-5). 112pp. The stories of six of the approximately 60,000 slaves who escaped from captivity in pre-Civil War America. (Rev: SLJ 4/04)

18562 Doeden, Matt. *The Battle of the Alamo* (4–6). Illus. Series: Graphic History. 2005, Capstone LB $26.60 (978-0-7368-3832-0). 32pp. An eye-catching and dramatically worded graphic presentation of the battle. [976]

18563 Draper, Charla L. *Cooking on Nineteenth-Century Whaling Ships* (4–7). Series: Exploring History Through Simple Recipes. 2000, Capstone LB $23.93 (978-0-7368-0602-2). 32pp. As well as learning about life on a whaling ship, this book provides a series of simple recipes. (Rev: BL 3/1/01; HBG 10/01; SLJ 4/01)

18564 Fischer, Laura. *Life in a Mississippi River Town* (2–4). Illus. Series: Picture the Past. 2003, Heinemann LB $24.22 (978-1-4034-3797-6). 32pp. A well-illustrated look at life along the Mississippi in the mid-19th century and the busy river's impact on society. (Rev: SLJ 6/04)

18565 Fradin, Dennis B. *The Alamo* (3–6). Series: Turning Points in U.S. History. 2006, Benchmark LB $29.93 (978-0-7614-2127-6). 45pp. A look at the famous battle, the events that led up to the fight for Texas's independence, the famous people involved, and its aftermath. (Rev: SLJ 3/07)

18566 Fradin, Dennis B. *Duel! Burr and Hamilton's Deadly War of Words* (3–6). Illus. by Larry Day. 2008, Walker $16.95 (978-0-8027-9583-0). 32pp. A fast-paced, dramatic account of the feud between Burr and Hamilton, with lots of information on the men's early lives and on their roles in the American Revolution. (Rev: BL 6/1–15/08; SLJ 7/08)

18567 Fradin, Dennis, and Judith Bloom Fradin. *The Price of Freedom: How One Town Stood Up to Slavery* (2–4). Illus. by Eric Velasquez. 2013, Walker $16.99 (978-080272166-2). 48pp. Fradin relates the true story of John Price, a slave who escaped by using the Underground Railroad only to be kidnapped by a Kentucky slave hunter two years later; the people of Oberlin, Ohio, staged a brave rescue despite the threat of imprisonment. (Rev: BL 2/1/13; LMC 3–4/13; SLJ 1/13*) [973.7]

18568 Gaines, Ann. *The Alamo: The Fight Over Texas* (4–6). Illus. Series: A Proud Heritage: The Hispanic Library. 2003, Child's World LB $28.50 (978-1-56766-

173-6). 40pp. An even-handed description of the history of the mission, its use as a fort, and the famous battle fought there. [976.4]

18569 Gay, Kathlyn, and Martin Gay. *War of 1812* (5–8). Series: Voices of the Past. 1995, Twenty-First Century LB $25.90 (978-0-8050-2846-1). Excerpts from letters, memoirs, and official reports highlight this well-illustrated history of the War of 1812 and its consequences. (Rev: BL 12/15/95; SLJ 3/96) [973.5]

18570 Green, Carl R. *The War of 1812* (4–6). Series: U.S. Wars. 2002, Enslow LB $25.26 (978-0-7660-5092-1). In addition to a concise discussion of the causes, progress, and resolution of the War of 1812, this book contains a lengthy listing of Web sites where students can find additional material on the subject. (Rev: BL 10/15/02; HBG 3/03)

18571 Gunderson, Mary. *Southern Plantation Cooking* (4–7). Illus. 2000, Capstone LB $23.93 (978-0-7368-0357-1). This book explores life on Southern plantations during the days of slavery with emphasis on the importance of food and food preparation. A few representative recipes are provided. (Rev: BL 8/00; HBG 10/00)

18572 Hansen, Joyce, and Gary McGowan. *Freedom Roads: Searching for the Underground Railroad* (5–8). Illus. by James Ransome. 2003, Cricket $18.95 (978-0-8126-2673-5). This look at the history of the Underground Railroad emphasizes how much of our knowledge consists of speculation and anecdotal material rather than hard evidence. (Rev: BL 5/1/03; HB 7–8/03; HBG 10/03; SLJ 9/03*) [973.7]

18573 Heinrichs, Ann. *The Underground Railroad* (3–5). Series: We the People. 2001, Compass Point LB $26.60 (978-0-7565-0102-0). 48pp. Heinrichs gives a clear explanation of the causes for the development of this route to freedom, details how it worked, and profiles key figures. (Rev: SLJ 7/01)

18574 Isaacs, Sally Senzell. *Life on a Southern Plantation* (1–3). Series: Picture the Past. 2000, Heinemann $21.36 (978-1-57572-316-7). A well-organized account that uses double-page spreads to describe life on a southern plantation before the Civil War with coverage of the lives of both the planters and the slaves. (Rev: HBG 3/01; SLJ 11/00)

18575 Jurmain, Suzanne. *Worst of Friends: Thomas Jefferson, John Adams and the True Story of an American Feud* (1–3). Illus. by Larry Day. 2011, Dutton $16.99 (978-0-525-47903-1). 32pp. The tumultuous friendship between Thomas Jefferson and John Adams is portrayed in this fascinating picture book. (Rev: BL 12/1/11*; LMC 3–4/12; SLJ 11/1/11*) [973.4]

18576 Kendall, Martha E. *The Erie Canal* (4–6). Illus. 2008, National Geographic $18.95 (978-1-4263-0022-6). 128pp. With period prints and photographs and a smooth narrative, Kendall tells the story of the building of the canal and how it helped shape westward expansion. (Rev: BL 1/1–15/08; SLJ 2/08)

18577 Kerley, Barbara. *Those Rebels, John and Tom* (2–4). Illus. by Edwin Fotheringham. 2012, Scholastic

$17.99 (978-054522268-6). 48pp. Thomas Jefferson and John Adams' divergent approaches to politics and philosophy are presented in this entertaining look at how our founding fathers excelled at compromise. (Rev: BL 12/1/11*; LMC 3–4/12; SLJ 9/12) [973.4]

18578 King, David C. *New Orleans* (5–8). Series: Battlefields Across America. 1998, Twenty-First Century LB $26.90 (978-0-7613-3010-3). The story of the famous 1815 battle in New Orleans in which the British were decisively defeated, including the background of the War of 1812, the role of Andrew Jackson, and the significance of this defeat to the British. (Rev: HBG 9/98; SLJ 8/98) [973.6]

18579 Leebrick, Kristal. *The United States Constitution* (3–8). Series: Let Freedom Ring. 2002, Capstone LB $23.93 (978-0-7368-1094-4). 48pp. James Madison's role in creating the constitution, the Constitutional Convention, and the ratification process are all covered here. Also use *The Declaration of Independence* (2002). (Rev: HBG 3/03; SLJ 7/02)

18580 Levy, Janey. *The Alamo: A Primary Source History of the Legendary Texas Mission* (5–8). Illus. Series: Primary Sources in American History. 2003, Rosen LB $29.25 (978-0-8239-3681-6). 64pp. Primary sources — including maps and paintings — tell the story of the Battle of the Alamo. (Rev: BL 5/15/03; SLJ 5/03)

18581 Levy, Janey. *The Erie Canal: A Primary Source History of the Canal That Changed America* (5–8). 2003, Rosen LB $29.25 (978-0-8239-3680-9). 64pp. The story of the construction of the Erie Canal and its impact on commerce is revealed through primary documents and many period illustrations. (Rev: SLJ 5/03)

18582 McGowen, Tom. *The Alamo* (3–6). Series: Cornerstones of Freedom, Second Series. 2003, Children's Pr. LB $26.00 (978-0-516-24208-8). 48pp. Background information provides context for the famous events at the Alamo; details of uniforms and weapons add to the picture. (Rev: SLJ 6/03)

18583 McKissack, Patricia C., and Fredrick McKissack. *Rebels Against Slavery: American Slave Revolts* (5–8). 1996, Scholastic paper $15.95 (978-0-590-45735-4). A fascinating account of the men and women who led revolts against slavery, including Toussaint L'Ouverture, Cinque, Harriet Tubman, and Nat Turner. (Rev: BCCB 6/96; BL 2/15/96; SLJ 3/96; VOYA 4/96) [970]

18584 McNeese, Tim. *Early National America: 1790–1850* (5–8). Illus. Series: Discovering U.S. History. 2010, Chelsea House $35 (978-1-60413-351-6). A satisfying survey of social and political developments in the early years of the United States, with illustrations, maps, photographs, and interesting sidebar feature **e** (Rev: LMC 11–12/10; SLJ 8/10) [973]

18585 Marquette, Scott. *War of 1812* (4–7). Series: America at War. 2002, Rourke LB $20.95 (978-1-58952-389-0). This book for middle-graders studies the war itself and the events that led up to it. (Rev: BL 10/15/02) [973.5]

18586 Martin, Michael. *Harriet Tubman and the Underground Railroad* (3–6). Illus. by Dave Hoover and Bill Anderson. Series: Graphic Library/Graphic History. 2004, Capstone LB $26.60 (978-0-7368-3829-0). 32pp. A graphic "novel" — factual, but embellished — about Tubman's role in the Underground Railroad; will appeal to reluctant readers. (Rev: SLJ 7/05)

18587 Moore, Cathy. *The Daring Escape of Ellen Craft* (1–3). Illus. by Mary O. Young. Series: On My Own History. 2002, Carolrhoda LB $23.93 (978-0-87614-462-6); paper $5.95 (978-0-87614-787-0). 48pp. This is the story, based on truth, of two slaves' 1848 journey from Georgia to safety in Philadelphia, the woman disguised as a white slave master. (Rev: HBG 10/02; SLJ 4/02)

18588 Morrison, Taylor. *Coast Mappers* (4–8). 2004, Houghton Mifflin $16.00 (978-0-618-25408-8). Science and biography are interwoven in this examination of the mid-19th-century mapping of the U.S. Pacific coastline. (Rev: BL 3/15/04; SLJ 5/04) [623.89]

18589 Nofi, Albert A. *The Underground Railroad and the Civil War* (4–8). Series: Untold History of the Civil War. 2000, Chelsea $25.00 (978-0-7910-5434-5). 64pp. A history of the dangers, devotion, excitement, and daring involved in this collaborative system that was developed to help fugitive Southern slaves reach freedom in the North or in Canada. (Rev: BL 5/15/00; HBG 10/00; SLJ 6/00)

18590 Olson, Kay Melchisedech. *Africans in America: 1619–1865* (4–6). Series: Coming to America. 2002, Capstone LB $23.93 (978-0-7368-1204-7). 32pp. The story of the forced migrations of Africans to America, their life of slavery, their culture and contributions, and information on famous African Americans. (Rev: BL 1/1–15/03; HBG 3/03)

18591 Paulson, Timothy J. *Days of Sorrow, Years of Glory, 1831–1850: From the Nat Turner Revolt to the Fugitive Slave Law* (5–9). Series: Milestones in Black American History. 1994, Chelsea paper $14.93 (978-0-7910-2552-9). An examination of the Underground Railroad, slave resistance, the Seminole Wars, and the abolition movement. (Rev: BL 11/1/94; SLJ 4/95; VOYA 12/94) [973]

18592 Ray, Kurt. *New Roads, Canals, and Railroads in Early-19th-Century America: The Transportation Revolution* (3–5). Illus. Series: Life in the New American Nation. 2004, Rosen LB $22.50 (978-0-8239-4036-3). 32pp. A look at the growth in transport-related construction in the early 19th century.

18593 Richards, Caroline Cowles. *A 19th Century Schoolgirl: The Diary of Caroline Cowles Richards, 1852–1855* (4–8). Ed. by Kerry Graves. Illus. Series: Diaries, Letters, and Memoirs. 2000, Capstone LB $23.93 (978-0-7368-0342-7). 32pp. This diary of a young girl living in western New York State in the early 1850s describes her daily life, schooling, and her reaction to the women's rights movement. (Rev: BL 10/15/00; HBG 10/00; SLJ 9/00)

18594 Santella, Andrew. *The Erie Canal* (4–6). Series: We the People. 2004, Compass Point LB $26.60 (978-0-

7565-0679-7). 48pp. Discusses the construction of this canal in the 19th century and its importance in transporting goods. (Rev: SLJ 2/05)

18595 Stefoff, Rebecca. *The War of 1812* (4–7). Illus. Series: North American Historical Atlases. 2000, Benchmark LB $27.07 (978-0-7614-1060-7). A clearly written text plus historical maps and reproductions are used to give an easy-to-read account of the War of 1812. (Rev: HBG 3/01; SLJ 1/01)

18596 Stewart, Mark. *The Alamo, February 23–March 6, 1836* (5–7). Series: American Battlefields. 2004, Enchanted Lion $14.95 (978-1-59270-026-4). This overview of the Battle of the Alamo offers a clear account of the conflict and an examination of the developments leading up to it; sidebars, illustrations, a timeline, and other features add to the narrative. (Rev: BL 11/1/04) [976.4]

18597 Turner, Glennette Tilley. *The Underground Railroad in Illinois* (5–8). 2001, Newman Educational paper $16.95 (978-0-938990-05-5). Using a question-and-answer format, this book focuses on the Underground Railroad in Illinois, the historical period, the problems, people who worked on the effort, and the many heroic deeds. (Rev: BL 2/15/01) [973.7]

18598 Uschan, Michael V. *The California Gold Rush* (5–8). Series: Landmark Events in American History. 2003, World Almanac LB $31.00 (978-0-8368-5374-2). An attractive account of the California gold rush, famous people involved, and its consequences. (Rev: BL 10/15/03) [979.4]

18599 Walker, Paul Robert. *Remember the Alamo: Texians, Tejanos, and Mexicans Tell Their Stories* (5–8). Illus. 2007, National Geographic $17.95 (978-1-4263-0010-3). 64pp. A detailed account of the siege of the Alamo, with explanation of the events leading up to the crisis and with many firsthand descriptions. (Rev: BL 5/15/07; SLJ 8/07)

18600 Whitcraft, Melissa. *Seward's Folly* (3–6). Series: Cornerstones of Freedom, Second Series. 2002, Children's Book Pr. LB $26.00 (978-0-516-22525-8). 48pp. An attractive account of the purchase of the Alaskan territory. (Rev: SLJ 12/02)

18601 Williams, Carla. *The Underground Railroad* (4–6). Series: Journey to Freedom. 2009, The Child's World LB $28.50 (978-1-60253-139-0). 32pp. A solid overview of the Underground Railroad told through personal stories, photographs, news accounts, and brief biographies. (Rev: SLJ 7/09)

PIONEER LIFE AND WESTWARD EXPANSION

18602 Ammon, Richard. *Conestoga Wagons* (2–5). Illus. 2000, Holiday House $17.95 (978-0-8234-1475-8). 32pp. This illustrated account gives the history of the vehicles used for long-distance hauling between 1750 and 1850 and discusses their construction, parts, uses, and the people who drove them. (Rev: BCCB 9/00; BL 10/1/00; HBG 3/01; SLJ 9/00)

18603 Anderson, Dale. *Westward Expansion* (5–8). Series: The Making of America. 2001, Raintree LB $28.54 (978-0-8172-5705-7). 96pp. An attractive, balanced history of the expansion of the United States to the Pacific with many biographies of pioneers given in sidebars. (Rev: BL 4/15/01; HBG 10/01)

18604 Bial, Raymond. *Cow Towns* (2–5). Series: American Community. 2004, Children's Pr. LB $29.00 (978-0-516-23706-0). 48pp. The daily lives of the people — cattlemen and prospectors, for example — who populated the towns of the early West are described plus detailed back matter and many illustrations. Also use *Frontier Settlements* and *Missions and Presidios* (both 2004). (Rev: SLJ 1/05)

18605 Bial, Raymond. *Ghost Towns of the American West* (3–5). Illus. 2001, Houghton $16.00 (978-0-618-06557-8). Several western ghost towns are presented, with pictures of how they looked then and look today and details of why they were abandoned. (Rev: BCCB 2/01; BL 1/1–15/01; HB 3/01; HBG 10/01; SLJ 2/01)

18606 Blashfield, Jean F. *The California Gold Rush* (3–6). Series: We the People. 2000, Compass Point LB $26.60 (978-0-7565-0041-2). 48pp. A straightforward account of why and how people traveled to California during the Gold Rush and of the lasting effects this migration had on western history. (Rev: SLJ 3/01)

18607 Blashfield, Jean F. *The Oregon Trail* (3–6). 2000, Compass Point LB $26.60 (978-0-7565-0045-0). 48pp. This book explains the building of the Oregon Trail, its uses, and travel conditions along it. Also use: *The Santa Fe Trail* (2000). (Rev: SLJ 3/01)

18608 Brill, Marlene T. *Bronco Charlie and the Pony Express* (2–4). Illus. by Craig Orback. Series: On My Own History. 2004, Carolrhoda LB $27.93 (978-1-57505-587-9); paper $5.95 (978-1-57505-618-0). 46pp. Bronco Charlie, 11, became the youngest rider for the Pony Express in 1861 and rode bravely through various dangers. (Rev: SLJ 8/04)

18609 Brown, Don. *Gold! Gold from the American River!* (2–4). Illus. by author. 2011, Roaring Brook $17.99 (978-159643223-9). 64pp. With quotations, maps, cartoon figures, and revealing vignettes about the lives of miners, this volume covers the California gold rush and the people involved. Lexile 1010L (Rev: BL 12/1/10; SLJ 2/1/11) [979.4]

18610 Burnett, Linda. *Pioneers: Adventure in a New Land* (4–6). Series: Trailblazers of the West. 2005, Children's Pr. LB $24.50 (978-0-516-25127-1); paper $6.95 (978-0-516-25097-7). 48pp. The hard life of pioneers on the western frontier is portrayed in short chapters suitable for reluctant readers. (Rev: SLJ 4/06)

18611 Calabro, Marian. *The Perilous Journey of the Donner Party* (5–8). 1999, Houghton Mifflin $20.00 (978-0-395-86610-8). The story of the ill-fated Donner Party, as seen through the eyes of 12-year-old Virginia Reed. (Rev: BL 4/1/99*; HB 5–6/99; SLJ 5/99; VOYA 2/00) [979.4]

18612 Coleman, Wim, and Pat Perrin. *What Made the Wild West Wild* (4–8). Illus. Series: The Wild History of the American West. 2006, Enslow LB $33.27 (978-1-59845-016-3). The myths and legends of the Wild West are debunked in this expansive overview of media portrayals and reality. (Rev: SLJ 1/07) [978]

18613 Collier, Christopher, and James Lincoln Collier. *Indians, Cowboys, and Farmers: And the Battle for the Great Plains* (5–8). Series: The Drama of American History. 2001, Marshall Cavendish LB $31.36 (978-0-7614-1052-2). This excellently written and illustrated account covers the history of the Great Plains from the end of the Civil War to 1910, by which time the Native Americans had been scattered and the ranchers and farmers had reached a truce. (Rev: BL 3/15/01; HBG 10/01; SLJ 7/01)

18614 Comport, Sally Wern. *The Great Expedition of Lewis and Clark: By Private Reubin Field, Member of the Corps of Discovery* (3–4). Illus. by author. 2003, Farrar $17.00 (978-0-374-38039-7). 40pp. Writing from the point of view of Reubin Field, Edwards gives a lively account of the famous expedition, its principal characters, and its dangers and delights. (Rev: BL 8/03; HBG 4/04; SLJ 11/03)

18615 Crewe, Sabrina, and Dale Anderson. *The California Gold Rush* (3–5). Series: Events That Shaped America. 2003, Gareth Stevens LB $26.00 (978-0-8368-3393-5). 32pp. This brief history of the mid-19th-century California Gold Rush covers the discovery of gold at Sutter's Mill and that event's impact on the state and the nation as a whole. (Rev: HBG 10/03; SLJ 10/03)

18616 Davis, Kenneth C. *Don't Know Much About the Pioneers* (3–5). Illus. by Renée Andriani. Series: Don't Know Much About. 2003, HarperCollins LB $16.89 (978-0-06-028618-7). 48pp. Quizzes, quotations, feature sidebars, and bright illustrations make this a volume for browsing. (Rev: HBG 10/03; SLJ 6/03)

18617 Dean, Arlan. *The Mormon Pioneer Trail: From Nauvoo, Illinois, to the Great Salt Lake, Utah* (2–4). Illus. Series: Famous American Trails. 2003, Rosen LB $19.95 (978-0-8239-6476-5). 24pp. For early readers and researchers, this title explores the 1,200-mile trail, providing lots of illustrations and maps. (Rev: SLJ 6/03)

18618 Dean, Arlan. *The Old Spanish Trail: From Santa Fe, New Mexico, to Los Angeles, California* (2–4). Series: Famous American Trails. 2003, Rosen LB $19.95 (978-0-8239-6480-2). 24pp. This attractive and informative survey for young readers includes maps, photographs, and illustrations. (Rev: SLJ 12/03)

18619 Dean, Arlan. *The Santa Fe Trail: From Independence, Missouri, to Santa Fe, New Mexico* (2–4). Illus. Series: Famous American Trails. 2003, Rosen LB $19.95 (978-0-8239-6481-9). 24pp. For early readers and researchers, this title explores the historic wagon trail, providing lots of illustrations and maps. (Rev: SLJ 6/03)

18620 Delgado, James P. *Shipwrecks from the Westward Movement* (5–7). Series: Shipwrecks. 2000, Watts LB $25.50 (978-0-531-20380-4). 64pp. A discussion and exploration of the shipwrecks — from small canoes to steam-powered riverboats — that occurred as European settlers moved across America. (Rev: BL 10/15/00)

18621 Domnauer, Teresa. *Life in the West* (2–4). Series: A True Book: Westward Expansion. 2010, Children's Press LB $26 (978-0-531-20583-9). 48pp. This volume answers such questions as "Why did so many people choose to move west?" and "What kinds of chores did pioneer children do?" as it explores life on ranches and the prairie. Also use *Westward Expansion* (2010). (Rev: LMC 8–9/10; SLJ 4/1/10) [978]

18622 Fine, Jil. *The Transcontinental Railroad: Tracks Across America* (4–6). Series: Trailblazers of the West. 2005, Children's Pr. LB $24.50 (978-0-516-25128-8); paper $6.95 (978-0-516-25098-4). This attractive title chronicles the building of the transcontinental railroad, an important step in opening up the American West, and the hardships suffered by those involved; short, well-illustrated chapters are suitable for reluctant readers. (Rev: SLJ 4/06)

18623 Freedman, Russell. *Children of the Wild West* (5–9). 1983, Clarion $18.00 (978-0-89919-143-0). A look at the life of the children of pioneers. (Rev: BL 1/1/90) [978]

18624 Freedman, Russell. *Cowboys of the Wild West* (5–8). 1990, Houghton Mifflin paper $9.95 (978-0-395-54800-4). Text and excellent historical photographs describe these romantic figures. (Rev: BCCB 12/85; HB 3–4/86) [978.02]

18625 Friedman, Mel. *The California Gold Rush* (2–4). Series: A True Book: Westward Expansion. 2010, Children's Press LB $26 (978-0-531-20581-5). 48pp. This volume answers such questions as "Why was travel to California so dangerous?" and "What was life like in a gold-mining camp?" as it explores life during the gold rush. (Rev: SLJ 4/1/10) [979.4]

18626 Galford, Ellen. *The Trail West: Exploring History Through Art* (5–8). Series: Picture That! 2004, Two-Can $19.95 (978-1-58728-442-7). Paintings serve as the vehicle to draw students into the story of westward expansion. (Rev: BL 11/1/04; SLJ 2/05) [978]

18627 Goldsmith, Connie. *Lost in Death Valley: The True Story of Four Families in California's Gold Rush* (5–8). Illus. 2001, Twenty-First Century LB $24.90 (978-0-7613-1915-3). 144pp. Using original sources, the author has re-created the story of an ill-fated pioneer trek and the shortcut that led them into Death Valley. (Rev: BL 4/1/01; HBG 10/01; SLJ 4/01; VOYA 10/01)

18628 Graves, Kerry A. *Going to School in Pioneer Times* (4–6). Illus. Series: Going to School in History. 2001, Capstone LB $23.93 (978-0-7368-0804-0). 32pp. Today's students will enjoy this look at the one-room schoolhouse of pioneer days, introduced by historical context and illustrated with period photographs. (Rev: BL 10/15/01; HBG 3/02; SLJ 1/02)

18629 Hailstone, Ruth. *The White Ox: The Journey of Emily Swain Squires* (2–5). Illus. by Dan Burr. 2009,

Boyds Mills $18.95 (978-1-59078-555-3). 40pp. Dramatic art extends this story of 10-year-old Emily, a Mormon, and her grueling journey to Salt Lake City; set in 1863, this is based on the experiences of an ancestor of the author. (Rev: BL 4/15/09)

18630 Hester, Sallie. *A Covered Wagon Girl: The Diary of Sallie Hester, 1849–1850* (4–6). Series: Diaries, Letters, and Memoirs. 2000, Capstone LB $23.93 (978-0-7368-0344-1). Diary entries by a young pioneer girl reveal everyday life on the American frontier. (Rev: BL 10/15/00; HBG 10/00; SLJ 9/00)

18631 Isaacs, Sally Senzell. *The Gold Rush* (4–6). Illus. Series: The American Adventure. 2003, Heinemann LB $25.65 (978-1-4034-2501-0). 32pp. An accessible account of the "Fortyniners" who thronged to California in the mid-18th century. (Rev: HBG 4/04; SLJ 6/04)

18632 Isaacs, Sally Senzell. *The Great Land Rush* (4–6). Illus. Series: The American Adventure. 2003, Heinemann LB $25.64 (978-1-4034-2505-8). 32pp. The story of the rush to settle land on the American frontier in the late 19th century, including its impact on the native people who already lived there. (Rev: HBG 4/04; SLJ 6/04)

18633 Isaacs, Sally Senzell. *The Lewis and Clark Expedition* (4–6). Illus. Series: The American Adventure. 2003, Heinemann LB $25.64 (978-1-4034-2503-4). The impact on the native peoples of the West and Pacific Northwest is one focus of this well-illustrated account. (Rev: HBG 4/04; SLJ 6/04)

18634 Isaacs, Sally Senzell. *Life on a Pioneer Homestead* (1–3). Series: Picture the Past. 2000, Heinemann LB $21.36 (978-1-57572-313-6). Using double-page spreads, this well-organized account covers such basic topics as pioneer food, clothing, and rearing of children. Also use from this series *Life on the Oregon Trail* (2000). (Rev: HBG 3/01; SLJ 11/00)

18635 January, Brendan. *Little Bighorn: June 25, 1876* (5–7). Series: American Battlefields. 2004, Enchanted Lion $14.95 (978-1-59270-028-8). This overview of the Battle of Little Bighorn offers a clear-cut account of the bloody conflict and an examination of the developments leading up to it; sidebars, illustrations, a timeline, and other features add to the narrative. (Rev: BL 11/1/04) [973]

18636 Johmann, Carol A., and Elizabeth J. Rieth. *Going West! Journey on a Wagon Train to Settle a Frontier Town* (3–6). Illus. by Michael Kline. Series: Kaleidoscope Kids. 2000, Williamson paper $14.25 (978-1-885593-38-2). 96pp. As well as information on wagon trains, this book gives good background history involving the opening up of the West and outlines projects that use the crafts and skills of the pioneers. (Rev: SLJ 1/01)

18637 Josephson, Judith P. *Growing up in Pioneer America: 1800 to 1890* (4–6). Series: Our America. 2002, Lerner LB $26.60 (978-0-8225-0659-1). The lives of children in this period are described with many quotations and excerpts from diaries, letter, and memoirs. (Rev: HBG 3/03; SLJ 2/03)

18638 Klausmeier, Robert. *Cowboy* (4–7). Series: American Pastfinder. 1996, Lerner LB $21.27 (978-0-8225-2975-0). This account focuses on the huge cattle drives and the men who led them in the years following the Civil War. (Rev: BL 3/1/96; SLJ 3/96) [636.2]

18639 Klobuchar, Lisa. *The History and Activities of the Wagon Trail* (3–5). Series: Hands-on American History. 2006, Heinemann LB $27.07 (978-1-4034-6055-4). An accessible and informative account of life on the westbound wagon trains is bolstered by illustrations and activities — a recipe, a toy, and a prairie schooner replica. (Rev: BL 9/1/06)

18640 Landau, Elaine. *The Pony Express* (2–4). Illus. Series: Westward Expansion (True Book). 2006, Children's Pr. LB $25.00 (978-0-516-25873-7). 48pp. The colorful — but brief — history of the Pony Express, launched to move mail from St. Joseph, Missouri, to San Francisco in a scant ten days, is chronicled in readable text, drawings, and maps. (Rev: BL 4/1/06)

18641 Landau, Elaine. *The Transcontinental Railroad* (5–8). Series: Watts Library: American West. 2005, Watts LB $25.50 (978-0-531-12326-3). The story behind the building of the Transcontinental Railroad, with illustrations, maps, a timeline, and sidebar features. (Rev: SLJ 12/05)

18642 Lassieur, Allison. *The Wild West: An Interactive History Adventure* (3–5). Illus. Series: You Choose. 2008, Capstone LB $20.99 (978-1-4296-2342-1). Put yourself right in the middle of the Wild West action as you choose between various actions; will you be a lawman or a gambler, for example? (Rev: BL 4/1/09)

18643 Leeper, David R. *The Diary of David R. Leeper: Rush for Gold* (3–6). Ed. by Connie Roop and Peter Roop. Illus. Series: My Own Words. 2000, Marshall Cavendish LB $27.07 (978-0-7614-1011-9). 64pp. This book, taken from Leeper's memoirs published in 1894, tells how he crossed the country by wagon train and his life as a prospector for gold in California. (Rev: BL 2/15/01; HBG 3/01; SLJ 3/01)

18644 Markel, Rita J. *Your Travel Guide to America's Old West* (4–6). Illus. Series: Passport to History. 2003, Lerner LB $26.60 (978-0-8225-3074-9). 96pp. Information about the Old West — everything from historical anecdotes to profiles of key individuals to details of dress and behavior — is conveyed in the style of a travel guide complete with photographs and prints. (Rev: BL 2/15/04; HBG 4/04; SLJ 4/04)

18645 Miller, Brandon Marie. *Buffalo Gals: Women of the Old West* (4–7). 1995, Lerner LB $30.35 (978-0-8225-1730-6). A realistic portrait of the hardships faced by women pioneers during the 19th century on the western frontier. (Rev: BCCB 7–8/95; BL 5/1/95; SLJ 6/95*) [978]

18646 O'Donnell, Kerri. *The Gold Rush: A Primary Source History of the Search for Gold in California* (4–8). Series: Primary Sources in American History. 2003, Rosen LB $29.25 (978-0-8239-3682-3). 64pp. Timelines and reproductions of period photographs and relevant items add to the narrative in this introduction to the Gold Rush, the life of the miners, and the lawless character of the West. (Rev: SLJ 5/03)

18647 Raabe, Emily. *Pioneers: Life as a Homesteader* (2–4). Series: Westward Ho! 2003, Rosen LB $19.95 (978-0-8239-6498-7). 24pp. An overview of what life was like for the men and women who opened up the American West. (Rev: SLJ 12/03)

18648 Randolph, Ryan P. *Frontier Schools and School-teachers* (3–5). Illus. Series: The Library of the Westward Expansion. 2003, Rosen LB $21.25 (978-0-8239-6295-2). 24pp. Historical artwork and "Did You Know" boxes enliven this overview of schools on the American frontier. (Rev: SLJ 10/03)

18649 Randolph, Ryan P. *Wild West Lawmen and Outlaws* (3–5). Illus. Series: The Library of the Westward Expansion. 2003, Rosen LB $21.25 (978-0-8239-6293-8). 24pp. Profiles the men who helped to put the "wild" in Wild West and the law enforcement officers who did their best to keep the peace. (Rev: SLJ 10/03)

18650 Ratliff, Tom. *You Wouldn't Want to Be a Pony Express Rider! A Dusty, Thankless Job You'd Rather Not Do* (3–5). Illus. by Mark Bergin. 2012, Scholastic LB $29 (978-053120872-4); paper $9.95 (978-053120947-9). 32pp. Ratliff presents a frank look at the life of a Pony Express rider and its many challenges. (Rev: BL 2/15/12) [383]

18651 Redmond, Shirley Raye. *Lewis and Clark: A Prairie Dog for the President* (1–3). Illus. by John Manders. Series: Step into Reading. 2003, Random LB $11.99 (978-0-375-81120-3); paper $3.99 (978-0-375-91120-0). 48pp. This entertaining history for beginning readers uses cartoon-style art to portray Lewis and Clark's efforts to find suitable presents to send back to President Jefferson. (Rev: BL 8/03; HBG 4/04)

18652 Ross, Stewart. *Cowboys* (5–7). Series: Fact or Fiction? 1995, Millbrook LB $26.90 (978-1-56294-618-0). The life of cowboys during the late 1800s is covered, with information that tries to separate fact from fable. (Rev: BL 7/95; SLJ 5/95) [978.02]

18653 Saffer, Barbara. *The California Gold Rush* (5–7). Series: The American West. 2002, Mason Crest LB $19.95 (978-1-59084-060-3). 64pp. Reluctant readers will be drawn to this attractive account of the hardships of traveling to California and the life in the mining camps. (Rev: SLJ 4/02)

18654 Salas, Laura Purdie. *The Wilderness Road, 1775* (4–6). Illus. Series: Let Freedom Ring. 2003, Capstone LB $23.93 (978-0-7368-1561-1). Tells the story of the building of the Wilderness Road, which opened the way into Kentucky for early American settlers; includes a chapter on Daniel Boone. (Rev: HBG 10/03; SLJ 12/03)

18655 Sanford, William R. *The Chisholm Trail in American History* (4–6). Series: In American History. 2000, Enslow LB $26.60 (978-0-7660-1345-2). 112pp. This book traces the history of the Chisholm Trail, the daily life of the cowboys who used it, and its eventual demise. (Rev: BL 7/00; HBG 3/01; SLJ 12/00)

18656 Schaffer, David. *The Louisiana Purchase: The Deal of the Century That Doubled the Nation* (5–8). Illus. Series: The Wild History of the American West. 2006, Enslow LB $33.27 (978-1-59845-018-7). Tells the story behind America's negotiations to buy the vast Louisiana Territory for $15 million, or less than 3 cents an acre; includes a list of carefully selected Web sites that offer additional information. (Rev: SLJ 12/06) [973.4]

18657 Schlaepfer, Gloria G. *The Louisiana Purchase* (5–8). Series: Watts Library: American West. 2005, Watts LB $25.50 (978-0-531-12300-3). The story behind the Louisiana Purchase and its role in America's westward expansion, with illustrations, maps, a timeline, and sidebar features. (Rev: SLJ 12/05)

18658 Schroeder, Lisa Golden. *California Gold Rush Cooking* (4–7). Series: Exploring History Through Simple Recipes. 2000, Capstone LB $23.93 (978-0-7368-0603-9). 32pp. This book discusses the California Gold Rush and everyday life of the period with details of the kinds of food eaten and some simple recipes. (Rev: BL 3/1/01; HBG 10/01; SLJ 4/01)

18659 Schwartz, Heather E. *Foul, Filthy American Frontier: The Disgusting Details About the Journey Out West* (4–8). Series: Fact Finders: Disgusting History. 2010, Capstone LB $25.32 (978-1-4296-3957-6). 32pp. Allen concentrates on the grosser side of life on the American frontier, describing poor sanitation, rotten food, bugs, medical horrors, and so forth. (Rev: LMC 11–12/10)

18660 Sheinkin, Steve. *Which Way to the Wild West?* (5–9). Illus. by Tim Robinson. 2009, Flash Point $19.95 (978-1-59643-321-2). 260pp. Useful for both researchers and browsers, this is a fact-filled but lively history of just what went on in the West. Lexile 940L (Rev: HB 9–10/09; LMC 10/09; SLJ 9/09)

18661 Sonneborn, Liz. *The Mormon Trail* (5–8). Series: Watts Library: American West. 2005, Watts LB $25.50 (978-0-531-12317-1). The story behind the westward trek of thousands of Mormons during the middle of the 19th century, with illustrations, maps, a timeline, and sidebar features. (Rev: SLJ 12/05)

18662 Sonneborn, Liz. *Women of the American West* (4–7). Series: Watts Library: American West. 2005, Watts LB $25.50 (978-0-531-12318-8). Excerpts from first-person accounts offer a glimpse into what life was like for the women who helped to open the American West. (Rev: BL 10/15/05) [978]

18663 Spradlin, Michael P. *Off Like the Wind! The First Ride of the Pony Express* (2–5). Illus. by Layne Johnson. 2010, Walker $17.99 (978-0-8027-9652-3). 40pp. A dramatic account of the exploits of the riders who faced many dangers as they delivered the mail. (Rev: BL 1/1/10; LMC 1–2/10; SLJ 2/1/10) [383]

18664 Spradlin, Michael P. *Texas Rangers: Legendary Lawmen* (2–4). Illus. by Roxie Munro. 2008, Walker $16.95 (978-0-8027-8096-6). 32pp. A picture-book history of the Texas Rangers (formed in 1823) and their exploits, this is more suitable for browsing than research. (Rev: BL 1/1–15/08; SLJ 4/08)

18665 Staton, Hilarie N. *Cowboys and the Wild West* (4–6). Illus. Series: All About America. 2011, Kingfisher LB $19.89 (978-0-7534-6582-0); paper $9.99 (978-0-7534-6510-3). 32pp. With many photographs, paintings, maps, and primary documents, this overview of the lives of cowboys and other residents of the Wild West will be useful for report writers. (Rev: BL 9/1/11; SLJ 8/11) [978]

18666 Stefoff, Rebecca. *First Frontier* (4–7). Series: North American Historical Atlases. 2000, Benchmark LB $24.21 (978-0-7614-1059-1). This book presents an illustrated view of the western expansion and its effects on Native Americans, frontiersmen, speculators, and soldiers. (Rev: HBG 3/01; SLJ 1/01)

18667 Stefoff, Rebecca. *The Opening of the West* (5–8). 2002, Benchmark LB $34.21 (978-0-7614-1201-4). 105pp. A collection of primary sources that includes excerpts from letters, newspaper articles, and journal entries commenting on different aspects of frontier life, exploration, and the plight of Native Americans. (Rev: HBG 10/03; SLJ 4/03)

18668 Stein, R. Conrad. *On the Old Western Frontier* (4–8). Series: How We Lived. 1999, Benchmark LB $28.50 (978-0-7614-0909-0). An interesting book that gives an overview of the history and living conditions on the American frontier with material on everyday life, farming and ranching, social life, religion, Native Americans, and slaves. (Rev: HBG 10/00; SLJ 3/00) [978]

18669 Stein, R. Conrad. *Spanish Missionaries: Bringing Spanish Culture to the Americas* (3–6). Series: A Proud Heritage. 2005, Child's World LB $28.50 (978-1-59296-387-4). A look at the missions found in various parts of the country and at key missionary leaders. (Rev: SLJ 6/05)

18670 Sundling, Charles W. *Cowboys of the Frontier* (4–6). Illus. Series: Frontier Land. 2000, ABDO $24.21 (978-1-57765-045-4). An accessible text that describes the daily life of hardworking cattle drivers, with emphasis on the second half of the 19th century. (Rev: BL 10/15/00; HBG 10/00; SLJ 7/00)

18671 Sundling, Charles W. *Explorers of the Frontier* (4–6). Series: Frontier Land. 2000, ABDO LB $24.21 (978-1-57765-044-7). 32pp. Using many easy-to-read maps and a fact-filled text, this book traces the exploits of the explorers who opened up the West. A companion volume is *Mountain Men of the Frontier* (2000). (Rev: BL 10/15/00; HBG 10/00)

18672 Sundling, Charles W. *Pioneers of the Frontier* (4–6). Series: Frontier Land. 2000, ABDO LB $24.21 (978-1-57765-047-8). 32pp. The day-to-day struggles of the early pioneers of the West are re-created in text and pictures. Also use *Women of the Frontier* (2000). (Rev: BL 10/15/00; HBG 10/00)

18673 Swanson, Wayne. *Why the West Was Wild* (5–8). 2004, Annick $12.95 (978-1-55037-837-5); paper $12.95 (978-1-55037-836-8). The excitement of the Old West is captured in this lavishly illustrated survey of the region's history during the second half of the 19th century. (Rev: BL 8/04; SLJ 6/04) [978]

18674 Thompson, Linda. *The Transcontinental Railroad* (4–6). Illus. Series: Expansion of America. 2005, Rourke LB $20.95 (978-1-59515-227-5). 48pp. The who, what, where, when, and how of the railroad, with background information linking the project to America's expansion. Among the other titles in this series by this author are *The Erie Canal*, *The Mississippi and West*, and *The Oregon Trail* (all 2005). (Rev: BL 4/1/05)

18675 Todras, Ellen H. *Wagon Trains and Settlers* (4–6). Illus. Series: All About America. 2011, Kingfisher paper $9.99 (978-0-7534-6-511-0). 32pp. With many photographs, paintings, maps, and primary documents, this overview of the lives of pioneers will be useful for report writers. (Rev: BL 9/1/11; SLJ 8/11) [973.8]

18676 Uschan, Michael V. *The Transcontinental Railroad* (4–7). Series: Landmark Events in American History. 2003, World Almanac LB $31.00 (978-0-8368-5382-7). In accessible language and with plenty of illustrations, this is the story of the railroad that spanned the nation. (Rev: SLJ 6/04) [385]

18677 Wadsworth, Ginger. *Words West: Voices of Young Pioneers* (5–8). 2003, Clarion $18.00 (978-0-618-23475-2). Excerpts from journals and other documents give a clear picture of the experiences of young people traveling west between 1840 and 1870. (Rev: HBG 4/04; SLJ 12/03) [917.804]

18678 Waldman, Stuart. *The Last River: John Wesley Powell and the Colorado River Exploring Expedition* (4–7). Illus. by Gregory Manchess. 2005, Mikaya $19.95 (978-1-931414-09-8). This is the exciting story of the three-month exploration of the Colorado River led by the one-armed John Wesley Powell in 1869; excerpts from journals and letters reveal details of the dangers faced. (Rev: BL 12/15/05; SLJ 2/06) [550.92]

18679 Walker, Paul Robert. *Gold Rush and Riches* (4–6). Illus. Series: All About America. 2011, Kingfisher LB $19.89 (978-0-7534-6584-4); paper $9.99 (978-0-7534-6512-7). 32pp. With many photographs, paintings, maps, and primary documents, this overview of the lives of men and women who headed west during the gold rush will be useful for report writers. (Rev: BL 9/1/11; SLJ 8/11) [978]

18680 Werther, Scott P. *The Donner Party* (5–7). Illus. 2002, Children's LB $24.50 (978-0-516-23901-9). 48pp. The fate of the Donner Party is described against the backdrop of life in America in the 1840s and the dangers of travel to the West and the Pacific. (Rev: SLJ 10/02)

18681 Woog, Adam. *A Cowboy in the Wild West* (3–5). Illus. Series: Daily Life. 2002, Gale LB $23.70 (978-0-7377-0990-2). 48pp. An information-packed review of a cowboy's daily routine, including material on clothing, trail drives and roundups, and the overall history of cowboys. (Rev: BL 12/1/02; SLJ 8/02)

18682 Yasuda, Anita. *Explore the Wild West! With 25 Great Projects* (2–4). Illus. by Alex Kim. 2012, Nomad paper $12.95 (978-19367497-1-3). 96pp. Projects and activities extend the interesting narratives about Native Americans, miners, cowboys, peacekeepers, lawbreakers, and pioneer life in general. (Rev: BL 8/12; SLJ 8/1/12) [978.02]

THE CIVIL WAR

18683 Abnett, Dan. *The Battle of Gettysburg: Spilled Blood on Sacred Ground* (4–6). Illus. by Dheeraj Verma. Series: Graphic Battles of the Civil War. 2007, Rosen LB $29.25 (978-1-4042-0777-6). 48pp. This graphic-novel treatment of the crucial battle has a dramatic style that seems to bring the reader close to the action. (Rev: SLJ 5/07)

18684 Allegra, Mike. *Sarah Gives Thanks: How Thanksgiving Became a National Holiday* (1–3). Illus. by David C. Gardner. 2012, Whitman $16.99 (978-0-8075-7239-9). 32pp. An engaging picture book about poet and magazine editor Sarah Josepha Hale, who played a key role in persuading Lincoln to proclaim Thanksgiving a national holiday. e Lexile AD730L (Rev: BL 10/1/12; LMC 11–12/12*; SLJ 8/12) [394.2649]

18685 Allen, Thomas B. *Harriet Tubman, Secret Agent: How Daring Slaves and Free Blacks Spied for the Union During the Civil War* (5–8). Illus. by Carla Bauer. 2006, National Geographic $16.95 (978-0-7922-7889-4). 191pp. The efforts of Tubman and other slaves to gather important information and pass it to the Union forces is the focus of this volume that includes examples of a code sometimes used. (Rev: BCCB 1/07; BL 12/1/06; HBG 4/07; LMC 5/07; SLJ 2/07*)

18686 Anderson, Dale. *The Causes of the Civil War* (4–6). 2004, World Almanac LB $31.00 (978-0-8368-5581-4); paper $11.95 (978-0-8368-5590-6). 48pp. A concise and readable overview of the underlying causes of the Civil War, with material on key individuals, interesting sidebar features, maps, and many appropriate illustrations. Also use *A Soldier's Life in the Civil War*, *The Aftermath of the Civil War*, and *The Union Victory: (July 1863–1865)*. (Rev: SLJ 3/05)

18687 Anderson, Dale. *The Civil War at Sea* (4–6). Series: World Almanac Library of the Civil War. 2004, World Almanac LB $31.00 (978-0-8368-5585-2). 48pp. A look at major battles at sea, with period photographs, maps, and sidebars about individuals. Also use in this series: *The Civil War in the East (1861–July 1863)*, *The Civil War in the West (1861–July 1863)*, and *The Home Fronts in the Civil War* (all 2004). (Rev: SLJ 7/04)

18688 Armentrout, David, and Patricia Armentrout. *The Emancipation Proclamation* (4–7). Series: Documents That Shaped the Nation. 2004, Rourke $20.95 (978-1-59515-233-6). 48pp. The reasons for the creation of this document and the results of its proclamation are thoroughly explored in concise text, accompanied by an array of maps and illustrations. (Rev: BL 10/15/04)

18689 Armstrong, Jennifer. *A Three-Minute Speech: Lincoln's Remarks at Gettysburg* (2–5). Series: Milestone Books. 2003, Aladdin paper $3.99 (978-0-689-85622-

8). 96pp. This appealing introduction to the Gettysburg Address provides extensive background information. (Rev: BL 9/1/03; HBG 4/04; SLJ 9/03)

18690 Arnold, James R., and Roberta Wiener. *Divided in Two: The Road to Civil War* (4–7). Series: The Civil War. 2002, Lerner LB $25.26 (978-0-8225-2312-3). A well-designed oversize book that describes the events of 1861 that led to the outbreak of the Civil War. (Rev: BL 10/15/02; HBG 10/02; SLJ 7/02) [973.7]

18691 Arnold, James R., and Roberta Wiener. *Life Goes On: The Civil War at Home* (4–7). Series: The Civil War. 2002, Lerner LB $25.26 (978-0-8225-2315-4). Many easy-to-follow maps and illustrations are used with a simple text to describe life on the home front in both South and North during the Civil War. (Rev: BL 10/15/02; HBG 10/02; SLJ 7/02) [973.7]

18692 Arnold, James R., and Roberta Wiener. *Lost Cause: The End of the Civil War* (4–7). Series: The Civil War. 2002, Lerner LB $25.26 (978-0-8225-2317-8). Beginning with the campaign of 1864, this well-illustrated account traces the Civil War to Appomattox and beyond. (Rev: BL 10/15/02; HBG 10/02; SLJ 6/02) [973.7]

18693 Arnold, James R., and Roberta Wiener. *On to Richmond: The Civil War in the East, 1861-1862* (4–7). Series: Civil War. 2002, Lerner LB $25.26 (978-0-8225-2313-0). Early battles in the Civil War are the subject of this volume for older readers that includes timelines, notes, and lists of Web sites and battlefields to visit. (Rev: BL 10/15/02; HBG 10/02; SLJ 6/02; VOYA 6/03) [973.7]

18694 Arnold, James R., and Roberta Wiener. *River to Victory: The Civil War in the West* (4–7). Series: The Civil War. 2002, Lerner LB $25.26 (978-0-8225-2314-7). The Civil War in the West from 1861 through 1863 is re-created in text and illustrations with many maps and sidebars on personalities and events. (Rev: BL 10/15/02; HBG 10/02; SLJ 6/02; VOYA 6/03) [973.7]

18695 Arnold, James R., and Roberta Wiener. *This Unhappy Country: The Turn of the Civil War* (4–7). Series: Civil War. 2002, Lerner LB $25.26 (978-0-8225-2316-1). Maps and other period illustrations flesh out the events of 1863, a pivotal year in the Civil War, in this volume for older readers. (Rev: BL 10/15/02; HBG 10/02; SLJ 7/02) [973.7]

18696 Ashby, Ruth. *Gettysburg* (5–8). Series: Civil War Chronicles. 2002, Smart Apple LB $28.50 (978-1-58340-186-6). 48pp. The three days of battle are covered in some detail, and the text and photographs convey the horrible conditions. (Rev: HBG 3/03; SLJ 2/03; VOYA 4/03)

18697 Beller, Susan P. *The Civil War* (5–8). Series: American Voices From. 2002, Benchmark LB $34.21 (978-0-7614-1204-5). 103pp. A collection of primary sources that includes speeches by Lincoln and Lee and represents people from all walks of life commenting on different aspects of the Civil War. (Rev: HBG 10/03; SLJ 4/03)

18698 Beller, Susan Provost. *Billy Yank and Johnny Reb: Soldiering in the Civil War* (5–8). 2000, Twenty-First Century LB $26.90 (978-0-7613-1869-9). Solid, interesting information is provided in this illustrated account that describes the everyday life of soldiers on both sides of the Civil War. (Rev: BL 10/15/00; HBG 3/01; SLJ 12/00; VOYA 2/01) [973.7]

18699 Berry, Carrie. *A Confederate Girl: The Diary of Carrie Berry, 1864* (4–6). Ed. by Christy Steel and Anne Todd. Series: Diaries, Letters, and Memoirs. 2000, Capstone LB $23.93 (978-0-7368-0343-4). These excerpts from the diary of a 10-year-old Confederate girl describe everyday life and problems behind the front lines and are supplemented by informative sidebars that give good background information. (Rev: BL 10/15/00; HBG 10/00; SLJ 9/00)

18700 Bolotin, Norman. *Civil War A to Z: A Young Reader's Guide to Over 100 People, Places, and Points of Importance* (4–8). Illus. 2002, Dutton $19.99 (978-0-525-46268-2). 160pp. An encyclopedia-style text on the Civil War, with brief entries on important battles; politicians, generals, and other key figures; and crucial issues of the time, with photographs, a glossary, a timeline, and information on further resources. (Rev: BL 7/02; SLJ 7/02)

18701 Brooks, Victor. *African Americans in the Civil War* (4–8). Illus. Series: Untold History of the Civil War. 2000, Chelsea $25.00 (978-0-7910-5435-2). 64pp. This book describes African American soldiers' roles in the Civil War, on both the Confederate and Union sides. (Rev: BL 5/15/00; HBG 10/00; SLJ 6/00)

18702 Brooks, Victor. *Civil War Forts* (4–8). Illus. Series: Untold History of the Civil War. 2000, Chelsea $25.00 (978-0-7910-5438-3). 64pp. Describes the important roles played by such forts as Fort Sumter and Fort Wagner in South Carolina, Fort Fischer in North Carolina, Fort Henry and Fort Donelson in Tennessee, and the city of Vicksburg, Mississippi. (Rev: BL 5/15/00; HBG 10/00; SLJ 7/00)

18703 Brooks, Victor. *Secret Weapons in the Civil War* (4–8). Series: Untold History of the Civil War. 2000, Chelsea $29.50 (978-0-7910-5433-8). 64pp. Covers such secret weapons and maneuvers as underwater transportation, advanced artillery, communications devices, and explosive materials. (Rev: BL 5/15/00; HBG 10/00; SLJ 7/00)

18704 Butzer, C. M. *Gettysburg: The Graphic Novel* (4–8). Illus. by author. 2009, HarperCollins $16.99 (978-0-06-156176-4); paper $9.99 (978-0-06-156175-7). 80pp. After a brief section on the Battle of Gettysburg, Butzer moves on to present Lincoln's famous address; the graphic novel format works well and he integrates words from primary sources including letters and diaries. (Rev: BL 12/1/08; LMC 10/09; SLJ 11/08) [973.7]

18705 Clinton, Catherine. *Scholastic Encyclopedia of the Civil War* (4–7). 1999, Scholastic paper $18.95 (978-0-590-37227-5). Using many black-and-white illustrations, this narrative gives a good chronological introduction to the Civil War, with interesting supplementary

information. (Rev: BL 1/1–15/00; HBG 3/00; SLJ 5/00) [973.7]

18706 Damon, Duane. *Growing Up In the Civil War: 1861 to 1865* (5–8). Series: Our America. 2002, Lerner LB $26.60 (978-0-8225-0656-0). The lives of children in this period are described with many quotations and excerpts from diaries, letters, and memoirs. (Rev: BL 2/15/03; HBG 3/03; SLJ 2/03) [973.7]

18707 Day, Nancy. *Your Travel Guide to Civil War America* (4–8). Series: Passport to History. 2000, Lerner LB $26.50 (978-0-8225-3078-7). 96pp. Using the format of a guide book, this account takes the reader back to the Civil War with coverage of topics including food, civil and military clothing, Lincoln's office, Gettysburg, and various battlefields. (Rev: BL 3/1/01; HBG 10/01; SLJ 4/01; VOYA 8/01)

18708 Dolan, Edward F. *The American Civil War: A House Divided* (5–8). 1997, Millbrook LB $29.90 (978-0-7613-0255-1). A chronologically arranged, well-organized account of the Civil War, beginning with the shots fired at Fort Sumter. (Rev: BL 3/1/98; HBG 3/98; SLJ 3/98) [973.7]

18709 Dosier, Susan. *Civil War Cooking: The Confederacy* (4–7). Series: Exploring History Through Simple Recipes. 2000, Capstone LB $23.93 (978-0-7368-0350-2). 32pp. As well as simple, authentic recipes of Civil War times, this book tells of customs, family roles, and everyday life during this period. Also use *Civil War Cooking: The Union* (2000). (Rev: BL 8/00; HBG 10/00; SLJ 9/00)

18710 Egger-Bovet, Howard, and Marlene Smith-Baranzini. *Book of the American Civil War* (5–7). Illus. by D. J. Simison. Series: Brown Paper School. 1998, Little, Brown paper $12.95 (978-0-316-22243-3). Facts, photographs, illustrations, stories and appealing activities are combined in this overview of the Civil War. (Rev: SLJ 12/98) [973.7]

18711 Feinberg, Barbara S. *Abraham Lincoln's Gettysburg Address: Four Score and More . . .* (4–8). Illus. 2000, Twenty-First Century LB $24.90 (978-0-7613-1610-7). 80pp. Illustrated with period photographs, this well-researched volume reveals surprising facts about the Gettysburg Address and its delivery. (Rev: BL 11/15/00)

18712 Ford, Carin T. *The American Civil War: An Overview* (5–8). Series: The Civil War Library. 2004, Enslow LB $23.93 (978-0-7660-2255-3). 48pp. This informative general overview of the war features maps, illustrations, and interesting sidebar features. Also use *Lincoln, Slavery, and the Emancipation Proclamation* (2004). (Rev: SLJ 3/05)

18713 Ford, Carin T. *The Battle of Gettysburg and Lincoln's Gettysburg Address* (4–6). Series: The Civil War Library. 2004, Enslow LB $23.93 (978-0-7660-2253-9). 48pp. Background information adds to the coverage of the battle itself and to an understanding of the importance of Lincoln's speech. (Rev: SLJ 1/05)

18714 Ford, Carin T. *Daring Women of the Civil War* (3–5). Series: The Civil War Library. 2004, Enslow LB $23.93 (978-0-7660-2250-8). 48pp. Primary-source quotations and reproductions add to the discussion of the role of women — from both the Union and the Confederacy — in America's Civil War. (Rev: BL 7/04; SLJ 8/04)

18715 Ford, Carin T. *Slavery and the Underground Railroad: Bound for Freedom* (3–5). Series: The Civil War Library. 2004, Enslow LB $23.93 (978-0-7660-2251-5). 48pp. Primary-source quotations and reproductions add to the discussion of the role of the Underground Railroad and the people involved in its success. (Rev: BL 7/04; SLJ 8/04)

18716 Friend, Sandra. *Florida in the Civil War: A State in Turmoil* (5–8). Illus. 2001, Millbrook LB $25.90 (978-0-7613-1973-3). 80pp. An account of Florida's involvement in the Civil War, with maps and photographs. (Rev: BL 10/15/01; HBG 3/02; SLJ 2/02; VOYA 12/01)

18717 *Gettysburg: Bold Battle in the North* (4–6). Series: The Civil War. 2005, Cobblestone $17.95 (978-0-8126-7903-8). 47pp. A richly illustrated overview of this important battle. (Rev: SLJ 3/06)

18718 Graves, Kerry A. *Going to School During the Civil War: The Confederacy* (4–6). Series: Going to School in History. 2001, Capstone LB $23.93 (978-0-7368-0802-6). 32pp. A look at schools in the South during the Civil War with information on subjects studied, the length of the school year, classroom materials, and typical activities and games. (Rev: BL 10/15/01; HBG 3/02)

18719 Graves, Kerry A. *Going to School During the Civil War: The Union* (4–6). Series: Going to School in History. 2001, Capstone LB $23.93 (978-0-7368-0801-9). 32pp. Details of school life in the northern states include curriculum, teaching methods, and subjects taught plus sidebars on crafts and games. (Rev: BL 10/15/01; HBG 3/03)

18720 Hama, Larry. *The Battle of Antietam: "The Bloodiest Day of Battle"* (4–6). Illus. by Scott Moore. Series: Graphic Battles of the Civil War. 2007, Rosen LB $29.25 (978-1-4042-0775-2). 48pp. Historically accurate and not overly gory, this graphic account of a key Civil War battle will hold the interest of researchers and browsers. (Rev: SLJ 5/07)

18721 Heinrichs, Ann. *The Emancipation Proclamation* (5–8). Series: We the People. 2002, Compass Point LB $26.60 (978-0-7565-0209-6). An accessible examination of the proclamation's creation that reveals Lincoln's careful attention to detail. (Rev: SLJ 7/02) [973.7]

18722 Herbert, Janis. *The Civil War for Kids: A History with 21 Activities* (4–8). 1999, Chicago Review paper $14.95 (978-1-55652-355-7). As well as supplying information about leaders, battles, daily life, and the contributions of women and African Americans, this book on the Civil War includes activities such as reenactments of battles, most of which are geared toward groups. (Rev: SLJ 12/99) [973.7]

18723 High, Linda Oatman. *The Cemetery Keepers of Gettysburg* (3–5). Illus. by Laura Francesca Filippucci. 2007, Walker $16.95 (978-0-8027-8094-2). 32pp. The battle of Gettysburg is presented from the perspective of the oldest boy of a family of cemetery keepers trying to survive the Civil War while the father is off fighting. (Rev: BL 3/15/07)

18724 Holford, David M. *Lincoln and the Emancipation Proclamation in American History* (5–8). Series: In American History. 2002, Enslow LB $26.60 (978-0-7660-1456-5). 128pp. A well-researched account that gives background material and traces the significance of this document. (Rev: BL 1/1–15/03; HBG 3/03)

18725 Hughes, Christopher. *Antietam* (5–8). Series: Battlefields Across America. 1998, Millbrook LB $26.90 (978-0-7613-3009-7). This book describes the battle at Antietam in detail, discusses its impact on the outcome of the war and on the future of the United States, profiles the major people involved, and provides information on where the history of this battle is preserved. (Rev: HBG 9/98; SLJ 8/98) [973.7]

18726 January, Brendan. *Gettysburg, July 1–3, 1863* (5–7). Series: American Battlefields. 2004, Enchanted Lion $14.95 (978-1-59270-025-7). This overview of the Battle of Gettysburg offers a clear account of the bloody conflict and an examination of the developments leading up to it; sidebars, illustrations, a timeline, and other features add to the narrative. (Rev: BL 11/1/04) [973]

18727 Johnson, Jennifer. *Gettysburg: The Bloodiest Battle of the Civil War* (4–6). Series: 24/7 Goes to War: On the Battlefield. 2009, Franklin Watts LB $27 (978-0-531-25528-5); paper $7.95 (978-0-531-25453-0). 64pp. The battle of Gettysburg is condensed into this slim though information-packed book that features soldiers' personal experiences as well as notes on battle strategy. (Rev: SLJ 2/10) [973]

18728 King, Wilma. *Children of the Emancipation* (2–5). Illus. Series: Picture the American Past. 2000, Carolrhoda $22.60 (978-1-57505-396-7). 48pp. This book covers the years 1860 through 1890 and examines the lives of children born as slaves, and how they fared before the Emancipation Proclamation, during the Civil War, and also during Reconstruction. (Rev: BL 6/1–15/00; HBG 10/00; SLJ 7/00)

18729 McComb, Marianne. *The Emancipation Proclamation* (4–7). Illus. Series: American Documents. 2006, National Geographic LB $23.90 (978-0-7922-7936-5). The background, nature, and impact of this important document are explained clearly, with photos and illustrations plus full texts of the Emancipation Proclamation, the Fugitive Slave Law of 1850, and Constitutional Amendments XIII through XV. (Rev: BL 2/1/06; SLJ 2/06; VOYA 8/06) [973.7]

18730 McNeese, Tim. *The Civil War Era 1851–1865* (5–8). Series: Discovering U.S. History. 2010, Chelsea House $35 (978-1-60413-352-3). 136pp. McNeese provides a succinct overview of the key events and issues of the Civil War, with a chronology and timeline plus illustrations and primary sources. (Rev: LMC 11–12/10) [973.7]

18731 Mountjoy, Shane. *Causes of the Civil War: The Differences Between the North and South* (5–8). Series: The Civil War: A Nation Divided. 2009, Chelsea House $35 (978-1-60413-036-2). 136pp. This volume looks at the political scene in the early 19th century and the rivalries that led to the outbreak of war. (Rev: SLJ 10/09) [973.711]

18732 Mountjoy, Shane. *Technology and the Civil War* (5–8). Series: The Civil War: A Nation Divided. 2009, Chelsea House $35 (978-1-60413-037-9). 136pp. In chapters covering railroads and the telegraph, weapons, ironclads, submarines, medicine, and photography, this volume documents the advances made during the war. (Rev: SLJ 8/09) [973.7301]

18733 Nofi, Albert A. *Spies in the Civil War* (5–8). Series: Untold History of the Civil War. 2000, Chelsea $25.00 (978-0-7910-5427-7). 64pp. In this account readers meet famous spies (including Allan Pinkerton and Belle Boyd) and lesser-known spies of the Civil War. (Rev: HBG 10/00; SLJ 7/00)

18734 O'Brien, Patrick. *Duel of the Ironclads: The Monitor vs. the Virginia* (2–6). Illus. 2003, Walker LB $18.85 (978-0-8027-8843-6). 40pp. A beautifully illustrated account of the battle between two state-of-the-art Civil War ships. (Rev: BL 3/15/03*; HBG 10/03; SLJ 5/03)

18735 Rappaport, Doreen. *United No More! Stories of the Civil War* (4–6). Illus. by Rick Reeves. 2006, HarperCollins $16.99 (978-0-06-050599-8). 144pp. Seven stories of Civil War personalities and events give readers a feeling for the conflict. (Rev: BL 2/15/06; SLJ 2/06)

18736 Savage, Douglas J. *Ironclads and Blockades in the Civil War* (4–8). Series: Untold History of the Civil War. 2000, Chelsea $25.00 (978-0-7910-5429-1). A clear text and period illustrations introduce the huge ships used in the Union and Confederate navies and their efforts to block different ports during the Civil War. (Rev: BL 7/00; HBG 10/00; SLJ 9/00)

18737 Savage, Douglas J. *Prison Camps in the Civil War* (4–8). Series: Untold History of the Civil War. 2000, Chelsea $25.00 (978-0-7910-5428-4). 64pp. This account describes the prisoner-of-war camps on both sides during the Civil War, the appalling conditions in them, and the acts of heroism that sometimes occurred. (Rev: BL 7/00; HBG 10/00; SLJ 9/00)

18738 Savage, Douglas J. *Women in the Civil War* (4–8). Series: Untold History of the Civil War. 2000, Chelsea $25.00 (978-0-7910-5436-9). 64pp. This book describes the roles played by women in the Civil War as nurses, suppliers of support services, and crusaders for issues including suffrage and abolition. (Rev: BL 7/00; HBG 10/00; SLJ 9/00)

18739 Schomp, Virginia. *The Civil War* (5–8). Series: Letters from the Homefront. 2001, Marshall Cavendish LB $29.93 (978-0-7614-1095-9). After placing the conflict in historical context, Schomp uses excerpts from let-

ters and other accounts that bring the period to life. (Rev: BL 10/15/01; HBG 3/02; SLJ 3/02) [973.7]

18740 Sheinkin, Steve. *Two Miserable Presidents: Everything Your Schoolbooks Didn't Tell You About the Civil War* (4–8). Illus. by Tim Robinson. 2008, Roaring Brook $19.95 (978-1-59643-320-5). This unusual take on the war and its leaders will attract reluctant history students. It focuses on the personalities but does not leave out the larger issues that led to the war and affected its outcome. (Rev: BL 4/15/08) [973.7]

18741 Sinnott, Susan. *Charley Waters Goes to Gettysburg* (3–5). Illus. 2000, Millbrook LB $22.90 (978-0-7613-1567-4). Told from the point of view of an 8-year-old boy who is visiting the Gettysburg battlefield with his parents, this book gives information on the battle and its reenactments. (Rev: BL 3/15/00; HBG 10/00; SLJ 6/00)

18742 Slavicek, Louise Chipley. *Women and the Civil War* (5–8). Series: The Civil War: A Nation Divided. 2009, Chelsea House $35 (978-1-60413-040-9). 128pp. Chapters cover women's roles as nurses, spies, soldiers, and scouts, and look at their work in the camps and on the home front in both North and South; there is also discussion of the situation of African American women. (Rev: SLJ 8/09) [973.7301]

18743 Smith, Carter, ed. *The Road to Appomattox: A Sourcebook on the Civil War* (5–8). Series: American Albums. 1993, Millbrook $25.90 (978-1-56294-264-9). The last battles of the Civil War are covered in this album that uses period illustrations and excerpts from first-person accounts. (Rev: BL 3/1/93) [973.7]

18744 Stanchak, John. *Civil War* (5–8). Illus. Series: Eyewitness Books. 2000, DK paper $15.99 (978-0-7894-6302-9). 64pp. This highly visual treatment presents topics related to the Civil War such as causes, battles, slavery, states' rights, weapons, and uniforms in a series of double-page spreads. (Rev: BL 1/1–15/01; HBG 3/01; SLJ 12/00)

18745 Stanley, George E. *The Crisis of the Union (1815–1865)* (5–8). Series: A Primary Source History of the United States. 2005, World Almanac LB $31.00 (978-0-8368-5826-6). A simple narrative links well-chosen primary sources documenting the key events of the Civil War. (Rev: BL 4/1/05)

18746 Stark, Ken. *Marching to Appomattox: The Footrace that Ended the Civil War* (4–6). Illus. by author. 2009, Putnam $17.99 (978-0-399-24212-0). 48pp. This volume offers a dramatic and highly readable account of six days in April 1865 as Southern troops worked doggedly to break out of the North's tightening noose. (Rev: BL 1/1–15/09; LMC 5/09; SLJ 1/09)

18747 Stille, Darlene R. *The Civil War through Photography* (4–6). Illus. Series: Documenting U.S. History. 2012, Raintree LB $48 (978-143296755-0); paper $8.99 (9781432967642). 48pp. This volume emphasizes the contributions photography has made to our knowledge of events during the Civil War. Lexile 830L (Rev: BLO 9/1/12) [973.7022]

18748 Sullivan, George. *The Civil War at Sea* (5–8). Illus. 2001, Twenty-First Century LB $27.90 (978-0-7613-1553-7). 64pp. This book tells of the struggle between the Union and Confederate forces in American bays, harbors, and rivers with material on famous ships and their commanders, important battles, and the daily life of the sailors. (Rev: BL 2/1/01; HBG 10/01; SLJ 3/01)

18749 Walker, Sally M. *Shipwreck Search: Discovery of the H. L. Hunley* (2–4). Illus. by Elaine Verstraete. Series: On My Own Science. 2006, Lerner $25.26 (978-1-57505-878-8). 48pp. Chronicles the successful search for the wreckage of the *H. L. Hunley*, a Confederate submarine that was sunk in Charleston Harbor during the Civil War. (Rev: BL 6/1–15/06; SLJ 6/06)

18750 Warren, Andrea. *Under Siege: Three Children at the Civil War Battle for Vicksburg* (5–8). Illus. 2009, Farrar $17.95 (978-0-374-31255-8). 176pp. Using the reminiscences of three children between the ages of 10 and 12 (including General Grant's son), this is an interesting account of the battle and of the plight of the city's residents who retreated to caves. (Rev: BL 4/15/09*; HB 5/09; SLJ 5/09) [973.7]

18751 Waryncia, Lou, and Sarah Elder Hale, eds. *Antietam: Day of Courage and Sacrifice* (4–6). Series: The Civil War. 2005, Cobblestone $17.95 (978-0-8126-7904-5). 48pp. Based on articles appearing in Cobblestone publications, this book consists of short chapters covering topics including the battle, the equipment used, the mascot dogs, and the role of Clara Barton. (Rev: BL 1/1–15/06)

18752 Weber, Michael. *Civil War and Reconstruction* (5–8). Series: The Making of America. 2001, Raintree LB $19.98 (978-0-8172-5707-1). Using many illustrations, interesting sidebars, and an accessible text, this is a concise history of the Civil War and its immediate aftermath. (Rev: BL 4/15/01)

18753 *Young Heroes of the North and South* (4–6). Series: The Civil War. 2005, Cobblestone $17.95 (978-0-8126-7901-4). A compelling look at the roles played by children on the home front and the battlefield, on both sides of the Civil War. (Rev: SLJ 3/06)

RECONSTRUCTION TO THE KOREAN WAR, 1865–1950

18754 Axelrod-Contrada, Joan. *The Lizzie Borden "Axe Murder" Trial: A Headline Court Case* (5–9). Series: Headline Court Cases. 2000, Enslow LB $26.60 (978-0-7660-1422-0). 128pp. A well-documented account of the famous 1892 trial, the events that led up to it, and its aftermath. (Rev: HBG 3/01; SLJ 1/01)

18755 Bartoletti, Susan Campbell. *Growing Up in Coal Country* (5–8). 1996, Houghton Mifflin $17.00 (978-0-395-77847-0). The life of child laborers in the coal mines of Pennsylvania 100 years ago is covered in this brilliant photoessay. (Rev: BCCB 2/97; BL 12/1/96*; SLJ 2/97*) [331.3]

18756 Bartoletti, Susan Campbell. *Kids on Strike!* (5–8). 1999, Houghton Mifflin $20.00 (978-0-395-88892-6).

This book chronicles the history of child labor in America during the 19th and early 20th centuries and features such personalities as William Randolph Hearst, Pauline Newman, and Mother Jones. (Rev: BCCB 12/99; BL 12/1/99; HBG 3/00; SLJ 12/99*; VOYA 2/00) [973.8]

18757 Bolden, Tonya. *FDR's Alphabet Soup: New Deal America, 1932–1939* (5–8). 2010, Knopf LB $22.99 (978-0-375-95214-2). 144pp. A lively review of FDR's presidency and in particular of the provisions of the New Deal and the impact it had on the American people. (Rev: BL 12/1/09; LMC 1–2/10; SLJ 1/10) [900]

18758 Brezina, Corona. *America's Political Scandals in the late 1800s: Boss Tweed and Tammany Hall* (5–8). Series: America's Industrial Society in the 19th Century. 2004, Rosen LB $22.50 (978-0-8239-4021-9). For reluctant readers, this overview of the political scandals of the late 19th century features large print and short chapters. (Rev: BL 4/1/04)

18759 Brill, Marlene Targ. *Annie Shapiro and the Clothing Workers' Strike* (2–4). Illus. by Jamel Akib. 2010, Millbrook LB $27.93 (978-1-58013-672-3). 48pp. This well-researched book tells the inspiring story of Hannah "Annie" Shapiro, the Russian girl who led a walkout at a Chicago clothing factory in 1910; includes a reader's theater section. (Rev: BL 10/1/10; LMC 1–2/11*; SLJ 12/1/10) [331.892]

18760 Brown, Harriet. *Welcome to Kit's World — 1934: Growing Up During America's Great Depression* (3–6). Illus. Series: American Girl. 2002, Pleasant $16.95 (978-1-58485-359-6). 60pp. Double-page spreads are used in this heavily illustrated volume to describe growing up in 1934 during the Great Depression. (Rev: BL 4/15/02; HBG 10/02; SLJ 7/02)

18761 Burgan, Michael. *The Great Depression* (4–6). Series: We the People. 2001, Compass Point LB $26.60 (978-0-7565-0152-5). 48pp. A basic overview of the causes of the Depression and the programs that were intended to alleviate its impact. (Rev: SLJ 1/02)

18762 Burgan, Michael. *The Haymarket Square Tragedy* (4–6). Series: We the People. 2005, Compass Point LB $26.60 (978-0-7565-1265-1). The story of the 1886 Haymarket Square riot in Chicago is placed in historical and social context, with period reproductions and photographs. (Rev: SLJ 2/06)

18763 Carter, Ron. *The Youngest Drover* (5–9). 1995, Harbour $19.95 (978-0-9643672-1-0); paper $14.95 (978-0-9643672-0-3). In 1923, when he was 15, the author's father participated in an exciting cattle drive from Alberta to Montana. (Rev: BL 1/1–15/96) [978]

18764 Collier, Christopher, and James Lincoln Collier. *Progressivism, the Great Depression, and the New Deal* (5–8). Illus. Series: The Drama of American History. 2001, Marshall Cavendish LB $31.36 (978-0-7614-1054-6). 96pp. A highly readable account that covers such topics as the stock market crash, the reformation of business practices, the Great Depression, and the social policies of the New Deal. (Rev: BL 3/15/01; HBG 10/01)

18765 Collier, Christopher, and James Lincoln Collier. *The United States Enters the World Stage: From the Alaska Purchase Through World War I* (5–8). Series: The Drama of American History. 2001, Marshall Cavendish LB $31.36 (978-0-7614-1053-9). Covering the years 1867 through 1918, this well-illustrated account traces America's emergence as a world power. (Rev: BL 3/15/01; HBG 10/01)

18766 Coombs, Karen Mueller. *Children of the Dust Days* (3–6). Illus. Series: Picture the American Past. 2000, Carolrhoda LB $22.60 (978-1-57505-360-8). 48pp. A mainly illustrated account of the hardships associated with the Dust Bowl and the journeys of many displaced farmers to California. (Rev: BL 4/1/00; HBG 10/00; SLJ 6/00)

18767 Cooper, Michael L. *Dust to Eat: Drought and Depression in the 1930s* (5–8). 2004, Clarion $17.00 (978-0-618-15449-4). First-person accounts and period photographs convey the hopelessness of those who were caught in the grip of the Depression and the drought in the Midwest. (Rev: BL 7/04; SLJ 9/04) [973.917]

18768 Costantino, Maria. *Fashions of a Decade: The 1930s* (5–10). 2007, Chelsea House LB $35.00 (978-0-8160-6719-0). 64pp. With illustrations, photographs, and a helpful chronology of trends and events, this book captures the fashions of the 1930s and relates them to the conditions of the times. (Rev: SLJ 7/07)

18769 Cryan-Hicks, Kathryn, ed. *Pride and Promise: The Harlem Renaisssance* (4–8). Series: Perspectives on History. 1994, Enterprises paper $6.95 (978-1-878668-30-1). The story of the great artistic awakening in New York's Harlem and of its many leaders, including Langston Hughes. (Rev: BL 8/94) [305.896]

18770 Davis, Barbara J. *The Teapot Dome Scandal: Corruption Rocks 1920s America* (5–8). Series: Snapshots in History. 2007, Compass Point LB $31.93 (978-0-7565-3336-6). 96pp. Davis traces the corruption in the Harding administration and the scandal that erupted over oil leasing without competitive bidding. (Rev: SLJ 1/08)

18771 Degezelle, Terri. *Franklin D. Roosevelt and the Great Depression* (2–4). Illus. Series: Heinemann First Library. 2007, Heinemann LB $17.75 (978-1-4034-9670-6); paper $7.99 (978-1-4034-9678-2). 32pp. A brief biography of Roosevelt precedes simple accounts of events including the 1929 stock market crash, the Depression itself, the New Deal, World War II and discussion of family life at that time. (Rev: BL 10/15/07; LMC 1/08; SLJ 1/08)

18772 Dolan, Edward F. *The Spanish-American War* (5–8). Illus. 2001, Millbrook LB $28.90 (978-0-7613-1453-0). 112pp. This chronological account of the Spanish-American War includes profiles of military personnel, maps, and historical photographs. (Rev: BL 11/1/01; HBG 3/02; SLJ 11/01)

18773 Duble, Kathleen Benner. *The Story of the Samson* (2–5). Illus. by Alexander Farquharson. 2008, Charlesbridge $16.95 (978-1-58089-183-7); paper $7.95 (978-1-58089-184-4). The importance of the *Samson*, a

schooner built in 1885 that played a part in many major events in maritime history, is revealed through conversations between a young boy, Sam, and his grandfather, who sailed aboard the ship. (Rev: BL 9/1/08)

18774 Feinstein, Stephen. *The 1910s: From World War I to Ragtime Music* (5–8). Series: Decades of the 20th Century. 2001, Enslow LB $22.60 (978-0-7660-1611-8). 64pp. The events of the 1910s are covered in chapters on lifestyle and fashion, arts and entertainment, sports, politics, and science, technology, and medicine. Also use *The 1920s: From Prohibition to Charles Lindbergh* (2001). (Rev: HBG 10/02; SLJ 2/02)

18775 Feinstein, Stephen. *The 1940s: From World War II to Jackie Robinson* (5–8). Illus. Series: Decades of the 20th Century. 2000, Enslow LB $22.60 (978-0-7660-1428-2). 64pp. A lively look at events of the 1940s, covering everything from fashion and fads to politics, science, technology, medicine, and sports. Also use *The 1930s: From the Great Depression to the Wizard of Oz* (2001) and *The 1950s: From the Korean War to Elvis* (2000). (Rev: HBG 3/01; SLJ 5/01)

18776 Ferrell, Claudine L. *Reconstruction* (5–10). Series: Greenwood Guides to Historic Events, 1500-1900. 2003, Greenwood $51.95 (978-0-313-32062-0). Covers key individuals involved in Reconstruction and the speeches, proclamations, and other primary documents that cast light on the events of the time. (Rev: SLJ 6/04) [973.8]

18777 Flanagan, Alice K. *The Buffalo Soldiers* (3–6). Illus. Series: We the People. 2005, Compass Point LB $26.60 (978-0-7565-0833-3). 48pp. An introduction to the first all-black regiments formed after the Civil War and nicknamed "Buffalo soldiers" by the Kiowa Indians. [973.7]

18778 Freedman, Russell. *Angel Island: Gateway to Gold Mountain* (4–7). Illus. 2014, Clarion $17.99 (978-054790378-1). 96pp. Freedman tells the story of the immigration station on the West Coast, where many Chinese arrivals were forced to live in horrible conditions for weeks or months, often to be denied entry to the United States. ❸ (Rev: BL 11/1/13*; HB 11–12/13; LMC 1–2/14; SLJ 9/13*) [979.4]

18779 Freedman, Russell. *Children of the Great Depression* (5–8). 2005, Clarion $20.00 (978-0-618-44630-8). The works of such notable photographers as Dorothea Lange and Walker Evans, moving quotations, and the accessible text of Freedman make this a memorable photoessay. (Rev: BCCB 12/05; BL 12/15/05*; HBG 4/05; LMC 3/06; SLJ 12/05*; VOYA 6/06) [305.23]

18780 Garland, Sherry. *Voices of the Dust Bowl* (4–7). Illus. by Judith Hierstein. Series: Voices of History. 2012, Pelican $16.99 (978-1-58980-964-2). 40pp. Sixteen moving first-person narratives convey how the drought and dust storms of the 1930s affected people in all walks of lives — even Bonnie and Clyde. (Rev: BL 5/15/12; LMC 10/12; SLJ 7/12) [973.917]

18781 Gonzales, Doreen. *The Secret of the Manhattan Project* (5–8). Illus. Series: Stories in American History.

2012, Enslow LB $31.93 (978-076603954-4). 128pp. Placing events in clear historical context, this is a compelling account of the development and deployment of the atomic bomb. (Rev: BL 4/1/12*; SLJ 4/12) [355.8]

18782 Graham, Ian. *You Wouldn't Want to Work on the Hoover Dam! An Explosive Job You'd Rather Not Do* (3–5). Illus. by David Antram. 2012, Scholastic LB $29 (978-053120871-7); paper $9.95 (978-053120946-2). 32pp. With cartoons and breezy text, this is a good introduction to the building of the Hoover Dam, the dangers involved, and the fact that few jobs were available during the Depression. (Rev: BL 2/15/12; SLJ 4/12) [627]

18783 Granfield, Linda. *97 Orchard Street, New York: Stories of Immigrant Life* (3–6). Photos by Arlene Alda. 2001, Tundra paper $15.00 (978-0-88776-580-3). 55pp. A detailed and appealing look at the immigrant experience through the stories of families who lived in the building that is now the Lower East Side Tenement Museum, with black-and-white photographs. (Rev: SLJ 12/01) [305.9]

18784 Graves, Kerry A. *Going to School During the Great Depression* (4–6). Series: Going to School in History. 2001, Capstone LB $16.95 (978-0-7368-0800-2). 32pp. School life during the 1930s and early '40s is covered with material on subjects studied, school supplies, and typical activities and games of the time. (Rev: BL 10/15/01)

18785 Green, Carl R. *The Spanish-American War* (4–6). Series: U.S. Wars. 2002, Enslow LB $25.26 (978-0-7660-5091-4). Preceding a brief history of the Spanish-American War, there is a lengthy section listing Internet sites that offer students additional material on the subject. (Rev: BL 10/15/02; HBG 3/03)

18786 Greene, Meg. *Into the Land of Freedom: African Americans in Reconstruction* (5–8). Series: People's History. 2004, Lerner LB $29.27 (978-0-8225-4690-0). Sepia-toned photographs and historical documents and interviews add to this portrait of the situation of African Americans during Reconstruction. (Rev: BL 2/15/04*; SLJ 5/04) [973]

18787 Heinrichs, Ann. *The Dust Bowl* (3–6). Illus. Series: We the People. 2005, Compass Point LB $26.60 (978-0-7565-0837-1). Describes the plight of people living in the Midwest during the long drought of the 1930s. [978]

18788 Herald, Jacqueline. *Fashions of a Decade: The 1920s* (5–10). 2007, Chelsea House LB $35.00 (978-0-8160-6718-3). 64pp. Photographs, illustrations, and timelines accompany text that relates the fashion of the 1920s to events and the culture of the times. (Rev: SLJ 7/07)

18789 Hoffman, Nancy. *Eleanor Roosevelt and the Arthurdale Experiment* (5–8). 2001, Linnet LB $22.50 (978-0-208-02504-3). Hoffman includes quotations and black-and-white photographs in her account of the story of Arthurdale, a government-planned community of the 1930s. (Rev: BL 10/15/01; HBG 3/02; SLJ 12/01) [975.4]

18790 Holiday, Billie, and Arthur Herzog. *God Bless the Child* (2–5). Illus. by Jerry Pinkney. 2004, HarperCollins $16.99 (978-0-06-028797-9). 32pp. The lyrics of Billie Holiday's signature song provide the framework for this moving portrait of a black family joining the great migration from the cotton fields of the Deep South to the streets of Chicago; a CD is included. (Rev: BL 2/15/04*; SLJ 2/04)

18791 Hopkinson, Deborah. *Shutting Out the Sky* (5–12). 2003, Scholastic $17.95 (978-0-439-37590-0). Five personal stories of young immigrants, striking photographs, and excerpts from primary documents form the backbone of this history of immigration to New York City in the late 19th century. (Rev: BL 11/1/03*; HBG 4/04; SLJ 12/03*; VOYA 6/04) [307.76]

18792 Houle, Michelle M. *Triangle Shirtwaist Factory Fire: Flames of Labor Reform* (4–6). Illus. Series: American Disasters. 2002, Enslow LB $23.93 (978-0-7660-1785-6). 48pp. A frank portrayal of the tragic 1911 fire and the impact it had on the labor movement. (Rev: HBG 3/03; SLJ 12/02)

18793 Isaacs, Sally Senzell. *Life in the Dust Bowl* (2–4). Illus. Series: Picture the Past. 2001, Heinemann LB $21.36 (978-1-58810-248-5). 32pp. A gripping introduction to the hardships of life on the plains in the 1930s, with information on society at the time. (Rev: SLJ 3/02)

18794 Jackson, Robert. *Meet Me in St. Louis: A Trip to the 1904 World's Fair* (4–7). Illus. 2004, HarperCollins $17.99 (978-0-06-009267-2). 144pp. Jackson beautifully evokes the excitement surrounding the 1904 St. Louis World's Fair, which attracted nearly 20 million people, many of them key figures of the day. (Rev: BL 2/15/04; SLJ 4/04)

18795 Jernegan, Laura. *A Whaling Captain's Daughter: The Diary of Laura Jernegan, 1868–1871* (4–6). Series: Diaries, Letters, and Memoirs. 2000, Capstone LB $22.60 (978-0-7368-0319-9). Excerpts from a young girl's diary introduce the reader to life ashore and aboard a whaling ship immediately after the Civil War. (Rev: BL 10/15/00; SLJ 9/00)

18796 Josephson, Judith P. *Growing Up in World War II* (5–8). Illus. Series: Our America. 2002, Lerner LB $26.60 (978-0-8225-0660-7). 64pp. A look at the lives of American children of different backgrounds and situations during World War II. (Rev: BL 2/1/03; HBG 3/03)

18797 Josephson, Judith Pinkerton. *Growing Up in a New Century* (5–8). Series: Our America. 2002, Lerner LB $26.60 (978-0-8225-0657-7). A look at the lives of American children of different backgrounds and situations at the dawn of the 20th century. (Rev: BL 2/1/03; HBG 3/03; SLJ 7/03) [973.91]

18798 King, David C. *Victorian Days: Discover the Past with Fun Projects, Games, Activities, and Recipes* (4–6). Illus. by Cheryl K. Noll. Series: American Kids in History. 2000, Wiley paper $14.95 (978-0-471-33122-3). 96pp. Through an interesting text and more than 30 activities like making paper flowers and shadow puppets and following some delicious recipes, young readers can re-create life in New York in the year 1893. (Rev: SLJ 4/00)

18799 King, David C. *World Wars and the Modern Age* (5–8). Series: American Heritage, American Voices. 2004, Wiley paper $12.95 (978-0-471-44392-6). A concise overview of the profound changes seen in the United States during the decades from 1870 to 1950, with excerpts from primary sources. (Rev: BL 2/1/05; SLJ 5/05) [973]

18800 Koehler-Pentacoff, Elizabeth. *Jackson and Bud's Bumpy Ride: America's First Cross-Country Automobile Trip* (1–3). Illus. by Wes Hargis. 2009, Millbrook LB $16.95 (978-0-8225-7885-7). 32pp. This is a compelling account of a 1903 cross-country adventure in a "horse-less buggy" accompanied by a dog called Bud; cartoon illustrations extend the narrative. (Rev: BL 4/15/09; LMC 10/09; SLJ 4/09)

18801 Lassieur, Allison. *The Dust Bowl: An Interactive History Adventure* (3–5). Illus. Series: You Choose. 2008, Capstone LB $20.99 (978-1-4296-2343-8). 112pp. The reader must choose among various alternatives — to stay and Kansas and try to farm despite the dust, to leave for California, to become a government photographer, and so forth. (Rev: BL 4/1/09)

18802 Littlefield, Holly. *Children of the Orphan Trains* (3–6). Illus. Series: Picture the American Past. 2001, Carolrhoda LB $22.60 (978-1-57505-466-7). 48pp. A brief, informative text is accompanied by moving photographs that dramatically tell the sad story of orphan children transported West to find work and homes. (Rev: BL 5/15/01; HBG 10/01)

18803 McHugh, Janet. *The Great Chicago Fire* (3–6). Series: Code Red. 2007, Bearport LB $23.96 (978-1-59716-360-6). 32pp. In chapters including "Where Is the Fire Department" "Looting in the Streets," No More Water!," and "Picking Up the Pieces," McHugh describes the 1871 catastrophe. (Rev: LMC 10/07; SLJ 10/07)

18804 McNeese, Tim. *The Gilded Age and Progressivism 1891–1913* (5–8). Series: Discovering U.S. History. 2010, Chelsea House $35 (978-1-60413-355-4). 136pp. McNeese provides a succinct overview of the key events and issues of this period of industrial progress and expanded immigration, with a chronology and timeline plus illustrations and primary sources. (Rev: LMC 11–12/10; SLJ 8/10)

18805 Marrin, Albert. *Years of Dust: The Story of the Dust Bowl* (5–8). 2009, Dutton $22.99 (978-0-525-42077-4). 128pp. This is a moving explanation of the nature of the Dust Bowl and its impact on agriculture and the population that lived there; personal accounts add depth, as do numerous sidebars and a warning about future events like this. ALA Notable Children's Book 2010. (Rev: BL 8/09*; LMC 10/09; SLJ 8/09) [978]

18806 Nardo, Don. *Migrant Mother: How a Photograph Defined the Great Depression* (5–8). Illus. Series: Captured History. 2011, Compass Point $33.99 (978-075654397-6). 64pp. Dorothea Lange's photograph of a Depression-era farm worker serves as the anchor for a

discussion of the Great Depression and Lange's contributions. (Rev: BL 4/1/11; LMC 10/11) [973.917]

18807 Nobleman, Marc Tyler. *The Hindenburg* (4–6). Series: We the People. 2005, Compass Point LB $26.60 (978-0-7565-1266-8). 48pp. The story of the *Hindenburg*, the German dirigible that burst into flames as it was landing at Lakehurst, New Jersey, in 1937, is placed in historical context. (Rev: SLJ 2/06)

18808 Porterfield, Jason. *Problems and Progress in American Politics: The Growth of the Democratic Party in the Late 1800s* (5–8). Series: America's Industrial Society in the 19th Century. 2004, Rosen LB $22.50 (978-0-8239-4026-4). For reluctant readers, this overview of the growth of the Democratic Party features large print and short chapters. (Rev: BL 4/1/04)

18809 Ransom, Candice F. *The Day of the Black Blizzard* (1–3). Illus. by Laurie Harden. Series: On My Own History. 2009, Millbrook $25.26 (978-0-8225-7895-6). 48pp. A fictionalized account of Black Sunday (April 14, 1935) featuring 10-year-old Orry and his younger stepsister as they find themselves far from home during the worst dust storm in the country's history. (Rev: BLO 1/14/09; SLJ 3/09)

18810 Rau, Dana Meachen. *The Harlem Renaissance* (4–6). Series: We the People. 2005, Compass Point LB $26.60 (978-0-7565-1264-4). A look at the key characters and the artistic creations of the Harlem Renaissance, an African American cultural movement during the 1920s and early 1930s. (Rev: SLJ 2/06)

18811 Rosenstock, Barb. *The Camping Trip That Changed America: Theodore Roosevelt, John Muir, and Our National Parks* (1–3). Illus. by Mordicai Gerstein. 2012, Dial $16.99 (978-080373710-5). 32pp. Theodore Roosevelt's inspirational camping trip with John Muir gave rise to the establishment of the national park system; this readable book chronicles the adventure. (Rev: BL 12/15/11; HB 1–2/12; LMC 8–9/12; SLJ 9/12)

18812 Ruth, Amy. *Growing Up in the Great Depression* (5–8). Series: Our America. 2002, Lerner LB $26.60 (978-0-8225-0655-3). 64pp. With many sidebars and quotations from original sources, this narrative re-creates the despair and courage of children growing up during the Great Depression. (Rev: BL 2/15/03; HBG 3/03)

18813 Sandler, Martin W. *The Dust Bowl Through the Lens: How Photography Revealed and Helped Remedy a National Disaster* (5–9). 2009, Walker $19.99 (978-0-8027-9547-2). 96pp. Sandler tells the devastating story of the American Dust Bowl through a series of photo-essays including period quotations and concise, engaging captions. (Rev: BL 11/1/09; HB 1–2/10; LMC 10/09; SLJ 10/09; VOYA 8/09) [973.917022]

18814 Sandler, Martin W. *The Impossible Rescue: The True Story of an Amazing Arctic Adventure* (5–8). Illus. 2012, Candlewick $22.99 (978-0-7636-5080-3). 176pp. The death-defying 1897–1898 rescue of nearly 300 sailors trapped in winter ice on Alaska's Point Barrow is described in this dramatic tale. (Rev: BL 5/15/12*;

HB 9–10/12; LMC 1–2/13; SLJ 9/12*; VOYA 8/12) [979.803]

18815 Sandler, Martin W. *Island of Hope: The Story of Ellis Island and the Journey to America* (5–7). 2004, Scholastic $19.99 (978-0-439-53082-8). Drawing heavily on first-hand accounts, Sandler traces immigrants' progress through the processing at Ellis Island and on into the cities and farms of their new country. (Rev: BL 4/15/04; SLJ 6/04) [304.8]

18816 Santella, Andrew. *Roosevelt's Rough Riders* (4–6). Series: We the People. 2005, Compass Point LB $26.60 (978-0-7565-1268-2). 48pp. Profiles the men from diverse walks of life who volunteered to fight as part of Roosevelt's Rough Riders during the Spanish-American War. (Rev: SLJ 2/06)

18817 Schaefer, Adam R. *The Triangle Shirtwaist Factory Fire* (4–7). Series: Landmark Events in American History. 2003, World Almanac LB $31.00 (978-0-8368-5383-4). 48pp. An accessible account of the tragic 1911 fire in New York City, with material on the horrible working conditions and the resulting reforms in labor law. (Rev: SLJ 6/04)

18818 Scher, Linda. *The Texas City Disaster* (3–6). Series: Code Red. 2007, Bearport LB $23.96 (978-1-59716-363-7). 32pp. Readers will learn of an explosion that killed 550 people in Texas City in 1947 and led to changes in industrial safety regulations. (Rev: LMC 10/07; SLJ 7/07)

18819 Schomp, Virginia. *World War II* (5–8). Illus. Series: Letters from the Homefront. 2001, Marshall Cavendish LB $29.93 (978-0-7614-1098-0). 96pp. Schomp uses letters written during World War II, accompanied by relevant illustrations, to give readers a real understanding of the difficulties of life on the homefront. (Rev: BL 10/15/01; HBG 3/02)

18820 Schwartz, Eric. *Crossing the Seas: Americans Form an Empire 1890–1899* (5–8). Series: How America Became America. 2005, Mason Crest LB $22.95 (978-1-59084-910-1). Schwartz explores America's turn to imperialism in the final decade of the 19th century. Also use *Super Power: Americans Today* (2005). (Rev: SLJ 11/05) [973]

18821 Stanley, George E. *An Emerging World Power (1900–1929)* (5–8). Series: A Primary Source History of the United States. 2005, World Almanac LB $31.00 (978-0-8368-5828-0). A simple narrative links well-chosen primary sources documenting the key events of the early 20th century. Also use *The Era of Reconstruction and Expansion (1865–1900)* and *The Great Depression and World War II (1929–1949)* (both 2005). (Rev: BL 4/1/05; SLJ 7/05)

18822 Staton, Hilarie N. *The Industrial Revolution* (4–6). Illus. Series: All About America. 2012, Kingfisher LB $19.89 (978-075346712-1); paper $9.99 (978-075346670-4). 32pp. In chapters such as "The First Mills," "Canals and Factories," and "Mass Production," Staton reviews technological developments in the United States from colonial times through the mid-1900s. (Rev: BL 4/15/12; SLJ 3/12) [338.0973]

18823 Stewart, Dave. *You Wouldn't Want to Sail on the Titanic! One Voyage You'd Rather Not Make* (4–6). Illus. by David Antram. Series: You Wouldn't Want To. 2001, Watts LB $29.00 (978-0-531-14604-0); paper $9.95 (978-0-531-16210-1). The uncomfortable opportunity to imagine yourself aboard the *Titanic*. (Rev: SLJ 3/02)

18824 Stites, Bill. *The Republican Party in the Late 1800s: A Changing Role for American Government* (5–8). Series: America's Industrial Society in the 19th Century. 2004, Rosen LB $22.50 (978-0-8239-4030-1). For reluctant readers, this overview of the growth of the Republican Party features large print and short chapters. (Rev: BL 4/1/04)

18825 Stone, Tanya L. *The Great Depression and World War II* (5–8). Series: Making of America. 2001, Raintree LB $28.54 (978-0-8172-5710-1). Concise text and attractive illustrations re-create the history of America from 1929 through World War II. (Rev: BL 9/15/01; HBG 10/01)

18826 Stone, Tanya L. *The Progressive Era and World War I* (5–8). Series: Making of America. 2001, Raintree LB $28.54 (978-0-8172-5709-5). 96pp. Roughly the first 20 years of the 20th century in American history are retold in this history that also looks at home life, culture, and entertainment. (Rev: BL 9/15/01; HBG 10/01; SLJ 6/01)

18827 Stroud, Bettye, and Virginia Schomp. *The Reconstruction Era* (5–8). Series: Drama of African-American History. 2006, Benchmark LB $23.95 (978-0-7614-2181-8). This volume traces the history of Reconstruction and the tensions remaining between the many factions after the Civil War. (Rev: SLJ 5/07) [973.8]

18828 Uschan, Michael V. *The 1940s* (5–10). Series: Cultural History of the United States. 1998, Lucent LB $28.70 (978-1-56510-554-6). Life at home and abroad during World War II dominate this book, which also discusses the Great Depression, the New Deal, events leading up to U.S. participation in the war, the beginnings of the Cold War, the growth of suburban living, and the rise of television, with sidebars on such topics as the Holocaust, the influences of radio, movies, and comics, 1940s slang, and the first computers. (Rev: SLJ 1/99) [973.9]

18829 Van Rynbach, Iris, and Pegi Deitz Shea. *The Taxing Case of the Cows: A True Story About Suffrage* (1–3). Illus. by Emily Arnold McCully. 2010, Clarion $16.99 (978-0-547-23631-5). 32pp. In 19th-century Connecticut sisters Abby and Julia Smith refuse to pay their taxes on the grounds that they are not allowed to vote. (Rev: BL 12/1/10; HB 1–2/11; LMC 5–6/11; SLJ 12/1/10) [324.6]

18830 Wadsworth, Ginger. *Camping with the President* (3–5). Illus. by Karen Dugan. 2009, Boyds Mills $16.95 (978-159078497-6). 32pp. Intricately tinted watercolor illustrations enliven this account of Teddy Roosevelt's 1903 camping trip in Yosemite with naturalist John Muir. (Rev: BL 9/15/09; LMC 11–12/09) [973.91]

18831 Weber, Valerie J., and Valerie Baker. *Traveling in Grandma's Day* (3–4). 2000, Carolrhoda LB $21.27 (978-1-57505-326-4). A nostalgic look at traveling in the 1930s and 1940s told through first-person narratives and plenty of photographs. Also use *School in Grandma's Day*, *Shopping in Grandma's Day*, and *Food in Grandma's Day* (all 2000). (Rev: HBG 10/00; SLJ 6/00)

18832 Wells, Donna. *America Comes of Age* (5–8). Series: The Making of America. 2001, Raintree LB $28.54 (978-0-8172-5708-8). 96pp. A handsomely illustrated account that traces U.S. history from Reconstruction to the beginning of the 20th century. (Rev: BL 4/15/01; HBG 10/01)

18833 Whitman, Sylvia. *Immigrant Children: Late 1800s to Early 1900s* (3–5). Series: Picture the American Past. 2000, Carolrhoda LB $22.60 (978-1-57505-395-0). 48pp. This book describes the lives of immigrant children who arrived in this country, many to work in mines, factories, or farms but all trying to get ahead. (Rev: HBG 10/00; SLJ 7/00)

18834 Winter, Jonah. *Born and Bred in the Great Depression* (2–4). Illus. by Kimberly Bulcken Root. 2011, Random House $17.99 (978-037586197-0); LB $20.99 (978-037596197-7). 40pp. The author describes his father's childhood in East Texas during the 1930s, the youngest of eight children. e (Rev: BL 11/15/11; HB 1–2/12; SLJ 1/12) [976.4]

18835 Worth, Richard. *The Harlem Renaissance: An Explosion of African-American Culture* (5–8). Illus. 2008, Enslow LB $23.95 (978-0-7660-2907-1). This attractive overview of the Harlem Renaissance traces the origins and spirit of the movement and profiles many of its writers, artists, musicians, and thinkers. (Rev: BL 2/1/09; LMC 11/08) [700.89]

18836 Wroble, Lisa A. *The New Deal and the Great Depression in American History* (5–8). Series: In American History. 2002, Enslow LB $26.60 (978-0-7660-1421-3). 128pp. A timeline, maps, chapter notes, and research topics are found in this well-researched account that concentrates on Roosevelt's economic policies during the 1930s. (Rev: BL 1/1–15/03; HBG 3/03)

THE 1950S TO THE PRESENT

18837 Anderson, Dale. *America into a New Millennium* (5–8). Series: Making of America. 2001, Raintree LB $28.54 (978-0-8172-5712-5). 96pp. This last part of a 12-volume series presents American history from the end of the Cold War to the beginning of the 21st century. (Rev: BL 9/15/01; HBG 10/01; SLJ 6/01)

18838 Anderson, Dale. *The Cold War Years* (5–8). Series: Making of America. 2001, Raintree LB $28.54 (978-0-8172-5711-8). 96pp. A concise, easy-to-understand text tells America's story from the end of World War II to the 1990s. (Rev: BL 9/15/01; HBG 10/01; SLJ 6/01)

18839 Aretha, David. *Sit-Ins and Freedom Rides* (5–8). Series: Civil Rights Movement. 2009, Morgan Reynolds LB $28.95 (978-1-59935-098-1). 128pp. Aretha offers a detailed, well-illustrated look at the grassroots efforts of

the early 1960s, with personal anecdotes, a helpful timeline, and lists of additional resources. (Rev: BL 2/1/10; SLJ 9/09) [323.1196]

18840 Bausum, Ann. *Marching to the Mountaintop: How Poverty, Labor Fights, and Civil Rights Set the Stage for Martin Luther King, Jr.'s Final Hours* (5–8). Illus. 2012, National Geographic $19.95 (978-142630939-7); LB $28.90 (978-142630940-3). 112pp. With succinct text, use of primary resources, gripping photographs, and attractive design, this is a compelling account — suitable for research and for browsing — of the 1968 Memphis sanitation workers strike and the death of Martin Luther King, Jr. e (Rev: BL 2/1/12; LMC 8–9/12; SLJ 3/12) [323.092]

18841 Britton, Tamara. *The World Trade Center* (3–5). Series: Symbols, Landmarks, and Monuments. 2003, ABDO LB $22.78 (978-1-57765-850-4). The design and construction of New York City's World Trade Center are described along with its destruction on September 11, 2001. (Rev: HBG 10/03; SLJ 10/03)

18842 Brown, Gene. *The Nation in Turmoil: Civil Rights and the Vietnam War (1960-1973)* (5–8). Series: First Person America. 1994, Twenty-First Century LB $20.90 (978-0-8050-2588-0). An overview of the civil rights movement and the Vietnam War, highlighting excerpts from letters, diaries, and speeches. (Rev: BL 5/15/94) [973.92]

18843 Burgan, Michael. *Spying and the Cold War* (4–6). Series: On the Front Line. 2005, Raintree LB $29.93 (978-1-4109-1465-1). This is an accessible overview of the Cold War, covering its roots and progress and looking in particular at the role of espionage; personal accounts add interest. (Rev: SLJ 12/05)

18844 Canwell, Diane, and Jon Sutherland. *African Americans in the Vietnam War* (5–8). Series: American Experience in Vietnam. 2005, World Almanac LB $31.00 (978-0-8368-5772-6). Personal stories and full-color photographs add to the information on black Americans' contributions to the conflict and the military's efforts toward integration. Also use *American Women in the Vietnam War* (2005). (Rev: BL 2/1/05) [959.705]

18845 Carter, E. J. *The Cuban Missile Crisis* (4–8). Series: 20th Century Perspectives. 2003, Heinemann LB $27.07 (978-1-4034-3806-5). 48pp. A review of the 1962 crisis in which Cuba secretly installed missiles capable of carrying nuclear warheads. (Rev: SLJ 5/04)

18846 Feinstein, Stephen. *The 1960s: From the Vietnam War to Flower Power* (4–7). Series: Decades of the Twentieth Century. 2000, Enslow LB $22.60 (978-0-7660-1426-8). An account of America's turbulent 1960s that includes lifestyles, politics, fashion, fads, and entertainment. (Rev: BL 10/15/00; HBG 3/01; SLJ 12/00) [973.92]

18847 Feinstein, Stephen. *The 1970s: From Watergate to Disco* (4–7). Series: Decades of the 20th Century. 2000, Enslow LB $22.60 (978-0-7660-1425-1). This book covers the people and events of the 1970s along with developments in such areas as politics, science, and sports. (Rev: BL 10/15/00; HBG 3/01; SLJ 12/00)

18848 Feinstein, Stephen. *The 1980s: From Ronald Reagan to MTV* (4–7). Series: Decades of the 20th Century. 2000, Enslow LB $22.60 (978-0-7660-1424-4). 64pp. Presents the decade's major events, important people, and developments in such areas as politics, science, the arts, and sports. (Rev: BL 10/15/00; HBG 10/00; SLJ 12/00)

18849 Feinstein, Stephen. *The 1990s: Fom the Persian Gulf War to Y2K* (5–8). Series: Decades of the Twentieth Century. 2001, Enslow LB $22.60 (978-0-7660-1613-2). The events of the 1990s are covered in chapters on lifestyle and fashion; arts and entertainment; sports; politics; and science, technology, and medicine. (Rev: HBG 10/02; SLJ 2/02) [973.9]

18850 Gard, Carolyn. *The Attack on the Pentagon on September 11, 2001* (4–8). Series: Terrorist Attacks. 2003, Rosen LB $27.95 (978-0-8239-3858-2). In addition to describing the attack itself, Gard looks at the organization of Al-Qaeda. (Rev: SLJ 2/04) [975.5]

18851 Green, Carl R. *The Vietnam War* (4–6). Illus. Series: U.S. Wars. 2003, Enslow LB $25.26 (978-0-7660-5147-8). 48pp. Supported by verified and updated Web links, this is a useful introduction to the Vietnam War. (Rev: HBG 4/04)

18852 Hampton, Wilborn. *Kennedy Assassinated! The World Mourns* (5–8). 1997, Candlewick $17.99 (978-1-56402-811-2). A gripping first-person account of John Kennedy's assassination by a veteran newspaper reporter who was in Dallas that day. (Rev: BL 9/15/97; HBG 3/98; SLJ 10/97) [364.1]

18853 Koestler-Grack, Rachel A. *The Kent State Tragedy* (4–7). Series: American Moments. 2005, ABDO LB $25.65 (978-1-59197-934-0). A concise overview of the deadly 1970 clash between National Guard troops and war protesters on the campus of Ohio's Kent State University. (Rev: BL 9/1/05; SLJ 11/05) [378.771]

18854 Koestler, Rachel. *Going to School During the Civil Rights Movement* (4–6). Illus. Series: Going to School in History. 2001, Capstone LB $23.93 (978-0-7368-0799-9). 32pp. Koestler explores the difficulties of attending school during segregation. (Rev: BL 10/15/01; HBG 3/02)

18855 McNeese, Tim. *Modern America: 1964–Present* (5–8). Illus. Series: Discovering U.S. History. 2010, Chelsea House $35 (978-1-60413-361-5). 144pp. Covering American history from LBJ through Obama, this is a satisfying survey of social and political developments with illustrations, maps, photographs, and interesting sidebar features. **e** (Rev: SLJ 8/10) [973.92]

18856 Mason, Andrew. *The Vietnam War: A Primary Source History* (5–8). Series: In Their Own Words. 2005, Gareth Stevens LB $27.00 (978-0-8368-5981-2). Primary sources — including letters, articles, speeches, and songs — deliver the views of combatants in Vietnam and people on the home front in this well-illustrated volume. (Rev: BL 10/15/05) [959.704]

18857 Niven, Felicia Lowenstein. *Fabulous Fashions of the 1970s* (4–7). Illus. Series: Fabulous Fashions of the Decades. 2011, Enslow LB $23.93 (978-076603826-4). 48pp. Looks at all aspects of fashion in the 1970s, from men's and women's clothing to hairstyles, accessories, and pop culture. (Rev: BL 4/1/12; VOYA 10/10) [746.9]

18858 Petersen, Christine. *The Iran-Contra Scandal* (4–6). Series: Cornerstones of Freedom. 2004, Children's Pr. LB $26.00 (978-0-516-24228-6). 48pp. Petersen offers a fascinating overview of the investigations into Reagan administration activities involving illegal arms sales to Iran. (Rev: SLJ 7/04)

18859 Poffenberger, Nancy. *September 11th, 2001: A Simple Account for Children* (PS–2). Illus. 2002, Fun paper $8.95 (978-0-938293-12-5). 16pp. Drawings by schoolchildren illustrate a straightforward presentation of the events of September 11. (Rev: BL 7/02)

18860 Santella, Andrew. *September 11, 2001* (4–6). Series: Cornerstones of Freedom, Second Series. 2002, Children's Book Pr. LB $26.00 (978-0-516-22692-7). 48pp. This presentation gives the basic facts on the attacks and the U.S. response. (Rev: SLJ 11/02)

18861 Schomp, Virginia. *The Vietnam War* (5–8). Series: Letters from the Homefront. 2001, Benchmark LB $29.93 (978-0-7614-1099-7). 96pp. Conditions on the home front during the Vietnam War are re-created through primary documents such as letters and period photographs. (Rev: BL 10/15/01; HBG 3/02; SLJ 3/02)

18862 Stein, R. Conrad. *The Cold War* (4–6). Series: U.S. Wars. 2002, Enslow LB $25.26 (978-0-7660-5095-2). 48pp. In addition to a concise history of the causes and progress of the Cold War, this volume includes a listing of pertinent Web sites where additional material such as maps, documents, and biographies can be found. (Rev: BL 10/15/02; HBG 3/03)

18863 Steins, Richard. *The Postwar Years: The Cold War and the Atomic Age (1950-1959)* (5–8). Series: First Person America. 1994, Twenty-First Century LB $20.90 (978-0-8050-2587-3). Coverage of the 1950s includes first-person material on the Cold War and the Korean conflict. (Rev: BL 5/15/94; SLJ 12/94) [973.92]

18864 Walsh, Frank. *The Montgomery Bus Boycott* (5–8). Series: Landmark Events in American History. 2003, World Almanac LB $31.00 (978-0-8368-5375-9). 48pp. The story of what happened when Rosa Parks refused to give up her seat on a Montgomery, Alabama, bus in 1955. (Rev: BL 10/15/03; SLJ 9/03)

18865 Wheeler, Jill C. *September 11, 2001: The Day That Changed America* (3–5). Illus. Series: War on Terrorism. 2002, ABDO $25.65 (978-1-57765-656-2). 64pp. This introductory volume covers the attacks, the rescue efforts, and the initial American response, with lots of photographs. Also use *Ground Zero* and *Heroes of the Day*. (Rev: BL 5/1/02; HBG 10/02; SLJ 6/02)

18866 Young, Jeff C. *The Korean War* (4–6). Illus. Series: U.S. Wars. 2003, Enslow LB $25.26 (978-0-7660-5148-5). 48pp. Supported by verified and updated Web links, this is a useful account of the Korean War. (Rev: HBG 4/04)

18867 Young, Jeff C. *Operation Iraqi Freedom* (4–6). Illus. Series: U.S. Wars. 2003, Enslow LB $25.26 (978-0-7660-5088-4). Supported by verified and updated Web links, this is a useful introduction to Operation Iraqi Freedom. (Rev: HBG 4/04)

18868 Zeinert, Karen. *The Valiant Women of the Vietnam War* (5–8). 2000, Millbrook LB $29.90 (978-0-7613-1268-0). Provides a good overview of the Vietnam War and highlights the contributions of women at home and abroad during this conflict. (Rev: BL 4/1/00; HBG 10/00; SLJ 5/00) [959.704]

Regions

MIDWEST

18869 Anderson, Reuben. *Uniquely Oklahoma* (4–7). Illus. Series: Heinemann State Studies. 2004, Heinemann LB $27.07 (978-1-4034-4658-9). 48pp. In addition to providing the facts necessary for report writers, this volume emphasizes the features that distinguish Oklahoma from its neighbors. (Rev: BL 10/15/03)

18870 Anderson, Reuben. *Uniquely South Dakota* (4–7). Illus. Series: Heinemann State Studies. 2004, Heinemann LB $31.36 (978-1-4034-4662-6). 48pp. In addition to providing the facts necessary for report writers, this volume emphasizes the features that distinguish South Dakota from its neighbors. (Rev: BL 10/15/03)

18871 Ash, Stephanie. *Uniquely Minnesota* (4–7). Series: Heinemann State Studies. 2004, Heinemann LB $27.07 (978-1-4034-4494-3). 48pp. In addition to providing the facts necessary for report writers, this volume emphasizes the features that distinguish Minnesota from its neighbors. (Rev: BL 4/1/04)

18872 Balcavage, Dynise. *Iowa* (5–8). Illus. Series: From Sea to Shining Sea, Second Series. 2002, Children's LB $30.50 (978-0-516-22481-7). 80pp. An attractive overview of Iowa's land, history, culture, economy, and people. (Rev: SLJ 3/03)

18873 Baldwin, Guy. *Oklahoma* (4–8). Series: Celebrate the States. 2000, Marshall Cavendish LB $148.29 (978-0-7614-1061-4). The beauties and hidden treasures of Oklahoma are covered in this colorful introduction to the state, its past, its present, and its people. (Rev: BL 12/15/00) [976.6]

18874 Bennett, Michelle. *Missouri* (4–8). Series: Celebrate the States. 2001, Benchmark LB $37.07 (978-0-7614-1063-8). A logically organized, thorough introduction to Missouri with material on such topics as history, people, landmarks, and famous natives. (Rev: BL 9/15/01; HBG 10/01) [977.8]

18875 Bial, Raymond. *Nauvoo: Mormon City on the Mississippi River* (4–7). Illus. 2006, Houghton $17.00 (978-0-618-39685-6). 48pp. This richly illustrated title profiles the Illinois city of Nauvoo and the important role it played in the history of the Church of Jesus Christ of Latter-day Saints. (Rev: BL 11/1/06; SLJ 12/06)

18876 Bjorklund, Ruth. *Kansas* (4–8). Series: Celebrate the States. 2000, Marshall Cavendish LB $37.07 (978-0-7614-0646-4). A broad introduction to Kansas — its geography and history, its government and people, its songs and folktales, and a few of its recipes. (Rev: BL 6/1–15/00; HBG 10/00) [978.1]

18877 Bodden, Valerie. *Mount Rushmore* (3–6). Series: Modern Wonders of the World. 2006, Creative Education LB $27.10 (978-1-58341-440-8). 32pp. This is an interesting history of the memorial at Mount Rushmore, with good photographs and discussion of its contemporary importance. (Rev: SLJ 12/06)

18878 Brezina, Corona. *Indiana: Past and Present* (3–6). Series: The United States: Past and Present. 2010, Rosen LB $26.50 (978-1-4358-3521-4). 48pp. Includes chapters on the geography, history, government, economy, and people of Indiana, with a timeline and "Indiana at a Glance." (Rev: SLJ 6/10) [977.2]

18879 Brill, Marlene Targ. *Illinois* (4–7). Series: Celebrate the States. 2005, Benchmark LB $37.07 (978-0-7614-1735-4). A revised edition of this introduction to the state — including its history, culture, famous sites, and important individuals — with updated illustrations. (Rev: SLJ 5/06) [913.73]

18880 Brill, Marlene Targ, and Elizabeth Kaplan. *Minnesota* (3–6). Series: It's My State! 2010, Marshall Cavendish LB $21.95 (978-1-60870-054-7). 80pp. This accessible survey covers geography, history, people and culture, government, and the economy and includes an introductory "quick look" and information about the state song, seal, and so forth. (Rev: SLJ 2/1/11) [917.76]

18881 Burgan, Michael. *Illinois* (5–8). Illus. Series: America the Beautiful: Third Series. 2007, Children's Press LB $38.00 (978-0-531-18559-9). This new edition of the classic series entry about the state features a new design and layout, definitions of difficult words in the margins, more history and mini biographies, and project ideas in writing, art, and science. (Rev: BL 2/1/08) [8. 977.3]

18882 Coury, Tina Nichols. *Hanging Off Jefferson's Nose: Growing Up on Mount Rushmore* (4–6). Illus. by Sally Wern Comport. 2012, Dial $16.99 (978-080373731-0). 40pp. Tells the fascinating story of the creation of Mount Rushmore; the project was started by Gutzon Borglum but finished by his son Lincoln, who is the focus of this book. (Rev: BL 4/15/12; SLJ 7/12) [730.92]

18883 Deinard, Jenny. *How to Draw Illinois' Sights and Symbols* (3–6). Illus. Series: Kid's Guide to Drawing America. 2002, Rosen LB $25.25 (978-0-8239-6069-9). 32pp. An eclectic mix of drawing exercises and basic facts about Illinois history, geography, demographics, and important features. Also use *How to Draw Missouri's Sights and Symbols* (2001). (Rev: BL 2/15/02; SLJ 7/02)

18884 Derzipilski, Kathleen. *Indiana* (3–6). Illus. Series: It's My State! 2007, Marshall Cavendish LB $20.95 (978-0-7614-1927-3). 80pp. Interesting facts and a pleasing design combine to make this an engaging introduction to the Hoosier state. (Rev: SLJ 8/07)

18885 Dornfeld, Margaret. *Wisconsin* (4–7). Series: It's My State! 2003, Marshall Cavendish LB $27.07 (978-0-7614-1524-4). 80pp. Using many quotations from various sources, this account supplies a basic introduction to Wisconsin, its people, and its past and present. (Rev: BL 9/15/03; HBG 4/04; SLJ 11/03)

18886 Dykstra, Mary. *Iowa* (2–4). Series: Portraits of the States. 2006, Gareth Stevens LB $24.00 (978-0-8368-4664-5). 32pp. Young report writers will find lots of useful information in this introduction to the state, with accessible text and graphic features that add interest. (Rev: SLJ 5/06)

18887 Edge, Laura B. *A Personal Tour of Hull-House* (4–7). Series: How It Was. 2001, Lerner LB $25.26 (978-0-8225-3583-6). A firsthand account of the settlement house founded in Chicago by Jane Addams. (Rev: BL 8/1/01) [977.3]

18888 Gedatus, Gus. *Minnesota* (2–4). Series: Portraits of the States. 2006, Gareth Stevens LB $24.00 (978-0-8368-4669-0). 32pp. Young report writers will find lots of useful information in this introduction to the state, with accessible text and graphic features that add interest. (Rev: SLJ 5/06)

18889 Hahn, Laura. *Mount Rushmore* (4–8). Illus. Series: American Symbols and Their Meanings. 2002, Mason Crest LB $18.95 (978-1-59084-027-6). 48pp. Hahn describes Gutzon Borglum's struggle to build his monument, with a helpful timeline and many illustrations. (Rev: SLJ 9/02)

18890 Heinrichs, Ann. *Illinois* (3–6). Series: This Land Is Your Land. 2002, Compass Point LB $25.26 (978-0-7565-0313-0). 48pp. An overview of the geography, history, government, economy, people, and attractions of Illinois. (Rev: SLJ 2/03)

18891 Heinrichs, Ann. *Michigan* (2–5). Illus. Series: This Land Is Your Land. 2003, Compass Point LB $25.26 (978-0-7565-0323-9). 48pp. For early researchers, this introduction to basic facts about the state and its history, geography, people, government, economy, and attractions includes plenty of photographs and maps. Also use *Ohio* (2003). (Rev: SLJ 7/03)

18892 Heinrichs, Ann. *Minnesota* (2–5). Illus. Series: This Land Is Your Land. 2003, Compass Point LB $25.26 (978-0-7565-0315-4). This brightly illustrated profile explores Minnesota's history, people, geography, government, economy, and attractions. Also use *Ohio* and *Wisconsin* (both 2003). (Rev: SLJ 7/03)

18893 Heinrichs, Ann. *Ohio* (3–5). Illus. by Matt Kania. Series: Welcome to the U.S.A. 2005, The Child's World LB $27.07 (978-1-59296-449-9). 40pp. Using an attractive scrapbook format featuring a family on vacation, this volume introduces the state's geography, history, people, major attractions, and state symbols. (Rev: SLJ 2/06)

18894 Heinrichs, Ann. *South Dakota* (3–5). Illus. by Matt Kania. Series: Welcome to the U.S.A. 2005, The Child's

World LB $27.07 (978-1-59296-483-3). 40pp. A basic introduction with maps, pertinent facts, discussion of the state's geography and history, plus popular destinations and cultural information. (Rev: SLJ 1/06)

18895 Jameson, W. C. *Buried Treasures of the Great Plains* (5–8). Series: Buried Treasure. 1997, August House $11.95 (978-0-87483-486-4). Stories of buried treasure are organized by the individual states of the Great Plains region. (Rev: SLJ 7/97) [977]

18896 Johnson, Robin. *What's in the Midwest?* (3–6). Illus. Series: All Around the U.S. 2011, Crabtree LB $19.95 (978-077871823-9); paper $8.95 (978-077871829-1). 32pp. Covers the history, geography, climate, industry, and culture of the midwestern United States, looking both at the rural areas and the cities of 12 states. (Rev: BL 10/1/11) [917.7]

18897 Kenney, Karen Latchana. *Mount Rushmore* (2–4). Illus. by Judith A. Hunt. Series: Our Nation's Pride. 2011, ABDO LB $28.50 (978-1-61641-153-4). 32pp. Kenney describes how Mount Rushmore was created and its importance as a symbol today. (Rev: SLJ 7/11) [978.3]

18898 King, David C. *Iowa* (3–6). Illus. Series: It's My State! 2007, Marshall Cavendish LB $20.95 (978-0-7614-1928-0). 80pp. A pleasant design and interesting information make this a useful resource for students writing reports on Iowa. (Rev: SLJ 8/07)

18899 Ling, Bettina. *Wisconsin* (4–6). Series: From Sea to Shining Sea. 2002, Children's Book Pr. LB $30.50 (978-0-516-22380-3). The state of Wisconsin is introduced through a lively text, many color photographs, maps, a glossary, a timeline, and other attractive features. (Rev: BL 4/15/02)

18900 Mader, Jan. *Michigan* (K–2). Series: Rookie Read-About Geography. 2003, Children's Pr. LB $20.50 (978-0-516-22736-8); paper $5.95 (978-0-516-27781-3). 31pp. A small-format, basic introduction to the state of Michigan suitable for beginning readers. (Rev: SLJ 10/03)

18901 Marsico, Katie. *The Mississippi River* (3–6). Illus. Series: It's Cool to Learn about America's Waterways. 2013, Cherry Lake LB $28.50 (978-162431011-9); paper $14.21 (9781624310355). 32pp. Presents the geography, wildlife, history, and environmental challenges facing this waterway, with activities. (Rev: BL 5/1/13; LMC 11–12/13) [977]

18902 Martin, Michael A. *Ohio: The Buckeye State* (4–7). Series: World Almanac Library of the States. 2002, World Almanac LB $31.00 (978-0-8368-5124-3). Facts, statistics, a pleasing layout, and color photographs make this a useful choice for report writers. Also use *Oklahoma: The Sooner State* (2002). (Rev: SLJ 9/02) [977.1]

18903 Murphy, Jim. *The Great Fire* (5–9). 1995, Scholastic paper $18.95 (978-0-590-47267-8). A dramatic re-creation of the great Chicago fire that combines documents, personal accounts, illustrations, photographs, and street maps to give an in-depth view of the disaster.

Margaret A. Edwards Award 2010. (Rev: BCCB 5/95; BL 6/1–15/95; HB 5–6/95, 9–10/95; SLJ 7/95) [977.3]

18904 Nobleman, Marc Tyler. *Chicago* (3–6). Series: Great Cities of the World. 2004, World Almanac LB $31.00 (978-0-8368-5036-9). 48pp. Chicago's history, geography, and economy are described, as are shopping and leisure attractions and the life of the city. (Rev: SLJ 4/05)

18905 Olien, Rebecca. *Kansas* (3–5). Illus. Series: Land of Liberty. 2003, Capstone LB $25.26 (978-0-7368-1584-0). 64pp. Bright illustrations — photographs, reproductions, charts, and maps — add to this overview of the state's geography, climate, history, people, lifestyle, economy, government, and flora and fauna. (Rev: SLJ 10/03)

18906 Opat, Jamie Stockman. *Uniquely Nebraska* (4–7). Illus. Series: Heinemann State Studies. 2004, Heinemann LB $27.07 (978-1-4034-4649-7). 48pp. In addition to providing the facts necessary for report writers, this volume emphasizes the features that distinguish Nebraska from its neighbors. (Rev: BL 10/15/03)

18907 Peterson, Sheryl. *Wisconsin* (3–8). Series: This Land Called America. 2010, Creative Education $28.50 (978-1-58341-802-4). 32pp. History, culture, and geography are all covered in this attractive slim volume that provides the vital facts report writers need. (Rev: LMC 8–9/10) [977.5]

18908 Pfeffer, Wendy. *The Big Flood* (K–3). Illus. by Vanessa Lubach. 2001, Millbrook LB $23.90 (978-0-7613-1653-4). Young Patti describes the Mississippi flood of 1993 and the way the neighbors worked together to try to avert disaster. (Rev: BL 6/1–15/01; HBG 10/01; SLJ 10/01)

18909 Price-Groff, Claire. *Illinois* (3–6). Illus. Series: It's My State! 2002, Benchmark LB $27.07 (978-0-7614-1422-3). 80pp. The usual state information — geography, history, government, people, and economy — is presented in an appealing layout and with an activity. (Rev: BL 3/1/03; HBG 10/03; SLJ 2/03)

18910 Redmond, Jim, and D. J. Ross. *Uniquely North Dakota* (4–7). Series: Heinemann State Studies. 2004, Heinemann LB $27.07 (978-1-4034-4657-2). 48pp. In addition to providing the facts necessary for report writers, this volume emphasizes the features that distinguish North Dakota from its neighbors. (Rev: BL 4/1/04)

18911 Riggs, Kate. *Mount Rushmore* (2–4). Illus. Series: Now That's Big! 2009, Creative Education LB $24.25 (978-1-58341-705-8). 24pp. A slim introduction to the mountain and its famous sculptures. (Rev: BLO 3/11/09)

18912 St. Antoine, Sara, ed. *Stories from Where We Live: The Great North American Prairie* (4–8). 2001, Milkweed $19.95 (978-1-57131-630-1). A collection of historical and contemporary stories, poems, essays, and journal entries about life on the prairie, with informative appendixes. (Rev: BL 5/15/01)

18913 Schonberg, Lisa. *People of Ohio* (4–7). Illus. Series: Heinemann State Studies. 2003, Heinemann LB $27.07 (978-1-4034-0668-2). 48pp. Schonberg looks at groups of Ohioans from the original native peoples to later arrivals and at individuals who have contributed to all fields of endeavor, with many color photographs. (Rev: BL 10/15/03; HBG 4/04; SLJ 10/03)

18914 Schonberg, Marcia. *Uniquely Ohio* (4–6). Illus. Series: Heinemann State Studies. 2003, Heinemann LB $27.07 (978-1-4034-0670-5). 48pp. Full of facts and figures about the people, places, and things that make Ohio "a one-of-a-kind place." (Rev: HBG 4/04; SLJ 10/03)

18915 Schwabacher, Martin. *Minnesota* (4–7). Series: Celebrate the States. 1999, Benchmark LB $37.07 (978-0-7614-0658-7). Minnesota is introduced in six chapters that cover history, geography, government and economy, people, achievements, and landmarks. (Rev: HBG 10/99; SLJ 10/99) [977.6]

18916 Somervill, Barbara. *Illinois* (4–6). Illus. Series: From Sea to Shining Sea. 2001, Children's Book Pr. LB $30.50 (978-0-516-22320-9). 80pp. A good resource for report writing, this book features historical facts, maps, and information about the governmental structure and the people of Illinois. (Rev: BL 3/15/02)

18917 Steele, Christy Lee. *Uniquely Wisconsin* (4–7). Series: Heinemann State Studies. 2004, Heinemann LB $27.07 (978-1-4034-4499-8). 48pp. In addition to providing the facts necessary for report writers, this volume emphasizes the features that distinguish Wisconsin from its neighbors. (Rev: BL 4/1/04)

18918 Sturm, Ellen. *Ohio* (3–5). Illus. Series: Land of Liberty. 2003, Capstone LB $25.26 (978-0-7368-1593-2). 64pp. Bright illustrations — photographs, reproductions, charts, and maps — add to this overview of the state's geography, climate, history, people, lifestyle, economy, government, and flora and fauna. (Rev: SLJ 10/03)

18919 Temple, Teri, and Bob Temple. *Welcome to Badlands National Park* (3–5). Series: Visitor Guides. 2006, The Child's World LB $27.07 (978-1-59296-693-6). 32pp. An attractively presented tour of the South Dakota park, with information on its geography, history, flora, fauna, and weather. (Rev: SLJ 2/07)

18920 Thomas, William David. *Kansas* (2–4). Series: Portraits of the States. 2006, Gareth Stevens LB $24.00 (978-0-8368-4665-2). 32pp. History, geography, economy, and other research needs — including some interesting trivia — are covered in this concise volume. (Rev: BL 7/06)

18921 Wills, Charles A. *A Historical Album of Michigan* (4–7). Series: Historical Albums. 1996, Millbrook LB $24.40 (978-0-7613-0036-6). Using many archival prints, drawings, photographs, and ample text, the history of Michigan is told. (Rev: BL 10/15/96) [977]

MOUNTAIN STATES

18922 Altman, Linda Jacobs, and Stephanie Fitzgerald. *Colorado* (3–6). Series: It's My State! 2010, Marshall Cavendish LB $21.95 (978-1-60870-046-2). 80pp. This accessible survey covers geography, history, people and culture, government, and the economy and includes an introductory "quick look," a recipe, and information about the state song, seal, and so forth. (Rev: SLJ 2/1/11) [978.8]

18923 Bauer, Marion Dane. *Yellowstone* (PS–2). Illus. by John Wallace. Series: Ready-to-Read Wonders of America. 2008, Aladdin LB $13.89 (978-1-4169-5405-7); paper $3.99 (978-1-4169-5404-0). 32pp. For beginning readers, this is an introduction to the geological and animals wonders of the first national park. (Rev: BL 5/15/08)

18924 Bograd, Larry. *Uniquely Wyoming* (4–7). Illus. Series: Heinemann State Studies. 2004, Heinemann LB $31.36 (978-1-4034-4666-4). 48pp. In addition to providing the facts necessary for report writers, this volume emphasizes the features that distinguish Wyoming from its neighbors. (Rev: BL 10/15/03)

18925 Dumas, Bianca, and D. J. Ross. *Uniquely Utah* (4–7). Series: Heinemann State Studies. 2004, Heinemann LB $27.07 (978-1-4034-4663-3). 48pp. In addition to providing the facts necessary for report writers, this volume emphasizes the features that distinguish Utah from its neighbors. (Rev: BL 4/1/04)

18926 Graf, Mike. *Montana* (3–5). Illus. Series: Land of Liberty. 2003, Capstone LB $25.26 (978-0-7368-2184-1). An accessible profile of Montana, covering its people, history, topography, climate, economy, and more, together with suggestions for further reading. (Rev: SLJ 3/04)

18927 Hall, M. C. *Glacier National Park* (K–4). Series: Symbols of Freedom: National Parks. 2005, Heinemann LB $25.36 (978-1-4034-6698-3). 32pp. Large color photographs and clear text introduce the history, geography, flora, and fauna of this park; useful for basic research and reports. (Rev: SLJ 12/05)

18928 Hall, M. C. *Grand Canyon National Park* (K–4). Series: Symbols of Freedom: National Parks. 2005, Heinemann LB $25.36 (978-1-4034-6699-0). 32pp. Large color photographs and clear text introduce the history, geography, flora, and fauna of this park; useful for basic research and reports. (Rev: SLJ 12/05)

18929 Hall, M. C. *Rocky Mountain National Park* (K–4). Series: Symbols of Freedom: National Parks. 2005, Heinemann LB $25.36 (978-1-4034-6701-0). 32pp. Large color photographs and clear text introduce the history, geography, flora, and fauna of this park; useful for basic research and reports. (Rev: SLJ 12/05)

18930 Hall, M. C. *Yellowstone National Park* (K–4). 2005, Heinemann LB $25.36 (978-1-4034-6702-7). 32pp. Large color photographs and clear text introduce the history, geography, flora, and fauna of this park; useful for basic research and reports. (Rev: SLJ 12/05)

18931 Hamilton, John. *Rocky Mountain National Park* (4–6). Series: National Parks. 2008, ABDO LB $17.95 (978-1-60453-094-0). 32pp. Very informative short chapters and dazzling photographs (some full-page) make up this book about the geology, landscape, and uses of this national park. Also use *Zion National Park* (2008). (Rev: SLJ 2/09)

18932 Heinrichs, Ann. *Colorado* (3–5). Illus. by Matt Kania. Series: Welcome to the U.S.A. 2005, The Child's World LB $24.21 (978-0-756503314). A basic introduction with maps, pertinent facts, discussion of the state's geography and history, plus popular destinations and cultural information. (Rev: SLJ 1/06)

18933 Heinrichs, Ann. *Utah* (3–5). Illus. by Matt Kania. Series: Welcome to the U.S.A. 2005, The Child's World LB $27.07 (978-1-59296-486-4). A basic introduction with maps, pertinent facts, discussion of the state's geography and history, plus popular destinations and cultural information. (Rev: SLJ 1/06)

18934 Higgins, Nadia. *Welcome to Glacier National Park* (3–5). Series: Visitor Guides. 2006, The Child's World LB $27.07 (978-1-59296-696-7). 32pp. An attractively presented tour of the Montana park, focusing on its geography, history, flora, fauna, and weather. (Rev: SLJ 2/07)

18935 Lorbiecki, Marybeth. *Welcome to Grand Teton National Park* (3–5). Illus. Series: Visitor Guides. 2006, Child's World LB $27.07 (978-1-59296-698-1). Despite confusing maps, this guide to the Wyoming park offers solid information for reports. (Rev: BL 10/15/06; SLJ 2/07)

18936 Lynch, Wayne, and Aubrey Lang. *Rocky Mountains* (4–7). Illus. by Wayne Lynch. Series: Our Wild World. 2006, NorthWord $16.95 (978-1-55971-948-3); paper $8.95 (978-1-55971-949-0). 64pp. An appealing introduction to the geography, animals, and plants of the region, with full-color photographs and first-person anecdotes. (Rev: BL 10/15/06; SLJ 1/07*)

18937 Mann, Elizabeth. *Hoover Dam* (3–6). Illus. by Alan Witschonke. Series: Wonders of the World. 2001, Mikaya $19.95 (978-1-931414-02-9). 48pp. The exciting story of Hoover Dam is presented in a well-designed package with personal anecdotes and an emphasis on the loss of life. (Rev: BL 12/1/01; HB 3/02; HBG 10/02; SLJ 12/01)

18938 Maynard, Charles W. *The Rocky Mountains* (2–5). Series: Great Mountain Ranges of the World. 2004, Rosen LB $21.25 (978-0-8239-6926-5). 24pp. Full-page, full-color photographs grace each spread of this slim volume that introduces the geology, climate, plants, animals, economy, peoples, and exploration of the Rockies, with discussion of environmental issues. (Rev: SLJ 8/04)

18939 Meister, Cari. *Yellowstone National Park* (2–4). Illus. Series: Going Places. 2000, ABDO $21.35 (978-1-57765-026-3). This tour of Yellowstone National Park includes material on history, its things to see and do, and the plants and animals. (Rev: HBG 10/00; SLJ 1/01)

18940 O'Connor, Rebecca K., and Dennis Myers. *Uniquely Nevada* (4–7). Illus. Series: Heinemann State Studies. 2004, Heinemann LB $27.07 (978-1-4034-4650-3). 48pp. In addition to providing the facts necessary for report writers, this volume emphasizes the features that distinguish Nevada from its neighbors. (Rev: BL 10/15/03)

18941 Patent, Dorothy Hinshaw. *When the Wolves Returned: Restoring Nature's Balance in Yellowstone* (3–5). Illus. by Cassie Hartman. 2008, Walker $17.95 (978-0-8027-9686-8). 40pp. Patent looks at the ecological harm caused by the disappearance of the wolf from Yellowstone, and the recovery that took place when they returned. (Rev: BL 2/15/08; HB 5/08; LMC 10/08; SLJ 6/08)

18942 Sanders, Doug. *Idaho* (4–6). Illus. Series: It's My State! 2004, Benchmark LB $27.07 (978-0-7614-1824-5). 80pp. Idaho's geography, wildlife, history, people, government, and natural resources are all covered here, with material on key individuals and famous events. (Rev: SLJ 5/05)

18943 Stefoff, Rebecca. *Idaho* (4–8). Series: Celebrate the States. 2000, Benchmark LB $37.07 (978-0-7614-0663-1). Interesting charts, graphs, and maps are used to illustrate such topics as the people, land, history, and culture of Idaho. (Rev: BL 1/1–15/00; HBG 10/00) [978.8]

18944 Stefoff, Rebecca. *Nevada* (4–8). Series: Celebrate the States. 2001, Benchmark LB $37.07 (978-0-7614-1073-7). This well-organized introduction to Nevada gives general information followed by a timeline and special material on tourist attractions, famous natives of Nevada, and local festivals. (Rev: BL 9/15/01; HBG 10/01) [979.3]

18945 Stefoff, Rebecca. *Utah* (4–8). Series: Celebrate the States. 2000, Marshall Cavendish LB $37.07 (978-0-7614-1064-5). 144pp. Utah's unique characteristics and places are highlighted in this account that also covers the state's history, geography, and government. (Rev: BL 12/15/00; HBG 3/01; SLJ 2/01)

18946 Trumbauer, Lisa. *Grand Canyon* (K–2). Series: Rookie Read-About Geography. 2005, Children's Pr. LB $20.50 (978-0-516-22747-4). This simple easy-reader covers the basic facts about the geographic wonder. (Rev: SLJ 7/05)

NORTHEAST

18947 Ashabranner, Brent. *Badge of Valor: The National Law Enforcement Officers Memorial* (5–8). Illus. 2000, Twenty-First Century LB $25.90 (978-0-7613-1522-3). 64pp. This history of the memorial, from the original proposal in the 1970s to its opening in 1991, also discusses what it stands for and reveals the heroic deeds of some important law enforcement officers. (Rev: BL 10/1/00; HBG 3/01; SLJ 1/01)

18948 Ashabranner, Brent. *A Date with Destiny: The Women in Military Service for America Memorial* (5–8). 2000, Twenty-First Century LB $25.90 (978-0-7613-1472-1). This book tells the story of the memorial outside Arlington National Cemetery that honors American women in the military and retells some of the stories of these servicewomen. (Rev: BL 2/1/00; HBG 10/00; SLJ 4/00) [355.1]

18949 Ashabranner, Brent. *No Better Hope: What the Lincoln Memorial Means to America* (4–8). Illus. Series: Great American Memorials. 2001, Twenty-First Century LB $25.90 (978-0-7613-1523-0). 64pp. As well as telling about Lincoln and his importance to the country, this volume describes the building of the memorial and the important events that have occurred on the site. (Rev: BL 3/1/01; HBG 10/01; SLJ 7/01; VOYA 10/01)

18950 Ashabranner, Brent. *On the Mall in Washington, D.C.: A Visit to America's Front Yard* (5–7). Illus. by Jennifer Ashabranner. 2002, Twenty-First Century LB $23.90 (978-0-7613-2351-8). 64pp. An entertaining and informative tour of the National Mall in Washington, D.C. (Rev: BL 3/15/02; HBG 10/02; SLJ 4/02)

18951 Ashabranner, Brent. *Remembering Korea: The Korean War Veterans Memorial* (4–8). Illus. by Jennifer Ashabranner. Series: Great American Memorials. 2001, Twenty-First Century LB $25.90 (978-0-7613-2156-9). 64pp. Ashabranner explains who the memorial honors, how much it cost, and what it represents. (Rev: BL 9/15/01; HBG 3/02; SLJ 12/01)

18952 Ashabranner, Brent. *The Washington Monument: A Beacon for America* (4–8). Illus. by Jennifer Ashabranner. Series: Great American Memorials. 2002, Millbrook LB $25.90 (978-0-7613-1524-7). 64pp. Ashabranner presents the story behind the monument, including its planning, design, and construction, with full-color photographs and black-and-white period reproductions. (Rev: BL 9/1/02; HBG 3/03; SLJ 11/02)

18953 Avakian, Monique. *A Historical Album of Massachusetts* (4–8). Series: Historical Albums. 1994, Millbrook LB $24.40 (978-1-56294-481-0). A history of Massachusetts that begins with the Native American culture and ends with the 1900s, including basic material on major events and personalities. (Rev: SLJ 2/95) [974.4]

18954 Backer, Miles. *Travels with Charlie: Travelin' the Northeast* (1–4). Illus. by Chuck Nitzberg. Series: A Search and Find Geography Book. 2006, Blue Apple $15.95 (978-1-59354-162-0). Charlie, a travel-loving mutt, takes readers on a light-hearted, seek-and-find hunt of the northeastern United States. (Rev: SLJ 2/07)

18955 Barenblat, Rachel. *Massachusetts: The Bay State* (4–7). Series: World Almanac Library of the States. 2002, World Almanac LB $31.00 (978-0-8368-5123-6). History, politics, government, culture, and state symbols are all covered, with charts, maps, photographs, biographical sketches, and a list of important events and attractions. (Rev: SLJ 6/02) [974.4]

18956 Bauer, Marion Dane. *Niagara Falls* (K–2). Illus. by John Wallace. Series: Ready-to-Read Wonders of America. 2006, Simon & Schuster LB $11.89 (978-0-689-86945-7); paper $3.99 (978-0-689-86944-0). 32pp. Basic information about the waterfall — geology and history, including daredevil feats — is presented in an attractive format suitable for beginning readers. (Rev: SLJ 6/06)

18957 Belanger, Jeff. *Who's Haunting the White House?* (4–7). Illus. by Rick Powell. 2008, Sterling $14.95 (978-1-4027-3822-7). 64pp. A history of the White House and paranormal incidents there, with period illustrations, paintings, drawings, and prints. (Rev: BL 12/15/08; SLJ 12/08) [133.1]

18958 Bial, Raymond. *Ellis Island: Coming to the Land of Liberty* (4–6). 2009, Houghton $18.00 (978-0-618-99943-9). 58pp. With both period and contemporary photographs, plus primary-source quotations, Bial looks at the history of the immigration center. (Rev: BCCB 9/09; BL 8/09; SLJ 6/09)

18959 Bial, Raymond. *Tenement: Immigrant Life on the Lower East Side* (5–8). 2002, Houghton Mifflin $16.00 (978-0-618-13849-4). Historic photographs complement the simple, descriptive text about life in New York City tenement housing in the late 1800s and early 1900s. (Rev: BL 10/15/02; HB 11–12/02; HBG 3/03; SLJ 9/02) [307.76]

18960 Bjorklund, Ruth, and Stephanie Fitzgerald. *Massachusetts* (3–6). Series: It's My State! 2010, Marshall Cavendish LB $21.95 (978-1-60870-053-0). 80pp. This accessible survey covers geography, history, people and culture, government, and the economy and includes an introductory "quick look" and information about the state song, seal, and so forth. (Rev: SLJ 2/1/11) [917.44]

18961 Braithwaite, Jill. *The Statue of Liberty* (K–2). Series: Pull Ahead Books. 2003, Lerner LB $22.60 (978-0-8225-3802-8); paper $5.95 (978-0-8225-3756-4). For beginning report writers, this is a simple, well-illustrated look at the statue and its symbolism. (Rev: SLJ 1/04)

18962 Britton, Tamara. *The Pentagon* (3–5). Series: Symbols, Landmarks, and Monuments. 2003, ABDO LB $22.78 (978-1-57765-849-8). 32pp. A brief history of the vast headquarters of the U.S. Department of Defense, covering the terrorist attack of September 11, 2001. (Rev: HBG 10/03; SLJ 10/03)

18963 Britton, Tamara. *The Smithsonian Institution* (3–5). Series: Symbols, Landmarks, and Monuments. 2004, ABDO LB $22.78 (978-1-59197-521-2). 32pp. An introduction to the history and contemporary importance of the museums that make up this venerable establishment. (Rev: SLJ 11/04)

18964 Britton, Tamara. *The Vietnam Veterans Memorial* (3–5). Series: Symbols, Landmarks, and Monuments. 2004, ABDO LB $22.78 (978-1-59197-523-6). 32pp. Explains the importance of this memorial and the story of its design. (Rev: SLJ 11/04)

18965 Burg, Ann K. *Times Square: A New York State Number Book* (2–5). Illus. by Maureen K. Brookfield. 2005, Sleeping Bear $16.95 (978-1-58536-195-3). Readers count to 100 while absorbing numerous facts — some little-known — about New York State. (Rev: SLJ 1/06)

18966 Burgan, Michael. *Connecticut* (4–7). Series: It's My State! 2003, Marshall Cavendish LB $27.07 (978-0-7614-1523-7). 80pp. This New England state is introduced with material on its people, geography, history, cities, products, and resources. (Rev: BL 9/15/03; HBG 4/04)

18967 Burgan, Michael. *Fort McHenry* (4–6). Series: Symbols of American Freedom. 2009, Chelsea Club-house $30 (978-1-60413-520-6). 48pp. Plenty of photographs, drawings, diagrams, and historical anecdotes enhance this portrait of the construction and history of Fort McHenry. (Rev: SLJ 4/10) [975.26]

18968 Clark, Diane C. *A Kid's Guide to Washington, D.C. Rev. ed.* (4–6). Ed. by Miriam Chernick. Illus. by Richard E. Brown. 2008, Harcourt paper $14.00 (978-0-15-206125-8). 160pp. This attractive, large-format book, an update of a 1989 edition, provides lots of age-appropriate information on the sites of the capital. (Rev: BL 6/1–15/08)

18969 Cotter, Kristin. *New York* (3–5). Illus. Series: From Sea to Shining Sea, Second Series. 2002, Children's Book Pr. LB $30.50 (978-0-516-22485-5). 80pp. This revision of an earlier title adds information and features that will enhance its appeal to report writers. Also use *Connecticut* and *Delaware* (both 2002). (Rev: SLJ 1/03)

18970 Cowan, Mary Morton. *Timberrr: A History of Logging in New England* (5–8). Illus. 2003, Millbrook LB $25.90 (978-0-7613-1866-8). 96pp. Cowan highlights timber's historical importance in many walks of life — trade, politics, and construction, for example — and looks at changes brought by new technologies and the impact on ecology and the environment. (Rev: BL 11/15/03; HBG 4/04)

18971 Curlee, Lynn. *Brooklyn Bridge* (3–6). Illus. 2001, Simon & Schuster $18.00 (978-0-689-83183-6). 40pp. The story of the construction of the Brooklyn Bridge with particular emphasis on the role played by the Roebling family. (Rev: BCCB 6/01; BL 4/15/01; HB 7/01; HBG 10/01; SLJ 5/01)

18972 Curlee, Lynn. *Capital* (2–5). Illus. 2003, Simon & Schuster $17.95 (978-0-689-84947-3). 48pp. Stories of five important Washington, D.C., buildings portray much of American history. (Rev: BCCB 2/03; BL 1/1–15/03; HBG 10/03; SLJ 1/03)

18973 Cytron, Barry. *Fire! The Library Is Burning* (4–7). 1988, Lerner LB $15.93 (978-0-8225-0525-9). How workers and volunteers helped to restore the Jewish Theological Seminary in New York City when it was nearly destroyed by fire. (Rev: BL 7/88; SLJ 9/88) [027.63]

18974 Degezelle, Terri. *Ellis Island* (K–2). Series: American Symbols. 2003, Capstone LB $21.26 (978-0-7368-2292-3). 24pp. A visit to Ellis Island in New York Harbor, the place of entry to the United States for millions of immigrants, with modern and archival photos. (Rev: SLJ 4/04)

18975 Deinard, Jenny. *How to Draw Massachusetts's Sights and Symbols* (3–6). Series: Kid's Guide to Drawing America. 2001, Rosen LB $25.25 (978-0-8239-6077-4). As well as basic facts on key sights and symbols of Massachusetts, clear instructions are given on how to draw the state seal, flag, bird, and so forth. (Rev: BL 4/15/02; SLJ 7/02)

18976 Doak, Robin. *New Jersey* (5–8). Series: Voices from Colonial America. 2005, National Geographic LB $32.90 (978-0-7922-6680-8). A compelling account of life in early New Jersey, from its initial settlement by the Dutch through the adoption of the Constitution. (Rev: BL 6/1–15/05; SLJ 1/06) [974.9]

18977 Doherty, Craig A., and Katherine M. Doherty. *Pennsylvania* (5–9). Series: The Thirteen Colonies. 2005, Facts on File LB $35.00 (978-0-8160-5413-8). Traces the history of Pennsylvania from the early settlers through 1787, with discussion of the Native American culture, the Quakers, and with excerpts from primary documents, maps, and profiles of key individuals. (Rev: SLJ 8/05) [973]

18978 Doherty, Craig A., and Katherine M. Doherty. *Rhode Island* (5–9). Series: The Thirteen Colonies. 2005, Facts on File LB $35.00 (978-0-8160-5415-2). Traces the history of Rhode Island from the early settlers through 1787, with discussion of the Native American culture and with excerpts from primary documents, maps, and profiles of key individuals. (Rev: SLJ 8/05) [973]

18979 Dornfeld, Margaret. *Maine* (4–8). Series: Celebrate the States. 2001, Benchmark LB $37.07 (978-0-7614-1071-3). 144pp. An attractive, fact-filled introduction to the state of Maine with material on history, famous places and people, and current concerns. (Rev: BL 9/15/01; HBG 10/01)

18980 Elish, Dan. *New York* (4–7). Illus. Series: My State. 2003, Marshall Cavendish $27.07 (978-0-7614-1419-3). 80pp. Color photographs accompany information on the state's topography, wildlife, climate, population, government, industries, and resources. (Rev: BL 3/1/03; HBG 10/03)

18981 Elish, Dan. *Washington, D.C.* (5–8). Series: Celebrate the States. 1998, Benchmark LB $37.07 (978-0-7614-0423-1). An attractive introduction to the people and government of the U.S. capital with material on parks, landmarks, history, economics, and racial problems. (Rev: HBG 10/98; SLJ 1/99) [975.3]

18982 Foster, Mark. *Whale Port: A History of Tuckanucket* (4–7). Illus. by Gerald Foster. 2007, Houghton $18.00 (978-0-618-54722-7). 64pp. The life and times of a fictitious New England town from 1683 to today reveal how changes in population, technology, commerce, and society all affect a town's growth; detailed illustrations. (Rev: BL 12/1/07; SLJ 11/07)

18983 Graham, Amy. *Maine* (4–7). Illus. Series: States. 2002, Enslow LB $25.26 (978-0-7660-5017-4). 48pp. This well-illustrated volume offers report writers basic information on the state's land, climate, economy, government, and history, plus recommendations of Web sites that will extend their knowledge. Also use *New York* (2002). (Rev: SLJ 9/02)

18984 Gray, Susan H. *The White House* (2–4). Series: Our Nation. 2001, Compass Point LB $19.93 (978-0-7565-0145-7). 24pp. An introduction to the interior of the executive mansion. (Rev: SLJ 1/02)

18985 Greene, Jacqueline D. *The Triangle Shirtwaist Factory Fire* (3–5). Illus. Series: Code Red. 2007, Bearport LB $25.27 (978-1-59716-359-0). 32pp. This study

of the tragic 1911 fire that killed 146 at a New York City clothing factory examines the disaster itself, the reasons for the heavy loss of life, and the lessons that were learned by city authorities. (Rev: BL 4/1/07)

18986 Hankins, Chelsey. *The Lincoln Memorial* (3–6). Series: Symbols of American Freedom. 2009, Chelsea Clubhouse $30 (978-1-60413-518-3). 48pp. With clear, simple language, this book looks at the history and contemporary importance of the Lincoln Memorial and includes photographs and excerpts from speeches as well as tips on making a successful visit. (Rev: LMC 3–4/10; SLJ 3/1/10) [975.3]

18987 Heinrichs, Ann. *Delaware* (3–5). Illus. by Matt Kania. Series: Welcome to the U.S.A. 2005, The Child's World LB $27.07 (978-1-59296-470-3). 40pp. Using an attractive scrapbook format featuring a family on vacation, this volume introduces the state's geography, history, people, major attractions, and state symbols. Also use *Maryland* (2005). (Rev: SLJ 2/06)

18988 Heinrichs, Ann. *Pennsylvania* (2–5). Illus. Series: This Land Is Your Land. 2003, Compass Point LB $25.26 (978-0-7565-0320-8). 48pp. A brightly illustrated introduction to Pennsylvania's history, people, geography, government, economy, and attractions. (Rev: SLJ 8/03)

18989 Hempstead, Anne. *The Statue of Liberty* (4–7). Series: Land of the Free. 2006, Heinemann LB $28.21 (978-1-4034-7004-1). With many illustrations and interesting sidebars, this history of the Statue of Liberty details key events and examines its significance as an American symbol. (Rev: SLJ 10/06) [974.7]

18990 Hempstead, Anne. *The Supreme Court* (4–7). Series: Land of the Free. 2006, Heinemann LB $28.21 (978-1-4034-7001-0). With many illustrations and interesting sidebars, this history of the U.S. Supreme Court details key events and examines its significance as an American symbol. Also use *The U.S. Capitol* and *The White House* (both 2006). (Rev: SLJ 10/06) [347]

18991 Herda, D. J. *Environmental America: The Northeastern States* (4–7). Series: American Scene. 1991, Millbrook LB $22.40 (978-1-878841-06-3). This volume discusses the condition of the environment and presents information on such topics as water and land pollution in the northeastern states. (Rev: BL 8/91; SLJ 7/91) [639.9]

18992 Hess, Debra. *The White House* (3–5). Series: Symbols of America. 2003, Benchmark LB $25.64 (978-0-7614-1712-5). 40pp. The history of the White House, residence of every U.S. president since 1792, and how it has changed over the years. (Rev: HBG 4/04; SLJ 3/04)

18993 Hicks, Terry Allan. *The Capitol* (3–5). Series: Symbols of America. 2006, Benchmark LB $28.50 (978-0-7614-2132-0). 40pp. A look at the U.S. Capitol, its history, and the important role it plays as the home of America's legislative branch of government. (Rev: SLJ 12/06)

18994 Hicks, Terry Allan. *Ellis Island* (3–5). Series: Symbols of America. 2006, Benchmark LB $28.50 (978-0-7614-2134-4). An overview of the history of Ellis Island and its importance as a symbol of the United States. (Rev: SLJ 12/06)

18995 Hicks, Terry Allan. *Washington, D.C.* (3–6). Illus. Series: It's My State! 2007, Marshall Cavendish LB $20.95 (978-0-7614-1929-9). 80pp. Interesting facts and a pleasing design combine to make this an engaging introduction to the United States capital. (Rev: SLJ 8/07)

18996 High, Linda O. *Under New York* (PS–3). Illus. by Robert Rayevsky. 2001, Holiday House $16.95 (978-0-8234-1551-9). 32pp. A richly illustrated picture book that takes the reader underground in New York City to a world of pipes, power lines, trains, and tunnels. (Rev: BL 3/1/01; HB 7/01; HBG 10/01)

18997 Hochain, Serge. *Building Liberty: A Statue Is Born* (3–6). Trans. from French by Camilla Bozzoli. Illus. by author. 2004, National Geographic LB $25.90 (978-0-7922-6969-4). The Statue of Liberty's story is told in four parts — design and construction, transportation across the Atlantic, fund-raising for the pedestal, and eventual erection — each involving a boy who plays a role. (Rev: SLJ 8/04)

18998 Ingram, Scott. *Pennsylvania: The Keystone State* (4–7). Series: World Almanac Library of the States. 2002, World Almanac LB $31.00 (978-0-8368-5120-5). Facts, statistics, a pleasing layout, and color photographs make this a useful choice for report writers. (Rev: SLJ 9/02) [974.8]

18999 Jameson, W. C. *Buried Treasures of New England: Legends of Hidden Riches, Forgotten War Loots, and Lost Ship Treasures* (4–8). Series: Buried Treasure. 1997, August House $11.95 (978-0-87483-485-7). This account describes how these treasures were amassed and lost, and furnishes maps to indicate their general location. (Rev: SLJ 10/97) [910.4]

19000 Kennedy, Marge. *The Story of the White House* (K–2). Series: Scholastic News Nonfiction Readers. 2009, Children's Pr. LB $20.00 (978-0-531-21094-9); paper $6.95 (978-0-531-22431-1). The White House's history and some interesting facts about the building are presented in an easy-to-read format. Also use *Having Fun at the White House* and *Time to Eat at the White House* (2009). (Rev: SLJ 5/09)

19001 Kenney, Karen Latchana. *Ellis Island* (2–4). Illus. by Judith A. Hunt. Series: Our Nation's Pride. 2011, ABDO LB $28.50 (978-1-61641-150-3). 32pp. Kenney looks at the history and importance of Ellis Island. (Rev: SLJ 7/11) [304.8]

19002 Kenney, Karen Latchana. *The White House* (2–4). Illus. by Judith A. Hunt. Series: Our Nation's Pride. 2011, ABDO LB $28.50 (978-1-61641-154-1). 32pp. Kenney describes how the site was chosen for the White House, the history of the building and the people who have lived and worked there, and what it's like to visit it. (Rev: SLJ 7/11) [975.3]

19003 Knox, Barbara. *New Hampshire* (3–5). Illus. Series: Land of Liberty. 2003, Capstone LB $25.26 (978-0-7368-2187-2). 64pp. A trip to Mount Monadnock opens this survey of New Hampshire, which provides all the material needed for a state report. (Rev: SLJ 2/04)

19004 Krensky, Stephen. *What's the Big Idea?* (4–6). Illus. 2008, Charlesbridge $18.95 (978-1-58089-310-7); paper $9.95 (978-1-58089-311-4). A brief history of Boston with mini-biographies of some of the city's major figures. (Rev: BL 3/1/08; LMC 11/08; SLJ 6/08)

19005 Leotta, Joan. *Massachusetts* (4–6). Series: From Sea to Shining Sea. 2001, Children's Book Pr. LB $30.50 (978-0-516-22486-2). As well as basic coverage on Massachusetts, this book includes interesting sidebars. (Rev: BL 4/15/02)

19006 Levert, Suzanne. *Massachusetts* (4–8). Series: Celebrate the States. 2000, Benchmark LB $37.07 (978-0-7614-0666-2). A fine introduction to the people and places of the Bay State that also includes recipes, folktales, and songs. (Rev: BL 1/1–15/00; HBG 10/00; SLJ 5/00)

19007 Louis, Nancy. *Ground Zero* (4–7). Series: War on Terrorism. 2002, ABDO LB $16.95 (978-1-57765-675-3). This heavily illustrated, factually accurate account describes the search, recovery, and cleanup that took place after September 11, 2001, in New York City. (Rev: BL 5/15/02) [974.7]

19008 Lourie, Peter. *Erie Canal: Canoeing America's Great Waterway* (5–8). 1997, Boyds Mills $17.95 (978-1-56397-669-8). This colorful book about a journey along the Erie Canal also supplies historical facts about its construction and uses. (Rev: BL 7/97; HBG 3/98; SLJ 9/97) [974.7]

19009 Low, William. *Old Penn Station* (2–4). Illus. 2007, Holt $16.95 (978-0-8050-7925-8). 32pp. This photoessay celebrates the grandeur of the New York City landmark that was demolished in the 1960s. (Rev: BL 3/15/07)

19010 McAuliffe, Emily. *Connecticut Facts and Symbols.* Rev. ed. (3–5). Illus. Series: The States and Their Symbols. 2003, Capstone LB $21.26 (978-0-7368-2237-4). A brief, illustrated overview of facts about Connecticut such as the state's nickname, motto, flag, and other symbols. (Rev: SLJ 1/04)

19011 McCurdy, Michael. *Walden Then and Now: An Alphabetical Tour of Henry Thoreau's Pond* (5–8). Illus. by author. 2010, Charlesbridge $16.95 (978-158089253-7). 32pp. "C is for the cabin Henry built with his own hands." This handsome book explores Walden Pond in Thoreau's time and today. (Rev: BL 9/1/10; LMC 1–2/11; SLJ 9/1/10) [818]

19012 McKendry, Joe. *One Times Square: A Century of Change at the Crossroads of the World* (5–8). Illus. by author. 2012, Godine $19.95 (978-1-56792364-3). 64pp. A fascinating and very visual history of Times Square, New York City. (Rev: BL 9/15/12; SLJ 8/1/12) [974.7]

19013 Mann, Elizabeth. *Statue of Liberty: A Tale of Two Countries* (4–6). Illus. by Alan Witschonke. Series: Wonders of the World. 2011, Mikaya $22.95 (978-1-931414-43-2). 48pp. This well-researched book chronicles the development, delivery, and worldwide impact of the Statue of Liberty. (Rev: BLO 11/15/11; LMC 11–12/11; SLJ 8/11) [974.7]

19014 Marcovitz, Hal. *The Liberty Bell* (4–8). Illus. Series: American Symbols and Their Meanings. 2002, Mason Crest LB $18.95 (978-1-59084-025-2). 48pp. The history and condition of the bell are presented through text, illustrations, and a useful timeline. Also use *The White House* (2002). (Rev: SLJ 9/02)

19015 Melman, Peter. *Uniquely New Hampshire* (4–7). Series: Heinemann State Studies. 2004, Heinemann LB $27.07 (978-1-4034-4651-0). 48pp. In addition to providing the facts necessary for report writers, this volume emphasizes the features that distinguish New Hampshire from its neighbors. (Rev: BL 4/1/04)

19016 Moose, Katherine B. *Uniquely Delaware* (4–7). Series: Heinemann State Studies. 2004, Heinemann LB $27.07 (978-1-4034-4644-2). 48pp. In addition to providing the facts necessary for report writers, this volume emphasizes the features that distinguish Delaware from its neighbors. (Rev: BL 4/1/04)

19017 Moose, Katherine B. *Uniquely Rhode Island* (4–7). Illus. Series: Heinemann State Studies. 2004, Heinemann LB $27.07 (978-1-4034-4660-2). 48pp. In addition to providing the facts necessary for report writers, this volume emphasizes the features that distinguish Rhode Island from its neighbors. (Rev: BL 10/15/03)

19018 Morgane, Wendy. *New Jersey* (4–8). Series: Celebrate the States. 2000, Benchmark LB $37.07 (978-0-7614-0673-0). This excellent introduction to New Jersey covers its history, land, government, economy, unique characteristics, and famous residents. (Rev: BL 1/1–15/00; HBG 10/00) [974.9]

19019 Mortensen, Lori. *Ellis Island* (K–2). Illus. by Matthew Skeens. Series: American Symbols. 2008, Picture Window $25.26 (978-1-4048-4705-7). 24pp. Simple text, engaging facts, and big illustrations make this a good entry-level read about Ellis Island. (Rev: BLO 10/7/08; SLJ 1/09)

19020 Nelson, Kristin L. *The Washington Monument* (K–2). Series: Pull Ahead Books. 2003, Lerner LB $22.60 (978-0-8225-0250-0); paper $5.95 (978-0-8225-3759-5). 32pp. For beginning report writers, this is a simple, well-illustrated look at the monument and its symbolism. (Rev: SLJ 1/04)

19021 *New York*. Rev. ed. (3–5). Series: One Nation. 2002, Capstone LB $22.60 (978-0-7368-1256-6). 48pp. A chapter on New York City's subways introduces an overview of the state's geography, history, people, lifestyle, economy, and tourist attractions. (Rev: HBG 3/03; SLJ 4/03)

19022 *Our White House: Looking In, Looking Out* (5–8). 2008, Candlewick $29.99 (978-0-7636-2067-7). Essays, historical fiction, and poetry from contemporary children's writers are combined with firsthand accounts from former presidents, their family members, and White House visitors to create this attractive, large-format look at the White House and its place in America's history. (Rev: BL 8/08; SLJ 9/08) [975.3]

19023 Pascoe, Elaine. *History Around You: A Unique Look at the Past, People, and Places of New York* (4–7). 2004, Gale LB $27.45 (978-1-4103-0490-2). Using a news-style format with maps, charts, and illustrations, Pascoe details the history of New York State and profiles famous individuals. (Rev: SLJ 3/05) [974.7]

19024 Peters, Stephen. *Pennsylvania* (4–7). Series: Celebrate the States. 2000, Marshall Cavendish LB $37.07 (978-0-7614-0644-0). 144pp. An overview of the history, geography, and culture of Pennsylvania with additional material on state symbols, industry, the people, and the economy. (Rev: BL 6/1–15/00; SLJ 9/00)

19025 Raabe, Emily. *Uniquely Vermont* (4–7). Series: Heinemann State Studies. 2005, Heinemann LB $31.36 (978-1-4034-4664-0). In addition to providing the facts necessary for report writers, this volume emphasizes the features that distinguish Vermont from its neighbors. (Rev: BL 10/15/03)

19026 Rappaport, Doreen. *Lady Liberty: A Biography* (2–5). Illus. by Matt Tavares. 2008, Candlewick $17.99 (978-0-7636-2530-6). 60pp. Free-verse accounts by individuals involved — including sculptor Auguste Bartholdi and poet Emma Lazarus — tell the story of the creation of the Statue of Liberty. (Rev: BL 4/15/08; HB 7/08; LMC 11/08; SLJ 5/08)

19027 Rau, Dana Meachen. *The Northeast* (3–5). Illus. Series: A True Book. 2012, Scholastic LB $28 (978-053124851-5); paper $6.95 (978-053128326-4). 48pp. History, people, geography, economy, and challenges are all covered in this overview of the 11 northeastern states that includes bright photographs, maps, and a timeline. (Rev: BL 4/1/12; LMC 10/12) [974]

19028 Rau, Dana Meachen. *The Statue of Liberty* (2–4). Series: Our Nation. 2001, Compass Point LB $19.93 (978-0-7565-0143-3). 24pp. An introduction to the statue with information on its history, symbolism, and location. (Rev: SLJ 1/02)

19029 Ross, D. J. *Uniquely Maine* (4–7). Series: Heinemann State Studies. 2004, Heinemann LB $27.07 (978-1-4034-4655-8). 48pp. In addition to providing the facts necessary for report writers, this volume emphasizes the features that distinguish Maine from its neighbors. (Rev: BL 4/1/04)

19030 Rubbino, Salvatore. *A Walk in New York* (2–5). Illus. by author. 2009, Candlewick $16.99 (978-0-7636-3855-9). 38pp. A boy and his father see the sights of New York City in this appealing volume with interesting bits of information and fold-out pages with city scenes. (Rev: HB 7/09; SLJ 5/09)

19031 Sanders, Mark. *The White House* (3–6). Series: American Government Today. 2000, Raintree LB $22.83 (978-0-7398-1791-9). 48pp. An account that gives a history of the White House, its construction and renovations, plus details on its rooms and offices. (Rev: HBG 10/00; SLJ 8/00)

19032 Schaefer, Ted, and Lola M. Schaefer. *Independence Hall* (1–3). Series: Symbols of Freedom. 2005, Heinemann LB $25.36 (978-1-4034-6664-8). 32pp.

Large color photographs and clear text introduce Philadelphia's Independence Hall and the important role it played in America's history; useful for basic research and reports. (Rev: SLJ 12/05)

19033 Schaefer, Ted, and Lola M. Schaefer. *The Vietnam Veterans Memorial* (1–3). Series: Symbols of Freedom. 2005, Heinemann LB $25.36 (978-1-4034-6659-4). Large color photographs and clear text introduce the Washington, D.C., memorial; useful for basic research and reports. (Rev: SLJ 12/05)

19034 Schnurnberger, Lynn. *Kids Love New York! The A-to-Z Resource Book* (4–8). 1990, Congdon & Weed paper $133.65 (978-0-312-92415-7). A group of suggestions for various activities in New York City.

19035 Schomp, Virginia. *New York* (4–7). Series: Celebrate the States. 2005, Benchmark LB $37.07 (978-0-7614-1738-5). A revised edition of this introduction to the Empire State — including its history, culture, famous sites, and distinguished New Yorkers — with updated illustrations. (Rev: SLJ 5/06) [917.47]

19036 Schuman, Michael. *Delaware* (4–8). Series: Celebrate the States. 2000, Marshall Cavendish LB $37.07 (978-0-7614-0645-7). Beginning with quotations about Delaware and its people, this account covers the basic topics plus information on folklore, food, and festivals. (Rev: BL 6/1–15/00; HBG 10/00) [975.1]

19037 Shea, Pegi Deitz. *Liberty Rising: The Story of the Statue of Liberty* (2–4). Illus. by Wade Zahares. 2005, Holt $17.95 (978-0-8050-7220-4). Bold illustrations highlight the story of the creation of the statue; also includes a timeline and pronunciation guide. (Rev: BL 8/05; SLJ 10/05)

19038 Slade, Suzanne. *The House That George Built* (K–3). Illus. by Rebecca Bond. 2012, Charlesbridge $16.95 (978-1-58089262-9). 32pp. Rhyming verse, accompanying background text, and detailed illustrations chronicle George Washington's work creating the White House; additional facts about the building are appended. **e** (Rev: BLO 8/12; LMC 3–4/13; SLJ 7/12) [975.3]

19039 Smith, Marie, and Roland Smith. *N Is for Our Nation's Capital: A Washington, DC Alphabet* (K–4). Illus. by Barbara Leonard Gibson. 2005, Sleeping Bear $17.95 (978-1-58556-148-3). An inventive alphabet book that introduces historical information about the capital and the people who have worked there. (Rev: SLJ 8/05)

19040 Somervill, Barbara. *Pennsylvania* (3–6). Illus. Series: From Sea to Shining Sea. 2003, Children's Pr. LB $30.50 (978-0-516-22388-9). 80pp. A photo-filled profile covering the state's geography, people, government, lifestyle, and attractions. (Rev: SLJ 8/03)

19041 Staib, Walter, and Jennifer Fox. *A Feast of Freedom: Tasty Tidbits from the City Tavern* (3–6). Illus. by Fernando Juarez. 2010, Running Press $15.95 (978-0-7624-3598-2). 48pp. The City Tavern in Philadelphia has been the venue for many political and business meetings over the years, and this picture book presents 14 vignettes — covering a private meeting between Washington and Lafayette, the writing of the Constitution, and

so forth — plus a recipe and information on the tavern today. (Rev: LMC 11–12/10; SLJ 8/10) [973.3]

19042 Staton, Hilarie. *Ellis Island* (4–6). Series: Symbols of American Freedom. 2009, Chelsea Clubhouse $30 (978-1-60413-519-0). 48pp. Tells the story of Ellis Island's importance as a first stage for many immigrants arriving in the United States, describes how its role has changed over the years, and explains its symbolism both for young researchers and students planning visits of their own. Also in this series: *Independence Hall* (2009). (Rev: SLJ 5/10) [304.8]

19043 Staton, Hilarie. *The Statue of Liberty* (3–6). Series: Symbols of American Freedom. 2009, Chelsea Clubhouse $30 (978-1-60413-516-9). 48pp. With clear, simple language, this book looks at the history and contemporary importance of the statue and includes photographs and excerpts from speeches as well as tips on making a successful visit. (Rev: LMC 3–4/10; SLJ 3/1/10) [974.7]

19044 Stevenson, Harvey. *Looking at Liberty* (3–5). Illus. by author. 2003, HarperCollins LB $17.89 (978-0-06-000101-8). 40pp. This artful blend of poetry, eye-catching artwork, and concise facts recounts the story behind the construction of the Statue of Liberty — a gift from the people of France to the people of the United States. (Rev: BL 10/1/03; HBG 10/03; SLJ 6/03)

19045 Tagliaferro, Linda. *Destination New York* (4–8). Series: Port Cities of North America. 1998, Lerner LB $23.93 (978-0-8225-2793-0). Written with a focus on New York's economic life and its handling of goods moving in and out of the port, this book also gives information on the city's history, geography, and daily life. (Rev: HBG 3/99; SLJ 1/99) [974.7]

19046 Talbott, Hudson. *River of Dreams: The Story of the Hudson River* (4–7). Illus. by author. 2009, Putnam $17.99 (978-0-399-24521-3). 40pp. An engaging history of the river, covering its role in early settlements, shipping and the Erie Canal, the pollution that afflicted the ecosystem and efforts to clean it up, and the river's influence on art. ALA Notable Children's Book. (Rev: BL 12/15/08; HB 3/09; SLJ 3/09) [974.7]

19047 Thomas, Pamela. *Brooklyn Pops Up* (3–10). Illus. 2000, Simon & Schuster $19.95 (978-0-689-84019-7). This pop-up book takes you on a tour of this borough of New York City, including visits to Coney Island and the Brooklyn Museum. (Rev: BL 12/1/00; HBG 3/01)

19048 Todras, Ellen H. *The Gettysburg Battlefield* (3–6). Series: Symbols of American Freedom. 2009, Chelsea Clubhouse $30 (978-1-60413-514-5). 48pp. With photographs and excerpts from speeches, this book explains the importance of this battlefield and provides tips for those planning a visit. (Rev: LMC 3–4/10; SLJ 3/1/10)

19049 Tougas, Joe. *New York* (3–8). Series: This Land Called America. 2010, Creative Education $28.50 (978-1-58341-785-0). 32pp. History, culture, and geography are all covered in this attractive slim volume that provides the vital facts report writers need. (Rev: LMC 8–9/10) [974.7]

19050 Walsh, Frank. *New York City* (3–6). Series: Great Cities of the World. 2003, World Almanac LB $31.00 (978-0-8368-5025-3). 48pp. An overview of one of the world's most famous cities, with detail on its history, its economy, and what it's like to live there. (Rev: SLJ 3/04)

19051 Warrick, Karen Clemens. *Independence National Historical Park* (5–8). Series: Virtual Field Trips. 2005, Enslow LB $25.26 (978-0-7660-5224-6). A visit to Independence Park, using both print and related Web sites, that covers its historical importance, including Independence Hall and the Liberty Bell. (Rev: SLJ 5/05)

19052 Wills, Charles A. *A Historical Album of Pennsylvania* (4–8). Series: Historical Albums. 1996, Millbrook LB $24.40 (978-1-56294-595-4). Beginning with its Native American origins and settlement by Europeans and the Quakers, this book traces the history of Pennsylvania from the First Continental Congress and the ratification of the United States Constitution, through the Battle of Gettysburg and President Lincoln's famous Gettysburg Address, and up to today. (Rev: BL 7/96; SLJ 7/96) [974.8]

19053 Yezerski, Thomas F. *Meadowlands: A Wetlands Survival Story* (1–3). Illus. by author. 2011, Farrar $17.99 (978-0-374-34913-4). 40pp. With lovely ink-and-watercolor illustrations, Yezerski traces the history of the Meadowlands, a wetlands area within sight of New York City that once was home to the Lenni Lenape and was gradually industrialized until conservation initiatives were finally implemented. (Rev: BL 3/1/11; LMC 5–6/11; SLJ 3/1/11) [577.6]

19054 Zschock, Martha, and Heather Zschock. *Journey Around New York from A to Z* (1–3). Illus. 2002, Commonwealth $17.95 (978-1-889833-32-3). 32pp. An alphabetical journey around New York that combines information on tourist attractions, history, neighborhoods, and public celebrations. (Rev: BL 6/1–15/02; SLJ 7/02)

PACIFIC STATES

19055 Aillaud, Cindy Lou. *Recess at 20 Below* (K–3). Illus. 2005, Alaska Northwest $15.95 (978-0-88240-604-6); paper $8.95 (978-0-88240-609-1). Though the temperature outside can be nearly 20 degrees below zero (Fahrenheit), Alaskan schoolchildren still find a way to play outdoors. (Rev: BL 12/15/05; HB 1/06; HBG 4/06; SLJ 3/06)

19056 Altman, Linda J. *California* (5–8). Series: Celebrate the States. 2005, Benchmark LB $37.07 (978-0-7614-1737-8). This revised edition updates facts and adds information on the government and economy plus new, full-color photographs. (Rev: SLJ 3/06) [979.4]

19057 Ansary, Mir Tamim. *People of California* (4–7). Series: Heinemann State Studies. 2003, Heinemann LB $27.07 (978-1-4034-0342-1). Ansary looks at groups of people who have settled in California and offers brief biographies of individuals who have contributed to all fields of endeavor, with many color photographs. (Rev: BL 10/15/03; HBG 4/04; SLJ 11/03) [305.8]

19058 Boekhoff, P. M., and Stuart A. Kallen. *California* (4–7). Illus. Series: Seeds of a Nation. 2002, Gale LB $23.70 (978-0-7377-0946-9). 48pp. The history of California before statehood is presented with material on Native Americans, missionaries, settlers, and prospectors. (Rev: BL 4/1/02)

19059 Britton, Tamara. *Pearl Harbor* (3–5). Series: Symbols, Landmarks, and Monuments. 2003, ABDO LB $22.78 (978-1-57765-851-1). From the attack in 1941 to the USS Arizona Memorial, this volume provides information that will be useful to report writers. (Rev: HBG 10/03; SLJ 10/03)

19060 Corral, Kimberly. *A Child's Glacier Bay* (4–8). 1998, Graphic Arts Center $15.95 (978-0-88240-503-2). A photoessay chronicling a three-week kayak trip in Alaska's Glacier Bay, told from the perspective of a 13-year-old girl. (Rev: BL 7/98; HBG 10/98; SLJ 8/98) [978.652]

19061 Cosson, M. J. *Welcome to Redwood National and State Parks* (3–5). Series: Visitor Guides. 2006, The Child's World LB $27.07 (978-1-59296-701-8). 32pp. An attractively presented tour of three California parks, focusing on their geography, history, flora, fauna, and weather. (Rev: SLJ 2/07)

19062 Covert, Kim. *Washington* (3–5). Illus. Series: Land of Liberty. 2003, Capstone LB $25.26 (978-0-7368-2203-9). 64pp. A profile of the state of Washington, covering everything from climate and topography to people and economy, with fast facts, a recipe, and other useful material at the end. (Rev: SLJ 3/04)

19063 Crewe, Sabrina. *Los Angeles* (4–6). Series: Great Cities of the World. 2004, World Almanac LB $31.00 (978-0-8368-5029-1). Report writers will find useful information on Los Angeles's history, culture, lifestyle, and current problems such as traffic congestion, smog, and water shortages. (Rev: SLJ 7/04)

19064 Dell, Pamela. *Welcome to Mount Rainier National Park* (3–5). Series: Visitor Guides. 2006, The Child's World LB $27.07 (978-1-59296-700-1). An attractively presented tour of the Washington state park, focusing on its geography, history, flora, fauna, and weather. (Rev: SLJ 2/07)

19065 Doak, Robin. *California 1542–1850* (5–8). Series: Voices from Colonial America. 2006, National Geographic $21.95 (978-0-7922-6391-3). 109pp. This well-illustrated title traces the history of California from its 1542 "discovery" by Juan Rodriguez Cabrillo to the frenzied Gold Rush years of the mid-19th century; maps and a timeline make this useful for research. (Rev: SLJ 1/07)

19066 Fandel, Jennifer. *Golden Gate Bridge* (3–6). Series: Modern Wonders of the World. 2006, Creative Education LB $27.10 (978-1-58341-437-8). 32pp. This is an attractive overview of the history of the famous bridge, the engineering challenges involved in its construction, and its importance today as a span and a symbol. (Rev: SLJ 12/06)

19067 Feeney, Stephanie. *Sun and Rain: Exploring Seasons in Hawaii* (K–3). Illus. 2007, Univ. of Hawaii $13.95 (978-0-8248-3088-5). 48pp. Hawaii's dry and wet seasons are explored with information about the weather, plants, and animals. (Rev: BL 12/15/07)

19068 Feinstein, Stephen. *Hawaii Volcanoes National Park* (4–8). Illus. Series: America's National Parks: Adventure, Explore, Discover. 2009, Enslow LB $33.27 (978-1-59845-094-1). 128pp. Links to Web sites add to the information provided here on the Hawaiian park and its geology and ecology, as well as its history and myths associated with it. Lexile 870 (Rev: SLJ 9/09)

19069 Frisch, Nate. *Death Valley National Park* (5–8). Illus. Series: Preserving America. 2013, Creative Education LB $24.95 (978-160818194-0). 48pp. Frisch introduces readers to Death Valley through magnificent photographs and readable text, delving into the history and characteristics of the park and providing descriptions of the animals and plants that live there. (Rev: BL 10/1/13; LMC 8–9/14) [979.4]

19070 Gaines, Ann Graham. *Hawaii* (3–6). Illus. Series: It's My State! 2007, Marshall Cavendish LB $20.95 (978-0-7614-1926-6). 32pp. Neatly designed and filled with color photographs, this overview of Hawaii provides information about the state's history, plants, animals, geography, economy, and so forth. (Rev: BL 5/15/07; SLJ 8/07)

19071 Gendell, Megan. *The Spanish Missions of California* (3–7). Series: A True Book. 2010, Children's Press LB $26 (978-0-531-20577-8). 48pp. An interesting survey of the history and structure of the Spanish mission buildings and their importance to society 500 years ago. (Rev: LMC 8–9/10) [979.4]

19072 Gill, Shelley. *Hawaii* (5–8). Illus. by Scott Goto. 2006, Charlesbridge paper $6.95 (978-0-88106-297-7). A boy and his father tour the state of Hawaii by kayak; as they pass each island the father tells his son a little about its history, geography, people, culture, and economy. (Rev: SLJ 8/06) [996.9]

19073 Gish, Melissa. *Washington* (3–8). Series: This Land Called America. 2010, Creative Education $28.50 (978-1-58341-800-0). 32pp. History, culture, and geography are all covered in this attractive slim volume that provides the vital facts report writers need. (Rev: LMC 8–9/10) [979.7]

19074 Goh, Geok Yian. *Uniquely Hawaii* (4–7). Illus. Series: Heinemann State Studies. 2004, Heinemann LB $27.07 (978-1-4034-4645-9). 48pp. In addition to providing the facts necessary for report writers, this volume emphasizes the features that make Hawaii unique. (Rev: BL 10/15/03)

19075 Goldberg, Jake. *Hawaii* (5–8). Series: Celebrate the States. 1998, Benchmark LB $37.07 (978-0-7614-0203-9). Using fine illustrations, fact boxes, graphs, and maps, this attractive book gives an excellent introduction to Hawaii, with the added bonus of a recipe and two songs. (Rev: HBG 10/98; SLJ 1/99) [996.9]

19076 Hall, M. C. *Hawaii Volcanoes National Park* (K–4). Series: Symbols of Freedom: National Parks. 2005, Heinemann LB $25.36 (978-1-4034-6700-3). 32pp. Large color photographs and clear text introduce the history, geography, flora, and fauna of this park; useful for basic research and reports. (Rev: SLJ 12/05)

19077 Hall, M. C. *Welcome to Denali National Park* (3–5). Series: Visitor Guides. 2006, The Child's World LB $27.07 (978-1-59296-695-0). 32pp. An attractively presented tour of the Alaskan park, focusing on its geography, history, flora, fauna, and weather. (Rev: SLJ 2/07)

19078 Harder, Dan, and Lawrence Migdale. *A Child's California* (2–4). Illus. 2000, Graphic Arts $15.95 (978-1-55868-520-8). 48pp. This introduction to California covers topics of particular interest to children and emphasizes the state's diversity and contrasts. (Rev: BL 2/1/01; SLJ 1/01)

19079 Heinrichs, Ann. *California* (2–4). Illus. Series: This Land Is Your Land. 2002, Compass Point LB $25.26 (978-0-7565-0308-6). 48pp. Simple text with age-appropriate language and good illustrations introduce the history, geography, culture, famous people, and attractions of California. (Rev: SLJ 1/03)

19080 Heinrichs, Ann. *The California Missions* (5–8). Series: We the People. 2002, Compass Point LB $26.60 (978-0-7565-0208-9). 48pp. An accessible, well-illustrated account of the creation of Spanish missions in California and the impact on the native peoples of the region. (Rev: SLJ 7/02)

19081 Heinrichs, Ann. *Oregon* (3–5). Illus. by Matt Kania. Series: Welcome to the U.S.A. 2005, The Child's World LB $27.07 (978-1-59296-479-6). 40pp. Using an attractive scrapbook format featuring a family on vacation, this volume introduces the state's geography, history, people, major attractions, and state symbols. (Rev: SLJ 2/06)

19082 Henry, Judy. *Uniquely Alaska* (4–7). Series: Heinemann State Studies. 2005, Heinemann LB $31.36 (978-1-4034-4642-8). In addition to providing the facts necessary for report writers, this volume emphasizes the features that make Alaska unique. (Rev: BL 10/15/03)

19083 Isaacs, Sally Senzell. *Life in San Francisco's Chinatown* (2–4). Illus. Series: Picture the Past. 2002, Heinemann LB $22.79 (978-1-58810-692-6). 32pp. A look at life in San Francisco for Chinese immigrants in the years from the Gold Rush through the early 20th century. (Rev: HBG 3/03; SLJ 3/03)

19084 Kennedy, Teresa. *California* (4–6). Series: From Sea to Shining Sea. 2001, Children's Book Pr. LB $30.50 (978-0-516-22309-4). This attractive, oversize volume includes material on the land, history, people, and lifestyle of California. (Rev: BL 4/15/02)

19085 Knapp, Ron. *Oregon* (4–7). Illus. Series: MyReportLinks.com. 2002, Enslow LB $25.26 (978-0-7660-5021-1). An introduction to the government, geography, and history of the state, with helpful Web sites. (Rev: BL 2/1/03; HBG 3/03; VOYA 4/03)

19086 Labella, Susan. *Washington* (K–2). Series: Rookie Read-About Geography. 2006, Scholastic LB $20.50 (978-0-516-24993-3); paper $5.95 (978-0-516-26455-4). A slim, square volume on Washington state that will be a good start for young researchers. (Rev: BL 7/06)

19087 Levinson, Nancy S. *Death Valley: A Day in the Desert* (2–3). Illus. by Diane D. Hearn. 2001, Holiday House $14.95 (978-0-8234-1566-3). 32pp. In this easily read book, Death Valley and its plants and animals are introduced with excellent drawings. (Rev: BL 4/15/01; HBG 10/01; SLJ 4/01)

19088 Mannis, Celeste Davidson. *Snapshots: The Wonders of Monterey Bay* (K–4). Photos by author. 2006, Viking $16.99 (978-0-670-06062-7). All about the varied plants and animals of California's spectacular Monterey Bay, with plenty of eye-catching photographs and clearly presented information. (Rev: SLJ 6/06*)

19089 Marsico, Katie. *Puget Sound* (3–6). Illus. Series: It's Cool to Learn about America's Waterways. 2013, Cherry Lake LB $28.50 (978-162431015-7); paper $14.21 (9781624310393). 32pp. Presents the geography, wildlife, history, and environmental challenges facing this waterway, with activities. (Rev: BL 5/1/13; LMC 11–12/13; SLJ 4/13) [551.46]

19090 Miller, Debbie S. *Big Alaska: Journey Across America's Most Amazing State* (2–4). Illus. by Jon Van Zyle. 2006, Walker $17.95 (978-0-8027-8069-0). 40pp. Sixteen of Alaska's most breathtaking natural wonders are shown in this large-format, photo-filled book that uses a bald eagle's flight as a unifying element; facts, state symbols, and Internet sites are appended. (Rev: BL 3/1/06; SLJ 5/06)

19091 Miller, Debbie S. *River of Life* (K–3). Illus. by Jon Van Zyle. 2000, Clarion $16.00 (978-0-395-96790-4). Realistic oil paintings are used to illustrate this book that describes a year in the life of an Alaskan river and the wildlife surrounding it. (Rev: BL 3/15/00; HBG 10/00; SLJ 7/00)

19092 Murphy, Claire Rudolf. *Children of Alcatraz: Growing Up on the Rock* (4–7). Illus. 2006, Walker $17.95 (978-0-8027-9577-9). 64pp. This is the story of the children who have grown up on Alcatraz Island over time — early Native American children, children of lighthouse keepers, children of prison authorities, and so forth — with archival photographs and a timeline. (Rev: BL 12/15/06; SLJ 11/06)

19093 Neri, P. J. *Hawaii* (3–6). Illus. Series: From Sea to Shining Sea, Second Series. 2003, Children's Pr. LB $30.50 (978-0-516-22383-4). A revised, photo-filled introduction to the Aloha State's geography, history, people, culture, and economy. (Rev: SLJ 12/03)

19094 Orr, Tamra. *California* (5–8). Illus. Series: America the Beautiful: Third Series. 2007, Children's Press LB $38.00 (978-0-531-18557-5). This new edition of the classic series entry about the state features a new design and layout, definitions of difficult words in the margins, more history and mini biographies, and project ideas in writing, art, and science. (Rev: BL 2/1/08) [979.4]

19095 Otfinoski, Steve. *Washington* (4–7). Series: It's My State! 2003, Marshall Cavendish LB $27.07 (978-0-7614-1522-0). 80pp. The state of Washington, its geography, history, people, and economic development are some of the topics covered in this introduction to this Pacific state. (Rev: BL 9/15/03; HBG 4/04)

19096 Quasha, Jennifer. *How to Draw California's Sights and Symbols* (3–6). Illus. Series: Kid's Guide to Drawing America. 2002, Rosen LB $25.25 (978-0-8239-6059-0). 32pp. An eclectic mix of California history, geography, demographics, and state sights and symbols. (Rev: BL 2/15/02; SLJ 7/02)

19097 Rice, Oliver D. *Lone Woman of Ghalas-Hat* (5–7). Illus. by Charles Zafuto. 1993, California Weekly LB $13.00 (978-0-936778-52-5); paper $6.00 (978-0-936778-51-8). The true story of the Indian woman who lived alone on a California island for 18 years. This was the basis of *Island of the Blue Dolphins*. A reissue. [979.7]

19098 Ryan, Pam Muñoz. *Our California* (PS–2). Illus. by Rafael Lopez. 2008, Charlesbridge $17.95 (978-1-58089-116-5); paper $7.95 (978-1-58089-117-2). 48pp. A rhyming text presents information about various locations in California, including Capistrano, San Francisco, Los Angeles, and Palm Springs. (Rev: BL 12/15/07; SLJ 6/08)

19099 Seibold, J. Otto, and Vivian Walsh. *Going to the Getty: A Book About the Getty Center in Los Angeles* (4–7). 1997, Getty Museum $17.50 (978-0-89236-493-0). This introduction to the Getty Museum in Los Angeles is a patchwork of impressions, photographs, drawings, and reproductions of artworks. (Rev: BL 2/15/98; HBG 10/98) [708]

19100 Stefoff, Rebecca. *Alaska* (4–6). Illus. Series: Celebrate the States. 2006, Benchmark LB $39.93 (978-0-7614-2153-5). 144pp. An updated edition that includes attractive photographs, maps, and graphs and covers Alaska's history, geography, government, economy, and natural and man-made landmarks; fun facts, famous people, and places to visit, plus a list of Web sites round out this useful volume. (Rev: SLJ 12/06)

19101 Stepanchuk, Carol. *Exploring Chinatown* (4–8). Illus. by Leland Wong. 2002, Pacific View LB $22.95 (978-1-881896-25-8). This "walk" through San Francisco's Chinatown explores the Chinese culture and customs, and offers historical facts as well as a few hands-on projects. (Rev: BL 8/02; SLJ 9/02) [305.8951073]

19102 Temple, Teri, and Bob Temple. *Welcome to Hawaii Volcanoes National Park* (3–5). Series: Visitor Guides. 2006, The Child's World LB $27.07 (978-1-59296-699-8). 32pp. An attractively presented tour of the Hawaiian state park, with information on its geography, history, flora, fauna, and weather plus discussion of the legend of Pele, the goddess of fire. (Rev: SLJ 2/07)

19103 Webster, Christine. *Washington* (3–6). Illus. Series: From Sea to Shining Sea. 2003, Children's Pr. LB $30.50 (978-0-516-22386-5). 80pp. This photo-filled overview provides all the information on the Pacific Northwest state that report writers need. (Rev: SLJ 9/03)

19104 Wills, Charles A. *A Historical Album of California* (4–8). Series: Historical Albums. 1994, Millbrook LB $24.40 (978-1-56294-479-7). A slim volume that covers the basic history of California, with material on major events and important personalities. (Rev: SLJ 3/95) [979.4]

19105 Young, Robert. *A Personal Tour of La Purisima* (4–7). Series: How It Was. 1999, Lerner LB $30.35 (978-0-8225-3576-8). A you-are-there visit to La Purisima — one of the 21 missions built by the Spanish in California — in which the reader experiences life in the mission as it was in 1820. (Rev: BL 6/1–15/99; HBG 10/99) [979.4]

SOUTH

19106 Alex, Nan. *North Carolina* (4–6). Series: From Sea to Shining Sea. 2001, Children's Book Pr. LB $30.50 (978-0-516-22487-9). An attractive, well-organized volume that introduces the land and people of North Carolina. Also use *Florida, Georgia, Kentucky,* and *Tennessee* (all 2001). (Rev: BL 4/15/02)

19107 Altman, Linda J. *Arkansas* (4–8). Series: Celebrate the States. 2000, Benchmark LB $37.07 (978-0-7614-0672-3). An broad introduction to the culture, land, government, history, and unique characteristics of Arkansas, with emphasis on its inhabitants. (Rev: BL 1/1–15/00; HBG 10/00) [976.7]

19108 Backer, Miles. *Travels with Charlie: Down South* (1–3). Illus. by Chuck Nitzberg. Series: Travels with Charlie. 2007, Blue Apple $15.95 (978-1-59354-594-9). Readers will learn about the southern United States as they search for a dog named Charlie. Trivia, fun facts, and maps packed with sites of interest make this a fun way to learn about geography. (Rev: SLJ 8/07)

19109 Bailey, Diane. *Tennessee: Past and Present* (3–6). Series: The United States: Past and Present. 2010, Rosen LB $26.50 (978-1-4358-3522-1). 48pp. Includes chapters on the geography, history, government, economy, and people of Tennessee, with a timeline and "Tennessee at a Glance." (Rev: SLJ 6/10) [976.8]

19110 Barrett, Tracy. *Virginia* (4–7). Series: Celebrate the States. 2005, Benchmark LB $37.07 (978-0-7614-1734-7). A revised edition of this introduction to the state — including its history, culture, famous sites, and important Virginians — with updated illustrations. (Rev: SLJ 5/06) [975.5]

19111 Bjorklund, Ruth. *Louisiana* (3–5). Illus. Series: It's My State. 2006, Benchmark LB $27.07 (978-0-7614-1863-4). Report writers will find all the facts they need on the history, geography, government, and economy of Louisiana — including information on the effects of Hurricane Katrina — plus a state-themed craft. (Rev: SLJ 6/06)

19112 Bredeson, Carmen, and Mary Dodson Wade. *Texas* (5–8). Series: Celebrate the States. 2005, Benchmark LB $37.07 (978-0-7614-1736-1). This revised edition

updates facts and adds information on the government and economy plus new, full-color photographs. (Rev: SLJ 3/06) [976.4]

19113 Cocke, William. *A Historical Album of Virginia* (4–8). Series: Historical Albums. 1995, Millbrook paper $6.95 (978-1-56294-856-6). A broad overview of Virginia's history, using many period prints and paintings, with equal space given to past and current events, and including general information on the state. (Rev: SLJ 1/96) [975.5]

19114 Coleman, Wim, and Pat Perrin. *Colonial Williamsburg* (5–8). Series: Virtual Field Trips. 2005, Enslow LB $25.26 (978-0-7660-5220-8). A visit to Williamsburg, using both print and related Web sites, that covers its historical importance and its portrayal of colonial life. (Rev: SLJ 5/05)

19115 Cribben, Patrick. *Uniquely West Virginia* (4–7). Series: Heinemann State Studies. 2005, Heinemann LB $31.36 (978-1-4034-4665-7). In addition to providing the facts necessary for report writers, this volume emphasizes the features that distinguish West Virginia from its neighbors. (Rev: BL 10/15/03)

19116 Doherty, Craig A., and Katherine M. Doherty. *North Carolina* (5–9). Series: The Thirteen Colonies. 2005, Facts on File LB $35.00 (978-0-8160-5412-1). Traces the history of North Carolina from the early settlers through 1787, with discussion of the Native American culture and with excerpts from primary documents, maps, and profiles of key individuals. (Rev: SLJ 8/05) [973]

19117 Gaines, Ann Graham. *Kentucky* (4–7). Series: It's My State! 2003, Marshall Cavendish LB $27.07 (978-0-7614-1525-1). Full-color photographs, trivia, and recipes and crafts are included along with the standard information required for reports. (Rev: BL 9/15/03; HBG 4/04; SLJ 9/03)

19118 Hamilton, John. *Everglades National Park* (4–6). Series: National Parks. 2005, ABDO LB $24.21 (978-1-59197-424-6). 32pp. Full-color photographs illustrate the information on the Everglades's history, ecosystem, geology, and wildlife, plus discussion of development of this area. Also use *Glacier National Park, Grand Canyon National Park,* and *Great Smoky Mountains National Park* (2005). (Rev: SLJ 6/05)

19119 Haywood, Karen Diane. *Georgia* (3–5). Illus. Series: It's My State! 2006, Benchmark LB $27.07 (978-0-7614-1862-7). 79pp. Report writers will find all the facts they need in this book that comes complete with a state-themed craft. (Rev: SLJ 6/06)

19120 Heinrichs, Ann. *Kentucky* (2–5). Illus. Series: This Land Is Your Land. 2003, Compass Point LB $25.26 (978-0-7565-0322-2). 48pp. Introduces readers to the geography, history, government, economy, and famous citizens of the Bluegrass State. (Rev: SLJ 8/03)

19121 Heinrichs, Ann. *Maryland* (2–5). Illus. Series: This Land Is Your Land. 2003, Compass Point LB $25.26 (978-0-7565-0348-2). 48pp. An attractive introduction to Maryland with plenty of photographs and accessible information for report writers. (Rev: SLJ 8/03)

19122 Heinrichs, Ann. *Tennessee* (2–5). Illus. Series: This Land Is Your Land. 2003, Compass Point LB $25.26 (978-0-7565-0319-2). 48pp. This brightly illustrated profile explores Tennessee's history, people, geography, government, economy, and attractions. (Rev: SLJ 7/03)

19123 Heinrichs, Ann. *Virginia* (2–4). Illus. Series: This Land Is Your Land. 2002, Compass Point LB $25.26 (978-0-7565-0310-9). 48pp. Simple text and good illustrations introduce the history, geography, culture, famous people, and attractions of Virginia. (Rev: SLJ 1/03)

19124 Heinrichs, Ann. *West Virginia* (3–5). Illus. by Matt Kania. 2005, The Child's World LB $27.07 (978-1-59296-490-1). Using an attractive scrapbook format featuring a family on vacation, this volume introduces the state's geography, history, people, major attractions, and state symbols. (Rev: SLJ 2/06)

19125 Herda, D. J. *Environmental America: The South Central States* (4–7). Series: American Scene. 1991, Millbrook LB $22.40 (978-1-878841-09-4). This account discusses the general state of the environment and presents information on animal species, pollution, waste, and urban sprawl for 10 states, including Georgia, Kansas, Missouri, and Texas. (Rev: BL 8/91; SLJ 7/91) [639.9]

19126 Hess, Debra. *Florida* (4–7). Series: It's My State! 2003, Marshall Cavendish LB $27.07 (978-0-7614-1527-5). 80pp. Products, resources, plants and animals, and important background material are some of the topics covered in this general introduction to Florida. (Rev: BL 9/15/03; HBG 4/04; SLJ 9/03)

19127 Higgins, Nadia. *Welcome to Everglades National Park* (3–5). 2006, The Child's World LB $27.07 (978-1-59296-702-5). 32pp. An attractively presented tour of the South Florida park, focusing on its geography, history, flora, fauna, and weather. (Rev: SLJ 2/07)

19128 Hoffman, Nancy. *South Carolina* (4–8). Series: Celebrate the States. 2000, Marshall Cavendish LB $37.07 (978-0-7614-1065-2). An interesting introduction to South Carolina, with material on its land and waterways, history, government, economy, landmarks, and success stories. (Rev: BL 12/15/00; HBG 3/01) [975.7]

19129 Kostyal, K. M. *1776: A New Look at Revolutionary Williamsburg* (4–8). 2009, National Geographic $27.90 (978-1-4263-0517-7). 48pp. The history of Williamsburg, Virginia, is told from the perspectives of a variety of period characters, who focus on everything from food and dress to slavery. (Rev: BL 10/15/09; LMC 11–12/09; SLJ 11/1/09) [973.3]

19130 La Doux, Rita C. *Louisiana. Rev. ed.* (3–5). Illus. Series: Hello U.S.A. 2001, Lerner LB $25.26 (978-0-8225-4065-6); paper $6.95 (978-0-8225-4145-5). 84pp. This revision of the 1993 edition features a more spacious layout and some expanded content. (Rev: SLJ 2/02)

19131 Leese, Jennifer. *Uniquely Maryland* (4–7). Series: State Studies. 2004, Heinemann LB $27.07 (978-1-4034-4493-6). 48pp. History, industry, tourism, and culture are among the highlights of this survey of Maryland and its characteristics. (Rev: BL 4/1/04)

19132 Lynch, Wayne. *The Everglades* (4–7). Illus. Series: Our Wild World. 2007, NorthWord $16.95 (978-1-55971-970-4); paper $8.95 (978-1-55971-971-1). With eye-catching color photographs and conversational narrative, Lynch introduces the flora and fauna of the Everglades and highlights the threats to this ecosystem. (Rev: BL 9/1/07; SLJ 11/07)

19133 MacAulay, Ellen. *Arkansas* (3–5). Illus. 2002, Children's Book Pr. LB $30.50 (978-0-516-22296-7). 80pp. This revision of an earlier title adds information and features that will enhance its appeal to report writers. (Rev: SLJ 1/03)

19134 McAuliffe, Emily. *Florida Facts and Symbols. Rev. ed.* (3–5). Illus. Series: The States and Their Symbols. 2003, Capstone LB $21.26 (978-0-7368-2239-8). 24pp. A brief, illustrated overview of facts about Florida such as the state's nickname, motto, flag, and other symbols. (Rev: SLJ 1/04)

19135 McAuliffe, Emily. *Georgia Facts and Symbols. Rev. ed.* (3–5). Illus. Series: The States and Their Symbols. 2003, Capstone LB $21.26 (978-0-7368-2240-4). A brief overview that will serve as a source of limited facts about the state. (Rev: SLJ 1/04)

19136 McClellan, Adam, and Martin Wilson. *Uniquely North Carolina* (4–7). Series: Heinemann State Studies. 2004, Heinemann LB $27.07 (978-1-4034-4653-4). 48pp. In addition to providing the facts necessary for report writers, this volume emphasizes the features that distinguish North Carolina from its neighbors. (Rev: BL 4/1/04)

19137 Marsico, Katie. *The Everglades* (3–6). Illus. Series: It's Cool to Learn about America's Waterways. 2013, Cherry Lake LB $28.50 (978-162431017-1); paper $14.21 (9781624310416). 32pp. Presents the geography, wildlife, history, and environmental challenges facing this waterway, with activities. (Rev: BL 5/1/13; LMC 11–12/13) [975.9]

19138 Martin, Michael A. *Alabama: The Heart of Dixie* (4–7). Series: World Almanac Library of the States. 2002, World Almanac LB $31.00 (978-0-8368-5127-4). Full-color photographs and graphic elements enhance this informative introduction to the state. Also use *Arizona: The Grand Canyon State* (2002). (Rev: SLJ 2/03) [976.1]

19139 Odinoski, Steve. *Georgia* (4–8). Series: Celebrate the States. 2000, Marshall Cavendish LB $37.07 (978-0-7614-1062-1). An informative, attractive introduction to Georgia with material on its land, history, people, social issues, and hidden treasures. (Rev: BL 12/15/00; HBG 3/01; SLJ 2/01) [975.8]

19140 Otfinoski, Steve. *Maryland* (3–6). Illus. Series: It's My State! 2002, Benchmark LB $27.07 (978-0-7614-1421-6). 80pp. The usual state information — geography, history, government, people, and economy — is presented in an appealing layout. (Rev: HBG 10/03; SLJ 2/03)

19141 Owens, Lisa. *Uniquely Missouri* (4–7). Series: Heinemann State Studies. 2004, Heinemann LB $27.07 (978-1-4034-4495-0). 48pp. In addition to providing the facts necessary for report writers, this volume emphasizes the features that distinguish Missouri from its neighbors. (Rev: BL 4/1/04)

19142 Pobst, Sandy. *Virginia, 1607–1776* (5–8). Series: Voices from Colonial America. 2005, National Geographic LB $32.90 (978-0-7922-6771-3). A thorough political and social history of early Virginia, with excellent illustrations. (Rev: BL 10/15/05; SLJ 11/05) [975.5]

19143 Rauth, Leslie. *Maryland* (5–9). Series: Celebrate the States. 1999, Benchmark LB $37.07 (978-0-7614-0671-6). This book explores Maryland with material on topics including land and waterways, government, economy, festivals, and people. (Rev: BL 1/1–15/00; HBG 10/00; SLJ 5/00) [975.2]

19144 Raven, Margot Theis. *Let Them Play* (2–5). Illus. by Chris Ellison. 2005, Sleeping Bear $16.95 (978-1-58536-260-8). In this fact-based tale from the mid-1950s, an African American Little League team from Charleston, South Carolina, is snubbed by the state's white teams and by officials of the Little League World Series. (Rev: SLJ 11/05)

19145 Santella, Andrew. *Mount Vernon* (4–6). Series: We the People. 2004, Compass Point LB $26.60 (978-0-7565-0682-7). 48pp. A look at George Washington's home, with discussion of its role as a plantation and of the slaves who worked there. (Rev: SLJ 2/05)

19146 Schaefer, Ted, and Lola M. Schaefer. *Arlington National Cemetery* (1–3). Series: Symbols of Freedom. 2005, Heinemann LB $25.36 (978-1-4034-6665-5). 32pp. The burial site for many Americans who served their country is introduced in simple text and archival and contemporary photographs; includes a "Fact File" and a timeline. (Rev: SLJ 12/05)

19147 Schaefer, Ted, and Lola M. Schaefer. *The Pentagon* (1–3). Series: Symbols of Freedom. 2005, Heinemann LB $25.36 (978-1-4034-6663-1). Large color photographs and clear text introduce the Pentagon's role as the headquarters of the U.S. Defense Department, also covering the terrorist attack of 2001; useful for basic research and reports. (Rev: SLJ 12/05)

19148 Sherrow, Victoria. *Uniquely South Carolina* (4–7). Series: Heinemann State Studies. 2005, Heinemann LB $31.36 (978-1-4034-4661-9). In addition to providing the facts necessary for report writers, this volume emphasizes the features that distinguish South Carolina from its neighbors. (Rev: BL 10/15/03)

19149 Shirley, David. *Alabama* (4–8). Series: Celebrate the States. 2000, Marshall Cavendish LB $37.07 (978-0-7614-0648-8). 141pp. An introduction to Alabama that covers its land and waterways; its history, government, and economy; and its culture and success stories. (Rev: BL 6/1–15/00; HBG 10/00)

19150 Shirley, David. *North Carolina* (4–8). Series: Celebrate the States. 2001, Benchmark LB $37.07 (978-0-7614-1072-0). A fine introduction to the land, history, economy, and people of North Carolina. (Rev: BL 9/15/01; HBG 10/01) [975.6]

19151 Smith, Karla. *Virginia* (4–6). Series: Heinemann State Studies. 2003, Heinemann LB $27.07 (978-1-4034-0361-2). 48pp. A useful overview of Virginia's geography, history, people, culture, and attractions. (Rev: HBG 4/04; SLJ 12/03)

19152 Smith, Karla. *Virginia History* (4–6). 2003, Heinemann LB $27.07 (978-1-4034-0362-9). 48pp. A useful overview of the history of Virginia. (Rev: HBG 4/04; SLJ 12/03)

19153 Stout, Mary. *Atlanta* (4–7). Series: Great Cities of the World. 2005, World Almanac LB $31.00 (978-0-8368-5042-0). Report writers will find useful information on Atlanta's history, culture, lifestyle, and current problems. (Rev: BL 4/15/04)

19154 Suben, Eric. *The Spanish Missions of Florida* (3–7). Series: A True Book. 2010, Children's Press LB $26 (978-0-531-20578-9). 48pp. A look at Spanish mission buildings in Florida, with beautiful color photographs and discussion of their history and the impact of the missions on the Native Americans. Lexile 910L (Rev: LMC 8–9/10) [975.9]

19155 Valzania, Kimberly. *Tennessee* (K–2). Series: Rookie Read-About Geography. 2003, Children's Pr. LB $20.50 (978-0-516-22699-6); paper $5.95 (978-0-516-27843-8). 31pp. For beginning readers, this is a useful introduction to Tennessee, covering the Volunteer State's geography, people, industry, agriculture, and recreation. (Rev: SLJ 10/03)

19156 Weatherford, Carole Boston. *Sink or Swim: African-American Lifesavers of the Outer Banks* (4–8). 1999, Coastal Carolina $15.95 (978-1-928556-01-5); paper $12.95 (978-1-928556-03-9). A history of the African Americans who participated in lifesaving efforts on the Outer Banks of North Carolina, known as "the graveyard of the Atlantic." (Rev: BL 12/15/99) [363.28]

19157 Wilson, Martin. *Uniquely Alabama* (4–7). Series: Heinemann State Studies. 2004, Heinemann LB $27.07 (978-1-4034-4485-1). In addition to providing the facts necessary for report writers, this volume emphasizes the features that distinguish Alabama from its neighbors. (Rev: BL 4/1/04)

19158 Wilson, Martin. *Uniquely Mississippi* (4–7). Illus. Series: Heinemann State Studies. 2004, Heinemann LB $27.07 (978-1-4034-4656-5). 48pp. In addition to providing the facts necessary for report writers, this volume emphasizes the features that distinguish Mississippi from its neighbors. (Rev: BL 10/15/03)

19159 Yolen, Jane. *Welcome to the River of Grass* (PS–3). Illus. by Laura Regan. 2001, Penguin $16.99 (978-0-399-23221-3). 32pp. Yolen examines the animal and plant life of the Everglades — and the perils the area faces — in rhythmic text accompanied by excellent illustrations. (Rev: BCCB 2/02; BL 10/1/01; HBG 3/02; SLJ 11/01)

SOUTHWEST

19160 Alter, Judy. *New Mexico* (4–7). Illus. Series: MyReportLinks.com. 2002, Enslow LB $25.26 (978-0-7660-5098-3). 48pp. An introduction to the government, geography, and history of the state, with helpful Web sites. (Rev: BL 2/1/03; SLJ 4/03; VOYA 4/03)

19161 Bauer, Marion Dane. *The Grand Canyon* (K–2). Illus. by John Wallace. Series: Ready-to-Read Wonders of America. 2006, Simon & Schuster LB $11.89 (978-0-689-86947-1); paper $3.99 (978-0-689-86946-4). How the Grand Canyon was formed, and what it's like to visit it, in a format for beginning readers with cartoon-like illustrations. (Rev: SLJ 7/06)

19162 Bjorklund, Ruth. *New Mexico* (4–7). Series: It's My State! 2003, Marshall Cavendish LB $27.07 (978-0-7614-1526-8). 80pp. Actual quotations from both famous and unknown residents of New Mexico are used to introduce this state, its people, history, wildlife, and resources. (Rev: BL 9/15/03; HBG 4/04)

19163 Corrick, James. *Uniquely Arizona* (4–7). Series: Heinemann State Studies. 2004, Heinemann LB $27.07 (978-1-4034-4486-8); paper $8.50 (978-1-4304-4501-2). 48pp. In addition to providing the facts necessary for report writers, this volume emphasizes the features that distinguish Arizona from its neighbors. (Rev: BL 4/1/04)

19164 Gendell, Megan. *The Spanish Missions of Texas* (3–7). Series: A True Book. 2010, Children's Press LB $26 (978-0-531-20580-8). 48pp. A look at the Spanish mission buildings of Texas, with beautiful color photographs and discussion of their history and their impact of the missions on the Native Americans. Lexile 940L (Rev: LMC 8–9/10) [976.4]

19165 Gibson, Karen Bush. *Oklahoma Facts and Symbols. Rev. ed.* (3–5). Illus. Series: The States and Their Symbols. 2003, Capstone LB $21.26 (978-0-7368-2266-4). A brief overview that will serve as a source of limited facts about the state. (Rev: SLJ 1/04)

19166 Hanson-Harding, Alexandra. *Texas* (4–6). Illus. Series: From Sea to Shining Sea. 2001, Children's Book Pr. LB $30.50 (978-0-516-22322-3). 80pp. A good resource for report writing, this book features historical facts, maps, and information about the governmental structure and the people of Texas. (Rev: BL 3/15/02)

19167 Heinrichs, Ann. *Oklahoma* (2–5). Illus. Series: This Land Is Your Land. 2003, Compass Point LB $25.26 (978-0-7565-0330-7). 48pp. This brightly illustrated profile explores Oklahoma's history, people, geography, government, economy, and attractions. (Rev: SLJ 7/03)

19168 Heinrichs, Ann. *Texas* (2–4). Illus. Series: This Land Is Your Land. 2002, Compass Point LB $25.26 (978-0-7565-0312-3). 48pp. Simple text with age-appropriate language and good illustrations introduce the history, geography, culture, famous people, and attractions of Texas. (Rev: SLJ 1/03)

19169 Herda, D. J. *Environmental America: The Southwestern States* (4–7). Series: American Scene. 1991, Millbrook LB $22.40 (978-1-878841-11-7). This account, which discusses the state of the environment and how it can be changed for the better, covers Arizona, California, Colorado, Nevada, New Mexico, and Utah. (Rev: BL 8/91; SLJ 7/91) [639.9]

19170 Hicks, Terry Allan. *Nevada* (3–5). Illus. Series: It's My State! 2006, Benchmark LB $27.07 (978-0-7614-1860-3). 80pp. Report writers will find all the facts they need in this book that comes complete with a state-themed craft. (Rev: SLJ 6/06)

19171 Lourie, Peter. *The Lost World of the Anasazi: Exploring the Mysteries of Chaco Canyon* (5–8). 2003, Boyds Mills $19.95 (978-1-56397-972-9). With many full-color photographs, the author describes his trip to the ruins of Chaco Canyon and discusses the mysterious disappearance of its Anasazi residents. (Rev: BL 9/1/03; HBG 4/04; SLJ 1/04) [978.9]

19172 Lynch, Wayne, and Aubrey Lang. *Sonoran Desert* (5–8). Series: Our Wild World Ecosystems. 2009, NorthWord $16.95 (978-1-58979-389-7). 64pp. The fascinating flora, fauna, topography, and climate of America's Sonoran Desert are described in chatty, well-written text and an abundance of eye-catching illustrations and color photographs. (Rev: SLJ 10/09) [77.5409791]

19173 Lyon, Robin. *The Spanish Missions of Arizona* (3–7). Series: A True Book. 2010, Children's Press LB $26 (978-0-531-20576-1). 48pp. A look at the Spanish mission buildings of Arizona, with beautiful color photographs and discussion of their history and the impact of the missions on the Native Americans. Also use *The Spanish Missions of New Mexico* (2010). Lexile 930L (Rev: LMC 8–9/10) [979.1]

19174 McDaniel, Melissa. *Arizona* (4–8). Series: Celebrate the States. 2000, Marshall Cavendish LB $37.07 (978-0-7614-0647-1). This introduction to Arizona discusses its land, history, economy, festivals, cultural diversity, and landmarks. (Rev: BL 6/1–15/00; HBG 10/00; SLJ 9/00) [979.1]

19175 Marcovitz, Hal. *The Alamo* (4–8). Series: American Symbols and Their Meanings. 2002, Mason Crest LB $18.95 (978-1-59084-037-5). A basic and readable introduction to the history of the Alamo and its importance to Americans, with illuminating illustrations and inset features. (Rev: SLJ 9/02) [976]

19176 Marsico, Katie. *The Rio Grande* (3–6). Illus. Series: It's Cool to Learn about America's Waterways. 2013, Cherry Lake LB $28.50 (978-162431012-6); paper $14.21 (9781624310362). 32pp. Presents the geography, wildlife, history, and environmental challenges facing this waterway, with activities. (Rev: BL 5/1/13; LMC 11–12/13) [978.8]

19177 Meister, Cari. *Grand Canyon* (2–4). Series: Going Places. 2000, ABDO LB $21.35 (978-1-57765-024-9). 24pp. This well-organized introduction to the Grand Canyon describes the geological formations and supplies material on the plants, animals, and interesting sights in the area. (Rev: HBG 10/00; SLJ 1/01)

19178 Melmed, Laura K. *Heart of Texas: A Lone Star ABC* (2–4). Illus. by Frane Lessac. 2009, HarperCollins $17.99 (978-0-06-114283-3). 48pp. An alphabetical tour of the history, landmarks, and people of Texas. (Rev: BL 5/1/09; SLJ 4/09)

19179 Munro, Roxie. *The Inside-Outside Book of Texas* (K–3). Illus. Series: Inside-Outside. 2001, North-South LB $16.88 (978-1-58717-051-5). 48pp. Some of the most famous places and landmarks in Texas are pictured in this attractive book with a minimum of text. (Rev: BL 4/1/01; HB 5/01; HBG 10/01; SLJ 6/01)

19180 Pelta, Kathy. *Texas. Rev. ed.* (3–5). Illus. Series: Hello U.S.A. 2001, Lerner LB $25.26 (978-0-8225-4064-9); paper $6.95 (978-0-8225-4142-4). This revision of a 1993 edition features a more spacious layout and some expanded content. (Rev: HBG 3/02; SLJ 2/02)

19181 Powell, John Wesley. *Conquering the Grand Canyon* (3–6). Series: In My Own Words. 2000, Marshall Cavendish LB $24.21 (978-0-7614-1013-3). 64pp. These excerpts from the writings of John Wesley Powell describe how he felt as the first white man to view the natural wonders of the Grand Canyon. (Rev: BL 3/1/01; HBG 3/01)

19182 Tweit, Susan J. *Meet the Wild Southwest: Land of Hoodoos and Gila Monsters* (4–8). 1996, Alaska Northwest paper $14.95 (978-0-88240-468-4). An impressive collection of facts and curiosities about the natural history of the Southwest, with many appendixes that supply more-traditional information. (Rev: BL 3/1/96) [508.79]

19183 Weintraub, Aileen. *The Grand Canyon: The Widest Canyon* (3–5). Illus. Series: Great Record Breakers in Nature. 2001, Rosen $21.25 (978-0-8239-5641-8). 24pp. Jam-packed with facts, this book takes readers on a word and photo tour of the formation, history, and appeal of one of the world's natural wonders. (Rev: BL 12/15/01; SLJ 7/01)

Social Institutions and Issues

Business and Economics

General

19184 Aaseng, Nathan. *Business Builders in Sweets and Treats* (5–8). Series: Business Builders. 2005, Oliver LB $24.95 (978-1-881508-84-7). This attractive title examines food companies that succeed through satisfying America's sweet tooth. (Rev: BL 12/1/05; HBG 4/06) [338.7]

19185 Adler, David A. *Money Madness* (PS–3). Illus. by Edward Miller. 2009, Holiday $16.95 (978-0-8234-1474-1). A picture-book introduction to money with a look at bartering and early forms of money such as rocks and feathers as well as today's coins, bills, and checks; features bright artwork and an interesting page showing foreign money. (Rev: BCCB 3/09; BL 1/1–15/09; HB 5/09; SLJ 5/09)

19186 Allman, Barbara. *Banking* (4–6). Illus. Series: How Economics Works. 2005, Lerner LB $25.26 (978-0-8225-2148-8). 48pp. An excellent overview of the banking system with cartoons and bright illustrations and sidebars; checking and savings accounts are among the topics covered and a glossary defines common banking terms. (Rev: BL 10/15/05)

19187 Caes, Charles J. *The Young Zillionaire's Guide to the Stock Market* (5–8). Series: Be a Zillionaire. 2000, Rosen LB $26.50 (978-0-8239-3265-8). Basic information on the inner workings of the stock market is presented with many examples from the corporate world. (Rev: HBG 10/01; SLJ 3/01) [332.6]

19188 Cipriano, Jeri. *How Do Mortgages, Loans, and Credit Work?* (5–8). Illus. Series: Economics in Action. 2010, Crabtree LB $26.60 (978-077874445-0); paper $8.95 (978-077874456-6). 32pp. Covers interest rates and borrowing and lending in general, with particular attention to credit cards. (Rev: BLO 8/10) [332.7]

19189 Condon, Daniel. *Playing the Market: Stocks and Bonds* (3–5). Series: Everyday Economics. 2004, Heine-mann LB $27.07 (978-1-58810-495-3). 48pp. Condon discusses savings and investment, stocks and bonds, interest rates, and the role of the government and the Federal Reserve. (Rev: SLJ 6/04)

19190 Cooper, Jason. *Around the World with Money* (2–4). Series: Money Power. 2002, Rourke LB $14.95 (978-1-58952-212-1). This brief, small-format overview introduces the currencies of Canada, Mexico, the United States, and Europe. Also use *Money Through the Ages* (2002), which looks at the history of money. (Rev: SLJ 4/03)

19191 Craats, Rennay. *Economy* (4–6). Illus. Series: USA Past, Present, Future. 2008, Weigl $29.05 (978-1-59036-980-7); paper $10.95 (978-1-59036-981-4). Although published before the current downturn, this volume — which examines the U.S. economy by decades from 1900 to the early 2000s provides good background material, profiles of key figures, and a running timeline. (Rev: BL 5/15/09; LMC 5/09)

19192 Craats, Rennay. *Fashion* (4–6). Illus. Series: USA Past, Present, Future. 2008, Weigl $29.05 (978-1-59036-972-2); paper $10.95 (978-1-59036-973-9). 48pp. A decade-by-decade look at a century of women's fashions, demonstrating the cyclical nature of the industry; includes profiles of key figures, and a running timeline. Also use *Trends* (2008). (Rev: BL 5/15/09; LMC 5/09)

19193 Downing, David. *Capitalism* (5–8). Series: Political and Economic Systems. 2002, Heinemann LB $28.50 (978-1-4034-0315-5). 64pp. In an attractive format, this book explains the capitalistic economic system, its history, key thinkers, and present status. (Rev: BL 1/1–15/03; HBG 3/03; SLJ 2/03)

19194 Downing, David. *Communism* (5–8). Series: Political and Economic Systems. 2002, Heinemann LB $28.50 (978-1-4034-0316-2). 64pp. The theoretical basis of communism is explained with material on its application, history, important thinkers and leaders, and different movements. (Rev: BL 1/1–15/03; HBG 3/03; SLJ 2/03)

19195 Drobot, Eve. *Money, Money, Money: Where It Comes From, How to Save It, Spend It, and Make It* (4–6). Illus. by Claudia Dávila. 2004, Maple Tree $19.95 (978-1-897066-10-2); paper $12.95 (978-1-897066-11-9). 96pp. Useful both for browsing and research, this accessible volume covers such fundamentals as the history of currency, banks and savings, credit cards, the stock market, and identity theft. (Rev: BL 1/1–15/05; SLJ 1/05)

19196 Firestone, Mary. *Earning Money* (K–3). Illus. Series: Learning About Money. 2004, Capstone LB $21.26 (978-0-7368-2639-6). 24pp. A simple introduction to the reasons why people want to earn money and how prices of goods are established. Also use *Saving Money* and *Spending Money* (both 2004). (Rev: BL 10/15/04)

19197 Firestone, Mary. *What Is Money?* (K–3). Series: Learning About Money. 2004, Capstone LB $21.26 (978-0-7368-2642-6). 24pp. Informative and attractive, this volume explains the basics of currency in clear text and covers such topics as bartering and the minting of new money. Also use *Earning Money* (2004), which explores ways of acquiring money and its relative worth. (Rev: BL 10/15/04)

19198 Furgang, Kathy, and Fred Hiebert. *Everything Money: A Wealth of Facts, Photos, and Fun!* (4–6). Illus. 2013, National Geographic LB $25.90 (978-142631027-0); paper $12.95 (9781426310263). 64pp. In four chapters this attractive, large-format book provides lots of information about money and how to make, spend, save, and enjoy it. (Rev: BL 6/13; LMC 1–2/14*) [332.4]

19199 Giesecke, Ernestine. *Your Money at Work: Taxes* (3–5). Series: Everyday Economics. 2004, Heinemann LB $27.07 (978-1-58810-494-6). 48pp. Introduces the principle of taxation, why it's necessary, different forms of taxation, and how the money collected is spent. (Rev: SLJ 6/04)

19200 Green, Meg. *The Young Zillionaire's Guide to Investments and Savings* (5–8). Series: Be a Zillionaire. 2000, Rosen LB $23.95 (978-0-8239-3261-0). 48pp. A guide to the investment markets and methods of saving with good use of examples and case studies. (Rev: HBG 10/01; SLJ 3/01)

19201 Hall, Margaret. *Credit Cards and Checks.* 2nd ed. (1–3). Series: Earning, Saving, Spending. 2007, Heinemann LB $28.21 (978-1-4034-9816-8). 32pp. An updated introduction to how we use checks, debit cards, and credit cards, with advice on using credit wisely. Also use *Banks* and *Money* (both 2007). (Rev: LMC 5/08; SLJ 12/07)

19202 Hall, Margaret. *Money* (3–5). Illus. Series: Earning, Saving, Spending. 2000, Heinemann $14.95 (978-1-57572-233-7). 32pp. This history of coins and paper money also discusses their value and uses and how people earn and spend money. (Rev: BL 10/15/00)

19203 Hamen, Susan E. *Google: The Company and Its Founders* (5–8). Illus. Series: Technology Pioneers. 2011, ABDO LB $34.22 (978-161714808-8). 112pp. Google's cofounders Sergey Brin and Larry Page trans-

formed a friendship into a thriving business; this profile of the company and its key players includes dynamic photographs and thorough back matter. (Rev: BL 4/1/11) [338.7]

19204 Harman, Hollis Page. *Money $ense for Kids! 2nd ed.* (4–7). 2004, Barron's paper $14.99 (978-0-7641-2894-3). Explains the basics of money and currency and of earning, saving, and investing, with exercises at the end of each chapter and a "Money Games" section. (Rev: SLJ 11/04) [332.024]

19205 Heinrichs, Ann. *The Great Recession* (4–7). Series: Cornerstones of Freedom. 2011, Scholastic LB $30 (978-053125035-8); paper $8.95 (978-053126560-4). 64pp. This visually appealing volume offers straightforward, age-appropriate information on the economic crisis of the first decade of the 21st century and its causes and impact on U.S. residents. (Rev: BL 10/1/11) [330.973]

19206 Johanson, Paula. *Making Good Choices About Fair Trade* (5–8). Series: Green Matters. 2010, Rosen LB $29.95 (978-1-4358-5315-7). 64pp. A thought-provoking introduction to international trade and the ways in which consumers can encourage fair trade practices, with real-life examples and discussion of labor laws. (Rev: BL 10/1/09; LMC 1–2/10) [381.3]

19207 Kummer, Patricia K. *Currency* (4–8). Series: Inventions That Shaped the World. 2004, Watts LB $30.50 (978-0-531-12341-6). 80pp. After looking at the nature of currency, this title discusses modern forms and the role of currency in our lives. (Rev: SLJ 2/05)

19208 Larson, Jennifer S. *What Can You Do with Money?: Earning, Spending, and Saving* (K–2). Series: Exploring Economics. 2010, Lerner LB $25.26 (978-0-7613-3910-6). 32pp. An easy-to-read introduction to earning and spending money, with explanations of the nature of income and goods and services. Also use *What Is Money, Anyway? Why Dollars and Coins Have Value* (2010). (Rev: SLJ 8/1/10) [331.2]

19209 Loewen, Nancy. *Cash, Credit Cards, or Checks: A Book About Payment Methods* (3–5). Illus. by Brad Fitzpatrick. Series: Money Matters. 2005, Picture Window LB $25.26 (978-1-4048-0951-2). 24pp. Shopping for school necessities forms the backdrop for information on money and banking. Also use *Save, Spend, or Donate?* (2005). (Rev: SLJ 9/05)

19210 McGowan, Eileen Nixon, and Nancy Lagow Dumas. *Stock Market Smart* (5–8). Illus. 2002, Millbrook LB $23.90 (978-0-7613-2113-2). 64pp. An accessible question-and-answer presentation on the stock market and different types of investors, with illustrations, tips on saving, activities, a glossary, and list of resources. (Rev: BL 9/1/02; HBG 3/03; SLJ 10/02)

19211 Mattern, Joanne. *The Mars Family: M and M Mars Candy Makers* (2–4). Illus. Series: Food Dudes. 2011, ABDO LB $25.65 (978-161613560-7). 32pp. This business profile explores the family legacy of the Mars company, which got its start when founder Franklin Mars began experimenting with candy while recovering from polio. (Rev: BL 4/1/11) [338.7]

19212 Rau, Dana Meachen. *Saving Money* (2–4). Series: Money and Banks. 2010, Gareth Stevens LB $22 (978-1-4339-3386-8). 24pp. A clear introduction to ways of saving money, from piggy banks to savings accounts and even stocks. Also use *Spending Money,* and *What Is a Bank?* (both 2010). (Rev: SLJ 6/1/10)

19213 Rau, Dana Meachen. *What Is a Bank?* (2–4). Illus. Series: Money and Banks. 2005, Weekly Reader LB $21.00 (978-0-8368-4873-1). An inside (small-format) look at how a bank operates, covering checking and savings accounts, safe-deposit boxes, ATMs, and money lending. (Rev: BL 10/15/05)

19214 Seidman, David. *The Young Zillionaire's Guide to Supply and Demand* (5–7). Series: Be a Zillionaire. 2000, Rosen LB $26.50 (978-0-8239-3264-1). The basic principles of supply and demand are explained, with information on how they are influenced by producers and consumers and how they help create economic conditions. (Rev: SLJ 2/01)

19215 Sylvester, Kevin, and Michael Hlinka. *Follow Your Money: Who Gets It, Who Spends It, Where Does It Go?* (5–8). Illus. by Kevin Sylvester. 2013, Annick $24.95 (978-155451481-6). 64pp. Using everyday examples and presenting information in digestible bits, this title describes various aspects of economics. (Rev: BLO 9/15/13; LMC 1–2/14; SLJ 12/13) [330]

19216 Thomas, Keltie. *The Kids Guide to Money Cent$* (4–7). Illus. by Stephen MacEachern. 2004, Kids Can $14.95 (978-1-55337-389-6); paper $7.95 (978-1-55337-390-2). 56pp. Readers follow three children — the Money Cent$ Gang — who join together to investigate the ins and outs of banking, credit, investment, and money making; quizzes and examples make the content clear and comic-strip scenes add appeal. (Rev: SLJ 7/04)

19217 Wilson, Antoine. *The Young Zillionaire's Guide to Distributing Goods and Services* (5–7). Series: Be a Zillionaire. 2000, Rosen LB $26.50 (978-0-8239-3259-7). This book explains how goods and services are distributed, the importance of retailing and wholesaling, how transportation affects prices and availability, and how the Internet might change these conditions. (Rev: SLJ 2/01) [330]

Consumerism

19218 Graydon, Shari. *Made You Look: How Advertising Works and Why You Should Know* (5–9). Illus. by Warren Clark. 2003, Annick $24.95 (978-1-55037-815-3); paper $14.95 (978-1-55037-814-6). The 8- to 14-year-old age group is an advertising target, and this title teaches readers to recognize the various techniques used and to assess products' value. (Rev: BL 12/1/03*; SLJ 12/03) [659.1]

19219 Larson, Jennifer S. *Who's Buying? Who's Selling? Understanding Consumers and Producers* (K–2). Series: Exploring Economics. 2010, Lerner LB $25.26 (978-0-7613-3912-0). 32pp. The concept of exchanging money for goods or services is explored in chapters on consumers, producers, vendors, supply and demand, and bartering. (Rev: SLJ 8/1/10) [381]

19220 Lewin, Ted. *How Much? Visiting Markets Around the World* (K–2). Illus. 2006, HarperCollins $16.99 (978-0-688-17552-8). 40pp. A large-format photographic tour of marketplaces on four continents, with text that enhances the images and offers the phrase "How much" in various languages. (Rev: BL 2/1/06; SLJ 1/06)

19221 Mayer, Cassie. *Markets* (PS–2). Illus. Series: Our Global Community. 2007, Heinemann LB $14.50 (978-1-4034-9404-7). 24pp. Simple, short text and photographs on each page make this a useful easy-reader introduction to markets around the world. (Rev: BL 7/07)

Money-Making Ideas and Budgeting

19222 Barkin, Carol, and Elizabeth James. *The New Complete Babysitter's Handbook* (5–7). 1995, Clarion paper $7.95 (978-0-395-66558-9). A fine manual that covers such topics as first aid, ways to amuse children, and how to get jobs baby sitting. (Rev: BL 5/1/95; SLJ 6/95) [649.1]

19223 Buckley, Annie. *Be a Better Babysitter* (5–6). Series: Girls Rock! 2006, The Child's World LB $25.64 (978-1-59296-740-7). 32pp. This introductory guide to baby-sitting explains the nature of the job, looks at its pros and cons and safety issues, and offers advice on doing a good job. (Rev: SLJ 2/07)

19224 Chassé, Jill D. *The Babysitter's Survival Guide: Fun Games, Cool Crafts, and How to Be the Best Babysitter in Town* (5–10). Illus. by Jessica Secheret. 2010, Sterling $12.95 (978-1-40274-654-3). 108pp. With information on how to assess job opportunities, this helpful guide offers plenty of activity ideas, advice for coping with difficult behaviors, and general tips on running a business. (Rev: SLJ 9/1/10) [649]

19225 Drew, Bonnie, and Noel Drew. *Fast Cash for Kids* (4–7). 1995, Career Pr. paper $13.99 (978-1-56414-154-5). The authors present a variety of possible ways to make money. (Rev: BL 6/15/87) [658.041]

19226 Hall, Margaret. *Your Allowance* (3–5). Illus. Series: Earning, Saving, Spending. 2000, Heinemann $21.36 (978-1-57572-234-4). This book looks seriously at budgeting one's allowance, at good consumer practices, savings accounts, and gifts to charity. (Rev: BL 10/15/00)

19227 Holyoke, Nancy. *A Smart Girl's Guide to Money: How to Make It, Save It, and Spend It* (4–7). Illus. by Ali Douglass. Series: A Smart Girl's Guide. 2006, Pleasant paper $9.95 (978-1-59369-103-5). 94pp. Shopping and investing are only two of the topics covered in this user-friendly guide. (Rev: BL 5/15/06; SLJ 5/06)

19228 Larson, Jennifer S. *Do I Need It? Or Do I Want It? Making Budget Choices* (K–2). Illus. 2010, Lerner LB $25.62 (978-076133914-4). 32pp. Young readers learn about the options they have regarding money — including donating it, saving it, and spending it right away — in this introduction to simple money management. (Rev: BL 4/1/10; LMC 5–6/10) [332.024]

19229 Loewen, Nancy. *Lemons and Lemonade: A Book About Supply and Demand* (3–5). Illus. by Brian Jensen. Series: Money Matters. 2005, Picture Window LB $25.26 (978-1-4048-0956-7). 24pp. Karly learns about managing a small business — and about the principle of supply and demand — in this humorous entry in the series. (Rev: SLJ 9/05)

19230 Salzmann, Mary Elizabeth. *Money for School* (2–4). Illus. Series: Your Piggy Bank: A Guide to Spending and Saving for Kids! 2010, ABDO LB $27.07 (978-1-61641-031-5). 24pp. Readers learn about money basics and help young Mason decide how to manage the little bit he has for school. Other titles in this series include *Money for Toys* and *Money for Food* (2011). (Rev: SLJ 5/1/11) [332.024]

19231 Weintraub, Aileen. *Everything You Need to Know About Being a Baby-Sitter: A Teen's Guide to Responsible Child Care* (5–8). 2000, Rosen LB $25.25 (978-0-8239-3085-2). This book covers all facets of baby-sitting from preparation, responsibilities, and safety precautions to employment opportunities. (Rev: SLJ 7/00) [649]

19232 Willson, Sarah. *Pet Peeves* (1–3). Illus. by John Nez. Series: Social Studies Connects. 2005, Kane paper $4.99 (978-1-57565-149-1). Children work together to become entrepreneurs in this story designed to support social studies. (Rev: SLJ 9/05)

Retail Stores and Other Workplaces

19233 Krull, Kathleen. *Supermarket* (K–3). Illus. by Melanie Hope Greenberg. 2001, Holiday House $16.95 (978-0-8234-1546-5). 32pp. This is a fascinating and stimulating overview of what you'll find in the supermarket and how it gets there, including material on the history of shopping from barter onward and lots of interesting tidbits. (Rev: BL 9/15/01; HBG 3/02; SLJ 10/01)

Ecology and Environment

General

19234 Anderson, Judith. *Sustaining the Environment* (4–7). Series: Working for Our Future. 2010, Black Rabbit LB $28.50 (978-1-59771-198-2). 32pp. This volume explains why the United Nations chose sustaining the environment as one of its eight Millennium Development goals and looks at the various obstacles challenging this mission. (Rev: BL 6/1/10; LMC 10/10; SLJ 4/10)

19235 Ansary, Mir T. *Earth Day* (2–3). Illus. Series: Holiday Histories. 2002, Heinemann LB $21.36 (978-1-58810-220-1). The author traces the history of the Earth and its natural resources, man's misappropriation of them, and the founding of Earth Day. (Rev: BL 2/1/02)

19236 Apte, Sunita. *Eating Green* (4–7). Series: Going Green. 2010, Bearport LB $25.27 (978-1-59716-965-3). 32pp. Things people can do to lessen damage to the environment are discussed in this book series, which is supported with a Web site featuring additional information and activities. (Rev: LMC 1–2/10)

19237 Arnold, Caroline. *A Warmer World: From Polar Bears to Butterflies, How Climate Change Affects Wildlife* (3–7). Illus. by Jamie Hogan. 2012, Charlesbridge $16.95 (978-1-58089-266-7); paper $7.95 (978-15808926-7-4). 32pp. Global warming's challenges to the animal kingdom are the focus of this cautionary book. ℮ (Rev: BL 2/15/12; LMC 11–12/12; SLJ 4/1/12) [363.738]

19238 Bailey, Jacqui. *What's the Point of Being Green?* (4–6). Illus. by Jan McCafferty. 2010, Barron's paper $12.99 (978-0-7641-4427-1). 96pp. Answering questions such as "Why are trees important?" and "How did it get so bad?," this appealing book presents many environmental challenges and explains what we can do to ameliorate the problems. (Rev: LMC 11–12/10; SLJ 8/10)

19239 Ballard, Carol. *The Search for Better Conservation* (4–7). Series: Science Quest. 2005, Gareth Stevens LB $26.00 (978-0-8368-4553-2). A look at how lack of conservation affects us, and what scientists are doing to tackle this problem. (Rev: BL 4/1/05)

19240 Barraclough, Sue. *Respecting Our World* (1–3). Series: Making a Difference. 2008, Sea-to-Sea LB $27.10 (978-1-59771-111-1). Clearly written information about saving water and energy and the importance of respecting nature is accompanied by facts, hints, suggestions, and photographs. (Rev: SLJ 9/08)

19241 Bellamy, Rufus. *Tourism* (4–7). Illus. Series: Sustaining Our Environment. 2010, Amicus LB $31.35 (978-160753138-8). 48pp. Takes a look at tourism's impact on the environment and the emergence of ecotourism, "slow travel," and other new trends. (Rev: BLO 2/14/11; LMC 8–9/11) [363.738]

19242 Boothroyd, Jennifer. *People and the Environment* (K–2). Illus. 2008, Lerner LB $18.60 (978-0-8225-8601-2). 24pp. A brief, simple look at how people, animals, and plants interact with each other — for good and for bad. (Rev: BL 2/15/08; LMC 3/08; SLJ 3/08)

19243 Bowden, Rob. *Water Supply: Our Impact on the Planet* (5–8). Illus. Series: 21st Century Debates. 2003, Raintree LB $28.56 (978-0-7398-5506-5). 64pp. A thought-provoking examination of the status of the world's water supply, predictions of a looming water crisis, and measures that could be taken to avert this. (Rev: BL 8/03; HBG 10/03)

19244 Burnie, David. *Endangered Planet* (4–8). Series: Kingfisher Knowledge. 2004, Kingfisher $11.95 (978-0-7534-5776-4). This volume looks at how human requirements threaten the flora, fauna, and resources of our planet. (Rev: BL 9/1/04; SLJ 1/05) [333.95]

19245 Caduto, Michael J. *Catch the Wind, Harness the Sun: 22 Super-Charged Science Projects for Kids* (5–8). Illus. 2011, Storey $26.95 (978-1-60342-971-9); paper $16.95 (978-1-60342-794-4). 224pp. Focusing on energy conservation and global warming, this book collects 22 empowering projects that can be undertaken by young people concerned about the environment. **e** (Rev: BL 5/1/11; SLJ 7/11*) [333.79]

19246 Chandler, Gary, and Kevin Graham. *Environmental Causes* (5–10). Series: Celebrity Activists. 1997, Twenty-First Century LB $25.90 (978-0-8050-5232-9). This book discusses how entertainers including Robert Redford, Sting, and Chevy Chase and other celebrities such as Al Gore, Ted Turner, and Jerry Greenfield support environmental causes. (Rev: SLJ 1/98) [363.7]

19247 Cherry, Lynne. *How We Know What We Know about Our Changing Climate: Scientists and Kids Explore Global Warming* (4–7). Illus. by Gary Braasch. 2008, Dawn $17.95 (978-1-58469-103-7). Children are called to be "citizen scientists" as they learn about the scientific evidence for global warming and are armed with specific strategies to help turn things around. (Rev: BL 2/15/08; SLJ 6/08) [551.6]

19248 Cole, Joanna. *The Magic School Bus and the Climate Challenge* (2–4). Illus. by Bruce Degen. 2010, Scholastic $16.99 (978-0-590-10826-3). 48pp. Ms. Frizzle takes her class on a global tour that demonstrates the effects of climate change. (Rev: BL 2/15/10; LMC 5–6/10; SLJ 2/1/10)

19249 Coley, Mary McIntyre. *Environmentalism: How You Can Make a Difference* (4–7). Series: Take Action. 2009, Capstone LB $25.32 (978-1-4296-2797-9). 32pp. This title provides directions for correctly researching an environmental problem, making a plan, and dealing with the rejection that sometimes accompanies speaking out. (Rev: SLJ 5/09) [333.72]

19250 Dalgleish, Sharon. *Protecting Wildlife* (4–6). Illus. Series: Our World: Our Future. 2002, Chelsea LB $28.00 (978-0-7910-7021-5). 32pp. The role of humans is emphasized in this look at the impact on wildlife of vanishing habitats and changes in the weather, and simple actions that children can take are suggested. Also use *Saving Our Water* (2002). (Rev: HBG 3/03; SLJ 1/03)

19251 David, Laurie, and Cambria Gordon. *The Down-to-Earth Guide to Global Warming* (4–7). Illus. 2007, Scholastic paper $15.99 (978-0-439-02494-5). The authors balance alarming information on climate change and its impact with practical ways in which readers can reduce their carbon footprint and details of new technologies that may help. (Rev: BL 9/15/07; SLJ 11/07) [363.738]

19252 Delano, Marfé Ferguson. *Earth in the Hot Seat: Bulletins from a Warming World* (4–6). Illus. 2009, National Geographic $16.95 (978-1-4263-0434-7). 64pp. A clear look at the subject of global warming, with information on the signs we are already seeing and the future consequences of inaction. (Rev: HB 7/09; SLJ 7/09)

19253 Ditchfield, Christin. *Oil* (2–5). Illus. Series: True Books — Natural Resources. 2002, Children's Book Pr. LB $25.00 (978-0-516-22343-8); paper $6.95 (978-0-516-29367-7). 48pp. This book discusses oil, its procurement and processing, and the environmental impact of using oil as fuel, with simple text and excellent photographs. (Rev: BL 10/15/02)

19254 Ditchfield, Christin. *Water* (2–5). Illus. Series: True Books — Natural Resources. 2002, Children's Book Pr. LB $25.00 (978-0-516-22345-2). 48pp. Ditchfield discusses water as a natural resource, covering in simple text and excellent photographs the forms of water, the water cycle, and the ways in which we use water. (Rev: BL 10/15/02)

19255 Farrell, Courtney. *Keeping Water Clean* (3–7). Series: Language Arts Explorer: Save the Planet. 2010, Cherry Lake LB $27.07 (978-1-60279-659-1). 32pp. Students are given a mission at the beginning of the book and must use creative thinking and problem solving to gather facts as they travel on a virtual trip researching water conservation. (Rev: LMC 8–9/10; SLJ 4/10) [363.7394]

19256 Goldsworthy, Steve. *The Top 10 Ways You Can Travel Green* (3–5). Illus. Series: Being Green. 2010, Weigl LB $28.55 (978-161690085-4); paper $12.95 (978-161690086-1). 32pp. Helpful and innovative suggestions for making transportation more green are sandwiched between a history of green travel and a look at what the future may hold. (Rev: BL 3/1/11) [333.79]

19257 Gorman, Jacqueline Laks. *Fossil Fuels* (5–8). Series: What If We Do Nothing? 2009, Gareth Stevens LB $31.00 (978-1-4339-0087-7). 48pp. A look at fossil fuels, how we use them, how they affect the climate, and the future of these fuels. (Rev: SLJ 6/09; VOYA 10/09)

19258 Gutman, Dan, ed. *Recycle This Book: 100 Top Children's Book Authors Tell You How to Go Green* (5–9). 2009, Random House paper $5.99 (978-0-385-73721-0). 267pp. In brief essays (and a poem) Laurie Halse Anderson, Lois Lowry, Rick Riordan, and 97 other authors children will recognize describe what they do to help the earth; some serious, some lighthearted, these pieces are grouped by location (home, school, community, and so forth) and usually include a practical suggestion. (Rev: LMC 5–6/09; SLJ 8/09) [640]

19259 Hanel, Rachael. *Climate Fever: Stopping Global Warming* (5–8). Series: Green Generation. 2010, Compass Point LB $31.99 (978-0-7565-4246-7). 64pp. Well organized and clearly written, this book is part of a series explaining about steps people can take to adjust their consumption and ease environmental impact, encouraging readers to spur change in their own communities. (Rev: LMC 1–2/10)

19260 Herzog, Brad. *S Is for Save the Planet: A How-to-Be-Green Alphabet* (2–4). Illus. by Linda Holt Ayriss. 2009, Sleeping Bear $17.95 (978-1-58536-428-2). 40pp. Simple eight-line poems deal with environmental topics from A to Z ("zero carbon footprint"), with informative sidebars. (Rev: BL 4/15/09; SLJ 5/09)

19261 Hirsch, Rebecca. *Protecting Our Natural Resources* (3–7). Series: Language Arts Explorer: Save the Planet. 2010, Cherry Lake LB $27.07 (978-1-60279-661-4). 32pp. Students are given a mission at the beginning of the book and must use creative thinking and problem solving to gather facts as they travel on a virtual trip through the various ways to protect natural resources. (Rev: LMC 8–9/10; SLJ 4/10) [333.72]

19262 Hollyer, Beatrice. *Our World of Water: Children and Water Around the World* (2–4). Illus. 2009, Henry Holt $16.95 (978-080508941-7). 48pp. Six stories of how different countries use and appreciate water are collected in this book, which features child narrators and color photographs. (Rev: BL 11/1/09; SLJ 8/1/09) [363.6]

19263 Ingram, W. Scott. *The Chernobyl Nuclear Disaster* (5–8). Series: Environmental Disasters. 2005, Facts on File $35.00 (978-0-8160-5755-9). Ingram assesses the continuing environmental fallout from the 1986 Chernobyl nuclear disaster. (Rev: SLJ 11/05) [333.79]

19264 Jakab, Cheryl. *Global Warming* (4–7). Series: Global Issues. 2009, Smart Apple Media LB $28.50 (978-1-59920-451-2). 32pp. Offering a global perspective, this volume covers warmer temperatures, declining ice cover, changing seasons and rainfall patterns, and the migration that will be caused by all these changes. (Rev: SLJ 2/10) [363.738]

19265 Jakubiak, David J. *What Can We Do About Acid Rain?* (3–5). Series: Protecting Our Planet. 2011, Rosen LB $21.25 (978-1-4488-4984-0); paper $8.25 (978-1-4488-5116-4). 24pp. This broad overview discusses what acid rain is, how it forms, and the harm it does to the environment, and looks at what can be done to prevent it — and the successes achieved so far. **e** (Rev: BL 2/15/12; SLJ 11/1/11) [363.738]

19266 Jakubiak, David J. *What Can We Do About Deforestation?* (3–5). Series: Protecting Our Planet. 2011, Rosen LB $21.25 (978-1-4488-4986-4); paper $8.25 (978-1-4488-5119-5). 24pp. This broad overview discusses the importance of trees and the harm that deforestation does to the environment, and looks at what can be done to reverse the damage. Also use *What Can We Do About Toxins in the Environment?* (2011). **e** (Rev: BL 2/15/12; SLJ 11/1/11) [634.9]

19267 Johnson, J. Angelique. *The Eco-Student's Guide to Being Green at School* (2–4). Illus. by Kyle Poling. Series: Point it Out! Tips for Green Living. 2010, Picture Window LB $25.99 (978-140486027-8). 24pp. Explores the various rooms in a school and the actions students can take to improve the eco-friendliness. (Rev: BL 3/1/11; LMC 3–4/11) [640]

19268 Juettner, Bonnie. *Energy* (5–8). Series: Our Environment. 2004, Gale LB $26.20 (978-0-7377-1821-8). Answers such questions as "How is energy managed?" and "Are we running out of energy?" in four chapters that feature many illustrations and large type. (Rev: SLJ 4/05) [333.79]

19269 Kaye, Cathryn Berger, and Philippe Cousteau. *Make a Splash! A Kid's Guide to Protecting Our Oceans, Lakes, Rivers, and Wetlands* (4–6). Illus. 2012, Free Spirit paper $13.99 (978-157542417-0). 128pp. Brightly colored photographs and drawings portray the many uses of water and the actions elementary children across the world have taken to protect their water from pollutants. (Rev: BL 2/15/13; SLJ 1/13) [577.7]

19270 Kelsey, Elin. *Not Your Typical Book About the Environment* (4–6). Illus. by Clayton Hanmer. 2010, OwlKids $22.95 (978-189734979-3); paper $10.95 (978-18973498-4-7). 64pp. This colorful book with comic-style illustrations describes how many options there are for consumers, looking at four areas in particular: fashion, food, technology, and energy. (Rev: BL 6/10; LMC 10/10; SLJ 6/10) [304.2]

19271 Kerley, Barbara. *A Cool Drink of Water* (PS–3). Illus. 2002, National Geographic $16.95 (978-0-7922-6723-2). 32pp. A series of beautiful photographs with minimal text show how water is collected and carried by people throughout the world. (Rev: BL 3/15/02; HBG 10/02; SLJ 4/02*) [363.738]

19272 Kirk, Ellen. *Human Footprint* (3–7). Illus. 2011, National Geographic paper $6.95 (978-1-4263-0-767-6). 32pp. Based on a National Geographic documentary and subtitled "Everything You Will Eat, Use, Wear, Buy, and Throw Out in your Lifetime," this attractive book looks at the average American's consumption. (Rev: BL 7/11; SLJ 6/11) [304.2]

19273 Langley, Andrew. *Avoiding Hunger and Finding Water* (5–8). Illus. Series: The Environment Challenge. 2011, Raintree LB $32 (978-141094298-2). 48pp. Famine and drought are the main focuses of this effective volume that also covers population growth, climate change, pollution, and so forth. (Rev: BL 2/15/12) [363.8]

19274 Langley, Andrew. *Bridging the Energy Gap* (5–8). Illus. Series: The Environment Challenge. 2011, Raintree LB $32 (978-141094297-5); paper $8.99 (978-141094304-0). 48pp. Langley explains the current sources of our energy, alternative options, and the importance of conserving energy. (Rev: BL 2/15/12) [333.79]

19275 Lishak, Antony. *Global Warming* (4–7). Illus. Series: What's That Got to Do with Me? 2007, Smart Apple Media LB $18.95 (978-1-59920-037-8). People from around the world who have been affected by climate change — and those who fear they may be — are interviewed to demonstrate various aspects of global warming. (Rev: BL 10/15/07; LMC 2/08) [363.738]

19276 Lorbiecki, Marybeth. *Planet Patrol* (3–5). Illus. by Nancy Meyers. 2005, Two-Can $15.95 (978-1-58728-514-1); paper $8.95 (978-1-58728-518-9). 48pp. This brightly illustrated title alerts readers to a wide range of environmental threats — pollution, overpopulation, climate change, deforestation, and species extinction — and what young people can do to help save the globe and reverse some of the damage. (Rev: BL 12/1/05; SLJ 12/05)

19277 McKenzie, Precious. *Cleaning Up the Earth* (1–3). Illus. Series: Green Earth Discovery Library. 2011, Rourke paper $7.95 (978-161741768-9). 24pp. After explaining pollution and global warming, this book discusses how young people can help to achieve progress. (Rev: BL 2/15/12; LMC 5–6/12) [363.7]

19278 McKenzie, Precious. *Our Organic Garden* (1–3). Illus. Series: Green Earth Discovery Library. 2011, Rourke paper $7.95 (978-161741767-2). 24pp. Introduces the principles of organic gardening and explains the benefits of this approach. (Rev: BL 2/15/12; LMC 5–6/12) [635.0]

19279 Mason, Paul. *How Big Is Your Clothing Footprint?* (5–9). Series: Environmental Footprints. 2010, Marshall Cavendish LB $28.50 (978-0-7614-4410-7). 32pp. Fibers (natural and artificial), cleaning techniques, fashion, shipping, and other aspects of the clothes we wear are discussed in this useful title. Other volumes in the series include *How Big Is Your Energy Footprint?*, *How Big Is Your Food Footprint?*, and *How Big Is Your Water Footprint?* (all 2010). (Rev: LMC 5–6/10; SLJ 11/1/09) [391]

19280 Metz, Lorijo. *What Can We Do About Invasive Species?* (3–5). Illus. Series: Protecting Our Planet. 2009, PowerKids LB $21.25 (978-140428084-7). 24pp. Providing information on a variety of invasive species from around the world — from camels and rabbits to kudzu — this book offers a thought-provoking glimpse into the consequences of human activities. (Rev: BL 2/15/10) [577]

19281 Minden, Cecilia. *Reduce, Reuse, and Recycle* (3–7). Series: Language Arts Explorer: Save the Planet. 2010, Cherry Lake LB $27.07 (978-1-60279-662-1). 32pp. Students are given a mission at the beginning of the book and must use creative thinking and problem solving to gather facts as they travel on a virtual trip through the various ways to minimize waste. (Rev: LMC 8–9/10; SLJ 4/10) [363.72]

19282 Morgan, Sally. *Ozone Hole* (3–5). Illus. Series: Earth SOS. 2009, Black Rabbit LB $28.50 (978-159771224-8). 32pp. Discusses the causes — natural and resulting from human activity — of the hole in the ozone layer and explains its importance using clear language and many visuals. (Rev: BL 2/15/10) [577.27]

19283 Munro, Roxie. *EcoMazes: Twelve Earth Adventures* (1–3). Illus. by author. 2010, Sterling $14.95 (978-1-4027-6393-9). 40pp. Twelve vibrantly colored ecosystem mazes from different biomes around the world present a variety of landforms, wildlife, and ecological facts. (Rev: BL 6/10; SLJ 6/1/10*) [577]

19284 Nakaya, Andrea C., ed. *The Environment* (5–9). Series: Introducing Issues with Opposing Viewpoints. 2006, Gale LB $33.70 (978-0-7377-3459-1). This thought-provoking study examines the delicate balance between the preservation of our natural environment and the need for energy to fuel economic growth. (Rev: SLJ 8/06)

19285 Olien, Rebecca. *Kids Care! 75 Ways to Make a Difference for People, Animals and the Environment* (3–6). Illus. by Michael Kline. Series: Williamson Kids Can! 2007, Williamson $16.99 (978-0-8249-6793-2); paper $12.99 (978-0-8249-6792-5). 128pp. In sections on people, pets, wildlife, the environment, and kids joining together, this volume presents practical ways in which children can improve life. (Rev: SLJ 10/07)

19286 Ostopowich, Melanie. *Greenpeace* (4–8). Series: International Organizations. 2002, Weigl LB $16.95

(978-1-59036-020-0). 32pp. An introduction to the goals, structure, members, and volunteers who work with this international organization. Also use *Peace Corps* (2003). (Rev: HBG 3/03; SLJ 4/03)

19287 Oxlade, Chris. *Global Warming* (5–7). Illus. Series: Our Planet in Peril. 2002, Capstone LB $22.60 (978-0-7368-1361-7). 32pp. Attractive double-page spreads explore the concern about global warning, its causes, and options for the future. Also use *Nuclear Waste* (2003). (Rev: HBG 3/03; SLJ 4/03)

19288 Parker, Janice, ed. *The Disappearing Forests* (5–8). Series: Understanding Global Issues. 2002, Smart Apple Media LB $19.95 (978-1-58340-168-2). A great deal of information about forest use, abuse, and conservation is packed into double-paged spreads with color illustrations. (Rev: BL 10/15/02; HBG 3/03; SLJ 12/02) [634.9]

19289 Parks, Peggy J. *Ecotourism* (5–8). Series: Our Environment. 2005, Gale LB $26.20 (978-0-7377-3048-7). All about how ecologically sensitive areas can be protected while being explored, with explanations of the advantages and disadvantages of this type of travel. (Rev: SLJ 5/06) [338.4]

19290 Parks, Peggy J. *Global Warming* (5–8). Series: Our Environment. 2004, Gale LB $26.20 (978-0-7377-1822-5). Answers such questions as "Caused by humans or caused by nature?" and "What can be done?" in four chapters that feature many illustrations and large type. (Rev: SLJ 4/05) [363.738]

19291 Parr, Todd. *The Earth Book* (PS–1). Illus. by author. 2010, Little, Brown $9.99 (978-0-316-04265-9). 40pp. Simple, accessible actions (turning off the tap when brushing teeth, using both sides of the paper) that protect the planet are the focus of this attractive book. (Rev: BL 3/1/10; SLJ 3/1/10) [333.72]

19292 Parry, Ann. *Greenpeace* (5–8). Series: Humanitarian Organizations. 2005, Chelsea House LB $25.00 (978-0-7910-8815-9). Maps, timelines, factboxes, and color photographs add to this account of Greenpeace's history and mission. (Rev: SLJ 12/05)

19293 Peters, Celeste, ed. *The Energy Dilemma* (5–8). Illus. Series: Understanding Global Issues. 2002, Smart Apple Media LB $19.95 (978-1-58340-169-9). 56pp. The information about energy sources, use, and conservation packed into these double-paged spreads with color illustrations will spark debate. (Rev: BL 10/15/02)

19294 Pringle, Laurence. *The Environmental Movement: From Its Roots to the Challenges of a New Century* (5–8). 2000, HarperCollins $16.95 (978-0-688-15626-8). This is a fine history of environmentalism in America, beginning with the conflicts between Native Americans and early settlers concerning natural resources and ending with current issues. (Rev: BL 4/1/00; HBG 10/00; SLJ 6/00) [363.7]

19295 Pringle, Laurence. *Global Warming: The Threat of Earth's Changing Climate* (4–8). 2001, NorthSouth $16.95 (978-1-58717-009-6). A straightforward account that covers topics including the causes of global warming, the signs that it is occurring, and possible solutions. (Rev: BL 4/1/01; HBG 10/01; SLJ 6/01) [363.738]

19296 Reilly, Kathleen M. *Planet Earth: 25 Environmental Projects You Can Build Yourself* (4–7). Series: Projects You Can Build Yourself. 2008, Nomad $21.95 (978-1-934670-05-7); paper $14.95 (978-1-934670-04-0). A worm composting castle and a wind-powered bubble machine are just two of the projects in this book that teaches about the environment and important environmental issues. (Rev: BL 5/1/08) [507.8]

19297 Rockwell, Anne. *Why Are the Ice Caps Melting? The Dangers of Global Warming* (2–4). Illus. by Paul Meisel. Series: Let's-Read-and-Find-Out Science. 2006, HarperCollins $15.99 (978-0-06-054669-4); paper $5.99 (978-0-06-054671-7). 33pp. The hot-button issue of global warming is discussed in easy-to-understand language, as are the greenhouse effect and the role of carbon dioxide emissions. (Rev: BL 12/15/06; SLJ 11/06)

19298 Rooney, Anne. *Is Our Climate Changing?* (4–8). Illus. Series: Global Questions. 2008, Arcturus LB $22.95 (978-1-84837-011-1). What is climate change? Has the climate changed in the past? This brief title answers these and other questions in clear text and color photographs, with a final chapter that looks at the future. (Rev: BL 12/1/08; LMC 5/09) [551.6]

19299 Royston, Angela. *Global Warming* (2–3). Illus. Series: Protect Our Planet. 2008, Heinemann LB $17.75 (978-1-4329-0924-6). 32pp. A basic introduction to global warming with discussion of climate change, the loss of ice at the poles, and measures we can take to protect the planet. (Rev: BL 9/1/08)

19300 Sayre, April P. *Trout Are Made of Trees* (K–2). Illus. by Kate Endle. 2008, Charlesbridge $15.95 (978-1-58089-137-0); paper $6.95 (978-1-58089-138-7). 32pp. Using very simple text, this book illustrates how the whole world is interconnected and that, in fact, trout are made from trees. (Rev: BL 2/15/08; HB 7/08; SLJ 4/08)

19301 Simon, Seymour. *Global Warming* (3–5). Illus. 2010, HarperCollins $17.99 (978-0-06-114250-5); LB $18.89 (978-0-06-114251-2). 32pp. A clear, comprehensive guide to the causes and effects of global warming and climate change, with many effective photographs. (Rev: BL 2/15/10; SLJ 3/1/10) [363.738]

19302 Sirett, Dawn. *Love Your World* (PS). Illus. 2009, DK $8.99 (978-0-7566-4590-8). 36pp. Advice for young environmentalists ranges from turning down the heat and brushing teeth without the water running to recycling and planting seeds. (Rev: BLO 4/14/09; SLJ 5/09)

19303 Solway, Andrew. *Biofuels* (5–8). Illus. Series: Energy for the Future and Global Warming. 2007, Gareth Stevens LB $26.60 (978-0-8368-8398-5); paper $9.95 (978-0-8368-8407-4). 32pp. A brief introduction to the use of alternatives to fossil fuels — ethanol, biogas, and so forth — with an explanation of how these could benefit the environment. (Rev: BL 10/15/07)

19304 Spilsbury, Louise, and Richard Spilsbury. *Water* (5–8). Series: Planet Under Pressure. 2006, Heinemann LB $31.43 (978-1-4034-8214-3). 48pp. Discusses the demand for water, its sources, and what's being done to conserve it. (Rev: SLJ 3/07)

19305 Spilsbury, Richard. *Climate Change Catastrophe* (4–8). Series: Can the Earth Survive? 2010, Rosen LB $26.50 (978-1-4358-5354-6). 48pp. With case studies and suggested strategies for the future, this volume looks at global warming problems around the world and the impact on everyday life. Additional titles in this series by this author are *Deforestation Crisis* and *Threats to Our Water Supply* (both 2010). (Rev: LMC 3–4/10; SLJ 1/10) [363.738]

19306 Stille, Darlene R. *Nature Interrupted: The Science of Environmental Chain Reactions* (5–7). Series: Headline Science. 2008, Compass Point LB $27.93 (978-0-7565-3949-8). 48pp. Through understandable text and helpful charts, this title clearly explains the fragile and important links between all things in the environment and how breaks in the chain can have detrimental, widespread results. (Rev: SLJ 2/09) [577.27]

19307 Strauss, Rochelle. *One Well: The Story of Water on Earth* (3–5). Illus. by Rosemary Woods. 2007, Kids Can $17.95 (978-1-55337-954-6). 32pp. The importance of water to life on earth and the connections between all uses of water are emphasized in this oversize picture book that also discusses water distribution and recycling and gives tips on conservation. (Rev: BL 2/15/07*)

19308 Suzuki, David, and Kathy Vanderlinden. *Eco-Fun* (5–8). 2001, Douglas & McIntyre paper $10.95 (978-1-55054-823-5). The activities in this collection reinforce some basic scientific concepts about air, water, earth, and fire, and encourage young readers to think about environmental issues and avoid pollution. (Rev: BL 6/1–15/01; SLJ 8/01) [577]

19309 Suzuki, David, and Kathy Vanderlinden. *You Are the Earth: Know Your World So You Can Help Make It Better* (4–8). Illus. by Wallace Edwards. 2011, Greystone paper $16.95 (978-1-55365-476-6). 144pp. This wide-ranging survey explores the importance of clean air, water, and soil and the interrelatedness of the sun's energy and plant, animal, and human life, with information on creation myths plus activities and experiments. (Rev: BL 3/1/11; SLJ 3/1/11*) [577]

19310 Taylor, Barbara. *How to Save the Planet* (3–6). Illus. by Scoular Anderson. Series: How To. 2001, Watts LB $16.00 (978-0-531-14640-8). 96pp. Experiments back up the concepts introduced in this discussion of global warming, pollution, future energy needs, and other important topics. (Rev: SLJ 4/02)

19311 Thomas, Keltie. *Animals That Changed the World* (4–8). Illus. 2010, Annick $21.95 (978-1-55451-243-0); paper $12.95 (978-1-55451-242-3). 112pp. A fascinating look at the ways in which animals impact life on earth and human history; the cat, dog, beaver, pigeon, and horse are profiled, and expressions involving animals are explained. (Rev: LMC 5–6/11; SLJ 1/1/11) [590]

19312 Toft, Kim Michelle. *The World That We Want* (PS–3). Illus. by author. 2005, Charlesbridge paper $6.95 (978-1-58089-115-8). The interconnectedness of animals, plants, and their habitats is emphasized in this book with beautiful illustrations and an environmental message. (Rev: SLJ 9/05)

19313 VanCleave, Janice. *Janice VanCleave's Ecology for Every Kid* (4–7). 1996, Wiley paper $12.95 (978-0-471-10086-7). Clear instructions and many diagrams introduce a series of experiments that highlight environmental issues. (Rev: BL 3/1/96; SLJ 4/96) [574.5]

19314 Walker, Jane. *Atmosphere in Danger* (4–6). 2005, Stargazer LB $27.10 (978-1-932799-12-5). Easy-to-understand language with helpful graphs, charts, and illustrations make this a useful introduction to the problems threatening the Earth's fragile atmosphere and the potential solutions. (Rev: SLJ 4/06)

19315 Walsh, Melanie. *10 Things I Can Do to Help My World: Fun and Easy Eco-Tips* (PS–2). Illus. by author. 2008, Candlewick $15.99 (978-0-7636-4144-3). 40pp. Simple actions — turning off the tap when you brush your teeth — are presented in this engaging can-do book. (Rev: BLO 9/24/08; HB 1/09)

19316 Webb, Barbara L. *What Does Green Mean?* (1–3). Illus. 2011, Rourke paper $7.95 (978-16174197-3-7). 24pp. This accessible offering gives young readers a chance to understand what it means to be "green," and examines a variety of actions that make this an achievable goal. (Rev: BL 2/15/12) [333.7]

19317 Wells, Robert E. *Polar Bear, Why Is Your World Melting?* (1–4). Illus. by author. 2008, Albert Whitman $16.99 (978-0-8075-6598-8); paper $6.99 (978-0-8075-6599-5). For young readers, this is an introduction to the dangers of global warming, with information on what can be done to ameliorate the situation. (Rev: BCCB 12/08; SLJ 11/08)

19318 Welsbacher, Anne. *Earth-Friendly Design* (4–8). Illus. Series: Saving Our Living Earth. 2008, Lerner LB $30.60 (978-082257564-1). 72pp. A straightforward look at the life cycle of the products we use daily (including vehicles and houses), examining how innovative thinking can lead to greener solutions. (Rev: BL 12/1/08; LMC 3–4/09; VOYA 12/08) [745.2]

19319 Whitman, Sylvia. *This Land Is Your Land: The American Conservation Movement* (5–7). 1994, Lerner LB $30.35 (978-0-8225-1729-0). A history of the conservation movement from its beginnings in 1870 when there were efforts to save Yellowstone and ending with today's major problems such as oil spills and trash disposal. (Rev: BL 12/15/94; HB 3–4/94; SLJ 12/94) [363.7]

19320 Wilson, Janet. *Our Earth: How Kids Are Saving the Planet* (2–5). Illus. by author. 2010, Second Story $18.95 (978-1-897187-84-5). 32pp. Wilson profiles young people around the world who have made significant contributions to solving environmental problems. (Rev: BL 1/1–15/11; SLJ 6/11) [333.72092]

19321 Woods, Michael, and Mary B. Woods. *Environmental Disasters* (4–7). Series: Disasters Up Close. 2008, Lerner LB $27.93 (978-0-8225-6774-5). Love Canal, Bhopal, the *Exxon Valdez* — these are only three of the disasters covered in this well-illustrated account of disasters that could have been avoided. (Rev: BL 2/15/08; SLJ 8/08) [363.7]

Cities

19322 Jakab, Cheryl. *Sustainable Cities* (4–7). Series: Global Issues. 2009, Smart Apple Media LB $28.50 (978-1-59920-454-3). 32pp. This volume discusses the factors that lead to unsustainable urban growth and the transportation and construction changes that could improve the situation. (Rev: SLJ 2/10) [307.76]

19323 Kent, Peter. *Peter Kent's City Across Time: From the Stone Age to the Distant Future* (2–4). Illus. by author. 2010, Kingfisher $16.99 (978-0-7534-6400-7). 48pp. An engaging look at how an imaginary European city evolved from the Stone Age to the 21st century, with detailed cross-section illustrations. (Rev: BL 5/1/10; LMC 10/10; SLJ 6/10) [307.76]

19324 Matsen, Bradford. *Go Wild in New York City* (4–6). Illus. 2005, National Geographic $16.95 (978-0-7922-7982-2). 80pp. Skippy the squirrel guides readers through the nature to be found in the urban landscape of New York City, with chapters on its flora and fauna, water, rocks, and air. (Rev: BL 3/15/05; SLJ 5/05)

19325 Pancella, Peggy. *City* (K–2). Series: Neighborhood Walk. 2005, Heinemann LB $25.36 (978-1-4034-6215-2). 32pp. After a discussion of a neighborhood as part of a larger community, this book looks at various aspects of life in the city, including work, recreation, transportation, and shopping. Also use *Farm Community, Military Base, Small Town,* and *Suburb* (all 2005). (Rev: SLJ 2/06)

Garbage and Waste Recycling

19326 Barraclough, Sue. *Recycling Materials* (1–3). Series: Making a Difference. 2008, Sea-to-Sea LB $27.10 (978-1-59771-108-1). Clearly written information about recycling paper, glass, metal, and plastic is accompanied by facts, hints, suggestions, and photographs. Also use *Reducing Garbage* (2008). (Rev: SLJ 9/08)

19327 Barraclough, Sue. *Reusing Things* (1–3). Series: Making a Difference. 2008, Sea-to-Sea LB $27.10 (978-1-59771-109-8). 32pp. Clearly written information about reusing paper, junk, clothing and other materials is accompanied by facts, hints, suggestions, and photographs. (Rev: SLJ 9/08)

19328 Bergen, Lara. *Don't Throw That Away! A Lift-the-Flap Book About Recycling and Reusing* (PS–K). Illus.

by Betsy Snyder. Series: Little Green Books. 2009, Simon & Schuster paper $6.99 (978-14169751-7-5). 14pp. Many simple and creative repurposing projects are presented in this lively book, which features bright illustrations against a paper-bag-brown background. (Rev: BLO 1/1/10) [363.72]

19329 Hall, Eleanor J. *Recycling* (5–8). Series: Our Environment. 2004, Gale LB $26.20 (978-0-7377-1517-0). Answers such questions as "What is recycling?" and "What does the future hold?" in four chapters that feature many illustrations and large type. (Rev: SLJ 4/05) [363.72]

19330 Love, Ann, and Jane Drake. *Trash Action: A Fresh Look at Garbage* (3–6). Illus. by Mark Thurman. 2006, Tundra paper $14.95 (978-0-88776-721-0). 76pp. Examples of trash on Mount Everest and in space draw readers into this information-packed book that looks at the growing problems of garbage and waste disposal and outlines steps that can be taken to address the situation. (Rev: SLJ 8/06)

19331 Morgan, Sally. *Waste and Recycling* (1–3). Series: Helping Our Planet. 2011, Cherrytree LB $28.50 (978-1-84234-608-2). 32pp. This book offers readers plenty of practical advice for reducing the amount of waste a household creates. (Rev: SLJ 8/1/11) [363.72]

19332 Porter, Esther. *What's Sprouting in My Trash? A Book about Composting* (1–3). Illus. Series: Earth Matters. 2013, Capstone LB $26.65 (978-162065047-9); paper $7.95 (9781620657454). 32pp. With plenty of photographs this is a succinct overview of composting and its benefits. (Rev: BL 4/1/13; LMC 1–2/14) [631.8]

19333 Spilsbury, Richard. *Waste and Recycling Challenges* (4–8). Series: Can the Earth Survive? 2010, Rosen LB $26.50 (978-1-4358-5355-3). 48pp. With case studies and suggested strategies for the future, this volume looks at waste disposal problems around the world and the impact on everyday life. (Rev: LMC 3–4/10; SLJ 1/10) [363.72]

19334 Winter, Jonah. *Here Comes the Garbage Barge!* (1–3). Illus. by Red Nose Studio. 2010, Random House LB $17.99 (978-0-375-95218-0). 40pp. This book tells the true story of a gigantic barge of garbage from Islip, NY, that was turned away from port after port all the way to Belize before finally turning back to its original home in 1987. Lexile AD670L (Rev: BL 2/15/10; LMC 3–4/10; SLJ 1/1/10*)

Pollution

19335 Ball, Jacqueline A. *Traveling Green* (2–5). Illus. Series: Going Green. 2009, Bearport LB $25.27 (978-159716964-6). 32pp. With many statistics and photographs, this is a good introduction to the types of transport that are kindest to the environment, explaining the dangers posed by pollution. (Rev: BL 2/15/10; LMC 1–2/10) [790.1]

19336 Bellamy, Rufus. *Clean Air* (4–6). 2005, Smart Apple LB $27.10 (978-1-58340-594-9). This book takes a somewhat optimistic tack on the problem of global air pollution, citing numerous examples of programs that either have been put in place or are being considered. (Rev: SLJ 4/06)

19337 Benoit, Peter. *The BP Oil Spill* (3–5). Series: A True Book: Disasters. 2011, Children's Press LB $28 (978-0-531-20630-0); paper $6.95 (978-0-531-28999-0). 48pp. Benoit examines the disaster and its aftermath and provides photographs, maps, timelines, and statistics. (Rev: LMC 3–4/12; SLJ 11/1/11) [363.738]

19338 Bouler, Olivia. *Olivia's Birds: Saving the Gulf* (3–6). Illus. by author. 2011, Sterling $14.95 (978-1-4027-8665-5). 32pp. Eleven-year-old Olivia's striking illustrations of birds fill the pages of this book, alongside her inspiring story of donating her artwork to help the Gulf recover from the 2010 oil spill. (Rev: BL 5/1/11; SLJ 6/11) [598]

19339 Bridges, Andrew. *Clean Air* (5–8). Series: Sally Ride Science. 2009, Roaring Brook paper $6.99 (978-1-59643-576-6). 40pp. A look at the importance of clean air and the ways in which it is threatened by human activity. Lexile 740 (Rev: SLJ 9/09) [363.739]

19340 Brown, Paul. *Global Pollution* (5–8). Illus. Series: Face the Facts. 2003, Raintree LB $28.56 (978-0-7398-6433-3). 56pp. The effects of pollution on the environment are described in understandable terms, and practical responses from young people are suggested. (Rev: BL 11/15/03; HBG 10/03; SLJ 9/03)

19341 Chapman, Matthew, and Rob Bowden. *Air Pollution* (5–8). Series: 21st Century Debates. 2002, Raintree LB $19.99 (978-0-7398-4874-6). 64pp. The causes of air pollution, the present situation, and possible future solutions are presented in this well-illustrated book that presents various points of view and offers topics for debate. (Rev: BL 6/1–15/02; SLJ 4/06)

19342 Coad, John. *Reducing Pollution* (4–9). Series: Why Science Matters. 2009, Heinemann-Raintree $32.86 (978-1-4329-2483-6). 56pp. Illustrating science's role in everyday life, this volume offers a comprehensive overview of the causes and consequences of pollution, and what we can do to reduce it. (Rev: LMC 11–12/09) [363.73]

19343 Geiger, Beth. *Clean Water* (5–8). Series: Sally Ride Science. 2009, Roaring Brook paper $6.99 (978-1-59643-577-3). 40pp. A look at the importance of clean water and the ways in which it is threatened by human activity. Lexile 740 (Rev: SLJ 9/09)

19344 Gifford, Clive. *Pollution* (4–7). Illus. Series: Planet Under Pressure. 2006, Heinemann LB $31.43 (978-1-4034-7742-2). 48pp. An overview of the various types of pollution, their sources and impact, and possible future remedies. (Rev: SLJ 6/06)

19345 Green, Jen. *Reducing Air Pollution* (4–6). 2005, Gareth Stevens LB $26.00 (978-0-8368-4428-3). This easy-to-understand overview of air pollution looks at what's causing the problem, including such factors as acid rain, ozone depletion, and global warming, and examines ways in which the world can reduce its dependence on fossil fuels. (Rev: SLJ 4/06)

19346 Landau, Elaine. *Oil Spill! Disaster in the Gulf of Mexico* (3–5). Illus. 2011, Millbrook LB $25.26 (978-0-7613-7485-5). 32pp. Tells the story of the 2010 oil spill, the struggle to stop the leak, and the impact on the environment, with a final chapter titled "What's to Be Done?" **e** Lexile 780L (Rev: BL 3/1/11*; SLJ 4/11) [363.738]

19347 Leacock, Elspeth. *The Exxon Valdez Oil Spill* (5–8). Series: Environmental Disasters. 2005, Facts on File $35.00 (978-0-8160-5754-2). A look at the environmental impact of the 1989 *Exxon Valdez* oil spill in Alaska's Prince William Sound. (Rev: SLJ 11/05) [363.7]

19348 McLeish, Ewan. *Population Explosion* (4–8). Series: Can the Earth Survive? 2010, Rosen LB $26.50 (978-1-4358-5356-0). 48pp. With case studies and suggested strategies for the future, this volume looks at population problems around the world and the impact on everyday life. (Rev: LMC 3–4/10; SLJ 1/10) [363.9]

19349 Morgan, Sally. *Pollution* (1–3). Series: Helping Our Planet. 2011, Cherrytree LB $28.50 (978-1-84234-607-5). 32pp. Morgan looks at the sources of air and water pollution, the impact of oil spills, dumping, and farming, and steps we can take to limit pollution. (Rev: SLJ 8/1/11) [363]

19350 Ostopowich, Melanie. *Water Pollution* (4–6). 2005, Weigl LB $24.45 (978-1-59036-307-2). This overview of water pollution explores the water cycle and various causes of pollution and includes a few experiments to help readers better understand the concepts involved. (Rev: SLJ 4/06)

19351 Person, Stephen. *Saving Animals from Oil Spills* (3–5). Illus. Series: Rescuing Animals from Disasters. 2011, Bearport LB $25.27 (978-161772288-2). 32pp. Looks at the impact on wildlife of such disasters as the *Exxon Valdez* spill in Alaska and the Deepwater Horizon explosion in the Gulf, introducing the people who risk their lives to save animals and the techniques they use. (Rev: BL 10/1/11) [628.1]

Population

19352 Anderson, Judith. *Ending Poverty and Hunger* (4–7). Series: Working for Our Future. 2010, Black Rabbit LB $28.50 (978-1-59771-195-1). 32pp. This volume explains why the United Nations chose eliminating poverty and hunger as one of its eight Millennium Development goals and looks at the various reasons why children are deprived of these basics and what can be done to

improve the situation. (Rev: BL 6/1/10; LMC 10/10; SLJ 4/10)

19353 Barber, Nicola. *Coping with Population Growth* (5–8). Illus. Series: Environment Challenge. 2011, Raintree LB $32 (978-141094296-8); paper $8.99 (978-141094303-3). 48pp. This book looks at the importance of population growth to our world and at the relationship between population and food supply, poverty, pollution, education, and so forth. (Rev: BL 2/15/12) [304.6]

19354 Bowden, Rob. *Food Supply* (5–8). Series: 21st Century Debates. 2002, Raintree LB $27.12 (978-0-7398-4871-5). 64pp. Trends and issues regarding the food supply, and possible solutions for shortages, are presented in this look at pros and cons. (Rev: BL 6/1–15/02)

19355 Bowden, Rob. *An Overcrowded World?* (5–8). Series: 21st Century Debates. 2002, Raintree LB $27.12 (978-0-7398-4872-2). 64pp. Using a well-organized text, plus sidebars for additional facts and statements of opinion, this colorfully illustrated volume explores the current problems of overpopulation and the dire strain it causes on the earth's supplies. (Rev: BL 6/1–15/02)

19356 Green, Robert. *Poverty* (4–8). Series: Global Perspectives. 2008, Cherry Lake LB $27.07 (978-1-60279-126-8). 32pp. An accessible look at poverty, how we measure it, its effects, and what can be done to curb this problem. (Rev: LMC 10/08; SLJ 11/08) [362.5]

19357 McLeish, Ewan. *Overcrowded World* (5–8). Illus. Series: What If We Do Nothing? 2009, Gareth Stevens LB $31.00 (978-1-4339-0088-4). 48pp. Overpopulation and the associated problems of famine, water shortages, poverty, and homelessness are addressed in this volume that looks at the past, the current status, and the future outlook. (Rev: BL 4/15/09; SLJ 6/09; VOYA 10/09) [363.9]

19358 Mason, Paul. *Population* (4–7). Series: Planet Under Pressure. 2006, Heinemann LB $31.43 (978-1-4034-7741-5). 48pp. The problems created by overpopulation are the focus of this book that also explores the underlying reasons and possible solutions. (Rev: SLJ 6/06)

19359 Smith, David J. *If the World Were a Village* (3–5). Illus. by Shelagh Armstrong. 2002, Kids Can $15.95 (978-1-55074-779-9). 32pp. By condensing the world's population to a "village" of 100 people, this book makes data and statistics more comprehensible — and more fascinating — for younger readers. (Rev: BL 3/1/02; HB 5/02; HBG 10/02; SLJ 5/02)

19360 Stearman, Kaye. *Why Do People Live on the Streets?* (5–7). Series: Exploring Tough Issues. 2001, Raintree LB $25.69 (978-0-7398-3232-5). 48pp. Among reasons given for homelessness are poverty and discrimination. (Rev: HBG 10/01; SLJ 7/01)

Government and Politics

Courts and the Law

19361 Anderson, Wayne. *Brown v. Board of Education: The Case Against School Segregation* (5–8). Series: Supreme Court Cases Through Primary Sources. 2004, Rosen LB $29.25 (978-0-8239-4009-7). Primary sources — photographs, police records, newspaper clippings, and court documents — provide details of the case and the narrative discusses the historical and social context. Also use *Plessy v. Ferguson: Legalizing Segregation* (2004). (Rev: SLJ 6/04) [345.73]

19362 Anderson, Wayne. *The Chicago Black Sox Trial: A Primary Source Account* (5–8). Series: Great Trials of the Twentieth Century. 2003, Rosen LB $29.25 (978-0-8239-3969-5). This is a detailed, readable account of the 1919 Chicago Black Sox scandal and the plot to fix the World Series. (Rev: BL 4/1/04; SLJ 6/04; VOYA 4/04) [796.357]

19363 Burnett, Betty. *The Trial of Julius and Ethel Rosenberg: A Primary Source Account* (5–8). Series: Great Trials of the Twentieth Century. 2004, Rosen LB $29.25 (978-0-8239-3976-3). Primary sources — photographs, original transcripts, quotations, and so forth — give depth to this compelling account of the complex trial. (Rev: BL 4/1/04; SLJ 10/04)

19364 Crewe, Sabrina, and Michael V. Uschan. *The Scottsboro Case* (4–7). Series: Events That Shaped America. 2005, Gareth Stevens LB $26.00 (978-0-8368-3407-9). A thorough and thought-provoking look at the infamous Scottsboro case in which nine young African Americans were accused of raping two white women. (Rev: BL 1/1–15/05; SLJ 3/05) [345.73]

19365 De Capua, Sarah. *Serving on a Jury* (3–5). Illus. Series: A True Book: Civics. 2012, Scholastic/Children's Press LB $29 (978-0-531-26042-5); paper $6.95 (978-0-531-26214-6). 48pp. What does it mean to be an upstanding citizen? Can jurors go home each night during a trial? Who can be the jury foreperson? This helpful book answers these and other key questions. Lexile 890L (Rev: BL 10/1/12; LMC 8–9/13; SLJ 2/13) [347.73]

19366 Donnelly, Karen. *Cruzan v. Missouri: The Right to Die* (5–7). Series: Supreme Court Cases Through Primary Sources. 2004, Rosen LB $29.25 (978-0-8239-4014-1). The lengthy legal battle for a patient's right to die is chronicled in this account of the Supreme Court's decision in Cruzan v. Missouri. (Rev: BL 6/1–15/04; SLJ 6/04) [344.73]

19367 Donovan, Sandy. *Making Laws: A Look at How a Bill Becomes a Law* (4–6). Illus. Series: How Government Works. 2003, Lerner LB $25.26 (978-0-8225-1346-9). 56pp. An easily understood explanation of how an idea (the example is banning school on Fridays) can become a bill and then a law. (Rev: SLJ 3/04)

19368 Dudley, Mark E. *Engel v. Vitale (1962): Religion and the Schools* (5–9). Series: Supreme Court Decisions. 1995, Twenty-First Century LB $25.90 (978-0-8050-3916-0). The story of the Supreme Court case on school prayer that originated with two Jewish youngsters who objected to being forced to pray every morning in a New York City school. (Rev: BL 11/15/95; SLJ 1/96; VOYA 4/96) [347]

19369 Gorman, Jacqueline Laks. *Judge* (2–4). Series: Know Your Government. 2009, Gareth Stevens LB $21.00 (978-1-4339-0092-1); paper $5.95 (978-1-4339-0120-1). With color photographs and clear text, Gorman introduces the various levels of judges, focusing mainly on the Supreme Court. (Rev: SLJ 6/09)

19370 Himton, Kerry. *The Trial of Sacco and Vanzetti: A Primary Source Account* (5–8). Series: Great Trials of the Twentieth Century. 2004, Rosen LB $29.25 (978-0-8239-3973-2). Primary sources — photographs, original transcripts, quotations, and so forth — give depth to this compelling account of the complex trial. (Rev: BL 4/1/04; SLJ 6/04)

19371 Hinton, KaaVonia. *Brown v. Board of Education of Topeka, Kansas, 1954* (5–8). Series: Monumental Milestones: Great Events of Modern Times. 2010, Mitchell

Lane LB $29.95 (978-1-58415-738-0). 48pp. Useful for research, this slim volume provides facts and biographical sketches key to this important ruling and supplies the necessary background to fully understand the issues involved. (Rev: BL 2/1/10; LMC 5–6/10; SLJ 1/10)

19372 Horn, Geoffrey M. *The Supreme Court* (5–8). Series: World Almanac Library of American Government. 2003, World Almanac LB $31.00 (978-0-8368-5459-6). An excellent introduction to the U.S. Supreme Court and the important role it plays in interpreting the laws of the land. (Rev: SLJ 1/04)

19373 Linz, Kathi. *Chickens May Not Cross the Road and Other Crazy (But True) Laws* (2–4). Illus. by Tony Griego. 2002, Houghton $16.00 (978-0-618-11257-9). 32pp. A compilation of silly laws ("no tying crocodiles to fire hydrants," "no donkeys in bathtubs") from cities across the United States, each with a cartoon illustration. (Rev: BL 9/1/02; HBG 3/03; SLJ 11/02)

19374 Naden, Corinne J., and Rose Blue. *Dred Scott: Person or Property?* (5–8). Series: Supreme Court Milestones. 2005, Benchmark LB $37.07 (978-0-7614-1841-2). The Supreme Court's 1857 Dred Scott decision, arguably the high court's most misguided ruling ever, is examined in detail. (Rev: BL 2/1/05) [342.7]

19375 Olson, Steven P. *The Trial of John T. Scopes: A Primary Source Account* (5–8). Series: Great Trials of the Twentieth Century. 2004, Rosen LB $29.25 (978-0-8239-3974-9). Primary sources — photographs, original transcripts, quotations, and so forth — give depth to this compelling account of the complex trial. (Rev: BL 4/1/04; SLJ 8/04) [344.73]

19376 Payment, Simone. *Roe v. Wade: The Right to Choose* (5–7). Illus. Series: Supreme Court Cases Through Primary Sources. 2004, Rosen LB $29.25 (978-0-8239-4012-7). 64pp. Illustrations are used to good effect in this overview of the issues raised in the Supreme Court's landmark decision. (Rev: BL 6/1–15/04; SLJ 6/04)

19377 Payment, Simone. *The Trial of Leopold and Loeb: A Primary Source Account* (5–8). Series: Great Trials of the Twentieth Century. 2004, Rosen LB $29.25 (978-0-8239-3970-1). Primary sources — photographs, original transcripts, quotations, and so forth — give depth to this compelling account of the complex trial. (Rev: BL 4/1/04; SLJ 6/04; VOYA 4/04)

19378 Roensch, Greg. *The Lindbergh Baby Kidnapping Trial: A Primary Source Account* (5–8). Series: Great Trials of the Twentieth Century. 2004, Rosen LB $29.25 (978-0-8239-3971-8). Primary sources — photographs, original transcripts, handwriting samples, and so forth — give depth to this account of this controversial trial. (Rev: BL 4/1/04; SLJ 8/04) [345.73]

19379 Scheppler, Bill. *The Mississippi Burning Trial: A Primary Source Account* (5–8). Series: Great Trials of the Twentieth Century. 2004, Rosen LB $29.25 (978-0-8239-3972-5). Primary sources — photographs, original transcripts, quotations, and so forth — give depth to

this compelling account of the complex trial. (Rev: BL 4/1/04; SLJ 10/04)

19380 Sonneborn, Liz. *Miranda v. Arizona: The Rights of the Accused* (5–8). Series: Supreme Court Cases Through Primary Sources. 2004, Rosen LB $29.25 (978-0-8239-4010-3). 64pp. Primary sources — photographs, police records, newspaper clippings, and court documents — provide details of the case and the narrative discusses the historical and social context. (Rev: BL 6/1–15/04; SLJ 6/04)

19381 Sorensen, Lita. *The Scottsboro Boys Trial: A Primary Source Account* (5–8). 2003, Rosen LB $29.25 (978-0-8239-3975-6). Sorensen dissects the sensational Scottsboro Boys rape case in Alabama that attracted media attention from around the globe. (Rev: BL 4/1/04) [345.761]

United Nations and International Affairs

19382 Anderson, Judith. *An Equal Chance for Girls and Women* (4–7). Series: Working for Our Future. 2010, Black Rabbit LB $28.50 (978-1-59771-196-8). 32pp. This volume explains why the United Nations chose equal opportunity for girls and women as one of its eight Millennium Development goals and looks at the various reasons why girls are deprived of opportunity and what can be done to improve the situation. (Rev: BL 6/10; LMC 10/10; SLJ 4/10) [323.3]

19383 Berg, Lois Anne. *An Eritrean Family* (4–7). Series: Journey Between Two Worlds. 1997, Lerner LB $22.60 (978-0-8225-3405-1); paper $8.95 (978-0-8225-9755-1). The story of the Kiklu family, which fled Eritrea in eastern Africa in 1978, spent 10 years in a refugee camp, and resettled in Minnesota. (Rev: BL 6/1–15/97; SLJ 8/97) [304.895]

19384 Bradman, Tony, ed. *Give Me Shelter: Stories About Children Who Seek Asylum* (5–8). 2007, Frances Lincoln $16.95 (978-1-84507-522-4). 220pp. These gripping stories of real children seeking refuge from countries torn apart by war or strife will capture readers' hearts. (Rev: SLJ 3/08)

19385 Connolly, Sean. *Theocracy* (5–8). Illus. Series: Systems of Government. 2012, Black Rabbit LB $35.65 (978-159920806-0). 48pp. Tackling such questions as "Is a Pure Theocracy Possible?" and "In God We Trust?," this is an interesting survey of religion's role in governments around the world. Also in this series: *Dictatorship, Democracy,* and *Communism* (all 2012). (Rev: BL 11/15/12*) [321]

19386 Downing, David. *Democracy* (5–8). Illus. Series: Political and Economic Systems. 2002, Heinemann LB $28.50 (978-1-4034-0317-9). 64pp. Downing explains the history of democracy and looks at its weaknesses and benefits. Also use *Dictatorship* (2002). (Rev: BL 1/1–15/03; HBG 3/03)

19387 Emsden, Katharine, ed. *Coming to America: A New Life in a New Land* (4–8). Series: Perspectives on History. 1993, Discovery paper $6.95 (978-1-878668-23-3). Diaries, journals, and letters of immigrants from many countries are used to provide insights into their lives. (Rev: BL 11/15/93) [325.73]

19388 *Every Human Has Rights: A Photographic Declaration for Kids* (4–8). Illus. 2009, National Geographic $17.95 (978-1-4263-0510-8). 48pp. Compelling photographs, accompanied by poems, illustrate the 30 rights covered in the Universal Declaration of Human Rights. (Rev: BL 12/15/08; SLJ 3/09) [300]

19389 Giesecke, Ernestine. *Governments Around the World* (3–5). Series: Kids' Guide. 2000, Heinemann $22.79 (978-1-57572-511-6). 32pp. This book explains different kinds of governments — democracies, communist and socialist states, monarchies, and other systems. (Rev: HBG 3/01; SLJ 10/00)

19390 Kerley, Barbara. *A Little Peace* (1–6). 2007, National Geographic $16.95 (978-1-4263-0086-8). Photographs of children performing simple acts of peace and kindness will inspire readers. (Rev: SLJ 5/07)

19391 Maddocks, Steven. *UNICEF* (5–8). Series: World Watch. 2004, Raintree LB $271.40 (978-0-7398-6617-7). 48pp. Introduces UNICEF's history, organization, and work on behalf of the world's children; sidebars provide key facts and relevant quotations. (Rev: BL 4/1/04; SLJ 6/04)

19392 *Making It Home: Real Life Stories from Children Forced to Flee* (5–8). Illus. 2006, Dial $17.99 (978-0-8037-3083-0); paper $6.99 (978-0-14-240455-3). 144pp. The horrific impact of war on children is documented in these first-person accounts, with many photographs, from children who were displaced from their homes in Afghanistan, Bosnia, Burundi, Congo, Iraq, Kosovo, Liberia, and Sudan. (Rev: BL 12/1/05; SLJ 2/06)

19393 Parry, Ann. *Red Cross* (4–6). Illus. Series: Humanitarian Organizations. 2005, Chelsea House LB $25.00 (978-0-7910-8814-2). 32pp. With many photographs, sidebars, and other features, this volume explores the history, mission, and core values of the Red Cross. (Rev: BL 10/15/05; SLJ 12/05)

19394 Radunsky, Vladimir. *What Does Peace Feel Like?* (PS–3). Illus. by author. 2004, Simon & Schuster $14.95 (978-0-689-86676-0). 24pp. Students at an international school in Rome imagine what peace looks, sounds, tastes, feels, and smells like. (Rev: BL 11/1/04; SLJ 1/05)

19395 Ring, Susan. *Greenpeace* (4–8). Series: International Organizations. 2003, Weigl LB $16.95 (978-1-59036-020-0). An introduction to the goals, structure, members, and volunteers who work with this international organization. Also use *Peace Corps* (2003). (Rev: HBG 3/03; SLJ 4/03) [333.72]

19396 Ross, Stewart. *United Nations* (5–8). Illus. Series: World Watch. 2004, Raintree LB $18.99 (978-0-7398-6616-0). 48pp. Ross explains the role of the United Na-

tions as an international watchdog and provides a brief review of its history and organization. (Rev: BL 4/1/04)

19397 Serres, Alain. *I Have the Right to Be a Child* (4–8). Trans. by Helen Mixter. Illus. by Aurelia Fronty. 2012, Groundwood $18.95 (978-155498149-6). 48pp. This colorful book encourages readers to think about the United Nations Convention on the Rights of the Child through simple text and eye-catching illustrations. (Rev: BL 7/12; LMC 1–2/13) [323.352]

19398 Smith, David J. *This Child, Every Child: A Book About the World's Children* (4–7). Illus. by Shelagh Armstrong. Series: CitizenKid. 2011, Kids Can $18.95 (978-1-55453-466-1). 36pp. The impact of the 1989 United Nations Convention on the Rights of the Child is outlined in this accessible, well-researched and thought-provoking volume. Lexile 1020L (Rev: BL 4/15/11; LMC 10/11; SLJ 5/1/11) [305.23]

19399 Suen, Anastasia. *Doctors Without Borders* (1–2). Series: Helping Organizations. 2002, Rosen LB $19.95 (978-0-8239-6002-6). 24pp. As well as giving a history of this humanitarian organization, this simple account describes how it works and the good work it accomplishes. (Rev: BL 6/1–15/02; SLJ 4/02)

19400 Suen, Anastasia. *The Red Cross* (1–2). Illus. Series: Helping Organizations. 2002, Rosen LB $19.95 (978-0-8239-6003-3). 24pp. This basic introduction to the Red Cross explains how it was formed and the work it does around the world. (Rev: BL 6/1–15/02)

19401 Suen, Anastasia. *UNICEF* (1–2). Illus. 2002, Rosen LB $19.95 (978-0-8239-6005-7). 24pp. This introduction to UNICEF and its mission also tells how volunteers can help and how youngsters can raise money to aid its programs. (Rev: BL 6/1–15/02; SLJ 3/02)

19402 Tames, Richard. *Monarchy* (5–8). Series: Political and Economic Systems. 2002, Heinemann LB $28.50 (978-1-4034-0320-9). 64pp. A description of the concept of monarchy, followed by a history of its application, its current status, and its various forms. (Rev: BL 1/1–15/03; HBG 3/03)

19403 *We Are All Born Free: The Universal Declaration of Human Rights in Pictures* (K–3). Illus. by John Burningham. 2008, Frances Lincoln $19.95 (978-1-84507-650-4). Effectively illustrated by a diverse group of well-known artists, this book presents the 30 articles of the Universal Declaration of Human Rights. (Rev: BL 12/1/08; SLJ 11/08)

United States

Civil Rights

19404 Adams, Colleen. *Women's Suffrage: A Primary Source History of the Women's Rights Movement in America* (5–8). Illus. Series: Primary Sources in American History. 2003, Rosen LB $29.25 (978-0-8239-3685-4). 64pp. Primary sources — including pamphlets and newspaper articles — tell the story of the women's rights movement in America. (Rev: BL 5/15/03)

19405 Bradley, David, and Shelley Fisher Fishkin, eds. *The Encyclopedia of Civil Rights in America* (5–10). 1997, Sharpe Reference $299.00 (978-0-7656-8000-6). This three-volume set contains 683 alphabetically arranged articles that explore the history, meaning, and application of civil rights issues in the United States. (Rev: BL 2/15/98; SLJ 5/98) [323]

19406 Brimner, Larry Dane. *Birmingham Sunday* (5–8). 2010, Boyds Mills LB $17.95 (978-1-59078-613-0). 48pp. This highly illustrated and moving account of the bombing in 1963 Alabama that killed four young girls places the tragedy in context of the civil rights turmoil of the time. Lexile NC1190L (Rev: BL 2/1/10; LMC 8–9/10; SLJ 4/10) [323.1196]

19407 Crewe, Sabrina, and Dale Anderson. *The Seneca Falls Women's Rights Convention* (3–5). Series: Events That Shaped America. 2005, Gareth Stevens LB $26.00 (978-0-8368-3408-6). 32pp. A simple, straightforward account of the 1848 convention featuring direct quotations, editorial cartoons, photographs, reproductions, and newspaper clippings. (Rev: SLJ 3/05)

19408 Davidson, Tish. *Prejudice* (4–8). Series: Life Balance. 2003, Watts LB $20.50 (978-0-531-12252-5); paper $6.95 (978-0-531-15572-1). This book explore the causes, types, and effects of prejudice, how it can change a person's mental health, and how it has influenced human history. (Rev: BL 10/15/03)

19409 Deutsch, Stacia, and Rhody Cohon. *Hot Pursuit: Murder in Mississippi* (5–8). Illus. by Craig Orback. 2010, Kar-Ben $17.95 (978-0-7613-3955-7). 40pp. A dramatic fictional story about civil rights activists who were murdered in Mississippi in 1964 is intertwined with informational chapters providing background context. (Rev: BL 4/1/10; LMC 8–9/10) [323.092]

19410 Edwards, Pamela Duncan. *The Bus Ride That Changed History: The Story of Rosa Parks* (K–2). Illus. by Danny Shanahan. 2005, Houghton $16.00 (978-0-618-44911-8). 32pp. The story of Rosa Parks's bus ride is told in cumulative "This Is the House That Jack Built" fashion with cartoon illustrations featuring children's questions in dialogue balloons. (Rev: BL 9/1/05; SLJ 10/05)

19411 Fitzgerald, Stephanie. *Struggling for Civil Rights* (4–6). Series: On the Front Line. 2005, Raintree LB $29.93 (978-1-4109-1467-5). 48pp. This is an accessible overview of the civil rights movement of the 1950s and 1960s, covering its roots and key events; personal profiles add interest. (Rev: SLJ 12/05)

19412 Freedman, Jeri. *America Debates Civil Liberties and Terrorism* (5–8). Series: America Debates. 2007, Rosen LB $29.25 (978-1-4042-1927-4). Presents facts and opinions on both sides of issues including governmental surveillance and homeland security. (Rev: LMC 2/08; SLJ 11/07) [323.4]

19413 Freedman, Jeri. *America Debates Privacy Versus Security* (5–8). Series: America Debates. 2007, Rosen LB $29.25 (978-1-4042-1929-8). Presents facts and opinions on both sides of issues including profiling and the right to privacy. (Rev: LMC 2/08; SLJ 11/07) [323.44]

19414 Freedman, Russell. *Freedom Walkers: The Story of the Montgomery Bus Boycott* (4–7). 2006, Holiday $18.95 (978-0-8234-2031-5). 114pp. First-person accounts enliven this history of the 381-day Montgomery Bus Boycott of the mid-1950s, which ended segregation on the buses. (Rev: BCCB 12/06; BL 9/15/06; HBG 4/07; LMC 3/07; SLJ 11/06*; VOYA 10/06)

19415 Good, Diane L. *Brown v. Board of Education* (4–6). Series: Cornerstones of Freedom. 2004, Children's Pr. LB $26.00 (978-0-516-24225-5). 48pp. A nicely presented examination of the Supreme Court's 1954 ruling against school segregation. (Rev: SLJ 7/04)

19416 Grant, Reg. *Slavery: Real People and Their Stories of Enslavement* (4–7). 2009, DK $24.99 (978-0-7566-5169-5). 192pp. The history of slavery around the world and information about its continued practice today is accompanied by firsthand accounts of people involved in slavery. (Rev: BL 7/09; LMC 11–12/09; SLJ 8/09) [306.362]

19417 Greenberg, Keith Elliot. *Adolescent Rights: Are Young People Equal Under the Law?* (5–8). Series: Issues of Our Time. 1995, Twenty-First Century LB $22.90 (978-0-8050-3877-4). This unbiased account of the controversial subject encourages readers to form their own conclusions. (Rev: SLJ 9/95) [323]

19418 Heinrichs, Ann. *The Ku Klux Klan: A Hooded Brotherhood* (4–7). Series: Journey to Freedom. 2002, Child's World LB $28.50 (978-1-56766-646-5). 40pp. This brief introduction to the Klan covers the group's origins and history, and touches on the Internet's role in spreading hate messages. (Rev: SLJ 12/02)

19419 Hollihan, Kerrie Logan. *Rightfully Ours: How Women Won the Vote* (5–8). Illus. 2012, Chicago Review paper $16.95 (978-1-883052-89-8). 130pp. After profiles of Lucy Stone, Elizabeth Cady Stanton, and Susan B. Anthony, Hollihan describes the long road to women's suffrage and offers activities, archival photographs, and sidebar features. e Lexile 1020L (Rev: BLO 8/29/12; LMC 5–6/13; SLJ 9/12) [324.6]

19420 Isler, Claudia. *The Right to Free Speech* (4–6). Series: Individual Rights and Civic Responsibility. 2001, Rosen LB $26.50 (978-0-8239-3234-4). The history of the first amendment is followed by information on sedition, protest, obscenity, symbolic speech, and hate speech. (Rev: SLJ 2/02)

19421 Kendall, Martha E. *Failure Is Impossible: The History of American Women's Rights* (5–8). Illus. Series: People's History. 2001, Lerner LB $30.35 (978-0-8225-1744-3). 96pp. The status of women in the United States is discussed from the time of the Puritans to the present, including information on life for slaves, Native American women, and mill girls, and on equal pay and equal opportunity. (Rev: BL 5/1/01; HBG 10/01; SLJ 6/01; VOYA 8/01)

19422 King, Casey. *Oh, Freedom! Kids Talk About the Civil Rights Movement with the People Who Made It Happen* (5–9). 1997, Random House paper $12.95 (978-0-679-89005-8). In 31 interviews, children ask family members, neighbors, and friends about the part they played in the civil rights movement. (Rev: BL 4/1/97; SLJ 6/97*) [973]

19423 King, David C. *Freedom of Assembly* (4–8). Series: Land of the Free. 1997, Millbrook LB $22.90 (978-0-7613-0064-9). This book covers this basic civil right with examples throughout U.S. history and landmark court cases that helped define its limits. (Rev: BL 5/15/97; SLJ 10/97) [342.73]

19424 King, Martin Luther, Jr. *I Have a Dream* (K–3). Illus. by Kadir Nelson. 2012, Random House $18.99 (978-0-375-85887-1). 40pp. A beautifully illustrated celebration of King's famous 1963 speech, with full text of the address at the back of the book. Coretta Scott King Honor Book. **e** (Rev: BL 9/1/12; HB 9–10/12; LMC 1–2/13*; SLJ 11/12*) [323.092]

19425 Kops, Deborah. *Women's Suffrage* (5–8). Illus. Series: People at the Center. 2004, Gale LB $24.95 (978-1-56711-772-1). This brief but fact-filled volume introduces key leaders in the women's suffrage movement in America. (Rev: BL 5/15/04; SLJ 9/04)

19426 Kramer, Ann. *Human Rights: Who Decides?* (5–8). Series: Behind the News. 2006, Heinemann LB $32.86 (978-1-4034-8832-9). With photographs and examples of news stories, this volume offers various viewpoints on the information we receive on human rights and asks readers how they will make up their minds. (Rev: SLJ 4/07) [323]

19427 Landau, Elaine. *The Civil Rights Movement in America* (3–5). Series: Cornerstones of Freedom. 2003, Children's Pr. LB $26.00 (978-0-516-24219-4). 48pp. A brief, well-illustrated history of the troubled race relations in the United States and the concerted drive for equality beginning with the U.S. Supreme Court finding that school segregation was unconstitutional. (Rev: SLJ 2/04)

19428 McKissack, Patricia C., and Fredrick McKissack. *Days of Jubilee: The End of Slavery in the United States* (5–8). 2003, Scholastic $19.99 (978-0-590-10764-8). A combination of clear, interesting narrative, relevant quotations from primary sources, thorough historical approach, and well-chosen illustrations make this a worthwhile volume on the gradual end of slavery. (Rev: BCCB 4/03; BL 5/15/03; HBG 10/03; LMC 8–9/03; SLJ 5/03; VOYA 4/03) [973.7]

19429 Meyers, Madeleine, ed. *Forward into Light: The Struggle for Woman's Suffrage* (4–8). Series: Perspectives on History. 1994, Discovery paper $6.95 (978-1-878668-25-7). The story of the long struggle for women's right to vote, including the contributions of Elizabeth Cady Stanton, Susan B. Anthony, Sojourner Truth, and other leaders. (Rev: BL 8/94) [324.6]

19430 Michelson, Richard. *As Good as Anybody: Martin Luther King Jr. and Abraham Joshua Heschel's Amaz-ing March Toward Freedom* (2–4). Illus. by Raúl Colón. 2008, Knopf $16.99 (978-0-375-83335-9). 40pp. A clear, well-written story about the collaboration between two civil rights leaders — one an African American Baptist and the other a Polish-born rabbi. (Rev: BL 2/1/08; LMC 3/08; SLJ 5/08)

19431 Miller, Jake. *The Montgomery Bus Boycott: Integrating Public Buses* (2–4). Series: The Library of the Civil Rights Movement. 2004, Rosen LB $21.25 (978-0-8239-6251-8). 24pp. Full of photographs, this is an accessible account of the major events of the bus boycott. Also use *Sit-Ins and Freedom Rides: The Power of Non-violent Resistance* and *The March from Selma to Montgomery: African Americans Demand the Vote* (bolth 2004). (Rev: SLJ 6/04)

19432 Morrison, Toni. *Remember: The Journey to School Integration* (5–12). 2004, Houghton Mifflin $18.00 (978-0-618-39740-2). With striking archival photographs and a fictionalized narrative based on historical fact, this fascinating book explores the impact of the American struggle for civil rights on the children who were often at its center. (Rev: BL 4/15/04; SLJ 6/04) [379.2]

19433 Parks, Rosa, and Gregory J. Reed. *Dear Mrs. Parks: A Dialogue with Today's Youth* (5–8). 1996, Lee & Low $16.95 (978-1-880000-45-8). This book contains a sampling of the thousands of letters sent to civil rights leader Rosa Parks and her replies. (Rev: BL 12/1/96; SLJ 12/96) [323]

19434 Pinkney, Andrea Davis. *Martin and Mahalia: His Words, Her Song* (2–4). Illus. by Brian Pinkney. 2013, Little, Brown $17.99 (978-0-316-07013-3). 40pp. Reviews the contributions to the civil rights movement of Martin Luther King Jr. and Mahalia Jackson. ALA Notable Children's Book; Booklist Editors' Choice: Books for Youth. (Rev: BL 4/1/13*; LMC 8–9/13; SLJ 7/13*)

19435 Pinkney, Andrea Davis. *Sit-In: How Four Friends Stood Up by Sitting Down* (2–4). Illus. by Brian Pinkney. 2010, Little, Brown $16.99 (978-0-316-07016-4). 40pp. When four young black men sat down at a whites-only lunch counter in Greensboro, North Carolina, their courage helped set the ball rolling toward integration. (Rev: BL 2/1/10*; LMC 10/10; SLJ 4/1/10*) [323.1196]

19436 Price, Sean. *When Will I Get In?* (4–6). Series: American History Through Primary Sources. 2006, Raintree LB $28.21 (978-1-4109-2414-8); paper $7.99 (978-1-4109-2425-4). An introduction for reluctant readers to the history of segregation and the important moments and people that were part of the fight for equal rights. (Rev: BL 2/1/07)

19437 Rappaport, Doreen. *Nobody Gonna Turn Me 'Round* (4–7). Illus. by Shane W. Evans. 2006, Candlewick $19.99 (978-0-7636-1927-5). 64pp. This concluding volume of a trilogy documenting the black experience in America focuses on the stormy decade between the Montgomery bus boycott and the signing of the Voting Rights Act in August 1965, providing profiles of key figures. (Rev: BL 8/06; SLJ 10/06)

19438 Rappaport, Doreen. *The School Is Not White!* (2–4). Illus. by Curtis James. 2005, Hyperion $16.99 (978-0-7868-1838-9). 32pp. This inspiring true story chronicles the courageous 1960s campaign by Mae Bertha and Matthew Carter, African American sharecroppers, to ensure that their children receive a quality education. (Rev: BL 2/1/05)

19439 Rossi, Ann. *Created Equal: Women Campaign for the Right to Vote, 1* (4–6). Series: Crossroads America. 2005, National Geographic LB $21.90 (978-0-7922-8285-3). 40pp. The campaign for women's right to vote is placed in historical context through period photographs, cartoons, and primary source material; biographical information is provided for key individuals. (Rev: SLJ 4/05)

19440 Rossi, Ann. *Freedom Struggle: The Anti-Slavery Movement in America, 1830–1865* (4–6). Series: Crossroads America. 2005, National Geographic LB $21.90 (978-0-7922-8061-3). 40pp. Efforts to abolish slavery in the mid-19th century are placed in historical context through period photographs, cartoons, and primary source material; biographical information is provided for key individuals. (Rev: BL 4/1/04; SLJ 4/05)

19441 Seidman, David. *Civil Rights* (4–6). Series: Individual Rights and Civic Responsibility. 2001, Rosen LB $26.50 (978-0-8239-3231-3). 128pp. Covers civil rights issues involving African Americans, women, Native Americans, immigrants, prisoners, and gays and lesbians. (Rev: BL 3/15/02; SLJ 2/02)

19442 Shore, Diane Z., and Jessica Alexander. *This Is the Dream* (2–4). Illus. by James Ransome. 2006, HarperCollins $16.99 (978-0-06-055519-1). Mixing archival photographs, newspaper clippings, original paintings, and rhythmic verse, the creators of this book tell the story of the civil rights movement in an unusual and effective way. (Rev: BL 2/1/06*; SLJ 1/06)

19443 Slade, Suzanne. *Climbing Lincoln's Steps: The African American Journey* (2–5). Illus. by Colin Bootman. 2010, Whitman $16.99 (978-0-8075-1204-3). 32pp. Using the Lincoln Memorial as a backdrop, this attractive picture book touches on key events in civil rights history — from the Emancipation Proclamation to the election of President Obama. (Rev: BL 9/15/10; LMC 11–12/10; SLJ 8/1/10) [305.800973]

19444 Stokes, John A., and Lois Wolfe. *Students on Strike: Jim Crow, Civil Rights, Brown, and Me* (5–8). 2008, National Geographic $15.95 (978-1-4263-0153-7). The author recounts his days on strike to protest the conditions at a black high school in Virginia in 1951 and explains how this strike helped lead to school desegregation in the 1960s. (Rev: BL 3/15/08; SLJ 4/08) [371.829]

19445 Tonatiuh, Duncan. *Separate Is Never Equal: Sylvia Mendez and Her Family's Fight for Desegregation* (2–5). Illus. by author. 2014, Abrams $18.95 (978-1-41971054-4). 40pp. Eight-year-old Sylvia Mendez, of Mexican and Puerto Rican heritage, played a key role in a 1946 desegregation case in California. (Rev: BL 5/1/14; SLJ 5/14*) [379.2]

19446 Turck, Mary C. *The Civil Rights Movement for Kids: A History with 21 Activities* (4–8). 2000, Chicago Review paper $14.95 (978-1-55652-370-0). The story of the civil rights movement with coverage of key events and personalities plus a number of related activities. (Rev: SLJ 10/00) [973.9]

19447 Venable, Rose. *The Civil Rights Movement* (4–6). Series: Journey to Freedom: The African American Library. 2001, Child's World LB $28.50 (978-1-56766-917-6). 40pp. An oversize, attractive volume that supplies details on the 20th-century civil rights movement in the United States, its leaders, and their accomplishments. (Rev: BL 12/15/01; HBG 3/02; SLJ 1/02)

19448 Walker, Paul Robert. *Remember Little Rock: The Time, the People, the Stories* (4–7). Illus. 2008, National Geographic $17.95 (978-1-4263-0402-6). 64pp. This title offers a dramatic and solidly researched account of the attempt to integrate an all-white school in Little Rock, Arkansas, in September 1957, with eyewitness accounts and news photography. (Rev: BL 2/1/09; SLJ 3/09*) [379.2]

19449 Welch, Catherine A. *Children of the Civil Rights Era* (3–6). Series: Picture the American Past. 2001, Carolrhoda LB $22.60 (978-1-57505-481-0). 48pp. Large historical photographs and a simple text are used to describe how young people participated in America's civil rights movement. (Rev: BL 6/1–15/01; HBG 10/01)

19450 Wilson, Reginald. *Think About Our Rights: Civil Liberties and the United States* (5–8). 1991, Walker LB $15.85 (978-0-8027-8127-7); paper $9.95 (978-0-8027-7371-5). The focus is on such civil rights questions as integration, affirmative action, and women's rights. (Rev: SLJ 1/92) [323.4]

Constitution

19451 Allen, Kathy. *The U.S. Constitution* (PS–2). Illus. 2006, Capstone $21.26 (978-0-7368-9594-1). This large-format picture book offers a child-friendly, very basic introduction to the U.S. Constitution. (Rev: BL 10/1/06)

19452 Baer, Nadja. *The United States Constitution: A Round Table Comic* (5–8). Illus. by Nathan Lueth. 2012, Round Table Comics paper $12.95 (978-16106602-5-9). 80pp. This fresh offering presents a graphic-novel take on the creation of the U.S. Constitution, and includes little-known facts and trivia. (Rev: BL 5/15/12; LMC 1–2/13*) [342.7302]

19453 Burgan, Michael. *The Bill of Rights* (4–6). Series: We the People. 2001, Compass Point LB $26.60 (978-0-7565-0151-8). 48pp. Burgan discusses the reasons behind the creation of the Bill of Rights, with paintings, maps, and documents. (Rev: SLJ 1/02)

19454 Catrow, David. *We the Kids* (PS–3). Illus. 2002, Dial $16.99 (978-0-8037-2553-9). 32pp. A visually engaging, straightforward interpretation of the constitution for young readers. (Rev: BL 3/15/02; HBG 10/02; SLJ 5/02)

19455 Eck, Kristin. *Drafting the Constitution: Weighing the Evidence to Draw Sound Conclusions* (5–8). Series: Critical Thinking in American History. 2005, Rosen LB $26.50 (978-1-4042-0412-6). This slim volume offers a review of the issues debated at the Constitutional Convention, plus study questions, a reading list, and a Web site with links to related online resources. (Rev: BL 10/15/05) [342.7302]

19456 Feinberg, Barbara S. *Constitutional Amendments* (5–8). Series: Inside Government. 1996, Twenty-First Century LB $22.40 (978-0-8050-4619-9). After presenting a brief history of the Constitution, this work examines the Bill of Rights and then covers the remaining amendments in chapters arranged by topic. (Rev: SLJ 12/96) [342.73]

19457 Finkelman, Paul. *The Constitution* (4–8). Series: American Documents. 2006, National Geographic LB $23.90 (978-0-7922-7975-4). An unusually attractive introduction to the Constitution, with reproductions, photographs, and profiles of key individuals. (Rev: SLJ 2/06; VOYA 8/06) [342.73]

19458 Freedman, Russell. *In Defense of Liberty: The Story of America's Bill of Rights* (5–10). 2003, Holiday $24.95 (978-0-8234-1585-4). 196pp. A succinct explanation of the history of the Bill of Rights, discussing each amendment in turn and its particular relevance to today's controversies, with many references to cases involving young people. (Rev: BCCB 10/03*; BL 10/1/03*; HB 9/03*; HBG 4/04; SLJ 10/03*; VOYA 4/04)

19459 Gerber, Larry. *The Second Amendment: The Right to Bear Arms* (5–8). Illus. Series: Amendments to the United States Constitution: The Bill of Rights. 2011, Rosen $29.95 (978-144881253-0). 64pp. This thorough, unbiased offering discusses the historical roots, political implications, and court cases pertaining to the Second Amendment. (Rev: BL 4/1/11) [344.7305]

19460 Gonzales, Doreen. *A Look at the Second Amendment: To Keep and Bear Arms* (4–7). Illus. Series: MyReportLinks.com. 2007, Enslow LB $24.95 (978-1-59845-061-3). Links to relevant Web sites enhance the text introducing students to the content and intent of the Second Amendment to the United States Constitution. (Rev: BL 10/15/07; LMC 11/07; SLJ 1/08) [344.7305]

19461 Graham, Amy. *A Look at the 18th and 21st Amendments: The Prohibition and Sale of Intoxicating Liquors* (5–8). Illus. Series: The Constitution of the United States. 2007, Enslow LB $33.27 (978-1-59845-063-7). 128pp. A clear overview of these two amendments with links to Web sites that offer additional information. (Rev: SLJ 1/08)

19462 Horn, Geoffrey M. *The Bill of Rights and Other Amendments* (5–8). Series: World Almanac Library of American Government. 2004, World Almanac LB $31.00 (978-0-8368-5475-6). 48pp. A thorough and detailed examination of the process of changing the Constitution and the issues underlying the various amendments. (Rev: SLJ 9/04)

19463 Hubbard-Brown, Janet. *How the Constitution Was Created* (5–8). Series: The U.S. Government: How It Works. 2007, Chelsea House LB $30.00 (978-0-7910-9420-4). 104pp. This is a thorough introduction to the Constitution, with interesting text and accompanying historical and biographical sidebars. (Rev: SLJ 1/08)

19464 Hudson, David L. *The Bill of Rights* (5–8). Illus. Series: The Constitution. 2002, Enslow LB $26.60 (978-0-7660-1903-4). 128pp. A look at the first 10 amendments to the Constitution and how they have affected the citizens of the United States. (Rev: BL 2/15/03; HBG 3/03)

19465 Hudson, David L. *The Fourteenth Amendment: Equal Protection Under the Law* (5–8). Illus. Series: The Constitution. 2002, Enslow LB $26.60 (978-0-7660-1904-1). What the 14th amendment to the Constitution entails and how it has affected the citizens of the United States. (Rev: BL 2/15/03; HBG 10/03)

19466 Krull, Kathleen. *A Kids' Guide to America's Bill of Rights: Curfews, Censorship, and the 100-Pound Giant* (5–8). 1999, Avon $16.99 (978-0-380-97497-9). After a description of the first 10 amendments, this book details famous court cases and what each amendment means to young people. (Rev: BL 12/1/99; HBG 3/00; VOYA 4/00) [342.73]

19467 Levert, Suzanne. *The Constitution* (2–5). Series: Kaleidoscope. 2002, Benchmark LB $25.64 (978-0-7614-1452-0). 48pp. An accessible overview of Constitution, its history, and its impact on the government of the united States. (Rev: HBG 3/03; SLJ 4/03)

19468 Sobel, Syl. *The U.S. Constitution and You* (3–5). Illus. by Denise Gilgannon. 2001, Barron's paper $6.95 (978-0-7641-1707-7). 48pp. Clear text and pen-and-ink sketches provide a concise look at the importance of the Constitution, with chapters on checks and balances and the rights of the people and of the states. (Rev: SLJ 8/01)

19469 Taylor-Butler, Christine. *The Bill of Rights* (3–5). Illus. Series: True Book: American History. 2007, Scholastic LB $26.00 (978-0-531-12627-1); paper $6.95 (978-0-531-14777-1). A visually engaging introduction to the basics of the Bill of Rights with fast facts, resource list, and glossary. (Rev: BL 1/1–15/08)

19470 Weidner, Daniel. *The Constitution: The Preamble and the Articles* (5–8). Series: The Constitution. 2002, Enslow LB $26.60 (978-0-7660-1906-5). 112pp. The history of the U.S. Constitution and its meanings are explored through personal stories and examples. (Rev: BL 2/15/03; HBG 3/03; SLJ 1/03)

19471 Weidner, Daniel. *Creating the Constitution: The People and Events That Formed the Nation* (5–8). Series: The Constitution. 2002, Enslow LB $26.60 (978-0-7660-1905-8). 112pp. This informative volume describes how the U.S. Constitution was written and the debates that preceded its adoption. (Rev: BL 2/15/03; HBG 3/03; SLJ 1/03)

Crime and Criminals

19472 Aaseng, Nathan. *Treacherous Traitors* (5–9). Series: Profiles. 1997, Oliver LB $19.95 (978-1-881508-38-0). This book profiles 12 Americans who were tried for treason, including Benedict Arnold, John Brown, Alger Hiss, Julius and Ethel Rosenberg, and Aldrich Ames. (Rev: SLJ 2/98) [355.3]

19473 Beres, D. B. *Dusted and Busted! The Science of Fingerprinting* (4–8). Illus. Series: 24/7: Science Behind the Scenes: Forensic Files. 2007, Watts LB $25.00 (978-0-531-11822-1); paper $7.95 (978-0-531-15457-1). Introduces the scientific process of fingerprinting through easy-to-read text, illustrations, and real-life examples. (Rev: SLJ 7/07)

19474 Beres, D. B. *Killer at Large* (3–6). Series: 24/7: Science Behind the Scenes. 2007, Watts LB $25.00 (978-0-531-12065-1); paper $7.95 (978-0-531-17526-2). 64pp. The profiling techniques used to track down murderers is explained in three real-life case studies. Readers meet people working in this field and learn how they got there. (Rev: SLJ 6/07)

19475 Blackwood, Gary L. *Gangsters* (4–7). Series: Bad Guys. 2001, Benchmark LB $28.50 (978-0-7614-1016-4). 72pp. Al Capone is just one of the evildoers profiled in this volume that gives historical context for each "bad guy." Also use *Outlaws* and *Highwaymen* (both 2001). (Rev: HBG 3/02; SLJ 1/02)

19476 Butterfield, Moira. *Pirates and Smugglers* (5–7). Series: Kingfisher Knowledge. 2005, Kingfisher paper $12.95 (978-0-7534-5864-8). A broad historical survey of outlaws on the high seas, from early smugglers to today's dealers in drugs and exotic animals. (Rev: SLJ 12/05)

19477 Dahl, Michael. *Computer Evidence* (4–8). Illus. Series: Forensic Crime Solvers. 2004, Capstone LB $23.93 (978-0-7368-2698-3). 32pp. After a story that draws the readers in, Dahl looks at the use of computer evidence in tracking down and convicting criminals. Also use *Poison Evidence* (2004). (Rev: BL 5/1/04)

19478 Denega, Danielle. *Gut-Eating Bugs: Maggots Reveal the Time of Death!* (3–6). Series: 24/7: Science Behind the Scenes. 2007, Watts LB $25.00 (978-0-531-11824-5); paper $7.95 (978-0-531-17525-5). 64pp. An obscure branch of forensics, forensic entomology, is explained here in a format that will interest many readers. (Rev: SLJ 6/07)

19479 Denega, Danielle. *Have You Seen This Face? The Work of Forensic Artists* (4–8). Illus. Series: 24/7: Science Behind the Scenes: Forensic Files. 2007, Watts LB $25.00 (978-0-531-11823-9); paper $7.95 (978-0-531-15458-8). 64pp. Introduces the work of forensic artists through easy-to-read text, illustrations, and real-life examples. (Rev: SLJ 7/07)

19480 Earnest, Peter, and Suzanne Harper. *The Real Spy's Guide to Becoming a Spy* (4–8). Illus. by Bret Bertholf. 2009, Abrams $16.95 (978-0-8109-8329-8). 144pp. This guide to spying covers skills and training, tactics, jargon, and true-life stories. (Rev: SLJ 10/09; VOYA 12/09) [27.1200]

19481 Farman, John. *The Short and Bloody History of Spies* (5–8). 2002, Lerner LB $19.93 (978-0-8225-0845-8); paper $5.95 (978-0-8225-0846-5). A witty and fascinating account of the intriguing lives of spies, with descriptions of spying techniques and gadgets. (Rev: BL 1/1–15/03; HBG 3/03) [327.12]

19482 Fridell, Ron. *Forensic Science* (4–7). Series: Cool Science. 2006, Lerner LB $25.25 (978-0-8225-5935-1). The history of forensic science from 1910 to today is accompanied by information on the professionals involved (medical examiners, forensic entomologists) and the equipment used; effective photographs add to the appeal. (Rev: SLJ 4/07) [363.25]

19483 Fridell, Ron. *Spy Technology* (4–7). Series: Cool Science. 2006, Lerner LB $26.60 (978-0-8225-5934-4). 48pp. A review of the kinds of technology available in the past and today — including gadgets used by the CIA and KGB and spy satellites — is followed by accounts of dangerous missions and discussion of future technologies. (Rev: SLJ 4/07) [623]

19484 Friedlander, Mark P., Jr., and Terry M. Phillips. *When Objects Talk: Solving a Crime with Science* (5–8). Illus. Series: Discovery! 2001, Lerner LB $27.93 (978-0-8225-0649-2). 120pp. A fictional mystery serves to introduce criminal investigation techniques such as fingerprints and DNA. (Rev: HBG 3/02; SLJ 2/02; VOYA 2/02)

19485 Gardner, Robert. *Who Forged This Document? Crime-Solving Science Project* (4–7). 2010, Enslow LB $23.93 (978-0-7660-3246-0). 48pp. After a review of the scientific method, this volume explores methods of analyzing handwriting, identifying types of paper, exposing counterfeit money, and so forth, with suggestions for science fair projects. (Rev: LMC 3–4/10; SLJ 7/10) [363.25]

19486 Gardner, Robert. *Whose Bones Are These? Crime-Solving Science Projects* (4–6). Illus. Series: Who Dunnit? Forensic Science Experiments. 2010, Enslow LB $23.93 (978-0-7660-3248-4). 48pp. After an introduction discussing science fairs and the scientific method, Gardner discusses various aspects of using bodies, blood, and other evidence to solve crimes and offers a related project for each. Also use *Whose Fingerprints Are These?* (2010). (Rev: LMC 3–4/10; SLJ 5/10) [614]

19487 Gifford, Clive. *Spies* (5–9). Series: Kingfisher Knowledge. 2004, Kingfisher LB $11.95 (978-0-7534-5777-1). Stories of notable espionage achievements are included along with brisk facts, plenty of high-interest illustrations, a history of spying, and discussion of the future of this field. (Rev: BL 9/1/04; SLJ 5/05)

19488 Gordon, Olivia. *Cold Case File: Murder in the Mountains* (5–8). Series: Crime Solvers. 2007, Bearport LB $25.27 (978-1-59716-547-1). After a description of the crime, the victim (a photographer who disappeared in the Rockies in the 1970s), and the accused, Gordon recounts the steps taken in the nearly 20-year effort to find the body and solve the crime. "Crime Solving Up Close" looks at forensic terminology. (Rev: LMC 1/08; SLJ 11/07)

19489 Graham, Ian. *Forensic Technology* (4–7). Illus. Series: New Technology. 2011, Black Rabbit LB $34.25 (978-159920532-8). 48pp. Describes the technology being used in investigating, deaths, fires and explosions, fakes and forgeries, and computer crimes, as well as the importance of print evidence and DNA profiling. (Rev: BL 10/15/11) [363.25]

19490 Head, Honor. *Famous Spies* (5–8). Series: Spies and Spying. 2010, Smart Apple $28.50 (978-1-59920-358-4). 32pp. Different types of espionage are explored in readable, eye-catching profiles with sidebars covering technology and codes. (Rev: LMC 1–2/10)

19491 Higgins, Melissa. *The Night Dad Went to Jail: What to Expect When Someone You Love Goes to Jail* (K–3). Illus. by Wednesday Kirwan. Series: Life's Challenges. 2011, Capstone LB $25.32 (978-140486679-9). 24pp. Policemen, social workers, and support groups are among the factors introduced in this explanation of what happens when someone has to go to jail. (Rev: BL 10/1/11) [362.82]

19492 Howard, Amanda. *Kidnapping File: The Graeme Thorne Case* (3–6). Series: Crime Solvers. 2007, Bearport LB $25.27 (978-1-59716-548-8). 32pp. An attention-grabbing account of the kidnapping of an 8-year-old boy, with details of the steps investigators took to solve the crime. Also use *Robbery File: The Museum Heist* (2007). (Rev: LMC 1/08; SLJ 11/07)

19493 Johnson, Julie. *Why Do People Join Gangs?* (5–8). Series: Exploring Tough Issues. 2001, Raintree LB $25.69 (978-0-7398-3236-3). 48pp. Johnson looks at gangs — who joins them and why, and how to get out of one — in the United States and abroad, and includes a chapter on dealing with bullies. Also use *Why Do People Fight Wars?* and *Why Are People Prejudiced?* (both 2002). (Rev: SLJ 11/01)

19494 Joyce, Jaime. *Bullet Proof! The Evidence That Guns Leave Behind* (5–10). Series: 24/7: Science Behind the Scenes. 2007, Watts LB $25.00 (978-0-531-11820-7); paper $7.95 (978-0-531-15455-7). 64pp. Joyce uses three real cases to illustrate how ballistics experts can help to solve crimes; reluctant readers will enjoy this. (Rev: SLJ 8/07)

19495 McDonald, Fiona. *You Wouldn't Want to Meet a Body Snatcher: Criminals and Murderers You'd Rather Avoid* (3–6). Illus. by David Antram. 2009, Scholastic LB $29.00 (978-0-531-20822-9); paper $9.95 (978-0-531-21046-8). 32pp. A lighthearted review of evildoers through the ages. (Rev: BLO 3/17/09)

19496 Mooney, Carla. *Forensics: Uncover the Science and Technology of Crime Scene Investigation* (4–7). Illus. by Samuel Carbaugh. 2013, Nomad $21.95 (978-161930188-7); paper $16.95 (978-16193018-4-9). 128pp. Blood evidence, bone analysis, and fingerprints are among the topics covered in this overview of foren-

sics that includes actiivities. ℮ (Rev: BL 7/13; SLJ 7/13) [363.25]

19497 Pentland, Peter, and Pennie Stoyles. *Forensic Science* (4–6). Illus. Series: Science and Scientists. 2002, Chelsea House LB $28.00 (978-0-7910-7010-9). 32pp. An overview of how blood types, fingerprints, and DNA profiling figure in forensic science, and of the career itself, with illustrations and interesting sidebars. (Rev: HBG 3/03; SLJ 4/03)

19498 Platt, Richard. *Forensics* (5–10). Series: Kingfisher Knowledge. 2005, Kingfisher paper $12.95 (978-0-7534-5862-4). This introduction to the use of the forensic sciences in crime investigation is presented in short blocks of text that will make it appealing to reluctant readers. (Rev: SLJ 11/05) [363.2]

19499 Prokos, Anna. *Guilty by a Hair! Real-Life DNA Matches!* (4–8). Illus. Series: 24/7: Science Behind the Scenes: Forensic Files. 2007, Watts LB $25.00 (978-0-531-11821-4); paper $7.95 (978-0-531-18733-3). 64pp. In clear, engaging prose with illustrations and real-life examples, this volume discusses the science behind DNA analysis used in crime investigations. (Rev: SLJ 7/07)

19500 Prokos, Anna. *Killer Wallpaper: True Cases of Deadly Poisonings* (5–10). Series: 24/7: Science Behind the Scenes. 2007, Watts LB $25.00 (978-0-531-12061-3); paper $7.95 (978-0-531-15459-5). 64pp. Prokos uses three real cases to illustrate the work of forensic toxicologists; reluctant readers will enjoy this. (Rev: SLJ 8/07)

19501 Rainis, Kenneth G. *Crime-Solving Science Projects: Forensic Science Experiments* (5–9). 2000, Enslow LB $26.60 (978-0-7660-1289-9). After defining forensic science, this book contains experiments and projects involving such areas as fingerprints, inks, writing samples, fibers, forgeries, and blood evidence. (Rev: HBG 10/01; SLJ 2/01) [363.2]

19502 Rainis, Kenneth G. *Forgery: Crime-Solving Science Experiments* (4–8). Series: Forensic Science Projects. 2006, Enslow LB $31.93 (978-0-7660-1961-4). Rainis explores how forensic scientists identify forgeries, with 10 interesting case studies. (Rev: SLJ 5/07) [363.25]

19503 Rollins, Barbara B., and Michael Dahl. *Ballistics* (4–7). Series: Edge Books, Forensic Crime Solvers. 2004, Capstone LB $23.93 (978-0-7368-2421-7). 32pp. Report writers and reluctant readers will be attracted to this brief, concise discussion of the science of ballistics. (Rev: BL 5/1/04; SLJ 8/04)

19504 Rollins, Barbara B., and Michael Dahl. *Blood Evidence* (4–8). Series: Forensic Crime Solvers. 2004, Capstone LB $23.93 (978-0-7368-2418-7). Reluctant readers will be attracted to the gruesome nature of the subject matter and the often lurid presentation of facts. (Rev: BL 5/1/04; SLJ 8/04) [363.25]

19505 Rollins, Barbara B., and Michael Dahl. *Cause of Death* (4–8). Series: Forensic Crime Solvers. 2004, Capstone LB $23.93 (978-0-7368-2420-0). This look at how crime scene technicians and medical examiners determine cause of death will draw in reluctant readers. (Rev: BL 5/1/04; SLJ 8/04) [614]

19506 Rollins, Barbara B., and Michael Dahl. *Fingerprint Evidence* (4–7). Series: Edge Books, Forensic Crime Solvers. 2004, Capstone LB $23.93 (978-0-7368-2419-4). After a story that draws the readers in, the authors describe the features of fingerprints and discusses their use in solving crimes. (Rev: BL 5/1/04; SLJ 8/04) [363.25]

19507 Ross, Stewart. *Spies and Traitors* (5–8). Series: Fact or Fiction? 1995, Millbrook LB $26.90 (978-1-56294-648-7). A history of the people who have placed themselves above their country in the dangerous game of espionage and betrayal. (Rev: BL 11/15/95; SLJ 3/96) [355.3]

19508 Schroeder, Andreas. *Robbers! True Stories of the World's Most Notorious Thieves* (4–8). Illus. by Remy Simard. 2012, Annick $21.95 (978-155451441-0); paper $12.95 (978-15545144-0-3). 160pp. Schroeder offers eight well-written accounts of criminal masterminds and their bank robberies, art thefts, and other heists. (Rev: BL 11/15/12; SLJ 2/13) [364.15]

19509 Schroeder, Andreas. *Scams!* (5–8). Series: True Stories from the Edge. 2004, Annick $18.95 (978-1-55037-853-5); paper $7.95 (978-1-55037-852-8). Ten stories reveal daring trickery, con jobs, and scams, including the 1938 radio broadcast of *War of the Worlds* that terrified millions of Americans and the baseless claim that a tribe of cavemen had been found living in a remote corner of the Philippines. (Rev: SLJ 8/04) [364.16]

19510 Schroeder, Andreas. *Thieves!* (5–10). Series: True Stories from the Edge. 2005, Annick $18.95 (978-1-55037-933-4); paper $8.95 (978-1-55037-932-7). Ten world-class crimes are described in compelling detail. (Rev: SLJ 3/06) [364]

19511 Spilsbury, Richard. *Bones Speak! Solving Crimes from the Past* (5–9). 2009, Enslow $23.93 (978-0-7660-3377-1). 48pp. Spilsbury provides a thorough overview of all things forensic, covering everything from insect evidence to careers in this field. (Rev: LMC 11–12/09; SLJ 11/1/09) [363.2]

19512 Spilsbury, Richard. *Zoom In on Crime Scenes* (4–7). Illus. 2013, Enslow LB $22.60 (978-076604311-4). 32pp. In chapters such as "Unique Fingerprints," "Hairy Hints," and "Details in the Dust," this volume looks at how the police investigate evidence at a crime scene. (Rev: BL 10/1/13; LMC 8–9/14) [363.25]

19513 Stiefel, Chana. *Fingerprints: Dead People Do Tell Tales* (5–7). Illus. Series: True Forensic Crime Stories. 2011, Enslow LB $31.93 (978-076603689-5). 104pp. Looking at what makes fingerprints unique, how they are located, and the ways in which criminals try to hide their fingerprints, this is a useful volume for young researchers. (Rev: BL 10/1/11) [363.25]

19514 Townsend, John. *Bone Detectives* (4–6). Series: Crabtree Contact. 2008, Crabtree LB $26.60 (978-0-7787-3806-0); paper $8.95 (978-0-7787-3828-2). 32pp.

A body is discovered and forensic scientists swing into action, examining the skeleton and seeking clues to the victim in fingerprints, teeth, and so forth. Also use *Forensic Evidence: Prints* (2008). (Rev: SLJ 3/09)

19515 Townsend, John. *Breakouts and Blunders* (5–8). Series: True Crime. 2005, Raintree LB $31.43 (978-1-4109-1427-9). Attempted and successful escapes through history are the subject of this book in the True Crime series, which features a scrapbook format with engaging photographs and graphics. Also use *Fakes and Forgeries* and *Kidnappers and Assassins* (both 2005). (Rev: SLJ 6/06) [365.641]

19516 Townsend, John. *Famous Forensic Cases* (5–7). Illus. Series: Amazing Crime Scene Science. 2011, Amicus LB $19.95 (978-160753169-2). 32pp. A chronological look at forensic science from early fingerprinting through DNA developments with case studies of particular interest. (Rev: BL 12/1/11) [363.25]

19517 Webber, Diane. *Do You Read Me? Famous Cases Solved by Handwriting Analysis!* (5–10). Series: 24/7: Science Behind the Scenes. 2007, Watts LB $25.00 (978-0-531-12066-8); paper $7.95 (978-0-531-15456-4). 64pp. Webber uses three real cases to illustrate ways in which the study of handwriting can help to solve crimes; reluctant readers will enjoy this. (Rev: SLJ 8/07)

19518 West, David. *Detective Work with Ballistics* (4–7). Illus. by Emanuele Boccanfuso. Series: Graphic Forensic Science. 2008, Rosen LB $21.95 (978-1-4042-1434-7). Graphic-novel-like depictions of actual cases in which ballistic evidence pointed to the culprit make this an interesting introduction to this forensic specialty. (Rev: BL 3/15/08) [363.25]

19519 Wiese, Jim. *Detective Science: 40 Crime-Solving, Case-Breaking, Crook-Catching Activities for Kids* (4–7). 1996, Wiley paper $12.95 (978-0-471-11980-7). Presents 40 experiments and activities that illustrate techniques in forensic science related to observing, collecting, and analyzing evidence. (Rev: BL 4/15/96; SLJ 6/96) [363.2]

19520 Winchester, Elizabeth Siris. *The Right Bite: Dentists as Detectives* (4–8). Series: Digital and Information Literacy. 2007, Scholastic LB $26.00 (978-0-531-12062-0); paper $7.95 (978-0-531-18734-0). Conversational text focuses on the work of forensic dentists and offers multiple (sometimes gruesome) examples of cases in which their findings identified victims and perpetrators; factual inserts add interest and a final section discusses the equipment used. (Rev: BL 4/1/07; SLJ 6/07) [001.4]

19521 Woodford, Chris. *Criminal Investigation* (4–8). Illus. Series: Science Fact Files. 2001, Raintree LB $27.12 (978-0-7398-1016-3). 45pp. A concise introduction to the forensic science with information on the newest equipment and techniques. (Rev: HBG 10/01; SLJ 1/02)

19522 Yaffe, Rebecca M., and Lonnie F. Hoade. *When a Parent Goes to Jail: A Comprehensive Guide for Counseling Children of Incarcerated Parents* (3–5). Illus. by Barbara S. Moody. 2000, Rayve $49.95 (978-1-877810-08-4). This book about adults in trouble with the law goes through the incarceration process from arrest to sentencing. (Rev: SLJ 12/00)

Elections and Political Parties

19523 Anderson, Dale. *The Democratic Party: America's Oldest Party* (5–8). Series: Snapshots in History. 2007, Compass Point LB $31.93 (978-0-7565-2450-0). This well-designed book provides a thorough, unbiased history of the Democratic Party and includes sidebars, charts, photographs, maps, and Web sites. (Rev: SLJ 7/07) [324.2736]

19524 Anderson, Dale. *The Republican Party: The Story of the Grand Old Party* (5–8). Series: Snapshots in History. 2007, Compass Point LB $31.93 (978-0-7565-2449-4). This history of the Republican Party presents a balanced view of the how the party formed, its values, and its highs and lows since its formation. (Rev: SLJ 7/07) [324.273]

19525 Andryszewski, Tricia. *The Reform Party* (5–8). Series: Headliners. 2000, Millbrook LB $25.90 (978-0-7613-1906-1). This book describes the formation of the Reform Party and highlights the work of Ross Perot, Pat Buchanan, and Jesse Ventura. (Rev: BL 8/00; HBG 10/01; SLJ 1/01)

19526 Ansary, Mir T. *Election Day* (2–3). Illus. Series: Holiday Histories. 2002, Heinemann LB $21.36 (978-1-58810-221-8). 32pp. A brief history and overview of the U.S. presidential election system. (Rev: BL 2/1/02)

19527 Christelow, Eileen. *Vote!* (2–5). 2003, Houghton LB $16.00 (978-0-618-24754-7). 48pp. A mayoral campaign — with comic-book style art and commentary by politically minded dogs — serves to illustrate the voting process and teach helpful lessons about such related issues as voting rights, registration, fund raising, and ballot recounts. (Rev: BL 11/1/03; HBG 4/04; SLJ 12/03)

19528 De Capua, Sarah. *Running for Public Office* (2–5). Series: True Books — Civics. 2002, Children's Book Pr. LB $25.00 (978-0-516-22333-9); paper $6.95 (978-0-516-27368-6). 48pp. A simple, large-type text and many photographs are used to introduce the positions open in public office and the steps in running for these positions, including campaigning and elections. (Rev: BL 6/1–15/02; SLJ 10/02)

19529 De Capua, Sarah. *Voting* (2–5). Series: True Books — Civics. 2002, Children's Book Pr. paper $6.95 (978-0-516-27365-5). 48pp. The election system is introduced in simple, large-type text with plenty of attractive color photographs. (Rev: BL 6/1–15/02)

19530 Donovan, Sandy. *Running for Office: A Look at Political Campaigns* (4–6). Illus. Series: How Government Works. 2004, Lerner LB $25.26 (978-0-8225-4700-6). 56pp. The fictional tale of Samantha Brown's campaign for election as a state senator serves as a framework for details about all aspects of electioneering. (Rev: BL 5/1/04; HBG 4/04)

19531 Giddens-White, Bryon. *National Elections and the Political Process* (4–6). Series: Our Government. 2005, Heinemann LB $28.21 (978-1-4034-6604-4). This explanation of how elections in the United States work will be useful for report writers. (Rev: SLJ 5/06)

19532 Gottfried, Ted. *The 2000 Election* (5–8). Illus. 2002, Millbrook LB $25.90 (978-0-7613-2406-5). 64pp. A well-designed and detailed look at the controversial presidential election of 2000, with background information, sidebars on important people, and an electoral map and other graphics. (Rev: BL 7/02; HBG 10/02; SLJ 4/02)

19533 Granfield, Linda. *America Votes: How Our President Is Elected* (4–6). 2003, Kids Can $16.95 (978-1-55337-086-4); paper $9.95 (978-1-55337-087-1). This is an appealing and clear explanation of the American presidential election process, from qualifications for voting through such issues as election fraud and the role of television. (Rev: BL 9/15/03; HBG 4/04; SLJ 12/03)

19534 Hamilton, John. *Running for Office* (3–5). Series: Government in Action! 2005, ABDO LB $22.78 (978-1-59197-822-0). 32pp. All about how one goes about being elected to public office, with discussion of the differences between the two major U.S. parties. (Rev: SLJ 7/05)

19535 Hewson, Martha S. *The Electoral College* (5–9). 2002, Chelsea $25.00 (978-0-7910-6790-1). Covers the history of the electoral college and details of elections of particular interest, including the 2000 Bush–Gore decision. (Rev: HBG 3/03; SLJ 2/03)

19536 Horn, Geoffrey M. *Political Parties, Interest Groups, and the Media* (5–8). Series: World Almanac Library of American Government. 2004, World Almanac LB $31.00 (978-0-8368-5478-7). An engaging introduction to the world of politics, the importance of money and lobbying, and the role of the press. (Rev: SLJ 9/04) [324]

19537 Landau, Elaine. *Friendly Foes: A Look at Political Parties* (4–6). Illus. Series: How Government Works. 2003, Lerner LB $25.26 (978-0-8225-1349-0). 56pp. Discusses the two major political parties in the United States, with an eye to their differences in such areas as the role of government in society; minority parties are mentioned in a final chapter. (Rev: HBG 4/04; SLJ 3/04)

19538 Landau, Elaine. *The 2000 Presidential Election* (2–5). Series: Cornerstones of Freedom, Second Series. 2002, Children's Book Pr. LB $26.00 (978-0-516-22527-2). 48pp. A timeline and informative text help to unravel the events between the 2000 election and Gore's concession speech. (Rev: SLJ 3/03)

19539 Lindop, Edmund. *Political Parties* (5–8). Series: Inside Government. 1996, Twenty-First Century LB $24.90 (978-0-8050-4618-2). This work traces the origins of political parties and the role they play in presidential elections. (Rev: BL 9/15/96; SLJ 12/96) [324.273]

19540 Lutz, Norma Jean. *The History of Third Parties* (4–6). Series: Your Government: How It Works. 2000, Chelsea LB $25.00 (978-0-7910-5541-0). 64pp. The Abolitionists, Liberty Party, Southern Democrats, Nativists, Prohibitionists, Socialists, and Reform Party are a few of the American third parties discussed here. (Rev: HBG 9/00; SLJ 8/00)

19541 Morris-Lipsman, Arlene. *Presidential Races: The Battle for Power in the United States* (5–8). Illus. Series: People's History. 2007, Lerner LB $30.60 (978-0-8225-6783-7). Political cartoons, photographs, and other memorabilia add to the text of this guide to the growth in importance of presidential election campaigns; the author gives pertinent background information on each election and provides a useful chart of election results. (Rev: BL 9/15/07; SLJ 10/07) [324.973]

19542 Murphy, Patricia. *Election Day* (PS–2). Series: Rookie Read-about Holidays. 2003, Children's Book Pr. paper $5.95 (978-0-516-27488-1). In very simple words and pictures, this book describes the activities that occur on the first Tuesday after the first Monday in November. (Rev: BL 3/15/03)

19543 Murphy, Patricia J. *Voting and Elections* (K–2). Series: Let's See. 2001, Compass Point LB $19.93 (978-0-7565-0144-0). 24pp. A simple introduction to the voting process and how you register to vote. (Rev: SLJ 1/02)

19544 Nelson, Robin, and Sandy Donovan. *Getting Elected: A Look at Running for Office* (3–5). Illus. Series: How Does Government Work? 2012, Lerner LB $27.93 (978-076136519-8). 40pp. Using a fictional mayor as a framework, this volume covers the ins and outs of conducting a successful political campaign; includes photographs of actual elections. e (Rev: BL 4/1/12) [324.70973]

19545 Nobleman, Marc Tyler. *Election Day* (1–3). Series: Let's See. 2004, Compass Point LB $19.93 (978-0-7565-0644-5). 24pp. Using a question-and-answer format, large print, and many illustrations, this small book introduces the American election process. (Rev: BL 10/15/04)

19546 Payan, Gregory. *The Federalists and Anti-Federalists: How and Why Political Parties Were Formed in Young America* (4–6). Illus. Series: Life in the New American Nation. 2004, Rosen LB $22.50 (978-0-8239-4038-7). 32pp. The evolution of political parties in America is chronicled from the close of the Constitutional Convention to the present. (Rev: BL 6/1–15/04)

19547 Santella, Andrew. *U.S. Presidential Inaugurations* (3–6). Series: Cornerstones of Freedom, Second Series. 2002, Children's Book Pr. LB $26.00 (978-0-516-22533-3). 48pp. Inaugural addresses, inaugural balls, and inaugural weather are the focus of this narrative, which also explains the role of the Electoral College and its part in the Gore-Bush presidential election. (Rev: SLJ 12/02)

19548 Staton, Hilarie. *The Progressive Party: The Success of a Failed Party* (5–8). Series: Snapshots in History. 2007, Compass Point LB $31.93 (978-0-7565-2451-7). This history of the Progressives is well-organized and shows how the party's agenda moved forward even

though the party itself didn't survive. (Rev: SLJ 7/07) [324.2732]

19549 Stier, Catherine. *If I Ran for President* (3–5). Illus. by Lynne Avril. 2007, Albert Whitman $15.95 (978-0-8075-3543-1). Through narration by six children, Stier explains the U.S. presidential election process in all its stages — from deciding to run through inauguration — with humor and cartoon illustrations. (Rev: BL 11/1/07; LMC 1/08; SLJ 9/07)

19550 Thomas, William David. *How Do We Elect Our Leaders?* (3–5). Illus. Series: My American Government. 2008, Gareth Stevens LB $23.93 (978-0-8368-8860-7); paper $8.95 (978-0-8368-8865-2). 32pp. A story about Ronald Reagan's candidacy introduces this informative volume that covers political parties, primaries and caucuses, conventions, and the election process. (Rev: BL 4/1/08; SLJ 6/08)

19551 Tracy, Kathleen. *The Historic Fight for the 2008 Democratic Presidential Nomination: The Clinton View* (5–8). Series: Monumental Milestones. 2009, Mitchell Lane LB $29.95 (978-1-58415-731-1). 48pp. A brief biography of Hillary Clinton accompanies a detailed account of the campaign to win the Democratic presidential nomination. (Rev: BL 4/1/09; SLJ 4/1/09) [973.931092]

19552 Wagner, Heather Lehr. *How the President Is Elected* (5–8). Series: The U.S. Government: How It Works. 2007, Chelsea House LB $30.00 (978-0-7910-9418-1). This is a thorough introduction to the presidential election process (using the drama of the 2000 election to draw readers in), with interesting text and accompanying historical and biographical sidebars. (Rev: SLJ 1/08)

Federal Government and Agencies

19553 Anderson, Dale. *The FBI Files: Successful Investigations* (5–8). Series: The FBI Story. 2009, Mason Crest LB $22.95 (978-1-4222-0561-7). 64pp. Anderson reviews several FBI success stories using accessible text full of illustrations. Also use *The FBI and White-Collar Crime, The FBI and Organized Crime*, and *The FBI and Civil Rights* (all 2009). (Rev: LMC 5–6/10) [363.25]

19554 Attebury, Nancy Garhan. *Out and About at the United States Mint* (1–3). Illus. by Zachary Trover. Series: Field Trips. 2005, Picture Window LB $26.60 (978-1-4048-1151-5). 24pp. Tour the U.S. Mint along with a group of children and learn about its operations and the money produced there. (Rev: SLJ 2/06)

19555 Bausum, Ann. *Our Country's Presidents* (5–8). 2005, National Geographic LB $45.90 (978-0-7922-9330-9). Full of interesting facts, quotations, and illustrations, this new edition has been extended with information on vice presidents, the Electoral College, and presidential security. (Rev: BL 5/15/05; SLJ 4/05) [973]

19556 Collard III, Sneed B. *The CIA and FBI: Top Secret* (4–7). Illus. Series: Freedom Forces. 2013, Rourke LB $29.95 (978-162169925-5); paper $8.95 (9781621698203). 32pp. Collard unravels some of the differences between these two organizations, examining their methods and roles both before 9/11 and afterward. **e** (Rev: BL 10/1/13) [327.1273]

19557 Crewe, Sabrina. *A History of the FBI* (5–8). Series: The FBI Story. 2009, Mason Crest LB $22.95 (978-1-4222-0563-1). 64pp. A succinct, highly illustrated account of the FBI's creation and significant achievements over the years. Also use *The FBI and Crimes Against Children* (2009) and other volumes in this series. (Rev: LMC 5–6/10; SLJ 4/10) [363.25]

19558 De Capua, Sarah. *Becoming a Citizen* (2–5). Illus. Series: True Books — Civics. 2002, Children's Book Pr. LB $25.00 (978-0-516-22331-5); paper $6.95 (978-0-516-27366-2). 48pp. This work describes the requirements for becoming a U.S. citizen and the steps one must take to become naturalized. (Rev: BL 6/1–15/02; SLJ check)

19559 Donovan, Sandy. *Protecting America: A Look at the People Who Keep Our Country Safe* (4–6). Illus. Series: How Government Works. 2003, Lerner LB $25.26 (978-0-8225-1345-2). 56pp. A look at the U.S. armed forces and at security agencies including the FBI and CIA, all from a post-September 11 vantage point. (Rev: HBG 4/04; SLJ 3/04)

19560 Feldman, Ruth Tenzer. *How Congress Works: A Look at the Legislative Branch* (4–6). Illus. Series: How Government Works. 2004, Lerner LB $25.26 (978-0-8225-1347-6). 56pp. An easily understood explanation of the roles of the two houses of the legislative branch.

19561 Giddens-White, Bryon. *The President and the Executive Branch* (4–6). Series: Our Government. 2005, Heinemann LB $28.21 (978-1-4034-6601-3). 32pp. This clear explanation of the executive power of the president of the United States will be useful for report writers. Also use *The Supreme Court and the Judicial Branch* (2005). (Rev: SLJ 5/06)

19562 Giesecke, Ernestine. *National Government* (3–5). Series: Kids' Guide. 2000, Heinemann $22.79 (978-1-57572-510-9). 32pp. A simple explanation of the three branches of government in the U.S. and the duties and responsibilities of each. (Rev: HBG 3/01; SLJ 10/00)

19563 Gorman, Jacqueline Laks. *Member of Congress* (2–4). Series: Know Your Government. 2009, Gareth Stevens LB $21.00 (978-1-4339-0094-5); paper $5.95 (978-1-4339-0122-5). 24pp. With color photographs and clear text, Gorman compares and contrasts members of the Senate and the House of Representatives. (Rev: SLJ 6/09)

19564 Gorman, Jacqueline Laks. *Vice President* (2–4). Series: Know Your Government. 2009, Gareth Stevens LB $21.00 (978-1-4339-0096-9); paper $5.95 (978-1-4339-0124-9). 24pp. With color photographs and clear text, Gorman introduces the job of vice president. (Rev: SLJ 6/09)

19565 Hamilton, John. *Becoming a Citizen* (3–5). Series: Government in Action! 2005, ABDO LB $22.78 (978-1-59197-642-4). The steps to citizenship are well explained and accompanied by photographs of documents,

sample questions, and the "Oath of Allegiance." (Rev: SLJ 7/05)

19566 Hamilton, John. *The FBI* (3–5). Series: Defending the Nation. 2007, ABDO LB $22.78 (978-1-59679-757-4). Students interested in the Federal Bureau of Investigation will find introductory information here, accompanied by photographs and sidebars. (Rev: SLJ 7/07)

19567 Hamilton, John. *How a Bill Becomes a Law* (3–5). Series: Government in Action! 2005, ABDO LB $22.78 (978-1-59197-646-2). 32pp. This look at the U.S. legislative system includes clear illustrations of the steps involved in a bill's passage. (Rev: SLJ 7/05)

19568 Hamilton, John. *The Navy* (3–5). 2007, ABDO LB $22.78 (978-1-59679-760-4). Students interested in the United States Navy will find introductory information here, accompanied by photographs and sidebars. (Rev: SLJ 7/07)

19569 Hamilton, John. *Special Forces* (3–5). Series: Defending the Nation. 2007, ABDO LB $22.78 (978-1-59679-759-8). 32pp. Students interested in the Army Rangers, Green Berets, Delta Force, Navy SEALs, Marine Corps Force Reconnaissance, and Air Force Special Operations will find introductory information here, accompanied by photographs and sidebars. (Rev: SLJ 7/07)

19570 Horn, Geoffrey M. *The Presidency* (5–8). Series: World Almanac Library of American Government. 2003, World Almanac LB $31.00 (978-0-8368-5458-9). Information on the first lady, the White House, and key presidents add to the coverage here, which includes primary sources as well as many photographs and statistics. (Rev: SLJ 1/04) [973]

19571 Kennedy, Edward M. *My Senator and Me: A Dog's Eye View of Washington D.C* (2–4). Illus. by David Small. 2006, Scholastic $16.99 (978-0-439-65077-9). 56pp. Senator Kennedy's dog Splash narrates the events of a busy day on Capitol Hill. (Rev: BL 8/06; SLJ 8/06*)

19572 Kowalski, Kathiann M. *A Balancing Act: A Look at Checks and Balances* (4–6). Illus. Series: How Government Works. 2004, Lerner LB $25.26 (978-0-8225-1350-6). 56pp. An easily understood explanation of the principle intended to ensure that the three branches of government share power. (Rev: HBG 4/04)

19573 Kule, Elaine A. *The U.S. Mail* (2–4). Series: Transportation and Communication. 2002, Enslow LB $23.93 (978-0-7660-1892-1). A history of the U.S. Postal Service from colonial days to the present, with material on how it works, its possible future uses, and people important in its development. (Rev: BL 9/15/02; HBG 3/03)

19574 Landau, Elaine. *The President's Work: A Look at the Executive Branch* (4–6). Illus. Series: How Government Works. 2004, Lerner LB $25.26 (978-0-8225-0811-3). 56pp. A look at the president's responsibilities, enhanced by interesting sidebars and photographs. (Rev: BL 5/1/04; HBG 4/04; SLJ 3/04)

19575 Levert, Suzanne. *The Congress* (2–5). Series: Kaleidoscope. 2002, Benchmark LB $25.64 (978-0-7614-1451-3). 48pp. An inside look at the inner workings of the House and Senate, with a description of the life of a piece of legislation, from introduction to passage. (Rev: HBG 3/03; SLJ 4/03)

19576 Price, Sean Stewart. *U.S. Presidents* (3–8). Illus. by Eldon Doty. Series: Truth and Rumors. 2010, Capstone LB $25.32 (978-1-4296-3952-1). 32pp. Did John Quincy Adams give an interview while naked? Was Jimmy Carter attacked by a rabbit? Price answers these and other questions and ends with a final chapter on how to tell the difference between fact and fiction. (Rev: LMC 11–12/10) [923.173]

19577 Robb, Don. *Hail to the Chief: The American Presidency* (3–5). Illus. by Alan Witschonke. 2000, Charlesbridge LB $16.95 (978-0-88106-392-9); paper $7.95 (978-0-88106-939-6). 31pp. In 14 double-page spreads, the office of the presidency is introduced with material on duties, responsibilities and powers plus coverage of some men who have held the office and changed its character. (Rev: HBG 3/01; SLJ 3/01)

19578 Rubel, David. *Scholastic Encyclopedia of the Presidents and Their Times. Rev. ed.* (4–8). 1997, Scholastic paper $18.95 (978-0-590-49366-6). This fine reference book introduces each of the presidents and his administration and supplies material on related historical events, movements, and personalities. (Rev: HBG 10/01; SLJ 5/97) [920]

19579 St. George, Judith. *So You Want to Be President?* (3–5). Illus. by David Small. 2000, Penguin $17.99 (978-0-399-23407-1). A delightful, lively compendium of facts about the presidency and the presidents covering such topics as favorite sports, appearance, pets, musical abilities, ages, and personalities. Caldecott Medal, 2001. (Rev: BCCB 7–8/00; BL 7/00*; HB 7/00; HBG 3/01; SLJ 8/00)

19580 Shea, Pegi Deitz. *The Impeachment Process* (4–6). Series: Your Government: How It Works. 2000, Chelsea LB $25.00 (978-0-7910-5538-0). 64pp. Beginning with the Watergate and Clinton scandals, this account traces the impeachment process and why the Constitution was written as it was. (Rev: HBG 9/00; SLJ 8/00)

19581 Smith, Carter, ed. *Presidents of a Divided Nation: A Sourcebook on the U.S. Presidency* (5–8). Series: American Albums. 1993, Millbrook $25.90 (978-1-56294-360-8). A visual sourcebook about the presidents during the Civil War and immediately after, from the Library of Congress collection on U.S. presidents. Also use *Presidents of a Growing Country.* (Rev: BL 12/1/93) [973.8]

19582 Smith, Carter, ed. *Presidents of a Growing Country: A Sourcebook on the U.S. Presidency* (5–8). Series: American Albums. 1993, Millbrook $25.90 (978-1-56294-358-5). Through extensive use of pictorials, a thorough timeline, and concise text, this attractive book traces the presidency from Hayes through McKinley. (Rev: BL 12/1/93; SLJ 4/94) [973.8]

19583 Smith, Carter, ed. *Presidents of a Young Republic: A Sourcebook on the U.S. Presidency* (5–8). Series: American Albums. 1993, Millbrook $25.90 (978-1-

56294-359-2). A well-illustrated account that traces U.S. history from the presidency of John Quincy Adams through James Buchanan. (Rev: BL 12/1/93; SLJ 4/94) [973.5]

19584 Stein, R. Conrad. *The National Archives* (4–6). Series: Watts Library: U.S. Government and Military. 2002, Watts LB $24.00 (978-0-531-13032-2); paper $8.95 (978-0-531-16602-4). This account presents in text and pictures a visit to the National Archives, a treasure trove that holds millions of American documents including the original Declaration of Independence. (Rev: BL 10/15/02)

19585 Suen, Anastasia. *The Peace Corps* (1–2). Series: Helping Organizations. 2002, Rosen LB $19.95 (978-0-8239-6001-9). 24pp. As well as a brief description of the history and activities of the Peace Corps, this beginning reader tells how youngsters can become involved. (Rev: BL 6/1–15/02)

19586 Teichmann, Iris. *Immigration and the Law* (5–8). Series: Understanding Immigration. 2006, Smart Apple LB $31.35 (978-1-58340-970-1). Covers all aspects of immigration including the laws granting admission, visas, and how to gain citizenship. (Rev: SLJ 3/07)

19587 Thomas, William David. *How to Become an FBI Agent* (5–8). Series: The FBI Story. 2009, Mason Crest LB $22.95 (978-1-4222-0571-6). 64pp. Readers learn about the process of applying to the FBI and the training that successful applicants receive. (Rev: LMC 5–6/10) [363.25]

19588 Townsend, Michael. *Where Do Presidents Come From? And Other Presidential Stuff of Super Great Importance* (3–6). Illus. by author. 2012, Dial $14.99 (978-080373748-8). 160pp. With humor and comic-book delivery, this book conveys lots of information about the American presidency and key events and places, answering questions such as "Why is the White House so awesome?" and "What do presidents actually do?" Lexile GN770L (Rev: BL 9/15/12*; LMC 1–2/13*; SLJ 9/12) [973.09]

19589 Ventura, Jesse, and Heron Marquez. *Jesse Ventura Tells It Like It Is: America's Most Outspoken Governor Speaks Out About Government* (5–8). Illus. 2002, Lerner LB $15.95 (978-0-8225-0385-9). 64pp. A look at the U.S. government and politicians from the viewpoint of wrestler-turned-Minnesota-governor Jesse Ventura. (Rev: BL 8/02; HBG 3/03; SLJ 9/02)

19590 Wagner, Heather Lehr. *The Central Intelligence Agency* (5–8). Illus. Series: The U.S. Government: How It Works. 2007, Chelsea House LB $30.00 (978-0-7910-9282-8). Provides information on the Central Intelligence Agency; its history, how it influences government policies, and the kinds of jobs available there. (Rev: BL 8/07) [327]

State Government and Agencies

19591 Armentrout, David, and Patricia Armentrout. *State Seals* (3–5). Illus. Series: The Rourke Guide to State

Symbols. 2001, Rourke LB $29.93 (978-1-58952-087-5). 48pp. Brief, large-print text explains the history and design of each state's seal. (Rev: SLJ 5/02)

19592 Giesecke, Ernestine. *State Government* (3–5). Series: Kids' Guide. 2000, Heinemann $22.79 (978-1-57572-513-0). 32pp. An appealing, simple account that discusses the structure of state governments in the U.S. and the responsibilities involved. (Rev: HBG 3/01; SLJ 10/00)

19593 Gorman, Jacqueline Laks. *Governor* (2–4). Illus. Series: Know Your Government. 2009, Gareth Stevens LB $21.00 (978-1-4339-0091-4); paper $5.95 (978-1-4339-0119-5). 24pp. An introductory look at the roles played by state governors, how governors are selected, and governors of note. (Rev: BL 3/1/09)

Municipal Government and Agencies

19594 Flanagan, Alice K. *Mayors* (1–3). Series: Community Workers. 2001, Compass Point LB $21.26 (978-0-7565-0064-1). This is an easily read introduction to the work of mayors, the skills and training required, and their contributions to the community. Also use *Teachers* (2001). (Rev: SLJ 5/01)

19595 Giesecke, Ernestine. *Local Government* (3–5). Series: Kids' Guide. 2000, Heinemann $22.79 (978-1-57572-512-3). 32pp. The functions of city, country, and school district governments are explained with material on duties and responsibilities. (Rev: HBG 3/01; SLJ 10/00)

19596 Gorman, Jacqueline Laks. *Mayor* (2–4). Series: Know Your Government. 2009, Gareth Stevens LB $21.00 (978-1-4339-0093-8); paper $5.95 (978-1-4339-0121-8). 24pp. With color photographs and clear text, Gorman introduces the job of mayor in both small towns and large cities. (Rev: SLJ 6/09)

Social Problems and Solutions

19597 Ajmera, Maya, and John D. Ivanko. *Be My Neighbor* (PS–2). Illus. 2004, Charlesbridge $15.95 (978-1-57091-504-8). 32pp. Observations from the late Fred Rogers open this appealing introduction to the concepts of community and neighborhood, presented on horizontal spreads with photographs depicting many environments. (Rev: BL 1/1–15/05; SLJ 1/05)

19598 Ancona, George. *Harvest* (4–7). Illus. 2001, Marshall Cavendish $15.95 (978-0-7614-5086-3). 48pp. This volume examines the difficult lives and work of Mexican migrant workers and the crops they harvest, ending with a look at the contributions of labor leader Cesar Chavez. (Rev: BL 1/1–15/02; HBG 3/02; SLJ 4/02)

19599 DeAngelis, Therese. *Blackout! Cities in Darkness* (4–8). Series: American Disasters. 2003, Enslow LB $23.93 (978-0-7660-2110-5). 48pp. This book chronicles the events and people involved in some of the important blackouts that have crippled America's cities. (Rev: BL 11/15/03)

19600 Ditchfield, Christin. *Serving Your Community* (3–5). Series: True Book. 2004, Children's Pr. LB $25.00 (978-0-516-22802-0). 47pp. The concept of volunteerism is introduced, with discussion of what young people can do to improve the quality of life in their communities. (Rev: SLJ 8/04)

19601 Donald, Rhonda Lucas. *Animal Rights: How You Can Make a Difference* (4–7). Series: Take Action. 2009, Capstone LB $25.32 (978-1-4296-2796-2). 32pp. Step-by-step instructions guide readers through formulating a plan of action, and profiles of activist teens describe their goals and strategies. (Rev: SLJ 5/1/09) [179.3]

19602 Fleming, Robert. *Rescuing a Neighborhood: The Bedford-Stuyvesant Volunteer Ambulance Corps* (4–8). 1995, Walker LB $16.85 (978-0-8027-8330-1). The story of how two determined, dedicated men organized emergency response services in their inner-city neighborhood. (Rev: BL 5/1/95; SLJ 9/95) [362]

19603 Gleason, Carrie. *Animal Rights Activist* (5–8). Series: Get Involved! 2009, Crabtree LB $26.60 (978-0-7787-4693-5); paper $8.95 (978-0-7787-4705-5). 32pp. Gleason explains animal rights and the nature of activism before discussing vegetarianism, animal testing, factory farming, and so forth, and giving tips on what young people can do to protect animals. (Rev: SLJ 2/10) [179]

19604 Gourley, Catherine. *Media Wizards: A Behind-the-Scenes Look at Media Manipulations* (5–9). 1999, Twenty-First Century LB $26.90 (978-0-7613-0967-3). An informative account of how the media can manipulate the truth. (Rev: HBG 3/00; SLJ 2/00; VOYA 4/00) [380.3]

19605 Grodin, Elissa D. *D Is for Democracy: A Citizen's Alphabet* (5–8). Illus. by Victor Juhasz. 2004, Sleeping Bear $16.95 (978-1-58536-234-9). From "Amendment" to "Zeitgeist," this is an exploration of key concepts, people, places, and things, with the emphasis on the United States. (Rev: BL 1/1–15/05; SLJ 10/04) [320.973]

19606 Harrison, Geoffrey C., and Thomas F. Scott. *Lethal Weapons* (5–8). Illus. Series: Great Debates. 2013, Norwood LB $29.27 (978-159953592-0). 48pp. Do all Americans have the right to bear arms? Are background checks an invasion of privacy? These and other questions are tackled in the frame of a debate. (Rev: BL 10/1/13; LMC 3–4/14) [363.330973]

19607 Hasday, Judy L. *Forty-Nine Minutes of Madness: The Columbine High School Shooting* (5–8). Illus. Series: Disasters: People in Peril. 2012, Enslow LB $23.93 (978-0-7660-4013-7). 48pp. Hasday examines the circumstances that led to the 1999 massacre, the event itself, the impact on the community, and related events. (Rev: BL 10/1/12; SLJ 12/12) [373.17]

19608 Hauser, Pierre. *Illegal Aliens* (5–8). Series: Immigrant Experience. 1996, Chelsea LB $14.95 (978-0-7910-3363-0). A history of attitudes toward immigration is followed by a discussion of illegal immigrants, where they come from, why they came, and the government's policy toward them. (Rev: SLJ 2/97) [932]

19609 Hovanec, Erin M. *Get Involved! A Girl's Guide to Volunteering* (5–8). Series: Girls' Guides. 1999, Rosen LB $27.95 (978-0-8239-2985-6). Two case studies of successful volunteers are given in this account that explains where to volunteer, how to approach organizations, and how to determine one's interests. (Rev: HBG 10/00; SLJ 1/00; VOYA 2/00) [361]

19610 Kuhn, Betsy. *Prying Eyes: Privacy in the Twenty-first Century* (5–8). 2008, Lerner LB $38.60 (978-0-8225-7179-7). From video cameras that can track our every move to personal data stored on computers, this book looks at security/privacy issues and court cases related to them to provide an overview of the important issues in this arena. (Rev: BL 1/1–15/08; LMC 10/08; SLJ 5/08) [323.44]

19611 Lewis, Barbara A. *The Kid's Guide to Social Action: How to Solve the Social Problems You Choose — and Turn Creative Thinking into Positive Action. Rev. ed.* (4–8). 1998, Free Spirit paper $18.95 (978-1-57542-038-7). An inspirational guide that shows how young people can make a difference by becoming involved in social action, such as instigating a cleanup of toxic waste, lobbying, or youth rights campaigns. (Rev: SLJ 1/99) [361.6]

19612 Luthringer, Chelsea. *So What Is Citizenship Anyway?* (5–8). Series: A Student's Guide to American Civics. 1999, Rosen LB $23.95 (978-0-8239-3097-5). Describes and defines the roles and responsibilities of citizens in a democracy and encourages young people to become active in political and social affairs and issues. (Rev: HBG 10/00; SLJ 3/00; VOYA 4/00) [323.6]

19613 McKissack, Patricia C., and Fredrick McKissack. *A Long Hard Journey* (5–9). 1989, Walker LB $18.85 (978-0-8027-6885-8). A 150-year saga of the organization of porters into the first black American union, the Brotherhood of Sleeping Car Porters. (Rev: BL 9/15/89; SLJ 1/90; VOYA 12/89) [331]

19614 Marsico, Katie. *Racism* (4–8). Series: Global Perspectives. 2008, Cherry Lake LB $27.07 (978-1-60279-134-3). 32pp. An accessible look at racism and its causes, history, and ways to alleviate this problem. (Rev: SLJ 11/08) [305.8]

19615 Mason, Paul. *Poverty* (4–7). Illus. Series: Planet Under Pressure. 2006, Heinemann LB $31.43 (978-1-4034-7743-9). A clear presentation of how poverty affects people around the world, with charts, photographs, and profiles. (Rev: BL 4/1/06; SLJ 6/06) [362.5]

19616 Newman, Shirlee P. *Child Slavery in Modern Times* (4–7). Illus. Series: Watts Library: History of Slavery. 2000, Watts LB $25.50 (978-0-531-11696-8). 64pp. From Europe to Asia and Africa, this book explores the deplorable lives of servitude forced on child laborers and slaves, and how some have escaped. (Rev: BL 2/15/01; SLJ 3/01)

19617 O'Brien, Anne Sibley, and Perry Edmond O'Brien. *After Gandhi* (4–7). Illus. by author. 2009, Charlesbridge $15.95 (978-1-58089-129-5). 192pp. Subtitled *One Hundred Years of Nonviolent Resistance,* this volume looks at Gandhi's legacy through the work of activists such as Martin Luther King, Jr., Nelson Mandela, and Cesar Chavez. (Rev: BL 2/15/09; SLJ 2/1/09)

19618 O'Neal, Claire. *Ways to Help in Your Community* (5–7). Series: How to Help: A Guide to Giving Back. 2010, Mitchell Lane LB $29.95 (978-1-58415-921-6). 48pp. Hosting a block party, organizing a neighborhood yard sale, feeding the hungry at a soup kitchen, and getting involved at your local library are among the approachable suggestions for volunteering in this well-organized book; lists of online resources are appended. Also use *Volunteering in Your School* (2010). (Rev: BL 4/1/11; SLJ 2/1/11) [361.3]

19619 Raatma, Lucia. *Citizenship* (4–6). Illus. Series: Cornerstones of Freedom. 2012, Scholastic LB $30 (978-053123064-0); paper $8.95 (978-053128164-2). 64pp. With many photographs and sidebars, Raatma explores the basics of becoming a U.S. citizen and some of the issues of current controversy. (Rev: BL 4/15/12) [323.60973]

19620 Reusser, Kayleen. *Celebrities Giving Back* (5–7). Series: How to Help: A Guide to Giving Back. 2010, Mitchell Lane LB $29.95 (978-1-58415-922-3). 48pp. Bono, Jimmy Carter, and Miley Cyrus are among the celebrities covered in this survey of the charitable activities of famous people. (Rev: BL 4/1/11; SLJ 2/1/11) [361.7]

19621 Robinson, J. Dennis. *Striking Back: The Fight to End Child Labor Exploitation* (5–8). Series: Taking a Stand. 2010, Compass Point LB $31.99 (978-0-7565-4297-9). 64pp. After an overview of child labor, this volume describes some of the dangers children faced and the movement to stop this exploitation, highlighting Mother Jones and others who had the courage to fight. Lexile 1000L (Rev: LMC 11–12/10; VOYA 8/10) [331.3]

19622 Rondeau, Amanda. *Do Something in Your Community* (K–2). Illus. Series: Do Something About It! 2004, ABDO LB $19.93 (978-1-59197-572-4). Photographs of people who contribute to the community — doctors and firefighters, for example — are accompanied by short descriptions of their roles. Also use *Do Something in Your Family* (2004). (Rev: BL 11/1/04)

19623 Rondeau, Amanda. *Volunteering* (1–3). 2003, ABDO LB $19.93 (978-1-57765-882-5). 24pp. Numerous examples of volunteer activities are shown in full-color photographs and simple text. (Rev: HBG 10/03; SLJ 6/03)

19624 Sanders, Lynn Bogen. *Social Justice: How You Can Make a Difference* (4–7). Series: Take Action. 2009, Capstone LB $25.32 (978-1-4296-2798-6). 32pp. Step-by-step instructions guide readers through formulating a plan of action, and profiles of activist teens describe their goals and strategies. (Rev: SLJ 5/1/09) [303.372]

19625 Saul, Laya. *Ways to Help Disadvantaged Youth* (5–7). Series: How to Help: A Guide to Giving Back. 2010, Mitchell Lane LB $29.95 (978-1-58415-918-6). 48pp.

Drives to collect books, toys, or school supplies and becoming involved in tutoring are among the approachable suggestions for volunteering in this well-organized book; lists of online resources are appended. (Rev: BL 4/1/11; SLJ 2/1/11) [362.74]

19626 Schwartz, Heather E. *Political Activism: How You Can Make a Difference* (4–7). Series: Take Action. 2009, Capstone LB $25.32 (978-1-4296-2799-3). 32pp. Personal profiles and practical advice are the hallmarks of books in this appealing series. (Rev: BL 4/1/09; SLJ 5/1/09) [322.40973]

19627 Siegel, Danny. *Mitzvah Magic: What Kids Can Do to Change the World* (3–8). Illus. by Naomi Eisenberger. 2002, Kar-Ben paper $8.95 (978-1-58013-034-9). 64pp. Siegel has amassed a large number of suggestions for children who want to help others. (Rev: BL 10/1/02)

19628 Solway, Andrew. *Graphing Immigration* (4–8). Illus. Series: Real World Data. 2010, Raintree LB $28.21 (978-143292617-5); paper $7.99 (978-143292626-7). 32pp. Solway uses charts, graphs, and tables — as well as interesting sidebars and photographs — to present trends in immigration and associated problems. (Rev: BL 2/1/10; SLJ 6/10) [304.802]

19629 Suen, Anastasia. *Habitat for Humanity* (1–2). Series: Helping Organizations. 2002, Rosen LB $19.95 (978-0-8239-6006-4). A beginning reader that describes how this organization provides housing for the poor and tells how such people as President Carter participate in its work. (Rev: BL 6/1–15/02; SLJ 3/02)

19630 Suvanjieff, Ivan, and Dawn Gifford Engle. *PeaceJam: A Billion Simple Acts of Peace* (5–10). 2008, Puffin paper $16.99 (978-0-14-241234-3). 208pp. This volume introduces the Nobel Peace laureates who are active in the work of the PeaceJam Foundation and describes their activism along with efforts by young people to support their causes. (Rev: SLJ 5/1/09; VOYA 12/08) [303.6]

19631 Wilson, Janet. *One Peace: True Stories of Young Activists* (4–7). Illus. by author. 2008, Orca $19.95 (978-1-55143-892-4). 48pp. In double-page spreads featuring children's poems, artwork, photos, and quotations, this picture book for older readers tells the stories of activists ages 8 to 15, who have often experienced atrocities. (Rev: BL 1/1/09; SLJ 2/1/09) [327.1]

Religion and Holidays

General and Miscellaneous

19632 Abrams, Judith Z. *The Secret World of Kabbalah* (5–9). Illus. 2006, Lerner paper $9.95 (978-1-58013-224-4). 80pp. This interesting introduction to Kabbalah defines this form of Jewish mysticism as "the journey to come as closely in touch with God as you can." (Rev: SLJ 12/06)

19633 Ajmera, Maya, and Cynthia Pon. *Faith* (1–3). Illus. 2009, Charlesbridge $16.95 (978-1-58089-177-6); paper $7.95 (978-1-58089-178-3). 48pp. An exploration of the many ways in which people practice their faiths around the world, with large photographs and brief captions. (Rev: BL 3/1/09; SLJ 3/09)

19634 Alexander, Cecil F. *All Things Bright and Beautiful* (PS–2). Illus. by Ashley Bryan. 2010, Atheneum $16.99 (978-1-4169-8939-4). 40pp. Cecil Alexander's well-known 19th-century hymn is presented here in a rich collages, with the musical score at the end. (Rev: BL 3/1/10*; LMC 8–9/10; SLJ 4/1/10) [264.23]

19635 Alexander, Cecil F. *All Things Bright and Beautiful* (PS–3). Illus. by Anna Vojtech. 2004, North-South LB $16.50 (978-0-7358-1893-4). A beautifully — and inventively — illustrated version of this 19th-century song. (Rev: SLJ 11/04)

19636 Ali-Karamali, Sumbul. *Growing Up Muslim: Understanding the Beliefs and Practices of Islam* (5–8). Illus. 2012, Delacorte $16.99 (978-0-385-74095-1); LB $19.99 (978-0-375-98977-3). 224pp. The Muslim author, who grew up in California, explains Muslim beliefs and customs — holidays, diet, clothing, praying, and so forth — and provides brief details on the history of Islam and the differences between the various sects. ❤ (Rev: BL 11/15/12; HB 9–10/12; LMC 11–12/12; SLJ 9/12; VOYA 6/12) [297]

19637 Baring-Gould, Sabine. *Now the Day Is Over* (PS–2). Illus. by Preston McDaniels. 2001, Morehouse $17.95 (978-0-8192-1868-1). Graceful illustrations of a little boy, animals, and angels accompany the four verses of the song. (Rev: BL 6/1–15/01)

19638 Barnes, Trevor. *Islam* (5–8). Series: World Faiths. 2005, Kingfisher paper $6.95 (978-0-7534-5882-2). Originally published in 1999 as part of *The Kingfisher Book of Religions: Festivals, Ceremonies, and Beliefs from Around the World*, this 40-page expanded volume provides a wide-ranging overview of Islam and its followers. (Rev: BL 10/1/05; SLJ 10/05; VOYA 6/06) [297]

19639 Bedard, Michael. *The Wolf of Gubbio* (2–4). Illus. 2001, Stoddart $15.95 (978-0-7737-3250-6). 24pp. The story of Saint Francis of Assisi and how his ability to talk to animals saved the city of Gubbio from a hungry wolf is retold through the voice of a young child. (Rev: BCCB 6/01; BL 4/15/01) [398.2]

19640 Borchard, Therese. *Taste and See: The Goodness of the Lord* (PS–K). Illus. by Phyllis V. Saroff. 2000, Paulist Press $9.95 (978-0-8091-6665-7). 32pp. With images that use the five senses, children are made to feel that God is everywhere and in all living things. (Rev: BL 10/1/00; HBG 3/01)

19641 Brown, Alan, and Andrew Langley. *What I Believe: A Young Person's Guide to the Religions of the World* (4–7). 1999, Millbrook LB $24.90 (978-0-7613-1501-8). Young people of eight major faiths explain their religion's principal tenets, rituals, holy days, and celebrations. (Rev: BL 10/1/99; HBG 3/00; SLJ 2/00) [291]

19642 Brown, Tricia. *Salaam: A Muslim American Boy's Story* (K–3). Photos by Ken Cardwell. 2006, Holt $17.95 (978-0-8050-6538-1). A young Muslim American boy explains the basic tenets of his faith and the customs and rituals associated with it; full of photographs, this also includes a glossary. (Rev: SLJ 12/06)

19643 Capek, Michael. *A Personal Tour of a Shaker Village* (4–7). Series: How It Was. 2001, Lerner LB $30.35 (978-0-8225-3584-3). An account of life in a Shaker village, seen through the eyes of people who lived there. (Rev: BL 8/1/01; HBG 10/01; SLJ 8/01) [289.8]

19644 Carew-Miller, Anna. *Buddha: Father of Buddhism* (2–5). Illus. by Paolo d'Altan. Series: Great Names. 2002, Mason Crest LB $19.95 (978-1-59084-137-2). This account of Buddha's life blends fact and fiction and conveys information on the religion as well as the man. (Rev: SLJ 8/03)

19645 Chaikin, Miriam. *Menorahs, Mezuzas, and Other Jewish Symbols* (5–9). 1990, Clarion $17.00 (978-0-89919-856-9). A Jewish historian explains some of the symbols of the faith. (Rev: BL 1/15/91; HB 5–6/91; SLJ 1/91) [296.4]

19646 Conover, Sarah, and Freda Crane. *Beautiful Signs/Ayat Jamilah: A Treasury of Islamic Wisdom for Children and Parents* (5–7). Illus. by Valerie Wahl. Series: Little Light of Mine. 2004, Eastern Washington Univ. paper $19.95 (978-0-910055-94-9). Muslim folktales, fables, stories from the Koran, and historic tales originate from countries around the world. (Rev: BL 10/15/04; SLJ 8/04) [297.1]

19647 Dalton, David. *Sikhism: Inderjeet's Story* (3–6). Illus. Series: Our World of Faith. 2013, New Forest LB $28.50 (978-184898617-6). 32pp. A personal narrative draws readers into this explanation of the traditions and rituals of Sikhism. (Rev: BL 4/1/13; LMC 11–12/13; SLJ 4/13) [294.6]

19648 Das, Rasamandala. *Hinduism* (4–6). Series: Religions of the World. 2005, World Almanac LB $31.00 (978-0-8368-5867-9). 48pp. A photo-filled introduction to Hinduism and its history, beliefs, rites, and holidays. (Rev: SLJ 1/06)

19649 David, Jo, and Daniel B. Syme. *The Book of the Jewish Life* (5–8). 1997, UAHC paper $13.95 (978-0-8074-0628-1). This book explores common Jewish traditions in such areas as birth and naming, religious schools, bar/bat mitzvahs, confirmation, marriage, and mourning. (Rev: SLJ 9/98) [296]

19650 Delval, Marie-Hélène. *Images of God for Young Children* (K–3). Illus. by Barbara Nascimbeni. 2011, Eerdmans $16.50 (978-0-8028-5391-2). 90pp. A nicely illustrated introduction to the concept that God can be found everywhere. (Rev: BL 4/15/11; SLJ 4/11) [231]

19651 Demi. *The Legend of St. Nicholas* (2–5). Illus. by author. 2003, Simon & Schuster $19.95 (978-0-689-84681-6). 40pp. Young readers will be fascinated by this beautifully illustrated biography of the real St. Nicholas, who devoted his life to relieving the suffering of others. (Rev: BL 10/1/03; HBG 4/04; SLJ 10/03)

19652 dePaola, Tomie. *Let the Whole Earth Sing Praise* (PS–K). Illus. by author. 2011, Putnam $15.99 (978-0-399-25478-9). 32pp. A biblically inspired celebration of all aspects of the natural world, drawing on the art of the Otomi people of Puebla, Mexico. (Rev: BL 3/1/11; LMC 5–6/11; SLJ 3/1/11) [231.7]

19653 Dillon, Leo, and Diane Dillon. *To Every Thing There Is a Season: Verses from Ecclesiastes* (4–7). 1998, Scholastic paper $16.95 (978-0-590-47887-8). Using verses from Ecclesiastes such as "A time to be born and a time to die," the artists have created a stunning pic-

ture book on the cycle of life. (Rev: BCCB 11/98; BL 10/1/98*; HB 9–10/98; HBG 3/99; SLJ 9/98) [223]

19654 Dineen, Jacqueline. *Births* (3–6). Series: Ceremonies and Celebrations. 2001, Raintree LB $25.69 (978-0-7398-3267-7). 32pp. Traditions surrounding births are explored in six major religions, covering topics from circumcision, baptism, and naming ceremonies to gifts, clothing, food, and horoscopes. Also use *Weddings* (2001). (Rev: SLJ 9/01)

19655 Douglass, Susan L. *Ramadan* (1–3). Series: On My Own Holidays. 2003, Carolrhoda LB $25.26 (978-0-87614-932-4); paper $5.95 (978-1-57505-584-8). 48pp. An excellent introduction to the holy month of fasting observed by Muslims each year, with helpful information about the basic beliefs and practices of Islam. (Rev: BL 10/15/03; HBG 4/04; SLJ 8/03)

19656 *A Faith Like Mine* (3–5). Illus. 2005, DK $19.99 (978-0-7566-1177-4). Children of different religious backgrounds describe the basics of their faith and what they like about their religion; includes background information on major and minor world religions. (Rev: BL 10/1/05; SLJ 11/05)

19657 Feinstein, Edward. *Tough Questions Jews Ask: A Young Adult's Guide to Building a Jewish Life* (5–7). 2003, Jewish Lights $14.99 (978-1-58023-139-8). Rabbi Feinstein effectively answers hypothetical questions posed by an imagined class of thoughtful young students. Sidney Taylor Book Honor 2003. (Rev: BL 4/1/03) [296.7]

19658 Ganeri, Anita. *Buddhism* (4–6). Series: Religions of the World. 2005, World Almanac LB $31.00 (978-0-8368-5865-5). 48pp. A photo-filled introduction to Buddhism and its history, beliefs, rites, and holidays. (Rev: SLJ 1/06)

19659 Ganeri, Anita. *Buddhist Stories* (1–6). Illus. by Tracey Fennell. Series: Traditional Religious Tales. 2006, Picture Window LB $26.60 (978-1-4048-1311-3). 32pp. The stories in this appealing collection chronicle the life of the Buddha, focusing in particular on his lifelong search for enlightenment. (Rev: SLJ 4/06)

19660 Ganeri, Anita. *Hindu Stories* (1–6). Illus. by Carole Gray. Series: Traditional Religious Tales. 2006, Picture Window LB $26.60 (978-1-4048-1309-0). 32pp. The seven stories in this collection are prime examples of classical Hindu mythology and include colorful tales about such deities and demons as Krishna the cowherd, Ganesh the elephant god, and Holika the demon princess. (Rev: SLJ 4/06)

19661 Ganeri, Anita. *Sikh Stories* (1–6). Illus. by Rachael Phillips. Series: Traditional Religious Tales. 2006, Picture Window LB $26.60 (978-1-4048-1314-4). This collection of stories documents incidents from the lives of Sikh spiritual leaders, emphasizing the moral lessons exemplified. (Rev: SLJ 4/06)

19662 Gellman, Marc. *And God Cried, Too: A Kid's Book of Healing and Hope* (2–5). Illus. by Harry Bliss. 2002, HarperCollins LB $17.89 (978-0-06-009887-2); paper $5.99 (978-0-06-009886-5). 128pp. A fictional story about a young angel-in-training opens this thought-provoking book that deals with questions that challenge faith. (Rev: BL 10/1/02; SLJ 12/02)

19663 Glossop, Jennifer. *The Kids Book of World Religions* (3–6). Illus. by John Mantha. 2003, Kids Can $15.95 (978-1-55074-959-5). 64pp. Students writing reports will find this a useful source of information on the basic tenets of the world's major religions. (Rev: BL 4/15/03; HBG 10/03; SLJ 4/03)

19664 Goodnough, David. *Cult Awareness: A Hot Issue* (5–8). Series: Hot Issues. 2000, Enslow LB $27.93 (978-0-7660-1196-0). 64pp. This book explains the nature of cults and how they differ as well as giving information on many groups including Jehovah's Witnesses, Unification Church, Hare Krishna, Shakers, Mormons, and Church of Scientology. (Rev: BL 6/1–15/00; HBG 10/00; SLJ 6/00)

19665 Gunderson, Cory. *Religions of the Middle East* (3–5). Series: World in Conflict: The Middle East. 2004, ABDO LB $25.65 (978-1-59197-412-3). 48pp. A comparative description of the major religion of the Middle East — Islam, Judaism, Christianity, Druze, and Hinduism. (Rev: SLJ 5/04)

19666 Hodges, Margaret. *The Legend of Saint Christopher* (3–6). Illus. by Richard Jesse Watson. 2002, Eerdmans $18.00 (978-0-8028-5077-5). 32pp. Hodges retells the story of how Saint Christopher got the name that means "Christ bearer." (Rev: BCCB 12/02; BL 10/1/02; HBG 3/03; SLJ 11/02)

19667 Hoffman, Lawrence A., and Wolfson Ron. *What You Will See Inside a Synagogue* (3–5). Illus. 2004, SkyLight Paths $17.99 (978-1-59473-012-2). 32pp. Introduces readers to the rituals and places of worship of three branches of American Judaism — Conservative, Reconstruction, and Reform. (Rev: BL 1/1–15/05; SLJ 2/05)

19668 *I Believe: The Nicene Creed* (1–3). Illus. by Pauline Baynes. 2004, Eerdmans $16.00 (978-0-8028-5258-8). 32pp. The Nicene Creed, a basic outline of Christian doctrine used by Eastern Orthodox, Roman Catholic, and most Protestant denominations, is examined line by line in this beautifully illustrated book. (Rev: BL 7/03; HBG 4/04; SLJ 11/03)

19669 Jani, Mahendra, and Vandana Jani. *What You Will See Inside a Hindu Temple* (4–6). Illus. by Neirah Bhargava. Series: What You Will See Inside. 2005, SkyLight Paths $17.99 (978-1-59473-116-7). 32pp. Attractive double-page spreads look inside a typical Hindu temple and introduce the fundamental beliefs, rituals, and ceremonies of Hinduism. (Rev: BL 1/1–15/06; SLJ 2/06)

19670 Jeffrey, Laura S. *Celebrate Ramadan* (5–8). Illus. Series: Celebrate Holidays. 2007, Enslow LB $23.95 (978-0-7660-2774-9). Report writers and others wanting to know about this Muslim holiday will find the facts they need here, as well as more general information about Islam in America. (Rev: BL 10/1/07; SLJ 11/07) [297.3]

19671 *Jesus Loves Me!* (K–2). Illus. by Tim Warnes. 2006, Simon & Schuster $12.95 (978-1-4169-0065-8). A happy family of bears living in a forest celebrate the classic Christian children's song; the music is appended. (Rev: SLJ 3/06)

19672 Johari, Harish, and Vatsala Sperling. *How Ganesh Got His Elephant Head* (1–4). Illus. by Pieter Weltevrede. 2003, Bear & Company $15.95 (978-1-59143-021-6). 32pp. Traditional illustrations highlight the Hindu story of how Ganesh got his elephant head, which is amplified with a tale of Ganesh's rivalry with his brother. (Rev: BL 12/1/03; SLJ 1/04)

19673 John Paul II, Pope. *Every Child a Light: The Pope's Message to Young People* (4–7). Ed. by Jerome M. Vereb. 2002, Boyds Mills $16.95 (978-1-56397-090-0). Using photographs and snippets from Pope John Paul II's writings for children and teens, this is an inspirational book of comments and advice for youngsters. (Rev: BL 6/1–15/02; HBG 10/02; SLJ 5/02) [248.8]

19674 Keane, Michael. *What You Will See Inside a Catholic Church* (3–6). Illus. 2002, SkyLight Paths $17.95 (978-1-893361-54-6). 32pp. Readers are introduced to the layout, ceremonies, and rituals of a Roman Catholic church. (Rev: BL 3/15/03; SLJ 9/03)

19675 Keene, Michael. *Judaism* (5–8). Series: Religions of the World. 2005, World Almanac LB $31.00 (978-0-8368-5869-3). A basic introduction to the beliefs and practices of Judaism around the world, with a chronology of important events. (Rev: SLJ 2/06) [296]

19676 Khan, Rukhsana. *Muslim Child: Understanding Islam Through Stories and Poems* (4–6). Illus. by Patty Gallinger. 2002, Whitman $16.99 (978-0-8075-5307-7). 104pp. A series of vignettes told by children about living as a Muslim in various countries around the world. (Rev: BL 2/15/02; HBG 10/02; SLJ 2/02)

19677 Kimmel, Eric A. *Brother Wolf, Sister Sparrow: Stories About Saints and Animals* (3–6). Illus. by John Winch. 2003, Holiday House $18.95 (978-0-8234-1724-7). 64pp. This collection of well-illustrated stories explores several saints' relationships with animals and includes the tale of a bargain Francis of Assisi struck with a wolf and an account of how angels helped Saint Brigid to replace the butter and milk she'd given to the needy. (Rev: BL 4/1/03; HBG 10/03; SLJ 5/03)

19678 Krishnaswami, Uma. *The Broken Tusk: Stories of the Hindu God Ganesha* (4–8). 1996, Linnet $19.95 (978-0-208-02242-4). A collection of tales about the elephant-headed Hindu god Ganesha, the god of good beginnings. (Rev: SLJ 7/97) [294.5]

19679 Kushner, Lawrence, and Karen Kushner. *Because Nothing Looks Like God* (PS–2). Illus. by Dawn Majewski. 2001, Jewish Lights $17.99 (978-1-58023-092-6). 32pp. The concept of God is explored in this picture book filled with paintings of nature scenes. (Rev: BL 1/1–15/01; SLJ 2/01)

19680 Le Joly, Edward, and Jaya Chaliha, eds. *Stories Told by Mother Teresa* (2–4). Illus. by Allan Drummond. 2000, Element Books $15.95 (978-1-902618-65-4).

These 11 moving stories derived from the personal experiences of Mother Teresa describe acts of sacrifice, faith, and devotion by ordinary people. (Rev: BL 3/15/00; HBG 9/00)

19681 Lehman-Wilzig, Tami. *Keeping the Promise: A Torah's Journey* (1–5). Illus. by Craig Orback. 2004, Lerner LB $16.95 (978-1-58013-117-9); paper $6.95 (978-1-58013-118-6). The story of a tiny Torah scroll that is passed from a Dutch rabbi to a young boy in Bergen-Belsen who years later gives it to Ilan Ramon, the Israeli astronaut, who took it with him on the tragic *Columbia* mission. (Rev: BCCB 4/04; SLJ 8/04)

19682 Lester, Julius. *When the Beginning Began: Stories About God, the Creatures, and Us* (4–8). 1999, Harcourt $17.00 (978-0-15-201138-3). Using parts of Genesis and creation stories from Jewish legends, this wondrous retelling adds thought-provoking human interest to the stories that end with Adam and Eve. (Rev: BL 4/15/99*; SLJ 5/99) [296.1]

19683 Levete, Sarah. *Death* (3–6). Illus. 2009, Rosen LB $26.50 (978-143585351-5). 48pp. Levete provides an overview of death and mourning traditions in religions around the world. (Rev: BL 4/1/10; LMC 1–2/10; SLJ 12/09) [203]

19684 Llewellyn, Claire. *Saints and Angels* (3–6). 2003, Houghton $14.95 (978-0-7534-5588-3). 64pp. This lushly illustrated book focuses primarily on the Christian saints — organized into such logical groups as martyrs, thinkers, and disciples — but also devotes a section to angels. (Rev: BL 10/1/03; HBG 4/04)

19685 Lutz, Norma Jean. *The History of the Black Church* (5–8). Illus. Series: African American Achievers. 2001, Chelsea $30.00 (978-0-7910-5822-0). 112pp. Historical and contemporary photographs illustrate this history of African American religious life and institutions. (Rev: BL 10/1/01; HBG 3/02; SLJ 12/01)

19686 Novesky, Amy. *Elephant Prince: The Story of Ganesh* (PS–2). Illus. by Belgin K. Wedman. 2004, Mandala $16.95 (978-1-886069-16-9). 32pp. A beautifully illustrated story of how the Hindu god Ganesh acquired his elephant head. (Rev: BL 1/1–15/05; SLJ 2/05)

19687 O'Connor, Frances. *The History of Islam* (5–8). Series: Understanding Islam. 2009, Rosen LB $29.25 (978-1-4358-5064-4). 64pp. After looking at the origins of Islam, this volume distinguishes between Sunnis and Shiites, discusses the Koran, describes Islam's spread through the world, and gives an overview of the practice of Islam today. (Rev: LMC 10/09*) [297.09]

19688 Paul, John. *For the Children: Words of Love and Inspiration from His Holiness John Paul II* (4–7). Illus. 2000, Scholastic paper $16.95 (978-0-439-14902-0). 32pp. Letters and speeches by Pope John Paul II and photographs of children from around the world are used to illustrate inspirational messages about such subjects as hope, faith, and school. (Rev: BL 3/1/00; HBG 10/00; SLJ 3/00)

19689 Rotner, Shelley, and Sheila M. Kelly. *Many Ways: How Families Practice Their Beliefs and Religions* (K–2). Illus. by Shelley Rotner. 2005, Millbrook $16.95 (978-0-7613-2873-5). 32pp. A simple child-friendly introduction to the customs followed by believers of six religions: Buddhism, Christianity, Hinduism, Islam, Judaism, and Sikhism. (Rev: BL 10/1/05)

19690 Schwartz, Howard. *Invisible Kingdoms: Jewish Tales of Angels, Spirits, and Demons* (3–5). Illus. by Stephen Fieser. 2002, HarperCollins LB $18.89 (978-0-06-027856-4). Schwartz retells nine varied tales peopled with angels, ghosts, and demons. (Rev: BL 10/1/02; HB 11/02; HBG 3/03; SLJ 10/02)

19691 Self, David. *Christianity* (5–8). Series: Religions of the World. 2005, World Almanac LB $31.00 (978-0-8368-5866-2). A basic introduction to the beliefs and practices of Christianity, with a chronology of important events. (Rev: SLJ 2/06)

19692 Stanton, Sue. *Child's Guide to the Mass* (PS–3). Illus. by H. M. Alan. 2001, Paulist Press $9.95 (978-0-8091-6682-4). Using a lighthearted approach, this book explains the parts of the Roman Catholic Mass and what each means. (Rev: BL 3/15/01; HBG 10/01)

19693 Teece, Geoff. *Christianity* (3–7). Illus. Series: Religion in Focus. 2004, Smart Apple LB $18.95 (978-1-58340-465-2). This slim, photo-filled volume introduces the history, beliefs, and practices of Christianity, covering festivals, sacred places, and a list of denominations. Also use *Buddhism* (2004). (Rev: BL 10/1/04)

19694 Thompson, Jan. *Islam* (5–8). Series: World Religions. 2005, Walrus paper $12.95 (978-1-55285-654-3). Using a question-and-answer format, this attractive introduction explores the history and beliefs of Islam; a first-person account by a 15-year-old Muslim boy in London starts the book. (Rev: BL 10/15/05) [297]

19695 Tompert, Ann. *Saint Nicholas* (2–4). Illus. 2000, Boyds Mills $15.95 (978-1-56397-844-9). 32pp. A retelling of the legends surrounding St. Nicholas and the attributes that made him one of the most beloved of all saints. (Rev: BCCB 10/00; BL 10/1/00; HBG 3/01)

19696 Visconti, Guido. *Clare and Francis* (4–7). Illus. by Bimba Landmann. 2004, Eerdmans $20.00 (978-0-8028-5269-4). Eye-catching artwork highlights the inspiring stories of saints Clare and Francis in this picture book for older readers. (Rev: BL 2/1/04*; SLJ 6/04) [270]

19697 Waldman, Neil. *The Promised Land: The Birth of the Jewish People* (4–7). 2002, Boyds Mills $21.95 (978-1-56397-332-1). Waldman interweaves information on religious tradition and the experiences of the Jewish people over time in this handsome volume. (Rev: BL 10/1/02; HBG 3/03; SLJ 9/02) [909]

19698 Wallace, Holly. *Islam: Budi's Story* (3–5). Illus. Series: This Is My Faith. 2007, Barron's paper $4.99 (978-0-7641-3475-3). 32pp. Budi, a young Indonesian Muslim, introduces his family and neighbors and describes the ways in which his religion affects his life. (Rev: BL 4/1/07)

19699 *What Do You Believe? Religion and Faith in the World Today* (5–8). Illus. 2011, DK $16.99 (978-0-

7566-7228-7). 96pp. The major world religions are introduced here — along with minor religions, spiritual movements, and atheism — with discussion of religious practices, morality, science and Creationism, and other related aspects. (Rev: BL 6/1/11; SLJ 6/11) [200]

19700 *What You Will See Inside a Mosque* (3–6). Series: What You Will See Inside. 2003, SkyLight Paths $16.95 (978-1-893361-60-7). 32pp. Two small New York mosques are featured in this introduction to the fundamentals of Islam and how and where Muslims worship. (Rev: BL 10/1/03; SLJ 2/04)

19701 Whiting, Jim. *The Role of Religion in the Early Islamic World* (5–7). Illus. Series: Life in the Early Islamic World. 2012, Crabtree LB $30.60 (978-077872169-7). 48pp. With excellent illustrations, this attractive volume provides a solid introduction to Islam and its importance to the overall culture of the time. (Rev: BL 8/12*; SLJ 8/12) [297.09]

19702 Wilkinson, Philip. *Buddhism* (5–8). Illus. 2003, DK $15.99 (978-0-7894-9833-5). 64pp. An attractive, well-illustrated overview of the teachings and symbols of Buddhism, with information on history, different forms, important sites, and art and artifacts. (Rev: BL 1/1–15/04)

19703 Wilson, Karma. *I Will Rejoice: Celebrating Psalm 118* (PS–2). Illus. by Amy June Bates. 2007, Zondervan $14.99 (978-0-310-71117-9). 32pp. Based on the psalm that reads "This is the day that the Lord has made, and I will rejoice and be glad in it," this book urges children to find happiness and joy in the world around them. (Rev: BL 10/1/06)

19704 Zarin, Cynthia. *Saints Among the Animals* (5–8). Illus. by Leonid Gore. 2006, Atheneum $17.95 (978-0-689-85031-8). 96pp. An attractive collection of ten stories about saints interacting with animals; brief biographies of the saints are appended. (Rev: BL 12/1/06; SLJ 1/07)

Bible Stories

19705 Alexander, Pat. *My First Bible* (PS–1). Illus. by Leon Baxter. 2002, Good Bks. $14.99 (978-1-56148-360-0). 480pp. A collection of more than 60 stories from the Old and New Testaments, with amusing, cartoon-style illustrations. (Rev: SLJ 12/02)

19706 Beneduce, Ann Keay. *Moses: The Long Road to Freedom* (2–4). Illus. by Gennady Spirin. 2004, Scholastic $16.95 (978-0-439-35225-3). 32pp. The striking artwork of Gennady Spirin enhances this retelling of the story of Moses and how he led his people out of Egypt to freedom. (Rev: BL 4/1/04; SLJ 3/04)

19707 Boroson, Martin. *Becoming Me* (K–3). Illus. by Christopher Gilvan-Cartwright. 2000, SkyLight Paths $16.95 (978-1-893361-11-9). 32pp. The Bible creation story as told from the standpoint of God. (Rev: BL 7/00; SLJ 10/00)

19708 Brett, Jan. *On Noah's Ark* (PS–1). Illus. by author. 2003, Penguin $16.99 (978-0-399-24028-7). Noah's granddaughter is the focus of this beautifully illustrated retelling with detailed watercolors of the ark's occupants. (Rev: BL 10/1/03; HBG 4/04; SLJ 9/03)

19709 Brunelli, Roberto. *A Family Treasury of Bible Stories: One for Each Week of the Year* (4–8). 1997, Abrams $24.95 (978-0-8109-1248-9). A collection of 52 short stories from the Old and New Testaments. (Rev: BL 10/1/97; SLJ 2/98) [220.9]

19710 Chancellor, Deborah, retel. *DK Children's Everyday Bible: A Bible Story for Every Day of the Year* (K–4). Illus. by Anna C. Leplar. 2002, DK $19.99 (978-0-7894-8858-9). 383pp. Retellings of Old and New Testament stories for each day of the year. (Rev: HBG 10/03; SLJ 12/02)

19711 Connolly, Sean. *New Testament Miracles* (5–10). Series: Art Revelations. 2004, Enchanted Lion $18.95 (978-1-59270-012-7). Presents brief retellings of 12 miracles performed by Jesus Christ, each illustrated by a well-known painting by an eminent artist, such as Rembrandt, El Greco, and Tintoretto. (Rev: SLJ 8/04) [226.7]

19712 Crossley-Holland, Kevin. *How Many Miles to Bethlehem?* (1–3). Illus. by Peter Malone. 2004, Scholastic LB $16.95 (978-0-439-67642-7). 32pp. Illustrations with a Renaissance flavor form a backdrop for the characters who introduce themselves and their role in the story of the Nativity. (Rev: BL 10/1/04; SLJ 10/04)

19713 Delval, Marie-Hélène. *The Bible for Young Children* (K–3). Illus. by Jean-Claude Gotting. 2010, Eerdmans $16.50 (978-0-8028-5383-7). 88pp. This attractively illustrated book presents nine Bible stories adapted for young readers. (Rev: BL 11/15/10; SLJ 3/1/11) [220.9]

19714 Demi. *Mary* (4–7). 2006, Simon & Schuster $19.95 (978-0-689-87692-9). 48pp. Traces the story of the mother of Jesus from the days preceding her birth through her ascension into heaven. (Rev: BL 10/1/06; SLJ 11/06) [232.91]

19715 Downey, Lynn. *This Is the Earth That God Made* (PS–1). Illus. by Benrei Huang. 2000, Augsburg $8.99 (978-0-8066-3960-4). In this good-natured look at the Creation, images such as mountains, fountains, seas, winds, animals, and bees gradually appear, ending with a human family giving thanks. (Rev: SLJ 9/00)

19716 Ehrlich, Amy. *With a Mighty Hand: The Story in the Torah* (5–8). Illus. by Daniel Nevins. 2013, Candlewick $35 (978-076364395-9). 224pp. An elegantly conceived adaptation of the five books of the Torah, introducing readers to the stories of the Adam and Eve, Abraham, Moses, and other key figures. ⋒ (Rev: BL 11/15/13*; SLJ 10/13*) [222]

19717 Fischer, Chuck, and Curtis Flowers. *In the Beginning: The Art of Genesis* (5–8). Illus. by Bruce Foster. 2008, Little, Brown $35.00 (978-0-316-11842-2). 12pp. This artful pop-up book highlights stories from the Book of Genesis, including the Garden of Eden, Noah's

Ark, the Tower of Babel, and Jacob's Ladder. (Rev: BL 2/1/09*) [222]

19718 Goble, Paul. *Song of Creation* (K–3). Illus. by author. 2004, Eerdmans $16.00 (978-0-8028-5271-7). 32pp. This richly illustrated celebration of God and the wonders of nature draws on *The Book of Common Prayer*. (Rev: BL 10/1/04; SLJ 10/04)

19719 Graham, Lorenz. *How God Fix Jonah* (3–5). Illus. 2000, Boyds Mills $17.95 (978-1-56397-698-8). 156pp. This collection of biblical-story poems contains tales from both the Testaments told from a West African native's viewpoint. (Rev: BL 10/1/00; HBG 10/01; SLJ 12/00)

19720 Grimes, Nikki. *Voices of Christmas* (3–6). Illus. by Eric Velasquez. 2009, Zondervan $16.99 (978-031071192-6). 32pp. A rich, lyrical telling of the Nativity story, giving voice to characters ranging from Mary and Joseph to Herod and the innkeeper. (Rev: BL 11/15/09; HB 11–21/09; SLJ 10/09) [232.92]

19721 Gunney, Lynn Tuttle. *Meet Jesus: The Life and Lessons of a Beloved Teacher* (K–3). Illus. by Jane Conteh-Morgan. 2007, Skinner $12.00 (978-1-55896-524-9). 36pp. A simple, clearly written introduction to the life of Jesus and his teachings and parables. (Rev: BL 10/1/07)

19722 Harrison, James. *My Very First Bible* (PS–2). Illus. by Diana Mayo. 2005, DK $12.99 (978-0-7566-0983-2). 80pp. Twenty-five key stories from both Testaments are told in clear prose and appealing illustrations. (Rev: BL 3/1/04; SLJ 5/05)

19723 Hodges, Margaret. *Moses* (3–5). Illus. by Barry Moser. 2006, Harcourt $16.00 (978-0-15-200946-5). 32pp. From his birth and placement in the bulrushes to his retrieval of the Ten Commandments, this handsome volume highlights Moses' achievements and the obstacles he faced. (Rev: BL 10/1/06; SLJ 12/06)

19724 Hoffman, Mary. *Kings and Queens of the Bible* (K–3). Illus. by Christina Balit. 2008, Holt $16.95 (978-0-8050-8837-3). 40pp. Retells the stories of Old Testament kings and queens (Moses, David, Soloman, Esther, Balkis, Jezebel, and Belshazzar); includes occasional violent scenes plus an appendix of the books of the Bible in which the figures appear. (Rev: BL 10/1/08; SLJ 11/08)

19725 Joslin, Mary. *The Paraclete Treasury of Angel Stories* (K–3). Illus. by Elena Temporin. 2008, Paraclete $18.95 (978-1-55725-572-3). 32pp. An accessible collection of Bible stories, verses, and prayers about angels. (Rev: BL 5/1/08)

19726 Jules, Jacqueline. *Abraham's Search for God* (K–3). Illus. by Natascia Ugliano. 2007, Kar-Ben $17.95 (978-1-58013-243-5). 32pp. Abraham came early to the belief that there was one God, according to this retelling of a legend based on the Bible. (Rev: BL 10/1/07; SLJ 9/07)

19727 Jules, Jacqueline. *Benjamin and the Silver Goblet* (K–3). Illus. by Natascia Ugliano. 2009, Lerner LB $17.95 (978-0-8225-8757-6); paper $8.95 (978-0-8225-

8758-3). Joseph, sold into slavery in Egypt but risen to become a powerful man, tests his brothers the honesty of his brothers in this Bible story. (Rev: SLJ 4/09)

19728 Jules, Jacqueline. *Miriam in the Desert* (K–3). Illus. by Natascia Ugliano. 2010, Lerner/Kar-Ben $17.95 (978-076134494-0); paper $8.95 (978-07613449-6-4). 32pp. The story of Moses's strong, comforting sister Miriam is given a warm, positive treatment in this updated Bible story. (Rev: BL 11/15/10) [222]

19729 Jules, Jacqueline. *Sarah Laughs* (PS–3). Illus. by Natascia Ugliano. 2008, Lerner $17.95 (978-0-8225-7216-9). 32pp. Sarah, the wife of Abraham and elderly mother of young Isaac, is the focus of this picture book that draws on legend as well as the Bible story. (Rev: BL 10/1/08; SLJ 6/08)

19730 Kimmel, Eric A. *Why the Snake Crawls on Its Belly* (K–3). Illus. by Allen Davis. 2001, Pitspopany $14.95 (978-1-930143-20-3). 32pp. This very readable pourquoi story relates how God punishes the snake for tempting Adam and Eve in the garden of Eden. (Rev: BL 10/1/01; HBG 3/02; SLJ 12/01)

19731 Koralek, Jenny. *The Coat of Many Colors* (PS–2). Illus. by Pauline Baynes. 2004, Eerdmans $16.00 (978-0-8028-5277-9). 32pp. The Old Testament story of Joseph is retold in a lively way and enhanced with art that evokes the time and the setting. (Rev: BL 10/15/04; SLJ 11/04)

19732 Koralek, Jenny. *The Moses Basket* (3–5). Illus. by Pauline Baynes. 2003, Eerdmans $16.00 (978-0-8028-5251-9). This beautifully realized retelling relates how Moses's mother gave up her infant son rather than see him killed. (Rev: HBG 4/04; SLJ 10/03)

19733 Lane, Leena. *Angels Among Us* (1–3). Illus. by Elena Baboni. 2007, Eerdmans $17.00 (978-0-8028-5321-9). 29pp. This oversize picture book contains 12 biblical stories in which angels appear to humans. (Rev: BL 10/1/07; SLJ 11/07)

19734 Lee, Young Shin. *Traitors, Kings, and the Big Break* (3–5). Illus. by Jung Sun Hwang. Series: Manga Bible. 2008, Zondervan paper $6.99 (978-0-310-71290-9). 208pp. King David and Solomon feature in this upbeat manga version of the first and second book of Kings from the Old Testament. (Rev: BLO 7/29/08)

19735 *The Lord Is My Shepherd* (PS–2). Illus. by Anne Wilson. 2003, Eerdmans $16.00 (978-0-8028-5250-2). 32pp. The 23rd psalm is accompanied by expressive art. (Rev: BL 2/1/03; HBG 10/03; SLJ 7/03)

19736 Lottridge, Celia B. *Stories from Adam and Eve to Ezekiel: Retold from the Bible* (4–7). Illus. by Gary Clement. 2004, Groundwood $24.95 (978-0-88899-490-5). Some of the best-loved stories from the Hebrew Bible are engagingly adapted in this attractively illustrated volume. (Rev: BL 10/1/04; SLJ 4/05) [220]

19737 Lottridge, Celia B. *Stories from the Life of Jesus* (5–7). Illus. by Linda Wolfsgruber. 2004, Douglas & McIntyre $24.95 (978-0-88899-497-4). Lottridge draws on the first four books of the New Testament for this illustrated collection of stories. (Rev: BL 5/1/04; HB 7–8/04; SLJ 11/04) [232.9]

19738 McCarthy, Michael. *The Story of Noah and the Ark* (PS–K). Illus. by Giuliano Ferri. 2001, Barefoot Bks. $16.99 (978-1-84148-361-0). 32pp. Wonderful illustrations show the animals arrayed around the decks, the roiling seas, and the arrival of the dove. (Rev: BL 10/1/01; HBG 3/02; SLJ 11/01)

19739 McCarthy, Michael, retel. *The Story of Daniel in the Lions' Den* (PS–3). Illus. by Giuliano Ferri. 2003, Barefoot Bks. $16.99 (978-1-84148-209-5). The Old Testament story is retold in rhyme in this beautifully illustrated picture book. (Rev: BL 6/1–15/03; HBG 10/03; SLJ 5/03)

19740 McGee, Marni. *The Colt and the King* (PS–3). Illus. by John Winch. 2002, Holiday House $16.95 (978-0-8234-1695-0). 32pp. Told from the standpoint of the donkey that carried Jesus into Jerusalem on Palm Sunday, this is a beautifully illustrated retelling of a Bible story. (Rev: BCCB 4/02; BL 4/1/02; HB 3/02; HBG 10/02; SLJ 4/02)

19741 Oberman, Sheldon. *The Wisdom Bird: A Tale of Solomon and Sheba* (K–4). Illus. by Neil Waldman. 2000, Boyds Mills $15.95 (978-1-56397-816-6). 32pp. Drawing on many sources, including the Bible, African folklore, and Jewish tales, this is the story of Sheba's request that Solomon build her a palace out of bird's beaks. (Rev: BCCB 10/00; BL 10/1/00; HBG 3/01; SLJ 10/00)

19742 *Paradise* (2–5). Illus. by Fiona French. 2004, Frances Lincoln $15.95 (978-1-84507-007-6). An eye-catching version of the Creation story, based on the King James translation of the Bible. (Rev: SLJ 6/04)

19743 Paterson, Katherine. *The Light of the World: The Life of Jesus for Children* (K–3). Illus. by François Roca. 2008, Scholastic $17.99 (978-0-545-01172-3). 48pp. Rich paintings accompany this telling of the life of Jesus, highlighting his disciples and some of the parables. (Rev: BCCB 2/08; BL 1/1–15/08; HB 5/08; SLJ 1/08)

19744 Pilling, Ann. *A Kingfisher Treasury of Bible Stories, Poems, and Prayers for Bedtime* (3–6). Illus. 2000, Kingfisher $18.95 (978-0-7534-5329-2). 96pp. Poetry, songs, and Bible stories from the Old and New Testaments are included in this anthology aimed at Christian children. (Rev: BL 10/1/00; HBG 10/01)

19745 Pinkney, Jerry. *Noah's Ark* (2–5). Illus. by author. 2002, North-South LB $16.50 (978-1-58717-202-1). Pinkney offers a fresh take on the popular story while keeping his narrative fairly close to the standard version. Caldecott Honor Book, 2004. (Rev: BCCB 1/03; BL 10/1/02; HB 1/03; HBG 3/03; SLJ 11/02*)

19746 Ray, Jane. *Adam and Eve and the Garden of Eden* (K–3). Illus. 2005, Eerdmans $17.00 (978-0-8028-5278-6). 32pp. A beautiful picture-book presentation of the story of the creation and fall of the first humans. (Rev: BL 4/1/05; SLJ 5/05)

19747 Rock, Lois, ed. *Words of Gold: A Treasury of Bible Poetry and Wisdom* (4–6). Illus. 2000, Eerdmans $18.00

(978-0-8028-5199-4). Using 22 double-page spreads, this book contains passages from the Old and New Testaments covering the story of the Jewish people from Abraham to Revelations. (Rev: BL 4/1/00; HBG 9/00; SLJ 9/00)

19748 Ross, Lillian H. *Daughters of Eve: Strong Women of the Bible* (5–7). Illus. 2000, Barefoot Bks. $19.99 (978-1-902283-82-1). Fictionalized accounts that expand on the material given in the Bible and Apocrypha about 12 strong women and their deeds. (Rev: BL 10/1/00; HBG 10/01; SLJ 11/00)

19749 Sasso, Sandy Eisenberg. *Adam and Eve's First Sunset: God's New Day* (K–4). Illus. by Joani Keller Rothenberg. 2003, Jewish Lights $17.95 (978-1-58023-177-0). 32pp. Based on a Talmudic lesson, this is the story of how God helped Adam and Eve build a fire on their first night in the Garden of Eden. (Rev: BL 1/1–15/04; SLJ 3/04)

19750 Sasso, Sandy Eisenberg. *Cain and Abel: Finding the Fruits of Peace* (K–3). Illus. by Joani Keller Rothenberg. 2001, Jewish Lights $16.95 (978-1-58023-123-7). 32pp. This retelling of a biblical parable encourages children to think about the harmful consequences of jealousy and anger. (Rev: BL 11/15/01; HBG 10/02; SLJ 2/02)

19751 Sasso, Sandy Eisenberg. *Naamah, Noah's Wife* (PS–K). Illus. by Bethanne Andersen. 2002, Jewish Lights $7.95 (978-1-893361-56-0). 24pp. This board-book version of *Noah's Wife: The Story of Naamah* (2002) shows Naamah gathering seeds and planting them aboard the ark, and then restocking the earth's plant life after the flood. (Rev: BL 1/1–15/03)

19752 Schmidt, Gary D, retel. *The Blessing of the Lord: Stories from the Old and New Testaments* (5–8). 1997, Eerdmans $20.00 (978-0-8028-3789-9). Using 25 Old and New Testament stories as a focus, these insightful accounts describe how biblical personalities react to such events as Daniel's struggle with the lions and Jesus causing nets to be filled with fish. (Rev: BL 11/1/97; HBG 3/98; SLJ 10/97) [222]

19753 Shaw, Luci. *The Genesis of It All* (K–3). Illus. by Sr. Huai-Kuang Miao. 2006, Paraclete $17.95 (978-1-55725-480-1). This child-friendly retelling of the creation story imagines what God was thinking as He gave form to the world and breathed life into man and beast; the beautiful art progresses from black and white to color, and the author emphasizes that the story is speculation not fact. (Rev: BL 10/1/06)

19754 Spirin, Gennady. *Gennady Spirin's Creation* (K–3). Illus. by author. Series: Master Illustrators. 2008, Zonderkidz $14.99 (978-0-310-71084-4). Handsome watercolors illustrate the creation story as told at the beginning of Genesis. (Rev: BL 6/1–15/08; SLJ 3/08)

19755 *Stories from the Bible* (5–7). Illus. by Lisbeth Zwerger. 2002, North-South $19.95 (978-0-7358-1413-4). 160pp. Sophisticated paintings illustrate verbatim excerpts from the King James version of both the Old and New Testaments. (Rev: BCCB 9/02; BL 4/1/02; HB 7/02; HBG 10/02; SLJ 5/02)

19756 *The Story of Noah and the Ark: According to the Book of Genesis: From the King James Bible* (3–5). Illus. by Gennady Spirin. 2004, Holt $18.95 (978-0-8050-6181-9). 32pp. This retelling of the bible story of Noah's Ark is set apart by Spirin's strikingly beautiful oil illustrations. (Rev: BL 4/15/04; HB 7/04; SLJ 4/04)

19757 Ward, Elaine. *Old Testament Women* (5–10). Series: Art Revelations. 2004, Enchanted Lion $18.95 (978-1-59270-011-0). Paintings by masters accompany stories about 18 women including Rachel, Ruth, and Bathsheba. (Rev: SLJ 8/04) [224]

19758 Watts, Murray. *The Bible for Children* (K–4). Illus. by Helen Cann. 2002, Good Bks. $23.99 (978-1-56148-362-4). Watts vividly retells more than 200 stories from both Old and New Testaments in this handsome volume that includes a map, a glossary, and indexes of people and places. (Rev: BL 10/1/02; HBG 3/03; SLJ 1/03)

19759 Wildsmith, Brian. *Jesus* (PS–3). Illus. 2000, Eerdmans $20.00 (978-0-8028-5212-0). 32pp. Using quotes from the four gospels, the illustrator covers the important incidents in the life of Jesus beginning with the Nativity story and ending with Jesus' death and resurrection. (Rev: BCCB 1/01; BL 2/1/01; HBG 10/01)

19760 Williams, Marcia. *God and His Creations: Tales from the Old Testament* (K–2). Illus. 2004, Candlewick $15.99 (978-0-7636-2211-4). Comic-strip interpretations make accessible several well-known Old Testament stories. (Rev: BL 3/15/04; SLJ 5/04)

19761 Winch, John. *Two by Two* (PS). 2004, Holiday House $16.95 (978-0-8234-1840-4). This retelling of the story of Noah's Ark, recounted in a lush blend of poetic narrative and detailed artwork, focuses on the flood itself and not the spiritual aspects of the Bible story. (Rev: BL 10/1/04; SLJ 10/04) [222]

Holidays and Holy Days

General and Miscellaneous

19762 Addasi, Maha. *The White Nights of Ramadan* (K–3). Illus. by Ned Gannon. 2008, Boyds Mills $16.95 (978-1-59078-523-2). 32pp. This is the story of how Noor, a young Kuwaiti girl, performs the rituals of Girgian, three days in the middle of the holy month of Ramadan. (Rev: BL 7/08; LMC 11/08; SLJ 9/08)

19763 Anderson, Sheila. *Kwanzaa* (PS–K). Illus. by Holli Conger. Series: Cultural Holidays. 2009, ABDO LB $18.95 (978-160270604-0). 32pp. A simple, brightly illustrated introduction to the customs and meaning of Kwanzaa. (Rev: BLO 11/1/09) [394.2612]

19764 Barner, Bob. *The Day of the Dead / El día de los muertos* (PS–1). Trans. by Teresa Mlawer. Illus. by author. 2010, Holiday House $16.95 (978-082342214-2). 32pp. Bright pastel illustrations and bilingual text describe the joy and festivity of the Mexican celebration. (Rev: BL 9/15/10; LMC 1–2/11) [394.264]

19765 Barner, Bob. *Parade Day: Marching Through the Calendar Year* (PS–1). Illus. 2003, Holiday House $16.95 (978-0-8234-1690-5). 32pp. A parade for each month — some for holidays, others (such as a pet parade) just for fun. (Rev: BL 2/15/03; HBG 10/03; SLJ 4/03)

19766 Batmanglij, Najmieh. *Happy Nowruz: Cooking with Children to Celebrate the Persian New Year* (4–8). 2008, Mage $40.00 (978-1-933823-16-4). This attractive spiral-bound book combines the history and customs of the Persian New Year with recipes. (Rev: BL 6/1–15/08) [641.59]

19767 Bennett, Kelly. *Flag Day* (PS–2). Series: Rookie Read-about Holidays. 2003, Children's Book Pr. LB $20.50 (978-0-516-22862-4); paper $5.95 (978-0-516-27755-4). An easy-to-read book that introduces the holiday celebrated on June 14, with details on its origin and observances. (Rev: BL 3/15/03)

19768 Blackwell, Amy Hackney. *Lent, Yom Kippur, and Other Atonement Days* (5–8). Series: Holidays and Celebrations. 2010, Knopf $19.99 (978-1-60413-100-0). 112pp. The customs of Lent, Yom Kippur, and the Buddhist holiday Rains Retreat are detailed and given historical context in this illustrated book. (Rev: BL 11/15/09; SLJ 1/10) [202]

19769 Brill, Marlene T. *Veterans Day* (1–3). Illus. Series: On My Own Holidays. 2005, Carolrhoda LB $25.26 (978-1-57505-699-9); paper $5.95 (978-1-57505-766-8). 48pp. The origins and traditions of Veterans Day are introduced with many illustrations and a short glossary.

19770 Bullard, Lisa. *Marco's Cinco de Mayo* (K–2). Illus. by Holli Conger. Series: Holidays and Special Days. 2012, Millbrook LB $23.93 (978-076135082-8); paper $6.95 (978-076138580-6). 24pp. A Mexican American boy explains the traditions of Cinco de Mayo and shows how his family celebrates. e (Rev: BL 4/1/12; SLJ 4/1/12) [972]

19771 Cooper, Jason. *Arbor Day* (1–3). Illus. Series: Holiday Celebrations. 2003, Rourke LB $20.64 (978-1-58952-217-6). 24pp. An attractive and informative overview of Arbor Day, the holiday's origins, and the contributions trees make to a healthy environment. (Rev: BL 4/1/03)

19772 Craats, Rennay. *Columbus Day: Observing the Day Christopher Columbus Came to the Americas* (3–6). Illus. Series: American Celebrations. 2010, Weigl LB $27.13 (978-160596775-2); paper $11.95 (978-160596933-6). 24pp. History, rituals, and symbols are among the topics covered in this accessible introduction to the holiday. (Rev: BL 1/1–15/11) [394.264]

19773 Dean, Sheri. *Flag Day / Día de la bandera* (K–2). Trans. by Tatiana Acosta and Guillermo Gutiérrez. Series: Our Country's Holidays / Las fiestas de nuestra nación. 2006, Weekly Reader LB $21.00 (978-0-8368-6518-9). 24pp. In English and Spanish, this is an introduction to the history behind Flag Day, with a look at the customs associated with the celebration. Also use *The Fourth of July / Cuatro de Julio, Martin Luther King Jr. Day / Día de Martin Luther King Jr.,*, and *Presidents' Day / Día de los presidentes* (all 2006). (Rev: SLJ 10/06)

19774 Dickmann, Nancy. *Ramadan and Id-ul-Fitr* (PS–1). Illus. Series: Holidays and Festivals. 2010, Acorn LB $21.50 (978-1-4329-4049-2); paper $5.99 (978-1-4329-4068-3). 24pp. With clear, simple text and effective illustrations, Dickmann introduces Islam's holy month and the celebration that takes place at its end. Lexile 230L (Rev: BL 11/15/10; SLJ 12/1/10) [297.3]

19775 Ditchfield, Christin. *Memorial Day* (2–4). Series: A True Book. 2003, Children's Pr. LB $25.00 (978-0-516-22783-2). 48pp. A concise look at Memorial Day (formerly known as Decoration Day) and the various ways in which it is observed. (Rev: SLJ 1/04)

19776 Doering, Amanda. *Cinco de Mayo: Day of Mexican Pride* (1–3). Series: First Facts: Holidays and Culture. 2005, Capstone LB $21.26 (978-0-7368-5387-3). 24pp. A craft, a story, and photographs accompany a brief introduction to the holiday and an explanation of why it is important; suitable for beginning readers. Also use *Day of the Dead* (2005). (Rev: SLJ 5/06)

19777 Erlbach, Arlene. *Happy New Year, Everywhere!* (K–3). Illus. by Sharon L. Holm. 2000, Millbrook LB $23.90 (978-0-7613-1707-4). Lavish double-page spreads introduce New Year celebrations in 20 countries, including Belgium, Haiti, Iran, and Israel. (Rev: BL 11/1/00; HBG 3/01; SLJ 12/00)

19778 Foran, Jill. *Martin Luther King Jr. Day: Recognizing the Life and Work of Martin Luther King Jr.* (3–5). Illus. Series: American Celebrations. 2010, Weigl LB $27.13 (978-160596772-1); paper $11.95 (978-160596779-0). 24pp. History, rituals, and symbols are among the topics covered in this accessible introduction to the holiday. (Rev: BL 1/1–15/11) [394.26]

19779 Freeman, Dorothy R. *St. Patrick's Day. Rev. ed.* (3–5). Illus. Series: Best Holiday Books. 2008, Enslow LB $23.93 (978-0-89490-383-0). 48pp. This easily read account describes the origins of St. Patrick's Day and how it is celebrated. (Rev: BL 10/1/92)

19780 Freeman, Dorothy R., and Dianne MacMillan. *Kwanzaa. Rev. ed.* (3–5). Illus. Series: Best Holiday Books. 2008, Enslow LB $23.93 (978-0-89490-381-6). 48pp. A full treatment of this African American holiday. (Rev: BL 10/1/92)

19781 Ganeri, Anita. *Hindu Festivals Throughout the Year* (3–6). Illus. Series: A Year of Festivals. 2003, Smart Apple LB $24.25 (978-1-58340-372-3). 30pp. After a short introduction to the religion, chronological chapters explain the origins and customs of the major festivals of Hinduism. Also use *Muslim Festivals Throughout the Year* (2003). (Rev: SLJ 12/03)

19782 Gibbons, Gail. *Groundhog Day* (PS–2). Illus. 2007, Holiday $16.95 (978-0-8234-2003-2). 32pp. This examination of the February holiday is accompanied by Gibbons's usual clear illustrations and augmented with information about groundhogs. (Rev: BL 1/1–15/07)

19783 Gilley, Jeremy. *Peace One Day: How September 21 Became World Peace Day* (4–6). Illus. by Karen Blessen. 2005, Putnam $16.99 (978-0-399-24330-1). British filmmaker Gilley tells the story behind World Peace Day, an annual observance he worked diligently to establish. (Rev: BL 10/1/05; SLJ 9/05)

19784 Gnojewski, Carol. *Cinco de Mayo: Celebrating Hispanic Pride* (3–5). Illus. Series: Finding Out About Holidays. 2002, Enslow LB $23.93 (978-0-7660-1575-3). 48pp. Simple text and colorful photographs cover many aspects of Cinco de Mayo, from its history to the way it is celebrated today. (Rev: BL 12/15/02; HBG 3/03; SLJ 11/02)

19785 Gnojewski, Carol. *Day of the Dead: A Latino Celebration of Family and Life* (3–5). Illus. Series: Finding Out About Holidays. 2005, Enslow LB $23.93 (978-0-7660-1780-1). A history of this Mexican holiday, with discussion of how it is celebrated today and its emphasis on family. (Rev: BL 6/1–15/05)

19786 Gnojewski, Carol. *Martin Luther King, Jr., Day: Honoring a Man of Peace* (2–4). Series: Finding Out About Holidays. 2002, Enslow LB $23.93 (978-0-7660-1574-6). 48pp. Information on the holiday and how it is celebrated follows a brief introduction to King's life. (Rev: HBG 3/03; SLJ 12/02)

19787 Gogerly, Liz. *Autumn* (2–4). Series: Holidays Around the World. 2004, Rourke $19.95 (978-1-59515-198-8). The holidays of September to November — and how they're celebrated in different parts of the globe — are profiled with many photographs. Also use *Spring* (2004). (Rev: BL 11/15/04)

19788 Hamilton, Lynn. *Presidents' Day: Honoring the Accomplishments of All U.S. Presidents* (3–5). Illus. Series: American Celebrations. 2010, Weigl LB $27.13 (978-160596773-8); paper $11.95 (978-160596931-2). 24pp. Describes the ways in which this holiday celebrates the history of the nation and its presidents. (Rev: BL 1/1–15/11) [394.261]

19789 Harris, Zoe, and Suzanne Williams. *Pinatas and Smiling Skeletons* (4–8). 1998, Pacific View LB $19.95 (978-1-881896-19-7). This book introduces six festivals celebrated in Mexico: the Feast of the Virgin of Guadalupe, Christmas, Carnaval, Corpus Christi, Independence Day, and the Day of the Dead. (Rev: BL 3/15/99; HBG 3/99; SLJ 3/99) [394.26972]

19790 Heiligman, Deborah. *Celebrate Diwali* (1–3). Series: Holidays Around the World. 2006, National Geographic $15.95 (978-0-7922-5922-0). 32pp. A look at the customs associated with the celebration of the Hindu holiday, in India and in four other countries. (Rev: SLJ 1/07)

19791 Heiligman, Deborah. *Celebrate Independence Day* (K–3). Series: Holidays Around the World. 2007, National Geographic $15.95 (978-1-4263-0074-5). 32pp. The author discusses how and why people around the United States celebrate the Fourth of July. A locator map shows where every photograph in the book was taken. (Rev: SLJ 8/07)

19792 Heiligman, Deborah. *Celebrate Ramadan and Eid al-Fitr* (1–3). Series: Holidays Around the World. 2006, National Geographic $15.95 (978-0-7922-5926-8). 32pp. A look at these Islamic observances and their religious significance as well as the associated customs and rituals. (Rev: SLJ 1/07)

19793 Heinrichs, Ann. *Chinese New Year* (K–3). Illus. by Benrei Huang. Series: Holidays, Festivals, and Celebrations. 2006, The Child's World LB $24.21 (978-1-59296-572-4). Examines the history, customs, and symbols of this holiday and includes a recipe and a craft. Also use *Saint Patrick's Day* (2006). (Rev: SLJ 9/06)

19794 Heinrichs, Ann. *Cinco de Mayo* (2–3). Illus. by Kathleen Petelinsek. Series: Holidays, Festivals, and Celebrations. 2006, The Child's World LB $24.21 (978-1-59296-573-1). Information about the holiday and how it is celebrated, plus photographs of the festivities, Spanish words, and a craft to try; also use *Día de los Muertos* (2006). (Rev: SLJ 5/06)

19795 Heinrichs, Ann. *Independence Day* (K–3). Illus. by Robert Squier. 2013, Child's World LB $25.64 (978-162323508-6). 32pp. Not only does this book about the Fourth of July discuss the beginnings of America, it also covers the Revolutionary War and offers tips for how to celebrate the holiday. (Rev: BL 11/1/13) [394.2634]

19796 Hoyt-Goldsmith, Diane. *Celebrating a Quinceañera: A Latina's 15th Birthday Celebration* (3–6). Photos by Lawrence Migdale. 2002, Holiday House $16.95 (978-0-8234-1693-6). 30pp. A detailed description of a young woman's preparations for and celebration of her quinceanera, the ritual coming of age at 15. (Rev: HBG 3/03; SLJ 9/02)

19797 Hoyt-Goldsmith, Diane. *Celebrating Ramadan* (2–5). Illus. by Lawrence Migdale. 2001, Holiday House $17.95 (978-0-8234-1581-6). 32pp. This informative picture-book introduction to Islam and the month of Ramadan features a fourth-grade New Jersey boy named Ibraheem. (Rev: BCCB 12/01; BL 10/1/01; HB 1/02; HBG 3/02; SLJ 8/01)

19798 Hoyt-Goldsmith, Diane. *Cinco de Mayo: Celebrating the Traditions of Mexico* (3–5). Illus. 2008, Holiday $16.95 (978-0-8234-2107-7). 32pp. Rosie and her Mexican American family enjoy the Cinco de Mayo celebration in their California community. (Rev: BL 3/15/08; SLJ 4/08)

19799 Hoyt-Goldsmith, Diane. *Three Kings Day: A Celebration at Christmastime* (2–5). Illus. by Lawrence Migdale. 2004, Holiday House $16.95 (978-0-8234-1839-8). 32pp. Dia de los Tres Reyes is seen from the point of view of a 10-year-old girl living in New York's Puerto Rican community. (Rev: BL 9/15/04; SLJ 10/04)

19800 Jackson, Ellen. *The Autumn Equinox: Celebrating the Harvest* (2–5). Illus. by Jan Davey Ellis. 2000, Millbrook LB $22.90 (978-0-7613-1354-0). Harvest festivals, past and present, from around the world are described with attractive craft projects, games, and recipes. (Rev: HBG 3/01; SLJ 11/00)

19801 Jackson, Ellen. *The Spring Equinox: Celebrating the Greening of the Earth* (3–5). Illus. by Jan Davey Ellis. 2002, Millbrook LB $24.90 (978-0-7613-1955-9). 32pp. Many of the holidays associated with spring — including Passover, Easter, Earth Day, and Holi — are highlighted in a series of illustrated double-page spreads. (Rev: BL 4/15/02; HBG 10/02; SLJ 6/02)

19802 Jango-Cohen, Judith. *Chinese New Year* (1–3). Illus. by Jason Chin. Series: On My Own Holidays. 2005, Carolrhoda LB $25.26 (978-1-57505-653-1); paper $5.95 (978-1-57505-763-7). 48pp. The origins and traditions of the Chinese New Year are introduced with many illustrations and a short glossary. (Rev: BL 1/1–15/05)

19803 Jordan, Denise M. *Juneteenth* (1–3). Series: Holiday Histories. 2003, Heinemann LB $22.79 (978-1-4034-3505-7). 32pp. The story of the unofficial holiday (June 19th) that celebrates the end of slavery. (Rev: SLJ 5/04)

19804 Kaplan, Leslie C. *Chinese New Year* (2–4). Series: Library of Holidays. 2004, Rosen LB $19.95 (978-0-8239-6658-5). 24pp. Brief, illustrated chapters introduce the history and traditions of this month-long holiday. (Rev: SLJ 8/04)

19805 Kaplan, Leslie C. *Cinco de Mayo* (2–4). Series: Library of Holidays. 2004, Rosen LB $19.95 (978-0-8239-6662-2). 24pp. A brief introduction to Cinco de Mayo, with information on history and tradition paired with full-page photographs. (Rev: SLJ 8/04)

19806 Kaplan, Leslie C. *Flag Day* (2–4). Series: Library of Holidays. 2004, Rosen LB $19.95 (978-0-8239-6659-2). 24pp. A brief introduction to the patriotic holiday, with information on history and tradition paired with full-page photographs. (Rev: SLJ 8/04)

19807 Katz, Karen. *My First Chinese New Year* (PS–K). Illus. 2004, Holt $14.95 (978-0-8050-7076-7). 32pp. A young girl and her family prepare for the annual celebration in this simple introduction. (Rev: BL 2/1/05)

19808 Krasno, Rena. *Floating Lanterns and Golden Shrines: Celebrating Japanese Festivals* (3–5). Illus. by Toru Sugita. 2000, Pacific View $19.95 (978-1-881896-21-0). 49pp. Important celebrations for both Japanese and Japanese Americans are covered in this attractive book. (Rev: HBG 9/00; SLJ 6/00)

19809 Krishnaswami, Uma. *Holi* (K–2). Illus. Series: Rookie Read-about Holidays. 2003, Children's Pr. LB $20.50 (978-0-516-22863-1). For beginning readers, this is a well-illustrated basic description of the Hindu festival of Holi. (Rev: BL 5/1/03; SLJ 6/03)

19810 Landau, Elaine. *Columbus Day — Celebrating a Famous Explorer* (3–6). Series: Finding Out About Holidays. 2001, Enslow LB $23.93 (978-0-7660-1573-9). 48pp. After introducing Christopher Columbus, this account describes the history of the holiday that honors him and tells how it is celebrated. (Rev: BL 9/15/01; HBG 3/02; SLJ 9/01)

19811 Landau, Elaine. *Earth Day: Keeping Our Planet Clean* (3–6). Series: Finding Out About Holidays. 2002, Enslow LB $23.93 (978-0-7660-1778-8). 48pp. A look at the founding of Earth Day in 1970 by Senator Gaylord Nelson and how Earth Day is observed today. (Rev: BL 7/02; HBG 10/02; SLJ 7/02)

19812 Landau, Elaine. *Independence Day: Birthday of the United States* (3–6). Series: Finding Out About Holidays. 2001, Enslow LB $23.93 (978-0-7660-1571-5). 48pp. Short chapters and plenty of color photographs introduce the history of the July 4th holiday and how it is celebrated today. (Rev: BL 9/15/01; HBG 3/02; SLJ 9/01)

19813 Landau, Elaine. *Mardi Gras: Parades, Costumes, and Parties* (3–6). Series: Finding Out About Holidays. 2002, Enslow LB $23.93 (978-0-7660-1776-4). The origins of Mardi Gras are explained, with material on how the holiday is observed in locations including New Orleans. (Rev: BL 7/02; HBG 10/02; SLJ 8/02)

19814 Landau, Elaine. *St. Patrick's Day: Parades, Shamrocks, and Leprechauns* (3–6). Series: Finding Out About Holidays. 2002, Enslow LB $23.93 (978-0-7660-1777-1). SaintPatrick is introduced along with material on the symbols connected with this holiday and ways it is observed. (Rev: BL 7/02; HBG 3/03; SLJ 10/02)

19815 Landau, Elaine. *Veteran's Day: Remembering Our War Heroes* (3–6). Series: Finding Out About Holidays. 2002, Enslow LB $23.93 (978-0-7660-1775-7). 48pp. Landau traces the origins of this holiday and details how it is observed across the United States. (Rev: BL 7/02; HBG 10/02)

19816 Landau, Elaine. *What Is St. Patrick's Day?* (K–2). Series: I Like Holidays! 2011, Enslow LB $21.26 (978-0-7660-3704-5); paper $6.95 (978-1-59845-291-4). 24pp. This straightforward overview for young children provides some cultural and historical background about St. Patrick's Day, and includes colorful photographs of contemporary celebrations and an activity. (Rev: SLJ 11/1/11) [394.2]

19817 Lowery, Linda. *Day of the Dead* (K–3). Illus. by Barbara Knutson. Series: On My Own Holidays. 2003, Carolrhoda LB $25.26 (978-0-87614-914-0); paper $5.95 (978-1-57505-581-7). 48pp. A lively, easy-reader introduction to the Mexican holiday. (Rev: HBG 4/04; SLJ 11/03)

19818 MacMillan, Dianne. *Martin Luther King, Jr. Day.* Rev. ed. (3–5). Illus. Series: Best Holiday Books. 2008, Enslow LB $23.93 (978-0-89490-382-3). 48pp. This easy-to-read book describes how Martin Luther King, Jr. Day originated and how it is celebrated in schools and towns. (Rev: BL 10/1/92; SLJ 1/93)

19819 Marx, David F. *Chinese New Year* (PS–1). Series: Rookie Read-about Holidays. 2002, Children's Book Pr. paper $5.95 (978-0-516-27375-4). An introduction for very young readers to the rituals of the Chinese New Year. Also use *Ramadan*. (Rev: SLJ 9/02)

19820 Mercer, Abbie. *Happy St. Patrick's Day* (2–4). Series: Holiday Fun. 2007, Rosen LB $21.25 (978-1-4042-3811-4). Along with historical information and discussion of the symbols and activities associated with this holiday, this volume includes a recipe and a craft. (Rev: SLJ 2/08)

19821 Mobin-Uddin, Asma. *The Best Eid Ever* (K–3). Illus. by Laura Jacobsen. 2007, Boyds Mills $16.95 (978-1-59078-431-0). 32pp. Aneesa and her grandmother celebrate Eid al-Adha, an Islamic holiday, and plan to help two girls who have escaped from a war-torn country; a glossary and pronunciation guide are helpful. (Rev: BL 1/1–15/08; LMC 3/08; SLJ 12/07)

19822 Murray, Julie. *Kwanzaa* (1–3). Illus. Series: Holidays. 2003, ABDO LB $21.35 (978-1-57765-955-6). 24pp. Examines Kwanzaa's adaptation from an African harvest festival and looks at some of the activities associated with the holiday. (Rev: HBG 10/03; SLJ 10/03)

19823 Murray, Julie. *Ramadan* (K–3). Series: Holidays. 2011, ABDO LB $25.65 (978-1-61783-041-9). 24pp. A simple introduction to the holiday and its traditions, with large photographs. (Rev: SLJ 12/1/11) [297]

19824 Nelson, Robin. *Constitution Day* (K–2). Illus. Series: First Step Nonfiction: American Holidays. 2009, Lerner LB $19.93 (978-0-7613-4930-3). 24pp. A simple look at the holiday that was enacted in 2005 and the reasons why we recognize this day. (Rev: BL 6/1–15/09)

19825 Nelson, Robin. *Juneteenth* (K–2). Illus. Series: First Step Nonfiction - American Holidays. 2009, Lerner LB $19.93 (978-0-7613-4934-1). Texas slaves heard about the Emancipation Proclamation two years late — on Juneteenth. (Rev: BL 6/1–15/09)

19826 Nelson, Vaunda Micheaux, and Drew Nelson. *Juneteenth* (2–4). Illus. by Mark Schroder. Series: On My Own Holidays. 2006, Lerner $25.26 (978-1-57505-876-4); paper $5.95 (978-0-8225-5974-0). 48pp. The story behind the Juneteenth holiday is told for beginning readers. (Rev: BL 2/1/06; SLJ 3/06)

19827 Nobleman, Marc Tyler. *Martin Luther King Jr. Day* (1–3). Series: Let's See. 2004, Compass Point LB $19.93 (978-0-7565-0646-9). 24pp. For young researchers, this is an introduction to this holiday, using questions as chapter headings. (Rev: SLJ 1/05)

19828 Otto, Carolyn. *Celebrate Chinese New Year: With Fireworks, Dragons, and Lanterns* (1–4). Illus. 2008, National Geographic $15.95 (978-1-4263-0381-4). Well-written narrative and color photographs show how Chinese New Year is celebrated in a variety of countries. (Rev: BL 12/15/08; SLJ 1/09)

19829 Otto, Carolyn. *Celebrate Cinco de Mayo with Fiestas, Music, and Dance* (1–4). Illus. Series: Holidays Around the World. 2008, National Geographic $15.95 (978-1-4263-0215-2). 32pp. An attractive account of the origins of and traditions associated with Cinco de Mayo both in the United States and south of the border, with lots of photographs, a bibliography, a glossary, and recipes. (Rev: BL 4/15/08; SLJ 4/08)

19830 Petelinsek, Kathleen, and E. Russell Primm. *Holidays and Celebrations / Días de fiesta y celebraciones* (K–2). Illus. by Nichole Day Diggins. Series: Talking Hands. 2006, The Child's World LB $21.36 (978-1-59296-453-6). 24pp. Students demonstrate simple holiday-related words using American Sign Language; the text is in both English and Spanish. (Rev: SLJ 6/06)

19831 Reynolds, Betty. *Japanese Celebrations: Cherry Blossoms, Lanterns and Stars!* (3–5). Illus. 2006, Turtle $16.95 (978-0-8048-3658-6). 48pp. A chronological survey of Japanese holidays throughout the year, covering food, dress, decoration, symbols, and so forth. (Rev: BL 12/1/06; SLJ 12/06)

19832 Rissman, Rebecca. *Martin Luther King, Jr. Day* (PS–K). Illus. Series: Holidays and Festivals. 2010, Heinemann LB $21.50 (978-143294055-3). 24pp. An introduction for very young children to the importance of this holiday and to the life of the man it honors. (Rev: BL 2/1/11) [394.261]

19833 Roberts, Russell. *Holidays and Celebrations in Colonial America* (4–6). Illus. Series: Building America. 2006, Mitchell Lane LB $29.95 (978-1-58415-467-9). 48pp. This attractive title, which features a timeline, glossary, and calendar, briefly profiles the holidays celebrated during America's colonial period and examines how those that are still observed today have changed over the years. (Rev: BL 11/1/06)

19834 Robinson, Fay. *Chinese New Year: A Time for Parades, Family, and Friends* (3–6). Illus. Series: Finding Out About Holidays. 2001, Enslow LB $23.93 (978-0-7660-1631-6). 48pp. This detailed account gives the history behind this traditional holiday and explains how Chinese Americans celebrate it. (Rev: BL 9/15/01; HBG 3/02; SLJ 1/02)

19835 Roop, Connie, and Peter Roop. *Let's Celebrate Earth Day* (1–3). Illus. by Gwen Connelly. 2001, Millbrook LB $22.90 (978-0-7613-1812-5). 32pp. Information on the history and purpose of Earth Day is presented in a question-and-answer format. (Rev: BL 5/1/01; HBG 10/01)

19836 Rosinsky, Natalie M. *Juneteenth* (1–3). Series: Let's See. 2004, Compass Point LB $19.93 (978-0-7565-0770-1). For young researchers, this is an introduction to this holiday, using questions as chapter headings. (Rev: SLJ 1/05)

19837 Rosinsky, Natalie M. *Presidents' Day* (1–3). Illus. Series: Let's See. 2004, Compass Point LB $19.93 (978-0-7565-0773-2). 24pp. Using a question-and-answer format, large print, and many illustrations, this small book discusses the history of Presidents' Day and how it honors Washington and Lincoln. (Rev: BL 10/15/04)

19838 San Vicente, Luis. *The Festival of Bones / El Festival de las Calaveras: The Little-Bitty Book for the Day of the Dead* (PS–3). Illus. by author. 2002, Cinco Puntos $14.95 (978-0-938317-67-8). 32pp. Dancing skeletons accompany the text describing the Mexican festival known as the Day of the Dead, or el Día de los Muertos. (Rev: HBG 3/03; SLJ 3/03)

19839 Schaefer, Lola M. *Chinese New Year* (PS–2). Series: Holidays and Celebrations. 2000, Capstone LB $17.26 (978-0-7368-0660-2). 24pp. A simple beginning reader that introduces the traditions and meaning behind the Chinese New Year. (Rev: HBG 3/01; SLJ 12/00)

19840 Schaefer, Lola M. *Cinco de Mayo* (PS–2). Series: Holidays and Celebrations. 2000, Capstone LB $17.26 (978-0-7368-0661-9). 24pp. The traditions and customs surrounding the Mexican Independence Day are outlined in this simple book for beginning readers. (Rev: HBG 3/01; SLJ 12/00)

19841 Schuh, Mari C. *Flag Day* (PS–2). Series: National Holidays. 2003, Capstone LB $17.26 (978-0-7368-1652-6). 24pp. For beginning readers, this is an introduction to Flag Day and its history. (Rev: HBG 10/03; SLJ 9/03)

19842 Schuh, Mari C. *Labor Day* (PS–2). Series: National Holidays. 2003, Capstone LB $17.26 (978-0-7368-1653-3). 24pp. For beginning readers, this is an introduction to Labor Day and its history. (Rev: HBG 10/03)

19843 Schuh, Mari C. *New Year's Day* (K–2). Series: Holidays and Celebrations. 2002, Capstone LB $17.26 (978-0-7368-1446-1). Double-page spreads with bright full-page photographs on the left and a brief text on the right introduce the history, traditions, and celebrations that surround New Year's Day. (Rev: BL 1/1–15/03; HBG 3/03)

19844 Schuh, Mari C. *St. Patrick's Day* (K–2). Illus. Series: Holidays and Celebrations. 2002, Capstone $17.26 (978-0-7368-1447-8). 24pp. This small, square book about Saint Patrick's Day includes discussion of the holiday's symbols and traditions and includes reference sources and a glossary. (Rev: BL 1/1–15/03; HBG 3/03)

19845 Senker, Cath. *Winter* (2–4). Illus. Series: Holidays Around the World. 2004, Rourke $19.95 (978-1-59515-199-5). Holidays that take place from December to February are included here, with Christmas in Zimbabwe and Id ul-Fitr in Canada among those featured; a chart lists dates through 2006. Also use *Summer* (2004). (Rev: BL 11/15/04)

19846 Shahan, Sherry. *Fiesta! A Celebration of Latino Festivals* (1–3). Illus. by Paula Barragán. 2009, August House $16.95 (978-0-87483-861-9). 32pp. A month-by-month look at various holidays celebrated in Latin American countries, including Mexico's Fiesta de San Antonio Abad and Brazil's Águas de Oxalá. (Rev: BL 4/1/09; LMC 8/09; SLJ 4/09)

19847 Sievert, Terri. *Ramadan: Islamic Holy Month* (K–2). Illus. Series: First Facts: Holidays and Culture. 2006, Capstone LB $21.26 (978-0-7368-5392-7). 24pp. This photo-filled title introduces young readers to the Islamic holiday, exploring its religious significance and traditions. (Rev: BL 4/1/06)

19848 Simonds, Nina, et al. *Moonbeams, Dumplings and Dragon Boats: A Treasury of Chinese Holiday Tales, Activities and Recipes* (4–6). Illus. by Meilo So. 2002, Harcourt $20.00 (978-0-15-201983-9). 80pp. This vibrantly illustrated book for older readers examines five Chinese holidays and includes stories, recipes, and crafts related to each. (Rev: BL 10/15/02; HBG 3/03; SLJ 11/02*)

19849 Tabor, Nancy María Grande. *Celebrations / Celebraciones* (PS–3). Illus. 2004, Charlesbridge $16.95 (978-1-57091-575-8). 32pp. Shared holidays and individual Mexican and U.S. holidays are introduced in both Spanish and English. (Rev: BL 3/1/04; SLJ 4/04)

19850 Tait, Leia. *Cinco de Mayo: Celebrating Mexican History and Culture* (3–5). Illus. Series: American Celebrations. 2010, Weigl LB $27.13 (978-160596776-9); paper $11.95 (978-160596934-3). 24pp. History, rituals, and symbols are among the topics covered in this accessible introduction to the Mexican holiday. (Rev: BL 1/1–15/11) [394.262]

19851 Taylor, Charles A. *Juneteenth: A Celebration of Freedom* (5–8). Illus. by author. 2002, Open Hand $19.95 (978-0-940880-68-9). A well-organized account of this holiday, which celebrates emancipation, with a discussion of the history of slavery. (Rev: SLJ 11/02) [394.2]

19852 Tokunbo, Dimitrea. *The Sound of Kwanzaa* (PS–2). Illus. by Lisa Cohen. 2009, Scholastic $16.99 (978-054501865-4). 32pp. The rituals and celebrations of Kwanzaa are presented along with a pronunciation guide and a recipe. (Rev: BL 11/1/09; LMC 1–2/10; SLJ 10/09) [394.261]

19853 Trueit, Trudi. *Kwanzaa* (1–3). Series: Rookie Read-about Holidays. 2006, Children's Pr. LB $20.50 (978-0-531-12458-1); paper $5.95 (978-0-531-11839-9). 32pp. This colorful introduction to the holiday examines its history and customs and provides a holiday-related recipe and craft. (Rev: SLJ 10/06)

19854 Verma, Jatinder. *The Story of Divaali* (1–3). Illus. by Nilesh Mistry. 2002, Barefoot Bks. $16.99 (978-1-84148-936-0). 40pp. Verma effectively retells the complex story, based on the Sanskrit *Ramayana*, of the lighting of lamps that started the celebration of the Hindu festival of Diwali. (Rev: BL 1/1–15/03; HBG 3/03; SLJ 11/02)

19855 Walsh, Kieran. *Chinese New Year* (2–3). Series: Holiday Celebrations. 2003, Rourke LB $20.64 (978-1-58952-215-2). 24pp. Provides basic information about how the holiday began and how it is celebrated. Also use *Cinco de Mayo* (2003). (Rev: BL 9/15/03; SLJ 1/03)

19856 Walsh, Kieran. *Cinco de Mayo* (1–3). Illus. Series: Holiday Celebrations. 2003, Rourke LB $20.64 (978-1-58952-221-3). 24pp. The Mexican holiday comes to life with discussions of the festivities that take place as well as the origin of the celebration. (Rev: BL 4/1/03)

19857 Whitman, Sylvia. *Under the Ramadan Moon* (PS–2). Illus. by Sue Williams. 2008, Albert Whitman $15.99 (978-0-8075-8304-3). 32pp. This rhythmic picture-book introduction to the Muslim month of Ramadan follows a family at home and at the mosque. (Rev: BL 10/1/08; SLJ 9/08)

Christmas

19858 Box, Su. *Behind the Scenes Christmas* (3–5). Illus. by Jo Blake. 2006, Abingdon $14.00 (978-0-687-49121-6). 29pp. Arranged in question-and-answer format and featuring excerpted Bible stories, this colorful book

pieces together the events surrounding the birth of Jesus Christ. (Rev: SLJ 10/06)

19859 *Christmas in Colonial and Early America* (4–7). 1996, World Book $19.00 (978-0-7166-0875-2). The evolution of Christmas celebrations is traced through more than 100 years of American history to the end of the 19th century. (Rev: BL 11/1/96) [394.26]

19860 *Christmas in Greece* (5–10). Series: Christmas Around the World. 2000, World Book $19.00 (978-0-7166-0859-2). This account focuses on the religious practices of the Greek Orthodox Church at Christmastime, which begins with a long fasting period. (Rev: BL 9/1/00) [398.2]

19861 Davis, Katherine, et al. *The Little Drummer Boy* (K–3). Illus. by Kristina Rodanas. 2001, Clarion $15.00 (978-0-395-97015-7). 32pp. An attractive rendering of the traditional Christmas song about the little boy and the value of gifts. (Rev: BL 9/1/01; HBG 3/02; SLJ 10/01)

19862 Erlbach, Arlene. *Christmas — Celebrating Life, Giving, and Kindness* (3–6). Series: Finding Out About Holidays. 2001, Enslow LB $23.93 (978-0-7660-1576-0). 48pp. In a series of short chapters that include many attractive color photographs, this book explores the history of Christmas and tells how it is observed in the United States. (Rev: BL 9/15/01; HBG 3/02; SLJ 10/01)

19863 Erlbach, Arlene, and Herb Erlbach. *Merry Christmas, Everywhere!* (K–2). Illus. by Sharon L. Holm. 2002, Millbrook $23.90 (978-0-7613-1956-6); paper $8.95 (978-0-7613-1699-2). 48pp. Fine illustrations and maps introduce Christmas traditions in countries around the world, accompanied by illustrations, recipes, and crafts. (Rev: BL 9/15/02; HBG 3/03; SLJ 10/02)

19864 Farmer, Jacqueline. *O Christmas Tree: Its History and Holiday Traditions* (1–4). Illus. by Joanne Friar. 2010, Charlesbridge $16.95 (978-158089238-4); paper $7.95 (978-15808923-9-1). 32pp. The history of the Christmas tree custom, from pagan and early Christian practices through current times, is the focus of this colorful book. (Rev: BL 9/1/10; HB 11–12/10; SLJ 10/10) [394.2663]

19865 Flanagan, Alice K. *Christmas* (2–3). Series: Holidays and Festivals. 2001, Compass Point LB $23.93 (978-0-7565-0085-6). 32pp. An easy-to-read picture book that describes the origins of Christmas and the many ways in which it is celebrated. (Rev: BL 10/15/01; SLJ 10/01)

19866 Foreman, Michael. *Michael Foreman's Christmas Treasury* (3–6). 2000, Pavilion $22.95 (978-1-86205-197-3). 124pp. A delightful collection of songs, stories, poems, and carols. (Rev: BL 12/1/00)

19867 French, Fiona. *Bethlehem* (PS–3). Illus. 2001, HarperCollins $15.95 (978-0-06-029623-0). 32pp. Stained-glass style illustrations illuminate the story of the first Christmas as told in the King James version of the gospels of St. Luke and St. Matthew. (Rev: BL 10/15/01; HBG 3/02; SLJ 10/01)

19868 Isadora, Rachel. *Twelve Days of Christmas* (1–3). Illus. by author. 2010, Putnam $16.99 (978-039925073-6). 32pp. Using text and rebuses, with bright collages, this picture book sets the traditional carol in Africa. (Rev: BL 10/15/10; HB 11–12/10; SLJ 10/10) [782.42]

19869 Jeffers, H. Paul. *Legends of Santa Claus* (4–7). Series: A&E Biography. 2000, Lucent LB $27.93 (978-0-8225-4983-3). 112pp. This book recounts the tales, legends, and myths about Santa Claus and sorts the truth from the fiction. (Rev: BL 12/15/00; HBG 3/01)

19870 Kelley, Emily. *Christmas Around the World. Rev. ed.* (2–3). Illus. by Joni Oeltjenbruns. Series: On My Own Holidays. 2003, Carolrhoda LB $25.26 (978-0-87614-915-7); paper $5.95 (978-1-57505-580-0). 48pp. This revised edition introduces young readers to Christmas traditions in Australia, China, Ethiopia, Germany, Lebanon, Mexico, Russia, and Sweden. (Rev: HBG 4/04; SLJ 10/03)

19871 Lankford, Mary D. *Christmas USA* (3–5). Illus. by Karen Dugan. 2006, HarperCollins $16.99 (978-0-688-15012-9). 48pp. A regional look at the various Christmas customs in the United States, including instructions for various crafts, recipes, and a timeline of popular Christmas toys over the years. (Rev: BL 11/15/06; SLJ 10/06)

19872 Mora, Pat. *A Piñata in a Pine Tree: A Latino Twelve Days of Christmas* (PS–3). Illus. by Magaly Morales. 2009, Clarion $16 (978-061884198-1). 32pp. With a pronunciation guide and a glossary, this adaptation of "The Twelve Days of Christmas" introduces many elements of Latino holiday celebrations. (Rev: BL 11/1/09; HB 11–12/09; SLJ 10/09) [782.42]

19873 Murray, Julie. *Christmas* (1–3). Series: Holidays. 2003, ABDO LB $21.35 (978-1-57765-951-8). 24pp. Explores the origins of the holiday, as well as many of the activities, foods, and customs associated with it. (Rev: HBG 10/03; SLJ 10/03)

19874 Nazoa, Aquiles. *A Small Nativity* (1–3). Trans. by Hugh Hazelton. Illus. by Ana Palmero Caceres. 2007, Groundwood $9.95 (978-0-88899-839-2). 44pp. Featuring contemporary characters but more traditional, rich artwork, this is an appealing retelling of the Nativity story. (Rev: BL 10/15/07; HB 11/07)

19875 Onyefulu, Ifeoma. *An African Christmas* (K–2). Illus. 2005, Frances Lincoln $15.95 (978-1-84507-387-9). 32pp. A young Nigerian boy Afam hopes to create his own mask and to dance in the traditional Mmo masquerade. (Rev: BL 11/1/05)

19876 Ross, Michael Elsohn. *A Mexican Christmas* (K–3). Photos by Felix Rigau. 2002, Carolrhoda LB $23.93 (978-0-87614-601-9). 40pp. Christmas customs in Oaxaca are described in text and photographs. (Rev: HBG 3/03; SLJ 10/02)

19877 Schuh, Mari C. *Christmas* (PS–2). Series: Holidays and Celebrations. 2002, Capstone LB $17.26 (978-0-7368-0979-5). 24pp. An overview of holiday traditions in the United States for beginning readers. (Rev: HBG 3/02; SLJ 10/02)

19878 Steiner, Joan. *Look-Alikes Christmas* (K–4). Photos by Ogden Gigli. 2003, Little, Brown $14.95 (978-0-316-81187-3). Challenges young readers to name the everyday objects that have been used to construct nine three-dimensional holiday scenes, including Santa's workshop, a cathedral, and a scene from the *Nutcracker* ballet. (Rev: HB 11/03; HBG 4/04; SLJ 10/03)

Easter

19879 Joslin, Mary. *On That Easter Morning* (K–3). Illus. by Helen Cann. 2006, Good Bks. $16.00 (978-1-56148-517-8). The biblical account of Jesus's last days on Earth, leading to his crucifixion and resurrection, is retold and accompanied by beautiful artwork. (Rev: SLJ 5/06)

19880 Knudsen, Shannon. *Easter Around the World* (1–3). Illus. Series: On My Own Holidays. 2005, Carolrhoda LB $25.26 (978-1-57505-655-5). 48pp. The origins and traditions of Easter are introduced with many illustrations and a short glossary.

19881 Landau, Elaine. *Easter: Parades, Chocolates, and Celebration* (2–5). Illus. Series: Finding Out About Holidays. 2004, Enslow LB $23.93 (978-0-7660-2172-3). 48pp. Informative text and colorful photographs present the history and religious significance of Easter, plus traditional symbols and contemporary ways of celebrating this holiday. (Rev: SLJ 4/05)

19882 Merrick, Patrick. *Easter Bunnies* (1–3). Illus. Series: Our Holiday Symbols. 2010, Child's World LB $24.21 (978-160253333-2). 24pp. Merrick explains the history and sometimes puzzling origins of the Easter Bunny. (Rev: BLO 3/1/10) [394.2667]

19883 Schuh, Mari C. *Easter* (K–2). Series: Holidays and Celebrations. 2002, Capstone LB $17.26 (978-0-7368-1445-4). This small, square book uses full-page photographs and a brief text to present the meaning of Easter, its symbols, celebrations, and importance. (Rev: BCCB 2/02; BL 1/1–15/03; HBG 3/03)

Halloween

19884 Flanagan, Alice K. *Halloween* (2–3). Series: Holidays and Festivals. 2001, Compass Point LB $23.93 (978-0-7565-0086-3). 32pp. An attractive picture book that describes the origins of Halloween and how it is celebrated by youngsters today. (Rev: BCCB 10/02; BL 10/15/01; SLJ 1/02)

19885 Gibbons, Gail. *Halloween Is . . .* (PS–2). Illus. 2002, Holiday House $17.95 (978-0-8234-1758-2). 32pp. A larger, revised version with new, enhanced illustrations of the 1984 *Halloween*, describing the holiday's history and traditions. (Rev: BL 9/15/02; HBG 3/03)

19886 Greene, Carol. *The Story of Halloween* (3–5). Illus. by Linda Bronson. 2004, HarperCollins LB $16.89 (978-0-06-029560-8). 40pp. The history of Halloween is covered from its origins in the Celtic festival of Samhain to present-day problems with trick-or-treating. (Rev: BL 9/1/04; SLJ 8/04)

19887 Lewis, Anne Margaret. *What Am I? Halloween* (PS–2). Illus. by Tom Mills. Series: My Look and See Holiday Book. 2011, Whitman $9.99 (978-0-8075-8959-5). Unpaged. "I can float through the air/and I like to shout, BOO!/What am I? What could I be?" Questions like this are answered on flaps: "I am a spooky ghost/on Halloween./That's me!" (Rev: SLJ 9/1/11) [394.2646]

19888 Mercer, Abbie. *Happy Halloween* (2–4). Series: Holiday Fun. 2007, Rosen LB $21.25 (978-1-4042-3806-0). 24pp. Along with discussion of the traditions and activities associated with this holiday, this volume includes a recipe and a craft. (Rev: SLJ 2/08)

19889 Rau, Dana Meachen. *Carving Pumpkins* (3–6). Illus. by Kathleen Petelinsek. Series: How-to Library. 2012, Cherry Lake LB $28.50 (978-161080470-7). 32pp. Covering everything from picking your pumpkin and the basic tools you will need to planning the personality of your pumpkin and tips on a carving, this is a useful volume. (Rev: BL 10/1/12) [745.594]

19890 Robinson, Fay. *Halloween — Costumes and Treats on All Hallows' Eve* (3–6). Series: Finding Out About Holidays. 2001, Enslow LB $23.93 (978-0-7660-1632-3). 48pp. The origins of Halloween are described, with material on how this holiday has evolved and how it is currently celebrated in the United States. (Rev: BL 9/15/01; HBG 3/02; SLJ 9/01)

19891 Zocchi, Judy. *On Halloween Night / La noche de Halloween* (2–4). Illus. by Rebecca Wallis. 2005, Dingles LB $15.50 (978-1-891997-76-1). A cartoon-filled bilingual introduction to the history and rituals of Halloween. (Rev: SLJ 2/06)

Jewish Holy Days and Celebrations

19892 Adler, David A. *The Story of Passover* (PS–1). Illus. by Jill Weber. 2014, Holiday $15.95 (978-082342902-8). 32pp. Tells the Exodus story in simplified form, with details of the horrors but without emphasizing them; with effective illustrations and an author's note about Passover traditions. (Rev: BL 3/1/14; SLJ 4/14) [296.4]

19893 Baum, Maxie. *I Have a Little Dreidel* (PS–K). Illus. by Julie Paschkis. 2006, Scholastic $9.99 (978-0-439-64997-1). Illustrations full of interesting details enhance this retelling of the traditional Hanukkah song. (Rev: BL 9/15/06; HB 11/06; HBG 4/07; SLJ 10/06)

19894 Ben-Zvi, Rebecca Tova. *Four Sides, Eight Nights: A New Spin on Hanukkah* (2–4). Illus. by Susanna Natti. 2005, Roaring Brook $16.95 (978-1-59643-059-4). Dreidels — their composition and rules and technique of the game — are the focus of this Hanukkah book that also touches on holiday food and the stories of Judith and Hannah. (Rev: BL 11/1/05; SLJ 10/05)

19895 Bernhard, Durga. *Around the World in One Shabbat: Jewish People Celebrate the Sabbath Together* (K–3). Illus. by author. 2011, Jewish Lights $18.99 (978-1-58023-433-7). 32pp. The rituals of Shabbat are

explained through a series of vignettes showing Jewish families around the world. ℮ (Rev: BL 4/15/11; SLJ 5/1/11) [296.4]

19896 Chaikin, Miriam. *Angels Sweep the Desert Floor: Bible Legends About Moses in the Wilderness* (4–7). Illus. by Alexander Koshkin. 2002, Clarion $19.00 (978-0-395-97825-2). This collection of stories mixes religious history and rabbinic literature to tell the story of the Israelites' 40 years in the wilderness. (Rev: BL 10/1/02; HB 11–12/02; HBG 3/03; SLJ 9/02) [296.1]

19897 Cone, Molly. *The Story of Shabbat* (2–5). Illus. 2000, HarperCollins LB $14.89 (978-0-06-027945-5). 40pp. A discussion of the weekly Jewish holiday — its history, customs, and such practices as abstaining from work and studying the Torah. (Rev: BL 4/1/00; HBG 9/00; SLJ 8/00)

19898 Cooper, Ilene. *Jewish Holidays All Year Round: A Family Treasury* (3–5). Illus. by Elivia Savadier. 2002, Abrams $18.95 (978-0-8109-0550-4). Details of the rituals that take place at home and in the synagogue are given in this overview of the holidays of the Jewish year, with an activity and recipe for each celebration. (Rev: HBG 3/03; SLJ 3/03)

19899 Fishman, Cathy Goldberg. *Hanukkah* (2–3). Illus. by Mary O'Keefe Young. Series: On My Own Holidays. 2003, Carolrhoda LB $25.26 (978-1-57505-195-6); paper $5.95 (978-1-57505-583-1). A simple history of the Jewish holiday, with a look at how it is celebrated today and instructions on how to play dreidel. (Rev: HBG 4/04; SLJ 10/03)

19900 Fishman, Cathy Goldberg. *On Sukkot and Simchat Torah* (K–3). Illus. by Melanie Hall. 2006, Lerner $17.95 (978-1-58013-165-0). 32pp. Follows a Jewish family preparing a sukkah for the Sukkot harvest festival, and enjoying the celebration that accompanies the completion of the Torah reading on Simchat Torah. (Rev: BL 10/1/06; SLJ 9/06)

19901 Goldin, Barbara D. *Ten Holiday Jewish Children's Stories* (K–3). Illus. by Jeffrey Allon. 2000, Pitspopany $16.95 (978-0-943706-47-4); paper $9.95 (978-0-943706-48-1). A lively collection of ten stories, each of which stems from a tradition or practice associated with a Jewish holiday. (Rev: BL 10/1/00)

19902 Groner, Judye, and Madeline Wikler. *All About Passover* (2–4). Illus. by Kinny Kreiswirth. 2000, Kar-Ben paper $5.95 (978-1-58013-060-8). 32pp. A concise guide to this holiday, with a summary of the Passover story, details on suitable preparations, including cooking the seder meal, and a description of the seder itself. (Rev: BL 10/1/00)

19903 Heiligman, Deborah. *Celebrate Hanukkah with Light, Latkes, and Dreidels* (1–3). Illus. Series: Holidays Around the World. 2006, National Geographic $15.95 (978-0-7922-5924-4). A colorful introduction to the history and traditions of Hanukkah, with photographs from countries around the world; appended materials include prayers, a recipe for latkes, a bibliography, and a glossary. (Rev: BL 10/15/06)

1112

19904 Heiligman, Deborah. *Celebrate Passover* (3–5). Illus. Series: Holidays Around the World. 2007, National Geographic LB $23.90 (978-1-4263-0019-6); paper $15.95 (978-1-4263-0018-9). 32pp. Introduces to the Jewish holiday and its religious significance, customs, and rituals in communities around the world. (Rev: BL 3/15/07)

19905 Heiligman, Deborah. *Celebrate Rosh Hashanah and Yom Kippur* (K–3). Series: Holidays Around the World. 2007, National Geographic $15.95 (978-1-4263-0076-9). 32pp. The author discusses how and why Jewish people around the world observe these High Holy Days. Includes a note for teachers and parents by Rabbi Shira Stern. (Rev: SLJ 8/07)

19906 Hoyt-Goldsmith, Diane. *Celebrating Passover* (2–5). Illus. 2000, Holiday House $16.95 (978-0-8234-1420-8). 32pp. A 9-year-old boy explains the origins of Passover and how he and his extended family celebrate it. (Rev: BL 5/1/00; HBG 9/00; SLJ 6/00)

19907 Kimmel, Eric A. *Wonders and Miracles: A Passover Companion* (4–8). 2004, Scholastic $18.95 (978-0-439-07175-8). In addition to a description of the holiday and its rituals, Kimmel provides stories, songs, prayers, poems, and recipes. Sidney Taylor Book Honor 2004. (Rev: BL 2/15/04*; SLJ 2/04) [296.4]

19908 Kropf, Latifa Berry. *It's Challah Time!* (PS–1). Illus. by Tod Cohen. 2002, Kar-Ben LB $12.95 (978-1-58013-036-3). 24pp. Color photographs show happy young children making challah for the Sabbath, singing blessings, and tasting the final product. (Rev: BL 10/1/02; HBG 3/03; SLJ 12/02)

19909 Kropf, Latifa Berry. *It's Purim Time!* (PS). Photos by Tod Cohen. 2005, Lerner LB $12.95 (978-1-58013-153-7). Preschool children enjoy a fun-filled Purim, selecting costumes, making noisemakers, and having traditional snacks. (Rev: SLJ 8/05)

19910 Kropf, Latifa Berry. *It's Shofar Time!* (1–3). Illus. by Tod Cohen. 2006, Kar-Ben $12.95 (978-1-58013-158-2). 24pp. Color photographs show children enjoying the traditions associated with the Jewish holiday of Rosh Hashanah. (Rev: BL 10/1/06)

19911 Metter, Bert. *Bar Mitzvah, Bat Mitzvah: The Ceremony, the Party, and How the Day Came to Be* (4–7). Illus. by Joan Reilly. 2007, Clarion $15.00 (978-0-618-76772-4); paper $5.95 (978-0-618-76773-1). This book about the coming-of-age ceremony for Jewish children (and now adults) covers its history but does not leave out the fun part — the party — and even includes details about the parties of some celebrities. (Rev: BL 7/07; SLJ 11/07)

19912 Murray, Julie. *Hanukkah* (1–3). Series: Holidays. 2003, ABDO LB $21.35 (978-1-57765-953-2). 24pp. Provides a brief history of the holiday as well as a look at some of the associated traditions. (Rev: HBG 10/03; SLJ 10/03)

19913 Podwal, Mark. *A Sweet Year: A Taste of the Jewish Holidays* (K–6). Illus. by author. 2003, Doubleday LB $14.99 (978-0-385-90869-6). Lyrical prose and striking artwork offer an excellent introduction to the traditions and foods of the Jewish holidays. (Rev: HBG 4/04; SLJ 8/03)

19914 Rosen, Michael J. *Chanukah Lights* (2–5). Illus. by Robert Sabuda. 2011, Candlewick $34.99 (978-076365533-4). 16pp. An intricate pop-up tour of the global Festival of Lights, this fragile yet engrossing volume will require adult participation for complete enjoyment and understanding. (Rev: BLO 10/15/11; HB 11–12/11; SLJ 10/1/11)

19915 Schuh, Mari C. *Passover* (K–2). Illus. Series: Holidays and Celebrations. 2002, Capstone $17.26 (978-0-7368-1448-5). 24pp. Colorful photographs and simple text explain the meaning, history, and traditions of the Passover celebration in this small, square book. (Rev: BL 1/1–15/03; HBG 3/03)

19916 Ziefert, Harriet. *Passover: Celebrating Now, Remembering Then* (PS–3). Illus. by Karla Gudeon. 2010, Blue Apple $17.99 (978-160905020-7). 40pp. Contrasting history, tradition, and contemporary practice, this is a handsome account of the Passover celebration. (Rev: BL 4/15/10) [296.4]

Thanksgiving

19917 Anderson, Laurie Halse. *Thank You, Sarah: The Woman Who Saved Thanksgiving* (K–3). Illus. by Matt Faulkner. 2002, Simon & Schuster $16.95 (978-0-689-84787-5). 40pp. Humorous illustrations accompany this true tale of a woman who campaigned for almost four decades to make Thanksgiving a national holiday. (Rev: BL 12/15/02; HBG 3/03; SLJ 12/02)

19918 Bruchac, Joseph. *Squanto's Journey: The Story of the First Thanksgiving* (4–8). Illus. by Greg Shed. 2000, Harcourt $17.00 (978-0-15-201817-7). A picture book for older readers about the Pilgrims, the first Thanksgiving, and the important role played by the Paluxet Indian Squanto in helping the colony survive. (Rev: BL 9/1/00; HBG 3/01; SLJ 11/00) [394.2]

19919 Colman, Penny. *Thanksgiving: The True Story* (5–8). Illus. 2008, Henry Holt $18.95 (978-080508229-6). 144pp. Colman presents a fascinating look at the origins, customs, and foods of America's Thanksgiving, drawing on survey responses as well as historical research. (Rev: BL 9/1/08; HB 11–12/08; SLJ 11/1/08; VOYA 8/08) [394.2649]

19920 Fink, Deborah F. *It's a Family Thanksgiving! A Celebration of an American Tradition for Children and Their Families* (K–4). Illus. by Kinny Kreiswirth. 2000, Harmony Hearth paper $9.95 (978-0-9678871-0-4). History, foods, and traditions are covered in this book about Thanksgiving that also contains recipes and craft projects. (Rev: BL 9/15/00)

19921 Grace, Catherine O'Neill, and Margaret M. Bruchac. *1621: A New Look at Thanksgiving* (K–4). Illus. by Sisse Brimberg and Cotton Coulson. 2001, National Geographic $17.95 (978-0-7922-7027-0). 48pp. This appealing and informative photoessay presents the historically correct story of the first Thanksgiving, as reenacted at the Plimoth Plantation. (Rev: BL 9/1/01; HBG 10/02; SLJ 9/01*)

19922 Heinrichs, Ann. *Thanksgiving* (K–3). Illus. by Charles Jordan. Series: Holidays, Festivals, and Celebrations. 2006, The Child's World LB $24.21 (978-1-59296-582-3). 32pp. Examines the history, customs, and symbols of this holiday and includes a recipe and a craft. (Rev: SLJ 9/06)

19923 Landau, Elaine. *Thanksgiving Day: A Time to Be Thankful* (3–6). Illus. Series: Finding Out About Holidays. 2001, Enslow LB $23.93 (978-0-7660-1572-2). 48pp. A general introduction to this traditional American holiday, its history, and how it is celebrated. (Rev: BL 9/15/01; HBG 3/02; SLJ 1/02)

19924 Mercer, Abbie. *Happy Thanksgiving* (2–4). Series: Holiday Fun. 2007, Rosen LB $21.25 (978-1-4042-3807-7). 24pp. Along with descriptions of typical Thanksgiving activities, traditions, and foods, this volume includes historical information, a recipe, and a craft. (Rev: SLJ 2/08)

19925 Paterson, Katherine. *Giving Thanks: Poems, Prayers, and Praise Songs of Thanksgiving* (4–7). Illus. by Pamela Dalton. 2013, Chronicle $18.99 (978-145211339-5). 56pp. Intricate cut-paper illustrations decorate poems, prayers, and meditations about giving thanks. (Rev: BL 10/1/13*; SLJ 11/13) [223]

19926 Schuh, Mari C. *Thanksgiving Day* (PS–1). Series: National Holidays. 2003, Capstone LB $17.26 (978-0-7368-1654-0). 24pp. This slim title examines the history of Thanksgiving Day, which was declared a national holiday in the 1860s. (Rev: HBG 10/03; SLJ 9/03)

Valentine's Day

19927 Farmer, Jacqueline. *Valentine Be Mine* (2–5). Illus. by Megan Halsey. 2013, Charlesbridge $17.95 (978-1-58089-389-3); paper $7.95 (978-1-58089-390-9). 32pp. Traces the history of Valentine's Day since its pagan origins, looks at Valentine cards and symbols, and includes many images as well as two crafts. (Rev: BL 12/15/12; SLJ 1/13) [394.2618]

19928 Flanagan, Alice K. *Valentine's Day* (2–4). Illus. by Shelley Dieterichs. Series: Holidays and Festivals. 2001, Compass Point LB $23.93 (978-0-7565-0088-7). 32pp. Flanagan tells readers about the origins of Valentine's Day (as a Roman festival) and details how we celebrate the holiday today. (Rev: BL 10/15/01; SLJ 1/02)

19929 Gibbons, Gail. *Valentine's Day Is . . .* (PS–1). Illus. 2006, Holiday $17.95 (978-0-8234-1852-7). 32pp. In spreads introduced by the title phrase, Gibbons explores the origins and customs of Valentine's Day. (Rev: BL 2/1/06; SLJ 3/06)

19930 Landau, Elaine. *Valentine's Day: Candy, Love, and Hearts* (3–6). Series: Finding Out About Holidays. 2002, Enslow LB $23.93 (978-0-7660-1779-5). 48pp. Material on Saint Valentine is included with information on the symbols connected with the holiday and the ways

in which it is celebrated. (Rev: BL 7/02; HBG 10/02; SLJ 10/02)

19931 Lynette, Rachel. *Let's Throw a Valentine's Day Party* (2–4). Illus. Series: Holiday Parties. 2011, Rosen LB $21.25 (978-144882570-7). 24pp. A useful, compact guide to holding a party, with suggestions for games, food, and decorations. (Rev: BL 12/15/11) [793.2]

19932 Speechley, Greta. *Valentine Crafts* (2–4). Illus. 2010, Gareth Stevens LB $28 (978-143393600-5). 32pp. A variety of everyday materials are employed in a dozen Valentine's Day craft projects. (Rev: BLO 11/15/10) [745.594]

19933 Trueit, Trudi. *Valentine's Day* (K–2). Illus. Series: Rookie Read-about Holidays. 2006, Scholastic LB $20.50 (978-0-531-12461-1). Brief information and stock photographs introduce beginning readers to Valentine's Day. (Rev: BL 1/1–15/07)

Prayers

19934 Brooks, Jeremy. *Let There Be Peace: Prayers from Around the World* (PS–3). Illus. by Jude Daly. 2009, Frances Lincoln $16.95 (978-184507530-9). 32pp. A collection of prayers from a variety of religions and countries are presented with beautiful illustrations. (Rev: BL 11/15/09) [242.82]

19935 Brooks, Jeremy. *My First Prayers* (K–2). Illus. by Laurie Fournier. 2009, Frances Lincoln $16.95 (978-1-84507-535-4). A collection of prayers from many nations. (Rev: SLJ 6/09)

19936 Brooks, Jeremy. *A World of Prayers* (PS–1). Illus. by Elena Gomez. 2006, Eerdmans $16.00 (978-0-8028-5285-4). A collection of more than 25 prayers from around the world, organized by category rather than religion. (Rev: BL 12/15/05; SLJ 2/06)

19937 Carlstrom, Nancy White. *Glory* (PS–2). Illus. by Debra R. Jenkins. 2001, Eerdmans $17.00 (978-0-8028-5143-7). 32pp. Animals — and one little girl — joyfully reflect the glory of God in this prayer with bright, bold illustrations. (Rev: BL 10/1/01; HBG 3/02; SLJ 12/01)

19938 *A Children's Treasury of Prayers* (PS–1). Illus. by Linda Bleck. 2006, Sterling $12.95 (978-1-4027-2982-9). 32pp. This child-friendly collection of prayers offers examples from a number of religions, including Christianity, Hinduism, Islam, and Judaism. (Rev: BL 10/1/06)

19939 Jelenek, Frank. X. *Journey to the Heart: Centering Prayer for Children* (1–4). Illus. by Ann Boyajian. 2007, Paraclete $14.95 (978-1-55725-482-5). 32pp. Jelenek introduces the concept of contemplative prayer to young children. (Rev: BL 10/1/07)

19940 Jordan, Deloris. *Baby Blessings: A Prayer for the Day You Are Born* (PS–K). Illus. by James E. Ransome. 2010, Simon & Schuster $16.99 (978-1-4169-5362-3). 32pp. A simple celebration of life as an African American baby grows to kindergarten age in an atmosphere of faith and love. (Rev: BL 11/15/09; SLJ 12/1/09) [242]

19941 Kangas, Juli. *A Child's Book of Prayers* (PS–K). Illus. by author. 2008, Dial $32.00 (978-0-8037-3054-0). 32pp. Families seeking blessings and meditations will appreciate this collection of 26 short prayers accompanied by colorful, child-centered illustrations. (Rev: BL 12/1/07; SLJ 7/08)

19942 Ladwig, Tim. *The Lord's Prayer* (PS–4). 2000, Eerdmans $17.00 (978-0-8028-5180-2). 32pp. Full-page paintings are used with the text of the Lord's Prayer to tell the story of an African American father and daughter who help an elderly neighbor. (Rev: BCCB 12/00; BL 10/1/00; SLJ 1/01)

19943 Lincoln, Frances. *A Family Treasury of Prayers* (4–8). 1996, Simon & Schuster $16.00 (978-0-689-80956-9). Classic art works illustrate this lovely collection of prayers from famous sources. (Rev: BL 10/1/96; SLJ 10/96; VOYA 6/97) [242]

19944 *The Lord Is My Shepherd* (PS–2). Illus. by Regolo Ricci. 2007, Tundra $18.95 (978-0-88776-776-0). 24pp. Illustrations of nature and the changing seasons accompany the words of the 23rd Psalm. (Rev: BL 10/1/07; SLJ 11/07)

19945 *The Lord Is My Shepherd: The Twenty-Third Psalm* (2–4). Illus. by Gennady Spirin. 2008, Philomel $17.99 (978-0-399-24527-5). 32pp. A handsomely illustrated version of the Old Testament psalm, with ornate scenes in lush colors. (Rev: BL 1/1–15/08; SLJ 5/08)

19946 Moser, Barry. *Psalm 23* (K–2). Illus. by author. 2008, Zondervan $14.99 (978-0-310-71085-1). The comfort and peace of this prayer is retained with fresh Caribbean island illustrations. (Rev: BL 1/1–15/08; SLJ 3/08)

19947 Paterson, Katherine. *Brother Sun, Sister Moon: Saint Francis of Assisi's Canticle of the Creatures* (2–5). Illus. by Pamela Dalton. 2011, Chronicle $17.99 (978-0-8118-7734-3). 36pp. Brother Francis's words celebrating the natural world are reimagined and enhanced with lush cut paper illustrations. e Lexile 740L (Rev: BL 8/11*; SLJ 7/11*)

19948 Piper, Sophie. *The Lion Book of Prayers to Read and Know* (2–4). Illus. by Anthony Lewis. 2010, Lion $12.99 (978-0-7459-6147-7). 96pp. Prayers from a variety of sources — including an 18th-century New England sampler — are illustrated in this accessible book for young readers. (Rev: SLJ 2/1/10) [242.8]

19949 Rock, Lois. *A Child's Book of Graces* (PS–2). Illus. by Allison Jay. 2006, Good Bks. $5.95 (978-1-56148-514-7). 28pp. Prayers for before (and after) meals from many sources, Christian and non-Christian. (Rev: BL 7/06)

19950 Rock, Lois, comp. *My Very First Prayers* (PS–2). Illus. by Alex Ayliffe. 2003, Good Bks. $14.99 (978-1-56148-371-6). 159pp. This collection of prayers covers family, friends, pets, holidays, love, nature, and the seasons. (Rev: SLJ 1/04)

19951 Simmons, Justine. *God, Can You Hear Me?* (PS–4). Illus. by Robert Papp. 2007, HarperCollins $16.99 (978-0-06-115397-6). Children ask God their tough questions in this book that reassures readers that God cares about the problems in their lives. The author appears on the MTV program "Run's House." (Rev: SLJ 8/07)

19952 Tickle, Phyllis. *This Is What I Pray Today: The Divine Hours Prayers for Children* (PS–1). Illus. by Elsa Warnick. 2007, Dutton $15.99 (978-0-525-47828-7). 32pp. This illustrated book offers three short simple prayers for different parts of each day of the week. (Rev: BL 10/1/07)

19953 Warren, Rick. *The Lord's Prayer* (PS–2). Illus. by Richard Jesse Watson. 2011, Zondervan $16.99 (978-0-310-71086-8). 40pp. This handsome volume provides a good, accessible interpretation of the Lord's Prayer in the King James version with line-by-line commentary. (Rev: BL 11/15/10; SLJ 2/1/11) [226.9]

19954 Winter, Rebecca. *Prayers for Children* (2–4). Illus. by Helen Cann. 2005, Good Bks. $14.99 (978-1-56148-470-6). 160pp. More than 200 prayers, traditional and new, come from different countries and cover a wide variety of subjects. (Rev: BL 6/1–15/05)

Social Groups

Ethnic Groups

19955 Adare, Sierra. *Mohawk* (4–8). 2003, Gareth Stevens LB $26.00 (978-0-8368-3665-3). An introduction to the history, culture, and current status of the Mohawk people, with photographs, maps, and interesting sidebar features that will be useful for reports. Also use *Apache* and *Nez Perce* (both 2003). (Rev: HBG 10/03; SLJ 9/03) [974.7004]

19956 Behnke, Alison. *Mexicans in America* (4–8). Series: In America. 2004, Lerner LB $27.93 (978-0-8225-3955-1). The reasons for Mexican migration to the United States and the life the newcomers find when they arrive are discussed in engaging narrative, with personal stories, notes on key figures, illustrations, and a timeline. (Rev: SLJ 3/05) [304.8]

19957 Binns, Tristan Boyer. *Chinese Americans* (3–5). Series: We Are America. 2003, Heinemann LB $24.22 (978-1-4034-0162-5). 32pp. Binns explores the challenges and hardships faced by Chinese immigrants to America and the many contributions they have made to society as a whole. Also use *Mexican Americans* (2003). (Rev: HBG 10/03; SLJ 8/03)

19958 Birdseye, Debbie H., and Tom Birdseye. *Under Our Skin: Kids Talk About Race* (4–8). 1997, Holiday $15.95 (978-0-8234-1325-6). In separate chapters, six 8th-grade students in Oregon from different racial and ethnic backgrounds talk about race and what racism means to them. (Rev: HBG 3/98; SLJ 4/98) [572.973]

19959 Bolden, Tonya. *Tell All the Children Our Story: Memories and Mementos of Being Young and Black in America* (4–8). 2002, Abrams $24.95 (978-0-8109-4496-1). From the first recorded birth of a black child in the United States to the Million Man March, this book describes the African American experience through both personal and historical accounts, using a scrapbook format. (Rev: BL 2/15/02; HB 3–4/02; HBG 10/02; SLJ 3/02*; VOYA 4/02) [973]

19960 Bryan, Nichol. *Haitian Americans* (3–5). Series: One Nation. 2004, ABDO LB $22.78 (978-1-57765-982-2). 32pp. A look at immigration from Haiti (both legal and illegal), the reasons behind it, what happens to the immigrants once they are in the United States, and the contributions they make to the culture in their new country. Also use *Mexican Americans* (2004). (Rev: HBG 4/04; SLJ 3/04)

19961 Burgan, Michael. *African Americans* (3–5). Illus. Series: Our Cultural Heritage. 2004, Child's World LB $27.07 (978-1-59296-012-5). 32pp. Covers migration from America to the United States, emphasizing that in the early years few came by choice, with material on native culture, ethnic background, and contributions to present-day American society. [973]

19962 Burgan, Michael. *Italian Immigrants* (5–8). Series: Immigration to the United States. 2004, Facts on File $35.00 (978-0-8160-5681-1). After an overview of the reasons underlying immigration in general, this illustrated volume looks at the circumstances of migrants from Italy, the group's history in the United States, and the contemporary situation, with sidebar features, a timeline, and a glossary. (Rev: SLJ 4/05)

19963 Cannarella, Deborah. *Cuban Americans* (3–5). Illus. Series: Our Cultural Heritage. 2004, Child's World LB $27.07 (978-1-59296-013-2). 32pp. Covers Cuban migration to the United States, with material on native culture, ethnic background, and the impact on present-day American society. [973]

19964 Catalano, Julie. *The Mexican Americans* (5–8). Series: Immigrant Experience. 1995, Chelsea LB $14.95 (978-0-7910-3359-3); paper $9.95 (978-0-7910-3381-4). This book traces the reasons for leaving Mexico, the immigrants' reception in the United States, and their contributions and achievements. (Rev: BL 11/15/95; SLJ 1/96) [973]

19965 Cavan, Seamus. *The Irish-American Experience* (5–7). Series: Coming to America. 1993, Millbrook LB $23.40 (978-1-56294-218-2). Beginning with the potato famine that forced millions of Irish to come to America, this is the story of the rise of Irish Americans to positions of prominence. (Rev: BCCB 4/93; BL 6/1–15/93) [973]

19966 Clinton, Catherine. *The Black Soldier: 1492 to the Present* (5–8). 2000, Houghton Mifflin $17.00 (978-0-395-67722-3). This history of African Americans in the army begins with colonial slaves who were given muskets to fight the Indians and continues through each of America's wars to the present with emphasis on the slow progress toward equality in the ranks. (Rev: BCCB 10/00; BL 9/15/00; HBG 3/01; SLJ 10/00; VOYA 2/01) [355]

19967 Cole, Harriette, and John Pinderhuges. *Coming Together: Celebrations for African American Families* (4–12). 2003, Hyperion $22.99 (978-0-7868-0753-6). Traditions surrounding celebrations including Christmas, Kwanzaa, and naming ceremonies are covered here, with accompanying crafts, menu suggestions, and activities. (Rev: BL 12/15/03; HBG 4/04; VOYA 2/04) [306.8]

19968 Cole, Melanie. *Famous People of Hispanic Heritage* (4–7). Series: Contemporary American Success Stories. 1997, Mitchell Lane LB $21.95 (978-1-883845-44-5); paper $12.95 (978-1-883845-43-8). This useful series, now in nine volumes, profiles famous Hispanics, past and present, from around the world. (Rev: BL 3/15/98; HBG 3/98) [920]

19969 Coleman, Lori. *Vietnamese in America* (4–8). Series: In America. 2004, Lerner LB $27.93 (978-0-8225-3951-3). The reasons for Vietnamese migration to the United States and the life the newcomers find when they arrive are discussed in engaging narrative, with personal stories, notes on key figures, illustrations, and a timeline. Also use *Koreans in America* (2004). (Rev: BL 11/15/04; SLJ 3/05) [973]

19970 Cunningham, Kevin. *Canadian Americans* (3–5). Illus. Series: Our Cultural Heritage. 2004, Child's World LB $27.07 (978-1-59296-178-8). 32pp. Covers Canadian migration to the United States, with material on native culture, ethnic background, and contributions to present-day American society.

19971 De Capua, Sarah. *Irish Americans* (3–5). Series: Spirit of America: Our Cultural Heritage. 2002, Child's World LB $27.07 (978-1-56766-155-2). 32pp. De Capua discusses the reasons for Irish migration to the United States and the lasting contributions this group has made. (Rev: BL 10/15/02)

19972 Di Franco, J. Philip. *The Italian Americans* (5–8). 1995, Chelsea LB $14.95 (978-0-7910-3353-1); paper $9.95 (978-0-7910-3375-3). A heavily illustrated discussion of the culture that Italian immigrants left behind and their contributions to American life. (Rev: BL 1/1/88) [973.0451]

19973 Doak, Robin. *Struggling to Become American: 1899–1940* (5–10). Series: Latino-American History. 2007, Chelsea House LB $35.00 (978-0-8160-6443-4). Doak looks at Latino immigration — especially from Puerto Rico, Cuba, and Mexico — and at the conditions

of Hispanic laborers in the United States during World War I and the Great Depression; includes photographs, sidebars, political cartoons, maps, and so forth. (Rev: SLJ 7/07)

19974 Feelings, Tom. *Tommy Traveler in the World of Black History* (5–8). 1991, Black Butterfly $13.95 (978-0-86316-202-2). A history of African Americans seen through the eyes of a boy who imagines himself participating in the important events. (Rev: BL 9/15/91; SLJ 2/92) [973]

19975 Fitterer, C. Ann. *German Americans* (3–5). Series: Spirit of America: Our Cultural Heritage. 2002, Child's World LB $27.07 (978-1-56766-151-4). Fitterer discusses German migration to the United States and the contributions of this community. (Rev: BL 10/15/02; SLJ 2/03)

19976 Fitterer, C. Ann. *Russian Americans* (3–5). Series: Spirit of America: Our Cultural Heritage. 2002, Child's World LB $27.07 (978-1-56766-158-3). 32pp. Russian migration to the United States is discussed in this richly illustrated account that includes material on famous immigrants. (Rev: BL 10/15/02; SLJ 12/02)

19977 Franchino, Vicky. *Italian Americans* (3–5). Series: Spirit of America: Our Cultural Heritage. 2002, Child's World LB $27.07 (978-1-56766-153-8). 32pp. How Italian immigrants changed American life is one of the topics discussed in this simple account of why and how they came to this country, their reception, and a rundown of famous Italian Americans. Also use *British Americans* and *Spanish Americans* (both 2002). (Rev: BL 10/15/02)

19978 Freeman, Dena. *How People Live* (3–6). 2003, DK $29.99 (978-0-7894-9867-0). 304pp. Organized by continent, this ambitious volume full of photographs explores many different cultures and is suitable for browsing. (Rev: HBG 4/04; SLJ 2/04)

19979 Frost, Helen. *Russian Immigrants: 1860–1915* (4–6). Series: Coming to America. 2002, Capstone LB $23.93 (978-0-7368-1209-2). 32pp. After a look at why Russians left their country to migrate to the United States, this account covers their destinations, culture, and contributions. (Rev: BL 1/1–15/03; HBG 3/03; SLJ 3/03)

19980 Gelber, Carol. *Love and Marriage Around the World* (5–7). 1998, Millbrook LB $23.90 (978-0-7613-0102-8). From courtship to the wedding, this book introduces marriage customs from around the world and among different ethnic groups. (Rev: BCCB 7–8/98; HBG 10/98; SLJ 6/98) [392]

19981 Goldstein, Margaret J. *Irish in America* (5–8). Series: In America. 2004, Lerner LB $27.93 (978-0-8225-3950-6). This overview of Irish migration to the United States looks at the underlying reasons for the exodus and explores the lives of the new arrivals and the traditions they maintained. (Rev: BL 11/15/04) [973]

19982 Goldstein, Margaret J. *Japanese in America* (4–7). Series: In America. 2006, Lerner LB $27.93 (978-0-8225-3952-0). The author discusses the history of U.S.-Japan relations and the course of Japanese immigration to America from the 1800s to today, including the internments during World War II; profiles of famous Japanese Americans are appended. (Rev: SLJ 5/06) [973.0495]

19983 Greenfield, Eloise, and Lessie Jones Little. *Childtimes: A Three-Generation Memoir* (5–8). Illus. by Jerry Pinkney. 1979, HarperCollins LB $16.89 (978-0-690-03875-0); paper $9.99 (978-0-06-446134-4). The childhoods of three generations of African American women.

19984 Haberle, Susan E. *Jewish Immigrants: 1880–1924* (4–6). Series: Coming to America. 2002, Capstone LB $23.93 (978-0-7368-1207-8). 32pp. A brief overview of why Jews left Europe, plus an account of where they settled in America, their cultural contributions, and a list of famous Jewish Americans. (Rev: BL 1/1–15/03; HBG 3/03)

19985 Harkrader, Lisa. *South Korea* (5–8). Illus. Series: Top Ten Countries of Recent Immigrants. 2004, Enslow LB $25.26 (978-0-7660-5181-2). 48pp. Information on South Korea — culture, history, climate, and people — accompanies an explanation of the reasons for migration to the United States and discussion of the contributions of this community; supported by Web links. (Rev: SLJ 3/05)

19986 Heinrichs, Ann. *French Americans* (3–5). Illus. Series: Our Cultural Heritage. 2004, Child's World LB $27.07 (978-1-59296-180-1). Covers French migration to the United States, with material on the group's native culture, ethnic background, and the impact they have had on present-day American society.

19987 Heinrichs, Ann. *Norwegian Americans* (3–5). Illus. Series: Our Cultural Heritage. 2004, Child's World LB $27.07 (978-1-59296-182-5). 32pp. Covers Norwegian migration to the United States, with material on the group's native culture, ethnic background, and the impact they have had on present-day American society.

19988 Herron, Carolivia. *Always an Olivia* (1–3). Illus. by Jeremy Tugeau. 2007, Lerner $17.95 (978-0-8225-7049-3). 32pp. Using a fictionalized framework in which Great-grandma Olivia tells Carol Olivia about their family's experiences beginning during the Spanish Inquisition, Herron traces her African American-Jewish roots. (Rev: BL 11/1/07; LMC 11/07; SLJ 10/07)

19989 Horton, Casey. *The Jews* (4–8). Series: We Came to North America. 2000, Crabtree LB $25.27 (978-0-7787-0187-3); paper $8.95 (978-0-7787-0201-6). As well as discussing the reasons why Jews left Europe, this account describes the trip across the Atlantic, reception in America, and the many contributions to the United States. (Rev: SLJ 10/00) [973]

19990 Hossell, Karen. *Pakistani Americans* (3–5). Series: We Are America. 2004, Heinemann LB $24.22 (978-1-4034-5023-4). A story about a young Pakistani's arrival in America introduces this overview of immigration from Pakistan that looks at history, cultural life, and contributions to the United States, with a map, a chart, and a timeline. (Rev: SLJ 11/04)

19991 Hunter, David. *Teen Life Among the Amish and Other Alternative Communities: Choosing a Lifestyle*

(5–8). Series: Youth in Rural North America. 2007, Mason Crest LB $22.95 (978-1-4222-0017-9). 96pp. Hunter introduces readers to the traditions and beliefs of Amish and other alternative communities found around the United States and Canada (including monasteries and kibbutzim), emphasizing how teens in these groupings cope with their different lifestyles; includes many photographs. (Rev: LMC 3/08; SLJ 2/08)

19992 Ingram, W. Scott. *Greek Immigrants* (5–8). Series: Immigration to the United States. 2004, Facts on File $35.00 (978-0-8160-5689-7). After an overview of the reasons underlying immigration in general, this illustrated volume looks at the circumstances of migrants from Greece, the group's history in the United States, and the contemporary situation, with sidebar features, a timeline, and a glossary. Also use *Japanese Immigrants* and *Polish Immigrants* (both 2004). (Rev: BL 4/1/04; HB 3–4/04; SLJ 4/05)

19993 Keedle, Jayne. *Americans from the Caribbean and Central America* (4–8). Series: New Americans. 2010, Marshall Cavendish LB $35.64 (978-0-7614-4302-5). 80pp. Part of a series that looks at the experiences of recent immigrants, this book discusses the challenges that new arrivals face and the impact they have on society; the citizenship process is explained and personal accounts add impact. Also use by this author *Mexican Americans* and *West African Americans* (2010). (Rev: LMC 3–4/10; SLJ 2/10)

19994 Knight, Margy B. *Who Belongs Here? An American Story* (4–7). Illus. by Anne S. O'Brien. 1993, Tilbury House $16.95 (978-0-88448-110-2). The story of ten-year-old Nari, who survived the killing fields of Cambodia and found a new life in the United States. (Rev: BL 3/1/94; SLJ 10/93) [305.895]

19995 Koenig, Angela T. *Pakistani Americans* (3–5). Series: Spirit of America: Our Cultural Heritage. 2003, Child's World LB $27.07 (978-1-59296-017-0). 32pp. Explores the history behind immigration to the United States from Pakistan, the influences this ethnic group has had on American culture, and life today. (Rev: SLJ 2/04)

19996 Kuropas, Myron B. *Ukrainians in America* (5–7). Series: In America. 1996, Lerner LB $19.93 (978-0-8225-1043-7). The story of Ukrainian immigrants to the United States, their cultural traditions, and their contributions to American life. (Rev: BL 3/15/96; SLJ 3/96) [973]

19997 Kyuchukov, Hristo, and Ian Hancock. *A History of the Romani People* (3–5). Illus. 2005, Boyds Mills $19.95 (978-1-56397-962-0). 48pp. An introductory overview of the history, culture, and language of the Roma or Gypsy people. (Rev: BL 12/1/05; SLJ 11/05)

19998 Levete, Sarah. *Being an Immigrant* (3–5). Series: Let's Talk About. 2007, Stargazer LB $27.10 (978-1-59604-084-7). 32pp. Readers will learn why immigrants come to the United States and what it's like to be part of an immigrant family. (Rev: SLJ 6/07)

19999 Lock, Donna. *The Polish Americans* (5–8). Illus. Series: We Came to America. 2002, Mason Crest LB

$19.95 (978-1-59084-112-9). 64pp. A look at the customs and contributions of this ethnic group, including information on famous Polish Americans, with a bibliography, glossary, timeline, and resources for tracing ancestors. (Rev: BL 7/02)

20000 McDaniel, Melissa. *Japanese Americans* (3–5). Series: Spirit of America: Our Cultural Heritage. 2002, Child's World LB $27.07 (978-1-56766-154-5). 32pp. The history of Japanese migration to the United States is discussed, with material on the the the discrimination the new citizens faced and the many ways in which they have changed American culture. (Rev: BL 10/15/02; SLJ 12/02)

20001 McQuinn, Anna. *My Friend Jamal* (PS–1). Illus. by author. Series: My Friend. 2008, Annick $17.95 (978-1-55451-123-5); paper $8.95 (978-1-55451-122-8). 32pp. Two immigrant boys — Jamal from Somalia and Joseph from Poland — enjoy a close friendship despite their different lives. (Rev: BL 6/1–15/08; SLJ 6/08)

20002 Morris, Ann. *Grandma Esther Remembers: A Jewish-American Family Story* (1–3). Series: What Was It Like, Grandma? 2002, Millbrook LB $22.90 (978-0-7613-2318-1). In double-page spreads (with a picture opposite a page of simple text), a Jewish American grandmother describes her life in the old country and her early experiences in the United States. (Rev: BL 9/15/02; HBG 10/02; SLJ 6/02)

20003 Morris, Ann. *Grandma Francisca Remembers: A Mexican-American Family Story* (1–3). Illus. by Peter Linenthal. Series: What Was It Like, Grandma? 2002, Millbrook LB $22.90 (978-0-7613-2315-0). 32pp. Some Spanish vocabulary, a recipe for stew, and instructions for making a sock doll accompany this account of the activities of a young Mexican American girl and her grandmother. (Rev: BL 2/15/02; HBG 10/02; SLJ 4/02)

20004 Morris, Ann. *Grandma Lai Goon Remembers: A Chinese-American Family Story* (1–3). Series: What Was It Like, Grandma? 2002, Millbrook LB $22.90 (978-0-7613-2314-3). 32pp. Activities such as making a Chinese doll, making Chinese buns, and playing a Chinese game complement the story of a Chinese American grandmother's life. (Rev: BL 9/15/02; HBG 10/02; SLJ 6/02)

20005 Morris, Ann. *Grandma Lois Remembers: An African-American Family Story* (1–3). Series: What Was It Like, Grandma? 2002, Millbrook LB $22.90 (978-0-7613-2316-7). 32pp. An African American grandmother tells the family history to her grandson, with appended activities and games. (Rev: BL 9/15/02; HBG 10/02; SLJ 3/02)

20006 Morris, Ann. *Grandma Susan Remembers: A British-American Family Story* (1–3). Series: What Was It Like, Grandma? 2002, Millbrook LB $22.90 (978-0-7613-2319-8). 32pp. A grandmother who was born in Britain recalls her childhood and the culture of the land she left. Activities are appended. (Rev: BL 9/15/02; HBG 10/02; SLJ 6/02)

20007 Nelson, Kadir. *Heart and Soul: The Story of America and African Americans* (3–7). Illus. by author. 2011, HarperCollins $19.99 (978-0-06-173074-0). 108pp. An elderly African American woman narrates the story of her people's struggle to be accepted and free in America in this compelling portrait with evocative full-page paintings. Coretta Scott King Author Winner 2012; ALA Notable Children's Book 2012. ⌒ ℮ Lexile 1050L (Rev: BL 8/11*; HB 11–12/11; SLJ 9/1/11*) [973]

20008 Nichols, Catherine. *African American Culture* (4–6). Series: Discovering the Arts. 2006, Advantage World LB $125.70 (978-1-59515-516-0). 48pp. A concise history of African American arts, introducing key figures and placing them in historical context. (Rev: BL 2/1/06)

20009 Ochoa, George. *The New York Public Library Amazing Hispanic American History: A Book of Answers for Kids* (4–9). 1998, Wiley paper $12.95 (978-0-471-19204-6). Using a question-and-answer format, this work explores such topics as Hispanic American identity and history, cultural groups, accomplishments, and immigrant experiences. (Rev: BL 12/1/98; SLJ 11/98) [973]

20010 O'Hara, Megan. *Irish Immigrants: 1840–1920* (4–6). Series: Coming to America. 2001, Capstone LB $23.93 (978-0-7368-0795-1). This account, complete with many reader activities, takes a quick look at Irish history, explains why the migrants left their country, and describes their reception in the United States and their contributions to American life. (Rev: BL 10/15/01; HBG 3/02; SLJ 1/02)

20011 Olson, Kay Melchisedech. *Chinese Immigrants: 1850–1900* (4–6). Series: Coming to America. 2001, Capstone LB $23.93 (978-0-7368-0793-7). 32pp. Using many sidebars, recipes, and suggested activities, this book tells how and why the Chinese originally came to the United States and the contributions they have made to American culture. (Rev: BL 10/15/01; HBG 3/02)

20012 Olson, Kay Melchisedech. *French Immigrants: 1840–1940* (4–6). Series: Coming to America. 2002, Capstone LB $23.93 (978-0-7368-1205-4). Covers the reasons why French citizens left their country for America and gives details of their struggle to retain their traditions, of their contributions, and the lives of famous immigrants and their descendants. (Rev: BL 1/1–15/03; HBG 3/03)

20013 Omoto, Susan. *Hmong Milestones in America: Citizens in a New World* (5–8). 2003, John Gordon Burke $27.00 (978-0-934272-57-5); paper $15.00 (978-0-934272-56-8). The author introduces the Hmong people's history and traditions and traces the steps of Hmong refugees who migrated to the United States, profiling five individuals who have found success in their new country. (Rev: BL 4/15/03) [973]

20014 Orr, Tamra. *The Korean Americans* (5–8). Illus. Series: Major American Immigration. 2009, Mason Crest LB $22.95 (978-1-4222-0612-6). 64pp. Orr provides a thorough overview of migration from Korea to the United States, with information on the history of Korea, the reasons for leaving the country, and the "picture brides" who arrived here in the early 20th century, plus profiles of key figures. (Rev: BL 5/15/09) [973]

20015 Parker, Lewis K. *Why Japanese Immigrants Came to America* (2–5). Series: Coming to America. 2003, Rosen LB $19.95 (978-0-8239-6463-5). 24pp. A brief overview of the experience of Japanese immigrants to America, the first major wave of whom arrived in Hawaii in 1885. (Rev: SLJ 10/03)

20016 Parker, Lewis K. *Why Mexican Immigrants Came to America* (2–5). Series: Coming to America. 2003, Rosen LB $19.95 (978-0-8239-6459-8). 24pp. Examines the reasons underlying Mexican immigration to the United States and the contributions this group has made to American society. (Rev: SLJ 10/03)

20017 Parker, Lewis K. *Why Vietnamese Immigrants Came to America* (2–5). Series: Coming to America. 2003, Rosen LB $19.95 (978-0-8239-6461-1). Focuses on the influx of Vietnamese immigrants that began in the 1960s, emphasizing the contributions this group has made to American society. (Rev: SLJ 10/03)

20018 Paulson, Timothy J. *Irish Immigrants* (5–8). Series: Immigration to the United States. 2004, Facts on File $35.00 (978-0-8160-5682-8). After an overview of the reasons underlying immigration in general, this illustrated volume looks at the circumstances of migrants from Ireland, the group's history in the United States, and the contemporary situation, with sidebar features, a timeline, and a glossary. (Rev: SLJ 4/05)

20019 Perl, Lila. *North Across the Border: The Story of the Mexican Americans* (5–9). Series: Great Journeys. 2001, Benchmark LB $32.79 (978-0-7614-1226-7). 112pp. The economic and social reasons for Mexican migration to the north through history are presented in text, quotations from primary sources, and many illustrations and maps. (Rev: BL 1/1–15/02; HBG 10/02; SLJ 3/02)

20020 Peterson, Tiffany. *Greek Americans* (3–5). Series: We Are America. 2004, Heinemann LB $24.22 (978-1-4034-5021-0). 32pp. A personal story introduces this overview of immigration from Greece that looks at history, cultural life, and contributions to the United States, with a map, a chart, and a timeline. Also use *Japanese Americans* (2004), which includes material on internment. (Rev: SLJ 11/04)

20021 Petrillo, Valerie. *A Kid's Guide to Asian American History: More than 90 Activities* (3–6). 2007, Chicago Review paper $14.95 (978-1-55652-634-3). 256pp. Crafts, games, and other activities introduce various aspects of Asian American cultures. (Rev: BL 4/15/07; SLJ 5/07)

20022 Petrillo, Valerie. *A Kid's Guide to Latino History: More Than 50 Activities* (4–8). Illus. 2009, Chicago Review paper $14.95 (978-1-55652-771-5). 208pp. This is a sweeping introduction to the history of Hispanic Americans in the United States, covering the countries they came from, the reasons they left, and their reception and contributions here, with profiles of key figures and discussion of such issues as bilingual education; activi-

ties include crafts, dancing, writing stories, and so forth. (Rev: BL 6/1–15/09; SLJ 8/09) [973]

20023 Pokiak, James, and Mindy Willett. *Proud to Be Inuvialuit / Quviahuktunga Inuvialuugama* (3–5). Photos by Tessa Macintosh. Illus. Series: The Land Is Our Storybook. 2010, Fifth House $16.95 (978-1-897252-59-8). 26pp. Pokiak presents his people and their way of life today, showing a modern whale harvest and explaining how ancient traditions have been retained. (Rev: BL 10/15/10; LMC 11–12/10; SLJ 5/11) [971.9]

20024 Raatma, Lucia. *Chinese Americans* (3–5). Illus. Series: Spirit of America: Our Cultural Heritage. 2002, Child's World LB $27.07 (978-1-56766-149-1). An overview of the Chinese American experience that includes maps, timelines, and other visuals. (Rev: BL 10/15/02)

20025 Raatma, Lucia. *Polish Americans* (3–5). Series: Spirit of America: Our Cultural Heritage. 2002, Child's World LB $27.07 (978-1-56766-157-6). 32pp. Provides a history of Polish migration to this country, with emphasis on the many contributions this group has made to American life and culture. (Rev: BL 10/15/02)

20026 Raatma, Lucia. *Swedish Americans* (3–5). Series: Spirit of America: Our Cultural Heritage. 2002, Child's World LB $27.07 (978-1-56766-159-0). 32pp. Swedish migration to the United States is the topic of this work, with material on the group's native culture, ethnic background, and the impact they have had on present-day American society. (Rev: BL 10/15/02)

20027 Rappaport, Doreen. *Free at Last! Stories and Songs of Emancipation* (4–8). Illus. by Shane W. Evans. 2004, Candlewick $19.99 (978-0-7636-1440-9). 64pp. First-hand accounts form the basis of this portrait of the black experience from emancipation to the 1954 Supreme Court decision declaring school segregation illegal. (Rev: BL 2/15/04*; HB 5/04; SLJ 2/04)

20028 Rappaport, Doreen. *No More! Stories and Songs of Slave Resistance* (4–7). Illus. by Shane W. Evans. 2002, Candlewick $17.99 (978-0-7636-0984-9). 64pp. A collection of narratives, prose, poetry, and songs that describe the African slave experience and the various forms of rebellion that took place. (Rev: BCCB 4/02; BL 2/15/02; HB 3/02; HBG 10/02; SLJ 2/02*)

20029 Rosenberg, Pam. *Jewish Americans* (3–5). Illus. Series: Our Cultural Heritage. 2004, Child's World LB $27.07 (978-1-59296-181-8). 32pp. Covers Jewish migration to the United States, with material on the group's native culture, ethnic background, and the impact they have had on present-day American society.

20030 Sanders, Nancy I. *D Is for Drinking Gourd: An African American Alphabet* (2–4). Illus. by E. B. Lewis. 2007, Sleeping Bear $17.95 (978-1-58536-293-6). 32pp. Four-line poems paired with watercolor paintings and historical information introduce African American topics from abolitionists through Harlem Renaissance, Malcolm X, and roots. (Rev: BL 9/1/07; LMC 1/08; SLJ 1/08)

20031 Sawyers, June S. *Famous Firsts of Scottish-Americans* (4–8). 1996, Pelican $13.95 (978-1-56554-122-1). Brief biographies of 30 Americans of Scottish descent, including Neil Armstrong, Alexander Calder, Herman Melville, and Patrick Henry. (Rev: BL 6/1–15/97) [920]

20032 Schouweiler, Thomas. *Germans in America* (5–7). Series: In America. 1994, Lerner LB $19.93 (978-0-8225-0245-6). The causes and results of German immigration to the United States are outlined, with good coverage of their contributions and important figures. (Rev: BL 1/15/95; SLJ 12/94) [973]

20033 Secakuku, Susan. *Meet Mindy: A Native Girl from the Southwest* (5–8). Photos by John Harrington. Series: My World: Young Native Americans Today. 2003, Beyond Words paper $15.95 (978-1-58270-091-5). A Hopi teen named Mindy talks about her life and heritage in this full-color photoessay. (Rev: BL 4/1/03; SLJ 3/03) [979.1004]

20034 Silverman, Robin L. *A Bosnian Family* (4–7). Series: Journey Between Two Worlds. 1997, Lerner LB $27.15 (978-0-8225-3404-4); paper $8.95 (978-0-8225-9754-4). The story of Velma Dusper, her homeland of Bosnia, and her journey with her family to freedom and a new home in North Dakota. (Rev: BL 6/1–15/97; SLJ 7/97) [304.8]

20035 Smith, Charles R., Jr. *I Am America* (1–3). Photos by author. 2003, Scholastic $14.95 (978-0-439-43179-8). Striking color photographs and simple text show children of multiple races and ethnicities. (Rev: HBG 4/04; SLJ 11/03)

20036 Straub, Deborah G., ed. *African American Voices* (5–8). 1996, Gale $126.00 (978-0-8103-9497-1). This is a collection of excerpts from important speeches delivered by a vast array of African Americans, past and present. (Rev: SLJ 2/97) [973]

20037 Taus-Bolstad, Stacy. *Puerto Ricans in America* (5–8). Series: In America. 2004, Lerner LB $27.93 (978-0-8225-3953-7). 80pp. This overview of Puerto Rican migration to the United States looks at the motivations for moving and explores the lives of the new arrivals and the traditions they maintained. (Rev: BL 11/15/04)

20038 Teitelbaum, Michael. *Chinese Immigrants* (5–8). Series: Immigration to the United States. 2004, Facts on File $35.00 (978-0-8160-5687-3). After an overview of the reasons underlying immigration in general, this illustrated volume looks at the circumstances of migrants from China, the group's history in the United States, and the contemporary situation, with sidebar features, a timeline, and a glossary. (Rev: SLJ 4/05)

20039 Temple, Bob. *The Arab Americans* (5–8). Illus. Series: We Came to America. 2002, Mason Crest LB $19.95 (978-1-59084-102-0). 64pp. Temple reviews the history of Arab immigration to North America, the group's customs and contributions, and famous Arab Americans, with the aid of photographs, a timeline, and glossary. (Rev: BL 7/02; SLJ 9/02)

20040 Todd, Anne M. *Italian Immigrants: 1880–1920* (4–6). Series: Coming to America. 2001, Capstone LB $23.93 (978-0-7368-0796-8). 32pp. The rich heritage and cultural contributions of Italian Americans are covered in this book that also explores why and how they came to the United States. (Rev: BL 10/15/01; HBG 3/02)

20041 Trumbauer, Lisa. *German Immigrants* (5–8). Series: Immigration to the United States. 2004, Facts on File $35.00 (978-0-8160-5683-5). After an overview of the reasons underlying immigration in general, this illustrated volume looks at the circumstances of migrants from Germany, the group's history in the United States, and the contemporary situation, with sidebar features, a timeline, and a glossary. Also use *Russian Immigrants* (2004). (Rev: SLJ 4/05)

20042 Walker, Paul Robert. *A Nation of Immigrants* (4–6). Illus. Series: All About America. 2012, Kingfisher LB $19.89 (978-075346713-8); paper $9.99 (978-075346671-1). 32pp. Illustrations, archival reproductions, and photographs add appeal to this survey of the various waves of immigrants to the United States from the earliest people to cross the land bridge from Siberia to the census of 2010. (Rev: BL 4/15/12; SLJ 3/12) [304.8]

20043 Wallner, Rosemary. *Greek Immigrants: 1890–1920* (4–6). Series: Coming to America. 2002, Capstone LB $23.93 (978-0-7368-1206-1). Using many primary sources, this book traces the causes of Greek immigration and provides information on the Greek immigrants' journeys, culture, integration, and contributions. (Rev: BL 1/1–15/03; HBG 3/03; SLJ 3/03)

20044 Wallner, Rosemary. *Japanese Immigrants: 1850–1950* (4–6). Series: Coming to America. 2001, Capstone LB $16.95 (978-0-7368-0797-5). 32pp. A century of Japanese migration to the United States is detailed with material on their contributions, cultural heritage, and treatment on arrival. (Rev: BL 10/15/01)

20045 Wallner, Rosemary. *Polish Immigrants: 1890–1920* (4–6). Series: Coming to America. 2002, Capstone LB $23.93 (978-0-7368-1208-5). 32pp. The exodus from Poland to America is traced through text, timelines, maps, and personal memoirs, with material on such topics as Polish culture, contributions to American life, and famous Polish Americans. (Rev: BL 1/1–15/03; HBG 3/03)

20046 Weatherford, Carole Boston. *The Beatitudes: From Slavery to Civil Rights* (2–4). Illus. by Tim Ladwig. 2010, Eerdmans $16.99 (978-0-8028-5352-3). 32pp. Weatherford uses the Beatitudes as the framework for a rich picture-book history of the African American experience, from slavery through the civil rights movement to the inauguration of Barack Obama. (Rev: BL 2/1/10; SLJ 3/1/10) [323.0973]

20047 Weber, Valerie J. *I Come from Afghanistan* (2–4). Illus. Series: This Is My Story. 2006, Gareth Stevens LB $21.00 (978-0-8368-7233-0). 24pp. Afghan American Bahishta, age 9, introduces readers to her family, Muslim faith, and cultural heritage in this series entry. (Rev: BL 1/1–15/07)

1121

20048 Weiss, Gail Garfinkel. *Americans from Russia and Eastern Europe* (5–8). Series: New Americans. 2009, Marshall Cavendish LB $24.95 (978-0-7614-4310-0). 80pp. This volume provides an overview of immigration past and present from these regions, providing census data and population maps and charts as well as discussing these immigrants' contributions to American culture. (Rev: LMC 3–4/10; SLJ 2/10) [305.8991]

20049 Williams, Jean Kinney. *Asian Indian Americans* (3–5). Series: Spirit of America: Our Cultural Heritage. 2003, Child's World LB $27.07 (978-1-59296-015-6). 32pp. A brief look at the history of Indian immigration to the United States and an assessment of the community's contributions to American culture and society. (Rev: SLJ 2/04)

20050 Wolf, Bernard. *Coming to America: A Muslim Family's Story* (3–5). Illus. 2003, Lee & Low $17.95 (978-1-58430-086-1); paper $7.95 (978-1-58430-177-6). 48pp. This bright photoessay offers useful insights into Islam and its adherents as it tells the story of a Muslim family's migration from Egypt to the United States. (Rev: BL 4/1/03; HB 5/03; HBG 10/03; SLJ 5/03)

20051 Worth, Richard. *Mexican Immigrants* (5–8). Series: Immigration to the United States. 2004, Facts on File $35.00 (978-0-8160-5690-3). After an overview of the reasons underlying immigration in general, this illustrated volume looks at the circumstances of migrants from Mexico, the group's history in the United States, and the contemporary situation, with sidebar features, a timeline, and a glossary. Also use *Jewish Immigrants* and *Africans in America* (both 2004). (Rev: SLJ 4/05) [304.8]

20052 Yoder, Carolyn P. *Asian Indian Americans* (3–5). Series: We Are America. 2003, Heinemann LB $24.22 (978-1-4034-0167-0). 32pp. Yoder explores the challenges and hardships faced by Indian immigrants to America and the many contributions they have made to society as a whole. Also use *Italian Americans* (2003). (Rev: HBG 10/03; SLJ 8/03)

Terrorism

20053 Bingley, Richard. *Terrorism* (5–9). Series: Face the Facts. 2003, Raintree LB $28.56 (978-0-7398-6852-2). 56pp. An examination of terrorism, its causes, and the efforts being made to combat it. (Rev: SLJ 4/04)

20054 Brown, Don. *America Is Under Attack: September 11, 2001: The Day the Towers Fell* (3–5). Series: Actual Times. 2011, Roaring Brook $16.99 (978-1-59643-694-7). 64pp. This balanced, straightforward account covers the events from the hijacking of the planes to the collapse of the towers. ALSC Notable Children's Book, 2012. Lexile 840L (Rev: BL 9/1/11; HB 11–12/11; LMC 1–2/12; SLJ 9/1/11*) [973.931]

20055 Burgan, Michael. *Terrorist Groups* (5–7). Series: Terrorism. 2010, Compass Point LB $27.99 (978-0-

7565-4311-2). 48pp. After providing a definition of terrorism, Burgan looks at various terrorist groups past and present: the IRA, Irgun, Fatah, ETA, Farc, Tamil Tigers, Hezbollah, Aum Shinrikyo, Hamas, and al-Qaeda. Lexile 990L (Rev: LMC 11–12/10) [363.325]

20056 Ching, Jacqueline. *Cyberterrorism* (5–8). Series: Doomsday Scenarios: Separating Fact from Fiction. 2010, Rosen LB $29.25 (978-1-4358-3565-8). 64pp. After describing cyberterrorists and their techniques, this volume describes some worst-case scenarios, assesses the scope of the threat, and looks at ways of fighting back. (Rev: LMC 11–12/10) [363.325]

20057 Deedy, Carmen A., and Wilson Kimeli Naiyomah. *14 Cows for America* (2–4). Illus. by Thomas Gonzalez. 2009, Peachtree $17.95 (978-1-56145-490-7). 36pp. A beautifully illustrated true story of an act of kindness and generosity from Africa to the United States after the tragedy of 9/11. (Rev: BL 7/09; LMC 11/09; SLJ 8/09*)

20058 Greene, Jacqueline D. *The 2001 World Trade Center Attack* (3–4). Series: Code Red. 2007, Bearport LB $23.96 (978-1-59716-365-1). This look at the terrorist attacks of September 11, 2001, describes what happened that day and how emergency workers responded. (Rev: SLJ 8/07)

20059 Hamilton, John. *Behind the Terror* (4–7). Series: War on Terrorism. 2002, ABDO LB $16.95 (978-1-57765-679-1). Using an accessible text and color photographs, this book reports on various international terrorist organizations, their leaders, and their tactics. (Rev: BL 5/15/02)

20060 Hamilton, John. *Operation Enduring Freedom* (4–7). Series: War on Terrorism. 2002, ABDO LB $25.65 (978-1-57765-665-4). Using many color photographs and a matter-of-fact text, this book covers various aspects of the U.S. war against terrorism. (Rev: BL 5/15/02; HBG 10/02) [973.9]

20061 Hamilton, John. *Operation Noble Eagle* (4–7). Series: War on Terrorism. 2002, ABDO LB $25.65 (978-1-57765-664-7). A look at U.S. efforts to police and defend its borders as part of the war on terroism. (Rev: BL 5/15/02; HBG 10/02) [973.9]

20062 Lalley, Patrick. *9.11.01: Terrorists Attack the U.S* (4–7). Illus. 2002, Raintree LB $31.40 (978-0-7398-6021-2). 48pp. A compact look at the terrorist attacks of September 11, 2001, their causes, the world of Islam, the history of the World Trade Center, and personal stories related to the attacks. (Rev: BL 4/1/02; HBG 10/02; SLJ 5/02; VOYA 8/02)

20063 Louis, Nancy. *Heroes of the Day* (4–7). Series: War on Terrorism. 2002, ABDO LB $25.65 (978-1-57765-658-6). This account of September 11, 2001, describes through pictures and case studies the gallant feats of firefighters, police, and those who fought back on Flight 93. (Rev: BL 5/15/02; HBG 10/02; SLJ 6/02) [973.9]

20064 Louis, Nancy. *United We Stand* (4–7). Series: War on Terrorism. 2002, ABDO LB $25.65 (978-1-57765-660-9). In text and pictures, this account describes the support offered to the victims of the terrorist attacks of September 11, 2001, and their families. (Rev: BL 5/15/02; HBG 10/02) [909.9]

20065 Margulies, Phillip. *Al-Qaeda: Osama Bin Laden's Army of Terrorists* (5–7). Series: Inside the World's Most Infamous Terrorist Organizations. 2003, Rosen LB $27.95 (978-0-8239-3817-9). Al-Qaeda's history, missions, methods, and structure are described, with a detailed profile of Osama Bin Laden. (Rev: BL 10/15/03) [973.93]

20066 Marquette, Scott. *America Under Attack* (4–7). Illus. Series: America at War. 2002, Rourke LB $20.95 (978-1-58952-386-9). 48pp. This book for middle graders explains in simple terms the September 11, 2001 attacks and other acts of terrorism against the United States, as well as discussing resulting legislation and changing opinions in America. (Rev: BL 10/15/02)

20067 Nardo, Don. *The History of Terrorism* (5–7). Series: Terrorism. 2010, Compass Point LB $27.99 (978-0-7565-4310-5). 48pp. A broad, well-illustrated survey of terrorism through time, looking at the governments, groups, and individuals that have sought to achieve their goals through violence and the various strategies they have used. (Rev: LMC 11–12/10) [363.3]

20068 Rosaler, Maxine. *Hamas: Palestinian Terrorists* (5–7). Illus. Series: Inside the World's Most Infamous Terrorist Organizations. 2003, Rosen LB $27.95 (978-0-8239-3820-9). 64pp. Hamas's history, missions, methods, and structure are described, with profiles of key figures. (Rev: BL 10/15/03)

20069 Stewart, Gail B. *Terrorism* (4–6). Illus. Series: Understanding Issues. 2002, Gale LB $26.20 (978-0-7377-1287-2). 48pp. Taking September 11, 2001, as a starting point, this account explores the causes and effects of terrorism and the measures taken to combat it. (Rev: BL 6/1–15/02; SLJ 9/02)

20070 Uschan, Michael V. *The Beslan School Siege and Separatist Terrorism* (5–8). Series: Terrorism in Today's World. 2005, World Almanac LB $186.00 (978-0-8368-6555-4). The deadly 2004 attack on a Russian school by Chechen Muslim terrorists is only the first of several attacks described in this volume on independence movements that use violence. (Rev: BL 4/1/06) [947.5]

20071 Wachtel, Alan. *September 11: A Primary Source History* (5–8). Illus. Series: In Their Own Words. 2009, Gareth Stevens LB $27.00 (978-1-4339-0048-8). 48pp. With narrative text and numerous photographs, plus excerpts from primary sources — including transcripts of phone conversations aboard the planes and firsthand accounts from responders and eyewitnesses — this volume covers the attack itself and the aftermath. (Rev: BL 4/1/09) [973.931]

Personal Development

Behavior

General

20072 Allen, Nancy Kelly. *Winning by Giving* (1–3). Illus. Series: Social Skills. 2013, Rourke LB $27.07 (978-162169910-1); paper $7.95 (9781621698050). 24pp. Offering your time to others is the subject of this addition to the series, allowing children the chance to better understand philanthropy and how they can help others. ℮ (Rev: BL 11/1/13; LMC 10/14; SLJ 11/4/13) [361.3]

20073 Andrews, Beth. *Why Are You So Scared? A Child's Book About Parents with PTSD* (1–4). Illus. by Katherine Kirkland. 2011, Magination $14.95 (978-143381045-9); paper $9.95 (978-14338104-4-2). 32pp. This book provides accessible information for children whose parents are coping with post-traumatic stress disorder. (Rev: BL 11/1/11) [616.85]

20074 Andrews, Linda Wasmer. *Intelligence* (4–8). Series: Life Balance. 2003, Watts paper $6.95 (978-0-531-16608-6). 80pp. This book explores the concept of intelligence, how it is measured, and how it affects daily life. (Rev: BL 10/15/03) [612]

20075 Andrews, Linda Wasmer. *Meditation* (3–6). Illus. Series: Life Balance. 2004, Watts LB $20.50 (978-0-531-12219-8). 79pp. Explores different forms of meditation, including yoga, zen, and transcendental meditation, and discusses how they can be used to reduce stress and improve mental well-being. (Rev: SLJ 7/04) [158.1]

20076 Barber, Nicola. *First Day of School* (K–1). Series: The Big Day! 2009, Rosen LB $21.25 (978-1-4358-2839-1). 24pp. This simple book looks at typical concerns about school — getting ready, saying goodbye, making friends, and so forth. (Rev: SLJ 7/09) [372.12]

20077 Barber, Nicola. *Moving to a New House* (K–1). Series: The Big Day! 2009, Rosen LB $21.25 (978-1-4358-2841-4). 24pp. Typical problems involved in moving — adjusting to a new neighborhood and finding new friends — are the focus of this volume. (Rev: SLJ 7/09) [648]

20078 Barron, T. A. *The Hero's Trail: A Guide for Heroic Life* (4–7). Illus. 2002, Putnam $15.99 (978-0-399-23860-4). 160pp. This collection of anecdotes about both real and fictional characters aims to define heroism, and explores how one can lead a heroic life. (Rev: BL 10/15/02; HBG 3/03; SLJ 12/02; VOYA 12/02) [170]

20079 Becker, Helaine. *Like a Pro: 101 Simple Ways to Do Really Important Stuff* (4–6). Illus. by Claudia Dávila. Series: Planet Earth News. 2006, Maple Tree $21.95 (978-1-897066-53-9); paper $9.95 (978-1-897066-54-6). 160pp. From changing a bike tire to telling jokes to making friends, this friendly, practical guide offers instructions and advice. (Rev: SLJ 6/06) [646.7]

20080 Borden, Sara, et al. *Middle School: How to Deal* (4–6). Illus. by Yuki Hatori. 2005, Chronicle LB $15.50 (978-0-8118-4845-9); paper $9.95 (978-0-8118-4497-0). 96pp. Advice from five 7th-grade girls on everything academic and social, with a dictionary of online chat conventions. (Rev: BL 6/1–15/05) [373.236]

20081 Buchholz, Rachel. *How to Survive Anything: Shark Attack, Lightning, Embarrassing Parents, Pop Quizzes, and Other Perilous Situations* (4–8). Illus. by Chris Philpot. 2011, National Geographic paper $14.95 (978-1-4263-0-774-4). 208pp. Full of humor, this survival guide covers everything from truly dangerous situations to public humiliation. (Rev: BLO 8/11; SLJ 7/11) [646.7]

20082 Buckley, Annie. *Hero Girls* (2–5). Series: Girls Rock! 2006, The Child's World LB $25.64 (978-1-59296-744-5). 32pp. Profiles American girls whose courage or other attributes can be classed as heroic; suitable for browsing by beginning readers. (Rev: SLJ 4/07) [305.2]

20083 Canfield, Jack, et al. *Chicken Soup for the Girl's Soul: Real Stories by Real Girls About Real Stuff* (4–6). 2005, Health Communications paper $14.95 (978-0-7573-0313-5). 345pp. Real-life stories tackle a wide variety of topics, including dealing with peer pressure, parental divorce, surviving middle school, first loves, and friendship. (Rev: SLJ 2/06) [158.1]

20084 Cindrich, Sharon. *A Smart Girl's Guide to Style: How to Have Fun with Fashion, Shop Smart, and Let Your Personal Style Shine Through* (4–7). Illus. by Shannon Laskey. Series: Be Your Best. 2010, American Girl paper $9.95 (978-1-59369-648-1). 119pp. With a light and breezy tone, this book outlines plenty of fashion dos and don'ts in chapters that define the difference between fashion and style, lay out the basics, and give shopping and storage advice. (Rev: SLJ 7/10) [562]

20085 Cordes, Helen. *Girl Power in the Classroom: A Book About Girls, Their Fears, and Their Future* (5–8). 2000, Lerner LB $30.35 (978-0-8225-2693-3). This book of personal guidance for girls describes how to conquer fears and cope with difficult situations at school. (Rev: BL 5/15/00; HBG 10/00; SLJ 5/00) [373.1822]

20086 Cordes, Helen. *Girl Power in the Mirror: A Book About Girls, Their Bodies, and Themselves* (5–8). 2000, Lerner LB $30.35 (978-0-8225-2691-9). This book for girls explains proper attitudes about appearance and gives coping strategies concerning pressures about one's looks. (Rev: BL 5/15/00; HBG 10/00; SLJ 5/00) [306.4]

20087 Damm, Antje. *Ask Me* (PS–3). Trans. from German by Doris Orgel. Illus. by author. 2003, Millbrook $14.95 (978-0-7613-1845-3). 220pp. This is a compilation of questions, ranging from the fairly basic to the thought-provoking and accompanied by imaginative illustrations, that can be used to prompt discussion. (Rev: BCCB 3/03; BL 4/1/03; HBG 10/03; SLJ 3/03) [306.874]

20088 Dawson, Mildred L. *Beauty Lab: How Science Is Changing the Way We Look* (5–10). 1997, Silver Moon $14.95 (978-1-881889-84-7). This work on health and hygiene contains chapters on skin, eyes, teeth, fitness, and hair. (Rev: SLJ 3/97) [613.7]

20089 Dee, Catherine, ed. *The Girls' Book of Wisdom: Empowering, Inspirational Quotes from Over 400 Fabulous Females* (5–8). Illus. by Lou M. Pollack. 1999, Little, Brown paper $8.95 (978-0-316-17956-0). A collection of quotations from more than 400 famous women grouped by such subjects as "Friends," "Happiness," and "Leadership." (Rev: SLJ 12/99; VOYA 4/00) [305.23]

20090 Doak, Robin. *Caring* (3–6). Series: Character Education. 2003, Raintree LB $24.26 (978-0-7398-5778-6). 32pp. Photographs and text illustrate the importance of compassion and caring. (Rev: HBG 3/03; SLJ 4/03)

20091 Doudna, Kelly. *Honestly!* (K–3). Illus. Series: Character Concepts. 2007, ABDO LB $13.95 (978-1-59928-735-5). 24pp. Examples of children behaving honestly — and a brief story about a boy who makes the decision to be honest — will help children grasp the concept and practice it in their lives. (Rev: SLJ 6/07)

20092 Doudna, Kelly. *Keep Your Cool!* (K–3). Illus. Series: Character Concepts. 2007, ABDO LB $13.95 (978-1-59928-736-2). 24pp. Stories of children nipping temper tantrums in the bud provide examples of good behavior. (Rev: SLJ 6/07)

20093 Dylan, Matthew. *Respect* (3–6). Series: Character Education. 2003, Raintree LB $24.26 (978-0-7398-5780-9). 32pp. This slim book examines respect from a number of points of view, including respect for authority, self, others, women, property rights, and the environment. (Rev: HBG 3/03; SLJ 4/03) [179]

20094 Edelman, Marian Wright. *I Can Make a Difference* (2–4). Illus. by Barry Moser. 2005, HarperCollins $20.89 (978-0-06-028052-9). 112pp. This oversize collection of poems, stories, songs, quotations, art, and folk tales, organized in 12 sections dealing with such topics as honesty, courage, and compassion, includes selections from a wide variety of sources that emphasize children's capacity to make a difference. (Rev: BL 11/1/05) [808.8]

20095 Erlbach, Arlene. *The Middle School Survival Guide* (5–7). Illus. by Helen Flook. 2003, Walker $16.95 (978-0-8027-8852-8); paper $8.95 (978-0-8027-7657-0). The author offers tips on a wide variety of topics of interest to this age group (homework, drugs, sex, and so forth), interspersed with advice from students themselves. (Rev: BL 9/15/03; SLJ 9/03) [373.18]

20096 Finn, Carrie. *Kids Talk About Bravery* (K–2). Illus. by Amy Bailey Muehlenhardt. Series: Kids Talk Jr. 2006, Picture Window LB $25.26 (978-1-4048-2314-3). 32pp. A question-and-answer format and simple language are used to discuss children's fears and ways of tackling them. (Rev: SLJ 1/07) [179]

20097 Fitzhugh, Karla. *Body Image* (5–9). Series: Health Issues. 2004, Steck-Vaughn LB $32.79 (978-0-7398-6891-1). Body image and such related issues as cosmetic surgery, piercing, tattooing, eating disorders, and physical culture are examined in appealing text with informative charts and sidebars. (Rev: SLJ 11/05) [155.2]

20098 Fleischman, Paul, ed. *Cannibal in the Mirror* (5–10). Photos by John Whalen. 2000, Twenty-First Century LB $24.90 (978-0-7613-0968-0). 64pp. This thought-provoking book takes 27 quotations that describe barbarous behavior of primitive societies and pairs each with a telling photograph of similar behavior in modern American society. (Rev: BL 4/15/00; HBG 10/00; SLJ 4/00) [150]

20099 Fox, Annie. *Real Friends vs the Other Kind* (5–8). Series: Middle School Confidential. 2009, Free Spirit paper $9.99 (978-1-57542-319-7). 90pp. The intricacies of middle school friendships, allegiances, and romances are examined here, with advice from real tweens about handing difficult situations. (Rev: SLJ 8/09) [177.62]

20100 Frost, Helen. *Feeling Angry* (PS–1). Series: Emotions. 2000, Capstone LB $17.26 (978-0-7368-0668-8). 24pp. Nine full-color photos and nine short sentences are used to illustrate anger. Others in the series are *Feeling Happy* and *Feeling Scared* (both 2000) (Rev: HBG 3/01; SLJ 1/01) [152.4]

20101 Graves, Sue. *But Why Can't I?* (PS–1). Illus. by Desideria Guicciardini. Series: Our Emotions and Behavior. 2011, Free Spirit $12.99 (978-1-57542-376-0). 25pp. Simple plot lines and real-life scenarios make this a useful discussion-starter about rules and their purpose in keeping us safe and healthy. Also use *I'm Not Happy, Not Fair, Won't Share,* and *Who Feels Scared?* (all 2011). (Rev: SLJ 8/1/11) [152.4]

20102 Guillain, Charlotte. *My First Sleepover* (K–2). Illus. Series: Growing Up. 2011, Heinemann LB $22 (978-1-4329-4802-3). 24pp. This reassuring book gives readers a sense of what to expect on their first sleepover. (Rev: BL 7/11; SLJ 6/11) [793.2]

20103 Hartman, Holly, ed. *Girlwonder: Every Girl's Guide to the Fantastic Feats, Cool Qualities, and Remarkable Abilities of Women and Girls* (4–8). 2003, Houghton Mifflin paper $9.95 (978-0-618-31939-8). A browsable look at famous women and their accomplishments, interspersed with information and advice on topics ranging from romance to fashion. (Rev: SLJ 5/04) [305.235]

20104 Holyoke, Nancy. *A Smart Girl's Guide to Boys: Surviving Crushes, Staying True to Yourself, and Other Love Stuff* (4–6). Illus. 2001, Pleasant $9.95 (978-1-58485-368-8). 112pp. Age-appropriate advice on dealing with boys, first kisses, and balancing friends and boyfriends is interwoven with magazine-style quizzes and letters from girls. (Rev: BL 8/01; SLJ 9/01) [305.23]

20105 Hughes, Monica. *First Day at School* (PS–2). Series: My First. 2004, Raintree LB $18.56 (978-1-4109-0643-4); paper $5.50 (978-1-4109-0669-4). Simple language introduces young readers to what happens on the first day of school — coatrooms, classrooms, playtime, and so forth. Also use *First Vacation* (2004). [371]

20106 Jackson, Donna M. *What's So Funny? Making Sense of Humor* (3–7). Illus. by Ted Stearn. 2011, Viking $16.99 (978-0-670-01244-2). 64pp. Jackson looks at the origins of humor, the physiology of laughter, animals and humor, and various other aspects of being funny. (Rev: BLO 8/11; SLJ 7/11) [152.4]

20107 Jackson, Ellen. *Sometimes Bad Things Happen* (PS–2). Photos by Shelley Rotner. 2002, Millbrook LB $22.90 (978-0-7613-2810-0); paper $7.95 (978-0-7613-1734-0). Children are reassured that while bad things do happen, there are ways to cope and people who will want to help. (Rev: BL 11/15/02; HBG 3/03; SLJ 2/03)

20108 Kevi. *Don't Talk to Strangers* (K–3). Illus. Series: Hip Kid Hop. 2003, Scholastic $13.95 (978-0-439-31385-8). This attractive title, packaged with an audio CD, uses a rap rhyme to teach young readers how to recognize and behave around strangers. (Rev: HBG 10/03; SLJ 9/03)

20109 King, Bart. *The Big Book of Girl Stuff* (4–8). Illus. by Jennifer Kalis. 2006, Gibbs Smith paper $19.99 (978-1-58685-819-3). A lighthearted, lightly organized guide to a great many topics of interest to growing girls, including why boys smell bad, etiquette, dieting, how to shop, and how to get a boy's attention. (Rev: SLJ 1/07) [646.7]

20110 Klingel, Cynthia A. *Friendliness* (K–3). 2007, The Child's World LB $21.36 (978-1-59296-669-1). 24pp. Using a question-and-answer format, Klingel discusses

friendliness and its benefits, with many pertinent examples. Also use *Generosity* (2007) (Rev: SLJ 11/07) [177]

20111 Lester, Julius. *Let's Talk About Race* (K–3). Illus. by Karen Barbour. 2005, HarperCollins LB $17.89 (978-0-06-028598-2). 32pp. Lester emphasizes that racial identity is only one of the many elements in an individual's makeup. (Rev: BL 2/1/05; SLJ 1/05) [305.8]

20112 Ljungkvist, Laura. *Follow the Line to School* (PS–1). Illus. by author. Series: Follow the Line. 2011, Viking $16.99 (978-0-670-01226-8). 32pp. As readers follow the line through this book, they are introduced to the various parts of a bright, well-equipped school and answer a variety of questions. (Rev: BL 8/11; HB 9–10/11; SLJ 7/11) [371]

20113 Lound, Karen. *Girl Power in the Family: A Book About Girls, Their Rights, and Their Voice* (5–10). Series: Girl Power. 2000, Lerner LB $30.35 (978-0-8225-2692-6). A book that explores the problems of growing up female today with material on gender roles, biases, and relationships. (Rev: HBG 10/00; SLJ 6/00) [303.6]

20114 Lyons, Shelly. *People in My Neighborhood* (PS–K). Illus. Series: My Neighborhood. 2013, Capstone LB $24.65 (978-162065099-8); paper $6.95 (9781620658833). 24pp. With simple text, large and bright photographs, and an oversize format, this entry in the series introduces all the different kinds of people found in a typical neighborhood. (Rev: BL 6/13; SLJ 4/13)

20115 MacGregor, Cynthia. *Think for Yourself: A Kid's Guide to Solving Life's Dilemmas and Other Sticky Problems* (3–6). Illus. by Susan Norberg Farias. 2003, Lobster paper $7.95 (978-1-894222-73-0). 96pp. Readers learn to identify problems and to work out solutions for themselves. (Rev: SLJ 2/04) [170]

20116 Madison, Lynda. *The Feelings Book: The Care and Keeping of Your Emotions* (4–6). Illus. by Norm Bendell. 2002, Pleasant paper $8.95 (978-1-58485-528-6). 104pp. Madison tackles the topic of the emotional upheavals that many youngsters experience as they near their teens and offers tips on identifying and coping with strong feelings. (Rev: BL 12/1/02; SLJ 10/02) [155.43]

20117 Marshall, Shelley. *Super Ben's Brave Bike Ride: A Book About Courage* (PS–K). Illus. by Ben Mahan. Series: Character Education with Super Ben and Molly the Great. 2010, Enslow $21.26 (978-0-7660-3515-7). 24pp. Young bear Ben finds the courage to get to his friend Molly the rabbit's house alone when his mother is busy, wearing his cape to bolster his confidence. Also use *Super Ben's Dirty Hands: A Book About Healthy Habits* (2010). (Rev: LMC 3/1/10; SLJ 5/1/10) [179]

20118 Mattern, Joanne. *Do You Share?* (PS–1). Illus. Series: Are You a Good Friend? 2007, Gareth Stevens LB $19.93 (978-0-8368-9275-8); paper $5.95 (978-0-8368-8280-3). 24pp. Photographs and a brief text illustrate many ways in which children enjoy sharing. (Rev: BL 10/15/07) [177]

20119 Mayer, Cassie. *Being Honest* (K–1). Series: Citizenship. 2007, Heinemann LB $20.71 (978-1-4034-

9484-9). 24pp. What is being honest? How can you be honest? This title answers such questions with simple vocabulary and helpful examples. (Rev: BL 9/1/07; SLJ 11/07) [179]

20120 Meiners, Cheri J. *Be Polite and Kind* (PS–1). Illus. by Meredith Johnson. 2004, Free Spirit paper $10.95 (978-1-57542-151-3). 40pp. This attractive picture book is designed to teach the simple virtues of courtesy and kindness. (Rev: BL 5/1/04; SLJ 8/04) [177]

20121 Meiners, Cheri J. *Join In and Play* (PS–1). Illus. by Meredith Johnson. 2004, Free Spirit paper $10.95 (978-1-57542-152-0). 40pp. The basic skills children need to interact happily with others are clearly communicated in this attractive picture book. (Rev: BL 5/1/04; SLJ 8/04) [790]

20122 *The Milestones Project: Celebrating Childhood Around the World* (PS–2). Photos by Richard Steckel and Michele Steckel. Illus. 2004, Tricycle $17.95 (978-1-58246-132-8). 64pp. Children around the world are shown in "milestone moments" — birthdays, losing a tooth, haircuts, playing with toys, and so forth. (Rev: BL 1/1–15/05; SLJ 11/04) [305.23]

20123 Montanari, Donata. *Children Around the World* (PS–K). Illus. by author. 2001, Kids Can $14.95 (978-1-55337-064-2). 32pp. Readers are introduced to children in countries around the world who describe their lives in simple sentences that highlight their similarities and differences. (Rev: HBG 3/02; SLJ 12/01) [390.083]

20124 Moore-Mallinos, Jennifer. *Do You Have a Secret?* (PS–3). Illus. by Marta Fàbrega. Series: Let's Talk About It! 2005, Barron's paper $6.95 (978-0-7641-3170-7). 31pp. Moore-Mallinos explains the difference between good secrets and bad ones, and gives advice on getting help from adults. (Rev: SLJ 10/05)

20125 Moss, Wendy L. *Being Me: A Kid's Guide to Boosting Confidence and Self-Esteem* (5–8). Illus. 2011, Magination $14.95 (978-143380883-8); paper $9.95 (978-14338088-4-5). 112pp. "Stand Up for Yourself" and "Hang Out with a Group" are two of the chapters in this book full of helpful and practical advice for building social confidence. (Rev: BL 1/1–15/11; SLJ 3/1/11) [155.4]

20126 Naik, Anita. *Read the Signals: The Body Language Handbook* (4–8). Series: Really Useful Handbooks. 2009, Crabtree LB $29.27 (978-0-7787-4388-0); paper $9.95 (978-0-7787-4401-6). This positive, often humorous book provides information on handling and interpreting a variety of tricky social situations — from bullying to shyness to flirtation — presented in digestible, bullet-point format. (Rev: BL 4/1/09; LMC 10/09; SLJ 6/1/09) [153.6]

20127 Navarra, Tova. *The Kids' Guidebook: Great Advice to Help Kids Cope. Rev. ed.* (4–6). Illus. by Tom Kerr. 2002, Barron's paper $12.99 (978-0-7641-2066-4). 128pp. Advice on coping with difficult situations, from power outages and dealing with strangers to the death of a loved one. (Rev: SLJ 3/03)

20128 Nelson, Robin. *Being a Leader* (K–1). Illus. Series: First Step Nonfiction: Citizenship. 2003, Lerner LB $18.60 (978-0-8225-1287-5). 23pp. A basic look at what it takes to be a leader and how to become a good leader at home, school, and in the community. (Rev: HBG 4/04; SLJ 11/03) [303.3]

20129 Nikola-Lisa, W. *How We Are Smart* (4–7). Illus. by Scan Quails. 2006, Lee & Low $16.95 (978-1-58430-254-4). A picture book for older readers that looks at different kinds of intelligence, using double-page spreads about 12 famous people to illustrate these concepts. (Rev: BL 4/1/06; SLJ 6/06) [811]

20130 Orr, Tamra. *Ways to Help the Elderly* (5–8). Series: How to Help: A Guide to Giving Back. 2010, Mitchell Lane LB $21.50 (978-1-58415-915-5). 48pp. Using real-life examples, this thoughtful book suggests many ways in which children can help elderly people. (Rev: SLJ 12/1/10) [305.26]

20131 Raatma, Lucia. *Determination* (2–4). Series: Character Education. 2002, Capstone LB $22.60 (978-0-7368-1387-7). 24pp. The characteristic is described, with examples of how to show determination and a famous person who exhibits it. Also use *Loyalty* and *Leadership* (both 2002) (Rev: HBG 3/03; SLJ 2/03)

20132 Raatma, Lucia. *Loyalty* (K–4). Illus. Series: 21st Century Junior Library Character Education. 2009, Cherry Lake LB $22.80 (978-1-60279-326-2). 24pp. An overview of what loyalty means, with specific examples illustrating how loyalty applies in the home, school, and community. (Rev: BL 4/1/09) [179]

20133 Roberts, Cynthia. *Tolerance* (K–2). Illus. Series: Learn About Values. 2007, Child's World LB $14.95 (978-1-59296-678-3). 24pp. Roberts shows the benefits of tolerant behavior in a variety of settings — at school, at home, with younger children. (Rev: BL 10/15/07) [179]

20134 Robinson, Sharon. *Jackie's Nine: Jackie Robinson's Values to Live By* (5–8). Illus. 2001, Scholastic paper $15.95 (978-0-439-23764-2). 183pp. A collection of inspirational writings, selected by baseball legend Jackie Robinson's daughter and organized under headings including "Courage" and "Determination," that include material by and about such well-known individuals as Christopher Reeve and Oprah Winfrey. (Rev: BL 7/01; HBG 10/01; SLJ 6/01; VOYA 8/01) [158]

20135 Rosenthal, Amy Krouse. *Cookies: Bite Size Life Lessons* (PS–1). Illus. by Jane Dyer. 2006, HarperCollins $12.99 (978-0-06-058081-0). 40pp. Baking cookies serves as the framework for defining words and concepts in this attractive and child-friendly book. (Rev: BCCB 9/06; BL 4/1/06*; HBG 10/06; SLJ 5/06) [179]

20136 Rotner, Shelley, and Sheila Kelly. *What Can You Do? A Book About Discovering What You Do Well* (PS–1). Photos by Shelley Rotner. Illus. 2001, Millbrook LB $22.90 (978-0-7613-2119-4). 24pp. With illustrations and text that show a variety of activities and talents, the authors ask readers to determine what they can do best. (Rev: BL 4/15/01; HBG 10/01; SLJ 9/01) [153.9]

20137 Salzmann, Mary Elizabeth. *I Am a Good Citizen* (K–2). Series: Building Character. 2003, ABDO LB $19.93 (978-1-57765-825-2). 23pp. A simple explanation of the character traits and behavior that make a good citizen. Also use *I Am Fair* (2003) (Rev: HBG 10/03; SLJ 9/03) [323.6]

20138 Scheunemann, Pam. *Patriotism* (1–3). Series: United We Stand. 2003, ABDO LB $19.93 (978-1-57765-880-1). 24pp. A look at pride in one's country, with simple text and relevant, multicultural photographs. (Rev: HBG 10/03; SLJ 6/03) [323.6]

20139 Schuette, Sarah L. *I Am Cooperative* (PS–2). Series: Character Values. 2002, Capstone LB $17.26 (978-0-7368-1439-3). 24pp. Photographs and simple text are used to explain how to be cooperative. Also use *I Am Honest, I Am Respectful,* and *I Am Responsible.* (Rev: HBG 3/03; SLJ 3/03)

20140 Schuette, Sarah L. *Soy bondadosa / I Am Caring* (PS–2). Trans. by Martin Luis Guzman Ferrer. Series: Pebble Bilingual Books. 2003, Capstone LB $17.26 (978-0-7368-2301-2). 24pp. Good, caring behavior is illustrated and described in English and Spanish. Also use *Soy respetuoso/I Am Respectful, Soy cooperativa/I Am Cooperative,* and *Soy responsable/I Am Responsible* (all 2003) (Rev: SLJ 4/04) [395]

20141 Sheindlin, Judy. *Judge Judy Sheindlin's You Can't Judge a Book by Its Cover: Cool Rules for School* (2–5). Illus. by Bob Tore. 2001, HarperCollins LB $14.89 (978-0-06-029484-7). Judge Judy looks at common choices young students have to make, presenting a range of possible decisions, some sensible and some clearly not. (Rev: HBG 10/01; SLJ 7/01) [170]

20142 Sherman, Joanne. *Because It's My Body!* (PS–2). Illus. by John S. Gurney. Series: Keep `em Safe. 2002, S.A.F.E. for Children paper $14.95 (978-0-9711735-0-7). 30pp. This text presents clear strategies for dealing with unwelcome attention, even from friends and family. (Rev: SLJ 12/02)

20143 Silverman, Robin L. *Reaching Your Goals* (4–8). Illus. Series: Life Balance. 2004, Watts LB $20.50 (978-0-531-12342-3); paper $6.95 (978-0-531-16691-8). 80pp. Practical advice on building self-confidence, making smart decisions, and focusing on achievable goals. (Rev: BL 10/15/03)

20144 Small, Mary. *Being a Good Citizen: A Book About Citizenship* (K–2). Illus. by Stacey Previn. Series: Way to Be! 2005, Picture Window LB $25.26 (978-1-4048-1050-1). 24pp. A slim overview of simple ways in which children can be good citizens and help improve their communities, such as picking up trash and planting flowers. (Rev: SLJ 12/05) [323.6]

20145 Small, Mary. *Being Fair: A Book About Fairness* (K–2). Illus. by Stacey Previn. Series: Way to Be! 2005, Picture Window LB $25.26 (978-1-4048-1051-8). 24pp. A slim overview of simple ways in which children can be fair in their dealings with others. Also use *Being Responsible, Being Respectful,* and *Being Trustworthy* (2005) (Rev: SLJ 12/05) [179]

20146 Spinelli, Eileen, and Jerry Spinelli. *Today I Will: A Year of Quotes, Notes, and Promises to Myself* (5–8). Illus. by Julia Rothman. 2009, Knopf $15.99 (978-0-375-84057-9); LB $18.99 (978-0-375-96230-1). 384pp. In this page-a-day advice book, the Spinellis offer accessible, often humorous quotes, advice, and affirmations from celebrities, historical figures, and popular literature. (Rev: BL 11/15/09; SLJ 10/09) [082]

20147 Szpirglas, Jeff. *You Just Can't Help It! Your Guide to the Wild and Wacky World of Human Behavior* (3–6). Illus. by Josh Holinaty. 2011, OwlKids $22.95 (978-1-926818-07-8); paper $12.95 (978-1-926818-08-5). 64pp. Plenty of hip trivia and an eye-catching layout add appeal to this book that explores the instincts behind human impulses and behavior. (Rev: LMC 8–9/11; SLJ 6/11; VOYA 2/11) [599.9]

20148 Thomas, Pat. *I'm Telling the Truth: A First Look at Honesty* (K–3). Illus. by Lesley Harker. Series: A First Look At. 2006, Barron's paper $6.99 (978-0-7641-3214-8). 29pp. Introduces the concept of honesty, explains its importance in dealing with others, and offers suggestions about how to incorporate this character trait into everyday life. (Rev: SLJ 9/06) [179.9]

20149 Thong, Roseanne. *Wish: Wishing Traditions Around the World* (K–3). Illus. by Elisa Kleven. 2008, Chronicle $16.99 (978-0-8118-5716-1). 44pp. Wishing traditions around the world — blowing dandelion fluff, tossing coins into fountains, and so forth — are the focus of this well-illustrated volume. (Rev: BL 12/1/08; SLJ 4/09) [398]

20150 Waber, Bernard. *Courage* (K–3). Illus. 2002, Houghton $12.00 (978-0-618-23855-2). 40pp. Waber introduces the concept of courage with amusing illustrations and examples that younger readers can understand. (Rev: BCCB 2/03; BL 12/15/02; HBG 3/03; SLJ 12/02) [179]

20151 Walker, Niki. *Why Do We Fight?* (5–8). 2013, Owl $16.95 (978-192697386-9). 80pp. This volume explores the nature of conflict, war, and peace using real-world examples and discussing the various triggers. (Rev: BLO 12/15/13; LMC 3–4/2014*; SLJ 9/13) [303.6]

20152 Waters, Jennifer. *Be a Good Friend!* (K–1). Series: Spyglass Books. 2002, Compass Point LB $19.93 (978-0-7565-0376-5). 24pp. For beginning readers, this book lists the qualities that make a good friend. Also use *Be a Good Sport!* (2002) (Rev: SLJ 1/03)

20153 Williams, Venus, and Serena Williams. *Venus and Serena: Serving from the Hip* (5–8). 2005, Houghton Mifflin paper $14.00 (978-0-618-57653-1). The successful Williams sisters offer practical advice on self-respect, friendship, financial security, and other pertinent topics. (Rev: BL 5/15/05; SLJ 4/05) [796.342]

20154 Zelinger, Laurie. *A Smart Girl's Guide to Liking Herself — Even on the Bad Days* (4–6). Illus. by Jennifer Kalis. Series: Be Your Best. 2012, American Girl paper $9.95 (978-1-59369-943-7). 96pp. The importance of high self-esteem is underlined in this guide that includes quizzes and advice on how to shake off negative feelings. (Rev: BL 4/15/12; SLJ 7/12) [155.43]

20155 Zemke, Deborah. *Don't Feed the Babysitter to Your Boa Constrictor: 43 Ridiculous Rules Every Kid Should Know* (2–3). Series: I'm Going to Read! 2006, Sterling paper $3.95 (978-1-4027-3429-8). 24pp. A funny, easy-reader collection of nonsensical rules for children — including "Never eat anything that's still moving" and "Don't eat spaghetti through your nose." (Rev: BL 11/1/06; SLJ 12/06) [818]

20156 Zimmerman, Bill. *100 Things Guys Need to Know* (5–9). 2005, Free Spirit paper $13.95 (978-1-57542-167-4). Effective graphic design will draw teenage boys into this self-help guide that touches on a wide variety of topics, including body image, dating, school, friendship, and family. (Rev: SLJ 11/05) [305.235]

Etiquette

20157 Arnold, Tedd, and Joe Berger, et al. *Manners Mash-Up: A Goofy Guide to Good Behavior* (2–4). Illus. by Tedd Arnold. 2011, Dial $16.99 (978-0-8037-3480-7). 40pp. Fourteen well-known children's book illustrators each present an amusing spread showing how to behave properly. (Rev: BL 1/1–15/11; HB 7–8/11; SLJ 3/1/11) [395.1]

20158 Cabot, Meg. *Princess Lessons* (5–7). Illus. by Chesley McLaren. Series: Princess Diaries. 2003, HarperCollins $12.99 (978-0-06-052677-1). Princess Mia gives lighthearted tips and often quite practical tips on behaving like a real princess. (Rev: BL 5/15/03; HBG 10/03; VOYA 10/03) [646.7]

20159 Doudna, Kelly. *Excuse Me* (PS–1). Series: Good Manners. 2001, ABDO LB $19.93 (978-1-57765-574-9). 24pp. Simple text suitable for beginning readers introduces the basic concept of apologizing, accompanied by illustrations of children in appropriate situations. Also in this series are *Please* and *Thank You*. (Rev: HBG 3/02; SLJ 4/02) [395.1]

20160 Doudna, Kelly. *Right on Time!* (K–3). Illus. Series: Character Concepts. 2007, ABDO LB $13.95 (978-1-59928-740-9). 24pp. This book shows the importance of punctuality through examples of children being on time. (Rev: SLJ 6/07)

20161 Dougherty, Karla. *The Rules to Be Cool: Etiquette and Netiquette* (5–9). Series: Teen Issues. 2001, Enslow LB $22.60 (978-0-7660-1607-1). 64pp. Respect and consideration for others are the key elements of Dougherty's rules of behavior, with an emphasis on politeness, kindness, and courtesy, on the Internet as well as at home and at school. (Rev: HBG 3/02; SLJ 10/01) [395]

20162 Finn, Carrie. *Manners in Public* (PS–2). Illus. by Chris Lensch. Series: Way to Be! 2007, Picture Window LB $23.93 (978-1-4048-3153-7). 24pp. This book gives examples of children behaving as they should, with photographs that emphasize that being polite makes every-

one happy. Also use *Manners on the Playground* (2007) (Rev: SLJ 6/07)

20163 Gibbs, Lynne. *Don't Slurp Your Soup! A First Guide to Letter Writing, E-Mail Etiquette, and Other Everyday Manners* (K–2). Illus. by John Eastwood. 2003, McGraw-Hill $14.95 (978-1-57768-556-2). 32pp. A lighthearted introduction to the basic rules of behavior, this guide covers table manners, party invitations, and phone etiquette. (Rev: BL 4/1/03; HBG 4/04; SLJ 8/03) [390]

20164 Goldberg, Whoopi. *Whoopi's Big Book of Manners* (K–3). Illus. by Olo. 2006, Hyperion $15.99 (978-0-7868-5295-6). A funny, chatty guide to proper etiquette. (Rev: SLJ 11/06) [395]

20165 Hample, Stoo. *Book of Bad Manners* (3–5). Illus. by author. 2006, Candlewick $15.99 (978-0-7636-2933-5). Examples of bad behavior are paired with lively drawings of the evil deeds, bound to amuse young readers. (Rev: SLJ 9/06) [395.12]

20166 Holyoke, Nancy. *A Smart Girl's Guide to Manners* (4–7). Illus. by Cathi Mingus. 2005, Pleasant paper $9.95 (978-1-58485-983-3). A nice mix of good manners that ranges from introductions to cell phone etiquette to how and when to write real thank-you notes. (Rev: BL 11/1/05; SLJ 1/06; VOYA 12/05) [395]

20167 James, Elizabeth, and Carol Barkin. *Social Smarts: Manners for Today's Kids* (4–7). 1996, Clarion paper $7.95 (978-0-395-81312-6). Table manners and responsible, appropriate public behavior are two topics covered. (Rev: BL 9/1/96; SLJ 9/96) [395]

20168 Lee, Sally. *Princes and Princesses* (K–2). Illus. Series: Pebble Plus: Royalty. 2013, Capstone LB $24.65 (978-162065124-7). 24pp. For beginning readers, this is an introduction to the concept of royalty and the lives and work of various princes and princesses. (Rev: BL 4/1/13; SLJ 4/13) [305.5]

20169 Lundsten, Apry. *A Smart Girl's Guide to Parties: How to Be a Great Guest, Be a Happy Hostess, and Have Fun at Any Party* (4–7). Illus. by Angela Martini. Series: Be Your Best. 2010, American Girl paper $9.95 (978-1-59369-645-0). 96pp. With a light and breezy tone, this book outlines party etiquette for both hosts and guests at affairs formal and informal, with advice on invitations, gifts, and so forth. (Rev: SLJ 7/10)

20170 Post, Peggy, and Cindy Post Senning. *Emily's Everyday Manners* (PS–2). Illus. by Steve Björkman. 2006, HarperCollins $16.99 (978-0-06-076174-5). 32pp. Emily and Ethan outline the basics of good behavior. (Rev: BL 10/15/06) [395.1]

20171 Raatma, Lucia. *Politeness* (K–2). Series: Character Education. 2002, Capstone LB $22.60 (978-0-7368-1134-7). 24pp. A how-to guide for the very young that provides a definition of politeness, shows how to display it, and offers some practice ideas. Also use *Self-Respect* and *Sportsmanship* (2002) (Rev: SLJ 6/02) [395.1]

20172 Senning, Cindy Post, and Peggy Post. *Emily Post's Table Manners for Kids* (4–8). Illus. by Steve Björkman. 2009, HarperCollins $15.99 (978-0-06-111709-1).

When can you eat with your fingers? Which fork do I use? Everything today's child needs to know about proper meal etiquette and just why these things matter. (Rev: BL 4/1/09) [395.5]

20173 Stewart, Marjabelle Young, and Ann Buchwald. *What to Do When and Why* (4–7). 1988, Luce $14.95 (978-0-88331-105-9). An easily read introduction to the basics of good manners and behavior.

20174 Thomas, Pat. *My Manners Matter: A First Look at Being Polite* (K–3). Illus. by Lesley Harker. 2006, Barron's paper $6.99 (978-0-7641-3212-4). 29pp. Introduces the concept of politeness, examines its importance in dealing with others, and offers suggestions about how to behave politely. (Rev: SLJ 9/06) [179.9]

20175 Verdick, Elizabeth. *Don't Behave Like You Live in a Cave* (4–6). Illus. by Steve Mark. Series: Laugh and Learn. 2010, Free Spirit paper $8.95 (978-1-57542-353-1). 120pp. A humorous, practical guide to good behavior, setting realistic goals, and exercise and nutrition, using a cartoon Cave Boy and Cave Girl as examples of poor etiquette. (Rev: SLJ 1/1/11) [395.1]

20176 Willems, Mo. *Time to Say "Please"!* (PS–3). Illus. by author. 2005, Hyperion $15.99 (978-0-7868-5293-2). Mice give children playful tips on correct behavior. (Rev: SLJ 8/05) [395.1]

Family Relationships

20177 Adamson, Heather. *Families in Many Cultures* (PS–2). Illus. Series: Life Around the World. 2007, Capstone LB $14.95 (978-1-4296-0019-4). 24pp. Families in eight countries around the world are shown enjoying time together in this simple volume suitable for beginning readers. (Rev: BL 10/15/07; LMC 5/08; SLJ 1/08) [306.85]

20178 Ajmera, Maya, and Sheila Kincade, et al. *Our Grandparents: A Global Album* (PS–1). 2010, Charlesbridge $16.95 (978-1-57091-458-4); paper $7.95 (978-1-57091-459-1). Unpaged. Multicultural youngsters and grandparents are shown engaging in simple, joyful activities together in this book celebrating the important bridge between generations. (Rev: LMC 11–12/10; SLJ 2/1/10)

20179 Ancona, George. *Mis abuelos / My Grandparents* (K–2). Photos by author. Illus. Series: Somos Latinos. 2005, Children's Pr. LB $21.00 (978-0-516-25294-0). 32pp. In this photo-filled bilingual picture book, Latino American children talk about their relationships with their grandparents. Also in this series: *Mis juegos / My Games, Mi música / My Music, Mis comidas / My Foods, Mis fiestas / My Celebrations*, and *Mis quehaceres / My Chores*. (Rev: SLJ 2/06) [977.5]

20180 Barber, Nicola. *A New Baby Arrives* (K–1). Series: The Big Day! 2009, Rosen LB $21.25 (978-1-4358-2842-1). 24pp. This simple book looks at typical concerns — sharing with a new baby, helping, bath time, and so forth. (Rev: SLJ 7/09) [306.875]

20181 Bingham, Jane. *Why Do Families Break Up?* (4–8). Series: Exploring Tough Issues. 2004, Raintree LB $29.93 (978-0-7398-6683-2). 48pp. Every member of the family is considered in this comprehensive examination of divorce and how individuals of different ages cope. (Rev: SLJ 2/05) [306.8]

20182 Cooper, Kay. *Where Did You Get Those Eyes? A Guide to Discovering Your Family History* (5–7). Illus. by Anthony Accardo. 1988, Walker LB $14.85 (978-0-8027-6803-2). A helpful guide for researching the family tree. (Rev: BCCB 11/88; BL 1/15/89; SLJ 2/89)

20183 Crist, James J., and Elizabeth Verdick. *Siblings: You're Stuck with Each Other, So Stick Together* (3–6). Illus. by Steve Mark. Series: Laugh and Learn. 2010, Free Spirit $8.95 (978-157542336-4). 128pp. Following information on the relationship between siblings (birth order and so forth), this book presents advice on avoiding friction and forging friendship. (Rev: BL 4/15/10; SLJ 6/10) [306.875]

20184 Dustman, Jeanne. *A Family's Story* (2–4). Illus. Series: Primary Source Readers: Content and Literacy in Social Studies. 2013, Teacher Created Materials paper $6.99 (978-14333699-2-6). 32pp. Following the family history of Sharon across four generations, this volume includes vintage photographs and will stimulate an interest in genealogy. (Rev: BL 10/1/13; LMC 8–9/14) [305]

20185 Fakhrid-Deen, Tina. *Let's Get This Straight: The Ultimate Handbook for Youth with LGBTQ Parents* (5–10). 2010, Seal $15.95 (978-1-58005-333-4). 174pp. This insightful book discusses the various challenges children with LGBTQ parents will face and offers excerpts from interviews, questionnaires, and a good list of resources. (Rev: SLJ 3/1/11) [306.8]

20186 Fox, Annie. *What's Up with My Family?* (5–8). Series: Middle School Confidential. 2010, Free Spirit paper $9.99 (978-1-57542-333-3). 96pp. Stories of children in difficult family situations alternate with advice for dealing with family issues and staying positive; a blend of fictional graphic novel stories and practical advice. (Rev: LMC 8–9/10; SLJ 4/10) [646.7]

20187 Gardner, Richard. *Boys and Girls Book About Divorce* (5–8). 1992, Bantam paper $6.99 (978-0-553-27619-0). A self-help book written for adolescents trying to cope with parental marriage problems. [306.8]

20188 Hoffman, Mary. *The Great Big Book of Families* (PS–2). Illus. by Ros Asquith. 2011, Dial $16.99 (978-0-8037-3516-3). 40pp. A compendium that celebrates all types of families and shows the many differences in the ways in which we live. (Rev: BL 3/15/11; LMC 10/11*; SLJ 5/1/11*) [306.85]

20189 Hughes, Monica. *First Brother or Sister* (PS–2). Series: My First. 2004, Raintree LB $18.56 (978-1-4109-0644-1). 24pp. Color photographs and simple narrative are tailor-made for only children whose families are awaiting the arrival of a new baby. (Rev: BL 4/1/04) [306.875]

20190 Isler, Claudia. *Caught in the Middle: A Teen Guide to Custody* (5–8). Series: The Divorce Resource. 2000, Rosen LB $27.95 (978-0-8239-3109-5). 64pp. This book about divorce uses many actual case histories to explore such questions as what happens to the children when parents divorce and whether grandparents get visitation rights. (Rev: SLJ 6/00) [306.8]

20191 Kinkade, Sheila. *My Family* (PS–2). Illus. by Elaine Little. 2006, Charlesbridge $16.95 (978-1-57091-662-5); paper $6.95 (978-1-57091-691-5). 32pp. In double-page spreads, this full-color photoessay shows the diversity and similarities of families around the world. (Rev: BL 1/1–15/06; SLJ 2/06) [306.85]

20192 Krementz, Jill. *How It Feels to Be Adopted* (5–8). 1988, Knopf paper $15.00 (978-0-394-75853-4). Interviews with 19 young people, ages 8 to 16, on how it feels to be adopted. [362.7]

20193 Krementz, Jill. *How It Feels When Parents Divorce* (4–8). 1988, Knopf paper $15.00 (978-0-394-75855-8). Boys and girls, ages 8 to 16, share their experiences with divorced parents. [306.8]

20194 Krohn, Katherine. *Everything You Need to Know About Birth Order* (5–9). Series: Need to Know Library. 2000, Rosen LB $27.95 (978-0-8239-3228-3). An interesting book that looks at a number of theories about how birth order affects people. (Rev: SLJ 12/00) [306.85]

20195 Krohn, Katherine. *You and Your Parents' Divorce* (5–8). Series: Family Matters. 2001, Rosen LB $26.50 (978-0-8239-3354-9). Krohn writes about the practicalities and emotional problems of divorce in a style suitable for reluctant readers. (Rev: SLJ 8/01) [155.44]

20196 Kuklin, Susan. *Families* (3–5). Illus. 2006, Hyperion $15.99 (978-0-7868-0822-9). 40pp. Kuklin explores the diversity of families in America through interviews of children who have single, mixed-race, divorced, immigrant, gay, and lesbian parents; photographs are included on the double-page spreads. (Rev: BL 12/15/05; SLJ 1/06*) [306.85]

20197 Leibowitz, Julie. *Finding Your Place: A Teen Guide to Life in a Blended Family* (5–8). 2000, Rosen LB $27.95 (978-0-8239-3114-9). This book explores possible problems and solutions for members of blended families. (Rev: SLJ 6/00) [645.7]

20198 Lindsay, Jeanne W. *Do I Have a Daddy? A Story About a Single-Parent Child* (PS–2). Illus. by Jami Moffett. 2000, Morning Glory $14.95 (978-1-885356-62-8); paper $7.95 (978-1-885356-63-5). 48pp. A single mother reassures her son that, although he does not have a father, his uncle and grandfather will be there to help him. (Rev: BL 5/15/00; HBG 9/00; SLJ 7/00) [306.85]

20199 MacGregor, Cynthia. *The Divorce Helpbook for Kids* (4–7). 2001, Impact paper $13.95 (978-1-886230-39-2). In this candid, honest book, a divorced mother gives advice to children about how to survive their parent's divorce. (Rev: BL 2/1/02; SLJ 3/02) [306.89]

20200 MacGregor, Cynthia. *Jigsaw Puzzle Family: The Stepkids' Guide to Fitting It Together* (5–8). Series: Rebuilding Books. 2005, Impact paper $12.95 (978-1-886230-63-7). Offers reassuring, practical advice — with an emphasis on talking through problems and seeking solutions — for stepchildren who are having difficulty adjusting to life in a blended family. (Rev: BL 9/1/05; SLJ 10/05) [306.874]

20201 McMahon, Patricia, and Conor Clarke McCarthy. *Just Add One Chinese Sister* (PS–2). Illus. by Karen A. Jerome. 2005, Boyds Mills $16.95 (978-1-56397-989-7). A compelling story of the adoption of a Chinese girl, conveyed through a scrapbook created by Claire and her American mother with contributions by her new big brother Conor. (Rev: BL 8/05; SLJ 2/05) [362.734]

20202 Moore-Mallinos, Jennifer. *When My Parents Forgot How to Be Friends* (PS–3). Illus. by Marta Fàbrega. Series: Let's Talk About It! 2005, Barron's paper $6.95 (978-0-7641-3172-1). 31pp. A girl talks about her unhappiness and uncertainty when her parents were preparing to separate; the situation improves when her dad moves out. (Rev: SLJ 10/05) [306.89]

20203 Morris, Ann. *Families* (PS–1). Illus. 2000, HarperCollins LB $17.89 (978-0-688-17199-5). 32pp. Different kinds of families around the world are introduced in this photo-essay that uses very little text. (Rev: BL 5/15/00; HBG 9/00; SLJ 5/00) [306.85]

20204 Murphy, Patricia J. *Divorce and Separation* (2–4). Illus. Series: Tough Topics. 2007, Heinemann LB $17.75 (978-1-4034-9775-8). 32pp. This title takes a frank but encouraging look at the lifestyle changes and emotional challenges associated with divorce and separation. (Rev: BL 1/1–15/08; LMC 3/08; SLJ 6/08) [306.89]

20205 Ollhoff, Jim. *Beginning Genealogy: Expert Tips to Help You Trace Your Own Ancestors* (3–6). Series: Your Family Tree. 2010, ABDO LB $18.95 (978-1-61613-460-0). 32pp. A helpful guide for young readers to family trees, the meanings of last names, and how to get started researching your background. Also use *Collecting Primary Records, DNA: Window to the Past: How Science Can Help Untangle Your Family Roots, Exploring Immigration: Discovering the Rich Heritage of America's Immigrants, Filling the Family Tree: Interviewing Relatives to Discover Facts and Stories,* and *Using Your Research: How to Check Your Facts and Use Your Information* (all 2010). (Rev: SLJ 3/1/11) [929.1]

20206 Raum, Elizabeth. *New Brothers and Sisters* (1–3). Series: Tough Topics. 2008, Heinemann LB $25.36 (978-1-4329-0820-1); paper $7.99 (978-1-4329-0825-6). 32pp. Raum provides guidance for siblings expecting a new baby in chapters with titles such as "Why Do I Have to Wait So Long?" and "What If I Feel Left Out?" (Rev: SLJ 11/08) [306.875]

20207 Rotner, Shelley, and Sheila Kelly. *Lots of Grandparents* (PS–1). Illus. 2001, Millbrook $23.90 (978-0-7613-2313-6). 24pp. A collection of color photographs showing grandparents of various ethnicities engaged in many activities. (Rev: BL 9/1/01; HBG 3/02; SLJ 9/01) [306.874]

20208 Rotner, Shelley, and Sheila M. Kelly. *I'm Adopted!* (PS–K). Illus. by Shelley Rotner. 2011, Holiday House

$16.95 (978-0-8234-2294-4). 32pp. Simple text with age-appropriate scenarios and close-up photographs showing a variety of conventional and unconventional families are features of this exploration of what adoption is and how it works. (Rev: BLO 9/1/11; SLJ 9/1/11) [362.734]

20209 Rubel, Nicole. *Twice As Nice: What It's Like to Be a Twin* (3–5). 2004, Farrar $16.50 (978-0-374-31836-9). 32pp. An entertaining exploration of the biology, psychology, and advantages and disadvantages of being — and parenting — a twin. (Rev: BL 11/15/04; SLJ 11/04) [306.875]

20210 Sanders, Pete, and Steve Myers. *Divorce and Separation* (4–8). Series: What Do You Know About. 1997, Millbrook LB $23.90 (978-0-7613-0574-3). An introduction to separation and divorce, with an emphasis on tips to help youngsters adjust and cope. (Rev: SLJ 10/97) [306.8]

20211 Schuette, Sarah L. *Adoptive Families* (PS–2). Series: My Family. 2009, Capstone LB $18.65 (978-1-4296-3977-4). 24pp. For very young readers, this book presents adoptive families of various ethnicities. Also use *Blended Families, Foster Families,* and *Single-Parent Families* (all 2009). (Rev: LMC 11–12/10; SLJ 5/1/10) [306.87]

20212 Sheldon, Annette. *Big Sister Now: A Story About Me and Our New Baby* (PS). Illus. by Karen Maizel. 2006, Magination $14.95 (978-1-59147-243-8); paper $9.95 (978-1-59147-244-5). 32pp. A little girl has some difficulty adjusting to the presence of her new baby brother; a note at the end gives parents advice on easing the transition. (Rev: BL 8/06; SLJ 2/07) [306.875]

20213 Simons, Rae. *Blended Families* (5–8). Illus. Series: The Changing Face of Modern Families. 2009, Mason Crest $22.95 (978-1-4222-1492-3). 64pp. This book about blended families provides statistics, information, and advice through graphs, newspaper articles, and questions for discussion. Also use *Grandparents Raising Kids* and *Single Parents*. (Rev: LMC 5–6/10; SLJ 3/10)

20214 Snow, Judith E. *How It Feels to Have a Gay or Lesbian Parent: A Book by Kids for Kids of All Ages* (5–8). 2004, Haworth $19.95 (978-1-56023-419-7); paper $12.95 (978-1-56023-420-3). Diverse reflections on what it means to have a gay or lesbian parent come from children, young adults, and adults (up to age 31). (Rev: BL 1/1–15/05; SLJ 10/04) [306.874]

20215 Stewart, Sheila. *What Is a Family?* (5–8). Illus. Series: The Changing Face of Modern Families. 2009, Mason Crest $22.95 (978-1-4222-1528-9). 64pp. Exploring what, exactly, makes a family a family, this book provides statistics, information, and advice through graphs, newspaper articles, and questions for discussion. Also use *Celebrity Families*. (Rev: LMC 5–6/10; SLJ 3/10)

20216 Tym, Kate, and Penny Worms. *Coping with Families: A Guide to Taking Control of Your Life* (5–8). Series: Get Real. 2004, Raintree LB $28.56 (978-1-4109-0574-1). Expert advice and case studies are presented in

an appealing format, plus a list of hotline numbers. Also use *Coping with Friends* (2004). (Rev: SLJ 5/05)

20217 Wolfman, Ira. *Climbing Your Family Tree: Online and Off-Line Genealogy for Kids*. Rev. ed. (5–9). Illus. by Tim Robinson. 2002, Workman paper $13.95 (978-0-7611-2539-6). 228pp. A wide-ranging look at genealogy and the ways of tracing family names through document research, interviews, and the World Wide Web. (Rev: SLJ 2/03; VOYA 10/03) [929]

Personal Problems and Relationships

20218 Allman, Toney. *Mean Behind the Screen: What You Need to Know About Cyberbullying* (5–8). Illus. Series: What's the Issue? 2008, Compass Point LB $20.99 (978-0-7565-4145-3). 48pp. A solid introduction to cyberbullying and its consequences. (Rev: BL 4/1/09; SLJ 10/09) [302.3]

20219 Cohen-Posey, Kate. *How to Handle Bullies, Teasers and Other Meanies: A Book That Takes the Nuisance out of Name Calling and Other Nonsense* (4–7). 1995, Rainbow paper $8.95 (978-1-56825-029-8). A practical book that offers useful suggestions on how to handle bullies. (Rev: BCCB 12/95; BL 11/15/95) [646.7]

20220 Crist, James J. *What to Do When You're Scared and Worried: A Guide for Kids* (5–8). Illus. by Michael Chesworth. 2004, Free Spirit paper $9.99 (978-1-57542-153-7). Reassuring words and sound advice for young people troubled by such diverse issues as school exams, bullies, terrorism, nightmares, monsters, and the dark. (Rev: SLJ 7/04) [152.4]

20221 Finn, Carrie. *Kids Talk About Bullying* (K–2). Illus. by Amy Bailey Muehlenhardt. Series: Kids Talk Jr. 2006, Picture Window LB $25.26 (978-1-4048-2315-0). 32pp. A question-and-answer format and simple language are used to discuss bullying and ways of coping with it. (Rev: SLJ 1/07) [303.6]

20222 Frankel, Erin. *Weird!* (1–3). Illus. by Paula Heaphy. 2012, Free Spirit $15.99 (978-1-57542-398-2). 48pp. Young Luisa describes how she used to try to change her behavior to avoid criticisms by Sam, who kept calling her "weird"; backmatter about dealing with bullying renders this book nonfiction. Also in this series are *Dare!* and *Tough!* (both 2012). **e** (Rev: BL 9/15/12; LMC 3–4/13; SLJ 2/13) [302.34]

20223 Greenberg, Judith E. *A Girl's Guide to Growing Up: Making the Right Choices* (5–8). Illus. 2000, Watts LB $24.00 (978-0-531-11592-3). 144pp. Lots of personal stories are quoted in this guidance book for preteen and teenage girls dealing with such subjects as school, risky behaviors, dating, sex, self-esteem, eating disorders, and cliques. (Rev: BL 2/15/01; SLJ 4/01; VOYA 6/01) [305.23]

20224 Halperin, Wendy A. *Love Is . . .* (PS–3). Illus. 2001, Simon & Schuster $16.00 (978-0-689-82980-2). 32pp. Different kinds of love are explored in this unusually beautiful picture book. (Rev: BL 1/1–15/01*; HBG 10/01; SLJ 2/01) [242]

20225 Jakubiak, David J. *A Smart Kid's Guide to Online Bullying* (2–5). Illus. Series: Kids Online. 2009, Rosen LB $21.25 (978-1-4042-8114-1). 24pp. This practical guide includes plenty of smart advice for kids who find themselves dealing with cyberbullies. (Rev: BL 4/1/10; SLJ 3/1/10) [302.3]

20226 Johnston, Marianne. *Let's Talk About Being Shy* (4–8). Series: Let's Talk. 1996, Rosen LB $19.95 (978-0-8239-2304-5). The causes and possible cures of shyness are covered in this straightforward discussion. Also use *Let's Talk About Being Afraid* (1996). (Rev: BL 3/15/97) [155.4]

20227 Kent, Susan. *Let's Talk About Needing Extra Help at School* (3–5). Series: Let's Talk. 2000, Rosen LB $19.95 (978-0-8239-5422-3). 24pp. Using actual cases and realistic photos, this book explores the many reasons why kids might need extra help at school and what they can do about it. (Rev: SLJ 2/01) [371.2]

20228 Kingston, Anna. *Respecting the Contributions of LGBT Americans* (2–5). Illus. Series: Stop Bullying Now! 2012, Rosen LB $22.60 (978-144887446-0). 24pp. Bullying of members of LGBT families is the focus of this book that includes some history of prejudice, facts about AIDS, and discussion of hate crimes. (Rev: BL 10/1/12; LMC 8–9/13) [306.76]

20229 McIntyre, Tom. *The Behavior Survival Guide for Kids: How to Make Good Choices and Stay out of Trouble* (4–7). Illus. by Chris Sharp. 2003, Free Spirit paper $14.95 (978-1-57542-132-2). This accessible guide offers concrete suggestions for dealing with behavior disorders and improving relations with teachers, family members, and friends. (Rev: SLJ 1/04) [649]

20230 Medina, Sarah. *Sad* (PS–K). Illus. Series: Feelings. 2007, Heinemann LB $21.36 (978-1-4034-9293-7). 24pp. In the form of questions and answers, this small volume tackles the topic of sadness and offers reassuring advice. (Rev: BL 4/15/07) [152.4]

20231 Moehn, Heather. *Everything You Need to Know About Cliques* (5–8). Series: Need to Know Library. 2001, Rosen LB $27.95 (978-0-8239-3326-6). Moehn uses first-person narratives to introduce such topics as making friends, peer pressure, bullies, insecurity, and popularity, with a look at how cliques continue after high school. (Rev: SLJ 12/01) [158.25]

20232 Moroney, Trace. *When I'm Feeling Angry* (PS). Illus. 2006, School Specialty $9.95 (978-0-7696-4424-0). 18pp. A bunny describes what makes him mad and what it's like to feel angry; readers learn when it's OK to feel angry and when they need to control their behavior. Also use *When I'm Feeling Scared* (2006). (Rev: BL 3/1/06) [152.4]

20233 Nelson, Robin. *Working with Others* (K–3). Series: Pull Ahead Books. 2006, Lerner LB $22.60 (978-0-8225-3488-4). 32pp. Easy-to-understand advice about how to work well with others, covering such topics as conflict resolution, respect for others' opinions, pa-

tience, and discussing all sides of an issue. (Rev: SLJ 8/06) [303.69]

20234 Polland, Barbara K. *We Can Work It Out: Conflict Resolution for Children* (K–3). Illus. by Craig DeRoy. 2000, Tricycle $13.95 (978-1-58246-031-4). 64pp. This book poses questions about various kinds of behavioral problems (e.g., teasing, poor sportsmanship) and enables children to solve these problems through self-direction. (Rev: BL 1/1–15/01; HBG 10/01) [303.6]

20235 Radabaugh, Melinda. *Sleeping Over* (PS–1). Series: First Time. 2003, Heinemann LB $18.50 (978-1-4034-0231-8). 24pp. Reassuring text and photographs introduce various kinds of sleepovers. (Rev: HBG 10/03; SLJ 9/03) [793.2]

20236 Raum, Elizabeth. *Bullying* (1–3). Series: Tough Topics. 2008, Heinemann LB $25.36 (978-1-4329-0818-8); paper $7.99 (978-1-4329-0823-2). 32pp. After defining bullying, Raum discusses what to do to avoid bullying and what to do if you see bullying taking place. Also use *Fighting* and *Peer Pressure* (both 2008). (Rev: SLJ 11/08) [302.3]

20237 Rechner, Amy. *The In Crowd: Dealing with Peer Pressure* (5–8). Series: What's the Issue? 2009, Compass Point $27.99 (978-0-7565-1891-2). 48pp. A compelling mix of direct quotes, real-life scenarios, quizzes, and short glossaries enhance this book about coping with peer pressure; suitable for reluctant readers. (Rev: LMC 10/09; SLJ 10/09) [303.3]

20238 Rimm, Sylvia. *See Jane Win for Girls: A Smart Girl's Guide to Success* (5–9). Illus. 2003, Free Spirit paper $13.95 (978-1-57542-122-3). 131pp. Rimm offers practical advice on social and academic achievement and general life skills, with quizzes, activities, and success stories. (Rev: LMC 10/03; SLJ 6/03) [305.235]

20239 Rivkin, Jennifer. *Physical Bullying* (5–8). Illus. Series: Take a Stand Against Bullying. 2013, Crabtree LB $22.95 (978-077877914-8); paper $10.95 (9780778779193). 48pp. Discusses the hows and whys of bullying, the kinds of behaviors involved, and the role of bystanders, as well as providing tips for victims. (Rev: BL 4/1/13; SLJ 7/13)

20240 Schwartz, John. *Short: Walking Tall When You're Not Tall at All* (4–8). 2010, Flash Point $16.99 (978-1-59643-323-6). 144pp. Short himself, journalist Schwartz explores various aspects of the importance of height (in terms of popularity, business success, and so forth); provides information on such topics as genetics and growth hormones; and takes aim at the media in this funny book that's part memoir, part self-help book. (Rev: BL 2/15/10; LMC 5–6/10; SLJ 3/10) [921]

20241 Shapiro, Ouisie. *Bullying and Me: Schoolyard Stories* (4–7). Illus. by Steven Vote. 2010, Whitman $16.99 (978-0-8075-0921-0). 32pp. A baker's dozen of stories describe physical abuse, verbal abuse, and online bullying, each followed by advice on how to deal with such situations. Lexile 740L (Rev: BL 8/10; LMC 11–12/10*; SLJ 10/1/10) [371.5]

20242 Thomas, Isabel. *Dealing with Feeling Worried* (K–2). Illus. Series: Dealing with Feeling. 2013, Raintree LB $22.65 (978-143297110-6); paper $6.49 (9781432971199). 24pp. Chapter headings include "Is it normal to feel worried?", "How can I deal with worries?", "What if I cannot talk about my feelings?", and "Make a worry toolbox." (Rev: BL 4/1/13; SLJ 4/13) [152.4]

20243 *Yikes! A Smart Girl's Guide to Surviving Tricky, Sticky, Icky Situations* (4–8). Illus. by Bonnie Timmons. Series: American Girl Library. 2002, Pleasant paper $8.95 (978-1-58485-530-9). Advice on everything from dealing with teachers and friends to coping with embarrassing situations and dangerous incidents. (Rev: SLJ 12/02) [305.23]

Careers

General and Miscellaneous

20244 Alagna, Magdalena. *War Correspondents: Life Under Fire* (5–10). Series: Extreme Careers. 2003, Rosen LB $26.50 (978-0-8239-3798-1). The dangers of wartime assignments are emphasized in this volume that also stresses job requirements that include a good education and broad knowledge of world events. (Rev: BL 9/15/03; SLJ 11/03) [808]

20245 Asher, Sandy. *Where Do You Get Your Ideas? Helping Young Writers Begin* (5–7). 1987, Walker LB $13.85 (978-0-8027-6691-5). Keeping a journal and other interesting ideas for would-be journalists. (Rev: BCCB 12/87; BL 9/15/87; SLJ 9/87) [808.02]

20246 Bauld, Jane Scoggins. *We Need Librarians* (PS–1). Series: Helpers in Our Schools. 2000, Capstone LB $13.25 (978-0-7368-0531-5). 24pp. The many roles of school librarians are discussed in this beginning reader. (Rev: HBG 9/00; SLJ 10/00) [027]

20247 Bauld, Jane Scoggins. *We Need Principals* (PS–1). Series: Helpers in Our Schools. 2000, Capstone LB $17.26 (978-0-7368-0532-2). 24pp. For beginning readers, this is a book about school principals and what they do. (Rev: HBG 9/00; SLJ 10/00) [371]

20248 Bentley, Nancy, and Donna Guthrie. *Writing Mysteries, Movies, Monster Stories, and More* (5–8). 2001, Millbrook LB $24.90 (978-0-7613-1452-3). This book gives solid information on all kinds of fictional writing, including novels, short stories, fantasy, science fiction, humor, and even movie scripts. (Rev: BL 3/15/01; HBG 10/01; SLJ 4/01; VOYA 8/01) [808]

20249 Binney, Greg A. *Careers in the Federal Emergency Management Agency's Search and Rescue Unit* (5–9). Series: Careers in Search and Rescue Operations. 2003, Rosen LB $26.50 (978-0-8239-3832-2). Starting with September 11, 2001, this volume explores the work of the teams that specialize in search and rescue after disasters such as tornadoes, hazardous materials spills,

and building collapses, with material on the training required. (Rev: BL 10/15/03) [363.3]

20250 Buckley, Annie & James Buckley, Jr. *Inside Photography* (3–5). Series: Reading Rocks! 2007, The Child's World LB $24.21 (978-1-59296-867-1). 32pp. This volume introduces three photographers — specializing in fashion, news, and animals — and looks at their techniques. (Rev: SLJ 1/08) [770]

20251 Cefrey, Holly. *Archaeologists: Life Digging Up Artifacts* (5–10). Series: Extreme Careers. 2004, Rosen LB $26.50 (978-0-8239-3963-3). 64pp. This is an introduction to the field of archeology, its problems, its opportunities, and its rewards. (Rev: BL 5/15/04) [930]

20252 Cohn, Jessica. *Animator* (4–6). Series: Cool Careers: Cutting Edge. 2010, Gareth Stevens LB $26 (978-1-4339-1953-4). 32pp. Explains the roles that animators play in cinematography and includes a "Career Fact File" that gives the career outlook, earnings, and training needed. (Rev: SLJ 8/10) [791.43]

20253 Crabtree, Marc. *Meet My Neighbor, the News Camera Operator* (K–3). Illus. Series: Meet My Neighbor. 2012, Crabtree LB $21.27 (978-077874560-0). 24pp. A Toronto cameraman gets ready for work, conducts interviews, and edits in the studio in this simple, colorful introduction. Also use *Meet My Neighbor, the Librarian* (2012). (Rev: BL 5/15/12) [777.092]

20254 Dolan, Edward F. *Careers in the U.S. Air Force* (5–8). Series: Military Service. 2009, Marshall Cavendish $24.95 (978-0-7614-4205-9). 80pp. This straightforward guide to the U.S. Air Force covers everything from training to joining requirements to salary; part of a recommended series that covers other branches of service. (Rev: BL 10/1/09; SLJ 3/10) [358.40023]

20255 Down, Susan Brophy. *Legally Green: Careers in Environmental Law* (5–8). Illus. Series: Green-Collar Careers. 2011, Crabtree LB $31.93 (978-077874857-1). 64pp. An accessible, well-illustrated guide to the options available in the field of environmental law, with profiles of lawyers and their work. (Rev: BL 2/15/12) [344.7304]

20256 *Fashion* (5–10). Illus. Series: Discovering Careers. 2011, Ferguson LB $24.95 (978-081608056-4). 118pp. With information on education and training, earnings potential, and so forth, this volume explores the work of everyone from fashion models and writers to retail sales workers and merchandise displayers. (Rev: BL 5/1/12) [746.9]

20257 Fletcher, Ralph. *How Writers Work: Finding a Process That Works for You* (4–8). 2000, HarperTrophy paper $4.99 (978-0-380-79702-8). Using a conversational style, the author explains the process of writing with material on brainstorming, rough drafts, revising, proofreading, and publishing. (Rev: SLJ 12/00) [808]

20258 *Food* (5–10). Illus. Series: Discovering Careers. 2012, Ferguson LB $30 (978-081608057-1). 122pp. With information on education and training, earnings potential, and so forth, this volume explores the work of everyone involved in the field, from farmers to chefs. (Rev: BL 5/1/12) [647.95023]

20259 Franks, Katie. *I Want to Be a Baseball Player* (2–4). Series: Dream Jobs. 2007, Rosen LB $21.25 (978-1-4042-3622-6). 24pp. Who wouldn't want to be a professional baseball player? Plenty of photographs and information about the career path to the pros will appeal to beginning and reluctant readers. (Rev: SLJ 7/07)

20260 Freedman, Jeri. *Careers in Emergency Medical Response Team's Search and Rescue Unit* (5–9). Series: Careers in Search and Rescue Operations. 2003, Rosen LB $26.50 (978-0-8239-3831-5). Starting with September 11, 2001, this volume explores the various roles played by emergency response teams, the use of equipment including helicopters and ambulances, and the training required. (Rev: BL 10/15/03) [616.0]

20261 Giacobello, John. *Bodyguards: Life Protecting Others* (5–10). Series: Extreme Careers. 2003, Rosen LB $26.50 (978-0-8239-3795-0). This book explores the duties and responsibilities of a bodyguard and includes information how to stay safe on the job and get ahead in this profession. (Rev: BL 9/15/03; SLJ 11/03) [340]

20262 Gibson, Karen Bush. *Child Care Workers* (K–3). Series: Community Helpers. 2000, Bridgestone LB $22.60 (978-0-7368-0622-0). 24pp. A solid introduction to various people who are involved in child care. (Rev: HBG 3/01; SLJ 2/01) [649]

20263 Gorman, Jacqueline Laks. *Librarian / El Bibliotecario* (PS–2). Photos by Gregg Andersen. Series: People in My Community/La Gente de Mi Comunidad. 2002, Gareth Stevens LB $21.00 (978-0-8368-3310-2). 24pp. Full-color photographs and single-sentence descriptions, in English and in Spanish, introduce various aspects of a librarian's job. (Rev: SLJ 3/03)

20264 Graham, Paula W. *Speaking of Journals: Children's Book Writers Talk About Their Diaries, Notebooks and Sketchbooks* (5–8). 1999, Boyds Mills paper $14.95 (978-1-56397-741-1). A book that discusses the how-tos and the rewards of keeping a personal journal, and features interviews with 27 writers including Jim Arnosky, Pam Conrad, and Jean George. (Rev: BL 3/1/99; SLJ 5/99; VOYA 2/00) [818]

20265 Greene, Meg. *Careers in the National Guards' Search and Rescue Unit* (5–9). Series: Careers in Search and Rescue Operations. 2003, Rosen LB $26.50 (978-0-8239-3836-0). This account describes the vital role that citizen-soldiers play in the line of defense and tells of the their search and rescue activities during the terrorist attacks of September 11, 2001. (Rev: BL 10/15/03; SLJ 4/04) [335]

20266 Hayhurst, Chris. *Astronauts: Life Exploring Outer Space* (4–7). Series: Extreme Careers. 2001, Rosen LB $26.50 (978-0-8239-3364-8). 64pp. A high-interest look at the extensive skills required to become an astronaut, with brief coverage of space exploration and profiles of astronauts. (Rev: SLJ 1/02) [629]

20267 *History* (4–8). Illus. Series: Discovering Careers for Your Future. 2001, Ferguson LB $21.95 (978-0-89434-391-9). 92pp. A useful introduction to the career opportunities in this field, with information on the skills required, potential earnings, and job outlook. (Rev: SLJ 11/01) [331.702]

20268 Hyland, Tony. *Miners and Drillers* (4–6). Series: Extreme Jobs. 2007, Smart Apple LB $27.10 (978-1-58340-741-7). 32pp. Readers interested in exciting, sometimes risky jobs will enjoy exploring what a miner or driller does and how to go about becoming one. Also use *Divers* (2007). (Rev: SLJ 8/07)

20269 Jackson, Donna M. *ER Vets: Life in an Animal Emergency Room* (5–8). 2005, Houghton Mifflin $17.00 (978-0-618-43663-7). With many photos, this is a behind-the-scenes look at life in a veterinary emergency clinic and the frustrations and joys to be found working there. (Rev: BL 11/1/05; SLJ 1/06*) [636.089]

20270 Kiland, Taylor Baldwin. *The U.S. Navy and Military Careers* (5–8). Series: U.S. Armed Forces and Military Careers. 2006, Enslow LB $31.93 (978-0-7660-2523-3). Straightforward and informative, this title provides a history of the Navy, looks at its role in the nation's defense, and details various jobs within this branch of the armed forces. (Rev: SLJ 6/07)

20271 Klein, Hilary Dole. *A Day with a Chef* (1–3). Illus. Series: Reading Rocks! 2007, Child's World LB $24.21 (978-1-59296-857-2). 32pp. Readers learn about the varied work involved in being a chef — planning menus, ordering supplies, managing the staff — as well as the training needed and the vocabulary of this trade. (Rev: BL 1/1–15/08; SLJ 1/08) [641.5092]

20272 Leboutillier, Nate. *A Day in the Life of a Zookeeper* (K–3). Series: First Facts: Community Helpers at Work. 2004, Capstone LB $21.26 (978-0-7368-2632-7). 24pp. Using a question-and-answer format and full-color photographs, this volume looks at the tasks a zookeeper performs. (Rev: SLJ 1/05) [636]

20273 Lee, Barbara. *Working in Sports and Recreation* (5–9). Series: Exploring Careers. 1996, Lerner LB $23.93 (978-0-8225-1762-7). Twelve people involved in careers related to sports and recreation talk candidly about their professions. (Rev: BL 2/15/97) [796]

20274 Lee, Barbara. *Working with Animals* (4–8). Series: Exploring Careers. 1996, Lerner LB $23.93 (978-0-8225-1759-7). Profiles of 12 careers involving animals, such as veterinarian, animal shelter worker, or pet sitter. (Rev: BL 2/15/97) [591]

20275 Libal, Joyce, and Rae Simons. *Professional Athlete and Sports Official* (5–9). Series: Careers with Character. 2003, Mason Crest LB $22.95 (978-1-59084-321-5). 90pp. The importance of character traits such as integrity, respect, fairness, and self-discipline when seeking careers in sports is emphasized here. (Rev: HBG 10/03; SLJ 4/03) [796]

20276 Liebman, Dan. *I Want to Be a Teacher* (K–2). Series: I Want to Be. 2001, Firefly LB $14.95 (978-1-55209-572-0). 24pp. A teacher's typical working day is described with a color photograph and two or three lines of text on each page in this easily read book. (Rev: BL 12/15/01; HBG 10/01) [371.1]

20277 Lowenstein, Felicia. *What Does a Teacher Do?* (K–2). Illus. Series: What Does a Community Helper Do? 2006, Enslow LB $21.26 (978-0-7660-2321-5). 24pp. Outlines in easy-to-understand language the job requirements and everyday responsibilities of a teacher. (Rev: SLJ 4/06) [371.1]

20278 Loy, Jessica. *When I Grow Up: A Young Person's Guide to Interesting and Unusual Occupations* (4–6). 2008, Holt $16.95 (978-0-8050-7717-9). Young people looking to the future will find interesting options here, among them master cheese maker, chocolatier, lobsterman, kite designer, and pet photographer. (Rev: LMC 1/09; SLJ 3/09) [331.702]

20279 Manley, Claudia B. *Secret Agents: Life as a Professional Spy* (4–7). Series: Extreme Careers. 2001, Rosen LB $26.50 (978-0-8239-3369-3). 64pp. A high-interest look at the extensive skills required to become an intelligence agent and the kinds of intelligence that are gathered (strategic, tactical, counterintelligence), with material on the history of espionage and on real-life and fictional spies. (Rev: SLJ 1/02) [327.12]

20280 Mara, Wil. *Information Security Analyst* (4–7). Illus. Series: Cool STEM Careers. 2013, Cherry Lake LB $28.50 (978-162431005-8). 32pp. Describes the work of these analysts, the activities in a typical day, and the careers of some well-known analysts. **e** (Rev: BL 4/1/13; LMC 11–12/13; SLJ 4/13) [005.8023]

20281 Marsico, Katie. *Working at the Library* (K–2). Series: 21st Century Junior Library. 2009, Cherry Lake LB $27.07 (978-1-60279-511-2). 24pp. Employees from librarians to shelvers to custodians are presented in this concise portrayal of what goes on at a library; suitable for beginning readers. (Rev: SLJ 2/1/10) [027]

20282 Marsico, Katie. *Working at the Post Office* (K–2). Series: 21st Century Junior Library. 2009, Cherry Lake LB $27.07 (978-1-60279-512-9). 24pp. Marsico presents an overview of all the functions undertaken at a post office; suitable for beginning readers. (Rev: SLJ 2/1/10) [383]

20283 Maze, Stephanie. *I Want to Be a Fashion Designer* (3–6). Illus. Series: I Want to Be. 2000, Harcourt $18.00 (978-0-15-201862-7); paper $9.00 (978-0-15-201938-9). 48pp. This large-format book uses double-page spreads to explore the world of fashion design and covers such topics as trade shows, education, and how a designer works. (Rev: BL 3/1/00; SLJ 4/00) [746.9]

20284 Minden, Cecilia. *Coaches* (1–2). Series: Neighborhood Helpers. 2006, The Child's World LB $24.21 (978-1-59296-561-8). 32pp. This attractive overview introduces young children to the role and responsibilities of a coach, plus the equipment and training needed. (Rev: SLJ 8/06) [796]

20285 Monroe, Judy. *A Day in the Life of a Librarian* (K–3). Series: First Facts: Community Helpers at Work. 2004, Capstone LB $21.26 (978-0-7368-2630-3). 24pp. Using a question-and-answer format and full-color photos, this volume looks at the tasks a librarian performs. (Rev: SLJ 1/05)

20286 Morris, Ann. *That's Our Librarian!* (K–3). Photos and illus. by Peter Linenthal. Series: That's Our School. 2003, Millbrook LB $22.90 (978-0-7613-2400-3). Readers are introduced to elementary school librarian Maria Rodriguez and all the responsibilities of her job. Also use *That's Our Teacher!* (2003). (Rev: HBG 4/04; SLJ 11/03) [027.8]

20287 Murdico, Suzanne J. *Bomb Squad Experts: Life Defusing Explosive Devices* (5–10). Series: Extreme Careers. 2004, Rosen LB $26.50 (978-0-8239-3968-8). A look at the career opportunities in bomb squads, with material on training, salaries, and working conditions. (Rev: BL 5/15/04) [363]

20288 Ollhoff, Jim. *Hazmat* (5–8). Illus. Series: Emergency Workers. 2012, ABDO LB $27.07 (978-161783514-8). 32pp. Describes the nine classes of hazardous materials and the training and equipment of the technicians who work to clean them up; includes an interview with a hazmat technician and a glossary. (Rev: BL 10/1/12; LMC 8–9/13) [363.17]

20289 Owen, Ruth. *Building Green Places: Careers in Planning, Designing, and Building* (5–8). Illus. Series: Green-Collar Careers. 2011, Crabtree LB $31.93 (978-077874852-6). 64pp. Looks at careers that involve designing and constructing eco-friendly buildings, cities, and parks. (Rev: BL 2/15/12) [720]

20290 Pasternak, Ceel. *Cool Careers for Girls with Animals* (5–8). Series: Cool Careers for Girls. 1998, Impact $19.95 (978-1-57023-108-7); paper $12.95 (978-1-57023-105-6). Veterinarian, pet sitter, bird handler, animal trainer, and horse-farm owner are among the careers covered, supplemented by interviews with women who work in each field. (Rev: SLJ 4/99; VOYA 8/99) [371.7]

20291 Pasternak, Ceel, and Linda Thornburg. *Cool Careers for Girls in Food* (5–10). Series: Cool Careers for Girls. 2000, Impact $19.95 (978-1-57023-127-8); paper $12.95 (978-1-57023-120-9). The 11 women featured in this book are involved in various aspects of the food industry such as cheese making, baking, wine making, selling health food, and cooking for the military. (Rev: SLJ 2/00) [641]

20292 Pasternak, Ceel, and Linda Thornburg. *Cool Careers for Girls in Sports* (5–10). Series: Cool Careers for Girls. 1999, Impact $19.95 (978-1-57023-107-0); paper $12.95 (978-1-57023-104-9). A golf pro, basketball player, ski instructor, sports broadcaster, trainer, sports psychologist, and athletic director are among the 10 women profiled in this overview of careers for women in sports. (Rev: SLJ 7/99; VOYA 8/99) [796]

20293 Payment, Simone. *Frontline Marines: Fighting in the Marine Combat Arms Units* (5–8). Series: Extreme Careers. 2007, Rosen LB $26.50 (978-1-4042-0946-6). Students looking for exciting careers may want to look into the combat arms units of the U.S. Marines, suggests this book, which tells readers what these units do and explains the training involved. (Rev: BL 7/07) [359.9]

20294 *Publishing* (5–9). Series: Discovering Careers for Your Future. 2005, Ferguson LB $21.95 (978-0-8160-5845-7). Education and training, salaries, and outlook for the field are all covered here along with a description of the kinds of daily activities found in various positions. (Rev: SLJ 1/06)

20295 Rau, Dana Meachen. *Baker* (PS–K). Series: Benchmark Rebus. 2007, Marshall Cavendish LB $15.95 (978-0-7614-2623-3). 24pp. For young children, this overview of the job of a baker contains an appealing mix of rebus, text, and image. (Rev: SLJ 12/07) [641.8]

20296 Reeves, Diane L. *Career Ideas for Kids Who Like Math* (4–8). Illus. by Nancy Bond. 2000, Facts on File $23.00 (978-0-8160-4095-7). 186pp. Presents an amazing array of careers available for the mathematically inclined, arranged alphabetically with good solid information on each. (Rev: HBG 10/00; SLJ 9/00) [510]

20297 Reeves, Diane Lindsey. *Career Ideas for Kids Who Like Art* (5–9). Series: Career Ideas for Kids Who Like. 1998, Facts on File $23.00 (978-0-8160-3681-3). An upbeat book that explores a variety of art-related careers, including many peripheral ones such as chef, animator, and photojournalist, with suggestions on how to test one's suitability for each area and reports from people working in the field. (Rev: SLJ 10/98; VOYA 8/98) [791]

20298 Reeves, Diane Lindsey. *Career Ideas for Kids Who Like Talking* (5–9). Illus. by Nancy Bond. Series: Career Ideas for Kids. 1998, Facts on File $23.00 (978-0-8160-3683-7); paper $12.95 (978-0-8160-3689-9). This is a guide to careers in communications, from hotel manager to publicist to broadcaster, with reports from people in the field, tests to check one's aptitude, and lists of resources. (Rev: SLJ 10/98) [331.7]

20299 Ring, Susan. *Animal Watch* (2–4). Series: On the Job. 2003, Chelsea Clubhouse LB $23.00 (978-0-7910-7409-1). 24pp. Explores three jobs that involve the study of animals: zoologist, entomologist, and ornithologist. (Rev: HBG 10/03; SLJ 10/03) [590]

20300 Rosenberg, Aaron. *Cryptologists: Life Making and Breaking Codes* (5–10). Series: Extreme Careers. 2004, Rosen LB $26.50 (978-0-8239-3965-7). After some background material on the history of codes, this volume discusses career opportunities as a cryptologist. (Rev: BL 5/15/04; SLJ 5/90) [410]

20301 Rotner, Shelley, and Ken Kreisler. *Everybody Works* (PS–1). Photos by Shelley Rotner. 2003, Millbrook LB $23.93 (978-0-7613-1751-7). In addition to jobs that interest youngsters — police, firefighters, and so forth — this book looks at lower-profile occupations and at volunteerism, hobbies, and even working animals. (Rev: HBG 10/03; SLJ 7/03) [331.7]

20302 Roza, Greg. *Careers in the Coast Guard's Search and Rescue Unit* (5–9). Series: Careers in Search and Rescue Operations. 2003, Rosen LB $26.50 (978-0-8239-3835-3). 64pp. This book covers the search and rescue operations involving the Coast Guard with particular emphasis on their vital role during the September 11, 2001, attacks. (Rev: BL 10/15/03; SLJ 4/04) [355]

20303 Schomp, Virginia. *If You Were a Farmer* (3–4). Series: If You Were A. 2000, Benchmark LB $22.79 (978-0-7614-1001-0). 32pp. The daily routines of a farmer and the equipment used are included in this simple career book. (Rev: BL 11/15/00; HBG 3/01; SLJ 3/01) [631]

20304 Simon, Charnan. *Lewis the Librarian* (K–2). Illus. by Rebecca Thornburgh. Series: Magic Door to Learning. 2006, The Child's World LB $21.36 (978-1-59296-624-0). 24pp. An inviting basic introduction to the role of a librarian. (Rev: SLJ 2/07) [020.92]

20305 Stein, R. Conrad. *The U.S. Marine Corps and Military Careers* (5–8). Series: U.S. Armed Forces and Military Careers. 2006, Enslow LB $31.93 (978-0-7660-2521-9). This overview of careers in the U.S. Marine Corps discusses expectations, duties, and pay scales as well as the Marines' role in national defense. (Rev: SLJ 6/07)

20306 Sweeney, Alyse. *Welcome to the Library* (K–2). Series: Scholastic News Nonfiction Readers. 2006, Children's Pr. LB $20.00 (978-0-531-16841-7). 24pp. Basic information for beginning readers about libraries and the work of librarians, with seven highlighted words that are featured in bold in the text. (Rev: SLJ 1/07) [027]

20307 Sweeney, Alyse. *Who Works at the Zoo?* (K–2). Series: Scholastic News Nonfiction Readers. 2006, Children's Pr. LB $20.00 (978-0-531-16842-4). 24pp. For beginning readers interested in working at a zoo, this book provides basic information. (Rev: SLJ 1/07) [590.73]

20308 Swinburne, Stephen R. *Whose Shoes? A Shoe for Every Job* (PS–2). Illus. by author. 2010, Boyds Mills $16.95 (978-159078569-0). 32pp. Readers guess a person's vocation based on the shoes he or she is wearing. (Rev: BL 2/1/10; HB 5–6/10; LMC 5–6/10) [331.702]

20309 Sylvester, Kevin. *Game Day: Meet the People Who Make It Happen* (5–8). 2010, Annick $21.95 (978-1-55451-251-5); paper $12.95 (978-1-55451-250-8).

136pp. Sylvester looks beyond the athletes to explore the roles of people behind the scenes of professional sports — a mechanic, a game scheduler, an umpire, a Zamboni driver, and so forth. **e** (Rev: BL 2/1/11; SLJ 1/1/11; VOYA 12/10) [796]

20310 Talbert, Marc. *Holding the Reins: A Ride Through Cowgirl Life* (5–7). Photos by Barbara Van Cleve. 2003, HarperCollins $16.99 (978-0-06-029255-3). 105pp. The demanding but exhilarating lives of modern-day cowgirls are shown here as the author follows four teens through the seasons. (Rev: BCCB 4/03; BL 1/1–15/03; HBG 10/03; SLJ 4/03) [978]

20311 Thompson, Lisa. *Creating Cuisine: Have You Got What It Takes to Be a Chef?* (5–8). Series: On the Job. 2008, Compass Point LB $19.95 (978-0-7565-3625-1). An inside look at professional kitchens and the training to become a restaurant cook. (Rev: BL 4/1/08) [641.5092]

20312 Turner, Chérie. *Adventure Tour Guides: Life on Extreme Outdoor Adventures* (5–10). Series: Extreme Careers. 2003, Rosen LB $26.50 (978-0-8239-3793-6). A look at the profession of tour guiding on excursions such as white-water rafting and mountain climbing, with material on qualifications and future possibilities. (Rev: BL 9/15/03) [908]

20313 Willett, Edward. *Careers in Outer Space: New Business Opportunities* (4–9). Series: The Career Resource Library. 2002, Rosen LB $31.95 (978-0-8239-3358-7). An interesting look at opportunities in the fields of science, math, engineering, technology, communication, and, of course, aeronautics, with information on required skills and training and on the pros and cons of working in the public and private sectors. (Rev: SLJ 6/02) [629.4]

Arts and Entertainment

20314 Aaseng, Nathan. *Wildshots: The World of the Wildlife Photographer* (5–8). Illus. 2001, Millbrook LB $29.90 (978-0-7613-1551-3). 80pp. This account describes the work of a wildlife photographer and tells exciting stories about unusual encounters. (Rev: BL 3/1/01*; HBG 10/01; SLJ 3/01; VOYA 10/01) [778.9]

20315 Amara, Philip. *So, You Wanna Be a Comic Book Artist?* (5–8). Illus. by Pop Mhan. 2001, Beyond Words paper $9.95 (978-1-58270-058-8). A comprehensive, engaging look at the world of comic-book illustration, with tips on everything from buying supplies to submitting work to publishers. (Rev: BL 1/1–15/02; SLJ 4/02) [808]

20316 *Art* (5–10). Illus. Series: Discovering Careers. 2011, Ferguson LB $24.95 (978-081608055-7). 122pp. With information on education and training, earnings potential, this volume explores the work of everyone involved in the field, from art dealers, teachers, and cu-

rators to artists, cartoonists, graphic designers, and so forth. Also use *Movies* (2011). (Rev: BL 5/1/12) [700.23]

20317 Burton, Marilee. *Artists at Work* (2–4). Series: On the Job. 2003, Chelsea Clubhouse LB $23.00 (978-0-7910-7410-7). 24pp. Introduces young readers to theatrical producer/costume designer Julie Taymor, architect/sculptor Maya Lin, and jazz trumpeter Wynton Marsalis. (Rev: HBG 10/03; SLJ 10/03) [700]

20318 Dubois, Muriel L. *I Like Music* (1–3). 2000, Bridgestone LB $22.60 (978-0-7368-0632-9). 24pp. Opposite each full-page photo, there is a description of a music-related occupation such as composer, conductor, sound engineer, or disc jockey. (Rev: HBG 3/01; SLJ 2/01) [780]

20319 Hyland, Tony. *Stunt Performers* (4–6). Series: Extreme Jobs. 2007, Smart Apple LB $27.10 (978-1-58340-739-4). 32pp. Readers interested in exciting, sometimes risky jobs will enjoy exploring what a stunt performer does and how to go about becoming one. (Rev: SLJ 8/07)

20320 Johnson, Marlys H. *Careers in the Movies* (5–9). Series: Career Resource Library. 2001, Rosen LB $31.95 (978-0-8239-3186-6). Job descriptions and qualifications are clearly laid out in this guide for aspiring filmmakers that also discusses the history of the industry and the basic steps in film production. (Rev: SLJ 8/01) [791.43]

20321 Lehn, Barbara. *What Is an Artist?* (PS–2). Illus. by Carol Krauss. 2002, Millbrook LB $21.90 (978-0-7613-2259-7). 32pp. An introduction of the concept of "artist," presented in a friendly format for younger readers. (Rev: BL 12/15/02; HBG 3/03) [709]

20322 McLaglen, Mary. *You Can Be a Woman Movie Maker* (4–8). Series: You Can Be a Woman. 2003, Cascade Pass $19.95 (978-1-880599-64-8); paper $14.95 (978-1-880599-63-1). Three women — a producer, an independent filmmaker, and an executive producer — talk about their jobs, how they got into the movie industry, and what a day on the job is like. Interviews and film clips are on an accompanying DVD. (Rev: SLJ 4/04) [791.43]

20323 Marsico, Katie. *Choreographer* (4–7). Illus. Series: Cool Arts Careers. 2011, Cherry Lake $18.95 (978-161080136-2). 32pp. Bright photos add appeal to this career guide, which gives readers a sense of what's required to be a professional choreographer. (Rev: BL 10/1/11) [792.82]

20324 Michael, Ted. *So You Wanna Be a Superstar? The Ultimate Audition Guide* (4–8). 2012, Running Press paper $10.95 (978-07624461-0-0). 152pp. With personality quizzes, dance terms, and audition tips, this is a useful guide to breaking into the entertainment industry. (Rev: BL 12/1/12; SLJ 2/13) [808.8245]

20325 Nathan, Amy. *Meet the Musicians: From Prodigy (or Not) to Pro* (5–8). Illus. 2006, Holt $17.95 (978-0-8050-7743-8). 156pp. Profiles of members of the New York Philharmonic give readers a good understanding of the different roles of various instruments and the careers of professional musicians. (Rev: BL 3/15/06; SLJ 5/06; VOYA 6/06) [750.92]

20326 Nathan, Amy. *The Young Musician's Survival Guide: Tips from Teens and Pros* (5–8). 2000, Oxford $21.99 (978-0-19-512611-2). A thorough study of how to break into the music world, with information on working with music teachers, conductors, and peers, and tips on practicing, choosing an instrument, and handling fears and frustrations. (Rev: BL 4/1/00; HBG 10/00; SLJ 6/00) [780]

20327 Parks, Peggy J. *Musician* (4–7). Series: Exploring Careers. 2004, Gale LB $26.20 (978-0-7377-2067-9). In addition to a description of the work that musicians (including DJs) do, there is a frank assessment of the opportunities available. (Rev: BL 3/15/04) [780]

20328 Parks, Peggy J. *Writer* (4–7). Series: Exploring Careers. 2004, Gale LB $26.20 (978-0-7377-2069-3). The ups and downs of a career in writing are frankly discussed in this slim guide. (Rev: BL 3/15/04) [808]

20329 *Radio and Television* (5–9). Series: Discovering Careers for Your Future. 2005, Ferguson LB $21.95 (978-0-8160-5846-4). Education and training, salaries, and outlook for the field are all covered here along with a description of the kinds of daily activities found in various positions. (Rev: SLJ 1/06)

20330 Schomp, Virginia. *If You Were a Musician* (3–4). Series: If You Were A. 2000, Benchmark LB $22.79 (978-0-7614-1002-7). 32pp. Using color photos and a simple text, this career book covers a typical day in the life of a musician. (Rev: BL 11/15/00; HBG 3/01; SLJ 3/01) [780]

20331 Sommers, Michael A. *Wildlife Photographers: Life Through a Lens* (5–10). Series: Extreme Careers. 2003, Rosen LB $26.50 (978-0-8239-3638-0). A concise explanation of the work of wildlife photographers, the attributes needed, and the training and tenacity required to enter this field. (Rev: BL 9/15/03; SLJ 5/03) [771]

20332 Thomas, Isabel. *Being a Stunt Performer* (4–6). Illus. Series: On the Radar: Awesome Jobs. 2012, Lerner $26.60 (978-076137776-4). 32pp. This lavishly illustrated volume explores the many roles of stunt performers and highlights some key figures and tricks of the trade. (Rev: BL 10/1/12; LMC 5–6/13) [791.4302]

Business

20333 *Advertising and Marketing* (5–9). Series: Discovering Careers for Your Future. 2005, Ferguson $21.95 (978-0-8160-5847-1). Education and training, salaries, and outlook for the field are all covered here along with a description of the kinds of daily activities found in various positions. (Rev: SLJ 1/06)

20334 Bernstein, Daryl. *Better Than a Lemonade Stand! Small Business Ideas for Kids* (5–8). 1992, Beyond Words paper $9.95 (978-0-941831-75-8). The author, a 15-year-old entrepreneur, provides ideas for starting 51

different small businesses and offers advice on start-up costs, billing, and customer relations. (Rev: BL 10/1/92; SLJ 1/93) [650.1]

Engineering, Technology, and Trades

20335 Boekhoff, P. M. *What Does a Construction Worker Do?* (K–2). Illus. Series: What Does a Community Helper Do? 2006, Enslow LB $21.26 (978-0-7660-2326-0). 24pp. Outlines in easy-to-understand language the job requirements and everyday responsibilities of a construction worker. (Rev: SLJ 4/06) [690]

20336 Brown, Marty. *Webmaster* (4–8). Series: Coolcareers.com. 2000, Rosen LB $23.95 (978-0-8239-3111-8). This volume describes a Web page, types of networks, servers, browsers, and protocols and introduces some careers in Web-related areas. (Rev: SLJ 6/00) [004]

20337 *Computers* (4–8). Series: Discovering Careers for Your Future. 2001, Ferguson LB $21.95 (978-0-89434-389-6). A useful introduction to the career opportunities in this field, with information on the skills required, potential earnings, and job outlook. (Rev: SLJ 11/01) [004.02373]

20338 Frew, Katherine. *Plumber* (5–8). Series: Great Jobs. 2004, Children's Pr. LB $24.50 (978-0-516-24088-6). 48pp. This appealing, photo-filled title focuses on the plumbing trade, looking at job requirements, training, and tools, as well as providing a history of the plumbing business and a look at a typical day at work. (Rev: SLJ 7/04) [696]

20339 Hovanec, Erin M. *Careers as a Content Provider for the Web* (5–8). Series: The Library of E-Commerce and Internet Careers. 2001, Rosen LB $26.50 (978-0-8239-3418-8). A basic guide to career opportunities in the high-tech sector, with personal stories, information on skills needed and how to get started, and lists of recommended resources, many of which are on the Web. Also use *E-Tailing: Careers Selling Over the Web* (2001). (Rev: SLJ 4/02) [004]

20340 Hyland, Tony. *Astronauts* (4–6). Series: Extreme Jobs. 2007, Smart Apple LB $27.10 (978-1-58340-743-1). 32pp. An interesting overview of what it takes to become an astronaut. (Rev: SLJ 8/07)

20341 Hyland, Tony. *High-Rise Workers* (4–6). Series: Extreme Jobs. 2007, Smart Apple LB $27.10 (978-1-58340-742-4). 32pp. Readers interested in exciting, sometimes risky jobs will enjoy exploring what high-rise workers do and how to go about becoming one. (Rev: SLJ 8/07)

20342 Jozefowicz, Chris. *Video Game Developer* (4–6). Series: Cool Careers: Cutting Edge. 2010, Gareth Stevens LB $26 (978-1-4339-1958-9). 32pp. Explains the roles of video game developers and the tools of the trade and includes a "Career Fact File" that gives the career outlook, earnings, and training needed. (Rev: SLJ 8/10) [794.8]

20343 McGinty, Alice B. *Software Designer* (4–8). Series: Coolcareers.com. 2000, Rosen LB $23.95 (978-0-8239-3149-1). This book explains what a software engineer does, the skills required, education needed, and future prospects. (Rev: SLJ 6/00) [004]

20344 Mazor, Barry. *Multimedia and New Media Developer* (4–8). Series: Coolcareers.com. 2000, Rosen LB $26.50 (978-0-8239-3102-6). This work explains the nature of multimedia careers, the training and skills necessary, and the job opportunities. (Rev: SLJ 6/00) [004]

20345 O'Donnell, Annie. *Computer Animator* (4–8). Series: Coolcareers.com. 2000, Rosen LB $23.95 (978-0-8239-3101-9). 44pp. This book gives a brief history of animation and explains how it is used today, the specialized roles of animators, educational requirements, and the future of the industry. (Rev: SLJ 6/00) [004]

20346 Oleksy, Walter. *Video Game Designer* (4–8). Series: Coolcareers.com. 2000, Rosen LB $23.95 (978-0-8239-3117-0). 47pp. This account explains how video games work and how they are designed, with material on the careers involved and the qualifications necessary. (Rev: SLJ 6/00) [794.8]

20347 Oleksy, Walter. *Web Page Designer* (4–8). Series: Coolcareers.com. 2000, Rosen LB $26.50 (978-0-8239-3112-5). 47pp. This well-illustrated account, which features case studies of several teenagers, gives information on Web page construction, what a designer does, the training required, and the job outlook. (Rev: SLJ 6/00) [004]

20348 Overcamp, David. *Electrician* (5–8). Series: Great Jobs. 2004, Children's Pr. LB $24.50 (978-0-516-24086-2); paper $6.95 (978-0-516-25924-6). 48pp. This appealing, photo-filled title focuses on the work of an electrician, looking at job requirements, training, and tools, as well as providing a history of the field and a look at a typical day at work. (Rev: SLJ 7/04) [621.3]

20349 Reeves, Diane Lindsey, and Peter Kent. *Career Ideas for Kids Who Like Computers* (5–9). Illus. by Nancy Bond. Series: Career Ideas for Kids. 1998, Facts on File $23.00 (978-0-8160-3682-0). An upbeat, breezy introduction to careers related to computers, providing aptitude tests and information on educational requirements, working conditions, activities, etc. (Rev: SLJ 6/99) [004]

20350 Spilsbury, Richard. *Design and Technical Art* (3–6). Illus. Series: Art off the Wall. 2006, Heinemann LB $32.86 (978-1-4034-8289-1). 56pp. Professional designers and engineers and their techniques using computer-aided design (CAD) are featured. Readers who would like to design cars will be especially interested in this book. (Rev: SLJ 5/07)

20351 Thomas, William David. *Environmental Engineer* (4–6). Series: Cool Careers: Cutting Edge. 2010, Gareth Stevens LB $26 (978-1-4339-1956-5). 32pp. Explains the roles that environmental engineers play in keeping our world as clean and unpolluted as possible and includes a "Career Fact File" that gives the career outlook, earnings, and training needed. (Rev: SLJ 8/10) [628]

20352 Weintraub, Aileen. *Auto Mechanic* (5–8). Series: Great Jobs. 2004, Children's Pr. LB $24.50 (978-0-516-24090-9). 48pp. This appealing, photo-filled title focuses on the work of an auto mechanic, looking at job requirements, training, and tools, as well as providing a history of the trade and a look at a typical day at work. (Rev: SLJ 7/04) [629.28]

20353 White, Katherine. *Oil Rig Workers: Life Drilling for Oil* (5–10). Series: Extreme Careers. 2003, Rosen LB $26.50 (978-0-8239-3797-4). 64pp. A look at the lives of oil rig workers and day-to-day activities on a rig. (Rev: BL 9/15/03) [665.5]

Health and Medicine

20354 Asher, Dana. *Epidemiologists: Life Tracking Deadly Diseases* (5–10). Series: Extreme Careers. 2003, Rosen LB $26.50 (978-0-8239-3633-5). A concise explanation of the work of epidemiologists, the history of this discipline, and the training required to enter this field, with a case study. (Rev: BL 5/15/03; SLJ 5/03) [614.4]

20355 Aylmore, Angela. *We Work at the Hospital* (PS–K). Series: Where We Work. 2006, Raintree LB $21.36 (978-1-4109-2246-5). 24pp. A basic introduction to what doctors, nurses, and other healthcare workers do, with color photographs and simple text. (Rev: SLJ 7/06) [362.1]

20356 Brill, Marlene T. *Doctors* (K–2). Series: Pull Ahead Books. 2004, Lerner LB $22.60 (978-0-8225-1689-7). The important role that doctors play in maintaining a healthy community is shown in brief text and and full-color photographs in this small-format book. (Rev: BL 10/15/04) [610]

20357 Fluet, Connie. *A Day in the Life of a Nurse* (K–3). Series: First Facts: Community Helpers at Work. 2004, Capstone LB $21.26 (978-0-7368-2631-0). 24pp. Using a question-and-answer format and full-color photos, Fluet looks at the tasks a nurse performs. (Rev: SLJ 1/05) [610]

20358 Gorman, Jacqueline Laks. *Dentist / El Dentista* (PS–2). Photos by Gregg Andersen. Series: People in My Community/La Gente de Mi Comunidad. 2002, Gareth Stevens LB $21.00 (978-0-8368-3307-2). 24pp. Full-color photographs and single-sentence descriptions, in English and in Spanish, introduce various aspects of a dentist's work. Also use *Doctor / El Medico* (2002). (Rev: HBG 3/03; SLJ 3/03)

20359 Kalman, Bobbie. *Hospital Workers in the Emergency Room* (1–4). Illus. Series: My Community and Its Helpers. 2004, Crabtree LB $25.27 (978-0-7787-2095-9); paper $8.95 (978-0-7787-2123-9). 32pp. A simple review of the tasks assigned to emergency room workers and the education necessary for a career in this field. (Rev: BL 5/1/04; SLJ 6/05)

20360 Liebman, Dan. *I Want to Be a Doctor* (PS–1). Illus. Series: I Want to Be. 2000, Firefly LB $14.95 (978-

1-55209-463-1); paper $3.99 (978-1-55209-461-7). 24pp. Using a simple text and many full-color photos, this book introduces the medical profession. (Rev: BL 9/15/00; HBG 9/00; SLJ 9/00) [610]

20361 Liebman, Dan. *I Want to Be a Nurse* (K–2). Series: I Want to Be. 2001, Firefly LB $14.95 (978-1-55209-568-3). 24pp. With color photographs and two or three lines of simple text on each page, the working day of a nurse is described. (Rev: BL 12/15/01; HBG 10/01) [610]

20362 Lowenstein, Felicia. *What Does a Doctor Do?* (1–3). Series: What Does a Community Helper Do? 2005, Enslow LB $21.26 (978-0-7660-2542-4). 24pp. This easy-reader chapter book looks at the important tasks that doctors perform to preserve the health of the communities in which they live and also examines career opportunities in the field of medicine. (Rev: SLJ 11/05)

20363 Miller, Heather. *What Does a Dentist Do?* (K–2). Illus. Series: What Does a Community Helper Do? 2006, Enslow LB $21.26 (978-0-7660-2323-9). 24pp. Outlines in easy-to-understand language the job requirements and everyday responsibilities of a dentist. (Rev: SLJ 4/06) [617.6]

20364 Minden, Cecelia. *Nurses* (1–2). Series: Neighborhood Helpers. 2006, The Child's World LB $24.21 (978-1-59296-566-3). 32pp. This attractive overview introduces young children to the role and responsibilities of a nurse, plus the equipment and training needed and the nature of the workplace. (Rev: SLJ 8/06) [610]

20365 Pasternak, Ceel, and Linda Thornburg. *Cool Careers for Girls in Health* (5–9). Series: Cool Careers for Girls. 1999, Impact $19.95 (978-1-57023-125-4); paper $12.95 (978-1-57023-118-6). This book describes health-related careers for girls — as doctors, nurses, dentists, personal trainers, medical technologists, physical therapists, and dietitians. (Rev: SLJ 10/99) [610]

20366 Schomp, Virginia. *If You Were a Doctor* (3–4). Series: If You Were A. 2000, Benchmark LB $22.79 (978-0-7614-1000-3). 32pp. Full-color photographs and an easy text are used to describe the daily routines of a doctor. (Rev: BL 11/15/00; HBG 3/01) [610]

20367 Simon, Charnan. *My Mother Is a Doctor* (K–2). Illus. by Patrick Girouard. Series: Magic Door to Learning. 2006, The Child's World LB $21.36 (978-1-59296-620-2). 24pp. An inviting basic introduction to doctors and their work, taking young readers through a typical day in a doctor's office. (Rev: SLJ 2/07) [610.69]

Police and Fire Fighters

20368 Aylmore, Angela. *We Work at the Fire Station* (PS–K). Series: Where We Work. 2006, Raintree LB $21.36 (978-1-4109-2243-4). 24pp. A basic introduction to what fire fighters do, with color photographs and simple text. (Rev: SLJ 7/06) [628.9]

20369 Bourgeois, Paulette. *Police Officers* (1–3). Series: Kids Can Read. 2004, Kids Can $14.95 (978-1-55337-742-9); paper $3.95 (978-1-55337-743-6). 32pp. After describing a fictional police investigation, Bourgeois moves on to discuss police duties and children's safety. (Rev: BL 11/15/04) [363.2]

20370 Crabtree, Marc. *Meet My Neighbor, the Police Officer* (K–3). Illus. Series: Meet My Neighbor. 2012, Crabtree LB $21.27 (978-077874561-7). 24pp. This accessible book follows a real police officer around on the job as she attends a meeting, stakes out a speed trap, and makes an arrest. (Rev: BL 5/15/12) [363.2]

20371 Croce, Nicholas. *Detectives: Life Investigating Crimes* (5–10). Series: Extreme Careers. 2003, Rosen LB $26.50 (978-0-8239-3796-7). As well as exploring the exciting side of detective work, this account explains the qualifications and training needed and the techniques that help do this job well. (Rev: BL 9/15/03) [340]

20372 Fall, Mitchell. *Careers in Fire Departments' Search and Rescue Unit* (5–9). Series: Careers in Search and Rescue Operations. 2003, Rosen LB $26.50 (978-0-8239-3833-9). 64pp. This account pays tribute to the heroism of fire departments' search and rescue operations particularly during the September 11, 2001 attacks and also gives a career guide to this occupation. (Rev: BL 10/15/03) [363]

20373 Fine, Jil. *Bomb Squad Specialist* (4–8). Series: Danger Is My Business. 2003, Children's Pr. LB $24.50 (978-0-516-24340-5). 48pp. An illustrated glimpse of the perilous life of a bomb squad member in an age of terrorism, including information on how bombs work and how they are detected and disarmed. (Rev: SLJ 3/04) [363.2]

20374 Ghione, Yvette. *This Is Daniel Cook at the Fire Station* (K–3). 2006, Kids Can $12.95 (978-1-55453-075-5); paper $4.95 (978-1-55453-076-2). In this companion to the popular Canadian-produced TV show, the young host invites readers to join him on a tour of a fire station. (Rev: SLJ 11/06) [628.9]

20375 Goldish, Meish. *Firefighters to the Rescue* (3–5). Illus. Series: Work of Heroes: First Responders in Action. 2011, Bearport LB $25.27 (978-161772284-4). 32pp. With information on training and gear, this is an overview of a fire fighter's job, with accounts of various notable incidents. (Rev: BL 10/1/11) [363.37023]

20376 Gorman, Jacqueline Laks. *Firefighter / El Bombero* (PS–2). Photos by Gregg Andersen. Series: People in My Community/La Gente de Mi Comunidad. 2002, Gareth Stevens LB $21.00 (978-0-8368-3309-6). 24pp. Full-color photographs and single-sentence descriptions, in English and in Spanish, introduce various aspects of a fire fighter's job. Also use *Police Officer / El Policía* (2002). (Rev: SLJ 3/03)

20377 Hayward, Linda. *A Day in the Life of a Firefighter* (PS–K). Series: Dorling Kindersley Readers: Jobs People Do. 2001, DK $14.99 (978-0-7894-7366-0); paper $3.99 (978-0-7894-7365-3). 32pp. In this beginning reader that uses a limited vocabulary and simple sentences, the daily life of a fire fighter is portrayed. (Rev: BL 8/1/01; HBG 10/01) [363]

20378 Horn, Geoffrey M. *FBI Agent* (4–8). Illus. Series: Cool Careers: Helping Careers. 2008, Gareth Stevens LB $24 (978-083689193-5). 32pp. What *do* FBI agents do? This book answers the question with facts about the training and responsibilities plus information on key cases. Lexile 760L (Rev: BL 10/15/08) [363.250973]

20379 Hubbell, Patricia. *Police: Hurry! Helping! Saving!* (PS–1). Illus. by Viviana Garofoli. 2008, Marshall Cavendish $14.99 (978-0-7614-5421-2). A lively, simple introduction to law enforcement jobs and roles. (Rev: SLJ 9/08) [363.2]

20380 Kalman, Bobbie. *Firefighters to the Rescue!* (1–4). Illus. Series: My Community and Its Helpers. 2004, Crabtree LB $25.27 (978-0-7787-2096-6); paper $8.95 (978-0-7787-2124-6). 32pp. A simple review of the work of fire fighters and the education necessary for a career in this field. (Rev: BL 5/1/04; SLJ 6/05) [363.37]

20381 Knudsen, Shannon. *Police Officers* (K–2). 2004, Lerner LB $22.60 (978-0-8225-1693-4). 32pp. The important role that police officers play in the community is shown in brief text and and full-color photographs in this small-format book. (Rev: BL 10/15/04) [363.2]

20382 Landau, Elaine. *Smokejumpers* (3–6). Illus. 2002, Millbrook LB $23.90 (978-0-7613-2324-2). 48pp. An excellent tribute to the life and work of the gallant men and women who jump from planes to fight forest fires. (Rev: BCCB 3/02; BL 6/1–15/02; HBG 10/02; SLJ 7/02) [634.9]

20383 Liebman, Dan. *I Want to Be a Police Officer* (PS–1). Illus. Series: I Want to Be. 2000, Firefly LB $14.95 (978-1-55209-467-9); paper $3.99 (978-1-55209-465-5). 24pp. Full-color photographs and a brief text introduce police officers and what they do. (Rev: BL 6/1–15/00; SLJ 9/00) [363.2]

20384 Nolan, Janet. *The Firehouse Light* (K–3). Illus. by Marie Lafrance. 2010, Tricycle $15.99 (978-1-58246-298-1). 32pp. Traces the evolution of firefighting equipment through the decades as a single four-watt bulb continues to glow for more than 100 years; based on a true story. Lexile AD990L (Rev: BL 6/10; SLJ 9/1/10*) [363.3]

20385 Plum, Jennifer. *Careers in Police Departments' Search and Rescue Unit* (5–9). Series: Careers in Search and Rescue Operations. 2003, Rosen LB $26.50 (978-0-8239-3834-6). 64pp. This account highlights the role of police officers in search and rescue operations, particularly their acts of heroism during the attacks of September 11, 2001. (Rev: BL 10/15/03) [363]

20386 Pohl, Kathleen. *What Happens at a Firehouse?* (PS–2). Series: Where People Work. 2006, Gareth Stevens LB $21.00 (978-0-8368-6887-6). 24pp. This small-format book combines cartoons and clear photographs with facts about day-to-day activities inside a firehouse. (Rev: BL 1/1–15/07) [628.9]

20387 Rau, Dana Meachen. *Firefighter* (PS–1). Illus. Series: Benchmark Rebus. 2007, Marshall Cavendish LB $15.95 (978-0-7614-2617-2). 24pp. Double-page spreads with large color photographs and simple large-type text introduce the work of a fire fighter; a small-format book suitable for young children. (Rev: BL 10/15/07; SLJ 12/07) [628.9]

20388 Rau, Dana Meachen. *Police Officer* (PS–K). Series: Benchmark Rebus. 2007, Marshall Cavendish LB $15.95 (978-0-7614-2618-9). 24pp. For young children, this overview of the job of a police officer contains an appealing mix of rebus, text, and image. (Rev: SLJ 12/07) [363.2]

20389 Simon, Charnan. *Firefighter Tom to the Rescue!* (K–2). Illus. by Joel Snyder. Series: Magic Door to Learning. 2006, The Child's World LB $21.36 (978-1-59296-621-9). 24pp. An inviting basic introduction to firefighters' role in the community and a typical day on the job. (Rev: SLJ 2/07) [628.9]

20390 Sweeney, Alyse. *A Very Busy Firehouse* (K–2). Series: Scholastic News Nonfiction Readers. 2006, Children's Pr. LB $20.00 (978-0-531-16840-0). 24pp. Basic information for beginning readers, with seven highlighted words that are featured in bold in the text. (Rev: SLJ 1/07) [628.9]

Science

20391 Collard, Sneed B., III. *A Firefly Biologist at Work* (4–6). Illus. Series: Wildlife Conservation Society. 2001, Watts LB $24.50 (978-0-531-11798-9). 48pp. Readers learn about the career of a firefly researcher, with information both about fireflies themselves and about the life and interests of a biologist. (Rev: BL 12/1/01; SLJ check) [595.7]

20392 Gaffney, Timothy R. *Storm Scientist: Careers Chasing Severe Weather* (4–8). Series: Wild Science Careers. 2009, Enslow LB $31.93 (978-0-7660-3050-3). 112pp. Full of tales of hard work and engaging action, this book presents an in-depth look at the real life, skills, and even salary expectations of scientists studying severe weather. (Rev: SLJ 10/09) [551.5023]

20393 Hammonds, Heather. *Geologists* (4–6). 2004, Smart Apple LB $27.10 (978-1-58340-543-7). 32pp. Following an overview of the science and its history, this volume discusses geology today, the duties of geologists and equipment used, the future of the profession, and how to become a geologist. (Rev: BL 10/15/04; SLJ 2/05) [551]

20394 Haydon, Julie. *Astronomers* (4–6). Illus. Series: Scientists at Work. 2004, Smart Apple LB $27.10 (978-1-58340-541-3). 32pp. Following an overview of the science and its history, this volume discusses astronomy today, the duties of astronomers and equipment used, the future of the profession, and how to become an astronomer. (Rev: BL 10/15/04; SLJ 2/05) [520]

20395 Hayhurst, Chris. *Arctic Scientists: Life Studying the Arctic* (5–10). Series: Extreme Careers. 2003, Rosen

LB $26.50 (978-0-8239-3794-3). 64pp. This guide to the life and work of Arctic scientists indicates exciting areas of research such as the plant and animal life and the effects of global warming. (Rev: BL 9/15/03; SLJ 11/03) [500]

20396 Hayhurst, Chris. *Volcanologists: Life Exploring Volcanoes* (5–10). Series: Extreme Careers. 2003, Rosen LB $26.50 (978-0-8239-3637-3). 64pp. This career guide explains what is necessary to become a serious student of volcanoes and what to expect when one becomes a volcanologist. (Rev: BL 9/15/03) [551.2]

20397 Jackson, Donna M. *Extreme Scientists: Exploring Nature's Mysteries from Perilous Places* (4–8). Illus. Series: Scientists in the Field. 2009, Houghton $18.00 (978-0-618-77706-8). 80pp. Jackson shows the work of scientists who face danger in the field — a meteorologist who flies into hurricanes, a biologist who goes deep into caves, an ecologist who climbs high into tall redwoods — and discusses their motivations. (Rev: BCCB 6/09; BL 5/15/09*; HB 7/09; SLJ 7/09) [509.2]

20398 McElroy, Lisa. *Meet My Grandmother: She's a Deep Sea Explorer* (2–4). Series: Grandmothers at Work. 2000, Millbrook LB $22.90 (978-0-7613-1720-3). 32pp. A young boy introduces his grandmother, Sylvia Earle, who regularly swims with sharks as she explores the ocean's depths. (Rev: BL 9/15/00; HBG 3/01; SLJ 1/01) [551.46]

20399 McGlone, Catherine. *Visiting Volcanoes with a Scientist* (1–3). Illus. Series: I Like Science! 2004, Enslow LB $21.26 (978-0-7660-2269-0). 24pp. Readers follow a volcanologist through work in the field and learn how to make a model volcano using everyday materials. (Rev: BL 4/1/04; SLJ 2/05) [551.21]

20400 Murdico, Suzanne J. *Forensic Scientists: Life Investigating Sudden Death* (5–12). Series: Extreme Careers. 2004, Rosen LB $26.50 (978-0-8239-3966-4). 64pp. A look at this rapidly growing science and the career opportunities offered. (Rev: BL 5/15/04) [363.2]

20401 Reeves, Diane Lindsey. *Career Ideas for Kids Who Like Science* (5–9). Illus. by Nancy Bond. Series: Career Ideas for Kids. 1998, Facts on File $23.00 (978-0-8160-3680-6); paper $12.95 (978-0-8060-3686-1). An upbeat, breezy introduction to 15 careers, providing aptitude tests and information on educational requirements, working conditions, activities, etc. (Rev: SLJ 9/98) [500]

20402 Swinburne, Stephen R. *The Woods Scientist* (4–8). Photos by Susan C. Morse. Series: Scientists in the Field. 2003, Houghton Mifflin $16.00 (978-0-618-04602-7). Swinburne describes his fascinating expeditions in the company of a conservationist and ecologist in the woods of Vermont, and provides lots of information on risks to wildlife. (Rev: BCCB 3/03; BL 3/15/03; HBG 10/03; SLJ 4/03) [591.73]

20403 Thomas, William David. *Marine Biologist* (4–6). Series: Cool Careers: Cutting Edge. 2010, Gareth Stevens LB $26 (978-1-4339-1957-2). 32pp. Explains the roles that marine biologists play in studying marine life in the oceans, lakes, and rivers and includes a "Career Fact File" that gives the career outlook, earnings, and training needed. (Rev: SLJ 8/10) [578.7]

20404 Willett, Edward. *Disease-Hunting Scientist: Careers Hunting Deadly Diseases* (4–8). Series: Wild Science Careers. 2009, Enslow LB $31.93 (978-0-7660-3052-7). 112pp. Full of real-life tales of hard work and engaging action, this book presents an in-depth look at the everyday activities, skills, and even salary expectations of scientists studying deadly epidemics. (Rev: SLJ 10/09) [614.4023]

20405 Williams, Judith. *Discovering Dinosaurs with a Fossil Hunter* (1–3). Illus. by Michael W. Skrepnick. Series: I Like Science! 2004, Enslow LB $21.26 (978-0-7660-2267-6). 24pp. Readers follow a paleontologist through work in the field and learn how to re-create a plant fossil. (Rev: BL 4/1/04; SLJ 2/05) [567.9]

Transportation

20406 Gorman, Jacqueline Laks. *Bus Driver / El Conductor del Autobús* (PS–2). Photos by Gregg Andersen. Series: People in My Community/La Gente de Mi Comunidad. 2002, Gareth Stevens LB $21.00 (978-0-8368-3306-5). 24pp. Full-color photographs and single-sentence descriptions, in English and in Spanish, introduce various aspects of a bus driver's job. (Rev: HBG 3/03; SLJ 3/03)

20407 Liebman, Dan. *I Want to Be a Truck Driver* (K–2). Series: I Want to Be. 2001, Firefly LB $14.95 (978-1-55209-576-8). 24pp. The daily life of a truck driver is described using a brief text and color photographs on each page. (Rev: BL 12/15/01; HBG 10/01) [629.24]

20408 Marsico, Katie. *Working at the Airport* (K–2). Series: 21st Century Junior Library. 2009, Cherry Lake LB $27.07 (978-1-60279-510-5). 24pp. Employees from baggage handlers to pilots are presented in this concise portrayal of what goes on at an airport; suitable for beginning readers. (Rev: SLJ 2/1/10) [387.7]

20409 Schomp, Virginia. *If You Were a Truck Driver* (3–4). Series: If You Were A. 2000, Benchmark LB $22.79 (978-0-7614-1003-4). 32pp. Covers the daily life of a truck driver, with information on the care and handling of trucks. (Rev: BL 11/15/00; HBG 3/01) [629.24]

20410 Trumbauer, Lisa. *What Does a Truck Driver Do?* (K–2). Illus. Series: What Does a Community Helper Do? 2006, Enslow LB $21.26 (978-0-7660-2324-6). 24pp. Outlines in easy-to-understand language the job requirements and everyday responsibilities of a truck driver. (Rev: SLJ 4/06) [388.324]

Veterinarians

20411 Aylmore, Angela. *We Work at the Vet's* (PS–K). Series: Where We Work. 2006, Raintree LB $21.36 (978-1-

4109-2245-8). 24pp. A basic introduction to what veterinarians and their assistants do, with color photographs and simple text. (Rev: SLJ 7/06) [636.089]

20412 Ermitage, Kathleen. *Veterinarian* (2–4). Series: Workers You Know. 2000, Raintree LB $25.70 (978-0-8172-5592-3). 32pp. Describes a day in the life of a vet, including routine diagnoses, emergency procedures, and follow-up activities. (Rev: HBG 9/00; SLJ 11/00) [636.089]

20413 Kalman, Bobbie. *Veterinarians Help Keep Animals Healthy* (1–4). Illus. Series: My Community and Its Helpers. 2004, Crabtree LB $25.27 (978-0-7787-2097-3); paper $8.95 (978-0-7787-2125-3). 32pp. A simple review of the work of veterinarians and the education necessary for a career in this field. (Rev: SLJ 6/05) [636]

20414 Leake, Diyan. *Vets* (PS–1). Illus. Series: People in Our Community. 2008, Heinemann LB $17.75 (978-1-4329-1192-8). 24pp. A basic introduction to the work of vets, with bright photographs. (Rev: BLO 7/31/08) [636.089]

20415 Liebman, Dan. *I Want to Be a Vet* (PS–1). Illus. Series: I Want to Be. 2000, Firefly LB $14.95 (978-1-55209-471-6); paper $3.99 (978-1-55209-469-3). 24pp. A very simple introduction to what veterinarians do and how they are prepared for their jobs. (Rev: BL 9/15/00; HBG 9/00; SLJ 2/01) [636]

20416 Minden, Cecelia. *Veterinarians* (1–2). Series: Neighborhood Helpers. 2006, The Child's World LB $24.21 (978-1-59296-571-7). 32pp. This attractive overview introduces young children to the role and responsibilities of a vet, plus the equipment and training needed. (Rev: SLJ 8/06) [636]

20417 Owen, Ann. *Caring for Your Pets: A Book About Veterinarians* (PS–3). Illus. by Eric Thomas. Series: Community Workers. 2004, Picture Window LB $25.26 (978-1-4048-0087-8). 24pp. A simple first look at the many tasks of veterinarians as they work with pets, livestock, and wild animals. (Rev: SLJ 4/04) [636]

20418 Patrick, Jean L. S. *Cows, Cats, and Kids: A Veterinarian's Family at Work* (3–6). Illus. by Alvis Upitis. 2003, Boyds Mills $17.95 (978-1-56397-111-2). 48pp. A rural vet's wife describes the family's love of animals and the ways in which her children are able to help their father. (Rev: BL 3/1/03; HBG 10/03; SLJ 4/03) [636.089]

20419 Simon, Charnan. *The Best Vet in the World* (K–2). Illus. by Carol Schwartz. Series: Magic Door to Learning. 2006, The Child's World LB $21.36 (978-1-59296-628-8). 24pp. An inviting basic introduction to the veterinary profession. (Rev: SLJ 2/07) [636]

Health and the Human Body

Aging and Death

20420 Dennison, Amy, and Allie Dennison. *Our Dad Died: The True Story of Three Kids Whose Lives Changed* (3–7). Illus. by authors. 2003, Free Spirit paper $9.95 (978-1-57542-135-3). 107pp. Three young siblings recount their initial reaction to the sudden and unexpected death of their father and how, with support from their mother, they learned to live with this loss. (Rev: SLJ 1/04) [155.9]

20421 Hyde, Margaret O., and Lawrence E. Hyde. *Meeting Death* (5–8). 1989, Walker LB $15.85 (978-0-8027-6874-2). After a history of how various cultures regard death, the authors discuss this phenomenon, the concept of grieving, and how to face death. (Rev: BL 1/1/90; SLJ 11/89) [306.9]

20422 Jackson, Aariane R. *Can You Hear Me Smiling? A Child Grieves a Sister* (2–4). Series: New Child and Family Press Titles. 2004, Child Welfare League of America $9.95 (978-0-87868-835-7). 40pp. Nine-year-old Aariane discusses the conflicting emotions she experienced after the sudden death of her older sister. (Rev: BL 7/04) [155.9]

20423 Krementz, Jill. *How It Feels When a Parent Dies* (4–7). 1988, Knopf paper $15.00 (978-0-394-75854-1). Eighteen experiences of parental death are recounted.

20424 Murphy, Patricia J. *Death* (PS–3). Series: Tough Topics. 2007, Heinemann LB $25.36 (978-1-4034-9778-9). 32pp. A sensitive discussion of the nature of death, why people die, funerals, and the ways people feel after a death. (Rev: SLJ 12/07) [155.9]

20425 Peacock, Carol Antoinette. *Death and Dying* (4–8). Illus. Series: Life Balance. 2004, Watts LB $20.50 (978-0-531-12370-6); paper $6.95 (978-0-531-16728-1). A practical guide to dealing with death and dying, with advice on seeking help when necessary. (Rev: BL 10/15/03)

20426 Rebman, Renee C. *Euthanasia and the "Right to Die": A Pro/Con Issue* (5–8). Illus. Series: Pro/Con Issues. 2002, Enslow LB $27.93 (978-0-7660-1816-7). 64pp. An objective examination of both sides of the issue of euthanasia. (Rev: BL 9/1/02; HBG 3/03) [179.7]

20427 Sanders, Pete, and Steve Myers. *When People Die* (3–6). Illus. by Mike Lacey. Series: Choices and Decisions. 2005, Stargazer LB $27.10 (1-59604-076-9). 32pp. This reassuring title covers with sensitivity the topics of death, grieving, and funerals, and also discusses euthanasia. (Rev: SLJ 4/06) [155.9]

20428 Stalfelt, Pernilla. *The Death Book* (2–4). Illus. 2002, Groundwood $15.95 (978-0-88899-482-0). 32pp. A straightforward yet lighthearted look at death, including the customs surrounding it, what might happen when we die, and an "interview" with a ghost. (Rev: BL 2/1/03; HBG 3/03; SLJ 8/03) [306.9]

20429 Wilson, Antoine. *You and a Death in Your Family* (5–8). Series: Family Matters. 2001, Rosen LB $26.50 (978-0-8239-3355-6). 48pp. Wilson provides concise, readable advice on coping with the death of a relative or pet and stresses that youngsters should seek help when necessary. (Rev: SLJ 8/01) [155.9]

Alcohol, Drugs, and Smoking

20430 Bailey, Jacqui. *Taking Action Against Drugs* (5–8). Series: Taking Action. 2010, Rosen LB $26.50 (978-1-4358-5492-5). 48pp. Bailey discusses the dangers of illegal drugs and the reasons why people choose to take them, along with their social and physical effects. (Rev: LMC 1–2/10)

20431 Green, Carl R. *Nicotine and Tobacco* (4–8). Series: Drugs. 2005, Enslow LB $25.26 (978-0-7660-5283-3). Fictional scenarios are combined with information on the addictive qualities of nicotine and the dangers of smoking and other forms of tobacco use; Web links extend the text. (Rev: SLJ 11/05) [362.2]

20432 Grosshandler-Smith, Janet. *Working Together Against Drinking and Driving* (4–8). Series: The Library of Social Activism. 1996, Rosen LB $16.95 (978-0-8239-2259-8). With an emphasis on prevention, the author presents a general discussion on drinking and driving and its consequences, followed by pointers on how to avoid embarrassing situations, how to handle peer pressure about drinking. (Rev: SLJ 2/97) [613.8]

20433 Hanan, Jessica. *When Someone You Love Is Addicted* (5–9). Series: Drug Abuse Prevention Library. 1999, Rosen LB $27.95 (978-0-8239-2831-6). A short book that begins with teenage case histories and then discusses treatments and resources for young people with drug problems. (Rev: SLJ 7/99) [362.29]

20434 Hyde, Margaret O. *Know About Drugs. 4th ed.* (5–8). 1995, Walker LB $15.85 (978-0-8027-8395-0). An introduction to drugs including marijuana, alcohol, PCP, inhalants, crack/cocaine, heroin, and nicotine. (Rev: BL 7/90; SLJ 3/96) [362.2]

20435 Hyde, Margaret O., and John F. Setaro. *Alcohol 101: An Overview for Teens* (5–10). 1999, Twenty-First Century LB $24.90 (978-0-7613-1274-1). Kinds of alcohol and their effects are described, with material on alcoholism and binge drinking. (Rev: HBG 3/00; SLJ 3/00; VOYA 12/00) [613.8]

20436 Landau, Elaine. *Hooked: Talking About Addiction* (5–10). 1995, Millbrook LB $22.90 (978-1-56294-469-8). This account defines addiction broadly — from use of alcohol and drugs to various forms of compulsive behavior — and gives suggestions for recovery. (Rev: BL 1/1–15/96; SLJ 1/96) [362.29]

20437 Lawler, Jennifer. *Drug Testing in Schools: A Pro/Con Issue* (5–8). Series: Hot Issues. 2000, Enslow LB $27.93 (978-0-7660-1367-4). 64pp. The pros and cons of drug testing in schools are presented in an unbiased manner with sections on methods of drug testing, policies of various organizations, and the opinions of students, teachers, and parents. (Rev: HBG 3/01; SLJ 12/00) [362.29]

20438 Levete, Sarah. *Drugs* (3–5). Series: Let's Talk About. 2007, Stargazer LB $27.10 (978-1-59604-090-8). 32pp. Questions and answers about drugs address their dangers in a straightforward way. Also use *Alcohol* (2007). (Rev: SLJ 8/07)

20439 Littell, Mary Ann. *Heroin Drug Dangers* (5–8). Series: Drug Dangers. 1999, Enslow LB $27.93 (978-0-7660-1156-4). A short, well-illustrated book that describes the physiological effects of heroin, the dangers of its use, and how to resist its temptations. (Rev: BL 9/15/99; HBG 3/00) [362.29]

20440 Murphy, Patricia J. *Avoiding Drugs* (1–3). Series: Pull Ahead. 2005, Lerner LB $22.60 (978-0-8225-2867-8); paper $5.95 (978-0-8225-2779-4). Alcohol, tobacco, and "non-medicinal" drugs are defined and discussed in clear text and photographs; a question-and-answer section offers practice in rejecting drug offers. (Rev: SLJ 3/06) [362.29]

20441 Nolan, Meghan, ed. *Let's Clear the Air: 10 Reasons Not to Start Smoking* (5–8). Illus. by Deanna Staffo. 2007, Lobster paper $14.95 (978-1-897073-66-7). In personal essays, young people reveal the reasons why they don't smoke — reasons ranging from the deaths of loved ones to the smell and the cost. (Rev: BL 1/1–15/08; LMC 2/08; SLJ 3/08) [613.85]

20442 Paris, Stephanie. *Straight Talk: Smoking* (3–5). Illus. Series: Time for Kids Nonfiction Readers. 2012, Teacher Created Materials paper $9.99 (978-14333485-8-7). 48pp. Answers questions about smoking, health risks, addiction, peer pressure, and advertising, with many sidebars and visual features. (Rev: BL 9/15/12; LMC 5–6/13) [610]

20443 Sanders, Pete. *Smoking* (4–7). Series: What Do You Know About. 1996, Millbrook LB $23.90 (978-0-7613-0536-1). Covers the effects of smoking and ways in which youngsters can avoid getting hooked. (Rev: SLJ 3/97) [362.2]

20444 Sanders, Pete, and Steve Myers. *Drinking Alcohol* (4–8). Series: What Do You Know About. 1997, Millbrook LB $23.90 (978-0-7613-0573-6). An introduction to alcohol use and abuse, with material on how alcohol affects the body and behavior. (Rev: SLJ 10/97) [613.8]

20445 Sherry, Clifford J. *Drugs and Eating Disorders* (5–10). Series: Drug Abuse Prevention Library. 1994, Rosen LB $17.95 (978-0-8239-1540-8). Shows how diet pills and other weight-loss products can lead to drug abuse and, in some cases, addiction. (Rev: BL 6/1–15/94; SLJ 6/94) [616.85]

20446 Sherry, Clifford J. *Inhalants* (5–10). 1994, Rosen LB $17.95 (978-0-8239-1704-4). A look at inhalants, where they are found, and how they affect the body. (Rev: BL 2/15/95; SLJ 3/95) [362.29]

20447 Weitzman, Elizabeth. *Let's Talk About Smoking* (4–8). Series: Let's Talk. 1996, Rosen LB $19.95 (978-0-8239-2307-6). This book explains why people smoke, its effects, and ways to avoid starting, with tips on how to give up. (Rev: BL 3/15/97; SLJ 1/97) [362.29]

20448 Westcott, Patsy. *Why Do People Take Drugs?* (5–7). Series: Exploring Tough Issues. 2001, Raintree LB $25.69 (978-0-7398-3231-8). 48pp. Drugs from caffeine to cocaine are explored, with discussion of society's attitudes toward drugs, legal issues, and the reasons some people are more tempted to abuse substances. (Rev: HBG 10/01; SLJ 7/01) [362.29]

Bionics and Transplants

20449 Beecroft, Simon. *Super Humans: A Beginner's Guide to Bionics* (5–7). Illus. by Ian Thompson and Stephen Sweet. Series: Future Files. 1998, Millbrook LB $23.40 (978-0-7613-0621-4). This work explores such futuristic topics as cloning humans, gene manipulation, electronic body parts, and life extension. (Rev: HBG 10/98; SLJ 10/98) [617.9]

20450 Fullick, Ann. *Rebuilding the Body* (5–8). Illus. Series: Science at the Edge. 2002, Heinemann LB $27.86 (978-1-58810-700-8). 64pp. An insightful volume about transplant procedures, including a section on how the organs of the body function and a discussion about ethics. (Rev: BL 10/15/02; HBG 3/03; SLJ 4/03) [617.9]

20451 Jango-Cohen, Judith. *Bionics* (4–6). 2006, Lerner LB $26.60 (978-0-8225-5937-5). 48pp. Covers the topic of bionics and how mechanical parts can replace human parts and can help the senses. (Rev: SLJ 3/07) [617]

20452 Rosaler, Maxine. *Bionics* (5–9). Series: Science on the Edge. 2003, Gale LB $24.95 (978-1-56711-784-4). 48pp. This account explores the science of fusing artificial parts with human parts to aid body functions and comments on the controversy surround this new science. (Rev: BL 10/15/03; SLJ 3/04) [174]

Disabilities, Physical and Mental

20453 Abeel, Samantha. *What Once Was White* (5–8). Illus. by Charles R. Murphy. 1993, Village $19.95 (978-0-941653-13-8). The author is a 13-year-old learning-disabled student who can't tell time but writes sensitive interpretations of a group of watercolor paintings. (Rev: SLJ 9/93*) [618.62]

20454 Baldwin, Carol. *Autism* (4–6). Illus. Series: Health Matters. 2002, Heinemann LB $24.22 (978-1-4034-0250-9). 32pp. Examines the causes and symptoms of autism and offers an inspiring profile of Scottish artist Richard Wawro, who has become world-famous despite his autism. (Rev: HBG 10/03; SLJ 5/03) [616.8]

20455 Bardhan-Quallen, Sudipta. *Autism* (3–6). Series: Understanding Diseases and Disorders. 2005, Gale LB $26.20 (978-0-7377-2167-6). 48pp. A well-presented look at the symptoms, diagnosis, treatment, and research relating to autism. (Rev: SLJ 8/05) [616.8]

20456 Cain, Barbara. *Autism, the Invisible Cord: A Sibling's Diary* (4–7). 2012, Magination $14.95 (978-143381191-3); paper $9.95 (978-14338119-2-0). 96pp. Fourteen-year-old Jenny describes her experiences with her autistic 11-year-old brother Ezra in this fictional story that is classified as nonfiction and includes pages of tips for siblings. (Rev: BL 11/15/12; SLJ 1/13) [618.92]

20457 Dendy, Chris A. Zeigler, and Alex Zeigler. *A Bird's-Eye View of Life with ADD and ADHD: Advice from Young Survivors* (5–9). 2003, Cherish the Children paper $19.95 (978-0-9679911-3-9). A guide to ADD and ADHD, written by a dozen teenagers with these disorders with the aim of helping others cope, with advice on succeeding in school, medication, driving, and so forth. (Rev: SLJ 4/04) [618.9]

20458 Dwight, Laura. *Brothers and Sisters* (K–3). Photos by author. 2005, Star Bright $15.95 (978-1-887734-80-6). Stories of children's lives with disabilities are told by siblings of the impaired and in some cases by the impaired children themselves. (Rev: SLJ 11/05)

20459 Fisher, Gary L., and Rhoda Woods Cummings. *The Survival Guide for Kids with LD (Learning Differences)* (5–8). 1990, Free Spirit paper $9.95 (978-0-915793-18-1). A book that explains various kinds of learning disabilities and how to cope with them. (Rev: BL 7/90; SLJ 6/90) [371.9]

20460 Giacobello, John. *Everything You Need to Know About Anxiety and Panic Attacks* (5–9). Series: Need to Know Library. 2000, Rosen LB $27.95 (978-0-8239-3219-1). This book explains anxiety attacks' causes, symptoms, and treatments in a reassuring tone. (Rev: SLJ 1/01) [616]

20461 Gray, Shirley W. *Good Mental Health* (2–4). Illus. Series: Living Well. 2003, Child's World LB $27.07 (978-1-59296-082-8). 32pp. Worry, stress, depression, and other mental problems are discussed. (Rev: SLJ 2/04) [616.89]

20462 Heelan, Jamee Riggio. *Can You Hear a Rainbow? The Story of a Deaf Boy Named Chris* (K–3). Illus. by Nicola Simmonds. 2002, Peachtree $14.95 (978-1-56145-268-2). Chris tells the reader how sign language and other aids help him to cope with his deafness. (Rev: HBG 10/02; SLJ 9/02) [362.42]

20463 Heelan, Jamee Riggio. *The Making of My Special Hand: Madison's Story* (PS–3). Photos by author. Illus. by Nicola Simmonds. 2000, Peachtree $14.95 (978-1-56145-186-9). Described the process of making a prosthesis for a girl who was born with one hand, from taking a plaster cast to connecting the electrode and battery and giving occupational therapy. (Rev: BL 4/1/00; HBG 3/01; SLJ 9/00) [617.5]

20464 Heelan, Jamee Riggio. *Rolling Along: The Story of Taylor and His Wheelchair* (PS–4). Illus. by Nicola Simmonds. 2000, Peachtree $14.95 (978-1-56145-219-4). 32pp. The true story of Taylor, who was born with cerebral palsy and uses a wheelchair. (Rev: BL 9/1/00; HBG 3/01; SLJ 12/00) [616.6]

20465 Kent, Deborah. *What Is Sign Language?* (3–5). Illus. Series: Overcoming Barriers. 2012, Enslow LB $23.93 (978-076603771-7). 48pp. This accessible book starts with a real-life story of sign language's applications before delving into the technology's history, invention, and modern use. Also in this series: *What Is Braille?*, *What Is it Like to Be Blind?*, and *What Is It Like to Be Deaf?* (all 2012). e (Rev: BL 8/12; LMC 1–2/13) [419]

20466 Kent, Susan. *Let's Talk About Stuttering* (3–5). Series: Let's Talk. 2000, Rosen LB $19.95 (978-0-8239-5423-0). 24pp. As well as explaining what causes stuttering and who is most likely to stutter, this book tells how to deal with teasing and how to get help. (Rev: SLJ 2/01) [616.85]

20467 Landau, Elaine. *Dyslexia* (3–6). Series: Life Balance. 2004, Watts LB $20.50 (978-0-531-12217-4). 79pp. An informative and practical guide that describes dyslexia and talks about ways to cope with the problem, mentioning famous people who have dealt with this "learning difference." (Rev: SLJ 7/04) [616.85]

20468 Landau, Elaine. *Schizophrenia* (4–8). Illus. Series: Life Balance. 2004, Watts LB $20.50 (978-0-531-12215-0); paper $6.95 (978-0-531-16614-7). 80pp. An overview of the causes, symptoms, and treatment of this mental condition, with true stories of sufferers. (Rev: BL 10/15/03)

20469 Lennard-Brown, Sarah. *Autism* (5–8). Illus. Series: Health Issues. 2003, Raintree LB $28.56 (978-0-7398-6422-7). 64pp. An in-depth introduction to autism, with attention to the difficulties people with autism face and what is being done to help them. (Rev: SLJ 5/04) [616.89]

20470 Levete, Sarah. *Learning Difficulties* (3–5). Series: Let's Talk About. 2007, Stargazer LB $27.10 (978-1-59604-089-2). 32pp. Dyslexia, autism, and ADHD are explained for elementary students who may know others with these conditions or have them themselves. Basic information and an airy design combine for a good introduction. (Rev: SLJ 6/07)

20471 McCully, Emily Arnold. *My Heart Glow: Alice Cogswell, Thomas Gallaudet and the Birth of American Sign Language* (1–3). Illus. by author. 2008, Hyperion $15.99 (978-1-4231-0028-7). 40pp. Alice Cogswell, who became deaf after suffering spotted fever, inspired neighbor Thomas Gallaudet to investigate methods of educating the deaf; imagined dialogue is intermingled with quotations and historical material. (Rev: BCCB 9/08; BL 6/1–15/08; HB 7/08; LMC 5/08; SLJ 7/08) [370]

20472 McMahon, Patricia. *Dancing Wheels* (3–7). Illus. 2000, Houghton $16.00 (978-0-395-88889-6). 48pp. Founded by a woman born with spina bifida, the Dancing Wheels project teaches people to "dance" from their wheelchairs. (Rev: BL 10/1/00; HBG 3/01; SLJ 11/00) [792.8]

20473 Moore-Mallinos, Jennifer. *It's OK to Be Me!* (K–3). Illus. by Marta Fàbrega. Series: Live and Learn. 2007, Barron's paper $6.99 (978-0-7641-3584-2). 32pp. A wheelchair-bound boy who feels isolated at school eventually makes the basketball team. (Rev: BL 5/15/07) [306.8]

20474 Pigache, Philippa. *ADHD* (4–8). Series: Just the Facts. 2004, Heinemann LB $27.07 (978-1-4034-5142-2). 56pp. The symptoms, causes, and treatment of attention deficit hyperactivity disorder are described, with discussion of continuing research. (Rev: SLJ 5/05)

20475 Quinn, Patricia O. *Attention, Girls! A Guide to Learn All About Your AD/HD* (3–8). Illus. by Carl Pearce. 2009, Magination $16.95 (978-1-4338-0447-2); paper $12.95 (978-1-4338-0448-9). 128pp. A readable, girl-centered look at ADHD with advice and tips from the author who is a physician living with ADHD. (Rev: BL 7/09; SLJ 10/09) [618.92]

20476 Rashkin, Rachel. *Feeling Better: A Kid's Book About Therapy* (4–8). Illus. by Bonnie Adamson. 2005, Magination paper $9.95 (978-1-59147-238-4). Present-ed in journal format, this volume uses 12-year-old Maya's experiences with a therapist to offer useful insights into the process and its value. (Rev: SLJ 11/05) [618.92]

20477 Resh, Kimberly, ed. *Our Friend Mikayla* (K–3). Illus. 2007, Bubel/Aiken Foundation $14.95 (978-1-4243-0734-0). 48pp. School children describe the experience of slowly welcoming Mikayla into their classroom and helping her to enjoy school despite her many disabilities. (Rev: SLJ 6/07)

20478 Riggs, Stephanie. *Never Sell Yourself Short* (3–6). Illus. 2001, Whitman $16.99 (978-0-8075-5563-7). 32pp. Through text and photographs, readers learn how Josh, a 14-year-old dwarf, enjoys his life despite obstacles. (Rev: BCCB 1/02; BL 9/1/01; HBG 3/02; SLJ 11/01) [618.92]

20479 Rissman, Rebecca. *We All Move* (PS–K). Illus. Series: Disabilities and Differences. 2009, Heinemann LB $14.50 (978-1-4329-2150-7). 24pp. Introduces physical and mental differences and looks at the ways in which people cope with various disabilities. (Rev: BL 4/1/09) [612]

20480 Rosenberg, Marsha Sarah. *Everything You Need to Know When a Brother or Sister Is Autistic* (5–9). Series: Need to Know Library. 2000, Rosen LB $27.95 (978-0-8239-3123-1). Autism is defined and described, with material on its diagnosis and treatment plus coverage of how this condition can affect other members of the family. (Rev: SLJ 8/00) [616.8]

20481 Rotner, Shelley, and Sheila Kelly. *The A.D.D. Book for Kids* (K–3). Illus. 2000, Millbrook LB $22.90 (978-0-7613-1722-7). 32pp. This photo-essay describes attention deficit disorder and its various symptoms and coping mechanisms. (Rev: BL 4/15/00; HBG 9/00; SLJ 7/00) [618.9]

20482 Sanders, Pete, and Steve Myers. *Dyslexia* (4–8). Illus. by Mike Lacy and Liz Sawyer. Series: What Do You Know About. 1999, Millbrook LB $23.90 (978-0-7613-0915-4). Using a case study, this book explores one boy's problems with dyslexia, its causes, symptoms, and treatment. (Rev: HBG 10/99; SLJ 10/99) [617.7]

20483 Shapiro, Ouisie. *Autism and Me: Sibling Stories* (3–6). Illus. by Steven Vote. 2009, Albert Whitman $16.99 (978-0-8075-0487-1). 32pp. Young siblings with brothers and sisters who have autism express the frustrations and rewards they feel. (Rev: BL 3/15/09; SLJ 5/09) [618.92]

20484 Silverstein, Alvin, et al. *Scoliosis* (3–5). Series: My Health. 2002, Watts LB $25.50 (978-0-531-12046-0); paper $6.95 (978-0-531-16639-0). 48pp. The causes of this abnormal curvature of the spine are covered with material on how it affects young people and how it can be treated. (Rev: BL 12/15/02) [616]

20485 Stefanski, Daniel. *How to Talk to an Autistic Kid* (2–6). Illus. 2011, Free Spirit $12.99 (978-1-57542-365-4). 48pp. Stefanski, an autistic 14-year-old, offers an insider's take on what it's like to have autism, and how others can make those with the affliction feel included and accepted. (Rev: BL 4/15/11; SLJ 6/11) [618.92]

20486 Taylor, John F. *The Survival Guide for Kids with ADD or ADHD* (3–5). Illus. by Tad Herr. 2006, Free Spirit paper $13.95 (978-1-57542-195-7). 119pp. This child-friendly guide to coping with ADD/ADHD offers information and advice on such topics as making friends, success at school, medications, eating sensibly, and so forth. (Rev: SLJ 12/06) [618.92]

20487 Thornton, Denise. *Physical Disabilities: The Ultimate Teen Guide* (5–10). Series: It Happened to Me. 2007, Scarecrow $42.00 (978-0-8108-5300-3). In interviews, teens with disabilities describe how they cope at school, with technology and tools, getting around, sports, and so forth. (Rev: SLJ 10/07) [362.40835]

20488 Trueit, Trudi. *ADHD* (3–6). Illus. Series: Life Balance. 2004, Watts LB $20.50 (978-0-531-12261-7). 79pp. Trueit looks at the learning and behavioral problems faced by children — and adults — who suffer from the disorder and discusses some of the more popular methods of treatment. (Rev: SLJ 7/04) [618.92]

20489 Verdick, Elizabeth, and Elizabeth Reeve. *The Survival Guide for Kids with Autism Spectrum Disorders (and Their Parents)* (4–8). Illus. by Nick Kobyluch. 2012, Free Spirit paper $16.99 (978-15754238-5-2). 240pp. This straightforward book provides background information on autism and famous people who have suffered from autism, and gives guidance on improving life at home and at school. (Rev: BL 4/15/12; SLJ 5/1/12; VOYA 6/12) [618.92]

20490 Wiltshire, Paula. *Dyslexia* (5–8). Illus. Series: Health Issues. 2002, Raintree LB $28.54 (978-0-7398-5221-7). 64pp. Color photographs and straightforward text introduce dyslexia's symptoms and treatment and explain how it affects learning, with tips on how to cope with the disability. (Rev: BL 12/15/02; HBG 3/03; SLJ 3/03) [616.85]

20491 Zucker, Faye. *Depression* (4–8). Series: Life Balance. 2003, Watts LB $20.50 (978-0-531-12259-4); paper $6.95 (978-0-531-15578-3). 80pp. This friendly, reassuring introduction explains the causes, diagnosis, and treatment of depression. (Rev: BL 10/15/03; SLJ 12/03) [616.85]

Disease and Illness

20492 Abrams, Liesa. *Chronic Fatigue Syndrome* (5–7). Series: Diseases and Disorders. 2003, Gale LB $32.45 (978-1-59018-039-6). The symptoms of and treatments for this mysterious condition and related medical problems are covered here, along with the research being undertaken. (Rev: SLJ 7/03) [616]

20493 Ali, Rasheda. *I'll Hold Your Hand So You Won't Fall: A Child's Guide to Parkinson's Disease* (2–4). Illus. 2005, Merit $19.95 (978-1-873413-13-5). 40pp. Rasheda Ali, daughter of Muhammad Ali, describes the disease that afflicts her father and its debilitating symptoms. (Rev: SLJ 10/05) [616.8]

20494 Anderson, Judith. *Fighting Disease* (4–7). Series: Working for Our Future. 2010, Black Rabbit LB $28.50 (978-1-59771-194-4). 32pp. This volume explains why the United Nations chose fighting disease as one of its eight Millennium Development goals and looks at the various reasons why people are deprived of good medical care and what can be done to improve the situation. (Rev: BL 6/10; LMC 10/10; SLJ 4/10) [362.196]

20495 Anonymous. *Quicksand: HIV/AIDS In Our Lives* (4–7). 2009, Candlewick $16.99 (978-076361589-5). 112pp. Part Q&A, part memoir, this book provides frank and supportive information about HIV/AIDS, dispelling myths in an age-appropriate manner. (Rev: BL 12/1/09; LMC 11–12/09; SLJ 11/09) [616.97]

20496 Baldwin, Carol. *Asthma* (4–6). Illus. Series: Health Matters. 2002, Heinemann LB $24.22 (978-1-4034-0248-6). 32pp. Examines the causes and symptoms of asthma and offers an inspiring profile of Olympic gold medalist Jackie Joyner-Kersee. (Rev: HBG 10/03; SLJ 5/03) [616.2]

20497 Baldwin, Carol. *Sickle Cell Disease* (4–6). Illus. Series: Health Matters. 2002, Heinemann LB $22.79 (978-1-4034-0252-3). 32pp. Examines the causes and symptoms of this disease and describes the condition of Rev. Jesse Jackson, who carries the genetic trait for this disease. (Rev: HBG 10/03; SLJ 5/03) [616.1]

20498 Ballard, Carol. *AIDS and Other Epidemics* (5–8). Illus. Series: What If We Do Nothing? 2009, Gareth Stevens LB $31.00 (978-1-4339-0085-3). 48pp. HIV/AIDS, SARS, and malaria are among the diseases addressed in this volume that looks at the past, the current status, and the future outlook. (Rev: BL 4/15/09; SLJ 6/09) [614.5]

20499 Bardhan-Quallen, Sudipta. *AIDS* (4–6). Illus. Series: Understanding Diseases and Disorders. 2005, Gale LB $26.20 (978-0-7377-2638-1). 48pp. This overview of HIV/AIDS examines the virus and its symptoms, diagnosis, and treatment; also covered are research and availability of medication in the Third World; full-color photographs and quotations from young patients add to the succinct text. (Rev: BL 7/05; SLJ 8/05) [616.97]

20500 Barnard, Bryn. *Outbreak! Plagues That Changed History* (5–8). Illus. by author. 2005, Crown LB $19.99 (978-0-375-92986-1). Information on microbes and the study of microorganisms precedes details of specific epidemics. (Rev: SLJ 2/06) [614.4]

20501 Beccia, Carlyn. *I Feel Better with a Frog in My Throat: History's Strangest Cures* (1–4). Illus. by author. 2010, Houghton Mifflin $17 (978-0-547-22570-8). 48pp. This guide to folk remedies offers readers the challenge of deciding which possible cure *really* works, with answers revealed at the end of the book. (Rev: BL 10/1/10; LMC 5–6/11; SLJ 11/1/10) [615.8]

20502 Bjorklund, Ruth. *Asthma* (4–7). Series: Health Alert. 2004, Benchmark LB $28.50 (978-0-7614-1803-0). In addition to describing the causes and treatment of asthma, this attractive title opens with a case history and also includes lists of famous people who suffer from the condition. (Rev: SLJ 5/05)

20503 Bjorklund, Ruth. *Food-Borne Illnesses* (4–7). Series: Health Alert. 2005, Marshall Cavendish LB $19.95 (978-0-7614-1917-4). This is a wide-ranging exploration of illnesses that can be caused by contaminated food — including those resulting from bacteria, poor hygiene, poor handling, and terrorism — and the treatments and preventions available. (Rev: SLJ 6/06) [615.9]

20504 Bowman-Kruhm, Mary. *Everything You Need to Know About Down Syndrome* (4–7). Series: Need to Know Library. 2000, Rosen LB $25.25 (978-0-8239-2949-8). Describes the causes, symptoms, and treatment of Down syndrome, and looks at the education and family life of individuals with this condition. (Rev: HBG 10/00; SLJ 3/00) [362.1]

20505 Bridge, Chris. *Andrew's Story: A Book About a Boy Who Beat Cancer* (2–4). Illus. 2001, Lerner LB $21.27 (978-0-8225-2587-5). 32pp. A straightforward account of a boy's battle with cancer written in a 9-year-old's voice. (Rev: BL 1/1–15/02; HBG 3/02; SLJ 12/01) [362.1]

20506 Brill, Marlene Targ. *Alzheimer's Disease* (4–7). Series: Health Alert. 2004, Benchmark LB $28.50 (978-0-7614-1799-6). In addition to describing the diagnosis and treatment of Alzheimer's disease, this attractive title opens with a case history and also includes lists of famous people who suffer from the condition. (Rev: SLJ 5/05) [362.19]

20507 Bryan, Jenny. *Asthma* (5–10). Illus. Series: Just the Facts. 2004, Heinemann LB $27.07 (978-1-4034-4599-5). 56pp. A well-organized explanation of asthma, illustrated with numerous color photographs and providing material on how air pollution and smoking are factors in causing or aggravating the disease. (Rev: SLJ 6/04) [616.2]

20508 Bryan, Jenny. *Diabetes* (5–10). Illus. Series: Just the Facts. 2004, Heinemann LB $27.07 (978-1-4034-4600-8). 56pp. An illustrated overview of the disease, including causes and treatments and the effects of diet and cultural factors. (Rev: SLJ 6/04) [616.4]

20509 Bueche, Shelley. *The Ebola Virus* (4–7). Series: Parasites. 2003, Gale LB $24.95 (978-0-7377-1780-8). Although it's part of the Parasites series, this book focuses on the Ebola virus, which causes an infectious illness and is found widely in Central Africa. (Rev: BL 3/1/04; SLJ 6/04) [616.9]

20510 Burnfield, Alexander. *Multiple Sclerosis* (5–8). Series: Just the Facts. 2004, Heinemann LB $27.07 (978-1-4034-4602-2). 56pp. An accessible explanation of multiple sclerosis, its symptoms, treatment, and the efforts being made to find new treatments and a cure. (Rev: SLJ 6/04) [616.8]

20511 Butler, Dori. *My Grandpa Had a Stroke* (K–2). Illus. by Nicole Wong. 2007, Magination $14.95 (978-1-59147-806-5); paper $8.95 (978-1-59147-807-2). 32pp. Ryan's safe world is shaken when his grandfather has a stroke and moves to Ryan's house, but the young boy

finds a way for the two to continue their fishing expeditions; this informative story conveys lots of information about strokes and depicts the young boy's fears. (Rev: BL 7/07; SLJ 7/07) [616.8]

20512 Carter, Alden R. *I'm Tougher than Diabetes!* (2–4). Illus. 2001, Whitman $16.99 (978-0-8075-1572-3). 32pp. A first-person account from the perspective of a pre-teen girl about the management of Type 1 diabetes, with color photographs and frequently asked questions. (Rev: BL 1/1–15/02; HBG 3/02; SLJ 5/02) [616.4]

20513 Casil, Amy Sterling. *Hantavirus* (4–6). Series: Epidemics. 2005, Rosen LB $27.95 (978-1-4042-0254-2). 64pp. Casil offers basic information, suitable for report writers, about the discovery of this virus; its carriers, symptoms, and prevention; outbreaks; and any dangers of its use in bioterrorism. (Rev: SLJ 10/05) [616.9]

20514 Cefrey, Holly. *Syphilis and Other Sexually Transmitted Diseases* (5–8). Series: Epidemics. 2001, Rosen LB $27.95 (978-0-8239-3488-1). Cefrey describes historic outbreaks and treatments, as well as the symptoms and cure, of syphilis and other sexually transmitted diseases. (Rev: BL 3/15/02) [616.95]

20515 Cefrey, Holly. *Yellow Fever* (5–8). Series: Epidemics. 2002, Rosen LB $27.95 (978-0-8239-3489-8). Yellow fever, spread by mosquitoes, was the cause of several epidemics in American cities during the 19th century before a cure was found by dedicated doctors who risked their lives. (Rev: BL 8/02) [616]

20516 Chilman-Blair, Kim, and John Taddeo. *Medikidz Explain HIV* (5–8). Series: Superheroes on a Medical Mission. 2010, Rosen LB $29.25 (978-143589458-7). 40pp. Using cartoon illustrations and a graphic novel format, this volume — and the Medikidz superheroes — explain the HIV virus and its dangers. Also use *Medikidz Explain Swine Flu, Medikidz Explain Depression,* and *Medikidz Explain Sleep Apnea* (all 2010). (Rev: BL 3/15/11; SLJ 5/1/11) [614.5]

20517 Chilman-Blair, Kim, and John Taddeo. *What's Up with Ella? Medikidz Explain Diabetes* (4–6). Illus. Series: Superheroes on a Medical Mission. 2010, Rosen LB $29.95 (978-143583538-2). 40pp. A young girl is taken on a tour of the pancreas in this light, superhero-inspired take on type 1 diabetes. (Rev: BL 3/15/10; LMC 10/10) [618.92]

20518 Chilman-Blair, Kim, and John Taddeo. *What's Up with Max? Medikidz Explain Asthma* (4–7). Series: Superheroes on a Medical Mission. 2010, Rosen LB $29.25 (978-1-4358-3534-4). 40pp. Multicultural young "superheroes" explain about asthma and its treatment and show readers around the relevant parts of the body. Also use *What's Up with Pam? Medikidz Explain Childhood Obesity, What's Up with Paulina? Medikidz Explain Food Allergies,* and *What's Up with Sean? Medikidz Explain Scoliosis* (all 2010) (Rev: LMC 10/10) [616.2]

20519 Cunningham, Kevin. *Pandemics* (3–5). Illus. Series: A True Book: Disasters. 2011, Scholastic LB $28 (978-053125423-3); paper $6.95 (978-053126628-1).

48pp. With statistics and Web resources, this volume covers everything from influenza to smallpox, cholera, and plague. (Rev: BL 11/15/11) [614.4]

20520 Davies, Nicola. *What's Eating You? Parasites — The Inside Story* (4–6). Illus. by Neal Layton. 2007, Candlewick $12.99 (978-0-7636-3460-5). 62pp. Fleas, lice, tapeworms, and other parasites are described in this book, which provides details about their life cycle and "host"/habitat. (Rev: BCCB 1/08; BL 12/1/07; HB 1/08; LMC 5/08; SLJ 3/08) [591.6]

20521 DerKazarian, Susan. *You Have Head Lice!* (PS–2). Illus. Series: Rookie Read-About Health. 2005, Children's Pr. LB $20.50 (978-0-516-25879-9); paper $5.95 (978-0-516-27920-6). 32pp. A small-format, matter-of-fact look at head lice and their transmission and treatment. (Rev: BL 6/1–15/05) [616.5]

20522 DiConsiglio, John. *When Birds Get Flu and Cows Go Mad!* (5–7). Illus. Series: 24/7 Science Behind the Scenes: Medical Files. 2007, Scholastic LB $26.00 (978-0-531-12069-9); paper $7.95 (978-0-531-17528-6). 64pp. A lively discussion of bird flu, mad cow disease, E. coli bacteria, and other food-borne and headline-grabbing illnesses. (Rev: BL 12/1/07; LMC 3/08) [616.9]

20523 Donnellan, William L. *The Miracle of Immunity* (5–8). Illus. Series: The Story of Science. 2002, Benchmark LB $29.93 (978-0-7614-1425-4). 79pp. A history of mankind's discoveries about diseases and about the body's vulnerabilities and abilities to fend off infections, from the earliest times through AIDS. (Rev: HBG 3/03; LMC 5/03; SLJ 5/03) [616.07]

20524 Donnelly, Karen. *Everything You Need to Know About Lyme Disease* (5–8). Series: Need to Know Library. 2000, Rosen LB $27.95 (978-0-8239-3216-0). This book explains how Lyme disease was discovered, how it is transmitted, its symptoms, and its treatments. (Rev: BL 12/1/00) [616.9]

20525 Donnelly, Karen. *Leprosy (Hansen's Disease)* (5–8). Series: Epidemics. 2002, Rosen LB $27.95 (978-0-8239-3498-0). This is the story of leprosy, the disease that created social outcasts of its victims, and of a man named Hansen who discovered an effective treatment. (Rev: BL 8/02) [616.9]

20526 Draper, Allison Stark. *Ebola* (5–8). Illus. Series: Epidemics. 2002, Rosen LB $27.95 (978-0-8239-3496-6). 64pp. Discusses the Ebola virus in both scientific and human terms. Also use *Mad Cow Disease* (2002). (Rev: BL 8/02; SLJ 6/02) [616.9]

20527 Faulk, Michelle. *The Case of the Flesh-Eating Bacteria: Annie Biotica Solves Skin Disease Crimes* (5–8). Illus. 2012, Enslow LB $23.93 (978-076603945-2). 48pp. Pinkeye, ringworm, chicken pox, and measles are all mentioned in this review of skin-related ailments. (Rev: BL 4/1/13; LMC 8–9/13) [616.5]

20528 Favor, Lesli J. *Bacteria* (5–8). Illus. Series: Germs: The Library of Disease-Causing Organisms. 2004, Rosen LB $26.50 (978-0-8239-4491-0). 48pp. An informative, illustrated discussion of bacteria, covering their

discovery, how they survive, and the dangers they pose to humans. (Rev: SLJ 1/05) [616]

20529 Foley, Ronan. *World Health: The Impact on Our Lives* (5–8). Series: 21st Century Debates. 2003, Raintree LB $28.56 (978-0-7398-5507-2). A thorough and thought-provoking exploration of the health status of countries around the world and the reasons for the wide disparity between wealthy and poor nations. (Rev: BL 8/03; HBG 10/03; SLJ 7/03) [362.1]

20530 Getz, David. *Purple Death: The Mysterious Flu of 1918* (3–5). Illus. 2000, Holt $16.00 (978-0-8050-5751-5). 86pp. This account describes the deadliest six months in human history — the 1918 flu epidemic that infected 2 billion people. (Rev: BCCB 12/00; BL 12/1/00; HBG 3/01; SLJ 2/01) [614.5]

20531 Gillie, Oliver. *Cancer* (5–8). Series: Just the Facts. 2004, Heinemann LB $27.07 (978-1-4034-5144-6). 56pp. Provides accessible explanations of cancer itself, plus the symptoms, diagnosis, and surgery, chemotherapy, and radiation involved in its treatment. (Rev: SLJ 2/05) [616.99]

20532 Gillie, Oliver. *Sickle Cell Disease* (5–8). Series: Just the Facts. 2004, Heinemann LB $27.07 (978-1-4034-4603-9). 56pp. An examination of sickle cell anemia presented in an accessible style, with coverage of symptoms, treatment, and research. (Rev: SLJ 6/04) [616.1]

20533 Gilman, Laura Anne. *Coping with Cerebral Palsy* (5–9). Series: Coping. 2001, Rosen LB $31.95 (978-0-8239-3150-7). This is a self-help book that looks at ways to deal with school, work, and travel as well as coping with other people and their attitudes. (Rev: SLJ 2/02) [616.836]

20534 Glaser, Jason. *Chicken Pox* (1–3). Series: First Facts: Health Matters. 2005, Capstone LB $21.26 (978-0-7368-4288-4). 24pp. Basic information on the causes, symptoms, and treatment of chickenpox is presented in simple text. Also use *Flu* and *Pinkeye* (both 2005). (Rev: SLJ 12/05) [618.92]

20535 Gold, Susan Dudley. *Attention Deficit Disorder* (4–8). Series: Health Watch. 2000, Enslow LB $23.93 (978-0-7660-1657-6). 48pp. This account focuses on one boy from childhood to college and how he coped with attention deficit disorder. Several young people are profiled in the companion volume *Bipolar Disorder and Depression* (2000). (Rev: HBG 10/01; SLJ 2/01) [618.92]

20536 Gold, Susan Dudley. *Sickle Cell Disease* (4–7). Illus. Series: Health Watch. 2001, Enslow LB $23.93 (978-0-7660-1662-0). 48pp. Readers are introduced to the symptoms and treatment of this disease through the true story of a young African American boy called Keone who received a successful stem-cell transplant. (Rev: HBG 3/02; SLJ 12/01) [616.1]

20537 Goldstein, Margaret J. *Everything You Need to Know About Multiple Sclerosis* (5–8). Series: Need to Know Library. 2001, Rosen LB $27.95 (978-0-8239-3292-4). An introduction to multiple sclerosis, its symptoms and treatment, and how it affects the nervous system, along with information on the importance of treating the emotional impact of this disease. (Rev: SLJ 5/01) [616]

20538 Gordon, Sherri Mabry. *Peanut Butter, Milk, and Other Deadly Threats: What You Should Know About Food Allergies* (5–9). Series: Issues in Focus Today. 2006, Enslow LB $31.93 (978-0-7660-2529-5). 112pp. This information-packed survey of food allergies identifies common culprit foods, explains the mechanics of allergic reactions, and also reports on medical research to find better treatments. (Rev: SLJ 11/06) [616.97]

20539 Gray, Susan H. *Living with Cystic Fibrosis* (3–5). Series: Living Well. 2002, Child's World LB $27.07 (978-1-56766-105-7). 32pp. The nature of cystic fibrosis is discussed with details on how it affects the body, its causes, and how to live with it, plus anecdotes from people who suffer from the illness. Also use *Living with Cerebral Palsy* (2002). (Rev: BL 10/15/02) [616]

20540 Gray, Susan H. *Living with Juvenile Rheumatoid Arthritis* (3–5). Illus. Series: Living Well. 2002, Child's World LB $27.07 (978-1-56766-104-0). 32pp. First-hand accounts from children with juvenile rheumatoid arthritis enhance the information on the disease, from diagnosis to treatment. (Rev: BL 10/15/02; SLJ 3/03) [618.92]

20541 Grossberg, Blythe. *Asperger's Rules! How to Make Sense of School and Friends* (5–8). 2012, Magination $14.95 (978-1-4338-1128-9); paper $9.95 (978-1-4338-1-127-2). 128pp. This helpful guide offers a selection of formats for young people interested in learning more about dealing with Asperger's, offering bulleted lists, quizzes, sample dialogues, multiple-choice and other tests, advice on body language, tips on making friends and coping with bullies, and so forth. (Rev: BL 8/12; SLJ 10/12) [618.92]

20542 Haney, Johannah. *Juvenile Diabetes* (4–7). Illus. Series: Health Alert. 2004, Benchmark LB $28.50 (978-0-7614-1798-9). 63pp. In addition to describing the treatment and possible complications of juvenile diabetes, this attractive title opens with a case history and also includes lists of famous people who suffer from the condition. (Rev: SLJ 5/05)

20543 Hawkins, Trisha. *Everything You Need to Know About Measles and Rubella* (4–8). Series: Need to Know Library. 2001, Rosen LB $27.95 (978-0-8239-3322-8). Simple text and photographs describe the diseases and methods of prevention and treatment, and discuss public-health issues. Also use *Everything You Need to Know About Chicken Pox and Shingles* (2001). (Rev: SLJ 8/01) [616.9]

20544 Hayhurst, Chris. *Cholera* (5–9). Series: Epidemics. 2001, Rosen LB $27.95 (978-0-8239-3345-7). In a readable style, Hayhurst discusses the history of cholera, formerly a deadly disease, and explains how its treatment was developed. Also use *Polio* and *Smallpox* (both 2001). (Rev: SLJ 7/01) [616.9]

20545 Hayhurst, Chris. *E. Coli* (4–7). Series: Epidemics. 2004, Rosen LB $27.95 (978-0-8239-4201-5). 64pp. A look at the transmission, treatment, and prevention of this bacterium, with an emphasis on the importance of washing hands and food before eating. (Rev: SLJ 8/04) [616.9]

20546 Hicks, Terry Allan. *Allergies* (4–8). Series: Health Alert. 2005, Benchmark LB $19.95 (978-0-7614-1918-1). All about what allergies are, what brings them on, and how they are treated, with colorful sidebars and features that add to the text. (Rev: SLJ 5/06) [616.97]

20547 Hirschmann, Kris. *Salmonella* (4–7). Series: Parasites. 2003, Gale LB $24.95 (978-0-7377-1785-3). This fascinating examination of Salmonella bacteria, responsible for a wide variety of illnesses in the United States and elsewhere, is supplemented with numerous photos and microscopic views of the title bacteria. (Rev: BL 3/1/04) [615.4]

20548 Hoffmann, Gretchen. *Mononucleosis* (4–8). Series: Health Alert. 2005, Benchmark LB $19.95 (978-0-7614-1915-0). All about what "mono" is, its symptoms, and its treatment, with graphic features that add to the text. (Rev: SLJ 5/06) [616.9]

20549 Hyde, Margaret O., and Elizabeth Forsyth. *Diabetes* (4–7). Illus. 2003, Watts LB $26.00 (978-0-531-12209-9). 96pp. Case studies of young people add to the easy-to-understand coverage of the disease, its different types, causes, symptoms, and popular methods of treatment. (Rev: SLJ 2/04) [616.4]

20550 Isle, Mick. *Everything You Need to Know About Food Poisoning* (4–8). Series: Need to Know Library. 2001, Rosen LB $27.95 (978-0-8239-3396-9). Safe ways to prepare food are the main focus of this book, which also describes the symptoms and treatment of food poisoning. (Rev: SLJ 10/01) [615.954]

20551 Jurmain, Suzanne. *The Secret of the Yellow Death: A True Story of Medical Sleuthing* (5–8). 2009, Houghton Mifflin $19 (978-0-618-96581-6). 112pp. As compelling as good fiction, this well-illustrated true story chronicles the fascinating methods used by scientists to discover the cause of yellow fever. (Rev: BL 9/15/09; HB 11–12/09; LMC 1–2/10; SLJ 9/09) [614.5]

20552 Kahn, Ada P., and Ronald M. Doctor. *Phobias* (4–8). Series: Life Balance. 2003, Watts LB $20.50 (978-0-531-12256-3); paper $6.95 (978-0-531-15575-2). 80pp. This book discusses the causes of phobias, the different types, how they affect people, and their treatment. (Rev: BL 10/15/03) [616.85]

20553 Lamb, Kirsten. *Cancer* (5–8). Series: Health Issues. 2002, Raintree LB $28.54 (978-0-7398-5219-4). 64pp. An informative account that covers various kinds of cancer, giving real-life stories, and also deals with issues and choices facing teens today. (Rev: BL 12/15/02; HBG 3/03; SLJ 3/03) [616.99]

20554 Landau, Elaine. *Allergies* (4–7). Series: Understanding Illness. 1994, Twenty-First Century LB $24.90 (978-0-8050-2989-5). After a case history that explores allergies in personal terms, an objective presentation is given of their causes, effects, and treatment. (Rev: BL 12/15/94; SLJ 2/95) [616.97]

20555 Landau, Elaine. *Cancer* (4–7). Series: Understanding Illness. 1994, Twenty-First Century LB $24.90 (978-0-8050-2990-1). This book explains the many types of cancer, their causes, present-day treatments, and possible developments in the future. (Rev: BL 12/15/95; SLJ 2/95) [616.99]

20556 Landau, Elaine. *Chickenpox* (1–3). Series: Head-to-Toe Health. 2009, Marshall Cavendish $19.95 (978-0-7614-3498-6). 32pp. The causes, symptoms, and experience of chickenpox are portrayed in this straightforward and useful guide. Also use *Food Allergies* (2009). (Rev: SLJ 1/1/10) [616.9]

20557 Lassieur, Allison. *Head Lice* (3–5). Illus. Series: My Health. 2000, Watts LB $25.50 (978-0-531-11624-1). 48pp. Using amazing photos taken with microscopes, this account introduces head lice, their physical characteristics, how they are transmitted, and how to get rid of them. (Rev: BL 6/1–15/00) [616.5]

20558 Lennard-Brown, Sarah. *Asthma* (5–8). Illus. Series: Health Issues. 2002, Raintree LB $28.54 (978-0-7398-5218-7). 64pp. Color photographs and straightforward text explain the symptoms, diagnosis, and treatment of asthma. (Rev: BL 12/15/02; HBG 3/03) [616.2]

20559 Levy, Joel. *Phobiapedia: All the Things We Fear the Most!* (3–6). Illus. 2011, Scholastic paper $8.99 (978-05453492-9-1). 80pp. An intriguing survey of 50-plus phobias, ranging from the well-known arachnophobia to the strange lutraphobia (fear of otters), with interesting facts about origins and etymology. (Rev: BL 12/1/11) [616.85]

20560 Lynette, Rachel. *Leprosy* (5–8). Series: Understanding Diseases and Disorders. 2005, Gale LB $26.20 (978-0-7377-3172-9). Straightforward text discusses the plight of leprosy patients around the world and through history; causes, treatments, and transmission are also discussed. (Rev: SLJ 6/06) [616.9]

20561 Margulies, Phillip. *Creutzfeldt-Jakob Disease* (4–7). Series: Epidemics. 2004, Rosen LB $27.95 (978-0-8239-4199-5). Examines the history and current state of knowledge about this rare disorder that affects the brain and is related to Mad Cow Disease. Also use *West Nile Virus* (2004). (Rev: SLJ 8/04) [616.8]

20562 Margulies, Phillip. *Diphtheria* (4–6). Series: Epidemics. 2005, Rosen LB $27.95 (978-1-4042-0253-5). 64pp. Suitable for report writers, this book covers the nature of diphtheria, important outbreaks of the disease, treatment, and efforts to prevent future epidemics. (Rev: SLJ 10/05) [616.9]

20563 Margulies, Phillip. *Everything You Need to Know About Rheumatic Fever* (5–8). Series: The Need to Know Library. 2004, Rosen LB $27.95 (978-0-8239-4509-2). After a brief history of the disease and the discovery of its cause, this volume discusses symptoms, treatment, and the concern that the disease may become more prevalent as bacteria develop resistance to antibiotics. (Rev: SLJ 4/05)

20564 Markle, Sandra. *Leukemia: True Survival Stories* (5–8). Series: Powerful Medicine. 2010, Lerner LB $27.93 (978-0-8225-8700-2). 48pp. Arresting full-color photographs, cross-sections, and personal stories are combined with facts about procedures and information about the medical personnel involved, (Rev: LMC 11–12/10) [616.99]

20565 Marrin, Albert. *Dr. Jenner and the Speckled Monster: The Search for the Smallpox Vaccine* (4–8). Illus. 2002, Dutton $19.99 (978-0-525-46922-3). 96pp. This highly readable and detailed account describes the impact of smallpox from the time of the Aztecs, major outbreaks over the years, the way the virus works, the work of Jenner in developing a vaccine, and the virus's potential as a weapon of mass destruction. (Rev: BL 11/15/02; HB 11/02; HBG 3/03; SLJ 1/03; VOYA 12/02) [614.5]

20566 Massari, Francesca. *Everything You Need to Know About Cancer* (5–9). Series: Need to Know Library. 2000, Rosen LB $27.95 (978-0-8239-3164-4). This book defines what cancer is and looks at its causes, prevention, symptoms, diagnosis, and treatment. (Rev: HBG 10/00; SLJ 8/00) [616.99]

20567 Moehn, Heather. *Everything You Need to Know When Someone You Know Has Leukemia* (5–10). Series: Need to Know Library. 2000, Rosen LB $27.95 (978-0-8239-3121-7). The basic facts about leukemia are covered with material on its various types and treatments, possible causes, and the emotional aspects of the illness. (Rev: SLJ 9/00) [616.99]

20568 Monroe, Judy. *Cystic Fibrosis* (5–9). Illus. Series: Perspectives on Disease and Illness. 2001, Capstone LB $25.26 (978-0-7368-1026-5). 64pp. A straightforward account of the symptoms, diagnosis, and treatment of this disease, with discussion of the impact on the life of the patient and other family members. Also use *Breast Cancer* (2001). (Rev: HBG 3/02; SLJ 3/02) [616.3]

20569 Moore-Mallinos, Jennifer. *I Have Asthma* (PS–2). Illus. by Rosa M. Curto. 2007, Barron's paper $6.99 (978-0-7641-3785-3). 32pp. At soccer practice a boy experiences his first asthma attack, is taken to the hospital where he learns how to deal with it, and returns to the playing field in this simple and informative picture book. (Rev: BL 11/1/07; SLJ 3/08) [616.238]

20570 Moragne, Wendy. *Allergies* (5–8). Series: Twenty-First Century Medical Library. 1999, Twenty-First Century LB $26.90 (978-0-7613-1359-5). After general material on allergies, their causes and treatment, this account describes specific allergies involving food, skin, rhinitis, drugs, and insects. (Rev: HBG 3/00; SLJ 3/00) [616.97]

20571 Morgan, Sally. *Germ Killers: Fighting Disease* (5–8). Series: Science at the Edge. 2002, Heinemann LB $27.86 (978-1-58810-699-5). 64pp. Current advances in fighting disease are outlined with their current applications and future possibilities. (Rev: BL 10/15/02; HBG 3/03) [616]

20572 Murphy, Patricia J. *Illness* (PS–3). Series: Tough Topics. 2007, Heinemann LB $25.36 (978-1-4034-

9777-2). 32pp. A sensitive discussion of the nature of illness, different kinds of illnesses, diagnosis, treatment, and how to cope when others are ill. (Rev: SLJ 12/07) [155.9]

20573 Nye, Bill, and Kathleen W. Zoehfeld. *Bill Nye the Science Guy's Great Big Book of Tiny Germs* (4–7). Illus. by Bryn Barnard. 2005, Hyperion $16.99 (978-0-7868-0543-3). Solid information on bacteria and viruses is presented in an appealing and lively format. (Rev: BL 6/1–15/05; SLJ 7/05) [579]

20574 Parker, Steve. *Allergies* (5–8). Series: Just the Facts. 2004, Heinemann LB $27.07 (978-1-4034-4598-8). 56pp. A comprehensive and accessible overview of allergies, their causes, symptoms, and treatment. (Rev: SLJ 6/04) [616.97]

20575 Pincus, Dion. *Everything You Need to Know About Cerebral Palsy* (4–7). Series: Need to Know Library. 2000, Rosen LB $27.95 (978-0-8239-2960-3). The causes and characteristics of cerebral palsy are discussed with material on the treatments and the daily life of those affected. (Rev: HBG 10/00; SLJ 3/00) [618.92]

20576 Powell, Jillian. *Asthma* (K–2). Illus. Series: Feeling Sick? 2008, Black Rabbit LB $18.95 (978-1-84234-472-9). 32pp. Powell looks at the causes, symptoms, and treatment of this common problem, and includes anecdotes about typical asthma experiences. (Rev: BL 4/1/08) [616.2]

20577 Ramen, Fred. *SARS (Severe Acute Respiratory Syndrome)* (4–6). Series: Epidemics. 2005, Rosen LB $27.95 (978-1-4042-0258-0). 64pp. Offers basic information, suitable for report writers, about the various outbreaks of Severe Acute Respiratory Syndrome and the symptoms, treatment, and research efforts. (Rev: SLJ 10/05) [614.5]

20578 Ramen, Fred. *Sleeping Sickness and Other Parasitic Tropical Diseases* (5–8). Series: Epidemics. 2002, Rosen LB $27.95 (978-0-8239-3499-7). After a history of parasitic diseases around the globe and the role played by bloodsucking killers like the tsetse fly, this account describes the treatments now available. (Rev: BL 8/02; SLJ 7/02) [616]

20579 Ray, Kurt. *Typhoid Fever* (5–8). Series: Epidemics. 2002, Rosen LB $27.95 (978-0-8239-3572-7). An introduction to the history and treatment of typhoid fever, including coverage of Typhoid Mary. (Rev: BL 3/15/02) [614.5]

20580 Reingold, Adam. *Smallpox: Is It Over?* (4–7). Illus. 2010, Bearport LB $25.27 (978-193608802-7). 32pp. This well-organized book presents a clear and balanced view of smallpox, from the biology of the virus itself, to symptoms, to its long and eventful history and purported "defeat" in 1980. (Rev: BL 10/1/10) [614.5]

20581 Romano, Amy. *Germ Warfare* (5–8). Series: Germs: The Library of Disease-Causing Organisms. 2004, Rosen LB $26.50 (978-0-8239-4493-4). An informative, illustrated overview of the history and current status of germ warfare, with discussion of what we can do to protect ourselves. (Rev: SLJ 1/05) [358]

20582 Rosaler, Maxine. *Botulism* (4–7). Series: Epidemics. 2004, Rosen LB $27.95 (978-0-8239-4197-1). A look at outbreaks of botulism and their causes and prevention. (Rev: SLJ 8/04) [614.5]

20583 Routh, Kristina. *Down Syndrome* (5–8). Series: Just the Facts. 2004, Heinemann LB $27.07 (978-1-4034-5145-3). 56pp. An informative overview of this disease and its diagnosis and treatment, stressing the individuality of children with the syndrome. (Rev: SLJ 2/05) [362.1]

20584 Routh, Kristina. *Epilepsy* (5–10). Illus. Series: Just the Facts. 2004, Heinemann LB $27.07 (978-1-4034-4601-5). 56pp. An overview of epilepsy, with attention to its effect on individuals when it comes to driving, sports, education, and employment. (Rev: SLJ 6/04) [616.8]

20585 Routh, Kristina. *Meningitis* (5–8). Illus. Series: Just the Facts. 2004, Heinemann LB $27.07 (978-1-4034-5146-0). 56pp. The symptoms of meningitis are provided along with a thorough explanation of the disease and its diagnosis and treatment. (Rev: SLJ 2/05)

20586 Roy, Jennifer. *Depression* (4–7). Illus. Series: Health Alert. 2004, Benchmark LB $28.50 (978-0-7614-1800-9). 64pp. In addition to describing the causes and treatment of depression, this attractive title opens with a case history and also includes lists of famous people who suffer from the condition. (Rev: SLJ 5/05)

20587 Royston, Angela. *Why Do My Eyes Itch? And Other Questions About Allergies* (3–5). Illus. Series: Body Matters. 2002, Heinemann LB $24.22 (978-1-4034-0207-3). 32pp. All kinds of allergies are introduced in concise, simple text with many illustrations. (Rev: SLJ 4/03) [616.97]

20588 Sanders, Pete, and Steve Myers. *Anorexia and Bulimia* (4–8). Illus. by Mike Lacy and Liz Sawyer. Series: What Do You Know About. 1999, Millbrook LB $23.90 (978-0-7613-0914-7). Using an actual case study as a beginning, this book explores the causes, effects, and treatment of these eating disorders and covers the behavioral patterns of those afflicted. (Rev: HBG 10/99; SLJ 10/99) [618.92]

20589 Schwartz, Robert H., and Peter M. G. Deane. *Coping with Allergies* (4–7). Series: Coping. 1999, Rosen LB $31.95 (978-0-8239-2511-7). After a rundown of the types and causes of allergies, this account describes their physical and emotional impact and current treatments. (Rev: BL 2/15/00) [616.97]

20590 Senker, Cath. *World Health Organization* (5–8). Series: World Watch. 2004, Raintree LB $18.99 (978-0-7398-6614-6). 48pp. The world's health problems and what is being done to combat them are the focus of this somber title, which looks at both the developing world and the wealthiest of nations. (Rev: BL 4/1/04; SLJ 3/04) [362.1]

20591 Sheen, Barbara. *Diabetes* (5–7). Illus. Series: Diseases and Disorders. 2003, Gale LB $32.45 (978-1-59018-244-4). 112pp. The symptoms of and treatments for diabetes are covered here, with discussion of alternative treatments, how diabetics manage their disease, and the research being undertaken. (Rev: SLJ 7/03) [616.4]

20592 Sherrow, Victoria. *Polio Epidemic: Crippling Virus Outbreak* (4–7). Series: American Disasters. 2001, Enslow LB $23.93 (978-0-7660-1555-5). 48pp. In this readable account, Sherrow looks at the history of polio, its treatment, the epidemic in the United States that started in 1952, and the creation of the polio vaccine. (Rev: HBG 3/02; SLJ 3/02) [362.1]

20593 Silverstein, Alvin. *The Asthma Update* (5–8). 2006, Enslow LB $31.93 (978-0-7660-2482-3). A thorough look at asthma, its symptoms, history, treatments, and the research being done in hopes of finding a cure. (Rev: BL 12/1/06) [616.2]

20594 Silverstein, Alvin. *The Food Poisoning Update* (5–8). Series: Disease Update. 2007, Enslow LB $23.95 (978-0-7660-2748-0). A clear introduction to what causes food poisoning, how it affects the body, and how it can be avoided. (Rev: BL 12/1/07; SLJ 2/08) [615.9]

20595 Silverstein, Alvin, and Virginia Silverstein. *The Breast Cancer Update* (5–9). Illus. Series: Disease Update. 2007, Enslow LB $31.93 (978-0-7660-2747-3). Symptoms, treatment, history, and new research are all included in this concise discussion of breast cancer. (Rev: SLJ 2/08)

20596 Silverstein, Alvin, and Virginia Silverstein. *Parkinson's Disease* (4–6). Illus. Series: Diseases and People. 2002, Enslow LB $26.60 (978-0-7660-1593-7). 128pp. Actor Michael J. Fox's diagnosis of Parkinson's serves as an introduction to the history, causes, symptoms, and treatment of this disease. (Rev: HBG 3/03; SLJ 12/02)

20597 Silverstein, Alvin, and Virginia Silverstein. *Vaccinations* (3–5). Series: My Health. 2002, Watts paper $6.95 (978-0-531-15564-6). 48pp. Using many visuals and a clear, simple text, this book describes how vaccinations were developed, how they work, and the various types. (Rev: BL 6/1–15/02; SLJ 8/02) [614.4]

20598 Silverstein, Alvin, et al. *The Flu and Pneumonia Update* (5–8). Illus. Series: Disease Update. 2006, Enslow LB $31.93 (978-0-7660-2480-9). 104pp. Symptoms, treatment, history, and new research are all included in this discussion of flu and pneumonia. (Rev: BL 4/1/06; SLJ 9/06) [616.2]

20599 Silverstein, Alvin, et al. *Lyme Disease* (4–7). Illus. 2000, Watts LB $25.50 (978-0-531-11751-4). 64pp. This book introduces Lyme disease, its symptoms, history, the tick that carries it, prevention, and treatments. (Rev: BL 10/15/00) [616.9]

20600 Simpson, Carolyn. *Everything You Need to Know About Asthma* (5–10). Series: Need to Know Library. 1998, Rosen LB $27.95 (978-0-8239-2567-4). Vital background information is given about the causes and effects, symptoms, and treatments of asthma. (Rev: SLJ 10/98) [616.2]

20601 Smart, Paul. *Everything You Need to Know About Mononucleosis* (5–9). Series: Need to Know Library. 1998, Rosen LB $27.95 (978-0-8239-2550-6). A straightforward presentation about the "kissing disease,"

which is often undiagnosed or mistaken for the flu and which requires long periods of rest for recovery. (Rev: SLJ 10/98) [616]

20602 Spray, Michelle. *Growing Up with Scoliosis: A Young Girl's Story* (5–9). Illus. by author. 2002, Book Shelf paper $12.95 (978-0-9714160-3-1). An autobiographical account of the treatment of scoliosis and the emotional impact on the patient, with clear illustrations. (Rev: SLJ 12/02) [362.19673]

20603 Stewart, Gail B. *Sleep Disorders* (5–8). Illus. Series: Diseases and Disorders. 2002, Gale LB $32.45 (978-1-56006-909-6). 112pp. Insomnia, narcolepsy, apnea, and night terrors are among the problems discussed here, with material on treatments, new research, and attitudes toward people who are always tired. (Rev: SLJ 3/03) [616.8498]

20604 Stone, Tanya Lee. *Medical Causes* (5–10). Series: Celebrity Activists. 1997, Twenty-First Century LB $25.90 (978-0-8050-5233-6). The contributions of such celebrity activists as Elizabeth Taylor, Elton John, Paul Newman, Jerry Lewis, and Linda Ellerbee to various medical causes are highlighted, with material on each of their causes. (Rev: SLJ 1/98) [616]

20605 Susman, Edward. *Multiple Sclerosis* (4–7). Series: Diseases and People. 1999, Enslow LB $26.60 (978-0-7660-1185-4). A description of this debilitating disease that attacks the nervous system. (Rev: HBG 3/00; SLJ 2/00) [616]

20606 Taylor-Butler, Christine. *Food Allergies* (3–5). Illus. Series: True Book: Health and the Human Body. 2008, Children's Pr. LB $26.00 (978-0-531-16858-5); paper $6.95 (978-0-531-20732-1). Peanuts, milk, and wheat are among the substances covered in this accessible and attractive overview that includes a useful "Hidden Dangers" spread. (Rev: BL 6/1–15/08; LMC 8/08) [618.92]

20607 Thomas, Pat. *Why Is It So Hard to Breathe?* (PS–2). Illus. by Lesley Harker. Series: A First Look At. 2008, Barron's paper $6.99 (978-0-7641-3898-0). 32pp. This title explains what asthma is and how it can be managed and features discussion questions for parents and children and colorful illustrations showing how a little boy learns to use his inhaler. (Rev: BLO 9/17/08) [616.2]

20608 Viegas, Jennifer. *Parasites* (5–8). Series: Germs: The Library of Disease-Causing Organisms. 2004, Rosen LB $26.50 (978-0-8239-4494-1). An informative, illustrated discussion of parasites, covering how they survive and the dangers they pose to humans. (Rev: SLJ 1/05) [574.5]

20609 Wainwright, Tabitha. *You and an Illness in Your Family* (5–8). Series: Family Matters. 2001, Rosen LB $26.50 (978-0-8239-3352-5). Concise, readable advice is accompanied by full-page photographs of young teens and the recommendation to seek help when necessary. (Rev: SLJ 8/01) [610]

20610 Ward, Brian. *Epidemic* (4–7). Illus. Series: Eyewitness Books. 2000, DK $15.99 (978-0-7894-6296-1). 64pp. This book covers the nature of epidemics, their causes, how they are spread and contained, and gives examples from history. (Rev: BL 12/1/00; HBG 10/01) [614.4]

20611 Watters, Debbie. *Where's Mom's Hair? A Family's Journey Through Cancer* (2–5). 2005, Second Story paper $10.95 (978-1-896764-94-8). 32pp. This photo-essay documents how family members lovingly supported a cancer-stricken mother as she underwent the rigors of chemotherapy. (Rev: BL 10/1/05; SLJ 7/05) [362.196]

20612 Whelan, Jo. *Diabetes* (5–8). Series: Health Issues. 2002, Raintree LB $28.54 (978-0-7398-5220-0). 64pp. Case histories of youngsters with diabetes are used to explain the nature of this disease, the problems it produces, and the treatments available. (Rev: BL 12/15/02; HBG 3/03) [616.4]

20613 Woolf, Alex. *Death and Disease* (5–8). Series: Medieval Realms. 2004, Gale LB $29.95 (978-1-59018-533-9). 48pp. Black Death, leprosy, and other diseases are discussed, with their impact on society, and the practice of medicine in general is described. (Rev: BL 4/1/04; SLJ 3/05) [610]

20614 Zonta, Pat. *Jessica's X-Ray* (2–5). Illus. by Clive Dobson. 2002, Firefly $19.95 (978-1—6); paper $8.95 (978-1-55297-577-0). 28pp. When Jessica breaks her arm, the doctor orders X-rays and the reader is introduced to the whys and hows of this diagnostic tool. (Rev: BL 5/1/02; HBG 10/02; SLJ check) [616.0750]

Doctors and Medicine

20615 Borenstein, Gerri. *Therapy* (4–8). Illus. Series: Life Balance. 2003, Watts paper $6.95 (978-0-531-15585-1). 80pp. This friendly, reassuring introduction explains what therapy consists of, the different kinds of professionals involved, and the ways in which privacy is maintained. (Rev: BL 10/15/03; SLJ 12/03) [616.89]

20616 Casterline, Linda. *Natural-born Killers: A Chapter Book* (3–7). Series: True Tales. 2004, Children's Pr. LB $22.50 (978-0-516-23725-1). 48pp. Discusses various poisonous plants and animals that have been used in modern medicine to save lives. (Rev: BL 12/1/04; SLJ 2/05) [578.6]

20617 Donovan, Sandy. *Does an Apple a Day Keep the Doctor Away? And Other Questions About Your Health and Body* (4–6). Illus. by Colin W. Thompson. Series: Is That a Fact? 2010, Lerner LB $26.60 (978-0-8225-9084-2). 40pp. Familiar sayings and old wives' tales about health are unraveled and examined with humor and eye-catching illustrations. Also use *Does It Really Take Seven Years to Digest Swallowed Gum? And Other Questions You've Always Wanted to Ask* (2010). (Rev: LMC 5–6/10; SLJ 7/10) [610]

20618 Dowswell, Paul. *Medicine* (5–8). Illus. Series: Great Inventions. 2001, Heinemann LB $25.64 (978-1-58810-213-3). 48pp. A chronological look at new medical instruments and procedures over the ages, with

diagrams and information on the inventors. (Rev: HBG 3/02; SLJ 2/02) [610]

20619 Freedman, Jeri. *Stem Cell Research* (5–8). Illus. Series: America Debates. 2007, Rosen LB $21.95 (978-1-4042-1928-1). 64pp. A technical and detailed examination of the issues surrounding stem cell research and the ethical questions that it provokes. (Rev: BL 12/1/07; LMC 1/08; SLJ 2/08) [616]

20620 Gorman, Jacqueline Laks. *Dentists* (K–2). Illus. Series: People in My Community. 2010, Gareth Stevens LB $22.60 (978-143393800-9). 24pp. A simple introduction to the work dentists do and what young children can expect on dental visits. (Rev: BL 3/15/11) [617.6]

20621 Green, Jen. *Medicine* (4–7). Illus. Series: Routes of Science. 2004, Gale LB $23.70 (978-1-4103-0168-0). 40pp. A look at the history of medicine and the scientific process, with profiles of key individuals and their discoveries, a chronology, and discussion of future advances. (Rev: SLJ 5/05)

20622 Guillain, Charlotte. *Visiting the Dentist* (PS–2). Series: Growing Up. 2011, Heinemann LB $22 (978-1-4329-4804-7); paper $6.49 (978-1-4329-4814-6). 24pp. This book for early readers answers such questions as "What Happens When I Go In?" and "Why Does the Dentist Wear a Mask and Gloves?" — and of course "Will Going to the Dentist Hurt?" (Rev: SLJ 6/11) [617.6]

20623 Hughes, Monica. *First Visit to the Dentist* (PS–2). Series: My First. 2004, Raintree LB $18.56 (978-1-4109-0645-8); paper $5.50 (978-1-4109-0671-7). 24pp. Simple language introduces young readers to what happens at the dentist — waiting rooms, examination, cleaning and polishing, and so forth.

20624 Ichord, Loretta Frances. *Toothworms and Spider Juice: An Illustrated History of Dentistry* (5–8). 2000, Millbrook LB $24.90 (978-0-7613-1465-3). A history of dentistry that reveals many of the barbaric treatments of the past and how superstition and ignorance gradually gave way to modern practices. (Rev: BCCB 2/00; BL 2/15/00; HBG 10/00; SLJ 2/00) [617.6]

20625 Jefferis, David. *Bio Tech: Frontiers of Medicine* (4–8). Series: Megatech. 2001, Crabtree paper $8.95 (978-0-7787-0061-6). An eye-catching look at future medical possibilities such as artificial body parts, enhanced use of robots, special foods, and so forth. (Rev: SLJ 6/02) [660.6]

20626 Lindsay, Judy. *The Story of Medicine: From Acupuncture to X Rays* (4–6). Illus. 2003, Oxford LB $26.50 (978-0-19-521984-5). 40pp. The history of medicine, from ancient times to the modern day, is presented in this lively and accessible book full of reproductions. (Rev: HBG 4/04; SLJ 4/04) [610]

20627 Manson, Ainslie. *House Calls: The True Story of a Pioneer Doctor* (3–6). Illus. by Mary Jane Gerber. 2001, Groundwood $15.95 (978-0-88899-446-2). 56pp. Though the narrator of this book is a fictional girl, the story details the real life of an early 19th-century rural

Canadian doctor with information on tools and treatment. (Rev: BL 2/1/02; HBG 3/02; SLJ 12/01) [610.92]

20628 Miller, Brandon Marie. *Just What the Doctor Ordered: The History of American Medicine* (5–8). Series: People's History. 1997, Lerner LB $30.35 (978-0-8225-1737-5). A history of American medicine from early Indian ceremonies and remedies to today's use of laser surgery, placing medical developments in a historical context, such as the role disease played in the Revolutionary and Civil Wars. (Rev: SLJ 5/97*) [610.9]

20629 Murphy, Patricia J. *Everything You Need to Know About Staying in the Hospital* (5–8). Series: Need to Know Library. 2001, Rosen LB $27.95 (978-0-8239-3325-9). This volume explains the basic hospital process from admission to discharge and follows a patient through a typical day. (Rev: SLJ 5/01) [362.1]

20630 Shepherd, Jodie. *A Day with Paramedics* (K–2). Illus. Series: Rookie Read-About: Community. 2012, Scholastic/Children's Press LB $23 (978-0-531-28954-9); paper $5.95 (978-0-531-29254-9). 32pp. Four short chapters look at the kinds of tasks performed by paramedics. Lexile 470L (Rev: BL 10/1/12; SLJ 1/13) [362.18]

20631 Townsend, John. *Scalpels, Stitches and Scars: A History of Surgery* (4–7). Series: A Painful History of Medicine. 2005, Raintree LB $32.86 (978-1-4109-1332-6). Gory it may be but this title conveys accurate facts and the eye-catching illustrations will entice browsers. (Rev: BL 5/15/05; SLJ 7/05) [617]

20632 Woods, Michael, and Mary B. Woods. *The History of Medicine* (5–8). Series: Major Inventions Through History. 2005, Twenty-First Century LB $26.60 (978-0-8225-2336-9). An attractive look at medical developments through time and their impact on our lives. (Rev: SLJ 1/06) [610]

Genetics

20633 Allan, Tony. *Understanding DNA: A Breakthrough in Medicine* (5–8). Illus. Series: Point of Impact. 2002, Heinemann LB $25.64 (978-1-58810-557-8). 32pp. A history of genetics with profiles of the important scientists and discussion of future uses of this knowledge in cloning, medicine, and production of food. (Rev: SLJ 9/02) [572.8609]

20634 Beatty, Richard. *Genetics* (4–8). Illus. Series: Science Fact Files. 2001, Raintree LB $27.12 (978-0-7398-1015-6). 42pp. Cells, chromosomes, genes, and genetic engineering are covered here, with profiles of key scientists. (Rev: HBG 10/01; SLJ 1/02) [660]

20635 Boskey, Elizabeth. *America Debates Genetic DNA Testing* (5–8). Series: America Debates. 2007, Rosen LB $29.25 (978-1-4042-1926-7). Presents facts and opinions on both sides of issues including prenatal and adult genetic testing. (Rev: LMC 2/08; SLJ 11/07) [362.196]

20636 Butterfield, Moira. *Genetics* (5–8). Illus. Series: 21st Century Science. 2003, Smart Apple LB $27.10 (978-1-58340-350-1). 44pp. An accessible, large-format volume on genetics, cloning, and the use of genes in medicine and food engineering, with attractive full-color photographs. (Rev: BL 12/1/03) [576.5.]

20637 Gallant, Roy A. *The Treasure of Inheritance* (5–8). Illus. Series: The Story of Science. 2002, Benchmark LB $29.93 (978-0-7614-1426-1). 78pp. A history of mankind's discoveries about genetics and heredity, starting with the earliest efforts to improve crops and animals, with material on today's and future genetic engineering and the mapping of the human genome. (Rev: HBG 3/03; LMC 5/03; SLJ 5/03) [576.5]

20638 George, Linda. *Gene Therapy* (5–9). Series: Science on the Edge. 2003, Gale LB $24.95 (978-1-56711-786-8). 48pp. This book explain how genetic engineering can not only have applications in health and industry but also can arouse a great deal of controversy. (Rev: BL 10/15/03) [660]

20639 Jefferis, David. *Cloning: Frontiers of Genetic Engineering* (5–7). Series: Megatech. 1999, Crabtree LB $25.27 (978-0-7787-0048-7). This account discusses the history of genetic discoveries and theories, cell reproduction, and the present and possible future of genetic engineering with plants, animals, and humans. (Rev: SLJ 9/99) [174.957]

20640 Lundgren, Julie K. *I Look Like My Mother* (3–5). Illus. Series: My Science Library. 2012, Rourke LB $27.07 (978-161810100-6); paper $7.95 (9781618102331). 24pp. This is a well-written introduction to the basics of genetics and heredity, ending with a "Show What You Know" quiz. (Rev: BL 9/15/12; SLJ Fall 2012 Series Guide) [576.5]

20641 Morgan, Sally. *Body Doubles: Cloning Plants and Animals* (5–8). Illus. Series: Science at the Edge. 2002, Heinemann LB $27.86 (978-1-58810-698-8). 64pp. A discussion of the scientific and ethical issues of cloning, with excellent diagrams. (Rev: BL 10/15/02; HBG 3/03) [660.6]

20642 Nardo, Don. *Cloning* (5–9). Illus. Series: Science on the Edge. 2003, Gale $24.95 (978-1-56711-782-0). 48pp. A concise overview of the techniques involved in cloning and the ways this science can be applied, with a balanced presentation of the pro and con arguments. (Rev: BL 10/15/03; SLJ 2/04) [660.6]

20643 Nicolson, Cynthia Pratt. *Baa! The Most Interesting Book You'll Ever Read About Genes and Cloning* (4–6). Illus. by Rose Cowles. Series: Mysterious You. 2001, Kids Can $14.95 (978-1-55074-856-7); paper $6.95 (978-1-55074-886-4). Nicolson provides succinct definitions and descriptions of genetics and cloning-related issues in an easy-to-read volume. (Rev: BL 1/1–15/02; HBG 3/02) [572.8]

20644 Phelan, Glen. *Double Helix: The Quest to Uncover the Structure of DNA* (5–8). Series: Science Quest. 2006, National Geographic $17.95 (978-0-7922-5541-3). From Mendel's early experiments with pea plants through Crick and Watson's race to solve the mystery of DNA, this is an accessible and informative history that also looks at the wide range of social and scientific areas influenced by the discovery. (Rev: SLJ 4/07) [572.8]

20645 Silverstein, Alvin, et al. *DNA* (4–8). Series: Science Concepts. 2002, Millbrook LB $26.90 (978-0-7613-2257-3). 64pp. This book examines the structure of DNA and clearly explains its components and functions and includes current topics such as the genome project, genetic engineering, gene therapy, and cloning. (Rev: BL 9/15/02; HBG 3/03; SLJ 11/02) [574.87]

20646 Simpson, Kathleen. *Genetics: From DNA to Designer Dogs* (4–6). Illus. Series: National Geographic Investigates. 2008, National Geographic $17.95 (978-1-4263-0361-6). 64pp. An absorbing introduction to genetics covering everything from Mendel's early work to what we know today about plant, animal, and human genetics and how this knowledge can help us in various ways. (Rev: BL 1/1–15/09) [576.5]

Hospitals

20647 Attebury, Nancy Garhan. *Out and About at the Hospital* (1–3). Illus. by Zachary Trover. Series: Field Trips. 2005, Picture Window LB $26.60 (978-1-4048-1148-5). 24pp. Takes readers on a tour of a typical hospital, explaining its purpose and the roles of people who work there. (Rev: SLJ 2/06) [362.11]

20648 Barber, Nicola. *Going to the Hospital* (K–1). Series: The Big Day! 2009, Rosen LB $21.25 (978-1-4358-2840-7). 24pp. This simple book looks at typical concerns — feeling sick, staying overnight, having an operation, visitors, and so forth. (Rev: SLJ 7/09) [362.11]

20649 Pascoe, Elaine, ed. *Crash: The Body in Crisis* (5–8). Illus. Series: Body Story. 2003, Gale LB $24.95 (978-1-4103-0062-1). 48pp. Two people are badly hurt in a car crash — he is unconscious, she has a ruptured spleen — and readers accompany them to the emergency room and the operating room as they fight for their lives. (Rev: SLJ 4/04) [617.1]

The Human Body

General

20650 Allison, Linda. *Blood and Guts: A Working Guide to Your Own Little Insides* (5–8). 1976, Little, Brown paper $14.99 (978-0-316-03443-2). An off-putting title but a fine explanation of the functions of the human body.

20651 Basher, Simon, and Dan Green. *Human Body: A Book with Guts* (5–8). Illus. by Simon Basher. 2011, Kingfisher $14.99 (978-0-7534-6628-5); paper $8.99 (978-0-7534-6-501-1). 128pp. An irreverent and enter-

taining look at the inner workings of the human body with Basher's cartoon illustrations. (Rev: BL 3/1/11; SLJ 9/1/11) [612]

20652 Batten, Mary. *Who Has a Belly Button?* (K–4). Illus. by Higgins Bond. 2004, Peachtree $15.95 (978-1-56145-235-4). All about belly buttons — what they are, where they come from, what animals' belly buttons are like, and so forth. (Rev: SLJ 5/04) [612.6]

20653 Berger, Melvin, and Gilda Berger. *You're Tall in the Morning but Shorter at Night and Other Amazing Facts About the Human Body* (2–5). Illus. Series: Speedy Facts. 2004, Scholastic paper $7.99 (978-0-439-62536-4). 48pp. An entertaining and lively presentation of amazing and informative facts about the human body. [611]

20654 Bradley, Timothy J. *Strange but True: Gross Anatomy* (3–5). Illus. Series: Time for Kids Nonfiction Readers. 2012, Teacher Created Materials $9.99 (978-1-43334860-0). 48pp. An appealing survey of the body's structure and systems, emphasizing their interconnectedness. Lexile 740L (Rev: BL 9/15/12; LMC 5–6/13) [611]

20655 Bruhn, Aron. *Inside Human Body* (4–6). Illus. by Joel Ito and Kathleen Kemly. 2010, Sterling $16.95 (978-1-4027-7091-3); paper $9.95 (978-1-4027-7779-0). 49pp. Gatefold features enhance this boldly colored overview of humans' internal workings. (Rev: LMC 1–2/11; SLJ 12/1/10*) [612]

20656 Calabresi, Linda. *Human Body* (4–7). Series: Insiders. 2008, Simon & Schuster $16.99 (978-1-4169-3861-3). Cross-sections, computer-aided graphics, and other visual wonders offer amazing views of the body in this large-format book that provides text information in snippets and sidebars. (Rev: BL 3/1/08; SLJ 5/08) [612]

20657 Cobb, Vicki. *Your Body Battles a Skinned Knee* (K–3). Illus. by Andrew N. Harris. 2009, Millbrook LB $25.26 (978-0-8225-6814-8). 32pp. A simple, accessible explanation — with cartoon illustrations and characters including Skin Cell and Platelet — of how the body heals after an injury. Also use *Your Body Battles a Stomachache* and *Your Body Battles a Cold* (2009). (Rev: BL 1/1–15/09; SLJ 4/09) [617.5]

20658 Darling, Kathy. *There's a Zoo on You!* (3–5). Illus. 2000, Millbrook LB $24.90 (978-0-7613-1357-1). 48pp. The supermagnified photographs in this book are of the bacteria, fungi, and other organisms that live in or on the human body. (Rev: BL 11/1/00; HBG 9/00; SLJ 7/00) [579]

20659 Donovan, Sandy. *Hawk and Drool: Gross Stuff in Your Mouth* (4–8). Illus. by Michael Slack. Series: Gross Body Science. 2010, Lerner LB $29.27 (978-0-8225-8966-2). 48pp. Cavities, canker sores, bacteria, and saliva are among the gross items causing smelly breath that are discussed here with close-up pictures. (Rev: LMC 1–2/10)

20660 Ewald, Wendy. *The Best Part of Me: Children Talk About Their Bodies in Pictures and Words* (1–3). Illus. 2001, Little, Brown $16.95 (978-0-316-70306-2). 32pp.

In their own words, youngsters describe what they like best about their bodies. (Rev: BL 9/1/01; HBG 3/02; SLJ 10/01) [810.8]

20661 Ganeri, Anita. *Alive: The Living, Breathing Human Body Book* (5–7). Illus. 2007, DK $24.99 (978-0-7566-3211-3). Visual and audio effects accompany amazing graphics and text in this comprehensive and attention-grabbing pop-up anatomy book. (Rev: SLJ 3/08)

20662 Gould, Francesca. *Why You Shouldn't Eat Your Boogers: Gross But True Things You Don't Want to Know about Your Body* (3–5). Illus. by JP Coovert. 2013, Putnam $8.99 (978-039925790-2). 128pp. A compendium of often gross facts about everything from hiccups and ear wax to creatures that live on and inside us. Lexile 612 (Rev: BL 4/1/13; LMC 10/13; SLJ 6/13)

20663 Harris, Robie H. *Who Has What? All About Girls' Bodies and Boys' Bodies* (PS–2). Illus. by Nadine Bernard Westcott. 2011, Candlewick $15.99 (978-0-7636-2931-1). 32pp. Young Nellie and Gus are at the beach with their parents and they explore the ways in which girls' and boys' bodies are different, and the same. (Rev: BL 9/1/11*; HB 11–12/11; SLJ 10/1/11*) [612.6]

20664 Hibbert, Clare. *I'm Tired and Other Body Feelings* (PS–2). Illus. by Simona Dimitri. Series: Feelings. 2011, Amicus LB $16.95 (978-160753175-3). 24pp. A simple guide to how it feels to be tired, hungry, sick, dizzy, and so forth, with relevant illustrations and text in speech balloons. (Rev: BL 10/1/11) [152.4]

20665 Hirschmann, Kris. *Reflections of Me: Girls and Body Image* (5–8). Series: What's the Issue? 2009, Compass Point $27.99 (978-0-7565-4132-3). 48pp. A compelling mix of direct quotes, real-life scenarios, quizzes, and short glossaries enhance this book about girls' body image problems; suitable for reluctant readers. (Rev: LMC 10/09; SLJ 10/09) [155.3]

20666 Jefferis, David. *Human Body* (3–6). Illus. Series: Record Breakers. 2003, Raintree LB $25.69 (978-0-7398-6322-0). 32pp. An attractively illustrated collection of fascinating trivia about the human body. (Rev: HBG 10/03; SLJ 7/03)

20667 Kim, Melissa L. *The Endocrine and Reproductive Systems* (5–10). Series: Human Body Library. 2003, Enslow LB $23.93 (978-0-7660-2020-7). Kim uses a conversational style to introduce detailed facts about these two body systems, with useful graphics and some practical advice. (Rev: BL 4/15/03; HBG 10/03) [612.4]

20668 Klingel, Cynthia, and Robert B. Noyed. *Feet* (PS–1). Photos by Gregg Andersen. Series: Let's Read About Our Bodies. 2002, Gareth Stevens LB $21.00 (978-0-8368-3064-4). 24pp. Full-page, full-color close-ups and minimal text present toes, feet, and shoes. Also use *Nose* and *Skin* (2002). (Rev: HBG 10/02; SLJ 5/02) [612.98]

20669 Levine, Shar, and Leslie Johnstone. *First Science Experiments: The Amazing Human Body* (PS–2). Illus. by Steve Harpster. 2006, Sterling LB $14.95 (978-1-4027-2437-4). 48pp. Simple activities using handy materials help students answer a wide range of questions, from "Do people with big ears hear better than people with small ears?" to "How can I tell how fast my heart is beating?" and "Why does my tummy growl or grumble when I am hungry?" (Rev: SLJ 11/06) [612.0078]

20670 Macnair, Patricia. *Everything You Need to Know About the Human Body* (3–5). Illus. 2011, Kingfisher $12.99 (978-075346686-5). 160pp. This overview provides clear, well-illustrated information on the various body parts and systems. (Rev: BL 11/1/11) [612]

20671 Manning, Mick, and Brita Granström. *Under Your Skin: Your Amazing Body* (1–3). Illus. by Mick Manning. 2007, Albert Whitman $16.95 (978-0-8075-8313-5). 32pp. This friendly introduction to the human body offers simple explanations written in a lively tone with an appealing lift-the-flap format. (Rev: BL 9/15/07; SLJ 6/08) [612]

20672 Murray, Julie. *The Body* (2–4). Illus. Series: That's Gross! A Look at Science. 2009, ABDO LB $17.95 (978-1-60453-554-9). 32pp. Snot, flatulence, farts, earwax — this exploration of all things icky about the body will attract an audience. (Rev: BL 5/15/09) [612]

20673 Myers, Jack. *On Top of Mount Everest: And Other Explorations of Science in Action* (4–6). Illus. by John Rice. 2005, Boyds Mills $17.95 (978-1-59078-252-1). 64pp. A collection of science-related articles that have appeared in the magazine *Highlights for Children*, most relating to interesting abilities of the human body. (Rev: SLJ 8/05)

20674 Parker, Steve. *Human Body: An Interactive Guide to the Inner Workings of the Body* (4–7). Series: Discoverology. 2008, Barron's $18.99 (978-0-7641-6083-7). Pop-ups, pullouts, gatefolds, cutaways, X-ray images, spinning wheels, and other visual elements make this guide to anatomy effective and interesting. (Rev: BL 6/1–15/08; SLJ 8/08) [612]

20675 Pascoe, Elaine, ed. *Out of Control: Brain Function and Immune Reactions* (5–8). Illus. Series: Body Story. 2003, Gale LB $24.95 (978-1-4103-0063-8). 48pp. This fact-packed book looks first at a baby's brain function, before and after birth, and how its capabilities grow as he learns, then traces the reaction of a young woman's immune system as it copes with a severe allergic reaction to a wasp sting. (Rev: SLJ 4/04) [612.8]

20676 Pinnington, Andrea, and Penny Lamprell. *My Body* (K–2). Illus. Series: Discover More. 2012, Scholastic $7.99 (978-054534514-9). 32pp. A useful and interesting introduction to the parts of the body (hair, skin, breathing, blood) and the senses. (Rev: BL 4/15/12) [612]

20677 Powell, Jillian. *Moving* (1–3). Series: The Body in Action. 2004, Smart Apple LB $18.95 (978-1-58340-437-9). 32pp. Powell explores human movement and explains the parts of the body involved in various activities and how injuries can occur. (Rev: BL 11/1/04) [612.7]

20678 Reilly, Kathleen M. *The Human Body: 25 Fantastic Projects* (5–9). Illus. by Shawn Braley. Series: Focus on Science. 2008, Nomad paper $15.95 (978-1-9346702-4-8). 120pp. Experiments (many of which need adult supervision) show how various processes of the human body work and are accompanied by excellent descriptions. (Rev: SLJ 2/09) [611]

20679 Ross, Michael Elsohn. *Body Cycles* (PS–1). Illus. by Gustav Moore. Series: Cycles. 2002, Millbrook LB $22.40 (978-0-7613-1816-3). Young readers are introduced to the ways in which the body uses oxygen, blood, and nutrients. (Rev: HBG 10/02; SLJ 8/02) [612]

20680 Saltz, Gail. *Amazing You! Getting Smart About Your Private Parts* (PS–2). Illus. by Lynne Cravath. 2005, Button $15.99 (978-0-525-47389-3). 32pp. Cheerful cartoons and straightforward text offer age-appropriate information about reproduction, birth, development, and the difference between boys' and girls' bodies. (Rev: BL 6/1–15/05; SLJ 5/05) [612.6]

20681 Seuling, Barbara. *From Head to Toe: The Amazing Human Body and How It Works* (3–4). Illus. by Edward Miller. 2002, Holiday House $16.95 (978-0-8234-1699-8). 32pp. An accessible overview of the various body systems, omitting reproduction, with clear illustrations and several experiments. (Rev: SLJ 11/02) [612]

20682 Simon, Seymour. *The Human Body* (4–7). Illus. 2008, HarperCollins $19.99 (978-006055541-2); LB $20.89 (978-006055542-9). 64pp. Drawing on earlier books, Simon presents a detailed overview of the human body with vivid illustrations and clear captions. (Rev: BL 10/15/08; HB 9–10/08; SLJ 11/1/08) [612]

20683 Stewart, David. *How Your Body Works: A Good Look Inside Your Insides* (1–3). Illus. by Carolyn Franklin. Series: Amaze. 2008, Children's Pr. LB $26.00 (978-0-531-20444-3); paper $8.95 (978-0-531-20455-9). 32pp. A bright and appealing introduction to the body, looking at the senses as well as internal organs and systems. (Rev: BL 4/1/08) [612]

20684 Swanson, Diane. *You Are Weird: Your Body's Peculiar Parts and Funny Functions* (2–4). Illus. by Kathy Boake. 2009, Kids Can $16.95 (978-1-55453-282-7); paper $7.95 (978-1-55453-283-4). Full of surprising, humorously delivered facts, this is an accessible introduction to the human body. (Rev: BL 3/15/09) [612]

20685 Szpirglas, Jeff. *Gross Universe: Your Guide to All Disgusting Things Under the Sun* (3–6). Illus. by Michael Cho. 2004, Maple Tree $21.95 (978-1-894379-64-9); paper $12.95 (978-1-894379-65-6). 64pp. Cartoon characters add details to the entertaining narrative about various bodily unpleasantnesses. (Rev: BCCB 5/04; SLJ 11/04) [612]

20686 Taylor-Butler, Christine. *Tiny Life on Your Body* (2–3). Series: Rookie Read-About Science. 2005, Children's Pr. LB $20.50 (978-0-516-25299-5); paper $4.95 (978-0-516-25480-7). 32pp. For beginning readers, this is an introduction to the kinds of bacteria — good and bad — that can be found on the human body. (Rev: SLJ 4/06) [612]

20687 VanCleave, Janice. *The Human Body for Every Kid: Easy Activities That Make Learning Science Fun* (5–7). Series: Science for Every Kid. 1995, Wiley paper $12.95 (978-0-471-02408-8). The various systems in the human body are introduced and decribed, with many projects and experiments. (Rev: BL 4/15/95; SLJ 5/95) [612]

20688 Walker, Richard. *Body* (4–7). 2005, DK $19.99 (978-0-7566-1371-6). With a spiral binding, acetate overlays, and computer-generated 3-D images, this volume gives an in-depth view of the human body; there is an accompanying CD. (Rev: BL 12/1/05; SLJ 3/06) [611]

20689 Walker, Richard. *How the Incredible Human Body Works . . . by the Brainwaves* (2–4). Illus. by Lisa Swerling. 2007, DK $19.99 (978-0-7566-3145-1). 64pp. Humorous illustrations add to this overview of the systems, organs, and operation of the human body. (Rev: BL 12/1/07; LMC 1/08; SLJ 11/07) [612]

20690 Walker, Richard. *Human Body* (5–9). Series: DK/Google e.guides. 2005, DK $17.99 (978-0-7566-1009-8). This highly illustrated guide introduces readers to the human body and provides a link to a Web site that serves as a gateway to additional resources. (Rev: SLJ 8/05) [612]

20691 Walker, Richard. *Ouch! How Your Body Makes It Through a Very Bad Day* (5–8). Illus. 2007, DK $16.99 (978-0-7566-2536-8). Wonderfully gross, this day starts with some sneezes and progresses through a variety of events including urinating, sweating, vomiting, and being stung by a bee; the accompanying CD-ROM adds an inside view to these processes. (Rev: LMC 10/07; SLJ 7/07)

20692 Waters, Jennifer. *All Kinds of People: What Makes Us Different* (K–2). Illus. Series: Spyglass Books. 2002, Compass Point LB $19.93 (978-0-7565-0377-2). 24pp. Eight spreads look at how people differ in physical appearance, personality, and ways of moving and communicating. (Rev: SLJ 4/03)

20693 Wiese, Jim. *Head to Toe Science: Over 40 Eye-Popping, Spine-Tingling, Heart-Pounding Activities That Teach Kids* (4–8). 2000, Wiley paper $12.95 (978-0-471-33203-9). A collection of experiments and projects that is arranged by body systems (e.g., nervous, digestive), accompanied by good instructions and scientific explanations. (Rev: BL 7/00; SLJ 7/00) [612]

20694 Winston, Robert M. L. *What Makes Me Me?* (4–6). 2004, DK $15.99 (978-0-7566-0325-0). 96pp. In this creative approach to human biology, full of questions and activities, Winston takes readers on a fascinating journey through the body and then concentrates on the mind. (Rev: BL 12/1/04) [612]

20695 Zoehfeld, Kathleen Weidner. *Human Body* (K–2). Illus. Series: Scholastic Reader. 2010, Scholastic paper $3.99 (978-05452375-2-9). 32pp. For beginning readers, this is a clear introduction to basic body parts (skin, senses, and so forth). Lexile 630L (Rev: BL 1/1–15/11) [612]

Circulatory System

20696 Corcoran, Mary K. *The Circulatory Story* (2–4). Illus. by Jef Czekaj. 2010, Charlesbridge $17.95 (978-1-

58089-208-7); paper $7.95 (978-1-58089-209-4). 44pp. Providing a humorous, accessible survey of the human circulatory system, Corcoran narrates as an eye-catching green imp goes tubing down a girl's bloodstream, making comical observations along the way. Lexile 850L (Rev: BL 1/1/10; LMC 10/10; SLJ 4/1/10) [612.1]

20697 Frost, Helen. *The Circulatory System* (K–2). Illus. Series: Human Body Systems. 2000, Capstone LB $17.26 (978-0-7368-0648-0). 24pp. A small-format, basic introduction for beginning readers. (Rev: HBG 10/01; SLJ 4/01) [612.1]

20698 Gray, Susan H. *The Circulatory System* (3–6). Illus. Series: The Human Body. 2003, Child's World LB $27.07 (978-1-59296-036-1). 32pp. A clear and detailed description of the functions of the circulatory system, using a child-friendly approach. (Rev: BL 2/1/04) [612.1]

20699 Markle, Sandra. *Faulty Hearts: True Survival Stories* (5–8). Series: Powerful Medicine. 2010, Lerner LB $27.93 (978-0-8225-8699-9). 48pp. Arresting full-color photographs, cross-sections, and personal stories are combined with facts about procedures and information about the medical personnel involved, (Rev: LMC 11–12/10; VOYA 10/10) [612.1]

20700 Newquist, H. P. *The Book of Blood: From Legends and Leeches to Vampires and Veins* (5–8). Illus. 2012, Houghton Harcourt $17.99 (978-0-547-31584-3). 149pp. A lively review of all things relating to blood, covering everything from ancient cultures' understanding of the body to modern knowledge about both human and animal blood and its amazing properties. (Rev: HB 9–10/12; SLJ 10/12) [612.1]

20701 Parker, Steve. *Heart, Lungs, and Blood* (5–9). Illus. Series: Our Bodies. 2004, Raintree LB $28.56 (978-0-7398-6621-4). 48pp. Details of the human body's circulatory system are accompanied by information on keeping them healthy. (Rev: BL 8/04) [612.1]

20702 Rau, Dana Meachen. *My Heart and Blood* (PS–3). Illus. Series: Bookworms: What's Inside Me? 2004, Benchmark LB $21.36 (978-0-7614-1779-8). 31pp. A simple overview of the circulatory system, with photographs, diagrams, and X-rays. (Rev: SLJ 2/05) [612]

20703 Romanek, Trudee. *Squirt! The Most Interesting Book You'll Ever Read About Blood* (4–7). Illus. by Rose Cowles. Series: Mysterious You. 2006, Kids Can $14.95 (978-1-55337-776-4); paper $7.95 (978-1-55337-777-1). This fascinating book with an engaging format discusses the human circulatory system, with information about other animals and their blood, too. (Rev: BL 5/15/06; HBG 10/06) [612.1]

20704 Showers, Paul. *A Drop of Blood* (K–2). Illus. by Edward Miller. Series: Let's Read-and-Find-Out. 2004, HarperCollins LB $5.99 (978-0-06-009110-1); paper $16.89 (978-0-06-009109-5). 128pp. This updated edition features a new, vampire slant and retains the earlier clear overview of blood and the human circulatory system. (Rev: BL 8/04; SLJ 7/04) [612]

20705 Showers, Paul. *Hear Your Heart* (2–5). Illus. by Holly Keller. Series: Let's-Read-and-Find-Out. 2001,

HarperCollins LB $15.89 (978-0-06-025411-7); paper $5.99 (978-0-06-445139-0). 32pp. An amusing introduction to the human heart accompanied by activities such as making a stethoscope, taking a pulse, and listening to heartbeats. (Rev: BL 1/1–15/01; HBG 10/01) [612.1]

20706 Viegas, Jennifer. *The Heart: Learning How Our Blood Circulates* (5–9). Illus. Series: 3-D Library of the Human Body. 2002, Rosen LB $27.95 (978-0-8239-3532-1). 48pp. An introduction to the anatomy and function of the human heart and the circulatory system that includes illustrations, diagrams, a glossary, and other aids. (Rev: BL 7/02) [612.1]

Digestive and Excretory Systems

20707 Bennett, Howard J. *Max Archer, Kid Detective: The Case of the Recurring Stomachaches* (2–5). Illus. by Spike Gerrell. Series: Max Archer, Kid Detective. 2012, Magination $14.95 (978-1-43381130-2); paper $9.95 (978-14338112-9-6). 48pp. Max helps children understand the process of digestion and common stomach problems for children (lactose intolerance, stress, and so forth) in this volume that combines a fictional story and nonfiction facts. (Rev: BL 9/1/12) [616.33]

20708 Brynie, Faith Hickman. *101 Questions About Food and Digestion That Have Been Eating at You . . . Until Now* (5–8). 2002, Millbrook LB $27.90 (978-0-7613-2309-9). A question-and-answer format succeeds in conveying lots of food for thought, with details on digestive functions, digestive disorders, food safety, fat cells, Mad Cow disease, vitamins, and so forth. (Rev: BL 1/1–15/03; HBG 3/03; SLJ 3/03) [612.3]

20709 Frost, Helen. *The Digestive System* (K–2). Illus. Series: Human Body Systems. 2000, Capstone LB $17.26 (978-0-7368-0649-7). 24pp. This is a simple introduction to the digestive system that includes clearly labeled diagrams and full-color photographs. (Rev: HBG 10/01; SLJ 4/01) [612.3]

20710 Goodman, Susan E. *Gee Whiz! It's All About Pee* (4–6). Illus. by Elwood H. Smith. 2006, Viking $15.99 (978-0-670-06064-1). 40pp. This companion to *The Truth About Poop* (2004) provides facts and trivia — often unexpected and humorous — about pee, with cartoon illustrations. (Rev: BL 11/1/06; SLJ 11/06) [612.4]

20711 Goodman, Susan E. *The Truth About Poop* (4–6). Illus. by Elwood H. Smith. 2004, Viking $15.99 (978-0-670-03674-5). 40pp. Cartoon artwork accompanies matter-of-fact information about human and animal waste and the history of toilets and sewage. (Rev: BL 5/15/04; SLJ 7/04) [612.3]

20712 Jakab, Cheryl. *Digestive System* (3–5). Illus. Series: Our Body. 2007, Smart Apple LB $27.10 (978-1-58340-737-0). 32pp. The anatomy and functions of this system of the body are covered, as well as diseases and conditions that can affect it and how to keep it healthy. (Rev: SLJ 7/07)

20713 Kolpin, Molly. *A Tour of Your Digestive System* (2–4). Illus. by Chris B. Jones. Series: First Graphics: Body Systems. 2012, Capstone LB $23.32 (978-142968430-9); paper $5.95 (9781429693240). 24pp. Peter Pea takes readers through a graphic-novel tour of the digestive tract. (Rev: BL 10/1/12) [612.3]

20714 Llewellyn, Claire. *Eating* (1–3). Series: Body in Action. 2004, Smart Apple LB $27.10 (978-1-58340-436-2). The digestive system, senses of smell and taste, the body's use of nutrients, and various types of food are all covered here, along with information on healthy eating and food allergies. (Rev: BL 11/1/04) [612.3]

20715 Parker, Steve. *Digestion* (5–9). Series: Our Bodies. 2004, Raintree LB $28.56 (978-0-7398-6620-7). Details of the human body's digestive system are accompanied by information on keeping them healthy. (Rev: BL 8/04) [612]

20716 Petrie, Kristin. *The Digestive System* (3–5). Illus. Series: The Human Body. 2006, ABDO LB $22.78 (978-1-59679-710-9). 32pp. Why and how we eat and how our bodies use food are all covered here, with diagrams, photographs, and interesting facts to keep readers engaged. (Rev: SLJ 5/07)

20717 Rau, Dana Meachen. *My Stomach* (PS–3). Illus. Series: Bookworms: What's Inside Me? 2004, Benchmark LB $21.36 (978-0-7614-1782-8). 31pp. A simple overview of the stomach's role in digestion, with photographs, diagrams, and X-rays. (Rev: SLJ 2/05) [612.3]

20718 Royston, Angela. *Why Do I Vomit? And Other Questions About Digestion* (3–5). Illus. Series: Body Matters. 2002, Heinemann LB $24.22 (978-1-4034-0206-6). 32pp. In easy-to-understand language and many illustrations, Royston gives an inside look at the gastrointestinal system and some of its most obvious manifestations. (Rev: HBG 10/03; SLJ 4/03) [612.3]

20719 Showers, Paul. *What Happens to a Hamburger?* (K–3). Illus. by Edward Miller. Series: Let's-Read-and-Find-Out Science. 2001, HarperCollins LB $15.89 (978-0-06-027948-6); paper $5.99 (978-0-06-445183-3). 32pp. A new edition of this interesting easy reader that explains the mysteries of digestion. (Rev: BL 4/15/01; HBG 10/01) [612.3]

20720 Simon, Seymour. *Guts: Our Digestive System* (5–8). 2005, HarperCollins LB $17.89 (978-0-06-054652-6). Photographs and straightforward yet fascinating text present the digestive system. (Rev: BL 3/1/05; SLJ 4/05) [612.3]

20721 Toriello, James. *The Stomach: Learning How We Digest* (5–9). Series: 3-D Library of the Human Body. 2002, Rosen LB $27.95 (978-0-8239-3536-9). Using outstanding diagrams and clear explanations, the digestive system is highlighted with material on each of its parts and their functions. (Rev: BL 7/02; SLJ 7/02) [612.3]

Nervous System

20722 Degezelle, Terri. *Your Brain* (K–2). Illus. Series: The Bridgestone Science Library. 2002, Capstone LB $22.60 (978-0-7368-1147-7). 24pp. An attractive, basic overview of the brain with "Fun Facts" and an easy activity. (Rev: SLJ 7/02) [612.8]

20723 Funston, Sylvia, and Jay Ingram. *It's All in Your Head: A Guide to Your Brilliant Brain. 2nd ed.* (3–6). Illus. by Gary Clement. 2005, Maple Tree $16.95 (978-1-897066-43-0); paper $9.95 (978-1-897066-44-7). 64pp. Answering questions in conversational text, this book explores the makeup and workings of the human brain, touches on brain research, and includes experiments and puzzles. (Rev: SLJ 1/06) [612.8]

20724 Hayhurst, Chris. *The Brain and Spinal Cord: Learning How We Think, Feel, and Move* (5–9). Series: 3-D Library of the Human Body. 2002, Rosen LB $27.95 (978-0-8239-3528-4). 48pp. Exceptional illustrations and a clear text are used to explain the composition of the brain with explanations of how it works and how emotions influence our thoughts. (Rev: BL 7/02; SLJ 7/02) [612.8]

20725 Jakab, Cheryl. *Nervous System* (3–5). Illus. Series: Our Body. 2007, Smart Apple LB $27.10 (978-1-58340-735-6). 32pp. The anatomy and functions of this system of the body are covered, as well as diseases and conditions that can affect it and how to keep it healthy. (Rev: SLJ 7/07)

20726 Nettleton, Pamela Hill. *Think, Think, Think: Learning About Your Brain* (K–3). Illus. by Becky Shipe. Series: The Amazing Body. 2004, Picture Window LB $25.26 (978-1-4048-0252-0). 24pp. A simple explanation of how the brain works, with an activity and discussion of protective gear and brain scans. (Rev: SLJ 11/04) [612.8]

20727 Newquist, H. P. *The Great Brain Book: An Inside Look at the Inside of Your Head* (5–8). Illus. by Keith Kasnot. 2005, Scholastic $18.95 (978-0-439-45895-5). The structure of the brain, its inner workings, and the history of our knowledge of this organ are all discussed in detail; interesting anecdotes add to the presentation. (Rev: BL 6/1–15/05; SLJ 9/05) [612.8]

20728 Parker, Steve. *The Brain and Nervous System* (5–9). Series: Our Bodies. 2004, Raintree LB $28.56 (978-0-7398-6619-1). Details of the human body's brain and nervous system are accompanied by information on keeping them healthy. (Rev: BL 8/04)

20729 Stewart, Melissa. *You've Got Nerve! The Secrets of the Brain and Nerves* (2–4). Illus. by Janet Hamlin. Series: Gross and Goofy Body. 2010, Marshall Cavendish LB $20.95 (978-076144157-1). 48pp. Detailed, compelling facts about the human and animal brains and nervous systems are presented in this clearly organized book. (Rev: BL 9/1/10) [612.8]

Respiratory System

20730 Frost, Helen. *The Respiratory System* (K–2). Illus. Series: Human Body Systems. 2000, Capstone LB $17.26 (978-0-7368-0652-7). 24pp. Simple, brief text introduces the respiratory system, with clearly labeled diagrams and full-color photographs. (Rev: HBG 10/01; SLJ 4/01) [612]

20731 Furgang, Kathy. *My Lungs* (K–3). Illus. Series: My Body. 2001, Rosen LB $21.25 (978-0-8239-5575-6). 24pp. A basic overview of the lungs, their anatomy, how they function, and diseases of the lung, with helpful illustrations. (Rev: SLJ 9/01) [612.2]

20732 Hayhurst, Chris. *The Lungs: Learning How We Breathe* (5–9). Series: 3-D Library of the Human Body. 2002, Rosen LB $27.95 (978-0-8239-3534-5). Amazing computer graphics are used to explain the composition of the lungs, how they work, and what keeps them healthy. (Rev: BL 7/02) [612.6]

20733 Jakab, Cheryl. *Respiratory System* (3–5). Illus. Series: Our Body. 2007, Smart Apple LB $27.10 (978-1-58340-736-3). 32pp. The anatomy and functions of this system of the body are covered, as well as diseases and conditions that can affect it and how to keep it healthy. (Rev: SLJ 7/07)

20734 Nettleton, Pamela Hill. *Breathe in, Breathe Out: Learning About Your Lungs* (K–3). Illus. by Becky Shipe. Series: The Amazing Body. 2004, Picture Window LB $25.26 (978-1-4048-0254-4). 24pp. A simple explanation of how the lungs work, with breathing activities and discussion of asthma and inhalers. (Rev: SLJ 11/04) [612.2]

20735 Simon, Seymour. *Lungs: Your Respiratory System* (3–6). Illus. 2007, Collins $16.99 (978-0-06-054654-0). 32pp. From simple breathing to coughing, hiccups, and other respiratory problems, this is a clear overview of the lungs and their importance to human life. (Rev: BL 12/1/06; SLJ 4/07) [612.2]

Senses

20736 Beck, Esther. *Cool Odor Decoders: Fun Science Projects About Smells* (4–6). 2008, ABDO LB $16.95 (978-1-59928-909-0). 32pp. Five high-interest experiments with detailed, illustrated instructions follow discussion about the scientific method, keeping a journal, and safety. (Rev: SLJ 2/08) [612.8]

20737 Cobb, Vicki. *Follow Your Nose: Discover Your Sense of Smell* (3–5). Illus. Series: Five Senses. 2000, Millbrook LB $22.90 (978-0-7613-1521-6). 32pp. This book blends facts and humor in an exploration of the sense of smell and also offers suggestions for easy experiments. (Rev: BL 11/15/00; HBG 3/01) [612.8]

20738 Cobb, Vicki. *Open Your Eyes: Discover Your Sense of Sight* (2–5). Illus. by Cynthia C. Lewis. Series: The Five Senses. 2002, Millbrook LB $22.90 (978-0-7613-1705-0). An appealing look at the eye, the parts of the eye, and how the eye works, with easy experiments and optical illusions. (Rev: HBG 10/02; SLJ 5/02) [612.84]

20739 Cobb, Vicki. *Perk up Your Ears: Discover Your Sense of Hearing* (3–6). Illus. by Cynthia C. Lewis. Series: The Five Senses. 2001, Millbrook LB $22.90 (978-0-7613-1704-3). An entertaining overview of hearing that encourages children to do lots of experimenting. (Rev: HBG 3/02; SLJ 4/02) [612.8]

20740 Cobb, Vicki. *Your Tongue Can Tell: Discover Your Sense of Taste* (3–5). Illus. Series: Five Senses. 2000, Millbrook LB $21.90 (978-0-7613-1473-8). 32pp. As well as giving an entertaining introduction to the sense of taste, this book supplies many ideas for activities and simple projects. (Rev: BL 11/15/00; HBG 3/01) [612.8]

20741 Furgang, Kathy. *My Ears* (K–3). Illus. Series: My Body. 2001, Rosen LB $21.25 (978-0-8239-5572-5). 24pp. A basic overview of the ears, their anatomy, how they function, and diseases of the ear, with helpful illustrations. (Rev: SLJ 9/01) [612.8]

20742 Gordon, Sharon. *Seeing* (1–2). Illus. Series: Rookie Read-About Health. 2001, Children's Book Pr. paper $5.95 (978-0-516-25990-1). 32pp. Very young readers are encouraged to think about their eyes and their ability to see. Also use *Smelling* (2001). (Rev: BL 12/1/01) [612.8]

20743 Markle, Sandra. *Lost Sight: True Survival Stories* (5–8). Series: Powerful Medicine. 2010, Lerner LB $27.93 (978-0-8225-8701-9). 48pp. Arresting full-color photographs, cross-sections, and personal stories are combined with facts about procedures and information about the medical personnel involved, (Rev: BL 10/1/10; LMC 11–12/10) [612.8]

20744 Murphy, Patricia J. *Hearing* (2–4). Illus. Series: A True Book. 2003, Children's Pr. paper $6.95 (978-0-516-26970-2). 47pp. A simple, large-print look at the ear and our sense of hearing. Also use *Taste* and *Touch* (both 2003). (Rev: SLJ 7/03) [612.8]

20745 Olien, Rebecca. *Hearing* (PS–1). Series: First Facts, The Senses. 2005, Capstone LB $21.26 (978-0-7368-4301-0). 24pp. This slim introduction to hearing includes an experiment to help young readers understand how this sense works. Also use *Tasting* and *Touching* (both 2005). (Rev: SLJ 1/06) [612.8]

20746 Parker, Steve. *The Senses* (5–9). Series: Our Bodies. 2004, Raintree LB $28.56 (978-0-7398-6624-5). Details of the human senses are accompanied by information on keeping them healthy. (Rev: BL 8/04) [612]

20747 Parker, Vic. *Having a Hearing Test* (K–2). Illus. Series: Growing Up. 2011, Heinemann LB $22 (978-143294799-6). 24pp. This reassuring book gives readers a sense of what to expect from a hearing test. (Rev: BL 7/11) [617.8]

20748 Schuette, Sarah L. *Taking Care of My Ears* (PS–1). Illus. Series: Keeping Healthy. 2005, Capstone LB $21.26 (978-0-7368-4259-4). 24pp. An easy-to-understand explanation of the sense of hearing plus basic information about ear care. (Rev: BL 10/15/05) [613]

20749 Schuh, Mari. *The Sense of Touch* (K–3). Series: Blastoff! Readers. The Senses. 2007, Children's Pr. LB $20.00 (978-0-531-14747-4). 24pp. With diagrams, clear text, and fun facts, Schuh introduces the sense of touch in both humans and animals. *The Sense of Hearing, The Sense of Sight, The Sense of Smell,* and *The Sense of Taste* (all 2007). (Rev: SLJ 2/08) [612.8]

20750 Sherman, Josepha. *The Ear: Learning How We Hear* (5–9). Series: 3-D Library of the Human Body. 2002, Rosen LB $26.50 (978-0-8239-3529-1). 48pp. Using amazing illustrations and clear explanations, Sherman introduces the ear, its anatomy, uses, operation, and problems that can develop. (Rev: BL 7/02) [612.8]

20751 Sideri, Simona. *Let's Look at Eyes* (PS–K). Illus. by Sheilagh Noble. Series: Let's Look At. 2004, Smart Apple LB $22.80 (978-1-58340-495-9). 30pp. Young children compare their eyes and sight with those of animals, including owls, eagles, camels, lobsters, and wasps. Also use *Let's Look at Feet* (2004). (Rev: BL 1/1–15/05) [573.8]

20752 Silverstein, Alvin, and Virginia Silverstein. *Earaches* (3–5). Series: My Health. 2002, Watts paper $6.95 (978-0-531-15562-2). 48pp. This book describes, in a simple text and many pictures, how the ear functions, what can cause earaches, and how to treat them. (Rev: BL 6/1–15/02) [612.8]

20753 Silverstein, Alvin, and Virginia Silverstein. *Smelling and Tasting* (4–6). Illus. by Anne Canevari Green. Series: Senses and Sensors. 2002, Twenty-First Century LB $25.90 (978-0-7613-1667-1). 64pp. Human and animal senses of smell and taste are covered in this well-organized and readable volume. Also use *Touching and Feeling* (2002). (Rev: BL 3/15/02; HBG 10/02; SLJ 8/02)

20754 Viegas, Jennifer. *The Eye: Learning How We See* (5–9). Series: 3-D Library of the Human Body. 2002, Rosen LB $27.95 (978-0-8239-3530-7). This volume on the anatomy and function of the human eye includes illustrations, diagrams, a glossary, and other aids. (Rev: BL 7/02) [612.8]

20755 Viegas, Jennifer. *The Mouth and Nose: Learning How We Taste and Smell* (5–9). Series: 3-D Library of the Human Body. 2002, Rosen LB $26.50 (978-0-8239-3535-2). 48pp. The mouth and nose are featured in this heavily illustrated account that covers their composition, functions, and how they work together. (Rev: BL 7/02) [612]

20756 Woodward, Kay. *Hearing* (1–4). Series: Our Senses. 2005, Gareth Stevens LB $23.00 (978-0-8368-4406-1). 24pp. A book on how the sense of hearing works in humans and animals, with simple text, eye-catching illustrations, and related activities. Also use *Touch, Taste, Smell,* and *Sight* (all 2005). (Rev: SLJ 7/05) [612.8]

Skeletal-Muscular System

20757 Arnold, Caroline. *The Skeletal System* (3–4). Illus. 2004, Lerner LB $25.26 (978-0-8225-5140-9). 48pp.

The skeleton and bones are introduced in simple, concise text. (Rev: SLJ 2/05) [612.7]

20758 Clements, Andrew. *The Handiest Things in the World* (PS–2). Illus. by Raquel Jaramillo. 2010, Atheneum $16.99 (978-1-4169-6166-6). 48pp. A simple celebration of all the things our hands can do and the tools we use with them. (Rev: BL 3/1/10; LMC 10/10; SLJ 5/1/10) [612]

20759 Cobb, Vicki. *Your Body Battles a Broken Bone* (3–6). Illus. by Andrew N. Harris. Series: Body Battles. 2009, Millbrook LB $25.26 (978-0-8225-7468-2). 32pp. This title explains and cleverly illustrates how the body's cells act like a troop to fix a broken bone, and additionally clarifies the concept through photomicrographs. (Rev: SLJ 5/09) [617.4]

20760 Degezelle, Terri. *Your Bones* (K–2). Illus. Series: The Bridgestone Science Library. 2002, Capstone LB $22.60 (978-0-7368-1146-0). 24pp. An attractive, basic overview of bones with "Fun Facts" and an easy activity. (Rev: SLJ 7/02) [612.7]

20761 Frost, Helen. *The Muscular System* (K–2). Illus. Series: Human Body Systems. 2000, Capstone LB $17.26 (978-0-7368-0650-3). 24pp. Short, simple text introduces the muscular system, accompanied by full-color illustrations. (Rev: HBG 10/01; SLJ 4/01) [612]

20762 Gold, Susan Dudley. *The Musculoskeletal System and the Skin* (5–10). Illus. Series: Human Body Library. 2003, Enslow LB $23.93 (978-0-7660-2023-8). 48pp. Gold uses a conversational style to introduce detailed facts about the skeletal system, with useful graphics and some practical advice. (Rev: BL 4/15/03; HBG 10/03; SLJ 10/03) [612.7]

20763 Jenkins, Steve. *Bones: Skeletons and How They Work* (2–5). Illus. by author. 2010, Scholastic $16.99 (978-0-545-04651-0). 48pp. Human and animal skeletons are explored in often humorous detail using concise text and cut-paper collages, with many comparisons and several gatefolds. (Rev: BL 5/15/10; HB 7–8/10; LMC 10/10; SLJ 7/10) [612]

20764 Johnson, Rebecca. *The Muscular System* (2–4). Series: Early Bird Body Systems. 2004, Lerner LB $25.26 (978-0-8225-1248-6). Photographs and diagrams add to the easy-to-understand text; a word list starts the book and print and Web resources are appended. (Rev: BL 10/15/04; SLJ 2/05) [612.7]

20765 Macnair, Patricia Ann. *Movers and Shapers* (3–5). Series: Bodyscope. 2004, Houghton $9.95 (978-0-7534-5791-7). 40pp. The importance of physical fitness is emphasized in this attractive overview of the musculoskeletal system. (Rev: BL 10/15/04) [612.7]

20766 Oleksy, Walter. *The Head and Neck: Learning How We Use Our Muscles* (5–9). Series: 3-D Library of the Human Body. 2002, Rosen LB $26.50 (978-0-8239-3531-4). 48pp. The muscles of the head and neck and their roles in controlling the sense organs, chewing and swallowing, facial expressions, and conveying emotions are explained in this well-illustrated account. (Rev: BL 7/02) [612.7]

20767 Parker, Steve. *The Skeleton and Muscles* (5–9). Series: Our Bodies. 2004, Raintree LB $28.56 (978-0-7398-6622-1). Details of the human body's skeletal and muscular systems are accompanied by information on keeping them healthy. (Rev: BL 8/04) [612.7]

20768 Rau, Dana Meachen. *My Bones and Muscles* (PS–3). Illus. Series: Bookworms: What's Inside Me? 2004, Benchmark LB $21.36 (978-0-7614-1777-4). 31pp. A simple overview of bones, skeleton, and muscles, with photographs, diagrams, and X-rays. (Rev: SLJ 2/05) [612.7]

20769 Sherman, Josepha. *The Upper Limbs: Learning How We Use Our Arms, Elbows, Forearms, and Hands* (5–9). Series: 3-D Library of the Human Body. 2002, Rosen LB $27.95 (978-0-8239-3537-6). 48pp. The parts of the arm and hand are examined with illustrated material on how the muscles in these areas function and receive support from the skeletal structure. (Rev: BL 7/02) [612.7]

20770 Silverstein, Alvin, et al. *Broken Bones* (3–5). Series: My Health. 2001, Watts LB $25.50 (978-0-531-11781-1). This book describes what happens when bones get broken, the causes, treatments available, and how mending takes place. (Rev: BL 1/1–15/02; SLJ 8/01) [612.7]

20771 Stewart, Melissa. *Give Me a Hand: The Secrets of Hands, Feet, Arms, and Legs* (2–4). Illus. by Janet Hamlin. Series: Gross and Goofy Body. 2010, Marshall Cavendish LB $20.95 (978-076144158-8). 48pp. Covering arms, legs, and feet in addition to hands, this is an interesting introduction to the function of human and animal body appendages. (Rev: BL 9/1/10) [591.4]

20772 Viegas, Jennifer. *The Lower Limbs: Learning How We Use Our Thighs, Knees, Legs, and Feet* (5–9). Series: 3-D Library of the Human Body. 2002, Rosen LB $26.50 (978-0-8239-3533-8). 48pp. The bones and muscles of the legs and feet and their functions are described in a clear text and exceptional illustrations. (Rev: BL 7/02; SLJ 7/02) [612.7]

Skin and Hair

20773 Baines, Becky. *Your Skin Holds You In: A Book About Your Skin* (1–2). Series: Zig Zag. 2008, National Geographic $14.95 (978-1-4263-0311-1). 32pp. Thirteen short sentences and large illustrations featuring children of diverse backgrounds convey key facts about skin. (Rev: HB 9/08; LMC 11/08; SLJ 11/08) [612.7]

20774 Degezelle, Terri. *Taking Care of My Hair* (PS–2). Series: Keeping Healthy. 2005, Capstone LB $21.26 (978-0-7368-4261-7). 24pp. Easy-to-understand advice about hair care, in an oversize format with large color photographs. Also use *Taking Care of My Skin* (2005). (Rev: SLJ 12/05) [646.7]

20775 Fromer, Liza, and Francine Gerstein. *My Itchy Body* (3–6). Illus. by Joe Weissmann. Series: Body Works. 2012, Tundra $12.95 (978-1-77049-312-4). 24pp. An accessible discussion of the various causes of itchiness and the most effective treatments. **e** (Rev: BL 12/1/12; SLJ 10/12) [612.7]

20776 Glaser, Jason. *Head Lice* (1–3). Series: First Facts: Health Matters. 2005, Capstone LB $21.26 (978-0-7368-4291-4). 24pp. In simple text, this basic title looks at the causes, symptoms, and treatment of head lice. (Rev: SLJ 12/05) [616.5]

20777 Kinch, Michael P. *Warts* (3–5). Illus. Series: My Health. 2000, Watts LB $25.50 (978-0-531-11625-8). 48pp. Different kinds of warts are discussed, with material and activities related to how they are transmitted, how they grow, and how they can be eliminated. (Rev: BL 6/1–15/00) [616.5]

20778 Radabaugh, Melinda. *Getting a Haircut* (PS–1). Series: First Time. 2003, Heinemann LB $18.50 (978-1-4034-0225-7). 24pp. Reasons for getting a haircut and the experiences involved are emploerd in simple, reassuring text plus pictures and a quiz. (Rev: HBG 10/03; SLJ 9/03) [646.7]

20779 Silverstein, Alvin, et al. *Is That a Rash?* (3–5). Illus. Series: My Health. 2000, Watts LB $25.50 (978-0-531-11637-1). 48pp. With many suggested activities and excellent color photos, this account introduces skin problems — their causes and treatments. (Rev: BL 6/1–15/00) [616.5]

20780 Stewart, Melissa. *Here We Grow: The Secrets of Hair and Nails* (2–4). Illus. by Janet Hamlin. Series: Gross and Goofy Body. 2010, Marshall Cavendish LB $20.95 (978-076144172-4). 48pp. Covering facial and body hair, nail, melanin, and so forth, this is an interesting introduction to the function of these organs in humans and animals. Also use *The Skin You're In: The Secrets of Skin* (2010). (Rev: BL 9/1/10) [612.7]

20781 Sutherland, Adam. *Body Decoration* (5–8). Illus. Series: On the Radar: Street Style. 2012, Lerner LB $26.60 (978-076137769-6). 32pp. With a history of body decoration since ancient times, this is an interesting survey of the various forms that are popular today. (Rev: BLO 3/15/12; SLJ 4/1/12) [391.6]

20782 Tyler, Michael. *The Skin You Live In* (PS–2). Illus. by David Lee Csicsko. 2005, Chicago Children's Museum $14.95 (978-0-9759580-0-1). Skin's physical properties and different shades are among the features explored in rhyming verse. (Rev: SLJ 5/05)

Teeth

20783 Cobb, Vicki. *Your Body Battles a Cavity* (3–6). Illus. by Andrew N. Harris. Series: Body Battles. 2009, Millbrook LB $25.26 (978-0-8225-7469-9). 32pp. This title explains and cleverly illustrates how the body's cells act like a troop to get rid of plaque and additionally clarifies the concept through photomicrographs. (Rev: SLJ 5/09) [617.6]

20784 Copeland, Cynthia L. *The Tooth Fairy Tells All* (K–3). Illus. by author. Series: Silly Millies. 2002, Millbrook LB $17.90 (978-0-7613-2805-6); paper $4.99 (978-0-7613-1785-2). 31pp. This gentle exchange between the Tooth Fairy and the Wisdom Tooth provides useful information about teeth — including the different types — and how best to care for them. (Rev: HBG 3/03; SLJ 8/03)

20785 Degezelle, Terri. *Taking Care of My Teeth* (PS–2). Series: Keeping Healthy. 2005, Capstone LB $21.26 (978-0-7368-4264-8). 24pp. Easy-to-understand advice about dental care, in an oversize format with large color photographs. Also use *Taking Care of My Skin* (2005). (Rev: SLJ 12/05) [617.6]

20786 Keller, Laurie. *Open Wide: Tooth School Inside* (2–4). Illus. 2000, Holt $16.95 (978-0-8050-6192-5). 32pp. A fun book that explores the different kinds of teeth, dental care, and the causes of tooth decay. (Rev: BCCB 9/00; BL 5/1/00; HB 5/00; HBG 9/00; SLJ 5/00) [617.6]

20787 Lee, Jordan. *Coping with Braces and Other Orthodontic Work* (4–9). Series: Coping. 1998, Rosen LB $31.95 (978-0-8239-2721-0). A book about braces, their purposes, and the problems they can cause. (Rev: SLJ 11/98) [612.3]

20788 Markle, Sandra. *What If You Had Animal Teeth!?* (1–3). Illus. by Howard McWilliam. 2013, Scholastic paper $3.99 (978-054548438-1). 32pp. Consider what would happen if your new teeth grew in as animal ones! The results would be funny and/or calamitous. (Rev: BL 1/13; LMC 5–6/13*) [610]

20789 Miller, Edward. *The Tooth Book: A Guide to Healthy Teeth and Gums* (K–3). Illus. by author. 2008, Holiday $16.95 (978-0-8234-2092-6). 32pp. Facts and advice are dispensed with a dollop of humor and history, plus engaging images. (Rev: BL 2/15/08; SLJ 2/08) [617.6]

20790 Murkoff, Heidi. *What to Expect When You Go to the Dentist* (1–3). Illus. by Laura Rader. Series: What To Expect Kids. 2002, HarperCollins $10.99 (978-0-694-01328-9). 32pp. Angus the dog gives good advice and some projects to prepare youngsters for their first visit to a dentist. (Rev: BL 6/1–15/02; HBG 10/02) [617.601]

Hygiene, Physical Fitness, and Nutrition

20791 Baptiste, Baron. *My Daddy Is a Pretzel* (PS–3). Illus. by Sophie Fatus. 2004, Barefoot Bks. $16.99 (978-1-84148-151-7). 48pp. An attractive introduction to basic yoga poses. (Rev: BL 10/15/04; SLJ 1/05) [613]

20792 Barraclough, Sue. *Wash and Clean* (2–4). Illus. 2012, Black Rabbit LB $24.25 (978-159771310-8). 24pp. Healthy human habits are compared with those of animals in this informative volume with chapter titles such as "Biting and Chewing" and "Hands, Nails, Claws." (Rev: BL 4/1/12) [613]

20793 Chryssicas, Mary Kaye. *I Love Yoga* (3–5). Photos by Angela Coppola. 2005, DK $12.99 (978-0-7566-1400-3). 48pp. Follows six children as they learn the

basic techniques and positions of hatha yoga. (Rev: BL 11/15/05; SLJ 5/06) [613.7]

20794 Cole, Babette. *The Sprog Owner's Manual (or How Kids Work)* (K–3). 2006, Trafalgar paper $9.99 (978-0-09-944765-8). 32pp. Tips on health and grooming issues for kids ("sprogs" is a British term), presented with lots of humor. (Rev: BL 5/1/06) [823.914]

20795 Crump, Marguerite. *Don't Sweat It! Every Body's Answers to Questions You Don't Want to Ask: A Guide for Young People* (5–9). Illus. by Chris Sharp. 2002, Free Spirit paper $12.95 (978-1-57542-114-8). Crump tackles potentially embarrassing questions about personal hygiene. (Rev: SLJ 1/03; VOYA 2/03) [613.0433]

20796 Curtis, Andrea. *What's for Lunch?: How Schoolchildren Eat Around the World* (1–4). Illus. by Sophie Casson. 2012, Red Deer paper $12.95 (978-0-88995-482-3). 40pp. Thirteen different countries are detailed in this informative book about the differences in what children eat at school each day, complete with facts about the countries as well as a discussion about the food or foods the children eat. (Rev: LMC 8–9/13*; SLJ 1/13) [371.7]

20797 D'Aluisio, Faith. *What the World Eats* (4–8). 2008, Tricycle $22.99 (978-1-5824-6246-2). 160pp. What do people eat around the world? This is a fascinating survey of expenses, ingredients, and meals shared with 25 families in 21 countries; with statistics on obesity, access to water, and other key factors. (Rev: BL 7/08*; SLJ 7/08) [641.300]

20798 Dalgleish, Sharon. *Exercise and Rest* (3–5). Illus. Series: Healthy Choices. 2007, Black Rabbit LB $18.95 (978-1-58340-755-4). 32pp. Square, colorful pages looks at the importance of both exercise and rest, recommending 30 minutes of exercise three or four times a week. (Rev: BL 4/1/07) [613.7]

20799 De Brunhoff, Laurent. *Babar's Yoga for Elephants* (2–4). Illus. 2002, Abrams $16.95 (978-0-8109-1021-8). 48pp. The sage elephant Babar re-creates yoga poses, which kids may be tempted to do as well, in this nonfiction book best read with an adult nearby. (Rev: BL 10/15/02; HBG 3/03; SLJ 4/03) [613.7]

20800 Edwards, Hazel, and Goldie Alexander. *Talking About Your Weight* (4–7). Illus. Series: Healthy Living. 2010, Gareth Stevens LB $26 (978-143393655-5). 32pp. Loaded topics such as eating disorders and obesity are presented in a clear, nonjudgmental fashion with emphasis on making better choices. (Rev: BL 4/1/10) [613]

20801 Ehrlich, Fred. *Does an Elephant Take a Bath?* (PS–K). Illus. by Emily Bolam. Series: Early Experiences. 2005, Blue Apple LB $13.50 (978-1-59354-111-8); paper $5.95 (978-1-59354-123-1). Illustrations of animals in bathtubs are followed by views of the animals using their natural methods of hygiene in this book that also shows how humans keep clean; a small, square book. (Rev: BL 10/15/05) [617.6]

20802 Feeney, Kathy. *Get Moving: Tips on Exercise* (K–3). Series: Your Health. 2001, Capstone LB $22.60 (978-0-7368-0973-3). 24pp. The importance of exercise is stressed through simple text and an activity pyramid. (Rev: HBG 3/02; SLJ 4/02) [613.7]

20803 Frost, Helen. *Drinking Water* (K–2). 2000, Capstone LB $17.26 (978-0-7368-0534-6). 24pp. This book explains simply why drinking water is a necessary part of one's diet. (Rev: HBG 9/00; SLJ 10/00) [613.2]

20804 Frost, Helen. *Eating Right* (K–2). Series: Food Guide Pyramid. 2000, Capstone LB $17.26 (978-0-7368-0535-3). 24pp. A very simple introduction to nutrition and the food pyramid. (Rev: HBG 9/00; SLJ 10/00) [613.2]

20805 Gordon, Sharon. *Exercise* (3–5). Series: Rookie Read-About Health. 2002, Children's Book Pr. paper $5.95 (978-0-516-26950-4). 32pp. This easy-reader explains how exercise builds strong muscles and shows how children can have fun while doing favorite activities. (Rev: BL 12/15/02) [613.7]

20806 Gordon, Sharon. *Keeping Clean* (3–5). Series: Rookie Read-About Health. 2002, Children's Book Pr. LB $20.50 (978-0-516-22572-2); paper $5.95 (978-0-516-26951-1). From bathing after exercise to washing one's hands before eating, this is a simple guide to personal hygiene and on how to keep germs from spreading. (Rev: BL 12/15/02) [613]

20807 Gordon, Sharon. *You Are What You Eat* (3–5). Series: Rookie Read-About Health. 2002, Children's Book Pr. LB $20.50 (978-0-516-22573-9); paper $5.95 (978-0-516-26952-8). 32pp. This book uses simple language to explain such nutritional facts as why breakfast is the most important meal of the day and why an apple is a better snack than potato chips. (Rev: BL 12/15/02) [613]

20808 Gray, Shirley W. *Exercising for Good Health* (2–4). Illus. Series: Living Well. 2003, Child's World LB $27.07 (978-1-59296-081-1). 32pp. Outlines the many benefits of regular exercise and describes the effects of specific activities on overall health. (Rev: SLJ 2/04) [613.7]

20809 Green, Emily K. *Fruits* (K–3). Illus. Series: New Food Guide Pyramid. 2006, Children's Pr. LB $18.50 (978-1-60014-005-1). 24pp. Explains the importance of fruit in the diet, referring to the new food guide pyramid. Also use *Grains; Meat and Beans; Oils; Milk, Yogurt, and Cheese; Vegetables,* and *Oils* (all 2006). (Rev: SLJ 5/07)

20810 King, Hazel. *Carbohydrates for a Healthy Body* (4–6). Illus. Series: Body Needs. 2003, Heinemann LB $27.07 (978-1-4034-0756-6). 48pp. A clearly written and well illustrated introduction to the role and value of carbohydrates in nutrition. (Rev: HBG 10/03; SLJ 4/04) [612.3]

20811 Koellhoffer, Tara, ed. *Food and Nutrition* (4–6). Series: Science News for Kids. 2006, Chelsea House $30.00 (978-0-7910-9121-0). 110pp. A wide-ranging collection of articles on food and nutrition that originally appeared on the Science News for Kids Web site. (Rev: BL 6/1–15/06) [613.2]

20812 Kuskowski, Alex. *Cool Relaxing: Healthy and Fun Ways to Chill Out* (4–6). Illus. Series: Cool Health

and Fitness. 2012, ABDO LB $27.07 (978-161783428-8). 32pp. Yoga, stretching, and meditation are among the relaxation strategies examined here. (Rev: BL 10/1/12) [613.7]

20813 Landau, Elaine. *A Healthy Diet* (4–7). Series: Watts Library. 2003, Watts LB $25.50 (978-0-531-12027-9). 63pp. Landau explains the basics of good nutrition; the benefits of vitamins, minerals, and exercise; and the dangers of fad diets. (Rev: SLJ 9/03) [613.2]

20814 Leedy, Loreen. *The Edible Pyramid: Good Eating Every Day. Rev. ed.* (PS–2). 2007, Holiday $17.95 (978-0-8234-2074-2); paper $6.95 (978-0-8234-2075-9). 32pp. This updated version of the 1994 guide retains the same charming animal characters and illustrations. (Rev: BL 5/1/07; SLJ 5/07) [613.2]

20815 Marsico, Katie. *Your Healthy Plate: Protein* (K–2). Illus. 2012, Cherry Lake LB $21.36 (978-161080349-6). 24pp. Answering such questions as "why do you need protein?" and "how much protein do you need?," this accessible guide provides readers with nutritious ways to fill their protein needs daily; colorful illustrations add appeal. Also use in this series: *Your Healthy Plate: Vegetables, Your Healthy Plate: Grains,* and *Your Healthy Plate: Dairy* (all 2012). (Rev: BL 8/12) [613.2]

20816 Miller, Edward. *The Monster Health Book: A Guide to Eating Healthy, Being Active and Feeling Great for Monsters and Kids!* (2–4). Illus. by author. 2006, Holiday $16.95 (978-0-8234-1956-2). 40pp. Basic health and nutrition facts and advice are presented in an enticing but brief format that may require amplification by adults. (Rev: BL 5/15/06; SLJ 6/06) [613.7]

20817 Mitchell, Melanie. *Eating Well* (K–3). Illus. Series: Pull Ahead Books. 2006, Lerner LB $22.60 (978-0-8225-2449-6). 32pp. An informative guide to the food pyramid and the fundamentals of healthy eating. (Rev: SLJ 8/06) [613.2]

20818 Nelson, Robin. *Staying Clean* (PS–1). Illus. Series: Pull-Ahead Books: Health. 2005, Lerner LB $22.60 (978-0-8225-2368-0); paper $5.95 (978-0-8225-2773-2). 32pp. Hand washing, brushing teeth, and avoiding head lice are among the topics addressed in simple text with full-color photographs. (Rev: BL 1/1–15/06) [613]

20819 Pascoe, Elaine, ed. *Spreading Menace: Salmonella Attack and the Hunger Craving* (5–8). Illus. Series: Body Story. 2003, Gale LB $24.95 (978-1-4103-0064-5). 48pp. Two stories show how the body can react to food — Mike is infected with salmonella, and George's hunger is giving him a weight problem. (Rev: SLJ 4/04) [615.9]

20820 Petrie, Kristin. *The Food Pyramid* (2–4). Illus. Series: Nutrition. 2004, ABDO LB $22.78 (978-1-59197-403-1). 32pp. A look at food groups, nutrition, serving sizes, and healthy eating in general, illustrated with photographs and other graphics. (Rev: HBG 4/04; SLJ 4/04) [613.2]

20821 Petrie, Kristin. *Nutrition Anyone?* (2–4). Illus. Series: Nutrition. 2004, ABDO LB $22.78 (978-1-59197-404-8). 32pp. Clear text and graphics introduce good nutrition and why it is necessary. (Rev: HBG 4/04; SLJ 4/04) [613.2]

20822 Petrie, Kristin. *Vitamins Are Vital* (2–4). Illus. Series: Nutrition. 2004, ABDO LB $22.78 (978-1-59197-406-2). 32pp. An exploration of the role of vitamins and minerals in nutrition, aimed at helping children have a healthful and balanced diet. (Rev: HBG 4/04; SLJ 4/04) [613.2]

20823 Rockwell, Lizzy. *The Busy Body Book: A Kid's Guide to Fitness* (PS–1). Illus. by author. 2004, Crown LB $17.99 (978-0-375-92203-9). Children of diverse backgrounds are shown in activities from yoga to roller-blading, and there is information on how the body works and the important role of exercise. (Rev: SLJ 1/04) [612]

20824 Royston, Angela. *Get Some Exercise!* (1–3). Series: Look After Yourself. 2003, Heinemann LB $22.79 (978-1-4034-4440-0). 32pp. The mechanics and benefits of exercise are clearly explained in easy-to-understand text. Also use *Get Some Rest!* (2003). (Rev: SLJ 2/04) [613.7]

20825 Royston, Angela. *Proteins for a Healthy Body* (4–6). Illus. Series: Body Needs. 2003, Heinemann LB $27.07 (978-1-4034-0759-7). 48pp. A description of the various types of proteins — hormones, antibodies, and enzymes — and how they are important in nutrition, with a look at how vegetarians can get enough of them on a restricted diet. (Rev: HBG 10/03; SLJ 4/04) [612.3]

20826 Royston, Angela. *Vitamins and Minerals for a Healthy Body* (4–6). Illus. Series: Body Needs. 2003, Heinemann LB $27.07 (978-1-4034-0758-0). 48pp. A look at the importance of vitamins and minerals in maintaining a healthy body, and at their role in preventing disease. (Rev: HBG 10/03; SLJ 4/04) [612.3]

20827 Schuh, Mari C. *Being Active* (PS–2). Series: Healthy Eating with MyPyramid. 2006, Capstone LB $21.26 (978-0-7368-5368-2). 24pp. This simple, bright volume focuses on activities that promote physical fitness, including bicycling, swimming, baseball, volleyball, taking care of pets, and playing with friends. Also use *Drinking Water* (2006). (Rev: SLJ 8/06) [613.7]

20828 Schuh, Mari C. *Healthy Snacks* (PS–2). Illus. by author. Series: Healthy Eating with MyPyramid. 2006, Scholastic LB $21.26 (978-0-7368-5369-9). 24pp. A companion to the new USDA food pyramid, explaining which snacks are best to eat in simple language and photographs. (Rev: BL 5/15/06; SLJ 8/06) [641.5]

20829 Schwartz, Ellen. *I'm a Vegetarian: Amazing Facts and Ideas for Healthy Vegetarians* (5–8). Illus. by Farida Zaman. 2002, Tundra paper $9.95 (978-0-88776-588-9). The social aspects of being a vegetarian are handled here with humor and sensitivity. (Rev: BL 7/02; SLJ 9/02) [613.2]

20830 Silverstein, Alvin, and Virginia Silverstein. *Physical Fitness* (3–5). Series: My Health. 2002, Watts paper $6.95 (978-0-531-15563-9). 48pp. Using photographs, cartoons, and other visuals plus a simple text, this book describes the importance of physical fitness and how to maintain it. (Rev: BL 6/1–15/02) [613.7]

20831 Silverstein, Alvin, et al. *Eat Your Vegetables! Drink Your Milk!* (3–5). Series: My Health. 2000, Watts paper $6.95 (978-0-531-16507-2). 48pp. This is a beginner's guide to nutrition and the part played by foods in maintaining a healthy body. (Rev: BL 9/15/00) [613]

20832 Simons, Rae. *I Eat When I'm Sad: Food and Feelings* (3–5). Illus. Series: Kids and Obesity. 2010, Mason Crest $19.95 (978-142221714-6); paper $7.95 (978-14222190-2-7). 48pp. This well-designed book takes a nonjudgmental and constructive look at the factors that motivate children to overeat. (Rev: BL 10/1/10; LMC 3–4/11) [616.85]

20833 Sullivan, Jaclyn. *What's in Your Chicken Nugget?* (3–5). Illus. Series: What's in Your Fast Food? 2012, Rosen LB $21.25 (978-144886208-5); paper $8.25 (978-144886375-4). 24pp. Books in this series explore the true contents of foods popular with children, explaining the science behind preservatives, fillers, and fats. e (Rev: BL 4/1/12; LMC 10/12) [641.6]

20834 Thornhill, Jan. *Who Wants Pizza? The Kids' Guide to the History, Science and Culture of Food* (5–8). 2010, Maple Tree paper $10.95 (978-1-897349-97-7). 64pp. Taking pizza as an example, this appealingly busy and well-illustrated book discusses the nutrients that food provides to the body and looks at various scientific (the chemistry of fertilizers, for example) and cultural aspects (a Bushman eating caterpillars) of food. (Rev: BL 12/1/10; LMC 11–12/10) [641.3]

20835 Tuminelly, Nancy. *Super Simple Bend and Stretch* (1–3). Illus. Series: Super Simple Exercise. 2011, ABDO LB $27.07 (978-161714959-7). 32pp. Introduces basic exercises as well as the benefits of healthy eating, and recommends tracking weekly progress. (Rev: BL 12/1/11) [613.7]

20836 VanCleave, Janice. *Janice VanCleave's Food and Nutrition for Every Kid: Easy Activities That Make Learning Science Fun* (4–8). Series: Science for Every Kid. 1999, Wiley paper $12.95 (978-0-471-17665-7). Each of the 25 chapters in this book contains information about food, including food groups, the relationship between energy and food, how to read nutrition labels, and vitamins and minerals, plus dozens of easily performed projects that demonstrate these facts and concepts. (Rev: SLJ 8/99) [641.3]

20837 Vestergaard, Hope. *Potty Animals: What to Know When You've Gotta Go!* (PS). Illus. by Valeria Petrone. 2010, Sterling $14.95 (978-1-4027-5996-3). 32pp. A colorful cast of animals illustrate different aspects of hygiene, cleanliness, privacy, and communication in this appealing guide to the potty. (Rev: BL 3/15/10; SLJ 5/1/10) [649.62]

20838 Watson, Stephanie. *Mystery Meat: Hot Dogs, Sausages, and Lunch Meats: The Incredibly Disgusting Story* (4–7). Illus. Series: Incredibly Disgusting Food. 2011, Rosen LB $26.50 (978-1-4488-1268-4); paper $11.75 (978-1-4488-2284-3). 48pp. Discusses the ingredients of "mystery meats" and the impact they can have on our bodies and minds, with some eye-catchingly off-putting photographs. Lexile 1220L (Rev: BL 4/1/11; SLJ 6/11) [664]

20839 Weiss, Stefanie Iris. *Everything You Need to Know About Being a Vegan* (5–8). Series: Need to Know Library. 1999, Rosen LB $27.95 (978-0-8239-2958-0). This book discusses vegans, people who do not eat or use animal products (usually for religious reasons), their lifestyles, diets, and possible social problems. (Rev: SLJ 1/00; VOYA 4/00) [613.2]

20840 Whitford, Rebecca. *Little Yoga: A Toddler's First Book of Yoga* (PS). Illus. by Martina Selway. 2005, Holt $9.95 (978-0-8050-7879-4). 28pp. Nine simple yoga exercises for children are shown in eye-catching spreads. (Rev: BL 10/1/05; SLJ 11/05) [613.7]

20841 Williams, Kara. *Frequently Asked Questions About MyPyramid: Eating Right* (5–8). Illus. 2007, Rosen LB $20.95 (978-1-4042-1974-8). Introduces the 2005 version of the food pyramid as well as information on diet, nutrition, the human body, and exercise. (Rev: BL 6/1–15/07; LMC 10/07) [613.2]

20842 Zahensky, Barbara A. *Diet Fads* (4–8). Series: Danger Zone. Dieting and Eating Disorders. 2007, Rosen LB $27.95 (978-1-4042-1999-1). Fad and crash diets and the dangers of overeating and excessive weight loss are the focus of this practical guide. (Rev: LMC 10/07; SLJ 9/07) [613.2]

Safety and Accidents

20843 Chaiet, Donna, and Francine Russell. *The Safe Zone: A Kid's Guide to Personal Safety* (4–7). 1998, Morrow paper $6.95 (978-0-688-16091-3). This book alerts youngsters to danger signs, gives advice on body language and self-esteem, and offers tips on how to avoid threatening situations. (Rev: BL 4/1/98; HBG 10/98) [613.6]

20844 Claybourne, Anna. *100 Deadliest Things on the Planet* (4–7). Illus. 2012, Scholastic paper $7.99 (978-05454343-7-9). 112pp. Dangerous animals, natural catastrophes, deadly diseases, poisonous plants — they're all here, with danger ratings. (Rev: BL 12/1/12) [591.65]

20845 Gale, Karen Buhler. *The Kids' Guide to First Aid: All About Bruises, Burns, Stings, Sprains and Other Ouches* (4–6). Illus. by Michael Kline. 2002, Williamson paper $14.25 (978-1-885593-58-0). 128pp. Readers learn to distinguish between situations they can handle and when they need to call for help, and gain useful information on stopping bleeding, applying bandages, and dealing with choking. (Rev: SLJ 4/02) [616.04]

20846 Gordon, Sharon. *Bruises* (1–2). Series: Rookie Read-About Health. 2002, Children's Book Pr. paper $5.95 (978-0-516-26872-9). 31pp. Readers learn why bruises change color and how to treat them, with reminders of the protection that proper clothing can offer. Also use *Cuts and Scrapes* (2001). (Rev: SLJ 8/02) [616.04]

20847 Gutman, Bill. *Be Aware of Danger* (5–8). Series: Focus on Safety. 1996, Twenty-First Century LB $24.90 (978-0-8050-4142-2). Situations that could be dangerous to young people are highlighted and preventive measures outlined. (Rev: BL 2/1/97; SLJ 2/97) [613.6]

20848 Gutman, Bill. *Recreation Can Be Risky* (4–8). Series: Focus on Safety. 1996, Henry Holt LB $24.90 (978-0-8050-4143-9). The author gives practical suggestions for enjoying such activities as baseball, biking, or hiking while also keeping safe through warm-up exercises, proper equipment, correct clothing, etc. (Rev: BL 7/96; SLJ 9/96; VOYA 10/96) [790]

20849 Herrington, Lisa M. *Stranger Safety* (PS–K). Illus. Series: Rookie Read About: Safety. 2012, Scholastic/Children's Press LB $23 (978-0-531-28972-3); paper $5.95 (9780531292747). 32pp. Beginning readers will find this book appealing as it discusses various strategies to remain safe in the presence of strangers. (Rev: BL 10/1/12; LMC 10/13; SLJ 3/13) [363.1]

20850 Hurley, Michael. *Surviving the Wilderness* (4–7). Series: Extreme Survival. 2011, Heinemann LB $33.50 (978-1-4109-3972-2). 56pp. Hurley explores the dangers posed in the mountains, forest, outback, desert, jungle, and wilderness as well as those we face at sea, and offers survival tips and advice. (Rev: SLJ 8/11) [613.6]

20851 Kyi, Tanya Lloyd. *Fifty Poisonous Questions: A Book with Bite* (4–7). Illus. by Ross Kinnaird. 2011, Annick $21.95 (978-1-55451-281-2); paper $12.95 (978-1-55451-280-5). 110pp. This luridly illustrated volume offers considerable information on poisons of all kinds, with humorous illustrations, interesting sidebars, and "Foul Facts." (Rev: LMC 11–12/11; SLJ 9/1/11) [615.9]

20852 Llewellyn, Claire. *Around Town* (PS–2). Illus. by Mike Gordon. Series: Watch Out! 2006, Barron's paper $5.99 (978-0-7641-3326-8). 32pp. Readers learn about some of the dangers they might face in an urban setting, such as dogs, getting lost, and construction sites. Also use *At Home, Near Water,* and *On the Road* (2006). (Rev: SLJ 10/06)

20853 Long, Denise. *Survivor Kid: A Practical Guide to Wilderness Survival* (5–8). Illus. 2011, Chicago Review paper $12.95 (978-15697670-8-5). 144pp. Personal anecdotes bolster the sensible advice presented here about staying safe in the woods. ℮ (Rev: BL 6/1/11) [613.6]

20854 Lyons, Shelly. *Safety in My Neighborhood* (PS–K). Illus. Series: My Neighborhood. 2013, Capstone LB $24.65 (978-162065102-5); paper $6.95 (9781620658871). 24pp. With simple text, large and bright photographs, and an oversize format, this entry in the series introduces various strategies that will keep young readers safe. (Rev: BL 6/13; SLJ 4/13) [363.1]

20855 Miller, Edward. *Fireboy to the Rescue! A Fire Safety Book* (K–2). Illus. by author. 2010, Holiday House $16.95 (978-0-8234-2222-7). 32pp. Flashy, cut-paper-style artwork enhances this superhero-inspired take on fire safety, which includes plenty of practical advice. Lexile AD640L (Rev: BL 1/1/10; SLJ 2/1/10) [628.9]

20856 O'Shei, Tim. *How to Survive on a Deserted Island* (4–6). Illus. 2008, Capstone LB $17.99 (978-1-4296-2282-0). 32pp. Building a shelter, finding water, building a fire, and finding food are just a few of the tasks you will learn to achieve in this handy guide. (Rev: BL 4/1/09) [613.6]

20857 Parker, Steve, and David West. *Human-Made Disasters* (5–8). Illus. by David West. Series: Science of Catastrophe. 2011, Crabtree LB $26.60 (978-077877575-1). 32pp. Not for the faint-hearted, this is a survey of events including the *Challenger* explosion, the Chernobyl meltdown, and the collapse of a bridge in Mississippi in 2007. (Rev: BL 4/1/12) [904]

20858 Pendziwol, Jean E. *Once Upon a Dragon: Stranger Safety Tips for Kids (and Dragons)* (PS–2). Illus. by Martine Gourbault. 2006, Kids Can $14.95 (978-1-55337-722-1); paper $6.95 (978-1-55337-969-0). 32pp. This companion to *No Dragons for Tea: Fire Safety for Kids (and Dragons)* uses fairy-tale characters as stand-ins for strangers, easing the scariness of this difficult topic. (Rev: BL 5/15/06; SLJ 6/06)

20859 Raatma, Lucia. *Bicycle Safety* (2–4). Illus. Series: Living Well. 2003, Child's World LB $27.07 (978-1-59296-085-9). 32pp. A simple story about a child riding a bicycle is followed by easy-to-understand safety rules. Also use *School Safety* and *Internet Safety* (both 2003). (Rev: SLJ 3/04) [796.6]

20860 Roberts, Robin. *Sports Injuries: How to Stay Safe and Keep on Playing* (5–8). Series: Get in the Game! With Robin Roberts. 2001, Millbrook LB $23.90 (978-0-7613-2116-3). 48pp. This general sports book that targets girls as a primary audience discusses safety in a variety of sports and how to cope with injuries. (Rev: BL 9/15/01; HBG 3/02; SLJ 1/02) [790]

Sleep and Dreams

20861 Feeney, Kathy. *Sleep Well: Why You Need to Rest* (K–3). Series: Your Health. 2001, Capstone LB $22.60 (978-0-7368-0970-2). 24pp. Simple text and illustrations stress the importance of sleep and discuss sleepwalking and nightmares. (Rev: HBG 3/02; SLJ 4/02) [612.82]

20862 Garfield, Patricia. *The Dream Book: A Young Person's Guide to Understanding Dreams* (5–8). 2002, Tundra paper $9.95 (978-0-88776-594-0). The author, a psychologist, explains the meanings of common (and uncommon) dreams and suggests how to use dreams to good effect. (Rev: BL 9/15/02; SLJ 9/02; VOYA 8/02) [154.6]

20863 Gordon, Sharon. *A Good Night's Sleep* (3–5). Series: Rookie Read-About Health. 2002, Children's Book Pr. LB $20.50 (978-0-516-22570-8). 32pp. After explaining the reasons why sleep is important, this easy-reader gives a few hints on how to fall asleep fast. (Rev: BL 12/15/02) [616.5]

20864 Romanek, Trudee. *Zzz . . .: The Most Interesting Book You'll Ever Read About Sleep* (3–6). Illus. by Rose Cowles. 2002, Kids Can $14.95 (978-1-55074-944-1); paper $7.95 (978-1-55074-946-5). 40pp. With lively, amusing illustrations and an interesting text, this book covers such topics related to sleep as REM sleep, dreams, sleep cycles, snoring, and yawning. (Rev: BL 6/1–15/02; HBG 10/02; SLJ 6/02) [612.8]

20865 Trueit, Trudi. *Dreams and Sleep* (4–8). Illus. Series: Life Balance. 2004, Watts LB $20.50 (978-0-531-12260-0). 80pp. Discusses why we dream and what dreams mean and gives advice on getting a good night's sleep. (Rev: BL 10/15/03) [616.5]

Sex Education and Reproduction

Babies

20866 Anderson, Judith. *Healthy Mothers* (4–7). Series: Working for Our Future. 2010, Black Rabbit LB $28.50 (978-1-59771-197-5). 32pp. This volume explains why the United Nations chose promoting healthy mothers as one of its eight Millennium Development goals. (Rev: BL 6/10; LMC 10/10; SLJ 4/10) [306.874.]

20867 Cole, Joanna. *When You Were Inside Mommy* (PS). Illus. by Maxie Chambliss. 2001, HarperCollins $7.99 (978-0-688-17043-1). 32pp. Basic facts about a child's development are presented in this small-format picture book. (Rev: BL 8/01; HBG 3/02; SLJ 12/01) [612.6]

20868 Heiligman, Deborah. *Babies: All You Need to Know* (K–2). Illus. by Laura Freeman. Series: Jump into Science. 2002, National Geographic $16.95 (978-0-7922-8205-1). 32pp. Young readers learn how babies grow, what they eat, how they learn, and so forth. (Rev: BCCB 10/02; BL 10/1/02; HBG 3/03; SLJ 10/02) [612.6]

20869 Murkoff, Heidi. *What to Expect When the New Baby Comes Home* (PS–K). Illus. by Laura Rader. 2001, HarperCollins $8.99 (978-0-694-01327-2). 32pp. Angus the Answer Dog guides readers through answers to such questions as "What do new babies eat?" and "Can I play with the new baby?" (Rev: BL 7/01; HBG 10/01; SLJ 6/01) [305.232]

20870 Sears, William, et al. *Baby on the Way* (K–3). Illus. by Renée Andriani. 2001, Little, Brown $12.95 (978-0-316-78767-3). 32pp. A reassuring, colorfully illustrated book that tells young children about the effects of pregnancy on the mother. (Rev: BL 9/15/01; HBG 3/02; SLJ 10/01) [618.2]

20871 Sears, William, et al. *What Baby Needs* (K–3). Illus. by Renée Andriani. 2001, Little, Brown $12.95 (978-0-316-78828-1). 32pp. A readable look at the changes boys and girls can expect when they become big brothers or sisters. (Rev: BL 9/15/01; HBG 3/02; SLJ 10/01) [649]

20872 Thomas, Shelley M. *A Baby's Coming to Your House!* (PS–1). Illus. by Eric Futran. 2001, Whitman $15.95 (978-0-8075-0502-1). 32pp. Using funny family pictures as illustrations, this book explains to youngsters the changes that take place when a new baby enters the house — like the appearance of high chairs and messy diapers. (Rev: BL 3/15/01; HBG 10/01) [305.2]

Reproduction

20873 Butler, Dori. *My Mom's Having a Baby!* (2–4). Illus. by Carol Thompson. 2005, Whitman $16.95 (978-0-8075-5344-2). 32pp. For children who are ready for a detailed treatment of intercourse, conception, gestation, and birth, this book discusses it all and is enhanced with cartoon-style illustrations. (Rev: BL 4/1/05; SLJ 5/05) [618.2]

20874 Fullick, Ann. *Test Tube Babies: In Vitro Fertilization* (5–8). Series: Science at the Edge. 2002, Heinemann LB $27.86 (978-1-58810-703-9). 64pp. This attractive book balances hard science with thought-provoking discussion on this controversial topic. (Rev: BL 10/15/02; HBG 3/03; SLJ 4/03) [613.9]

20875 Orr, Tamra. *Test Tube Babies* (5–9). Series: Science on the Edge. 2003, Gale LB $24.95 (978-1-56711-788-2). 48pp. This book discusses in vitro fertilization, and how it has helped many but also caused a great deal of controversy. (Rev: BL 10/15/03; SLJ 3/04) [612]

20876 Overend, Jenni. *Welcome with Love* (1–3). Illus. by Julie Vivas. 2000, Kane $15.95 (978-0-916291-96-9). 32pp. A direct, graphic treatment of childbirth showing the members of a close family participating in a home delivery. (Rev: BCCB 6/00; BL 3/15/00; HBG 9/00; SLJ 4/00) [618.4]

20877 Parker, Steve. *Reproduction* (5–9). Illus. Series: Our Bodies. 2004, Raintree LB $28.56 (978-0-7398-6623-8). 48pp. Details of the human body's reproductive organs and how they function are accompanied by information on keeping them healthy. (Rev: BL 8/04) [612.6]

Sex Education and Puberty

20878 Arredia, Joni. *Sex, Boys, and You: Be Your Own Best Girlfriend* (5–9). 1998, Perc paper $15.95 (978-0-9653203-2-0). A self-help book for younger teen girls with advice on how to accept oneself, when to say "no" to sex, how to assess one's strengths and weaknesses, and how to develop healthy relationships with boys. (Rev: SLJ 10/98) [305.23]

20879 Bailey, Jacqui. *Sex, Puberty and All That Stuff: A Guide to Growing Up* (5–10). Illus. by Jan McCafferty. 2004, Barron's paper $12.99 (978-0-7641-2992-6). In this comprehensive volume full of lighthearted illustrations, Bailey covers the wide range of changes that affect young people, emphasizing the individual's right to choose and the need to resist peer pressure. (Rev: SLJ 1/05) [613.9]

20880 Dunham, Kelli. *The Boy's Body Book: Everything You Need to Know for Growing Up YOU* (4–7). Illus. by Steven Björkman. 2007, Sterling paper $9.95 (978-1-933662-74-9). This is a straightforward review of the changes to expect during puberty; it also discusses stress, friendship, peer pressure, and family problems such as divorce. (Rev: LMC 2/08; SLJ 10/07) [612.6]

20881 Dunham, Kelli. *The Girl's Body Book: Everything You Need to Know for Growing Up You* (4–7). Illus. by Laura Tallardy. 2008, Applesauce paper $9.95 (978-1-60433-004-5). 128pp. This friendly introduction to puberty covers physical and emotional changes and offers practical guidance. (Rev: LMC 1/09; SLJ 11/08) [612]

20882 Feinmann, Jane. *Everything a Girl Needs to Know About Her Periods* (5–9). 2003, Ronnie Sellers paper $14.95 (978-1-56906-555-6). This useful and reassuring guide to the female body changes of puberty focuses largely on the menstrual cycle. (Rev: BL 2/1/04) [618.083]

20883 Foltz, Linda Lee. *Kids Helping Kids: Break the Silence of Sexual Abuse* (4–9). 2003, Lighthouse Point $21.95 (978-0-9637966-8-4); paper $14.95 (978-0-9637966-9-1). Personal stories from young people and adults who suffered abuse as children illustrate the guilt and shame typically experienced and show how to get help. (Rev: SLJ 9/03) [362.7]

20884 Gravelle, Karen, and Nick Castro. *What's Going on Down There? Answers to Questions Boys Find Hard to Ask* (5–10). Illus. by Robert Leighton. 1998, Walker paper $8.95 (978-0-8027-7540-5). Straightforward information for boys covers such topics as physical changes, sexual intercourse, peer pressure, and pregnancy and

birth. (Rev: BL 11/1/98; HB 1–2/99; HBG 3/99; SLJ 12/98) [613]

20885 Harris, Robie H. *It's Not the Stork! A Book About Girls, Boys, Babies, Bodies, Families, and Friends* (K–3). Illus. by Michael Emberley. 2006, Candlewick $16.99 (978-0-7636-0047-1). 64pp. A frank, sensitive, and inevitably controversial discussion of gender differences, human anatomy, sexuality, and reproduction. (Rev: BCCB 10/06; BL 6/1–15/06; HBG 4/07; LMC 1/07; SLJ 9/06*) [613.9]

20886 Johnson, Eric W. *People, Love, Sex, and Families: Answers to Questions That Preteens Ask* (5–8). 1985, Walker LB $14.85 (978-0-8027-6605-2). Based on the results of a survey of 1,000 preteens, this book covers a broad range of topics, from sexual abuse to venereal disease to divorce and incest. (Rev: BL 3/15/86) [306.707]

20887 Jukes, Mavis. *Growing Up: It's a Girl Thing: Straight Talk About First Bras, First Periods and Your Changing Body* (4–8). 1998, Knopf paper $10.00 (978-0-679-89027-0). Essential information about the changes girls experience during puberty, with half the book devoted to what to expect and how to plan for their first period, presented in an easy, big-sister style. (Rev: BL 11/1/98; SLJ 11/98) [612]

20888 Jukes, Mavis. *It's a Girl Thing: How to Stay Healthy, Safe, and in Charge* (5–9). 1996, Knopf paper $12.00 (978-0-679-87392-1). This guide to puberty for girls discusses such topics as menstruation, drinking and drugs, body changes, contraceptives, sexually transmitted diseases, and sexual abuse and harassment. (Rev: SLJ 6/96*) [612.6]

20889 Jukes, Mavis, and Lilian Cheung. *Be Healthy! It's a Girl Thing: Food, Fitness, and Feeling Great* (5–8). Illus. by Debra Ziss. 2003, Crown LB $18.99 (978-0-679-99029-1); paper $12.95 (978-0-679-89029-4). 160pp. The authors take a matter-of-fact, motivational approach to changes that arrive with puberty and the steps girls can take to be healthy and avoid weight gain and eating disorders. (Rev: BL 1/1–15/04; SLJ 12/03) [613]

20890 Katz, Anne. *Girl in the Know: Your Inside-and-Out Guide to Growing Up* (4–8). Illus. by Monika Melnychuk. 2010, Kids Can $18.95 (978-1-55453-303-9). 112pp. A straightforward, conversational, and wide-ranging introduction to the physical and emotional changes that accompany puberty. (Rev: BL 4/1/10; LMC 8–9/10; SLJ 5/10) [613]

20891 Kemp, Kristen. *Healthy Sexuality* (5–10). Illus. Series: Life Balance. 2004, Watts LB $20.50 (978-0-531-12336-2); paper $6.95 (978-0-531-16689-5). 80pp. Covering both boys and girls, this easy-to-understand volume looks at physical and emotional changes and provides practical tips on handling difficult decisions and confusing feelings. (Rev: BL 10/15/03; SLJ 4/05)

20892 Larimore, Walt. *The Ultimate Guys' Body Book: Not-So-Stupid Questions About Your Body* (5–8). Illus. by Guy Francis. 2012, Zondervan paper $7.99 (978-03107232-3-3). 192pp. Answering such questions as "I've got BO — what's a guy to do?" and "My acne is scary! What's wrong with my face?," this book offers a Christian perspective on puberty. (Rev: BL 4/15/12; SLJ 5/1/12; VOYA 6/12) [613]

20893 Loulan, JoAnn, and Bonnie Worthen. *Period: A Girl's Guide to Menstruation with a Parent's Guide.* Rev. ed. (5–7). 2001, Book Peddlers paper $9.99 (978-0-916773-96-0). This practical guide to menstruation is arranged by such questions as "What do I do when I get my first period?" and "What kind of exercise can I do?" (Rev: BL 2/1/01; HBG 10/01) [612.6]

20894 Madaras, Lynda. *On Your Mark, Get Set, Grow! A "What's Happening to My Body?" Book for Younger Boys* (4–6). Illus. by Paul Gilligan. 2008, Newmarket $22.00 (978-1-55704-780-0); paper $12.00 (978-1-55704-781-6). 119pp. For boys, this companion book to the *Ready, Set, Grow* also takes a humorous and accessible look at puberty and contains many questions and quotations from boys themselves. (Rev: BL 5/15/08; SLJ 5/08) [613]

20895 Madaras, Lynda. *Ready, Set, Grow! A "What's Happening to My Body?" Book for Younger Girls* (2–5). Illus. by Linda Davick. 2003, Newmarket $22.00 (978-1-55704-587-4); paper $12.00 (978-1-55704-565-2). 125pp. This spin-off guide to puberty is aimed at the girls who are now going through this experience at a younger age and includes medical tips and upbeat discussion. (Rev: HBG 4/04; SLJ 11/03) [612.6]

20896 Mar, Jonathan, and Grace Norwich. *The Body Book for Boys* (5–8). Illus. by Ming Sung Ku. 2010, Scholastic paper $8.99 (978-05452375-1-2). 128pp. This straightforward book presents information on subjects of concern to middle-school boys, from hygiene to the opposite sex. (Rev: BL 12/1/10) [613]

20897 Mosatche, Harriet S., and Karen Unger. *Too Old for This, Too Young for That! Your Survival Guide for the Middle-School Years* (5–8). Illus. 2000, Free Spirit

paper $14.99 (978-1-57542-067-7). 200pp. This guide to the early years of puberty contains material on self-esteem, family relationships, friendships, and activities; also included is a lengthy section on bodily changes and such events as the onset of menstruation, erections, and ejaculation. (Rev: BL 7/00; SLJ 9/00) [646.7]

20898 Movsessian, Shushann. *Puberty Girl* (4–7). 2005, Allen & Unwin paper $15.95 (978-1-74114-104-7). A frank and friendly guide covering such topics as body changes, conflict resolution, and personal boundaries, as well as the changes that puberty brings in the opposite sex. (Rev: BL 10/15/05; SLJ 10/05; VOYA 10/05) [612.6]

20899 Pascoe, Elaine, ed. *Teen Dreams: The Journey Through Puberty* (5–8). Illus. Series: Body Story. 2003, Gale LB $24.95 (978-1-4103-0061-4). 48pp. Puberty and the many changes it brings are the topic of this arresting and informative book, seen from the points of view of a teenage boy and girl. (Rev: SLJ 4/04) [612.6]

20900 Pfeifer, Kate Gruenwald. *Boy's Guide to Becoming a Teen* (4–7). 2006, Jossey-Bass paper $12.95 (978-0-7879-8343-7). A guide to handling the physical, emotional, and social changes that accompany puberty in boys. (Rev: BL 5/15/06; SLJ 5/07) [613]

20901 Pfeifer, Kate Gruenwald. *Girl's Guide to Becoming a Teen* (4–7). Ed. by Amy B. Middleman. 2006, Jossey-Bass paper $12.95 (978-0-7879-8344-4). A guide to handling the physical, emotional, and social changes that accompany puberty in girls. (Rev: BL 5/15/06; SLJ 5/07) [613]

20902 Price, Geoff. *Puberty Boy* (5–8). 2006, Allen & Unwin paper $15.95 (978-1-74114-563-2). A frank and friendly guide with an Australian accent that covers the important physical and emotional changes that accompany puberty. (Rev: BL 7/06; SLJ 9/06; VOYA 8/06) [612]

Physical and Applied Sciences

General Science

Miscellaneous

20903 Aaseng, Nathan. *Yearbooks in Science: 1930–1939* (5–8). Series: Yearbooks in Science. 1995, Twenty-First Century LB $22.90 (978-0-8050-3433-2). An overview of the accomplishments in science in the 1930s arranged by such divisions as physics and chemistry. (Rev: BL 12/1/95; SLJ 1/96) [609]

20904 Aaseng, Nathan. *Yearbooks in Science: 1940–1949* (5–8). Series: Yearbooks in Science. 1995, Twenty-First Century LB $22.90 (978-0-8050-3434-9). An important decade in scientific discovery is chronicled, with emphasis on the impact of these advances on society. (Rev: BL1/1–15/96; SLJ 5/96) [609]

20905 Arnold, Nick. *The Stunning Science of Everything: Science with the Squishy Bits Left In!* (4–8). Illus. by Tony De Saulles. 2006, Scholastic $10.99 (978-0-439-87777-0). This lighthearted look at science, brightly illustrated with cartoons, examines such diverse topics as the Big Bang theory, atoms, insects, humans, dinosaurs, and the universe. (Rev: HBG 4/07; LMC 3/07; SLJ 2/07; VOYA 2/07) [500]

20906 Bryson, Bill. *A Really Short History of Nearly Everything* (5–8). Illus. 2009, Delacorte $19.99 (978-0-385-73810-1). 170pp. A junior edition of his popular book for adults, this volume tackles many scientific topics with humor and cheer. ℮ Lexile 1190L (Rev: BL 11/15/09; SLJ 2/10) [900]

20907 Day, Trevor. *Genetics* (4–7). Illus. Series: Routes of Science. 2004, Gale LB $24.95 (978-1-4103-0301-1). 40pp. A detailed examination of the development of genetics as a science, with profiles of key individuals and their discoveries, a chronology, and discussion of future advances. (Rev: SLJ 5/05)

20908 Dotlich, Rebecca Kai. *What Is Science?* (PS–2). Illus. by Sachiko Yoshikawa. 2006, Holt $16.95 (978-0-8050-7394-2). 32pp. A trio of children and their dog get a simple, poetic tour of the world of science. (Rev: BL 9/15/06; SLJ 11/06) [500]

20909 Fridell, Ron. *Genetic Engineering* (4–6). Illus. Series: Cool Science. 2005, Lerner LB $26.60 (978-0-8225-2633-9). 48pp. With many interesting examples and an attractive layout, this introduction explores how this cutting-edge branch of science is paving the way for new species of plant and animal life and also helping to deal with human health problems. (Rev: SLJ 12/05) [660.6]

20910 Gutfreund, Geraldine M. *Yearbooks in Science: 1970–1979* (5–8). Series: Yearbooks in Science. 1995, Twenty-First Century LB $22.90 (978-0-8050-3437-0). A decade of new scientific concepts and inventions is discussed, with profiles of the scientists behind them. (Rev: BL 1/1–15/96; SLJ 5/96) [609]

20911 Hicks, Kelli. *I Can Prove It! Investigating Science* (3–5). Illus. Series: My Science Library. 2012, Rourke LB $27.07 (978-161810111-2); paper $7.95 (9781618102447). 24pp. From initial hypothesis to communicating results, this is a well-written introduction to the scientific method, ending with a "Show What You Know" quiz. (Rev: BL 9/15/12; SLJ Fall 2012 Series Guide) [500]

20912 Hoyt, Beth Caldwell, and Erica Ritter. *The Ultimate Girls' Guide to Science: From Backyard Experiments to Winning the Nobel Prize!* (4–8). 2004, Beyond Words paper $9.95 (978-1-58270-092-2). Designed to pique girls' interest in the study of science, this attractive title offers brief profiles of famous female scientists as well as the major branches of science and also provides instructions for a number of scientific experiments. (Rev: SLJ 8/04) [500]

20913 McGowen, Tom. *The Beginnings of Science* (5–8). 1998, Twenty-First Century LB $26.90 (978-0-7613-3016-5). Beginning with primitive people and their use of magic, fire, counting, writing, and astronomy, this book traces the history of science up to the 16th century. (Rev: BL 12/1/98; HBG 3/99) [509]

20914 McGowen, Tom. *Yearbooks in Science: 1900–1919* (5–8). Series: Yearbooks in Science. 1995, Twenty-First Century LB $22.90 (978-0-8050-3431-8). An overview of human achievements in science and technology during the first 20 years of the 20th century, how they helped humanity, and the men and women involved. (Rev: BL 12/1/95; SLJ 1/96) [609]

20915 McGowen, Tom. *Yearbooks in Science: 1960–1969* (5–8). Series: Yearbooks in Science. 1996, Twenty-First Century LB $22.90 (978-0-8050-3436-3). Developments in the history of science and technology during the 1960s are covered in an exciting step-by-step approach. (Rev: BL 1/1–15/96; SLJ 5/96) [609]

20916 Martin, Paul D. *Science: It's Changing Your World* (5–8). 1985, National Geographic LB $12.50 (978-0-87044-521-7). An overview of the science field today, crediting computers and lasers with the vast growth of scientific information. (Rev: BL 9/15/85; SLJ 10/85) [500]

20917 Masoff, Joy. *Oh, Yuck! The Encyclopedia of Everything Nasty* (4–8). Illus. by Terry Sirrell. 2001, Workman paper $14.95 (978-0-7611-0771-2). This unsavory, fact-filled look at smells, noises, creepy-crawlies, toilets, and other fascinating topics even includes some suitably gross experiments. (Rev: SLJ 5/01) [031.02]

20918 Murphy, Glenn. *Why Is Snot Green?* (3–6). Illus. by Mike Phillips. 2009, Roaring Brook paper $9.95 (978-1-59643-500-1). 240pp. Facts and fun are combined in this conversational, question-and-answer look at scientific topics ranging from outer space ("What is space made of?") to animals ("Do rabbits fart?"), the human body, and the future. (Rev: BCCB 6/09; BL 3/1/09; SLJ 6/09) [500]

20919 Murray, Julie. *Home* (2–4). Series: That's Gross! A Look at Science. 2009, ABDO LB $17.95 (978-1-60453-555-6). 32pp. A look at all the icky stuff in our homes — from bacteria and bugs to the spray of a flushing toilet. Also use *Icky, Sticky, Gross Stuff in Your School* (2009). (Rev: BL 5/15/09) [577.5]

20920 Newton, David E. *Yearbooks in Science: 1920–1929* (5–8). Series: Yearbooks in Science. 1995, Twenty-First Century LB $22.90 (978-0-8050-3432-5). The history of scientific advances in the 1920s, with chapters on various fields that explain the breakthroughs, how they helped humanity, and the scientists involved. (Rev: BL 12/1/95; SLJ 1/96) [609]

20921 Nye, Bill. *Bill Nye the Science Guy's Big Blast of Science* (5–8). 1993, Addison-Wesley paper $16.00 (978-0-201-60864-9). Matter, heat, light, electricity, magnetism, weather, and space are among the topics introduced in this quick and entertaining tour of the world of science. (Rev: BL 2/15/94) [507.8]

20922 Parker, Steve. *What About . . . Science and Technology?* (5–8). Illus. Series: Answering Q&A Questions. 2009, Mason Crest $19.95 (978-1-4222-1565-4). 40pp. Using a question-and-answer format, two-page spreads look at subjects ranging from matter and magnetism to sound and transportation. (Rev: LMC 5–6/10; SLJ 4/10) [500]

20923 Pentland, Peter, and Pennie Stoyles. *Kitchen Science* (4–6). Illus. Series: Science and Scientists. 2002, Chelsea House LB $27.00 (978-0-7910-7014-7). 32pp. A clear overview of the scientific phenomena involved in basic foodstuffs as well as the various ways in which they are prepared and preserved, with illustrations, interesting sidebars, and information on careers in kitchen science. Also use *Party Science* and *Toy and Game Science* (both 2002). (Rev: HBG 3/03; SLJ 4/03) [641.5]

20924 Raab, Brigitte. *Where Does Pepper Come From? And Other Fun Facts* (K–3). Trans. from German by J. Alison James. Illus. by Manuela Olten. 2006, North-South $15.95 (978-0-7358-2070-8). A humorous and lively question-and-answer format provides answers to a wide variety of science questions. (Rev: SLJ 10/06)

20925 Richardson, Gillian. *Kaboom! Explosions of All Kinds* (4–7). 2009, Annick $22.95 (978-1-55451-204-1); paper $12.95 (978-1-55451-203-4). 83pp. Loud noises of all kinds are covered here — natural explosions (in the earth and outer space, in plants and animals) and manmade explosions (dynamite, fireworks, internal combustion engine, and so forth). (Rev: BL 12/1/09; SLJ 12/09) [541]

20926 Rosinsky, Natalie M. *How Scientists Work* (3–5). Series: Simply Science. 2004, Compass Point LB $21.26 (978-0-7565-0596-7). 32pp. Introduces readers to the scientific method of research. (Rev: SLJ 8/04) [507]

20927 Ross, Michael Elsohn. *Re-Cycles* (K–2). Illus. by Gustav Moore. 2002, Millbrook LB $22.90 (978-0-7613-1818-7). 32pp. Readers learn how water and soil are constantly being recycled for reuse, and how humans can contribute to nature's efforts. (Rev: BL 11/1/02; HBG 3/03; SLJ 1/03) [551.3]

20928 Schwartz, David M. *Q Is for Quark: A Science Alphabet Book* (4–9). Illus. by Kim Doner. 2001, Tricycle $15.95 (978-1-58246-021-5). An entertaining and informative alphabet book from atom to Zzzzzzzz that doesn't hesitate to tackle difficult topics. (Rev: HBG 3/02; SLJ 11/01) [500]

20929 *Science Detectives: How Scientists Solved Six Real-Life Mysteries* (3–5). Illus. by Rose Cowles. 2006, Kids Can $15.95 (978-1-55337-994-2); paper $8.95 (978-1-55337-995-9). 48pp. An interesting selection of mysteries that were eventually solved through scientific means — including a typhoid outbreak in New York and a plunge in the number of vultures in central Asia. (Rev: BL 10/15/06) [501]

20930 Shields, Carol Diggory. *BrainJuice: Science, Fresh Squeezed!* (4–7). Illus. by Richard Thompson. 2003, Handprint $14.95 (978-1-59354-005-0). A humorous, rhyming look at grade-school science with appealing illustrations and useful mnemonic devices. (Rev: SLJ 3/04) [500]

20931 Silverstein, Herma. *Yearbooks in Science: 1990 and Beyond* (5–8). Series: Yearbooks in Science. 1995, Twenty-First Century LB $22.90 (978-0-8050-3439-4).

The final volume in this series not only traces recent developments in science and technology but also presents the challenges of the future. (Rev: BL 1/1–15/96) [609]

20932 Stein, Sara Bonnett. *The Science Book* (4–8). Illus. by author. 1980, Workman paper $9.95 (978-0-89480-120-4). A whole-earth approach to strange and fascinating science facts.

20933 Sullivan, Navin. *Time* (4–7). Series: Measure Up! 2006, Marshall Cavendish LB $20.95 (978-0-7614-2321-8). This entertaining volume provides a history of the way humans have measured time, up to the present day and including the new rule for Daylight Saving Time. (Rev: LMC 8–9/07; SLJ 6/07) [529]

20934 Swanson, Diane. *Nibbling on Einstein's Brain* (5–8). Illus. by Warren Clark. 2001, Firefly paper $14.95 (978-1-55037-686-9). 112pp. Swanson looks at "bad" science and examines the difference between sound scientific theory and hype, teaching kids how to ask the right questions when analyzing advertisers' claims. (Rev: BL 2/15/02; HBG 3/02; SLJ 11/01) [507.2]

20935 Swanson, Diane. *Turn It Loose: The Scientist in Absolutely Everybody* (4–6). Illus. by Warren Clark. 2004, Annick $29.95 (978-1-55037-851-1); paper $14.95 (978-1-55037-850-4). Swanson offers activities to help young people polish their scientific skills and profiles a number of scientists and others who have demonstrated scientific thinking. (Rev: BL 6/1–15/04; SLJ 6/04) [500]

20936 Tocci, Salvatore. *Experiments with Magic* (2–4). Illus. Series: A True Book. 2003, Children's Pr. LB $25.00 (978-0-516-22788-7). 48pp. Basic scientific principles are demonstrated through "magic" tricks in this attractive book that is suitable for beginning readers. (Rev: SLJ 4/04) [507.8]

20937 Weakland, Mark. *Bubbles Float, Bubbles Pop* (1–3). Illus. Series: Science Starts. 2011, Capstone LB $25.99 (978-142965250-6); paper $7.95 (978-142966141-6). 32pp. A succinct guide to the nature of bubbles and how they are formed. (Rev: BL 4/1/11; LMC 10/11) [530.4]

20938 Wollard, Kathy. *How Come?* (5–9). 1993, Workman paper $12.95 (978-1-56305-324-5). Provides answers to some common and not-so-common questions about ordinary things. (Rev: BL 5/1/94) [500]

20939 Wollard, Kathy. *How Come Planet Earth?* (4–7). Illus. by Debra Solomon. 1999, Workman paper $12.95 (978-0-7611-1239-6). This book contains 125 science questions asked by children involving subjects such as warts, dust, cholesterol, and volcanoes. (Rev: SLJ 5/00) [500]

Experiments and Projects

20940 Bardhan-Quallen, Sudipta. *Championship Science Fair Projects: 100 Sure-to-Win Experiments* (5–9). 2005, Sterling $19.95 (978-1-4027-1138-1). Clearly defined science projects (more than 100 at varying levels of difficulty) are accompanied by lists of materials, illustrations, and extension activities. (Rev: BL 8/05; SLJ 9/05; VOYA 8/05) [507]

20941 Bardhan-Quallen, Sudipta. *Kitchen Science Experiments: How Does Your Mold Garden Grow?* (4–7). Illus. by Edward Miller. Series: Mad Science. 2010, Sterling $12.95 (978-140272413-8). 64pp. Eighteen activities introduce basics of biology and chemistry through recipes that can be used in everyday kitchens. (Rev: BL 12/1/10; LMC 5–6/11; SLJ 2/1/11) [579]

20942 Bardhan-Quallen, Sudipta. *Last-Minute Science Fair Projects* (4–7). Illus. 2007, Sterling $19.95 (978-1-4027-1690-4). A guide to science experiments that can be done in a short amount of time using common household materials. (Rev: BL 5/15/07) [507.8]

20943 Bardhan-Quallen, Sudipta. *Nature Science Experiments: What's Hopping in a Dust Bunny?* (4–6). Illus. by Edward Miller. 2010, Sterling LB $12.95 (978-1-4027-2412-1). 64pp. Diverse experiments, some of which require specialized equipment, mostly involve everyday objects and are presented in clear text with scientific explanations. (Rev: SLJ 9/1/10) [570.78]

20944 Benbow, Ann, and Colin Mably. *Awesome Animal Science Projects* (2–4). Illus. by Tom LaBaff. Series: Real Life Science Experiments. 2009, Enslow LB $23.93 (978-0-7660-3148-7). 48pp. Focuses on easy experiments that illustrate characteristics of backyard animals and animal behavior, answering questions such as "What Seeds Do Different Birds Like?" and "Are Earthworms Attracted to Light?" (Rev: BL 8/09; SLJ 1/1/10) [590.78]

20945 Blobaum, Cindy. *Explore Night Science! With 25 Great Projects* (1–4). Illus. by Bryan Stone. Series: Explore Your World. 2012, Nomad paper $12.95 (978-1-61930-156-6). 96pp. This accessible volume, which includes both "Words to Know" and humorous cartoons, looks at how our senses react to the night and provides simple activities. e (Rev: BLO 11/15/12; LMC 5–6/13; SLJ 6/13) [508.078]

20946 Boring, Mel, and Leslie Dendy. *Guinea Pig Scientists: Bold Self-Experimenters in Science and Medicine* (5–9). Illus. by C. B. Mordan. 2005, Henry Holt $19.95 (978-0-8050-7316-4). Scientists who served as their own guinea pigs — demonstrating their passion for science and often their foolhardiness — are the topic of this appealing volume. (Rev: BL 7/05*; SLJ 7/05*; VOYA 6/05) [616]

20947 Brown, Jordan D. *Crazy Concoctions: A Mad Scientist's Guide to Messy Mixtures* (4–7). Illus. by Anthony Owsley. 2012, Imagine $14.95 (978-193614051-0). 80pp. For budding scientists with a love of glop and viscosity, this volume proposes a number of experiments involving such ingredients as cornstarch and raisins and with names such as "bogus barf." (Rev: BL 2/15/12; SLJ 4/12) [540.76]

20948 Burns, Loree Griffin. *Citizen Scientists: Be a Part of Scientific Discovery from Your Own Backyard* (3–6).

Illus. by Ellen Harasimowicz. 2012, Henry Holt $19.99 (978-0-8050-9062-8); paper $12.99 (978-0-8050-9-517-3). 80pp. Shows young readers various scientific studies they can do around the year in the backyard involving butterflies, birds, frogs, and ladybugs; with excellent photographs. (Rev: BL 4/1/12; HB 5–6/12; SLJ 7/12*) [590.72]

20949 Buttitta, Hope. *It's Not Magic, It's Science! 50 Science Tricks that Mystify, Dazzle and Astound!* (4–6). Illus. by Tom LaBaff and Orrin Lundgren. 2005, Sterling $14.95 (978-1-57990-622-1). 80pp. Each "magic track" in this book demonstrates a scientific principle, making it a fun exploration of basic concepts. (Rev: SLJ 9/05) [793.8]

20950 Calhoun, Yael. *Plant and Animal Science Fair Projects Using Beetles, Weeds, Seeds, and More* (5–8). Series: Biology! Best Science Projects. 2005, Enslow LB $26.60 (978-0-7660-2368-0). Great ideas for biology-based science fair projects, with plenty of information for performing and presenting each activity correctly plus helpful charts and graphs. (Rev: SLJ 7/06) [570]

20951 Calhoun, Yael. *Plant and Animal Science Fair Projects, Revised and Expanded Using the Scientific Method* (5–8). Series: Science Projects Using the Scientific Method. 2010, Enslow LB $34.60 (978-0-7660-3421-1). 160pp. With a focus on the basics of scientific investigation, this well-organized and attractive volume gives an overview of the topic and provides experiments that support various hypotheses. (Rev: LMC 8–9/10; SLJ 9/1/10) [570.78]

20952 Cobb, Vicki. *See for Yourself: More Than 100 Experiments for Science Fairs and Projects* (3–8). Illus. by Dave Klug. 2001, Scholastic $16.95 (978-0-439-09010-0); paper $7.95 (978-0-439-09011-7). 192pp. A collection of experiments and activities arranged by topic, with a notation of the level of difficulty. (Rev: HBG 10/02; SLJ 3/02) [507.8]

20953 Cobb, Vicki, and Kathy Darling. *We Dare You! Hundreds of Science Bets, Challenges, and Experiments You Can Do at Home* (3–7). Illus. by True Kelley and Meredith Johnson. 2008, Skyhorse $19.95 (978-1-60239-225-0). 321pp. More than 200 well-explained experiments are presented in chapters with headings such as "Energy Entrapments" and "Mathematical Duplicity." (Rev: SLJ 9/08) [507.8]

20954 Cole, Joanna. *The Magic School Bus and the Science Fair Expedition* (2–4). Illus. by Bruce Degen. Series: Magic School Bus. 2006, Scholastic $15.99 (978-0-590-10824-9). 32pp. Ms. Frizzle and her students travel on the bus to a nearby museum in search of inspiration for the upcoming science fair. (Rev: BL 9/15/06) [507.8]

20955 Connolly, Sean. *The Book of Potentially Catastrophic Science: 50 Experiments for Daring Young Scientists* (5–8). Illus. 2010, Workman $13.95 (978-0-7611-5687-1). 256pp. Each chapter of this compelling book presents a scientific milestone, starting with Stone Age tools and ending with the Hadron Collider, and provides the historical context and related activities. (Rev: BL 6/10; HB 3–4/11; SLJ 9/1/10) [507.8]

20956 Duensing, Edward. *Talking to Fireflies, Shrinking the Moon: Nature Activities for All Ages* (5–9). 1997, Fulcrum paper $15.95 (978-1-55591-310-6). More than 40 nature activities are included in this volume, including how to hypnotize a frog, weave a daisy chain, and whistle for woodchucks. (Rev: VOYA 10/97) [507]

20957 Fox, Tom. *Snowball Launchers, Giant-Pumpkin Growers, and Other Cool Contraptions* (5–8). Illus. by Joel Holland. 2006, Sterling paper $9.95 (978-0-8069-5515-5). A collection of 20 creative projects with clear instructions and explanations of scientific principles. (Rev: BL 1/1–15/07; SLJ 3/07)

20958 Gardner, Robert. *Genetics and Evolution Science Fair Projects, Revised and Expanded Using the Scientific Method* (5–8). Series: Biology Science Projects Using the Scientific Method. 2010, Enslow LB $34.60 (978-0-7660-3422-8). 160pp. With a focus on the basics of scientific investigation, this well-organized and attractive volume gives an overview of the topic and provides experiments that support various hypotheses. (Rev: LMC 8–9/10; SLJ 9/1/10) [576.078]

20959 Graham, John, et al. *Hands-On Science* (4–6). Illus. by David Le Jars. Series: Hands-On. 2002, Kingfisher paper $10.95 (978-0-7534-5440-4). 160pp. More than 100 easy-to-follow, nicely presented experiments teach students about basic science concepts. (Rev: SLJ 8/02)

20960 Haduch, Bill. *Science Fair Success Secrets: How to Win Prizes, Have Fun, and Think Like a Scientist* (5–8). Illus. by Philip Scheuer. 2002, Dutton paper $10.99 (978-0-525-46534-8). 128pp. A handy and appealing introduction to how to conduct a science experiment, with examples of award-winning projects, a list of ideas, and metric conversion tables. (Rev: BL 12/1/02; SLJ 3/03) [507]

20961 Harris, Elizabeth Snoke. *First Place Science Fair Projects for Inquisitive Kids* (4–7). 2005, Sterling LB $19.95 (978-1-57990-493-7). Project ideas in biology, chemistry, and physics mostly involve everyday materials and are presented in accessible text with an eight-week schedule and clear photographs. (Rev: SLJ 3/06) [507]

20962 Harris, Elizabeth Snoke. *Yikes! Wow! Yuck! Fun Experiments for Your First Science Fair* (4–7). Illus. by Nora Thompson. 2008, Sterling $12.95 (978-1-57990-930-7). The breezy, lighthearted tone of this book will appeal to young scientists looking for simple but interesting projects. (Rev: BL 4/15/08; SLJ 6/08) [507.8]

20963 Hartzog, John Daniel. *Everyday Science Experiments in the Kitchen* (PS–3). Series: Science Suprises. 2000, Rosen $21.25 (978-0-8239-5456-8). 24pp. Eight simple experiments are outlined from using lemon juice to shine a penny to creating a celery straw. (Rev: SLJ 9/00) [509]

20964 Hurd, Will. *Changing States: Solids, Liquids, and Gases* (3–6). Illus. 2009, Heinemann LB $22.00 (978-1-4329-2312-9). 48pp. Experiments with easy-to-obtain materials and parental warnings. (Rev: BL 6/1–15/09) [530.4]

20965 Lawrence, Ellen. *Color* (1–3). Illus. Series: FUNdamental Experiments. 2013, Bearport LB $23.93 (978-161772738-2). 24pp. This picture book offers seven projects that extend understanding of colors, how they can be mixed, properties relating to heat, rainbows, and how animals can use color. Also use *Dirt, Motion,* and *Water*(all 2013). (Rev: BL 5/1/13; SLJ 4/13) [535.6]

20966 Lempke, Donald B., and Thomas K. Adamson. *Lessons in Science Safety with Max Axiom, Super Scientist* (5–8). Illus. by Tod Smith. Series: Graphic Science. 2006, Capstone LB $18.95 (978-0-7368-6834-1). This graphic-novel approach to teaching safe science procedures features an appealing adult. (Rev: BL 3/15/07) [507.8]

20967 Levine, Shar. *Sports Science* (3–5). Illus. by Leslie Johnstone. 2006, Sterling $19.95 (978-1-4027-1520-4). 80pp. A collection of 26 science experiments, each with a sports connection, that illustrate such scientific principles as gravity, aerodynamics, and buoyancy. (Rev: BL 12/1/06; SLJ 12/06) [507.8]

20968 Margles, Samantha. *Mythbusters Science Fair Book* (4–8). Illus. 2011, Scholastic paper $9.99 (978-05452374-5-1). 128pp. A collection of science projects that answer common questions (can we believe the five-second rule?) using proper scientific methods. (Rev: BL 4/15/11) [507.8]

20969 Mercer, Bobby. *The Leaping, Sliding, Sprinting, Riding Science Book: 50 Super Sports Science Activities* (4–7). Illus. by Tom LaBaff. 2007, Sterling $14.95 (978-1-57990-785-3). Sports moves are used to illustrate scientific principles in this activity book with step-by-step instructions, discussions of the science, and lots of lively illustrations. (Rev: BL 5/1/07; SLJ 5/07) [796]

20970 Murphy, Pat. *Exploratopia* (4–7). Illus. 2006, Little, Brown $29.99 (978-0-316-61281-4). From San Francisco's Exploratorium, this is an interesting selection of facts, activities, and hands-on experiments that encourage students to learn about and explore the world around them. (Rev: BL 12/1/06; SLJ 1/07) [507.8]

20971 Newcomb, Rain, and Bobby Mercer. *Crash It! Smash It! Launch It!* (5–8). Illus. by Rain Newcomb. 2006, Sterling $14.95 (978-1-57990-795-2). More than 40 experiments provide great entertainment as well as scientific knowledge. (Rev: BL 11/1/06; SLJ 12/06) [507.8]

20972 Reilly, Kathleen M. *Natural Disasters: Investigate Earth's Most Destructive Forces with 25 Projects* (2–4). Illus. by Tom Casteel. Series: Build It Yourself. 2012, Nomad paper $15.95 (978-1-61930-146-7). 128pp. From earthquakes and tsunamis to tornadoes, wildfires, and blizzards and avalanches, this book provides basic information and safe projects that illustrate the destructive forces involved. **e** (Rev: BL 12/1/12; SLJ 3/13) [363.34]

20973 Ross, Michael Elsohn. *Toy Lab* (4–6). Illus. by Tim Seeley. Series: You Are the Scientist. 2002, Carolrhoda LB $23.93 (978-0-87614-456-5). 48pp. Toys such as slinkies, silly putty, frisbees, and blocks are all put to good use as readers learn about gravity, flight, motion, and other basic concepts. (Rev: HBG 3/03; SLJ 2/03)

20974 Rybolt, Thomas R., and Leah M. Rybolt. *Science Fair Success with Scents, Aromas, and Smells* (5–8). Series: Science Fair Success. 2002, Enslow LB $26.60 (978-0-7660-1625-5). 112pp. Several science fair projects using the sense of smell are presented with clear instructions and easy-to-find materials. (Rev: BL 5/15/02; HBG 10/02; SLJ 11/02) [507]

20975 *Science Fairs: Ideas and Activities* (4–8). 1998, World Book $15.00 (978-0-7166-4498-9). Using many diagrams and logical step-by-step explanations, this work offers science projects in such areas as space, earth science, geology, botany, and machines. (Rev: SLJ 1/99) [507]

20976 Spangler, Steve. *Naked Eggs and Flying Potatoes: Unforgettable Experiments That Make Science Fun* (3–6). Illus. 2010, Greenleaf paper $14.95 (978-16083206-0-8). 160pp. With experiments organized under headings such as "The Power of Air" and "Gooey Wonders," this volume presents child-friendly projects that may require adult help. (Rev: BL 12/1/10; SLJ 12/1/10) [507.8]

20977 Tocci, Salvatore. *Experiments with Sports* (2–4). Illus. Series: True Books. 2003, Children's Pr. paper $6.95 (978-0-516-27807-0). 48pp. A book of experiments that demonstrate how basic scientific principles apply to sports. (Rev: SLJ 4/04) [507.8]

20978 Tocci, Salvatore. *Science Fair Success in the Hardware Store* (5–8). Series: Science Fair Success. 2000, Enslow LB $26.60 (978-0-7660-1287-5). 128pp. A group of science fair projects that use materials and objects found in a hardware store, with clear explanations of the scientific principles behind each project. (Rev: BL 4/15/00; HBG 10/00) [507]

20979 Tocci, Salvatore. *Science Fair Success Using Supermarket Products* (5–8). Series: Science Fair Success. 2000, Enslow LB $26.60 (978-0-7660-1288-2). 128pp. Using common items found in a supermarket, this work outlines a number of excellent science projects that demonstrate important scientific principles. (Rev: BL 4/15/00; HBG 10/00; SLJ 4/00) [507]

20980 Tocci, Salvatore. *Using Household Products* (5–8). Series: Science Fair Success. 2002, Enslow LB $26.60 (978-0-7660-1626-2). This useful volume outlines a number of science fair projects that can be done using materials found around the house. (Rev: BL 4/15/02; HBG 10/02) [509]

20981 UNESCO. *700 Science Experiments for Everyone* (5–8). 1964, Doubleday $19.95 (978-0-385-05275-7). An excellent collection of experiments, noted for its number of entries and breadth of coverage.

20982 VanCleave, Janice. *Janice VanCleave's Biology for Every Kid: 101 Easy Experiments That Really Work* (4–7). 1989, Wiley paper $12.95 (978-0-471-50381-1). This book outlines simple experiments that use readily available equipment and supplies. (Rev: BL 2/15/90) [574]

20983 VanCleave, Janice. *Janice VanCleave's Guide to More of the Best Science Fair Projects* (4–8). 2000,

Wiley paper $14.95 (978-0-471-32627-4). After general information about the scientific method, research, and presentation, this book outlines about 50 projects in the areas of astronomy, biology, earth science, engineering, physical science, and mathematics. (Rev: SLJ 5/00) [509]

20984 VanCleave, Janice. *Janice VanCleave's 203 Icy, Freezing, Frosty, Cool and Wild Experiments* (4–7). 1999, Wiley paper $12.95 (978-0-471-25223-8). An excellent book filled with easily performed experiments in such areas as biology, chemistry, earth science, and physics. (Rev: SLJ 4/00) [507.8]

20985 VanCleave, Janice. *Step-By-Step Science Experiments in Ecology* (5–8). Series: Janice VanCleave's First-Place Science Fair Projects. 2012, Rosen Central LB $33.25 (978-1-4488-6980-0). 80pp. An updated volume with step-by-step instructions for 22 experiments mostly using easily found materials. (Rev: SLJ 10/12) [577.078]

Astronomy

20986 Asimov, Isaac. *The Birth of Our Universe* (5–8). Series: Isaac Asimov's 21st Century Library of the Universe. 2005, Gareth Stevens LB $26.00 (978-0-8368-3964-7). This is an update of a 1995 edition on the origins of the universe, with illustrations and photographs. (Rev: BL 3/1/05) [523.1]

20987 Bortz, Fred. *Collision Course! Cosmic Impacts and Life on Earth* (4–7). Illus. 2001, Millbrook LB $25.90 (978-0-7613-1403-5). 72pp. A straightforward discussion of an intriguing subject that includes material on past collisions and on detecting and perhaps deflecting future "near Earth objects." (Rev: BL 5/1/01; HBG 10/01; SLJ 5/01) [523.44]

20988 Brake, Mark. *Really, Really Big Questions About Space and Time* (4–7). Illus. by Nishant Choksi. 2010, Kingfisher $16.99 (978-075346502-8). 64pp. Presents lighthearted and thoughtful answers to questions children ask about space and time, with a section on "How to Think Like a Scientist and Apply the Scientific Method." (Rev: BL 11/1/10; LMC 3–4/11) [523.1]

20989 Bredeson, Carmen. *What Do Astronauts Do?* (1–3). Illus. Series: I Like Space! 2008, Enslow LB $22.60 (978-0-7660-2942-2). 32pp. "What do astronauts eat and how do they go to the bathroom?" Simple design and text with a question-and-answer format and color photographs present fascinating space-related facts. (Rev: SLJ 9/08) [629.45]

20990 Campbell, Ann-Jeanette. *The New York Public Library Amazing Space: A Book of Answers for Kids* (5–8). 1997, Wiley paper $12.95 (978-0-471-14498-4). This question-and-answer book introduces space exploration, the solar system, individual planets, galaxies, and related phenomena. (Rev: SLJ 7/97) [523]

20991 Carson, Mary Kay. *Beyond the Solar System: Exploring Galaxies, Black Holes, Alien Planets, and More; A History with 21 Activities* (5–8). Illus. 2013, Chicago Review $18.95 (978-161374544-1). 144pp. In chapters covering prehistory to 1600, the 1600s, the 1700s to 1915, 1900 to 1940, the 1930s to 1970s, and the 1980s to 2010s, this chronological history looks at significant developments in the science of astronomy and provides activities that reinforce readers' understanding. (Rev: BL 7/13*; SLJ 8/13) [520.9]

20992 Carson, Mary Kay. *Far-Out Guide to Asteroids and Comets* (4–6). Illus. Series: Far-Out Guide to the Solar System. 2010, Enslow LB $23.93 (978-0-7660-3188-3); paper $7.95 (978-1-59845-191-7). 48pp. A lively and well-illustrated introduction to asteroids and comets and their threats to Earth. (Rev: SLJ 12/1/10) [523.44]

20993 Cole, Michael D. *Eye on the Universe: The Incredible Hubble Space Telescope* (5–8). Illus. Series: American Space Missions: Astronauts, Exploration, and Discovery. 2012, Enslow LB $23.93 (978-0-7660-4077-9). 48pp. This volume looks at how the telescope works (and why), the problems it encountered initially, and the images it has sent home since then and what we can learn from them. (Rev: BL 11/15/12; LMC 5–6/13; SLJ 12/12) [522]

20994 Cole, Michael D. *Hubble Space Telescope: Exploring the Universe* (4–7). Series: Countdown to Space. 1999, Enslow LB $23.93 (978-0-7660-1120-5). This close-up look at the Hubble space telescope covers its parts, uses, problems, and photographs that the telescope has sent back to earth. (Rev: BL 2/1/99; HBG 10/99) [522]

20995 Davis, Kenneth C. *Don't Know Much About Space* (3–7). Illus. by Sergio Ruzzier. Series: Don't Know Much About. 2001, HarperCollins LB $19.89 (978-0-06-028602-6); paper $6.99 (978-0-06-440835-6). 144pp. An entertaining, informal, question-and-answer introduction to astronomy. (Rev: BL 9/15/01; HBG 3/02; SLJ 8/01) [520]

20996 DeCristofano, Carolyn Cinami. *A Black Hole Is Not a Hole* (4–6). Illus. by Michael Carroll. 2012, Charlesbridge $9.99 (978-157091783-7). 80pp. With humor, lively text, and dramatic illustrations, this book introduces important information about black holes in an appealing and understandable fashion. ⌂ (Rev: BL 2/1/12*; LMC 11–12/12; SLJ 4/12*) [523.8]

20997 Delafosse, Claude, et al. *Hidden World: Space* (PS–2). Series: First Discovery. 2000, Scholastic $12.95 (978-0-439-14826-9). 24pp. For the very young, this is a colorful, well-illustrated introduction to space and what it means. (Rev: BL 8/00) [523]

20998 Dyer, Alan. *Space* (5–8). Illus. Series: Insiders. 2007, Simon & Schuster $16.99 (978-1-4169-3860-6). An introduction to the big bang, the solar system, stars and nebulas, galaxies, and so forth, with eye-catching illustrations. (Rev: LMC 10/07; SLJ 12/07) [520]

20999 Fleisher, Paul. *The Big Bang* (5–8). Series: Great Ideas in Science. 2005, Twenty-First Century LB $27.93 (978-0-8225-2133-4). Students with a real interest in science will benefit most from this overview of theories about the creation of the universe, from creation myths onward. (Rev: BL 12/1/05; SLJ 12/05) [523.1]

21000 Fox, Karen C. *Older Than the Stars* (2–6). Illus. by Nancy Davis. 2010, Charlesbridge $15.95 (978-1-57091-787-5). Unpaged. The formation of the universe is broken down into small, accessible bits of information in this lively book full of eye-catching illustrations. (Rev: LMC 11–12/10; SLJ 2/1/10) [523.1]

21001 Gardner, Robert. *Far-Out Science Projects About Earth's Sun and Moon* (3–6). Illus. by Tom LaBaff. Series: Rockin' Earth Science Experiments. 2007, Enslow LB $23.93 (978-0-7660-2736-7). 48pp. A book of basic projects that show how the sun and moon affect our planet. (Rev: SLJ 8/07) [523.7078]

21002 Gifford, Clive. *The Kingfisher Facts and Records Book of Space: The Ultimate Information Database* (4–6). Illus. 2001, Kingfisher $14.95 (978-0-7534-5363-6). 64pp. Among the topics covered in this fact-packed volume are the solar system, the Milky Way and other galaxies, astronomical equipment, and man's journeys into space. (Rev: HBG 10/02; SLJ 12/01) [520]

21003 Goldsmith, Mike. *Universe: Journey into Deep Space* (4–7). Illus. by Mark A. Garlick. 2012, Kingfisher $17.99 (978-075346876-0). 48pp. A visually pleasing and accessible introduction to the Milky Way and other galaxies. (Rev: BL 12/15/12) [523.1]

21004 Grady, Monica. *Stardust from Space* (K–3). Illus. by Lucia deLeiris. 2007, Frances Lincoln $16.95 (978-1-84507-570-5). 32pp. The formation of planets and other objects in the solar system is explored and accompanied by large, appealing illustrations. (Rev: BL 12/1/07; SLJ 4/08) [523.1125]

21005 Graham, Ian. *Voyage Through Space* (4–6). Illus. by Sebastian Quigley and Gary Slater. Series: Discoverology. 2007, Barron's $18.99 (978-0-7641-6062-2). 30pp. With wheels, pull-tabs, flaps, and pop-ups, this effective volume gives a nice introduction to the solar system, stars, and galaxies, as well as details of human exploration; more suitable for display than circulation. (Rev: SLJ 1/08) [520]

21006 Graun, Ken, and Suzanne Maly. *Our Galaxy and the Universe* (4–6). Illus. Series: 21st Century Astronomy. 2002, Ken Pr. $15.95 (978-1-928771-08-1). 36pp. Excellent illustrations add to the appeal of this look at the stars. (Rev: SLJ 12/02)

21007 Gustafson, John. *Planets, Moons and Meteors: The Young Stargazer's Guide to the Galaxy* (4–8). 1992, Simon & Schuster LB $12.95 (978-0-671-72534-1); paper $6.95 (978-0-671-72535-8). This guidebook tells how and when to observe the solar system and provides basic information about the planets. (Rev: BL 11/1/92) [523]

21008 Halpern, Paul. *Faraway Worlds: Planets Beyond Our Solar System* (3–6). Illus. by Lynette R. Cook. 2004, Charlesbridge $16.95 (978-1-57091-616-8); paper $6.95 (978-1-57091-617-5). 32pp. This strikingly illustrated slim volume looks at planets exising beyond our solar system and discusses how they are studied by scientists. (Rev: BL 8/04; SLJ 3/05) [523.2]

21009 Hartland, Jessie. *How the Meteorite Got to the Museum* (K–3). Illus. by author. 2013, Blue Apple $17.99 (978-160905252-2). 40pp. Using a cumulative form, this book tells the fascinating story of how a meteorite that crashed into a car in Peekskill, New York, made its way to the American Museum of Natural History. (Rev: BL 11/1/13; SLJ 1/1/14*) [523.5]

21010 Hicks, Terry Allan. *Earth and the Moon* (4–8). Series: Space! 2010, Marshall Cavendish LB $32.79 (978-0-7614-4254-7). 64pp. After an overview of Earth and its moon, Hicks looks at our growing understanding over time and the missions to explore our moon. Also use *Saturn* (2010). ℮ (Rev: LMC 3–4/10; SLJ 2/10) [525]

21011 Jackson, Ellen. *The Mysterious Universe: Supernovae, Dark Energy, and Black Holes* (5–8). Series: Scientists in the Field. 2008, Houghton Mifflin $18.00 (978-0-618-56325-8). Astronomer Alex Filippenko and his work at key observatories is the focus of this book that also describes such phenomena as supernovae and black holes in accessible text with informative diagrams and spectacular photographs. (Rev: BL 6/1–15/08; SLJ 6/08) [523.8]

21012 Jefferis, David. *Black Holes and Other Bizarre Space Objects* (5–8). Illus. Series: Science Frontiers. 2006, Crabtree LB $26.60 (978-0-7787-2856-6); paper $8.95 (978-0-7787-2870-2). 32pp. Double-page spreads with color photographs and informative sidebars explore the life of stars, black holes, gamma-ray bursts, space telescopes, and so forth. (Rev: BL 4/1/06) [523.8]

21013 Jefferis, David. *Star Spotters: Telescopes and Observatories* (4–6). Illus. Series: Our Solar System. 2009, Crabtree LB $26.60 (978-0-7787-3725-4); paper $8.95 (978-0-7787-3742-1). A brief, attractive, and easy-to-understand overview of telescopes and observatories — both on Earth and orbiting far above — and of the important information they provide; with a "Young Astronomer" section. Also use *Space Probes: Exploring Beyond Earth* and *Galaxies: Immense Star Islands* (both 2009). (Rev: LMC 10/09; SLJ 5/09) [522]

21014 Love, Ann, and Jane Drake. *The Kids' Book of the Night Sky* (4–6). Illus. by Heather Collins. 2004, Kids Can $19.95 (978-1-55337-357-5). 144pp. The authors offer a potpourri of basic astronomy facts, sky folklore, charts, and suggestions for art and science projects, leavened with light humor and helpful illustrations. (Rev: BL 4/15/04; SLJ 7/04) [520]

21015 Macy, Sue. *Are We Alone? Scientists Search for Life in Space* (4–8). 2004, National Geographic $18.95 (978-0-7922-6567-2). Modern scientific efforts to find extraterrestrial life are discussed along with the popularity of flying saucers, crop circles, and other theories. (Rev: BL 10/1/04; SLJ 12/04*) [001.9]

21016 Miller, Ron. *Earth and the Moon* (5–7). Series: Worlds Beyond. 2003, Twenty-First Century LB $25.90 (978-0-7613-2358-7). NASA photographs and computer-generated images are used throughout this account of the origin, composition, and evolution the Earth and its moon. (Rev: HBG 10/03; SLJ 8/03) [525]

21017 Oleksy, Walter. *Mapping the Skies* (5–7). Series: Watts Library: Geography. 2002, Watts LB $25.50 (978-0-531-12031-6); paper $8.95 (978-0-531-16635-2). 64pp. From the ancient Greeks and Romans through Galileo to astronomers today, this is a history of how the stars, planets, and space have been mapped. (Rev: BL 10/15/02) [520]

21018 Orr, Tamra. *The Telescope* (4–8). Series: Inventions That Shaped the World. 2004, Watts LB $30.50 (978-0-531-12344-7). 80pp. Describes the invention of the telescope, the impact of the knowledge imparted, and future possibilities. (Rev: BL 4/1/04; SLJ 2/05) [522]

21019 Portman, Michael. *Are There Other Earths?* (3–5). Illus. Series: Space Mysteries. 2013, Gareth Stevens LB $25.25 (978-143398257-6). 32pp. Brief chapters with diagrams and photographs cover galaxies and stars, the solar system, the Goldilocks zone, and exoplanets, as well as discussing telescopes and the search for new discoveries. (Rev: BL 4/1/13; LMC 1–2/14*; SLJ 4/13) [523.2]

21020 Rau, Dana Meachen. *Black Holes* (3–5). Illus. Series: Our Solar System. 2005, Compass Point $23.93 (978-0-7565-0849-4). 32pp. Good coverage of a tricky topic, describing black holes' nature and formation, with photographs and illustrations adding to the appeal. (Rev: SLJ 8/05) [523.8]

21021 Roza, Greg. *The Incredible Story of Telescopes* (3–6). Illus. Series: A Kid's Guide to Incredible Technology. 2004, Rosen LB $19.95 (978-0-8239-6715-5). 24pp. The history and technology of telescopes are discussed in concise terms, with material on Hubble and on future developments. (Rev: SLJ 2/05) [681]

21022 Schorer, Lonnie Jones. *Kids to Space: A Space Traveler's Guide* (5–9). Illus. 2006, Apogee paper $29.95 (978-1-894959-42-1). Organized in almost 100 categories, this volume includes thousands of questions about space posed by children and answered by experts including NASA engineers, former astronauts, and astronomy professors. (Rev: SLJ 12/06) [500.5]

21023 Scott, Elaine. *Space, Stars, and the Beginning of Time: What the Hubble Telescope Saw* (5–8). Illus. 2011, Clarion $17.99 (978-0-547-24189-0). 66pp. This inspiring tribute to the Hubble Space Telescope features a discussion of the history of astronomy, and how the Hubble contributed to our understanding of the universe. ALA Notable Children's Book 2012. (Rev: HB 3–4/11; SLJ 3/1/11) [522]

21024 Sherman, Josepha. *Asteroids, Meteors, and Comets* (5–7). Series: Space! 2009, Marshall Cavendish LB $22.95 (978-0-7614-4252-3). 64pp. Good for research, this volume presents facts clearly and concisely with many photos and other illustrations. (Rev: LMC 3–4/10; SLJ 2/10) [523]

21025 Sparrow, Giles. *Cosmic! The Ultimate 3-D Guide to the Universe* (3–6). Illus. by Richard Ferguson. 2008, DK $24.99 (978-0-7566-4021-7). 16pp. Pop-up illustrations, gatefold pages, lift-flaps, illustrations, and text present information on the universe. (Rev: BLO 12/16/08) [523.1]

21026 Stott, Carole. *Astronomy* (4–6). Illus. 2003, Kingfisher $16.95 (978-0-7534-5582-1). 64pp. This engaging introduction to astronomy explores the history of the science, how the universe was viewed by earlier civilizations, and the tools of the astronomer. (Rev: HBG 4/04; SLJ 11/03) [520]

21027 VanCleave, Janice. *Step-By-Step Science Experiments in Astronomy* (5–8). Series: Janice VanCleave's First-Place Science Fair Projects. 2012, Rosen Central LB $33.25 (978-1-4488-6978-7). 80pp. An updated volume with step-by-step instructions for 22 experiments mostly using easily found materials. (Rev: SLJ 10/12) [520.78]

21028 Vogt, Gregory L. *Deep Space Astronomy* (5–8). 1999, Twenty-First Century LB $25.90 (978-0-7613-1369-4). This look beyond our own star system covers such topics as the development of space-based detectors, information-gathering techniques, and recent discoveries. (Rev: BL 1/1–15/00; HBG 3/00; SLJ 2/00) [520]

21029 Weakland, Mark. *The Lonely Existence of Asteroids and Comets* (3–5). Illus. by Carlos Aon. Series: Adventures in Science. 2012, Capstone $29.99 (978-142967546-8); paper $7.95 (978-14296798-7-9). 32pp. Weakland uses a graphic-novel format to explore the small bodies that zoom around in space. (Rev: BL 3/15/12; LMC 11–12/12) [523.44]

21030 Whitfield, David. *Northern Lights* (2–4). Illus. Series: Science Matters. 2006, Weigl $24.45 (978-1-59036-413-0). 24pp. Readers will be fascinated to learn about the phenomenon of the northern lights and the science behind it. Photographs and other graphics, as well as related information and activities, add to this book's appeal. (Rev: SLJ 5/07)

21031 Williams, Brian. *What About . . . the Universe?* (5–8). Illus. Series: Answering Q&A Questions. 2009, Mason Crest $19.95 (978-1-4222-1566-1). 40pp. Using a question-and-answer format, two-page spreads look at subjects ranging from the Big Bang to space missions and the solar system. (Rev: LMC 5–6/10; SLJ 4/10) [520]

21032 Wills, Susan, and Steven Wills. *Astronomy: Looking at the Stars* (5–8). Series: Innovators. 2001, Oliver $21.95 (978-1-881508-76-2). A good starting point for research into astronomy, with profiles of individuals including Ptolemy, Copernicus, Galileo, and Newton. (Rev: HBG 10/02; SLJ 2/02) [520.922]

Earth

21033 Bailey, Jacqui. *Sun Up, Sun Down: The Story of Day and Night* (2–4). Illus. by Matthew Lilly. Series: Science Works. 2004, Picture Window LB $26.60 (978-1-4048-0567-5). 31pp. A clear and attractive look at the Earth's rotation and the changes in light, explaining how light rays travel, how shadows are formed, and so forth. (Rev: SLJ 8/04) [525.35]

21034 Carson, Mary Kay. *Far-Out Guide to Earth* (4–6). Illus. Series: Far-Out Guide to the Solar System. 2010, Enslow LB $23.93 (978-0-7660-3182-1); paper $7.95 (978-1-59845-183-2). 48pp. A lively and well-illustrated introduction to our planet with information on the technology used to study it. (Rev: SLJ 12/1/10) [525]

21035 Davis, Kenneth C. *Don't Know Much About Planet Earth* (3–6). Illus. by Tom Bloom. Series: Don't Know Much About. 2001, HarperCollins LB $19.89 (978-0-06-028600-2); paper $7.99 (978-0-06-440834-9). 144pp. A question-and-answer format with cartoon-like drawings makes an attractive backdrop for this overview of the earth's physical and environmental features, as well as today's political divisions and a timeline of historical highlights. (Rev: BL 12/15/01; HBG 3/02; SLJ 8/01) [910]

21036 Gilpin, Dan. *Planet Earth* (3–5). Illus. by Peter Bull. Series: Explorers. 2011, Kingfisher $10.99 (978-075346591-2). 32pp. An inviting mix of text, sidebars, captions, fact lists, and more add read-appeal to this well-illustrated book about Earth, its position in space, and its geology, environment, and inhabitants. (Rev: BL 2/15/12) [550]

21037 Goldsmith, Mike. *Earth: The Life of Our Planet* (4–7). Illus. by Mark A. Garlick. 2011, Kingfisher $17.99 (978-075346625-4). 48pp. This broad overview of the big events that have shaped Earth's climate and topography begins with the planet's formation and ends with space exploration and possibilities for the future. (Rev: BLO 10/15/11; LMC 5–6/12) [550]

21038 Karas, G. Brian. *On Earth* (K–3). Illus. 2005, Penguin $16.99 (978-0-399-24025-6). 32pp. Large double-page spreads featuring attractive illustrations discuss the passage of time, the seasons, and the Earth's obit, rotation, and tilt. (Rev: BL 5/1/05; SLJ 5/05) [525]

21039 Kerrod, Robin. *Planet Earth* (4–6). Series: Planet Library. 2000, Lerner LB $21.27 (978-0-8225-3902-5). 32pp. This book discusses the earth's formation, its jour-

ney through space, its drifting continents, its waters and weather, and its many forms of life. (Rev: BL 10/15/00; HBG 3/01) [525]

21040 Nadeau, Isaac. *Learning About Earth's Cycles with Graphic Organizers* (3–6). 2005, Rosen LB $21.25 (978-1-4042-2807-8). This title uses a wide variety of graphic organizers, including concept webs, compare/contrast charts, Venn diagrams, graphs, timelines, and KWL charts, to introduce readers to Earth's natural cycles, including tidal ebb and flow; seasonal changes; and day and night. (Rev: SLJ 11/05)

21041 Pettigrew, Mark. *Planet Earth* (3–6). Series: Science World. 2004, Stargazer LB $27.10 (978-1-932799-28-6). 32pp. Basic facts about the Earth — its structure, movement, atmosphere, and so forth — are introduced in concise text with good diagrams, photographs, and a project, all presented in picture-book format. (Rev: BL 12/1/04) [551]

21042 Ross, Michael E. *Earth Cycles* (1–3). Illus. by Gustav Moore. 2001, Millbrook $22.40 (978-0-7613-1815-6). 32pp. The earth's rotation pattern is described with material on the reasons for night and day and the causes of seasons, plus why the moon appears to change shape during a lunar month. (Rev: BL 1/1–15/01; HBG 10/01) [525]

21043 Wells, Robert E. *What's So Special About Planet Earth?* (1–3). Illus. by author. 2009, Whitman $16.99 (978-0-8075-8815-4). 32pp. In a lighthearted fashion, Wells explores the benefits of living on Earth and compares conditions here with those on the other planets. (Rev: BL 9/15/09; LMC 11–12/09; SLJ 9/1/09) [525]

21044 Whitehouse, Patricia. *The Earth* (2–4). Illus. Series: Space Explorer. 2004, Heinemann LB $24.21 (978-1-4034-5150-7). 32pp. A slim overview of the Earth, discussing its composition, axis, and rotation, with fascinating photographs from space and final Earth facts. [550]

Moon

21045 Branley, Franklyn M. *What the Moon Is Like* (1–3). Illus. by True Kelley. Series: Let's-Read-and-Find-Out. 2000, HarperCollins LB $15.89 (978-0-06-027993-6). 40pp. An updated version of this standard title that includes important new material about the moon and its composition. (Rev: BL 6/1–15/00; HBG 9/00; SLJ 7/00) [559.9]

21046 Crelin, Bob. *Faces of the Moon* (2–4). Illus. by Leslie Evans. 2009, Charlesbridge $16.95 (978-1-57091-785-1). 36pp. The moon's phases are explained through poetry, prose, and illustrations. (Rev: BL 7/09; SLJ 7/09) [523.3]

21047 Kerrod, Robin. *The Moon* (4–6). Series: Planet Library. 2000, Lerner LB $21.27 (978-0-8225-3900-1). 32pp. The moon's formation, history, orbit, and makeup are covered, plus material on the moon landing. (Rev: BL 10/15/00; HBG 3/01; SLJ 11/00) [523.3]

21048 Ross, Stewart. *Moon: Science, History, and Mystery* (4–6). 2009, Scholastic LB $18.99 (978-0-545-12732-5). 128pp. An oversize, information-packed book celebrating the moon's history, mythology, influence on culture generally, and human exploration. (Rev: LMC 11–12/09; SLJ 12/09) [523.3]

21049 Simon, Seymour. *The Moon* (2–4). 2003, Simon & Schuster $17.95 (978-0-689-83563-6). 32pp. This revised edition adds new photographs and color reproductions. (Rev: BL 10/15/03; SLJ 1/04) [559.9]

21050 Siy, Alexandra. *Footprints on the Moon* (3–5). Illus. 2001, Charlesbridge $16.95 (978-1-57091-408-9). 32pp. This heavily illustrated book covers human fascination with the moon throughout history and then focuses on Project Apollo and the moon landings. (Rev: BL 2/1/01; HBG 10/01; SLJ 2/01) [629.45]

21051 Tomecek, Steve. *Moon* (K–3). Illus. by Lisa Chauncy Guida. Series: Jump into Science. 2005, National Geographic LB $25.90 (978-0-7922-8304-1). 32pp. An entertaining introduction to the moon for young children. (Rev: BL 3/1/05) [523.3]

21052 Whitehouse, Patricia. *The Moon* (2–4). Illus. Series: Space Explorer. 2004, Heinemann LB $24.21 (978-1-4034-5152-1). 32pp. A slim overview of the moon, covering topics including its size, composition, climate, and different phases. (Rev: BL 7/02; HBG 10/02) [523.3]

Planets

21053 Allyn, Daisy. *Jupiter: The Largest Planet* (K–2). Illus. Series: Our Solar System. 2010, Gareth Stevens LB $22.60 (978-1-4339-3821-4); paper $8.15 (978-1-4339-3822-1). 24pp. Bright images and clear information about Jupiter are presented in a small, square format. Lexile 420 (Rev: BL 1/1–15/11; SLJ 11/1/10) [523.45]

21054 Arlon, Penelope, and Tory Gordon Harris. *Planets* (3–5). Illus. Series: Discover More. 2012, Scholastic paper $12.99 (978-05453302-8-2). 80pp. A visually appealing overview of the planets, with information on related aspects such as asteroids and space travel plus the ability to download a digital book that offers interactivity and links to other features. (Rev: BL 3/1/12; SLJ 4/1/12) [523.4]

21055 Bjorklund, Ruth. *Venus* (4–8). Series: Space! 2010, Marshall Cavendish LB $32.79 (978-0-7614-4251-6). 64pp. In chapters covering the discovery of Venus, its features, missions to the planet, and handy quick facts, this accessible title features useful, well-presented material. ℮ (Rev: LMC 3–4/10; SLJ 2/10) [523.42]

21056 Bortolotti, Dan. *Exploring Saturn* (4–8). 2003, Firefly $19.95 (978-1-55297-766-8); paper $9.95 (978-1-55297-765-1). This highly visual volume with readable text presents facts about Saturn, explains how and

when we acquired this knowledge, and looks at the Cassini-Huygens mission, scheduled to reach the planet in 2004. (Rev: BL 12/1/03; SLJ 5/04) [523.46]

21057 Capaccio, George. *Jupiter* (4–8). Series: Space! 2010, Marshall Cavendish LB $32.79 (978-0-7614-4244-8). 64pp. Capaccio looks at the physical features of Jupiter, the history of its discovery and what we have since learned about it, and speculates about future missions. Also use *The Sun* and *Neptune* (both 2010). ℮ (Rev: LMC 3–4/10; SLJ 2/10) [523.45]

21058 Carson, Mary Kay. *Far-Out Guide to Jupiter* (4–6). Illus. 2010, Enslow LB $23.93 (978-0-7660-3184-5); paper $7.95 (978-1-59845-186-3). 48pp. A lively and well-illustrated introduction to the planet and its moons. Also use *Far-Out Guide to the Icy Dwarf Planets* (2010). (Rev: SLJ 12/1/10) [523.45]

21059 Colligan, L. H. *Mercury* (4–8). Series: Space! 2010, Marshall Cavendish LB $32.79 (978-0-7614-4239-4). 64pp. Colligan looks at how planets were formed, the history of Mercury's discovery and what we have since learned about it, and speculates about its future importance. ℮ (Rev: LMC 3–4/10; SLJ 2/10) [523.41]

21060 Feinstein, Stephen. *Saturn* (4–7). Series: Solar System. 2005, Enslow LB $25.26 (978-0-7660-5304-5). Useful for reports, this clearly written title includes links to Web sites for further research. (Rev: SLJ 12/05) [523.46]

21061 Gallant, Roy A. *Planets* (2–4). Illus. Series: Kaleidoscope. 2000, Marshall Cavendish LB $25.64 (978-0-7614-1033-1). 48pp. With colorful illustrations, each of the planets of our solar system is introduced with a brief descriptive text. (Rev: BL 1/1–15/01; HBG 10/01) [523.4]

21062 Gibbons, Gail. *The Planets. Rev. ed.* (K–2). Illus. by author. 2005, Holiday House $16.95 (978-0-8234-1957-9). There are few changes in this revised edition of the popular introductory guide to the planets that was first published in 1993. (Rev: SLJ 11/05) [523.4]

21063 Gifford, Clive. *How to Live on Mars* (3–6). Illus. by Scoular Anderson. Series: How To. 2001, Watts LB $16.00 (978-0-531-14647-7). 96pp. Experiments back up the concepts introduced in this discussion of the possibilities of traveling to and living on Mars. (Rev: SLJ 4/02) [523.4]

21064 Goldstein, Margaret J. *Uranus* (2–3). Illus. Series: Our Universe. 2003, Lerner LB $22.60 (978-0-8225-4654-2). 32pp. This solid introduction to Uranus examines the huge planet's physical characteristics, distance from the sun, rotation axis, and 15 moons. Also use *Saturn* and *Venus* (both 2003). (Rev: SLJ 1/04) [523.47]

21065 James, Lincoln. *Mercury: The Iron Planet* (K–2). Illus. Series: Our Solar System. 2010, Gareth Stevens LB $22.6 (978-143393827-6). 24pp. Bright images and clear information about Mercury are presented in a small, square format. Lexile 420 (Rev: BL 1/1–15/11; SLJ 11/1/10) [523.41]

21066 Kerrod, Robin. *Jupiter* (4–6). Illus. Series: Planet Library. 2000, Lerner $21.27 (978-0-8225-3907-0). 32pp. Jupiter, the largest of the planets, is presented in text and pictures with material on its formation, makeup, atmosphere, and the space probes that have gathered information about it. Two others in this series are *Mars* and *Mercury and Venus*. (Rev: BL 10/15/00; HBG 3/01) [523.45]

21067 Kerrod, Robin. *Saturn* (4–6). Series: Planet Library. 2000, Lerner LB $21.27 (978-0-8225-3909-4). 32pp. Breathtaking photographs and a clear text introduce Saturn, the planet of swirling clouds, bright rings, and 18 moons. (Rev: BL 10/15/00; HBG 3/01; SLJ 1/01) [523.4]

21068 Kerrod, Robin. *Uranus, Neptune, and Pluto* (4–6). Series: Planet Library. 2000, Lerner LB $21.27 (978-0-8225-3908-7). 32pp. An exploration of the planets on the edge of our solar system, beginning with the ringed gas giants, Uranus and Neptune, and ending with mysterious Pluto. (Rev: BL 10/15/00; HBG 3/01; SLJ 1/01) [513.4]

21069 Landau, Elaine. *Pluto: From Planet to Dwarf* (2–4). Illus. Series: True Books: Space. 2008, Scholastic LB $26.00 (978-0-531-12566-3). 48pp. Pluto's changed status to dwarf planet is clearly explained along with information about a space probe scheduled to reach Pluto in 2015. (Rev: BL 12/1/07) [523.48]

21070 Leedy, Loreen, and Andrew Schuerger. *Messages from Mars* (2–4). 2006, Holiday $16.95 (978-0-8234-1954-8). 40pp. In 2106, six children take a trip to Mars, tour the planet, visit the sites of century-old landings, and send messages home reporting on their travels and discoveries. (Rev: BL 9/15/06; SLJ 10/06) [523.43]

21071 Lew, Kristi. *The Dwarf Planet Pluto* (4–8). Series: Space! 2010, Marshall Cavendish LB $32.79 (978-0-7614-4243-1). 64pp. The author discusses Pluto's composition, its new status as a dwarf planet, missions to Pluto, and pertinent facts. e (Rev: LMC 3–4/10; SLJ 2/10) [523.482]

21072 McGranaghan, John. *Meet the Planets* (2–4). Illus. by Laurie Allen Klein. 2011, Sylvan Dell $16.95 (978-1-60718-123-1); paper $8.95 (978-1-60718-133-0). Unpaged. A lighthearted introduction to the planets, with cartoonish caricatures and plenty of facts and information on science and astronomy. e (Rev: LMC 11–12/11; SLJ 7/11) [523.4]

21073 Miller, Ron. *Jupiter* (5–8). Series: Worlds Beyond. 2002, Millbrook LB $25.90 (978-0-7613-2356-3). An excellent oversize volume that explores the largest of the planets with amazing full-page color illustrations and a detailed text. Also use *Venus* (2002). (Rev: BL 8/02; HBG 3/03; SLJ 8/02) [523.4]

21074 Miller, Ron. *Mercury and Pluto* (5–8). Series: Worlds Beyond. 2003, Millbrook LB $25.90 (978-0-7613-2361-7). 80pp. Information on these planets and their discoveries is presented clearly, with helpful illustrations. Also use *Saturn* (2003). (Rev: BL 11/15/03; SLJ 12/03) [523.4]

21075 Miller, Ron. *Saturn* (5–8). Series: Worlds Beyond. 2003, Millbrook LB $25.90 (978-0-7613-2360-0). A colorful volume that describes the discovery of the solar system and supplies details about the planet Saturn and its many rings. (Rev: BL 11/15/03; SLJ 12/03) [523.4]

21076 Miller, Ron. *Seven Wonders of the Gas Giants and Their Moons* (5–8). Illus. Series: Seven Wonders. 2011, Twenty-First Century LB $33.26 (978-0-7613-5449-9). 80pp. Saturn's rings, the great red spot of Jupiter, and the auroras of Saturn are among the seven wonders explored in this interesting volume. Also use *Seven Wonders of the Rocky Planets and Their Moons* (2011). e (Rev: BL 3/1/11; SLJ 2/1/11) [523.4]

21077 Miller, Ron. *Uranus and Neptune* (5–7). Series: Worlds Beyond. 2003, Twenty-First Century LB $25.90 (978-0-7613-2357-0). NASA photographs and computer-generated images are used throughout this account of the discovery and exploration of these two planets and what we know about their origin, composition, and evolution. (Rev: HBG 10/03; SLJ 8/03) [523.47]

21078 Mist, Rosalind. *Jupiter and Saturn* (K–2). Illus. 2012, Amicus/QEB LB $17.95 (978-1-60992321-1). 24pp. For beginning readers, this slim volume introduces the main characteristics of these two planets. Lexile AD630L (Rev: BL 12/1/12) [523.45]

21079 O'Connell, Kim A. *Mercury* (4–7). Series: Solar System. 2005, Enslow LB $25.26 (978-0-7660-5209-3). A blend of easy-to-understand narrative, vivid color photographs, and links to related online resources introduce Mercury. Also use *Pluto* (2005). (Rev: SLJ 12/05) [523.4]

21080 Rau, Dana Meachen. *Jupiter* (3–5). Illus. Series: Our Solar System. 2002, Compass Point LB $23.93 (978-0-7565-0198-3). 32pp. An appealing introduction to the planet, with large photographs. Also use *Mars*, *Mercury*, and *Venus* (all 2002). (Rev: BL 5/15/02; SLJ 7/02) [523.45]

21081 Ring, Susan. *Dwarf Planets* (3–5). Illus. Series: Our Solar System. 2013, Weigl LB $20.71 (978-162127262-5). 24pp. NASA photographs and other vibrant images of the five dwarf planets enhance this brief discussion of how these planets were named, discovered, and their positions within the solar system. (Rev: BL 10/1/13) [523.49]

21082 Roza, Greg. *Uranus: The Ice Planet* (K–2). Illus. Series: Our Solar System. 2010, Gareth Stevens LB $22.60 (978-143393842-9). 24pp. Bright images and clear information about Uranus are presented in a small, square format. Lexile 420 (Rev: BL 1/1–15/11; SLJ 11/1/10) [523.47]

21083 Scherer, Glenn, and Marty Fletcher. *Neptune* (4–6). Illus. Series: The Solar System. 2005, Enslow LB $25.26 (978-0-7660-5211-6). 48pp. A useful overview of our knowledge about Neptune (including its planetoid, Sedna), with 30 recommended Internet links. (Rev: SLJ 11/05)

21084 Scherer, Glenn, and Marty Fletcher. *Uranus* (4–6). Illus. Series: The Solar System. 2005, Enslow LB

$25.26 (978-0-7660-5307-6). 48pp. A useful overview of our knowledge about Uranus, with 30 recommended Internet links. (Rev: SLJ 11/05) [523.4]

21085 Scott, Elaine. *Mars and the Search for Life* (5–8). Illus. 2008, Clarion $17.00 (978-0-618-76695-6). 60pp. Is there water on the Red Planet? Scott addresses this and other questions while discussing what we know about the planet, the various explorations that have already taken place, and possible future missions. (Rev: BCCB 12/08; BL 12/1/08; HB 1/09; SLJ 1/09) [576.8]

21086 Scott, Elaine. *When is a Planet Not a Planet?* (3–6). Illus. 2007, Clarion $17.00 (978-0-618-89832-9). 40pp. Pluto's reclassification serves as the introduction for a discussion of astronomy and the discovery of planets and other celestial bodies. (Rev: BL 9/1/07; HB 11/07; LMC 1/08; SLJ 10/07) [523.48]

21087 Sherman, Josepha. *Neptune* (5–7). Series: Space! 2009, Marshall Cavendish LB $22.95 (978-0-7614-4246-2). 64pp. Good for research, this volume presents facts clearly and concisely with many photos and other illustrations. (Rev: LMC 3–4/10; SLJ 2/10) [523.4]

21088 Sherman, Josepha. *Uranus* (4–8). Series: Space! 2010, Marshall Cavendish LB $32.79 (978-0-7614-4248-6). 64pp. The author discusses the discovery of this planet, mysteries surrounding it, Voyager 2's expedition, and other key facts in this easily understood volume. Also use *Mars* (2010). e (Rev: LMC 3–4/10; SLJ 2/10) [523.47]

21089 Simon, Seymour. *Planets Around the Sun* (1–3). Series: See More Readers. 2002, North-South $13.95 (978-1-58717-145-1); paper $3.95 (978-1-58717-146-8). 32pp. The plants and the solar system are introduced in this beginning reader. (Rev: BL 7/02; HBG 10/02; SLJ 6/02) [523.2]

21090 Stefoff, Rebecca. *Pluto* (3–5). Illus. Series: Blast-off. 2003, Marshall Cavendish LB $28.50 (978-0-7614-1404-9). 64pp. A fascinating, well-illustrated account of the discovery of the planet Pluto and the continuing scientific debate about whether it is a true planet or not. (Rev: BL 4/1/03; HBG 3/03) [523.48]

21091 Stone, Tanya L. *Mercury* (3–5). Illus. Series: Blastoff. 2003, Marshall Cavendish LB $28.50 (978-0-7614-1403-2). 64pp. Stone explains the history of our knowledge of Mercury and what we may learn from new expeditions to the planet; a glossary, bibliography, and list of Web sites follow the text. (Rev: BL 4/1/03; HBG 3/03) [523.41]

21092 Vogt, Gregory L. *Jupiter* (3–4). Series: Galaxy. 2000, Capstone LB $22.60 (978-0-7368-0512-4). 24pp. This book and the others listed cover basic facts and material on atmospheres, rings, physical features, and moons. Others are *Neptune, Pluto,* and *Uranus* (all 2000). (Rev: HBG 9/00; SLJ 9/00) [523.4]

21093 Weitekamp, Margaret A., and David DeVorkin. *Pluto's Secret: An Icy World's Tale of Discovery* (1–4). Illus. by Diane Kidd. 2013, Abrams $16.95 (978-1-4197-0423-9). 40pp. Published in association with the Smithsonian National Air and Space Museum, this is an accessible, entertaining, and informative introduction to Pluto's rise to full planethood and subsequent change in status. (Rev: BL 3/1/13; SLJ 4/13) [523.49]

Solar System

21094 Aguilar, David A. *11 Planets: A New View of the Solar System* (5–8). 2008, National Geographic $16.95 (978-1-4263-0236-7). The author includes the eight planets and three dwarf planets in his calculation of the main celestial bodies in the solar system; attractive color paintings and photographs accompany the text. (Rev: BL 5/1/08; SLJ 9/08) [523]

21095 Bredeson, Carmen. *What Is the Solar System?* (1–3). Illus. Series: I Like Space! 2008, Enslow LB $22.60 (978-1-7660-2944-6). 32pp. "Is Pluto a planet?" Simple design and text with a question-and-answer format and color photographs present fascinating space-related facts. (Rev: SLJ 9/08) [523.2]

21096 Croswell, Ken. *Ten Worlds: Everything That Orbits the Sun* (4–6). 2006, Boyds Mills $19.95 (978-1-59078-423-5). 56pp. A large-format exploration of the solar system with striking images of the planets. (Rev: BL 8/06; SLJ 7/06) [523.4]

21097 Farndon, John. *Exploring the Solar System* (4–9). Series: Why Science Matters. 2009, Heinemann-Raintree $32.86 (978-1-4329-2484-3). 56pp. This appealing guide to the solar system emphasizes the importance of scientific understanding to everyday life. (Rev: LMC 11–12/09) [523.4]

21098 Gallan, Roy. *Comets, Asteroids, and Meteorites* (2–4). Series: Kaleidoscope. 2000, Marshall Cavendish LB $25.64 (978-0-7614-1034-8). 48pp. An up-to-date account that combines good visuals with an exciting text in this examination of these visitors from space. (Rev: BL 1/1–15/01; HBG 10/01) [523]

21099 Goldsmith, Mike. *Solar System* (1–3). Illus. Series: Discover Science. 2010, Kingfisher $9.99 (978-075346447-2). 56pp. This lively solar system overview contains plenty of glossy photos, intriguing facts, activities, and comprehensive back matter. (Rev: BL 10/1/10; LMC 11–12/10) [523.2]

21100 Goldsmith, Mike. *Solar System* (K–3). Series: Kingfisher Young Knowledge. 2004, Kingfisher $8.95 (978-0-7534-5773-3). 47pp. Using two-page chapters with large text and eye-catching photographs, planets, asteroids, comets, and meteoroids are introduced. (Rev: SLJ 4/05) [523.4]

21101 Graun, Ken. *Our Earth and the Solar System* (4–6). Illus. 2001, Ken Pr. $15.95 (978-1-928771-02-9). 36pp. A large-format, interesting guide to the solar system that also looks at the equipment we use to look at these bodies. (Rev: BL 5/1/01; SLJ 6/01) [523.2]

21102 Jenkins, Alvin. *Next Stop Neptune: Experiencing the Solar System* (2–5). Illus. by Steve Jenkins. 2004, Houghton $16.00 (978-0-618-41603-5). 40pp. Colorful collage illustrations subsitute for photographs in this well-written introduction to the solar system. (Rev: BL 10/15/04; SLJ 10/04) [523.2]

21103 Kerrod, Robin. *Asteroids, Comets, and Meteors* (4–6). Series: Planet Library. 2000, Lerner LB $21.27 (978-0-8225-3905-6). 32pp. This book explores the smallest members of the solar system and tells how they were formed, how they shaped the surface of the planets and moons, and how they sometimes light up our sky. (Rev: BL 10/15/00; HBG 3/01) [523.4]

21104 Kerrod, Robin. *The Solar System* (4–6). Illus. Series: Planet Library. 2000, Lerner $21.27 (978-0-8225-3903-2). 32pp. A discussion on the formation of the sun, the planets, their moons, and the asteroid belt is followed by additional coverage of topics such as orbiting stars, space exploration, and the search for extraterrestrial life. (Rev: BL 10/15/00; HBG 3/01; SLJ 11/00) [523.3]

21105 Kudlinski, Kathleen V. *Boy, Were We Wrong About the Solar System!* (1–3). Illus. by John Rocco. 2008, Dutton $15.99 (978-0-525-46979-7). 32pp. Kudlinski provides a lighthearted overview of some of the scientific concepts of the universe that have proved quite wrong. (Rev: BCCB 11/08; BL 12/1/08; LMC 1/09; SLJ 11/08) [523.2]

21106 Mitton, Jacqueline. *The Planet Gods: Myths and Facts About the Solar System* (2–4). Illus. by Christina Balit. 2008, National Geographic LB $25.90 (978-1-4263-0449-1); paper $7.95 (978-1-4263-0448-4). Gorgeous artwork is just one of the highlights of this title about space that includes lush language, poetic references, solid facts, and information on mythology. (Rev: BLO 1/13/09) [523.2]

21107 Peddicord, Jane Ann. *Night Wonders* (2–4). Illus. 2005, Charlesbridge paper $6.95 (978-1-57091-878-0). 32pp. Eye-catching full-color images of the moon, sun, stars, and planets are paired with appealing verse and brief descriptive narrative. (Rev: SLJ 4/05) [523]

21108 Rau, Dana Meachen. *The Solar System* (2–3). 2000, Compass Point LB $21.26 (978-0-7565-0036-8). 32pp. After discussing the sun, the author conducts a quick tour of the solar system including meteors, comets, and moons. (Rev: SLJ 2/01) [523.4]

21109 Theodorou, Rod. *Across the Solar System* (2–4). Series: Amazing Journeys. 2000, Heinemann LB $22.79 (978-1-57572-486-7). 32pp. In this journey into outer space there are double-page spreads with information on each planet including distance from the sun, size, and length of a day and year. (Rev: HBG 3/01; SLJ 7/00) [523.4]

21110 Tourville, Amanda Doering. *Exploring the Solar System* (4–7). Illus. Series: Let's Explore Science. 2010, Rourke LB $32.79 (978-161590323-8). 48pp. With information on the sun and moon, planets, comets, and asteroids, this is an introduction to the solar system and how scientists study it. (Rev: BL 9/1/10) [523.2]

21111 Trammel, Howard K. *The Solar System* (3–5). Illus. Series: True Book: Space. 2010, Children's Press LB $26 (978-053116898-1). 48pp. A beautifully illus-

trated introduction to the solar system with fascinating sidebars. (Rev: BL 11/1/09*; LMC 1–2/10) [523.2]

21112 VanCleave, Janice. *Janice VanCleave's Solar System: Mind-Boggling Experiments You Can Turn into Science Fair Projects* (4–6). Illus. by Laurel Aiello. Series: Spectacular Science Projects. 2000, Wiley paper $10.95 (978-0-471-32204-7). 90pp. Twenty interesting experiments involving the solar system are outlined with material on how to turn them into science projects. (Rev: SLJ 6/00) [523.4]

21113 Whitehouse, Patricia. *The Planets* (2–4). Illus. Series: Space Explorer. 2004, Heinemann LB $24.21 (978-1-4034-5153-8). 32pp. A slim survey of the solar system and the individual planets, defining what makes a planet and ending with a listing of quick facts.

Stars

21114 Abramson, Andra Serlin, and Mordecai-Mark Mac Low. *Inside Stars* (5–8). Illus. 2011, Sterling paper $9.95 (978-14027816-2-9). 48pp. A dramatic presentation of information about the Big Bang, the formation and death of stars, the sun, and so forth, with many photographs and gatefolds. (Rev: BL 11/1/11) [523.8]

21115 Aguilar, David A. *Super Stars: The Biggest, Hottest, Brightest, Most Explosive Stars in the Milky Way* (4–8). 2010, National Geographic LB $25.90 (978-1-4263-0602-0). 48pp. An exciting, engaging look at different types of stars (for example, G Stars, planetary nebulae, and brown dwarfs), with beautiful photographs and art. Lexile NC1160L (Rev: BL 4/15/10; LMC 8–9/10; SLJ 4/10) [523.8]

21116 Asimov, Isaac. *The Life and Death of Stars* (5–8). Series: Isaac Asimov's 21st Century Library of the Universe. 2005, Gareth Stevens LB $26.00 (978-0-8368-3967-8). A revised, well-illustrated edition of a previously published book, this discusses the birth of stars, profiles different types of stars, and looks at the future of our Sun. Also in this series: *Black Holes, Pulsars, and Quasars*, *The Milky Way and Other Galaxies*, *Our Planetary System*, and *Comets and Meteors* (all 2005). (Rev: BL 3/1/05; SLJ 8/05)

21117 Croswell, Ken. *The Lives of Stars* (5–8). Illus. 2009, Boyds Mills $19.95 (978-159078582-9). 75pp. Using easy-to-understand language and striking images, Croswell describes the different kinds of stars and how they are formed, live, and eventually die. (Rev: BLO 11/1/09; LMC 11–12/09; SLJ 11/09) [523.8]

21118 Croswell, Ken. *See the Stars* (4–8). 2000, Boyds Mills $16.95 (978-1-56397-757-2). Twelve constellations are introduced in double-page spreads, with material on where and when to look for them. (Rev: BL 11/1/00; HBG 3/01; SLJ 10/00) [523]

21119 Forest, Christopher. *The Kids' Guide to the Constellations* (3–5). Illus. Series: Kids' Guides. 2011, Capstone LB $26.65 (978-142966007-5). 32pp. With "Fun

Facts" and "Gazing Guides," this is an accessible introduction focusing on 11 constellations and explaining the myths associated with them. (Rev: BL 2/15/12) [523.8]

21120 Gallan, Roy. *Stars* (2–4). Series: Kaleidoscope. 2000, Marshall Cavendish LB $25.64 (978-0-7614-1036-2). 48pp. This book introduces stars, how they are born and die, and their constellations. (Rev: BL 1/1–15/01; HBG 10/01) [523]

21121 Gibbons, Gail. *Galaxies, Galaxies!* (2–3). Illus. by author. 2006, Holiday House $16.95 (978-0-8234-2002-5). 32pp. In addition to describing five forms of galaxies, Gibbons discusses telescopes and the study of astronomy. (Rev: SLJ 12/06) [523.1]

21122 Kim, F. S. *Constellations* (3–5). Illus. Series: True Book: Space. 2010, Children's Press LB $26 (978-053116895-0); paper $6.95 (978-053122802-9). 48pp. Science, history, and mythology are all covered in this well-illustrated and clearly explained introduction to the constellations, who discovered them, and their importance today. (Rev: BL 11/1/09*; LMC 1–2/10) [523.8]

21123 MacKall, Dandi Daley. *Seeing Stars* (PS–K). Illus. by Claudine Gevry. 2006, Simon & Schuster $9.99 (978-1-4169-0361-1). 16pp. An introduction to the constellations for very young children, with sparkling gold outlining stars that shine above people of many backgrounds. (Rev: BL 5/1/06) [520]

21124 Miller, Ron. *Seven Wonders Beyond the Solar System* (5–8). Series: Seven Wonders. 2011, Twenty-First Century LB $33.26 (978-0-7613-5454-3). 80pp. Miller discusses how stars and galaxies are formed and looks at significant nebulas and superclusters as well as the search for an Earthlike planet; readers are challenged to choose an eighth wonder. e (Rev: BL 3/1/11; SLJ 2/1/11) [523.8]

21125 Mitton, Jacqueline. *Once Upon a Starry Night: A Book of Constellations* (K–4). Illus. by Christina Balit. 2004, National Geographic $16.95 (978-0-7922-6332-6). 26pp. Ten brief, richly illustrated tales about the constellations are drawn from the mythology of ancient Greece and Rome. (Rev: BL 1/1–15/04; SLJ 1/04) [523.8]

21126 Mitton, Jacqueline. *Zodiac* (2–4). Illus. by Christina Balit. 2005, Frances Lincoln $16.95 (978-1-84507-074-8). 44pp. This is an attractive introduction to the 12 constellations that make up the zodiac, also providing information on the fundamentals of astronomy and on the mythology surrounding these stars. (Rev: BL 11/15/05; SLJ 1/06) [133.5]

21127 Nicolson, Cynthia Pratt. *Discover the Stars* (1–3). Illus. by Bill Slavin. Series: Kids Can Read. 2006, Kids Can $14.95 (978-1-55337-898-3); paper $3.95 (978-1-55337-899-0). 32pp. Using a question-and-answer format, this easy reader introduces basic information about the stars, including constellations, galaxies, the typical life cycle of a star, and how we observe them. (Rev: BL 3/15/06; SLJ 8/06) [523.8]

21128 Pearce, Q. L. *The Stargazer's Guide to the Galaxy* (4–8). Illus. by Mary Ann Fraser. 1991, Tor paper $6.99

(978-0-8125-9423-2). In this introduction to star gazing in the Northern Hemisphere, material covered includes a look at the night sky in each of the four seasons. (Rev: SLJ 12/91) [523]

21129 Purslow, Frances. *Constellations* (2–4). Illus. Series: Science Matters. 2006, Weigl $24.45 (978-1-59036-410-9). 24pp. An introduction to the constellations for the young reader or researcher, with photographs and other graphics as well as an astronomy-related craft. (Rev: SLJ 5/07)

21130 Rau, Dana Meachen. *The Milky Way and Other Galaxies* (3–5). Illus. Series: Our Solar System. 2005, Compass Point $23.93 (978-0-7565-0853-1). 32pp. After a discussion of our own galaxy, Rau describes others including quasars, clusters, and superclusters; photographs and illustrations add to the appeal. (Rev: SLJ 8/05) [523.1]

21131 Rey, H. A. *Find the Constellations* (5–7). 1976, Houghton Mifflin LB $20.00 (978-0-395-24509-5); paper $9.95 (978-0-395-24418-0). Through clear text and illustrations, the reader is helped to recognize stars and constellations in the northern United States. Also use *The Stars: A New Way to See Them* (1973).

21132 Rey, H. A. *Find the Constellations. 2nd ed.* (4–6). Illus. by author. 2008, Houghton $20.00 (978-0-547-13140-5); paper $9.99 (978-0-547-13178-8). 72pp. This updated version includes an explanation of why Pluto is no longer a planet, new data for all the planets, charts, and a list of current books for further reading. (Rev: SLJ 2/09) [523.8]

21133 Sasaki, Chris. *Constellations: A Glow-in-the-Dark Guide to the Night Sky* (1–4). Illus. by Alan Flinn. 2006, Sterling $12.95 (978-1-4027-0385-0). 48pp. Introduces some of the best-known constellations, with the mythology behind them, and glow-in-the-dark outlines that will show when the lights are turned off. (Rev: SLJ 8/06) [523.8]

21134 Than, Ker. *Stars* (3–5). Illus. Series: True Book: Space. 2010, Children's Press LB $26 (978-053116899-8); paper $6.95 (978-053122806-7). 48pp. A beautifully illustrated introduction to the life of stars, what happens when they die, and how and why we study them. (Rev: BL 11/1/09*; LMC 1–2/10) [523.8]

21135 Tomecek, Steve. *Stars* (K–3). Illus. by Sachiko Yoshikawa. 2003, National Geographic $16.95 (978-0-7922-6955-7). 32pp. A boy introduces young readers to the stars in this book that includes a star activity. (Rev: BL 2/1/03; HBG 10/03; SLJ 5/03) [523.8]

21136 Whitehouse, Patricia. *The Stars* (2–4). Illus. Series: Space Explorer. 2004, Heinemann LB $24.21 (978-1-4034-5156-9). 32pp. A slim overview of stars, looking at the Milky Way and other galaxies, the ways in which stars are born and grow, and the changing night sky. [523.8]

Sun and the Seasons

21137 Anderson, Maxine. *Explore Spring! 25 Great Ways to Learn About Spring* (1–4). Illus. by Alexis Frederick-Frost. 2007, Nomad paper $12.95 (978-0-9785037-4-1). 92pp. This activity book with good solid science, engaging experiments, and humorous illustrations looks at such topics as the seasons, spring's role in the growth of plants and trees, and spring weather. (Rev: LMC 11/07; SLJ 10/07)

21138 Dolan, Graham. *The Greenwich Guide to the Seasons* (3–6). Illus. Series: Greenwich Guide To. 2001, Heinemann LB $22.79 (978-1-58810-044-3). 32pp. Color photographs and clear text introduce the seasons, with a glossary and other aids. (Rev: BL 10/15/01) [525]

21139 Esbaum, Jill. *Everything Spring* (PS–K). Series: Picture the Seasons. 2010, National Geographic paper $5.95 (978-1-4263-0607-5). 16pp. A variety of young animals experience the joys of spring in this simple book full of photographs. (Rev: LMC 8–9/10; SLJ 5/1/10) [508.2]

21140 Felix, Rebecca. *What Do Animals Do in Fall?* (PS–1). Illus. Series: Let's Look at Fall. 2013, Cherry Lake LB $22.79 (978-161080907-8). 24pp. Beginning readers learn about hibernation, migration, food storage, and other strategies for preparing for winter. Also use *We Harvest Pumpkins in Fall, We Harvest Apples in Fall*, and *How's the Weather in Fall?* (all 2013). (Rev: BL 6/13) [591.5]

21141 Glaser, Linda. *It's Fall!* (2–4). Illus. by Susan Swan. 2001, Millbrook $21.90 (978-0-7613-1758-6). 32pp. A young boy observes the changes that occur in nature in the fall, with suggested nature activities for the season. (Rev: BL 9/15/01; HBG 3/02; SLJ 10/01)

21142 Goldstone, Bruce. *Awesome Autumn: All Kinds of Fall Facts and Fun* (1–3). Illus. by author. 2012, Henry Holt $16.99 (978-0-8050-9210-3). 48pp. A colorful, large-format introduction to all aspects of fall and its impact on flora, fauna, and people. ∩ ℮ Lexile AD690L (Rev: BL 9/1/12; SLJ 8/12) [508.2]

21143 Hicks, Terry Allan. *Why Do Leaves Change Color?* (2–4). Series: Tell Me Why, Tell Me How. 2010, Marshall Cavendish LB $20.95 (978-0-7614-4827-3). 32pp. With chapters such as "A Sign of the Times" and "The Colors of Life," this volume introduces essential concepts in easy-to-read text and lots of helpful illustrations. (Rev: BL 3/1/11; SLJ 2/1/11) [575.5]

21144 Jackson, Ellen. *The Summer Solstice* (2–4). Illus. 2001, Millbrook LB $21.90 (978-0-7613-1623-7). 32pp. An attractive resource that explains the summer solstice, why it is the longest day of the year, and its cultural significance. (Rev: BL 4/1/01; HBG 10/01; SLJ 5/01) [394.263]

21145 James, Lincoln. *The Sun: Star of the Solar System* (K–2). Illus. Series: Our Solar System. 2010, Gareth Stevens LB $22.60 (978-143393848-1). 24pp. Bright images and clear information about the sun are presented in a small, square format. Lexile 420 (Rev: BL 1/1–15/11; SLJ 11/1/10) [523.7]

21146 Kerrod, Robin. *The Sun* (4–6). Series: Planet Library. 2000, Lerner LB $21.27 (978-0-8225-3901-8). 32pp. This work explains how the sun was formed, its role in the solar system, in the galaxy, and beyond, and what the future holds. (Rev: BL 10/15/00; HBG 3/01; SLJ 1/01) [523.7]

21147 Latta, Sara. *What Happens in Spring?* (PS–2). Illus. Series: I Like the Seasons! 2006, Enslow LB $21.26 (978-0-7660-2419-9). 24pp. Answers a parade of questions about spring ("What are the first signs . . ."), and provides an experiment and a glossary of seasonally related terms. Also use *What Happens in Winter?* (2006). (Rev: SLJ 12/06) [508.2]

21148 Lin, Grace, and Ranida T. McKneally. *Our Seasons* (1–3). Illus. by Grace Lin. 2006, Charlesbridge $15.95 (978-1-57091-360-0). 32pp. Questions and answers about the seasons, with paintings and haiku to accompany the factual information. (Rev: BL 7/06; SLJ 8/06) [508.2]

21149 Martin, Bill, Jr., and Michael Sampson. *I Love Our Earth* (PS–2). Illus. by Dan Lipow. 2006, Charlesbridge $14.95 (978-1-58089-106-6). 32pp. Impressive color photographs and minimal text celebrate the wonders of nature and the changing seasons. (Rev: BL 2/1/06; SLJ 2/06) [525]

21150 Meyer, Mary L. *Spring* (2–3). Series: Seasons. 2002, Smart Apple LB $21.35 (978-1-58340-143-9). 24pp. The weather, animals, plants, and activities of spring are presented in concise text with attractive full-color photographs. Also use *Fall* (2002). (Rev: HBG 10/03; SLJ 2/03)

21151 Miller, Ron. *The Sun* (5–8). Series: Worlds Beyond. 2002, Millbrook LB $25.90 (978-0-7613-2355-6). Miller explores the nature and structure of the sun and the importance of solar energy. (Rev: BL 4/1/02; HBG 10/02; SLJ 5/02) [523.7]

21152 Pfeffer, Wendy. *The Longest Day: Celebrating the Summer Solstice* (1–3). Illus. by Linda Bleck. 2010, Dutton $17.99 (978-0-525-42237-2). 40pp. For young readers, this is an introduction to the summer solstice, how it has been celebrated through the centuries, and the differences in time zones; with activities. (Rev: BL 4/15/10; SLJ 6/1/10) [394.263]

21153 Pfeffer, Wendy. *A New Beginning: Celebrating the Spring Equinox* (1–3). Illus. by Linda Bleck. 2008, Dutton $17.99 (978-0-525-47874-4). 40pp. Learn about the arrival of spring and how it is celebrated in different cultures. (Rev: BL 12/1/07; SLJ 3/08) [394.26]

21154 Pfeffer, Wendy. *The Shortest Day: Celebrating the Winter Solstice* (K–4). Illus. by Jesse Reisch. 2003, Dutton $16.99 (978-0-525-46968-1). History and astronomy are combined in this easy-to-understand overview of the winter landmark. (Rev: HBG 4/04; SLJ 9/03) [394.261]

21155 Pfeffer, Wendy. *We Gather Together: Celebrating the Harvest Season* (1–3). Illus. by Linda Bleck. 2006, Dutton $17.99 (978-0-525-47669-6). 40pp. This companion to *The Shortest Day: Celebrating the Winter Solstice* provides information on the autumnal equinox, ways in which humans and animals prepare for the winter during this season; facts on the harvest and its many celebrations around the world, plus experiments and activities. (Rev: BL 12/1/06; SLJ 11/06) [508.2]

21156 Pipe, Jim. *The Sun* (3–5). Illus. Series: Earthwise. 2004, Stargazer LB $27.10 (978-1-932799-46-0). 32pp. An excellent introduction to the sun and its energy, this attractively illustrated volume supplements its facts and figures with suggested activities. (Rev: BL 10/15/04) [523.7]

21157 Rau, Dana Meachen. *Seasons* (PS–2). Series: Bookworms. Natures Cycles. 2009, Marshall Cavendish $15.95 (978-0-7614-4098-7). 24pp. The concept of how the Earth's tilt results in different seasons in different parts of the world is captured in this simple book suitable for beginning readers. (Rev: LMC 1–2/10; SLJ 4/1/10) [508.2]

21158 Rockwell, Anne. *Four Seasons Make a Year* (K–2). Illus. by Megan Halsey. 2004, Walker $15.95 (978-0-8027-8883-2). 32pp. A young girl on a farm guides readers through the seasons, following the progress of a sunflower she planted in spring. (Rev: BL 2/15/04; SLJ 4/04) [508]

21159 Schuette, Sarah L. *Let's Look at Spring* (K–2). Series: Investigate the Seasons. 2006, Capstone LB $19.93 (978-0-7368-6707-8). 24pp. The attractive and simple design will draw young readers into this introduction. Also use *Let's Look at Fall, Let's Look at Summer,* and *Let's Look at Winter* (all 2006). (Rev: SLJ 5/07)

21160 Wells, Robert E. *Why Do Elephants Need the Sun?* (2–4). Illus. by author. 2010, Whitman $16.99 (978-0-8075-9081-2). 32pp. Playful illustrations enhance this exploration of the sun's importance to everything on Earth, covering photosynthesis, gravity, and nuclear fusion as well as the sun's impact on weather and water. (Rev: BL 9/15/10*; LMC 11–12/10; SLJ 10/1/10) [599.67]

21161 Whitehouse, Patricia. *The Sun* (2–4). Illus. Series: Space Explorer. 2004, Heinemann LB $24.21 (978-1-4034-5157-6). 32pp. A slim overview of the sun and its composition, size, and temperature, with material on solar flares, eclipses, and solar wind. [523.7]

Biological Sciences

General

21162 Arnold, Caroline. *Too Hot? Too Cold? Keeping Body Temperature Just Right* (1–4). Illus. by Annie Patterson. 2013, Charlesbridge $17.95 (978-1-58089-276-6); paper $7.95 (978-1-58089-277-3). 32pp. This is an attractive, browsable guide to how humans and animals deal with various temperature extremes. (Rev: BL 4/1/13; LMC 11–12/13; SLJ 3/13) [612]

21163 Arnold, Katya. *Let's Find It! My First Nature Guide* (PS–1). Illus. 2002, Holiday House $16.95 (978-0-8234-1539-7). 32pp. Young readers search for plants and animals in painted scenes of habitats in this colorful introduction to nature. (Rev: BL 8/02; HBG 3/03; SLJ 10/02) [570]

21164 Batten, Mary. *Aliens from Earth: When Animals and Plants Invade Other Ecosystems* (3–5). Illus. by Beverly J. Doyle. 2003, Peachtree $15.95 (978-1-56145-236-1). 32pp. A narrative overview of the results of animal and plant migrations to new home ecosystems, with full-page illustrations. (Rev: BL 3/1/03; HBG 10/03; SLJ 5/03) [577]

21165 Bottone, Frank G, Jr. *The Science of Life: Projects and Principles for Beginning Biologists* (5–8). 2001, Chicago Review paper $14.95 (978-1-55652-382-3). Twenty-five projects introduce readers to the basics of biology and the rigors of scientific research. (Rev: SLJ 11/01) [570.78]

21166 Cheshire, Gerard. *Living World* (1–4). Illus. by Janet Baker, et al. Series: World of Wonder. 2008, Children's Pr. LB $29.00 (978-0-531-24026-7); paper $9.95 (978-0-531-23822-6). 32pp. Answering such questions as "What's the Deadliest Creature on Earth," this book looks at various forms of life on our planet and includes acetate overlays. (Rev: SLJ 3/09)

21167 Collard, Sneed B. *Science Warriors: The Battle Against Invasive Species* (5–8). Series: Scientists in the Field. 2008, Houghton Mifflin $17 (978-0-618-75636-

0). 48pp. Collard balances often grotesque images with weighty scientific fact in this examination of invasive species — plant and animal — that cost the United States $137 billion annually. Lexile 1110L (Rev: BL 12/1/08; HB 1–2/09; SLJ 1/1/09) [578.6]

21168 *DK Nature Encyclopedia* (5–8). 1998, DK paper $29.99 (978-0-7894-3411-1). A browsable reference book that covers topics including classification of living things, ecology, the origins and evolution of life, specific animal and plant groups, and the inner workings of plants and animals, all in a series of beautifully illustrated double-page spreads. (Rev: BL 12/1/98; SLJ 2/99) [574]

21169 Drake, Jane, and Ann Love. *Alien Invaders: Species That Threaten Our World* (4–6). Illus. by Mark Thurman. 2008, Tundra $19.95 (978-0-88776-798-2). 56pp. This title presents a variety of natural disasters that occur when invaders in the form of plants, animals, bacteria, and viruses are introduced into a new habitat. (Rev: BL 3/15/08; SLJ 6/08) [578.6]

21170 Early, Bobbi. *Tiny Life in a Puddle* (2–3). Series: Rookie Read-About Science. 2005, Children's Pr. LB $20.50 (978-0-516-25272-8); paper $4.95 (978-0-516-25475-3). 32pp. For beginning readers, this is an introduction to the kinds of bacteria — good and bad — that can be found in a small puddle of water. (Rev: SLJ 4/06) [579.176]

21171 Gallant, Roy A. *The Wonders of Biodiversity* (5–8). Series: The Story of Science. 2002, Benchmark $29.93 (978-0-7614-1427-8). Gallant discusses the importance of biodiversity, the plight of species that are affected by loss of habitat and other environmental factors, and species interdependence. (Rev: HBG 3/03; SLJ 2/03) [578]

21172 Goodman, Susan E. *Nature Did It First!* (PS–2). Illus. 2003, Millbrook LB $21.90 (978-0-7613-2413-3). 24pp. This attractive picture book teaches younger children about everyday products and processes that have their roots in nature. (Rev: BL 5/1/03; HBG 10/03) [508]

21173 Green, Dan. *Extreme Biology* (4–7). Illus. by Simon Basher. Series: Basher Science. 2013, Kingfisher $12.99 (978-075347051-0); paper $7.99 (978-07534705-0-3). 64pp. In chapters titled "Hard-core Herd," "Gene Genies," "Biohacker Crew," and "Medical Mavericks," this engaging book with cartoon characters covers microorganisms that can deal with harsh environments, genetics, cutting-edge molecules, and new medical technologies. (Rev: BLO 4/1/13; LMC 8–9/13)

21174 Green, Jen. *In a Backyard* (2–5). Illus. Series: Small World. 2002, Crabtree LB $25.27 (978-0-7787-0141-5); paper $8.95 (978-0-7787-0155-2). 32pp. This book for younger readers takes a close look at the creatures that might be found in a backyard, and how plant and animal life coexist there. (Rev: BL 10/15/02) [591.75]

21175 Jackson, Cari. *Alien Invasion: Invasive Species Become Major Menaces* (4–6). Illus. Series: Current Science. 2009, Gareth Stevens LB $31 (978-1-4339-2057-8). 48pp. Invasive species from around the world — plants and animals — are profiled in this engaging title, which focuses on humankind's role in spreading or maintaining the problem. (Rev: SLJ 4/10) [577]

21176 Johnson, Rebecca. *Mighty Animal Cells* (5–7). Illus. by Jack Desrocher. Series: Microquests. 2007, Lerner LB $29.27 (978-0-8225-7137-7). 48pp. Animal cell structure and cell division, followed by human cells, are discussed in chapters such as "Meet the Organelles," "What Cells Do," and "Cells with Special Talents" in this reader-friendly but information-packed book with cartoon illustrations to spice up the text. (Rev: BL 10/15/07; HB 1/08*; SLJ 11/07) [571.6]

21177 Jones, Jennifer B. *Who Lives in the Snow?* (PS–3). Illus. by Consie Powell. 2001, Court Wayne $15.95 (978-1-57098-287-3). 32pp. Cutaway illustrations give young readers a glimpse below the surface of a snowy meadow to see what happens to plants, insects, and animals during winter. (Rev: BL 11/15/01) [591.4]

21178 Kalman, Bobbie. *Forest Food Chains* (2–4). Illus. Series: Food Chains. 2004, Crabtree LB $25.27 (978-0-7787-1943-4); paper $6.95 (978-0-7787-1989-2). 32pp. All about the dynamics of food chains and food webs in the forest. (Rev: BL 3/15/05) [577.3]

21179 Kelsey, Elin. *Strange New Species: Astonishing Discoveries of Life on Earth* (5–8). 2005, Maple Tree $24.95 (978-1-897066-31-7). A large-format, well-illustrated introduction to plant and animal classification and to newly discovered species. (Rev: BL 10/15/05; SLJ 2/06) [578]

21180 Knight, Tim. *Dramatic Displays* (3–5). Series: Amazing Nature. 2003, Heinemann LB $24.22 (978-1-4034-0721-4). 32pp. An attractive look at nature's use of camouflage, mimicry, and brilliant color displays, more suitable for browsers than for report writers. Also use *Ferocious Fighters* and *Fantastic Feeders* (2003). (Rev: HBG 10/03; SLJ 7/03) [591.4]

21181 Knight, Tim. *Super Survivors* (3–5). Series: Amazing Nature. 2003, Heinemann LB $24.22 (978-1-4034-

0723-8). 32pp. How plants and animals adapt to their surroundings in order to survive and thrive is the subject of this photo-illustrated volume. Also in this series is *Incredible Life Cycles* (2003), which looks at the more unusual features of the life cycles of plants and animals. (Rev: HBG 4/04; SLJ 3/04) [578.4]

21182 Latham, Donna. *Backyard Biology: Investigate Habitats Outside Your Door with 25 Projects* (4–7). Illus. by Beth Hetland. Series: Build It Yourself. 2013, Nomad $15.95 (978-161930151-1). 128pp. Experiments and activities extend basic information on microbiology and cells, botany, life cycles, conservation, and adaptations. (Rev: BL 2/15/13; LMC 10/13; SLJ 5/13) [570]

21183 Lindstrom, Karin. *Tiny Life on Plants* (2–3). Series: Rookie Read-About Science. 2005, Children's Pr. LB $20.50 (978-0-516-25297-1); paper $4.95 (978-0-516-25478-4). For beginning readers, this is an introduction to the kinds of bacteria — good and bad — that thrive on the surface of plants. (Rev: SLJ 4/06) [577.852]

21184 MacAulay, Kelley, and Bobbie Kalman. *Backyard Habitats* (K–2). Illus. Series: Introducing Habitats. 2006, Crabtree LB $25.27 (978-0-7787-2957-0); paper $6.95 (978-0-7787-2985-3). 32pp. For beginning readers, this inviting volume introduces the diversity of animal and plant life that can be found in many backyards. (Rev: BL 10/15/06) [577.5]

21185 McNamara, Ken. *It's True: We Came from Slime* (4–6). Illus. by Andrew Plant. Series: It's True. 2006, Annick $19.95 (978-1-55037-953-2); paper $5.95 (978-1-55037-952-5). 96pp. Eye-catching artwork highlights this fascinating look at the origins of life on Earth — from primordial ooze through evolution across more than 3.5 billion years of history. (Rev: BL 4/1/06) [576.8]

21186 Manning, Mick, and Brita Granström. *Snap!* (PS–2). Illus. by authors. 2006, Frances Lincoln $14.95 (978-1-84507-408-1). A lighthearted look at the food chain in which one creature after another is gobbled up by a larger animal. (Rev: SLJ 11/06) [577.16]

21187 Mattern, Joanne. *What Grassland Animals Eat* (1–2). Illus. Series: Nature's Food Chains. 2007, Weekly Reader LB $19.93 (978-0-8368-6872-2); paper $5.95 (978-0-8368-6879-1). Beginning readers learning about food chains will find this book on the food chain on a grassland helpful. Also use *What River Animals Eat, What Sea Animals Eat,* and *What Polar Animals Eat* (all 2007). (Rev: SLJ 8/07)

21188 Morrison, Gordon. *Nature in the Neighborhood* (2–5). Illus. 2004, Houghton $16.00 (978-0-618-35215-9). 32pp. This attractively illustrated title introduces readers to the abundance of plant and animal life that can be found in areas ranging from their own backyards to train tracks and vacant lots. (Rev: BL 12/1/04; SLJ 10/04) [508]

21189 Murray, Julie. *Backyard* (2–5). Illus. Series: That's Gross! A Look at Science. 2009, ABDO $17.95 (978-1-60453-553-2). 32pp. A look at all the icky stuff in the backyard — centipedes, worms, poop of all kinds, and so forth. (Rev: BL 5/15/09) [591.75]

21190 Parker, Steve. *Survival and Change* (4–7). Series: Life Processes. 2001, Heinemann LB $21.36 (978-1-57572-340-2). 32pp. Parker considers how organisms evolve and looks at how species behave under threat and the origin of new species in this concise book with diagrams, charts, and color photographs. (Rev: HBG 10/01; SLJ 7/01) [578.4]

21191 Peters, Lisa Westberg. *Our Family Tree: An Evolution Story* (K–3). Illus. by Lauren Stringer. 2003, Harcourt $17.00 (978-0-15-201772-9). This oversize picture book, with conversational text and many bright illustrations, is fairly successful in its ambitious mission; adults may want to explain the timeline and final notes. (Rev: BL 3/15/03; HBG 10/03; SLJ 5/03) [576.8]

21192 Quinlan, Susan E. *The Case of the Monkeys That Fell from the Trees: And Other Mysteries in Tropical Nature* (5–8). 2003, Boyds Mills $15.95 (978-1-56397-902-6). Quinlan introduces plant and animal mysteries in South and Central American tropical forests and shows how scientists approached solving them. (Rev: BL 3/1/03; HBG 10/03; SLJ 3/03; VOYA 10/03) [508.313]

21193 Rau, Dana Meachen. *Food Chains* (PS–2). Illus. Series: Bookworms. Natures Cycles. 2009, Marshall Cavendish $15.95 (978-0-7614-4095-6). 24pp. The concept of how energy is transferred from food to animals to crops and back again is captured in this simple book suitable for beginning readers. (Rev: LMC 1–2/10; SLJ 4/1/10) [577]

21194 Rockwell, Anne. *Growing Like Me* (PS–K). Illus. by Holly Keller. 2001, Harcourt $15.00 (978-0-15-202202-0). 24pp. This simple book about change and development in the plant and animal world shows an organism on one page and what it becomes on the next (e.g., a caterpillar and then a butterfly). (Rev: BL 3/1/01; HB 9/01; HBG 3/02) [571.8]

21195 Ross, Michael Elsohn. *Life Cycles* (2–4). Illus. by Gustav Moore. 2001, Millbrook LB $22.40 (978-0-7613-1817-0). 32pp. Young readers are introduced to the concept of life cycles through the stories of a sunflower, a mushroom, and a grasshopper. (Rev: BL 8/01; HBG 3/02; SLJ 1/02) [571.8]

21196 Salas, Laura Purdie. *Are You Living? A Song About Living and Nonliving Things* (PS–2). Illus. by Viviana Garofoli. Series: Science Songs. 2008, Picture Window LB $18.99 (978-1-4048-5302-7). 24pp. This variation on the "Are You Sleeping?" song explores the characteristics of living and nonliving things, looking at characteristics such as locomotion and nutrition. (Rev: BL 4/1/09; SLJ 5/09) [570]

21197 Schwartz, David M., and Yael Schy. *What in the Wild? Mysteries of Nature Concealed . . . and Revealed* (2–4). Photos by Dwight Kuhn. Series: In the Wild. 2010, Tricycle $16.99 (978-1-58246-310-0). 44pp. Readers are challenged to guess the identity of natural objects presented in color photographs accompanied by brief verses; the answers are hidden behind flaps. (Rev: BL 9/15/10; SLJ 9/1/10) [508]

21198 Shea, John. *Viruses Up Close* (5–8). Illus. Series: Under the Microscope. 2013, Gareth Stevens LB $26.60 (978-143398354-2). 32pp. With close-up photographs and an attractive layout,, this is a useful overview of the world of viruses. (Rev: BL 12/1/13; LMC 5–6/14*)

21199 Singer, Marilyn. *What Stinks?* (4–6). 2006, Darby Creek $17.95 (978-1-58196-035-8). 64pp. The use of scent in the animal and plant kingdoms — to mark territory, to attract mates, and so forth — is presented in an entertaining format full of wordplay and illustrations. (Rev: BL 5/1/06) [591.5]

21200 Strauss, Rochelle. *Tree of Life: The Incredible Biodiversity of Life on Earth* (3–6). Illus. by Margot Thompson. 2004, Kids Can $16.95 (978-1-55337-669-9). 40pp. This large-format book presents a visual representation — using the branches of a tree — of the diversity of species, from bacteria on up. (Rev: BL 12/1/04; SLJ 10/04) [578]

21201 Thomas, Keltie. *Nature Shockers* (4–6). Illus. by Greg Hall. Series: Planet Earth News. 2005, Maple Tree $16.95 (978-1-897066-29-4); paper $9.95 (978-1-897066-30-0). 64pp. Oddities of nature — including everything from a tree that's wrapped itself around a bicycle to the discovery of a strange-looking salamander — are reported in tabloid style. (Rev: BL 10/15/05; SLJ 1/06) [508]

21202 Triefeldt, Laurie. *Plants and Animals* (4–8). Illus. Series: World of Wonder. 2007, Quill Driver $19.95 (978-1-884956-72-0). By the author of a nationally syndicated newspaper column called World of Wonder, this book, a companion to *People and Places*, covers a huge amount of material and will be helpful to report writers. (Rev: BL 4/1/08) [570]

21203 Trumbauer, Lisa. *Tiny Life in Your Home* (2–3). 2005, Children's Pr. LB $20.50 (978-0-516-25274-2); paper $4.95 (978-0-516-25477-7). 32pp. This fascinating title gives a close-up look at the diversity of microscopic life forms — mostly bacteria — that can be found in the average home. (Rev: SLJ 4/06) [579.1755]

21204 Turner, Pamela S. *Life on Earth — and Beyond* (5–8). 2008, Charlesbridge $19.95 (978-1-58089-133-2); paper $11.95 (978-1-58089-134-9). Readers follow NASA astrobiologist Chris McKay as he searches for microbes in extreme environments on Earth — in hopes of determining if life can survive in extreme environments in space. (Rev: BL 2/1/08; SLJ 3/08) [571.0919]

21205 VanCleave, Janice. *Step-By-Step Science Experiments in Biology* (5–8). Series: Janice VanCleave's First-Place Science Fair Projects. 2012, Rosen Central LB $33.25 (978-1-4488-6982-4). 80pp. An updated volume with step-by-step instructions for 22 experiments mostly using easily found materials. (Rev: SLJ 10/12) [570]

21206 Wallace, Holly. *Classification* (4–7). Series: Life Processes. 2006, Heinemann LB $20.50 (978-1-4034-8845-9). A clear and colorful introduction to the classification of plants and animals. (Rev: BL 10/15/06) [570.1]

21207 Winston, Robert. *Life As We Know It* (3–7). Illus. 2012, DK $16.99 (978-075669169-1). 96pp. Covering everything from cells to the six kingdoms, evolution, photosynthesis, habitats, migration, and ecosystems, this is a visually appealing book organized into five sections such as "Living Together" and "Secrets of Survival." (Rev: BL 6/12; SLJ 8/1/12) [001]

Animal Life

General

21208 Aaseng, Nathan. *Nature's Poisonous Creatures* (5–9). Series: Scientific American Sourcebooks. 1997, Twenty-First Century LB $28.90 (978-0-8050-4690-8). After a general introduction to animal poisons, why they are produced, and their composition, this book devotes separate chapters to such venom-bearing vertebrates and invertebrates as sea wasps, blue-ringed octopi, African killer bees, and marine toads. (Rev: BL 2/1/98; SLJ 8/98) [591.6]

21209 Ablow, Gail. *A Horse in the House and Other Strange but True Animal Stories* (2–4). Illus. by Kathy Osborn. 2007, Candlewick $17.99 (978-0-7636-2838-3). 40pp. Truth really *is* stranger than fiction as each of these 16 tales proves; source notes document authenticity. (Rev: BL 9/15/07; LMC 1/08) [590]

21210 Armentrout, David, and Patricia Armentrout. *Animals* (PS–2). Series: 50 Words About. 2002, Rourke LB $19.95 (978-1-58952-341-8). 32pp. Simple definitions are given for 50 words about animals (camouflage, extinct, and so forth), along with a sentence that includes the word. (Rev: SLJ 3/03) [590]

21211 Arnold, Caroline. *Australian Animals* (1–3). 2000, HarperCollins LB $15.89 (978-0-688-16767-7). 48pp. Seventeen Australian animals are introduced in four sections that represent individual biomes. (Rev: HBG 3/01; SLJ 10/00) [591]

21212 Aston, Dianna. *An Egg Is Quiet* (PS–2). Illus. by Sylvia Long. 2006, Chronicle $16.95 (978-0-8118-4428-4). 32pp. This exploration of eggs — from fish eggs to bird eggs — offers a blend of factual and poetic text plus detailed illustrations. (Rev: BL 4/15/06; SLJ 6/06) [591.4]

21213 Aston, Dianna. *Mama's Wild Child / Papa's Wild Child* (PS–2). Illus. by Nora Hilb. 2006, Charlesbridge $14.95 (978-1-57091-590-1). In this appealing "flip-me-over" book, a mother and father separately tell their child how various parents in the animal kingdom take care of their offspring. (Rev: SLJ 3/06) [591.56]

21214 Barrow, Lloyd H. *Science Fair Projects Investigating Earthworms* (5–8). Series: Science Fair Success. 2000, Enslow LB $26.60 (978-0-7660-1291-2). 104pp. This book contains a fascinating number of experiments involving earthworms, with very explicit directions and explanations of the scientific principles behind each project. (Rev: BL 4/15/00; HBG 10/00) [595.1]

21215 Berger, Gilda, and Melvin Berger. *Why Do Zebras Have Stripes?* (2–4). Illus. 2013, Scholastic paper $4.99 (978-05455632-3-9). 48pp. Using photographs and facts to engage the reader, Berger poses and then answers 20 questions about mammals, such as "why do cats purr?" and "do bears hibernate?" **e** (Rev: BL 10/1/13) [591.03]

21216 Berger, Melvin, and Gilda Berger. *Do Tarantulas Have Teeth? Questions and Answers About Poisonous Creatures* (3–5). Illus. by Jim Effler. Series: Scholastic Question and Answer. 2000, Scholastic $14.95 (978-0-439-09578-5); paper $5.95 (978-0-439-14877-1). Using a question-and-answer format and bright, realistic illustrations, this title presents information on the methods poisonous animals use to inject their venom, how they hunt and feed, and their physical characteristics. (Rev: HBG 3/01; SLJ 5/01) [591]

21217 Berger, Melvin, and Gilda Berger. *101 Animal Records* (2–5). Illus. 2013, Scholastic paper $8.99 (978-05454279-6-8). 112pp. A browsable, well-illustrated collection of interesting facts such as the "Loudest Insect," the "Most Useful Insect," "Most Successful Hunter," and "Champion Migrator." (Rev: BLO 3/15/13; LMC 10/13) [591.03]

21218 Bial, Raymond. *A Handful of Dirt* (3–5). Photos by author. 2000, Walker $16.95 (978-0-8027-8698-2). 32pp. This set of photographs with accompanying text examines life found underground from invertebrates to the mammals and reptiles that burrow into the earth. (Rev: BCCB 5/00; HBG 9/00; SLJ 4/00) [591]

21219 Bishop, Nic. *Backyard Detective: Critters Up Close* (1–3). Illus. 2002, Scholastic $16.95 (978-0-439-17478-7). 48pp. Photographic collages show "life-sized" animals and insects found in backyards across the United States, along with two pages of informational text about each and a section of nature projects. (Rev: BL 10/15/02; HBG 3/03; SLJ 10/02) [591.75]

21220 Bloom, Steve. *Untamed: Animals Around the World* (4–7). Illus. by Emmanuelle Zicot. 2005, Abrams $18.95 (978-0-8109-5956-9). Enthralling photographs of wild animals are accompanied by brief facts and an environmentalist message. (Rev: BL 12/1/05) [636]

21221 Bradley, Timothy J. *Strange but True: Tiny Creatures* (3–5). Illus. Series: Time for Kids Nonfiction Readers. 2012, Teacher Created Materials paper $9.99 (978-14333486-2-4). 48pp. An appealing survey of tiny creatures (ticks, dust mites, stinging ants, nematode worms, and so forth) that can have large impacts on humans. Lexile 730L (Rev: BL 9/15/12; LMC 5–6/13) [579]

21222 Browning, Bel. *Animal Welfare* (5–8). Illus. Series: Face the Facts. 2003, Raintree LB $28.56 (978-0-7398-6430-2). 56pp. Hot issues in animal protection such as whaling, intensive farming, and zoos are discussed, and practical responses from young people are suggested. (Rev: BL 11/15/03; HBG 10/03) [364.1]

21223 Callery, Sean. *Desert* (3–5). Illus. Series: Life Cycles. 2012, Kingfisher $12.99 (978-075346811-1). 32pp. A large-format, richly illustrated exploration of the

Kalahari Desert, the Australian Outback, and the Mojave Desert, with a focus on three or four species each. Also use *River, Mountain,* and *Forest* (2012). (Rev: BL 10/15/12) [591.754]

21224 Carle, Eric, ed. *What's Your Favorite Animal?* (PS–3). Illus. 2014, Henry Holt $17.99 (978-080509641-5). 40pp. Fourteen picture-book illustrators depict and describe their favorite animals in this diverse and eye-catching collection. (Rev: BL 12/1/13; LMC 10/14*; SLJ 2/14*) [746]

21225 Cassie, Brian. *Say It Again* (1–3). Illus. by David Mooney. 2000, Charlesbridge LB $16.95 (978-0-88106-341-7); paper $6.95 (978-0-88106-342-4). This unusual animal book features, in picture and text, 12 creatures whose names involve a repetitive sound, such as a killy-killy and a caracara. (Rev: HBG 9/00; SLJ 3/00) [591]

21226 Crenson, Victoria. *Horseshoe Crabs and Shorebirds: The Story of a Food Web* (2–4). Illus. by Annie Cannon. 2003, Marshall Cavendish $16.95 (978-0-7614-5115-0). 32pp. Wildlife on the Delaware Bay is the focus of this informative picture-book exploration full of attractive and atmospheric paintings. (Rev: BL 11/1/03; HBG 4/04; SLJ 12/03)

21227 Curtis, Jennifer Keats. *Animal Helpers: Wildlife Rehabilitators* (PS–2). Illus. 2012, Sylvan Dell $17.95 (978-1-60718-671-7); paper $9.95 (978-1-60718-672-4). 32pp. This heavily illustrated book looks at centers that nurse injured animals back to health and freedom. **e** (Rev: BL 10/1/12; SLJ 12/12) [639.9]

21228 de la Bedoyere, Camilla. *Wild Animals* (3–6). Illus. Series: Ripley's Believe It or Not! Twists. 2010, Mason Crest LB $19.95 (978-142221835-8). 48pp. Characteristics of wild animals are introduced through a lively blend of conversational text, snappy sidebars, and innovative design elements, with a focus on the unusual. Lexile IG1010L (Rev: BL 4/15/11) [590]

21229 Donovan, Sandra. *Animals of Rivers, Lakes, and Ponds* (2–4). Series: Animals of the Biomes. 2003, Raintree LB $25.70 (978-0-7398-5690-1). 48pp. The great blue heron, giant water bugs, raccoons, and snapping turtles are featured in this introduction. Also use *Desert Animals,* which looks at roadrunners, scorpions, camels, and Gila monsters. (Rev: HBG 3/03; SLJ 2/03)

21230 Doris, Ellen. *Meet the Arthropods* (4–7). 1996, Thames & Hudson $16.95 (978-0-500-19010-4). Such arthropods as the horseshoe crab, potato beetle, and praying mantis are introduced with photographs and activities. (Rev: BL 10/15/96) [595.2]

21231 Ehrlich, Fred. *Does a Seal Smile?* (PS–2). Illus. by Emily Bolam. Series: Early Experiences. 2006, Blue Apple $13.50 (978-1-59354-168-2); paper $5.95 (978-1-59354-169-9). 32pp. An entertaining look at the different ways in which humans and animals communicate. (Rev: BL 8/06) [153.6]

21232 Fielding, Beth. *Animal Tails* (2–4). Illus. 2011, Charlesbridge $14.95 (978-0-9797455-8-4). 36pp. Fielding explores the wide variety of kinds of animal tails and their different functions — balancing, warn-

ing, swimming, wagging, and so forth. Lexile NC1060L (Rev: BLO 8/11; SLJ 10/1/11) [573.9]

21233 Fredericks, Anthony D. *Fearsome Fangs* (4–6). Illus. Series: Watts Library. 2002, Watts LB $25.50 (978-0-531-11966-2). 63pp. Animals with alarming teeth — including some prehistoric beasts — are profiled here, with information on physical features, behavior, distribution, habitat, prey, and relationship with humans. (Rev: SLJ 1/03) [591.47]

21234 Ganeri, Anita. *Animal Life Cycles* (K–3). Illus. Series: Nature's Patterns. 2005, Heinemann LB $16.95 (978-1-4034-5894-0). 32pp. In simple languge, this volume introduces the life cycles of reptiles, insects, mammals, and amphibians. (Rev: SLJ 6/05)

21235 Glassman, Jackie. *Amazing Arctic Animals* (K–3). Illus. by Lisa Bonforte. Series: All Aboard Science Reader. 2002, Grosset paper $3.99 (978-0-448-42844-4). 48pp. Animals including the polar bear, arctic tern, caribou, snowy owl, and arctic fox are introduced with colored illustrations. (Rev: SLJ 6/03) [591.7]

21236 Goldish, Meish. *Wildlife Rehabilitators to the Rescue* (3–5). Illus. Series: The Work of Heroes: First Responders in Action. 2013, Bearport LB $25.27 (978-1-61772-748-1). 32pp. This is an interesting account of the work of people — often volunteers — who help to rehabilitate injured wildlife. Also use *Animal Control Officers to the Rescue* (2013). (Rev: BL 7/13; SLJ 6/13) [639.9]

21237 Gordon, Sharon. *Guess Who Grabs* (K–2). Series: Bookworms: Guess Who. 2003, Benchmark LB $21.36 (978-0-7614-1557-2). 31pp. Young readers are challenged to identify an animal that "grabs" (an octopus), with clues about characteristics, habitat, and so forth. Also use *Guess Who Changes* and *Guess Who Hides* (both 2003). (Rev: HBG 4/04; SLJ 4/04)

21238 Grayson, Robert. *Military* (4–7). Series: Working Animals. 2010, Marshall Cavendish LB $19.95 (978-1-60870-164-3). 64pp. Describes the varied roles that animals — ranging from rats and pigeons to dogs, dolphins, and horses — have played in military operations. (Rev: SLJ 12/1/10) [355.424]

21239 Grubman, Steve, and Jill Davis. *Orangutans Are Ticklish: Fun Facts from an Animal Photographer* (2–4). Illus. by Steve Grubman. 2010, Random House $16.99 (978-0-375-85886-4); LB $19.99 (978-0-375-95886-1). 40pp. Large, clearly focused photographs accompany fascinating facts about wild animals. (Rev: BL 8/10; SLJ 8/1/10) [590.22]

21240 Halfmann, Janet. *Life in a Garden* (5–7). Photos by David Liebman. 2000, Creative LB $22.60 (978-1-58341-072-1). This book explores such life forms found in a garden as fungi, beetles, slugs, snails, and aphids. (Rev: SLJ 8/00) [635]

21241 Hansen, Rosanna. *Caring Animals* (2–4). Illus. Series: True Tales. 2003, Children's Pr. LB $22.50 (978-0-516-22912-6); paper $4.95 (978-0-516-24603-1). Introduces animals that help people, from dolphins to a seeing-eye horse. (Rev: BL 1/1–15/04) [362.404]

21242 Haven, Kendall. *Animal Mummies* (4–8). 2010, Scholastic $19.99 (978-0-545-03460-9). 112pp. A fascinating overview of the practice of mummifying animals, with large, eye-catching photographs. (Rev: LMC 10/10)

21243 Heller, Ruth. *"Galápagos" Means "Tortoises"* (3–5). Illus. by author. 2000, Sierra Club $14.95 (978-0-87156-917-2). 41pp. The animals and birds of the Galapagos Islands are described in this book of rhymes and accompanying realistic paintings. (Rev: SLJ 3/01) [985]

21244 Hile, Lori. *Animal Survival* (4–7). Series: Extreme Survival. 2011, Heinemann LB $33.50 (978-1-4109-3973-9). 56pp. Hile tells stories of animals that have beaten the odds and survived disasters. (Rev: SLJ 8/11)

21245 Hodge, Deborah. *Polar Animals* (PS–1). Illus. by Pat Stephens. Series: Who Lives Here? 2008, Kids Can LB $14.95 (978-1-55453-043-4); paper $5.95 (978-1-55453-044-1). A simple introduction to polar animals including penguins, foxes, and whales, with eye-catching photographs. (Rev: BL 4/1/08; LMC 10/08) [591.75]

21246 Hodgkins, Fran. *Animals Among Us: Living with Suburban Wildlife* (5–8). 2000, Linnet LB $19.50 (978-0-208-02478-7). This book discusses the behavior and lifestyles of animals such as deer, coyotes, bears, skunks, and bats that live in suburbs, close to their original haunts. (Rev: BL 6/1–15/00; HB 7–8/00; HBG 10/00; SLJ 9/00; VOYA 12/00) [591.7]

21247 Ipcizade, Catherine. *Big Predators* (K–2). Series: Big. 2009, Capstone LB $21.32 (978-1-4296-3316-1). 24pp. Simple text and eye-catching, close-up photographs describe predators in action — big, bigger, and biggest — in this wide-format photoessay. (Rev: LMC 3–4/10; SLJ 2/1/10) [591.5]

21248 Jackson, Donna. *The Wildlife Detectives: How Forensic Scientists Fight Crimes Against Nature* (3–7). Illus. 2000, Houghton $17.00 (978-0-395-86976-5). 48pp. This book introduces the forensic scientists who track down criminals who harm wild animals. (Rev: BL 4/1/00; HBG 9/00; SLJ 7/00) [363.28]

21249 Jefferis, David. *Animal Kingdom* (3–6). Illus. Series: Record Breakers. 2003, Raintree LB $25.69 (978-0-7398-6321-3). 32pp. Good for browsing, this attractive volume identifies such animal record-holders as the smallest bird, largest sea creature, longest migrator, best camouflage, and so forth. (Rev: HBG 10/03; SLJ 7/03) [591]

21250 Jenkins, Steve. *Actual Size* (1–3). Illus. 2004, Houghton $16.00 (978-0-618-37594-3). 32pp. Striking cut-paper collages portray animals — and parts of animals — in real size, so that an earthworm appears in full size while only the eyes of a giant squid can be accommodated. (Rev: BL 5/15/04; HB 5/04; SLJ 6/04) [591.4]

21251 Jenkins, Steve. *The Animal Book: A Collection of the Fastest, Fiercest, Toughest, Cleverest, Shyest—and Most Surprising—Animals on Earth* (1–5). Illus. by author. 2013, Houghton Mifflin $24.99 (978-0-547-55799-1). 208pp. Visually compelling, this is a rich and browsable compendium of information on animals organized

by themes. Notable Children's Books: 2014. (Rev: BL 10/1/13*; LMC 1–2/14; SLJ 10/13) [599]

21252 Jenkins, Steve, and Robin Page. *What Do You Do with a Tail Like This?* (PS–2). Illus. 2003, Houghton $15.00 (978-0-618-25628-0). 32pp. The tails, mouths, and other parts of different animals are rendered in cut paper, illustrating interesting animal facts. Caldecott Honor Book, 2004. (Rev: BCCB 3/03; BL 2/15/03*; HBG 10/03; SLJ 3/03) [573.8]

21253 Kalman, Bobbie. *Food Chains and You* (2–4). Illus. Series: Food Chains. 2004, Crabtree LB $25.27 (978-0-7787-1942-7); paper $6.95 (978-0-7787-1988-5). 32pp. A simple look at the relationship between producers and consumers of energy (both herbivores and carnivores), with discussion of humans' food choices.

21254 Kaner, Etta. *Animals at Work: How Animals Build, Dig, Fish and Trap* (2–4). Illus. by Pat Stephens. 2001, Kids Can $10.95 (978-1-55074-673-0); paper $5.95 (978-1-55074-675-4). Activities, a game, and a quiz are provided in this basic look at the work various animals have to do to find food, shelter, and mates. (Rev: HBG 3/02; SLJ 10/01) [591.5]

21255 Kneidel, Sally. *Slugs, Bugs, and Salamanders: Discovering Animals in Your Garden* (5–7). Illus. by Anna-Maria L. Crum. 1997, Fulcrum paper $16.95 (978-1-55591-313-7). As well as introducing backyard insects and other small creatures, this account gives a number of tips on growing healthy flowers and vegetables. (Rev: SLJ 10/97) [595.7]

21256 Kratter, Paul. *The Living Rain Forest: An Animal Alphabet* (PS–2). Illus. 2004, Charlesbridge $17.95 (978-1-57091-603-8). 64pp. Striking acrylic-and-watercolor illustrations introduces 26 animals of the rain forest. (Rev: BL 2/1/04; SLJ 4/04) [591.734]

21257 Laidlaw, Rob. *On Parade: The Hidden World of Animals in Entertainment* (3–6). 2010, Fitzhenry & Whiteside $19.95 (978-1-55455-143-9). 53pp. An interesting, and sad, look at how animals are abused in circuses, on movies and TV programs, in zoos, and in sporting events, with suggestions for animal sanctuaries and other improvements. (Rev: BL 2/1/11; SLJ 3/1/11; VOYA 2/11) [636.088]

21258 Lundgren, Julie K. *Skeletons and Exoskeletons* (3–5). Illus. Series: My Science Library. 2012, Rourke LB $27.07 (978-161810088-7); paper $7.95 (9781618102218). 24pp. This is a well-written introduction to the basics of internal and external skeletons, ending with a "Show What You Know" quiz. (Rev: BL 9/15/12; SLJ Fall 2012 Series Guide) [611.71]

21259 Marrin, Albert. *Little Monsters: The Creatures That Live on Us and in Us* (4–7). Illus. 2011, Dutton $19.99 (978-052542262-4). 160pp. Not for the faint of heart, this book discusses — and shows in graphic detail — parasites that live on or in the human body (leeches, tapeworms, and so forth). (Rev: BLO 2/15/12) [578.6]

21260 Martin, James W. R. *In a House* (2–5). Series: Small World. 2002, Crabtree LB $25.27 (978-0-7787-0140-8); paper $8.95 (978-0-7787-0154-5). 32pp. From bugs and rodents to insects and worms, this is a rundown of the animal life that can be found inside a house. (Rev: BL 10/15/02) [591]

21261 Maze, Stephanie, ed. *Beautiful Moments in the Wild: Animals and Their Colors* (PS–K). Series: Moments in the Wild. 2002, Moonstone $15.00 (978-0-9707768-7-7). 32pp. An attractive picture book showing the diversity of animal colors in full-color shots. (Rev: SLJ 3/03)

21262 Mezzanotte, Jim. *Police* (4–7). Series: Working Animals. 2010, Marshall Cavendish LB $19.95 (978-1-60870-166-7). 64pp. Animals' varied roles in police operations — search-and-rescue, tracking, bomb sniffing, and so forth — are described in this attractive, informative book. (Rev: SLJ 12/1/10) [363.2]

21263 Miles, Victoria. *Wild Science: Amazing Encounters Between Animals and the People Who Study Them* (5–8). Series: Scientists in the Field. 2004, Raincoast paper $18.95 (978-1-55192-618-6). 168pp. This photo-filled volume introduces readers to scientists who study animals and describes memorable moments with animals in the wilderness. (Rev: BL 12/1/04; SLJ 12/04) [591.68]

21264 Mitton, Tony. *Rainforest Romp* (PS–1). Illus. by Ant Parker. Series: Amazing Animals. 2009, Kingfisher $9.99 (978-0-7534-6298-0). 24pp. Rabbit, Mouse, and Bird study a variety of animals in the rain forest; rhyming text highlights various characteristics. (Rev: BL 4/1/09) [578.734]

21265 Murawski, Darlyne A. *Animal Faces* (PS–2). Photos by author. 2005, Sterling LB $12.95 (978-1-4027-2295-0). A nature photographer offers close-up views of the faces of a wide variety of animals, introduced by brief poems. (Rev: SLJ 3/06) [590]

21266 Myers, Jack, ed. *The Puzzle of the Platypus and Other Explorations of Science in Action* (3–5). Illus. by John Rice. 2008, Boyds Mills $17.95 (978-1-59078-556-0). 64pp. Each story in this collection of eleven short essays reprinted from *Highlights* magazine tells how a scientist was able to unravel a mystery about some kind of animal; resource list. (Rev: BL 3/1/08; LMC 3/08; SLJ 6/08) [590]

21267 Palazzo, Tony. *The Biggest and the Littlest Animals* (4–7). Illus. by author. 1973, Lion LB $13.95 (978-0-87460-225-8). Many ways of comparing animals, including size and mobility, are explored.

21268 Pascoe, Elaine, ed. *Into Wild California* (3–6). Series: The Jeff Corwin Experience. 2004, Gale LB $24.95 (978-1-56711-858-2). 48pp. In a spin-off of his Animal Planet TV series, Corwin introduces such creatures as bears, snakes, sea otters, and bobcats that make California their home. (Rev: SLJ 4/04) [591.9]

21269 Pascoe, Elaine, ed. *Into Wild Madagascar* (3–6). Series: The Jeff Corwin Experience. 2004, Gale LB $24.95 (978-1-56711-855-1). 48pp. Jeff Corwin of television's Animal Planet is the "host" for this survey of the threatened wildlife of Madagascar, from chameleons to lemurs. (Rev: SLJ 4/04) [591.9]

21270 Patkau, Karen. *Creatures: Yesterday and Today* (2–4). Illus. by author. 2008, Tundra $18.95 (978-0-88776-833-0). 32pp. Using double-page spreads with bold computer-generated graphics and simple text Patkau looks at prehistoric animals and their modern-day descendants. (Rev: BL 4/1/08; SLJ 6/08) [591.38]

21271 Pfeffer, Wendy. *Icy Antarctic Waters* (3–5). Series: Living on the Edge. 2002, Benchmark LB $25.64 (978-0-7614-1438-4). 40pp. The Weddell seal, emperor penguin, and minke whale are highlighted in this colorful, easy-to-read overview of Antarctic animals. (Rev: HBG 10/03; SLJ 6/03) [591.77]

21272 Pittau, Francesco, and Bernadette Gervais. *Out of Sight* (K–2). Illus. by authors. 2010, Chronicle $19.99 (978-0-8118-7712-1). 16pp. This large, lift-the-flap and pop-up book features a wide range of hidden animals. (Rev: SLJ 2/1/11*) [590]

21273 Presnall, Judith Janda. *Animal Actors* (4–6). Series: Animals with Jobs. 2002, Gale LB $23.70 (978-0-7377-0934-6). 48pp. Animals that work in television and movies are profiled here with information on their training and care. Also use *Navy Dolphins* (2002). (Rev: SLJ 3/02) [791.43]

21274 Pye, Claire. *The Wild World of the Future* (4–8). Illus. 2003, Firefly $24.95 (978-1-55297-727-9); paper $14.95 (978-1-55297-725-5). 96pp. This lively, attractive volume speculates on the animals of the future, basing the projections on previous evolutionary development. (Rev: BL 7/03; SLJ 6/03) [576.8]

21275 Ruurs, Margriet. *Amazing Animals: The Remarkable Things That Creatures Do* (2–4). Illus. by W. Allan Hancock. 2011, Tundra $17.95 (978-0-88776-973-3). 32pp. Suited for browsing more than research, this highly illustrated volume introduces 44 animals from around the world and their interesting characteristics and behaviors. (Rev: BL 5/1/11; SLJ 6/11) [591.5]

21276 Ruurs, Margriet. *Wild Babies* (PS–2). Illus. by Andrew Kiss. 2003, Tundra $14.95 (978-0-88776-627-5). 32pp. Young animals and birds found in a North American forest are shown in lush, detailed paintings that provide intriguing hints of the next animal. (Rev: HBG 10/03; SLJ 2/03)

21277 Shields, Amy. *Saving Animal Babies* (K–2). Illus. 2013, National Geographic LB $13.90 (978-142631041-6); paper $3.99 (9781426310409). 32pp. A compelling, well-illustrated account of the ways in which vets, zookeepers, and other rescuers help baby animals in need. (Rev: BL 6/13) [591.3]

21278 Silverman, Buffy. *Can an Old Dog Learn New Tricks? And Other Questions About Animals* (4–6). Illus. by Colin W. Thompson. Series: Is That a Fact? 2010, Lerner LB $26.60 (978-0-8225-9083-5). 40pp. Familiar sayings and old wives' tales about animals are unraveled and examined with humor and eye-catching illustrations. (Rev: LMC 5–6/10; SLJ 7/10) [590]

21279 Singer, Marilyn. *A Strange Place to Call Home: The World's Most Dangerous Habitats and the Animals That Call Them Home* (K–3). Illus. by Ed Young. 2012,

Chronicle $16.99 (978-1-4521-0120-0). 44pp. A poetic tribute to 14 animals that live in unusually inhospitable habitats. (Rev: BL 10/15/12; SLJ 9/12) [571.1]

21280 Siwanowicz, Igor. *Animals Up Close* (4–8). Illus. by author. 2009, DK $16.99 (978-0-7566-4513-7). 96pp. Dramatic close-up photographs display the features of small creatures of all kinds; fascinating for browsing, this book also offers enough information for reports. (Rev: BLO 5/27/09; SLJ 8/09) [500]

21281 Spada, Ada. *Fangs, Claws and Talons: Animal Predators* (3–6). Trans. by Amy Gulick. Illus. by Filippo Cappellini. 2007, Sterling $9.95 (978-1-60059-150-1). 48pp. This large-format book describes a variety of predators including snakes, raptors, big cats, and even tyrannosaurs. (Rev: BL 12/1/07; LMC 1/08) [591.5]

21282 Squire, Ann O. *African Animals* (2–3). Series: True Books — Animals. 2001, Children's Book Pr. LB $23.00 (978-0-516-22186-1). 48pp. A compact guide to the most common animals of Africa is presented in a simple text with color photographs on each page. (Rev: BL 12/15/01) [599]

21283 Stetson, Emily. *Kids' Easy-to-Create Wildlife Habitats* (2–5). Illus. by J. Susan Stone. Series: Quick Starts for Kids! 2004, Williamson paper $12.95 (978-0-8249-8665-0). 128pp. Offering solid information, illustrations, and activities, this wide-format book introduces the wildlife found in many communities and the foods that may bring them into the open. (Rev: BL 12/1/04; SLJ 3/05) [639.9]

21284 Stewart, Melissa. *Why Are Animals Orange?* (K–3). Illus. Series: Rainbow of Animals. 2009, Enslow LB $16.95 (978-0-7660-3250-7). 32pp. Butterflies can be orange, as can tigers, fish, and other animals. This photo-essay looks at the reasons why this coloring can be beneficial. (Rev: BL 4/1/09) [591.47]

21285 Suen, Anastasia. *ASPCA* (1–2). Series: Helping Organizations. 2002, Rosen LB $19.95 (978-0-8239-6004-0). 24pp. As well as a history of this organization, this easily read account describes how it works and how young people can get involved. (Rev: BL 6/1–15/02; SLJ 4/02) [179.3]

21286 Thornhill, Jan. *I Found a Dead Bird: The Kids' Guide to the Cycle of Life and Death* (3–6). Illus. 2006, Maple Tree $21.95 (978-1-897066-70-6); paper $9.95 (978-1-897066-71-3). 64pp. An attractive, thought-provoking approach to such sensitive topics as death and decomposition that covers scientific and social aspects. (Rev: SLJ 10/06)

21287 Tildes, Phyllis L. *Eye Guess: A Foldout Guessing Game* (PS–2). Illus. 2005, Charlesbridge $9.95 (978-1-57091-650-2). 36pp. Each of eight foldouts shows close-ups of an animal's eye and part of the face; there are a few facts about each animal and a tantalizing glimpse of the next animal. (Rev: BL 9/1/05) [590]

21288 Votaw, Carol. *Waking Up Down Under* (PS–1). Illus. by Susan Banta. 2007, NorthWord $15.95 (978-1-55971-976-6). Rhyming verses describe 12 Australian animals and how they greet the day (or night). (Rev: SLJ 12/07) [591.994]

21289 Wadsworth, Ginger. *River Discoveries* (2–4). Illus. by Paul Kratter. 2002, Charlesbridge $16.95 (978-1-57091-418-8); paper $6.95 (978-1-57091-419-5). 32pp. An introduction to the varied wildlife that surrounds and depends on a river, describing the activities of 13 types of animals over a 24-hour period. (Rev: BL 9/15/02; HBG 3/03; SLJ 8/02) [591.76]

21290 Ward, Jennifer. *Forest Bright, Forest Night* (K–3). Illus. by Jamichael Henterly. Series: Sharing Nature with Children. 2005, Dawn $16.95 (978-1-58469-066-5); paper $8.95 (978-1-58469-067-2). Diurnal animals go about daytime errands in the first part of this attractive book; readers flip it over to find these animals asleep and the nocturnal residents of the forest moving about. (Rev: SLJ 10/05) [591.5]

21291 Webb, Sophie. *Far from Shore: Chronicles of an Open Ocean Voyage* (4–6). Illus. by author. 2011, Houghton Mifflin $17.99 (978-0-618-59729-1). 80pp. Webb documents her research work with dolphins in the Pacific Ocean and the many other birds and animals she saw during a four-month trip, with notes on scientific methods and research techniques. (Rev: BL 9/1/11; HB 9–10/11; LMC 1–2/12; SLJ 9/1/11) [591.77]

21292 Werner, Sharon, and Sarah Forss. *Alphasaurs and Other Prehistoric Types* (1–3). Illus. by Sharon Werner. 2012, Blue Apple $22.99 (978-1-60905-193-8). 56pp. An inventive use of typography, foldouts, and informative text makes this an engaging alphabetical introduction. (Rev: BL 12/15/12; SLJ 1/13*) [567.9]

Amphibians and Reptiles

GENERAL AND MISCELLANEOUS

21293 Allen, Nancy Kelly. *Whose Food Is This: A Look at What Animals Eat — Seeds, Bugs, and Nuts* (PS–2). Illus. by Derrick Alderman and Denise Shea. Series: Whose Is It? 2004, Picture Window LB $25.26 (978-1-4048-0607-8). 24pp. Rhythmic question-and-answer format and colorful collages introduce the wide variety of foods that animals eat. Also use *Whose Sound Is This? A Look at Animal Noises — Chirps, Clicks, and Hoots* (2004). (Rev: BL 11/1/04) [591.5]

21294 Arnosky, Jim. *Slither and Crawl: Eye to Eye with Reptiles* (2–4). Illus. by Jim Aronsky. 2009, Sterling $14.95 (978-1-4027-3986-6). 32pp. A large-format look at reptiles—mostly North American—with eye-catching life-size paintings and details of physical features, diet, hibernation, and so forth. (Rev: BL 4/1/09; LMC 8/09; SLJ 6/09) [597.9]

21295 Behler, John. *National Audubon Society First Field Guide: Reptiles* (4–8). 1999, Scholastic $17.95 (978-0-590-05467-6); paper $11.95 (978-0-590-05487-4). This richly illustrated manual discusses common characteristics of North American reptiles, then presents individual species under four groups: crocodiles, turtles, lizards, and snakes. (Rev: BL 3/15/99; SLJ 7/99) [597.9]

21296 Borgert-Spaniol, Megan. *Salamanders* (K–2). Illus. Series: Backyard Wildlife. 2012, Children's Press LB $21.95 (978-160014723-4). 24pp. A slim, colorful introduction to salamanders and their lives. (Rev: BL 9/15/12) [597.8]

21297 Bredeson, Carmen. *Fun Facts About Salamanders!* (1–3). Series: I Like Reptiles and Amphibians! 2007, Enslow LB $21.26 (978-0-7660-2790-9). 24pp. The crisp narrative uses a question-and-answer format to provide basic information about salamanders; illustrated with color photographs. (Rev: SLJ 10/07) [597.6]

21298 Dennard, Deborah. *Reptiles* (5–7). Illus. by Jennifer Owings Dewey. Series: Our Wild World. 2004, NorthWord $16.95 (978-1-55971-880-6). A compilation of four shorter books published by NorthWord in 2003, this volume examines the physical characteristics, natural habitat, diet, and behavior of alligators, crocodiles, lizards, snakes, and turtles. (Rev: SLJ 8/04) [597.9]

21299 Holub, Joan. *Why Do Snakes Hiss? And Other Questions About Snakes, Lizards, and Turtles* (1–2). Illus. by Anna DiVito. Series: Easy-to-Read. 2004, Penguin $14.99 (978-0-8037-3000-7). 48pp. Using an attractive question-and-answer format, this volume explores the characteristics and behavior of the reptile family. (Rev: BL 11/1/04; SLJ 11/04) [597.9]

21300 Hutchinson, Mark. *Reptiles* (4–7). Illus. Series: Insiders. 2011, Simon & Schuster $16.99 (978-144243276-5). 64pp. With dramatic 3-D illustrations, this volume offers a general overview of reptiles and then focuses on 12 specific animals, exploring their anatomy, behavior, and other characteristics. (Rev: BL 9/15/11; LMC 1–2/12) [597.9]

21301 Jango-Cohen, Judith. *Desert Iguanas* (PS–2). Series: Pull Ahead Books. 2001, Lerner LB $22.60 (978-0-8225-3635-2). 32pp. A color photograph and two lines of simple text are found on each page of this attractive basic introduction to these desert reptiles. (Rev: BL 6/1–15/01; HBG 10/01) [597.9]

21302 Llewellyn, Claire. *Question Time: Reptiles* (3–5). Illus. Series: Question Time. 2002, Kingfisher $11.95 (978-0-7534-5451-0); paper $6.95 (978-0-7534-5463-3). 32pp. Topics covered in a question-and-answer format include the different types of reptiles, and their characteristics, habitat, and defense mechanisms. (Rev: HBG 3/03; SLJ 2/03)

21303 Miller, Ruth. *Reptiles* (4–6). Series: Animal Kingdom. 2004, Raintree LB $32.79 (978-1-4109-1052-3). 64pp. The common characteristics of reptiles are explained, followed by descriptions of various orders of reptiles and selected specific species plus discussion of endangered status and evolution. Also use *Amphibians* (2004). (Rev: BL 5/1/04; SLJ 6/05)

21304 Murray, Peter. *Amphibians* (3–6). Series: Science Around Us. 2004, Child's World LB $27.07 (978-1-59296-271-6). 32pp. Eye-catching photographs and interesting "Did You Know?" features draw the reader into this overview of amphibians. Also use *Reptiles* (2004). (Rev: SLJ 3/05) [597.8]

21305 Pascoe, Elaine, ed. *Into Wild Louisiana* (3–6). Series: The Jeff Corwin Experience. 2004, Gale LB $24.95 (978-1-4103-0060-7). 48pp. Readers visit the swamp creatures of backwoods Louisiana, from alligators to frogs, guided by Jeff Corwin of TV's *Animal Planet*. (Rev: SLJ 4/04)

21306 Savage, Stephen. *Amphibians* (2–4). Series: What's the Difference? 2000, Raintree LB $25.69 (978-0-7398-1359-1). 32pp. This book introduces a number of amphibians that live on water, land, or both. (Rev: BL 10/15/00; HBG 3/01) [597.6]

21307 Savage, Stephen. *Reptiles* (2–4). Series: What's the Difference? 2000, Raintree LB $25.69 (978-0-7398-1358-4). 32pp. This book explores the similarities and differences in the class known as reptiles and introduces such creatures as crocodiles, rattlesnakes, and tortoises. (Rev: BL 10/15/00; HBG 3/01; SLJ 1/01) [597.96]

21308 Sill, Cathryn. *About Amphibians: A Guide for Children* (PS–2). Illus. by John Sill. 2001, Peachtree $15.95 (978-1-56145-234-7). 40pp. An introduction for young children that has colorful, realistic paintings facing brief text. (Rev: BL 5/15/01; HBG 10/01; SLJ 6/01) [597.8]

21309 Spilsbury, Richard, and Louise Spilsbury. *Classifying Reptiles* (4–6). Series: Classifying Living Things. 2003, Heinemann LB $24.22 (978-1-4034-0848-8). 32pp. This title examines the scientific classification of reptiles, including identification of the phylum, class, and order of different types of reptiles. (Rev: HBG 10/03; SLJ 11/03) [597.9]

21310 Spilsbury, Richard, and Louise Spilsbury. *The Life Cycle of Amphibians* (3–5). Illus. Series: From Egg to Adult. 2003, Heinemann LB $24.22 (978-1-4034-0785-6). 32pp. A brief overview of amphibians, examining the creatures' physical characteristics, habitat, diet, and life cycle. (Rev: HBG 4/04; SLJ 10/03) [597.8]

21311 Squire, Ann O. *Chinese Giant Salamander: The World's Biggest Amphibian* (K–2). Illus. Series: SuperSized! 2007, Bearport LB $21.28 (978-1-59716-386-6). 24pp. Report writers will get lots of mileage from this introduction to the Chinese giant salamander, filled with facts about and photographs of the big amphibian. (Rev: SLJ 8/07)

21312 Stewart, Melissa. *Amphibians* (2–3). Series: True Books — Animals. 2001, Children's Book Pr. LB $25.00 (978-0-516-22037-6). 48pp. In this colorful, simple volume, a variety of amphibians are introduced with material on their appearance, habits, and distinctive characteristics. (Rev: BL 12/15/01) [597.6]

21313 Wilkes, Sarah. *Amphibians* (5–9). Series: World Almanac Library of the Animal Kingdom. 2006, World Almanac LB $31.00 (978-0-8368-6208-9). This colorful guide identifies common species of amphibians and examines their physical characteristics, habitats, diets, behaviors, and life cycles. (Rev: SLJ 12/06) [597.5]

21314 Wilson, Hannah. *Life-Size Reptiles* (3–6). Illus. 2007, Sterling $9.95 (978-1-4027-4542-3). 28pp. From lizards to turtles, geckos to Komodo dragons, this is a large-format introduction to things reptile with fold-out illustrations. (Rev: BL 6/1–15/07; SLJ 8/07) [597.9]

21315 Winner, Cherie. *Everything Reptile: What Kids Really Want to Know About Reptiles* (3–5). 2004, North-Word $10.95 (978-1-55971-146-3); paper $7.95 (978-1-55971-164-7). 63pp. A basic introduction, using a question-and-answer format with plenty of photographs. (Rev: SLJ 11/04) [597.9]

21316 Zabludoff, Marc. *The Reptile Class* (5–9). Series: Family Trees. 2005, Benchmark LB $32.79 (978-0-7614-1820-7). Habits, habitats, and other aspects of this varied class of animals; an engaging book with plenty of facts for report-writers. (Rev: SLJ 6/06) [597.9]

ALLIGATORS AND CROCODILES

21317 Arnosky, Jim. *Crocodile Safari* (2–5). Illus. by author. 2009, Scholastic $21.99 (978-0-439-90356-1). 40pp. Arnosky sprinkles informative text about crocodiles with anecdotes about his own experiences in the mangrove swamps of Florida. (Rev: BL 12/1/08; LMC 5/09; SLJ 2/09) [597.98]

21318 Bodden, Valerie. *Crocodiles* (K–2). Illus. Series: Amazing Animals. 2010, Creative Education $16.95 (978-158341806-2). 24pp. A simple overview of the characteristics of crocodiles, with eye-catching photographs. (Rev: BL 7/10) [597.98]

21319 Clarke, Ginjer L. *Baby Alligator* (1–3). Illus. by Neecy Twinem. 2000, Penguin paper $3.99 (978-0-448-42095-0). 48pp. For beginning readers, this is a simple introduction to alligators that traces the life cycle from hatching from an egg in the spring to waiting out the winter in a dark tunnel. (Rev: BL 7/00; HBG 9/00) [597.98]

21320 Feigenbaum, Aaron. *American Alligators: Freshwater Survivors* (3–5). Series: America's Animal Comebacks. 2008, Bearport LB $25.27 (978-1-59716-503-7). 32pp. With eye-catching photographs and an appealing format, this volume looks at the reasons for the decline in the alligator population (hunting, pollution, loss of habitat) and the measures that succeeded in bring them back from the brink of extinction. (Rev: SLJ 2/08) [597.98]

21321 Fitzgerald, Patrick J. *Croc and Gator Attacks* (4–7). Series: Animal Attack! 2000, Children's paper $6.95 (978-0-516-23514-1). 48pp. Aimed at the reluctant reader, this book tells true stories of attacks by crocodiles and alligators and gives information about these species and their differences. (Rev: SLJ 2/01) [597.98]

21322 Hamilton, Sue. *Attacked by a Crocodile* (4–7). Series: Close Encounters of the Wild Kind. 2010, ABDO LB $27.07 (978-1-60453-929-5). 32pp. Exciting stories and graphic photographs add high-interest appeal to the information about crocodiles and advice on avoiding and surviving such an attack. (Rev: LMC 10/10; SLJ 5/10) [597.98]

21323 Harasymiw, Mark. *Alligators Are Not Pets!* (3–5). Illus. Series: When Pets Attack! 2013, Gareth Stevens LB $26.60 (978-143399278-0). 32pp. Fascinating and informative text combined with extraordinary photo-

graphs present information about alligators, including their habitat, diet, speed when pursuing prey, and other characteristics. ℮ (Rev: BL 10/1/13; LMC 5–6/14) [597.98]

21324 Jango-Cohen, Judith. *Crocodiles* (5–8). Series: AnimalWays. 2000, Marshall Cavendish LB $31.36 (978-0-7614-1136-9). This book examines the habitat, range, classification, evolution, anatomy, behavior, and endangered status of the crocodile. (Rev: BL 1/1–15/01; HBG 3/01) [597.98]

21325 Jango-Cohen, Judith. *Crocodiles* (4–6). Series: Animals Animals. 2002, Benchmark LB $25.64 (978-0-7614-1446-9). 48pp. This is an oversize book filled with excellent photographs and text covering the anatomy, habits, food, and habitats of crocodiles. (Rev: BL 12/15/02; HBG 3/03; SLJ 2/03) [597.98]

21326 Kallen, Stuart A., and P. M. Boekhoff. *Alligators* (4–6). Series: Nature's Predators. 2002, Gale LB $23.70 (978-0-7377-0642-0). Color photographs are used with a simple text to describe characteristics of alligators and their habitats, with coverage on how they kill their prey and how they also are hunted. (Rev: BL 1/1–15/02; SLJ 6/02) [597.98]

21327 Llewellyn, Claire. *Crocodile* (PS–3). Illus. by Simon Mendez. Series: Starting Life. 2004, NorthWord $16.95 (978-1-55971-900-1). 23pp. On pages that grow progressively wider, the stages of a crocodile's development are traced, with information on such topics as habitat, diet, and predatory behavior plus realistic illustrations. (Rev: SLJ 11/04) [597.98]

21328 Marisco, Katie. *Saltwater Crocodiles* (3–5). Illus. Series: Nature's Children. 2013, Scholastic/Children's Press LB $28 (978-053123361-0); paper $6.95 (9780531251591). 48pp. With full-page photographs and clear text this book explores the characteristics and behaviors of these animals, their life cycle, their history, and relationship with humans. (Rev: BL 11/15/13) [597.98]

21329 Markle, Sandra. *Crocodiles* (2–5). Illus. Series: Animal Predators. 2004, Carolrhoda LB $25.26 (978-1-57505-726-2). 40pp. Concise text and clear, full-page photographs introduce the life cycle of the crocodile and its physical characteristics, habitat, diet, and predatory behavior. (Rev: BL 9/15/04; SLJ 10/04) [597.98]

21330 Noonan, Diana. *The Crocodile* (2–4). Illus. Series: Life Cycles. 2002, Chelsea LB $23.00 (978-0-7910-6964-6). 32pp. Handsome photographs and simple text describe the life cycle, habitat, appearance, and predators of the crocodile, in a small, square, photo-essay format. (Rev: BL 1/1–15/03; HBG 3/03) [597.98]

21331 Riggs, Kate. *Alligators* (K–3). Illus. Series: Amazing Animals. 2012, Creative Education LB $17.95 (978-160818104-9). 24pp. For new or reluctant readers, this is a good introduction to the alligator's physical characteristics, habitat, and behavior, and includes a story from folklore explaining why alligators and dogs don't get along. (Rev: BL 3/1/12) [599.98]

21332 Rockwell, Anne. *Who Lives in an Alligator Hole?* (K–3). Illus. by Lizzy Rockwell. Series: Let's-Read-and-Find-Out Science. 2006, HarperCollins $15.99 (978-0-06-028530-2); paper $4.99 (978-0-06-445200-7). 40pp. This informational picture book gives facts on the history and habitat of alligators; it also discusses threats to their existence, how their surroundings have changed, conservation efforts, and their key role in helping other species to survive. (Rev: BL 12/1/06; SLJ 11/06) [597.98]

21333 Scherer, Glenn, and Marty Fletcher. *The American Crocodile: Help Save This Endangered Species!* (5–7). Illus. Series: Saving Endangered Species. 2007, Enslow $33.27 (978-1-59845-041-5). Report writers will welcome the information included in this volume and at the recommended Web links. (Rev: SLJ 11/07) [597.98]

21334 Snyder, Trish. *Alligator and Crocodile Rescue: Changing the Future for Endangered Wildlife* (4–8). Series: Firefly Animal Rescue. 2006, Firefly LB $19.95 (978-1-55297-920-4); paper $9.95 (978-1-55297-919-8). 64pp. Examines the work being done to protect alligators and crocodiles in their natural habitats and also looks at the physical characteristics, diets, behaviors, and life cycles of these reptiles. (Rev: SLJ 12/06) [597.98]

21335 Spilsbury, Richard. *Alligator* (4–6). Illus. Series: Animals Under Threat. 2004, Heinemann LB $18.95 (978-1-4034-4857-6). 48pp. The life cycle of the alligator and threats to its survival are explored in this blend of narrative and eye-catching color photography.

21336 Tourville, Amanda Doering. *A Crocodile Grows Up* (1–3). Illus. by Michael Denman and William J. Huiett. Series: Wild Animals. 2006, Picture Window LB $25.26 (978-1-4048-3157-5). 24pp. A crocodile's development from birth to full independence is described in brief text and realistic illustrations. (Rev: SLJ 4/07) [597.98]

21337 Walker, Sally M. *Crocodiles* (4–6). Illus. Series: Nature Watch. 2003, Lerner LB $25.26 (978-1-57505-345-5). 48pp. An attractive introduction to crocodiles, how and where they live, and their life cycle. (Rev: HBG 4/04)

FROGS AND TOADS

21338 Aloian, Molly, and Bobbie Kalman. *Endangered Frogs* (3–5). Illus. Series: Earth's Endangered Animals. 2006, Crabtree LB $25.27 (978-0-7787-1872-7). 32pp. Large text and clear color photographs focus on threatened frog species, presenting basic information about physical characteristics, diet, habitat, and behavior, and discussing the specific threats they face. (Rev: SLJ 1/07) [597.8]

21339 Arnosky, Jim. *All About Frogs* (2–4). Illus. Series: All About. 2002, Scholastic $16.95 (978-0-590-48164-9). 32pp. Excellent illustrations accompany the in-depth information about the anatomy and habitats of various species of frogs in this book for younger readers. (Rev: BL 2/1/02; HB 3/02; HBG 10/02; SLJ 3/02) [597.8]

21340 Bishop, Nic. *Nic Bishop Frogs* (2–4). Illus. 2008, Scholastic $17.99 (978-0-439-87755-8). 48pp. Compelling photographs and clear text — covering anatomy, diet, reproduction, and so forth — make this a very appealing volume. (Rev: BL 1/1–15/08; HB 3/08; LMC 3/08; SLJ 2/08*) [597.8]

21341 Bredeson, Carmen. *Fun Facts About Frogs!* (PS–2). Series: I Like Reptiles and Amphibians! 2007, Enslow LB $21.26 (978-0-7660-2788-6). 24pp. Eye-catching photographs and clear text make this a useful introduction for beginning readers. (Rev: SLJ 1/08) [597.8]

21342 Bredeson, Carmen. *Poison Dart Frogs Up Close* (1–3). Series: Zoom in on Animals! 2008, Enslow LB $21.26 (978-0-7660-3077-0). 24pp. Simple text and close-up color photographs introduce body parts, babies, and other important characteristics. (Rev: SLJ 11/08) [597.87]

21343 Chrustowski, Rick. *Hop Frog* (PS–3). Illus. by author. 2003, Holt $15.95 (978-0-8050-6688-3). The life cycle of a leopard frog is told in an entertaining narrative. (Rev: HBG 10/03; SLJ 5/03) [597.8]

21344 Crump, Marty. *The Mystery of Darwin's Frog* (3–5). Illus. by Steve Jenkins. 2013, Boyds Mills $16.95 (978-159078864-6). 33pp. An account of Darwin's discovery of this particular breed of frog and the later, surprising discovery that the male frog of the species nurtures the young; now this fascinating animal is in danger of extinction. (Rev: BL 6/13; LMC 11–12/13; SLJ 5/13*) [597.8]

21345 Ganeri, Anita. *From Tadpole to Frog* (1–3). Illus. Series: How Living Things Grow. 2006, Heinemann LB $25.36 (978-1-4034-7859-7). 32pp. How a tadpole grows to be a frog, presented in an easy-to-read format. (Rev: SLJ 6/06) [597.8]

21346 Godwin, Sam. *The Trouble with Tadpoles: A First Look at the Life Cycle of a Frog* (K–1). Illus. Series: First Look: Science. 2004, Picture Window LB $25.26 (978-1-4048-0654-2). 32pp. In simple language with cartoon-style illustrations, this volume describes the life cycle of frogs.

21347 Greenberg, Dan. *Frogs* (5–8). Series: Animal-Ways. 2000, Marshall Cavendish LB $31.36 (978-0-7614-1138-3). 112pp. As well as chapters devoted to the amazing variety of frogs, this book discusses their anatomy, habits, and survival skills. (Rev: BL 1/1–15/01; HBG 3/01) [597.8]

21348 Guiberson, Brenda. *Frog Song* (K–3). Illus. by Gennady Spirin. 2013, Henry Holt $17.99 (978-080509254-7). 40pp. This volume focuses on 11 varieties of frogs across the world and the different sounds they make. (Rev: BL 1/13; LMC 8–9/13*; SLJ 3/13*) [597.8]

21349 Hawes, Judy. *Why Frogs Are Wet* (K–3). Illus. by Mary Ann Fraser. Series: Let's-Read-and-Find-Out. 2000, HarperCollins LB $15.89 (978-0-06-028162-5); paper $5.99 (978-0-06-445195-6). 40pp. The physical characteristics, life cycle, evolution, and behavior of frogs are introduced in this revision of the 1968 title. (Rev: BL 9/15/00; HBG 3/01) [597.8]

21350 Llewellyn, Claire. *Frog* (K–4). Illus. by Simon Mendez. Series: Starting Life. 2003, NorthWord $16.95 (978-1-55971-869-1). 23pp. A look at the life cycle of a frog, from egg to tadpole to adult, and the environment in which frogs live. (Rev: SLJ 4/04) [597.8]

21351 Magloff, Lisa. *Watch Me Grow: Frog* (PS–2). Series: Watch Me Grow. 2003, DK $7.99 (978-0-7894-9629-4). 24pp. This attractive title provides a close-up look — from the perspective of the animal — at the early life cycle of a frog from the tadpole stage. (Rev: BL 10/15/03) [597.8]

21352 Markle, Sandra. *The Case of the Vanishing Golden Frogs: A Scientific Mystery* (4–6). Illus. 2011, Millbrook LB $29.27 (978-0-7613-5108-5). 48pp. One scientist's crusade against a fungus killing off Panamanian golden frogs is described in this attractive volume. (Rev: BL 9/15/11*; SLJ 11/1/11*) [597.8]

21353 Markle, Sandra. *Hip-Pocket Papa* (K–3). Illus. by Alan Marks. 2010, Charlesbridge $15.95 (978-1-57091-708-0). 32pp. Markle introduces the life and characteristics of the hip-pocket frog of Australia's temperate rainforest — and the role of the father — in this beautifully illustrated picture book. Lexile AD1060L (Rev: BL 1/1/10; LMC 10/10; SLJ 3/1/10) [597.8]

21354 Markle, Sandra. *Slippery, Slimy Baby Frogs* (3–5). 2006, Walker $16.95 (978-0-8027-8062-1). 32pp. This compelling photo-essay pairs interesting facts about frogs and their development with beautiful photographs, including some great close-ups. (Rev: BL 5/1/06; SLJ 5/06) [597.8]

21355 Marsico, Katie. *American Bullfrogs* (3–5). Illus. Series: Nature's Children. 2012, Scholastic/Children's Press LB $28 (978-053126832-2); paper $6.95 (9780531254776). 48pp. Simple text and many photographs present basic information about these animals' anatomy and behavior as well as their environment and history. (Rev: BL 3/1/13) [597.8]

21356 Miller, Sara S. *Frogs and Toads: The Leggy Leapers* (3–5). Series: Animals in Order. 2000, Watts LB $26.50 (978-0-531-11632-6). 48pp. A brief introduction to animal classification is followed by a description of frogs and toads, their similarities, differences, and life cycles. (Rev: BL 10/15/00) [597.8]

21357 Netherton, John. *Red-Eyed Tree Frogs* (2–3). Series: Early Bird Nature Books. 2000, Lerner LB $25.26 (978-0-8225-3037-4). 48pp. An introduction to these colorful rain forest amphibians — with their orange feet, lime green skin, blue stripes, and big red eyes. (Rev: BL 7/00; HBG 3/01) [597.8]

21358 Noonan, Diana. *The Frog* (2–4). Series: Life Cycles. 2002, Chelsea LB $23.00 (978-0-7910-6966-0). 32pp. This account follows the life cycle of this amphibian from egg to tadpole and finally the growth of lungs and legs needed to live on land. (Rev: BL 12/15/02; HBG 3/03) [597.8]

21359 Pringle, Laurence. *Frogs! Strange and Wonderful* (2–5). Illus. by Meryl Henderson. 2012, Boyds Mills $16.95 (978-1-59078-371-9). 32pp. With clear writing and beautiful watercolor illustrations, this book offers extensive information on frogs and toads, covering everything from anatomy, habitat, location, and diet to sounds, metamorphosis, and conservation. Lexile 980L (Rev: BL 4/15/12; LMC 11–12/12; SLJ 7/12) [597.8]

21360 Rau, Dana Meachen. *The Frog in the Pond* (PS–1). Series: Benchmark Rebus. 2006, Benchmark LB $22.79 (978-0-7614-2310-2). 24pp. With its child-friendly blend of rebuses and easy-to-understand text, this easy reader describes the physical characteristics, life cycle, and daily activities of frogs. (Rev: SLJ 12/06) [597.8]

21361 Rau, Dana Meachen. *Guess Who Jumps* (PS–K). Series: Bookworms. Guess Who. 2009, Marshall Cavendish $15.95 (978-0-7614-2908-1). 32pp. Fun for browsing, this book asks readers to identify a frog using the clues in the text and images. (Rev: SLJ 6/09) [597.8]

21362 Robinson, Fay. *Fantastic Frogs* (1–2). Illus. by Jean Cassels. Series: Hello Reader! 2000, Scholastic paper $3.99 (978-0-590-52269-4). 32pp. Different varieties of frogs like brown, green, and jungle frogs are introduced in this beginning reader with material on their looks and behavior. (Rev: BL 2/15/01) [597.8]

21363 Somervill, Barbara. *Cane Toad* (3–6). Series: Animal Invaders. 2008, Cherry Lake LB $26.26 (978-1-60279-115-2). 32pp. A solid introduction to the invasive cane toad and the threat it presents in Australia, with color photographs and maps. (Rev: SLJ 9/08) [597.8]

21364 Spilsbury, Louise. *Frog* (K–2). Series: Life Cycles. 2005, Heinemann LB $20.64 (978-1-4034-6772-0). 24pp. Brief text consisting of questions and answers suitable for beginning readers and bold photographs focus on the life cycle of the frog. (Rev: SLJ 7/05) [597.8]

21365 Stewart, Melissa. *A Place for Frogs* (K–3). Illus. by Higgins Bond. 2010, Peachtree $16.95 (978-1-56145-521-8). Unpaged. A richly illustrated tour of frogs' life, endangered status, and measures we can take to save them. (Rev: SLJ 5/1/10) [597.8]

21366 Stone, Tanya L. *Toads* (3–5). Series: Wild America. 2002, Gale LB $24.94 (978-1-56711-646-5). 24pp. A close-up look at these amphibians that gives material on where they live and their physical features, life cycle, and habits. (Rev: BL 10/15/02) [597.8]

21367 Tagholm, Sally. *The Frog* (2–3). Illus. by Bert Kitchen. Series: Animal Lives. 2000, Kingfisher $9.95 (978-0-7534-5215-8). 32pp. After a series of pictures depicting the daily activities of a frog and its mating procedures, this account focuses on the development of an egg to adulthood. (Rev: BL 5/15/00; HBG 3/01; SLJ 8/00) [597.8]

21368 Turner, Pamela S. *The Frog Scientist* (5–9). Photos by Andy Comins. Series: Scientists in the Field. 2009, Houghton Mifflin $18 (978-0-618-71716-3). 58pp. Why are frog populations disappearing at an alarming rate? This fascinating book recounts the research of African American biologist Tyrone Hayes and explains the advances he has made in this environmentally sensitive field. ALA Notable Children's Book 2010. Lexile 950L (Rev: BL 8/09*; HB 9–10/09; SLJ 9/09) [597.8]

21369 Wechsler, Doug. *Bullfrogs* (3–6). Series: The Really Wild Life of Frogs. 2002, Rosen LB $21.25 (978-0-8239-5855-9). 24pp. The bullfrog's physical characteristics, habitat, diet, predators, and so forth are presented with close-up photographs and boxed features. Also use *Leopard Frogs, Treefrogs,* and *Wood Frogs* (all 2002). (Rev: SLJ 5/02) [597.89]

21370 Whiting, Jim. *Frogs in Danger* (3–5). Series: A Robbie Reader. On the Verge of Extinction: Crisis in the Environment. 2007, Mitchell Lane LB $25.70 (978-1-58415-585-0). 32pp. After explaining what is happening to frogs, Whiting discusses the impact of global warming and other threats and looks ahead to the future; a "What You Can Do" section will help emerging activists. (Rev: LMC 1/08; SLJ 11/07)

21371 Winer, Yvonne. *Frogs Sing Songs* (PS–3). Illus. by Tony Oliver. 2003, Charlesbridge $16.95 (978-1-57091-548-2); paper $6.95 (978-1-57091-549-9). 32pp. Frogs and their sounds are presented in a lyrical text combined with realistic watercolor illustrations and a strong environmental message. (Rev: BL 4/1/03; HBG 10/03; SLJ 7/03) [597.8]

21372 Zollman, Pam. *A Tadpole Grows Up* (K–1). Series: Scholastic News Nonfiction Readers. 2005, Children's Pr. LB $20.00 (978-0-516-24947-6). 24pp. This photo-filled book introduces the life cycle of frogs and toads, focusing in particular on survival strategies of tadpoles. (Rev: SLJ 4/06) [597.8]

LIZARDS

21373 Bishop, Nic. *Lizards* (2–4). Illus. by author. 2010, Scholastic $17.99 (978-0-545-20634-1). 48pp. Wildlife photographer Nic Bishop presents a compelling look at the lizard world in this book that includes plenty of succinct scientific information. (Rev: BL 12/1/10*; HB 11–12/10; SLJ 10/1/10*) [597.95]

21374 Bodden, Valerie. *Komodo Dragons* (1–3). Illus. Series: Amazing Animals. 2013, Creative Education LB $17.95 (978-160818087-5). 24pp. An eye-catching introduction to these animals that will appeal to young and reluctant readers; includes a story from folklore. Lexile 597.95 (Rev: BL 4/15/13; LMC 10/13*)

21375 Collard, Sneed B. *Lizards* (4–7). Illus. 2012, Charlesbridge $16.95 (978-158089324-4); paper $7.95 (978-15808932-5-1). 48pp. A clear, well-designed introduction to lizards and their life cycle, habitats, diets, and so forth, with plenty of close-up photographs. e (Rev: BL 1/1/12; LMC 11–12/12; SLJ 5/1/12) [597.95]

21376 Cowley, Joy. *Chameleon, Chameleon* (K–2). Illus. 2005, Scholastic $16.95 (978-0-439-66653-4). 32pp. The panther chameleon of Madagascar is the focus of this compelling photo-essay. (Rev: BL 2/15/05; SLJ 4/05) [597.95]

21377 Crump, Marty. *Mysteries of the Komodo Dragon: The Biggest, Deadliest Lizard Gives Up Its Secrets*

(3–5). Illus. 2010, Boyds Mills $18.95 (978-159078757-1). 40pp. With fascinating facts, lively text, and color photographs, this volume describes the life of the lizard, scientific study of the animal, and conservation efforts. (Rev: BL 11/1/10; LMC 1–2/11; SLJ 11/1/10) [597.95]

21378 Gish, Melissa. *Komodo Dragons* (5–8). Illus. Series: Living Wild. 2011, Creative Education LB $23.95 (978-160818080-6). 48pp. Gish looks at komodo dragons' habitats, physical characteristics, behaviors, relationships with humans, endangered status, and role in folklore. (Rev: BL 12/1/11) [597.95]

21379 Kalman, Bobbie. *Endangered Komodo Dragons* (3–5). Illus. Series: Earth's Endangered Animals. 2004, Crabtree LB $25.27 (978-0-7787-1857-4); paper $6.95 (978-0-7787-1903-8). 32pp. In addition to discussion of their endangered status, this volume covers these animals' habitat, behavior, life cycle, and so forth. (Rev: SLJ 6/05)

21380 Lunis, Natalie. *Komodo Dragon: The World's Biggest Lizard* (K–2). Illus. Series: SuperSized! 2007, Bearport LB $21.28 (978-1-59716-392-7). 24pp. A fact-filled introduction to the big lizard, with eye-catching photographs. (Rev: SLJ 8/07)

21381 Macken, JoAnn Early. *Gila Monsters / Monstruos de Gila* (2–4). Trans. by Tatiana Acosta and Guillermo Gutiérrez. Series: Animals That Live in the Desert / Animales del desierto. 2005, Weekly Reader LB $21.00 (978-0-8368-4841-0). 24pp. A beginning book with facts about gila monsters in both English and Spanish. (Rev: SLJ 6/06) [597.95]

21382 Marsico, Katie. *Geckos* (3–5). Illus. Series: Nature's Children. 2013, Scholastic/Children's Press LB $28 (978-053123357-3); paper $6.95 (9780531251553). 48pp. With full-page photographs and clear text this book explores the characteristics and behaviors of these animals, their life cycle, their history, and relationship with humans. (Rev: BL 11/15/13) [597.95]

21383 Marsico, Katie. *A Komodo Dragon Hatchling Grows Up* (1–2). 2007, Children's Pr. LB $19.00 (978-0-531-17477-7). 24pp. The development of a Komodo dragon is the topic of this vocabulary-building book with interesting photographs. (Rev: SLJ 7/07)

21384 Mattern, Joanne. *Lizards* (3–6). Series: Animals, Animals. 2001, Benchmark LB $25.64 (978-0-7614-1259-5). 48pp. In addition to describing physical characteristics, behavior, habitat, and so forth of more than two dozen species, Mattern looks at related folklore and at the animals' relationship with humans. (Rev: HBG 10/02; SLJ 6/02) [597.95]

21385 Maynard, Thane. *Komodo Dragons* (3–4). Series: New Naturebooks. 2006, The Child's World LB $27.07 (978-1-59296-642-4). 32pp. An introductory overview of this large lizard, with vivid color photographs. (Rev: SLJ 2/07) [597.95]

21386 Welsbacher, Anne. *Komodo Dragons* (3–5). Series: Predators in the Wild. 2002, Capstone LB $23.93 (978-0-7368-1066-1). 32pp. Basic information about the komodo dragon's life, habitat, diet, and endangered status is presented in a format that will suit both browsers and report writers. (Rev: SLJ 8/02) [597.95]

SNAKES

21387 Behler, Deborah, and John Behler. *Snakes* (5–8). Series: AnimalWays. 2001, Marshall Cavendish LB $31.36 (978-0-7614-1265-6). 112pp. Brilliant photographs highlight this fine introduction to snakes, their habitats, behavior, species, evolution, and anatomy. (Rev: BL 3/15/02; HBG 10/02) [597.96]

21388 Bishop, Nic. *Nic Bishop Snakes* (2–4). Illus. by author. 2012, Scholastic $17.99 (978-0-545-20638-9). 48pp. Fascinating close-up photographs are accompanied by descriptions of snakes' anatomy and characteristics. Lexile 850L (Rev: BL 11/15/12; HB 1–2/13; SLJ 10/12*) [597.96]

21389 Blobaum, Cindy. *Awesome Snake Science! 40 Activities for Learning About Snakes* (5–8). Illus. 2012, Chicago Review paper $14.95 (978-1-56976-807-5). 130pp. Students learn about snakes and their biology through text, experiments, art projects, and games. e (Rev: LMC 5–6/13; SLJ 7/12) [597.96071]

21390 Bredeson, Carmen. *Fun Facts About Snakes!* (PS–2). Series: I Like Reptiles and Amphibians! 2007, Enslow LB $21.26 (978-0-7660-2787-9). 24pp. Eye-catching photographs and clear text make this a useful introduction for beginning readers. (Rev: SLJ 1/08) [597.96]

21391 de la Bedoyere, Camilla. *Snakelet to Snake* (1–3). Illus. Series: Life Cycles. 2012, Amicus/QEB LB $17.95 (978-160992046-3). 24pp. Double-page spreads with clear images trace snakes' life cycles. (Rev: BL 11/1/12) [597.96156]

21392 Editors of Time for Kids. *Snakes!* (1–3). Illus. Series: Time For Kids Science Scoops. 2005, HarperCollins $14.99 (978-0-06-057637-0); paper $3.99 (978-0-06-057636-3). 32pp. Simple text suitable for beginning readers and bright illustrations present basic information on snakes, plus a profile of a scientist who works with them.

21393 Feldman, Heather. *Cottonmouths* (3–5). Series: The Really Wild Life of Snakes. 2004, Rosen LB $21.25 (978-0-8239-6722-3). 24pp. The behavior, physical characteristics, and habitat of the cottonmouth are featured in this colorfully illustrated account. Also use *Diamondbacks* and *Milk Snakes* (both 2004). (Rev: SLJ 2/05) [597.96]

21394 Fiedler, Julie. *Vipers* (2–4). Series: Scary Snakes. 2007, Rosen LB $21.25 (978-1-4042-3833-6). 24pp. A basic introduction to vipers' characteristics, habitat, diet, and so forth, suitable for beginning report writers. Also use *Rattlesnakes* and *Boas* (2007). (Rev: SLJ 4/08) [597.96]

21395 Gibbons, Gail. *Snakes* (1–3). Illus. by author. 2008, Holiday $16.95 (978-0-8234-2122-0). 32pp. Snake basics are delivered in straightforward style and illustrated with dozens of different species. (Rev: BL 2/15/08; SLJ 4/08) [597.96]

21396 Greenaway, Theresa. *Snakes* (4–7). Series: The Secret World of . . . 2001, Raintree LB $18.98 (978-0-7368-3510-7). A look at the world of snakes with material on their structure, habitats, behavior, food, mating habits, and enemies. (Rev: BL 10/15/01) [597.96]

21397 Hamilton, Sue. *Bitten by a Rattlesnake* (4–7). Series: Close Encounters of the Wild Kind. 2010, ABDO LB $27.07 (978-1-60453-930-1). 32pp. Exciting stories and graphic photographs add high-interest appeal to the information about these snakes and advice on avoiding and surviving such an attack. (Rev: LMC 10/10; SLJ 5/10) [597.96]

21398 Macken, JoAnn Early. *Rattlesnakes / Serpientes de cascabel* (2–4). Trans. by Tatiana Acosta and Guillermo Gutiérrez. Series: Animals That Live in the Desert / Animales del desierto. 2005, Weekly Reader LB $21.00 (978-0-8368-4843-4). 24pp. A beginning book with facts about rattlesnakes in both English and Spanish. (Rev: SLJ 6/06) [597.96]

21399 Mason, Adrienne. *Snakes* (2–4). Illus. by Nancy Gray Ogle. Series: Wildlife. 2005, Kids Can $10.95 (978-1-55337-627-9); paper $6.95 (978-1-55337-628-6). 32pp. In addition to introducing the physical characteristics and behavior of snakes, this overview discusses their usefulness to humans and the reasons why people are afraid of snakes. (Rev: BL 5/1/05; SLJ 6/05) [597.96]

21400 Montgomery, Sy. *The Snake Scientist* (5–8). Series: Scientists in the Field. 1999, Houghton Mifflin $16.00 (978-0-395-87169-0). This account captures the excitement of scientific discovery by focusing on a zoologist and young students who are studying the red-sided garter snake in Canada. (Rev: BCCB 4/99; BL 2/15/99; HB 7–8/99; HBG 9/99; SLJ 5/99) [597.96]

21401 Munro, Roxie. *Slithery Snakes* (1–4). Illus. by author. 2013, Amazon/Two Lions $17.99 (978-147781658-5). Full of facts and illustrations, this title introduces nine different types of snakes and challenges readers to guess which they are. e (Rev: BL 10/1/13; LMC 5–6/14; SLJ 11/13) [597.96]

21402 Pascoe, Elaine, ed. *Into Wild Arizona* (3–6). Series: The Jeff Corwin Experience. 2004, Gale LB $24.95 (978-1-4103-0058-4). 48pp. Jeff Corwin of TV's *Animal Planet* guides a tour of the wildlife of Arizona, concentrating on its snakes. (Rev: SLJ 4/04)

21403 Patent, Dorothy Hinshaw. *Slinky Scaly Slithery Snakes* (K–3). Illus. by Kendahl Jan Jubb. 2000, Walker LB $17.85 (978-0-8027-8744-6). 32pp. This colorful introduction to snakes explains how they move, their body parts, where they live, and how they can eat animals larger than themselves. (Rev: BL 12/1/00; HBG 3/01; SLJ 3/01) [597.96]

21404 Pipe, Jim. *The Giant Book of Snakes and Slithery Creatures* (4–8). 1998, Millbrook LB $27.90 (978-0-7613-0804-1). This richly illustrated, oversize volume contains details about snakes, lizards, and amphibians. (Rev: BL 8/98; HBG 9/98; SLJ 12/98) [597.9]

21405 Pringle, Laurence. *Snakes! Strange and Wonderful* (2–5). Illus. by Meryl Henderson. Series: Strange and

Wonderful. 2004, Boyds Mills $15.95 (978-1-59078-003-9). 32pp. Realistic illustrations and lively, concise text present an interesting and fact-filled introduction to snakes and their diverse behaviors. (Rev: BL 12/1/04*; SLJ 9/04) [597.96]

21406 Ruth, Maria Mudd. *Snakes* (3–6). Series: Animals, Animals. 2001, Benchmark LB $25.64 (978-0-7614-1262-5). 48pp. In addition to describing physical characteristics, behavior, habitat, locomotion, and so forth of more than a dozen species, Mattern looks at related folklore and at the animals' relationship with humans. (Rev: HBG 10/02; SLJ 6/02) [597.96]

21407 Smith, Molly. *Green Anaconda: The World's Heaviest Snake* (K–2). Illus. Series: SuperSized! 2007, Bearport LB $21.28 (978-1-59716-391-0). 24pp. Report writers will get lots of mileage from this introduction to the anaconda, filled with facts about and photographs of the scary snake. (Rev: SLJ 7/07)

21408 Thomson, Sarah L. *Amazing Snakes!* (K–2). Illus. Series: I Can Read Book. 2006, HarperCollins $15.99 (978-0-06-054462-1). 32pp. This photo-filled beginning reader introduces young students to snakes, offering easy-to-understand basic information about the reptiles' physical characteristics and behavior. (Rev: BL 12/15/05; SLJ 7/06) [597.96]

21409 Welsbacher, Anne. *Anacondas* (3–6). Series: Predators in the Wild. 2001, Capstone LB $23.93 (978-0-7368-0785-2). 32pp. Myths about the anaconda are presented along with facts in this general introduction to the snake's characteristics and habitat. (Rev: HBG 10/01; SLJ 1/02) [597.96]

TURTLES AND TORTOISES

21410 Bredeson, Carmen. *Fun Facts About Turtles!* (1–3). Series: I Like Reptiles and Amphibians! 2007, Enslow LB $21.26 (978-0-7660-2785-5). 24pp. The crisp narrative uses a question-and-answer format to provide basic information about turtles; illustrated with color photographs. (Rev: LMC 11/07; SLJ 10/07) [597.92]

21411 Cerullo, Mary. *Sea Turtles: Ocean Nomads* (3–6). Photos by Jeffrey L. Rotman. Illus. 2003, Dutton $17.99 (978-0-525-46649-9). 32pp. A handsome photo-essay on these endangered animals and their fascinating lives. (Rev: BL 5/15/03; HBG 10/03; SLJ 7/03) [597.92]

21412 Christopherson, Sara Cohen. *Top 50 Reasons to Care About Marine Turtles* (5–8). Series: Top 50 Reasons to Care About Endangered Animals. 2010, Enslow LB $31.93 (978-0-7660-3455-6). 104pp. Threats to marine turtles' survival are the main focus of this volume that also discusses the animals' biology, habitat, and behavior. Also use *Top 50 Reasons to Care About Whales and Dolphins* (2010). (Rev: LMC 3–4/10) [597.928]

21413 Chrustowski, Rick. *Turtle Crossing* (1–3). Illus. 2006, Holt $16.95 (978-0-8050-7498-7). 32pp. A painted turtle's life is portrayed in large-scale art and a simple narrative that offers a satisfying circular structure. (Rev: BL 3/1/06; SLJ 6/06) [597.92]

21414 Cooper, Jason. *Loggerhead Turtle* (1–3). Series: Life Cycles. 2002, Rourke LB $17.95 (978-1-58952-354-8). 24pp. Handsome photographs and simple text describe the life cycle, habitat, appearance, and behavior of these animals. (Rev: SLJ 12/02) [597.92]

21415 Davies, Nicola. *One Tiny Turtle* (PS–4). Illus. by Janet Chapman. 2001, Candlewick $15.99 (978-0-7636-1549-9). 32pp. An appealing overview of the loggerhead sea turtle, introduced by the story of one turtle's life from hatching to laying her own eggs on the beach of her birth. (Rev: BCCB 11/01; BL 12/1/01; HBG 3/02; SLJ 12/01) [597.92]

21416 Hall, Kirsten. *Leatherback Turtle: The World's Heaviest Reptile* (K–2). Illus. Series: SuperSized! 2007, Bearport LB $21.28 (978-1-59716-393-4). 24pp. Report writers will get lots of mileage from this introduction to the leatherback turtle, filled with facts about and photographs of this big reptile. (Rev: SLJ 7/07)

21417 Hickman, Pamela. *Turtle Rescue: Changing the Future for Endangered Wildlife* (4–8). Series: Firefly Animal Rescue. 2006, Firefly $19.95 (978-1-55297-916-7); paper $9.95 (978-1-55297-915-0). 64pp. Hickman provides a detailed but accessible overview of the dangers facing turtles around the world and what is being done to protect them. (Rev: SLJ 6/06) [597.92]

21418 Jacobs, Lee. *Turtles* (3–5). Series: Wild America. 2003, Gale LB $24.94 (978-1-56711-571-0). 24pp. A brief and basic introduction to turtles and their habitat, diet, physical appearance, and behavior. (Rev: SLJ 11/03) [597.92]

21419 Kalman, Bobbie. *The Life Cycle of a Sea Turtle* (2–4). Illus. Series: The Life Cycle. 2001, Crabtree LB $25.27 (978-0-7787-0652-6); paper $6.95 (978-0-7787-0682-3). 32pp. After a general description of the sea turtle, the author clearly explains its life cycle and discusses what can be done to curb human encroachment. (Rev: SLJ 6/02) [597.92]

21420 Korman, Susan. *Box Turtle at Silver Pond Lake* (K–3). Illus. by Stephen Marchesi. Series: Smithsonian Backyard. 2001, Smithsonian Institution $15.95 (978-1-56899-860-2). 32pp. A female box turtle's daily life is presented in simple text with realistic illustrations. (Rev: BL 9/15/01; HBG 10/01; SLJ 8/01)

21421 Lang, Aubrey. *Baby Sea Turtle* (PS–1). Illus. Series: Nature Babies. 2007, Fitzhenry & Whiteside $13.95 (978-1-55041-728-9); paper $7.95 (978-1-55041-746-3). 32pp. This volume full of eye-catching photographs provides fascinating information about the leatherback sea turtle's life cycle. (Rev: BL 5/15/07; SLJ 7/07) [597.92]

21422 Laskey, Elizabeth. *Sea Turtles* (4–6). Illus. Series: Sea Creatures. 2003, Heinemann LB $22.79 (978-1-4034-0962-1). 32pp. A clear overview of sea turtles and their lives, using a question-and-answer format. (Rev: HBG 10/03; SLJ 11/03) [597.9]

21423 Lockwood, Sophie. *Sea Turtles* (4–7). Illus. Series: World of Reptiles. 2006, Child's World LB $29.93 (978-1-59296-550-2). In addition to the kind of information needed for reports, Lockwood discusses conservation, how scientists track turtles, and the turtle's appearances in folklore and art. (Rev: BL 4/1/06) [597.92]

21424 Mason, Janeen. *Ocean Commotion: Sea Turtles* (3–5). Illus. 2006, Pelican $15.95 (978-1-58980-434-0). 32pp. Follow the journey of a female loggerhead sea turtle from the time she hatches on a Florida beach to the day she returns to mate and lay eggs of her own. (Rev: BL 12/1/06; SLJ 12/06) [597.92]

21425 Monroe, Mary Alice. *Turtle Summer: A Journal for My Daughter* (2–3). Photos by Barbara J. Bergwerf. Illus. by Lisa Downey. 2007, Sylvan Dell $15.95 (978-0-9777423-5-6); paper $8.95 (978-0-9777423-7-0). In a scrapbook format, a mother organizes photos and information about the sea turtles that she and her daughter observe on the beach. Readers are encouraged to compile their own scrapbooks about what they observe in nature. (Rev: SLJ 6/07)

21426 Noonan, Diana. *The Green Turtle* (2–4). Series: Life Cycles. 2002, Chelsea LB $23.00 (978-0-7910-6967-7). 32pp. The story of this endangered reptile that lives and mates in the sea is told with material on how the female goes ashore to lay her eggs and what happens when the young hatch. (Rev: BL 12/15/02; HBG 3/03) [597.92]

21427 Rathmell, Donna. *Carolina's Story: Sea Turtles Get Sick Too!* (2–4). Illus. 2005, Sylvan Dell $15.95 (978-0-9764943-0-0). 32pp. A sick loggerhead turtle's rehabilitation in South Carolina is documented in sensitive text and photographs. (Rev: BL 8/05; SLJ 11/05)

21428 Rebman, Renee C. *Turtles and Tortoises* (3–5). Series: Animals, Animals. 2006, Benchmark LB $19.95 (978-0-7614-2239-6). 48pp. An introduction to the anatomy, behavior, and habitat of turtles and tortoises, in addition to other aspects of these animals and their lives. Color photographs give readers a close-up look. (Rev: SLJ 5/07)

21429 Sayre, April P. *Turtle, Turtle, Watch Out!* (PS–2). Illus. by Lee Christiansen. 2000, Orchard LB $17.99 (978-0-531-33285-6). 32pp. A lovely nature book with some fictional touches that covers the life cycle of a sea turtle and how a boy protected one turtle's eggs so they could hatch. (Rev: BL 8/00; HBG 3/01; SLJ 10/00) [597.92]

21430 Stefoff, Rebecca. *Turtles* (4–8). Illus. Series: AnimalWays. 2007, Marshall Cavendish LB $23.95 (978-0-7614-2539-7). Report writers will find plenty of valuable information about turtles' anatomy, habitat, evolution, and appearances in literature and legend as well as discussion of conservation efforts and many attractive photographs. (Rev: BL 2/8/08) [597.92]

21431 Stewart, Melissa. *A Place for Turtles* (1–4). Illus. by Higgins Bond. 2013, Peachtree $16.95 (978-1-56145-693-2). 32pp. In addition to an overview of turtles and their characteristics, Stewart provides interesting information on ecological challenges to their survival. (Rev: BL 3/15/13; SLJ 5/13) [597.92]

21432 Theodorou, Rod. *Leatherback Sea Turtle* (2–4). Illus. Series: Animals in Danger. 2001, Heinemann LB $21.36 (978-1-57572-272-6). 32pp. Basic information about the sea turtle and its endangered status. (Rev: BL 7/01; HBG 10/01) [597.2]

Animal Behavior and Anatomy

GENERAL

21433 Allman, Toney. *Animal Life in Groups* (5–8). Series: Animal Behavior. 2009, Chelsea House $32.95 (978-1-60413-142-0). 110pp. Examining the reasons why animals choose to live in groups, this volume discusses safety in numbers and various ways animals can cooperate, looking in particular at colonies, schools and flocks, herds, predator groups, and primate societies. (Rev: LMC 11–12/09) [591.5]

21434 Arndt, Ingo. *Best Foot Forward: Exploring Feet, Flippers, and Claws* (1–3). Trans. by J. Alison James. Illus. by author. 2013, Holiday $16.95 (978-082342857-1). 32pp. Part guessing game, part instructional, this is an eye-catching exploration of animal feet and their functions. (Rev: BL 9/15/13; SLJ 10/13) [591.47]

21435 Arnold, Caroline. *Did You Hear That? Animals with Super Hearing* (3–5). Illus. by Cathy Trachok. 2001, Charlesbridge $16.95 (978-1-57091-404-1). 32pp. This book full of color pictures introduces bats' and dolphins' echolocation skills, rhinos' ability to communicate over long distances, and other facts to do with animal hearing. (Rev: BL 12/1/01; HBG 3/02; SLJ 8/01) [591.59]

21436 Arnosky, Jim. *Wild Tracks! A Guide to Nature's Footprints* (1–3). Illus. by author. 2008, Sterling $14.95 (978-1-4027-3985-9). 32pp. With full-color paintings, pencil sketches, fold-out pages, and accessible text, Arnosky provides information about the tracks of a variety of North American animals. (Rev: BL 4/1/08; SLJ 6/08) [591.47]

21437 Aruego, Jose, and Ariane Dewey. *Weird Friends: Unlikely Allies in the Animal Kingdom* (1–3). Illus. 2002, Harcourt $16.00 (978-0-15-202128-3). 40pp. Fourteen symbiotic relationships among animals are explained and brightly illustrated. (Rev: BL 5/15/02; HBG 10/02; SLJ 4/02) [577.8]

21438 Barner, Bob. *Animal Baths* (PS–K). Illus. by author. 2011, Chronicle $15.99 (978-1-4521-0056-2). Unpaged. Barner illustrates how a variety of animals clean themselves. e (Rev: LMC 3–4/12; SLJ 12/1/11) [591.5]

21439 Batten, Mary. *Please Don't Wake the Animals: A Book About Sleep* (PS–3). Illus. by Higgins Bond. 2008, Peachtree $16.95 (978-1-56145-393-1). 32pp. A look at how a variety of animals sleep (by day, by night; in danger, in safety), with information on hibernation too. (Rev: BL 7/08; LMC 5/08; SLJ 8/08) [591.5]

21440 Berkes, Marianne. *Going Home: The Mystery of Animal Migration* (K–2). Illus. by Jennifer DiRubbio. 2010, Dawn $16.95 (978-1-58469-126-6); paper $8.95 (978-1-58469-127-3). 32pp. Poems relate various animals' migratory experiences and are supported by extensive back matter including maps. (Rev: BLO 2/15/10; LMC 10/10; SLJ 5/1/10) [591.56]

21441 Black, Sonia. *Animal Mysteries: A Chapter Book* (3–5). Series: True Tales. 2005, Children's Pr. LB $22.50 (978-0-516-25187-5). 48pp. This interesting book looks at examples of amazing animal behavior, such as the loggerhead turtle's ability to navigate by using the ocean's magnetic fields. (Rev: SLJ 1/06) [590]

21442 Bonnett-Rampersaud, Louise. *How Do You Sleep?* (PS). Illus. by Kristin Kest. 2005, Marshall Cavendish $14.95 (978-0-7614-5231-7). 32pp. A look at the sleeping habits of seven creatures, including human siblings, bears, and birds. (Rev: BL 10/1/05; SLJ 11/05) [573.8]

21443 Bonsignore, Joan. *Stick Out Your Tongue! Fantastic Facts, Features, and Functions of Animal and Human Tongues* (2–3). Illus. by John T. Ward. 2001, Peachtree $15.95 (978-1-56145-230-9). 32pp. A look at how animals of all kinds use their tongues with comparisons to similar human behavior. (Rev: BL 8/01; HBG 3/02; SLJ 11/01) [612.8]

21444 Burnie, David. *How Animals Work: Why and How Animals Do the Things They Do* (5–8). Illus. 2010, DK $24.99 (978-0-7566-5897-7). 192pp. This highly visual, oversize volume covers everything from animal anatomy, locomotion, diet, and habitat to evolution and communication. (Rev: BL 9/1/10; SLJ 12/1/10) [571.1]

21445 Butler, John. *Can You Cuddle Like a Koala?* (PS). Illus. by author. 2003, Peachtree $15.95 (978-1-56145-298-9). In this charming blend of rhyming text and colorful artwork, young readers will learn how various animals move. (Rev: HBG 4/04; SLJ 1/04)

21446 Carlson-Voiles, Polly. *Someone Walks By: The Wonders of Winter Wildlife* (K–3). Illus. by author. 2008, Raven $18.95 (978-0-9801045-5-4); paper $12.95 (978-0-9801045-6-1). This attractive picture book follows a variety of animals as they adapt to winter living in the northern woods. (Rev: BL 12/1/08; SLJ 6/09) [591.723]

21447 Carney, Elizabeth. *Great Migrations: Whales, Wildebeests, Butterflies, Elephants, and Other Amazing Animals on the Move* (3–5). Illus. 2010, National Geographic $18.95 (978-142630700-3); LB $27.90 (978-142630701-0). 48pp. The migration stories of eight diverse animals, ranging from army ants to Mali elephants, are presented in this attractive book with maps, facts, and clear text. (Rev: BL 12/15/10) [591.56]

21448 Collard, Sneed B. *Animals Asleep* (PS–3). Illus. by Anik McGrory. 2004, Houghton $15.00 (978-0-618-27697-4). 32pp. Readers can choose between brief, large-print information and more detailed smaller text in this chatty overview of animals' sleeping habits. (Rev: BL 3/1/04; SLJ 5/04) [591.56]

21449 Collard, Sneed B. *Teeth* (1–3). Illus. by Phyllis V. Saroff. 2008, Charlesbridge $16.95 (978-1-58089-120-2); paper $7.95 (978-1-58089-121-9). 32pp. Animal teeth are the focus of this informative and colorful large-format picture book. (Rev: BL 3/1/08; SLJ 2/08) [591.4]

21450 Collard, Sneed B., III. *Leaving Home* (PS–3). Illus. by Joan Dunning. 2002, Houghton $15.00 (978-0-618-

11454-2). 32pp. This unique book for younger readers explores the various ways in which animals leave their homes upon maturation. (Rev: BL 3/1/02; HBG 10/02; SLJ 4/02) [591.5]

21451 Cooper, Jason. *Antlers and Horns* (K–2). Series: Let's Look at Animals. 2007, Rourke LB $21.35 (978-1-60044-168-4). 24pp. Photos of animals that have antlers and horns are accompanied by brief text explaining what they are used for. (Rev: SLJ 6/07)

21452 Cooper, Jason. *Hooves and Claws* (K–2). Series: Let's Look at Animals. 2007, Rourke LB $21.35 (978-1-60044-173-8). 24pp. Photos of animals' hooves and claws are accompanied by brief text explaining what they are used for. (Rev: SLJ 6/07)

21453 Crump, Donald J., ed. *How Animals Behave: A New Look at Wildlife* (5–8). 1984, National Geographic LB $12.50 (978-0-87044-505-7). A general, colorful introduction to why and how animals perform such functions as courting, living together, and caring for their young. [591.5]

21454 Crump, Donald J., ed. *Secrets of Animal Survival* (4–8). 1983, National Geographic LB $12.50 (978-0-87044-431-9). The survival tactics of animals in five geographical environments are discussed.

21455 Dale, Jay. *Top 10 Minibeasts* (3–6). Illus. Series: Deadly and Incredible Animals. 2012, Black Rabbit LB $27.10 (978-159920411-6). 32pp. This books looks at the 10 deadliest small animals, starting with the Japanese giant hornet and counting down through spiders, bees, worms, and scorpions. (Rev: BLO 3/1/12) [595]

21456 Davies, Nicola. *Extreme Animals: The Toughest Creatures on Earth* (3–5). Illus. by Neal Layton. 2006, Candlewick $12.99 (978-0-7636-3067-6). 58pp. Reveals some of the world's most resilient creatures and how they've adapted to habitats that humans couldn't last minutes in. (Rev: BL 12/1/06; SLJ 12/06*) [590]

21457 de la Bedoyere, Camilla. *100 Things You Should Know About Nocturnal Animals* (4–6). Illus. Series: 100 Things You Should Know About. 2009, Mason Crest $19.95 (978-1-4222-1523-4). 48pp. Good for browsers, this volume looks at the distinctive senses of nocturnal animals (sight, smell, and so forth) and provides photographs, quizzes, activities, and brain teasers. (Rev: LMC 5–6/10; SLJ 2/10) [591.5]

21458 de la Bedoyere, Camilla. *Smartest and Silliest* (2–5). Illus. Series: Animal Opposites. 2010, Black Rabbit LB $27.10 (978-159566761-8). 32pp. A fascinating, well-designed introduction to animal intelligence in all its amazing forms. (Rev: BLO 3/14/11; LMC 5–6/11) [590]

21459 Eamer, Claire. *Spiked Scorpions and Walking Whales: Modern Animals, Ancient Animals, and Water* (4–6). 2009, Annick $19.95 (978-1-55451-206-5); paper $9.95 (978-1-55451-205-8). 100pp. Four categories of animals that bridge the gap between terrestrial and aquatic are explored in this adaptation-focused book. (Rev: BLO 11/5/09; SLJ 2/10; VOYA 6/10) [591.3]

21460 Ehrlich, Fred. *You Can't Use Your Brain If You're a Jellyfish* (K–3). Illus. by Amanda Haley. 2005, Blue Apple $15.95 (978-1-59354-090-6). 44pp. A lighthearted but fact-packed look at the brains of a diverse range of creatures — from invertebrates to humans. (Rev: BL 12/1/05; SLJ 11/05) [612.8]

21461 Feldman, Thea. *Strangest Animals* (1–3). Illus. 2013, Sterling $9.95 (978-145490636-0). 32pp. Using simple sentence structures and high-quality colored photographs, Feldman explains and describes various animals and their strange talents, from a frog with a see-through body to a mimic octopus that transforms into a flounder. (Rev: BL 10/1/13) [591]

21462 Flegg, Jim. *Animal Movement* (4–7). Illus. by David Hosking. Series: Wild World. 1991, Millbrook LB $17.90 (978-1-878137-21-0). Various ways animals move and at what speeds are discussed in this well-illustrated book. (Rev: BL 1/1/91; SLJ 2/92) [591.18]

21463 Ganeri, Anita. *Animals* (4–7). Series: Inside and Outside Guide. 2006, Heinemann LB $29.29 (978-1-4034-9084-1). This attractive guide provides in-depth introductions to 12 animals, with double-page spreads focusing on each animal's identifying characteristics and behaviors. (Rev: BL 10/15/06) [571.3]

21464 Gilpin, Daniel. *Life-Size Killer Creatures* (3–6). Illus. 2006, Sterling $9.95 (978-1-4027-2701-6). 28pp. This oversized book with numerous eye-catching foldouts shows life-size illustrations of several predatory animals and offers basic facts on each. (Rev: BL 12/1/06; SLJ 12/1/06) [590]

21465 Goldstein, Natalie. *Animal Hunting and Feeding* (5–8). Series: Animal Behavior. 2009, Chelsea House $32.95 (978-1-60413-143-7). 110pp. Examining the ways in which animals hunt and feed, this volume discusses waiting for food, sharing and taking, plant-eating animals, generalists and specialists, and scavengers and decomposers. (Rev: LMC 11–12/09) [591.5]

21466 Goodman, Susan E. *Claws, Coats, and Camouflage: The Ways Animals Fit into Their World* (2–5). Illus. by Michael Doolittle. 2001, Millbrook $22.90 (978-0-7613-1865-1). 48pp. The ways in which animals (and finally, humans) adapt to their worlds are presented in broad categories with brief text and photographs. (Rev: BL 12/1/01; HBG 3/02; SLJ 1/02) [591.4]

21467 Gould, Francesca, and David Haviland. *Why Dogs Eat Poop: Gross but True Things You Never Knew about Animals* (1–4). Illus. by JP Coovert. 2013, Putnam paper $8.99 (978-03991653-0-6). 176pp. A collection of facts and information about little-known animal behaviors depicted through cartoon images and formatted in a question-and-answer style. e (Rev: BL 10/1/13) [591.5]

21468 Hall, Kirsten. *Tracking Animals: A Chapter Book* (3–5). Series: True Tales. 2005, Children's Pr. LB $22.50 (978-0-516-25186-8). 48pp. An interesting exploration of scientists' ability to track animals and study their behavior using technology. (Rev: SLJ 1/06) [591.5]

21469 Hartley, Karen, and Chris Macro. *Hearing in Living Things* (K–2). Series: Sense. 2000, Heinemann LB $21.36 (978-1-57572-246-7). 32pp. An overview that explains hearing in animals and uses as examples such animals as bats, frogs, insects, owls, elephants, and humans. Also use *Tasting in Living Things* (2000). (Rev: HBG 3/01; SLJ 8/00) [591]

21470 Hickman, Pamela. *Animals Eating* (3–5). Illus. 2001, Kids Can $10.95 (978-1-55074-577-1); paper $5.95 (978-1-55074-579-5). 40pp. After a general discussion of animal mouths, tongues, and teeth, this book explains how various animals eat and drink. It also gives a number of interesting simple activities. (Rev: BL 3/15/01; HBG 10/01) [591.5]

21471 Hickman, Pamela. *Animals in Motion: How Animals Swim, Jump, Slither and Glide* (3–5). Illus. 2000, Kids Can $10.95 (978-1-55074-573-3); paper $5.95 (978-1-55074-575-7). 40pp. This book on animal locomotion classifies animals by how they move — running, hopping, slipping, swimming, and climbing, for example. (Rev: BL 5/1/00; HBG 9/00; SLJ 9/00) [573.7]

21472 Hirschi, Ron. *When Morning Comes* (1–4). Photos by Thomas D. Mangelsen. 2000, Boyds Mills $16.95 (978-1-56397-767-1). Using striking photographs, this book on nature study shows various forms of wildlife in the morning. A companion volume is *When Night Comes* (2000). (Rev: BL 10/15/00; HBG 3/01; SLJ 12/00) [508]

21473 Hirschi, Ron. *When Night Comes* (1–3). Illus. by Thomas D. Mangelsen. 2000, Boyds Mills $16.95 (978-1-56397-766-4). 32pp. The activities of such animals as otters, raccoons, and coyotes at night are described in excellent photos and a simple text. (Rev: BL 10/15/00; HBG 3/01; SLJ 12/00) [591.5]

21474 Hulbert, Laura. *Who Has These Feet?* (PS–2). Illus. by Erik Brooks. 2011, Henry Holt $16.99 (978-0-8050-8907-3). 42pp. Animals' feet and their function are the focus of this well-illustrated book that uses a guessing game format. (Rev: BL 8/11; LMC 11–12/11; SLJ 9/1/11) [590]

21475 Hulbert, Laura. *Who Has This Tail?* (PS–2). Illus. by Erik Brooks. 2012, Henry Holt $16.99 (978-0-8050-9429-9). 44pp. Readers are challenged to identify the animals that own nine tails. e (Rev: BLO 9/15/12; LMC 5–6/13; SLJ 1/13) [590]

21476 James, Ray. *Teeth and Fangs* (K–2). Series: Let's Look at Animals. 2007, Rourke LB $21.35 (978-1-60044-174-5). 24pp. Photos of animals' teeth — and, in some cases, fangs — are accompanied by brief text explaining what they are used for. (Rev: SLJ 6/07)

21477 Jenkins, Steve, and Robin Page. *Animals in Flight* (PS–3). Illus. by Steve Jenkins. 2001, Houghton $16.00 (978-0-618-12351-3). 32pp. The wonder of flight is explained in simple prose and sensational cut-paper collages. (Rev: BCCB 12/01; BL 12/15/01; HBG 3/02; SLJ 11/01) [573.7]

21478 Jenkins, Steve, and Robin Page. *How to Clean a Hippopotamus: A Look at Unusual Animal Partnerships* (K–3). Illus. by Steve Jenkins. 2010, Houghton Mifflin $16 (978-0-547-24515-7). 32pp. A compelling, close-up look at symbiotic relationships between animals. **e** Lexile GN950L (Rev: BL 3/15/10*; SLJ 4/1/10*) [591.7]

21479 Jenkins, Steve, and Robin Page. *Move!* (PS–2). Illus. 2006, Houghton $16.00 (978-0-618-64637-1). 32pp. This engaging picture book shows diverse members of the animal kingdom in motion. (Rev: BL 3/15/06; SLJ 6/06*) [573.7]

21480 Jenkins, Steve, and Robin Page. *Time for a Bath* (K–3). Illus. by Steve Jenkins. 2011, Houghton Mifflin $12.99. (978-0-547-25037-3). 24pp. Well, how do animals take baths? Eye-catching illustrations show various surprising techniques. Also use *Time to Sleep* (2011). **e** (Rev: LMC 10/11; SLJ 6/11) [591.56]

21481 Jenkins, Steve, and Robin Page. *Time to Eat* (PS–3). Illus. by Steve Jenkins. 2011, Houghton Mifflin $12.99 (978-0-547-25032-8). 24pp. This small, square book with beautiful collage illustrations explores the eating habits of a variety of animals, including a baby blue whale, an anaconda, and an ostrich. (Rev: BL 2/15/11*; SLJ 5/1/11) [591.5]

21482 Jocelyn, Marthe. *Eats* (K–1). Illus. by Tom Slaughter. 2007, Tundra $15.95 (978-0-88776-820-0). A simple look at who eats what — worms eat apples, birds eat worms — with appealing illustrations. (Rev: SLJ 12/07)

21483 Johnson, Rebecca L. *Zombie Makers: True Stories of Nature's Undead* (4–8). Illus. 2012, Millbrook LB $30.60 (978-076138633-9). 48pp. A variety of different parasitic creatures that turn their hosts into some form of "zombie" are profiled in this fascinating title. ALA Notable Children's Book. **e** (Rev: BLO 10/1/12; SLJ 10/12*; VOYA 2/13) [578.6]

21484 Kalman, Bobbie. *How Do Animals Adapt?* (1–3). Series: Science of Living Things. 2000, Crabtree LB $25.27 (978-0-86505-980-1); paper $6.95 (978-0-86505-957-3). 32pp. This beginning science book on animal adaptations includes camouflage, hibernation, and migration. (Rev: SLJ 11/00) [591]

21485 Kalman, Bobbie. *How Do Animals Find Food?* (2–4). Illus. Series: The Science of Living Things. 2001, Crabtree LB $25.27 (978-0-86505-986-3); paper $6.95 (978-0-86505-963-4). Colorful illustrations present details of animals of various kinds and their ways of killing and devouring their prey. (Rev: SLJ 12/01) [591.5]

21486 Kaner, Etta. *Animal Groups: How Animals Live Together* (K–3). Illus. by Pat Stephens. 2004, Kids Can $10.95 (978-1-55337-337-7); paper $5.95 (978-1-55337-338-4). For browsers, this is an interesting introduction to how animals behave, from hunting to grooming to raising young. (Rev: SLJ 5/04) [591.56]

21487 Karwoski, Gail. *River Beds: Sleeping in the World's Rivers* (1–3). Illus. by Connie McLennan. 2008, Sylvan Dell $16.95 (978-0-9777423-4-9); paper $8.95 (978-1-934359-31-0). 32pp. It's evening and a boy goes around the world in a rowboat visiting animals who make their homes in or near the water. (Rev: BL 8/08; LMC 10/08) [591.76]

21488 Karwoski, Gail. *Water Beds: Sleeping in the Ocean* (PS–1). Illus. by Connie McLennan. 2005, Sylvan Dell $15.95 (978-0-9764943-1-7). 32pp. An educational and attractive bedtime book that conveys facts about the sleeping habits of water mammals. (Rev: SLJ 6/06) [599.5]

21489 Kenah, Katherine. *Predator Attack!* (K–2). Illus. Series: Extreme Readers. 2004, McGraw-Hill paper $3.95 (978-0-7696-3176-9). 32pp. This photo-filled book introduces, with drama, such predators as the shark, tiger, alligator, cheetah, and polar bear. (Rev: BL 4/15/04) [591.5]

21490 Kenney, Karen Latchana. *Animal Tracks* (PS–2). Illus. Series: Our Animal World. 2011, Amicus $16.95 (978-160753142-5). 24pp. For beginning readers, this simple text with photographs discusses animal tracks and what they tell us. (Rev: BL 10/15/11) [591.47]

21491 Kudlinski, Kathleen V. *The Sunset Switch* (PS–2). Illus. by Lindy Burnett. 2005, NorthWord $15.95 (978-1-55971-916-2). Some animals settle in for the night while their nocturnal friends set off to hunt in this book that can double as a bedtime story and inspiration to learn more about animals. (Rev: SLJ 7/05) [591.5]

21492 McGrath, Susan. *The Amazing Things Animals Do* (4–7). 1989, National Geographic $8.95 (978-0-87044-709-9). Unusual animal behavior is shown in such areas as communication, motion, raising young, and survival. (Rev: SLJ 2/90) [591.5]

21493 McPhee, Margaret. *Show-Offs* (2–4). Illus. Series: Animal Planet: Weird and Wonderful. 2011, Kingfisher $12.99 (978-075346722-0). 64pp. Looks at the how different animals use posture, plumage, movements, and so forth to attract and repel other animals. (Rev: BL 10/1/11) [591]

21494 Markle, Sandra. *Animal Heroes: True Rescue Stories* (4–7). 2009, Lerner LB $29.27 (978-0-8225-7884-0). 64pp. A compelling collection of stories of animals saving human lives — from a dog on 9/11 to a gorilla, a cat, and dolphins; with factual information about each animal. (Rev: BL 7/08; LMC 3–4/09) [636.088]

21495 Marsh, Laura. *Amazing Animal Journeys* (2–4). Illus. 2010, National Geographic LB $11.90 (978-1-4263-0742-3); paper $3.99 (978-1-4263-0741-6). 48pp. Zebras, red crabs, and walruses are featured in this colorful account of unusual animal migrations. (Rev: BL 12/1/10; LMC 5–6/11; SLJ 3/1/11) [591.56]

21496 Matero, Robert. *Animals Asleep* (3–6). Illus. 2000, Millbrook LB $25.90 (978-0-7613-1652-7). 80pp. Covers the sleep and rest habits of humans and animals, including bears, woodchucks, bats, hummingbirds, lobsters, and frogs. (Rev: BL 11/1/00; HBG 3/01; SLJ 2/01) [579.5]

21497 Mayo, Margaret. *Roar!* (K–2). Illus. by Alex Ayliffe. 2007, Carolrhoda $15.95 (978-0-7613-9473-0). 32pp. A rhyming celebration of wild animals and their behaviors — climbing, prowling, stretching, fishing, jumping . . . (Rev: BL 1/1–15/08; SLJ 10/07) [590]

21498 Miller, Debbie S. *Survival at 40 Below* (2–4). Illus. by Jon Van Zyle. 2010, Walker $17.99 (978-0-8027-9815-2); LB $18.89 (978-080279816-9). 40pp. Arctic animals' fascinating techniques and adaptations for winter survival are the focus of this nicely illustrated book. (Rev: BL 12/1/09; LMC 1–2/10; SLJ 1/1/10) [591.75]

21499 Morlock, Lisa. *Track That Scat!* (K–3). Illus. by Carrie Anne Bradshaw. 2012, Sleeping Bear $15.95 (978-158536536-4). 32pp. Finn and her dog explore the woods, noting — and sometimes stepping in — a variety of different animal droppings. (Rev: BL 4/15/12; LMC 11–12/12; SLJ 5/1/12) [591.47]

21500 Moses, Brian. *Winking, Blinking, Wiggling, and Waggling* (2–3). Illus. Series: Eyewitness Reader. 2000, DK paper $3.99 (978-0-7894-5413-3). 32pp. This book for beginning readers describes fascinating facts about animals that have unusual eyes and ears. (Rev: BL 4/15/00; HBG 9/00; SLJ 8/00) [573.8]

21501 Mostue, Trude. *Wild About Animals: A Book of Beastly Behaviour* (4–6). 2000, Madcap $24.95 (978-0-233-99684-4). 112pp. A total of 26 mammals — some familiar, like the elephant, and others not so, like the hyrax — are introduced with four-page descriptions of each animal, its habits, and habitats. (Rev: SLJ 1/01) [591]

21502 Myers, Jack. *How Dogs Came from Wolves: And Other Explorations of Science in Action* (3–6). Illus. by John Rice. 2001, Boyds Mills $17.95 (978-1-56397-411-3). 64pp. A professor of zoology presents 12 fascinating animal abilities and adaptations, such as elephant "speech" and dog domestication. (Rev: BL 9/15/01; HBG 3/02; SLJ 10/01) [590]

21503 Myers, Jack. *What Happened to the Mammoths? And Other Explorations of Science in Action* (4–6). Illus. 2000, Boyds Mills $17.95 (978-1-56397-801-2). 64pp. A collection of articles from *Highlights for Children* magazine that explores such aspects of animal behavior as the seal's ability to dive and the cat's purr. (Rev: BL 3/1/00; HBG 9/00; SLJ 6/00) [591]

21504 Nichols, Catherine. *Animal Masterminds: A Chapter Book* (2–5). Series: True Tales. 2003, Children's Pr. LB $22.50 (978-0-516-22913-3). 48pp. Four animals with amazing abilities are the focus of this appealing volume that introduces new terms with care. (Rev: SLJ 1/04) [591.5]

21505 Nunn, Daniel. *Ears* (PS–2). Series: Spot the Difference. 2006, Heinemann LB $20.71 (978-1-4034-8473-4). 24pp. Compares the ears of a cricket, chimpanzee, and bat, with color photographs illustrating the differences. (Rev: SLJ 2/07) [591.44]

21506 Nunn, Daniel. *Eyes* (PS–2). Series: Spot the Difference. 2006, Heinemann LB $20.71 (978-1-4034-8474-1). 24pp. Color photographs allow readers to compare the eyes of such animals ranging from moles to gorillas. (Rev: SLJ 2/07)

21507 Page, Robin, and Steve Jenkins. *Sisters and Brothers: Sibling Relationships in the Animal World* (2–4). Illus. by Steve Jenkins. 2008, Houghton $16.00 (978-0-618-37596-7). 32pp. From termites and spiders to bears and elephants, this book offers an attractive peek into the

many varied relationships among animal siblings. (Rev: BL 4/1/08; HB 5/08; LMC 11/08; SLJ 7/08) [591]

21508 Patkau, Karen. *Creatures Great and Small* (K–3). Illus. by author. 2006, Tundra LB $17.95 (978-0-88776-754-8). Large and small animals are juxtaposed on spreads that show relative sizes and give a good impression of the environments they inhabit. (Rev: SLJ 11/06) [591.4]

21509 Pattison, Darcy. *Desert Baths* (K–2). Illus. by Kathleen Rietz. 2012, Sylvan Dell $17.95 (978-1-60718-525-3); paper $9.95 (978-1-60718-534-5). 32pp. Explores the interesting strategies desert animals use to keep clean. (Rev: BL 10/15/12; LMC 1–2/13; SLJ 9/12) [591.754]

21510 Ross, Michael Elsohn. *Mama's Milk* (PS–1). Illus. by Ashley Wolff. 2007, Tricycle $12.95 (978-1-58246-181-6). Human and animal mothers are shown nursing their babies in this book that is perfect for little ones who are curious about breast-feeding. (Rev: SLJ 5/07)

21511 Rylant, Cynthia. *The Journey: Stories of Migration* (2–4). Illus. by Lambert Davis. 2006, Scholastic $16.99 (978-0-590-30717-8). 48pp. Migrations of the desert locust, the blue whale, the American silver eel, the monarch butterfly, the caribou, and the Arctic tern are described in separate chapters in this large-format, well-illustrated book. (Rev: BL 12/1/05; SLJ 3/06) [591.56]

21512 Sayre, April P. *Splish! Splash! Animal Baths* (PS–1). Illus. 2000, Millbrook LB $21.90 (978-0-7613-1821-7). 32pp. Lots of photos and a spare text are used to introduce unusual grooming techniques in the animal kingdom, such as chimpanzees picking fleas off each other. (Rev: BL 4/1/00; HBG 9/00; SLJ 5/00) [591.56]

21513 Schaefer, Lola M. *Just One Bite* (PS–2). Illus. by Geoff Warning. 2010, Chronicle $17.99 (978-081186473-2). 40pp. Using life-size illustrations (sometimes showing only a part of a head), this colorful, large-format book shows 11 animals — from earthworm up to sperm whale — and how much they eat in just one bite. (Rev: BL 11/1/10; LMC 1–2/11; SLJ 11/10) [591.5]

21514 Schueller, Gretel H., and Sheila K. Schueller. *Animal Migration* (5–8). Series: Animal Behavior. 2009, Chelsea House $32.95 (978-1-60413-127-7). 110pp. Examining how and why animals migrate, this volume discusses birds, whales and other marine animals, animals that migrate on foot, sea turtles and salmon, and so forth. (Rev: LMC 11–12/09) [591.5]

21515 Settel, Joanne. *Exploding Ants: Amazing Facts About How Animals Adapt* (4–8). 1999, Simon & Schuster $16.00 (978-0-689-81739-7). Lurid details of animal life, such as predatory fireflies, regurgitating birds, and bloodsuckers, are presented in this attention-getting collection of biological facts. (Rev: BCCB 3/99; BL 4/15/99; HBG 10/99; SLJ 4/99) [591.5]

21516 Shalev, Zahavit. *Water Hole* (3–5). Illus. Series: 24 Hours. 2005, DK $12.99 (978-0-7566-1126-2). 48pp. A colorful and information-packed look at the animals — elephants, giraffes, wildebeest, hawks, and so forth —

that use a water hole over a 24-hour period. (Rev: BL 5/15/05) [591.74]

21517 Singer, Marilyn. *Eggs* (1–4). Illus. by Emma Stevenson. 2008, Holiday House $16.95 (978-0-8234-1727-8). 32pp. Realistic paintings and smooth text introduce eggs of many shapes and sizes and explain their functions. (Rev: BL 4/1/08; HB 5/08; LMC 10/08; SLJ 4/08) [591.4]

21518 Singer, Marilyn. *A Pair of Wings* (2–3). Illus. by Anne Wertheim. 2001, Holiday House $16.95 (978-0-8234-1547-2). 32pp. A fascinating introduction to all the ways in which animals' wings are used in addition to simple flying. (Rev: BL 5/15/01; HBG 10/01; SLJ 6/01) [591.47]

21519 Singer, Marilyn. *Venom* (5–8). Illus. 2007, Darby Creek $19.95 (978-1-58196-043-3). Poisonous animals and insects of the land, sea, and air are featured in this book, with plenty of strange facts and weird photographs. (Rev: BL 10/1/07; SLJ 11/07) [592.16]

21520 Souza, D. M. *Look What Feet Can Do* (2–4). Illus. Series: Look What Animals Can Do. 2006, Lerner LB $22.60 (978-0-7613-9460-0). 48pp. An interesting look at all the ways in which animals — from slugs to ostriches — can use their feet. (Rev: BL 10/15/06) [573.9]

21521 Souza, D. M. *Look What Mouths Can Do* (2–4). Series: Look What Animals Can Do. 2006, Lerner LB $22.60 (978-0-7613-9462-4). 48pp. This photo-filled, chatty volume with large type shows the varied ways in which animals use their mouths. Also use *Look What Tails Can Do* and *Look What Whiskers Can Do* (both 2006). (Rev: SLJ 12/06) [573.9]

21522 Stewart, Melissa. *Animal Grossapedia* (3–6). Illus. 2012, Scholastic paper $8.99 (978-05454334-8-8). 112pp. With bright photographs and a conversational style, this volume looks at gross behaviors in the animal kingdom. Lexile 870L (Rev: BL 11/15/12) [591]

21523 Stewart, Melissa. *When Rain Falls* (PS–2). Illus. by Constance R. Bergum. 2008, Peachtree $16.95 (978-1-56145-438-9). What do animals do when the rain falls? Stewart looks at the various fascinating actions they take. (Rev: LMC 10/08; SLJ 4/08) [591.72]

21524 Stockdale, Susan. *Stripes of All Types* (PS–1). Illus. by author. 2013, Peachtree $15.95 (978-156145695-6). 32pp. An attractive look at striped animals with appended information on the reasons why animals have these features. (Rev: BLO 5/15/13; LMC 11–12/13; SLJ 4/13) [591.47]

21525 Stockland, Patricia M. *Red Eyes or Blue Feathers: A Book About Animal Colors* (K–2). Illus. Series: Animal Wise. 2005, Picture Window LB $25.26 (978-1-4048-0931-4). 24pp. With color photographs, this volume introduces the varied colors found in animals and the ways in which they enable survival. Also use *Pointy, Long or Round: A Book About Animal Shapes, Strange Dances and Long Flights: A Book About Animal Behaviors,* and *Stripes, Spots, or Diamonds: A Book About Animal Patterns* (all 2005

21526 Swanson, Diane. *Animals Can Be So Playful* (K–1). Illus. by Rose Cowles. Series: Animals Can Be So. 2002, Douglas & McIntyre $10.95 (978-1-55054-900-3). 24pp. Various animals are seen at play in a series of excellent color photographs and an accompanying simple text. (Rev: BL 4/1/02) [591.5]

21527 Swanson, Diane. *Headgear That Hides and Plays* (2–4). Series: Up Close. 2001, Greystone $9.95 (978-1-55054-819-8). 32pp. Beginning with the human skull, this book describes the head structure of a number of animals from birds to the musk ox and tells how their heads help them to compete, court, and defend themselves. (Rev: BL 8/1/01; SLJ 1/02) [591]

21528 Swanson, Diane. *Noses That Plow and Poke* (2–4). Series: Up Close. 2000, Greystone $9.95 (978-1-55054-715-3). 30pp. A colorful, well-organized book that examines — up-close — noses on a number of animals and their uses beyond breathing. Also use *Tails That Talk and Fly, Feet That Suck and Feed,* and *Teeth That Stab and Grind.* (Rev: HB 7/03; HBG 10/03; SLJ 4/00) [591]

21529 Swanson, Diane. *Skin That Slimes and Scares* (2–4). Series: Up Close. 2001, Greystone $9.95 (978-1-55054-817-4). 32pp. This interesting science book starts with the human skin and then describes the outer coverings of different animals, from the armored skin of an African rhino to the poison-packed needles on the back of a red lionfish. (Rev: BL 8/1/01; SLJ 1/02) [591]

21530 Thimmesh, Catherine. *Friends: True Stories of Extraordinary Animal Friendships* (4–8). Illus. 2011, Houghton Mifflin $16.99 (978-0-547-39010-9). 32pp. Thirteen short real-life stories of unlikely animal friendships — a basset hound and an owl, for example. (Rev: BL 9/1/11; SLJ 7/11) [591.5]

21531 Thornhill, Jan. *Is This Panama? A Migration Story* (1–3). Illus. by Soyeon Kim. 2013, OwlKids $16.95 (978-192697388-3). 40pp. A Wilson's warbler named Sammy finds himself alone on his first migration to Panama. (Rev: BL 9/15/13; LMC 1–2/14*; SLJ 11/13) [591.56]

21532 Took, Atif. *Animal Encounters: A Chapter Book* (3–5). Series: True Tales. 2005, Children's Pr. LB $22.50 (978-0-516-25190-5). 48pp. This title examines encounters — friendly and dangerous — between humans and animals. (Rev: SLJ 1/06) [590]

21533 Walker, Niki, and Bobbie Kalman. *How Do Animals Move?* (1–3). Series: Science of Living Things. 2000, Crabtree LB $25.27 (978-0-86505-981-8); paper $6.95 (978-0-86505-958-0). 32pp. Using pictures and a very simple text, this book introduces such forms of animal locomotion as swimming, running, flying, and jumping. (Rev: SLJ 11/00) [591]

21534 *Who's That Roaring?* (PS). Illus. 2013, Kingfisher $5.99 (978-075346970-5). 14pp. Roaring, buzzing, bleating. This board book teaches young readers about animal sounds and other characteristics. (Rev: BL 11/15/13) [591.59]

21535 Woelfle, Gretchen. *Animal Families, Animal Friends* (1–3). Illus. by Robert Hynes. 2005, NorthWord

$15.95 (978-1-55971-901-8). Animal relationships are explored in three areas: parent-child, family group or pack, and larger communities. (Rev: LMC 10/05; SLJ 5/05)

BABIES

21536 Ashman, Linda. *Babies on the Go* (PS–2). Illus. by Jane Dyer. 2003, Harcourt $16.00 (978-0-15-201894-8). 32pp. This beautiful picture book looks at the diverse ways in which animal mothers — including humans — transport their young from one place to another. (Rev: BL 5/1/03; HBG 10/03; SLJ 5/03) [591.56]

21537 Batten, Mary. *Hey, Daddy! Animal Fathers and Their Babies* (K–3). Illus. by Higgins Bond. 2002, Peachtree $15.95 (978-1-56145-272-9). 32pp. Detailed illustrations are paired with descriptive text to introduce animal fathers that share in parenting. (Rev: BL 10/1/02; HBG 3/03; SLJ 12/02) [591.56]

21538 Bentley, Dawn. *Busy Little Beaver* (PS–2). Illus. by Beth Stover. Series: Read-and-Discover Atlantic Wilderness Adventures. 2003, Soundprints paper $3.95 (978-1-59249-011-0). 48pp. This appealing book follows a male beaver as he prepares a suitable home for his mate and the new babies that are soon to arrive. (Rev: SLJ 1/04)

21539 Bredeson, Carmen. *Baby Animals of the Grasslands* (K–2). Series: Nature's Baby Animals. 2008, Enslow LB $15.95 (978-0-7660-3006-0). 24pp. Engaging photographs show baby animals at home in the grasslands. (Rev: BLO 2/9/09; LMC 1/09) [591.74]

21540 Bredeson, Carmen. *Baby Animals of the Seashore* (K–3). Illus. Series: Nature's Baby Animals. 2011, Enslow LB $21.26 (978-076603565-2). 24pp. With clear information and close-up photographs, this title introduces king penguin chicks, harbor seal pups, and other baby animals. (Rev: BL 5/1/11) [591.769]

21541 Bull, Schuyler. *Crocodile Crossing* (K–4). Illus. by Alan Male. Series: Amazing Animal Adventures. 2003, Soundprints $15.95 (978-1-59249-051-6); paper $6.95 (978-1-59249-052-3). 27pp. A Nile crocodile waits for her hatchlings to emerge from the egg and then tries to protect them from the multiple threats around the waterhole. (Rev: HBG 4/04; SLJ 2/04) [597.98]

21542 Butler, John. *Whose Baby Am I?* (PS). Illus. 2001, Viking $10.99 (978-0-670-89683-7). 24pp. Nine animal babies ask "Whose baby am I?" and the answer is found by turning the page. (Rev: BL 6/1–15/01; HBG 10/01; SLJ 7/01) [591.39]

21543 Feldman, Thea. *Baby Animals* (K–3). Illus. 2012, Kingfisher paper $3.99 (978-07534675-4-1). 32pp. From puppies and kittens to a wide range of species, this book for beginning readers introduces baby animals and associated vocabulary. (Rev: BL 4/1/12) [591.3]

21544 Fraser, Mary Ann. *How Animal Babies Stay Safe* (PS–1). Illus. Series: Let's-Read-and-Find-Out Science. 2002, HarperCollins $15.95 (978-0-06-028803-7). 40pp. An introduction to the many ways in which nature pro-

tects baby animals, from camouflage to parental supervision. (Rev: BL 2/1/02; HBG 10/02; SLJ 2/02) [591.56]

21545 Greve, Meg. *Tap, Tap, Tap: What's Hatching?* (PS). Illus. Series: Rourke Board Books. 2009, Rourke $5.99 (978-1-60472-430-1). 16pp. Attractive color photographs and rhymed sentences provide a few easily absorbed facts about animals that hatch from eggs. (Rev: BL 5/15/09) [591.4]

21546 Hickman, Pamela. *Animals and Their Young: How Animals Produce and Care for Their Babies* (3–5). Illus. by Pat Stephens. 2003, Kids Can $10.95 (978-1-55337-061-1); paper $5.95 (978-1-55337-062-8). 40pp. This picture-book-format account shows animals' reproductive habits and care of the young. (Rev: BL 3/1/03; HBG 10/03; SLJ 6/03) [591.56]

21547 Jenkins, Steve, and Robin Page. *My First Day: What Animals Do on Day One* (PS–2). Illus. by Steve Jenkins. 2013, Houghton Mifflin $16.99 (978-0-547-73851-2). 32pp. A fascinating and eye-catching look at the wide variations between animals' abilities soon after birth. (Rev: BL 11/1/12; SLJ 1/13*) [591.3]

21548 Kajikawa, Kimiko. *Close to You: How Animals Bond* (PS–1). Illus. 2008, Holt $16.95 (978-0-8050-8123-7). 32pp. Photographs of baby animals bonding with adult animals are paired with brief descriptions ("Porcupines brush with a prickly nose"). (Rev: BL 5/1/08; SLJ 5/08) [591.3]

21549 Maze, Stephanie, ed. *Tender Moments in the Wild: Animals and Their Babies* (PS–2). 2001, Moonstone $15.00 (978-0-9707768-0-8). Adult animals caring for their young are shown in attractive spreads with minimal text. (Rev: SLJ 12/01)

21550 Owen, Ruth. *Squirrel Kits* (K–3). Illus. Series: Wild Baby Animals. 2011, Bearport LB $19.96 (978-161772160-1). 24pp. Using simple text and bright photographs, this volume introduces baby squirrels, what they eat, and how they learn to live on their own. Also use *Skunk Kits, Raccoon Cubs,* and *Polar Bear Cubs* (2011). (Rev: BL 7/11) [599.36]

21551 Reasoner, Charles. *Animal Babies!* (PS). Illus. by author. 2011, Rourke $5.99 (978-161236054-6). 10pp. For the very young, this is a simple, sturdy introduction to animal babies. (Rev: BLO 12/15/11) [591.3]

21552 Schofield, Jennifer. *Animal Babies in Ponds and Rivers* (PS–K). Illus. Series: Animal Babies. 2004, Kingfisher $7.95 (978-0-7534-5790-0). 32pp. Using a simple question-and-answer format that involves young readers, this volume introduces seven baby animals found in ponds and rivers. Also use *Animal Babies in Grasslands.* (Rev: BL 4/1/04; SLJ 10/04) [591.76]

21553 Simon, Seymour. *Baby Animals* (1–3). Series: See More Readers. 2002, North-South paper $3.95 (978-1-58717-171-0). 32pp. Double-page spreads containing a brief text opposite a color photograph introduce a number of different baby animals with material on how they are raised. (Rev: BL 7/02; HBG 3/03; SLJ 10/02) [591.3]

21554 Squire, Ann O. *Animal Babies* (2–3). Series: True Books — Animals. 2001, Children's Book Pr. LB $25.00

(978-0-516-22188-5). 48pp. The young of many species are presented in colorful pictures and simple text. (Rev: BL 12/15/01) [591.3]

21555 Stockdale, Susan. *Carry Me! Animal Babies on the Move* (PS–2). Illus. 2005, Peachtree $15.95 (978-1-56145-328-3). 32pp. Bright illustrations show how 14 varied animals — including a baboon and an alligator — carry their young. (Rev: BL 5/1/05; SLJ 4/05) [591.56]

21556 Wallace, Karen. *Wild Baby Animals* (K–3). Illus. Series: Eyewitness Reader. 2000, DK $12.99 (978-0-7894-5420-1); paper $3.99 (978-0-7894-5419-5). 32pp. Beginning readers will enjoy this book on various animal babies, their body parts, behavior, protection, and diet. (Rev: BL 7/00; HBG 9/00) [591.3]

CAMOUFLAGE

21557 Helman, Andrea. *Hide and Seek: Nature's Best Vanishing Acts* (2–4). Illus. 2008, Walker $16.95 (978-0-8027-9690-5). 40pp. With a wide format and high-quality photographs, this is an arresting collection of examples of animal camouflages. (Rev: BL 3/1/08; HB 3/08; LMC 3/08*; SLJ 7/08) [591.47]

21558 Holmes, Anita. *Can You Find Us?* (1–2). Illus. 2000, Benchmark $21.36 (978-0-7614-1108-6). 32pp. A beginner reader that explores animal camouflage and challenges children to find small animals hidden in their surroundings. (Rev: BL 12/1/00; HBG 3/01; SLJ 2/01) [591.47]

21559 Kalman, Bobbie. *What Are Camouflage and Mimicry?* (2–4). Illus. Series: The Science of Living Things. 2001, Crabtree LB $25.27 (978-0-86505-985-6); paper $6.95 (978-0-86505-962-7). 32pp. Dramatic close-up photographs with informative captions accompany details of animals' efforts to become invisible. (Rev: SLJ 12/01) [591]

21560 Kenney, Karen Latchana. *How Animals Hide* (PS–2). Illus. Series: Our Animal World. 2011, Amicus $16.95 (978-160753143-2). 24pp. For beginning readers, this simple text with photographs discusses animal camouflage techniques. (Rev: BL 10/15/11) [591.47]

21561 Schwartz, David M., and Yael Schy. *Where Else in the Wild? More Camouflaged Creatures Concealed . . . and Revealed* (1–4). Photos by Dwight Kuhn. 2009, Tricycle $16.99 (978-1-58246-283-7). Unpaged. Eleven well-camouflaged creatures are introduced by way of poetry and photography in this nicely designed, interactive book. (Rev: BL 10/15/09; LMC 3–4/10; SLJ 10/1/09) [591.47]

21562 Schwartz, David M., and Yael Schy. *Where in the Wild?* (1–3). Illus. by Dwight Kuhn. 2007, Tricycle $15.95 (978-1-58246-207-3). 32pp. Combining poetry, photography, and gatefolds with facts, this clever book challenges readers to find animals against their camouflage. (Rev: BL 11/1/07; LMC 1/08; SLJ 8/07) [590]

21563 Stevenson, Emma. *Hide-and-Seek Science: Animal Camouflage* (K–3). Illus. by author. 2013, Holiday $16.95 (978-082342293-7). 32pp. Stevenson explains how animals use camouflage in different areas of the world and allows children to identify them on hide-and-seek pages. (Rev: BL 11/1/13; SLJ 10/13) [591.47]

21564 Swanson, Diane. *Animals Can Be So Hard to See* (K–1). Illus. by Rose Cowles. Series: Animals Can Be So. 2002, Douglas & McIntyre $10.95 (978-1-55054-901-0). 24pp. Using double-page spreads with a color photograph on one side and simple text on the other, the camouflaging abilities of a variety of animals are explored. (Rev: BL 4/1/02; SLJ 8/02) [591.47]

21565 Weber, Belinda. *Animal Disguises* (K–3). Illus. Series: Kingfisher Young Knowledge. 2004, Kingfisher $8.95 (978-0-7534-5772-6). 47pp. Using two-page chapters with large text and eye-catching photographs, Weber introduces camouflage and the various animals that use this disguise. (Rev: BL 4/15/04*; SLJ 4/05) [591]

COMMUNICATION

21566 Davies, Nicola. *Talk, Talk, Squawk!* (3–5). Illus. by Neal Layton. 2011, Candlewick $14.99 (978-0-7636-5088-9). 64pp. Explores ways in which animals communicate with each other using colors, patterns, smells, movements, vibrations, sounds, and electricity. Lexile NC1220L (Rev: BL 11/15/11; HB 1–2/12; LMC 3–4/12; SLJ 11/1/11) [591.59]

21567 Jenkins, Steve. *Slap, Squeak, and Scatter: How Animals Communicate* (K–3). Illus. 2001, Houghton $16.00 (978-0-618-03376-8). 48pp. An introduction to the many wonderful ways in which animals communicate with each other. (Rev: BL 5/15/01; HBG 10/01; SLJ 5/01) [591.59]

21568 Kaner, Etta. *Animal Talk: How Animals Communicate Through Sight, Sound and Smell* (2–4). Illus. by Greg Douglas. 2002, Kids Can $10.95 (978-1-55074-982-3); paper $5.95 (978-1-55074-984-7). 40pp. Double-page spreads with photographs and original artwork explain how a variety of animals communicate through smell, sound, and body language. (Rev: BL 4/15/02; HBG 10/02; SLJ 7/02) [581.59]

21569 Sayre, April Pulley. *Secrets of Sound: Studying the Calls and Songs of Whales, Elephants, and Birds* (4–7). 2002, Houghton Mifflin $17.00 (978-0-618-01514-6). Fascinating profiles of scientists who study animal sounds serve to introduce readers to a number of scientific concepts. (Rev: BL 12/1/02; HB 9–10/02; HBG 3/03; SLJ 10/02) [559.159]

21570 Schlein, Miriam. *Hello, Hello!* (K–2). Illus. by Daniel Kirk. 2002, Simon & Schuster $16.95 (978-0-689-83435-6). 32pp. This simple picture book shows how different animals greet each other. (Rev: BL 6/1–15/02; HB 7/02; HBG 10/02; SLJ 7/02) [591.59]

DEFENSES

21571 Jenkins, Steve. *Never Smile at a Monkey* (K–3). Illus. by author. 2009, Houghton Mifflin $16 (978-0-618-96620-2). Unpaged. Animals can be dangerous — and this fascinating book explores how 18 animals react to perceived threats. (Rev: BL 10/15/09; LMC 3–4/10*; SLJ 9/1/09*) [591.6]

21572 Kenney, Karen Latchana. *Spiny Animals* (PS–2). Illus. Series: Our Animal World. 2011, Amicus $16.95 (978-160753144-9). 24pp. For beginning readers, this simple text with photographs discusses the defense mechanisms of animals like sea urchins and porcupines. (Rev: BL 10/15/11) [591.47]

21573 Page, Robin, and Steve Jenkins. *How Many Ways Can You Catch a Fly?* (PS–3). Illus. by Steve Jenkins. 2008, Houghton $16.00 (978-0-618-96634-9). 32pp. A close and engaging look at how a variety of animals escape danger, avoid predators, and survive and thrive. (Rev: BL 9/1/08) [591.5]

21574 Souza, D. M. *Packed with Poison! Deadly Animal Defenses* (1–3). Illus. by Jack Harris. Series: On My Own Science. 2006, Millbrook LB $25.26 (978-1-57505-877-1). 48pp. For new readers, an introduction to several animals — spiders, scorpions, jellyfish, and so forth — that use poison as a defense. (Rev: SLJ 6/06) [591.65]

HIBERNATION

21575 Ganeri, Anita. *Hibernation* (K–3). Series: Nature's Patterns. 2005, Heinemann LB $16.95 (978-1-4034-5895-7). 32pp. In simple languge, this volume introduces the stages of animal hibernation. (Rev: SLJ 6/05)

21576 Hickman, Pamela. *Animals Hibernating: How Animals Survive Extreme Conditions* (3–5). Illus. by Pat Stephens. Series: Animal Behavior. 2005, Kids Can $12.95 (978-1-55337-662-0); paper $5.95 (978-1-55337-663-7). 40pp. Hickman explains the reasons for hibernation and distinguishes between animals that go into true hibernation and those that merely retreat into deep sleep. (Rev: BL 11/1/05; SLJ 10/05) [591.56]

HOMES

21577 Cobb, Allan B. *Super Science Projects About Animals and Their Habitats* (4–8). Series: Psyched for Science. 2000, Rosen LB $26.50 (978-0-8239-3175-0). Six hand-on activities are introduced to help children observe animals and to study their adjustments to climate, habitat, and food. (Rev: SLJ 9/00) [591]

21578 Gregoire, Elizabeth. *Whose House Is This? A Look at Animal Homes — Webs, Nests, and Shells* (PS–2). Illus. by Derrick Alderman and Denise Shea. Series: Whose Is It? 2004, Picture Window LB $25.26 (978-1-4048-0608-5). 24pp. Rhythmic question-and-answer format and colorful collages introduce a wide variety of animal habitats. (Rev: BL 11/1/04) [591.56]

21579 Ham, Catherine. *Step Inside! A Look Inside Animal Homes* (K–3). Illus. 2012, EarlyLight $14.95 (978-0-9832014-2-7). 32pp. Compelling photographs accompany rhymed poems about a variety of animal homes, from treetop nests to underground burrows. **e** (Rev: BL 3/15/12; SLJ 4/1/12) [591.56]

21580 Hickman, Pamela. *It's Moving Day!* (PS–2). Illus. by Geraldo Valério. 2008, Kids Can $16.95 (978-1-55453-074-8). 32pp. A single burrow is home to a revolving variety of creatures and often their young — first a woodchuck, then a rabbit, followed by a salamander, and so forth. (Rev: BL 5/1/08; LMC 5/08; SLJ 6/08) [591.56]

21581 Jenkins, Steve, and Robin Page. *I See a Kookaburra! Discovering Animal Habitats Around the World* (K–3). Illus. by Steve Jenkins. 2005, Houghton $16.00 (978-0-618-50764-1). A bright I Spy game that introduces six habitats — the American Southwest, an English coastal tide pool, the Amazon rain forest, African grasslands, an Australian forest, and a Midwest pond — and the wildlife found there. (Rev: BCCB 5/05; BL 8/05; HB 5/05; SLJ 5/05) [591]

21582 Lauber, Patricia. *Fur, Feathers, and Flippers: How Animals Live Where They Do* (4–8). 1994, Scholastic paper $4.95 (978-0-590-45072-0). Using various habitats such as the grasslands of East Africa as examples, this photoessay describes how animals have adapted to their different environments. (Rev: BL 12/1/94*; SLJ 12/94) [591.5]

21583 Phillips, Dee. *Chipmunk's Hole* (K–3). Illus. Series: Hole Truth! Underground Animal Life. 2012, Bearport LB $23.93 (978-161772407-7). 24pp. Readers learn about the lives, habitat, diet, and life cycle of eastern chipmunks. (Rev: BL 4/1/12) [599.36]

21584 Shields, Carol Diggory. *Homes* (PS–3). Illus. by Svjetlan Junakovic. Series: Animagicals. 2001, Handprint $9.95 (978-1-929766-27-7). 32pp. Rhyming riddles give clues about animal homes hidden under the flaps in this tall-format picture book. (Rev: BL 2/1/02; HBG 3/02; SLJ 2/02) [811]

21585 Squire, Ann O. *Animal Homes* (2–3). Series: True Books — Animals. 2001, Children's Book Pr. LB $25.00 (978-0-516-22189-2). 48pp. Various kinds of animal homes are presented with well-captioned color pictures on each page plus a few lines of accompanying text. (Rev: BL 12/15/01) [591.56]

21586 Stockland, Patricia M. *Sand, Leaf, or Coral Reef: A Book About Animal Habitats* (K–2). Illus. Series: Animal Wise. 2005, Picture Window LB $25.26 (978-1-4048-0932-1). 24pp. With color photographs, this volume introduces the varied places where animals make their homes.

REPRODUCTION

21587 Cusick, Dawn, and Joanne O'Sullivan. *Animal Eggs: An Amazing Clutch of Mysteries and Marvels!* (3–5). Illus. 2011, EarlyLight $14.95 (978-0-9797455-3-9). 48pp. This informative and highly illustrated survey takes a conversational approach to unveiling the marvels and mysteries of eggs — amphibian, reptile, insect, and bird. Lexile NC1010L (Rev: BL 4/15/11; SLJ 4/11) [591.468]

21588 Gill, Shelley. *The Egg* (K–3). Illus. by Jo-Ellen Bosson. 2001, Charlesbridge $16.95 (978-1-57091-377-

8). 32pp. A fact-filled book about eggs and egg-bearers with attractive illustrations and humorous text. (Rev: BCCB 2/01; BL 11/1/01; HBG 3/02; SLJ 7/01) [591.4]

21589 Hickman, Pamela. *Animals and Their Mates: How Animals Attract, Fight for and Protect Each Other* (2–5). Illus. by Pat Stephens. 2004, Kids Can $5.95 (978-1-55337-546-3). 40pp. A broad range of mating rituals — many involving unexpected behaviors — are presented. (Rev: BL 10/15/04) [591.56]

21590 Kenney, Karen Latchana. *Who Lays Eggs?* (PS–2). Illus. Series: Our Animal World. 2011, Amicus $16.95 (978-160753146-3). 24pp. For beginning readers, this simple text with photographs discusses animals that lay eggs such as birds, spiders, and crocodiles. (Rev: BL 10/15/11) [591.4]

21591 Posada, Mia. *Guess What Is Growing Inside This Egg* (K–3). Illus. 2007, Millbrook $15.95 (978-0-8225-6192-7). 32pp. On the first spread of each pair, a close-up of an egg is accompanied by a rhyming clue; on the second spread, the answer is given as well as basic information about the animal in question. (Rev: BL 4/1/07) [591.4]

Animal Species

GENERAL AND MISCELLANEOUS

21592 Anderson, Jill. *Zebras* (PS–2). Series: Wild Ones. 2005, NorthWord $12.95 (978-1-55971-926-1); paper $6.95 (978-1-55971-927-8). With lots of photographs, many of them close-ups, this simple text introduces basic facts about zebras. (Rev: HBG 4/06; SLJ 1/06) [599.72]

21593 Arnold, Caroline. *A Zebra's World* (PS–2). Illus. by author. Series: Caroline Arnold's Animals. 2006, Picture Window LB $26.60 (978-1-4048-1324-3). 24pp. A baby zebra grows up and learns to fend for himself in this appealing fact-packed title. (Rev: LMC 11/06; SLJ 6/06) [599.72]

21594 Barbé-Julien, Colette. *Little Hippopotamuses* (1–3). Series: Born to Be Wild. 2005, Gareth Stevens LB $23.00 (978-0-8368-4736-9). 24pp. A close-up look at what life is like for baby hippopotamuses, including their relationships with their parents; suitable for browsers. (Rev: SLJ 2/06) [599.63]

21595 Barnes, Julia. *Camels and Llamas at Work* (3–5). Series: Animals at Work. 2006, Gareth Stevens LB $24.00 (978-0-8368-6222-5). 32pp. Camels and llamas are not only used as pack animals; full-color photographs show them in various roles and the text discusses the animals' physical characteristics and relationship with humans. (Rev: SLJ 1/07) [636.2]

21596 Bodden, Valerie. *Bison* (1–3). Illus. Series: Amazing Animals. 2013, Creative Education LB $17.95 (978-160818085-1). 24pp. An eye-catching introduction to these animals that will appeal to young and reluctant readers; includes a story from folklore. (Rev: BL 4/15/13; LMC 10/13*) [599.64]

21597 Borgert-Spaniol, Megan. *Weasels* (K–2). Illus. Series: Backyard Wildlife. 2012, Children's Press LB $21.95 (978-160014725-8). 24pp. A slim, colorful introduction to weasels and their lives. (Rev: BL 9/15/12) [599.76]

21598 Burnie, David. *Mammals* (3–6). Illus. Series: Navigators. 2011, Kingfisher $12.99 (978-075346610-0). 48pp. An illustrated overview of mammals, from deserts and rain forests to grasslands and frozen tundra, with information on life cycles, habitats, diet, and homes. (Rev: BL 12/15/11) [599]

21599 Caper, William. *American Bison: A Scary Prediction* (3–4). Series: America's Animal Comebacks. 2007, Bearport LB $25.27 (978-1-59716-504-4). 32pp. With eye-catching photographs and an appealing design, Caper looks at how the iconic American bison almost disappeared and at efforts being made to help them on the comeback trail. (Rev: LMC 1/08; SLJ 12/07) [599.64]

21600 Carson, Mary Kay. *Emi and the Rhino Scientist* (5–8). Illus. Series: Scientists in the Field. 2007, Houghton $18.00 (978-0-618-64639-5). 64pp. Emi, a rhinoceros at the Cincinnati Zoo, gives birth in captivity (which is unusual for a rhino) thanks to the help of scientist Terri Roth in this exciting and informative account. (Rev: BL 12/1/07; HB 11/07; SLJ 11/07) [599.66]

21601 Clarke, Ginjer L. *Platypus!* (PS–1). Illus. by Paul Mirocha. Series: Step into Reading. 2004, Random paper $3.99 (978-0-375-82417-3). 32pp. This friendly introduction to the platypus provides simple, engaging text and close-up illustrations. (Rev: BL 7/04) [599.2]

21602 Cohn, Scotti. *Big Cat, Little Kitty* (PS–3). Illus. by Susan Detwiler. 2011, Sylvan Dell $16.95 (978-1-60718-124-8); paper $8.95 (978-1-60718-134-7). Unpaged. Cohn describes the similarities and differences between domestic and wild cats, exploring the various habitats of the latter. e (Rev: LMC 11–12/11; SLJ 8/1/11) [599.75]

21603 Collard, Sneed B., III. *In the Rain Forest Canopy* (3–6). Series: Science Adventures. 2005, Benchmark LB $25.64 (978-0-7614-1954-9). 43pp. Readers meet a scientist who studies creatures that live high in the canopy of the rain forest. (Rev: SLJ 5/06) [578.734]

21604 Collard, Sneed B., III. *A Platypus, Probably* (K–3). Illus. by Andrew Plant. 2005, Charlesbridge $16.95 (978-1-57091-583-3); paper $6.95 (978-1-57091-584-0). 32pp. An accessible and attractive introduction to the platypus. (Rev: BL 9/15/05; SLJ 9/05) [599.2]

21605 Cooke, Lucy. *A Little Book of Sloth* (2–4). Illus. by author. 2013, Simon & Schuster $16.99 (978-1-4424-4557-4). 64pp. Meet appealing baby sloths in a Costa Rican sanctuary in this volume full of color photographs and engaging text. e (Rev: BL 12/15/12; LMC 10/13; SLJ 3/13) [599.3]

21606 de la Bedoyere, Camilla. *Why Why Why — Are Orangutans Hairy?* (4–6). Illus. 2009, Mason Crest $18.95 (978-142221570-8). 32pp. Goofy and accessible, this book uses cartoons and sketches — as well as facts — to answer questions about mammals. (Rev: BL 1/1/10) [599]

21607 Eamer, Claire. *Lizards in the Sky: Animals Where You Least Expect Them* (3–5). Illus. 2010, Annick $21.95 (978-155451265-2); paper $12.95 (978-15545126-4-5). 104pp. This interesting volume with close-up photographs presents brief profiles of birds and spiders that live underwater, shrimp living in the desert, climbing fish, and other animals with unusual characteristics. (Rev: BL 12/1/10; LMC 3–4/11; SLJ 12/1/10) [591.4]

21608 FitzSimmons, David. *Curious Critters, Vol. 2* (1–4). Illus. 2014, Wild Iris $19.95 (978-193660770-9). 32pp. Photographs against white backgrounds, accompanied by informative text, highlight 20 unusual animals. (Rev: BL 3/1/14; LMC 10/14*; SLJ 2/14) [591]

21609 Fredericks, Anthony D. *Zebras* (2–3). Series: Early Bird Nature Books. 2000, Lerner LB $25.26 (978-0-8225-3043-5). 48pp. A fact-filled text and amazing color photos explore how zebras live and grow in their native Africa or in zoos around the world. (Rev: BL 7/00; HBG 3/01) [599.72]

21610 Ganeri, Anita. *Meerkat* (PS–2). Series: A Day in the Life: Desert Animals. 2011, Heinemann LB $22 (978-1-4329-4773-6); paper $6.49 (978-1-4329-4782-8). 24pp. Answering questions such as "What do meerkats look like?" and "What do meerkats do during the day?," Ganeri presents the physical characteristics and life of this desert animal. (Rev: SLJ 6/11) [599.74]

21611 Gardner, Jane P. *African Wild Dogs* (K–2). Illus. Series: Wild Canine Pups. 2013, Bearport LB $21.32 (978-161772932-4). 24pp. Statistics, maps, and vivid photographs various African canines as they grow up from cute pups to intimidating adults. e (Rev: BL 10/1/13; LMC 8–9/14) [599.77]

21612 George, Jean Craighead. *The Buffalo Are Back* (3–5). Illus. by Wendell Minor. 2010, Dutton $16.99 (978-0-525-42215-0). 32pp. A stirring history of the American buffalo, from Native Americans' sustainable herd management techniques, to mass slaughter, to 20th-century preservation efforts. (Rev: BL 4/15/10; SLJ 7/1/10) [599.64]

21613 Gish, Melissa. *Bison* (5–8). Illus. Series: Living Wild. 2011, Creative Education LB $23.95 (978-1-60818-077-6). 48pp. Gish looks at the bison's habitats, physical characteristics, behaviors, relationships with humans, protected status, importance to Native Americans, and status as a symbol of the American West. (Rev: BL 12/1/11; SLJ 11/1/11) [599.64]

21614 Gish, Melissa. *Camels* (4–6). Illus. Series: Living Wild. 2012, Creative Education LB $24.95 (978-160818166-7). 48pp. Useful for reports, this volume covers the animals' anatomy, habitat, life cycle, reproduction, position on the food chain, adaptations, and threats to survival. Lexile NC1250L (Rev: BL 12/15/12) [599.63]

21615 Glaser, Linda. *Hello Squirrels! Scampering Through the Seasons* (K–2). Illus. by Gay Holland. 2006, Millbrook LB $22.60 (978-0-7613-2887-2). 32pp.

An appealing look at the first year of a squirrel's life, narrated from the perspective of a young child and including realistic drawings. (Rev: BL 4/15/06) [599.36]

21616 Green, Jen, and David Burnie. *Mammal* (5–9). Series: DK/Google e.guides. 2005, DK $17.99 (978-0-7566-1139-2). This highly illustrated guide introduces readers to the evolution and diversity of mammals and provides a link to a Web site that serves as a gateway to additional resources. (Rev: SLJ 8/05) [599]

21617 Guidoux, Valérie. *Little Zebras* (1–3). Series: Born to Be Wild. 2005, Gareth Stevens LB $23.00 (978-0-8368-4741-3). 24pp. This attractive title introduces the physical and behavioral characteristics of zebras and examines the role of zebra parents in feeding their young and protecting them from predators. (Rev: SLJ 2/06) [599.72]

21618 Haas, Robert B. *African Critters* (3–5). Illus. 2008, National Geographic $17.95 (978-1-4263-0317-3). 96pp. Wildlife photographer Haas shows real life for animals from antelope to zebra in clear text and arresting photographs. (Rev: BL 7/08; SLJ 9/08)

21619 Halls, Kelly Milner. *Wild Horses: Galloping Through Time* (4–7). Illus. by Mark Hallet. 2008, Darby Creek $18.95 (978-1-58196-065-5). 72pp. Gorgeous photographs and clear text tell the history of horses and document the presence of wild horses worldwide. (Rev: BLO 7/29/08; SLJ 10/1/08) [599.665]

21620 Hatkoff, Isabella, and Craig Hatkoff. *Owen and Mzee: The Language of Friendship* (K–4). Photos by Peter Greste. 2007, Scholastic $16.99 (978-0-439-89959-8). This appealing sequel to *Owen and Mzee: The True Story of a Remarkable Friendship* continues the story of the bond between the baby hippo orphaned by the Indian Ocean tsunami and an ancient tortoise, focusing on how the two creatures communicate with one another. (Rev: BL 12/15/06*; SLJ 2/07*) [599.63]

21621 Hatkoff, Isabella, and Craig Hatkoff. *Owen and Mzee: The True Story of a Remarkable Friendship* (1–3). Illus. by Peter Greste. 2006, Scholastic $16.99 (978-0-439-82973-1). 32pp. A baby hippo and a giant tortoise form an unlikely bond following the hippo's rescue from the 2004 tsunami; photographs bring the unusual situation to life. (Rev: BL 5/15/06; SLJ 5/06*) [599.63]

21622 Jango-Cohen, Judith. *Camels* (3–6). Illus. Series: Animals, Animals. 2004, Benchmark $25.64 (978-0-7614-1750-7). 47pp. A well-written overview of these animals, providing all the information needed for report writing plus additional material of interest. (Rev: BL 3/15/04; SLJ 2/05) [599.63]

21623 Jango-Cohen, Judith. *Hippopotamuses* (3–5). Illus. Series: Animals, Animals. 2006, Marshall Cavendish LB $28.50 (978-0-7614-2238-9). 47pp. This series entry combines full-color photographs and facts about hippos, including a chapter about interaction with humans. (Rev: BL 1/1–15/07) [599.63]

21624 Jango-Cohen, Judith. *Rhinoceroses* (3–6). Illus. Series: Animals, Animals. 2004, Benchmark $25.64 (978-0-7614-1753-8). 47pp. A well-written overview of these animals, providing all the information needed for report writing plus additional material of interest. (Rev: BL 4/15/04; HB 3/04; SLJ 2/05) [599.72]

21625 Joubert, Beverly, and Dereck Joubert. *African Animal Alphabet* (K–3). Photos by Beverly Joubert. 2011, National Geographic $16.95 (978-1-4263-0781-2); LB $26.90 (978-1-4263-0782-9). 48pp. With alliterative text, facts, and eye-catching full-color photographs, this is an appealing alphabetical introduction to African animals from antelope to zebra. (Rev: SLJ 5/1/11) [591.96]

21626 Kalman, Bobbie. *The Life Cycle of a Beaver* (2–4). Illus. Series: Life Cycle. 2006, Crabtree LB $25.20 (978-0-7787-0628-1); paper $6.95 (978-0-7787-0702-8). 32pp. Report writers will find this a useful and interesting resource. Diet, habitat, behavior, and other aspects of beavers are covered. Photographs and illustrations accompany the text, and vocabulary words appear in bold font. (Rev: SLJ 5/07)

21627 Kaner, Etta. *And the Winner Is . . .: Amazing Animal Athletes* (K–3). Illus. by David Anderson. 2013, Kids Can $16.95 (978-1-55453-904-8). 32pp. A walrus and a cockatoo emcee the World Animals Games in this instructive and humorous survey of which animals are the best athletes in various sports. (Rev: BL 4/1/13; SLJ 3/13) [591]

21628 Komiya, Teruyuki. *Life-Size Zoo* (PS–2). Illus. by Toyofumi Fukuda. 2009, Seven Footer $17.95 (978-1-934734-20-9). 48pp. This oversize book presents excellent, proportionally sized photographs of animals or parts of animals — a whole meerkat but a tiger's head — and encourages readers to notice salient features; facts are appended. (Rev: BL 4/15/09; LMC 10/09; SLJ 6/09) [500]

21629 Lambilly-Bresson, Élisabeth de. *Animals in the Desert* (PS–2). Series: Animal Show and Tell. 2007, Gareth Stevens LB $17.27 (978-0-8368-8204-9). 16pp. In simple first-person narratives, desert animals describe their key characteristics and behaviors; with eye-catching full-page photographs. Also use *Animals in the Jungle, Animals of the Mountains,* and *Animals of the Ocean* (all 2007). (Rev: SLJ 3/08)

21630 Landau, Elaine. *Raccoons: Scavengers of the Night* (2–3). Series: Animals after Dark. 2007, Enslow LB $22.60 (978-0-7660-2767-1). 32pp. Photographs of raccoons accompany information about their nocturnal behavior and their scavenging habits. (Rev: SLJ 8/07)

21631 Lang, Aubrey. *Baby Ground Squirrel* (2–4). Photos by Wayne Lynch. Series: Nature Babies. 2004, Fitzhenry & Whiteside $13.95 (978-1-55041-797-5); paper $5.95 (978-1-55041-799-9). 36pp. Full-color photographs follow the development of a litter of baby ground squirrels on the Western Canadian prairie. (Rev: BCCB 7–8/04; SLJ 2/05)

21632 Lang, Aubrey. *Baby Porcupine* (1–4). Photos by Wayne Lynch. Series: Nature Babies. 2006, Fitzhenry & Whiteside $13.95 (978-1-55041-560-5); paper $6.95 (978-1-55041-562-9). 36pp. Filled with photographs of a baby porcupine's growth until it's able to survive without its mother's protection and guidance. (Rev: SLJ 6/06) [599.35]

21633 Lang, Aubrey. *Baby Sloth* (1–4). Photos by Wayne Lynch. Series: Nature Babies. 2005, Fitzhenry & Whiteside $13.95 (978-1-55041-825-5); paper $5.95 (978-1-55041-827-9). 36pp. After a fascinating account of their trip to Panama's rain forests, the authors supply basic information on baby sloths — habitat, diet, relationship with their mothers, and so forth. (Rev: SLJ 4/05)

21634 Latta, Jan. *Rudy the Rhinoceros* (K–4). Series: Wild Animal Families. 2006, Gareth Stevens LB $23.93 (978-0-8368-7771-7). 24pp. In a first-"person" account, Rudy describes what it's like to be a rhinoceros, giving readers facts about his species in an enjoyable and engaging format. (Rev: SLJ 5/07)

21635 Lynette, Rachel. *Kinkajous* (K–3). Illus. Series: Jungle Babies of the Amazon Rain Forest. 2013, Bearport LB $21.32 (978-161772752-8). 24pp. Beginning readers will be fascinated by information on these small, long-tailed mammals and their lives. (Rev: BL 4/1/13; LMC 1–2/14; SLJ 4/13) [599.76]

21636 Macken, JoAnn Early. *Jackrabbits / Liebres americanas* (2–4). Trans. by Tatiana Acosta and Guillermo Gutiérrez. Series: Animals That Live in the Desert / Animales del desierto. 2005, Weekly Reader LB $21.00 (978-0-8368-4842-7). 24pp. A beginning book with facts about jackrabbits in both English and Spanish. (Rev: SLJ 6/06) [599.32]

21637 Markle, Sandra. *Musk Oxen* (K–4). Series: Animal Prey. 2007, Lerner LB $25.26 (978-0-8225-6064-7). 40pp. Eye-catching photographs and clear, readable text discuss musk oxen, their social structure, and how they deal with predators, mainly wolves that target the young or weak. (Rev: SLJ 4/07) [599.64]

21638 Marrin, Albert. *Saving the Buffalo* (5–7). 2006, Scholastic $18.99 (978-0-439-71854-7). This well-written, well-illustrated history traces the fortunes of the American bison from the days when huge herds covered the plains to near extinction at the end of the 19th century and then to an amazing recovery over the past century or so. (Rev: SLJ 12/06*) [599.64]

21639 Mason, Adrienne. *Skunks* (2–4). Illus. by Nancy Gray Ogle. 2006, Kids Can LB $10.95 (978-1-55337-733-7); paper $6.95 (978-1-55337-734-4). This picture-book introduction to skunks covers the often-maligned creature's physical characteristics, diet, habitat, behavior, and interaction with humans. (Rev: SLJ 9/06) [599.74]

21640 Merrick, Patrick. *Raccoons* (3–4). Series: New Naturebooks. 2006, The Child's World LB $27.07 (978-1-59296-647-9). 32pp. An introductory overview of this nocturnal mammal, with vivid color photographs. (Rev: SLJ 2/07) [599.76]

21641 Montgomery, Sy. *Quest for the Tree Kangaroo: An Expedition to the Cloud Forest of New Guinea* (5–8). Illus. by Nic Bishop. 2006, Houghton $18.00 (978-0-618-49641-9). 80pp. Join researchers on a challenging expedition to the cloud forests of Papua New Guinea to learn more about the rare Matschie's tree kangaroo. Sibert Honor Book, 2007. (Rev: BL 12/1/06; SLJ 12/06*) [599.2]

21642 Montgomery, Sy. *The Tapir Scientist: Saving South America's Largest Mammal* (5–8). Illus. by Nic Bishop. Series: Scientists in the Field. 2013, Houghton Mifflin $18.99 (978-054781548-0). 80pp. A fascinating account of research into the lives of these gentle herbivorous mammals that live in the wetlands of Brazil. (Rev: BL 8/13*; HB 11–12/13; SLJ 9/13*) [599.66]

21643 Moore, Heidi. *A Mob of Meerkats* (3–5). Series: Animal Groups. 2004, Heinemann LB $24.22 (978-1-4034-4694-7). 32pp. A basic introduction to the animal and its characteristics, using a question-and-answer format and including color close-ups. (Rev: SLJ 9/04)

21644 Morgan, Ben. *DK Guide to Mammals: A Wild Journey with These Extraordinary Beasts* (4–6). Illus. 2003, DK $15.99 (978-0-7894-9581-5). 64pp. For browsers, an excellent overview of mammals, covering topics from the purely physical to the social — "Urban Living," for example. (Rev: HBG 4/04; SLJ 1/04) [599]

21645 Murray, Peter. *Rhinos* (4–7). Series: The World of Mammals. 2005, Child's World LB $29.93 (978-1-59296-502-1). Arresting photographs and engaging text introduce the anatomy, behavior, habitat, and life cycle of the rhinoceros as well as the threats to the animal's survival in the wild. (Rev: SLJ 3/06) [599.72]

21646 Nelson, Kristin L. *Clever Raccoons* (PS–2). Series: Pull Ahead Books. 2000, Lerner LB $22.60 (978-0-8225-3763-2); paper $5.95 (978-0-8225-3644-4). This simple science book covers raccoons — their homes, when they are active, and how they use their paws. (Rev: BL 9/15/00; HBG 3/01) [599.32]

21647 Nelson, Kristin L. *Spraying Skunks* (2–3). Series: Pull Ahead Books. 2003, Lerner LB $22.60 (978-0-8225-4670-2); paper $5.95 (978-0-8225-3598-0). 32pp. An introduction to skunks and their habits that contains many color photographs and a map activity. (Rev: BL 3/15/03; HBG 10/03) [599.74]

21648 Older, Jules. *Pig* (K–3). Illus. by Lyn Severance. 2004, Charlesbridge paper $6.95 (978-0-88106-110-9). 32pp. Children will enjoy browsing through the pages of this colorfully illustrated introduction to pigs and their place in the world. (Rev: BL 8/04; SLJ 9/04) [636.4]

21649 Otfinoski, Steven. *Raccoons* (4–6). 2010, Marshall Cavendish LB $20.95 (978-0-7614-4841-9). 46pp. This volume covers the animal's habitat, diet, reproduction, life span, adaptability, and relationship with humans. (Rev: SLJ 1/1/11) [599.76]

21650 Otfinoski, Steven. *Skunks* (4–6). Series: Animals Animals. 2008, Marshall Cavendish LB $20.95 (978-0-7614-2929-6). 48pp. *Skunks* is packed with information regarding habitat, adaptations, and humanity's impact and includes excellent photographs. (Rev: SLJ 2/09) [599.76]

21651 Penny, Malcolm. *Black Rhino* (3–6). Illus. Series: Natural World. 2001, Raintree LB $27.12 (978-0-7398-4438-0). 48pp. A fine guide to the black rhinoceros with

accessible text, memorable photographs, a glossary, and list of Web sites. (Rev: BL 12/15/01; HBG 10/02) [599.66]

21652 Perry, Phyllis J. *Buffalo* (3–5). Illus. Series: Animals, Animals. 2005, Benchmark LB $17.95 (978-0-7614-1866-5). 48pp. Report writers will find plenty of clear photographs and maps plus well-organized information about the bison and its physical characteristics, diet, habitat, and behavior. (Rev: SLJ 2/06) [599.64]

21653 Phillips, Dee. *Badger's Burrow* (2–4). Illus. Series: The Hole Truth! Underground Animal Life. 2013, Bearport LB $23.93 (978-161772745-0). 24pp. An effective to badgers and their characteristics and behavior, with clear photographs and boxed fun facts. Also use *Armadillo's Burrow* (2013). (Rev: BL 9/1/13)

21654 Pringle, Laurence. *Strange Animals, New to Science* (4–7). Illus. 2002, Marshall Cavendish $16.95 (978-0-7614-5083-2). 112pp. The results of scientists' efforts to discover new animal species are presented here, with color photographs and coverage of the reasons behind disappearing habitats. (Rev: BCCB 9/02; BL 7/02; HBG 10/02; SLJ 8/02) [591.68]

21655 Pyers, Greg. *Why Am I a Mammal?* (3–5). Illus. Series: Classifying Animals. 2005, Raintree LB $27.50 (978-1-4109-2016-4); paper $7.85 (978-1-4109-2023-2). 32pp. Introduces readers to the process of scientific classification and then examines the unique characteristics of mammals. (Rev: SLJ 4/06) [599]

21656 Rake, Jody Sullivan. *Meerkats* (PS–2). Illus. Series: Pebble Plus: African Animals. 2008, Capstone LB $14.95 (978-1-4296-1249-4). 32pp. Rake uses close-up photographs and limited-vocabulary text to introduce the meerkat and its behavior, anatomy, habitat, and diet. (Rev: BL 4/1/08) [599.74]

21657 Rau, Dana Meachen. *Guess Who Grunts* (PS–K). Series: Bookworms. Guess Who. 2009, Marshall Cavendish $15.95 (978-0-7614-2906-7). 32pp. Fun for browsing, this book asks readers to identify a pig using the clues in the text and images. (Rev: SLJ 6/09) [636.4]

21658 Rau, Dana Meachen. *The Rabbit in the Garden* (PS–1). Series: Benchmark Rebus. 2006, Benchmark LB $22.79 (978-0-7614-2308-9). 24pp. This colorful easy reader, which features a blend of rebuses and easy-to-understand text, follows a typical day in the life of a rabbit and describes physical characteristics, habitat, diet, and behavior. (Rev: SLJ 12/06) [599.32]

21659 Rebman, Renee C. *Anteaters* (3–5). Series: Animals, Animals. 2006, Benchmark LB $19.95 (978-0-7614-2234-1). 48pp. An introduction to the anatomy, behavior, diet, and habitat of anteaters. Color photographs give readers a close-up look. (Rev: SLJ 5/07)

21660 Ring, Susan. *Project Hippopotamus* (3–6). Illus. Series: Zoo Life. 2002, Weigl LB $15.15 (978-1-59036-013-2). 32pp. This volume looks at both the good and bad aspects of raising hippopotamuses in zoos, and discusses their natural habitat, physiology, and so forth, using color photographs and featured sidebars. (Rev: BL 12/15/02; HBG 3/03) [599.63]

21661 Robbins, Ken. *Thunder on the Plains: The Story of the American Buffalo* (3–5). Illus. 2001, Simon & Schuster $16.00 (978-0-689-83025-9). 32pp. An introduction to the American buffalo, its place in American history, and why its population went from 50 million to near extinction. (Rev: BL 12/1/00; HBG 10/01; SLJ 3/01) [599.64]

21662 Rockwood, Leigh. *Tell Me the Difference between a Porcupine and a Hedgehog* (3–5). Illus. Series: How Are They Different? 2013, Rosen LB $22.60 (978-144889637-0). 24pp. Compares these two animals and their physical characteristics, behavior, diets, habitats, etc. **e** (Rev: BL 4/1/13; LMC 1–2/14; SLJ 4/13) [599.35]

21663 Rodriguez, Ana María. *Secret of the Singing Mice . . . and More!* (4–6). Series: Animal Secrets Revealed! 2008, Enslow LB $23.93 (978-0-7660-2956-9). 48pp. Full-color pictures and interesting information about how scientists discovered and proved their theories about mice, bats, and other small animals. (Rev: SLJ 2/09) [599]

21664 Royer, Anne. *Little Marmots* (3–5). Illus. Series: Born to Be Wild. 2005, Gareth Stevens LB $23.00 (978-0-8368-4439-9). 24pp. A simply worded look at young marmots and their lives, with large photographs.

21665 *Savage Safari: Extreme Encounters with Animal Warriors* (2–5). Illus. 2010, Kingfisher $14.99 (978-0-7534-6456-4). 48pp. Lions, wild dogs, eagles, cheetahs, elephants, cobras, and leopards are among the animals profiled in this overview of the many fierce animals found in Africa. (Rev: BL 6/10; LMC 10/10; SLJ 6/10) [591.4]

21666 Savage, Stephen. *Mammals* (2–4). Illus. Series: What's the Difference? 2000, Raintree $25.69 (978-0-7398-1354-6). 32pp. This book reveals common characteristics and differences among mammals and discusses habitats, babies, food, and locomotion. (Rev: BL 10/15/00; HBG 3/01) [599]

21667 *Savanna Animals: Fun Facts and Stuff to Do* (PS–K). Illus. Series: Padded Animal Board Books. 2006, ME Media $7.95 (978-1-58925-798-6). 24pp. This richly illustrated board book introduces young readers to the animals of the African savanna, including elephants and chimpanzees. (Rev: BL 10/15/06) [591.74]

21668 Schlaepfer, Gloria G. *Hyenas* (4–6). 2010, Marshall Cavendish LB $20.95 (978-0-7614-4838-9). 48pp. This volume covers the animal's habitat, diet, reproduction, life span, adaptability, and the dangers it faces. (Rev: SLJ 1/1/11) [599.74]

21669 Souza, D. M. *Skunks Do More Than Stink!* (3–5). Illus. 2002, Millbrook LB $21.90 (978-0-7613-2503-1). 32pp. This volume is filled with photographs and easily understandable text about the lives of skunks. (Rev: BL 3/1/02; HBG 10/02; SLJ 3/02) [599.76]

21670 Spilsbury, Richard. *Black Rhino* (4–6). Illus. Series: Animals Under Threat. 2004, Heinemann LB $27.07 (978-1-4034-4859-0); paper $8.50 (978-1-4034-5433-1). The rhinoceros and its characteristics are de-scribed before discussion of poaching, relocation, tourism, and other environmental concerns. (Rev: SLJ 1/05) [599.66]

21671 Spilsbury, Richard, and Louise Spilsbury. *A Mob of Kangaroos* (3–5). Series: Animal Groups. 2004, Heinemann LB $24.22 (978-1-4034-4690-9). 32pp. A basic introduction to the animal and its characteristics, using a question-and-answer format and including color close-ups. (Rev: SLJ 9/04)

21672 Stewart, Melissa. *Hippopotamuses* (2–3). Series: Animals. 2002, Children's Book Pr. LB $25.00 (978-0-516-22200-4). 48pp. The anatomy, life cycle, and habits of the hippopotamus are covered in a simple, large-type text and many color photographs. Also use *Rhinoceroses* and *Zebras* (both 2002). (Rev: BL 8/02) [599.63]

21673 Stone, Tanya L. *Skunk* (3–5). Series: Wild America. 2002, Gale LB $21.20 (978-1-56711-641-0). 24pp. A photo-essay on this much-shunned animal with material on its appearance, unusual abilities, food, and life cycle. (Rev: BL 10/15/02; SLJ 2/03) [599.74]

21674 Swanson, Diane. *Skunks* (2–4). Series: Welcome to the World of Animals. 2002, Gareth Stevens LB $24.00 (978-0-8368-3317-1). 32pp. A slim volume that provides information on the animal's home, diet, communication, and lifestyle. (Rev: HBG 3/03; SLJ 3/03) [599.74]

21675 Swinburne, Stephen. *Armadillo Trail* (K–3). Illus. by Bruce Hiscock. 2009, Boyds Mills $16.95 (978-1-59078-463-1). 32pp. This engaging picture book follows a mother armadillo as she gives birth to four pups and raises them to start families of their own. (Rev: BL 2/1/09; SLJ 3/09) [599.3]

21676 Theodorou, Rod. *Black Rhino* (K–2). Illus. Series: Animals in Danger. 2000, Heinemann LB $21.36 (978-1-57572-262-7). 32pp. The endangered black rhino is introduced, with information on diet, habitat, life cycle, and so on, as well as the reasons why the animal is imperiled. (Rev: HBG 10/03; SLJ 4/01) [599]

21677 Webber, Desiree Morrison. *The Buffalo Train Ride* (4–7). Illus. by Sandy Shropshire. 1999, Eakin $14.95 (978-1-57168-275-8). This is a history of the American buffalo, how it was hunted to near extinction, and the modern efforts to make sure it survives, with special attention to the work of William Hornaday. (Rev: HBG 3/00; SLJ 3/00) [591.52]

21678 Winter, Jeanette. *Mama: A True Story in Which a Baby Hippo Loses His Mama During a Tsunami, but Finds a New Home and a New Mama* (K–2). Illus. 2006, Harcourt $16.00 (978-0-15-205495-3). 32pp. In this affecting, well-illustrated picture book, a baby hippo is separated from his mother during a tsunami and later, at a wildlife preserve, adopts a giant tortoise as a surrogate parent. (Rev: BL 4/1/06; SLJ 5/06) [599.63]

APE FAMILY

21679 Barker, David. *Top 50 Reasons to Care About Great Apes* (5–8). Series: Top 50 Reasons to Care About Endangered Animals. 2010, Enslow LB $31.93 (978-0-7660-3456-3). 104pp. Readers learn about apes' biology and habitat, behavior, and threats to their survival; activities in which young people can contribute to apes' welfare are listed. (Rev: LMC 3–4/10) [599.88]

21680 Bredeson, Carmen. *Orangutans Up Close* (1–3). Series: Zoom in on Animals! 2008, Enslow LB $21.26 (978-0-7660-3078-7). 24pp. Simple text and close-up color photographs introduce body parts, babies, and other important characteristics. (Rev: SLJ 11/08) [599.88]

21681 Climo, Shirley. *Monkey Business: Stories from Around the World* (3–5). Illus. by Erik Brooks. 2005, Holt $18.95 (978-0-8050-6392-9). 128pp. Climo has gathered monkey-related folktales, proverbs, historical facts, and scientific information in one entertaining volume. (Rev: BL 5/15/05; SLJ 6/05) [599.8]

21682 Eason, Sarah. *Save the Orangutan* (1–3). Illus. by Andrew Geeson and Marijke Veldhoven. Series: Save the . . . 2009, Rosen LB $23.95 (978-1-4358-2811-7). 32pp. Colorful spreads present answers to common questions in this solid introduction to the endangered orangutan. (Rev: SLJ 6/09) [599.883]

21683 Eszterhas, Suzi. *Orangutan* (PS–2). Illus. by author. Series: Eye on the Wild. 2013, Frances Lincoln $15.99 (978-1-84780-316-0). 28pp. Appealing photographs and simple text chronicle the life of a young orangutan. (Rev: BL 4/1/13; SLJ 5/13) [599.88]

21684 Fleisher, Paul. *Gorillas* (5–8). Illus. Series: AnimalWays. 2000, Marshall Cavendish LB $28.50 (978-0-7614-1140-6). 104pp. Color photographs and clear text introduce gorillas, their scientific classification, physical and behavioral characteristics, and relationship to humans. (Rev: BL 1/1–15/01; HBG 3/01) [599.884]

21685 Gibbons, Gail. *Gorillas* (K–3). Illus. by author. 2011, Holiday House $17.95 (978-0-8234-2236-4). 32pp. A concise and appealing introduction to gorillas and their lives in Africa. Lexile AD820L (Rev: BL 4/15/11; SLJ 4/11) [599.884]

21686 Goodall, Jane. *The Chimpanzees I Love: Saving Their World and Ours* (5–8). 2001, Scholastic paper $18.95 (978-0-439-21310-3). Jane Goodall combines details of her own life researching chimpanzees with fact-filled descriptions of the animals' behavior and a cry for chimpanzee protection. (Rev: BL 12/1/01; HB 1–2/02; HBG 3/02; SLJ 9/01*) [599]

21687 Green, Carl R. *The Gorilla* (3–7). Series: Endangered and Threatened Animals. 2004, Enslow LB $25.26 (978-0-7660-5060-0). 48pp. Supplemented by a lengthy list of links to online resources, this overview of the gorilla explores its behavior and physical characteristics, as well as the threats it faces. (Rev: BL 6/1–15/04)

21688 Hatkoff, Craig, and Juliana Hatkoff. *Looking for Miza: The True Story of the Mountain Gorilla Family Who Rescued One of Their Own* (2–5). Illus. by Peter Greste. 2008, Scholastic $16.99 (978-0-545-08540-3). 40pp. This moving photo-essay tells the story of a father gorilla going to rescue his young daughter when the mother disappears in the Democratic Republic of Congo's Virunga National Park. (Rev: BCCB 12/08; BL 12/15/08; LMC 5/09; SLJ 2/09) [599.884]

21689 Hirsch, Rebecca. *Top 50 Reasons to Care About Polar Bears* (5–8). Series: Top 50 Reasons to Care About Endangered Animals. 2010, Enslow LB $31.93 (978-0-7660-3458-7). 104pp. Threats to polar bears' survival are the main focus of this volume that also discusses the animals' biology, habitat, and behavior. (Rev: LMC 3–4/10) [599.74]

21690 Jango-Cohen, Judith. *Gorillas* (4–6). Series: Animals Animals. 2002, Benchmark LB $25.64 (978-0-7614-1444-5). 48pp. The world of the giant gorilla is explored in this volume that covers topics including physical characteristics, habitat, care of the young, food, and social life. (Rev: BL 12/15/02; HBG 3/03) [599.884]

21691 Jenkins, Martin. *Ape* (K–3). Illus. by Vicky White. 2007, Candlewick $16.99 (978-0-7636-3471-1). 45pp. Compelling illustrations combine with interesting text to introduce the orangutan, chimpanzee, bonobo, and gorilla, showing their daily lives and family relationships and including a final section about threats to their survival and comparisons with human beings. (Rev: HB 1/08; LMC 5/08*; SLJ 3/08) [599.88]

21692 Kalman, Bobbie. *Endangered Mountain Gorillas* (3–5). Illus. Series: Earth's Endangered Animals. 2004, Crabtree LB $25.27 (978-0-7787-1855-0); paper $6.95 (978-0-7787-1901-4). In addition to discussion of their endangered status, this volume covers these animals' habitat, behavior, life cycle, and so forth. (Rev: SLJ 6/05) [599.884]

21693 Kalman, Bobbie, and Hadley Dyer. *Endangered Chimpanzees* (3–5). Illus. Series: Earth's Endangered Animals. 2005, Crabtree LB $25.27 (978-0-7787-1859-8); paper $6.95 (978-0-7787-1905-2). 32pp. After giving a clear overview of the chimpanzee's physical characteristics, life cycle, and behavior, the authors discuss the reasons the animal is endangered and measures being taken to reduce the threat. (Rev: SLJ 12/05) [599.885]

21694 Kane, Karen. *Mountain Gorillas* (2–3). Series: Early Bird Nature Books. 2001, Lerner LB $22.60 (978-0-8225-3040-1). 48pp. An easy-to-read text and numerous color photographs highlight this introduction to mountain gorillas that covers their life cycle, habits, anatomy, and habitats. (Rev: BL 8/1/01) [599.884]

21695 Kendell, Patricia. *Gorillas* (K–2). Series: In the Wild. 2003, Raintree LB $25.70 (978-0-7398-5497-6). 32pp. Designed for beginning readers, this colorfully illustrated book provides a basic overview of gorillas, including their habitat, diet, behavior, and the reasons the species is endangered. (Rev: HBG 10/03; SLJ 10/03) [599.8]

21696 Laman, Tim. *Face to Face with Orangutans* (3–5). Illus. by Cheryl Knott. Series: Face to Face with Animals. 2009, National Geographic $16.95 (978-1-4263-0464-4). 32pp. Striking photo spreads are combined with crisp text and fast facts, with information on the threats this animal faces. (Rev: BL 4/1/09) [599.88]

21697 Lewin, Ted, and Betsy Lewin. *Gorilla Walk* (4–8). 1999, Lothrop LB $17.89 (978-0-688-16510-9). A beautifully illustrated book about the Lewins' trip to Uganda to study mountain gorillas. (Rev: BL 8/99; HBG 4/00; SLJ 9/99) [599.8]

21698 Lockwood, Sophie. *Baboons* (4–7). Series: The World of Mammals. 2005, Child's World LB $29.93 (978-1-59296-497-0). Arresting photographs and engaging text introduce the anatomy, behavior, habitat, and life cycle of the baboon as well as the threats to the animal's survival in the wild. (Rev: SLJ 3/06) [599.8]

21699 McLeese, Don. *Gorillas* (1–3). Illus. Series: Eye to Eye with Endangered Species. 2010, Rourke LB $27.07 (978-161590274-3). 24pp. With eye-catching photographs, this book looks at gorillas' lives and the threats they face. (Rev: BL 3/1/11) [599.884]

21700 Martin, Patricia A. *Chimpanzees* (3–5). Series: True Books. 2000, Children's Book Pr. LB $21.50 (978-0-516-24013-8). 48pp. Large text and color photos introduce chimpanzees, their habits, food, and homes. (Rev: BL 5/15/00) [599.88]

21701 Orme, David. *Orangutan* (4–6). Illus. Series: Animals Under Threat. 2005, Heinemann LB $29.93 (978-1-4034-5586-4). 48pp. The life cycle of the orangutan and threats to its survival are explored in this blend of narrative and eye-catching color photography.

21702 Pimm, Nancy Roe. *Colo's Story: The Life of One Grand Gorilla* (4–6). Series: The Columbus Zoo Books for Young Readers. 2011, Columbus Zoo and Aquarium $18.95 (978-0-9841554-4-6); paper $8.95 (978-0-9841554-5-3). 78pp. The inspiring story of Colo, the first gorilla born in captivity, is told in this interesting book that shows changes in zoo management and primate conservation since the 1950s. (Rev: SLJ 7/11) [599.884]

21703 Pimm, Nancy Roe. *The Heart of the Beast: Eight Great Gorilla Stories* (4–7). 2007, Darby Creek $18.95 (978-1-58196-054-9). True stories about famous gorillas provide information on their mental and physical development, behavior, and diet. (Rev: BL 6/1–15/07; SLJ 12/07) [599.884]

21704 Powzyk, Joyce. *In Search of Lemurs: My Days and Nights in a Madagascar Rain Forest* (4–7). 1998, National Geographic $17.95 (978-0-7922-7072-0). The author describes and illustrates her journey into the wilds of Madagascar and the many animals, plants, and birds she encountered, culminating in the elusive lemur. (Rev: BL 9/15/98; HBG 3/99; SLJ 10/98) [599.8]

21705 Riggs, Kate. *Gorillas* (K–3). Illus. Series: Amazing Animals. 2012, Creative Education LB $17.95 (978-160818107-0). 24pp. For new or reluctant readers, this is a good introduction to the gorilla's physical characteristics, habitat, and behavior, and includes a story from folklore explaining why all they do is eat and sleep. (Rev: BL 3/1/12) [599.884]

21706 Sayre, April Pulley. *Meet the Howlers!* (PS–2). Illus. by Woody Miller. 2010, Charlesbridge $16.95 (978-1-57091-733-2). 32pp. Full-bleed illustrations and a monkey-call refrain enhance this accessible introduction to howler monkeys. (Rev: BL 3/15/10; SLJ 3/1/10) [599.8]

21707 Spilsbury, Richard, and Louise Spilsbury. *A Troop of Chimpanzees* (3–5). Series: Animal Groups. 2003, Heinemann LB $24.22 (978-1-4034-0746-7). 32pp. This photo-filled overview of chimpanzees looks at behavior, diet, habitat, physical appearance, and social structure. (Rev: HBG 10/03; SLJ 9/03) [599.885]

21708 Stefoff, Rebecca. *Chimpanzees* (4–7). Illus. Series: AnimalWays. 2003, Benchmark LB $31.36 (978-0-7614-1579-4). 112pp. A richly illustrated look at chimpanzees, from their physiology to their interaction with humans. (Rev: SLJ 3/04)

21709 Stefoff, Rebecca. *The Primate Order* (5–9). Series: Family Trees. 2005, Benchmark LB $32.79 (978-0-7614-1816-0). Habits, habitats, and human-like aspects of this order of animals; an engaging book with plenty of facts for report-writers. (Rev: SLJ 6/06) [599.8]

21710 Taylor, Marianne. *Mountain Gorilla* (4–6). Illus. Series: Animals Under Threat. 2004, Heinemann LB $27.07 (978-1-4034-4861-3); paper $8.50 (978-1-4034-5435-5). 48pp. The mountain gorilla and its characteristics are described before discussion of problems with habitat, tourism, and conservation. (Rev: SLJ 1/05) [599.884]

21711 Thomson, Sarah L. *Amazing Gorillas!* (K–2). Illus. Series: I Can Read. 2005, HarperCollins LB $16.89 (978-0-06-054460-7). 32pp. Close-up color photographs add to the simple text in this informative introduction that looks at gorillas and their diet, habitat, physical characteristics, and endangered status. (Rev: BL 5/1/05) [599.884]

21712 Turner, Pamela S. *Gorilla Doctors: Saving Endangered Great Apes* (3–5). Illus. Series: Scientists in the Field. 2005, Houghton $17.00 (978-0-618-44555-4). 48pp. Exciting accounts of real events add drama to this exploration of the work of veterinarians in east central Africa. (Rev: BL 6/1–15/05) [333.95]

21713 Zabludoff, Marc. *Monkeys* (3–6). Series: AnimalWays. 2007, Marshall Cavendish LB $23.95 (978-0-7614-2535-9). 108pp. After an overview of monkey history, this volume looks at monkey anatomy, behavior, relationship with humans, and so forth. (Rev: SLJ 5/08) [599.8]

BATS

21714 Gerber, Carole. *Little Red Bat* (1–3). Illus. by Christina Wald. 2010, Sylvan Dell $16.95 (978-1-60718-069-2); paper $8.95 (978-160718-0-80-7.). 32pp. An endearing little bat ponders whether to fly south for the winter or stay put as she considers preparations her woodland friends have made for winter in this informational book with a fictional feel. (Rev: BL 4/15/10; LMC 11–12/10; SLJ 6/1/10) [599.4]

21715 Greenaway, Theresa. *The Secret Life of Bats* (4–7). Series: The Secret World of . . . 2002, Raintree LB $27.12 (978-0-7398-4982-8). 48pp. An accessible, attractive volume that begins with little-known facts about bats and continues with information on their structure, habits, food, and habitats. (Rev: BL 8/02) [599.4]

21716 Landau, Elaine. *Bats: Hunters of the Night* (2–3). Series: Animals after Dark. 2007, Enslow LB $22.60 (978-0-7660-2772-5). 32pp. Photographs of bats accompany information about their nocturnal behavior and their peculiar habits and abilities. (Rev: LMC 10/07; SLJ 8/07)

21717 Markle, Sandra. *Bats: Biggest! Littlest!* (K–3). Illus. 2013, Boyds Mills $16.95 (978-1-59078-952-0). 40pp. An attractive overview of bats from the giant flying fox to the tiny bumblebee bat, and their characteristics and behaviors. (Rev: BL 3/15/13; SLJ 6/13) [599.4]

21718 Pringle, Laurence. *Bats! Strange and Wonderful* (3–5). 2000, Boyds Mills $15.95 (978-1-56397-327-7). 32pp. This book gives basic information about various types of bats and their habitats and lifestyles, and exposes popular myths about these misunderstood mammals. (Rev: BCCB 4/00; BL 3/15/00; HBG 9/00; SLJ 6/00) [599.4]

21719 Ruff, Sue, and Don E. Wilson. *Bats* (5–8). Series: AnimalWays. 2000, Marshall Cavendish LB $31.36 (978-0-7614-1137-6). 112pp. Some of the topics that are covered include anatomy, habits, range, classification, habitats, evolution, and survival skills. (Rev: BL 1/1–15/01; HBG 3/01) [599.4]

21720 Schuetz, Kari. *Bats* (K–2). Illus. Series: Backyard Wildlife. 2012, Children's Press LB $21.95 (978-160014720-3). 24pp. Young readers learn the basics about bats: where they live, where and when they sleep, and what they eat. (Rev: BL 9/15/12) [599.4]

21721 Simon, Seymour. *Amazing Bats* (1–3). Series: See-More Readers. 2005, Chronicle Bks. LB $14.50 (978-1-58717-261-8); paper $3.95 (978-1-58717-262-5). This photo-filled title provides beginning readers with an attractive overview of bats' physical characteristics, habitat, diet, and behavior. (Rev: SLJ 11/05)

21722 Stewart, Melissa. *A Place for Bats* (PS–3). Illus. by Higgins Bond. 2012, Peachtree $16.95 (978-156145624-6). 32pp. Introduces the bats of North America with photographs and information on habitat and threats to their survival. (Rev: BL 2/1/12; SLJ 5/1/12) [599.4]

21723 Vogel, Julia. *Bats* (2–4). Illus. Series: Our Wild World. 2007, NorthWord $10.95 (978-1-55971-968-1); paper $7.95 (978-1-55971-969-8). 48pp. This easy-to-understand and eye-catching guide to bats introduces a variety of different species, as well as general information about the flying mammals' physical characteristics, habitat, diet, predators, prey, and behavior. (Rev: BL 3/15/07) [599.4]

21724 Welsbacher, Anne. *Vampire Bats* (3–6). Series: Predators in the Wild. 2001, Capstone LB $23.93 (978-0-7368-0787-6). 32pp. Myths about the vampire bat are presented along with facts in this general introduction to the animal's characteristics and habitat. (Rev: HBG 10/01; SLJ 1/02) [599.4]

21725 Wheeler, Jill C. *Bumblebee Bats* (3–5). Illus. Series: Bats, Set II. 2005, ABDO LB $21.35 (978-1-59679-320-0). 24pp. Introduces the bumblebee bat,

which is found in Thailand and is the world's smallest bat species. (Rev: SLJ 2/06) [599.4]

BEARS

21726 Arnold, Caroline. *A Polar Bear's World* (K–2). Illus. by author. Series: Animals. 2010, Capstone LB $25.32 (978-140485743-8). 24pp. This book presents engaging information about polar bears — how far they can swim without stopping, for example — with effective artwork. (Rev: BL 9/15/10) [599.786]

21727 Bodden, Valerie. *Polar Bears* (K–2). Illus. Series: Amazing Animals. 2010, Creative Company $16.95 (978-158341811-6). 24pp. A simple overview of the characteristics of polar bears, with eye-catching photographs. (Rev: BL 7/10) [599.786]

21728 Brett, Jeannie. *Wild About Bears* (K–3). Illus. by author. 2014, Charlesbridge $17.95 (978-158089418-0); paper $7.95 (978-15808941-9-7). 32pp. With double-page watercolors and informative text, Brett profiles the eight species of bears and shows them in typical bear activities. **e** (Rev: BL 3/1/14; SLJ 3/14) [599.78]

21729 Calabro, Marian. *Operation Grizzly Bear* (5–8). 1989, Macmillan $13.95 (978-0-02-716241-7). An account by two naturalists on a 12-year study of silvertip bears in Yellowstone Park. (Rev: BL 3/15/90; VOYA 4/90) [599.74]

21730 Daly, Timothy M. *Black Bears* (3–5). Illus. Series: Nature's Children. 2012, Scholastic/Children's Press LB $28 (978-053126831-5); paper $6.95 (9780531254769). 48pp. Simple text and many photographs present basic information about these animals' anatomy and behavior as well as their environment and history. Lexile 1010L (Rev: BL 3/1/13) [599.78]

21731 Davies, Nicola. *Ice Bear: In the Steps of the Polar Bear* (K–2). Illus. by Gary Blythe. 2005, Candlewick $16.99 (978-0-7636-2759-1). 32pp. Basic information about polar bears — and admiration for their survival — is delivered in a friendly narrative that also touches on what the Inuit have learned from these animals. (Rev: BL 12/1/05; SLJ 2/06) [599.796]

21732 Deady, Kathleen W. *Grizzly Bears* (3–5). Series: Predators in the Wild. 2002, Capstone LB $23.93 (978-0-7368-1063-0). 32pp. Basic information about grizzly bears' lives, habitat, diet, and endangered status is presented in a format that will suit both browsers and report writers. (Rev: SLJ 8/02) [599.74]

21733 Eason, Sarah. *Save the Polar Bear* (1–3). Illus. by Andrew Geeson and Marijke Veldhoven. Series: Save the . . . 2009, Rosen LB $23.95 (978-1-4358-2810-0). 32pp. Colorful spreads present answers to common questions in this solid introduction to the endangered polar bear. (Rev: SLJ 6/09) [599.786]

21734 Eszterhas, Suzi. *Brown Bear* (PS–2). Illus. Series: Eye on the Wild. 2012, Frances Lincoln $15.99 (978-184780302-3). 32pp. Excellent color photographs show a pair of brown bear cubs as they grow up in Alaska. (Rev: BL 11/1/12) [599.784]

21735 Fraggalosch, Audrey. *Great Grizzly Wilderness: A Story of the Pacific Rain Forest* (K–3). Illus. by Donald G. Eberhart. Series: Habitats. 2000, Soundprints $15.95 (978-1-56899-838-1). This highly pictorial account traces one year in the lives of a British Columbia grizzly bear and her cubs. (Rev: HBG 3/01; SLJ 1/01) [599.7]

21736 Gaines, Richard Marshall. *When Bears Attack!* (4–6). Series: When Wild Animals Attack! 2006, Enslow LB $23.93 (978-0-7660-2669-8). 48pp. Readers will come away from this book with a healthy respect for bears and their wild ways. The author also discusses conservation of bear habitats. (Rev: SLJ 7/07)

21737 Gibbons, Gail. *Grizzly Bears* (K–4). Illus. by author. 2003, Holiday House $16.95 (978-0-8234-1793-3). All about grizzly bears — where they live, what they eat, and what's being done to protect them. (Rev: HBG 4/04; SLJ 3/04) [599.7]

21738 Gibbons, Gail. *Polar Bears* (2–4). Illus. 2001, Holiday House $16.95 (978-0-8234-1593-9). 32pp. An accessible, nicely illustrated introduction to the habitat, behavior, diet, and anatomy of the polar bear. (Rev: BL 9/15/01; HBG 3/02; SLJ 9/01) [599.786]

21739 Greene, Jacqueline D. *Grizzly Bears: Saving the Silvertip* (3–4). Series: America's Animal Comebacks. 2007, Bearport LB $25.27 (978-1-59716-533-4). 32pp. With eye-catching photographs and an appealing design, Greene looks at threats to the grizzly and at efforts to bring them back from the brink of extinction. (Rev: SLJ 12/07) [599.7]

21740 Guiberson, Brenda Z. *Moon Bear* (PS–3). Illus. by Ed Young. 2010, Henry Holt $16.99 (978-0-8050-8977-6). 32pp. Guiberson portrays the life of the Southeast Asian moon bear and explains the threats that it faces; with eye-catching illustrations and an informative author's note. Lexile AD780L (Rev: BL 1/1/10; SLJ 4/1/10*) [599.78]

21741 Guidoux, Valérie. *Little Polar Bears* (1–3). Series: Born to Be Wild. 2005, Gareth Stevens LB $23.00 (978-0-8368-4739-0). 24pp. This colorful overview of polar bear cubs focuses on the role that their parents play in finding food for their offspring and protecting them from predators. (Rev: SLJ 2/06) [599.786]

21742 Hamilton, Sue. *Mauled by a Bear* (4–7). Series: Close Encounters of the Wild Kind. 2010, ABDO LB $27.07 (978-1-60453-932-5). 32pp. Exciting stories and graphic photographs add high-interest appeal to the information about bears and advice on avoiding and surviving such an attack. (Rev: LMC 10/10; SLJ 5/10) [599.7]

21743 Hatkoff, Juliana, and Isabella Hatkoff. *Knut: How One Little Polar Bear Captivated the World* (2–4). Illus. 2007, Scholastic $16.99 (978-0-545-04716-6). 40pp. Enchanting photographs of Knut, a polar bear born in a German zoo and abandoned by his mother, accompany a text describing the role of the zookeeper who raised him. (Rev: BCCB 12/07; BL 12/15/07; SLJ 1/08) [599.786]

21744 Hirschi, Ron. *Our Three Bears* (3–5). Illus. 2008, Boyds Mills $16.95 (978-1-59078-015-2). 32pp. An at-

tractive introduction to the bears — black, grizzly, and polar — that live in North America. (Rev: BL 11/15/08; LMC 1/09; SLJ 10/08) [599.78]

21745 Hirschi, Ron. *Searching for Grizzlies* (3–5). Illus. 2005, Boyds Mills $15.95 (978-1-59078-014-5). 32pp. Beautiful photographs, factual text, and excerpts from notebooks make this a fascinating introduction to the grizzly bear, with enough information for report writers. (Rev: BL 9/1/05; SLJ 9/05) [599.784]

21746 Hunt, Joni Phelps. *A Band of Bears: The Rambling Life of a Lovable Loner* (5–8). Series: Jean-Michel Cousteau Presents. 2007, London Town paper $8.95 (978-0-9766134-5-9). With eye-catching photographs and stories of close encounters with these animals, this book looks at bears' characteristics, behavior, intelligence, and the threats to their survival. (Rev: SLJ 11/07) [599.78]

21747 Lang, Aubrey. *The Adventures of Baby Bear* (K–2). Illus. by Wayne Lynch. Series: Nature Babies. 2001, Fitzhenry & Whiteside $13.95 (978-1-55041-670-1). 28pp. Readers accompany two young bear cubs from birth to adolescence, in a photographic presentation with simple text and a page of facts. (Rev: BL 12/15/01; SLJ 2/02) [599.78]

21748 Lang, Aubrey. *Baby Grizzly* (2–4). Photos by Wayne Lynch. Series: Nature Babies. 2006, Fitzhenry & Whiteside $13.95 (978-1-55041-577-3); paper $6.95 (978-1-55041-579-7). 36pp. This photo-filled title follows the development of three grizzly cubs as they stay by their mother's side in the wilds of Alaska. (Rev: SLJ 11/06) [599.784]

21749 Lang, Aubrey. *Baby Polar Bear* (2–3). Illus. by Wayne Lynch. Series: Nature Babies. 2008, Fitzhenry & Whiteside $15.95 (978-1-55455-101-9); paper $7.95 (978-1-55455-102-6). 36pp. A handsome portrayal of a female polar bear looking after her two cubs. (Rev: BL 9/15/08) [599.786]

21750 Leathers, Dan. *Polar Bears on the Hudson Bay* (3–6). Illus. Series: A Robbie Reader: On the Verge of Extinction: Crisis in the Environment. 2007, Mitchell Lane LB $17.95 (978-1-58415-586-7). 32pp. Global warming and growth in tourism are two of the threats described in this overview of the animals and their habitat; there are close-up photographs and "What You Can Do" sections. (Rev: BL 10/15/07; LMC 1/08; SLJ 11/07) [599.786]

21751 Lockwood, Sophie. *Polar Bears* (5–8). Series: World of Mammals. 2005, Child's World LB $29.93 (978-1-59296-501-4). This slim but richly illustrated title looks at polar bears' physical characteristics, behavior, diet, relationship with the Inuit people, and the growing threats to their survival. (Rev: BL 10/15/05) [599.786]

21752 McAllister, Ian, and Nicholas Read. *The Salmon Bears: Giants of the Great Bear Rainforest* (5–8). Illus. by Ian McAllister. 2010, Orca paper $18.95 (978-15546920-5-7). 89pp. Introduces grizzly, black, and spirit bears as they experience the seasons in the Great Bear Rainforest of British Columbia, and their relationship with the salmon in the rivers. (Rev: BL 6/10; SLJ 7/10) [599.78]

21753 Markle, Sandra. *Polar Bears* (3–7). Series: Animal Predators. 2004, Carolrhoda LB $25.26 (978-1-57505-730-9). 40pp. Describes the life of a female polar bear in the Arctic — behavior, diet, communication, life cycle, and so forth. (Rev: SLJ 1/05) [599.786]

21754 Montgomery, Sy. *Search for the Golden Moon Bear: Science and Adventure in the Asian Tropics* (5–9). 2004, Houghton Mifflin $17.00 (978-0-618-35650-8). Nature writer Montgomery describes her search across war-torn Southeast Asia for the elusive golden moon bear. (Rev: BL 12/1/04; SLJ 12/04) [599.78]

21755 Murray, Julie. *Black Bears* (2–3). Illus. Series: Animal Kingdom. 2005, ABDO LB $21.35 (978-1-59197-302-7). 24pp. For beginning readers, this is an introduction to the black bear and its physical characteristics, habitat, and diet. (Rev: SLJ 5/05) [599]

21756 Murray, Julie. *Grizzly Bears* (1–3). Illus. Series: Animal Kingdom. 2002, ABDO LB $21.35 (978-1-57765-715-6). 24pp. For beginning readers, this photo-filled book offers a basic introduction to the life of the grizzly bear. (Rev: SLJ 4/03) [599.784]

21757 Newman, Mark. *Polar Bears* (K–3). Photos by author. 2010, Henry Holt $16.99 (978-0-8050-8999-8). Unpaged. Appealing photographs and simple text introduce the lives of polar bears — physical characteristics, life cycle, and so forth — and discuss the challenges they face as their habitat is disappearing. (Rev: HB 1–2/11; LMC 5–6/11; SLJ 2/1/11) [599.786]

21758 Patent, Dorothy Hinshaw. *A Polar Bear Biologist at Work* (4–6). Series: Wildlife Conservation Society. 2001, Watts LB $24.50 (978-0-531-11850-4). 48pp. Basic information on polar bears is enlivened by the portrayal of biologist Chuck Jonkel at work and by his comments on bears and the environment. (Rev: SLJ 11/01) [599.786]

21759 Patent, Dorothy Hinshaw. *Polar Bears* (3–6). Series: Nature Watch. 2000, Carolrhoda $25.26 (978-1-57505-020-1). 48pp. The biggest and strongest animal of the arctic, the polar bear is the subject of this simple science book that contains outstanding color photographs. (Rev: BL 3/15/00; HBG 9/00; SLJ 7/00) [599.78]

21760 Penny, Malcolm. *Polar Bear* (2–4). Series: Natural World. 2000, Raintree LB $27.12 (978-0-7398-1060-6). 48pp. This fine introduction to the polar bear, with clear photos and a good layout, covers topics including appearance, life cycle, mating, food, and habits. (Rev: HBG 9/00; SLJ 7/00) [599.7]

21761 Preston-Mafham, Rod. *The Secret Life of Bears* (4–7). Series: The Secret World of . . . 2002, Raintree LB $27.12 (978-0-7398-4983-5). 48pp. In this attractive volume readers learn why bears behave as they do, how they feed, communicate, and reproduce, and what dangers face their future. (Rev: BL 8/02) [599.74]

21762 Robinson, Jill, and Marc Bekoff. *Jasper's Story: Saving Moon Bears* (2–5). Illus. by Gijsbert van Frankenhuyzen. 2013, Sleeping Bear $16.99 (978-1-58536-

798-6). 40pp. The sad but true story of a Chinese moon bear that lived in a tiny cage for years before being rescued by a team called Animals Asia. (Rev: BL 3/15/13; LMC 1–2/14; SLJ 4/13) [599.78]

21763 Rosing, Norbert. *Polar Bears* (3–5). Illus. 2010, Firefly $19.95 (978-1-55407-599-7); paper $9.95 (978-1-55407-623-9). 56pp. Close-up photographs with informative captions show the lives of polar bears through the four seasons. (Rev: BL 12/1/10; SLJ 2/1/11) [599.786]

21764 Ryder, Joanne. *A Pair of Polar Bears: Twin Cubs Find a Home at the San Diego Zoo* (K–2). Illus. 2006, Simon & Schuster $16.95 (978-0-689-85871-0). 32pp. This engaging photo-essay chronicles the story of two orphaned polar bear cubs who find a home at the San Diego Zoo. (Rev: BL 2/1/06; SLJ 3/06) [599.786]

21765 Sartore, Joel. *Face to Face with Grizzlies* (2–5). Illus. Series: Face to Face with Animals. 2007, National Geographic $16.95 (978-1-4263-0050-9). 32pp. This close-up look at the grizzly bear describes the author/photographer's encounters with these huge animals and introduces readers to their physical characteristics, habitat, diet, behavior, and the threats to their survival. (Rev: BL 4/1/07) [599.784]

21766 Shea, Therese. *Bears* (PS–2). 2006, Rosen LB $19.95 (978-1-4042-3524-8). 24pp. An up-close look at various bears, with facts on their physical characteristics, the food they eat, their habitat, caring for their young, and their enemies. (Rev: SLJ 3/07) [599.78]

21767 Stefoff, Rebecca. *Bears* (5–8). Series: Animal-Ways. 2001, Marshall Cavendish LB $31.36 (978-0-7614-1268-7). 112pp. Various species of bears are introduced in text and color photographs with additional material on their location, anatomy, habits, and behavior. (Rev: BL 3/15/02; HBG 10/02) [599.74]

21768 Stone, Jason, and Jody Stone. *Grizzly Bear* (2–4). Illus. 2000, Blackbirch $21.20 (978-1-56711-342-6). 24pp. Striking photos and a straightforward text are used to introduce grizzly bears, their physical characteristics, habits, hibernation, food, and habitats. (Rev: BL 12/15/00; HBG 3/01) [599.784]

21769 Stone, Jason, and Jody Stone. *Polar Bear* (2–4). Series: Wild Bears! 2000, Blackbirch LB $24.94 (978-1-56711-344-0). 24pp. This stunningly illustrated book describes the physical characteristics and homes of the polar bear, its food, mating, care of young, and interaction with humans. (Rev: BL 12/15/00; HBG 3/01) [599.7]

21770 Swinburne, Stephen. *Black Bear: North America's Bear* (3–4). 2003, Boyds Mills $15.95 (978-1-59078-023-7). 32pp. This comprehensive, photo-filled overview covers the black bear's habitat, diet, and behavior, looks at the bear's history in Yellowstone, and clears up some common misconceptions. (Rev: BL 1/1–15/04; HBG 4/04; SLJ 11/03) [599.78]

21771 Thomas, Keltie. *Bear Rescue: Changing the Future for Endangered Wildlife* (4–8). Series: Firefly Animal Rescue. 2006, Firefly LB $19.95 (978-1-55297-922-8); paper $9.95 (978-1-55297-921-1). Focuses on work that's being done on behalf of threatened bear species, including Indian sloth bears, Chinese black bears, and polar bears. (Rev: SLJ 12/06) [599.78]

BIG CATS

21772 Becker, John E. *Wild Cats: Past and Present* (5–8). Illus. by Mark Hallett. 2008, Darby Creek $18.95 (978-1-58196-052-5). Lions, tigers, jaguars, and cheetahs are among the wild cats covered in this well-illustrated, large-format book that covers history, environmental threats, and conservation and will attract both researchers and browsers. (Rev: BL 3/15/08; SLJ 6/08) [599.75]

21773 Bodden, Valerie. *Jaguars* (1–3). Illus. Series: Amazing Animals. 2013, Creative Education LB $17.95 (978-160818086-8). 24pp. An eye-catching introduction to these animals that will appeal to young and reluctant readers; includes a story from folklore. (Rev: BL 4/15/13; LMC 10/13*) [599.75]

21774 Bortolotti, Dan. *Tiger Rescue: Changing the Future for Endangered Wildlife* (3–8). Series: Firefly Animal Rescue. 2003, Firefly LB $19.95 (978-1-55297-599-2); paper $9.95 (978-1-55297-558-9). 64pp. A look at how and why tigers are an endangered species and what can be done to help them, with profiles of some of the people involved in the effort. (Rev: BL 1/1–15/04; SLJ 4/04) [333.9]

21775 Chancellor, Deborah. *Tiger Tales: And Big Cat Stories* (2–4). Illus. by Peter Dennis. Series: Eyewitness Reader. 2000, DK $14.99 (978-0-7894-5424-9); paper $3.99 (978-0-7894-5423-2). 48pp. A beginning reader that features lions, tigers, and other big cats and incidents in which they clash with humans. (Rev: HBG 9/00; SLJ 7/00) [599.74]

21776 Chottin, Ariane. *Little Leopards* (3–5). Illus. Series: Born to Be Wild. 2005, Gareth Stevens LB $23.00 (978-0-8368-4438-2). 24pp. A simply worded look at young leopards and their lives, with large photographs.

21777 Costello, Emily. *Realm of the Panther: A Story of South Florida's Forests* (K–3). Illus. by Wes Siegrist. Series: Habitats. 2000, Soundprints $15.95 (978-1-56899-847-3). A richly illustrated account that focuses on a pair of yearling panthers in the Big Cypress National Preserve in Florida. (Rev: HBG 3/01; SLJ 1/01) [599.74]

21778 Darling, Kathy. *Lions* (3–6). Series: Nature Watch. 2000, Carolrhoda $25.26 (978-1-57505-404-9). 48pp. The unique life of the lion is described in this simple book that contains a wealth of attention-getting color photographs. (Rev: BL 3/15/00; HBG 9/00) [599.74]

21779 de la Bedoyere, Camilla. *100 Things You Should Know About Big Cats* (3–6). Illus. Series: Remarkable Man and Beast: Facing Survival. 2010, Mason Crest LB $19.95 (978-142221965-2). 48pp. With plenty of lively photographs and illustrations woven together with cohesive text, this is a useful introduction to big cats. (Rev: BL 10/15/10; LMC 3–4/11) [599.75]

21780 Eason, Sarah. *Save the Tiger* (1–3). Illus. by Andrew Geeson and Marijke Veldhoven. Series: Save the

. . . 2009, Rosen LB $23.95 (978-1-4358-2813-1). 32pp. Colorful spreads present answers to common questions in this solid introduction to the endangered tiger. (Rev: SLJ 6/09) [599.74]

21781 Estigarribia, Diana. *Cheetahs* (3–6). Illus. Series: Animals, Animals. 2004, Benchmark $25.64 (978-0-7614-1749-1). 46pp. A well-written overview of these animals, providing all the information needed for report writing plus additional material of interest. (Rev: SLJ 2/05) [599.74]

21782 Eszterhas, Suzi. *Cheetah* (PS–2). Illus. Series: Eye on the Wild. 2012, Frances Lincoln $15.99 (978-184780301-6). 28pp. With beautiful photographs, this large-format book follows cheetah cubs and shows their close bonds with their mothers. (Rev: BL 4/15/12; LMC 11–12/12; SLJ 5/1/12) [599.759]

21783 Gaines, Richard Marshall. *When Tigers Attack!* (4–6). Series: When Wild Animals Attack! 2006, Enslow LB $23.93 (978-0-7660-2665-0). 48pp. Readers will come away from this book with a healthy respect for tigers and their wild ways. The author also discusses conservation of tiger habitats. (Rev: LMC 3/07; SLJ 7/07)

21784 Gallimard Jeunesse, et al. *Lions* (PS–2). Series: First Discovery. 2000, Scholastic $12.95 (978-0-439-14824-5). 24pp. A beginner's look at lions in a heavily illustrated book that presents their physical characteristics, homes, and family life. (Rev: BL 8/00; HBG 3/01) [599.74]

21785 Gish, Melissa. *Cougars* (4–6). Illus. Series: Living Wild. 2012, Creative Education LB $24.95 (978-160818167-4). 48pp. Useful for reports, this volume covers the animals' anatomy, habitat, life cycle, reproduction, position on the food chain, adaptations, and threats to survival. Lexile NC1370L (Rev: BL 12/15/12) [599.75]

21786 Greenberg, Dan. *Leopards* (4–6). Series: Animals Animals. 2002, Benchmark LB $25.64 (978-0-7614-1448-3). 48pp. This simple introduction to leopards examines, in text and photographs, their anatomy, habitats, behavior, and eating habits. (Rev: BL 12/15/02; HBG 3/03) [599.6]

21787 Hamilton, Sue. *Ambushed by a Cougar* (4–7). Series: Close Encounters of the Wild Kind. 2010, ABDO LB $27.07 (978-1-60453-928-8). 32pp. Exciting stories and graphic photographs add high-interest appeal to the information about cougars and advice on avoiding and surviving such an attack. (Rev: LMC 10/10; SLJ 5/10) [599.73]

21788 Hansen, Rosanna. *Caring for Cheetahs: My African Adventure* (3–6). Illus. 2007, Boyds Mills $16.95 (978-1-59078-387-0). 32pp. Cheetahs saved by the Cheetah Conservation Fund in Namibia are featured in beautiful color photos, along with plenty of information about the big cats in general and one rescued cheetah in particular. (Rev: BCCB 4/07; BL 2/15/07; SLJ 3/07) [599.75]

21789 Hatkoff, Craig, and Juliana Hatkoff, et al. *Leo the Snow Leopard: The True Story of an Amazing Rescue*

(1–3). 2010, Scholastic $17.99 (978-0-545-22927-2). Unpaged. The story of an orphaned snow leopard that is rescued from the mountains in Pakistan and finds a home at the Bronx Zoo. (Rev: BL 10/15/10; SLJ 10/1/10) [599.75]

21790 Hewitt, Joan. *A Tiger Cub Grows Up* (1–3). Series: Baby Animals. 2001, Carolrhoda LB $21.27 (978-1-57505-163-5); paper $6.95 (978-0-8225-0089-6). 32pp. For beginning readers, this colorful account describes the youth of a tiger cub in a brief, simple text. (Rev: BL 10/15/01; HBG 3/02; SLJ 10/01) [599.74]

21791 Hughes, Monica. *Tiger Cub* (K–2). Illus. Series: I Love Reading. 2006, Bearport LB $19.96 (978-1-59716-155-8). 24pp. Facts about tigers — their physical appearance, habitat, endangered status, and behavior — are given in concise answers to questions posed on colorful double-page spreads; a small-format book suitable for beginning readers. (Rev: BL 4/1/06) [599.756]

21792 Joubert, Beverly, and Dereck Joubert. *Face to Face with Leopards* (3–6). Series: Face to Face with Animals. 2009, National Geographic $16.95 (978-1-4263-0636-5); LB $25.90 (978-1-4263-0637-2). 32pp. The story of the two authors meeting a days-old leopard cub is illustrated with ample close-up photographs. (Rev: SLJ 11/09) [599.75]

21793 Joubert, Beverly, and Dereck Joubert. *Face to Face with Lions* (4–8). Illus. by author. 2008, National Geographic $16.95 (978-142630207-7). 32pp. Lions' biology, habitat, diet, and reproduction are vividly portrayed in this photographic guide that also provides engaging firsthand experiences, Lexile 820L (Rev: BL 11/15/08) [599.757]

21794 Kendell, Patricia. *Leopards* (K–2). Series: In the Wild. 2003, Raintree LB $25.70 (978-0-7398-5496-9). 32pp. Designed for beginning readers, this photo-filled overview of leopards provides basic information about the big cat's habitat, diet, behavior, and how it raises its young. (Rev: HBG 10/03; SLJ 10/03) [599.7]

21795 Landau, Elaine. *Big Cats: Hunters of the Night* (2–3). 2007, Enslow LB $22.60 (978-0-7660-2770-1). 32pp. Photographs of big cats accompany information about their nocturnal behavior and their hunting abilities. (Rev: SLJ 8/07*)

21796 Landau, Elaine. *Fierce Cats* (3–5). Illus. Series: Fearsome, Scary, and Creepy Animals. 2003, Enslow LB $23.93 (978-0-7660-2062-7). 48pp. Landau offers a dramatic overview of the fierce behavior of leopards, cheetahs, and other big cats and documents some real-life attacks on humans. (Rev: BL 10/15/03; HBG 4/04) [599.7]

21797 Latta, Jan. *Timba the Tiger* (K–4). Series: Wild Animal Families. 2006, Gareth Stevens LB $23.93 (978-0-8368-7772-4). 24pp. In a first-"person" account, Timba describes what it's like to be a tiger, giving readers facts about these big cats in an enjoyable and engaging format. Also use *Lisa the Lion* (2006). (Rev: SLJ 5/07)

21798 Macken, JoAnn Early. *Cougars* (K–2). Series: Animals That Live in the Mountains. 2010, Weekly

Reader LB $22 (978-1-4339-2411-8). 24pp. Close-up photographs and bright backgrounds enliven this book about the life and habitat of cougars. (Rev: SLJ 8/1/10) [599.75]

21799 Macken, JoAnn Early. *Cougars / Puma* (2–4). Trans. by Tatiana Acosta and Guillermo Gutiérrez. Series: Animals That Live in the Mountains / Animales de las montañas. 2006, Weekly Reader LB $21.00 (978-0-8368-6448-9). 24pp. A beginning book with facts about cougars in both English and Spanish. (Rev: SLJ 6/06) [599.75]

21800 Macken, JoAnn Early. *Tigers* (K–2). Series: Animals I See at the Zoo. 2002, Gareth Stevens LB $21.00 (978-0-8368-3276-1). 24pp. Large type and clear pictures make this introduction appealing to beginning readers. (Rev: HBG 3/03; SLJ 2/03)

21801 Markle, Sandra. *Lions* (2–5). Illus. Series: Animal Predators. 2004, Carolrhoda LB $25.26 (978-1-57505-727-9). Concise text and clear, full-page photographs introduce the life cycle of the lion and its physical characteristics, habitat, diet, and predatory behavior. (Rev: BL 9/15/04; SLJ 10/04) [599.757]

21802 Markle, Sandra. *Outside and Inside Big Cats* (2–4). Series: Outside Inside. 2003, Simon & Schuster $16.95 (978-0-689-82299-5). 40pp. This overview of the big cats, including cougars, leopards, lions, and tigers, looks in particular at their predatory characteristics. (Rev: BL 10/1/03; HB 7/03; HBG 4/04; SLJ 8/03) [599.75]

21803 Markle, Sandra. *Snow School* (1–3). Illus. by Alan Marks. 2013, Charlesbridge $16.95 (978-158089410-4). 32pp. Watercolor paintings and lyrical prose depict the story of two snow leopard cubs as they learn how to fend for themselves in the Hindu Kush. ℮ (Rev: BL 2/15/13; LMC 11–12/13; SLJ 3/13) [599.75]

21804 Montgomery, Sy. *Saving the Ghost of the Mountain: An Expedition Among Snow Leopards in Mongolia* (4–7). Photos by Nic Bishop. Series: Scientists in the Field. 2009, Houghton Mifflin $18 (978-0-618-91645-0). 74pp. This compelling and thoughtful account of an (ultimately unsuccessful) expedition to find a snow leopard features eye-catching photographs and a handsome layout. (Rev: BLO 8/09; HB 11–12/09; SLJ 10/09) [599.75]

21805 O'Brien, Patrick. *Sabertooth* (2–4). Illus. by author. 2008, Holt $16.95 (978-0-8050-7105-4). 32pp. This large-format volume looks at the prehistoric cats with long, sharp teeth; illustrations compare sizes with modern tigers. (Rev: BL 8/08; LMC 8/08; SLJ 7/08) [569.74]

21806 Otfinoski, Steven. *Jaguars* (4–6). Series: Animals Animals. 2010, Marshall Cavendish LB $20.95 (978-0-7614-4839-6). 48pp. This volume covers the animal's habitat, diet, reproduction, life span, adaptability, and relationship with humans. (Rev: SLJ 1/1/11) [599.75]

21807 Patent, Dorothy Hinshaw. *Big Cats* (2–4). Illus. by Kendahl Jan Jubb. 2005, Walker $16.95 (978-0-8027-8968-6). 32pp. An excellent overview — covering physical characteristics, diet, habitat, and behavior — of the world's big cat species, including the cheetah, cougar, jaguar, leopard, lion, and tiger. (Rev: BL 11/15/05; SLJ 12/05) [599.75]

21808 Raatma, Lucia. *Snow Leopards* (3–5). Illus. Series: Nature's Children. 2013, Scholastic/Children's Press LB $28 (978-053123362-7); paper $6.95 (9780531251607). 48pp. With full-page photographs and clear text this book explores the characteristics and behaviors of these animals, their life cycle, their history, and relationship with humans. (Rev: BL 11/15/13) [599.75]

21809 Riggs, Kate. *Cheetahs* (K–3). Illus. Series: Amazing Animals. 2011, Creative Education $16.95 (978-158341988-5). 24pp. Riggs provides clear, interesting facts enhanced by large, eye-catching photographs and retells an African folktale about cheetahs' tear lines. (Rev: BL 4/15/11) [599.75]

21810 Schafer, Susan. *Tigers* (3–5). Illus. Series: Animals, Animals. 2000, Benchmark LB $25.64 (978-0-7614-1170-3). 48pp. Color photographs and brief, readable text introduce these big cats and their anatomy, behavior, diet, reproduction, and so on. Also use *Lions* (2000). (Rev: HBG 3/01; SLJ 7/01) [599.756]

21811 Schneider, Jost. *Lynx* (4–7). 1994, Carolrhoda LB $28.75 (978-0-87614-844-0). The life cycle, habits, and behavior of the lynx are described. (Rev: BL 1/15/95; SLJ 3/95) [599.74]

21812 Spilsbury, Louise, and Richard Spilsbury. *Save the Bengal Tiger* (2–4). Series: Save Our Animals! 2006, Heinemann LB $25.36 (978-1-4034-7803-0). 32pp. Information about the threats to these tigers and the decline in their population is accompanied by information on their diet, habitat, and so forth, and on the ways in which readers can help. Also use *Save the Black Rhino, Save the Giant Panda, Save the Blue Whale,* and *Save the Florida Manatee* (all 2006). (Rev: SLJ 9/06) [599.75]

21813 Spilsbury, Louise, and Richard Spilsbury. *Watching Lions in Africa* (1–3). Series: Wild World. 2006, Heinemann LB $25.36 (978-1-4034-7222-9). 32pp. Provides details about lions' characteristics, diet, reproduction, predators, and so forth, with photographs, a world map, and a "Tracker's Guide." (Rev: SLJ 7/06) [599.757]

21814 Spilsbury, Richard. *Bengal Tiger* (4–6). Illus. Series: Animals Under Threat. 2004, Heinemann LB $27.07 (978-1-4034-4858-3). 48pp. The life cycle of the threatened Bengal tiger is explored in this blend of narrative and eye-catching color photography. (Rev: BL 8/04; SLJ 1/05) [599.756]

21815 Squire, Ann O. *Cheetahs* (2–4). Illus. Series: True Book. 2005, Children's Pr. LB $25.00 (978-0-516-22792-4); paper $6.95 (978-0-516-27932-9). 48pp. An appealing look at the cheetah and its characteristics, with discussion of its endangered status and plenty of arresting color photographs. (Rev: BL 6/1–15/05) [599.759]

21816 Suen, Anastasia. *A Tiger Grows Up* (K–2). Illus. by Michael L. Denman and William J. Huiett. Series: Wild Animals. 2005, Picture Window LB $25.26 (978-1-4048-0987-1). 24pp. Minimal text paired with vivid

paintings, in an oversize format, follow a Bengal tiger and her three cubs as they learn to fend for themselves. (Rev: BL 10/15/05) [599.756]

21817 Sullivan, Jody. *Cheetahs: Spotted Speedsters* (1–3). Illus. Series: Wild World of Animals. 2002, Capstone LB $22.60 (978-0-7368-1393-8). 24pp. Facts about the fleet-footed cheetah include habitat, reproduction, behavior, and physical characteristics. (Rev: BL 1/1–15/03; HBG 3/03) [599]

21818 Swinburne, Stephen. *Bobcat: North America's Cat* (3–6). Illus. 2001, Boyds Mills $15.95 (978-1-56397-843-2). 32pp. Using a first-person narrative, the author describes his encounters with the bobcat and gives many background facts about this animal. (Rev: BL 4/1/01; HBG 10/01; SLJ 8/01) [599.75]

21819 Taylor, Bonnie Highsmith. *Ezra: A Mountain Lion* (3–5). Illus. Series: Cover-to-Cover Books. 2000, Perfection Learning $16.95 (978-0-7807-9313-2); paper $8.95 (978-0-7891-5166-7). 56pp. The reader learns through text and color photos about the life cycle of a mountain lion named Ezra. (Rev: BL 2/1/01) [599.75]

21820 Theodorou, Rod. *Bengal Tiger* (K–2). Illus. Series: Animals in Danger. 2000, Heinemann LB $21.36 (978-1-57572-267-2). 32pp. A look at the Bengal tiger and its life cycle, habitat, habits, and diet, with a section on its endangered status and efforts to save the species. (Rev: HBG 3/01; SLJ 4/01) [599.756]

21821 Thompson, Sharon E. *Built for Speed: The Extraordinary, Enigmatic Cheetah* (5–8). 1998, Lerner LB $27.93 (978-0-8225-2854-8). The habits and lifestyle of this endangered animal are introduced with full-color illustrations. (Rev: BL 6/1–15/98; HBG 10/98) [599.75]

21822 Tourville, Amanda Doering. *A Jaguar Grows Up* (1–3). Illus. by Michael Denman and William J. Huiett. Series: Wild Animals. 2006, Picture Window LB $25.26 (978-1-4048-3159-9). 24pp. A jaguar's development from birth to full independence is described in brief text and realistic illustrations. (Rev: SLJ 4/07) [599.75]

21823 Von Zumbusch, Amelie. *Cheetahs* (PS–2). Series: Safari Animals. 2007, Rosen LB $21.25 (978-1-4042-3614-1). 24pp. The photographs are the focus of this simple introduction to these big cats. (Rev: SLJ 5/07)

21824 Von Zumbusch, Amelie. *Lions* (PS–2). Series: Safari Animals. 2007, Rosen LB $21.25 (978-1-4042-3612-7). 24pp. The photographs are the focus of this simple introduction to these big cats. (Rev: SLJ 5/07)

21825 Walker, Sarah, ed. *Big Cats* (3–5). Series: Eye Wonder. 2002, DK paper $9.99 (978-0-7894-8548-9). 48pp. A brilliantly illustrated look at tigers, lions, and other big cats and how and where they live. (Rev: BL 6/1–15/02; HBG 10/02) [599.74]

COYOTES, FOXES, AND WOLVES

21826 Bailey, Jill. *Gray Wolf* (4–6). Illus. Series: Animals Under Threat. 2005, Heinemann LB $29.93 (978-1-4034-5583-3). 48pp. The life cycle of the gray wolf and threats to its survival are explored in this blend of narrative and eye-catching color photography.

21827 Chottin, Ariane. *Little Foxes* (3–5). Illus. Series: Born to Be Wild. 2005, Gareth Stevens LB $23.00 (978-0-8368-4435-1). 24pp. A simply worded look at young foxes and their lives, with large photographs.

21828 Ganeri, Anita. *Fennec Fox* (PS–2). Series: A Day in the Life: Desert Animals. 2011, Heinemann LB $22 (978-1-4329-4771-2); paper $6.49 (978-1-4329-4780-4). 24pp. "What do fennec foxes look like?" Ganeri answers this and other basic questions and provides large photographs. (Rev: BLO 3/14/11; SLJ 6/11) [599.776]

21829 George, Jean Craighead. *The Wolves Are Back* (3–5). Illus. by Wendell Minor. 2008, Dutton $16.99 (978-0-525-47947-5). 32pp. Lovely paintings and clear text describe how the wolf was reintroduced into Yellowstone Park in the mid-1990s and the effect this has had on the whole ecosystem. (Rev: BL 4/1/08; HB 5/08; LMC 5/08; SLJ 3/08) [599.773]

21830 Goldish, Meish. *Gray Wolves: Return to Yellowstone* (3–4). Series: America's Animal Comebacks. 2007, Bearport LB $25.27 (978-1-59716-502-0). 32pp. With eye-catching photographs and an appealing design, Goldish looks at how the gray wolf almost disappeared and at efforts to bring them back to Yellowstone. (Rev: SLJ 12/07) [599.773]

21831 Goldish, Meish. *Red Wolves: And Then There Were (Almost) None* (3–6). Series: America's Animal Comebacks. 2009, Bearport LB $25.27 (978-1-59716-742-0). 32pp. Goldish traces the red wolf's struggle to survive and scientists' efforts to bring this animal back into its natural habitat. (Rev: SLJ 5/09) [599.74]

21832 Green, Emily. *Wolves* (K–2). Illus. Series: Backyard Wildlife. 2011, Children's Press LB $21.95 (978-160014563-6). 24pp. A simple introduction with simple text and bright photographs that will appeal to emerging readers. (Rev: BL 6/1/11) [599.773]

21833 Greenaway, Theresa. *Wolves, Wild Dogs, and Foxes* (4–7). Illus. Series: Secret World Of. 2001, Raintree LB $27.12 (978-0-7398-3507-4). 48pp. Report writers will find information here about wolves, wild dogs, and foxes, including their diet, habitat, and behavior, with photographs and interesting facts. (Rev: BL 10/15/01; HBG 3/02; SLJ 1/02) [599.77]

21834 Greenberg, Dan. *Wolves* (4–6). Series: Animals Animals. 2002, Benchmark LB $25.64 (978-0-7614-1447-6). 48pp. A colorful introduction to wolves, their physical characteristics, social behavior, and hunting strategies. (Rev: BL 12/15/02; HBG 3/03) [599.773]

21835 Gunzi, Christiane. *The Best Book of Wolves and Wild Dogs* (3–5). Illus. by Mike Rowe. 2003, Kingfisher $12.95 (978-0-7534-5574-6). 31pp. Young dog lovers will delight in this richly illustrated overview of wild canines, including African wild dogs, gray wolves of North America, Australian dingoes, and the jackals of southern Europe. (Rev: HBG 10/03; SLJ 11/03) [599.773]

21836 Harrington, Fred H. *The Ethiopian Wolf* (2–4). Series: The Library of Wolves and Wild Dogs. 2002, Rosen LB $21.25 (978-0-8239-5767-5). 24pp. Basic information about this wolf is accompanied by full-page photographs. Also use *The Dingo* and *The African Wild Dog* (2002). (Rev: SLJ 6/02)

21837 Johnson, Sylvia A., and Alice Aamodt. *Wolf Pack: Tracking Wolves in the Wild* (5–8). 1985, Lerner paper $27.93 (978-0-8225-9526-7). Fascinating details of the lives of these animals that travel in packs and share hunting, raising the young, and protection. (Rev: BCCB 12/85; BL 2/1/86; SLJ 1/86) [599.74442]

21838 Kalman, Bobbie. *Endangered Wolves* (3–5). Illus. Series: Earth's Endangered Animals. 2004, Crabtree LB $25.27 (978-0-7787-1854-3); paper $6.95 (978-0-7787-1900-7). 32pp. In addition to discussion of their endangered status, this volume covers these animals' habitat, behavior, life cycle, and so forth. (Rev: SLJ 6/05) [599.74]

21839 Kalman, Bobbie, and Amanda Bishop. *The Life Cycle of a Wolf* (2–5). Illus. by Margaret Amy Reiach. Series: The Life Cycle. 2002, Crabtree LB $25.27 (978-0-7787-0657-1); paper $6.95 (978-0-7787-0687-8). 32pp. Report writers and browsers will find value in this easily read account of the life and habits of wolves that includes plenty of illustrations. (Rev: SLJ 10/02)

21840 Lang, Aubrey. *Baby Fox* (1–3). Photos by Wayne Lynch. Series: Nature Babies. 2002, Fitzhenry & Whiteside $13.95 (978-1-55041-688-6). 36pp. Browsers will enjoy following the story of a female fox finding a mate, giving birth to pups, and rearing them. (Rev: SLJ 12/02)

21841 McLeese, Don. *Gray Wolves* (1–3). Illus. Series: Eye to Eye with Endangered Species. 2010, Rourke LB $27.07 (978-161590271-2). 24pp. With eye-catching photographs, this book looks at gray wolves' lives and the threats they face. (Rev: BL 3/1/11) [599.733]

21842 Mara, Wil. *Coyotes* (4–6). Series: Animals Animals. 2008, Marshall Cavendish LB $20.95 (978-0-7614-2928-9). 48pp. *Coyotes* is packed with information regarding habitat, adaptations, and humanity's impact and includes excellent photographs. (Rev: SLJ 2/09) [599.77]

21843 Markle, Sandra. *Jackals* (2–5). Series: Animal Scavengers. 2005, Lerner LB $25.26 (978-0-8225-3197-5). 40pp. A well-written overview of jackals and their physical characteristics, diet, habitat, and behavior, with a focus on foraging for food. (Rev: SLJ 2/06) [599.77]

21844 Markle, Sandra. *Wolverines* (2–5). Series: Animal Scavengers. 2005, Lerner LB $25.26 (978-0-8225-3198-2). 40pp. A well-written overview of wolverines and their physical characteristics, diet, habitat, and behavior, with a focus on foraging for food. (Rev: SLJ 2/06) [599.76]

21845 Markle, Sandra. *Wolves* (3–6). Illus. Series: Animal Predators. 2004, Carolrhoda LB $25.26 (978-1-57505-732-3). 40pp. Concise text and clear, full-page photographs introduce the life cycle of the wolf and its physical characteristics, habitat, diet, and predatory behavior. (Rev: SLJ 10/04) [599.74]

21846 Martin, Patricia A. Fink. *Gray Wolves* (2–3). Series: Animals. 2002, Children's Book Pr. paper $6.95 (978-0-516-27472-0). 48pp. An attractive, well-designed beginning chapter book that introduces gray wolves, their social life, habits, homes, and food. (Rev: BL 8/02) [599.773]

21847 Montardre, Helene. *Little Wolves* (3–5). Illus. Series: Born to Be Wild. 2005, Gareth Stevens LB $23.00 (978-0-8368-4440-5). 24pp. A simply worded look at young wolves and their lives, with large photographs.

21848 Murdico, Suzanne J. *Coyote Attacks* (4–7). 2000, Children's paper $6.95 (978-0-516-23513-4). 48pp. As well as covering the causes of coyote attacks on animals and humans, this account gives basic information on coyotes, their habitat, survival techniques, behavior, and preferred food. (Rev: SLJ 3/01) [599.74]

21849 Read, Tracy C. *Exploring the World of Coyotes* (4–6). Series: Exploring the World of . . . 2011, Firefly $16.95 (978-1-55407-795-3); paper $6.95 (978-1-55407-795-3). 24pp. Introduces the physical characteristics, mating choices, communication, and family life of coyotes. (Rev: SLJ 8/11) [599.7]

21850 Silverstein, Alvin. *The Red Wolf* (4–8). Series: Endangered Species. 1994, Millbrook LB $24.90 (978-1-56294-416-2). The story of the red wolf, once thought to have become extinct in the United States, and the recent efforts to reintroduce it in North Carolina. (Rev: BL 4/15/95) [333.95]

21851 Swanson, Diane. *Coyotes* (2–4). Series: Welcome to the World of Animals. 2002, Gareth Stevens LB $24.00 (978-0-8368-3313-3). 32pp. A slim volume that provides information on the animal's home, diet, communication, and lifestyle. (Rev: SLJ 3/03)

21852 van Frankenhuyzen, Robbyn Smith. *Saving Samantha: A True Story* (K–2). Illus. by Gijsbert van Frankenhuyzen. 2004, Sleeping Bear $17.95 (978-1-58536-220-2). 48pp. A fox pup named Samantha is the focus of this frank story about rehabilitating animals and returning them to the wild. (Rev: BL 7/04; SLJ 9/04) [599.775]

DEER FAMILY

21853 DuTemple, Lesley A. *North American Moose* (3–6). Series: Nature Watch. 2000, Carolrhoda LB $25.26 (978-1-57505-426-1). 48pp. An introduction to these gentle giants of the north, how and where they live, and their life cycle. (Rev: BL 5/15/00; HBG 10/01) [599.73]

21854 Estigarribia, Diana. *Moose* (3–5). Illus. Series: Animals, Animals. 2005, Benchmark LB $17.95 (978-0-7614-1870-2). 48pp. Report writers will find plenty of clear photographs and maps plus well-organized information about the moose and its physical characteristics, diet, habitat, and behavior. (Rev: SLJ 2/06) [599.65]

21855 Ganeri, Anita. *Arabian Oryx* (PS–2). Series: A Day in the Life: Desert Animals. 2011, Heinemann LB $22 (978-1-4329-4769-9); paper $6.49 (978-1-4329-4778-1). 24pp. Answering questions such as "What do Arabian oryxes look like?" and "What do Arabian oryxes do

at night?," Ganeri presents the physical characteristics and life of this desert animal. (Rev: SLJ 6/11) [599.6]

21856 Heuer, Karsten. *Being Caribou: Five Months on Foot with a Caribou Herd* (3–6). Illus. 2007, Walker $17.95 (978-0-8027-9565-6). 48pp. Heuer tells the fascinating story of a five-month trip with a caribou herd whose Arctic birthing grounds are threatened by oil drilling. (Rev: BCCB 2/07; BL 4/15/07; HBG 10/07) [599.65]

21857 Hinshaw Patent, Dorothy. *White-Tailed Deer* (2–4). Series: Early Bird Nature Books. 2004, Lerner LB $25.26 (978-0-8225-3052-7). This engaging overview ntroduces early readers to the white-tailed deer's physical characteristics, habitat, diet, behavior, and life cycle. (Rev: BL 12/15/04)

21858 Hiscock, Bruce. *The Big Caribou Herd: Life in the Arctic National Wildlife Refuge* (2–5). Illus. 2003, Boyds Mills $16.95 (978-1-59078-010-7). 32pp. Beautiful watercolor paintings illustrate this account of a caribou herd's migration through Alaska's Arctic National Wildlife Refuge. (Rev: BL 2/1/03; HBG 10/03; SLJ 3/03) [599.73]

21859 Kawa, Katie. *Fawns* (PS–K). Illus. Series: Cute and Cuddly: Baby Animals. 2011, Gareth Stevens LB $22.60 (978-143395542-6). 24pp. A very simple book featuring brief text and adorable photographs of baby deer, with basic information about their lives. (Rev: BL 2/15/12) [599.65]

21860 Love, Pamela. *A Moose's Morning* (K–3). Illus. by Lesia Sochor. 2007, Down East $15.95 (978-0-89272-733-9). In a gentle style, this book takes the reader along as a young moose and his mother spend their day in the wild. (Rev: SLJ 6/07)

21861 Mara, Wil. *Deer* (4–6). Series: Animals Animals. 2008, Marshall Cavendish LB $20.95 (978-0-7614-2926-5). 48pp. *Deer* is packed with information regarding habitat, adaptations, and humanity's impact and includes excellent photographs. (Rev: SLJ 2/09) [599.65]

21862 Stefoff, Rebecca. *Deer* (3–6). Series: Animal-Ways. 2007, Marshall Cavendish LB $23.95 (978-0-7614-2534-2). 108pp. After looking at the physical characteristics of deer (sharp senses, unique antlers), this volume discusses their history, classification, diet, family life, and so forth as well as looking at particular kinds of deer and their conservation status. (Rev: SLJ 5/08) [599.65]

21863 Stewart, Melissa. *Antelope* (2–3). Series: Animals. 2002, Children's Book Pr. LB $25.00 (978-0-516-22198-4). 48pp. An attractively designed beginning chapter book that introduces the antelope, its life cycle, and how and where it lives. (Rev: BL 8/02) [599.73]

21864 Sullivan, Jody. *Deer: Graceful Grazers* (1–3). Series: Wild World of Animals. 2002, Capstone LB $22.60 (978-0-7368-1394-5). 24pp. Using a simple text, colorful images, and large type, this is a beginner's introduction to the world of the deer. (Rev: BL 1/1–15/03; HBG 3/03) [599.73]

21865 Urbigkit, Cat. *Path of the Pronghorn* (2–4). Illus. by Mark Gocke. 2010, Boyds Mills $17.95 (978-159078756-4). 32pp. This large-format volume with excellent color photographs and clear text introduces readers to the habitat and habits of pronghorn antelope, the fastest land mammals in North America. Lexile AD1100L (Rev: BL 12/15/10; SLJ 11/1/10) [599.63]

21866 Zobel, Derek. *Deer* (PS–1). Series: Blastoff! Readers: Backyard Wildlife. 2010, Bellwether Media LB $15.95 (978-1-60014-440-0). 24pp. With chapters including "What Are Deer?," "What Deer Look Like," and "Food and Seasons," this is a very simple introduction for early readers. (Rev: SLJ 1/1/11) [599.65]

ELEPHANTS

21867 Arnold, Katya. *Elephants Can Paint Too!* (1–3). Illus. 2005, Simon & Schuster $16.95 (978-0-689-86985-3). 40pp. Asian elephants' ability to paint is compared with the author's young human students in this affecting and informative picture book; the unemployed elephants' plight is explained, and additional facts are provided. (Rev: BCCB 11/05; BL 8/05; HBG 4/06; LMC 1/06; SLJ 9/05) [599.67]

21868 Barnes, Julia. *Elephants at Work* (3–5). Series: Animals at Work. 2006, Gareth Stevens LB $24.00 (978-0-8368-6224-9). 32pp. Full-color photographs show elephants being used in various roles and the text discusses the animal's physical characteristics, ability to learn commands, and relationship with humans. (Rev: SLJ 1/07) [636.9]

21869 Buckley, Carol. *Just for Elephants* (3–6). 2006, Tilbury House $16.95 (978-0-88448-283-3). This is the moving story of an aging circus elephant finding refuge after years of performing and then neglect in a zoo; the author's elephant sanctuary in Tennessee is the real star of this true story. (Rev: BL 12/15/06; SLJ 1/07) [639.97]

21870 Buckley, Carol. *Travels with Tarra* (3–5). Illus. 2002, Tilbury House $16.95 (978-0-88448-241-3). 40pp. Buckley tells the story of Tarra, the elephant she trained to do circus acts before creating an elephant sanctuary for Tarra's retirement. (Rev: BL 10/1/02; HBG 3/03) [599.67]

21871 Darling, Kathy. *The Elephant Hospital* (3–5). Illus. by Tara Darling. 2002, Millbrook LB $23.90 (978-0-7613-1723-4). 40pp. This is the story of a hospital for sick elephants that was founded in Thailand in 1994. (Rev: BCCB 7–8/02; BL 4/15/02; HBG 10/02; SLJ 4/02) [636.9]

21872 de la Bedoyere, Camilla. *100 Things You Should Know About Elephants* (3–6). Illus. Series: Remarkable Man and Beast: Facing Survival. 2010, Mason Crest LB $19.95 (978-142221968-3). 48pp. With plenty of lively photographs and illustrations woven together with cohesive text, this is a useful introduction to elephants. (Rev: BL 10/15/10; LMC 3–4/11) [599.67]

21873 Hall, Kirsten. *African Elephant: The World's Biggest Land Mammal* (K–2). Illus. Series: SuperSized! 2007, Bearport LB $21.28 (978-1-59716-387-3). 24pp. Report writers will get lots of mileage from this introduction to the African elephant, filled with facts about and photographs of the largest land mammal. (Rev: LMC 10/07; SLJ 8/07)

21874 Helfer, Ralph. *The World's Greatest Elephant* (1–3). Illus. by Ted Lewin. 2006, Philomel $16.99 (978-0-399-24190-1). 48pp. The amazing true story of the lifelong relationship between a boy and an elephant, who performed in circuses in Germany and the United States and had many adventures. (Rev: BCCB 4/06; BL 2/1/06*; HBG 10/06; SLJ 2/06) [791.3]

21875 Jonas, Ann. *Little Elephants* (3–5). Illus. Series: Born to Be Wild. 2005, Gareth Stevens LB $23.00 (978-0-8368-4434-4). 24pp. A simply worded look at young elephants and their lives, with large color photographs.

21876 Kalman, Bobbie. *Endangered Elephants* (3–5). Illus. Series: Earth's Endangered Animals. 2005, Crabtree LB $25.27 (978-0-7787-1860-4); paper $6.95 (978-0-7787-1906-9). 32pp. The dangers elephants face are highlighted in this photo-essay that also covers physical characteristics, diet, behavior, habitat, and life cycle. (Rev: BL 9/15/05; SLJ 12/05) [599.67]

21877 Latta, Jan. *Ella the Elephant* (K–4). Series: Wild Animal Families. 2006, Gareth Stevens LB $23.93 (978-0-8368-7768-7). 24pp. In a first-"person" account, Ella describes what it's like to be an elephant, giving readers facts about her species in an enjoyable and engaging format. (Rev: SLJ 5/07)

21878 Lewin, Ted, and Betsy Lewin. *Balarama: A Royal Elephant* (2–5). Illus. by Ted Lewin. 2009, Lee & Low $19.95 (978-1-60060-265-8). 56pp. The Lewins describe their encounters with Indian parade elephants; with facts about the elephants and their training. (Rev: BL 11/15/09; LMC 11–12/09; SLJ 9/1/09) [636.9670954]

21879 Lewin, Ted, and Betsy Lewin. *Elephant Quest* (4–9). Illus. by authors. 2000, HarperCollins $15.95 (978-0-688-14111-0). 47pp. This account of the flora and fauna of Botswana's Moremi Reserve also describes the authors' search for elephants. (Rev: HB 1/01; HBG 3/01; SLJ 9/00) [599.67]

21880 Magloff, Lisa. *Elephant* (1–2). Illus. Series: Watch Me Grow. 2005, DK $7.99 (978-0-7566-1155-2). 24pp. An appealing look at how elephants develop, with eye-catching illustrations.

21881 Marsh, Laura. *Elephants* (K–3). Series: Great Migrations. 2010, National Geographic LB $11.90 (978-1-4263-0744-7); paper $3.99 (978-1-4263-0743-0). 48pp. Focusing on African elephants, this volume discusses their habitat and diet, their migration patterns, and the dangers they face. (Rev: SLJ 3/1/11) [599.67]

21882 Morgan, Jody. *Elephant Rescue: Changing the Future for Endangered Wildlife* (4–7). Series: Firefly Animal Rescue. 2005, Firefly $19.95 (978-1-55297-595-4); paper $9.95 (978-1-55297-594-7). This photo-filled book documents the many threats facing the world's remaining herds of African and Asian elephants, and discusses elephant physiology, behavior, and habitat. (Rev: BL 2/15/05; SLJ 5/05) [599.67]

21883 Murray, Julie. *Elephants* (2–3). Illus. Series: Animal Kingdom. 2005, ABDO LB $21.35 (978-1-59197-314-0). 24pp. For beginning readers, this is an introduction to the elephant and its physical characteristics, habitat, and diet. (Rev: SLJ 5/05) [599.6]

21884 Overbeck, Cynthia. *Elephants* (4–7). 1981, Lerner LB $22.60 (978-0-8225-1452-7). Elephants and their life cycle and habitats are discussed in this well-illustrated volume. [599]

21885 Ring, Susan. *Project Elephant* (3–6). Illus. Series: Zoo Life. 2002, Weigl LB $15.15 (978-1-59036-016-3). 32pp. Ring looks at elephants born in captivity and at the good and bad aspects of being raised in a zoo, with information on the animals' natural habitat and physiology. (Rev: BL 12/15/02; HBG 3/03) [599.67]

21886 Schlaepfer, Gloria G. *Elephants* (5–9). Illus. Series: AnimalWays. 2003, Marshall Cavendish $31.36 (978-0-7614-1390-5). 112pp. In addition to material on physical characteristics, behavior, habitats, and threats, Schlaepfer touches on the animal's roles in history, mythology, religion, and literature. (Rev: BL 3/15/03; HBG 3/03) [599.67]

21887 Schwabacher, Martin. *Elephants* (4–6). Illus. 2000, Marshall Cavendish LB $25.64 (978-0-7614-1168-0). 32pp. A useful volume that describes the physical structure of the elephant and gives coverage on its habitats, behavior, mating habits, life cycle, and food. (Rev: BL 3/15/01; HBG 3/01) [599.67]

21888 Sobol, Richard. *An Elephant in the Backyard* (PS–2). Illus. 2004, Penguin $17.99 (978-0-525-47288-9). 32pp. A 4-year-old elephant is the focus of this photo-essay about elephants' roles in the everyday life of a Thai village. (Rev: BL 6/1–15/04; SLJ 7/04) [636.9]

21889 Stewart, Melissa. *Elephants* (2–3). Series: Animals. 2002, Children's Book Pr. LB $25.00 (978-0-516-22199-1); paper $6.95 (978-0-516-26990-0). 48pp. This beginning chapter book uses attractive color photographs and a simple text to introduce the elephant and explain where and how it lives and raises its family. (Rev: BL 8/02) [599.6]

21890 Turner, Matt. *Asian Elephant* (4–6). Illus. Series: Animals Under Threat. 2005, Heinemann LB $29.93 (978-1-4034-5581-9). 48pp. The life cycle of the Asian elephant and threats to its survival are explored in this blend of narrative and eye-catching color photography.

21891 Zimmer, Tracie Vaughn. *Cousins of Clouds: Elephant Poems* (K–3). Illus. by Megan Halsey. 2011, Clarion $16.99 (978-0-618-90349-8). 32pp. Elephants' biology, behavior, and importance in ancient mythology are described in text, poems, and mixed-media collages. (Rev: BL 4/15/11; SLJ 4/11) [599.67]

GIRAFFES

21892 Anderson, Jill. *Giraffes* (PS–K). Illus. Series: Wild Ones. 2005, North Word $12.95 (978-1-55971-928-5); paper $6.95 (978-1-55971-929-2). 24pp. This photo-filled title chronicles a day in the life of a giraffe and provides basic information about the animal's physical appearance, habitat, diet, and behavior. (Rev: BL 10/15/05; HBG 4/06; SLJ 1/06) [599.665]

21893 Jango-Cohen, Judith. *Giraffes* (3–5). Illus. Series: Animals, Animals. 2001, Benchmark LB $25.64 (978-0-7614-1258-8). 48pp. In addition to the usual information on the species, this book discusses the giraffe's discovery and naming, and its relationship with humans. (Rev: HBG 10/02; SLJ 2/02) [599.638]

21894 Leach, Michael. *Giraffe* (3–6). Illus. Series: Natural World. 2001, Raintree LB $27.12 (978-0-7398-4435-9). 48pp. Fascinating facts about giraffes are expressed in breezy, clear terms, with memorable close-up photographs, a glossary, and a list of Web sites. (Rev: BL 12/15/01; HBG 10/02) [599.638]

21895 Marie, Christian. *Little Giraffes* (3–5). Illus. Series: Born to Be Wild. 2005, Gareth Stevens LB $23.00 (978-0-8368-4436-8). 24pp. A simply worded look at young giraffes and their lives, with large color photographs.

21896 Parker, Barbara Keevil. *Giraffes* (4–6). Illus. Series: Nature Watch. 2003, Lerner LB $25.26 (978-1-57505-346-2). 48pp. An attractive introduction to these long-necked animals, how and where they live, and their life cycle. (Rev: HBG 4/04)

21897 St. George, Judith. *Zarafa: The Giraffe Who Walked to the King* (1–3). Illus. by Britt Spencer. 2009, Philomel $16.99 (978-0-399-25049-1). 40pp. In 1824 an elegant and good-natured giraffe called Zarafa — a gift from one ruler to another — started a long journey from Egypt to Paris, making friends and impressing crowds along the way. (Rev: BL 5/1/09; LMC 10/09; SLJ 6/09) [599.638092]

21898 Tourville, Amanda Doering. *A Giraffe Grows Up* (1–3). Illus. by Michael Denman and William J. Huiett. Series: Wild Animals. 2006, Picture Window LB $25.26 (978-1-4048-3158-2). 24pp. A giraffe's development from birth to full independence is described in brief text and realistic illustrations. (Rev: SLJ 4/07) [599.638]

21899 Underwood, Deborah. *Watching Giraffes in Africa* (1–3). Series: Wild World. 2006, Heinemann LB $25.36 (978-1-4034-7230-4). 32pp. Provides details about giraffes' characteristics, diet, reproduction, predators, and so forth, with photographs, a world map, and a "Tracker's Guide." (Rev: SLJ 7/06) [599.638]

MARSUPIALS

21900 Anderson, Jill. *Kangaroos* (PS–2). Series: Wild Ones. 2006, NorthWord $12.95 (978-1-55971-935-3); paper $6.95 (978-1-55971-936-0). This photo-filled title offers an excellent visual introduction to kangaroos and is appropriate for preschoolers and early elementary students. (Rev: HBG 10/06; SLJ 8/06)

21901 Arnold, Caroline. *A Wombat's World* (K–3). Illus. by author. Series: Caroline Arnold's Animals. 2008, Picture Window LB $19.95 (978-1-4048-3986-1). 24pp. This title follows the events in a wombat's life over the course of a year as she gives birth and raises her young to maturity. (Rev: BL 3/15/08; SLJ 8/08) [599.24]

21902 Bredeson, Carmen. *Kangaroos Up Close* (1–3). Series: Zoom in on Animals! 2008, Enslow LB $21.26 (978-0-7660-3079-4). 24pp. Simple text and close-up color photographs introduce body parts, babies, and other important characteristics. (Rev: SLJ 11/08) [599.2]

21903 Burt, Denise. *Kangaroos* (3–6). Series: Nature Watch. 2000, Carolrhoda $25.26 (978-1-57505-388-2). 48pp. This attractive volume uses a number of color photos to introduce the kangaroo, its physical characteristics, habits, and homes. (Rev: BL 3/15/00; HBG 9/00) [599.2]

21904 Collard, Sneed B. *Pocket Babies and Other Amazing Marsupials* (4–7). Illus. 2007, Darby Creek $18.95 (978-1-58196-046-4). A large-format introduction to marsupials around the world — including the opossum, kangaroo, koala, and wombat — and to the efforts being made to save the many endangered marsupials. (Rev: BL 9/15/07; SLJ 10/07) [599.2]

21905 Dennard, Deborah. *Koala Country: The Story of an Australian Eucalyptus Forest* (2–4). Illus. Series: Wild Habitat. 2001, Soundprints $15.95 (978-1-56899-887-9). 32pp. An appealing look at a day in the life of a koala, covering the animal's diet, habitat, and nocturnal and reproductive activities. (Rev: BL 6/1–15/01; HBG 10/01; SLJ 11/01) [599.1]

21906 French, Jackie. *How to Scratch a Wombat: Where to Find It . . . What to Feed It . . . Why It Sleeps All Day* (3–5). Illus. by Bruce Whatley. 2009, Clarion $15.00 (978-0-618-86864-3). 86pp. All about wombats and their physical characteristics and behavior, with engaging anecdotes and advice on dealing with these Australian marsupials. (Rev: BL 2/1/09; SLJ 3/09) [599.2]

21907 Green, Emily. *Opossums* (K–2). Illus. Series: Backyard Wildlife. 2011, Children's Press LB $21.95 (978-160014561-2). 24pp. A simple introduction with simple text and bright photographs that will appeal to emerging readers. (Rev: BL 6/1/11) [599.2]

21908 Heos, Bridget. *What to Expect When You're Expecting Joeys: A Guide for Marsupial Parents (and Curious Kids)* (1–3). Illus. by Stéphane Jorisch. 2011, Millbrook LB $25.26 (978-0-7613-5859-6). 32pp. This humorous and informative book provides information on marsupial babies. **e** (Rev: LMC 3–4/12; SLJ 10/1/11) [599.2]

21909 Hewett, Joan. *A Kangaroo Joey Grows Up* (1–3). Illus. by Richard Hewett. Series: Baby Animals. 2001, Lerner LB $21.27 (978-1-57505-165-9); paper $6.95 (978-0-8225-0091-9). 32pp. Beginning readers will enjoy this basic book about a young kangaroo joey. (Rev: BL 10/15/01; HBG 3/02; SLJ 10/01) [599.2]

21910 Inskipp, Carol. *Koala* (4–6). Illus. Series: Animals Under Threat. 2005, Heinemann LB $29.93 (978-1-4034-5585-7). 48pp. The life cycle of the koala and threats to its survival are explored in this blend of narrative and eye-catching color photography. [599.1]

21911 Kalman, Bobbie. *The Life Cycle of a Koala* (2–4). Illus. Series: The Life Cycle. 2001, Crabtree LB $25.27 (978-0-7787-0655-7); paper $6.95 (978-0-7787-0685-

4). After a general description of the koala, the author clearly explains its life cycle and discusses what can be done to curb human encroachment. (Rev: SLJ 6/02) [599.1]

21912 Kalman, Bobbie, and Heather Levigne. *What Is a Marsupial?* (1–3). Series: Science of Living Things. 2000, Crabtree LB $25.27 (978-0-86505-978-8); paper $6.95 (978-0-86505-955-9). 32pp. This beginning science book introduces in text and pictures such marsupials as the kangaroo, koala, and opossum. (Rev: SLJ 11/00) [599.1]

21913 Lang, Aubrey. *Baby Koala* (K–3). Illus. Series: Nature Babies. 2005, Fitzhenry & Whiteside $13.95 (978-1-55041-874-3); paper $5.95 (978-1-55041-876-7). 36pp. This appealing photo-essay follows a koala mother and baby as they browse on eucalyptus in an Australian forest. (Rev: BL 2/1/05; SLJ 4/05) [599.25]

21914 Levine, Michelle. *Jumping Kangaroos* (K–2). Illus. Series: Pull Ahead Books. 2005, Lerner LB $22.60 (978-0-8225-2421-2); paper $5.95 (978-0-8225-2440-3). 32pp. All about kangaroos, their behavior and habitat, designed for the beginning reader. (Rev: BL 3/15/05) [599.2]

21915 Markle, Sandra. *Finding Home* (K–3). Illus. by Alan Marks. 2008, Charlesbridge $15.95 (978-1-58089-122-6). 32pp. The story of a mother koala who manages to survive raging bushfires and protect her young joey in the face of multiple challenges. (Rev: BL 2/15/08; HB 3/08; LMC 10/08; SLJ 2/08) [599.2]

21916 Markle, Sandra. *Tasmanian Devils* (2–5). Series: Animal Scavengers. 2005, Lerner LB $25.26 (978-0-8225-3199-9). 40pp. A well-written overview of the ill-tempered Tasmanian devil and its physical characteristics, diet, habitat, and behavior, with a focus on foraging for food. (Rev: SLJ 2/06) [599.2]

21917 Marsico, Katie. *A Kangaroo Joey Grows Up* (1–2). 2007, Children's Pr. LB $19.00 (978-0-531-17476-0). 24pp. The development of a baby kangaroo is the topic of this vocabulary-building book with interesting photographs. (Rev: SLJ 8/07)

21918 Murray, Peter. *Kangaroos* (4–7). Series: The World of Mammals. 2005, Child's World LB $29.93 (978-1-59296-499-4). Arresting photographs and engaging text introduce the anatomy, behavior, habitat, and life cycle of the kangaroo as well as the threats to the animal's survival in the wild. (Rev: SLJ 3/06) [599.2]

21919 Noonan, Diana. *The Kangaroo* (2–4). Illus. Series: Life Cycles. 2002, Chelsea LB $23.00 (978-0-7910-6968-4). 32pp. Handsome images and simple text describe the life cycle, habitat, appearance, and predators of the kangaroo, in a small, square, photo-essay format. (Rev: BL 1/1–15/03; HBG 3/03) [599.2]

21920 Otfinoski, Steven. *Koalas* (2–5). Illus. Series: Animals Animals. 2007, Marshall Cavendish LB $23.95 (978-0-7614-2526-7). 48pp. Reference aids including a glossary and additional resources make this overview on koalas useful for research. (Rev: BL 12/1/07) [599.2]

21921 Penny, Malcolm. *The Secret Life of Kangaroos* (4–7). Series: The Secret World of . . . 2002, Raintree LB $27.12 (978-0-7398-4986-6). 48pp. A visually interesting look at the world of the kangaroo with material on behavior, anatomy, reproduction, and how pollution and habitat destruction have affected these animals. (Rev: BL 8/02) [599.2]

21922 Rose, Deborah Lee, and Susan Kelly. *Jimmy the Joey: The True Story of an Amazing Koala Rescue* (K–3). Illus. by Susan Kelly. 2013, National Geographic $16.95 (978-1-4263-1371-4). 32pp. This is a compelling story, beautifully illustrated with large photographs, of the rescue of a young koala injured in an accident; informative backmatter provides context. (Rev: BL 7/13; LMC 11–12/13; SLJ 7/13) [599.2]

21923 Sill, Cathryn. *About Marsupials: A Guide for Children* (K–2). Illus. by John Sill. 2006, Peachtree $15.95 (978-1-56145-358-0). 48pp. Kangaroos, wombats, and wallabies are only three of the marsupials covered in this useful, well-illustrated guide. (Rev: BL 2/15/06; SLJ 5/06) [599.2]

21924 Spilsbury, Louise, and Richard Spilsbury. *Watching Kangaroos in Australia* (1–3). Series: Wild World. 2006, Heinemann LB $25.36 (978-1-4034-7225-0). 32pp. Provides details about kangaroos' characteristics, diet, reproduction, predators, and so forth, with photographs, a world map, and a "Tracker's Guide." (Rev: SLJ 7/06) [599.2]

21925 Swan, Erin Pembrey. *Meat-Eating Marsupials* (3–5). Series: Animals in Order. 2002, Watts LB $26.50 (978-0-531-11628-9). 48pp. After a general introduction to these pouched animals, individual species are featured in descriptive text and striking color photographs. (Rev: BL 3/15/02) [599.1]

21926 Theodorou, Rod. *Koala* (2–4). Illus. Series: Animals in Danger. 2001, Heinemann LB $21.36 (978-1-57572-271-9). 32pp. Basic information about the koala and its endangered status. (Rev: BL 7/01; HBG 10/01) [599.2]

PANDAS

21927 Arnold, Caroline. *A Panda's World* (PS–2). Illus. by author. Series: Caroline Arnold's Animals. 2006, Picture Window LB $26.60 (978-1-4048-1322-9). 24pp. A baby panda grows up and learns to fend for himself in this appealing fact-packed title. (Rev: LMC 11/06; SLJ 6/06) [[599.789]

21928 Bortolotti, Dan. *Panda Rescue: Changing the Future for Endangered Wildlife* (3–8). Series: Firefly Animal Rescue. 2003, Firefly LB $19.95 (978-1-55297-598-5); paper $9.95 (978-1-55297-557-2). 64pp. Threats to the panda's survival and efforts to protect them from extinction are examined in detail, with profiles of some of the key individuals involved. (Rev: BL 1/1–15/04; SLJ 4/04) [599.789]

21929 Bredeson, Carmen. *Giant Pandas Up Close* (PS–3). Series: Zoom in on Animals. 2006, Enslow LB $21.26 (978-0-7660-2496-0). 24pp. Eye-catching full-color close-ups show key physical characteristics of the panda, and the text gives basic details on diet, habitat, life cycle, and so forth. (Rev: SLJ 11/06) [599.789]

21930 Claybourne, Anna. *Giant Panda* (4–6). Illus. Series: Animals Under Threat. 2005, Heinemann LB $29.93 (978-1-4034-5582-6). 48pp. The life cycle of the giant panda and threats to its survival are explored in this blend of narrative and eye-catching color photography. [599.74]

21931 Crossingham, John, and Bobbie Kalman. *Endangered Pandas* (3–5). Illus. Series: Earth's Endangered Animals. 2005, Crabtree LB $25.27 (978-0-7787-1858-1); paper $6.95 (978-0-7787-1904-5). 32pp. After giving a clear overview of the giant panda's physical characteristics, life cycle, and behavior, the authors discuss the reasons the animal is endangered and measures being taken to reduce the threat. (Rev: SLJ 12/05) [599.789]

21932 Eason, Sarah. *Save the Panda* (1–3). Illus. by Andrew Geeson and Marijke Veldhoven. Series: Save the . . . 2009, Rosen LB $23.95 (978-1-4358-2812-4). 32pp. Colorful spreads present answers to common questions in this solid introduction to the endangered panda. (Rev: SLJ 6/09) [599.789]

21933 Gibbons, Gail. *Giant Pandas* (K–3). Illus. 2002, Holiday House $16.95 (978-0-8234-1761-2). 32pp. Simple text and watercolors introduce facts about pandas in the wild and in zoos. (Rev: BL 1/1–15/03; HBG 10/03; SLJ 12/02) [599.789]

21934 Green, Carl R. *The Giant Panda* (3–7). Series: Endangered and Threatened Animals. 2004, Enslow LB $25.26 (978-0-7660-5061-7). 48pp. Supplemented by a lengthy list of links to online resources, this overview of the giant panda explores its behavior and physical characteristics, as well as the threats it faces. (Rev: BL 6/1–15/04) [599.789]

21935 Jiguang, Xin, and Markus Kappeler. *The Giant Panda* (5–7). Trans. by Noel Simon. 1984, China Books paper $9.95 (978-0-8351-1388-5). China's giant panda is introduced in its natural habitat. (Rev: BL 12/15/86; HB 1–2/87; SLJ 12/86) [599]

21936 Leeson, Tom, and Pat Leeson. *Panda* (2–4). Illus. Series: Wild Bears! 2000, Blackbirch $24.94 (978-1-56711-341-9). 24pp. Using a direct text and quality photos, this book covers topics related to pandas, such as the world population, physical characteristics, behavior, diet, and endangered status. (Rev: BL 12/15/00; HBG 3/01) [599.789]

21937 Nagda, Ann Whitehead. *Panda Math: Learning About Subtraction from Hua Mei and Mei Sheng* (3–5). Illus. 2005, Holt $16.95 (978-0-8050-7644-8). 32pp. Using two giant panda siblings at the San Diego Zoo as the framework, this book teaches the fundamentals of subtraction as it considers topics including bamboo consumption, sleep habits, weight, and life expectancy. (Rev: BL 9/15/05; SLJ 9/05) [513.2]

21938 Penny, Malcolm. *Giant Panda* (2–4). Series: Natural World. 2000, Raintree LB $27.12 (978-0-7398-1063-7). 48pp. Clear photos and a good layout distinguish this book about the giant panda, its habitat, mating, diet, and endangered status. (Rev: HBG 9/00; SLJ 7/00) [599.74]

21939 Ryder, Joanne. *Little Panda* (K–3). Illus. 2001, Simon & Schuster $16.95 (978-0-689-84310-5). 32pp. This photo-essay chronicles the birth and early life of Hua Mei, a panda born at the San Diego Zoo. (Rev: BL 4/15/01; HB 5/01; HBG 10/01; SLJ 7/01*) [599.789]

21940 Ryder, Joanne. *Panda Kindergarten* (PS–3). Illus. by Katherine Feng. 2009, HarperCollins $17.99 (978-0-06-057850-3). 32pp. A photo-essay about panda cubs at a Chinese zoo. (Rev: BCCB 9/09; BL 6/1–15/09; HB 9/09) [599.789]

RODENTS

21941 Bastian, Lois Brunner. *Chipmunk Family* (3–5). Illus. Series: Wildlife Conservation Society Books. 2000, Watts LB $24.50 (978-0-531-11683-8). 48pp. Photographed in the author's backyard in New Jersey, this is a stunning book that focuses on a mother chipmunk and how she raises her brood. (Rev: BL 2/15/01) [599.36]

21942 Conniff, Richard. *Rats! The Good, the Bad, and the Ugly* (3–5). Illus. 2002, Crown $15.95 (978-0-375-81207-1). 37pp. A volume packed with information, anecdotes, and color photographs covering the biology, mythology, and history of rats. (Rev: BCCB 12/02; BL 12/15/02; HBG 3/03; SLJ 1/03) [599.35]

21943 Gallagher, Kristin Ellersbusch. *Cottontail Rabbits* (PS–2). Series: Pull Ahead Books. 2000, Lerner LB $22.60 (978-0-8225-3617-8); paper $5.95 (978-0-8225-3623-9). 32pp. Using many questions built into the text, this attractive easy reader introduces the cottontail rabbit, its physical characteristics, habits, food, and habitats. (Rev: BL 8/00; HBG 3/01) [599.32]

21944 Green, Emily. *Beavers* (K–2). Illus. Series: Backyard Wildlife. 2011, Children's Press LB $21.95 (978-160014560-5). 24pp. A simple introduction with simple text and bright photographs that will appeal to emerging readers. Also use *Porcupines* (2011). (Rev: BL 6/1/11) [599.37]

21945 Hipp, Andrew. *The Life Cycle of a Mouse* (PS–2). Illus. by Dwight Kuhn. Series: Life Cycle Of. 2002, Rosen LB $19.95 (978-0-8239-5866-5). 24pp. This book for beginning readers follows the life of a mouse from conception to adulthood. (Rev: BL 12/15/02) [599.35]

21946 Holub, Joan. *Why Do Rabbits Hop?* (K–2). Illus. 2003, Dial paper $3.99 (978-0-14-230120-3). 48pp. An interesting introduction to rabbits in a question-and-answer format for beginning readers. (Rev: BL 11/15/02; HBG 10/03; SLJ 2/03) [636.9]

21947 Jacobs, Lee. *Beaver* (3–5). Series: Wild America. 2003, Gale LB $24.94 (978-1-56711-566-6). 24pp. This colorful volume introduces young readers to the beaver, examining the toothy creature's physical characteristics, habitat, and behavior. (Rev: SLJ 11/03) [599.37]

21948 Jango-Cohen, Judith. *Porcupines* (3–5). Illus. Series: Animals, Animals. 2005, Benchmark LB $17.95 (978-0-7614-1868-9). 48pp. Report writers will find

plenty of clear photographs and maps plus well-organized information about the porcupine and its physical characteristics, diet, habitat, and behavior. (Rev: SLJ 2/06) [599.35]

21949 Lorbiecki, Marybeth. *Prairie Dogs* (2–4). Illus. Series: Our Wild World. 2004, NorthWord $10.95 (978-1-55971-883-7). 48pp. This photo-filled book dramatizes the plight of prairie dogs, facing increasing pressure from the rapid spread of human development into their habitat. (Rev: BL 3/15/04; SLJ 10/04) [599.36]

21950 Lunis, Natalie. *Capybara: The World's Largest Rodent* (2–4). Illus. Series: More SuperSized. 2010, Bearport LB $22.61 (978-193608731-0). 24pp. Large glossy photos and clear, concise text make an accessible introduction to the world's largest rodent. (Rev: BL 4/1/10) [599.35]

21951 Markle, Sandra. *Porcupines* (K–4). Series: Animal Prey. 2007, Lerner LB $25.26 (978-0-8225-6439-3). 40pp. Eye-catching photographs and clear, readable text discuss how porcupines, nocturnal rodents, repel predators with their sharp quills. (Rev: SLJ 4/07) [599.35]

21952 Marrin, Albert. *Oh, Rats! The Story of Rats and People* (3–5). Illus. by C. B. Mordan. 2006, Dutton $16.99 (978-0-525-47762-4). 48pp. All about rats and everything they do to both assist and annoy people, with red-accented illustrations. (Rev: BL 7/06; SLJ 8/06*) [599.35]

21953 Miller, Sara Swan. *Rabbits, Pikas, and Hares* (3–5). Series: Animals in Order. 2002, Watts LB $26.50 (978-0-531-11634-0). 48pp. Following a general explanation of animal classification, this attractive volume describes in text and color photographs several species of rabbits and related animals. (Rev: BL 3/15/02) [599.32]

21954 Old, Wendie. *The Groundhog Day Book of Facts and Fun* (K–3). Illus. by Paige Billin-Frye. 2004, Whitman LB $16.99 (978-0-8075-3066-5). 40pp. Punxsutawney Phil, groundhogs in general, and information on other animal forecasters around the world are all included in this volume. (Rev: BL 12/15/04; SLJ 1/05)

21955 Pascoe, Elaine. *Mice* (3–6). Illus. by Dwight Kuhn. Series: Nature Close-Up. 2005, Gale LB $24.95 (978-1-4103-0537-4). 48pp. The life cycle of mice, as well as their physical characteristics, different breeds, diet, and behavior, are examined in this book full of eye-catching photographs that also addresses the care of pet mice. (Rev: BL 2/1/06) [599.35]

21956 Richardson, Adele D. *Groundhogs: Woodchucks, Marmots, and Whistle Pigs* (1–3). Illus. Series: Wild World of Animals. 2002, Capstone LB $22.60 (978-0-7368-1397-6). 24pp. A simple introduction to the groundhog's appearance, behavior, and other basic facts is followed by a glossary and list of resources. Also use *Beavers* (2002). (Rev: BL 1/1–15/03; HBG 3/03; SLJ 4/03) [599]

21957 Savage, Stephen. *Mouse* (3–6). Illus. Series: Animal Neighbors. 2008, Rosen LB $23.95 (978-1-4358-4990-7). 32pp. This title includes details about a mouse's life and habitat and has clear, easy text and large photographs which help explain a mouse's anatomy. Also use *Rat* (2008). (Rev: SLJ 5/09) [599.35]

21958 Sill, Cathryn. *About Rodents: A Guide for Children* (K–3). Illus. by John Sill. 2008, Peachtree $15.95 (978-1-56145-454-9). 32pp. Each rodent in this attractive picture book — which introduces everything from mice and squirrels to chinchillas and capybaras — gets a full spread with a watercolor painting and a sentence or two of text, with additional information at the back of the book. (Rev: BL 9/15/08) [599.35]

21959 Stone, Tanya L. *Rabbits* (3–5). Series: Wild America. 2002, Gale LB $24.94 (978-1-56711-645-8). 24pp. Rabbits in the wild are featured in this picture-filled account that describes appearance, life cycle, food, and survival skills. Also use *Squirrels* (2002). (Rev: BL 10/15/02) [599.32]

21960 Tagholm, Sally. *The Rabbit* (2–3). Illus. by Bert Kitchen. Series: Animal Lives. 2000, Kingfisher $9.95 (978-0-7534-5214-1). 32pp. After a description of the daily routines of a rabbit and its mating habits, this account details the building of a nest by the female, the birth of little rabbits, and their care until adulthood. (Rev: BL 5/15/00; HBG 3/01; SLJ 8/00) [599.32]

SHEEP AND GOATS

21961 Green, Emily. *Goats* (PS–2). Illus. Series: Blastoff! Readers. 2007, Scholastic LB $18.50 (978-0-531-17552-1). 24pp. Short descriptions of goats and their characteristics make this book useful for beginning readers. (Rev: BL 5/15/07; SLJ 6/07) [636.3]

21962 Kawa, Katie. *Lambs* (PS–K). Illus. Series: Cute and Cuddly: Baby Animals. 2011, Gareth Stevens LB $22.60 (978-143395546-4). 24pp. A very simple book featuring brief text and adorable photographs of baby sheep, with basic information about their lives. (Rev: BL 2/15/12) [636.3]

21963 Lang, Aubrey. *Baby Mountain Sheep* (K–3). Illus. 2008, Fitzhenry & Whiteside $15.95 (978-1-55455-042-5); paper $6.95 (978-1-55455-043-2). 36pp. With many color photographs, this attractive volume traces the first year in the life of a young Dall's sheep, born in the Alaskan mountains. (Rev: BL 2/15/08; SLJ 3/08) [599.649]

21964 Macken, JoAnn Early. *Bighorn Sheep* (K–2). Series: Animals That Live in the Mountains. 2010, Weekly Reader LB $22 (978-1-4339-2409-5). 24pp. Close-up photographs and bright backgrounds enliven this book about the life and habitat of bighorn sheep. Also use *Mountain Goats* (2010). (Rev: SLJ 8/1/10) [599.649]

21965 Macken, JoAnn Early. *Bighorn Sheep / Carnero de Canadá* (2–4). Trans. by Tatiana Acosta and Guillermo Gutiérrez. Series: Animals That Live in the Mountains / Animales de las montañas. 2006, Weekly Reader LB $21.00 (978-0-8368-6446-5). 24pp. A beginning book with facts about bighorn sheep in both English and Spanish; also use *Mountain Goats / Cabra montés* (2006). (Rev: SLJ 6/06) [599.649]

21966 Urbigkit, Cat. *The Shepherd's Trail* (2–4). Illus. 2008, Boyds Mills $16.95 (978-1-59078-509-6). 32pp.

Urbigkit follows the migration of sheep herds in the U.S. West, explaining why they change habitats, how they move, and when breeding and shearing take place. (Rev: BL 1/1–15/08; SLJ 3/08) [636.300978]

Birds

GENERAL AND MISCELLANEOUS

21967 Alderfer, Jonathan. *National Geographic Kids Bird Guide of North America* (5–8). Illus. 2013, National Geographic LB $23.90 (978-142631095-9); paper $15.95 (9781426310942). 176pp. With information on more than 100 species, this volume is divided by habitats such as "City Streets and Parks," "Deserts," and "Southern Swamp and Bayou." (Rev: BL 5/1/13) [598.097]

21968 Arnold, Caroline. *Birds: Nature's Magnificent Flying Machines* (3–4). Illus. by Patricia J. Wynne. 2003, Charlesbridge $16.95 (978-1-57091-516-1); paper $6.95 (978-1-57091-572-7). 32pp. Arnold take a close look at the physical mechanics behind birds' flight, examining such topics as taking off, hovering, gliding, altering direction, soaring, and landing. (Rev: BL 6/1–15/03; HBG 4/04; SLJ 12/03) [598]

21969 Aziz, Laurel. *Hummingbirds: A Beginner's Guide* (5–8). 2002, Firefly LB $19.95 (978-1-55209-487-7); paper $9.95 (978-1-55209-374-0). This heavily illustrated book offers a great deal of information about hummingbirds, including their bills, metabolism, flight, nesting, and migration. (Rev: BL 6/1–15/02; HBG 10/02) [598.7]

21970 Bateman, Robert. *Bateman's Backyard Birds* (4–7). 2005, Barron's $14.99 (978-0-7641-5882-7). Wildlife artist Bateman introduces readers to numerous North American species of birds and the joys of birding in this beautifully illustrated guide. (Rev: BL 10/15/05) [598]

21971 Berendt, John. *My Baby Blue Jays* (PS–3). Illus. by author. 2011, Viking $16.99 (978-0-670-01290-9). 32pp. The author documents in words and photographs the blue jays that built a nest on the balcony of his New York apartment, and the ensuing eggs and growing baby birds. (Rev: BL 5/1/11; SLJ 5/1/11) [598.8]

21972 Bjorklund, Ruth. *Parrots* (3–5). Illus. Series: Nature's Children. 2012, Scholastic/Children's Press LB $28 (978-053126836-0); paper $6.95 (9780531254813). 48pp. Simple text and many photographs present basic information about these birds' anatomy and behavior as well as their environment and history. (Rev: BL 3/1/13) [598.7]

21973 Carney, Margaret. *Where Does a Tiger-Heron Spend the Night?* (PS–1). Illus. by Melanie Watt. 2002, Kids Can $15.95 (978-1-55337-022-2). 32pp. Rhyming text, rich acrylic artwork, and a lift-the-flap format combine to present facts about birds for younger readers. (Rev: BCCB 9/02; BL 3/15/02; HBG 10/02; SLJ 5/02) [598]

21974 Cate, Annette LeBlanc. *Look Up! Bird-Watching in Your Own Backyard* (3–5). Illus. by author. 2013, Candlewick $15.99 (978-076364561-8). 64pp. Using vivid ink-and-watercolor illustrations and descriptive text, Cate shares her love for birds and bird-watching, describing various birds' characteristics, habitats, classifications, migration, and calls, while also teaching readers how to sketch birds and how to become a bird-watcher. ALA Notable Children's Book. (Rev: BL 2/1/13; LMC 10/13; SLJ 3/13*) [598]

21975 Chrustowski, Rick. *Blue Sky Bluebird* (1–3). 2004, Holt $16.95 (978-0-8050-7104-7). 32pp. This overview of the bluebird's physical characteristics, diet, mating habits, and migratory patterns includes vivid and detailed illustrations. (Rev: BL 8/04; SLJ 4/04) [598.8]

21976 Cleary, Brian P. *Sparrow, Eagle, Penguin, and Seagull: What Is a Bird?* (K–3). Illus. by Martin Goneau. Series: Animal Groups Are CATegorical. 2012, Millbrook $26.60 (978-076136207-4); paper $7.95 (978-14677034-0-6). 32pp. An attractive series that provides a lot of basic information while entertaining the reader with cartoon scenes. e (Rev: BL 10/15/12; LMC 5–6/13; SLJ Fall 2012) [598]

21977 Collard, Sneed B., III. *Beaks!* (K–3). Illus. by Robin Brickman. 2002, Charlesbridge $16.95 (978-1-57091-387-7); paper $6.95 (978-1-57091-388-4). Striking artwork and engrossing text about birds and their beaks will fascinate younger readers. (Rev: BL 8/02; HBG 3/03; SLJ 8/02) [573.3]

21978 Collard, Sneed B., III. *Wings* (3–5). Illus. by Robin Brickman. 2008, Charlesbridge $16.95 (978-1-57091-611-3); paper $7.95 (978-1-57091-612-0). 32pp. This is a fascinating look at the many animals that have wings, wing design, and the freedom of movement that these wings provide. (Rev: LMC 10/08; SLJ 2/08) [591.47]

21979 Copeland, Cynthia L., and Alexandra P. Lewis. *Funny Faces, Wacky Wings, and Other Silly Big Bird Things* (K–3). Series: Silly Millies. 2002, Millbrook LB $17.90 (978-0-7613-2863-6); paper $4.99 (978-0-7613-1788-3). 28pp. This overview of the world of big birds looks at the physical characteristics and behavior of such creatures as the ostrich, penguin, and bustard in an appealing blend of colorful illustrations and easy-to-read narrative. (Rev: HBG 3/03; SLJ 8/03)

21980 Dewey, Jennifer O. *Paisano, the Roadrunner* (4–6). Illus. by Wyman Meinzer. 2002, Millbrook LB $23.90 (978-0-7613-1250-5). 48pp. The author relates — in photographs, diary entries, and narrative — her experiences with a roadrunner she named "Paisano." (Rev: BCCB 9/02; BL 5/15/02; HB 7/02; HBG 10/02; SLJ 8/02) [598.7]

21981 Doris, Ellen. *Ornithology* (4–7). Series: Real Kids Real Science. 1994, Thames & Hudson $16.95 (978-0-500-19008-1). An excellent manual on how to study birds in their natural habitats, with accompanying activities for all seasons. (Rev: BL 9/1/94) [598]

21982 Gish, Melissa. *Hummingbirds* (5–8). Illus. Series: Living Wild. 2011, Creative Education LB $23.95 (978-160818078-3). 48pp. Gish looks at hummingbirds' habitats, physical characteristics, behaviors, relation-

ships with humans, and symbolic importance in some cultures. (Rev: BL 12/1/11) [598.7]

21983 Goodman, Susan E. *Saving the Whooping Crane* (2–5). Illus. by Phyllis V. Saroff. Series: On My Own Science. 2007, Millbrook LB $25.26 (978-0-8225-6748-6). 48pp. How a group of scientists went to extreme measures to rear baby whooping cranes. (Rev: SLJ 10/07) [598.3]

21984 Guiberson, Brenda Z. *Mud City: A Flamingo Story* (K–3). Illus. 2005, Holt $16.95 (978-0-8050-7177-1). 32pp. From egg through mating and having a chick, this volume follows the life cycle of a flamingo. (Rev: BL 5/15/05; SLJ 5/05) [598.3]

21985 Guibert, Francoise de. *Sing, Nightingale, Sing!* (3–5). Illus. by Chiaki Miyamoto. 2006, Kane $13.95 (978-1-929132-98-0). 48pp. This brightly illustrated guide translated from French introduces 51 bird species, each with an illustration and a paragraph of text, and is accompanied by an audio CD of the birds' songs. (Rev: BL 4/1/06) [598]

21986 Hall, Kirsten. *Great Bustard: The World's Heaviest Flying Bird* (K–2). Illus. Series: SuperSized! 2007, Bearport LB $21.28 (978-1-59716-390-3). 24pp. Report writers will get lots of mileage from this introduction to the bustard, filled with facts about and photographs of the big bird. (Rev: SLJ 7/07)

21987 Haus, Robyn. *Make Your Own Birdhouses and Feeders* (3–6). Illus. Series: Quick Starts for Kids! 2001, Williamson paper $8.95 (978-1-885593-55-9). 64pp. A detailed guide for younger readers to feeding and providing shelter for wild birds. (Rev: BL 2/15/02; SLJ 12/01) [690]

21988 Herkert, Barbara. *Birds in Your Backyard* (K–3). Illus. by author. Series: A Sharing Nature with Children Book. 2001, Dawn $17.95 (978-1-58469-026-9); paper $8.95 (978-1-58469-025-2). 35pp. Tips on attracting birds to your backyard, instructions for building a birdhouse, and advice on binoculars accompany descriptions of a variety of birds and maps showing birds commonly found in North America. (Rev: HBG 3/02; SLJ 5/02) [598]

21989 Hewitt, Joan. *A Flamingo Chick Grows Up* (1–3). Series: Baby Animals. 2001, Carolrhoda LB $21.27 (978-1-57505-164-2); paper $6.95 (978-0-8225-0090-2). 32pp. Using excellent photographs, short sentences, large print, and simple vocabulary, this attractive book describes a flamingo chick's growth to adulthood. (Rev: BL 10/15/01; HBG 3/02; SLJ 10/01) [598]

21990 Hickman, Pamela. *Starting with Nature Bird Book* (2–4). Illus. by Heather Collins. Series: Starting with Nature. 2000, Kids Can $12.95 (978-1-55074-471-2); paper $5.95 (978-1-55074-810-9). 32pp. An introduction to birds that gives basic material on species, homes, migration, songs, and banding as well as advice to bird watchers and a series of activities including making a birdhouse. (Rev: HBG 9/00; SLJ 7/00) [598]

21991 Hoose, Phillip. *The Race to Save the Lord God Bird* (5–8). 2004, Farrar $20.00 (978-0-374-36173-0).

The sad tale of the ivory-billed woodpecker's decline is interwoven with discussion of the scientific and sociological implications. (Rev: BL 6/1–15/04; SLJ 9/04) [598.7]

21992 Jango-Cohen, Judith. *Hovering Hummingbirds* (2–3). Series: Pull Ahead Books. 2003, Lerner LB $22.60 (978-0-8225-4666-5). 32pp. In this book, ideal for beginning readers, author Judith Jango-Cohen examines the life cycle, physical characteristics, behavior, and habitat of hummingbirds. (Rev: BL 11/15/03; HBG 10/03)

21993 Johnson, Sylvia A. *Crows* (4–6). Illus. Series: Nature Watch. 2004, Carolrhoda LB $25.26 (978-1-57505-628-9). Along with information on the crow's habitat, diet, behavior, migratory patterns, and life cycle, this photo-filled overview discusses West Nile virus and crows' increasing taste for city dwelling. (Rev: BL 12/1/04; SLJ 4/05) [598.8]

21994 Kelly, Irene. *It's a Hummingbird's Life* (1–3). Illus. 2003, Holiday House $16.95 (978-0-8234-1658-5). 32pp. An appealing look at a year in the life of the ruby-throated hummingbird, including its annual migration south in search of warmer weather. (Rev: BL 4/1/03; HBG 10/03; SLJ 6/03) [598.7]

21995 Kenyon, Linda. *Rainforest Bird Rescue: Changing the Future for Endangered Wildlife* (4–8). Series: Firefly Animal Rescue. 2006, Firefly LB $19.95 (978-1-55407-153-1); paper $9.95 (978-1-55407-152-4). 64pp. This book discusses the threats to the tropical bird species that live in the world's rain forests, habitat that is rapidly disappearing, and profiles the men and women who are crusading to save them. (Rev: SLJ 12/06) [598.1734]

21996 Kirby, Pamela F. *What Bluebirds Do* (K–3). Illus. 2009, Boyds Mills $18.95 (978-1-59078-614-7). 32pp. Excellent images document the lives of a family of Eastern Bluebirds. (Rev: BL 4/15/09; SLJ 5/09) [598.8]

21997 Larson, Jeanette, and Adrienne Yorinks. *Hummingbirds: Facts and Folklore from the Americas* (4–6). Illus. by Adrienne Yorinks. 2011, Charlesbridge $16.95 (978-1-58089-332-9); paper $8.95 (978-1-58089-333-6). 64pp. Interweaving facts, folklore, collage artwork, and extensive back matter, this volume gives readers a good overview of these birds and their anatomy, flight, habitat, diet, migration, and predators. e (Rev: BL 3/1/11; LMC 10/11; SLJ 3/1/11) [598.7]

21998 London, Jonathan. *Flamingo Sunset* (K–3). Illus. by Kristina Rodanas. 2008, Marshall Cavendish $16.99 (978-0-7614-5384-0). 32pp. Readers follow a flamingo family through a year during which a chick grows up; with attractive illustrations and discussion of conservation efforts. (Rev: BL 4/15/08; LMC 8/08; SLJ 7/08) [598.3]

21999 London, Jonathan. *Gone Again Ptarmigan* (K–3). Illus. by Jon Van Zyle. 2001, National Geographic $16.95 (978-0-7922-7561-9). 32pp. The life cycle of the Arctic ptarmigan is covered in this picture book that shows how its feathers change color to offer camouflage

in both winter and summer. (Rev: BL 1/1–15/01; HBG 10/01) [598.6]

22000 Macken, JoAnn Early. *Roadrunners / Correcaminos* (2–4). Trans. by Tatiana Acosta and Guillermo Gutiérrez. Series: Animals That Live in the Desert / Animales del desierto. 2005, Weekly Reader LB $21.00 (978-0-8368-4844-1). 24pp. A beginning book with facts about roadrunners in both English and Spanish. (Rev: SLJ 6/06) [598.7]

22001 Mania, Cathy, and Robert Mania. *Woodpecker in the Backyard* (3–5). Series: Wildlife Conservation Society Books. 2000, Watts LB $24.50 (978-0-531-11799-6). 48pp. A heavily illustrated book that describes the physical characteristics of the woodpecker and gives material on its habits, lifestyle, food, and homes. (Rev: BL 3/15/01) [598]

22002 Markle, Sandra. *Vultures* (3–5). Illus. Series: Animal Scavenger. 2005, Lerner LB $25.26 (978-0-8225-3195-1). 40pp. Vultures' role as scavengers is the focus of this volume full of dramatic photographs that looks in particular at the vultures of the African savannah, the Gulf Coast of Florida, and the Peruvian jungle. (Rev: BL 12/1/05) [598.9]

22003 Marsico, Katie. *A Peachick Grows Up* (1–2). 2007, Children's Pr. LB $19.00 (978-0-531-17480-7). 24pp. The development of a baby peacock is the topic of this vocabulary-building book with interesting photographs. (Rev: SLJ 8/07)

22004 Martin, Gilles. *Birds* (5–8). 2005, Abrams $18.95 (978-0-8109-5878-4). An oversize book full of color photographs of birds, plus watercolor sketches and brief, quite advanced text that comments on various aspects of the birds. (Rev: BL 5/1/05; SLJ 5/05) [598.22]

22005 Martin, Patricia A. Fink. *California Condors* (2–3). Series: Animals. 2002, Children's Book Pr. LB $25.00 (978-0-516-22161-8). 48pp. With a color photograph on almost every page and large type throughout, this is a simple but informative introduction to the California condor. (Rev: BL 8/02) [598.9]

22006 Maynard, Thane. *Ostriches* (3–4). Series: New Naturebooks. 2006, The Child's World LB $27.07 (978-1-59296-645-5). 32pp. An introductory overview of this huge bird, with vivid color photographs. (Rev: SLJ 2/07) [598.5]

22007 Miller, Sara Swan. *Wading Birds: From Herons to Hammerheads* (3–5). Series: Animals in Order. 2001, Watts LB $26.50 (978-0-531-11630-2). 32pp. The traits and behavior of wading birds are discussed with full-color photographs of various species and a simple text. (Rev: BL 6/1–15/01) [598.3]

22008 Miller, Sara Swan. *Woodpeckers, Toucans, and Their Kin* (4–6). Series: Animals in Order. 2003, Watts LB $26.50 (978-0-531-12243-3). 47pp. Introduces readers to birds that are members of the piciforme order, with information on representative species and their habitats. (Rev: SLJ 7/03) [598]

22009 Montgomery, Sy. *Kakapo Rescue: Saving the World's Strangest Parrot* (4–7). Illus. by Nic Bishop.

2010, Houghton Mifflin $18 (978-061849417-0). 80pp. The quest to save New Zealand's endangered Kakapo parrot is the focus of this inspiring conservation book. Sibert Medal 2011; ALA Notable Children's Book 2011. (Rev: BL 4/15/10*; SLJ 6/10) [639.9]

22010 Munro, Roxie. *Hatch!* (PS–3). Illus. by author. 2011, Marshall Cavendish $17.99 (978-0-7614-5882-1). 40pp. Readers guess the identities of birds based on pictures of their eggs in this volume that provides facts on birds including the great horned owl, emperor penguin, ostrich, and bald eagle. (Rev: BL 3/15/11; HB 5–6/11; LMC 8–9/11; SLJ 5/1/11) [598]

22011 Parker, Edward. *Birds* (5–8). Photos by author. Series: Rain Forest. 2003, Raintree LB $27.12 (978-0-7398-5239-2). 48pp. Birds that are found in rain forests are the topic of this overview that describes the dangers posed by humans through hunting, pollution, and agriculture. (Rev: HBG 3/03; SLJ 1/03) [598]

22012 Pericoli, Matteo. *The True Story of Stellina* (K–3). Illus. 2006, Knopf $15.95 (978-0-375-83273-4). 40pp. In lyrical text and appealing art, Pericoli describes his wife's care for a baby finch she rescued from a busy New York City intersection. (Rev: BCCB 4/06; BL 2/1/06*; HBG 10/06; LMC 5/06; SLJ 4/06) [636.6]

22013 Posada, Mia. *Robins: Songbirds of Spring* (K–3). Illus. by author. 2004, Carolrhoda LB $15.95 (978-1-57505-615-9). After a description in rhyming text of the life cycle of the American robin and its migratory and other behaviors, a detailed section gives additional facts and tips. (Rev: SLJ 5/04) [598.8]

22014 Post, Hans, and Kees Heij. *Sparrows* (PS–2). Illus. by Irene Goede. 2008, Boyds Mills $16.95 (978-1-59078-570-6). 32pp. An appealing and informative large-format look at the life cycle of the house sparrow. (Rev: BL 8/08; LMC 10/08) [598.8]

22015 Pringle, Laurence. *Crows! Strange and Wonderful* (2–4). Illus. by Bob Marstall. 2002, Boyds Mills $15.95 (978-1-56397-899-9). 32pp. This is an absorbing, well-illustrated account of the life and behavior of the crow, showing the bird's intelligence, adaptability, and amazing ability to communicate. (Rev: BCCB 12/02; BL 11/1/02; HBG 3/03; SLJ 9/02) [598.964]

22016 Pyers, Greg. *Why Am I a Bird?* (3–5). Illus. Series: Classifying Animals. 2005, Raintree LB $27.50 (978-1-4109-2014-0); paper $7.85 (978-1-4109-2021-8). 32pp. Introduces readers to the process of scientific classification and then examines the unique physical characteristics — such as feathers, wings, and hollow bones — of birds as a class. (Rev: SLJ 4/06) [598]

22017 Rau, Dana Meachen. *The Robin in the Tree* (PS–1). 2006, Benchmark LB $22.79 (978-0-7614-2304-1). 24pp. With its child-friendly blend of rebuses and easy-to-understand text, this easy reader follows a typical day in a robin's life, providing basic information about the bird's physical characteristics, habitat, diet, behavior, and life cycle. (Rev: SLJ 12/06) [598.8]

22018 Rauzon, Mark J. *Parrots Around the World* (3–5). Series: Animals in Order. 2001, Watts LB $26.50 (978-0-531-11688-3). 32pp. Following a discussion of the parrot family, various species are introduced through color photographs and a brief text that describes anatomy, habits, and habitats. Also use *Pelicans, Cormorants, and Their Kin* (2002). (Rev: BL 6/1–15/01) [598.71]

22019 Rebman, Renee C. *Vultures* (3–5). Illus. Series: Animals Animals. 2011, Marshall Cavendish LB $20.95 (978-076144880-8). 48pp. Rebman examines the vulture's anatomy, scavenging habits, flight, and life cycle, with discussion of threats to their long-term survival. (Rev: BL 10/15/11) [598.9]

22020 Robinson, Fay. *Singing Robins* (PS–2). Series: Pull Ahead Books. 2000, Lerner $22.60 (978-0-8225-3641-3). 32pp. With four lines of simple text and a color photo on each page, this book tells of the bird with the beautiful orange breast feathers and the pretty blue eggs. (Rev: BL 5/15/00; HBG 9/00) [598.8]

22021 Roth, Susan L., and Cindy Trumbore. *Parrots Over Puerto Rico* (2–5). Illus. by Susan L. Roth. 2013, Lee & Low $19.95 (978-162014004-8). 48pp. Using vivid illustrations, this history of parrots in Puerto Rico also incorporates the history of the Puerto Rican people, focusing not only on how close to extinction the parrot was in the 1960s and the resulting Puerto Rican Parrot Recovery Program initiated by America and Puerto Rico, but also the history of the island before and after the first human settlers. Sibert Medal; ALA Notable Children's Book; Booklist Editors' Choice: Books for Youth. Lexile AD560 (Rev: BL 11/15/13*; HB 1–2/14; SLJ 10/13*) [597]

22022 Savage, Stephen. *Birds* (2–4). Illus. Series: What's the Difference? 2000, Raintree $25.69 (978-0-7398-1356-0). 32pp. A most attractive volume that presents a number of different birds and explains their common characteristics, along with material on their nests, food, and how they care for their young. (Rev: BL 10/15/00; HBG 3/01) [598]

22023 Sayre, April P. *The Hungry Hummingbird* (K–3). Illus. by Gay Holland. 2001, Millbrook LB $22.90 (978-0-7613-1951-1). 32pp. A hungry little hummingbird searches for food in this beautifully illustrated book. (Rev: BL 11/15/01; HBG 3/02; SLJ 11/01) [598.7]

22024 Sexton, Colleen. *Puffins* (K–3). Series: Blastoff! Readers: Oceans Alive. 2009, Children's Pr. LB $20.00 (978-0-531-21714-6). 24pp. With color photographs and clearly defined scientific terms, this simple book introduces beginning readers to the puffin. (Rev: SLJ 6/09) [598.3]

22025 Sill, Cathryn. *About Hummingbirds: A Guide for Children* (K–3). Illus. by John Sill. Series: About . . . 2011, Peachtree $16.95 (978-1-56145-588-1). Unpaged. Simple text and bright watercolor illustrations introduce these fascinating birds and their characteristics. (Rev: SLJ 9/1/11) [598.7]

22026 Spilsbury, Richard, and Louise Spilsbury. *A Murder of Crows* (3–5). Series: Animal Groups. 2003, Heinemann LB $24.22 (978-1-4034-0742-9). 32pp. In this attractively illustrated book readers learn about the crow's habitat, diet, hierarchical social structure, and behavior in groups. (Rev: HBG 10/03; SLJ 9/03) [598.8]

22027 Spinner, Stephanie. *Alex the Parrot: No Ordinary Bird* (2–5). Illus. by Meilo So. 2012, Knopf $17.99 (978-0-375-86846-7). 48pp. This accessible book tells the story of an African grey parrot that showed an ability not only to use words but to identify colors, shapes, materials, and numbers, displaying the intellect of a 5-year-old child. ℮ Lexile 680L (Rev: BL 10/1/12; HB 9–10/12; LMC 1–2/13; SLJ 10/12) [636.6]

22028 Stewart, Melissa. *A Place for Birds* (K–3). Illus. by Higgins Bond. 2009, Peachtree $16.95 (978-1-56145-474-7). 28pp. This attractive title highlights the ways in which humans threaten the lives of birds, recommends environmentally conscious behavior, and includes species maps of North America. (Rev: BL 3/15/09; SLJ 5/09) [598]

22029 Stockdale, Susan. *Bring on the Birds* (PS–1). Illus. by author. 2011, Peachtree $15.95 (978-1-56145-560-7). 32pp. A rhyming, brightly illustrated introduction to familiar and exotic birds, focusing on 21 diverse species. (Rev: BL 3/15/11; LMC 8–9/11; SLJ 4/11) [598]

22030 Taylor, Kenny. *Puffins* (5–9). Series: WorldLife Library. 1999, Voyageur paper $16.95 (978-0-89658-419-8). Outstanding photographs and conservation awareness are highlights of this introduction to puffins, their characteristics, habitats, and habits. (Rev: BL 8/99) [598.3]

22031 Townsend, Emily Rose. *Woodpeckers* (PS–2). 2004, Capstone LB $17.26 (978-0-7368-2070-7). 24pp. Presents basic information on woodpeckers in a small format with brief text facing full-color close-up photographs. (Rev: SLJ 8/04) [598]

22032 Underwood, Deborah. *Colorful Peacocks* (2–3). Series: Pull Ahead Books. 2006, Lerner LB $22.60 (978-0-8225-5930-6). 32pp. This colorful introduction to peacocks examines the birds' physical characteristics, diet, behavior, and habitat, and looks at how peacock parents care for their young. (Rev: SLJ 9/06) [598.6]

22033 Vogel, Carole G. *The Man Who Flies with Birds* (4–8). 2009, Kar-Ben $18.95 (978-0-8225-7643-3). 64pp. This is the fascinating story of Yossi Leshem, an Israeli ornithologist whose research on bird migration resulted in air space restrictions that reduce the number of bird-airplane collisions. (Rev: HB 11–12/09; LMC 1–2/10; SLJ 12/09) [598.0956]

22034 Wilkes, Angela. *Question Time: Birds* (3–5). Illus. Series: Question Time. 2002, Kingfisher $11.95 (978-0-7534-5450-3); paper $6.95 (978-0-7534-5462-6). 32pp. Topics covered in a question-and-answer format include the different types of birds, and their characteristics, habitat, and defense mechanisms. (Rev: HBG 3/03; SLJ 2/03)

22035 Willis, Nancy Carol. *Red Knot: A Shorebird's Incredible Journey* (2–4). 2006, Birdsong $15.95 (978-0-9662761-4-5); paper $6.95 (978-0-9662761-5-2). 32pp. Using the form of journal entries, this picture book follows the red knot shorebird on its incredible 20,000-mile annual migration. (Rev: BL 6/1–15/06; SLJ 7/06) [598.3]

22036 Winner, Cherie. *Everything Bird: What Kids Really Want to Know About Birds* (3–4). 2007, NorthWord LB $10.95 (978-1-55971-962-9); paper $7.95 (978-1-55971-963-6). 64pp. Questions and answers about birds provide plenty of interesting information about these feathered friends. With photographs. (Rev: SLJ 8/07)

22037 Winner, Cherie. *Woodpeckers* (3–6). Series: Nature Watch. 2000, Carolrhoda LB $25.26 (978-1-57505-445-2). 48pp. This colorful introduction to the varieties of woodpeckers explains why they tap holes in wood. (Rev: BL 7/00; HBG 10/01) [598]

22038 Wolf, Sallie. *The Robin Makes a Laughing Sound: A Birder's Journal* (4–8). Illus. by author. 2010, Charlesbridge $11.95 (978-1-58089-318-3). 43pp. The author's journal — with sketches, watercolors, poems, and notes — documents bird visitors throughout the year, from geese to woodpeckers, robins, and cardinals. (Rev: SLJ 6/10) [598]

22039 Zim, Herbert S., and Ira N. Gabrielson. *Birds* (5–8). 1991, Western paper $21.27 (978-0-307-64053-6). A guide to the most commonly seen birds, with accompanying illustrations and basic materials. [598]

BEHAVIOR

22040 Johnson, Sylvia A. *Songbirds: The Language of Song* (3–6). Series: Nature Watch. 2000, Carolrhoda LB $25.26 (978-1-57505-483-4). 48pp. This book introduces a number of songbirds and describes their songs. (Rev: BL 3/1/01; HBG 10/01) [598]

22041 Kelly, Irene. *Even an Ostrich Needs a Nest: Where Birds Begin* (1–3). Illus. by author. 2009, Holiday $16.95 (978-0-8234-2102-2). 32pp. An appealing and informative look at bird nests, the materials used, and how they are constructed. (Rev: BL 3/1/09; SLJ 6/09) [598.156]

22042 Markle, Sandra. *The Long, Long Journey: The Godwit's Amazing Migration* (K–3). Illus. by Mia Posada. 2013, Millbrook LB $26.60 (978-076135623-3). 32pp. Tells the story of the bar-tailed godwit's amazing annual migration from Alaska to New Zealand, flying more than 7,000 miles nonstop. ℮ (Rev: BL 3/15/13; HB 7–8/13; LMC 10/13*; SLJ 3/13*) [598.3]

22043 Winer, Yvonne. *Birds Build Nests* (PS–3). Illus. by Tony Oliver. 2002, Charlesbridge $16.95 (978-1-57091-500-0); paper $6.95 (978-1-57091-501-7). 32pp. A lovely book of poetic text and beautiful, realistic illustrations that introduces the nesting habits of various species of birds to younger readers. (Rev: BL 3/1/02; HBG 10/02; SLJ 3/02) [598.156]

DUCKS, GEESE, AND SWANS

22044 Cooper, Jason. *Canada Goose* (1–3). Series: Life Cycles. 2002, Rourke LB $17.95 (978-1-58952-351-7). 24pp. Handsome photographs and simple text describe the life cycle, habitat, appearance, and behavior of these animals. (Rev: SLJ 12/02)

22045 Helget, Nicole. *Swans* (4–7). Series: Living Wild. 2008, Smart Apple LB $32.80 (978-1-58341-659-4). 48pp. With excellent color photographs and extensive explanatory text this book looks at the seven species of swans, including humanity's influence on and involvement with the birds. (Rev: SLJ 2/09) [598.4]

22046 Hipp, Andrew. *The Life Cycle of a Duck* (PS–2). Illus. by Dwight Kuhn. Series: Life Cycle Of. 2002, Rosen LB $19.95 (978-0-8239-5868-9). 24pp. This book for beginning readers follows the life of a duck from conception to adulthood. (Rev: BL 12/15/02) [598.4]

22047 Kawa, Katie. *Ducklings* (PS–K). Illus. Series: Cute and Cuddly: Baby Animals. 2011, Gareth Stevens LB $22.60 (978-143395538-9). 24pp. A very simple book featuring brief text and adorable photographs of baby ducks, with basic information about their lives. (Rev: BL 2/15/12) [598.4]

22048 Llewellyn, Claire. *Duck* (K–3). Illus. by Simon Mendez. Series: Starting Life. 2004, NorthWord $16.95 (978-1-55971-878-3). 32pp. An innovative picture-book layout enhances the journey of the mallard duck from egg to adult. (Rev: BL 4/15/04; SLJ 11/04) [598.4]

22049 Mara, Wil. *Ducks* (4–6). Series: Animals Animals. 2008, Marshall Cavendish LB $20.95 (978-0-7614-2927-2). 48pp. *Ducks* clearly defines various types of ducks, their habits and habitats, and how humans affect them. (Rev: SLJ 2/09) [598.4]

22050 Osborn, Elinor. *Project UltraSwan* (3–6). Illus. 2002, Houghton $16.00 (978-0-618-14528-7). 64pp. This is a fascinating and readable account of how scientists using ultralight aircraft are working to help trumpeter swans to rediscover their migratory routes. (Rev: BCCB 12/02; BL 12/15/02; HB 1/03; HBG 3/03; SLJ 6/03) [598.4]

22051 Savage, Stephen. *Duck* (3–6). Illus. Series: Animal Neighbors. 2008, Rosen LB $23.95 (978-1-4358-4988-4). 32pp. This title includes details about a duck's life and habitat and has clear easy text and large photographs which help explain a duck's anatomy. (Rev: SLJ 5/09) [598.4]

22052 Sayre, April P. *Honk, Honk, Goose! Canada Geese Start a Family* (K–3). Illus. by Huy Voun Lee. 2009, Holt $16.95 (978-0-8050-7103-0). 32pp. A pair of geese mate mate, build a nest, protect the eggs, and nurture the young; detailed information appears at the back of the book. (Rev: BL 3/1/09; HB 5/09; SLJ 4/09)

22053 Spilsbury, Louise. *Duck* (K–2). Series: Life Cycles. 2005, Heinemann LB $20.64 (978-1-4034-6771-3). 24pp. Simple easy-reader questions and answers about ducks and how they grow are accompanied by color photographs. (Rev: SLJ 7/05) [598.4]

22054 Stockland, Patricia M. *On the Duck Pond* (K–2). Illus. by Todd Ouren. Series: Barnyard Buddies. 2008, ABDO LB $17.95 (978-1-60270-027-7). 24pp. Simple facts about ducks are presented in two formats — information about a fictional family of ducks in larger type, with specific features highlighted in smaller type alongside; clear illustrations and a labeled diagram are also included. (Rev: BL 10/15/07; SLJ 2/08) [636.5]

22055 Watts, Barrie. *Duck* (K–3). Illus. 2002, Smart Apple LB $24.25 (978-1-58340-197-2). 32pp. This easy-to-read book about ducks includes loads of facts and excellent photography. (Rev: BL 10/15/02; HBG 3/03) [598.4]

EAGLES, HAWKS, AND OTHER BIRDS OF PREY

22056 Arnosky, Jim. *Thunder Birds: Nature's Flying Predators* (2–5). Illus. by author. 2011, Sterling $14.95 (978-1-4027-5661-0). 32pp. Arnosky introduces a variety of birds of prey with succinct text, large paintings, and pencil drawings in this attractive volume with fold-out pages. (Rev: BL 6/1/11; SLJ 6/11*) [598.153]

22057 Bailey, Jill. *The Secret Life of Falcons* (4–7). Series: The Secret World of . . . 2002, Raintree LB $27.12 (978-0-7398-4985-9). 48pp. This book describes the anatomy and habits of the falcon with material on how they feed, communicate, and reproduce. (Rev: BL 8/02) [598.9]

22058 Bardhan-Quallen, Sudipta. *Flying Eagle* (K–3). Illus. by Deborah Kogan Ray. 2009, Charlesbridge $15.95 (978-1-57091-671-7). 32pp. A tawny eagle soars over the Serengeti in search of food for his young, giving readers a view of the wildlife below and the dangers of life there; effective watercolors are accompanied by simple rhymes. (Rev: BL 4/1/09; SLJ 3/09) [598.9]

22059 Colman, C. H. *The Bald Eagle's View of American History* (1–4). Illus. by Joanne Friar. 2006, Charlesbridge paper $5.95 (978-1-58089-301-5). 48pp. Postage-stamp depictions of the bald eagle illustrate this history of the bird, threats to its existence, and its importance as a symbol. (Rev: SLJ 1/07) [929.9]

22060 Evert, Laura, and Wayne Lynch. *Birds of Prey* (3–6). Illus. by Sherry Neidigh and John F. McGee. Series: Our Wild World. 2005, NorthWord $16.95 (978-1-55971-925-4). 191pp. An attractive, well-organized and easily accessible introduction to the four major subdivisions of raptors: eagles, falcons, owls, and vultures. (Rev: SLJ 11/05)

22061 George, Jean Craighead. *The Eagles Are Back* (2–4). Illus. by Wendell Minor. 2013, Dial $16.99 (978-0-8037-3771-6). 32pp. Blending fact and fiction, this is a tribute to the successful efforts to save the bald eagle from extinction. (Rev: BL 11/15/12; LMC 8–9/13; SLJ 3/13) [598.9]

22062 Goldish, Meish. *Bald Eagles: A Chemical Nightmare* (3–5). Series: America's Animal Comebacks. 2008, Bearport LB $25.27 (978-1-59716-505-1). 32pp. With eye-catching photographs and an appealing format, this volume looks at the reasons for the decline in the eagle population (mainly hunting and pesticides) and the measures that succeeded in bring them back from the brink of extinction. (Rev: LMC 1/08; SLJ 2/08) [598.9]

22063 Goldish, Meish. *California Condors: Saved by Captive Breeding* (3–6). Series: America's Animal

Comebacks. 2009, Bearport LB $25.27 (978-1-59716-741-3). 32pp. Goldish traces the condor's struggle to survive and scientists' efforts to bring this animal back into its natural habitat. (Rev: SLJ 5/09)

22064 Hodge, Deborah. *Eagles* (2–5). Illus. Series: Kids Can! 2000, Kids Can $10.95 (978-1-55074-715-7); paper $5.95 (978-1-55074-717-1). After a general look at eagles around the world, this account focuses on two American breeds and gives information on their habitats, food, physical characteristics, flight, behavior, and young. (Rev: BL 11/1/00; HBG 3/01) [598.9]

22065 Laubach, Christyna. *Raptor! A Kid's Guide to Birds of Prey* (4–7). 2002, Storey paper $14.95 (978-1-58017-445-9). A large-format treasure trove of facts about raptors, with information on individual species, identification, habits, habitat, range maps, and so forth. (Rev: BL 12/1/02; HBG 3/03; SLJ 10/02) [598.9]

22066 Lunis, Natalie. *Peregrine Falcon: Dive, Dive, Dive!* (1–3). Illus. Series: Blink of an Eye: Superfast Animals! 2010, Bearport LB $22.61 (978-193608793-8). 24pp. Clear action photographs enhance this profile of the world's fastest animal. (Rev: BL 10/1/10) [598.9]

22067 Lynch, Wayne. *Falcons* (3–5). Photos by author. Illus. by Sherry Neidigh. Series: Our Wild World. 2005, NorthWord $10.95 (978-1-55971-911-7); paper $7.95 (978-1-55971-912-4). With eye-catching photographs and readable text, this book discusses the physical characteristics, life cycle, diet, habitat, and family life of the falcons of North America. Also use *Vultures* (2005) (Rev: SLJ 8/05) [598.9]

22068 McCarthy, Meghan. *City Hawk: The Story of Pale Male* (PS–3). Illus. by author. 2007, Simon & Schuster $15.99 (978-1-4169-3359-5). Bird watchers follow a red-tailed hawk as he and his mate make a nest and raise their young on a Central Park building in 1991. (Rev: BCCB 10/07; LMC 1/08; SLJ 10/07) [598.9]

22069 Macken, JoAnn Early. *Golden Eagles* (K–2). Series: Animals That Live in the Mountains. 2010, Weekly Reader LB $22 (978-1-4339-2413-2). 24pp. Close-up photographs and bright backgrounds enliven this book about the life and habitat of golden eagles. (Rev: SLJ 8/1/10) [598.9]

22070 Macken, JoAnn Early. *Golden Eagles / Águila real* (2–4). Trans. by Tatiana Acosta and Guillermo Gutiérrez. Series: Animals That Live in the Mountains / Animales de las montañas. 2006, Weekly Reader LB $21.00 (978-0-8368-6450-2). 24pp. A beginning book with facts about golden eagles in both English and Spanish. (Rev: SLJ 6/06) [598.9]

22071 Martin-James, Kathleen. *Soaring Bald Eagles* (PS–2). Series: Pull Ahead Books. 2001, Lerner LB $22.60 (978-0-8225-3636-9). 32pp. A few lines of simple text plus a color photograph on each page present the world of bald eagles to beginning readers. (Rev: BL 6/1–15/01; HBG 10/01) [598.9]

22072 Patent, Dorothy Hinshaw. *The Bald Eagle Returns* (4–8). 2000, Clarion $16.00 (978-0-395-91416-8). This book not only discusses the successful efforts to save the bald eagle but also gives material on its anatomy, habitats, mating, and behavior. (Rev: BCCB 1/01; BL 10/15/00; HBG 10/01; SLJ 11/00) [598.9]

22073 Povey, Karen D. *Falcons* (4–6). Illus. Series: Nature's Predators. 2005, Gale LB $26.20 (978-0-7377-2347-2). 48pp. In four brief chapters, the lives of falcons are explored with material on the food they eat and how they catch it.

22074 Rauzon, Mark. *Golden Eagles of Devil Mountain* (3–5). Series: Wildlife Conservation Society Books. 2000, Watts LB $24.50 (978-0-531-11787-3). 48pp. The golden eagle is introduced, with material on its anatomy, behavioral patterns, life cycle, and habitat. (Rev: BL 3/15/01) [598.9]

22075 Riggs, Kate. *Eagles* (K–3). Illus. Series: Amazing Animals. 2012, Creative Education LB $17.95 (978-160818106-3). 24pp. For new or reluctant readers, this is a good introduction to the eagle's physical characteristics, habitat, and behavior, and includes a story from folklore explaining why people respect eagles. (Rev: BL 3/1/12) [598.9]

22076 Sayre, April P. *Vulture View* (K–2). Illus. by Steven Jenkins. 2007, Holt $16.95 (978-0-8050-7557-1). 32pp. Brief, rhyming text and brilliant-colored collage backgrounds show the lives of vultures, ending with a more-detailed informational spread about "nature's cleanup crew." (Rev: BCCB 11/07; BL 11/1/07; HB 11/07; SLJ 12/07) [598.9]

22077 Schulman, Janet. *Pale Male: Citizen Hawk of New York City* (1–3). Illus. by Meilo So. 2008, Knopf $16.99 (978-0-375-84558-1). 40pp. The story of a red-tailed hawk who nested on a ledge of an exclusive New York City building and the resulting clash between residents and environmentalists. (Rev: BL 2/15/08; HB 3/08; LMC 3/08; SLJ 1/08) [598.9]

22078 Unwin, Mike. *Peregrine Falcon* (4–6). Illus. Series: Animals Under Threat. 2004, Heinemann LB $18.95 (978-1-4034-4862-0). 48pp. The life cycle of the peregrine falcon and threats to its survival are explored in this blend of narrative and eye-catching color photography.

GULLS AND OTHER SEA BIRDS

22079 Bentley, Dawn. *Welcome Back, Puffin!* (PS–2). Illus. by Beth Stover. Series: Read-and-Discover Atlantic Wilderness Adventures. 2003, Soundprints paper $3.95 (978-1-59249-009-7). 48pp. This appealing title follows a female puffin and her mate as they make their annual visit to an island; soon after they arrive, the female lays a single egg, and she and her mate keep it warm until it hatches, after which they're kept busy gathering food for the hatchling that eats ten times a day. (Rev: SLJ 1/04)

22080 Dunning, Joan. *Seabird in the Forest: The Mystery of the Marbled Murrelet* (K–3). Illus. 2011, Boyds Mills $17.95 (978-1-59078-715-1). 32pp. A fascinating, lyrical account of the life of a Pacific Coast seabird that chooses to nest and raise its young far inland. (Rev: BL 4/15/11; SLJ 5/1/11) [598]

22081 Lewin, Ted. *Puffling Patrol* (2–4). Illus. by Betsy Lewin. 2012, Lee & Low $19.95 (978-160060424-9). 56pp. On an island off the coast of Iceland, two children volunteer to help fledgling puffins that took the wrong direction and have become stranded in town; handsome illustrations add appeal to the natural drama. Lexile 910L (Rev: BL 4/1/12; LMC 11–12/12; SLJ 7/12) [598.3]

22082 Metz, Lorijo. *Discovering Seagulls* (3–5). Series: Along the Shore. 2011, Rosen LB $21.25 (978-1-4488-4995-6). 24pp. A clear introduction that provides information on habitat, physical characteristics, diet, relationship with humans, and so forth. ℮ (Rev: SLJ 12/1/11) [598.3]

22083 Miller, Sara S. *Shorebirds: From Stilts to Sanderlings* (3–5). Illus. Series: Animals in Order. 2000, Watts LB $26.50 (978-0-531-11596-1). 48pp. Introductory material on animal classification is followed by an overview of shorebirds, their varieties, habits, structure, and care of young. (Rev: BL 9/15/00) [598.29]

22084 Webb, Sophie. *Looking for Seabirds: Journal from an Alaskan Voyage* (4–6). Illus. 2004, Houghton $16.00 (978-0-618-21235-4). 48pp. The author conveys the excitement of research in this fact-filled account of a shipboard bird-counting expedition. (Rev: BL 4/15/04; HB 5/04; SLJ 5/04) [598.177]

22085 Zecca, Katherine. *A Puffin's Year* (PS–3). Illus. 2007, Down East $15.95 (978-0-89272-742-1). 32pp. Clearly written and well designed, this appealing book about puffins' life cycle includes a conservation message from the National Audubon Society. (Rev: BL 5/1/07; SLJ 8/07) [598.3]

OWLS

22086 Bodden, Valerie. *Owls* (1–3). Illus. Series: Amazing Animals. 2013, Creative Education LB $17.95 (978-160818088-2). 24pp. An eye-catching introduction to these animals that will appeal to young and reluctant readers; includes a story from folklore. (Rev: BL 4/15/13; LMC 10/13*) [598.9]

22087 Curtis, Jennifer Keats. *Baby Owl's Rescue* (3–4). Illus. by Laura Jacques. 2009, Sylvan Dell $16.95 (978-1-934359-95-2); paper $8.95 (978-1-607180-40-1). Unpaged. A baby owl is lucky enough to tumble out of its nest and into the backyard of young Maddie and Max, whose mother is a wildlife rehabilitator and teaches them how to treat the bird. (Rev: LMC 1–2/10; SLJ 12/1/09) [598.9]

22088 Gibbons, Gail. *Owls* (K–3). Illus. 2005, Holiday House $16.95 (978-0-8234-1880-0). 32pp. All about the owls that are native to North America, with watercolor illustrations and a section about an owl family. (Rev: BL 3/15/05; SLJ 4/05) [598.9]

22089 Gish, Melissa. *Owls* (5–8). Illus. Series: Living Wild. 2011, Creative Education LB $23.95 (978-160818081-3). 48pp. Gish looks at owls' habitats, physical characteristics, behaviors, relationships with humans, protected status, and role in folklore. (Rev: BL 12/1/11) [598.9]

22090 Hiscock, Bruce. *Ookpik: The Travels of a Snowy Owl* (K–3). Illus. by author. 2008, Boyds Mills $16.95 (978-1-59078-461-7). 32pp. A snowy owl hatches in the arctic tundra and migrates to a farm in the Adirondacks, facing many challenges along the way; with a final page of facts. (Rev: BL 1/1–15/08; LMC 3/08; SLJ 6/08) [598.9]

22091 Landau, Elaine. *Owls: Hunters of the Night* (2–4). Illus. Series: Animals after Dark. 2007, Enslow LB $16.95 (978-0-7660-2768-8). 32pp. Large color photographs accompany basic facts about owls' physical characteristics and behavior. (Rev: BL 5/15/07; LMC 10/07; SLJ 8/07) [598.9]

22092 Lang, Aubrey. *Baby Owl* (1–3). Photos by Wayne Lynch. Series: Nature Babies. 2004, Fitzhenry & Whiteside $11.95 (978-1-55041-796-8); paper $5.95 (978-1-55041-798-2). 36pp. Full-color photographs follow the development of three baby great horned owls from hatching to independence. (Rev: SLJ 2/05) [598.9]

22093 Lynch, Wayne. *Owls* (3–5). Photos by author. Illus. by Sherry Neidigh. Series: Our Wild World. 2005, NorthWord $10.95 (978-1-55971-914-8); paper $7.95 (978-1-55971-915-5). 47pp. With eye-catching photographs and readable text, this book discusses the physical characteristics, life cycle, diet, habitat, and family life of the owls of North America. (Rev: SLJ 8/05) [598.9]

22094 Markle, Sandra. *Owls* (3–6). Illus. Series: Animal Predators. 2004, Carolrhoda LB $25.26 (978-1-57505-729-3). 40pp. Concise text and clear, full-page photographs introduce the life cycle of the owl and its physical characteristics, habitat, diet, and predatory behavior. (Rev: SLJ 12/04)

22095 Richardson, Adele D. *Owls: Flat-Faced Flyers* (1–3). Series: Wild World of Animals. 2002, Capstone LB $22.60 (978-0-7368-1396-9). 24pp. For beginning readers, this is an attractive introduction to owls, their appearance, habits, care of young, and habitats. (Rev: BL 1/1–15/03; HBG 3/03) [598.9]

22096 Townsend, Emily Rose. *Owls* (PS–2). Series: Woodland Animals. 2004, Capstone LB $17.26 (978-0-7368-2068-4). 24pp. Presents basic information on owls in a small format with brief text facing full-color close-up photographs. (Rev: SLJ 8/04) [598]

22097 Warhol, Tom. *Owls* (3–6). Series: AnimalWays. 2007, Marshall Cavendish LB $23.95 (978-0-7614-2537-3). 112pp. Information on owl lore and legend precedes details of owl evolution; types of owls; owl anatomy, characteristics, behavior, and reproduction; and threats to their survival. (Rev: SLJ 5/08) [598.9]

PENGUINS

22098 Arnold, Caroline. *A Penguin's World* (PS–2). Illus. Series: Caroline Arnold's Animals. 2006, Picture Window LB $26.60 (978-1-4048-1323-6). 24pp. With an accessible blend of paper collage artwork and easy-to-understand text, this picture book introduces basic facts about Adelie penguins and their family life. (Rev: BL 4/1/06; LMC 11/06; SLJ 6/06) [598.47]

22099 Barner, Bob. *Penguins, Penguins, Everywhere!* (PS–2). Illus. 2007, Chronicle $14.95 (978-0-8118-5664-5). 32pp. Basic information about penguins is couched in appealing rhyming text accompanied by bold illustrations. (Rev: BL 4/1/07) [598.47]

22100 Bodden, Valerie. *Penguins* (K–2). Illus. Series: Amazing Animals. 2010, Creative Company/Creative Education LB $16.95 (978-158341810-9). 24pp. A simple overview of the characteristics of penguins, with eye-catching photographs. (Rev: BL 7/10) [598.47]

22101 Bredeson, Carmen. *Emperor Penguins Up Close* (PS–3). Series: Zoom in on Animals! 2006, Enslow LB $21.26 (978-0-7660-2497-7). 24pp. Eye-catching full-color close-ups show key physical characteristics of the penguins, and the text gives basic details on diet, habitat, life cycle, and so forth. (Rev: SLJ 11/06) [598.47]

22102 Daigle, Evelyne. *The World of Penguins* (4–6). Trans. from French by Geneviève Wright. Illus. by Daniel Grenier. 2007, Tundra $18.95 (978-0-88776-799-9). 48pp. Penguins' habitat, diet, anatomy, behavior, and distribution are all covered here, along with information about the author's 2003 trip to Antarctica to view the penguins. With photographs and illustrations. (Rev: SLJ 5/07)

22103 Guiberson, Brenda Z. *The Emperor Lays an Egg* (K–3). Illus. by Joan Paley. 2001, Holt $16.95 (978-0-8050-6204-5). 32pp. Colorful text and lovely collages depict a year in the life of a family of emperor penguins, showing the father's incredible care for the egg, the necessary swimming skills, and the struggle to stay warm in the frigid air. (Rev: BL 12/1/01; HB 1/02; HBG 3/02; SLJ 12/01*) [598.47]

22104 Hanel, Rachael. *Penguins* (4–7). Series: Living Wild. 2008, Smart Apple LB $32.80 (978-1-58341-658-7). 48pp. With excellent color photographs and extensive explanatory text this book looks at the 17 species of penguins, including humanity's influence on and involvement with the birds. (Rev: SLJ 2/09) [598.47]

22105 Jacquet, Luc. *March of the Penguins* (3–5). Illus. by Jerome Maison. 2005, National Geographic $30.00 (978-0-7922-6190-2). 160pp. A companion to the movie, this book also tells the story of emperor penguins' life cycle, and features many striking images; back matter includes a behind-the-scenes look at the making of the movie and additional information about the emperor penguins that were its stars. (Rev: BL 11/15/05) [598.47]

22106 Jango-Cohen, Judith. *Penguins* (3–5). Illus. Series: Animals, Animals. 2001, Benchmark LB $25.64 (978-0-7614-1260-1). 48pp. In addition to the usual information on the species, this book discusses the penguin's discovery and naming, and its relationship with humans. (Rev: HBG 10/02; SLJ 2/02) [598.47]

22107 Johnson, Sylvia A. *Penguins* (4–7). 1981, Lerner LB $22.60 (978-0-8225-1453-4). Handsome photographs enliven the text of this introduction to penguins and their habitats. [598]

22108 Jonas, Ann. *Little Penguins* (1–3). Series: Born to Be Wild. 2005, Gareth Stevens LB $23.00 (978-0-8368-

4738-3). 24pp. This colorful title introduces the physical and behavioral characteristics of penguins and examines how adult birds feed their offspring and protect them from predators. (Rev: SLJ 2/06) [598.4]

22109 Kalman, Bobbie. *The Life Cycle of an Emperor Penguin* (2–4). Illus. Series: Life Cycle. 2006, Crabtree LB $25.20 (978-0-7787-0630-4); paper $6.95 (978-0-7787-0704-2). 32pp. Report writers will find this a useful and interesting resource. Diet, habitat, behavior, and other aspects of emperor penguins are covered. Photographs and illustrations accompany the text, and vocabulary words appear in bold font. (Rev: SLJ 5/07)

22110 Lang, Aubrey. *Baby Penguin* (K–2). Illus. by Wayne Lynch. Series: Nature Babies. 2001, Fitzhenry & Whiteside $13.95 (978-1-55041-675-6). 28pp. Excellent photographs and a brief text present young penguins from birth to adolescence. (Rev: BL 12/15/01; SLJ 2/02) [598.47]

22111 London, Jonathan. *Little Penguin: The Emperor of Antarctica* (PS–2). Illus. by Julie Olson. 2011, Marshall Cavendish $17.99 (978-0-7614-5954-5). Unpaged. Two penguins take turns caring for their fluffy hatchling in this sweet and informative look at the birds' family life. e (Rev: LMC 1–2/12; SLJ 9/1/11) [598]

22112 Lynch, Wayne. *Penguins!* (4–7). 1999, Firefly LB $19.95 (978-1-55209-421-1); paper $9.95 (978-1-55209-424-2). An appealing book that introduces penguins and their various species with coverage of their evolution, food, life cycle, habits, and habitats. (Rev: BCCB 12/99; BL 9/15/99; HBG 3/00) [598.47]

22113 Markert, Jenny. *Penguins* (1–3). Illus. Series: New Naturebooks. 2007, Child's World LB $18.95 (978-1-59296-850-3). 32pp. Easily read text and large bright photographs introduce facts about penguins. (Rev: BL 10/1/07; SLJ 2/08) [598.47]

22114 Markle, Sandra. *A Mother's Journey* (K–3). Illus. by Alan Marks. 2005, Charlesbridge $16.95 (978-1-57091-621-2). 32pp. This handsome picture book chronicles the arduous journey of a female Emperor penguin from laying an egg through hunting for food for the newborn chick. (Rev: BL 9/1/05; SLJ 9/05) [598.47]

22115 Marzollo, Jean. *Pierre the Penguin: A True Story* (PS–2). Illus. by Laura Regan. 2010, Sleeping Bear $15.95 (978-1-58536-485-5). Unpaged. A biologist at the California Academy of Sciences helps an African penguin who loses his feathers and becomes alienated from the other penguins. (Rev: SLJ 8/1/10) [598.47]

22116 Momatiuk, Yva, and John Eastcott. *Face to Face with Penguins* (3–6). Photos by authors. Series: Face to Face with Animals. 2009, National Geographic $16.95 (978-1-4263-0561-0); LB $25.90 (978-1-4263-0562-7). 32pp. With beautiful photographs, this attractive volume looks at the nesting habits, diet, and social lives of penguins, as well as the threats to their survival. (Rev: SLJ 11/09) [598.47]

22117 Noonan, Diana. *The Emperor Penguin* (2–4). Series: Life Cycles. 2002, Chelsea LB $23.00 (978-0-7910-6965-3). 32pp. This account covers the life cycle of the Antarctic emperor penguin and how these animals grow, mate, incubate their eggs, and feed their chicks. (Rev: BL 12/15/02; HBG 3/03) [598.42]

22118 Pringle, Laurence. *Penguins!* (3–7). Series: Strange and Wonderful. 2007, Boyds Mills $16.95 (978-1-59078-090-9). 32pp. Report writers will find plenty of material in this book that covers the 17 species of penguins and their behavior, with realistic double-page watercolor illustrations. (Rev: BL 2/15/07; SLJ 4/07) [516]

22119 Raatma, Lucia. *Penguins* (2–4). Series: First Reports. 2001, Compass Point LB $22.60 (978-0-7565-0058-0). 48pp. Young report writers will quickly find basic information on penguins here. (Rev: HBG 4/04; SLJ 7/01) [598]

22120 Rau, Dana Meachen. *Guess Who Swims* (PS–K). Series: Bookworms. Guess Who. 2009, Marshall Cavendish $15.95 (978-0-7614-2974-6). 32pp. Fun for browsing, this book asks readers to identify a penguin using the clues in the text and images. (Rev: SLJ 6/09) [598.47]

22121 Rodriguez, Ana María. *Secret of the Puking Penguins . . . and More!* (5–7). Illus. Series: Animal Secrets Revealed! 2008, Enslow LB $17.95 (978-0-7660-2955-2). 48pp. Unusual habits of a variety of animals are revealed along with the ways in which scientists establish these facts. (Rev: BL 12/1/08; SLJ 3/09) [597.9]

22122 Sill, Cathryn. *About Penguins: A Guide for Children* (PS–2). Illus. by John Sill. 2009, Peachtree $15.95 (978-1-56145-488-4). 48pp. Covering 17 species of penguins, this beautifully illustrated book describes key characteristics. (Rev: BL 9/15/09; SLJ 9/1/09) [598.47]

22123 Simon, Seymour. *Penguins* (2–4). Illus. 2007, HarperCollins $16.99 (978-0-06-028395-7). 32pp. Eye-catching, full-page photographs accompany clear text about penguins and their lives. (Rev: BL 9/15/07; SLJ 10/07) [598.47]

22124 Spilsbury, Louise, and Richard Spilsbury. *Watching Penguins in Antarctica* (1–3). Series: Wild World. 2006, Heinemann LB $25.36 (978-1-4034-7223-6). 32pp. Provides details about penguins' characteristics, diet, reproduction, predators, and so forth, with photographs, a world map, and a "Tracker's Guide." (Rev: SLJ 7/06) [598.47]

22125 Spilsbury, Richard, and Louise Spilsbury. *A Rookery of Penguins* (3–5). Illus. Series: Animal Groups. 2004, Heinemann LB $24.22 (978-1-4034-4691-6). 32pp. Easy-to-understand narrative and plenty of color photographs provide a good overview of penguins and their behaviors and habitats. (Rev: BL 4/15/04; SLJ 9/04) [598.47]

22126 Stefoff, Rebecca. *Penguins* (4–8). Series: Animal-Ways. 2005, Benchmark LB $21.95 (978-0-7614-1743-9). Beautiful photographs enrich this well-organized volume that provides basic information on the penguin's characteristics, habits, and habitat. (Rev: SLJ 5/06) [598.4]

22127 Tatham, Betty. *Penguin Chick* (2–3). Illus. by Helen K. Davie. Series: Let's-Read-and-Find-Out Sci-

ence. 2002, HarperCollins $16.99 (978-0-06-028594-4); paper $5.99 (978-0-06-445206-9). 40pp. An account for younger readers of an emperor penguin chick's survival in an often ruthless habitat. (Rev: BL 3/1/02; HB 5/02; HBG 10/02; SLJ 3/02) [598.47]

22128 Teitelbaum, Michael. *Baby Penguin Slips and Slides* (PS–1). Illus. Series: Photo Adventure Book. 2009, Treasure Bay $9.95 (978-1-60115-285-5); paper $4.99 (978-1-60115-286-2). 24pp. Color photographs show penguins as they make their way through the day. (Rev: BL 6/1–15/09)

22129 Webb, Sophie. *My Season with Penguins: An Antarctic Journal* (4–8). Illus. by author. 2000, Houghton Mifflin $15.00 (978-0-395-92291-0). Journal entries plus effective drawings show the joys and tribulations of a two-month stay in the Antarctic studying penguins and their behavior. (Rev: HB 11–12/00; HBG 3/01; SLJ 12/00) [598]

Conservation of Endangered Species

22130 Astorga, Amalia, and Gary Paul Nabhan. *Efrain of the Sonoran Desert: A Lizard's Life Among the Seri People* (2–6). Illus. by Janet K. Miller. 2001, Cinco Puntos $15.95 (978-0-938317-55-5). 32pp. The fascinating story of how an endangered lizard can flourish within a special community. (Rev: BL 12/15/01; HBG 3/02; SLJ 12/01) [305.8975]

22131 Barnes, Simon. *Planet Zoo* (4–7). 2001, Orion $29.95 (978-1-85881-488-9). An overview of 100 endangered species that conveys information in a conversational manner. (Rev: BL 8/01; SLJ 8/01) [578.68]

22132 Casterline, Linda. *Rare Animals: A Chapter Book* (2–5). Series: True Tales. 2003, Children's Pr. LB $22.50 (978-0-516-22914-0). 48pp. Written in simple language, this volume introduces four endangered animals — the whopping crane, elephant, monk seal, and polar bear — and discusses what is being done to protect them. (Rev: SLJ 2/04) [591.68]

22133 Collard, Sneed B., III. *In the Wild* (3–6). Series: Science Adventures. 2005, Benchmark LB $28.50 (978-0-7614-1955-6). 43pp. Readers meet scientists at Zoo Atlanta who work with endangered primates. (Rev: SLJ 5/06) [599.8]

22134 Feinstein, Stephen. *The Jaguar: Help Save This Endangered Species!* (4–7). Series: Saving Endangered Species. 2008, Enslow LB $24.95 (978-1-59845-065-1). Part of the MyReportLinks.com series, this introduction to jaguars and the threats they face features Web sites that report writers can access for more information. (Rev: BL 2/15/08) [599.75]

22135 Firestone, Mary. *Top 50 Reasons to Care About Elephants* (5–8). Series: Top 50 Reasons to Care About Endangered Animals. 2010, Enslow LB $31.93 (978-0-7660-3454-9). 104pp. Readers learn about elephants' biology and habitat, behavior, and threats to their survival; activities in which young people can contribute to elephant welfare are listed. Also in this series by this author are *Top 50 Reasons to Care About Giant Pandas, Top 50 Reasons to Care About Rhinos,* and *Top 50 Reasons to Care About Tigers* (all 2010). (Rev: LMC 3–4/10) [599.67]

22136 Fletcher, Marty, and Glenn Scherer. *The Green Sea Turtle: Help Save This Endangered Species!* (5–7). Series: Saving Endangered Species. 2006, Enslow LB $33.27 (978-1-59845-033-0). A well-illustrated look at the plight of the endangered green sea turtle, with an overview of its physical characteristics, diet, habitat, and behavior. (Rev: SLJ 9/06) [597.92]

22137 Fowler, Allan. *It Could Still Be Endangered* (K–2). Illus. Series: Rookie Readers. 2000, Children's Book Pr. $20.50 (978-0-516-21208-1). 32pp. Full-page colors photos introduce the concept of endangerment and introduce several animals large and small that are on the endangered list. (Rev: BL 1/1–15/01) [333.95]

22138 Hirsch, Rebecca. *Helping Endangered Animals* (3–7). Series: Language Arts Explorer: Save the Planet. 2010, Cherry Lake LB $27.07 (978-1-60279-658-4). 32pp. Students are given a mission at the beginning of the book and must use creative thinking and problem solving to gather facts as they travel on a virtual trip researching the plight of animals including pandas and elephants. (Rev: LMC 8–9/10; SLJ 4/10) [591.68]

22139 Hirschi, Ron. *Lions, Tigers, and Bears: Why Are Big Predators So Rare?* (3–6). Illus. by Thomas D. Mangelsen. 2007, Boyds Mills $16.95 (978-1-59078-435-8). 32pp. Hirschi explains the many and varied threats facing cougars, polar bears, lions, cheetahs, tigers, grizzly bears, and killer whales; the wide format and eye-catching photographs make this a compelling book. (Rev: BL 10/15/07; LMC 1/08; SLJ 9/07) [591.3]

22140 Jenkins, Martin. *Can We Save the Tiger?* (2–4). Illus. by Vicky White. 2011, Candlewick $16.99 (978-0-7636-4909-8). 56pp. A beautifully illustrated book about extinct and endangered animals and humans' impact on their environment past and future. ALSC Notable Children's Book, 2012. Lexile 970L (Rev: BLO 2/14/11; SLJ 3/1/11*) [333.9]

22141 Jenkins, Steve. *Almost Gone: The World's Rarest Animals* (1–3). Illus. Series: Let's-Read-and-Find-Out Science. 2006, HarperCollins $16.99 (978-0-06-053598-8); paper $5.99 (978-0-06-053600-8). 40pp. Striking cut-paper collages and brief text introduce 21 animal species that are endangered. (Rev: BL 12/1/05; SLJ 2/06*) [574.529]

22142 Kendell, Patricia. *WWF* (5–8). Series: World Watch. 2004, Raintree LB $27.14 (978-0-7398-6615-3). 48pp. Introduces the World Wildlife Fund's history, organization, and work on behalf of the endangered animals; sidebars provide key facts and relevant quotations. (Rev: BL 4/1/04; SLJ 6/04) [333.95]

22143 McDaniel, Melissa. *Mysterious Nature: A Chapter Book* (3–6). Series: True Tales. 2005, Children's Pr. LB $22.50 (978-0-516-25183-7); paper $4.95 (978-0-516-25453-1). Scientists discuss the causes of mysterious

animal extinctions around the world; clear illustrations add to the easy-reading text. (Rev: SLJ 5/06) [591.68]

22144 McLimans, David. *Gone Fishing: Ocean Life by the Numbers* (2–4). Illus. by author. 2008, Walker $16.99 (978-0-8027-9770-4). 40pp. Endangered marine creatures and their habitats are introduced along with "Ocean Facts by the Numbers"; illustrations are numbers made up of creatures' bodies. (Rev: BL 12/1/08; LMC 11/08; SLJ 10/08) [591.77]

22145 Martin, Jacqueline Briggs. *The Chiru of High Tibet: A True Story* (1–3). Illus. by Linda Wingerter. 2010, Houghton Harcourt $17.99 (978-0-618-58130-6). 40pp. One researcher's quest to protect the endangered chiru (small antelope) of Tibet is chronicled in this inspiring story. ⊖ (Rev: HB 9–10/10; LMC 3–4/11*; SLJ 10/1/10) [599.64]

22146 Morgan, Sally. *Animal Rescue* (1–3). Series: Helping Our Planet. 2011, Cherrytree LB $28.50 (978-1-84234-606-8). 32pp. Morgan introduces the kinds of animals that are endangered, the reasons for their status, and what can be done to protect them. (Rev: SLJ 8/1/11) [333.95]

22147 Nirgiotis, Nicholas, and Theodore Nigiortis. *No More Dodos: How Zoos Help Endangered Wildlife* (5–8). 1996, Lerner LB $23.93 (978-0-8225-2856-2). An introduction to the many organizations that are trying to protect and preserve endangered wildlife worldwide. (Rev: BCCB 2/97; BL 2/15/97; SLJ 2/97) [639.9]

22148 Penny, Malcolm. *Endangered Species* (5–8). Series: 21st Century Debates. 2002, Raintree LB $27.12 (978-0-7398-4873-9). 64pp. Topics covered in this well-illustrated book include a history of conservation, how species become endangered, methods for protection such as captive breeding, and saving habitats. (Rev: BL 6/1–15/02) [591]

22149 Radley, Gail. *Forests and Jungles* (2–5). Illus. by Jean Sherlock. Series: Vanishing From. 2001, Carolrhoda LB $22.60 (978-1-57505-405-6); paper $6.95 (978-1-57505-567-1). The plight of endangered species as humans threaten their habitats serves as an introduction to double-page spreads about specific animals. Also use *Grasslands and Deserts* and *The Skies* (both 2001). (Rev: HBG 3/02; SLJ 10/01) [591]

22150 Salmansohn, Pete, and Stephen W. Kress. *Saving Birds: Heroes Around the World* (4–7). 2003, Tilbury House $16.95 (978-0-88448-237-6). Efforts to save endangered bird species are detailed in informative text and arresting, full-color photographs. (Rev: BL 3/15/03; HBG 10/03; SLJ 5/03) [333.95]

22151 Sheehan, Sean. *Endangered Species* (5–8). Illus. Series: What If We Do Nothing? 2009, Gareth Stevens LB $31.00 (978-1-4339-0086-0). 48pp. The threats to both plants and animals, along with factors such as ecotourism and the exotic pet market, are addressed in this volume that looks at the past, the current status, and the future outlook. (Rev: BL 4/15/09; SLJ 6/09) [333.95]

22152 Silhol, Sandrine, and Gaelle Guerive. *Extraordinary Endangered Animals* (5–8). Illus. by Marie

Doucedame. 2011, Abrams $24.95 (978-1-4197-0034-7). 160pp. Two-page spreads introduce species in six geographical groupings and describe habitat, location, feeding, hibernation, reproduction, and adaptations to the environment; with maps, large photographs, and discussion of threats to survival. (Rev: BL 11/15/11; LMC 3–4/12; SLJ 11/1/11) [333.95]

22153 Thomas, Peggy. *Big Cat Conservation* (5–8). Series: Science of Saving Animals. 2000, Twenty-First Century LB $25.90 (978-0-7613-3231-2). This book focuses on seven species, including panthers, cheetahs, and tigers, and discusses wildlife conservation programs, challenges, and successes. (Rev: BL 6/1–15/00; HBG 10/00; SLJ 7/00) [333.95]

22154 Thomas, Peggy. *Bird Alert* (5–8). Series: The Science of Saving Animals. 2000, Twenty-First Century LB $25.90 (978-0-7613-1457-8). This book discusses conservation programs designed to save endangered bird species and tells how youngsters can get involved in saving birds. (Rev: BL 10/15/00; HBG 10/01; SLJ 12/00) [591.52]

22155 Thomas, Peggy. *Marine Mammal Preservation* (5–8). Series: The Science of Saving Animals. 2000, Twenty-First Century LB $25.90 (978-0-7613-1458-5). 64pp. Focuses on endangered marine mammals and describes a wide range of conservation programs. (Rev: BL 10/15/00; HBG 10/01; SLJ 1/01) [574.92]

22156 Thomas, Peggy. *Reptile Rescue* (5–8). Illus. Series: Science of Saving Animals. 2000, Twenty-First Century LB $25.90 (978-0-7613-3232-9). 64pp. A description of various conservation programs and how they operate in relation to several reptile species, including tortoises, crocodiles, and snakes. (Rev: BL 6/1–15/00; HBG 10/00; SLJ 7/00) [333.95]

Insects and Arachnids

GENERAL AND MISCELLANEOUS

22157 Aloian, Molly. *Where Do Insects Live?* (1–3). Illus. Series: Close-Up. 2013, Crabtree LB $16.95 (978-077871280-0); paper $7.95 (9780778712848). 24pp. *Where Do Insects Live?* answers the question posed by the title through simple sentences and close-up photographs, with discussion of six-legged creatures living underground, in burrows, and in hives, nests, and the water. (Rev: BL 10/1/13) [595.7]

22158 Arnosky, Jim. *Creep and Flutter: The Secret World of Insects and Spiders* (3–5). Illus. by author. 2012, Sterling $14.95 (978-1-4027-7766-0). 40pp. With six fold-out pages, this large-format book is an informative and well-illustrated exploration of a variety of insects and spiders. (Rev: BL 4/15/12; SLJ 4/1/12) [595.7]

22159 Ashley, Susan. *Fireflies* (1–4). Series: Let's Read About Insects. 2004, Weekly Reader LB $21.00 (978-0-8368-4053-7); paper $5.95 (978-0-8368-4060-5). 24pp. The life cycle of fireflies is described in small-format, easy-to-read text with close-up photographs. (Rev: SLJ 2/05)

22160 *Ask a Bug* (2–5). Illus. 2011, DK $9.99 (978-075667230-0). 48pp. Many frequently asked questions about insects — "why do crickets sing" and "why don't spiders get stuck to their own webs," for example — are answered in this appealing and informative book that will attract browsers. **e** (Rev: BLO 3/14/11; LMC 10/11) [595.7]

22161 Baker, Nick. *Bug Zoo* (2–4). Illus. 2010, DK $12.99 (978-0-7566-6166-3). 64pp. Baker showing how to catch and care for 13 different kinds of common insects is the focus of this compelling book with close-up photos and clear instructions. (Rev: BLO 10/1/10; SLJ 7/1/10) [500]

22162 Barner, Bob. *Bug Safari* (1–3). Illus. 2004, Holiday House $16.95 (978-0-8234-1707-0). 32pp. In this colorful journey into the world of insects, a young boy follows a trail of ants and discovers an alternative perspective on a picnic lunch. (Rev: BL 4/15/04; SLJ 3/04) [595.7]

22163 Beccaloni, George. *Biggest Bugs Life-Size* (3–7). Illus. 2010, Firefly $19.95 (978-155407699-4). 88pp. Thirty-five bugs of unusual sizes are presented in this fascinating book full of close-up photographs. (Rev: BL 12/1/10; SLJ 12/1/10) [595.714]

22164 Becker, Helaine. *The Insecto-Files* (3–6). Illus. by Claudia Dávila. 2009, Maple Tree $22.95 (978-1-897349-46-5); paper $10.95 (978-1-897349-47-2). 64pp. This is a bright, lively introduction to insects and their important characteristics, including facts, interesting sidebars, quizzes, experiments, and activities. (Rev: LMC 10/09; SLJ 7/09) [595.7]

22165 Berger, Melvin. *Buzz! A Book About Insects* (1–2). Illus. 2000, Scholastic $3.99 (978-0-439-08748-3). 40pp. This easy-to-read science book uses color photographs to introduce various insects, explain their physical characteristics, and show the changes from caterpillar to butterfly. (Rev: BL 10/1/00) [595.7]

22166 Blobaum, Cindy. *Insectigations! 40 Hands-on Activities to Explore the Insect World* (3–6). Illus. by Gail Rattray. 2005, Chicago Review paper $12.95 (978-1-55652-568-1). 133pp. From collecting and drawing insects to raising mealworms, keeping a scientific journal, and gardening for butterflies, this useful volume offers both activities and facts. (Rev: SLJ 1/06) [595.7]

22167 Bodden, Valerie. *Cockroaches* (K–3). Illus. Series: Creepy Creatures. 2013, Creative Education LB $17.95 (978-160818232-9). 24pp. Bodden introduces young readers to these surprisingly varied creatures using large and vivid photographs and simple text to describe their diet, habitat, growth, and unique abilities, such as holding their breath for extended periods. (Rev: BL 2/15/13; LMC 10/13*) [595.7]

22168 Bodden, Valerie. *Crickets* (K–1). Illus. Series: Creepy Creatures. 2011, Creative Education $16.95 (978-158341993-9). 24pp. A basic introduction to crickets and their anatomy and behavior. (Rev: BL 4/1/11; LMC 8–9/11) [595.7]

22169 Bulion, Leslie. *Hey There, Stink Bug!* (4–6). 2006, Charlesbridge $12.95 (978-1-58089-304-6). 48pp. Poems about bugs full of dramatic and often gross details are designed to fascinate the older elementary student. (Rev: BL 7/06; SLJ 7/06) [595.7]

22170 Burnie, David. *Bug Hunter* (4–6). Illus. Series: Nature Activities. 2005, DK paper $9.99 (978-0-7566-1030-2). 72pp. Bright, attractive double-page spreads explore the study of bugs (insects, spiders, and some worms) and provide activities. (Rev: BL 7/05) [595.7]

22171 Burnie, David. *Insect* (5–9). Series: DK/Google e.guides. 2005, DK $17.99 (978-0-7566-1010-4). This highly illustrated guide introduces readers to the life cycle, behavior, diet, and habitat of insects and provides a link to a Web site that serves as a gateway to additional resources. (Rev: SLJ 8/05)

22172 Burris, Judy, and Wayne Richards. *The Secret Lives of Backyard Bugs* (4–6). Illus. 2011, Storey $24.95 (978-1-60342-985-6); paper $14.95 (978-1-60342-563-6). 128pp. Lightning bugs, ladybugs, dragonflies, stick insects, bees, cicadas, aphids, and luna moths are among the bugs covered in this attractive volume that also outlines a garden's seasonal cycles and the life cycles of plants, soil, and insects and spiders. e (Rev: LMC 11–12/11; SLJ 11/1/11) [595.7]

22173 Crowley, Ned. *Ugh! A Bug!* (K–2). Series: Silly Millies. 2005, Millbrook LB $18.60 (978-0-7613-3450-7); paper $4.99 (978-0-7613-2475-1). This photo-filled title with rhyming text introduces young readers to 25 kinds of insects, provides some fascinating facts, and includes a "pictionary" index. (Rev: SLJ 11/05)

22174 DiTerlizzi, Angela. *Some Bugs* (PS–1). Illus. by Brendan Wenzel. 2014, Simon & Schuster $17.99 (978-144245880-2). 32pp. Butterflies, moths, cicadas, and spiders are among the creatures featured in this attractive title with rhyming text. e (Rev: BL 3/1/14; LMC 8–9/14; SLJ 3/14) [571.4]

22175 Dixon, Norma. *Focus on Flies* (3–6). Illus. 2008, Fitzhenry & Whiteside $18.95 (978-1-55005-128-5). 32pp. Dixon provides an engaging, conversational introduction to insects including houseflies, fruit flies, and mosquitoes, covering their history, physical characteristics, metamorphosis, role in pollination, and so forth, plus their ability to spread disease. (Rev: BL 12/15/08; SLJ 4/09) [595.77]

22176 Frost, Helen. *Praying Mantises* (PS–3). Series: Insects. 2001, Capstone LB $17.26 (978-0-7368-0853-8). 24pp. Spare text and full-page color photographs — often close-up shots — offer basic information on praying mantises. Also use *Walkingsticks* (2001) (Rev: HBG 3/02; SLJ 9/01) [959.7]

22177 Gilpin, Daniel. *Centipedes, Millipedes, Scorpions and Spiders* (4–6). Illus. Series: Animal Kingdom Classification. 2005, Compass Point LB $29.26 (978-0-7565-1254-5). 48pp. Spiders and other members of the arachnid family, including mites, scorpions, and ticks, are introduced in informative spreads with eye-catching illustrations. (Rev: BL 11/1/05) [595.6]

22178 Glaser, Linda. *Dazzling Dragonflies: A Life Cycle Story* (K–3). Illus. by Mia Posada. 2008, Lerner LB $22.60 (978-0-8225-6753-0). 32pp. The life cycle of the dragonfly is clearly presented for younger readers. (Rev: BL 12/1/07; LMC 10/08; SLJ 8/08) [595.7]

22179 Glaser, Linda. *Not a Buzz to Be Found: Insects in Winter* (2–4). Illus. by Jaime Zollars. 2011, Millbrook LB $25.26 (978-0-7613-5644-8). 32pp. Glaser explores the wintertime state of 12 insects including the monarch butterfly, woolly bear caterpillar, and the praying mantis. (Rev: BL 11/1/11; SLJ 11/1/11) [595.7]

22180 Gleason, Carrie. *Feasting Bedbugs, Mites, and Ticks* (3–6). Illus. Series: Creepy Crawlies. 2010, Crabtree LB $26.60 (978-0-7787-2500-8); paper $8.95 (978-0-7787-2507-7). 32pp. With plenty of close-up color photographs, this title explores the characteristics of tiny insects that share our environment. (Rev: BL 10/1/10; SLJ 2/1/11) [614.4]

22181 Gray, Leon. *Walking Sticks: The World's Longest Insects* (1–4). Illus. Series: Even More Supersized! 2013, Bearport LB $23.93 (978-161772733-7). 24pp. A detailed, well-illustrated introduction to these fascinating animals and their habitat, diet, life cycle, behavior, and so forth. e (Rev: BL 4/1/13; LMC 11–12/13) [595.7]

22182 Gray, Susan H. *Emerald Ash Borer* (3–6). Series: Animal Invaders. 2008, Cherry Lake LB $26.26 (978-1-60279-112-1). 32pp. A solid introduction to the invasive borer and the threat it presents to ash trees, with color photographs and maps. (Rev: SLJ 9/08) [595.76]

22183 Greenaway, Theresa. *Ants* (4–7). Series: The Secret World of . . . 2001, Raintree LB $18.98 (978-0-7368-3511-4). After presenting interesting and unusual facts about ants, this book examines their structure, homes, behavior, and enemies. (Rev: BL 10/15/01) [595.79]

22184 Hansen, Amy S. *Bugs and Bugsicles: Insects in the Winter* (2–4). Illus. by Robert Clement Kray. 2010, Boyds Mills $17.95 (978-1-59078-269-9); paper $11.95 (978-1-59078-763-2). 32pp. How do insects survive winter? A colorful answer to this question, exploring the lives of insects including a praying mantis, a ladybug, a monarch butterfly, and a woolly bear caterpillar. (Rev: BL 3/1/10; LMC 5–6/10; SLJ 4/1/10) [595.714]

22185 Hartley, Karen, et al. *Fly* (1–4). Illus. Series: Bug Books. 2000, Heinemann LB $21.36 (978-1-57572-548-2). 32pp. Traces the life cycle of the fly, with illustrations and text that also cover its habitats and food. (Rev: BL 7/00) [595.77]

22186 Hartley, Karen, et al. *Head Louse* (1–4). Illus. Series: Bug Books. 2000, Heinemann LB $21.36 (978-1-57572-549-9). 32pp. Close-up photos are used to introduce the life cycle of the head louse, its food, and habits. (Rev: BL 7/00) [616.5]

22187 Heinrichs, Ann. *Grasshoppers* (2–4). Series: Nature's Friends. 2002, Compass Point LB $22.60 (978-0-7565-0166-2). 32pp. Grasshoppers, their anatomy and life cycle, and their relationship to humans are covered in simple text and clear close-up photographs. (Rev: SLJ 7/02) [595.7]

22188 Himmelman, John. *Noisy Bug Sing-Along* (PS–2). Illus. by author. 2013, Dawn paper $8.95 (978-1-58469-192-1). 30pp. Close-up illustrations and phonetic descriptions enhance this exploration of insect calls. (Rev: BL 6/13; LMC 11–12/13; SLJ 6/13) [595.715]

22189 Hipp, Andrew. *Orchid Mantises* (3–5). Series: The Really Wild Life of Insects. 2003, Rosen LB $21.25 (978-0-8239-6239-6). 24pp. Mantises that can mimic the flower of an orchid are the focus of this interesting, well-illustrated volume. (Rev: SLJ 1/04) [595.7]

22190 Hipp, Andrew. *Peanut-Head Bugs* (3–5). Series: The Really Wild Life of Insects. 2003, Rosen LB $21.25 (978-0-8239-6242-6). 24pp. An excellent overview of members of the Fulgoridae family, found throughout much of Latin America and commonly called peanut-head bugs. (Rev: SLJ 1/04) [595.7]

22191 Hirschmann, Kris. *Lice* (4–6). Illus. Series: Parasites. 2003, Gale LB $24.95 (978-0-7377-1784-6). 32pp. The physical and behavioral characteristics of lice are introduced, with information on how they spread disease to humans. (Rev: SLJ 6/04) [614.4]

22192 Holland, Gay. *Look Closer: An Introduction to Bug-Watching* (1–4). Illus. 2003, Millbrook LB $22.90 (978-0-7613-2664-9). 32pp. Aphids, spittlebugs, and dragonflies are among the bugs introduced in this guide that combines realistic illustrations with easy-to-read text. (Rev: BL 6/1–15/03; HBG 10/03; SLJ 9/03) [595.7]

22193 Holmes, Anita. *Insect Detector* (1–2). Illus. Series: We Can Read About — Nature! 2000, Benchmark $21.36 (978-0-7614-1110-9). 32pp. A beginning reader that defines the characteristics of an insect and asks if particular creatures such as a scorpion or a spider would meet these criteria. (Rev: BL 12/1/00; HBG 3/01; SLJ 2/01) [595.7]

22194 Hughes, Monica. *Pill Bugs* (PS–2). Illus. Series: Creepy Creatures. 2003, Raintree LB $18.56 (978-1-4109-0624-3). 24pp. A close-up look at the diet, anatomy, habitat, and life cycle of pill bugs, for beginning readers. (Rev: BL 2/15/04) [595.3]

22195 Jackson, Donna. *The Bug Scientists* (4–7). Illus. Series: Scientists in the Field. 2002, Houghton $16.00 (978-0-618-10868-8). 48pp. In addition to describing a variety of professional jobs related to insects, this colorful volume presents excellent information about insects and how they live. (Rev: BCCB 6/02; BL 4/1/02; HB 5/02; HBG 10/02; SLJ 4/02) [595.7]

22196 Jarrow, Gail. *Chiggers* (4–6). Series: Parasites. 2003, Gale LB $24.95 (978-0-7377-1778-5). 32pp. A close-up look at these tiny bloodsucking mites, with color photographs and first-person accounts of chigger encounters. (Rev: SLJ 6/04) [616.9]

22197 Johnson, Jinny. *Insects and Creepy-Crawlies* (3–5). Illus. by Peter Bull. Series: Explorers. 2011, Kingfisher $10.99 (978-075346592-9). 32pp. An inviting mix of text, sidebars, captions, fact lists, and more add read-

appeal to this well-illustrated book about insects and their habitats. (Rev: BL 2/15/12) [595.7]

22198 Karapetkova, Holly. *Katydid? Katy Didn't!* (PS). Illus. Series: Rourke Board Books. 2009, Rourke $5.99 (978-1-60472-427-1). 16pp. Attractive color photographs and chanting wordplay provide a few easily absorbed facts about katydids. (Rev: BL 5/15/09) [595.7]

22199 Kite, L. Patricia. *Cockroaches* (2–3). Series: Early Bird Nature Books. 2001, Lerner LB $25.26 (978-0-8225-3046-6). 48pp. Using a simple text and color photographs on each page, this book effectively introduces the life cycle of the cockroach with material on its habits, anatomy, and homes. Also use *Fireflies* (2001) (Rev: BL 8/1/01; HBG 10/01) [595.7]

22200 Kite, L. Patricia. *Insect: Facts and Folklore* (3–6). Illus. 2001, Millbrook LB $29.90 (978-0-7613-1822-4). 80pp. Fascinating information (mixing facts, folklore, and interesting anecdotes) about insects, all colorfully presented. (Rev: BL 9/1/01; HBG 3/02; SLJ 10/01) [595.7]

22201 Lockwood, Sophie. *Dragonflies* (4–6). Series: The World of Insects. 2007, The Child's World LB $29.93 (978-1-59296-821-3). 40pp. Crisp writing and sharp photographs offer substantive insight into various aspects of dragonfly life. Also use *Flies* (2007) (Rev: SLJ 3/08) [595.7]). (Rev: SLJ 3/08) [595.7]

22202 Markle, Sandra. *Insects* (1–3). Illus. Series: Biggest! Littlest! 2009, Boyds Mills $16.95 (978-1-59078-512-6). 24pp. Looking at insects both tiny and large, Markle identifies the characteristics that make them successful. (Rev: BCCB 4/09; BL 3/15/09; LMC 8/09; SLJ 3/09) [595.7]

22203 Markle, Sandra. *Mites: Master Sneaks* (4–7). Illus. Series: Arachnid World. 2012, Lerner LB $29.27 (978-076135046-0). 48pp. With large color photographs and concise text, this book introduces the life cycle, characteristics, and behavior of the mite. (Rev: BL 3/1/12; SLJ 2/12) [595.4]

22204 Markle, Sandra. *Praying Mantises: Hungry Insect Heroes* (2–4). Illus. 2008, Lerner LB $27.93 (978-0-8225-7300-5). 48pp. With clear, eye-catching photographs, an animated text, and numerous sidebars, this is a thorough and interesting overview of the praying mantis. (Rev: BL 4/1/08; SLJ 2/08) [595.7]

22205 Markle, Sandra. *Termites: Hardworking Insect Families* (2–5). Series: Insect World. 2008, Lerner LB $27.93 (978-0-8225-7301-2). 48pp. Eye-catching illustrations and simple diagrams are combined with interestingly presented facts about these insects and two activities. (Rev: LMC 10/08; SLJ 2/08) [595.7]

22206 Markle, Sandra. *Ticks: Dangerous Hitchhikers* (3–5). Illus. 2011, Lerner LB $29.27 (978-076135041-5). 48pp. With close-up photographs, this volume introduces ticks, their anatomy, life cycle, and diet, and the dangers they pose to humans and pets. (Rev: BL 4/1/11) [595.4]

22207 Meister, Cari. *Mosquitoes* (2–4). Illus. Series: Checkerboard Science and Nature Library: Insects.

2001, ABDO LB $21.35 (978-1-57765-464-3). 24pp. An introduction to mosquitoes and their structure, diet, habitat, and habits. (Rev: BL 10/15/01; HBG 10/01) [595.77]

22208 Miller, Sara Swan. *Grasshoppers and Crickets of North America* (3–5). Series: Animals in Order. 2002, Watts $26.50 (978-0-531-12170-2). 48pp. This colorful volume explores insect jumpers of the orthopteran order, which includes grasshoppers, crickets, and katydids. (Rev: BL 9/15/02) [595]

22209 Munro, Roxie. *Busy Builders* (K–3). Illus. by author. 2012, Marshall Cavendish $17.99 (978-076146105-0). 40pp. An oversize exploration of eight insects and one spider and the structures they build as their homes. (Rev: BL 4/15/12; HB 5–6/12; LMC 11–12/12; SLJ 5/1/12) [595.7156]

22210 Murawski, Darlyne A. *Bug Faces* (K–4). Illus. 2000, National Geographic $16.95 (978-0-7922-7557-2). 32pp. Huge, sometimes scary photographs in gorgeous color show close-up views of such creatures as a spider, cockroach, bumblebee, deer fly, and weevil. (Rev: BL 11/15/00; HBG 3/01; SLJ 11/00) [595.7]

22211 Nathan, Emma. *What Do You Call a Group of Butterflies? And Other Insect Groups* (3–5). Illus. 2000, Blackbirch LB $21.20 (978-1-56711-359-4). 24pp. This simple science book uses questions and answers to give basic facts about insects and to reveal each one's group name, such as a colony of ants. (Rev: BL 12/1/00; HBG 3/01) [595.7]

22212 Needham, Karen, and Launi Lucas. *Strange Beginnings* (K–2). Illus. by Launi Lucas. 2002, Tradewind paper $6.95 (978-1-896580-11-1). An attractive introduction to the various insects that emerge from water to spend their often brief adult lives in the air. (Rev: SLJ 9/02) [595.7176]

22213 Pascoe, Elaine. *Ant Lions and Lacewings* (4–8). Photos by Dwight Kuhn. Series: Nature Close-Up. 2005, Gale LB $24.95 (978-1-4103-0310-3). Eye-catching close-ups illustrate information on these insects' life cycles and eating habits. Also use *Mantids and Their Relatives* (2005). (Rev: SLJ 6/05)

22214 Pascoe, Elaine. *Flies* (4–7). Series: Nature Close-Up. 2000, Blackbirch LB $27.44 (978-1-56711-149-1). 48pp. This introduction to flies uses stunning photographs and text to describe their body parts, life cycle, and how to observe them; a few focused experiments are also included. (Rev: BL 4/15/00; HBG 3/01; SLJ 9/00) [595.7]

22215 Pascoe, Elaine. *Spittlebugs: And Other Sap Tappers* (3–5). Photos by Dwight Kuhn. Series: Nature Close-Up. 2003, Gale LB $24.95 (978-1-56711-430-0). 48pp. A close-up study, with eye-catching photographs, of the insect order Homoptera, covering life cycle, behavior, characteristics, and how they may be harmful or beneficial. (Rev: SLJ 3/04) [595.7]

22216 Pipe, Jim. *The Giant Book of Bugs and Creepy Crawlies* (4–8). 1998, Millbrook LB $27.90 (978-0-7613-0716-7). Exotic and common insects and spiders

are presented in this oversize book with eye-catching pictures and fascinating text. (Rev: BL 8/98) [595.7]

22217 Pringle, Laurence. *Cicadas! Strange and Wonderful* (2–4). Illus. by Meryl Henderson. 2010, Boyds Mills $16.95 (978-1-59078-673-4). 32pp. An attractive picture-book introduction to these insects and their life cycle, habitat, and behavior. (Rev: BL 12/1/10; LMC 1–2/11*; SLJ 1/1/11) [595.7]

22218 Pringle, Laurence. *A Dragon in the Sky: The Story of a Green Darner Dragonfly* (3–5). Illus. 2001, Scholastic $18.95 (978-0-531-30315-3). 64pp. The reader follows a green darner from egg to mating in this attractive, large-format book. (Rev: BL 6/1–15/01; HB 7/01; HBG 10/01; SLJ 8/01) [595.7]

22219 Pyers, Greg. *Grasshoppers up Close* (2–4). Illus. Series: Minibeasts Up Close. 2005, Raintree LB $27.50 (978-1-4109-1529-0). 32pp. A simple introduction to grasshoppers and their physical characteristics, habitat, senses, locomotion, and reproduction, with large-scale color photographs.

22220 Pyers, Greg. *Why Am I an Insect?* (3–5). Illus. Series: Classifying Animals. 2005, Raintree LB $27.50 (978-1-4109-2019-5); paper $7.85 (978-1-4109-2026-3). 32pp. Introduces readers to the process of scientific classification and then examines the unique characteristics of insects. (Rev: SLJ 4/06) [595.7]

22221 Rockwell, Anne. *Bugs Are Insects* (K–3). Illus. by Steve Jenkins. Series: Let's-Read-and-Find-Out Science. 2001, HarperCollins $15.95 (978-0-06-028568-5); paper $17.89 (978-0-06-028569-2). 32pp. Rockwell makes clear the distinctions between insects and spiders and the characteristics of bugs and beetles. (Rev: BCCB 7–8/01; BL 5/1/01; HB 9/01; HBG 3/02; SLJ 10/01) [595.7]

22222 Savage, Stephen. *Insects* (2–4). Series: What's the Difference? 2000, Raintree LB $25.69 (978-0-7398-1355-3). 32pp. This book points out similar characteristics among insects — such as the three parts of their bodies — but also shows how they can differ in size, color, and shape. (Rev: BL 10/15/00; HBG 3/01; SLJ 1/01) [595.7]

22223 Sayre, April P. *Ant, Ant, Ant: An Insect Chant* (K–3). Illus. by Trip Park. 2005, NorthWord $15.95 (978-1-55971-922-3). With a rhyming chant as its narrative line, this colorful and humorous picture book introduces 60 American insects and highlights their unusual features; a companion to *Trout, Trout, Trout! A Fish Chant* (2004). (Rev: SLJ 12/05) [595.7]

22224 Schuh, Mari. *Crickets* (PS–1). Illus. Series: Insect World. 2013, Bullfrog LB $25.65 (978-162031054-0). 24pp. Explores the world of crickets, their diets, their habitats, the sounds they make, and so forth. Also use *Ladybugs* (2013). (Rev: BL 12/15/13; LMC 10/14*)

22225 Sexton, Colleen. *Cicadas* (1–3). Series: Blast Off! Readers: World of Insects. 2007, Children's Pr. LB $18.50 (978-0-531-17567-5). 24pp. Facts about cicadas are accompanied by close-up photographs, making this a useful book for beginning report writers. (Rev: SLJ 8/07)

22226 Sexton, Colleen. *Praying Mantises* (1–3). Series: Blast Off! Readers: World of Insects. 2007, Children's Pr. LB $18.50 (978-0-531-17569-9). 24pp. Facts about praying mantises are accompanied by close-up photographs, making this a useful book for beginning report writers. (Rev: SLJ 8/07)

22227 Sill, Cathryn. *About Arachnids: A Guide for Children* (PS–2). Illus. by John Sill. 2003, Peachtree $15.95 (978-1-56145-038-1). 40pp. Clear simple sentences and naturalistic paintings present basic information about arachnids. (Rev: BL 3/1/03) [595.4]

22228 Sill, Cathryn. *About Insects: A Guide for Children* (PS–2). Illus. by John Sill. Series: About Books. 2000, Peachtree $15.95 (978-1-56145-207-1). 48pp. Naturalistic paintings present several insects and their characteristics. (Rev: BL 2/1/00; HBG 9/00; SLJ 7/00) [595.7]

22229 Siy, Alexandra. *Mosquito Bite* (2–4). Illus. by Dennis Kunkel. 2005, Charlesbridge $15.95 (978-1-57091-591-8). 32pp. Information on the mosquito is presented within the framework of a story about children playing outside on a summer night; arresting magnified photographs show the insect and its parts. (Rev: BL 6/1–15/05) [595.77]

22230 Smithyman, Kathryn, and Bobbie Kalman. *Insects in Danger* (3–5). Illus. Series: The World of Insects. 2006, Crabtree LB $25.27 (978-0-7787-2344-8). 32pp. This brightly illustrated volume considers the dangers facing certain insect species, including the pressure put on some insects by the migratory patterns of other animals. (Rev: SLJ 1/07) [595.7168]

22231 Solway, Andrew. *Classifying Insects* (4–6). Series: Classifying Living Things. 2003, Heinemann LB $24.22 (978-1-4034-0849-5). 32pp. This introduction to the scientific classification of animals provides an overview of the ways in which insects differ from other animals and also how different insect species differ from each other; among the insects examined are ants, butterflies, bees, dragonflies, cockroaches, and grasshoppers. (Rev: HBG 10/03; SLJ 11/03) [595.7]

22232 Spilsbury, Richard, and Louise Spilsbury. *The Life Cycle of Insects* (3–5). Illus. Series: From Egg to Adult. 2003, Heinemann LB $24.22 (978-1-4034-0786-3). 32pp. This overview of insect life looks at where they live, what they eat, and how they differ from other types of animals. (Rev: HBG 4/04; SLJ 10/03) [595.7]

22233 Stewart, Melissa. *Maggots, Grubs, and More: The Secret Lives of Young Insects* (4–6). 2003, Millbrook LB $24.90 (978-0-7613-2658-8). 63pp. This photo-filled look at the world of insects details the life cycles of more than 20 insect species, including ants, mosquitoes, and yellow jackets. (Rev: HBG 4/04; SLJ 1/04) [595.7]

22234 Swanson, Diane. *Bugs Up Close* (3–5). Photos by Paul Davidson. 2007, Kids Can $16.95 (978-1-55453-138-7); paper $8.95 (978-1-55453-139-4). Full of useful information, this large-format volume also provides huge close-ups of insects and their parts, and discusses each part in turn — legs, wings, eyes, antennae, and so forth. (Rev: LMC 11/07*; SLJ 11/07) [595.7]

22235 Tokuda, Yukihisa. *I'm a Pill Bug* (PS–2). Illus. by Kiyoshi Takahashi. Series: Nature: A Child's Eye View. 2006, Kane paper $7.95 (978-1-929132-95-9). 28pp. This attractive picture book provides a wealth of information about pill bugs, including what they eat, how they defend themselves, their reproductive habits, why they live near people, and why they shed their shells. (Rev: BL 4/1/06*) [595.372]

22236 Voake, Steve. *Insect Detective* (PS–1). Illus. by Charlotte Voake. 2010, Candlewick $16.99 (978-0-7636-4447-5). 32pp. Portrays a variety of familiar insects communicating with each other, building homes, eating, and defending themselves from predators, and encourages young readers to observe the natural world. (Rev: BL 5/1/10; LMC 10/10; SLJ 6/1/10*) [595.7]

22237 Werner, Sharon, and Sarah Forss. *Bugs by the Numbers* (4–6). 2011, Blue Apple $19.99 (978-1-60905-061-0). Unpaged. Interesting facts about insects are combined with counting features in this visually appealing book with several liftable flaps. (Rev: SLJ 7/11) [595.7]

22238 Wilkes, Sarah. *Insects* (5–9). Series: World Almanac Library of the Animal Kingdom. 2006, World Almanac LB $31.00 (978-0-8368-6211-9). A helpful introduction to members of the insect kingdom, this guide looks at physical characteristics that help to define this group as a whole, as well as specific species, habitats, diets, behaviors, and life cycles. (Rev: SLJ 12/06) [595.7]

22239 Winner, Cherie. *Everything Bug: What Kids Really Want to Know About Insects and Spiders* (3–6). Series: Kids' FAQs. 2004, North Word $10.95 (978-1-55971-890-5). 64pp. In a question-and-answer format, this compendium of facts is suitable for browsing. (Rev: BL 2/15/04; SLJ 7/04) [595]

22240 York, Penelope, ed. *Bugs* (3–5). 2002, DK LB $17.99 (978-0-7894-8553-3). 48pp. A colorful introduction to insects, their characteristics, life cycles, habitats, and varieties. (Rev: BL 6/1–15/02; HBG 10/02) [595.7]

22241 Young, Karen Romano. *Bug Science: 20 Projects and Experiments About Arthropods: Insects, Arachnids, Algae, Worms, and Other Small Creatures* (4–8). Illus. by David Goldin. Series: Science Fair Winners. 2009, National Geographic LB $24.90 (978-1-4263-0520-7); paper $12.95 (978-1-4263-0519-1). 80pp. Divided into workshops that focus on specific bugs, this is an appealing compendium of projects that are properly documented and explained. (Rev: LMC 3–4/10; SLJ 3/10; VOYA 4/10) [595.7]

22242 Zabludoff, Marc. *The Insect Class* (5–9). Series: Family Trees. 2005, Benchmark LB $29.93 (978-0-7614-1819-1). Habits, habitats, and other aspects of this varied class of animals; an engaging book with plenty of facts for report-writers. (Rev: SLJ 6/06) [595.7]

22243 Zuchora-Walske, Christine. *Leaping Grasshoppers* (PS–2). Series: Pull Ahead Books. 2000, Lerner $22.60 (978-0-8225-3634-5). 32pp. This simple, colorful introduction to grasshoppers explains the reasons why they hop: to find food, to avoid predators, and to find mates. (Rev: BL 5/15/00; HBG 9/00) [595.7]

ANTS

22244 Allen, Judy. *Are You an Ant?* (PS–1). Series: Backyard Books. 2002, Kingfisher $9.95 (978-0-7534-5365-0). 32pp. A young ant faces many challenges on the road to adulthood in this beginning science book. (Rev: BL 6/1–15/02; SLJ 7/02) [595.79]

22245 Fleisher, Paul. *Ants* (5–8). Series: AnimalWays. 2001, Marshall Cavendish LB $31.36 (978-0-7614-1269-4). 112pp. This introduction to ants and their habits and habitats also includes fine color images and material on species identification, anatomy, and classification. (Rev: BL 3/15/02; HBG 10/02) [595.79]

22246 Gomel, Luc. *The Ant: Energetic Worker* (3–6). Illus. by Remy Amann and Dominique Stoffell. Series: Face-to-Face. 2001, Charlesbridge $9.95 (978-1-57091-451-5). 32pp. This is a detailed look at ants and the ant world, with arresting photographs. (Rev: BL 10/15/01; HBG 3/02) [595.79]

22247 Greve, Meg. *Can an Ant Carry Me?* (PS). Illus. 2009, Rourke $5.99 (978-1-60472-425-7). 16pp. Attractive color photographs and rhymed sentences provide a few easily absorbed facts about ants. (Rev: BL 5/15/09) [595.79]

22248 Hodge, Deborah. *Ants* (1–3). Illus. Series: Denver Museum of Nature and Science. 2004, Kids Can $14.95 (978-1-55337-066-6). 32pp. Simple narrative and detailed photographs combine to offer young readers an introduction to the world of ants; instructions for three related projects are included. (Rev: BL 4/1/04; SLJ 6/04) [595.79]

22249 Lockwood, Sophie. *Ants* (4–6). Series: The World of Insects. 2007, The Child's World LB $29.93 (978-1-59296-817-6). 40pp. Crisp writing and sharp photographs offer substantive insight into various aspects of ant life. (Rev: SLJ 3/08) [595.79]

22250 Micucci, Charles. *The Life and Times of the Ant* (1–4). Illus. 2003, Houghton $16.00 (978-0-618-00559-8). 32pp. Micucci provides an impressive amount of information about the life and physique of the ant in a brightly illustrated picture-book format. (Rev: BL 4/15/03; HB 5/03; HBG 10/03; SLJ 5/03) [595.79]

22251 Morris, Ting. *Ant* (2–4). Illus. by Desiderio Sanzi. Series: Creepy Crawly World. 2004, Smart Apple LB $27.10 (978-1-58340-376-1). 32pp. Introduces ants' characteristics, habitat, diet, defense mechanisms, and life cycle, using realistic paintings and diagrams. (Rev: HB 11/96; SLJ 6/05)

22252 Nirgiotis, Nicholas. *Killer Ants* (2–5). Illus. by Emma Stevenson. 2009, Holiday House $17.95 (978-0-8234-2034-6). 32pp. Army ants, driver ants, and fire ants are among the dangerous varieties discussed in this informative, eye-catching volume. (Rev: BL 9/15/09; LMC 1–2/10; SLJ 9/1/09) [595.79]

22253 Rissman, Rebecca. *Ants* (PS–K). Illus. Series: Creepy Critters. 2012, Raintree LB $24.50 (978-141094801-4); paper $8.95 (9781410948144). 24pp. Readers learn about ants through rhyming text, photographs, and cartoon backgrounds. (Rev: BL 11/15/12) [595.79]

22254 Sayre, April P. *Army Ant Parade* (PS–2). Illus. by Rick Chrustowski. 2002, Holt $16.95 (978-0-8050-6353-0). 32pp. This beautifully illustrated book for younger readers gives a detailed description of an army ant swarm in a Central American jungle. (Rev: BCCB 3/02; BL 3/1/02; HB 9/02; HBG 3/03; SLJ 5/02) [595.79]

22255 Schuh, Mari. *Ants* (PS–1). Illus. Series: Insect World. 2013, Bullfrog LB $25.65 (978-162031050-2). 24pp. Explores the world of ants, their diets, their habitats, their communities, and so forth. (Rev: BL 12/15/13; LMC 10/14*) [595.79]

BEES AND WASPS

22256 Ang, Karen. *Inside the Bees' Hive* (K–2). Illus. Series: Snug as a Bug: Where Bugs Live. 2013, Bearport LB $23.93 (978-161772905-8). 24pp. Ang takes young readers into a bee hive and presents information about bees' habitats, behavior, and diet through large photographs and large-print text. (Rev: BL 10/1/13; LMC 10/14) [595.79]

22257 Ashley, Susan. *Bees* (1–3). Series: Let's Read About Insects. 2004, Weekly Reader LB $21.00 (978-0-8368-4051-3); paper $5.95 (978-0-8368-4058-2). 24pp. The life cycle of bees is described in small-format, easy-to-read text with close-up photographs. (Rev: SLJ 2/05) [595.79]

22258 de la Bedoyere, Camilla. *Egg to Bee* (1–3). Illus. Series: Life Cycles. 2012, Amicus/QEB LB $17.95 (978-160992050-0). 24pp. Double-page spreads with clear images trace an insect's life cycle from egg to larva to pupa to adult. (Rev: BL 11/1/12) [595.79]

22259 Glaser, Linda. *Brilliant Bees* (K–3). Illus. by Gay Holland. 2003, Millbrook LB $22.90 (978-0-7613-2670-0); paper $8.95 (978-0-7613-1943-6). A young girl looks at bees' behavior and habits in simple text and large colored pictures; four pages at the back of the book add factual information. (Rev: HBG 4/04; SLJ 1/04) [595.799]

22260 Guidoux, Valérie. *Little Bees* (3–5). Illus. Series: Born to Be Wild. 2005, Gareth Stevens LB $16.50 (978-0-7368-4433-8). 32pp. A simply worded look at young bees and their lives, with large color photographs.

22261 Hamilton, Sue. *Swarmed by Bees* (4–7). Series: Close Encounters of the Wild Kind. 2010, ABDO LB $27.07 (978-1-60453-933-2). 32pp. Exciting stories and graphic photographs add high-interest appeal to the information about bees and advice on avoiding and surviving such an attack. (Rev: LMC 10/10; SLJ 5/10) [595.79]

22262 Hodge, Deborah. *Bees* (1–3). Illus. Series: Denver Museum of Nature and Science. 2004, Kids Can $14.95

(978-1-55337-065-9). 32pp. Suggestions for simple projects supplement this attractive examination of the life cycle of bees. (Rev: BL 4/1/04; SLJ 6/04) [595.79]

22263 Jango-Cohen, Judith. *Bees* (3–5). Series: Animals, Animals. 2006, Benchmark LB $19.95 (978-0-7614-2235-8). 48pp. An introduction to the anatomy, behavior, and habitat of bees, in addition to other aspects of these insects and their lives. Color photographs give readers a close-up look. (Rev: SLJ 5/07)

22264 Landau, Elaine. *Killer Bees* (4–6). Series: Fearsome, Scary, and Creepy Animals. 2003, Enslow LB $23.93 (978-0-7660-2061-0). 48pp. Landau offers a dramatic overview of killer bees and documents some real-life attacks on humans. (Rev: BL 10/15/03; HBG 10/03; SLJ 2/04) [595.79]

22265 Markle, Sandra. *The Case of the Vanishing Honeybees: A Scientific Mystery* (3–6). Illus. 2013, Millbrook $29.27 (978-146770592-9). 48pp. Using eye-catching photographs and simple language, Markle describes how honeybees live and work, their environment and development, and the causes of a strange disease called colony collapse disorder (CCD). **e** (Rev: BL 10/1/13; SLJ 9/13*) [595.79]

22266 Markle, Sandra. *Hornets: Incredible Insect Architects* (2–5). Series: Insect World. 2008, Lerner LB $27.93 (978-0-8225-7297-8). 48pp. Eye-catching illustrations and simple diagrams are combined with interestingly presented facts about these insects and two activities. (Rev: LMC 10/08; SLJ 2/08) [595.79]

22267 Milton, Joyce. *Honeybees* (1–3). Illus. by Pete Mueller. Series: All Aboard Science Reader. 2003, Grosset paper $3.99 (978-0-448-42846-8). 48pp. An accessible introduction to honeybees for beginning readers, including information on how their community works and where honey comes from. (Rev: BL 5/15/03; HBG 10/03) [595.79]

22268 Rau, Dana Meachen. *Guess Who Stings* (PS–K). Series: Bookworms. Guess Who. 2009, Marshall Cavendish $15.95 (978-0-7614-2973-9). 32pp. Fun for browsing, this book asks readers to identify a honeybee using the clues in the text and images. (Rev: SLJ 6/09) [595.79]

22269 Riley, Joelle. *Buzzing Bumblebees* (2–3). Series: Pull Ahead Books. 2003, Lerner LB $22.60 (978-0-8225-4668-9). 32pp. An excellent introduction to the physical characteristics, behavior, and life cycle of the bumblebee, this book is suitable for beginning readers. (Rev: BL 11/15/03; HBG 10/03)

22270 Rissman, Rebecca. *Bees* (PS–K). Illus. Series: Creepy Critters. 2012, Raintree LB $24.50 (978-141094802-1); paper $8.95 (9781410948151). 24pp. Readers learn about bees through rhyming text, photographs, and cartoon backgrounds. (Rev: BL 11/15/12) [595.79]

22271 Rotner, Shelley, and Anne Woodhull. *The Buzz on Bees: Why Are They Disappearing?* (1–3). Illus. by Shelley Rotner. 2010, Holiday House $16.95 (978-0-8234-2247-0). 32pp. Emphasizing bees' importance to humans, this bright, readable book about Colony Collapse Disorder offers advice on ways to attract and assist the pollinators. (Rev: BL 5/15/10; LMC 11–12/10; SLJ 6/1/10) [638]

22272 Sayre, April P. *The Bumblebee Queen* (1–3). Illus. by Patricia J. Wynne. 2005, Charlesbridge $14.95 (978-1-57091-362-4). 32pp. The life of a bumblebee queen, accompanied by additional bee information and detailed watercolor illustrations. (Rev: BL 3/1/05; SLJ 4/05) [595.79]

22273 Starosta, Paul. *The Bee* (2–4). Illus. Series: Animal Close-Ups. 2005, Charlesbridge paper $6.95 (978-1-57091-629-8). 28pp. Plenty of close-up photographs accompany information about the life cycle of honeybees and the important role they play in nature. (Rev: BL 9/15/05) [575.79]

BEETLES

22274 Allen, Judy. *Are You a Ladybug?* (PS–1). Illus. by Tudor Humphries. Series: Backyard Books. 2000, Kingfisher $9.95 (978-0-7534-5241-7). 32pp. A beginner's book that explains in text and pictures what a ladybug is, what it eats, and how it grows from egg to first flight. (Rev: BL 5/15/00; HBG 3/01; SLJ 9/00) [595.76]

22275 Ashley, Susan. *Ladybugs* (1–4). Series: Let's Read About Insects. 2004, Weekly Reader LB $21.00 (978-0-8368-4055-1); paper $5.95 (978-0-8368-4062-9). 24pp. The life cycle of ladybugs is described in small-format, easy-to-read text with close-up photographs. (Rev: SLJ 2/05) [595.76]

22276 Chrustowski, Rick. *Bright Beetle* (PS–2). Illus. 2000, Holt $15.95 (978-0-8050-6058-4). 32pp. The life cycle of the ladybug, its habits, and physical characteristics are covered in this good introduction for beginning scientists. (Rev: BL 6/1–15/00; HBG 9/00; SLJ 5/00) [595.76]

22277 Gibbons, Gail. *Ladybugs* (K–3). Illus. by author. 2012, Holiday House $17.95 (978-0-8234-2368-2). 32pp. With concise text and colorful art, this is an accessible and informative introduction to the ladybug and its anatomy, diet, life cycle, habitat, defenses, and threats to survival. (Rev: BL 4/15/12; LMC 8–9/12; SLJ 4/1/12) [595.76]

22278 Jango-Cohen, Judith. *Hungry Ladybugs* (2–3). Series: Pull Ahead Books. 2003, Lerner LB $22.60 (978-0-8225-4667-2). 32pp. The life cycle and physical characteristics of the ladybird beetle, one of nature's most efficient pest-killers and commonly known as the ladybug, is explored in this short book suitable for beginning readers. (Rev: BL 11/15/03; HBG 10/03)

22279 Jenkins, Steve. *The Beetle Book* (3–5). Illus. by author. 2012, Houghton Mifflin $16.99 (978-054768084-2). 40pp. With bright illustrations and accessible snippets of fact and trivia, this title offers readers a bug's-eye view of the dazzling world of beetles. (Rev: BL 4/1/12*; LMC 10/12*; SLJ 4/12*) [595.76]

22280 Llewellyn, Claire. *Ladybug* (PS–3). Illus. by Simon Mendez. Series: Starting Life. 2004, NorthWord

$16.95 (978-1-55971-892-9). 23pp. On pages that grow progressively wider, the stages of a ladybug's development are traced, with information on such topics as habitat and diet plus realistic illustrations. (Rev: SLJ 11/04) [595.76]

22281 Lockwood, Sophie. *Beetles* (4–6). Illus. Series: World of Insects. 2007, Child's World LB $20.95 (978-1-59296-819-0). 40pp. All about beetles — their life cycle, anatomy, diversity, and ubiquity — with a look at their relationship with humans. (Rev: BL 10/15/07) [595.76]

22282 McEvey, Shane F. *Beetles* (3–5). Series: Insects and Spiders. 2001, Chelsea LB $28.00 (978-0-7910-6600-3). 32pp. Beetle facts of all kinds are amplified by information on how scientists collect and study them and by tips on keeping beetles as pets. Also use *Bugs* (2001). (Rev: HBG 3/02; SLJ 2/02) [595.76]

22283 Murray, Peter. *Beetles* (1–4). Series: Naturebooks. 2003, Child's World LB $25.64 (978-1-56766-976-3). 32pp. Large-print text and close-up photographs explore beetles' many varieties, physical characteristics, habitat, diet, and behavior. (Rev: SLJ 12/03) [595.76]

22284 Pallotta, Jerry. *The Beetle Alphabet Book* (PS–2). Illus. by David Biedrzycki. 2004, Charlesbridge $16.95 (978-1-57091-551-2). 32pp. An arresting alphabet of bugs, providing brightly illustrated information with a dollop of humor. (Rev: BL 2/1/04; SLJ 5/04) [595.76]

22285 Posada, Mia. *Ladybugs: Red, Fiery, and Bright* (PS–2). Illus. by author. 2002, Carolrhoda LB $15.95 (978-0-87614-334-6). A rhythmic look at ladybugs and their life cycle and behavior. (Rev: HBG 10/02; SLJ 5/02) [595.7]

22286 Pyers, Greg. *Ladybugs up Close* (2–4). Illus. Series: Minibeasts Up Close. 2005, Raintree LB $27.50 (978-1-4109-1530-6). 32pp. A simple introduction to ladybugs and their physical characteristics, habitat, senses, and reproduction, with large-scale color photographs.

22287 Schuh, Mari. *Beetles* (PS–1). Illus. Series: Insect World. 2013, Bullfrog LB $25.65 (978-162031052-6). 24pp. Explores the world of beetles, their diets, their habitats, their unusual characteristics, and so forth. (Rev: BL 12/15/13; LMC 10/14*)

22288 Sexton, Colleen. *Beetles* (1–3). Series: Blast Off! Readers: World of Insects. 2007, Children's Pr. LB $18.50 (978-0-531-17566-8). 24pp. Facts about beetles are accompanied by close-up photographs, making this a useful book for beginning report writers. (Rev: SLJ 8/07)

22289 Smith, Sian. *Ladybugs* (PS–K). Illus. Series: Creepy Critters. 2012, Raintree LB $24.50 (978-141094809-0); paper $8.95 (9781410948229). 24pp. Readers learn about ladybugs through rhyming text, photographs, and cartoon backgrounds. (Rev: BL 11/15/12) [595.76]

22290 Tracqui, Valerie. *Face-to-Face with the Ladybug* (3–6). Series: Face-to-Face. 2002, Charlesbridge $9.95 (978-1-57091-453-9). 32pp. The physical characteristics, habits, life cycle, and habitats of the industrious,

colorful ladybug are featured in this attractive volume. (Rev: BCCB 10/02; BL 9/15/02; HBG 3/03) [595.76]

CATERPILLARS, BUTTERFLIES, AND MOTHS

22291 Allen, Judy. *Are You a Butterfly?* (PS–1). Illus. by Tudor Humphries. Series: Backyard Books. 2000, Kingfisher $9.95 (978-0-7534-5240-0). 32pp. By allowing the child to imagine that he or she is the insect discussed, this simple book goes through the stages of growth from egg and caterpillar to chrysalis and butterfly. (Rev: BL 10/15/00; HBG 10/01) [544.2]

22292 Aston, Dianna Hutts. *A Butterfly Is Patient* (2–4). Illus. by Sylvia Long. 2011, Chronicle $16.99 (978-0-8118-6479-4). 40pp. A handsome presentation showing butterflies and their metamorphosis, camouflage, protective mechanisms, wonderful patterns, and other characteristics. Lexile AD1040L (Rev: BLO 7/11; LMC 11–12/11*; SLJ 7/11*) [595.78]

22293 Bishop, Nic. *Nic Bishop Butterflies and Moths* (2–4). Illus. by author. 2009, Scholastic $17.99 (978-0-439-87757-2). 48pp. Fine color photos and well-written text make this title a fly away winner. (Rev: BCCB 5/09; BL 6/1–15/09; HB 7/09; SLJ 6/09) [595.78]

22294 Ehlert, Lois. *Waiting for Wings* (PS–1). Illus. 2001, Harcourt $17.00 (978-0-15-202608-0). 38pp. Using a short rhyming text and glowing illustrations, this book covers the life cycle of the butterfly, with information on physical characteristics, diet, and behavior. (Rev: BL 3/1/01*; HB 5/01; HBG 10/01) [595.78]

22295 Frost, Helen. *Monarch and Milkweed* (PS–2). Illus. by Leonid Gore. 2008, Atheneum $17.99 (978-1-4169-0085-6). 40pp. The interdependent life cycles of the monarch butterfly and the milkweed plant are presented with maps and illustrations. (Rev: BL 1/1–15/08; SLJ 1/08) [595.78]

22296 Frost, Helen. *Moths* (PS–3). Series: Insects. 2001, Capstone LB $17.26 (978-0-7368-0852-1). 24pp. Spare text and full-page color photographs — often close-up shots — offer basic information on moths. (Rev: HBG 3/02; SLJ 9/01) [595.78]

22297 Glaser, Linda. *Magnificent Monarchs* (K–3). Illus. by Gay Holland. 2000, Millbrook LB $21.40 (978-0-7613-1700-5). This is a very attractive work on monarch butterflies and their amazing lives and migrations. (Rev: HBG 10/01; SLJ 1/01) [595.78]

22298 Kalman, Bobbie. *The Life Cycle of a Butterfly* (2–4). Illus. Series: The Life Cycle. 2001, Crabtree LB $25.27 (978-0-7787-0650-2); paper $6.95 (978-0-7787-0680-9). 32pp. After a general description of the butterfly, the author clearly explains the stages of its life cycle and discusses what can be done to curb human encroachment. (Rev: SLJ 6/02) [595.789]

22299 Kalman, Bobbie, and Robin Johnson. *Endangered Butterflies* (3–5). Illus. Series: Earth's Endangered Animals. 2006, Crabtree LB $25.27 (978-0-7787-1870-3). 32pp. Large text and clear color photographs focus on endangered butterfly species, presenting basic information about physical characteristics, diet, habitat, behavior, and discussing the specific threats they face. (Rev: SLJ 1/07) [595.78]

22300 Lawrence, Ellen. *A Butterfly's Life* (1–3). Illus. Series: Animal Diaries: Life Cycles. 2012, Bearport LB $23.93 (978-161772413-8). 24pp. A young boy's diary entries follow butterflies as they mate, migrate away, and return the next summer; with photographs, maps, and illustrations. (Rev: BL 4/1/12) [595.78]

22301 List, Ilka Katherine. *Moths and Butterflies of North America* (3–5). Series: Animals in Order. 2002, Watts LB $26.50 (978-0-531-11597-8). 48pp. After a general discussion of animal classification, this book describes in words and pictures 15 species of moths and butterflies that live in North America. (Rev: BL 3/15/02) [595.78]

22302 Llewellyn, Claire. *Butterfly* (K–4). Illus. by Simon Mendez. Series: Starting Life. 2003, NorthWord $16.95 (978-1-55971-868-4). 23pp. The life cycle of a butterfly is detailed in words and paintings, together with a combined glossary and index; the unusual graduated page sizes add appeal. (Rev: SLJ 4/04) [595.78]

22303 Loewen, Nancy. *Flying Colors: Butterflies in Your Backyard* (PS–2). Illus. by Rick Peterson. Series: Backyard Bugs. 2005, Picture Window LB $25.26 (978-1-4048-1143-0). 24pp. Butterflies' importance as plant pollinators is emphasized in this large, horizontal volume that includes an activity and a craft project. (Rev: BL 12/1/05) [595.78]

22304 Markle, Sandra. *Luna Moths: Masters of Change* (2–5). Series: Insect World. 2008, Lerner LB $27.93 (978-0-8225-7302-9). 48pp. Eye-catching illustrations and simple diagrams are combined with interestingly presented facts about these insects and two activities. (Rev: LMC 10/08; SLJ 2/08) [595.78]

22305 Marsh, Laura. *Butterflies* (K–3). Series: Great Migrations. 2010, National Geographic LB $11.90 (978-1-4263-0740-9); paper $3.99 (978-1-4263-0739-3). 48pp. Focusing on the monarch butterfly, this volume discusses their incredible migrations, the reasons why they undertake these long trips, and the dangers they face. (Rev: LMC 5/1/11; SLJ 3/1/11) [595.7]

22306 Meister, Cari. *Butterflies* (2–4). Illus. Series: Checkerboard Science and Nature Library: Insects. 2001, ABDO LB $21.35 (978-1-57765-459-9). 24pp. This is an attractive, basic introduction to butterflies. (Rev: BL 10/15/01; HBG 10/01) [595.78]

22307 Morris, Ting. *Butterfly* (2–4). Illus. by Desiderio Sanzi. Series: Creepy Crawly World. 2004, Smart Apple LB $27.10 (978-1-58340-379-2). 32pp. Introduces butterflies' characteristics, habitat, diet, defense mechanisms, and life cycle, using realistic paintings and diagrams. (Rev: SLJ 6/05)

22308 Murawski, Darlyne A. *Face to Face with Caterpillars* (3–6). Photos by author. Series: Face to Face. 2007, National Geographic $16.95 (978-1-4263-0052-3). 32pp. Close-up photographs by the author provide a new perspective on caterpillars, with facts suitable for report writers. (Rev: SLJ 6/07)

22309 Noonan, Diana. *The Butterfly* (2–4). Series: Life Cycles. 2002, Chelsea LB $23.00 (978-0-7910-6963-9). 32pp. Full-color illustrations show the various stages in the life cycle of the butterfly from egg to caterpillar and pupa to the mature butterfly. (Rev: BL 12/15/02; HBG 3/03) [595.78]

22310 Patent, Dorothy Hinshaw. *Fabulous Fluttering Tropical Butterflies* (1–3). Illus. by Kendahl Jan Jubb. 2003, Walker LB $17.85 (978-0-8027-8839-9). 32pp. With bright illustrations, this book describes tropical butterflies' life cycles and looks at individual species and at butterflies' lives in the rainforest and in zoos. (Rev: BL 5/1/03; HBG 10/03; SLJ 5/03) [595.78]

22311 Preston-Mafham, Rod. *The Secret Life of Butterflies and Moths* (4–7). Series: The Secret World of . . . 2002, Raintree LB $27.12 (978-0-7398-4984-2). 48pp. Beginning with little-known facts about butterflies and moths, this book explores their life cycles, behavior, mating habits, enemies, food, and habitats. (Rev: BL 8/02) [595.78]

22312 Pyers, Greg. *Butterflies up Close* (2–4). Illus. Series: Minibeasts Up Close. 2005, Raintree LB $27.50 (978-1-4109-1528-3). 32pp. A simple introduction to butterflies and their physical characteristics, habitat, senses, and reproduction, with large-scale color photographs.

22313 Rabe, Tish. *My, Oh My — a Butterfly! All About Butterflies* (1–2). Illus. by Aristides Ruiz and Joe Mathieu. Series: The Cat in the Hat's Learning Library. 2007, Random $11.99 (978-0-375-82882-9). 45pp. Rhyming, Dr. Seuss-style text introduces facts about different types of butterflies in an engaging way. (Rev: SLJ 8/07)

22314 Rea, Ba. *Monarch! Come Play with Me* (K–2). Illus. by author. 2006, Bas Relief paper $10.95 (978-0-9657472-5-7). 32pp. A young girl's conversation with a monarch caterpillar that is concentrating on metamorphosis offers insights into the process. (Rev: SLJ 8/06) [595]

22315 Rockwell, Anne. *Becoming Butterflies* (PS–2). Illus. by Megan Halsey. 2002, Walker LB $16.85 (978-0-8027-8798-9). 32pp. The story of the metamorphosis of monarch butterflies is told in a clear, concise manner for young readers. (Rev: BCCB 5/02; BL 3/15/02; HBG 10/02; SLJ 3/02) [595.78]

22316 Schlaepfer, Gloria G. *Butterflies* (4–8). Series: AnimalWays. 2005, Benchmark LB $21.95 (978-0-7614-1745-3). Beautiful photographs of butterfly specimens enrich this well-organized volume that provides basic information on the butterfly's characteristics, habits, and habitat. (Rev: SLJ 5/06) [595.78]

22317 Simon, Seymour. *Butterflies* (2–4). Illus. 2011, HarperCollins $17.99 (978-006191493-5). 32pp. Simon uses the story of the monarch butterfly to draw children into this exploration of the world of moths and butterflies, encouraging participation in activities relating to these insects. (Rev: BL 10/15/11*) [595.78]

22318 Singer, Marilyn. *Caterpillars* (2–4). Illus. 2011, Charlesbridge $14.95 (978-0-9797455-7-7). 40pp. Rhymed text guides readers through a brightly illustrated exploration of caterpillars. (Rev: BLO 8/11; SLJ 11/1/11) [595.78]

22319 Spilsbury, Louise. *Butterfly* (K–2). Series: Life Cycles. 2005, Heinemann LB $20.64 (978-1-4034-6770-6). 24pp. Brief text and bold photographs suitable for beginning readers focus on the life cycle of the butterfly. (Rev: SLJ 7/05) [595.78]

22320 Stewart, Melissa. *Butterflies* (4–7). Illus. by Andrew Recher. Series: Our Wild World. 2007, NorthWord LB $10.95 (978-1-55971-966-7); paper $7.95 (978-1-55971-967-4). 48pp. The behavior, physical characteristics and life cycles of butterflies are presented in great detail with many photographs. (Rev: SLJ 7/07) [595.78]

22321 Stewart, Melissa. *A Place for Butterflies* (K–3). Illus. by Higgins Bond. 2006, Peachtree $16.95 (978-1-56145-357-3). 32pp. This richly illustrated book takes readers on a tour of butterfly habitats where human intervention has helped the insects to survive. (Rev: BL 3/15/06; SLJ 6/06) [595.7]

22322 Swinburne, Stephen. *A Butterfly Grows* (PS–1). Illus. Series: Green Light Readers. 2009, Houghton $12.99 (978-0-15-206422-8). 24pp. For beginning readers, this simple and colorful book follows the development of a butterfly. (Rev: BL 5/1/09; SLJ 10/09) [595.78]

22323 Swinburne, Stephen. *Wings of Light: The Migration of the Yellow Butterfly* (K–3). Illus. by Bruce Hiscock. 2006, Boyds Mills $15.95 (978-1-59078-082-4). 32pp. Traces the migration of the cloudless sulphur butterfly from its winter home in Mexico's Yucatan to its summer range in the northeastern United States. (Rev: BL 4/1/06; SLJ 5/06) [595.78]

22324 Wallace, Nancy Elizabeth. *Fly, Monarch! Fly!* (K–2). Illus. by author. 2008, Marshall Cavendish $16.99 (978-0-7614-5425-0). 40pp. A rabbit family — mother, father, Minna, and Pip — visit Butterfly Place and learn all about monarch butterflies' life cycle through a series of exhibits; a craft, tips for a butterfly garden, and additional facts close this attractive book. (Rev: BL 6/1–15/08; LMC 10/08; SLJ 8/08) [595.78]

22325 Waxman, Laura Hamilton. *Monarch Butterflies* (2–3). Series: Pull Ahead Books. 2003, Lerner LB $22.60 (978-0-8225-4669-6). 32pp. Suitable for beginning readers, this book follows the beautiful monarch butterfly through each stage of its life cycle. (Rev: BL 11/15/03; HBG 10/03)

22326 Wilner, Yvonne. *Butterflies Fly* (2–5). Illus. by Karen Lloyd-Jones. 2001, Charlesbridge LB $16.95 (978-1-57091-446-1). 32pp. A poetic text with large illustrations shows butterflies of the world in their natural habitats. (Rev: BL 2/15/01; HBG 10/01; SLJ 2/01) [595.78]

22327 Zemlicka, Shannon. *From Egg to Butterfly* (K–2). Series: Start to Finish. 2003, Lerner LB $18.60 (978-0-8225-0713-0). 24pp. Full of photographs, this basic in-

troduction suitable for beginning readers follows the life cycle of a butterfly. (Rev: SLJ 9/03) [595.78]

SPIDERS AND SCORPIONS

22328 Allen, Judy. *Are You a Spider?* (PS–1). Illus. by Tudor Humphries. Series: Backyard Books. 2000, Kingfisher $9.95 (978-0-7534-5243-1). 32pp. The reader becomes a newly hatched spider and learns how to spin threads, make webs, and watch out for dangers such as birds. (Rev: BL 10/15/00; HBG 10/01) [595.4]

22329 Allman, Toney. *From Spider Webs to Man-Made Silk* (4–7). Series: Imitating Nature. 2005, Gale LB $24.95 (978-0-7377-3124-8). An introduction to scientists' attempts to replicate spider silk in the laboratory. (Rev: BL 10/15/05; LMC 3/06) [595.4]

22330 Berger, Melvin. *Spinning Spiders* (K–4). Illus. by S. D. Schindler. Series: Let's-Read-and-Find-Out Science. 2003, HarperCollins LB $16.89 (978-0-06-028697-2); paper $5.99 (978-0-06-445207-6). 33pp. The differences between arachnids and insects are clearly explained, and five types of spiders are profiled with full-color illustrations. (Rev: HBG 10/03; SLJ 9/03) [595.4]

22331 Berger, Melvin, and Gilda Berger. *Do All Spiders Spin Webs? Questions and Answers About Spiders* (3–5). Illus. by Roberto Osti. Series: Scholastic Question and Answer. 2000, Scholastic $14.95 (978-0-439-09586-0); paper $6.99 (978-0-439-14881-8). 48pp. The authors give informative answers to such questions as "What happens when an enemy bites off a spider's leg?" Also use *Tarantulas* (2001). (Rev: HBG 3/01; SLJ 5/01) [595.4]

22332 Bishop, Nic. *Nic Bishop Spiders* (3–5). Photos by author. 2007, Scholastic $16.99 (978-0-439-87756-5). 48pp. Striking close-up photographs and conversational text introduce more than 15 arachnids and their behavior. (Rev: BCCB 10/07; HB 3/08; SLJ 11/07)

22333 Bishop, Nic. *Spiders* (PS–2). Illus. Series: Scholastic Reader Level 2. 2012, Scholastic paper $3.99 (978-05452375-7-4). 32pp. With many large photographs and simple text, this easy reader introduces a variety of spiders and their behavior; it is not to be confused with 2007's award-winning *Nic Bishop Spiders*, which is intended for students in grades 2 to 4. (Rev: BL 10/15/12) [596]

22334 Bredeson, Carmen. *Tarantulas Up Close* (1–3). Series: Zoom in on Animals! 2008, Enslow LB $21.26 (978-0-7660-3076-3). 24pp. A simple introduction to tarantulas with sharp, close-up color photographs and clear text. (Rev: SLJ 9/08) [595.4]

22335 Dinaberg, Leslie. *Spider Life* (2–5). Series: Boys Rock! 2006, The Child's World LB $25.64 (978-1-59296-737-7). 32pp. A good choice for beginning and reluctant readers (girls as well as boys), this colorful volume looks at spiders' physical and behavioral characteristics, habitat, diet, predators, and life cycle. (Rev: SLJ 2/07) [595.4]

22336 Ganeri, Anita. *From Egg to Spider* (1–3). Illus. Series: How Living Things Grow. 2006, Heinemann LB

$25.36 (978-1-4034-7860-3). 32pp. The life cycle of the garden spider, presented in an easy-to-read format. (Rev: SLJ 6/06) [595.4]

22337 Ganeri, Anita. *Scorpion* (PS–2). Series: A Day in the Life: Desert Animals. 2011, Heinemann LB $22 (978-1-4329-4776-7); paper $6.49 (978-1-4329-4785-9). 24pp. Answering questions such as "What do scorpions look like?" and "What do scorpions do at night?," Ganeri presents the physical characteristics and life of this desert animal. (Rev: SLJ 6/11) [595.4]

22338 Greenaway, Theresa. *Spiders* (4–7). Series: The Secret World of . . . 2001, Raintree LB $18.98 (978-0-7368-3509-1). An information-crammed text and attractive illustrations introduce spiders, how and where they live, and their behavior. (Rev: BL 10/15/01) [595.4]

22339 Gregory, Josh. *Wolf Spiders* (3–5). Illus. Series: Nature's Children. 2013, Scholastic/Children's Press LB $28 (978-053123363-4); paper $6.95 (9780531251614). 48pp. With full-page photographs and clear text this book explores the characteristics and behaviors of these animals, their life cycle, their history, and relationship with humans. (Rev: BL 11/15/13) [595.4]

22340 Hughes, Monica. *Spiders* (PS–2). Illus. 2003, Raintree LB $18.56 (978-1-4109-0622-9). 24pp. A close-up look at the diet, anatomy, habitat, and life cycle of spiders, for beginning readers. (Rev: BL 2/15/04) [595.4]

22341 Kallen, Stuart A. *Spiders* (4–6). Illus. Series: Nature's Predators. 2001, Gale LB $23.70 (978-0-7377-0630-7). 48pp. Spiders' methods of hunting, catching, and eating their prey are presented, with illustrations. (Rev: BL 10/15/01) [595.4]

22342 Lasky, Kathryn. *Silk and Venom: Searching for a Dangerous Spider* (5–8). Photos by Christopher G. Knight. 2011, Candlewick $16.99 (978-0-7636-4222-8). 64pp. A scientist's research trips to study the dangerous brown recluse spider are documented in this compelling book, which includes plenty of photographs and factual material about spiders. Lexile 1050L (Rev: BL 2/15/11; HB 3–4/11; LMC 5–6/11; SLJ 3/1/11) [595.4]

22343 McGinty, Alice B. *The Jumping Spider* (3–6). 2001, Rosen LB $18.75 (978-0-8239-5568-8). 24pp. Two-page chapters with arresting photographs discuss topics such as the spider's anatomy, behavior, habitat, and relationship to humans. Other titles in this series include *The Black Widow* and *The Tarantula* (both 2001). (Rev: SLJ 3/02) [595.4]

22344 Markle, Sandra. *Sneaky, Spinning Baby Spiders* (2–5). Illus. 2008, Walker $16.99 (978-0-8027-9697-4). 32pp. Featuring clear photographs, this volume focuses on baby spiders and how their mothers care (or fail to care) for them. (Rev: BCCB 11/08; BL 12/1/08; HB 1/09; LMC 1/09; SLJ 10/08) [595.4]

22345 Markle, Sandra. *Wind Scorpions: Killer Jaws* (4–7). Illus. Series: Arachnid World. 2012, Lerner LB $29.27 (978-076135048-4). 48pp. With large color photographs and concise text, this book introduces the life cycle, characteristics, and behavior of the wind scorpion.

Also use *Tarantulas: Supersized Predators* (2012). **e** (Rev: BL 3/1/12; SLJ 2/12) [595.4]

22346 Montgomery, Sy. *The Tarantula Scientist* (4–7). Photos by Nic Bishop. Series: Scientists in the Field. 2004, Houghton Mifflin $18.00 (978-0-618-14799-1). This informative, photo-filled book chronicles the day-to-day field work of arachnologist Sam Marshall as he searches for tarantulas in the French Guianan rain forest. (Rev: BL 3/15/04; HB 7–8/04; SLJ 5/04) [595.4]

22347 Morley, Christine. *Freaky Facts About Spiders* (2–4). Illus. Series: Freaky Facts About. 2007, Two-Can $13.95 (978-1-58728-596-7); paper $8.95 (978-1-58728-597-4). A colorful introduction to spiders and their weirder characteristics, full of graphic elements that will appeal to reluctant readers. (Rev: BL 3/15/07) [595.4]

22348 Murawski, Darlyne. *Spiders and Their Webs* (2–5). 2004, National Geographic $16.95 (978-0-7922-6979-3). 32pp. Dramatic telephoto shots of spiders are paired with basic facts and information on unusual behaviors. (Rev: BL 12/1/04; SLJ 3/05) [595.4]

22349 Murray, Peter. *Spiders and Scorpions* (3–6). Series: Science Around Us. 2004, Child's World LB $27.07 (978-1-59296-273-0). 32pp. Eye-catching photographs and interesting "Did You Know?" features draw the reader into this overview of spiders and scorpions. (Rev: SLJ 3/05) [595.4]

22350 Otfinoski, Steven. *Scorpions* (3–5). Illus. Series: Animals Animals. 2011, Marshall Cavendish LB $20.95 (978-076144878-5). 48pp. With good photographs and clear text, this volume looks at the scorpion's anatomy and sting, its dangerous mating habits, its predatory nature, and its relationship with humans. (Rev: BL 10/15/11) [595.4]

22351 Ross, Michael E. *Spiderology* (3–6). Illus. 2000, Carolrhoda LB $19.93 (978-1-57505-387-5); paper $6.95 (978-1-57505-438-4). After describing how to collect and observe spiders humanely, this book suggests a number of activities to learn more about them. (Rev: BL 5/15/00; HBG 9/00; SLJ 7/00) [595.4]

22352 Simon, Seymour. *Spiders. Rev. ed.* (3–6). 2007, Collins $16.99 (978-0-06-089104-6); paper $6.99 (978-0-06-089103-9). 32pp. A new edition of the guide to spiders that provides stunning photographs and smooth, informative text, making it a browsing pleasure as well as a resource for reports. (Rev: HB 11/03; SLJ 3/08) [595.4]

22353 Squire, Ann O. *Spiders of North America* (3–5). Series: Animals in Order. 2000, Watts LB $26.50 (978-0-531-11516-9). 48pp. This book explains the animal classification system and then goes on to describe arachnids and introduce different varieties of spiders and their behavior. (Rev: BL 4/15/00) [595.4]

22354 Time For Kids Eds., and Nicole Iorio. *Spiders!* (2–3). Illus. Series: Time For Kids Science Scoops. 2005, HarperCollins $14.99 (978-0-06-057635-6); paper $3.99 (978-0-06-057634-9). 48pp. Simple text suitable for beginning readers and bright illustrations present basic information on spiders, plus a profile of a scientist who works with them. (Rev: SLJ 3/05) [595.4]

22355 Zabludoff, Marc. *Spiders* (4–8). Series: Animal-Ways. 2005, Benchmark LB $21.95 (978-0-7614-1747-7). Beautiful photographs enrich this well-organized volume that provides basic information on the insect's characteristics, habits, and habitat. (Rev: SLJ 5/06) [595.4]

22356 Zollman, Pam. *A Spiderling Grows Up* (K–1). Series: Scholastic News Nonfiction Readers. 2005, Children's Pr. LB $20.00 (978-0-516-24946-9). 24pp. Covers the life cycle of a spider, with a focus on spider eggs and young spiderlings and their survival tactics. (Rev: SLJ 4/06) [595.4]

Land Invertebrates

22357 Allen, Judy. *Are You a Snail?* (PS–1). Illus. by Tudor Humphries. Series: Backyard Books. 2000, Kingfisher $9.95 (978-0-7534-5242-4). 32pp. An introduction to snails that discusses their appearance, food, and how they grow from egg to adult. (Rev: BL 5/15/00; HBG 3/01; SLJ 9/00) [594]

22358 Blaxland, Beth. *Annelids: Earthworms, Leeches, and Sea Worms* (3–5). Illus. Series: Invertebrates. 2002, Chelsea LB $28.00 (978-0-7910-6993-6). 32pp. Close-up photographs, straightforward text, and an enticing layout introduce the annelid invertebrates. Also use *Cephalopods: Octopuses, Squids, and Their Relatives* and *Myriapods: Centipedes, Millipedes, and Their Relatives* (2002). (Rev: BL 12/1/02; HBG 3/03) [592]

22359 Campbell, Sarah C. *Wolfsnail: A Backyard Predator* (PS–2). Illus. by author. 2008, Boyds Mills $16.95 (978-1-59078-554-6). 32pp. Simple text and close-up photographs introduce the tiny wolfsnail, which eats smaller snails and slugs. (Rev: BL 4/1/08; HB 7/08; LMC 10/08; SLJ 5/08) [594]

22360 Dell'Oro, Suzanne Paul. *Tunneling Earthworms* (PS–2). Series: Pull Ahead Books. 2000, Lerner LB $22.60 (978-0-8225-3762-5). 32pp. A lavishly illustrated book that introduces the earthworm, its anatomy, food, and how it is able to move through earth. (Rev: BL 3/1/01; HBG 10/01) [595]

22361 Dixon, Norma. *Lowdown on Earthworms* (2–4). Illus. 2005, Fitzhenry & Whiteside $16.95 (978-1-55041-114-0). 32pp. This attractive title digs into the anatomy, behavior, and habitat of earthworms and describes worm-related projects. (Rev: BL 9/1/05) [592.64]

22362 Fredericks, Anthony D. *Slugs* (2–3). Series: Early Bird Nature Books. 2000, Lerner LB $25.26 (978-0-8225-3041-1). 48pp. A beginning science book that describes, in pictures and text, what a slug looks like, where it lives, how it reproduces, and how it survives in spite of predators. (Rev: BL 5/15/00; HBG 9/00) [595]

22363 Hartley, Karen, et al. *Centipede* (1–3). Illus. 2006, Heinemann LB $17.75 (978-1-4034-8295-2). 31pp. A simple question-and-answer format and eye-catching photographs introduce the life cycle of the centipede, as

well as the invertebrate's physical characteristics, diet, habitat, and predators. (Rev: BL 9/15/06) [595.6]

22364 Heinrichs, Ann. *Worms* (1–3). Illus. Series: Nature's Friends. 2004, Compass Point LB $22.60 (978-0-7565-0589-9). 32pp. Worms' anatomy and life cycle are covered in simple text and clear close-up photographs. (Rev: SLJ 5/06) [595.4]

22365 Johnson, Sylvia A. *Silkworms* (4–7). 1982, Lerner paper $5.95 (978-0-8225-9557-1). The life cycle of the silkworm, told in text and striking color pictures. [595.78]

22366 Knudsen, Michelle. *A Slimy Story* (K–2). Illus. by Paige Billin-Frye. Series: Science Solves It! 2004, Kane paper $4.99 (978-1-57565-144-6). 32pp. Dan can't think what he can give his mother for her birthday until he realizes that earthworms are the perfect present for a gardener; scientific facts are interwoven into the text. (Rev: SLJ 1/05) [595]

22367 Miller, Ruth. *Arthropods* (4–6). Series: Animal Kingdom. 2004, Raintree LB $25.70 (978-1-4109-1049-3). 64pp. The common characteristics of arthropods are explained, followed by descriptions of various orders of arthropods and selected specific species plus discussion of endangered status and evolution. (Rev: SLJ 6/05)

22368 Parker, Steve. *Nematodes, Leeches and Other Worms* (4–6). Illus. Series: Animals Kingdom Classification. 2006, Compass Point LB $29.26 (978-0-7565-1615-4). 48pp. Concise, well-written text, color photographs, diagrams, and charts cover the physical characteristics, habitat, diet, and behavior of worms. (Rev: SLJ 11/06) [592]

22369 Pfeffer, Wendy. *Wiggling Worms at Work* (K–3). Illus. by Steve Jenkins. Series: Let's-Read-and-Find-Out Science. 2004, HarperCollins $15.99 (978-0-06-028448-0). 40pp. Solid information on the earthworm and its characteristics are followed by advice on observing worms in their native habitat. (Rev: BL 2/15/04; SLJ 3/04) [592]

22370 Ross, Michael E. *Millipedeology* (3–6). Illus. Series: Backyard Buddies. 2000, Carolrhoda LB $19.93 (978-1-57505-398-1); paper $6.95 (978-1-57505-436-0). 48pp. This book shows how to collect and humanely study millipedes, with experiments that can be performed to learn more about them. (Rev: BL 5/15/00; HBG 9/00; SLJ 7/00) [595.6]

Marine and Freshwater Life

GENERAL AND MISCELLANEOUS

22371 Allen, Judy. *Whales and Dolphins* (1–3). Illus. by Mike Bostock. Series: I Wonder Why: Flip the Flaps. 2008, Kingfisher $7.95 (978-0-7534-6225-6). 32pp. This attractive introduction to whales and dolphins features half-page flaps. (Rev: BL 4/1/08) [599.5]

22372 Bang, Molly, and Penny Chisholm. *Ocean Sunlight: How Tiny Plants Feed the Seas* (K–3). Illus. by Molly Bang. 2012, Scholastic $18.99 (978-054527322-0). 48pp. The sun narrates this interesting and accessible book, which explains how ocean plankton captures energy, creates food, and lays the foundation of a whole ecosystem. (Rev: BL 5/15/12*; HB 5–6/12; LMC 8–9/12; SLJ 6/1/12) [571.4]

22373 Batten, Mary. *The Winking, Blinking Sea: All About Bioluminescence* (3–5). 2000, Millbrook LB $20.90 (978-0-7613-1550-6). Large photos of 11 bioluminescent sea creatures are presented opposite a paragraph or two of descriptive text. (Rev: BCCB 6/00; HBG 9/00; SLJ 7/00) [591.92]

22374 Becker, Helaine. *The Big Green Book of the Big Blue Sea* (3–5). Illus. by Willow Dawson. 2012, Kids Can $15.95 (978-155453746-4); paper $9.95 (978-15545374-7-1). 80pp. After discussing the ocean and its vulnerability to pollution and other changes, Becker looks at marine life and various strategies for survival, providing illustrative experiments. (Rev: BL 2/15/12; LMC 10/12; SLJ 6/1/12) [577.7]

22375 Berger, Melvin. *Dive! A Book of Deep-Sea Creatures* (1–2). Illus. Series: Hello Reader! 2000, Scholastic $3.99 (978-0-439-08747-6). 40pp. This easy reader introduces the marine life found on the ocean floor, with color photographs mostly at a close range. (Rev: BL 10/1/00) [591.77]

22376 Blake, Carly. *Why Why Why — Do Dolphins Squeak?* (4–6). Illus. 2009, Mason Crest LB $18.95 (978-142221581-4). 32pp. Goofy and accessible, this book uses cartoons and sketches — as well as facts — to answer questions about dolphins and whales. (Rev: BL 1/1/10) [599.53]

22377 Butterworth, Chris. *Sea Horse: The Shyest Horse in the Sea* (K–2). Illus. by John Lawrence. 2006, Candlewick $16.99 (978-0-7636-2989-2). 32pp. Lovely, detailed illustrations and appealing narrative combined with facts trace the life cycle of an endangered sea horse. (Rev: BCCB 10/06; BL 4/15/06*; HB 7/06; HBG 10/06; SLJ 6/06*) [597]

22378 Cerullo, Mary. *The Truth About Dangerous Sea Creatures* (3–5). Photos by Jeffrey L. Rotman. Illus. by Michael Wertz. 2003, Chronicle $15.95 (978-0-8118-4050-7). 46pp. The dangers posed by jellyfish, giant squid, sharks, octopi, and other marine animals are examined in text and illustrations. (Rev: SLJ 12/03) [591.77]

22379 Cerullo, Mary M. *Sea Soup: Zooplankton* (4–7). Illus. by Bill Curtsinger. 2001, Tilbury House $16.95 (978-0-88448-219-2). An inviting introduction to the world of tiny drifting animals known as zooplankton, with intriguing photographs. (Rev: BL 7/01; HBG 10/01; SLJ 8/01) [592.1776.]

22380 Collard, Sneed B, III. *On the Coral Reefs* (4–7). Series: Science Adventures. 2005, Marshall Cavendish LB $25.64 (978-0-7614-1953-2). In addition to a profile of a marine biologist who studies fish that eat parasites living on other fish, Collard presents information on scientific research methods and on global warming and other environmental threats. (Rev: BL 2/1/06; SLJ 5/06) [577.8]

22381 Collard, Sneed B., III. *In the Deep Sea* (3–6). Illus. Series: Science Adventures. 2005, Benchmark LB $25.64 (978-0-7614-1952-5). 43pp. Readers meet a scientist who studies creatures of the deep sea that use bioluminescence. (Rev: SLJ 5/06) [572]

22382 Earle, Sylvia A. *Sea Critters* (1–4). Illus. by Wolcott Henry. 2000, National Geographic $16.95 (978-0-7922-7181-9). 32pp. Color photos and a lyrical text are used to introduce such unusual sea creatures as Christmas-tree worms, sea squirts, sponges, and moray eels. (Rev: BL 11/1/00; HBG 3/01; SLJ 9/00) [591.7]

22383 Ganeri, Anita. *Whales and Dolphins* (3–5). Illus. by Peter Bull. Series: Explorers. 2013, Kingfisher $10.99 (978-075346815-9). 32pp. With large text, bright spreads, and the ability to move around the book using buttons, this is an informative and appealing guide. (Rev: BL 7/13) [599.5]

22384 Grupper, Jonathan. *Destination: Deep Sea* (1–4). 2000, National Geographic $16.95 (978-0-7922-7693-7). 31pp. A beautiful collection of photographs and informative text present many sea creatures, from the inhabitants of coral reefs to dolphins, whales, and sea otters. (Rev: BL 10/15/00; HBG 3/01; SLJ 9/00) [591.92]

22385 Halfmann, Janet. *Life in the Sea* (5–7). Series: LifeViews. 2000, Creative LB $22.60 (978-1-58341-074-5). All life in the sea is discussed with a focus on the tiniest — plankton, algae, sea spiders, coral, and worms. (Rev: SLJ 8/00) [591.92]

22386 Hirschmann, Kris. *Moray Eels* (4–6). Illus. Series: Creatures of the Sea. 2003, Gale LB $23.70 (978-0-7377-0985-8). 48pp. Introduces the moray eel, with color photographs and readable text. (Rev: SLJ 3/03) [597]

22387 Hoyt, Erich. *Weird Sea Creatures* (4–8). Illus. 2013, Firefly $19.95 (978-177085197-9); paper $9.95 (978-17708519-1-7). 64pp. A well illustrated survey of the species found in the deep ocean, with information on characteristics and on the conditions they live in. (Rev: BL 7/13; LMC 3–4/14; SLJ 7/13*) [578.77]

22388 Jenkins, Steve. *Down, Down, Down: A Journey to the Bottom of the Sea* (2–4). Illus. by author. 2009, Houghton $17.00 (978-0-618-96636-3). 40pp. Starting with the surface and the birds and the sea animals that emerge into the air, Jenkins explores deeper and deeper into the ocean, identifying the animals that live at each layer. (Rev: BCCB 7–8/09; BL 4/1/09; HB 5/09; SLJ 4/09) [591.779]

22389 Johnson, Jinny. *Simon and Schuster Children's Guide to Sea Creatures* (4–7). 1998, Simon & Schuster $19.95 (978-0-689-81534-8). This book contains broad coverage of the invertebrates, birds, mammals, and fish found in various parts of the oceans and their shores. (Rev: HBG 10/98; SLJ 5/98) [591]

22390 Johnson, Rebecca L. *Journey into the Deep: Discovering New Ocean Creatures* (5–8). 2010, Millbrook $31.93 (978-0-7613-4148-2). 64pp. Documenting the Census of Marine Life, which was conducted between 2000 and 2001, this book provides facts, pithy quotes, and vivid photographs captured from the mission. Lexile 920L (Rev: BL 12/1/10; LMC 1–2/11; SLJ 10/1/10) [591.77]

22391 Kramer, Jennifer Evans. *Ocean Hide and Seek* (K–3). Illus. by Gary R. Phillips. 2009, Sylvan Dell $16.95 (978-1-934359-91-4); paper $8.95 (978-1-60718-036-4). Large illustrations and four-line verses show how marine animals use various forms of camouflage for protection. (Rev: BL 3/15/09; SLJ 6/09) [591.77]

22392 Kurtz, Kevin. *A Day in the Deep* (K–3). Illus. by Erin E. Hunter. 2013, Sylvan Dell $17.95 (978-160718617-5); paper $9.95 (978-16071862-9-8). 32pp. Using accurate illustrations of sea creatures and their various deep-ocean habitats, in addition to engaging rhyming prose, Kurtz informs readers of how various fish and sea creatures survive in the darkest depths of the ocean. (Rev: BL 11/15/13; SLJ 11/13) [591.77]

22393 Leardi, Jeanette. *Southern Sea Otters: Fur-tas-trophe Avoided* (3–4). Series: America's Animal Comebacks. 2007, Bearport LB $25.27 (978-1-59716-534-1). 32pp. With eye-catching photographs and an appealing design, Leardi looks at threats to the sea otters that lived off the coast of California and at efforts to bring them back from the brink. (Rev: SLJ 12/07) [599.769]

22394 Lindeen, Carol K. *Sea Horses* (K–3). Series: Under the Sea. 2004, Capstone LB $21.26 (978-0-7368-3662-3). 24pp. A simple, easy-to-read description of the sea horse, with bright photographs. (Rev: SLJ 7/05) [597]

22395 Moore, Heidi. *Ocean Food Chains* (4–7). Series: Protecting Food Chains. 2010, Heinemann LB $32 (978-1-4329-3859-8); paper $8.99 (978-1-4329-3866-6). 48pp. With chapter headings that ask questions such as "What Are the Producers in Oceans?" and "What Are the Decomposers in Oceans?," this volume explores food chains within an ocean habitat and discusses why we need to protect them. (Rev: SLJ 11/1/10) [577.7]

22396 O'Neill, Michael Patrick. *Ocean Magic* (1–4). Photos by author. 2008, Batfish $19.95 (978-0-9728653-5-7). 45pp. Mainly for browsers, this book features eye-catching photographs of underwater life in diverse environments and discusses the need for conservation. (Rev: LMC 5/08; SLJ 3/08)

22397 Parker, Steve. *Ocean and Sea* (4–7). Illus. Series: Scholastic Discover More. 2012, Scholastic paper $15.99 (978-05453302-2-0). 112pp. In five chapters — "All About Oceans," "Oceans of the World," "Life in the Ocean," "People and Oceans," and "Oceans Under Threat" — this attractive print book offers bright images and succinct text; an accompanying digital companion, *Shark Spotter,* offers additional detail on that species and includes videos. (Rev: BL 3/1/12) [551.46]

22398 Parker, Steve. *Sponges, Jellyfish and Other Simple Animals* (4–6). Illus. Series: Animal Kingdom Classification. 2006, Compass Point LB $29.26 (978-0-7565-1614-7). 48pp. Concise, well-written text, color photographs, diagrams, and charts cover the physical characteristics, habitat, diet, and behavior of animals

such as sea anemones, corals, sponges, and jellyfish. (Rev: SLJ 11/06) [592]

22399 Redmond, Shirley Raye. *Tentacles! Tales of the Giant Squid* (1–3). Illus. by Bryn Barnard. Series: Step into Reading. 2003, Random LB $11.99 (978-0-375-91307-5); paper $3.99 (978-0-375-81307-8). 48pp. For beginning readers, facts and myths about the giant squid are presented with photographs and paintings. (Rev: BL 7/03; HBG 4/04) [594]

22400 Rhodes, Mary Jo, and David Hall. *Partners in the Sea* (2–4). Photos by David Hall. Series: Undersea Encounters. 2005, Children's Pr. LB $27.00 (978-0-516-24397-9). 48pp. This photo-filled title explores the symbiotic relationship between different forms of marine life. (Rev: BL 10/15/05) [591.77]

22401 Rizzo, Johnna. *Oceans: Dolphins, Sharks, Penguins, and More!* (4–7). 2010, National Geographic $14.95 (978-1-4263-0686-0). 64pp. This large-format volume full of eye-catching photographs and easy-to-find factoids covers 15 types of marine animals and will inspire browsers to investigate further. (Rev: BLO 6/10; LMC 10/10; SLJ 6/10) [551.46]

22402 Rustad, Martha E. H. *Stingrays* (PS–1). Series: Blastoff! Readers: Oceans Alive. 2007, Children's Pr. LB $18.50 (978-0-531-17570-5). 24pp. Basic information about stingrays is accompanied by photographs in this introduction for young students. (Rev: SLJ 6/07)

22403 Sheather, Allan. *Neptune's Nursery* (2–3). Illus. by Kim Michelle Toft. 2000, Charlesbridge LB $16.95 (978-1-57091-391-4); paper $6.95 (978-1-57091-392-1). A rhyming text and stunning paintings introduce a number of marine animals and their young. (Rev: BL 12/15/00; HBG 3/01; SLJ 10/00) [591.77]

22404 Stone, Lynn M. *The Food Chain* (2–4). Illus. Series: Under the Sea Discovery Library. 2001, Rourke LB $20.64 (978-1-58952-113-1). 24pp. A look at how food is used to provide energy and at the structure of the food chain found in the underwater world. (Rev: BL 12/15/01; SLJ 3/02) [577.7]

22405 Stone, Lynn M. *Getting Around* (2–3). Series: Under the Sea. 2001, Rourke LB $20.64 (978-1-58952-110-0). 24pp. Text and full-page color photographs provide a simple introduction to the locomotion of various sea animals. (Rev: BL 3/15/02; SLJ 3/02) [591.7]

22406 Stone, Lynn M. *Life of the Kelp Forest* (2–3). Series: Under the Sea. 2001, Rourke LB $20.64 (978-1-58952-112-4). 24pp. The vegetation and marine life found in an ocean kelp forest are introduced with simple text and full-page photographs. (Rev: BL 3/15/02; SLJ 2/02) [589.4]

22407 Stone, Lynn M. *Partners* (2–4). Illus. Series: Under the Sea Discovery Library. 2001, Rourke LB $20.64 (978-1-58952-114-8). 24pp. Underwater partnerships such as parasites and symbiotic relationships are the focus of this slim volume with full-color double-page spreads. (Rev: BL 12/15/01; SLJ 2/02) [591.77]

22408 Taylor-Butler, Christine. *A Home in the Coral Reef* (1–3). 2006, Children's Pr. LB $20.00 (978-0-516-

25344-2). 24pp. This easy-to-understand introduction to the coral reef looks at the nature of the coral, its climate, flora, and the animals that call it home. (Rev: SLJ 2/07) [574.9]

22409 Treat, Rose. *The Seaweed Book: How to Find and Have Fun with Seaweed* (4–7). 1995, Star Bright paper $5.95 (978-1-887724-00-5). The identification, collection, and preservation of various kinds of seaweed. (Rev: BL 2/1/96) [589.45]

22410 Vogel, Carole G. *Ocean Wildlife* (5–9). Series: The Restless Sea. 2003, Watts LB $30.50 (978-0-531-12324-9); paper $12.95 (978-0-531-16681-9). 95pp. A thorough examination of marine life, from algae to whales, with an emphasis on those species facing extinction through pollution, overfishing, and other manmade threats. (Rev: SLJ 3/04) [591.77]

22411 Zabludoff, Marc. *The Protoctist Kingdom* (5–9). Series: Family Trees. 2005, Benchmark LB $32.79 (978-0-7614-1818-4). Habits, habitats, and other aspects of this newly classified kingdom of animals that includes algae; an engaging book with plenty of facts for report-writers. (Rev: SLJ 6/06) [579]

CORALS AND JELLYFISH

22412 Chin, Jason. *Coral Reefs* (K–3). Illus. by author. 2011, Roaring Brook $16.99 (978-1-59643-563-6). 32pp. Facts about coral reefs are presented alongside a story about a young girl studying them. (Rev: BL 8/11; HB 9–10/11; LMC 11–12/11; SLJ 10/1/11) [577.7]

22413 Collard, Sneed B. *Lizard Island: Science and Scientists on Australia's Great Barrier Reef* (5–7). Illus. 2000, Watts LB $26.00 (978-0-531-11719-4). 144pp. A lively and absorbing description of the work of scientists studying the forms of life on the Great Barrier Reef. (Rev: BL 2/1/01; SLJ 5/01; VOYA 12/01) [577.7]

22414 Collard, Sneed B. *One Night in the Coral Sea* (3–5). Illus. by Robin Brickman. 2005, Charlesbridge $15.95 (978-1-57091-389-1). 32pp. Collard describes a unique spawning of millions of eggs by the coral of the Great Barrier Reef. (Rev: BL 5/15/05) [593.6]

22415 Earle, Sylvia A. *Coral Reefs* (K–2). Illus. by Bonnie Matthews. Series: Jump into Science. 2003, National Geographic $16.95 (978-0-7922-6953-3). 32pp. A young swimmer describes the passing world of a coral reef, explaining its ecology, plants, and sea life, illustrated by vivid paintings and accompanied by a map and an activity. (Rev: BL 1/1–15/03; HBG 10/03; SLJ 5/03) [577.7]

22416 Furgang, Kathy. *Let's Take a Field Trip to a Coral Reef* (3–5). Illus. Series: Neighborhoods in Nature. 2000, Rosen LB $21.25 (978-0-8239-5445-2). 24pp. This book looks at the formation of coral reefs, the types of plants and animals found there, and the impact of human activities. (Rev: SLJ 4/01) [574.9]

22417 George, Twig C. *Jellies: The Life of Jellyfish* (K–3). Illus. 2000, Millbrook LB $21.90 (978-0-7613-1659-6). 32pp. Handsome photographs introduce jellyfish,

their many varieties, special features, and beauty. (Rev: BL 5/1/00; HBG 9/00; SLJ 8/00) [593.5]

22418 Gibbons, Gail. *Coral Reefs* (K–3). Illus. by author. 2007, Holiday $16.95 (978-0-8234-2080-3). 32pp. With her signature style — watercolor pictures, text boxes, labels, definitions, maps, and more — Gibbons takes the reader on an exploration of the ecology of coral reefs. (Rev: BL 12/1/07; SLJ 1/08) [577.7]

22419 Green, Jen. *A Coral Reef* (2–5). Series: Small World. 2002, Crabtree LB $25.27 (978-0-7787-0138-5); paper $8.95 (978-0-7787-0152-1). The variety of life found in a coral reef is described in a simple text with stunning pictures. (Rev: BL 10/15/02; SLJ 8/02) [574.5]

22420 Herriges, Ann. *Jellyfish* (K–3). Series: Blastoff! Readers: Oceans Alive! 2006, Children's Pr. LB $16.95 (978-1-60014-018-1). 24pp. Habitat, anatomy, and characteristics of the jellyfish are covered in large text accompanied by eye-catching photographs. (Rev: SLJ 2/07) [593.5]

22421 Johansson, Philip. *The Coral Reef: A Colorful Web of Life* (3–5). Illus. Series: Wonderful Water Biomes. 2007, Enslow LB $17.95 (978-0-7660-2813-5). 48pp. A colorful look at coral reefs and the varied plants and animals found within them. (Rev: BL 10/1/07; LMC 11/07) [577.7]

22422 Lunis, Natalie. *Gooey Jellyfish* (1–3). Series: No Backbone! The World of Invertebrates. 2007, Bearport LB $21.28 (978-1-59716-510-5). 24pp. An engaging overview of these animals' physical characteristics, habitat, diet, and behavior, with excellent photographs, appealing layout, useful glossary, and accompanying, informative Web site. (Rev: LMC 3/08; SLJ 12/07) [593.5]

22423 Martin-James, Kathleen. *Floating Jellyfish* (PS–2). Series: Pull Ahead Books. 2001, Lerner LB $22.60 (978-0-8225-3766-3). 32pp. Each page contains two lines of simple text and a color photograph in this introduction to jellyfish for beginning readers. (Rev: BL 6/1–15/01; HBG 10/01) [593.5]

22424 Metz, Lorijo. *Discovering Jellyfish* (3–5). Series: Along the Shore. 2011, Rosen LB $21.25 (978-1-4488-4997-0). 24pp. A clear introduction that provides information on habitat, physical characteristics, diet, predators, and so forth. **e** (Rev: SLJ 12/1/11)

22425 Pyers, Greg. *Coral Reef Explorer* (2–4). Illus. Series: Perspectives: Habitat Explorer. 2004, Raintree LB $25.70 (978-1-4109-0515-4). 32pp. This photo-filled exploration of Australia's Great Barrier Reef and other reefs offers readers important information about coral reefs, the abundant life found there, and their fragility. (Rev: BL 4/1/04) [577.7]

22426 Rhodes, Mary Jo, and David Hall. *Life on a Coral Reef* (4–6). Photos by David Hall. Series: Undersea Encounters. 2006, Children's Pr. LB $27.00 (978-0-516-24395-5). 48pp. A look at life on a coral reef, with facts on life cycles, reproduction, and threats from pollution. (Rev: SLJ 3/07) [574]

22427 Schomp, Virginia. *24 Hours on a Coral Reef* (5–8). Illus. Series: A Day in an Ecosystem. 2013, Cavendish

Square LB $29.93 (978-160870892-5). 48pp. This attractive book takes the reader through a full 24 hours of life on a coral reef, with information about how the reefs began, the variety of species that dwell within them, the threats to the ecosystem, and so forth. **e** (Rev: BL 10/1/13; LMC 5–6/14) [577.7]

22428 Simon, Seymour. *Coral Reefs* (2–4). Illus. 2013, HarperCollins $17.99 (978-0-06-191495-9). 32pp. A clear and colorful introduction to the variety of life on coral reefs. (Rev: BL 6/13; SLJ 6/13) [577.7]

CRUSTACEANS

22429 Blaxland, Beth. *Crustaceans: Crabs, Crayfishes, and Their Relatives* (4–6). Series: Invertebrates. 2002, Chelsea LB $28.00 (978-0-7910-6994-3). 32pp. Blaxland defines crustaceans and describes their physical characteristics, life cycles, habitats, senses, food, and means of self-defense. (Rev: HBG 3/03; SLJ 1/03)

22430 Greenaway, Theresa. *Crabs* (4–6). Illus. Series: The Secret World Of. 2001, Raintree LB $27.12 (978-0-7398-3506-7). 48pp. An attractive, well-organized account of the life cycle, anatomy, and habits of the crab, with information on the animal's place in the ecosystem and interesting material on peculiar features or unusual subspecies. (Rev: BL 10/15/01; HBG 3/02; SLJ 1/02) [595.3]

22431 Grimm, Phyllis W. *Crayfish* (2–3). Series: Early Bird Nature Books. 2000, Lerner LB $25.26 (978-0-8225-3030-5). 48pp. A look at this unusual sea creature that has eight legs, two large claws, four antennae, and many mouth parts. (Rev: BL 10/15/00; HBG 3/01; SLJ 2/01) [595.3]

22432 Lunis, Natalie. *Crawling Crabs* (1–3). Series: No Backbone! The World of Invertebrates. 2007, Bearport LB $21.28 (978-1-59716-509-9). 24pp. An engaging overview of crabs' physical characteristics, habitat, diet, and behavior, with excellent photographs, appealing layout, useful glossary, and accompanying, informative Web site. (Rev: LMC 3/08; SLJ 12/07) [595.3]

22433 Marsico, Katie. *A Baby Lobster Grows Up* (1–2). 2007, Children's Pr. LB $19.00 (978-0-531-17475-3). 24pp. The development of a lobster is the topic of this vocabulary-building book with interesting photographs. (Rev: SLJ 7/07)

22434 Sexton, Colleen. *Shrimp* (K–3). 2009, Children's Pr. LB $20.00 (978-0-531-21716-0). 24pp. With color photographs and clearly defined scientific terms, this simple book introduces beginning readers to the characteristics and behavior of shrimp. (Rev: SLJ 6/09) [595.3]

22435 Sill, Cathryn. *About Crustaceans: A Guide for Children* (PS–2). Illus. by John Sill. Series: About . . . 2004, Peachtree $15.95 (978-1-56145-301-6). 40pp. Brief, large-print text and precise watercolor paintings introduce the world of crustaceans, including barnacles, crabs, and lobsters. (Rev: BL 5/1/04; SLJ 6/04) [595.3]

DOLPHINS AND PORPOISES

22436 Barnes, Julia. *The Secret Lives of Dolphins* (3–5). Illus. Series: The Secret Lives of Animals. 2007, Gareth Stevens LB $17.95 (978-0-8368-7656-7). 32pp. Characteristics common to most dolphins are the focus of this clearly written volume. (Rev: BL 5/15/07; LMC 11/07) [599.53]

22437 Crisp, Marty. *Everything Dolphin: What Kids Really Want to Know About Dolphins* (3–5). 2004, NorthWord $10.95 (978-1-55971-042-8); paper $7.95 (978-1-55971-049-7). 63pp. A basic introduction, using a question-and-answer format with plenty of photographs. (Rev: SLJ 11/04) [599.5]

22438 Greenaway, Theresa. *Whales* (4–7). Illus. Series: Secret World Of. 2001, Raintree LB $27.12 (978-0-7398-3508-1). 48pp. A look at whales' diet, habitat, and behavior, with photographs and interesting facts. (Rev: BL 10/15/01; HBG 3/02) [599.5]

22439 Greenberg, Dan. *Whales* (5–9). Illus. Series: AnimalWays. 2003, Marshall Cavendish $31.36 (978-0-7614-1389-9). 110pp. In addition to material on physical characteristics, behavior, habitats, and threats, Greenberg touches on the animal's roles in history, mythology, religion, and literature. (Rev: BL 3/15/03; HBG 3/03) [599.5]

22440 Hirschi, Ron. *Dolphins* (4–6). Series: Animals Animals. 2002, Benchmark LB $25.64 (978-0-7614-1443-8). 48pp. An oversize book filled with excellent photographs and a simple text that introduces dolphins and their structure, habits, and homes. (Rev: BL 12/15/02; HBG 3/03) [599.5]

22441 Pfeffer, Wendy. *Dolphin Talk: Whistles, Clicks, and Clapping Jaws* (1–2). Illus. by Helen K. Davie. Series: Let's-Read-and-Find-Out Science. 2003, HarperCollins LB $16.89 (978-0-06-028802-0); paper $5.99 (978-0-06-445210-6). 33pp. Dolphins' many ways of communicating are conveyed in understandable text. (Rev: HBG 4/04; SLJ 1/04) [599.53]

22442 Riggs, Kate. *Dolphins* (K–3). Illus. Series: Amazing Animals. 2011, Creative Education $16.95 (978-158341989-2). 24pp. Riggs provides clear, interesting facts enhanced by large, eye-catching photographs and retells a Greek myth about dolphins' relationship with humans. (Rev: BL 4/15/11) [599.53]

22443 Simon, Seymour. *Dolphins* (1–4). Illus. 2009, HarperCollins $17.99 (978-0-06-028393-3). 32pp. With full-page color photographs, Simon looks at dolphins, their relationship to porpoises and whales, their anatomy and characteristics, and their experiences with humans. (Rev: BL 4/1/09; HB 7/09; SLJ 5/09) [599.53]

22444 Spilsbury, Richard, and Louise Spilsbury. *A School of Dolphins* (3–5). Illus. Series: Animal Groups. 2004, Heinemann LB $24.22 (978-1-4034-4692-3). 32pp. Easy-to-understand narrative and plenty of color photographs provide a good overview of dolphins and their behaviors and habitats. (Rev: BL 4/15/04) [599.53]

22445 Thomson, Sarah L. *Amazing Dolphins!* (K–3). Series: I Can Read. 2006, HarperCollins $16.99 (978-

0-06-054453-9). 32pp. For beginning readers, this introduces the world of dolphins, discussing their physical characteristics, communications, habitat, behavior, and how they care for their young. (Rev: BL 6/1–15/06; SLJ 7/06) [599.53]

22446 Turner, Pamela S. *The Dolphins of Shark Bay* (5–8). Illus. Series: Scientists in the Field. 2013, Houghton Mifflin $18.99 (978-054771638-1). 80pp. The author describes the work of biologist Janet Mann, who is studying dolphin intelligence in the wild, and the wide-reaching implications of this project. (Rev: BL 11/1/13; LMC 5–6/14; SLJ 11/13*) [599.53]

FISH

22447 Curtis, Jennifer Keats. *Seahorses* (PS–3). Illus. by Chad Wallace. 2012, Henry Holt $16.99 (978-0-8050-9239-4). 32pp. This is a very attractive account of a sea horse's fascinating life cycle. Outstanding Science Trade Books for Students K–12, 2013. **e** Lexile AD1100L (Rev: BL 11/15/12; LMC 5–6/13; SLJ 10/12) [597]

22448 de la Bedoyere, Camilla. *Fry to Sea Horse* (1–3). Illus. Series: Life Cycles. 2012, Amicus/QEB LB $17.95 (978-160992049-4). 24pp. Double-page spreads with clear images trace the animal's life cycle, explaining the unusual role of the fathers. (Rev: BL 11/1/12) [597]

22449 Einhorn, Kama. *My First Book About Fish* (PS–1). Illus. by Christopher Moroney. Series: Sesame Subjects. 2006, Random paper $7.99 (978-0-375-83513-1). Muppets Grover and Elmo, the latter accompanied by his pet goldfish, team up to introduce basic information about fish, including their physical characteristics, habitat, diet, and behavior. (Rev: SLJ 12/06) [597]

22450 Gish, Melissa. *Piranhas* (4–6). Illus. Series: Living Wild. 2012, Creative Education LB $24.95 (978-1-60818-168-1). 48pp. Useful for reports, this volume covers the fishes' anatomy, habitat, life cycle, reproduction, position on the food chain, adaptations, and threats to survival. Lexile NC1320L (Rev: BL 12/15/12; SLJ 12/12) [597]

22451 Herriges, Ann. *Sea Horses* (K–3). Series: Blastoff! Readers: Oceans Alive! 2006, Children's Pr. LB $16.95 (978-1-60014-020-4). 24pp. Habitat, anatomy, and characteristics of sea horses are covered in large text accompanied by eye-catching photographs. Also use *Sea Stars* (2006). (Rev: SLJ 2/07) [597]

22452 Hirschi, Ron. *Salmon* (3–6). Series: Nature Watch. 2000, Carolrhoda LB $25.26 (978-1-57505-482-7). 48pp. Amazing photos and a clear text describe how salmon change from egg to fry to grown fish that then complete the cycle by making a journey upstream to reproduce. (Rev: BL 10/15/00; HBG 10/01) [597.55]

22453 Hirschmann, Kris. *Rays* (4–7). Illus. 2003, Gale LB $23.70 (978-0-7377-0988-9). 48pp. Hirschmann presents basic information about the ray's anatomy, movement, feeding, defense, reproduction, and man's fascination with this fish. (Rev: BL 3/1/03) [597.3]

22454 Hodge, Deborah. *Salmon* (3–5). Illus. by Nancy Gray Ogle. Series: Wildlife. 2002, Kids Can $10.95

(978-1-55074-961-8); paper $5.95 (978-1-55074-963-2). 32pp. Atlantic and Pacific salmon are covered along with subspecies in a flowing text and detailed paintings. (Rev: HBG 10/02; SLJ 7/02) [597.56]

22455 Jango-Cohen, Judith. *Clinging Sea Horses* (PS–2). Series: Pull Ahead Books. 2000, Lerner LB $22.60 (978-0-8225-3764-9); paper $5.95 (978-0-8225-3767-0). 32pp. Stunning underwater photos bring to life this unique fish whose young grow in a pouch on the father's body. (Rev: BL 8/00; HBG 3/01; SLJ 1/01) [597]

22456 Kurlansky, Mark. *The Cod's Tale* (3–5). Illus. by S. D. Schindler. 2001, Penguin $17.99 (978-0-399-23476-7). 48pp. Kurlansky looks at the surprisingly fascinating relationship between cod and humans, presenting basic facts about the fish itself (including how to cook it) and exploring its importance throughout history. (Rev: BCCB 10/01; BL 12/1/01; HB 11/01; HBG 3/02; SLJ 10/01) [639.2]

22457 Laskey, Elizabeth. *Seahorses* (4–6). Series: Sea Creatures. 2003, Heinemann LB $22.79 (978-1-4034-0963-8). 32pp. Examines the tiny marine animal's physical characteristics, habitat, diet, and behavior. (Rev: HBG 10/03; SLJ 11/03) [597]

22458 Pascoe, Elaine. *Freshwater Fish* (4–8). Photos by Dwight Kuhn. Series: Nature Close-Up. 2005, Gale LB $24.95 (978-1-4103-0308-0). Eye-catching close-ups illustrate information on the life cycles and eating habits of freshwater fish. (Rev: SLJ 6/05)

22459 Pyers, Greg. *Why Am I a Fish?* (3–5). Illus. Series: Classifying Animals. 2005, Raintree LB $27.50 (978-1-4109-2015-7); paper $7.85 (978-1-4109-2022-5). 32pp. Introduces readers to the process of scientific classification and then examines the unique physical characteristics — such as fins, gills, and a streamlined body — of fish as a class. (Rev: SLJ 4/06) [597]

22460 Rodriguez, Ana María. *Secret of the Suffocating Slime Trap . . . and More!* (4–6). 2008, Enslow LB $23.93 (978-0-7660-2954-5). 48pp. How scientists discovered fish species that use secretions for many purposes is explained though interesting text and photographs. (Rev: SLJ 2/09) [597]

22461 Royston, Angela. *Life Cycle of a Salmon* (PS–3). Series: Life Cycle. 2000, Heinemann LB $21.36 (978-1-57572-212-2). 32pp. From egg to adult, this book explains the life cycle of a salmon, using a simple text and full-color photos on each page. (Rev: BL 5/15/00; HBG 3/01) [597.55]

22462 Rustad, Martha E. H. *Parrotfish* (K–3). Series: Blastoff! Readers: Oceans Alive. 2007, Children's Pr. LB $20.00 (978-0-531-14739-9). 24pp. For beginning readers, this is an easily read, colorful introduction to these fish. Also use *Sharks* (2007). (Rev: SLJ 2/08) [597]

22463 Savage, Stephen. *Fish* (2–4). Series: What's the Difference? 2000, Raintree LB $25.69 (978-0-7398-1357-7). 32pp. Fish can be as different as a goldfish and a shark, but this book points out their common features (e.g., gills) as well as salient differences. (Rev: BL 10/15/00; HBG 3/01) [597]

22464 Schach, David. *Sea Dragons* (PS–1). Series: Blastoff! Readers: Oceans Alive. 2007, Children's Pr. LB $18.50 (978-0-531-17563-7). 24pp. This entry in the series covers this fish by briefly discussing habitat, diet, behavior, and so on, with bright photographs and resources for additional information. (Rev: SLJ 6/07)

22465 Sexton, Colleen. *Clown Fish* (PS–1). 2007, Children's Pr. LB $18.50 (978-0-531-17562-0). 24pp. Briefly discusses habitat, diet, behavior, and so on, with bright photographs and resources for additional information. (Rev: SLJ 6/07)

22466 Sexton, Colleen. *Lionfish* (K–3). Series: Blastoff! Readers: Oceans Alive. 2009, Children's Pr. LB $20.00 (978-0-531-21713-9). 24pp. With color photographs and clearly defined scientific terms, this book introduces beginning readers to the lionfish, an interesting predator. (Rev: SLJ 6/09) [597]

22467 Sill, Cathryn. *About Fish: A Guide for Children* (PS–1). Illus. by John Sill. 2002, Peachtree $15.95 (978-1-56145-256-9). 40pp. Watercolor illustrations and simple text describe for preschoolers how fish live and move. Also use *About Amphibians* (2001). (Rev: BL 3/1/02; HBG 10/02; SLJ 6/02) [597]

22468 Spilsbury, Richard, and Louise Spilsbury. *Classifying Fish* (4–6). Series: Classifying Living Things. 2003, Heinemann LB $24.22 (978-1-4034-0846-4). 32pp. The principles of scientific classification are covered along with an introduction to some of the many groupings of fish. (Rev: HBG 10/03; SLJ 11/03) [597]

22469 Spilsbury, Richard, and Louise Spilsbury. *The Life Cycle of Fish* (3–5). Illus. Series: From Egg to Adult. 2003, Heinemann LB $24.22 (978-1-4034-0783-2). 32pp. A photo-filled overview of the life cycle of fish, with material on habitat, diet, and life expectancy. (Rev: HBG 4/04; SLJ 10/03) [597]

22470 Stewart, Melissa. *Fishes* (2–3). Series: True Books. 2001, Children's Book Pr. LB $25.00 (978-0-516-22038-3). 48pp. This book looks at a number of kinds of fish and points out similarities as well as differences. (Rev: BL 3/15/01) [597]

22471 Stewart, Melissa. *How Do Fish Breathe Underwater?* (2–4). Series: Tell Me Why, Tell Me How. 2006, Marshall Cavendish LB $28.50 (978-0-7614-2109-2). 32pp. In brief chapters with easy-to-understand text and eye-catching full-color photos, the author discusses how fish breathe. (Rev: BL 10/15/06; SLJ 12/06) [573.2]

22472 Stewart, Melissa. *A Place for Fish* (K–3). Illus. by Higgins Bond. 2011, Peachtree $16.95 (978-1-56145-562-1). 32pp. Rich illustrations showcase a variety of endangered fishes in their native habitats, and the text emphasizes in simple language the threats that humans pose; "Fascinating Fish Facts" and vocabulary words are included. Lexile AD940L (Rev: BL 4/15/11; SLJ 3/1/11) [597.17]

22473 Stockdale, Susan. *Fabulous Fishes* (PS–3). Illus. by author. 2008, Peachtree $15.95 (978-1-56145-429-7). 32pp. Fishes of all kinds are introduced in simple rhymes and clear illustrations. (Rev: BL 4/1/08; LMC 3/08; SLJ 4/08) [597]

22474 Stone, Lynn M. *Ocean Hunters* (2–3). Series: Under the Sea. 2001, Rourke LB $20.64 (978-1-58952-111-7). 24pp. A basic introduction to various sea animals and how they find, kill, and eat their food. (Rev: BL 3/15/02) [597]

22475 Turner, Pamela S. *Project Seahorse* (5–8). Illus. by Scott Tuason. Series: Scientists in the Field. 2010, Houghton Mifflin $18 (978-0-547-20713-1). 64pp. Sea horses and the scientists who study these beguiling creatures are the focus of this book, which contains the story of fishermen and biologists working together to protect a reef where they live. (Rev: BL 7/10; HB 9–10/10; SLJ 8/10) [596]

22476 Walker, Sally M. *Fossil Fish Found Alive: Discovering the Coelacanth* (5–8). 2002, Carolrhoda LB $17.95 (978-1-57505-536-7). An engaging look at the search for and study of coelacanths, a fish believed to be extinct until 1938. (Rev: BL 3/15/02; HB 1–2/03; HBG 3/03; SLJ 5/02*) [597.3]

22477 Walker, Sally M. *Sea Horses* (2–4). Series: Early Bird Nature Books. 2003, Lerner LB $25.26 (978-0-8225-3051-0). 48pp. Newly independent readers will enjoy this basic introduction to the life cycle of the sea horse, covering habitat, diet, and reproduction. (Rev: HBG 4/04; SLJ 11/03) [597]

22478 Walker, Sally M. *Seahorse Reef: A Story of the South Pacific* (1–3). Illus. by Steven J. Petruccio. Series: Smithsonian Oceanic. 2001, Smithsonian Institution $15.95 (978-1-56899-869-5). 32pp. Information about the sea horse — behavior, habitat, and reproduction — is presented through the story of one sea horse and his mate. (Rev: BL 9/15/01; HBG 10/01; SLJ 8/01) [597]

22479 Weber, Valerie J. *Anglerfish* (3–5). Series: Weird Wonders of the Deep. 2005, Gareth Stevens LB $23.00 (978-0-8368-4560-0). 24pp. A look at the unusual anglerfish and its ability to swallow prey much larger than itself. (Rev: SLJ 8/05) [597]

22480 Weber, Valerie J. *Coelacanth: The Living Fossil* (3–5). Series: Weird Wonders of the Deep. 2005, Gareth Stevens LB $23.00 (978-0-8368-4561-7). 24pp. An introduction to a interesting fish that lived 400 million years ago and had no backbone — and still exists today. (Rev: SLJ 8/05) [597.3]

22481 Wilkes, Sarah. *Fish* (5–9). Series: World Almanac Library of the Animal Kingdom. 2006, World Almanac LB $31.00 (978-0-8368-6210-2). This brightly illustrated guide to fish introduces specific species, physical characteristics, habitats, diets, behaviors, and life cycles. (Rev: SLJ 12/06) [597]

22482 Winkelman, Barbara Gaines. *Puffer's Surprise* (2–3). 2005, Soundprints $15.95 (978-1-59249-032-5); paper $6.95 (978-1-59249-034-9). 32pp. A fascinating day in the life of a tiny puffer fish is chronicled in beautiful illustratations and simple but detailed text. (Rev: BL 12/1/03; HBG 4/04)

22483 Zim, Herbert S., and Hurst H. Shoemaker. *Fishes* (5–8). Illus. by James G. Irving. 1991, Western paper $21.27 (978-0-307-64059-8). This is a basic guide to both fresh and saltwater species.

OCTOPUS

22484 Herriges, Ann. *Octopuses* (K–3). Series: Blastoff! Readers: Oceans Alive! 2006, Children's Pr. LB $16.95 (978-1-60014-019-8). 24pp. Habitat, anatomy, and characteristics of the octopus are covered in large text accompanied by eye-catching photographs. (Rev: SLJ 2/07) [594]

22485 Hirschi, Ron. *Octopuses* (3–6). Series: Nature Watch. 2000, Carolrhoda $25.26 (978-1-57505-386-8). 48pp. An informative text about the octopus, its daily life, and how it uses its eight arms for swimming, eating, catching prey, and even tasting food. (Rev: BL 3/15/00; HBG 9/00; SLJ 7/00) [594]

22486 Lindeen, Carol K. *Octopuses* (K–3). Series: Under the Sea. 2004, Capstone LB $21.26 (978-0-7368-3661-6). 24pp. A simple, easy-to-read description of the octopus, with bright photographs. (Rev: SLJ 7/05) [594]

22487 Markle, Sandra. *Octopuses* (3–5). Illus. Series: Animal Prey. 2007, Lerner $25.26 (978-0-8225-6063-0). 40pp. Stunning color photography highlights this well-written introduction to the octopus that covers its physical characteristics, habitat, diet, behavior, and life cycle. (Rev: BL 4/1/07) [594]

22488 Matsen, Brad. *The Incredible Hunt for the Giant Squid* (4–6). Illus. Series: Incredible Deep-Sea Adventures. 2003, Enslow LB $23.93 (978-0-7660-2192-1). 48pp. An engaging overview of what is known about the mysterious creature, focusing primarily on efforts to track down the elusive squid in its deep habitat. (Rev: HBG 4/04; SLJ 1/04) [594]

22489 Spirn, Michele. *Octopuses* (3–6). Series: Smart Animals. 2006, Bearport LB $25.27 (978-1-59716-250-0). 32pp. The octopus's intelligence and ability to solve problems are discussed here; a facts page gives details about physical characteristics and so forth and a diagram labels body parts. (Rev: SLJ 1/07) [594]

MOLLUSKS, SPONGES, STARFISH

22490 Blaxland, Beth. *Echinoderms: Sea Stars, Sea Urchins, and Their Relatives* (4–6). Series: Invertebrates. 2002, Chelsea LB $28.00 (978-0-7910-6996-7). 32pp. Blaxland defines echinoderms and describes their physical characteristics, life cycles, habitats, senses, food, and means of self-defense. (Rev: HBG 3/03; SLJ 1/03)

22491 Bodden, Valerie. *Slugs* (K–3). Illus. Series: Creepy Creatures. 2013, Creative Education LB $17.95 (978-160818233-6). 24pp. Simple text and compelling photographs will draw young readers to an unlikely fascination with slugs. (Rev: BL 2/15/13; LMC 10/13*) [594]

22492 Cerullo, Mary M., and Clyde F. E. Roper. *Giant Squid: Searching for a Sea Monster* (4–6). Illus. 2012, Capstone LB $26.86 (978-142967541-3); paper $8.95

(978-142968023-3). 48pp. This title describes undersea expeditions to learn about the mysterious giant squid, and documents what little we do know about them. (Rev: BL 3/15/12; LMC 3–4/13; SLJ 5/1/12) [594]

22493 Gilpin, Daniel. *Snails, Shellfish and Other Mollusks* (4–6). Illus. Series: Animal Kingdom Classification. 2006, Compass Point LB $29.26 (978-0-7565-1613-0). 48pp. Concise, well-written text, color photographs, diagrams, and charts cover the physical characteristics, habitat, diet, and behavior of mollusks. (Rev: SLJ 11/06)

22494 Halfmann, Janet. *Star of the Sea: A Day in the Life of a Starfish* (K–2). Illus. by Joan Paley. 2011, Henry Holt $16.99 (978-0-8050-9073-4). Unpaged. Readers learn about the characteristics and life of a starfish or sea star in this beautifully illustrated book. (Rev: LMC 10/11; SLJ 7/11) [593.9]

22495 Lunis, Natalie. *Prickly Sea Stars* (1–3). Series: No Backbone! The World of Invertebrates. 2007, Bearport LB $21.28 (978-1-59716-508-2). 24pp. An engaging overview of these animals' physical characteristics, habitat, diet, and behavior, with excellent photographs, appealing layout, useful glossary, and accompanying, informative Web site. (Rev: LMC 3/08; SLJ 12/07) [593.9]

22496 Morgan, Sally. *Sponges and Other Minor Phyla* (4–6). Series: Animal Kingdom. 2004, Raintree LB $32.79 (978-1-4109-1053-0). 64pp. The common characteristics of sponges and other minor phyla are explained, followed by descriptions of various orders within this classification and selected specific species, plus discussion of endangered status and evolution. (Rev: SLJ 6/05)

22497 Newquist, H. P. *Here There Be Monsters: The Legendary Kraken and the Giant Squid* (5–8). Illus. 2010, Houghton Mifflin $18 (978-0-547-07678-2). 80pp. Explores the history and mystery of the giant squid, with many illustrations, historical maps, and scientific facts. (Rev: BL 9/1/10; HB 11–12/10; SLJ 9/1/10) [594]

22498 Rustad, Martha E. H. *Sea Urchins* (K–3). Series: Blastoff! Readers: Oceans Alive. 2007, Children's Pr. LB $20.00 (978-0-531-14741-2). 24pp. For beginning readers, this is an easily read, colorful introduction to these marine animals. (Rev: SLJ 2/08) [593.9]

22499 Sill, Cathryn. *About Mollusks: A Guide for Children* (K–2). Illus. by John Sill. 2005, Peachtree $15.95 (978-1-56145-331-3). A simple introduction to mollusks, with large, realistic watercolors. (Rev: BL 2/1/04; HB 5/04; SLJ 4/05)

22500 Zuchora-Walske, Christine. *Spiny Sea Stars* (PS–2). Series: Pull Ahead Books. 2001, Lerner LB $22.60 (978-0-8225-3765-6). 32pp. A variety of starfish and their habits and habitats are presented with a simple, basic text and attractive color photographs. (Rev: BL 6/1–15/01; HBG 10/01) [593.9]

SEA MAMMALS

22501 Arnold, Caroline. *Super Swimmers* (2–4). Illus. by Patricia J. Wynne. 2007, Charlesbridge $16.95 (978-1-

57091-588-8); paper $6.95 (978-1-57091-589-5). 32pp. A wide variety of marine mammals are introduced in this clear text with well-chosen illustrations. (Rev: BL 2/1/07) [599.5]

22502 Arnosky, Jim. *All About Manatees* (K–3). Illus. by author. 2008, Scholastic paper $5.99 (978-0-439-90361-5). 32pp. For young readers, this is a clear introduction to manatees — their physical characteristics, habitat, and endangered status — with eye-catching illustrations. (Rev: BL 6/1–15/08; LMC 10/08; SLJ 8/08) [599.55]

22503 Boyle, Doe. *Otter on His Own: The Story of a Sea Otter. 2nd ed.* (K–2). Illus. by Robert Lawson. 2002, Soundprints $15.95 (978-1-56899-129-0); paper $6.95 (978-1-931465-53-3). 31pp. A revision of the exciting story of an otter pup's childhood, with plenty of facts about sea otters. (Rev: HBG 3/03; SLJ 11/02) [599.74]

22504 Eszterhas, Suzi. *Sea Otter* (1–3). Illus. 2013, Frances Lincoln $15.99 (978-1-84780-300-9). 32pp. Appealing full-page photographs of mother and child add to the appeal of this readable account of an otter's first year of life; there is no index or bibliography. (Rev: BLO 3/15/13; SLJ 5/13) [599]

22505 Fetty, Margaret. *Sea Lions* (3–6). Series: Smart Animals. 2006, Bearport LB $25.27 (978-1-59716-274-6). 32pp. Sea lions' intelligence is clearly shown in stories of their ability to communicate and their work for the U.S. Navy; a facts page gives details about physical characteristics and so forth. (Rev: SLJ 1/07) [599.79]

22506 Gish, Melissa. *Sea Lions* (4–6). Illus. Series: Living Wild. 2012, Creative Education LB $24.95 (978-1-60818-169-8). 48pp. Useful for reports, this volume covers the animals' anatomy, habitat, life cycle, reproduction, position on the food chain, adaptations, and threats to survival. Lexile NC1300L (Rev: BL 12/15/12; SLJ 12/12) [599.79]

22507 Goldish, Meish. *Florida Manatees: Warm Water Miracles* (2–4). Illus. Series: America's Animal Comebacks. 2007, Bearport LB $18.95 (978-1-59716-507-5). 32pp. Goldish recounts the manatee's recovery from near-extinction and looks at the many challenges the animal still faces and at today's conservation efforts. (Rev: BL 10/15/07) [599.5509]

22508 Hall, Howard. *A Charm of Dolphins: The Threatened Life of a Flippered Friend* (5–8). Series: Jean-Michel Cousteau Presents. 2007, London Town paper $8.95 (978-0-9766134-8-0). With eye-catching photographs and stories of close encounters with these animals, this book looks at dolphins' characteristics, behavior, intelligence, and the threats to their survival. (Rev: SLJ 11/07) [599.53]

22509 Harvey, Jeanne Walker. *Astro the Steller Sea Lion* (1–3). Illus. by Shennen Bersani. 2010, Sylvan Dell $16.95 (978-1-60718-076-0); paper $8.95 (978-1-60718-087-6). 32pp. An orphaned sea lion raised at California's Marine Mammal Center returns to his laboratory home each time his handlers try to release him. (Rev: BL 11/1/10; LMC 1–2/11*; SLJ 9/1/10) [599.79]

22510 Hewett, Joan. *A Harbor Seal Grows Up* (1–3). Illus. by Richard Hewett. Series: Baby Animals. 2001, Lerner LB $21.27 (978-1-57505-166-6); paper $6.95 (978-0-8225-0092-6). 32pp. A book for beginning readers about a baby harbor seal being raised in captivity. (Rev: BL 10/15/01; HBG 3/02; SLJ 10/01) [599.79]

22511 Hirschi, Ron. *Seals* (4–6). Series: Animals Animals. 2002, Benchmark LB $25.64 (978-0-7614-1445-2). 48pp. Pictures and text present these animals' anatomy, diet, habits, and social interactions. (Rev: BL 12/15/02; HBG 3/03; SLJ 2/03) [599.74]

22512 Hodgkins, Fran. *Andre: The Famous Harbor Seal* (K–3). Illus. by Yetti Frenkel. 2003, Down East $16.95 (978-0-89272-594-6). 32pp. The real-life story of Andre the harbor seal traces the animal's life from its 1961 adoption as a pup by a Maine harbormaster to its death in 1986. (Rev: SLJ 1/04) [599.79]

22513 Kawa, Katie. *Baby Seals* (PS–K). Illus. Series: Cute and Cuddly: Baby Animals. 2011, Gareth Stevens LB $22.60 (978-143395534-1). 24pp. A very simple book featuring brief text and adorable photographs of baby seals, with basic information about their habits and habitat. **e** (Rev: BL 2/15/12) [599.79]

22514 Leon, Vicki. *A Raft of Sea Otters: The Playful Life of a Furry Survivor. 2nd ed.* (4–7). Illus. 2005, London Town paper $7.95 (978-0-9666490-4-8). 48pp. This accessible introduction to the sea otter and its physical characteristics, behavior, diet, habitat, life cycle, and conservation threats is a picture-book-size revision of an earlier edition and contains excellent photographs. (Rev: BL 7/05) [599.7695]

22515 Lindeen, Carol K. *Seals* (K–3). Series: Under the Sea. 2004, Capstone LB $21.26 (978-0-7368-3663-0). 24pp. A simple, easy-to-read description of the seal, with bright photographs. (Rev: SLJ 7/05) [599.79]

22516 Lourie, Peter. *The Manatee Scientists: Saving Vulnerable Species* (4–7). Illus. Series: Scientists in the Field. 2011, Houghton Mifflin $18.99 (978-0-547-15254-7). 80pp. Lourie looks at research scientists' work on manatees around the world, where these mammals face quite different dangers depending on the environment and priorities of the human population. (Rev: BL 5/1/11; SLJ 7/11) [599.55092]

22517 Marsico, Katie. *A Manatee Calf Grows Up* (PS–2). Illus. Series: Scholastic News Nonfiction Readers: Life Cycles. 2007, Children's Pr. LB $20.00 (978-0-531-17479-1). 24pp. This photo-filled title traces the life cycle of a female manatee, introducing young readers to the marine mammal's physical and behavioral characteristics, habitat, and diet. (Rev: BL 3/15/07) [599.55]

22518 Marsico, Katie. *Manatees* (3–5). Illus. Series: Nature's Children. 2012, Scholastic/Children's Press LB $28 (978-053126835-3); paper $6.95 (9780531254806). 48pp. Simple text and many photographs present basic information about these animals' anatomy and behavior as well as their environment and history. (Rev: BL 3/1/13) [599.55]

1272

22519 Martin, Patricia A. Fink. *Manatees* (2–3). Series: Animals. 2002, Children's Book Pr. paper $6.95 (978-0-516-27473-7). 48pp. Color photographs on almost every page and large-type text are used to introduce these endangered sea mammals and explain their life cycle, habits, and habitats. (Rev: BL 8/02) [599.5]

22520 Owen, Ruth. *Sea Otter Pups* (K–3). Illus. Series: Water Babies. 2012, Bearport LB $21.32 (978-161772601-9). 24pp. An appealing introduction to young sea otters and their families. (Rev: BLO 9/1/12; LMC 8–9/13) [599.769]

22521 Person, Stephen. *Walrus: Tusk, Tusk* (3–5). Illus. Series: Built for Cold: Arctic Animals. 2011, Bearport LB $25.27 (978-161772133-5). 32pp. Dramatic photographs add appeal to this book, which explores the biology, habitat, and threats facing walruses. (Rev: BL 4/1/11) [599.79]

22522 Read, Andrew. *Porpoises* (5–8). Series: WorldLife Library. 1999, Voyageur paper $16.95 (978-0-89658-420-4). With many color illustrations and large print, this book introduces porpoises, their characteristics, behavior, habitats, and how humans study them. (Rev: BL 8/99; VOYA 2/00) [599.53]

22523 Read, Tracy C. *Exploring the World of Seals and Walruses* (4–6). Series: Exploring the World of . . . 2011, Firefly $16.95 (978-1-55407-784-7); paper $6.95 (978-1-55407-784-7). 24pp. Introduces the physical characteristics, habitat, family life, and behaviors of these sea mammals. (Rev: SLJ 8/11) [599.79]

22524 Rebman, Renee C. *Walruses* (3–5). Illus. Series: Animals Animals. 2011, Marshall Cavendish LB $20.95 (978-076144881-5). 48pp. Rebman examines the walrus's anatomy, diet, and life cycle, with discussion of threats to long-term survival. (Rev: BL 10/15/11) [599.79]

22525 Richardson, Adele D. *Manatees: Peaceful Plant-Eaters* (1–3). Series: Wild World of Animals. 2002, Capstone LB $22.60 (978-0-7368-1395-2). 24pp. This endangered aquatic mammal is introduced with many color photographs, large type, and simple language. (Rev: BL 1/1–15/03; HBG 3/03) [599.55]

22526 Rinard, Judith E. *Amazing Animals of the Sea* (5–8). 1981, National Geographic LB $12.50 (978-0-87044-387-9). Whales, dolphins, sea otters, sea lions, seals, manatees, and other marine mammals are described.

22527 Sexton, Colleen. *Seals* (PS–1). Series: Blastoff! Readers: Oceans Alive. 2007, Children's Pr. LB $18.50 (978-0-531-17564-2). 24pp. This entry covers seals by briefly discussing habitat, diet, behavior, and so on, with bright photos and resources for additional information. (Rev: SLJ 6/07)

22528 Sexton, Colleen. *Walruses* (K–3). Series: Blastoff! Readers: Oceans Alive. 2007, Children's Pr. LB $20.00 (978-0-531-14742-9). 24pp. For beginning readers, this is an easily read, colorful introduction to these sea mammals. (Rev: SLJ 2/08) [599.79]

22529 Silverstein, Alvin. *The Manatee* (4–7). Series: Endangered in America. 1995, Millbrook LB $24.90 (978-1-56294-551-0). A profile of this sea creature, its lifestyle and habits, and how it became an endangered species. (Rev: BL 10/15/95; SLJ 1/96) [599.5]

22530 Staub, Frank. *Sea Lions* (2–3). Series: Early Bird Nature Books. 2000, Lerner LB $25.26 (978-0-8225-3018-3). 48pp. This simple introduction to the California sea lion covers its habitat, appearance, behavior, and the dangers it faces. (Rev: BL 5/15/00; HBG 9/00) [599]

22531 Stille, Darlene R. *I Am a Seal: The Life of an Elephant Seal* (K–3). Illus. by Todd Ouren. Series: I Live in the Ocean. 2004, Picture Window LB $25.26 (978-1-4048-0598-9). 24pp. An elephant seal describes its life — diet, activities, and so forth. (Rev: SLJ 1/05) [599.74]

22532 Swinburne, Stephen. *Saving Manatees* (4–6). 2006, Boyds Mills $16.95 (978-1-59078-319-1). 40pp. This tour of Florida's manatee country includes discussions with biologists and park rangers and a class of fourth-graders swimming with manatees, as well as information on the mammal's physical appearance, diet, behavior, and habitat, plus the threats it faces. (Rev: BL 9/1/06; SLJ 11/06) [599.5]

22533 Tatham, Betty. *Baby Sea Otter* (PS–2). Illus. by Joan Paley. 2005, Holt $16.95 (978-0-8050-7504-5). 32pp. With some tender and some exciting moments, this book follows the life of a sea otter from birth through mating and caring for its own pups. (Rev: BL 11/1/05; SLJ 9/05) [599.769]

22534 Theodorou, Rod. *Florida Manatee* (K–2). Illus. Series: Animals in Danger. 2000, Heinemann LB $21.36 (978-1-57572-265-8). 32pp. This is an introductory overview of the manatee, with basic information on the animal, its diet and habitat, and the reasons it is endangered. (Rev: HBG 3/01; SLJ 4/01) [599.5]

22535 Weber, Valerie J. *Squids* (2–4). Illus. Series: Weird Wonders of the Deep. 2005, Gareth Stevens LB $23.00 (978-0-8368-4564-8). 24pp. A small-format but informative introduction to the many types of squid and their characteristics. (Rev: BL 5/1/05) [594]

SHARKS

22536 Arnosky, Jim. *All About Sharks* (1–4). Illus. by author. Series: All About. 2003, Scholastic $15.95 (978-0-590-48166-3). Easy-to-understand text and attractive illustrations present facts about sharks in an accessible manner. (Rev: BL 7/03; HBG 4/04; SLJ 6/03) [597.3]

22537 Bodden, Valerie. *Sharks* (K–2). Illus. Series: Amazing Animals. 2010, Creative Company/Creative Education LB $16.95 (978-158341812-3). 24pp. A simple overview of the characteristics of sharks, with eye-catching photographs. (Rev: BL 7/10) [597.3]

22538 Brusha, Joe. *Top 10 Deadliest Sharks* (4–7). Illus. by Anthony Spay. 2010, Silver Dragon paper $9.99 (978-09827507-2-8). 200pp. Facts about sharks are presented along with assessments of their threats to humans. (Rev: BL 3/15/11) [741.5]

22539 Burnham, Brad. *The Hammerhead Shark* (1–4). Illus. Series: Underwater World of Sharks. 2001, Rosen LB $18.75 (978-0-8239-5584-8). 24pp. A fact-filled, easy-to-read book about the odd-looking hammerhead shark, with full-color photographs and a list of Web sites. (Rev: BL 12/15/01) [597.3]

22540 Burnie, David. *Sharks* (2–4). Illus. Series: Discover More. 2013, Scholastic paper $12.99 (978-05454956-1-5). 80pp. With many effective photographs, this book looks at the various kinds of sharks, their locomotion and other characteristics, and their endangered status. Also available in Spanish. (Rev: BL 7/13) [597.3]

22541 Cerullo, Mary M. *The Truth About Great White Sharks* (4–7). 2000, Chronicle $14.95 (978-0-8118-2467-5). A fascinating account with excellent underwater photographs that explores such topics about sharks as physical characteristics, behavior, feeding habits, and the difficulty of studying them. (Rev: BL 4/1/00; SLJ 7/00) [597.3]

22542 Ellwood, Nancy, and Margaret Parrish. *Sharkpedia* (4–6). Illus. 2008, DK $12.99 (978-0-7566-3761-3). 124pp. Conversational yet thorough, this attractive volume offers lots of information on sharks present and past, their physical characteristics and behavior, shark mythology and appearances in literature, and so forth. (Rev: BLO 8/28/08) [500]

22543 Hamilton, Sue. *Eaten by a Shark* (4–7). Series: Close Encounters of the Wild Kind. 2010, ABDO LB $27.07 (978-1-60453-931-8). 32pp. Exciting stories and graphic photographs add high-interest appeal to the information about sharks and advice on avoiding and surviving such an attack. (Rev: LMC 10/10; SLJ 5/10) [597.3]

22544 Johnston, Marianne. *Sharks Past and Present* (3–5). Illus. 2000, Rosen LB $21.25 (978-0-8239-5206-9). 24pp. The shark's anatomy is discussed, as well as its 400-million-year history and why it has changed so little during that time. (Rev: BL 12/1/00) [567.3]

22545 McKay, Sindy. *Sharks!* (1–2). Illus. by Judith Hunt. Series: We Both Read. 2012, Treasure Bay $9.95 (978-160115261-9); paper $4.99 (978-16011526-2-6). 44pp. With eye-catching illustrations and basic information, this text presents parallel texts for parents and children. ⌒ (Rev: BLO 8/12; SLJ 6/1/12)

22546 McMillan, Beverly, and John A. Musick. *Sharks* (3–7). Illus. Series: Insiders. 2008, Simon & Schuster $16.99 (978-1-4169-3867-5). 64pp. Close-up views introduce everything shark delivered in an easy conversational tone, with double-page spreads, detailed diagrams, photographs, and a glossary. (Rev: BL 9/15/08; SLJ 9/08) [597.3]

22547 Mallory, Kenneth. *Swimming with Hammerhead Sharks* (3–7). Illus. Series: Scientists in the Field. 2001, Houghton $16.00 (978-0-618-05543-2). 48pp. Vivid photographs and first-person narrative depict the excitement of swimming with sharks and describe this creature of the deep. (Rev: BL 4/1/01; HB 7/01; HBG 10/01; SLJ 7/01*) [597.3]

22548 Markle, Sandra. *Great White Sharks* (3–6). Illus. Series: Animal Predators. 2004, Carolrhoda LB $25.26 (978-1-57505-731-6). 40pp. Concise text and clear, full-page photographs introduce the life cycle of the great white shark and its physical characteristics, habitat, diet, and predatory behavior. (Rev: SLJ 12/04) [597]

22549 Markle, Sandra. *Tough, Toothy, Baby Sharks* (4–6). Illus. 2007, Walker $16.95 (978-0-8027-9593-9). 32pp. Eye-catching photographs and easy-to-understand text make this an unusually appealing book about baby sharks and how they mature. (Rev: BL 9/1/07; LMC 1/08; SLJ 12/07) [597.3]

22550 Nelson, Kristin L. *Hunting Sharks* (2–3). Series: Pull Ahead Books. 2003, Lerner LB $22.60 (978-0-8225-4671-9). 32pp. This fascinating book explores the physical characteristics, behavior, and life cycle of the shark and is suitable for beginning readers. (Rev: BL 11/15/03; HBG 10/03)

22551 O'Neill, Michael Patrick. *Shark Encounters* (2–4). Illus. 2008, Batfish $19.95 (978-0-9728653-4-0). 45pp. Eye-catching photographs make this an appealing introduction to sharks, more suitable for browsing than for research although it does discuss sharks' importance to the ecosystem and the threats they face. (Rev: BLO 6/17/08; LMC 3/08; SLJ 3/08) [597.3]

22552 Pringle, Laurence. *Sharks! Strange and Wonderful* (3–5). Illus. 2001, Boyds Mills $15.95 (978-1-56397-863-0). 32pp. A picture book for older children that explains the shark's anatomy and habits, and introduces several different species. (Rev: BL 4/15/01; HBG 10/01; SLJ 8/01) [597.3]

22553 Rockwell, Anne. *Little Shark* (K–2). Illus. by Megan Halsey. 2005, Walker $15.95 (978-0-8027-8955-6). Readers follow the growth and maturing of a baby blue shark in this simple text with pertinent facts presented in bubbles. (Rev: BL 2/1/04*; SLJ 4/05) [597]

22554 *Sharks: Facts at Your Fingertips* (5–8). Illus. Series: Pocket Genius. 2012, DK $7.99 (978-075669286-5). 160pp. In encyclopedic fashion, this well-illustrated volume profiles more than 150 sharks and rays, with information on reproduction, migration, threats, and so forth. (Rev: BL 8/12) [597.3]

22555 Shea, Therese. *Sharks* (PS–2). Series: Big Bad Biters. 2006, Rosen LB $19.95 (978-1-4042-3519-1). 24pp. A look at the world of sharks and learn about their physical characteristics, habitat, what they eat, how they raise their young, and their enemies in the sea. (Rev: SLJ 3/07) [597.3]

22556 Sieswerda, Paul L. *Sharks* (5–8). Series: Animal-Ways. 2001, Marshall Cavendish LB $31.36 (978-0-7614-1267-0). 112pp. Photographs, maps, and text introduce many species of sharks, their behavior, anatomy, and habitats. (Rev: BL 3/15/02; HBG 10/02) [597.31]

22557 Smith, Miranda. *Sharks* (4–7). Illus. Series: Kingfisher Knowledge. 2010, Kingfisher paper $8.99 (978-07534640-5-2). 64pp. An eye-catching overview of sharks' physical characteristics, habit, diet, and behavior, with spreads on *Jaws* and on shark attacks as well as information on their history and myths about these animals. (Rev: BL 2/15/10; SLJ 9/1/08) [597.3]

22558 Spilsbury, Richard. *Great White Shark* (4–6). Illus. Series: Animals Under Threat. 2004, Heinemann LB $31.43 (978-1-4034-4860-6). 48pp. Striking color photographs enhance this overview of the great white shark and the environmental threats it faces. (Rev: BL 8/04) [597.3]

22559 Stille, Darlene R. *I Am a Shark: The Life of a Hammerhead Shark* (K–3). Illus. by Todd Ouren. Series: I Live in the Ocean. 2004, Picture Window LB $25.26 (978-1-4048-0599-6). 24pp. A hammerhead shark describes its life — diet, activities, and so forth. (Rev: SLJ 1/05) [597]

22560 Strong, Mike. *Shark! The Truth Behind the Terror* (4–6). Series: High Five Reading. 2002, Capstone LB $23.93 (978-0-7368-9547-7). 48pp. The combination of simple text describing sharks and shark attacks plus eye-catching photographs will attract reluctant readers. (Rev: HBG 10/03; SLJ 5/03) [597.3]

22561 Thomas, Elizabeth. *Goblin Sharks* (3–5). Illus. Series: Exploring Our Oceans. 2013, Cherry Lake LB $28.50 (978-162431444-5); paper $14.21 (9781624314827). 32pp. Colored photographs and clear prose inform readers about goblin sharks, discussing the basic facts about the deep-sea dwelling creatures such as their physical characteristics, diet, and habitat. (Rev: BL 10/1/13; SLJ 11/13) [597.3]

22562 Thomson, Sarah L. *Amazing Sharks!* (K–2). Illus. Series: I Can Read. 2005, HarperCollins $15.99 (978-0-06-054458-4). 32pp. Short sentences and bright photographs make this overview of sharks and shark behavior suitable for beginning readers. (Rev: BL 10/1/05; SLJ 1/06) [597.3]

22563 Troll, Ray. *Sharkabet: A Sea of Sharks from A to Z* (2–4). Illus. 2002, Graphic Arts paper $8.95 (978-1-55868-519-2). 40pp. From angel sharks to zebra sharks (and including some non-shark species), Troll includes many interesting shark facts in this unusual and beautifully illustrated alphabet book. (Rev: BL 9/1/02; HBG 10/02; SLJ 5/02) [597.3]

22564 Tuchman, Gail. *Shark Attack!* (K–3). Illus. Series: Discover More Readers. 2013, Scholastic paper $3.99 (978-05455337-7-5). 32pp. With eye-catching photographs, factoids, and large type, this is an interesting introduction to the lives of sharks. (Rev: BLO 11/15/13) [597.3]

22565 Vadon, Catherine. *Meet the Shark* (K–4). Illus. by Vincent Boyer and Charles Dutertre. 2007, Two-Can $15.95 (978-1-58728-598-1). 45pp. Using cartoon characters and clear, interesting text, Vadon covers sharks' anatomy, behavior, and reproduction, and emphasizes the grave threats to their survival, dispelling myths about their violent character. (Rev: LMC 1/08; SLJ 12/07) [597.3]

22566 Woods, Bob. *Shark Attack!* (2–5). Series: Boys Rock! 2006, The Child's World LB $25.64 (978-1-59296-734-6). 32pp. A non-alarmist overview of the

danger posed by sharks, suitable for beginning and reluctant readers (girls as well as boys). (Rev: SLJ 2/07) [597.3]

22567 Zollman, Pam. *A Shark Pup Grows Up* (K–1). Series: Scholastic News Nonfiction Readers. 2005, Children's Pr. LB $20.00 (978-0-516-24945-2). 24pp. Covers the life cycle of a shark, with a focus on newborn pups and their survival tactics. (Rev: SLJ 4/06) [597.3]

SHELLS

22568 Berkes, Marianne. *Seashells by the Seashore* (PS–2). Illus. by Robert Noreika. 2002, Dawn $16.95 (978-1-58469-035-1); paper $8.95 (978-1-58469-034-4). Using rhyme and lovely illustrations, this picture book combines a lesson in counting with a lesson in seashell identification. (Rev: BL 3/1/02; HBG 10/02; SLJ check) [594.147]

22569 Cassie, Brian. *Shells* (4–6). Series: National Audubon Society First Field Guides. 2000, Scholastic $17.95 (978-0-590-64233-0); paper $8.95 (978-0-590-64258-3). 160pp. With more than 450 color photographs, this attractive volume focuses on about 50 of the most easily found shells and their characteristics. (Rev: BL 8/00; SLJ 1/01) [591]

WHALES

22570 Arnold, Caroline. *A Killer Whale's World* (PS–2). Illus. by author. Series: Caroline Arnold's Animals. 2006, Picture Window LB $26.60 (978-1-4048-1321-2). 24pp. A baby killer whale grows up and learns to fend for himself in this appealing fact-packed title. (Rev: LMC 11/06; SLJ 6/06) [599.53]

22571 Collard, Sneed B. *A Whale Biologist at Work* (3–5). Illus. Series: Wildlife Conservation Society Books. 2000, Watts LB $24.50 (978-0-531-11786-6). 48pp. This book focuses on a marine biologist's observations of humpback and blue whales off the Pacific coast of North America. (Rev: BL 2/15/01; SLJ 3/01) [578.77]

22572 Greenberg, Dan. *Whales* (4–6). Illus. Series: Animals Animals. 2000, Marshall Cavendish LB $25.64 (978-0-7614-1167-3). 32pp. A useful book that introduces several types of whales and supplies information on their habitats, mating habits, structure, and behavior. (Rev: BL 3/15/01; HBG 3/01) [599.5]

22573 Hodgkins, Fran. *The Whale Scientists: Solving the Mystery of Whale Strandings* (5–8). Illus. Series: Scientists in the Field. 2007, Houghton Mifflin $18.00 (978-0-618-55673-1). A look at scientists' efforts to understand why whales sometimes strand themselves on beaches, seemingly waiting for death; with accounts of efforts to rescue these huge mammals. (Rev: BL 12/1/07; HB 1–2/08; SLJ 12/07) [599.5]

22574 Hodson, Sally. *Granny's Clan: A Tale of Wild Orcas* (K–3). Illus. by Ann Jones. 2012, Dawn paper $8.95 (978-15846917-2-3). 32pp. A 100-year-old orca guides two new members of her superpod through the basics of their lives. (Rev: BL 12/1/12; LMC 5–6/13; SLJ 3/13) [599.53]

22575 Hopkins, Ellen. *Orcas: High Seas Supermen* (3–7). Illus. 2000, Perfection Learning $17.95 (978-0-7807-9670-6); paper $8.96 (978-0-7891-5258-9). 56pp. For reluctant readers, this attractive book introduces different species of whales, their habitats, food, and methods of communication. (Rev: BL 11/1/00) [599.5]

22576 Hoyt, Erich. *Whale Rescue: Changing the Future for Endangered Wildlife* (4–6). Illus. Series: Animal Rescue. 2005, Firefly $19.95 (978-1-55297-601-2); paper $9.95 (978-1-55297-600-5). 64pp. An interesting discussion of international efforts to conserve the world's whales, with coverage of the various species and their characteristics plus information on whale researchers. (Rev: BL 8/05; SLJ 12/05) [599.5]

22577 Inskipp, Carol. *Killer Whale* (4–6). Illus. Series: Animals Under Threat. 2005, Heinemann LB $29.93 (978-1-4034-5584-0). 48pp. The life cycle of the killer whale and threats to its survival are explored in this blend of narrative and eye-catching color photography.

22578 Kant, Tanya. *The Migration of a Whale* (K–3). Illus. by Mark Bergin. Series: Amaze. 2008, Children's Pr. LB $26.00 (978-0-531-24049-6); paper $8.95 (978-0-531-23803-5). 32pp. "What Do Whales Eat? Why Do Whales Migrate? What Happens After Mating?" This simple introduction to whale migration, with colorful illustrations and well-organized chapters, includes a "Words to Remember" section. (Rev: SLJ 3/09)

22579 Kelsey, Elin. *Finding Out About Whales* (4–8). Series: Science Explorers. 1998, Owl $19.95 (978-1-895688-79-5); paper $9.95 (978-1-895688-80-1). This book discusses how information is gathered about whales and introduces five different species: blue, humpback, beluga, gray, and killer. (Rev: BL 3/1/99; SLJ 3/99) [595.5]

22580 Kurth, Linda Moore. *Keiko's Story: A Killer Whale Goes Home* (4–6). 2000, Millbrook $24.90 (978-0-7613-1500-1). 72pp. An informative, enjoyable read about Keiko, the killer whale who played in the movie *Free Willy* and the efforts to return him to the wild. (Rev: HBG 4/04; SLJ 9/00) [595.5]

22581 Leon, Vicki. *A Pod of Killer Whales: The Mysterious Life of the Intelligent Orca* (5–8). Series: Jean-Michel Cousteau Presents. 2007, London Town paper $8.95 (978-0-9766134-7-3). With eye-catching photographs and stories of close encounters with these animals, this book looks at killer whales' characteristics, behavior, intelligence, and the threats to their survival. (Rev: SLJ 11/07) [599.53]

22582 Lockwood, Sophie. *Whales* (4–7). Series: World of Mammals. 2008, Child's World LB $20.95 (978-1-59296-930-2). Well-suited to report writers, this surprisingly comprehensive title discusses whale behavior and physiology and includes information on conservation. (Rev: BL BLO 6/17/08; SLJ 6/08) [599.5]

22583 Lourie, Peter. *Whaling Season: A Year in the Life of an Arctic Whale Scientist* (4–8). Series: Scientists

in the Field. 2009, Houghton Mifflin $18 (978-0-618-77709-9). 80pp. Lourie follows the work of Arctic whale scientist John Craighead George (son of the well-known children's author) in this fascinating account of George's everyday work, the research process, his subjects, and his ways of relaxing at the end of the day. Lexile NC1150L (Rev: BL 12/1/09*; SLJ 2/10) [599.5]

22584 Markle, Sandra. *Killer Whales* (3–6). Series: Animal Predators. 2004, Carolrhoda LB $25.26 (978-1-57505-728-6). The killer whale's skill as a hunter is emphasized in this attractive overview. (Rev: BL 12/1/04; SLJ 1/05) [599.53]

22585 Marsh, Laura. *Whales* (K–3). Series: Great Migrations. 2010, National Geographic LB $11.90 (978-1-4263-0746-1); paper $3.99 (978-1-4263-0745-4). 48pp. Focusing on sperm whales, this volume discusses their anatomy and diet, their migration patterns, and the dangers they face. (Rev: SLJ 3/1/11) [599.5]

22586 Pringle, Laurence. *Whales! Strange and Wonderful* (3–5). Illus. by Meryl Henderson. 2003, Boyds Mills $15.95 (978-1-56397-439-7). 32pp. Whales and their physical and behavioral characteristics are introduced, with brief information on whaling history and current conservation efforts. (Rev: BL 3/15/03; HBG 10/03; SLJ 4/03) [599.53]

22587 Rau, Dana Meachen. *Guess Who Hunts* (PS–K). Series: Bookworms. Guess Who. 2009, Marshall Cavendish $15.95 (978-0-7614-2907-4). 32pp. Fun for browsing, this book asks readers to identify a whale using the clues in the text and images. (Rev: SLJ 6/09) [599.5]

22588 Reiter, Chris. *The Blue Whale* (4–7). Series: Endangered and Threatened Animals. 2003, Enslow LB $25.26 (978-0-7660-5055-6). 48pp. Standard information on the blue whale and its endangered status is accompanied by links to Web sites for further research. (Rev: HBG 10/03; SLJ 6/03) [599.5]

22589 Riggs, Kate. *Killer Whales* (K–3). Illus. Series: Amazing Animals. 2012, Creative Education LB $17.95 (978-160818109-4). 24pp. For new or reluctant readers, this is a good introduction to the killer whale's physical characteristics, habitat, and behavior, and includes a story from Canadian folklore. (Rev: BL 3/1/12) [599.53]

22590 Simon, Seymour. *Killer Whales* (1–3). Series: See More Readers. 2002, North-South paper $3.95 (978-1-58717-142-0). 32pp. Stunning photographs placed opposite a few lines of text give basic information about killer whales in this beginning reader. (Rev: BL 7/02; HBG 10/02; SLJ 4/02) [599.5]

22591 Skerry, Brian. *A Whale on Her Own: The True Story of Wilma the Beluga Whale* (3–4). Photos by author. 2000, Blackbirch LB $26.19 (978-1-56711-431-7). 32pp. This true story tells of the friendly relationship that developed between a diver and a beluga whale in Chedabucto Bay, Nova Scotia. (Rev: HBG 9/00; SLJ 10/00) [595.5]

22592 Sobol, Richard. *Adelina's Whales* (2–5). Illus. 2003, Penguin $17.99 (978-0-525-47110-3). 32pp. Readers meet 10-year-old Adelina, who lives in a simple home in Baja California and each winter awaits the arrival of gray whales in the lagoon — and of the tourists who watch them; facts about the gray whale and a foreword about protectionist efforts accompany this photoessay. (Rev: BL 7/03; HBG 10/03; SLJ 9/03) [639]

22593 Stille, Darlene R. *I Am a Whale: The Life of a Humpback Whale* (K–3). Illus. by Todd Ouren. Series: I Live in the Ocean. 2004, Picture Window LB $25.26 (978-1-4048-0600-9). 24pp. A humpback whale describes its life — diet, activities, and so forth. (Rev: SLJ 1/05) [599.5]

22594 Thomson, Sarah L. *Amazing Whales!* (1–3). Illus. Series: I Can Read! 2005, HarperCollins LB $17.89 (978-0-06-054466-9). 32pp. Simple, easy-reader text introduces blue whales, killer whales, sperm whales, dolphins, and porpoises and their characteristics, communication, and endangered status. (Rev: BL 5/15/05; SLJ 1/05) [599.5]

Microscopes and Microbiology

22595 Brown, Jordan D. *Micro Mania: A Really Close-Up Look at Bacteria, Bedbugs and the Zillions of Other Gross Little Creatures That Live In, On and All Around You!* (4–6). 2009, Imagine $19.95 (978-0-9823064-2-0). 80pp. Close-up gross-out photographs of bacteria, microbes, fungi, and other parasites are presented here along with information about the scientists who study them plus some activities. Lexile 1010L (Rev: SLJ 3/10) [500]

22596 Kramer, Stephen. *Hidden Worlds: Looking Through a Scientist's Microscope* (4–7). Series: Scientists in the Field. 2001, Houghton Mifflin $16.00 (978-0-618-05546-3). Striking photographs, mostly taken with electron microscopes by scientist Dennis Kunkel, serve to illustrate this explanation of how scientists use microscopes in their work. (Rev: BL 8/01; HB 1–2/02; HBG 3/02; SLJ 9/01*) [570]

22597 Latta, Sara L. *The Good, the Bad, the Slimy: The Secret Life of Microbes* (5–8). Photos by Dennis Kunkel. 2006, Enslow LB $31.93 (978-0-7660-1294-3). Bright photography and clear explanations will engage browsers and please report writers. (Rev: LMC 4–5/07; SLJ 8/07)

22598 Lee, Kimberly Fekany. *Cells* (4–6). Illus. Series: Mission: Science. 2008, Compass Point LB $26.60 (978-0-7565-3954-2). 40pp. An appealing exploration of the structure of plant and animal cells, cell movement, and cell reproduction; also includes many photographs and illustrations plus an activity. (Rev: LMC 3/09; SLJ 6/09) [571.6]

22599 Levine, Shar, and Leslie Johnstone. *The Ultimate Guide to Your Microscope* (5–9). 2008, Sterling paper $9.95 (978-1-4027-4329-0). 144pp. After covering the basics of using a microscope, this volume presents 41 hands-on activities. (Rev: LMC 10/08; SLJ 11/08) [570.28]

22600 Silverstein, Alvin. *Cells* (4–8). Series: Science Concepts. 2002, Millbrook LB $26.90 (978-0-7613-2254-2). The functions and components of plant and animal cells are discussed along with such topics as cloning, cell fusion, and stem cell research. (Rev: BL 9/15/02; HBG 3/03) [574.87]

22601 Thomas, Peggy. *Bacteria and Viruses* (5–8). Series: Lucent Library of Science and Technology. 2005, Gale LB $29.95 (978-1-59018-438-7). Introduces the scientists who discovered bacteria and viruses and how we fight ones that harm us and attempt to use others to our benefit. (Rev: BL 1/05)

22602 Walker, Richard. *Microscopic Life* (4–8). Series: Kingfisher Knowledge. 2004, Kingfisher $11.95 (978-0-7534-5778-8). A well-illustrated look at the tiniest living things — bacteria, viruses, mites, fungi, and molds, for example — and how we study them and attempt to use them to our benefit. (Rev: BL 9/1/04; SLJ 1/05) [579]

Oceanography

GENERAL

22603 Berger, Melvin, and Gilda Berger. *What Makes an Ocean Wave? Questions and Answers About Oceans and Ocean Life* (3–6). Illus. 2001, Scholastic $14.95 (978-0-439-09588-4). 48pp. In question-and-answer format, this title tackles topics of interest both to browsers and report writers. (Rev: BL 7/01; HBG 10/01) [551.46]

22604 Castaldo, Nancy F. *Oceans: An Activity Guide for Ages 6–9* (3–5). Illus. 2002, Chicago Review paper $14.95 (978-1-55652-443-1). 134pp. All about the world's oceans, including their plant and animal life, folklore, and currents and tides, with related crafts and experiments. (Rev: BL 5/15/02; SLJ 3/02) [372.3]

22605 Chambers, Catherine. *Oceans and Seas* (3–5). Series: Mapping Earthforms. 2000, Heinemann LB $21.36 (978-1-57572-526-0). 32pp. A basic overview that describes the characteristics of oceans and seas, life within them, and how environmental factors like global warming affect them. (Rev: HBG 3/01; SLJ 8/00) [551.46]

22606 Cobb, Allan B. *Super Science Projects About Oceans* (4–7). Series: Psyched for Science. 2000, Rosen LB $26.50 (978-0-8239-3174-3). Although the format is unattractive, this book contains six fine experiments that explore concepts involving the ocean. (Rev: SLJ 7/00) [551.46]

22607 Davies, Nicola. *Oceans and Seas* (K–3). Series: Kingfisher Young Knowledge. 2004, Houghton $8.95 (978-0-7534-5758-0). 48pp. Attractive double-page spreads with many illustrations and diagrams present basic information on salt water, tides, and marine plants and animals and the dangers they face. (Rev: BL 9/1/04) [551.46]

22608 Gray, Samantha. *Ocean* (3–5). Illus. Series: Eye Wonder. 2001, DK LB $17.99 (978-0-7894-8180-1); paper $9.99 (978-0-7894-7852-8). 48pp. The ocean, marine animals, and marine research are among the topics tackled in this fact-filled book. (Rev: BL 12/1/01; HBG 3/02) [591.77]

22609 Hague, Bradley. *Alien Deep: Revealing the Mysterious Living World at the Bottom of the Ocean* (4–7). Illus. 2012, National Geographic $17.95 (978-1-4263-1067-6); LB $26.90 (978-1-4263-1068-3). 48pp. Hague explores hydrothermal vents and the creatures that live in them in this engaging volume. Outstanding Science Trade Book for Students K-12. (Rev: BL 10/15/12; SLJ 4/13) [551.2]

22610 Harrison, David L. *Oceans: The Vast, Mysterious Deep* (2–3). Illus. by Cheryl Nathan. Series: Earthworks. 2003, Boyds Mills $15.95 (978-1-59078-018-3). 32pp. The oceans, their movement, and the life they support are shown in bright illustrations and brief, informative text. (Rev: BL 1/1–15/04; HBG 4/04; SLJ 1/04) [577.7]

22611 Hirschi, Ron. *Ocean Seasons* (1–3). Illus. by Kirsten Carlson. 2007, Sylvan Dell $15.95 (978-0-9777423-2-5); paper $8.95 (978-1-9343591-6-7). An engaging exploration of the ways in which the seasons affect the oceans and ocean wildlife, looking in particular at marine and land ecology in the Pacific Northwest; with attractive illustrations and well-written text. (Rev: LMC 11/07; SLJ 10/07) [577.7]

22612 Hodge, Susie. *Ocean Survival* (4–6). Illus. Series: Extreme Habitats. 2007, Gareth Stevens LB $25.27 (978-0-8368-8247-6). 32pp. This well-designed title combines high visual appeal and accessible facts to make an attractive and informative overview of the oceans, the plants and animals that live there, how people use the oceans, and the threats the oceans face. (Rev: LMC 1/08; SLJ 12/07) [551.46]

22613 Hynes, Margaret. *Oceans and Seas* (4–6). Illus. by Thomas Bayley. Series: Navigators. 2010, Kingfisher $12.99 (978-0-7534-6415-1). 48pp. This attractive volume introduces all aspects of the marine environment, covering everything from tides and waves to pollution, preservation, marine archaeology, and future threats and opportunities. (Rev: BL 9/1/10; SLJ 10/1/10) [551.46]

22614 Kalman, Bobbie. *The ABCs of Oceans* (2–4). Illus. Series: ABCs of the Natural World. 2007, Crabtree LB $26.60 (978-0-7787-3412-3); paper $7.95 (978-0-7787-3432-1). Butterfly fish, camouflage, dolphins, and eels are among the topics covered in this alphabetical look at the oceans that also includes krait, nudibranchs, and zones of the ocean. (Rev: BL 10/15/07; LMC 5/08) [591.77]

22615 Littlefield, Cindy A. *Awesome Ocean Science!* (3–5). Illus. by Sarah Rakitin. Series: Kids Can. 2003, Williamson paper $12.95 (978-1-885593-71-9). 120pp. This informative book looks at the water cycle, the oceans and their animal life, and at conservation, and provides simple projects that illustrate or reinforce some of the basic concepts. (Rev: BL 1/1–15/03; SLJ 5/03) [551.46]

22616 McMillan, Beverly, and John A. Musick. *Oceans* (5–8). Illus. Series: Insiders. 2007, Simon & Schuster $16.99 (978-1-4169-3859-0). An introduction to Earth's oceans, marine life, ocean migrations, sea vents, coastal

and polar seas, and so forth, with eye-catching illustrations. (Rev: LMC 10/07; SLJ 12/07) [551.46]

22617 Pyers, Greg. *Ocean Explorer* (2–4). Illus. Series: Habitat Explorer. 2004, Raintree LB $25.70 (978-1-4109-0510-9). 32pp. This photo-filled exploration of oceans looks at the plants and animals found there, plus environmental threats posed by pollution and development.

22618 Stone, Lynn M. *Oceans* (1–3). Illus. Series: Biomes of North America. 2003, Rourke $20.64 (978-1-58952-686-0). 24pp. For young researchers, this is an excellent introduction to this biome, with clear, simple text, photographs, and maps. (Rev: BL 10/15/03) [577.7]

22619 VanCleave, Janice. *Janice VanCleave's Oceans for Every Kid: Easy Activities That Make Learning Science Fun* (5–7). Series: Science for Every Kid. 1996, Wiley paper $12.95 (978-0-471-12453-5). This book gives good background information about oceans plus a number of entertaining and instructive projects and activities. (Rev: BL 4/15/96; SLJ 5/96) [551.46]

22620 Vogel, Carole G. *Dangerous Crossings* (5–8). Illus. Series: The Restless Sea. 2003, Watts LB $30.50 (978-0-531-12325-6); paper $12.95 (978-0-531-16679-6). 79pp. Ranging widely from tales of endurance at sea to pirates and problems created by global warming, this is an arresting account. (Rev: BL 1/1/04; SLJ 1/04) [910.4]

22621 Vogel, Carole G. *Human Impact* (5–9). Series: The Restless Sea. 2003, Watts LB $30.50 (978-0-531-12323-2). 95pp. An examination of how mankind is endangering the sea and its creatures through activities including coastal development, global warming, and oil spills. (Rev: SLJ 3/04) [333.91]

22622 Woodward, John. *Oceans Atlas: An Amazing Aquatic Adventure* (4–6). Illus. 2007, DK $19.99 (978-0-7566-2557-3). 96pp. Readers will enjoy the photographs and maps of the world's oceans and their features. Facts about ocean exploration, oceanographers, conservation efforts, and the 2004 tsunami add interest. With transparent overlays and an interactive CD-ROM. (Rev: SLJ 5/07)

22623 Young, Karen Romano. *Across the Wide Ocean: The Why, How, and Where of Navigation for Humans and Animals at Sea* (5–7). Illus. by author. 2007, HarperCollins $18.99 (978-0-06-009086-9). Before satellite global positioning technology, humans had to use many different methods to navigate at sea, and this book creatively explores many of these methods as well as those of sea creatures including turtles and whales. (Rev: SLJ 7/07) [623.89]

22624 Zim, Herbert S., and Lester Ingle. *Seashores* (5–8). 1991, Western $21.27 (978-0-307-64496-1). This is a guide to animals and plants found along the beaches.

CURRENTS, TIDES, AND WAVES

22625 Adamson, Thomas K. *Tsunamis* (2–4). Illus. 2005, Capstone LB $22.60 (978-0-7368-5248-7). 24pp. This volume, which explores the causes and destructive capacities of tsunamis, includes information on the December 26, 2004, tragedy. (Rev: BL 6/1–15/05) [551.40]

22626 Allen, Judy. *Higher Ground* (5–8). 2006, Chrysalis paper $8.99 (978-1-84458-581-6). First-person accounts of survivors and rescue workers mixed with fictional treatments based on fact portray the impact on children of the deadly Indian Ocean tsunami of December 2004. (Rev: BCCB 5/06; BL 2/1/06; SLJ 3/06) [363.349]

22627 Fine, Jil. *Tsunamis* (3–5). Illus. Series: Natural Disaster. 2006, Children's Pr. LB $24.50 (978-0-531-12444-4). 48pp. A photo-filled exploration of tsunamis and the geological events that can cause these massive tidal waves, focusing in particular on the deadly Indian Ocean tsunami of December 2004. (Rev: BL 11/1/06) [551.46]

22628 Hamilton, John. *Tsunamis* (3–4). Series: Nature's Fury. 2005, ABDO LB $24.21 (978-1-59679-333-0). 32pp. Well-chosen color photographs and clear text explore tsunamis, their causes and impact, and specific tidal waves of the past. (Rev: SLJ 3/06) [551.55]

22629 Karwoski, Gail. *Tsunami: The True Story of an April Fools' Day Disaster* (4–7). Illus. by John MacDonald. 2006, Darby Creek $17.95 (978-1-58196-044-0). Karwoski tells the story of a devastating 1946 tsunami, and expands the coverage to other destructive waves and their causes, effects, and the measures being taken to alert residents to their arrival. (Rev: SLJ 1/07) [363.34]

22630 Mara, Wil. *How Do Waves Form?* (2–4). Series: Tell Me Why, Tell Me How. 2010, Marshall Cavendish LB $20.95 (978-0-7614-4829-7). 32pp. With information on such topics as the relationship between wind and waves and how tsunamis are formed, this volume introduces essential concepts in easy-to-read text and lots of helpful illustrations. (Rev: BL 3/1/11; SLJ 2/1/11) [551.46]

22631 Morris, Ann, and Heidi Larson. *Tsunami: Helping Each Other* (2–4). 2005, Millbrook $15.95 (978-0-7613-9501-0). 48pp. Focusing on the experiences of two Thai brothers, 8-year-old Chaiya and 12-year-old Chaipreak, who lose their father to the tsunami, this is a more personal treatment than many of the books about tsunamis and includes many photographs of the disaster and the progress toward recovery. (Rev: BL 12/1/05; SLJ 7/06) [959.304]

22632 Morrison, Taylor. *Tsunami Warning* (4–6). Illus. 2007, Houghton $17.00 (978-0-618-73463-4). 32pp. Morrison discusses the tsunamis of 1946 and 1957 in this overview of warning systems and how they work. (Rev: BL 2/1/07) [551.47]

22633 Spilsbury, Louise, and Richard Spilsbury. *Sweeping Tsunamis* (3–6). Series: Awesome Forces of Nature. 2010, Heinemann LB $29 (978-1-4329-3785-0). 32pp. "Where do tsunamis happen?" "Who helps when tsunamis happen?" These and other questions are answered — and case studies look at famous events — in this eye-catching volume. (Rev: LMC 11–12/10; SLJ 9/1/10) [551.46]

22634 Steele, Christy. *Tsunamis* (3–5). Illus. 2001, Raintree LB $22.83 (978-0-7398-4706-0). 32pp. The authors look at our knowledge of tidal waves and their causes, and discuss the ways in which we can protect ourselves from danger. (Rev: HBG 3/02; SLJ 2/02) [551.55]

22635 Stewart, Gail B. *Catastrophe in Southern Asia: The Tsunami of 2004* (5–8). Series: Overview. 2005, Gale LB $29.95 (978-1-59018-831-6). An information-packed review of the tsunami itself, the human costs of the disaster, and the reconstruction efforts. (Rev: SLJ 12/05)

22636 Torres, John A. *Disaster in the Indian Ocean: Tsunami 2004* (5–8). Series: Monumental Milestones: Great Events of Modern Times. 2005, Mitchell Lane LB $29.95 (978-1-58415-344-3). This slim volume, uneven in its coverage, nonetheless offers a chilling overview of the devastating Indian Ocean tsunami of December 2004 and includes a number of eyewitness accounts. (Rev: BL 10/15/05; SLJ 12/05) [909]

22637 Vogel, Carole G. *Savage Waters* (5–8). Illus. Series: The Restless Sea. 2003, Watts LB $30.50 (978-0-531-12321-8); paper $12.95 (978-0-531-16682-6). 79pp. An entertaining and attractive discussion of the origins of the world's oceans and seas and the forces that influence waves, tides, and tsunamis. Also use *Shifting Shores* (2003). (Rev: BL 1/1/04; SLJ 1/04) [551.46]

22638 Wade, Mary Dodson. *Tsunami: Monster Waves* (4–8). Series: American Disasters. 2002, Enslow LB $23.93 (978-0-7660-1786-3). 48pp. This book explains in photographs and text how these giant sea swells are created, how they are tracked, and their effects. (Rev: BL 6/1–15/02; HBG 10/02; SLJ 10/02) [551.55]

SEASHORES AND TIDAL POOLS

22639 Arnosky, Jim. *Beach Combing: Exploring the Seashore* (PS–2). 2004, Penguin $15.99 (978-0-525-47104-2). 32pp. Arnosky explores the wonders of a tropical beach and its wildlife. (Rev: BL 7/04; SLJ 7/04) [578.769]

22640 Arnosky, Jim. *Following the Coast* (3–5). Illus. 2004, HarperCollins $15.99 (978-0-688-17117-9). 32pp. The life and landmarks of the salt marshes of the Atlantic Coast, from Florida northward to Delaware, are the focus of this attractive blend of narrative and artwork. (Rev: BL 2/15/04; SLJ 5/04) [591.769]

22641 Brenner, Barbara. *One Small Place by the Sea* (2–4). Illus. by Tom Leonard. 2004, HarperCollins $16.99 (978-0-688-17182-7). 32pp. The abundant life in a tidal pool is explored in accessible text and realistic illustrations. (Rev: BL 3/1/04; SLJ 4/04) [577.69]

22642 Davidson, Avelyn. *Beach Biology* (3–5). Illus. 2007, Children's Pr. LB $25.00 (978-0-531-17764-8); paper $6.95 (978-0-531-15495-3). 36pp. A well-designed introduction to topics including tides, waves and currents, rocky and sandy shores, coral reefs, and so forth. (Rev: LMC 1/08; SLJ 11/07) [577.5]

22643 Hunter, Anne. *What's in the Tide Pool?* (K–2). Illus. 2000, Houghton $5.95 (978-0-618-01510-8). 32pp.

Ten animals that live in tidal pools, such as the sea anemone, herring gull, hermit crab, and barnacle, are introduced in this little book. (Rev: BL 9/15/00; HBG 3/01) [578.769]

22644 Johansson, Philip. *The Seashore: A Saltwater Web of Life* (4–6). Illus. Series: Wonderful Water Biomes. 2007, Enslow LB $23.93 (978-0-7660-2811-1). 48pp. After an account of a midnight search for a leatherback turtle on a tropical beach, this title looks at the plants and animals that live on seashores. (Rev: SLJ 1/08) [577.69]

22645 Kudlinski, Kathleen V. *The Seaside Switch* (K–2). Illus. by Lindy Burnett. 2007, NorthWord $16.95 (978-1-55971-964-3). 32pp. An appealing look at the changing of the tides and the seashore and the effects on the varied life there. (Rev: BL 3/15/07) [577.69]

22646 Pringle, Laurence. *Come to the Ocean's Edge* (K–3). Illus. by Michael Chesworth. 2003, Boyds Mills $15.95 (978-1-56397-779-4). 32pp. Watercolor paintings depict the shoreline and the wildlife found there in daytime and at night. (Rev: BL 2/1/04; HBG 4/04; SLJ 10/03) [577.7]

22647 Serafini, Frank. *Looking Closely Along the Shore* (PS–3). Illus. 2008, Kids Can $15.95 (978-1-55453-141-7). 40pp. Close-up photographs and an interactive format make this an appealing introduction to seashore plants and animals. (Rev: BLO 6/17/08; LMC 10/08; SLJ 4/08) [578.769]

22648 Theodorou, Rod. *Along the Seashore* (2–4). Series: Amazing Journeys. 2000, Heinemann LB $22.79 (978-1-57572-483-6). 32pp. This brief overview of seashores focuses on several specific plants and animals found there. (Rev: HBG 3/01; SLJ 7/00) [591]

22649 Waldron, Melanie. *Coasts* (3–5). Series: Mapping Earthforms. 2007, Heinemann LB $28.21 (978-1-4034-9605-8). 32pp. With maps, diagrams, tables, and color photographs, this title looks at how coasts were formed, the action of tides and waves, erosion, plants and animals, and important examples (one chapter is titled "A Way of Life — Iceland"). (Rev: SLJ 10/07) [508.314]

22650 Wechsler, Doug. *Marvels in the Muck: Life in the Salt Marshes* (3–6). Illus. by author. 2008, Boyds Mills $17.95 (978-1-59078-588-1). 48pp. This year in the life of a salt marsh follows the seasons in text and photographs. (Rev: BL 12/1/08; LMC 3/09; SLJ 12/08) [578.769]

22651 Wilson, Hannah. *Seashore* (PS–1). Illus. by Simon Mendez. Series: Flip the Flaps. 2010, Kingfisher $9.99 (978-0-7534-6445-8). 32pp. With a single question-and-answer flap per spread, this appealing book presents various types of seashore with large-font text and realistic paintings. (Rev: BL 2/1/11; SLJ 4/11) [551.458]

UNDERWATER EXPLORATION

22652 Collard, Sneed B., III. *The Deep-Sea Floor* (2–4). Illus. by Gregory Wenzel. 2003, Charlesbridge $16.95 (978-1-57091-402-7); paper $6.95 (978-1-57091-403-4). A look at the amazing discoveries gleaned from the exploration of the deep-sea floor, including plant and animal life and geologic finds, with watercolor illustrations. (Rev: BL 2/1/03; HBG 10/03; SLJ 7/03) [591.779]

22653 Lindop, Laurie. *Venturing the Deep Sea* (4–8). Series: Science on the Edge. 2005, Twenty-First Century LB $27.93 (978-0-7613-2701-1). A behind-the-scenes look at the technology employed by modern-day undersea explorers, with a clear explanation of the types of knowledge these researchers are seeking. (Rev: SLJ 8/06; VOYA 4/06) [551.46]

22654 Mallory, Kenneth. *Adventure Beneath the Sea: Living in an Underwater Science Station* (5–8). Illus. by Brian Skerry. 2010, Boyds Mills $18.95 (978-159078607-9). 48pp. This readable book describes life in an underwater science station on a reef off the Florida Keys, with discussion of the training required, the living conditions, and the tasks performed. (Rev: BL 12/1/10; LMC 1–2/11; SLJ 11/1/10) [551.46]

22655 Mallory, Kenneth. *Diving to a Deep-Sea Volcano* (4–7). Illus. 2006, Houghton Mifflin $17.00 (978-0-618-33205-2). Take a dive with marine biologists as they explore deep-sea volcanoes and the creatures that live and thrive around them; scientific method, adventure, biography, and insight into a career are intertwined in this portrait of a marine biologist's work in an underwater habitat. (Rev: BL 12/1/06; SLJ 2/07) [551.2]

22656 Matsen, Brad. *The Incredible Record-Setting Deep-Sea Dive of the Bathysphere* (4–6). Series: Incredible Deep-Sea Adventures. 2003, Enslow LB $23.93 (978-0-7660-2188-4). 48pp. An attractive look at early bathyspheres and undersea discoveries. Also use *The Incredible Submersible Alvin Discovers a Strange Deep-Sea World* (2003), about more-recent explorations. (Rev: HBG 4/04; SLJ 1/04) [551.46]

22657 Pitkin, Linda. *Journey Under the Sea* (3–6). Illus. 2003, Oxford $19.95 (978-0-19-521972-2). 48pp. In words and pictures, marine photographer Pitkin paints a vivid portrait of her visit to coral reefs off the coast of Indonesia. (Rev: BL 2/15/04; HBG 4/04) [578]

22658 Platt, Richard. *Shipwreck* (4–9). Series: Eyewitness Books. 1997, Knopf LB $20.99 (978-0-679-98569-3). An overview of the causes and consequences of the world's most famous maritime disasters. (Rev: BL 12/15/97) [387.2]

22659 Sandler, Michael. *Oceans: Surviving in the Deep Sea* (3–5). Illus. Series: X-treme Places. 2005, Bearport LB $25.27 (978-1-59716-087-2). 32pp. This overview of the deep ocean environment is given added punch by the first-person account of marine biologist Dr. Sylvia Earle, who has explored the ocean depths in submersibles and pressurized suits. (Rev: SLJ 1/06) [551.46]

22660 *Sunk! Exploring Underwater Archaeology* (5–8). Series: Buried Worlds. 1994, Lerner LB $28.75 (978-0-8225-3205-7). Provides a general overview of how archaeologists interpret underwater discoveries to learn about aspects of ancient trade, commerce, and history. (Rev: BL 10/15/94; SLJ 9/94) [930.1]

Pets

GENERAL AND MISCELLANEOUS

22661 Altman, Linda J. *Parrots* (4–6). Illus. Series: Perfect Pets. 2000, Marshall Cavendish LB $25.64 (978-0-7614-1102-4). 32pp. Full-color photographs and accessible text introduce parrots, their physical characteristics, and how to care for them. (Rev: BL 3/15/01; HBG 3/01) [636.6]

22662 Barnes, Julia. *Pet Guinea Pigs* (2–5). 2006, Gareth Stevens LB $24.00 (978-0-8368-6779-4). 32pp. This handy guide full of advice on caring for a guinea pig also examines the qualities that make them desirable pets, looks at how they communicate, and explores the guinea pig's roots in the wild. Also use *Pet Rabbits* (2006). (Rev: SLJ 2/07) [636.9]

22663 Barnes, Julia. *Pet Parakeets* (2–5). 2006, Gareth Stevens LB $24.00 (978-0-8368-6780-0). 32pp. This handy guide full of advice on caring for a parakeet also examines the qualities that make them such popular pets, looks at how they communicate, and explores their roots in the wild. (Rev: SLJ 12/06) [636.6]

22664 Bjorklund, Ruth. *Rabbits* (2–4). Series: Great Pets. 2007, Marshall Cavendish LB $19.95 (978-0-7614-2708-7). 48pp. A solid introduction to the pleasures and responsibilities of caring for rabbits. (Rev: LMC 8/08; SLJ 4/08) [636.932]

22665 Bozzo, Linda. *My First Bird* (1–3). Series: My First Pet Library from the American Humane Association. 2007, Enslow LB $22.60 (978-0-7660-2749-7). 32pp. New pet owners will learn all the facts about caring for birds and will enjoy looking at the pictures of birds and their owners. (Rev: SLJ 6/07)

22666 Buckmaster, Marjorie L. *Freshwater Fishes* (2–4). Series: Great Pets. 2007, Marshall Cavendish LB $19.95 (978-0-7614-2712-4). 48pp. A solid introduction to the pleasures and responsibilities of caring for fish. (Rev: LMC 8/08; SLJ 4/08) [639.34]

22667 Davis, Kathryn Gibbs. *Wacky White House Pets* (2–4). Illus. by David Johnson. 2004, Scholastic LB $16.95 (978-0-439-44373-9). 48pp. Presidential pets have included John Quincy Adam's alligator, Reagan's First Fish, and Coolidge's raccoon; all White House occupants are mentioned in the appendix to this entertaining book. (Rev: BL 10/1/04; SLJ 11/04) [636.088]

22668 Doudna, Kelly. *Frisky Ferrets* (K–2). Illus. by C. A. Nobens. Series: Perfect Pets. 2007, ABDO LB $19.93 (978-1-59928-748-5). 24pp. Caring for ferrets looks like fun in this book that combines photographs and drawings of ferrets and their happy owners. (Rev: SLJ 7/07)

22669 Fritzsche, Peter. *Hamsters* (2–5). Illus. Series: Complete Pet Owner's Manual. 2008, Barron's paper $7.99 (978-0-7641-3927-7). 64pp. A comprehensive introduction to the care of hamsters, with information on their physical characteristics and behavior. (Rev: BLO 7/31/08) [636.935]

22670 Ganeri, Anita. *Guinea Pigs* (1–3). Series: A Pet's Life. 2003, Heinemann LB $22.79 (978-1-4034-3996-3). 32pp. All about pet guinea pigs and how to care for them, with detailed information on their physiology and life cycle. (Rev: SLJ 6/04) [636.9]

22671 Ganeri, Anita. *Hamsters* (1–3). Series: A Pet's Life. 2003, Heinemann LB $22.79 (978-1-4034-3997-0). 32pp. Presents clear information on hamsters and their physiology, habits, and care and feeding; suitable for beginning readers. (Rev: SLJ 6/04) [636.9]

22672 Ganeri, Anita. *Rabbits* (1–3). Series: A Pet's Life. 2003, Heinemann LB $22.79 (978-1-4034-3995-6). 32pp. A book on keeping rabbits as pets, with help on their care and feeding, habits, and physiology. (Rev: SLJ 6/04) [636.9]

22673 Gelman, Amy. *My Pet Ferrets* (2–5). Photos by Andy King. Series: All About Pets. 2000, Lerner LB $22.60 (978-0-8225-2264-5). 64pp. The care and feeding of ferrets are covered in this book that also gives details on grooming, bathing, and even litter-box training. (Rev: BL 1/1–15/01; HBG 3/01; SLJ 11/00) [636]

22674 Gibbons, Gail. *Rabbits, Rabbits and More Rabbits!* (K–3). Illus. 2000, Holiday House $16.95 (978-0-8234-1486-4). 32pp. Simple text and colored drawings introduce different types of rabbits, their physical characteristics, habits, behavior, and how to care for them. (Rev: BCCB 3/00; BL 1/1–15/00; HBG 9/00; SLJ 3/00) [636.9]

22675 Gutman, Bill. *Adopting Pets: How to Choose Your New Best Friend* (3–6). Illus. by Anne Canevari Green. Series: Pet Friends. 2001, Millbrook LB $22.90 (978-0-7613-1863-7). 64pp. This book gives special tips on choosing a pet with attention to topics such as the kind of home and food it will need and the attention required. (Rev: BCCB 3/01; BL 3/1/01; HBG 10/01) [636]

22676 Gutman, Bill. *Becoming Best Friends with Your Iguana, Snake, or Turtle* (3–6). Illus. by Anne Canevari Green. Series: Pet Friends. 2001, Millbrook LB $24.90 (978-0-7613-1862-0). 64pp. Explains the special needs of reptiles that are kept as pets. (Rev: BL 3/1/01; HBG 10/01) [636]

22677 Hamilton, Lynn. *Caring for Your Bird* (3–5). Illus. 2002, Weigl LB $16.95 (978-1-59036-037-8). 32pp. A guide to choosing and looking after a feathered pet with information on different avian breeds. (Rev: BL 12/1/02; HBG 3/03) [636.6]

22678 Hamilton, Lynn. *Ferret* (3–5). Illus. Series: My Pet. 2009, Weigl LB $26 (978-160596096-8). 32pp. Facts about ferrets, including "Ferret Firsts," are combined with tips on choosing and caring for these animals. (Rev: BL 4/1/10) [636.976]

22679 Haney, Johannah. *Turtles* (2–4). Series: Great Pets. 2007, Marshall Cavendish LB $19.95 (978-0-7614-2709-4). 48pp. A solid introduction to the pleasures and responsibilities of caring for turtles. (Rev: LMC 8/08; SLJ 4/08) [639.3]

22680 Hansen, Rosanna. *Animal Rescuers: A Chapter Book* (2–5). Series: True Tales. 2003, Children's Pr. LB

$22.50 (978-0-516-22915-7). 48pp. Heroic animals featured in these four tales include the guide dog named Salty that led his owner from the World Trade Center on 9/11. (Rev: SLJ 1/04) [636.088]

22681 Heos, Bridget. *Do You Really Want a Bird?* (PS–1). Illus. by Katya Longhi. Series: Do You Really Want a Pet? 2013, Amicus $18.95 (978-160753205-7). 24pp. A practical guide to the responsibilities and joys of owning a pet bird. (Rev: BL 10/1/13) [636.6]

22682 Hernandez-Divers, Sonia. *Geckos* (4–8). Illus. Series: Keeping Unusual Pets. 2003, Heinemann LB $25.64 (978-1-4034-0282-0). 48pp. An appealing and informative introduction to geckos that provides much practical guidance on actually keeping one as a pet. Also use *Chinchillas, Ferrets, Snakes* (all 2002), and *Rats* (2003). (Rev: BL 3/15/03; HBG 10/03; SLJ 4/03) [639.3]

22683 Hinds, Kathryn. *Hamsters and Gerbils* (4–6). Illus. Series: Perfect Pets. 2000, Marshall Cavendish LB $25.64 (978-0-7614-1104-8). 32pp. Gives tips on housing, feeding, training, and keeping these pets safe. (Rev: BL 3/15/01; HBG 3/01) [636]

22684 Jenkins, Steve. *Dogs and Cats* (1–3). Illus. 2007, Houghton $16.00 (978-0-618-50767-2). 40pp. Start at one end and you read about dogs and their characteristics; from the other end you have cats; and in the middle of this appealing and informative package, a portrait of a dog and cat happily coexisting. (Rev: BCCB 6/07; BL 5/1/07; HB 5/07; SLJ 5/07) [636.7]

22685 Keenan, Sheila. *Animals in the House: A History of Pets and People* (4–6). Illus. by author. 2007, Scholastic $17.99 (978-0-439-69286-1). 112pp. This eye-catching volume provides a history of how humans began to keep pets, chapters on specific animals, and finally a chapter about how humans have dealt with the death of pets throughout the ages. (Rev: BL 7/07; SLJ 7/07) [636.088]

22686 Kennedy, Marge. *Pets at the White House* (PS–1). Illus. Series: Scholastic News Nonfiction Readers. 2009, Scholastic LB $20.00 (978-0-531-21096-3); paper $6.95 (978-0-531-22433-5). 24pp. A cheerful collective overview of presidential pets, which include seven goats and a herd of sheep, with highlighted vocabulary and opportunities to practice counting. (Rev: BL 4/1/09; SLJ 5/09) [975.3]

22687 Kent, Deborah. *Animal Helpers for the Disabled* (5–7). Illus. Series: Watts Library: Disability. 2003, Watts LB $25.50 (978-0-531-12017-0). 64pp. Stories of animal accomplishments draw readers into this account, which covers the history of service animals, the kinds of animals used, and the training they undergo. (Rev: BL 10/15/03; LMC 11/03; SLJ 9/03) [636.08]

22688 Leavitt, Amie Jane. *Care for a Pet Chimpanzee* (2–4). 2007, Mitchell Lane LB $25.70 (978-1-58415-607-9). 32pp. Is a chimpanzee the right pet for your family? Probably not, but this straightforward book will help readers understand the pros and cons of chimp ownership. Also use *Care for a Pet Tarantula* and *Care for*

a Pet Mouse (both 2007). (Rev: LMC 1/08; SLJ 10/07) [636.9885]

22689 Love, Ann, and Jane Drake. *Talking Tails: The Incredible Connection Between People and Their Pets* (4–6). Illus. by Bill Slavin. 2010, Tundra $22.95 (978-0-88776-884-2). 80pp. Human-animal relationships from familiar (dogs and cats) to less common (reptiles, for example) are explored, with information on body language and pet care. (Rev: BL 4/15/10; SLJ 3/10) [636.088]

22690 McKay, Sindy. *About Pets* (K–2). Series: We Both Read. 2003, Treasure Bay $7.99 (978-1-891327-41-4). 40pp. Designed to be read together by a child and an adult, this book looks at what's involved in caring for a pet. (Rev: HBG 10/03; SLJ 7/03) [636.088]

22691 McNicholas, June. *Ferrets* (3–6). Series: Keeping Unusual Pets. 2002, Heinemann LB $25.64 (978-1-4034-0281-3). 48pp. A pratical, no-nonsense guide to the choice of and responsibilities of caring for such a pet. (Rev: HBG 10/03; SLJ 4/03) [636.9]

22692 Moberg, Julia. *Presidential Pets: The Weird, Wacky, Little, Big, Scary, Strange Animals That Have Lived in the White House* (4–7). Illus. by Jeff Albrecht Studios. 2012, Charlesbridge $14.95 (978-193614079-4). 176pp. With poems, bulleted facts, and lively illustrations, this is a solid introduction to animal residents of the White House from Washington to Obama. Lexile NC920L (Rev: BL 7/12; LMC 3–4/13; SLJ 7/12) [973]

22693 Nelson, Robin. *Pet Frog* (PS). Series: Classroom Pets. 2002, Lerner LB $18.60 (978-0-8225-1271-4). 24pp. With only a few sentences of text and full-page color illustrations, this book introduces the frog as a pet and describes its care and feeding. Also use *Pet Guinea Pig, Pet Hamster,* and *Pet Hermit Crab* (all 2002). (Rev: BL 10/15/02; HBG 3/03; SLJ 10/02) [597.8]

22694 Nelson, Robin. *Pet Hamster* (PS–K). Illus. Series: Classroom Pets. 2002, Lerner LB $18.60 (978-0-8225-1269-1). 24pp. A preschooler's introduction to the care and feeding of classroom hamsters, with relevant facts, a glossary, and an index. Also use *Pet Guinea Pig* (2002). (Rev: BL 10/15/02; HBG 3/03) [636.9]

22695 Nelson, Robin. *Pet Hermit Crab* (PS–K). Illus. Series: Classroom Pets. 2002, Lerner LB $18.60 (978-0-8225-1270-7). 24pp. A preschooler's introduction to the care and feeding of classroom hermit crabs, with relevant facts, a glossary, and an index. (Rev: HBG 3/03)

22696 Niven, Felicia Lowenstein. *Learning to Care for Small Mammals* (2–4). Series: Beginning Pet Care with American Humane. 2010, Enslow LB $23.93 (978-0-7660-3195-1). 48pp. After a brief history of small mammals (rabbits, ferrets, and so forth), this book describes the environment you need to provide for them and the various problems and challenges you will face. (Rev: SLJ 3/1/11) [636.9]

22697 Rayner, Matthew. *Hamster* (2–4). Photos by Frank Greenaway. Series: I Am Your Pet. 2004, Gareth Stevens LB $24.00 (978-0-8368-4104-6). 32pp. Practical information on selecting and caring for a hamster is presented in clear text with dialogue bubbles giving the hamster's point of view plus colorful fact boxes. (Rev: SLJ 8/04) [636]

22698 Richardson, Adele. *Caring for Your Hamster* (K–3). Illus. Series: First Facts, Positively Pets. 2006, Capstone LB $21.26 (978-0-7368-6387-2). 24pp. Hamster selection, care and feeding, health, safety, relations in the wild, and behavior are all covered in this attractive, concise title that includes commentary by a cartoon hamster. (Rev: SLJ 12/06) [636]

22699 Richardson, Adele. *Caring for Your Hermit Crab* (K–3). Illus. Series: First Facts, Positively Pets. 2006, Capstone LB $21.26 (978-0-7368-6388-9). 24pp. Hermit crab selection, care and feeding, health, safety, and roots in the wild are all covered in this attractive, concise title that includes commentary by a cartoon crab. (Rev: SLJ 12/06) [639]

22700 Rockwell, Anne. *My Pet Hamster* (K–2). Illus. by Bernice Lum. Series: Let's-Read-and-Find-Out Science. 2002, HarperCollins LB $17.89 (978-0-06-028565-4). 33pp. Facts about hamsters blend easily with the text about a young girl selecting, looking after, and playing with her pet. (Rev: HBG 3/03; SLJ 12/02) [636]

22701 Ross, Veronica. *My First Hamster* (K–2). Illus. Series: My First Pet. 2002, Thameside LB $24.25 (978-1-930643-75-8). 32pp. A basic guide to caring for a hamster, with information on diet and hygiene. (Rev: BL 3/1/03) [636.935]

22702 Salzmann, Mary Elizabeth. *Brilliant Birds* (K–2). Illus. by C. A. Nobens. Series: Perfect Pets. 2007, ABDO LB $19.93 (978-1-59928-744-7). 24pp. Caring for birds looks like fun in this book that combines photographs and drawings of birds and their happy owners. (Rev: SLJ 7/07)

22703 Salzmann, Mary Elizabeth. *Goofy Guinea Pigs* (K–2). Illus. by C. A. Nobens. 2007, ABDO LB $19.93 (978-1-59928-749-2). 24pp. Information on guinea pigs is paired with photographs and drawings of these furry animals and their happy owners. (Rev: SLJ 7/07)

22704 Schafer, Susan. *Lizards* (4–6). Series: Perfect Pets. 2000, Marshall Cavendish LB $25.64 (978-0-7614-1103-1). 32pp. History, folklore, and practical tips are included in this introduction to the care, feeding, and raising of pet lizards. (Rev: BL 3/15/01; HBG 3/01) [595.95]

22705 Silverstein, Alvin, and Virginia Silverstein, et al. *Poison Dart Frogs* (3–5). Illus. Series: Far-Out and Unusual Pets. 2012, Enslow LB $23.93 (978-076603881-3). 48pp. Factual information on these frogs is combined with tips on keeping one as a pet and discussion of their pros and cons in the home. (Rev: BL 4/15/12) [639.3]

22706 Silverstein, Alvin, and Virginia Silverstein, et al. *Rats* (3–5). Illus. Series: Far-Out and Unusual Pets. 2012, Enslow LB $23.93 (978-076603882-0). 48pp. Factual information on rats is combined with tips on keeping one as a pet and discussion of their pros and cons in the home. (Rev: BL 4/15/12) [636.935]

22707 Starosta, Paul. *Face-to-Face with the Hamster* (3–4). Photos by author. Series: Face-to-Face. 2004,

Charlesbridge $9.95 (978-1-57091-456-0). 25pp. Colorful photographs accompany bright text on the characteristics and care of hamsters. (Rev: SLJ 2/05) [636]

22708 Stevens, Kathryn. *Parakeets* (PS–2). Illus. Series: Pet Care for Kids. 2009, Child's World LB $21.36 (978-1-60253-186-4). 24pp. With large color photographs and simple text, this is an introduction to the care of parakeets. (Rev: BL 4/1/09) [636.6]

22709 Tracy, Kathleen. *The Hamster in Our Class* (1–3). Illus. 2012, Mitchell Lane LB $25.70 (978-158415980-3). 32pp. Solid information on hamster care is woven into a simple story about a class caring for its pet, Hamlet. (Rev: BL 4/1/12) [636.935]

22710 Urbigkit, Cat. *The Guardian Team: On the Job with Rena and Roo* (K–3). Illus. 2011, Boyds Mills $16.95 (978-1-59078-770-0). 32pp. The fascinating story of an orphaned wild burro (Roo) and a puppy (Rena), the runt of the litter, who bond with each other as they are trained to guard the sheep on a Wyoming ranch; a companion to *Brave Dogs, Gentle Dogs* (2005). (Rev: BL 12/1/11; LMC 5–6/12; SLJ 10/1/11) [636.737]

22711 Verdick, Elizabeth. *Tails Are Not for Pulling* (PS). Illus. by Marieka Heinlen. 2005, Free Spirit $7.95 (978-1-57542-180-3). Preschoolers will learn the right and wrong way to play with a pet from this simple board book. (Rev: SLJ 6/06) [636.088]

CATS

22712 Arnold, Caroline. *Cats: In from the Wild* (4–7). Photos by Richard Hewett. 1993, Carolrhoda LB $19.93 (978-0-87614-692-7). Domestic and wild cats are highlighted with comparisons and contrasts. (Rev: BL 8/93) [636.8]

22713 Barnes, Julia. *Pet Cats* (3–5). Illus. Series: Pet Pals. 2006, Gareth Stevens $24.00 (978-0-8368-6776-3). 32pp. This guide to cats provides tips about care and feeding as well as exploring cat behavior, human-feline interaction, and the diversity of cat breeds. (Rev: BL 10/15/06; SLJ 2/07) [636.8]

22714 Bearce, Stephanie. *Care for a Kitten* (3–6). Series: A Robbie Reader. How to Convince Your Parents You Can. 2010, Mitchell Lane LB $18.50 (978-1-58415-803-5). 32pp. For beginning readers, this book outlines the pros and cons of getting a kitten and provides tips on preparing the house. (Rev: SLJ 5/1/10) [636.8]

22715 Bidner, Jenni. *Is My Cat a Tiger? How Your Pet Compares to Its Wild Cousins* (3–5). Illus. 2007, Sterling $9.95 (978-1-57990-815-7). 64pp. Clearly written and illustrated with crisp photos, this book examines cats' behavior in relationship to the larger cat family, presenting information about the body language and curious antics of these pets. (Rev: BL 1/1–15/07) [636.8]

22716 Bozzo, Linda. *My First Cat* (K–2). Illus. Series: My First Pet Library. 2007, Enslow LB $16.95 (978-0-7660-2750-3). 32pp. Provides very basic information about choosing and caring for a cat. (Rev: BL 9/1/07; SLJ 8/07) [636.8]

22717 George, Jean Craighead. *How to Talk to Your Cat* (2–4). Illus. by Paul Meisel. 2000, HarperCollins LB $13.89 (978-0-06-027969-1). 40pp. After a history of the domestication of cats, this account tells how and what they communicate with humans. (Rev: BCCB 4/00; BL 12/15/99; HB 3/00; HBG 9/00; SLJ 2/00) [636.8]

22718 Hart, Joyce. *Cats* (2–4). Series: Great Pets. 2007, Marshall Cavendish LB $19.95 (978-0-7614-2710-0). 48pp. A solid introduction to the pleasures and responsibilities of caring for cats. (Rev: LMC 8/08; SLJ 4/08) [636.8]

22719 Holub, Joan. *Why Do Cats Meow?* (1–2). Illus. Series: Easy-to-Read. 2001, Dial paper $3.99 (978-0-14-056788-5). 48pp. This informative, easy-to-read book, with many photos and cartoons, discusses behavioral traits of cats and provides material on breeds and their characteristics. (Rev: BCCB 2/01; BL 2/15/01) [636.8]

22720 Jeffrey, Laura S. *Cats: How to Choose and Care for a Cat* (3–5). Illus. Series: American Humane Pet Care Library. 2004, Enslow LB $23.93 (978-0-7660-2516-5). 48pp. Offers a wide array of information on cats and their care, including tips on selecting the right cat, steps to prevent the loss of a pet, cat allergies, and how to cope with feline misbehavior. (Rev: BL 10/15/04; SLJ 2/05) [636.8]

22721 Mattern, Joanne. *The American Shorthair Cat* (4–7). Series: Learning About Cats. 2002, Capstone LB $23.93 (978-0-7368-1300-6). Beautiful photographs of frisky felines are accompanied by data about the physical characteristics and personality, with a glossary, bibliography, and lists of addresses and Web sites. Also use *The Manx Cat* (2002). (Rev: BL 12/1/02; HBG 3/03) [636.8]

22722 Quasha, Jennifer. *The Manx: The Cat with No Tail* (2–4). Illus. Series: Kids Can! 2000, Rosen LB $21.25 (978-0-8239-5512-1). 24pp. Many color close-ups are used to present the Manx cat, its characteristics, habits, and the myth about how it lost its tail. (Rev: BL 10/15/00) [636.8]

22723 Quasha, Jennifer. *Shorthaired Cats in America* (2–4). Illus. 2000, Rosen LB $18.75 (978-0-8239-5513-8). 24pp. This is a general book about cats that covers American attitudes toward them, their history from the Mayflower to today, their part in the Salem witch trials, and similar material. (Rev: BL 10/15/00) [636.8]

22724 Rau, Dana Meachen. *Guess Who Purrs* (PS–K). Series: Bookworms. Guess Who. 2009, Marshall Cavendish $15.95 (978-0-7614-2972-2). 32pp. Fun for browsing, this book asks readers to identify a cat using the clues in the text and images. (Rev: SLJ 6/09) [636.8]

22725 Rayner, Matthew. *Cat* (2–4). Photos by Jane Burton. Series: I Am Your Pet. 2004, Gareth Stevens LB $24.00 (978-0-8368-4102-2). 32pp. Practical information on selecting and caring for a cat is presented in clear text with dialogue bubbles giving the cat's point of view plus colorful fact boxes. (Rev: SLJ 8/04) [636.8]

22726 Ring, Susan. *Caring for Your Cat* (3–5). Illus. 2002, Weigl LB $16.95 (978-1-59036-032-3). 32pp. A detailed introduction to the various breeds of cat and how to care for one — in more than the strict physical sense — with photographs and a list of relevant Web sites. (Rev: BL 12/1/02; HBG 3/03) [636.8]

22727 Roca, Núria. *Let's Take Care of Our New Cat* (K–3). Illus. by Rosa M. Curto. Series: Let's Take Care of. 2006, Barron's paper $6.99 (978-0-7641-3452-4). 35pp. An appealing introduction to the care and feeding of a cat, with watercolor illustrations. (Rev: SLJ 2/07) [636.8]

22728 Ross, Veronica. *My First Cat* (K–2). Illus. Series: My First Pet. 2002, Thameside LB $24.25 (978-1-930643-72-7). 32pp. A basic guide to choosing and caring for a cat. (Rev: BL 3/1/03; HBG 3/03) [636.8]

22729 Simon, Seymour. *Cats* (2–3). Illus. 2004, HarperCollins $16.99 (978-0-06-028940-9). 40pp. Full-color photographs and clear text explore basic facts about cats — breeds, intelligence, diet, and so forth. (Rev: BL 3/15/04; SLJ 6/04) [599.75]

22730 Singer, Marilyn. *Cats to the Rescue* (4–7). Illus. by Jean Cassels. 2006, Henry Holt $16.95 (978-0-8050-7433-8). This collection of true cat stories focuses on feats ranging from catching tens of thousands of mice to detecting a gas leak. (Rev: BL 9/15/06; SLJ 11/06) [636.8]

22731 Stefoff, Rebecca. *Cats* (4–7). Series: AnimalWays. 2003, Benchmark LB $31.36 (978-0-7614-1577-0). 112pp. A well-illustrated study of cats, their evolution, behavior, and human attitudes toward them. (Rev: SLJ 3/04) [636.8]

22732 Whitehead, Sarah. *How to Speak Cat!* (4–8). 2008, Scholastic paper $6.99 (978-0-545-02079-4). 96pp. Amply illustrated, this book offers advice on building a relationship with a pet cat through body language cues and mutual respect. (Rev: SLJ 6/1/09) [599.75]

DOGS

22733 Adams, Michelle Medlock. *Care for a Puppy* (3–6). Series: A Robbie Reader. How to Convince Your Parents You Can. 2010, Mitchell Lane LB $18.50 (978-1-58415-802-8). 32pp. For beginning readers, this book outlines the pros and cons of getting a puppy and offers a chapter titled "Perfecting the Puppy Pitch to Your Parents." (Rev: SLJ 5/1/10) [636.7]

22734 Ajmera, Maya, and Alex Fisher. *A Kid's Best Friend* (1–3). Illus. 2002, Charlesbridge $15.95 (978-1-57091-513-0); paper $6.95 (978-1-57091-514-7). 32pp. Photographs of children and their dogs show that dogs are friends and helpers everywhere in the world. (Rev: BL 9/1/02; HBG 3/03; SLJ 8/02) [636.7]

22735 Altman, Linda J. *Big Dogs* (4–6). Series: Perfect Pets. 2000, Marshall Cavendish LB $25.64 (978-0-7614-1101-7). 32pp. Filled with historical and factual material, this book introduces several breeds of large dogs and gives tips for raising and caring for them. (Rev: BL 3/15/01; HBG 3/01) [636.7]

22736 Anderson, Bendix. *Security Dogs* (2–4). Illus. Series: Dog Heroes. 2005, Bearport LB $25.27 (978-1-59716-015-5). 32pp. Features dogs who work to keep people safe, with photographs and factoids emphasizing their helpfulness to humans. (Rev: SLJ 8/05) [363.2]

22737 Baines, Becky. *Everything Dogs* (3–6). Illus. 2012, National Geographic paper $12.95 (978-14263102-4-9). 64pp. The subtitle says it all: "All the canine facts, photos, and fun that you can get your paws on!" Lexile 1000L (Rev: BL 12/1/12) [636.7]

22738 Barnes, Julia. *Pet Dogs* (2–5). 2006, Gareth Stevens LB $24.00 (978-0-8368-6777-0). 32pp. This handy guide full of advice on caring for a dog also examines the qualities that make cats such popular pets, looks at how they communicate, and explores the dog's roots in the wild. (Rev: SLJ 2/07) [636.7]

22739 Bial, Raymond. *Rescuing Rover: Saving America's Dogs* (4–7). Illus. 2011, Houghton Mifflin $16.99 (978-0-547-34125-5). 80pp. Cruelty to animals, puppy mills, dogfighting, dog rescue services, and animal shelters are all discussed in this wide-ranging survey that also includes a personal account of adopting a rescue dog. Lexile NC1230L (Rev: BL 6/1/11; LMC 1–2/12; SLJ 7/11) [636.08]

22740 Bidner, Jenni. *Is My Dog a Wolf? How Your Dog Compares to Its Wild Cousin* (4–6). 2006, Sterling $9.95 (978-1-57990-732-7). 64pp. Using many vivid photographs, this is a fascinating look at the similarities — and differences — between domestic dogs and wild wolves. (Rev: BL 9/1/06; SLJ 10/06) [636.7]

22741 Bozzo, Linda. *Guide Dog Heroes* (2–4). Series: Amazing Working Dogs with American Humane. 2010, Enslow LB $23.93 (978-0-7660-3198-2). 48pp. With large, simple text and many photographs, this book starts with a true story and follows with information on guide dog breeds, training, working tasks, and status as heroes. Also use *Police Dog Heroes* and *Service Dog Heroes* (both 2010). (Rev: SLJ 3/1/11) [362.4]

22742 Bozzo, Linda. *My First Dog* (1–3). Series: My First Pet Library from the American Humane Association. 2007, Enslow LB $22.60 (978-0-7660-2754-1). 32pp. New pet owners will learn all the facts about caring for dogs and will enjoy looking at the pictures of dogs and their owners. (Rev: SLJ 6/07)

22743 Calmenson, Stephanie. *May I Pet Your Dog? The How-to Guide for Kids Meeting Dogs (and Dogs Meeting Kids)* (PS–2). Illus. by Jan Ormerod. 2007, Clarion $9.95 (978-0-618-51034-4). 32pp. A dachshund named Harry patiently explains how to approach an unfamiliar dog. (Rev: SLJ 4/07)

22744 Collard, Sneed B., III. *Shep: Our Most Loyal Dog* (2–4). Illus. by Joanna Yardley. 2006, Sleeping Bear $16.95 (978-1-58536-259-2). This is the moving story of Shep, a sheepdog that watched its master's coffin being loaded onto a train in Montana and met every passenger train arriving at that station from that day until his death more than five years later. (Rev: SLJ 8/06) [636.737]

22745 Coren, Stanley. *Why Do Dogs Have Wet Noses?* (2–4). Illus. 2006, Kids Can $12.95 (978-1-55337-657-6). 64pp. The famous dog expert offers a wealth of doggy facts in an appealing format suited more to browsing than report writing. (Rev: BL 4/15/06; SLJ 5/06) [636.7]

22746 Crisp, Marty. *Everything Dog: What Kids Really Want to Know About Dogs* (2–5). 2003, NorthWord $9.95 (978-1-55971-839-4); paper $6.95 (978-1-55971-854-7). 64pp. Friendly and attractive, this is nonetheless a fact-filled volume suitable for browsing. (Rev: BL 5/15/03; SLJ 6/03) [636.7]

22747 Crosby, Jeff, and Shelley Jackson. *Little Lions, Bull Baiters and Hunting Hounds* (2–4). Illus. by Jeff Crosby. 2008, Tundra $19.95 (978-0-88776-815-6). 72pp. Best for browsers, this is an attractive introduction to a variety of breeds of dogs, with painted portraits that occasionally show confrontations with other animals. (Rev: BL 6/1–15/08; SLJ 5/08) [636.7]

22748 Feldman, Heather. *The Story of the Golden Retriever* (2–4). Illus. Series: Dogs Throughout History. 2000, Rosen $21.25 (978-0-8239-5514-5). 24pp. This history of the golden retriever also describes its physical characteristics and its roles in rescue missions and as a guide dog. (Rev: BL 10/15/00) [636.752]

22749 Fetty, Margaret. *Seizure-Alert Dogs* (3–5). Illus. Series: Dog Heroes. 2009, Bearport LB $25.27 (978-159716865-6). 32pp. Describes how dogs can help people anticipate and deal with seizures. (Rev: BL 11/1/09) [362.196]

22750 Flowers, Pam, and Ann Dixon. *Big-Enough Anna: The Little Sled Dog Who Braved the Arctic* (PS–3). Illus. by Bill Farnsworth. 2003, Alaska Northwest $15.95 (978-0-88240-577-3); paper $8.95 (978-0-88240-580-3). In this inspiring real-life story, Anna, a sled dog that was the runt of her litter, takes over as lead dog on an arduous journey across the North American Arctic. (Rev: HBG 4/04; SLJ 1/04) [636.73]

22751 Gewirtz, Elaine Waldorf. *The Chihuahua* (4–8). Illus. Series: Our Best Friends. 2011, Eldorado Ink LB $34.95 (978-193290475-8). 112pp. An attractive introduction to these small dogs and their pros and cons as pets. (Rev: BL 4/15/11) [636.76]

22752 Gewirtz, Elaine Waldorf. *Fetch This Book: Train Your Dog to Do Almost Anything* (4–8). Series: Our Best Friends. 2010, Eldorado Ink $34.95 (978-1-932904-60-4). 112pp. In clearly written chapters such as "What Your Dog Thinks About Training," "Establishing Who's in Charge," and "Making Your Dog a Champion," this is a practical guide to dog training from the basics to advanced opportunities in service roles. (Rev: BL 8/10*; SLJ 9/1/10) [636.7]

22753 Goldish, Meish. *Baghdad Pups* (3–5). Illus. Series: Dog Heroes. 2011, Bearport LB $25.27 (978-1-61772-150-2). 32pp. The dogs that work with soldiers in war zones are the focus here. Also use *Prison Puppies* (2011), about dogs trained by inmates for various tasks. (Rev: BL 5/1/11; SLJ 6/11) [956.7044]

22754 Goldish, Meish. *Ground Zero Dogs* (3–5). Illus. Series: Dog Heroes. 2012, Bearport LB $25.27 (978-161772576-0). 32pp. A moving account of the contributions dogs made on and after 9/11, with information on the care the humans take with these brave and tireless animals. Also use *Surf Dog Miracles* (2012), about dogs' feats on the waves, even helping the disabled to surf. Lexile IG990L (Rev: BL 11/1/12*; LMC 8–9/13) [636.7]

22755 Goldish, Meish. *Pest-Sniffing Dogs* (3–5). Illus. Series: Dog Heroes. 2012, Bearport LB $25.27 (978-161772454-1). 32pp. Dogs trained to detect bed bugs, termites, and more are the focus of this title, which includes information on the dogs' training regimen and visually appealing photographs. (Rev: BL 4/15/12) [636.73]

22756 Goldish, Meish. *Science Dogs* (3–5). Illus. Series: Dog Heroes. 2013, Bearport LB $25.27 (978-161772887-7). 32pp. Goldfish tells of the roles that dogs have played in scientific achievements, including dogs that can smell the presence of cancer and a dachshund that regains the use of his back legs after scientists transplant the cells from his nose into his injured spine. Also use *Shelter Dogs* (2013). ℮ (Rev: BL 11/15/13) [636.7]

22757 Gorrell, Gena K. *Working Like a Dog: The Story of Working Dogs Through History* (4–8). 2003, Tundra $16.95 (978-0-88776-589-6). A comprehensive and very appealing look at dogs' services to man throughout history — as hunters and trackers, bomb sniffers, guide dogs, and companions, to name but a few. (Rev: BL 11/1/03; SLJ 12/03) [636.73]

22758 Grogan, John. *Marley: A Dog Like No Other* (4–7). Illus. 2007, HarperCollins $16.99 (978-0-06-124033-1). An adaptation of Grogan's book for adults, *Marley & Me,* this story of a hopelessly out-of-control but lovable dog who dies too soon will touch young readers. ∩ (Rev: BL 7/07; SLJ 7/07) [636.752]

22759 Guy, Foglesong Ginger. *Perros! Perros! / Dogs! Dogs! A Story in English and Spanish* (PS–K). Illus. by Sharon Glick. 2006, Greenwillow $16.99 (978-0-06-083574-3). 32pp. Dogs of all sizes and shapes are the focus of this simple bilingual book. (Rev: BL 9/1/06; SLJ 10/06) [468.1]

22760 Halls, Kelly Milner. *Wild Dogs: Past and Present* (4–7). 2005, Darby Creek $18.95 (978-1-58196-027-3). A wide-ranging introduction to dogs and their history, with attractive design, many photographs, and lots of factboxes about dogs both wild and domestic. (Rev: BL 12/1/05; SLJ 11/05) [599.77]

22761 Hart, Joyce. *Big Dogs* (2–4). Series: Great Pets. 2007, Marshall Cavendish LB $19.95 (978-0-7614-2707-0). 48pp. A solid introduction to the pleasures and responsibilities of caring for large dogs. (Rev: LMC 8/08; SLJ 4/08) [636.7]

22762 Hengel, Katherine. *Brainy Brittanys* (2–3). Illus. Series: Dog Daze. 2009, ABDO LB $16.95 (978-1-60453-616-4). 24pp. For beginning readers, this volume offers a blend of facts, stories, photographs, and art relating to Brittany spaniels. (Rev: BL 4/1/09) [636.752]

22763 Houston, Dick. *Bulu: African Wonder Dog* (5–8). 2010, Random House LB $18.99 (978-0-375-94720-9). 336pp. The true story of an African terrier with an unusual personality and a protective attitude toward other animals. Lexile 700L (Rev: BL 3/15/10; LMC 8–9/10; SLJ 5/10) [636.7]

22764 Hubbell, Patricia. *Shaggy Dogs, Waggy Dogs* (PS–2). Illus. by Donald Wu. 2011, Marshall Cavendish $17.99 (978-0-7614-5957-6). Unpaged. A rhymed celebration of all things doggy. ℮ (Rev: SLJ 9/1/11) [636.7]

22765 Jackson, Emma. *A Home for Dixie: The True Story of a Rescued Puppy* (2–4). Illus. by Bob Carey. 2008, HarperCollins $16.99 (978-0-06-144962-8). 40pp. A young girl finds the pet she has been longing for in this affecting photo-essay. (Rev: BL 6/1–15/08; SLJ 5/08) [636.7]

22766 Jeffrey, Laura S. *Dogs: How to Choose and Care for a Dog* (2–5). Illus. Series: American Humane Pet Care Library. 2004, Enslow LB $23.93 (978-0-7660-2520-2). 48pp. Appealing full-color photographs accompany advice on choosing and caring for a dog. (Rev: SLJ 2/05) [636.7]

22767 Kirk, Daniel. *Dogs Rule!* (3–5). Illus. by author. 2003, Disney $18.99 (978-0-7868-1949-2). 48pp. In this large-format collection of dog-related poetry and accompanying CD, Kirk manages to celebrate just about every aspect of canine behavior. (Rev: BL 10/15/03; HBG 4/04; SLJ 12/03)

22768 Laidlaw, Rob. *No Shelter Here: Making the World a Kinder Place for Dogs* (3–6). Illus. 2012, Pajama $21.95 (978-098694955-5). 64pp. Laidlaw provides solid advice on caring for a dog, but the emphasis here is on how dogs are mistreated and on the work of "Dog Champions" who are seeking better conditions for all dogs. (Rev: BL 4/15/12; LMC 11–12/12; SLJ 4/12) [636.7]

22769 Lauber, Patricia. *The True-or-False Book of Dogs* (1–3). Illus. by Rosalyn Schanzer. 2003, HarperCollins $15.99 (978-0-06-029767-1). 32pp. This brightly illustrated book uses a true-or-false format to convey a wide range of facts and figures about dogs and their history. (Rev: BL 11/1/03; HBG 4/04; SLJ 12/03)

22770 Lawrenson, Diana. *Guide Dogs: From Puppies to Partners* (4–6). 2002, Allen & Unwin paper $7.95 (978-1-86508-246-2). 32pp. The breeding, care, and training of guide dogs are covered in this title from Australia, with profiles of several dogs and their partners and an interesting chart of commands. (Rev: SLJ 10/02)

22771 Lendroth, Susan. *Calico Dorsey: Mail Dog of the Mining Camps* (PS–3). Illus. by Adam Gustavson. 2010, Tricycle $16.99 (978-1-58246-318-6); LB $19.99 (978-1-58246-367-4). Unpaged. In 1885 California a border collie named Dorsey is trained to deliver mail to miners across the desert. (Rev: BL 10/15/10; LMC 3–4/11; SLJ 9/1/10) [636.7]

22772 McCarthy, Meghan. *The Incredible Life of Balto* (2–4). Illus. by author. 2011, Knopf $16.99 (978-0-375-

84460-7). 40pp. This nonfiction picture book tells the story of the sled dog who delivered anti-diptheria serum to Nome, Alaska, in 1925 and became famous in the process. (Rev: BL 7/11; SLJ 6/11) [636.73]

22773 McDaniel, Melissa. *Disaster Search Dogs* (2–4). Illus. Series: Dog Heroes. 2005, Bearport LB $25.27 (978-1-59716-012-4). 32pp. Dogs that work to find people in trouble are the focus of this photo-filled volume. Also use *Guide Dogs* (2005). (Rev: SLJ 8/05) [363.2]

22774 Mehus-Roe, Kristin. *Dogs for Kids! Everything You Need to Know About Dogs* (4–7). Illus. 2007, Bowtie paper $14.95 (978-1-931993-83-8). From a history of dogs to information on breeds, anatomy, and behavior to advice on care and training — as the title says, this book is all you need. (Rev: BL 2/15/08; SLJ 6/07) [636.7]

22775 Meister, Cari. *Basset Hounds* (3–5). Series: Dogs. 2001, ABDO $21.35 (978-1-57765-478-0). 24pp. A simple colorful introduction to this breed of dog that describes its physical and behavioral characteristics and gives tips on proper care. Other titles in this series include *Boxers*, *Greyhounds*, and *Saint Bernards* (all 2001). (Rev: BL 12/15/01; HBG 3/02) [636.7]

22776 Meister, Cari. *Bulldogs* (3–5). Series: Dogs. 2001, ABDO $21.35 (978-1-57765-476-6). 24pp. Attractive color photographs show bulldogs playing, eating, and sleeping, and a simple text describes the breed, its many varieties, and its characteristics. (Rev: BL 12/15/01; HBG 3/02) [636.7]

22777 Miles, Ellen. *The Puppy Place: Guide to Puppies* (2–4). Illus. 2013, Scholastic paper $5.99 (978-05454843-3-6). 80pp. From initial planning through basic training and vet checkups, this guide asks readers to consider various factors before deciding on a puppy. (Rev: BL 3/1/13) [636.7]

22778 Morn, September. *The Doberman Pinscher* (4–7). Illus. Series: Our Best Friends. 2011, Eldorado Ink LB $34.95 (978-193290477-2). 112pp. An attractive introduction to these popular dogs and their pros and cons as pets. (Rev: BL 4/15/11) [636.73]

22779 Mulvany, Martha. *The Story of the Boxer* (2–4). Illus. Series: Dogs Throughout History. 2000, Rosen $21.25 (978-0-8239-5519-0). 24pp. This history of the boxer also describes its physical characteristics and its reputation for loyalty and courage. (Rev: BL 10/15/00) [636.73]

22780 Newman, Aline Alexander, and Gary Weitzman. *How to Speak Dog: A Guide to Decoding Dog Language* (4–7). Illus. 2013, National Geographic paper $12.95 (978-14263137-3-8). 176pp. Dog behaviors are covered in detail in this book, offering young readers a chance to understand their dog's body language and why certain behaviors, such as eating grass, are so common. (Rev: BL 9/15/13) [636.7]

22781 O'Sullivan, Robyn. *More than Man's Best Friend: The Story of Working Dogs* (2–4). Illus. Series: National Geographic Science Chapters. 2006, National Geographic $17.90 (978-0-7922-5940-4). 40pp. Six chapters look at the different kinds of jobs performed by working dogs; photos and easy vocabulary make this suitable for young readers. (Rev: BL 10/15/06) [636.7]

22782 Patent, Dorothy Hinshaw. *Dogs on Duty: Soldiers' Best Friends on the Battlefield and Beyond* (3–6). Illus. 2012, Walker $16.99 (978-0-80272-845-6). 48pp. With many full-color photographs, this appealing volume chronicles the history of military working dogs from ancient history forward, documenting their contributions to both World Wars and to more recent conflicts and profiling some individual dogs. ALA Notable Children's Book. (Rev: BL 9/1/12*; HB 11–12/12; LMC 1–2/13; SLJ 9/12) [355.4]

22783 Patent, Dorothy Hinshaw. *Right Dog for the Job: Ira's Path from Service Dog to Guide Dog* (3–5). 2004, Walker $16.95 (978-0-8027-8915-0). 32pp. A puppy's training to be a guide dog is followed in loving detail in this appealing and informative photo-essay. (Rev: BL 6/1–15/04; SLJ 6/04)

22784 Patent, Dorothy Hinshaw. *Saving Audie: A Pit Bull Puppy Gets a Second Chance* (2–4). Illus. by William Munoz. 2011, Walker $17.99 (978-0-8027-2272-0). 40pp. A pit bull formerly part of NFL star Michael Vick's dogfighting ring undergoes rehabilitation and finds a happy home with a family in San Francisco. (Rev: BL 3/1/11; SLJ 5/1/11*) [636.755]

22785 Paulsen, Gary. *My Life in Dog Years* (5–10). 1998, Delacorte $15.95 (978-0-385-32570-7). The famous novelist tells about eight wonderful dogs that he has known and loved over the years. (Rev: BCCB 3/98; BL 1/1–15/98; SLJ 3/98; VOYA 4/98) [636.7]

22786 Prap, Lila. *Doggy Whys?* (2–4). Illus. by author. 2011, NorthSouth $14.95 (978-0-7358-4014-0). 40pp. "Why do dogs wag their tails?" Prap answers these and other doggy questions with humor and facts, describing particular breeds and their pros and cons. (Rev: BL 6/1/11; LMC 8–9/11; SLJ 5/1/11) [636.7]

22787 Presnall, Judith Janda. *Police Dogs* (4–7). Illus. Series: Animals with Jobs. 2002, Gale LB $23.70 (978-0-7377-0631-4). 48pp. This well-illustrated account describes the various ways in which dogs are used to fight crime. (Rev: BL 4/1/02) [363.2]

22788 Presnall, Judith Janda. *Rescue Dogs* (4–6). Series: Animals with Jobs. 2002, Gale LB $23.70 (978-0-7377-1361-9). 48pp. Individual rescue dogs are profiled in this well-written overview of these animals and their training. (Rev: SLJ 9/03) [636.7]

22789 Rappaport, Jill. *Jack and Jill: The Miracle Dog with a Happy Tail to Tell* (2–4). Photos by Linda Solomon. 2009, HarperCollins $17.99 (978-0-06-173136-5). A German Shepherd loses a leg and survives cancer in this moving story that will help children facing a similar situation. (Rev: SLJ 6/09) [636.737]

22790 Rayner, Matthew. *Dog* (2–4). Photos by Jane Burton. Series: I Am Your Pet. 2004, Gareth Stevens LB $24.00 (978-0-8368-4103-9). 32pp. Practical information on selecting and caring for a dog is presented in clear text with dialogue bubbles giving the dog's point of view plus colorful fact boxes. (Rev: SLJ 8/04) [636.7]

22791 Roca, Núria. *Let's Take Care of Our New Dog* (K–3). Illus. by Rosa M. Curto. Series: Let's Take Care of . . . 2006, Barron's paper $6.99 (978-0-7641-3455-5). 35pp. An appealing introduction to the care and feeding of a dog, with watercolor illustrations. (Rev: SLJ 2/07) [636.7]

22792 Rogers, Tammie. *4-H Guide to Dog Training and Dog Tricks* (5–12). 2010, Voyageur paper $18.99 (978-0-7603-3629-8). 176pp. Learn how to train your dog to master the basics and then move on to competition skills and even emptying the dryer! (Rev: SLJ 5/10) [636.7]

22793 Rosenthal, Lisa. *A Dog's Best Friend: An Activity Book for Kids and Their Dogs* (4–7). Illus. by Bonnie Matthews. 1999, Chicago Review paper $12.95 (978-1-55652-362-5). This book that gives hints on how to choose a dog and care for a puppy offers 60 projects related to these subjects including crafts, recipes, and games. (Rev: SLJ 1/00) [636.7]

22794 Ross, Veronica. *My First Dog* (PS–2). Series: My First. 2002, Raintree LB $24.95 (978-1-930643-71-0). 32pp. Simple language introduces young readers to dogs and their care. (Rev: HBG 3/03)

22795 Royston, Angela. *Life Cycle of a Dog* (PS–3). Series: Life Cycle. 2000, Heinemann LB $21.36 (978-1-57572-209-2). 32pp. This book describes a dog's life cycle with a simple text and color photos on each page. (Rev: BL 5/15/00; HBG 3/01) [636.7]

22796 Schweitzer, Karen. *The Cocker Spaniel* (4–7). Illus. Series: Our Best Friends. 2011, Eldorado Ink LB $34.95 (978-193290476-5). 112pp. An attractive introduction to these dogs and their pros and cons as pets. (Rev: BL 4/15/11) [636.752]

22797 Silverstein, Alvin. *Different Dogs* (4–7). Series: What a Pet! 2000, Twenty-First Century LB $23.90 (978-0-7613-1371-7). Several different breeds of dogs are introduced in pictures and text plus information on cost, food, housing, and training. (Rev: HBG 10/00; SLJ 5/00) [636.7]

22798 Simon, Seymour. *Dogs* (2–3). Illus. 2004, HarperCollins $16.99 (978-0-06-028942-3). 40pp. Full-color photographs and clear text explore basic facts about dogs — breeds, intelligence, diet, and so forth. (Rev: BL 3/15/04; SLJ 6/04) [636.7]

22799 Singer, Marilyn. *A Dog's Gotta Do What a Dog's Gotta Do* (3–6). Illus. 2000, Holt $16.00 (978-0-8050-6074-4). 86pp. This book on working dogs includes material on their roles as defenders, herders, detectives, rescuers, and entertainers. (Rev: BCCB 11/00; BL 11/15/00; HBG 3/01; SLJ 2/01) [636.7]

22800 Stamper, Judith Bauer. *Eco Dogs* (3–5). Illus. Series: Dog Heroes. 2011, Bearport LB $25.27 (978-1-61772-152-6). 32pp. A fascinating look at dogs that work with wildlife scientists to help endangered animals and habitats. (Rev: BL 5/1/11; SLJ 6/11) [636.7]

22801 Stone, Lynn M. *Beagles* (K–2). Series: Eye to Eye with Dogs. 2002, Rourke LB $17.95 (978-1-58952-325-8). 24pp. From puppyhood to adult status, this is an introduction to beagles and their behavior, characteris-

tics, and care. Other titles in this series include *German Shepherds*, *Golden Retrievers*, *Labrador Retrievers*, and *Poodles* (all 2002). (Rev: BL 10/15/02) [636.7]

22802 Stone, Lynn M. *Dachshunds* (K–2). Series: Eye to Eye with Dogs. 2002, Rourke LB $17.95 (978-1-58952-326-5). 24pp. The five short sections in this simple book give information on dachshunds' characteristics, history, appearance, and care, and discuss how dachshunds help people. (Rev: BL 10/15/02) [636.7]

22803 Tagliaferro, Linda. *Therapy Dogs* (2–4). Illus. Series: Dog Heroes. 2005, Bearport LB $25.27 (978-1-59716-018-6). 32pp. Features dogs that work to help people with special needs, with photographs and factoids emphasizing their helpfulness to humans. (Rev: SLJ 8/05) [363.2]

22804 Temple, Bob. *Chihuahuas* (3–5). Series: Dogs. 2000, ABDO LB $21.35 (978-1-57765-419-3). 24pp. This heavily illustrated book covers the history of this breed, its structure, habits, and required care and feeding. Also use from the same series: *Pugs*, *Scottish Terriers*, and *Shih Tzus* (all 2000). (Rev: BL 3/15/01; HBG 3/01) [636.7]

22805 Temple, Bob. *Jack Russell Terriers* (3–5). Illus. Series: Dogs. 2000, ABDO $21.35 (978-1-57765-424-7). 24pp. This book introduces terriers, their physical characteristics, habits, how to care for them, and their special needs. Similar material is found in *Siberian Huskies* (2000). (Rev: BL 3/15/01; HBG 3/01) [636.755]

22806 Tracqui, Valerie. *The Dog: Loyal Companion* (2–4). Trans. from French by Lisa Laird. Photos by Marie-Luce Hubert and Jean-Louis Klein. Series: Face-to-Face. 2002, Charlesbridge $9.95 (978-1-57091-452-2). 32pp. A celebration of dogs' relationship with humans, their ability to follow commands, and their contributions to the lost and handicapped. (Rev: SLJ 8/02) [636.7]

22807 Turner, Pamela S. *Hachiko: The True Story of a Loyal Dog* (1–3). Illus. by Yan Nascimbene. 2004, Houghton $16.00 (978-0-618-14094-7). 32pp. This small-format picture book tells the moving story of Hachiko, the devoted dog who spent nearly 10 years at a Tokyo train station, waiting in vain for the return of his dead master. (Rev: BL 4/15/04*; HB 7/04; SLJ 5/04) [636.7]

22808 Urbigkit, Cat. *Brave Dogs, Gentle Dogs: How They Guard Sheep* (K–2). Illus. 2005, Boyds Mills $15.95 (978-1-59078-317-7). 32pp. Photographs of Wyoming ranch dogs accompany the text on guardian dogs, trained to tend and protect flocks of sheep. (Rev: BL 3/1/05; SLJ 3/05) [636.737]

22809 Wahman, Wendy. *Don't Lick the Dog: Making Friends with Dogs* (PS–2). Illus. by author. 2009, Holt $16.95 (978-0-8050-8733-8). 32pp. A humorous, rhyming guide to meeting and interacting with dogs. (Rev: BL 3/15/09; SLJ 5/09) [636.7]

22810 Weatherford, Carole Boston. *First Pooch: The Obamas Pick a Pet* (PS–2). Illus. by Amy June Bates. 2009, Marshall Cavendish $16.99 (978-0-7614-5636-0). 32pp. The story of the Obamas' dog Bo is given a family focus and enhanced with plenty of facts about other presidential pets and promises. (Rev: BL 11/15/09; LMC 5–6/10; SLJ 12/1/09) [973.932]

22811 Wheeler, Jill C. *Portuguese Water Dogs* (3–5). Illus. 2010, ABDO LB $16.95 (978-160453784-0). 24pp. A concise introduction to the current White House canine incumbent, with information on anatomy, personality, and so forth. Also use *Boston Terriers, Welsh Corgis,* and *Weimaraners* (all 2010). (Rev: BL 9/1/10) [636.73]

22812 Williams, Chris. *One Incredible Dog! Kizzy* (1–5). Illus. by Judith Friedman. 2006, Keene LB $15.95 (978-0-9766805-5-0). This photo-essay documents a day in the life of Kizzy, a therapy dog that offers a kind and interested ear to children and adults practicing reading and speaking. (Rev: SLJ 2/07) [636.7]

22813 Wood, Selina. *Dog* (4–6). Illus. Series: Owning a Pet. 2008, Black Rabbit LB $18.95 (978-1-59771-056-5). 32pp. Wood offers sensible advice on the selection, care, and training of dogs. (Rev: BL 4/1/08) [636.7]

FISH

22814 Barnes, Julia. *Pet Goldfish* (2–5). Series: Pet Pals. 2006, Gareth Stevens LB $24.00 (978-0-8368-6778-7). 32pp. This handy guide full of advice on caring for goldfish also examines their history. (Rev: SLJ 12/06) [639.3]

22815 Nelson, Robin. *Pet Fish* (PS–K). Illus. Series: Classroom Pets. 2002, Lerner LB $18.60 (978-0-8225-1267-7). 24pp. A preschooler's introduction to the care and feeding of classroom fish, with fish facts, a glossary, and an index. (Rev: BL 10/15/02; HBG 3/03) [639.34]

22816 Niven, Felicia Lowenstein. *Learning to Care for Fish* (2–4). Series: Beginning Pet Care with American Humane. 2010, Enslow LB $23.93 (978-0-7660-3193-7). 48pp. After a brief history of fish, this book describes the environment you need to provide to pet fish and the various problems and challenges you will face. (Rev: SLJ 3/1/11) [639.34]

22817 Richardson, Adele. *Caring for Your Fish* (K–3). Illus. Series: First Facts, Positively Pets. 2006, Capstone LB $21.26 (978-0-7368-6386-5). 24pp. Fish selection, care and feeding, health, and safety are all covered in this attractive, concise title that includes commentary by a cartoon fish. (Rev: SLJ 12/06) [639.34]

22818 Salzmann, Mary Elizabeth. *Flashy Fish* (K–2). Illus. by C. A. Nobens. 2007, ABDO LB $19.93 (978-1-59928-747-8). 24pp. Caring for fish looks like fun in this book that combines photographs and drawings of fish and their happy owners. (Rev: SLJ 7/07)

HORSES AND PONIES

22819 Arnosky, Jim. *Wild Ponies* (PS–3). Illus. by author. Series: One Whole Day. 2002, National Geographic $16.95 (978-0-7922-7121-5). 32pp. Bright illustrations and simple rhyming text introduce the small ponies of Assateague Island and the other animals that live there. (Rev: HBG 3/03; SLJ 10/02)

22820 Barnes, Julia. *Horses at Work* (3–5). Series: Animals at Work. 2006, Gareth Stevens LB $24.00 (978-0-8368-6225-6). 32pp. Full-color photographs show horses working in many roles and the text discusses the animal's physical characteristics, ability to learn commands, and relationship with humans. (Rev: SLJ 1/07) [636.1]

22821 Budd, Jackie. *Seasons of the Horse: A Practical Guide to Year-Round Equine Care* (5–12). 2007, T.F.H. $29.95 (978-0-7938-0611-9). Well-organized and visually pleasing, this book provides a complete guide to caring for a horse, including nutrition and exercise. (Rev: SLJ 3/08)

22822 Budiansky, Stephen. *The World According to Horses: How They Run, See, and Think* (4–8). 2000, Henry Holt $17.95 (978-0-8050-6054-6). This book explores horses' behavior — such as their sight and thinking powers — and goes on to explain how this knowledge was gained through observation and experiments. (Rev: BCCB 5/00; BL 3/1/00; HB 5–6/00; HBG 10/00; SLJ 7/00; VOYA 6/00) [636.1]

22823 Crisp, Marty. *Everything Horse: What Kids Really Want to Know About Horses* (3–5). Series: Kids' FAQs. 2005, NorthWord $10.95 (978-1-55971-920-9); paper $7.95 (978-1-55971-921-6). 63pp. Answers to frequently asked questions about horses, with photographs and a diagram of a horse's body. (Rev: SLJ 9/05)

22824 Dell, Pamela. *Thoroughbreds* (2–4). Illus. Series: Majestic Horses. 2007, Child's World LB $17.95 (978-1-59296-786-5). 24pp. This introduction to Thoroughbred horses covers their history, their physical characteristics, and their achievements. (Rev: BL 5/1/07) [636.1]

22825 Draper, Judith. *My First Horse and Pony Book* (2–4). Illus. 2005, Kingfisher $9.95 (978-0-7534-5878-5). 48pp. All about looking after and riding horses and ponies, with details of the animals' physical characteristics and discussion of Western and English riding, proper clothing, jumping, and so forth. (Rev: BL 7/05; SLJ 8/05) [636.1]

22826 Dubowski, Cathy E., and Mark Dubowski. *A Horse Named Seabiscuit* (2–4). Illus. by Mark Rowe. Series: All Aboard Reading. 2003, Grosset paper $3.99 (978-0-448-43342-4). 47pp. The story of the famous Depression-era race horse is told in lively, well-illustrated narrative. (Rev: BL 1/1–15/04; HBG 4/04; SLJ 4/04) [636.1]

22827 Funny Cide Team. *A Horse Named Funny Cide* (2–4). Illus. by Barry Moser. 2006, Putnam $16.99 (978-0-399-24462-9). 32pp. This is a beautifully illustrated tribute to the little race horse that overcame a number of obstacles to win both the Kentucky Derby and Preakness in 2003. (Rev: BL 4/15/06; SLJ 5/06) [798.4]

22828 Gibbons, Gail. *Horses!* (K–3). Illus. by author. 2003, Holiday House $16.95 (978-0-8234-1703-2). Browsers and report writers will enjoy Gibbons's exploration of horses' history, physical characteristics and breeds, life cycle, and care and grooming. (Rev: HBG 4/04; SLJ 12/03) [636.1]

22829 Hansen, Rosanna. *Panda: A Guide Horse for Ann* (3–5). Illus. by Neil Soderstrom. 2005, Boyds Mills $19.95 (978-1-59078-184-5). 48pp. This photo-essay presents the heartwarming story of Panda, a miniature horse trained to be a guide for a blind woman. (Rev: BL 1/1–15/06; SLJ 10/05) [362.40483]

22830 Hayden, Kate. *Horse Show* (1–3). Series: Dorling Kindersley Readers. 2001, DK $12.99 (978-0-7894-7372-1); paper $3.99 (978-0-7894-7371-4). An introduction to gymkhanas and the preparations that horses and riders undergo, for beginning readers. (Rev: HBG 10/01; SLJ 6/01) [798.24]

22831 Henry, Marguerite. *Album of Horses* (5–8). Illus. by Wesley Dennis. 1951, Macmillan paper $11.99 (978-0-689-71709-3). A beautifully illustrated guide to 20 breeds of horses.

22832 Hill, Cherry. *Horse Care for Kids* (4–8). Illus. 2002, Storey $23.95 (978-1-58017-476-3); paper $16.95 (978-1-58017-407-7). 128pp. A very practical guide for young horse lovers and their parents using clear prose and topnotch illustrations to cover everything from selecting a horse and instructor to proper care and equine psychology. (Rev: BL 12/1/02; HBG 3/03; SLJ 1/03) [636.1]

22833 Holub, Joan. *Why Do Horses Neigh?* (K–2). Illus. Series: Dial Easy-to-Read. 2003, Dial paper $3.99 (978-0-14-230119-7). 48pp. Beginning readers will enjoy this introduction to horses that presents interesting material in a question-and-answer format. (Rev: BL 11/15/02; HBG 10/03; SLJ 2/03) [636.1]

22834 Jeffrey, Laura S. *Horses: How to Choose and Care for a Horse* (3–5). Illus. Series: American Humane Pet Care Library. 2004, Enslow LB $23.93 (978-0-7660-2519-6). 48pp. This helpful guide to horses and their care offers tips on selecting the right breed for your needs and on grooming, housing, and diet. (Rev: BL 10/15/04; SLJ 2/05) [636.1]

22835 Joyce, Gare. *Northern Dancer: King of the Racetrack* (5–8). Illus. 2012, Fitzhenry & Whiteside $22.95 (978-155455163-7); paper $9.95 (978-1-55041-496-7). 72pp. An interesting biography of the racehorse that overcame an inauspicious appearance to win the Derby and Preakness and sire many other winners. (Rev: BL 7/12; SLJ 7/12) [798.40092]

22836 Jurmain, Suzanne. *Once Upon a Horse: A History of Horses and How They Shaped Our History* (5–9). 1989, Lothrop $15.95 (978-0-688-05550-9). A history of the horse and how it has been domesticated and used by humans. (Rev: BL 12/15/89; SLJ 1/90; VOYA 4/90) [636.1]

22837 Kelley, Brent. *Horse Breeds of the World* (4–8). Series: Horse Library. 2001, Chelsea $25.00 (978-0-7910-6652-2). 64pp. In addition to basic facts about nearly 40 types of horses around the world, this account looks briefly at the horse's evolutionary history and related species. (Rev: HBG 3/02; SLJ 3/02) [636.1]

22838 Lewin, Ted. *Stable* (K–3). Illus. by author. 2010, Roaring Brook $17.99 (978-1-59643-467-7). 40pp.

Evocative watercolor illustrations enhance this passage-of-time story about Brooklyn's Kensington stable, which has been in use since the 1800s. (Rev: BL 10/15/10; LMC 1–2/11; SLJ 10/1/10) [636.1]

22839 Libby, Barbara M. *I Rode the Red Horse: Secretariat's Belmont Race* (1–3). Illus. by author. 2003, Blood-Horse $16.95 (978-1-58150-096-7). 32pp. Triple Crown-winner Secretariat's victory at the Belmont Stakes in 1973 is told in the words of jockey Ron Turcotte. (Rev: BL 7/03; HBG 10/03) [798.4]

22840 McKerley, Jennifer. *Man O' War: Best Racehorse Ever* (1–3). Illus. by Terry Widener. Series: Step into Reading. 2005, Random LB $11.99 (978-0-375-93164-2); paper $3.99 (978-0-375-83164-5). 48pp. The exciting story of the famous, independent-minded racehorse who was the grandfather of Seabiscuit. (Rev: BL 11/1/05; SLJ 1/06) [798.4]

22841 Momatiuk, Yva, and John Eastcott. *Face to Face with Wild Horses* (5–8). Illus. Series: Face to Face with Animals. 2009, National Geographic $16.95 (978-1-4263-0466-8). 32pp. Riveting close-up photographs show wild horses in their own environment; back matter includes sections on How You Can Help, It's Your Turn, and Facts at a Glance. (Rev: BL 4/1/09) [599.665]

22842 Patent, Dorothy Hinshaw. *Horses* (2–3). Series: Early Bird Nature Books. 2001, Lerner LB $25.26 (978-0-8225-3045-9). 48pp. With color photographs on each page and a simple text, this book introduces the life cycle of the horse with material on its anatomy, habits, and relationship to humans. (Rev: BL 8/1/01; HBG 10/01) [636.1]

22843 Penny, Malcolm. *The Secret Life of Wild Horses* (4–7). Series: The Secret World of . . . 2002, Raintree LB $27.12 (978-0-7398-4987-3). 48pp. A page of little-known facts about wild horses introduces this book that explores the horse's life, habits, mating, behavior, and threats to its future. (Rev: BL 8/02) [636.1]

22844 Peterson, Chris. *Wild Horses* (3–8). Illus. 2003, Boyds Mills $16.95 (978-1-56397-745-9). 32pp. Peterson presents photographs of and information about the horses living in the Wild Horse Sanctuary in the Black Hills of South Dakota. (Rev: BL 2/15/03; HBG 10/03; SLJ 3/03) [599.665]

22845 Presnall, Judith Janda. *Horse Therapists* (4–7). Illus. Series: Animals with Jobs. 2002, Gale LB $23.70 (978-0-7377-0615-4). 48pp. Numerous photographs show how horses are used in various therapeutic situations including exercise for people with physical and mental disabilities. (Rev: BL 4/1/02; SLJ 3/02) [636.1]

22846 Price, Steven D. *The Kids' Book of the American Quarter Horse* (3–5). Illus. 2000, Lyons paper $19.95 (978-1-55821-975-5). 159pp. As well as telling how to choose, care for, and ride quarter horses, this account tells their history and explains the functions of the American Quarter Horse Association. (Rev: BL 2/1/00) [636.1]

22847 Pritchard, Louise. *I Love Ponies: A First Pony Guide* (2–4). Illus. 2007, Barron's paper $11.99 (978-0-

7641-3790-7). 64pp. Cartoon and color photos illustrate this introduction to ponies. (Rev: SLJ 4/08)

22848 Ransford, Sandy. *Horse and Pony Breeds* (3–5). Photos by Bob Langrish. Series: Kingfisher Riding Club. 2003, Kingfisher $14.95 (978-0-7534-5575-3). 64pp. An attractive guide to horse and pony breeds from around the world. (Rev: HBG 10/03; SLJ 7/03) [636.1]

22849 Ransford, Sandy. *The Kingfisher Illustrated Horse and Pony Encyclopedia* (4–8). Photos by Bob Langrish. 2004, Kingfisher $24.95 (978-0-7534-5781-8). After describing the history and various breeds of horses, this comprehensive and highly illustrated volume explains how to care for horses and how to ride them well and safely. (Rev: BL 3/1/05; SLJ 1/05) [636.1]

22850 Richter, Judy. *Riding for Kids* (4–8). 2003, Storey $23.95 (978-1-58017-511-1); paper $16.95 (978-1-58017-510-4). An introduction to horsemanship, from caring for horses and riding equipment to advice on safety, showing, and jumping. (Rev: BL 1/1–15/04; SLJ 3/04) [798.2]

22851 Scanlan, Lawrence. *The Big Red Horse: The Story of Secretariat and the Loyal Groom Who Loved Him* (4–8). Photos by Raymond Woolfe. 2010, HarperTrophy paper $7.99 (978-0-00-639352-8). 170pp. Prized racehorse Secretariat's inspiring story is portrayed in this biography, which features a variety of compelling anecdotes and black-and-white pictures. (Rev: SLJ 3/1/11)

22852 Simon, Seymour. *Horses* (2–4). Illus. 2006, HarperCollins $16.99 (978-0-06-028944-7). 40pp. Basic facts about horses — their history, physical characteristics, breeds, and so forth — are accompanied by eye-catching photographs. (Rev: BL 12/1/05; SLJ 2/06) [636.1]

22853 Stefoff, Rebecca. *Horses* (5–8). Series: Animal-Ways. 2000, Marshall Cavendish LB $31.36 (978-0-7614-1139-0). A well-illustrated account that describes the physical and behavioral characteristics of horses, their place in the classification system, and their relationships with humans. (Rev: BL 1/1–15/01) [599.884]

22854 Tracqui, Valerie. *The Horse: Faster Than the Wind* (3–6). Illus. by Gilles Delaborde. Series: Face-to-Face. 2001, Charlesbridge $9.95 (978-1-57091-450-8). 32pp. Clear text and photographs introduce the horse, with information on habitat, behavior, and reproduction. (Rev: BL 10/15/01; HBG 3/02) [599.665]

22855 van der Linde, Laurel. *From Mustangs to Movie Stars: Five True Horse Legends of Our Time* (4–7). 1995, Millbrook LB $24.40 (978-1-56294-456-8). Biographies of five famous horses are recounted, from the racer Native Dancer to Cass Olé, who was the star of the film *The Black Stallion*. (Rev: BCCB 12/95; SLJ 12/95) [636.1]

22856 Vogel, Julia. *Wild Horses* (2–4). Illus. 2004, North-Word $10.95 (978-1-55971-881-3). 48pp. Vogel examines the threats facing the last remaining herds of wild mustangs roaming the western United States. (Rev: BL 3/15/04; SLJ 10/04) [599.665]

22857 Wilsdon, Christina. *For Horse-Crazy Girls Only: Everything You Want to Know About Horses* (3–8). Illus. by Alecia Underhill. 2010, Feiwel & Friends $14.99 (978-0-312-60323-6). 150pp. A lighthearted survey of all things horse, from horse jokes and lore to information on markings and ailments to practical tips on working with horses. (Rev: SLJ 4/11) [636.1]

22858 Yerxa, Leo. *Ancient Thunder* (K–3). Illus. by author. 2006, Groundwood $18.95 (978-0-88899-746-3). This handsome book with a spare text and illustrations that appear to be painted shirts celebrates the wild horses that roamed the Great Plains and their contributions to the Native Americans living there. (Rev: SLJ 11/06) [599.665]

Zoos and Marine Aquariums

22859 Bleiman, Andrew, and Chris Eastland. *Zoo Borns! Zoo Babies from Around the World* (PS–3). Photos by authors. 2010, Simon & Schuster $12.99 (978-1-4424-1272-9). 160pp. With appealing photographs and simple first-person text, this book introduces baby animals including a hyena, a mongoose, an ocelot, and a fennec fox. (Rev: SLJ 10/1/10) [591.3]

22860 Halls, Kelly Milner, and William Sumner. *Saving the Baghdad Zoo: A True Story of Hope and Heroes* (4–7). Illus. by William Sumner. 2010, Greenwillow $17.99 (978-0-06-177202-3). 64pp. American soldiers work together with Iraqi citizens to protect and provide for the animals of the Baghdad zoo in this inspiring story of cooperation. (Rev: BL 2/15/10; SLJ 6/10) [590.73]

22861 Komiya, Teruyuki. *More Life-Size Zoo* (PS–2). Trans. by Junko Miyakoshi. Illus. by Toshimitsu Matsuhashi. 2010, Seven Footer $18.95 (978-1-934734-19-3). 48pp. In this sequel to *Life-Size Zoo* (2009), Komiya offers up more vivid life-size photographs, fold-outs, and quirky facts for a variety of zoo animals. (Rev: BLO 8/10; SLJ 9/1/10) [591.4]

22862 Laidlaw, Rob. *Wild Animals in Captivity* (4–7). Illus. 2008, Fitzhenry & Whiteside $19.95 (978-1-55455-025-8). 48pp. Animal rights emerge front and center in this passionate, well-researched and convincing case for replacing zoos with wildlife sanctuaries and conservation centers. (Rev: BLO 2/5/09; SLJ 7/08) [636.088]

22863 Morecroft, Richard, and Alison Mackay. *Zoo Album* (3–5). Illus. by Karen Lloyd-Diviny. 2004, Enchanted Lion $17.95 (978-1-59270-032-5). 48pp. Vivid artwork and an easy-to-follow narrative introduce animals in Australian zoos, with interesting anecdotes by caretakers. (Rev: BL 12/1/04; SLJ 2/05) [590.73]

22864 Nagda, Ann Whitehead, and Cindy Bickel. *Tiger Math* (3–6). Illus. 2000, Holt $16.00 (978-0-8050-6248-9). 30pp. This account traces the growth and maturation of a Siberian tiger cub who was cared for at the Denver Zoo after his mother died when he was only ten weeks old. (Rev: BCCB 9/00; BL 10/1/00; HBG 3/01; SLJ 10/00) [511]

22865 Rinard, Judith E. *Zoos Without Cages* (5–8). 1981, National Geographic LB $12.50 (978-0-87044-340-4). A description of the new zoos that strive to reproduce the natural habitat of the enclosed animals. [590.74]

Botany

General and Miscellaneous

22866 Bang, Molly, and Penny Chrisholm. *Living Sunlight: How Plants Bring the Earth to Life* (PS–3). Illus. by Molly Bang. 2009, Scholastic $16.99 (978-0-545-04422-6). 40pp. Bang offers a clear explanation of photosynthesis and its importance. (Rev: BCCB 4/09; BL 12/1/08; HB 5/09; LMC 5/09; SLJ 2/09) [572]

22867 Ganeri, Anita. *Plant Life Cycles* (K–3). Series: Nature's Patterns. 2005, Heinemann LB $16.95 (978-1-4034-5896-4). 32pp. In simple languge, this volume introduces the life cycles of plants. (Rev: SLJ 6/05)

22868 Kudlinski, Kathleen V. *What Do Roots Do?* (K–3). Illus. by David Schuppert. 2005, NorthWord $15.95 (978-1-55971-896-7). This colorfully illustrated picture book explores in rhyming verse the role of roots in the lives of plants, flowers, and trees. (Rev: SLJ 12/05) [581.4]

22869 Murphy, Patricia J. *Peeking at Plants with a Scientist* (1–3). Series: I Like Science! 2004, Enslow LB $21.26 (978-0-7660-2266-9). 24pp. The work of a botanist is portrayed in question-and-answer format and many photographs. (Rev: SLJ 8/04) [580]

22870 Patent, Dorothy Hinshaw. *Plants on the Trail with Lewis and Clark.* (5–8). Photos by William Muñoz. 2003, Clarion $18.00 (978-0-618-06776-3). This introduction to the trees and plants seen by Lewis and Clark also discusses Lewis's training as a botanist and his contributions to the field. (Rev: BL 3/1/03; HBG 10/03; SLJ 5/03) [581.978]

22871 Schaefer, Lola M. *Pick, Pull, Snap! Where Once a Flower Bloomed* (PS–1). Illus. by Lindsay Barrett George. 2003, Greenwillow $16.99 (978-0-688-17834-5). 32pp. Attractively illustrated flaps and fold-outs add to the appeal of this introduction to the basics of plant growth. (Rev: BL 5/1/03; HBG 10/03; SLJ 7/03) [571.8]

22872 Silverstein, Alvin. *Photosynthesis* (5–9). Series: Science Concepts. 1998, Twenty-First Century LB $26.90 (978-0-7613-3000-4). Photosynthesis is explained, with a history of the discoveries about the process and material on related issues including acid rain and the greenhouse effect. (Rev: HBG 3/99; SLJ 2/99) [581.1]

Flowers

22873 Farndon, John. *Flowers* (2–5). Illus. Series: World of Plants. 2006, Gale LB $23.70 (978-1-4103-0423-0). 24pp. Diagrams and photographs supplement the clear text describing flowers and the role they play in the overall life of the plant. (Rev: SLJ 2/07)

22874 Holmes, Anita. *Flowers and Friends* (K–2). Series: We Can Read About — Science! 2000, Benchmark LB $21.36 (978-0-7614-1113-0). 32pp. An easy-to-read book that describes the process of pollination through the perception of various creatures. (Rev: HBG 3/01; SLJ 2/01) [582]

22875 Hood, Susan, and National Audubon Society, eds. *Wildflowers* (5–8). 1998, Scholastic paper $17.95 (978-0-590-05464-5). Fifty common wildflowers are pictured and described, along with information on what equipment to use and what to look for to observe and study wildflowers (leaves, blooms, habitat, height, range). (Rev: BL 8/98; SLJ 8/98) [583]

22876 Johnson, Sylvia A. *Morning Glories* (4–7). 1985, Lerner LB $22.60 (978-0-8225-1462-6). Color photographs display the stages of this plant's development. (Rev: BCCB 3/86; BL 4/15/86; SLJ 4/86)

22877 Pascoe, Elaine. *Flowers* (3–5). Photos by Dwight Kuhn. Series: Nature Close-Up. 2003, Gale LB $24.95 (978-1-56711-432-4). 48pp. Beautiful photographs of flowering plants are accompanied by introductory information on their importance to ecology and their usefulness to mankind. (Rev: SLJ 3/04) [575.6]

22878 Ryden, Hope. *Wildflowers Around the Year* (4–6). Illus. 2001, Clarion $17.00 (978-0-395-85814-1). 48pp. A handsome book on wildflowers that gives details on characteristics, uses in food or medicine, and fertilization. (Rev: BL 3/1/01; HB 3/01; HBG 10/01) [582.13]

22879 Souza, D. M. *Freaky Flowers* (4–7). Series: Watts Library. 2002, Watts LB $25.50 (978-0-531-11981-5). 64pp. Flowering plants are the main focus in this discussion of basic botany, the ways in which flowers attract pollinators, and the environmental dangers plants are facing. (Rev: SLJ 7/02) [582]

22880 Wade, Mary Dodson. *Flowers Bloom!* (K–2). Series: I Like Plants! 2009, Enslow LB $21.26 (978-0-7660-3157-9). 24pp. Using a question-and-answer format, this book provides a simple explanation of how flowers grow and bloom, with color photographs and an activity. (Rev: SLJ 4/09) [582.13]

22881 Weiss, Ellen. *From Bulb to Daffodil* (1–2). Series: Scholastic News Nonfiction Reader. 2007, Children's Pr. LB $20.00 (978-0-531-18534-6); paper $6.95 (978-0-531-18787-6). 24pp. For beginning readers, this is an easy-to-follow explanation of how bulbs grow into flowers. (Rev: SLJ 12/07) [635.9]

Foods and Farming

GENERAL

22882 Arlon, Penelope, and Tory Gordon Harris. *Farm* (PS–K). Illus. Series: Discover More. 2012, Scholastic $7.99 (978-054536571-0). 32pp. This print picture book offers an overview of types of farms and the animals and equipment found there, and is supported by a digital companion with additional features. (Rev: BLO 3/1/12) [630]

22883 Artley, Bob. *Once Upon a Farm* (4–9). Illus. by author. 2000, Pelican $21.95 (978-1-56554-753-7). Fine watercolors accompany a readable look at the seasons as experienced by the author while growing up on a farm in Iowa. (Rev: SLJ 12/00) [630]

22884 Bell, Rachael. *Cows* (K–3). Series: Farm Animals. 2000, Heinemann LB $21.36 (978-1-57572-529-1). 32pp. Using double-page spreads, this book introduces cows and their uses as a source of meat and milk. Also use *Pigs* (2000). (Rev: HBG 3/01; SLJ 7/00) [630]

22885 Bial, Raymond. *The Farms* (4–7). Photos by author. Illus. Series: Building America. 2001, Benchmark LB $27.07 (978-0-7614-1332-5). 56pp. An interesting, beautifully illustrated look at the ways in which farms developed in America, with information on their structure and significance to the country as a whole. Also use *The Mills* (2001). (Rev: HBG 3/02; SLJ 2/02*) [630]

22886 Bowden, Rob. *Food and Farming* (5–8). Illus. Series: Sustainable World. 2004, Gale LB $26.20 (978-0-7377-1899-7). 48pp. Bowden looks at conventional methods of farming and at the new focus on sustainable agriculture, providing lots of facts and statistics and highlighting choices we all can make that may improve the future. (Rev: BL 4/15/04; SLJ 10/04) [338]

22887 Chandler, Gary, and Kevin Graham. *Natural Foods and Products* (4–8). Series: Making a Better World. 1996, Twenty-First Century LB $25.90 (978-0-8050-4623-6). This work discusses genetically engineered foods, safe eco-friendly methods of growing crops, and companies that engage in safe practices. (Rev: BL 12/15/96; SLJ 1/97) [333.76]

22888 Chapman, Garry, and Gary Hodges. *Coffee* (5–8). Illus. Series: World Commodities. 2010, Black Rabbit LB $28.50 (978-159920584-7). 32pp. Explores the cultural, environmental, and political story of coffee. (Rev: BL 10/1/10; LMC 5–6/11) [338.1]

22889 Damerow, Gail. *Your Chickens: A Kid's Guide to Raising and Showing* (4–7). 1993, Storey paper $14.95 (978-0-88266-823-9). A straightforward, practical guide on raising prize-winning chickens that is both thorough and filled with information. (Rev: BL 5/15/94; SLJ 1/94) [636.5]

22890 Damerow, Gail. *Your Goats: A Kid's Guide to Raising and Showing* (4–7). 1993, Storey paper $14.95 (978-0-88266-825-3). This is a complete guide to raising, breeding, and showing goats, with many useful tips and helpful illustrations. (Rev: BL 5/15/94; SLJ 1/94) [636.3]

22891 Dyer, Hadley. *Potatoes on Rooftops: Farming in the City* (4–7). Illus. 2012, Annick $24.95 (978-1-55451-425-0); paper $14.95 (978-1-55451-424-3). 84pp. An appealing overview of the various — environmental, psychological, health — benefits of rooftop and container gardening and of school and community gardens. Lexile 1090L (Rev: BL 12/1/12; SLJ 12/12*) [630]

22892 Eagen, Rachel. *The Biography of Bananas* (4–7). Series: How Did That Get Here? 2005, Crabtree LB $26.60 (978-0-7787-2483-4). This richly illustrated title offers a wealth of information about the science and business of producing bananas. (Rev: BL 3/1/06) [634]

22893 Feldman, Thea. *Who You Callin' Chicken?* (3–5). Photos by Stephen Green-Armytage. 2003, Abrams $14.95 (978-0-8109-4593-7). Chickens of all kinds feature in this lively photographic survey. (Rev: HBG 4/04; SLJ 12/03) [636.5]

22894 Ghione, Yvette. *This Is Daniel Cook at the Farm* (K–3). 2006, Kids Can $12.95 (978-1-55453-077-9); paper $4.95 (978-1-55453-078-6). In this companion to the popular Canadian-produced TV show, the young host invites readers to join him on a journey of discovery around a busy farmyard. (Rev: SLJ 11/06) [636]

22895 Gibbons, Gail. *Chicks and Chickens* (1–3). Illus. by author. 2003, Holiday House $16.95 (978-0-8234-1700-1). Using cartoon illustrations and simple narrative, Gibbons examines the life cycle of chickens. (Rev: HBG 10/03; SLJ 7/03) [636.5]

22896 Hughes, Meredith S. *Tall and Tasty: Fruit Trees* (5–8). Series: Plants We Eat. 2000, Lerner LB $31.95 (978-0-8225-2837-1). 80pp. This book explores the world of apples, peaches, mangoes, and other fruits that grow on trees and explains each one's life cycle, and how the fruit has migrated during its history. (Rev: BL 4/15/00; HBG 10/00) [641.3]

22897 Kant, Tanya. *How an Egg Grows into a Chicken* (K–3). Illus. by Carolyn Franklin. Series: Amaze. 2008, Children's Pr. LB $26.00 (978-0-531-24047-2); paper $8.95 (978-0-531-23801-1). "Why do chickens lay eggs? Why do they sit on them?" This simple introduction to a chicken's life cycle, with colorful illustrations and well-organized chapters, includes two experiments. (Rev: SLJ 3/09) [636.5]

22898 Lasky, Kathryn. *Sugaring Time* (4–7). 1998, Center for Applied Research paper $4.95 (978-0-87628-350-9). Through photographs and text, the process of maple sugar production in New England is described.

22899 Miller, Sara S. *Chickens* (2–3). Series: True Books. 2000, Children's Book Pr. LB $25.00 (978-0-516-21576-1). 32pp. A simple introduction to chickens that describes their anatomy, uses, homes, and habits. (Rev: BL 1/1–15/01) [636.5]

22900 Miller, Sara S. *Cows* (2–3). Illus. Series: True Books. 2000, Children's Book Pr. LB $25.00 (978-0-516-21577-8). 48pp. Covers dairy cows and their domestication as well as giving information on dairy products and life on a dairy farm. (Rev: BL 1/1–15/01) [636.3]

22901 Miller, Sara S. *Pigs* (2–3). Series: True Books. 2000, Children's Book Pr. LB $25.00 (978-0-516-21579-2). 32pp. Using colorful pictures and a minimum of text, this farm animal is introduced with material on its anatomy, habits, and uses. (Rev: BL 1/1–15/01) [636.3]

22902 Miller, Sara S. *Sheep* (2–3). Illus. Series: True Books. 2000, Children's Book Pr. LB $25.00 (978-0-516-21580-8). 48pp. This book introduces sheep and sheep farming with material on the animal's use both for food and wool. (Rev: BL 1/1–15/01) [636.3]

22903 Morck, Irene. *Old Bird* (2–4). Illus. by Muriel Wood. 2003, Fitzhenry & Whiteside $15.95 (978-1-55041-695-4). 32pp. An aging horse named Bird is determined to prove she can pull her weight around the farm in this novel based on a true story. (Rev: SLJ 10/03) [813]

22904 Munro, Roxie. *Ranch* (2–4). 2004, Bright Sky $16.95 (978-1-931721-37-0). 36pp. Readers are introduced to all aspects of a cattle ranch and the people who work there. (Rev: BL 7/04; SLJ 9/04) [636.2]

22905 Peterson, Chris. *Amazing Grazing* (3–5). Illus. by Alvis Upitis. 2002, Boyds Mills $16.95 (978-1-56397-942-2). 32pp. Color photographs and a lucid text show how three Montana cattle ranchers are using environment-friendly practices. (Rev: BL 4/1/02; HBG 10/02; SLJ 4/02) [636.0845]

22906 Peterson, Chris. *Clarabelle: Making Milk and So Much More* (1–3). Illus. 2007, Boyds Mills $16.95 (978-1-59078-310-8). 32pp. A look at the dairy industry, featuring a day in the life of Clarabelle the cow; color photographs add to the informative text. (Rev: BL 9/1/07; SLJ 10/07) [636.2]

22907 Pipe, Jim. *Farm Animals* (PS–1). Illus. Series: Read and Play. 2007, Stargazer LB $22.80 (978-1-59604-112-7). 32pp. Very basic facts about farm animals are presented with eye-catching photographs and a "Let's Play" section with easy games. (Rev: BL 4/15/07) [636]

22908 Powell, Jillian. *From Calf to Cow* (PS–3). Series: How Do They Grow? 2001, Raintree LB $25.69 (978-0-7398-4426-7). 32pp. Brief text and large, full-color photographs follow calves through birth and growth. Also use *From Chick to Chicken* and from *From Piglet to Pig* (both 2001). (Rev: HBG 3/02; SLJ 1/02) [636.2]

22909 Reilly, Kathleen M. *Food: 25 Amazing Projects Investigate the History and Science of What We Eat* (4–6). Illus. by Farah Rizvi. 2010, Nomad paper $15.95 (978-1-934670-59-0). 124pp. Activities reinforce the information presented on food in general and around the world, farming, packaging, and healthy choices. (Rev: SLJ 2/1/11) [641.3]

22910 Rendon, Marcie, and Cheryl Walsh Bellville. *Farmer's Market: Families Working Together* (4–6). Illus. 2001, Carolrhoda $23.93 (978-1-57505-462-9). 48pp. A look at truck farming and the sale of the produce at farmers' markets, with profiles of two Midwest families. (Rev: BL 5/1/01; HBG 10/01) [635]

22911 Rockwell, Lizzy. *Plants Feed Me* (PS–K). Illus. by author. 2014, Holiday $16.95 (978-082342526-6). 32pp. With detailed illustrations, diagrams, and simple text, this title looks at plants that we eat and how they grow. (Rev: BL 3/1/14; SLJ 3/14) [581.6]

22912 Rosen, Michael J. *Our Farm: Four Seasons with Five Kids on One Family's Farm* (3–7). Photos by author. 2008, Darby Creek $18.95 (978-1-58196-067-9). 144pp. An interesting photo-essay covering a year on an Ohio family farm. (Rev: SLJ 9/08) [630]

22913 Schuh, Mari C. *Chickens on the Farm* (PS–2). Series: On the Farm. 2001, Capstone LB $17.26 (978-0-7368-0991-7). 24pp. Spare text and full-color photographs convey simple facts about chickens. Also use *Pigs on the Farm* and *Sheep on the Farm* (both 2001). (Rev: HBG 3/02; SLJ 1/02) [636.5]

22914 Sklansky, Amy E. *Where Do Chicks Come From?* (K–2). Illus. by Pam Paparone. Series: Let's-Read-and-Find-Out. 2005, HarperCollins LB $16.89 (978-0-06-028893-8); paper $5.99 (978-0-06-445212-0). 40pp. Follows the development of a chick from the moment of fertilization until it hatches from the egg roughly three weeks later. (Rev: BL 2/1/05; SLJ 2/05) [636.5]

22915 Sweeney, Alyse. *Let's Visit a Dairy Farm* (K–2). Series: Scholastic News Nonfiction Readers. 2006, Children's Pr. LB $20.00 (978-0-531-16843-1). 24pp. Basic information for beginning readers, with seven highlighted words that are featured in bold in the text. (Rev: SLJ 1/07) [069]

22916 Urbigkit, Cat. *A Young Shepherd* (1–3). Illus. 2006, Boyds Mills $15.95 (978-1-59078-364-1). 32pp. This photo-essay documents a year in the life of a 12-year-old boy who tends his own sheep on a Wyoming ranch. (Rev: BL 2/15/06; SLJ 5/06) [636]

22917 Vogel, Julia. *Local Farms and Sustainable Food* (3–7). Series: Language Arts Explorer: Save the Planet. 2010, Cherry Lake LB $27.07 (978-1-60279-660-7). 32pp. Students are given a mission at the beginning of the book and must use creative thinking and problem solving to gather facts as they travel on a virtual trip through the process of growing and distributing organic food. (Rev: LMC 8–9/10; SLJ 4/10) [630]

22918 Wolfman, Judy. *Life on a Cattle Farm* (4–6). Illus. by David Lorenz Winston. Series: Life on a Farm. 2001, Carolrhoda LB $23.93 (978-1-57505-516-9). 48pp. A photo-illustrated look at activities on a Pennsylvania cattle farm, told from a teenager's point of view. Also use *Life on a Crop Farm*, *Life on a Goat Farm*, and *Life on a Horse Farm* (all 2001). (Rev: BL 11/15/01; HBG 3/02; SLJ 11/01) [636.2]

FARMS, RANCHES, AND FARM ANIMALS

22919 Bailer, Darice. *Donkeys* (3–5). Illus. 2011, Marshall Cavendish LB $20.95 (978-0-7614-4875-4). 48pp. Bailer looks at how and why we keep donkeys, their anatomy and life cycle, abuse of donkeys, and the relationship between donkeys and people. (Rev: BL 10/15/11; SLJ 11/1/11) [636.1]

22920 Katz, Jon. *Lenore Finds a Friend* (PS–1). Illus. by author. 2012, Henry Holt $15.99 (978-080509220-2). 15.99pp. This sequel to *Meet the Dogs of Bedlam Farm* (2011) tells the true story of the unlikely friendship between black lab Lenore and a ram named Brutus. Lexile AD460L (Rev: BL 10/15/12) [636.7309747]

22921 Katz, Jon. *Meet the Dogs of Bedlam Farm* (K–2). Photos by author. 2011, Henry Holt $16.99 (978-0-8050-9219-6). 32pp. With many pictures and appealing text, Katz introduces the four dogs that live with him on an upstate New York farm, and the jobs that they do each day. Lexile AD600L (Rev: BL 2/1/11; LMC 5–6/11; SLJ 3/1/11*) [636.7]

22922 Martin, Claudia. *Farming* (4–7). Series: Working Animals. 2010, Marshall Cavendish LB $19.95 (978-1-60870-162-9). 64pp. Animals' varied roles in agriculture are described in this attractive, informative book. Also use *Helpers* (2010), about animals that help the blind and deaf. (Rev: SLJ 12/1/10) [636]

22923 Olney, Ross R. *The Farm Combine* (4–8). 1984, Walker LB $10.85 (978-0-8027-6568-0). The development of the reaper and thrasher is discussed, with information on today's combine harvester.

22924 Stiefel, Chana. *Chickens on the Family Farm* (K–3). Illus. Series: Animals on the Family Farm. 2013, Enslow LB $21.26 (978-0-7660-4204-9). 24pp. A basic introduction to chickens and how they live, with bright photographs and boldface vocabulary words. The series also includes *Turkeys on the Family Farm, Pigs on the Family Farm,* and *Goats on the Family Farm* (all 2013). (Rev: BL 6/13; SLJ 5/13) [636.5]

22925 Webber, Desiree Morrison. *Bone Head: Story of the Longhorn* (4–7). Illus. by Sandy Shropshire. 2003, Eakin $16.95 (978-1-57168-763-0). The longhorn's characteristics and the reasons for its early success but decline with the arrival of the railroad are explored in appealing text and archival photographs. (Rev: SLJ 2/04) [636.2]

FOODS

22926 Allen, Nancy Kelly. *Whose Work Is This? A Look at Things Animals Make-Pearls, Milk, and Honey* (PS–2). Illus. Series: Whose Is It? Science. 2004, Picture Window LB $25.26 (978-1-4048-0612-2). 24pp. A rhythmic question-and-answer format and colorful collages introduce the wide variety of foods that animals produce.

22927 Ancona, George. *Come and Eat!* (PS–1). Illus. 2011, Charlesbridge $16.95 (978-1-58089-366-4); paper $7.95 (978-1-58089-367-1). 48pp. A lively overview of food customs around the world, with appetizing color photographs. (Rev: BL 6/1/11; SLJ 7/11) [394.1]

22928 Bial, Raymond. *The Super Soybean* (4–6). Illus. 2007, Albert Whitman $16.95 (978-0-8075-7549-9). 32pp. This well-organized title with many photographs introduces the history and characteristics of the soybean and looks at the surprising number and variety of soy products. (Rev: BL 9/1/07; LMC 1/08; SLJ 10/07) [633.3]

22929 Burleigh, Robert. *Chocolate: Riches from the Rainforest* (3–6). Illus. 2002, Abrams $16.95 (978-0-8109-5734-3). 40pp. Traces the rich history of choco-

late, from the Aztecs to Hershey's. (Rev: BL 3/1/02; HBG 10/02; SLJ 4/02) [641.3]

22930 Butterworth, Chris. *How Did That Get in My Lunchbox? The Story of Food* (K–3). Illus. by Lucia Gaggiotti. 2011, Candlewick $12.99 (978-0-7636-5005-6). 32pp. Butterworth presents an appealing tour of a typical child's lunch and the origins of the ingredients. (Rev: BL 4/15/11; HB 3–4/11; LMC 8–9/11; SLJ 4/11) [641.3]

22931 Calì, Davide. *I Love Chocolate* (K–3). Illus. by Evelyn Daviddi. 2009, Tundra $12.95 (978-0-88776-912-2). A delicious exploration of all the good things about chocolate. (Rev: SLJ 4/09) [641.3]

22932 Cobb, Vicki. *Junk Food* (3–5). Illus. by Michael Gold. Series: Where's the Science Here? 2005, Millbrook LB $23.93 (978-0-7613-2773-8). 48pp. Candy, corn chips, and soda are among the popular products explored here; clear text and easy projects will grab attention. (Rev: BL 10/15/05; HBG 4/06; SLJ 2/06) [664]

22933 Fleisher, Paul. *Ice Cream Treats: The Inside Scoop* (4–6). Photos by David O. Saunders. 2001, Carolrhoda LB $23.93 (978-1-57505-268-7). 48pp. This is an appealing overview of the history of ice cream, with a tour of a factory and a few simple recipes. (Rev: HBG 10/01; SLJ 7/01) [641.8]

22934 Frost, Helen. *The Grain Group* (K–2). Series: Food Guide Pyramid. 2000, Capstone LB $17.26 (978-0-7368-0538-4). 24pp. This text for beginning readers introduces different grains and explains their importance in the food pyramid. (Rev: HBG 9/00; SLJ 10/00) [633.1]

22935 Gibbons, Gail. *Ice Cream: The Full Scoop* (K–2). 2006, Holiday $16.95 (978-0-8234-2000-1). 32pp. A delicious history of ice cream from the days of Marco Polo to the present, with a tour of a contemporary factory. (Rev: BL 6/1–15/06; SLJ 8/06) [641.8]

22936 Greenstein, Elaine. *Ice-Cream Cones for Sale!* (K–2). Illus. 2003, Scholastic $15.95 (978-0-439-32728-2). 32pp. Greenstein tells the "real" story behind the ice-cream cone, taking care to delineate the boundaries between known fact and speculative fiction. (Rev: BL 5/1/03; HB 9/03; HBG 4/04; SLJ 9/03) [637.4]

22937 Hartzog, John Daniel. *Everyday Science Experiments with Food* (PS–3). 2000, Rosen $21.25 (978-0-8239-5460-5). 24pp. The eight projects outlined in this simple science book include recipes for making butter and homemade soda. (Rev: SLJ 9/00) [641.3]

22938 Hughes, Meredith S. *Flavor Foods: Spices and Herbs* (5–8). Series: Plants We Eat. 2000, Lerner LB $26.60 (978-0-8225-2835-7). 88pp. This book explains how roots, leaves, flowers, seeds, fruit, and bark of some plants are transformed in the seasonings that flavor so many dishes. (Rev: BL 7/00; HBG 10/00) [633.8]

22939 Hughes, Meredith S. *Glorious Grasses: The Grains* (5–8). Series: Plants We Eat. 1999, Lerner LB $26.60 (978-0-8225-2831-9). A description of the history, cultivation, processing, and dietary importance of wheat, rice, corn, millet, barley, oats, and rye, plus recipes and activities. (Rev: BL 7/99; HBG 10/99; SLJ 8/99) [633.1]

22940 Jango-Cohen, Judith. *The History of Food* (5–8). Series: Major Inventions Through History. 2005, Twenty-First Century LB $26.60 (978-0-8225-2484-7). Addresses inventions in the food industry such as canning, pasteurization, and genetically modified crops. (Rev: SLJ 2/06)

22941 Jones, Carol. *Cheese* (4–7). Illus. Series: From Farm to You. 2002, Chelsea $28.00 (978-0-7910-7005-5). 32pp. This is an absorbing account of the techniques used in manufacturing cheese and the history of cheese, with an overview of the many varieties and a map of cheese eating around the world. Also use *Pasta and Noodles* (2002). (Rev: BL 11/1/02; HBG 3/03) [641.3]

22942 Keller, Kristin Thoennes. *From Maple Trees to Maple Syrup* (1–3). Series: First Facts: From Farm to Table. 2004, Capstone LB $21.26 (978-0-7368-2634-1). 24pp. This easy-reader traces the various steps involved in the production of maple syrup and includes a simple recipe. Also use *From Oranges to Orange Juice* and *From Peanuts to Peanut Butter* (both 2004). (Rev: SLJ 2/05) [641.3]

22943 Landau, Elaine. *Popcorn!* (2–4). Illus. by Brian Lies. 2003, Charlesbridge $16.95 (978-1-57091-442-3); paper $6.95 (978-1-57091-443-0). 32pp. An entertaining look at the history of the popular snack, with humorous illustrations. (Rev: BL 2/1/03; HBG 10/03; SLJ 4/03) [646.6]

22944 Levenson, George. *Bread Comes to Life: A Garden of Wheat and a Loaf to Eat* (PS–1). 2004, Tricycle $15.95 (978-1-58246-114-4). 32pp. All kinds of bread feature in this rhythmic and appetizing volume. (Rev: BL 10/1/04) [641.8]

22945 Morgan, Sally. *Superfoods: Genetic Modification of Foods* (5–8). Series: Science at the Edge. 2002, Heinemann LB $27.86 (978-1-58810-702-2). 64pp. A look at the history and genetic alteration of foods, with discussion of the controversy this has created. (Rev: BL 10/15/02; HBG 3/03; SLJ 4/03) [174.957]

22946 Morris, Neil. *Do You Know Where Your Food Comes From?* (4–7). Illus. 2006, Heinemann LB $32.86 (978-1-4034-8575-5). In this informative book students learn all about the global food market, where and how their food is produced, and how to make good food choices. (Rev: BL 12/1/06; SLJ 4/07) [363.8]

22947 Nelson, Robin. *From Cocoa Bean to Chocolate* (K–3). Illus. Series: Start to Finish: Food. 2012, Lerner LB $23.93 (978-0-7613-6560-0). 24pp. Bold, full-page photographs add appeal to this account of how cocoa beans get turned into chocolate, starting with the farmer and ending with the wrapper. Also use *From Peanut to Peanut Butter* (2012). (Rev: BL 5/15/12; SLJ 8/12) [664]

22948 Nelson, Robin. *From Flower to Honey* (K–2). Series: Start to Finish. 2003, Lerner LB $18.60 (978-0-8225-0717-8). 24pp. Full of photographs, this basic introduction suitable for beginning readers follows the cycle of honey creation. (Rev: HBG 3/03; SLJ 9/03) [638]

22949 Older, Jules. *Ice Cream* (3–6). Illus. by Lyn Severance. 2002, Charlesbridge $16.95 (978-0-88106-111-6); paper $6.95 (978-0-88106-112-3). 32pp. A fact-packed, colorful, and lighthearted book about the history of ice cream and important ice cream inventions, such as the cone and the banana split. (Rev: BL 2/15/02; HBG 10/02; SLJ 5/02) [641.8]

22950 Polin, C. J. *The Story of Chocolate* (2–4). Illus. Series: DK Readers. 2004, DK $14.99 (978-0-7566-0991-7); paper $3.99 (978-0-7566-0992-4). From harvesting of beans to production of candy bars, this is a simple introduction to chocolate and its history. (Rev: BL 2/1/05) [641.3]

22951 Reynolds, Jan. *Cycle of Rice, Cycle of Life: A Story of Sustainable Farming* (4–7). Illus. 2009, Lee & Low $19.95 (978-1-60060-254-2). 48pp. This photo-essay describes Balinese rice farming and its importance to the community. (Rev: BL 6/1–15/09; SLJ 6/09) [633.1]

22952 Ridley, Sarah. *A Chocolate Bar* (3–5). Illus. Series: How It's Made. 2006, Gareth Stevens LB $24.00 (978-0-8368-6293-5). 32pp. This attractive volume traces the history of a chocolate bar from a cacao farm in Ghana to the factory in which the final product is made; suitable both for reports and browsing. (Rev: BL 4/1/06) [664]

22953 Robbins, Ken. *Food for Thought: The Stories Behind the Things We Eat* (2–4). Illus. by author. 2009, Roaring Brook $17.95 (978-1-59643-343-4). 48pp. A luscious compilation of facts and legends about the fruit and vegetables that we eat. (Rev: BCCB 5/09; BL 3/15/09; HB 5/09; LMC 8/09; SLJ 5/09) [641.3]

22954 Rotner, Shelley, and Gary Goss. *Where Does Food Come From?* (PS–2). Illus. 2006, Millbrook LB $22.60 (978-0-7613-2935-0). 32pp. The origins of the foods we eat — and the many varieties available — are presented in simple, informative text and color photographs. (Rev: BL 3/1/06; SLJ 5/06) [664]

22955 Royston, Angela. *How Is Chocolate Made?* (2–4). Illus. Series: How Are Things Made? 2005, Heinemann LB $24.21 (978-1-4034-6641-9). 32pp. Follows the chocolate manufacturing process from the harvesting of cacao beans to the delivery of the finished product to a retailer's shelves. (Rev: BL 9/15/05) [641.3]

22956 Swain, Ruth Freeman. *How Sweet It Is (and Was): The History of Candy* (1–3). Illus. by John O'Brien. 2003, Holiday House $16.95 (978-0-8234-1712-4). 32pp. This entertaining, illustrated history of sugary delights includes anecdoes, facts, a timeline, recipes, and a bibliography. (Rev: BL 10/15/03; HBG 4/04; SLJ 11/03)

22957 Sylver, Adrienne. *Hot Diggity Dog: The History of the Hot Dog* (K–3). Illus. by Elwood H. Smith. 2010, Dutton $16.99 (978-0-525-47897-3). 32pp. So who did invent the hot dog and who propagated it? This overview covers early origins in ancient Rome, popularity in Europe, star role in the United States, and role as astronaut food. (Rev: BL 4/15/10; SLJ 6/1/10) [641.3]

22958 Taus-Bolstad, Stacy. *From Milk to Ice Cream* (K–3). Illus. Series: Start to Finish: Food. 2012, Lerner LB $23.93 (978-1580139687). 24pp. Bold, full-page photographs add appeal to this account of how milk gets turned into ice cream. *From Grass to Milk* explains how the grass a cow eats becomes nutritious milk (2012). (Rev: BL 5/15/12; SLJ 8/12) [637]

22959 Thomas, Ann. *Dairy Products* (K–4). Series: Food. 2002, Chelsea Clubhouse LB $23.00 (978-0-7910-6980-6). 32pp. A simple introduction to milk (including goat and soy milks), cheese, yogurt, and other dairy products. Also use *Meat and Protein* and *Vegetables* (both 2002). (Rev: HBG 3/03; SLJ 2/03)

22960 Wardlaw, Lee. *We All Scream for Ice Cream: The Scoop on America's Favorite Dessert* (4–7). Illus. by Sandra Forrest. 2000, HarperTrophy paper $4.95 (978-0-380-80250-0). 216pp. A history of this frozen dessert from ancient times to the present with a concentration on modern times and such variations as Eskimo pies and the Good Humor business. (Rev: SLJ 11/00) [637]

FRUITS

22961 Anderson, Sara. *Fruit* (PS–1). Illus. by author. 2007, Handprint $8.95 (978-1-59354-188-0). A bright board-book introduction to various types of fruit. (Rev: SLJ 2/08)

22962 Farmer, Jacqueline. *Apples* (3–5). Illus. by Phyllis L. Tildes. 2007, Charlesbridge $16.95 (978-1-57091-694-6); paper $6.95 (978-1-57091-695-3). 32pp. From pollination and grafting to apple juice and cider, this is an information-filled overview of apples. (Rev: BL 6/1–15/07; SLJ 9/07) [634]

22963 Farmer, Jacqueline. *Pumpkins!* (1–3). Illus. by Phyllis L. Tildes. 2004, Charlesbridge paper $6.95 (978-1-57091-558-1). 32pp. Facts about pumpkins are followed by instructions for cooking and carving them and interesting tidbits such as world pumpkin records. (Rev: BL 8/04; SLJ 7/04) [635]

22964 Frost, Helen. *The Fruit Group* (K–2). Series: Food Guide Pyramid. 2000, Capstone LB $17.26 (978-0-7368-0537-7). 24pp. This easy-to-read guide to good health through eating properly introduces the fruit group and gives examples. (Rev: HBG 9/00; SLJ 10/00) [634]

22965 Ganeri, Anita. *From Seed to Apple* (1–3). Illus. Series: How Living Things Grow. 2006, Heinemann LB $25.36 (978-1-4034-7862-7). 32pp. How a Red Delicious apple grows from a seed, presented in an easy-to-read format. (Rev: SLJ 6/06) [583]

22966 Gibbons, Gail. *Apples* (2–3). Illus. 2000, Holiday House $16.95 (978-0-8234-1497-0). 32pp. This introduction to apples includes information on their history, varieties, parts, and development from blossom to fruit. (Rev: BL 8/00; HBG 3/01; SLJ 9/00) [634]

22967 Gibbons, Gail. *The Berry Book* (PS–2). Illus. 2002, Holiday House $16.95 (978-0-8234-1697-4). 32pp. A well-illustrated introduction to North American berries, including a few simple recipes. (Rev: BL 3/1/02; HBG 10/02; SLJ 3/02) [634]

22968 Harris, Calvin. *Apple Harvest* (PS–2). Series: All About Fall. 2007, Capstone LB $19.93 (978-1-4296-0023-1). 24pp. With attractive illustrations, this book for beginning readers looks at growing, picking, and eating apples. (Rev: SLJ 4/08) [634]

22969 Hubbell, Will. *Apples Here!* (PS–1). Illus. 2002, Whitman $16.99 (978-0-8075-0397-3). 32pp. The life of apples, from buds to blossoms to fruit, is the subject of this informative book. (Rev: BL 10/15/02; HBG 3/03; SLJ 9/02) [634.11]

22970 Maestro, Betsy. *How Do Apples Grow?* (5–8). Illus. by Giulio Maestro. Series: Let's-Read-and-Find-Out. 1992, HarperCollins LB $16.89 (978-0-06-020056-5). The development of the apple from bud to fruit. (Rev: BL 12/15/91; HB 1–2/92; SLJ 2/92) [582]

22971 Pfeffer, Wendy. *From Seed to Pumpkin* (PS–2). Illus. by James G. Hale. Series: Let's-Read-and-Find-Out Science. 2004, HarperCollins LB $5.99 (978-0-06-445190-1); paper $17.89 (978-0-06-028039-0). 40pp. Children watch a pumpkin grow from seed to maturity; two activities round out this volume for beginning readers. (Rev: BL 10/1/04; SLJ 10/04) [583]

22972 Robbins, Ken. *Pumpkins* (PS–2). 2006, Roaring Brook $14.95 (978-1-59643-184-3). 32pp. Full of dramatic color photographs, this celebration of the pumpkin traces its growing cycle and offers step-by-step instructions for carving a jack-o'-lantern. (Rev: BL 9/1/06; SLJ 8/06) [635]

22973 Smucker, Anna Egan. *Golden Delicious: A Cinderella Apple Story* (1–3). Illus. by Kathleen Kemly. 2008, Albert Whitman $16.99 (978-0-8075-2987-4). 32pp. A hundred years ago, the Stark brothers dreamed of cultivating the perfect apple and this is the delicious true story of how they did it. (Rev: BL 8/08) [634.11]

22974 Watts, Barrie. *Pumpkin* (K–3). Illus. 2002, Smart Apple LB $24.25 (978-1-58340-199-6). 32pp. This easy-to-read book about pumpkins includes lots of facts and excellent photography. Also use *Bean* (2002). (Rev: BL 10/15/02; HBG 3/03; SLJ 2/03) [635]

22975 Weiss, Ellen. *From Pit to Peach Tree* (1–2). Series: Scholastic News Nonfiction Reader. 2007, Children's Pr. LB $20.00 (978-0-531-18538-4); paper $6.95 (978-0-531-18791-3). 24pp. For beginning readers, this is an easy-to-follow explanation of how peaches grow. (Rev: SLJ 12/07) [634]

22976 Ziefert, Harriet. *One Red Apple* (PS–2). Illus. by Karla Gudeon. 2009, Blue Apple $16.99 (978-1-934706-67-1). Unpaged. Follows the life of an apple from harvest to store, to picnic, to seed, and to sapling and tree. (Rev: SLJ 11/1/09) [583.73]

NUTRITION

22977 Roth, Ruby. *That's Why We Don't Eat Animals: A Book About Vegans, Vegetarians, and All Living Things* (3–6). Illus. by author. 2009, North Atlantic $16.95 (978-1-55643-785-4). 48pp. Roth describes animals' lives in factory farms, and compares this with their lives in the wild in this affecting introduction vegetarianism and veganism. (Rev: BL 4/15/09) [641.5]

VEGETABLES

22978 Anderson, Sara. *Vegetables* (PS–1). Illus. by author. 2007, Handprint $8.95 (978-1-59354-189-7). A bright board-book introduction to various types of vegetables. (Rev: SLJ 2/08)

22979 Fowler, Allan. *Taking Root* (1–2). Series: Rookie Readers. 2000, Children's Book Pr. LB $20.50 (978-0-516-21591-4). 32pp. This simple science book introduces taproots that we eat including carrots, beets, and radishes. (Rev: BL 4/15/00) [641.6]

22980 Gibbons, Gail. *Corn* (K–3). Illus. by author. 2008, Holiday $16.95 (978-0-8234-2169-5). 32pp. From the ancient Mayans and the Pilgrims to today's multiple uses of corn, this is a clearly written overview. (Rev: BL 11/15/08; SLJ 10/08) [633.1]

22981 Hughes, Meredith S. *Cool as a Cucumber, Hot as a Pepper* (5–8). Series: Foods We Eat. 1999, Lerner LB $26.60 (978-0-8225-2832-6). This lively book on vegetables gives botanical information, details on growing and harvesting, the history of many of these plants, and a number of mouth-watering recipes. (Rev: BL 7/99; HBG 10/99; SLJ 8/99) [635]

22982 Nelson, Robin. *From Kernel to Corn* (PS–2). Illus. Series: Start to Finish. 2003, Lerner $18.60 (978-0-8225-4659-7). 24pp. This small, colorful picture book uses simple language to describe corn's progress from initial planting to delivery to market. (Rev: BL 4/15/03; HBG 10/03; SLJ 7/03) [633.1]

22983 Sayre, April Pulley. *Rah, Rah, Radishes! A Vegetable Chant* (PS–1). Photos by author. 2011, Simon & Schuster $14.99 (978-1-4424-2141-7). 32pp. A celebration of all things vegetable, with attractive photographs and rhyming text. (Rev: BL 5/1/11; SLJ 6/11*) [641.3]

22984 Weiss, Ellen. *From Eye to Potato* (1–2). Series: Scholastic News Nonfiction Reader. 2007, Children's Pr. LB $20.00 (978-0-531-18535-3); paper $6.95 (978-0-531-18788-3). 24pp. For beginning readers, this is an easy-to-follow explanation of how potatoes grow. (Rev: SLJ 12/07) [635]

Fungi

22985 Royston, Angela. *Life Cycle of a Mushroom* (PS–3). Series: Life Cycle. 2000, Heinemann LB $21.36 (978-1-57572-210-8). 32pp. Using a color photo and four or five lines of text on each page, this book describes different mushrooms and gives their basic life cycle. (Rev: BL 5/15/00; HBG 3/01) [589.2]

Leaves and Trees

22986 Brenner, Barbara. *One Small Place in a Tree* (2–4). Illus. by Tom Leonard. 2004, HarperCollins $16.99 (978-0-688-17180-3). 32pp. The abundant life found in a single tree is captured in easy-to-understand narrative and realistic artwork. (Rev: BL 3/1/04; SLJ 4/04) [577.3]

22987 Bulla, Clyde Robert. *A Tree Is a Plant* (PS–1). Illus. by Stacey Schuett. Series: Let's-Read-and-Find-Out Science. 2001, HarperCollins LB $5.99 (978-0-06-445196-3); paper $15.89 (978-0-06-028172-4). Vivid paintings grace this new version of the book first published in 1960 that portrays the life cycle of an apple tree and discusses how the different parts of a tree work. (Rev: BL 12/15/01; HBG 10/02; SLJ 11/01) [583]

22988 de la Bedoyere, Camilla. *Acorn to Oak Tree* (1–3). Illus. Series: Life Cycles. 2012, Amicus/QEB LB $17.95 (978-160992045-6). 24pp. Double-page spreads with clear images trace the life cycle of an oak tree. (Rev: BL 11/1/12) [583]

22989 Farndon, John. *Leaves* (2–5). Illus. 2006, Gale LB $23.70 (978-1-4103-0422-3). 24pp. Diagrams and photographs supplement the clear text describing leaves and the role they play in the overall life of the plant. (Rev: SLJ 2/07)

22990 Fowler, Allan. *Maple Trees* (1–2). Series: Rookie Read-About Science. 2001, Children's Book Pr. LB $20.50 (978-0-516-21684-3). 32pp. For beginning readers, a simple text with color illustrations introduces trees, their varieties, parts, and growth cycles. (Rev: BL 1/1–15/02) [582.16]

22991 Gerber, Carole. *Leaf Jumpers* (PS–1). Illus. by Leslie Evans. 2004, Charlesbridge $15.95 (978-1-57091-497-3). 32pp. The leaves of eight common trees — including the red maple, birch, and ginkgo — are introduced in simple, lyrical text and striking autumnal colors. (Rev: BL 9/1/04; SLJ 8/04) [575.5]

22992 Gerber, Carole. *Spring Blossoms* (1–3). Illus. by Leslie Evans. 2013, Charlesbridge $16.95 (978-1-58089-412-8). 32pp. Rhyming couplets and clear illustrations introduce trees that flower in the spring. (Rev: BL 3/1/13; SLJ 8/13) [582.13]

22993 Gerber, Carole. *Winter Trees* (PS–2). Illus. by Leslie Evans. 2008, Charlesbridge $15.95 (978-1-58089-168-4). 32pp. A little boy and his dog appreciate the beauty of bare trees in the snow in this beautifully illustrated book that melds fact and poetry. (Rev: BL 7/08) [582.16]

22994 Gibbons, Gail. *Tell Me, Tree: All About Trees for Kids* (PS–3). Illus. 2002, Little, Brown $15.95 (978-0-316-30903-5). 32pp. An oversize basic guide that introduces different kinds of trees, and explains their parts and how each operates. (Rev: BL 4/1/02; HB 7/02; HBG 10/02; SLJ 3/02) [582.16]

22995 Godwin, Sam. *From Little Acorns: A First Look at the Life Cycle of a Tree* (K–1). Illus. by Simone Abel. Series: First Look : Science. 2004, Picture Window LB $25.26 (978-1-4048-0658-0). 32pp. In simple language with cartoon-style illustrations, a mother squirrel and her babies discuss how an oak tree grows. (Rev: BL 10/15/04; SLJ 3/05) [571.8]

22996 Guillain, Charlotte. *Leaves* (PS–K). Illus. Series: Spot the Difference. 2008, Heinemann LB $14.50 (978-1-4329-0944-4). 24pp. Basic facts about leaves are presented attractively in this small, horizontal book. (Rev: BL 4/1/08; LMC 10/08) [581.4]

22997 Llewellyn, Claire. *Tree* (K–3). Illus. by Simon Mendez. 2004, NorthWord $16.95 (978-1-55971-879-0). 32pp. An innovative picture-book layout chronicles the life cycle of an apple tree, tracing its progress from seedling to a mature, fruit-bearing adult. (Rev: BL 4/15/04; SLJ 11/04) [634]

22998 Miller, Debbie S. *Are Trees Alive?* (K–3). Illus. by Stacey Schuett. 2002, Walker LB $17.85 (978-0-8027-8802-3). 32pp. This colorful picture book explains how trees live and survive in different environments. (Rev: BL 6/1–15/02; HBG 10/02; SLJ 5/02) [582.16]

22999 Morrison, Gordon. *Oak Tree* (4–6). Illus. 2000, Houghton $16.00 (978-0-395-95644-1). 32pp. A year in the life of an oak tree is described in this appealing account that uses a picture-book format. (Rev: BL 3/1/00; HBG 9/00; SLJ 6/00) [583]

23000 Pascoe, Elaine. *The Ecosystem of a Fallen Tree* (3–5). Photos by Dwight Kuhn. Series: The Library of Small Ecosystems. 2003, Rosen LB $22.50 (978-0-8239-6308-9). 32pp. In this photo-filled overview of the plant and animal life that can be sustained in the remains of a downed tree, students will learn that ecosystems come in all sizes. (Rev: SLJ 11/03) [577]

23001 Pascoe, Elaine. *The Ecosystem of an Apple Tree* (3–5). Photos by Dwight Kuhn. Series: The Library of Small Ecosystems. 2003, Rosen LB $22.50 (978-0-8239-6304-1). 32pp. An overview of the animal and plant life associated with the apple tree. (Rev: SLJ 11/03) [577]

23002 Pascoe, Elaine. *Leaves and Trees* (4–7). Series: Nature Close-Up. 2001, Blackbirch LB $23.70 (978-1-56711-474-4). 32pp. Easy projects and a simple text are used to introduce the nature of trees and leaves and the living processes involved. (Rev: BL 9/15/01; HBG 3/02) [582.16]

23003 Preus, Margi. *CelebriTrees: Historic and Famous Trees of the World* (2–5). Illus. by Rebecca Gibbon. 2011, Henry Holt $16.99 (978-0-8050-7829-9). 40pp. An interesting history of 14 trees around the world that are important for their size, longevity, or as witness of important historical or cultural events. Lexile 1020L (Rev: BL 5/1/11; HB 3–4/11; SLJ 2/1/11) [582.16]

23004 Royston, Angela. *Life Cycle of an Oak Tree* (PS–3). Series: Life Cycle. 2000, Heinemann LB $21.36 (978-1-57572-211-5). 32pp. From acorn to giant oak, this book describes the life cycle of an oak tree using a few lines of text and a color photo on each page. (Rev: BL 5/15/00; HBG 3/01) [583]

23005 Souza, D. M. *Wacky Trees* (3–6). Series: Watts Library. 2003, Watts LB $25.50 (978-0-531-12210-5). 63pp. The oddities of the tree world, including such giants as the sequoia and the baobab, are examined in this illustrated work. (Rev: SLJ 4/04) [582.16]

23006 Spicer, Maggee, and Richard Thompson. *We'll All Go Exploring* (PS–1). Illus. by Kim LaFave. 2003, Fitzhenry & Whiteside $16.95 (978-1-55041-732-6).

36pp. Three young explorers find out about different kinds of trees and the wildlife found near them in this lively rhyming-text picture book. (Rev: BL 5/1/03; SLJ 5/03) [811]

23007 Zim, Herbert S., and Alexander C. Martin. *Trees* (5–8). 1991, Western paper $21.27 (978-0-307-64056-7). A small, handy volume packed with information and color illustrations that help identify our most important trees. [582.16]

Plants

23008 Farndon, John. *Roots* (2–5). Illus. 2006, Gale LB $23.70 (978-1-4103-0421-6). 24pp. Diagrams and photographs supplement the clear text describing roots and the role they play in the overall life of the plant. Also use *Stems* (2006). (Rev: SLJ 2/07)

23009 Godwin, Sam. *A Seed in Need: A First Look at the Plant Cycle* (K–1). Illus. Series: First Look: Science. 2004, Picture Window LB $25.26 (978-1-4048-0920-8). 32pp. In simple language with cartoon-style illustrations, this volume describes the life cycle of plants.

23010 Goodman, Emily. *Plant Secrets* (PS–2). Illus. by Phyllis L. Tildes. 2009, Charlesbridge $16.95 (978-1-58089-204-9). 40pp. Goodman explores the life cycles of four plants — the rose, the oak, the pea, and the tomato — identifying "secrets" at key stages of development (seed, plant, flower, and fruit). (Rev: BCCB 4/09; BL 3/15/09; SLJ 3/09) [580]

23011 Goodman, Susan E. *Seeds, Stems, and Stamens: The Ways Plants Fit into Their World* (2–4). Illus. by Michael Doolittle. 2001, Millbrook LB $22.90 (978-0-7613-1874-3). 48pp. A clear look at how plants adapt to their environments, with stunning photographs and questions to stimulate investigation. (Rev: BL 9/15/01; HBG 3/02; SLJ 11/01) [581.4]

23012 Halfmann, Janet. *Plant Tricksters* (3–6). Series: Watts Library. 2003, Watts LB $25.50 (978-0-531-12278-5); paper $8.95 (978-0-531-16371-9). 63pp. With plenty of close-up photographs, this is a study of the unusual mechanisms by which some plants survive — from being unusually smelly to trying to fool the eye. (Rev: SLJ 4/04) [581.4]

23013 Hickman, Pamela. *Starting with Nature Plant Book* (2–4). Illus. by Heather Collins. Series: Starting with Nature. 2000, Kids Can $12.95 (978-1-55074-483-5); paper $5.95 (978-1-55074-812-3). 32pp. This introductory account describes groups of plants and plant parts and gives material on state flowers, endangered plants, and outlines of several related activities. (Rev: HBG 9/00; SLJ 7/00) [581]

23014 Lawrence, Ellen. *Meat-Eating Plants: Toothless Wonders* (1–3). Illus. Series: Plant-ology. 2012, Bearport LB $23.93 (978-161772589-0). 24pp. An informative and colorful introduction to carnivorous plants such as the Venus flytrap, butterwort, and pitcher plant. (Rev: BL 10/1/12) [575.9]

23015 Lerner, Carol. *Cactus* (4–7). 1992, Morrow LB $14.89 (978-0-688-09637-3). After explaining the parts of the cactus and how it can exist in near-waterless environments, this account describes different species. (Rev: BCCB 10/92; HB 1–2/93; SLJ 12/92) [635.7]

23016 Lundgren, Julie K. *Plants as Food, Fuel, and Medicine* (3–5). Illus. Series: My Science Library. 2012, Rourke LB $27.07 (978-161810102-0); paper $7.95 (9781618102355). 24pp. This is a well-written introduction to the importance of plants to existence on our planet, ending with a "Show What You Know" quiz. (Rev: BL 9/15/12; SLJ Fall 2012 Series Guide) [581.63]

23017 Mooney, Carla. *Sunscreen for Plants* (4–7). Illus. Series: A Great Idea! Going Green. 2009, Norwood LB $18.95 (978-159953344-5). 48pp. Discusses how exposure to the sun affects plants and posits potential inventions that could reduce the problem of sun damage. (Rev: BL 2/15/10) [632]

23018 Pascoe, Elaine. *The Ecosystem of a Milkweed Patch* (3–5). Photos by Dwight Kuhn. Series: The Library of Small Ecosystems. 2003, Rosen LB $22.50 (978-0-8239-6309-6). 32pp. Introduces the animals and plants that live within a milkweed patch and also to the ways in which they interact. (Rev: SLJ 11/03) [577.4]

23019 Posada, Mia. *Dandelions: Stars in the Grass* (PS–2). Illus. by author. 2000, Carolrhoda LB $15.95 (978-1-57505-383-7). The life cycle of a dandelion is covered in bright acrylic illustrations and a text that includes unusual facts and a recipe for dandelion salad. (Rev: HBG 9/00; SLJ 5/00) [581]

23020 Silvey, Anita. *The Plant Hunters: True Stories of Their Daring Adventures to the Far Corners of the Earth* (5–8). Illus. 2012, Farrar $19.99 (978-037430908-4). 96pp. A fascinating account of the work of botanists around the world, mainly during the 19th and 20th centuries. Lexile 1170L (Rev: BL 4/15/12; LMC 10/12; SLJ 6/12) [580.75]

23021 Souza, D. M. *Plant Invaders* (3–6). Series: Watts Library. 2003, Watts LB $25.50 (978-0-531-12211-2). 63pp. An illustrated look at invasive plants, such as kudzu, that spread widely and pose a significant threat to the ecosystem. (Rev: SLJ 4/04) [581.6]

23022 Wade, Mary Dodson. *Plants Live Everywhere!* (K–2). 2009, Enslow LB $21.26 (978-0-7660-3155-5). 24pp. Using a question-and-answer format, this book provides a simple explanation of plant habitats of all kinds, with color photographs and an activity. Also use *People Need Plants* and *Plants Grow!* (both 2009). (Rev: SLJ 4/09)

Seeds

23023 Aston, Dianna. *A Seed Is Sleepy* (PS–2). Illus. by Sylvia Long. 2007, Chronicle $16.95 (978-0-8118-5520-4). 32pp. Using poetic text and lush watercolors, this picture book explores the mysteries of seeds and how they are transformed into colorful plants and flowers of very varying sizes. (Rev: BL 3/15/07) [581.4]

23024 Burns, Diane L. *Berries, Nuts and Seeds* (4–7). Illus. by John F. McGee. 1996, NorthWord paper $7.95 (978-1-55971-573-7). Each page in this guide is devoted to a description of a single berry, nut, or seed. (Rev: BL 2/15/97) [582.13]

23025 Farndon, John. *Seeds* (2–5). Illus. 2006, Gale LB $23.70 (978-1-4103-0419-3). 24pp. Diagrams and photographs supplement the clear text describing seeds and the role they play in the overall life of the plant. (Rev: SLJ 2/07)

23026 Galbraith, Kathryn O. *Planting the Wild Garden* (PS–3). Illus. by Wendy Anderson Halperin. 2011, Peachtree $15.95 (978-1-56145-563-8). 32pp. This celebration of seed dispersal encourages wonder and appreciation for all the ways nature ensures new generations of flowers. Lexile AD490L (Rev: BL 4/15/11; LMC 11–12/11; SLJ 6/11) [581.467]

23027 Macken, JoAnn Early. *Flip, Float, Fly: Seeds on the Move* (K–3). Illus. by Pam Paparone. 2008, Holiday $16.95 (978-0-8234-2043-8). 32pp. Seeds of all kinds are shown benefiting from their abilities to float, roll, stick to clothing, drift on water, and so forth. (Rev: BL 4/15/08; LMC 11/08; SLJ 5/08) [581.4]

23028 Pascoe, Elaine. *Plants with Seeds* (2–5). Photos by Dwight Kuhn. Series: A Kid's Guide to the Classification of Living Things. 2003, Rosen LB $22.50 (978-0-8239-6314-0). 32pp. A richly illustrated, slim guide to plants that use seeds to reproduce, with color photographs and a useful glossary. Also use *Plants Without Seeds* (2003). (Rev: SLJ 7/03) [580]

23029 Peterson, Cris. *Seed Soil Sun: Earth's Recipe for Food* (K–3). Photos by David R. Lundquist. 2010, Boyds Mills $17.95 (978-1-59078-713-7). Unpaged. The roles of seeds, soil, and sunlight are explained along with the mechanism of photosynthesis in this attractive and accessible book. (Rev: BL 11/1/10; LMC 1–2/11; SLJ 11/1/10) [581.4]

23030 Richards, Jean. *A Fruit Is a Suitcase for Seeds* (PS–2). Illus. by Anca Hariton. 2002, Millbrook LB $21.90 (978-0-7613-1622-0). 32pp. An accessible and very visual introduction to seeds and how they are dispersed. (Rev: HBG 10/02; SLJ 5/02) [581.467]

23031 Sayre, April Pulley. *Let's Go Nuts! Seeds We Eat* (PS–2). Illus. by author. 2013, Simon & Schuster $16.99 (978-144246728-6). 32pp. Continuing the theme from her well-received *Rah, Rah, Radishes!* and *Go, Go, Grapes!*, the author uses beautiful photographs and rhythmic text to present the luscious diversity of edible seeds, nuts, grains, and spices; includes a reference section at the end of the book. e (Rev: BL 9/1/13; LMC 1–2/14; SLJ 8/13) [641.3]

23032 Wade, Mary Dodson. *Seeds Sprout!* (K–2). 2009, Enslow LB $21.26 (978-0-7660-3154-8). 24pp. Using a question-and-answer format, this book provides a simple explanation of seeds and how they create plants, with color photographs and an activity. (Rev: SLJ 4/09) [581.4]

Chemistry

23033 Aloian, Molly. *Mixtures and Solutions* (3–5). Series: Why Chemistry Matters. 2009, Crabtree LB $26.60 (978-0-7787-4243-2). 32pp. A slim introduction to the various types of mixtures and solutions, how they are formed, and how we use them. (Rev: LMC 8–9/09) [541.34]

23034 Angliss, Sarah. *Gold* (4–8). Series: The Elements. 1999, Marshall Cavendish LB $25.64 (978-0-7614-0887-1). Easy-to-follow diagrams, fact boxes, and color illustrations accompany an informative text that introduces gold, where it is mined and processed, its properties, value, and uses. (Rev: BL 2/15/00; HBG 10/00) [546]

23035 Baxter, Roberta. *Chemical Reaction* (4–8). Series: The Kidhaven Science Library. 2004, Gale LB $26.20 (978-0-7377-2072-3). Clear, concise text, supported by full-color photographs and diagrams, describes many types of reactions — oxidation and photosynthesis, for example — and discusses their uses. (Rev: SLJ 6/05)

23036 Beatty, Richard. *Copper* (4–8). Series: The Elements. 2000, Marshall Cavendish LB $25.64 (978-0-7614-0945-8). This book identifies the element copper, defines its properties and describes its uses in everyday life, especially in electrical cables. (Rev: BL 1/1–15/01; HBG 10/01; SLJ 2/01) [546]

23037 Beatty, Richard. *The Lanthanides* (4–8). Series: The Elements. 2007, Marshall Cavendish LB $19.95 (978-0-7614-2687-5). This detailed and thorough overview of the 15 metal elements in the Lanthanides provides fact boxes and clear explanations in a graphically pleasing format. (Rev: SLJ 3/08)

23038 Beatty, Richard. *Manganese* (5–8). Illus. Series: The Elements. 2004, Marshall Cavendish LB $25.64 (978-0-7614-1813-9). 32pp. Easy-to-follow diagrams, fact boxes, and color illustrations accompany an informative text that introduces manganese and its properties, value, and uses. (Rev: BL 12/1/04)

23039 Beatty, Richard. *Phosphorus* (4–8). Series: The Elements. 2000, Marshall Cavendish LB $25.64 (978-0-7614-0946-5). This book describes this nonmetallic element, lists its properties, tells how it behaves, and discusses such uses as matches and fertilizers. (Rev: BL 1/1–15/01; HBG 10/01; SLJ 2/01) [546]

23040 Beatty, Richard. *Sulfur* (4–8). Series: The Elements. 2000, Marshall Cavendish LB $25.64 (978-0-7614-0948-9). Introduces this nonmetallic element, its characteristics, various compounds, and uses in everyday life, with color photographs, easy-to-follow diagrams, fact boxes, and a clear text. (Rev: BL 1/1–15/01; HBG 10/01; SLJ 2/01) [546]

23041 Brandolini, Anita. *Fizz, Bubble and Flash! Element Explorations and Atom Adventures for Hands-On Science Fun!* (4–7). Illus. by Michael Kline. Series: Kids Can! 2003, Williamson paper $14.25 (978-1-885593-83-2). A friendly narrative and cartoon-style drawing present activities that illustrate basic scientific concepts. (Rev: BL 1/1–15/04; SLJ 11/03) [546]

23042 Brent, Lynnette. *Acids and Bases* (3–5). Series: Why Chemistry Matters. 2009, Crabtree LB $26.60 (978-0-7787-4239-5). 32pp. A slim introduction to the properties of acids and bases, explaining how they exist in our bodies and in the environment. Also use *Chemical Changes, States of Matter,* and *Elements and Compounds* (all 2009). (Rev: LMC 8–9/09) [546.24]

23043 Cobb, Allan B. *Cadmium* (4–8). Series: The Elements. 2007, Marshall Cavendish LB $19.95 (978-0-7614-2686-8). This well-designed overview of cadmium is thorough and also includes a section on how the element relates to the health of human beings. (Rev: SLJ 3/08)

23044 Cooper, Chris. *Arsenic* (4–8). Illus. Series: The Elements. 2006, Benchmark LB $19.95 (978-0-7614-2203-7). A basic guide to arsenic's properties and uses (including as a poison and in industrial applications). (Rev: SLJ 5/07) [546]

23045 Farndon, John. *Aluminum* (4–8). Series: The Elements. 2000, Marshall Cavendish LB $25.64 (978-0-7614-0947-2). This silvery, metallic element is introduced, with material on its individual characteristics, how it behaves, and its many uses in everyday life. (Rev: BL 1/1–15/01; HBG 10/01) [546]

23046 Farndon, John. *Chemicals* (3–6). Series: Science Experiments. 2002, Marshall Cavendish LB $25.64 (978-0-7614-1466-7). 32pp. Simple experiments with easy-to-follow instructions explore the nature and properties of chemicals. (Rev: BL 12/15/02; HBG 3/03; SLJ 4/03) [540]

23047 Farndon, John. *Oxygen* (5–8). Series: The Elements. 1998, Benchmark LB $25.64 (978-0-7614-0879-6). Oxygen, its properties, uses, and various chemical combinations are covered in this informative text that also discusses the ozone layer. (Rev: HBG 10/99; SLJ 2/99) [540]

23048 Gray, Leon. *Iodine* (5–8). Series: Elements (Group 7). 2004, Marshall Cavendish $25.64 (978-0-7614-1812-2). 2004, Marshall Cavendish $25.64 (978-0-7614-1812-2). This introduction to iodine examines the importance of this substance to body chemistry, as well as how it was discovered, where it is found, and its physical characteristics. (Rev: BL 12/1/04) [546]

23049 Jackson, Tom. *Lithium* (4–8). Illus. Series: The Elements. 2006, Benchmark LB $19.95 (978-0-7614-2199-3). A basic guide to lithium's properties and uses in batteries and pharmaceuticals. (Rev: SLJ 5/07) [546]

23050 Lepora, Nathan. *Molybdenum* (4–8). Illus. Series: The Elements. 2006, Benchmark LB $19.95 (978-0-7614-2201-3). A basic guide to molybdenum's properties and uses (including its medical applications). (Rev: SLJ 5/07) [546]

23051 O'Daly, Anne. *Sodium* (4–8). Series: The Elements. 2001, Marshall Cavendish LB $25.64 (978-0-7614-1271-7). Diagrams and full-color illustrations are used to introduce sodium and its characteristics and importance in everyday life. (Rev: BL 3/15/02; HBG 3/02) [546]

23052 Richards, Jon. *Chemicals and Reactions* (3–6). Illus. 2000, Millbrook LB $21.90 (978-0-7613-1160-7). 32pp. Using common household items, experiments involving chemical reactions are accompanied with sidebars that explain how each works. (Rev: BL 8/00; HBG 3/01) [540]

23053 Roza, Greg. *Calcium* (5–8). Illus. Series: Understanding the Elements of the Periodic Table. 2007, Rosen LB $26.50 (978-1-4042-1963-2). This reader-friendly volume contains a full overview of calcium, including basic information and interesting sidebar features such as the amount of calcium found in different foods. (Rev: SLJ 3/08)

23054 Saucerman, Linda. *Chlorine* (5–8). Illus. Series: Understanding the Elements of the Periodic Table. 2007, Rosen LB $26.50 (978-1-4042-1962-5). Little-known facts interspersed among basic details make this book about chlorine an interesting read. (Rev: SLJ 3/08)

23055 Sommers, Michael A. *Phosphorus* (5–8). Illus. 2007, Rosen LB $26.50 (978-1-4042-1960-1). An easy to understand overview of phosphorus, including attrac-

tive graphics and interesting, little known facts (includes charts, diagrams, illustrations, photos, reproductions, bibliography, further reading, glossary, index and Web sites). (Rev: SLJ 3/08)

23056 Sparrow, Giles. *Nickel* (5–8). Illus. Series: The Elements. 2004, Marshall Cavendish LB $25.64 (978-0-7614-1811-5). 32pp. Easy-to-follow diagrams, fact boxes, and color illustrations accompany an informative text that introduces nickel and its properties, value, and uses. (Rev: BL 12/1/04)

23057 Stimola, Aubrey. *Sulfur* (5–8). Illus. 2007, Rosen LB $26.50 (978-1-4042-1961-8). This basic overview of sulfur is well-organized and easy to understand, and contains interesting facts such as the use of sulfur in medicine (includes charts, diagrams, illustrations, photos, reproductions, bibliography, further reading, glossary, index and Web sites). (Rev: SLJ 3/08)

23058 Thomas, Jens. *Silicon* (4–8). Series: The Elements. 2001, Marshall Cavendish LB $25.64 (978-0-7614-1274-8). 32pp. Thomas introduces this important element and its origins, discovery, and many uses. (Rev: BL 3/15/02; HBG 3/02) [546]

23059 Tocci, Salvatore. *Carbon* (2–3). Illus. Series: True Book - Elements. 2004, Children's Pr. LB $25.00 (978-0-516-22828-0); paper $6.95 (978-0-516-27848-3). 48pp. An exploration of the characteristics of carbon and what makes it special. Also use *Calcium* and *Nitrogen* (both 2004

23060 Tocci, Salvatore. *The Periodic Table* (2–3). Illus. Series: True Book - Elements. 2004, Children's Pr. LB $25.00 (978-0-516-22833-4). 48pp. Introduces the periodic table, how it was developed, and how it is organized, with some fun facts at the end. [546.8]

23061 Uttley, Colin. *Magnesium* (4–8). Series: The Elements. 1999, Marshall Cavendish LB $25.64 (978-0-7614-0889-5). This book explores magnesium, a silvery metallic element important in living organisms, and explains its place in the periodic table, as well as its forms, uses, and properties. (Rev: BL 2/15/00; HBG 10/00) [546]

23062 Van Gorp, Lynn. *Elements* (4–6). Illus. Series: Mission: Science. 2008, Compass Point LB $26.60 (978-0-7565-3951-1). 40pp. An appealing exploration of matter and the elements, the periodic table, reactions, and so forth; also includes many photographs and illustrations plus an activity. (Rev: LMC 3/09; SLJ 6/09) [540]

23063 VanCleave, Janice. *Step-By-Step Science Experiments in Chemistry* (5–8). Series: Janice VanCleave's First-Place Science Fair Projects. 2012, Rosen Central LB $33.25 (978-1-4488-6981-7). 80pp. An updated volume with step-by-step instructions for 22 experiments mostly using easily found materials. (Rev: SLJ 10/12) [540.78]

23064 Watt, Susan. *Chlorine* (4–8). Series: The Elements. 2001, Marshall Cavendish LB $25.64 (978-0-7614-1272-4). 32pp. Using diagrams, photographs, and a concise text, this book introduces this active, nonmetallic element with material on its composition, characteristics, and many uses — including as a disinfectant and in water purification. (Rev: BL 3/15/02; HBG 3/02) [546]

23065 Watt, Susan. *Cobalt* (4–8). Illus. Series: The Elements. 2006, Benchmark LB $19.95 (978-0-7614-2200-6). A basic guide to cobalt's properties and uses. (Rev: SLJ 5/07) [546]

23066 Watt, Susan. *Lead* (4–8). Series: The Elements. 2001, Marshall Cavendish LB $25.64 (978-0-7614-1273-1). Explores the history, origins, discovery, characteristics, and uses of this heavy metallic element in everyday life. (Rev: BL 3/15/02; HBG 3/02) [546]

23067 Watt, Susan. *Mercury* (5–8). Illus. Series: The Elements. 2004, Marshall Cavendish LB $25.64 (978-0-7614-1814-6). 32pp. Easy-to-follow diagrams, fact boxes, and color illustrations accompany an informative text that introduces mercury and its properties, value, and uses. (Rev: BL 12/1/04)

23068 Watt, Susan. *Silver* (4–8). Illus. Series: The Elements. 2002, Benchmark LB $25.64 (978-0-7614-1464-3). 32pp. A concise introduction to this element, its history, where it is found and how it is mined, and its many uses. Also in this series is *Potassium* (2002). (Rev: HBG 3/03; LMC 5/03; SLJ 4/03) [546]

23069 Watt, Susan. *Zirconium* (4–8). Series: The Elements. 2007, Marshall Cavendish LB $19.95 (978-0-7614-2688-2). This volume covers all aspects of zirconium including its use in dating some rocks and minerals. (Rev: SLJ 3/08)

23070 West, Krista. *Bromine* (4–8). Series: The Elements. 2007, Marshall Cavendish LB $19.95 (978-0-7614-2685-1). The element bromine is covered in detail in this attractively designed volume. (Rev: SLJ 3/08)

Geology and Geography

Earth and Geology

23071 Bailey, Jacqui. *The Birth of the Earth* (3–5). Illus. by Matthew Lilly. Series: Cartoon History of the Earth. 2001, Kids Can $16.95 (978-1-55337-071-0); paper $7.95 (978-1-55337-080-2). 32pp. A comic-book-style presentation of the origin of the planet. (Rev: BL 10/15/01; HBG 3/02; SLJ 1/02) [523.1]

23072 Blobaum, Cindy. *Geology Rocks! 50 Hands-On Activities to Explore the Earth* (4–6). Illus. by Michael Kline. Series: A Kaleidoscope Kids Book. 2000, Williamson paper $14.25 (978-1-885593-29-0). 96pp. Each chapter introduces a different concept in geology with accompanying projects and plenty of sidebars to furnish interesting information on geologists, land formations, the scientific method, etc. (Rev: SLJ 3/00) [551]

23073 Calhoun, Yael. *Earth Science Fair Projects Using Rocks, Minerals, Magnets, Mud, and More* (5–8). Series: Earth Science! Best Science Projects. 2005, Enslow LB $26.60 (978-0-7660-2363-5). More than 20 geology-related projects are introduced with clear instructions and interesting background information. (Rev: BL 11/1/05) [550]

23074 Campbell, Ann-Jeanette, and Ronald Rood. *The New York Public Library Incredible Earth: A Book of Answers for Kids* (4–7). 1996, Wiley paper $14.95 (978-0-471-14497-7). Questions and answers involving science, collected from the reference department of the New York Public Library. (Rev: BL 9/15/96; SLJ 1/97) [550]

23075 Coady, Christopher, and Meredith Hooper. *The Island That Moved* (3–5). 2004, Penguin $16.99 (978-0-670-05882-2). An imaginary island off the coast of Antarctica serves as the focus for an exploration of geologic and climate change, continental drift, and plate tectonics. (Rev: BL 8/04; SLJ 12/04) [551.1]

23076 Downs, Sandra. *Shaping the Earth: Erosion* (5–8). Series: Exploring Planet Earth. 2000, Twenty-First Century LB $24.90 (978-0-7613-1414-1). 64pp. This book explores the force of erosion and how such phenomena as wind, waves, floods, rain, acid rain, freezing, and thawing can change the face of the land. (Rev: HBG 10/00; SLJ 7/00) [551]

23077 Gardner, Robert. *Planet Earth Science Fair Projects, Revised and Expanded Using the Scientific Method* (5–8). Series: Earth Science Projects Using the Scientific Method. 2010, Enslow LB $34.60 (978-0-7660-3423-5). 160pp. With a focus on the basics of scientific investigation, this well-organized and attractive volume gives an overview of the topic and provides experiments that support various hypotheses. (Rev: LMC 8–9/10) [550]

23078 Gardner, Robert. *Super Science Projects About Earth's Soil and Water* (3–5). Illus. Series: Rockin' Earth Science Experiments. 2007, Enslow LB $23.93 (978-0-7660-2735-0). 48pp. The experiments and projects outlined here teach important lessons about soil and water, touching on such topics as the makeup of soil, evaporation, and pollution of aquifers; scientific principles are reinforced, and symbols flag projects especially suited to science fairs. (Rev: BL 4/1/07) [631.4078]

23079 George, Linda. *Plate Tectonics* (4–9). Illus. 2003, Gale LB $23.70 (978-0-7377-1405-0). 48pp. Concise information on the movement of continents, the formation of mountains, and volcanic and earthquake activity is presented with full-color photographs and diagrams. (Rev: SLJ 10/03) [551.1]

23080 Gilpin, Dan. *Planet Earth: What Planet Are You On?* (5–8). Illus. by Simon Basher. 2010, Kingfisher paper $8.99 (978-0-7534-6412-0). 128pp. Geological features of the Earth (such as the core, crust, and volcanoes) are personified as cartoon characters in this informational and entertaining overview of earth science. (Rev: BL 5/15/10; LMC 8–9/10) [550]

23081 Patent, Dorothy Hinshaw. *Shaping the Earth* (4–7). 2000, Clarion $18.00 (978-0-395-85691-8). The evolution of the earth is traced in this compelling book that describes how the surface has changed and continues to change, with coverage of plate tectonics, ice ages, natural disasters, and descriptions of its natural wonders. (Rev: BL 3/15/00; HBG 10/00; SLJ 4/00) [550]

23082 Pellant, Chris. *Rocks and Fossils* (K–3). Series: Kingfisher Young Knowledge. 2003, Kingfisher $8.95 (978-0-7534-5619-4). 47pp. Bright, clear photographs and easy-to-read text convey information on rocks and fossils, crystals, and erosion, plus suggested activities. (Rev: HBG 4/04; SLJ 4/04) [552]

23083 Redfern, Martin. *The Kingfisher Young People's Book of Planet Earth* (4–8). 1999, Kingfisher $21.95 (978-0-7534-5180-9). A useful, enjoyable look at the earth's geology, atmosphere, and weather. (Rev: HBG 10/00; SLJ 2/00) [525]

23084 Redmond, Jim, and Ronda Redmond. *Landslides and Avalanches* (3–5). Illus. Series: Nature on the Rampage. 2001, Raintree LB $22.83 (978-0-7398-4704-6). 32pp. The authors look at our knowledge of landslides and avalanches and their causes, and discuss the ways in which we can protect ourselves from danger. (Rev: HBG 3/02; SLJ 2/02) [551.3]

23085 Robson, Pam. *Mountains and Our Moving Earth* (2–4). Illus. by Tony Kenyon. Series: Geography for Fun. 2001, Millbrook LB $22.90 (978-0-7613-2166-8). 32pp. Step-by-step instructions for projects that reinforce the information given here on geology, weather and erosion, and earthquakes and volcanoes. (Rev: HBG 10/01; SLJ 9/01) [551.43]

23086 Storad, Conrad J. *Earth's Crust* (2–4). Series: Early Bird Earth Science. 2006, Lerner $25.26 (978-0-8225-5944-3). 48pp. This attractive, readable overview of the earth's geological makeup examines the structure of the planet, changes in its crust, plate tectonics, and such features as mountains, volcanoes, and faults. (Rev: BL 9/1/06; SLJ 1/07) [851.1]

23087 Twist, Clint, and Lisa Regan, et al. *Extreme Earth* (3–6). Illus. Series: Ripley's Believe It or Not! Twists. 2010, Mason Crest LB $19.95 (978-142221829-7). 48pp. The basics of earth science are introduced through a lively blend of conversational text, snappy sidebars, and innovative design elements, with a focus on record-breaking earthquakes, hurricanes, volcanic explosions, and so on. Lexile IG1100L (Rev: BL 4/15/11) [550]

23088 VanCleave, Janice. *Janice VanCleave's A+ Projects in Earth Science: Winning Experiments for Science Fairs and Extra Credit* (5–10). 1999, Wiley paper $12.95 (978-0-471-17770-8). Thirty projects varying in complexity are included in this exploration of topography, minerals, atmospheric composition, the ocean floor, and erosion. (Rev: BL 12/1/98; SLJ 6/99) [550]

23089 VanCleave, Janice. *Step-By-Step Science Experiments in Earth Science* (5–8). Series: Janice VanCleave's First-Place Science Fair Projects. 2012, Rosen Central LB $33.25 (978-1-4488-6983-1). 80pp. An updated volume with step-by-step instructions for 22 experiments mostly using easily found materials. (Rev: SLJ 10/12) [550.78]

23090 Williams, Brian. *Earth Time* (4–6). Series: About Time. 2002, Smart Apple LB $24.25 (978-1-58340-210-8). 32pp. An exploration of geologic and evolutionary time that looks at the forms of life appearing in each era. (Rev: HBG 3/03; SLJ 12/02)

Earthquakes and Volcanoes

23091 Aronin, Miriam. *Earthquake in Haiti* (3–5). Series: Code Red. 2010, Bearport LB $25.27 (978-1-936088-66-9). 32pp. This picture book tells the story of the 2010 disaster, referring frequently to the experiences of two survivors, and describes the ongoing recovery efforts. Lexile 910L (Rev: LMC 5–6/11; SLJ 5/1/11)

23092 Bauer, Marion Dane. *Natural Disasters: Earthquake!* (PS–2). Illus. by John Wallace. Series: Ready-to-Read Natural Disasters. 2009, Aladdin paper $3.99 (978-1-4169-2551-4). 32pp. Bauer looks at what causes earthquakes and explores traditional beliefs, what scientists know now, and what remains a mystery; for beginning readers. (Rev: BLO 6/19/09) [551.22]

23093 Benoit, Peter. *The Haitian Earthquake of 2010* (3–5). Illus. Series: A True Book: Disasters. 2011, Scholastic LB $28 (978-053125420-2); paper $6.95 (978-053126625-0). 48pp. With statistics and Web resources, this volume covers the disaster and the aftermath. (Rev: BL 11/15/11) [972.94]

23094 Berger, Melvin, and Gilda Berger. *Why Do Volcanoes Blow Their Tops?* (3–5). Series: Scholastic Question and Answer. 2000, Scholastic LB $14.95 (978-0-439-09580-8). 48pp. Answers basic questions about volcanoes and earthquakes with plenty of eye-catching illustrations. (Rev: BL 12/15/00; HBG 3/01; SLJ 2/01) [551.2]

23095 Branley, Franklyn M. *Earthquakes* (K–3). Illus. by Megan Lloyd. Series: Let's-Read-and-Find-Out Science. 2005, HarperCollins LB $16.89 (978-0-06-028009-3); paper $5.99 (978-0-06-445188-8). 40pp. An update of the 1990 edition, with photographs and diagrams of what happens when earthquakes strike. (Rev: BL 3/1/05; SLJ 4/05) [551.22]

23096 Branley, Franklyn M. *Volcanoes* (PS–2). Illus. by Megan Lloyd. Series: Let's-Read-and-Find-Out. 2008, HarperCollins $16.99 (978-0-06-028011-6); paper $5.99 (978-0-06-445189-5). 32pp. This new edition of a 1985 title features new artwork, a page of facts, and directions for making a baking soda and vinegar eruption. (Rev: BLO 3/3/08; SLJ 8/08) [551.21]

23097 Bunce, Vincent. *Volcanoes* (4–6). Series: Restless Planet. 2000, Raintree LB $27.12 (978-0-7398-1327-0). 48pp. Different volcanic landforms are illustrated and explained, along with various kinds of eruptions, their effects, and disaster relief efforts. (Rev: HBG 9/00; SLJ 12/00) [551.2]

23098 Burleigh, Robert. *Volcanoes: Journey to the Crater's Edge* (5–9). Adapted by Robert Burleigh. Illus. by

David Giraudon. Photos by Philippe Bourseiller. 2003, Abrams $14.95 (978-0-8109-4590-6). Volcanoes, lava lakes, ash plumes, and other related phenomena are beautifully illustrated in this oversized photoessay. (Rev: BL 1/1–15/04; SLJ 12/03) [550]

23099 Challen, Paul. *Volcano Alert!* (4–6). Illus. Series: Disaster Alert! 2004, Crabtree LB $26.60 (978-0-7787-1570-2); paper $8.95 (978-0-7787-1602-0). 32pp. In addition to describing volcanoes, there is colorfully presented material on early beliefs and myths associated with them, discussion of advances in predicting eruptions, tips on staying safe, and an experiment. (Rev: SLJ 3/05) [551.2]

23100 Claybourne, Anna. *Volcanoes* (3–6). Illus. 2007, Kingfisher $16.95 (978-0-7534-6137-2). 64pp. This well-designed, oversized volume arranges information about volcanoes in chapters titled "World of Volcanoes," "Exploding Earth," "Famous Eruptions," "Changing Landscapes," "Volcanoes and People," "Studying Volcanoes," and "Volcano Data." (Rev: SLJ 10/07) [551.2]

23101 Fradin, Judy, and Dennis Fradin. *Volcanoes* (4–6). Illus. Series: Witness to Disaster. 2007, National Geographic $16.95 (978-0-7922-5376-1). 48pp. This volume is filled with compelling facts, photographs, and accounts of famous volcanoes and eruptions. (Rev: BL 6/1–15/07; SLJ 10/07) [551.21]

23102 Harper, Kristine C. *The Mount St. Helens Volcanic Eruptions* (5–8). Series: Environmental Disasters. 2005, Facts on File $35.00 (978-0-8160-5757-3). The environmental impact of Mount St. Helens' eruptions is examined in this title from the Environmental Disasters series. (Rev: SLJ 11/05)

23103 Harrison, David L. *Earthquakes: Earth's Mightiest Moments* (K–3). Illus. by Cheryl Nathan. Series: Earthworks. 2004, Boyds Mills $15.95 (978-1-59078-243-9). After a dramatic account of an 1811 earthquake in Missouri, Harrison presents clear, reader-friendly explanations of plate tectonics and the study of earthquakes. (Rev: SLJ 11/04) [551.2]

23104 Harrison, David L. *Volcanoes: Nature's Incredible Fireworks* (1–3). Illus. by Cheryl Nathan. Series: Earthworks. 2002, Boyds Mills $15.95 (978-1-56397-996-5). 32pp. The forces underlying volcanic eruptions are discussed here, with rich and informative illustrations. (Rev: BL 7/02; HBG 3/03; SLJ 9/02) [551.21]

23105 Higgins, Nadia. *Natural Disasters through Infographics* (3–5). Illus. by Alex Sciuto. Series: Super Science Infographics. 2013, Lerner LB $26.60 (978-146771287-3); paper $8.99 (9781467715935). 32pp. Vivid graphics, timelines, diagrams, and charts all serve to make this an appealing nonfiction read full of facts and details about natural disasters such as earthquakes, volcanoes, and tsunamis. **e** (Rev: BL 10/1/13; LMC 5–6/14) [363.34]

23106 Lindop, Laurie. *Probing Volcanoes* (5–8). Illus. Series: Science on the Edge. 2003, Millbrook LB $26.90 (978-0-7613-2700-4). 80pp. A lively introduction to the history of volcanoes and eruptions, the scientists who

dare to study volcanoes, and techniques for collecting data and forecasting volcanic activity. (Rev: BL 12/1/03; SLJ 1/04) [551.21]

23107 Mara, Wil. *Why Do Earthquakes Happen?* (2–4). Series: Tell Me Why, Tell Me How. 2010, Marshall Cavendish LB $20.95 (978-0-7614-4826-6). 32pp. With easy-to-read text and lots of helpful illustrations, this volume introduces essential concepts relating to tectonic plates and seismic waves. (Rev: BL 3/1/11; SLJ 2/1/11) [551.22]

23108 Maslin, Mark. *Earthquakes* (4–6). Series: Restless Planet. 2000, Raintree LB $27.12 (978-0-7398-1328-7). 48pp. This book explains the causes, measurement, hazards, and effects of both earthquakes and tsunamis. (Rev: HBG 9/00; SLJ 12/00) [551.2]

23109 Mehta-Jones, Shilpa. *Earthquake Alert!* (4–6). Illus. Series: Disaster Alert! 2004, Crabtree LB $26.60 (978-0-7787-1572-6); paper $8.95 (978-0-7787-1604-4). In addition to describing earthquakes, there is colorfully presented material on early beliefs and myths associated with them, discussion of advances in predicting events, tips on staying safe, and an experiment. (Rev: SLJ 3/05) [551.2]

23110 Nicolson, Cynthia Pratt. *Earthquake!* (3–6). Illus. 2002, Kids Can $14.95 (978-1-55074-949-6); paper $6.95 (978-1-55074-968-7). 32pp. Using double-page spreads that contain concise text and dramatic photographs, various aspects of earthquakes and their causes and effects are covered. (Rev: BL 5/1/02; HBG 10/02; SLJ 5/02) [551.2]

23111 Nicolson, Cynthia Pratt. *Volcano!* (2–5). Illus. Series: Disaster. 2001, Kids Can $14.95 (978-1-55074-908-3); paper $6.95 (978-1-55074-966-3). 32pp. A tabloid-style format with sensational headlines draws attention to this survey of volcanoes, famous volcanic eruptions, and the work of volcanologists. (Rev: BL 12/1/01; HBG 3/02) [551.21]

23112 Person, Stephen. *Devastated by a Volcano!* (3–5). Illus. Series: Disaster Survivors. 2010, Bearport LB $25.27 (978-193608750-1). 32pp. Firsthand accounts bring immediacy to the factual information on the causes and characteristics of volcanic eruptions and our efforts to predict them. (Rev: BL 4/1/10; LMC 10/10) [551.21]

23113 Prager, Ellen. *Earthquakes* (K–3). Illus. by Susan Greenstein. Series: Jump into Science. 2002, National Geographic $16.95 (978-0-7922-8202-0). 32pp. This is a colorful book that explains simply what earthquakes are, where and why they occur, and their effects. (Rev: BL 6/1–15/02; HBG 10/02) [551.22]

23114 Reed, Jennifer. *Earthquakes: Disaster and Survival, 2005* (4–7). Series: Disaster and Survival. 2005, Enslow LB $23.93 (978-0-7660-2381-9). Major earthquakes and their effects are detailed in text and personal accounts, with a chapter devoted to the December 2004 Asian tsunami. (Rev: BL 5/1/05; SLJ 10/05) [363.34]

23115 Rubin, Ken. *Volcanoes and Earthquakes* (4–7). Illus. Series: Insiders. 2007, Simon & Schuster $16.99 (978-1-4169-3862-0). Vivid illustrations accompany informative text, charts, and graphs introducing earthquakes and volcanoes and some of the important disasters that have taken place. (Rev: SLJ 10/07) [551.21]

23116 Rusch, Elizabeth. *Eruption! Volcanoes and the Science of Saving Lives* (5–8). Illus. Series: Scientists in the Field. 2013, Houghton Mifflin $18.99 (978-054750350-9). 80pp. With a focus on the difficulties of predicting volcanic eruptions and two particularly difficult challenges — Mount Pinatubo and Mount Merapi — this is a compelling and informative account. ALA Notable Children's Book. (Rev: BLO 7/13; HB 11–12/13; SLJ 8/13*) [363.34]

23117 Rusch, Elizabeth. *Will It Blow? Become a Volcano Detective at Mount St. Helens* (4–6). Illus. by K. E. Lewis. 2007, Sasquatch $18.95 (978-1-57061-510-8); paper $13.95 (978-1-57061-509-2). 46pp. Readers will learn how scientists predict whether a volcano will erupt as they read about the "clues" that lead to this conclusion. Cartoon drawings, experiments, and case studies add interest. (Rev: SLJ 7/07)

23118 Simon, Seymour. *Danger! Earthquakes* (1–3). Illus. Series: SeeMore Readers. 2002, North-South paper $3.95 (978-1-58717-140-6). 32pp. Double-page spreads that use color photographs and diagrams explain the causes and impact of earthquakes. (Rev: BL 4/15/02; HBG 10/02; SLJ 3/02) [551.22]

23119 Simon, Seymour. *Danger! Volcanoes* (1–3). Series: See More Readers. 2002, North-South $13.95 (978-1-58717-181-9). 32pp. Outstanding pictures and a brief, simple text are the highlights in this first reader that explores the world of volcanoes. (Rev: BL 7/02; HBG 3/03; SLJ 8/02) [551.2]

23120 Spilsbury, Louise, and Richard Spilsbury. *Shattering Earthquakes* (3–6). Series: Awesome Forces of Nature. 2010, Heinemann LB $29 (978-1-4329-3784-3). 32pp. "What happens in an earthquake?" "Can earthquakes be predicted?" These and other questions are answered — and case studies look at famous tremors — in this eye-catching volume. (Rev: LMC 11–12/10; SLJ 9/1/10) [551.22]

23121 Stewart, Melissa. *Inside Earthquakes* (5–8). Illus. by Cynthia Shaw. Series: Inside. 2011, Sterling $16.95 (978-140275877-5); paper $9.95 (978-14027816-3-6). 48pp. A dramatic presentation of information about what causes earthquakes and their impact on the population and environment, with many photographs and gatefolds. (Rev: BL 11/1/11) [551.22]

23122 Stewart, Melissa. *Inside Volcanoes* (5–8). Illus. by Cynthia Shaw. Series: Inside. 2011, Sterling $16.95 (978-140275876-8); paper $9.95 (978-14027816-4-3). 48pp. A dramatic presentation of information about the different kinds of volcanoes and eruptions and their impact on the population and environment, with many photographs and gatefolds. (Rev: BL 11/1/11) [551.21]

23123 VanCleave, Janice. *Janice VanCleave's Volcanoes: Mind-Boggling Experiments You Can Turn into Science Fair Projects* (4–7). 1994, Wiley paper $10.95 (978-0-471-30811-9). Twenty experiments that explore the

properties of erupting volcanoes using simple materials that can often be found around the house. (Rev: BL 7/94; SLJ 8/94) [551.2]

23124 Waldron, Melanie. *Volcanoes* (3–5). Series: Mapping Earthforms. 2007, Heinemann LB $28.21 (978-1-4034-9606-5). 32pp. With maps, diagrams, tables, and color photographs, this title looks at how volcanoes were formed, what happens during an eruption, the impact on population and wildlife, and important examples (one chapter is titled "A Way of Life — Montserrat"). (Rev: SLJ 10/07) [551.21]

23125 Watson, Nancy. *Our Violent Earth* (4–8). 1982, National Geographic LB $12.50 (978-0-87044-388-6). A discussion of such phenomena as earthquakes, volcanoes, and floods. [363.3]

23126 Winchester, Simon. *The Day the World Exploded: The Earthshaking Catastrophe at Krakatoa* (5–8). Adapted by Dwight Jon Zimmerman. Illus. by Jason Chin. 2008, HarperCollins $22.99 (978-0-06-123982-3). 96pp. After looking at volcanoes and the reasons for eruptions plus the culture and economy of the region at the time, Winchester describes the 1883 disaster and its aftermath; an adaptation of a book for adults titled *Krakatoa* (2003). (Rev: SLJ 11/08; VOYA 8/08) [363.3495]

23127 Woods, Michael, and Mary B. Woods. *Volcanoes* (4–6). Series: Disasters Up Close. 2006, Lerner LB $27.93 (978-0-8225-4715-0). 64pp. With charts, photographs, and quotes from survivors, this book clearly demonstrates the devastating power of volcanic eruptions, and provides information on the formation of volcanoes and the ways we measure their activity. (Rev: SLJ 1/07) [551.21]

23128 Worth, Richard. *The San Francisco Earthquake* (5–8). Series: Environmental Disasters. 2005, Facts on File $35.00 (978-0-8160-5756-6). Worth examines how the San Francisco earthquake of 1906 affected the region's environment. (Rev: SLJ 11/05) [363.34]

Icebergs and Glaciers

23129 Bundey, Nikki. *Ice and the Earth* (3–5). Series: The Science of Weather. 2000, Carolrhoda LB $21.27 (978-1-57505-472-8). 32pp. Along with some interesting experiments, this book describes how ice affects the earth, how it is created, and what would happen if there was no ice on the earth. Also use a companion work *Ice and People* (2000). (Rev: BL 12/15/00; HBG 3/01) [551.3]

23130 Harrison, David L. *Glaciers: Nature's Icy Caps* (1–3). Illus. by Cheryl Nathan. Series: Earthworks. 2006, Boyds Mills $15.95 (978-1-59078-372-6). 32pp. A solid introduction to glaciers, with digital illustrations and large maps. (Rev: BL 4/1/06; SLJ 8/06) [551.31]

23131 Love, Donna. *The Glaciers Are Melting!* (PS–1). Illus. by Shennen Bersani. 2011, Sylvan Dell $16.95

(978-1-6071-8126-2); paper $8.95 (978-1-6071-8136-1). Unpaged. Presents facts about climate change as animals discuss their worries about the melting glaciers and what can be done about it. **e** Lexile AD680L (Rev: LMC 11–12/11; SLJ 8/1/11) [551.31]

Physical Geography

General and Miscellaneous

23132 Baldwin, Carol. *Living in the Tundra* (3–6). Series: Living Habitats. 2003, Heinemann LB $24.22 (978-1-4034-2991-9). 32pp. The plants and animals of the tundra are presented in question-and-answer format, with brief discussion of human interference. (Rev: HBG 4/04; SLJ 2/04) [577.5]

23133 Burnie, David. *Shrublands* (5–8). Series: Biomes Atlases. 2003, Raintree LB $31.42 (978-0-7398-5514-0). 64pp. This comprehensive overview of shrublands describes the climate, flora and fauna, people, and future of these areas, and includes good maps. (Rev: SLJ 9/03) [577.3]

23134 Casil, Amy Sterling. *The Creation of Canyons* (5–9). Series: Land Formation: The Shifting, Moving, Changing Earth. 2010, Rosen LB $29.95 (978-1-4358-5296-8). 64pp. Part of a series that addresses how landforms are created and the ways in which scientists seek to understand them, this volume includes useful examples and provides interesting career information. (Rev: LMC 1–2/10)

23135 Harrison, David L. *Caves: Mysteries Beneath Our Feet* (1–3). Illus. by Cheryl Nathan. 2001, Boyds Mills $15.95 (978-1-56397-915-6). 32pp. A general discussion of caves follows the story of the discovery of New York's Howe Caverns in 1842. (Rev: BL 9/15/01; HBG 3/02; SLJ 10/01) [551.447]

23136 Jennings, Terry. *Coasts and Islands* (3–6). Illus. Series: Restless Earth. 2003, Thameside LB $24.25 (978-1-931983-18-1). 32pp. Diagrams, photographs, and paintings combine with the text to illustrate how islands, coral reefs, and atolls are created and how water and earth interact. (Rev: BL 12/1/02; HBG 3/03) [551.457]

23137 Johansson, Philip. *The Frozen Tundra: A Web of Life* (3–5). Illus. Series: World of Biomes. 2004, Enslow LB $23.93 (978-0-7660-2176-1). 48pp. Plants and animals of the tundra are introduced here, along with information on the climate and seasons and the cycle of life. (Rev: BL 4/1/04) [577.5]

23138 Johansson, Philip. *Marshes and Swamps: A Wetland Web of Life* (4–6). Illus. Series: Wonderful Water Biomes. 2007, Enslow LB $23.93 (978-0-7660-2814-2). 48pp. After an account of a herpetologist's expedition into the New Jersey salt marshes, this title looks at the plants and animals that live in such habitats. (Rev: SLJ 1/08) [577.68]

23139 Johnson, Rebecca. *A Journey into a Wetland* (3–6). Illus. by Phyllis V. Saroff. Series: Biomes of North America. 2004, Lerner LB $23.93 (978-1-57505-593-0). 48pp. This appealing blend of easy-to-understand narrative and colorful illustrations explores the plants and animals found in and around a wetlands habitat. (Rev: BL 5/1/04) [577.68]

23140 Marsico, Katie. *A Home on the Tundra* (1–3). 2006, Children's Pr. LB $20.00 (978-0-516-25345-9). 24pp. This easy-to-understand introduction to the tundra as a natural habitat looks at the nature of the land itself, its climate, flora, and the animals that call it home. (Rev: SLJ 2/07) [577.5]

23141 Marx, Trish. *Everglades Forever: Restoring America's Great Wetland* (3–5). Illus. 2004, Lee & Low $17.95 (978-1-58430-164-6). 40pp. A Florida fifth-grade class's exploration of the Everglades serves as an appealing framework for information on this ecosystem and the perils it faces. (Rev: BL 2/1/05; SLJ 1/05) [508.759]

23142 Quigley, Mary. *Wetlands Explorer* (2–4). Illus. Series: Habitat Explorer. 2004, Raintree LB $25.70 (978-1-4109-0514-7). 32pp. This photo-filled exploration of wetlands looks at the plants and animals found there, plus environmental threats posed by pollution and development.

23143 Sayres, Meghan Nuttall. *The Shape of Betts Meadow: A Wetlands Story* (K–3). Illus. by Joanne Friar. 2002, Millbrook LB $22.90 (978-0-7613-2115-6). 32pp. A stunning picture book set in Washington State that shows how a local doctor purchased a dry meadow and restored it to its original condition as a wetland. (Rev: BL 6/1–15/02; HBG 10/02; SLJ 4/02) [333.91]

23144 Stone, Lynn M. *Wetlands* (1–3). Illus. Series: Biomes of North America. 2003, Rourke LB $20.64 (978-1-58952-688-4). 24pp. For young researchers, this is an excellent introduction to this biome, with clear, simple text, photographs, and maps. [574.5]

23145 Warhol, Tom. *Chaparral and Scrub* (5–8). Series: Earth's Biomes. 2006, Marshall Cavendish LB $32.79 (978-0-7614-2195-5). Report writers will appreciate this attractive introduction to the characteristics of this biome and its plants and animals; also use *Tundra* (2006). (Rev: LMC 8–9/07; SLJ 8/07) [577.3]

23146 Wojahn, Rebecca Hogue, and Donald Wojahn. *A Tundra Food Chain: A Who-Eats-What Adventure in the Arctic* (3–6). Illus. Series: Follow That Food Chain. 2009, Lerner LB $30.60 (978-0-8225-7500-9). 64pp. Polar animals are introduced in this attractive "choose your own adventure" introduction to plant and animal life on the tundra. (Rev: SLJ 6/09) [577.5]

23147 Zollman, Pam. *Gulf of Mexico* (1–2). Series: Rookie Read-About Geography. 2006, Children's Pr. LB $20.50 (978-0-516-25035-9). 32pp. Geographical and geological facts about this body of water are presented in an airy format that will appeal to beginning readers. (Rev: SLJ 6/06) [911.6364]

Deserts

23148 Benduhn, Tea. *Living in Deserts* (3–4). Series: Life on the Edge. 2007, Gareth Stevens LB $19.93 (978-0-8368-8341-1). 24pp. After an introduction to deserts and the desert climate, Benduhn looks at the people of desert areas, the life they lead, and the problems they face. (Rev: LMC 1/08; SLJ 12/07) [910.915]

23149 Brown, John. *Journey into the Desert* (3–6). 2003, Oxford LB $19.95 (978-0-19-515777-2). 48pp. A camping trip forms the backdrop for a photo-filled introduction to the landscape, plants, and wildlife of the Sonoran Desert. (Rev: HBG 10/03; SLJ 8/03) [508.3154]

23150 Ceceri, Kathy. *Discover the Desert: The Driest Place on Earth* (4–6). Illus. by Samuel Carbaugh. Series: Discover Your World. 2009, Nomad paper $16.95 (978-1-9346704-6-0). 112pp. A large-format look at deserts and their topography and human and animal inhabitants, with information on famous explorers and preparations you need to make for a desert expedition. (Rev: BL 2/15/10; SLJ 3/10) [910.9154]

23151 Chambers, Catherine. *Deserts* (3–5). Series: Mapping Earthforms. 2000, Heinemann LB $21.36 (978-1-57572-522-2). 32pp. Deserts and desert life plus environmental factors that affect deserts are introduced in a large, bold text and numerous illustrations. (Rev: HBG 3/01; SLJ 8/00) [574.5]

23152 Donald, Rhonda Lucas. *Deep in the Desert* (1–3). Illus. by Sherry Neidigh. 2011, Sylvan Dell $16.95 (978-1-60718-125-5); paper $8.95 (978-1-60718-135-4). Unpaged. Donald offers new lyrics for well-known children's songs, describing the desert and the animals that live there; includes facts and activities. ℮ (Rev: LMC 11–12/11; SLJ 7/11) [577.54]

23153 Fredericks, Anthony D. *Around One Cactus: Owls, Bats and Leaping Rats* (K–4). Illus. by Jennifer DiRubbio. Series: Sharing Nature with Children. 2003, Dawn $16.95 (978-1-58469-051-1); paper $7.95 (978-1-58469-052-8). A cumulative tale, told in verse, about the natural life surrounding a Saguaro cactus, colorfully illustrated with detailed drawings. (Rev: HBG 4/04; SLJ 4/04) [591.754]

23154 Hyde, Natalie. *Desert Extremes* (2–5). Illus. Series: Extreme Nature. 2008, Crabtree LB $26.60 (978-0-7787-4500-6); paper $8.95 (978-0-7787-4517-4). Clear photographs accompany informative text describing the plants, animals, and people of deserts around the world. (Rev: BLO 3/11/09) [578.754]

23155 Johnson, Rebecca. *A Walk in the Desert* (2–5). Illus. by Phyllis V. Saroff. Series: Biomes of North America. 2001, Carolrhoda LB $23.93 (978-1-57505-152-9). 48pp. As well as the climate of the desert, this account covers its flora and fauna and their interactions. (Rev: HBG 10/01; SLJ 3/01) [574.5]

23156 Lazaroff, David. *Correctamundo! Prickly Pete's Guide to Desert Facts and Cactifracts* (K–3). Illus. by Preston Neel. 2001, Arizona-Sonora Desert Museum paper $14.95 (978-1-886679-17-7). A bright, lively question-and-answer introduction to desert plants and animals, conducted by a packrat named Prickly Pete. (Rev: SLJ 8/01) [574.5]

23157 Le Rochais, Marie-Ange. *Desert Trek: An Eye-Opening Journey Through the World's Driest Places* (3–5). Trans. by George L. Newman. Illus. 2001, Walker LB $18.85 (978-0-8027-8766-8). 40pp. Dramatic spreads and brief text show the diversity of desert landscapes around the world, with features ranging from plants, animals, and oases to people hunting and working. (Rev: BL 6/1–15/01; HBG 10/01; SLJ 9/01) [577.54]

23158 Mora, Pat. *Listen to the Desert / Oye al Desierto* (PS–2). Illus. by Francisco Mora. 1994, Clarion $16.00 (978-0-395-67292-1). Using double-page spreads, this book in English and Spanish introduces the animals and sounds found in a Southwestern desert. (Rev: HBG 4/04; SLJ 10/94) [574.5]

23159 Moss, Miriam. *This Is the Oasis* (K–2). Illus. by Adrienne Kennaway. 2005, Kane $14.95 (978-1-929132-76-8). Lush illustrations enhance this large-format introduction to the people, plants, and animals of a Saharan oasis. (Rev: SLJ 3/06) [574.5]

23160 Patent, Dorothy Hinshaw. *Life in a Desert* (5–8). Series: Ecosystems in Action. 2003, Lerner LB $26.60 (978-0-8225-2140-2). This account explores the plant and animal life in deserts and how human intervention has changed this ecosystem. (Rev: BL 9/15/03; HBG 10/03) [574.5]

23161 Pfeffer, Wendy. *Hot Deserts* (3–5). Series: Living on the Edge. 2002, Benchmark LB $25.64 (978-0-7614-1440-7). 40pp. This easy-to-read overview of the animals and plants that flourish in desert climates opens with a map. (Rev: HBG 10/03; SLJ 6/03) [577.54]

23162 Pipe, Jim. *Desert Survival* (4–6). Illus. Series: Extreme Habitats. 2007, Gareth Stevens LB $25.27 (978-0-8368-8245-2). 32pp. This well-designed title combines high visual appeal and accessible facts to make an attractive and informative overview of deserts, the plants and animals that live there, how people use deserts, and the threats the deserts face. (Rev: LMC 1/08; SLJ 12/07) [577.54]

23163 Pratt-Serafini, Kristin Joy. *Saguaro Moon: A Desert Journal* (3–6). Illus. 2002, Dawn $16.95 (978-1-58469-037-5); paper $7.95 (978-1-58469-036-8). 32pp. Factual information about desert plant and animal life is presented in the form of a nature journal written by a girl named Megan, who has recently moved to Arizona. (Rev: BL 10/15/02; HBG 3/03; SLJ 9/02) [508.3154]

23164 Pyers, Greg. *Desert Explorer* (2–4). Illus. Series: Habitat Explorer. 2004, Raintree LB $25.70 (978-1-4109-0507-9). 32pp. This photo-filled exploration of deserts looks at the plants and animals found there, plus environmental threats to this habitat.

23165 Salzmann, Mary Elizabeth. *In the Desert* (K–1). Illus. Series: What Do You See? 2001, ABDO LB $19.93 (978-1-57765-564-0). 24pp. Colorful double-page spreads introduce the desert in simple language for beginning readers. (Rev: HBG 3/02; SLJ 3/02) [577.54]

23166 Sandler, Michael. *Deserts: Surviving in the Sahara* (3–5). Illus. Series: X-treme Places. 2005, Bearport LB $25.27 (978-1-59716-085-8). 32pp. A compelling overview of deserts and the challenges to their human and animal inhabitants is given added punch by the inclusion of the story of René Caillié, who crossed the Sahara in 1828. (Rev: SLJ 1/06) [916.6]

23167 Sayre, April Pulley. *Desert* (4–7). Series: Exploring Earth's Biomes. 1994, Twenty-First Century LB $25.90 (978-0-8050-2825-6). After a general introduction to deserts, a specific one is explored in brief chapters with excellent illustrations. (Rev: BL 1/1/95*; SLJ 1/95) [574.5]

23168 Sill, Cathryn. *Deserts* (1–4). Illus. by John Sill. Series: About Habitats. 2007, Peachtree $16.95 (978-1-56145-390-0). 48pp. The landscape, flora, and fauna of the desert are introduced in appealing illustrations and accessible text. (Rev: BL 4/1/07) [577.54]

23169 Silverman, Buffy. *Desert Food Chains* (4–7). Series: Protecting Food Chains. 2010, Heinemann LB $32 (978-1-4329-3856-7); paper $8.99 (978-1-4329-3863-5). 48pp. With chapter headings that ask questions such as "What Are the Producers in Deserts?" and "What Are the Decomposers in Deserts?," this volume explores species and food chains in deserts and discusses why we need to protect them. (Rev: SLJ 11/1/10) [577.5]

23170 Stone, Lynn M. *Deserts* (1–3). Illus. Series: Biomes of North America. 2003, Rourke LB $20.64 (978-1-58952-683-9). 24pp. For young researchers, this is an excellent introduction to this biome, with clear, simple text, photographs, and maps. [574.5]

23171 Warhol, Tom. *Desert* (5–8). Series: Earth's Biomes. 2006, Marshall Cavendish LB $32.79 (978-0-7614-2194-8). Report writers will appreciate this attractive introduction to the characteristics of this biome and its plants and animals. (Rev: SLJ 8/07) [577.54]

Forests and Rain Forests

23172 Art, Henry W., and Michael W. Robbins. *Woods Walk* (4–6). Illus. 2003, Storey $21.95 (978-1-58017-477-0); paper $14.95 (978-1-58017-452-7). 128pp. A broad overview of the plants and animals found in the woodlands of the eastern and western United States. (Rev: HBG 4/04; SLJ 6/03) [508.352]

23173 Baldwin, Carol. *Living in a Rain Forest* (3–6). Series: Living Habitats. 2003, Heinemann LB $24.22 (978-1-4034-2992-6). 32pp. The plants and animals of the rain forest are presented in question-and-answer format, with brief discussion of human interference. (Rev: HBG 4/04; SLJ 2/04) [577.34]

23174 Baldwin, Carol. *Living in the Taiga* (3–6). Series: Living Habitats. 2003, Heinemann LB $24.22 (978-1-4034-2994-0). 32pp. The plants and animals of the taiga are presented in question-and-answer format, with brief discussion of human interference. (Rev: HBG 4/04; SLJ 2/04) [577.3]

23175 Benduhn, Tea. *Living in Tropical Rain Forests* (3–4). Series: Life on the Edge. 2007, Gareth Stevens LB $19.93 (978-0-8368-8344-2). 24pp. After an introduction to rain forests and the climate of these areas, Benduhn looks at the people who live there, the life they lead, and the problems they face. (Rev: LMC 1/08; SLJ 12/07) [910.915]

23176 Bishop, Nic. *Forest Explorer: A Life-Size Field Guide* (K–4). Photos by author. 2004, Scholastic $17.95 (978-0-439-17480-0). 48pp. An attractive introductory guide to the trees and animal life found in deciduous forests. (Rev: BL 1/1–15/04; SLJ 3/04) [591.734]

23177 Castaldo, Nancy F. *Rainforests: An Activity Guide for Ages 6–9* (2–6). Illus. 2003, Chicago Review paper $14.95 (978-1-55652-476-9). 133pp. This engaging collection of resources and activities is designed to help young readers gain a better understanding of the different types of rainforests and the animals and plants that are common to each. (Rev: SLJ 11/03) [577.34]

23178 Chinery, Michael. *Poisoners and Pretenders* (5–8). Series: Secrets of the Rainforests. 2000, Crabtree LB $25.27 (978-0-7787-0219-1); paper $7.95 (978-0-7787-0229-0). After a brief description of a rain forest, this book looks at animals found there and their mimicry, camouflage, venom, natural selection, and adaptation to the environment. Also use *Predators and Prey* (2000). (Rev: SLJ 2/01) [574.5]

23179 Cobb, Vicki. *This Place Is Wet: An Imagine Living Here Book* (2–4). Illus. by Barbara Lavallee. 2013, Walker paper $8.99 (978-08027340-0-6). 32pp. An updated edition of a volume originally published in 1989, this offers improved coverage of what it's like to live in the Amazon rain forest. (Rev: BL 3/15/13) [577.34]

23180 Cole, Melissa. *Forests* (3–6). Photos by Tom Leeson and Pat Leeson. Series: Wild America Habitats. 2003, Gale LB $21.20 (978-1-56711-802-5). 24pp. Describes the unique characteristics of the forest habitat and the plants and animals that thrive within it. Also use *Rain Forests* (2003). (Rev: SLJ 2/04) [577.3]

23181 Collard, Sneed B. *The Forest in the Clouds* (2–4). Illus. by Michael Rothman. 2000, Charlesbridge $16.95 (978-0-88106-985-3); paper $6.95 (978-0-88106-986-0). 32pp. In double-page spreads, the Monteverde Cloud Forest in Costa Rica is introduced with material on its climate, animals, and plants. (Rev: BL 6/1–15/00; HBG 3/01; SLJ 8/00) [577.34]

23182 Fleisher, Paul. *Forest Food Webs* (2–5). Illus. Series: Early Bird Food Webs. 2007, Lerner LB $26.60 (978-0-8225-6729-5). 48pp. This book describes the interrelationship between plants and animals in the forest. (Rev: BL 12/1/07) [577.3]

23183 Ganeri, Anita. *Rainforests* (3–5). Illus. by Peter Bull. Series: Explorers. 2011, Kingfisher $10.99 (978-075346590-5). 32pp. An inviting mix of text, sidebars, captions, fact lists, and more add read-appeal to this well-illustrated book about rain forests and the flora and fauna found there. (Rev: BL 2/15/12) [577.34]

23184 Godkin, Celia. *Fire!* (1–3). 2006, Fitzhenry & Whiteside $17.95 (978-1-55041-889-7). 40pp. Double-page spreads show the role fire plays in forest ecology, with a frightening blaze followed by returning animals and plants. (Rev: BL 8/06; SLJ 11/06) [577.24]

23185 Guiberson, Brenda Z. *Life in the Boreal Forest* (2–5). Illus. by Gennady Spirin. 2009, Holt $16.99 (978-0-8050-7718-6). 40pp. Beautiful illustrations and compelling text describe the taigas of the northern hemisphere, the plants and animals that live there, the threats they face, and their importance to the environment. (Rev: BL 7/09; LMC 10/09; SLJ 9/09) [578.73]

23186 Guiberson, Brenda Z. *Rain, Rain, Rainforest* (K–3). Illus. by Steve Jenkins. 2004, Holt $16.95 (978-0-8050-6582-4). 32pp. Basic information on day-to-day life and survival in the rain forest is conveyed in an attractive blend of picturesque narrative and colorful paper-cut collages. (Rev: BL 5/1/04; HB 7/04; SLJ 6/04) [577.34]

23187 Jackson, Kay. *Rain Forests* (4–7). Illus. Series: Our Environment. 2007, Gale LB $23.70 (978-0-7377-3624-3). This well-illustrated volume explores why rain forests are important; what people, plants, and animals live there; why these areas are endangered; and what their future may hold. (Rev: BL 12/1/07) [577.34]

23188 Jackson, Tom. *Tropical Forests* (5–8). Series: Biomes Atlases. 2003, Raintree LB $31.42 (978-0-7398-5250-7). 64pp. This comprehensive overview of tropical forests describes the climate, flora and fauna, people, and future of these areas, and includes good maps. (Rev: SLJ 9/03) [577.34]

23189 Johanasen, Heather, and Sindy McKay. *About the Rain Forest* (1–2). Illus. Series: We Both Read. 2000, Treasure Bay $7.99 (978-1-891327-23-0); paper $3.99 (978-1-891327-24-7). 44pp. Using side-by-side texts, one for adults and the other for children, this book introduces the rain forest, its climate, ecosystem, and animals. (Rev: BL 7/00) [574.5]

23190 Johansson, Philip. *The Dry Desert: A Web of Life* (3–5). Illus. Series: A World of Biomes. 2004, Enslow LB $23.93 (978-0-7660-2200-3). 48pp. An engaging introduction to the flora and fauna of the desert and to the work of the scientists who study the biome.

23191 Johansson, Philip. *The Forested Taiga: A Web of Life* (3–6). Illus. Series: A World of Biomes. 2004, Enslow LB $23.93 (978-0-7660-2197-6). 48pp. Introduces readers to the physical characteristics, climate, flora, and fauna of the forested taiga, a vast subpolar region dominated by conifers. (Rev: SLJ 8/04) [577.3]

23192 Johansson, Philip. *The Temperate Forest: A Web of Life* (3–5). Illus. Series: World of Biomes. 2004, Enslow LB $23.93 (978-0-7660-2198-3). 48pp. A biologist's interest in a black bear in North Carolina serves as an introduction to this study of plant and animal interaction in temperate forests. (Rev: BL 4/1/04; SLJ 8/04) [577.3]

23193 Johansson, Philip. *The Tropical Rain Forest: A Web of Life* (3–6). Illus. Series: World of Biomes. 2004, Enslow LB $23.93 (978-0-7660-2199-0). 48pp. An en-

gaging introduction to the flora and fauna of the rain forest and to the work of the scientists who study the biome. (Rev: SLJ 8/04) [577.34]

23194 Johnson, Rebecca. *A Walk in the Boreal Forest* (2–4). Illus. by Phyllis V. Saroff. Series: Biomes of North America. 2000, Carolrhoda LB $23.93 (978-1-57505-156-7). 48pp. This book takes the reader to a forest of tall conifers and tells about its plants and animals and their interdependence. (Rev: BL 10/15/00; HBG 3/01; SLJ 3/01) [574.5]

23195 Johnson, Rebecca. *A Walk in the Rain Forest* (2–5). Illus. by Phyllis V. Saroff. Series: Biomes of North America. 2001, Carolrhoda LB $23.93 (978-1-57505-154-3). 48pp. Examines the climate of the rain forest and its flora and fauna. (Rev: HBG 10/01; SLJ 3/01) [574.5]

23196 Knight, Tim. *Journey into the Rainforest* (3–5). Illus. by Juan Pablo Moreiras and Tim Knight. 2001, Oxford $19.95 (978-0-19-521751-3). 48pp. Readers take a colorful tour through a rain forest, observing the vegetation and wildlife as they go and learning about the ecosystem's intricacies and endangered status. (Rev: BL 9/15/01; HBG 3/02; SLJ 10/01) [577.34]

23197 Lasky, Kathryn. *The Most Beautiful Roof in the World: Exploring the Rainforest Canopy* (5–8). 1997, Harcourt paper $9.00 (978-0-15-200897-0). The canopy of plants and animals found in the rain forest of Belize is explored by the author, a biologist, who also explains the methods scientists use to conduct research in this environment, sometimes under extremely difficult conditions. (Rev: BL 4/1/97; SLJ 4/97) [574.5]

23198 Levinson, Nancy S. *Rain Forests* (K–2). Illus. by Diane D. Hearn. 2008, Holiday $15.95 (978-0-8234-1899-2). 40pp. A useful introduction to rain forests around the world and the animals and plants found in them. (Rev: BL 5/1/08; SLJ 5/08) [577.34]

23199 Levy, Janey. *Discovering Rain Forests* (3–5). Series: World Habitats. 2007, Rosen LB $23.95 (978-1-4042-3782-7). 32pp. With photographs and fast facts, this volume covers location, climate, plants and animals, people, threats and conservation efforts, and so forth. (Rev: LMC 3/08; SLJ 1/08) [577.34]

23200 MacMillan, Dianne M. *Life in a Deciduous Forest* (5–8). Series: Ecosystems in Action. 2003, Lerner LB $26.60 (978-0-8225-4684-9). This book explores the ecosystem, its flora and fauna, where trees shed their leaves in autumn. (Rev: BL 9/15/03; HBG 10/03) [574.5]

23201 Montgomery, Sy. *Encantado: Pink Dolphin of the Amazon* (5–8). Illus. by Diane Taylor Snow. 2002, Houghton Mifflin $18.00 (978-0-618-13103-7). The author describes the flora and fauna of the South American rain forest seen in her unsuccessful journey to locate the encantado, the elusive pink dolphin. (Rev: BL 4/1/02; HB 7–8/02; HBG 10/02; SLJ 5/02*) [599.53]

23202 Moore, Heidi. *Rain Forest Food Chains* (4–7). Series: Protecting Food Chains. 2010, Heinemann LB $32 (978-1-4329-3860-4); paper $8.99 (978-1-4329-3867-3). 48pp. With chapter headings that ask questions such as "What Are the Producers in Rain Forests?" and "What Are the Decomposers in Rain Forests?," this volume explores species and food chains within rain forests and discusses why we need to protect them. (Rev: SLJ 11/1/10) [577.3]

23203 Morrison, Taylor. *Wildfire* (4–6). Illus. 2006, Houghton $17.00 (978-0-618-50900-3). 48pp. Explores the contradiction between the destruction caused by wildfires and their beneficial impact on forests; with descriptions of the roles of firefighters, scientists, and foresters. (Rev: BL 4/1/06; SLJ 5/06) [634.9]

23204 Mutel, Cornelia F., and Mary M. Rodgers. *Our Endangered Planet: Tropical Rain Forests* (4–7). Series: Our Endangered Planet. 1991, Lerner LB $27.15 (978-0-8225-2503-5); paper $8.95 (978-0-8225-9629-5). Describes tropical rain forests and the environmental threats they face. (Rev: BL 6/15/91; SLJ 5/91) [333]

23205 O'Hare, Ted. *Vanishing Rain Forest* (1–3). Photos by Lynn M. Stone. Series: Rain Forests Today. 2005, Rourke LB $14.95 (978-1-59515-156-8). 24pp. An attractive introduction to the threats to world's rain forests from pollution and wholesale deforestation. Other titles in this series include *Animals of the Rain Forest*, *Plants of the Rain Forest*, and *People of the Rain Forest* (all 2005). (Rev: BL 1/1–15/05) [333.75]

23206 Parker, Edward. *People* (5–8). Photos by author. Series: Rain Forest. 2003, Raintree LB $27.12 (978-0-7398-5242-2). 48pp. An introduction to the various peoples of the rain forest. (Rev: HBG 3/03; SLJ 1/03) [304.2]

23207 Parker, Edward. *Rain Forest Mammals* (5–9). Illus. Series: Rain Forest. 2002, Raintree LB $27.12 (978-0-7398-5241-5). 48pp. Mammals of the rain forest and the importance of preserving their habitat are introduced in close-up color photographs and a catchy layout, with a glossary, bibliography, and list of related organizations. Also use *Rain Forest Reptiles and Amphibians* (2002). (Rev: BL 12/1/02; HBG 3/03) [599]

23208 Pyers, Greg. *Forest Explorer* (2–4). Illus. Series: Habitat Explorer. 2004, Raintree LB $25.70 (978-1-4109-0508-6). 32pp. This photo-filled exploration of forests looks at the plants and animals found there, plus environmental threats posed by pollution and development. Also use *Rain Forest Explorer* (2004

23209 Rapp, Valerie. *Life in an Old Growth Forest* (5–8). Series: Ecosystems in Action. 2002, Lerner LB $26.60 (978-0-8225-2135-8). In pictures and text, this book introduces life in an established forest with material on the interdependence of organisms there, and how human intervention has changed this ecosystem. (Rev: BL 12/15/02; HBG 3/03; SLJ 2/03) [574.5]

23210 Sandler, Michael. *Rain Forests: Surviving in the Amazon* (3–5). Illus. Series: X-treme Places. 2005, Bearport LB $25.27 (978-1-59716-089-6). 32pp. This colorful overview of the world's rain forests includes the harrowing survival story of Yossi Ghinsberg, who became lost in the wilds of the Amazon basin. (Rev: SLJ 1/06) [578.734]

23211 Sayre, April Pulley. *Tropical Rain Forest* (4–7). Series: Exploring Earth's Biomes. 1994, Twenty-First Century LB $25.90 (978-0-8050-2826-3). The structure and contents of rain forests are explored with information on the plants, animals, and people that exist in this habitat. (Rev: BL 1/1/95; SLJ 1/95) [574.5]

23212 Serafini, Frank. *Looking Closely Through the Forest* (K–3). Photos by author. 2008, Kids Can $15.95 (978-1-55453-212-4). Guessing game questions draw readers through the forest with answers and facts revealed at the turn of each page. (Rev: LMC 10/08; SLJ 4/08) [578.73]

23213 Simon, Seymour. *Tropical Rainforests* (2–5). Illus. 2010, HarperCollins $16.99 (978-0-06-114253-6); LB $17.89 (978-006114254-3). 32pp. This visually appealing book provides oversize text and excellent color photographs of the flora and fauna of tropical rain forests, some of the products that originate there, and the problem of their destruction. (Rev: BL 10/15/10; SLJ 9/1/10) [578.734]

23214 Stone, Lynn M. *Forests* (1–3). Illus. Series: Biomes of North America. 2003, Rourke LB $20.64 (978-1-58952-684-6). 24pp. For young researchers, this is an excellent introduction to this biome, with clear, simple text, photographs, and maps. [574.5]

23215 Welsbacher, Anne. *Life in a Rainforest* (5–8). Series: Ecosystems in Action. 2003, Lerner LB $26.60 (978-0-8225-4685-6). This illustrated account covers the plant and animal life in rain forests and explains how human intervention has changed, and often endangered, this ecosystem. (Rev: BL 9/15/03; HBG 10/03) [574.5]

Mountains

23216 Benduhn, Tea. *Living in Mountains* (3–4). Series: Life on the Edge. 2007, Gareth Stevens LB $19.93 (978-0-8368-8342-8). 24pp. After an introduction to mountains and the climate of these areas, Benduhn looks at the people of mountain areas, the life they lead, and the problems they face. (Rev: LMC 1/08; SLJ 12/07) [910.914]

23217 Chambers, Catherine. *Mountains* (3–5). Series: Mapping Earthforms. 2000, Heinemann LB $21.36 (978-1-57572-525-3). 32pp. A basic overview of mountains presented in double-page spreads illustrated with photographs, maps, and charts. (Rev: HBG 3/01; SLJ 8/00) [551.4]

23218 Gill, Shelley. *Up on Denali* (2–4). Illus. by Shannon Cartwright. 2006, Sasquatch $16.95 (978-1-57061-366-1); paper $10.95 (978-1-57061-365-4). Explores the geology and plants and animals of Denali, North America's tallest mountain, in an appealing and humorous blend of fact and fiction. (Rev: BL 6/1–15/06) [551.43]

23219 Grupper, Jonathan. *Rocky Mountains* (4–6). Series: Destination. 2001, National Geographic LB $16.95 (978-0-7922-7722-4). 32pp. This book introduces the Rockies, how they were formed, their composition, and their animals and plants. (Rev: BL 3/1/01; HBG 10/01) [978]

23220 Harrison, David L. *Mountains: The Tops of the World* (1–3). Illus. by Cheryl Nathan. 2005, Boyds Mills $16.95 (978-1-59078-326-9). 32pp. Explores the ways in which mountains were created and provides explanations for such puzzling phenomena as the discovery of a fish fossil on a mountaintop. (Rev: BL 11/1/05; SLJ 10/05) [551.43]

23221 Jennings, Terry. *Mountains* (3–6). Illus. 2003, Thameside LB $24.25 (978-1-931983-19-8). 32pp. Vivid photographs help to explain how mountains are formed and eroded, their importance in our climate, and the kind of life there. (Rev: BL 12/1/02; HBG 3/03) [551.432]

23222 Levy, Janey. *Discovering Mountains* (3–5). Series: World Habitats. 2007, Rosen LB $23.95 (978-1-4042-3785-8). 32pp. With photographs and fast facts, this volume covers location, climate, plants and animals, people, threats and conservation efforts, and so forth. (Rev: LMC 3/08; SLJ 1/08) [551.4]

23223 Locker, Thomas. *Mountain Dance* (K–4). Illus. by author. 2001, Harcourt $17.00 (978-0-15-202622-6). Verse and oil paintings describe various kinds of mountains and how they were formed, in an informative combination that appends additional details. (Rev: BCCB 2/02; HBG 3/02; SLJ 10/01) [551.4]

23224 Maynard, Charles W. *The Appalachians* (2–5). Series: Great Mountain Ranges of the World. 2004, Rosen LB $21.25 (978-0-8239-6695-0). 24pp. Geology, history, climate, flora and fauna, and economy are all discussed in this easy-to-read, large-format volume. (Rev: SLJ 8/04) [917.4]

23225 Maynard, Charles W. *The Himalayas* (2–5). Series: Great Mountain Ranges of the World. 2004, Rosen LB $21.25 (978-0-8239-6694-3). 24pp. Geology, history, climate, flora and fauna, and economy are all discussed in this easy-to-read, large-format volume. (Rev: SLJ 8/04) [915.496]

23226 Pyers, Greg. *Mountain Explorer* (2–4). Illus. Series: Habitat Explorer. 2004, Raintree LB $25.70 (978-1-4109-0509-3). 32pp. This photo-filled exploration of mountains looks at the plants and animals found there, plus environmental threats posed by pollution and development.

23227 Rotter, Charles. *Mountains: The Towering Sentinels* (4–6). Series: LifeViews. 2002, Creative Editions LB $24.25 (978-1-58341-123-0). 32pp. The various types of mountains are detailed, with information on climate, ecosystems, and environmental concerns. (Rev: HBG 3/03; SLJ 1/03)

23228 Sandler, Michael. *Mountains: Surviving on Mt. Everest* (3–5). Series: X-treme Places. 2005, Bearport LB $25.27 (978-1-59716-086-5). 32pp. The first-person account of Temba Tsheri Sherpa, a Nepalese climber who lost fingers to frostbite during a successful assault on Mount Everest, gives added punch to this overview of mountain climbing. (Rev: SLJ 1/06) [796.52]

23229 Sill, Cathryn. *Mountains* (K–4). Illus. by John Sill. Series: About Habitats. 2009, Peachtree $16.95 (978-1-56145-469-3). Simple, descriptive text and detailed illustrations of the plants and animals that inhabit various mountain locations combine to create an appealing volume. (Rev: SLJ 5/09) [577.5]

23230 Tocci, Salvatore. *Alpine Tundra: Life on the Tallest Mountain* (4–7). Series: Biomes and Habitats. 2005, Watts LB $25.50 (978-0-531-12365-2). Introduces the climate, flora, and fauna found high above sea level on the world's highest mountains. Also use *Arctic Tundra: Life at the North Pole* (2005). (Rev: SLJ 7/05) [577.5]

Ponds, Rivers, and Lakes

23231 Arnosky, Jim. *The Brook Book: Exploring the Smallest Streams* (K–3). Illus. by author. 2008, Dutton $15.99 (978-0-525-47716-7). 32pp. Beautiful watercolor artwork enhances this exploration of the ecology of brooks and streams. (Rev: BL 12/1/07; HB 3/08; LMC 10/08; SLJ 1/08) [574.5]

23232 Baron, Robert. *Hudson: The Story of a River* (2–5). Illus. by Thomas Locker. 2004, Fulcrum $17.95 (978-1-55591-512-4). 32pp. Breathtaking landscape paintings bring this natural history of the Hudson River Valley to life. (Rev: BL 5/15/04; SLJ 6/04) [974.7]

23233 Bauer, Marion Dane. *The Mighty Mississippi* (1–2). Illus. by John Wallace. Series: Wonders of America. 2007, Simon & Schuster LB $11.89 (978-0-689-86951-8); paper $3.99 (978-0-689-86950-1). An introduction to the Mississippi River, with pleasing color illustrations and simple phrases for the beginning reader. (Rev: SLJ 5/07)

23234 Bryan, Dale-Marie. *The Colorado River* (1–2). Series: Rookie Read-About Geography. 2006, Children's Pr. LB $20.50 (978-0-516-25033-5). 32pp. Beginning readers and report writers will get all the facts about this grand river in this well-designed book. (Rev: SLJ 6/06) [917.91]

23235 Castaldo, Nancy F. *River Wild: An Activity Guide to North American Rivers* (4–7). Illus. 2006, Chicago Review $14.95 (978-1-55652-585-8). From a general introduction to the water cycle and watersheds, this volume narrows in on specific rivers in North America and the flora and fauna found there, even offering profiles of riverkeepers. (Rev: BL 3/1/06; SLJ 6/06) [372.8991]

23236 Chambers, Catherine, and Nicholas Lapthorn. *Rivers. Rev. ed.* (3–5). Series: Mapping Earthforms. 2007, Heinemann LB $28.21 (978-1-4034-9604-1). 32pp. With maps, diagrams, tables, and color photographs, this title looks at how rivers are formed; river landscapes, plants, and animals; the future of rivers; and important examples (one chapter is titled "A Way of Life — Bangladesh") (Rev: SLJ 10/07) [508.316]

23237 Gilpin, Daniel. *The Snake River* (4–8). Illus. Series: Rivers of North America. 2003, Gareth Stevens LB $26.00 (978-0-8368-3761-2). 32pp. Following the course of the Snake RIver in the Northwestern United

States, with attention to the plant and animal life along it and its role in history. (Rev: SLJ 3/04)

23238 Gray, Leon. *The Missouri River* (4–8). Series: Rivers of North America. 2003, Gareth Stevens LB $26.00 (978-0-8368-3758-2). A trip along the Missouri, the longest river in the United States, from its source to its confluence with the Mississippi, with a look at the history that has been made on its banks. (Rev: SLJ 3/04)

23239 Harris, Tim. *The Mackenzie River* (4–8). Series: Rivers of North America. 2003, Gareth Stevens LB $26.00 (978-0-8368-3756-8). A visit to the Mackenzie River in Canada's Northwest Territories and the people, plants, and animals who have lived along it. (Rev: SLJ 3/04)

23240 Harrison, David L. *Rivers: Nature's Wondrous Waterways* (K–3). Illus. by Cheryl Nathan. 2002, Boyds Mills $15.95 (978-1-56397-968-2). 32pp. Using verse and color illustrations, this basic science book explains how rivers are formed, how they support life, and their importance in conservation and pollution. (Rev: BL 4/1/02; HBG 10/02; SLJ 5/02) [551.48]

23241 Hawkes, Steve. *The Tennessee River* (4–8). Series: Rivers of North America. 2003, Gareth Stevens LB $26.00 (978-0-8368-3763-6). A trip along the length of the Tennessee River, with information on its history, natural attributes, and its effect on the people who live along its path. (Rev: SLJ 3/04)

23242 Heinz, Brian J. *Butternut Hollow Pond* (2–4). Illus. by Bob Marstall. 2000, Millbrook LB $22.90 (978-0-7613-0268-1). 32pp. This beautiful study of a day and night on a pond introduces many forms of animal life and demonstrates the food chain and the interdependence of creatures. (Rev: BL 1/1–15/01*; HBG 3/01; SLJ 3/01) [591.763]

23243 Himmelman, John. *Frog in a Bog* (PS–2). Illus. 2004, Charlesbridge $15.95 (978-1-57091-517-8). 32pp. A detailed and colorful look at life in a bog, for frogs and for all the other plants and animals found there. (Rev: BL 2/15/04; SLJ 3/04) [591.76]

23244 Jackson, Tom. *The Arkansas River* (4–8). Series: Rivers of North America. 2003, Gareth Stevens LB $26.00 (978-0-8368-3752-0). Tracing the Arkansas River its entire length of nearly 1,500 miles, with coverage of the people who have lived along it over the centuries and its importance to them. (Rev: SLJ 3/04)

23245 Jackson, Tom. *The Ohio River* (4–8). Series: Rivers of North America. 2003, Gareth Stevens LB $26.00 (978-0-8368-3759-9). Following the Ohio River from Pittsburgh to its confluence with the Mississippi at Cairo, Illinois, with material on the people and places found along its banks. (Rev: SLJ 3/04)

23246 Johnson, Rebecca. *A Journey into a Lake* (3–6). Illus. by Phyllis V. Saroff. Series: Biomes of North America. 2004, Lerner LB $23.93 (978-1-57505-594-7). 48pp. The flora and fauna found in and around lakes are clearly described in striking text and illustrations that will please report writers and browsers. (Rev: BL 5/1/04) [577.63]

23247 Kalman, Bobbie, and Hadley Dyer. *Wetland Food Chains* (3–5). Illus. Series: Food Chains. 2006, Crabtree paper $6.95 (978-0-7787-1999-1). An introduction to this biome, the plants and animals that live there, and how their interconnection functions. (Rev: SLJ 6/07)

23248 Morrison, Gordon. *Pond* (3–6). Illus. 2002, Houghton $16.00 (978-0-618-10271-6). 32pp. Wonderful watercolors, descriptive text, and detailed insets show life in and around a pond through the seasons of the year. (Rev: BL 1/1–15/03; HBG 3/03; SLJ 10/02) [577.63]

23249 Pyers, Greg. *River Explorer* (2–4). Illus. Series: Habitat Explorer. 2004, Raintree LB $25.70 (978-1-4109-0512-3). 32pp. This photo-filled exploration of rivers looks at the plants and animals found in and around them, plus environmental threats posed by pollution and development.

23250 Rapp, Valerie. *Life in a River* (5–8). Series: Ecosystems in Action. 2002, Lerner LB $26.60 (978-0-8225-2136-5). The first title in a new series about ecosystems, this volume uses the example of the Columbia River to explain the concept and the interrelationship of rivers, animals, and humans. (Rev: BL 10/15/02; HBG 3/03; SLJ 1/03; VOYA 2/03) [577.6]

23251 Sayre, April Pulley. *Lake and Pond* (4–7). Series: Exploring Earth's Biomes. 1996, Twenty-First Century LB $25.90 (978-0-8050-4089-0). A colorful introduction to lake and pond habitats and the life forms found within them. (Rev: BL 6/1–15/96; SLJ 6/96) [574.05]

23252 Sayre, April Pulley. *River and Stream* (4–7). Series: Exploring Earth's Biomes. 1996, Twenty-First Century LB $25.90 (978-0-8050-4088-3). In a clearly written, informative style, this book presents material on rivers and streams, their ecology, and the various creatures and plants living in and around them. (Rev: BL 6/1–15/96; SLJ 6/96) [574.5]

23253 Schulte, Mary. *Great Salt Lake* (1–2). Series: Rookie Read-About Geography. 2006, Children's Pr. LB $20.50 (978-0-516-25034-2). 32pp. Beginning readers and report writers will get all the facts about this unusual lake in this well-designed book. (Rev: SLJ 6/06) [979.2]

23254 Sill, Cathryn. *Wetlands* (K–3). Illus. by John Sill. 2008, Peachtree $16.95 (978-1-56145-432-7). 32pp. From swamp to marsh to meadow to bog, this title covers the variety, features and environmental significance of wetlands. (Rev: BLO 3/3/08; SLJ 5/08) [578.768]

23255 Stewart, Melissa. *Life in a Lake* (5–8). Series: Ecosystems in Action. 2002, Lerner LB $26.60 (978-0-8225-2138-9). The diversity and interdependence of life in a typical lake are introduced with material on how this ecosystem works and how man's interference has changed the balance of nature. (Rev: BL 12/15/02; HBG 3/03) [551.48]

23256 Viera, Linda. *The Mighty Mississippi: The Life and Times of America's Greatest River* (3–5). Illus. by Higgins Bond. 2005, Walker LB $17.85 (978-0-8027-8944-0). 32pp. Viera explores the geology and history of

America's mighty Mississippi River. (Rev: BL 10/1/05; SLJ 11/05) [917.7]

23257 Walker, Sally M. *Life in an Estuary* (5–8). Series: Ecosystems in Action. 2002, Lerner LB $26.60 (978-0-8225-2137-2). A look at life at the tidal mouths of rivers and the diversity of life in these areas, its interdependence, the balance of nature, and how human interaction has changed this ecosystem. (Rev: BL 12/15/02; HBG 3/03; SLJ 2/03) [574]

23258 Wechsler, Doug. *Frog Heaven: Ecology of a Vernal Pool* (3–6). 2006, Boyds Mills $17.95 (978-1-59078-253-8). 48pp. This is a vivid, richly illustrated, and thorough exploration of life in a vernal pool in Delaware over the period of a year. (Rev: BL 11/1/06*; HBG 4/07; LMC 3/08; SLJ 11/06) [577.63]

23259 Zollman, Pam. *Lake Tahoe* (1–2). Series: Rookie Read-About Geography. 2006, Children's Pr. LB $20.50 (978-0-516-25036-6). 32pp. Geographical and geological facts about this body of water are presented in an airy format that will appeal to beginning readers. (Rev: SLJ 6/06) [917.9438]

Prairies and Grasslands

23260 Cole, Melissa. *Prairies* (3–6). Photos by Tom Leeson and Pat Leeson. Series: Wild America Habitats. 2003, Gale LB $22.45 (978-1-56711-807-0). 24pp. Examines the overall ecology and climate of the prairie, as well as the specific plant and animal species that flourish there. (Rev: SLJ 2/04) [577.4]

23261 Collard, Sneed B. *The Prairie Builders: Reconstructing America's Lost Grasslands* (5–8). 2005, Houghton Mifflin $17.00 (978-0-618-39687-0). This wide-format look at a project to regenerate tallgrass prairie and populate it with native plants and animals includes excellent photographs. (Rev: BL 6/1–15/05; SLJ 8/05*) [635.9]

23262 Himmelman, John. *Mouse in a Meadow* (PS–2). Illus. 2005, Charlesbridge $15.95 (978-1-57091-250-4); paper $6.95 (978-1-57091-521-5). 32pp. A close-up view of wildlife in a typical North American meadow. (Rev: BL 3/1/05; SLJ 5/05) [578.74]

23263 Hoare, Ben. *Temperate Grasslands* (5–8). Series: Biomes Atlases. 2003, Raintree LB $31.42 (978-0-7398-5249-1). 64pp. This comprehensive overview of grasslands describes the climate, flora and fauna, people, and future of these areas, and includes good maps. (Rev: SLJ 9/03) [577.4]

23264 Hunter, Anne. *What's in the Meadow?* (K–2). Illus. 2000, Houghton $5.95 (978-0-618-01512-2). 32pp. Ten animals that live in meadows — including the woolly bear caterpillar, spittlebug, firefly, and meadowlark — are introduced with material on this habitat. (Rev: BL 9/15/00; HBG 3/01) [591.74]

23265 Johansson, Philip. *The Wide Open Grasslands: A Web of Life* (3–5). Illus. Series: A World of Biomes. 2004, Enslow LB $23.93 (978-0-7660-2201-0). 48pp. An engaging introduction to the flora and fauna of the

grasslands and to the work of the scientists who study the biome. [577.4]

23266 Kalman, Bobbie, and Hadley Dyer. *Australian Outback Food Chains* (3–5). Illus. Series: Food Chains. 2006, Crabtree LB $25.20 (978-0-7787-1950-2); paper $6.95 (978-0-7787-1996-0). 32pp. An introduction to this habitat, the plants and animals that live there, and how their interconnection functions. (Rev: SLJ 6/07)

23267 Kalman, Bobbie, and Hadley Dyer. *Savanna Food Chains* (3–5). Illus. Series: Food Chains. 2006, Crabtree LB $25.20 (978-0-7787-1952-6); paper $6.95 (978-0-7787-1998-4). An introduction to this biome, the plants and animals that live there, and how their interconnection functions. (Rev: SLJ 6/07)

23268 Levy, Janey. *Discovering the Tropical Savanna* (3–5). Series: World Habitats. 2007, Rosen LB $23.95 (978-1-4042-3783-4). 32pp. With photographs and fast facts, this volume covers location, climate, plants and animals, people, threats and conservation efforts, and so forth. (Rev: LMC 3/08; SLJ 1/08) [304.2]

23269 Lion, David C. *A Home on the Prairie* (1–3). Series: Scholastic News Nonfiction Readers. 2006, Children's Pr. LB $20.00 (978-0-516-25346-6). 24pp. This easy-to-understand introduction to the prairie as a natural habitat looks at the nature of the land itself, its climate, flora, and the animals that call it home. (Rev: SLJ 2/07) [574.5]

23270 Lunde, Darrin. *After the Kill* (2–4). Illus. by Catherine Stock. 2011, Charlesbridge $16.95 (978-1-57091-743-1); paper $7.95 (978-1-57091-744-8). Unpaged. A grisly and vivid account of predators and prey on the Serengeti Plain. **e** (Rev: HB 7–8/11; SLJ 7/11) [599.7]

23271 Patent, Dorothy Hinshaw. *Life in a Grassland* (5–8). Series: Ecosystems in Action. 2002, Lerner LB $26.60 (978-0-8225-2139-6). Using excellent pictures and a clear text, this volume explores the flora and fauna of different kinds of grasslands, with material on conservation. (Rev: BL 12/15/02; HBG 3/03) [574.5]

23272 Quigley, Mary. *Prairie Explorer* (2–4). Illus. Series: Habitat Explorer. 2004, Raintree LB $25.70 (978-1-4109-0513-0). 32pp. This photo-filled exploration of prairies looks at the plants and animals found there, plus environmental threats posed by pollution and development.

23273 Sayre, April Pulley. *Grassland* (4–7). Series: Exploring Earth's Biomes. 1994, Twenty-First Century LB $25.90 (978-0-8050-2827-0). A well-organized, clearly written account that explains what grasslands are and where they exist and the interaction of the creatures who live in this biome. (Rev: BL 1/15/95; SLJ 2/95) [574.5]

23274 Sill, Cathryn. *Grasslands* (2–5). Illus. by John Sill. Series: About Habitat. 2011, Peachtree $16.95 (978-156145559-1). 48pp. Sills introduces the environment, plants, and animals found in grasslands around the world using appealing illustrations and accessible text. (Rev: BL 4/15/11) [577.4]

23275 Stone, Lynn M. *Grasslands* (1–3). Illus. Series: Biomes of North America. 2003, Rourke LB $20.64 (978-

1-58952-685-3). 24pp. For young researchers, this is an excellent introduction to this biome, with clear, simple text, photographs, and maps. [574.5]

23276 Toupin, Laurie Peach. *Life in the Temperate Grasslands* (4–7). Series: Biomes and Habitats. 2005, Watts LB $25.50 (978-0-531-12385-0). Introduces the climatic conditions, plants, and wildlife of the world's temperate grasslands. Also use *Savannas: Life in the Tropical Grasslands* (2005). (Rev: SLJ 7/05) [577.4]

Rocks, Minerals, and Soil

23277 Bourgeois, Paulette. *The Dirt on Dirt* (3–6). Illus. by Martha Newbigging. 2008, Kids Can $15.95 (978-1-55453-101-1); paper $7.95 (978-1-55453-102-8). 32pp. An appealing introduction to dirt in all its forms, with experiments and activities. (Rev: BL 3/1/08; LMC 3/08; SLJ 5/08) [631.4]

23278 Ditchfield, Christin. *Soil* (2–5). Series: True Books — Natural Resources. 2002, Children's Book Pr. LB $25.00 (978-0-516-22344-5); paper $6.95 (978-0-516-29368-4). This book covers such topics as how soil is formed, what it is made of, what it's used for, and how we can protect this important resource. (Rev: BL 10/15/02) [631.5]

23279 Eid, Alain. *1000 Photos of Minerals and Fossils* (5–9). Photos by Michel Viard. 2000, Barron's paper $24.95 (978-0-7641-5218-4). 127pp. An oversized, nicely illustrated volume that introduces minerals in their natural and refined states with material on sites, fossils, and jewelry. (Rev: SLJ 10/00) [548]

23280 Estigarribia, Diana. *Learning About Rocks, Weathering, and Erosion with Graphic Organizers* (3–6). Series: Graphic Organizers in Science. 2005, Rosen LB $21.25 (978-1-4042-2806-1). 24pp. This title uses a wide variety of graphic organizers, including concept webs, compare/contrast charts, Venn diagrams, graphs, timelines, and KWL charts, to illustrate geological concepts. (Rev: SLJ 11/05)

23281 Farndon, John. *Rock and Mineral* (5–9). Series: DK/Google e.guides. 2005, DK $17.99 (978-0-7566-1140-8). This highly illustrated guide introduces readers to the basics of geology and provides a link to a Web site that serves as a gateway to additional resources. (Rev: SLJ 8/05) [552]

23282 Farndon, John. *Rocks and Minerals* (3–6). Series: Science Experiments. 2002, Marshall Cavendish LB $25.64 (978-0-7614-1468-1). 32pp. Clear illustrations and good step-by-step instructions are used to present a series of experiments that reveal the nature and properties of rocks and minerals. (Rev: BL 12/15/02; HBG 3/03; SLJ 4/03) [552]

23283 Faulkner, Rebecca. *Igneous Rock* (4–6). Series: Geology Rocks! 2007, Raintree LB $31.43 (978-1-4109-2747-7). 48pp. Categories of rocks, minerals, identification, and formation are among the topics cov-

ered in this appealing and well-organized, high-interest introduction to igneous rock, with color photographs. (Rev: LMC 10/08; SLJ 3/08) [552]

23284 Faulkner, Rebecca. *Sedimentary Rock* (4–6). Series: Geology Rocks! 2007, Raintree LB $31.43 (978-1-4109-2748-4); paper $8.99 (978-1-4109-2756-9). 48pp. Rock formation and fossils are among the topics covered in this appealing and well-organized, high-interest introduction to sedimentary rock, with color photographs. (Rev: LMC 10/08; SLJ 3/08) [552]

23285 Flanagan, Alice K. *Rocks* (2–3). Series: Simply Science. 2000, Compass Point LB $21.26 (978-0-7565-0033-7). 32pp. This book explains how the three types of rocks are formed with examples of each as well as information on erosion and how to be a rock hound. (Rev: SLJ 2/01) [552]

23286 Franchino, Vicky. *Junior Scientists: Experiment with Soil* (3–5). Illus. Series: Science Explorer Junior. 2010, Cherry Lake LB $27.07 (978-160279837-3). 32pp. Beginning with an overview of the scientific method, this book features soil experiments done with everyday materials. (Rev: BL 10/1/10; LMC 3–4/11) [631]

23287 Friend, Sandra. *Sinkholes* (4–7). 2002, Pineapple $18.95 (978-1-56164-258-8). This volume uncovers the geological and ecological causes of sinkholes, holes in the earth's surface that occur naturally, sometimes with devastating consequences. (Rev: BL 8/02; HBG 10/02) [551.44]

23288 Gallant, Roy A. *Minerals* (3–5). Illus. Series: Kaleidoscope. 2000, Marshall Cavendish $25.64 (978-0-7614-1039-3). 48pp. An interesting look at minerals and rocks that begins with simple material and moves on to more complex topics such as mineral replacement. (Rev: BL 2/1/01; HBG 3/01) [549]

23289 Gallant, Roy A. *Rocks* (5–8). Series: Earth Sciences. 2000, Marshall Cavendish LB $25.64 (978-0-7614-1042-3). 48pp. Illustrations and full-spread diagrams introduce rocks and minerals and their properties, forms, and uses. (Rev: BL 3/1/01; HBG 3/01; SLJ 3/01) [552.2]

23290 Green, Dan, and Simon Basher. *Rocks and Minerals: A Gem of a Book!* (5–8). Illus. by Simon Basher. Series: Basher Science. 2009, Kingfisher paper $8.99 (978-0-7534-6314-7). 128pp. Friendly cartoon characters narrate this informative and appealing introduction to rocks, gems, crystals, fossils, and so forth. (Rev: BL 9/15/09; SLJ 10/09) [500]

23291 Kallen, Stuart A. *Gems* (4–7). Illus. Series: Wonders of the World. 2003, Gale LB $23.70 (978-0-7377-1028-1). 48pp. The formation of precious stones, their mining, and individual stones of note are all covered here. (Rev: BL 5/1/03) [553.8]

23292 Milne, Jean. *The Story of Diamonds* (5–8). 2000, Linnet LB $21.50 (978-0-208-02476-3). 113pp. A book that explains where diamonds are found and how they are mined, evaluated, cut, polished, and used as jewels or in industry. (Rev: BL 2/1/00; HBG 10/00; SLJ 6/00; VOYA 4/01) [553.8]

23293 Oxlade, Chris. *Rock* (2–3). Series: Materials, Materials, Materials. 2002, Heinemann LB $22.79 (978-1-58810-585-1). 32pp. Using a few lines of text and a color picture on each page, this is a simple introduction to rocks, their composition, structure, and uses. (Rev: BL 6/1–15/02) [552]

23294 Oxlade, Chris. *Soil* (2–3). Series: Materials, Materials, Materials. 2002, Heinemann LB $22.79 (978-1-58810-587-5). 32pp. The composition of soil and its properties, uses, and formation are topics covered in this easily-read beginning science book. (Rev: BL 6/1–15/02) [631.5]

23295 Ricciuti, Edward R., ed. *National Audubon Society First Field Guide: Rocks and Minerals* (5–8). 1998, Scholastic paper $17.95 (978-0-590-05463-8). A guide to equipment and techniques for observation and general information on geology, followed by an examination of 50 common rocks, their composition, texture, color, and environment. (Rev: BL 8/98; SLJ 8/98) [552]

23296 Richardson, Adele D. *Rocks* (2–4). Illus. Series: The Bridgestone Science Library. 2001, Capstone LB $22.60 (978-0-7368-0953-5). 24pp. Rock types, rock formation, and the Mohs scale of hardness are covered in this slim volume. (Rev: HBG 3/02; SLJ 2/02) [552]

23297 *Rocks and Minerals* (5–8). Illus. Series: Pocket Genius. 2012, DK $7.99 (978-075669285-8). 160pp. In encyclopedic fashion, this well-illustrated volume introduces profiles different rocks and minerals. (Rev: BL 8/12) [552]

23298 Spickert, Diane Nelson. *Earthsteps: A Rock's Journey Through Time* (3–6). Illus. 2000, Fulcrum $17.95 (978-1-55591-986-3). 32pp. The story of a rock and its transformation over 250 million years to a grain of sand. (Rev: BL 1/1–15/01; SLJ 1/01) [551.3]

23299 Staedter, Tracy. *Rocks and Minerals* (4–8). Series: Reader's Digest Pathfinders. 1999, Reader's Digest $16.99 (978-1-57584-290-5). An outstanding introduction to geology is organized in three sections — "Rocks," "Minerals," and "Collecting Rocks and Minerals" — with "discovery paths" featuring personal accounts, hands-on activities, vocabulary, and facts. (Rev: SLJ 11/99) [552]

23300 Stewart, Melissa. *Extreme Rocks and Minerals! Q & A* (3–6). 2007, Collins $16.99 (978-0-06-089982-0); paper $6.99 (978-0-06-089981-3). 48pp. Well-designed and on-target, this title offers a clearly organized and well-illustrated overview of rocks and minerals. (Rev: SLJ 4/08) [552]

23301 Tomecek, Steve. *Dirt* (1–3). Illus. by Nancy Woodman. Series: Jump into Science. 2002, National Geographic $16.95 (978-0-7922-8204-4). 31pp. This discussion of soil's composition, inhabitants, and uses combines scientific fact with appealing humor. (Rev: BCCB 11/02; HBG 3/03; SLJ 10/02) [631.5]

23302 Tomecek, Steve. *Rocks and Minerals* (1–3). Illus. by Kyle Poling. Series: Jump into Science. 2010, National Geographic $16.95 (978-4-4263-0538-2); LB $25.90 (978-1-4263-0539-9). 32pp. Part geology, part examination of rocks' cultural significance throughout the world, this picture book offers interesting facts with plenty of colorful computer graphics. (Rev: BL 1/1–15/11; SLJ 4/11) [552]

23303 Trueit, Trudi. *Rocks, Gems, and Minerals* (4–7). Series: Watts Library. 2003, Watts LB $25.50 (978-0-531-12195-5); paper $8.95 (978-0-531-16241-5). 63pp. This attractive volume introduces readers to rocks, gems, and minerals and examines the natural forces that created them. (Rev: SLJ 1/04) [552]

23304 Walker, Sally M. *Rocks* (2–4). Series: Early Bird Earth Science. 2006, Lerner LB $25.26 (978-0-8225-5947-4). 48pp. This attractive, readable overview of rocks and crystals examines the three families into which rocks are divided and also how they're formed. (Rev: BL 9/1/06; SLJ 1/07) [352]

23305 Wallace, Nancy Elizabeth. *Rocks! Rocks! Rocks!* (PS–2). Illus. by author. 2009, Marshall Cavendish $17.99 (978-0-7614-5528-8). 48pp. Mama and Buddy Bear study rocks at the Nature Center and learn about bedrock, erosion, and so forth. (Rev: BL 4/1/09; SLJ 6/09) [552]

Mathematics

General

23306 Aber, Linda Williams. *Who's Got Spots?* (2–3). Illus. by Gioia Fiammenghi. Series: Math Matters. 2000, Kane paper $4.95 (978-1-57565-099-9). 32pp. In this early math book, there is an outbreak of chicken pox and kids use this opportunity to create charts and graphs to record who has been sick and predict who will stay well. (Rev: SLJ 2/01) [001.4]

23307 Aboff, Marcie. *Mike's Mystery* (1–3). Illus. by Amy Bailey Muehlenhardt. Series: Read It! Readers: Math. 2007, Picture Window LB $19.93 (978-1-4048-3667-9). 32pp. Mike and his friends count down as they gather books toward their final donation goal. How many are left to go? Will they win a pizza party? (Rev: SLJ 2/08) [513.2]

23308 Adler, David A. *Fractions, Decimals, and Percents* (3–5). Illus. by Edward Miller. 2010, Holiday House $16.95 (978-082342199-2). 32pp. Using the framework of a county fair, this brightly illustrated book shows how to move comfortably between fractions, decimals, and percents. (Rev: BL 3/1/10) [513.2]

23309 Adler, David A. *Mystery Math: A First Book of Algebra* (2–4). Illus. by Edward Miller. 2011, Holiday House $16.95 (978-0-8234-2289-0). 32pp. A haunted house setting and comic-creepy premise add appeal to this algebra book for beginners. (Rev: BL 10/1/11; SLJ 9/1/11) [512]

23310 Adler, David A. *Working with Fractions* (1–3). Illus. by Edward Miller. 2007, Holiday $32.00 (978-0-8234-2010-0). 32pp. With a birthday party as the setting, Adler uses such items as pizza, cake, children, and balloons to illustrate properties of fractions. (Rev: BL 11/15/07; LMC 1/08; SLJ 10/07) [513.2]

23311 Arroyo, Sheri L. *How Crime Fighters Use Math* (4–6). Series: Math in the Real World. 2009, Chelsea Clubhouse $28 (978-1-60413-602-9). 32pp. Measurement, estimation, data analysis, and problem solving are all used in this examination of crime-fighting activities. (Rev: SLJ 3/10)

23312 Bodach, Vijaya Khisty. *Bar Graphs* (PS–2). 2007, Capstone LB $23.93 (978-1-4296-0040-8). 32pp. Using simple text and child-friendly examples, this book leads readers through the process of sorting items and representing quantity on a graph. Also use *Pictographs* and *Tally Charts* (both 2007). (Rev: LMC 1/08; SLJ 2/08) [510]

23313 Bodach, Vijaya Khisty. *Pie Graphs* (K–2). Illus. 2007, Capstone LB $17.95 (978-1-4296-0042-2). 32pp. Eight child-friendly examples illustrate the usefulness of pie charts and show how to create them. (Rev: BL 10/15/07; LMC 1/08; SLJ 2/08) [510]

23314 Bruce, Sheila. *Everybody Wins!* (2–3). Illus. by Paige Billin-Frye. Series: Math Matters. 2001, Kane paper $4.95 (978-1-57565-101-9). 32pp. Readers learn the usefulness of math skills as they see friends agreeing to share. Also use *Keep Your Distance*. (Rev: SLJ 12/01) [513]

23315 Caron, Lucille, and Philip M St. Jacques. *Fractions and Decimals* (4–8). Illus. Series: Math Success. 2000, Enslow LB $22.60 (978-0-7660-1430-5). 64pp. Many examples accompany explanations of how to add, subtract, multiply, and divide fractions and decimals. Also use *Addition and Subtraction* (2001). (Rev: HBG 3/01; SLJ 7/01) [513.2]

23316 Cleary, Brian P. *The Action of Subtraction* (K–4). Illus. by Brian Gable. Series: Math Is CATegorical. 2006, Millbrook LB $15.95 (978-1-76139-461-4). 32pp. Cartoon-style illustrations and a rap-style rhyming text introduce subtraction with child-friendly examples. (Rev: SLJ 11/06) [513.2]

23317 Cleary, Brian P. *A Dollar, a Penny, How Much and How Many?* (K–3). Illus. by Brian Gable. Series: Math Is CATegorical. 2012, Millbrook $16.95 (978-082257882-6). 32pp. With cartoons and clear examples, the signature cats explain the basics of coins and bills and how to count them. Lexile 890L (Rev: BL 11/1/12) [332.4]

23318 Cleary, Brian P. *A Fraction's Goal — Parts of a Whole* (K–3). Illus. by Brian Gable. Series: Math Is CATegorical. 2011, Millbrook $16.95 (978-082257881-9). 32pp. Uses humor and charts to introduce fractions (parts of pizzas and groups of people) and their usefulness. (Rev: BL 10/1/11) [513.2]

23319 Clemson, Wendy, and David Clemson. *Digging for Dinosaurs* (2–3). Illus. Series: Math Adventures. 2007, Gareth Stevens LB $25.27 (978-0-8368-7838-7); paper $8.95 (978-0-8368-8137-0). 32pp. Readers will learn that math does come in handy in the real world as they explore how paleontologists manipulate data in their study of dinosaurs. (Rev: SLJ 5/07)

23320 Clemson, Wendy, and David Clemson. *Firefighters to the Rescue* (2–3). Illus. Series: Math Adventures. 2007, Gareth Stevens LB $25.27 (978-0-8368-7839-4); paper $8.95 (978-0-8368-8138-7). 32pp. Would-be firefighters will be fascinated to learn how math is used in this job. Photographs of real-world heroes using math will inspire reluctant students. (Rev: SLJ 5/07)

23321 Clemson, Wendy, and David Clemson. *Ocean Giants* (2–3). Illus. Series: Math Adventures. 2007, Gareth Stevens LB $25.27 (978-0-8368-7840-0); paper $8.95 (978-0-8368-8139-4). Readers will be fascinated to learn that even scuba divers use math. The photographs of deep-sea divers will inspire even reluctant students of mathematics. (Rev: SLJ 5/07)

23322 Clemson, Wendy, and David Clemson. *Rocket to the Moon* (2–3). Illus. Series: Math Adventures. 2007, Gareth Stevens LB $25.27 (978-0-8368-7841-7); paper $8.95 (978-0-8368-8140-0). 32pp. Math is essential to space exploration, as readers will discover in this book. Photographs of astronauts and explanations of how data are used by them will spur a new interest in math. (Rev: SLJ 5/07)

23323 Day, Eileen M. *I'm Good at Math* (PS–1). Series: I'm Good At. 2003, Heinemann LB $18.50 (978-1-4034-0901-0). 24pp. Basic mathematical skills, from counting to measuring, are introduced with large photographs. (Rev: HBG 4/04; SLJ 4/04) [510]

23324 Dobson, Christina. *The Pizza Counting Book* (1–3). Illus. by Matthew Holmes. 2004, Charlesbridge $16.95 (978-0-88106-338-7); paper $6.95 (978-0-88106-339-4). Pizzas and their toppings are used to teach young readers such basic mathematical concepts as fractions, large numbers, addition, and subtraction. (Rev: BL 8/03; HBG 4/04; SLJ 11/03) [513.2]

23325 Dodds, Dayle Ann. *Full House: An Invitation to Fractions* (K–3). Illus. by Ann Carter. 2007, Candlewick $16.99 (978-0-7636-2468-2). 32pp. A rhyming text and humorous illustrations frame this story about fractions set at Miss Bloom's guest house, Strawberry Inn. (Rev: BL 12/1/07; SLJ 12/07) [513.6]

23326 Dugan, Christine. *Pack It Up: Surface Area and Volume* (3–5). Illus. 2012, Teacher Created Materials paper $8.99 (978-14333346-1-0). 32pp. Readers are invited to practice their understanding of surface area and volume in this story about a family moving. Also use *Tonight's Concert: Using Data and Graphs, A Sense of Art: Perimeter and Area,* and *Hurricane Hunters: Measures of Central Tendency* (all 2012). (Rev: BL 5/15/12) [510]

23327 Ellis, Julie. *Pythagoras and the Ratios* (4–7). Illus. by Phyllis Hornung Peacock. 2010, Charlesbridge $16.95 (978-1-57091-775-2); paper $7.95 (978-1-57091-776-9). 32pp. An entertaining picture book that explains ratios as young Pythagoras establishes that Octavius's pipes are the wrong length to make melodious music. (Rev: LMC 10/10; SLJ 2/10) [516.2]

23328 Gifford, Scott. *Piece = Part = Portion: Fractions = Decimals = Percents* (3–5). 2004, Tricycle $14.95 (978-1-58246-102-1). 32pp. A strong visual approach enhances clear explanations of the relationships between various mathematical concepts. (Rev: BL 12/15/03; HBG 4/04; SLJ 11/03)

23329 Goldstone, Bruce. *Great Estimations* (2–4). 2006, Holt $16.95 (978-0-8050-7446-8). 32pp. Through eye-catching photographs of well-arranged items, readers learn progressively to recognize larger and larger quantities, from groupings of 10 to 100 to 1000, and then to estimate amounts. (Rev: BL 9/1/06; SLJ 11/06) [519.5]

23330 Goldstone, Bruce. *Greater Estimations* (2–4). Illus. 2008, Holt $16.95 (978-0-8050-8315-6). 32pp. Readers who have mastered *Great Estimations* (2006) can now tackle groupings up to 10,000 and learn strategies for estimating length, weight, volume, and so forth. (Rev: BLO 7/29/08; LMC 3/09; SLJ 9/08) [519.5]

23331 Goldstone, Bruce. *That's a Possibility! A Book about What Might Happen* (1–4). Illus. by author. 2013, Henry Holt $16.99 (978-0-8050-8998-1). 32pp. A brightly illustrated introduction to the concept of probability. ℮ (Rev: BL 6/13; LMC 11–12/13; SLJ 8/13*) [519.2]

23332 Harris, Trudy. *Splitting the Herd: A Corral of Odds and Evens* (K–2). Illus. by Russell Julian. 2008, Lerner $16.95 (978-0-8225-7466-8). 32pp. Miss Emma's cattle keep straying onto Cowboy Kirby's land, causing problems. Whose cows are whose? And how to sort them out? Their first effort at division in not a success in this entertaining introduction to a mathematical concept. (Rev: BLO 10/7/08; LMC 1/09; SLJ 10/08) [513]

23333 Haven, Kendall. *Marvels of Math: Fascinating Reads and Awesome Activities* (5–8). 1998, Teacher Ideas paper $23.50 (978-1-56308-585-7). This book chronicles 16 turning points in the history of mathematics, including the discovery of zero and the story of the first female to become a professor of mathematics. (Rev: VOYA 4/99) [510]

23334 Hense, Mary. *How Astronauts Use Math* (4–8). Illus. Series: Math in the Real World. 2009, Chelsea Clubhouse $28 (978-1-60413-610-4). 32pp. A look at how astronauts use math in their everyday activities. Also use *How Fighter Pilots Use Math* (2009). (Rev: SLJ 4/10) [629.45]

23335 Holub, Joan. *Riddle-Iculous Math* (2–5). Illus. by Regan Dunnick. 2003, Whitman $16.99 (978-0-8075-4996-4). 32pp. Puns, rhymes, jokes, and cartoons add appeal to learning basic mathematical tasks. (Rev: BL 10/15/03; HBG 4/04; SLJ 3/04)

23336 Hyland, Tony. *Multiplying and Dividing at the Bake Sale* (3–5). Illus. Series: Real World Math. 2010, Capstone $25.32 (978-142965244-5). 32pp. Corey and his grandfather bake muffins for the school bake sale, and Corey works out how much money is made; the fictional story is followed by a problem-solving activity. (Rev: BL 1/1–15/11; LMC 3–4/11) [641.8]

23337 Lee, Cora, and Gillian O'Reilly. *The Great Number Rumble: A Story of Math in Surprising Places* (4–6). Illus. by Virginia Gray. 2007, Annick $24.95 (978-1-55451-032-0); paper $14.95 (978-1-55451-031-3). 104pp. Who wouldn't want to get rid of math? Sam, upset when his school district wants to cut math from the curriculum, expounds on the value and applications of mathematics. (Rev: SLJ 6/07)

23338 Leech, Bonnie Coulter. *Mesopotamia: Creating and Solving Word Problems* (4–8). Series: Math for the Real World. 2007, Rosen LB $23.95 (978-1-4042-3357-7). Ancient number systems are among the mathematical concepts highlighted in this overview of the civilization of Mesopotamia that covers its people, buildings, writings, and calendars. (Rev: SLJ 2/07) [510]

23339 Leedy, Loreen. *It's Probably Penny* (1–3). Illus. 2007, Holt $16.95 (978-0-8050-7389-8). 32pp. Lisa uses her dog Penny to anchor her probability calculations — for example, Will Penny want to go for a walk? (Rev: BL 4/1/07) [519.2]

23340 Littlefield, Cindy A. *Real-World Math for Hands-On Fun!* (3–5). Illus. by Michael Kline. Series: A Williamson Kids Can! Book. 2001, Williamson paper $12.95 (978-1-885593-51-1). 128pp. Numbers, shapes, measurements, time, probability, and money are all discussed here, with puzzles, activities, and experiments that include a water clock, a pyramid of clay, and a pendulum made from a plastic bottle. (Rev: SLJ 3/02) [510]

23341 Long, Ethan. *The Wing Wing Brothers Math Spectacular!* (PS–2). Illus. by author. 2012, Holiday $15.95 (978-0-8234-2320-0). 32pp. Ducks Wilber, Wendell, Willy, Walter, and Woody demonstrate various math basics (addition, subtraction, greater than, lesser than, equal to) as they juggle plates and pies. (Rev: BL 10/1/12; SLJ 10/12) [372.7]

23342 Long, Lynette. *Dazzling Division: Games and Activities That Make Math Easy and Fun* (2–5). Illus. 2000, Wiley $12.95 (978-0-471-36983-7). 122pp. A large-format book that explains division and outlines many activities that explore this concept. (Rev: BL 12/15/00; SLJ 1/01) [513]

23343 Long, Lynette. *Fabulous Fractions: Games and Activities that Make Math Easy and Fun* (2–6). Illus. 2001, Wiley $12.95 (978-0-471-36981-3). 128pp. Games and projects are used to teach youngsters the na-

ture of fractions and how they can be manipulated. (Rev: BL 4/1/01; SLJ 7/01) [513.2]

23344 Long, Lynette. *Great Graphs and Sensational Statistics: Games and Activities That Make Math Easy and Fun* (4–7). 2004, Wiley paper $12.95 (978-0-471-21060-3). The games and activities in this large-format paperback will give new insights into the value of statistics and graphs and how the latter can be used to visually represent the former. (Rev: BL 5/1/04; SLJ 11/04) [372.7]

23345 Long, Lynette. *Marvelous Multiplication: Games and Activities That Make Math Easy and Fun* (2–5). Illus. 2000, Wiley $12.95 (978-0-471-36982-0). 122pp. Multiplication is explained in this large-format paperback with cheerful drawings and a number of related activities. (Rev: BL 12/15/00) [513.2]

23346 Marzollo, Jean. *Help Me Learn Subtraction* (K–1). Illus. by Chad Phillips. 2012, Holiday $15.95 (978-082342401-6). 32pp. Using bright photographs and rhyming text that incorporates light humor, this volume introduces the basics of subtraction. (Rev: BL 9/1/12) [513.2]

23347 Murphy, Stuart J. *Probably Pistachio* (1–3). Illus. by Marsha Winborn. Series: MathStart. 2001, HarperCollins LB $15.89 (978-0-06-028029-1); paper $5.99 (978-0-06-446734-6). 40pp. Throughout his day, Stuart makes predictions based on sound reasoning in this entertaining concept book about probability. Also use *Betcha!* (1997), about estimating; *Safari Park* (2002), about finding unknowns; and *Same Old Horse* (2005), about prediction theory. (Rev: BL 2/15/01; HBG 10/01; SLJ 3/01) [519.2]

23348 Murphy, Stuart J. *The Sundae Scoop* (1–3). Illus. by Cynthia Jabar. 2003, HarperCollins paper $5.99 (978-0-06-446250-1). 40pp. A story of the various flavor combinations available at an ice-cream booth illustrates a basic math concept in a way sure to appeal. (Rev: BL 1/1–15/03; HBG 10/03) [511]

23349 Nagda, Ann Whitehead. *Cheetah Math: Learning About Division from Baby Cheetahs* (3–5). 2007, Holt $16.95 (978-0-8050-7645-5). 32pp. A clever way to introduce a math concept to animal lovers, this book combines photographs of cheetahs, math problems, and animal facts. (Rev: SLJ 8/07)

23350 Nagda, Ann Whitehead, and Cindy Bickel. *Polar Bear Math: Learning About Fractions from Klondike and Snow* (3–5). Illus. 2004, Holt $16.95 (978-0-8050-7301-0). 29pp. The care of two polar bears cubs, Klondike and Snow, is used as a way to introduce fractions — looking at such topics as milk consumption, polar bear weight, and so forth. (Rev: SLJ 9/04) [513.2]

23351 Nelson, Robin. *Let's Make a Bar Graph* (K–2). Illus. Series: Graph It! 2012, Lerner LB $22.60 (978-076138972-9). 24pp. Part of the larger First Step Nonfiction series, this is one of the titles that introduces basic graphing concepts, in this case using a story about a girl who decides to document her classmates' pets. Also use

Let's Make a Circle Graph (2012). e (Rev: BL 8/12; LMC 1–2/13*) [001.4]

23352 Neuschwander, Cindy. *Sir Cumference and the Great Knight of Angleland: A Math Adventure* (1–4). Illus. by Wayne Geehan. 2001, Charlesbridge LB $16.95 (978-1-57091-170-5); paper $6.95 (978-1-57091-169-9). 32pp. The pun-full exploits of Radius, son of Sir Cumference and Lady Di of Ameter, involve the mastery of angles, squares, circles, and so forth, in this story that can be read on several levels. (Rev: HBG 3/02; SLJ 2/02) [516]

23353 Neuschwander, Cindy. *Sir Cumference and the Isle of Immeter: A Math Adventure* (3–6). Illus. by Wayne Geehan. 2006, Charlesbridge paper $6.95 (978-1-57091-681-6). 32pp. Per pays a visit to her uncle and aunt — Sir Cumference and Lady Di of Ameter — and with her cousin Radius uses skills of establishing perimeter and area to solve a riddle about the Isle of Immeter. (Rev: SLJ 8/06) [516]

23354 Noonan, Diana. *Collecting Data in Animal Investigations* (3–5). Illus. Series: Real World Math. 2010, Capstone LB $25.32 (978-142965237-7). 32pp. A class of 4th-graders collect data on animals they see in the park and organize the information in diagrams, charts, and graphs; the fictional stories are followed by a problem-solving activity. (Rev: BL 1/1–15/11; LMC 3–4/11) [590.72]

23355 Orr, Tamra. *Wildfires* (5–8). Illus. Series: Real World Math: Natural Disasters. 2012, Cherry Lake LB $27.07 (978-161080329-8). 32pp. Math problems ranging in difficulty are integrated into this account of wildfires and their causes and impact. (Rev: BL 4/1/12) [363.37]

23356 Penner, Lucille R. *Clean-Sweep Campers* (2–3). Illus. by Paige Billin-Frye. Series: Math Matters. 2000, Kane paper $4.95 (978-1-57565-096-8). 32pp. Using a story about a messy cabin at summer camp, this book effectively introduces fractions. (Rev: SLJ 2/01) [513.2]

23357 Perritano, John. *Mummies in the Library: Divide the Pages* (2–4). Illus. Series: iMath Readers. 2013, Norwood LB $23.73 (978-159953558-6). 32pp. Division problems are woven into a story about a young boy researching mummies in this illustrated book designed to meet STEM and Common Core standards. (Rev: BL 4/1/13; SLJ 4/13) [513.2]

23358 Pistoia, Sara. *Counting* (1–3). Illus. Series: Mighty Math. 2002, Child's World LB $24.21 (978-1-56766-114-9). 24pp. Counting by fives and tens is shown with clear examples and advice from cartoon character Math Mutt. Also use *Money*, which discusses counting change. (Rev: SLJ 3/03)

23359 Reisberg, Joanne A. *Zachary Zormer: Shape Transformer* (2–4). Illus. by David Hohn. Series: Math Adventures. 2006, Charlesbridge paper $6.95 (978-1-57091-876-6). 32pp. A forgetful but resourceful student comes up with some ingenious ways to measure area, perimeter, length, and width. (Rev: SLJ 8/06) [516]

23360 Ribke, Simone T. *Grouping at the Dog Show* (1–2). Series: Rookie Read-about Math. 2006, Children's Pr. LB $20.50 (978-0-516-24959-9). 32pp. For beginning readers, an introduction to the concept of grouping, using different attributes of different breeds of dogs. (Rev: SLJ 6/06) [511.3]

23361 Ribke, Simone T. *Pet Store Subtraction* (K–2). Series: Rookie Read-about Math. 2006, Children's Pr. LB $20.50 (978-0-516-29673-9). 32pp. A pet store employee uses subtraction skills to determine how many new animals and supplies she needs to order. (Rev: SLJ 12/06) [513.2]

23362 Robinson, Tom. *Basketball: Math on the Court* (4–6). Illus. Series: Math in Sports. 2013, Child's World LB $27.07 (978-161473408-6). 32pp. Basketball fans will enjoy the focus here on basics of the sport, score keeping, statistics, points and percentages, and so forth. e (Rev: BL 4/1/13; SLJ 4/13) [796.357]

23363 Roy, Jennifer, and Gregory Roy. *Graphing in the Desert* (2–4). Series: Math All Around. 2006, Benchmark LB $28.50 (978-0-7614-2262-4). 32pp. Introduces different types of graphs and uses them to convey information about the Sonoran Desert and its flora and fauna. (Rev: SLJ 12/06) [518]

23364 Roy, Jennifer, and Gregory Roy. *Multiplication on the Farm* (2–4). Illus. Series: Math All Around. 2006, Benchmark LB $28.50 (978-0-7614-2268-6). 32pp. This title focuses on multiplication and gives multiple examples of how it can be used to make important calculations on the farm. (Rev: SLJ 12/06) [513.2]

23365 Roy, Jennifer, and Gregory Roy. *Subtraction at School* (K–3). Series: Math All Around. 2005, Benchmark LB $25.64 (978-0-7614-2003-3). 32pp. Everyday situations are used to illustrate the principles of subtraction. Also use *Sorting at the Ocean* and *Patterns in Nature* (both 2005). (Rev: SLJ 3/06)

23366 Sargent, Brian. *Guess the Order* (1–2). Series: Rookie Read-about Math. 2006, Children's Pr. LB $20.50 (978-0-516-24963-6). 32pp. An introduction to the mathematical concept of placing things in order using pictures from a day at a carnival; for beginning readers. (Rev: SLJ 6/06) [513.2]

23367 Sargent, Brian. *Slumber Party Problem Solving* (1–2). Series: Rookie Read-about Math. 2006, Children's Pr. LB $20.50 (978-0-516-24962-9). 32pp. For beginning readers, this book has a girl using basic math to plan a slumber party. (Rev: SLJ 6/06) [513]

23368 Shea, Therese. *America's Electoral College: Choosing the President: Comparing and Analyzing Charts, Graphs, and Tables* (4–8). Series: Math for the Real World. 2007, Rosen LB $23.95 (978-1-4042-3358-4). 32pp. Results of various elections, including the controversial 2000 polls, are used to demonstrate fundamental mathematical principles. (Rev: SLJ 2/07) [324.6097]

23369 Shea, Therese. *The Great Barrier Reef: Using Graphs and Charts to Solve Word Problems* (4–8). Series: Math for the Real World. 2007, Rosen LB $23.95 (978-1-4042-3359-1). Charts and graphs are used to show the number of species found on the reef, the percentages of coral, the number of visitors, and so forth. (Rev: SLJ 2/07) [510]

23370 Shea, Therese. *The Transcontinental Railroad: Using Proportions to Solve Problems* (4–8). Series: Math for the Real World. 2007, Rosen LB $23.95 (978-1-4042-3361-4). The cost of laying the track, number of rails laid in a period, and other interesting aspects of construction of the railroad are considered using ratios, proportions, and other mathematical techniques. (Rev: SLJ 2/07) [513.24]

23371 Skinner, Daphne. *Tightwad Tod* (1–3). Illus. by John Nez. Series: Math Matters. 2001, Kane paper $4.95 (978-1-57565-109-5). 32pp. Tod has $20 to spend, and the story follows his purchases and deducts the amounts spent, in this book that includes three math problems. (Rev: SLJ 1/02) [512.9]

23372 Stewart, Melissa. *Giraffe Graphs* (K–2). Series: Rookie Read-about Math. 2006, Children's Pr. LB $20.50 (978-0-516-23798-5). 32pp. Students on a class trip to the zoo use graphs and charts to keep track of the animals they've seen. (Rev: SLJ 12/06) [511]

23373 Tang, Greg. *The Best of Times: Math Strategies That Multiply* (2–3). Illus. by Harry Briggs. 2002, Scholastic $16.95 (978-0-439-21044-7). 32pp. A rhyming approach to remembering the multiplication tables from one to ten. (Rev: BL 11/1/02; HBG 3/03; SLJ 9/02) [513.2]

23374 Tang, Greg. *Math-Terpieces* (2–4). 2003, Scholastic $16.95 (978-0-439-44388-3). 32pp. The paintings of 12 great artists are used in exercises that develop mathematics problem-solving skills. (Rev: BL 7/03; HBG 4/04; SLJ 8/03) [510]

23375 Townsend, Donna. *Apple Fractions* (1–2). Series: Rookie Read-about Math. 2004, Scholastic LB $5.95 (978-0-516-24670-3). 32pp. Using apples and apple muffins as examples, author Donna Townsend introduces beginning readers to the concept of fractions. (Rev: BL 10/15/04)

23376 Wingard-Nelson, Rebecca. *Division Made Easy* (1–4). Illus. by Tom LaBaff. Series: Making Math Easy. 2005, Enslow LB $23.93 (978-0-7660-2511-0). 48pp. An easy-to-understand introduction to the fundamentals of division. Also use *Multiplication Made Easy* and *Word Problems Made Easy* (2005). (Rev: SLJ 1/06) [513.2]

23377 Wingard-Nelson, Rebecca. *Graphing and Probability Word Problems: No Problem!* (5–8). Illus. Series: Math Busters Word Problems. 2010, Enslow LB $27.93 (978-076603372-6). 64pp. Bar graphs, histograms, line graphs, circle graphs, Venn diagrams — they are all covered here with explanations of how data, graphs, and probability are used in word problems. (Rev: BL 4/1/11) [519.2]

23378 Woods, Mary B., and Michael Woods. *Ancient Computing: From Counting to Calendars* (5–8). Series: Ancient Technologies. 2000, Runestone LB $25.26 (978-0-8225-2997-2). From the invention of the abacus and sundials to the creation of calculators and comput-

ers, this is a history of counting with material on the development of the calendar. (Rev: BL 9/15/00; HBG 3/01; SLJ 1/01) [510]

23379 Wyatt, Valerie. *The Math Book for Girls and Other Beings Who Count* (3–6). Illus. 2000, Kids Can $14.95 (978-1-55074-830-7); paper $9.95 (978-1-55074-584-9). 64pp. A well-organized, cheerful book that introduces such math concepts as proportion in an entertaining way. (Rev: BCCB 11/00; BL 2/15/01; HBG 10/01; SLJ 11/00) [510.8]

23380 Yoder, Eric, and Natalie Yoder. *Sixty-five Short Mysteries You Solve with Math!* (3–6). Series: One Minute Mysteries. 2010, Science, Naturally paper $9.95 (978-0-9678020-0-8). 176pp. One-page scenarios set in the home, outdoors, and at camp and sports fields present real-world problems that involve math skills and some creative thought. **e** (Rev: LMC 10/10; SLJ 1/1/11) [793.74]

23381 Zaslavsky, Claudia. *Number Sense and Nonsense: Building Math Creativity and Confidence Through Number Play* (3–6). Illus. 2001, Chicago Review paper $14.95 (978-1-55652-378-6). 120pp. Readers are encouraged to develop "number sense" rather than learning by rote, in chapters that introduce mathematical concepts, look at money and measurement, and provide puzzles, games, and some history. (Rev: SLJ 7/01) [510]

Geometry

23382 Leedy, Loreen. *Seeing Symmetry* (1–4). Illus. by author. 2012, Holiday House $17.95 (978-0-8234-2360-6). 32pp. This engaging, large-format book introduces different kinds of symmetry with clear explanations and examples; includes activities. (Rev: BL 4/15/12; HB 7–8/12; LMC 11–12/12*; SLJ 4/1/12) [516]

23383 Roy, Jennifer, and Gregory Roy. *Shapes in Transportation* (2–4). Illus. Series: Math All Around. 2006, Benchmark LB $28.50 (978-0-7614-2265-5). 32pp. Using traffic signs, bridges, buildings, and other transport-related items, this volume introduces shapes of all kinds and discusses such topics as angles and dimensions. (Rev: SLJ 12/06) [516]

23384 Sargent, Brian. *Grandfather's Shape Story* (K–2). Series: Rookie Read-about Math. 2006, Children's Pr. LB $20.50 (978-0-516-29919-8). 32pp. A grandfather entertains his granddaughter with tangrams while telling her a story. (Rev: SLJ 12/06) [793.74]

Mathematical Puzzles

23385 Adler, David A. *You Can, Toucan, Math: Word Problem-Solving Fun* (1–3). Illus. by Edward Miller. 2006, Holiday $16.95 (978-0-8234-1919-7). 32pp. This collection of 20 bird-themed word problems — rhyming riddles posing math questions — covers the basics of addition, subtraction, multiplication, and division. (Rev: BL 8/06; HBG 4/07; SLJ 10/06) [511.3]

23386 Ball, Johnny. *Go Figure! A Totally Cool Book About Numbers* (4–7). 2005, DK $15.99 (978-0-7566-1374-7). A fascinating volume for math-minded youngsters and adults, introducing number-related games and puzzles as well as more sophisticated mathematical disciplines, such as chaos theory, fractals, and topology. (Rev: BL 10/15/05; SLJ 1/06) [510]

23387 Barber, Patti. *First Number Book* (PS–1). Illus. by Mandy Stanley. 2001, Kingfisher $12.95 (978-0-7534-5338-4). 48pp. More than a counting book, this brightly illustrated guide also looks at shapes and sizes and addition and subtraction and includes beginning mathematical puzzles and exercises. (Rev: BL 10/1/01; SLJ 7/01) [513.2]

23388 Burns, Marilyn. *The I Hate Mathematics! Book* (5–8). Illus. by Martha Hairston. 1975, Little, Brown paper $14.99 (978-0-316-11741-8). A lively collection of puzzles and other mind stretchers that illustrate mathematical concepts.

23389 Ferris, Julie. *Galaxy Getaway: A Math Puzzle Adventure* (2–4). Series: Math for Martians. 2000, Larousse paper $5.95 (978-0-7534-5276-9). 32pp. Zeno, a young Martian, must solve a number of math problems and decipher codes in order to rescue a pet. Also use: *Planet Omicron: A Math Puzzle Adventure* (2000). (Rev: SLJ 9/00) [793.7]

23390 Fisher, Valorie. *How High Can a Dinosaur Count? And Other Math Mysteries* (1–3). Illus. 2006, Random $16.95 (978-0-375-83608-4). 40pp. Fifteen entertaining math mysteries are presented with interesting text and eye-catching illustrations. (Rev: BL 1/1–15/06; SLJ 2/06*) [513]

23391 Gardner, Martin. *Perplexing Puzzles and Tantalizing Teasers* (4–7). Illus. by Laszlo Kubinyi. 1988, Dover paper $7.95 (978-0-486-25637-5). An assortment of math problems, visual teasers, and tricky questions to challenge young, alert minds; perky drawings. [793.73]

23392 Larochelle, David. *1+1=5: And Other Unlikely Additions* (K–3). Illus. by Brenda Sexton. 2010, Sterling $14.95 (978-1-4027-5995-6). Unpaged. This arithmetic book challenges foregone conclusions about simple number problems by presenting creative scenarios where one plus one doesn't equal two. (Rev: BL 9/15/10; LMC 11–12/10; SLJ 9/1/10) [513.2]

23393 Lewis, J. Patrick. *Arithme-Tickle: An Even Number of Odd Riddle-Rhymes* (2–4). Illus. by Frank Remkiewicz. 2002, Harcourt $16.00 (978-0-15-216418-8). 32pp. A book of puzzles and problems that entertain while testing elementary mathematics skills, with illustrations. (Rev: BL 5/15/02; HBG 10/02; SLJ 4/02) [513]

23394 Salvadori, Mario, and Joseph P. Wright. *Math Games for Middle School: Challenges and Skill-Builders for Students at Every Level* (5–8). 1998, Chicago Review paper $14.95 (978-1-55652-288-8). After explaining the concepts involved in such mathematical

areas as geometry, arithmetic, graphing, and linear equations, this work presents a series of puzzles for readers to solve. (Rev: BL 11/1/98) [510]

23395 Slade, Suzanne. *What's the Difference? An Endangered Animal Subtraction Story* (1–3). Illus. by Joan C. Waites. 2010, Sylvan Dell $16.95 (978-1-60718-070-8); paper $8.95 (978-1-60718-081-4). Unpaged. Part math practice, part animal interest book, this volume introduces 12 endangered species with a rhyming math word problem, a picture, and a paragraph about its population in the wild. (Rev: LMC 10/10; SLJ 6/1/10) [591.68]

23396 Tang, Greg. *The Grapes of Math: Mind-Stretching Math Riddles* (3–5). Illus. by Harry Briggs. 2001, Scholastic $16.99 (978-0-439-21033-1). Each riddle and the rhyming clues that accompany it, can be answer by applying simple math skills like adding, subtracting, and multiplying. (Rev: BCCB 3/01; HBG 10/01; SLJ 3/01) [793.7]

23397 Tang, Greg. *Math Appeal: Mind-Stretching Math Riddles* (2–4). Illus. by Harry Briggs. 2003, Scholastic $16.95 (978-0-439-21046-1). 40pp. Counting and adding puzzles encourage children to find answers in creative ways. (Rev: BL 2/15/03; HBG 10/03; SLJ 2/03) [510]

23398 Tang, Greg. *Math for All Seasons: Mind-Stretching Math Riddles* (1–3). Illus. by Harry Briggs. 2002, Scholastic $16.95 (978-0-439-21042-3). 40pp. Each spread of this book for younger readers features a different math riddle, as well as clues to counting in different ways. (Rev: BL 2/1/02; HBG 10/02; SLJ 3/02) [513]

23399 Tang, Greg. *Math Potatoes: Mind-Stretching Brain Food* (3–5). Illus. by Harry Briggs. 2005, Scholastic $16.99 (978-0-439-44390-6). 40pp. Games involving humorous rhymes and appealing illustrations teach readers how to approach grouping numbers efficiently. (Rev: BL 7/05; SLJ 8/05) [793.74]

23400 Zaslavsky, Claudia. *More Math Games and Activities from Around the World* (3–7). Illus. 2003, Chicago Review paper $14.95 (978-1-55652-501-8). 160pp. More than 70 inventive math games and activities are accompanied by historical background. (Rev: SLJ 1/04) [793.7]

Metric System

23401 Murphy, Stuart J. *Polly's Pen Pal* (PS–3). Illus. by Rémy Simard. Series: MathStart. 2005, HarperCollins $15.99 (978-0-06-053168-3); paper $5.99 (978-0-06-053170-6). 33pp. Polly's (e-mail) pen pal lives in Canada, and through her Polly learns about the metric system. (Rev: SLJ 7/05)

Numbers and Number Systems

23402 Adler, David A. *Fun with Roman Numerals* (2–4). Illus. by Edward Miller. 2008, Holiday $16.95 (978-0-8234-2060-5). 32pp. A bright and accessible introduction to roman numerals, with attractive illustrations. (Rev: BLO 10/7/08; SLJ 11/08) [513.5]

23403 Adler, David A. *Millions, Billions, and Trillions: Understanding Big Numbers* (K–3). Illus. by Edward Miller. 2013, Holiday $17.95 (978-0-8234-2403-0). 32pp. Adler gives a clear explanation of the nature of large quantities, how and when we use them, and how their meanings differ around the world. (Rev: BL 3/1/13; LMC 11–12/13; SLJ 5/13) [513]

23404 Murphy, Stuart J. *Coyotes All Around* (1–3). Illus. by Steve Björkman. Series: MathStart. 2003, HarperCollins paper $5.99 (978-0-06-051531-7). 31pp. The concept of rounding is introduced in a western setting. (Rev: HBG 4/04; SLJ 2/04) [519.5]

23405 Murphy, Stuart J. *Earth Day — Hooray!* (1–3). Illus. by Renée Andriani. Series: MathStart. 2004, HarperCollins $16.99 (978-0-06-000127-8); paper $5.99 (978-0-06-000129-2). 40pp. Readers learn about place value as well as the benefits of recycling in this accessible and humorous book. Also use *More or Less* (2005), about comparing numbers. (Rev: BL 1/1–15/04) [513]

23406 Schwartz, Joanne. *City Numbers* (3–7). Illus. by Matt Beam. 2011, Groundwood $18.95 (978-1-55498-081-9). 60pp. An unusual look at numbers of all kinds seen in an urban landscape. (Rev: BL 6/1/11; LMC 11–12/11; SLJ 5/1/11) [971.3]

Statistics

23407 Leedy, Loreen. *The Great Graph Contest* (2–4). Illus. 2005, Holiday $16.95 (978-0-8234-1710-0). 32pp. Gonk the toad and Beezy the lizard compete in a graph contest in a lively tale displaying all kinds of graphs and methods of gathering data. (Rev: BL 8/05; SLJ 9/05*)

23408 Nechaev, Michelle Wagner. *Making Graphs* (PS–1). Illus. Series: I Can Do Math. 2004, Gareth Stevens LB $22.00 (978-0-8368-4111-4). 24pp. A question-and-answer format and abundant photographs introduce the use of graphs to visually represent different characteristics. (Rev: BL 4/1/04) [001.4]

Time, Clocks, and Calendars

23409 Adler, David A. *Time Zones* (2–4). Illus. by Edward Miller. 2010, Holiday House $16.95 (978-0-8234-2201-2). 32pp. Discusses the need for time zones and the history behind the division of the world into 24 zones;

with charts, maps, and photographs. (Rev: BL 12/15/10; SLJ 9/1/10) [389]

23410 Bernhard, Durga. *While You Are Sleeping: A Lift-the-Flap Book of Time Around the World* (PS–3). Illus. by author. 2011, Charlesbridge $14.95 (978-1-57091-473-7). 24pp. Flaps are used to show how time zones work, with illustrations of different activities taking place in different countries around the world. Lexile NC480L (Rev: BL 4/15/11; HB 5–6/11; SLJ 3/1/11) [389]

23411 Cobb, Annie. *The Long Wait* (1–3). Illus. by Liza Woodruff. Series: Math Matters. 2000, Kane paper $4.59 (978-1-57565-094-4). 32pp. Introduces the concept of estimating time, using a simple easy-to-read story about two boys waiting in line for a thrill ride. (Rev: SLJ 6/00)

23412 Dolan, Graham. *The Greenwich Guide to Day and Night* (3–6). Illus. Series: Greenwich Guide To. 2001, Heinemann LB $22.79 (978-1-58810-042-9). 32pp. Dolan explains how day becomes night, with photographs, a glossary, and other aids. Also use *The Greenwich Guide to Measuring Time* (2001). (Rev: BL 10/15/01) [525]

23413 Farndon, John. *Time* (3–6). Series: Science Experiments. 2002, Marshall Cavendish LB $25.64 (978-0-7614-1470-4). 32pp. Through simple experiments using common household objects, the nature and properties of time are explored. (Rev: BL 12/15/02; HBG 3/03) [529]

23414 Formichelli, Linda, and W. Eric Martin. *Timekeeping: Explore the History and Science of Telling Time with 15 Projects* (4–7). Illus. by Samuel Carbaugh. Series: Build It Yourself. 2012, Nomad $21.95 (978-161930136-8); paper $15.95 (978-16193003-3-0). 128pp. Projects that range in difficulty bolster readers' understanding of time and how we measure it. (Rev: BL 12/1/12; SLJ 6/13) [529]

23415 Jenkins, Martin. *The Time Book: A Brief History from Lunar Calendars to Atomic Clocks* (4–7). Illus. by Richard Holland. 2009, Candlewick $18.99 (978-0-7636-4112-2). 62pp. A clearly written history of how humans have measured the passage of time from ancient calendars through Einstein's theory of relativity. Lexile NC1200L (Rev: BL 5/1/09; LMC 10/09; SLJ 9/09) [529]

23416 Jenkins, Steve. *Just a Second* (4–7). Illus. by author. 2011, Houghton Mifflin $16.99 (978-0-618-70896-3). 40pp. Jenkins explores time, looking at the amazing things that can take place in a second, a minute, an hour, a month, and a year. (Rev: BL 11/1/11; SLJ 12/1/11) [529]

23417 Koscielniak, Bruce. *About Time: A First Look at Time and Clocks* (2–5). Illus. 2004, Houghton $16.00 (978-0-618-39668-9). 32pp. After a general discussion of the basic concepts of time, Koscielniak traces the development of clocks from sundials onward. (Rev: BL 12/1/04; SLJ 11/04) [529.7]

23418 Kummer, Patricia K. *The Calendar* (5–8). Series: Inventions That Shaped the World. 2005, Watts LB $30.50 (978-0-531-12340-9). Traces the development of calendars from prehistoric times, with period and contemporary illustrations, lists of recommended resources, and a calendar. (Rev: BL 5/15/05) [529]

23419 Nagda, Ann Whitehead, and Cindy Bickel. *Chimp Math: Learning About Time from a Baby Chimpanzee* (2–5). Illus. 2002, Holt $16.95 (978-0-8050-6674-6). 32pp. This is a delightful and effective combination, presenting both the story of young chimp Jiggs being raised by humans and the various methods of timekeeping — clocks, calendars, timelines, charts — that recorded his growth and development. (Rev: BL 11/1/02; HB 9/02; HBG 3/03; SLJ 9/02) [529]

23420 Older, Jules. *Telling Time* (PS–2). Illus. by Megan Halsey. 2000, Charlesbridge $16.95 (978-0-88106-396-7); paper $6.95 (978-0-88106-397-4). As well as exploring the concept of time, this picture book explains ways in which it is measured and covers topics including how to tell time, calendars, and different kinds of numbers. (Rev: BL 3/1/00; HBG 9/00; SLJ 3/00) [529]

23421 Richards, Kitty. *It's About Time, Max!* (1–3). Illus. by Gioia Fiammenghi. Series: Math Matters. 2000, Kane paper $4.95 (978-1-57565-088-3). 32pp. After losing his digital watch, a young boy must learn how to tell time using analog timepieces in this easy-to-read concept book. (Rev: SLJ 6/00)

23422 Skurzynski, Gloria. *On Time: From Seasons to Split Seconds* (2–5). Illus. 2000, National Geographic $17.95 (978-0-7922-7503-9). 48pp. This heavily illustrated book discusses time and seasons, years, months, and days, with additional coverage on the development of clocks and calendars. (Rev: BL 3/1/00; HBG 9/00; SLJ 7/00) [529]

23423 Somervill, Barbara. *The History of the Calendar* (3–6). Series: Our Changing World: The Timeline Library. 2006, The Child's World LB $27.07 (978-1-59296-436-9). 32pp. Two students and their teacher explore how different cultures have measured days, months, and years through the ages. (Rev: SLJ 7/06) [529]

23424 Wells, Robert E. *How Do You Know What Time It Is?* (2–5). Illus. 2002, Whitman $16.99 (978-0-8075-7939-8); paper $6.95 (978-0-8075-7940-4). In picture-book format, the author traces the history of timekeeping — from sundials to quartz crystals, from lunar and solar calendars to the one we know today. (Rev: BL 12/1/02; HBG 3/03; SLJ 1/03) [529]

23425 Whiting, Jim. *Space and Time* (5–8). Illus. Series: Mysteries of the Universe. 2012, Creative Education LB $24.95 (978-160818192-6). 48pp. "Is space expanding or contracting?" "Is time travel possible?" Whiting answers these and many other questions as he considers our strategies for keeping time. Lexile NC1270L (Rev: BL 12/1/12; LMC 5–6/13) [530.11]

23426 Williams, Brian. *Calendars* (4–6). Series: About Time. 2002, Smart Apple LB $24.25 (978-1-58340-207-8). 32pp. The need for keeping time and the various methods used over the centuries are explained in text and illustrations. (Rev: HBG 3/03; SLJ 12/02) [909.83]

Weights and Measures

23427 Adamson, Thomas K., and Heather Adamson. *How Do You Measure Length and Distance?* (PS–2). Series: Measure It! 2010, Capstone LB $25.99 (978-1-4296-4456-3). 32pp. This visually appealing book guides readers through the ways we measure and the tools we use. Also in this series: *How Do You Measure Liquids?*, *How Do You Measure Time?*, and *How Do You Measure Weight?* (Rev: SLJ 4/11) [530.8]

23428 Adler, David A. *Perimeter, Area, and Volume: A Monster Book of Dimensions* (2–4). Illus. by Edward Miller. 2012, Holiday House $16.95 (978-0-8234-2290-6). 32pp. Appealing monsters guide young readers through the principles of dimensions, showing how to measure area and calculate volume. (Rev: BL 3/15/12; LMC 8–9/12; SLJ 4/1/12) [516]

23429 Chrismer, Melanie. *Math Tools* (1–2). Series: Rookie Read-about Math. 2006, Children's Pr. LB $20.50 (978-0-516-24961-2). 32pp. For beginning readers, an introduction to the tools used to measure distance, time, volume, and other quantities. (Rev: SLJ 6/06) [681]

23430 Cleary, Brian P. *On the Scale, a Weighty Tale* (K–4). Illus. by Brian Gable. Series: Math Is CATegorical. 2008, Lerner $15.95 (978-0-8225-7851-2). 32pp. A lighthearted introduction to systems of measuring weight. (Rev: BLO 9/17/08) [530.8]

23431 Gresko, Marcia S. *Measuring* (PS–1). Illus. Series: I Can Do Math. 2004, Gareth Stevens LB $22.00 (978-0-8368-4112-1). 24pp. A question-and-answer format and abundant photographs introduce the concept of measurement and the various standards that are used to measure height, weight, length, temperature, and time. (Rev: BL 4/1/04) [530.8]

23432 Long, Lynette. *Measurement Mania: Games and Activities that Make Math Easy and Fun* (2–6). Illus. 2001, Wiley $12.95 (978-0-471-36980-6). 128pp. Forty activities are outlined, such as measuring the length of a smile, in this entertaining book that teaches the rudiments of measurement. (Rev: BL 4/1/01; SLJ 7/01) [513.2]

23433 Loughran, Donna. *How Long Is It?* (1–2). Series: Rookie Read-about Math. 2004, Scholastic LB $5.95 (978-0-516-24671-0). 32pp. Photographs and brief text introduce linear measures and the use of rulers. (Rev: BL 10/15/04)

23434 Murphy, Stuart J. *Bigger, Better, Best!* (K–3). Illus. by Marsha Winborn. Series: MathStart. 2002, Harper-Collins paper $5.99 (978-0-06-446247-1). 33pp. A story of siblings choosing rooms in a new house is a backdrop for teaching about measurements and area. Also use *Room for Ripley* (1999), which introduces liquid measurements. (Rev: HBG 3/03; SLJ 1/03) [516]

23435 Robbins, Ken. *For Good Measure: The Ways We Say How Much, How Far, How Heavy, How Big, How*

Old (4–7). 2010, Flash Point $17.99 (978-1-59643-344-1). 48pp. Robbins takes an unusual, highly illustrated approach to explaining various measurements, including the metric system. (Rev: BLO 4/1/10; HB 5–6/10; LMC 5–6/10; SLJ 4/10) [510]

23436 Roy, Jennifer, and Gregory Roy. *Measuring at Home* (2–4). Series: Math All Around. 2006, Benchmark LB $28.50 (978-0-7614-2263-1). 32pp. Everyday items such as a ruler, thermometer, and measuring cup are used to introduce the concepts of measuring area, weight, volume, and time. (Rev: SLJ 12/06) [516]

23437 Schwartz, David M. *Millions to Measure* (1–4). Illus. by Steven Kellogg. 2003, HarperCollins LB $18.89 (978-0-06-623784-8). 40pp. Marvelosissimo the Mathematical Magician explains the history of measures and measurement (with an appendix on the metric system) in this informative and entertaining book. (Rev: BL 2/1/03*; HB 3/03; HBG 10/03; SLJ 3/03) [530.8]

23438 Scott, Janine. *Why We Measure* (K–2). Illus. 2003, Compass Point LB $19.93 (978-0-7565-0449-6). 24pp. Introduces the concept of measurement and the various tools that can be used to gauge length, weight, speed, and quantity. (Rev: SLJ 12/03) [530.8]

23439 Sullivan, Navin. *Area, Distance, and Volume* (4–7). Illus. Series: Measure Up. 2006, Marshall Cavendish LB $20.95 (978-0-7614-2323-2). Includes information on the history of measuring area, distance, and volume along with how to measure each and the devices used. (Rev: BL 2/15/07; SLJ 6/07) [598.47]

Meteorology

General

23440 Cassino, Mark, and Jon Nelson. *The Story of Snow: The Science of Winter's Wonder* (2–4). Illus. by Nora Aoyagi. 2009, Chronicle $16.99 (978-0-8118-6866-2). 34pp. Dazzling close-up photographs enhance this book about snow crystals and their beautiful diversity. (Rev: BL 12/1/09*; LMC 1–2/10; SLJ 11/1/09) [551.57]

23441 Gardner, Robert. *Stellar Science Projects About Earth's Sky* (3–6). Illus. by Tom LaBaff. Series: Rockin' Earth Science Experiments. 2007, Enslow LB $23.93 (978-0-7660-2732-9). 48pp. A book of basic projects involving the earth's atmosphere for beginning researchers. (Rev: SLJ 8/07) [551.5078]

23442 Locker, Thomas. *Cloud Dance* (3–5). Illus. 2000, Harcourt $17.00 (978-0-15-202231-0). 32pp. This picture book for older readers is a mixture of fiction, science, and art as it describes the beauty of the sky during the different seasons. (Rev: BL 10/1/00; HBG 3/01; SLJ 11/00) [551.5]

23443 Malone, Peter. *Close to the Wind: The Beaufort Scale* (4–8). Illus. by author. 2007, Putnam $16.99 (978-0-399-24399-8). An informative picture book that explains the history and use of the Beaufort scale that measures wind force at sea. (Rev: BL 6/1–15/07; LMC 11/07; SLJ 5/07) [551.51]

23444 Smith, Trevor. *Earth's Changing Climate* (5–8). Series: Understanding Global Issues. 2003, Smart Apple $19.95 (978-1-58340-358-7). 56pp. Topics including global warming are discussed in this well-organized look at the world's climate, how it is gradually changing, and what can be done about it. (Rev: BL 11/15/03; SLJ 12/03) [551.6]

23445 Sullivan, Navin. *Temperature* (4–7). Series: Measure Up! 2006, Marshall Cavendish LB $20.95 (978-0-7614-2322-5). This well-designed book about temperature includes at-home experiments and easy-to-follow charts. (Rev: LMC 8–9/07; SLJ 6/07)

23446 Vogel, Carole G. *Nature's Fury: Eyewitness Reports of Natural Disasters* (3–6). Illus. 2000, Scholastic $16.95 (978-0-590-11502-5). 128pp. Taken from historical archives and newspapers, this book features 13 eyewitness accounts of 13 disasters including flash floods, earthquakes, blizzards, and tornadoes. (Rev: BL 12/15/00; HBG 3/01) [551]

Air

23447 Bauer, Marion Dane. *Wind* (K–2). Illus. by John Wallace. Series: Ready-to-Read. 2003, Simon & Schuster paper $3.99 (978-0-689-85443-9). 32pp. For beginning readers, this is an attractively illustrated simple introduction to wind and its properties. (Rev: HBG 4/04; SLJ 1/04) [551.51]

23448 Bundey, Nikki. *Wind and People* (3–5). Series: The Science of Weather. 2000, Carolrhoda LB $21.27 (978-1-57505-495-7). 32pp. This book, which contains some simple experiments, shows how wind affects our lives — from causing snowdrifts and sandstorms to powering sailboats and creating energy. (Rev: BL 12/15/00; HBG 3/01) [551.5]

23449 Cobb, Vicki. *I Face the Wind* (PS–2). Illus. by Julia Gorton. Series: Vicki Cobb Science Play. 2003, HarperCollins LB $17.89 (978-0-688-17841-3). For beginning readers, Cobb explains the properties of wind and suggests appropriate demonstrations. (Rev: HB 7/03; HBG 10/03; SLJ 8/03) [551.51]

23450 Friend, Sandra. *Earth's Wild Winds* (5–8). Series: Exploring Planet Earth. 2002, Twenty-First Century LB $24.90 (978-0-7613-2673-1). Report writers will find good material in this attractively presented coverage of all kinds of winds that also looks at the ways in which humans have attempted to harness wind power. (Rev: HBG 3/03; SLJ 10/02) [551.518]

23451 Gallant, Roy A. *Atmosphere: Sea of Air* (4–8). Illus. Series: Earthworks. 2003, Marshall Cavendish $29.93 (978-0-7614-1366-0). 80pp. An intriguing and well-presented look at how changes in the atmosphere affect us — from storms to beautiful rainbows and sunsets — and how we affect the atmosphere. (Rev: BL 3/15/03; HBG 3/03; SLJ 4/06) [551.51]

23452 Hoff, Mary, and Mary M. Rodgers. *Atmosphere* (4–7). Series: Our Endangered Planet. 1995, Lerner LB $27.15 (978-0-8225-2509-7). This account describes the atmosphere and current threats including the ozone layer problem. (Rev: BL 8/95; SLJ 12/95) [363.73]

23453 Kaner, Etta. *Who Likes the Wind?* (PS–2). Illus. by Marie Lafrance. Series: Exploring the Elements. 2006, Kids Can $14.95 (978-1-55337-839-6). 32pp. Children's questions about the wind are answered in attractive illustrations using foldout pages. Also use *Who Likes the Rain?* (2007). (Rev: BL 4/1/06) [551.51]

23454 Vogt, Gregory L. *The Atmosphere: Planetary Heat Engine* (5–8). Illus. Series: Earth's Spheres. 2007, Lerner $29.27 (978-0-7613-2841-4). 80pp. Examines a wide array of topics, including the composition of our air, weather and climate, and the use of satellites and other tools to study the atmosphere. (Rev: BL 4/1/07; SLJ 5/07) [551.5]

Storms

23455 Bailer, Darice. *Why Does It Thunder and Lightning?* (2–4). Series: Tell Me Why, Tell Me How. 2010, Marshall Cavendish LB $20.95 (978-0-7614-4825-9). 32pp. Answering such questions as "What Makes Thunderstorm Clouds?" and "How Does a Thunderstorm Begin?," this volume introduces essential concepts in easy-to-read text and lots of helpful illustrations. (Rev: BL 3/1/11; SLJ 2/1/11) [551.55]

23456 Benoit, Peter. *Hurricane Katrina* (3–5). Illus. Series: A True Book: Disasters. 2011, Scholastic LB $28 (978-053125421-9); paper $6.95 (978-053126626-7). 48pp. With statistics and Web resources, this volume covers the disaster and the aftermath. (Rev: BL 11/15/11) [976.3]

23457 Berger, Melvin, and Gilda Berger. *Hurricanes Have Eyes but Can't See and Other Amazing Facts About Wild Weather* (2–5). Illus. Series: Speedy Facts. 2004, Scholastic paper $7.99 (978-0-439-62534-0). 48pp. An entertaining and lively presentation of amazing and informative facts about storms.

23458 Boskey, Madeline. *Natural Disasters: A Chapter Book* (2–5). Series: True Tales. 2003, Children's Pr. LB $22.50 (978-0-516-22918-8). 48pp. This imaginative overview of natural disasters transports reluctant readers into the eye of the storm on a hurricane hunter plane, to the edge of a volcano that may erupt at any moment, and into a truck chasing tornadoes. (Rev: SLJ 2/04) [904]

23459 Carson, Mary Kay. *Inside Hurricanes* (5–8). Illus. 2010, Sterling $16.95 (978-140275880-5); paper $9.95 (978-14027778-0-6). 48pp. Inventive, eye-catching fold-outs and dramatic photographs enhance this engaging book about hurricanes. (Rev: BL 10/1/10; LMC 1–2/11; SLJ 12/1/10*) [551.552]

23460 Carson, Mary Kay. *Inside Tornadoes* (4–6). 2010, Sterling $16.95 (978-1-4027-5879-9); paper $9.95 (978-1-4027-7781-3). 49pp. Gatefold features enhance this boldly colored overview of tornadoes, how they are formed, and their destructive force. Also use *Inside Hurricanes* (2010). (Rev: SLJ 12/1/10*) [551.55]

23461 Ceban, Bonnie J. *Tornadoes: Disaster and Survival* (4–7). Series: Deadly Disasters. 2005, Enslow LB $23.93 (978-0-7660-2383-3). Explores the science behind tornadoes and offers advice about how to prepare for and survive such natural disasters. (Rev: SLJ 10/05) [551.5]

23462 Challen, Paul. *Hurricane and Typhoon Alert!* (4–6). Illus. Series: Disaster Alert! 2004, Crabtree LB $26.60 (978-0-7787-1575-7); paper $8.95 (978-0-7787-1607-5). 32pp. In addition to describing hurricanes and typhoons, there is colorfully presented material on early beliefs and myths associated with them, discussion of advances in predicting storms, tips on staying safe, and an experiment. (Rev: SLJ 3/05) [551.5]

23463 Demarest, Chris L. *Hurricane Hunters! Riders on the Storm* (2–4). Illus. 2006, Simon & Schuster $17.95 (978-0-689-86168-0). 40pp. Pastel paintings introduce the work of the pilots and planes that fly into hurricanes on weather reconnaissance missions. (Rev: BL 2/1/06; SLJ 6/06) [551.55]

23464 Doeden, Matt. *Hurricanes* (K–3). Illus. Series: Pull Ahead Books: Forces of Nature. 2008, Lerner LB $22.60 (978-0-8225-7906-9). 32pp. An overview of hurricanes, cyclones, and typhoons, looking at how they form, when and where they strike, and how we can prepare for them. (Rev: BL 4/1/08; LMC 5/08) [551.55]

23465 Fradin, Judith Bloom, and Dennis B. Fradin. *Tornado! The Story Behind These Twisting, Turning, Spinning, and Spiraling Storms* (4–6). Illus. 2011, National Geographic $16.95 (978-1-4263-0779-9); LB $26.90 (978-1-4263-0780-5). 64pp. Eyewitness stories, newspaper reports, photographs, and statistics make this an exciting and informative survey of U.S. tornadoes through the years. Lexile 1120L (Rev: BL 7/11; LMC 3–4/12*; SLJ 10/1/11) [551.55]

23466 Gibbons, Gail. *Tornadoes* (1–3). Illus. by author. 2009, Holiday $16.95 (978-0-8234-2216-6). 32pp. A dramatic, fact-filled introduction to tornadoes and the destruction they cause, highlighting two spectacular events, and providing tips on keeping safe. (Rev: BL 6/1–15/09; SLJ 6/09) [551.55]

23467 Gibson, Karen Bush. *The Fury of Hurricane Andrew, 1992* (3–5). Illus. Series: Robbie Reader: Natural Disasters. 2006, Mitchell Lane LB $25.70 (978-1-58415-416-7). 32pp. Explores the economic and social impact of the devastating 1992 hurricane, with photographs, personal stories, and resources for further research. (Rev: BL 4/1/06; SLJ 5/06) [363.34]

23468 Godkin, Celia. *Hurricane!* (3–4). Illus. by author. 2008, Fitzhenry & Whiteside $19.95 (978-1-55455-080-7). Godkin looks at how people and animals in a fictional Florida town prepare for a storm, the storm itself, and the aftermath as residents assess the damage. (Rev: LMC 5/09; SLJ 11/08) [551.55]

23469 Goin, Miriam Busch. *Storms!* (PS–2). Illus. 2009, National Geographic LB $11.90 (978-1-4263-0395-1); paper $3.99 (978-1-4263-0394-4). Color photos add drama to this absolutely furious weather narrative. (Rev: BL 6/1–15/09) [551.55]

23470 Gow, Mary. *Johnstown Flood: The Day the Dam Burst* (4–8). Series: American Disasters. 2003, Enslow LB $23.93 (978-0-7660-2109-9). 48pp. The story of the terrible Pennsylvania flood of 1889 that resulted in more than 2,000 deaths. (Rev: BL 11/15/03; HBG 10/03) [973.8]

23471 Harper, Kristine C. *Hurricane Andrew* (5–8). Series: Environmental Disasters. 2005, Facts on File $35.00 (978-0-8160-5759-7). The impact of 1992's Hurricane Andrew on Florida's wetlands is seen as a warning about the need to be more prepared. (Rev: SLJ 11/05) [551.5]

23472 Hayden, Kate. *Twisters!* (2–3). Illus. Series: DK Readers. 2000, DK $12.99 (978-0-7894-5708-0); paper $3.99 (978-0-7894-5709-7). 32pp. An easy reader that uses a story about Rob, a farmer in Texas, to explain the causes, characteristics, and effects of tornadoes. (Rev: BL 10/1/00; HBG 3/01; SLJ 1/01) [551.55]

23473 Langley, Andrew. *Hurricanes, Tsunamis, and Other Natural Disasters* (4–6). Series: Kingfisher Knowledge. 2006, Kingfisher $12.95 (978-0-7534-5975-1). 64pp. This well-illustrated volume examines a wide range of natural disasters and looks at the ways in which humans respond and what they are doing to better predict or prevent these disasters in the future. (Rev: BL 9/1/06; SLJ 10/06) [363.34]

23474 Larson, Kirby, and Mary Nethery. *Two Bobbies: A True Story of Hurricane Katrina, Friendship, and Survival* (K–3). Illus. by Jean Cassels. 2008, Walker $16.99 (978-0-8027-9754-4). 32pp. The inspiring story of a cat and a dog who survived Hurricane Katrina through mutual devotion and the help of a volunteer shelter. (Rev: BL 9/1/08; SLJ 9/08) [636.08]

23475 Lindop, Laurie. *Chasing Tornadoes* (5–8). Illus. Series: Science on the Edge. 2003, Millbrook LB $26.90 (978-0-7613-2703-5). 80pp. A lively introduction to tornadoes, the scientists who dare to study them, and techniques for collecting data and forecasting tornado activity. (Rev: BL 12/1/03; SLJ 1/04) [551.55]

23476 McGrath, Barbara Barbieri, comp. *The Storm: Students of Biloxi, Mississippi, Remember Hurricane Katrina* (3–8). Illus. 2006, Charlesbridge $18.95 (978-1-58089-172-1). 64pp. Artwork and writings show the impact of the storm on K–12 students in Biloxi; the book

is divided into four sections: "Evacuation," "Storm," "Aftermath," and "Hope." (Rev: SLJ 12/06) [976.2]

23477 Miller, Mara. *Hurricane Katrina Strikes the Gulf Coast* (5–8). Series: Deadly Disasters. 2006, Enslow LB $23.93 (978-0-7660-2803-6). The story of Hurricane Katrina and its disastrous impact on the Gulf Coast in 2005 is accompanied by personal stories plus information on other deadly storms. (Rev: BL 7/06; SLJ 9/06) [363.34]

23478 Nicolson, Cynthia Pratt. *Tornado!* (3–6). Illus. 2003, Kids Can $14.95 (978-1-55337-951-5); paper $6.95 (978-1-55337-972-0). 32pp. The nature and power of tornadoes are described in this oversize volume that includes easy experiments and accounts of notable tornadoes. (Rev: BL 4/1/03) [551.55]

23479 Oxlade, Chris. *Why Why Why — Do Tornadoes Spin?* (4–6). Illus. 2009, Mason Crest $18.95 (978-142221586-9). 32pp. Goofy and accessible, this book uses cartoons and sketches — as well as facts — to answer questions about tornadoes. (Rev: BL 1/1/10) [551.55]

23480 Prokos, Anna. *Tornadoes* (4–6). Series: The Ultimate 10 Natural Disasters. 2008, Gareth Stevens LB $31.00 (978-0-8368-9153-9). 48pp. Prokos looks at 10 significant tornadoes and the destruction they caused, with color photographs, eyewitness accounts, maps and charts, and statistics; a final section covers ways to prepare for such events. (Rev: LMC 3/09; SLJ 3/09) [551.55]

23481 Raum, Elizabeth. *Can You Survive Storm Chasing? An Interactive Survival Adventure* (3–5). Series: You Choose: Survival. 2011, Capstone LB $30.65 (978-1-4296-6587-2); paper $6.95 (978-1-4296-7347-1). 112pp. In this choose-your-own adventure with many endings, readers' decisions will govern their ultimate survival. (Rev: SLJ 12/1/11) [613.6]

23482 Rebman, Renee C. *How Do Tornadoes Form?* (2–4). Series: Tell Me Why, Tell Me How. 2010, Marshall Cavendish LB $20.95 (978-0-7614-4828-0). 32pp. With easy-to-read text and lots of helpful illustrations, this volume introduces essential concepts relating to the formation of tornadoes. (Rev: SLJ 2/1/11) [551.55]

23483 Rotter, Charles. *Hurricanes: Storms of the Sea* (4–6). Series: LifeViews. 2002, Creative Editions LB $24.25 (978-1-58341-020-2). 32pp. A revised edition with updated text and new photographs that describes hurricanes and their causes and includes two projects. (Rev: HBG 3/03; SLJ 1/03) [551.5]

23484 Royston, Angela. *Floods* (2–4). Illus. Series: Wild Weather. 2009, Black Rabbit LB $18.95 (978-1-59566-584-3). 32pp. What causes floods, the kinds of floods and mudslides that occur, their destructive power, and what can be done to prevent and prepare for these disasters are all covered here. (Rev: BL 4/1/09) [500]

23485 Ryback, Carol, and Jayne Keedle. *Hurricanes* (4–6). Series: The Ultimate 10 Natural Disasters. 2008, Gareth Stevens LB $31.00 (978-0-8368-9152-2). 48pp. This volume looks at 10 significant hurricanes and the destruction they caused, with color photographs, eye-witness accounts, maps and charts, and statistics; a final section covers ways to prepare for such events. (Rev: LMC 3/09; SLJ 3/09) [551.55]

23486 Scavuzzo, Wendy. *Tornado Alert!* (4–6). Illus. Series: Disaster Alert! 2004, Crabtree LB $26.60 (978-0-7787-1571-9); paper $8.95 (978-0-7787-1603-7). 32pp. In addition to describing tornadoes, there is colorfully presented material on early beliefs and myths associated with them, discussion of advances in predicting storms, tips on staying safe, and an experiment. (Rev: SLJ 3/05) [551.55]

23487 Simon, Seymour. *Hurricanes. Rev. ed.* (3–5). 2007, Collins $16.99 (978-0-06-117072-0); paper $6.99 (978-0-06-117071-3). 32pp. An updated edition of the 2003 volume, with colorful photographs, thorough explanations of how hurricanes are formed and behave, and details of important storms. (Rev: LMC 3/04; SLJ 5/08) [551.55]

23488 Simon, Seymour. *Super Storms* (1–3). Series: See More Readers. 2002, North-South $13.95 (978-1-58717-137-6); paper $3.95 (978-1-58717-138-3). 32pp. Violent storms and their causes are covered in this beginning reader that uses double-page spreads consisting each of a large color picture opposite a few lines of text. (Rev: BL 7/02; HBG 10/02) [551.5]

23489 Simon, Seymour. *Tornadoes* (4–8). 1999, Morrow LB $16.89 (978-0-688-14647-4). Well-organized text discusses the weather conditions that give rise to tornadoes, how they form, where they are most likely to occur, and how scientists predict and track them, supplemented by large, riveting photographs showing meteorologists at work, a variety of tornadoes, and the devastation caused by major tornadoes. (Rev: BCCB 4/99; BL 5/99; HBG 9/99; SLJ 6/99) [551.55]

23490 Spilsbury, Louise, and Richard Spilsbury. *Howling Hurricanes* (3–6). Series: Awesome Forces of Nature. 2010, Heinemann LB $29 (978-1-4329-3781-2). 32pp. "Where do hurricanes happen?" "Can people prepare for hurricanes?" These and other questions are answered — and case studies look at famous storms — in this eye-catching volume. (Rev: LMC 11–12/10; SLJ 9/1/10) [551.55]

23491 Stewart, Mark. *Blizzards and Winter Storms* (4–6). Series: The Ultimate 10 Natural Disasters. 2008, Gareth Stevens LB $31.00 (978-0-8368-9150-8). 48pp. Stewart looks at 10 significant blizzards and the destruction they caused, with color photographs, eyewitness accounts, maps and charts, and statistics; a final section covers ways to prepare for such events. (Rev: LMC 3/09; SLJ 3/09) [551.55]

23492 Stewart, Melissa. *Inside Lightning* (5–8). Illus. by Cynthia Shaw. Series: Inside. 2011, Sterling $16.95 (978-140275878-2). 48pp. A dramatic presentation of information about what causes lightning and its impact on the population and environment, with many photographs and gatefolds. (Rev: BL 11/1/11*) [551.55]

23493 Torres, John A. *Hurricane Katrina and the Devastation of New Orleans* (4–7). Series: Monumental Milestones. 2006, Mitchell Lane $29.95 (978-1-58415-473-0). An interview with a newlywed couple who lost everything in the storm draws readers into this account of the devastation. (Rev: BL 9/1/06) [363.34]

23494 Webster, Christine. *Storms* (2–4). Illus. 2006, Weigl $24.45 (978-1-59036-418-5). 24pp. An engaging and detailed introduction to storms, their meteorological origins, extreme phenomena such as hail and tornadoes, and the technologies that allow us to predict and track them. (Rev: BL 12/1/06) [551.55]

23495 Woods, Michael, and Mary B. Woods. *Hurricanes* (4–6). Series: Disasters Up Close. 2006, Lerner LB $27.93 (978-0-8225-4710-5). 64pp. With charts, photographs, and quotes from survivors, this book clearly demonstrates the power of hurricanes, and provides quick facts plus tips on preparing for a storm. (Rev: SLJ 1/07) [551.5]

23496 Woods, Michael, and Mary B. Woods. *Tornadoes* (5–8). Illus. Series: Disasters Up Close. 2006, Lerner $27.93 (978-0-8225-4714-3). Eyewitness accounts add to this well-illustrated overview of tornadoes and the destruction they can cause. (Rev: BL 10/15/06) [551.55]

23497 Zelch, Patti R. *Ready, Set . . . WAIT! What Animals Do Before a Hurricane* (PS–3). Illus. by Connie McLennan. 2010, Sylvan Dell $16.95 (978-1-60718-072-2); paper $8.95 (978-1-60718-083-8). Unpaged. Compares human and animal preparations for an approaching storm. (Rev: BL 12/1/10; SLJ 9/1/10) [591.512]

Water

23498 Bauer, Marion Dane. *Snow* (K–2). Illus. by John Wallace. Series: Ready to Read. 2003, Simon & Schuster paper $3.99 (978-0-689-85437-8). 31pp. Facts about snow become part of this gentle story about a child and dog enjoying a wintry day. (Rev: HBG 4/04; SLJ 1/04) [551.57]

23499 Bundey, Nikki. *Rain and People* (3–5). Illus. Series: Science of Weather. 2000, Carolrhoda $21.27 (978-1-57505-494-0). 32pp. This volume describes how fresh water and rain are involved in health, agriculture, construction, and power. A companion volume *Rain and the Earth* (2000), discusses the water cycle, clouds, water pollution, and ecosystems. (Rev: BL 10/15/00; HBG 3/01) [551.57]

23500 Bundey, Nikki. *Snow and the Earth* (3–5). Series: The Science of Weather. 2000, Carolrhoda LB $21.27 (978-1-57505-471-1). 32pp. This account, with a few experiments, shows how important snow is to the well-being of the earth and its people, animals, and plants. (Rev: BL 12/15/00; HBG 3/01) [551.57]

23501 Cobb, Vicki. *Squirts and Spurts: Science Fun with Water* (3–6). Illus. 2000, Millbrook LB $24.90 (978-0-7613-1572-8). 48pp. The mechanics behind hydraulics, vacuum pressure, and other forms of moving water are explored in this entertaining activity book that uses a cartoon format. (Rev: BCCB 11/00; BL 10/15/00; HBG 3/01; SLJ 3/01) [507.8]

23502 Farndon, John. *Water* (3–6). Series: Science Experiments. 2000, Marshall Cavendish LB $25.64 (978-0-7614-1087-4). 32pp. Covers the properties of water, its three states, and the ways it can be manipulated, along with related experiments and projects. (Rev: BL 3/15/01; HBG 3/01) [553.7]

23503 Gallant, Roy A. *Water* (5–8). Series: Earth Sciences. 2000, Marshall Cavendish LB $25.64 (978-0-7614-1040-9). 48pp. This work introduces the importance of water on the earth, its three states, and the water cycle. (Rev: BL 3/1/01; HBG 3/01; SLJ 5/01) [551.57]

23504 Gallant, Roy A. *Water: Our Precious Resource* (4–8). Series: Earthworks. 2003, Marshall Cavendish $29.93 (978-0-7614-1365-3). A thought-provoking and well-presented overview of the sources of water; the ways in which we use, misuse, and recycle water; and efforts to preserve this vital natural resource. (Rev: BL 3/15/03; HBG 3/03; SLJ 2/03) [553.7]

23505 Godwin, Sam. *The Drop Goes Plop: A First Look at the Water Cycle* (K–1). Illus. by Simone Abel. Series: First Look : Science. 2004, Picture Window LB $25.26 (978-1-4048-0657-3). 32pp. In simple language with cartoon-style illustrations, a mother bird explains to her baby how a single drop of water fits into the water cycle. (Rev: BL 10/15/04) [551.48]

23506 Hamilton, Kersten. *This Is the Ocean* (PS–2). Illus. by Lorianne Siomades. 2001, Boyds Mills $14.95 (978-1-56397-890-6). 32pp. Using rhyming couplets and lovely three-dimensional collages, this book presents the water cycle to a young audience. (Rev: BL 4/15/01; HBG 10/01; SLJ 6/01) [551.46]

23507 Lyon, George Ella. *All the Water in the World* (PS–K). Illus. by Katherine Tillotson. 2011, Atheneum $15.99 (978-1-4169-7130-6). 40pp. Simple text and appealing illustrations introduce the water cycle and what we can do to save water and keep it clean. (Rev: BL 3/15/11*; HB 5–6/11; LMC 10/11*; SLJ 5/1/11*) [551.48]

23508 Morgan, Sally, and Adrian Morgan. *Water* (4–7). Series: Designs in Science. 1994, Facts on File $23.00 (978-0-8160-2982-2). The importance and uses of water are described, with information on water storage, filtering, and conservation, plus activities and experiments. (Rev: BL 7/94) [533.7]

23509 Morrison, Gordon. *A Drop of Water* (K–3). 2006, Houghton $16.00 (978-0-618-58557-1). 32pp. A gentle account of the water cycle, following the path of a drop of rainwater as it makes its way downhill past different settings, plants, and animals. (Rev: BL 8/06; SLJ 10/06) [508]

23510 Nadeau, Isaac. *Learning About the Water Cycle with Graphic Organizers* (3–6). Series: Graphic Organizers in Science. 2005, Rosen LB $21.25 (978-1-4042-2808-5). 24pp. This title uses a wide variety of graphic

organizers, including concept webs, compare/contrast charts, Venn diagrams, graphs, timelines, and KWL charts, to introduce readers to the water cycle. (Rev: SLJ 11/05)

23511 Nelson, Robin. *We Use Water* (PS–K). Illus. Series: First Step Nonfiction: Water. 2003, Lerner LB $18.60 (978-0-8225-4594-1). 24pp. This introduction for beginning readers to the properties and uses of water looks at familiar scenarios such as hand washing, fire fighting, and ice cubes. Also use *Where Is Water?* (2003). (Rev: BL 10/15/03; HBG 4/04) [553.7]

23512 Oxlade, Chris. *Water* (2–3). Series: Materials, Materials, Materials. 2002, Heinemann LB $22.79 (978-1-58810-588-2). 32pp. Color photographs and an easy text are used to introduce water, its properties, and its uses. (Rev: BL 6/1–15/02) [533.7]

23513 Rau, Dana Meachen. *Water* (PS–2). Illus. Series: Bookworms. Nature's Cycles. 2009, Marshall Cavendish $15.95 (978-0-7614-4099-4). 24pp. The concept of how water goes from liquid to vapor to clouds to rain and back again is captured in this simple book suitable for beginning readers. (Rev: SLJ 4/1/10) [508.2]

23514 Royston, Angela. *Water: Let's Look at a Puddle* (K–3). Illus. Series: Read and Learn: Material Detectives. 2005, Heinemann LB $14.95 (978-1-4034-7676-0). 24pp. Examples from daily life — What happens to a frozen puddle? What makes a puddle dry up? — make basic science concepts clear. (Rev: BL 12/1/05) [553.7]

23515 Salas, Laura Purdie. *Water Can Be . . .* (K–2). Illus. by Violeta Dabija. 2014, Millbrook $17.95 (978-146770591-2). 32pp. "A poetic exploration of water throughout the year," this richly illustrated volume considers roles ranging from "kid drencher" to "snowman former." **e** (Rev: BL 3/1/14; SLJ 3/14) [553.7]

23516 Schaefer, Lola M. *This Is the Rain* (PS–1). Illus. by Jane Wattenberg. 2001, Greenwillow LB $16.89 (978-0-688-17040-0). 32pp. Simple, rhythmic text echoes the movement of water through its cycle from sea to sky to streams in this book with inventive illustrations. (Rev: BCCB 10/01; BL 12/15/01; HBG 3/02; SLJ 9/01) [551]

23517 Seuling, Barbara. *Drip! Drop! How Water Gets to Your Tap* (K–2). Illus. by Nancy Tobin. 2000, Holiday House $15.95 (978-0-8234-1459-8). After describing the water cycle, this concise account tells how reservoir water is collected, filtered, and sent through a water-treatment plant before reaching houses and apartments. (Rev: BCCB 1/01; HBG 10/01; SLJ 2/01) [546]

23518 Stewart, Melissa. *The Wonders of Water* (2–4). Illus. Series: Investigate Science. 2004, Compass Point LB $21.26 (978-0-7565-0637-7). 32pp. Text, illustrations, and activities introduce the characteristics and importance of water. (Rev: SLJ 3/05) [553.7]

23519 Swanson, Diane. *The Wonder in Water* (3–5). 2006, Annick $19.95 (978-1-55037-937-2); paper $8.95 (978-1-55037-936-5). 44pp. The many faces of water — from beads of human perspiration to raindrops to the world's largest oceans — are explored in conversational text with lots of interesting sidebars, photographs, and diagrams. (Rev: BL 1/1–15/06) [553.7]

23520 Waldman, Neil. *The Snowflake: A Water Cycle Story* (1–5). Illus. by author. 2003, Millbrook LB $23.90 (978-0-7613-1762-3). This beautiful overview follows a single drop of water from snowflake through the entire water cycle and back to snowflake. (Rev: BL 11/1/03; HBG 4/04; SLJ 12/03) [551.48]

23521 Wells, Robert E. *Did a Dinosaur Drink This Water?* (1–3). Illus. by author. 2006, Albert Whitman $16.99 (978-0-8075-8839-0); paper $6.95 (978-0-8075-8840-6). This cartoon-style introduction to the water cycle takes readers on a world tour to explore a wide variety of issues, including water's importance in sustaining the life of plants and animals; its three states; water use policies; conservation efforts; and water pollution. (Rev: BL 12/1/06; SLJ 2/07) [551.48]

Weather

23522 Armentrout, David, and Patricia Armentrout. *Weather* (PS–2). Illus. 2002, Rourke LB $19.95 (978-1-58952-346-3). 32pp. Simple definitions are given for 50 words about weather (arid, breeze, and so forth), along with a sentence that includes the word. (Rev: HBG 3/03; SLJ 3/03)

23523 Arnold, Caroline. *El Niño: Stormy Weather for People and Wildlife* (4–8). 1998, Clarion $16.00 (978-0-395-77602-5). A brief overview of El Niño, its causes and history, and how tracking and forecasting are used to make predictions. (Rev: BL 10/1/98; HBG 10/99; SLJ 12/98) [551.6]

23524 Banqueri, Eduardo. *Weather* (4–8). Illus. by Estudio Marcel Socías and Gabi Marfil. Series: Field Guides. 2006, Enchanted Lion $16.95 (978-1-59270-059-2). This information-packed guide explores a broad array of weather-related topics, including seasonal change, climatic zones, the science of meteorology, clouds, winds, storms, and the atmosphere. (Rev: SLJ 1/07) [551.5]

23525 Bredeson, Carmen. *El Niño and La Niña: Deadly Weather* (4–8). Series: American Disasters. 2002, Enslow LB $23.93 (978-0-7660-1551-7). A well-researched account of these two weather phenomena, their effects, and how they can be traced. (Rev: BL 6/1–15/02; HBG 10/02; SLJ 6/02) [551.6]

23526 Breen, Mark, and Kathleen Friestad. *The Kids' Book of Weather Forecasting* (3–5). Illus. Series: Kids Can! 2000, Williamson paper $14.25 (978-1-885593-39-9). 140pp. This book explains the complex subject of weather forecasting and includes such activities as making a barometer, a rain gauge, and a tornado. (Rev: BL 2/1/01; SLJ 1/01) [551.63]

23527 Brotak, Edward. *Wild About Weather: 50 Wet, Windy and Wonderful Activities* (3–6). 2004, Lark Books $19.95 (978-1-57990-468-5). 128pp. In addition to 50 activities with clear instructions, Brotak provides lots

of entertainingly presented facts, diagrams, and photographs. (Rev: BL 12/1/04) [551.6]

23528 Carson, Mary Kay. *Weather Projects for Young Scientists* (4–7). 2007, Chicago Review paper $14.95 (978-1-55652-629-9). A detailed look at weather basics is intertwined with more than 40 projects, many appropriate for science fairs, and a few career profiles. (Rev: BL 12/1/06; SLJ 3/08) [551.5078]

23529 Cobb, Allan B. *Weather Observation Satellites* (5–9). Series: The Library of Satellites. 2003, Rosen LB $26.50 (978-0-8239-3856-8). 64pp. This book shows how the development of satellites from the 1960s on has provided us with clear weather observations and accurate forecasts. (Rev: BL 11/15/03) [551.6]

23530 Drake, Jane, and Ann Love. *Snow Amazing: Cool Facts and Warm Tales* (3–5). Illus. by Mark Thurman. 2004, Tundra $19.95 (978-0-88776-670-1). 80pp. Snow lore and facts are at the center of this compendium of diverse facts, figures, and folktales, including details of the animals that inhabit arctic regions. (Rev: BL 2/1/05; SLJ 12/04) [551.57]

23531 Estigarribia, Diana. *Learning About Weather with Graphic Organizers* (3–6). Series: Graphic Organizers in Science. 2005, Rosen LB $21.25 (978-1-4042-2803-0). 24pp. This title uses a wide variety of graphic organizers, including concept webs, compare/contrast charts, Venn diagrams, graphs, timelines, and KWL charts, to introduce topics such as global warming, the greenhouse effect, seasonal change, and weather forecasting. (Rev: SLJ 11/05)

23532 Farndon, John. *Weather* (3–6). Illus. Series: Science Experiments. 2000, Marshall Cavendish LB $25.64 (978-0-7614-1089-8). 32pp. In addition to material on topics including sunlight, winds, clouds, and storms, this book outlines such projects as making a rain gauge and a weather vane. (Rev: BL 3/15/01; HBG 3/01) [551.6]

23533 Gardner, Robert. *Weather Science Fair Projects, Revised and Expanded Using the Scientific Method* (5–8). Series: Earth Science Projects Using the Scientific Method. 2010, Enslow LB $34.60 (978-0-7660-3424-2). 160pp. With a focus on the basics of scientific investigation, this well-organized and attractive volume gives an overview of the topic and provides experiments that support various hypotheses. (Rev: LMC 8–9/10) [551.63]

23534 Gardner, Robert. *Wild Science Projects About Earth's Weather* (4–6). Illus. by Tom LaBaff. Series: Rockin' Earth Science Experiments. 2007, Enslow LB $23.93 (978-0-7660-2734-3). 48pp. These projects concerning weather are appropriate for science fairs and are accompanied by safety precautions and detailed directions. (Rev: SLJ 6/07)

23535 Gibbons, Gail. *It's Snowing!* (K–3). Illus. by author. 2011, Holiday House $17.95 (978-0-8234-2237-1). 32pp. The formation of snowflakes, typical locations of snowstorms, record snowfalls, and definitions of various degrees of severity are all presented here, along with illustrations of how we behave before, during, and after snowstorms. (Rev: BL 9/15/11; SLJ 11/1/11) [551.57]

23536 Kahl, Jonathan D. *Weather Watch: Forecasting the Weather* (5–8). Series: How's the Weather? 1996, Lerner LB $21.27 (978-0-8225-2529-5). This work provides basic information on weather systems, maps, and forecasting tools, the history of weather forecasting and keeping weather records, and directions for making a weather station. (Rev: BL 6/1–15/96; SLJ 6/96) [551.6]

23537 Kaner, Etta. *Who Likes the Snow?* (PS–2). Illus. by Marie Lafrance. Series: Exploring the Elements. 2006, Kids Can $14.95 (978-1-55337-842-6). This slim book uses questions and flaps to offer interesting information about snow. (Rev: SLJ 12/06) [551.51]

23538 Marsico, Katie. *Snowy Weather Days* (K–2). Series: Scholastic News Nonfiction Readers. 2006, Children's Pr. LB $20.00 (978-0-531-16773-1). 24pp. Basic information for beginning readers, with seven highlighted words that are featured in bold in the text. Also use *Wild Weather Days* (2006). (Rev: SLJ 1/07) [551.57]

23539 Michaels, Pat. *W Is for Wind: A Weather Alphabet* (1–4). Illus. by Melanie Rose. 2005, Sleeping Bear $16.95 (978-1-58536-237-0). A rhyming alphabet book about the weather with useful information for young elementary students. (Rev: SLJ 7/05) [428.1]

23540 Nelson, Robin. *A Rainy Day* (PS–1). Illus. Series: Weather. 2001, Lerner LB $17.27 (978-0-8225-0173-2); paper $4.25 (978-0-8225-1962-1). In a small format for beginning readers, some simple facts about rainy days are accompanied by bold illustrations. Also use *A Snowy Day* and *A Sunny Day* (both 2001). (Rev: HBG 3/02; SLJ 4/02) [551.57]

23541 Pipe, Jim. *Weather* (3–5). Illus. Series: Earthwise. 2004, Stargazer LB $27.10 (978-1-932799-47-7). 32pp. An excellent introduction to the forces that create our weather, this attractively illustrated volume supplements its facts and figures with suggested activities. (Rev: BL 10/15/04) [551.5]

23542 Rockwell, Anne. *Clouds* (PS–1). Illus. by Frane Lessac. Series: Let's-Read-and-Find-Out Science Stage 1. 2008, Collins $16.99 (978-0-06-445220-5); paper $5.99 (978-0-06-029101-3). 40pp. For beginning readers, this is a simple picture-book introduction to clouds and the kinds of weather they accompany. (Rev: BL 12/15/08; SLJ 12/08) [551.57]

23543 Rodgers, Alan, and Angella Streluk. *Cloud Cover* (3–6). Illus. Series: Measuring the Weather. 2002, Heinemann LB $22.79 (978-1-58810-686-5). 32pp. Fog, ultraviolet radiation, types of cloud, and cloud cover in itself are all discussed — with their benefits and potential dangers — in this attractive titles. (Rev: HBG 3/03; SLJ 4/03) [551.5]

23544 Rodgers, Alan, and Angella Streluk. *Forecasting the Weather* (3–6). Illus. Series: Measuring the Weather. 2002, Heinemann LB $22.79 (978-1-58810-687-2). 32pp. Many of the tools used by meteorologists are examined here. Also use *Wind and Air Pressure* (2002). (Rev: HBG 3/03; SLJ 4/03) [551.6]

23545 Rosenberg, Pam. *Sunny Weather Days* (K–2). Series: Scholastic News Nonfiction Readers. 2006, Chil-

dren's Pr. LB $20.00 (978-0-531-16770-0). 24pp. This colorful picture book introduces young readers to the properties of the sun and introduces seven weather-related vocabulary words. (Rev: SLJ 1/07) [551.5]

23546 Rupp, Rebecca. *Weather! Watch How Weather Works* (4–8). 2003, Storey paper $14.95 (978-1-58017-420-6). A well-illustrated and appealing introduction to the science of weather, with numerous experiments and projects. (Rev: SLJ 5/04) [551.6]

23547 Rustad, Martha E. H. *Today Is Hot* (PS–3). 2005, Capstone LB $21.26 (978-0-7368-5343-9). 24pp. A very basic introduction to climate and weather, emphasizing aspects that affect a child's life. Also in this series: *Today Is Cold, Today Is Rainy,* and *Today Is Snowy* (all 2005). (Rev: SLJ 7/06) [551.5]

23548 Saunders-Smith, Gail. *La lluvia / Rain* (K–2). Trans. by Mart'n Luis Guzm n Ferrer. Series: Pebble Bilingual Books. 2003, Capstone LB $17.26 (978-0-7368-2309-8). 24pp. An introduction to rain and rainstorms in English and Spanish, illustrated with photographs. (Rev: SLJ 4/04) [551.5]

23549 Sayre, April Pulley. *El Niño and La Niña: Weather in the Headlines* (4–8). 2000, Twenty-First Century LB $25.90 (978-0-7613-1405-9). An exploration of this complex Pacific Ocean phenomenon that produces unusual weather conditions that affect the entire world. (Rev: BL 9/15/00; HBG 3/01) [551.6]

23550 Silverstein, Alvin. *Weather and Climate* (4–7). Series: Science Concepts. 1998, Twenty-First Century LB $26.90 (978-0-7613-3223-7). This book introduces weather by explaining earth's atmosphere, rotation, and different climates with material on air and water movements, cloud formation, and recent climate changes. (Rev: BL 5/1/99; HBG 10/99) [551.5]

23551 Solway, Andrew. *A Pirate Adventure: Weather* (3–6). Illus. Series: Raintree Fusion. 2005, Raintree LB $28.21 (978-1-4109-1926-7). 32pp. An exciting voyage on an 18th-century ship serves as the backdrop for information about wind, weather, and weather forecasting. (Rev: SLJ 5/06) [551.6]

23552 Stein, Paul. *Forecasting the Climate of the Future* (5–7). Series: The Library of Future Weather and Climate. 2001, Rosen LB $29.25 (978-0-8239-3413-3). A fascinating, well-organized account that looks at long-range weather predictions and at the use and accuracy of computer models in forecasting future weather patterns, especially with regard to global warming. Also use *Storms of the Future* (2001), which looks at whether global warming might cause stronger storms. (Rev: SLJ 4/02) [551.5]

23553 Stein, Paul. *Ice Ages of the Future* (5–7). Series: The Library of Future Weather and Climate. 2001, Rosen LB $29.25 (978-0-8239-3415-7). A look at the possibility that the greenhouse effect and other factors could in fact cause a wave of colder rather than warmer air. (Rev: SLJ 11/01) [551.6]

23554 Vogel, Carole G. *Weather Legends: Native American Lore and the Science of Weather* (4–8). Illus. 2001,

Millbrook LB $29.90 (978-0-7613-1900-9). 80pp. Native American weather myths are paired with scientific information about actual weather phenomena. (Rev: BL 9/1/01; HBG 3/02; SLJ 10/01) [398.2]

23555 Williams, Judith. *How Does the Sun Make Weather?* (1–3). Illus. Series: I Like Weather! 2005, Enslow LB $21.26 (978-0-7660-2317-8). 24pp. Preceded by a glossary and using questions as most chapter headers, this volume introduces the sun's influence on our weather. Also use: *Why Is It Raining?* and *Why Is It Windy?* (2005). (Rev: BL 4/1/05) [551.6]

23556 Williams, Zella, ed. *Experiments on the Weather* (3–5). Series: Do-It-Yourself Science. 2007, Rosen LB $23.95 (978-1-4042-3663-9). 24pp. Young scientists will find these weather-related projects informative. Instructions are included for an anemometer, a barometer, and a thermometer, as well as other activities. (Rev: SLJ 5/07)

23557 Wills, Susan, and Steven Wills. *Meteorology: Predicting the Weather* (5–7). Series: Innovators. 2004, Oliver LB $21.95 (978-1-881508-61-8). 144pp. Introduces seven scientists who have made substantial contributions to the science of meteorology. (Rev: SLJ 7/04) [920]

23558 Wyatt, Valerie. *FAQ Weather* (4–6). Illus. by Brian Share. 2000, Kids Can $12.95 (978-1-55074-582-5); paper $6.95 (978-1-55074-815-4). Using a question-and-answer format, this book covers many aspects of weather including winds, clouds, precipitation, and global warming. (Rev: SLJ 8/00) [551.6]

Physics

General

23559 Adler, David A. *Things That Float and Things That Don't* (PS–2). Illus. by Anna Raff. 2013, Holiday $16.95 (978-082342862-5). 32pp. Through inventive illustrations and practical hands-on activities, this volume offers a useful overview of the concept of density with numerous experiments. (Rev: BL 9/1/13*; SLJ 8/13) [532]

23560 Bonnet, Bob, and Dan Keen. *Science Fair Projects: Physics* (4–7). Illus. 2000, Sterling $17.95 (978-0-8069-0707-9). 96pp. This large-format book presents 47 projects demonstrating concepts in physics and using common materials as equipment. (Rev: BL 2/1/00; SLJ 4/00) [530]

23561 Boothroyd, Jennifer. *What Is a Liquid?* (K–2). Illus. Series: States of Matter. 2007, Lerner LB $17.27 (978-0-8225-6838-4). 24pp. A very basic introduction to the liquid state of matter, with brief text and large photographs. (Rev: SLJ 5/07)

23562 Boothroyd, Jennifer. *What Is a Solid?* (K–2). Illus. Series: States of Matter. 2007, Lerner LB $17.27 (978-0-8225-6836-0). 24pp. A very basic introduction to the solid state of matter, with brief text and large photographs. (Rev: SLJ 5/07)

23563 Claybourne, Anna. *Gut-Wrenching Gravity and Other Fatal Forces* (3–6). Illus. Series: Disgusting and Dreadful Science. 2013, Crabtree LB $20.70 (978-077870950-3); paper $9.95 (9780778709572). 32pp. A dramatic introduction to various aspects of gravity, more for browsing and inspiration than research. (Rev: BL 4/1/13) [531]

23564 Claybourne, Anna. *The Nature of Matter* (4–6). Illus. Series: Gareth Stevens Vital Science: Physical Science. 2007, Gareth Stevens LB $26.60 (978-0-8368-8088-5); paper $11.95 (978-0-8368-8097-7). 48pp. A straightforward look at various forms of matter and their properties. (Rev: SLJ 1/08) [530]

23565 Cook, Trevor. *Experiments with States of Matter* (3–7). Series: Science Lab. 2009, Rosen LB $25.25 (978-1-4358-2805-6). 32pp. A variety of science experiments using simple materials from around the house; each one illustrates a key concept pertaining to the varying states of matter. (Rev: LMC 11–12/09) [530.4]

23566 Cregan, Elizabeth R. *The Atom* (4–6). Illus. Series: Mission: Science. 2008, Compass Point LB $26.60 (978-0-7565-3953-5). 40pp. An appealing exploration of the structure of the atom, cathode rays and electrons, radioactivity, the future, and key scientists involved in research; also includes many photographs and illustrations plus an activity. (Rev: LMC 3/09; SLJ 6/09) [539.7]

23567 Evans, Neville. *The Science of Gravity* (5–8). Illus. Series: Science World. 2000, Raintree LB $25.69 (978-0-7398-1323-2). 32pp. Explores the force of gravity and how it affects our lives, with additional material on air resistance, mass, and invisible forces. (Rev: BL 9/15/00; HBG 10/00) [531]

23568 Farndon, John. *Buoyancy* (3–6). Series: Science Experiments. 2002, Marshall Cavendish LB $25.64 (978-0-7614-1467-4). 32pp. The nature of buoyancy is explained through a simple text, color photographs, and an explanatory experiment in each chapter. (Rev: BL 12/15/02; HBG 3/03) [530]

23569 Gardner, Robert. *Melting, Freezing, and Boiling Science Projects with Matter* (3–5). Series: Fantastic Physical Science Experiments. 2006, Enslow LB $23.93 (978-0-7660-2589-9). 48pp. Nine science projects that explore the properties of matter are introduced in double-page spreads, with discussion of the principles demonstrated. Also use *Sizzling Science Projects with Heat and Energy* (2006). (Rev: BL 9/15/06) [507]

23570 Goodstein, Madeline. *Fish Tank Physics Projects* (5–8). Series: Science Fair Success. 2002, Enslow LB $26.60 (978-0-7660-1624-8). 112pp. Using a common fish tank and its contents, various aspects of laws of physics are presented in the form of science fair projects. (Rev: BL 5/15/02; HBG 10/02; SLJ 11/02) [621.9]

23571 Hammond, Richard. *Can You Feel the Force?* (5–8). Illus. 2006, DK $15.99 (978-0-7566-2033-2). Light, matter, friction, gravity, velocity — these and other basic physics principles are explained in a reader-friendly format that includes experiments, captions, sidebars, and other eye-catching elements. (Rev: SLJ 10/06) [530]

23572 Hopwood, James. *Cool Gravity Activities: Fun Science Projects About Balance* (4–6). Series: Cool Science. 2008, ABDO LB $16.95 (978-1-59928-908-3). 32pp. Five high-interest experiments with detailed, illustrated instructions follow discussion about the scientific method, keeping a journal, and safety. Also use *Cool Dry Ice Devices: Fun Science Projects with Dry Ice* and *Cool Distance Assistants: Fun Science Projects to Propel Things* (both 2008). (Rev: LMC 5/08; SLJ 2/08) [531]

23573 Jerome, Kate Boehm. *Atomic Universe: The Quest to Discover Radioactivity* (5–8). Series: Science Quest. 2006, National Geographic $17.95 (978-0-7922-5543-7). An attractive and informative history of radioactivity, profiling key figures and placing the discovery and subsequent developments in scientific and social context. (Rev: SLJ 4/07) [539.7]

23574 Juettner Fernandes, Bonnie. *The Large Hadron Collider* (4–7). Illus. Series: A Great Idea. 2013, Norwood LB $19.95 (978-159953600-2). 48pp. Using simple and concise language, detailed diagrams, and color photographs, this volume explains how the Large Hadron Collider is used to learn more about how the universe was created. (Rev: BL 10/1/13; LMC 5–6/14) [539.7]

23575 Juettner, Bonnie. *Molecules* (4–8). 2004, Gale LB $26.20 (978-0-7377-2076-1). Clear, concise text, supported by full-color photographs and diagrams, describes the characteristics of atoms and molecules. (Rev: SLJ 6/05)

23576 McGrath, Susan. *Fun with Physics* (5–9). 1986, National Geographic LB $12.50 (978-0-87044-581-1). An introduction to physics that uses everyday situations as examples and supplies a smattering of experiments. (Rev: SLJ 6/87) [530]

23577 Mason, Adrienne. *Motion, Magnets, and More: The Big Book of Primary Science* (K–2). Illus. by Claudia Davila. 2011, Kids Can $18.95 (978-155453707-5). 128pp. Materials, structures, states of matter, and forces of motion are covered in this well-illustrated volume that includes experiments that reinforce basic concepts. (Rev: BL 12/1/11; LMC 1–2/12) [500.2]

23578 Mason, Adrienne. *Touch It! Materials, Matter and You* (K–2). Illus. by Claudia Dávila. Series: Primary Physical Science. 2005, Kids Can $12.95 (978-1-55337-760-3); paper $5.95 (978-1-55337-761-0). 32pp. This easy-to-understand approach to science introduces the various properties of matter and suggests simple activities and projects. (Rev: BL 10/15/05) [530]

23579 Morgan, Sally, and Adrian Morgan. *Materials* (4–7). Series: Designs in Science. 1994, Facts on File $23.00 (978-0-8160-2985-3). Basic properties of matter

and materials are explored in a series of experiments using everyday materials. (Rev: BL 7/94) [620.1]

23580 Parker, Barry. *The Mystery of Gravity* (5–8). Illus. Series: The Story of Science. 2002, Benchmark $29.93 (978-0-7614-1428-5). 78pp. Parker traces our understanding of gravity from the early Greek philosophers through Einstein and Hubble, with discussion of the Big Bang theory and black holes. (Rev: HBG 3/03; SLJ 2/03) [531]

23581 Rosinsky, Natalie M. *Sinking and Floating* (3–5). Series: Simply Science. 2004, Compass Point LB $21.26 (978-0-7565-0598-1). 32pp. Rosinsky examines why some objects float while others sink, looking in detail at such scientific principles as water displacement and density. (Rev: SLJ 8/04) [532]

23582 Silverstein, Alvin, and Virginia Silverstein. *Forces and Motion* (4–8). Illus. Series: Science Concepts, Second Series. 2008, Twenty-First Century LB $31.93 (978-0-8225-7514-6). 112pp. With photographs, diagrams, and examples that attract young readers, this volume provides clear explanations of forces, motion, gravity, and simple machines. Also use *Matter* (2008). (Rev: SLJ 12/08) [531]

23583 Snedden, Robert. *Forces and Motion* (4–6). Illus. Series: Gareth Stevens Vital Science: Physical Science. 2007, Gareth Stevens LB $26.60 (978-0-8368-8087-8); paper $11.95 (978-0-8368-8096-0). 48pp. Speed, acceleration, gravity, and friction are among the topics covered in this straightforward overview that includes features on Galileo, Newton, and Pascal. (Rev: SLJ 1/08) [531]

23584 Solway, Andrew. *Sports Science* (4–9). Series: Why Science Matters. 2009, Heinemann-Raintree $32.86 (978-1-4329-2480-5). 56pp. Geared towards illuminating science's role in our everyday lives, this title provides a thorough, well-researched look at the science of sports. (Rev: LMC 11–12/09)

23585 Spilsbury, Richard. *What Are Solids, Liquids, and Gases? Exploring Science with Hands-on Activities* (3–4). Illus. Series: In Touch with Basic Science. 2008, Enslow LB $22.60 (978-0-7660-3094-7). 32pp. Introduces solids, liquids, and gases, with activities that demonstrate scientific principles. (Rev: SLJ 3/09) [530.4078]

23586 Stille, Darlene R. *Physical Change: Reshaping Matter* (5–8). Series: Exploring Science. 2005, Compass Point LB $27.93 (978-0-7565-1257-6). An attractive format with plenty of graphics adds to the appeal of this brief discussion of the states of matter. (Rev: SLJ 7/06) [530]

23587 Stille, Darlene R. *Solids, Liquids, and Gases* (2–4). Illus. Series: Science Around Us. 2004, Child's World LB $27.07 (978-1-59296-225-9). 32pp. In simple, easy-to-understand language supplemented by bright photographs, Stille introduces readers to the differences between the three basic states of matter. (Rev: BL 11/1/04) [530.4]

23588 Stringer, John. *The Science of a Spring* (5–8). Illus. Series: Science World. 2000, Raintree LB $25.69

(978-0-7398-1322-5). 32pp. Leaf and coil springs are introduced as well as the balance of forces in physics, the limits of springs, and their uses in such common objects as staplers. (Rev: BL 9/1/00; HBG 10/00; SLJ 8/00) [531]

23589 Sullivan, Navin. *Weight* (4–7). Illus. Series: Measure Up! 2006, Marshall Cavendish LB $20.95 (978-0-7614-2324-9). Topics such as gravity and buoyancy are covered in this well-designed book about weight. (Rev: LMC 8–9/07; SLJ 6/07)

23590 Taylor-Butler, Christine. *Think Like a Scientist in the Gym* (3–5). Illus. Series: Science Explorer Junior. 2011, Cherry Lake LB $27.07 (978-161080163-8). 32pp. Using the gym and sports as a framework, this book demonstrates how running, throwing, jumping, breathing, and so forth involve principles of physics; with related experiments. (Rev: BL 12/1/11) [507.8]

23591 Tiner, John Hudson. *Gravity* (4–7). Series: Understanding Science. 2002, Smart Apple $24.25 (978-1-58340-157-6). 32pp. Through a number of simple projects, colorful illustrations, and a clear text, the fundamentals of gravity are explored. (Rev: BL 3/15/03; HBG 3/03) [531]

23592 Twist, Clint. *Light and Sound* (K–1). Illus. Series: Check It Out! 2005, Bearport LB $19.96 (978-1-59716-060-5). 24pp. Presents the basics of the science behind light and sound. (Rev: BL 10/15/05) [535]

23593 VanCleave, Janice. *Step-By-Step Science Experiments in Energy* (5–8). Series: Janice VanCleave's First-Place Science Fair Projects. 2012, Rosen Central LB $33.25 (978-1-4488-6972-4). 80pp. An updated volume with step-by-step instructions for 22 experiments mostly using easily found materials. (Rev: SLJ 10/12) [531.6078]

23594 Williams, Zella, ed. *Experiments with Physical Science* (3–5). Series: Do-It-Yourself Science. 2007, Rosen LB $23.95 (978-1-4042-3659-2). 24pp. Young scientists will find these physics-related projects informative. Instructions are included to investigate sound waves, vibrations, friction, and gravity, as well as other phenomena. (Rev: SLJ 5/07)

Energy and Motion

General

23595 Asimov, Isaac. *How Did We Find Out About Solar Power?* (5–8). Illus. by David Wool. 1981, Walker LB $12.85 (978-0-8027-6423-2). An explanation of how man has benefited from solar power from the earliest time until today. [621.47]

23596 Boyle, Jordan. *Examining Geothermal Energy* (4–7). Illus. Series: Examining Energy. 2013, Oliver LB $24.95 (978-193454549-2). 48pp. A survey of geothermal energy and past, present, future uses of this source

of power. **e** (Rev: BL 4/1/13; LMC 8–9/13; SLJ 4/13) [621.44]

23597 Bradley, Kimberly Brubaker. *Energy Makes Things Happen* (1–3). Illus. by Paul Meisel. Series: Let's-Read-and-Find-Out Science. 2003, HarperCollins LB $16.89 (978-0-06-028909-6); paper $5.99 (978-0-06-445213-7). 40pp. An entertaining introduction to energy and its sources and uses, for young readers. (Rev: BL 2/1/03; HBG 10/03; SLJ 1/03) [531]

23598 Bradley, Kimberly Brubaker. *Forces Make Things Move* (1–3). Illus. by Paul Meisel. Series: Let's-Read-and-Find-Out Science. 2005, HarperCollins $15.99 (978-0-06-028906-5); paper $5.99 (978-0-06-445214-4). Using a toy car as an example, this is a basic exploration of the physics of motion and such related concepts as inertia, friction, and gravity. (Rev: BL 9/15/05) [531]

23599 Cobb, Vicki. *I Fall Down* (PS–1). Illus. by Julia Gorton. Series: Science Play. 2004, HarperCollins LB $17.89 (978-0-688-17843-7). 40pp. Exercises introduce the concept of gravity. (Rev: BL 2/1/05) [531]

23600 Cobb, Vicki. *Whirlers and Twirlers: Science Fun with Spinning* (3–5). Illus. by Steve Haefele. 2001, Millbrook LB $24.90 (978-0-7613-1573-5). 64pp. A lighthearted introduction to the physics involved in the motion of spinning, with experiments with tops, pinwheels, and other objects. (Rev: BL 10/15/01; HBG 3/02; SLJ 1/02) [531]

23601 Cruden, Gabriel. *Energy Alternatives* (5–8). Series: Lucent Library of Science and Technology. 2005, Gale LB $29.95 (978-1-59018-530-8). A look at the importance of finding alternatives to existing energy sources, covering such technologies as solar, wind, and geothermal power. (Rev: BL 1/05)

23602 de Pinna, Simon. *Transfer of Energy* (4–6). Illus. Series: Gareth Stevens Vital Science: Physical Science. 2007, Gareth Stevens LB $26.60 (978-0-8368-8091-5); paper $11.95 (978-0-8368-8100-4). A straightforward overview of the nature of energy, its forms, and its sources. (Rev: SLJ 1/08) [531]

23603 Doherty, Paul, and Don Rathjen. *The Spinning Blackboard and Other Dynamic Experiments on Force and Motion* (4–8). Series: Exploratorium Science Snackbook. 1996, Wiley paper $13.95 (978-0-471-11514-4). The many activities in this well-organized, attractive book reveal important characteristics of force and motion. (Rev: BL 4/15/96; SLJ 6/96) [531]

23604 Driscoll, Laura. *Slow Down, Sara!* (1–3). Illus. by Page Eastburn O'Rourke. Series: Science Solves It! 2003, Kane paper $4.99 (978-1-57565-125-5). 32pp. This appealing title from the Science Solves It! series focuses on the principle of friction and its impact on speed; young Sara has a need for speed, but she discovers that sometimes it makes sense to slow down. (Rev: SLJ 10/03)

23605 Drummond, Allan. *Energy Island: How One Community Harnessed the Wind and Changed Their World* (1–3). Illus. by author. 2011, Farrar $16.99 (978-0-374-32184-0). 40pp. The inspiring story of the Danish island of Samsø's successful efforts to become energy independent, a project started by a visionary teacher and supported by his students and then the whole population. Lexile AD920L (Rev: BL 3/1/11*; LMC 5–6/11; SLJ 3/1/11*) [333.9]

23606 Egendorf, Laura K., ed. *Energy Alternatives* (5–9). Series: Introducing Issues with Opposing Viewpoints. 2006, Gale LB $33.70 (978-0-7377-3458-4). Presents basic information about alternatives to fossil fuel-driven energy, along with diverse views on the feasibility and practicality of these alternative energy sources. (Rev: SLJ 8/06) [333.79]

23607 Farndon, John. *Energy* (3–6). Series: Science Experiments. 2002, Marshall Cavendish LB $25.64 (978-0-7614-1469-8). 32pp. The nature and forms of energy are introduced through a series of easy-to-follow experiments and a simple explanatory text with many color photographs and diagrams. (Rev: BL 12/15/02; HBG 3/03) [531.6]

23608 Farndon, John. *Motion* (3–6). Series: Science Experiments. 2002, Marshall Cavendish LB $25.64 (978-0-7614-1471-1). 32pp. The properties of motion are revealed to the young scientist through several easy-to-follow activities using common household materials. (Rev: BL 12/15/02; HBG 3/03) [531]

23609 Farrell, Courtney. *Using Alternative Energies* (3–7). Series: Language Arts Explorer: Save the Planet. 2010, Cherry Lake LB $27.07 (978-1-60279-663-8). 32pp. Students are given a mission at the beginning of the book and must use creative thinking and problem solving to gather facts as they travel on a virtual trip researching solar power, wind power, and other alternatives. (Rev: LMC 8–9/10) [333.79]

23610 Gardner, Robert. *Energy Experiments: Using Ice Cubes, Springs, Magnets, and More* (4–7). Series: Last Minute Science Projects. 2012, Enslow LB $23.93 (978-076603959-9). 48pp. Eighteen projects that use everyday objects demonstrate basic concepts of energy and how matter changes from a solid to a liquid to a gas. (Rev: BL 12/1/12; LMC 5–6/13)

23611 Goodman, Polly. *Understanding Wind Power* (5–8). Illus. Series: The World of Energy. 2010, Gareth Stevens LB $31.95 (978-143394133-7). 48pp. Different kinds of wind power, and pros and cons of their construction and use, are discussed in this slim volume. (Rev: BLO 2/14/11; LMC 5–6/11) [621.4]

23612 Gray, Susan H. *Experiments with Motion* (4–6). Illus. Series: True Book: Experiments. 2011, Scholastic LB $28 (978-053126346-4). 48pp. Readers learn about laws governing motion and scientific investigation before tackling experiments using everyday materials. (Rev: BL 12/1/11) [531]

23613 Jakab, Cheryl. *Renewable Energy* (4–7). Series: Global Issues. 2009, Smart Apple Media LB $28.50 (978-1-59920-453-6). 32pp. Offering a global perspective, this volume discusses the benefits of renewable energy and the various challenges the technology faces. (Rev: SLJ 2/10) [333.79]

23614 Landau, Elaine. *The History of Energy* (5–8). Series: Major Inventions Through History. 2005, Twenty-First Century LB $26.60 (978-0-8225-3806-6). An attractive look at developments through time in the use of various forms of energy (fire, wind, water, coal, steam, oil and gasoline, electricity, and so forth) and their application in transportation and other sectors. (Rev: SLJ 1/06)

23615 Leedy, Loreen. *The Shocking Truth About Energy* (K–3). Illus. by author. 2010, Holiday House $17.95 (978-0-8234-2220-3). 32pp. An imaginary bolt of energy named Erg narrates this accessible, engaging book, which offers an introduction to basic energy concepts, explaining the various forms, how they are generated, and pros and cons of each alternative. (Rev: BL 4/15/10; LMC 10/10; SLJ 5/1/10) [333.79]

23616 Lew, Kristi. *Goodbye, Gasoline: The Science of Fuel Cells* (5–7). Series: Headline Science. 2008, Compass Point LB $27.93 (978-0-7565-3521-6). 48pp. Understandable text and helpful charts educate readers as they delve into the science of fuel cells as alternative, clean energy and learn about the negative impact that gasoline has on our environment. (Rev: LMC 5/09*; SLJ 2/09) [621.31]

23617 McLeish, Ewan. *Challenges to Our Energy Supply* (4–8). Series: Can the Earth Survive? 2010, Rosen LB $26.50 (978-1-4358-5357-7). 48pp. With case studies and suggested strategies for the future, this volume looks at energy shortages around the world and the impact on everyday life. (Rev: LMC 3–4/10; SLJ 1/10) [333.79]

23618 Mulder, Michelle. *Brilliant! Shining a Light on Sustainable Energy* (4–6). Illus. 2013, Orca $19.95 (978-145980221-6). 48pp. A thought-provoking look at nontraditional, renewable sources of energy and the environmental concerns we face in the future. ℮ (Rev: BL 9/15/13; LMC 3–4/14) [333.79]

23619 Petersen, Christine. *Wind Power* (3–5). Illus. Series: True Book (Environment and Conservation). 2004, Children's Pr. LB $25.00 (978-0-516-22809-9). 48pp. This thought-provoking look at at the potential of wind power discusses current and future uses of the technology. (Rev: BL 6/1–15/04) [621.31]

23620 Silverstein, Alvin. *Energy* (4–7). Series: Science Concepts. 1998, Twenty-First Century LB $26.90 (978-0-7613-3222-0). Photographs, diagrams, and illustrations help to introduce six types of energy: electrical, magnetic, light, heat, sound, and nuclear. (Rev: BL 5/1/99; HBG 10/99) [621.042]

23621 Spilsbury, Richard, and Louise Spilsbury. *What Are Forces and Motion? Exploring Science with Hands-on Activities* (3–4). Illus. Series: In Touch with Basic Science. 2008, Enslow LB $22.60 (978-0-7660-3095-4). 32pp. Introduces Newton's laws of motion and some simple machines, with activities that demonstrate scientific principles. (Rev: LMC 1/09; SLJ 3/09)

23622 Stille, Darlene R. *Waves: Energy on the Move* (5–8). Series: Exploring Science. 2005, Compass Point LB $27.93 (978-0-7565-1259-0). An attractive format with plenty of graphics adds to the appeal of this brief discussion of waves in water, light, air, and other media. (Rev: SLJ 7/06) [531]

23623 Sullivan, Navin. *Speed* (4–7). Illus. Series: Measure Up! 2006, Marshall Cavendish LB $20.95 (978-0-7614-2325-6). In addition to providing an overview of the science of speed, this volume includes high-quality graphics, information about historical versus modern methods, and at-home experiments. (Rev: LMC 8–9/07; SLJ 6/07)

23624 Walker, Niki. *Generating Wind Power* (5–8). Illus. Series: Energy Revolution. 2007, Crabtree LB $25.20 (978-0-7787-2913-6); paper $8.95 (978-0-7787-2927-3). 32pp. Wind is explored as an alternative energy source in this well-designed volume. Also use *Harnessing Power from the Sun* and *Biomass: Fueling Change* (both 2007). (Rev: SLJ 7/07)

23625 Woodford, Chris. *Energy* (4–7). Illus. Series: See for Yourself. 2007, DK $14.99 (978-0-7566-2561-0). This introductory guide to energy provides an easy-to-understand definition, offers examples of both kinetic and potential energy, identifies major energy sources, explains the processes through which energy is released, and discusses the problems inherent in energy usage. (Rev: BL 4/1/07) [333.79]

Coal, Gas, and Oil

23626 Ditchfield, Christin. *Coal* (2–5). Series: True Books — Natural Resources. 2002, Children's Book Pr. LB $25.00 (978-0-516-22342-1). 48pp. This simple introduction to coal explains how it is formed, where it is found, how it is used, and how it affects our environment. (Rev: BL 10/15/02) [622]

Nuclear Energy

23627 Benoit, Peter. *Nuclear Meltdowns* (3–5). Illus. 2011, Scholastic LB $28 (978-053125422-6); paper $6.95 (978-053126627-4). 48pp. With statistics and Web resources, this volume covers everything from how power plants to work to the accidents at Three Mile Island and Chernobyl. (Rev: BL 11/15/11) [363.17]

23628 Cole, Michael D. *Three Mile Island: Nuclear Disaster* (4–8). Series: American Disasters. 2002, Enslow LB $23.93 (978-0-7660-1556-2). 48pp. An informative, well-researched account of the disaster that affected the development of nuclear power plants in this country. (Rev: BL 6/1–15/02; HBG 10/02; SLJ 6/02) [621.48]

23629 Jakubiak, David J. *What Can We Do About Nuclear Waste?* (3–5). Illus. Series: Protecting Our Planet. 2011, Rosen LB $21.25 (978-144884983-3). 24pp. After a basic description of how nuclear energy works, this book looks at our choices for storing and disposing of dangerous nuclear waste. e (Rev: BL 2/15/12) [363.72]

Solar Energy

23630 Petersen, Christine. *Solar Power* (3–5). Illus. Series: True Book (Environment and Conservation). 2004, Children's Pr. LB $25.00 (978-0-516-22807-5). 48pp. The energy of the sun and its potential as a source of power are eplored in this photo-filled, small-format book. (Rev: BL 6/1–15/04) [612.47]

Light and Color

23631 Bang, Molly. *My Light* (1–3). Illus. 2004, Scholastic $16.95 (978-0-439-48961-4). 48pp. Highly visual and accessible, this picture book introduces four ways of making electricity and explores the energy provided by the sun. (Rev: BL 2/1/04*; HB 5/04; SLJ 4/04) [621]

23632 Farndon, John. *Color* (3–6). Illus. Series: Science Experiments. 2000, Marshall Cavendish LB $25.64 (978-0-7614-1092-8). 32pp. Topics covered include the spectrum, primary colors, pigment, mixing colors, and color blindness, with many interesting activities such as making a color wheel and creating a spectrum. (Rev: BL 3/15/01; HBG 3/01) [535.6]

23633 Farndon, John. *Lights and Optics* (3–6). Series: Science Experiments. 2000, Marshall Cavendish LB $25.64 (978-0-7614-1090-4). 32pp. Explores properties of light and optics and outlines projects that apply the principles established. (Rev: BL 3/15/01; HBG 3/01) [535]

23634 Gardner, Robert. *Dazzling Science Projects with Light and Color* (4–6). Illus. by Tom LaBaff. Series: Fantastic Physical Science Experiments. 2006, Enslow LB $23.93 (978-0-7660-2587-5). 48pp. Experiments involving readily available materials demonstrate the properties of light and color and how the two interact; advice on developing these into science fair projects follows. (Rev: SLJ 8/06) [535]

23635 Gardner, Robert. *Science Projects About Light* (4–8). Series: Science Projects. 1994, Enslow LB $26.60 (978-0-89490-529-2). This project book contains a wealth of demonstrations that explain the basic principles of light. (Rev: SLJ 1/95) [535]

23636 Sitarski, Anita. *Cold Light: Creatures, Discoveries, and Inventions that Glow* (4–7). Illus. 2007, Boyds Mills $16.95 (978-1-59078-468-6). An interesting introduction to the phenomenon of luminescence — found in animals that glow but also in light-emitting diodes — this will appeal to report writers and browsers. (Rev: BL 12/1/07; LMC 1/08; SLJ 10/07) [535.35]

23637 Stille, Darlene R. *Manipulating Light: Reflection, Refraction, and Absorption* (5–8). Series: Exploring Science. 2005, Compass Point LB $27.93 (978-0-7565-1258-3). An attractive format with plenty of graphics adds to the appeal of this brief discussion of the nature of light. (Rev: SLJ 7/06) [535]

23638 Tocci, Salvatore. *Experiments with Colors* (2–4). Illus. Series: A True Book. 2003, Children's Pr. LB $25.00 (978-0-516-22785-6). 48pp. A simple and attractive explanation of what creates color, how we perceive it, and how optical illusions work. (Rev: SLJ 4/04) [535.6]

23639 Trumbauer, Lisa. *All About Light* (PS–1). Series: Rookie Read-About Science. 2004, Scholastic LB $4.95 (978-0-516-25842-3). 31pp. Simple text and color photographs introduce beginning readers to the concept of light, including its sources and basic characteristics. (Rev: BL 9/1/04) [535]

23640 Whitfield, David. *Rainbows* (2–4). Illus. Series: Science Matters. 2006, Weigl $24.45 (978-1-59036-414-7). 24pp. Readers will be fascinated to learn about the science behind rainbows. Photographs and other graphics, as well as related information and activities, add to this book's appeal. (Rev: SLJ 5/07)

Magnetism and Electricity

23641 Bartholomew, Alan. *Electric Mischief* (4–7). Series: Kids Can Do It. 2002, Kids Can $12.95 (978-1-55074-923-6); paper $5.95 (978-1-55074-925-0). 48pp. An activity book that outlines simple, safe experiments with electricity. (Rev: BL 3/15/03; HBG 3/03; SLJ 12/02) [537]

23642 Dreier, David. *Electrical Circuits: Harnessing Electricity* (5–7). Illus. Series: Exploring Science: Physical Science. 2007, Compass Point LB $19.95 (978-0-7565-3267-3). A user-friendly introduction to electricity and how we use it, with good graphics and interesting sidebar features. (Rev: BL 12/1/07; LMC 2/08) [537]

23643 Evans, Neville. *The Science of a Light Bulb* (5–8). Illus. Series: Science World. 2000, Raintree LB $25.69 (978-0-7398-1325-6). 32pp. This work explains how Edison invented the light bulb, describes its parts, and tells how light is produced and how we see it. (Rev: BL 9/15/00; HBG 10/00) [535]

23644 Farndon, John. *Electricity* (3–6). Series: Science Experiments. 2000, Marshall Cavendish LB $25.64 (978-0-7614-1086-7). 32pp. Each chapter contains information on different aspects and applications of electricity plus experiments that illustrate key principles. (Rev: BL 3/15/01; HBG 3/01) [537]

23645 Good, Keith. *Zap It! Exciting Electricity Activities* (3–7). Series: Design It! 2000, Lerner LB $21.27 (978-0-8225-3565-2). 30pp. An activity book that explores concepts in electricity and contains projects involving electric circuits, pressure pads, and different kinds of switches. (Rev: HBG 9/00; SLJ 6/00) [537]

23646 Levine, Shar, and Leslie Johnstone. *Magnet Power!* (2–4). Illus. by Steve Harpster. Series: First Science Experiments. 2006, Sterling $14.95 (978-1-4027-2438-1). 48pp. Clearly explained experiments and activities demonstrate the properties of magnets. (Rev: BL 11/1/06) [538]

23647 Nankivell-Aston, Sally, and Dorothy Jackson. *Science Experiments with Electricity* (3–6). Series: Science Experiments. 2000, Watts paper $6.95 (978-0-531-15443-4). 32pp. This book of simple electricity projects includes building simple switches and circuits with additional material on scientific method and safety. (Rev: SLJ 3/01) [537]

23648 Parker, Steve. *Electricity and Magnetism* (4–6). Illus. Series: Gareth Stevens Vital Science: Physical Science. 2007, Gareth Stevens LB $26.60 (978-0-8368-8085-4); paper $11.95 (978-0-8368-8094-6). 48pp. A straightforward introduction to electricity and magnetism and their importance in our lives. (Rev: SLJ 1/08) [537]

23649 Rau, Dana Meachen. *Electricity and Magnetism* (2–4). Illus. Series: Real World Science. 2009, Cherry Lake LB $27.07 (978-1-60279-459-7). 32pp. With bright illustrations and clear text, this title looks at static and current electricity and the relationship between electricity and magnets. (Rev: BL 4/1/09) [537]

23650 Seuling, Barbara. *Flick a Switch: How Electricity Gets to Your Home* (1–3). Illus. by Nancy Tobin. 2003, Holiday House $16.95 (978-0-8234-1729-2). 32pp. An easy-to-understand narrative is combined with bright cartoon illustrations to help young readers learn some basics about electricity — where it comes from and how it gets to where it's needed. (Rev: BL 9/1/03; HBG 4/04; SLJ 11/03)

23651 Solway, Andrew. *Generating and Using Electricity* (4–9). Series: Why Science Matters. 2009, Heinemann-Raintree $32.86 (978-1-4329-2481-2). 56pp. This appealing guide offers a look at the key role electricity plays in our lives. (Rev: LMC 11–12/09) [537]

23652 Spilsbury, Richard. *What Is Electricity and Magnetism? Exploring Science with Hands-on Activities* (3–4). Illus. Series: In Touch with Basic Science. 2008, Enslow LB $22.60 (978-0-7660-3096-1). 32pp. Motors, generators, and electromagnetism are among the topics discussed, with activities that demonstrate scientific principles. (Rev: SLJ 3/09) [537]

23653 Tiner, John Hudson. *Magnetism* (4–7). Series: Understanding Science. 2002, Smart Apple LB $24.25 (978-1-58340-158-3). 32pp. Using clear explanations, simple projects, and good illustrations, the concept of magnetism is introduced. (Rev: BL 3/15/03; HBG 3/03) [538.4]

23654 VanCleave, Janice. *Janice VanCleave's Electricity: Mind-Boggling Experiments You Can Turn into Science Fair Projects* (5–7). 1994, Wiley paper $10.95 (978-0-471-31010-5). As well as providing a discussion on the nature of electricity, this book offers 20 informative experiments that move from the very simple to the more complex. (Rev: BL 12/1/94; SLJ 11/94) [537]

23655 Walker, Sally M. *Electricity* (3–5). Photos by Andy King. Illus. Series: Early Bird Energy. 2005, Lerner LB $25.26 (978-0-8225-2919-4). 48pp. After a basic explanation of how electricity works, this volume looks at static electricity, currents, circuits, and so forth and suggests a number of activities that use materials including batteries, light bulbs, and aluminum foil. (Rev: BL 12/1/05) [537]

23656 Woodford, Chris, and Martin Clowes. *Electricity* (4–7). Illus. 2004, Gale LB $23.70 (978-1-4103-0165-9). 40pp. A detailed examination of the development of electricity, with profiles of key individuals and their discoveries, a chronology, and discussion of future advances. (Rev: SLJ 5/05)

Optical Illusions

23657 Illusionworks. *Amazing Optical Illusions* (3–5). Illus. 2005, Firefly LB $16.95 (978-1-55297-961-7); paper $5.95 (978-1-55237-962-2). 32pp. Twenty-nine optical illusions challenge readers. (Rev: SLJ 8/05) [152]

Simple Machines

23658 Armentrout, David, and Patricia Armentrout. *An Inclined Plane* (1–3). Illus. Series: How Can I Experiment With . . .? 2002, Rourke LB $19.95 (978-1-58952-333-3). 32pp. This volume teaches younger readers, through illustration, narrative, and experimentation, about inclined planes. Other titles in this series include *A Lever*, *A Screw*, *A Wedge*, and *A Wheel* (all 2002). (Rev: BL 10/15/02; SLJ 3/03) [621.8]

23659 Gardner, Robert. *Sensational Science Projects with Simple Machines* (4–6). Illus. by Tom LaBaff. Series: Fantastic Physical Science Experiments. 2006, Enslow LB $23.93 (978-0-7660-2585-1). 48pp. The experiments and projects in this volume are designed to help readers understand the workings of simple machines — such as inclined planes, levers, and pulleys — and to incorporate them in exciting science fair projects. (Rev: SLJ 8/06) [621.8]

23660 Good, Keith. *Gear Up! Marvelous Machine Projects* (3–7). Series: Design It! 2000, Lerner LB $21.27 (978-0-8225-3566-9). 30pp. Simple machines like pulleys, levers, crankshafts, gear wheels, and conveyor belts are explored in this book of projects that apply the principles behind these machines. (Rev: HBG 9/00; SLJ 6/00) [621.8]

23661 Oxlade, Chris. *Levers* (K–2). Illus. Series: Useful Machines. 2003, Heinemann LB $22.79 (978-1-4034-3662-7). 32pp. Information on how these simple machines work are followed by illustrations of levers in action in everyday situations. Also use *Pulleys* (2003). (Rev: BL 2/15/04) [021.8]

23662 Royston, Angela. *Screws* (2–4). Illus. Series: Machines in Action. 2000, Heinemann LB $22.79 (978-1-57572-322-8). 32pp. An easy-to-read introduction to

how screws work and the different kinds of screws we find in objects all around us. Also use *Springs* (2000). (Rev: HBG 3/01; SLJ 4/01) [621.8]

23663 Solway, Andrew. *Castle Under Siege! Simple Machines* (3–5). Illus. 2005, Raintree LB $28.21 (978-1-4109-1918-2). 32pp. Covering the construction of a medieval castle and its forms of defense, this book also introduces simple machines — wedges, inclined planes, levers, and so forth. (Rev: SLJ 4/06) [621.8]

23664 Sugiura, Kuniko. *Pulleys to the Rescue* (2–3). Illus. Series: First Facts: Simple Machines to the Rescue. 2006, Capstone LB $21.26 (978-0-7368-6748-1). 24pp. Readers will learn that pulleys are simple machines that make simple tasks easier in this introduction that includes photographs, fast facts, and an easy experiment. Also use *Screws to the Rescue* and *Wedges to the Rescue* (both 2006). (Rev: SLJ 8/07)

23665 Thales, Sharon. *Inclined Planes to the Rescue* (2–3). Series: Simple Machines to the Rescue. 2006, Capstone LB $21.26 (978-0-7368-6752-8). 24pp. A simple introduction to a simple machine using real-world examples is accompanied by an easy-to-perform experiment. Also use *Levers to the Rescue and Wheels* and *Axles to the Rescue* (both 2006). (Rev: SLJ 5/07)

23666 Tieck, Sarah. *Inclined Planes* (2–4). Series: Buddy Books: Simple Machines. 2006, ABDO $21.35 (978-1-59679-818-2). 32pp. A concise explanation of inclined planes and their importance, with illustrations that aid comprehension. (Rev: BL 10/15/06) [621.8]

23667 Walker, Sally M., and Roseann Feldmann. *Inclined Planes and Wedges* (2–4). Photos by Andy King. 2001, Lerner LB $25.26 (978-0-8225-2221-8). 47pp. A concise explanation of these simple machines, that increases in complexity as the reader progresses through the book, with simple experiments and clear illustrations. Also use *Pulleys* and *Wheels and Axles* (both 2001). (Rev: HBG 3/02; SLJ 2/02) [621.8]

23668 Walker, Sally M., and Roseann Feldmann. *Put Wheels and Axles to the Test* (3–5). Illus. Series: How Do Simple Machines Work? 2011, Lerner LB $27.93 (978-076135326-3). 40pp. With chapters titled "Work," "Machines," "Friction," "Parts of a Wheel and Axle," and "Gears," this book explains concepts and provides simple experiments. (Rev: BL 12/1/11) [621.8078]

23669 Welsbacher, Anne. *Wedges* (2–3). Illus. Series: Understanding Simple Machines. 2000, Capstone $22.60 (978-0-7368-0614-5). 24pp. This book introduces wedges, their parts, and how they are used in axes, knives, scissors, doorstops, and zippers. (Rev: BL 12/1/00; HBG 3/01; SLJ 12/00) [621.8]

23670 Yasuda, Anita. *Explore Simple Machines! 25 Great Projects, Activities, Experiments* (2–4). Illus. by Bryan Stone. Series: Explore Your World. 2011, Nomad paper $12.95 (978-19363138-2-2). 96pp. Levers, inclined planes, pulleys, screws, wedges, and wheels and axles are introduced and then demonstrated in kid-friendly projects (a crane, a drawbridge, a whirligig, and so forth). (Rev: BL 12/1/11) [621.8]

Sound

23671 Cobb, Vicki. *Bangs and Twangs: Science Fun with Sound* (3–6). Illus. 2000, Millbrook LB $24.90 (978-0-7613-1571-1). 48pp. Using a cartoon format, this lively activity book explores different aspects of sound including pitch and the physiology of hearing. (Rev: BCCB 11/00; BL 10/15/00; HBG 3/01; SLJ 3/01) [534.078]

23672 Farndon, John. *Sound and Hearing* (3–6). Series: Science Experiments. 2000, Marshall Cavendish LB $25.64 (978-0-7614-1091-1). 32pp. The properties of sound and the process of hearing are explored with a series of experiments to illustrate different concepts and applications. (Rev: BL 3/15/01; HBG 3/01) [534]

23673 Morgan, Sally, and Adrian Morgan. *Using Sound* (4–7). Series: Designs in Science. 1994, Facts on File $23.00 (978-0-8160-2981-5). The properties of sound and their relation to everyday life are covered in the text

and a number of experiments using readily available materials. (Rev: BL 7/94) [534]

23674 Parker, Steve. *The Science of Sound: Projects and Experiments with Music and Sound Waves* (4–7). Series: Tabletop Scientist. 2005, Heinemann LB $29.29 (978-1-4034-7281-6). The 12 experiments and projects in this collection demonstrate the basic scientific principles of sound waves. (Rev: SLJ 12/05)

23675 Trumbauer, Lisa. *All About Sound* (PS–1). Series: Rookie Read-About Science. 2004, Scholastic LB $4.95 (978-0-516-25847-8). 31pp. Simple text and color photographs introduce beginning readers to the basic characteristics of sound. (Rev: BL 9/1/04) [534]

23676 Wright, Lynne. *The Science of Noise* (5–8). Series: Science World. 2000, Raintree LB $25.69 (978-0-7398-1324-9). This account describes how sound is produced, how it travels, how we hear it, and how it can be changed. (Rev: BL 9/1/00; HBG 10/00; SLJ 8/00) [534]

Space Exploration

23677 Aldrin, Buzz. *Look to the Stars* (1–3). Illus. by Wendell Minor. 2009, Putnam $17.99 (978-0-399-24721-7). 40pp. The *Apollo 11* astronaut presents an interesting overview of aviation and space flight from early theories of Newton and Galileo through the developments by such figures as the Wright brothers and Robert Goddard to concepts for colonies on Mars. (Rev: BL 12/1/08; HB 5/09; SLJ 4/09) [629.409]

23678 *The Amazing International Space Station* (4–6). Illus. by Rose Cowles. 2003, Kids Can $15.95 (978-1-55337-380-3); paper $8.95 (978-1-55337-523-4). An appealing, highly visual and information-packed look at life aboard the International Space Station. (Rev: HBG 4/04; SLJ 4/04) [629.44]

23679 Angliss, Sarah. *Cosmic Journeys: A Beginner's Guide to Space and Time Travel* (5–7). Illus. by Alex Pang, et al. Series: Future Files. 1998, Millbrook LB $23.90 (978-0-7613-0620-7). This book explores such topics as traveling to other solar systems, time travel, black holes, and parallel universes. (Rev: HBG 10/98; SLJ 10/98) [629.4]

23680 Barter, James. *Space Stations* (5–8). Series: Lucent Library of Science and Technology. 2005, Gale LB $29.95 (978-1-59018-106-5). Explores the space stations that have been used for many years as medical laboratories and platforms for space study. (Rev: BL 1/05)

23681 Baxter, Roberta. *The Challenger Explosion* (4–7). Illus. 2013, ABDO LB $32.79 (978-161783954-2). 48pp. Baxter describes the general hazards of traveling in space before discussing what caused the Challenger explosion in 1986, using photographs, timelines, charts, diagrams, and maps to explain how this disaster occurred. (Rev: BL 10/1/13) [363.12]

23682 Berger, Melvin, and Gilda Berger. *Can You Hear a Shout in Space? Questions and Answers About Space Exploration* (3–6). Illus. 2001, Scholastic $14.95 (978-0-439-09582-2); paper $5.95 (978-0-439-14879-5). 48pp. In question-and-answer format, this title tackles

topics of interest both to browsers and report writers. (Rev: BL 7/01; HBG 10/01) [629.4]

23683 Beyer, Mark. *Crisis in Space: Apollo 13* (3–4). Illus. Series: Survivor. 2002, Children's Book Pr. LB $24.50 (978-0-516-23903-3). 48pp. A suspenseful account of the problems encountered on the *Apollo 13* mission and the dangers the astronauts faced. (Rev: SLJ 6/02) [629.45]

23684 Bortz, Fred. *Seven Wonders of Space Technology* (5–8). Illus. 2011, Lerner LB $33.26 (978-076135453-6). 80pp. Observatories, satellites, the International Space Station, and the Mars Rovers are among the pieces of space technology covered in this volume that also looks at the future. (Rev: BL 3/1/11) [629.4]

23685 Bredeson, Carmen. *John Glenn Returns to Orbit: Life on the Space Shuttle* (4–7). Series: Countdown to Space. 2000, Enslow LB $23.93 (978-0-7660-1304-9). 48pp. This is the story of John Glenn, now a famous politician, his return to space, and the different conditions he encountered. (Rev: BL 8/00; HBG 10/00) [629.4]

23686 Bredeson, Carmen. *NASA Planetary Spacecraft: Galileo, Magellan, Pathfinder, and Voyager* (4–7). Series: Countdown to Space. 2000, Enslow LB $23.93 (978-0-7660-1303-2). 48pp. This gives a good rundown on the NASA spacecraft used to explore planets, their individual missions, and their findings. (Rev: BL 9/15/00; HBG 10/01) [629.4]

23687 Britton, Tamara. *NASA* (3–5). Series: Symbols, Landmarks, and Monuments. 2005, ABDO LB $22.78 (978-1-59197-836-7). 32pp. American space exploration and the key role of the National Aeronautics and Space Administration are the focus of this informative book that includes photographs and graphics. (Rev: SLJ 9/05) [354.79]

23688 Burleigh, Robert. *One Giant Leap* (1–3). Illus. by Mike Wimmer. 2009, Philomel $16.99 (978-0-399-23883-3). 40pp. Using rich language and eye-catching illustrations, Burleigh describes the moon landing on

July 20, 1969; an author's note adds historical context. (Rev: BCCB 7–8/09; BL 12/1/08; SLJ 4/09) [629.45]

23689 Caper, William. *The Challenger Space Shuttle Explosion* (3–4). 2007, Bearport LB $23.96 (978-1-59716-367-5). 32pp. Part of the Code Red series, this book looks at the terrible shuttle accident of 1986, how it happened, and the effects that it had on the space program. (Rev: SLJ 8/07)

23690 Chaikin, Andrew, and Victoria Kohl. *Mission Control, This is Apollo: The Story of the First Voyages to the Moon* (5–8). Illus. by Alan Bean. 2009, Viking $23.99 (978-0-670-01156-8). 128pp. A compelling wide-format account of the Apollo program, with interesting anecdotes, informative sidebars, excellent photographs, and paintings by former astronaut Bean. (Rev: BL 5/1/09; HB 7/09*; SLJ 5/09; VOYA 6/09) [900]

23691 Cole, Michael D. *NASA Space Vehicles: Capsules, Shuttles, and Space Stations* (4–7). Series: Countdown to Space. 2000, Enslow LB $23.93 (978-0-7660-1308-7). 48pp. Gives a rundown on these specialized vehicles plus a description of space stations and how they operate, with full-color photographs and clear, readable text. (Rev: BL 5/15/00; HBG 10/00; SLJ 12/00) [629.4]

23692 Cole, Michael D. *Space Emergency: Astronauts in Danger* (4–8). Illus. Series: Countdown to Space. 2000, Enslow LB $23.93 (978-0-7660-1307-0). 48pp. An explosion on the command module of *Apollo 13* and a faulty landing bag on *Friendship 7* are two of the emergencies described in this book on crises in space exploration. (Rev: BL 2/1/00; HBG 10/00; SLJ 12/00) [629.45]

23693 Cole, Michael D. *Space Launch Disaster: When Liftoff Goes Wrong* (4–7). Series: Countdown to Space. 2000, Enslow LB $23.93 (978-0-7660-1309-4). 48pp. This is a rundown of problems that can occur during the liftoff of space vehicles, with examples of actual disasters, many caught on camera. (Rev: BL 3/15/00; HBG 10/00; SLJ 8/00) [629]

23694 Dyer, Alan. *Mission to the Moon* (5–7). 2009, Simon & Schuster $19.99 (978-1-4169-7935-7). 80pp. This well-organized package of clear narrative, color photographs, quotations, and DVD of video clips presents a good overview of the space race and the U.S. Apollo missions. (Rev: LMC 10/09; SLJ 4/09) [629.45]

23695 Dyson, Marianne J. *Home on the Moon: Living on a Space Frontier* (5–8). 2003, National Geographic $18.95 (978-0-7922-7193-2). Dyson, a former NASA mission controller, discusses the resources available on the moon, explores the possibilities of building facilities there, and suggests activities. (Rev: BL 7/03; HBG 10/03; SLJ 9/03) [919.91]

23696 Dyson, Marianne J. *Space Station Science: Life in Free Fall* (4–7). 1999, Scholastic paper $16.95 (978-0-590-05889-6). Written by a former member of a NASA control team, this work explores living and working in space including details on a space station bathroom. (Rev: BL 11/15/99; HBG 10/00; SLJ 12/99) [629.45]

23697 English, June A., and Thomas D. Jones. *Mission: Earth: Voyage to the Home Planet* (4–7). 1996, Scholastic paper $16.95 (978-0-590-48571-5). The space program is introduced, with special coverage of the flights of the shuttle *Endeavor* in 1994 and its environmental studies. (Rev: BL 10/15/96; SLJ 10/96) [550]

23698 Fallen, Anne-Catherine. *USA from Space* (4–7). 1997, Firefly LB $19.95 (978-1-55209-159-3); paper $7.95 (978-1-55209-157-9). Excellent satellite pictures of parts of the earth are contained in this book, which also explains the value of satellite imagery in tracking pollution, population, and natural disasters. (Rev: BL 3/1/98; SLJ 12/97) [917.3]

23699 Farbman, Melinda, and Frye Gaillard. *Spacechimp: NASA's Ape in Space* (4–7). Series: Countdown to Space. 2000, Enslow LB $23.93 (978-0-7660-1478-7). 48pp. The story of how animals in general have helped the space program and how one chimp's voyage into space contributed to progress. (Rev: BL 8/00; HBG 10/00) [629.4]

23700 Feldman, Heather. *Dennis Tito: The First Space Tourist* (2–3). Series: Space Firsts. 2003, Rosen LB $21.25 (978-0-8239-6249-5). 24pp. The true story of a 60-year-old man who paid a reported $20 million to spend a week aboard the International Space Station. (Rev: SLJ 3/04) [910]

23701 Feldman, Heather. *Skylab: The First American Space Station* (2–3). Series: Space Firsts. 2003, Rosen LB $21.25 (978-0-8239-6248-8). 24pp. An interesting look at Skylab and its significance in space exploration. (Rev: SLJ 3/04) [629.44]

23702 Feldman, Heather. *Sputnik: The First Satellite* (2–3). Series: Space Firsts. 2003, Rosen LB $21.25 (978-0-8239-6244-0). 24pp. An ideal choice for young readers with no memory of the race for space between the Soviet Union and the United States, this book profiles the Soviets' Sputnik 1, the first satellite to be launched into space by humans. (Rev: SLJ 11/03) [629.46]

23703 Gaffney, Timothy R. *Secret Spy Satellites: America's Eyes in Space* (4–7). Series: Countdown to Space. 2000, Enslow LB $23.93 (978-0-7660-1402-2). With sharp illustrations and a strong narrative, this book describes U.S. spy satellites, their purposes, and findings. (Rev: BL 9/15/00; HBG 10/01) [629.4]

23704 Gallant, Roy A. *Space Stations* (2–4). Illus. Series: Kaleidoscope. 2000, Marshall Cavendish LB $25.64 (978-0-7614-1035-5). 48pp. This account briefly covers, in text and color pictures, space stations *Salyut*, *Skylab*, and *Mir* with a little information on the International Space Station. (Rev: BL 1/1–15/01; HBG 10/01) [629.44]

23705 Goldsmith, Mike. *Space* (4–7). Series: Kingfisher Voyages. 2005, Kingfisher $14.95 (978-0-7534-5910-2). An appealing overview of space exploration, with concise text, good photographs, and a foreword and comments by astronaut Sally Ride. (Rev: BL 10/15/05) [629.45]

23706 Goodman, Susan E. *Ultimate Field Trip 5: Blasting Off to Space Academy* (3–5). Illus. Series: Ultimate Field Trip. 2001, Simon & Schuster $17.00 (978-0-689-83044-0). 48pp. This book follows 16 young people through a week-long training session at the U.S. Space Academy and includes the children's own comments and some space facts. (Rev: BL 5/1/01; HBG 10/01; SLJ 6/01) [629.45]

23707 Green, Carl R. *Apollo 11 Rockets to First Moon Landing: A MyReportLinks.com Book* (4–6). Illus. Series: Space Flight Adventures and Disasters. 2004, Enslow LB $25.26 (978-0-7660-5164-5). 48pp. Thorough chapter notes support this well-researched account of the dramatic story; Web links extend the book. Also use *The Gemini 4 Spacewalk Mission* (2004). (Rev: BL 10/1/04; SLJ 1/05) [029.45]

23708 Green, Carl R. *Spacewalk: The Astounding Gemini 4 Mission* (5–8). Illus. Series: American Space Missions: Astronauts, Exploration, and Discovery. 2012, Enslow LB $23.93 (978-0-7660-4075-5). 48pp. Tells the story of the first American to walk in space and the technology that made this possible. (Rev: BL 11/15/12; LMC 5–6/13; SLJ 12/12)

23709 Hilliard, Richard. *Ham the Astrochimp* (3–5). Illus. by author. 2007, Boyds Mills $16.95 (978-1-59078-459-4). Young readers will fascinated to learn that a chimpanzee was sent into space in 1961 as part of the Mercury space program. Illustrated by the author, who also wrote *Godspeed, John Glen, Neil, Buzz and Mike Go to the Moon*, and *Lucky 13: Survival in Space*. (Rev: LMC 11/07; SLJ 8/07)

23710 Holden, Henry M. *The Coolest Job in the Universe: Working Aboard the International Space Station* (5–8). Illus. Series: American Space Missions: Astronauts, Exploration, and Discovery. 2012, Enslow LB $23.93 (978-0-7660-4074-8). 48pp. The dangers and wonders of the International Space Station are explained in this review of how it was built, what life is like onboard, and the kinds of work performed there. (Rev: BL 11/15/12; LMC 5–6/13; SLJ 12/12) [629.44]

23711 Holden, Henry M. *Danger in Space: Surviving the Apollo 13 Disaster* (5–8). Illus. Series: American Space Missions: Astronauts, Exploration, and Discovery. 2012, Enslow LB $23.93 (978-0-7660-4072-4). 48pp. What went wrong? This straightforward volume lays out the mission and the problems that occurred. (Rev: BL 11/15/12; LMC 5–6/13; SLJ 12/12) [629.45]

23712 Holden, Henry M. *Living and Working Aboard the International Space Station: A MyReportLinks.com Book* (4–6). Series: Space Flight Adventures and Disasters. 2004, Enslow LB $25.26 (978-0-7660-5168-3). 48pp. This inside look at space station is supported by thorough chapter notes and extended by Web links. (Rev: BL 10/1/04; SLJ 2/05) [029.44]

23713 Holden, Henry M. *The Tragedy of the Space Shuttle Challenger* (4–8). Series: Space Flight Adventures and Disasters. 2004, Enslow LB $25.26 (978-0-7660-5165-2). An account of the ill-fated *Challenger* mission, backed up by a list of Web sites that provide additional information. (Rev: BL 10/1/04; SLJ 2/05) [629.5]

23714 Jemison, Mae, and Dana Meachen Rau. *The 100 Year Starship* (3–5). Illus. Series: True Book. 2013, Scholastic/Children's Press LB $29 (978-053125500-1); paper $6.95 (9780531240601). 48pp. The first woman of color in space is a coauthor of this book about the design of a starship and the challenges it and its passengers will face. (Rev: BL 4/1/13; LMC 11–12/13; SLJ 4/13) [629.45]

23715 Johnson, Rebecca. *Satellites* (4–6). Illus. Series: Cool Science. 2005, Lerner LB $26.60 (978-0-8225-2908-8). 48pp. With many interesting examples and an attractive layout, this introduction explores the history and science of the artificial satellites that orbit the earth and gather all sorts of data. (Rev: SLJ 12/05) [629.46]

23716 Kerrod, Robin. *Dawn of the Space Age* (5–7). Series: The History of Space Exploration. 2005, World Almanac LB $31.00 (978-0-8368-5705-4). A well-illustrated history of space exploration, from the ideas of Cyrano de Bergerac to the modern Mars probes. Also recommended in this series are *Space Probes*, *Space Shuttles*, and *Space Stations* (all 2004). (Rev: SLJ 3/05) [629.4]

23717 Kupperberg, Paul. *Spy Satellites* (4–8). Series: Library of Satellites. 2003, Rosen LB $26.50 (978-0-8239-3854-4). The author discusses the history of U.S. spy satellites and how the country has used the information they have gleaned. (Rev: BL 5/15/03; SLJ 1/04) [327.1273]

23718 McCarthy, Meghan. *Astronaut Handbook* (K–3). Illus. by author. 2008, Knopf $16.99 (978-0-375-84459-1). 40pp. Aspiring astronauts will enjoy this lighthearted introduction to the training required before taking off for space. (Rev: BCCB 7–8/08; BL 6/1–15/08; HB 7/08; LMC 8/08; SLJ 7/08) [629.45]

23719 Markle, Sandra. *Pioneering Space* (5–8). 1992, Atheneum LB $14.95 (978-0-689-31748-4). A look at space travel and how people may succeed in living in space. (Rev: BL 9/1/92; SLJ 2/93) [629.4]

23720 Mason, Paul. *Space Race* (3–5). Series: Space Busters. 2002, Raintree LB $25.69 (978-0-7398-4851-7). 32pp. The Apollo Program is the major focus of this look at efforts to win the space competition. (Rev: HBG 10/02; SLJ 4/02) [629.45]

23721 Murphy, Patricia J. *Exploring Space with an Astronaut* (1–3). Series: I Like Science! 2004, Enslow LB $21.26 (978-0-7660-2268-3). 24pp. In addition to a discussion of life in space, this title introduces readers to an astronaut and offers a night sky activity. (Rev: SLJ 2/05) [629.5]

23722 Nardo, Don. *Destined for Space: Our Story of Exploration* (3–5). Illus. 2012, Capstone LB $31.86 (978-142967540-6); paper $8.95 (978-142968024-0). 64pp. The history of space exploration is narrated in simple text accompanied by bright illustrations. (Rev: BLO 2/27/12) [629.45]

23723 Nicolson, Cynthia P. *Exploring Space* (3–5). Illus. Series: Starting with Space. 2000, Kids Can $12.95 (978-1-55074-711-9). 40pp. A basic book that covers the huge topic of space exploration in a clear, well-organized way. (Rev: BL 12/1/00; HBG 10/01) [629.4]

23724 O'Brien, Patrick. *You Are the First Kid on Mars* (K–3). Illus. by author. 2009, Putnam $16.99 (978-0-399-24634-0). 32pp. This compelling, well-illustrated imagining of a trip to Mars conveys lots of information about science and space travel. (Rev: BL 5/1/09; SLJ 7/09) [919.9]

23725 Platt, Richard. *Moon Landing: A Pop-Up Celebration of Apollo 11* (3–5). Illus. by David Hawcock. 2008, Candlewick $29.99 (978-0-7636-4046-0). 10pp. Pop-ups of a rocket, a lunar module, a spaceship, and the moon are bolstered by many fold-out flaps and pull-out minibooks that present lots of information about the Apollo program. (Rev: BLO 12/16/08; SLJ 1/09) [629.45]

23726 Rusch, Elizabeth. *The Mighty Mars Rovers: The Incredible Adventures of Spirit and Opportunity* (5–8). Illus. Series: Scientists in the Field. 2012, Houghton Mifflin $18.99 (978-0-547-47881-4). 80pp. With profiles of the scientists involved, and of the rovers *Spirit* and *Opportunity*, and their joint achievements, this is an effective and informative celebration of NASA's efforts on Mars. (Rev: BL 6/12*; HB 9–10/12*; LMC 1–2/13; SLJ 7/12*) [523.43]

23727 Schyffert, Bea Uusma. *Man Who Went to the Far Side of the Moon* (3–6). 2003, Chronicle $14.95 (978-0-8118-4007-1). 80pp. With scrapbook-style illustrations and fascinating details, this story of astronaut Michael Collins, who circled the moon while fellow astronauts Neil Armstrong and Buzz Aldrin walked on its surface, is full of tension and suspense. (Rev: BL 11/1/03; HBG 4/04; SLJ 10/03)

23728 Sherman, Josepha. *Deep Space Observation Satellites* (4–8). Illus. Series: Library of Satellites. 2003, Rosen LB $26.50 (978-0-8239-3852-0). 64pp. The author discusses the history of U.S. observation satellites and how the country has benefited from their discoveries. (Rev: BL 5/15/03) [522]

23729 Siy, Alexandra. *Cars on Mars: Roving the Red Planet* (5–8). Illus. by author. 2009, Charlesbridge $18.95 (978-1-57091-462-1). The fascinating story of the Mars rovers built to last for three months but still exploring the Martian terrain more than five years later. (Rev: BL 8/09*; LMC 11/09; SLJ 7/09) [919.9]

23730 Stone, Jerry. *One Small Step: Celebrating the First Men on the Moon* (4–8). 2009, Roaring Brook $24.95 (978-1-59643-491-2). This "scrapbook" offers a wealth of perspectives on the first moon landing. (Rev: SLJ 6/09)

23731 Sullivan, George. *The Day We Walked on the Moon: A Photo History of Space Exploration* (5–8). 1990, Scholastic paper $4.95 (978-0-685-58532-0). The history of U.S. space exploration, showing the accomplishments of both the United States and the Soviet Union. (Rev: BL 9/1/90; SLJ 2/91) [629.4]

23732 Thimmesh, Catherine. *Team Moon: How 400,000 People Landed Apollo 11 on the Moon* (5–10). 2006, Houghton Mifflin $19.95 (978-0-618-50757-3). A breathless account of all the behind-the-scenes work that went into the Apollo space program, with plenty of photographs. Sibert Medal 2007. (Rev: SLJ 6/06) [629.45]

23733 Vogt, Gregory L. *Apollo Moonwalks: The Amazing Lunar Missions* (4–7). Series: Countdown to Space. 2000, Enslow LB $23.93 (978-0-7660-1306-3). 48pp. This account focuses on the moonwalks during the *Apollo 11* expedition and details what was found. (Rev: BL 8/00; HBG 10/00) [629.4]

23734 Vogt, Gregory L. *Disasters in Space Exploration. Rev. ed.* (5–8). 2003, Millbrook LB $25.90 (978-0-7613-2895-7). 79pp. An illustrated survey of serious accidents that have befallen the U.S. and Russian space programs, what caused them, and what was learned from them. This revised edition includes the *Columbia* space shuttle disaster of February 2003. (Rev: SLJ 3/04) [363.12]

23735 Vogt, Gregory L. *Spacewalks: The Ultimate Adventures in Orbit* (4–7). Series: Countdown to Space. 2000, Enslow LB $23.93 (978-0-7660-1305-6). This gives a history of spacewalks, tells who were the pioneers, and explains their purpose. (Rev: BL 8/00; HBG 10/00) [629.4]

23736 Whitehouse, Patricia. *Space Travel* (2–4). Illus. Series: Space Explorer. 2004, Heinemann LB $24.21 (978-1-4034-5155-2). 32pp. A brief introduction to space travel, with lots of photographs, short paragraphs, and large type. (Rev: BL 1/1–15/05; SLJ 2/05) [910]

23737 Whitehouse, Patricia. *Working in Space* (1–3). Illus. Series: Space Explorer. 2004, Heinemann LB $24.21 (978-1-4034-5158-3); paper $6.95 (978-1-4034-5662-5). 32pp. For young readers, this is a colorful introduction to the kind of work carried out in space. Companion books are *Space Equipment* and *Living in Space* (both 2004). (Rev: SLJ 2/05) [629]

23738 Woodford, Chris. *Space Dramas* (3–5). Illus. Series: Space Busters. 2002, Raintree LB $25.69 (978-0-7398-4850-0). 32pp. Natural space events such as comet collisions are described along with disasters that have hit manned and unmanned missions outside our atmosphere. (Rev: HBG 10/02; SLJ 4/02) [629.45]

Technology, Engineering, and Industry

General and Miscellaneous Industries and Inventions

23739 Allman, Toney. *From Fish Gills to Underwater Breathing* (4–6). Series: Imitating Nature. 2006, Gale LB $22.45 (978-0-7377-3608-3). 32pp. All about an inventor's attempts to design a diving vest that would mimic fish gills. Part of an interesting series that helps readers to see the practical applications of scientific principles that also includes *From Octopus Eyes to Powerful Lenses* (2006). (Rev: SLJ 5/07)

23740 Arato, Rona. *Design It! The Ordinary Things We Use Every Day and the Not-So-Ordinary Ways They Came to Be* (4–6). Illus. by Claudia Newell. 2010, Tundra paper $20.95 (978-0-88776-846-0). 72pp. The inspiration and design behind many commonly used and taken-for-granted objects are explored in this well-organized volume that asks readers to consider function, usability, ergonomics, aesthetics and environmental impact of objects. (Rev: LMC 3–4/11; SLJ 1/1/11) [745.2]

23741 Baker, Christopher W. *A New World of Simulators: Training with Technology* (5–8). Illus. 2001, Millbrook LB $23.90 (978-0-7613-1352-6). 48pp. An introduction to the uses of simulators and their importance in training workers who operate complex technologies such as those found in airplanes, ships, and nuclear power plants. (Rev: BL 8/01; HBG 3/02; SLJ 8/01) [003]

23742 Becker, Helaine. *What's the Big Idea: Inventions That Changed Life on Earth* (3–6). Illus. by Steve Attoe. 2009, Maple Tree $29.95 (978-189734960-1); paper $19.95 (978-18973496-1-8). 96pp. This appealing, conversational book looks at inventions throughout history that met various human needs, looking in particular at design and at high-interest facts; suitable for browsing. (Rev: BL 2/1/10; LMC 3–4/10) [609]

23743 Bodden, Valerie. *Carousels* (K–3). Illus. Series: Thrill Rides. 2012, Creative Education $17.95 (978-

160818112-4). 24pp. A history of merry-go-rounds, with beautiful photographs and emphasis on the fact that even the smallest children are allowed aboard. (Rev: BL 4/1/12) [791.06]

23744 Boothroyd, Jennifer. *From Marbles to Video Games: How Toys Have Changed* (K–3). Illus. Series: Comparing Past and Present. 2011, Lerner LB $25.26 (978-076136746-8); paper $7.95 (978-076137841-9). 32pp. Charting the evolution of toys from jacks to Pokémon, this book provides readers with many thought-provoking comparisons as it examines changes in materials, marketing, and habits. (Rev: BL 10/1/11) [790.1]

23745 *CDs, Super Glue, and Salsa Series 2: How Everyday Products Are Made* (5–10). 1996, Gale LB $126.00 (978-0-7876-0870-5). This two-volume set tells how 30 everyday products are made, including air bags, bungee cords, contact lenses, ketchup, pencils, soda bottles, and umbrellas. (Rev: SLJ 8/97) [658.5]

23746 Cobb, Vicki. *Fireworks* (4–8). Photos by Michael Gold. Series: Where's the Science Here? 2005, Lerner LB $23.93 (978-0-7613-2771-4). A well-illustrated, engaging text covers the history and science of pyrotechnics; experiments require adult supervision. Also recommended in this series are *Junk Food* and *Sneakers* (both 2005). (Rev: SLJ 2/06)

23747 Collicutt, Paul. *This Rocket* (PS–2). Illus. 2005, Farrar $16.00 (978-0-374-37484-6). 32pp. A colorful overview of rockets and spacecraft ranging from Fourth of July fireworks to the space shuttle. (Rev: BL 12/1/05; SLJ 9/05) [621.43]

23748 Colman, Penny. *Toilets, Bathtubs, Sinks, and Sewers: A History of the Bathroom* (5–8). 1994, Atheneum $16.00 (978-0-689-31894-8). A fascinating look at sanitation systems and inventions related to personal hygiene from ancient times to the present. (Rev: BCCB 2/95; BL 1/1/95; SLJ 3/95) [643]

23749 Cooper, Elisha. *Ice Cream* (1–3). Illus. 2002, HarperCollins LB $15.89 (978-0-06-001424-7). 40pp. An entertaining look at the production of ice cream, tracing its way from cow to consumer. (Rev: BL 5/15/02; HB 5/02; HBG 10/02; SLJ 5/02) [637.4]

23750 Crump, Donald J., ed. *How Things Work* (5–7). 1984, National Geographic LB $12.50 (978-0-87044-430-2). A handsome volume that explains the mechanics of a variety of objects from toasters to space shuttles. [600]

23751 Ditchfield, Christin. *Wood* (2–5). Series: True Books — Natural Resources. 2002, Children's Book Pr. LB $25.00 (978-0-516-22346-9). 48pp. This simple account shows the importance of wood in such industries as building and paper-making, and tells how we can protect this resouce from forest fires and pollution. (Rev: BL 10/15/02) [674]

23752 Englart, Mindi Rose. *Pens* (3–5). Series: Made in the USA. 2002, Gale LB $23.70 (978-1-56711-487-4). 32pp. The evolution of writing pens is described along with a detailed view of how they are made today. (Rev: BL 9/15/02) [681]

23753 *Fantastic Feats and Failures* (4–8). Illus. by Jane Kurisu. 2004, Kids Can paper $9.95 (978-1-55337-634-7). Highs and lows of engineering (the Brooklyn Bridge in the first category, for example, and the Tacoma Narrows in the latter) are reviewed in this fascinating large-format book. (Rev: BL 9/15/04) [624.1]

23754 Feigenbaum, Aaron. *Emergency at Three Mile Island* (3–6). Series: Code Red. 2007, Bearport LB $23.96 (978-1-59716-364-4). 32pp. Part of a series on the causes and costs of disasters, this book discusses the accident at this nuclear power plant and how it could have been much more serious. (Rev: SLJ 7/07)

23755 Gates, Phil. *Nature Got There First: Inventions Inspired by Nature* (3–6). Illus. 2010, Kingfisher $16.99 (978-075346410-6). 64pp. Gates explores similarities between nature and technology in this attractive volume suitable for browsing. (Rev: BL 9/1/10; LMC 11–12/10) [508]

23756 Goldberg, Jan. *Earth Imaging Satellites* (5–9). Series: The Library of Satellites. 2003, Rosen LB $26.50 (978-0-8239-3853-7). A survey of the various satellites and how their images of the earth's surface measure pollution, locate forest fires, find earthquake faults, and measure the size of polar caps. (Rev: BL 11/15/03) [629.46]

23757 Graham, Ian. *Machines and Inventions* (1–4). Illus. by David Antram, et al. Series: World of Wonder. 2008, Children's Pr. LB $29.00 (978-0-531-24027-4); paper $9.95 (978-0-531-23823-3). 32pp. Answering such questions as "How Do People Keep Clean," this book looks at devices that make our lives easier and includes acetate overlays with cutaway details. (Rev: SLJ 3/09)

23758 Harper, Charise Mericle. *Imaginative Inventions* (2–4). Illus. 2001, Little, Brown $14.95 (978-0-316-34725-9). 32pp. An imaginative look at the origins of products ranging from chewing gum and doughnuts to roller skates and high-heeled shoes. (Rev: BL 12/15/01; HBG 3/02; SLJ 10/01) [609]

23759 Kassinger, Ruth G. *Iron and Steel: From Thor's Hammer to the Space Shuttle* (5–7). Series: Material World. 2003, Millbrook LB $25.90 (978-0-7613-2111-8). The different ways in which humans have used and processed iron and steel through the ages is the focus of this book. (Rev: BL 5/15/03; HBG 10/03; SLJ 1/04) [669]

23760 Kent, Peter. *Technology* (4–7). Illus. Series: Navigators. 2009, Kingfisher $12.99 (978-075346307-9). 48pp. For browsers and those interested in learning about exciting technologies — everything from new developments in computers and electronics to nanotechnology, wave farming, and superstructures, this is a well-designed informative volume. (Rev: BLO 11/1/09; LMC 1–2/10) [500]

23761 Kerrod, Robin. *New Materials: Present Knowledge, Future Trends* (5–9). Illus. Series: 21st Century Science. 2003, Smart Apple LB $27.10 (978-1-58340-353-2). 44pp. Numerous diagrams, photographs, and drawings help to explain the processing of raw materials and the need to conserve our limited resources. (Rev: SLJ 1/04) [620.11]

23762 Koscielniak, Bruce. *Looking at Glass Through the Ages* (3–6). Illus. by author. 2006, Houghton $16.00 (978-0-618-50750-4). From the earliest faience of ancient Egypt to today's optical fiber, this is a fascinating review of glassmaking, covering everything from magnifying lenses to stained glass, lead crystal, and neon tubes. (Rev: SLJ 8/06) [666]

23763 Landau, Elaine. *The History of Everyday Life* (5–8). Series: Major Inventions Through History. 2005, Twenty-First Century LB $26.60 (978-0-8225-3808-0). Fireplaces, washing machines, and microwave ovens are among the inventions discussed here that have improved our everyday lives. (Rev: SLJ 2/06)

23764 Lee, Dora. *Biomimicry: Inventions Inspired by Nature* (3–6). Illus. by Margot Thompson. 2011, Kids Can $18.95 (978-1-55453-467-8). 40pp. A fascinating, large-format and well-illustrated survey of facets of nature that have inspired human inventions and may do so in the future, organized in such chapters as "Medical Marvels" and "Magic Materials"; suitable for browsing. (Rev: BL 9/15/11; SLJ 11/1/11) [608]

23765 Llewellyn, Claire. *Paper* (2–4). Series: Material World. 2002, Watts LB $24.00 (978-0-531-14629-3). 30pp. A well-illustrated look at paper and the ways it is used; with "Fast Facts," related activities, and a glossary. (Rev: SLJ 5/03) [620.1]

23766 Lockie, Mark. *Biometric Technology* (5–8). Series: Science at the Edge. 2002, Heinemann LB $27.86 (978-1-58810-701-5). 64pp. Lockie explores the study of biometry and its applications in such areas as voice-speaker identification and facial recognition. (Rev: BL 10/15/02; HBG 3/03) [609]

23767 Macaulay, David, and Sheila Keenan. *Toilet: How It Works* (K–3). Illus. by David Macaulay. 2013, Roaring Brook $15.99 (978-159643779-1); paper $3.99 (978-15964378-0-7). 32pp. Macaulay's ink and watercolor illustrations provide cutaways, details, and designs of toilets, sewer systems, septic tanks, and wastewater treatment plants in this exploration of why humans have waste, but also how it works and where it all goes. (Rev: BL 9/1/13; SLJ 10/13*) [696]

23768 *Machines and Inventions* (5–9). Series: Understanding Science and Nature. 1993, Time-Life $17.95 (978-0-8094-9704-1). Using a question-and-answer format, double-page spreads look at a variety of inventions including the box camera, printing press, and dynamite. (Rev: BL 1/15/94; SLJ 6/94) [621.8]

23769 Mara, Wil. *From Locusts to . . . Automobile Anti-Collision Systems* (4–7). Illus. Series: 21st Century Skills Innovation Library: Innovations from Nature. 2012, Cherry Lake LB $28.50 (978-161080501-8). 32pp. An interesting exploration of how the science of biomimicry can be put to practical application, in this case in the design of collision avoidance systems based on locusts' swarming strategies. (Rev: BL 10/1/12; SLJ 11/12) [629.2]

23770 Nelson, Robin. *From Wax to Crayon* (1–3). Series: Start to Finish. 2003, Lerner LB $18.60 (978-0-8225-4660-3). 24pp. Traces the creation of a crayon, full-page color photographs. (Rev: HBG 10/03; SLJ 8/03) [741.2]

23771 Nobleman, Marc Tyler. *The Telephone* (2–4). Series: Fact Finders: Great Inventions. 2003, Capstone LB $23.93 (978-0-7368-2218-3). 32pp. A simple and attractive introduction to the invention of the telephone, how it works, and the effect it has had on society, ending with instructions for making a phone with cups and string. (Rev: SLJ 6/04) [621.385]

23772 Nomad Press . *Nylon* (K–1). Illus. Series: Investigate Materials. 2012, Nomad $16.95 (978-193631397-6). 24pp. A clean, spare layout and bright photographs add appeal to this exploration of where nylon comes from and how it's used. (Rev: BL 4/1/12)

23773 Oxlade, Chris. *Glass* (2–3). Series: Materials, Materials, Materials. 2001, Heinemann LB $21.36 (978-1-58810-154-9). 32pp. Though in a compact format, this book contains lots of information about how glass is manufactured, its history, forms, and uses. (Rev: BL 10/15/01) [666]

23774 Oxlade, Chris. *Paper* (2–3). Series: Materials, Materials, Materials. 2001, Heinemann LB $21.36 (978-1-58810-156-3). 32pp. An attractive, introductory look at paper, how it is produced, its uses, and its recycling and conservation. (Rev: BL 10/15/01) [676]

23775 Oxlade, Chris. *Plastic* (2–3). Series: Materials, Materials, Materials. 2001, Heinemann LB $21.36 (978-1-58810-157-0). 32pp. Using a compact format with a color illustration and text on each page, this introductory work explains what plastics are, how they are made, their uses, and their role in conservation. (Rev: BL 10/15/01) [547.7]

23776 Oxlade, Chris. *Rubber* (2–3). Series: Materials, Materials, Materials. 2002, Heinemann LB $22.79 (978-1-58810-586-8). 32pp. This book provides a simple, clear introduction to rubber, its properties, where

it comes from, and its uses in everyday life. (Rev: BL 6/1–15/02) [633.8]

23777 Oxlade, Chris. *Wood* (2–3). Illus. Series: Materials, Materials, Materials. 2001, Heinemann LB $21.36 (978-1-58810-158-7). 32pp. A discussion of where wood comes from and how it is made into products we use, with photographs. (Rev: BL 10/15/01) [674]

23778 Packard, Mary. *High-Tech Inventions: A Chapter Book* (3–7). Series: True Tales. 2004, Children's Pr. LB $22.50 (978-0-516-23728-2). 48pp. A clear and attractive look at the history of computers and at new and future developments, such as a cockroach that might be used for search-and-rescue operations. (Rev: SLJ 2/05) [004]

23779 Rau, Dana Meachen. *Fireworks* (2–4). Illus. Series: Surprising Science. 2010, Marshall Cavendish LB $20.95 (978-076144868-6). 24pp. Discusses the history of fireworks and how they are made, and includes safety information. (Rev: BL 4/1/11; LMC 8–9/11) [662]

23780 Raum, Elizabeth. *The Story Behind Toilets* (2–4). Illus. Series: True Stories. 2009, Raintree LB $19.75 (978-1-4329-2350-1). 32pp. A fascinating look at the history of toilets — with a great timeline — and contemporary debates about pay toilets, waste treatment, and sanitation in general. (Rev: BL 4/1/09; SLJ 10/09) [696]

23781 Rocker, Megan. *How It Happens at the Fireworks Factory* (K–3). Illus. Series: How It Happens. 2005, Oliver $19.95 (978-1-881508-97-7). 32pp. An inside look at the operation of a factory. Also use *How It Happens at the Cereal Company* (2005

23782 Romanek, Trudee. *Switched On, Flushed Down, Tossed Out: Investigating the Hidden Workings of Your Home* (3–5). Illus. by Stephen MacEachern. 2005, Annick paper $12.95 (978-1-55037-902-0). 48pp. Casey, who has a vivid imagination, is curious about the workings of all kinds of household features — plumbing, electricity, thermostats, phones — and his funny theories are balanced by clear explanations of the real thing. (Rev: BL 7/05; SLJ 12/05) [643]

23783 Romanek, Trudee, and Pat Cupples. *The Technology Book for Girls: And Other Advanced Beings* (3–6). 2001, Kids Can $14.95 (978-1-55074-936-6); paper $8.95 (978-1-55074-619-8). 56pp. The workings of a variety of everyday items — remote controls, smoke detectors, lasers, and so forth — are detailed in this lighthearted book that also profiles women with science-based careers. (Rev: HBG 10/01; SLJ 6/01) [604.83]

23784 Roslund, Samantha, and Kristin Fontichiaro. *Maker Faire* (4–7). Illus. Series: Makers as Innovators. 2013, Cherry Lake LB $28.50 (978-162431136-9); paper $14.21 (9781624312687). 32pp. A look at Maker Faires and the opportunities they offer for learning and for displaying technological innovations. **e** (Rev: BL 11/1/13; LMC 5–6/14; SLJ 3/14) [607]

23785 St. George, Judith. *So You Want to Be an Inventor?* (3–5). Illus. by David Small. 2002, Penguin $16.99 (978-0-399-23593-1). 56pp. A spirited and informative look at inventors and their inventions with eye-catching and amusing illustrations. (Rev: BCCB 10/02; BL 8/02; HB 9/02; HBG 3/03; SLJ 9/02) [608]

23786 Scott, Elaine. *Buried Alive! How 33 Miners Survived 69 Days Deep under the Chilean Desert* (4–7). Illus. 2012, Clarion $17.99 (978-054770778-5). 80pp. Scott recounts the experiences of the miners trapped deep beneath the ground in 2010, the ways in which they collaborated, the rescue efforts, and the intense media coverage. Lexile 1060L (Rev: BL 5/1/12; LMC 11–12/12; SLJ 5/1/12) [363.11]

23787 Skurzynski, Gloria. *Almost the Real Things: Simulation in Your High Tech World* (5–8). 1991, Macmillan LB $16.95 (978-0-02-778072-7). Skurzynski explains how engineers and scientists simulate events from weightlessness to complex animation. (Rev: BCCB 10/91; BL 10/15/91; HB 11–12/91; SLJ 10/91) [620]

23788 Slavin, Bill. *Transformed: How Everyday Things Are Made* (4–7). 2005, Kids Can $24.95 (978-1-55337-179-3). A behind-the-scenes look at the manufacturing process for a wide array of everyday products. (Rev: BL 10/15/05; SLJ 1/06) [670]

23789 Smith, Elizabeth Simpson. *Paper* (4–8). 1984, Walker LB $10.85 (978-0-8027-6569-7). An exploration of the manufacture and use of paper.

23790 Smith, Ryan A. *Trading Cards: From Start to Finish* (3–5). Illus. Series: Made in the U.S.A. 2005, Gale LB $23.70 (978-1-4103-0374-5). 48pp. A behind-the-scenes glimpse at how trading cards are manufactured and distributed. (Rev: BL 9/15/05) [976]

23791 Taylor, Barbara. *Be an Inventor* (5–9). 1987, Harcourt $11.95 (978-0-15-205950-7); paper $7.95 (978-0-15-205951-4). A discussion of the process of invention and some examples plus coverage of entries in a *Weekly Reader* invention contest. (Rev: BL 12/15/87; SLJ 3/88) [608]

23792 Taylor, Barbara. *I Wonder Why Zippers Have Teeth and Other Questions about Inventions* (K–3). Illus. 2012, Kingfisher paper $6.99 (978-07534680-1-2). 32pp. "Why were Band-Aids invented?," "Who first flushed the toilet?," "Who invented raincoats?" — these and other important questions about inventions are answered in this wide-ranging volume. (Rev: BL 12/1/12) [608]

23793 Thimmesh, Catherine. *Girls Think of Everything* (4–7). 2000, Houghton Mifflin $16.00 (978-0-395-93744-0). A fresh, breezy account about women whose inventions include the windshield wiper, chocolate chip cookies, and Glo-paper. (Rev: BCCB 5/00; BL 3/15/00; HB 5–6/00; HBG 10/00; SLJ 4/00) [609.2]

23794 Tomecek, Steve. *What a Great Idea! Inventions That Changed the World* (3–6). Illus. by Dan Stuckenschneider. 2003, Scholastic $18.95 (978-0-590-68144-5). 128pp. This attractively illustrated chronology — divided into five time periods — identifies the major inventions of human civilization from the hand axe and wheel to the airplane and computer. (Rev: BL 4/1/03; HBG 10/03; SLJ 4/03) [609]

23795 Whiting, Jim. *James Watt and the Steam Engine* (5–8). Series: Uncharted, Unexplored, and Unexplained: Scientific Advancements of the 19th Century. 2006, Mitchell Lane LB $29.95 (978-1-58415-371-9). Brief biographical information about Watt is accompanied by a more detailed discussion of his invention and its importance. (Rev: SLJ 5/06) [621]

23796 Williams, Marcia. *Hooray for Inventors!* (3–5). Illus. 2005, Candlewick $16.99 (978-0-7636-2760-7). 40pp. This attractive large-format book tells the stories behind some of the world's most notable inventions and their creators, pairing a lighthearted text full of asides and snippets of dialogue. (Rev: BL 12/1/05; SLJ 12/05) [609.2]

23797 Woodford, Chris, and Jon Woodcock. *Cool Stuff 2.0 and How It Works* (4–8). Illus. by Darren Awuah, et al. 2007, DK $24.99 (978-0-7566-3207-6). More than 100 new "cool" items are featured in this updated edition full of things that appeal to kids, such as robot cars and "silent flight" aircraft. (Rev: SLJ 3/08)

23798 Woods, Michael, and Mary B. Woods. *The History of Communication* (5–8). Series: Major Inventions Through History. 2005, Twenty-First Century LB $26.60 (978-0-8225-3807-3). An attractive look at developments through time in methods of communication — the printing press, telephone, radio, television, and the Internet — and the impact on our lives. (Rev: SLJ 1/06) [302.2]

23799 Woods, Samuel. *Recycled Paper* (3–5). Series: Made in the USA. 2000, Blackbirch LB $24.94 (978-1-56711-395-2). 32pp. The process of recycling paper is covered from the collection of old paper to the production of new paper. (Rev: BL 12/15/00; HBG 3/01; SLJ 12/00) [686.2]

23800 Wyatt, Valerie. *Inventions* (3–5). Illus. by Matthew Fernandes. Series: Frequently Asked Questions. 2003, Kids Can $12.95 (978-1-55337-403-9); paper $6.95 (978-1-55337-404-6). 40pp. A bright question-and-answer format is used to present information about a variety of inventions. (Rev: HBG 10/03; SLJ 7/03) [608]

23801 Ye, Ting-Xing. *The Chinese Thought of It: Amazing Inventions and Innovations* (5–8). Illus. 2009, Annick LB $19.95 (978-155451196-9); paper $9.95 (978-155451195-2). 48pp. Famous inventions from 37 centuries of Chinese history are presented in this well-organized book. (Rev: BLO 11/15/09) [609.51]

23802 Zuckerman, Amy, and James Daly. *2030: A Day in the Life of Tomorrow's Kids* (K–3). Illus. by John Manders. 2009, Dutton $16.99 (978-0-525-47860-7). 32pp. This light look at the future follows a boy through a typical day featuring a talking dog, a smart wristwatch, magnetically hovering skateboards, and other wonders. (Rev: BCCB 4/09; BL 1/1–15/09; LMC 5/09; SLJ 3/09) [601]

Aeronautics and Airplanes

23803 Benoit, Peter. *The Hindenburg Disaster* (3–5). Series: A True Book: Disasters. 2011, Children's Press LB $28 (978-0-531-20626-3); paper $6.95 (978-0-531-28995-2). 48pp. Benoit examines the disaster and provides a history of airships, photographs, maps, and statistics. (Rev: LMC 3–4/12; SLJ 11/1/11) [363.124]

23804 Berliner, Don. *Aviation: Reaching for the Sky* (5–8). Series: Innovators. 1997, Oliver LB $21.95 (978-1-881508-33-5). A thorough history of aviation, beginning with early hot-air balloons and dirigibles and continuing through the Wright Brothers and Sikorsky's helicopter to supersonic jets. (Rev: BL 5/1/97; SLJ 7/97) [629.133]

23805 Bingham, Caroline. *Big Book of Airplanes* (2–5). Illus. 2001, DK $14.99 (978-0-7894-6521-4). 32pp. A stunning fact-filled picture book about all kinds of planes, from jumbo jets to the tiny "Gee Bee" and the space plane X-33. (Rev: BL 3/1/01; HBG 10/01) [629.133]

23806 Britton, Tamara. *Air Force One* (3–5). Series: Symbols, Landmarks, and Monuments. 2004, ABDO LB $22.78 (978-1-59197-520-5). 32pp. A look at the aircraft that have been used to transport the president, especially Air Force One, which has become a symbol of the office itself. (Rev: SLJ 11/04) [387.7]

23807 Carson, Mary Kay. *The Wright Brothers for Kids: How They Invented the Airplane: 21 Activities Exploring the Science and History of Flight* (4–8). Illus. by Laura D'Argo. 2003, Chicago Review paper $14.95 (978-1-55652-477-6). After an account of the achievements of the Wrights and other early airplane enthusiasts, 21 activities allow readers to investigate some of the basic principles and to learn about equipment and means of communication. (Rev: SLJ 6/03) [629.13]

23808 Feigenbaum, Aaron. *The Hindenburg Disaster* (3–6). Series: Code Red. 2007, Bearport LB $23.96 (978-1-59716-361-3). 32pp. In chapters including "Why Airships Can Fly," "A Floating Hotel," "The Crash," and "What Happened?," Feigenbaum describes the 1937 catastrophe. (Rev: LMC 10/07; SLJ 10/07) [363.12]

23809 Finkelstein, Norman H. *Three Across: The Great Transatlantic Air Race of 1927* (5–8). Illus. 2008, Boyds Mills $17.95 (978-159078462-4). 136pp. Finkelstein focuses on the first three fliers to make it across the Atlantic Ocean in this interesting account that conveys the flavor of the Roaring Twenties. (Rev: BL 9/1/08; LMC 11–12/08; SLJ 11/1/08; VOYA 12/08) [629.130]

23810 Gaffney, Timothy R. *Hurricane Hunters* (4–7). Series: Aircraft. 2001, Enslow LB $23.93 (978-0-7660-1569-2). Information on the planes that investigate hurricanes is accompanied by quotations from the pilots and scientists who fly in them. (Rev: HBG 3/02; SLJ 2/02) [551.55]

23811 Ghione, Yvette. *This Is Daniel Cook on a Plane* (K–3). 2006, Kids Can $12.95 (978-1-55453-081-6); paper $4.95 (978-1-55453-082-3). In this companion to the popular Canadian-produced TV show, the young host takes readers on a flight in a small airplane, introducing them to the parts of the airplane, flying techniques, and safety procedures. (Rev: SLJ 11/06) [629.13]

23812 Graham, Ian. *Aircraft* (3–5). Illus. Series: How Machines Work. 2008, Smart Apple LB $18.95 (978-1-59920-292-1). 32pp. Fast facts, drawings, diagrams, and photographs accompany text explaining how the engines, wings, controls, and so forth work. (Rev: BL 12/1/08) [629.133]

23813 Graham, Ian. *You Wouldn't Want to Be on the Hindenburg! A Transatlantic Trip You'd Rather Skip* (3–5). Illus. by David Antram. 2009, Scholastic LB $29.00 (978-0-531-20823-6); paper $9.95 (978-0-531-21049-9). 32pp. This detailed cartoon account of the design, construction, and dangers of airships also described the disaster. (Rev: BLO 3/17/09) [900]

23814 Hansen, Ole Steen. *Amazing Flights: The Golden Age* (4–7). Series: The Story of Flight. 2003, Crabtree LB $25.27 (978-0-7787-1202-2); paper $8.95 (978-0-7787-1218-3). Double-page spreads present text, feature sidebars, color photographs, and paintings on the people and events of flying after World War I — air races, barnstormers, Lindbergh, and more. (Rev: BL 10/15/03) [629.13]

23815 Hansen, Ole Steen. *Commercial Aviation* (4–7). Series: The Story of Flight. 2003, Crabtree $25.27 (978-0-7787-1205-3). The history and development of airlines and other forms of commercial aviation are discussed with coverage of present-day problems. (Rev: BL 10/15/03) [629.13]

23816 Hansen, Ole Steen. *Modern Military Aircraft* (4–7). Series: The Story of Flight. 2003, Crabtree LB $25.27 (978-0-7787-1204-6); paper $8.95 (978-0-7787-1220-6). A highly visual overview of military aircraft since World War II, with a spotter's guide. (Rev: BL 10/15/03) [623.]

23817 Hill, Lee S. *The Flyer Flew! The Invention of the Airplane* (2–4). Illus. by Craig Orback. Series: On My Own Science. 2006, Millbrook LB $25.26 (978-1-57505-758-3). 48pp. This easy-reader chapter book tells the story of the Wright brothers' invention, discusses their scientific approach, and explains terms such as pitch and air pressure. (Rev: SLJ 8/06) [629.13]

23818 Hodgkins, Fran. *How People Learned to Fly* (1–3). Illus. by True Kelley. Series: Let's-Read-and-Find-Out Science. 2007, Collins $15.99 (978-0-06-029558-5); paper $5.99 (978-0-06-445221-2). 33pp. An introduction to the history of aircraft and the scientific principles that keep them aloft. (Rev: SLJ 10/07) [629.133]

23819 Homan, Lynn M., and Thomas Reilly. *Women Who Fly* (5–8). Illus. by Rosalie M. Shepherd. 2004, Pelican $14.95 (978-1-58980-160-8). Women's efforts to establish a foothold in the male-dominated field of aviation are recounted in this book that is suitable for browsers. (Rev: BL 7/04; SLJ 9/04) [629.13]

23820 Hunter, Ryan Ann. *Into the Air: A Timeline of Flight* (2–4). 2003, National Geographic $16.95 (978-

0-7922-5120-0). 48pp. Hunter reaches way back in history to begin her beautifully illustrated history of flight, starting with prehistory's flying reptiles and continuing through the ages to the developments of human flight. (Rev: BL 12/15/03; HBG 4/04)

23821 Hunter, Ryan Ann. *Take Off!* (PS–1). Illus. by Edward Miller. 2000, Holiday House $15.95 (978-0-8234-1466-6). 32pp. All kinds of airplanes — from the Wright brothers' craft to the 1,000-seat plane of the future — are introduced in this brightly illustrated volume that ends with directions on making a paper airplane. (Rev: BCCB 7–8/00; BL 2/15/00; HBG 9/00; SLJ 9/00) [629.13]

23822 Malam, John. *Airport: Behind the Scenes, Check-in to Take-off* (3–5). Illus. Series: Building Works. 2000, Bedrick $16.95 (978-0-87226-586-8). 32pp. This book supplies an illustrated guided tour of an airport and its facilities plus a history of airports and a glossary of terms. (Rev: BL 7/00; HBG 9/00) [387.7]

23823 Masters, Nancy Robinson. *The Airplane* (4–8). Series: Inventions That Shaped the World. 2004, Watts LB $30.50 (978-0-531-12360-7). 80pp. An interesting overview of the discovery and development of flight, with discussion of its impact on our lives today and in the future. (Rev: SLJ 2/05) [629.13]

23824 Maynard, Chris. *Aircraft* (5–8). Series: Need for Speed. 1999, Lerner LB $23.93 (978-0-8225-2485-4); paper $7.95 (978-0-8225-9855-8). Using double-page spreads, this work introduces high-speed aircraft. (Rev: BL 1/1–15/00; HBG 3/00; SLJ 2/00) [629.133]

23825 Millspaugh, Ben. *Aviation and Space Science Projects* (5–8). 1992, TAB paper $9.95 (978-0-8306-2156-9). The principles of flight are explored in 19 projects that vary in difficulty and complexity. (Rev: BL 1/15/92; SLJ 6/92) [629.1]

23826 Molzahn, Arlene Bourgeois. *Airplanes* (2–4). Illus. Series: Transportation and Communication. 2003, Enslow LB $23.93 (978-0-7660-2026-9). 48pp. An easy-to-read history of airplanes and their use in enabling various forms of communication. Also use *Ships and Boats* (2003). (Rev: HBG 10/03)

23827 Mooney, Carla. *Pilotless Planes* (5–7). Illus. Series: A Great Idea. 2010, Norwood LB $25.27 (978-1-59953-381-0). 48pp. An interesting account of the development and potential uses of "drones" in military and civilian situations. (Rev: BL 11/1/10; SLJ 1/1/11) [623.74]

23828 O'Brien, Patrick. *Fantastic Flights: One Hundred Years of Flying on the Edge* (3–6). 2003, Walker $17.95 (978-0-8027-8880-1); paper $18.85 (978-0-8027-8881-8). 40pp. Seventeen significant flights — from Otto Lilienthal's glider experiments to the landing of the spacecraft Pathfinder on Mars — are introduced in colorful spreads. (Rev: BL 9/1/03; HBG 4/04; SLJ 11/03) [629.13]

23829 Old, Wendie. *To Fly: The Story of the Wright Brothers* (3–5). Illus. by Robert Andrew Parker. 2002, Clarion $16.00 (978-0-618-13347-5). 48pp. An attractive, large-format introduction to the brothers and their

accomplishments with good coverage of the basic principles of flight. (Rev: BL 10/1/02; HB 11/02; HBG 3/03; SLJ 10/02) [629.13]

23830 Oxlade, Chris. *Airplanes: Uncovering Technology* (4–8). Illus. Series: Uncovering. 2006, Firefly $16.95 (978-1-55407-134-0). A well-illustrated survey of developments in air travel, with four overlay pages and a look at future possibilities. (Rev: SLJ 2/07) [629.133]

23831 Oxlade, Chris. *Plane* (4–6). Series: Take It Apart. 2002, Thameside $24.25 (978-1-930643-95-6). 32pp. Readers get an inside look at the various parts of a plane with cutaway illustrations, in-depth diagrams, and fact boxes. (Rev: BL 1/1–15/03; HBG 3/03) [629.133]

23832 Parker, Vic. *My First Trip on an Airplane* (K–2). Illus. Series: Growing Up. 2011, Heinemann LB $22 (978-1-4329-4801-6). 24pp. This reassuring book gives first-time plane passengers a sense of what to expect on the ground and in the air. (Rev: BL 7/11; SLJ 6/11) [387.7]

23833 Priceman, Marjorie. *Hot Air: The (Mostly) True Story of the First Hot-Air Balloon Ride* (K–3). Illus. 2005, Simon & Schuster $16.95 (978-0-689-82642-9). 40pp. The Montgolfier brothers' first successful hot-air balloon flight is detailed with humor, great illustrations, and a little embellishment. Caldecott Honor Book, 2006. (Rev: BL 7/05; SLJ 7/05) [629.133]

23834 Riehle, Mary Ann McCabe. *A Is for Airplane: An Aviation Alphabet* (2–4). Illus. by David Craig. 2009, Sleeping Bear $16.95 (978-1-58536-358-2). 32pp. This attractive alphabet book provides lots of history, science, and biographical information. (Rev: BLO 3/5/09) [629.1]

23835 Rinard, Judith E. *The Story of Flight* (3–6). Illus. 2002, Firefly $16.95 (978-1-55297-642-5); paper $8.95 (978-1-55297-694-4). From balloon travel to possible manned space flights to Mars, this well-illustrated overview of the history of flight was published in cooperation with the National Air and Space Museum. (Rev: BL 12/15/02; HBG 3/03; SLJ 12/02) [629.1]

23836 Roberts, Cynthia. *Rescue Helicopters* (2–4). Series: Machines at Work. 2007, The Child's World LB $21.36 (978-1-59296-835-0). 24pp. Beginning and reluctant readers will enjoy this introduction to these helicopters and how they are used to rescue people in distress. Features many photographs. (Rev: SLJ 8/07)

23837 Santella, Andrew. *Air Force One* (4–7). 2003, Millbrook LB $24.90 (978-0-7613-2617-5). An overview of the aircraft that have transported United States presidents, with an inside look at today's Air Force One. (Rev: BL 2/15/03; HBG 10/03; SLJ 8/03) [387.7]

23838 Sherrow, Victoria. *The Hindenburg Disaster: Doomed Airship* (4–8). Series: American Disasters. 2002, Enslow LB $23.93 (978-0-7660-1554-8). 48pp. Excellent illustrations and a clear text are used to tell the story of the destruction of the mighty German dirigible. (Rev: BL 6/1–15/02; HBG 10/02; SLJ 6/02) [629.133]

23839 Silverman, Buffy. *How Do Hot Air Balloons Work?* (2–4). Illus. Series: How Flight Works. 2013, Lerner LB $25.26 (978-076138969-9). 32pp. A basic intro-duction to the mechanics of flying in hot air balloons and the safety measures that are necessary. (Rev: BL 4/1/13; LMC 8–9/13)

23840 Verstraete, Larry. *Surviving the Hindenburg* (3–5). Illus. by David Geister. 2012, Sleeping Bear $16.95 (978-1-58536-787-0). 32pp. The true story of the Hindenburg disaster is told here from the perspective of 14-year-old cabin boy Werner Franz, and includes detailed illustrations. (Rev: BL 4/1/12; LMC 11–12/12; SLJ 8/12) [363.12]

Building and Construction

General

23841 Aldridge, Rebecca. *The Hoover Dam* (5–8). Series: Building America: Then and Now. 2009, Chelsea House $35 (978-1-60413-069-0). 120pp. This book about the Hoover Dam includes illustrative maps, primary source documents, Web sites, a timeline, and glossary. (Rev: LMC 10/09) [627]

23842 Ardagh, Philip. *A Hole in the Road* (PS–K). Illus. by Tig Sutton. Series: British Mighty Machines. 2003, Thameside LB $24.25 (978-1-931983-02-0). 32pp. A burst water pipe causes a hole in the road and a great deal of digging, earth moving, and paving involving a variety of large machines. (Rev: BL 12/1/02; HBG 3/03) [621.8]

23843 Bailey, Gerry. *Towering Homes* (3–6). Illus. by Moreno Chiacchiera. Series: Young Architect. 2013, Crabtree LB $20.70 (978-077870289-4); paper $9.95 (9780778702993). 32pp. Using facts, cartoon illustrations, and large photographs, Bailey describes to the young reader the steps and challenges involved in building tall structures. **e** (Rev: BL 10/1/13; LMC 10/14) [728]

23844 Barker, Geoff. *Incredible Skyscrapers* (5–7). Illus. Series: Superstructures. 2010, Amicus LB $19.95 (978-160753133-3). 32pp. Sky-scraping structures from around the world are profiled in this book, which offers technical explanations of the engineering feats required in building such a structure. (Rev: BL 7/11) [720]

23845 Britton, Tamara. *The Empire State Building* (3–5). Series: Symbols, Landmarks, and Monuments. 2005, ABDO LB $22.78 (978-1-59197-834-3). 32pp. All about the famous New York landmark, with information on its history, construction, and importance. (Rev: SLJ 9/05)

23846 Britton, Tamara. *The Golden Gate Bridge* (3–5). Series: Symbols, Landmarks, and Monuments. 2005, ABDO LB $22.78 (978-1-59197-835-0). 32pp. All about the famous California landmark, with information on its history, its construction, and its importance. (Rev: SLJ 9/05) [624]

23847 Caney, Steven. *Steven Caney's Ultimate Building Book* (4–8). Illus. by Lauren House. 2006, Running Press $29.95 (978-0-7624-0409-4). Starting with a history of construction and the basic techniques involved, Caney looks at the ways design and technology intersect and suggests a wide range of kid-tested building projects. (Rev: SLJ 1/07*) [624]

23848 Donovan, Sandy. *The Channel Tunnel* (4–7). Series: Great Building Feats. 2003, Lerner LB $27.93 (978-0-8225-4692-4). 96pp. Using many black-and-white illustrations, diagrams, and maps, this is the exciting story of the underwater engineering marvel that links England and France. (Rev: BL 11/15/03; HBG 10/03; SLJ 11/03) [624.1]

23849 Dreyer, Francis. *Lighthouses* (4–7). Photos by Philip Plisson. 2005, Abrams $18.95 (978-0-8109-5958-3). A fascinating and strikingly beautiful overview of lighthouses — of the past and present — and of the courage and loneliness of the men and women who tend them. (Rev: BL 1/1–15/06) [387.1]

23850 DuTemple, Lesley A. *The Hoover Dam* (4–7). Series: Great Building Feats. 2003, Lerner LB $27.93 (978-0-8225-4691-7). This story traces the dam's construction from the planning stages through its technically difficult and dangerous construction and places this impressive structure in historical context. (Rev: BL 11/15/03; HBG 10/03; SLJ 11/03) [627]

23851 Farbman, Melinda. *Bridges* (2–4). Series: Transportation and Communication. 2001, Enslow LB $23.93 (978-0-7660-1647-7). 48pp. Basic facts are given on the history of bridges and their present-day construction in this heavily illustrated volume. (Rev: BL 3/15/02; HBG 3/02) [624]

23852 Goldish, Meish. *Amazing Amusement Park Rides* (1–5). Illus. Series: So Big Compared to What? 2011, Bearport LB $22.61 (978-161772304-9). 24pp. A look at amazing structures around the world, with colorful photographs, statistics, and size comparisons. (Rev: BL 1/1/12; SLJ 2/12) [791.06]

23853 Goldish, Meish. *Spectacular Skyscrapers* (1–5). Illus. Series: So Big Compared to What? 2011, Bearport LB $22.61 (978-161772303-2). 24pp. With dramatic photographs, statistics, and size comparisons, this volume introduces some of the tallest buildings in the world and provides historical context. (Rev: BL 1/1/12; SLJ 2/12) [720]

23854 Gonzales, Doreen. *Seven Wonders of the Modern World* (4–7). Series: Seven Wonders of the World. 2005, Enslow LB $25.26 (978-0-7660-5292-5). Profiles seven marvels of modern construction, including the Panama Canal, Toronto's CN Tower, and the Empire State Building in New York City; the text is extended by constantly updated links to Web sites. (Rev: SLJ 11/05)

23855 Good, Keith. *Build It! Activities for Setting Up Super Structures* (3–7). Series: Design It! 2000, Lerner LB $21.27 (978-0-8225-3567-6). 30pp. This book of projects explores ideas for bridges, domes, structures that collapse, and pop-ups in a clear format with good directions. (Rev: HBG 9/00; SLJ 6/00) [624]

23856 Goodman, Susan E. *Skyscraper* (2–5). 2004, Knopf $18.99 (978-0-375-91309-9). 40pp. The myriad details involved in designing and building a skyscraper are accompanied by personal stories that draw the reader into the process. (Rev: BL 12/1/04*; SLJ 2/05) [720]

23857 Graham, Ian. *Amazing Stadiums* (5–7). Series: Superstructures. 2010, Amicus LB $28.50 (978-1-60753-131-9). 32pp. With discussion of stadiums past and future, this book looks at nine specific structures around the world and gives information on the architects and the challenges they faced. (Rev: BL 7/11; SLJ 11/1/10) [725]

23858 Graham, Ian. *Fabulous Bridges* (5–7). Series: Superstructures. 2010, Amicus LB $28.50 (978-1-60753-132-6). 32pp. With discussion of bridges past and future, this book looks at nine specific structures around the world and gives information on the architects and the challenges they faced. Also use *Tremendous Tunnels* (2010). (Rev: BL 7/11; SLJ 11/1/10) [624.2]

23859 Greene, Meg. *The Eiffel Tower* (5–8). Series: Building World Landmarks. 2004, Gale LB $24.95 (978-1-56711-315-0). 48pp. The story of the construction of the Eiffel Tower, which when completed in 1899 was the tallest human-made structure in the world. (Rev: SLJ 7/04) [725]

23860 Hill, Lee S. *Monuments Help Us Remember* (1–3). Illus. Series: Building Blocks Books. 2000, Carolrhoda $21.27 (978-1-57505-475-9). 32pp. This simple book takes the reader on a tour of the world's most famous monuments, including the Statue of Liberty. (Rev: BL 9/15/00; HBG 3/01) [720]

23861 Hill, Lee S. *Tunnels Go Underground* (1–3). Illus. Series: Building Blocks Books. 2000, Carolrhoda $14.60 (978-1-57505-429-2). 32pp. Many different kinds of tunnels are covered, from mining tunnels in Pennsylvania to the tunnel that runs under the English Channel. (Rev: BL 9/15/00; HBG 3/01) [725]

23862 Hudson, Cheryl W. *Construction Zone* (K–3). Illus. by Richard Sobol. 2006, Candlewick $15.99 (978-0-7636-2684-6). 32pp. A fascinating behind-the-scenes glimpse of the construction of a building designed by noted architect Frank Gehry, featuring eye-catching photographs and definitions of specialized vocabulary. (Rev: BL 9/1/06; SLJ 6/06) [690]

23863 Jefferis, David. *Megastructures* (3–6). Series: Record Breakers. 2003, Raintree LB $25.69 (978-0-7398-6324-4). 32pp. In this overview of large-scale structures, part of the Record Breakers series, author David Jefferis looks at massive tunnels, bridges, castles, and domes. (Rev: HBG 10/03; SLJ 7/03)

23864 Kirkwood, Jon. *The Fantastic Cutaway Book of Giant Buildings* (4–7). 1997, Millbrook paper $9.95 (978-0-7613-0629-0). Using double-page spreads, outstanding graphics, and many fact boxes, this book features a wide variety of structures including the Statue of Liberty, the pyramids, the Colosseum, churches, operas

houses, Grand Central Station, Munich's Olympic stadium, and skyscrapers. (Rev: BL 4/1/98; HBG 10/98) [720]

23865 Leboutillier, Nate. *Eiffel Tower* (3–6). Series: Modern Wonders of the World. 2006, Creative Education LB $27.10 (978-1-58341-438-5). 32pp. Leboutillier tells the story of the construction of the tower — in the face of much protest and technical challenges — and documents its history, including many unusual feats, and its contemporary importance as a symbol. (Rev: SLJ 12/06) [725]

23866 Levy, Debbie. *The World Trade Center* (4–6). Illus. Series: Great Structures in History. 2005, Gale LB $26.20 (978-0-7377-2071-6). 48pp. Chronicles the six-year construction project — including design and excavation, their symbolism, and the eventual destruction of the towers. (Rev: BL 12/1/05) [720]

23867 Macaulay, David. *Unbuilding* (5–8). Illus. by author. 1980, Houghton Mifflin $19.00 (978-0-395-29457-4); paper $6.95 (978-0-395-45360-5). A book that explores the concept of tearing down the Empire State Building.

23868 Macaulay, David. *Underground* (5–10). Illus. by author. 1983, Houghton Mifflin $19.00 (978-0-395-24739-6); paper $9.95 (978-0-395-34065-3). An exploration in text and detailed drawings of the intricate network of systems under city streets. [624]

23869 Macken, JoAnn Early. *Digging Tunnels* (PS–1). Illus. 2008, Capstone LB $14.95 (978-1-4296-1234-0). 32pp. Macken uses full-page color photographs and large, simple text to show types of tunnels and how they are built. (Rev: BL 8/08; SLJ 8/08) [624.1]

23870 Mann, Elizabeth. *The Brooklyn Bridge* (4–7). Series: Wonders of the World. 1996, Mikaya $19.95 (978-0-9650493-0-6). The story of the building of the Brooklyn Bridge is told through the eyes of a family. (Rev: BL 2/1/97; SLJ 6/97*) [624]

23871 Mann, Elizabeth. *Empire State Building* (3–8). Illus. by Alan Witschonke. Series: Wonders of the World Books. 2003, Mikaya $19.95 (978-1-931414-06-7). 48pp. With a four-page foldout, period photographs, and full-color illustrations, this story of the skyscraper's construction will please both browsers and report writers. (Rev: BL 2/1/04; SLJ 4/04) [974.7]

23872 Mattern, Joanne. *The Chunnel* (5–8). Series: Building World Landmarks. 2004, Gale LB $24.95 (978-1-56711-301-3). 48pp. The story of the long delays and eventual construction of the tunnel under the English Channel, linking England and France, with a focus on the new technology involved. (Rev: SLJ 7/04) [624.1]

23873 Murray, Julie. *Golden Gate Bridge* (2–3). Illus. Series: All Aboard America. 2003, ABDO LB $21.35 (978-1-57765-672-2). 24pp. A brief history of the huge San Francisco suspension bridge. (Rev: HBG 10/03; SLJ 11/03) [624]

23874 Neumann, Dietrich. *Joe and the Skyscraper: The Empire State Building in New York City* (2–4). Illus. Series: Where We Live. 2000, Prestel $14.95 (3-7913-

2103-X). Seen through the eyes of a 16-year-old water-boy, this is the story of the construction of the Empire State Building. (Rev: BL 4/15/00*; SLJ 4/00) [720.483]

23875 Owens, Thomas S. *Football Stadiums* (5–8). Series: Sports Palaces. 2001, Millbrook LB $25.90 (978-0-7613-1764-7). Rather than highlighting individual stadiums, this book covers general topics such as their design, replacement, funding, amenities, and history. (Rev: BL 4/1/01; HBG 10/01; SLJ 4/01) [796.332]

23876 Oxlade, Chris. *Skyscrapers* (3–5). Series: Building Amazing Structures. 2000, Heinemann LB $22.79 (978-1-57572-278-8). 32pp. This colorful book introduces skyscrapers and describes their construction, materials, and functions with many examples of historical and contemporary buildings. Also use *Stadiums* and *Tunnels* (both 2000). (Rev: HBG 10/01; SLJ 3/01) [720.4]

23877 Oxlade, Chris. *Skyscrapers: Uncovering Technology* (4–6). Series: Uncovering. 2006, Firefly $16.95 (978-1-55407-136-4). 52pp. This overview of the world's skyscrapers — past, present, and future — looks briefly at some of the most notable structures, as well as the design and technological challenges involved in building them, and offers several mylar overlays. (Rev: BL 10/15/06; SLJ 2/07) [720]

23878 Roza, Greg. *The Incredible Story of Skyscrapers* (3–6). Illus. Series: A Kid's Guide to Incredible Technology. 2004, Rosen LB $21.25 (978-0-8239-6716-2). 24pp. Discusses the challenges and techniques of building skyscrapers, with a look at some famous buildings and at the potential size of future ones. (Rev: SLJ 2/05) [720]

23879 Sandler, Michael. *Freaky-Strange Buildings* (1–5). Illus. Series: So Big Compared to What? 2011, Bearport LB $22.61 (978-161772305-6). 24pp. Unusual structures featured here include the Burj Al Arab Hotel in Dubai, which resembles the sail of an Arab boat, and the Guggenheim Museum in Bilboa, Spain. Also use *Stupendous Sports Stadiums* (2011). (Rev: BL 1/1/12; SLJ 2/12) [720]

23880 Severance, John B. *Skyscrapers: How America Grew Up* (5–9). Illus. 2000, Holiday $18.95 (978-0-8234-1492-5). 96pp. Beginning with an explanation of the architectural breakthroughs that made the building of skyscrapers possible, this account traces the construction of these buildings from 1851 to the end of the 20th century. (Rev: BL 6/1–15/00; HB 9/00; HBG 10/00; SLJ 7/00; VOYA 4/01) [720]

23881 Stone, Lynn M. *Bridges* (3–5). Illus. Series: How Are They Built? 2001, Rourke LB $29.93 (978-1-58952-135-3). 48pp. How, why, and where bridges are built, with photographs, a glossary, and other features. Also use *Dams* (2001). (Rev: BL 10/15/01) [624]

23882 Stone, Lynn M. *Roads and Highways* (3–5). Series: How Are They Built? 2001, Rourke LB $29.93 (978-1-58952-138-4). 48pp. Following information on the history of roads, this book gives details on highway construction today, the materials used, and the techniques employed. (Rev: BL 10/15/01) [625.7]

23883 Stone, Lynn M. *Skyscrapers* (3–5). Series: How Are They Built? 2001, Rourke LB $29.93 (978-1-58952-139-1). 48pp. Background material on skyscrapers is followed by coverage of how they are built, their design, materials used, and present-day practices and concerns. (Rev: BL 10/15/01) [720]

23884 Sullivan, George. *Built to Last: Building America's Amazing Bridges, Dams, Tunnels, and Skyscrapers* (5–8). 2005, Scholastic $18.99 (978-0-439-51737-9). Seventeen marvels of American engineering — including the Erie Canal, Hoover Dam, Brooklyn Bridge, and Boston's "Big Dig" — are presented in chronological chapters with good illustrations and fact boxes that add historical and technological context. (Rev: BL 12/1/05; SLJ 3/06*; VOYA 8/06) [624]

23885 Wearing, Judy, and Tom Riddolls. *Golden Gate Bridge* (4–7). Illus. Series: Structural Wonders. 2009, Weigl LB $18.20 (978-160596136-1). 32pp. Looks at the history, construction, and design of the bridge, with period photographs and information on key individuals. (Rev: BL 9/15/09; SLJ 11/09) [624.2]

23886 Woods, Mary B., and Michael Woods. *Ancient Construction: From Tents to Towers* (5–8). Illus. Series: Ancient Technologies. 2000, Runestone LB $25.26 (978-0-8225-2998-9). 88pp. From Stonehenge and the Colosseum to the Eiffel Tower and the Golden Gate Bridge, this is a history of building and construction. (Rev: BL 9/15/00; HBG 3/01; SLJ 1/01) [720]

23887 Yuan, Margaret Speaker. *The Royal Gorge Bridge* (5–8). Series: Building World Landmarks. 2004, Gale LB $24.95 (978-1-56711-352-5). 48pp. Examines the engineering and construction challenges involved in the 1929 construction of Colorado's Royal Gorge Bridge. (Rev: SLJ 7/04) [624.2]

23888 Zaunders, Bo. *The Great Bridge-Building Contest* (3–5). Illus. by Roxie Munro. 2004, Abrams $16.95 (978-0-8109-4929-4). 32pp. With fine illustrations, this is the story of 19th-century cabinetmaker Lemuel Chenoweth's successful bid to design a bridge. (Rev: BL 12/1/04; SLJ 3/05) [624.2]

Houses

23889 Andersen, Jenna. *How It Happens at the Building Site* (K–3). Illus. Series: How It Happens. 2004, Oliver $19.95 (978-1-881508-95-3). 32pp. An inside look at the work that goes into the construction of a home. (Rev: BL 1/1–15/05) [690]

23890 Bial, Raymond. *The Houses* (4–8). Illus. Series: Building America. 2001, Marshall Cavendish LB $27.07 (978-0-7614-1335-6). 56pp. A history of different types of housing in the United States that includes excellent photographs and drawings. (Rev: BL 3/1/02; HBG 3/02) [392.3]

23891 Gustafson, Angela. *Imagine a House: A Journey to Fascinating Houses Around the World* (2–5). Illus. 2003, Out of the Box $16.95 (978-0-9726849-0-3). 32pp. A dozen houses around the world serve as examples of the diversity of architecture and creativity. (Rev: SLJ 2/04) [392.3]

23892 Hill, Lee S. *Homes Keep Us Warm* (1–3). Illus. Series: Building Blocks Books. 2000, Carolrhoda $21.27 (978-1-57505-430-8). 32pp. This book explores all kinds of homes, from huts made with animal skins to city apartments, farmhouses, and bungalows. (Rev: BL 9/15/00; HBG 3/01) [690]

23893 Komatsu, Yoshio. *Wonderful Houses Around the World* (3–5). Trans. from Japanese by Katy Bridges and Naoko Amemiya. Photos by author. Illus. by Akira Nishiyama. 2004, Shelter $14.95 (978-0-936070-35-3); paper $8.95 (978-0-936070-34-6). 43pp. A Mongolian yurt, a Chinese circular tulou, and a Tunisian underground home are among the 10 houses included, with cutaway diagrams and information on decor and inhabitants. (Rev: SLJ 4/05)

23894 Laroche, Giles. *If You Lived Here: Houses of the World* (K–3). Illus. by author. 2011, Houghton Mifflin $16.99 (978-0-547-23892-0). 32pp. Attractive cut-paper collages invite readers to explore 16 very different kinds of homes around the world. **e** Lexile NC1170L (Rev: BL 10/15/11; HB 9–10/11; SLJ 9/1/11*) [392.3]

23895 Newhouse, Maxwell. *The House That Max Built* (PS–2). Illus. by author. 2008, Tundra $18.95 (978-0-88776-774-6). 24pp. A detailed look at how houses are constructed, covering all phases from design through foundation, framing, siding, plumbing, and so forth, ending with landscaping and a glossary of the tradesmen involved. (Rev: BL 4/15/08; SLJ 5/08) [690]

23896 Stone, Lynn M. *Houses* (3–5). Series: How Are They Built? 2001, Rourke LB $19.95 (978-1-58952-137-7). 48pp. After some historical material, this book describes how houses are built today and the materials used. (Rev: BL 10/15/01) [690]

Clothing, Textiles, and Jewelry

23897 Carlson, Laurie. *Queen of Inventions: How the Sewing Machine Changed the World* (3–5). Illus. 2003, Millbrook LB $22.90 (978-0-7613-2706-6). 32pp. The history of the sewing machine and its impact on home and commercial garment-making, with illustrations and photographs. (Rev: BL 2/15/03; HBG 10/03; SLJ 4/03) [681]

23898 Elgin, Kathy. *France* (3–5). Series: Costume Around the World. 2008, Chelsea Clubhouse LB $28.00 (978-0-7910-9766-3). 32pp. Elgin introduces the traditional costumes of France and discusses the influences of climate, culture, religion, and so forth. (Rev: LMC 11/08; SLJ 9/08)

23899 Hoobler, Dorothy, and Thomas Hoobler. *Vanity Rules: A History of American Fashion and Beauty* (5–8). Illus. 2000, Twenty-First Century LB $28.90 (978-0-7613-1258-1). 160pp. From the painted bodies of early Native Americans to today's body piercing, this is a his-

tory of the quest for personal beauty in America. (Rev: BL 4/1/00; HBG 10/00; SLJ 5/00) [391]

23900 Kyi, Tanya Lloyd. *The Lowdown on Denim* (5–8). Illus. by Clayton Hanmer. 2011, Annick $21.95 (978-155451355-0); paper $12.95 (978-15545135-4-3). 112pp. A history of denim is accompanied by a graphic-novel story of two students investigating dungarees as part of their detention project. (Rev: BLO 11/15/11; SLJ 2/12) [391]

23901 Llewellyn, Claire. *Silk* (2–4). Illus. Series: Material World. 2002, Watts LB $24.00 (978-0-531-14630-9). 30pp. A well-illustrated look at silk, how it is manufactured, and the various types; with "Fast Facts," related activities, and a glossary. (Rev: SLJ 5/03) [677]

23902 Nelson, Robin. *From Cotton to T-Shirt* (PS–2). Illus. Series: Start to Finish. 2003, Lerner $18.60 (978-0-8225-4661-0). 24pp. This colorful picture book traces the production of a T-shirt from the picking of the cotton that will be its main ingredient through each step of the manufacturing process. (Rev: BL 4/15/03; HBG 10/03; SLJ 7/03) [633.5]

23903 Nelson, Robin. *From Sheep to Sweater* (1–3). Series: Start to Finish. 2003, Lerner LB $18.60 (978-0-8225-0716-1). 24pp. This accessible overview follows the process of a wool sweater's creation from shearing of the sheep to finished product. (Rev: HBG 10/03; SLJ 8/03) [746.43]

23904 Oxlade, Chris. *Cotton* (2–3). Series: Materials, Materials, Materials. 2002, Heinemann LB $22.79 (978-1-58810-584-4). 32pp. With a color picture and brief text on each page, this is a basic introduction to cotton and how it is grown, processed, and made into other things. (Rev: BL 6/1–15/02) [633.5]

23905 Oxlade, Chris. *Wool* (2–3). Illus. Series: Materials, Materials, Materials. 2001, Heinemann LB $21.36 (978-1-58810-159-4). 32pp. Photographs accompany detailed information about where wool comes from and how it is made into products we use. (Rev: BL 10/15/01) [677]

23906 Reynolds, Helen. *Jewelry and Accessories* (3–8). Illus. Series: A Fashionable History of Costume. 2003, Raintree LB $25.70 (978-1-4109-0029-6). 32pp. Traces the evolution of accessories and jewelry from the beginning of recorded history to the present. (Rev: HBG 10/03; SLJ 9/03) [391.4]

23907 Reynolds, Helen. *The Shoe* (3–8). Illus. Series: A Fashionable History of Costume. 2003, Raintree LB $25.70 (978-1-4109-0027-2). 32pp. Traces the evolution of footwear from the beginning of recorded history to the present. (Rev: HBG 10/03; SLJ 9/03) [391.4]

23908 Shaffer, Jody Jensen. *Blue Jeans Before the Store* (1–3). Illus. by Dan McGeehan. Series: Before the Store. 2012, Child's World LB $28.50 (978-160973628-6). 32pp. This well-designed title encourages readers to consider how a pair of jeans is made — from how the cotton is grown, to the fabric created at the textile mill, to the sewing in a factory, and eventually the selling in a store. (Rev: BL 4/1/12) [338.47687]

23909 Shaskan, Kathy. *How Underwear Got Under There: A Brief History* (5–8). Illus. by Regan Dunnick. 2007, Dutton $16.99 (978-0-525-47178-3). Shaskan takes a lighthearted look at the history of nether garments, looking at their various roles (protection, warmth, modesty, support, and so forth) and at changes in fashion and social attitudes; a lack of sources makes this most suitable for browsing. (Rev: BCCB 9/07; LMC 11–12/07; SLJ 8/07) [391.4]

23910 Smith, Elizabeth Simpson. *Cloth* (5–8). 1985, Walker LB $10.85 (978-0-8027-6577-2). The discovery of fiber and how cloth is made. (Rev: BL 8/85; SLJ 11/85) [677.02864]

23911 Walton, Ruth. *Let's Get Dressed: Find Out About Clothes and Fashion* (1–3). Illus. by author. Series: Let's Find Out. 2013, Black Rabbit LB $28.50 (978-159771383-2). 32pp. Underwear, outerwear, fabrics, and fasteners are all discussed in this attractive and accessible volume. (Rev: BL 4/1/13; LMC 11–12/13) [391]

23912 Weaver, Janice. *From Head to Toe: Bound Feet, Bathing Suits, and Other Bizarre and Beautiful Things* (5–8). Illus. by Francis Blake. 2003, Tundra paper $16.95 (978-0-88776-654-1). History and culture are interwoven in this account of fashion fads over the years, mostly in the West. (Rev: SLJ 2/04) [391]

23913 Whitty, Helen. *Protective Clothing* (3–8). Illus. Series: Clothing. 2001, Chelsea LB $22.95 (978-0-7910-6574-7). 32pp. An interesting look at apparel that includes aprons, armor, firefighting suits, and space suits. Also use *You Are What You Wear* and *Underwear* (both 2001). (Rev: HBG 3/02; SLJ 12/01) [745]

23914 Woods, Samuel G. *Kids' Clothes from Start to Finish* (3–5). Series: Made in the USA. 2001, Blackbirch LB $23.70 (978-1-56711-483-6). 32pp. The steps in the manufacture of children's clothing from design to finished product are discussed in this colorful, easily read account. (Rev: BL 3/15/02; HBG 3/02) [687]

Computers and Automation

23915 Bailey, Diane. *Cyber Ethics* (4–6). Illus. Series: Cyber Citizenship and Cyber Safety. 2008, Rosen LB $19.95 (978-1-4042-1349-4). 48pp. Privacy, plagiarism, and bullying are among the topics discussed in this accessible volume. (Rev: BL 4/1/08; LMC 10/08; SLJ 7/08) [175]

23916 Baker, Christopher W. *Robots Among Us: The Challenges and Promises of Robotics* (5–8). Series: New Century Technology. 2002, Millbrook LB $23.90 (978-0-7613-1969-6). A lavishly illustrated account that describes the science of robotics, current developments, and what might be expected in the future. (Rev: BL 6/1–15/02; HBG 10/02; SLJ 9/02) [629.8]

23917 Baker, Christopher W. *Scientific Visualization: The New Eyes of Science* (5–8). Illus. Series: New Century Technology. 2000, Millbrook LB $23.90 (978-0-7613-1351-

9). This book explores the ways in which computers enable scientists to study the universe and simulate events such as the creation of a black hole. (Rev: BL 4/1/00; HBG 3/01; SLJ 6/00) [507.2]

23918 Bingham, Jane. *Internet Freedom: Where Is the Limit?* (5–8). Series: Behind the News. 2006, Heinemann LB $32.86 (978-1-4034-8833-6). Short news stories highlight the problems involved in the freedom we find on the Internet and chapters discuss how to evaluate the stories behind the news and the pros and cons of Internet regulation. (Rev: SLJ 4/07)

23919 Brasch, Nicolas. *The Technology Behind the Internet* (5–8). Illus. 2011, Black Rabbit LB $28.50 (978-159920567-0). 32pp. This thorough, well-designed book addresses such pertinent subjects as how the Internet works, email, blogs, Web pages, Twitter, and chat-room safety. (Rev: BL 4/1/11) [004.67]

23920 Chorlton, Windsor. *The Invention of the Silicon Chip: A Revolution in Daily Life* (5–8). Series: Point of Impact. 2002, Heinemann LB $25.64 (978-1-58810-554-7). 32pp. Chorlton explores computers before and after the invention of the chip, introduces key players in the field, and discusses the impact of this new technology on society. (Rev: SLJ 9/02) [621.3815]

23921 Cindrich, Sharon. *A Smart Girl's Guide to the Internet* (3–7). Illus. by Ali Douglass. 2009, American Girl paper $9.95 (978-1-59369-599-6). 96pp. This colorful and appealing volume is subtitled *How to Connect with Friends, Find What You Need, and Stay Safe Online* and provides relevant guidance to games, blogs, games, music, and so forth along with quizzes, lists, and other features. (Rev: LMC 1–2/10; SLJ 11/09) [004.67]

23922 Domaine, Helena. *Robotics* (4–6). Illus. Series: Cool Science! 2005, Lerner LB $26.60 (978-0-8225-2112-9). 48pp. An attractive, colorful exploration of the history of robotics and the ways in which this technology is likely to affect life in the future. (Rev: BL 9/1/05; SLJ 12/05) [629.8]

23923 Douglas, Julie. *The Internet* (2–4). Series: Transportation and Communication. 2002, Enslow LB $23.93 (978-0-7660-1889-1). 48pp. A basic introduction to the Internet that supplies material on what it is, its history, people behind it, safety while online, and possible future developments. (Rev: BL 9/15/02; HBG 3/03) [004]

23924 Fritz, Sandy. *Robotics and Artificial Intelligence* (5–10). Illus. Series: Hot Science. 2003, Smart Apple LB $28.50 (978-1-58340-364-8). 48pp. After describing robots' contributions in space, in the workplace, in danger spots, and in medicine, Fritz speculates on the future possibilities. (Rev: BL 12/1/03; HBG 4/04; SLJ 4/04) [629.8]

23925 Gallimard Jeunesse, et al. *Internet* (PS–2). Series: First Discovery. 2000, Scholastic $12.95 (978-0-439-14825-2). 24pp. A beginning look at computers and the Internet with large illustrations and clear, simple explanations. (Rev: BL 8/00; HBG 3/01; SLJ 11/00) [004]

23926 Graham, Ian. *Robot Technology* (4–7). Illus. Series: New Technology. 2011, Black Rabbit LB $34.25

(978-159920533-5). 48pp. Describes the kinds of robots being used in various environments (space, military, factories, hospitals) and the technology evolutions taking place. (Rev: BL 10/15/11) [629.8]

23927 Herumin, Wendy. *Censorship on the Internet: From Filters to Freedom of Speech* (5–12). Series: Issues in Focus. 2004, Enslow LB $26.60 (978-0-7660-1946-1). A look at the various ways we restrict the free exchange of information over the Internet and the pros and cons of doing so. (Rev: SLJ 4/04) [303.48]

23928 Jefferis, David. *Internet: Electronic Global Village* (4–8). Series: Megatech. 2001, Crabtree paper $8.95 (978-0-7787-0062-3). An eye-catching look at the development of the Internet and the World Wide Web and their uses in communication and commerce. (Rev: SLJ 6/02) [4.678]

23929 Jones, David. *Mighty Robots: Mechanical Marvels That Fascinate and Frighten* (5–8). Illus. 2006, Annick $24.95 (978-1-55037-929-7); paper $14.95 (978-1-55037-928-0). 126pp. Artificial intelligence, mobility, and various robot roles are discussed in this look at the past, present, and future of robots. (Rev: BL 2/1/06) [629.8]

23930 Jortberg, Charles A. *The Internet* (4–6). Illus. Series: Kids and Computers. 1997, ABDO LB $24.21 (978-1-56239-727-2). 38pp. A history of the Internet, how to use it, and a listing of important sites for kids. (Rev: BL 6/1–15/97; HBG 3/98) [004.6]

23931 Knittel, John, and Michael Soto. *Everything You Need to Know About the Dangers of Computer Hacking* (5–8). 2000, Rosen LB $25.25 (978-0-8239-3034-0). This book points out the differences between a hacker and a cracker and, through this, discusses beneficial and harmful computer actions and how to avoid the latter. (Rev: BL 4/1/00; SLJ 5/00) [364.16]

23932 Lawler, Jennifer. *Cyberdanger and Internet Safety: A Hot Issue* (5–10). Series: Hot Issues. 2000, Enslow LB $27.93 (978-0-7660-1368-1). 64pp. As well as introducing the Internet, this account explains how people abuse it with hidden identities, threatening or obscene material, loss of privacy, hacking, con tricks, pranks, and hoaxes. (Rev: HBG 3/01; SLJ 1/01; VOYA 4/01) [004.6]

23933 Lemke, Donald. *Steve Jobs, Steve Wozniak, and the Personal Computer* (4–6). Illus. by Tod Smith. Series: Graphic Library: Inventions and Discovery. 2006, Capstone LB $26.60 (978-0-7368-6488-6). 32pp. A graphic-novel presentation of the story of Apple Computer, profiling its two young creators; the art has less value than the information presented but will attract some students to this history. (Rev: BL 10/15/06) [621.39092]

23934 Lindsay, Dave. *Dave's Quick 'n' Easy Web Pages: An Introductory Guide to Creating Web Sites. 2nd ed.* (5–9). Illus. by Sean Lindsay. 2001, Erin $11.95 (978-0-9690609-8-7). Young Dave, Webmaster of the popular Redwall site, gives good, basic information on HTML coding and Web page design. (Rev: SLJ 8/01) [005.7]

23935 Loughran, Donna. *Using the Internet Safely* (3–5). Series: Technology and You. 2003, Raintree LB $27.12

(978-0-7398-4697-1). 48pp. A guide to avoiding the pitfalls of the Web, with diagrams and "Techno Tips." (Rev: HBG 10/03; SLJ 4/03) [004.67]

23936 MacDonald, Joan Vos. *Cybersafety: Surfing Safely Online* (5–7). Illus. Series: Teen Issues. 2001, Enslow LB $22.60 (978-0-7660-1580-7). 64pp. Various dangers of venturing online are covered, from viruses and other problems that can infect your computer to activities such as hacking, cyberstalking, and copying software illegally. (Rev: HBG 3/02; SLJ 12/01) [004.6]

23937 Mason, Adrienne, ed. *Robots: From Everyday to Out of This World* (3–7). Illus. 2008, Kids Can $16.95 (978-1-55453-203-2). 32pp. A fascinating introduction to robots at work and at play with snappy text, easy reading sidebars, cartoon graphics, and color photographs. (Rev: BL 9/1/08) [629.8]

23938 Masura, Shauna. *Digital Badges* (4–7). Illus. Series: Makers as Innovators. 2013, Cherry Lake LB $28.50 (978-162431143-7); paper $14.21 (9781624312755). 32pp. A brief and understandable introduction to digital badges and how to use them and display them. (Rev: BL 11/1/13; LMC 5–6/14) [371.5]

23939 O'Neill, Terence, and Josh Williams. *3D Printing* (4–7). Illus. Series: Makers as Innovators. 2013, Cherry Lake LB $28.50 (978-162431138-3); paper $14.21 (9781624312700). 32pp. After explaining the technology involved, this volume discusses how they are being used and how to set about designing 3D objects made from plastic. **e** (Rev: BL 11/1/13; LMC 5–6/14; SLJ 3/14) [681]

23940 Oxlade, Chris. *My First E-Mail Guide* (K–2). Illus. Series: My First Computer Guides. 2007, Heinemann LB $25.36 (978-1-4329-0017-5). 32pp. An easy-to-read introduction to everything email — writing messages, correct etiquette, adding attachments, junk mail, and so forth. Also use *My First Internet Guide* (2007). (Rev: SLJ 12/07) [004.692]

23941 Oxlade, Chris. *Robots* (3–5). Illus. by Peter Bull. Series: Explorers. 2013, Kingfisher $10.99 (978-075346816-6). 32pp. With interactive "buttons" that allow readers to explore the book from different perspectives, this is a comprehensive survey of robots and the jobs they do in the house, in industry, in outer space, and so forth. Lexile y (Rev: BL 7/13) [629.8]

23942 Perry, Robert L. *Personal Computer Communications* (4–7). Illus. Series: Watts Library: Computer Science. 2000, Watts paper $8.95 (978-0-531-16483-9). 64pp. This work covers such topics as modems, networks, satellite and wireless technology, and the future of communications. (Rev: BL 10/15/00) [004.16]

23943 Raum, Elizabeth. *The History of the Computer* (2–3). Series: Inventions That Changed the World. 2007, Heinemann LB $25.36 (978-1-4034-9649-2). 32pp. After looking at the equipment we used before the invention of the computer, Raum traces developments from the early monster machines to today's notebooks and examines how the Internet has changed our lives. (Rev: SLJ 11/07) [004]

23944 Rooney, Anne. *Computers: Faster, Smaller, and Smarter* (5–9). Series: The Cutting Edge. 2005, Heinemann LB $32.86 (978-1-4034-7426-1). Looks at the technology behind computers of the past, present, and future; a high-tech design completes the package. (Rev: SLJ 6/06) [004]

23945 Roza, Greg. *The Incredible Story of Computers and the Internet* (3–6). Illus. Series: A Kid's Guide to Incredible Technology. 2004, Rosen LB $21.25 (978-0-8239-6717-9). 24pp. The structure of the Internet and the technology of accessing it are explained in concise terms, with discussion of safe behavior and future developments. (Rev: SLJ 2/05) [004.67]

23946 Selfridge, Benjamin, and Peter Selfridge. *A Kid's Guide to Creating Web Pages for Home and School* (5–10). 2004, Chicago Review paper $19.95 (978-1-56976-180-9). Simple instructions on creating Web pages using HTML are accompanied by helpful illustrations and sample finished pages. (Rev: SLJ 2/05) [005.7]

23947 Severance, Charles R., and Kristin Fontichiaro. *Raspberry Pi* (4–7). Illus. Series: Makers as Innovators. 2013, Cherry Lake LB $28.50 (978-162431139-0); paper $14.21 (9781624312717). 32pp. Raspberry Pi, a tool used to teach children programming, is the subject of this book, which discusses how Raspberry Pi can be used to help children become technology inventors and provides inspiring sidebars. (Rev: BL 11/1/13; LMC 5–6/14) [5.13]

23948 Spangenburg, Ray, and Kit Moser. *Savvy Surfing on the Internet: Searching and Evaluating Web Sites* (5–8). Series: Issues in Focus. 2001, Enslow LB $26.60 (978-0-7660-1590-6). Readers are encouraged to view much of the information on the Internet with healthy suspicion and are given advice on efficient searching for and assessment of Web sites. (Rev: HBG 3/02; SLJ 12/01) [004.6]

23949 Thomas, Peggy. *Artificial Intelligence* (5–8). Series: Lucent Library of Science and Technology. 2005, Gale LB $29.95 (978-1-59018-437-0). An interesting overview of progress in efforts to create machines that can think like humans. (Rev: BL 1/05) [004]

23950 Truesdell, Ann. *Get to the Right Site* (3–5). Illus. Series: Information Explorer Junior. 2012, Cherry Lake LB $27.07 (978-161080365-6). 32pp. This research-friendly guide provides solid advice on how to evaluate Web sites. (Rev: BL 4/1/12; LMC 8–9/13*) [025.042]

23951 Wan, Guofang. *Virtually True: Questioning Online Media* (4–7). Illus. Series: Fact Finders. Media Literacy. 2006, Capstone LB $22.60 (978-0-7368-6767-2). 32pp. Designed to awaken skepticism about online media, this book discusses the motivations of those who produce online content and the influence this media has on society. (Rev: SLJ 6/07)

23952 Ward-Johnson, Chris. *Computers: A Magic Mouse Guide* (1–4). Illus. Series: Magic Mouse Guides. 2003, Enslow LB $22.60 (978-0-7660-2263-8). 32pp. Suitable for beginners, this basic guide is presented in the form

of a story about Ben, Liza, and Hari, who are learning to use a computer. (Rev: HBG 4/04; SLJ 8/03) [004]

23953 Ward-Johnson, Chris. *E-mail: A Magic Mouse Guide* (1–4). Illus. Series: Magic Mouse Guides. 2003, Enslow LB $22.60 (978-0-7660-2261-4). 32pp. Ben and Hari learn to communicate electronically in this attractive and informative volume for beginners. Also use *Internet* (2003). (Rev: HBG 4/04; SLJ 8/03) [004.692]

23954 Williams, Brian. *Computers* (5–8). Illus. Series: Great Inventions. 2001, Heinemann LB $25.64 (978-1-58810-210-2). 48pp. A chronological look at computers and their predecessors, from the abacus onward, with diagrams and information on the inventors. (Rev: HBG 3/02; SLJ 2/02) [004]

23955 Wolinsky, Art. *Internet Power Research Using the Big6 Approach. Rev. ed.* (3–8). Illus. Series: The Internet Library. 2005, Enslow LB $22.60 (978-0-7660-1563-0). 64pp. Shows readers how to apply the "Big6" method to research done on the Internet; a revision of a 2002 title. (Rev: SLJ 11/05) [025.04]

23956 Wolinsky, Art. *Safe Surfing on the Internet* (4–8). 2003, Enslow LB $22.60 (978-0-7660-2030-6). Wolinksy presents information on safe use of the Internet and topics including proper use of language, copyright, privacy, and plagiarism. (Rev: HBG 10/03; LMC 8–9/03; SLJ 7/03) [004.67]

23957 Woodford, Chris. *Digital Technology* (4–7). Series: Science in Focus. 2006, Chelsea House LB $27.00 (978-0-7910-8861-6). A clear introduction to the world of digital technology, covering topics including smart cards, computer-aided design, mobile phones, and so forth in easy-to-understand language. (Rev: BL 10/15/06) [621.381]

23958 Worland, Gayle. *The Computer* (2–4). Series: Fact Finders: Great Inventions. 2003, Capstone LB $23.93 (978-0-7368-2215-2). 32pp. An introduction to computers — how they came to be, how they work, and how they have changed daily life — with a final page of facts and an activity (writing a message in binary code). (Rev: SLJ 6/04) [004]

Electronics

23959 Kaplan, Arie. *The Epic Evolution of Video Games* (5–8). Illus. Series: Games and Gamers. 2013, Lerner LB $26.60 (978-146771248-4). 32pp. An eye-catching survey of the evolution of computer games, putting them into historical, creative, and cultural context. **e** (Rev: BL 10/1/13; LMC 3–4/14) [794.809]

23960 Oxlade, Chris. *Electronics: MP3s, TVs, and DVDs* (5–9). Series: The Cutting Edge. 2005, Heinemann LB $32.86 (978-1-4034-7427-8). Looks at the technology behind popular electronic devices and at predictions about gadgets of the future; a high-tech design completes the package. (Rev: SLJ 6/06)

23961 Oxlade, Chris. *Gaming Technology* (4–7). Illus. Series: New Technology. 2011, Black Rabbit LB $34.25 (978-159920531-1). 48pp. An attractive (if soon dated) introduction to the technology used in creating video games. (Rev: BL 10/15/11) [794.8]

23969 Ridley, Sarah. *A Metal Can* (2–4). Illus. Series: How It's Made. 2006, Gareth Stevens $24.00 (978-0-8368-6702-2). 32pp. This photo-filled title traces the life cycle of an aluminum soda can from the mining of the raw material — bauxite — to the recycling bin. (Rev: BL 10/15/06) [670]

Machinery

23962 Low, William. *Machines Go to Work* (PS–1). Illus. by author. 2009, Holt $14.95 (978-0-8050-8759-8). 42pp. With motion, bright images, and fold-outs that expose additional images, this is a satisfying look at powerful machines (a helicopter, a tugboat, a cement mixer, and so forth). (Rev: BL 3/15/09; HB 7/09; SLJ 5/09*) [621.8]

23963 Mitchell, Joyce Slayton. *Knuckleboom Loaders Load Logs: A Trip to the Sawmill* (K–3). Illus. 2003, Overlook $14.95 (978-1-58567-368-1). 40pp. This feast of powerful machines used in the harvesting, hauling, and processing of forest products will appeal to the big-truck crowd. (Rev: BL 2/1/04; HBG 4/04; SLJ 3/04) [634]

23964 Peterson, Cris. *Fantastic Farm Machines* (1–3). Illus. by David R. Lundquist. 2006, Boyds Mills $17.95 (978-1-59078-271-2). 32pp. Peterson gives readers a personal tour of the high-tech equipment used on today's farms. (Rev: BL 2/15/06; SLJ 3/06) [631.3]

23965 Silverman, Buffy. *Simple Machines* (3–6). Illus. 2009, Heinemann LB $22.00 (978-1-4329-2310-5). 48pp. Examples and experiments in building simple machines with parental guidance advised. (Rev: BL 6/1–15/09) [621.8]

23966 Wallace, Karen. *Big Machines* (K–2). Series: Eyewitness Reader. 2000, DK LB $14.99 (978-0-7894-5412-6); paper $3.99 (978-0-7894-5411-9). 32pp. This book presents pictures and text on such big machines as a crane, a bulldozer, a front loader, a dump truck, and an excavator. (Rev: HBG 9/00; SLJ 7/00) [621.8]

23967 Whitehouse, Patty. *Moving Machines* (K–2). Illus. 2006, Rourke LB $14.95 (978-1-60044-192-9). 24pp. This attractive title explores the wide range of machines used to move materials, ranging from simple pulleys, shovels, and wheelbarrows to cherry pickers and scissor lifts. (Rev: BL 10/15/06) [621.8]

Metals

23968 Oxlade, Chris. *Metal* (2–3). Series: Materials, Materials, Materials. 2001, Heinemann LB $21.36 (978-1-58810-155-6). 32pp. With color photographs and brief text on each page, the story of what metals are is covered plus where they are found and extracted, and their uses in everyday life. (Rev: BL 10/15/01) [669]

Telegraph, Telephone, and Telecommunications

23970 Byers, Ann. *Communications Satellites* (5–9). Series: The Library of Satellites. 2003, Rosen LB $26.50 (978-0-8239-3851-3). From the first important communications satellites launched in 1962, this account traces the growth of this technology and its possible future developments. (Rev: BL 11/15/03; SLJ 1/04) [001.51]

23971 Hegedus, Alannah, and Kaitlin Rainey. *Bleeps and Blips to Rocket Ships: Great Inventions in Communications* (5–9). Illus. by Bill Slavin. 2001, Tundra paper $17.95 (978-0-88776-452-3). This is a fact-packed and appealing look at the field of communications, with information on history and inventors and inventions as well as suggested activities. (Rev: SLJ 8/01) [609.71]

23972 Maddison, Simon. *Telecoms: Present Knowledge, Future Trends* (5–9). Series: 21st Century Science. 2003, Smart Apple Media LB $27.10 (978-1-58340-352-5). Numerous diagrams, photographs, and drawings add to this overview of the history of telecommunications and the status of current technology. (Rev: SLJ 1/04) [384]

23973 Mattern, Joanne. *From Radio to the Wireless Web* (2–4). Series: Transportation and Communication. 2002, Enslow LB $23.93 (978-0-7660-1893-8). 48pp. This book explains the development of telecommunications, present uses, possible future developments, and people involved in its history. (Rev: BL 9/15/02; HBG 10/02) [384]

23974 Mattern, Joanne. *Telephones* (2–4). Series: Transportation and Communication. 2002, Enslow LB $23.93 (978-0-7660-1888-4). 48pp. From Alexander Graham Bell to the cell phones of today, this is the history of the telephone with material on how it works and possible future developments. (Rev: BL 9/15/02; HBG 10/02) [384.6]

23975 Nelson, Robin. *Communication* (3–6). Series: First Step Nonfiction. 2003, Lerner LB $18.60 (978-0-8225-4638-2). 24pp. For beginning readers, old and new in the field of communication are paired to good effect on double-page spreads. (Rev: BL 11/15/03; HBG 4/04; SLJ 12/03)

23976 Raum, Elizabeth. *The History of the Telephone* (2–3). Series: Inventions That Changed the World. 2007, Heinemann LB $25.36 (978-1-4034-9650-8). 32pp. After looking at the status quo before the invention of the telephone, Raum traces the history of this service from party lines to cell phones. (Rev: SLJ 11/07) [621.385]

23977 Streissguth, Thomas. *Communications: Sending the Message* (5–8). Series: Innovators. 1997, Oliver LB $21.95 (978-1-881508-41-0). A compact, easy-to-understand history of communication from earliest times, through Gutenberg, Edison, and Marconi, to the present "information highway." (Rev: SLJ 2/98) [001.51]

Television, Motion Pictures, Radio, and Recording

23978 Abraham, Philip. *Television and Movies* (4–7). Illus. Series: American Pop Culture. 2004, Children's Pr. LB $24.50 (978-0-516-24074-9); paper $6.95 (978-0-516-25946-8). 48pp. Traces the technological and cultural development of TV and movies in the United States. (Rev: SLJ 1/05)

23979 Feeney, Kathy. *Television* (2–4). Series: Transportation and Communication. 2001, Enslow LB $23.93 (978-0-7660-1644-6). 48pp. A simple, well-illustrated volume on the history of television, its development, and its many uses. (Rev: BL 3/15/02; HBG 3/02) [384.55]

23980 Gilbert, Sara. *The Story of CNN* (5–8). Illus. Series: Built for Success. 2012, Creative Education $24.95 (978-160818175-9). 48pp. Tells the story of the creation of the first 24-hour all-news cable network, its success, and some of the events it has covered. Also in this series: *The Story of Amazon.com, The Story of Facebook,* and *The Story of Fedex* (all 2012). Lexile NC1330L (Rev: BL 9/15/12; LMC 5–6/13) [070.4]

23981 Glassbourg, Michael. *Learn to Speak Film: A Guide to Creating, Promoting and Screening Your Movies* (5–8). Illus. by Jeff Kulak. 2013, OwlKids $22.95 (978-192697384-5); paper $14.95 (978-19269738-5-2). 96pp. Taking the reader through the steps of film production to distribution, this text provides an overview of everything you need to know about the creative process of making and editing your own films and offers tips from professionals. (Rev: BL 9/1/13; SLJ 9/13) [791.43]

23982 Hamilton, Jake. *Special Effects: In Film and Television* (4–8). 1998, DK $17.95 (978-0-7849-2813-4). This is an intriguing glimpse at special effects in film and television, using double-page spreads that each focus on a different aspect of production, such as storyboards, makeup, and stunts. (Rev: BCCB 9/98; BL 8/98; VOYA 10/98) [791.43]

23983 Hirschmann, Kris. *HDTV: High Definition Television* (4–6). Series: Great Idea. 2010, Norwood LB $25.27 (978-1-59953-379-7). 48pp. Hirschmann looks at the development of high-definition television, how it works, and how it changes the way we watch TV, with "Did You Know" boxes, photographs, and useful Web sites. (Rev: SLJ 1/1/11) [384.55]

23984 Kinney, Jeff. *The Wimpy Kid Movie Diary: How Greg Heffley Went Hollywood* (4–8). Illus. 2010, Abrams $14.95 (978-081099616-8). 208pp. Kinney offers a behind-the-scenes glimpse at the making of *Diary of a Wimpy Kid: The Movie* in this engrossing book. Lexile 1000L (Rev: BLO 3/15/10) [791.43]

23985 Mattern, Joanne. *The History of Radio* (2–4). Illus. Series: Transportation and Communication. 2002, Enslow LB $23.93 (978-0-7660-2027-6). 48pp. An easy-to-read account of the invention and long popularity of radio. (Rev: HBG 10/03) [621]

23986 Raum, Elizabeth. *The History of the Camera* (2–3). Series: Inventions That Changed the World. 2007, Heinemann LB $25.36 (978-1-4034-9647-8). 32pp. After looking at the images we used before the development of the camera, Raum traces the camera's history from early daguerrotypes to today's digital and cellphone cameras. (Rev: SLJ 11/07) [771.309]

23987 Somervill, Barbara. *The History of the Motion Picture* (3–6). Series: Our Changing World: The Timeline Library. 2006, The Child's World LB $27.07 (978-1-59296-440-6). 32pp. From moving shadows to computer video clips, this book traces the evolution of moving images and looks forward into the future. (Rev: SLJ 7/06) [791.43]

23988 Spilsbury, Richard. *Cartoons and Animation* (4–7). Illus. Series: Art off the Wall. 2006, Heinemann LB $23.00 (978-1-4034-8287-7). Surveys the history, techniques, and movie applications of cartooning and animation, and includes bold color illustrations of familiar characters and animators at work. (Rev: BL 1/1–15/07; SLJ 5/07) [741.5]

23989 Worland, Gayle. *The Radio* (2–4). Series: Fact Finders: Great Inventions. 2003, Capstone LB $23.93 (978-0-7368-2217-6). 32pp. A basic history of radio — how it works, who its pioneers were, and the impact it has had on civilization. (Rev: SLJ 6/04) [621.384]

Transportation

General

23990 Abramson, Andra Serlin. *Heavy Equipment Up Close* (2–4). Illus. Series: Up Close. 2008, Sterling $9.95 (978-1-4027-4799-3). 24pp. Full-color photographs show construction equipment (dump trucks, dozers, tractors, cranes, and so forth) up close in this large-format book that also provides the correct terminology and lots of interesting facts. (Rev: BL 4/1/08; LMC 8/08) [623.74]

23991 Anderson, Catherine. *Fire Truck Factory* (PS–2). Illus. Series: Read and Learn. 2005, Heinemann LB $18.50 (978-1-4034-6162-9). 24pp. The construction of a fire truck is shown in clear photographs and short, simple sentences. (Rev: BL 5/1/05; SLJ 5/05) [629.225]

23992 Askew, Amanda. *Loaders* (PS–2). Illus. Series: Mighty Machines. 2010, Firefly paper $5.95 (978-15540770-6-9). 24pp. How loaders work — and why we use them — are explored in this clear early reader.

Also use *Cranes* and *Diggers* (both 2010). (Rev: BL 10/15/10) [621.8]

23993 Bial, Raymond. *The Canals* (4–8). Illus. Series: Building America. 2001, Marshall Cavendish LB $27.07 (978-0-7614-1336-3). 56pp. This history of the U.S. canal system and how it works includes excellent photographs and illustrations that help to explain the technical aspects of canals. (Rev: BL 3/1/02; HBG 3/02; SLJ 2/02*) [386]

23994 Bridges, Sarah. *I Drive a Bulldozer* (PS–2). Illus. by Derrick Alderman and Denise Shea. Series: Working Wheels. 2004, Picture Window LB $25.26 (978-1-4048-0613-9). 24pp. A large-format volume that shows a bulldozer driver day at work. Also use *I Drive a Dump Truck* and *I Drive a Snowplow* (2004). (Rev: SLJ 3/05) [621.8]

23995 Brimner, Larry Dane. *Subway: A Brief History of Underground Mass Transit* (3–6). Illus. by Neil Waldman. 2004, Boyds Mills $15.95 (978-1-59078-176-0). 32pp. This attractively illustrated overview explores the history of New York City's century-old subway, the forces behind its development, and the impact it had on the city. (Rev: BL 10/15/04; SLJ 3/05) [388.4]

23996 Cooper, Wade. *On the Road* (PS–1). Illus. Series: Scholastic Reader. 2008, Scholastic LB $3.99 (978-0-545-00720-7). 32pp. Vehicles from cement mixers to sports cars are presented in photographs and rhymes geared to brand-new readers. (Rev: BL 1/1–15/08) [629.046]

23997 Coppendale, Jean. *Fire Trucks and Rescue Vehicles* (PS–2). Illus. Series: QEB First Book Of. 2007, Black Rabbit LB $16.95 (978-1-59566-342-9). 24pp. This title features trucks and fireboats, urgent action, and big color pictures. (Rev: BLO 3/3/08) [629.225]

23998 David, Jack. *Motocross Racing* (3–5). Series: Torque: Action Sports. 2007, Children's Pr. LB $20.00 (978-0-531-18491-2). 24pp. With lots of clear, bright photographs and simple text, this volume looks at the equipment and experiences of this sport. Also use *Enduro Motocycles, Cruisers,* and *Choppers* in the companion Torque: Motorcycles series (all 2007). (Rev: SLJ 7/08) [796.7]

23999 Dittmer, Lori. *The Future of Transportation* (5–8). Illus. Series: What's Next? 2012, Creative Education LB $24.95 (978-160818224-4). 48pp. This thought-provoking volume first surveys earlier advances in transportation before looking at developments that may have success in the future. (Rev: BL 10/1/12; LMC 5–6/13) [629.04]

24000 DuTemple, Lesley A. *New York Subways* (4–7). Illus. Series: Great Building Feats. 2003, Lerner LB $27.93 (978-0-8225-0378-1). 80pp. DuTemple presents the history of the subway system with details of its difficult construction, continuing financial problems, and the damage caused in the destruction of the World Trade Center. (Rev: BL 1/1–15/03; HBG 10/03) [388.4]

24001 Francis, Dorothy. *Our Transportation System* (3–4). Illus. Series: I Know America. 2002, Millbrook LB $24.90 (978-0-7613-2366-2). 48pp. A historical look at

transportation in the United States, from roads to rail, water, and air. (Rev: BL 2/1/02; HBG 10/02) [388]

24002 Frisch, Aaron. *Dump Trucks* (PS–1). Illus. Series: Seedlings. 2013, Creative Education $17.95 (978-160818341-8). 24pp. Large photographs and simple text provide an overview of the functions, equipment, and design of dump trucks. Also use *Diggers, Cranes,* and *Bulldozers* (all 2013). (Rev: BL 9/1/13; SLJ 10/13) [629.225]

24003 Ganeri, Anita. *Things That Go* (K–2). Illus. by Mark Bergin. Series: Flip the Flaps. 2010, Kingfisher $9.99 (978-0-7534-6409-0). 32pp. With a single question-and-answer flap per spread, this appealing book presents various kinds of transportation with large-font text. (Rev: BL 2/1/11; SLJ 4/11) [629]

24004 Gifford, Clive. *Things That Go* (3–5). Illus. by Peter Bull. Series: Explorers. 2011, Kingfisher $10.99 (978-075346593-6). 32pp. An inviting mix of text, sidebars, captions, fact lists, and more add read-appeal to this well-illustrated book about vehicles including cars, planes, boats, and rockets. (Rev: BL 2/15/12)

24005 *Go! The Whole World of Transportation* (5–10). Illus. 2006, DK $26.99 (978-0-7566-2224-4). This wide-ranging, visually fascinating journey through the world of transportation touches on everything from buses and ferries to speedboats and fighter jets. (Rev: SLJ 2/07*) [388]

24006 Goodman, Susan. *Choppers!* (K–2). Photos by Michael J. Doolittle. Series: Step into Reading. 2004, Random LB $11.99 (978-0-375-92517-7); paper $3.99 (978-0-375-82517-0). 48pp. For beginning readers, a look at the history and uses of helicopters. (Rev: SLJ 5/05)

24007 Goodman, Susan E. *Motorcycles!* (PS–2). Illus. by Michael Doolittle. Series: Step into Reading. 2007, Random LB $11.99 (978-0-375-94116-0); paper $3.99 (978-0-375-84116-3). 48pp. Beginning readers will imagine themselves riding the motorcycles and racing bikes featured in this photograph-filled book. (Rev: BL 6/1–15/07; SLJ 10/07) [629.227]

24008 Hamilton, John. *Transportation: A Pictorial History of the Past One Thousand Years* (4–7). Series: The Millennium. 2000, ABDO LB $25.65 (978-1-57765-361-5). A history of 1,000 years of transportation that includes animals, ships, trains, bicycles, motorcycles, cars, airplanes, and spacecraft. (Rev: BL 7/00; HBG 10/00; SLJ 10/00) [388.21]

24009 Herbst, Judith. *The History of Transportation* (5–8). Series: Major Inventions Through History. 2005, Twenty-First Century LB $26.60 (978-0-8225-2496-0). From the wheel to the airplane, technological innovations involving transport have had a profound impact on our lives as shown in this attractive, well-written volume. (Rev: SLJ 2/06) [973]

24010 Isaacs, Sally Senzell. *Stagecoaches and Railroads* (4–6). Illus. Series: All About America. 2012, Kingfisher LB $19.89 (978-075346696-4); paper $9.99 (978-075346516-5). 32pp. In 13 highly illustrated spreads, this informative book looks at the transportation system that made it possible to develop the West — steamboats, stagecoaches, and of course the railroads. (Rev: BL 4/15/12; SLJ 3/12) [388]

24011 Jango-Cohen, Judith. *Dump Trucks* (2–3). Series: Pull Ahead Books. 2002, Lerner LB $22.60 (978-0-8225-0688-1); paper $5.95 (978-0-8225-0602-7). 32pp. This colorful account introduces dump trucks, explains their parts, tells how they work, and describes their functions. (Rev: BL 8/02; HBG 3/03) [629.224]

24012 Jango-Cohen, Judith. *Fire Trucks* (2–3). Series: Pull Ahead Books. 2002, Lerner LB $22.60 (978-0-8225-0077-3); paper $5.95 (978-0-8225-0604-1). After describing the parts of a fire truck in text and pictures, this book explains how they work and the jobs they do. (Rev: BL 8/02; HBG 3/03) [629.255]

24013 Johnstone, Mike. *Monster Trucks* (5–8). Series: Need for Speed. 2002, Lerner LB $23.93 (978-0-8225-0388-0). 32pp. In stunning action-filled text and pictures, this book highlights huge trucks that weigh thousands of pounds and stand more than 10 feet high. (Rev: BL 8/02; HBG 10/02; SLJ 7/02) [629.225]

24014 Kilby, Don. *On the Road* (PS–K). Illus. 2003, Kids Can $14.95 (978-1-55337-379-7). 24pp. Double-page spreads show bright illustrations of a variety of trucks and tractors at work. (Rev: BL 5/1/03; HBG 10/03; SLJ 5/03) [629.224]

24015 *Let's Get to Work! / ¡Vamos a trabajar!* (PS–2). Illus. by Gaétan Evrard. 2005, Two-Can $6.95 (978-1-58728-512-7). This attractive bilingual board book introduces young readers to a variety of vehicles and their names in both English and Spanish; also use *Let's Go! / ¡Vamos a Viajar!* (2005). (Rev: SLJ 10/05)

24016 Macaulay, David, and Sheila Keenan. *Jet Plane: How It Works* (K–2). Illus. by David Macaulay. 2012, Roaring Brook $15.99 (978-1-59643-764-7); paper $3.99 (978-1-59643-767-8). 32pp. A simple and yet detailed introduction to the experience of flying on a jet plane, with the usual cutaway illustrations; suitable for beginning readers. Lexile 560L (Rev: BL 11/15/12; HB 1–2/13; SLJ 2/13) [629.133]

24017 McKendry, Joe. *Beneath the Streets of Boston: Building America's First Subway* (3–5). Illus. 2005, Godine $19.95 (978-1-56792-284-4). 48pp. A fascinating and detailed look at America's first subway and the social and technical issues surrounding it. (Rev: BL 6/1–15/05) [625.4]

24018 Maynard, Christopher. *Extreme Machines* (3–6). Series: Eyewitness Reader. 2000, DK paper $3.99 (978-0-7894-5417-1). 48pp. A visually appealing book that looks at machines from drag cars to helicopters. (Rev: HBG 9/00; SLJ 8/00) [629.04]

24019 Mayo, Margaret. *Choo Choo Clickety-Clack!* (PS–K). Illus. by Alex Ayliffe. 2005, Carolrhoda $14.95 (978-1-57505-819-1). 32pp. Brightly colored pages with eye-catching graphics and lively words introduce various modes of transportation. (Rev: BL 2/15/05; SLJ 5/05) [629]

24020 Mayo, Margaret. *Dig Dig Digging* (PS). Illus. by Alex Ayliffe. 2002, Holt $14.95 (978-0-8050-6840-5). 32pp. A rhyming book, with illustrations, about tractors, fire engines, helicopters, and other favorite vehicles. (Rev: BL 5/15/02; HBG 10/02; SLJ 5/02) [629.225]

24021 Molzahn, Arlene Bourgeois. *Fire Engines* (2–4). Illus. Series: Transportation and Communication. 2001, Enslow LB $23.93 (978-0-7660-1643-9). 48pp. The ever-popular fire engine is featured here, with photographs of vehicles past and present, a timeline, a glossary, and lists of further resources. (Rev: BL 10/15/01; HBG 3/02) [628.9]

24022 Molzahn, Arlene Bourgeois. *Highways and Freeways* (2–4). Series: Transportation and Communication. 2002, Enslow LB $23.93 (978-0-7660-1891-4). 48pp. This book traces the development of road transportation, how networks developed, their importance, and possible future developments. (Rev: BL 9/15/02; HBG 3/03) [388.11]

24023 Mulder, Michelle. *Pedal It! How Bicycles Are Changing the World* (4–7). Illus. 2013, Orca $19.95 (978-145980219-3). 48pp. An engaging overview of bicycles, their history, and their diverse uses around the world. (Rev: BL 6/13; LMC 1–2/14; SLJ 7/13) [629.227]

24024 Murphy, John. *The Eisenhower Interstate System* (5–8). Series: Building America: Then and Now. 2009, Chelsea House $35 (978-1-60413-067-6). 120pp. This book about the Eisenhower Interstate System includes illustrative maps, primary source documents, Web sites, a timeline, and glossary. (Rev: LMC 10/09)

24025 Nelson, Kristin L. *Farm Tractors* (2–3). Series: Pull Ahead Books. 2002, Lerner LB $22.60 (978-0-8225-0690-4); paper $5.95 (978-0-8225-0607-2). 32pp. Farm tractors are introduced with many photographs and large-type text and coverage is given on the jobs they do like towing a plow, seed drill, or a mower. (Rev: BL 8/02; HBG 3/03; SLJ 10/02) [621.8]

24026 Nelson, Robin. *Transportation* (3–6). Series: First Step Nonfiction. 2003, Lerner LB $18.60 (978-0-8225-4636-8). 24pp. Suitable for beginning readers, this book uses double-page spreads to show how transportation has changed over the years. (Rev: BL 11/15/03; HBG 4/04; SLJ 12/03)

24027 Prince, April Jones. *What Do Wheels Do All Day?* (PS–2). Illus. by Giles Laroche. 2006, Houghton $16.00 (978-0-618-56307-4). 32pp. This oversized picture book explores wheels of every size and description and the wide range of tasks they perform. (Rev: BL 4/15/06; SLJ 6/06) [621.8]

24028 Richards, Julie. *Canals and Aqueducts* (4–6). Illus. Series: Smart Structures. 2003, Smart Apple LB $24.25 (978-1-58340-347-1). 32pp. The science and history of canals, from Venice to Panama, is explored in this well-illustrated book. (Rev: SLJ 3/04) [627]

24029 Roberts, Cynthia. *Tow Trucks* (PS). Illus. Series: Machines at Work. 2007, Child's World LB $22.79 (978-1-59296-836-7). 24pp. With close-up photographs and dramatic photographs, this small book looks at the different tasks these vehicles can perform and the equipment they use to do the job. (Rev: BL 4/15/07) [629.225]

24030 Tourville, Amanda Doering. *Bulldozers* (PS–2). Illus. by Zachary Trover. Series: Mighty Machines. 2009, Magic Wagon LB $18.95 (978-1-60270-621-7). 32pp. For machinery fans, this offers bright images and details of key working parts. (Rev: BL 4/1/09) [629.225]

24031 Whitman, Sylvia. *Get Up and Go! The History of American Road Travel* (5–8). 1996, Lerner LB $30.35 (978-0-8225-1735-1). From primitive pathways to modern superhighways, this is a history of American roads and the vehicles that traveled them. (Rev: BL 10/15/96; SLJ 10/96; VOYA 2/97) [388.1]

Automobiles and Trucks

24032 Anderson, Jenna. *How It Happens at the Truck Plant* (1–3). Photos by Bob Wolfe and Diane Wolfe. Series: How It Happens. 2002, Oliver LB $19.95 (978-1-881508-93-9). 32pp. How trucks are manufactured is described in text and photographs. (Rev: HBG 10/02; SLJ 12/02) [629]

24033 Bearce, Stephanie. *All About Electric and Hybrid Cars and Who's Driving Them* (4–7). Series: Tell Your Parents. 2010, Mitchell Lane LB $29.95 (978-1-58415-763-2). 48pp. With photographs and graphics, this is an attractive introduction to the mechanics and benefits of hybrid and electric cars. (Rev: BL 10/1/09; LMC 1–2/10)

24034 Benjamin, Daniel. *Prius* (4–6). Series: Green Cars. 2010, Marshall Cavendish LB $19.95 (978-1-60870-011-0). 48pp. Benjamin introduces the technology used in the Toyota hybrid and discusses the environmental benefits of this eco-friendly car. (Rev: SLJ 1/1/11) [629.22]

24035 Burgan, Michael. *The World's Fastest Cars* (3–8). Illus. Series: Built for Speed. 2000, Capstone LB $23.93 (978-0-7368-0570-4). 48pp. Dragsters, Indie 500 race cars, and other fast automobiles are covered in this visually appealing account that will be attractive to reluctant readers. (Rev: HBG 10/01; SLJ 6/01) [629.228]

24036 Collicutt, Paul. *This Truck* (PS–1). Illus. by author. 2004, Farrar $15.00 (978-0-374-37496-9). From the front endpapers showing vintage models to the back endpapers' contemporary examples, this is an appealing and colorful look at big rigs. (Rev: SLJ 7/04) [629.224]

24037 Flammang, James M. *Cars* (2–4). Illus. Series: Transportation and Communication. 2001, Enslow LB $23.93 (978-0-7660-1646-0). 48pp. Car lovers will enjoy this easy-reading look at automobiles past and present with black-and-white and color photographs, a timeline, a glossary, and lists of further resources. (Rev: BL 10/15/01; HBG 3/02) [629.222]

24038 Hubbell, Patricia. *Cars: Rushing! Honking! Zooming!* (PS–2). Illus. by Megan Halsey. 2006, Marshall Cavendish $14.99 (978-0-7614-5296-6). 32pp. Rhyming text and intricate illustrations introduce everything from family cars to limousines and hot rods. (Rev: BL 11/1/06; SLJ 11/06)

24039 Juettner, Bonnie. *Hybrid Cars* (4–7). Illus. Series: A Great Idea!: Going Green. 2009, Norwood House LB $18.95 (978-1-59953-193-9). 48pp. Juettner places the development of hybrid cars in historical context and discusses research into alternative fuels; the photographs will attract browsers. (Rev: BL 4/1/09) [629.22]

24040 Levinson, Nancy S. *Cars: A Holiday House Reader, Level 2* (1–3). Trans. and illus. by Jacqueline Rogers. Series: Holiday House Reader. 2004, Holiday House $14.95 (978-0-8234-1614-1). 32pp. Benz, Daimler, and Ford are among the prominent names in this overview for beginning readers of the early days of the automobile. (Rev: BL 11/15/04) [629.2]

24041 Lew, Kristi. *Volt* (4–6). Series: Green Cars. 2010, Marshall Cavendish LB $19.95 (978-1-60870-013-4). 48pp. Lew reviews the battery technology used in the Chevrolet Volt and the future of electric cars. (Rev: SLJ 1/1/11) [629.22]

24042 Lichtenheld, Tom. *Everything I Know About Cars: A Collection of Made-Up Facts, Educated Guesses, and Silly Pictures About Cars, Trucks, and Other Zoomy Things* (2–4). Illus. by author. 2005, Simon & Schuster $16.95 (978-0-689-84382-2). A zany, large-format introduction to cars and car parts, with some facts and some fake facts plus lots of cartoons and good advice on drawing cars. (Rev: BCCB 4/05; BL 1/1–15/05; SLJ 5/05) [388.3]

24043 Lindeen, Mary. *Trucks* (PS–3). 2007, Children's Pr. LB $18.50 (978-1-60014-063-1). 24pp. The basics about trucks for young readers, clearly presented and accompanied by engaging photographs. (Rev: SLJ 7/07)

24044 McKenna, A. T. *Corvette* (5–7). Series: Ultimate Car. 2000, ABDO LB $24.21 (978-1-57765-127-7). This introduction to this famous sports car includes material on its design, construction, and records it has broken. Similar material appears in companion books *Ferrari*, *Jaguar*, *Lamborghini*, *Mustang*, and *Porsche* (all 2000). (Rev: BL 3/1/01; HBG 10/01) [629]

24045 Mitchell, Joyce Slayton. *Crashed, Smashed, and Mashed* (1–3). Illus. by Steven Borns. 2001, Tricycle $14.95 (978-1-58246-034-5). 32pp. Photos and text show an automobile junkyard and describe what happens to old cars when they are recycled. (Rev: BL 3/15/01; HBG 10/01) [629.2]

24046 Mitchell, Joyce Slayton. *Tractor-Trailer Trucker: A Powerful Truck Book* (2–5). Illus. 2000, Tricycle $14.95 (978-1-58246-010-9). 40pp. Written like a manual, this book gives detailed instructions on how to drive and care for a big rig. (Rev: BL 4/1/00; HBG 9/00; SLJ 8/00) [629.2844]

24047 Mitton, Tony. *Cool Cars* (PS–3). Illus. by Ant Parker. 2005, Kingfisher $9.95 (978-0-7534-5802-0). Introduces all kinds of cars — family cars, taxis, race cars, and so forth — with an appealing blend of rhyming text and dynamic artwork. (Rev: BL 7/05; SLJ 6/05) [629.222]

24048 Molzahn, Arlene Bourgeois. *Police and Emergency Vehicles* (2–4). Series: Transportation and Communication. 2002, Enslow LB $23.93 (978-0-7660-1890-7). 48pp. Various kinds of emergency vehicles are presented with background history, details of people who were important in their development, and potential future improvements. (Rev: BL 9/15/02; HBG 3/03) [629.04]

24049 Nelson, Kristin L. *Monster Trucks* (2–3). Series: Pull Ahead Books. 2002, Lerner LB $22.60 (978-0-8225-0691-1); paper $5.95 (978-0-8225-0605-8). 32pp. The world of monster trucks is introduced in color photographs and a simple text with material on their structure and functions such as heavy towing. (Rev: BL 8/02; HBG 3/03) [629.225]

24050 Newhouse, Maxwell. *Let's Go for a Ride* (K–4). Illus. by author. 2006, Tundra $16.95 (978-0-88776-748-7). From the earliest automobiles through the "glory days" of the 1950s, this friendly, first-person overview gives a good feeling of the joys of driving as they change over time. (Rev: SLJ 4/06) [629.222]

24051 Nielsen, L. Michelle. *Vintage Cars: 1919–1930* (4–6). Series: Automania! 2006, Crabtree LB $25.20 (978-0-7787-3011-8); paper $8.95 (978-0-7787-3033-0). 32pp. Plenty of photographs of cool cars from the 1920s will draw in readers. The text discusses which models were most popular and how cars evolved during this time. (Rev: SLJ 8/07)

24052 Oxlade, Chris. *Car* (4–6). Illus. Series: Take It Apart. 2002, Thameside $24.25 (978-1-930643-94-9). 32pp. The mechanically minded will particularly enjoy this look at cars that uses cutaways and detailed diagrams to show its major parts. (Rev: BL 1/1–15/03; HBG 3/03) [629.222]

24053 Power, Bob. *Dodge Vipers* (3–6). Illus. Series: Wild Wheels. 2011, Gareth Stevens LB $26.60 (978-143395822-9). 32pp. With a V-10 engine, the Viper is one the fastest cars available today; learn all about the car's history, horsepower, and track performance here. Also use *Ferraris, Maseratis,* and *Lamborghinis* (all 2011). (Rev: BL 12/1/11) [629.222]

24054 Rau, Dana Meachen. *Cars* (PS–1). Series: Bookworms. We Go! 2009, Marshall Cavendish $15.95 (978-0-7614-4078-9). 24pp. A very basic introduction to cars and trucks and their uses, suitable for beginning readers. (Rev: SLJ 4/1/10) [629.22]

24055 Raum, Elizabeth. *The History of the Car* (2–3). Series: Inventions That Changed the World. 2007, Heinemann LB $25.36 (978-1-4034-9648-5). 32pp. After looking at the transport we used before the invention of the car, Raum traces developments from the earliest automobiles to new fuel alternatives and examines how cars have changed our lives. (Rev: SLJ 11/07) [629.22209]

24056 Simon, Seymour. *Seymour Simon's Book of Trucks* (K–4). 2000, HarperCollins LB $16.89 (978-0-06-028481-7). A highly appealing book that contains pictures and information on a large number of trucks and the various jobs they do. (Rev: HBG 9/00; SLJ 7/00) [629.28]

24057 Steggall, Susan. *The Life of a Car* (PS–2). Illus. by author. 2008, Holt $16.95 (978-0-8050-8747-5). 32pp. A very simple look at a car's life from construction through recycling, with minimal text. (Rev: BL 4/15/08; SLJ 5/08) [629.222]

24058 Swanson, Jennifer. *How Hybrid Cars Work* (4–6). Illus. by Glen Mullaly. Series: How Things Work. 2011, Child's World LB $18.95 (978-160973217-2). 32pp. Cartoon characters — a caveman and a robot — narrate this overview of the technology and environmental benefits involved in hybrid cars. (Rev: BL 10/1/11*) [629.222]

24059 Warhol, Tom. *Aptera* (4–6). Series: Green Cars. 2010, Marshall Cavendish LB $19.95 (978-1-60870-008-0). 48pp. Warhol looks at the technology used in the Aptera, a futuristic car that appeared in a Star Trek movie. (Rev: SLJ 1/1/11) [629.22]

24060 Wheeler, Jill C. *Alternative Cars* (3–5). Illus. Series: Checkerboard Science Library: Eye on Energy. 2008, ABDO LB $16.95 (978-1-59928-803-1). 32pp. After a discussion of the internal combustion engine and its disadvantages, this title looks at hybrid, diesel, hydrogen fuel-cell, electric, and other alternatives. (Rev: BL 2/15/08) [629.22]

24061 Wright, David K. *The Story of Chevy Impalas* (1–3). Illus. Series: Classic Cars. 2002, Gareth Stevens LB $23.00 (978-0-8368-3190-0). 24pp. Young automobile enthusiasts will enjoy seeing how the Impala has changed over the years. (Rev: BL 10/15/02; HBG 3/03) [629.222]

24062 Wright, David K. *The Story of Ford Thunderbirds* (1–3). Series: Classic Cars. 2002, Gareth Stevens LB $23.00 (978-0-8368-3191-7). 24pp. The history of the legendary Ford Thunderbird is told with bright full-page photographs and a simple text. (Rev: BL 10/15/02; HBG 3/03) [629]

24063 Wright, David K. *The Story of Model T Fords* (1–3). Series: Classic Cars. 2002, Gareth Stevens LB $23.00 (978-0-8368-3192-4). 24pp. The Model T Ford holds a unique position in the history of the automobile. Its story is told here in beginning text and many pictures. (Rev: BL 10/15/02; HBG 3/03) [639]

24064 Wright, David K. *The Story of Porsches* (1–3). Series: Classic Cars. 2002, Gareth Stevens LB $23.00 (978-0-8368-3193-1). 24pp. The story of this pioneering European automobile is told in full-page color pictures and a beginning-reader text. (Rev: BL 10/15/02; HBG 3/03) [629]

24065 Wright, David K. *The Story of Volkswagen Beetles* (1–3). Illus. Series: Classic Cars. 2002, Gareth Stevens LB $23.00 (978-0-8368-3194-8). 24pp. Traces the history of the Volkswagen Beetle, from its inception in the 1930s to its revival in the 1990s. (Rev: BL 10/15/02; HBG 3/03) [629.222]

24066 Zabludoff, Marc. *Ebox* (4–6). Series: Green Cars. 2010, Marshall Cavendish LB $19.95 (978-1-60870-009-7). 48pp. Zabludoff reviews the technology used in the eBox and the future of electric cars. (Rev: SLJ 1/1/11) [629.22]

24067 Zronik, John. *Street Cred* (4–6). Series: Automania! 2006, Crabtree LB $25.20 (978-0-7787-3006-4); paper $8.95 (978-0-7787-3028-6). 32pp. Slick, souped-up cars are the focus of this book that includes plenty of photographs of customized rides. (Rev: SLJ 8/07)

Railroads

24068 Crowther, Robert. *Trains: A Pop-Up Railroad Book* (2–4). Illus. by author. 2006, Candlewick $17.99 (978-0-7636-3082-9). Suitably linear pop-ups supply a lot of information about train history and engineering. (Rev: SLJ 10/06) [625]

24069 Curlee, Lynn. *Trains* (4–6). Illus. by author. 2009, Atheneum $19.99 (978-1-4169-4848-3). 48pp. A history of railroads from the earliest steam engines to today's new technologies. (Rev: BCCB 5/09; BL 4/1/09; SLJ 6/09) [385.09]

24070 Floca, Brian. *Locomotive* (K–3). Illus. by author. 2013, Atheneum $17.99 (978-1-4169-9415-2). 64pp. A beautifully illustrated account of a journey on the Transcontinental Railroad in 1869. Caldecott Medal; Sibert Honor; ALA Notable Children's Book; Top of the List; Booklist Editors' Choice. **e** (Rev: BL 7/13*; HB 9–10/13; LMC 1–2/14; SLJ 7/13*) [385.0973]

24071 Houghton, Gillian. *The Transcontinental Railroad: A Primary Source History of America's First Coast-to-Coast Railroad* (4–8). Series: Primary Sources in American History. 2003, Rosen LB $29.25 (978-0-8239-3684-7). 64pp. Timelines and reproductions of period photographs and relevant items add to the narrative in this introduction to the planning and construction of the railroad in the mid-19th century. (Rev: SLJ 5/03) [385]

24072 Lindeen, Mary. *Trains* (PS–3). 2007, Children's Pr. LB $18.50 (978-1-60014-062-4). 24pp. The basics about trains for young readers, clearly presented and accompanied by engaging photographs. (Rev: SLJ 7/07)

24073 Maynard, Chris. *High-Speed Trains* (5–8). Series: Need for Speed. 2002, Lerner LB $23.93 (978-0-8225-0387-3). 32pp. This action-packed book looks at fast trains from around the world, propelled by steam, oil, magnets, and electricity. (Rev: BL 8/02; HBG 10/02) [625.1]

24074 O'Brien, Patrick. *Steam, Smoke, and Steel: Back in Time with Trains* (K–2). Illus. 2000, Charlesbridge $16.95 (978-0-88106-969-3); paper $6.95 (978-0-88106-972-3). 32pp. A boy describes the different trains driven by six generations of his family in this history of railroads and trains. (Rev: BL 7/00; HBG 3/01; SLJ 8/00) [385]

24075 Perry, Phyllis. *Trains* (2–4). Series: Transportation and Communication. 2001, Enslow LB $23.93 (978-0-7660-1645-3). 32pp. In an attractive format, this book supplies information on the history, development, and use of trains in North America. (Rev: BL 10/15/01; HBG 3/02) [625.1]

24076 Rau, Dana Meachen. *Trains* (PS–1). Series: Bookworms. We Go! 2009, Marshall Cavendish $15.95 (978-0-7614-4081-9). 24pp. A very basic introduction to trains and their uses, suitable for beginning readers. (Rev: SLJ 4/1/10) [625.2]

24077 Simon, Seymour. *Seymour Simon's Book of Trains* (PS–3). Illus. 2002, HarperCollins LB $18.89 (978-0-06-028476-3). 40pp. An oversized volume with striking photographs of trains coupled with simple but fascinating information ranging from early steam locomotives to today's high-speed trains. (Rev: BCCB 3/02; BL 2/15/02; HB 5/02; HBG 10/02; SLJ 5/02) [385]

24078 Steele, Philip. *Trains: The Slide-Out, See-Through Story of World-Famous Trains and Railroads* (K–6). Illus. by Sebastian Quigley and Nicholas Forder. Series: Legendary Journeys. 2010, Kingfisher $19.99 (978-0-7534-6465-6). 32pp. Readers explore railroads in spreads covering the history, some of the most famous trains, and even the architecture of key stations; with photographs, diagrams, maps, and interactive features. (Rev: BL 12/15/10; SLJ 5/1/11) [385.09]

24079 Stille, Darlene R. *Freight Trains* (K–2). Illus. Series: Transportation. 2001, Compass Point LB $21.26 (978-0-7565-0148-8). 32pp. Simple descriptions and an attractive layout will appeal to young train fans. (Rev: BL 12/15/01) [625.1]

24080 Weitzman, David. *A Subway for New York* (4–7). 2005, Farrar $17.00 (978-0-374-37284-2). The story behind the early-20th-century construction of New York City's first subway is presented in picture-book format. (Rev: BL 12/1/05; SLJ 2/06) [625.4]

24081 Yancey, Diane. *Camels for Uncle Sam* (4–7). 1995, Hendrick-Long $16.95 (978-0-937460-91-7). The story of the experiment that involved importing camels to the Southwest in the 1850s to help in railroad construction. (Rev: BL 9/15/95) [357]

24082 Zimmermann, Karl. *All Aboard! Passenger Trains Around the World* (4–7). Illus. 2006, Boyds Mills $19.95 (978-1-59078-325-2). Photo-filled double-page spreads show the excitement of travel by train and interweave history, geography, commerce, and technology. (Rev: BL 2/15/06; SLJ 6/06) [385]

24083 Zimmermann, Karl. *Steam Locomotives: Whistling, Chugging, Smoking Iron Horses of the Past* (4–8). 2004, Boyds Mills $19.95 (978-1-59078-165-4). Informative and photo-filled, this is an appealing history of steam engines. (Rev: BL 2/1/04; SLJ 7/04) [625.26]

24084 Zimmermann, Karl. *The Stourbridge Lion: America's First Locomotive* (1–3). Illus. by Steven Walker. 2012, Boyds Mills $16.95 (978-1-59078-859-2). 32pp. Tells the story of the first locomotive, brought to America from England, to haul coal from the Pennsylvania coalfields to the canals. (Rev: BL 4/1/12; LMC 11–12/12; SLJ 8/12) [388]

Ships, Boats, and Lighthouses

24085 Ardagh, Philip. *All at Sea* (PS–K). Illus. by Tig Sutton. Series: British Mighty Machines. 2003, Thameside LB $24.25 (978-1-931983-04-4). 32pp. Young boat lovers will enjoy the parade of yachts, submarines, aircraft carrier, hovercraft, ferry, and other vessels portrayed here in bright illustrations and simple words. (Rev: BL 12/1/02; HBG 3/03) [387.2]

24086 Beech, Linda Ward. *The Exxon Valdez's Deadly Oil Spill* (3–4). Series: Code Red. 2007, Bearport LB $23.96 (978-1-59716-366-8). 32pp. Part of the Code Red series, this book looks at how the 1989 spill happened, how it was contained and cleaned, and the effects that it had on wildlife. (Rev: LMC 10/07; SLJ 8/07)

24087 Benoit, Peter. *The Titanic Disaster* (3–5). Illus. Series: True Book: Disasters. 2011, Children's Press LB $26 (978-0-531-20627-0); paper $6.95 (978-0-531-28996-9). 48pp. A clear account of the disaster, covering the construction of the vessel, the safety measures, and the mistakes made by the crew. (Rev: BL 4/1/11; SLJ 11/1/11) [910.916]

24088 Bornhoft, Simon. *High Speed Boats* (5–8). Series: Need for Speed. 1999, Lerner LB $23.93 (978-0-8225-2488-5). Using a jazzy, attention-getting format with action photographs, sidebars with statistics and interesting facts, and different type sizes, this book covers present and future speedboats. (Rev: BL 1/1–15/00; HBG 3/00) [629.222]

24089 Burgan, Michael. *The Titanic* (3–6). Illus. Series: We the People. 2004, Compass Point LB $26.60 (978-0-7565-0614-8). 48pp. This entry in the We the People series chronicles the tragic history of the *Titanic* from the construction of the mammoth ocean liner through its ill-fated encounter with a North Atlantic iceberg to the discovery of its remains on the ocean floor in the mid-1980s. (Rev: BL 5/1/04) [910]

24090 Burgan, Michael. *Titanic* (3–8). Illus. by Eldon Doty. Series: Truth and Rumors. 2010, Capstone LB $25.32 (978-1-4296-3951-4). 32pp. Burgan clarifies certain aspects of the construction and final voyage of the *Titanic*, answering questions like "Was the *Titanic* disaster predicted before 1912?" and "Did an officer kill a passenger?," and finishes with a chapter on how to tell the difference between fact and fiction. (Rev: LMC 11–12/10) [910.45]

24091 Callery, Sean. *Titanic* (4–8). Illus. 2014, Scholastic $15.99 (978-054550512-3). 112pp. With chapters on the engineering involved in building the ship, the interest in its sailing, and the voyage itself and the sinking, this is an engaging title full of interesting photographs and documents, encouraging readers to consider various aspects of the tragedy. (Rev: BL 3/1/14) [910.916]

24092 Caper, William. *Nightmare on the Titanic* (3–6). Series: Code Red. 2007, Bearport LB $23.96 (978-1-59716-362-0). 32pp. Could the sinking of the *Titanic* have been prevented? This book, part of the Code Red series, looks at the facts surrounding this tragedy, a popular subject with young readers. (Rev: SLJ 7/07)

24093 Cerullo, Mary M. *Shipwrecks: Exploring Sunken Cities Beneath the Sea* (5–8). 2009, Dutton $18.99 (978-0-525-47968-0). 64pp. Cerullo looks at two well-preserved shipwrecks, describing the sinkings themselves, the state of the wrecks today which are home to a variety of marine life, and the technology used to explore these environments. (Rev: BL 12/1/09; SLJ 1/10; VOYA 12/09) [930.1028]

24094 Collicutt, Paul. *This Boat* (PS–3). Illus. 2001, Farrar $15.00 (978-0-374-37495-2). 32pp. A number of different boats are presented in this picture book, including sailboats, paddle-powered riverboats, a submarine, and an aircraft carrier. (Rev: BL 3/15/01; HBG 10/01) [623.8]

24095 Delgado, James P. *Wrecks of American Warships* (5–7). Series: Shipwrecks. 2000, Watts LB $25.50 (978-0-531-20376-7). 64pp. This book describes how underwater archaeologists have discovered and explored such warships as the *Constitution, Philadelphia, Alabama,* and *Arizona.* (Rev: BL 10/15/00) [623.8]

24096 Denenberg, Barry. *Titanic Sinks!* (5–8). Illus. 2011, Viking $19.99 (978-0-670-01243-5). 80pp. Blending fact and fiction, this oversize volume infuses real information about the sinking with imagined sensationalistic newspaper articles, written by a victim of the disaster, that add energy and drama. (Rev: BL 10/15/11*; HB 3–4/12; LMC 3–4/12; SLJ 11/1/11*) [910.9163]

24097 Doeden, Matt. *The Sinking of the Titanic* (3–5). Illus. Series: Graphic History. 2005, Capstone LB $26.60 (978-0-7368-3834-4). 32pp. An eye-catching and dramatically worded presentation of the sinking. (Rev: BL 2/1/05) [910]

24098 Frederick, Dawn. *How It Happens at the Boat Factory* (1–3). Photos by Bob Wolfe and Diane Wolfe. Series: How It Happens. 2002, Oliver LB $19.95 (978-1-881508-90-8). 32pp. How boats are manufactured is described in text and photographs. (Rev: HBG 10/02; SLJ 12/02)

24099 Gunderson, Jessica. *Your Life as a Cabin Attendant on the Titanic* (3–6). Illus. by Rachel Dougherty. Series: The Way It Was. 2012, Picture Window LB $25.99 (978-140487158-8); paper $7.95 (978-140487248-6). 32pp. Follows the experiences of a 20-year-old cabin attendant, one of only 18 female stewards, as the *Titanic* sails toward its doom. (Rev: BL 4/15/12) [910.9163]

24100 Hopkinson, Deborah. *Titanic: Voices from the Disaster* (4–8). Illus. 2012, Scholastic $17.99 (978-054511674-9). 304pp. With diagrams, maps, charts, and period photographs, this account also draws on survivor letters as well as newspaper and other reports. Sibert Honor 2013; ALA Notable Children's Book 2013. ∩ (Rev: BL 12/1/11; HB 3–4/12; LMC 5–6/12; SLJ 2/12*; VOYA 4/12) [910.9163]

24101 Houghton, Gillian. *The Wreck of the Andrea Gail: Three Days of a Perfect Storm* (4–6). 2003, Rosen LB $25.25 (978-0-8239-3677-9). 48pp. This account of the

1991 loss of the fishing boat *Andrea Gail,* featured in the film *Perfect Storm,* examines possible causes. (Rev: SLJ 9/03) [910]

24102 Hubbell, Patricia. *Boats: Speeding! Sailing! Cruising!* (PS–1). Illus. by Megan Halsey. 2009, Marshall Cavendish $17.99 (978-0-7614-5524-0). 32pp. Boats and ships of all kinds — from canoes to aircraft carriers — are shown in varied illustrations with rhyming text. (Rev: BCCB 4/09; BL 3/15/09; SLJ 3/09)

24103 Hunter, Nick. *Shipwrecks* (4–6). Illus. Series: Treasure Hunters. 2013, Raintree LB $31.43 (978-141094954-7); paper $8.99 (9781410949615). 48pp. The wrecks of the *Mary Rose* (1545) and the *Titanic* (1912) are among those discussed in this survey of shipping disasters and how the wrecks are discovered. (Rev: BL 4/1/13; SLJ 4/13) [910.45]

24104 Jenkins, Martin. *Titanic* (4–6). Illus. by Brian Sanders. 2007, Candlewick $29.99 (978-0-7636-3468-1). An impressive *Titanic* pop-up is accompanied by a text account of the disaster. (Rev: SLJ 10/07) [910.9163]

24105 Kalman, Maira. *Fireboat: The Heroic Adventures of the John J. Harvey* (2–6). Illus. 2002, Penguin $16.99 (978-0-399-23953-3). 48pp. A beautifully and sensitively presented account of the work of the *John J. Harvey* fireboat, from its launch in 1931 through its restoration in the 1990s and its role in fighting fires in New York City on September 11, 2001. (Rev: BL 9/1/02; HB 9/02*; HBG 3/03; SLJ 9/02*) [974.71044]

24106 Kently, Eric. *The Story of the Titanic* (4–8). Illus. by Steve Noon. 2001, DK paper $17.99 (978-0-7894-7943-3). 32pp. Details of life aboard ship, double-page spreads, cutaways and cross-sections, facts and trivia, and a well-designed layout are just a few of the features of this beautifully designed large-format book. (Rev: BL 12/15/01; HBG 3/02; SLJ 12/01) [363.1]

24107 Lassieur, Allison. *Can You Survive the Titanic? An Interactive Survival Guide Adventure* (3–5). Series: You Choose: Survival. 2011, Capstone LB $30.65 (978-1-4296-6586-5); paper $6.95 (978-1-4296-7351-8). 112pp. In this choose-your-own adventure offering, readers make choices in a number of situations that ultimately determine whether or not they would have survived the shipwreck; in the process they learn details of the ship, the circumstances, and the social differences among passengers. (Rev: HB 3–4/12; SLJ 12/1/11) [910.9163]

24108 Macaulay, David. *Ship* (5–8). 1993, Houghton Mifflin $19.95 (978-0-395-52439-8). A fictional caravel is featured in this exploration of historical seagoing vessels and the work of underwater archaeologists. (Rev: BCCB 11/93; BL 10/15/93*; SLJ 11/93) [387.2]

24109 Matsen, Brad. *The Incredible Search for the Treasure Ship Atocha* (4–6). Series: Incredible Deep-Sea Adventures. 2003, Enslow LB $23.93 (978-0-7660-2193-8). 48pp. This is the detailed story of the discovery of the wreck of the Spanish treasure ship *Nuestra Señora de Atocha* that sank in a hurricane in 1622. (Rev: HBG 4/04; SLJ 3/04) [909]

24110 Mayell, Hillary. *Shipwrecks* (5–8). Series: Man-Made Disasters. 2004, Gale LB $29.95 (978-1-59018-058-7). Period photographs enhance the impact of stories of shipwrecks of all kinds — from fishing boats to luxury liners — during the 19th and 20th centuries. (Rev: SLJ 7/04) [910.4]

24111 Rau, Dana Meachen. *Boats* (PS–1). Series: Bookworms. We Go! 2009, Marshall Cavendish $15.95 (978-0-7614-4076-5). 24pp. A very basic introduction to boats and their uses, suitable for beginning readers. (Rev: SLJ 4/1/10) [623.82]

24112 Sherrow, Victoria. *Titanic* (2–4). Series: Scholastic History Readers. 2002, Scholastic paper $3.99 (978-0-439-26706-9). 48pp. First-person accounts enliven this illustrated account for beginning readers. (Rev: SLJ 4/03) [910]

24113 Sutherland, John, and Diane Canwell. *Aircraft Carriers* (4–6). Illus. Series: Amazing Ships. 2007, Gareth Stevens LB $23.93 (978-0-8368-8376-3). 32pp. An attractive, basic introduction to these large vessels, with detailed drawings, photographs, and statistics. Also use *Container Ships and Oil Tankers* and *Cruise Ships* (both 2007). (Rev: SLJ 1/08) [623.825]

24114 Van Rynbach, Iris. *Safely to Shore: America's Lighthouses* (3–5). Illus. by author. 2003, Charlesbridge $16.95 (978-1-57091-434-8); paper $6.95 (978-1-57091-435-5). 32pp. Twenty-two of the most famous American lighthouses are profiled, with information on equipment, history, and keepers. (Rev: HBG 4/04; SLJ 1/04) [387.1]

24115 Wargin, Kathy-Jo. *The Edmund Fitzgerald: The Song of the Bell* (K–3). Illus. by Gijsbert van Frankenhuyzen. 2003, Sleeping Bear $17.95 (978-1-58536-126-7). The bell that was retrieved from the *Edmund Fitzgerald* after it sank in Lake Superior in 1975 brings immediacy to this narrative and poem about the storm that took the sailors' lives. (Rev: BL 1/1/04; HBG 4/04; SLJ 2/04) [917.74]

24116 Wilkinson, Philip. *Ships* (4–7). 2000, Kingfisher $16.95 (978-0-7534-5280-6). Straightforward text and handsome illustrations cover maritime history from the earliest sailing ships and discuss piracy, the slave trade, and superstitions about the sea. (Rev: BL 2/1/01; HBG 10/01; SLJ 1/01) [623.8]

24117 Wishinsky, Frieda. *Remembering the Titanic* (2–4). Illus. Series: Scholastic Reader. 2012, Scholastic paper $3.99 (978-05453584-4-6). 32pp. Archival photographs, reproductions, and underwater images of the wreck add drama to this account. (Rev: BL 3/1/12) [910.916]

24118 Zimmermann, Karl. *Steamboats: The Story of Lakers, Ferries, and Majestic Paddle-Wheelers* (4–7). Illus. 2007, Boyds Mills $19.95 (978-1-59078-434-1). Carefully researched by an aficionado, this detailed examination of the history, purpose, and engineering of steamboats contains biographical information and excellent archival and modern illustrations. (Rev: BL 1/1–15/07; SLJ 4/07) [623.82]

Weapons, Submarines, and the Armed Forces

24119 Aaseng, Nathan. *The Marine Corps in Action* (4–8). Series: U.S. Military Branches and Careers. 2001, Enslow LB $26.60 (978-0-7660-1637-8). 128pp. An attractive introduction to all aspects of the Marine Corps that looks at the future of this military branch and the number of women and minorities included. (Rev: HBG 3/02; SLJ 4/02) [359.9]

24120 Alvarez, Carlos. *AC-130H/U Gunships* (4–6). Illus. Series: Military Machines. 2010, Children's Press LB $19.95 (978-160014493-6). 24pp. A dynamic layout and plenty of action shots enhance this detailed, technical profile of the enormous air force plane that acts as a shield for ground troops; suitable for reluctant readers. Also use *AH-1W Super Cobras, MH-53E Sea Dragons,* and *Strykers* (all 2010). (Rev: BL 11/15/10) [623.74]

24121 Benson, Michael. *The U.S. Army* (4–6). Illus. Series: U.S. Armed Forces. 2004, Lerner LB $26.60 (978-0-8225-1645-3). 64pp. An introductory overview of the Army and its history, recruitment and training, equipment, and day-to-day routines. (Rev: BL 1/1–15/05; SLJ 3/05) [355]

24122 Benson, Michael. *The U.S. Marine Corps* (4–7). Series: U.S. Armed Forces. 2004, Lerner LB $26.60 (978-0-8225-1648-4). Introduces the history of the Marine Corps, followed by information on recruitment, training, and daily life. (Rev: BL 1/05; SLJ 3/05) [359.6]

24123 Bledsoe, Karen, and Glen Bledsoe. *Helicopters: High-Flying Heroes* (4–6). Series: Mighty Military Machines. 2006, Enslow LB $23.93 (978-0-7660-2663-6). 48pp. Describes how military helicopters are used in a variety of tasks that display their nimbleness and versatility. (Rev: SLJ 4/07) [358.4]

24124 Bodden, Valerie. *Tanks* (2–4). Illus. Series: Built for Battle. 2012, Creative Education LB $17.95 (978-160818129-2). 24pp. This volume looks at the history of tanks, some famous tanks, how they perform in battle, and their parts and crews. (Rev: BL 4/1/12) [623.7]

24125 Boos, Ben. *Swords: An Artist's Devotion* (4–7). Illus. by author. 2008, Candlewick $24.99 (978-076363148-2). 96pp. In this large-format book, masterfully crafted swords used by everyone from peasants to sultans and in many countries over many centuries are illustrated and described in detail. (Rev: BLO 11/1/08; LMC 3–4/09; SLJ 10/1/08) [623.4]

24126 Byers, Ann. *America's Star Wars Program* (5–7). Series: The Library of Weapons of Mass Destruction. 2005, Rosen LB $27.95 (978-1-4042-0287-0). Photographs and text document the development of 20th-century missiles and America's controversial "Star Wars" strategy. (Rev: SLJ 11/05) [623]

24127 Demarest, Chris L. *Mayday! Mayday! A Coast Guard Rescue* (K–2). Illus. by author. 2004, Simon & Schuster $16.95 (978-0-689-85161-2). 40pp. Rhyming

text and eye-catching illustrations follow a Coast Guard helicopter team as it locates a yacht in trouble and rescues everybody aboard. (Rev: BL 9/1/04; SLJ 7/04) [303.12]

24128 Doeden, Matt. *Can You Survive in the Special Forces? An Interactive Survival Adventure* (4–6). Illus. Series: You Choose: Survival. 2012, Capstone LB $31.32 (978-142968582-5); paper $6.95 (9781429694803). 112pp. Readers must make crucial decisions as they take part in Green Beret, Army Ranger, and Navy SEAL missions. (Rev: BL 12/15/12) [356]

24129 Donovan, Sandy. *The U.S. Air Force* (4–7). Illus. Series: U.S. Armed Forces. 2004, Lerner LB $26.60 (978-0-8225-1436-7). 64pp. Introduces the history of the Air Force, followed by information on recruitment, training, and daily life. Also use *U.S. Air Force Special Operations* (2004). (Rev: BL 1/05; SLJ 3/05) [358.4]

24130 Egan, Tracie. *Weapons of Mass Destruction and North Korea* (5–7). Series: The Library of Weapons of Mass Destruction. 2005, Rosen LB $27.95 (978-1-4042-0296-2). Explores what the West knows about North Korea's efforts to build stockpiles of biological, chemical, and — potentially — nuclear weapons. (Rev: SLJ 11/05) [623]

24131 Gartman, Gene. *Life in Army Basic Training* (4–6). Illus. Series: On Duty. 2000, Children's Book Pr. LB $24.50 (978-0-516-23347-5). 48pp. Written by a man who served in the military, this book goes through the routines and demands of basic training with information on weapons and various fitness programs. (Rev: BL 2/1/01) [355.5]

24132 Goldberg, Jan. *Green Berets: The U.S. Army Special Forces* (5–7). Series: Inside Special Operations. 2003, Rosen LB $26.50 (978-0-8239-3808-7). 64pp. An overview of the history, mission, training, and equipment of the Special Forces. (Rev: BL 7/03) [356]

24133 Goldish, Meish. *Coast Guard: Civilian to Guardian* (4–7). Illus. Series: Becoming a Soldier. 2010, Bearport LB $22.61 (978-193608812-6). 24pp. Recent recruits' journeys from enlistment through placement, conditioning, training, and graduation are presented in this true-to-life book that doesn't gloss over the rigors of military life. (Rev: BL 10/1/10) [363.28]

24134 Goldish, Meish. *Horses, Donkeys, and Mules in the Marines* (3–5). Illus. 2012, Bearport LB $23.93 (978-161772453-4). 24pp. Explores the roles of animals in the Marine Corps over the years, the training they undergo, and their current missions. (Rev: BLO 3/1/12) [359.9]

24135 Gonen, Rivka. *Charge! Weapons and Warfare in Ancient Times* (5–8). 1993, Lerner LB $23.93 (978-0-8225-3201-9). A look at the development of weapons from sticks and stones to battering rams. (Rev: BCCB 12/93; BL 2/1/94; SLJ 2/94) [355.8]

24136 Graham, Ian. *You Wouldn't Want to Be in the First Submarine! An Undersea Expedition You'd Rather Avoid* (3–5). Illus. by David Antram. 2008, Scholastic LB $29.00 (978-0-531-20702-4); paper $9.95 (978-0-531-

21912-6). 32pp. A historical look at submarines highlighting the dangerous *Hunley*, built by the Confederates during the Civil War. (Rev: BL 12/1/08) [973.7]

24137 Gurstelle, William. *The Art of the Catapult: Build Greek Ballistae, Roman Onagers, English Trebuchets, and More Ancient Artillery* (5–12). 2004, Chicago Review paper $14.95 (978-1-55652-526-1). Information on history, physics, and military tactics, plus step-by-step instructions for the construction of 10 working catapults. (Rev: SLJ 11/04) [623.4]

24138 Hamilton, John. *Armed Forces* (4–7). Series: War on Terrorism. 2002, ABDO LB $25.65 (978-1-57765-674-6). An introduction to the U.S. military and the roles these services play in protecting the country, with color photographs, a glossary, and list of Web sites. (Rev: BL 8/02; HBG 10/02) [355]

24139 Hamilton, John. *Weapons of War* (4–7). Series: War on Terrorism. 2002, ABDO LB $25.65 (978-1-57765-673-9). This account describes the weapons currently available to U.S. military personnel, including fighter planes, bombers, helicopters, bombs, missiles, and ships. (Rev: BL 5/1/02; HBG 10/02) [623.4]

24140 Hamilton, John. *Weapons of War: A Pictorial History of the Past One Thousand Years* (4–7). Series: The Millennium. 2000, ABDO LB $25.65 (978-1-57765-362-2). In a short space, this book traces 1,000 years of weapons including small weaponry, ships, firearms, military airplanes, tanks, missiles, and bombs. (Rev: BL 7/00; HBG 10/00; SLJ 10/00) [623.4]

24141 Hasan, Tahara. *Anthrax Attacks Around the World* (4–8). Series: Terrorist Attacks. 2003, Rosen LB $27.95 (978-0-8239-3859-9). Examines the use of anthrax as a terrorist weapon and includes accounts of its use in Japan, the Soviet Union, and the United States. (Rev: SLJ 2/04) [303.6]

24142 Herbst, Judith. *The History of Weapons* (5–8). Series: Major Inventions Through History. 2005, Twenty-First Century LB $26.60 (978-0-8225-3805-9). An attractive look at the evolution of weapons from rocks and sticks to today's weapons of mass destruction. (Rev: SLJ 1/06) [623.4]

24143 Hibbert, Adam. *Chemical and Biological Warfare* (5–9). Series: Face the Facts. 2003, Raintree LB $28.56 (978-0-7398-6847-8). 56pp. Part of a series on international issues, this volume examines the powers and dangers of chemical and biological weapons. (Rev: SLJ 4/04) [358]

24144 Kennedy, Robert C. *Life as an Army Demolition Expert* (4–6). Illus. Series: On Duty. 2000, Children's Book Pr. LB $24.50 (978-0-516-23346-8); paper $6.95 (978-0-516-23546-2). 48pp. This work gives historical background plus an explanation of work today in this specialized area of the U.S. Army. (Rev: BL 2/1/01) [358]

24145 Kennedy, Robert C. *Life with the Navy Seals* (4–7). Series: On Duty. 2000, Children's LB $24.50 (978-0-516-23351-2). 48pp. A look at this special branch of the U.S. Navy with material on its responsibilities, training, and career opportunities. (Rev: BL 3/1/01) [359]

24146 Myers, Walter Dean. *USS Constellation: Pride of the American Navy* (4–8). 2004, Holiday House $16.95 (978-0-8234-1816-9). 86pp. Myers presents the colorful history of the *USS Constellation,* the last of America's all-sail fighting ships, in this volume with extensive illustrations and other materials. (Rev: BL 7/04; HB 7/04; SLJ 8/04) [359.8]

24147 Nardo, Don. *Special Operations: Paratroopers* (5–8). Illus. Series: Military Experience. 2012, Morgan Reynolds LB $27.45 (978-159935360-9). 64pp. Readers learn about the demanding training and dramatic combat adventures of special ops paratroopers. (Rev: BL 10/1/12)

24148 Payan, Gregory, and Alexander Guelke. *Life on a Submarine* (4–6). Illus. Series: On Duty. 2000, Children's Book Pr. LB $24.50 (978-0-516-23349-9). 48pp. The glamorous and arduous aspects of life aboard a navy submarine are covered, including exercise and sleeping arrangements. (Rev: BL 2/1/01) [359.9]

24149 Pelta, Kathy. *The U.S. Navy* (5–7). 1990, Lerner LB $23.93 (978-0-8225-1435-0). A look at the history and present status and activities of the U.S. Navy. (Rev: BL 12/1/90) [359]

24150 Peppas, Lynn. *Powerful Armored Vehicles* (2–4). Illus. Series: Vehicles on the Move. 2011, Crabtree LB $26.60 (978-077872750-7). 32pp. This detail-rich title provides readers with photographs of armored vehicles of various nations. Also use *Military Helicopters: Flying into Battle, Fighter Jets: Defending the Skies,* and *Aircraft Carriers: Runways at Sea* (all 2012). (Rev: BL 3/1/12) [623.74]

24151 Richie, Jason. *Weapons: Designing the Tools of War* (5–10). 2000, Oliver LB $21.95 (978-1-881508-60-1). Using separate chapters for different categories of weapons — for example, submarines, battleships, and tanks — this is a history of the development of weaponry from 300 B.C. to today. (Rev: BL 5/1/00; HBG 10/00; SLJ 8/00) [623]

24152 Roza, Greg. *The Incredible Story of Aircraft Carriers* (3–6). Illus. Series: A Kid's Guide to Incredible Technology. 2004, Rosen LB $21.25 (978-0-8239-6714-8). 24pp. A concise look at how and why aircraft carriers are built and at the role they play and the planes they carry, with a layout diagram and discussion of the future for these huge ships. (Rev: SLJ 2/05) [359.9]

24153 Rudolph, Jessica. *Marine Scout Snipers in Action* (4–7). Illus. Series: Special Ops II. 2013, Bearport LB $26.60 (978-161772891-4). 32pp. A high-interest look at the training, equipment, and skills of these snipers, with vivid action photographs. (Rev: BL 10/1/13) [359.9]

24154 Schwartz, Heather E. *Women of the U.S. Air Force: Aiming High* (3–7). Series: Snap: Women in the U.S. Armed Forces. 2011, Capstone LB $26.65 (978-1-4296-5449-4). 32pp. A real-life story of a female Air Force recruit adds personal appeal to this title that explores women's history and growing presence and importance in the U.S. Air Force. Also use *Women of the U.S. Navy: Making Waves* (2011). (Rev: SLJ 6/11) [358.4]

24155 Sutherland, John, and Diane Canwell. *Submarines* (4–6). Illus. Series: Amazing Ships. 2007, Gareth Stevens LB $23.93 (978-0-8368-8379-4). 32pp. An attractive, basic introduction to these underwater vessels, with detailed drawings, photographs, and statistics. (Rev: SLJ 1/08) [623.825]

24156 Thompson, Gare. *The Monitor: The Iron Warship that Changed the World* (2–4). Series: All Aboard Reading. 2003, Penguin paper $3.99 (978-0-448-43245-8). 48pp. This fascinating book recounts not only the Civil War history of the ironclad *Monitor* but also the successful 20th-century search for its underwater wreck site. (Rev: BL 12/15/03; HBG 4/04)

24157 Wolny, Philip. *Weapons Satellites* (5–9). Series: The Library of Satellites. 2003, Rosen LB $26.50 (978-0-8239-3855-1). This account explores the growing technology of weapon satellites that are capable of knocking out enemies' satellites, and launching attacks from outer space. (Rev: BL 11/15/03; SLJ 1/04) [629.46]

24158 Woods, Mary B., and Michael Woods. *Ancient Warfare: From Clubs to Catapults* (5–8). Series: Ancient Technologies. 2000, Runestone LB $25.26 (978-0-8225-2999-6). 96pp. The weaponry of ancient civilizations including Greece and China. (Rev: BCCB 12/00; BL 9/15/00; HBG 3/01; SLJ 1/01) [623]

24159 Yomtov, Nel. *Navy SEALS in Action* (3–6). Illus. Series: Special Ops. 2008, Bearport LB $18.95 (978-1-59716-630-0). 32pp. An overview of the SEALS' history, training, equipment, and operations, with plenty of color photographs. (Rev: BL 4/1/08) [359.9]

24160 Zeinert, Karen, and Mary Miller. *The Brave Women of the Gulf Wars: Operation Desert Storm and Operation Iraqi Freedom* (5–8). Series: Women at War. 2005, Twenty-First Century LB $30.60 (978-0-7613-2705-9). Highlights women's roles in the Persian Gulf military campaigns. (Rev: BL 10/1/05; SLJ 11/05) [956.7]

Recreation

Crafts

General and Miscellaneous

24161 Bell-Rehwoldt, Sheri. *The Kids' Guide to Duct Tape Projects* (3–5). Illus. 2011, Capstone LB $26.65 (978-142966010-5). 32pp. The title says it all: here are step-by-step instructions for a variety of practical projects. (Rev: BL 2/15/12) [745.5]

24162 Bell, Samantha. *How to Make Stuff with Duct Tape* (2–4). Illus. by Kelsey Oseid. Series: Make Your Own Fun. 2013, Child's World LB $27.07 (978-162323563-5). 24pp. A pencil holder, a visor, and a wallet are among the items made here. ℮ (Rev: BL 10/1/13) [745.5]

24163 Birdseye, Tom. *A Kids' Guide to Building Forts* (5–8). Illus. by Bill Klein. 1993, Harbinger paper $11.95 (978-0-943173-69-6). A guide to the building of 19 kinds of forts, from the very simple to the more complex, some of which can be turned into clubhouses. (Rev: SLJ 9/93) [745.5]

24164 Blake, Susannah. *Crafts for Pampering Yourself* (4–6). Illus. Series: Eco Chic. 2013, Enslow $22.60 (978-076604314-5). 32pp. In this craft book about how to make your own beauty products, Blake addresses issues such as renewable resources and eco-friendliness, while detailing how to create different products with step-by-step instructions. (Rev: BL 10/1/13) [745.5]

24165 Blanchette, Peg, and Terri Thibault. *Really Cool Felt Crafts* (3–5). Illus. Series: Quick Starts for Kids! 2002, Williamson paper $8.95 (978-1-885593-80-1). 64pp. This book of easy-to-make felt projects includes instructions accompanied by drawings, and a section of full-sized templates. (Rev: BL 12/15/02; SLJ 1/03) [746]

24166 Bledsoe, Karen. *Chinese New Year Crafts* (K–5). Illus. Series: Fun Holiday Crafts Kids Can Do! 2005, Enslow LB $22.60 (978-0-7660-2347-5). 32pp. The ten crafts presented use everyday materials and include a dragon-streamer puppet, a ribbon lantern, and Chinese zodiac pictures. (Rev: SLJ 6/05) [394.261]

24167 Boonyadhistarn, Thiranut. *Fingernail Art: Dazzling Fingers and Terrific Toes* (4–8). Illus. Series: Snap Books: Crafts. 2006, Capstone LB $25.26 (978-0-7368-6474-9). 32pp. This colorful, well-thought-out guide offers interesting tips on decorating nails. (Rev: SLJ 2/07) [646.7]

24168 Boonyadhistarn, Thiranut. *Stamping Art: Imprint Your Designs* (4–8). Illus. Series: Snap Books: Crafts. 2006, Capstone LB $25.26 (978-0-7368-6477-0). Simple, step-by-step instructions guide readers through a variety of stamping projects that use accessible materials. (Rev: SLJ 2/07) [761]

24169 Boston, Lisa. *Sing! Play! Create! Hands-On Learning for 3- to 7-Year-Olds* (PS–2). Illus. by Sarah Cole. Series: A Williamson Little Hands Book. 2006, Williamson $14.95 (978-0-8249-6781-9); paper $12.95 (978-0-8249-6780-2). 126pp. Crafts, poems, and songs are among the activities suggested here and centered around a pond, garden, zoo, and farm. (Rev: SLJ 8/06) [372.21]

24170 Broida, Marian. *Projects About Nineteenth-Century Chinese Immigrants* (3–5). Illus. Series: Hands-on History. 2005, Benchmark LB $18.95 (978-0-7614-1978-5). 48pp. Crafts — a miner's scale, an abacus, a fan — plus recipes and other projects are accompanied by historical and cultural information. (Rev: SLJ 5/06)

24171 Broida, Marian. *Projects About Nineteenth-Century European Immigrants* (3–5). Illus. Series: Hands-on History. 2005, Benchmark LB $18.95 (978-0-7614-1980-8). 47pp. Through the varied projects in this book, students will learn the details of the sometimes-difficult lives of 19th-century immigrants from Europe; cultural and historical notes precede the activities. (Rev: SLJ 5/06) [973.5085]

24172 Brownrigg, Sheri. *Hearts and Crafts* (4–8). 1995, Tricycle paper $9.95 (978-1-883672-28-7). Clear instructions show how to complete a variety of Valentine's Day projects, including making necklaces and candles. (Rev: BL 3/1/96; SLJ 3/96) [745.5]

24173 Castaldo, Nancy F. *Winter Day Play! Activities, Crafts, and Games for Indoors and Out* (PS–3). Illus. 2001, Chicago Review paper $13.95 (978-1-55652-381-6). 161pp. The more than 70 suggested activities range from scientific projects and artistic endeavors to parties and cooking. (Rev: SLJ 12/01) [790]

24174 Check, Laura. *Create Your Own Candles: 30 Easy-to-Make Designs* (5–8). Illus. by Norma Jean Martin-Jourdenais. 2004, Williamson paper $8.95 (978-0-8249-8663-6). 61pp. Safety is stressed in this guide to exciting (and complex) candle creations. (Rev: SLJ 11/04) [745.593]

24175 Craig, Rebecca. *Gorgeous Gifts* (3–6). Photos by Andy Crawford. Series: Ecocrafts. 2007, Kingfisher paper $7.95 (978-0-7534-5967-6). 48pp. With clear instructions and photographs, this book shows how to use recyclables to create attractive gifts. Also use *Dream Bedroom* (2007). (Rev: SLJ 2/08) [745.5]

24176 D'Cruz, Anna-Marie. *Make Your Own Musical Instruments* (3–4). Series: Do It Yourself Projects! 2009, Rosen LB $23.95 (978-1-4358-2854-4). 24pp. Castanets, bongo drums, washboard, and maracas are among the instruments featured in this guide that provides color photographs and clear directions. Also use *Make Your Own Puppets* (2009). (Rev: SLJ 7/09) [784.192]

24177 Dall, Mary Doerfler. *Little Hands Create! Art and Activities for Kids Ages 3 to 6* (PS–2). Illus. by Sarah Rakitin. 2004, Williamson paper $12.95 (978-0-8249-8664-3). 120pp. Children will need help with these activities, most of which — egg-carton boats and twisted-paper jewelry, for example, use everyday materials. (Rev: BL 1/1–15/05) [745.5]

24178 Dickins, Rosie. *Art Treasury: Pictures, Paintings, and Projects* (4–7). 2007, Usborne LB $19.99 (978-0-7945-1452-5). Each of the art projects in this exciting collection is inspired by an existing work of art. (Rev: BL 4/1/07) [709]

24179 Dickinson, Gill, and Cheryl Owen. *Creative Crafts for Kids: Over 100 Projects for Two to Ten Year Olds* (4–10). 2007, Sterling LB $24.95 (978-0-600-61590-3). 256pp. Paper crafts, jewelry, holiday decorations, food crafts, and even good-smelling crafts for children and their teachers or adult friends are presented in a pleasant format. Materials lists and step-by-step instructions make this user-friendly. (Rev: SLJ 5/07)

24180 Drake, Jane, and Ann Love. *The Kids Winter Handbook* (3–5). Illus. by Heather Collins. 2001, Kids Can $18.95 (978-1-55337-033-8); paper $12.95 (978-1-55074-969-4). Crafts, recipes, games, and other activities are geared to indoor and outdoor winter entertainment. (Rev: HBG 3/02; SLJ 11/01) [790.1]

24181 Erlbach, Arlene, and Herb Erlbach. *Mother's Day Crafts* (3–5). Illus. Series: Fun Holiday Crafts Kids Can Do! 2005, Enslow LB $22.60 (978-0-7660-2348-2). 32pp. Ten original gifts for Mom that students will enjoy making; photographs help them picture the finished product. (Rev: SLJ 8/05) [745.594]

24182 Freixenet, Anna. *Creating with Mosaics* (3–6). Series: Crafts for All Seasons. 2000, Blackbirch LB $23.70 (978-1-56711-440-9). 32pp. This appealing craft book shows how to create attractive mosaics using items like beads, balls of aluminum foil, beans, seeds, and buttons. (Rev: SLJ 2/01) [745]

24183 Friday, Megan. *Pet Crafts: Everything You Need to Become Your Pet's Craft Star!* (4–6). Photos by Steve Giraud. Illus. by Diana Fisher. Series: Craft Star. 2009, Walter Foster paper $8.95 (978-1-60058-600-2). 64pp. A collection of 15 easy-to-make projects for pets — toys, clothing, treats, and so forth. (Rev: SLJ 6/09) [745.5]

24184 *Fun-to-make Crafts for Easter* (3–6). 2005, Boyds Mills $15.95 (978-1-59078-340-5); paper $7.95 (978-1-59078-365-8). 64pp. Greeting cards, holiday decorations, and clothing are among the 150 crafts suggested. Also use *Fun-to-Make Crafts for Every Day* (2005). (Rev: SLJ 6/05)

24185 *Fun-to-Make Crafts for Halloween* (3–6). 2005, Boyds Mills $15.95 (978-1-59078-343-6); paper $7.95 (978-1-59078-368-9). 63pp. The crafts and projects here include edible treats, masks, decorations, gifts, and other goodies for Halloween and the entire harvest season. (Rev: SLJ 9/05)

24186 Furstinger, Nancy. *Creative Crafts for Critters* (2–4). Illus. by Philippe Beha. 2001, Stoddart paper $8.95 (978-0-7737-6135-3). 48pp. Pet lovers will find lots of craft ideas for animal toys, clothing, and nutrition. (Rev: SLJ 1/02) [745.5]

24187 Gabriel, Faith K. *Nifty Thrifty Animal Crafts* (1–3). Illus. Series: Nifty Thrifty Crafts for Kids. 2007, Enslow LB $22.60 (978-0-7660-2779-4). 32pp. These simple, animal-themed crafts use readily available materials, and each includes some facts about the featured animal. (Rev: SLJ 5/07)

24188 Garner, Lynne. *African Crafts: Fun Things to Make and Do from West Africa* (4–6). Illus. 2008, Chicago Review $12.95 (978-1-55652-748-7). 48pp. Ghana is the main focus of this crafts book that also includes information on history and culture. (Rev: BL 5/1/08; SLJ 10/08) [745.5]

24189 Gessat, Audrey. *Crafts from Salt Dough* (2–4). Trans. from French by Cheryl L. Smith. Series: Step by Step. 2002, Capstone LB $22.60 (978-0-7368-1475-1). 32pp. Tips on working with dough accompany instructions for making items including a candleholder and a clown pencil. Also use *Crafts from Felt* and *Crafts from Modeling Clay* (both 2002). (Rev: HBG 3/03; SLJ 2/03)

24190 Gillman, Claire, and Sam Martin. *The Kids' Winter Fun Book* (3–5). Illus. 2011, Barron's paper $12.99 (978-07641472-6-5). 128pp. This is a comprehensive guide to cold-weather activities, with ideas divided into four sections: crafting, outdoor play, indoor play, and feasting. (Rev: BL 12/15/11; SLJ 1/12) [745.5]

24191 Glenn, Joshua, and Elizabeth Foy Larsen. *Unbored: The Essential Field Guide to Serious Fun* (5–8). Illus. 2012, Bloomsbury $25.00 (978-1-60819-641-8). 352pp. Bursting with creative ideas, this book encourages kids to make fun happen inside, outside, and in the community. (Rev: SLJ 9/12) [790]

24192 Gnojewski, Carol. *Cinco de Mayo Crafts* (K–5). Illus. Series: Fun Holiday Crafts Kids Can Do! 2005, Enslow LB $22.60 (978-0-7660-2344-4). 32pp. The ten crafts presented use everyday materials and include a sombrero and a paper poncho. (Rev: SLJ 6/05)

24193 Gould, Roberta. *Kidtopia: 'Round the Country and Back Through Time in 60 Projects* (2–7). 2000, Tricycle paper $13.95 (978-1-58246-026-0). 152pp. Divided into sections that cover American history and geography, this book contains many related projects, crafts, party ideas, and games. (Rev: SLJ 12/00) [745]

24194 Griffith, Saul, and Nick Dragotta. *Howtoons: The Possibilities Are Endless* (5–8). Illus. by Nick Dragotta. 2007, HarperCollins paper $15.99 (978-0-06-076158-5). A comic book and a project book in one, this will appeal to readers who are reluctant to pick up ordinary craft books; the "crafts" go beyond origami and include a marshmallow shooter, a tree swing, a rocket, and a flute. (Rev: BL 12/15/07; SLJ 5/08) [741.5]

24195 Halls, Kelly Milner, ed. *Look What You Can Make with Craft Sticks: Over 80 Pictured Crafts and Dozens of Other Ideas* (2–4). Photos by Hank Schneider. 2002, Boyds Mills paper $5.95 (978-1-56397-997-2). 48pp. Younger children may need help with some of the projects here, which use everyday materials to make a wide variety of items. Also use *Look What You Can Make with Plastic Bottles and Tubs: Over 80 Pictured Crafts and Dozens of Other Ideas* (2002). (Rev: SLJ 4/02) [745.5]

24196 Halls, Kelly Milner, ed. *Look What You Can Make with Plastic-Foam Trays: Over 90 Pictured Crafts and Dozens of Other Ideas* (K–3). Illus. 2003, Boyds Mills paper $5.95 (978-1-59078-078-7). 48pp. Child-friendly ideas for using plastic-foam trays in a variety of inventive ways. (Rev: SLJ 2/03)

24197 Hankin, Rosie. *Crafty Kids: Fun Projects for You and Your Toddler* (K–2). Illus. by author. 2006, Barron's paper $8.99 (978-0-7641-3542-2). 64pp. Adults and young children work together on the 28 simple projects here, many of them created from paper plates with a variety of adornments. (Rev: BL 1/1–15/07; SLJ 12/06) [745.5]

24198 Hauser, Jill F. *Little Hands Celebrate America! Learning About the U.S.A. Through Crafts and Activities* (K–5). Illus. by Michael Kline. Series: A Williamson Little Hands Book. 2004, Williamson paper $14.29 (978-1-885593-93-1). 128pp. Easy projects and activities introduce American symbols, sights, traditions, and holidays. (Rev: SLJ 11/04) [973]

24199 Hendry, Linda. *Cat Crafts* (4–6). Illus. Series: Kids Can Do It! 2002, Kids Can $12.95 (978-1-55074-964-9); paper $5.95 (978-1-55074-921-2). 40pp. Using double-page spreads, this book outlines 17 cat-related projects. (Rev: BL 4/1/02; HBG 10/02; SLJ 6/02) [745.5]

24200 Hendry, Linda. *Dog Crafts* (4–6). Illus. Series: Kids Can Do It! 2002, Kids Can $12.95 (978-1-55074-960-1); paper $5.95 (978-1-55074-962-5). 40pp. Sev-

enteen projects, such as making jewelry and toys, and all related to dogs, are presented in double-page spreads with easy-to-follow instructions. (Rev: BL 4/1/02; HBG 10/02; SLJ 6/02) [745.5]

24201 Hendry, Linda. *Making Gift Boxes* (4–8). Illus. by author. Series: Kids Can! 1999, Kids Can paper $5.95 (978-1-55074-503-0). The 14 boxes included in this fine craft book with clear instructions include a photo box, a garden box to grow seeds, a box for storing CDs, and a treasure box with false compartments. (Rev: SLJ 12/99) [745]

24202 Henry, Sally, and Trevor Cook. *Eco-Crafts* (4–8). Photos by authors. Series: Make Your Own Art. 2011, Rosen LB $25.25 (978-1-4488-1582-1); paper $11.75 (978-1-4488-1611-8). 32pp. Craft projects here — glow jars, a bird feeder, cat bookends, and so forth — feature natural or reused materials or support wildlife in some way. Also recommended in this series: *Making Mosaics* (2011). (Rev: SLJ 7/11) [745.5]

24203 Henry, Sandi. *Kids' Art Works! Creating with Color, Design, Texture and More* (K–5). Illus. by Norma Jean Martin-Jourdenais. Series: A Williamson Kids Can! Book. 2000, Williamson paper $12.95 (978-1-885593-35-1). 138pp. Sixty artistic creations using household materials; for example, a pasta fish, a Swiss cheese candle, and a sandpaper relief print. (Rev: SLJ 3/00) [745]

24204 *Holiday and Everyday Projects: Festive and Fun Creations* (2–5). Illus. Series: Crafty Kids. 2003, McGraw-Hill $12.95 (978-1-57768-528-9). 48pp. Projects for Easter, Halloween, and Mother's Day are among those included in this volume with easy-to-follow instructions and illustrations. (Rev: HBG 4/04; SLJ 12/03) [745.5]

24205 Hollow, Michele C. *Nifty Thrifty Sports Crafts* (1–3). Illus. Series: Nifty Thrifty Crafts for Kids. 2007, Enslow LB $22.60 (978-0-7660-2782-4). 32pp. Crafts for children who enjoy playing and watching sports. Easy-to-find, inexpensive materials make this teacher- and parent-friendly. (Rev: SLJ 8/07)

24206 Hosking, Wayne. *Asian Kites* (3–6). Illus. Series: Asian Arts and Crafts for Creative Kids. 2005, Tuttle $12.95 (978-0-8048-3545-9). 63pp. A thorough how-to guide to making 15 kites from China, Japan, Korea, Malaysia, and Thailand, with historical and cultural background. (Rev: SLJ 9/05)

24207 Hunter, Dette. *38 Ways to Entertain Your Grandparents* (K–2). Illus. by Deirdre Betteridge. 2002, Annick LB $19.95 (978-1-55037-749-1); paper $9.95 (978-1-55037-748-4). Hunter deftly interweaves Sarah's story of all the entertaining things she does with her grandparents with instructions for young readers to do likewise, including rules for games, recipes, and craft projects. (Rev: BL 12/1/02; HBG 3/03; SLJ 4/03) [793]

24208 Icanberry, Mark. *LooLeDo: Extraordinary Projects from Ordinary Objects* (K–3). Illus. 2010, LooLeDo $12.95 (978-189332712-2). 96pp. The creator of the Web site LooLeDo presents 31 easy-to-follow, well-illustrated projects using household and recycled materials. (Rev: BLO 11/15/10) [746.5]

24209 Irvin, Christine M. *Egg Carton Mania* (2–4). Illus. Series: Craft Mania. 2002, Children's Book Pr. LB $23.50 (978-0-516-22277-6). 32pp. Projects using egg cartons range from finger puppets to a double-decker bus. (Rev: BL 1/1–15/03; SLJ check) [745.5]

24210 Jocelyn, Marthe. *Sneaky Art: Crafty Surprises to Hide in Plain Sight* (3–5). Illus. 2013, Candlewick $12.99 (978-0-7636-5648-5). 64pp. A collection of crafts using everyday materials that are intended to be put on public display and to be easily removed. (Rev: BL 12/15/12*; SLJ 3/13) [745]

24211 Johnson, Ginger. *Make Your Own Christmas Ornaments* (3–5). Illus. by Norma Jean Martin-Jourdenais. Series: Quick Starts for Kids! 2002, Williamson paper $8.95 (978-1-885593-79-5). 64pp. A collection of 25 ornaments with clear instructions and photographs of finished products. (Rev: BL 12/15/02; SLJ 10/02)

24212 Jovinelly, Joann, and Jason Netelkos. *The Crafts and Culture of a Medieval Monastery* (4–8). Illus. Series: Crafts of the Middle Ages. 2006, Rosen LB $29.25 (978-1-4042-0759-2). Crafts and history are interwoven in this interesting that looks at the history of monasteries, life within them, and the work that took place in scriptoria, gardens, and hospitals; crafts include prayer beads and a plague mask. Also use *The Crafts and Culture of a Medieval Town* (2006). (Rev: SLJ 4/07) [271.0094]

24213 Kimble-Ellis, Sonya. *Traditional African American Arts and Activities* (3–7). Illus. Series: Celebrating Our Heritage. 2002, Wiley paper $12.95 (978-0-471-41046-1). 120pp. The projects featured in this title will teach students something about traditional culture, foods, holidays, crafts, and games. (Rev: SLJ 8/02)

24214 Kranz, Linda. *Let's Rock! Rock Painting for Kids* (1–6). Illus. 2003, NorthWord paper $11.95 (978-1-55971-870-7). 48pp. A comprehensive introduction to rock painting, including recommendations for the best kinds of rocks and paint to use, painting techniques, and special designs. (Rev: SLJ 10/03) [751.4]

24215 Lipsey, Jennifer. *I Love to Collage* (2–4). Illus. Series: My Favorite Art Book. 2006, Sterling $9.95 (978-1-57990-770-9). 48pp. Provides lots of practical, well-described ideas for making collages from materials ranging from leaves to candy wrappers to pasta. (Rev: BL 12/15/06; SLJ 12/06) [702]

24216 Love, Ann, and Jane Drake. *Kids and Grandparents: An Activity Book* (3–6). Illus. by Heather Collins. 2000, Kids Can $17.95 (978-1-55074-784-3); paper $10.95 (978-1-55074-492-7). 160pp. A collection of over 90 games, crafts, recipes, and activities for children and their grandparents together with a "Making Memories" section on creating a memory book, a relative map, and a family tree. (Rev: HBG 10/00; SLJ 5/00) [745]

24217 Luxbacher, Irene. *The Jumbo Book of Outdoor Art* (3–6). Photos by Ray Boudreau and Doug Hall. Illus. by author. 2006, Kids Can paper $16.95 (978-1-55337-680-4). 144pp. This large-format volume provides step-by-

step instructions for nearly 60 outdoor art projects and activities. (Rev: SLJ 11/06) [704.9]

24218 McGraw, Sheila. *Gifts Kids Can Make* (4–8). Photos by Sheila McGraw and Joy von Tiedemann. 1994, Firefly paper $9.95 (978-1-895565-35-5). A craft book that gives directions for making 14 simple gifts, such as a cotton sock doll and a hobby horse, using easily obtainable materials. (Rev: SLJ 12/94) [745]

24219 MacLeod, Elizabeth. *Gifts to Make and Eat* (4–7). Illus. by June Bradford. Series: Kids Can Do It! 2001, Kids Can $12.95 (978-1-55074-956-4); paper $6.95 (978-1-55074-958-8). 40pp. Kids learn through step-by-step instructions how to make an array of edible and craft gifts. (Rev: BL 11/1/01; HBG 3/02; SLJ 2/02) [641.5]

24220 Martin, Laura C. *Nature's Art Box: From T-Shirts to Twig Baskets, 65 Cool Projects for Crafty Kids to Make with Natural Materials You Can Find Anywhere* (4–8). Illus. by David Cain. 2003, Storey paper $16.95 (978-1-58017-490-9). These projects use natural materials such as twigs, moss, gourds, stones, shells, flowers, and leaves to make articles including wreaths, necklaces, and a chess set. (Rev: HBG 10/03; SLJ 8/03*) [745.5]

24221 Martin, Laura C. *Recycled Crafts Box* (3–7). Illus. 2004, Storey Kids $19.95 (978-1-58017-523-4). 96pp. A craft book with an environmental twist, this volume offers great project ideas plus information on recycling and the history of trash. (Rev: BL 3/15/04; SLJ 7/04) [363.72]

24222 Merrill, Yvonne Y. *Hands-On Latin America: Art Activities for All Ages* (4–8). Series: Hands-On. 1998, Kits paper $20.00 (978-0-9643177-1-0). A collection of 30 interesting, affordable arts and crafts projects inspired by the ancient cultures of Latin America. (Rev: BL 9/1/98; SLJ 8/98) [980.07]

24223 Mitchell, Mari Rutz. *Creating Clever Castles and Cars (from Boxes and Other Stuff): Kids Ages 3–8 Make Their Own Pretend Play Spaces* (PS–3). Illus. by Michael Kline. 2006, Williamson $14.95 (978-0-8249-6783-3); paper $12.95 (978-0-8249-6782-6). 128pp. Directions for making pretend-play items such as a fairy house, a barn, a fire engine, and a pyramid; the crafts are of varying levels of difficulty and all include illustrations and a list of needed supplies. (Rev: SLJ 7/06) [745.5]

24224 Monaghan, Kathleen, and Hermon Joyner. *You Can Weave! Projects for Young Weavers* (4–7). 2001, Sterling $19.95 (978-0-87192-493-3). Step-by-step instructions and photographs guide young crafters through weaving projects of varying complexity. (Rev: BL 11/1/01) [746.41]

24225 Monaghan, Kimberly. *Organic Crafts: 75 Earth-Friendly Art Activities* (3–5). Illus. 2007, Chicago Review $14.95 (978-1-55652-640-4). 160pp. The crafts, games, and activities in this collection use natural, renewable materials such as leaves and twigs, pebbles and shells. (Rev: BL 4/1/07) [745.5]

24226 Mooney, Carla. *Amazing Africa Projects You Can Build Yourself* (4–7). Illus. by Megan Stearns. Series: Build It Yourself. 2010, Nomad paper $15.95 (978-1-

9346704-1-5). Unpaged. Full of information about all aspects of Africa, this volume includes 25 projects — such as a mask, a basket, and rock paintings — made with everyday materials. **e** Lexile IG930L (Rev: BL 5/15/10; SLJ 10/1/10) [745.5096]

24227 Mueller, Stephanie R., and Ann E. Wheeler. *101 Great Gifts from Kids: Fabulous Gifts Every Child Can Make* (PS–3). Illus. 2002, Gryphon House paper $14.95 (978-0-87659-279-3). 174pp. Gift ideas that vary in difficulty and may require some adult help are accompanied by line drawings of the process involved and the end product. (Rev: SLJ 9/02) [745.5]

24228 Murillo, Kathy Cano. *The Crafty Diva's Lifestyle Makeover: Awesome Ideas to Spice Up Your Life!* (5–12). Illus. by Carrie Wheeler. 2005, Watson-Guptill paper $12.95 (978-0-8230-1008-0). The Crafty Diva is back with this collection of easy-to-follow instructions for 50 projects that cover everything from room makeovers to fashion accessories. (Rev: SLJ 9/05)

24229 Niven, Felicia Lowenstein. *Nifty Thrifty Music Crafts* (1–3). Illus. Series: Nifty Thrifty Crafts for Kids. 2007, Enslow LB $22.60 (978-0-7660-2784-8). 32pp. Crafts for children who enjoy playing and listening to music. Easy-to-find, inexpensive materials make this teacher- and parent-friendly. (Rev: SLJ 8/07)

24230 Oldham, Todd. *Kid Made Modern* (3–6). Illus. 2009, AMMO $22.95 (978-1-934429-36-5). 192pp. In addition to acquainting readers with modern design, this book includes a variety of child-friendly craft projects, including paper lanterns and jewelry, that require varying levels of skill. (Rev: BL 12/15/09; SLJ 2/10) [700]

24231 Otten, Jack. *Watch Me Make a Bird Feeder* (PS–2). Series: Making Things. 2002, Children's Book Pr. paper $4.95 (978-0-516-23497-7). 24pp. The process of making a bird feeder is simply explained in language that will suit challenged early readers. Also use *Watch Me Plant a Garden* (2002). (Rev: SLJ 6/02) [690.89]

24232 Owen, Cheryl. *Gifts for Kids to Make* (2–4). 2006, Sterling $14.95 (978-0-600-61502-6). 128pp. More than 50 projects involve sewing, art, clay and dough, and other materials, some of which require adult supervision. (Rev: BL 1/1–15/07; SLJ 12/06) [745.5083]

24233 Phillips, Matt. *Make Your Own Fun Frames!* (3–6). Illus. by Stan Jaskiel. 2001, Williamson paper $8.95 (978-1-885593-64-1). 63pp. Basic instructions for making frames and matting, cropping photographs, and hanging frames are accompanied by design suggestions using a variety of everyday materials. (Rev: SLJ 6/02) [749.7]

24234 Ponte, June. *Fun and Simple Southeastern State Crafts* (2–4). Illus. Series: Fun and Simple State Crafts. 2008, Enslow LB $17.95 (978-0-7660-2935-4). 48pp. Crafts associated with West Virginia, Virginia, North Carolina, South Carolina, Georgia, and Florida are accompanied by pages of facts. (Rev: BL 12/15/08) [745.50975]

24235 Powell, Michelle. *Beadwork* (3–5). Illus. Series: Step-by-Step. 2002, Heinemann LB $25.64 (978-1-

4034-0696-5). 32pp. Color photographs show each step in creating beadwork projects. (Rev: BL 12/15/02; HBG 3/03) [745.58]

24236 Powell, Michelle. *Mosaics* (4–7). Series: Step-by-Step. 2001, Heinemann LB $24.22 (978-1-57572-332-7). 32pp. A number of fascinating projects creating mosaics are described with step-by-step instructions and many colorful illustrations. (Rev: BL 8/1/01; HBG 10/01; SLJ 10/01) [745]

24237 Powell, Michelle, and Judy Balchin. *Crafty Activities: Over 50 Fun and Easy Things to Make* (4–7). Illus. 2007, Search paper $19.95 (978-1-84448-250-4). Fifty crafts involving mosaics, printing, lettering, papier-mâché, card-making, and origami, attractively and clearly presented for the young crafter. (Rev: BL 12/15/07; SLJ 1/08) [745]

24238 Press, Judy. *All Around Town: Exploring Your Community Through Craft Fun* (PS–3). Illus. Series: Little Hands. 2002, Williamson paper $12.95 (978-1-885593-68-9). 128pp. Projects using everyday materials that will introduce youngsters to community institutions such as schools, libraries, and gas stations are shown with instructions and illustrations. (Rev: BL 1/1–15/03; SLJ 4/03) [307]

24239 Press, Judy. *Around-the-World Art and Activities: Visiting the 7 Continents Through Craft Fun* (PS–2). Illus. by Betsy Day. Series: Little Hands. 2001, Williamson paper $14.29 (978-1-885593-45-0). 128pp. Activities, which are coded by level of difficulty, include making travel-related items such as a passport and suitcase, and cultural items such as totem poles, leis, nesting Russian dolls, gaucho belts, and Korean drums. (Rev: SLJ 5/01) [745]

24240 Press, Judy. *ArtStarts for Little Hands! Fun and Discoveries for 3- to 7-Year-Olds* (PS–2). Illus. by Karol Kaminski. 2000, Williamson paper $12.95 (978-1-885593-37-5). 118pp. A fresh and amusing book that presents simple activities using everyday materials under such themes as animals, seasons, transportation, colors, and gardens. (Rev: SLJ 10/00) [745]

24241 Press, Judy. *At the Zoo: Explore the Animal World with Craft Fun* (PS–3). Illus. by Jenny Campbell. Series: A Little Hands Book. 2002, Williamson paper $12.95 (978-1-885593-61-0). 126pp. Crafts using widely available materials are grouped in broad categories such as "African Safari" and "Tropical Forest" that are introduced by a map and brief general information, followed by individual animal projects. (Rev: SLJ 8/02)

24242 Price, Pam. *Cool Rubber Stamp Art* (4–6). Illus. Series: Cool Crafts. 2005, ABDO LB $22.78 (978-1-59197-743-8). 32pp. A terra-cotta flowerpot, wrapping paper, and a canvas beach bag are among the projects shown, with advice on safety, creativity, and seeking help from adults. Also use *Cool Scrapbooks* (2005). (Rev: SLJ 6/05)

24243 *Recyclables* (4–6). Trans. from Spanish by Colleen Coffey. Series: Let's Create! 2004, Gareth Stevens LB $24.00 (978-0-8368-4018-6). 32pp. Projects using recyclables — cardboard, paper, and plastic, in particular — include a milk-carton cow and an egg-carton tree. (Rev: SLJ 11/04) [745.5]

24244 Rhatigan, Joe. *Soapmaking: 50 Fun and Fabulous Soaps to Melt and Pour* (4–6). Series: Kids' Crafts. 2003, Lark Books $19.95 (978-1-57990-416-6). 112pp. More than 50 diverse soap projects follow basic information and are accompanied by tips for budding entrepreneurs. (Rev: BL 12/15/03; SLJ 6/04)

24245 Rhodes, Vicki. *Pumpkin Decorating* (4–8). 1997, Sterling $10.95 (978-0-8069-9574-8). Clear directions and full-color photographs demonstrate more than 80 designs for pumpkins. (Rev: SLJ 12/97) [745.5]

24246 Robinson, Fay. *Father's Day Crafts* (3–5). Illus. 2005, Enslow LB $22.60 (978-0-7660-2343-7). 32pp. Ten original gifts for Dad that students will enjoy making. Photographs help them picture the finished product. (Rev: SLJ 8/05)

24247 Robinson, Fay. *Halloween Crafts* (3–5). Illus. Series: Fun Holiday Crafts Kids Can Do! 2004, Enslow LB $22.60 (978-0-7660-2236-2). 32pp. Ten craft ideas that involve easily found, inexpensive materials are shown with simple instructions. (Rev: SLJ 7/04) [745.594]

24248 Robinson, Fay. *Hispanic-American Crafts Kids Can Do!* (3–5). Series: Multicultural Crafts Kids Can Do! 2006, Enslow LB $22.60 (978-0-7660-2459-5). 32pp. Easy-to-follow instructions are provided for ten crafts that originated in various corners of Latin America. (Rev: BL 8/06) [745.5089]

24249 Ross, Kathy. *All New Crafts for Kwanzaa* (K–3). Illus. by Sharon L. Holm. 2006, Lerner LB $25.26 (978-0-7613-3401-9); paper $7.95 (978-0-8225-3435-8). 48pp. This new version of a 1994 title by the same authors includes additional projects related to the holiday. (Rev: BL 1/1–15/07; SLJ 10/06) [745.594]

24250 Ross, Kathy. *All New Crafts for Thanksgiving* (3–5). Illus. by Sharon L. Holm. 2005, Millbrook LB $25.26 (978-0-7613-2922-0); paper $7.95 (978-0-7613-2398-3). 48pp. More than 20 Thanksgiving-themed craft ideas use readily available materials and vary in difficulty. (Rev: BL 10/1/05) [745.594]

24251 Ross, Kathy. *All New Crafts for Valentine's Day* (1–3). Illus. by Barbara Leonard. 2002, Millbrook LB $23.90 (978-0-7613-2553-6); paper $7.95 (978-0-7613-1576-6). 48pp. Easy crafts are accompanied by step-by-step instructions and bright watercolor paintings. (Rev: HBG 3/03; SLJ 11/02) [745.594]

24252 Ross, Kathy. *All-Girl Crafts* (2–4). Illus. by Elaine Garvin. Series: Girl Crafts. 2005, Lerner LB $25.26 (978-0-7613-2776-9); paper $7.95 (978-0-7613-2391-4). Clear directions and lists of required items are a strong feature of this collection of 22 craft projects designed to appeal to elementary-school girls and including doll furniture, a change purse, fancy envelopes, and a pillow-doll pajama bag. (Rev: BL 12/15/05; SLJ 10/05) [745.5]

24253 Ross, Kathy. *Christmas Presents Kids Can Make* (4–6). Illus. by Sharon L. Holm. 2001, Millbrook LB

$24.40 (978-0-7613-1754-8). 64pp. The author provides new ideas for 29 creative Christmas gifts using everyday items. (Rev: BL 9/15/01; HBG 3/02; SLJ 10/01) [745.5]

24254 Ross, Kathy. *Community Workers* (K–2). Illus. by Jan Barger. Series: Crafts for Kids Who Are Learning About. 2005, Millbrook LB $25.26 (978-0-7613-2743-1). 48pp. Twenty crafts introduce children to the activities of various community workers, including firefighters, dentists, shopkeepers, and librarians. (Rev: SLJ 1/06) [745.5]

24255 Ross, Kathy. *Crafts for All Seasons* (3–5). Illus. 2000, Millbrook $19.95 (978-0-7613-1346-5). 176pp. Drawing widely on the material in the author's four seasonal craft books, this spiral-bound volume contains 80 projects with clear instructions. (Rev: BL 10/15/00; HBG 10/01) [745.5]

24256 Ross, Kathy. *Crafts for Christian Values* (K–4). Illus. by Sharon L. Holm. 2000, Millbrook LB $24.90 (978-0-7613-1618-3). 63pp. A book of 28 craft projects, each related to a particular Christian value — such as a bookmark that honors one's parents. (Rev: HBG 10/01; SLJ 2/01) [745]

24257 Ross, Kathy. *Crafts from Your Favorite Bible Stories* (3–5). Illus. 2000, Millbrook LB $24.90 (978-0-7613-1619-0). 64pp. Using simple materials such as lunch bags and pipe cleaners, this book offers 27 craft projects from both the Old and New Testaments such as making Noah's ark or Joseph's coat of many colors. (Rev: BL 6/1–15/00; HBG 10/00; SLJ 8/00) [268]

24258 Ross, Kathy. *Crafts from Your Favorite Children's Songs* (PS–2). Illus. by Vicky Enright. 2001, Millbrook LB $24.40 (978-0-7613-1912-2). 47pp. Crafts designed to accompany familiar songs are presented with simple instructions. (Rev: HBG 10/01; SLJ 5/01) [745.5]

24259 Ross, Kathy. *Crafts from Your Favorite Children's Stories* (1–4). Illus. by Elaine Garvin. 2001, Millbrook LB $24.90 (978-0-7613-1772-2). 47pp. Young children may need help with some of these projects, which include a "Bear Hug Puppet," a spinning Dorothy house on its way to Oz, and a Sourdough Sam. (Rev: HBG 3/02; SLJ 9/01) [745.5]

24260 Ross, Kathy. *Crafts from Your Favorite Nursery Rhymes* (3–5). Illus. by Elaine Garvin. 2002, Millbrook LB $24.90 (978-0-7613-2523-9); paper $8.95 (978-0-7613-1589-6). 48pp. Simple directions and clear illustrations accompany projects of varying difficulty; young children will need some help with these activities related to popular rhymes. (Rev: BL 1/1–15/03; HBG 3/03; SLJ 12/02) [745.5]

24261 Ross, Kathy. *Crafts to Celebrate God's Creation* (3–5). Illus. 2001, Millbrook LB $24.90 (978-0-7613-1621-3). 64pp. Using the creation story in Genesis as a focus, this craft book gives directions for making such items as a "sunrise puppet," flying birds, and a beaded pin in the shape of a cross. (Rev: BL 1/1–15/01; HBG 10/01) [268.432]

24262 Ross, Kathy. *Earth-Friendly Crafts: Clever Ways to Reuse Everyday Items* (3–6). Illus. by Celine Malepart.

2009, Millbrook LB $26.60 (978-0-8225-9099-6). 48pp. A collection of projects that encourage kids to reduce, reuse, and recycle. (Rev: BL 12/15/08) [745.5]

24263 Ross, Kathy. *Girlfriends' Get-Together Craft Book* (1–5). Illus. by Nicole in den Bosch. Series: Girl Crafts. 2007, Millbrook LB $25.26 (978-0-7613-3408-8). 48pp. Filled with great ideas for girls who like wearable and decorative crafts, this book will inspire fun sleepover projects. (Rev: SLJ 6/07)

24264 Ross, Kathy. *Kathy Ross Crafts Numbers* (PS–1). Illus. by Jan Barger. Series: Learning Is Fun! 2003, Millbrook LB $23.90 (978-0-7613-2105-7); paper $7.95 (978-0-7613-1697-8). 48pp. Numbers and the ways they are used in everyday life form the central theme of this large-format collection of crafts; included among the simple projects are a birthday cake pin, a toy alarm clock, and playing-card counters. (Rev: BL 4/15/03; HBG 10/03) [745.5]

24265 Ross, Kathy. *Kathy Ross Crafts Triangles, Rectangles, Circles, and Squares* (PS–1). Illus. by Jan Barger. Series: Learning Is Fun! 2002, Millbrook LB $23.90 (978-0-7613-2104-0); paper $7.95 (978-0-7613-1696-1). Projects that introduce basic geometric shapes include puppets, jewelry, games, and hanging objects. (Rev: HBG 3/03; SLJ 1/03)

24266 Ross, Kathy. *One-of-a-Kind Stamps and Crafts* (3–6). Illus. by Nicole in den Bosch. 2010, Millbrook $25.26 (978-0-8225-9216-7); paper $7.95 (978-1-58013-885-7). 48pp. Offers clear instructions on creating 20 stamps using beads, buttons, foam shapes, coins, and so forth. (Rev: SLJ 4/1/10) [761]

24267 Ross, Kathy. *Play-Doh Animal Fun* (K–4). Illus. by Sharon Hawkins Vargo. 2002, Millbrook LB $24.40 (978-0-7613-2506-2). 48pp. Twenty animals to make with play-doh range from simple clams to a rattlesnake with a rattle. Also use *Play-Doh Art Projects* (2002). (Rev: HBG 10/02; SLJ 5/02) [745.5]

24268 Ross, Kathy. *The Scrapbooker's Idea Book* (3–5). Illus. by Nicole in den Bosch. Series: Girl Crafts. 2006, Millbrook LB $25.26 (978-0-7613-2777-6). 48pp. An excellent introduction to scrapbooking, with step-by-step instructions for 22 projects. (Rev: SLJ 9/06)

24269 Ross, Kathy. *Star-Spangled Crafts* (4–6). Illus. by Sharon L. Holm. 2003, Millbrook LB $23.90 (978-0-7613-2853-7). 48pp. Twenty-two crafts with patriotic themes include an American eagle magnet and an Uncle Sam tissue box. (Rev: HBG 10/03; SLJ 7/03)

24270 Ross, Kathy. *Step-by-Step Crafts for Summer* (3–4). Illus. by Jennifer Emery. 2007, Boyds Mills $15.95 (978-1-59078-360-3). 48pp. Twenty summer-themed crafts include projects for picnics, parades, patios, playgrounds, and more. (Rev: SLJ 7/07)

24271 Ross, Kathy. *Step-by-Step Crafts for Winter* (K–3). Illus. by Jennifer Emery. 2006, Boyds Mills $15.95 (978-1-59078-449-5); paper $6.95 (978-1-59078-358-0). 48pp. Step-by-step instructions for 20 winter-themed crafts using everyday materials include projects appro-

priate for Christmas, Kwanzaa, Hanukkah, Lincoln's Birthday, and Valentine's Day. (Rev: SLJ 12/06) [745]

24272 Ross, Kathy, ed. *Look What You Can Make with Dozens of Household Items!* (4–6). Photos by Hank Schneider. Series: Look What You Can Make With. 2003, Boyds Mills $24.99 (978-1-59078-058-9). 384pp. Common household items are used to create a wide range of crafts. (Rev: BL 12/15/02) [745]

24273 Sadler, Judy Ann. *Christmas Crafts from Around the World* (4–6). 2003, Kids Can $12.95 (978-1-55337-427-5); paper $6.95 (978-1-55337-428-2). 40pp. This guide offers step-by-step instructions for making 17 Christmas crafts with origins in countries around the world. (Rev: BL 12/15/03; HBG 4/04; SLJ 10/03)

24274 Sadler, Judy Ann. *Jumbo Book of Easy Crafts* (3–5). Illus. 2001, Kids Can $14.95 (978-1-55074-811-6). 208pp. Crafts using everyday items — paper plates, popsicle sticks, aluminum foil, beans, beads, and so forth — are arranged by type of material. (Rev: BL 6/1–15/01; SLJ 7/01) [745.5]

24275 Schwarz, Renee. *Funky Junk* (4–7). Series: Kids Can Do It! 2002, Kids Can $12.95 (978-1-55337-387-2); paper $5.95 (978-1-55337-388-9). Using easily found materials, this craft book supplies details on how to make unusual conversation pieces. (Rev: BL 3/15/03; HBG 10/03; SLJ 4/03) [745.5]

24276 Simons, Robin. *Recyclopedia: Games, Science Equipment and Crafts from Recycled Materials* (5–8). Illus. by author. 1976, Houghton Mifflin paper $13.95 (978-0-395-59641-8). Clear directions complemented by good illustrations characterize this book of interesting projects using waste materials.

24277 Souter, Gillian. *Holiday Handiworks* (3–6). Illus. Series: Handy Crafts. 2002, Gareth Stevens LB $26.00 (978-0-8368-3050-7). 48pp. A well-organized collection of crafts with clear instructions, aimed at holidays including Easter, Passover, Kwanzaa, and Chinese New Year. Also use *Rainy Day Fun* and *Terrific Toys* (both 2002). (Rev: HBG 10/02; SLJ 6/02) [745.5]

24278 Stetson, Emily, and Vicky Congdon. *Little Hands Fingerplays and Action Songs: Seasonal Rhymes and Creative Play for 2- to 6-Year-Olds* (PS–1). Illus. by Betsy Day. Series: Little Hands. 2001, Williamson paper $12.95 (978-1-885593-53-5). 128pp. Suggestions for songs, games, and crafts are organized by season and accompanied by brief facts and short reading lists. (Rev: SLJ 11/01) [793.4]

24279 Temko, Florence. *Traditional Crafts from China* (5–7). Series: Culture Crafts. 2001, Lerner LB $23.93 (978-0-8225-2939-2). After a few words about crafts in general, this volume carefully outlines a number of projects relating to Chinese culture, including instructions for picture scrolls and tanagrams. (Rev: BL 2/15/01; HBG 10/01; SLJ 4/01) [745]

24280 Temko, Florence. *Traditional Crafts from Japan* (3–5). Illus. by Randall Gooch. Series: Culture Crafts. 2001, Lerner LB $23.93 (978-0-8225-2938-5). 64pp. Eight traditional Japanese handicrafts are presented with instructions for making them and explanations of their significance in Japanese culture. (Rev: HBG 10/01; SLJ 4/01) [745]

24281 Temko, Florence. *Traditional Crafts from the Caribbean* (5–7). Series: Culture Crafts. 2001, Lerner LB $23.93 (978-0-8225-2937-8). Step-by-step instructions with clear diagrams are given for a number of craft projects relating to Caribbean culture including yarn dolls, Puerto Rican masks, and metal cutouts. (Rev: BL 2/15/01; HBG 10/01; SLJ 4/01) [745]

24282 Torres, Laura. *Best Friends Forever! 199 Projects to Make and Share* (5–8). Illus. 2004, Workman paper $13.95 (978-0-7611-3274-5). 148pp. Craft ideas that will appeal to young teens — bracelets, key chains, picture frames, and so forth — are clearly explained and organized into chapters such as "Cool Notes" and "Home and School." (Rev: SLJ 2/05) [745.5]

24283 Trottier, Maxine. *Native Crafts: Inspired by North America's First Peoples* (3–6). Illus. 2000, Kids Can $12.95 (978-1-55074-854-3); paper $5.95 (978-1-55074-549-8). 40pp. Sixteen projects (all requiring adult help) from the traditional arts and crafts of Native Americans are presented with step-by-step instructions and pictures of the finished products. (Rev: BL 7/00; HBG 10/00; SLJ 6/00) [745.5]

24284 Van Vleet, Carmella. *Great Ancient Egypt Projects You Can Build Yourself* (4–6). Illus. 2006, Nomad paper $14.95 (978-0-9771294-5-4). 122pp. More than two dozen hands-on activities explore life in ancient Egypt — everything from hieroglyphs and papyrus to perfume and pyramids — and are supplemented by background information. (Rev: SLJ 2/07) [932]

24285 Wagner, Lisa. *Cool Melt and Pour Soap* (4–7). Photos by Kelly Doudna. Series: Cool Crafts. 2005, ABDO LB $22.78 (978-1-59197-741-4). Coloring, fragrance, and packaging are all covered in this guide to projects using soap. (Rev: SLJ 7/05)

24286 Wagner, Lisa. *Cool Painted Stuff* (4–6). Illus. Series: Cool Crafts. 2005, ABDO LB $22.78 (978-1-59197-742-1). 32pp. A fancy flowerpot and a mini-tote are among the projects shown, with advice on safety, creativity, and seeking help from adults. (Rev: SLJ 6/05)

24287 Walsh, Danny, et al. *The Cardboard Box Book: 25 Things to Make and Do with Empty Boxes* (3–5). Photos by Martin Norris. Illus. by Josh Halloran. 2006, Watson-Guptill paper $12.95 (978-0-8230-0610-6). 112pp. The authors — a father and sons — offer a number of kid-tested ways to convert empty boxes to better use. (Rev: SLJ 2/07) [745.54]

24288 Warwick, Ellen. *Stuff for Your Space* (4–6). Series: Kids Can Do It! 2004, Kids Can $12.95 (978-1-55337-398-8). 40pp. Well-illustrated advice and instructions for boys and girls on decorating their individual living spaces. (Rev: BL 2/15/04; SLJ 4/04) [745]

24289 White, Linda. *Haunting on a Halloween* (5–7). Illus. by Fran Lee. 2002, Gibbs Smith paper $9.95 (978-1-58685-112-5). Everything young party planners need to host a Halloween get-together, with instructions for crafts, food, decorations, and costumes. (Rev: BL 9/15/02) [745.594]

24290 Zakarin, Debra Mostow. *Happening Hanukkah: Creative Ways to Celebrate* (4–6). Illus. by Amanda Haley. 2002, Grosset paper $5.99 (978-0-448-42869-7). 64pp. A treasure trove of Hanukkah gift ideas plus suggestions for parties, food, and games. (Rev: SLJ 10/02)

American Historical Crafts

24291 Beard, D. C. *The American Boys' Handy Book: What to Do and How to Do It* (5–7). 1983, Godine paper $12.95 (978-0-87923-449-2). A facsimile edition of a manual first published in 1882. [790.194]

24292 Broida, Marian. *Projects About Plantation Life* (3–5). Series: Hands-on History. 2003, Benchmark LB $27.07 (978-0-7614-1605-0). 48pp. Introduced by appropriate background, illustrations, and maps, this book offers detailed instructions on re-creating things from the period — from crafts to recipes. Also use *Projects About Westward Expansion* (2003). (Rev: BL 2/15/04; HBG 4/04; SLJ 3/04)

24293 Kuntz, Lynn. *Celebrate the USA: Hands-on History Activities for Kids* (3–5). Illus. by Mark A. Hicks. 2007, Gibbs Smith paper $7.95 (978-1-58685-846-9). 80pp. Twenty-five activities accompany information about America's history, people, landscape, holidays, songs, and more, presented in an engaging format. (Rev: SLJ 7/07)

24294 Merrill, Yvonne Y. *Hands-On Rocky Mountains: Art Activities About Anasazi, American Indians, Settlers, Trappers, and Cowboys* (4–8). 1996, Kits paper $16.95 (978-0-9643177-2-7). Historical groups from the Rocky Mountain region — early people, American Indians, trappers, settlers, and cowboys — are introduced and, for each, a series of craft projects is outlined. (Rev: BL 1/1–15/97; SLJ 4/97) [745.5]

24295 Mooney, Carla. *George Washington: 25 Great Projects You Can Build Yourself* (4–7). Illus. by Samuel Carbaugh. Series: Build It Yourself. 2010, Nomad paper $15.95 (978-1-934670-63-7). 128pp. Part Washington biography, part colonial crafts book, this volume provides plenty of historical information while also giving clear instructions for activities such as making swords and wigs. (Rev: BL 3/1/11; SLJ 3/1/11) [973.4]

Clay and Other Modeling Crafts

24296 Arima, Elaine. *The Kids 'n' Clay Ceramics Book: HandBuilding and Wheel-Throwing Projects from the Kids 'N' Clay Pottery Studio* (3–8). Illus. 2000, Tricycle paper $16.95 (978-1-883672-89-8). 128pp. A ceramic project book for middle and junior high grades that involves creating both handmade and wheel-thrown objects including a breakfast bowl, bookends, and a porcupine. (Rev: BL 3/1/00; SLJ 8/00) [738]

24297 Carlson, Maureen. *Clay Characters for Kids* (3–8). Photos by author. 2003, North Light paper $12.99 (978-1-58180-286-3). 79pp. This photo-filled guide to modeling figures out of polymer clay outlines 30 projects that will require a degree of adut supervision. (Rev: SLJ 12/03) [731.4]

24298 *Clay* (3–6). Series: Let's Create! 2003, Gareth Stevens LB $24.00 (978-0-8368-3746-9). 32pp. This plentifully illustrated primer on working creatively with clay details a dozen projects, with suggestions for further reading and a list of Web resources. (Rev: SLJ 4/04) [738]

24299 Cuxart, Bernadette. *Modeling Clay Animals: Easy-to-Follow Projects in Simple Steps* (1–4). Illus. 2010, Barron's paper $9.99 (978-0-7641-4-579-7). 96pp. Cuxart introduces a few basic shapes that can be repeated to form different animals in this clear guide. (Rev: BL 12/15/10; SLJ 12/1/10) [731.42]

24300 Good, Keith. *Shape It! Magnificent Projects for Molding Materials* (3–7). Series: Design It! 2000, Lerner LB $21.27 (978-0-8225-3568-3). 30pp. This is a book of craft projects that involve molding materials such as salt dough, plaster, air-drying clay, and edible materials like cookie dough. (Rev: HBG 10/00; SLJ 6/00) [745.5]

24301 Ross, Kathy. *Play-Doh Fun and Games* (K–4). Illus. by Sharon Vargo. Series: Play-Doh Fun. 2003, Millbrook LB $24.90 (978-0-7613-2507-9). 48pp. Detailed instructions for 20 game and toy projects that can be made using Play-Doh and/or other readily available materials. (Rev: HBG 10/03; SLJ 6/03)

24302 Scheunemann, Pam. *Cool Clay Projects* (4–7). Photos by Anders Hanson. Series: Cool Crafts. 2005, ABDO LB $22.78 (978-1-59197-740-7). Clear, step-by-step instructions for a number of clay projects are accompanied by full-color photos and tips about safety. (Rev: SLJ 7/05) [731.4]

24303 Speechley, Greta. *Clay Modeling* (3–6). Series: Step-by-Step. 2000, Heinemann LB $24.22 (978-1-57572-326-6). 32pp. This book shows how to create figures including a cat, a tiger, a flowerpot, and a bowl using air-drying clay. (Rev: BL 10/15/00; HBG 10/01; SLJ 12/00) [745.5]

Costume and Jewelry Making

24304 Baker, Diane. *Jazzy Jewelry: Power Beads, Crystals, Chokers, and Illusion and Tattoo Styles* (5–9). Illus. by Alexandra Michaels. 2001, Williamson paper $12.95 (978-1-885593-47-4). 144pp. Jewelry projects for bead lovers include chokers, headbands, and bobby pins, all presented with black-and-white line drawings and guidance on color choice, clasps and knots, and proper storage. (Rev: SLJ 7/01) [745.594]

24305 Baker, Diane. *Make Your Own Hairwear: Beaded Barrettes, Clips, Dangles and Headbands* (4–8). Illus. by Alexandra Michaels. 2001, Williamson paper $8.95 (978-1-885593-63-4). 63pp. Easy instructions guide readers through the steps of making hair accessories using beads, shells, rhinestones, and other materials. (Rev: SLJ 4/02) [745.58]

24306 Boonyadhistarn, Thiranut. *Beading: Bracelets, Barrettes, and Beyond* (4–8). Illus. Series: Snap Books: Crafts. 2006, Capstone LB $25.26 (978-0-7368-6472-5). 32pp. Simple, step-by-step instructions guide readers through a variety of fashion accessories that use accessible materials. (Rev: SLJ 2/07) [745.58]

24307 Di Salle, Rachel, and Ellen Warwick. *Junk Drawer Jewelry* (4–7). Photos by Ray Boudreau. Illus. by Jane Kurisu. Series: Kids Can Do It. 2006, Kids Can $12.95 (978-1-55337-965-2); paper $6.95 (978-1-55337-966-9). 40pp. This innovative craft book offers step-by-step instructions for making jewelry using odds and ends found in the junk drawer at home. (Rev: SLJ 11/06) [745.5]

24308 Newcomb, Rain. *Girls' World Book of Jewelry: 50 Cool Designs to Make* (5–8). Series: Kids Crafts. 2004, Lark Books paper $14.95 (978-1-57990-473-9). Up-to-date designs are accompanied by well-thought-out instructions and advice in this large-format volume. (Rev: BL 12/15/04; SLJ 4/05)

24309 Sadler, Judy Ann. *Beading: Bracelets, Earrings, Necklaces and More* (4–8). Series: Kids Can! 1998, Kids Can paper $6.95 (978-1-55074-338-8). Using photographs and simple instructions, directions are given for making a simple beading loom and creating necklaces and bracelets. (Rev: BL 5/15/98) [745.594]

24310 Sadler, Judy Ann. *Hemp Jewelry* (4–7). Series: Kids Can Do It! 2005, Kids Can $12.95 (978-1-55337-774-0); paper $6.95 (978-1-55337-775-7). Sixteen projects for boys and girls using hemp, with drawings and photographs to illustrate the steps and the results. (Rev: BL 3/15/05; SLJ 5/05) [746.4]

24311 Scheunemann, Pam. *Cool Beaded Jewelry* (4–7). Photos by Anders Hanson. Series: Cool Crafts. 2005, ABDO LB $22.78 (978-1-59197-739-1). Step-by-step instructions and full-color photographs guide the user through beaded jewelry projects. (Rev: SLJ 7/05) [745]

Drawing and Painting

24312 Ames, Lee J. *Draw Fifty Baby Animals: The Step-by-Step Way to Draw Kittens, Lambs, Chicks, and Other Adorable Offspring* (3–5). Illus. by author. 2003, Broadway paper $8.95 (978-0-7679-1284-6). In this step-by-step guide, author Lee J. Ames shows young readers how to draw pictures of baby animals — both wild and domesticated. (Rev: SLJ 11/03) [743.6]

24313 Ames, Lee J. *Draw Fifty Cats* (4–7). 1986, Doubleday paper $8.95 (978-0-385-24640-8). Step-by-step ways of drawing different breeds and poses of cats. Also use *Draw Fifty Holiday Decorations* (1987). (Rev: BL 11/15/86) [743.69752]

24314 Artell, Mike. *Funny Cartooning for Kids* (3–6). Illus. by author. 2007, Sterling LB $17.95 (978-1-4027-2260-8). 128pp. This guide emphasizes the importance of humor in cartooning and explains the basics — exaggeration, simplification, anthropomorphism, and so forth. (Rev: SLJ 4/07) [741.5]

24315 Balchin, Judy. *Creative Lettering* (4–7). Series: Step-by-Step. 2001, Heinemann LB $24.22 (978-1-57572-331-0). 32pp. Using easy-to-find materials, this craft book gives clear directions for several fascinating lettering projects. (Rev: BL 8/1/01; HBG 10/01) [745.6]

24316 Balchin, Judy. *Decorative Painting* (4–7). Series: Step-by-Step. 2001, Heinemann LB $24.22 (978-1-57572-330-3). 32pp. With easy-to-follow directions and illustrations that describe each step, this colorful book contains a number of simple projects that decorate with paints. (Rev: BL 8/1/01; HBG 10/01; SLJ 10/01) [745]

24317 Baron, Nancy. *Getting Started in Calligraphy* (5–8). 1979, Sterling paper $13.95 (978-0-8069-8840-5). This well-organized text shows how to draw letters with beauty and grace. [745.6]

24318 Barr, Steve. *1-2-3 Draw Cartoon Aliens and Space Stuff: A Step-by-Step Guide* (3–6). Illus. by author. 2003, Peel paper $8.99 (978-0-939217-71-7). 62pp. Easy-to-follow instructions show progressively difficult drawings first in black-and-white and finally in color. Also use *1-2-3 Draw Cartoon Wildlife* (2003). (Rev: SLJ 5/03) [741.5]

24319 Barr, Steve. *1-2-3 Draw Cartoon Animals* (2–5). Illus. 2002, Peel paper $8.99 (978-0-939217-48-9). 64pp. Easy, step-by-step directions guide budding young artists to draw a variety of animals using a cartoon style. Also use *1-2-3 Draw Cartoon Faces* and *1-2-3 Draw Cartoon People* (both 2002). (Rev: BL 1/1–15/03) [741.5]

24320 Bergin, Mark. *How to Draw Pets* (4–7). Illus. Series: How to Draw. 2011, Rosen LB $25.25 (978-144884511-8). 32pp. Cats, dogs, and rabbits are among the animals featured in this slim volume that shows how to use pencils, ink, charcoal, and pastels. (Rev: BL 11/1/11) [743.6]

24321 Bergin, Mark. *Robots* (5–8). Illus. by author. Series: How to Draw. 2008, PowerKids LB $18.95 (978-1-4358-2521-5). 32pp. After discussion of perspective, tools, and materials, Bergin shows how to draw droids and robots, showing the progression of a drawing from its basic shape and form to the final detailing and shading. Lexile IG1140L (Rev: BLO 10/7/08) [743]

24322 Besel, Jennifer M. *A Christmas Drawing Wonderland* (2–5). Illus. by Lucy Makuc. 2013, Capstone LB $24.65 (978-147653092-5). 24pp. Step-by-step instructions help young artists with Christmas creations. (Rev: BL 11/1/13) [743]

24323 Brooks, Susie. *Get Into Art! Animals: Discover Great Art — Create Your Own!* (3–6). Illus. by author. 2013, Kingfisher $12.99 (978-075347058-9). 32pp. With works by famous artists as examples, this inspiring book organized by subject urges readers to create their own masterpieces. (Rev: BL 6/13*; LMC 3–4/2014*)

24324 Butterfield, Moira. *Fun with Paint* (4–8). Series: Creative Crafts. 1994, Random House paper $6.99 (978-0-679-83942-2). This simple introduction to painting covers various media and a number of creative projects, including making your own paints. (Rev: SLJ 3/94) [745]

24325 Clay, Kathryn. *How to Draw Mythical Creatures* (4–6). Illus. by Anne Timmons. 2009, Capstone $25.32 (978-142962307-0). 32pp. Mermaids, dragons, pixies, unicorns — all these and more are presented with black-and-white sketches followed by a full-color illustration; useful for relatively experienced young artists. (Rev: BLO 11/15/09) [743]

24326 ComicsKey Staff. *How to Draw Kung Fu Comics* (4–8). 2004, ComicsOne paper $19.95 (978-1-58899-394-6). Cheung's instructions on creating architecture and perspective are particularly valuable. (Rev: BL 8/04) [741.5]

24327 Court, Rob. *How to Draw Cars and Trucks* (4–6). Illus. Series: The Scribbles Institute. 2005, Child's World LB $24.21 (978-1-59296-148-1). 32pp. In addition to introducing the basics, Court focuses readers on the composition and purpose of the objects they are drawing. Also use *How to Draw Dinosaurs* (2005). (Rev: BL 4/1/05) [743]

24328 DuBosque, Doug. *Draw! Grassland Animals: A Step-by-Step Guide* (4–7). Illus. by author. 1996, Peel paper $8.99 (978-0-939217-25-0). A step-by-step description of how to draw 31 animals from grasslands around the world. (Rev: SLJ 9/96) [741]

24329 DuBosque, Doug. *Draw Insects* (4–8). 1997, Peel paper $8.99 (978-0-939217-28-1). A carefully constructed drawing book that gives simple directions for drawing more than 80 insects, including millipedes, ticks, and spiders. (Rev: SLJ 6/98) [741.2]

24330 DuBosque, Doug. *Draw 3-D: A Step-by-Step Guide to Perspective Drawing* (4–9). Illus. by author. 1999, Peel paper $8.99 (978-0-939217-14-4). Using easy-to-follow sketches, the author introduces the techniques of 3-D drawing, beginning with basic concepts involving depth and progressing to more difficult areas such as multiple vanishing points. (Rev: SLJ 5/99; VOYA 8/99) [741.2]

24331 DuBosque, Doug. *Learn to Draw Now!* (5–8). Illus. by author. Series: Learn to Draw. 1991, Peel paper $8.99 (978-0-939217-16-8). A simple, easily followed manual on how to draw that contains many interesting practice exercises. (Rev: SLJ 8/91) [743]

24332 Durkin, Kath. *Paint It!* (3–5). Illus. 2012, Amicus/QEB LB $19.95 (978-160992275-7). 32pp. Twelve projects such as a self-portrait, a gift card, snowflakes, and a patchwork landscape teach budding artists about different painting techniques (watercolors, acrylics, and so forth). (Rev: BL 11/1/12; LMC 5–6/13) [745.5]

24333 Eason, Sarah. *Drawing Baby Animals* (2–5). Illus. by Jorge Santillan. Series: Learn to Draw. 2013, Gareth Stevens LB $26.60 (978-143399524-8). 32pp. A lively guide to drawing simplified baby animals with large doe eyes. (Rev: BL 11/1/13; SLJ 11/4/13) [743.6]

24334 Gonyea, Mark. *A Book About Color* (2–5). Illus. by author. 2010, Henry Holt $19.99 (978-0-8050-9055-0). 96pp. An introduction to primary and secondary colors, the color wheel, and properties such as warmth. (Rev: BL 2/15/10; HB 5–6/10; SLJ 3/1/10) [700]

24335 Gray, Peter. *Heroes and Villains* (5–8). Series: Kid's Guide to Drawing. 2006, Rosen LB $25.25 (978-1-4042-3330-0). 32pp. Shows clearly how to draw manga heroes and villains and offers guidance on getting facial expressions just right. (Rev: BL 9/1/06; SLJ 9/06) [741.5]

24336 Hart, Christopher. *The Cartoonist's Big Book of Drawing Animals* (2–6). Illus. by author. 2008, Watson-Guptill paper $21.95 (978-0-8230-1421-7). 224pp. Dogs, cats, horses, bears, and penguins are among the animals featured in this step-by-step approach to drawing cartoon figures with many facial expressions. (Rev: SLJ 3/09) [741.5]

24337 Hart, Christopher. *Drawing the New Adventure Cartoons: Cool Spies, Evil Guys & Action Heroes* (4–8). Illus. by author. 2008, Sixth & Spring paper $19.95 (978-1-933027-60-9). 128pp. Both entertaining and educational, this book gives detailed instructions, and amusing side notes, that show how to create adventure characters. (Rev: SLJ 2/09) [741.5]

24338 Hart, Christopher. *Kids Draw Anime* (4–8). 2002, Watson-Guptill paper $10.95 (978-0-8230-2690-6). Instructions on how to draw anime (Japanese cartoons) characters, with many colorful examples. (Rev: BL 2/1/03; SLJ 11/02) [741.5]

24339 Hart, Christopher. *Kids Draw Funny and Spooky Holiday Characters* (3–6). Illus. by author. 2001, Watson-Guptill paper $10.95 (978-0-8230-2626-5). 64pp. Cartoon drawing for Halloween and Christmas are the focus of this guide that covers the basic principles of showing movement and good positioning of characters. (Rev: SLJ 9/01) [741.5]

24340 Hart, Christopher. *Kids Draw Manga* (3–8). Illus. by author. Series: Kids Draw. 2004, Watson-Guptill paper $10.95 (978-0-8230-2623-4). 64pp. For beginners, this is a guide to the basics of manga, showing how to draw a number of characters, poses, and action moves. (Rev: SLJ 9/04) [741.5]

24341 Hart, Christopher. *Manga Mania: How to Draw Japanese Comics* (5–9). 2001, Watson-Guptill paper $19.95 (978-0-8230-3035-4). Hart looks at the techniques for drawing typical Japanese comic characters and animals, providing examples of published manga along with an introduction to the various genres of manga and an interview with a manga publisher. (Rev: BL 7/01; SLJ 7/01) [741.5]

24342 Hart, Christopher. *Manga Mania Chibi and Furry Characters: How to Draw the Adorable Mini-People*

and Cool Cat-Girls of Japanese Comics (5–12). Illus. 2006, Watson-Guptill paper $19.95 (978-0-8230-2977-8). 144pp. Fans of these super-cute manga characters will appreciate the step-by-step directions in this informative book. (Rev: SLJ 5/06) [741.5]

24343 Hart, Christopher. *Mecha Mania: How to Draw the Battling Robots, Cool Spaceships, and Military Vehicles of Japanese Comics* (4–8). 2002, Watson-Guptill paper $19.95 (978-0-8230-3056-9). Instructions on how to draw the high-tech, scary, fanciful machines and weapons that fill the pages of Japanese comic books. (Rev: BL 2/1/03; SLJ 4/03) [741.5]

24344 Hart, Christopher. *Xtreme Art: Draw Manga Monsters!* (1–4). Illus. by author. Series: Xtreme Art. 2005, Watson-Guptill paper $6.95 (978-0-8230-0372-3). 64pp. A simple guide to drawing in the manga style for children; also use *Draw Mini Manga!* (2005). (Rev: SLJ 9/05) [741.5]

24345 Hart, Christopher. *You Can Draw Cartoon Animals: A Simple Step-by-Step Drawing Guide* (2–6). Illus. by author. Series: Just for Kids! 2009, Walter Foster paper $12.99 (978-1-60058-611-8). 120pp. Simple instructions help readers learn to draw a variety of wild and domestic animals. (Rev: SLJ 4/10) [741.5]

24346 Hart, Chrisropher. *Kids Draw Animals* (3–6). Illus. by author. Series: Kids Draw. 2003, Watson-Guptill paper $10.95 (978-0-8230-2631-9). 64pp. Organized by topics, this is an easy-to-understand, step-by-step guide to drawing cartoons of animals. (Rev: SLJ 11/03) [743.6]

24347 Hodge, Anthony. *Drawing* (4–8). Series: Mastering Art. 2004, Stargazer LB $.00 (978-1-932799-01-9). 32pp. Along with basic information on materials, colors, and techniques, this slim volume looks at drawing the human body. Also use *Painting* (2004). (Rev: BL 11/1/04) [741.2]

24348 Kesselring, Susan. *Five Steps to Drawing Faces* (3–6). Illus. by Dana Regan. 2011, Child's World LB $25.64 (978-160973197-7). 32pp. This straightforward drawing book helps children draw a variety of different faces and expressions. (Rev: BL 11/1/11) [743.4]

24349 LaBaff, Stephanie. *Draw Aliens and Space Objects in 4 Easy Steps: Then Write a Story* (3–5). Illus. by Tom LaBaff. Series: Drawing in 4 Easy Steps. 2012, Enslow LB $23.93 (978-076603841-7). 48pp. A wildly imaginative gallery of astronauts, aliens, robots, spacecraft is combined with advice on incorporating the images into a story. (Rev: BL 4/1/12) [743]

24350 Lee, Frank. *Telling the Story in Your Graphic Novel* (4–6). Illus. Series: How to Draw Your Own Graphic Novel. 2012, Rosen LB $12.30 (978-144886453-9). 32pp. This series volume helps readers to conceive story lines and create drama suitable for graphic novels. (Rev: BL 3/15/12) [741.5]

24351 Levin, Freddie. *1-2-3 Draw: Cars, Trucks, and Other Vehicles* (3–5). Illus. 2002, Peel paper $8.99 (978-0-939217-43-4). 64pp. A large-format paperback that shows how to draw 24 vehicles including a race car, cement truck, and a school bus. (Rev: BL 4/15/02; SLJ 7/02) [743]

24352 Levin, Freddie. *1-2-3 Draw: Dinosaurs and Other Prehistoric Animals: A Step by Step Guide* (1–5). Illus. by author. 2000, Peel paper $8.95 (978-0-939217-41-0). 64pp. Using three basic shapes — circles, ovals, and eggs — the author shows how to draw 24 different prehistoric animals. The same techniques are applied in *1-2-3-Draw: Pets and Farm Animals* (2000). (Rev: SLJ 3/01) [742]

24353 Lewis, Amanda. *Lettering: Make Your Own Cards, Signs, Gifts and More* (4–8). 1997, Kids Can paper $6.95 (978-1-55074-232-9). This book describes calligraphy and gothic lettering techniques, covering such topics as typefaces, displays, types of pens to purchase, how to determine pen size, and how to use pens, as well as explaining how to make letterhead stationery and newsletters on the computer. (Rev: BL 10/15/97; SLJ 1/98) [745.6]

24354 Lipsey, Jennifer. *I Love to Finger Paint!* (1–3). Series: My Very Favorite Art Book. 2006, Sterling $9.95 (978-1-57990-771-6). 48pp. This attractive guide to finger painting lists essential supplies, explores various techniques, and describes several projects. (Rev: BL 6/1–15/06) [751.4]

24355 Lipsey, Jennifer. *I Love to Paint!* (3–5). Illus. 2006, Lark $9.95 (978-1-57990-630-6). 48pp. Finger painting, watercolors, scratch art, and sponge painting are among the painting techniques introduced in this attractive and well-organized guide. (Rev: BL 2/15/06) [751.4]

24356 Luxbacher, Irene. *The Jumbo Book of Art* (3–8). Illus. by author. 2003, Kids Can paper $14.95 (978-1-55074-762-1). 208pp. Drawing, use of color, sculpting, and mixed media are the focus of this book full of interesting art projects. (Rev: SLJ 11/03) [701]

24357 Luxbacher, Irene. *1-2-3 I Can Draw!* (1–3). Illus. by author. Series: Starting Art. 2008, Kids Can $14.95 (978-1-55453-039-7); paper $5.95 (978-1-55453-152-3). 24pp. This friendly book offers clear, easy directions for drawing such items as faces, features, expressions, and figures. (Rev: SLJ 4/08) [741.2]

24358 Luxbacher, Irene. *1-2-3 I Can Paint!* (1–3). Illus. Series: Starting Art. 2007, Kids Can LB $12.95 (978-1-55453-037-3); paper $5.95 (978-1-55453-150-9). 24pp. Mixing colors, perspective, and brush techniques are among the topics discussed in this introduction to painting. (Rev: BL 10/15/07; SLJ 10/07) [751.4]

24359 Masiello, Ralph. *Ralph Masiello's Ancient Egypt Drawing Book* (3–6). Illus. by author. 2008, Charlesbridge $16.95 (978-1-57091-533-8); paper $7.95 (978-1-57091-534-5). A step-by-step guide to drawing Egyptian symbols and pictures — each with its own commentary. (Rev: SLJ 9/08)

24360 Masiello, Ralph. *Ralph Masiello's Dragon Drawing Book* (3–6). Illus. by author. 2007, Charlesbridge $16.95 (978-1-57091-531-4); paper $7.95 (978-1-57091-532-1). Eleven cool dragons and other mythical creatures from cultures around the world are included

in this well-designed, step-by-step drawing guide. (Rev: BL 7/07; SLJ 9/07) [743.6]

24361 Masiello, Ralph. *Ralph Masiello's Farm Drawing Book* (1–4). Illus. by author. Series: Drawing Book. 2012, Charlesbridge $16.95 (978-157091537-6); paper $7.95 (978-15709153-8-3). 32pp. Clear instructions for drawing farm animals and fixtures are appended with bits of folk trivia, songs, information, and farm crafts. **e** (Rev: BL 12/15/11) [743.6]

24362 Masiello, Ralph. *Ralph Masiello's Robot Drawing Book* (2–5). Illus. by author. 2011, Charlesbridge $16.95 (978-1-57091-535-2); paper $7.95 (978-1-57091-536-9). 32pp. Step-by-step directions for drawing ten colorful robots. (Rev: BLO 7/11; SLJ 8/1/11) [743]

24363 Mayne, Don. *Draw Your Own Cartoons* (3–8). Illus. by author. 2001, Williamson paper $8.95 (978-1-885593-76-4). 64pp. A cartoon-like atmosphere prevails in this guide that teaches readers to draw characters. (Rev: SLJ 6/01) [741.5]

24364 Mayne, Don. *Drawing Horses (That Look Real)* (4–8). Illus. by author. Series: Quick Starts for Kids! 2002, Williamson paper $8.95 (978-1-885593-74-0). 64pp. Cartoonlike instructions take young artists step by step through using basic shapes to draw horses and to show movement and character. (Rev: SLJ 4/03) [743.6]

24365 Murawski, Laura. *How to Draw Cats* (2–5). Illus. by author. Series: A Kid's Guide to Drawing. 2001, Rosen LB $21.25 (978-0-8239-5549-7). 24pp. Information about each breed precedes instructions on how to draw it in stages that begin with basic shapes and proceed to add details. Also use *How to Draw Dogs* (2001). (Rev: SLJ 8/01) [741]

24366 *Paper and Paint: Hands-on Crafts for Everyday Fun* (2–5). Illus. Series: Crafty Kids. 2003, McGraw-Hill $12.95 (978-1-57768-527-2). 48pp. Paper and paint projects that may need adult help are included in this volume with easy-to-follow instructions and illustrations. (Rev: HBG 4/04; SLJ 12/03) [745.54]

24367 Peffer, Jessica. *DragonArt: How to Draw Fantastic Dragons and Fantasy Creatures* (5–12). Illus. by author. 2005, Impact paper $19.99 (978-1-58180-657-1). Beautiful creatures from the author's imagination fill the pages of this well-written book and will inspire young artists to develop their own fantasy style. (Rev: SLJ 5/06) [743]

24368 Peot, Margaret. *Inkblot: Drip, Splat, and Squish Your Way to Creativity* (4–6). Illus. by author. 2011, Boyds Mills $19.95 (978-1-59078-720-5). 56pp. A large-format introduction to creating inkblot art and using them to develop ideas. (Rev: BL 5/1/11; SLJ 5/11*) [751.4]

24369 Peterson, Tiffany. *Watercraft* (3–6). Series: Draw It! 2003, Heinemann LB $24.22 (978-1-4034-0214-1). 32pp. Author Tiffany Peterson offers guidance for drawing and painting pictures of various watercraft, including jet skis, river boats, and sailing ships. Also in this series are *Sports Stars*, *Fashion Design*, and *Sea Crea-*

tures (both 2003). (Rev: BL 11/15/03; HBG 10/03; SLJ 10/03)

24370 Reinagle, Damon J. *Draw! Medieval Fantasies* (4–8). 1995, Peel paper $8.99 (978-0-939217-30-4). A how-to drawing book that gives simple instructions on creating such medieval subjects as dragons and castles. (Rev: BL 1/1–15/96; SLJ 3/96) [743]

24371 Reinagle, Damon J. *Draw Sports Figures* (4–8). 1997, Peel paper $8.99 (978-0-939217-32-8). In six chapters arranged by sport or sports category, the author gives easy-to-follow instructions on how to draw action figures. (Rev: SLJ 6/98) [742]

24372 Robins, Deri. *Painting* (2–5). Illus. Series: Learn Art. 2004, QEB LB $27.10 (978-1-59566-046-6). 32pp. Creativity is emphasized in this look at how colors interact and the various techniques for applying them. (Rev: SLJ 4/05) [750]

24373 Robins, Deri. *Special Effects* (3–5). Series: QEB Learn Art. 2004, QEB LB $27.10 (978-1-59566-047-3). 32pp. Using glitter paint and making mosaics and collages are among the projects presented here with clear step-by-step directions. (Rev: BL 11/1/04; SLJ 4/05) [741.2]

24374 Roche, Art. *Art for Kids: Comic Strips: Create Your Own Comic Strips from Start to Finish* (4–8). Illus. by author. 2007, Sterling LB $17.95 (978-1-57990-788-4). This is a practical guide to creating a comic strip, with tips on story ideas, design, creating characters, and writing jokes. (Rev: BCCB 5/07; LMC 8–9/07; SLJ 5/07) [741.5]

24375 Roche, Art. *Cartooning: The Only Cartooning Book You'll Ever Need to Be the Artist You've Always Wanted to Be* (3–6). Illus. by author. Series: Art for Kids. 2005, Sterling $17.95 (978-1-57990-623-8). 111pp. An engaging guide to the basics of cartooning, encouraging young artists to seek their own style. (Rev: SLJ 7/05) [741.5]

24376 Roza, Greg. *Drawing Dracula* (3–6). Illus. Series: Drawing Movie Monsters Step-by-Step. 2010, Windmill LB $25.65 (978-1-61533-015-7); paper $12.85 (978-1-61533-021-8). 24pp. Straightforward step-by-step instructions teach readers how to recreate the famous vampire. Also use *Drawing Frankenstein, Drawing Godzilla,* and *Drawing King Kong* (2010). e (Rev: SLJ 5/11) [743]

24377 Ryall, Jeanette. *Junk Art* (3–6). Illus. Series: Awesome Art. 2012, Windmill LB $26.50 (978-1-4488-8087-4). 32pp. Double-page spreads introduce 11 art projects using items that may have been consigned to the trash. e (Rev: BL 12/15/12; LMC 8–9/13; SLJ 11/12) [745.5]

24378 Sikorski, Joy, and Nick Sunday. *How to Draw a Happy Witch and 99 Things That Go Bump in the Night* (K–3). Illus. by Joy Sikorski. 2011, Sterling paper $9.95 (978-1-4027-5-708-2). 96pp. This drawing book includes instructions for Halloween-inspired items (a witch, a jack-o-lantern) within a story about a nighttime

expedition visit through wetlands and on to a jazz club. (Rev: BL 11/1/11; SLJ 10/1/11) [741.2]

24379 Silver, Patricia. *Face Painting* (1–4). Illus. by Louise Phillips. 2000, Kids Can $12.95 (978-1-55074-845-1); paper $6.95 (978-1-55074-689-1). A fine introduction to face painting that includes 16 of the most commonly requested faces with rules for safety and cleanup tips. (Rev: BL 9/15/00; SLJ 10/00) [745.5]

24380 Stephens, Jay. *Heroes!* (4–7). Illus. by author. 2007, Sterling $12.95 (978-1-57990-934-5). How to draw superheroes, masks, action moves, and so forth, with lots of great examples. (Rev: BL 12/1/07; SLJ 8/07) [741.5]

24381 Stephens, Jay. *Monsters! Draw Your Own Mutants, Freaks and Creeps* (4–6). Illus. by author. 2007, Sterling LB $12.95 (978-1-57990-935-2). 64pp. The author guides readers in developing their own artistic style while supplying plenty of inspiration. (Rev: SLJ 8/07)

24382 Tecco, Betsy Dru. *How to Draw Egypt's Sights and Symbols* (3–6). Illus. Series: A Kid's Guide to Drawing the Countries of the World. 2004, Rosen LB $26.50 (978-0-8239-6682-0). 48pp. After background information on Egypt, step-by-step instructions guide readers through sketching scenes including a camel, a date palm, a pyramid, and the mask of King Tut. Also use *How to Draw France's Sights and Symbols* and *How to Draw Japan's Sights and Symbols* (both 2004). (Rev: SLJ 3/05) [743]

24383 Temple, Kathryn. *Drawing* (5–8). Series: Art for Kids. 2005, Sterling $17.95 (978-1-57990-587-3). A comprehensive and clearly written guide to equipment and techniques, with useful illustrations and practical exercises at the end of each section. (Rev: BL 5/1/05; SLJ 9/05) [741.2]

24384 Tullet, Herve. *The Big Book of Art* (PS–1). Illus. by author. 2013, Phaidon $24.95 (978-071486349-8). 86pp. Young people are offered the opportunity to be artists with the unique page layout of this book, which allows readers to turn half a page at a time, creating endless combinations of shapes and lines. (Rev: BL 11/1/13; SLJ 12/13) [700]

24385 Wallace, Mary. *I Can Make Art* (4–8). Series: I Can Make. 1997, Firefly paper $6.95 (978-1-895688-65-8). Art and crafts are combined in these 12 projects involving such techniques as watercolor, still life, chalk drawing, print making, and collage. (Rev: SLJ 12/97) [741.2]

24386 Walsh, Patricia. *Aircraft* (3–6). Illus. Series: Draw It! 2000, Heinemann LB $22.79 (978-1-57572-347-1). 32pp. From the Wright brothers' flying machine to a modern Bell JetRanger helicopter, this chronologically arranged book describes aircraft and gives directions for sketching them. (Rev: BL 2/1/01; HBG 10/01) [743]

24387 Walsh, Patricia. *Cars* (3–6). Series: Draw It! 2000, Heinemann LB $22.79 (978-1-57572-348-8). 32pp. Using colored lines to show each step, this book shows how to draw cars in six easy steps. Also use from the same art series: *Dinosaurs*, *Space Vehicles*, and *Wild Animals* (all 2000). (Rev: BL 3/1/01; HBG 10/01) [741.2]

24388 Walsh, Patricia. *Woodland Animals* (3–6). Illus. 2000, Heinemann LB $22.79 (978-1-57572-352-5). 32pp. Introducing a single animal per double-page spread, this book describes such animals as the skunk, woodpecker, and porcupine with clear instructions on how to draw each. (Rev: BL 2/1/01; HBG 10/01; SLJ 2/01) [743]

24389 Wellford, Lin. *Painting on Rocks for Kids* (K–3). Illus. 2002, North Light paper $12.99 (978-1-58180-255-9). 64pp. Step-by-step instructions and tips on technique accompany ideas for making cars, flowers, dinosaurs, fish, food, and other items from painted stones and rocks. (Rev: SLJ 1/03) [745.7]

24390 Wheeler, Annie. *Painting on a Canvas: Art Adventures for Kids* (5–8). Illus. by Debra Spina Dixon. 2006, Gibbs Smith $9.95 (978-1-58685-839-1). These projects are designed to get children's creative juices flowing and to introduce them to some of the techniques used by such world-famous artists as Matisse, Michelangelo, and Picasso. (Rev: SLJ 11/06) [701]

24391 Zemke, Deborah. *Doodle a Zoodle* (3–5). 2006, Blue Apple $12.95 (978-1-59354-140-8). Gives step-by-step instructions for drawing 39 "zoodles" — animals, such as squirrels and jackrabbits, that have double letters in their names; brief information is provided on each animal. (Rev: SLJ 12/06) [743]

24392 Zemke, Deborah. *2 Is for Toucan: Oodles of Doodles from 0 to 42* (3–5). Illus. by author. 2005, Handprint $12.95 (978-1-59354-075-3). Step-by-step instructions show how to do creative doodles integrating art and numbers; a spiral binding allows the book to open flat. (Rev: SLJ 9/05) [741]

Masks and Mask Making

24393 D'Cruz, Anna-Marie. *Make Your Own Masks* (3–4). Series: Do It Yourself Projects! 2009, Rosen LB $23.95 (978-1-4358-2853-7). 24pp. Step-by-step directions show how to make a selection of masks from diverse cultures. (Rev: SLJ 7/09) [646.4]

24394 Henry, Sally, and Trevor Cook. *Making Masks* (4–8). Photos by authors. Series: Make Your Own Art. 2011, Rosen LB $25.25 (978-1-4488-1583-8); paper $11.75 (978-1-4488-1613-2). 32pp. Color photographs and clear instructions add appeal to this book detailing a variety of creative mask projects. (Rev: SLJ 7/11) [731.785]

24395 Schwarz, Renee. *Making Masks* (4–6). Series: Kids Can Do It! 2002, Kids Can $12.95 (978-1-55074-929-8); paper $5.95 (978-1-55074-931-1). A basic volume on making masks from a various of easily obtained materials. (Rev: BL 9/15/02; HBG 3/03; SLJ 12/02) [731.785]

Paper Crafts

24396 Alexander, Chris. *Sort-of-Difficult Origami* (2–5). Illus. 2008, Capstone LB $18.95 (978-1-4296-2023-9). 32pp. Moderately difficult origami models include a tulip and stem, a penguin, a seal, and a goldfish. (Rev: BL 12/15/08) [736]

24397 Balchin, Judy. *Papier Mâché* (4–7). Illus. Series: Step-by-Step. 2000, Heinemann LB $24.22 (978-1-57572-328-0). 32pp. Combines easy-to-follow projects with information on how papier-mâché has been used over the centuries, including applications in construction and furniture. (Rev: BL 10/15/00; HBG 10/01; SLJ 12/00) [745.54]

24398 Blanchette, Peg, and Terri Thibault. *Make Your Own Cool Cards: 40 Awesome Notes and Invitations!* (2–4). Series: Quick Starts for Kids! 2004, Ideals Publications paper $8.95 (978-1-885593-96-2). 64pp. Sixteen projects that use easy-to-obtain materials are presented in detail with clear illustrations. (Rev: BL 12/15/03)

24399 Carter, Tamsin. *Handmade Cards* (3–5). Illus. Series: Step-by-Step. 2002, Heinemann LB $25.64 (978-1-4034-0698-9). 32pp. This volume provides simple instructions, explained one step at a time, for creating and decorating greeting cards. (Rev: BL 12/15/02; HBG 3/03) [745.594]

24400 Castleforte, Brian. *Papertoy Monsters: 50 Cool Papertoys You Can Make Yourself!* (4–7). Illus. by Robert James. 2011, Workman paper $16.95 (978-0-7611-5882-0). 124pp. Fifty different paper craft projects are contained within this punch-out-and-assemble collection. (Rev: BL 12/15/10; SLJ 4/11) [745]

24401 Check, Laura. *The Kids' Guide to Making Scrapbooks and Photo Albums! How to Collect, Design, Assemble, Decorate* (4–6). Illus. by Betsy Day. 2002, Williamson paper $12.95 (978-1-885593-59-7). 128pp. Check discusses the best ways to use images to tell stories as well as giving practical instructions for creating scrapbooks and albums. (Rev: SLJ 7/02) [745.593]

24402 Harbo, Christopher L. *The Kids' Guide to Paper Airplanes* (4–7). Illus. 2009, Capstone LB $23.93 (978-1-4296-2274-5). 32pp. Detailed, step-by-step directions show how to make a variety of arrows, missiles, and planes, with tips on increasing flight time. (Rev: BL 12/15/08; SLJ 5/09) [745.592]

24403 Henry, Sally. *Paper Folding* (3–6). Illus. Series: Make Your Own Art. 2008, PowerKids LB $18.95 (978-1-4358-2507-9). 32pp. This fold-your-own title offers an introduction to techniques and equipment followed by a number of inventive projects. (Rev: BL 12/15/08) [736]

24404 Henry, Sally, and Trevor Cook. *Origami* (4–8). Photos by authors. Series: Make Your Own Art. 2011, Rosen LB $25.25 (978-1-4488-1586-9); paper $11.75 (978-1-4488-1619-4). 32pp. Color photographs and clear instructions detail a variety of origami projects such as a bird, a lotus flower, a windmill, and a butterfly. Also use *Papier-Mâché* (2011). (Rev: SLJ 7/11) [745.592]

24405 Hufford, Deborah. *Greeting Card Making: Send Your Personal Message* (3–5). Illus. Series: Snap Books Crafts. 2005, Capstone LB $25.26 (978-0-7368-4385-0). 32pp. Clear directions will help readers create a variety of greeting cards, including pop-ups, collage cards, mosaic cards, and photo cards. (Rev: BL 12/15/05) [745.594]

24406 Irvin, Christine M. *Paper Plate Mania* (K–2). Illus. Series: Craft Mania. 2002, Children's Book Pr. LB $23.50 (978-0-516-21675-1). 32pp. Masks and sun catchers are among the many inventive uses for paper plates suggested in this book that emphasizes the importance of recycling. Also use *Paper Cup Mania* (2002). (Rev: SLJ 9/02) [745.54]

24407 Jackson, Paul. *Origami Toys: That Tumble, Fly, and Spin* (4–6). Illus. by author. Photos by Avi Valdman. 2010, Gibbs Smith paper $19.99 (978-1-4236-0524-9). 128pp. Clear diagrams guide readers through creating origami objects with moving parts; projects are rated by difficulty. (Rev: SLJ 4/10) [736.9]

24408 Jackson, Paul, and Miri Golan. *Origami Zoo: 25 Fun Paper Animal Creations!* (1–6). Illus. by Paul Jackson. Photos by Avi Valdman. 2011, Gibbs Smith paper $19.99 (978-1-4236-2016-7). 128pp. Clear illustrations add appeal to this collection of 25 different origami projects involving animals (koalas, monkeys, and butterflies, for example), which vary in difficulty from very simple to challenging. (Rev: SLJ 5/1/11) [736]

24409 Johnson, Ginger. *Paper-Folding Fun! 50 Awesome Crafts to Weave, Twist and Curl* (3–5). Illus. Series: Kids Can. 2002, Williamson paper $12.95 (978-1-885593-67-2). 128pp. Step-by-step directions accompany each idea for making objects from paper, including jewelry, mobiles, and books. (Rev: BL 11/1/02) [745.54]

24410 Lafosse, Michael G. *Making Origami Christmas Decorations Step by Step* (2–4). Illus. by author. Series: Kid's Guide to Origami. 2002, Rosen LB $21.25 (978-0-8239-5874-0). 24pp. Nine projects related to Christmas are suitable for beginning folders. (Rev: SLJ 10/02)

24411 Lafosse, Michael G. *Making Origami Masks Step by Step* (2–6). Illus. Series: A Kid's Guide to Origami. 2004, Rosen LB $21.25 (978-0-8239-6703-2). 24pp. Well-explained projects are suitable for different levels of expertise. Also use *Making Origami Puzzles Step by Step* and *Making Origami Science Experiments Step by Step* (both 2004). (Rev: SLJ 11/04) [745.592]

24412 Lafosse, Michael G. *Origami Activities* (4–6). Illus. Series: Asian Arts and Crafts for Creative Kids. 2004, Tuttle $12.95 (978-0-8048-3497-1). 64pp. Step-by-step instructions guide readers through 15 increasingly difficult projects. (Rev: SLJ 8/04) [736]

24413 Lassus, Irene, and Marie-Anne Voituriez. *Papier Mâché* (2–5). Series: I Made It Myself! 2005, Gareth Stevens LB $23.00 (978-0-8368-5966-9). 24pp. Following an introduction to the properties of papier mâché and

the ways to work with it, nine projects include beads, candy, and a crocodile. (Rev: SLJ 2/06) [745.54]

24414 Lewis, Amanda. *The Jumbo Book of Paper Crafts* (3–6). Illus. by Jane Kurisu. 2002, Kids Can paper $14.95 (978-1-55074-940-3). 160pp. Easy, illustrated techniques and instructions teach older children how to create a multitude of crafts with paper and cardboard. (Rev: BL 12/15/02; SLJ 12/02) [745]

24415 Llimós, Anna. *Easy Cardboard Crafts in 5 Steps* (2–4). Series: Easy Crafts in Five Steps. 2008, Enslow LB $22.60 (978-0-7660-3083-1). 32pp. A notebook, a drum, and a hang-glider are among the 14 projects provided here. Also use *Easy Cloth Crafts in Five Steps* (2008). (Rev: SLJ 4/08) [745.54]

24416 McGee, Randel. *Paper Crafts for Christmas* (2–5). Illus. Series: Paper Craft Fun for Holidays. 2009, Enslow LB $17.95 (978-0-7660-2952-1). 48pp. A brief history of the holiday and its traditions precedes such projects as a holly wreath, snowflake ornaments, a paper plate angel, and a pop-up chimney card. (Rev: BL 4/1/09) [745.594]

24417 McGee, Randel. *Paper Crafts for Halloween* (2–5). Illus. Series: Paper Craft Fun for Holidays. 2009, Enslow LB $17.95 (978-0-7660-2947-7). 48pp. A brief history of the holiday and its traditions precedes such projects as a flying bat, a haunted house, a black cat, and a skull headdress. (Rev: BL 4/1/09; SLJ 4/09) [745.594]

24418 McGee, Randel. *Paper Crafts for Valentine's Day* (2–5). Illus. 2008, Enslow LB $17.95 (978-0-7660-2948-4). 48pp. This craft book opens with an introduction to Valentine's Day followed by eight simple projects. (Rev: BL 12/15/08; SLJ 11/08) [745.594]

24419 Newell, Keith. *Look and Make with Paper* (4–5). Photos by Steve Shott. Illus. by Michael Evans. Series: Look and Make. 2004, Sea-to-Sea LB $27.10 (978-1-932889-24-6). 32pp. Well-designed projects — such as paper sandals — use paper and glue and are presented with clear instructions and a photograph of the final product. (Rev: SLJ 4/05) [745.54]

24420 Nguyen, Duy. *Monster Origami* (5–7). Illus. 2007, Sterling paper $9.95 (978-1-4027-4014-5). This how-to origami book provides easy-to-understand instructions on creating amazing paper monsters. (Rev: SLJ 3/08)

24421 Owen, Ruth. *Valentine's Day Origami* (3–6). Illus. Series: Holiday Origami. 2012, Rosen LB $26.50 (978-144887865-9). 32pp. Step-by-step instructions guide readers through creating a heart, a rose, a heart box, and other Valentine's Day items. (Rev: BL 12/15/12) [736]

24422 *Paper* (3–6). Series: Let's Create! 2003, Gareth Stevens LB $24.00 (978-0-8368-3747-6). 32pp. An attractive introduction to paper crafts, including 12 projects and additional suggested resources. (Rev: SLJ 4/04) [745.54]

24423 *Papier-Mâché* (3–4). Illus. Series: Let's Create! 2004, Gareth Stevens LB $24.00 (978-0-8368-4017-9). 32pp. Simple projects created by children may still require some adult help. Also use *Stones and "Stuff"* and *Metal* (both 2004). (Rev: BL 6/1–15/04; SLJ 11/04) [745.5]

24424 Powell, Michelle. *Printing* (4–7). Illus. Series: Step-by-Step. 2000, Heinemann LB $24.22 (978-1-57572-329-7). 32pp. Various easy-to-follow printing projects are presented along with material on printing methods from ancient Egypt onward. (Rev: BL 10/15/00; HBG 10/01) [761]

24425 Ransom, Candice. *Scrapbooking Just for You! How to Make Fun, Personal, Save-Them-Forever Keepsakes* (4–9). Illus. 2010, Sterling $14.95 (978-1-4027-4096-1). 128pp. Plenty of innovative ideas for a variety of different scrapbooking projects — including magnets, frames, and cards — are collected in this well-designed title that also has instructions for hosting a scrapbooking party. (Rev: BLO 11/15/10; SLJ 6/10) [745.5]

24426 Ross, Kathy, ed. *Look What You Can Make with Newspapers, Magazines, and Greeting Cards: Over 80 Pictured Crafts and Dozens of Other Ideas* (2–4). Photos by Hank Schneider. 2002, Boyds Mills paper $5.95 (978-1-56397-566-0). 48pp. Final products include dolls with clothes, boxes, banks, signs and cards, and mobiles; the illustrations enhance the written instructions. (Rev: SLJ 4/02) [745.54]

24427 Schwarz, Renee. *Papier-Mâché* (4–6). Illus. by author. Series: Kids Can! 2000, Kids Can $12.95 (978-1-55074-833-8); paper $6.95 (978-1-55074-727-0). 40pp. This work outlines 11 projects in papier-mâché with tips on getting the proper supplies, preparing the paste, and sanding and fixing mistakes. (Rev: HBG 10/00; SLJ 6/00) [745.5]

24428 Seix, Victoria. *Creating with Papier-Mâché* (3–6). Series: Crafts for All Seasons. 2000, Blackbirch LB $23.70 (978-1-56711-439-3). 32pp. Fifteen projects using either paper strips or paper pulp are outlined in this attractive craft book. (Rev: SLJ 2/01) [745.5]

24429 Stevens, Clive. *Paperfolding* (4–7). Series: Step-by-Step. 2001, Heinemann LB $24.22 (978-1-57572-333-4). 32pp. Easy-to-find materials are used in a number of exciting paper folding projects, each of which is described in clear, detailed directions with step-by-step illustrations. (Rev: BL 8/1/01; HBG 10/01; SLJ 10/01) [745.5]

24430 Watson, David. *Papermaking* (4–7). Series: Step-by-Step. 2000, Heinemann LB $24.22 (978-1-57572-327-3). 32pp. This book shows how you can use old paper to make new paper and create a number of wonderful art objects following simple step-by-step directions. (Rev: BL 10/15/00; HBG 10/01) [745.5]

Printmaking

24431 Luxbacher, Irene. *1-2-3 I Can Make Prints!* (PS–3). Illus. by author. 2008, Kids Can LB $14.95 (978-1-55453-040-3); paper $5.95 (978-1-55453-153-0). 24pp. This volume offers easy kid-friendly printmaking proj-

ects with step-by-step instructions. (Rev: BLO 3/3/08; SLJ 4/08) [760.28]

Sewing and Needle Crafts

24432 Blanchette, Peg, and Terri Thibault. *12 Easy Knitting Projects* (3–6). Illus. by Norma Jean Martin-Jourdenais. Series: Quick Starts for Kids! 2006, Williamson $12.95 (978-0-8249-6784-0); paper $8.95 (978-0-8249-6785-7). 63pp. Offering features for both beginners and more advanced knitters, this book provides basic information about knitting and step-by-step instructions for 12 projects of differing complexity, including a scarf, doggy turtleneck sweater, and a poncho. (Rev: SLJ 8/06) [746.4]

24433 Bradberry, Sarah. *Kids Knit! Simple Steps to Nifty Projects* (4–8). Photos by Michael Hnatov. Illus. by Kim Coxey. 2004, Sterling $14.95 (978-0-8069-7733-1). 96pp. Simple, clear instructions and illustrations add to the value of this book full of appealing projects. (Rev: BL 12/15/04; SLJ 2/05)

24434 Clewer, Carolyn. *Kids Can Knit: Fun and Easy Projects for Small Knitters* (3–7). 2003, Barron's paper $16.95 (978-0-7641-2718-2). 128pp. The reader gradually moves from simple beginnings to more sophisticated projects. (Rev: BL 12/15/03; SLJ 3/04)

24435 Gibbons, Gail. *The Quilting Bee* (K–2). Illus. by author. 2004, HarperCollins $17.99 (978-0-688-16397-6). Adults and children participate in a quilting circle, from initial planning to displaying the final product; historical information is included as is a concept for an author and illustrator quilt. (Rev: SLJ 5/04) [746.46]

24436 Guy, Lucinda. *Kids Learn to Crochet* (2–4). Illus. by Francois Hall. 2008, Trafalgar paper $15.95 (978-1-57076-395-3). 96pp. Presented with lists of materials, templates for felt pieces, and tips, the projects here include flowers, a bag, and a pen topper. (Rev: SLJ 3/09) [745.5]

24437 Guy, Lucinda. *Kids Learn to Knit* (2–4). Illus. by Francois Hall. 2007, Trafalgar $14.95 (978-1-57076-335-9). 96pp. After basic instructions for beginners, this book includes six simple projects suitable for this age group, with clear instructions and advice on troubleshooting problems such as dropped stitches. (Rev: BL 12/15/06) [746.43]

24438 Kinsler, Gwen Blakley, and Jackie Young. *Crocheting* (4–7). Series: Kids Can Do It! 2003, Kids Can $12.95 (978-1-55337-176-2); paper $6.95 (978-1-55337-177-9). 48pp. A simple introduction to crocheting with many easily followed diagrams and clear directions. (Rev: BL 3/15/03; HBG 10/03; SLJ 4/03) [745.5]

24439 Mahren, Sue. *Make Your Own Teddy Bears and Bear Clothes* (3–6). Illus. by Stan Jaskiel. Series: Quick Starts for Kids! 2001, Williamson paper $8.95 (978-1-885593-75-7). 64pp. Patterns for two teddy bears are followed by patterns for clothing that are clear and easy to follow using only scissors, needle, and thread. Also use *Kids' Easy Knitting Projects* and *Kids' Easy Quilting Projects* (both 2001). (Rev: SLJ 7/01) [745.592]

24440 Nicholas, Kristin, and John Gruen. *Kids' Embroidery: Projects for Kids of All Ages* (3–7). 2004, Stewart, Tabori & Chang $19.95 (978-1-58479-366-3). 144pp. Step-by-step instructions guide readers through 15 colorful embroidery projects. (Rev: BL 12/15/04)

24441 Okey, Shannon. *Knitgrrl: Learn to Knit with 15 Fun and Funky Projects* (5–8). Photos by Shannon Fagan. 2005, Watson-Guptill paper $9.95 (978-0-8230-2618-0). Up-to-date designs are shown clearly and explained in detail. (Rev: BL 12/15/05*; SLJ 11/05; VOYA 12/05) [746.43]

24442 Okey, Shannon. *Knitgrrl 2: Learn to Knit with 16 All-New Patterns* (4–7). 2006, Watson-Guptill paper $9.99 (978-0-8230-2619-7). This sequel to *Knitgrrl* (2005) offers step-by-step instructions for 16 new projects, including bracelets, a sports bottle holder, and a cardigan. (Rev: BL 6/1–15/06; SLJ 6/06) [746]

24443 Plumley, Amie Petronis, and Andria Lisle. *Sewing School: 21 Sewing Projects Kids Will Love to Make* (3–6). Photos by Justin Fox Burks. 2010, Storey paper $16.95 (978-1-60342-578-0). 144pp. This attractive, large-format volume presents child-friendly projects that teach children various skills and increase in sophistication as the book progresses. (Rev: BL 12/15/10; SLJ 2/1/11) [646.2]

24444 Ronci, Kelli. *Kids Crochet: Projects for Kids of All Ages* (4–8). Illus. by Lena Corwin. Photos by John Gruen. 2005, Stewart, Tabori & Chang $19.95 (978-1-58479-413-4). A poncho, a quilt, and a tool pouch are among the 15 crocheting projects presented, which are introduced by detailed coverage of techniques. (Rev: BL 5/15/04; SLJ 6/05) [745.5]

24445 Sadler, Judy Ann. *Corking* (4–8). Series: Kids Can! 1998, Kids Can paper $5.95 (978-1-55074-265-7). Provides directions for a handmade knitting device that is used to create knit tubes or corks popular in toys and headbands. (Rev: BL 5/15/98) [746.4]

24446 Sadler, Judy Ann. *Embroidery* (4–8). Illus. by June Bradford. Series: Kids Can Do It! 2004, Kids Can $12.95 (978-1-55337-616-3); paper $6.95 (978-1-55337-617-0). 40pp. In addition to a thorough introduction to embroidery and various stitches, Sadler provides nine projects that progress in difficulty. (Rev: SLJ 8/04) [746.44]

24447 Sadler, Judy Ann. *The Jumbo Book of Needlecrafts* (4–7). Illus. by Esperança Melo, et al. 2005, Kids Can paper $16.95 (978-1-55337-793-1). After advice on getting started, step-by-step directions guide readers through a range of needlecraft projects. (Rev: SLJ 5/05)

24448 Sadler, Judy Ann. *Knitting* (4–6). Series: Kids Can Do It! 2002, Kids Can $12.95 (978-1-55337-050-5); paper $6.95 (978-1-55337-051-2). 40pp. The basic stitches in knitting are described in text and color illustrations, followed by a series of easily accomplished knitting

projects. (Rev: BL 9/15/02; HBG 3/03; SLJ 11/02) [746.43]

24449 Sadler, Judy Ann. *Making Fleece Crafts* (4–7). Illus. by June Bradford. 2000, Kids Can $12.95 (978-1-55074-847-5); paper $6.95 (978-1-55074-739-3). 40pp. Fifteen colorful and inviting projects using fleece including mittens, a scarf, and a jester's hat. (Rev: BL 9/15/00; SLJ 9/00) [745]

24450 Sadler, Judy Ann. *Quick Knits* (5–8). Illus. by Esperanca Melo. 2006, Kids Can $12.95 (978-1-55337-963-8); paper $6.95 (978-1-55337-964-5). 40pp. Clear instructions, appealing projects, and suggestions for personalizing these are features of this introduction to knitting. (Rev: BL 1/1–15/07; SLJ 12/06) [746.43]

24451 Sadler, Judy Ann. *Simply Sewing* (4–8). Illus. by Jane Kurisu. Series: Kids Can Do It! 2004, Kids Can $12.95 (978-1-55337-659-0); paper $6.95 (978-1-55337-660-6). 48pp. Detailed instructions for 12 projects — a makeup bag and a jeans skirt, for example — follow basic information on sewing by hand and by machine. (Rev: BL 12/15/04; SLJ 11/04)

24452 Storms, Biz. *All-American Quilts* (4–7). Illus. by June Bradford. Series: Kids Can Do It! 2003, Kids Can paper $6.95 (978-1-55337-539-5). Instructions are provided for making quilts with American themes — eagles, flags, and so forth. (Rev: BL 12/15/03; SLJ 1/04) [746.46]

24453 Storms, Biz. *Quilting* (4–7). Illus. by June Bradford. Series: Kids Can Do It! 2001, Kids Can $12.95 (978-1-55074-967-0); paper $5.95 (978-1-55074-805-5). 40pp. Easy-to-follow, step-by-step instructions take kids through quilting projects of varying difficulty. (Rev: BL 11/1/01; HBG 3/02; SLJ 2/02) [746.46]

24454 Warwick, Ellen. *Injeanuity* (5–8). Illus. by Bernice Lum. 2006, Kids Can $12.95 (978-1-55337-681-1). Seventeen projects involving jeans and a sewing machine are shown with clear directions. (Rev: BL 6/1–15/06; SLJ 6/06) [746.9]

24455 Wenger, Jennifer. *Teen Knitting Club: Chill Out and Knit Some Cool Stuff* (5–9). 2004, Artisan $17.95 (978-1-57965-244-9). Children who already know how to know will derive the most benefit from this collection of 35 appealing projects. (Rev: BL 12/15/04; SLJ 2/05)

24456 Willing, Karen Bates, and Julie Bates Dock. *Fabric Fun for Kids: Step-by-Step Projects for Children (and Their Grown-ups)* (4–9). 1997, Now & Then LB $17.95 (978-0-9641820-4-2); paper $12.95 (978-0-9641820-5-9). From simple sewing projects to more complex quilting work, this book gives good step-by-step instructions, provides a rundown on necessary sewing tools and materials, and discusses methods for putting designs on fabrics. (Rev: SLJ 4/98) [746.46]

24457 Wilson, Sule Greg C. *African American Quilting: The Warmth of Tradition* (4–7). Series: Library of African American Arts and Culture. 1999, Rosen LB $27.95 (978-0-8239-1854-6). This book traces African influences on textile patterns and techniques particularly as they have been applied to quilting by African Americans. (Rev: BL 2/15/00; SLJ 9/99) [746.46]

Toys and Dolls

24458 Cunningham, Kevin. *Toys* (5–8). Illus. Series: Calling All Innovators: A Career for You. 2013, Scholastic/Children's Press LB $30 (978-053126522-2); paper $8.95 (9780531220108). 64pp. An engaging discussion of toys over the years, evolution in terms of materials used, the process of creating them, and future possibilities. **e** (Rev: BL 10/1/13)

24459 Hall, Patricia. *The Real-for-Sure Story of Raggedy Ann* (PS–3). Illus. by Joni Gruelle Wannamaker. 2001, Pelican $15.95 (978-1-56554-763-6). 32pp. A story about the origins of the doll, portraying the details of her clothes and the way the first dolls were made. (Rev: HBG 10/01; SLJ 11/01) [688.7]

24460 Henry, Sally, and Trevor Cook. *Making Puppets* (4–8). Photos by authors. Series: Make Your Own Art. 2011, Rosen LB $25.25 (978-1-4488-1584-5); paper $11.75 (978-1-4488-1615-6). 32pp. Color photographs and clear instructions add appeal to this book detailing a variety of creative puppet projects. (Rev: BL 12/15/11; SLJ 7/11) [791.5]

24461 Polacco, Patricia. *Betty Doll* (3–5). Illus. 2001, Penguin $16.99 (978-0-399-23638-9). 32pp. In this picture book for older children, Polacco tells the story of her mother's precious Betty Doll, which accompanied her mother on many journeys until her death, when the doll was passed on to her daughter. (Rev: BL 8/01; HBG 10/01; SLJ 4/01) [973.4]

24462 Sadler, Judy Ann. *Beanbag Buddies and Other Stuffed Toys* (4–7). Illus. by June Bradford. Series: Kids Can! 1999, Kids Can paper $5.95 (978-1-55074-590-0). Using clear directions and many step-by-step illustrations, this book offers many ideas on how to create a variety of stuffed toys. (Rev: SLJ 10/99) [745]

Woodworking

24463 Ellenwood, Everett. *Woodcarving* (4–7). Illus. Series: Kidcrafts. 2009, Fox Chapel paper $14.95 (978-1-56523-366-9). 122pp. A succinct look at this craft and the wood, tools, and techniques involved, with seven woodcarving projects. (Rev: SLJ 7/09) [736]

24464 Robertson, J. Craig, and Barbara Robertson. *The Kids' Building Workshop: 15 Woodworking Projects for Kids and Parents to Build Together* (3–7). Illus. 2004, Storey Kids paper $12.95 (978-1-58017-488-6). 136pp. After discussing tools and techniques, 15 projects — a bird house, a stool, for example — are presented in order of increasing difficulty. (Rev: SLJ 2/05) [684]

24465 Schwarz, Renee. *Birdhouses* (4–7). Series: Kids Can Do It! 2005, Kids Can $12.95 (978-1-55337-549-4); paper $6.95 (978-1-55337-550-0). Nine different birdhouse projects for children to tackle, with illustrated instructions and photographs of the finished products. (Rev: BL 4/1/05; SLJ 5/05) [690]

24466 Walker, Lester. *Housebuilding for Children* (4–7). 1977, Overlook paper $16.95 (978-0-87951-332-0). The construction of six different kinds of houses, including a tree house, is clearly described in text and pictures.

Hobbies

General and Miscellaneous

24467 Blakey, Nancy. *Go Outside! Activities for Outdoor Adventures* (3–7). Photos by Dana Dean Doering. 2002, Tricycle paper $14.95 (978-1-58246-064-2). 144pp. Double-page spreads suggest outdoor activities for each of the seasons, some for learning and some for pure fun. (Rev: BL 4/15/02; SLJ 9/02) [796]

24468 Brent, Lynnette R. *At Play: Long Ago and To-day* (2–4). Series: Times Change. 2003, Heinemann LB $24.22 (978-1-4034-4532-2). 32pp. A look at how various everyday activities have changed over the past century or so, with photographs illustrating "then" and "now." (Rev: SLJ 5/04) [790.1]

24469 Burgess, Ron. *Be a Clown! Techniques from a Real Clown* (K–3). Illus. by Heather Barberie. 2001, Williamson paper $8.95 (978-1-885593-57-3). 63pp. Aspiring clowns will appreciate this guide to clown costumes and makeup, actions and gags, and magic tricks, along with some historical information about traditional clowns and clowning. (Rev: SLJ 10/01) [791.3]

24470 Burnie, David. *Bird Watcher* (3–6). Illus. Series: Smithsonian Nature Activity Guides. 2005, DK paper $9.99 (978-0-7566-1029-6). 72pp. All sorts of fun and facts for children fascinated by birds, including experiments, crafts, and photographs. (Rev: SLJ 8/05) [598]

24471 Hunter, Dette. *38 Ways to Entertain Your Babysitter* (2–4). Illus. by Stephen MacEachern. 2003, Annick LB $19.95 (978-1-55037-795-8); paper $9.95 (978-1-55037-794-1). A story about two siblings' efforts to keep their babysitter happy provides the framework for a collection of three dozen or so entertaining activities, each accompanied by easy-to-follow instructions. (Rev: SLJ 1/04) [793]

24472 Kenney, Karen Latchana. *Cool Holiday Parties: Perfect Party Planning for Kids* (3–6). Illus. Series: Cool Parties. 2011, ABDO LB $27.07 (978-1-61714-974-0). 32pp. Bright photographs and practical advice enhance

this activity-filled book about holiday party planning. Other titles in this series include *Cool Family Parties, Cool Slumber Parties,* and *Cool Theme Parties* (all 2011). (Rev: SLJ 12/1/11) [793.2]

24473 Kenney, Sean. *Cool Castles* (PS–3). Illus. 2012, Henry Holt $12.99 (978-080509539-5). 32pp. Shows young readers how to create medieval structures using LEGO toys, (Rev: BL 10/15/12) [688.7]

24474 Latno, Mark. *The Paper Boomerang Book: Build Them, Throw Them, and Get Them to Return Every Time* (5–8). 2010, Chicago Review paper $12.95 (978-1-56976-282-0). 128pp. Everything you need to know about boomerangs and their construction and use, with a surprising depth of kid-friendly physics. **℮** (Rev: SLJ 7/10; VOYA 12/10) [629.133]

24475 Ralston, Birgitta. *Snow Play: How to Make Forts and Slides and Winter Campfires, Plus the Coolest Loch Ness Monster and 23 Other Brrrilliant Projects in the Snow* (4–12). Photos by Vegard Fimland. 2010, Artisan $14.95 (978-1-57965-405-4). 112pp. Ralston presents a variety of compelling snow projects, ranging from small ornaments to an LED-illuminated birthday cake to a snow cave. (Rev: SLJ 4/11) [796.9]

24476 Stetson, Emily. *Knots to Know: 40 Hitches, Loops, Bends and Bindings* (3–6). Illus. by Marc Nadel and Sarah Rakitin. 2002, Williamson paper $8.95 (978-1-885593-70-2). 64pp. A simple guide to the types and uses of knots, with step-by-step instructions on how to tie them. (Rev: BL 8/02; SLJ 9/02) [623.88]

24477 Swain, Ruth Freeman. *Hairdo! What We Do and Did to Our Hair* (K–2). Illus. by Cat B. Smith. 2002, Holiday House $16.95 (978-0-8234-1522-9). 32pp. Entertaining facts about hair and hairstyles through the ages. (Rev: BL 12/15/02; HBG 3/03; SLJ 10/02) [391.5]

24478 Taylor, Maureen. *Through the Eyes of Your Ancestors: A Step-by-Step Guide to Uncovering Your Family's History* (5–9). 1999, Houghton Mifflin paper $8.95 (978-0-395-86982-6). Budding researchers learn how to investigate family history, from conducting interviews to visiting genealogical libraries. (Rev: BCCB 5/99; BL 3/1/99; HB 5–6/99; HBG 10/99; SLJ 5/99) [929.1]

24479 Trusty, Brad, and Cindy Trusty. *The Kids' Guide to Balloon Twisting* (4–8). Illus. Series: Kids' Guides. 2012, Capstone LB $26.65 (978-142965444-9). 32pp. A variety of twisted-balloon projects are presented with easy-to-follow directions. (Rev: BL 9/1/11) [745.594]

Cooking

24480 Amari, Suad. *Cooking the Lebanese Way. Rev. ed.* (5–10). Series: Easy Menu Ethnic Cookbooks. 2003, Lerner LB $25.26 (978-0-8225-4116-5). 72pp. Revised to include low-fat and vegetarian foods, this introduction to Lebanese cooking contains about 40 recipes, clearly explained and well-illustrated. (Rev: BL 9/15/02; HBG 3/03) [641.5]

24481 Bacon, Josephine. *Cooking the Israeli Way. Rev. ed.* (5–10). Series: Easy Menu Ethnic Cookbooks. 2002, Lerner LB $25.26 (978-0-8225-4112-7). 72pp. After a general introduction to Israel, this book discusses cooking terms and ingredients, and then gives a series of tantalizing recipes with clear instructions. (Rev: BL 7/02; HBG 10/02) [641]

24482 Barker, Geoff. *Mexico* (3–6). Series: A World of Food. 2010, Clara House $24.95 (978-1-934545-13-3). 32pp. With color photographs, information on the country's history, agriculture, and culture, this book covers Mexican holidays and provides simple recipes suitable for this age group. (Rev: LMC 10/10; SLJ 5/10) [641.3]

24483 Barlow, Melissa. *Noodlemania! 50 Playful Pasta Recipes* (5–8). Illus. by Alison Oliver. 2013, Quirk paper $15.95 (978-15947461-7-8). 112pp. Creative recipes are presented in chapters such as "Totally Tubular," "Twisted & Twirly," "Super Skinny," and "Very Stuffed." (Rev: BL 5/1/13; SLJ 10/13) [641.822]

24484 Bastyra, J., and C. Bradley. *Look and Make Cooking* (4–5). Photos by Howard Allman. Illus. by Michael Evans. Series: Look and Make. 2004, Sea-to-Sea LB $27.10 (978-1-932889-22-2). 32pp. Well-designed recipes are introduced by reminders about safety and the importance of gathering ingredients and equipment in advance. (Rev: SLJ 4/05)

24485 Bisignano, Alphonse. *Cooking the Italian Way. Rev. ed.* (5–10). Series: Easy Menu Ethnic Cookbooks. 2001, Lerner $25.26 (978-0-8225-4113-4); paper $7.95 (978-0-8225-4161-5). 72pp. A revised edition that now includes vegetarian and low-fat recipes as well as an expanded introductory section on the country, the people, and the culture. (Rev: HBG 3/02; SLJ 9/01) [641]

24486 Blaxland, Wendy. *Mexican Food* (5–8). Illus. Series: I Can Cook! 2012, Smart Apple Media LB $28.50 (978-1-59920-668-4). 32pp. Introduces the food of Mexico, with appealing recipes and clear photographs, along with information on the culture and geography of the country. Also in this series, use *Chinese Food,* *French Food,* and *Middle Eastern Food* (all 2011). (Rev: BL 1/1/12; SLJ 12/1/11) [641.5956]

24487 Blaxland, Wendy. *Middle Eastern Food* (5–8). Illus. Series: I Can Cook! 2011, Black Rabbit LB $28.50 (978-1-59920-672-1). 32pp. With recipes that will need adult supervision, this book places Middle Eastern food and ingredients in historical and cultural perspective. (Rev: BL 1/1/12; SLJ 12/1/11) [641.5956]

24488 Brash, Lorna. *Professor Cook's Smashing Snacks* (4–6). Illus. 2013, Enslow LB $22.60 (978-076604304-6). 32pp. Kid-friendly recipes are accompanied by useful scientific information. Also use *Professor Cook's Mind-Blowing Baking, Professor Cook's Fruity Desserts,* and *Professor Cook's Dynamite Dinners* (all 2013). (Rev: BL 11/1/13) [641.5]

24489 Brennan, Georgeanne. *Green Eggs and Ham Cookbook* (3–6). Photos by Frankie Frankeny. 2006, Random $16.95 (978-0-679-88440-8). 64pp. Diverse recipes requiring different levels of skill and varied ingredients (no green coloring) are featured here. (Rev: SLJ 2/07) [641.5]

24490 Chung, Okwha, and Judy Monroe. *Cooking the Korean Way. Rev. ed.* (5–10). Illus. Series: Easy Menu Ethnic Cookbooks. 2003, Lerner LB $25.26 (978-0-8225-4115-8). 48pp. Tempting recipes and a brief look at where they come from. (Rev: BL 8/88; HBG 3/03; SLJ 9/88) [641.59519]

24491 Cornell, Kari. *Holiday Cooking Around the World. Rev. ed.* (5–10). Series: Easy Menu Ethnic Cookbooks. 2002, Lerner LB $25.26 (978-0-8225-4128-8); paper $7.95 (978-0-8225-4159-2). Beginning cooks will appreciate the clear instructions and varied options in this appealing book that includes cultural and social information. (Rev: BL 1/1–15/02; HBG 10/02; SLJ 5/02) [641.5]

24492 Cornell, Kari. *Slurpable Smoothies and Drinks* (3–5). Illus. Series: You're the Chef. 2013, Millbrook LB $26.60 (978-076136639-3). 32pp. Learn to make smoothies and drinks from a kiwi colada to a yogurt drink, with safety tips, photographs, and diagrams. Also use *Awesome Snacks and Appetizers* (2013). (Rev: BL 9/1/13; SLJ 8/13)

24493 Coronado, Rosa. *Cooking the Mexican Way. Rev. ed.* (5–10). Series: Easy Menu Ethnic Cookbooks. 2002, Lerner LB $25.26 (978-0-8225-4117-2). Recipes organized by type of meal are preceded by a section that covers the geography, culture, and festivals and by information on equipment, ingredients, and eating customs. Other titles in this series include *Cooking the East African Way* and *Cooking the Spanish Way* (both 2001). (Rev: HBG 3/02; SLJ 2/02) [641]

24494 D'Amico, Joan, and Karen Eich Drummond. *The Science Chef Travels Around the World: Fun Food Experiments and Recipes for Kids* (4–8). 1996, Wiley paper $12.95 (978-0-471-11779-7). An entertaining combination of simple science experiments and international cooking, with recipes from 14 countries and activities that demonstrate scientific principles of various cooking and baking processes. (Rev: BL 2/1/96; SLJ 3/96) [641.5]

24495 D'Amico, Joan, and Karen Eich Drummond. *The United States Cookbook: Fabulous Foods and Fascinating Facts from All 50 States* (4–6). Illus. by Jeff Cline and Tina Cash-Walsh. 2000, Wiley paper $12.95 (978-0-471-35839-8). 186pp. This cookbook, which is divided into seven regions and then individual states, gives basic information about each state followed by tempting recipes and food and cooking tips. (Rev: BL 5/15/00; SLJ 5/00) [641]

24496 Dahl, Roald, and Felicity Dahl. *Roald Dahl's Even More Revolting Recipes* (4–6). Illus. by Quentin Blake. 2001, Viking $17.99 (978-0-670-03515-1). 64pp. A follow-up to *Revolting Recipes* (1994), this volume includes 31 new recipes inspired by Dahl's books. (Rev: BL 2/1/02; HBG 3/02; SLJ 11/01) [641.5]

24497 Deen, Paula, and Martha Nesbit. *Paula Deen's Cookbook for the Lunch-Box Set* (3–6). Illus. by Susan Mitchell. 2009, Simon & Schuster $21.99 (978-1-4169-8268-5). 192pp. With recipes for bake sales, sleepovers, pool parties, and more, this is a cookbook with an old-fashioned appeal. (Rev: SLJ 12/09) [641]

24498 Dunnington, Rose. *The Greatest Cookies Ever: Dozens of Delicious, Chewy, Chunky, Fun and Foolproof Recipes* (4–8). Photos by Stewart O'Shields. 2005, Sterling $9.95 (978-1-57990-627-6). More than 70 recipes are included in this spiral-bound guide to cookie making, with useful information about measuring, substitutions, types of mixers, and safety. (Rev: BL 1/1–15/06; SLJ 2/06) [641.8]

24499 Engfer, Lee, ed. *Desserts Around the World. Rev. ed.* (4–6). Series: Easy Menu Ethnic Cookbooks. 2003, Lerner LB $18.45 (978-0-8225-0926-4). 72pp. This expanded edition gives recipes and background material on simple desserts as prepared in different countries and cultures and features low-fat recipes. (Rev: BL 6/15/92) [641.8]

24500 Fauchald, Nick. *Holy Guacamole!* (1–3). Illus. by Rick Peterson. Series: Kids Dish. 2008, Picture Window LB $18.95 (978-1-4048-3995-3). 32pp. After an introductory section with tips on cooking, equipment, and healthy eating, Fauchald provides simple recipes for snacks and drinks including pita chips with hummus, quesadilla bites, fruit kabobs, milkshakes, and of course guacamole. (Rev: BL 4/1/08) [641.5]

24501 Frankeny, Frankie, and Wesley Martin. *The Star Wars Cookbook II: Darth Malt and More Galactic Recipes* (3–5). Photos by Frankie Frankeny. 2000, Chronicle $15.95 (978-0-8118-2803-1). 62pp. A delightful cookbook with 29 recipes in five categories: breakfasts, snacks, main courses, desserts, and drinks. (Rev: SLJ 11/00) [641]

24502 Gillies, Judi, and Jennifer Glossop. *The Jumbo Vegetarian Cookbook* (4–8). 2002, Kids Can paper $14.95 (978-1-55074-977-9). An introduction to the vegetarian lifestyle, including nutrition and recipes. (Rev: BCCB 7–8/02; BL 3/1/02; SLJ 7/02) [641.5]

24503 Gillies, Judi, and Jennifer Glossop. *The Kids Can Press Jumbo Cookbook* (5–8). 2000, Kids Can paper $14.95 (978-1-55074-621-1). After a few cooking tips, this book provides recipes that range from the simple (scrambled eggs) to the difficult (crepes and carrot cake). (Rev: BL 5/1/00; SLJ 6/00) [641.8]

24504 Gioffre, Rosalba. *The Young Chef's French Cookbook* (4–7). Series: I'm the Chef! 2001, Crabtree LB $25.27 (978-0-7787-0282-5); paper $8.95 (978-0-7787-0296-2). This oversize book uses double-page spreads to present 15 appetizing French recipes along with good background material, clear directions, and excellent illustrations. (Rev: BL 10/15/01) [641]

24505 Gioffre, Rosalba. *The Young Chef's Italian Cookbook* (4–7). Series: I'm the Chef! 2001, Crabtree LB $25.27 (978-0-7787-0279-5). 32pp. Along with good background material, clear instructions are presented for 15 Italian dishes in this well-illustrated, oversize book. (Rev: BL 10/15/01; SLJ 11/01) [641]

24506 Gold, Rozanne. *Kids Cook 1-2-3: Recipes for Young Chefs Using Only 3 Ingredients* (3–6). Illus. by Sara Pinto. 2006, Bloomsbury $17.95 (978-1-58234-735-6). 144pp. A beginner's cookbook offering 125 recipes that use only three ingredients for each meal of the day. (Rev: BL 12/1/06; SLJ 3/07)

24507 Goldish, Meish. *Bug-a-licious* (2–5). Illus. Series: Extreme Cuisine. 2009, Bearport LB $16.96 (978-1-59716-757-4). 24pp. Goldish explores global insect delicacies — termites, grasshoppers, dragonflies, and so forth — with full-page illustrations. (Rev: BL 4/1/09; SLJ 6/09) [641.6]

24508 Hargittai, Magdolna. *Cooking the Hungarian Way. Rev. ed.* (5–10). Series: Easy Menu Ethnic Cookbooks. 2002, Lerner LB $25.26 (978-0-8225-4132-5). After an introduction to Hungary and its cuisine, there are about 40 clearly presented recipes from appetizers through desserts. (Rev: BL 9/15/02; HBG 3/03) [641.5]

24509 Harrison, Supenn, and Judy Monroe. *Cooking the Thai Way. Rev. ed.* (5–10). Series: Easy Menu Ethnic Cookbooks. 2002, Lerner LB $25.26 (978-0-8225-4124-0); paper $7.95 (978-0-8225-0608-9). The country of Thailand is introduced followed by general information on its foods and several easy-to-follow recipes. (Rev: BL 9/15/02) [641.5]

24510 Hill, Barbara W. *Cooking the English Way. Rev. ed.* (5–10). Series: Easy Menu Ethnic Cookbooks. 2002, Lerner LB $25.26 (978-0-8225-4105-9). The land and people of England are briefly introduced followed by material on their favorite dishes and easy-to-follow recipes. (Rev: BL 9/15/02) [641.5]

24511 Hill, Mary. *Let's Make Pizza* (PS–1). Series: In the Kitchen. 2002, Children's Book Pr. paper $4.95 (978-0-516-24020-6). 24pp. For beginning readers, this is a simple introduction to the ingredients of a pizza and the technique for making one. Also use *Let's Make Tacos* (2002). (Rev: SLJ 2/03)

24512 Hopkinson, Deborah. *Fannie in the Kitchen: The Whole Story from Soup to Nuts of How Fannie Farmer*

Invented Recipes with Precise Measurements (K–3). Illus. by Nancy Carpenter. 2001, Simon & Schuster $16.00 (978-0-689-81965-0). 40pp. Fannie Farmer teaches a young girl to cook in this fictionalized account that is interspersed with excerpts from Farmer's cookbook. (Rev: BCCB 6/01; BL 5/15/01*; HB 5/01; HBG 10/01; SLJ 5/01*) [641.5]

24513 Ichord, Loretta Frances. *Double Cheeseburgers, Quiche, and Vegetarian Burritos: American Cooking from the 1920s Through Today* (5–8). Illus. by Jan Davey Ellis. 2007, Lerner $25.26 (978-0-8225-5969-6). This title traces American cuisine from 1920 to the present, with chapters highlighting such trends as TV dinners, fast food, and the rise of organic foods; recipes round out a volume useful for both reports and browsing. (Rev: BL 1/1–15/07; SLJ 5/07) [394.1]

24514 Ichord, Loretta Frances. *Pasta, Fried Rice, and Matzoh Balls: Immigrant Cooking in America* (3–5). Illus. by Jan Davey Ellis. 2006, Millbrook LB $25.26 (978-0-7613-2913-8). 64pp. French, Italian, Jewish, Polish, Portuguese, Spanish, and Swedish immigrant recipes are included, as well as a few foreign phrases and customs. (Rev: SLJ 5/06) [394.1]

24515 Ichord, Loretta Frances. *Skillet Bread, Sourdough, and Vinegar Pie: Cooking in Pioneer Days* (3–5). Illus. by Jan Davey Ellis. 2003, Millbrook LB $24.90 (978-0-7613-1864-4). 64pp. This fascinating overview of pioneer cuisine features a number of classic recipes as well as a look at unique food preparation challenges faced by early Americans. (Rev: HBG 10/03)

24516 Jacques, Brian. *The Redwall Cookbook* (3–7). Illus. by Christopher Denise. 2005, Philomel paper $24.99 (978-0-399-23791-1). 96pp. "Hare's Pawspring Vegetable Soup" and "Savoury Squirrel Bakes" are among the recipes grouped by season and introduced by a tale about preparations for a feast; the recipes themselves are quite complex. (Rev: SLJ 1/06)

24517 Katzen, Mollie. *Salad People and More Real Recipes* (PS–2). Illus. 2005, Ten Speed $17.95 (978-1-58246-141-0). 96pp. Healthy, kid-tested recipes for a range of tastes include instructions for children and for adults. (Rev: BL 11/15/05*; SLJ 11/05*) [641.5]

24518 Kaufman, Cheryl Davidson. *Cooking the Caribbean Way. Rev. ed.* (5–10). Illus. Series: Easy Menu Ethnic Cookbooks. 2002, Lerner $25.26 (978-0-8225-4103-5). 72pp. A variety of dishes featuring the spices and fresh fruits that come from these islands are provided in this expanded edition that includes low-fat and vegetarian foods. (Rev: BL 8/88; SLJ 9/88) [641.59729]

24519 La Penta, Marilyn. *Way Cool Drinks* (2–5). Illus. Series: Yummy Tummy Recipes. 2011, Bearport LB $22.61 (978-161772163-2). 24pp. Slushies, smoothies, and shakes feature large in this guide to drinks with names like "Red Lava Volcano." (Rev: BL 10/1/11) [641.8]

24520 Lagasse, Emeril. *Emeril's There's a Chef in My Family! Recipes to Get Everybody Cooking* (5–10). Photos by Quentin Bacon. Illus. by Charles Yuen. 2004, HarperCollins $22.99 (978-0-06-000439-2). 209pp. Seventy-six recipes are presented with clear instructions that focus on the enjoyment of cooking. (Rev: SLJ 7/04) [641.5]

24521 Lagasse, Emeril. *Emeril's There's a Chef in My Soup: Recipes for the Kid in Everyone* (5–8). Illus. by Charles Yuen. 2002, HarperCollins $22.99 (978-0-688-17706-5). The famed TV chef presents a series of simple recipes for main dishes, pasta, desserts, breakfast and lunch items, and salads. (Rev: BL 5/1/02; HBG 10/02) [641.5]

24522 Lagasse, Emeril. *Emeril's There's a Chef in My World!* (5–8). Illus. 2006, HarperCollins $22.99 (978-0-06-073926-3). The famous chef adds to his successful series with a basic introduction to sandwiches, meals, snacks, and more from around the world, with sections on basic skills, safety, and equipment for beginners; cultural facts accompany each recipe. (Rev: BL 12/1/06; SLJ 2/07) [641.59]

24523 LaPenta, Marilyn. *Winter Punches to Nut Crunches* (3–5). Illus. Series: Yummy Tummy Recipes: Seasons. 2013, Bearport LB $23.93 (978-161772743-6). 24pp. A collection of recipes — such as cranberry punch, hot chocolate, butternut squash soup, and ginger cookies — to enjoy during the winter months. (Rev: BL 4/1/13; SLJ 4/13) [641.5]

24524 Larson, Jennifer S. *Yummy Soup and Salad Recipes* (4–7). Illus. Series: You're the Chef. 2013, Millbrook LB $26.60 (978-076136633-1). 32pp. Chicken wonton soup, cucumber soup, corn chowder, taco salad, pizza pasta salad — there's lots of choice in this well-organized cookbook with safety and other tips. Also use *Perfect Pizza Recipes, Meaty Main Dishes* and *Delicious Vegetarian Main Dishes* (all 2013). e (Rev: BL 5/1/13; SLJ 4/13) [641.81]

24525 Lee, Frances. *The Young Chef's Chinese Cookbook* (4–7). Series: I'm the Chef! 2001, Crabtree LB $25.27 (978-0-7787-0280-1); paper $8.95 (978-0-7787-0294-8). Fifteen child-friendly recipes for Chinese dishes are presented with step-by-step directions and photographs. (Rev: BL 10/15/01; SLJ 11/01) [641.5951]

24526 Lewis, Sara. *Kids' Baking: 60 Delicious Recipes for Children to Make* (4–7). 2006, Sterling $12.95 (978-0-600-61561-3). Well-illustrated recipes for cakes, cookies, and breads are suitable for children working with adult help. (Rev: BL 12/1/06) [641.8]

24527 Llewellyn, Claire, and Clare O'Shea. *Cooking with Fruits and Vegetables* (5–8). Series: Cooking Healthy. 2011, Rosen LB $27.95 (978-1-4488-4844-7). 48pp. Basic cooking terms and techniques are defined and illustrated in this accessible guide to cooking fruits and vegetables. Also use *Cooking with Meat and Fish* (2011). (Rev: SLJ 12/1/11) [641.3]

24528 Locricchio, Matthew. *The Cooking of Greece* (5–10). Photos by Jack McConnell. Illus. Series: Superchef. 2004, Benchmark LB $29.93 (978-0-7614-1729-3). 80pp. Recipes follow an informative overview of regional cuisines in Greece and the ingredients commonly used. (Rev: SLJ 4/05)

24529 Locricchio, Matthew. *The Cooking of India* (4–8). Photos by Jack McConnell. Illus. Series: Superchef. 2004, Benchmark $29.93 (978-0-7614-1730-9). 80pp. Clear instructions guide readers through the steps involved in making dishes from various areas of India; fresh ingredients are recommended and safety is emphasized. Also use *The Cooking of Thailand* (2004). (Rev: SLJ 2/05) [641.5954]

24530 McCulloch, Julie. *The Caribbean* (3–6). Illus. Series: World of Recipes. 2001, Heinemann LB $25.64 (978-1-58810-153-2). 48pp. Recipes, arranged by difficulty, follow information on the region and typical food choices. (Rev: BL 8/01; HBG 10/01) [641.59]

24531 McCulloch, Julie. *China* (3–6). Illus. Series: World of Recipes. 2001, Heinemann LB $25.64 (978-1-58810-152-5). 48pp. Recipes, arranged by difficulty, follow information on China and the kinds of foods eaten there. (Rev: BL 8/01; HBG 10/01; SLJ 10/01) [641.5951]

24532 McCulloch, Julie. *India* (4–6). Illus. Series: A World of Recipes. 2001, Heinemann LB $25.64 (978-1-58810-085-6). 48pp. A discussion of the history and traditions of Indian food is accompanied by a selection of typical recipes, most of which require adult participation. Also use *Mexico*. (Rev: HBG 10/01; SLJ 12/01) [641.5954]

24533 McCulloch, Julie. *Japan* (4–6). Illus. by Nicholas Beresford-Davies. Series: A World of Recipes. 2001, Heinemann LB $25.64 (978-1-58810-087-0). 48pp. Step-by-step instructions clearly show how to make dishes that are typical of Japanese cuisine, accompanied by advice on handling chopsticks. Also use *China* (2001). (Rev: HBG 10/01; SLJ 10/01) [641.5952]

24534 MacLeod, Elizabeth. *Bake and Make Amazing Cakes* (4–6). Illus. by June Bradford. Series: Kids Can Do It! 2001, Kids Can $12.95 (978-1-55074-849-9); paper $5.95 (978-1-55074-848-2). 40pp. A collection of child-friendly cake recipes with easy-to-follow instructions. (Rev: SLJ 6/01) [641.8653]

24535 MacLeod, Elizabeth. *Bake and Make Amazing Cookies* (3–8). Illus. by June Bradford. Series: Kids Can Do It! 2004, Kids Can $12.95 (978-1-55337-631-6); paper $6.95 (978-1-55337-632-3). 40pp. Organized under headings such as "Holidays" and "Seasons," these are simple recipes for a wide variety of enticing cookies. (Rev: SLJ 2/05) [641.8]

24536 Madavan, Vijay. *Cooking the Indian Way* (5–8). 1985, Lerner LB $19.93 (978-0-8225-0911-0). Cultural information is detailed plus both vegetarian and nonvegetarian recipes. (Rev: SLJ 9/85) [641.5954]

24537 Marchant, Kerena. *Hindu Cookbook* (3–5). Photos by Zul Mukhida. Series: Holiday Cookbooks from Around the World. 2001, Raintree LB $25.69 (978-0-7398-3264-6). 32pp. Marchant looks at three Hindu holidays (Holi, Divali, and Ganesh Chaturthi), describes how they are celebrated, and provides appropriate reci-

pes, with appealing photographs. Also use *Chinese Cookbook* (2001). (Rev: SLJ 8/01) [641.5]

24538 Mattern, Joanne. *Recipe and Craft Guide to China* (4–7). Illus. Series: World Crafts and Recipes. 2010, Mitchell Lane LB $24.50 (978-158415937-7). 64pp. Mattern looks at foods and crafts found in various geographic regions around China, with recipes and activities; a glossary and vocabulary words are included. (Rev: BL 1/1/10) [641.591]

24539 Mendez, Sean. *One World Kids Cookbook: Easy, Healthy and Affordable Family Meals* (5–8). 2011, Interlink $20 (978-1-56656-866-1). 96pp. Recipes from around the world are presented alongside snippets of trivia and relevant food proverbs. (Rev: SLJ 12/1/11) [641.5]

24540 Montgomery, Bertha Vining, and Constance Nabwire. *Cooking the West African Way. Rev. ed.* (5–10). Series: Easy Menu Ethnic Cookbooks. 2002, Lerner LB $25.26 (978-0-8225-4163-9). An appealing introduction to West African cuisine, with information on the land, people, and culture, and several low-fat and vegetarian recipes. (Rev: HBG 10/02; SLJ 5/02) [641.5966]

24541 Munsen, Sylvia. *Cooking the Norwegian Way. Rev. ed.* (5–10). Series: Easy Menu Ethnic Cookbooks. 2002, Lerner LB $25.26 (978-0-8225-4118-9). 72pp. A revised edition of an earlier publication that gives information on the country and culture in addition to a selection of typical recipes. (Rev: BL 7/02; SLJ 9/02) [641.59]

24542 Nguyen, Chi, and Judy Monroe. *Cooking the Vietnamese Way* (5–10). Illus. Series: Easy Menu Ethnic Cookbooks. 2002, Lerner $25.26 (978-0-8225-4125-7). 72pp. The authors introduce the land and people of Vietnam before giving recipes for regional dishes, including low-fat and vegetarian selections. (Rev: BL 9/15/85; SLJ 9/85) [641]

24543 Orr, Tamra. *The Food of China* (4–7). Illus. Series: Flavors of the World. 2011, Marshall Cavendish LB $21.95 (978-160870234-3). 64pp. Introduces the five major cuisines of China, the kinds of foods that are eaten and the way they are cooked, and festive dishes, with recipes and photographs. (Rev: BL 10/1/11) [394.1]

24544 Osseo-Asare, Fran. *A Good Soup Attracts Chairs: A First African Cookbook for American Kids* (5–9). 1993, Pelican $18.95 (978-0-88289-816-2). A basic cookbook for youngsters that explores African cooking past and present and gives more than 35 recipes. (Rev: BL 10/15/93; SLJ 8/93) [641.5966]

24545 Parnell, Helga. *Cooking the German Way. Rev. ed.* (5–10). Illus. Series: Easy Menu Ethnic Cookbooks. 2002, Lerner $25.26 (978-0-8225-4107-3). 72pp. This expanded edition now includes low-fat and vegetarian recipes as well as such treats as Black Forest torte and apple cake. (Rev: BL 8/88) [641.5943]

24546 Parnell, Helga. *Cooking the South American Way. Rev. ed.* (5–10). Series: Easy Menu Ethnic Cookbooks. 2002, Lerner LB $25.26 (978-0-8225-4121-9). The continent of South America is introduced followed by about

40 clearly presented recipes from several countries. (Rev: BL 9/15/02; HBG 3/03) [641.5]

24547 Plotkin, Gregory, and Rita Plotkin. *Cooking the Russian Way. Rev. ed.* (5–10). Series: Easy Menu Ethnic Cookbooks. 2002, Lerner LB $25.26 (978-0-8225-4120-2). Included along with history and information are such recipes as Russian honey spice cake. (Rev: BL 10/15/86) [641.5947]

24548 Price, Pam. *Cool Pet Treats: Easy Recipes for Kids to Bake* (3–6). Illus. 2010, ABDO LB $17.95 (978-160453777-2). 32pp. This guide to cooking up treats for pets features plenty of basic cooking information and advice about equipment and ingredients. (Rev: BL 10/1/10) [636.7]

24549 Raabe, Emily. *An Easter Holiday Cookbook* (2–5). Series: Festive Foods for the Holidays. 2001, Rosen LB $19.50 (978-0-8239-5624-1). 24pp. Spring holidays and their foods are presented with large print and colorful illustrations. Also use *A Passover Holiday Cookbook* (2001). (Rev: SLJ 2/02) [641.568]

24550 Ralph, Judy, and Ray Gompf. *The Peanut Butter Cookbook for Kids* (5–7). 1995, Hyperion paper $10.95 (978-0-7868-1028-4). An amazing collection of recipes involving peanut butter, including soups, snacks, and main dishes. (Rev: BL 10/1/95; SLJ 9/95) [641.6]

24551 Sanger, Amy Wilson. *Yum Yum Dim Sum* (PS–K). Illus. by author. 2003, Tricycle $6.95 (978-1-58246-108-3). This appealing blend of rhyming text and mixed-media artwork introduces children to dim sum. (Rev: SLJ 1/04)

24552 Shannon, George. *Who Put the Cookies in the Cookie Jar?* (PS–1). Illus. by Julie Paschkis. 2013, Henry Holt $16.99 (978-0-8050-9197-7). 32pp. From the milk and butter to the wheat, eggs, and sugar, simple rhyming text describes the ingredients of cookies and how they are made and distributed. (Rev: BL 3/1/13; HB 3–4/13; LMC 10/13*; SLJ 2/13) [641.86]

24553 Sheen, Barbara. *Foods of Brazil* (4–6). Illus. 2007, Gale LB $32.45 (978-0-7377-3773-8). 64pp. After a history of the food eaten in Brazil, this volume explores the dishes of different regions and the specialties made for feasts. Also use *Foods of Ethiopia, Foods of Spain,* and *Foods of the Caribbean* (2007). (Rev: SLJ 5/08) [641.5981]

24554 Sheen, Barbara. *Foods of Greece* (4–6). Illus. Series: Taste of Culture. 2005, Gale LB $27.45 (978-0-7377-3033-3). 64pp. Eight recipes introduce the cuisine of Greece, with sidebars that add information plus a map, Web sites, and other features. (Rev: BL 1/1–15/06; SLJ 4/06) [394.1]

24555 Sheen, Barbara. *Foods of Italy* (4–8). Series: A Taste of Culture. 2005, Gale LB $27.45 (978-0-7377-3034-0). Cultural and historical notes add to the simple, traditional recipes provided. Also use *Foods of Mexico* (2005). (Rev: SLJ 2/06) [641]

24556 Townsend, Sue, and Caroline Young. *Indonesia* (5–8). Illus. Series: A World of Recipes. 2003, Heinemann LB $27.07 (978-1-4034-0976-8). 48pp. After a discussion of Indonesian food and ingredients, clear directions, with illustrations, are given for recipes that are graded by ease of preparation. Also use *Russia* and *Vietnam* (both 2003). (Rev: HBG 4/04; SLJ 9/03)

24557 Vaughan, Jenny, and Penny Beauchamp. *Christmas Foods* (3–7). Series: A World of Recipes. 2004, Heinemann LB $30.00 (978-1-4034-4697-8). 48pp. Christmas dishes from around the world have straightforward directions and color photographs. (Rev: BL 6/1–15/04) [641.5]

24558 Vaughan, Jenny, and Penny Beauchamp. *Festival Foods* (3–7). Series: World of Recipes. 2004, Heinemann LB $30.00 (978-1-4034-4699-2). 48pp. The easy-to-follow recipes here focus on dishes for festive occasions worldwide. (Rev: BL 6/1–15/04) [745.594]

24559 Villios, Lynne W. *Cooking the Greek Way. Rev. ed.* (5–10). Illus. Series: Easy Menu Ethnic Cookbooks. 2003, Lerner LB $25.26 (978-0-8225-4131-8). 52pp. The young cook is introduced to the cuisine of Greece, with a chapter covering utensils and ingredient needs and a glossary of basic cooking terms. Recipes are varied and easy to prepare. (Rev: BL 7/02; SLJ 9/02) [641]

24560 Wagner, Lisa. *Cool Cuisine for Super Sleepovers: Easy Recipes for Kids to Cook* (4–6). Series: Cool Cooking. 2007, ABDO LB $15.95 (978-1-59928-721-8). 32pp. Easy-to-follow, tasty recipes will inspire young cooks to treat their friends to superior sleepover fare. (Rev: SLJ 7/07)

24561 Wagner, Lisa. *Cool Foods for Fun Fiestas: Easy Recipes for Kids to Cook* (4–6). Series: Cool Cooking. 2007, ABDO LB $15.95 (978-1-59928-722-5). 32pp. This collection of Mexican-inspired party foods will help young cooks prepare for a fiesta; clear photographs and instructions will allow them to work mostly independently. (Rev: SLJ 7/07)

24562 Wagner, Lisa. *Cool Lunches to Make and Take: Easy Recipes for Kids to Cook* (4–6). Series: Cool Cooking. 2007, ABDO LB $15.95 (978-1-59928-723-2). 32pp. Children will enjoy preparing and packing their own lunches if they use this easy-to-follow guide with photographs. (Rev: SLJ 7/07)

24563 Wagner, Lisa. *Cool Meals to Start Your Wheels: Easy Recipes for Kids to Cook* (3–6). Series: Cool Cooking. 2007, ABDO LB $22.78 (978-1-59928-724-9). 32pp. Interesting, tasty, and healthy breakfast recipes for children. Many require no baking or little preparation, so students may work somewhat independently. (Rev: SLJ 8/07)

24564 Wagner, Lisa. *Cool Pizza to Make and Bake: Easy Recipes for Kids to Cook* (3–6). 2007, ABDO LB $22.78 (978-1-59928-725-6). 32pp. Recipes for many variations on this favorite food are featured, along with tips on technique and safety precautions. (Rev: SLJ 8/07)

24565 Wagner, Lisa. *Cool Sweets and Treats to Eat: Easy Recipes for Kids to Cook* (3–6). Series: Cool Cooking. 2007, ABDO LB $22.78 (978-1-59928-726-3). 32pp. Snacks and treats for after school and summer days are featured here. Many require no baking or little preparation, so students may work somewhat independently. (Rev: SLJ 8/07)

24566 Waldee, Lynne Marie. *Cooking the French Way* (5–10). Illus. 2002, Lerner LB $25.26 (978-0-8225-4106-6). 48pp. A nicely illustrated introduction to French recipes including breads and sauces. (Rev: HBG 3/02; SLJ 2/02) [641.5944]

24567 Walker, Barbara M. *The Little House Cookbook* (5–7). Illus. by Garth Williams. 1979, HarperCollins paper $9.99 (978-0-06-446090-3). Frontier food, such as green pumpkin pie from the Little House books, served up in tasty, easily used recipes.

24568 Weston, Reiko. *Cooking the Japanese Way. Rev. ed.* (5–8). Series: Easy Menu Ethnic Cookbooks. 2002, Lerner LB $25.26 (978-0-8225-4114-1). Directions for preparing traditional foods are given along with lists of terms, ingredients, and utensils. (Rev: HBG 3/02) [641.5952]

24569 Williamson, Sarah A. *Bake the Best-Ever Cookies!* (3–6). Illus. by Tom Ernst. Series: Quick Starts for Kids! 2001, Williamson paper $8.95 (978-1-885593-56-6). 64pp. Simple recipes follow basic information on equipment and ingredients and a number of frequently asked questions. (Rev: SLJ 11/01) [641.8654]

24570 Yolen, Jane, and Heidi Stemple. *Fairy Tale Feasts: A Literary Cookbook for Young Readers and Eaters* (K–3). Illus. by Philippe Beha. 2006, Interlink $24.95 (978-1-56656-643-8). 224pp. A tasty, oversized collection of 20 fairy tales accompanied by kid-friendly recipes, presented in four sections: breakfast, lunch, dinner, and desert. (Rev: BL 11/1/06; SLJ 11/06) [641.5]

24571 Yu, Ling. *Cooking the Chinese Way. Rev. ed.* (5–10). Illus. Series: Easy Menu Ethnic Cookbooks. 2001, Lerner LB $25.26 (978-0-8225-4104-2). 72pp. From appetizers to desserts, with attractive illustrations, this is a revised and expanded edition. (Rev: HBG 3/02) [641.5]

24572 Zamojska-Hutchins, Danuta. *Cooking the Polish Way. Rev. ed.* (5–10). Illus. Series: Easy Menu Ethnic Cookbooks. 2002, Lerner LB $25.26 (978-0-8225-4119-6). 52pp. Simple Polish recipes include traditional dishes such as pierogi. Glossary of terms, plus listing of utensils and ingredients used. (Rev: BL 7/02; HBG 10/02) [641.5]

24573 Zanzarella, Marianne. *The Good Housekeeping Illustrated Children's Cookbook* (5–8). 1997, Morrow $17.95 (978-0-688-13375-7). A visually appealing cookbook containing a number of excellent recipes, some of which require adult supervision. (Rev: BL 12/15/97; HBG 3/98; SLJ 1/98) [641.5]

Gardening

24574 Barker, David. *Compost It* (3–7). Series: Language Arts Explorer: Save the Planet. 2010, Cherry Lake LB $27.07 (978-1-60279-656-0). 32pp. Students are given a mission at the beginning of the book and must use creative thinking and problem solving to gather facts as they travel on a virtual trip researching how gardeners create and use compost. (Rev: BL 4/1/10; LMC 8–9/10; SLJ 4/10) [631.8]

24575 Gourley, Robbin. *First Garden: The White House Garden and How It Grew* (1–4). Illus. by author. 2011, Clarion $16.99 (978-0-547-48224-8). 48pp. With recipes and gardening tips, this engaging volume traces the history of growing food at the White House, from John Adams to Michelle Obama. (Rev: BL 4/15/11; LMC 10/11; SLJ 6/11) [712.09753]

24576 Hengel, Katherine. *Cool Basil from Garden to Table: How to Plant, Grow, and Prepare Basil* (3–6). Illus. Series: Cool Garden to Table. 2012, ABDO LB $27.07 (978-161783182-9). 32pp. Accessible guidance on planting, growing, harvesting, and eating basil is presented clearly, with six recipes. (Rev: BL 4/1/12) [583]

24577 Hirsch, Rebecca. *Growing Your Own Garden* (3–7). Series: Language Arts Explorer: Save the Planet. 2010, Cherry Lake LB $27.07 (978-1-60279-657-7). 32pp. Readers use creative thinking and problem solving to gather facts as they travel on a virtual trip researching vegetable gardening. (Rev: LMC 8–9/10; SLJ 4/10) [635]

24578 Houle, Michelle E. *Lindsey Williams: Gardening for Impoverished Families* (4–7). Illus. Series: Young Heroes. 2007, Gale LB $27.45 (978-0-7377-3867-4). 48pp. Young author Williams has won many awards for her agricultural activism; here she talks about ways to have good food without spending a fortune and about the importance and rewards of volunteering. (Rev: BL 2/15/08) [363.8]

24579 Lay, Richard. *A Green Kid's Guide to Garden Pest Removal* (3–5). Illus. by Laura Zarrin. Series: A Green Kid's Guide to Gardening! 2013, ABDO LB $27.07 (978-161641944-8). 24pp. Young gardeners receive tips on avoiding pesticides, encouraging good bugs and dealing with bad ones, and building a frog house. (Rev: BL 4/1/13; SLJ 4/13) [635.9]

24580 Leavitt, Amie Jane. *A Backyard Vegetable Garden for Kids* (4–7). Illus. Series: Gardening for Kids. 2008, Mitchell Lane LB $20.95 (978-158415634-5). 48pp. Young people learn to reap the rewards of their very own backyard garden — or container garden — in this helpful volume that offers simple, practical advice. (Rev: BL 10/15/08) [635]

24581 Lock, Deborah, ed. *Grow It, Cook It: Simple Gardening Projects and Delicious Recipes* (3–6). Illus. 2008, DK $15.99 (978-0-7566-3367-7). 80pp. Covering everything from plant and gardening basics (growth cycles, soil, pests, and so forth) to individual fruits and vegetables to recipes and projects, this is a handy and appealing volume. (Rev: BL 5/1/08) [641.5]

24582 Maurer, Tracy Nelson. *Growing Flowers* (1–4). Series: Green Thumb Guides. 2000, Rourke LB $23.93 (978-1-55916-251-7). 24pp. A very simple gardening guide that includes material on what, where, and when to plant plus information on weeding, watering, and other gardening tips. Also use *Growing House Plants* and *Growing Vegetables* (both 2000). (Rev: SLJ 1/01) [635]

24583 Morris, Karyn. *The Kids Can Press Jumbo Book of Gardening* (3–6). Illus. 2000, Kids Can $14.95 (978-1-55074-690-7). 240pp. Some of the topics covered in this information-packed volume include fruit, vegetable, and flower gardens; native plants; gardens that attract wildlife; and group projects. (Rev: BL 7/00) [635]

24584 Nichol, Barbara. *One Small Garden* (3–6). Illus. by Barry Moser. 2001, Tundra $17.95 (978-0-88776-475-2). 56pp. A Toronto garden is the focus of this lyrical narrative describing plants, animals, and even the people who have enjoyed it. (Rev: BL 12/15/01; HBG 3/02; SLJ 12/01) [635]

Magic

24585 Becker, Helaine. *Magic Up Your Sleeve: Amazing Illusions, Tricks, and Science Facts You'll Never Believe* (4–7). Illus. by Claudia Dávila. 2010, Maple Tree paper $10.95 (978-1-897349-76-2). 64pp. Thirty sleights of hand incorporating various scientific properties are collected in this clear, easy-to-follow book. (Rev: BLO 5/15/10; SLJ 4/10) [793.8]

24586 Burgess, Ron. *Kids Make Magic: The Complete Guide to Becoming an Amazing Magician* (3–6). Illus. by Marie Ferrante-Doyle and Sarah Rakitin. Series: Kids Can! 2003, Williamson paper $12.95 (978-1-885593-87-0). 127pp. Step-by-step tips for aspiring magicians, from the tricks themselves to advice on setting up a magic show. Includes a detailed resource guide. (Rev: SLJ 3/04) [793.8]

24587 Clibbon, Meg. *Imagine You're a Wizard!* (K–4). Illus. by Lucy Clibbon. Series: Imagine This! 2003, Annick $19.95 (978-1-55037-793-4); paper $7.95 (978-1-55037-792-7). All about wizards and how to become one, with ideas for projects. (Rev: SLJ 3/04) [133.4]

24588 Colbert, David. *The Magical Worlds of Harry Potter: A Treasury of Myths, Legends, and Fascinating Facts* (5–9). 2001, Lumina $14.95 (978-0-9708442-0-0). Information on more than 50 topics in Harry's universe — such as alchemy, Grindylows, and Voldemort — arranged in alphabetical order. (Rev: SLJ 2/02) [823]

24589 Jones, Richard. *That's Magic! 40 Foolproof Tricks to Delight, Amaze and Entertain* (5–8). Illus. 2001, New Holland $19.95 (978-1-85974-668-4). 112pp. Simple instructions and photographs teach the beginning magician a few tricks. (Rev: BL 1/1–15/02; SLJ 1/02) [793.8]

24590 Keable, Ian. *The Big Book of Magic Fun* (5–9). Photos by Steve Tanner. 2005, Barron's paper $14.99 (978-0-7641-3222-3). Step-by-step instructions, with photographs, are given for 40 tricks plus discussion of suitable props and a history of different kinds of magic and famous performers. (Rev: SLJ 3/06) [793.8]

24591 McMaster, Shawn. *Magic Tricks: Absolutely Everything You Need to Know About Magic!* (3–6). Illus. by Mike Moran. 2000, Lowell House paper $9.95 (978-0-7373-0231-8). 119pp. As well as a number of tricks, this book gives a history of sleight-of-hand performances and spells out the skills required to become a magician. (Rev: SLJ 8/00) [793.8]

24592 Tremaine, Jon. *Pocket Tricks* (4–6). Illus. by Mark Turner. 2010, Black Rabbit LB $28.50 (978-159566853-0). 32pp. A book of simple magic tricks with items you might find in your pocket. Also use *Paper Tricks, Magical Illusions,* and *Magic with Numbers* (all 2010). (Rev: BL 5/1/11) [793.8]

24593 Wenzel, Angela. *Do You See What I See? The Art of Illusion* (5–8). Trans. from German by Rosie Jackson. 2001, Prestel $14.95 (978-3-7913-2488-3). Tricks with perspective and color, coded messages, and hidden images are all presented in this attractive volume that makes for excellent browsing. (Rev: HBG 3/02; SLJ 2/02) [152]

24594 *Wizardology: The Book of the Secrets of Merlin* (5–8). 2005, Candlewick $19.99 (978-0-7636-2895-6). This follow-up to *Dragonology* offers a variety of information for wannabe wizards. (Rev: BL 10/15/05)

24595 Zenon, Paul. *Simple Sleight-of-Hand: Card and Coin Tricks for the Beginning Magician* (4–7). Illus. 2007, Rosen LB $21.95 (978-1-4042-1070-7). Written by a practicing magician, this book walks the reader through 13 tricks that will astound and amaze; photographs provide additional explanation. (Rev: BL 11/15/07; SLJ 1/08) [793.8]

Model Making

24596 Kenney, Sean. *Cool Robots* (K–4). Illus. 2010, Henry Holt $12.99 (978-0-8050-8763-5). 32pp. LEGO aficionado Kenney shows off some of his most inspiring creations and provides instructions, tips, and designs. Also use *Cool City* (2011). (Rev: BLO 8/10; SLJ 11/1/10) [629.8]

Photography and Filmmaking

24597 Friedman, Debra. *Picture This: Fun Photography and Crafts* (4–7). Series: Kids Can Do It! 2003, Kids Can $12.95 (978-1-55337-046-8); paper $5.95 (978-1-55337-047-5). 48pp. An easy-to-follow project book that combines photographs and crafts. (Rev: BL 3/15/03; HBG 10/03; SLJ 4/03) [770]

24598 Morgan, Terri, and Shmuel Thaler. *Photography: Take Your Best Shot* (5–8). Series: Media Workshop. 1991, Lerner LB $21.27 (978-0-8225-2302-4). A comprehensive and well-put-together guide to photography that covers cameras, film, developing, composition, lighting, and special effects, as well as discussing career opportunities. (Rev: BL 10/1/91; SLJ 11/91) [771]

24599 Price, Susanna, and Tim Stephens. *Click! Fun with Photography* (4–8). 1997, Sterling $14.95 (978-0-8069-9541-0). A fine introduction to photography that covers both beginning and advanced subjects, including the operation of various cameras, exposure, lighting, different types of photography, and filters. (Rev: SLJ 8/97) [771]

24600 Shulman, Mark, and Hazlitt Korg. *Attack of the Killer Video Book: Tips and Tricks for Young Directors* (5–8). Illus. by Martha Newbigging. 2004, Annick $24.95 (978-1-55037-841-2); paper $12.95 (978-1-55037-840-5). Practical advice on all aspects of movie making will be helpful for aspiring directors. (Rev: BL 5/15/04; SLJ 6/04) [778.59]

24601 Sullivan, George. *Click Click Click! Photography for Children* (5–8). Illus. 2012, Prestel $14.95 (978-379137079-8). 96pp. A brief history of photography begins this user-friendly guide to getting started taking effective, well-composed pictures. (Rev: BL 1/1/12; SLJ 2/12) [771]

Stamp, Coin, and Other Types of Collecting

24602 Dyson, Cindy. *Rare and Interesting Stamps* (5–8). Series: Costume, Tradition, and Culture: Reflecting on the Past. 1998, Chelsea $19.75 (978-0-7910-5171-9). The stories behind 25 rare and unusual stamps start with Britain's first one-penny stamp, which bore a portrait of Queen Victoria. (Rev: BL 3/15/99; HBG 10/99) [769.56]

24603 Hubley, Dan, and Mary Hubley. *Kids Collect: Amazing Collections for Fun, Crafts, and Science Fair Projects* (3–6). Illus. 2002, Bluefish Bay paper $13.95 (978-0-9707267-1-1). 176pp. Provides tips on the selection of an item to collect; the development of the collection itself through buying, trading, and selling; and using the collection as part of a science fair or other school project. (Rev: SLJ 3/03)

24604 Owens, Thomas S. *Collecting Baseball Cards: 21st Century Edition. Rev. ed.* (4–8). 2001, Millbrook LB $26.90 (978-0-7613-1708-1). 80pp. An entertaining introduction to collecting baseball cards, with information on the history of the industry, on how to determine the condition of cards, and how to use the Internet to buy and sell. (Rev: HBG 10/01; SLJ 7/01) [796]

24605 Owens, Thomas S. *Collecting Comic Books: A Young Person's Guide* (5–8). 1995, Millbrook LB $26.90 (978-1-56294-580-0). A beginner's guide to comic book collecting, with sections on kinds of collections, sources, and organizations. (Rev: BL 2/1/96; SLJ 1/96) [741.5]

24606 Owens, Thomas S. *Collecting Stock Car Racing Memorabilia* (4–8). 2001, Millbrook LB $26.90 (978-0-7613-1853-8). NASCAR fans in particular will appreciate this practical and detailed guide to collecting, which includes extensive lists of useful addresses. (Rev: BL 12/15/01; HBG 3/02; SLJ 11/01) [796.72]

24607 Reid, Margarette S. *Lots and Lots of Coins* (K–3). Illus. by True Kelley. 2011, Dutton $16.99 (978-0-525-47879-9). 32pp. A boy and his father share their interest in coin collecting and the history of money in this appealing book. (Rev: BL 2/15/11; SLJ 3/1/11) [737.4]

Jokes and Riddles, Puzzles, Word Games

24608 Becker, Helaine. *Boredom Blasters: Brain Bogglers, Awesome Activities, Cool Comics, Tasty Treats, and More . . .* (4–6). Illus. by Claudia Dávila. 2004, Maple Tree $21.95 (978-1-897066-02-7); paper $9.95 (978-1-897066-03-4). Cures for boredom include stories, jokes and riddles, tricks, games, and foods. (Rev: SLJ 1/05) [818]

24609 Becker, Helaine. *Funny Business: Clowning Around, Practical Jokes, Cool Comedy, Cartooning, and More* (5–8). Illus. by Claudia Dávila. 2005, Maple Tree $21.95 (978-1-897066-40-9). Tips on body language, stand-up routines, clowning, and so forth are accompanied by discussion of various types of humor, a self-quiz, and recipes for delights including "Moose Droppings." (Rev: SLJ 1/06) [808.7]

24610 Bell-Rehwoldt, Sheri. *The Kids' Guide to Pranks, Tricks, and Practical Jokes* (3–6). Illus. 2008, Capstone LB $23.99 (978-1-4296-2275-2). 32pp. This well-illustrated book gives instructions for harmless tricks and jokes such as "fake vomit" and "rattlesnake eggs." (Rev: SLJ 5/09) [793.8]

24611 Boynton, Sandra. *Amazing Cows! A Book of Bovinely Inspired Misinformation* (2–4). Illus. by author. 2010, Workman paper $9.95 (978-0-7611-6-214-8). 80pp. With wordplay, knock-knock jokes, limericks, ads, anecdotes, and more, this is a silly celebration of all things bovine. (Rev: BL 2/15/11; SLJ 4/11) [636.2]

24612 Brewer, Paul. *You Must Be Joking!* (3–5). Illus. 2003, Cricket $15.95 (978-0-8126-2661-2). 128pp. More than 200 jokes are accompanied by tips for effective delivery. (Rev: BL 2/1/04; HBG 4/04; SLJ 2/04) [818]

24613 Calmenson, Stephanie. *Kindergarten Kids: Riddles, Rebuses, Wiggles, Giggles, and More!* (PS–K). Illus. by Melissa Sweet. 2005, HarperCollins LB $16.89 (978-0-06-000714-0). 32pp. This well-illustrated collec-

tion of riddles and rhymes celebrates typical kindergarten activities. (Rev: BL 8/05; SLJ 8/05) [811]

24614 Chmielewski, Gary. *The Classroom Zone: Jokes, Riddles, Tongue Twisters and "Daffynitions"* (3–5). Illus. by Jim Caputo. Series: The Funny Zone. 2008, Norwood House LB $19.95 (978-1-59953-145-8). 24pp. A collection of funny school-themed jokes and riddles, many of them new, with tips on creating your own. Also use *Let's Eat in the Funny Zone, Let's Go in the Funny Zone,* and *The Science Zone* (all 2008). (Rev: LMC 10/08; SLJ 7/08) [818]

24615 Dahl, Michael. *Chuckle Squad: Jokes About Classrooms, Sports, Food, Teachers, and Other School Subjects* (K–3). Illus. by Anne Haberstroh. Series: Michael Dahl Presents Super Funny Joke Books. 2011, Picture Window LB $23.99 (978-140485773-5); paper $6.95 (978-140486370-5). 80pp. Full of humorous illustrations, this is an accessible book of jokes on all topics relating to schools. Lexile AD360L (Rev: BLO 1/1–15/11) [818]

24616 Eisenberg, Lisa. *Silly School Riddles* (1–3). Illus. by Elwood H. Smith. 2008, Dial $14.99 (978-0-8037-3165-3). 40pp. A slightly uneven collection of jokes, riddles, and puns. (Rev: BL 8/08) [398.6]

24617 Fisher, Doris. *Happy Birthday to Whooo? A Baby Animal Riddle Book* (K–3). Illus. by Lisa Downey. 2006, Sylvan Dell $15.95 (978-0-9768823-1-2). Birth announcements give relevant details about new animal arrivals, and readers must turn the page to find out the animal in question. (Rev: SLJ 10/06)

24618 Hall, Katy, and Lisa Eisenberg. *Piggy Riddles* (PS–2). Illus. by Renée Andriani. Series: Dial Easy-to-Read. 2004, Dial $14.99 (978-0-8037-2855-4). 40pp. The unifying theme throughout this brightly illustrated book of riddles is pigs. (Rev: BL 3/1/04; SLJ 7/04) [818]

24619 Hall, Katy, and Lisa Eisenberg. *Simms Taback's Great Big Book of Spacey, Snakey, Buggy Riddles* (K–3). Illus. by Simms Taback. 2008, Viking $17.99 (978-0-670-01121-6). 64pp. A very lively collection of riddles enhanced by illustrations that offer clues. (Rev: BL 9/1/08) [818]

24620 Helmer, Marilyn. *Critter Riddles* (1–3). Illus. by Eric Parker. Series: Kids Can Read. 2003, Kids Can $14.95 (978-1-55337-445-9); paper $3.95 (978-1-55337-411-4). Animal-themed jokes and riddles teach vocabulary and wordplay. Also use the food-related *Yummy Riddles* (2003). (Rev: HBG 10/03; SLJ 5/03) [818]

24621 Helmer, Marilyn. *Yucky Riddles* (K–2). Illus. by Eric Parker. Series: Kids Can Read. 2003, Kids Can $14.95 (978-1-55337-448-0); paper $3.95 (978-1-55337-414-5). 32pp. Cartoon art accompanies jokes and riddles that feature both humor and suitable grossness. (Rev: BL 1/1–15/04; HBG 4/04) [818.54]

24622 Helmer, Marilyn, and Jane Kurisu. *Funtime Riddles* (2–3). Series: Kids Can Read. 2004, Kids Can $14.95 (978-1-55337-579-1). 32pp. This collection of pun-filled riddles and jokes focuses on athletics and other leisure activities. (Rev: BL 6/1–15/04; SLJ 5/04) [818.5]

24623 Helmer, Marilyn, and Jane Kurisu. *Recess Riddles* (2–3). Series: Kids Can Read. 2004, Kids Can $14.95 (978-1-55337-577-7). 32pp. Easy-to-read school-related riddles and jokes include many puns. (Rev: BL 6/1–15/04; SLJ 5/04) [818.5]

24624 Hills, Tad. *Knock, Knock! Who's There? My First Book of Knock-Knock Jokes* (PS–1). Illus. by author. 2000, Simon & Schuster $6.99 (978-0-689-83413-4). Using flaps to conceal answers, this is an amusing collection of old and new knock-knock jokes. (Rev: SLJ 8/00) [818]

24625 Holub, Joan. *Geogra-fleas! Riddles All over the Map* (1–3). Illus. by Regan Dunnick. 2004, Whitman LB $16.99 (978-0-8075-2818-1). Funny facts and riddles are presented by a little brown dog. (Rev: SLJ 11/04) [398.6]

24626 Joyce, Susan, comp. and ed. *ABC School Riddles* (2–5). Illus. by Freddie Levin. 2001, Peel $13.95 (978-0-939217-54-0). This simple book presents one riddle for each letter of the alphabet. (Rev: HBG 10/01; SLJ 1/01)

24627 Lewis, J. Patrick. *Scien-Trickery: Riddles in Science* (1–4). Illus. by Frank Remkiewicz. 2004, Harcourt $16.00 (978-0-15-216681-6). 32pp. Eighteen brain-teasing riddles feature colorful illustrations that provide hints and humor. (Rev: BL 2/15/04; SLJ 4/04) [811]

24628 Lewis, J. Patrick. *Spot the Plot: A Riddle Book of Book Riddles* (K–2). Illus. by Lynn Munsinger. 2009, Chronicle $15.99 (978-0-8118-4668-4). Unpaged. Challenges young readers to identify books based on scenarios such as a pumpkin coach pulled by mice, a princess with unbelievably long hair, and a spider that weaves words into her web. (Rev: HB 11–12/09; LMC 1–2/10; SLJ 11/1/09) [811]

24629 Lupton, Hugh. *Riddle Me This! Riddles and Stories to Challenge Your Mind* (4–6). Illus. by Sophie Fatus. 2003, Barefoot Bks. $19.99 (978-1-84148-169-2). 64pp. Riddles and riddle-related stories and poems, of-

ten with a humorous twist, are accompanied by folk-art illustrations. (Rev: BL 12/1/03; HBG 4/04; SLJ 4/04)

24630 Martin, Jannelle. *ABC Math Riddles* (1–4). Illus. by Freddie Levin. 2003, Peel $13.95 (978-0-939217-57-1). Colorfully illustrated riddles introduce key mathematical terms. (Rev: HBG 4/04; SLJ 2/04) [510]

24631 Morrison, Lillian. *Guess Again! Riddle Poems* (K–3). Illus. by Christy Hale. 2006, August House $16.95 (978-0-87483-730-8). 48pp. A collection of 23 rhyming riddles — some simple some challenging — with colorful illustrations. (Rev: BL 5/1/06; SLJ 6/06) [811]

24632 Musgrave, Ruth A. *Just Joking 3: 300 Hilarious Jokes about Everything, Including Tongue Twisters, Riddles, and More!* (2–5). Illus. 2013, National Geographic paper $7.95 (978-14263109-8-0). 208pp. In bright pages featuring animal photographs, readers can browse a large collection of jokes that are also accessible by topic. (Rev: BL 4/1/13) [818]

24633 Roop, Peter, and Connie Roop. *Holiday Howlers: Jokes for Punny Parties!* (1–3). Illus. by Brian Gable. Series: Make Me Laugh! 2003, Carolrhoda LB $19.93 (978-1-57505-645-6); paper $4.95 (978-1-57505-705-7). 32pp. Very corny jokes are tied to holidays and other important calendar dates, from Thanksgiving to Election Day. (Rev: HBG 4/04) [793]

24634 Rosenberg, Pam. *Sports Jokes* (2–5). Illus. by Mernie Gallagher-Cole. 2010, Child's World LB $22.79 (978-160253521-3). 24pp. Where do ghosts go swimming? Why is tennis such a noisy game? Plenty of humorous wordplay is on offer in this zany joke book full of cartoon-style illustrations. Also use *Space Jokes, Doctor Jokes,* and *Holiday Jokes* (all 2010). (Rev: BL 12/15/10) [818]

24635 Rosenberg, Pam, comp. *Baseball Jokes* (2–3). Illus. by Patrick Girouard. Series: Laughing Matters. 2007, The Child's World LB $22.79 (978-1-59296-705-6). 24pp. Simple, silly jokes for the early elementary set on a fun and familiar topic. Bright, goofy illustrations add to the humor. Also use *Bug Jokes, Gross-Out Jokes, Monster Jokes,* and *Outdoor Jokes* (all 2007) plus *Historical Jokes* and *School Jokes* (both 2005). (Rev: SLJ 5/07)

24636 Rosenbloom, Joseph. *School Jokes* (2–4). Illus. by Steve Harpster. Series: Giggle Fit. 2003, Sterling $12.95 (978-0-402-70440-9). 48pp. This entertaining title is loaded with knock-knock jokes, puns, joke dialogues, and riddles.

24637 Schultz, Sam. *Animal Antics: The Beast Jokes Ever!* (K–4). Illus. by Brian Gable. 2003, Carolrhoda LB $19.93 (978-1-57505-640-1); paper $4.95 (978-1-57505-702-6). 31pp. Animal-themed jokes and wordplay will entertain young readers. (Rev: SLJ 1/04) [972.91]

24638 Schultz, Sam. *Monster Mayhem: Jokes to Scare You Silly!* (1–3). Illus. by Brian Gable. Series: Make Me Laugh! 2003, Carolrhoda LB $19.93 (978-1-57505-642-5); paper $4.95 (978-1-57505-708-8). 32pp. Lots of silly jokes and riddles about monsters, with bright cartoon illustrations. (Rev: HBG 4/04) [793]

24639 Shields, Carol Diggory. *Sports* (PS–3). Illus. by Svjetlan Junakovic. Series: Animagicals. 2001, Handprint $9.95 (978-1-929766-28-4). 32pp. Rhyming riddles give clues about animals hidden under the flaps in this tall-format picture book. (Rev: BL 2/1/02; HBG 3/02; SLJ 2/02) [811]

24640 Teitelbaum, Michael. *Halloween Howlers: Frightfully Funny Knock-Knock Jokes* (PS–2). Illus. by Jannie Ho. 2011, HarperCollins $6.99 (978-006180891-3). 16pp. Interactive features add to the fun in this spooky collection of Halloween knock-knock jokes. (Rev: BLO 9/15/11) [818]

Puzzles

24641 Brookes, Olivia. *Uncover History* (K–2). Illus. by Peter Kent. Series: Hide-and-Seek Visual Adventures. 2010, Windmill LB $22.80 (978-1-60754-653-5). 24pp. Concise fact-filled text and detailed illustrations of buildings of the past with cutaway walls showing the activities inside make this seek-the-hidden-object book informative and entertaining. Also use *Uncover Nature* and *Uncover Technology* (both 2010). (Rev: LMC 11–12/10; SLJ 6/1/10) [909]

24642 Chedru, Delphine. *Spot It Again!* (K–2). Illus. by author. 2011, Abrams $14.95 (978-0-8109-9736-3). 40pp. Sixteen eye-catching seek-and-find illustrations, some behind flaps, conceal abstract animal shapes. (Rev: BLO 6/15/11; SLJ 5/1/11) [793.73]

24643 Garland, Michael. *The Great Easter Egg Hunt* (PS–2). Illus. Series: Look Again. 2005, Dutton $15.99 (978-0-525-47357-2). 32pp. Rhyming clues lead Tommy and readers to more than 200 objects hidden in the elaborate collage artwork. (Rev: BL 2/15/05; SLJ 2/05) [793.73]

24644 Kidslabel. *Spot 7 School* (K–4). 2006, Chronicle $12.95 (978-0-8118-5324-8). Readers are challenged to identify objects in photographs and at the same time to solve riddles that continue throughout the book. (Rev: SLJ 10/06)

24645 Ljungkvist, Laura. *Follow the Line Through the House* (K–3). Illus. by author. 2007, Viking $16.99 (978-0-670-06225-6). Children will enjoy this combination of hide-and-seek and treasure hunt in which line drawings against patterned designs guide readers to hidden objects. (Rev: HB 7/07; SLJ 6/07)

24646 Maidment, Stella. *Cowboy Puzzles* (PS–2). Illus. by Daniela Dogliani. Series: Puzzle Adventures. 2012, Amicus/QEB LB $19.95 (978-160992271-9). 32pp. Readers solve a variety of picture puzzles as they follow the exploits of cowboy Rocky, his horse Grace, and his dog Bob. (Rev: BL 10/1/12) [793.73]

24647 Marks, Jennifer L. *School Times: A Spot-It Challenge* (PS–2). 2009, Capstone LB $23.99 (978-1-4296-

2218-9). 32pp. Similar to *I Spy* books, this volume provide visual challenges in a school setting. Also use *Fun and Games: A Spot-It Challenge* and *Mean Machines: A Spot-It Challenge* (both 2009). (Rev: SLJ 5/09)

24648 Marzollo, Jean. *I Spy: Extreme Challenger: A Book of Picture Riddles* (K–3). Photos by alter Wick. 2000, Scholastic $13.99 (978-0-439-19900-1). 40pp. This book contains 12 double-page picture puzzles with accompanying riddles. (Rev: BL 10/1/00; HBG 3/01; SLJ 12/00) [793.73]

24649 Marzollo, Jean. *I Spy A to Z: A Book of Pictures and Riddles* (PS–2). Illus. by Walter Wick. 2009, Scholastic $13.99 (978-0-545-10782-2). 56pp. Elements of phonics and letter recognition are introduced to this familiar series while standard observation skills are engaged. (Rev: BLO 6/16/09; SLJ 7/09)

24650 Marzollo, Jean. *I Spy an Apple* (K–2). Photos by Walter Wick. Series: Scholastic Reader. 2011, Scholastic $3.99 (978-054522095-8). 32pp. For beginning readers, this I Spy teaches words and visual recognition in bright photographs of objects. (Rev: BLO 7/11) [793.73]

24651 Marzollo, Jean. *I Spy an Egg in a Nest* (K–2). Photos by Walter Wick. Series: Scholastic Reader. 2011, Scholastic paper $3.99 (978-05452209-3-4). 32pp. For beginning readers, this I Spy book combines simple phrases with eye-catching photographs. (Rev: BL 1/1–15/11) [793.73]

24652 Marzollo, Jean. *I Spy Funhouse: A Book of Picture Riddles* (PS–3). Photos by Walter Wick. 1993, Scholastic $13.99 (978-0-590-46293-8). 40pp. This entertaining book consists of a series of picture puzzles involving an amusement park fun house and of a series of rhyming word clues. (Rev: BL 5/15/93; SLJ 4/93) [793]

24653 Marzollo, Jean. *I Spy Year-Round Challenger! A Book of Picture Riddles* (PS–2). Illus. by Walter Wick. 2001, Scholastic $13.99 (978-0-439-31634-7). 40pp. A book of double-page picture puzzles with holiday themes, one for each of the 12 months. (Rev: BL 2/1/02; HBG 10/02; SLJ 4/02) [793.73]

24654 Onishi, Satoru. *Who's Hiding?* (PS–2). Illus. by author. 2007, Kane $14.95 (978-1-933605-24-1). 32pp. A hide-and-seek book in which a different animal is partially hidden on each page, making for an entertaining but not too difficult challenge for little ones. (Rev: SLJ 5/07)

24655 Phillips, Dee. *Find It at the Beach* (K–3). Series: Can You Find It? 2005, Gareth Stevens LB $23.00 (978-0-8368-6298-0). 24pp. This hunt for animals and objects found at the beach will prompt children to study the detailed photographs. Also use *Find It in a Rain Forest*, *Find It in the Desert*, and *Find It on the Farm* (all 2005). (Rev: SLJ 6/06) [578.7699]

24656 Philpot, Lorna, and Graham Philpot. *Find Anthony Ant* (PS–1). Illus. by Lorna Philpot. 2006, Sterling $12.95 (978-1-905417-10-0). 24pp. Children will enjoy hunting for Anthony on each spread of this detailed book featuring "The Ants Go Marching." (Rev: BL 5/15/06)

24657 Raffin, Deborah. *Mitzi's World: Seek and Discover More Than 150 Details in 15 Works of Folk Art* (K–3). Illus. by Jane Wooster Scott. 2009, Abrams $17.95 (978-0-8109-8004-4). 32pp. A black-and-white dog explores diverse American scenes full of objects to discover. (Rev: BLO 11/1/09; LMC 3–4/10; SLJ 9/1/09) [793.73]

24658 Riedler, Isabella. *Tricky Puzzles for Clever Kids* (2–5). Illus. 2001, Sterling paper $5.95 (978-0-8069-6753-0). 128pp. A collection of challenging visual puzzles illustrated in black and white. (Rev: BL 2/15/02) [793.73]

24659 Sheppard, Kate. *Animal I Spy: What Can You Spot?* (PS). Illus. by author. 2010, Kingfisher $6.99 (978-0-7534-6395-6). 18pp. This find-and-seek board book combines challenging clues and dynamic illustrations in six different animal-related spying games. (Rev: BL 5/1/10; SLJ 6/1/10) [590]

24660 Staake, Bob. *Look! A Book! A Zany Seek-and-Find Adventure* (PS–3). Illus. by author. 2011, Little, Brown $16.99 (978-0-316-11862-0). 40pp. Easy-to-read rhyming text offers clues to the searching and counting tasks on each page. (Rev: BL 2/15/11; SLJ 2/1/11*) [793.73]

24661 White, Graham. *Secrets of the Pyramids: A Maze Adventure* (3–6). Illus. 2002, National Geographic paper $8.95 (978-0-7922-6938-0). 32pp. Fans of mazes will enjoy helping 12-year-old Hemon look for his father in the pyramid, and will learn about ancient Egypt in the process. (Rev: SLJ 11/02) [793.7]

24662 Whybrow, Ian. *Faraway Farm* (PS–K). Illus. by Alex Ayliffe. 2006, Carolrhoda LB $14.95 (978-1-57505-938-9). Rhyming text encourages readers to locate specific animals and inanimate objects in the illustrations that chronicle a day in the life of Farmer Flat and his family. (Rev: SLJ 11/06)

24663 Wick, Walter. *Can You See What I See? Cool Collections: Picture Puzzles to Search and Solve* (K–2). 2004, Scholastic $13.95 (978-0-439-61772-7). 40pp. In this colorful assortment of picture puzzles, Wick focuses on some of the diverse objects that people collect, including seashells, buttons, stuffed animals, and model cars. (Rev: BL 12/1/04; SLJ 10/04) [793.73]

24664 Wick, Walter. *Can You See What I See? Dream Machine: A Picture Adventure to Search and Solve* (PS–2). Photos by author. 2003, Scholastic $13.99 (978-0-439-39950-0). 35pp. A dozen picture puzzles each offer multiple challenges, including search-and-find quests, mazes, and matching games. (Rev: HBG 4/04; SLJ 11/03) [793.73]

24665 Wick, Walter. *Can You See What I See? Once Upon a Time* (PS–2). Illus. by author. 2006, Scholastic $13.99 (978-0-439-61777-2). 40pp. Twelve classic fairy tales are the setting for this new picture puzzle book; each spread comes with a list of items to find in each fairy tale scene. (Rev: BL 12/1/06; SLJ 2/07) [793.3]

24666 Wick, Walter. *Can You See What I See? Out of This World* (PS–2). Illus. by author. 2013, Scholastic $13.99 (978-054524468-8). 40pp. A princess in a castle and a robot in a spaceship are the main features in this search-and-find addition to the series. (Rev: BL 4/1/13) [793.73]

24667 Wick, Walter. *Can You See What I See? Picture Puzzles to Search and Solve* (K–3). Illus. 2002, Scholastic $13.95 (978-0-429-16391-3). 40pp. A collection of clever picture puzzles that test the visual perception of young readers. (Rev: BL 4/15/02; HBG 10/02; SLJ 3/02) [792.73]

24668 Wick, Walter. *Can You See What I See? Seymour Makes New Friends* (PS–K). Illus. Series: Seymour. 2006, Scholastic $8.99 (978-0-439-61780-2). 32pp. Readers must seek out specific objects on the spreads while Seymour makes a seesaw and two rabbits. (Rev: BL 2/1/06; SLJ 2/06) [793.73]

24669 Wick, Walter. *Can You See What I See? Treasure Ship* (K–3). Illus. by author. Series: Can You See What I See? 2010, Scholastic $13.99 (978-043902643-7). 40pp. Shipwrecks and beach combing are the focus of this addition to the popular series. Also use *Can You See What I See? Toyland Express* (2011). (Rev: BLO 2/1/10)

Word Games

24670 McCall, Francis, and Patricia Keeler. *A Huge Hog Is a Big Pig: A Rhyming Word Game* (K–3). Illus. 2002, HarperCollins LB $16.89 (978-0-06-029766-4). 32pp. "A wet hound is . . . a soggy doggy!" and other wondrous rhymes are accompanied by photographs of children from a mix of races and of the appropriate animals. (Rev: BL 12/15/01; HBG 10/02; SLJ 2/02)

24671 Steig, William. *CDB! Rev. ed.* (PS–4). Illus. 2000, Simon & Schuster $16.00 (978-0-689-83160-7). 48pp. The great word-game book of 30 years ago is now reissued with color drawings. (Rev: BL 4/1/00; HBG 10/00) [793.734]

Mysteries, Monsters, Curiosities, and Trivia

24672 Allman, Toney. *Werewolves* (4–7). Series: Monsters. 2004, Gale LB $26.20 (978-0-7377-2620-6). An examination of the origins of the werewolf, with references to and illustrations from movie and TV appearances by these monsters. (Rev: SLJ 4/05) [398]

24673 Arnosky, Jim. *Monster Hunt: Exploring Mysterious Creatures with Jim Arnosky* (2–5). Illus. by author. 2011, Hyperion/Disney $16.99 (978-1-4231-3028-4). 32pp. Arnosky looks at mysterious creatures from the Loch Ness Monster to the prehistoric carcharodon; large, realistic paintings accompany the narrative. Lexile NC1090L (Rev: BL 6/1/11; LMC 11–12/11; SLJ 7/11) [001.944]

24674 Asimov, Isaac. *Is There Life in Outer Space?* (3–5). Illus. Series: Isaac Asimov's 21st Century Library of the Universe. 2004, Gareth Stevens LB $26.00 (978-0-8368-3950-0). 32pp. A revised, well-illustrated edition of a previously published book, this offers thoughtful discussion of the possibility of alien life, with material on the development of life on Earth and on exploration of Mars. (Rev: SLJ 3/05) [576.8]

24675 Aslan, Madalyn. *What's Your Sign? A Cosmic Guide for Young Astrologers* (5–9). Illus. by Jennifer Kalis. 2002, Grosset $12.99 (978-0-448-42693-8). A lively, spiral-bound guide to the 12 signs of the zodiac and the personality traits they represent, with information on the underlying mythology and lists of famous people born under each sign. (Rev: SLJ 9/02) [133.5]

24676 Bardhan-Quallen, Sudipta. *The Real Monsters* (5–8). Illus. by Josh Cochran. Series: Mysteries Unwrapped. 2008, Sterling paper $5.95 (978-1-4027-3776-3). 88pp. This volume looks into stories about ghosts, werewolves, vampires, mummies, zombies, and other monsters. (Rev: SLJ 6/09) [001.944]

24677 Becker, Helaine. *Are You Psychic? The Official Guide for Kids* (4–6). Illus. by Claudia Dávila. 2005, Maple Tree $16.95 (978-1-897066-20-1); paper $9.95 (978-1-897066-21-8). 64pp. Telepathy, mind reading, and fortune telling are among the psychic abilities in-

troduced in this breezy volume that includes activities. (Rev: SLJ 5/05) [001.9]

24678 Belanger, Jeff. *What It's Like to Climb Mount Everest, Blast Off into Space, Survive a Tornado, and Other Extraordinary Stories* (5–8). Illus. 2011, Sterling paper $9.95 (978-14027671-1-1). 136pp. First-person accounts describe a variety of exciting, extreme adventures in this compilation that will appeal to reluctant readers. Lexile 1250 (Rev: BL 4/15/11) [179]

24679 *The Book of Why? 50 Questions and All the Answers* (K–3). Illus. by Kath Grimshaw. 2010, Kingfisher paper $7.99 (978-0-7534-6396-3). 64pp. Answers to pressing questions such as why elephants have trunks and why your legs look shorter underwater are presented in this eye-catching book. Also use *The Book of How* (2010). (Rev: BL 4/1/10; SLJ 9/1/10) [500]

24680 Burns, Jan. *Crop Circles* (4–6). Series: Wonders of the World. 2005, Gale LB $26.20 (978-0-7377-3063-0). 48pp. A slim overview of the history of crop circles over the past century, with discussion of the various theories about these strange phenomena. (Rev: SLJ 12/05) [001.94]

24681 Campbell, Peter A. *Alien Encounters* (5–7). 2000, Millbrook LB $23.90 (978-0-7613-1402-8). An overview of eight supposed encounters between humans and aliens. (Rev: BL 7/00; HBG 10/00; SLJ 4/00) [001.9]

24682 Crisp, Tony. *Super Minds: People with Amazing Mind Power* (4–7). Illus. by Mary Kuper. 1999, Element Books paper $4.95 (978-1-901881-03-5). A survey of near-death experiences, feral children's case histories, and instances of strange mental powers. (Rev: SLJ 5/99) [001.9]

24683 Delrio, Martin. *The Loch Ness Monster* (3–5). Series: Unsolved Mysteries. 2002, Rosen LB $25.25 (978-0-8239-3564-2). 48pp. Here is a rundown on the many sightings and stories surrounding the Lock Ness monster, including the expeditions that tried and failed to find the truth. (Rev: BL 10/15/02) [001.9]

24684 Demolay, Jack. *Atlantis: The Mystery of the Lost City* (3–5). Illus. by author. Series: Jr. Graphic Mysteries. 2006, Rosen LB $22.50 (978-1-4042-3407-9). 24pp. Readers will be fascinated by the mystery of Atlantis, presented here with engaging artwork and background information. (Rev: SLJ 5/07)

24685 Doft, Tony. *Nostradamus* (3–6). Illus. Series: Unexplained. 2011, Children's Press LB $21.95 (978-160014584-1). 24pp. This appealing survey of theories and stories pertaining to Nostradamus will appeal to reluctant readers. Lexile 710L (Rev: BL 4/15/11) [133.3092]

24686 Donkin, Andrew. *Atlantis: The Lost City?* (2–4). Illus. Series: DK Readers. 2000, DK $14.99 (978-0-7894-6681-5). 48pp. The first part of this book discusses the legend of Atlantis; the second half tells of the search for this lost city at sites around the world. (Rev: BL 12/15/00; HBG 10/01) [001.94]

24687 Donkin, Andrew. *Bermuda Triangle* (2–4). Series: Eyewitness Reader. 2000, DK paper $3.99 (978-0-7894-5415-7). 48pp. An easily read study of the Bermuda Triangle that favors explanations leaning toward the supernatural — blaming UFOs or the lost continent of Atlantis. (Rev: HBG 10/00; SLJ 8/00) [001.9]

24688 Donovan, Sandy. *Does It Really Take Seven Years to Digest Swallowed Gum? And Other Questions You've Always Wanted to Ask* (4–6). Illus. 2010, Lerner LB $26.60 (978-082259085-9). 40pp. This book applies science to the investigation of childhood myths, including whether a penny on a railroad track can derail a train and if it's really possible to swing in a circle over a swingset. (Rev: BL 4/1/10; LMC 5–6/10; SLJ 7/10) [610]

24689 Dumont-Le Cornec, Elisabeth. *Wonders of the World: Natural and Man-Made Majesties* (5–9). Illus. by Laureen Topalian. 2007, Abrams $24.95 (978-0-8109-9417-1). Seventy-one striking sites around the world, both natural and man-made and featured on the UNESCO World Heritage list, are shown in beautiful photographs. (Rev: BL 12/15/07) [031.02]

24690 Erickson, Justin. *Alien Abductions* (3–6). Illus. Series: Unexplained. 2011, Children's Press LB $21.95 (978-160014582-7). 24pp. This appealing survey of theories and stories pertaining to alien abductions will appeal to reluctant readers. Lexile 780L (Rev: BL 4/15/11) [001.942]

24691 Farman, John. *The Short and Bloody History of Ghosts* (4–6). Illus. by author. Series: Short and Bloody Histories. 2002, Lerner LB $19.93 (978-0-8225-0837-3); paper $5.95 (978-0-8225-0838-0). 96pp. Ghosts and other supernatural beings are the focus of this overview of sightings around the world today and in the past, with most of the events occurring in Britain. (Rev: HBG 3/03; SLJ 2/03)

24692 Fecher, Sarah, and Clare Oliver. *Freaky Facts About Natural Disasters* (3–5). Illus. Series: Freaky Facts. 2006, Two-Can $13.95 (978-1-58728-539-4); paper $8.95 (978-1-58728-542-4). Great for browsing, this is an overview of the impact of events ranging from extreme weather to earthquakes and volcanic eruptions. (Rev: BL 4/15/06) [363.34]

24693 French, Jackie. *The Little Book of Big Questions* (3–6). Illus. by Martha Newbigging. 2000, Annick $19.95 (978-1-55037-655-5); paper $9.95 (978-1-55037-654-8). 127pp. Fifteen subject-oriented chapters cover such areas as the universe, animal intelligence, extraterrestrials, and mortality. (Rev: HBG 3/01; SLJ 11/00) [001.9]

24694 Frisch, Aaron. *Zombies* (1–4). Illus. Series: That's Spooky! 2013, Creative Education $17.95 (978-160818251-0). 24pp. This hi-low introduction to the nature of zombies relies heavily on movie stills and other illustrations. (Rev: BL 4/1/13; SLJ 4/13) [398.21]

24695 Gilman, Laura Anne. *Yeti, the Abominable Snowman* (3–5). Illus. Series: Unsolved Mysteries. 2002, Rosen LB $26.50 (978-0-8239-3565-9). 48pp. The author presents historical accounts of the elusive yeti of the Himalayas. (Rev: BL 10/15/02) [001.944]

24696 Gorman, Jacqueline Laks. *The Bermuda Triangle* (3–5). Illus. Series: X Science: An Imagination Library. 2002, Gareth Stevens LB $23.00 (978-0-8368-3196-2). 24pp. An introduction to the mysterious Bermuda Triangle, with discussion of theories, evidence, and research. Also use *Bigfoot* and *The Loch Ness Monster* (both 2002). (Rev: HBG 3/03; SLJ 2/03) [001.9]

24697 Grace, N. B. *UFO Mysteries* (2–5). Series: Boys Rock! 2006, The Child's World LB $25.64 (978-1-59296-738-4). 32pp. A good choice for beginning and reluctant readers (girls as well as boys), this is a photo-filled exploration of the search for life outside our solar system and of the possibility that other life forms have visited earth. (Rev: SLJ 2/07) [001.942]

24698 Halls, Kelly Milner. *Alien Investigation: Searching for the Truth About UFOs and Aliens* (5–8). Illus. by Rick C. Spears. 2012, Millbrook $20.95 (978-0-7613-6204-3). 64pp. Halls explores reports of alien encounters, with interviews of witnesses and discussion of hoaxes. ℮ (Rev: BL 4/1/12; LMC 10/12*; SLJ 10/12; VOYA 6/12) [001.942]

24699 Halls, Kelly Milner. *Tales of the Cryptids: Mysterious Creatures That May or May Not Exist* (4–7). Illus. by Rick Spears. 2006, Darby Creek $18.95 (978-1-58196-049-5). A fun, close-up look at cryptozoology, the study of legendary animals (that may or may not be real) such as the Loch Ness Monster and Bigfoot. (Rev: BL 11/15/06; SLJ 12/06) [001.944]

24700 Helstrom, Kraig. *Crop Circles* (3–6). Illus. Series: Unexplained. 2011, Children's Press LB $21.95 (978-160014583-4). 24pp. Reluctant readers will be attracted to this account of various hoaxes. (Rev: BL 4/1/11; SLJ 4/11) [001.94]

24701 Herbst, Judith. *Hoaxes* (3–4). Illus. Series: The Unexplained. 2004, Lerner LB $26.60 (978-0-8225-1629-3). 48pp. Crop circles, fairy photographs, moon-men, and other famous and less-well-known hoaxes and publicity stunts are described. Also in this series is *Monsters* (2004). (Rev: SLJ 2/05) [001.9]

24702 Hillman, Ben. *How Big Is It?* (3–5). Illus. Series: What's the Big Idea? 2007, Scholastic $14.99 (978-0-439-91808-4). 48pp. Twenty-two giant items — a polar bear, a huge spider, an airship, a redwood — are juxtaposed with other objects to illustrate their size; conversational narrative provides key information. (Rev: BL 11/15/07; SLJ 2/08) [153.7]

24703 Hirschmann, Kris. *Demons* (5–8). Illus. Series: Monsters and Mythical Creatures. 2011, ReferencePoint $26.95 (978-160152147-7). 80pp. Demons and evil spirits' prevalence throughout world cultures is explored here, with eye-catching illustrations and discussion of topics such as exorcism and demonic possession. (Rev: BL 8/11; SLJ 4/11) [133.4]

24704 Ho, Oliver. *Mutants and Monsters* (4–6). Illus. by Josh Cochran. Series: Mysteries Unwrapped. 2008, Sterling paper $5.95 (978-1-4027-3642-1). 96pp. Bigfoot, the Jersey Devil, and Nessie are among the beings included in this survey of curiosities that is good for browsing. (Rev: BL 7/08; SLJ 7/08) [001.944]

24705 Howe, John. *Lost Worlds* (4–6). Illus. by author. 2009, Kingfisher $16.99 (978-0-7534-6107-5). 96pp. Real and legendary "lost worlds" — the Garden of Eden, Pompeii, Atlantis, and Camelot, for example — are the focus of this attractive volume that mixes history and myth. (Rev: BL 11/1/09; LMC 1–2/10; SLJ 6/10) [813.6]

24706 Huang, Chungliang Al. *The Chinese Book of Animal Powers* (5–7). 1999, HarperCollins LB $16.89 (978-0-06-027729-1). The 12 animals of the Chinese zodiac are introduced in double-page spreads, and the characteristics and powers of each are outlined. (Rev: BCCB 12/99; BL 1/1–15/00; HBG 3/00) [133.5]

24707 Hubbard, Ben. *Top 10 Biggest* (3–6). 2010, Crabtree LB $26.60 (978-0-7787-7487-7); paper $8.95 (978-0-7787-7508-9). 32pp. A nice variety of natural and man-made records — from the biggest hamburger and food fight to the biggest flower, swimming pool, and tomb — are covered in this browsable volume. (Rev: SLJ 7/10) [152.14]

24708 Jones, Jen. *Cancer, Scorpio, and Pisces: All About the Water Signs* (4–6). Illus. Series: Zodiac Fun. 2009, Capstone LB $26.65 (978-1-4296-4015-2). 32pp. A light introduction to the water signs of the zodiac, with a personality profile, compatibility with other signs, and sketches of celebrities. Also use *Gemini, Libra, and Aquarius: All About the Air Signs* (2010). (Rev: BLO 3/1/10; LMC 11–12/10; SLJ 4/10) [133.5]

24709 Kallen, Stuart A. *Atlantis* (4–7). Illus. Series: Mysterious Encounters. 2011, Kidhaven LB $27.50 (978-073775534-3). 48pp. Kallen covers the legend of Atlantis in readable text with relevant illustrations. (Rev: BL 3/1/12) [398.23]

24710 Kallen, Stuart A. *Dreams* (4–8). Illus. Series: The Mystery Library. 2004, Gale LB $29.95 (978-1-59018-288-8). 112pp. In this volume in the Mystery Library, Kallen examines topics including dream science, the interpretation of dreams, and telepathic dreaming. Also

use *Ghosts, Possessions and Exorcisms*, and *Shamans* (all 2004). (Rev: BL 5/15/04) [154.6]

24711 Kallen, Stuart A. *Fortune-Telling* (4–8). Series: Mystery Library. 2004, Gale LB $29.95 (978-1-59018-289-5). This exploration of the history and mystery of fortune-telling separates fact from fiction. (Rev: BL 5/15/04) [133.3]

24712 Kallen, Stuart A. *The Loch Ness Monster* (3–6). Illus. Series: Mysteriousand Unknown. 2008, Reference Point LB $25.95 (978-1-60152-059-3). 104pp. Kallen chronicles sightings of Nessie, the various expeditions to find the monster, and looks at the many hoaxes that have been perpretrated. (Rev: BLO 3/5/09) [001.944]

24713 Kerns, Ann. *Wizards and Witches* (4–7). Illus. Series: Fantasy Chronicles. 2009, Lerner LB $27.93 (978-0-8225-9983-8). 48pp. Kerns touches on everything from King Arthur's court to Middle Earth in her tour of primarily European and American witches and wizards. (Rev: BL 10/1/09; LMC 11–12/09; SLJ 1/10) [133.4]

24714 Krensky, Stephen. *Frankenstein* (4–7). Illus. Series: Monster Chronicles. 2006, Lerner LB $26.60 (978-0-8225-5923-8). A survey of the folklore and fiction featuring Frankenstein's monster, including excerpts from the famous Mary Shelley novel. Also use *Vampires* and *Werewolves* (both 2006). (Rev: SLJ 2/07) [823]

24715 Krull, Kathleen. *Big Wig: A Little History of Hair* (3–6). Illus. by Peter Malone. 2011, Scholastic $18.99 (978-0-439-67640-3). 48pp. A broad survey, full of bizarre facts, of hairstyles and head coverings through the ages. (Rev: BL 9/1/11; LMC 10/11; SLJ 7/11) [391.5]

24716 Kyi, Tanya Lloyd. *Fifty Underwear Questions: A Bare-All History* (4–7). Illus. by Ross Kinnaird. 2011, Annick $21.95 (978-155451353-6); paper $12.95 (978-15545135-2-9). 116pp. Everything you wanted to know about underwear through the ages, with some fascinating pieces of trivia — all delivered with humor and even some games. (Rev: BL 12/15/11; SLJ 2/12) [391.4]

24717 Law, Stephen. *Really, Really Big Questions About the Weird, the Wonderful, and Everything Else* (5–8). Illus. by Nishant Choksi. 2009, Kingfisher $16.99 (978-0-75346-309-3). 64pp. What is nothing? Is my mind my brain? How important is happiness? Is time travel possible? These are only a few of the questions posed here as Law tackles some weighty problems in an accessible manner. (Rev: BL 12/15/09; LMC 1–2/10; SLJ 1/10) [100]

24718 Lunis, Natalie. *Haunted Caves* (4–7). Illus. Series: Scary Places. 2012, Bearport LB $25.27 (978-1-61772-456-5). 32pp. This volume looks at 11 caves around the world with spooky features. (Rev: BL 9/1/12; SLJ 7/12) [133.10914]

24719 Lynette, Rachel. *Curses* (4–7). Illus. Series: Mysterious Encounters. 2011, Greenhaven LB $27.50 (978-073775422-3). 48pp. Lynette presents details of various famous curses (the Chicago Cubs' curse, the Hope diamond, to name just two) in readable text with relevant illustrations. (Rev: BL 3/1/12) [398]

24720 McDonald, Megan. *Stink It Up! A Guide to the Gross, the Bad, and the Smelly* (2–4). Illus. by Peter H. Reynolds. 2013, Candlewick paper $5.99 (978-07636594-2-4). 128pp. Judy Moody's younger brother Stink guides readers through a disgusting litany of things such as unappetizing recipes, weird things to eat, bodily functions, and more. (Rev: BLO 9/15/13) [31.02]

24721 Marks, Jennifer L. *Aries, Leo, and Sagittarius: All About the Fire Signs* (4–6). Illus. Series: Zodiac Fun. 2009, Capstone LB $26.65 (978-1-4296-4014-5). 32pp. A light introduction to the fire signs of the zodiac, with a personality profile, compatibility with other signs, and sketches of celebrities. (Rev: LMC 11–12/10; SLJ 4/10) [133.5]

24722 Messenger, Norman. *Imagine* (3–5). Illus. 2005, Candlewick $17.99 (978-0-7636-2757-7). 32pp. This inventively constructed book, with folds, wheels, and flaps, offers a variety of visual stimuli and puzzles. (Rev: BL 1/1–15/06) [793.73]

24723 Michels, Troy. *Atlantis* (3–6). Illus. Series: Unexplained. 2011, Children's Press LB $21.95 (978-160014585-8). 24pp. This appealing survey of theories and stories pertaining to the lost continent will appeal to reluctant readers. Lexile 800L (Rev: BL 4/15/11) [001.94]

24724 Miller, Karen. *Monsters and Water Beasts: Creatures of Fact or Fiction?* (4–6). Illus. by Sergio Ruzzier. 2007, Holt $17.95 (978-0-8050-7902-9). 88pp. Legends of creatures such as Bigfoot and sea serpents are thoroughly described in this book, along with scientific information that could possibly rule out the creatures' existence. (Rev: BL 5/1/07; SLJ 7/07) [398.24]

24725 Miller, Raymond H. *Vampires* (4–7). Series: Monsters. 2004, Gale LB $26.20 (978-0-7377-2619-0). An examination of the origins of the vampire, with references to and illustrations from movie and TV appearances by these monsters. (Rev: SLJ 4/05) [398]

24726 Murphy, Glenn. *How Loud Can You Burp? More Extremely Important Questions (and Answers!)* (4–7). Illus. by Mike Phillips. 2009, Flash Point paper $10.99 (978-1-59643-506-3). 284pp. Bizarre and often funny questions gleaned from Murphy's Web site are answered in a casual and engaging manner in this compendium of facts and trivia. (Rev: BLO 8/09; SLJ 10/09) [500]

24727 Murphy, Glenn. *Stuff That Scares Your Pants Off! A Book of Scary Things (and How to Avoid Them)* (4–8). Illus. by Mike Phillips. 2011, Roaring Brook paper $14.99 (978-1-59643-633-6). 192pp. This reassuring and humorous book examines the fears we harbor about wild animals, natural disasters, doctors, dentists, snakes, spiders, and so forth. **e** Lexile 1210L (Rev: LMC 5–6/11; SLJ 9/1/11) [001.9]

24728 Murphy, Jim. *The Giant and How He Humbugged America* (5–8). Illus. 2012, Scholastic $19.99 (978-0-439-69184-0). 112pp. Murphy chronicles the story of the Cardiff Giant, a hoax in 1869 upstate New York involving the body of a 10-foot-tall figure. Lexile 1210L (Rev: BL 6/12*; SLJ 9/12*) [974.7]

24729 Myers, Janet Nuzum. *Strange Stuff: True Stories of Odd Places and Things* (5–8). 1999, Linnet LB $19.50 (978-0-208-02405-3). A collection of curiosities — items about zombies, quicksand, scorpions, poisonous snakes, black holes, Bigfoot, mermaids, voodoo, the Bermuda Triangle, and feral children raised by wolves. (Rev: HBG 3/00; SLJ 7/99; VOYA 2/00) [001.9]

24730 Nardo, Don. *Atlantis* (5–8). Series: The Mystery Library. 2004, Gale LB $29.95 (978-1-59018-287-1). The author examines whether the ancient story of the lost continent of Atlantis — as described by Plato — could be true. (Rev: BL 5/15/04; SLJ 4/04) [001.94]

24731 Nardo, Don, and Bradley Steffens. *Medusa* (4–7). Series: Monsters. 2004, Gale LB $26.20 (978-0-7377-2617-6). Describes the mythological personage, telling the story of Perseus killing Medusa, and showing her role in paintings, sculptures, movie stills, and computer games. Also use *Cyclops* (2004). (Rev: SLJ 4/05) [398.2]

24732 O'Meara, Stephen James. *Are You Afraid Yet? The Science Behind Scary Stuff* (5–8). Illus. by Jeremy Kaposy. 2009, Kids Can $17.95 (978-1-55453-294-0); paper $9.95 (978-1-55453-295-7). 80pp. A humorous yet macabre exploration of "mysteries" that include vampires, werewolves, ghosts, UFOs — with scientific explanations. (Rev: BL 3/15/09; LMC 10/09; SLJ 8/09) [001.944]

24733 Owen, Ruth. *Top 10 Fastest* (3–6). Series: Crabtree Contact. 2010, Crabtree LB $26.60 (978-0-7787-7488-4); paper $8.95 (978-0-7787-7509-6). 32pp. A nice variety of natural and man-made records — from the fastest car and motorbike to the fastest growing plant and fastest mammal — are covered in this browsable volume. (Rev: SLJ 7/10) [531]

24734 Pascoe, Elaine. *Fooled You! Fakes and Hoaxes Through the Years* (4–6). Illus. by Laurie Keller. 2005, Holt $16.95 (978-0-8050-7528-1). 96pp. Pascoe tells the stories behind some of the world's most infamous hoaxes, including the Cardiff Giant, Bigfoot, crop circles, and Piltdown Man. (Rev: BL 9/15/05; SLJ 11/05) [001.9]

24735 Pearce, Q. L. *Ghost Hunters* (5–7). Illus. Series: Mysterious Encounters. 2011, Kidhaven LB $27.50 (978-073775290-8). 48pp. Case studies, historical facts, and scientific explorations ground this satisfying book about haunted houses and the people who investigate them. (Rev: BL 8/11) [133.1]

24736 Pearce, Q. L. *Mysterious Disappearances* (4–7). Illus. Series: Mysterious Encounters. 2011, Kidhaven LB $27.50 (978-073775840-5). 48pp. Roanoke and Amelia Earhart are among the mysteries presented here in readable text with relevant illustrations. (Rev: BL 3/1/12) [001.94]

24737 *Pick Me Up* (4–8). Illus. 2006, DK $29.99 (978-0-7566-2159-9). This attractive, child-friendly compilation of facts and figures offers information on a wide variety of topics, including nature, fashion, math, politics, popular culture, geography, music, movies, and technology. (Rev: SLJ 12/06) [900]

24738 Redmond, Shirley Raye. *Oak Island Treasure Pit* (4–7). Illus. Series: Mysterious Encounters. 2011, Kidhaven LB $27.50 (978-073775140-6). 48pp. Redmond presents details of the pit in Nova Scotia that is reputed to house Captain Kidd's gold. (Rev: BL 3/1/12) [971.6]

24739 Reinhart, Matthew, and Robert Sabuda. *Dragons and Monsters* (2–5). Illus. by authors. Series: Encyclopedia Mythologica. 2011, Candlewick $29.99 (978-0-7636-3173-4). 12pp. Grotesque and fearsome monsters from myths and traditions around the world are depicted in this beautifully executed pop-up book. (Rev: BL 9/1/11; HB 5–6/11; SLJ 8/1/11*) [398]

24740 Reynolds, Helen. *Makeup and Body Decoration* (3–8). Illus. Series: A Fashionable History of Costume. 2003, Raintree LB $25.70 (978-1-4109-0028-9). 32pp. Chronicles the history of body decoration and makeup from the beginning of recorded history to the present. (Rev: HBG 10/03; SLJ 9/03) [391.6]

24741 *Ripley's Believe It or Not!* (4–7). Illus. 2004, Ripley $25.95 (978-1-893951-73-0). 256pp. Packed with fascinating trivia and fun for browsing, this appealing volume focuses on weird and amazing facts. (Rev: SLJ 2/05) [031.02]

24742 Roleff, Tamara L., ed. *Black Magic and Witches* (5–8). Series: Fact or Fiction? 2003, Gale paper $18.70 (978-0-7377-1319-0). 127pp. A good starting point for debate over witchcraft, with essays for and against witches, magic, and Harry Potter, and some history of persecution of witches. (Rev: SLJ 3/03) [133.43]

24743 Rosen, Michael J. *Balls! Round 2* (4–7). Illus. by John Margeson. Series: Balls! 2008, Darby Creek $18.95 (978-1-58196-066-2). This sequel to *Balls!* (2006) introduces even more balls — bocce, croquet, meatballs, even the Magic Eight ball — with all kinds of facts, puzzles, experiments, and fun. (Rev: BL BLO 6/17/08; SLJ 7/08) [796.3]

24744 Rosenthal, Amy Krouse. *The Wonder Book* (2–4). Illus. by Paul Schmid. 2010, HarperCollins $17.99 (978-0-06-142974-3). 80pp. Puns, poems, palindromes, puzzles, and quirky kid-friendly questions abound in this light compendium made for browsing. (Rev: BL 1/1/10; SLJ 3/1/10)

24745 Savage, Candace. *Wizards: An Amazing Journey Through the Last Great Age of Magic* (5–8). 2003, Greystone $17.95 (978-1-55054-943-0). An appealing, oversize book full of information on witchcraft and wizardry in the late 17th century, when science and sorcery were not far apart. (Rev: BL 6/1–15/03; VOYA 8/03) [133]

24746 Schroeder, Andreas. *Duped! True Stories of the World's Best Swindlers* (4–7). Illus. by Remy Simard. 2011, Annick $21.95 (978-155451351-2); paper $12.95 (978-15545135-0-5). 144pp. With graphic-novel flair, this is a lighthearted but informative exploration of hoaxes in modern times. (Rev: BL 12/15/11; SLJ 1/12) [364.16]

24747 Shulman, Mark. *Are You "Normal"? More Than 100 Questions That Will Test Your Weirdness* (5–8).

2011, National Geographic paper $12.95 (978-1-4263-0837-6). 176pp. Can you roll your tongue? Where do you bite a chocolate bunny first? Which ice cream flavor do you like best? These and many other questions are posed here with subliminal statistical lessons hidden in the final answers. Lexile 570L (Rev: BL 12/1/11; SLJ 3/12) [155.2]

24748 Slade, Arthur. *Monsterology: Fabulous Lives of the Creepy, the Revolting, and the Undead* (5–8). Illus. by Derek Mah. 2005, Tundra paper $8.95 (978-0-88776-714-2). Dracula, Medusa, Dr. Jekyll/ Mr. Hyde, and Sasquatch are among the characters profiled in this entertaining volume, each with a list of loves and hates, favorite saying, and fashion rating. (Rev: SLJ 2/06; VOYA 2/06)

24749 Spirn, Michele Sobel. *Mysterious People: A Chapter Book* (3–6). Series: True Tales. 2005, Children's Pr. LB $22.50 (978-0-516-25181-3); paper $4.95 (978-0-516-25454-8). 48pp. A compelling account of four people who met mysterious fates — Queen Nefertiti, Kaspar Hauser, Ishi, and a 5,000-year-old corpse called Otzi — and how they were discovered. (Rev: SLJ 5/06) [920]

24750 Stiekel, Bettina, ed. *The Nobel Book of Answers: The Dalai Lama, Mikhail Gorbachev, Shimon Peres, and Other Nobel Prize Winners Answer Some of Life's Most Intriguing Questions for Young People* (3–6). 2003, Simon & Schuster $14.95 (978-0-689-86310-3). 272pp. Some of life's most intriguing questions are addressed — if not answered — in this collection of writings by 22 Nobel Price winners, including Bishop Desmond Tutu, mathematician Enrico Bombieri, and geneticist Richard J. Roberts. (Rev: BL 10/15/03; HBG 4/04; SLJ 11/03)

24751 Stirling, Janet. *UFOs* (3–5). Illus. Series: Unsolved Mysteries. 2002, Rosen LB $25.25 (978-0-8239-3566-6). 48pp. An account of UFO sightings over time, from early glimpses of Army blimps to the continuing flying saucer reports. (Rev: BL 10/15/02) [001.942]

24752 Szpirglas, Jeff. *They Did What?! Your Guide to Weird and Wacky Things People Do* (3–6). Illus. by Dave Whamond. 2005, Maple Tree $16.95 (978-1-897066-22-5); paper $9.95 (978-1-897066-23-2). 64pp. A fascinating look at weird human behavior and inventions (think pet rocks, hoaxes, air-guitar competitions, and so forth). (Rev: SLJ 3/06) [031.02]

24753 Terry, Paul. *Top 10 for Boys* (5–8). Illus. 2013, Firefly $24.95 (978-177085223-5). 320pp. A collection of lists, pictures, and facts ranging from top 10 biggest cities and airports to deadly animals and insects, deadly storms, and fastest pitchers. (Rev: BL 11/15/13; SLJ 1/14) [796.332092]

24754 Thomas, Lyn. *What? What? What? Astounding, Weird, Wonderful and Just Unbelievable Facts* (3–5). Illus. by Dianne Eastman. 2003, Maple Tree $19.95 (978-1-894379-51-9); paper (978-1-894379-52-6). 128pp. This cleverly illustrated collection of trivia is loaded with facts and figures about a little bit of everything, from animals and human anatomy to haunted houses and inventions. (Rev: BL 6/1–15/03) [031.02]

24755 Tibballs, Geoff. *Ripley's Believe It or Not! Enter If You Dare!* (5–7). 2010, Ripley Entertainment $28.95 (978-1-893951-63-1). 254pp. A compendium of odd information organized in such chapters as "Animal Antics," "Extreme Sports," "Incredible Feats," "Fantastic Food," and "Amazing Science." (Rev: BL 11/1/10; SLJ 12/1/10) [031.02]

24756 Watkins, Graham. *Ghosts and Poltergeists* (3–5). Series: Unsolved Mysteries. 2002, Rosen LB $26.50 (978-0-8239-3563-5). 48pp. This book explores actual case histories of hauntings and poltergeist activity, as well as a look into the way a real ghost hunter works. (Rev: BL 10/15/02) [133.1]

24757 Wells, Robert E. *What's Older Than a Giant Tortoise?* (PS–3). Illus. 2004, Whitman LB $16.99 (978-0-8075-8831-4); paper $6.95 (978-0-8075-8832-1). A giant tortoise takes young readers on a wide-ranging tour of items that are even older than he is; included are a giant sequoia tree, the pyramids of Egypt, and Mount Everest. (Rev: BL 10/15/04; SLJ 1/05) [500]

24758 Wetzel, Charles. *Haunted U.S.A* (5–8). Illus. by Josh Cochran. Series: Mysteries Unwrapped. 2008, Sterling paper $5.95 (978-1-4027-3735-0). 86pp. An eerie look at ghosts and apparitions, haunted houses, and mysteries across the United States, including on the Hollywood screen. (Rev: SLJ 6/09) [133.1]

24759 Williams, Dinah. *Dark Mansions* (4–7). Illus. Series: Scary Places. 2012, Bearport LB $25.27 (978-1-61772-457-2). 32pp. This volume describes 11 houses that are apparently haunted, including one in Indianapolis where a group of Underground Railroad fugitives died in a fire. (Rev: BL 9/1/12; SLJ 7/12) [133.1]

24760 Williams, Dinah. *Monstrous Morgues of the Past* (4–6). Illus. Series: Scary Places. 2011, Bearport LB $25.27 (978-161772149-6). 32pp. This effective book describes 11 morgues that were the site of hair-raising stories. (Rev: BL 3/15/11) [133.1]

Sports and Games

General and Miscellaneous

24761 Ajmera, Maya, and John D. Ivanko. *Come Out and Play* (PS–2). Series: It's a Kid's World. 2001, Charlesbridge LB $15.95 (978-1-57091-385-3); paper $6.95 (978-1-57091-386-0). Photographs and simple text show the differences and similarities in children's play around the world. (Rev: HBG 10/01; SLJ 8/01) [790]

24762 Ajmera, Maya, and Michael Regan. *Let the Games Begin!* (3–5). Illus. 2000, Charlesbridge LB $16.95 (978-0-88106-067-6); paper $6.95 (978-0-88106-068-3). 32pp. This book examines the philosophy of sports and sportsmanship with double-page spreads on topics such as practice, teamwork, competition, and rules. (Rev: BL 4/1/00; HBG 10/00; SLJ 5/00) [796]

24763 Alexander, Kyle. *Pro Wrestling's Most Punishing Finishing Moves* (4–7). Series: Pro Wrestling Legends. 2000, Chelsea $25.00 (978-0-7910-5833-6). 64pp. This book describes the most effective finishing moves in the sport of wrestling and fighters who use them. (Rev: BL 3/1/01; HBG 3/01) [796.8]

24764 Alexander, Kyle. *The Women of Pro Wrestling* (4–7). Illus. Series: Pro Wrestling Legends. 2000, Chelsea $25.00 (978-0-7910-5839-8); paper $25.00 (978-0-7910-5840-4). After introducing several famous women pro wrestlers, this account describes women's roles in this sport in and out of the ring. (Rev: BL 10/15/00; HBG 3/01) [796.812]

24765 Athans, Sandra K. *Tales from the Top of the World: Climbing Mount Everest with Pete Athans* (5–8). Illus. 2012, Millbrook LB $31.93 (978-076136506-8). 64pp. An exciting account of Pete Athans's ascents of the mountain and the dangers and challenges that climbers face. ⓔ (Rev: BL 8/12; LMC 3–4/13; SLJ 9/12) [796.522095496]

24766 Bell-Rehwoldt, Sheri. *The Kids' Guide to Classic Games* (3–6). Series: Edge Books: Kids' Guides. 2008, Capstone LB $23.99 (978-1-4296-2273-8). 32pp. Offers clear instructions for many traditional games such as Old Maid and Red Rover. (Rev: SLJ 5/09) [790.1]

24767 Bell-Rehwoldt, Sheri. *The Kids' Guide to Jumping Rope* (4–8). Illus. Series: Kids' Guides. 2012, Capstone LB $26.65 (978-142965443-2). 32pp. A variety of jump rope tricks and rhymes are presented with easy-to-follow directions. (Rev: BL 9/1/11) [796.2]

24768 Birkemoe, Karen. *Strike a Pose: The Planet Girl Guide to Yoga* (5–10). Illus. by Heather Collett. Series: Planet Girl. 2007, Kids Can paper $12.95 (978-155337004-8). 96pp. This is a practical, easy-going guide to yoga poses, breathing, meditation, and uses in sports. (Rev: SLJ 8/07) [613.7]

24769 Burgess, Ron. *Yo-Yo! Tips and Tricks from a Pro* (3–6). Illus. by author. 2001, Williamson paper $8.95 (978-1-885593-54-2). 64pp. Burgess shows simple and complex yo-yo techniques in easy-to-follow line drawings. (Rev: SLJ 1/02) [796.2]

24770 Caldwell, Michaela. *The Girls' Yoga Book: Stretch Your Body, Open Your Mind, and Have Fun!* (4–6). Illus. by Claudia Dávila. 2005, Maple Tree $16.95 (978-1-897066-24-9); paper $9.95 (978-1-897066-25-6). 64pp. This book emphasizes the psychological benefits of yoga in a bright and vibrant format. (Rev: SLJ 5/06) [613.7]

24771 Campbell, Guy. *The Boys' Book of Survival: How to Survive Anything, Anywhere* (4–7). Illus. by Simon Ecob. 2009, Scholastic paper $9.99 (978-0-545-08536-6). 128pp. How to deal with everything from avalanches to zombie invasions. (Rev: BLO 3/16/09) [796.54]

24772 Catel, Patrick. *Surviving Stunts and Other Amazing Feats* (4–7). Series: Extreme Survival. 2011, Heinemann LB $33.50 (978-1-4109-3969-2). 56pp. Catel describes amazing feats performed by stuntmen and daredevils. (Rev: SLJ 8/11) [613.6]

24773 Chapman, Garry. *Air* (3–5). Series: Extreme Sports. 2001, Chelsea LB $28.00 (978-0-7910-6609-6). 32pp. Sky diving, bungee jumping, sky surfing, and other aerial sports are covered in this attractively illustrated volume. (Rev: BL 10/15/01; HBG 3/02) [796]

24774 Chapman, Garry. *Mountains* (3–5). Series: Extreme Sports. 2001, Chelsea LB $28.00 (978-0-7910-6610-2). 32pp. Mountain climbing, adventure racing, mountain biking, and extreme hiking are highlighted in this book that also covers weather conditions, safety precautions, and competitions. (Rev: BL 10/15/01; HBG 3/02; SLJ 12/01) [796.5]

24775 Chapman, Garry. *Rivers* (3–5). Illus. Series: Extreme Sports. 2001, Chelsea LB $28.00 (978-0-7910-6608-9). 32pp. This account looks at "extreme" water sports (such as white-water kayaking and riverboarding), with information on required gear, terminology, and stunts, accompanied by photographs. (Rev: BL 10/15/01; HBG 3/02; SLJ 12/01) [797.1]

24776 Chapman, Garry. *Snow* (3–5). Series: Extreme Sports. 2001, Chelsea LB $16.95 (978-0-7910-6606-5). 32pp. A variety of snow sports such as skiing and sledding are presented, with descriptions of unique winter environments. (Rev: BL 10/15/01) [796.95]

24777 Chapman, Garry. *Streets* (3–5). Illus. Series: Extreme Sports. 2001, Chelsea LB $28.00 (978-0-7910-6612-6). 32pp. "Extreme" sports such as BMX riding, luge racing, and inline skating that can be practiced on the street are covered here, with information on required gear, terminology, and stunts, accompanied by photographs. (Rev: BL 10/15/01; HBG 3/02) [796.2]

24778 Cleare, John. *Epic Climbs* (5–8). Illus. Series: Epic Adventures. 2011, Kingfisher $19.99 (978-0-7534-6473-8). 64pp. The Eiger, K2, Everest, McKinley, and the Matterhorn are featured in this browsable volume full of photographs, maps, diagrams, and details of climbs, equipment, and so forth. (Rev: BL 4/1/11; SLJ 5/11; VOYA 6/11) [796.52]

24779 Connolly, Helen. *Field Hockey: Rules, Tips, Strategy, and Safety* (4–8). Series: Sports from Coast to Coast. 2005, Rosen LB $26.50 (978-1-4042-0182-8). This title puts the spotlight on field hockey, including a brief history of the sport as well as a look at its rules, equipment, training, and so forth. (Rev: SLJ 10/05)

24780 Corbett, Doris, and John Cheffers, eds. *Unique Games and Sports Around the World: A Reference Guide* (4–9). 2001, Greenwood $85.00 (978-0-313-29778-6). More than 300 games and sports are organized by continent and then by country, with details of the number of players, equipment, rules, and so forth, and indications of whether this is a suitable game for the classroom or playground. (Rev: SLJ 8/01) [790.1]

24781 Crossingham, John. *Cheerleading in Action* (4–7). Series: Sports in Action. 2003, Crabtree LB $25.27 (978-0-7787-0333-4); paper $6.95 (978-0-7787-0353-2). This is a colorful, attractive introduction to cheerleading, the cheers, costumes, duties, and its importance in sports. (Rev: BL 11/15/03) [791]

24782 Crossingham, John. *In-Line Skating in Action* (4–7). Series: Sports in Action. 2002, Crabtree LB $25.27 (978-0-7787-0328-0); paper $6.95 (978-0-7737-0348-3). A fine introduction to this fast-growing sport with easy-to-follow descriptions of moves and techniques. (Rev: BL 1/1–15/03; SLJ 10/03) [796.9]

24783 Crossingham, John. *Lacrosse in Action* (4–7). Series: Sports in Action. 2002, Crabtree LB $25.27 (978-0-7787-0329-7); paper $6.95 (978-0-7737-0349-0). A clear, concise introduction to lacrosse that discusses techniques, equipment, rules, and safety precautions. (Rev: BL 1/1–15/03) [796.34]

24784 Crossingham, John. *Spike It Volleyball* (2–4). Illus. Series: Sports Starters. 2008, Crabtree LB $18.95 (978-0-7787-3143-6). 32pp. This introduction to volleyball explains scoring, tactics, basic moves, and other important factors in a well-designed easy-to-read format. (Rev: BL 9/1/08) [796.325]

24785 Crossingham, John. *Wrestling in Action* (4–7). Series: Sports in Action. 2003, Crabtree LB $25.27 (978-0-7787-0336-5); paper $6.95 (978-0-7787-0356-3). This introduction to wrestling describes basic moves, skills, and rules. (Rev: BL 11/15/03) [796.8]

24786 Crossingham, John, and Bobbie Kalman. *Skiing in Action* (3–5). Illus. Series: Sports in Action. 2004, Crabtree LB $25.27 (978-0-7787-0337-2); paper $6.95 (978-0-7787-0357-0). 32pp. For beginning skiers, this is an attractive and useful introduction to equipment, technique, and vocabulary. (Rev: BL 4/1/04; SLJ 6/05) [796.93]

24787 Ditchfield, Christin. *Wrestling* (2–4). Illus. Series: True Books. 2000, Children's Book Pr. LB $25.00 (978-0-516-21611-9). 48pp. This simple introduction to wrestling contains material on its history and how it is played and judged. (Rev: BL 9/15/00) [796.8]

24788 Doeden, Matt. *Can You Survive Extreme Mountain Climbing? An Interactive Survival Adventure* (4–6). Illus. Series: You Choose: Survival. 2012, Capstone LB $31.32 (978-142968583-2); paper $6.95 (9781429694780). 112pp. Readers must make crucial decisions as they climb Kilimanjaro, the Matterhorn, and Everest (with companions). e (Rev: BL 12/15/12) [796.522]

24789 Donkin, Andrew. *Danger on the Mountain: Scaling the World's Highest Peaks* (2–4). Illus. Series: Dorling Kindersley Readers. 2001, DK $14.99 (978-0-7894-7386-8); paper $3.99 (978-0-7894-7385-1). Donkin presents details of some famous expeditions as well as discussing the hazards involved and the way climbing equipment has changed over the years. (Rev: HBG 10/01; SLJ 11/01) [796.52]

24790 Eckart, Edana. *I Can Bowl* (K–2). Series: Sports. 2002, Children's Book Pr. paper $4.95 (978-0-516-24028-2). 24pp. This slim volume for beginning readers shows Emma bowling with her father and discusses equipment and safety. Also use *I Can Swim*, *I Can Play Soccer*, and *I Can Ride a Bike* (all 2002). (Rev: SLJ 9/02) [794.6]

24791 Edwardes, Dan. *Parkour* (4–7). Illus. 2009, Crabtree LB $19.95 (978-0-7787-3821-3); paper $8.95 (978-0-7787-3842-8). 32pp. A fascinating look at the athletes who use urban environments as their gyms. (Rev: BL 6/1–15/09) [796.04]

24792 Egan, Tracie. *Water Polo: Rules, Tips, Strategy, and Safety* (4–8). Series: Sports from Coast to Coast. 2005, Rosen LB $26.50 (978-1-4042-0186-6). Introduces readers to the sport of water polo, along with its rules, training, and equipment. (Rev: SLJ 10/05)

24793 Gay, Kathlyn. *They Don't Wash Their Socks! Sports Superstitions* (3–5). Illus. by John Kerschbaum. 1990, Walker LB $14.85 (978-0-8027-6917-6). 114pp. Superstitions from many sports are highlighted. (Rev: SLJ 6/90) [796]

24794 Gedatus, Gus. *In-Line Skating for Fitness* (4–7). Series: Nutrition and Fitness. 2001, Capstone LB $25.26 (978-0-7368-0707-4). 64pp. Inline skating is introduced with an emphasis on fitness benefits and the necessity of a healthy diet. (Rev: BL 9/15/01; HBG 10/01) [796]

24795 Giddens, Sandra, and Owen Giddens. *Volleyball: Rules, Tips, Strategy, and Safety* (4–8). Series: Sports from Coast to Coast. 2005, Rosen LB $26.50 (978-1-4042-0185-9). Introduces the sport of volleyball — including its rules, equipment, and strategies. (Rev: SLJ 10/05) [796.32]

24796 Gifford, Clive. *Golf: From Tee to Green — The Essential Guide for Young Golfers* (5–8). Illus. 2010, Kingfisher $16.99 (978-075346399-4). 64pp. This informative guide covers everything from gear and techniques to clothing and the achievements of golfing greats. (Rev: BL 9/1/10) [796.352]

24797 Gigliotti, Jim. *Barefoot Waterskiing* (5–8). Illus. Series: Extreme Sports. 2011, Child's World LB $27.07 (978-160973177-9). 32pp. This extreme sports offering boasts dynamic photographs alongside historical and safety information about barefoot waterskiing. (Rev: BL 1/1/12) [797.3]

24798 Gordon, John. *The Kids Book of Golf* (3–6). Illus. 2001, Kids Can $14.95 (978-1-55337-017-8); paper $7.95 (978-1-55074-617-4). History, equipment, technique, rules, competitions, and humorous anecdotes are all included here, along with diagrams and full-color photographs showing children and famous golfers. (Rev: HBG 10/01; SLJ 7/01) [796.352]

24799 Green, Sara. *Cheerleading Camp* (4–7). Illus. Series: Kick, Jump, Cheer! 2011, Children's Press LB $22.95 (978-160014647-3). 24pp. This breezy book offers a behind-the-scenes glimpse into what takes place at cheerleading camp. (Rev: BL 10/1/11) [791.6]

24800 Griffin, Margot. *The Sleepover Book* (2–7). Illus. by Jane Kurisu. 2001, Kids Can paper $14.95 (978-1-55074-522-1). 144pp. These sleepover activities range from making a music video, cooking midnight snacks, treasure hunts, games and crafts, and, of course, telling scary stories. (Rev: SLJ 6/01) [793.21]

24801 Gryski, Camilla. *Cat's Cradle, Owl's Eyes: A Book of String Games* (4–7). Illus. by Tom Sankey. 1984, Morrow LB $15.93 (978-0-688-03940-0); paper $6.95 (978-0-688-03941-7). Explanations of 21 string figures, plus variations. [793.9]

24802 Gurtler, Janet. *Small Game* (5–8). Illus. Series: Outdoor Hunting Guide. 2012, Weigl LB $27.13 (978-161913504-8). 24pp. Covering the history of this sport as well as tracking, equipment, safety, and ethics, this is a useful volume for those contemplating hunting everything from skunks and woodchucks to grouse and beavers. (Rev: BL 10/1/12) [799.2]

24803 Hamilton, S. L. *White Water* (4–6). Illus. Series: Xtreme Sports. 2010, ABDO LB $25.65 (978-161613006-0). 32pp. With plenty of exciting photographs, Hamilton introduces the thrills of whitewater canoeing, kayaking, and rafting. (Rev: BL 9/1/10) [796.04]

24804 Hayhurst, Chris. *Wakeboarding! Throw a Tantrum* (4–8). Series: Extreme Sports. 2000, Rosen LB $26.50 (978-0-8239-3008-1). This new water sport is described with material on the equipment needed and the necessary safety precautions. (Rev: BL 6/1–15/00; SLJ 8/00) [797.1]

24805 Herzog, Brad. *P Is for Putt* (3–6). Illus. by Bruce Langton. 2005, Sleeping Bear $16.95 (978-1-58536-252-3). 40pp. An alphabetical format is used to introduce various facts about the game of golf. (Rev: BL 5/1/05) [796.352]

24806 Hile, Kevin. *Video Games* (5–8). Series: Technology 360. 2009, Lucent $32.45 (978-1-4205-0170-4). 104pp. An attractive and informative look at video games and how they are created, with discussion of their history and impact on culture plus a glossary and lists of material for further research. (Rev: BL 4/1/10; LMC 8–9/10) [794.8]

24807 Hile, Lori. *Surviving Extreme Sports* (4–7). Series: Extreme Survival. 2011, Heinemann LB $33.50 (978-1-4109-3968-5). 56pp. Starting with a chapter titled "Are You Nuts!?," Hile tells stories of extreme sports including diving, skateboarding, mountaineering, and skydiving. (Rev: SLJ 8/11) [796.046]

24808 Hort, Lenny. *Treasure Hunts! Treasure Hunts! Treasure and Scavenger Hunts to Play with Friends and Family* (3–6). 2000, HarperCollins $15.95 (978-0-688-17245-9); paper $7.95 (978-0-688-17177-3). 80pp. This book supplies information for all sorts of treasure-hunting games with material on number of players, and where, when, and how to play. (Rev: BL 6/1–15/00; HBG 10/00; SLJ 11/00) [796.1]

24809 Howell, Brian. *Golf* (4–6). Illus. Series: Best Sport Ever. 2012, ABDO LB $22.95 (978-161783143-0). 64pp. With a history of the game, profiles of some of the best players, key accomplishments and important courses, and interesting sidebars, this is an appealing introduction for young players. (Rev: BL 9/1/12; SLJ 3/12) [796.352]

24810 Howes, Chris. *Caving* (4–8). Series: Radical Sports. 2003, Heinemann LB $25.64 (978-1-58810-626-1). Technique, safety, gear, and other vital aspects are covered in this introduction to the sport. (Rev: BL 2/15/03; HBG 3/03) [796.52]

24811 Hunter, Matt. *Pro Wrestling's Greatest Tag Teams* (4–7). Series: Pro Wrestling Legends. 2000, Chelsea $25.00 (978-0-7910-5835-0). 64pp. This title covers such tag teams as the Road Warriors, the Midnight Express, the Nasty Boys, Public Enemy, and Harlem Heat. (Rev: BL 10/15/00; HBG 3/01) [796.8]

24812 Hunter, Matt. *Ric Flair: The Story of the Wrestler They Call "The Natural Boy"* (4–7). Series: Pro Wrestling Legends. 2000, Chelsea $25.00 (978-0-7910-5825-1). 64pp. The story of the wrestler who has been at the top of his sport for most of the last three decades. (Rev: BL 10/15/00; HBG 3/01) [796.8]

24813 Jaffe, Elizabeth Dana. *Dominoes* (1–4). Illus. Series: Games Around the World. 2001, Compass Point LB $22.60 (978-0-7565-0132-7). 32pp. Variations of dominoes games are presented with instructions and diagrams, along with a section on using them to create a domino effect. (Rev: SLJ 10/01) [795.3]

24814 Jaffe, Elizabeth Dana. *Juggling* (3–5). Series: Games Around the World. 2002, Compass Point LB $22.60 (978-0-7565-0191-4). 32pp. This work contains a history of juggling and describes equipment and basic techniques, using colorful illustrations. (Rev: BL 5/15/02; SLJ 7/02) [793.8]

24815 Jones, Jen. *Cheer Tryouts: Making the Cut* (3–7). Illus. Series: Snap Books Cheerleading. 2005, Capstone LB $25.26 (978-0-7368-4361-4). 32pp. The focus here is on preparation — from good nutrition and regular stretching to practicing drills and a good attitude; part of a series that also includes *Cheer Squad: Building Spirit and Getting Along* (2005). (Rev: SLJ 1/06) [791.6]

24816 Jones, Patrick. *The Main Event: The Moves and Muscle of Pro Wrestling* (4–8). Illus. Series: Spectacular Sports. 2012, Millbrook LB $31.93 (978-076138635-3). 64pp. A look at the history and strategies of wrestling, with profiles of athletes. **e** (Rev: BL 10/1/12; SLJ 5/13) [796.812]

24817 Jones, Patrick. *Ultimate Fighting: The Brains and Brawn of Mixed Martial Arts* (5–8). Illus. 2013, Millbrook LB $31.93 (978-146770934-7). 64pp. This volume traces the history and evolution of combat sports from ancient Olympic games to wrestling to martial arts and eventually to mixed martial arts and the Ultimate Fighting Championship; it includes many photographs but is not a how-to book. (Rev: BL 9/1/13; LMC 8–9/14) [796.8]

24818 Kaiman, Bobbie, and Sarah Dann. *Badminton in Action* (4–7). Series: Sports in Action. 2003, Crabtree LB $25.27 (978-0-7787-0334-1); paper $6.95 (978-0-7787-0354-9). This basic introduction to badminton includes material on racquets, courts, rules, and strategies. (Rev: BL 11/15/03) [796.34]

24819 Kalman, Bobbie. *Extreme Wakeboarding* (3–10). Illus. Series: Extreme Sports: No Limits! 2006, Crabtree LB $25.27 (978-0-7787-1680-8); paper $6.95 (978-0-7787-1726-3). 32pp. The history wakeboarding is covered here, as well as the fundamental techniques, equipment, and safety considerations. (Rev: SLJ 2/07) [797.3]

24820 Kalman, Bobbie, and John Crossingham. *Extreme Skydiving* (3–10). Illus. Series: Extreme Sports: No Limits! 2006, Crabtree LB $25.27 (978-0-7787-1684-6); paper $6.95 (978-0-7787-1730-0). 32pp. This colorful introduction to skydiving chronicles the sport's long history, which can be traced back to the late 18th century, and describes its different disciplines and required equipment. (Rev: SLJ 2/07)

24821 Kalman, Bobbie, and John Crossingham. *Extreme Sports* (4–8). Series: Extreme Sports No Limits! 2004, Crabtree LB $25.27 (978-0-7787-1673-0). All manner of extreme sports are covered in this overview. (Rev: BL 9/1/04)

24822 Kalman, Bobbie, and Sarah Dann. *Bowling in Action* (4–7). Series: Sports in Action. 2003, Crabtree LB $25.27 (978-0-7787-0335-8); paper $6.95 (978-0-7787-0355-6). 32pp. This well-illustrated introduction to bowling includes material on equipment, techniques, rules, and bowling alleys. (Rev: BL 11/15/03) [794.6]

24823 Kaminker, Laura. *In-Line Skating! Get Aggressive* (5–8). Series: Extreme Sports. 1999, Rosen LB $26.50 (978-0-8239-3012-8). This book provides information for both beginning and advanced inline skaters and covers topics including equipment, history, techniques, and safety tips. (Rev: SLJ 4/00) [796]

24824 Kent, Deborah. *Athletes with Disabilities* (5–7). Illus. Series: Watts Library: Disabilities. 2003, Watts LB $25.50 (978-0-531-12019-4). 64pp. Achievements of disabled athletes are accompanied by the history of such events as the Special Olympics and by information on new games, equipment, and techniques that widen horizons. (Rev: BL 10/15/03; SLJ 9/03) [371.9]

24825 Klein, Adam G. *Hunting* (2–4). Illus. Series: Checkerboard Adventure Library: Outdoor Adventure! 2008, ABDO LB $16.95 (978-1-59928-960-1). 32pp. A general overview of hunting's history, the reasons why people hunt, equipment, and so forth. (Rev: BL 4/1/08) [799.2]

24826 Klingel, Cynthia, and Robert B. Noyed. *Yo-Yo Tricks* (3–5). Series: Games Around the World. 2002, Compass Point LB $22.60 (978-0-7565-0193-8). 32pp. The development of the yo-yo is covered in this volume, along with colorful illustrations and diagrams that describe techniques and moves. (Rev: BL 5/15/02; SLJ 7/02) [796]

24827 Lehn, Barbara. *What Is an Athlete?* (PS–2). Illus. by Carol Krauss. 2002, Millbrook LB $21.90 (978-0-7613-2258-0). 32pp. An introduction of the concept of "athlete," presented in a friendly format for younger readers. (Rev: BL 12/15/02; HBG 3/03) [796]

24828 Lewin, Ted. *At Gleason's Gym* (4–7). Illus. by author. 2007, Roaring Brook $17.95 (978-159643231-4). 40pp. The history of the famous Gleason's Gym (where Muhammad Ali and Jake La Motta trained) is told as readers follow the progress of 9-year-old Sugar Boy Younan, already showing great promise as a boxer. ALA Notable Children's Book 2008. (Rev: BL 9/1/07*; SLJ 10/07) [796.83]

24829 Lindeen, Carol K. *Let's Downhill Ski!* (PS–1). Series: Sports and Activities. 2006, Capstone LB $21.26 (978-0-7368-6359-9). 24pp. A large-format, simply written introduction that covers basic techniques, equipment, and safety and includes color photographs. (Rev: SLJ 2/07) [796.9]

24830 Lowe, Ayana, ed. *Come and Play: Children of Our World Having Fun* (K–3). Illus. 2008, Bloomsbury $16.95 (978-1-59990-245-6). 64pp. Full-page photographs of children playing in diverse settings around the world are accompanied by simple verses by New York City children. (Rev: BL 7/08; SLJ 8/08) [808.81]

24831 MacAulay, Kelley, and Bobbie Kalman. *Extreme Skiing* (3–9). Illus. Series: Extreme Sports: No Limits! 2006, Crabtree LB $25.27 (978-0-7787-1682-2); paper $6.95 (978-0-7787-1728-7). 32pp. This slim, well-illustrated volume looks at freestyle skiing, offering a brief history of the sport and touching on such topics as skiing styles, equipment, and competition rules. (Rev: SLJ 2/07) [797.937]

24832 Manley, Claudia B. *Competitive Volleyball for Girls* (4–7). Illus. Series: Sportsgirl. 2001, Rosen LB $26.50 (978-0-8239-3404-1). 64pp. An introduction to the rules of volleyball, the training necessary, and the special opportunities for girls, with material on nutrition and the dangers of overtraining. (Rev: SLJ 3/02) [796.325]

24833 Mason, Paul. *Skiing* (4–8). Illus. 2003, Heinemann LB $25.64 (978-1-58810-628-5). 32pp. Technique, safety, gear, and profiles of famous skiers are all covered in this introduction to the sport. (Rev: BL 2/15/03; HBG 3/03) [796.93]

24834 Payan, Gregory. *Essential Snowmobiling for Teens* (5–9). Series: Outdoor Life. 2000, Children's paper $6.95 (978-0-516-23558-5). 48pp. The invention of the snowmobile is covered plus material on license requirements, trail permits, equipment, clothing, safety, driving techniques, and maintenance. (Rev: SLJ 2/01) [796.94]

24835 Peters, Craig. *Chants, Cheers, and Jumps* (5–8). Series: Let's Go Team. 2003, Mason Crest $19.95 (978-1-59084-535-6). Readers will learn the difference between cheers and chants and how to do various jumps. Also use *Competitive Cheerleading* (2003). (Rev: BL 10/15/03; SLJ 9/03) [791.6]

24836 Peters, Craig. *Cheerleading Stars* (5–8). Series: Let's Go Team. 2003, Mason Crest LB $19.95 (978-1-59084-533-2). This book highlights the careers and accomplishments of a select group of star cheerleaders. (Rev: BL 10/15/03; HBG 4/04) [791]

24837 Peters, Craig. *Techniques of Dance for Cheerleading* (5–8). Series: Let's Go Team. 2003, Mason Crest LB $19.95 (978-1-59084-531-8). 64pp. The importance of stretching and safety measures are emphasized in this volume that discusses choreography and the similarities and differences between cheerleading and dancing. (Rev: SLJ 9/03) [791.6]

24838 Price, Sean Stewart. *The Kids' Guide to Pro Wrestling* (3–5). Illus. Series: Kids' Guides. 2011, Capstone LB $26.65 (978-142966008-2). 32pp. Pro wrestling trivia, history, information, and even some choice moves are presented here. (Rev: BL 2/15/12) [796.812]

24839 Ripoll, Oriol. *Play with Us: 100 Games from Around the World* (3–5). Illus. 2005, Chicago Review paper $16.95 (978-1-55652-594-0). 128pp. Ball games, card games, checkers, hopscotch — these are only a few of the 100 games, both indoor and outdoor, included in this international collection that is indexed by continent. (Rev: BL 11/15/05; SLJ 1/06) [793]

24840 Roberts, Jeremy. *Rock and Ice Climbing! Top the Tower* (4–8). Series: Extreme Sports. 2000, Rosen LB $26.50 (978-0-8239-3009-8). This book on climbing covers the dangers, different climbing styles, equipment, techniques, and venues, and profiles some young climbers. (Rev: BL 3/15/00; SLJ 8/00) [796.52]

24841 Roberts, Robin. *Sports for Life: How Athletes Have More Fun* (5–8). Illus. Series: Get in the Game! 2000, Millbrook LB $23.90 (978-0-7613-1407-3). 48pp. This account, mainly for girls, explains how to enjoy sports through applying discipline, patience, cooperation, health, and the sheer fun of competition. (Rev: BL 1/1–15/01; HBG 3/01) [796]

24842 Roberts, Robin. *Which Sport Is Right for You?* (5–8). Series: Get in the Game! 2001, Millbrook LB $23.90 (978-0-7613-2117-0). 48pp. Written with girls in mind, this short book explores how to choose a sport that is right for one's capabilities and interests. (Rev: BL 9/15/01; HBG 3/02; SLJ 1/02) [796]

24843 Roper, Ingrid. *Yo-Yos: Tricks to Amaze Your Friends* (3–6). 2001, HarperCollins $15.95 (978-0-688-14663-4). 64pp. A guide to different kinds of yo-yos and yo-yo technique that starts with the basic and progresses to the more advanced. (Rev: BL 5/15/01; HBG 10/01; SLJ 8/01) [796.2]

24844 Rosen, Michael J. *Balls!* (4–7). 2006, Darby Creek $18.95 (978-1-58196-030-3). Balls used in all sorts of sports and their history, choice of shape, and method of construction are the topic of lighthearted discussion. (Rev: BL 6/1–15/06) [796.3]

24845 Ross, Dan. *Pro Wrestling's Greatest Wars* (4–7). Illus. Series: Pro Wrestling Legends. 2000, Chelsea $25.00 (978-0-7910-5837-4); paper $25.00 (978-0-7910-5838-1). Some of the great feuds in wrestling history, such as Harlem Heat vs. the Nasty Boys, are described in this fast read. (Rev: BL 10/15/00; HBG 3/01) [796.812]

24846 Ross, Stewart. *Sports Technology* (4–7). Illus. Series: New Technology. 2011, Black Rabbit LB $34.25 (978-159920534-2). 48pp. Technology's importance in all aspects of sports — equipment, judging and timing, surfaces and stadiums, clothing, machinery, training and cheating — is discussed in this attractive book. (Rev: BL 10/15/11) [688.76]

24847 Ryan, Pat. *Rock Climbing* (4–7). Illus. Series: World of Sports. 2000, Smart Apple LB $16.95 (978-1-887068-57-4). 32pp. In addition to covering the origins and evolution of rock climbing, this book discusses the basics of the sport, equipment, and star athletes. (Rev: BL 9/15/00) [796.52]

24848 Schindler, John E. *Hang Gliding and Parasailing* (2–5). Series: Extreme Sports: An Imagination Library Series. 2005, Gareth Stevens LB $23.00 (978-0-8368-4540-2); paper $5.95 (978-0-8368-4547-1). An introduction to this "extreme" sport, with brief text and colorful photographs suitable for reluctant readers. (Rev: SLJ 9/05) [797.5]

24849 Schindler, John E. *Skydiving* (2–5). 2005, Gareth Stevens LB $23.00 (978-0-8368-4543-3); paper $5.95 (978-0-8368-4550-1). A basic introduction to this "extreme" sport, with brief text and colorful photographs that will appeal to reluctant readers. (Rev: SLJ 9/05) [797.5]

24850 Schindler, John E. *Triathlons* (2–5). 2005, Gareth Stevens LB $23.00 (978-0-8368-4544-0); paper $5.95 (978-0-8368-4551-8 24pp.A basic introduction to this "extreme" sport, with brief text and colorful photographs that will appeal to reluctant readers. (Rev: SLJ 9/05) [796.42]). A basic introduction to this "extreme" sport, with brief text and colorful photographs that will appeal to reluctant readers. (Rev: SLJ 9/05) [796.42]

24851 Schwartz, Ellen. *I Love Yoga: A Guide for Kids and Teens* (5–12). Illus. by Ben Hodson. 2003, Tundra paper $9.95 (978-0-88776-598-8). Illustrated instructions for 18 basic poses are accompanied by breathing and relaxation exercises, discussion of the benefits of yoga, and a description of the different types of yoga practiced around the world. (Rev: SLJ 12/03; VOYA 10/03) [613.7]

24852 Seeberg, Tim. *Rock Climbing* (3–5). Illus. Series: Kids' Guides to the Outdoors. 2004, Child's World LB $25.64 (978-1-59296-033-0). 32pp. A useful guide for young people new to this sport, this book is loaded with tips about equipment and what to expect. [796.5]

24853 Sheely, Robert, and Louis Bourgeois. *Sports Lab: How Science Has Changed Sports* (4–7). Series: Science Lab. 1994, Silver Moon $14.95 (978-1-881889-49-6). Traces the effect on sports of applying findings from such branches of science as aerodynamics, psychology, and medicine. (Rev: SLJ 9/94) [617.1]

24854 Sherman, Josepha. *Barrel Racing* (4–6). Series: Rodeo. 2000, Heinemann LB $21.36 (978-1-57572-503-1). 32pp. Barrel racing training, skills, equipment, and schedules are covered here. Three other titles on rodeo events are *Bronc Riding*, *Bull Riding* and *Steer Wrestling* (all 2000). (Rev: BL 10/15/00; HBG 3/01; SLJ 8/00) [791.8]

24855 Sherman, Josepha. *Ropers and Riders* (4–6). Series: Rodeo. 2000, Heinemann LB $21.36 (978-1-57572-506-2). 32pp. A colorful book that features these stars of the rodeo, their skills, training, and lifestyles. (Rev: BL 10/15/00; HBG 3/01; SLJ 9/00) [791.8]

24856 Sherman, Josepha. *Welcome to the Rodeo!* (4–6). Illus. Series: Rodeo. 2000, Heinemann $21.36 (978-1-57572-508-6). 32pp. An introduction to rodeos with material on the various riding and roping competitions and

on famous rodeo stars. (Rev: BL 10/15/00; HBG 3/01; SLJ 9/00) [791.8]

24857 Silas, Elizabeth, and Diane Goodney. *Yoga* (4–8). Illus. Series: Life Balance. 2003, Watts LB $20.50 (978-0-531-12258-7); paper $6.95 (978-0-531-15577-6). 80pp. Information on the spiritual and philosophical aspects of yoga follows chapters on basic yoga moves. (Rev: BL 10/15/03) [613.7]

24858 Skreslet, Laurie, and Elizabeth MacLeod. *To the Top of Everest* (5–9). Illus. 2001, Kids Can $16.95 (978-1-55074-721-8). 56pp. Skreslet relates his lifelong ambition to climb Everest and his actual experiences doing so, with many facts about the mountain and the dangers involved and stunning photographs of his adventure. (Rev: BCCB 10/01; BL 9/15/01; HBG 3/02; SLJ 9/01*) [796.52]

24859 Smith, Graham. *Karting* (4–8). Series: Radical Sports. 2002, Heinemann LB $25.64 (978-1-58810-624-7). 32pp. The sport of karting is introduced with discussion of equipment selection, basic skills, fitness and training, and safety. (Rev: BL 2/15/03; HBG 3/03) [796.7]

24860 Smolka, Bo. *Lacrosse* (5–8). Illus. Series: Girls Play to Win. 2011, Norwood LB $27.93 (978-159953463-3). 64pp. Along with the history and rules of the sport, this volume discusses how women's lacrosse differs from men's. (Rev: BL 12/15/11) [796.34]

24861 Steiner, Andy. *Girl Power on the Playing Field: A Book About Girls, Their Goals, and Their Struggles* (5–10). Series: Girl Power. 2000, Lerner LB $30.35 (978-0-8225-2690-2). This book explains women's roles in sports with good personal guidance for young girls on participation and goals. (Rev: HBG 10/00; SLJ 6/00) [796]

24862 Steiner, Andy. *A Sporting Chance: Sports and Gender* (4–8). Series: Sports Issues. 1995, Lerner LB $28.75 (978-0-8225-3300-9). An overview of the hurdles that female athletes have had to overcome and the persistent inequality between men and women in sports at all levels, from Little League to the pros. (Rev: BL 1/1–15/96; SLJ 1/96) [796]

24863 Sullivan, George. *Any Number Can Play: The Numbers Athletes Wear* (4–8). 2000, Millbrook LB $23.90 (978-0-7613-1557-5). A fascinating glimpse at players' devotion to their assigned numbers, along with information on retired and banned numbers and who uses the number 13. (Rev: BL 12/15/00; HBG 3/01; SLJ 2/01; VOYA 2/01) [796]

24864 Sullivan, George. *Don't Step on the Foul Line: Sports Superstitions* (4–8). Illus. 2000, Millbrook LB $23.90 (978-0-7613-1558-2). 80pp. This is an intriguing look at superstitions, customs, and traditions associated with many different sports. (Rev: BL 12/15/00; HBG 3/01; SLJ 2/01; VOYA 2/01) [796.357]

24865 Szwast, Ursula. *Cheerleading* (3–6). Series: Get Going! Hobbies. 2005, Heinemann LB $27.79 (978-1-4034-6116-2). 32pp. This guide reviews basic moves and positions and discusses both competitive cheerleading and the history of cheerleading. (Rev: SLJ 3/06) [791.6]

24866 Takeda, Pete. *Climb! Your Guide to Bouldering, Sport Climbing, Trad Climbing, Ice Climbing, Alpinism, and More* (4–9). Series: Extreme Sports. 2002, National Geographic paper $8.95 (978-0-7922-6744-7). An attractive guide to climbing of all types — sport, wall, ice, alpine, and so forth — and to the equipment, techniques, and dangers. (Rev: SLJ 1/03) [796.5223]

24867 Valliant, Doris. *Going to College* (5–8). Series: Let's Go Team. 2003, Mason Crest LB $19.95 (978-1-59084-541-7). 64pp. This well-illustrated, breezy account describes the function of cheerleading in college sports activities. (Rev: BL 10/15/03; SLJ 1/04) [791]

24868 Valliant, Doris. *The History of Cheerleading* (5–8). Series: Let's Go Team. 2003, Mason Crest LB $19.95 (978-1-59084-534-9). Using many illustrations, this slim volume describes the history and function of cheerleading at various levels in this country. (Rev: BL 10/15/03; HBG 4/04; SLJ 1/04) [791]

24869 Wells, Don. *For the Love of Golf* (3–5). Illus. Series: For the Love of Sports. 2005, Weigl LB $24.45 (978-1-59036-296-9). 24pp. Colorful double-page spreads present the fundamentals of golf, as well as the history of the game and information on famous players. (Rev: BL 9/1/05) [796.352]

24870 Wells, Garrison. *Brazilian Jiujitsu: Ground-Fighting Combat* (5–8). Illus. Series: Martial Arts Sports Zone. 2012, Lerner LB $26.60 (978-076138456-4). 32pp. A compact introduction to the techniques involved in this form of judo. (Rev: BL 9/1/12) [796.81520981]

24871 Willard, Keith. *Ballooning* (4–7). Illus. Series: World of Sports. 2000, Smart Apple LB $16.95 (978-1-887068-51-2). 32pp. This brief introduction to ballooning mentions star balloonists, different kinds of ballooning, the origins of this sport, and how one becomes proficient at it. (Rev: BL 9/15/00) [797.5]

24872 Willker, Joshua D. G. *Everything You Need to Know About the Dangers of Sports Gambling* (5–10). Series: Need to Know Library. 2000, Rosen LB $27.95 (978-0-8239-3229-0). This brief, well-written book surveys the world of gambling on sports, its legal and illegal aspects, and how it has ruined the careers of many fine athletes. (Rev: BL 1/1–15/01) [796]

24873 Wiseman, Blaine. *Ultimate Fighting* (4–7). Series: Sporting Championships. 2011, Weigl $26 (978-1616901301). This is an appealing, colorful introduction to the world of mixed martial arts and the championship competition that features athletes trained in boxing, wrestling, karate, and so forth. (Rev: LMC 11–12/10) [796.815]

24874 Woods, Bob. *Snowmobile Racers* (4–6). Illus. Series: Kid Racers. 2010, Enslow LB $23.93 (978-076603487-7). 48pp. Reluctant readers will enjoy the illustrations and information on the equipment and techniques of safe snowmobile racing. (Rev: BL 9/1/10) [796.94]

24875 Wulffson, Don L. *Toys! Amazing Stories Behind Some Great Inventions* (4–6). Illus. 2000, Holt $15.95 (978-0-8050-6196-3). 136pp. The story behind such toys as Mr. Potato Head, Slinky, Silly Putty, kites, checkers, and Parcheesi is told in 25 illustrated chapters each dealing with a different game or toy. (Rev: BCCB 6/00; BL 6/1–15/00; HBG 3/01; SLJ 9/00) [688.7]

24876 Wurdinger, Scott, and Leslie Rapparlie. *Ice Climbing* (5–9). Series: Adventure Sports. 2006, Creative Education LB $31.35 (978-1-58341-393-7). This well-designed guide to ice climbing familiarizes readers with the sport's history, equipment, competitions, and safety measures. (Rev: SLJ 12/06) [796.52]

Automobile Racing

24877 Braun, Eric. *Hot Rods* (3–5). Illus. Series: Motor Mania. 2006, Lerner LB $26.60 (978-0-8225-3531-7). 48pp. A basic introduction to these customized cars and how they're raced as well as information on their history, how they're built, and what they look like. (Rev: BL 10/1/06; SLJ 3/07) [629.228]

24878 Buckley, James. *NASCAR* (5–8). Series: Eyewitness Books. 2005, DK LB $19.99 (978-0-7566-1193-4). A visual pleasure for NASCAR fans, full of information about people, places, individual races, engineering advances, and so forth. (Rev: BL 9/1/05) [796.72]

24879 Caldwell, Dave. *Speed Show: How NASCAR Won the Heart of America* (5–8). 2006, Kingfisher $16.95 (978-0-7534-6011-5). The history of NASCAR, the basics of stock car racing, its famous drivers, its fans, and so forth are all described in this very readable book by a *New York Times* sports writer. (Rev: BL 11/15/06; SLJ 3/07) [796.720973]

24880 Doeden, Matt. *NASCAR's Wildest Wrecks* (3–6). Series: Edge Books/NASCAR Racing. 2004, Capstone LB $23.93 (978-0-7368-3775-0). 32pp. An overview of famous NASCAR crashes, complete with color photographs, and of the safety measures prompted by these accidents. (Rev: SLJ 7/05) [796.72]

24881 Doeden, Matt. *Stock Cars* (3–5). Illus. Series: Motor Mania. 2006, Lerner LB $26.60 (978-0-8225-3530-0). 48pp. Describes stock cars and their history, racing, and famous drivers. (Rev: SLJ 3/07) [796.72]

24882 Dooling, Michael. *The Great Horse-less Carriage Race* (2–4). Illus. 2002, Holiday House $16.95 (978-0-8234-1640-0). 32pp. Car lovers will particularly appreciate this lively picture-book presentation of the country's first car race, which took place in Chicago in 1895, with competitors reaching the heady average speed of 7 mph. (Rev: BCCB 2/03; BL 11/15/02; HBG 3/03; SLJ 12/02) [796.72]

24883 Eagen, Rachel. *NASCAR* (4–7). Series: Automania. 2006, Crabtree $26.60 (978-0-7787-3007-1). An excellent, photo-filled overview of NASCAR's history, rules, safety measures, cars, and leading drivers. (Rev: BL 9/1/06) [796.720973]

24884 Egan, Erin. *Hottest Race Cars* (4–6). Illus. Series: Wild Wheels! 2007, Enslow LB $17.95 (978-0-7660-2871-5). 48pp. All about "open-wheel" cars and drivers, race strategy, and traditions with full-color photographs. (Rev: BL 10/15/07) [796.72]

24885 Franks, Katie. *I Want to Be a Race Car Driver* (3–5). Illus. Series: Dream Jobs. 2007, Rosen LB $15.95 (978-1-4042-3623-3). 24pp. Safety, pits stops, and famous races and drivers are all covered in this brief introduction to stock-car racing. (Rev: BL 6/1–15/07; SLJ 7/07) [796.72]

24886 Herzog, Brad. *R Is for Race: A Stock Car Alphabet* (3–5). 2006, Sleeping Bear $16.95 (978-1-58536-272-1). 32pp. The variety of formats in this A to Z of auto racing will suit readers of different ages and needs. (Rev: BL 8/06) [796.72]

24887 Howell, Brian. *Amazing Auto Racing Records* (3–5). Illus. Series: Amazing Sports Records. 2013, Child's World LB $27.07 (978-161473400-0). 32pp. Useful for report writers, this attractive volume provides both history and facts. (Rev: BL 5/1/13) [796.72]

24888 Johnstone, Mike. *NASCAR* (5–8). Series: Need for Speed. 2002, Lerner LB $23.93 (978-0-8225-0389-7). 32pp. A look at the fast-growing sport of NASCAR auto racing, with detailed descriptions of the drivers, their cars, and the circuits. (Rev: BL 8/02; HBG 10/02; SLJ 7/02) [796.7]

24889 Kelley, K. C. *Hottest NASCAR Machines* (5–7). Series: Wild Wheels! 2007, Enslow LB $23.93 (978-0-7660-2869-2). Colorful photographs and helpful fact boxes highlight interesting information on cars used on the NASCAR circuit. Also use *Hottest Muscle Cars* and *Hottest Sports Cars* (both 2007). (Rev: SLJ 4/08)

24890 Miller, Tim. *Vroom!* (4–6). 2006, Tundra paper $17.95 (978-0-88776-755-5). 64pp. A large-format introduction to the many different types of auto racing, featuring facts and history on each and plenty of action photographs. (Rev: BL 11/15/06) [796]

24891 Morganelli, Adrianna. *Formula One* (4–6). Series: Automania! 2006, Crabtree LB $25.20 (978-0-7787-3009-5); paper $8.95 (978-0-7787-3031-6). 32pp. The Grand Prix races in Europe and their amazing cars are the focus here. The photographs will thrill race fans. (Rev: SLJ 8/07)

24892 Parr, Danny. *Lowriders* (4–7). Series: Wild Rides! 2001, Capstone LB $23.93 (978-0-7368-0928-3). This volume on "lowrider" cars discusses the types of vehicles that are popular, the history of this trend, and the competitions that are held. (Rev: BL 10/15/01; HBG 3/02) [628.28]

24893 Pearce, Al. *Famous Tracks* (4–8). Series: Race Car Legends: Collector's Edition. 2005, Chelsea House LB $25.00 (978-0-7910-8692-6). Four well-known racetracks are the focus of this readable title full of photographs. (Rev: SLJ 5/06; VOYA 4/06) [796.72]

24894 Piehl, Janet. *Formula One Race Cars* (3–5). Illus. 2006, Lerner LB $26.60 (978-0-8225-5929-0). 48pp. Describes Formula One racing cars and their history and famous drivers. (Rev: SLJ 3/07)

24895 Pimm, Nancy Roe. *The Daytona 500: The Thrill and Thunder of the Great American Race* (5–8). Series: Spectacular Sports. 2011, Millbrook $29.27 (978-0-7613-6677-5). 64pp. This visually appealing book features lots of information about the early days of NASCAR racing, including tragedies and rivalries. e (Rev: BL 3/1/11; SLJ 5/11) [796.7]

24896 Schaefer, A. R. *The Daytona 500* (4–7). Illus. Series: NASCAR Racing. 2004, Capstone LB $23.93 (978-0-7368-2423-1). 32pp. This slim volume celebrates one of America's most famous automobile racing venues and some of the illustrious drivers who achieved fame there. (Rev: BL 4/1/04) [790.72]

24897 Schaefer, A. R. *Racing with the Pit Crew* (3–6). Series: Edge Books/NASCAR Racing. 2005, Capstone paper $7.95 (978-0-7368-5235-7). 32pp. A look at the work performed by the pit crew and the safety and other concerns they must monitor. Also use *The History of NASCAR* (2005). (Rev: SLJ 7/05) [796.72]

24898 Stewart, Mark, and Mike Kennedy. *NASCAR at the Track* (4–6). Series: The Science of NASCAR. 2008, Lerner LB $27.93 (978-0-8225-8741-5). 48pp. Stewart explores the differences between the various NASCAR tracks in this eye-catching volume that includes problems to solve. Also use *NASCAR in the Pits* (2008). (Rev: LMC 10/08; SLJ 4/08) [796.72]

24899 Stewart, Mark, and Mike Kennedy. *NASCAR in the Driver's Seat* (4–6). Illus. Series: Science of NASCAR. 2008, Lerner LB $27.93 (978-0-8225-8737-8). 48pp. NASCAR racing scenarios are used to introduce basic mathematical and physical principles in this accessible and visually pleasing book that includes problems to solve and experiments. (Rev: BL 4/1/08; SLJ 4/08) [796.72]

Baseball

24900 Aretha, David. *Power in Pinstripes: The New York Yankees* (4–7). Series: Sensational Sports Teams. 2007, Enslow LB $24.95 (978-1-59845-044-6). Fans of this winning team will enjoy this book that includes the ball club's history, its top players, its World Series achievements, and lots of links to Web sites. (Rev: BL 7/07) [796.357]

24901 Bildner, Phil. *The Unforgettable Season: The Story of Joe DiMaggio, Ted Williams, and the Record-Setting Summer of '41* (2–4). Illus. by S. D. Schindler. 2011, Putnam $16.99 (978-0-399-25501-4). 32pp. A handsome tribute to the talents of the baseball greats of 1941. Lexile AD980L (Rev: BLO 5/1/11; HB 5–6/11; SLJ 3/1/11*) [796.357]

24902 Bowen, Fred. *No Easy Way: The Story of Ted Williams and the Last .400 Season* (1–3). Illus. by Charles S. Pyle. 2010, Dutton $16.99 (978-0-525-47877-5). 32pp. A picture-book celebration of the baseball great, his lasting dreams, and his determination to win. (Rev: BL 12/15/09; LMC 3–4/10; SLJ 1/1/10) [921]

24903 Brown, Jonatha A. *Baseball* (1–3). Series: My Favorite Sport. 2005, Weekly Reader LB $21.00 (978-0-8368-4337-8). 24pp. For beginning readers, this is an introduction to the history and sport of baseball, defining key terms. (Rev: SLJ 5/05)

24904 Buckley, James, Jr. *Ultimate Guide to Baseball* (4–7). Illus. by Mike Arnold. Series: Scholastic Ultimate Guides. 2010, Scholastic LB $30 (978-0-531-20750-5). 160pp. An appealing review of key events, teams, athletes, slang, and all other aspects of baseball. (Rev: BL 6/10; SLJ 5/10; VOYA 8/10) [796.357]

24905 Burke, Jim. *Take Me Out to the Ball Game* (2–4). Illus. 2006, Little, Brown $16.99 (978-0-316-75819-2). 32pp. Burke uses the classic song as the backdrop for the story of a famous 1908 game between the New York Giants and the Chicago Cubs. (Rev: BL 4/1/06; SLJ 4/06) [796.357]

24906 Coleman, Janet Wyman, and Elizabeth V. Warren. *Baseball for Everyone: Stories from the Great Game* (4–6). 2003, Abrams $16.95 (978-0-8109-4580-7). 48pp. Based on an exhibition at the American Folk Art Museum, this attractively illustrated volume uses many interesting anecdotes in chronicling the history of baseball. (Rev: BL 9/1/03; HBG 4/04; SLJ 10/03) [796.357]

24907 Cook, Sally, and James Charlton. *Hey Batta Batta Swing!* (3–5). Illus. by Ross MacDonald. 2007, Simon & Schuster $17.99 (978-1-4169-1207-1). 56pp. This buoyant history of baseball's early years provides fascinating facts about team names, players' numbers, equipment, and so forth; antique typography and colorful illustrations recalling early cartoons complement the lively text. (Rev: BL 1/1–15/07) [796.3]

24908 Curlee, Lynn. *Ballpark: The Story of America's Baseball Fields* (4–6). Illus. 2005, Simon & Schuster $17.95 (978-0-689-86742-2). 48pp. All about baseball stadiums, both the loved and the not-so-loved, from the mid-1800s through today. (Rev: BL 3/15/05; SLJ 3/05) [796.357]

24909 Driscoll, Laura. *Negro Leagues: All-Black Baseball* (3–5). Illus. by Tracy Mitchell. Series: Smart About History. 2002, Grosset paper $5.99 (978-0-448-42684-6). 32pp. Through Emily's report on her visit to the National Baseball Hall of Fame, readers learn about the history of the Negro Leagues and the famous African American players. (Rev: BL 9/1/02; HBG 3/03; SLJ 12/02) [796.35764]

24910 Fuerst, Jeffrey B. *The Kids' Baseball Workout: A Fun Way to Get in Shape and Improve Your Game* (5–8). Illus. by Anne Canevari Green. 2002, Millbrook LB $24.90 (978-0-7613-2307-5). This book offers exercises, stretches, and skills that will help young base-ball players improve their game. (Rev: BL 9/1/02; HBG 10/02; SLJ 7/02) [796.357]

24911 Gardner, Robert, and Dennis Shortelle. *The Forgotten Players: The Story of Black Baseball in America* (5–8). 1993, Walker LB $13.85 (978-0-8027-8249-6). A discussion of the challenges that faced the players of the Negro Leagues. (Rev: BL 2/15/93; SLJ 4/93) [769.357]

24912 Gibbons, Gail. *My Baseball Book* (PS–3). Illus. 2000, HarperCollins $6.99 (978-0-688-17137-7). 24pp. An attractive introduction to baseball that describes the playing field, positions, equipment, and game plays. (Rev: BCCB 4/00; BL 5/1/00; HBG 10/00; SLJ 6/00) [796.357]

24913 Glaser, Jason. *Catcher* (4–7). Illus. Series: Play Ball: Baseball. 2011, Gareth Stevens LB $31.95 (978-143394483-3). 48pp. Explaining the difficult role of catcher — which demands intellectual qualities as well as physical strength and flexibility — this book also profiles well-known catchers and gives tips on how to ace the position. (Rev: BL 4/1/11; SLJ 4/1/11) [796.357]

24914 Goodman, Michael E. *The Story of the Boston Red Sox* (5–8). Illus. 2011, Creative Education LB $23.95 (978-160818034-9). 48pp. The star-studded history of the Boston Red Sox is chronicled in this statistics-filled title full of archival and contemporary photographs. (Rev: BL 2/1/12)

24915 Goodman, Michael E. *The Story of the San Francisco Giants* (5–8). Illus. 2011, Creative Education LB $23.95 (978-160818055-4). 48pp. The city-hopping history of the San Francisco Giants is chronicled in this statistics-filled title full of archival and contemporary photographs. (Rev: BL 2/1/12)

24916 Grabowski, John. *The Boston Red Sox Baseball Team* (4–6). Series: Great Sports Teams. 2001, Enslow $23.93 (978-0-7660-1488-6). 48pp. This introduction to the Boston Red Sox gives lively information on the team's past, present, and future prospects. (Rev: BL 9/15/01; HBG 10/01) [796.357]

24917 Howell, Brian. *Amazing Baseball Records* (3–5). Illus. Series: Amazing Sports Records. 2013, Child's World LB $27.07 (978-161473401-7). 32pp. Useful for report writers, this attractive volume provides both history and facts. (Rev: BL 5/1/13) [796.357]

24918 Isadora, Rachael. *Nick Plays Baseball* (2–4). Illus. 2001, Penguin $15.99 (978-0-399-23231-2). 32pp. Using a fictional story about Nick and his team as a framework, this oversize picture book gives information on batting, pitching, equipment, playing positions, and the rules of the game. (Rev: BCCB 2/01; BL 2/15/01; HBG 3/02) [796.357]

24919 Kellogg, David. *True Stories of Baseball's Hall of Famers* (4–8). 2000, Bluewood $8.95 (978-0-912517-41-4). Using a chronological approach, this book profiles 60 Hall of Famers and tells why each is there. (Rev: BL 10/15/00; VOYA 8/01) [796.357]

24920 Kennedy, Mike. *Baseball* (2–4). Series: True Books — Sports. 2002, Children's Book Pr. LB $25.00 (978-0-516-22334-6). 48pp. Using large type and many color photographs, this is a simple introduction to baseball, its history, and how it is played. (Rev: BL 9/1/02; SLJ check) [796.357]

24921 Kisseloff, Jeff. *Who Is Baseball's Greatest Pitcher?* (5–7). 2003, Cricket $15.95 (978-0-8126-2685-8). The author presents profiles of 33 pitchers, with relevant statistics, and challenges the reader to choose the best and justify this decision. (Rev: BL 7/03; HBG 10/03; SLJ 5/03) [796.359]

24922 Krasner, Steven. *Play Ball Like the Pros: Tips for Kids from 20 Big League Stars* (5–9). 2002, Peachtree paper $12.95 (978-1-56145-261-3). Each chapter features a professional player talking about the position he plays and giving tips to the young athlete. (Rev: BL 5/1/02; SLJ 6/02; VOYA 10/03) [796.357]

24923 LeBoutillier, Nate. *The Story of the Los Angeles Dodgers* (5–8). Illus. 2011, Creative Education LB $23.95 (978-160818045-5). 48pp. The city-hopping history of the Los Angeles Dodgers is chronicled in this statistics-filled title full of archival and contemporary photographs. (Rev: BL 2/1/12)

24924 Mackin, Bob. *Record-Breaking Baseball Trivia* (5–8). 2000, Douglas & McIntyre $6.95 (978-1-55054-757-3). Questions, answers, and quizzes cover topics including baseball history, team play, World Series facts, and trivia from the plate and mound. (Rev: BL 9/15/00) [796.357]

24925 Nelson, Kadir. *We Are the Ship: The Story of Negro League Baseball* (5–8). Illus. by author. 2008, Hyperion $18.99 (978-0-7868-0832-8). Beautiful illustrations accompany a history of the league told by an anonymous but proud former player. (Rev: BL 2/1/08; SLJ 1/08) [796.357]

24926 Nevius, Carol. *Baseball Hour* (1–3). Illus. by Bill Thomson. 2008, Marshall Cavendish $16.99 (978-0-7614-5380-2). 32pp. Photorealistic art and brief rhyming text bring a baseball practice session to life. (Rev: BL 4/1/08; LMC 10/08; SLJ 6/08) [796.357]

24927 Nitz, Kristin Wolden. *Softball* (5–9). Series: Play-by-Play. 2000, Lerner paper $23.93 (978-0-8225-9875-6). 80pp. Good basic information about softball is given including history, rules, equipment, and positions. (Rev: SLJ 9/00) [796.357]

24928 Omoth, Tyler. *The Story of the Chicago Cubs* (3–6). Illus. Series: Baseball: The Great American Game. 2007, Creative Education $22.95 (978-1-58341-482-8). 48pp. Omoth offers a history of the Chicago baseball team, including details of the many defeats the team has suffered in recent years. (Rev: BL 10/15/07) [796.357]

24929 Patrick, Jean L. S. *The Girl Who Struck Out Babe Ruth* (2–3). Illus. by Jeni Reeves. 2000, Lerner $23.93 (978-1-57505-397-4); paper $5.95 (978-1-57505-455-1). In 1931, 17-year-old Jackie Mitchell, a pitcher in the minor leagues, played in an exhibition game in which she struck out Babe Ruth and Lou Gehrig. (Rev: BCCB 6/00; BL 4/15/00; HBG 10/00; SLJ 8/00) [796.357]

24930 Pietrusza, David. *The Baltimore Orioles Baseball Team* (4–6). Series: Great Sports Teams. 2000, Enslow LB $23.93 (978-0-7660-1283-7). 48pp. Covers the history of the Baltimore Orioles, the team's best players, and its performance today and tomorrow. (Rev: BL 5/15/00; HBG 10/00) [796.357]

24931 Pietrusza, David. *The Cleveland Indians Baseball Team* (4–6). Series: Great Sports Teams. 2001, Enslow $23.93 (978-0-7660-1491-6). 48pp. Using fast-paced writing and many photographs, Pietrusza supplies a good thumbnail sketch of the team, its famous players, and outstanding games. (Rev: BL 9/15/01; HBG 3/02) [796.357]

24932 Pietrusza, David. *The San Francisco Giants Baseball Team* (4–6). Series: Great Sports Teams. 2000, Enslow LB $23.93 (978-0-7660-1284-4). 48pp. Plenty of sports action is included in this introduction to the past, present, and future of the San Francisco Giants. (Rev: BL 5/15/00; HBG 10/00) [795.357]

24933 Pietrusza, David. *The St. Louis Cardinals Baseball Team* (4–6). Series: Great Sports Teams. 2001, Enslow $23.93 (978-0-7660-1490-9). 48pp. An exciting introduction to the team with material on its history, key players, exciting seasons, and present status. (Rev: BL 9/15/01; HBG 3/02)

24934 Preller, James. *McGwire and Sosa: A Season to Remember* (4–7). 1998, Simon & Schuster paper $5.99 (978-0-689-82871-3). An oversize paperback that traces the baseball season that brought Sosa and McGwire to the nation's attention and made them sports heroes. (Rev: BL 1/1–15/99) [796.357]

24935 Sandler, Michael. *Baseball: The 2004 Boston Red Sox* (3–5). Illus. Series: Upsets and Comebacks. 2006, Bearport LB $25.27 (978-1-59716-165-7). 32pp. Full of photographs, this tells the story of Red Sox' triumphant 2004 season; with trivia, timeline, bibliography, glossary, and Web sites. (Rev: BL 4/1/06; SLJ 7/06) [796.357]

24936 Shaughnessy, Dan. *The Legend of the Curse of the Bambino* (2–4). Illus. by C. F. Payne. 2005, Simon & Schuster $16.95 (978-0-689-87235-8). 32pp. A father tells his daughter about Babe Ruth and the "curse" that kept the Boston Red Sox from winning the World Series until 2004. (Rev: BL 3/15/05; SLJ 5/05) [796.357]

24937 Stewart, Mark, and Mike Kennedy. *Long Ball: The Legend and Lore of the Home Run* (3–5). Illus. 2006, Millbrook LB $22.60 (978-0-7613-2779-0). 64pp. Containing photographs and reproductions of baseball cards and magazine covers, this attractive book chronicles the history of the home run and profiles some of baseball's most notable long-ball hitters. (Rev: BL 4/1/06; SLJ 6/06; VOYA 6/06) [796.357]

24938 Suen, Anastasia. *The Story of Baseball* (1–3). Illus. Series: Sports History. 2002, Rosen LB $19.95 (978-0-8239-6000-2). 24pp. A basic, easy-to-read introduction to the sport. (Rev: BL 5/15/02) [796.357]

24939 Sullivan, George. *Baseball's Boneheads, Bad Boys, and Just Plain Crazy Guys* (5–8). Illus. by Anne Canevari Green. 2003, Millbrook LB $23.90 (978-0-7613-2321-1); paper $8.95 (978-0-7613-1928-3). 64pp. An amusing collection of anecdotes that show the humor, superstitions, and general nuttiness of baseball players. (Rev: BL 7/03; HBG 10/03; SLJ 11/03) [790.357]

24940 Teitelbaum, Michael. *Baseball* (4–7). Illus. Series: Innovation in Sports. 2008, Cherry Lake LB $18.95 (978-160279255-5). 32pp. Teitelbaum tells the story of baseball by focusing not on the athletes but on the development of the rules, equipment, and training and profiling lesser-known figures — such as the man who invented box scoring — who made important contributions. (Rev: BL 9/1/08) [796.357]

24941 Thomas, Keltie. *How Baseball Works* (3–6). Illus. by Greg Hall. 2004, Maple Tree $19.95 (978-1-894379-60-1). 64pp. A detailed overview of baseball and its history and techniques, plus information on famous players. (Rev: BL 5/15/04; SLJ 11/04) [796]

24942 Thomas, Ron, and Joe Herran. *Getting into Baseball* (2–4). Illus. by Nives Porcellato and Andy Craig. Series: Getting into Sports. 2005, Chelsea House LB $28.00 (978-0-7910-8808-1). After a brief history of the game, this book covers rules, equipment, clothing, and competitions and provides color photographs, useful diagrams, and interesting trivia. (Rev: SLJ 12/05) [796.357]

24943 Tocher, Timothy. *Odd Ball: Hilarious, Unusual, and Bizarre Baseball Moments* (3–6). Illus. by Stacy Curtis. 2011, Marshall Cavendish $15.99 (978-0-7614-5813-5). 64pp. A fascinating and humorous collection of baseball trivia. (Rev: BL 4/15/11; SLJ 6/11) [796.357]

24944 Vernick, Audrey. *Brothers at Bat: The True Story of An Amazing All-Brother Baseball Team* (1–3). Illus. by Steven Salerno. 2012, Clarion $16.99 (978-054738557-0). 40pp. The true story of a passionate baseball-playing New Jersey family — the Acerras — whose children form their own semipro team in 1938 and became the longest-running all-brother team in history. Lexile AD780L (Rev: BL 4/15/12*; HB 3–4/12; LMC 10/12; SLJ 4/12) [796.35709749]

24945 Weatherford, Carole Boston. *A Negro League Scrapbook* (2–4). Illus. 2005, Boyds Mills $19.95 (978-1-59078-091-6). 48pp. The colorful history of baseball's Negro Leagues is documented in an interesting scrapbook format. (Rev: BL 2/1/05; SLJ 3/05) [796.357]

24946 Will, Sandra. *Baseball for Fun!* (2–4). Illus. Series: Sports for Fun. 2003, Compass Point LB $25.26 (978-0-7565-0428-1). 48pp. Covering rules, necessary skills, and key figures, this is an attractive introduction for beginning readers. (Rev: SLJ 6/03) [796.357]

24947 Wong, Stephen. *Baseball Treasures* (4–7). Illus. by Susan Einstein. 2007, HarperCollins $16.99 (978-0-06-114464-6). An inside look at the Smithsonian Institution's collection of baseball memorabilia, revealing how much the equipment has changed since the early days of the game. (Rev: BL 12/15/07) [796.3570]

24948 Woodyard, Janelle Valido. *A Girl's Guide to Softball* (3–5). Illus. Series: Get in the Game. 2012, Capstone LB $27.32 (978-142967672-4). 32pp. After a quiz that assesses their knowledge, this book guides readers through the rules, positions, and techniques of the game

as well as providing advice on general fitness and working with others. (Rev: BL 9/1/12) [796.357]

24949 Young, Robert. *A Personal Tour of Camden Yards* (4–7). Series: How It Was. 1999, Lerner LB $30.35 (978-0-8225-3578-2). Designed to remind fans of famous old ballparks, this book visits Camden Yards, home of the Baltimore Orioles. The reader inspects the field, visits the old warehouse, and views the game from a skybox. (Rev: BL 6/1–15/99; HBG 10/99) [796.357]

Basketball

24950 Aretha, David. *The Detroit Pistons Basketball Team* (4–6). Series: Great Sports Teams. 2001, Enslow LB $23.93 (978-0-7660-1487-9). 48pp. In narrative and pictures, this volume highlights the history and achievements of the Detroit Pistons with material on their key players and important seasons, past and present. (Rev: BL 12/15/01; HBG 3/02) [796.323]

24951 Coleman, Lori. *Girls' Basketball: Making Your Mark on the Court* (3–6). Series: Girls Got Game. 2006, Capstone LB $25.26 (978-0-7368-6821-1). 32pp. Especially for girls, this overview of basketball will get readers excited about the sport. (Rev: SLJ 7/07)

24952 Gibbons, Gail. *My Basketball Book* (K–2). Illus. 2000, HarperCollins $6.99 (978-0-688-17140-7). 24pp. This small-format paperback book contains the basics of basketball with coverage of equipment, positions, and rules. (Rev: BL 9/15/00; HBG 3/01; SLJ 11/00) [796.323]

24953 Gifford, Clive. *Basketball: From Warm-up to Final Whistle — The Essential Guide* (4–6). Illus. 2012, Kingfisher $15.99 (978-075346872-2). 64pp. Introduces the basics of basketball play, with discussion of college and professional teams as well as international competition. (Rev: BL 9/1/12) [796.323]

24954 Glenn, Mike. *Lessons in Success from the NBA's Top Players* (5–7). 1998, Visions 3000 paper $14.95 (978-0-9649795-5-0). This noted sportsman tells about his career in the NBA while introducing each of the NBA teams and its strengths. (Rev: BL 7/98) [796.323]

24955 Hoblin, Paul. *Amazing Basketball Records* (3–5). Illus. Series: Amazing Sports Records. 2013, Child's World LB $27.07 (978-161473402-4). 32pp. Useful for report writers, this attractive volume provides both history and facts. (Rev: BL 5/1/13) [796.323]

24956 Kelley, James S. *The Central Division* (3–5). Illus. Series: Above the Rim. 2008, Child's World LB $19.95 (978-1-59296-982-1). 40pp. Basketball's Central Division — its history, players, and interesting facts and figures — is the focus of this slim volume with full-color photographs. (Rev: BL 4/1/08) [796.323]

24957 Kennedy, Mike. *Basketball* (3–5). Series: True Books — Sports. 2002, Children's Book Pr. LB $25.00 (978-0-516-22335-3). 48pp. Covers the basic elements of basketball, its history, and superstars, with color photographs on each page plus large type and simple text. (Rev: BL 1/1–15/03) [796.323]

24958 Lannin, Joanne. *A History of Basketball for Girls and Women: From Bloomers to the Big Leagues* (5–9). Series: Sports Legacy. 2000, Lerner LB $26.63 (978-0-8225-3331-3); paper $9.95 (978-0-8225-9863-3). From the creation of basketball in 1891 to today, this account describes women's roles. (Rev: BL 1/1–15/01; HBG 3/01; SLJ 2/01; VOYA 4/01) [796.323]

24959 Macy, Sue. *Basketball Belles: How Two Teams and One Scrappy Player Put Women's Hoops on the Map* (3–5). Illus. by Matt Collins. 2011, Holiday House $16.95 (978-0-8234-2163-3). 32pp. The first all-female intercollegiate basketball game is described from the perspective of Stanford's Agnes Morley, a guard in the historic game against Berkeley in 1896. (Rev: BL 3/15/11*; LMC 8–9/11; SLJ 4/11) [796.3]

24960 Owens, Thomas S. *Basketball Arenas* (5–8). Illus. Series: Sports Palaces. 2002, Millbrook LB $25.90 (978-0-7613-1766-1). 64pp. Lots of basketball lore and history are included in a visit to the Boston Garden, Chicago Stadium, and the old Madison Square Garden. (Rev: BL 6/1–15/02; HBG 10/02) [796.323]

24961 Parselle, Matt. *Basketball: Learn How to Be a Star Player* (3–5). Illus. by Mel Pickering. Series: Sports Club. 2000, Two-Can $9.95 (978-1-58728-000-9). 32pp. This basic book on basketball explains different kinds of passes and the rules of the game, as well as giving some history and profiles of a few important players. (Rev: SLJ 3/01) [796.323]

24962 Roberts, Robin. *Basketball Year: What It's Like to Be a Woman Pro* (4–6). Illus. Series: Get in the Game! 2000, Millbrook $21.90 (978-0-7613-1406-6). 48pp. This account follows women of the WNBA as they train, travel, play games, and try to lead normal lives. (Rev: BL 9/1/00; HBG 10/00; SLJ 8/00) [796.323]

24963 Schulz, Randy. *The New York Knicks Basketball Team* (4–6). Series: Great Sports Teams. 2000, Enslow LB $23.93 (978-0-7660-1281-3). 48pp. The New York Nicks are profiled with material on the team's history, greatest players, and most exciting games. (Rev: BL 9/15/00; HBG 10/01) [796.323]

24964 Silverman, Steve. *The Story of the Indiana Pacers* (5–8). Illus. Series: The NBA: A History of Hoops. 2010, Creative Education $23.95 (978-158341946-5). 48pp. With plenty of action-packed photographs this volume tells the story of this team, its key players, and best games. (Rev: BL 9/1/10) [796.323]

24965 Skogen, J. M. *Oklahoma City Thunder* (2–4). Illus. Series: On the Hardwood. 2013, Lerner LB $27.93 (978-161570515-3); paper $8.95 (9781615705146). 48pp. Tells the story of the creation of the Thunder basketball team, its relationship with Oklahoma City, and its successes on the court. (Rev: BL 4/1/13; SLJ 4/13) [796]

24966 Stewart, Mark. *The Georgetown Hoyas* (4–7). Illus. Series: Team Spirit: College Basketball. 2010, Norwood LB $26.60 (978-159953364-3). 48pp. A look at the history of university's basketball team, the key play-

ers and coaches, uniform, and so forth, with lots of photographs and statistics. (Rev: BL 9/1/10) [796.323]

24967 Stewart, Mark. *The Miami Heat* (3–5). Illus. Series: Team Spirit. 2006, Norwood House LB $18.95 (978-0-599-53009-6). 48pp. An attractive profile of professional basketball's Miami Heat, examining the team's brief history, its standout players, and performance. (Rev: BL 4/1/06) [796.323]

24968 Stewart, Mark. *The NBA Finals* (5–10). Series: Watts History of Sports. 2003, Watts LB $34.50 (978-0-531-11955-6). 95pp. National Basketball Association finals over more than half a century are detailed year by year, with ample information on the teams and the players. (Rev: SLJ 3/04) [797]

24969 Stewart, Mark, and Mike Kennedy. *Swish: The Quest for Basketball's Perfect Shot* (5–8). Illus. 2009, Millbrook LB $25.26 (978-0-8225-8752-1). This wide-ranging volume covers basketball history, famous shots, key players, remarkable plays, scoring, and so forth. (Rev: BL 1/1–15/09; SLJ 5/09) [796.3230973]

24970 Thomas, Keltie. *How Basketball Works* (5–8). 2005, Maple Tree $16.95 (978-1-897066-18-8); paper $6.95 (978-1-897066-19-5). A lively overview of basketball's history, equipment, training, and skills, with interesting anecdotes and factoids. (Rev: BL 5/15/05) [796.323]

24971 Yancey, Diane. *Basketball* (5–10). Series: Science Behind Sports. 2011, Gale LB $33.45 (978-1-4205-0293-0). 112pp. This volume looks at all aspects of the sport, focusing in particular on the physics involved and the mental attitude required for success. **e** (Rev: SLJ 9/1/11) [796.3]

Bicycles

24972 Bach, Julie. *Bicycling* (4–7). Illus. Series: World of Sports. 2000, Smart Apple LB $16.95 (978-1-887068-53-6). 32pp. A brief introduction to bicycling that gives material on the origins and evolution of the sport, equipment, and techniques, plus coverage of the sport's star athletes. (Rev: BL 9/15/00) [796.6]

24973 Buckley, Annie. *Be a Better Biker* (5–6). Series: Girls Rock! 2006, The Child's World LB $25.64 (978-1-59296-741-4). 32pp. As well as advice on safety and maintenance, this volume (which is suitable for boys too) covers the history of bicycles and the various types available today. (Rev: SLJ 2/07) [796.6]

24974 Cole, Steve. *Kids' Easy Bike Care: Tune-Ups, Tools and Quick Fixes* (5–9). Illus. by Sarah Rakitin. Series: Quick Starts for Kids! 2003, Williamson paper $8.95 (978-1-885593-86-3). 64pp. A detailed and accessible guide to the parts of a bicycle and their maintenance, bicycle safety, and preparing an emergency kit, with cartoon illustrations. (Rev: SLJ 12/03) [629.28]

24975 Crossingham, John. *Cycling in Action* (4–7). Illus. by Bonna Rouse. Series: Sports in Action. 2002,

Crabtree LB $25.27 (978-0-7787-0118-7); paper $6.95 (978-0-7787-0124-8). 32pp. Photographs and drawings illustrate important concepts in this introduction to the sport of cycling that covers equipment and technique. (Rev: BL 9/1/02) [796.4]

24976 Deady, Kathleen W. *BMX Bikes* (4–7). Series: Wild Rides! 2001, Capstone LB $23.93 (978-0-7368-0925-2). Bicycle motocross fans will enjoy the color photographs and concise text that explains the equipment and skills needed for BMX (bicycle motocross) racing. (Rev: BL 10/15/01; HBG 3/02) [629.22]

24977 Dick, Scott. *BMX* (4–8). Series: Radical Sports. 2002, Heinemann LB $25.64 (978-1-58810-623-0). 32pp. This introduction to bicycle motocross gives material on equipment, skills, training, and safety. (Rev: BL 2/15/03; HBG 3/03) [796.6]

24978 Freeman, Gary. *Motocross* (4–8). Series: Radical Sports. 2002, Heinemann LB $25.64 (978-1-58810-627-8). 32pp. The sport of cross-country racing on motorcycles is introduced, with an emphasis on safety and skill development. (Rev: BL 2/15/03; HBG 3/03) [796.7]

24979 Haduch, Bill. *Go Fly a Bike! The Ultimate Book About Bicycle Fun, Freedom, and Science* (4–8). Illus. by Chris Murphy. 2004, Dutton $16.99 (978-0-525-47024-3). Packed with facts and cartoon illustrations, this comprehensive guide covers everything from the history of bicycling to practical tips for bike care and repair. (Rev: BL 2/1/04; SLJ 3/04) [796.6]

24980 Hayhurst, Chris. *Bicycle Stunt Riding!* (4–8). Series: Extreme Sports. 2000, Rosen LB $26.50 (978-0-8239-3011-1). In this book, readers will learn about stunts like the vert and mega spin as well as finding out about the bikes and the safety equipment needed to start this sport. (Rev: BL 6/1–15/00) [629]

24981 Hayhurst, Chris. *Mountain Biking: Get on the Trail* (4–8). Series: Extreme Sports. 2000, Rosen LB $26.50 (978-0-8239-3013-5). Stressing safety throughout, this book covers topics including the history of mountain biking, why mountain bikes are different than others, and riding techniques. (Rev: BL 3/15/00; SLJ 8/00) [796.6]

24982 Hinman, Bonnie. *Extreme Cycling with Dale Holmes* (2–4). Illus. Series: Robbie Reader: Extreme Sports. 2006, Mitchell Lane LB $16.95 (978-1-58415-487-7). 32pp. This high-interest volume combines information on extreme cycling with a biographical profile of British-born BMX bike racer Dale Holmes. (Rev: BL 10/15/06) [796.6]

24983 Maurer, Tracy Nelson. *BMX Freestyle* (3–6). Series: Radsports. 2001, Rourke LB $29.93 (978-1-58952-102-5). 48pp. Safety is emphasized in this account of BMX history, equipment, and techniques. (Rev: SLJ 5/02) [796.62]

24984 Pinchuk, Amy. *The Best Book of Bikes* (4–7). Illus. 2003, Maple Tree paper $12.95 (978-1-894379-44-1). 64pp. Diagrams, color photographs, and fascinating facts add to the appeal of the maintenance advice, racing

strategies, and stunts provided. (Rev: BCCB 9/03; SLJ 9/03) [629.227]

24985 Robinson, Laura. *Cyclist Bikelist: The Book for Every Rider* (4–6). Illus. by Ramon K. Perez. 2010, Tundra paper $17.95 (978-08877678-4-5). 80pp. Vivid, cartoon-style illustrations and a wealth of practical advice enhance this comprehensive guide for young cyclists that covers equipment, safety, and so forth. (Rev: BL 6/10; SLJ 9/1/10) [796.6]

24986 Schoenherr, Alicia, and Rusty Schoenherr. *Mountain Biking* (4–6). Series: Kids' Guides. 2005, The Child's World LB $25.64 (978-1-59296-209-9). 32pp. An introduction to mountain biking, describing its history and equipment and key athletes and competitions, with plenty of photographs and a glossary. (Rev: SLJ 7/05) [796.6]

24987 Wurdinger, Scott, and Leslie Rapparlie. *Mountain Biking* (5–9). Series: Adventure Sports. 2006, Creative Education LB $31.35 (978-1-58341-396-8). Using many eye-catching photographs, this slim volume introduces the popular sport's history, equipment, competitions, and safety measures. (Rev: SLJ 12/06) [796.6]

Camping and Backpacking

24988 Brunelle, Lynn. *Camp Out! The Ultimate Kids' Guide* (5–12). Illus. by Brian Biggs and Elara Tanguy. 2007, Workman paper $11.95 (978-0-7611-4122-8). This volume is packed with information about camping out, covering equipment, planning, and skills, and offering games, activities, recipes, nature tips, and so forth. (Rev: SLJ 2/08)

24989 Champion, Neil. *Finding Your Way* (4–7). Illus. 2010, Amicus LB $28.50 (978-1-60753-038-1). 32pp. Plenty of interactive quizzes and eye-catching photographs enhance this survival guide with an emphasis on navigation techniques — both technological and natural. (Rev: BL 10/1/10; SLJ 11/1/10) [613.6]

24990 Ching, Jacqueline. *Camping: Have Fun, Be Smart* (3–6). Series: Explore the Outdoors. 2000, Rosen LB $27.95 (978-0-8239-3173-6). 64pp. A basic introduction to camping that includes material on setting up a camp, gear and clothing, and different types of tents. (Rev: SLJ 1/01) [796.54]

24991 Drake, Jane, and Ann Love. *The Kids Campfire Book* (4–8). 1998, Kids Can paper $12.95 (978-1-55074-539-9). This manual describes how to select a location, build safe campfires, and later douse them, suggests fireside activities, including some science demonstrations, and offers safe cooking tips. (Rev: BL 3/15/98; HBG 9/98; SLJ 4/98) [796.54]

24992 George, Jean Craighead, and Twig C. George. *Pocket Guide to the Outdoors: Based on My Side of the Mountain* (5–8). 2009, Dutton paper $9.99 (978-0-525-42163-4). 138pp. This companion piece to George's *My Side of the Mountain* provides information on identifying edible plants, building shelters, catching fish, orienteering, and so forth. (Rev: SLJ 3/10; VOYA 6/10)

24993 Ghione, Yvette. *This Is Daniel Cook on a Hike* (K–3). 2006, Kids Can $12.95 (978-1-55453-079-3); paper $4.95 (978-1-55453-080-9). In this companion to the popular Canadian-produced TV show, the young host takes readers on a walk in the woods, introducing them to hiking equipment, safety precautions, and the animals and plants they encounter. (Rev: SLJ 11/06) [796.51]

24994 Kalman, Bobbie, and John Crossingham. *Extreme Climbing* (4–8). Series: Extreme Sports No Limits! 2004, Crabtree LB $25.27 (978-0-7787-1671-6). Explores the full spectrum of climbing sports, looking at the specific challenges of each and offering readers valuable advice about equipment, climbing techniques, locations, and difficulty ratings, as well as profiles of notable climbers. (Rev: BL 9/1/04)

24995 Loy, Jessica. *Follow the Trail: A Young Person's Guide to the Great Outdoors* (2–6). Illus. 2003, Holt $18.95 (978-0-8050-6195-6). 48pp. This slim volume uses the story of a camping trip to convey information about identifying wildflowers and trees, building a campfire, and avoiding such perils as poison ivy, snakes, and bears. (Rev: BL 4/1/03; HBG 10/03; SLJ 6/03) [796.54]

24996 Mader, Jan. *Let's Go Camping!* (PS–1). Series: Sports and Activities. 2006, Capstone LB $21.26 (978-0-7368-6360-5). 24pp. A large-format, simply written introduction that covers basic techniques, equipment, and safety and includes color photographs. (Rev: SLJ 2/07) [796.54]

24997 Oxlade, Chris. *Rock Climbing* (4–8). Series: Extreme Sports. 2003, Lerner LB $22.60 (978-0-8225-1240-0). An appealing introduction to the history, equipment, techniques, safety concerns, and challenges of this sport. (Rev: BL 3/1/04; SLJ 5/04) [790.52]

24998 Seeberg, Tim. *Camping* (3–5). Illus. Series: Kids' Guides to the Outdoors. 2004, Child's World LB $25.64 (978-1-59296-032-3). 32pp. For children with no experience of camping, the tips on safety, equipment, and advance planning provided here will be helpful. (Rev: BL 5/15/04) [796.54]

24999 Weber, Sandra. *Two in the Wilderness: Adventures of a Mother and Daughter in the Adirondack Mountains* (3–5). Photos by Carl E. Heilman. Illus. 2005, Boyds Mills $19.95 (978-1-59078-182-1). 48pp. This photoessay covers a 12-day journey the author took with her preteen daughter through New York's Adirondack Mountains, describing various physical and meteorological challenges as well as the geological and historical sights along the way; excerpts from daughter Marcy's journal add another perspective. (Rev: BL 7/05; SLJ 11/05) [508.747]

25000 Wurdinger, Scott, and Leslie Rapparlie. *Rock Climbing* (5–9). Series: Adventure Sports. 2006, Creative Education LB $31.35 (978-1-58341-394-4). Using many eye-catching photographs, this slim volume introduces rock climbing and examines the sport's history,

equipment, competitions, and safety measures. (Rev: SLJ 12/06) [796.5]

Chess

25001 Basman, Michael. *Chess for Kids* (4–8). 2001, DK paper $12.99 (978-0-7894-6540-5). A guide to the game of chess that includes everything from the basic moves and important strategies to information on the game's origins and the roles the game has played in arenas ranging from literature to history. (Rev: BL 7/01; HBG 10/01) [794.1]

25002 Kidder, Harvey. *The Kids' Book of Chess* (4–8). Illus. by Kimberly Bulcken. 1990, Workman paper $15.95 (978-0-89480-767-1). Using their origins in the Middle Ages as a focus, this book explains the role of each chess piece and the basics of the game. (Rev: SLJ 2/91) [794.1]

Fishing

25003 Arnosky, Jim. *Hook, Line, and Seeker: A Beginners Guide to Fishing, Boating, and Watching Water Wildlife* (4–6). Illus. 2005, Scholastic $12.95 (978-0-439-45584-8). 192pp. Outdoorsman (and illustrator) Arnosky draws on personal experience in this information-packed guide to boating, fishing, and wildlife watching. (Rev: BL 8/05; VOYA 4/06) [799.1]

25004 Schmidt, Gerald D. *Let's Go Fishing: A Book for Beginners* (4–7). Illus. by Brian W. Payne. 1990, Roberts Rinehart paper $11.95 (978-0-911797-84-8). This practical guide to freshwater fishing includes material on tackle and kinds of fish. (Rev: BL 3/1/91; SLJ 5/91) [799.1]

25005 Seeberg, Tim. *Freshwater Fishing* (3–5). Illus. Series: Great Outdoors. 2004, Child's World LB $25.64 (978-1-59296-035-4). 32pp. A useful guide for young people planning their first fishing trip, this book is loaded with tips about equipment and what to expect. Also use *Fly-Fishing* (2004). (Rev: BL 5/15/04) [799.1]

25006 Solomon, Dane. *Fishing: Have Fun, Be Smart* (3–6). Illus. Series: Explore the Outdoors. 2000, Rosen $26.50 (978-0-8239-3168-2). This introduction to fishing includes material on fresh and salt water varieties and the equipment needed. (Rev: SLJ 1/01) [799.1]

Football

25007 Devaney, John. *Winners of the Heisman Trophy. Rev. ed.* (5–8). 1990, Walker LB $15.85 (978-0-8027-6907-7). A history of the award is given, with profiles of 15 past winners. (Rev: SLJ 6/90) [796.332]

25008 Frisch, Aaron. *New York Giants* (K–3). Illus. Series: Super Bowl Champions. 2011, Creative Company $16.95 (978-160818023-3). 24pp. For young children, this is a visually appealing profile of the New York Giants, with short, straightforward text and a child-friendly glossary. This 18-volume series covers other teams around the country. (Rev: BL 2/1/11) [796.332]

25009 Gibbons, Gail. *My Football Book* (K–2). Illus. 2000, HarperCollins $6.99 (978-0-688-17139-1). 24pp. Equipment, the playing field, positions, and basic rules are covered in this small-format paperback introduction to football. (Rev: BL 9/15/00; HBG 3/01; SLJ 11/00) [796.332]

25010 Gitlin, Marty. *Football Skills* (4–6). Illus. Series: How to Play Like a Pro. 2008, Enslow LB $17.95 (978-0-7660-3203-3). 48pp. This introduction to football basics looks at separate skills — passing, receiving, and so forth — and highlights the importance of good sportsmanship and safety. (Rev: BLO 2/9/09) [796.332]

25011 Goin, Kenn. *Football for Fun!* (2–4). Illus. Series: Sports for Fun. 2003, Compass Point LB $25.26 (978-0-7565-0430-4). 48pp. Covering rules, necessary skills, and key figures, this is an attractive introduction for beginning readers. (Rev: SLJ 6/03) [796.332]

25012 Herzog, Brad. *T Is for Touchdown: A Football Alphabet* (3–5). Illus. by Mark Braught. 2004, Sleeping Bear $16.95 (978-1-58536-233-2). Football facts abound in this informative, alphabetical picture book, written in easy rhymes, that covers history, rules, teams and players, and famous plays. (Rev: SLJ 2/05)

25013 Kennedy, Mike. *Football* (3–5). Series: True Books — Sports. 2002, Children's Book Pr. LB $25.00 (978-0-516-22336-0). 48pp. Large type and a simple text plus plenty of well-captioned color photographs are highlights of this basic introduction to football, its history, rules, and key players. (Rev: BL 1/1–15/03) [796.332]

25014 Latimer, Clay. *VIP Pass to a Pro Football Game: From the Locker Room to the Press Box* (2–4). Illus. Series: Sports Illustrated Kids: Game Day. 2011, Capstone LB $26.65 (978-142965461-6). 32pp. Readers learn about all aspects of a pro game, introducing the people involved and the actions that take place. (Rev: BLO 3/14/11) [796.332]

25015 LeBoutillier, Nate. *The Story of the Chicago Bears* (5–8). Illus. 2009, Creative Education LB $22.95 (978-158341750-8). 48pp. With eye-catching photographs and a pleasing design and interesting text, this is a fascinating history of a football team. (Rev: BL 10/1/09*) [796.323]

25016 Macnow, Glen. *The Denver Broncos Football Team* (4–6). Series: Great Sports Teams. 2001, Enslow $23.93 (978-0-7660-1489-3). 48pp. A simple account that gives information on the history of the team, its star players, and most exciting seasons. (Rev: BL 9/15/01; HBG 3/02) [796.332]

25017 Madden, John, and Bill Gutman. *John Madden's Heroes of Football: The Story of America's Game* (5–8). 2006, Dutton $18.99 (978-0-525-47698-6). The former NFL coach and popular football commentator chronicles the history of professional football, looking at how the game has changed over the years and profiling some of its best-known players and coaches. (Rev: BL 9/1/06; SLJ 2/07) [796.332092]

25018 Mader, Jan. *Let's Play Football!* (PS–1). Series: Sports and Activities. 2006, Capstone LB $21.26 (978-0-7368-6361-2). 24pp. A large-format, simply written introduction that covers basic techniques, equipment, and safety and includes color photographs. (Rev: SLJ 2/07) [796.332]

25019 Molzahn, Arlene Bourgeois. *The San Francisco 49ers Football Team* (4–6). Series: Great Sports Teams. 2000, Enslow LB $23.93 (978-0-7660-1280-6). 48pp. As well as giving a history of this great team, this short book describes the team's best players. (Rev: BL 9/15/00; HBG 10/01) [796.48]

25020 O'Shei, Tim. *The Chicago Bears Football Team* (4–6). Series: Great Sports Teams. 2001, Enslow LB $23.93 (978-0-7660-1285-1). 48pp. The history of the Chicago Bears is given in text and pictures with coverage of key seasons, important players, and future outlook. (Rev: BL 12/15/01; HBG 3/02) [796.48]

25021 Stewart, Mark. *The Michigan Wolverines* (4–6). Illus. Series: Team Spirit-College Football. 2009, Norwood House LB $19.95 (978-1-59953-278-3). 48pp. For football fans, this volume traces the history of the famous team and looks at key games and players. (Rev: BL 4/1/09) [796.332]

25022 Stewart, Mark, and Mike Kennedy. *Touchdown: The Power and Precision of Football's Perfect Play* (5–8). 2009, Lerner LB $27.93 (978-0-8225-8751-4). 64pp. Full of action photographs, trading cards, and period prints, this engaging book provides a history of American football, its heroes, bloopers, and most thrilling moments. (Rev: BL 9/1/09; SLJ 1/10) [796.33]

25023 Thomas, Keltie. *How Football Works* (3–5). Illus. by Stephen MacEachern. 2010, OwlKids $22.95 (978-189734987-8); paper $12.95 (978-18973498-8-5). 64pp. History, rules, equipment, players, and famous games are all covered here with photographs and information packaged in small bites. (Rev: BL 11/1/10; SLJ 3/1/11) [796.332]

25024 Woods, Bob. *NFC North* (4–6). Series: Inside the NFL. 2005, Child's World LB $28.50 (978-1-59296-513-7). 48pp. Introduces the four teams that make up the NFC North division of the National Football League, with discussion of their history and famous games and players. (Rev: BL 9/1/05) [796.332]

Gymnastics

25025 Bray-Moffatt, Naia. *I Love Gymnastics* (K–3). Photos by avid Handley. Illus. 2005, DK $12.99 (978-0-7566-1011-1). 48pp. Excellent photographs show a young girl's introduction to the world of gymnastics, showing both basic and advanced moves. (Rev: BL 9/1/05; SLJ 5/06) [796.44]

25026 Ditchfield, Christin. *Gymnastics* (2–4). Illus. Series: True Books. 2000, Children's Book Pr. LB $25.00 (978-0-516-21063-6). 48pp. A simple introduction to gymnastics that describes some of the events, their history, and the equipment. (Rev: BL 9/15/00) [796.44]

25027 Kalman, Bobbie, and John Crossingham. *Gymnastics in Action* (4–7). Series: Sports in Action. 2002, Crabtree LB $25.27 (978-0-7787-0330-3); paper $6.95 (978-0-7737-0350-6). Various branches of gymnastics are introduced in text and pictures with coverage of techniques, equipment, and basic movements. (Rev: BL 1/1–15/03) [796.44]

Horsemanship

25028 Bolt, Betty. *Jumping* (4–8). Series: Horse Library. 2001, Chelsea $25.00 (978-0-7910-6657-7). 64pp. Show jumping, eventing, and steeplechase riding are all covered in detail here. Also use *Western Riding*. (Rev: HBG 3/02; SLJ 3/02) [798.4]

25029 Davis, Caroline. *The Young Equestrian* (5–8). Illus. 2000, Firefly $29.95 (978-1-55209-495-2); paper $19.95 (978-1-55209-484-6). 128pp. With a generous use of color photographs, this account devotes chapters to riding aids and techniques, choosing schools and proper equipment, buying and caring for a horse, and competitions. (Rev: BL 2/15/01; SLJ 2/01; VOYA 2/01) [798.2]

25030 Dowdy, Penny. *Dressage* (3–5). Illus. Series: Horsing Around. 2009, Crabtree LB $26.60 (978-077874978-3). 32pp. Featuring plenty of action photos and a layout evocative of barns and stables, this book communicates the importance of a strong connection between horse and rider, highlighting some famous competitors. (Rev: BL 1/1/10) [798.2]

25031 Haas, Jessie. *Safe Horse, Safe Rider: A Young Rider's Guide to Responsible Horsekeeping* (4–7). 1994, Storey paper $16.95 (978-0-88266-700-3). This guide to horsemanship stresses safety and covers such topics as understanding horse behavior. (Rev: BL 1/1/95) [636.1]

25032 Johnson, Robin. *Show Jumping* (3–5). Illus. Series: Horsing Around. 2009, Crabtree LB $26.60 (978-077874979-0). 32pp. Featuring plenty of action photos and a layout evocative of barns and stables, this book looks at the training, skills, and rituals of show jumping, highlighting some famous riders and horses. Also use *Rodeo* (2009). (Rev: BL 1/1/10) [798.2]

25033 Kimball, Cheryl. *Horse Showing for Kids* (4–8). 2004, Storey paper $16.95 (978-1-58017-501-2). A comprehensive guide to showing horses, covering preparations for both horse and rider/handler, plus advice on safety, sportsmanship, and appropriate attire (for animals and humans). (Rev: SLJ 2/05) [798.2]

25034 Kirksmith, Tommie. *Ride Western Style: A Guide for Young Riders* (4–8). 1991, Howell Book House $16.95 (978-0-87605-895-4). Background information and step-by-step instructions for young people interested in learning to ride Western style. (Rev: BL 4/1/92; SLJ 7/92) [798.2]

25035 Mickle, Shelley Fraser. *Barbaro: America's Horse* (4–8). 2007, Simon & Schuster LB $16.89 (978-1-4169-4866-7); paper $8.99 (978-1-4169-4865-0). 147pp. The tragic story of racehorse Barbaro is told in straightforward but moving text, with lots of details about horses, racing, and genetic choices, plus many photographs. (Rev: SLJ 7/07) [636.1]

25036 Ransford, Sandy. *First Riding Lessons* (3–7). Illus. 2002, Kingfisher $14.95 (978-0-7534-5454-1). 64pp. This no-nonsense book takes young horse fans through choosing a riding instructor, learning about different types of mounts, basic lessons and exercises, and a brief view of equine competitions. (Rev: BL 1/1–15/03; HBG 3/03; SLJ 12/02) [798.2]

25037 Tate, Nikki. *Behind the Scenes: The Racehorse* (5–8). 2008, Fitzhenry & Whiteside $22.95 (978-1-55455-018-0); paper $12.95 (978-1-55455-032-6). Readers get an inside look at horse racing — breeding, training, jockeys and grooms, and so forth — and learn about both the glamor and the sometimes dangerous and harsh realities. (Rev: BL 2/1/08; SLJ 2/08) [798]

25038 Wiseman, Blaine. *Kentucky Derby* (4–7). Illus. Series: Sporting Championships. 2011, Weigl LB $27.13 (978-161690121-9); paper $10.95 (9781616901226). 32pp. This is an appealing, colorful introduction to the sport of thoroughbred racing and to its premier event. (Rev: BL 4/1/11; LMC 11–12/10) [798.4]

Ice Hockey

25039 Adelson, Bruce. *Hat Trick Trivia: Secrets, Statistics, and Little-Known Facts About Hockey* (4–7). 1998, Lerner LB $23.93 (978-0-8225-3315-3). History, statistics, and trivia are combined in this lively discussion of hockey and its players. (Rev: BL 1/1–15/99) [796.962]

25040 Brown, Jonatha A. *Hockey* (1–3). Series: My Favorite Sport. 2005, Weekly Reader LB $21.00 (978-0-8368-4340-8). 24pp. For beginning readers, this is an introduction to the history and sport of hockey, defining key terms. (Rev: SLJ 5/05)

25041 Carson, Paul, and Sean Rossiter. *Hockey the NHL Way: Tips from the Pros* (4–6). Illus. 2001, Sterling paper $9.95 (978-1-55054-864-8). 64pp. Excellent photographs accompany advice on skills and sportsmanship for young hockey fans from professional players and coaches. (Rev: BL 2/1/02) [796.962]

25042 Kennedy, Mike. *Ice Hockey* (5–7). Series: Watts Library. 2003, Watts LB $25.50 (978-0-531-12273-0). 64pp. This overview explores the history of the sport, its rules, and styles of play, and provides information on some of the key players. (Rev: SLJ 2/04) [796.962]

25043 McFarlane, Brian. *Real Stories from the Rink* (5–8). Illus. by Steve Nease. 2002, Tundra paper $14.95 (978-0-88776-604-6). Entertaining true stories give insight into ice hockey's history, rules, and players. (Rev: BL 2/15/03; SLJ 4/03) [796.962]

25044 McKinley, Michael, and Suzanne Levesque. *Ice Time: The Story of Hockey* (5–8). Illus. 2006, Tundra $18.95 (978-0-88776-762-3). This history of ice hockey focuses mainly on the development and current status of the game in Canada, also covering international stars. (Rev: BL 12/1/06; SLJ 1/07) [796.962]

25045 O'Shei, Tim. *The Detroit Red Wings Hockey Team* (4–6). Series: Great Sports Teams. 2000, Enslow LB $23.93 (978-0-7660-1282-0). 48pp. Profiles the Detroit Red Wings, their history, great moments from the past, and famous players. (Rev: BL 9/15/00; HBG 10/01) [796.962]

25046 Stewart, Mark, and Mike Kennedy. *Score! The Action and Artistry of Hockey's Magnificent Moment* (5–8). Illus. 2010, Millbrook LB $29.27 (978-0-8225-8753-8). 64pp. Not for beginning players, this is a book about strategy and technique, with information about key players. **e** (Rev: BL 9/1/10; SLJ 4/11) [796.355]

25047 Wilson, Stacy. *The Hockey Book for Girls* (4–7). Illus. 2000, Kids Can $12.95 (978-1-55074-860-4); paper $6.95 (978-1-55074-719-5). 40pp. This book, by the former captain of Canada's women's Olympic hockey team, introduces ice hockey's rules, positions, strategies, and training and includes interviews with star players. (Rev: BL 3/1/01; HBG 3/01; SLJ 12/00) [796.962]

25048 Wiseman, Blaine. *Stanley Cup* (4–7). Series: Sporting Championships. 2011, Weigl $26 (978-1-61690-128-8). This is an appealing, colorful introduction to the sport of ice hockey and to its premier event. (Rev: LMC 11–12/10) [796.962]

Ice Skating

25049 Helmer, Diana Star, and Thomas S. Owens. *The History of Figure Skating* (2–4). Series: Sports Throughout History. 2000, Rosen LB $19.95 (978-0-8239-5472-8). 24pp. This book gives a history of figure skating and information on equipment, along with biographical details on famous skaters. (Rev: SLJ 12/00) [796.91]

25050 Lindeen, Carol K. *Let's Ice-Skate!* (K–2). Series: Sports and Activities. 2005, Capstone LB $21.26 (978-0-7368-5360-6). 24pp. An attractive introduction to the sport for beginning readers. (Rev: SLJ 6/06) [796.91]

25051 Macnow, Glen. *The Philadelphia Flyers Hockey Team* (4–6). Series: Great Sports Teams. 2000, Enslow LB $23.93 (978-0-7660-1279-0). 48pp. With a generous number of color and black-and-white photos, this slim book traces the history of the Philadelphia Flyers,

their star players, and their greatest successes. (Rev: BL 3/15/00; HBG 10/00) [796.964]

25052 Schwartz, Heather E. *Girls' Figure Skating: Ruling the Rink* (3–6). Series: Girls Got Game. 2006, Capstone LB $25.26 (978-0-7368-6822-8). 32pp. An introduction to a popular sport, with tips on form, safety, terminology, and more, including profiles of famous skaters and lots of color photographs. (Rev: SLJ 7/07)

25053 Wilkes, Debbi. *The Figure Skating Book: A Young Person's Guide to Figure Skating* (4–8). 2000, Firefly LB $19.95 (978-1-55209-444-0); paper $12.95 (978-1-55209-445-7). The author, an Olympic silver medalist, gives practical advice on figure skating from buying skates to simple and complicated skating techniques. (Rev: BL 7/00; SLJ 4/00) [796.9]

Indoor Games

25054 Bonner, Lori. *Putting on a Party: Adventure Parties for Kids* (3–6). Illus. by Fran Lee. 2004, Gibbs Smith paper $9.95 (978-1-58685-232-0). 63pp. Provides creative ideas for invitations, decorations, games and activities, and party foods with adventure themes — a polar expedition and a safari, for example. (Rev: SLJ 7/04) [793.2]

25055 Klingel, Cynthia, and Robert B. Noyed. *Card Tricks* (3–5). Series: Games Around the World. 2002, Compass Point LB $22.60 (978-0-7565-0190-7). 32pp. After background material on playing cards, this illustrated book highlights several baffling card tricks and shows how to perform them. (Rev: BL 5/15/02; SLJ 7/02) [795.4]

25056 Sheinwold, Alfred. *101 Best Family Card Games* (5–12). 1993, Sterling paper $5.95 (978-0-8069-8635-7). A book filled with games enjoyed by many age groups. (Rev: BL 2/15/93) [795.4]

Motor Bikes and Motorcycles

25057 Maurer, Tracy Nelson. *ATV Riding* (4–6). Illus. Series: Radsports. 2002, Rourke LB $20.95 (978-1-58952-276-3). 48pp. A jargon- and action-filled introduction to a "radical" sport, with photographs and Web sites. (Rev: BL 2/15/03) [796.7]

25058 Raby, Philip, and Simon Nix. *Motorbikes* (5–8). Series: Need for Speed. 1999, Lerner LB $23.93 (978-0-8225-2486-1); paper $23.93 (978-0-8225-9854-1). A variety of motorbikes are introduced including dirt, motorcross, and land speed bikes. (Rev: BL 1/1–15/00; HBG 3/00; SLJ 2/00) [629.227]

25059 Sandler, Michael. *Mighty MotoXers* (3–6). Illus. Series: X-Moves. 2009, Bearport LB $16.96 (978-159716951-6). 24pp. Sandler highlights the history, equipment, and thrills of motocross racing, providing gravity-defying photographs. (Rev: BL 1/1/10) [796.7]

25060 Smedman, Lisa. *From Boneshakers to Choppers: The Rip-Roaring History of Motorcycles* (5–8). Illus. 2007, Annick $24.95 (978-1-55451-016-0); paper $14.95 (978-1-55451-015-3). 120pp. Covering all types of motorcycles, as well as all types of riders, this well-illustrated book will be popular with fans of transportation, extreme sports, history, and American popular culture. (Rev: BL 11/15/07) [629.227]

25061 Stuart, Dee. *Motorcycles* (2–4). Series: Transportation and Communication. 2001, Enslow LB $23.93 (978-0-7660-1648-4). 48pp. Using simple language and many illustrations, this short book describes the history and present developments related to motorcycles and their uses. (Rev: BL 3/15/02; HBG 3/02) [7796.7]

Olympic Games

25062 Fischer, David. *The Encyclopedia of the Summer Olympics* (4–8). Illus. Series: Watts Reference. 2003, Watts LB $37.00 (978-0-531-11886-3). 160pp. Events from archery to wrestling are organized in alphabetical order, with historical information from the first games to the forthcoming 2004 games, profiles of athletes, lists of gold medal winners, information on rules and equipment, and fast facts. (Rev: SLJ 12/03) [796.4]

25063 Gaff, Jackie. *Ancient Olympics* (3–6). Series: The Olympics. 2003, Heinemann LB $24.22 (978-1-4034-4676-3). 32pp. A concise look at the Ancient Olympics, with many illustrations and graphics, sidebars, and explanations of what the games involved as far back as 776 B.C. (Rev: SLJ 5/04) [796.48]

25064 Hoblin, Paul. *Amazing Olympic Records* (3–5). Illus. Series: Amazing Sports Records. 2013, Child's World LB $27.07 (978-161473405-5). 32pp. Useful for report writers, this attractive volume provides both history and facts. (Rev: BL 5/1/13; SLJ 4/13) [796.48]

25065 Middleton, Haydn. *Modern Olympics* (4–8). Series: The Olympics. 2003, Heinemann LB $16.95 (978-1-4034-4677-0). 32pp. A concise look at the modern games, with many illustrations, graphics, and sidebars, plus discussion of terrorism incidents, drug use, the choice of host cities, and the Paralympics. (Rev: SLJ 5/04) [796.48]

Running and Jogging

25066 Griffis, Molly Levite. *The Great American Bunion Derby* (5–10). 2003, Eakin $15.95 (978-1-57168-801-9); paper $9.95 (978-1-57168-810-1). The story of a poor part-Cherokee farm boy who joined a marathon run across the United States in the late 1920s and won

the $25,000 top prize. (Rev: BL 1/1–15/04; SLJ 3/04) [796.42]

25067 Hughes, Morgan. *Track and Field: The Jumps: Instructional Guide to Track and Field* (4–8). Series: Compete Like a Champion. 2001, Rourke LB $27.93 (978-1-57103-290-4). 48pp. This book includes material on the long jump, the triple jump, the high jump, and the pole vault, along with training tips. Also use in the same series *Track and Field: Middle and Long Distance Runs* and *Track and Field: The Sprints* (both 2001). (Rev: SLJ 3/01) [796.42]

25068 Manley, Claudia B. *Competitive Track and Field for Girls* (4–7). Series: Sportsgirl. 2001, Rosen LB $26.50 (978-0-8239-3408-9). An introduction to the rules of track and field competitions, the training necessary, and the special opportunities for girls, with material on nutrition and the dangers of overtraining. (Rev: SLJ 3/02) [796.42]

25069 Wiseman, Blaine. *Boston Marathon* (4–7). Illus. Series: Sporting Championships. 2011, Weigl LB $27.13 (978-161690124-0); paper $10.95 (9781616901257). 32pp. This is an appealing, colorful introduction to the the sport of long-distance running and the history and modern technology of one of the key races in the United States. (Rev: BL 4/1/11; LMC 11–12/10) [796.425]

Sailing and Boating

25070 Bass, Scott. *Kayaking* (4–6). Series: Kids' Guides. 2005, The Child's World LB $25.64 (978-1-59296-208-2). 32pp. An introduction to kayaking, describing its history and equipment and key athletes and competitions, with plenty of photographs and a glossary. (Rev: SLJ 7/05) [797.12]

25071 Ditchfield, Christin. *Kayaking, Canoeing, Rowing, and Yachting* (2–4). Illus. Series: True Books. 2000, Children's Book Pr. LB $25.00 (978-0-516-21610-2). 48pp. Introduces a range of water sports in a simple text with many color photos. (Rev: BL 9/15/00) [797.1]

Self-Defense

25072 Ancona, George. *Capoeira: Game! Dance! Martial Art!* (2–4). Illus. 2007, Lee & Low $18.95 (978-1-58430-268-1). 32pp. Capoeira — a Brazilian blend of dance, martial art, and game — is shown in eye-catching photographs of students practicing in California. (Rev: BL 4/15/07) [793.3]

25073 Atwood, Jane. *Capoeira: A Martial Art and a Cultural Tradition* (5–8). Series: The Library of African American Arts and Culture. 1999, Rosen LB $27.95 (978-0-8239-1859-1). Capoeira, a unique martial art developed by African slaves in Brazil, is described, along with its history and preparations for its debut in the 2004 Olympic games. (Rev: SLJ 8/99) [796.8]

25074 Ellis, Carol. *Judo and Jujitsu* (5–7). Illus. 2011, Marshall Cavendish LB $20.95 (978-076144933-1). 48pp. This title offers information about the history, practice, and philosophy of judo and jujitsu. (Rev: BL 2/1/12; SLJ 4/12)

25075 Haney-Withrow, Anna. *Tae Kwon Do* (5–7). Illus. 2011, Marshall Cavendish LB $20.95 (978-076144940-9). 48pp. This interesting title covers the history, practice, and philosophy of tae kwon do. (Rev: BL 2/1/12; SLJ 4/12)

25076 Mack, Gail. *Kickboxing* (5–7). Illus. 2011, Marshall Cavendish LB $20.95 (978-076144936-2). 48pp. This title offers information about the history, practice, and philosophy of kickboxing. (Rev: BL 2/1/12; SLJ 4/12)

25077 Nakashima, Maiko. *Etiquette, Equipment, and the Dojo* (5–7). Trans. by Chiaki Hasegawa. Illus. Series: Karate Made Simple. 2013, Oliver LB $24.95 (978-193454517-1). 32pp. Full of color photographs, this volume teaches basic karate etiquette, training, and history. (Rev: BL 4/1/13; LMC 10/13; SLJ 4/13) [796.815]

25078 Rielly, Robin L. *Karate for Kids* (5–8). Series: The Martial Arts for Kids. 2004, Tuttle paper $13.95 (978-0-8048-3534-3). After an overview of the history of karate, this appealing volume with clear illustrations looks at the moves, rules and etiquette, uniform and belts, and so forth. (Rev: BL 9/1/04; SLJ 2/05) [796.815]

25079 Scandiffio, Laura. *The Martial Arts Book* (3–5). Illus. by Nicolas Debon. 2003, Firefly paper $9.95 (978-1-55037-776-7). 64pp. The focus of this overview is the origins and evolution of various martial arts, looking at the spiritual aspects and overall benefits. (Rev: BL 4/15/03) [796.8]

Skateboarding

25080 Burke, L. M. *Skateboarding! Surf the Pavement* (5–8). Series: Extreme Sports. 1999, Rosen LB $26.50 (978-0-8239-3014-2). This book supplies information for beginning and advanced skateboarders with coverage of history, techniques, equipment, and safety considerations. (Rev: SLJ 4/00) [796]

25081 Crossingham, John. *Skateboarding in Action* (4–7). Series: Sports in Action. 2002, Crabtree LB $25.27 (978-0-7787-0117-0); paper $6.95 (978-0-7787-0123-1). A well-illustrated introduction to skateboarding with good material on equipment and injury prevention. (Rev: BL 9/1/02; SLJ 11/02) [795.2]

25082 Dieterich, Alice. *Tony Hawk and Andy MacDonald Ride* (2–3). Series: All Aboard Science Reader Station Stop. 2003, Penguin paper $3.99 (978-0-448-43160-4). 48pp. Skateboarding stars Tony Hawk and Andy MacDonald share some of their boarding experiences with readers. (Rev: BL 10/15/03; HBG 4/04; SLJ 1/04)

25083 Freimuth, Jeri. *Extreme Skateboarding Moves* (4–7). Illus. Series: Behind the Moves. 2001, Capstone LB $23.93 (978-0-7368-0783-8). 32pp. Skateboard slang is just one appealing part of this account of proper equipment and technique, with safety tips and some tricks. (Rev: BL 6/1–15/01; HBG 10/01; SLJ 9/01) [796.22]

25084 Hocking, Justin. *Awesome Obstacles: How to Build Your Own Skateboard Ramps and Ledges* (4–6). Illus. Series: Skateboarder's Guide to Skate Parks, Half-Pipes, Bowls, and Obstacles. 2005, Rosen LB $26.50 (978-1-4042-0337-2). 48pp. Along with advice on safety, this volume provides plans for the construction of six wooden ramps and boxes. (Rev: BL 9/1/05) [796.22]

25085 Horsley, Andy. *Skateboarding* (4–7). Series: To the Limit. 2001, Raintree LB $25.69 (978-0-7398-3163-2). A brief history of skateboarding is included here along with material on equipment, moves, and some advice on turning pro. (Rev: BL 6/1–15/01) [796.22]

25086 Loizos, Constance. *Skateboard! Your Guide to Street, Vert, Downhill, and More* (4–9). Series: Extreme Sports. 2002, National Geographic paper $8.95 (978-0-7922-8229-7). An attractive guide to skateboarding equipment, technique, rules, etiquette, jargon, and safety. (Rev: SLJ 1/03) [796.22]

25087 Maurer, Tracy Nelson. *Skateboarding* (3–6). Series: Radsports. 2001, Rourke LB $29.93 (978-1-58952-104-9). 48pp. Safety is emphasized in this account of skateboarding's history, equipment, and techniques that includes "Pro Spotlights." (Rev: SLJ 5/02) [796.22]

25088 Spencer, Russ. *Skateboarding* (4–6). Series: Kids' Guides. 2005, The Child's World LB $25.64 (978-1-59296-210-5). 32pp. An introduction to skateboarding, describing its history and equipment and key athletes and competitions, with plenty of photographs and a glossary. (Rev: SLJ 7/05) [796.2]

25089 Werner, Doug. *Skateboarder's Start-Up: A Beginner's Guide to Skateboarding* (4–8). 2000, Tracks paper $11.95 (978-1-884654-13-8). 144pp. Using a question-and-answer format, this introduction to skateboarding covers such subjects as equipment, history, and basic skating and technical tricks. (Rev: SLJ 12/00) [795.2]

Snowboarding

25090 Barr, Matt, and Chris Moran. *Snowboarding* (4–8). Series: Extreme Sports. 2003, Lerner LB $22.60 (978-0-8225-1242-4). An appealing introduction to the history, equipment, techniques, safety concerns, and stars of this increasingly popular sport. (Rev: BL 3/1/04; SLJ 5/04; VOYA 6/04) [790.9]

25091 Brown, Gillian C. P. *Snowboarding* (5–8). Illus. Series: X-treme Outdoors. 2003, Children's LB $24.50 (978-0-516-24322-1); paper $6.95 (978-0-516-24383-2). 48pp. Equipment, technique, competition, and safety are covered here, as well as a history of this sport. (Rev: BL 4/15/03; SLJ 10/03) [796.9]

25092 Crossingham, John. *Snowboarding in Action* (4–7). Illus. by Bonna Rouse. Series: Sports in Action. 2002, Crabtree LB $25.27 (978-0-7787-0119-4); paper $6.95 (978-0-7787-0125-5). 32pp. Aspiring snowboarders will find much of interest here, including basic techniques. (Rev: BL 9/1/02; SLJ 11/02) [796.9]

25093 Degezelle, Terri. *Let's Snowboard!* (K–2). Series: Sports and Activities. 2005, Capstone LB $21.26 (978-0-7368-5366-8). 24pp. An attractive introduction to the sport for beginning readers, with emphasis on equipment and safety. (Rev: SLJ 6/06) [796.9]

25094 Hayhurst, Chris. *Snowboarding! Shred the Powder* (5–8). Series: Extreme Sports. 1999, Rosen LB $26.50 (978-0-8239-3010-4). The book supplies both beginning and advanced information on this sport, including material on history, equipment, techniques, and safety considerations. (Rev: SLJ 4/00; VOYA 6/00) [796.9]

25095 Herran, Joe, and Ron Thomas. *Snowboarding* (5–8). Series: Action Sports. 2003, Chelsea LB $28.00 (978-0-7910-7003-1). Basic information on this sport's gear and performance is accompanied by biographical details about snowboarding champions. (Rev: BL 4/15/03; HBG 10/03) [796.9]

25096 Sandler, Michael. *Cool Snowboarders* (3–6). Illus. Series: X-Moves. 2009, Bearport LB $16.96 (978-159716949-3). 24pp. With dramatic photographs, Sandler offers an overview of the history of snowboarding, the thrills of the sport, and the amazing accomplishments of the champions. (Rev: BL 1/1/10) [796.939]

25097 Schwartz, Heather E. *Snowboarding* (5–10). Series: Science Behind Sports. 2011, Gale LB $33.45 (978-1-4205-0322-7). 104pp. After reviewing the history of snowboarding, this book discusses training and other preparations, glides and turns, jumps and rails, and aerial moves before looking at psychological aspects. **℮** (Rev: SLJ 9/1/11) [796.9]

25098 Woods, Bob. *Snowboarding* (4–6). Series: Kids' Guides. 2005, The Child's World LB $25.64 (978-1-59296-211-2). 32pp. An introduction to snowboarding, describing its history and equipment and key athletes and competitions, with plenty of photographs and a glossary. (Rev: SLJ 7/05) [796.9]

Soccer

25099 Brown, Jonatha A. *Soccer* (1–3). Series: My Favorite Sport. 2005, Weekly Reader LB $21.00 (978-0-8368-4341-5). 24pp. For beginning readers, this is an introduction to the history and sport of soccer, defining key terms. (Rev: SLJ 5/05)

25100 Buckley, James, Jr. *Soccer Superstars* (2–5). Series: Boys Rock! 2006, The Child's World LB $25.64 (978-1-59296-736-0). 32pp. A good choice for beginning and reluctant readers (girls as well as boys), this colorful book looks at the status of soccer and profiles some of the game's most popular players. (Rev: SLJ 2/07) [796.3]

25101 Buckley, James, Jr. *Soccer Superwomen* (1–3). Series: Girls Rock! 2006, The Child's World LB $25.64 (978-1-59296-750-6). 32pp. Introduces readers to some of the world's best female soccer players and looks at the overall popularity of soccer. (Rev: SLJ 2/07) [796.3]

25102 Capucilli, Alyssa Satin. *My First Soccer Game* (PS–K). Illus. by Leyah Jensen. 2011, Simon & Schuster $9.99 (978-1-4424-2747-1). 14pp. This board book offers a simple introduction to the basics of soccer (Rev: BLO 8/11; SLJ 12/1/11) [796.334]

25103 Coleman, Lori. *Girls' Soccer: Going for the Goal* (3–6). Series: Girls Got Game. 2006, Capstone LB $25.26 (978-0-7368-6823-5). 32pp. Especially for girls, this overview of soccer will get readers excited about the sport. (Rev: SLJ 7/07)

25104 Coleman, Lori. *Soccer* (5–9). Series: Play-by-Play. 2000, Lerner paper $23.93 (978-0-8225-9876-3). A fine introduction to the rules, equipment, and tactics of soccer with historical coverage through 1999. (Rev: SLJ 9/00) [796.334]

25105 Diehl, David. *Goal!* (PS–1). Illus. by author. 2008, Sterling $5.95 (978-1-60059-241-6). 28pp. A board book primer introducing the basics of soccer. (Rev: BLO 8/28/08) [796.3]

25106 Gibbons, Gail. *My Soccer Book* (PS–3). Illus. 2000, HarperCollins $6.99 (978-0-688-17138-4). 24pp. This accessible guide describes the playing field, equipment, rules, and the method of scoring. (Rev: BCCB 4/00; BL 5/1/00; HBG 10/00; SLJ 6/00) [796.334]

25107 Gifford, Clive. *The Kingfisher Book of Soccer Skills* (5–8). Illus. 2012, Kingfisher $15.99 (978-075346873-9). 64pp. A practical guide to various soccer moves, techniques of offense and defense, types of passes, and so forth, with color photographs. (Rev: BL 6/12; SLJ 6/12) [796.334]

25108 Gifford, Clive. *My First Soccer Book* (2–5). Illus. 2012, Kingfisher $12.99 (978-075346783-1). 48pp. Covering equipment, the field, and rules first, this book then looks at preparation and basic skills and provides many helpful photographs and tips. (Rev: BL 5/15/12; LMC 10/10; SLJ 6/1/12) [796.334]

25109 Gifford, Clive. *Soccer Players and Skills* (3–6). Series: Spotlight on Soccer. 2010, Rosen LB $23.95 (978-1-61532-611-2); paper $10 (978-1-61532-612-9). 32pp. The different roles and skill sets of various soccer field positions are discussed in depth. Also use (all 2010) *Soccer Rules and Regulations, Teamwork in Soccer,* and *The Business of Soccer,* which discusses the management of soccer teams and franchising. (Rev: SLJ 2/1/11) [796.334]

25110 Goin, Kenn. *Soccer for Fun!* (2–4). Illus. Series: Sports for Fun. 2003, Compass Point LB $25.26 (978-0-7565-0431-1). 48pp. Covering rules, necessary skills, and key figures, this is an attractive introduction for beginning readers. (Rev: SLJ 6/03) [796.334]

25111 Helmer, Diana Star, and Thomas S. Owens. *The History of Soccer* (2–4). Series: Sports Throughout History. 2000, Rosen LB $18.75 (978-0-8239-5467-4). In addition to a history of soccer, this book profiles some championship players. (Rev: SLJ 12/00) [796.334]

25112 Kennedy, Mike, and Mark Stewart. *Soccer in Asia* (2–4). Illus. Series: Smart About Sports: Soccer. 2011, Norwood LB $21.27 (978-159953448-0). 24pp. Plenty of bright, clearly focused photographs add appeal to this survey of soccer's influence and importance in Asian culture, with details of history, stadiums, player statistics, and so forth. Also use *Soccer in the British Isles, Soccer in Africa,* and *Soccer in South America* (all 2011). (Rev: BL 7/11; LMC 11–12/11) [796.334095]

25113 Lineker, Gary. *Soccer* (3–8). Series: Superguides. 2000, DK $9.99 (978-0-7894-5425-6). 44pp. Bright clear photographs and a straightforward text explain the fundamentals of soccer and give sound advice on improving one's game. (Rev: BL 6/1–15/00; HBG 10/00; SLJ 8/00) [796.334]

25114 Mackin, Bob. *Soccer the Winning Way: Play Like the Pros* (4–7). Illus. 2002, Douglas & McIntyre paper $10.95 (978-1-55054-825-9). 62pp. A guide to mastering crucial soccer skills, with photographs and words of wisdom from the pros. (Rev: BL 5/15/02) [796]

25115 Otten, Jack. *Soccer* (1–6). Series: Sports Training. 2002, Rosen LB $19.95 (978-0-8239-5972-3). 24pp. A brief and basic introduction to the sport that will be useful for reluctant readers and ESL students. (Rev: SLJ 3/02) [796.334]

25116 Owens, Thomas S., and Diana Star Helmer. *Soccer* (5–8). Series: Game Plan. 2000, Twenty-First Century LB $26.90 (978-0-7613-1400-4). 64pp. This introduction to soccer covers the different positions, game strategy, and memorable games and players of the past. (Rev: HBG 10/00; SLJ 7/00) [796.334]

25117 Page, Jason. *Soccer: Learn How to Be a Star Player* (3–5). Illus. by Mel Pickering. Series: Sports Club. 2000, Two-Can $9.95 (978-1-58728-001-6). 32pp. Soccer rules are explained along with some important plays and techniques, a little history, and profiles of important players. (Rev: SLJ 3/01) [796.334]

25118 Saunders, Catherine. *Play Soccer* (3–6). Photos by Russell Sadur. 2006, DK LB $12.99 (978-0-7566-2032-5). 63pp. This is a practical book that will help soccer players improve their passing and control of the ball; photographs demonstrate techniques. (Rev: SLJ 7/06) [796.334]

25119 Sherman, Josepha. *Competitive Soccer for Girls* (4–7). Series: Sportsgirl. 2001, Rosen LB $26.50 (978-0-8239-3405-8). 64pp. An introduction to the rules of soccer, the training necessary, and the special opportunities for girls, with material on nutrition and the dangers of overtraining. (Rev: SLJ 3/02) [796.334]

25120 Stewart, Mark. *The World Cup* (5–10). Series: The Watts History of Sports. 2003, Watts LB $34.50 (978-0-531-11957-0). 96pp. An overview of the international soccer championship that takes place every four years,

this volume, which will be useful for reports, starts with the 1930 games and includes information on teams and players. (Rev: SLJ 3/04) [796.3]

25121 Stewart, Mark, and Mike Kennedy. *Goal! The Fire and Fury of Soccer's Greatest Moment* (5–8). 2010, Millbrook LB $27.93 (978-0-8225-8754-5). 64pp. Famous goals are the main focus of this book that also explores the history of the game and the scoring rules. (Rev: BL 3/1/10; SLJ 5/10) [796.334]

25122 Suen, Anastasia. *The Story of Soccer* (1–3). Illus. Series: Sports History. 2002, Rosen LB $19.95 (978-0-8239-5998-3). 24pp. A basic, easy-to-read introduction to the sport. (Rev: BL 5/15/02; SLJ 3/02) [796.334]

25123 Thomas, Ron, and Joe Herran. *Getting into Soccer* (2–4). Illus. by Nives Porcellato and Andy Craig. Series: Getting into Sports. 2005, Chelsea House LB $28.00 (978-0-7910-8806-7). After a brief history of the game, this book covers rules, equipment, clothing, and competitions and provides color photographs, useful diagrams, and interesting trivia. (Rev: SLJ 12/05) [796.334]

25124 Venturini, Tisha Lea, and Judith Cohen. *You Can Be a Woman Soccer Player* (2–5). Illus. 2000, Cascade Pass $13.95 (978-1-880599-49-5); paper $7.00 (978-1-880599-48-8). 40pp. This is basically a biography of Venturini, a World Cup soccer player, plus tips on how to play the game and a brief history of the sport. (Rev: BL 10/1/00) [796.334]

Surfing

25125 Chapman, Garry. *Surf* (3–5). Series: Extreme Sports. 2001, Chelsea LB $28.00 (978-0-7910-6611-9). 32pp. This book covers the history of surfing, safety in the surf, and the extreme sports that began as spin-offs of traditional surfing. (Rev: BL 10/15/01; HBG 3/02; SLJ 12/01) [797.2]

25126 Maurer, Tracy Nelson. *Surfing* (4–6). Illus. Series: Radsports. 2002, Rourke LB $20.95 (978-1-58952-280-0). 48pp. A jargon- and action-filled introduction to a "radical" sport, with photographs and Web sites. (Rev: BL 2/15/03) [797.3]

25127 Sandler, Michael. *Super Surfers* (3–6). Illus. Series: X-Moves. 2009, Bearport $16.95 (978-159716953-0). 24pp. Sandler highlights the history, equipment, and thrills of surfing, providing photographs of daring feats. (Rev: BL 1/1/10) [797.3]

Swimming and Diving

25128 Crossingham, John, and Niki Walker. *Swimming in Action* (4–7). Series: Sports in Action. 2002, Crabtree LB $25.27 (978-0-7787-0331-0); paper $6.95 (978-0-7737-0351-3). Color photographs and many diagrams are used with a clear text to describe swimming basics, with tips on various strokes and safety. (Rev: BL 1/1–15/03; SLJ 10/03) [977.2]

25129 Lourie, Peter. *First Dive to Shark Dive* (5–8). Illus. 2006, Boyds Mills $17.95 (978-1-59078-068-8). This attractive, interesting photoessay documents a 12-year-old girl's introduction to scuba diving among sharks. (Rev: BL 2/15/06; SLJ 6/06) [797.2]

25130 Romanek, Trudee. *Splash It Swimming* (K–3). Illus. Series: Sports Starters. 2012, Crabtree LB $26.60 (978-077873152-8). 32pp. Covering major forms of competitive swimming (freestyle, breaststroke, backstroke, and butterfly), this volume also introduces contemporary swimmers of note. (Rev: BL 9/1/12) [797.2]

25131 Vander Hook, Sue. *Scuba Diving* (4–7). Illus. Series: World of Sports. 2000, Smart Apple LB $16.95 (978-1-887068-59-8). 32pp. After a section on star scuba divers, this account describes the origins and evolution of the sport, its equipment, hazards, and techniques. (Rev: BL 9/15/00) [797.2]

Tennis

25132 Crossingham, John. *Tennis in Action* (4–7). Series: Sports in Action. 2002, Crabtree LB $25.27 (978-0-7787-0116-3); paper $6.95 (978-0-7787-0122-4). A fine introduction to tennis told through a concise text with easy-to-follow descriptions and material on equipment, rules, and techniques. (Rev: BL 9/1/02; SLJ 11/02) [796.342]

25133 Ditchfield, Christin. *Tennis* (1–3). Series: A True Book. 2003, Children's Pr. LB $25.00 (978-0-516-22589-0). 48pp. Rules, scoring, and other basics of the game are outlined in simple text and photographs, plus profiles of some of the key players. (Rev: SLJ 6/03) [796.342]

25134 Muskat, Carrie. *The Composite Guide to Tennis* (5–7). Series: Composite Guide. 1998, Chelsea LB $12.95 (978-0-7910-4728-6). Past and present tennis stars are mentioned along with a general introduction to the game. (Rev: HBG 10/98; SLJ 9/98) [796.342]

25135 Rutledge, Rachel. *The Best of the Best in Tennis* (4–7). 1998, Millbrook LB $24.90 (978-0-7613-1303-8). Using a lively text and many color photographs, this work gives a history of women in tennis and a rundown of today's most important female players. (Rev: BL 2/15/99; HBG 10/99; SLJ 3/99) [796.342]

Track and Field

25136 Crossingham, John, and Bobbie Kalman. *Track Events in Action* (3–5). Illus. by Bonna Rouse. Series: Sports in Action. 2004, Crabtree LB $25.27 (978-0-7787-0339-6). 32pp. For beginning sprinters, steeplechasers, and other track enthusiasts, this is an attractive and useful introduction to equipment, technique, and vocabulary. (Rev: SLJ 6/05) [796.42]

25137 Kalman, Bobbie. *Field Events in Action* (3–5). Illus. Series: Sports in Action. 2004, Crabtree LB $25.27 (978-0-7787-0340-2); paper $6.95 (978-0-7787-0360-0). 32pp. For beginning enthusiasts of high and long jumps, pole vault, javelin throwing, and other field events, this is an attractive and useful introduction to equipment, technique, and vocabulary. (Rev: SLJ 6/05) [796.42]

25138 Knotts, Bob. *Track and Field* (2–4). Illus. Series: True Books. 2000, Children's Book Pr. LB $25.00 (978-0-516-21066-7). 48pp. Various track and field events are introduced in a simple text with material on their history and how they are judged. (Rev: BL 9/15/00) [796.42]

Author and Illustrator Index

Authors and illustrators are arranged alphabetically by last name, followed by book titles — which are also arranged alphabetically — and the text entry number. Book titles may refer to those that appear as a main entry or as an internal entry mentioned in the annotation. Fiction titles are indicated by (F) following the entry number.

Aamodt, Alice. *Wolf Pack*, 21837
Aardema, Verna. *The Lonely Lioness and the Ostrich Chicks*, 12166
  Rabbit Makes a Monkey of Lion, 12167
  Sebgugugu the Glutton, 12168
Aardema, Verna (ed.). *Why Mosquitoes Buzz in People's Ears*, 12169
Aardema, Verna (retel.). *Bringing the Rain to Kapiti Plain*, 12170
Aaseng, Nathan. *Business Builders in Computers*, 15519
  Business Builders in Fast Food, 15520
  Business Builders in Oil, 15521
  Business Builders in Sweets and Treats, 19184
  Construction, 15522
  The Marine Corps in Action, 24119
  Michael Jordan, 15969
  Nature's Poisonous Creatures, 21208
  The Peace Seekers, 16119
  Treacherous Traitors, 19472
  Wildshots, 20314
  Yearbooks in Science: 1930–1939, 20903
  Yearbooks in Science: 1940–1949, 20904
  You Are the Explorer, 17114
Abbot, Judi. *The Biggest Kiss*, 302(F)
Abbott, Jason. *The Ravioli Kid*, 3905(F)
Abbott, Tony. *City of the Dead*, 8694(F)
  Firegirl, 10483(F)
  Kringle, 8695(F)
  Lunch-Box Dream, 11322(F)
Abdel-Fattah, Randa. *Where the Streets Had a Name*, 10857(F)
Abdul-Jabbar, Kareem. *Sasquatch in the Paint*, 12013(F)
  What Color Is My World? The Lost History of African-American Inventors, 10533(F)
Abeel, Samantha. *What Once Was White*, 20453
Abel, Simone. *The Drop Goes Plop*, 23505
  From Little Acorns, 22995
Abela, Deborah. *The Ghosts of Gribblesea Pier*, 8696(F)
  Mission, 7716(F)
Aber, Linda Williams. *Carrie Measures Up*, 366(F)
  Grandma's Button Box, 164
  Who's Got Spots?, 23306
Abercrombie, Barbara. *The Show-and-Tell Lion*, 5623(F)
Abeya, Elisabet. *Hansel and Gretel / Hansel y Gretel*, 12171

Abley, Mark. *Ghost Cat*, 5062(F)
Ablow, Gail. *A Horse in the House and Other Strange but True Animal Stories*, 21209
Abnett, Dan. *The Battle of Gettysburg*, 18683
Aboff, Marcie. *Mike's Mystery*, 23307
Abolafia, Yossi. *It's Snowing! It's Snowing! Winter Poems*, 13990
  It's Valentine's Day, 13843
Abolivier, Aurelie. *Gran, You've Got Mail!*, 3262(F)
Abouraya, Karen Leggett. *Hands around the Library*, 17540
Abraham, Denise Gonzales. *Cecilia's Year*, 11155(F)
Abraham, Philip. *Television and Movies*, 23978
Abraham, Susan Gonzales. *Cecilia's Year*, 11155(F)
Abraham-Podietz, Eva. *Ten Thousand Children*, 17422
Abrahams, Peter. *Giving to the Poor*, 7332(F)
  Into the Dark, 7717(F)
  Quacky Baseball, 1492(F)
  Robbie Forester and the Outlaws of Sherwood Street, 7333(F)
Abrams, Douglas Carlton. *God's Dream*, 2995(F)
Abrams, Judith Z. *The Secret World of Kabbalah*, 19632
Abrams, Liesa. *Chronic Fatigue Syndrome*, 20492
Abramson, Andra Serlin. *Heavy Equipment Up Close*, 23990
  Inside Stars, 21114
Abramson, Andra Serlin (et al). *Inside Dinosaurs*, 16928
Abramson, Beverley. *Off We Go!*, 165
Abramson, Jill. *Obama*, 15335
Accardo, Anthony. *Benito's Sopaipillas / La sopaipillas de Benito*, 909(F)
  César Chávez, 14981
  Chiles for Benito / Chiles para Benito, 3065(F)
  The Last Doll / La Ultima Muneca, 5947(F)
  Where Did You Get Those Eyes? A Guide to Discovering Your Family History, 20182
Acedera, Kei. *Liesl and Po*, 9586(F)
  Secrets of the Crown, 9043(F)
Ackerman, Karen. *Bean's Big Day*, 3757(F)
  Song and Dance Man, 3041(F)
Ada, Alma Flor. *Dancing Home*, 11803(F)
  I Love Saturdays y Domingos, 3042(F)

  Love, Amalia, 7334(F)
  Tales Our Abuelitas Told, 12173
  The Three Golden Oranges, 12172
  With Love, Little Red Hen, 891(F)
  Yes! We Are Latinos, 11970(F)
Ada, Alma Flor (sel.). *Pio Peep! Traditional Spanish Nursery Rhymes/Rimas Tradicionles en Espanol*, 13253
Adam, Paul. *Max Cassidy*, 7718(F)
Adam, Beth. *Confessions of a Former Bully*, 10381(F)
Adams, Colleen. *Women's Suffrage*, 19404
Adams, Diane. *I Can Do It Myself!*, 3043(F)
  I Want to Help!, 5624(F)
Adams, Jean Ekman. *Clarence Goes Out West and Meets a Purple Horse*, 1493(F)
Adams, Lynn. *Chickens on the Move*, 394
  How Many Feet? How Many Tails? A Book of Math Riddles, 433
  Where's That Bone?, 261(F)
Adams, McCrea. *Tipi*, 18271
Adams, Michelle Medlock. *Care for a Puppy*, 22733
Adams, Sean. *Tim Duncan*, 15960
Adams, Simon. *Alexander*, 16150
  Ancient Egypt, 17223
  Elizabeth I, 16192
  The Presidents of the United States, 14797
  World War II, 17400
Adams, Steve. *The Boy Who Grew Flowers*, 1479(F)
  The Boy Who Wanted to Cook, 4859(F)
  Lost Boy, 14617
Adams, W. Royce. *Me and Jay*, 7719(F)
Adamson, Bonnie. *Feeling Better*, 20476
Adamson, Heather. *Ancient Egypt*, 17224
  Families in Many Cultures, 20177
  How Do You Measure Length and Distance?, 23427
  How Do You Measure Liquids?, 23427
  How Do You Measure Time?, 23427
  How Do You Measure Weight?, 23427
Adamson, Thomas K. *How Do You Measure Length and Distance?*, 23427
  How Do You Measure Liquids?, 23427
  How Do You Measure Time?, 23427
  How Do You Measure Weight?, 23427
  Lessons in Science Safety with Max Axiom, Super Scientist, 20966
  Tsunamis, 22625
Adare, Sierra. *Mohawk*, 19955
Addasi, Maha. *Time to Pray*, 2583(F)
  The White Nights of Ramadan, 19762

Paxmann, Christine. *From Mud Huts to Skyscrapers*, 16392
Payan, Gregory. *Essential Snowmobiling for Teens*, 24834
The Federalists and Anti-Federalists, 19546
Life on a Submarine, 24148
Marquis de Lafayette, 16244
Paye, Won-Ldy. *Head, Body, Legs*, 12854
Paye, Won-Ldy (retel.). *Mrs. Chicken and the Hungry Crocodile*, 12855
The Talking Vegetables, 12856
Payment, Simone. *Buck Leonard*, 15910
Frontline Marines, 20293
Roe v. Wade, 19376
The Trial of Leopold and Loeb, 19377
Payne, Adam. *Four in All*, 259
Payne, Brian W. *Let's Go Fishing*, 25004
Payne, C. C. *Lula Bell on Geekdom, Freakdom, and the Challenges of Bad Hair*, 7617(F)
Something to Sing About, 7618(F)
Payne, C. F. *Brave Harriet*, 14173
Casey at the Bat, 14033
Hide and Squeak, 673(F)
The Legend of the Curse of the Bambino, 24936
Meet Molly, 11454(F)
Mighty Jackie, 15916
Mousetronaut Goes to Mars, 1955(F)
Pop's Bridge, 4464(F)
Shoeless Joe and Black Betsy, 4443(F)
The Shot Heard 'Round the World, 4444
To Dare Mighty Things, 15364
Turkey Bowl, 6386(F)
Payne, Henry. *Where Did Daddy's Hair Go?*, 3426(F)
Payne, Nina. *Four in All*, 259
Payne, Tom. *Cats!*, 6472(F)
Payson, Dale. *The Lucky Stone*, 8486(F)
Paz, Grizelle. *Ruben's Jungle / La selva de Ruben*, 1115(F)
Ruben's Rainbow / El Arco Iris de Ruben, 324
Peacock, Carol Antoinette. *Death and Dying*, 20425
Red Thread Sisters, 7619(F)
Peacock, Phyllis Hornung. *Pythagoras and the Ratios*, 23327
Pearce, Al. *Famous Tracks*, 24893
Pearce, Carl. *Attention, Girls! A Guide to Learn All About Your AD/HD*, 20475
The No-Dogs-Allowed Rule, 3534(F)
Pearce, Clemency. *Frangoline and the Midnight Dream*, 1327(F)
Pearce, Emily Smith. *Isabel and the Miracle Baby*, 8628(F)
Slowpoke, 4112(F)
Pearce, Philippa. *A Finder's Magic*, 9603(F)
The Squirrel Wife, 12857
Tom's Midnight Garden, 9604(F)
Pearce, Q. L. *Ghost Hunters*, 24735
James Quadrino, 15796
Mysterious Disappearances, 24736
Red Bird Sings, 15219
The Stargazer's Guide to the Galaxy, 21128
Pearl, Norman. *The Bald Eagle*, 18252
Pearsall, Shelley. *All of the Above*, 7620(F)
All Shook Up, 8629(F)
Crooked River, 11090(F)
Jump into the Sky, 11420(F)
Pearson, Debora. *Alphabeep*, 123
Jungle Islands, 17753
Leo's Tree, 3452(F)
Sophie's Wheels, 2894(F)
Pearson, Luke. *Hilda and the Bird Parade*, 7219(F)
Hilda and the Midnight Giant, 7219(F)
Hildafolk, 7219(F)
Pearson, Maggie. *The Fox and the Rooster and Other Tales*, 12858

The Headless Horseman and Other Ghoulish Tales, 12859
Pearson, Mike Parker. *If Stones Could Speak*, 17086
Pearson, Ridley. *The Bridge to Never Land*, 8791(F)
The Challenge, 8124(F)
Peter and the Secret of Rundoon, 8792(F)
Peter and the Shadow Thieves, 8793(F)
Peter and the Sword of Mercy, 8794(F)
Science Fair, 11531(F)
Pearson, Susan. *Eagle-Eye Ernie Comes to Town*, 6851(F)
Hooray for Feet!, 260
How to Teach a Slug to Read, 2895(F)
Squeal and Squawk, 13773
We're Going on a Ghost Hunt, 1328(F)
Who Swallowed Harold?, 13774
Pearson, Susan (ed.). *The Drowsy Hours*, 13595
Pearson, Tracey Campbell. *Guinea Pigs Add Up*, 461(F)
Little Miss Muffet, 13300
The Moon, 14006
My Brother Bert, 3975(F)
Peck, Beth. *Abbie in Stitches*, 4502(F)
How Many Days to America? A Thanksgiving Story, 6388(F)
Just Like Josh Gibson, 4625(F)
Music for the End of Time, 14418
Peck, Ira. *Elizabeth Blackwell*, 15583
Peck, Jan. *Giant Peach Yodel!*, 4113(F)
The Green Mother Goose, 12860
Way Far Away on a Wild Safari, 1329(F)
Way Up High in a Tall Green Tree, 753(F)
Peck, Richard. *Fair Weather*, 11271(F)
The Ghost Belonged to Me, 9605(F)
Here Lies the Librarian, 11272(F)
A Long Way from Chicago, 11422(F)
The Mouse with the Question Mark Tail, 9606(F)
On the Wings of Heroes, 11421(F)
Past Perfect, Present Tense, 12006(F)
A Season of Gifts, 11422(F)
Secrets at Sea, 9607(F)
A Year Down Yonder, 11422(F)
Peck, Robert Newton. *Arly*, 11273(F)
Higbee's Halloween, 11720(F)
Peddicord, Jane Ann. *Night Wonders*, 21107
Pedersen, Janet. *Baby for Sale*, 1990(F)
Thea's Tree, 3981(F)
What to Do? What to Do?, 3748(F)
Pedlar, Elaine. *A Shelter in Our Car*, 4951(F)
Peel, Yana (ed.). *Faces for Baby*, 16393
Peers, Judi. *Shark Attack*, 12125(F)
Peet, Bill. *Big Bad Bruce*, 1330(F)
The Caboose Who Got Loose, 1331(F)
Cowardly Clyde, 2187(F)
Eli, 2188(F)
Farewell to Shady Glade, 2187(F)
The Luckiest One of All, 2187(F)
No Such Things, 2187(F)
Pamela Camel, 2187(F)
The Wump World, 4377(F)
Peet, Mal. *Cloud Tea Monkeys*, 10641(F)
Peete, Holly Robinson. *My Brother Charlie*, 3453(F)
Peete, Ryan Elizabeth. *My Brother Charlie*, 3453(F)
Peffer, Jessica. *DragonArt*, 24367
Peirce, Lincoln. *Big Nate*, 11721(F)
Big Nate Flips Out, 4114(F)
Big Nate on a Roll, 7621(F)
Big Nate Strikes Again, 11927(F)
Pellant, Chris. *Rocks and Fossils*, 23082
Pellegrini, Nancy. *Beijing*, 17634
Pellegrini, Nina. *Families Are Different*, 3454(F)
Pelleschi, Andrea. *Neil and Nan Build Narrative Nonfiction*, 16647

Olivia and Oscar Build an Opinion Piece, 16647
Pelley, Kathleen T. *Inventor McGregor*, 3455(F)
Magnus Maximus, A Marvelous Measurer, 4759(F)
Raj the Bookstore Tiger, 5456(F)
Pellowski, Michael J. *Super Sports Star Latrell Sprewell*, 15989
Pels, Winslow. *Ali and the Magic Stew*, 4750(F)
Cricket at the Manger, 6065(F)
Stone Soup, 12736
Pelta, Kathy. *Rediscovering Easter Island*, 17766
Texas. Rev. ed., 19180
The U.S. Navy, 24149
Pelton, Mindy L. *When Dad's at Sea*, 3456
Pelzel, Vernise Elaine. *Hugs on the Wind*, 1513(F)
Pemberton, Bonnie. *The Cat Master*, 9608(F)
Pendziwol, Jean. *No Dragons for Tea*, 1332(F)
Pendziwol, Jean E. *Marja's Skis*, 4760(F)
Once Upon a Dragon, 20858
The Red Sash, 4761(F)
Pendziwol, Jean K. *Once Upon a Northern Night*, 754(F)
Penn, Audrey. *Mystery at Blackbeard's Cove*, 8125(F)
Pennell, Christopher. *The Mysterious Woods of Whistle Root*, 9609(F)
Penner, Fred. *The Cat Came Back*, 16719
Penner, Lucille R. *Clean-Sweep Campers*, 23356
Dragons, 13196
Ice Wreck, 18189
Where's That Bone?, 261(F)
X Marks the Spot!, 262
Penney, Rich. *Raptor*, 16989
Penny, Malcolm. *Black Rhino*, 21651
Endangered Species, 22148
Giant Panda, 21938
Polar Bear, 21760
The Secret Life of Kangaroos, 21921
The Secret Life of Wild Horses, 22843
Pennypacker, Sara. *Clementine*, 10057(F)
Clementine and the Family Meeting, 8630(F)
Clementine, Friend of the Week, 10058(F)
Clementine's Letter, 6852(F)
The Mount Rushmore Calamity, 8860(F)
Pierre in Love, 2189(F)
Sparrow Girl, 4762(F)
Stuart Goes to School, 9610(F)
Stuart's Cape, 9610(F)
The Talented Clementine, 11722(F)
Penrose, Antony. *The Boy Who Bit Picasso*, 14332
Pentland, Peter. *Forensic Science*, 19497
Kitchen Science, 20923
Party Science, 20923
Toy and Game Science, 20923
Peot, Margaret. *Inkblot*, 24368
Peppas, Lynn. *Aircraft Carriers: Runways at Sea*, 24150
Cultural Traditions in Greece, 17881
Fighter Jets: Defending the Skies., 24150
M. I. A., 14539
Military Helicopters: Flying into Battle, 24150
Powerful Armored Vehicles, 24150
Percy, Graham. *A Cup of Starshine*, 13345
Percy, Graham (retel.). *The Ant and the Grasshopper*, 12861
The Lion and the Mouse, 12861
Perdomo, Willie. *¡Clemente!*, 15890
Visiting Langston, 13596

Wacky Trees, 23005
Spackman, Jeff. *Boo! Halloween Poems and Limericks*, 6260
Spada, Ada. *Fangs, Claws and Talons*, 21281
Spain, Susan Rosson. *The Deep Cut*, 11150(F)
Spalding, Andrea. *Bottled Sunshine*, 3551(F)
The Keeper and the Crows, 9798(F)
Me and Mr. Mah, 5034(F)
The Most Beautiful Kite in the World, 3552(F)
Spangenburg, Ray. *Edward Hopper*, 14282
Georgia O'Keeffe, 14324
Savvy Surfing on the Internet, 23948
Spangler, Brie. *The Caped 6th Grader*, 9645(F)
The Grumpy Dump Truck, 1425(F)
Spangler, Steve. *Naked Eggs and Flying Potatoes*, 20976
Spanyol, Jessica. *Little Neighbors on Sunnyside Street*, 2331(F)
Sparrow, Giles. *Cosmic! The Ultimate 3-D Guide to the Universe*, 21025
Nickel, 23056
Spay, Anthony. *Top 10 Deadliest Sharks*, 22538
Spearing, Craig. *The Great Big Wagon That Rang*, 4805(F)
Spears, Rick. *Dinosaur Mummies*, 16986
Tales of the Cryptids, 24699
Spears, Rick C. *Alien Investigation*, 24698
Speck, Katie. *Maybelle in the Soup*, 1426(F)
Speechley, Greta. *Clay Modeling*, 24303
Valentine Crafts, 19932
Speidel, Sandra. *Songs for the Seasons*, 13968
Speir, Nancy. *Check It Out! Reading, Finding, Helping*, 2759(F)
My First Airplane Ride, 5837(F)
Speirs, John. *Animal Tracks*, 13743
The Little Boy's Christmas Gift, 6175(F)
Spellman, Susan. *A Small Treasury of Easter*, 13844
Way to Go! Sports Poems, 14025
Spelman, Cornelia Maude. *When I Feel Jealous*, 5035(F)
When I Feel Worried, 5036(F)
Spencer, Ann. *Song of the Sea*, 13027
Spencer, Britt. *Fleas!*, 4204(F)
Make Your Mark, Franklin Roosevelt, 15356
Zarafa, 21897
Spencer, Lauren. *Hank Aaron*, 15882
Spencer, Mariko Ando. *A Crash of Rhinos, A Party of Jays*, 16599
Spencer, Octavia. *The Case of the Time-Capsule Bandit*, 8200(F)
Spencer, Russ. *Skateboarding*, 25088
Spengler, Kenneth J. *How Jackrabbit Got His Very Long Ears*, 1921(F)
Spengler, Kremena. *Chile*, 18153
France, 17815
Germany, 17827
Iraq, 18010
Israel, 17975
Russia, 17901
Spengler, Margaret. *Little Loon and Papa*, 5135(F)
Storm Is Coming!, 2383(F)
Sper, Emily. *The Kids' Fun Book of Jewish Time*, 288
Sperling, Vatsala. *How Ganesh Got His Elephant Head*, 19672
Sperring, Mark. *The Fairytale Cake*, 5992(F)
Find-a-Saurus, 1427(F)
Mermaid Dreams, 1428(F)
The Sunflower Sword, 1429(F)
Wanda's First Day, 1430(F)
Sperry, Armstrong. *Call It Courage*, 8201(F)
Spetter, Jung-Hee. *Lily and Trooper's Fall*, 2963(F)
Lily and Trooper's Winter, 2963(F)

Spicer, Maggee. *We'll All Go Exploring*, 23006
We'll All Go Flying, 289
When They Are Up . . ., 13310
Spickert, Diane Nelson. *Earthsteps*, 23298
Spiegel, Beth. *First Grade Stinks!*, 5781(F)
Rosa's Room, 3666(F)
Will It Be a Baby Brother?, 3119(F)
Spiegelman, Art. *Jack and the Box*, 7280(F)
Little Lit: Folklore and Fairy Tale Funnies, 7281(F)
Spiegelman, Art (ed.). *Little Lit: Strange Stories for Strange Kids*, 12008(F)
The TOON Treasury of Classic Children's Comics, 7283(F)
Little Lit: It Was a Dark and Silly Night, 7282(F)
Spiegelman, Nadja. *Zig and Wikki in Something Ate My Homework*, 7284(F), 7285(F)
Zig and Wikki in The Cow, 7285(F)
Spiegle, Dan. *Historical Adventure*, 7010(F)
Murder and Mystery, 7178(F)
Spieled, Sandra. *What's Wrong with Timmy?*, 3742(F)
Spielman, Gloria. *Janusz Korczak's Children*, 16240
Marcel Marceau, 14541
Spiers, John. *Three Swords for Granada*, 9541(F)
Spillman, Fredrika. *Year of the Black Pony*, 8394(F)
Spilsbury, Louise. *Butterfly*, 22319
Classifying Fish, 22468
Classifying Reptiles, 21309
Duck, 22053
Frog, 21364
Howling Hurricanes, 23490
The Life Cycle of Amphibians, 21310
The Life Cycle of Fish, 22469
The Life Cycle of Insects, 22232
Living on the Ganges River, 17660
A Mob of Kangaroos, 21671
A Murder of Crows, 22026
A Rookery of Penguins, 22125
Save the Bengal Tiger, 21812
Save the Black Rhino, 21812
Save the Blue Whale, 21812
Save the Florida Manatee, 21812
Save the Giant Panda, 21812
A School of Dolphins, 22444
Shattering Earthquakes, 23120
Sweeping Tsunamis, 22633
A Troop of Chimpanzees, 21707
Watching Kangaroos in Australia, 21924
Watching Lions in Africa, 21813
Watching Penguins in Antarctica, 22124
Water, 19304
What Are Forces and Motion? Exploring Science with Hands-on Activities, 23621
Spilsbury, Richard. *Alligator*, 21335
Bengal Tiger, 21814
Black Rhino, 21670
Bones Speak! Solving Crimes from the Past, 19511
Cartoons and Animation, 23988
Classifying Fish, 22468
Classifying Reptiles, 21309
Climate Change Catastrophe, 19305
Comics and Graphic Novels, 16417
Deforestation Crisis, 19305
Design and Technical Art, 20350
Great White Shark, 22558
Howling Hurricanes, 23490
Jay-Z, 14516
The Life Cycle of Amphibians, 21310
The Life Cycle of Fish, 22469
The Life Cycle of Insects, 22232
Living on the Ganges River, 17660

A Mob of Kangaroos, 21671
A Murder of Crows, 22026
On the Film Set, 16840
Pop Art, 16464
A Rookery of Penguins, 22125
Save the Bengal Tiger, 21812
Save the Black Rhino, 21812
Save the Blue Whale, 21812
Save the Florida Manatee, 21812
Save the Giant Panda, 21812
A School of Dolphins, 22444
Settlements of the Ganges River, 17661
Shattering Earthquakes, 23120
Sweeping Tsunamis, 22633
Threats to Our Water Supply, 19305
A Troop of Chimpanzees, 21707
Waste and Recycling Challenges, 19333
Watching Kangaroos in Australia, 21924
Watching Lions in Africa, 21813
Watching Penguins in Antarctica, 22124
Water, 19304
What Are Forces and Motion? Exploring Science with Hands-on Activities, 23621
What Are Solids, Liquids, and Gases? Exploring Science with Hands-on Activities, 23585
What Is Electricity and Magnetism? Exploring Science with Hands-on Activities, 23652
Zoom In on Crime Scenes, 19512
Spinelli, Eileen. *The Best Time of Day*, 2964(F)
A Big Boy Now, 2332(F)
Buzz, 2333(F)
Callie Cat, Ice Skater, 2334(F)
Cold Snap, 2965(F)
The Dancing Pancake, 8653(F)
Do You Have a Cat?, 4809(F)
Do You Have a Dog?, 5540(F)
Heat Wave, 4810(F)
Hero Cat, 5541(F)
In My New Yellow Shirt, 5993(F)
Miss Fox's Class Earns a Field Trip, 2335(F)
Miss Fox's Class Shapes Up, 2336(F)
Peace Week in Miss Fox's Class, 2337(F)
The Perfect Thanksgiving, 6412(F)
Polar Bear, Arctic Hare, 14005
Princess Pig, 2338(F)
Silly Tilly, 4202(F)
Someday, 2966(F)
Song for the Whooping Crane, 13791
Sophie's Masterpiece, 1431(F)
Tea Party Today, 13661
Today I Will, 20146
Together at Christmas, 6176(F)
Wanda's Monster, 5037(F)
When No One Is Watching, 5038(F)
When Papa Comes Home Tonight, 792(F)
When You Are Happy, 3553(F)
Spinelli, Jerry. *Eggs*, 10450(F)
I Can Be Anything, 2967(F)
Jake and Lily, 8654(F)
Knots in My Yo-Yo String, 14746
The Library Card, 11771(F)
Loser, 11945(F)
Maniac Magee, 7664(F)
Third Grade Angels, 11946(F)
Today I Will, 20146
Wringer, 10451(F)
Spinner, Stephanie. *Alex the Parrot*, 22027
Aliens for Breakfast, 9045(F)
It's a Miracle, 6367(F)
Paddywack, 6935(F)
Spiotta-Dimare, Loren. *Rockwell*, 4811(F)
Spires, Ashley. *Binky Takes Charge*, 7286(F)
Binky the Space Cat, 7287(F)
Binky to the Rescue, 7288(F)
Binky Under Pressure, 7289(F)

Title Index

This index contains both main entry titles and internal titles cited within entries. References are to entry numbers, not page numbers. Fiction titles are indicated by (F) following the entry number.

Subject/Grade Level Index

All entries are listed by subject and then according to grade level suitability (see the key at the foot of pages for grade level designations). Subjects are arranged alphabetically and subject heads may be subdivided into nonfiction (e.g., "Airplanes") and fiction (e.g., "Airplanes — Fiction"). References to entries are by entry number, not page number.

P = Primary; PI = Primary-Intermediate; I = Intermediate; IJ = Intermediate-Junior High

P = Primary; PI = Primary-Intermediate; I = Intermediate; IJ = Intermediate-Junior High

Authors
IJ: 16629

Authors — African American
IJ: 16497

Authors — Asian American
IJ: 14209

Authors — Biography
P: 3160, 14153, 14607, 14611, 14644, 14665, 14668, 14701, 14721, 14733, 14761, 14765, 14783, 14793
PI: 14602, 14604, 14608–09, 14617, 14619, 14621–22, 14625–26, 14631, 14635–36, 14641, 14646–49, 14651–53, 14659–60, 14664, 14667, 14669–71, 14674, 14678, 14680–82, 14685, 14690, 14698, 14700, 14709, 14716, 14722, 14735, 14740, 14742–44, 14747, 14751, 14757, 14760, 14762–63, 14767, 14773, 14785, 14788, 14794–95, 14971, 15429
I: 14639, 14675, 14683, 14688–89, 14702, 14712, 14723–24, 14726, 14752, 14769, 14771
IJ: 14193–96, 14199, 14207, 14211–12, 14339, 14605–06, 14610, 14613–16, 14624, 14627–29, 14632–34, 14637–38, 14640, 14642–43, 14654–55, 14657–58, 14661, 14672–73, 14676, 14684, 14691–97, 14703, 14707–08, 14715, 14717–20, 14727–28, 14730–32, 14736–39, 14741, 14745–46, 14748–50, 14753–55, 14758–59, 14764, 14766, 14768, 14770, 14772, 14776–79, 14781, 14784, 14786–87, 14792, 14796, 14972, 15124–25, 15189

Authors — Careers
IJ: 14613, 20328

Authors — Fiction
P: 5615
PI: 7463, 10031
I: 7338, 10649
IJ: 11629

Authorship
PI: 16639

Autism
PI: 20485
I: 20454–55, 20483
IJ: 20456, 20469, 20480, 20489

Autism — Biography
IJ: 15440

Autism — Fiction
P: 3453, 4926, 5682, 5746
PI: 3049
IJ: 7551, 8668, 10228, 10399, 11181

Autobiographies
IJ: 14732

Automobile accidents — Fiction
P: 5863

Automobile industry — Biography
IJ: 15699

Automobile racing
See also NASCAR
P: 5866
PI: 24882, 24885–87, 24894
I: 24884, 24890–91, 24899
IJ: 24606, 24888–89, 24893

Automobile racing — Biography
PI: 15869
I: 15871
IJ: 15870, 15872, 15875–79

Automobile racing — Fiction
I: 12110

Automobile travel — Fiction
PI: 4218
IJ: 7498, 10096

Automobiles
P: 15696, 18800, 24038, 24040, 24045, 24047, 24054, 24057, 24061–65
PI: 15695, 24037, 24042, 24050, 24055, 24060
I: 24034, 24041, 24051–53, 24058–59, 24066–67
IJ: 24031, 24035, 24039, 24044, 24892

Automobiles — Biography
P: 15700
I: 15694
IJ: 15575, 15697–98

Automobiles — Careers
P: 5842
IJ: 20352

Automobiles — Drawing and painting
PI: 24351

Automobiles — Fiction
P: 1515, 2544, 2688, 2739, 3057, 3801, 3914, 5828, 5850, 5855, 5863, 5875
I: 9075

Automobiles — Poetry
P: 13532

Autumn
P: 99, 21140, 21142, 21155
PI: 19800, 21141

Autumn — Fiction
P: 2388, 2823, 3596, 4134, 4371, 6779

Autumn — Poetry
P: 13940
PI: 13954

Avalanches
PI: 23084

Avalanches — Fiction
IJ: 10849

Avalon — Fiction
IJ: 9540

Avery, Oswald
IJ: 15559

Avi (author)
IJ: 14615–16

Aviation
See also Airplanes; Airships
P: 23677
PI: 23834
IJ: 23804, 23809, 23814, 23816, 23819, 23830

Axles
PI: 23665

Aymara (South American people)
I: 18131

Azerbaijan
I: 17898

Aztecs
PI: 12619, 17188, 17333
I: 17334, 17338
IJ: 17194, 17326, 17332, 18060, 18072

Aztecs — Crafts
IJ: 18066

Aztecs — Folklore
PI: 12831
IJ: 13155

Aztecs — Mythology
PI: 12636
I: 13171
IJ: 7326, 13194

B

Babies
P: 237, 3249, 13630, 20180, 20189, 20206, 20212, 20867–72, 21510

Babies — Fiction
P: 170, 253, 306, 1251, 1325, 1402, 1845–46, 2056, 2435, 2451, 2585, 2682, 2706, 2729, 2772, 2791, 2822, 2853–54, 2879, 2889, 2980, 3045, 3061, 3095, 3101, 3119–20, 3124, 3143, 3208, 3230–31, 3265, 3268, 3321, 3328, 3337, 3353, 3392, 3401, 3413, 3419–20, 3428, 3485–86, 3531, 3535, 3557, 3563, 3566, 3574, 3583, 3585, 3597, 3603, 3605, 3617, 3621, 3626, 3880, 3892, 3901, 3903, 3943–44, 4045, 4051, 4104, 4140, 4262, 4589, 4821, 5581, 5642, 6671
PI: 3044, 3570, 3636, 8649, 10018, 11709
I: 10123, 10168
IJ: 10075, 10240

Babies — Poetry
P: 3060, 13334, 13342, 13370

Baboons
IJ: 21698

Baboons — Fiction
PI: 8400

Babylon
IJ: 17988

Babysitting
PI: 24471
I: 19223
IJ: 19222, 19224, 19231

Babysitting — Fiction
P: 2002, 2134, 2356, 2403, 2748, 2764, 3243, 6600, 6629, 6755
PI: 10453
I: 7191, 7305
IJ: 8147, 9967, 11632, 11685

Bach, Johann Sebastian
P: 14397

Bach, Johann Sebastian — Fiction
P: 4474, 4642

Backyards
PI: 21189

Bacon, Roger — Fiction
IJ: 10567

Bacteria
PI: 20686, 20919, 21170, 21183, 21203
I: 22595
IJ: 20528, 20547, 20573, 22601

Badgers
PI: 21653

Badgers — Fiction
P: 5180, 6656–57
IJ: 9277

Badges
IJ: 23938

Badminton
IJ: 24818

Baer, Ralph
PI: 15560

Baghdad (Iraq)
I: 18012
IJ: 22860

Bagpipes — Fiction
IJ: 7861

Bahamas
I: 18115

Baird, John Logie
I: 15561

Baker, Josephine
P: 14446

Baking
See also specific baking products, e.g., Cupcakes
P: 24552

Baking — Careers
P: 20295

Baking — Fiction
P: 2340, 2888, 2927, 3090, 6081, 6365, 9583
PI: 1765, 9188, 11367

P = Primary; PI = Primary-Intermediate; I = Intermediate; IJ = Intermediate-Junior High

Coyotes — Fiction
P: 2067
I: 8435

Coyotes — Folklore
I: 13039

Crabs
P: 22432
I: 22430

Crafts
See also specific crafts,
e.g., Paper crafts
P: 3675, 3716, 4473, 24169,
24173, 24177, 24196–97,
24207–08, 24223, 24227,
24229, 24231, 24238–41,
24249, 24251, 24254, 24258,
24264–65, 24278, 24389
PI: 16748, 17023, 18639,
19932, 24161, 24165–66,
24170, 24176, 24180, 24186,
24189, 24192, 24195, 24198,
24203–04, 24209, 24211,
24214–15, 24225, 24232,
24234–35, 24248, 24250,
24252, 24255–57, 24259–61,
24263, 24267–68, 24274,
24280, 24287, 24292, 24301,
24393, 24415–18, 24471
I: 12787, 16830, 17432,
18302, 18798, 20021, 24164,
24175, 24182–84, 24184–85,
24188, 24193, 24199–200,
24213, 24216–17, 24221,
24230, 24242–44, 24262,
24269, 24272–73, 24277,
24283, 24286, 24288, 24290,
24300, 24377, 24395, 24439,
24467, 24800
IJ: 16960, 17201, 17245,
17304, 17651, 17675, 17812,
17871, 17919, 18066, 24163,
24168, 24172, 24174,
24178–79, 24191, 24194,
24201–02, 24212, 24218–20,
24222, 24224, 24226, 24228,
24236–37, 24245, 24275–76,
24279, 24281–82, 24285,
24291, 24294–96, 24304–07,
24315–16, 24394, 24449,
24453, 24460, 24463

Crandall, Prudence
P: 14876
IJ: 14875

Crane, Stephen
IJ: 14637

Cranes
P: 24002

Cranes (bird) — Fiction
P: 916, 10650

Cranes (bird) — Poetry
P: 13791

Crayfish
PI: 22431

Crayons
P: 23770

Crayons — Fiction
P: 6687

Crazy Horse (Sioux chief)
PI: 15176
I: 15174, 15177

IJ: 15175, 15178

Crazy Horse (Sioux chief) — Fiction
PI: 10863

Creation stories
P: 977, 1377, 19707
PI: 10558, 12194, 12233,
13058
I: 12760
IJ: 19682

Creative writing
PI: 16660
IJ: 16636

Creative writing — Fiction
P: 2893
PI: 11706, 11896
IJ: 11783

Credit
IJ: 19188

Credit cards
P: 19201

Cree Indians
I: 18049

Cree Indians — Fiction
P: 3099

Creek Indians
PI: 18325, 18350

Creesy, Eleanor
P: 14095

Creutzfeldt-Jakob disease
IJ: 20561

Crews, Donald
P: 3160

Crick, Francis
IJ: 15523

Crickets
P: 22168, 22224
PI: 22208

Crickets — Fiction
P: 1632, 6024
I: 9754

Crime and criminals
See also specific crimes,
e.g., Stealing
PI: 19522
I: 19495
IJ: 17121, 19472, 19475,
19484, 19509–10, 19515,
19521

Crime and criminals — Fiction
P: 11021
PI: 4621
I: 8013
IJ: 7517, 8076, 8078, 8162,
8262, 10354, 10436, 10769,
11591

Crimean War — Biography
I: 16276

Criminal justice
IJ: 19381

Criminals
See Crime and criminals

Croatian Americans — Fiction
IJ: 11198

Crocheting
PI: 24436
IJ: 24438, 24444

Crockett, Davy
P: 14098
PI: 14096–97

Crockett, Davy — Fiction
P: 1394

Crocodiles
See Alligators and crocodiles

Crop circles
I: 24680, 24700

Cross-dressing — Fiction
IJ: 10469

Crow Indians
PI: 18321

Crow Indians — Biography
IJ: 15179

Crow, Joseph Medicine
IJ: 15179

Crows
PI: 22015, 22026

Crows — Fiction
P: 2892, 4383, 5315, 5530
PI: 12259
IJ: 8340

Crows — Folklore
P: 13080

Crows — Poetry
PI: 13788

Crum, George
PI: 15623

Crusades
IJ: 17946

Crustaceans
P: 22435
I: 22429

Crutcher, Chris
IJ: 14638

Cruz, Celia
PI: 14469

Cryptograms
See Codes and ciphers

Cryptozoology
IJ: 24699

Cub Scouts
See Scouts and scouting

Cuba
PI: 18093, 18095, 18109,
18111
I: 18104
IJ: 18100

Cuba — Biography
IJ: 14437, 16173–74

Cuba — Fiction
P: 3510, 4556
PI: 7695
IJ: 10093, 10841, 11352

Cuba — Folklore
I: 12509

Cuban Americans
PI: 19963

Cuban Americans — Fiction
P: 4488
I: 11193

Cuban Missile Crisis
IJ: 18845

Cuban Missile Crisis — Fiction
IJ: 11446, 11470

Culpepper, Daunte
PI: 16017
IJ: 16016

Cults
IJ: 19664

Cultural Revolution (China)
IJ: 14396

Culture
I: 19978

Cuna Indians — Art
IJ: 16442

Cunxin, Li
PI: 16186

Cupcakes — Fiction
P: 1114, 6697

Curie, Marie
P: 15628–29
PI: 15631, 15633
I: 15626
IJ: 15624–25, 15627, 15630,
15632

Curie, Pierre
PI: 15633

Curiosities and wonders
PI: 24701, 24720, 24754
I: 16910, 24693, 24734,
24749–50, 24752
IJ: 17146, 20917, 24682,
24717, 24729, 24732, 24753,
24755

Curiosity — Fiction
P: 2123, 2992

Curses
IJ: 24719

Curses — Fiction
IJ: 7435

Curtis, Christopher Paul
I: 14639

Custer, George Armstrong
IJ: 15034–35

Cutlery — Fiction
P: 1383

Cyberbullying
PI: 20225
IJ: 20218

Cyberterrorism
IJ: 20056

Cycles (nature)
P: 20927
I: 21040

P = Primary; PI = Primary-Intermediate; I = Intermediate; IJ = Intermediate-Junior High

Cycling
See Bicycles

Cyprus
IJ: 17779

Cyr, Louis
PI: 16187

Cyrus, Miley
I: 14470

Cystic fibrosis
PI: 20539
IJ: 20568

Cystic fibrosis — Fiction
IJ: 8616

Czech Americans — Fiction
I: 11262

Czechoslovakia
IJ: 17407, 17431

Czechoslovakia — Fiction
IJ: 10722

Czechoslovakia — Folklore
I: 13103

D

D-Day (World War II)
IJ: 17418

D-Day (World War II) — Fiction
IJ: 11411

da Gama, Vasco
IJ: 14099–01, 17935

da Vinci, Leonardo
P: 14249
I: 14250
IJ: 14248, 14251–56, 16355

da Vinci, Leonardo — Fiction
P: 4868
PI: 10666
I: 10753

Dachshunds
P: 22802

Dadaism — Fiction
PI: 4619

Daffodils
P: 22881

Dahl, Roald
PI: 14641
IJ: 14640, 14642

Dairy cattle
P: 22906
PI: 22900

Dairy farms
P: 22915, 23749
PI: 22900

Dairy products
P: 20809

Dairying
See Cattle

Dakota Indians
See Sioux Indians

Dakota Indians — Fiction
See Sioux Indians — Fiction
IJ: 10873, 11094

Dalai Lama
I: 16188
IJ: 16189

Dali, Salvador
IJ: 14257

Dalmatians — Fiction
PI: 9783

Damadian, Raymond
IJ: 15634

Damon, Matt
IJ: 14471

Dams
PI: 23881
IJ: 23850

Dance
See also specific types of dance, e.g., Ballet
P: 16810
PI: 16811, 16820
IJ: 16805, 16828

Dance — Biography
PI: 14445, 14451, 14533
I: 14522
IJ: 14201, 14436, 14477, 14487, 14544

Dance — Fiction
P: 331, 476, 937, 1669, 1866, 1985, 2108, 2257, 2744, 3041, 3072, 3451, 3692, 3696, 4921, 5000, 6466, 6892
PI: 4467, 4687
IJ: 7013, 10233

Dance — Folklore
PI: 13143

Dance — Poetry
P: 13332
PI: 13382

Dancing Wheelchairs
I: 20472

Dandelions
P: 23019

Dangerous animals
IJ: 20844

Danziger, Paula
IJ: 14643

Daredevils
IJ: 24772

Daredevils — Biography
PI: 14159

d'Arezzo, Guido
PI: 14404

Darwin, Charles
PI: 15641, 15643
I: 15637–38, 15644
IJ: 15635–36, 15639–40, 15642, 15645–47

Darwin, Charles — Fiction
P: 4602

Dating (social) — Fiction
I: 8456

Dakota Indians — Fiction
IJ: 7001, 7417, 7684, 9998, 10415, 10419, 11641, 11643

Dave (1834–1864)
P: 14259

David-Neel, Alexandra
P: 17690

Davis, Jefferson
PI: 15037
IJ: 15036

Davis, Miles
IJ: 14472

Davis, Terrell
IJ: 16018

Dawes, Dominique
IJ: 16078

Dawn — Poetry
PI: 13343

Day, Dorothy
I: 15433

Day of the Dead
P: 157, 5927, 19764, 19776, 19817, 19838
PI: 19785, 19794

Day of the Dead — Fiction
P: 5914, 5918

Days — Folklore
PI: 12447

de Aviles, Pedro Menendez
IJ: 18394

de Kooning, Willem
I: 14260

de Portola, Gaspar
IJ: 14987

de Soto, Hernando
I: 14102
IJ: 14103

de Zavala, Lorenzo
IJ: 15038

Deaf
P: 20462, 20471
PI: 4476, 16541, 20465

Deaf — Biography
P: 15446, 15450
PI: 15448, 15452–53, 15455, 15457
I: 15449, 15454, 15456
IJ: 15425, 15451

Deaf — Fiction
P: 4819, 4989–90, 5022
PI: 4840, 4988, 8665, 11882
I: 10518, 10522
IJ: 7362, 8431, 10524, 11426, 11439

Death
See also Euthanasia
P: 3391, 17593, 20424
PI: 20422, 20428
I: 19683, 20420, 20427
IJ: 17113, 19366, 20421, 20423, 20425, 20429

Death — Fiction
P: 925, 1773, 2066, 3055, 3103, 3114, 3121, 3127, 3182, 3206, 3255, 3394, 3468, 3540, 3546, 3551, 3624, 4579, 4950, 4996, 5006, 5020, 5040, 5050, 5132, 5159, 5320, 5455, 5584, 5598, 5639, 5921, 6511, 11842
PI: 7548, 7617, 9918, 10142, 10165, 10355, 10430
I: 7520, 7560, 7701, 7803, 8678, 10097, 10104, 10275, 10348, 10390, 10464, 10503, 10530
IJ: 7351, 7369, 7422, 7478, 7629, 7638, 7641, 7656, 7901, 8130, 8315, 8343, 8448, 8492, 8664, 9111, 9631, 10073, 10112, 10116–17, 10137, 10140, 10153, 10169, 10173, 10176, 10178, 10185, 10189, 10191–92, 10197, 10207, 10244, 10247, 10309, 10357, 10406, 10434, 10486, 10512, 10517, 11387, 11988

Death — Poetry
PI: 13892
I: 13706

Death Valley National Park
PI: 19087
IJ: 18627, 19069

Declaration of Independence (U.S.)
P: 18537
PI: 121, 18514, 18516, 18541, 18550
I: 18509, 18511
IJ: 15122, 18496, 18513, 18579

Deep-sea animals
IJ: 22387

Deep-sea vents
PI: 22652

Deer
P: 21859, 21864, 21866
PI: 21857
I: 21861–62

Deer -- Fiction
P: 5543

Deer — Fiction
P: 6796
IJ: 8420

Deere, John
PI: 15648

Defecation
P: 2722

Deforestation
PI: 19266

Degas, Edgar
PI: 14261, 16407, 16823
I: 16424

Delacroix, Eugene
P: 14262

Delano, Poli
I: 14705

Delaware (state)
PI: 18969, 18987
IJ: 19016, 19036

Delaware (state) — History
PI: 18422
IJ: 18442, 18479

P = Primary; PI = Primary-Intermediate; I = Intermediate; IJ = Intermediate-Junior High

P = Primary; PI = Primary-Intermediate; I = Intermediate; IJ = Intermediate-Junior High

P = Primary; PI = Primary-Intermediate; I = Intermediate; IJ = Intermediate-Junior High

P = Primary; PI = Primary-Intermediate; I = Intermediate; IJ = Intermediate-Junior High

PI: 18564, 18602, 18604–05, 18616–17, 18619, 18621, 18639, 18642, 18647–48, 18681–82, 21661
I: 18607, 18610, 18628, 18630, 18632, 18636–37, 18643, 18654–55, 18665, 18670–72, 18675
IJ: 18603, 18611, 18613, 18620, 18623, 18627, 18645, 18659–60, 18662, 18666–68, 18677, 18680

Frontier life (U.S.) — Biography
P: 14065, 14098, 15128
PI: 14060, 14096–97, 14549–50
I: 14062, 14064, 14551, 14836
IJ: 14061, 14063, 14552, 14817, 15087, 15442

Frontier life (U.S.) — Crafts
I: 18636

Frontier life (U.S.) — Fiction
P: 3824, 4423, 4459, 4471, 4578, 4606–07, 4633–34, 4636, 4667, 4731, 6087, 6187, 6469, 11034, 11112
PI: 4567, 6712, 7310, 10974, 11041, 11043–44, 11050–52, 11067, 11076, 11082–83, 11096, 11099, 11102, 11104, 11113
I: 8129, 8554, 10966, 10982, 11032–33, 11036, 11057, 11059, 11062, 11064, 11069–71, 11075, 11078, 11090, 11093, 11101, 11108–09
IJ: 8459, 8677, 10869–70, 10977, 11011, 11017–18, 11020, 11024–25, 11027, 11030–31, 11037–38, 11040, 11045–46, 11055, 11060, 11066, 11068, 11072–74, 11079–80, 11084, 11086, 11088, 11092, 11094, 11100, 11105–07, 11110, 11255

Frontier life (U.S.) — Plays
I: 16879

Frost, Robert
P: 14662
IJ: 14663

Fruits
See specific types of fruits, e.g., Apples
P: 20809, 22961, 22964, 22967
PI: 12686
IJ: 22896

Fuel cells
IJ: 23616

Fulton, Robert
PI: 15706, 15708
IJ: 15707

Funerals
I: 19683

Funerals — Fiction
I: 11570

Fur trade — Fiction
P: 4761

Future — Fiction
IJ: 8213

G

Gac-Artigas, Alejandro
IJ: 14988

Gág, Wanda
PI: 14267

Gagarin, Yuri
PI: 14121

Gagne, Eric
I: 15896

Galapagos Islands
PI: 18018, 18123
IJ: 18154

Galapagos Islands — Animals
PI: 21243

Galapagos Islands — Fiction
P: 5328, 5351

Galaxies
See also Stars
PI: 21130

Galileo
PI: 15712
I: 15709, 15714
IJ: 15710–11, 15713

Galileo — Fiction
P: 4379

Gallaudet, Thomas
P: 20471

Gambling — Fiction
IJ: 10969

Gambling — Sports
IJ: 24872

Game reserves — Fiction
IJ: 9715

Games
See also Picture puzzles; Puzzles; Sports; Word games and puzzles; and specific games, e.g., Chess
P: 13321, 20179, 24278
PI: 24180, 24471, 24813, 24839
I: 18249, 18302, 24608, 24766, 24800, 24808, 24875
IJ: 24780, 25056

Games — Experiments and projects
I: 20923

Games — Fiction
P: 2767–68, 3018, 13130
PI: 1456

Ganci, Peter J.
PI: 15064

Gandhi, Mahatma
PI: 16210–11
I: 16208–09, 16213
IJ: 16212, 16214

Ganesha (Hindu deity) — Fiction
P: 4586

Ganges River
PI: 17660–61
IJ: 17647

Gantos, Jack
PI: 14664

Garages — Fiction
P: 2789

Garbage
P: 19326, 19334
I: 19330
IJ: 19333

Garbage — Fiction
P: 2707

Garbage trucks — Fiction
P: 1259, 2162

Gardens and gardening
P: 464, 16797, 19278
PI: 158, 24575, 24579, 24582
I: 22172, 24574, 24576–77, 24581, 24583–84
IJ: 21240, 21240, 21255, 22891, 24578, 24580

Gardens and gardening — Biography
PI: 16156

Gardens and gardening — Fiction
P: 9, 1124, 1651, 1745, 2292, 2502, 2588, 2629, 2649, 2680, 2702, 2765, 2906, 3058, 3113, 3127, 3248, 3323, 3545, 3596, 3700, 3896, 4281, 4322, 4342, 4367, 4410, 4561, 4610, 4936, 5424, 13317
PI: 4724, 7472, 7536, 8136
I: 10004
IJ: 7421, 7614

Gardens and gardening — Poetry
P: 13966, 13995
PI: 13950

Garfield, James A.
IJ: 15255

Garnett, Kevin
PI: 15963
IJ: 15962

Garter snakes
IJ: 21400

Gases (physics)
I: 20964

Gases (physics) — Experiments and projects
PI: 23585

Gates, Bill
I: 15715–16, 15719
IJ: 15717–18, 15720

Gates, Bill and Melinda
IJ: 15721

Gaudi, Antoni
P: 14268

Gauguin, Paul
P: 14216
IJ: 14269

Gawain (legendary character) — Fiction
PI: 10804

Gay and lesbian parents
IJ: 20185, 20214

Gay and lesbian parents — Fiction
P: 3215, 3408, 3408–10, 3427

Gay men and lesbians
See also Gay and lesbian parents
PI: 20228, 20228
IJ: 20214

Gay men and lesbians — Fiction
P: 3607, 4999
PI: 3469
I: 8283
IJ: 10174, 10174

Gay youth — Fiction
IJ: 7584

Geckos
PI: 21382
IJ: 22682

Gee, Maggie
PI: 15065

Geese
See Ducks and geese

Gehrig, Lou
IJ: 15897–98

Gehry, Frank
IJ: 14270

Geisel, Theodor
P: 14665
PI: 14667, 14669–71
IJ: 14666

Gellar, Sarah Michelle
PI: 14484

Gemini 4 (spacecraft)
IJ: 23708

Gems
IJ: 23291, 23303

Genealogy
PI: 20184
I: 20205
IJ: 20182, 20217, 24478, 24478

Genealogy — Fiction
I: 8477

Generals (U.S.) — Biography
PI: 15027

Generosity
P: 20072

Generosity — Fiction
P: 1247, 1963, 2602, 2625, 4564, 4878
I: 6060

IJ: 17302

Gladiators (Rome) — Fiction
IJ: 10743

Glass
PI: 23773
I: 23762

Glass blowing — Fiction
P: 4558

Glenn, John
P: 15066
PI: 15069
I: 15067–68
IJ: 15070, 23685

Glenn, Mike
IJ: 24954

Global warming
P: 19277
PI: 19297, 19299, 19301, 19317
I: 19237, 19252, 19310, 19314
IJ: 18193, 19247, 19251, 19264, 19287, 19290, 19295, 23444, 23552

Global warming — Fiction
IJ: 8082

Globe Theatre (London)
PI: 17834
IJ: 14734, 16445

Globe Theatre (London) — Fiction
PI: 4548
IJ: 10761, 10824

Globes
See Maps and globes

Gnomes — Folklore
P: 12468

Goals — Fiction
PI: 2810

Goat farmers
PI: 2624

Goats
P: 21961, 22924
I: 22918
IJ: 22890

Goats — Fiction
P: 2302, 3928, 4694, 5161, 6058

Goats — Folklore
P: 12206, 12428

Goblins
P: 1402, 6332

God
P: 19650, 19679

God — Fiction
P: 1123
IJ: 7642

God — Poetry
P: 13333

Goddard, Robert
IJ: 15722

Gods and goddesses
PI: 13176
IJ: 13190, 13203

Gogh, Vincent van — Fiction
P: 4421

Gold
IJ: 23034

Gold miners — Fiction
P: 4414

Gold Rush (Alaska and Yukon)
IJ: 18033, 18036

Gold Rush (Alaska and Yukon) — Fiction
P: 4668
PI: 11053
I: 11317
IJ: 7957

Gold Rush (California)
PI: 18609, 18615, 18625
I: 18606, 18631, 18643, 18679
IJ: 18598, 18646, 18653, 18658

Gold Rush (California) — Cookbooks
IJ: 18658

Gold Rush (California) — Fiction
P: 4630, 4635, 4666
PI: 11016
IJ: 10954, 10988, 11039, 11061, 11111

Golden Gate Bridge
PI: 23846, 23873
I: 19066
IJ: 23885

Golden Gate Bridge — Fiction
P: 4464

Golden retrievers
PI: 22748

Goldfish — Fiction
P: 2010

Golem
I: 12929, 13123

Golem — Fiction
IJ: 9959

Golf
PI: 24869
I: 24798, 24805, 24809
IJ: 24796

Golf — Biography
PI: 16109, 16111
I: 16115
IJ: 16091, 16112–14

Golf — Fiction
P: 4987

Gonzalez, Tony
PI: 16022
I: 16021

Goodall, Jane
P: 15724
PI: 15725
IJ: 15723

Goodall, Jane — Fiction
P: 4702

Google (company)
IJ: 19203

Gordon, Jeff
I: 15871
IJ: 15872

Gorillas
P: 21685, 21695, 21699, 21705, 21711
PI: 21688, 21692, 21694, 21712
I: 15701, 21687, 21690, 21702, 21710
IJ: 15820, 21684, 21697, 21703

Gorillas — Biography
PI: 15704

Gorillas — Fiction
P: 1583, 3768
IJ: 9056

Gorman, R. C.
IJ: 14273

Gossip — Fiction
P: 2083, 13089

Gould, Glenn
PI: 14486

Governesses — Fiction
I: 10825

IJ: 10827

Government (U.S.)
See United States — Government and politics

Government and politics
See also Municipal government (U.S.); State government (U.S.); United States — Government and politics
P: 19594
PI: 19389
IJ: 19385–86, 19589

Government and politics — Biography
IJ: 14863, 15118

Government and politics — Fiction
I: 7779
IJ: 7388

Government and politics (U.S.)
PI: 19549, 19593

Government and politics (U.S.) — Biography
PI: 15485, 15501
I: 15113, 15430
IJ: 14967, 15131, 15155, 15165, 15189

Governors (U.S.)
PI: 19593

Gownley, Jimmy
J: 14274

Goya, Francisco
I: 14275

Graffiti
IJ: 16329

Graffiti — Fiction
I: 7689

Graham, Katharine
PI: 15439

Graham, Martha
IJ: 14487

Grains
P: 20809, 22934, 23031
IJ: 22939

Grammar
See parts of speech, e.g., Conjunctions
P: 16572

Grammar — Fiction
PI: 2657

Grammar
PI: 16564–65, 16570, 16590, 16597, 16605
IJ: 16554, 16594, 16598, 16628

Grammar — Fiction
P: 981, 5772

Grand Canyon
P: 18946, 19161
PI: 19183
I: 19181

Grand Canyon — Fiction
P: 3859

Grand Canyon National Park
PI: 18928, 19177
I: 19118

Grand Teton National Park
PI: 18935

Grandfathers — Fiction
P: 796, 915, 1451, 1506, 1513, 1737, 1888, 2575, 2765, 2801, 2945, 3041, 3055, 3063, 3103, 3152, 3175, 3193, 3216, 3219, 3229, 3250, 3257, 3280, 3293, 3323, 3362, 3403, 3468, 3512, 3540, 3546, 3599, 3609, 3624, 3629, 3643, 4463, 4553, 4820, 4867, 5040, 5042, 5571, 6410, 6493, 6813, 6888, 8457
PI: 3446, 3511, 3967, 4943, 5115, 6277, 8464, 8561, 8598, 8659
I: 8493, 8632, 10555
IJ: 7369, 7640, 7905, 8041, 8266, 8492, 8507, 8626, 8670, 9242, 10096, 10253, 10523, 10670, 11236, 11462, 12148

Grandfathers — Folklore
IJ: 12275

Grandin, Temple
IJ: 15440

Grandmothers — Fiction
P: 1028, 1978, 2491, 2513, 2583, 2730, 2862, 2954, 3039, 3079, 3082, 3097, 3100, 3116, 3118, 3121–22, 3126–27, 3133, 3148, 3164, 3234, 3254, 3294, 3296, 3298–99, 3312, 3319, 3329, 3344, 3367, 3371, 3402, 3412, 3414, 3440, 3442, 3451, 3458, 3472, 3476, 3484, 3520, 3536, 3544, 3551, 3582, 3584,

3606, 3611, 3622, 3641, 3650, 3734, 3941, 3961, 4136, 4473, 4579, 4731, 4766, 4816, 4835, 5921, 6205, 6756, 6951, 11870
PI: 953, 3050, 3204, 3446, 3594, 4725, 6327, 7617, 8486, 8599, 8652, 11156
I: 3262, 8453, 8477, 8552, 8666, 8973, 10097, 10390
IJ: 7649, 8482, 8556, 8636, 8669, 8681, 10084, 10294, 10325, 10414, 10850

Grandparents
See also Grandfathers; Grandmothers
P: 3160, 20179, 20207

Grandparents — Crafts
I: 24216

Grandparents — Fiction
P: 275, 1998, 3059, 3112, 3145, 3206–07, 3248, 3255, 3260, 3267, 3304, 3422, 3502, 3527, 3615, 3642, 4262, 4900, 5649, 6755
PI: 3359, 10188
IJ: 7652, 10211, 10440

Grandparents — Games
I: 24216

Grandparents — Poetry
PI: 13559
I: 13456

Grant, Ulysses S.
IJ: 15256–58

Graphic design
PI: 16360

Graphic novels
PI: 24344
I: 24350
IJ: 7228, 16652, 17843, 24335, 24342

Graphic novels
I: 16417

Graphic novels — Biography
IJ: 16249

Graphic novels — Fairy tales
P: 7117

Graphic novels — Fiction
P: 1098, 1317, 2924, 6635, 6925, 7006, 7009, 7011, 7015, 7024, 7026, 7037–40, 7046, 7049, 7060, 7062–63, 7071–72, 7079, 7111–14, 7116, 7152, 7155–58, 7169, 7171, 7173, 7175, 7179–81, 7185, 7199, 7215, 7227, 7249, 7260, 7276, 7280, 7284–85, 7299, 7311, 7314, 7319, 7322
PI: 7000, 7002, 7005, 7008, 7012, 7020–23, 7025, 7028, 7041–42, 7045, 7050, 7052, 7061, 7065–66, 7082–83, 7089–91, 7100–01, 7104, 7118–19, 7122–23, 7131, 7138, 7140–41, 7160–64, 7167–68, 7172, 7176, 7182–84, 7190, 7193–94, 7196, 7200, 7202, 7204, 7207–08, 7216, 7219–20, 7226, 7231, 7239–40, 7244,

7253–54, 7259, 7262–64, 7273–74, 7278, 7286–91, 7298, 7302, 7304, 7308, 7310, 7318, 7325, 7327, 7762, 8165, 9899
I: 7018, 7027, 7029, 7035, 7048, 7054, 7056, 7073–74, 7081, 7084, 7092–93, 7095–96, 7103, 7105, 7108–10, 7120–21, 7125–27, 7129, 7133, 7148, 7165–66, 7174, 7177, 7186, 7191, 7212, 7214, 7217, 7229–30, 7243, 7246, 7258, 7265, 7268, 7283, 7295, 7301, 7305, 7324, 7329, 7889, 12573
IJ: 7001, 7001, 7004, 7007, 7010, 7013–14, 7016–17, 7019, 7030, 7032–34, 7044, 7047, 7051, 7053, 7055, 7057, 7064, 7067–70, 7075–78, 7080, 7085–88, 7094, 7097, 7106–07, 7115, 7130, 7132, 7134–37, 7139, 7142–47, 7149–51, 7154, 7159, 7170, 7178, 7187, 7189, 7192, 7195, 7197–98, 7203, 7205–06, 7209, 7211, 7213, 7218, 7221–25, 7232, 7236–38, 7241–42, 7245, 7247–48, 7256–57, 7266–67, 7269–70, 7275, 7277, 7279, 7281, 7293–94, 7296–97, 7300, 7303, 7306–07, 7312–13, 7315, 7317, 7320, 7323, 7328, 7330–31, 9255, 9578, 10784, 11296, 11994

Graphic novels — Mythology
I: 13184
IJ: 7201, 7326, 13237

Graphic novels — Plays
IJ: 16897–99

Graphs
P: 23312, 23351, 23372, 23408
PI: 23306, 23363, 23407
IJ: 23344

Grasshoppers
P: 22243
PI: 22187, 22208, 22219

Grasslands
P: 21187, 23264, 23275
PI: 17514, 23265, 23267–68, 23274
IJ: 23263, 23271, 23273, 23276

Gratitude — Fiction
P: 249, 2721, 3027

Grave robbing — Fiction
IJ: 10985

Gravity
P: 23599
I: 23563
IJ: 23567, 23580, 23591

Gravity — Experiments and projects
I: 23572

Great Barrier Reef
PI: 22425
I: 17750
IJ: 22413, 23369

Great Britain
See also England; Northern Ireland; Scotland; Wales; United Kingdom
I: 17851
IJ: 17838–39, 17844

Great Britain — Biography
I: 16282
IJ: 14104–05, 16177–79, 16181, 16190, 16281, 16283

Great Britain — Fiction
IJ: 8995, 10782, 10813

Great Britain — Folklore
P: 12205, 12212, 12217–18, 12257, 12270, 12276, 12289, 12401, 12414, 12416, 12423–25, 12427, 12429, 12611, 12620, 12723, 12726, 12735, 13009, 13015, 13028, 13081, 13109, 13160
PI: 12310, 12329, 12476, 12521, 12531
I: 12534, 12562–63
IJ: 12903, 13049

Great Depression
PI: 18771, 18782, 18793, 18834
I: 18760–61, 18766, 18784
IJ: 18764, 18767, 18779, 18805–06, 18812, 18825, 18836

Great Depression — Fiction
P: 4415, 4446, 4566, 4603, 4612, 4779, 4779, 4815, 11215
PI: 4447, 8487, 11223, 11256, 11264, 11279, 11297, 11299–02
I: 7864, 11193, 11197, 11203, 11225, 11303, 11320
IJ: 8298, 8399, 8682, 9292, 10492, 11168, 11174, 11176, 11186, 11200–01, 11240, 11251, 11261, 11274, 11276, 11280, 11287, 11307, 11314–16

***Great Expectations* — Adaptations**
IJ: 7088

Great Plains
See Plains (U.S.)

Great Salt Lake
P: 23253

Great Smoky Mountains National Park
I: 19118

Great Wall (China)
I: 17630
IJ: 17619, 17624

Greece
P: 17274, 17883
PI: 10565, 10693, 17273, 17276, 17286–87, 17862, 17864, 17881
I: 17275, 17277–80, 17282, 17285, 17288
IJ: 16432, 16437–38, 16438, 17197, 17281, 17283–84, 17859, 17865–66, 17868–69,

17871, 17875–76, 17878, 19860

Greece — Art
IJ: 16436–37

Greece — Biography
PI: 16296
IJ: 15558, 16151, 16160, 16295

Greece — Cookbooks
I: 24554
IJ: 24528, 24559

Greece — Crafts
IJ: 17871

Greece — Fiction
P: 4844
I: 10688
IJ: 10670, 10726, 11341

Greece — Folklore
P: 12178, 12274, 12502, 12693, 12808, 12837, 12861, 13132
PI: 12176, 12279, 12379, 13020
I: 12177, 12209, 12706

Greece — Graphic novels
I: 7251

Greece — Mythology
P: 12456, 12889, 13096, 13208, 13216, 13229, 13248
PI: 12700, 12875, 13187, 13211, 13213–14, 13218, 13220, 13226–27, 13235, 13245, 13249
I: 13210, 13217, 13221, 13230, 13233–34, 13241, 13243, 13251
IJ: 7201, 7270, 9877, 9879, 13209, 13223–25, 13231–32, 13236–37, 13246, 24731

Greece — Mythology — Fiction
IJ: 9880, 11569, 11759

Greed — Fiction
P: 1166

Greed — Folklore
PI: 12333
I: 12168

Greek Americans
PI: 20020
I: 20043
IJ: 19992

Greek Americans — Fiction
P: 4463

Green movement — Fiction
IJ: 7452

Green turtles
PI: 21426

Greenberg, Hank
P: 15900
IJ: 15901

Greene, Nathanael
IJ: 15071

Greenhouse effect
IJ: 19295

P = Primary; PI = Primary-Intermediate; I = Intermediate; IJ = Intermediate-Junior High

I: 16081

Hamsters
P: 22671, 22693–94, 22698, 22700–01, 22709
PI: 22669, 22697, 22707
I: 22683

Hamsters — Fiction
P: 3996, 5330, 5506, 5522, 6693
PI: 9658, 11541–42

Hancock, John
PI: 15079, 15082
IJ: 15080–81

Handel, George Frideric
I: 14409
IJ: 14410

Handler, Daniel
I: 14675

Hands
P: 20758
PI: 20771
IJ: 20769

Hands — Fiction
P: 230, 251

Handwriting — Fiction
P: 5684

Hang gliding
PI: 24848

Hanh, Thich Nhat
I: 16221

Hannibal
IJ: 16222

Hanson (musical group)
IJ: 14488

Hantavirus
I: 20513

Hanukkah
P: 6322, 19903, 19912
PI: 19894, 19899, 19914
I: 24290

Hanukkah — Fiction
P: 4108, 5892, 6314–18, 6324, 6326, 6329–33, 6335, 6337, 6339, 6341–43, 6348, 6350–51, 6353, 6359, 6367–68, 6376–77
PI: 6334, 6338, 6355, 11486, 11497, 11509
I: 11484, 11490

Hanukkah — Songs
P: 19893

Happiness — Fiction
P: 2686, 2848, 4970

Hardaway, Penny
PI: 15964

Hares — Fiction
P: 5481
IJ: 9277

Harlem (NY) — Fiction
P: 2655, 4718, 4829
PI: 4467, 11249
IJ: 7588, 7590

Harlem (NY) — Poetry
P: 13588
PI: 13429

Harlem Renaissance
PI: 13579
I: 18810
IJ: 18769, 18835

Harlem Renaissance — Fiction
P: 4581
I: 18211
IJ: 11295

Harmonicas — Fiction
P: 4040

Harrison, John
PI: 15728–29

Harrison, William Henry
PI: 15260
I: 15259

Hart, Melissa Joan
PI: 14489

Harvest
P: 21155

Harvest festivals
PI: 19800

Harvey, William
IJ: 15730

Hats — Colonial period (U.S.)
I: 18427

Hats — Fiction
P: 327, 1407, 2756, 2793, 2867, 3580, 3641, 3679, 4162, 4194, 4646, 4966

Hatshepsut, Queen of Egypt
I: 16223

Haunted houses
PI: 18228
I: 7801
IJ: 24758–59

Haunted houses — Fiction
P: 6529
I: 9636

Haunted places
IJ: 24718

Haunted places — Fiction
IJ: 9849

Hausa (African people)
IJ: 17595

Hawaii
P: 19067
PI: 19059, 19102
I: 19070, 19093
IJ: 17448, 19072, 19074–75

Hawaii — Biography
I: 16083

Hawaii — Fiction
P: 2058, 3299, 4539
PI: 7644–45, 8419, 8689, 11937
IJ: 7500, 10445, 11430

Hawaii — Folklore
P: 12713
PI: 12827
IJ: 12256

Hawaii Volcanoes National Park
PI: 19076
IJ: 19068

Hawkins, Waterhouse
PI: 17002

Hawks
P: 22068, 22077

Hawks — Fiction
PI: 5516, 8309

Haydn, Franz Joseph
IJ: 14411

Haydn, Joseph — Fiction
PI: 4475

Hayes, Ira
PI: 15184

Haymarket Square Riot
I: 18762

Hayslip, Le Ly
IJ: 15083

Hazardous substances
IJ: 20288

Head lice
P: 20521, 20776
PI: 20557, 22186

Health and health care
See also Exercise; Nutrition
P: 20794
I: 20617
IJ: 20088, 20529, 20590, 20819, 20841

Health and health care — Careers
IJ: 20365

Health and health care — Fiction
P: 2336
PI: 10599

Hearing
See also Deaf
P: 20462, 20745, 20747–48
PI: 20744, 20756
I: 20739
IJ: 20750

Hearing — Experiments and projects
P: 20745
I: 23672

Heart
See also Circulatory system
PI: 20705
IJ: 20706

Heart — Fiction
P: 2738

Heart disease — Fiction
IJ: 7369, 8525

Heart transplants — Biography
I: 15564

Heart transplants — Fiction
IJ: 10509

Heat — Fiction
P: 3462, 4810

Heaven — Fiction
P: 5505

Hedgehogs
PI: 21662

Hedgehogs — Fiction
P: 4170, 5507

Height — Fiction
P: 2086
PI: 6764
IJ: 11413

Heisman Trophy
IJ: 25007

Helicopters
P: 24006
PI: 15812, 23836, 24150
I: 24120, 24123

Hell — Fiction
IJ: 11534

Helpfulness — Fiction
P: 197, 1594, 3314

Hemsworth, Liam
I: 14490

Hendrix, Jimi
PI: 14491

Henry, Patrick
IJ: 15084

Henry the Navigator
IJ: 14122

Henson, Jim
PI: 14492
IJ: 14493

Henson, Matthew
P: 14123
PI: 14126–27
IJ: 14124–25

Hepburn, Audrey
P: 14494

Heredity
IJ: 20182

Hermit crabs
P: 22693, 22695

Hermit crabs — Pets
P: 22699

Heroes
IJ: 14816, 20078

Heroes — Fiction
PI: 4660
I: 10423
IJ: 7221

Heroes — Graphic novels
I: 7235

Heroes — Poetry
IJ: 13523

Heroin
IJ: 20439

Herons — Fiction
P: 5366

Herons — Poetry
I: 13799

Hershiser, Orel
IJ: 15902

P = Primary; PI = Primary-Intermediate; I = Intermediate; IJ = Intermediate-Junior High

P = Primary; PI = Primary-Intermediate; I = Intermediate; IJ = Intermediate-Junior High

Kipsigis (African people)
IJ: 17513

Kirby, Jack
IJ: 14291

KISS (rock group)
IJ: 14521

Kisses — Fiction
P: 293, 302, 806, 3032

Kites
I: 24206

Kites — Fiction
P: 930, 2226, 3284, 3334, 3552, 3609, 3883, 3986, 4491, 4554
PI: 4643, 4749
I: 10634

Kittens — Fiction
P: 4913, 6904

Klee, Paul
IJ: 14292

Klimt, Gustav — Fiction
P: 4469

Knight, Margaret
P: 15750
PI: 15749

Knights
PI: 17339, 17358, 17371
I: 17345, 17349, 17362
IJ: 17350, 17359

Knights — Fiction
P: 1010, 1277, 1709, 6957
PI: 7327, 8166, 8965, 9449–50, 10678, 10804–05
IJ: 9144, 10574, 10679, 10806–09

Knights — Folklore
PI: 12476, 12531
I: 12530, 12534
IJ: 12765, 12903

Knitting
PI: 24437
I: 24432, 24434, 24448
IJ: 24433, 24441–42, 24445, 24447, 24450, 24455

Knitting — Fiction
P: 11228
PI: 2933

Knot tying
I: 24476

Knox, Henry
PI: 15110

Knox, Henry — Fiction
P: 10927

Ko, Alex
I: 14522

Koalas
P: 21913, 21915, 21922
PI: 21905, 21911, 21920, 21926
I: 21910

Koalas — Fiction
P: 1811, 1863

Kolff, Willem
IJ: 15751

Kollek, Teddy
IJ: 16237

Komodo dragons
P: 21374, 21380, 21383
PI: 21377, 21379, 21385–86
IJ: 21378

Korczak, Janusz
P: 16240
PI: 16238
IJ: 16239

Korea
See also North Korea; South Korea; Korean War
P: 33
PI: 17692

Korea — Fiction
P: 4484, 4754–58, 4879
PI: 7208
I: 10631, 10634
IJ: 9596, 10635–37

Korea — Folklore
P: 12294, 12449, 12495, 12517, 12850–51, 12951
PI: 12708, 12952, 12984

Korea — Poetry
I: 13593

Korean Americans
IJ: 19969, 19985, 20014

Korean Americans — Biography
PI: 14709, 16109
IJ: 16085

Korean Americans — Fiction
P: 2630, 3251, 3253, 3440, 3442, 3454, 3609, 4754, 5944, 6150, 6238
PI: 8579, 10328
IJ: 8431, 10056, 10473, 11442, 11878

Korean language
PI: 12540

Korean War
I: 18866
IJ: 17150, 17492

Korean War Veterans Memorial
IJ: 18951

Korman, Gordon
I: 14689

Kosciuszko, Thaddeus
PI: 16148

Kosovo
IJ: 17783

Kossman, Nina
IJ: 16241

Kouanchao, Malichansouk
P: 16242

Koufax, Sandy
PI: 15909

Krakatoa (Indonesia)
IJ: 23126

Ku Klux Klan
IJ: 19418

Ku Klux Klan — Fiction
PI: 6942
IJ: 10141, 11169, 11258, 11277

Kublai Khan
PI: 16243

Kung fu — Fiction
PI: 4599

Kurds
I: 18002

Kuwait
P: 19762
IJ: 18004

Kwan, Michelle
I: 16008

Kwanzaa
P: 5907, 5913, 19763, 19822, 19852–53
PI: 19780

Kwanzaa — Crafts
P: 24249

Kwanzaa — Fiction
P: 5923, 5939

Kwolek, Stephanie
PI: 15752

Kyrgyzstan
I: 17895

L

La Brea Tar Pits (CA)
IJ: 17051

La Niña (weather)
IJ: 23525, 23549

La Purisima Mission
IJ: 19105

La Salle, Cavelier de
I: 14142
IJ: 14141

Labonte, Terry and Bobby
IJ: 15875

Labor — Biography
PI: 14995

Labor Day
P: 19842

Labor movements
PI: 18759
IJ: 18208

Labor movements — Biography
P: 15460
PI: 14979
I: 14994

Labor movements — Fiction
P: 2652

Labor problems
PI: 16494

Labor problems — Fiction
IJ: 11212

Labor unions
I: 18762
IJ: 19613

Labor unions — Biography
PI: 14986
IJ: 14985

Labor unions — Fiction
IJ: 11269

Labyrinths
PI: 17141

Lacrosse
IJ: 24783, 24860

Lacrosse — Fiction
IJ: 12038

Ladders — Fiction
P: 1356

LaDuke, Winona
IJ: 15189

Lady Gaga
IJ: 14523

Ladybugs
P: 22224, 22274, 22276–77, 22280, 22285, 22289
PI: 22278, 22286
I: 22290

Ladybugs — Fiction
P: 1625, 6578

Lafayette, Marquis de
IJ: 16244

Laffite, Jean
PI: 15111

Lagasse, Emeril
IJ: 15753

Lake Tahoe
P: 23259

Lakes
I: 23246
IJ: 23251, 23255

Lakota Indians
See Sioux Indians

Lamarr, Hedy
PI: 15754

Lambke, Bryan
All: 16245

Lamborghini
I: 24053

Lambs — Fiction
P: 6346

Lancelot (knight)
PI: 12806
IJ: 13055

Landmines — Fiction
IJ: 10595

Landslides
PI: 23084

Lange, Dorothea
PI: 14293

Language
IJ: 16478, 16480, 16549, 16601

Language and languages
See also Dictionaries; Word books; and specific

P = Primary; PI = Primary-Intermediate; I = Intermediate; IJ = Intermediate-Junior High

I: 10235

**Long Island (NY) —
Fiction**
IJ: 10236

Longworth, Alice Roosevelt
P: 15465

Loons — Fiction
P: 3338, 5250

Lopez, Jennifer
PI: 14536–37
IJ: 14535

The Lord's Prayer
PI: 19942

Lorenz, Konrad
P: 15760

**Los Alamos (NM) —
Fiction**
IJ: 11380–81

Los Angeles (CA)
I: 19063

**Los Angeles (CA) —
Fiction**
PI: 8558
IJ: 7526, 7532, 8559, 11476

Los Angeles (CA) — Poetry
P: 13940

**Los Angeles riot (1992) —
Fiction**
P: 2630

Loss — Fiction
P: 5276
I: 10077
IJ: 10461

Lost — Fiction
P: 2751, 5150, 6293

Lost and found — Fiction
P: 5698

**Lost and found possessions
— Fiction**
P: 1534, 1609, 1792, 1973,
2608, 2684, 2756, 4056, 5056,
6947

Lost children — Fiction
P: 2874, 6555

**Lou Gehrig's disease —
Fiction**
IJ: 10659

Louis, Joe
P: 16005
PI: 16004

Louis, Joe — Fiction
IJ: 11274

Louisiana
PI: 18433, 19111, 19130
I: 21305

Louisiana — Fiction
P: 5068
I: 8264, 10158
IJ: 8583, 11990

Louisiana — Folklore
I: 12377–78

Louisiana Purchase
IJ: 18555, 18557, 18656–57

Love
See also Romance
P: 282, 303, 20224

Love — Fiction
P: 517, 1997, 2189, 2786,
2888, 3066, 3419, 3553, 3575,
3940
PI: 8998, 10736
IJ: 7587, 11205, 11792, 12405

Love — Poetry
P: 13550
IJ: 13393, 13514, 13729

Lovecraft, H. P.
IJ: 14694

Low, Juliette Gordon
PI: 15466
IJ: 15467

Lowry, Lois
IJ: 14695–96

Loyalty
PI: 20132

Loyie, Larry
I: 15190

Lucas, George
IJ: 14538

Luck — Fiction
P: 4794
PI: 923
IJ: 12015

Ludington, Sybil
PI: 18489

Lullabies
P: 617, 725, 13609, 16678,
16690, 16722, 16729
IJ: 16715

Lullabies — Fiction
P: 730

Luminescence
IJ: 23636

Lungs
P: 20731, 20734
I: 20735
IJ: 20732

Luo (African people)
IJ: 17512

Lusitania **(ship)**
IJ: 17394

Lyme disease
IJ: 20524, 20599

Lynx
IJ: 21811

Lyon, Maritcha Rémond
IJ: 14919

M

Maasai (African people)
P: 17530
PI: 17514
I: 17518
IJ: 17528, 17552

**Maasai (African people) —
Biography**
IJ: 16247

**Maasai (African people) —
Fiction**
P: 3302

Maathai, Wangari
P: 16251–53
PI: 16250

MacArthur, Douglas
IJ: 15115–16

Macbeth **(play)**
IJ: 16855, 16883

Machiavelli, Niccolò
IJ: 16254

Machinery
See also Simple machines
P: 5833, 23962–64, 23966–67,
23992, 24020
PI: 23757, 23897
IJ: 22923, 23768

**Machinery — Experiments
and projects**
I: 23660

Machinery — Fiction
P: 5812, 5851, 5854, 5890

Machu Picchu (Peru)
PI: 17331, 17335
I: 17337

Mackenzie River
IJ: 23239

Madagascar
P: 17564
IJ: 21704

Madagascar — Animals
I: 21269
IJ: 21704

Madison, Dolley
P: 15468
PI: 15469

IJ: 15471

Madison, James
PI: 15327–28
IJ: 15325–26

Madison, James and Dolley
P: 15329
IJ: 15330

Magee, John
IJ: 14697

Magellan, Ferdinand
PI: 14150
I: 14145, 14147
IJ: 14146, 14148–49, 14151

Magic and magicians
P: 12595
PI: 24587
I: 24586, 24591–92
IJ: 9096, 24588–90, 24594

**Magic and magicians —
Biography**
P: 14498
PI: 14499
I: 14505

Maasai (African people) —

IJ: 14500, 14502–03, 14506,
14519

**Magic and magicians —
Fiction**
P: 866, 1012, 1062, 1132,
1198, 1349, 1409, 1729, 1812,
1958, 2523, 3377, 3466, 4004,
4520, 5150, 5901, 5953, 6634
PI: 6518, 7308, 7761, 8944,
9188, 9376, 9496, 9500, 9563,
9567, 9591, 10685, 11594,
11811
I: 7084, 7353, 7468, 8975,
9101, 9353, 9431, 9551, 9559,
9565, 9793, 9947, 9984, 11856
IJ: 7333, 7397, 8023, 8112,
8701, 8703, 8840, 8927, 8933,
9098, 9227–28, 9312, 9360,
9372–73, 9391, 9481, 9580,
9582, 9639, 9689, 9706, 9792,
9903, 9991, 10010

**Magic and magicians —
Folklore**
IJ: 13004

Magic tricks
IJ: 24585, 24595

Magnesium
IJ: 23061

Magnetism
PI: 23649, 23652
I: 23648
IJ: 23653

**Magnetism — Experiments
and projects**
PI: 23646

Magritte, Rene
IJ: 16425

Mahjong — Fiction
P: 3339

Maid Marian — Fiction
IJ: 10795

Mail — Fiction
P: 2345, 2999

Maiman, Theodore H.
PI: 15761

Maine
IJ: 18979, 18983, 19029

Maine — Fiction
P: 3350, 4039, 5090, 5282,
5457
PI: 3123, 4359, 7440
I: 11226
IJ: 7552, 8560, 8581, 9161,
10294, 10900, 11005

Malamutes — Fiction
IJ: 8667

Malaria
IJ: 20498

Malawi
IJ: 17519, 17529

Malawi — Biography
P: 16236

Malawi — Fiction
IJ: 10242, 10584, 10598

Malaysia
P: 17700

I: 24395
IJ: 17130, 24394

Mason, Biddy
I: 14925

Mass (church)
P: 19692

Mass media
IJ: 16466, 16493, 16841, 19426, 23918, 23951

Massachusetts
PI: 18416
I: 18960, 18975, 19005
IJ: 18953, 18955, 19006

Massachusetts — Fiction
P: 4748
I: 11713
IJ: 10921, 10993, 11012, 11269

Mastodons
PI: 17028
IJ: 16939

Materials
P: 23577
IJ: 23579, 23761

Mathematics
See also Counting books; branches of mathematics, e.g., Algebra
P: 23313, 23323–24, 23341, 23348, 23358, 23367, 23371, 23375, 23403–04
PI: 23308, 23319–22, 23326, 23336, 23340, 23352, 23354, 23357, 23359, 23374, 23383, 24630
I: 23311, 23337, 23353, 23362, 23379–81, 24899
IJ: 17168, 23333–34, 23338, 23355, 23368–70, 23377

Mathematics — Biography
P: 15683
PI: 15690
I: 15714
IJ: 15557–58, 15675, 15677

Mathematics — Careers
IJ: 20296

Mathematics — Experiments and projects
P: 23387

Mathematics — Fiction
P: 486, 533, 1041, 1368, 2085, 2105, 2928, 3183, 3968, 5638, 5683, 5737, 6560
PI: 7413, 10298, 11673, 11873
IJ: 7545, 11750

Mathematics — Games
PI: 23343

Mathematics — Jokes and riddles
PI: 23397

Mathematics — Puzzles
P: 23385, 23390, 23392, 23395, 23398
PI: 23335, 23389, 23393, 23396, 23399

I: 23400
IJ: 23386, 23388, 23391, 23394

Mathematics — Puzzles — Fiction
PI: 5786

Matisse, Henri
P: 273, 14300, 14302, 14305
PI: 14303, 16387
IJ: 14301, 14304

Matisse, Henri — Fiction
P: 4669

Matter (physics)
P: 23577–78
PI: 23569, 23587
I: 23564–65
IJ: 23579, 23582, 23586

Matter (physics) — Fiction
PI: 7762

Mauritania — Fiction
P: 4507

Mayan Indians
P: 18081
PI: 17204
I: 17336
IJ: 17098, 17104, 17194, 17203, 17207, 17328, 18086

Mayan Indians — Biography
IJ: 15191

Mayan Indians — Fiction
PI: 9739
IJ: 9907, 10838

Mayan Indians — Folklore
P: 12388, 12692, 12796, 12799–800
PI: 7141
IJ: 12797

Mayan Indians — Mythology
IJ: 7326, 13175, 13194

Mayflower (ship)
See also Pilgrims (U.S.) — Fiction
I: 18378, 18412
IJ: 18375–76, 18485

Mayflower (ship) — Fiction
IJ: 10910, 10912

Mayflower Compact
IJ: 18485

Mayors
P: 19594
PI: 19596

Mays, Willie
PI: 15915

Mazes
PI: 16543, 17141
I: 24661

McCain, John
IJ: 15118

McClellan, George
PI: 15120

McClintock, Barbara
IJ: 15764

McCoy, Elijah
P: 15765

McGwire, Mark
IJ: 24934

McNabb, Donovan
PI: 16030

McNair, Ronald E. — Fiction
P: 4733

Mead, Margaret
IJ: 15766

Meade, George Gordon
PI: 15121

Meadowlands (NJ)
P: 19053

Meadows
P: 23264

Meadows — Animals
P: 23262

Meadows — Plants
P: 23262

Meadows — Poetry
PI: 13996

Mealtime — Fiction
PI: 3211

Measures and measurement
See Concept books — Measurement; Weights and measures

Meat
P: 20809
IJ: 20838

Medici, Lorenzo de
IJ: 16259

Medicine
See also Diseases and illness
P: 6939
PI: 18457, 20501
I: 20616–17, 20626–27
IJ: 17168, 17221, 17359, 20449, 20604, 20613, 20618, 20621, 20625, 20628, 20631–32, 20649, 22845

Medicine — Biography
I: 15581, 15667
IJ: 15526, 15543, 15751, 15777, 15807

Medicine — Careers
P: 20355

Medicine — Fiction
PI: 10599

Medicine — Women
I: 15581

Medieval times
See Middle Ages

Meditation
I: 20075

Mediterranean Sea
IJ: 17215

Medusa
IJ: 24731

Meerkats
P: 21610, 21656
PI: 21643

Megalodon
I: 16932

Mekong River
IJ: 17603

Memoirs
J: 14274
All: 16245
P: 14388, 14906, 14973
PI: 14647–48, 14660, 14722, 14902, 16186
I: 14756, 15190, 16224, 16287
IJ: 14265, 14382, 14581, 14645, 15179, 15191, 15517, 16219–20, 16248–49, 16293, 16304

Memoirs — Fiction
PI: 10028

Memorial Day
PI: 19775

Memory — Fiction
P: 3164, 3193
PI: 3050
I: 10210

Menchu, Rigoberta
IJ: 15191, 18092

Mendel, Gregor
PI: 15768
IJ: 15767

Mendeleyev, Dmitri
IJ: 15769

Meningitis
IJ: 20585

Mennonites — Fiction
P: 3578
I: 10324
IJ: 10342, 10438

Menominee Indians
IJ: 18283, 18309

Menstruation
IJ: 20882, 20893

Mental disabilities — Fiction
IJ: 8662

Mental illness
See also specific disorders, e.g., Depression (mental state)
P: 20477, 20479

Mental illness — Fiction
I: 11313
IJ: 10146

Mental problems
PI: 20461
I: 20075
IJ: 20459

Mental problems — Biography
IJ: 15851

Mental problems — Fiction
P: 3742, 4935
IJ: 10489, 10526–27

P = Primary; PI = Primary-Intermediate; I = Intermediate; IJ = Intermediate-Junior High

P = Primary; PI = Primary-Intermediate; I = Intermediate; IJ = Intermediate-Junior High

Middleton, Kate
IJ: 16316

A Midsummer Night's Dream — Adaptations
IJ: 16897

Midway, Battle of
IJ: 17479

Midwest (U.S.)
See also specific states, e.g., Indiana
I: 18896
IJ: 15086, 18895

Midwest (U.S.) — Biography
IJ: 14818

Midwest (U.S.) — Fiction
I: 11676
IJ: 11191

Midwest (U.S.) — Poetry
PI: 13642

Migrant workers
IJ: 19598

Migrant workers — Biography
P: 14992
PI: 14806

Migrant workers — Fiction
P: 3556, 3578
IJ: 8557, 8562, 10850, 11273, 11368

Migration
P: 22042
IJ: 17116, 21514

Migration — Fiction
P: 5220, 5468
PI: 8325

Migrations (bird)
PI: 22035

Migrations (bird) — Fiction
P: 5484

Milano, Alyssa
PI: 14543

Military (U.S.) — Careers
PI: 19569

Military bases
P: 19325

Military history
IJ: 17160, 17466

Military history — Fiction
IJ: 11054

Military vehicles
PI: 24150

Milk
P: 22958

Milk — Fiction
P: 365

Milk shakes — Fiction
P: 3840

Miller, Norma
IJ: 14544

Million Man March — Fiction
P: 2819

Millionaires — Fiction
PI: 7345

Millipedes
PI: 22358
I: 22370

Millman, Isaac
IJ: 16260

Mills
IJ: 16458, 22885

Mills, Florence
P: 14545

Mimes — Biography
PI: 14540

Minerals
See Rocks and minerals
See Rocks and minerals

Mines and mining
PI: 16714
IJ: 18118

Mines and mining — Accidents
IJ: 23786

Mines and mining — Careers
I: 20268

Mines and mining — Fiction
I: 11159

Ming, Yao
PI: 15979
I: 15980
IJ: 15978

Minneapolis (MN) — Fiction
PI: 7559

Minnesota
PI: 18888, 18892
I: 18880
IJ: 16423, 18871, 18915

Minnesota — Fiction
P: 3131
PI: 11098–99
IJ: 10414, 11018, 11416

Minnesota — Folklore
PI: 12583
I: 12938

Minotaur (mythology)
I: 13221, 13247

Minutemen (U.S.)
I: 18536

Miracles — Fiction
P: 4746, 4856

Mirrors — Fiction
IJ: 9115

Missing children — Fiction
IJ: 8997

Missing persons — Fiction
P: 2325
IJ: 7752, 8279, 8285

Missionaries — Biography
IJ: 14191

Missionaries — Fiction
IJ: 8141

Missions
I: 18391, 18669, 19071, 19154, 19164, 19173

Mississauga Indians — Folklore
PI: 12316

Mississippi (state)
IJ: 19158, 19409

Mississippi (state) — Fiction
IJ: 2541, 11168, 11258, 11399

Mississippi River
P: 18908, 23233
PI: 18204, 18241, 18253, 18256, 18564, 23256
I: 18901

Mississippi River — Biography
IJ: 14141

Mississippi River — Fiction
PI: 4531
I: 9762

Missouri (state)
I: 18883
IJ: 18874, 19141

Missouri (state) — Fiction
I: 11070–71

Missouri River
IJ: 23238

Mistral, Gabriela
P: 14699

Misunderstandings — Fiction
P: 3856

Mitchell, Jackie
P: 15916
PI: 24929

Mites
IJ: 22203

Mittens — Fiction
P: 1092, 4125

Miwok Indians — Folklore
PI: 12960

Mixtures — Poetry
PI: 13637

Model car racing — Fiction
PI: 7700

Model T Ford (automobile)
P: 24063

Modeling crafts
I: 24300

Modern art
IJ: 16375

Modoc Indian War — Fiction
IJ: 11068

Mohammed
IJ: 16269

Mohapatra, Jyotirmayee
IJ: 16261

Mohawk Indians
P: 13050
IJ: 18319, 19955

Mohawk Indians — Fiction
P: 2873

Molasses — Fiction
P: 3381

Mold — Fiction
P: 4353

Moldova
IJ: 17900

Moles — Fiction
IJ: 10783

Moles — Folklore
IJ: 12389

Mollusks
P: 22499
I: 22493

Molybdenum
IJ: 23050

Monarch butterflies
P: 22314

Monarch butterflies — Fiction
P: 4364

Monarchy
IJ: 19402

Monet, Claude
P: 16385
PI: 14310, 14312–13
IJ: 14309, 14311, 14314

Monet, Claude — Fiction
P: 4422
I: 10708

Money
P: 2646, 19185, 19196–97, 19201, 19208, 19554, 23317, 23358
PI: 19190, 19202, 19209, 19212
I: 19195, 19198
IJ: 19204, 19207, 19227

Money — Fiction
P: 2884, 6971
PI: 2028

Money making — Fiction
I: 8443

Money management — Fiction
P: 1638
PI: 7347

Money-making ideas
P: 19232
PI: 19229
IJ: 19225, 19227, 20334

Money-making ideas — Fiction
P: 2335, 2774
PI: 7367, 7403, 11592
IJ: 7659, 10416, 10475, 11717–18, 11744

Mongolia
PI: 17714
IJ: 17724, 21804

Mongolia — Biography
IJ: 16216

Mongolia — Fiction
PI: 4431

Mongolia — Folklore
P: 12849

Mongols
IJ: 17605

Mongols — Biography
PI: 16243
IJ: 16215, 16218

Mongooses — Fiction
P: 1180

Monkeys
PI: 21681
I: 21713

Monkeys — Fiction
P: 128, 450–51, 2226, 4194, 5216
PI: 2225
I: 11663

Monkeys — Folklore
P: 12426, 12430

Monks — Fiction
P: 4564

Monologues
IJ: 16887, 16891–92

Mononucleosis
IJ: 20548, 20601

Monplaisir, Sharon
IJ: 16088

Monroe, James
PI: 15331–32

Monsoons — Fiction
P: 4659

Monsters
PI: 24673, 24739
I: 24376, 24704, 24724
IJ: 13188, 24676, 24699, 24714, 24748

Monsters — Fiction
P: 95, 120, 305, 661, 748, 817, 899, 957, 991, 1005, 1035, 1054, 1074, 1098, 1117, 1127, 1161, 1240, 1243–44, 1252–53, 1295, 1312, 1390, 1392–93, 1403, 1433, 1435, 2374, 3397, 3831, 3888, 3969, 4090, 4147, 4190, 4216, 4255, 4985, 5037, 5691, 6591, 6843, 7049
PI: 2028, 7042, 7264, 9047, 9414
I: 8824, 8884, 8943, 9124
IJ: 7788, 9040, 9204, 9772, 9799, 9846, 9994

Monsters — Mythology
PI: 13220
I: 13221

Monsters — Poetry
P: 13387, 13905–06
PI: 13696, 13921

Monsters — Songs
P: 16706

Montana
PI: 18926, 18934, 22905

Monterey Bay (California)
PI: 19088

Monteverde Cloud Forest (Costa Rica)
PI: 23181

Montezuma
PI: 12619

Montezuma, Carlos
PI: 15192

Montgolfier brothers
P: 23833

Montgomery bus boycott
PI: 19431
IJ: 18864, 19414

Montgomery, Lucy Maud
P: 14701
PI: 14700

Months — Fiction
P: 4180

Months — Poetry
P: 13502

Montreal
I: 18052

Monuments
P: 23860
IJ: 18952

Moodiness — Fiction
P: 1820

Moon
P: 4404, 21042, 21045, 21051, 23688
PI: 21046, 21049–50, 21052
I: 21047–48
IJ: 21010, 21016, 23690, 23694–95, 23731, 23733

Moon — Fiction
P: 631, 734, 979, 1063, 1091, 1095, 1151, 1292, 1365, 1401, 1516, 1961, 2057, 2954, 3152, 3790, 4321, 4576, 4708, 5849
PI: 13068

Moon — Folklore
PI: 12330
I: 13017

Moon — Poetry
P: 13970, 14006
PI: 13391, 14004

Moore, Marianne — Fiction
P: 4460

Moose
P: 21860
PI: 21854
I: 21853

Moose — Fiction
P: 398, 2153, 5492, 5524, 6994

Moran, Thomas
P: 14315

Moray eels
I: 22386

Moreno, Luisa
I: 14994

Morgan, Ann
PI: 15772

Morgan, Julia
PI: 14316

Morgues
I: 24760

Mormons
PI: 18617, 18629
IJ: 18661, 18875

Mormons — Biography
PI: 15169
IJ: 15170

Mormons — Fiction
P: 4570

Morning — Fiction
P: 2627

Morocco
PI: 17557

Morocco — Fiction
P: 823, 4417, 4614

Morris, Esther
PI: 15473

Morris, Gouverneur
IJ: 15122

Morrison, Toni
I: 14702

Morse, Samuel
PI: 15773

Mortgage loans
IJ: 19188

Mosaics
I: 16363
IJ: 24202

Mosaics — Crafts
I: 24182
IJ: 24236

Moscow
I: 17902

Moscow — Fiction
P: 5542

Moses (Bible)
PI: 19706, 19723, 19732

Moses, Grandma
P: 14317

Mosques
I: 19700

Mosques — Fiction
PI: 4631

Mosquitoes
PI: 22207, 22229

Mosquitoes — Fiction
P: 4352

Mosquitoes — Folklore
P: 12169

Moss, Randy
PI: 16032
IJ: 16031

Mother and child — Fiction
P: 1780, 3138, 3242, 4388, 6711

Mother Goose
P: 13256, 13287, 13293–94, 13296, 13298, 13304, 13312

Mother's Day — Fiction
P: 5922

Mothers — Fiction
P: 2256, 2474, 2777, 3053, 3064, 3066, 3102, 3105, 3110, 3124, 3159, 3169, 3186, 3328, 3373, 3444, 3613, 3645, 5020, 5604
PI: 3469, 3852
IJ: 11471

Mothers — Folklore
I: 12403

Mothers — Poetry
P: 3060, 13561
PI: 13714

Mothers and daughters — Fiction
P: 2543, 3314, 3326, 3347, 3356, 3372, 3509, 3523–24, 3577, 4776, 12014
I: 10158, 10204
IJ: 7337, 7469, 8574, 9403, 10182, 10659, 11235

Mothers and daughters — Poetry
IJ: 13653

Mothers and sons — Fiction
P: 1117, 2073, 2293, 2492, 3101, 3226, 3434, 3634, 5168
PI: 7327
I: 8381

Mothers and sons — Poetry
P: 13689

Mother's Day — Crafts
PI: 24181

Mother's Day — Fiction
P: 5896, 5904, 5935

Mothers of presidents (U.S.) — Biography
PI: 14825

Moths
See Butterflies and moths

Motion
P: 20965

Motion (physics) — Experiments and projects
P: 23577, 23598, 23604
PI: 23621
I: 23583, 23608, 23612
IJ: 23582, 23603

Motion pictures
I: 16831, 16834, 16840, 23987
IJ: 14264, 23978, 23981, 23984

Motion pictures — Biography
PI: 14518
I: 14458, 14601
IJ: 14206, 14463–64, 14529–30, 14538, 14571, 14586–87

Motion pictures — Careers
IJ: 14613, 20316, 20320, 20322, 24600

Motion pictures — Fiction
P: 2856

P = Primary; PI = Primary-Intermediate; I = Intermediate; IJ = Intermediate-Junior High

P = Primary; PI = Primary-Intermediate; I = Intermediate; IJ = Intermediate-Junior High

Muslim Americans
P: 19642

**Muslim Americans —
Fiction**
IJ: 8614

Muslims
See also Islam
PI: 19797

Muslims — Fiction
P: 4565
I: 8367

Mustangs (horses)
PI: 22856

**Mustangs (horses) —
Fiction**
IJ: 8348

**Mutes and mutism —
Fiction**
PI: 10379
IJ: 8006, 9858, 10267

My Lai Massacre
IJ: 17486

Myanmar (Burma)
I: 17705
IJ: 16162, 17746

**Myanmar (Burma) —
Fiction**
IJ: 10642, 11441

**Myanmar (Burma) —
Folklore**
P: 12419

Mysteries
IJ: 24736

Mystery stories — Fiction
P: 1992, 2328, 2564, 3878,
4118, 5724, 6419, 6434–35,
6494, 6529–31, 6742, 6766,
6857, 6886, 6919–20, 6940,
7319, 7798–99, 8087, 8156
PI: 1076, 1836, 2571, 4138,
6505, 6637, 6705, 6823–24,
6851, 6874, 6889–90, 7052,
7090, 7131, 7160, 7162–64,
7176, 7239–40, 7244, 7318,
7720–27, 7761, 7769, 7783,
7785, 7790, 7797, 7805, 7810,
7814, 7816, 7818, 7835, 7855,
7859, 7876, 7892–94, 7923,
7931, 7935, 7940–41, 7958,
7975, 7977, 7985–87, 7989,
7995, 8030, 8032, 8048–49,
8055–56, 8069, 8073, 8081,
8088–90, 8105, 8108–09,
8136, 8154–55, 8164, 8174,
8196, 8211, 8224, 8237, 8246,
8269–72, 8288, 9165, 9167–68,
9170, 9221, 9410, 9669, 9971,
10943, 11637, 11872
I: 7035, 7174, 7177, 7268,
7742–43, 7746, 7748, 7754–60,
7765, 7768, 7780–82, 7784,
7793, 7801, 7801–04, 7804,
7815, 7817, 7819, 7839–40,
7858, 7864, 7869–70, 7873,
7895–97, 7899–900, 7908–09,
7911, 7925, 7946–47, 7968,
7973, 7994, 7996, 8003, 8011,
8019, 8027, 8031, 8033–34,
8037, 8039, 8047, 8050, 8059,
8070, 8099, 8106, 8132, 8135,

8158, 8179, 8194–95, 8197,
8200, 8215, 8221, 8235,
8241–42, 8256, 8258, 8264,
8267, 8275–76, 8283, 8290,
8384, 8502, 8733, 8753, 8811,
8987, 9046, 9166, 9169, 9171,
9252, 9326, 9357, 9408, 9483,
9736, 9749, 10819, 11033,
11320, 11333, 11630, 11651,
11698
IJ: 7019, 7178, 7211, 7213,
7222, 7242, 7332, 7404,
7444, 7528, 7561, 7707,
7717–18, 7732–35, 7737–39,
7745, 7750–52, 7763–64,
7766–67, 7775–76, 7778,
7789, 7794–95, 7800, 7809,
7811, 7813, 7820–24, 7827,
7830–32, 7836–37, 7842–44,
7846, 7848–49, 7857, 7860–62,
7865–66, 7871, 7874–75,
7877, 7881, 7888, 7890–91,
7898, 7906, 7910, 7913–14,
7916–17, 7921, 7929–30,
7933–34, 7937, 7939, 7943,
7945, 7954, 7960, 7962–65,
7972, 7979–81, 7984, 7990–91,
7997–99, 8002, 8004, 8006–07,
8009, 8012, 8015, 8022, 8024,
8028–29, 8040, 8042, 8046,
8052–54, 8058, 8060–61, 8064,
8066–68, 8071, 8075, 8083–84,
8095–96, 8098, 8101, 8112–13,
8128, 8133, 8137, 8140, 8145,
8147–48, 8151–52, 8159–60,
8167–68, 8173, 8176, 8178,
8180–81, 8192–93, 8202–05,
8207, 8209–10, 8217–18, 8223,
8225–28, 8230, 8239, 8239,
8244, 8247–52, 8259, 8266,
8273, 8277–79, 8281, 8284,
8286–87, 8289, 8293, 8427,
8720, 8749, 8898, 9038, 9055,
9216–18, 9325, 9331, 9372,
9501–02, 9589, 9678, 9737,
9794, 9829, 9868, 9970, 10314,
10619, 10714–15, 10766,
10796, 10811, 10817, 10847,
10905, 10990, 11028, 11182,
11195, 11332, 11438, 11549,
11602, 11633, 11715, 11766,
11835, 11941, 12080, 12124

Mythology
See also specific mythological beings, e.g., Athena
(Greek deity); as subdivision under other subjects,
e.g., Animals — Mythol-
ogy; and as subdivision
of specific countries, e.g.,
Greece — Mythology
PI: 13173–74, 13176–77,
13196, 13218, 21106
I: 13166, 13171, 13210
IJ: 13167–70, 13178,
13180–83, 13188, 13190,
13197, 13203, 13205, 13215,
13219, 13223, 13228, 13240,
13250, 24731

Mythology — Anthologies
I: 13217, 13230, 13241
IJ: 13179, 13225

Mythology — Art
PI: 13204

Mythology — Australia
PI: 13189

Mythology — Aztecs
IJ: 7326, 13194

Mythology — British
IJ: 13202

Mythology — Classical
PI: 21125
IJ: 13252

Mythology — Egypt
PI: 13206
I: 13184
IJ: 13191, 13198

Mythology — Fiction
I: 9224
IJ: 8991, 9673

Mythology — Greece
See also specific gods, e.g.,
Athena (Greek deity)
P: 12456, 12889, 13208,
13216, 13222, 13229, 13242
PI: 12700, 12875, 13187,
13211, 13213, 13226–27,
13235, 13245, 13249
I: 13251
IJ: 7201, 7270, 9050, 9202,
9672, 9801, 9877, 9880, 13209,
13224, 13231, 13236–37,
13246

Mythology — India
IJ: 13192

**Mythology — Iroquois
Indians**
PI: 13201

Mythology — Japan
IJ: 13193

**Mythology — Mayan
Indians**
IJ: 7326, 13175, 13194

Mythology — Middle East
IJ: 13195

**Mythology — Native
American**
IJ: 13199

Mythology — Norse
I: 13186

Mythology — Plays
I: 16877

Mythology — Rome
IJ: 13244

Mythology — Scandinavia
IJ: 13200

N

Nagasaki, Japan
IJ: 17409

Nail art
IJ: 24167

Nails
PI: 20780

Naismith, James
PI: 15982

Nakahama, Manjiro
PI: 16271
IJ: 16270

Names — Fiction
P: 2366, 3213, 7063

Nannies — Fiction
P: 3559
PI: 8470, 8548
I: 8547

Nantucket (MA) — Fiction
IJ: 11002

Napster — Biography
IJ: 15685

Narcolepsy — Fiction
P: 6493

NASCAR
PI: 24881
I: 24880, 24897–98
IJ: 15870, 15878, 24878–79,
24883, 24895–96

NASCAR — Biography
PI: 15861
I: 15873–74

Nash, Kevin
IJ: 16090

Nast, Thomas
IJ: 14319

Natchez Trail — Fiction
IJ: 11017

Nation, Carry A.
IJ: 15474

**Nation of Islam —
Biography**
PI: 14922

**National Aeronautics and
Space Administration
(U.S.)**
PI: 23687

National Archives (U.S.)
I: 19584

**National Guard (U.S.) —
Careers**
IJ: 20265

**National Law Enforcement
Officers Memorial
(Washington, DC)**
IJ: 18947

National parks (U.S.)
See also specific national
parks, e.g., Yellowstone
National Park
P: 18811
PI: 18919, 18927–30, 18934–
35, 19061, 19064, 19076–77,
19102, 19127
I: 18931
IJ: 19068

**National parks (U.S.) —
Fiction**
IJ: 7918

P = Primary; PI = Primary-Intermediate; I = Intermediate; IJ = Intermediate-Junior High

O

IJ: 22619

Oceans — Fiction
P: 4370
IJ: 8201

Oceans — Folklore
PI: 22604
I: 12450

Oceans — Poetry
PI: 14012

Ochoa, Ellen
PI: 14155–56
IJ: 14154, 14157

O'Connor, Sandra Day
P: 15476
I: 15475, 15477

Octopuses
P: 22484, 22486
PI: 22487
I: 22485, 22489

Odetta
PI: 14554

O'Donnell, Rosie
IJ: 14548

Odysseus (Greek mythology)
IJ: 13238

Odysseus (Greek mythology) — Fiction
IJ: 13239

Oglala Sioux Indians — Folklore
P: 13061

Oglethorpe, James
I: 15123
IJ: 18437

Ohio
PI: 18892–93, 18918
I: 18356, 18914, 22912
IJ: 18902, 18913

Ohio — Fiction
I: 10966
IJ: 8543

Ohio River
IJ: 23245

Ohr, George E.
I: 14326

Oil
PI: 19253

Oil industry
IJ: 17489

Oil industry — Biography
IJ: 15521, 15800

Oil industry — Careers
IJ: 20353

Oil pollution
PI: 19346
I: 19338

Oil spills
See also Exxon Valdez oil spill
PI: 19337, 19346

Oil spills — Fiction
P: 5483

Oils
P: 20809, 20809

Ojibwa Indians
PI: 18299
IJ: 18331

Ojibwa Indians — Fiction
PI: 3594
IJ: 10868–70

Ojibwa Indians — Folklore
P: 4690, 13084

O'Keeffe, Georgia
P: 14323
PI: 14321–22, 14324

O'Keeffe, Georgia — Fiction
PI: 7539

Oklahoma
PI: 19165, 19167
IJ: 18869, 18873, 18902

Oklahoma — Fiction
PI: 11096
I: 8435
IJ: 8399, 8670, 10164

Oklahoma City Thunder
PI: 24965

Olympic Games
PI: 73, 16057, 25064
I: 25063
IJ: 25062, 25065

Olympic Games — Biography
PI: 16096, 16106
I: 15895, 16007, 16060
IJ: 15850, 16099, 16108

Olympic Games — Fiction
PI: 13245

Oman
I: 17998

Omidyar, Pierre
IJ: 15784

O'Neal, Shaquille
I: 15984
IJ: 15983

Oneida Indians
IJ: 18332

Only children — Fiction
P: 3091

Opera
I: 16890
IJ: 16676

Opera — Fiction
P: 5593
PI: 8691

Opera houses — Fiction
PI: 9971

Operation Iraqi Freedom
I: 18867
IJ: 17488, 24160

Operation Moses — Fiction
P: 4803

Operetta — Fiction
P: 4874

Opossums
P: 21907

Opossums — Fiction
P: 1812, 1863, 12382

Oppenheimer, J. Robert
IJ: 15785

Opposites — Fiction
P: 1265

Optical illusions
PI: 23638, 23657, 24722
I: 16330
IJ: 24593

Optics — Experiments and projects
I: 23633

Optimism — Fiction
P: 196

Oracle Corp. — Biography
IJ: 15681

Orange juice
P: 22942

Oranges — Fiction
P: 4280

Orangutans
P: 21680, 21682–83
PI: 21696
I: 21701

Orangutans — Fiction
P: 5067, 5252

Orchestras
PI: 16752
I: 16688
IJ: 16684, 16750

Orchestras — Fiction
P: 1918

Order (mathematics)
P: 23366

Oregon
PI: 19081
IJ: 19085

Oregon — Fiction
PI: 11044
I: 11565
IJ: 7611, 7970, 8394, 10182, 11042, 11055

Oregon — Poetry
I: 13520

Oregon Trail
P: 18634
I: 18607

Oregon Trail — Fiction
P: 2557
PI: 11050
I: 7329, 18211
IJ: 11037, 11065, 11087

Organ donation — Fiction
PI: 10165

Organ transplants
See also Heart transplants
IJ: 20450

Organisms
I: 21169

Orienteering
IJ: 24989

Origami
PI: 24396, 24408, 24410–11
I: 24407, 24412, 24421
IJ: 24404, 24420

Origami — Fiction
P: 2944, 4665, 5959
I: 11806
IJ: 10144

Origami — Poetry
P: 13406

Orkney Islands
IJ: 17085

Ornithology — Careers
PI: 20299

Orphan Train
I: 18802

Orphan Train — Biography
IJ: 14866

Orphan Train — Fiction
PI: 11204
IJ: 11188

Orphans — Fiction
P: 993, 4741
PI: 7345, 9128, 10545, 10633, 11156
I: 7378, 7399, 7467, 7922, 8472, 8476, 8958, 10118, 10262, 10742, 11222, 11286
IJ: 7625, 7652, 7828, 8168, 8839, 8997, 9114, 9311, 9644, 10615, 10758–60, 10847, 10914, 10989, 11023, 11035, 11121, 11191, 11254, 11275, 11416, 11462, 11468, 11767

Oryx
P: 21855

Osage Indians
PI: 18351

Osceola (Seminole chief)
I: 15193

Ostriches
PI: 22006

Ostriches — Fiction
P: 4017, 5433
I: 8368

Otero, Katherine Stinson
P: 14158

Otis, Elisha
P: 15786

Otters
P: 22503

Otters — Fiction
P: 2447, 5147–48, 5349, 5450

Ottoman Empire
IJ: 17172

Outdoor life
PI: 24995
IJ: 24992

Outdoor life — Jokes and riddles
PI: 24635

P = Primary; PI = Primary-Intermediate; I = Intermediate; IJ = Intermediate-Junior High

P = Primary; PI = Primary-Intermediate; I = Intermediate; IJ = Intermediate-Junior High

IJ: 20169, 24289

Parties — Fiction
P: 1991, 2913, 2941, 3089, 3655, 4157, 4640, 5152
PI: 7432, 10284
I: 7354, 10754

Passover
P: 6323, 6371, 19892, 19915–16
PI: 19902, 19904, 19906
IJ: 19907

Passover — Cookbooks
PI: 24549

Passover — Crafts
P: 6378

Passover — Fiction
P: 6325, 6344–47, 6352, 6354, 6358, 6361, 6364, 6374, 6378–79
PI: 6349, 6356
I: 11919

Passover — Folklore
P: 12637

Pasteur, Louis
PI: 15788
I: 15787, 15790
IJ: 15789, 15791

Patagonia — Fiction
P: 4438

Patch, Sam
PI: 14159

Paterson, Katherine
IJ: 14710–11

Patience — Fiction
P: 5215

Patrick, Danica
IJ: 15876

Patriotism
P: 20138

Patriotism — Fiction
P: 3021, 3542

Patterns (mathematics)
P: 23365

Patton, George S., Jr.
PI: 15129

Paul, Les
I: 14555

Pauling, Linus
I: 15792

Paulsen, Gary
I: 14712
IJ: 14713–15

Pavlov, Ivan
IJ: 15793

Pavlova, Anna
PI: 16823
I: 14556

Pawnee Indians — Folklore
P: 12299

Payton, Gary
PI: 15986

Peace
See also Pacifists and pacifism
P: 2790, 16782, 19394
PI: 19390
IJ: 19630–31, 20151

Peace — Folklore
IJ: 12724

Peace — Poetry
PI: 13455
I: 13500

Peace Corps
P: 19585
IJ: 19286, 19395

Peace movements
IJ: 16149

Peaches
P: 22975

Peaches — Fiction
P: 4484

Peaches — Folklore
P: 12634

Peacocks
P: 22003
PI: 22032

Peacocks — Fiction
P: 5338

Peale, Charles Willson
PI: 17028

Peanut butter
P: 22942, 22947
IJ: 24550

Peanut butter — Fiction
P: 3028

Peanuts
P: 22947

Peanuts — Biography
PI: 15605

Peanuts — Fiction
P: 5719

Peanuts (comic strip)
PI: 14365

Pearl Harbor
PI: 19059
I: 17463
IJ: 17402, 17425, 17445, 17448, 17473–74

Peary, Marie Ahnighito
IJ: 15130

Peary, Robert E.
IJ: 14160

Pebbles — Fiction
P: 1286

Peer pressure
P: 20236
IJ: 20237

Peer pressure — Fiction
IJ: 7416

Pegasus (Mythology)
I: 13233

Pei, I. M.
PI: 14328

Pele (soccer player)
P: 16092–93

Pelicans
PI: 22018

Pelicans — Fiction
P: 5483

Pelosi, Nancy
IJ: 15131

Pen pals — Fiction
P: 964, 1956, 3706, 3726
I: 10348
IJ: 10035

Pencils — Fiction
P: 892

Penguins
P: 21979, 22098–100, 22103, 22108, 22110–11, 22113–15, 22120, 22122, 22124, 22128
PI: 22105–06, 22109, 22117, 22119, 22123, 22125, 22127
I: 22102, 22116, 22118
IJ: 22104, 22107, 22112, 22126, 22129

Penguins — Fiction
P: 370, 486, 1150, 2364, 2510, 3701, 5416, 5460, 5485, 5603
I: 11522

Penguins — Poetry
P: 13787

Penmanship — Fiction
IJ: 10961

Penn, William
PI: 15132
IJ: 18441

Pennsylvania
PI: 18988
I: 19040
IJ: 18441, 18977, 18998, 19024, 19052, 23470

Pennsylvania
PI: 15132

Pennsylvania — Fiction
P: 6018
IJ: 10945, 11194

Pennsylvania Station (NY)
PI: 19009

Penraat, Jaap
IJ: 17472

Pens — Fiction
I: 9793

Pens (writing)
PI: 23752

Pentagon (Washington, DC)
P: 19147
PI: 18962

Pequot Indians
PI: 18328

Perception
P: 363

Perception — Fiction
P: 2726

Peregrine falcons
P: 22066

Peregrine falcons — Fiction
P: 5226
PI: 5227

Periodic table
PI: 23060
IJ: 23037, 23043, 23053–55, 23057, 23069–70

Perseverance — Fiction
P: 3076

Persia
See also Iran
PI: 10565
IJ: 17190, 17199

Persia — Biography
IJ: 14729

Persia — Fiction
P: 4750

Persia — Folklore
P: 13162
PI: 13163–64
I: 13127

Persian Gulf War
See Gulf War (1991)

Persian New Year
IJ: 19766

Personal finances
P: 19228
PI: 19226, 19230
I: 19195
IJ: 19216

Personal guidance
P: 20137, 20142
I: 20079–80, 20090, 20104, 20127, 20154, 23921
IJ: 16501, 16526, 20081, 20084, 20089, 20095, 20099, 20134, 20143, 20146, 20153, 20186, 20200, 20220, 20231, 20880, 20887–88, 20890, 20897

Personal guidance — Boys
IJ: 20156

Personal guidance — Fiction
P: 1670

Personal guidance — Girls
I: 20083
IJ: 20085–86, 20109, 20113, 20166, 20223, 20238, 20243, 20878

Personal problems
See also topics such as Bullies and bullying; Death; Divorce; Moving
P: 20234
PI: 20227
IJ: 20216, 20231

Personal problems — Fiction
P: 2260, 4893–96, 4902, 4907–08, 4915, 4919, 4921, 4927–28, 4930–31, 4933, 4957, 4964, 4966, 4983, 4996–97, 4999, 5010, 5013, 5017, 5020, 5025, 5027, 5039–40, 5042, 5050–51, 5054, 5059, 5661, 6447, 6465

P = Primary; PI = Primary-Intermediate; I = Intermediate; IJ = Intermediate-Junior High

Puzzles — Poetry
IJ: 13674

Pyramids
P: 17237
IJ: 16433, 17231, 17236, 17243, 17246, 17255

Pythagoras
IJ: 23327

Q

Quadrino, James
IJ: 15796

Quadruplets — Fiction
IJ: 8508

Quakers — Fiction
P: 6471

Quan, Elizabeth
PI: 14722

Quarlls, Caroline
I: 14936

Quarter horses
PI: 22846

Quebec — Folklore
I: 12277

Questions and answers — Fiction
P: 2704

Quezada, Juan
PI: 16324

Quicksand — Fiction
P: 4311

Quiet — Fiction
P: 299

Quilting — Fiction
IJ: 11026

Quilts and quilting
P: 3180, 24435
IJ: 24452–53, 24456–57

Quilts and quilting — Fiction
P: 965, 2785, 3449, 4530, 4688, 6511
PI: 3363, 4883

Quimby, Harriet
P: 14174
PI: 14173

Quinceanera (coming-of-age ritual)
I: 19796

Quinceanera (coming-of-age ritual) — Fiction
P: 3352, 5947

Quinn, Anthony
IJ: 14560

Quotations
IJ: 16610, 16655

R

Rabbits
P: 21658, 21943, 21946, 22672, 22674
PI: 21953, 21959–60, 22662, 22664, 22697

Rabbits — Fiction
P: 1604, 2001, 2208, 2536, 2737, 3896–97, 3988, 4089, 5150, 5271, 5300, 5324, 5521, 6216, 6464, 6849
PI: 499, 1603, 9955
I: 9482, 11628
IJ: 9390

Rabbits — Folklore
P: 12167, 12178, 12511, 12715, 12754
PI: 12500
I: 13106

Raccoons
P: 5602, 21550, 21646
PI: 21630, 21640
I: 21649

Raccoons — Fiction
P: 5392, 5527, 5610
PI: 8917
IJ: 8321

Race — Fiction
IJ: 10420

Race relations — Fiction
P: 3099, 4790
PI: 4656, 12161
I: 7712, 11359
IJ: 11200, 11248, 11399, 11915

Racial prejudice
IJ: 14875, 19364

Racially mixed people — Biography
P: 14417
I: 14416
IJ: 14454

Racially mixed people — Fiction
P: 2851, 3289, 3396, 6908
I: 8429, 8526–27, 10338
IJ: 7457, 7652, 8636, 8687, 10043, 10301, 10723

Racing — Fiction
P: 1703
PI: 7486

Racism
P: 20111
PI: 19144
IJ: 19614, 19958

Racism — Biography
PI: 15880

Racism — Fiction
P: 4537, 4719, 5024
PI: 4660
I: 11306
IJ: 7502, 8514, 9140, 10093, 10213, 10755, 11199, 11338, 11346, 11423

Radio
PI: 23985, 23989

Radio — Fiction
IJ: 11325

Radioactive waste
PI: 23629

Radioactivity
IJ: 23573

Radium
IJ: 15630

Radium — Biography
I: 15626
IJ: 15625

Railroads and trains
P: 26, 5819, 5841, 24072, 24074, 24076–77, 24079
PI: 18592, 24068, 24075, 24078
I: 18674, 24010, 24069
IJ: 18641, 18676, 24071, 24073, 24081–83

Railroads and trains — Fiction
P: 1129, 1331, 1366, 2666, 3853, 3877, 4478, 4646, 5467, 5807, 5811, 5814–15, 5818, 5822, 5829, 5835, 5838, 5845, 5850, 5859, 5862, 5867, 5871, 5884, 5888–89, 5891, 6186, 6658, 6848

Rain
P: 21523
PI: 23499

Rain — Fiction
P: 2619, 2662, 2780, 3031, 4560

Rain — Folklore
P: 12170

Rain forests
P: 16716, 23186, 23189, 23198, 23205, 24655
PI: 23175, 23177, 23179, 23183, 23195–96, 23199, 23208, 23210, 23213
I: 18158, 23173, 23180, 23193
IJ: 12811, 21995, 22011, 23178, 23187, 23197, 23201–02, 23204, 23206, 23211, 23215

Rain forests — Animals
P: 182, 21256, 23186
PI: 23177
I: 21603
IJ: 23178, 23207

Rain forests — Fiction
P: 424, 4298, 5425, 21264
PI: 2562, 4858

Rain forests — Folklore
P: 12711

Rain forests — Poetry
PI: 13975

Rainbows
PI: 23640

Rains Retreat
IJ: 19768

Rainy days — Fiction
P: 7173

Raleigh, Sir Walter
I: 14175

Raleigh, Sir Walter — Fiction
IJ: 10757

Rama (Hindu deity) — Fiction
IJ: 9209

Ramadan
P: 19655, 19762, 19774, 19792, 19819, 19823, 19847, 19857
PI: 19797
IJ: 19670

Ramadan — Fiction
P: 5915, 5925, 5933
PI: 5912

Ramayana — Folklore
P: 13107
I: 12226

Ramon, Ilan
IJ: 14176

Ranches and ranch life
PI: 22905

Ranches and ranch life — Fiction
P: 5195
I: 8414, 8421
IJ: 10422, 10431

Rankin, Jeannette
PI: 15485

Rap music
IJ: 16664

Rap music — Biography
PI: 14475
I: 14585
IJ: 14514–15, 14525, 14532, 14580

Rap music — Fiction
P: 1684

Raspberry Pi (computer)
IJ: 23947

Ratio and proportion
IJ: 23327

Rats
PI: 21942, 21952, 22706
I: 21957
IJ: 22682

Rats — Fiction
P: 5343
PI: 11575
I: 8811, 8929
IJ: 8841, 8931, 8954, 9581, 10783

Rattlesnakes
PI: 21394, 21398
IJ: 21397

Rattlesnakes — Fiction
P: 3945, 12211

Rawlings, Marjorie Kinnan
I: 14723

P = Primary; PI = Primary-Intermediate; I = Intermediate; IJ = Intermediate-Junior High

17317
I: 17137, 17296–97, 17303,
17306, 17308, 17310–11,
17313–14, 17318–19, 17321,
17324
IJ: 16431, 17197, 17289–90,
17290, 17292–94, 17299,
17302, 17304, 17309, 17315,
17320, 17322–23, 17323,
17860, 17873–74

Rome — Art
IJ: 16431, 16436

Rome — Biography
IJ: 16273

Rome — Crafts
IJ: 17304

Rome — Fiction
P: 4712, 5373, 6566
PI: 10750
I: 10563, 10731
IJ: 10668, 10714–15, 10743

Rome — Graphic novels
I: 7252

Rome — Mythology
See Mythology — Classical

***Romeo and Juliet* (play)**
IJ: 16882

Romo, Tony
PI: 16036

Room decoration
I: 24288

Roosevelt, Eleanor
PI: 15486–87, 15489, 15494
I: 15493, 15495
IJ: 15488, 15490–92,
15496–98, 18789

Roosevelt, Franklin D.
P: 15357
PI: 15355–56, 18771
IJ: 14842, 15349–54, 18757,
18764, 18836

**Roosevelt, Franklin D. and
Eleanor**
IJ: 15358

Roosevelt, Theodore
P: 15359, 15365, 15465,
18811
PI: 15361, 15364, 15366–67,
18830
I: 18816
IJ: 14840, 15360, 15362–63

**Roosevelt, Theodore —
Fiction**
PI: 11903
I: 11159

Roots
P: 22868
PI: 23008

Rope jumping
IJ: 24767

Rose, Derrick
PI: 15988

Rosenfeld, Fanny Bobbie
IJ: 16099

Rosetta Stone
PI: 16175

Rosh Hashanah
P: 19905, 19910

Rosh Hashanah — Fiction
P: 5814, 6320, 6336, 6340,
6362, 6373

Ross, Betsy
I: 15151, 15153
IJ: 15152, 15154

Rothschild, Walter
P: 15802

Rousseau, Henri
P: 14359
PI: 14360

Rowling, J. K.
I: 14726
IJ: 14727–28

**Royal Canadian Mounted
Police**
I: 18043

**Royal Canadian Mounted
Police — Fiction**
P: 2545

Royalty
P: 20168
IJ: 16122, 17366

Royalty — Biography
IJ: 16127

Royalty — Fiction
I: 10696
IJ: 8986

Rubber
PI: 23776

Rubber stamps
I: 24266

Rudolph, Wilma
P: 16059
PI: 16062
I: 16060–61

Rugs — Fiction
P: 4614

Rulers
IJ: 17149

Rules — Fiction
P: 2711

Rumi
IJ: 14729

Rumors — Fiction
PI: 10411

Runaways
See Running away

Running and jogging
IJ: 25066

Running and jogging
IJ: 25069

**Running and jogging —
Fiction**
P: 4425
IJ: 8041, 8545, 12127

Running away — Fiction
P: 1604, 4903, 5049
PI: 10007

I: 7736, 9484
IJ: 7540, 8662, 9494, 10083,
10108, 10222, 10267, 10474,
10524, 11185

Rural life
PI: 18028
IJ: 19991

Rural life — Fiction
P: 2379, 3063, 3256
PI: 8633
I: 8612
IJ: 7556, 7616, 10598

Russell, Keri
PI: 14574

Russia
P: 17892–93
PI: 17901
IJ: 16241, 17890, 17899,
17904

Russia — Biography
P: 14607
PI: 14121
IJ: 16285

Russia — Cookbooks
IJ: 24547, 24556

Russia — Fiction
PI: 10736, 10744
IJ: 10669, 10695, 10710,
10724, 10732, 10734, 11218

Russia — Folklore
P: 4766, 12201, 12324,
12336, 12519, 12535, 12560,
12599–600, 12657, 12705,
12769, 12887, 12912, 13030,
13043, 13070, 13139, 13165
PI: 12538, 12757, 12911,
12923
I: 12614
IJ: 12897, 12909

Russia — Mythology
IJ: 13170

Russian Americans
PI: 19976
I: 19979
IJ: 20041

**Russian Revolution —
Fiction**
IJ: 10724

Rustin, Bayard
IJ: 14937

Ruth, Babe
P: 15936
PI: 15935, 15938
IJ: 15934, 15937

Ruth, Babe — Fiction
P: 3720, 4415
I: 12081
IJ: 9137

Rwanda
PI: 17520
IJ: 19550

Rwanda — Fiction
PI: 6519

Rwanda — Folklore
I: 12168

Ryder, Winona
PI: 14575

S

Sabbath (Jewish)
P: 19895
I: 12565

Sabbath (Jewish) — Fiction
P: 3505

Sabertooth tigers
PI: 21805

Sacagawea
PI: 15203–04, 15206
I: 15205, 15207, 18388

Sacagawea — Fiction
P: 4735
IJ: 11086

Sachar, Louis
IJ: 14730

Sadat, Anwar
IJ: 16288

Sadness
P: 20230

Sadness — Fiction
P: 4974

Safety
See also Fire safety; Safety
education; Sports —
Safety
P: 20108, 20849, 20852,
20854
IJ: 20843, 20847–48, 20853

Safety — Fiction
P: 2492, 2677, 2939

Safety education
P: 20858
PI: 20859
IJ: 20966

Sagan, Carl
IJ: 15803–04

Saguaro cactus
PI: 23153

Sahara Desert
PI: 17553, 17558, 23166

Sailing and boating
See also Ships and boats
IJ: 14714

**Sailing and boating —
Fiction**
P: 1156
IJ: 8220

Sailors — Biography
P: 14095

Saints
P: 12783
PI: 19651
I: 19677, 19684
IJ: 19696, 19704

Saints — Biography
P: 16140, 16303

P = Primary; PI = Primary-Intermediate; I = Intermediate; IJ = Intermediate-Junior High

P = Primary; PI = Primary-Intermediate; I = Intermediate; IJ = Intermediate-Junior High

P = Primary; PI = Primary-Intermediate; I = Intermediate; IJ = Intermediate-Junior High

P = Primary; PI = Primary-Intermediate; I = Intermediate; IJ = Intermediate-Junior High

P = Primary; PI = Primary-Intermediate; I = Intermediate; IJ = Intermediate-Junior High

Turkey — Fiction
P: 4565
IJ: 10677

Turkey — Folklore
P: 12989
IJ: 13090

Turkeys
P: 22924

Turkeys — Fiction
P: 5109, 6389, 6392, 6403, 6975

Turner, Joseph
PI: 14375

Turnips — Folklore
PI: 12333

Turtles and tortoises
P: 21410, 21413–14, 21416, 21420, 21429
PI: 21418–19, 21426, 21428, 21431–32, 21620, 22679
I: 21411, 21422
IJ: 21417, 21430

Turtles and tortoises — Fiction
P: 2553, 3163, 5119, 5128, 5149, 5351
I: 9762

Turtles and tortoises — Folklore
P: 12178, 12430, 12597

Tuskegee Airmen
I: 17410, 17416
IJ: 14820, 17429

Tuskegee Airmen — Fiction
P: 4598, 4628

Tutankhamen, King
PI: 17227
I: 16312, 17229, 17260
IJ: 16311, 17248

Tutsi (African people)
IJ: 17549

Twain, Mark
P: 14761, 14765
PI: 14760, 14762–63, 14767
I: 14769
IJ: 14759, 14764, 14766, 14768

Twain, Mark — Fiction
PI: 8569

Twain, Shania
IJ: 14592

Tweed, William "Boss"
IJ: 15163

20th century
IJ: 17183

Twins
P: 16012
PI: 20209
I: 16009

Twins — Fiction
P: 242, 3276, 3593, 3635, 3999, 6245, 6262, 6700, 6728, 6738–39
PI: 8345, 8625, 9032, 10216, 12128

I: 7748, 7922, 8527, 8613, 8654, 8753, 9225, 9588, 11537, 11827
IJ: 7918, 8182, 8533, 8563, 8771, 8900, 9420, 9613, 10092, 10116, 10331, 10492, 10852, 11172, 11584, 11794, 12016, 12062, 12105

Tyler, John
PI: 15374
I: 15373

Tyler, Liv
PI: 14593

Typhoid fever
IJ: 20579

Typhoons
I: 23462

Tyrannosaurus rex
P: 17067

U

UFOs
PI: 24697, 24751
IJ: 24681, 24698

UFOs — Fiction
PI: 7647

Uganda
PI: 17542
IJ: 17532, 21697

Uganda — Fiction
P: 4551, 4694, 4876

Uganda — Folklore
P: 12916

Ukraine
IJ: 17888, 17891, 17897

Ukraine — Folklore
P: 12213, 12250, 12454, 12602, 12621, 12627

Ukrainian Americans
IJ: 19996

Ultimate Fighting Championship
IJ: 24873

Uluru
IJ: 17749

Umbrellas — Fiction
P: 3029

Uncle Sam
PI: 18232

Uncles — Fiction
P: 3342, 3710
PI: 8175, 8693, 9188, 11479
IJ: 10192, 10203

Underground areas — Fiction
IJ: 8076, 8078

Underground life
P: 21177

Underground Railroad
PI: 18573, 18715
I: 14957, 18586, 18601

IJ: 14955, 14961, 17101, 18572, 18589, 18591, 18597

Underground Railroad — Biography
P: 14956
I: 14936, 15032
IJ: 14958, 14960

Underground Railroad — Fiction
P: 4534, 4573, 4587, 4604, 4738, 4818, 4873, 6471, 10992
PI: 832, 4527, 10984, 10991, 11014–15
I: 7853, 10967, 11144
IJ: 10968, 10973, 10986–87, 10994, 11004

Underground Railroad — Poetry
IJ: 13635

Underwater archaeology
IJ: 17110, 18300, 24093

Underwater exploration
PI: 22608
I: 22656
IJ: 22653–55, 22660, 24108

Underwater exploration — Biography
P: 15622
I: 15618, 15620–21
IJ: 15654–55

Underwater exploration — Careers
PI: 20398

Underwater life
PI: 22404

Underwear
PI: 17180
IJ: 23909, 24716

Underwear — Fiction
P: 3904

Unemployment — Fiction
IJ: 10147

UNESCO World Heritage
IJ: 24689

UNICEF
P: 19401
IJ: 19391

Unicorns
PI: 13177
IJ: 8949

Unicorns — Fiction
P: 1125, 1363
PI: 6556–58
I: 9233

Unidentified flying objects
See UFOs

United Arab Emirates
I: 18006
IJ: 17979

United Farm Workers — Biography
IJ: 14990

United Kingdom
See also England; Great Britain; Northern Ireland; Scotland; Wales
IJ: 17830

United Kingdom — Biography
PI: 16180
IJ: 15588, 16316

United Nations
IJ: 16490, 19234, 19352, 19382, 19396, 20494, 20866

United Nations — Biography
PI: 14873

United States
See also specific regions, states, and cities, e.g., Midwest (U.S.); California; New York (NY)
P: 18250
PI: 18217
I: 18225
IJ: 18218, 18912

United States — Aerial views
IJ: 23698

United States — Alphabet books
PI: 31

United States — Civil War
See Civil War (U.S.)

United States — Colonial period
See Colonial period (U.S.)

United States — Congress
See Congress (U.S.)

United States — Constitution
See Constitution (U.S.)

United States — Fiction
See specific topics, e.g., Frontier life (U.S.) — Fiction
P: 1615

United States — Folklore
P: 12325, 12328, 12422, 12497, 12507, 12548, 12580, 12585, 12625, 12777, 12977, 13117, 13131
PI: 12300, 12498, 12500, 12524, 12644, 12959
I: 12363, 12377–78, 12493, 12873
IJ: 12492, 12561, 12917, 12972–73

United States — Frontier life
See Frontier life (U.S.)

United States — Geography
All: 18203
P: 2877, 18202, 18224, 19108
PI: 18254, 18269
I: 18213
IJ: 17128, 18263

P = Primary; PI = Primary-Intermediate; I = Intermediate; IJ = Intermediate-Junior High

P = Primary; PI = Primary-Intermediate; I = Intermediate; IJ = Intermediate-Junior High

P = Primary; PI = Primary-Intermediate; I = Intermediate; IJ = Intermediate-Junior High

P = Primary; PI = Primary-Intermediate; I = Intermediate; IJ = Intermediate-Junior High

11447, 11449, 11451, 11457, 11461–62, 11464–66, 11472–73, 11481–82

World Wide Web
See also Internet
PI: 23935, 23943
IJ: 15576, 20336, 23928, 23934, 23946

World Wide Web — Careers
IJ: 20336, 20347

World Wildlife Fund
IJ: 22142

Worms
P: 22360, 22364
I: 22368
IJ: 22365

Worms — Experiments and projects
IJ: 21214

Worms — Fiction
P: 2049, 5127
I: 11747
IJ: 9079

Worry
P: 20242

Worry — Fiction
P: 5036

Wozniak, Steve
PI: 15549
I: 23933
IJ: 15830

Wrestling
PI: 24787, 24838
IJ: 24763–64, 24785, 24811, 24816, 24845

Wrestling — Biography
IJ: 16077, 16090, 16102–03, 16105, 24812

Wrestling — Fiction
PI: 12068
I: 12069
IJ: 10206

Wrestling — Folklore
P: 12512

Wright, Elsie
IJ: 17848

Wright, Frank Lloyd
IJ: 14392–93

Wright, Richard — Fiction
PI: 4722

Wright, Wilbur and Orville
P: 15843
PI: 15831–33, 15836–38, 15841, 15844, 16895, 23817, 23829
IJ: 15529, 15834–35, 15839–40, 15842, 23807

Wright, Wilbur and Orville — Fiction
PI: 6923
IJ: 11177, 11210

Writers
See Authors

Writing
See also Creative writing
P: 16619, 16621
PI: 4, 16516, 16613, 16642–43
I: 16624, 16626, 16640, 16647–48, 24368
IJ: 14618, 16549, 16609, 16614, 16616, 16627, 16637–38, 16645, 16652, 16657–58, 20245, 20248, 20257

Writing — Egyptian
PI: 16175

Writing — Fiction
P: 1526, 2140, 3787, 4953, 4980, 5330
PI: 6508, 8478, 10031, 11805, 11838, 11888
I: 9230, 12114
IJ: 7390, 7525, 7586, 10250, 10358

Writing — Handbooks
IJ: 16620, 16628, 16636, 16661

Writing — Poetry
PI: 13359

Writing — Skills
PI: 16611
IJ: 16622, 16644, 16651, 16653

Writings
IJ: 20264

Wu Daozi
P: 14394

Wyoming
P: 22916
IJ: 18924

Wyoming — Fiction
IJ: 8459, 11073

X

X-rays
PI: 20614

X-rays — Biography
I: 15801

Xerography — Biography
I: 15593

Xiaoping, Deng
IJ: 16317

Y

Yaccarino, Dan
P: 14793

Yahoo! (computers) — Biography
IJ: 15546

Yang, Jerry
IJ: 15546

Yangtze River
PI: 17627
IJ: 17613

Yanomami (people)
PI: 18159
I: 18155

Yao (African people) — Fiction
PI: 10588

Yard sales — Fiction
P: 6828

Yawning — Fiction
P: 2621

Yeboah, Emmanuel Ofosu
IJ: 16318

Yellow fever
IJ: 20515, 20551

Yellowstone National Park
P: 14315, 18923
PI: 18930, 18939, 18941
IJ: 21729

Yellowstone National Park — Fiction
IJ: 8181

Yemen
I: 18007
IJ: 17995, 18016

Yep, Laurence
PI: 14794

Yeti
See also Big Foot
PI: 24695

Yo-yos
PI: 24826
I: 24769, 24843

Yoga
P: 20791, 20840
PI: 13705, 20793, 20799
I: 24770
IJ: 24768, 24851, 24857

Yoga — Fiction
P: 5720

Yolen, Jane
PI: 14795

Yom Kippur
P: 19905
IJ: 19768

Yom Kippur — Fiction
P: 6336

York (c. 1775-1815)
PI: 14976

Yorktown, Battle of
IJ: 18546

Yoruba (African people) — Folklore
P: 12440

Yosemite National Park
PI: 18830

Young, Brigham
PI: 15169
IJ: 15170

Young, Ed
PI: 14395

Yugoslavia
IJ: 17783

Z

Zaharias, Babe Didrikson
PI: 16116
IJ: 16117–18

Zambia — Biography
IJ: 22763

Zambia — Fiction
P: 5190

Zambia — Folklore
P: 12268

Zanzibar — Poetry
P: 13868

Zebras
P: 21592–93, 21617
PI: 21609, 21672

Zedong, Mao
IJ: 17623

Zenimura, Kenichi
PI: 15947

Zeus (Greek deity)
PI: 13227

Zeus (mythology)
IJ: 13237

Zhang, Ange
IJ: 14396

Zheng He
PI: 16319
I: 16320

Zimbabwe
IJ: 17566, 17572, 17574

Zimbabwe — Fiction
P: 4816
IJ: 9714

Zindel, Paul
IJ: 14796

Zion National Park (UT)
I: 18931

Zion National Park (UT) — Fiction
I: 8179

Zirconium
IJ: 23069

Zitkala-Sa
PI: 15219

Zodiac (astrology)
I: 24708, 24721

Zombies
PI: 24694

Zombies — Fiction
P: 3871, 11681
I: 7922, 9438, 9822, 11545
IJ: 7346, 9011–12, 9222, 9358, 9532, 11515

P = Primary; PI = Primary-Intermediate; I = Intermediate; IJ = Intermediate-Junior High

About the Authors

CATHERINE BARR is the author of other volumes in the Best Books series (*Best Books for Middle School and Junior High Readers* and *Best Books for High School Readers*) and of *Popular Series Fiction for K–6 Readers*, *Popular Series Fiction for Middle School and Teen Readers*, and *High/Low Handbook: Best Books and Web Sites for Reluctant Teen Readers*, 4th Edition.

DR. JAMIE CAMPBELL NAIDOO is an endowed associate professor at the University of Alabama School of Library and Information Studies where he teaches and researches in the areas of early childhood literacy, culturally diverse children's literature, and library services to diverse populations. He is active in REFORMA, the United States Board on Books for Young People (USBBY), and the Association for Library Services to Children (ALSC) and has served on and chaired multiple book award committees. Jamie is also the editor of *Celebrating Cuentos: Promoting Latino Children's Literature and Literacy in Classrooms and Libraries*, and author of *Rainbow Family Collections: Selecting and Using Children's Books with Lesbian, Gay, Bisexual, Transgender, and Queer Content* and *Diversity Programming for Digital Youth: Promoting Cultural Competence in the Children's Library*.